*Concise English
Dictionary*

The Wordsworth
Concise English Dictionary

—

Edited by
G. W. Davidson, M. A. Seaton and J. Simpson

Wordsworth Reference

This edition published 1994 by Wordsworth Editions Ltd.
Cumberland House, Crib Street, Ware, Hertfordshire SG12 9ET.

Wordsworth® is a registered trade mark of
Wordsworth Editions Ltd

ISBN 1-85326-328-1

Printed and bound in Great Britain by Mackays of Chatham PLC.

Contents

Using the dictionary

The Arrangement of Entries

Words which are derived from the same root have often been grouped together under one headword. This applies not only to words which simply add a suffix to the headword, e.g. **coolness,** which is under **cool,** but also to words which are more radically different from the root word. Thus, for example, **bronchitis** is entered under **bronchus, conclusion** under **conclude,** and **laborious** under **labour.**

Cross-references have been given in many cases in order to make the entries easier to find whilst still preserving the etymological "nesting" system, e.g. **invasion** see **invade, donor** see **donation, liar** see **lie.**

The derivatives given under a headword are arranged alphabetically in three categories. The direct derivatives of the headword, i.e. those words which are formed by adding a suffix or ending to the headword or root word, are given immediately after the various meanings of the headword. After these come the compounds, some of which are hyphenated, some of which are one word and some of which are two words—where no grammatical label has been given at compounds they are to be assumed to be nouns. Those compounds which do not begin with the headword or derivative of the headword are listed under the third category, the phrases.

Labels

A label relating to grammatical form, e.g. *n., v.t., adj.,* appears before the word or meaning(s) to which it applies. A label relating to classification (e.g. *coll., slang, obs., chem., elect., psych.*) precedes the list of meanings where it applies to all the meanings given. Where a label applies to only one meaning of a word it immediately follows that meaning.

Foreign Words

Words in the text which are still regarded as foreign words, rather than as naturalised English words, have been labelled accordingly, e.g. (Fr.),(Ger.) etc. German nouns have been spelt with a capital letter as they are in their country of origin.

Etymologies

The etymology is given in square brackets at the end of each entry. The sign — indicates 'derived from'. Where the derivation is not included, it is either self-evident or of unknown or uncertain origin.

Hyphenation

Where the hyphen separating the elements of a hyphenated compound word in bold type occurs at the end of a line this has been shown by the symbol = to distinguish it from the ordinary hyphen which indicates a line-break.

Detailed chart of pronunciation

Respelling is a rough method of showing pronunciation compared with the use of phonetic symbols, but it has two merits — it is intelligible to a large number of people who do not know phonetic symbols, and it allows for more than one interpretation so that each user of the dictionary may choose a pronunciation in keeping with his speech.

Vowels and Diphthongs in Accented Syllables

Symbol		Examples	Pronunciation
ā	as in	name, aid, rein, tare, wear, hair, heir, fairy	nām, ād, rān, tār, wār, hār, ār, făr'i
ä	„	grass, path, palm, harm, heart	gräs, päth, päm, härm, härt
a	„	sat, bad, have, marry	sat, bad, hav, mar'i
ē	„	lean, keel, dene, chief, seize, gear, sheer, here, bier, query	lēn, kēl, dēn, chēf, sēz, gēr, shēr, hēr, bēr, kwē'ri
e	„	red, thread, said, bury	red, thred, sed, ber'i
ī	„	side, shy, dye, height, hire, byre, fiery	sīd, shī, dī, hīt, hīr, bīr, fīr'i
i	„	pin, busy, hymn	pin, biz'i, him
ō	„	bone, road, foe, low, dough, more, soar, floor, port, Tory (For alternative pronunciation of port, more, etc., see ō)	bōn, rōd, fō, lō, dō, mōr, sōr, flōr, pōrt, tō'ri
ō	„	haul, lawn, fall, bought, swarm, more, soar, floor, port, Tory (For alternative pronunciation of port, more, etc., see ō)	hōl, lōn, fōl, bōt, swōrm, mōr, sōr, flōr, pōrt, tōr'i
o	„	got, shot, shone	got, shot, shon
ōō	„	fool, sou, boor, tour	fōōl, sōō, bōōr, tōōr
ŏŏ	„	good, full, would	gŏŏd, fŏŏl, wŏŏd
ū	„	tune, due, newt, view, endure, fury	tūn, dū, nūt, vū, in-dūr', fū'ri
u	„	bud, run, love	bud, run, luv
û	„	heard, bird, world, absurd, bury	hûrd, bûrd, wûrld, ab-sûrd, bûr'i
ow	„	mount, frown, sour	mownt, frown, sowr
oi	„	toy, buoy, soil	toi, boi, soil

Stress

In words of more than one syllable, the syllable with the main accent is shown by a stress mark ′ following that syllable, both in the respellings (e.g. äf′tər, bi-gin′) and in entries in bold-faced type (e.g. af′ter, begin′er).

Note the difference in pronunciation, as shown by the position of the stress mark, between blessed′ (blest) and bless′ed (bles′id), refined′ (ri-fīnd′) and refin′edly (ri-fīn′id-li).

Vowels in Unaccented Syllables

Neutral vowels in unaccented syllables are usually shown by ə (schwa)
e.g. el′ə-mənt, in′fənt, ran′dəm, pre′shəs (precious), nā′chər (nature).

In certain cases, they are more exactly represented by i
e.g. ē′vil, bi-hōld′, bles′id, man′ij, di-ment′.

Vowels followed by r

In certain accents, for example in Scots, Irish, General American, r is pronounced wherever it occurs in the spelling and this is the form adopted in the dictionary.

In certain other accents, for example Received Pronunciation or what is sometimes called the BBC accent, it is pronounced only when it occurs before a vowel. Elsewhere the following rules apply:

ār	is pronounced as		eə	ō	is pronounced as		ō or ōə
är	„	„	ä	ōōr	„	„	ōōə
ēr	„	„	iə	ūr	„	„	ūə
er	„	„	eə	ûr	„	„	û
īr	„	„	īə	owr	„	„	owə

Consonants

Symbol		Examples	Pronunciation
b	as in	hob, rabbit	hob, rab'it
ch	„	church, much, match	chûrch, much, mach
d	„	ado, dew	ə-dōō', dū
dh	„	then, father	dhen, fä'dhər
f	„	faint, phase, rough	fānt, fāz, ruf
g	„	gold, guard, ghastly	gōld, gärd, gäst'li
gz	„	exact	igz-akt'
h	„	happy, home	hap'i, hōm
hh	„	loch, leprechaun	lohh, lep'rə-hhön
hl	„	pennill, (W.) llan	pen'ihl, hlan
(h)w	„	whale, which	(h)wāl, (h)wich
j	„	jack, gentle, ledge, region	jak, jen'tl, lej, rē'jən
k	„	keep, cat, chorus	kēp, kat, kōr'əs (kōr')
ks	„	lax, vex	laks, veks
kw	„	quite, coiffeur	kwīt, kwä-fœr'
l	„	lamp, collar	lamp, kol'ər
m	„	meat, palm, stammer	mēt, päm, stam'ər
n	„	net, gnome, knee, dinner	net, nōm, nē, din'ər
ng	„	fling, longing	fling, long'ing
ngg	„	single, longer, languor	sing'gl, long'gər, lang'gər
ngk	„	monkey, precinct	mungk'i, prē'singkt
p	„	peat, apple	pēt, ap'l
r	„	rest, wreck, arrive	rest, rek, ə-rīv'
s	„	sad, city, circuit, scene, mass, psalm	sad, sit'i, sûr'kit, sēn, mas, säm
sh	„	shine, machine, sure, militia, acacia	shīn, mə-shēn, shōōr, mi-lish'ə, ə-kā'sh(y)ə
t	„	tape, nettle, thyme	tāp, net'l, tīm
th	„	thin, three	thin, thrē
v	„	valid, river	val'id, riv'ər
w	„	was, one, twig	woz, wun, twig
y	„	young, bastion	yung, bast'yən
z	„	zoo, was, roads	zōō, woz, rōdz
zh	„	azure, measure, congé, lesion	azh'ər (or ā'zhûr), mezh'ər, kɔ̃-zhā, lē'zhən

Additional Sounds in Foreign and Dialect Words

Symbol		Examples	Pronunciation
ø	as in	deux, feu, peu	dø, fø, pø
œ	„	fleur, leur, cœur	floer, lœr, koer
ü	„	(1) Fr. sur, luminaire	sür, lü-mē-ner
		(2) Ger. über, Führer	üb'ər, fü'rər
		(3) Scots bluid, buik	blüd, bük

Nasalised vowels

Symbol		Examples	Pronunciation
ä	as in	sang, temps, dent	sä, tä, dä
ɛ̃	„	faim, vin, plein	fɛ̃, vɛ̃, plɛ̃
ɔ̃	„	tomber, long, sonde	tɔ̃-bä, lɔ̃, sɔ̃d
œ̃	„	lundi, humble, un	lœ̃-dē, œ̃bl', œ̃

An apostrophe is used to mark such pronunciations as t'h (representing the sound of two separate consonants, t followed by h) to distinguish this from the sound th (as in thin). It is also used in words such as timbre (tɛ̃br'), maître (metr') and humble (œ̃bl') in the pronunciation of which a final ə (e.g. tɛ̃-brə) is possible.

Vowels in Bold-faced Entries

A breve, ˘, is used to show the pronunciation of certain short vowels in bold-faced entries. These vowels are to be pronounced as follows:

Symbol	Pronunciation	Symbol	Pronunciation
ă	a, ə	ĭ, ў̆	i
ĕ	e	ŏ	o

The long vowels ā, ē, ī, ō, ū have the values ä, ē, ī, ō, ū; ȳ is to be pronounced ī.

Notes on American English

Despite increased contact and communication between Britain and America there are still major differences in the forms of English spoken and written in the two countries.

Spelling differences in a number of individual words (e.g. *maneuver, defense,* and *practice* as a verb) have been noted in the dictionary. Groups of words in which the spelling is different are as follows:

Brit.	U.S.	
our	or	American spellings such as *color, humor,* have often been noted in the text.
re	er	*center, meter, reconnoiter, saltpeter, theater,* etc.
		But, to show the hard sound of *c* or *g: acre, lucre, massacre, ogre,* etc.
ll	l	Americans have single *l* in all derivatives in *-ed, -ing, -er* (or *-or*) of words ending in an *l: canceled, -ing, caroled, -ing, chiseled, -ing, counseled, -ing, -or, disheveled, -ing, equaled, -ing, imperiled, -ing, jeweled, -ing, -er, libeled, -ing, -er, reveled, -ing, -er, traveled, -ing, -er, victualed, -ing, -er,* etc. Also *woolen, marvelous.*
l or ll	ll	*enroll, enthrall, instill, thralldom.*
l	ll	In *fulfill, skillful, willful.*
		In nouns in *-ment: enrollment, enthrallment, fulfillment, installment.*
pp	p	*kidnaped, -ing, -er, worshiped, -ing, -er.*
tt	t	*carbureted, -er, sulfureted.*
ae, oe or e	e	The tendency to replace *ae* and *oe* in words from Greek or Latin by *e* is more strongly developed in the United States than in Britain: e.g. *etiology, hemoglobin, esophagus.*
ise or ize	ize	In verbs and their derivatives that may be spelt *-ise* or *-ize.* Americans prefer *-ize.*

American pronunciation is naturally not the same in all areas and in all classes, but generally speaking it shows differences from British English pronunciation in the following respects (not specifically noted in the dictionary):

Brit.	U.S.
ă	Various shorter forms of the vowel are common in place of English *ä.*
i	Where British English has *i* in final position, as in *happy,* Americans tend to pronounce the vowel *ē.*
ŏ	Alternative form *ä* is common in words such as *haunt, launch, saunter, taunt, vaunt.*
o	A longer vowel than the normal British one is heard in *coffee, long, officer, soft,* etc., (mostly words in which the vowel is followed by *f, th, s, r, g, ng*); *ä* also is widely used in these words. *Block, pond, probable, top,* etc., always have *ä.*
ū	In British English this is a diphthong; in American English it often loses its diphthongal character when preceded by *t, d, n, l,* or *s,* becoming *ōō.*
-il	In the commoner words Americans pronounce *-il,* as *agile (aj'il), fertile, fragile, futile, hostile, versatile.* In *infantile* and *juvenile,* both *-il* and *-īl* are heard; *gentile* is always pronounced *-īl; mercantile* is usually pronounced *-ēl.*
t	In words such as *batter, butter, writing,* the *-tt-/-t-* is pronounced with a sound similar or identical to that of the *-dd-/-d-* of *madder, shudder, riding.*

Vowels and diphthongs before *r*

ā	In America, this is commonly pronounced as a diphthong, the first element of which approaches a lengthened form of *e.*
	Sometimes the second element, *ə,* is not pronounced when the diphthong occurs in initial or medial position in a word; for example, the usual pronunciation of *Maryland* is *mer'i-lənd.*
a	Some Americans tend to make a sound approaching *e,* so that *marry,* for instance, approximates to *merry.*
i	The sound heard in *squirrel, stirrup,* and commonly also in *syrup,* approaches *û.*
u	In English speech, when *ur* is followed by a vowel, the sound of the *u* is not *û,* but Americans tend to pronounce the same vowel in *her* and *hurry.* Other examples are *occurring, worry,* and *courage.*
är spelt er	In words such as *clerk* and *Derby* where English speech preserves an older pronunciation *är,* American speech follows the spelling, pronouncing the words *klûrk, dûr'bi,* etc.
-ə-ri	Americans tend to give words in *-ary* and *-ory* a stronger secondary accent and to pronounce *-er'ē* and *-ôr'ē.* Examples are *necessary, monetary, secondary, temporary, obligatory, peremptory, respiratory.*

Some individual differences in the sounds of certain words and prefixes are noted in the dictionary, e.g. *tomato, schedule, simultaneous, anti-.*

Some variations in vocabulary and meaning between British English and American English are indicated in the dictionary, e.g. *bonnet, hood; braces, suspenders.* A few words used only in the U.S. are likewise indicated, e.g. *sidewalk.*

List of abbreviations used in the dictionary

abbrev.	abbreviation	*deriv.*	derivative	*lit.*	literal(ly)
abl.	ablative	*derog.*	derogatory,	*Linc.*	Lincolnshire
acc.	according		derogatorily	*log.*	logic
accus.	accusative	*dial.*	dialect(al)		
adj(s).	adjective(s)	*Dict.*	Dictionary	*m.*	masculine
adv(s).	adverb(s)	*dim.*	diminutive	*mach.*	machinery
Aen.	Aeneid	*dub.*	doubtful	*masc.*	masculine
aero.	aeronautics			*math.*	mathematics
agri.	agriculture	*E.*	East	*mech.*	mechanics
alch.	alchemy	*eccles.*	ecclesiastical	*med.*	medicine
alg.	algebra	*econ.*	economics	*metaph.*	metaphysics
anat.	anatomy	*e.g.*	(L. *exempli gratia*)	*meteor.*	meteorology
anc.	ancient(ly)		for example	*mil.*	military
ant.	antiquities	*elect.*	electricity,	*Milt.*	Milton
anthrop.	anthropology		electrical	*min.*	mineralogy
aor.	aorist	*entom.*	entomology	*mod.*	modern
app.	apparently	*erron.*	erroneous(ly)	*mus.*	music
approx.	approximately	*esp.*	especially	*myth.*	mythology
arch.	archaic	*ety.*	etymology		
archaeol.	archaeology	*euph.*	euphemistic(ally)	*N.*	North
archit.	architecture	*exc.*	except	*n(s).*	noun(s)
arith.	arithmetic			*nat. hist.*	natural history
astrol.	astrology	*f.*	feminine	*naut.*	nautical
astron.	astronomy	*facet.*	facetiously	*N.E. Bible*	New English Bible
at. numb.	atomic number	*fam.*	familiar,	*neg.*	negative
attrib.	attributive(ly)		family	*neut.*	neuter
augm.	augmentative	*fem.*	feminine	*nom.*	nominative
A.V.	Authorised	*fig.*	figurative(ly)	*North.*	Northern
	Version	*fl.*	floruit	*n.pl.*	noun plural
		fol.	followed,	*n.sing.*	noun singular
			following	*N.T.*	New Testament
B.	Bible (A.V.)	*form.*	formerly		(A.V.)
biol.	biology	*fort.*	fortification	*nuc.*	nucleonics,
bookk.	bookkeeping	*freq.*	frequentative		nuclear
bot.	botany	*F.Q.*	Faerie Queene		
Bucks.	Buckinghamshire	*fut.*	future	*obs.*	obsolete
				opp.	opposed,
c.	(L. *circa*) about	*gen.*	genitive		opposite
cap.	capital	*gener.*	generally	*opt.*	optics
cent.	century	*geog.*	geography	*org.*	organic
cf.	(L. *confer*)	*geol.*	geology	*orig.*	original(ly),
	compare	*geom.*	geometry		origin
chem.	chemistry,	*ger.*	gerundive	*O.S.*	Old Style
	chemical	*gram.*	grammar	*O.T.*	Old Testament
Ch. of Eng.	Church of England	*Gr. Ch.*	Greek Church		(A.V.)
cog.	cognate				
coll.	colloquial(ly)	*her.*	heraldry	*p.*	participle
collec.	collectively	*hist.*	history	*p.adj.*	participial
comp.	composition	*hort.*	horticulture		adjective
compar.	comparative	*hyperb.*	hyperbolically	*paint.*	painting
comput.	computers,			*palaeog.*	palaeography
	computing	*i.e.*	(L. *id est*) that is	*pa.p.*	past participle
conj(s).	conjunction(s)	*illit.*	illiterate	*part.*	participle
conn.	connected,	*imit.*	imitative	*pass.*	passive
	connection	*imper.*	imperative	*pa.t.*	past tense
contr.	contracted,	*impers.*	impersonal(ly)	*path.*	pathology
	contraction	*incl.*	including	*perf.*	perfect
cook.	cookery	*indic.*	indicative	*perh.*	perhaps
corr.	corruption,	*infin.*	infinitive	*pers.*	person(al)
	corresponding	*infl.*	influenced	*petr.*	petrology
crystal.	crystallography	*intens.*	intensive	*pfx.*	prefix
		interj(s).	interjection(s)	*philol.*	philology
dat.	dative	*interrog.*	interrogative(ly)	*philos.*	philosophy
demons.	demonstrative	*intrans.*	intransitive	*phon.*	phonetics
der.	derived,	*iron.*	ironic	*phot.*	photography
	derivation	*irreg.*	irregular(ly)	*phys.*	physics

physiol.	physiology	*redup.*	reduplication	*term.*	termination
pl.	plural	*refl.*	reflexive(ly)	*theat.*	theatre,
poet.	poetical	*rel.*	related, relative		theatrical
pol. econ.	political economy	*rhet.*	rhetoric	*theol.*	theology
pop.	popular(ly)	*R.V.*	Revised Version	*trans.*	transitive,
poss.	possessive,				translation
	possibly			*trig.*	trigonometry
Pr. Bk.	Book of Common			*TV*	television
	Prayer	*S*	South		
pr.p.	present participle	*sculp.*	sculpture		
prep(s).	preposition(s)	*Shak.*	Shakespeare	*ult.*	ultimately
pres.	present	*sig.*	signifying	*usu.*	usually
pret.	preterite	*sing.*	singular		
print.	printing	*South.*	Southern		
priv.	privative	*specif.*	specifically	*vb(s).*	verb(s)
prob.	probably	*Spens.*	Spenser	*v(s).i.*	verb(s)
pron(s).	pronoun(s)	*subj.*	subjective		intransitive
pron.	pronunciation	*suff.*	suffix	*voc.*	vocative
prop.	properly	*superl(s).*	superlative(s)	*v(s).t.*	verb(s) transitive
pros.	prosody	*surg.*	surgery	*vulg.*	vulgar
psych.	psychology	*s.v.*	(L. *sub verba*)		
			under the word		
q.v., qq.v.(pl.) which see		*symb.*	symbol	*W.*	West
®	registered	*telecomm.*	telecommunica-	*Yorks.*	Yorkshire
	trademark		tions		
R.C.	Roman Catholic	*teleg.*	telegraphy		
		Tenn.	Tennyson	*zool.*	zoology

A.Fr.	Anglo-French	*Hind.*	Hindustani	*O.N.,*	Old Norse
Afrik.	Afrikaans	*Hung.*	Hungarian	*O.N.Fr.*	Old Northern
Amer.	American				French
Angl.	Anglian	*Icel.*	Icelandic	*O.Sax.*	Old Saxon
Ar.	Arabic		(Modern)		
Assyr.	Assyrian	*Ind.*	Indian		
Austr.	Australian	*Ir.*	Irish	*Pers.*	Persian
		It.	Italian	*Peruv.*	Peruvian
Bav.	Bavarian			*Pol.*	Polish
Beng.	Bengali	*Jap.*	Japanese	*Port.*	Portuguese
Bohem.	Bohemian	*Jav.*	Javanese	*Prov.*	Provençal
Braz.	Brazilian				
Brit.	British	*L.*	Latin		
		L.G(er).	Low German	*Rom.*	Roman
Can.	Canadian	*Lith.*	Lithuanian	*Russ.*	Russian
Celt.	Celtic	*L.L.*	Low or Late		
Chin.	Chinese		Latin		
Copt.	Coptic			*S.Afr.*	South African
Corn.	Cornish	*M.Du.*	Middle Dutch	*Sans.*	Sanskrit
		M.E.	Middle English	*Scand.*	Scandinavian
Dan.	Danish	*Mex.*	Mexican	*Scot.*	Scottish
Du.	Dutch	*M.Flem.*	Middle Flemish		(Broad Scots)
		M.Fr.	Middle French	*Serb.*	Serbian
Egypt.	Egyptian	*M.H.G.*	Middle High	*Sinh.*	Sinhalese
Eng.	English		German	*Slav.*	Slavonic
		M.L.G.	Middle Low	*Sp.*	Spanish
Finn.	Finnish		German	*Sw.*	Swedish
Flem.	Flemish				
Fr.	French	*Norm.*	Norman	*Turk.*	Turkish
Fris.	Frisian	*Norw.*	Norwegian		
		N.Z.	New Zealand	*U.K.*	United Kingdom
Gael.	Gaelic			*U.S.*	United States
Ger.	German	*O.E.*	Old English		(often includes
Gmc.	Germanic	*O.Fr.*	Old French		Canadian)
Goth.	Gothic	*O.Fris.*	Old Frisian		
Gr.	Greek	*O.H.G.*	Old High		
			German	*W.*	Welsh
Heb.	Hebrew	*O.Ir.*	Old Irish	*W.S.*	West Saxon

A

A, a *ā, n.* the first letter in our alphabet (see **alpha**): in music, the major sixth of the scale of C: first class or order, or a class arbitrarily designated A: see **blood-group**: in road-classification, followed by a number, indicating a major, or trunk, road. —**A1** (*ā wun*) the symbol for a first-class vessel in Lloyd's Register: hence first-rate; **A'-bomb** atomic bomb; **A'-level** (*n., adj.*) (an examination at the end of a school course) demanding an advanced knowledge of a school subject:~a pass in an A-level; **A'-road** a trunk or a principal road.—**from A to B** from one point or place to another; **from A to Z** from beginning to end.

a¹ *a,* also (esp. emphatic) *ā, adj.* the indefinite article, a broken down form of **an** used before a consonant sound. [O.E. *ān,* one.]

a² *a.* A reduced form of the O.E. prep. *an, on,* on, in, at, chiefly used as a prefix, as *abroad, asleep,* occasionally used separately as a preposition, as *once a year.*

aardvark *ärt'färk'* (S.Afr.), *ärd'värk, n.* the ant-bear, a South African edentate. [Du. *aarde,* earth, *vark* (now *varken*), pig.]

aardwolf *ärt'volf'* (S.Afr.), *ärd'wŏŏlf, n.* a hyena-like South African carnivore. [Du. *aarde,* earth, *wolf,* wolf.]

Aaronic, -al *ā-ron'ik, -l, adjs.* pertaining to Aaron, the Jewish high-priest: pontifical.—**Aaron's beard** a saxifrage: the great St John's wort, or other plant; **Aaron's rod** mullein, golden-rod, or other plant.

ab- *ab-, pfx.* used to indicate a centimetre-gram-second electromagnetic unit (e.g. **abam'pere** equivalent to 10 amperes). [**absolute.**]

aba, abba *a'ba,* or **abaya** *a-bä'ya, ns.* a Syrian cloth, of goat's or camel's hair, usually striped: an outer garment made of it. [Ar. *'abā, 'abāya.*]

abaca *ä-bä-kä', n.* a plantain grown in the Philippine Islands: its fibre, called Manila hemp. [Tagálog.]

abaci. See **abacus.**

aback *a-bak', adv.* backwards: said of sails pressed backward against the mast by the wind (*naut.*)—hence (*fig.*) **taken aback** taken by surprise. [O.E. *on bæc,* on back.]

abacus *ab'a-kas, n.* a counting-frame:—*pl.* **ab'aci** (*-sī*), **ab'acuses.** [L. *abacus*—Gr. *abax, -akos.*]

abaft *a-bäft',* (*naut.*) *adv.* and *prep.* behind. [Prep. **a** and O.E. *bæftan,* after—pfx. *be-, æftan.* See **aft.**]

abalone *ab-a-lō'nä, n.* an edible shellfish. [Amer. Sp. *abulón.*]

abampere. See **ab-.**

abandon *a-ban'dan, v.t.* to give up: to desert: to yield (oneself) without restraint: to give up all claims to.—*n.* (sometimes as Fr. *ä-bä-dõ*) the condition of letting oneself go: careless freedom of action.—*adj.* **aban'-doned** completely deserted: given up, as to a vice: profligate: very wicked.—*adv.* **aban'donedly.**—*ns.* **abandonee'** (*law*) an insurer to whom a wreck has been abandoned; **aban'donment.** [O.Fr. *abandoner,* to put at one's disposal or in one's control (*à bundon*); see **ban.**]

abase *a-bäs', v.t.* to lower: to cast down: to humble: to degrade.—*adj.* **abased'** lowered.—*n.* **abase'ment.** [O.Fr. *abaissier*—L. *ad,* to, L.L. *bassus,* low.]

abash *a-bash', v.t.* to strike with shame: to put out of countenance: to astound: to confound.—*adjs.*

abashed'; abash'less shameless: unabashed.—*n.* **abash'ment.** [O.Fr. *esbahir*—pfx. *es-* (L. *ex,* out), *bahir,* to astound.]

abate *a-bät', v.t.* to put an end to (*law*): to nullify, to bring down (*law*): to lessen: to deduct (with *of*): to mitigate: to blunt.—*v.i.* to grow less: to subside: to be abated (*law*).—*adjs.* **abāt'able; abāt'ed** blunted: diminished: lowered: subdued: beaten down or cut away, as the background of relief.—*n.* **abate'ment** the act or process of abating: the sum or quantity abated: the state of being abated. [O.Fr. *abatre,* to beat down—L. *ab,* from, and L.L. *batĕre,* for L. *batuĕre,* to beat.]

abattoir *ab'a-twär, n.* a public slaughterhouse. [Fr.; see **abate.**]

abaya, abba. See **aba.**

abbacy *ab'a-si, n.* the office or jurisdiction of abbot: the time during which one is abbot: an abbey.—*adj.* **abbatial** (*ab-ä'shl*). [App. orig. Scot.: L.L. *abbātia,* abbey.]

abbé *ab'ā, n.* a courtesy title for a priest, an ecclesiastic in minor orders, or for a tutor or holder of a benefice, even if a layman. [Fr., orig. abbot.]

abbess *ab'es, n.* a woman who is head of an abbey. [L.L. *abbātissa,* fem. of *abbās,* abbot.]

abbey *ab'i, n.* a convent under an abbot or abbess, or (*loosely*) a prior or prioress: the church now or formerly attached to it: a name often retained by an abbatial building that has become a private house:—*pl.* **abb'eys.** [O.Fr. *abaïe* (Fr. *abbaye*)—L.L. *abbātia.* See **abbacy.**]

abbot *ab'at, n.* a male head of an abbey:—*fem.* **abb'ess.**—*n.* **abb'otship.** [L.L. *abbās, abbātis*—Aramaic *abbā.*]

abbreviate *a-brē'vi-āt, v.t.* to shorten: to contract: to abridge.—*adj.* shortened.—*ns.* **abbrēviā'tion** an act of shortening: a shortened form, esp of a word; **abbrē'viātor.**—*adj.* **abbrē'viatory** (*-a-tor-i*). [L. *abbreviāre, -ātum*—*ab,* intens., *brevis,* short.]

ABC *ā-bē-sē', n.* the alphabet, from its first letters: first rudiments: anything arranged alphabetically.

abdabs. See **habdabs.**

abdicate *ab'di-kāt, v.t.* and *v.i.* formally to renounce or give up (office or dignity).—*adjs.* **ab'dicable; ab'dicant.**—*n.* **abdicā'tion.** [L. *ab,* from or off, *dicāre, -ātum,* to proclaim.]

abdomen *ab'd-man, ab-dō'man, n.* the belly: in mammals, the part between diaphragm and pelvis: in arthropods, the hind-body.—*adj.* **abdominal** (*-dom'*).—*adv.* **abdom'inally.**—*adj.* **abdom'inous** pot-bellied. [L. *abdōmen, -inis.*]

abduce *ab-dūs', v.t.* an earlier form of **abduct.**—*adj.* **abdūc'ent** drawing back: separating.—*v.t.* **abduct** (*-dukt'*) to take away by fraud or violence: to kidnap.—*ns.* **abduction** (*-duk'shan*) the carrying away, esp. of a person by fraud or force: muscular action drawing one part away from another; **abduc'tor** one who abducts: a muscle that draws away. [L. *abducĕre*—*ab,* from, *ducĕre, ductum,* to draw, lead.]

abeam *a-bēm',* (*naut.*) *adv.* on the beam, or in a line at right angles to a vessel's length. [Prep. **a,** and **beam.**]

abecedarian *ā-bi-sē-dā'ri-an, adj.* pertaining to the ABC: rudimentary: arranged in the manner of an acrostic.—*n.* a learner of the ABC, a beginner. [ABC.]

abed *a-bed'*, *adv.* in bed. [Prep. **a**, and **bed¹**.]

abele *a-bēl'*, *ā'bl*, *n.* the white poplar-tree. [Du. *abeel*—O.Fr. *abel*, *aubel*—L.L. *albellus*—L. *albus*, white.]

Aberdeen *ab-ər-dēn'*, sometimes *ab'*, *adj.* of or originating in *Aberdeen* or Aberdeenshire.—*n.* (in full **Aberdeen terrier**) a coarse-haired kind of Scottish terrier.—*adj.* **Aberdō'nian** of Aberdeen.—Also *n.*—**Aberdeen Angus** (*ang'gəs*) a breed of polled cattle.

Abernethy biscuit *ab-ər-neth'i*, *-nēth'i*, or *ab'*, *bis'kit* a hard biscuit, apparently originally with caraway seeds. [Poss. after Dr John *Abernethy* (1764–1831).]

aberrate *ab'ər-āt*, *v.i.* to wander or deviate from the right way.—*ns.* **aberrance** (*-er'*), **aberr'ancy.**—*adj.* **aberr'ant** wandering: having characteristics not strictly in accordance with type (*bot.*, *zool.*).—*n.* **aberra'tion** (*-ər-*) a deviation from the usual, normal, or right: a wandering of the intellect, mental lapse: a non-convergence of rays (*opt.*): displacement of a star (*astron*). [L. *aberrāre*, *-ātum*—*ab*, from, *errāre*, to wander.]

abet *a-bet'*, *v.t.* to incite by encouragement or aid (used chiefly in a bad sense):—*pr.p.* **abett'ing;** *pa.t.* **abett'ed.**—*ns.* **abet'ment; abett'er,** (esp. *legal*) **abett'or.** [O.Fr. *abeter*—*à* (L. *ad*, to), and *beter*, to bait; see **bait**.]

abeyance *a-bā'əns*, *n.* a state of suspension or temporary inactivity: the state of being without a claimant (as a peerage).—Also **abey'ancy.** [O.Fr. *abeance*—*à* (L. *ad*, to), and *beer*, *baer*, to gape, open wide.]

abhor *ab-hör'*, *v.t.* to shrink from with horror: to detest: to loathe:—*pr.p.* **abhorr'ing;** *pa.t.* and *pa.p.* **abhorred'.**—*n.* **abhorr'ence** (*-hor'*) extreme hatred: a thing abhorred.—*adj.* **abhorr'ent** detesting: repugnant: strongly opposed: out of keeping: detestable: detested.—*adv.* **abhorr'ently.**—*ns.* **abhorr'er; abhorr'ing** repugnance: an object of abhorrence. [L. *abhorrēre* —*ab*, from, and *horrēre*, to bristle, shudder.]

abide *a-bīd'*, *v.t.* to bide or wait for: to meet, face, sustain: to endure: to tolerate.—*v.i.* to remain: to dwell or stay: to conform, adhere (with *by*):—*pa.t.* **abode'**, also **abid'ed;** *pa.p.* **abode'**, **abid'ed**, also **abidd'en.**—*n.* **abid'ance.**—*adj.* **abid'ing** continual, permanent.—*adv.* **abid'ingly.** [O.E. *ābīdan*—pfx. *ā-*, and *bīdan*, to wait.]

à bientôt *a byē-tō*, (Fr.) see you again soon.

Abies *ab'i-ēz*, *n.* the genus of the true firs: (without *cap.*) a tree of the genus.

abigail *ab'i-gāl*, *n.* a lady's-maid. [From *Abigail*, in Beaumont and Fletcher's *Scornful Lady*, or 1 Sam. xxv.]

ability *a-bil'i-ti*, *n.* the quality or fact of being able (to): power (physical and mental): strength: skill. [O.Fr. *ableté* (Fr. *habileté*), remodelled on its source, L. *habilitās*, *-ātis*—*habēre*, to have, hold; see **able**.]

ab initio *ab in-ish'i-ō*, *-it'i-ō*, (L.) from the beginning.

abiosis *ā-bī-ō'sis*, *n.* absence of life.—*adj.* **abiot'ic** without life: inanimate. [Gr. *a-*, neg., *biotikos*—*bios*, life.]

abject *ab'jekt*, *adj.* cast away: mean: worthless: grovelling: base.—*n.* an outcast: a base slave.—*n.* **abjec'tion** abjectness: casting forth: forcible expulsion of spores (*bot.*).—*adv.* **abject'ly.**—*n.* **abject'ness.** [L. *abjicĕre*, *abjectum*—*ab*, from, *jacĕre*, to throw.]

abjure *ab-jōōr'*, *v.t.* to renounce on oath or solemnly: to recant: to repudiate.—*ns.* **abjura'tion; abjur'er.** [L. *ab*, from, *jurāre*, *-ātum*, to swear.]

ablactation *ab-lak-tā'shən*, *n.* a weaning. [L. *ab*, from, *lactāre*, to suckle—*lac*, milk.]

ablation *ab-lā'shən*, *n.* removal: decrease by melting, evaporation, weathering.—*v.t.* **ablate** (*ab-lāt'*).—

adj. **ab'lative** (*-la-tiv*) pertaining to ablation: in or belonging to a case which in Indo-European languages originally expressed *direction from*, or *time when*, later extended to other functions (*gram.*).—*n.* the ablative case: a word in the ablative.—*adj.* **ablati'val** —*n.* **abla'tor** for the heat shield of a spacecraft. [L. *ab*, from, *lātum*, used as supine of *ferre*, to take.]

ablaut *āp'lowt*, *ab'lowt*, (*philol.*) *n.* a variation in root vowel as in sing, sang, song, sung. [Ger., *ab*, off, *Laut*, sound.]

ablaze *a-blāz'*, *adv.* and *adj.* in a blaze, on fire: gleaming brightly. [Prep. **a**, and **blaze**.]

able *ā'bl*, *adj.* having enough strength, power or means (to do a thing): skilful.—*adj.* **a'ble-bod'ied** free from disability, etc.: robust.—*adv.* **a'bly.**—**able seaman**, **able-bodied seaman**, rating (abbrev. A.B.) one able to perform all the duties of seamanship and having a higher rating than the ordinary sailor. [See **ability**.] -**able** *-ə-bl*, *adj. suff.* capable of being.—*n. suff.* **-ability.**—*adv. suff.* **-ably.**—See also **-ible.**

ablution *a-blōō'shən*, *n.* (often in *pl.*) the act of washing, esp. the body: ceremonial washing: (*sing.*) the wine and water used to rinse the chalice, drunk by the officiating priest.—*adj.* **ablu'tionary.** [L *ablūtiō*, *-ōnis*—*ab*, away, *luĕre*, to wash.]

abnegate *ab'ni-gāt*, *v.t.* to deny: to renounce —*ns.* **abnega'tion; ab'negator.** [L. *ab*, away, *negāre*, to deny.]

abnormal *ab-nör'ml*, *adj.* not normal.—*ns.* **abnor'malism; abnormality** (*-nör-mal'i-ti*).—*adv.* **abnor'mally.**—*n.* **abnor'mity.** [Fr. *anormal*—L.L. *anormalus*—Gr. *anōmalos* (see **anomaly**).]

abo. See **aborigine**.

aboard *a-börd'*, *-börd'*, *adv.* or *prep.* on board: in or into a ship, railway train, etc.: alongside. [Prep. **a**, on, and **board**.]

abode *a-bōd'*, *n.* a dwelling-place: a stay.—*v.t.* and *v.i.*, *pa.t.* and *pa.p.* of **abide**.—**of no fixed abode** having no permanent address (*legal*).

ab officio et beneficio *ab o-fish'i-ō* (*-fik'*) *et ben-e-fish'i-ō* (*-fik'*), (L.L.) from office and benefice—of a clergyman suspended.

abolish *a-bol'ish*, *v.t.* to put an end to.—*adj.* **abol'ishable.**—*ns.* **abol'ishment** (*rare*); **aboli'tion.**—*adjs.* **aboli'tional, aboli'tionary.**—*ns.* **aboli'tionism; aboli'tionist** one who seeks to abolish anything, e.g. slavery, capital punishment. [L. *abolēre*, *-itum*, partly through Fr.]

abomasum *ab-ō-mā'səm*, *n.* the fourth or true stomach of ruminants.—Also **aboma'sus.** [L. *ab*, away from, *omāsum*, tripe, paunch.]

abominate *a-bom'in-āt*, *v.t.* to abhor: to detest.—*adj.* **abom'inable** hateful: detestable.—*n.* **abom'inableness.**—*adv.* **abom'inably.**—*ns.* **abomina'tion** extreme aversion: an object of detestation; **abom'inator.**—**abominable snowman** a mythical hairy manlike creature supposed to live in the snows of Tibet—also **yeti.** [L. *abōmināri*, *-ātus*, to turn from as of bad omen; see **omen**.]

abundance. See **abundance**.

ab origine *ab ō-rij'in-e*, *-rēg'in-e*, (L.) from the very first, from the source.

aborigine *ab-ə-rij'i-nē*, *-ni*, *n.* an original or native inhabitant of a country, esp. (often with *cap.*) Australia.—*offensive abbrev.* **abo** (*ab'ō*):—*pl.* **abos.**—*adj.* **aborig'inal** (often with *cap.*) earliest, primitive, indigenous.—*n.* (often with *cap.*) an aborigine.—*n.* **aboriginality** (*-al'i-ti*).—*adv.* **aborig'inally.** [L. (*pl.*) *aborigines*—*ab*, from *origō*, *-inis* beginning.]

abort *a-bört'*, *v.i.* to miscarry in birth: to come to nothing.—*v.t.* to cause to abort: to check, stop or call off (an attack, the flight of a rocket, a mission, etc.) at an early stage.—*n.* an instance of abortion (esp. of rocket).—*n.* **aborticide** (*-i-sīd*) foeticide.—*adj.* **abortifacient** (*-i-fā'shənt, -shi-ənt*) causing abortion. —*n.* means of causing abortion.—*n.* **abor'tion** the premature expulsion of an embryo or a foetus, or the procuring of this, esp. in the first three months of pregnancy: anything that fails in course of coming into being or completion; **abor'tionist.**—*adj.* **abor'tive** unsuccessful: brought forth in an imperfect condition: checked in development.—*adv.* **abort'ively.** —*n.* **abort'iveness.**—**contagious abortion** contagious bacterial infections of cattle and of horses, causing abortion. [L. *aborīrī, abortus*—pfx. *ab-*, reversing the meaning, *orīrī*, to rise.]

aboulia, abulia *a-bōō'li-ə, -bow', -bū', n.* loss of willpower: inability to make decisions [Gr. *a-*, priv., *boulē,* will.]

abound *ə-bownd', v.i.* to be in great plenty: to be rich (with *in*): to be filled (with *with*).—*adj.* **abound'ing.** [O.Fr. *abunder*—L. *abundāre,* to overflow—*ab,* from, *unda,* a wave.]

about *ə-bowt', prep.* round on the outside of: around: here and there in: near in place, time, size, etc.: on the person of: connected with: concerning: engaged in.—*adv.* around: halfway round, in the opposite direction (e.g. *to face about*): nearly: here and there: on the opposite tack: in motion or activity.—**about's face** a complete change of opinion, attitude, etc.— Also *v.i.*—Also **about'-turn.**—**about to** (do, etc.), on the point of (doing etc.); **be about** to be astir; **bring about** to cause to take place; **come about** to happen in the course of time; **go about** to prepare to do; **turn about** alternately: in rotation. [O.E. *onbūtan—on,* in, *būtan,* without.]

above *ə-buv', prep.* over: in or to a position higher than that of: beyond in degree, amount, etc.: too magnanimous or proud for.—*adv.* overhead: in a higher position, order, or power: in an earlier passage: in heaven.—*adj.* mentioned, etc. in an earlier passage. —*adjs.* **above'-board** open, without deception; **above'-mentioned; above'-named.**—**above oneself** elated: conceited. [Late O.E. *ābufan*—O.E. *ā-,* on, *bufan,* above.]

abracadabra *ab-rə-kə-dab'rə, n.* a magic word: a spell or conjuring word: gibberish. [Found in a 2nd-cent. poem.]

abrade *ə-brād', v.t.* to wear down or off.—*adj.* and *n.* **abra'dant.** [L. *ab,* from, *rādēre, rāsum,* to scrape.]

abranchiate *ə-brang'ki-āt, adj.* without gills. [Gr. *a-,* priv., *branchia,* gills.]

abrasion *ə-brā'zhən, n.* a wearing away: a worn-down or grazed place.—*adj.* **abra'sive** (*-ziv, -siv*) tending to abrade: harsh: of a person, tending to irritate or annoy.—*n.* a substance used to remove matter by scratching and grinding. [See **abrade.**]

abraxas *ə-braks'əs, n.* a mystic word, or a gem engraved therewith, often bearing a mystical figure of combined human and animal form, used as a charm. [Said to express 365 by addition of the numerical values of the Greek letters.]

abreaction *ab-rē-ak'shən,* (*psych.*) *n.* the resolution of a neurosis by reviving forgotten or repressed ideas of the event first causing it.—*v.i.* **abreact'.** [L. *ab,* from, and **reaction.**]

abreast *ə-brest', adv.* with fronts in line: side by side: keeping pace with (with *of*). [Prep **a,** on, and **breast.**]

abridge *ə-brij', v.t.* to shorten: to epitomise: to curtail —*ns.* **abridg'er; abridg'ment** (sometimes **abridge'-ment**) contraction: shortening: an epitome or synopsis. [O.Fr. *abregier*—L. *abbreviāre.*]

abroad *ə-bröd', adv.* over a wide area: out of doors: at large: current: in or to another country: astray. [Prep. **a,** and **broad.**]

abrogate *ab'rō-gāt, v.t.* to annul.—*n.* **abroga'tion.**— *adj.* **ab'rogative.**—*n.* **ab'rogator.** [L. *ab,* away, *rogāre, -ātum,* to ask, or to propose a law.]

abrupt *ə-brupt', adj.* truncated: as if broken off: sudden: unexpected: precipitous: (of manners) short, rude.—*n.* **abrup'tion** (*-shən*) a breaking off—*adv.* **abrupt'ly.**—*n.* **abrupt'ness.** [L. *abruptus*—*ab,* from, *rumpĕre, ruptum,* to break.]

abscess *ab'ses, -sis, n.* a collection of pus in a cavity. [L. *abscessus*—*abs,* from, *cēdĕre, cessum,* to go, retreat.]

abscind *ab-sind', v.t.* to cut off —*n.* **abscissa** (*-sis'ə*), also **absciss, abscisse** (*ab'sis*) the intercept between a fixed point and the foot of an ordinate: the *x*-co-ordinate in analytical geometry:—*pl.* **abscissae** (*ab-sis'ē, -sis'ī*), **absciss'as, ab'scisses.**—*n.* **abscission** (*-sizh'ən*) an act of cutting off, or state of being cut off: organised shedding of a part (*bot.*). [L. *abscin-dĕre, abscissum,* to cut off—*ab,* from, *scindĕre,* to cut.]

abscond *ab-skond', v.i* to hide, or get out of the way, esp. to escape a legal process.—*ns.* **abscond'ence; abscond'er.** [L. *abscondĕre*—*abs,* from, *condĕre,* to hide.]

abseil *ap'zīl, ab-sīl', v.i* to let oneself down a rock face using a double rope.—*n.* **abseiling.** [Ger *ab,* down, *Seil,* rope.]

absent *ab'sənt, adj.* not present: inattentive.—*v.t.* (*ab-sent'*; usu. *refl.*) to keep away.—*ns.* **ab'sence** the state of being not present: want: non-existence: inattention; **absentee'** one who is absent: one who makes a habit of living away from his estate or his office; **absentee'ism** the practice of absenting oneself from duty, etc.—*adv.* **ab'sently.**—*adj.* **ab'sent-mind'ed** inattentive to surroundings: preoccupied.— *adv.* **ab'sent-mind'edly.**—*n.* **ab'sent-mind'edness.** [L. *absēns, -sentis,* pr.p. of *abesse*—*ab,* away from, *esse,* to be.]

absinth(e) *ab'sinth, n.* wormwood: a liqueur containing (orig. at all events) extract of wormwood. [Fr. *absinthe*—Gr. *apsinthion.*]

absolute *ab'sal-ōōt, -ūt, adj.* free from limits, restrictions, or conditions: certain, positive: complete: unlimited: free from mixture: independent of relation to other things: peremptory: unrestricted by constitutional checks: out of ordinary syntactic relation (*gram.*): existing in and by itself without necessary relation to anything else (*philos.*).—*n.* (with **the;** often *cap.*) that which is absolute, self-existent, uncaused.—*adv.* **ab'solutely** separately, by itself: unconditionally: positively: completely—as a colourless but emphatic affirmative (*-lōōt'li, -lūt'*). —*ns.* **ab'soluteness; absolu'tion** release from punishment: acquittal: remission of sins, declared officially by a priest; **ab'solutism** government by a ruler without restriction: adherence to the doctrine of the Absolute; **ab'solutist.**—Also *adj.*—*adj.* **absolutory** (*ab-sol'ū-tər-i*) of, or giving, absolution.—**absolute alcohol** water-free alcohol; **absolute magnitude** the magnitude that a star would have at a standard distance of 10 parsecs; **absolute majority** a majority, in an election, etc., which is greater than the total number of votes for all other candidates; **absolute pitch** (recognition of) the pitch of a note as determined by the number of vibrations per second; **absolute privilege** (*law*) a privilege that protects members of a law-making body, in making (even malicious) statements from the floor, from possible charges under the laws of slander; **absolute temperature** temperature measured on the Kelvin scale or Rankine scale; **absolute zero** the zero of the absolute scale of temperature (approx. – 273°C). [L. *absolūtus,* pa.p. of *absolvĕre;* see **absolve.**]

absolve *ab-zolv'*, *-solv'*, *v.t.* to loose or set free (from): to pardon: to give absolution to or for: to acquit: to discharge (from).—*n.* **absolv'er.** [L. *absolvēre*—*ab*, from, *solvĕre*, to loose.]

absorb *ab-sörb'*, *-zörb'*, *v.t.* to suck in: to swallow up: to imbibe: to take in: to incorporate: to take up and transform (energy) instead of transmitting or reflecting: to engage wholly.—*n.* **absorbabil'ity.**—*adj.* **absorb'able.**—*adj.* **absorbed** swallowed up: entirely occupied.—*adv.* **absorb'edly.**—*n.* **absorb'ency.**—*adj.* **absorb'ent** absorbing: able to absorb.—*n.* that which absorbs.—*n.* **absorb'er.**—*adj.* **absorb'ing** engrossing the attention.—*adv.* **absorb'ingly.**—*n.* **absorp'tion** the act of absorbing: entire occupation of mind.—*adj.* **absorp'tive** having power to absorb. —*ns.* **absorp'tiveness, absorptiv'ity.**—**absorption bands, lines** dark bands, lines, interrupting a spectrum. [L. *ab*, from, *sorbēre, sorptum*, to suck in.]

abstain *ab-stān'*, *v.i.* to hold or refrain (from).—*ns.* **abstain'er** one who abstains, esp. from alcoholic drinks; **absten'tion.** [Fr. *abstenir*—L. *abs*, from, *tenēre*, to hold.]

abstemious *ab-stē'mi-əs*, *adj.* sparing in food, drink, or enjoyments.—*adv.* **abstē'miously.**—*n.* **abstē'miousness.** [L. *abstēmius*—*abs*, from, *tēmētum*, strong wine.]

absterge *ab-stûrj'*, *v.t.* to wipe: to cleanse: to purge.—*adj.* **absterg'ent.**—*n.* a cleansing agent.—*n.* **abster'sion.**—*adj.* **abster'sive** having the quality of cleansing: purgative.—Also *n.* [L. *abstergēre, -tersum*, to wipe away—*abs*, from, *tergēre*, to wipe.]

abstinent *ab'stin-ənt*, *adj.* abstaining: temperate.—*ns.* **ab'stinence** an abstaining or refraining, especially from some indulgence (with *from*); **ab'stinency** the quality of being abstinent.—*adv.* **ab'stinently.** [L. *abstinēns, -entis*, pr.p. of *abstinēre*; see **abstain.**]

abstract *ab-strakt'*, *v.t.* to separate: to remove quietly: to purloin: to summarise: to form a general concept from consideration of particular instances.—*n.* (*ab'strakt*) a summary, abridgment: that which represents the essence: an abstraction.—*adj.* (*ab'strakt*) abstracted: existing only as a mental concept—opp. to *concrete*: theoretical: (of terms) denoting a quality of a thing apart from the thing, as 'redness': representing ideas in geometric and other designs (*paint.* and *sculp.*).—*adj.* **abstract'ed** drawn off (with *from*): removed: absent in mind.—*adv.* **abstract'edly.**—*ns.* **abstract'edness; abstrac'ter, abstrac'tor; abstrac'tion** the act or process of abstracting: the state of being abstracted: abstract quality or character: absence of mind: a thing existing only in idea: a theory: an abstract term: an abstract composition (*paint.* and *sculp.*).—*adj.* **abstrac'tional.**—*n.* **abstrac'tionist** one dealing in abstractions or unrealities.—*adj.* **abstrac'tive** able or tending to abstract: formed by or pertaining to abstraction.—*n.* anything abstractive: an abstract.—*adv.* **ab'stractly.**—*n.* **ab'stractness.—in the abstract** as an abstraction: in theory. [L. *abs*, away from, *trahĕre, tractum*, to draw.]

abstrict *ab-strikt'*, (*biol.*) *v.t.* to set free (spores, etc.), esp. by constriction of the stalk.—*n.* **abstric'tion.** [L. *ab*, from, *stringĕre, strictum*, to tie.]

abstruse *ab-strōōs'*, *adj.* remote from apprehension: difficult to understand.—*adv.* **abstruse'ly.**—*n.* **abstruse'ness.** [L. *abstrūsus*, thrust away—*abs*, away, *trūdĕre, trūsum*, to thrust.]

absurd *ab-sûrd'*, *adj.* opposed to reason: ridiculous.—*ns.* **absurd'ity, absurd'ness.**—*adv.* **absurd'ly.** [L. *absurdus*—*ab*, from, *surdus*, deaf, indistinct.]

abulia. See **aboulia.**

abundance *ə-bund'əns*, *n.* ample sufficiency: great plenty: a call of nine tricks (*solo whist*): also **abun-**dance (*-bund'*)).—*n.* **abund'ancy.**—*adj.* **abund'ant.**—*adv.* **abund'antly** enough: fully. [See **abound.**]

abuse *ə-būz'*, *v.t.* to make a bad use of: to take undue advantage of: to betray (as confidence): to revile: to maltreat: to violate.—*ns.* **abusage** (*ə-bū'sij*) wrong use, esp. of words or grammar; **abuse** (*ə-būs'*) wrong use: an evil or corrupt practice: hurt: betrayal (of confidence): ill usage: **abuser** (*ə-bū'zər*); **abū'sion** (*-zhən*), misuse: deception: wrong: outrage: reviling. —*adj.* **abū'sive** (*-siv*) wrong: containing, giving, of the nature of, abuse: coarsely reviling.—*adv.* **abū'sively.**—*n.* **abū'siveness.** [L. *ab*, from, *ūti, ūsus*, to use.]

abut *ə-but'*, *v.i.* to end or lean (on, upon, against).—*v.t.* to border:—*pr.p.* **abutt'ing**; *pa.t.* and *pa.p.* **abutt'ed.**—*ns.* **abut'ment** an endwise meeting or junction: that which a limb of an arch ends or rests against (*archit.*): a place of abutting; **abutt'al** abutment: (in *pl.*) boundaries; **abutt'er** one whose property abuts.—*adj.* **abutt'ing** confronting. [O.Fr. *abouter*, to touch by an end, and O.Fr. *abuter*, to touch at the end; cf. also Fr. *aboutir*, to end at—*à*, to, *bout, but*, end; see **butt⁴**.]

abysmal *ə-biz'məl*, *adj.* bottomless: unfathomable: very deep: very bad (*coll.*).—*adv.* **abys'mally.** [O.Fr. *abisme*, an abyss from a L.L. superl. of *abyssus*; see **abyss.**]

abyss *ə-bis'*, *n.* a bottomless gulf: hell: anything very deep: the depths of the sea: a measureless chasm.—*adj.* **abyss'al.** [Gr. *abyssos*, bottomless —*a-*, priv., *byssos*, depth, bottom.]

acacia *ə-kā'sh(y)ə*, *n.* a wattle, any plant of the genus *Acacia*: also applied to the *false acacia* (of the genus *Robinia*). [L.—Gr. *akakiā*.]

academy *ə-kad'ə-mi*, *n.* (orig.) Plato's school of philosophy: a higher or specialised school, or a university: a riding-school: a society for the promotion of science or art.—*adj.* **academic** (*-dem'*) of the philosophical school of Plato: of an academy or university: sceptical: scholarly: formal: theoretical only.—*n.* a Platonic philosopher: one studying or teaching at a university, esp. one who has scholarly tastes.—*adj.* **academ'ical** academic.—*n.* (in *pl.*) university garb. —*n.* **academ'icalism** close adherence to formal academic teaching.—*adv.* **academ'ically.**—*ns.* **academician** (*ə-kad-ə-mish'ən*) a member of an academy esp. of the French Academy or the R.A. or R.S.A.; **academ'icism, academ'icalism; acad'emist** an academic: an academician. [Gr. *Akadēmeiā*, the garden, outside Athens, where Plato taught.]

Acadian *ə-kā'di-ən*, *adj.* and *n.* Nova Scotian. [Fr. *Acadie*, Nova Scotia—Micmac Ind. *ākāde*, abundance.]

acajou *ak'ə-zhōō, -zhōō'*, *n.* the cashew tree or its fruit or gum: a kind of mahogany. [See **cashew.**]

acanaceous *ak-ə-nā'shəs*, (*bot.*) *adj.* prickly. [L. *acanos*, a kind of thistle—Gr. *akanos*—*akē*, a point.]

acanth *ə-kanth'*, *n.* acanthus.—*n.* **acanth'a** a thorn, prickle: a spinous process.—*adj.* **acanthā'ceous** prickly.—*n.* **acanth'in** strontium sulphate in skeletons of Radiolaria.—*adj.* **acanth'ine** of, like, ornamented with, acanthus.—*adj.* **acanth'oid** like acanthus; **acanth'ous** spiny.—*n.* **acanth'us** any plant of the prickly-leaved genus **Acanthus**: a conventionalised representation of an acanthus leaf, as in Corinthian capitals. [Gr. *akantha*, prickle, *akanthos*, acanthus—*akē*, point.]

acarus *ak'ə-rəs*, *n.* a mite:—*pl.* **ac'ari.**—*adj.* **acā'rian.** —*ns.* **acari'asis** disease due to mites; **acaricide** (*ə-kar'i-sid*), a mite killer; **ac'arid** one of the Acarida.—*n.pl.* **Acar'ida** the order of Arachnida to which mites and ticks belong.—*adjs.* and *ns.* **acar'idan, acarid'ean, acarid'ian.**—*adjs.* **ac'arine; ac'aroid** mite-like.—*ns.* **scarol'ogist; scarol'ogy.** [Gr. *akari,* a mite—*akarēs,* too short to cut—*a-,* priv., *keirein,* to cut.]

acatalectic *a-kat-ə-lek'tik,* (*pros.*) *adj.* having the full number of syllables.—*n.* an acatalectic verse. [Gr. *akatalēktos—a-,* priv.; see **catalectic.**]

acaudal *ā-kö'dl, adj.* tailless.—Also **acau'date.** [Gr. *a-,* priv., and **caudal.**]

acaulescent *ak-ö-les'ənt, adj.* having a very short stem. [Gr. *a-,* priv., L. *caulis,* stem, and suff. *-escent.*]

accede *ək-sēd', v.i.* to come to office or dignity: to join up, become a party, hence agree or assent (with *to*).—*ns.* **accēd'ence; accēd'er.** [L. *accēdĕre, accēssum,* to go near—*ad,* to, *cēdĕre,* to go; see **cede.**]

accelerando *ak-sel-ər-an'dō,* It. *ät-chel-er-än'dō,* (*mus.*) adj. and adv. with increasing speed. [It.]

accelerate *ək-sel'ər-āt, v.t.* to increase the speed of: to hasten the progress or occurrence of.—*v.i.* to become faster.—*ns.* **accel'erant** an accelerating agent (also *adj.*); **accelerā'tion** increase of speed: rate of change of velocity: a cumulative advance ahead of the normal or theoretical: the power or means of accelerating.—*adj.* **accel'erative** quickening.—*n.* **accel'erātor** any person or thing that accelerates, esp. a substance that accelerates chemical action, a nerve or muscle that increases rate of action, an apparatus for changing the speed of a machine, or one for imparting high energies to atomic particles.—*adj.* **accel'eratory.** [L. *accelerāre, -ātum—ad,* to, *celer,* swift.]

accent *ak'sənt, n.* stress on a syllable, word, or note: a mark used to direct this stress: a mark over a letter to indicate differences of stress, pitch, length, etc.: any mode of utterance characteristic of a region, a class, or an individual: a distinguishing mark: a significant word, or words generally (*poet.*): emphasis: a touch bringing out some particular effect (*paint.*): (*pl.*) speech, language.—*v.t.* (*ək-sent'*) to express or mark the accent of: to utter: to accentuate.—*adj.* **accent'ual.**—*n.* **accentual'ity.**—*adv.* **accent'ually.**—*v.t.* **accent'uate** to mark, play, or pronounce with accent: to emphasise.—*n.* **accentuā'tion.** [L. *accentus—ad,* to, *cantus,* song.]

accentor *ak-sent'òr, -ər, n.* a member of the hedge-sparrow genus. [L., one who sings with another—*ad,* to, *cantor,* singer.]

accept *ək-sept', v.t.* to take (something offered): to receive: to reply to, engaging to comply: to understand.—*adj.* **accept'able** worth accepting: welcome, pleasing: capable of being accepted: satisfactory, adequate.—*n.* **accept'ableness.**—*adv.* **accept'ably.**—*ns.* **acceptabil'ity; accept'ance** accepting: favourable reception: acceptableness: an agreeing to terms: an accepted bill: acceptation; **accept'ancy; accept'ant** one who accepts.—*adj.* ready to receive.—*ns.* **accepta'tion** sense in which a word, etc., is understood; **accept'er; accept'or** one who accepts, esp. a bill of exchange: an impurity in semiconductor material which increases the conductivity of the material. [L. *acceptāre—accipĕre, acceptum—ad,* to, *capĕre,* to take.]

access *ak'ses, n.* approach: admittance: a way of opportunity, of approach or entrance: addition, accession: onset or attack of illness: a fit (of illness or passion).—*v.t.* to locate or retrieve information (*comput.*).—*n.* and *adj.* **access'ary** accessory (esp. in legal senses).—*adj.* **accessibil'ity.**—*adj.* **access'ible** within reach: approachable: easily comprehensible.—*adv.* **access'ibly.**—*n.* **accession** (*ak-sesh'ən*) the act or event of acceding: a coming, esp. to office or dignity, or as an addition: that which is added: assent.—*v.t.* to enter in a book as an accession to a library.—

adj. **access'ory** additional: subsidiary: adventitious: aiding, participating in, a crime (*law*) or misdeed, but not as principal.—*n.* anything that is secondary, additional, or non-essential: one who aids a crime.—*adj.* **accessor'ial.**—*adv.* **access'orily.**—**accessary before or after the fact** one who helps a criminal before or after the committing of a crime; **access broadcasting, access television** radio or television programmes put out independently by groups of people who want to bring their points of view to public notice; **Access® card** a credit card issued by a group of banks; **access time** the time needed for information stored in a computer to be retrieved. [See **accede.**]

accidence *ak'sid-əns, n.* the part of grammar treating of the 'accidents', *i.e.* inflexions of words.—*n.* **ac'cident** an unforeseen or unexpected event: a chance: a mishap.—*adj.* **accidental** (*-dent'*) happening by chance: not essential.—*n.* a sharp, flat, or natural not in the key-signature (*mus.*).—*ns.* **accident'alism** the state or quality of being accidental; **accidental'ity.**—*adv.* **accident'ally.**—*adj.* **ac'cident-prone** more than normally liable to have accidents.—**a chapter of accidents** a series of accidents. [L. *accidēns, -entis,* pr.p. of *accidĕre,* to happen—*ad,* to, *cadĕre,* to fall.]

accidie *ak'si-di, n.* acedia. [O.Fr. *accide*—L.L. *acēdia;* see **acedia.**]

accipitrine *ak-sip'i-trīn, -trin, adj.* pertaining to hawks. [L. *accipiter,* a hawk.]

acclamation *ak-lə-mā'shən, n.* a shout of applause or assent.—*v.t.* **acclaim** (*ə-klām'*) to hail or declare by acclamation.—*n.* acclamation.—*adj.* **acclamatory** (*ə-klam'ə-tər-i*). [L. *acclāmāre—ad,* to, *clāmāre, -ātum,* to shout; see **claim.**]

acclimatise, -ize *ə-klī'mə-tīz, v.t.* to inure to a new climate.—Also **accli'mate** (or *ak'lī, -li-*), **cli'matise, -ize.**—*n.* **acclimatisā'tion, -z-.**—Also **acclimatā'tion, acclima'tion** (*ak-lī-, -li-*). [Fr. *acclimater—à,* to, *climat,* climate.]

acclivity *ə-kliv'i-ti, n.* an upward slope.—*adjs.* **accliv'itous, accli'vous.** [L. *ad,* to, *clīvus,* a slope.]

accolade *ak'ə-lād, -ād', ak-ol-ād', n.* the action used in conferring knighthood, formerly an embrace, a kiss, now a tap on each shoulder with the flat of a sword: high award, or praise publicly given. [Fr.,—L. *ad,* to, *collum,* neck.]

accommodate *ə-kom'ə-dāt, v.t.* to adapt: to adjust: to harmonise: to furnish or supply (with): to find or afford room, etc., for: to oblige.—*v.i.* to come to terms: to make adjustment.—*adjs.* **accomm'odable; accomm'odating** ready to make adjustment: obliging.—*n.* **accommodā'tion** adaptation: adjustment, esp. of the eye to change of distance: settlement or compromise: a convenience: lodgings, quarters: space for what is required: a loan of money.—*adj.* **accomm'odative.**—*ns.* **accomm'odativeness; accomm'odātor.**—**accommodation address** an address to which mail may be sent but which is not that of the addressee's home or office; **accommodation ladder** a stairway outside of a ship for entering and leaving boats. [L. *accommodāre, -ātum—ad,* to, *commodus,* fitting.]

accompany *ə-kum'pə-ni, v.t.* to go or be in company with: to attend: to go along with: to perform an accompaniment to or for: to associate, join, or couple.—*ns.* **accom'panier; accom'paniment** that which accompanies: a subsidiary part or parts supporting a solo (*mus.*); **accom'panist** (also **accom'panyist**) a player of accompaniments. [Fr. *accompagner;* see **company.**]

accomplice *ə-kom'plis,* or *-kum', n.* an associate in crime. [L. *complex, -icis,* joined; pfx. unexplained.]

accomplish *ə-kom'plish,* or *-kum',* *v.t.* to complete: to fulfil: to achieve: to equip.—*adjs.* **accom'plishable;**

accom'plished complete, finished, or highly skilled in acquirements: polished.—*ns.* **accom'plisher; accom'plishment** completion: an achievement: rendering accomplished: a skilled acquirement in matters of culture or social grace. [O.Fr. *accomplir* —L. *ad*, to, *complēre*, to fill up; see **complete**.]

accord *ə-kord'*, *v.i.* to agree: to be in correspondence (with).—*v.t.* to cause to agree: to reconcile: to grant (to a person).—*n.* agreement: harmony: grant: assent.—*adj.* **accord'able**.—*ns.* **accord'ance, accord'ancy** agreement: conformity: a granting.—*adj.* **accord'ant**.—*adv.* **accord'antly**.—*n.* **accord'er**. —*adj.* **accord'ing** in accordance.—*adv.* **accord'ingly** suitably: in agreement (with what precedes): therefore.—**according as** in proportion as: depending on whether; **according to** in accordance with, or agreeably to: as asserted by; **of one's own accord** of one's own spontaneous motion; **with one accord** with spontaneous unanimity. [O.Fr. *acorder*—L. *ad*, to, *cor, cordis*, the heart.]

accordion *ə-kör'di-ən*, *n.* a musical instrument consisting of folding bellows, keyboard, and free metal reeds.—*n.* **accord'ionist**. [accord.]

accost *ə-kost'*, *v.t.* to approach and address: to speak first to: to solicit as a prostitute.—*adj.* **accost'able**. [O.Fr. *acoster*—L. *ad*, to, *costa*, a rib, a side.]

accouchement *a-kōō sh'mä, -mənt*, *n.* delivery in childbed. [Fr.]

account *ə-kownt'*, *v.t.* to reckon: to judge, value.—*v.i.* to reckon: to keep accounts: to give a reason or explanation: to give a statement of money dealings: to answer as one responsible.—*n.* reckoning: a reckoning of money or other responsibilities: a statement of money owing: a business relationship involving the provision of goods or services in return for money: value: estimation: consideration: sake: a descriptive report: a performance.—*n.* **accountabil'ity**.—*adj.* **account'able** responsible: explicable.—*n.* **account'ableness**.—*adv.* **account'ably**.—*ns.* **account'ancy** the office, work, or profession of an accountant; **account'ant** one who keeps, or is skilled in, accounts; **account'antship**.—*n. and adj.* **account'ing**.—**account'-book** a book for keeping accounts in—**bring, call, to account** to demand of someone an explanation or justification of what they have done: to reprimand; **by all accounts** according to general opinion; **give a good account of oneself** to give a good performance: to do well; **hold to account** to hold responsible; **on** or **to account as** an instalment or interim payment; **on account of** because of; **on no account** not for any reason; **on one's own account** on one's own responsibility; **take into account** to take into consideration; **take no account of** to overlook; **turn to (good) account** to turn to advantage. [O.Fr. *acconter*—L. *ad*, to, *computāre*, to reckon; see **compute, count²**.]

accoutre *ə-kōō'tər*, *v.t.* to dress or equip (esp. a warrior).—*n.* **accou'trement** (*-tər-* or *-trə-*) equipping: (usu. in *pl.*) dress: military equipments. [Fr. *accoutrer*, earlier *accoustrer*.]

accredit *ə-kred'it*, *v.t.* to show to be true or correct: to accept as true: to furnish or send with credentials: to certify: to attribute (to): to ascribe to (*with* the thing attributed).—*n.* **accredita'tion**.—*adj.* **accred'ited** furnished with credentials: certified officially: (of livestock) certified free from a particular disease, e.g. brucellosis. [Fr. *accréditer—à*, to, *crédit*, credit.]

accrescent *ə-kres'ənt*, *adj.* growing: ever-increasing.—*n.* **accresc'ence**.—*v.i.* **accrēte'** to grow together: to become attached.—*v.t.* to unite: to form or gather round itself.—*n.* **accrē'tion** continued growth: the

growing together of parts externally: an extraneous addition.—*adj.* **accrē'tive**. [L. *accrēscĕre, accrētum—ad*, to, *crēscĕre*, to grow.]

accrue *ə-krōō'*, *v.i.* to come as an accession, increment, or product: to fall (to one) by way of advantage: to fall due.—*n.* **accru'al**. [O.Fr. *acrewe*, what grows up to the profit of the owner—*acreistre* —L. *accrēscĕre*.]

acculturation *ə-kul-char-ā'shan*, *n.* the assimilation of another culture.—*adj.* **accul'tural**—*v.t.* and *v.i.* **accul'turate**. [L. *ad*, and **culture**.]

accumulate *ə-kūm'ūl-āt*, *v.t.* to heap or pile up.—*v.i.* to increase greatly: to go on increasing.—*adj.* heaped up.—*n.* **accūmū'lation** heaping up: a heap or mass.—*adj.* **accūm'ūlative** growing by progressive addition: cumulative.—*n.* **accūm'ūlator** a thing or person that accumulates: a means of storing energy, esp. an electric battery that can be recharged: in a computer, etc., a device that performs arithmetical operations and stores the results.— **accumulator (bet)** a bet on four or more races, original stake and winnings from each race being laid on the next race. [L. *ad*, to, *cumulus*, a heap.]

accurate *ak'ū-rit*, *adj.* exact.—*n.* **acc'uracy** (*-ə-si*) correctness: exactness.—*adv.* **acc'urately**.—*n.* **acc'urateness**. [L. *accūrātus*, performed with care —*ad*, to, *cūra*, care.]

accurse *ə-kûrs'*, *v.t.* to curse: to devote to misery or destruction.—*adj.* **accurs'ed** (or *-kûrst'*) subjected to or worthy of a curse. [O.E. pfx. *ā-*, and *cursian*, to curse.]

accuse *ə-kūz'*, *v.t.* to bring a charge against (with *of*).—*adj.* **accūs'able**.—*ns.* **accūs'al** accusation; **accūsa'tion** the act of accusing: a charge brought.—*adj.* **accūs'ative** accusing: in or belonging to a grammatical case which expresses the direct object of transitive verbs.—*n.* (a word in) the accusative case.—*adjs.* **accūsati'val; accūsatō'rial; accūs'atory** containing accusation.—*adj.* **accused'**.—*n.* (*sing.* or *pl.*) the person or persons accused.—*n.* **accūs'er**. [L. *accūsāre, -ātum—ad*, to, *causa*, cause, partly through O.Fr. *accuser*.]

accustom *ə-kus'təm*, *v.t.* to make familiar by custom (with *to*): to habituate.—*adj.* **accus'tomary**.—*adj.* **accus'tomed** usual: frequent: habituated: in the habit.—*n.* **accus'tomedness**. [O.Fr. *acostumer— à*, to, *costume, coustume*; see **custom**.]

ace *ās*, *n.* a unit: the one in dice, cards, dominoes, etc.: a single point: a hole in one (see under **hole¹**; *golf*): a winning serve (*tennis*): a jot: a person of distinguished achievement (*coll.*).—*adj.* of highest quality: outstanding.—*v.t.* to serve an ace against (an opponent) (*tennis*): to play (a hole) in one stroke (*golf*).—**an ace up one's sleeve** a decisive but hidden advantage; **play one's ace** to use one's best weapon, resource, etc.; **within an ace of** within a hair's-breadth of. [Fr. *as*—L. *as*, unity.]

acedia *ə-sē'di-ə*, *n.* listlessness: torpor: sloth. [Gr. *akēdia, akēdeia—a-*, priv., *kēdos*, care. See **accidie**.]

acephalous *a-, ā-, ə-sef'ə-ləs*, *adj.* headless. [Gr. *akephalos—a-*, priv., *kephalē*, head.]

acerbic *ə-sûr'bik*, *adj.* bitter and sour.—*v.t.* **acerbate** (*as'ər-bāt*) to embitter: to irritate.—*n.* **acerb'ity**. [L. *acerbus*.]

acerous *a-sē'rəs*, *adj.* without horns, antennae, tentacles. [Gr. *a-*, priv. *keras*, horn.]

acet-, aceto- *as'it-(ō-), a-, ə-set'-(ō-), a-sēt'-(ō-)*, in composition, vinegar.—*ns.* **ac'etal** a liquid formed by oxidation of alcohol, etc. which this is the type; **ac'etate** a salt of acetic acid.—*adj.* **acetic** (*-sēt', -set'*) of, of the nature of, producing, vinegar (**acetic acid** the sour principle in vinegar).—*n.* **acetifi-**

câ'tion (-*set*-).—*v.t.* and *v.i.* **acet'ify** to turn into vinegar.—*n.* **ac'etone** a ketone.—*adjs.* **ac'etose** acetous; **acē'tous** like, or producing, vinegar: sour.—*ns.* **acetyl** (*as'i-til*, -*til*, or *a-sē'*) the radical of acetic acid (**acetyl-salicylic acid** aspirin); **acetylene** (-*set'*) a gas used in welding, synthesising acetic acid, illumination, etc. [L. *acētum*, vinegar.]

acetabulum *as-et-ab'ū-ləm*, -*ēt*-, *n.* the hollow that receives the head of the thigh-bone: the cavity that receives a leg in the body of insects: in various animals, a sucker:—*pl.* **acetab'ūla**.—*adj* **acetab'ūlar**. [L. *acētábulum*, a vinegar cup.]

Achaean *ə-kē'ən*, **Achaian** -*kī'*, -*kā'*, *adj.* belonging to *Achâiâ*, in the Peloponnese, or to Greece generally. —Also *n.*

ache *āk*, *n.* a continued pain.—*v.i.* to be in or be the site of continued pain: to long (for).—*n.* **ach'ing**.— *adj.* **ach'y.** [The verb was properly *ake*, the noun *ache*, as in *speak*, *speech*.—O.E. *acan* (*vb.*), *æce* (*n.*).]

achene *a-kēn'*, *n.* a dry, one-seeded fruit, formed of one carpel, as in the buttercup.—*adj.* **achē'nial.** [From Gr. *a-*, priv., and *chainein*, to gape.]

Acheron *ak'ər-on*, (*Gr. myth.*) *n.* one of the rivers of the infernal regions.—*adj.* **Acheron'tic.** [Gr. *Acherōn.*]

achieve *ə-chēv'*, *v.t.* to perform: to accomplish: to win. —*adj.* **achiev'able.**—*n.* **achieve'ment** achieving: something achieved: an exploit: an escutcheon or armorial shield granted in memory of some achievement: escutcheon, armour, etc., hung over a tomb. [Fr. *achever*, from *à chief* (*venir*)—L.L. *ad caput*, to a head; see **chief, hatchment.**]

Achillean *ak-il-ē'ən*, *adj.* like *Achilles*, the great Greek hero in the Trojan war, invulnerable except in the heel, by which his mother held him when she dipped him in the Styx.—**Achilles' heel, heel of Achilles** a person's most vulnerable point; **Achilles' tendon** the attachment of the muscles of the calf of the leg to the heel-bone.

achondroplasia *ak-on-drō-plā'zhi-ə*, *n.* dwarfism characterised by shortness of the arms and legs.— *adj.* **achondroplastic** (-*plas'tik*). [Gr. *a-*, priv., *chondros*, cartilage, *plassein*, to make.]

achromatic *ak-rō-mat'ik*, *adj.* transmitting light without much chromatic aberration: without colour.— *adv.* **achromat'ically.**—*v.t.* **achro'matise**, -**ize** to render achromatic.—*ns.* **achro'matism** the state of being achromatic; **achromatopsia** (*ə-krō-mə-top'si-ə*; Gr. *ops*, eye) total colour blindness. [Gr. *a-*, priv., *chrōma*, -*atos*, colour.]

acicular *as-ik'ū-lər*, *adj.* needle-shaped: slender and sharp-pointed.—*adj.* **acic'ulate** marked as if with needle-scratches. [L. *acicula*, dim. of *acus*, a needle.]

acid *as'id*, *adj.* sharp: sour: of soil, having an acid reaction: biting, keen (*fig.*): ill-natured, morose (*fig.*): pertaining to, of the nature of, having the properties of, an acid (*chem.*).—*n.* a substance with a sour taste: in chemistry, variously considered as:—any of a class of substances which turn vegetable blues (e.g. litmus) red, and combine with bases, certain metals, etc., to form salts; any of a class of substances that dissolve in water with the formation of hydrogen ions; any of a class of substances that can transfer a proton to another substance; etc.: something harsh, biting, sarcastic (*fig.*): LSD or other hallucinogenic drug (*slang*).—*adjs.* **acid'ic**; **acidifi'able**.—*n.* **acidification**.—*v.t.* **acid'ify** to make acid: to convert into an acid.—*v.i.* to become acid:—*pr.p.* **acid'ifying**; *pa.t.* and *pa.p.* **acid'ified**.—*ns.* **acid'ity** the quality of being acid or sour; **acidō'sis** (*med.*) the presence of acids in the blood beyond normal limits.—*v.t.*

acid'ūlate to make slightly acid.—*adj.* **acid'ūlous** slightly sour: caustic, sharp (*fig.*).—**acid drop** a sweet flavoured with tartaric acid; **acid rain** precipitation containing sulphur and nitrogen compounds and other pollutants; **acid test** a test for gold by acid: a searching test (*fig.*). L. *acidus*, sour—*acēre*, to be sour.]

acierate *as'i-ər-āt*, *v.t.*, to turn into steel.—*n.* **ac'ierage** the covering of a metal plate with a film of iron. [Fr. *aciérer—acier*, steel.—L.L. *aciárium* (*ferrum*), lit. edging (iron)—L. *aciēs*, edge.]

acinus *as'i-nəs*, *n.* one of the small fruits that compose an aggregate fruit, as in the raspberry: an aggregate fruit: a pip:—*pl.* **ac'ini.**—*adjs.* **acinā'ceous**; **acin'i-form.** [L. *acinus*, berry, pip.]

ack-ack *ak-ak*, *adj.* anti-aircraft.—*adv.* **ack-emm'a** ante meridiem. [Formerly signallers' names for the letters AA, AM.]

acknowledge *ək-nol'ij*, *v.t.* to own as true, or genuine, or valid, or one's own: to confess: to own with thanks: to intimate receipt of.—*adj.* **acknowl'edgeable.**—*n.* **acknowl'edgment** (sometimes **acknowl'edgement**) recognition: admission: confession: thanks: an intimation of receipt. [See **knowledge.**]

acme *ak'mi*, *n.* the top or highest point: the culmination or perfection in the career of anything: the crisis, as of a disease (*arch.*).—*n.* **ac'mite** a soda pyroxene whose crystals often show a steep pyramid [Gr. *akmē—akē*, a point.]

acne *ak'ni*, *n.* inflammation of the sebaceous follicles, as on the nose. [Perh. Gr. *akmē*, a point.]

acolyte *ak'ə-līt*, **ac'olyth**-*lith*-, *ns.* one in minor orders, next below subdeacon (*R.C. Church*): an inferior church officer: an attendant or assistant: a faithful follower. [Gr. *akolouthos*, an attendant.]

aconite *ak'ə-nīt*, *n.* wolf's-bane or monk's-hood (*Aconitum*): poison got from it, or (*poet.*) deadly poison in general (often **aconi'tum**).—*adj.* **aconit'ic.** —*n.* **aconitine** (-*kon'*) a poisonous alkaloid from aconite.—**winter aconite** an early-flowering ranunculaceous plant. [L. *aconītum*—Gr. *akonīton*.]

acorn *ā'körn*, *n.* the fruit of the oak.—*adj.* **ā'corned.** —**ā'corn-cup'** the woody cup-shaped involucre of an acorn; **ā'corn-shell** a cirripede of the genus Balanus (L., acorn). O.E. *æcern*; form influenced by confusion with **corn'** and perh. **oak** (Northern *aik*, O.E. *āc*).]

acotyledon *a-kot-i-lē'dən*, *n.* a cryptogam.—*adj.* **acotylē'donous.** [Gr. *a-*, priv., and **cotyledon.**]

acoustic, -al *ə-kōōs'tik*, -*əl*, *adjs.* pertaining to the sense of hearing or to the theory of sounds: used in hearing: operated by sound vibrations: (of musical instruments) not electric.—*n.* **acous'tic** acoustic properties.—*adv.* **acous'tically.**—*ns.* **acoustician** (-*ti'shən*); **acous'tics** (*sing.*) the science of sound: (as *pl.*) acoustic properties. [Gr. *akoustikos—akouein*, to hear.]

acquaint *ə-kwānt'*, *v.t.* to let know: to inform.—*ns.* **acquaint'ance** knowledge, esp. falling short of intimacy: a person (sometimes persons) known slightly; **acquaint'anceship** slight knowledge.—*adj.* **acquaint'ed** personally known: having personal knowledge of (usu. with *with*). [O.Fr. *acointer*—L. *ad*, to, *cognitus*, known.]

acquiesce *ak-wi-es'*, *v.i.* to rest satisfied or without making opposition: to assent (with *in*).—*n.* **acquiesc'ence** quiet assent or submission.—*adj.* **acquiesc'ent** acquiescing.—*n.* one who acquiesces.— *advs.* **acquiesc'ently**, **acquiesc'ingly.** [L. *acquiéscère* —*ad*, to, *quiēs*, rest.]

acquire *ə-kwīr'*, *v.t.* to gain: to attain to.—*n.* **acquirability.**—*adj.* **acquir'able** that may be acquired.— *n.* **acquir'al.**—*adj.* **acquired'.**—*ns.* **acquire'ment**

acquisition: something learned or got by effort, not a gift of nature; **acquisition** (*ak-wi-zish'ən*) the act of acquiring: that which is acquired.—*adj.* **acquisitive** (*ə-kwiz'*) able, desiring or ready to acquire.—*n.* **acquis'itiveness.**—**acquired taste** a liking that comes after some experience: a thing so liked (often ironically); **Acquired Immune Deficiency Syndrome** (also known as AIDS *ādz*) a condition brought about by a virus which causes the body's immunity system to become deficient, leaving the sufferer very vulnerable to infection. [L. *acquirĕre, -quisītum—ad,* to, *quaerĕre,* to seek.]

acquit *ə-kwit'*, *v.t.* to free: to release: to discharge, as a debt: to discharge (oneself of a duty): hence to behave, conduct (oneself): to prove (oneself): to release from an accusation:—*pr.p.* **acquitt'ing;** *pa.t.* and *pa.p.* **acquitt'ed.**—*ns.* **acquitt'al** a judicial discharge from an accusation; **acquitt'ance** a discharge from an obligation or debt: a receipt in evidence of such a discharge. [O.Fr. *aquiter*—L. *ad,* to, *quiĕtāre,* to quiet, settle; see **quit.**]

acre *ā'kər, n.* a measure of 4840 sq. yards: (in *pl.*) lands, estates.—*n.* **acreage** (*ā'kər-ij*) area in acres. [O.E. *æcer,* field.]

acrid *ak'rid, adj.* biting: pungent.—*n.* **acrid'ity.** [L. *ācer, ācris,* sharp, keen; noun suffix perh. as in imitation of *acid.*]

acridin(e) *ak'ri-dēn, -din, n.* a compound found in coaltar, a parent substance of dyes and anti-bacterial drugs.—*n.* **scriflavin(e)** (*-flā'vēn, -vin; acridine* and *flavin(e)*) an antiseptic. [**acrid,** and n. suff. *-ine.*]

acrimony *ak'ri-mən-i, n.* bitterness of feeling or language.—*adj.* **acrimō'nious.**—*adv.* **acrimō'niously.** [L. *ācrimōnia—ācer,* sharp.]

acro- *ak-rō-,* in composition, tip, point, summit. [Gr. *akron,* tip, end, *akros,* highest, outermost.]

acrobat *ak'rō-bat, n.* a rope-dancer: a tumbler: a performer of gymnastic feats.—*adj.* **acrobat'ic.**—*n.pl.* **acrobat'ics** acrobatic performances (esp. *fig.*). [Gr. *akrobatēs,* acrobat, *akrobatos,* walking on tiptoe—*akron,* point, and the root of *bainein,* to go.]

acrogen *ak'rō-jən, n.* a cryptogam with growing-point at the tip—a fern or moss.—*adj.* **acrogenous** (*ə-kroj'inas*). [Gr. *akron, -genēs,* born.]

acromegaly *ak-rō-meg'ə-li, n.* a disease characterised by overgrowth, esp. of the face and extremities.—*adj.* **acromegal'ic.** [Gr. *akron,* point, *megas, megalos,* great.]

acronychal *ə-kron'ik-əl, adj.* at nightfall (of the rising or setting of stars).—*adv.* **acron'ychally.** [Gr. *akronychos,* at nightfall—*akron,* point, *nychos, -eos,* night.]

acronym *ak'rō-nim, n.* a word formed from the initial letters of other words, as *radar.*—*n.* **acronymā'nia** a craze for forming acronyms.—*adjs.* **acronym'ic,** **acron'ymous.** [**acro-,** and Gr. *onyma,* name.]

acropetal *ə-krop'i-tl, adj.* (*bot.*) towards the apex.—*adv.* **acrop'etally.** [Gr. *akron,* L. *petĕre,* to seek.]

acrophobia *ak-rō-fō'bi-ə, n.* fear of heights. [Gr. *akron,* tip, *akros,* highest, *phobos,* fear.]

acropolis *ə-krop'ol-is, ə-krop'ə-lis, n.* a citadel, esp. that of Athens. [Gr. *akropolis—akros,* highest, *polis,* a city.]

acrospire *ak'rō-spīr,* (*bot.*) *n.* the first leaf that sprouts from a germinating seed. [M.E. *akerspire*—O.E. *æhher,* ear, *spire*[1].]

across *ə-kros', prep.* from side to side of: on or to the other side of: crosswise.—Also *adv.*—*adj.* **across's the-board** of wage increases, etc., applying in all cases (*adverbially* **across the board**).—**come across** to alight upon, meet: to hand over information, confession, money, etc., in answer to demand or inducement (*coll.*); **get** or **come across** to take effect (on the audience across the footlights, and so generally); **get it**

across to make acceptable, to bring to a successful issue; **put it across** (someone), to deceive (him). [Prep. **a,** and **cross.**]

acrostic *ə-kros'tik, n.* a poem or puzzle in which the first (or last) letters of each line spell a word or sentence: an acronym. [Gr. *akros,* extreme, *stichos,* a line.]

acrylic *ə-kril'ik, n.* a synthetic fibre.—Also *adj.*—**acrylic acid** a very reactive acid belonging to the series of oleic acids; **acrylic resins** thermoplastic resins derived from acrylic acid. [*acrolein,* Gr. *hylē,* matter.]

act *akt, v.i.* to produce an effect: to behave oneself: to perform, as on the stage: to feign.—*v.t.* to perform: to imitate or play the part of.—*n.* something done or doing: the process of doing: a decree: a legislative enactment: a distinct main section of a play: an individual performance, as in variety.—*n.* **actabil'ity;** **act'ing** action: the act or art of performing an assumed or a dramatic part: feigning.—*adj.* performing some duty temporarily, or for another.—*n.* **act'or** one who acts: a stage-player:—*fem.* **act'ress.**—**act** as to perform the duties of; **act of God** a result of natural forces, unexpected and not preventable by human foresight; **act of grace** a favour, esp. a pardon granted by a sovereign; **act on** to exert an influence on: to act in accordance with; **act out** to play as an actor; **act up** (*coll.*) to behave badly; **act up to** to come in practice up to the standard of: to fulfil; **get in on the act** (*coll.*) to start participating in something apparently profitable already taking place in order to share in the benefits; **put on an act** to make a pretence: to show off. [L. *āctus, -ūs,* an action, doing, *āctum,* a thing done, *āctor,* a doer, actor; *agĕre, āctum,* to do, drive.]

actin(o)- *ak-tin-(o-),* in composition, ray.—*adj.* **actinal** (*ak-tī'nəl,* or *ak'ti-nəl*) belonging to the radiating bands on the body of an echinoderm where the tubelike feet are, or to the region of the mouth and tentacles in Anthozoa.—*n.* **actinia** (*-tin'*) a sea-anemone:—*pl.* **actin'iae** or **actin'ias.**—*n.* and *adj.* **actin'ian.**—*adj.* **actin'ic** of or showing actinism.—*ns.* **ac'tinide, actinoid** any element of a group from atomic number 89 (actinium) upwards; **ac'tinism** the chemical action of radiant energy; **actin'ium** a radioactive metal (atomic number 89; symbol Ac) found in pitchblende; **actin'olite** (Gr. *lithos,* a stone) a green amphibole; **actinom'eter** an instrument for measuring the heat-intensity or the actinic effect of light rays.—*adj.* **actinomor'phic** (Gr. *morphē,* form; (*biol.*) radially symmetrical.—*ns.* **Actinomyces** (*-mī'sēz;* Gr. *mykēs,* fungus) the ray-fungus, a genus of minute fungi or filamentous bacteria with radiating mycelium; **actinomycosis** (*-kō'sis*) lumpy-jaw in cattle, etc., or other disease caused by Actinomyces; **ac'tinon** actinium emanation, an isotope of radon.—**actinic rays** those rays that have a marked chemical action, esp. the ultraviolet. [Gr. *aktīs, aktīnos,* ray.]

action *ak'shən, n.* acting: activity: behaviour: a deed: an operation: a gesture: fighting: a battle: a lawsuit, or proceedings in a court: the movement of events in a drama, novel, etc.: the mechanism, esp. of a keyboard instrument.—*adj.* **ac'tionable** giving ground for a lawsuit.—*n.* **ac'tionist** an activist.—**action committee** or **group** members of an organisation who are chosen to take active measures; **action painting** an American version of tachism concerned with the physical manipulation of paint; **action replay** on television, the repeating of a piece of film, e.g. the scoring of a goal in football, usu. in slow motion; **action stations** posts to be manned during or preparatory to battle (often *fig.*). [Fr.,—L. *āctiō, -ōnis.*]

active *ak'tiv, adj.* acting: in actual operation: given to action: brisk: busy: nimble: practical, as opp. to speculative: effective: of that voice in which the subject of the verb represents the doer of the action (*gram.*).— *v.t.* **ac'tivate** to make active: to increase the energy of: to make radioactive.—*ns.* **activa'tion; ac'tivator**.—*adv.* **ac'tively**.—*ns.* **ac'tiveness; ac'tivism** a philosophy of creative will: a policy of vigorous action esp. in politics; **ac'tivist** a believer in or supporter of activism; **activ'ity** quality, state, or fact of being active: (esp. in *pl.*) doings.—**active immunity** immunity due to the making of antibodies within the organism; **active list** a list of full-pay officers engaged in or available for service; **active service** service in the battle area. [L. *āctīvus*.]

actor, actress. See under **act**.

actual ak'tū-əl, ak'chōō-əl, *adj.* real: existing in fact: at the time being.—*v.t.* **ac'tualise, -ize** to make actual: to realise in action.—*ns.* **actuali'sa'tion, -z-; ac'tualist** one who looks to actual facts; **actuality** (-*al'i-ti*) the fact or state of being actual: realism: a newsreel or current affairs programme (also **actualités** ak- tū-al-ē-tā, Fr.).—*adv.* **ac'tually** as a matter of fact: truly. [Fr. *actuel*—L.L. *āctuālis*.]

actuary ak'tū-ər-i, *n.* one who makes the calculations connected with insurance.—*adj.* **actuarial** (-*ā'ri-əl*).—*adv.* **actuā'rially**. [L. *āctuārius* (*scriba*), a clerk.]

actuate ak'tū-āt, *v.t.* to put into, or incite to, action.— *v.i.* to act.—*ns.* **actua'tion; ac'tuator**. [L. *āctus*, action; see **act**.]

acuity ə-kū'i-ti, *n.* sharpness. [L.L. *acuitās, -ātis*—L. *acus*, needle.]

acumen ə-kū'men, ak'ū-mən, *n.* quickness of perception.—*v.t.* **acū'minate** to sharpen: to give a point to.—*adj.* (*bot.*) tapering to a point (also **acū'minated**).—*n.* **acūmina'tion**. [L. *acūmen, -inis*, a point.]

acupuncture ak'ū-pungk-chər, *n.* the science of puncturing the skin with needles to effect anaesthesia, relieve symptoms, etc. [L. *acus*, needle, **puncture**.]

acute ə-kūt, *adj.* sharp: sharp-pointed: keen: piercing: finely discriminating: shrewd: urgently pressing: of a disease, coming to a crisis, as opp. to *chronic*.—*n.* an acute accent.—*adv.* **acute'ly**.—*n.* **acute'ness**.— **acute accent** a mark (´) over letters, used for various purposes; **acute angle** one less than a right angle. [L. *acūtus*, pa.p. of *acuēre*, to sharpen.]

acyclic ā-, a-sī'klik, *adj.* not periodic. [Gr. *a-*, priv., *kyklos*, a wheel.]

ad ad, *n.* coll. for **advertisement**.

adage ad'ij, *n.* an old saying: a proverb. [Fr.,—L. *adagium*—ad, to, and root of *āiō*, I say.]

adagio ə-dä'j(y)ō, (*mus.*) *adv.* slowly.—*adj.* slow.— *n.* a slow movement:—*pl.* **ada'gios**. [It.,—*ad agio*, at ease.]

Adam ad'əm, *n.* the first man, according to Genesis.— *adjs.* **Adam** applied to a style of architecture, interior decoration and furniture, designed by Robert and James Adam in the 18th century; **Adamic, -al** (ə-dam'ik, -əl) of or like Adam: naked.—*n.* **Ad'amite** a descendant of Adam: one who goes naked.—*adjs.* **Adamit'ic, -al**.—*n.* **Ad'amitism**.—**Adam's ale** or **wine** water; **Adam's apple** the projection of the thyroid cartilage in front of the throat.—**not know someone from Adam** (*coll.*) not to know someone, or who someone is. [Heb. *Ādām*.]

adamant ad'əm-ənt, -ant, *n.* a name formerly applied to various hard substances, e.g. steel.—*adjs.* **ad'amant** unyielding; **adaman'tine**. [Gr. *adamas, -antos*, prob. orig. steel, also diamond—*a-*, priv., and *damaein*, to tame, overcome.]

adapt ə-dapt', *v.t.* to make fit or suitable.—*n.* **adaptabil'ity**.—*adj.* **adapt'able**.—*n.* **adaptation** (ad-əp-tā'shən) the fact, act, process, or result of adapting.—*adjs.* **adapt'ative; adapt'ed** modified to suit: suitable.—*ns.* **adapt'er, -or**, one who, or that which,

adapts: an attachment or accessory enabling a piece of apparatus to be used for a purpose, or in conditions, other than that, or those, for which it was orig. intended; **adap'tion** adaptation.—*adj.* **adapt'ive**.—*adv.* **adapt'ively**.—*n.* **adapt'iveness**. [Fr. *adapter*—L. *adaptāre*—*ad*, to, and *aptāre*, to fit.]

adaxial ad-aks'i-əl, (*bot.*) *adj.* next to or towards the axis. [L. *ad*, to.]

add ad, *v.t.* to put, join, or annex (to something else): to sum up, compute the sum of: to say further.—*v.i.* to make an addition: to increase (with *to*): to find the total of numbers, etc.—*ns.* **add'er** one who adds: a machine for adding; **addi'tion** the act of adding: a thing added.—*adj.* **addi'tional** added.—*adv.* **addi'tionally**.—*adjs.* **additi'tious** increasing; **add'itive** characterised by addition: to be added.—*n.* a substance added to foodstuffs, etc., for a special purpose.—**adding machine** an apparatus for performing basic arithmetical calculations; **add up to** amount on adding: to be consistent: to point to a reasonable conclusion. [L. *addĕre, additum*—*ad*, to, *dăre*, to put.]

addax ad'aks, *n.* a large African antelope with long slightly twisted horns. [L., from an African word.]

addend ad'end, ə-dend', *n.* a number or quantity added. [addendum.]

addendum ə-den'dəm, *n.* a thing to be added, as supplementary material to a book, etc.:—*pl.* **adden'da**. [L. gerundive of *addĕre*; see **add**.]

adder ad'ər, *n.* the only venomous British snake, a viper (q.v.).—**ad'der's-wort, add'erwort** the bistort, or snakeweed, supposed to cure snake-bite. [O.E. *nǣdre* (*an adder* for *a nadder*).]

addict ə-dikt', *v.t.* to give up (to), devote, apply habitually (to).—*n.* (*ad'ikt*) a slave to a habit or vice, esp. drugs.—*adj.* **addict'ed** inclined or given up (to).— *ns.* **addict'edness; addic'tion** the state of being addicted: a habit that has become impossible to break.—*adj.* **addict'ive** tending to cause addiction: habit-forming.—**drug of addiction** a habit-forming drug. [L. *addīcĕre, addictum*—*ad*, to, *dīcĕre*, to declare.]

Addison's disease ad'i-sənz diz-ēz', a disease characterised by wasting, weakness, low blood-pressure, and pigmentation of the skin (bronzed skin). [Dr Thomas *Addison* (1793–1860), who investigated it.]

addle ad'l *adj.* bad (as an egg): empty: muddled.— *v.t.* and *v.i.* to make or become addle.—*adj.* **addl'ed**.—*n.* **add'lement**.—*adjs.* **add'le-brained, -headed, -pated** muddle- headed. [O.E. *adela*, mud.]

address ə-dres', *v.t.* to apply or devote (oneself; with *to*): to apply oneself to: to direct: to aim: to speak directly to: to send: to put a indication of destination upon.—*n.* act or mode of addressing: deportment: adroitness: a formal communication in writing: a speech: a place to which letters may be directed: a place where one may be found: a name, label or number that identifies the location of a stored item of data, etc. (*comput.*): (in *pl.*) attentions of the nature of courtship.—*adj.* **addressed'** aimed: directed.— *ns.* **addressee'** the person to whom a communication is addressed; **address'er, -or**.—*n.* **Addressograph®** (ə-dres'ō-gräf) a machine for printing addresses automatically, on envelopes, etc.—**address book** a notebook, usu. with alphabetical thumb-index, in which names and addresses can be entered. [Fr. *adresser*—L.L. *addīrectiare*—L. *ad*, to, *directum*, straight; see **dress, direct**.]

adduce ə-dūs', *v.t.* to bring forward in discussion, to cite or quote.—*adj.* **adduc'ent** drawing inward or together, as a muscle.—*n.* **adduc'er**.—*adj.* **adduc'ible**.—*v.t.* **adduct** (ə-dukt') to draw inward or together.—*n.* **adduc'tion** the act of adducing or of adducting.—*adj.* **adduc'tive** tending to bring

forward.—*n.* **adduc'tor** an adducent muscle. [L. *addūcĕre, adductum—ad,* to, and *dūcĕre,* to bring.]
à demi *a da-mē,* (Fr.) by halves, half.

aden- *ad'an,* in composition, gland.—*n.* **adenitis** (*ad-an-ī'tis*) inflammation of glands.—*adj.* **ad'enoid** glandlike: glandular.—*n.* (usu. in *pl.*) enlargement of glandular tissue at the back of the nose.—*adj.* **adenoid'al** of adenoids: affected by, or as if by, adenoids (as a voice).—*n.* **adeno'ma** a benign tumour like, or originating in, a gland:—*pl.* **adeno'mata** or **-mas.**—*adj.* **adenō'matous.** [Gr. *adēn,* gland.]
adept *ad'ept, a-dept', a-dept', adj.* completely skilled (at, in).—*n.* (*ad'ept, a-dept', a-dept'*) [L. *adeptus* (*artem*), having attained (an art), pa.p. of *adipīscī,* to attain.]

adequate *ad'i-kwit, -kwāt, adj.* sufficient: competent —*adv.* **ad'equately.**—*ns.* **ad'equateness, ad'equacy** (*-kwa-si*). [L. *adaequātus,* made equal—*ad,* to, and *aequus,* equal.]
à deux *a dø,* (Fr.) of two, between two, two-handed; **à deux mains** (*mē*) with both hands: for two hands.
adharma *a-dār'mä, a-dûr'ma, n.* unrighteousness— opposite of **dharma.** [Sans.]

adhere *ad-, ad-hēr', v.i.* to stick (to): to remain fixed or attached (to): to cleave (as to a party, a leader, a doctrine): to agree.—*n.* **adhēr'ence** state of adhering. —*adj.* **adhēr'ent** sticking: concrescent and unlike.— *n.* one who adheres: a follower: a partisan.—*n.* **adhēr'er.** [L. *ad,* to, *haerēre, haesum,* to stick.]
adhesion *ad-hē'zhon, n.* the act of adhering or sticking: reunion of separated surfaces (*surg.*): abnormal union of parts that have been inflamed (*path.*): (often in *pl.*) a band of fibrous tissue joining such parts.—*adj.* **adhē'sive** (*-siv, -ziv*) sticky: apt to adhere.—*n.* a substance used for sticking things together.—*adv* **adhē'sively.**—*n.* **adhē'siveness.** [See **adhere.**]
adhibit *ad-hib'it, v.t.* to apply: to attach: to admit: to administer.—*n.* **adhibi'tion.** [L. *adhibēre, -itum— ad,* to, *habēre,* to hold.]
ad hoc *ad hok,* (L.) for this special purpose (used as *adj.*).
ad hominem *ad hom'in-em,* (L.) to the man, addressed to the feelings or prejudices of the hearer or reader: dealing with an opponent by attacking his character instead of answering his argument.
adiabatic *ad-i-a-bat'ik, adj.* without transference of heat.—*adv.* **adiabat'ically.** [Gr. *a-,* priv., *dia,* through, *batos,* passable.]
adiaphoron *ad-i-af'a-ron, n.* in theology and ethics, any tenet or usage considered non-essential:—*pl.* **adiaph'ora.**—*ns.* **adiaph'orism; adiaph'orist.**—*adj.* **adiaph'orous.** [Gr., from *a-,* priv., *diaphoros,* differing—*dia,* apart, *pherein,* to carry.]
adieu *a-dū, interj.* (I commend you) to God: farewell.— *n.* a farewell:—*pl.* **adieus** or **adieux** (*a-dūz'*). [Fr. *à Dieu,* to God.]
ad infinitum *ad in-fin-īt'am, -ēt'ōōm,* (L.) to infinity
ad interim *ad in'tar-im,* (L.L.) for the meantime.
adiós *ad-ē-os',* (Sp.; lit. 'to God') *interj.* good-bye.
adipocere *ad'i-pō-sēr,* or *-sēr', n.* a fatty, waxy substance resulting from the decomposition of animal bodies in moist places or under water, but not exposed to air. [L. *adeps, adipis,* soft fat, and *cēra,* wax.]
adipose *ad'i-pōs, adj.* fatty.—*n.* **adiposity** (*-pos'i-ti*) — **adipose tissue** the structure in the animal body which contains the fat. [L. *adeps, adipis,* soft fat.]
adit *ad'it, n.* an opening or passage, esp. into a mine. [L. *aditus—ad,* to, *ire, itum,* to go.]
adjacent *a-jā'sant, adj.* lying near or next (to).—*n.* **adja'cency.**—*adv.* **adja'cently.** [L. *ad,* to, *jacēns, -entis,* pr.p. of *jacēre,* to lie.]
adjective *aj'ik-tiv, adj.* added: (of dyes) requiring a mordant.—*n.* a word added to a noun to qualify it.—

adjectival (*-tīv'l*).—*advs.* **adjecti'vally; ad'jectively.** [L. *adjectīvum* (*nōmen*), added (word)— *adjicĕre, -jectum,* to add—*ad,* to, *jacĕre,* to throw]
adjoin *a-join', v.t* to join on: to lie next to.—*v.i.* to be in contact.—*adj.* **adjoin'ing.** [L. *adjungĕre—ad,* to, *jungĕre,* to join.]
adjourn *a-jûrn', v.t.* to put off to another day: to postpone: to discontinue (a meeting) in order to reconstitute it at another time or place.—*v.i.* to suspend proceedings and disperse.—*n.* **adjourn'ment.** [O.Fr. *ajorner*—L L. *adiurnāre*—L. *ad,* to, *diurnus,* daily; cf. **journal.**]
adjudge *a-juj', v.t.* to decide: to assign: to award.—*n.* **adjudg'ment** (sometimes **adjudge'ment**). [O.Fr. *ajuger*—L. *adjūdicāre;* cf. **judge.**]
adjudicate *a-jōō'di-kāt, v.t.* to determine judicially: to pronounce: to award.—*v.i.* to pronounce judgment. to act as judge in a competition between amateurs in one of the arts, e.g. music.—*ns.* **adjudi'cā'tion** act or process of adjudicating; **adju'dicātor.** [L. *adjūdicāre, -ātum.*]
adjunct *aj'ung(k)t, adj.* joined or added.—*n.* a thing or person joined or added, subordinate or not essentially a part: any word or clause enlarging the subject or predicate (*gram.*).—*n.* **adjunction** (*a-jungk'shan*).— *adj.* **adjunct'ive.**—*advs.* **adjunct'ively; ad'junct'ly.** [L. *adjunctus* pa.p. of *adjungĕre,* to join.]
adjure *a-jōō'r', v.t.* to charge on oath or solemnly.—*n.* **adjurā'tion** (*aj-*)—*adjs.* **adjur'atory; adjur'ing.** [L. *adjūrāre—ad,* to, *jūrāre, -ātum,* to swear.]
adjust *a-just', v.t.* to regulate: to settle.—*v.i.* to adapt oneself (to).—*adj.* **adjust'able.**—*ns.* **adjust'er** one who adjusts: see **average, loss; adjust'ment; adjust'or** an organ or faculty that determines behaviour in response to stimuli. [L.L. *adjuxtāre,* to put side by side—L. *juxtā,* near; confused by association with *jūstus,* right]
adjutant *aj'ōō-tant, n.* an officer specially appointed to assist a commanding officer: a large Indian stork or crane.—*n.* **ad'jutancy** the office of an adjutant: assistance.—**ad'jutant-gen'eral** head of a department of the general staff: the executive officer of a general:— *pl.* **ad'jutants-gen'eral.** [L. *adjūtāns, -antis,* pr.p. of *adjūtāre,* freq. of *adjūvāre—ad,* to, *jūvāre,* to assist.]
adjuvant *aj'ōō-vant, adj.* helping.—*n.* a help.—*n.* **ad'juvancy.** [Fr —L *ad,* to, *jūvāre,* to help.]
ad lib. See **ad libitum.**
ad libitum *ad lib'i-tam, -tōōm,* (L.) at pleasure — Abbrev. **ad lib.**—**ad-lib** (*ad-lib'*) (*coll.*) *v.t.* and *v.i.* to extemporise, esp. to fill up time.—*ns* **ad-lib'ber;** **ad-libb'ing.**
ad-man. See under **advertise.**
admin. See under **administer.**
administer *ad-min'is-tar, v.t.* to govern: to manage as a steward, substitute, or executor: to dispense (justice, rites): to tender (an oath, medicine)—*v.t.* to minister.—*adj.* **admin'istrable.**—*adj.* and *n.* **admin'istrant.**—*v.t.* **admin'istrate** to administer.—*n.* **administrā'tion** (*coll.* shortening **ad'min**) the act of administering: management: dispensation of sacraments: the government.—*adj.* **admin'istrative** concerned with administration.—*n.* **admin'istrātor** one who manages or directs: the person to whom is committed the administration or distribution of the personal estate of a deceased person, in default of an executor: one empowered to act for a person legally incapable of acting for himself (*Scots law*):— *fem* **admin'istratrix.**—*n.* **admin'istratorship.** [L *administrāre, -ātum—ad,* to, *ministrāre,* to minister]
admirable, admire. See **admire.**
admiral *ad'mar-al, n* the chief commander of a navy: a naval officer ranking with a general in the army (**admiral of the fleet** with field-marshal): an admiral's

flagship: the chief ship in a fleet of merchantmen or fishing boats: a cone-shell: a butterfly of certain kinds (see **red, white**).—*ns.* **ad'miralship**; **Ad'miralty** the board administering navy (since 1964 under Ministry of Defence): the building where it transacts business. [O.Fr. *a(d)miral*—Ar. *amīr-al-bahr*, a lord of the sea, confused with L. *admīrābilis* (see **admire**).]

admire *ad-mīr'*, *v.t.* to have (or express) a high opinion of.—*adj.* **ad'mirable** worthy of being admired.—*n.* **ad'mirableness.**—*adv.* **ad'mirably.**—*n.* **admirā'tion** the act of admiring: wonder, together with esteem, love, or veneration.—*adj.* **ad'mirative.**—*n.* **admir'er** one who admires: a lover.—*adv.* **admir'ingly.** [Fr. *admirer*—L. *ad*, at, *mīrāri*, to wonder.]

admissible, etc. See **admit**.

admit *ad-mit'*, *v.t.* to allow to enter (with *into* or *to*): to let in: to concede: to acknowledge: to be capable of (also *v.i.* with *of*):—*pr.p.* **admitt'ing**; *pa.p.* **admitt'ed.**—*n.* **admissibil'ity.**—*adj.* **admiss'ible** that may be admitted or allowed (generally, or specially as legal proof).—*n.* **admission** (*-mish'ən*) the act of admitting: anything admitted or conceded: leave to enter.—*adjs.* **admiss'ive**; **admitt'able** that may be admitted.—*n.* **admitt'ance** admission: the property of an electric circuit by virtue of which a current flows under the action of a potential difference (*elect.*).—*adj.* **admitt'ed.**—*adv.* **admitt'edly.** [Partly through Fr.,—L. *admittĕre*, *-missum—ad*, to, *mittĕre*, *missum*, to send.]

admix *ad-*, *ad-miks'*, *v.t.* to mix with something else.—*n.* **admix'ture** the action of mixing: what is added to the chief ingredient of a mixture. [L. *ad*, to, and **mix**.]

admonish *ad-mon'ish*, *v.t.* to warn: to reprove mildly.—*n.* **admon'ishment** admonition. [O.Fr. *amonester*—L.L. *admonestāre*—L. *admonēre—ad*, to, *monēre*, to warn.]

admonition *ad-mon-ish'ən*, or *-mən-*, *n.* reproof: counsel: advice: ecclesiastical censure.—*adjs.* **admonitive** (*-mon'*), **admon'itory** containing admonition.—*n.* **admon'itor.** [L. *admonitiō*, *-ōnis*; cf. **admonish**.]

ad nauseam *ad nö'zi-am*, *-shi-*, *now'si-*, (L.) to the pitch of producing disgust.

ado *ə-dōō'*, *n.* a to-do: bustle: trouble: difficulty: stir or fuss:—*pl.* **ados'.** [**at do**, Northern English infin. with **at** instead of **to**, borrowed from Scand.]

adobe *ə-dō'bi*, *n.* a sun-dried brick: a house made of such bricks: (also **adobe clay**) a name for any kind of mud which, when mixed with straw, can be sun-dried into bricks.—Also *adj.* [Sp.,—*adobar*, to plaster.]

adolescent *ad-ō-les'ənt*, *adj.* passing from childhood to maturity: belonging to, typical of, this state.—Also *n.* —*n.* **adolesc'ence** the state or time of being adolescent. [L. *adolēscēns*, *-entis*, pr.p. of *adolēscĕre*, to grow up.]

Adonai *ə-dōn'ī*, *ə-don-ā'i*, *n.* a name of the Deity in the O.T., usu. translated 'Lord'. See also *Jehovah*. [Heb. *adōnāi*, my lord.]

Adonis *ə-dō'nis*, *n.* a youth beloved by Aphrodite: a beautiful youth: a beau or dandy. [Gr. *Adōnis*—Phoenician *adōn*, lord.]

adopt *ə-dopt'*, *v.t.* to take voluntarily as one's own child, with the rights of a child: to take into any relationship: to take as one's own: to take up: to take over: to take (a precaution, etc.): to choose formally (e.g. a candidate): to endorse, approve (e.g. a resolution, minutes).—*adj.* **adopt'ed** taken by adoption.—*ns.* **Adoptianism, Adoptionism** (*ə-dop'shən-izm*; often **adoptianism**) the doctrine that Christ, as man, is the adopted son of God; **adop'tianist, adop'tionist; adop'tion.**—*adj.* **adopt'ive** that adopts or is adopted. [L. *adoptāre—ad*, to, *optāre*, to choose.]

adore *ə-dōr'*, *-dor'*, *v.t.* to worship: to love or reverence

intensely.—*adj.* **ador'able.**—*n.* **ador'ableness.**—*adv.* **ador'ably.**—*ns.* **adorā'tion; ador'er.**—*adv* **ador'ingly.** [L. *ad*, to, *ōrāre*, to pray.]

adorn *ə-dörn'*, *v.t.* to deck or dress: to embellish.—*n.* **adorn'ment** ornament: decoration. [O Fr. *äorner*, *adorner*—L. *adōrnāre—ad*, to, *örnāre*, to furnish.]

ad referendum *ad ref-er-en'dum*, *-dōōm*, (L.) to be further considered.

ad rem *ad rem* (L.) to the point: to the purpose.

adren(-o)- *ə-dren(-ō-)*, *-drēn(-ō-)*, in composition, adrenal, adrenal glands, adrenalin.—*adj.* **adrenal** (*ə-drē'nəl*) beside the kidneys: of, relating to the adrenal glands.—*n.* an adrenal gland.—*n.* **adrenaline** (*ə-dren'ə-lin*, *-lēn*) a hormone secreted by the adrenal glands that causes constriction of the arteries, so increasing blood pressure and stimulating the heart muscle; also produced synthetically (as **Adrenalin®**) for this property.—*adj.* **adre'nocorticotrop(h)ic** (*kör'tikō-trop'ik*, *-trof'ik*; **cortex** and Gr. *trophē*, food) stimulating the activity of the adrenal cortex.—*ns.* **adrenocorticotrop(h)ic hormone**, also **adrenocorticotrop(h)in** (*-trof'in*, *-trop'in*, *trō'*) a hormone having this action, secreted by the pituitary gland, also produced synthetically e.g. as a treatment for rheumatoid arthritis:—abbrev. **ACTH.**—**adrenal glands** two small ductless glands over the kidneys which secrete adrenaline and steroids [L *ad*, to, *rēnēs*, kidneys.]

adrift *ə-drift'*, *adj.* or *adv.* drifting: loose from moorings: left to one's own resources, without help, guidance, or contacts: cut loose. [Prep. **a**, and **drift**.]

adroit *ə-droit'*, *adj.* dexterous: skilful: ingenious.—*adv.* **adroit'ly.**—*n.* **adroit'ness.** [Fr. *à droit*, according to right—L. *directus*, straight; see **direct**.]

adsorb *ad-sörb'*, *v.t.* of a solid, to take up a vapour on its surface (cf. **absorb**).—*ns.* **adsorb'ate** the vapour adsorbed; **adsorb'ent** a solid (as charcoal) that adsorbs a vapour in contact with it; **adsorp'tion.** [L *ad*, to, *sorbēre*, to suck in.]

adsuki bean. Same as **adzuki bean.**

ad summum *ad sum'um*, *sōōm'oō m*, (L.) to the highest point.

aduki bean. Same as **adzuki bean.**

adulate *ad'ū-lāt*, *v.t.* to fawn upon, to flatter —*ns.* **adūlā'tion**; **ad'ūlātor.**—*adj.* **ad'ūlatory.** [L. *adūlārī*, *adūlātus*, to fawn upon.]

adult *ad'ult*, *ə-dult'*, *adj.* grown-up: mature: of or for adults.—*n.* a grown-up person.—*n.* **ad'ulthood.** [L. *adultus*, pa.p. of *adolēscĕre*, to grow up; see **adolescent**.]

adulterate *ə-dult'ər-āt*, *v t* to debase, falsify, by mixing with something inferior or spurious.—*adj.* defiled by adultery: spurious: corrupted by base elements —*ns.* **adult'erant** that with which anything is adulterated, **adulterā'tion** the act of adulterating: the state of being adulterated; **adult'erātor** one who adulterates a commodity; **adult'erer** one guilty of adultery:—*fem.* **adult'eress.**—*adj.* **adult'erine** resulting from adultery: spurious.—*adj* **adult'erous** pertaining to, of the nature of, guilty of, adultery.—*adv.* **adult'erously.**—*n.* **adult'ery** violation of the marriage-bed, whether one's own or another's: unchastity generally (*B.*): applied opprobriously, esp. by theologians to marriages disapproved of: image-worship. [L. *adulterāre*, *-ātum*, prob. from *ad*, to, and *alter*, another Some forms come from Fr., remodelled later on Latin.]

adumbrate *ad'um-brāt*, or *-um'*, *v.t.* to give a faint shadow of: to shadow forth: to foreshadow: to overshadow.—*n.* **adumbrā'tion.** [L *adumbrāre*, *-ātus—ad*, to, *umbra*, a shadow.]

ad valorem *ad val-ör'əm*, *-ör'*, *wal-ör'-em*, (L.) according, in proportion, to value.

For other sounds see detailed chart of pronunciation.

advance ǝd-väns, v.t. to put forward: to promote: to further: to raise in price: to supply beforehand: to pay before due time: to lend, esp. on security.—v.i. to move or go forward: to approach esp. aggressively (with on): to make progress: to rise in rank or in value.—n. a forward move: progress: an increase: a rise in price, value, wages: payment beforehand: a loan: an approach, overture, move towards agreement, favour, etc.—adj. before in place: made, given, etc., ahead of time.—adj. **advanced** at, appropriate to, a far-on stage (of education, thought, emancipation, life, etc.).—n. **advance'ment** promotion: furthering: payment in advance.—**advance factory** one built to encourage development, in the belief that a firm will take it over; **advance(d) guard** a guard or party in front of the main body; **advanced level** same as A-level.—**in advance** before: in front. [O.Fr. avancer—L.L. abante (Fr. avant)—L. ab ante, from before; the prefix refashioned later as if from ad.]

advantage ǝd-vänt'ij, n. superiority over another: a favouring condition or circumstance: gain or benefit: the first point after deuce (tennis).—v.t. and v.i. to benefit or profit.—adj. **advantageous** (ad-vǝn-tā'jǝs) of advantage: useful (with to and for).—adv. **advanta'geously.**—n. **advanta'geousness.—advantage rule** in games, a rule under which an infringement and its penalty are overlooked when this is to the advantage of the non-offending side.—**advantage server,** **striker** the server, the striker has gained the first point after deuce; **have the advantage of** to recognise without being recognised; **take advantage of** to avail oneself of: to make undue use of an advantage over; **to advantage** so that the merits are readily perceived. [Fr. avantage—avant, before; see **advance**.]

advection ad-vek'shǝn, (meteor.) n. movement horizontally of air or atmospheric conditions. [L. advectio—ad, vehěre, to carry.]

advene ad-věn', v.i. to be superadded.—n. **advent** (ad'vǝnt, -vent) a coming or arrival: (with cap.) the first or the second coming of Christ: the period immediately before the festival of the Nativity, including four Sundays.—n. **Ad'ventist** one who expects a second coming of Christ: a millenarian.—adj. **adventitious** (ad-vǝn-tish'ǝs; L. adventicius, extraneous) accidental: additional: foreign: appearing casually: developed out of the usual order or place.—adv. **adventi'tiously.** [L. advenire, adventum, to approach, happen—ad, to, venire, to come; adventus, arrival.]

adventure ǝd-ven'chǝr, n. a remarkable incident: an enterprise a commercial speculation: an exciting experience: the spirit of enterprise.—n. **adven'turer** one who engages in hazardous enterprises: a soldier of fortune, or speculator: one who pushes his fortune, esp. by unscrupulous means:—fem. **adven'turess** (chiefly in bad sense).—adj. **adven'turesome** adventurous.—n. **adven'turism** the practice of engaging in hazardous and ill-considered enterprises: in foreign policy, opportunism employed in the service of expansionism.—n. and adj. **adven'turist.**—adj. **adven'turous** enterprising: ready to incur risk.—adv. **adven'turously.**—n. **adven'turousness.—adventure playground** a playground with objects that can be used by children for building, to climb on, etc. [L. adventūrus, fut. p. of advenīre, to approach, happen—ad, to, venīre, to come; partly through Fr.]

adverb ad'vûrb, n. a word added to a verb, adjective, or other adverb to express some modification of the meaning or an accompanying circumstance.—adj **adverb'ial** (ǝd-).—adv. **adverb'ially.** [L. adverbium—ad, to, verbum, a word (a trans. of Gr. epirrēma, lit. that which is said afterwards).]

adverbum ad vûr'bǝm, wer'bŏŏm, (L.) to a word: word for word.

adversary ad'vǝr-sǝr-i, n. an opponent.—adjs. **adversative** (ǝd-vûrs') denoting opposition, contrariety, or variety; **ad'verse** (-vûrs) contrary (with to): opposed: unfavourable: facing the main axis (bot.).—adv. **ad'versely.**—ns. **ad'verseness; advers'ity** adverse circumstances: misfortune. [L. adversus—ad, to, and vertěre, versum, to turn.]

advert¹ ad-vûrt', v.i. (with to) to turn one's attention: to refer.—ns. **advert'ence, advert'ency** attention: heedfulness: regard.—adj. **advert'ent** attentive: heedful.—adv. **advert'ently.** [L. advertěre—ad, to, vertěre, to turn.]

advert². See **advertise.**

advertise ad'vǝr-tīz, -tīz', v.t. to give notice of: to give public information about merits claimed for: to draw attention to: to offer for sale by public notice, printed or broadcast.—v.i. to issue advertisements: to ask (for) by means of public notice, e.g. in a newspaper. —ns. **advertisement** (ǝd-vûr'tis-mǝnt) the act of advertising: a public notice (coll. short forms **ad**, **ad'vert**): any device for obtaining public favour or notoriety; **advertiser** (ad', or -tīz'); **ad'vertising.—ad-man** (ad'-man) one who takes part in advertising. [Fr. avertir, avertiss—L. advertěre; see **advert**.]

advice ǝd-vis', n. counsel: information (usu. in pl.): formal official intelligence about anything: specially skilled opinion, as of a physician or lawyer. [O.Fr. advis—L. ad visum, according to what is seen or seems best.]

advise ǝd-vīz', v.t. to counsel: to recommend: to inform: to announce.—v.i. to consult (with).—n. **advisabil'ity**—adj. **advis'able** to be recommended: expedient: open to advice.—n. **advis'ableness.**—adv. **advis'ably.**—adjs. **advis'atory** (rare) advisory; **advised** having duly considered: considered: deliberate: apprised: amenable to advice.—adv. **advis'edly** (-id-li) after consideration: intentionally: wisely, prudently.—ns. **advis'edness** deliberate consideration: prudent procedure; **advis'er, advis'or** one who advises: a teacher appointed by an education authority to advise on the teaching and development of his subject; **advis'ership.**—n. **advis'orate** the body of advisers appointed by an education authority.—adj. **advis'ory** having the attribute or function of advising. [O.Fr. aviser, and L.L. advisāre; cf. **advice**.]

advocaat ad'vō-kät, n. a liqueur containing eggs and flavourings: a medicinal drink of eggs, rum, and lemon-juice. [Du. advokaatenborrel, advocate's dram, as a clearer of the throat.]

advocate ad'vǝ-kit, ad'vǝ-kāt, n. an intercessor or defender: one who pleads the cause of another: one who is qualified to plead before the higher courts of law—the ordinary name in Scotland and some other countries, corresponding to barrister in England: one who recommends or urges something e.g. a certain reform, method, etc.—v.t. (ad'vǝ-kāt) to plead in favour of: to recommend.—Also v.i. (with for).—ns. **ad'vocacy** (-kǝ-si) the function of an advocate: a pleading for: defence; **advoca'tion; ad'vocator.—**adj. **ad'vocatory.—Lord Advocate** the first law-officer of the crown and public prosecutor of crimes for Scotland. [O.Fr. avocat and L. advocātus—advocāre, -ātum, to call in—ad, to, vocāre, to call.]

adytum ad'i-tǝm, n. the most sacred part of a temple: the chancel of a church:—pl. **ad'yta.** [Latinised from Gr. adyton—a-, priv., dyein, to enter.]

adze adz, n. a cutting tool with an arched blade which is set at right angles to the handle. [O.E. adesa.]

adzuki bean ad-zŏŏ'ki bēn, a type of kidney bean

grown esp. in China and Japan.—Also **adsuki bean** (ad-sōō'ki), **aduki bean** (a-dōō'ki). [Jap. azuki.]

aecidium ə-sid'i-əm, n. a cup-shaped fructification in rust fungi.—Also **aecium** (ē'si-əm):—pls. **aecid'ia**, **aec'ia**.—ns. **aecid'iospore**, **aec'iospore** spore produced in it. [Gr. (dim. of) aikiā, injury.]

aedile ē'dīl, n. a magistrate in ancient Rome who had the charge of public buildings, games, markets, police, etc.—n. **ae'dileship**. [L. aedīlis—aedēs, -is, a building.]

aegis ē'jis, n. orig. a shield belonging to Zeus, or to Pallas: protection: patronage. [Gr. aigis.]

aegrotat ē-grō'tat, or ē', n. in universities, a medical certificate of illness, or a degree granted on it. [L. aegrōtat, is sick, 3rd pers. sing. pres. indic. of aegrōtāre—aeger, sick.]

aeluro-. See all(o)ur(o)-.

aeolian ē-ō'li-ən, adj. pertaining to, acted on by, or due to the agency of, the wind: aerial.—**aeolian** (or with cap.) harp a sound-box with strings tuned in unison, sounding harmonics in a current of air; **aeolian rocks** (geol.) those deposited by wind, as desert sands. [L. Aeolus—Gr. Aiolos, god of the winds.]

aeolotropy ē-əl-ot'rə-pi, n. variation in physical properties according to direction.—adj. **aeolotrop'ic**. [Gr. aiolos, changeful, tropē, a turn.]

aeon, eon ē'on, n. a vast age: eternity: the largest, or a very large division of geological time.—adj. **aeō'nian** eternal. [L. aeon—Gr. aiōn.]

Aepyornis ē-pi-ör'nis, n. a gigantic Recent fossil wingless bird of Madagascar. [Gr. aipys, tall, ornis, bird.]

aerate ā'ər-āt, v.t. to put air into: to charge with air or with carbon dioxide or other gas (as **aerated waters**): to excite, perturb (coll.).—ns. **aera'tion** exposure to the action of air: mixing or saturating with air or other gas: oxygenation of the blood by respiration; **ā'erator** an apparatus for the purpose.—**aerated concrete** lightweight concrete made by a process which traps gas bubbles in the mix. [L. āēr, air.]

aerial ā-ē'ri-əl, also -er', adj. of, in, belonging to, the air: airy: unreal: lofty: (for the following meanings usu. ā'(ə)ri-əl) atmospheric: elevated: connected with aircraft, e.g. used in, against, aircraft: using aircraft (as aerial support, reconnaissance, warfare): carried out from aircraft: growing in air (biol.).—n. (all ā'(ə)ri-əl) a wire, rod, etc. exposed to receive or emit electromagnetic waves: an antenna.—ns. **aer'ialist** one who performs on the high wire or trapeze; **aeriality** (-al'i-ti).—adv. **aer'ially.—aerial railway**, ropeway one for overhead conveyance. [L. āērius—āēr, air.]

aerie. Same as eyrie.

aeriform ā'(ə)r-i-förm, adj. gaseous: unreal. [L. āēr, air, and fōrma, form.]

aero- ā'(ə)r-ō-, in combination, air.—n. sing. **aerobat'ics** (Gr. bateein, to tread) the art of performing stunts in the air: aerial acrobatics.—n. **a'erobe** (Gr. bios, life) an organism that requires free oxygen for respiration.—adjs. **aerobic** (-ōb', -ob') requiring free oxygen for respiration: effected by aerobes, as a biochemical change: involving the activity of aerobes: of, relating to, aerobics.—adv. **aerob'ically.**—n. sing. **aerob'ics** a system of exercising, by means of such rhythmic activities as walking, swimming, cycling, etc., that aims to improve physical fitness through increased oxygen consumption.—Also **Aerobics®.—aerobi'ont** an aerobe; **a'erobus** an airbus: a passenger helicopter; **a'erodrome** an area, with its buildings, etc., used for the take-off and landing of aircraft.—adjs. **aerodynam'ic, -al.**—adv. **aerodynam'ically.**—n. sing. **aerodynam'ics** the dynamics of gases.—ns. **aeroem'bolism** an airman's

condition similar to caisson disease, caused by rapid ascent to high altitudes; **a'ero-engine** an aircraft engine; **a'erofoil** a body (e.g. wing, tail plane) shaped so as to produce an aerodynamic reaction (lift) normal to its direction of motion, for a small resistance (drag) in that plane; **a'erogram**, **a'erogramme**, **aérogramme** an air letter: a sheet of thin paper, with postage stamp imprinted, to be folded and sent by airmail at a special low rate; **a'erolite**, **a'erolith** a meteoric stone or meteorite (Gr. lithos, a stone).—adjs. **aerolit'ic**; **aerolog'ical.**—ns. **aerol'ogist**; **aerol'ogy** the branch of science that treats of the atmosphere; **a'eronaut** (Gr. nautēs, a sailor) a balloonist or airman.—adjs. **aeronaut'ic, -al.**—n. sing. **aeronaut'ics** the science or art of aerial navigation.—ns. **aeron'omist**; **aeron'omy** the science of the earth's atmosphere.—adj. **aerophōb'ic** (or -fōb').—ns. **a'erophyte** an epiphyte (Gr. phyton, a plant); **a'eroplane** any heavier-than-air power-driven flying-machine, with fixed wings: a small plane for aerostatic experiments (see plane²); **a'erosol** a colloidal system, such as a mist or a fog, in which the dispersion medium is a gas: a liquid, e.g. insecticide, in a container under pressure: the container; **a'erospace** the earth's atmosphere together with space beyond: the branch of technology or of industry concerned with the flight of spacecraft through this (as adj. pertaining to, or capable of operating in, air and/or space). [Gr. āēr, air.]

aery. Same as eyrie.

Aesculapian ēs-kū-lā'pi-ən, or es-, adj. pertaining to Aesculapius, and so to the art of healing. [L. Aesculāpius, Gr. Asklēpios, god of healing.]

aesthesia, in U.S. es-, es-thēz'i-ə, ēs-, **aesthēsis** ns. feeling: sensitivity.—n. **aesthēs'iogen** something producing sensation, esp. a stimulus or suggestion producing a sensory effect on a subject under hypnosis.—adj. **aesthēsiogen'ic.**—n. **aes'thete** (-thēt) a professed disciple of aestheticism: one who affects an extravagant love of art.—adjs. **aesthetic** (es-thet'ik, is-, ēs-) orig. relating to perception by the senses: generally relating to possessing, or pretending to, a sense of beauty; artistic or affecting to be artistic; **aesthet'ical** pertaining to aesthetics.—adv. **aesthet'-ically.**—n. **aesthetician** (-tish'ən) one devoted to or versed in aesthetics.—v.t. **aesthet'icise, -ize** (-sīz) to render aesthetic.—ns. **aesthet'icism** the principles of aesthetics: the cult of the beautiful, applied esp. to a late 19th-century movement to bring art into life, which developed into affectation: **aesthet'icist.**—n. sing. **aesthet'ics** the principles of taste and art: the philosophy of the fine arts. [Gr. aisthētikos, perceptive—aisthanesthai, to feel or perceive.]

aestival, in U.S. es-, ēs-tī'vəl, or es-, adj. of summer.—v.i. **aes'tivate** (-ti-vāt) to pass the summer.—n. **aestivā'tion** a spending of the summer: manner of folding in the flower-bud (bot.): arrangement of foliage leaves relative to one another in the bud (bot.): dormancy during the dry season (zool. and bot.). [L. aestīvus, aestīvālis, relating to summer, aestīvāre, to pass the summer—aestās, summer.]

aetatis suae ē-tat'is sū'ē, ī-tāt'is sōō'ī, (L.) of his (or her) age.

aether ē'thər, n. Same as ether (but not generally used in the chemical sense).

aetiology, in U.S. et-, ē-ti-ol'ə-ji, n. the science or philosophy of causation: an inquiry into the origin or causes of anything, esp. a disease.—adj. **aetiolog'ical.** [Gr. aitiologiā—aitiā, cause, logos, discourse.]

afar ə-fär', adv. from a far distance (usually from afar): at or to a distance (usually afar off). [of and on, far.]

affable *af'ə-bl, adj.* easy to speak to: courteous, esp. towards inferiors: pleasant, friendly.—*n.* **affabil'ity.** —*adv.* **aff'ably.** [Fr.,—L. *affābilis—affārī,* to speak to—*ad,* to, and *fārī,* to speak.]

affair *ə-fār', n.* that which is to be done: business: any matter, occurrence, etc.: a minor battle: a matter of intimate personal concern: a thing (*coll.*): a romantic intrigue, a love affair: (*pl.*) transactions in general: public concerns. [O.Fr. *afaire* (Fr. *affaire*)—*à* and *faire*—L. *ad,* to, *facĕre,* to do; cf. **ado.**]

affaire *a-fer,* (Fr.) *n.* liaison, intrigue: (usu. with name of chief person involved following or preceding) an episode, incident, arousing speculation and scandal **affaire d'honneur** *a-fer do-nœr,* affair of honour (a duel).

affect *ə-fekt', v.t.* to act upon: to infect or attack as disease: to influence: to move the feelings of: (in *pass.* only) to assign, allot.—*n.* (*af'ekt*) the emotion that lies behind action (*psych.*): pleasantness or unpleasantness of, or complex of ideas involved in, an emotional state (*psych.*).—*adjs.* **affect'ed; affect'ing** having power to move the emotions.—*adv.* **affect'-ingly.**—*adj.* **affect'ive** of, arising from, or influencing, emotion.—*adv.* **affect'ively.**—*n.* **affectivity** (*af-ek-tiv'i-ti*). [L. *afficĕre, affectum—ad,* to, *facĕre,* to do.]

affect *ə-fekt', v.t.* to make a show of preferring: to do, wear, inhabit, by preference: to assume: to assume the character of: to make a show or pretence of.— *v.i.* to incline, tend.—*n.* **affecta'tion** (*af-ik-*) assumption of or striving after an appearance of what is not natural or real: pretence.—*adj.* **affect'ed** full of affectation: feigned.—*adv.* **affect'edly.**—*ns.* **'affect'edness; affect'er.** [L. *affectāre, -ātum,* freq. of *afficĕre;* see **affect¹** above.]

affection *ə-fek'shən, n.* the act of influencing: emotion: disposition: inclination: love: attachment: an attribute or property: a disease.—*adjs.* **affec'tional; affec'tionate** full of affection: loving.—*adv.* **affec'-tionately.**—*n.* **affec'tionateness.** [L. *affectiō, -ōnis.*]

affenpinscher *af'en-pinsh-ər, n.* a small dog related to the Brussels griffon, having tufts of hair on the face. [Ger.—*Affe,* monkey, *Pinscher,* terrier.]

afferent *af'ər-ənt, adj.* bringing inwards, as the nerves that convey impulses to the central nervous system. [L. *afferēns, -entis—ad,* to, and *ferre,* to carry.]

affiance *ə-fi'əns, v.t.* to betroth.—*n.* faith pledged: contract of marriage: trust.—*adj.* **affi'anced** betrothed. [O.Fr *afiance.*]

affidavit *af-i-dā'vit, n.* a written declaration on oath. [L.L. *affidāvit,* 3rd pers. sing. perf. of *affidāre,* to pledge one's faith.]

affiliate *ə-fil'i-āt, v.t.* to adopt or attach as a member or branch: to impute paternity of: to assign the origin of.—*v.i.* to become closely connected, to associate: to fraternise.—*n.* (*-ət*) an affiliated person, an associate: a branch, unit, or subsidiary of an organisation.—*n.* **affilia'tion.**—*adj.* **affil'iable.** [L. *af-filiātus,* adopted—*ad,* to, *filius,* a son.]

affine *a-fin', a', n.* a relation, esp. by marriage.—*adj.* **affined'** related: bound by some tie.—*n.* **affinity** (*ə-fin'i-ti*) relationship by marriage: relation of sponsor and godchild: natural or fundamental relationship, esp. common origin: attraction, esp chemical attraction· a spiritual attraction between two persons: a person whose attraction for another is supposed to be of this kind.—*adj* **affin'itive.** [O.Fr. *affin*—L. *affīnis,* neighbouring—*ad,* to, at, *finis,* a boundary.]

affirm *ə-fûrm', v.t.* to assert confidently or positively: to ratify (a judgment): to confirm or stand by (one's own statement): to state in the affirmative (*log*)· to

declare formally, without an oath (*law*).—*v.i.* to make an affirmation.—*adj.* **affirm'able.**—*n.* **affirm'-ance** affirmation: assertion: confirmation.—*adj.* and *n.* **affirm'ant.**—*n.* **affirmation** (*af-ər-mā'shən, -ûr-*) assertion: that which is affirmed: a positive judgment or proposition: a solemn declaration in lieu of an oath.—*adj.* **affirm'ative** affirming or asserting: positive, not negative: dogmatic.—*n.* the affirmative mode: an affirmative word, proposition or utterance.—*adv.* **affirm'atively.**—*adj.* **affirm'atory.**—*n.* **affirm'er.**—*adv.* **affirm'ingly.—affirmative action** (chiefly *U.S.*) positive steps taken to ensure that minority groups and women are not discriminated against, esp. as regards employment. [O.Fr. *afer-mer*—L. *affirmāre—ad,* to, *firmus,* firm.]

affix *ə-fiks', v.t* to fix to something: to subjoin: to attach: to append: to add (to something).—*n.* (*af'iks*) an addition to a root, stem, or word, to modify its meaning or use, whether *prefix* or *suffix:* any appendage or addition. [L. *affigĕre, -fixum—ad,* to, *figĕre,* to fix.]

afflict *ə-flikt', v.t.* to distress grievously: to harass: to vex.—*adj.* **afflict'ed** harassed by disease of body or mind (with *with*): suffering.—*n.* and *adj* **afflict'ing** distressing.—*n.* **afflic'tion** state or cause of grievous distress.—*adj.* **afflict'ive** causing distress. [L. *afflīgĕre, -flictum,* to overthrow, cast down—*ad,* to, *flīgĕre,* to dash to the ground.]

affluent *af'lōō-ənt, adj.* inflowing: abounding: wealthy. —*n.* an inflowing stream.—*n.* **aff'luence** inflow: abundance: wealth.—*adv.* **aff'luently.**—*n.* **aff'luent-ness.—affluent society** a society in which the ordinary person can afford many things once regarded as luxuries. [L. *affluĕre—ad,* to, *fluĕre, fluxum,* to flow.]

afforce *ə-fōrs', ə-fors', (law) v.t.* to strengthen (e g. a jury by addition of skilled persons).—*n.* **afforce'-ment.** [O.Fr. *aforcer*—L.L. *exfortiāre*—L. *ex, out, fortis,* strong.]

afford *ə-fōrd', ə-ford', v.t.* to yield, give, provide: to bear the expense, or disadvantage, of (having the necessary money or other resources or security of position). [M.E. *aforthen*—O.E. *geforthian,* to further or cause to come forth.]

affray *ə-frā', n.* a disturbance, breach of the peace: a brawl, fight, fray. [O.Fr. *afrayer, esfreer* (Fr. *ef-frayer*)—L.L. *exfridāre,* to break the king's peace—L. *ex,* out of, O.H.G. *fridu* (Ger. *Friede*), peace.]

affricate *af'ri-kət, -kāt n.* consonant sound beginning as a plosive and passing into the corresponding fricative (*phon.*).—*adjs.* **affric'ative; aff'ricated.**—*n* **affrica'tion.** [L. *affricāre, -ātum,* to rub against—*ad,* to, *fricāre,* to rub.]

affright *ə-frīt, v.t.* to frighten. [O.E. *āfyrhtan—ā-,* intens., *fyrhtan,* to frighten]

affront *ə-frunt', v.t.* to meet face to face: to face: to confront: to insult to one's face.—*n* a contemptuous treatment: an open insult: indignity.—*adj.* **affront'ed** insulted or offended, esp. in public.— *n.* and *adj.* **affront'ing.**—*adv.* **affront'ingly.**—*adj.* **affront'ive.** O.Fr. *afronter,* to slap on the forehead —L.L. *affrontāre*—L. *ad,* to, *frōns, frontis,* forehead.]

Afghan *af'gan, n* a native or citizen, or the language, of Afghanistan: (without *cap*) a heavy knitted or crocheted woollen blanket or shawl —**Afghan hound** an ancient hunting and sheep dog of Afghanistan and northern India, kept as a pet in the West.

aficionado *a-fish-yo-na'dō, a-fē-thyō-na'dhō,* (Sp.) *n.* an amateur: an ardent follower, fan:—*pl.* **aficiona'dos.**

afield *ə-fēld', adv.* to, in, or on the field· to or at a distance. [**on, field.**]

afire ə-fīr', *adj.* and *adv.* on fire: in a state of inflammation. [on, **fire**.]

aflame ə-flām', *adj.* and *adv.* in a flaming or glowing state. [on, **flame**.]

afloat ə-flōt', *adv.* and *adj.* in a floating state: at sea: unfixed: in circulation. [on, **float**.]

afoot ə-fŏŏt', *adv.* and *adj.* on foot: astir: actively in being. [on, **foot**.]

afore ə-fōr', -för', *prep.* in front of, before.—*adv.* beforehand, previously.—*adv.* **afore'hand** beforehand: before the regular time for accomplishment: in advance.—*adjs.* **afore'mentioned** previously mentioned, aforesaid; **afore'said** said or named before; **afore'thought** thought of or meditated before: premeditated.—*n.* premeditation. [O.E. *onforan* —*on, foran;* see **before**.]

a fortiori ā för-ti (or -shi)-ör'ī, ä för-ti-ör'ē, (L.) with stronger reason.

afraid ə-frād', *adj.* struck with fear, fearful (with *of*): timid: reluctantly inclined to think (that): regretfully admitting. [Pa.p. of **affray**.]

afreet. See **afrit.**

afresh ə-fresh', *adv.* anew. [Pfx. *a*-, **fresh.**]

African af'rik-ən, *adj.* of Africa.—*n.* a native of Africa: a Negro or other person of black race, esp. one whose people live now, or lived recently, in Africa.—*n.* **Africanisa'tion, -z-.**—*v.t.* **Af'ricanise, -ize** to make African: to exclude people of other races from, replacing them with Africans.—Also *v.i.*— *ns.* **Af'ricanism** an African characteristic; **Af'ricanist** one learned in matters relating to Africa.—*ns.* **Afrikaans** (af-ri-käns') one of two official languages of S. Africa; it developed from 17th cent. Dutch; **Afrikan'er** (formerly **African'er, African'der, Afrikan'der**) one born in South Africa of white parents (esp. of Dutch descent).—Also *adj.*— **African coast fever** see **East Coast** fever; **African violet** a plant from tropical Africa (*Saintpaulia ionantha*), commonly with violet-coloured flowers but not related to the violet. [L. *Africānus.*]

afrit, afreet ä-frēt', af'rēt, *n.* an evil demon in Arabian mythology. [Ar.'*ifrīt*, a demon.]

Afro af'rō, (*coll.*, sometimes without *cap.*) *adj.* a shortening for African: (of a hairstyle) characterised by thick, bushy curls standing out from the head, as worn by some negroes (also *n.*).—**Afro-** in composition, African (and).—*adj.* **Afro-American** pertaining to American(s) of African descent.—Also *n.*—*adj.* **Afro-Asian** (-äzh'yən) of, consisting of, Africans and Asians: of Asian origin but African citizenship: of mixed Asian and African blood: (of language) belonging to a group spoken in southwest Asia and north Africa.

aft äft, *adj.* or *adv.* behind: near or towards the stern of a vessel. [O.E. *æftan.*]

after äf'tər, *prep.* and *adv.* behind in place: later in time than: following in search of: in imitation of: in proportion to, or in agreement with: concerning: subsequent to, or subsequently, afterwards: in the manner of, or in imitation of: according to: in honour of: with the name, or a name derived from the name, of.—*adj.* behind in place: later in time: more towards the stern (in this sense as if the *comp.* of **aft**).— *conj.* later than the time when.—*n.pl.* **af'ters** (*coll.*) the dessert or other course following a main course. —*advs.* **af'terward** (chiefly *U.S.*), **af'terwards** at a later time: subsequently.—**af'terbirth** the placenta and membranes expelled from the uterus after a birth: a posthumous birth; **af'terburner** the device used in afterburning; **af'terburning** reheat; **af'tercare** care subsequent to a period of treatment, corrective training, etc.—Also *adj.*—**af'ter-crop** a second crop from the same land in the same year; **after-dinn'er** the time following dinner.—*adj.* belonging to that time, esp. before leaving the table.—**af'ter-effect** an effect that comes after an interval; **af'tergame** a second game played in the hope of reversing the issue of the first: means employed after the first turn of affairs; **af'terglow** a glow in the sky after sunset; **af'tergrowth** a later growth: an aftermath; **af'ter-image** an image that persists for a time after one looks at an object; **af'ter-life** a future life: later life: a life after death; **af'termath** a second mowing of grass in the same season: later consequences, esp. if bad (*fig.*); **af'ternoon** the time between noon and evening.—Also *adj.* **af'ternoon.**—**af'tershave** a lotion for men, for use after shaving; **af'tertaste** a taste that remains or comes after eating or drinking; **af'terthought** a thought or thing thought of after the occasion: a later thought or reflection or modification; **af'terword** an epilogue.—**after a fashion** see **fashion; after all** when everything is taken into account: in spite of everything. [O.E. *æfter,* in origin a comparative from *af* (*æf*), **off.**]

aftermost äf'tər-mōst, -məst, **aftmost** äft', *adjs.* superl. of **aft,** nearest the stern: hindmost. [O.E. *æftemest,* a double superlative.]

afterward(s). See under **after.**

aga, agha ä'gə, ä-gä', *n.* a Turkish commander or chief officer.—**Aga Khan** (kän) the head of the Ismaili Muslims. [Turk. *aga, aghā.*]

again, ə-gen', also ə-gān', *adv.* once more: in return: in response or consequence: back: further: on the other hand: to the same amount in addition.—**again and again** repeatedly. [O.E. *ongēan, ongegn.*]

against ə-genst', also ə-gānst', *prep.* opposite to: in opposition or resistance to: in protection from: in or into contact or collision with or pressure upon: in anticipation of: in contrast or comparison with: in exchange for: instead of. [**again,** with gen. ending *-es,* and *-t* as in **whilst, betwixt, amongst.**]

agamic a-gam'ik, **agamous** ag'ə-məs, *adjs.* asexual: parthenogenetic.—**agamogenesis** (-jen') reproduction without sex, as in lower animals and in plants. [Gr. *a-,* priv., *gamos,* marriage.]

Agapanthus a-gə-pan'thəs, *n.* a genus of lily native to South Africa: (without *cap.*) a plant of the genus. [Gr. *agape,* love, *anthos,* flower.]

agape[1] ag'ə-pē, ə. a love-feast, held by the early Christians at communion time, when contributions were made for the poor: selfless Christian brotherly love: the love of God for man:—*pl.* **ag'apae** (-pē). [Gr. *agapē,* love.]

agape[2] ə-gāp', *adj.* or *adv.* with gaping mouth. [Prep. **a,** and **gape.**]

agar-agar ä'gär-ä'gär, ä'gär-ä'gär, *n.* a jelly prepared from seaweeds of various kinds used in bacteriaculture, medicine, glue-making, silk-dressing, and cooking: any of the seaweeds concerned.—Also **a'gar.** [Malay.]

agaric ag'ər-ik, or əg-ar'ik, *n.* a fungus, properly one of the mushroom family, but loosely applied.—*adj.* **agar'ic.** [Gr. *agarikon.*]

agate ag'it, -ät, *n.* a banded variegated chalcedony: a marble used in games, made of this material or of variegated glass. [Fr.—Gr. *achātēs,* said to be so called because first found near the river *Achates* in Sicily.]

Agave a-gā'vē, *n.* an aloe-like American genus of amaryllids: (without *cap.*) a plant of this genus.—Also called American aloe, maguey, century-plant. [L. *Agāvē,* Gr. *Agauē,* daughter of Cadmus, fem. of *agauos,* illustrious.]

age āj, *n.* duration of life: the time during which a person or thing has lived or existed: time of life reached: mature years: legal maturity: the time of being old: equivalence in development to the average of an actual age: a period of time: any great division of world, human, or individual history: a generation: a century: (often *pl.*) a long time, however short (*coll.*).—*v.i.* to grow old: to develop the characteristics of old age.—*v.t.* to make to seem old or to be like the old: to mature:—*pr.p.* **aging** or **ageing** (*āj'ing*); *pa.t.* and *pa.p.* **aged** (*ājd*).—*adj.* **aged** (*āj'id*) advanced in age: (*ājd*) of the age of.—*n. pl.* (*āj'id*; usu. with *the*) old people.—*ns.* **agedness** (*āj'id-nis*) the condition of being aged; **age(e)'ing** the process of growing old or developing qualities of the old: maturing: change in properties that occurs in certain metals at atmospheric temperature after heat treatment or cold working; **age'ism** discrimination on grounds of age.—*n.* and *adj.* **age'ist**.—*adjs.* **age'less** never growing old, perpetually young: timeless; **age'long** lasting an age.—*age'-bracket** the people between particular ages, taken as a group; **age group** a group of people of a similar age.—**be, act your age!** don't be childish; **of age** old enough to be deemed legally mature (with respect to voting, crime, contracts, marriage, etc.); **over age** too old; **under age** too young: not yet of age. [O.Fr. *aåge* (Fr. *âge*)—L. *aetās*, *-ātis*, for *aevitās*—L. *aevum*, age.]

agency. See **agent**.

agenda *ɔ-* or *a-jen'dɔ*, *n.pl.* things to be done—programme of business for a meeting (often treated as a *sing.*). [L. neuter pl. of *agendus*, to be done, gerundive of *agēre*, to do.]

agent *ā'jɔnt*, *n.* a person or thing that acts or exerts power: any natural force acting on matter: one authorised or delegated to transact business for another: a paid political party worker: a secret agent, spy.—*adj.* acting: of an agent.—*n.* **agency** (*ā'jɔn-si*) the operation or action of an agent: instrumentality: the office or business of an agent: such a business putting employers and those requiring employment in contact with each other.—*adj.* **agen'tial** (*-shɔl*) pertaining to an agent or agency.—**agency shop**, a shop in which the union usu. by agreement with the management represents all workers whether they are members of it or not. [L. *agēns*, *-entis*, pr.p. of *agēre*, to do.]

agent provocateur *a-zhā prō-vo-ka-tœr*, (Fr.) one employed to lead others, by pretended sympathy, into acts incurring penalties.

agglomerate *ɔ-glom'ɔr-āt*, *v.t.* to make into a ball: to collect into a mass.—*v.i.* to grow into a mass.—*adj.* (*-rɔt*, *-rāt*) agglomerated: clustered: gathered in a head (*bot.*).—*n.* (*-rɔt*, *-rāt*) a volcanic rock consisting of irregular fragments.—*adj.* **agglom'erated**.—*n.* **agglomerā'tion**.—*adj.* **agglom'erative**. [L. *agglomerāre*, *-ātum*—ad, to, L. *glomus*, *glomeris*, a ball.]

agglutinate *ɔ-glōō'ti-nāt*, *v.t.* to glue together: to cause to cohere or clump.—*v.i.* to cohere as if glued: to clump.—*adj.* (*-nɔt*, *-nāt*) agglutinated.—*adjs.* **agglut'inable; agglut'inant**.—*n.* an agglutinating agent.—*n.* **agglutinā'tion** the act of agglutinating: an agglutinated mass: the clumping of bacteria, blood corpuscles, protozoa, etc. (*biol.*): a type of word-formation process in which words are inflected by the addition of one or more meaningful elements to a stem, each of which elements expresses one single element of meaning (*linguistics*).—*adj.* **agglut'inative** tending, or having power, to agglutinate.—**agglutinating, agglutinative languages** languages in which words are inflected by agglutination. [L. *agglûtinâre*—ad, to, *glūten*, *-inis*, glue.]

aggrandise, -ize *ɔ-gran'dīz*, *ag'rɔn-*, *v.t.* to make

greater.—*n.* **aggrandisement, -z-** (*ɔg-ran'diz-mɔnt*). [Fr. *agrandir*, *agrandiss-*—L. *ad*, to, *grandis*, large.]

aggravate *ag'rɔ-vāt*, *v.t.* to make more grievous or worse: to irritate (*coll.*).—*adj.* **agg'ravating**.—*adv.* **agg'ravatingly**.—*n.* **aggravā'tion**. [L. *aggravāre*, *-ātus*—ad, to, *gravis*, heavy.]

aggregate *ag'ri-gāt*, *v.t.* to collect into a mass or whole: to assemble: to add as a member to a society: to amount to (*coll.*).—*v.i.* to accumulate.—*adj.* (*-gɔt*, *-gāt*) formed of parts that combine to make a whole: gathered in a mass or whole: united in a colonial organism: formed from an apocarpous gynaeceum (*bot.*).—*n.* (*-gɔt*, *-gāt*) an assemblage: a mass: a total: any material mixed with cement to form concrete: a collection of elements having a common property that identifies the collection (*math.*).—*adv.* **agg'regately**.—*n.* **aggregā'tion**.—*adj.* **agg'regative**. [L. *aggregāre*, *-ātum*, to bring together, as a flock—ad, to, *grex*, *gregis*, a flock.]

aggress *ɔ-gres'*, *v.i.* to make a first attack: to begin a quarrel: to intrude.—*n.* **aggression** (*-gresh'ɔn*) a first act of hostility or injury: the use of armed force by a state against the sovereignty, territorial integrity or political independence of another state: self-assertiveness, either as a good characteristic or as a sign of emotional instability.—*adj.* **aggress'ive** making the first attack, or prone to do so: discourteously hostile or self-assertive: offensive as opposed to defensive: showing energy and initiative.—*adv.* **aggress'ively**.—*ns.* **aggress'iveness; aggress'or** one who attacks first. [L. *aggredī*, *-gressus*—ad, to, *gradī*, to step.]

aggrieve *ɔ-grēv'*, *v.t.* to press heavily upon: to pain or injure.—*adj.* **aggrieved'** injured: having a grievance. [O.Fr. *agrever*—L. *ad*, to, *gravis*, heavy.]

aggro *ag'rō*, *n.* slang short form of **aggravation**, also associated with **aggression**, meaning aggressive behaviour or trouble-making, esp. between gangs, racial groups, etc.

agha. See **aga**.

aghast *ɔ-gäst'*, *adj.* stupefied with horror. [Pa.p. of obs. *agast*—O.E. intens. pfx. *ā-*, and *gǣstan*, to terrify.]

agile *aj'īl*, in U.S. *-ɔl*, *adj.* nimble.—*adv.* **ag'ilely**.—*n.* **agility** (*ɔ-jil'i-ti*) nimbleness. [Fr.,—L. *agilis*—agēre, to do or act.]

agin *ɔ-gin'*, (*dial.*, esp. Ir.) *prep.* against. [**again**.]

agio *aj'(i)ō*, *āj'*, *n.* the sum payable for the convenience of exchanging one kind of money for another, as silver for gold, paper for metal: the difference in exchange between worn or debased coinage and coinage of full value: the amount of deviation from the fixed par of exchange between the currencies of two countries: the discount on a foreign bill of exchange: money-changing:—*pl.* **ag'ios.**—*n.* **agiotage** (*aj'ɔ-tij*) agio: money-changing: stock-jobbing: speculative manoeuvres in stocks. [The word used in It. is *aggio*, a variant of *agio*, convenience.]

agitate *aj'i-tāt*, *v.t.* to keep moving: to stir violently: to disturb: to perturb: to excite: to discuss, or keep up the discussion of.—*v.i.* to stir up public feeling.—*adj.* **ag'itated**.—*adv.* **ag'itatedly**.—*n.* **agitā'tion**.—*adj.* **ag'itative**.—*n.* **ag'itator** one who excites or keeps up a social or political agitation: an apparatus for stirring. [L. *agitāre*, freq. of *agēre*, to put in motion.]

agitato *aj-i-tä'tō*, (*mus.*) *adj.* agitated.—*adv.* agitatedly. [It.,—L. *agitāre*, to agitate.]

agitprop *aj'it-prop'*, *n.* (often *cap.*) (department, person, engaged in) *agit*ation and *prop*aganda, esp. pro-Communist.—Also *adj.*

aglee. See **agley**.

aglet, aiglet, aiguillette *ag'lit, ăg'lit, ā-gwi-let'*, *ns.* the metal tag of a lace or string: an ornamental tag or other metal appendage: anything dangling: (usu. **aiguillette**) a tagged point of braid hanging from the shoulder in some uniforms. [Fr. *aiguillette*, dim. of *aiguille*, a needle—from L. *acūcula*, dim. of *acus*, a needle.]

agley, aglee *ə-gli'*, *ə-glē'*, (*Scot.*) *adv.* askew: awry. [Prep. **a**, and Scot. *gley*, squint.]

aglitter *ə-glit'ər*, *adj.* and *adv.* in a glitter. [Prep. **a**, and **glitter**.]

aglow *ə-glō'*, *adj.* and *adv.* in a glow. [Prep. **a**, and **glow**.]

agnail *ag'nāl*, *n.* a torn shred of skin beside the nail. [O.E. *angnægl*, corn—*ange*, *enge*, compressed, painful, *nægl*, nail (for driving in), confused with *hang*, *anger*, and (finger-) *nail*.]

agnate *ag'nāt*, *adj.* related on the father's side or (*Roman law*) through males only: allied.—*n.* a person so related.—*adjs.* **agnatic** (*-nat'*), **-al**.—*adv.* **agnat'ically**.—*n.* **agna'tion**. [L. *agnātus—ad*, to, (*g*)*nāscī*, to be born. See **cognate**.]

agnomen *ag-*, *əg-nō'mən*, *n.* a name added to the family name, generally on account of some great exploit, as *Africanus* to Publius Cornelius Scipio [L., —*ad*, to, and (*g*)*nōmen*, a name.]

agnostic *ag-*, *əg-nos'tik*, *n.* one who holds that we know nothing of things beyond material phenomena—that a First Cause and an unseen world are things unknown and (some would add) apparently unknowable.— Also *adj.*—*n.* **agnos'ticism**. [Coined by T. H. Huxley in 1869 from Gr. *agnostos*, unknown, unknowable —*a-*, priv., *gnostos*, known, knowable, and *-ic*.]

agnus dei *ag'nəs dē'ī*, *ăg'nŏŏs dā'ē*, a part of the mass beginning with these words: music for it: a figure of a lamb emblematic of Christ, bearing the banner of the cross: a cake of wax stamped with such a figure, and blessed by the Pope. [L. *agnus Dēī*, lamb of God.]

ago *ə-gō'*, *adv.* gone: past: since. [O.E. *āgān*, pa.p. of *āgān*, to pass away—intens. pfx. *ā-*, and *gān*, to go.]

agog *ə-gog'*, *adj.* and *adv.* in excited eagerness. [Perh. connected with O.Fr. *en gogues*, frolicsome.]

agonic *ə-gon'ik*, *adj.* making no angle.—**agonic line** the line of no magnetic variation, along which the magnetic needle points directly north and south. [Gr. *agōnos*—*a-*, priv., *gōniā*, angle.]

agony *ag'ə-ni*, *n.* conflict in games: a violent struggle: extreme suffering: the death struggle: Christ's anguish in Gethsemane.—*v.i.* **ag'onise**, **-ize** to struggle, contend: to suffer agony: to worry (*coll.*).—*v.t.* to subject to agony.—*adj.* **ag'onised**, **-z-** suffering or expressing anguish.—*adv.* **ag'onisedly**, **-z-** (*-iz-id-li*). —*adj.* **ag'onising**, **-z-** causing agony.—*adv.* **ag'onisingly**, **-z-**.—**agony column** the part of a newspaper containing special advertisements, as for missing friends and the like: the part of a newspaper or magazine in which readers submit, and receive advice about, personal problems. [Gr. *agōniā*, contest, agony—*agōn*, meeting, contest.]

agora¹ *ag'ə-ra*, *n.* an assembly, place of assembly, market-place.—*n.* **agorapho'bia** morbid fear of (crossing) open places.—*adj.* and *n.* **agorapho'bic** (or *-fob'*). [Gr. *agora*, assembly, market-place, *phobos*, fear.]

agora² *ag-ə-ra'*, *n.* a monetary unit of Israel, worth 1/100 of an Israeli pound:—*pl.* **agorot** (*-rot'*). [Heb. *agōrāh—āgōr*, to collect.]

agouti, aguti *ə-gōō'tē*, *n.* a small South American rodent allied to the guinea-pig. [Fr.,—Sp. *aguti*—Guaraní *acuti*.]

agraffe *ə-graf'*, *n.* a hooked clasp. [Fr. *agrafe*—*à*, to, *grappe*—L.L. *grappa*—O.H.G. *chrapfo* (Ger. *krappen*), hook.]

agraphia *a-graf'i-ə*, *n.* loss of power of writing, from brain disease or injury.—*adj.* **agraph'ic**. [Gr. *a-*, priv., *graphein*, to write.]

agrarian *əg-rā'ri-ən*, *adj.* relating to land, or its management or distribution.—*n.* **agra'rianism** equitable division of lands: a political movement in favour of change in conditions of property in land. [L. *agrārius —ager*, a field.]

agravic *ə-grav'ik*, *ā-grav'*, *adj.* pertaining to a condition or place where the effect of gravity is zero.

agree *ə-grē'*, *v.i.* to be, or come to be, of one mind (with): to suit, do well (with): to concur (with *with* and *in*, on or *about*): to accede, assent (to): to be consistent (with): to harmonise: to get on together: to be in grammatical concord, take the same gender, number, case, or person (with *with*).—*v.t.* to arrange with consent of all: to concede (that): to decide jointly (to do, that): to consent (to do):—*pr.p.* **agree'ing**; *pa.t.* and *pa.p.* **agreed'**.—*n.* **agreeabil'ity**.—*adj.* **agree'able** suitable: pleasant: in harmony: conformable: willing, consenting (*coll.*).—*adv.* in accordance.—*n.* **agree'ableness**.—*adv.* **agree'ably**.—*n.* **agree'ment** concord: conformity: harmony: a compact, contract, treaty. [O. Fr. *agréer*, to accept kindly—L. *ad*, to, and *grātus*, pleasing.]

agrément *a-grā-mā*, (Fr.) *n.* approval by state of diplomatic representative sent to it:—*n.pl.* **agréments** amenities (also **agrémens**): courtesies, charms, blandishments: embellishments, as grace notes and trills (*mus.*).

agrestic *ə-gres'tik*, *adj.* of the fields: rural: unpolished. [L. *agrestis—ager*, a field.]

agri-, agribusiness, etc. See under **agriculture**.

agriculture *ag'ri-kul-chər*, *n.* the art or practice of cultivating the land.—*adj.* **agricult'ural**.—*n.* **agricult'urist** one skilled in agriculture: a farmer.— Also **agricult'uralist**.—**agri-, agro-** (*-rō-*) in composition, pertaining to fields, land use, or agriculture. —*ns.* **ag'ribusiness**, **ag'robusiness** all the operations of supplying the market with farm produce taken together, including growing, provision of farm machinery, distribution, etc.; **agrobiol'ogy** the study of plant nutrition and soil yields.—*adj.* **agrobiolog'ical**.—*ns.* **agrobiol'ogist**; **agrochem'ical** a chemical intended for agricultural use.—Also *adj.*— *n.* **agroind'ustry** the area of production that serves the needs of both agriculture and industry.—*adj.* **agroindust'rial**.—*n.* **agron'omy** (Gr. *nemein*, to administer, dispense) rural economy.—*adjs.* **agronō'mial**; **agronom'ic**.—*n.sing.* **agronom'ics** the science dealing with the management and productivity of land. [L. *ager*, (Gr. *agros*) field, *cultūra*, cultivation.]

agrimony *ag'ri-mən-i*, *n.* a genus (*Agrimonia*) of the rose family, with small yellow flowers and bitter taste: extended to other plants, especially **hemp-agrimony** (*Eupatorium cannabinum*), a composite. [L. *agrimōnia* (a blunder or misreading)—Gr. *argemōnē*, long prickly-headed poppy.]

agro-, agrobiology, etc. See under **agriculture**.

agrostology *ag-ros-tol'ə-ji*, *n.* the study of grasses.— *adj.* **agrostological** (*-tə-loj'i-kl*).—*n.* **agrostol'ogist**. [Gr. *agrōstis*, dog's-tooth grass.]

aground *ə-grownd'*, *adv.* in or to a stranded condition: on the ground. [Prep. **a**, and **ground**.]

ague *ā'gū*, *n.* a fever with hot and cold fits: malaria: a shivering fit.—*adjs.* **agued** (*ā'gūd*) struck with ague: shivering: cold; **a'guish**.—*adv.* **a'guishly**. [O.Fr. (*fièvre*) *ague*—L. (*febris*) *acūta*, sharp (fever).]

aguti. See **agouti**.

ah *a*, *interj.* expressing surprise, joy, pity, complaint, objection, etc. [Perh. O.Fr. *ah*.]

aha *ə-hä'*, *interj.* of exultation, pleasure, surprise, or contempt [**ah**, and **ha**.]

ahead ə-hed', *adv.* further on: in advance: forward: headlong. [Prep. **a**, and **head**.]

ahem ə-h(e)m', *interj.* a lengthened form of hem².

ahimsa ə-him'sa, *n* duty of sparing animal life: non-violence. [Sans. *ahimsā.*]

ahistorical ā-his-tor'i-kəl, *adj.* not historical: taking no account of, or not related to, history. [Gr. *a-*, priv., and **historical**.]

-aholic, -oholic *-ə-hol'ik, (facet.) suffix* having an addiction to (something) as in *workaholic, clothesoholic.*—**ahol'ism, -ohol'ism** (*-izm*) noun suffix. [By analogy, from *alcoholic, alcoholism.*]

ahorse ə-hörs', *(arch.) adv.* on horseback. [Prep. **a.**]

ahoy ə-hoi', *(naut.) interj.* used in hailing. [**ah** and **hoy.**]

ai ā'ē, *n.* the three-toed sloth. [Tupí *ai*, representing the animal's cry.]

aia. Same as **ayah.**

aid ād, *v.t.* to help.—*n.* help: succour: assistance, as in defending an action: that which helps: an auxiliary: a helper: an apparatus, etc., that gives help, e.g. *hearing-aid, navigational aid*: money, etc., donated to relieve poor or disaster-stricken countries.—*adj.* **aid'ed.**—*n.* **aid'er.**—*adjs.* **aid'ful; aid'ing; aid'less.** —**aid and abet** (*law*) to assist and encourage usu. the commission of a crime; **in aid of** (*coll.*) intended to achieve: in support of. [O.Fr *aider*—L. *adjūtāre*, freq. of *adjuvāre—jùvāre, jūtum*, to help]

aide ād, *n.* a confidential assistant to a person of senior rank e.g. an ambassador or president: an aide-de-camp.—**aide-de-camp** (*ed-, ād'də-kä*) an officer who carries the orders of a general and acts as secretary: an officer attending a king, governor, etc.:—*pl.* **aides-de-camp** (*ed-, ād'-*). [Fr., assistant, assistant on the field.]

aide-mémoire *ed-mā-mwär*, (Fr.) *n.* an aid to the memory: a reminder: a memorandum-book: a written summary of a diplomatic document

AIDS. See under **acquire.**

aiery. A variant of **eyrie.**

aiglet. Same as **aglet.**

aigre-doux *egr'-dōō* (*fem.* **-douce** *-dōōs*), (Fr.) *adj* bitter-sweet, sourish.

aigrette ā'gret, ā-gret', *n.* an egret: an egret plume: a plume: a tuft: a pappus: a spray of jewels: a savoury cooked in deep fat. [Fr.]

aiguille ā-gwēl', *n.* a sharp, needle-like peak of rock: a slender boring-tool.—*n.* **aiguillette'** see **aglet.** [Fr.]

aikido ī-kē'dō, *n.* a Japanese combative sport using locks and pressure against joints.

ail āl, *v.t. (impers.)* to trouble, afflict, be the matter with: to have the matter with one.—*v.i.* to be sickly, indisposed.—*adj.* **ail'ing** unwell: in poor health.—*n.* **ail'ment** pain: indisposition: disease, esp. if not very serious. [O.E. *eglan*, to trouble.]

aileron āl, el'ə-rə, *-ron*, *n.* a flap on an aeroplane wing-tip for lateral balancing. [Fr. dim. of *aile*—L. *āla*, a wing.]

ailouro(o)-, ailuro(o)- ī-lōō r'(ə)-, **aelur(o)-** ē-lōō r', *t-*, in composition, cat —*ns* **ail(o)ur'ophile** (*-fīl*) a cat lover or fancier; **ail(o)urophilia** (*-fil'i-ə*); **ail(o)ur'ophobe** (*-fōb*) a cat hater: one with an abnormal fear of cats; **ail(o)uroph'obia.** [Gr *ailouros*, cat.]

aim ām, *v.t.* to place: to point, level, direct, with (or as if with) a view to hitting an object: to purpose or try (to do).—*v.t.* (with *at*) to direct a course: to level a weapon: to direct a blow or missile: to direct an utterance with personal or special application: to direct one's intention and endeavours with a view to attainment —*n.* an act or manner of aiming: an object or purpose aimed at: design. intention.—*adj*

aim'less without fixed aim.—*adv.* **aim'lessly.**—*n* **aim'lessness.**—**aim off** to aim slightly off the target to allow for wind or other factor; **take aim** to aim deliberately. [Prob. partly O.Fr. *esmer* (Picardian *amer*)—L. *aestimāre*, partly O.Fr. *aesmer*—L. *adaestimāre*; cf. **esteem, estimate.**]

ainé (*fem.* **ainée**), *e-nā*, (Fr.) *adj.* elder, senior

ain't ānt, (*coll*) contracted form of *are not*, used also for *am* or *is not*: also of *have not*.

Ainu ī'nōō, *n* a people of Japan: their language

air är, *n.* the gaseous mixture (chiefly nitrogen and oxygen) of which the atmosphere is composed: the medium through which sound-waves travel (*radio*): the medium in which aircraft operate: a light breeze: effluvium: the aura or atmosphere that invests anything: bearing, outward appearance, manner, look: an assumed or affected manner: (in *pl.*) affectation of superiority: exposure, noising abroad: melody, tune: the chief, usually upper, part or tune.—*adj.* of, pertaining to, the air: affecting, regulating, (the) air: by means of (the) air: operated by air: of aircraft: carried out, or conveyed, by aircraft.—*v.t.* to expose to the air: to ventilate: to warm and dry: to give an airing to: to wear openly, display: to publish abroad.—*v.i.* to take an airing: to become aired.—*n.* **air'er** one who airs: a frame on which clothes are dried.—*adv.* **air'ily** in an airy manner: jauntily.—*ns.* **air'iness; air'ing** exposure to air or heat or to general notice: a short excursion in the open air.—*adj.* **air'less** without air: without free communication with the outer air: without wind: stuffy.—*advs.* **air'ward, air'wards** up into the air —*adj.* **air'y** consisting of or relating to air: open to the air: having sufficient (fresh) air: like air: unsubstantial: sprightly: offhand.—**air'-am'bulance** an aircraft used to take patients from remote places to hospital; **air'-arm** the branch of the fighting services that uses aircraft; **air bag** a safety device in a motor-car, etc. consisting of a bag that inflates to protect the occupants in a collision: an air-filled bag for another purpose e.g. raising sunken craft; **air'-base** a base of operations for aircraft; **air'-bed** an inflated mattress.—*adj.* **air'borne** carried by air: borne up in the air.—**air'-brake** a brake worked by compressed air: a means of checking the speed of an aircraft; **air'-brush** a device for spraying paint by compressed air; **air'-bubble** a bubble of air, specif. one causing a spot on a photograph; **air'burst** the explosion of a bomb, etc in the air; **air'-bus** a very large passenger jet aircraft used for short flights; **air'-chief-mar'shal** an air-force officer ranking with an admiral or general; **air'-comm'odore** an air-force officer ranking with a commodore or brigadier; **air'-compress'or** a machine which draws in air at atmospheric pressure, compresses it, and delivers it at higher pressure —*v t.* **air'-condi'tion** to equip, e g. a building, with devices for air-conditioning.—*adj.* **air'-condi'tioned** —*n.* **air'-condi'tioning** the bringing of air to the desired state of purity, temperature and humidity; **air'-corr'idor** in an area where flying is restricted, a narrow strip along which flying is allowed; **air'-cov'er** protection given by fighter aircraft to other forces during a military operation: the protecting aircraft; **aircraft, sing.** (also *pl.*) any structure or machine for navigating the air; **air'craft-carrier** a vessel from which aircraft can take off and on which they may alight; **air'craftman** an air force member of lowest rank.—Also **air'craftsman; air'craft(s)woman** lowest rank in the W.R.A.F.; **air'-crew'** the crew of an aircraft; **air'-cushion** a cushion that can be inflated: protective barrier, e g between a hovercraft and land or water, formed by down-driven air; **air'-drop** (*mil*) a landing of men or supplies by parachute, **air'field** an open expanse where aircraft may land and take off; **air force** a force organised for warfare in the air; **air'frame** the body of an aircraft as opposed to its engines; **air'-gun** a gun that discharges missiles by means of compressed air: **air'hole** a hole for the passage of air: a hold in ice where animals come up to breathe: an airpocket; **air-hostess see hostess; air'-lane'** a route normally taken by aircraft because of steady winds; **air letter** a letter sent by air mail; **air'lift** a transport operation carried out by air.—Also v.t.—**air line** a route or system of traffic by aircraft; **air'liner** a large passenger aircraft: an aircraft plying in an air line; **air'-lock** a small chamber in which pressure of air can be raised or lowered, through which communication is made between a caisson where the air is compressed and the outer air: a bubble in a pipe obstructing flow of liquid, **air mail** mail conveyed by air; **air'man** an aviator:—fem. **air'woman; air'manship** the art of handling aircraft; **air'-mar'shal** an air-force officer ranked with a vice-admiral or a lieutenant-general; **air'-mechan'ic** one who tends and repairs aircraft, **air'plane** (chiefly U.S.) an aeroplane; **air'-pocket** a region of rarefied or down-flowing air, in which aircraft drop, **air'port** an aerodrome with a custom-house, used as a station for international transport of passengers and cargo; **air'-power** military power in respect of aircraft; **air'-pump** an instrument for pumping air out or in; **air'-raid** an attack on a place by aircraft; **air rifle** one discharging missiles by means of compressed air; **air'-sac** an alveolus, or the cluster of alveoli, at the termination of a bronchiole in the lungs: an outgrowth of the lung in birds, helping respiration or lightening the body; **air'screw** the propeller of an aircraft; **Air Scout** a member of a branch of the Scouts with special interest in air activities; **air'ship** a mechanically driven dirigible aircraft, lighter than air; **air'-sickness** nausea affecting travellers by air.—adj. **air'sick.**—**air'space** the part of the atmosphere above a particular territory, state, etc.: the space used, or required by, an aircraft in manoeuvring; **air'-strike'** an attack with aircraft; **air'strip** a temporary or emergency landing-place for aircraft: a runway; **air terminal** a terminus to or from which passengers are conveyed from or to an airport.—adj. **air'tight** impermeable to air: impenetrable (fig.).—**air'time** the amount of broadcasting time on radio or television allotted to a particular topic, type of material, commercial advertisement, etc.: the time at which the broadcasting of a programme, etc. is due to begin; **air'-vice-mar'shal** an air-force officer ranking with a rear-admiral or major-general; **air'wave** a channel for broadcasting; **air'way** a passage for air: a radio channel: an organised route for air travel; **air'worthiness.**—adjs. **air'worthy** in fit condition for safe flying; **air'y-fair'y** fanciful: delicate.—**air-sea rescue** combined use of aircraft and high-speed launches in sea rescue; **air-traffic control** system of regional centres and airport units which instruct aircraft exactly about route to follow, height at which to fly, etc.; **give oneself airs** to affect superiority; **(go) up in the air** (to become) excited or angry; **in the air** prevalent in an indefinite form; **off the air** not broadcasting, or being broadcast, for a period of time; **on the air** broadcast by radio: in the act of broadcasting; **take the air** to have an airing. [O.Fr. (and Fr.) air—L. āēr, āēris —Gr. āēr, āeros, air.]

Airedale ār'dāl, n. (in full **Airedale terrier**) a large terrier of a breed from Airedale in Yorkshire.

airt ārt, (Scot.) n. direction, quarter. [Perh. Gael. aird, point (of compass).]

aisle īl, n. a side division of the nave or other part of a church or similar building, generally separated off by pillars: (loosely) any division of a church, or a small building attached: (loosely) a passage between rows of seats.—adj. **aisled** (īld) having aisles. [O.Fr. ele —L. āla, a wing; confused with isle and alley.]

aitch āch, n. the eighth letter of the alphabet (H, h).— **drop one's aitches** to fail to pronounce initial aitches, formerly considered a sign of lack of education [O.Fr. ache, from which L.L. ahha is inferred.]

aitchbone āch'bōn, n the bone of the rump: the cut of beef over it. [An aitchbone is for a nachebone— O.Fr. nache—L. natis, buttock; and bone.]

ajar ə-jar', adv. and adj partly open. [O.E. on, on, cerr, a turn.]

akene a-kēn', n. Same as achene.

akimbo ə-kim'bō, adj. and adv. with hand on hip and elbow out [M.E. in kenebow; poss. in a keen (sharp) bow or bend; other suggestions are can-bow (i.e. canhandle), and O.N. kengboginn, bent into a crook—kengr, kink, boginn, bowed]

akin ə-kin', adv. by kin: of nature —adj. related by blood: of like nature. [Prep. a, and kin¹.]

akinesia ā-kin-ē'zi-ə, -ē'sha, (path) n. the lack, loss, or impairment of the power of voluntary movement.— Also **akinesis** (-ē'sis). [Gr. akinesia, lack of motion; a-, priv., kinein, to move.]

Akkadian ə-kād'i-ən, n. the Semitic language of the ancient Middle-Eastern kingdom of Akkad. a native of this kingdom.—Also adj. [City of Agade.]

akvavit. Same as aquavit.

à la a la, prep. in the manner of, e.g à la James Joyce; in cooking, prepared with, in the manner of (a person or place). e.g. à la Dubarry, with cauliflower, à la Florentine, with spinach, etc. [Fr.—contraction of à la mode de.]

ala ā'lə, n a membranous outgrowth on a fruit (bot.): a side petal in the pea family (bot.)· a large side sepal in the milkworts (bot.)· a leafy expansion running down the stem from a leaf (bot.): any flat winglike process, esp. of bone (zool.):—pl. **alae** (ā'lē).—adjs. **a'lar,** **a'lary** pertaining to a wing; **a'late, -d** winged, having an ala. [L. āla, wing.]

à l'abandon a la-bā-dõ, (Fr.) neglected, uncared for. (in Eng.) carelessly, recklessly.

alabaster al'ə-bás-tər, or bas', n. a semi-transparent massive gypsum.—adj. of or like alabaster. [Gr. alabastros, said to be from Alabastron, a town in Egypt.]

à la carte a la kärt, ä lä kart, (Fr.) according to the bill of fare: with each dish charged individually at the price shown on the menu.

alack ə-lak', arch. interj. denoting regret. [Prob. ah, and lack¹.]

alacrity ə-lak'ri-ti, n. briskness: cheerful readiness: promptitude [L alacritās, -ātis—alacer. alacris, brisk.]

Aladdin's cave ə-lad'inz kāv, a place of immense treasure.—**Aladdin's lamp** a charmed object able to grant all one's desires. [Aladdin, a character in Arabian Nights.]

alae. See ala.

alalia ə-lā'li-ə, n. loss of speech [Gr. a-, priv., and laleein, to talk.]

à la maître d'hôtel a la metr' dō-tel, (Fr) in the style of a house-steward, of a hotel-keeper.

à la mode a la mod(ə), **alamode** a-lə-mōd', advs. and adjs. according to the fashion, fashionable; in cooking, of beef, larded and stewed with vegetables: of desserts, served with ice-cream (U.S.) [Fr. à la mode.]

alar, alary. See ala.

alarm ə-lärm', n. a call to arms: notice of danger: a mechanical contrivance for arousing, warning, or giving notice: the noise made by it: a fearstricken state: apprehension of danger —v.t to arouse: to

strike with fear.—*adj.* **alarmed'**.—*adv.* **alarm'edly.**
—*adj.* **alarm'ing.**—*adv* **alarm'ingly.**—*n.* **alarm'ist**
a scaremonger.—Also *adj.*—**alarm'-bell; alarm'-
clock'** a clock that can be set to ring an alarm at
a chosen time; **alarm'-radio** a clock radio.—**sound
the alarm** to give the signal to prepare for an
emergency. [Ō.Fr. (Fr.) *alarme*—It. *all'arme*, to
(the) arms.]

alas *ə-läs'*, *interj.* expressive of grief. [O.Fr. *ha las, a
las* (mod. Fr. *hélas*); *ha*, ah, and *las, lasse*, wretched,
weary—L. *lassus*, wearied]

alate. See **ala.**

a latere *ä la'tə-rē, a la'tə-rā*, (L.) lit from the side:
confidential (of legate sent by the Pope)

alb *alb*, *n.* a long white tight-sleeved vestment.
[O.E *albe*—L.L. *alba*—L. *albus*, white]

albacore *al'bə-kōr, -kor, n.* a large tunny: a species of
mackerel (*S Afr.*).—Also written **al'bicore.** [Port.
albacor—Ar. *al*, the, *bukr*, young camel.]

Alban *al'bən*, **Albany** *-i*, **Albion** *-i-ən, ns.* ancient names
for the island of Great Britain, now used poetically
for Britain, England, or esp. Scotland.—**Alban** the
ancient kingdom of the Picts and (Celtic) Scots, which
the addition of Lothian and Strathclyde transformed
into Scotland.—**Albany herald** one of the Scottish
heralds. [Celtic.]

Albanian *al-bā'ni-ən, adj.* of or pertaining to the S.E.
European Republic of *Albania.*—*n.* a native or citizen thereof: the language thereof.

albatross *al'bə-tros, n.* a large, long-winged sea-bird of
remarkable powers of flight: a hole in three below par
(*golf*): used symbolically to mean an oppressive and
inescapable fact, influence, etc. (from the dead bird
hung round the neck of the sailor in Coleridge's
Ancient Mariner). [Perh. influenced by L. *albus*,
white.]

albedo *al-bē'dō, n.* whiteness: the proportion of incident light reflected, as by a planet:—*pl.* **albe'dos.** [L
albēdō, whiteness—*albus*, white.]

albeit *öl-bē'it, conj* although it be (that): even if,
although. [**all be it.**]

albescent *al-bes'ənt, adj.* becoming white: whitish.—
n. **albesc'ence.** [L *albēscēns, -entis*, pr.p. of *al-
bēscēre*, to grow white—*albus*, white]

albicore. See **albacore.**

Albigensian *al-bi-jen'si-ən, adj* of the town of *Albi* or
its district (the *Albigeois*), in the S. of France: of a
Catharist or Manichaean sect or of the 13th-century
crusade (beginning in the Albigeois) by which, with
the Inquisition, the Catholic Church stamped it out in
blood.—Also *n.*—*n.pl.* **Albigen'sēs.**—*n.* **Albigen'-
sianism.** [L.L. *Albigēnsēs.*]

albino *al-bē'nō*, in U.S. *-bī'*, *n.* a person or other
animal with abnormally white skin and hair and pink
pupils: a plant lacking in pigment:—*pl.* **albi'nos:—
fem. **albiness** (*al'bin-es*).—*ns.* **al'binism** (*-bin-*), **al'-
binoism** (*-bē'*)—*adj.* **albinotic** (*al-bin-ot'ik*)
[Port. *albino*, white Negro or albino—L. *albus*,
white.]

Albion. See **Alban.**

albugo *al-bū'gō, n* leucoma—*adj* **albugineous**
(*-jin'i-əs*) like the white of an egg or of the eye [L
albūgō, -inis, whiteness—*albus*, white.]

album *al'bəm, n.* a blank book for the insertion of
photographs, autographs, poetical extracts, scraps,
postage-stamps, or the like: a printed book of selections, esp. of music: a book-like container for gramophone records. a long-playing gramophone record: a
visitors' book (*U.S.*)—*pl.* **al'bums.—al'bum-leaf**
(trans. of Ger. *Albumblatt*) a short musical composition. [L. neut. of *albus*, white.]

albumen *al-bū'mən, -min*, or *al'*, *n.* white of egg: the
nutritive material surrounding the yolk in the eggs of

higher animals, a mixture of proteins (*zool.*): any
tissue within the seed-coat other than the embryo
itself—endosperm and perisperm, a store of food for
the young plant, no matter what its chemical nature
(*bot.*).—*v.t.* **albū'menise, albū'minise, -ize** (*phot.*)
to cover or impregnate with albumen or an albuminous solution.—*n* **albū'min** (or *al'*) a protein of various kinds soluble in pure water, the solution coagul-
able by heat —*adj* **albū'minous** like or containing
albumen or albumin: insipid —*n.* **albūminūr'ia** presence of albumin in the urine [L. *albūmen, -inis*—
albus, white.]

albumin. See **albumen.**

alburnum *al-bûrn'əm, n.* sapwood, the soft wood
between inner bark and heartwood. [L *albus*,
white.]

alcaide, alcayde *al-kād', al-kī'dhä, -dä*, (Sp) *n* governor of a fortress; a gaoler. [Sp. *alcaide*—Ar
al-qā'id—*al*, the, *qā'id*, leader—*qāda*, to lead.]

alcalde *al-kal'dä*, (Sp.) *n.* a judge. [Sp ,—Ar *al-
qādī*—*qada*, to judge.]

alchemy *al'ki-mi, kə-, n.* the infant stage of chemistry,
its chief pursuit the transmutation of other metals
into gold, and the elixir of life: transmuting potency
(*fig.*).—*adjs.* **alchemic** (*-kem'ik*), **-al.**—*n.* **al'-
chemist.** [Ar. *al-kīmiā*—*al*, the, and *kīmiā*—late
Gr. *chēmeiā, chȳmeiā*, variously explained as the
Egyptian art (*Khēmiä*, 'black-land', Egypt, from the
Egyptian name), the art of *Chymēs* (its supposed
inventor), or the art of pouring (*chȳma*, fluid; cf.
cheein, to pour).]

alcohol *al'kə-hol, n.* a liquid generated by the fermentation of sugar or other saccharine matter and
forming the intoxicating element of fermented liquors: a general term for a class of hydrocarbon compounds analogous to common (or ethyl) alcohol, in
which a hydroxyl group is substituted for an atom of
hydrogen —*adj* **alcohol'ic** of, like, containing, or
due to alcohol —*n* one addicted to excessive
drinking of alcohol.—*n.* **alcholisā'tion, -z-.**—*v t.*
al'coholise, -ize to convert into or saturate with alcohol —*ns.* **al'coholism** alcoholic poisoning: condition
suffered by an alcoholic, **alcoholom'eter** an instrument for measuring the proportion of alcohol in
solutions, **alcoholom'etry.** [Ar. *al-koh'l*—*al*, the,
koh'l, antimony powder used in the East to stain the
eyelids]

alcove *al'kōv, n.* a recess in a room: any recess: a shady
retreat [Sp *alcoba*, a place in a room railed off to
hold a bed—Ar. *al*, the, *qobbah*, a vault.]

Alcyonium *al-si-ō'ni-əm, n* a genus of Anthozoa growing in masses of polyps called dead men's fingers.
[Gr *alkyoneion*, an organism said to resemble a halcyon's nest—*alkyōn*, halcyon, kingfisher]

aldehyde *al'di-hīd, n.* a volatile fluid with a suffocating
smell, obtained by the oxidation of alcohol. a
compound differing from an alcohol in having two
atoms fewer of hydrogen [Contr for *alcohol dē-
hydrogenātum*, alcohol deprived of hydrogen.]

al dente *al den'tä*, (It) of pasta, firm to the teeth

alder *ol'dər, n.* any tree of the genus *Alnus*, related to
the birches, usually growing in moist ground: extended to various other trees or shrubs —*adj* **al'-
dern** made of alder [O.E. *alor*]

alderman *ol'dər-mən, n.* in O E times a nobleman of
highest rank, a governor of a shire or district, a high
official: later, head of a guild: in English boroughs, a
civic dignitary next in rank to the mayor, elected by
fellow councillors (chiefly *hist*): a superior member
of an English county council (chiefly *hist*)· a member of the governing body of a borough or of its
upper house, elected by popular vote (*U.S*):—*pl.*
al'dermen.—*adj* **aldermanic** (*-man'ik*) —*adjs* **al'-**

dermanlike, al'dermanly pompous and portly.—ns. al'dermanry; al'dermanship. [O.E aldorman (W.S. ealdorman)—aldor (ealdor), a chief—ald (eald) old, and noun-forming suffix -or.]

Alderney öl'dər-ni, n. a small dairy-cow, formerly of a breed kept in Alderney, now loosely including Jersey and Guernsey.—Also adj.

aldose al'dōs, n. any of a class of monosaccharide sugars of aldehyde constitution. [aldehyde.]

aldrin al'drin, n. a chlorinated hydrocarbon, used as a contact insecticide. [From K. Alder, German chemist (1902–58).]

ale āl, n. a beverage made from an infusion of malt by fermentation—name applied to beers in brewing of which yeast ferments on the top of the liquid: a festival, from the liquor drunk (arch.).—ale'cost costmary (used in flavouring ale); ale'-house a house in which ale is sold;ale'wife a woman who sells ale: a fish akin to the herring, common off the N.E. of America (perhaps from its corpulent shape, but perhaps a different word):—pl. ale'wives. [O.E. (Anglian) alu (W.S. ealu); O.N. öl.]

aleatory ā'li-ə-tər-i, adj. depending on contingencies: used of the element of chance in poetic composition, etc: of music, aleatoric.—n. aleatoric music.—adj. aleatoric (ā-li-ə-tör'ik) in which chance influences choice of notes (mus.): aleatory. [L. āleātōrius—ālea, a die.]

alecost. See ale.

alee ə-lē', adv. on or toward the lee-side. [O.N. ā, on, hlē, lee.]

Alemannic al-ə-man'ik, adj. of the Alemannen (L. Alamanni, Alemanni), an ancient people of S.W. Germany, or their dialect.—n. the High German dialect of Switzerland, Alsace, etc.

alepine al'i-pēn, n. a mixed fabric of wool and silk or mohair and cotton. [Perh. Aleppo.]

alert ə-lûrt', adj. watchful: wide-awake: brisk.—n. a sudden attack or suprise: a danger warning: the time for which it lasts: condition of preparedness.—v.t. to make alert.—adv. alert'ly.—n. alert'ness.—on, upon the alert upon the watch: wakefully attentive. [Fr. alerte—It. all'erta, on the erect—erto—L. ērēctus, erect.]

alevin al'i-vin, n. a young fish, esp. a salmonid. [Fr., —O.Fr. alever, to rear—L. ad, to, levāre, to raise.]

alexanders al-ig-zän'dərz, n. an umbelliferous plant (genus Smyrnium) formerly used as celery is. [O.E. alexandre; L. olus atrum, olusatrum, lit. 'black herb, vegetable', has been suggested as source.]

Alexandrian al-ig-zän'dri-ən, adj. relating to Alexandria in Egypt, its school of philosophy, its poetry, or the general character of its culture and taste, erudite and critical rather than original in inspiration—sometimes with a suggestion of decadence: relating to Alexander the Great or other of the name.—Also n. —n. and adj. Alexan'drine Alexandrian.—n. alexan'drine a verse of six iambs (as in English), or in French of 12 and 13 syllables in alternate couplets (perhaps from a poem on Alexander the Great by Alexandre Paris).—Also adj.—n. alexan'drite a dark green chrysoberyl discovered on the day of majority of the Cesarevich later Alexander II.

alexia a-lek'si-ə, n. loss of power to read: word-blindness.—adj. alex'ic. [Gr. a-, priv., legein, to speak, confused with L. legēre, to read.]

alexin a-lek'sin, n. a body present in the blood serum, which uniting with an anti-serum gives protection against disease. [Gr. alexein, to ward off, alexipharmakos—pharmakon, poison.]

alfalfa al-fal'fə, n. a variety of, or (esp. U.S) another name for, lucerne. [Sp. alfalfa—Ar. alfaçfaçah.]

alfresco al-fresk'ō, adv. and adj. on fresh or moist plaster: in the fresh or cool air. [It.; see fresco, fresh.]

alga al'gə, n. a seaweed: any member of the Algae:—pl. algae (al'jē).—n.pl. algae (bot.) the seaweeds and allied forms.—adj. al'gal (-gəl).—ns. al'gicide (-ji-sīd) a substance used to destroy algae; al'gin (-jin) sodium alginate, a gummy nitrogenous organic compound got from seaweeds; al'ginate a salt of alginic acid.—adjs. algin'ic (as alginic acid, an acid obtained from certain seaweeds, used in plastics, medicine, as a food-thickening agent, etc.); al'goid (-goid) of the nature of, resembling, an alga; algolog'ical.—ns. algol'ogist; algol'ogy phycology. [L. alga, seaweed.]

algebra al'ji-brə, n. a method of calculating by symbols —by means of letters employed to represent quantities, and signs to represent their relations, thus forming a kind of generalised arithmetic: in modern mathematics, any of a number of systems using symbols and involving reasoning about relationships and operations.—adjs. algebraic (-brā'ik), -al.—adv. algebraically.—n. algebra'ist one skilled in algebra. [It. and Sp.,—Ar. al-jebr, resetting (of anything broken), hence combination—jabara, to reunite.]

Algerian al-jē'ri-ən, adj. of Algeria or Algiers.—n. a native of Algeria.

algesia al-jē'zi-ə, or -si-, n. sensitiveness to pain.—n. alge'sis sensation of pain. [Mod. L.—Gr. algēsis—algein, to suffer.]

-algia al'ji-ə, in composition, denoting pain (in a particular part or because of a particular thing). [Gr. algos, pain.]

algicide. See alga.

algid al'jid, adj. cold, chill—esp. applied to a cold fit in disease.—n. algid'ity. [L. algidus, cold.]

alginate, algology, etc. See alga.

Algol al'gol, n. a type of computer language. [Al-go(rithmic) l(anguage).]

Algonkian al-gong'ki-ən, Algonquian also -kwi-, n. a family of North American Indian languages, including Natick, Shawnee, Ojibwa, Cheyenne, etc., spoken over a wide area: a member of a tribe speaking one of these languages.—Also adj. [Amer. Eng.— Algonquin.]

Algonquin al-gong'kwin, Algonkin -kin, n. a leading group of Indian tribes in the valley of the Ottawa and around the northern tributaries of the St Lawrence: a member of this group: their language.—Also adj. [Micmac Indian algoomaking, at the place of spearing fish.]

algorism al'gə-rizm, n. the Arabic system of numeration: arithmetic.—Also al'gorithm (-ridhm). [L.L. algorismus—Ar. al-Khwārazmi, the native of Khwārazm (Khiva), i.e. the 9th-cent. mathematician Abu Ja'far Mohammed ben Musa.]

algorithm al'gə-ridhm, n. a rule for solving a mathematical problem in a finite number of steps: a set of prescribed computational procedures for solving a problem or achieving a result (comput.): a step-by-step method for solving a problem.—adj. algorith'-mic.—algorithmic language see Algol. [algorism.]

Alhambra al-ham'brə, n. the palace of the Moorish kings of Granada in Spain.—adj. Alhambresque (-bresk'). [Ar. al-hamrā', the red (house).]

alias ā'li-əs, (L. a'li-ás) adv. otherwise.—n. an assumed name:—pl. a'liases. [L. aliās, at another time, otherwise—alius, other.]

alibi al'i-bī, (L. äl'-i-bē) n the plea in a criminal charge of having been elsewhere at the material time: the fact of being elsewhere: an excuse for failure (coll.). [L. alibī, elsewhere, orig. locative—alius, other.]

Alice *al'is, n.* the main character in the children's fantasies *Alice's Adventures in Wonderland* (1865) and *Through the Looking-glass* (1872) by Lewis Carroll —**Alice band** a wide hair-band of coloured ribbon (as worn by Alice in Tenniel's illustrations to *Through the Looking-glass*).—*adj* **Al'ice-in-Won'derland** as if happening in a dream or fantasy: unreal

alicyclic *al-i-sīk'lik, adj.* having properties of aliphatic organic compounds but containing a ring of carbon atoms instead of an open chain [aliphatic, cyclic.]

alidad *al'i-dad*, or *-dad'*, **alidade** *-dād, ns.* a revolving index for reading the graduations of an astrolabe, quadrant, or similar instrument, or for taking the direction of objects [Ar. *al 'idādah*, the revolving radius—*'adid*, humerus.]

alien *ā'li-ən, -lyən, adj.* belonging to something else: foreign: from elsewhere: extraneous: repugnant: inconsistent (with *to*): incompatible: estranged.—*n.* a foreigner: a resident neither native-born nor naturalised: an outsider: a plant introduced by man but maintaining itself.—*v.t.* to alienate: to transfer: to estrange.—*n.* **alienabil'ity**.—*adj.* **a'lienable** capable of being transferred to another.—*v.t.* **a'lienate** to transfer: to estrange.—*ns.* **alienā'tion** estrangement: insanity: the state of not being involved: the critical detachment with which, according to Bertolt Brecht, audience and actors should regard a play, considering action and dialogue and the ideas in the drama without emotional involvement; **a'lienātor**.—*ns* **alienee'** one to whom property is transferred; **al'ienism** the position of being a foreigner: study and treatment of mental diseases; **a'lienist** one who specially studies or treats mental diseases; **a'lienor** (*law*) one who transfers property. [L. *aliēnus*—*alius*, other.]

alight[1] *ə-līt', v.i.* to dismount, descend: to perch, settle: to land: to come to rest: to come by chance (upon something): to fall, strike.—*pa.t* and *pa.p* **alight'ed** (or **alit'**). [O.E. *ālīhtan*. See **light**[2].]

alight[2] *ə-līt, adj.* on fire: lighted up [Prep. a, and **light**[1].]

align *ə-līn', v.t.* to regulate by a line: to arrange in line. —Rarely **aline'**.—*n.* **align'ment** a laying out by a line: setting in a line or lines: the ground-plan of a railway or road: a row, as of standing-stones, taking of side, or side taken, politically, etc.—Rarely **aline'ment**.—**alignment chart** a nomogram, esp. one comprising three scales in which a line joining values on two determines a value on the third. [Fr *aligner* —L. *ad*, to, *līneāre*, to line.]

alike *ə-līk', adj.* the same in appearance or character —*adv.* equally. [O.E. *gelīc*, combined with O N *ālīkr*, O E. *onlīc*; see **like**[1].]

aliment *al'i-mənt, n.* nourishment: food: provision for maintenance, alimony.—*v.t.* to support, sustain: to provide aliment for.—*adjs* **alimental** (*-ment'l*) supplying food; **aliment'ary** pertaining to aliment nutritive.—*n.* **alimentā'tion**.—*adj* **aliment'ative**. —**alimentary canal** the passage from mouth to anus. [L. *alimentum*—*alēre*, to nourish.]

alimony *al'i-mən-i, n* an allowance for support made by one spouse to the other pending or after their divorce or legal separation [L *alimōnia*—*alēre*, to nourish]

aline, alinement. See align.

alineation. See allineation.

aliphatic *al-i-fat'ik, (chem.) adj* fatty. belonging to the open-chain class of organic compounds, or methane derivatives (opp to *aromatic*) [Gr *aleiphar, aleiphatos,* oil.]

aliquant *al'i-kwənt, adj.* such as will not divide a number without a remainder, thus 5 is an aliquant part of 12 [L *aliquantum,* somewhat]

aliquot *al'i-kwot, adj.* such as will divide a number without a remainder. [L *aliquot,* some, several.]

alit. See alight[1].

aliunde *ā-li-un'de, (law) adv.* from another source.— Also *adj.* [L , from elsewhere]

alive *ə-līv', n* in life: in vigour: in being. lively: of a wire, etc., live: sensitive, cognisant (with *to*) —**alive and kicking** strong and active. full of vigour; **alive with** swarming with, **look alive** be brisk. hurry up [O.E. *on līfe* (dat. of *līf,* life), in life.]

alkali *al'kə-li,* or *-lī,* (*chem.*) *n.* a substance which in aqueous solution has more hydroxyl ions than hydrogen ions, and has strong basic properties:—*pl.* **al'kali(e)s**.—*adj.* of, pertaining to, containing, forming, an alkali.—*ns* **alkalesc'ence, alkalesc'ency**.—*adj.* **alkalesc'ent** tending to become alkaline: slightly alkaline —*adj.* **al'kaline** (*-līn, -lin*) having the properties of an alkali: containing much alkali.—*n.* **alkalinity** (*-lin'*) quality of being alkaline: extent to which a solution is alkaline.—*n.* **al'kaloid** any of various nitrogenous organic bases found in plants, having specific physiological action.—*adj.* pertaining to, resembling, alkali.—*n.* **al'kyl** (*-kil*) general name for monovalent hydrocarbon radicals. —**alkali metals** the univalent metals of first group of periodic system, lithium, sodium, potassium, rubidium, caesium, francium, forming strong basic hydroxides; **alkaline earth** an oxide of any of the alkaline earth metals. an alkaline earth metal, **alkaline earth metals** the bivalent metals of the second group, calcium, strontium, barium, and sometimes magnesium and radium. [Ar. *alqalīy,* the calcined ashes.]

alkane *al'kān, n* the general name of hydrocarbons of the methane series, of general formula C_nH_{2n+2}.

alkanet *al'kə-net, n.* a Mediterranean boraginaceous plant (genus *Alkanna*). a red dye got from its root: extended to various kindred plants (*Anchusa*, etc.). [Sp *alcaneta,* dim.—Ar. *al-hennā,* the henna.]

alkyd *al'kid, n.* any of a group of synthetic resins used in paints and protective coatings and in adhesives.— Also **alkyd resin** (*rez'in*). [*alkyl* and acid.]

alkyl. See alkali.

all *ol, adj.* comprising every individual one (e g. *all men*): comprising the whole extent, etc., of (e.g. *all winter*) any whatever: (preceding 'the') as many as there are, or as much as there is (e.g. *all the men, all the cheese*): also used following *pl. pers pron* , or sometimes *pl. n* (e g. *we all laughed, the guests all came*) the greatest possible (e.g. *with all haste, in all sincerity*) every —*n.* the whole: everybody. everything. the totality of things—the universe: one's whole possessions (formerly often in *pl.*).—*adv* wholly: entirely: quite. without limit, infinitely. on all sides: on each side, apiece: even, just (passing into a mere intensive, as in *all on a summer's day*, or almost into a conjunction by omission of *if* or *though*) —In composition, infinite. infinitely: universal. completely wholly. by all having all for object —Possible compounds are without limit: only a selection can be given.—*adj* **all'-Amer'ican** representative of the whole of America, esp in some admirable quality. typically American (in behaviour, appearance, etc)· chosen to represent the United States' consisting entirely of U S or American members —**All Blacks** the New Zealand international rugby team, **all'-clear'a** signal that the reason for sheltering, or (*fig*) for inactivity, is past —*adjs* **all'-day** lasting all day, **all'-elec'tric** using only electricity for heating and lighting **all'-fired** (*coll* orig. U S) infernal (perh for hell-fired) — *adv* **all'-firedly**.—*interj* **all-hail** a greeting. *lit.* all health —*n* a salutation of 'All hail' —*v t* to greet with 'All hail'.—**All-hall'owmass** the feast of All Saints; **All-Hall'ows** All Saints' Days; **all'heal** the great valerian or other plant thought to have healing properties, e.g. self-heal; **all-hid'** hide-and-seek — *adjs.* **all'-import'ant** essential: crucial; **all'-in'** including everything: of a school, etc , comprehensive; **all'night** lasting, open, etc. all night; **all'-or- noth'ing** that must be gained, accepted, etc completely or not at all; **all'-out** using maximum effort: of a strike, with everyone participating, **all'- ov'er** over the entire surface, body, etc.; **all-ô'verish** having an indefinite sense of indisposition, discomfort, or malaise.—*n.* **all-ô'verishness.**—*adjs.* **all- pow'erful** supremely powerful: omnipotent; **all'- pur'pose** that can be used for any purpose, in any circumstances, etc.; **all'-risks'** (of insurance) covering all risks except a number specifically excluded (as e.g. war risks, damage due to depreciation, etc.), **all'- round'** including, applying to, all: adequate, complete, or competent on all sides.—**all'-round'er** one who shows ability in many sports, many aspects of a particular sport, esp. cricket, or many kinds of work, etc.; **all'-round'ness; all'spice** pimento or Jamaica pepper, supposed to combine the flavours of cinnamon, nutmeg, and cloves (see also **Calycanthus**) —*adjs.* **all'-star'** having a cast or team all of whom are stars; **all'-time** of all time to date.—*n., adj.* **all'-up** (of loaded aircraft) total (weight).—**all'work** all kinds of work (esp. domestic).—**after all** when everything has been considered: in spite of all that. nevertheless; **all along** everywhere along: all the time; **all at once** suddenly; **all but** everything short of, almost; **All Fools' Day** the day of making April fools, 1st April; **all for** (*coll.*) in favour of, **all found** (usu. of a price) all in, with everything included; **All Hallows' Day** All Saints' Day; **all in** all exhausted; everything included; **all in all** all things in all respects, all or everything together: that which one is wholly wrapped up in; **all-in** wrestling wrestling with almost no holds barred as against the rules; **all of** (*coll.*) as long, far, etc. as: the whole distance, time, etc. of; **all out** at full power or speed: completely exhausted; **all over** everywhere: over the whole of. covered with (*coll.*): thoroughly, entirely: very characteristically, **all over with** finished, done with, completely at an end with; **all right** a coll. phrase expressing assent or approbation, **All Saints' Day** 1st November, a festival in honour of the saints collectively; **all's one** it is just the same; **All Soul's Day** 2nd November, a R.C. day of prayer for souls in Purgatory; **all systems go** everything (is) in working order, starting up, etc. (also *fig.*): **all the best** phrase used to wish someone good luck, etc ; **all there** completely sane: alert; **all the same** see same; **all-time high, low** a high, low, level never before reached, **all-time record** a record exceeding all others in all times, all times, all told including every person, thing, etc.: taking everything into account; **all up with** at an end with: beyond any hope for; **and all** as well as the rest; **and all that** and all the rest of it, *et cetera*; **at all** in the least degree: in any way: in any circumstances. used also merely to give emphasis; **be all over someone** to irk someone, or treat someone, with too much show of friendliness; **for all** notwithstanding; **for good and all** finally; **in all** all told: in total; **once (and) for all** once and once only, finally; **when all is said and done** after all: all things considered. [O E (Anglian) *all*, (W.S. *eall*); Ger *all*.]

alla breve a'lə, al'la brā'vā, (*mus.*) in quick common time. [It., according to the breve, there being orig. a breve to the bar.]

Allah al'ä, *n.* among Muslims, God [Ar *allāh— alilāh*, the God.]

allantois a-lan'tō-is, *n.* a membranous sac-like appendage for effecting oxygenation in the embryos of mammals, birds, and reptiles.—*adjs.* **allanto'ic; allan'toid** (*-toid*), sausage-shaped, pertaining to the allantois.—*n* the allantois. [Irregularly formed from Gr. *allās, -āntos*, a sausage, *eidos*, form.]

allay ə-lā', *v.t.* to put down: to quell: to calm: to alleviate: to abate· to reduce: to alloy.—*v.i* to abate —*n.* **allay'er; allay'ing; allay'ment**. [O.E. *ālecgan*—pfx. ā-, intens., *lecgan*, to lay.]

allay ə-lā', *v.t* to alloy· to mix with something inferior. to dilute: to debase to abate or detract from the goodness of.—*n.* alloy: alloying: dilution: abatement: impairment. [See **alloy**]

allege ə-lej', *v.t.* to assert with a view to subsequent proof, hence without proof. to bring forward in argument or plea: to adduce —*n.* **allegation** (*al-i-gā'shən*) the act of alleging: that which is alleged: an unproved or unaccepted assertion.—*adj.* **alleged** (ə-lejd').—*adv.* **allegedly** (-lej'əd-li). [O.Fr. *es- ligier*, to clear at law—L. *ex*, from, *lītigāre*, to sue]

allegiance ə-lē'jəns, *n.* the relation or obligation of liegeman to liege-lord or of subject to sovereign or state: loyalty (to a person or cause). [L. *ad*, to, and **liege**.]

allegory al'i-gər-i, *n.* a narrative to be understood symbolically: symbolical narration.—*adjs.* **allegoric** (-gor'ik), **-al**.—*adv.* **allegor'ically**.—*v.t.* **all'egorise, -ize** to put in form of an allegory: to treat as allegory. —*v t* to use allegory.—*ns.* **allegorisa'tion, -z-; all'egoriser, -z-; all'egorist**. [Gr. *allēgoriā—allos*, other, *agoreuein*, to speak.]

allegro a-lā'grō (It *al-lā'grō*), (*mus.*) *adv., adj.* with brisk movement.—*n.* an allegro piece or movement: —*pl.* **alle'gros.**—*adv* and *adj.* **allegret'to** somewhat brisk.—Also *n.* (*pl.* **allegret'tos**) [It ,—L. *alacer*, brisk.]

allele, allel al-ēl', *n.* shortened forms of **allelomorph** (*al-ēl'ō-morf*) any one of the two or more possible forms of a gene: a gene considered as the means of transmission of an allele.—*adj* **allelomor'phic.**—*n.* **allelomor'phism.** [Gr *allēlôn*, of one another, *morphē*, form.]

alleluia, alleluiah al-i-lōō'ya. Same as **hallelujah**.

allemande al'(i-)mand, al-mäd, *n.* a smooth-running suite movement of moderate tempo, in common time, coming after the prelude (of German origin): a Swabian dance in triple time: a German dance in 2–4 time: a movement affecting change of order in a dance. [Fr. *allemande* (*fem.*), German.]

allergy al'ər-ji, *n.* an altered or acquired state of sensitivity: abnormal reaction of the body to substances normally harmless: hypersensitivity to certain antigens or other exciting substances (*coll.*) antipathy.—*n.* **all'ergen** any substance that induces an allergic reaction.—*adjs* **allergen'ic** causing an allergic reaction; **allergic** (ə-lûr'jik) (of the body) reacting in an abnormally sensitive manner suffering from an allergy (to). [Gr *allos*, other, *ergon*, work.]

alleviate ə-lēv'i-āt, *v.t.* to make light: to mitigate.— *ns.* **allevia'tion; allev'iātor.**—*adjs.* **allev'iative; allēvia'tory.** [L.L. *alleviāre, -ātum*—L. *ad*, to, *levis*, light]

alley al'i, *n.* a walk in a garden or shrubbery: a passage: a narrow lane: a back-lane a long narrow enclosure, or rink, for bowls or skittles:—*pl* **all'eys.** —**all'eyway** a narrow passage. a corridor. [O Fr *alee* (Fr *allée*), a passage. from *aller*, to go.]

alley, **ally** al'i, *n.* a choice taw or large marble.—*n.* **all'(e)y-taw'**, **-tor'**. [Prob originally made of **alabaster**.]

allheal. See **all**.

alliaceous al-i-ā'shəs, adj garlic-like. [L allium, garlic.]

alliance. See ally.

alligator al'i-gā-tər, n. a reptile of a mainly American family differing from crocodiles in the broader snout and other characteristics.—**alligator pear** see avocado. [Sp. el, the (L. ılle), lagarto, lizard (L. lacertus).]

allineation, alineation a-lin-i-ā'shən, n. position in a straight line: alignment. [L. ad, to, lineāre, -ātum, to draw a line—līnea, line.]

alliteration ə- or a-lit-ər-ā'shən, n. the recurrence of the same initial sound (not necessarily letter) in words in close succession, as 'Sing a Song of Sixpence'.—v.i. **allit'erate** to begin with the same sound: to constitute alliteration: to practise alliteration.—adj. **allit'erative.** [L. ad, to, and litera, littera, a letter.]

Allium al'i-əm, n. the plant genus to which onions, leeks, garlic, etc. belong. [L., garlic.]

allo-, a'lō-, a'lə, in composition, other: denoting one of a group constituting a structural unit: different: from outside.—ns. **all'omorph** (-mörf) one of two or more forms of the same morpheme; **all'ophone** (-fōn) one of two or more forms of the same phoneme.—adj. **allophonic** (-fon').—n. **all'oplasm** protoplasm differentiated to perform a special function.—adj. **alloplas'tic** affected by, or affecting, external factors. [Gr. allos, other.]

allocarpy al'ō-kär-pi, (bot.) n. fruiting after cross-fertilisation. [Gr. karpos, fruit.]

allocate al'ō-kāt, al'ə-kāt, v.t. to place: to locate: to apportion.—adjs. **all'ocable, allocāt'able.**—n. **allocā'tion** act of allocating: a share allocated: allotment: apportionment: an allowance made upon an account [L. allocāre—ad, to, locāre, -ātum, to place—locus, a place.]

allocution al-ō-kū'shən, n. an exhortation: a formal address. [L. allocūtiō, -ōnis—ad, to, and loquī, locūtus, to speak.]

allogamy al-og'ə-mi, (bot) n. cross-fertilisation—adj. **allog'amous.** [Gr. allos, other, gamos, marriage.]

allograph al'ō-graf, n. a writing made by one person on behalf of another. [Gr. graphē, writing.]

allomorph. See allo-.

allonge al-3zh, n. a piece of paper attached to a bill of exchange for further endorsement. [Fr.]

allopathy al-op'ə-thi, n. orthodox medical practice, treatment of diseases by drugs, etc., whose effect on the body is the opposite of that of the disease, distinguished from homoeopathy.—n. **all'opath.**—adj. **allopathic** (al-ō-path'ik).—n. **allop'athist** [Ger. Allopathie, coined by Hahnemann (1755–1843)—Gr. allos, other, pathos, suffering.]

allophone, allophonic, alloplasm, alloplastic. See allo-.

Allosaurus al-ə-sör'əs, n. a genus of large, lizard-hipped, carnivorous dinosaurs.—n. **all'osaur** a member of this genus. [Mod. L.—Gr. allos, other, sauros, lizard.]

allot al-ot, v.t. to divide as by lot: to distribute in portions: to parcel out: to assign:—pr.p. **allott'ing;** pa.t. and pa.p. **allott'ed.**—ns allot'ment act of allotting: a part or share allotted: a piece of ground let out for spare-time cultivation under a public scheme. [O.Fr. aloter—à, to, and the Gmc root of lot.]

allotropy al-ot'rə-pi, n. the property (esp. in chemical elements, as carbon) of existing in more than one form.—n. allotrope (al'ə-trōp) an allotropic form.—adj. allotrop'ic.—n. allot'ropism. [Gr. allos, other, and tropos, turn, habit.]

allow ə-low', v t. to concede: to conclude, hence to assert (U.S.): to permit· to accord as due: to assign: to grant or give, esp periodically: to abate: to assume as an element in calculation or as something to be taken into account.—v ı. to admit of: to make allowance for.—adj. **allow'able** that may be allowed: permissible: excusable —n. **allow'ableness.**—adv. **allow'ably.**—n. **allow'ance** that which is allowed: a limited portion or amount allowed, allotted, granted: a ration or stint: money allowed to meet expenses or in consideration of special conditions: abatement: a sum periodically granted: a taking into account in calculation or excuse, as, e.g., in make allowances for.—v.t. to put upon an allowance: to supply in limited quantities.—adj. **allowed'** permitted: licensed: acknowledged. [O.Fr. alouer, to praise, bestow, of double origin: (1) L. allaudāre—ad, to, laudāre, to praise; (2) L. ad, locāre, to place.]

alloy al'oi, ə-loi', n. a mixture of metals: extended to a mixture of metal with non-metal: the baser ingredient in such a mixture (esp. in gold or silver): any admixture that impairs or debases: fineness, standard, of gold or silver —v.t. to mix (metal): to mix with a less valuable metal: to impair or debase by being present: to temper, qualify.—v.i. to become alloyed. [Fr. aloi (n.), aloyer (vb.)—O.Fr. alei, aleier—L. allıgāre—ad, to, lıgāre, to bind.]

allspice. See under all.

allude ə-lōōd', -lūd', v.i. (with to) to convey an indirect reference in passing: to refer without explicit mention, or with suggestion of further associations: to refer.—n. **allu'sion** (-zhən) indirect reference.—adj. **allu'sive** (-siv) alluding: hinting: referring indirectly.—adv. **allu'sively.**—n. **allu'siveness.** [L. allūdēre—ad, at, lūdēre, lūsum, to play.]

allure ə-lūr', -lōōr', v.t. to entice.—ns. **allure', allure'ment.**—adj **allur'ing.**—adv. **allur'ingly.** [O.Fr. alurer—à, to, lurer, to lure.]

allusion, etc. See allude.

alluvion ə-lōō'vi-ən, -lū', n land gradually gained from a river or the sea by the washing up of sand and earth: a flood: alluvium. [L. alluviō, -ōnis, see alluvium.]

alluvium ə-lōō'vi-əm, -lū', n. matter transported in suspension and deposited by rivers or floods:—pl. **allu'via.**—adj. **allu'vial.** [L. neut. of alluvius, washed up—ad, to, luēre, to wash]

ally ə-lī', v.t. to join in relation of marriage, friendship, treaty, co-operation, or assimilation:—pr.p. **ally'ing;** pa.t. and pa.p. **allied'.**—n. **a'lly** (formerly, and still by some, ə-lī') a member of or party to an alliance: a state or sovereign joined in league for co-operation in a common purpose: anything that co-operates or helps: anything near to another in classification or nature:—pl. **a'llies** (or -līz').—n. **alli'ance** the state of being allied: union, or combination by marriage, treaty, etc.: kinship: a group of allies or kindred: a subclass or group of families (bot.).—adj. **a'llied** (or -līd') [O.Fr. alier—L. allıgāre.]

ally², ally-taw. See alley².

allyl al'il, (chem.) n. an organic radical (C_3H_5) whose sulphide is found in oil of garlic [L. allium, garlic, and Gr. hylē, matter]

almacantar, almucantar al-mə-kan'tər, -mū-, ns. a circle of altitude, parallel to the horizon: an instrument for determining a star's passage across an almacantar. [Ar. almuqantarāt, the sundials—al, the, qantarah, bridge.]

alma mater al'mə mā'tər, al'ma ma'ter, (L.) benign mother—applied by alumni to their university

almanac ol'mə-nak, n a register of the days, weeks, and months of the year, with astronomical events, anniversaries, etc. [App. from an Ar word almanākh.]

almandine al'man-dīn, -dēn, n. precious (red iron-alumina) garnet. [L.L. alabandīna—Alabahda, a town in Caria, where it was found.]

almery. See ambry.

almighty ōl-mīt'i, adj. omnipotent: irresistible: invincible: mighty.—Also adv.—the Almighty God. [O.E. ælmihtig.]

almond ä'mənd, n. the fruit, and esp. the kernel, of a tree akin to the peach, with a dry husk instead of flesh: anything of the shape of an almond (an ellipse pointed at one end), as a tonsil, a rock-crystal ornament.—adj. al'mond-eyed' with apparently almond-shaped eyes. [O.Fr. almande (Fr amande)—L amygdala—Gr. amygdalē.]

almoner ä'mən-ər, al'mən-ər, n. a distributor or (arch.) giver of alms: a medical social worker attached to a hospital (no longer official title). [O.Fr. aumoner, aumonier (Fr. aumônier)—L.L. eleēmosynārius (adj.); see alms.]

almost ōl'mōst, -məst, adv. very nearly. [all, most (in sense of nearly).]

alms amz, n. sing. and pl. relief given out of pity to the poor.—alms'-house a house endowed for the support and lodging of the poor. [O.E. ælmysse, through L.L. from Gr. eleēmosynē—eleos, compassion.]

almucantar. See almacantar.

Alnus. See alder.

Aloe al'ō-ē, n. a liliaceous genus, mainly South African, mostly trees and shrubs: (without cap.; al'ō) any member of the genus extended to the so-called American aloe (see Agave), also (often pl.) to aloeswood or its resin: (without cap.; usu. in pl. form but treated as sing.) a bitter purgative drug, the inspissated juice of the leaves of various species of Aloe. [Directly and through O.E. aluwan, alewan (pl.)—L. aloē—Gr. aloē.]

aloft ə-loft', -loft', adv. on high: overhead: above: on the top: high up: up the mast: in or to heaven. [O.N. ā lopt (pron. loft), of motion; ā lopti, of position—ā, on, in, to, lopt (see loft).]

alogia ə-lōj'ē-ə, n. inability to speak, due to brain lesion. [Gr. a-, priv., and logos, speech.]

alogical a-loj'i-kl, or ā-, adj. outside the domain of logic. [Gr. a-, priv., and logical.]

aloha ä-lō'ə, -lō'ha, n. love: kindness.—interj. greetings: farewell. [Hawaiian.]

alone ə-lōn', adj. single: solitary: unaccompanied: without any other: by oneself: unique.—adv. singly.—n. alone'ness.—go it alone (coll.) to act on one's own, without help. [all and one.]

along ə-long, adv. by or through the length: lengthwise: at full length: throughout: onward: together, in company or conjunction.—prep. lengthwise by, through, or over: by the side of.—adj. alongshore' see longshore.—prep. and adv. along'side beside: side by side (with): close to the side (of). [O.E. andlang—pfx. and-, against, and lang, long[1].]

aloof ə-lōōf', adv. some way off (from): apart: with avoidance or detachment: without participation: with reserve suggesting consciousness of superiority.—adj. distant, withdrawn.—adv. aloof'ly.—n. aloof'-ness. [Prep. a, and loof (luff).]

alopecia al-ō-pē'si-ə, -sh(y)ə, n. baldness. [Gr alōpekiā, fox-mange, a bald spot,—alōpēx, fox.]

aloud ə-lowd', adv. loudly: audibly. [Prep. a, and loud.]

alp alp, n. a high mountain: a mountain pasture: (pl.; with cap.) specially applied to the lofty ranges of Switzerland and neighbouring countries.—adj. Alp'ine, alp'ine (-īn) of the Alps or other mountains: growing on mountain tops.—n. an alpine plant: a member of the Alpine race.—ns. alp'inism (-in-) the art or practice of mountain-climbing; alp'inist.—

alp'enhorn, alp'horn a long powerful horn, of wood and bark, used chiefly by Alpine cowherds; alp'enstock a mountain traveller's long spiked staff.—Alpine race one of the principal races of white men, characterised by broad head, sallow skin, moderate stature. [L. Alpēs, the Alps; perh. Celtic.]

alpaca al-pak'ə, n. a domesticated animal akin to the llama: cloth made of its long silken wool. [Sp., prob. from Quechua.]

alpha al'fə, n. the first letter of the Greek alphabet (A, α): the first or brightest star of a constellation: the beginning: in classification, the first or one of the first grade—n. alpha-fětōprō'tein a protein whose presence in excessive quantities in amniotic fluid has been found to correlate with certain foetal abnormalities, e.g. those leading to spina bifida.—adjs. alpha(nū)mer'ic, -al consisting of, or (of a machine) using, both letters and numbers.—adv. alpha(nū)mer'ically.—al'pha-block'er a drug used to produce vasodilatation, esp. in muscle; alpha particle a helium nucleus given off by radioactive substances; alpha rays streams of alpha particles.—alpha and omega beginning and end. [Gr. alpha—Heb. āleph.]

alphabet al'fə-bit, -bet, n. a system of letters, esp. arranged in conventional order: first elements.—adjs. alphabet'ic, -al relating to or in the order of an alphabet.—adv. alphabet'ically.—v.t. al'phabetise, -ize to arrange alphabetically. [Gr. alphabētos—alpha, bēta, the first two Greek letters.]

already ol-red'i, adv. previously, or by the time in question. [all, ready.]

alright ol-rīt'. An alternative, less acceptable, spelling of all right.

Alsatia al-sā'sh(y)ə, n. a district long disputed by Ger many and France—Alsace.—adj. Alsa'tian of Alsatia: a German sheep-dog of wolf-like breed, often used by police and security officers because of its strength and fierceness (in U.S. German Shepherd dog, German Police dog).—Also n.

alsike al'sik, n. a white or pink-flowered clover. [From Alsike, near Uppsala, a habitat]

also ol'sō, adv. likewise: further.—al'so-ran a horse that also ran in a race but did not get a 'place': a person of like degree of importance. [O.E. all (W.S. eall) swā, all so.]

Alstroemeria al-strə-mē'ri-ə, n. a South American genus of amaryllids with inverted leaves: (without cap.) a plant of the genus [C. Alströmer, 18th-cent. Swedish botanist.]

alt alt, n. a high tone, in voice or instrument.—in alt in the octave above the treble stave beginning with G: in an exalted and high-flown mood. [L. altus, high]

Altaic al-tā'ik, n a family of languages, forming one branch of Ural-Altaic, and consisting of Turkic, Mongolic and Tungusic.—Also adj.

altar ol'tər, n. a block or table for making sacrifices on: a table used for mass or the eucharist (by those who regard it as a sacrifice): sometimes, without such implication, the communion table: a scene of worship or marriage ceremony (fig): a ledge on a dry-dock wall.—alt'ar-cloth the covering of the altar; al'-tarpiece a work of art placed above and behind an altar; alt'ar-rails rails separating the sacrarium from the rest of the chancel, alt'ar-stone a stone serving as an altar: a consecrated slab forming, or inserted in, the top of an altar —family altar the symbol or place of family worship; high altar the principal altar, lead to the altar to marry (a woman). [L. altāre—altus, high]

alter ol'tər, v t to make different· to modify —v.i. to become different.—n. alterabil'ity.—adjs. al'ter-able; al'terant altering· having the power of pro-

ducing changes.—*n.* an alternative.—*n* **altera'tion.**
—*adj.* **al'terative** having power to alter.—*n.* a medicine that makes a change in the vital functions.—
p.adj. **al'tered** (of a rock) changed in mineral composition by natural forces. [L. *alter*, one of two]
alter ego (*al'ter eg'ō, ol'tər ē'gō*) one's second self (see **second**). [L., other.]
altercate *ol'tər-kāt, v.i.* to bandy words, wrangle.—*n.*
alterca'tion.—*adj.* **al'tercative.** [L. *altercārī, -ātus*
—*alter*, other.]
alternate *ol'tər-nāt*, also *al', v.t.* to cause to follow by turns or one after the other (prop. of two things) —
v.i. to follow or interchange (with each other: prop. of two things): to happen by turns, change by turns.
—*n.* a deputy, substitute: an alternative.—*adj.*
alter'nate (*-tûr'*; in the U S. *ol'*) arranged or coming one after the other by turns: every other or second: of leaves, placed singly with change of side at each node of floral whorls, each occupying, in ground plan, the spaces of the next: of angles, placed one after the other on either side of a line (*geom*).—*adv*
alter'nately.—*ns.* **alter'nance** (or *al'*-) alternation,
alter'nant (or *al'*-) a spelling or sound variant that does not affect meaning (allomorph or allophone): a type of determinant (*math*).—*adj* **al'ternating.**—
ns. **alterna'tion** the act of alternating: alternate succession: interchange: reading or singing antiphonally;
alter'native (*-na-tiv*) a pair (loosely a set) of possibilities (esp. of choice) excluding all others: a choice between them: one of them, esp. other than the one in question.—*adj.* possible as an alternative: disjunctive. considered by some as preferable to the existing state or form of something, very often with the connotation of being less conventional, less materialistic, more in harmony with the environment and the natural order of things, etc., as *alternative society, alternative technology, alternative medicine,* etc.—*adv.* **alter'natively** with an alternative: by way of alternative.—*n.* **alt'ernātor** a generator of alternating current.—**alternating current** an electric current that periodically reverses its direction; **alternative vote** a system of voting whereby, if an elector's favourite candidate is out of the running, his vote is transferred to the candidate he has marked next in order of preference. [L *alternāre, -ātum—alter,* one or other of two.]
alterne *al-tûrn', n.* one of two or more plant communities adjoining but differing greatly. [Fr. *alterne,* alternate—L *alternus*]
Althaea *al-thē' ə, n.* the marsh-mallow and hollyhock genus: (without *cap.*) a plant of this genus: sometimes extended to the hibiscus genus and applied (without *cap.*) esp. to the Rose of Sharon. [Gr. *althaiā,* marsh-mallow.]
althorn *alt'hôrn, n.* a tenor saxhorn. [**alt.**]
although *ol-dhō', conj.* though (esp., but not necessarily, in stating matter of fact) [**all, though.**]
altimeter *al-tim'i-tər, al'ti-mē-tər, ol', n* an instrument for measuring heights, by means of differences in atmospheric pressure, or (*radio altimeter*) by means of time taken for radio wave from an aircraft to be reflected back [L. *altus,* high. and **meter¹**.]
altissimo *al-tis'(s)i-mō, (mus.) adj.* very high.—**in altissimo** in second octave above treble stave. beginning with G. [It., superl. of *alto,* high.]
altitude *al'ti-tūd, n.* height: angle of elevation above the horizon: perpendicular from vertex upon base·high rank or eminence: a high point or position: (in *pl.*) exalted mood, passion, or manner.—*adj*
altitud'inal pertaining to altitude· found at high level. [L. *altitūdō, -inis.—altus,* high]
alto *al'tō, (mus) n.* properly counter-tenor, the highest male voice: extended to contralto. the lowest female

voice; the part sung by a counter-tenor or contralto: an instrument of corresponding compass: the possessor of a counter-tenor or contralto voice:—*pl.* **al'tos.**
—Also *adj* [It ,—L *altus,* high]
altogether *ol-tōō-gedh'ər,* or *-tə-, adv* wholly: completely: without exception· in total: all things considered —**the altogether** (*coll*) the nude. [**all** and **together.**]
alto-rilievo *al'tō-rēl-yā'vō, n.* high relief: figures projected by at least half their thickness from the background on which they are sculptured.—Partly anglicised as **al'to-relie'vo** (*al-tō-ri-lē'vō*). [It See **relief.**]
altrices *al-trī'sēz, n.pl* birds whose young are hatched very immature and have to be fed in the nest by the parents —*adj.* **altricial** (*-trish'l*). [L *altrīcēs* (pl of *altrix*), feeders, nurses.]
altruism *al'trōō-izm, n* the principle of living and acting for the interest of others —*n.* **al'truist.**—*adj*
altruist'ic.—*adv.* **altruist'ically.** [Fr. *altruisme,* formed by Comte from It *altrui,* someone else—L *alterī huic,* to this other]
alula *al'ū-lə, n* the bastard-wing. [L dim of *āla,* wing.]
alum *al'əm, n.* double sulphate of aluminium and potassium, with 24 molecules of water, crystallising in transparent octahedra: any like compound of a trivalent metal (especially aluminium) and a univalent metal or radical —*n.* **alumina** (*ə-lū'* or *ə-lōō'mi-nə*) oxide of aluminium.—*v.t* **alum'inise,**
-ize to treat (a metal) so as to form an aluminium alloy on its surface: to coat (e g. glass) with aluminium.—
n. **alumin'ium** (*al-ū-* or *al-ōō-*) an element (symbol Al; at. numb. 13), a remarkably light silvery metal first named (though not then isolated) by Sir Humphry Davy **alu'mium,** then (as still *U.S)* **alum'inum.**—*adj.* **alu'minous** of the nature of, or containing, alum or alumina. [L. *alūmen, -inis,* alum.]
alumnus *al-um'nəs, n* a former pupil or student:—*pl.*
alum'ni:—*fem.* **alum'na** (*pl* **alum'nae** *-nē*) [L., foster-son, pupil—*alēre,* to nourish.]
alveolus *al-vē'ə-ləs, al'vi-, n* a pit, small depression or dilatation· a tooth-socket· one of the clustered cells at the termination of a bronchiole in the lungs:—*pl.*
alveoli.—*adjs.* **alve'olar** (or *-ōl',* or *al'*) of an alveolus: produced with the tongue against the roots of the upper teeth (*phon.*): pitted; **alvé'olate** (or *al'vi-*) pitted: honeycombed: inserted in an alveolus.—*n.*
al'veole an alveolus —**alveolar arch** the part of the jaw in which the teeth are inserted. [L *alveolus,* dim of *alveus,* a hollow]
alway *ol'wā, (arch.) adv* through all time: always.—
adv **al'ways** every time· ever· continually: in any case. [**ail** and **way²**—O.E *eaine weg* (accus.) and M.E. *alles weis* (gen)]
Alyssum *al'is-əm, ə-lis', n* a genus of cruciferous plants with white or yellow flowers. grown in rock-gardens (without *cap.*) a plant of this genus· (without *cap.*) a mass of such plants.—**sweet alyssum** a white scented perennial of a related genus. [Gr. *alysson,* a plant reputed to cure madness—*a-,* priv., and *lyssa,* madness.]
Alzheimer's disease *alts'hī-mərz diz-ēz', a form of premature senile decay
am *am, əm,* used as 1st person sing of the verb *to be*
[O E (Anglian) *am, eam* (W.S *eom*), a relic of the verbs in *-mi,* from the root *es-,* cf Gr. *eimi* (for *esmi*) L. *sum,* Sans *asmi*]
amadavat *am-ə-də-vat', n.* an Indian songbird akin to the weaver-birds —Now usu. **avadavat'.** [From *Ahmadabad,* whence they were sent to Europe]
amadou *am' ə-dōō, n* tinder made from fungi (genu

amah 27 **amble**

Polyporus) growing on trees, used also as a styptic [Fr., of doubtful origin.]

amah *ä'mə, (Oriental) n.* a native maidservant or child's nurse, esp. wet-nurse. [Port.]

amalgam *ə-mal'gəm, n.* a mixture of mercury with other metal: any soft mixture: an intimate mixture: an ingredient.—*v.t.* **amal'gamate** to mix with mercury: to merge.—*v.i.* to unite in an amalgam: to come together as one: to blend.—*n.* **amalgamā'tion** a blending or merging: a union of diverse elements.—*adj.* **amal'gamative.** [L.L. *amalgama*, perh —Gr *malagma*, an emollient.]

Amanita *am-ən-i'tə, n.* a genus of toadstools, near akin to the mushroom, including the fly agaric and other poisonous kinds: (without *cap.*) a toadstool of this genus. [Gr. *amānītai* (pl.), a kind of fungus.]

amanuensis *ə-man-ū-en'sis, n.* one who writes to dictation: a copying secretary:—*pl.* **amanuen'sēs.** [L. *āmanuēnsis—ā,* from, *manus,* hand.]

amarant(h) *am'ər-ant(h), ns.* a fabled never-fading flower, emblem of immortality: any species of **Amarant(h)'us,** the love-lies-bleeding genus, with richly coloured spikes, long in withering: (**amaranth**) a type of dye used for colouring foodstuffs [Gr. *amarantos—a-,* priv., *marainein,* to wither; the *th* forms from confusion with *anthos,* flower.]

amaryllis *am-ə-ril'is, n* the belladonna lily. [*Amaryllis,* a girl's name, in the Gr. and L. poets, and others.]

amass *ə-mas', v.t.* and *v.i.* to gather in great quantity: to accumulate.—*adj.* **amass'able.**—*n.* **amass'ment.** [Fr. *amasser*—L. *ad,* to, and *massa,* a mass.]

amateur *am'ə-tər, -tūr, -tûr, n.* an enthusiast, admirer: one who cultivates a study or art for the love of it, and not professionally, often implying that he is superficial, trifling, dilettantish, or inexpert: one who engages in sport purely for pleasure (opp. to *professional*).—Also *adj.*—*adj.* **amateur'ish** imperfect and defective, as the work of an amateur rather than a professional hand.—*adv.* **amateur'ishly.**—*ns.* **amateur'ishness; am'ateurism; am'ateurship.** [Fr.,— L. *amātor, -ōris,* a lover—*amāre,* to love.]

Amati *ə-mä'tē, n.* a violin or cello made by the *Amati* family (c. 1550–1700) of Cremona.

amative *am'ə-tiv, adj.* inclined towards love.—*n.* **am'ativeness** propensity to love or to sexuality. [L. *amāre, -ātum,* to love.]

amatol *am'ə-tol, n.* a high explosive composed of ammonium nitrate and trinitrotoluene.

amatory *am'ə-tər-i, adj.* relating to or causing love: amorous.—*adj.* **amatō'rial** (or *tō'*).—*adv.* **amato'rially.**—*adjs.* **amatō'rian; amatō'rious.** [L. *amātōrius.*]

amaurosis *am-o-rō'sis, n.* blindness without outward change in the eye.—*adj.* **amaurotic** (*-rot'ik*). [Gr. *amaurōsis—amauros,* dark.]

amaze *ə-māz', v.t.* to confound with astonishment or wonder.—*n.* extreme astonishment.—*adv.* **amaz'edly.**—*ns.* **amaz'edness** (*rare*), **amaze'ment** astonishment mingled with wonder.—*adj.* **amaz'ing.**—*adv.* **amaz'ingly** (often hyperbolically). [O.E. *āmasian* (found in the pa.p. *āmasod*).]

Amazon *am'ə-zon, -zən, n.* in Greek story, one of a nation of women warriors, located in Asia or Scythia: the great river of South America (Port. *Amazonas,* Amazons, perh. based on a misunderstood Tupí-Guaraní word *amassona, amaçunu,* tidal bore, connected with records of Amazons living on its banks). an Indian of the Amazons: (the following usu. without *cap.*) a female soldier a warlike, manlike, strong, or vigorous woman.—Also *adj.*—*adj.* **Amazō'nian** (also without *cap.*). [Gr. *Amāzōn, -onos,* in folk-etymology referred to *a-,* priv., *māzos,* breast, with

the explanation that Amazons cut off the right breast lest it should get in the way of the bowstring.]

ambages *am-bä'jēz, n.pl.* windings: roundabout ways: delays.—Also *n.sing.* **ambage** (*am'bij*) with *pl.* **am'bages.**—*adj.* **ambagious**(*-bä'jəs*) tortuous: circumlocutory. [L. *ambāgēs* (pl.)—*ambi-,* about, *agěre,* to drive, lead.]

ambassador *am-bas'ə-dər, n.* a diplomatic minister of the highest order: a messenger or agent:—*fem* **ambass'adress.**—*adj.* **ambassadorial** (*-dō'ri-əl, -do'*).—*n.* **ambass'adorship.**—**ambass'ador-at-large'** an ambassador not accredited to any particular foreign government; **ambassador extraordinary** an ambassador sent on a special occasion, as distinguished from the ordinary or resident ambassador. [Fr *ambassadeur*—L. *ambactus,* a slave or servant.]

amber *am'bər, n.* a yellowish fossil resin.—*adj.* made of amber· amber-hued—clear brownish yellow.—*adjs.* **am'berous; am'bery.**—*n.* **am'broid** or **am'beroid** pressed amber, a synthetic amber formed by heating and compressing pieces of natural amber too small to be of value in themselves, sometimes along with other resins [Fr. *ambre*—Ar. *'anbar,* ambergris]

ambergris *am'bər-grēs, n.* an ash-grey strongly-scented substance, found floating or cast up, and in the intestines of the spermaceti whale, where it originates. [Fr. *ambre gris,* grey amber.]

ambiance. See **ambient.**

ambidext(e)rous *am-bi-deks'trəs, -tər-əs, adj.* able to use both hands alike: on both sides: double-dealing.—*n.* **ambidexterity** (*-ter'i-ti*). [L. *ambi-,* on both sides, *dexter,* right.]

ambient *am'bi-ənt, adj.* going round: surrounding: investing.—*n.* that which encompasses: the air or sky. —*n.* **ambience** (*am'bi-əns*) environment: surrounding influence: atmosphere: (also **ambiance** (*ä-bē-äs*)) the use or disposition of accessories in art. [L. *ambiēns, -entis,* pr.p. of *ambīre*—pfx. *ambi-,* about, *īre,* to go.]

ambiguous *am-big'ū-əs, adj.* doubtful: undetermined: of intermediate or doubtful nature: indistinct: wavering: admitting of more than one meaning: equivocal —*n.* **ambigū'ity** doubtful or double meaning: an equivocal expression.—*adv.* **ambig'uously.**—*n.* **ambig'uousness.** [L. *ambiguus—ambigěre,* to go about, waver—pfx. *ambi-,* both ways, *agěre,* to drive.]

ambisonics *am-bi-son'iks, n. sing.* a system of high-fidelity sound reproduction which electronically reproduces the natural ambience of the sound. [L. pfx. *ambi-,* about, and **sonics.**]

ambit *am'bit, n.* circuit: scope: compass: precincts: confines. [L. *ambitus,* a going round—pfx. *ambi-,* round, *itus,* going—*īre, itum,* to go.]

ambition *am-bish'ən, n.* aspiration after success or advancement: the object of aspiration.—*adjs.* **ambi'tionless; ambitious** (*am-bish'əs*), full of ambition: strongly desirous (of, to do): aspiring: indicating ambition: pretentious.—*adv.* **ambi'tiously.**—*n* **ambi'tiousness.** [L. *ambitiō, -ōnis,* canvassing—pfx. *ambi,* about, and *īre, itum,* to go.]

ambivalence *am-biv'ə-ləns,* **ambivalency** *-i, ns.* co-existence in one person of opposing emotional attitudes towards the same object.—*adj* **ambiv'alent.** [L. pfx. *ambi-,* on both sides, *valēns, -entis,* pr.p. of *valēre,* to be strong.]

amble *am'bl, v.i.* to move, as a horse, by lifting together both legs on one side alternately with those on the other side: to move at an easy pace: to go like an ambling horse. to ride an ambling animal —*n.* an ambling pace.—*n* **am'bler.**—*n.* and

For other sounds see detailed chart of pronunciation

adj. **am'bling.** [Fr. *ambler*—L. *ambulāre*, to walk about.]

amblyopia *am-bli-ō'pi-ə*, *n.* (partial) blindness or dullness of sight without any apparent damage to the eye [Gr *amblyōpiā*—*amblys*, dull, *ops*, eye.]

Amblystoma *am-blis'to-mə*, *n.* a genus of tailed amphibians in the gill-less or salamandroid suborder, in the larval stage called axolotl. [Gr. *amblys*, blunt, *stoma*, mouth.]

ambroid. See **amber.**

ambrosia *am-brō'z(h)i-ə*, *-z(h)yə*, *n.* the food (later, the drink) of the Greek gods, which conferred everlasting youth and beauty: the anointing oil of the gods: any finely flavoured beverage: something sweet and pleasing: bee-bread —*adj.* **ambrō'sial** fragrant delicious immortal: heavenly.—*adv.* **ambrōs'ially.** —*adj.* **ambrō'sian.** [Gr *ambrosiā*—*ambrotos*, immortal—*a-*, priv., and *brotos*, for *mbrotos*, mortal; cf Sans. *amṛta*, immortal]

ambry, aumbry, almery *am'*, *om'(b)ri*, *ns* a recess for church vessels: a cupboard· a pantry· a dresser· a safe [O.Fr. *almerie*—L *armārium*, a chest, safe—*arma*, arms, tools]

ambulance *am'bū-ləns*, *n.* a vehicle or (**air ambulance**) helicopter, etc , for conveying sick or injured: a movable field hospital.—*adj.* **am'bulant** walking· moving from place to place: allowing or calling for walking.—*n* a walking patient.—*adj* **am'bulatory** (*-ə-tər-i*) of or for walking: moving from place to place, not stationary mutable.—**am'bulance-chaser** a lawyer on the look-out for accidents in order to instigate actions for damages (*U S*) [L *ambulāre*, *-ātum*, to walk about.]

ambuscade *am-bəs-kād'*, *n* an ambush. [Fr *embuscade* or Sp *emboscada*; see **ambush.**]

ambush *am'boosh*, *n.* a lying, or laying, in wait to attack by surprise: a place of lying in wait: a body (or person) lying in wait.—*v.t.* to lay in wait: to waylay.—*v.t.* to lie in wait.—*n* **am'bushment** ambush. [O Fr. *embusche* (Fr. *embûche*)—*embuscher*—L L. *imboscāre*—*im*, in, *boscus* (see **bush**[1]).]

âme damnée *am da-nā*, (Fr.) lit damned soul, a tool or agent blindly devoted to one's will; **âme perdue** (*per-du*) lit. lost soul, a desperate character.

ameer. See **amir.**

amelia *a-mēl'i-ə*, *-mel'*, or *-yə*, *n* the condition where one or more limbs are completely absent [Gr *a-*, priv., and *melos*, limb.]

ameliorate *ə-mē'lyə-rāt*, *v t* to make better. to improve.—*v.i.* to grow better.—*n* **amēliorā'tion.** —*adj.* **amē'liorative.** [Fr *améliorer*—L *ad*, to, *melior*, better.]

amen *a-men'*, *ā-men'*, *interj.* so let it be. [Heb *āmēn*, true, truly, retained in Gr and English translations]

amenable *ə-mēn'ə-bl*, *adj.* ready to be led or won over. liable or subject —*ns.* **amenabil'ity, amen'ableness.** —*adv.* **amen'able.** [Fr. *amener*, to lead—*à*—L. *ad*, to, and *mener*, to lead—L L *mināre*, to lead, to drive (as cattle)—L. *mināri*, to threaten]

amend *ə-mend'*, *v.t.* to free from fault or error· to correct: to improve: to alter in detail, with a view to improvement. as a bill before parliament: to rectify to cure· to mend.—*v.i* to grow or become better· to reform: to recover.—*adjs.* **amend'able; amend'atory** corrective —*ns.* **amend'er; amend'ment** correction: improvement. an alteration proposed on a bill under consideration: a counter-proposal put before a meeting. a counter-motion —**make amends** to supply a loss: to compensate (for). [Fr *amender*—L *ēmendāre*—*ē*, out of, and *mendum*, a fault]

amene *ə-mēn'*, *adj.* (now *rare*) pleasant —*n* **amenity** (*-men'*, *-men'*) pleasantness, as in situation, climate, manners, disposition. a pleasing feature, object,

characteristic: a facility (*usu.* *pl*): civility. [L *amoenus*, pleasant.]

amenorrhoea *a-*, *ā-men-ō-rē'ə*, *n.* failure of menstruation. [Gr *a-*, priv., *mēn*, month, *rhoiā*, a flowing]

ament *ā'mənt*, *ə-ment'*, *n* one who is mentally defective by failure to develop: a sufferer from amentia.— *n* **amentia** (*a-*, *ā-men'shi-ə*) mental deficiency. [L. *āmēns*, *-entis*—*ā*, from, *mēns*, *mentis*, mind.]

amentum *a-men'təm*, *n.* a catkin—*pl.* **amen'ta.**— Also **a'ment.** [L , thong]

amerce *ə-mûrs'*, *v.t.* to fine (esp. at discretion): to deprive. to punish —*ns* **amerce'ment, amerc'iament** infliction of a fine: a fine.—*adj* **amerc'iable.** [A Fr *amercier*—*à merci*, at mercy]

American *ə-mer'i-kən*, *adj* pertaining to America, esp to the United States —*n.* a native or citizen of America: the English language as spoken in America. —*v.t* **Amer'icanise, -ize** to render American —*ns* **Amer'icanism** a custom, characteristic, word, phrase, or idiom characteristic of Americans: condition of being an American citizen· devotion to American institutions —**American aloe** Agave; **American Express® card** a type of credit card issued by a commercial company, **American football** an American game of football, somewhat resembling British rugby football; **American Indian** a member of the native race of America [From *America*, perh so called from Richard *Ameryk*, Sheriff of Bristol, who financed John Cabot's voyage, also said to be from Amerigo (L *Americus*) Vespucci]

americium *am-ər-ish'i-əm*, *n.* a radioactive metallic element (at numb 95; symbol Am), obtained artificially in *America*

Amerind *am'ər-ind*, *n* and *adj.* American Indian.— Also **Amerind'ian.**

amethyst *am'ə-thist*, *n.* a bluish violet quartz anciently supposed to prevent drunkenness its colour.—*adj* of, or coloured like, amethyst. [Gr *amethystos*—*a-*, priv , and *methyein*, to be drunken—*methy*, wine.]

Amharic *am-har'ik*, *n* an Ethiopic language, the official language of Ethiopia —Also *adj* [*Amhara* district.]

amiable *ām'i-ə-bl*, *adj* lovable of sweet and friendly disposition —*ns.* **āmiabil'ity, ām'iableness.**—*adv* **ām'iably.** [O Fr *amiable*, friendly—L. *amicābilis* —*amicus*, friend, confused in meaning with O Fr *amable* (Fr *aimable*)—L *amābilis*—*amāre*, to love]

amianthus *am-i-anth'əs*, more correctly **amientus** (*-ant'əs*), *n.* the finest fibrous asbestos, which can be made into cloth readily cleansed by fire [Gr *amiantos* (*lithos*), undefiled (stone)—*a-*, priv , and *miainein*, to soil]

amicable *am'ik-ə-bl*, *adj.* in friendly spirit —*ns.* **amicabil'ity, am'icableness.**—*adv* **am'icably.** [L *amicābilis*—*amicus*, a friend—*amāre*, to love]

amice[1], *am'is*, *n.* a strip of fine linen, worn formerly on the head, now on the shoulders, by a priest at mass: a cloak, wrap [O Fr *amit*—L. *amictus*, cloak— *amb-*, about, and *jacēre*, to throw]

amice[2], *am'is*, *n* a furred hood with long ends hanging down in front, originally a cap or covering for the head, afterwards a hood, or cape with a hood, later a mere college hood [O Fr *aumuce*]

amicus curiae *a-mī'kus kū'ri-ē*, *a-mē'koōskoō'ri-ī*, (L) a friend of the law-court· formerly, in Scots law, a disinterested adviser, not a party to the case in Eng law, counsel acting for a person who is interested in the outcome of a case he is not personally involved in (wrongly) a friend in high quarters —*pl* **ami'ci** (or *-mē'kē*)

amid *ə-mid'*, *prep* in the midst of among —*adv*

amid'ships in, near, towards, the middle of a ship lengthwise (from gen. of **ship**).—*adv.* and *prep.*
amidst' amid. [O.E. *on middan* (dat. of adj.), in middle; the *s* is a later adverbial genitive ending, the *t* as in **amongst, betwixt**, etc.]
amide *am'īd, n.* a derivative of ammonia in which an acid radical takes the place of one or more of the three hydrogen atoms.—*n.* **amido-group** (*ə-mē'dō*) the group NH₂ in such combination. [From **ammonia**.]
amine *am'īn, -ēn, n.* a derivative of ammonia (NH₂) in which one or more hydrocarbon radicals take the place of one or more of the three hydrogen atoms.—*ns.* **amino-a'cid** (*a-mē'nō-*) a fatty acid in which the amino-group takes the place of a hydrogen atom of the hydrocarbon radical; **ami'no-group'** the group NH₂ in such combination. [From **ammonia**.]
aminobutene *a-mē'nō-bū'tēn, n.* a pain-relieving drug, less addiction-forming than morphine. [**amine** and **butene**.]
amir, ameer *a-mēr', ə-mēr', n.* the title borne by certain Muslim princes. [Ar. *amīr*; see **admiral, emir**.]
amiss *ə-mis', adv.* astray: wrongly: improperly: faultily.—*adj.* out of order: wrong: unsuitable: to be objected to.—*n.* an evil: a misdeed.—**come amiss** to be unwelcome, untoward; **take amiss** to take offence at (strictly, by misinterpretation). [Prep. **a**, and **miss¹**.]
amitosis *am-ı-tō'sis,* (*biol.*) *n.* cell-division without mitosis.—*adj.* **amitotic** (*-tot'ik*).—*adv.* **amitot'ically.** [Gr. *a-*, priv., and *mitos*, thread.]
amity *am'i-ti, n.* friendship: goodwill: friendly relations. [Fr. *amitié*—L. *amicus*, a friend.]
ammeter *am'i-tər, n.* an instrument for measuring electric current. [From **ampere**, and Gr. *metron*, measure.]
ammo *am'ō, n.* a familiar contraction of **ammunition**.
Ammon *am'on, n.* the ancient Egyptian ram-headed god *Amûn, Amen: (without cap.*) the argali (from its gigantic horns).—*n.* **ammonia** (*a-, ə-mō'ni-ə*) a pungent compound of nitrogen and hydrogen (NH₃) first obtained in gaseous form from *sal-ammoniac*: its solution in water, strictly ammonium hydroxide (*liquid ammonia,* long known as spirits of hartshorn).—*adjs.* **ammō'niac, ammoni'acal** of ammonia.—*adj.* **ammō'niated** combined, impregnated, with ammonia.—*ns.* **amm'onite** a fossil cephalopod of many kinds, with coiled chambered shell like Ammon's horn; **ammō'nium** a univalent radical, NH₄, resembling the alkali metals in chemical behaviour. [Gr. *Ammōn, -ōnos.*]
ammunition *am-ū-nish'ən, n.* orig. military stores generally: things used for charging fire-arms—missiles, propellants (*coll.* **am'mo**): explosive military devices: anything that can be used in fighting (*lit.* and *fig.*).—*adj.* for ammunition: supplied from army stores.—*v.t.* to supply with ammunition. [Obs. Fr. *amunition,* app. from *l'amunition* for *la munition*; see **munition**.]
amnesia *am-nē'zh(y)ə, n.* the loss of memory.—*n.* **amne'siac** one who suffers from amnesia.—Also *adj.*—*adj.* and *n.* **amne'sic.** [Gr. *amnēsiā.*]
amnesty *am'nes-ti, n.* a general pardon: an act of oblivion.—*v.t.* to give amnesty to. [Gr. *amnēstiā,* forgetfulness.]
amnion *am'ni-ən, n.* the innermost membrane enveloping the embryo of reptiles, birds, and mammals:—*pl.* **am'nia.**—**amnio-** in composition, amnion: amniotic.—*n.* **amniocentesis** (*am-ni-ō-sin-tē'sis*) the insertion of a hollow needle into the uterus of a pregnant woman to withdraw a sample of the amniotic fluid to test for foetal abnormalities, etc.—*adj.* **amniot'ic.**—**amniotic fluid** the fluid within the

amnion in which the embryo is suspended [Gr.]
amoeba *ə-mē'bə, n.* a protozoon of ever-changing shape:—*pl.* **amoebae** (*-bē, -bi*).—*adjs.* **amoe'bic; amoe'biform; amoe'boid.** [Gr. *amoibē,* change.]
amok *ə-mok',* **amuck** *ə-muk', adjs.* and *advs* in a frenzy, esp. in phrase **to run amok,** to run forth murderously assailing all who come in the way (also *fig*). [Malay *amoq,* frenzied.]
among *ə-mung',* **amongst** *ə-mungst', preps.* of the number of: amidst. [O.E. *on-gemang,* lit. in mixture, crowd—*gemengan,* to mingle: for *-st* see **against**.]
amontillado *ā-mon-til-(y)ä'dō, n.* a slightly sweet sherry of light colour and body, orig. from *Montilla*:—*pl.* **amontilla'dos.** [Sp.]
amoral *a-mor'əl,* also *ā-, adj.* non-moral, outside the domain of morality —*ns.* **amor'alism** refusal to recognise the validity of any system of morality; **amor'alist.** [Gr. *a-,* priv., and **moral**.]
amorist *am'ər-ist, n.* a lover: a gallant: one who writes of love: a seeker of sexual adventures or experiences.—*n.* **am'orism.** [L. *amor,* love.]
amoroso *am-or-ō'sō,* (*mus.*) *adj.* tender.—Also *adv.*—*n.* a lover: a gallant:—*pl.* **amoro'sos:**—*fem.* **amoro'sa.** [It.]
amorous *am'ər-əs, adj.* inclined to love: in love: fond: amatory: relating to love.—*adv.* **am'orously.**—*n.* **am'orousness.** [O.Fr. *amorous* (Fr. *amoureux*)—L.L. *amōrōsus—amor,* love.]
amorphous *ə-mör'fəs, adj.* without definite shape or structure: shapeless: without crystalline structure.—*n.* **amor'phism.** [Gr. *amorphos,* shapeless—*a-,* priv., *morphē,* form.]
amortise, -ize *ə-mör'tīz, -tiz, v.t.* to alienate in mortmain or convey to a corporation: to wipe out esp. through a sinking-fund.—*n.* **amortisã'tion, -z-.** [L.L. *a(d)mortizāre*—Fr. *à,* to, *mort,* death.]
amount *ə-mownt', v.i.* to come in total: to come in meaning or substance (with *to*).—*n.* the whole sum: principal and interest together: quantity: value, import, equivalence. [O.Fr. *amonter,* to ascend—L. *ad,* to, *mōns, montis,* a mountain.]
amour *ə-mōō'r', n.* a love affair (now usu. discreditable): a loved one. [Fr.,—L. *amor, amōris,* love.]
amour-propre *a-mōō'r-pro-pr', (*Fr.*) *n.* self-esteem: sometimes in exaggerated form, shown in readiness to take offence at slights.
amp *amp, n.* short for **ampere**.
ampelopsis *am-pi-lop'sis, n.* a plant of the genus *Ampelopsis:* (*form.* and *rarely*) any of certain related plants such as the Virginia creeper:—*pl.* **ampelop'ses** (*-sēz*). [Gr. *ampelos,* vine, *opsis,* appearance.]
ampere, ampère *am'per, -pēr', ā-per,* (*elect.*) *n.* the SI and MKSA unit of current, defined as that which, flowing in two parallel conductors, each infinitely thin and long, one metre apart in a vacuum, will produce a force between the conductors of 2×10^{-7} newtons per metre length (**international ampere** a unit formerly defined by means of the rate of deposition of silver from a solution of silver nitrate and slightly less than the practical unit in use; now the same as the unit just defined).—*n.* **am'perage** current in amperes. [From A. M. *Ampère* (1775–1836), French physicist.]
ampersand *am'pars-and, n.* the character (&; originally ligatured *E* and *T,* for L. *et*) representing *and.* [*and per se and*—that is, &, by itself, 'and'.]
amphetamine *am-fet'ə-mēn, n.* C₉H₁₃N, or its sulphate or phosphate, a synthetic drug used to relieve nasal congestion or taken internally to stimulate the central nervous system. [**alpha** methyl *phen*ethyl + **amine**]
amphibious *am-fib'i-əs, adj.* leading two lives: living, or adapted to life, or use, on land and in or on water: of military operations, in which troops are conveyed

across the sea or other water in landing barges, assault-craft, etc., and land on enemy-held territory: of double, doubtful, or ambiguous nature.—*n.pl* **Amphib'ia** a class of vertebrates typically gill-breathing in the larval state and lung-breathing or skin-breathing as adults—frogs, toads, newts, salamanders, caecilians.—*adj.* **amphib'ian** amphibious: of the Amphibia.—*n.* a member of the Amphibia: an aeroplane designed to alight on land or water: a vehicle for use on land or water [Gr. *amphibios*—*amphi*, on both sides, *bios*, life.]

amphibole *am'fi-bōl, n.* any mineral of a group including hornblende, actinolite, tremolite, etc.—*n.* **amphib'olite** a rock composed essentially of amphibole [Gr. *amphibolos*, ambiguous, on account of the resemblance between hornblende and tourmaline.]

amphibology *am-fi-bol'ə-ji, n.* a phrase or sentence ambiguous not in its individual words but in its construction: the use of such ambiguities.—*adjs.* **amphibol'ic; amphibological** (*-bō-loj'*), **amphib'olous** (*-ə-ləs*).—*n* **amphib'oly** amphibology. [Gr. *amphibolos*—*amphi*, on both sides, *ballein*, to throw.]

amphimixis *am-fi-mik'sis, n* fusion of gametes: sexual reproduction: combination of characters from both parents.—*adj.* **amphimic'tic.** [Gr. *amphi*, on both sides, *mixis*, intercourse, mixing.]

amphioxus *am-fi-oks'əs, n* a lancelet of the genus *Amphioxus* or *Branchiostoma.* [Gr. *amphi*, at both ends, and *oxys*, sharp.]

amphipod *am'fi-pod, n.* one of the **Amphip'oda**, an order of small sessile-eyed crustaceans with swimming feet and jumping feet—sand-hoppers, etc.—*adj.* **amphip'odous.** [Gr. *amphi*, both ways, *pous*, *podos*, a foot.]

amphitheatre *am'fi-thē-ə-tər, n.* a building with rows of seats one above another, around an open space: a similar configuration of hill slopes: one of the galleries in a theatre.—*adjs.* **amphithe'atral; amphitheatrical** (*-at'ri-kl*).—*adv.* **amphitheat'rically.** [Gr *amphitheātron*—*amphi*, theatre, theatre.]

ampholyte *am'fō-līt, n.* an *amphoteric* electrolyte.

amphora *am'fə-rə, n.* a two-handled jar used by the Greeks and Romans for holding liquids:—*pl.* **am'phorae** (*-rē; -rī*). [L. *amphora*—Gr *amphoreus*, *amphiphoreus*—*amphi*, on both sides, and *phoreus*, a bearer.]

amphoteric *am-fō-ter'ik, adj.* of both kinds: acting both ways, e.g. as acid and base, electropositive and electronegative. [Gr. *amphoteros*, both.]

ample *am'pl, adj.* spacious: wide: large enough: abundant: liberal: copious: full or somewhat bulky in form.—*ns.* **am'pleness; amplifica'tion** enlargement; **am'plifier** one who amplifies: a lens that enlarges the field of vision: a device for giving greater loudness.—*v.t.* **am'plify** (*-fī*) to make more copious in expression: to add to: to increase loudness of (sound), strength of (current), etc.:—*pr.p.* **am'plifying;** *pa.p.* and *pa.t.* **am'plified.**—*n.* **am'plitude** largeness: abundance: width: range: extent of vibratory movement (from extreme to extreme, or from mean to extreme): the angular distance from the east point of the horizon at which a heavenly body rises, or from the west point at which it sets —*adv.* **am'ply** (*-pli*). —**amplitude modulation** (*telecomm.*) modulation in radio transmission by varying the amplitude of the carrier wave—cf. *frequency modulation.* [Fr *ample, amplifier, amplitude*—L. *amplus, amplificāre, amplitūdo.*]

amplification, etc. See **ample.**

amplosome *am'plə-sōm, n* the short, or stocky, type of human figure [L *amplus*, large, Gr *sōma*, body.]

ampoule *am'pōōl* (also *-pōō l'*)*, n.* a small glass etc. container for a hypodermic dose, etc —Also **am'pul, am'pule** (*-pūl*). [Fr.; see **ampulla.**]

ampulla *am-pōōl'ə, n* a small two-handled flask: a pilgrim's bottle: a vessel for holy oil, as at coronations cruet for the wine and water used at the altar: any small membranous vesicle (*biol.*): the dilated end of a semicircular canal in the ear:—*pl.* **ampull'ae** (*-ē*).—See also **ampoule.** [L. irregular dim of *amphora*, a flagon; partly directly from L, partly through O.E *ampulle*, O.Fr. *ampo(u)le*, and It *ampolla.*]

amputate *am'pūt-āt, v.t.* to cut off, as a limb —*ns.* **amputa'tion; am'putātor; amputee'.** [L *amputāre, -ātum—amb-*, around, and *putāre, -ātum*, to lop.]

amrit *am'rət, n.* a sacred sweetened water used in the Sikh baptismal ceremony the ceremony itself [Punjabi,—Sans. *amrta*, immortal.]

amtrack *am'trak, n.* an amphibious tracked military motor landing-vehicle [**am** for *amphibious*, and **track**[1].]

amuck *ə-muk'.* See **amok.**

amulet *am'ū-let, -lit, n.* a charm carried about the person: a medicine supposed to have occult operation.—*adj.* **amulet'ic.** [L. *amulētum.*]

amuse *ə-mūz', v.t* to occupy pleasantly: to entertain, divert: to excite mirth in —*adjs.* **amus'able; amused'.**—*adv.* **amus'edly.**—*ns* **amuse'ment** distraction of attention: a pleasant feeling of the ludicrous that which amuses: recreation, pastime, **amus'er.** —*adj.* **amus'ing** affording amusement: entertaining. —*adv.* **amus'ingly.**—**amusement arcade** a public hall, etc. with mechanical gambling machines, etc. [Fr. *amuser—à*, to, *muser*, to stare.]

amyl *am'il, n.* an alcohol radical, C_5H_{11}.—*ns.* **am'ylase** (*-ās*) any of the enzymes that play a part in hydrolysis of starch and similar substances; **am'ylene** a hydrocarbon of composition C_5H_{10}.—**amyl nitrate** a liquid added to diesel fuel to improve its ignition quality, also inhaled to heighten sexual pleasure; **amyl nitrite** a fruity-smelling, amber-coloured liquid; inhaled medicinally as a vasodilator. [From the first syllable of Gr. *amylon*, starch, fine meal, and *hylē*, matter, from having been first got from fusel-oil made from starch.]

amylum *am'il-əm,* (*chem.*) *n.* starch.—*adjs* **amyla'ceous; am'yloid; amyloid'al.** [Gr. *amylon*, the finest flour, starch; literally unmilled—*a-*, priv., *mylē*, a mill.]

an *an, ən, adj* one: the indefinite article, used before a vowel sound, and by some (now rarely) before an unstressed syllable beginning with a sounded *h* [O.E. ān; see **one.**]

-ana *-a'nə, -ā'nə,* also **-iana** *suff.* things belonging to, or typical of, such as sayings, anecdotes, small objects, etc, e.g. Johnson*iana*, Victor*iana* (gener. used in reference to the time of Queen Victoria rather than to Victoria herself) —**ana** *n.pl* or *collective sing.* (with *pl* **ana's, anas**) a collection of someone's table-talk or of gossip, literary anecdotes or possessions. [L. neut. pl ending of adjs in *-anus.*]

anabaptist *an-ə-bap'tist, n.* a name given by opponents to one holding that baptism should be of adults only and therefore that those baptised in infancy must be baptised again: (with *cap.*) one of a Protestant sect of German origin (1521) rejecting infant baptism and seeking establishment of a Christian communism. [Gr *ana-*, again, and *baptizein*, to dip.]

Anabas *an'a-bas, n.* the genus to which belongs the climbing perch, an East Indian fish that often leaves the water: (without *cap*) a fish of this genus [Gr. *anabās*, aor part of *anabainein*, to climb—*ana*, up, *bainein*, to go.]

anabasis *an-ab'ə-sis, n* a going up: a military advance up-country, such as that of Cyrus the younger (401 B.C.) related (with the subsequent katabasis or retreat of the 10,000) by Xenophon in his *Anabasis* [Gr., *ana*, up, *basis*, going.]

anabiosis *an-ə-bī-ō'sis*, *n.* (the power of) returning to life after apparent death: a state of suspended animation.—*adj.* **anabio'tic.** [Gr. *anabiōsis—ana*, up, back, *bios*, life.]

Anableps *an'ə-bleps*, *n.* a genus of bony fishes with open air-bladders, and projecting eyes divided in two for vision in air and water: (without *cap.*) a fish of this genus. [Gr. *ana*, up, *blepein*, to look.]

anabolism *an-ab'əl-izm*, *n.* chemical upbuilding of complex substances in living matter (opp. to *katabolism*).—*adj.* **anabolic** (*an-ə-bol'ik*)—**anabolic steroids** steroids used to increase the build-up of body tissue, esp. muscle; illegally used by some athletes. [Gr. *anabolē*, a heaping up—*ana*, up, *bolē*, a throw.]

Anacharis *ən-ak'ə-ris*, *n.* a genus of water-plants including *Anacharis helodea* or *Elodea canadensis*, a North American weed found in Britain in 1842, soon clogging canals and rivers by vegetative growth: (without *cap.*) a plant of this genus. [Gr. *ana*, up, and *charis*, grace.]

anachronism *ə-nak'rə-nizm*, *n.* an error assigning a thing to an earlier or (less strictly) to a later age than it belongs to: anything out of keeping with chronology.—*adjs.* **anachron'ic, anachronist'ic, anach'ronous.**—*advs.* **anachron'ically, anachronist'ically, anach'ronously.** [Gr. *ana-*, backwards, *chronos*, time.]

anacoluthia *an-ə-ko-lōō'thi-ə, -lū-*, *n.* want of syntactical sequence, when the latter part of a sentence does not grammatically fit the earlier —*n.* **anacolu'thon** an instance of anacoluthia: anacoluthia:—*pl.* **anacolu'tha.** [Gr. *anakolouthiā, anakolouthon—an-*, priv., *akolouthos*, following.]

anaconda *an-ə-kon'də*, *n.* a gigantic South American water-boa. [Perhaps from a Sinhalese name for another snake in Sri Lanka.]

anacoustic zone *an-ə-kōō st'ik zōn*, a zone of absolute silence in space. [Gr. *an-*, priv.; **acoustic.**]

anacrusis *an-ə-krōō'sis, (pros.) n.* one or more short syllables introductory to the normal rhythm of a line —*pl.* **anacru'ses** (*-sēz*)—*adj.* **anacrustic** (*-krus'tik*). [Gr. *anakrousis*, a pushing back, striking up a tune—*ana*, up, back, *krouein*, to strike]

anadromous *an-ad'rə-məs, adj* of fish, ascending rivers to spawn (opp. to *catadromous*). [Gr. *anadromos*, running up—*ana*, up, *dromos*, a run.]

anaemia, in U.S. **anemia,** *an-ēm'i-ə*, *n.* bloodlessness: lack of red blood corpuscles or of haemoglobin—a condition marked by paleness and languor.—*adj.* **anaem'ic** suffering from anaemia: sickly, spiritless, washed-out, lacking in body (*fig.*) —**pernicious anaemia** a severe form of anaemia characterised by abnormalities in the red blood corpuscles, etc [Gr *anaimiā—an-*, priv, *haima*, blood.]

anaerobe *an'ā(ə)r-ōb*, *n.* an organism that lives in absence of free oxygen.—Also **anaero'biont.**—*adjs* **anaerobic** (*-ob'ik, -ōb'ik*), **anaerobiotic** (*-ō-bī-ot'ik*) living in the absence of free oxygen: of a process, etc , requiring the absence, or not requiring the presence, of free oxygen: effected by anaerobes, as a biochemical change involving the activity of anaerobes —*advs.* **anaerob'ically, anaerobiot'ically.**—*n* **anaerobio'sis** life in the absence of oxygen. [Gr. *an-*, priv., *āēr*, air, *bios*, life.]

anaesthesia, in U.S. **anesthesia,** *an-əs-thē'zi-ə, -zyə* or *-ēs-*, **anaesthesis** *-sis*, *ns.* loss of feeling: insensibility, general or local.—*adj.* **anaesthetic** (*-thet'ik, -thēt'ik*) producing or connected with insensibility —*n* an anaesthetic agent.—*adv.* **anaesthet'ically.**—*n sing*

anaesthet'ics the science of anaesthesia —*n.* **anaesthetisā'tion, -z-.**—*v.t.* **anaes'thetise, -ize.**—*n.* **anaesthetist** (*-ēs'thə-tist,* or *-es'*) one who administers anaesthetics.—**general anaesthetic** one which produces insensibility in the whole body, usually causing unconsciousness; **local anaesthetic** one producing insensibility in only the relevant part of the body. [Gr. *anaisthēsiā*, insensibility, *anaisthētos*, insensible —*an-*, priv., *aisthanesthai*, to perceive.]

anaglyph *an'ə-glif*, *n.* an ornament in low relief: a picture composed of two prints, in complementary colours, seen stereoscopically through spectacles of these colours.—*adj.* **anaglyph'ic.**—*n* **anaglypta** (*a-na-glip'tə*) a type of plain, white wallpaper that has a heavily embossed pattern (orig a proprietary name).—Also *adj.*—*adj.* **anaglyp'tic.** [Gr. *anaglyphos, anaglyptos*, in low relief—*ana*, up, back, *glyphein*, to engrave, carve.]

anagoge *an-ə-gō'ji*, *n.* mystical interpretation.—Also **an'agogy.**—*adjs.* **anagogic** (*-goj'ik*) pertaining to mystical interpretation: of the strivings in the unconscious towards morally high ideals; **anagog'ical.**—*adv.* **anagog'ically.** [Gr. *anagōgē*, leading up, elevation—*ana*, up, *agein*, to lead.]

anagram *an'ə-gram*, *n.* word or phrase formed by the letters of another in different order.—*adjs.* **anagrammat'ic; anagrammat'ical.**—*adv* **anagrammat'ically.** [Gr. *ana-*, back, *gramma*, letter.]

anal. See **anus.**

analects *an'ə-lekts*, **analecta** *-lek'tə*, *ns.pl.* collected literary fragments —*adj.* **analec'tic.** [Gr. (*pl.*) *analekta—ana*, up, *legein*, to gather.]

analeptic *an-ə-lep'tik*, *adj.* restorative: comforting. [Gr *analēptikos*, restorative—*ana*, up, and the root *lab* of *lambanein*, to take]

analgesia *an-al-jē'zi-ə*, *n.* painlessness: insensibility to pain.—*n.* **analgesic** (*-jē'sik*) an anodyne.—*adj.* producing analgesia. [Gr. *analgēsiā—an-*, priv., and *algeein*, to feel pain.]

analogy *an-al'ə-ji*, *n.* an agreement or correspondence in certain respects between things otherwise different: a resemblance of relations: parallelism: relation in general: a likeness: proportion, or the equality of ratios (*math.*): agreement in function, as distinguished from *homology* or agreement in origin (*biol*): a resemblance by virtue of which a word may be altered on the model of another class of words, as *strove, striven*, remodelled upon *drove, driven, throve, thriven*, etc (*philol.*).—*adjs* **analogic** (*an-ə-loj'ik; rare*); **analog'ical.**—*adv* **analog'ically.**—*adj.* **anal'ogous** (*-gəs*) having analogy: bearing some correspondence or resemblance: similar in certain circumstances or relations (with *to*). positively electrified by heating.—*adv* **anal'ogously.**—*ns* **anal'ogousness; an'alogue** (*-log;* in U.S also **analog**) that which is analogous to something else, e g protein substances prepared to resemble meat: that which is of like function (distinguished from a *homologue*) (*biol.*). a variable physical quantity which is similar to some other variable in that variations in the former are in the same proportional relationship as variations in the latter, often being used to record or represent such changes (also *adj*): a watch with the traditional face and hands (also *adj* ; opp to *digital*)—**analogue computer** a type of computer in which varying electrical currents or voltages, etc., are used to represent proportionally other quantities (e g., forces, speeds) in working out problems about these qualities; **analogue transmission** (*telecomm*) the transmission of signals and messages by means of radio waves, without first converting them to a computerised form as in *digital transmission*. [Gr *analogiā—ana*, according to, and *logos*, ratio.]

analysis *ən-al'is-is, n.* a resolving or separating of a thing into its elements or component parts. ascertainment of those parts: a table or statement of the results of this: the tracing of things to their source, and so discovering the general principles underlying individual phenomena: resolution of a sentence into its syntactic elements (*gram.*): use of algebraical methods. psychoanalysis:—*pl.* anal'yses (*-sēz*).— Opp. to *synthesis.*—Spellings with *-z-* in following words are chiefly U.S.—*adj.* analysable, -zable (*an-ə-līz'ə-bl*).—*v t.* an'alyse, -yze (*-līz*) to subject to analysis.—*ns.* analys'er, -yz'er one who analyses: in a polariscope the nicol (or substitute) through which the polarised light passes: a device that analyses; an'alyst (*-list*) one skilled in or practising analysis, esp. chemical or economic: a psychoanalyst.—*adj.* analytic (*-lit'ik*) pertaining to, performing, or inclined to analysis: resolving into first principles. —*n.* (often *pl.* in form) analytical logic: analytical geometry.—*adj.* analyt'ical.—*adv.* analyt'ically.— analytical chemistry (*loosely* analysis) chemistry concerned with determination of the constituents of chemical compounds, or mixtures of compounds; analytical geometry co-ordinate geometry; analytical languages those that use separate words instead of inflexions; analytical logic logic which is concerned with analysis.—in the last analysis when all inessentials are excluded from the problem, or the situation. [Gr. *analysis*—*analȳein,* to unloose, *ana,* up, *lȳein,* to loose.]

anamnesis *an-am-nēs'is, n.* the recalling to memory of things past; a patient's medical history:—*pl.* anamnē'ses (*-sēz*).—*adj.* anamnēs'tic. [Gr. *anamnēsis* —*ana,* up, back, *mimnēskein,* to remind, recall to memory.]

ananas *ə-nā'nas, n.* the pineapple (*Ananas sativus*): the pinguin (*Bromelia pinguin*), or its fruit.—Also an'ana. [From an American Indian language]

anandrous *an-an'drəs,* (*bot.*) *adj.* lacking stamens. [Gr. *anandros,* lacking men—*an-,* priv., *anēr, andros,* a man.]

ananthous *an-an'thəs,* (*bot.*) *adj.* lacking flowers. [Gr. *ananthēs*—*an-,* priv., *anthos,* a flower.]

anapaest, in U.S. anapest, *an'ə-pēst,* (*pros.*) *n.* a foot of two short (or unstressed) syllables followed by a long (or stressed) syllable—a dactyl reversed.—*adjs.* anapaes'tic, -al. [Gr. *anapaistos,* struck back—*ana,* back, *paiein,* to strike.]

anaphora *ən-af'ə-rə, n.* the rhetorical device of beginning successive sentences, lines, etc., with the same word or phrase: the use of a word (such as *it, do*) to avoid repetition of a preceding word or group of words: the offering of the Eucharistic elements.— *adjs.* anaphoric (*an-ə-for'ik*). -al referring to a preceding word or group of words.—*adv.* anaphor'ically. [Gr. *anaphorā,* a carrying back, reference—*ana,* back, *pherein,* to bear.]

anaphrodisiac *an-af-rō-diz'i-ak, adj.* tending to diminish sexual desire.—*n.* an anaphrodisiac agent. [Gr. *an-,* priv., *aphrodisiakos,* sexual.]

anaphylaxis *an-ə-fil-aks'is, n.* an increased susceptibility to injected foreign material, protein or nonprotein, brought about by a previous introduction of it. —Also anaphylax'y.—*adj.* anaphylac'tic. [Gr *ana,* back, *phylaxis,* protection.]

anaplasty *an'ə-plas-ti, n.* the reparation of superficial lesions by the use of adjacent healthy tissue, as by transplanting a portion of skin.—*adj.* anaplas'tic. [Gr. *ana,* again, *plassein,* to form.]

anaptyxis *an-əp-tik'sis,* (*phon.*) *n.* the development of a vowel between consonants.—*adj.* anaptyc'tic. [Gr. *anaptyxis,* gape—*ana,* back, *ptyssein,* to fold]

anarak. See anorak.

anarchy *an'ər-ki, n.* complete absence of law or gov-

ernment: a harmonious condition of society in which government is abolished as unnecessary: utter lawlessness: chaos: complete disorder —*adjs.* anarch'-ic, -al.—*adv* anarch'ically.—*ns.* an'archism the teaching of the anarchists; an'archist one whose ideal of society is one without government of any kind: one who seeks to advance such a condition by terrorism. —Also *adj* —*adj.* anarchist'ic. [Gr *anarchiā,* leaderlessness, lawlessness—*an-,* priv., *archē,* government.]

anastigmat *an-as'tig-mat,* or *-stig', n.* an anastigmatic lens.—*adj.* anastigmat'ic (*an-ə-*) not astigmatic.—*n.* anastig'matism. [Gr. *an-,* priv., and astigmatic.]

anastomosis *an-as-tə-mō'sis, n.* communication by cross-connections to form a network:—*pl* anastomō'ses (*-sēz*).—*v.i.* anas'tomose to intercommunicate in such a way.—*adj.* anastomōt'ic. [Gr. *anastomōsis,* outlet—*ana,* back, *stoma,* mouth.]

anastrophe *a-* or *ə-nas'trə-fi,* (*rhet.*) *n.* inversion. [Gr. *anastrophē*—*ana,* back, and *strephein,* to turn.]

anathema *a-* or *ə-nath'i-mə, n* a solemn ecclesiastical curse or denunciation involving excommunication: a curse, execration: a person or thing cursed ecclesiastically or generally: an object of abhorrence:—*pl* anath'emas.—*adj.* anathematical (*-mat'i-kl*).—*n.* anathematisation, *-z-* (*-mə-tī-zā'shən*).—*v.t.* and *v.i.* anath'ematise, -ize. [Gr. *anathēma,* a thing dedicated or accursed, for *anathēma,* a votive offering.—*ana,* up, and the root of *tithenai,* to place.]

Anatolian *an-ə-tōl'i-ən, adj.* of Anatolia, now the major part of Turkey: of or denoting any or all of an extinct family of languages belonging to, or closely related to, the Indo-European family.—*n.* a native or inhabitant of Anatolia: the Anatolian family of languages.

anatomy *ə-nat'ə-mi, n.* the art of dissecting any organised body: the science of the structure of the body learned by dissection bodily frame or structure: dissection: analysis.—*adjs.* anatomic (*an-ə-tom'ik*), -al.—*adv.* anatom'ically.—*v.t.* anat'omise, -ize to dissect: to lay open minutely (*fig.*).—*n* anat'omist one skilled in anatomy. [Gr. *anatomē,* dissection— *ana,* up, *tomē,* a cutting.]

anatta, anatto. See annatto.

anbury *an'bər-i, n.* a soft bloody wart on horses, etc.: a disease in turnips, cabbages, etc., due to a slime-fungus. [Perh. for *angberry*—O.E. *ange,* narrow, painful, and *berry.*]

ancestor *an'sis-tər, n.* one from whom a person is descended: a forefather:—*fem.* an'cestress.—*adjs* ances'tral (*-ses'*); ancestorial (*-sis-tō'ri-əl, -to'*)—*n* an'cestry a line of ancestors: lineage —an'cestorwor'ship. [O.Fr. *ancestre*—L. *antecēssor*—*ante,* before, *cēdēre, cēssum,* to go.]

anchor *ang'kər, n.* an implement for retaining a ship by chaining it to the bottom, or for holding a balloon to the ground, or the like: anything that gives stability or security (*fig.*).—*v.t.* to fix by an anchor: to fasten.— *v.i.* to cast anchor: to stop, or rest.—*n.* anch'orage the act of anchoring. a place of or for anchoring: rest or support to the mind (*fig.*) duty imposed for anchoring.—*adj.* anch'orless.—anchor escapement or recoil escapement a clock escapement in which the pallets push the escape-wheel slightly backwards at the end of each swing, causing a recoil of the pendulum; anch'or-hold the hold of an anchor upon the ground. security (*fig.*); anchor (man) the man at the back of a team in a tug-of-war: the man who runs the last stage of a relay-race: (or anch'orman) a person on whom the success of an activity depends, esp., on television, the person responsible for smooth running of a dialogue or discussion between or among others; anch'or-stock the cross-bar of an anchor, which causes one or other of the flukes to turn to the bottom.—**at anchor** anchored; **cast anchor** to let down the anchor; **weigh anchor** to take up the anchor. [O.E. *ancor*—L. *ancŏra;* cf. Gr. *ankȳra—ankos,* a bend; conn. with **angle.**]

anchorite *ang'kər-īt, n.* a man or woman who has withdrawn from the world, especially for religious reasons: a recluse.—*ns.* **anch'orage** a recluse's cell; **anch'oress,** *anc'ress* a female anchorite.—*adjs.* **anchoret'ic, -al, anchorit'ic, -al.** [Gr *anachōrētēs —ana,* apart, *chōreein,* to withdraw.]

anchovy *an'chə-vi,* or *-chō-, an-chō'vi, n.* a small Mediterranean fish of the herring family, used for pickling, and making sauce, paste, etc.—**an'chovy-pear** the fruit of a W. Indian tree, often pickled. [Sp. and Port. *anchova.*]

anchylose, etc. See **ankylose,** etc.

ancien régime *ā-syē rā-zhēm,* (Fr.) the old order (esp. before the French Revolution).

ancient *ān'shənt, adj.* very old: of former times: of long standing: belonging or relating to times long past, esp. before the downfall of the Western Roman Empire (A.D. 476).—*n.* an aged man: an elder or senior: one who lived in ancient times—usu. in *pl.* and applied esp. to the Greeks and Romans.—*adv.* **an'ciently.**—*n.* **an'cientness.**—**ancient history** (*coll. fig.*) information, news or gossip which, contrary to the expectations of the teller, one is already well aware of: something no longer of importance. [Fr. *ancien*—L.L. *antiānus,* former, old—L. *ante,* before.]

ancillary *an-sil'ər-i, an'sil-ər-i, adj.* subserving: ministering: auxiliary: supplementary: subsidiary: subordinate.—Also *n.* [L. *ancilla,* a maid-servant.]

ancipitous *an-sip'i-təs,* (*bot.*) *adj.* two-edged and flattened.—Also **ancip'ital.** [L. *anceps, -cipitis,* two-edged, double—*ambi-,* on both sides, *caput, capitis,* head.]

and[1] *and, ənd, ən, n, conj.* indicating addition: also: also of another kind: used to introduce a consequence or aim: used to introduce a question expressive of surprise, realisation, wonder, incredulity, etc.: even if, although: as if.—**and all** not without; **and how** (*coll.*) I should think so indeed. [O.E. *and, ond.*]

and[2] *and, n.* the sign ampersand: a use of the word 'and': something added.

Andalusian *an-də-lōō'(or-lū')z(h)yən, -s(h)yən, n.* a native of *Andalusia* (Sp. *Andalucía*), in Spain.

andante *an-dan'tā,* (*mus.*) *adv.* and *adj.* moving with moderately slow, even expression.—*n.* a movement or piece composed in andante time.—*adj., adv.* and *n.* **andantino** (*mus.; an-dan-tē'nō*) (a movement, etc.) somewhat slower than andante: now more usu. intended for somewhat quicker:—*pl.* **-nos.** [It., *pr.p.* of *andare,* to go.]

Andean *an-dē'ən,* **Andine** *an'dīn, adjs.* of, or like, the Andes Mountains.

Anderson shelter *and'ər-sən shel'tər,* a small air-raid shelter consisting of an arch of corrugated iron, built partially under ground, used in Britain during World War II.—Also **And'erson.** [Sir John *Anderson,* Home Secretary 1939–1940.]

andiron *and'ī-ərn, n.* an iron bar to support the end of a log in a fire: a fire-dog. [O.Fr. *andier* (Fr. *landier = l'andier*); origin unknown; early confused with **iron.**]

Andrew *an'drōō, n.* one of the twelve Apostles, patron Saint of Scotland.—**St Andrew's cross** a saltire, or cross of equal shafts crossed diagonally: the saltire of Scotland, white on a blue ground.

andro-, *andr- an-dr(ō)-, an-dro',* in composition, man: male.—*adj.* **androdiecious** (*-dī-ē'shəs*) having hermaphrodite and male flowers on separate plants (see **dioecious**).—*ns.* **androdioe'cism; androecium** (*an-*

drē'shi-əm, or *-si-əm*) stamens collectively (Gr. *oikion,* house); **androgen** (*an'drō-jən*) any one of the male sex-hormones: a synthetic compound with similar effect.—*adjs.* **androgen'ic** pertaining to an androgen; **androgynous** (*an-droj'i-nəs,* or *-drog'*) having the characteristics of both male and female in one individual: hermaphrodite: having an inflorescence of both male and female flowers (*bot.*).—*ns.* **androg'yny** hermaphroditism (Gr. *gynē,* woman); **an'droid** a robot in human form; **androl'ogy** the branch of medicine which deals with the functions and diseases peculiar to men.—*adj.* **andromonoecious** (*an-drō-mon-ē'shəs*) having hermaphrodite and male flowers on the same plant (see **monoecious**).—*ns.* **andromonoe'cism; androsterone** (*ən-dros'tə-rōn, an-dro-stē'rōn;* from *sterol*) a male sex-hormone, found in the testes and in urine. [Gr. *anēr, andros,* man, *andro-.*]

Andromeda *an-drom'i-də, n.* a genus of shrubs of the heath family: (*without cap.*) a plant of this genus: a northern constellation.—*n.* **andromedotoxin** (*an-drom'i-dō-tok'sin*) a vegetable drug got from Andromeda, used in relief of high blood pressure. [*Andromeda,* in Greek myth, a maiden delivered by Perseus from a sea-monster.]

anecdote *an'ik-dōt, n.* a short narrative of an incident of private life.—*ns.* **an'ecdotage** anecdotes collectively; **an'ecdotist.**—*adj.* **anecdot'al.**—*adv.* **anecdot'ally.**—*adj.* **anecdot'ical.** [Gr. *an-,* priv., *ekdotos,* published—*ek,* out, *didonai,* to give.]

anechoic *an-ək-ō'ik, adj.* echoless. [Gr. *an-,* priv., and **echoic.**]

anele *ə-nēl', v.t.* to anoint (*arch.*): to administer extreme unction to. [O.E. *an,* on, *ele,* oil.]

anemia, anemic, etc. Same as **anaemia,** etc.

anemo- *ə-nem'ō-, an-i-mo'-,* in composition, wind.—*ns.* **anemogram** (*ə-nem'o-gram*) an anemographic record; **anem'ograph** (*-graf*) an instrument for measuring and recording the pressure and velocity of the wind.—*adj.* **anemographic** (*-graf'ik*).—*ns.* **anemology** (*an-i-mol'ə-ji*) the science of the winds; **anemometer** (*-mom'i-tər*) a wind-gauge.—*adj.* **anemometric** (*-mō-met'rik*).—*ns.* **anemom'etry; anemone** (*ə-nem'ə-ni*) windflower—any member of the genus *Anemone* of the crowfoot family: a sea-anemone (Gr. *anemōnē.*). [Gr. *anemos,* wind; cf. L. *animus, anima*]

anencephaly *an-ən-sef'ə-li, -kef',* n. congenital absence of all or part of the brain.—Also **anencephal'ia** (*-āl'yə*).—*adj.* **anencephal'ic.** [Gr. *an-,* priv.; see **encephalon.**]

aneroid *an'ə-roid, adj.* dispensing with the use of liquid.—*n.* an aneroid barometer. [Fr. *anéroïde*—Gr. *a-,* priv., *nēros,* wet, *eidos,* form.]

anesthesia, etc. Same as **anaesthesia,** etc.

anetic *a-net'ik,* (*med.*) *adj.* soothing. [L. *aneticus*—Gr. *anetikos,* abating sickness.]

aneurin *an'ū-rin, ə-nū'rin, n.* vitamin B₁, deficiency of which affects the nervous system.—Also called **thiamine.** [Gr. *a-,* priv., *neuron,* nerve.]

aneurysm *an'ūr-izm, n.* dilatation of an artery (*path.*): any abnormal enlargement.—*adj.* **aneurys'mal.**—Also **aneurism, -al.** [Gr. *aneurysma—ana,* up, *eurys,* wide.]

anew *ə-nū',* in U S *-nōō', adv.* afresh: again [of and new.]

anfractuous *an-frakt'ū-əs, adj.* winding, involved, circuitous.—*n.* **anfractuosity** (*-os'i-ti*). [L. *anfractuōsus—ambi-,* about, *frangĕre,* to break.]

Angaraland *ang-ga-rä'land,* (*geol.*) *n.* the primitive nucleus of N E. Asia. [*Angara* River.]

angary *ang'gər-i, n.* a belligerent's right to seize and use neutral or other property (subject to compensation). [Gr. *angareiā*, forced service—*angaros*, a courier—a Persian word—Assyrian *agarru*, hired labourer.]

angel *ān'jl, n.* a divine messenger: a ministering spirit: an attendant or guardian spirit: a person possessing the qualities attributed to these—gentleness, purity, etc.: a dead person regarded as received into heaven: in the Catholic Apostolic Church, one who corresponds in a limited sense to a bishop: a radar echo of unknown origin: a financial backer or adviser (*coll*): a rich man who is an easy victim for those in search of money (*coll.*).—*n.* **ān'gelhood.**—*adjs.* **angelic** (*an-jel'ik*), **-al.**—*adv* **angel'ically.**—*ns.* **Angel'ica** a genus of umbelliferous plants with large leaves and double-winged fruit, once highly reputed as a defence against poison and pestilence· (without *cap.*) a garden plant by some included in the genus as *A.archangelica*, by others called *Archangelica officinalis*: its candied leaf-stalks and midribs—**an'gel-cake, an'gel-food** a cake made of flour, sugar, and white of egg; **angel dust** (*coll.*) the drug phencyclidine, a hallucinogen; **an'gel-fish** a tropical American river-fish (*Pterophyllum*) of the family Cichlidae, much compressed, almost circular in body but crescent-shaped owing to the long fin filaments, the whole banded with changing black vertical stripes· applied also to and several other fishes; **ang'els-on-horse'back** oysters and bacon on toast.—**on the side of the angels** basically in sympathy with traditional virtues and virtuous aims. [Gr *angelos*, a messenger.]

angelus *an'ji-ləs, n* a short devotional exercise in honour of the Incarnation, repeated three times daily· the bell rung in Roman Catholic countries at morning, noon, and sunset, to invite the faithful to recite it. [From the introductory words,·*Angelus* domini nuntiavit Mariae'.]

anger *ang'gər, n.* hot displeasure, often involving a desire for retaliation: wrath: inflammation (now dial) —*v t.* to make angry: to irritate.—*adv.* **ang'rily.**—*n.* **ang'riness.**—*adj* **ang'ry** excited with anger: inflamed: of threatening or lowering aspect.— **angry young man** a young man loud in disgust at what his elders have made of society (from *Look Back in Anger*, play, 1956, by John Osborne, one of a group of writers of the period to whom the term was applied) [O N. *angr*]

Angevin *ang'ji-vin, adj.* of *Anjou*, in France: relating to the Plantagenet house that reigned in England from 1154 to 1485, descended from Geoffrey V, Count of Anjou.—*n.* a native of Anjou: a member of the house of Anjou

angina *an-jī'nə, n* any inflammatory affection of the throat, as quinsy, croup, etc —*adj.* **anginal** (*an-jī'nl*).—**angina pec'toris** a disease of the heart marked by paroxysms of intense pain, radiating from the breastbone mainly towards the left shoulder and arm [L. *angina*, see **anguish.**]

angiogram *an'ji-ō-gram, n.* a photograph made by angiography —*ns* **angiog'raphy** the art or process of making X-ray photographs of blood-vessels by injecting the vessels with a substance opaque to the rays; **angioma** (*an-ji-ō'mə*) a benign tumour composed of blood or lymph vessels:—*pl* **angiō'mas, angiō'mata.** [Gr. *angeion*, a case, vessel]

angiosperm *an'ji-ō-spûrm, n* a plant of the **Angiosperm'ae,** one of the main divisions of flowering plants, in which the seeds are in a closed ovary, not naked as in gymnosperms.—*adjs* **angiosperm'al;** **angiosperm'ous.** [Gr *angeion*, case, *sperma*, seed]

angle¹ *ang'gl, n* a corner: the point from which lines or surfaces diverge: the inclination of two straight lines, or of two curves measured by that of their tangents, or of two planes measured by that of perpendiculars to

their intersection (*geom*). the spread of a cone, a number of meeting planes or the like, measured by the area on the surface of a sphere subtending it at the centre (*geom*): an outlying corner or nook: a point of view, a frame (*snooker*, etc.) —*v.t.* to put in a corner: to corner: to put in the jaws of a billiard pocket: to move, drive, direct, turn, adjust, present, at an angle. to present (news, etc) in such a way as to serve a particular end —*v.t.* to proceed at an angle or by an angular course —*adj* **ang'led** having angles· biased —*adv* **ang'lewise.**—*adj.* **ang'ular** (*ang'gū-lər*) having an angle or corner: measured by an angle: stiff in manner, the opposite of easy or graceful (*fig.*): bony and lean in figure —*n* **angularity** (*-lar'i-ti*).—**angle iron** an L-shaped piece of iron or steel used in structural work [Fr.—L *angulus*, cog with Gr *ankylos*, both from root *ank*, to bend, seen also in **anchor, ankle.**]

angle² *ang'gl,* to fish with rod and line (for): to try to gain by some artifice (with *for*).—*v.t* to angle for -- *ns* **ang'ler** one who fishes with rod and line, esp for sport· the devil-fish or fishing-frog, a wide-mouthed voracious fish (*Lophius piscatorius*) that attracts its prey by waving filaments attached to its head: extended to related kinds, some of them remarkable for the dwarf males parasitic on the female; **ang'ling.** [O E *angul*, hook.]

Angle *ang'gl, n.* a member or descendant of the German tribe (O.E. *Engle*) from Schleswig that settled in Northumbria, Mercia, and East Anglia.—*adj.* **Ang'lian** of the Angles —*n* an Angle: the English dialect of the Angles.—*adj.* **Ang'lican** of or characteristic of the Church of England and churches in communion with it: English (esp *U.S.*).—Also *n.*— *ns.* **Ang'licanism** the principles of the Church of England: attachment to English institutions, esp the English Church; **anglicisa'tion, -z-.**—*v.t* **ang'licise, -ize** (*-sīz*) to make English.—*v.t* to assume or conform to English ways —*ns.* **ang'licism** (*-sizm*) an English idiom or peculiarity; **ang'licist, ang'list** one who has a scholarly knowledge of the English language, literature, and culture —*adj.* **Anglo** (*ang'glō*) of British extraction.—**Anglo-** in composition, English: British: esp. conjointly English or British and something else.—*n.* **Anglo-Cath'olic** one who regards himself as a Catholic of Anglican pattern: a High-Churchman —Also *adj.*—*ns* **Anglo-Cathol'icism; Anglo-I'rish** the English language as spoken in Ireland: Irish people of English descent· people of mixed English and Irish descent.—*adj.* of England or Britain and Ireland: of the Anglo-Irish people or speech.—*ns.* **angloma'nia** (with *cap.*) a craze, or indiscriminate admiration, for what is English; **angloma'niac.** (All the following also with *cap.*) *n.* **ang'lophil** (*-fil*), also **-phile** (*-fil*) a friend and admirer of England and things English (Gr *philos*, friend) —Also *adj.*—*n.* **anglophil'ia.**—*adj.* **anglophil'ic.**—*n.* **ang'lophobe** one who fears or dislikes England and things English (Gr *phobos*, fear) —Also *adj* —*n.* **anglophō'bia.**—*adjs.* **anglophō'biac, -phobic** (*-fōb'*, *-fob'*); **Ang'lophone** (sometimes without *cap.*) of a state, person, etc., speaking or using English, esp as opp. to French, in everyday affairs.—*n* an English-speaking, esp. as opp to French-speaking, person, esp. in a state, etc. where English is not the only language spoken —*adj* **Anglophōn'ic** (sometimes without *cap*)—*n.* **Anglo-Sax'on** Old English (q.v): one of the Germanic settlers in England and Scotland, including Angles, Saxons, and Jutes, or of their descendants: a Saxon of England, distinguished from the Old Saxons of the Continent: anybody of English speech —Also *adj.*—*n.* **Anglo-Sax'ondom.** [L. *Anglus*]

Anglican, etc , **Anglo-,** etc. See **Angle.**

Angora *ang-gō'rə, -gō', adj.* of *Ang'ŏra* (Gr. *Ankȳra*; in later times *Angora, Ankara*) a town of ancient Galatia, now capital of Turkey. (sometimes without *cap.*) of an Angora breed, yarn, etc.—*n.* (in all meanings sometimes without *cap.*) an Anatolian goat: its long silky wool (the true mohair) cloth made from it: a silky-haired rabbit: an Angora cat: yarn or material partly or wholly of Angora rabbit hair.—**Angora cat** a silky-haired kind of cat similar to the Persian and possibly no longer existing as a pure breed, the term now being treated by some as an obsolete term for Persian cat.

Angostura *ang-gos-tū'rə, n* a town (now Ciudad Bolivar) on the narrows (Sp. *angostura*) of the Orinoco in Venezuela.—**Angostura bitters®** a brand of aromatic bitters first made in Angostura.

angry. See **anger.**

Angst, angst *angst, n.* anxiety, esp a general feeling of anxiety produced by awareness of the uncertainties and paradoxes inherent in the state of being human. —*adj.* **Angst'-, angst'-ridden.** [Ger. *Angst*, Dan. *angst*, fear, anxiety.]

Ångstrom, angstrom *ang'* or *ong'strəm, n.* a unit (10⁻¹⁰ metres) used in expressing wavelengths of light, ultraviolet rays, X-rays, molecular and atomic distances.—Formerly, but not now usu., **Ång-, angstrom unit.** [Anders J. *Ångström* (1814–74), Swedish physicist.]

anguish *ang'gwish, n.* excessive pain of body or mind: agony.—*v.t.* to afflict with anguish.—*v.i* to suffer anguish.—*adj.* **ang'uished.** [O.Fr. *angoisse*, choking—L. *angustia*, tightness, narrowness.]

angular. See under **angle.¹**

anhelation *an-hi-lā'shən, n.* shortness of breath [L. *anhēlātiō, -ōnis—anhēlāre*, to gasp.]

anhydride *an-hī'drīd, n.* a compound representing in its composition an acid *minus* water.—*n.* **anhy'drite** a mineral, anhydrous calcium sulphate.—*adj.* **anhy'drous** free from water. [Gr. *an-*, priv., *hydōr*, water.]

aniconic *an-ī-kon'ik, adj.* symbolising without aiming at resemblance: pertaining to aniconism.—*ns.* **ani'conism** (-*kən-izm*) worship or veneration of an object that represents a god without being an image of him; **ani'conist.** [Gr. *an-*, priv., *eikōn*, image.]

anil *an'il, n.* indigo, plant or dye. [Port. *anil*—Ar. *an-nil*, the indigo plant—Sans. *nilī*, indigo.]

anile *an'il, ān'il, adj.* old-womanish: imbecile.—*n* **anility** (*a-* or *ə-nil'i-ti*) old-womanishness: imbecile dotage. [L. *ānus, -ūs*, an old woman.]

aniline *an'il-ēn, -in,* or *-īn, n.* a product of coal tar extensively used in dyeing and other industrial arts, first obtained from *anil.*—Also *adj.* (as in *aniline dye*)

animadvert *an-im-ad-vûrt', v.i.* to take cognisance (*law*; usu. with *on, upon*): to take note: to comment critically (on): to express censure.—*ns.* **animadver'sion; animadvert'er.** [L. *animus*, the mind, *ad*, to, and *vertēre*, to turn.]

animal *an'i-məl, n.* an organised being having life, sensation, and voluntary motion—typically distinguished from a plant, which is organised and has life, but apparently not sensation or voluntary motion: often, a lower animal—one below man: a mammal: a brutish or sensual man: loosely or colloquially, a person, thing, organisation, etc.—*adj.* of, of the nature of, derived from, or belonging to an animal or animals: brutal, sensual.—*ns.* **an'imalism** exercise or enjoyment of animal life, as distinct from intellectual: the state of being actuated by mere animal appetites: brutishness, sensuality: the theory that man is a mere animal being; **an'imalist** one who practises or believes in animalism; **animality** (-*al'i-ti*) animal nature or life: status of an animal or of a lower

animal.—*adv.* **an'imally** physically.—**animal magnetism** see under **magnet; animal spirits** nervous force: exuberance of health and life: cheerful buoyancy of temper; **an'imal-worship; -worshipper.** [L. *animal—anima*, air, breath, life, soul.]

animalcule *an-im-al'kūl, n* a small animal: (now) one that cannot be seen by the naked eye—*pl.* **animal'-cūles, animal'cūla.**—*adj.* **animal'cūlar.** [L. *animalculum*, dim. of *animal.*]

animate *an'im-āt, v t* to give life to: to enliven: to inspirit: to actuate—*adj.* (-*mit*) living: having animal life.—*adj* **animated** lively: full of spirit: endowed with life: moving as if alive—*adv* **an'imatedly.**—*adj.* **an'imating.**—*adv* **an'imatingly.**—*ns.* **anima'tion** the act of animating: the state of being alive: liveliness: vigour; **an'imatism** primitive attribution of life to natural phenomena and natural objects, but not, as in *animism*, belief that spirits reside in them; **an'imator** an artist who makes drawings for animated cartoons —**animated cartoon** a motion picture produced from drawings, each successive drawing showing a very slight change of position so that a series of them gives the effect of a definite movement. [L. *animāre, -ātum—anima*, air, breath, life]

animism *an'im-izm, n.* the attribution of a soul to natural objects and phenomena.—*n* **an'imist.**—*adj* **animis'tic.** [L. *anima*, the soul]

animosity *an-im-os'i-ti, n.* strong dislike: enmity [L *animōsitās*, fullness of spirit]

animus *an'im-əs, n.* intention: actuating spirit: hostility. [L. *animus*, spirit, soul]

anion *an'ī-ən, n.* an ion that seeks the anode: an electronegative ion —*adj* **anion'ic.** [Gr *ana*, up, *iōn*, going, pr p neut. of *ienai*, to go]

anise *an'is, n* an umbelliferous plant (*Pimpinella*) whose aromatic seeds are used in making cordials — *ns.* **an'iseed** the seed of anise. anisette; **anisette** (*an-i-zet'*) a cordial or liqueur prepared from anise seed [Gr. *anīson*, anise]

aniso- *an-ī'sō-,* or -*so', in* composition. unequal —*adj* **anisotrop'ic** not isotropic, showing differences of property or of effect in different directions.—*n* **anisot'ropy.** [Gr. *anīsos*, unequal—*an-*, priv , *isos*, equal.]

ankh *angk, n* an ansate cross—T-shaped with a loop above the horizontal bar—symbol of life. [Egypt , life]

ankle *angk'l, n.* the joint connecting the foot and leg —*adj.* **ank'led** having ankles —*n.* **ank'let** (-*lit*) an ornamental or supporting ring or chain for the ankle. —**ank'le-boot, ank'le-jack** a boot reaching above the ankle; **ankle sock** a sock reaching to and covering the ankle. [O.E. *ancléow*; cf. **angle.**]

Ankole *ang-kō'lē, n* a breed of large cattle with long horns.—Also *adj.* [*Ankole*, plateau region in Uganda]

ankylosaur *ang'kə-lə-sór, n.* any of the **Ankylosauria** (-*sor'i-ə*), a suborder of bird-hipped plant-eating dinosaurs of the Cretaceous period, with short legs and flattened heavily-armoured bodies, including **Ankylosaur'us** which gave name to the suborder. [Mod. L.—Gr. *ankylos*, crooked, *sauros*, lizard.]

ankylosis, anchylosis *ang-ki-lō'sis, n.* the fusion of bones or skeletal parts: the fixation of a joint by fibrous bands or union of bones —*v t.* and *v.t.* **ank'ylose, anch'ylose** to stiffen or fuse, as a joint or bones.—*adj* **ank'ylosed, anch'ylosed.** [Gr. *ankylōsis*, stiffening of a joint—*ankyloein*, to crook]

ankylostomiasis, anchylostomiasis *ang-ki-lō-sto-mī'ə-sis, n* hookworm disease or miner's anaemia, caused by a parasitic nematode (*Ankylostomum duodenale* or other)   [Gr *ankylos*, crooked, *stoma*, mouth.]

anlage *an'la-gə*, (*biol.*) *n.* the primordium or first rudiment of an organ. [Ger.]

anna *an'ə*, *n.* a former coin of India, Pakistan, and Bangladesh, the sixteenth part of a rupee. (Decimal coinage introduced India, 1957, Pakistan, 1961.) [Hind. *ānā*.]

annal *an'əl*, *n.* a year's entry in a chronicle: (in *pl.*) records of events under the years in which they happened: historical records generally: year-books.—*v.t.* **ann'alise, -ize** to record.—*n.* **ann'alist** a writer of annals.—*adj.* **annalist'ic.** [L. *annālis*, yearly—*annus*, a year.]

annates *an'āts*, *n.pl.*, the first-fruits, or one year's income of a benefice, paid to the Pope . [L.L. *annāta*—L. *annus*, a year.]

an(n)atto *a*- or *ə-nat'ō*, **an(n)atta** -*ə*, **arnotto** *ār-not'ō*, *ns.* a bright orange colouring matter got from the fruit pulp of a tropical American tree, *Bixa orellana* (fam *Bixaceae*):—*pl.* **-s.** [Supposed to be of Carib origin.]

anneal *ə-nēl'*, *v.t.* to heat and cool gradually (glass, metals), usu. in order to soften: to heat in order to fix colours on, as glass.—Also *v.i.*—*ns.* **anneal'er; anneal'ing.** [Pfx. *an-*, on, and O.E. *ǣlan*, to burn.]

annelid *an'ə-lid*, *n.* a member of the **Annelida** (*ə-nel'i-də*) a class comprising the red-blooded worms, having a long body composed of numerous rings. [L. *annellus*, *ānellus*, dim. of *ānulus*, a ring.]

annex *ə-neks'*, *v.t.* to add to the end: to join or attach: to take permanent possession of: to purloin, appropriate (*coll.*): to affix: to append.—*n.* (*an'eks*) something added: a supplementary building—sometimes (as Fr.) **annexe** (*a-neks'*, *an'eks*).—*n.* **annexa'tion** (*an-*). [L. *annectēre*, *annexum—ad*, to, *nectēre*, to tie.]

annihilate *ə-nī'(h)il-āt*, *v.t.* to reduce to nothing: to put out of existence: to crush or wither by look or word (*fig.*): to defeat completely (*coll. fig.*): to cause to annihilate (*phys.*).—*v.i.* to undergo annihilation (*phys.*).—*n.* **annihila'tion** reduction to nothing: the process by which a particle and its corresponding antiparticle, e.g. an electron and a positron, combine and are spontaneously transformed into radiation (**annihilation radiation**) (*phys.*)—*adj.* **anni'hilative.**—*n.* **anni'hilātor.** [L. *annihilāre*, *-ātum—ad*, to, *nihil*, nothing.]

anniversary *an-i-vûrs'ə-ri*, *n.* the day of the year on which an event happened or is celebrated as having happened in a previous year: the celebration proper to recurrence, esp. a mass or religious service. [L. *anniversārius—annus*, a year, and *vertēre*, *versum*, to turn.]

anno *an'ō*, (L.) in the year; **anno Domini** *dom'in-ī*, *-ē*, in the year of our Lord (used as *n.* for 'advancing old age'); **anno urbis conditae** *ûr'bis kon'dit-ē*, *ōōr'bis kon'dit-ī*, in the year of the founding of the city (i.e. Rome, 753 B.C.).

annotate *an'ō-tāt*, *v.t.* to make notes upon.—*v.i.* to append notes.—*ns.* **annotā'tion** the making of notes: a note of explanation: comment; **ann'otātor.** [L. *annotāre—ad*, to, *notāre*, *-ātum*, to mark.]

announce *ə-nowns'*, *v.t.* to declare: to give public notice of: to make known.—*ns.* **announce'ment; announc'er** one who announces: in radio and television, one who reads the news and announces other items in the programme. [O.Fr. *anoncer—*L. *annuntiāre—ad*, to, *nuntiāre*, to report.]

annoy *ə-noi'*, *v.t.* and *v.i.* to trouble: to vex: to tease: to harm, esp. in military sense.—*n.* **annoy'ance** that which annoys: the act of annoying: the state of being annoyed.—*adj.* **annoyed'** (with *at*, *with*).—*adv.* **annoy'ingly.** [O.Fr. *anoier* (noun *anoi*, mod. *ennui*)—L.L. *inodiāre—*L. phrase, *in odiō*, as in 'est mihi *in odiō*' = it is to me hateful.]

annual *an'ū-əl*, *adj.* yearly: coming every year: lasting or living for a year: requiring to be renewed every year: performed in a year: being, or calculated as, the total for one year.—*n.* a plant that lives for one year only: a publication appearing yearly, esp. an illustrated gift-book: a year-book.—*v.t.* **annualise, -ize** to convert to a yearly rate, amount, etc.—*adv.* **ann'ually.** [L.L. *annuālis—annus*, a year.]

annuity *ə-nū'i-ti*, *n.* a payment (generally of uniform amount) falling due in each year during a given term, such as a period of years or the life of an individual, the capital sum not being returnable.—*n.* **annu'itant** one who receives an annuity. [Fr. *annuité—*L.L. *annuitās*, *-ātis—*L. *annus*, year.]

annul *ə-nul'*, *v.t.* to make null: to reduce to nothing: to abolish:—*pr.p.* **annull'ing;** *pa.t.* and *pa.p.* **annulled'.**—*n* **annul'ment.** [Fr. *annuler—*L.L. *annūlāre—*L. *ad*, to, *nūllus*, none.]

annular *an'ū-lər*, *adj.* ring-shaped: cutting in a ring: ring-bearing.—*n.* the ring-finger.—*n.* **annūlarity** (*-lar'i-ti*).—*adjs.* **ann'ūlate, -d** ringed.—*n.* **ann'ūlet** a little ring: a small flat fillet encircling a column, etc. (*archit.*). [L. *annulāris*, for *ānulāris—ānulus*, a ring—dim. of *ānus*, a rounding or ring.]

annunciate, annuntiate *ə-nun's(h)i-āt*, *v.t.* to proclaim. —*ns.* **annuncia'tion** (*-si-*) proclamation: esp. (*cap.*) that of the angel to the Virgin Mary, or its anniversary, 25th March (**Annuncia'tion-day** Lady-day).—*adj* **annun'ciative.**—*n.* **annun'ciator** a device giving audible or visual information, e.g. indicating where a bell or telephone is being rung. [L. *annuntiāre*, *-ātum—ad*, to, *nuntiāre—nuntius*, a messenger; *c* from mediaeval spelling of Latin; cf. **announce.**]

annus mirabilis *an'əs mir-ab'il-is*, *an'ōōs mēr-āb'il-is*, (L.) year of wonders—applied to 1666 (year of plague and fire of London), etc.

anode *an'ōd*, *n.* the electrode by which an electric current enters an electrolyte or gas (opp. to *cathode*): in high vacuum, the electrode to which electrons flow. —*v.t.* **an'odise, -ize** to give a protective or decorative coat to (a metal) by using it as an anode in electrolysis—*adjs.* **anōd'al** (or *an'od-əl*), **anodic** (*an-od'ik*) of an anode: upwards on the genetic spiral (*bot.*). [Gr. *anodos*, way up—*ana*, up, *hodos*, way.]

anodyne *an'ō-dīn*, *n.* a medicine that allays pain: something that relieves mental distress: something that prevents or avoids argument or controversy.—Also *adj.* [Gr. *anōdynos—an-*, priv., and *ŏdynē*, pain.]

anoint *ə-noint'*, *v.t.* to smear with ointment or oil: to consecrate with oil.—*n.* **anoint'ment.** [Fr. *enoint*, pa.p. of *enoindre—*L. *inungēre*, *inunctum—in*, on, *ung(u)ĕre*, to smear.]

anomaly *ə-nom'ə-li*, *n.* irregularity: deviation from rule: the angle measured at the sun between a planet in any point of its orbit and the last perihelion (*astron.*).—*adjs.* **anomalis'tic, -al** anomalous: departing from established rules: irregular.—*adv.* **anomalis'tically.**—*adj.* **anom'alous** irregular: deviating from rule: of vision, relatively insensitive to one or more colours. [Gr. *anōmalos—an-*, priv., and *homalos*, even—*homos*, same.]

anomie *an'ə-mē*, *n.* in society or in an individual, a condition of hopelessness caused by breakdown of rules of conduct, and loss of belief and sense of purpose.—Also **an'omy.**—*adj.* **anomic** (*ə-nom'ik*). [Fr.—Gr. *anomia*, or *-iē*, lawlessness—*ā-*, priv., *nomos*, law.]

anon *ə-non'*, *adv.* immediately. soon: at another time: coming (in reply to a call) [O.E. *on*, in, *ān*, one.]

anonymous *ə-non'i-məs*, *adj.* wanting a name: without name of author, real or feigned: lacking distinctive features or individuality—*ns.* **anonym** (*an'*) a person whose name is not given: a pseudonym; **anonym'**

ity.—*adv.* **anon'ymously.** [Gr. *anōnymos—an-*, priv., and *onyma = onoma*, name.]

Anopheles *an-of'əl-ēz*, *n.* a genus of germ-carrying mosquitoes: (without *cap.*) a mosquito of this genus. —*adj.* **anoph'eline** relating to Anopheles —*n.* a mosquito of this genus. [Gr. *anōphelēs*, hurtful—*an-*, priv., *ophelos*, help.]

Anoplura *an-o-plōō'rə*, *n.pl.* an order or suborder of insects, the bugs [Gr. *anoplos*, unarmed, *ourā*, tail.]

anorak, anarak *an'ə-rak*, *n.* a Greenlander's fur coat: a usu. hooded waterproof outer jacket. [Greenland Eskimo word.]

anorexia *an-or-ek'si-ə*, **anorexy** *an'or-ek-si* (or *-ek'*), *ns.* lack of appetite: anorexia nervosa.—*adj.* **anorec'-tic** causing a lack of appetite: relating to, or suffering from, anorexia (nervosa).—*n.* an anorectic substance.—Also *n.* and *adj.* **anoret'ic.**—*adj.* **anorex'ic** relating to, or suffering from, anorexia (nervosa): relating to anorexics.—*n.* a person suffering from anorexia (nervosa).—**anorexia nervosa** *(nər-vō'sə, -zə; psych.* or *med.*) a condition characterised by loss of appetite and aversion to food due to emotional disturbance, normally leading to marked emaciation, etc. [Gr. *an-*, priv., *orexis*, longing—*oregein*, to reach out.]

anosmia *an-oz'mi-ə*, *n.* the loss of sense of smell.

another *ə-nudh'ər*, *adj.* and *pron.* a different or distinct (thing or person): one more: a second: one more of the same kind: any other.—**one another** a compound reciprocal pronoun usu. regarded as interchangeable with 'each other', but by some restricted to cases where more than two individuals are involved; only **with another** taken all together, taken on an average. [Orig. **an other.**]

anoxia *an-ok'si-ə*, *n.* deficient supply of oxygen to the tissues.—*adj.* **anox'ic.** [Gr. *an-*, priv., *oxygen*, *-ia.*] **ansate, -d** *an'sāt, -id*, *adjs.* having a handle.—**ansate cross** see **ankh.** [L. *ansātus—ansa*, handle.]

Anschluss *an'shlōōs*, (Ger.) *n.* union, esp. the political union of Germany and Austria in 1938.

anserine *an'sər-īn*, *adj.* of the goose or the goose family: stupid. [L. *anserīnus—anser*, goose.]

answer *än'sər*, *n.* that which is said, written, or done in meeting a charge, combating an argument, objection, or attack: that which is called for by a question or questioning state of mind: the solution of a problem: an acknowledgment: a return in kind: anything given, sent or said in return: an immediate result or outcome in definite relation to the act it follows: a repetition or echo of a sound: restatement of a theme by another voice or instrument *(mus.).*—*v.t.* to speak, write, or act in answer to or against: to say or write as an answer: to give, send, afford, or be an answer to: to behave in due accordance with: to be in proportion to or in balance with: to give a conclusive or satisfactory answer to: to serve the purpose of: to fulfil: to recompense satisfactorily: to be punished for.—*v.i.* to give an answer: to behave in answer: to be responsible: to suffer the consequences: to be in conformity: to serve the purpose: to succeed: to react.—*adj.* **an'swerable** able to be answered: accountable: suitable: equivalent: in due proportion.—*n.* **an'swerabil'ity.** —*adv.* **an'swerably.**—*n.* **an'swerer.**—**answer back** *(coll.)* to answer one who expects silent submission: to answer pertly; **answering service** a commercial service which answers telephone calls, takes messages, etc. for its clients when they are not available. —**answer to (the name of)** to show sign of accepting as one's name: to have as one's name *(coll.).* [O.E. *andswaru* (n.), *andswarian* (vb.)—*and-*, against, *swerian*, to swear.]

ant *ant*, *n.* a small hymenopterous insect (of the

Formicidae), of proverbial industry: loosely, a termite.—*n.* **ant'ing** the introduction by birds of live ants or other stimulants into their plumage, possibly as a pleasurable means of cleaning it and their skin.— **ant'bear** the great ant-eater, found in swampy regions in S. America: the aardvark of S. Africa, **ant'-eater** any one of a S. American family of edentates, feeding chiefly on ants: a pangolin: an aardvark: an echidna. —*n pl.* **ant(s')'-eggs** pupae of ants.—**ant'-hill** hillock raised as nest by ants or by termites; **ant'-lion** a neuropterous insect (*Myrmeleon*) whose larva traps ants in a funnel-shaped sand-hole.—**have ants in one's pants** *(coll.)* to be restless, impatient, needlessly hurrying. [O.E. *æmete*; cf. **emmet.**]

antacid *ant-as'id*, *adj.* counteracting acidity of the stomach.—*n.* a medicine that counteracts acidity. [Gr. *anti*, against, and **acid.**]

antagonist *an-tag'ə-nist*, *n.* one who contends or struggles with another: an opponent: a muscle that opposes the action of another: in an organism, something that has an opposite effect.—Also *adj.*—*n.* **antagonisā'tion, -z-.**—*v.t.* **antag'onise, -ize** to counteract the action of: to arouse opposition in.—*n.* **antag'onism** opposition: hostility: production of opposing effects, e.g. in a living body: interference with the growth of another organism, as by using up the food supply or producing an antibiotic substance.—*adj.* **antagonist'ic.**—*adv.* **antagonis'tically.** [Gr. *antagōnistēs—anti*, against, *agōn*, contest. See **agony.**]

Antarctic *ant-ärk'tik*, *adj.* opposite the Arctic: of, near, or relating to the south pole.—*n.* the south polar regions.—**Antarctic Circle** the parallel of latitude 66°32' S, bounding the region of the earth surrounding the south terrestial pole. [Gr. *antarktikos* —*anti*, opposite, and *arktikos*; see **Arctic.**]

ante- *ant'i-*, *pfx.* before. [L *ante*, old form *anti*; conn. with Gr. **anti-.**]

ante *an'ti*, *n.* a fixed stake put down by a poker player, usu. before the deal: advance payment.—*v.t.* to stake: to pay.—**up, raise, the ante** *(coll. fig.)* to increase the costs or risks involved in, or the demands requiring to be met before, some action. [L., before.]

antecedent *an-ti-sē'dənt*, *adj.* going before in time: prior.—*n.* that which precedes in time: an ancestor: the noun or its equivalent to which a relative pronoun refers *(gram.)*: the conditional part of a hypothetical proposition *(logic)*: the numerator term of a ratio *(math.)*: (in *pl.*) previous principles, conduct, history, etc.—*n.* **antece'dence.**—*adv.* **antece'dently.** [L. *antecēdēns, -entis—ante*, before, *cēdēre*, to go.]

antechamber *an'ti-chām-bər*, *n.* a chamber or room leading to a more important apartment. [Fr. *anti-chambre*—L. *ante*, before, and *camera*, a vault.]

antechoir *an'ti-kwīr*, *n.* the space in front of the choir in a church. [L. *ante*, before, and **choir.**]

antedate *an'ti-dāt*, *n.* a date assigned which is earlier than the actual date.—*v.t.* to date before the true time: to assign to an earlier date: to bring about at an earlier date: to be of previous date to: to accelerate: to anticipate. [L. *ante*, before, and **date[1]**.]

antediluvian *an-ti-di-lōō'vi-ən, -lū'*, *adj.* existing or happening before Noah's Flood: resembling the state of things before the Flood: very old-fashioned, primitive.—*n.* one who lived before the Flood: one who lives to be very old.—*adj.* **antedilu'vial.**—*adv.* **antedilu'vially.** [L. *ante*, before, *dīlūvium*, flood.]

antefix *an'ti-fiks*, *n.* (usu. in *pl.*) an ornament concealing the ends of roofing tiles:—*pl.* **an'tefixes, antefix'a** (L.).—*adj.* **antefix'al.** [L. *ante*, before, in front, and *fīgĕre, fīxum*, to fix.]

antelope *an'ti-lōp*, *n.* any one of a group of hollow-horned ruminants closely related to goats. [O Fr. *antelop*—mediaeval L. *antalopus*—Late Gr. *antholops*, of unknown origin.]

ante meridiem *an-te mer-id'i-em, mer-ēd'*, (L.) before noon.

antenatal *an-ti-nā'tl, adj.* before birth.—**antenatal clinic** a clinic for the purpose of treating and giving advice to pregnant women. [L. *ante*, before, *nātālis*, natal, *nātus*, born.]

antenna *an-ten'ə, n.* a feeler or horn in insects, crustaceans, and myriapods: in wireless communication, a structure for sending out or receiving electric waves. an aerial:—*pl.* **antenn'ae** (*-ē*), **antenn'as** (radio). [L. *antemna, antenna,* yard (of a mast)]

antependium *an-ti-pend'i-əm, n.* a frontlet, or forecloth, for an altar: a frontal. [L. *ante,* before, and *pendēre,* to hang.]

antepenult *an-ti-pen-ult', n.* the last syllable but two. —*adj.* **antepenult'imate** last but two [L. *ante,* before, and **penult.**]

ante-post *an'ti-pōst, adj* of betting, beginning before the runners' numbers are posted. [L. *ante,* before, and post.]

anterior *an-tē'ri-ər, adj.* before, in time or place: in front: towards the bract or away from the axis (*bot.*) —*n* **anteriority** (*-or'i-ti*)—*adv.* **antē'riorly.** [L *antērior* (compar.)—*ante,* before.]

anteroom *an'ti-rōōm, n.* a room leading into another larger one: a waiting-room: an officers' mess sitting-room. [L *ante,* before, and **room.**]

anteversion *an-ti-vûr'shən, (med.) n.* the tipping forward of a bodily organ.—*v.t.* **antevert'.** [L. *ante,* before, and *vertēre, versum,* to turn]

anthelion *an-thē'li-an, -lyən, n.* a luminous coloured ring seen on a cloud or fog-bank opposite the sun:— *pl* **anthe'lia.** [Gr *ant(h)ēlios, -on,—anti,* opposite, *hēlios,* the sun.]

anthelminthic, anthelmintic *an-thel-min'thik, -tik, adj.* destroying or expelling worms.—*n* a drug used for that purpose. [Gr. *anti,* against, and *helmins, helminthos,* a worm.]

anthem *an'thəm, n* a composition for a church choir, commonly with solo passages, usually set to a passage from the Bible. any song of praise or gladness: loosely applied to an officially recognised national hymn or song (as *national anthem*). [O.E. *antefn*—Gr *antiphōna* (*pl.*) sounding in answer—*anti,* in return. *phōnē,* voice. See **antiphon.**]

anther *an'thər, n.* that part of a stamen that contains the pollen.—*n.* **antherid'ium** (*bot.*) the gametangium in which male gametes are produced:—*pl.* **antherid'ia.** [Gr. *anthēra,* a medicine made from flowers, esp. their inner parts—*anthos,* flower.]

antho- *an'tho-, an'thə-,* in composition, flower.—*n* **anthocarp** (*an'thō-karp;* Gr. *karpos,* fruit) a fruit resulting from many flowers, as the pineapple: a fruit of which the perianth or the torus forms part.—*adj.* **anthocarp'ous.**—*v.t.* and *v.i.* **anthologise, -ize** (*an-thol'ə-jīz*).—*ns.* **anthol'ogist; anthol'ogy** a flower-gathering (*lit.*): a choice collection of writings, songs, paintings, etc (orig. of Greek epigrams).—*adj* **anthophilous** (*an-thof'i-ləs*) loving, frequenting, or feeding on flowers.—*ns.* **an'thophore** (*-thō-fōr, -fór*) an elongation of the receptacle between calyx and corolla.—*n.pl.* **Anthozō'a** (Gr. *zōia,* animals) a class of coelenterates including sea-anemones, corals, etc. [Gr. *anthos,* flower.]

anthologise, etc., **anthology.** See **antho-.**

Anthony *an'tən-i, n.* a 4th-century saint —St **Anthony's cross** a tau-cross; St **Anthony's fire** (*pop.*) erysipelas; St **Anthony's nut** earthnut or pignut

anthophilous, etc. See **antho-.**

anthrax *an'thraks, n.* a carbuncle, malignant boil: a deadly disease due to a bacillus, most common in sheep and cattle but communicable to men. —*adj* **anthracic** (*an-thras'ik*).—*ns.* **anthracene** (*an'thrə-sēn*) a product of coal-tar distillation ($C_{14}H_{10}$), a source of dye-stuffs; **an'thracite** (*an'thrə-sīt*) hard lustrous coal that burns nearly without flame or smoke, consisting almost entirely of carbon.—*adj.* **anthracitic** (*-thrə-sit'ik*) of, of the nature of. anthracite.—*adj.* **anthracoid** (*an'thrə-koid*) like anthrax.—*n.* **anthracosis** (*-kō'sis*) a diseased state of the lung due to breathing coal-dust [Gr. *anthrax, -akos,* charcoal, coal, carbuncle (stone or boil).]

anthropo-, anthropo- in composition, man, human.— *adjs.* **anthropic** (*an-throp'ik*), **-al** human.—*adj.* **anthropocentric** (*an-thrō-pō-sent'rik;* Gr. *kentron,* centre) centring the universe in man.—*adj.* **an'thropoid** (or *-thrŏp';* Gr. *eidos,* form) man-like: applied esp. to the highest apes—gorilla, chimpanzee, orang-utan, gibbon, but also to the higher Primates generally—man, apes, monkeys, but not lemurs.—*n.* an anthropoid ape.—*adj.* **anthropoid'al.**—*adj.* **anthropological** (*-loj'*).—*adv* **anthropolog'ically.**—*ns.* **anthropol'ogist; anthropol'ogy** the science of man in its widest sense.— *adj.* **anthropomet'ric.**—*ns.* **anthropometry** (*-pom'i-tri;* Gr. *metreein,* to measure) measurement of the human body; **anthropomorph'ism** conception or representation of a god as having the form, personality, or attributes of man: ascription of human characteristics to what is not human—*adj.* **anthropomorph'ous** formed like or resembling man. —*ns.* **anthropoph'agy** (*-ə-ji*) cannibalism; **anthropos'ophist; anthropos'ophy** (Gr *sophiā,* wisdom) the knowledge of the nature of men: human wisdom: esp. the spiritualistic doctrine of Rudolf Steiner (1861–1925). [Gr. *anthrōpos,* man (in general sense).]

Anthurium *an-thū'ri-əm, n.* a genus of tropical American plants with showy leaves and flowers. (without *cap.*) a member of the genus. [Gr. *anthos,* flower, *oura,* tail.]

anti *an'ti,* in U.S. also *an'tī, prep.* opposed to, against. —*n.* and *adj.* (one who is) opposed to anything. [Gr. *anti,* against, instead of, etc]

anti- *an'ti,* in U.S also *an'tī, pfx.* (1) acting against, counteracting: (2) opposed to: (3) opposite or reverse [Gr *anti,* against.]

anti-aircraft *an'ti-ār'krȧft, adj.* intended for use against hostile aircraft [Pfx. **anti-** (1)]

antiballistic *an-ti-bə-lis'tik, adj.* (of a missile, etc.) designed to destroy a ballistic missile.—Also **A.B.M.** [Pfx. **anti-** (1).]

antibiosis *an-ti-bī-ō'sis, n* antagonistic relation between associated organisms: inhibition of growth by a substance produced by another organism.—*adj* **antibiotic** (*-ot'ik*) inimical to life: inhibiting the growth of another organism. used esp. of a substance produced by micro-organisms which, in dilute solution, has the capacity to inhibit the growth of, or to destroy, micro-organisms causing infectious diseases: pertaining to antibiosis.—*n.* an antibiotic substance. [Pfx **anti-** (1), Gr *biosis,* way of life; adj *biōtikos—bios,* life]

antibody *an'ti-bod-i, n.* a defensive substance produced in an organism in response to the action of a foreign body such as the toxin of a parasite [Pfx. **anti-** (1).]

antic *ant'ik,* (usu. in *pl.*) a fantastic action or trick: a caper —*v.i* to cut capers —See also **antique.** [It *antico,* ancient—L *antiquus*; orig used of the fantastic decorations found in the remains of ancient Rome]

anticathode *an-tı-kath'ŏd, n.* the target of an X-ray tube, on which the cathode rays are focused and from which X-rays are emitted. [Pfx. **anti-** (3)]

anticatholic *an-tı-kath'ə-lık, adj.* opposed to the Catholic or the Roman Catholic Church, to Catholics, or to what is catholic [Pfx. **anti-** (2).]

Antichrist *an'tı-krīst, n* an opponent of Christ. the great opposer of Christ and Christianity expected by the early Church, applied by some to the Pope and others.—*adj.* **antichristian** (*-krıs'*) relating to Antichrist: opposed to Christianity. [Gr *Antıchrıstos—antı-*, against, *Chrıstos*, Christ.]

anticipate *an-tıs'ıp-āt, v.t.* to forestall (a person or thing): to preoccupy to use, spend, deal with in advance or before the due time· to realise beforehand: to foresee or count upon as certain. to expect: to precede· to advance to an earlier time, bring on sooner.—*v ı* to be before the normal time to do anything before the appropriate time.—*adj.* **antic'ıpant** anticipating, anticipative —Also *n.*—*n.* **anticipā'tion** act of anticipating assignment to too early a time: introduction of a tone or tones of a chord before the whole chord (*mus.*). intuition foretaste previous notion: presentiment: prejudice· imagining beforehand: expectation.—*adjs.* **antı'cipātive, antı'cipatory.**—*advs* **antı'cipātively, antı'cipatorily.**—*n* **antic'ipātor.** [L. *antıcıpāre, -ātum—ante,* before, *capēre,* to take]

anticlerical *an-tı-kler'ı-kl, adj.* opposed to the clergy or their power —*n.* a member of an anticlerical party —*n* **anticler'icalism.** [Pfx anti- (2).]

anticlimax *an-tı-klī'maks, n* the opposite of climax: a ludicrous drop in impressiveness after a progressive rise —*adj.* **anticlimac'tic.**—*adv.* **anticlimac'tically.** [Pfx. **anti-** (3).]

anticline *an'tı-klīn,* (geol.) *n.* an arch-like fold dipping outwards from the fold-axis.—*adj.* **anticlin'al** sloping in opposite directions: perpendicular to the surface near the growing-point (*bot.*).—*n.* an anticline [Pfx. **anti-** (1), Gr. *klıneın,* to lean.]

anticlockwise *an-tı-klok'wīz, adv.* in the opposite direction to that of the hands of a clock. [Pfx. **anti-** (3).]

anticoagulant *an-tı-kō-ag'ū-lənt, n* a drug that hinders clotting of blood.—Also *adj.* [Pfx **anti-** (1)]

anticonvulsant *an-tı-kən-vul'sənt, n* a drug used to control epilepsy, etc.—Also *adj.* [Pfx. **anti-** (1)]

anticyclone *an-tı-sī'klōn, n.* a rotatory outflow of air from an area of high pressure.—*adj.* **anticyclonic** (*-klon'ık*). [Pfx. **anti-** (3).]

antidepressant *an-tı-dı-pres'ənt, n.* a drug used to counteract depression.—Also *adj.* [Pfx. **anti-** (1).]

antidisestablishmentarianism *an-tı-dıs-es-tab-lısh-mən-tār'ı-ən-ızm, n.* a movement against the removing of state recognition of an established church, esp. the Anglican church in the nineteenth century.—*adj.* **antidisestablishmenta'rian.** [Pfx. **anti-** (1).]

antidote *an'tı-dōt, n.* that which counteracts poison. anything that prevents an evil (with *against, for, to*) (*fig.*).—*adj.* **antido'tal.** [Gr. *antıdotos—dıdonaı,* to give.]

anti-establishment *an-tı-es-tab'lısh-mənt, adj.* opposed to the opinions and values of the establishment in society.—*n.* the people who are opposed to such opinions, etc [Pfx **anti-** (1).]

antifouling *an-tı-fowl'ing, adj.* intended to prevent fouling of ships' bottoms. [Pfx. **anti-** (1).]

antifreeze *an'tı-frēz, n.* a substance, as ethylene glycol, with low freezing point put into the radiator of an internal-combustion engine to prevent freezing up. [Pfx. **anti-** (1).]

antigen *an'tı-jen, n.* any substance that stimulates the production of an antibody [Pfx **anti-** (1), Gr *gennaein,* to engender.]

anti-hero *an'tı-hē'rō, n.* a principal character who lacks noble qualities and whose experiences are without tragic dignity:—*fem* **anti-heroine** (*her'ō-ın*) —*adj.* **anti-heroic** (*hı-rō'ık*). [Pfx **anti-** (3)]

antihistamine *an-tı-hıs'tə-mēn, n.* any of a group of drugs that prevents the action of histamines in allergic conditions. [Pfx. **anti-** (1).]

antiknock *an-tı-nok', n* a substance that prevents knock or detonation in internal-combustion engines [Pfx **anti-** (1)]

antilogarithm *an-tı-log'ə-rıdhm, -rıthm, n.* a number of which a particular number is the logarithm:—*contr.* **an'tilog.** [Pfx anti- (3)]

antilogy *an-tıl'ə-jı, n* a contradiction —*adj* **antil'ogous** (*-gəs*) of the contrary kind. negatively electrified by heating [Gr *antılogıā,* contradiction]

antilymphocyte serum *an-tı-lım'fə-sīt sē'rəm,* serum used to prevent defensive action of lymphocytes, e.g in cases where they would reject an organ transplanted into the body. [Pfx **anti-** (1)]

antimacassar *an-tı-mək-as'ər, n* a covering for chairbacks, etc , to protect them from macassar oil or other grease in the hair, or for ornament [Pfx. **anti-** (1)]

anti-marketeer *an-tı-mar-kı-tēr', n* a person who opposes Britain's entry into or membership of the European Common Market. [Pfx **anti-** (1)]

anti-matter *an'tı-mat'ər, n.* hypothetical extraterrestrial matter that would consist of particles similar to those of terrestrial matter but of opposite electrical charge or, in the case of the neutron, reversed magnetic polarity [Pfx **anti-** (3)]

antimony *an'tı-mən-ı, n* a brittle, bluish-white element (at. numb. 51, symbol Sb, for stibium) of metallic appearance.—*adjs* **antimonial** (*-mō'nı-əl*) pertaining to, or containing, antimony, **antimonic** (*-mon'ık*) containing pentavalent antimony, **antimō'nious** containing trivalent antimony [L L. *antımōnıum,* of unknown origin, prob. from some Arabic word.]

antinephritic *an-tı-ne-frıt'ık, adj.* acting against diseases of the kidney [Pfx. **anti-** (1)]

antineutrino *an-tı-nū-trē'nō, n.* the antiparticle of the neutrino.—*n* **antineu'tron** (*-tron*) an uncharged particle that combines with the neutron with mutual annihilation and emission of energy [Pfx. **anti-** (3).]

anting. See **ant.**

antinode *an'tı-nōd,* (phys.) *n* a point of maximum disturbance midway between nodes —*adj.* **antinōd'al.** [Pfx **anti-** (3)]

antinomian *an-tı-nō'mı-ən, n* one who denies the obligatoriness of moral law: one who believes that the Christians are emancipated by the gospel from the obligation to keep the moral law, faith alone being necessary —Also *adj.*—*n* **antino'mianism.**—*adjs.* **antinomic** (*-nom'ık*), **-al** pertaining to, of the nature of, or involving, antinomy.—*n.* **antinomy** (*an-tın'ə-mı*) a contradiction in a law: a conflict of authority: conclusions discrepant though apparently logical. [Pfx. **anti-** (1), Gr *nomos,* law.]

anti-novel *an'tı-nov'l, -nuv'l, n.* a type of novel of the mid-twentieth century which largely discards plot and character and concerns itself with tiny inner dramas on the border of consciousness. [Pfx **anti-** (3)]

antipapal *an-tı-pā'pəl, adj.* opposed to the pope or the papal system.—See also **antipope.** [Pfx. **anti-** (2).]

antiparticle *an'tı-par'tı-kl, n.* the 'pair' of an elementary particle, particle and antiparticle being mutually destructive. [Pfx **anti-** (3)]

---

antibil'ious *adj.* anti- (1).   **antimalā'rial** *adj* anti- (1)   **antimon'archist** *n* anti- (2).
antifric'tion *adj.* anti- (1).   **antimonarch'ical** *adj* anti- (2).   **anti-na'tional** *adj* anti- (2).

antipasto *an'ti-päs'tō*, (It.) *n* an hors d'œuvre, a whet. [Cf. **antepast**.]

antipathy *an-tip'əth-i*, *n.* opposition in feeling: aversion: repugnance: incompatibility: mutual opposition: an object of antipathy.—*adjs.* **antipathet'ic**, **-al**.—*adv.* **antipathet'ically.**—*adj.* **antipathic** (*an-ti-path'ik*) belonging to antipathy: opposite: contrary.—*n.* **antip'athist** one possessed by an antipathy. [Pfx. **anti-** (1), Gr. *pathos*, feeling.]

anti-personnel *an'ti-pûr-sən-el'*, *adj.* intended to destroy military personnel and other persons. [Pfx. **anti-** (1).]

antiperspirant *an-ti-pûr'spi-rənt*, *n.* a substance helping to stop perspiration.—Also *adj.* [Pfx. **anti-** (1).]

antiphlogistic *an-ti-floj-ist'ik*, *adj.* acting against heat, or inflammation.—*n.* a medicine to allay inflammation. [Pfx. **anti-** (1).]

antiphon *an'ti-fon*, *n.* alternate chanting or singing: a species of church music sung by two parties each responding to the other—also **antiph'ony** (*-ən-i*).—*adj.* **antiph'onal.**—*n.* a book of antiphons or of anthems.—Also **antiph'onary** and **antiph'oner.**—*adv.* **antiph'onally.**—*adjs.* **antiphonic** (*-fon'*), **-al** mutually responsive.—*adv.* **antiphon'ically.** [Gr. *anti*, in return, and *phōnē*, voice.]

antiphrasis *an-tif'rə-sis*, (*rhet.*) *n.* the use of words in a sense opposite to the literal one.—*adjs.* **antiphrastic** (*an-ti-fras'tik*), **-al** involving antiphrasis: ironical. [Gr., *-anti*, against, *phrasis*, speech.]

antipodes *an-tip'ə-dēz*, *n.pl.* (also *sing.*) those who live on the other side of the globe, or on opposite sides, standing feet to feet: a point or place diametrically opposite to another on the surface of the earth or of any globular body or sphere: a pair of points or places so related to each other: the exact opposite of a person or a thing.—*adjs.* **antip'ōdal, antipōdē'an.** [Gr. *antipōdēs*, pl. of *antipous*, with feet opposite—*pous*, *podos*, a foot.]

antipole *an'ti-pōl*, *n.* the opposite pole: direct opposite. [Pfx. **anti-** (3).]

antipope *an'ti-pōp*, *n.* a pontiff set up in opposition to one asserted to be canonically chosen, as those who resided at Avignon in the 13th and 14th centuries.—See also **antipapal.** [**anti-** (3).]

antiproton *an-ti-prō'ton*, *n.* a particle comparable to the proton but negatively charged. [Pfx. **anti-** (3).]

antipruritic *an-ti-proō-rit'ik*, *n.* a substance that reduces itchiness.—Also *adj.* [Pfx. **anti-** (1).]

antipyretic *an-ti-pī-ret'ik*, *adj.* counteracting fever.—*n.* an antipyretic agent. [Gr. *anti-*, against, *pyretos*, fever—*pŷr*, fire.]

antiquark *an'ti-kwärk*, *n.* the hypothetical antiparticle corresponding to the quark. [Pfx. **anti-** (3)]

antiquary *an'ti-kwər-i*, *n.* one who studies, collects, or deals in relics of the past, but not usually very ancient things—curiosities rather than objects of serious archaeological interest.—*adj.* **antiquarian** (*-kwā'ri-ən*) connected with the study of antiquities. —*n.* an antiquary.—*n.* **antiquā'rianism.** [L. *antiquārius—antīquus*, old.]

antique *an-tēk'*, *adj.* ancient· of a good old age, olden: old-fashioned: savouring of bygone times: after the manner of the ancients.—*n.* anything very old: an old relic: a piece of old furniture or other object sought by collectors.—*v.t.* to alter the appearance of (wood, leather, etc.) so that it seems very old.—*v.t.* **antiquate** (*an'ti-kwāt*) to make antique, old, or obsolete. to put out of use.—*adj.* **an'tiquated.**—*n.* **antique'ness.**—*ns.* **antiquitarian** (*an-tik-wi-tā'ri-ən*) one attached to old ways or beliefs; **antiq'uity** ancient times, esp the times of the ancient Greeks and Romans. great age: ancient style: the people of old time: a relic of the past.—See also **antic.** [L. *antīquus*, old, ancient—*ante*, before; influenced by Fr. *antique*.]

Antirrhinum *an-ti-rī'nəm*, *n.* the snapdragon genus: (without *cap.*) a plant of the genus. [Latinised from Gr. *antirrīnon*, snapdragon—*anti*, like, mimicking, *rhīs*, *rhīnos*, nose.]

antiscorbutic *an-ti-skór-būt'ik*, *adj.* acting against scurvy.—*n.* a remedy or preventive for scurvy. [Pfx. **anti-** (1).]

anti-Semite *an'ti-sem'īt*, *-sēm'*, *n.* a hater of Semites, esp. Jews, or of their influence.—*adj.* **anti-Semitic** (*-sim-it'*).—*n.* **anti-Semitism** (*-sem'*, *-sēm'*). [Pfx. **anti-** (2).]

antisepsis *an-ti-sep'sis*, *n.* destruction, or inhibition of growth, of bacteria.—*adj.* **antisep'tic.**—*n.* an antiseptic agent.—*n.* **antisep'ticism** (*-sizm*) antiseptic treatment.—*adv.* **antisep'tically.**—*v.t.* **antisep'ticise**, **-ize** (*-sīz*). [Gr. *anti-*, against, *sēpsis*, putrefaction.]

antiserum *an'ti-sēr-əm*, *n.* a serum which contains antibodies:—*pl.* **antiser'ums, antiser'a.** [*antī*body and **serum.**]

antisocial *an-ti-sō'shl*, *adj.* opposed to the good of society, or the principles of society: disinclined to mix in society. without social instincts.—*adv.* **antisoc'ially.**—*ns.* **antiso'cialism; antiso'cialist** (formerly) unsociable person: now opponent of socialism; **antisociality** (*-shi-al'i-ti*) unsociableness: opposition to the principles of society. [Pfx. **anti-** (2).]

antispasmodic *an-ti-spaz-mod'ik*, *adj.* opposing spasms or convulsions.—*n.* a remedy for spasms [Pfx. **anti-** (1).]

antistatic *an-ti-stat'ik*, *adj.* having the property of counteracting static electricity.—Also **antistat** (*an'* or *-stat'*).—Also *n.* [Pfx. **anti-** (1).]

antithesis *an-tith'i-sis*, *n.* a figure in which thoughts or words are balanced in contrast: a thesis or proposition opposing another: opposition: the direct opposite:—*pl.* **antith'eses** (*-sēz*).—*adjs* **antithet'ic**, **-al**.—*adv.* **antithet'ically.** [Gr. *antithesis—thesis*, placing.]

antitoxin *an-ti-tok'sin*, *n.* a substance that neutralises toxin formed in the body.—*adj.* **antitox'ic.** [Pfx. **anti-** (1).]

antitrade *an'ti-trād*, *n.* a wind that blows in the opposite direction to the trade wind—that is, in the northern hemisphere from south-west, and in the southern hemisphere from north-west. [Pfx. **anti-** (3).]

anti-trust *an-ti-trust'*, *adj* of legislation, etc , directed against the adverse effects of monopolies on commerce. [Pfx. **anti-** (1).]

antitussive *an-ti-tus'iv*, *adj.* tending to alleviate or suppress coughing.—*n.* an antitussive agent. [Pfx. **anti-** (1), L. *tussis*, a cough]

antitype *an'ti-tīp*, *n.* that which corresponds to the type: that which is prefigured by the type —*adjs* **antityp'al, -typic** (*-tip'ik*), **-al.** [Pfx. **anti-** (3).]

antivenin *an-ti-ven'in*, *n.* an antitoxin counteracting esp snake venom [Pfx. **anti-** (1).]

anti-vivisection *an'ti-viv-i-sek'shən*, *n.* opposition to vivisection.—*ns.* **anti-vivisec'tionism; anti-vivisec'- tionist.** [Pfx. **anti-** (2).]

antler *ant'lər*, *n.* a bony outgrowth from the frontal bone of a deer: orig. the lowest branch of a stag's horn, then any branch, then the whole.—*adj.* **ant'- lered.**—**ant'ler-moth** a noctuid moth with antler-like markings on the wings, its larvae very destructive to pastures. [O.Fr. *antoullier*.]

antonomasia *ant-on-o-mā'zi-ə*, *n.* use of an epithet, or the name of an office or attributive, for a person's proper name, e.g. his lordship for an earl; and conversely, e.g. a Napoleon for a great conqueror. [Gr. *antonomasiā—onomazein*, to name, *onoma*, a name.]

antonym *ant'ō-nim*, *n.* a word opposite in meaning to another. [Gr. *onyma* = *onoma*, a name.]

antrorse *an-trörs'*, *adj.* turned up or forward. [From *anterus*, hypothetical positive of L. *anterior*, front, and L. *versus*, turned.]

anuria *an-ū'ri-ə*, *n.* failure in secretion of urine. [Gr. *an-*, priv., *ouron*, urine.]

anus *ā'nəs*, *n.* the opening of the alimentary canal by which undigested residues are voided.—*adj.* **ā'nal.** [L. *ānus*, *-ī*, a ring.]

anvil *an'vil*, *n.* an iron block on which smiths hammer metal into shape: the incus of the ear. [O.E. *anfilte*, *onfilti*.]

anxious *ang(k)'shəs*, *adj.* uneasy with fear and desire regarding something doubtful: solicitous: eager (for something, to do something).—*n.* **anxiety** (*ang(g)-zī'i-ti*) state of being anxious: a state of chronic apprehension as a symptom of mental disorder — *adj.* **anxiolytic** (*angk-si-ō-lit'ik*) of a drug, reducing anxiety and tension.—Also *n.*—*adv.* **an'xiously.**—*n.* **an'xiousness.** [L. *anxius—angĕre*, to press tightly. See **anger, anguish.**]

any *en'i*, *adj.* and *pron.* one indefinitely: some whichever, no matter which.—*adv.* at all, to an appreciable extent.—*n.* and *pron.* **an'ybody** any single person: a person of any account.—*adv.* **an'yhow** in any way whatever: in any case, at least: indifferently, carelessly.—*n.* and *pron.* **an'yone** (or **any one**) anybody at all: anybody whatever.—*adv.* **an'yroad** (*dial.*) anyway.—*n.* and *pron.* **an'ything** a thing indefinitely, as opposed to nothing.—*adv.* any whit, to any extent.—*adv.* **an'ytime** at any time; **an'yway, an'yways** in any manner: anyhow: in any case; **an'ywhere** in or to any place; **an'ywise** in any manner, to any degree.—**any amount** a lot (*coll.*); **any day** in any circumstances; **any more** any longer; **any old how** without any special care; **anyone else** any other person; **at any rate** whatever may happen: at all events; **like anything** very much: with great vigour [O.E. *ænig—ān*, one.]

Anzac *an'zak*, *n.* an Australasian expeditionary soldier (1914 *et seq.*).—Also *adj.*—**Anzac Day** April 25, a public holiday in Australia and New Zealand in memory of the Anzac landing in Gallipoli (1915) [Coined from the initials of *Australian-New-Zealand Army Corps.*]

aorist *ā'ər-ist*, *n.* a tense, esp. in Greek, expressing simple past time, with no implications of continuance, repetition, or the like.—*adj* **aorist'ic.** [Gr. *aoristos*, indefinite—*a-*, priv., and *horistos*, limited.]

aorta *ā-ör'tə*, *n.* the great arterial trunk that carries blood from the heart.—*adjs.* **aor'tal, aor'tic.**—*n* **aorti'tis** inflammation of the aorta [Gr. *aortē—aeirein*, to raise up.]

aoudad *ä'ŏŏ-dad*, *n.* a North African wild sheep. [Native name in French spelling.]

apace *ə-pās'*, *adv* at a quick pace: swiftly. [Prep. **a**, and **pace.**]

Apache *ə-pa'chi*, *n.* a Red Indian of a group of tribes in Arizona, New Mexico, etc.: (**apache**, *ə-pash'*) a lawless ruffian or hooligan in Paris or elsewhere. [Perh. Zuñi *āpachu*, enemy.]

apagoge *ap-ə-gō'jē*, *n.* reduction to absurdity, indirect proof by showing the falsehood of the opposite.—*adjs.* **apagogic** (*-goj'ik*), **-al.**—*adv* **apagog'ically.** [Gr. *apagōgē*, leading away, *apagein*, to lead off.]

apanage. See **appanage.**

apart *ə-pärt'*, *adv.* separately: aside: asunder, parted:

separate: out of consideration.—*n.* **apart'ness.**—**set apart** to separate: to devote; **take apart** (*slang*) to reprimand severely; **tell apart** to distinguish, see the difference between. [Fr. *à part*—L. *ad partem*, to the side.]

apartheid *a-pärt'hāt, -pär'tīd*, *n.* segregation and separate development (of races). [Afrikaans.]

apartment *ə-pärt'mənt*, *n.* a separate room in a house occupied by a particular person or party: a suite or set of such rooms (*arch* and *U.S.*)—now in this sense in the *pl.*—*adj.* **apartmental** (*-ment'əl*). [Fr *appartement*, a suite of rooms forming a complete dwelling—L. *ad*, to, and *partīre*, *partīrī*, to divide—*pars*, *partis*, part.]

apatetic *ap-ə-tet'ik*, *adj.* of an animal's coloration or marking which closely resembles that of another species or of its surroundings. [Gr. *apatētikos*, deceitful.]

apathy *ap'əth-i*, *n.* want of feeling, passion, or interest: indifference.—*adjs.* **apathet'ic, -al.**—*adv.* **apathet'ically.** [Gr. *apatheia—a-*, priv., *pathos*, feeling.]

Apatosaurus *ə-pat-ō-sor'əs*, *n* the scientific name for Brontosaurus. [Gr. *apatē*, deceit, *sauros*, lizard.]

ape *āp*, *n.* a monkey: a large monkey without a tail or with a very short one: a mimic: an imitator.—*v.t.* to mimic: to imitate.—*ns.* **ape'dom; ape'hood; ap'ery** conduct of one who apes: any ape-like action: a colony of apes.—*adj.* **ap'ish** like an ape: imitative: foppish.—**ape'man** any of several extinct primates thought to have been intermediate in development between man and the higher apes.—**go ape** (*U.S slang*) to go crazy (with *over* or *for*). [O.E. *apa*.]

apepsy *a-pep'si*, **apepsia** *a-pep'si-ə*, *ns* weakness of digestion [Gr. *apepsiā*, indigestion; *a-*, priv , *peptein*, to digest.]

aperçu *a-per-su*, *n.* a summary exposition: a brief outline: a glimpse: an immediate intuitive insight. [Fr. *aperçu*, survey, sketch—lit (pa.p of *apercevoir*) perceived.]

aperient *ə-pē'ri-ənt*, *n.* and *adj.* laxative.—*adj.* **aperitive** (*ə-per'i-tiv*) laxative.—*n.* (usu. as Fr. **apéritif**, *ə-pā-rē-tēf*) a (liquid) appetiser [L *aperīre*, *apertum*, to open]

aperiodic *ā-pē-ri-od'ik*, *adj* not periodic: coming to rest without oscillation.—*n* **aperiodicity** (*-ə-dis'i-ti*) [Gr *a-*, priv , and **periodic.**]

apéritif, aperitive. See **aperient.**

aperture *ap'ər-chər*, *n* an opening: a hole: the diameter of the opening through which light passes in an optical instrument. [L. *apertura—aperīre*, to open.]

apery. See **ape.**

apetalous *ə-pet'əl-əs*, *adj.* (*bot.*) without petals.—*n.* **apet'aly.** [Gr. *a-*, priv., and *petalon*, a leaf]

apex *ā'peks*, *n* summit, tip, or point: a vertex (*geom.*): the culminating point, climax of anything:—*pl.* **a'pexes, apices** (*āp'*, or *ap'i-sēz*). [L *āpex*, *āpicis*, a tip]

apfelstrudel *ap-fəl-s(h)trŏŏ'del*, *n.* a sweet pastry containing apples, spices, etc [Ger]

aphaeresis, apheresis *a-fē'ri-sis*, *n* (*gram.*) the taking away of a sound or syllable at the beginning of a word. [Gr *aphairesis*, a taking away, *apo*, away, and *hairecin*, to take]

aphagia *a-fā'j(i)-ə*, *n* inability to swallow. (of imago of certain insects) inability to feed [Gr. *a-*, priv., *phagia—phagein*, to eat.]

aphasia *a-fā'z(h)i-ə*, *n* inability to press thought in words, or inability to understand thought as expressed in the spoken or written words of others, by reason of some brain disease —*n* and *adj.* **apha'siac.** —*adj* **aphasic** (*a-fā'zik, -a-faz'ik*) [Gr *a-*, priv., *phasis*, speech—*phanai*, to speak.]

aphelion *a-fē'li-ən, n.* a planet's furthest point in its orbit from the sun:—*pl.* **aphe'lia.**—*adjs* **aphe'lian, aphe'lic.** [Gr. *apo,* from, *hēlios,* sun.]

apheliotropic *a-fē-li-ō-trop'ik, adj.* turning away from the sun —*n.* **apheliot'ropism.** [Gr. *apo,* from, *hēlios,* sun, and *tropikos,* belonging to turning]

apheresis. Same as **aphaeresis.**

aphesis *af'i-sis, n.* the gradual and unintentional loss of an unaccented vowel at the beginning of a word, as in *squire* from *esquire*—a special form of aphaeresis —*adj.* **aphetic** (*ə-fet'ik*).—*v.t.* **aph'etise, -ize.** [Gr *aphesis,* letting go—*apo,* from, *hienai,* to send.]

aphis *af'is, āf'is,* **aphid** *af'id, ns* a plant-louse or green-fly, a small insect that sucks plant juices:—*pl.* **aph'ides** (-*i-dēz*), **aph'ids.**—*adj.* **aphid'ical.**—*ns.* **aph'icide, aphid'icide** (-*sīd*) an aphis killer.

aphonia *a-fō'ni-ə,* **aphony** *af'ə-ni, ns.* loss of voice from hysteria, disease of larynx or vocal cords, etc.—*adjs.* **aphonic** (-*fon'*), **aphonous** (*af'ə-nəs*) voiceless. [Gr. *a-,* priv, *phōnē,* voice]

aphorism *af'ər-izm, n.* a concise statement of a principle in any science: a brief, pithy saying: an adage —*v.i.* **aph'orise, -ize.**—*ns.* **aph'oriser, -z-; aph'orist.**—*adj.* **aphoris'tic.**—*adv.* **aphorist'ically.** [Gr. *aphorizein,* to define—*apo,* from, *horos,* a limit]

aphotic *a-fō'tik, adj.* lightless. [Gr. *a-,* priv, *phōs, phōtos,* light.]

aphrodisiac *af-rō-diz'i-ak, -rə-, adj.* exciting sexually —*n.* that which so excites.—*n.* **aphrodis'ia** sexual desire, esp. violent.—*adj.* **Aphrodis'ian** belonging to Aphrodite. [Gr *aphrodisiakos—Aphroditē,* the goddess of love.]

aphtha *af'thə, n.* the disease thrush: a small whitish ulcer on the surface of a mucous membrane:—*pl* **aph'thae** (-*thē*).—*adj.* **aph'thous.** [Gr. *aphtha,* mostly in pl. *aphthai.*]

aphyllous *a-fil'əs,* (*bot.*) *adj.* without foliage, leaves.—*n.* **aphyll'y.** [Gr. *a-,* priv., *phyllon,* a leaf]

apian *ā'pi-ən, adj.* relating to bees.—*adj.* **apiarian** (-*ā'ri-ən*) relating to beehives or bee-keeping.—*ns.* **ā'piarist** a bee-keeper; **a'piary** (-*ər-i*) a place where bees are kept; **a'piculture** bee-keeping; **apicul'turist.** [L. *āpis,* a bee, *āpiārium,* a bee-house]

apical *ap',* or *āp'ik-l, adj* of or at the apex: denoting a sound articulated with the tip of the tongue (*phon.*) —*adv.* **ap'ically.**—*n.pl* **ap'ices** see apex. [See apex.]

apiculture. See apian.

apiece *ə-pēs', adv.* for each piece, thing, or person: to each individually. [**a¹,** piece.]

apish. See ape.

aplacental *a-pla-sen'tl, adj.* without placenta [Gr. *a-,* priv , and placental.]

aplasia *a-plā'z(h)i-ə, n.* imperfect development or absence of an organ or part.—*adj* **aplastic** (-*plas'*) —**aplastic anaemia** a form of anaemia caused by malfunctioning of the bone marrow. [Gr *a-,* priv , and Mod. L. -*plasia*—Gr *plasis,* moulding.]

aplenty *ə-plen'ti,* (*dial.*) *adv.* in plenty [**a³,** plenty.]

aplomb *ə-plom',* Fr *a-plɔ̃, n.* perpendicularity: self-possession, coolness [Fr *aplomb—à plomb,* according to plummet.]

apnoea, apnea *ap-nē'ə, n.* a cessation of breathing [Gr *apnoia—a-,* priv., *pno(i)ē,* breath.]

Apocalypse *a-pok'əl-ips, n.* the last book of the New Testament, otherwise the Revelation of St John: (without *cap.*) any book purporting to reveal the future or last things: a revelation or disclosure.—*adjs.* **apocalypt'ic** pertaining to the Apocalypse: prophetic of disaster or of the end of the world; **apocalypt'-ical.**—*adv.* **apocalypt'ically.** [Gr. *apokalypsis,* an uncovering—*apo,* from, *kalyptein,* to cover.]

apocarpous *ap-ō-kar'pəs,* (*bot.*) *adj* having the carpels separate [Gr. *apo,* from, *karpos,* fruit]

apochromatic *ap-ō-krō-mat'ik, adj* relatively free from chromatic and spherical aberration.—*ns.* **ap'ochromat** an apochromatic lens or instrument; **apochro'matism.** [Gr. *apo,* from, *chrōma, -atos,* colour.]

apocope *ə-pok'ō-pē, n.* the cutting off of the last sound or syllable of a word.—*v.t.* **apoc'opate.**—*n.* **apocop-ā'tion.** [Gr. *apokopē—apo,* off, *koptein,* to cut]

apocrypha *ə-pok'rif-ə, n.pl* hidden or secret things applied specially to certain books or parts of books included in the Septuagint and Vulgate translations of the Old Testament but not accepted as canonical by Jews or Protestants, and to later books (Apocrypha of the New Testament) never accepted as canonical or authoritative by any considerable part of the Christian Church:—*sing.* **apoc'ryphon.**—*adj.* **apoc'ryphal** of the Apocrypha: of doubtful authority: spurious: fabulous [Gr., things hidden—*apo,* from, *kryptein,* to hide.]

apodictic *ap-ō-dik'tik,* **apodeictic** -*dīk', adjs.* necessarily true: demonstrative without demonstration: beyond contradiction.—*adj.* **apod(e)ic'tical.**—*adv.* **apod(e)ic'tically.** [Gr *apodeiktikos—apodeik-nynai* (*apo* and *deiknynai*), to demonstrate.]

apodosis *ə-pod'ə-sis,* (gram.) *n* the consequent clause in a conditional sentence:—opp. *protasis.* [Gr *apodosis—apo,* back, *didonai,* to give.]

apogaeic See apogee.

apogamy *ə-pog'ə-mi,* (*bot.*) *n* omission of the sexual process in the life-history—the sporophyte developing either from an unfertilised egg-cell or some other cell —*adj.* **apog'amous.**—*adv* **apog'amously.** [Gr. *apo,* from, *gamos,* marriage.]

apogee *ap'ō-jē, n.* a heavenly body's point of greatest distance from the earth: culmination (*fig.*).—opp. to *perigee.*—*adjs* **apogaeic** (-*jē'ik*), **apoge'al, apoge'an.** [Gr *apogaion—apo,* from, *gaia,* or *gē,* the earth]

apograph *ap'ō-graf, n.* an exact copy. [Gr. *apogra-phon,* a copy—*apo,* from, and *graphein,* to write.]

apolitical *a-pal-it'ik-əl,* also *ā-, adj.* indifferent to political affairs: uninvolved in politics.—*adv.* **apolit'ically.**—*ns.* **apolitical'ity, apolit'icism.** [Gr *a-,* priv., and political.]

Apollo *ə-pol'o, n.* the Greek sun-god, patron of poetry and music, medicine, archery, etc. (sometimes without *cap.*) an extremely handsome young man:—*pl.* **apoll'os.** [Gr *Apollōn, -ōnos,* L *Apollō, -inis.*]

apologetic *ə-pol-ə-jet'ik, adj.* (primarily) vindicatory, defensive: (now usu.) regretfully acknowledging fault.—*n.* a defence, vindication.—*adj.* **apologet'-ical.**—*adv* **apologet'ically.**—*n. sing* **apologet'ics** the defensive argument or method, esp the defence of Christianity.—*n.* **apologia** (*ap-o-lō'ji-ə*) a written defence or vindication.—*v.t* **apologise, -ize** (*ə-pol'-ə-jīz*) to put forward a defence: (now usu.) to express regret for a fault —*ns.* **apol'ogist** (-*jist*) a defender by argument; **apology** (*ə-pol'ə-ji*) a defence, justification, apologia: an explanation with expression of regret: a regretful acknowledgment of a fault: a poor specimen hardly worthy of its name. [Gr *apologia,* defence, *apologos,* a tale—*apo,* off, *logos,* speaking.]

apomixis *ap-ō-miks'is, n* omission of sexual fusion in reproduction, as in parthenogenesis, or in apogamy —*adjs.* **apomictic** (-*mik'tik*), **-ai.**—*adv.* **apomic'-tically.** [Gr *apo,* from, *mixis,* mingling, intercourse]

aponeurosis *ap-ō-nū-rō'sis, n.* a flat thin tendon —*adj* **aponeurotic** (-*rot'ik*) [Gr *aponeurōsis—apo,* off, *neuron,* tendon.]

apophatic *a-pō-fat'ik,* (*theol*) *adj* (of a description of God) using negatives, i e , saying what God is not.

apophlegmatic *ap-ō-fleg-mat'ik, adj.* promoting the discharge of mucus —*n* an apophlegmatic agent. [Gr *apophlegmatikos—apo,* off: see phlegm.]

apophthegm, apothegm *ap'ō-them, n.* a pithy saying, more short, pointed, and practical than the aphorism need be.—*adjs.* **apo(ph)thegmat'ic, -al** (*-theg-*).—*adv.* **apo(ph)thegmat'ically.** [Gr. *apophthegma*—*apo*, forth, and *phthengesthai*, to utter]

apophyge *a-pof'i-jē, n.* the curve where a column merges in its base or capital. [Gr. *apophygē*, escape.]

apophysis *a-pof'i-sis, -zis, n.* an outgrowth or protuberance, esp. on a bone, on the end of a pine-cone scale, on a moss stalk below the capsule (*biol.*): a branch from a mass of igneous rock (*geol.*):—*pl.* **apoph'yses.** [Gr., offshoot—*apo*, off, *phyein*, to grow.]

apoplexy *ap'ō-pleks-i, n.* sudden loss of sensation and motion, generally the result of haemorrhage or thrombosis in the brain.—*adjs.* **apoplec'tic, -al.** [Gr. *apoplēxiā*—*apo-*, expressing completeness, *plēssein*, to strike.]

aport *a-pört', -pört, adv.* on or towards the port side.

aposematic *ap-ō-sē-mat'ik, adj.* (of animal coloration) warning. [Gr. *apo*, away from, *sēma*, *sēmatos*, sign.]

aposiopesis *a-pos-i-ō-pē'sis, ap-ō-si-, n.* a sudden breaking off in the midst of a sentence. [Gr. *aposiō-pēsis*—*apo*, off, and *siōpē*, silence.]

apospory *a-pos'po-ri, (bot.) n.* omission of spore-formation in the life-history—the gametophyte developing vegetatively from the sporophyte.—*adj.* **apos'porous.** [Gr. *apo*, away from, and **spore.**]

apostasy *a-post'a-si, n.* abandonment of one's religion, principles, or party: a revolt from ecclesiastical obedience, from a religious profession, or from holy orders: defection.—*n.* **apost'ate** (*-āt, -it*) one who has apostatised: a renegade.—Also *adj.*—*adjs.* **apostatic** (*ap-ō-stat'ik*), **-al.**—*v.i.* **apostatise, -ize** (*a-pos'ta-tīz*). [Gr. *apostasiā*, a standing away—*apo*, from, *stasis*, a standing.]

a posteriori *ā pos-tē-ri-ō'rī, -o'rī, ā pos-ter-i-ō'rē, adj.* applied to reasoning from experience, from effect to cause: inductive: empirical: gained from experience:—opp. to *a priori.*—Also *adv.* [L. *ā*, from, *posteri-ōrī*, abl. of *posterior*, coming after.]

apostle *a-pos'l, n.* one sent to preach the gospel: esp. one of Christ's twelve: a first introducer of Christianity in a country: a principal champion or supporter of a new system, or of a cause: the highest in the fourfold ministry of the Catholic Apostolic Church: one of the twelve officials forming a presiding high council in the Mormon Church.—*ns.* **apos'tleship; apost'olate** (*a-post'a-lāt*) the office of an apostle: leadership in a propaganda.—*adjs.* **apostolic** (*ap-as-tol'ik*), **-al.**—*adv.* **apostol'ically.**—*ns.* **apostol'icism** (*-i-sizm*), **apostolicity** (*a-post-a-lis'i-ti*) the quality of being apostolic.—**Apostles' Creed** the oldest form of Christian creed that exists, early ascribed to the apostles; **apostle spoons** silver spoons with handles ending in figures of the apostles, once a common baptismal present; **apostolical succession** the derivation of holy orders by unbroken chain of transmission from the apostles through bishops—the theory of the Catholic Church: the assumed succession of a ministry so ordained to apostolic powers and privileges; **apostolic fathers** the immediate disciples and fellow-labourers of the apostles, more especially those who have left writings (Barnabas, Clement of Rome, Ignatius, Hermas, Polycarp); **apostolic see** the see of Rome; **apostolic vicar** the cardinal representing the Pope in extraordinary missions. [Gr. *apostolos*, one sent away, *apo*, away, *stellein*, to send.]

apostrophe¹ *a-pos'tra-fi, n.* (in *rhet.*) a sudden turning away from the ordinary course of a speech to address some person or object present or absent.—*adj.* **apostrophic** (*ap-ō-strof'ik*).—*v.t.* **apos'trophise, -ize** to

address by apostrophe. [Gr. *apo*, from, and *strophē*, a turning.]

apostrophe² *a-pos'tra-fi, n.* a mark (') showing (among other uses) the omission of a letter or letters in a word: a sign of the modern Eng genitive or possessive case—orig. marking the dropping of *e*. [Gr. *apostrophos*, turning away, elision; confused with foregoing.]

apothecary *a-poth'i-kar-i, n.* a druggist or pharmacist (*arch.*)—still a legal description for licentiates of the Society of Apothecaries: a medical practitioner of an inferior branch, who often kept a shop for drugs (*obs.*).—**apothecaries' measure** liquid units of capacity (fluid ounce, etc) used by pharmacists before 1969; **apothecaries' weight** a pre-1969 system based on the troy ounce. [L L *apothēcarius*—Gr. *apothēkē*, a storehouse—*apo*, away, and *tithenai*, to place.]

apothegm, etc See **apophthegm.**

apothem *ap'a-them, n.* the perpendicular from the centre to any of the sides of a regular polygon. [Gr *apo*, away from, *thema*, that which is placed.]

apotheosis *a-po-thi-ō'sis, n.* a deification: glorification:—*pl.* **apotheo'ses** (*-sēz*)—*v.t* **apoth'eosise, -ize** (or *a-pō-thē'ō-sīz*). [Gr. *apotheōsis*—*apo-*, expressing completion, *theos*, a god.]

appal *a-pol', v.t.* to horrify, dismay:—*pr.p.* **appall'ing;** *pa.t.* and *pa.p.* **appalled'.**—*adj.* **appall'ing.**—*adv.* **appall'ingly.** [Perh. from O Fr. *apalir, apallir,* to wax pale, make pale. See **pall and pale.**]

Appaloosa *a-pa-lōō'sa, n.* a North American breed of horse, usu. white or grey with dark spots. [Prob. the *Palouse* Indians.]

appanage, apanage *ap'an-ij, n.* a provision for maintenance, esp of a king's younger child: dependent territory: a perquisite: an adjunct or attribute. [Fr. *apanage*—L. *ad*, and *panis*, bread]

apparat *a'pa-rat, n.* the political machine of the Communist party.—*n.* **apparatchik** (*á-pa-rách'ik*) a member of the Soviet bureaucracy. [Russ , *apparatus.*]

apparatus *ap-a-rā'tas, -ra'tas, n.* things prepared or provided, material: set of instruments, tools, natural organs, etc: materials (as various readings) for the critical study of a document (**apparatus criticus** *ap-a-rā'tas krit'i-kas, ap-a-rā'tōōs krit'i-kŏōs*):—*pl.* **appara'tuses** or **appara'tus** (L. *appārātūs*). [L. *appārātus, -ūs, -ad,* to, *pārāre, -ātum,* to prepare.]

apparel *a-par'l, v.t.* to dress, clothe: to adorn:—*pr.p.* **appar'elling;** *pa.t.* and *pa.p.* **appar'elled.**—*n.* attire, dress.—*n.* **appar'elment.** [O.Fr. *apareiller*—L *ad,* to, *pār,* equal.]

apparent *a-par'ant,* or *-pār', adj.* that may be seen: obvious: conspicuous: seeming: obtained by observation without correction, distinguished from *true* or from *mean.*—*n.* **appar'ency** apparentness: position of being heir-apparent.—*adv.* **appar'ently.**—*n.* **appar'entness.** [L. *appārens, -entis,* pr.p. of *appārēre,* see **appear.**]

apparition *ap-a-rish'an, n* an appearing: an appearance: reappearance after occultation: that which appears: a phantom: a ghost.—*adj.* **appari'tional.** [See **appear.**]

apparitor *a-par'i-tar, n.* an officer in attendance on an ecclesiastical court: a university beadle. [L. *appāritor.* See **appear.**]

appeal *a-pēl', v.i.* to call upon, have recourse to (with *to*): to refer (to a witness or superior authority): to make supplication or earnest request (to a person for a thing): to resort for verification or proof (to some principle or person): to make a demand on the feelings that comes home: to attract one's interest or enjoyment: to demand another judgment by a higher court: to remove to another court: to ask for the umpire's decision esp. as to whether a player is out (*cricket*).—*v.t.* to remove to a higher court (*arch.* except in U.S.).—*n.* recourse: an act of appealing: a supplication: removal of a cause to a higher tribunal: an evocation of sympathetic feeling.—*adjs.* **appeal'-able; appeal'ing** making an appeal: imploring: calling forth sympathy —*adv.* **appeal'ingly.**—*n.* **appeal'ingness.**—**Court of Appeal** a section of the English High Court of Justice; **Court of Criminal Appeal** an English Court created in 1907 for appeal in criminal cases. [O Fr. *apeler*—L. *appellāre*, *-ātum*, to address, call by name; also to appeal to, impeach.]

appear *ə-pēr'*, *v.i.* to become visible: to present oneself formally before an authority or tribunal, hence to act as the representative or counsel for another: to come into view, to come before the public, be published· to be manifest: to seem —*ns.* **appear'-ance** the act of appearing, e.g in court to prosecute or answer a charge: the publication of a book: the effect of appearing conspicuously, show, parade: the condition of that which appears, form, aspect: outward look or show: a natural phenomenon: an apparition; **appear'er.**—**keep up appearances** to keep up an outward show, often with intent to conceal absence of the inward reality; **put in an appearance** to appear in person; **to all appearance(s)** so far as appears to any one. [O.Fr. *apareir*—L. *appārēre*—ad, to, *pārēre*, *pāritum*, to come forth.]

appease *ə-pēz'*, *v.i.* to pacify: to propitiate by concessions: to satisfy: to quiet: to allay.—*adj* **appeas'able.**—*n* **appease'ment.**—*adv.* **appeas'ingly.** [O.Fr. *apeser*, to bring peace—L. *ad*, to, *pāx*, *pācis*, peace.]

appellant *ə-pel'ənt*, *n.* one who appeals: one who impeaches.—*adj.* **appell'ate** relating to appeals.—*n.* **appellation** (*ap-ə-lā'shən*) that by which anything is called: name, esp. one attached to a particular person —*adj.* **appellā'tional.**—*n.* **appell'ative** (*ə-pel'ə-tiv*) a common as distinguished from a proper name: a designation.—*adj.* common (as distinguished from proper): of or pertaining to the giving of names.—*adv.* **appell'atively.** [L. *appellāre*, *-ātum*, to call.]

appellation (**d'origine**) **contrôlée** *a-pel-a-syō'* (*dor-ə-zhēn*) *cō-trō-lā*, (Fr.) in the labelling of French wines a guarantee that the wine conforms to certain specified conditions of origin, strength, etc

append *ə-pend'*, *v.t.* to hang on (to something): to add.—*n.* **append'age** something appended: esp. one of the paired jointed structures of arthropods—antennae, jaws, legs —*adj.* **append'ant** attached, annexed, consequent.—*n.* an adjunct, quality.—*ns* **appendec'tomy**, more commonly **appendicec'tomy** (*-dis-*), removal of the vermiform appendix (Gr *ektomē*, cutting out); **appendici'tis** inflammation of the vermiform appendix.—*adj.* **appendicular** (*ap-en-dik'ū-lər*) of the nature of, or belonging to, an appendix.—*n.* **appendix** (*ə-pen'diks*) something appended or added: a supplement: an addition to a book or document, containing matter explanatory, but not essential to its completeness: a process, prolongation, or projection, esp. the vermiform appendix (*anat.*):—*pl.* **append'ixes**, **append'ices** (*-sēz*, *-siz*).—**appendix** vermiformis or **vermiform appendix** a blind process terminating the caecum. [L *ad*, to, *pendēre*, to hang.]

apperception *ap-ər-sep'shən*, *n.* the mind's perception of itself as a conscious agent: an act of voluntary consciousness, accompanied with self-consciousness the assimilation of a new sense-experience to a mass already in the mind —*adj's* **appercep'tive; ap-**

percipient (*-sip'i-ənt*).—*v.t.* **apperceive** (*-sēv'*). [L. *ad*, to, and **perception, perceive.**]

appertain *ap-ər-tān'*, *v.i.* to belong, as a possession, a right, or attribute.—*adj.* **appertain'ing** proper, appropriate (with *to*).—*adj.* **apper'tinent** appertaining. [O.Fr. *apartenir*, *apertenir*—L. *ad*, to, *pertinēre*, to belong.]

appetent *ap'i-tənt*, *adj.* eagerly desirous: craving: longing.—*ns.* **app'etence**, **app'etency.** [L. *appetēns*, *-entis*, pr.p. of *appetēre*—ad, to, *petēre*, to seek.]

appetite *ap'i-tīt*, *n.* physical craving, accompanied with uneasy sensation (hunger, thirst, sex): natural desire: inclination: desire for food: hunger (with *for*).—*n.* **app'etiser**, *-z-* something to whet the appetite.—*adj.* **appetis'ing**, *-z-*.—*adv.* **appetis'ingly**, *-z-*. [O.Fr. *apetit*—L. *appetitus*—*appetēre*; see foregoing]

applaud *ə-plöd'*, *v.t.* to express approbation of by clapping the hands or otherwise: to extol: to commend.—*v.i.* to clap the hands or otherwise express approval —*n.* **applaud'er.**—*adj.* **applaud'ing.**—*adv.* **applaud'ingly.**—*n.* **applause** (*-ploz'*) clapping of hands or other sign of approval: general approbation: loud praise: acclamation. [L. *applaudēre*, *-plausum*—ad, to, *plaudēre*, to clap; cf. **explode.**]

apple *ap'l*, *n.* the fruit of the apple-tree: extended to other fruits (as pineapple, custard-apple), or even galls (oak-apple): the fruit of the forbidden tree in the Garden of Eden.—**app'le-blossom; app'le-cart; app'le-jack** (*U.S.*) apple brandy, distilled from fermented apple juice; **app'le-pie** a pie made with apples; **apple-tart** a tart made with apples; **app'le-tree** a tree (*Pyrus malus*) of the rose family, closely related to the pear-tree; **app'le-wife**, **app'le-woman** a woman who sells apples at a stall.—**apple of the eye** the pupil of the eye: something especially dear; **apple-pie bed** a bed prepared playfully, e.g. with sheets doubled up, so as to be impossible or painful to get into; **apple-pie order** perfect order; **upset the apple-cart** to throw plans into confusion. [O E. *æppel*.]

Appleton layer *ap'l-tən lā'ər*, an ionised region in the atmosphere, about 150 miles up, that acts as a reflector of radio waves. [From the physicist Sir Edward *Appleton*]

appliqué *a-plē'kā*, *-kā'*, Fr *a-plē-kā*, *n* work applied to, or laid on, another material, either of metalwork or of lace or the like —Also *adj.* [Pa.p. of Fr. *appliquer*, to apply.]

apply *ə-pli'*, *v.t.* to lay or put in contact: to administer: to bring to bear: to put to use: to show the reference or relevance of: to assign: to wield or ply: to direct: to devote (to a pursuit): to lay on as appliqué: to cover with appliqué.—*v.i* to suit or agree: to have recourse: to offer oneself as a candidate: to make or lodge a request: to be relevant: to hold good: to give close attention;—*pr.p.* **apply'ing;** *pa.t.* and *pa.p.* **applied'.**—*adj.* **appli'able** applicable.—*ns.* **appli'ance** application: apparatus; **applicability** (*ap-li-kə-bil'i-ti*) —*adj.* **app'licable** (now also -*plik'* in adj. and adv.) that may be applied: suitable.—*adv.* **app'licably.**—*n.* **app'licant** one who applies: a petitioner: a candidate for a post.—*adj* **app'licate** put to practical use, applied.—*n* **applica'tion** the act of applying, administering, or using: a thing applied: a formal request for a post, etc.: an appeal or petition: diligence: close thought or attention: employment, use of anything in special regard to something else: a bringing to bear: the lesson or moral of a fable: employment of a word with assignment of meaning: a kind of needlework, appliqué.—*adj* **app'licative** put into actual use in regard to anything: practical.—*n* **app'licator** a device or tool for applying something —*adj.* **app'licatory** (*-ko-tor-i*) having the property of applying.—*adj.* **applied** (*ə-plīd'*) placed with a flat surface against or close to something: turned to use —**applied mathematics** mathematics applied to observed facts of nature, or to practical life; **applied science** science put to use for a purpose, generally utilitarian, other than its own end (opposed to *pure*). [O.Fr. *aplier*, and its source, L *applicāre, -ātum—ad,* to, *plicāre,* to fold.]

appoggiatura *ap-pod-jä-tōō'ra, n* a leaning note—a grace-note written in smaller size taking its time at the expense of the following note: a similar note with a stroke through the tail, played very quickly. [It —*appoggiare,* to lean upon; same root as *appui.*]

appoint *ə point', v.t.* to fix: to settle: to assign, grant: to fix the time of: to engage to meet. to name to an office: to ordain: to prescribe: to destine, devote: to equip (*obs.* except in *pa p*).—*adj.* **appoint'ed** fixed: furnished.—*n* **appointee'** a person appointed to a job, position or office.—*adj* **appoint'ive** (*U.S.*) filled by appointment.—*n.* **appoint'ment** engagement, esp for a meeting, consultation, etc.: direction: nomination: an office to which one is or may be nominated: (now usu. in *pl.*) equipment: article of equipment. [O.Fr. *apointer—à point,* to (the) point]

apportion *ə-pōr'shən, -pōr', v.t.* to portion out: to divide in just shares: to adjust in due proportion.—*n.* **appor'tionment.** [L. *ad,* to, and **portion.**]

appose *ə-pōz', v.t.* to apply, e.g. a seal to a document: to place side by side. [Fr. *apposer—*L. *ad,* to, *pausāre,* to cease, rest; confused and blended in meaning with words from *pōnĕre, pōsitum,* to put.]

apposite *ap'ə-zit, adj.* apt: to the purpose.—*adv.* **app'-ositely.**—*ns.* **app'ositeness; apposition** (*-zish'ən*) application: juxtaposition: the position of a word parallel to another in syntactic relation (*gram.*): growth by deposition on the surface (*bot.*).—*adjs.* **apposi'tional; appositive** (*ə-poz'*) placed in apposition. [L. *appŏsitus,* pa.p. of *appōnĕre,* to put to— *ad,* to, *pōnĕre,* to put.]

appraise *ə-prāz', v.t.* to set a price on. to value with a view to sale or (in U.S.) payment of customs duty: to estimate the worth of.—*adj.* **apprais'able.**—*ns.* **apprais'al** appraisement; **appraise'ment** a valuation: estimation of quality; **apprais'er** one who values property: one who estimates quality. [Later form of **apprize.**]

appreciate *ə-prē'shi-āt, v.t.* to estimate justly: to be fully sensible of all the good qualities in: to estimate highly: to perceive: to raise in value, to advance the quotation or price of, as opposed to *depreciate.*—*v.i.* to rise in value.—*adj.* **appre'ciable** capable of being estimated: perceptible.—*adv.* **appre'ciably.**—*n.* **apprecia'tion** the act of setting a value, especially on a work of literature or art: just—and also favourable —estimation: a sympathetic critical essay: increase in value.—*adj.* **appre'ciative** characterised by, implying appreciation.—*adv.* **appre'ciatively.**—*n.* **appre'ciator** one who appreciates, or estimates justly.—*adj.* **appre'ciatory** (*-shyə-tər-i*). [L.L. *ap-pretiāre, -ātum—ad,* to, and *pretium,* price.]

apprehend *ap-ri-hend', v.t.* to lay hold of: to arrest: to be conscious of by the senses: to lay hold of by the intellect: to catch the meaning of: to understand: to recognise: to consider: to look forward to, esp. with fear.—*n.* **apprehensibil'ity.**—*adj.* **apprehens'ible.** —*n.* **apprehen'sion** act of apprehending or seizing: arrest: conscious perception: conception: ability to understand: fear.—*adj.* **apprehens'ive** pertaining to the laying hold of sensuous and mental impressions:

intelligent, clever: having an apprehension or notion: fearful: anticipative of something adverse.—*adv.* **apprehens'ively.**—*n.* **apprehens'iveness.** [L. *ap-praehendĕre—ad,* to, *praehendĕre, -hēnsum,* to lay hold of.]

apprentice *ə-prent'is, n* one bound to another to learn a craft: a mere novice.—Also *adj.*—*v.t.* to bind as an apprentice.—*ns.* **apprent'icement; apprent'iceship** the state of an apprentice: a time of training for a trade, or for any activity.—**serve an apprenticeship to** undergo the training of an apprentice. [O.Fr. *aprentis—aprendre,* to learn—L. *appraehendĕre;* see **apprehend.**]

apprise *ə-prīz', v.t.* to give notice to: to inform. [Fr. *apprendre,* pa.p *appris;* see **apprehend.**]

apprize, -ise *ə-prīz', v t.* to value, appreciate. [O.Fr. *appriser, aprisier—à,* to, and *prisier,* to price, prize See **appraise.**]

appro. See **approbation, approve.**

approach *ə-prōch', v t.* to bring near: to come near to in any sense: to come into personal relations or seek communication with: to resemble—*v i.* to come near.—*n.* a drawing near: in golf, play on drawing near the putting-green (also **approach-stroke, -shot,** etc.): access: an avenue or means of access: approximation: attitude towards, way of dealing with: (usu. *pl.*) advances towards personal relations: (*pl.*) trenches, etc., by which besiegers strive to reach a fortress, or routes into any area of military importance. —*n.* **approachabil'ity.**—*adj.* **approach'able.** [O.Fr. *aprochier,* L.L. *adpropiāre*—L. *ad,* to, *prope,* near.]

approbation *ap-rō-bā'shən, n.* a formal sanction: approval.—**on approbation** (*coll.* **appro** *ap'rō*) on approval [L. *approbāre, -ātum;* see **approve**[1].]

appropriate *ə-prō'pri-āt, v.t.* to make to be the private property of any one: to take to oneself as one's own: to filch: to set apart for a purpose, assign: to suit (with *to*).—*adj.* set apart for a purpose: peculiar (with *to*): suitable (with *to* or *for*).—*adv* **appro'priately.**—*ns.* **appro'priateness; appropria'tion.**—*adj.* **appro'pria-tive.**—*ns.* **appro'priativeness; appro'priator.** [L. *appropriāre, -ātum—ad,* to, *proprius,* one's own; see **proper.**]

approve *ə-prōō'v', v.t.* to show, demonstrate (esp. *refl.*): to confirm: to sanction or ratify: to think well of, to be pleased with: to commend.—*v.i.* to judge favourably, to be pleased (with *of*).—*adj.* **approv'-able** deserving approval.—*n.* **approv'al** approbation.—*adv.* **approv'ingly.**—**approved school** (1933 (Scotland 1937) to 1969) a state boarding school for young people who have broken the law or who are pronounced to be in need of care and protection.—**on approval** (*coll.* **appro** (*ap'rō*)) subject to approval: without obligation to buy. [O.Fr. *aprover*—L. *ap-probāre—ad,* to, and *probāre,* to test or try—*probus,* good.]

approximate *ə-proks'im-it, adj.* close together: nearest or next: approaching correctness (**very approximate** very nearly exact; but by some used to mean very rough).—*v.t.* (*-āt*) to bring near: to come or be near to.—*v.i.* to come near (to), approach.—*adj.* **approx'imal** close together: next to.—*adv.* **approx'i-mately** (abbrev. **approx'**).—*n.* **approxima'tion** an approach: an imprecise account, calculation, etc.: a result in mathematics not rigorously exact, but so near the truth as to be sufficient for a given purpose. —*adj.* **approx'imative** (*-i-mā-tiv,-i-mə-tiv*) approaching closely. [L. *approximāre, -ātum—ad,* to, *prox-imus,* nearest, superl. adj.—*prope,* near.]

appui *a-pwē', n.* support: the reciprocal action between horse's mouth and rider's hand. [Fr.— O.Fr. *apuyer*—assumed L.L *appodiāre*—L *ad,* to, *podium,* support.]

appurtenance *ə-pûr'tən-əns, n.* that which appertains an appendage or accessory. a right belonging to a property (*law*).—*adj.* and *n.* **appur'tenant.** [A.Fr. *apurtenance*—O Fr. *apertenance*—*apertenir.* See **appertain.**]

apraxia *a-praks'ı-ə, n.* an inability, not due to paralysis, to perform voluntary purposeful movements of parts of the body, caused by brain lesion [Gr , inaction]

après-ski, apres- *a-pre-skē, -prā-, n* (evening period of, or clothes, etc suitable for) amusements after skiing —Also *adj* [Fr.]

apricot *ā'prı-kot, -kət,* or *a', n* a fruit of the plum genus, roundish, pubescent, orange-coloured, of a rich aromatic flavour. its colour. the tree that bears it. [Port *albrıcoque*—Ar *al-bırqūq*—*al,* the, Late Gr. *praıkokıon*—L *praecoquum* or *praecox,* early ripe]

April *ā'prıl, -prəl, n.* the fourth month of the year — **April fool** one hoaxed, deceived, or sent upon a bootless errand on the first of April [L *Aprīlis.*]

a priori *ā prī-ō'rī, -o', L a prē-ōr'ē,* the term applied to reasoning from what is prior, logically or chronologically, e.g reasoning from cause to effect, from a general principle to its consequences, even from observed fact to another fact or principle not observed, or to arguing from pre-existing knowledge, or even cherished prejudices; from the forms of cognition independent of experience (*Kant*) —*ns* **aprió'rism; apriority** (*-or'ı-tı*) [L. *ā,* from, *prıōrī* (abl), preceding.]

apron *ā'prən, n* a cloth or piece of leather or the like worn in front: an English bishop's short cassock anything resembling an apron in shape or use. a timber behind the stem of a ship a stage or part of stage in front of the proscenium arch, projecting to greater or less extent into the auditorium (also **a'pron-stage**)· a rim, border, etc.: ground-surface at entrance to a hangar, lock, etc . an extent of e g. gravel, sand, spread outward from a source (*geol.*).—**a'pron-string** a string by which an apron is tied —**tied to a woman's apron-strings** bound as a child to its mother. [M.E *napron*—O Fr *naperon*—*nappe,* cloth, tablecloth—L *mappa,* a napkin (*an apron* from *a napron,* cf **adder**)]

apropos *a-prō-pō', -prə-, adv* to the purpose appropriately in reference to (with *of*). by the way, incidentally.—*adj* to the purpose. [Fr *à propos* See **propose, purpose.**]

apse *aps, n.* a semicircular or polygonal recess, esp at the east end of a church choir —*adj.* **ap'sidal** of an apse or apsis —*n* **aps'is** in an orbit, the point of greatest or least distance from the central body. an apse —*pl* **aps'idēs** (*-z,* or *-id-ēz*) [L. *apsıs, -īdıs*— Gr *hapsıs* (*apsıs*), *-idos,* a felly, wheel, arch, loop— *haptein,* to fit, connect]

apso. See **Lhasa apso.**

apt *apt, adj.* fitting fit. suitable: apposite tending (to) liable: ready or prone· open to impressions. ready to learn (often with *at*). likely (to).—*n.* **ap'titude** fitness tendency (with *to*) natural ability, readiness to learn (with *for*)—*adv* **apt'ly.**—*n* **apt'ness.** [L *aptus,* fit, suitable]

apterous *ap'tər-əs, adj* wingless [Gr *a-,* priv , *pteron,* feather, wing. side-wall]

Apteryx *ap'tər-ıks, n* a genus of birds, the kiwis (without *cap*) a member of the genus.—*pl.* **ap'teryxes.** [Gr *a-,* priv , *pteryx, -ygos,* wing]

aqua *ak'wə,* (L) *n.* water.—**aqua-for'tis, aquafor'tis** nitric acid. etching with nitric acid (L *fortıs,* strong), **aquafor'tist** an etcher or engraver who uses aqua-fortis, **aqua-regia** (*rē'jyə,* L *rā'gı-a*) a mixture of nitric and hydrochloric acids, which dissolves the

royal (L *rēgius, -a, -um*) metal, gold, **aqua-vitae** (*vī'tē, wē'tı,* of life) alcohol: brandy, whisky, etc [L. *aqua,* water.]

aqua- *ak'wə-, ak'wa-,* in composition. water —*ns.* **a'quaculture, a'quiculture** the practice of using the sea, lakes, rivers, etc. for fish-farming, shellfish cultivation, the growing of plants, etc., **a'quafer** aquifer, **a'qualung** a lightweight, self-contained diving apparatus with compressed-air supply carried on the back, **a'quaplane** a board on which one stands and is towed behind a motor-boat —*v ı.* to ride on an aquaplane· (of a car, etc.) to travel or skid on a film of water which has built up between the tyres and the road surface —*ns* **a'quaplaner; a'quaplaning; aquifer** (*ak'wı-fer*), **aquafer** (*geol.*) any formation containing water sufficient to supply wells, etc [L *aqua,* water]

aquamarine *ak-wə-mə-rēn', n.* a pale green beryl —*adj* bluish-green [L. *aqua marina,* sea water—*mare,* the sea.]

aquaplane, etc. See **aqua-.**

aquarelle *ak-wə-rel', n.* water-colour painting. a painting in (transparent) water-colours.—*n* **aquarell'ist.** [Fr ,—It *acquerella, acquarella*—*acqua*—L. *aqua.*]

aquarium *ə-kwā'rı-əm, n.* a tank or (a building containing) a series of tanks for keeping aquatic animals or plants.—*pl.* **aquā'riums, aquā'ria.**—*adj* **aquā'rian.**—*n.* one who keeps an aquarium —*ns.* **aquā'riist, aquā'rist** (or *a'kwə-*) an aquarian.—*n.* **Aquā'rius** the Water-bearer, a sign of the zodiac, and a constellation once coincident with it [L *aquārıus, -a, -um, adj* —*aqua,* water.]

aquatic *ə-kwat'ık, -kwot', adj* living, growing, practising sports, taking place, in or on water —*n.* an aquatic plant, animal, or sportsman. (in *pl.*) water sports. [L. *aquātıcus*—*aqua,* water]

aquatint *ak'wə-tınt, n.* a mode of etching on copper with resin and nitric acid.—Also **aquatint'a.**—*v ı* and *v.ı.* a'**quatint** to engrave in aquatint [It. *acqua tınta,* dyed water—L. *aqua,* water, and *tıngĕre, tınctum,* to dye.]

aquavit *ak'wə-vēt, ak', n.* a Scandinavian spirit flavoured with caraway seeds —Also **ak'vavit.** [Dan , Sw , Norw *akvavıt*—Mediaeval L *aqua vītae*]

aqueduct *ak'wı-dukt, n.* an artificial channel or pipe for conveying water, most commonly understood to mean a bridge across a valley· a bridge carrying a canal a small passage in an animal body [L *aqua,* water, *dūcĕre, ductum,* to lead]

aqueous *ā'kwı-əs, adj* of water. watery. deposited by water. [L *aqua,* water]

aquiculture, aquifer. See **aqua-.**

Aquila *ak'wı-lə, n.* the golden eagle genus —*adj* **aq'uiline** (*-līn*) of the eagle hooked like an eagle's beak [L *aquıla,* eagle]

Arab *ar'əb, n* one of the Semitic people inhabiting Arabia and neighbouring countries: an Arabian horse a neglected or homeless boy or girl (usu. **street** or **city Arab**).—*adj* Arabian —*adj* **Arabian** (*ə-rā'bı-ən, -byən*) of or belonging to Arabia or the Arabs —*n.* a native of Arabia —*adj.* **Arabic** (*ar'əb-ık*) relating to Arabia, or to its language —*n.* the language of the Arabs see also **gum.**—*v ı* **ar'abise, -ize** to make Arab —*n.* **arabisā'tion, -z-.**— *ns.* **Ar'abism** an Arabic idiom, **Ar'abist** one learned in, or studying, Arabic culture, history, language, etc , **Ar'aby** a poetical form of *Arabia* —**Arabian camel** a one-humped camel, **Arabian** or **Arabic numerals** the numerals in ordinary use in arithmetic, transmitted from India to Europe by the Arabs [L *Arabs, Arabıs*—Gr. *Araps, Arabos.*]

arabesque *ur-ə-besk', adj* after the manner of Arabian

designs.—*n.* a fantastic painted or sculptured ornament among the Spanish Moors, consisting of foliage and other forms curiously intertwined: a musical composition with analogous continuity: a posture in ballet dancing in which one leg is stretched out backwards parallel with the ground and the body is bent forward from the hips. [Fr.,—It. *arabesco; -esco* corresponding to Eng *-ish*]

arabise, Arabism, etc. See **Arab.**

arable *ar'ə-bl, adj.* fit for ploughing or tillage. [L *arābilis—arāre*]

Araby. See **Arab.**

Araceae, araceous. See **Arum.**

Arachnida *a-rak'ni-də, n.pl.* a class of Arthropoda, embracing spiders, scorpions, mites, etc.—*n.* **arach'nid** any member of the class.—*n.* and *adj.* **arach'-nidan.**—*adj.* **arach'noid** like a cobweb.—*n* the arachnoid membrane.—*adjs.* **arachnoi'dal; arach-nolog'ical.**—*ns* **arachnol'ogist** one who studies the Arachnida; **arachnol'ogy.—arachnoid membrane** one of the three coverings of the brain and spinal cord, between the dura-mater and pia-mater, nonvascular, transparent, thin [Gr *arachnē,* spider.]

arak. Once *obs.,* now more usu., spelling of **arrack.**

Aralia *ə-rā'li-ə, n* a genus of the ivy family, **Aralia'ceae,** much grown as decorative plants: (without *cap.*) a plant of the genus.—*adj.* **aralia'ceous.** [Perh. American Indian origin.]

Aramaic *ar-ə-mā'ik, adj.* relating to Aramaea, or Aram (roughly, modern Syria), or to its language—also **Aramaean** (-*mē'ən*).—*n.* any of a group of Semitic languages (including that spoken by Christ) once used in this and neighbouring areas in commerce and government —*n.* **Aramā'ism** an Aramaic idiom. [Gr *Aramaios.*]

Aran *a'rən, adj.* (of knitwear) made in a style or with a pattern that originated in the *Aran* Islands, off the south-west of Ireland.

arapaima *ar-ə-pī'mə, n* a gigantic South American river-fish, chief food-fish of the Amazon, reaching sometimes 4 cwt. [Tupi origin.]

Araucaria *a-ro-kā'ri-ə, n.* the monkey-puzzle genus, coniferous trees of S. America and Australasia (without *cap.*) a tree of the genus. [*Arauco,* in S Chile]

arbalest *ar'bəl-est, n* a crossbow. a cross-staff.—Also **ar'balist.**—*ns* **ar'balester, ar'balister** a crossbowman. [L. *arcuballista—arcus,* bow, *ballista* (see **ballista**), partly through O E *arblast*—O Fr *arbaleste.*]

arbiter *ar'bi-tər, n* a judge. an umpire one chosen by parties to decide between them one who has absolute control:—*fem* **ar'bitress.**—*adj* **ar'bitrable.**—*ns* **ar'bitrage** (*-trij*) arbitration: traffic in bills or exchange or stocks to profit by different prices in different markets.—*n* **arbit'rament** (now less usu **arbit'rement**) the decision of an arbiter. determination. power of decision —*v i* and *v t* **ar'bitrate** to decide, determine to refer to arbitration· to judge as arbiter —*ns.* **arbitra'tion** (submission to) the decision of an arbiter, **ar'bitrator** arbiter [L] **arbiter elegantiarum** *ar'bit-er el-e-gan-shi-ār'əm, el-e-gan-ti-ar'ōōm,* (L) judge of taste.

arbitrary *ar'bi-trər-i, adj.* not bound by rules. despotic, absolute. capricious: arising from accident rather than from rule —*adv* **ar'bitrarily.**—*n.* **ar'bitrariness.** [L *arbitrārius—arbiter*]

arbor *ar'bər, n.* a tree: a shaft or beam· a spindle or axis —*adjs* **arborā'ceous** tree-like: wooded, **arboreal** (*arbō'ri-əl, -bo'*) of, of the nature of, trees· tree-dwelling, **arbo'reous** of or belonging to trees: tree-like: in the form of a tree wooded —*n* **arbor-esc'ence,** a tree-like growth a tree-like crystalline

formation.—*adj.* **arboresc'ent** growing, formed, branched, like a tree: approaching the character of a tree.—*n.* **arbore'tum** (L. *àr-bor-ā'tōōm*) a botanic garden of trees:—*pl.* **arbore'ta.**—*adj.* **arboricul'-tural.**—*ns.* **ar'boriculture** forestry, the culture of trees, esp. timber-trees; **arboricul'turist; arboris-ā'tion, -z-** an arborescence; **ar'borist** one who studies trees.—**arbor vitae** (L., tree of life; *vi'tē, wē'ti*) a coniferous tree of the genus Thuja, akin to cypress· a tree-like appearance seen when the human cerebellum is cut vertically [L. *arbor,* tree.]

arbour *ar'bər, n.* a retreat or bower of trees or climbing plants [A F. *herber*—L *herbārium—herba,* grass, herb, meaning changed through confusion with L. *arbor,* tree.]

arc *ark, n.* a part of the circumference of a circle or other curve· a luminous discharge of electricity across a gap between two conductors or terminals.—*v i.* to form an arc:—*pr.p.* **arc(k)'ing;** *pa.t.* and *pa.p.* **arc(k)ed'.**—*n* **arc(k)'ing.**—*ns.* **arc-lamp, arc-light** a lamp whose source of light is an electric arc between carbon electrodes; **arc-welding** see **weld**[2]. [L *arcus,* a bow.]

arcade *ar-kād', n* a row of arches, open or closed, on columns or pilasters: a walk arched over. a covered passageway lined with shops —*adj.* **arcād'ed.**—*n.* **arcād'ing.** [Fr.,—L.L *arcāta,* arched, see **arch**[1].]

Arcadian *ar-kād'i-ən, adj.* of *Arcadia* (*poet.* **Arcady** *ar'kə-di*), a district in Greece whose people were primitive in manners and given to music and dancing· pastoral: simple, innocent.—Also *n —n.* **Arcad'ianism.**

arcanum *ar-kān'əm, n* a secret. a mystery: a secret remedy or elixir:—*pl* **arcan'a.**—*adj.* **arcane'** secret: mysterious —*adv* **arcane'ly.**—*n.* **arcane'ness.** [L., neut. of *arcānus—arca,* a chest]

arch[1] *arch, n* a structure of wedge-shaped stones or other pieces supporting each other by mutual pressure and able to sustain a superincumbent weight. anything of like form. an archway the part from heel to toes of the bony structure of the foot, normally having an upward curve.—*v.t.* to cover or furnish with an arch —*v t* and *v i.* to bend in the form of an arch —*adj.* **arched** having the form of an arch. covered with an arch.—*adv.* **arch'wise** in the manner of an arch —**arch'way** an arched or vaulted passage —**dropped** or **fallen arch** a flattened foot arch [O Fr *arche*—L *arcus,* bow (as if *arca*)]

arch[2] *arch, adj* cunning waggish roguish shrewd —*adv* **arch'ly.**—*n* **arch'ness.** [From the prefix *arch-,* in words such as *arch-*rogue, etc]

arch- *arch-* (*ark-* in direct borrowings from Greek), *pfx* first or chief· often an intensive in an odious sense.—*ns* **arch'-druid** a chief or presiding druid; **arch'-en'emy** a chief enemy. Satan—also **arch's fiend'; arch'-priest'** a chief priest. in early times, a kind of vicar to the bishop—later, a rural dean a superior appointed by the Pope to govern the secular priests sent into England from the foreign seminaries during the period 1598–1621, **arch-stone** see **voussoir; arch'-vill'ain** one supremely villainous [O.E *arce-, ærce-,* through L. from Gr. *archi-—archos,* chief]

Archaean *ar-kē'ən,* (geol) *adj* and *n* (of or relating to) the oldest geological period, early Pre-Cambrian [Gr *archaios,* ancient—*archē,* beginning.]

archaeology, archeology *ark-i-ol'ə-ji, n.* the scientific study of human antiquities, usu as discovered by excavation —*adj* **archaeological** (*-ə-loj'i-kl*) —*adv* **archaeolog'ically.**—*n.* **archaeol'ogist.** [Gr *archaios,* ancient—*archē,* beginning, *logos,* discourse]

archaeopteryx *ar-ki-op'tər-iks, n* a Jurassic fossil bird

For other sounds see detailed chart of pronunciation

of the Archaeopteryx genus, with a long bony tail [Gr *orchaios*, ancient, *pteryx*, wing]

archaic *ar-kā'ık, adj.* ancient: savouring of the past: not absolutely obsolete but no longer in general use: old-fashioned.—*adv.* archā'ically.—*n.* archā'icism. —*v.i* ar'chāise, -ıze to imitate the archaic —*ns.* ar'chāiser, -z-; ar'chāism inclination to archaic: an archaic word or phrase; ar'chāist.—*adj.* archāist'ic affectedly or imitatively archaic. [Gr *archaikos*— *archaios*, ancient—*archē*, beginning]

archangel *ark'ān-jl,* or *-ān',* *n.* an angel of the highest order.—*adj.* **archangelic** (*-an-jel'*) [Gr *archangelos*—*archos,* chief, *angelos,* messenger]

archbishop *arch-bısh'əp,* or *arch',* *n.* a metropolitan bishop who superintends the bishops in his province, and also exercises episcopal authority in his own diocese.—*n* **archbish'opric** the office or jurisdiction of, or area governed by, an archbishop [O E. *ærce-biscop,* see **arch-,** and **bishop.**]

archdeacon *arch-dē'kn,* or *arch',* *n.* a chief deacon: the ecclesiastical dignitary having the chief supervision of a diocese or part of it, next under the bishop —*n.* **archdeac'onry** the office, jurisdiction, or residence of an archdeacon [O E *ærcediacon*; see **arch-,** and **deacon.**]

archdiocese *ärch-dī'ə-sıs, -sēs, n* an archbishop's diocese.

archduke *ärch'dūk, ärch'dūk', (hist.) n.* the title of certain early reigning dukes of importance, and of princes of the imperial house of Austria:—*fem.* **archduchess** (*ärch'duch'is*).—*adj.* **arch'dū'cal.**—*ns.* **arch'duch'y, arch'duke'dom.** [**arch-,** chief, and **duke.**]

archegonium *ärk-i-gō'ni-əm, n.* the flask-shaped female reproductive organ of mosses and ferns, and (in a reduced form) of flowering plants:—*pl* **archego'nia.** [Gr. *archegonos,* founder of a race.]

archer *ärch'ər, n.* one who shoots with a bow and arrows: (with *the*) the constellation and sign of the zodiac Sagittarius:—*fem.* **arch'eress.**—*n.* **arch'ery** the art or sport of shooting with the bow: a company of archers.—**arch'er-fish** an Indian fish that catches insects by shooting water at them from its mouth. [O.Fr. *archier*—L *arcārius*—*arcus,* a bow.]

archetype *ark'i-tīp, n.* the original pattern or model, prototype.—*adjs* **archetyp'al, archetyp'ical.** [Gr *archetypon, arche-, archi-,* and *typos,* a model.]

Archichlar.ydeae *är-ki-klə-mid'i-ē, (bot.) n.pl.* one of the main divisions of the Dicotyledons, in which the petals, if present, are in general not united.—*adj* **archichlamyd'eous.** [Gr. pfx. *archi-* denoting primitiveness, *chlamys, -ydos,* mantle]

archidiaconal *är-ki-dī-ak'ə-nl, adj.* of an archdeacon. [Gr *archidiakonos*; see **deacon.**]

archiepiscopal *är-ki-i-pis'kə-pl, adj.* of an archbishop. —*ns.* **archiepis'copacy, archiepis'copate** dignity or province of an archbishop.—**archiepiscopal cross** a patriarchal cross. [Gr. *archiepiskopos,* archbishop]

archil *är'chıl, -kıl, n.* a red or violet dye made from various lichens: a lichen yielding it, esp. species of Roccella —Also **orchel** (*or'chəl*), **orchella** (*-chel'ə*), **or'chil, orchill'a.** [O.Fr. *orchel, orseil* (Fr. *orseille*) —It. *orcello,* origin undetermined.]

Archimedean *ark-i-mē-dē'ən,* or *-mē'di-ən, adj.* pertaining to *Archimedes,* a celebrated Greek mathematician of Syracuse (*c.* 287-212 в c.) —**Archimedean screw** a machine for raising water. etc., in simplest form a tube bent spirally turning on its axis; **Archimedean spiral** the curve described by a point moving uniformly along a uniformly revolving radius vector, its polar equation being $r = a\theta$; **principle of**

Archimedes that a body weighed when immersed wholly or partly in a fluid shows a loss of weight equal to the weight of fluid it displaces

Archipelago *ark-i-pel'ə-gō, n.* the Aegean Sea: (without *cap*) a sea abounding in islands, hence a group of islands.—*pl* archipel'ago(e)s.—*adj* archipelagic (*-pi-laj'ik*) [An Italian compound *arcipelago* from Gr *archi-,* chief, *pelagos,* sea, with pfx. restored to Gr form]

architect *ark'i-tekt, n* a designer of buildings: a designer of ships (*naval architect*): a maker a contriver.—*v.t* to plan or design as an architect.—*adj.* **architecton'ic** pertaining to architecture. constructive controlling, directing: pertaining to the arrangement of knowledge —*n.* (often in *pl.* form) the science of architecture the systematic arrangement of knowledge —*adj.* **architec'tural** (*-chər-əl*) —*n.* **arch'itecture** the art or science of building: structure: in specific sense, one of the fine arts, the art of designing buildings: style of building: the overall design of the hardware and software of a computer, particularly of the former [Gr. *architektōn,* master-builder—*archi-,* chief, and *tektōn,* a builder.]

architrave *ark'i-trāv, (archit)* *n* the lowest division of the entablature resting immediately on the abacus of the column: collective name for the various parts, jambs, lintels, etc , that surround a door or window: moulding round an arch.—*adj* **arch'itraved.** [It. *architrave*—Gr. *archi-,* chief, and L *trabs, trabis,* a beam.]

archive *ärk'īv, n.* (usu in *pl.*) a repository of public records or of records and monuments generally: public records: (rare in *sing*) a document, monument.—*adj* **archiv'al** (or *ark'i-vəl*) —*n.* **archivist** (*ark'i-vıst*) a keeper of archives or records. [Fr.—L.L. *archī(v)um*—Gr. *archeion,* magisterial residence—*archē,* government]

archivolt *ar'ki-vōlt, n.* the under-curve of an arch. moulding on it. [It *archivolto*—*arco* (L. *arcus,* an arch) and *volta,* vault]

archon *ärk'on, -ən, n.* one of nine chief magistrates of ancient Athens.—*ns* **arch'onship; arch'ontate** the archon's tenure of office.—*adj.* **archontic** (*-ont'ik*). [Gr. *archōn, -ontos,* pr.p. of *archein,* to be first, to rule.]

arco saltando *är'kō säl-tán'dō, (mus.)* with rebounding bow.—*n.* a quick staccato.—**(coll')** **arco** (*mus*) with the bow, a direction marking the end of a pizzicato passage [It]

Arctic, arctic *ark'tık, adj.* relating to the Great Bear, or to the north: extremely cold.—*n.* (usu *cap.* and with the) the area lying north of the Arctic Circle or north of the timber line.—*adj.* **arc'toid** bear-like.—**Arctic Circle** the parallel of latitude 66°32'N, bounding the region of the earth surrounding the north terrestrial pole. [Gr. *arktos,* a bear.]

arctophile *ärk'tə-fīl, n.* a lover or collector of teddy-bears. [Gr *arktos,* bear, and **-phile.**]

arcuate *ar'kū-āt,* **arcuated** *-id, adjs.* arched —*n.* **arcua'tion.** [L *arcuātus,* pa p. of *arcuāre,* to bend like a bow—*arcus,* a bow]

ardent *ärd'ənt, adj.* burning. fiery: fervid: combustible, inflammable (*obs.* except in **ardent spirits,** distilled alcoholic liquors, whisky, brandy, etc).—*n.* **ard'ency.**—*adv.* **ard'ently.**—*n.* **ard'our** warmth of passion or feeling: eagerness: enthusiasm (with *for*). [L *ardēns, -entis,* pr p. of *ardēre,* to burn.]

arduous *ard'ū-əs, adj* steep, difficult to climb: difficult to accomplish: laborious —*adv.* **ard'u-ously.**—*n.* **ard'uousness.** [L. *arduus,* steep, high.]

are [1] *ar, n.* the unit of the metric land measure, 100 sq. metres [Fr .—L *ārea,* a site, space, court.]

are[2] *ār*, used as plural of the present indicative of the verb *to be*. [Old Northumbrian *aron*, which ousted the usual O.E. *sind, sindon*; both from the root *es-*.]

area *ā′ri-ə*, *n.* a space or piece of ground: a portion of surface: a region (*lit.* and *fig.*): the floor of a theatre, etc.: a sunken space alongside the basement of a building: superficial extent.—*adj.* **ā′real**.—**area code** (*U.S.*) a three-digit number used before the local telephone number when dialling long-distance telephone calls. [L. *ārea*, an open empty place, etc.]

Areca *ar′i-kə, ə-rē′, n.* the betel-nut genus of palms: (without *cap.*) a tree of the genus.—**areca-nut** betel-nut, the nut of *Areca catechu*, chewed by the Malays, southern Indians, etc., with lime in a betel-pepper leaf. [Port.,—Malayalam *adekka*.]

arena *ə-rē′nə, n.* part of the ancient amphitheatre strewed with sand for combats: any place of public contest: any sphere of action.—*adj.* **arenaceous** (*ar-i-nā′shəs*) sandy: composed of sand or quartz grains: with shell of agglutinated sand-grains: sand-growing. —**arena stage** a stage which can have audience all round it (see **theatre-in-the-round** under **theatre**). [L. *arēna*, sand]

aren't *ärnt*. Contraction of **are not.**

areola *a-rē′ō-lə, n.* a small area: a small space marked off by lines, or a slightly sunken spot (*biol.*): an interstice in a tissue (*physiol.*): any circular spot such as that around the nipple (*physiol.*): the part of the iris of the eye bordering on the pupil (*physiol.*):—*pl.* **arē′olae** (*-lē*).—*adjs.* **arē′olar; arē′olate, arē′olated** divided into small areas.—*ns.* **arēolā′tion** division into areolae; **areole** (*ar′i-ōl*) an areola: a spiny or hairy spot on a cactus. [L. *āreola*, dim. of *ārea*.]

Areopagus *ar-i-op′əg-əs, n.* the Hill of Arēs, on which the supreme court of ancient Athens was held: the court itself: any important tribunal.—*n.* **Areop′agite** (*-gīt, -jīt*), a member of the Areopagus. [Latinised from Gr. *Areios pagos*, hill of Arēs (identified with Roman Mars).]

arête *a-ret′, n.* a sharp ridge: esp. in French Switzerland, a rocky edge on a mountain. [Fr.,—L. *arista*, an ear of corn, fish-bone, spine.]

Aretinian *ar-i-tin′i-ən, adj.* pertaining to Guido of Arezzo (d 1050).—**Aretinian syllables** the initial syllables of the half-lines of a hymn to John the Baptist, which, falling on successive notes of the diatonic scale, were used (apparently by Guido) as names for the notes:—*Ut* queant laxis *resonare* fibris *Mi*ra gestorum *famu*li tuorum, *Sol*ve polluti *labi*i reatum, Sancte Ioannes. See **gamut.** [L. *Arētīnus, Arrētinus,* of Arrētium or Arezzo.]

argala *ar′gə-lə, n.* the adjutant stork. [Hind. *hargīla*.]

argali *ar′gə-li, n.* the great wild sheep (*Ovis ammon*) of Asia. [Mongol.]

argent *arj′ənt, adj.* and *n.* silver: silvery-white: white (*her.*).—*adjs.* **argentif′erous** silver-bearing; **ar′gentine** (*-īn*) of or like silver: sounding like silver: (with *cap*) of, or belonging to, Argentina or its people.—*n.* white metal coated with silver: spongy tin: a small smelt with silvery sides: (with *cap.*) a native or citizen of Argentina (also **Argentino** *-tē′nō*, Sp. *ar-hhen-tē′nō*).—*n.* **ar′gentite** silver-glance, native sulphide of silver. [Fr.,—L. *argentum,* silver; the republic is named from the Rio de la Plata (silver river).]

argie-bargie. See under **argue.**

argil *är′jil, n.* potter's clay: pure clay or alumina.—*adj.* **argillā′ceous** clayey.—*n.* **ar′gillite** an indurated clay rock. [L. *argilla,* Gr *argillos,* white clay—*argēs,* white.]

arginine *ar′ji-nin, n.* one of the basic amino acids.

Argive *ar′gīv, -jīv, adj.* belonging to *Argos:* Greek.— Also *n.*

argle-bargle. See under **argue.**

argol *ar′gol, n.* a hard crust formed on the sides of wine-vessels, from which cream of tartar and tartaric acid are obtainable—generally reddish. [Prob. conn. with Gr. *argos,* white.]

argon *ar′gon, n.* a colourless, odourless inert gas (at. numb. 18; symbol Ar) discovered in the atmosphere in 1894 by Rayleigh and Ramsay. [Gr. *ārgon* (neut.) inactive—*a-,* priv., *ergon,* work.]

Argonaut *ar′gō-not, n.* one of those who sailed in the ship Argo in search of the golden fleece: (without *cap.*) the paper nautilus (*Argonauta*).—*adj.* **argonaut′ic.** [Gr *Argō,* and *nautēs,* a sailor.]

argot *ar′gō, n.* slang, originally that of thieves and vagabonds: cant. [Fr.; of unknown origin.]

argue *arg′ū, v.t.* to prove or indicate: to give reason to believe: to seek to show by reasoning: to discuss with reasoning: to persuade or bring by reasoning (into or out of course of action).—*v.i.* to offer reasons: to contend with reasoning: to contradict.—*adj.* **arg′ū-able** capable of being maintained: capable of being disputed.—*adv.* **ar′gūably.**—*n.* **arg′ūer.**—*v.i.* **ar′gūfy** (*coll.*) to bandy arguments: to wrangle.—*v.t.* to beset with wrangling.—*ns.* **ar′gūment** proof: evidence: a reason or series of reasons offered or possible towards proof or inducement (with *for* or *against*): exchange of such reasons: debate: matter of debate or contention: a summary of subject-matter: a quantity upon which another depends, or under which it is to be sought in a table (*math.*): the angle between a vector and its axis of reference (*math.*); **argūmentā′tion** reasoning: sequence or exchange of arguments.—*adj.* **argūment′ative** controversial: addicted to arguing.—*adv.* **argūment′atively.**—*n.* **argūment′ativeness.**—*v.t.* **ar′gy-bar′gy, ar′gie-bar′gie, ar′gle-bar′gle** (*orig. Scot.*) to argue tediously or vexatiously.—*n.* a bandying of argument. [Fr. *arguer*—L. *argūtāre,* freq. of *argūere,* to show, accuse; *argūmentum,* proof, accusation, summary of contents.]

Argus *ar′gəs, n.* in Greek mythology, Io's guardian, whose hundred eyes Hera transferred to the peacock's tail: a vigilant watcher: (without *cap.*) an East Indian pheasant (**argus pheasant**) of the genus *Argusianus.* (without *cap.*) a butterfly with many eye-spots on the wings (as some *Lycaenidae* and *Satyridae*): (without *cap.*) an ophiuroid with much-divided coiling arms.—*adj.* **Ar′gus-eyed′.** [Gr. *Argos,* lit , bright.]

argute *ar-gūt′, adj.* shrill: keen shrewd.—*adv.* **argute′ly.**—*n.* **argute′ness.** [L. *argūtus.*]

argy-bargy. See under **argue.**

arhythmia, arhythmic. See **arrhythmic.**

aria *ä′ri-ə,* (*mus.*) *n.* an air or melody, esp. an accompanied vocal solo in a cantata, oratorio, or opera: a regular strain of melody followed by another in contrast and complement, and then repeated *da capo.* [It., from root of **air.**]

Arian *ā′ri-ən, adj.* pertaining to, or following, *Arius* of Alexandria (d. 336)—*n.* one who adheres to the doctrines of Arius: a Unitarian.—*n.* **A′rianism.**

arid *ar′id, adj.* dry: parched: barren: jejune.—*ns.* **arid′ity, ar′idness**—*adv.* **ar′idly.** [L. *aridus.*]

ariel *ā′ri-əl, n.* a kind of gazelle. [Ar. *aryil.*]

Aries *ā′ri-ēz, n.* the Ram, a constellation giving name to, and formerly coinciding with, a sign of the zodiac. —**first point of Aries** the intersection of equator and ecliptic passed by the sun in (the northern) spring, now actually in Pisces. [L. *ariēs, -etis,* ram.]

arietta *ar-i-et′ə,* (*mus*) *n.* a little aria or air.—Also (Fr.) **ariette** (*-et′*). [It. *arietta,* dim. of *aria.*]

aright *ə-rīt′, adv.* in a right way: rightly: on or to the right. [Prep. **a,** and **right.**]

aril *ar′il, n.* a covering or appendage of some seeds, an outgrowth of the funicle: sometimes, a caruncle (*false aril*).—*adjs.* **ar'illary, ar'illate, ar'illated** having an aril.—*n.* **ar'illode** a caruncle or false aril, from near the micropyle. [L.L. *arillus*, raisin.]

arioso *a-rı-ō'sō, adj.* and *adv.* in the melodious manner of an aria, or between aria and recitative.—Also *n*.. —*pl.* **arıo'sos, -si** (*-sē*). [It. *aria*.]

arise *a-rīz', v.ı.* to rise up: to take rise, originate (with *from, out of*): to come into being, view, or activity: —*pa.t.* **arose** (*a-rōz'*);*pa.p.* **arisen** (*a-riz'n*). [Pfx *a-*, up, out, and **rise**.]

arista *a-ris'ta, n.* an awn: a bristle-like appendage on some insects' antennae.—*adj.* **aris'tate** (or *ar'*) awned. [L. *arista*, an awn.]

aristocracy *ar-is-tok'ra-sı, n.* government by, or political power of, a privileged order: a state so governed: a nobility or privileged class: an analogous class in respect of any quality.—*n.* **aristocrat** (*ar'is-ta-krat*, or *a-ris'*; sometimes (*coll.*) shortened to **aristo** (*a'ris-tō* or *a-ris'tō:—pl.* **aristos**)) a member of an aristocracy: one who has the characteristics of or attributed to an aristocracy: a haughty person: one of the, or the, best of its kind.—*adjs.* **aristocrat'ic, -al** belonging to aristocracy: having the character that belongs to, or is thought to befit, aristocracy —*adv* **aristocrat'ically.**—*n.* **aristocratism** (*-tok'ra-tızm*) the spirit of, or belief in, aristocracy [Gr *aristokratiā—aristos*, best, and *kratos*, power.]

aristology *ar-is-tol'a-ji, n.* the science or art of dining. [Gr. *ariston*, breakfast, luncheon, *logos*, discourse.]

Aristotelian *ar-is-to-tē'li-an,* **Aristotelean** *ar-is-tot-i-lē'an, adj.* relating to Aristotle (Gr. *Aristotelēs*) or to his philosophy.—*n.* a follower of Aristotle —*ns.* **Aristote'lianism, Aristot'elism.**

arithmetic *a-rith'ma-tık, n.* the science of numbers: the art of reckoning by figures: a treatise on reckoning.— *adjs.* **arithmetic** (*ar-ith-met'ik*), **-al.**—*adv.* **arith-met'ically.**—*n.* **arithmetician** (*-ma-tish'n,* or *ar'*) one skilled in arithmetic.—**arithmetical progression** a series increasing or diminishing by a common difference, as 7, 10, 13, 16, 19, 22; or 12, 10½, 9, 7½, 6. [Gr. *arithmētikē* (*technē,* art), of numbers— *arithmos*, number.]

ark *ärk, n.* a chest or coffer: in Jewish history, the wooden coffer in which the Tables of the Law were kept: a large floating vessel, as Noah's in the Deluge (Gen. vi-viii): a toy representing Noah's ark. [O.E *arc* (*earc*)—L. *arca*, a chest—*arcēre*, to guard.]

arkose *är-kōs', n.* a sandstone rich in feldspar grains, formed from granite, etc.

arm¹ *ärm, n.* the fore-limb from shoulder to hand, esp. when used for purposes other than locomotion: a tentacle: a narrow projecting part: an inlet: a branch: a rail or support for the arm as on a chair: power (*fig.*).—*v.t.* to take in the arms: to conduct arm-in-arm.—*adj.* **armed** (usu. in composition) having an arm or arms, as *one-armed.*—*n* **arm'ful.**—*adj.* **arm'less.**—*n.* **arm'let** a little arm: a ring or band round the arm.—**arm'band** a band of cloth worn round the sleeve; **arm'chair'** a chair with arms.—*adj.* **arm'chair** amateur: stay-at-home: doctrinaire.— **arm'hole** the hole in a garment through which the arm is put.—*adv.* **arm'-in-arm'** with arms interlinked.— **arm'pit** the hollow under the shoulder.—**at arm's length** at a distance (*lit., fig.*), not showing friendliness or familiarity: (of negotiations, etc.) in which each party preserves its independent ability to bargain; **in arms** carried as a child: young enough for this; **right arm** the main support or assistant; **secular arm** the civil authority, opp. to the spiritual or ecclesiastical; **the long arm of the law** the far-reaching power and influence of the law—esp. the police force: **(with)in arm's reach** able to be reached easily.

i.e. from where one is sitting; **with open arms** with hearty welcome [O.E. *arm* (*earm*)]

arm² *arm, n.* a weapon: a branch of the fighting forces. —in *pl.* weapons of offence and defence: hostilities: fighting: soldiering: heraldic devices.—*v t* to furnish with weapons, means of protection, armature, or (*fig.*) equipment: to make (a bomb, etc.) ready to explode: to strengthen with a plate or otherwise — *v.i.* to take arms.—*ns* **ar'mament** a force equipped for war total means of making war: munitions, esp. for warships: act of arming or equipping for war: defensive equipment; **ar'mature** armour: any apparatus for defence: a wooden or wire support around which a sculpture, model, etc., is constructed: a piece of iron set across the poles of a magnet· a moving part in a magnetic circuit to indicate the presence of electric current: that part of a direct-current machine in which, in the case of a generator, the electromotive force is produced, or, in the case of a motor, the torque is produced.—*adj.* **armed** furnished with arms: provided with means of defence: thorny.— **arms race** competition among nations in building up armaments —**bear arms** to serve as a soldier· (also **give arms**) to show armorial bearings; **in arms** armed: quartered (*her.*); **lay down one's arms** to surrender, submit; **take (up) arms** to resort to fighting; **under arms** armed; **up in arms** in readiness to resist· protesting hotly [Fr *armes*, from L. *arma* (*pl.*); L. *armamenta*, tackle, equipment, *armātūra*, armour].

armada *ar-mä'da,* (sometimes *-mā'*), *n.* a fleet of armed ships, esp that sent by Philip II of Spain against England in 1588 [Sp , fem. pa p of *armar* —L. *armāre*, to arm.]

armadillo *arm-a-dil'ō, n* an American edentate armed with bands of bony plates:—*pl* **armadill'os.** [Sp , dim. of *armado*, armed; see foregoing.].

Armageddon *ar-ma-ged'n, n.* the great symbolical battlefield of the Apocalypse, scene of the final struggle between the powers of good and evil. a great war or battle of nations [*Harmagedōn* or *Armaged-dōn* given as Heb. name in Rev. xvi. 16]

Armagnac *ar-ma-nyak, n.* a dry brandy distilled in S.W. France [Name of district.]

armament, armature. See under **arm².**

Armenian *ar-mē'nyan, adj* belonging to *Armenia,* in Western Asia, or its people or language, or their branch of the Christian Church—*n* native of Armenia: one of the Armenian people: the language of the Armenians.

armiger *ar'mı-jar, n.* one entitled to a coat-of-arms· an esquire —*adjs.* **armi'geral, armi'gerous.** [L., an armour-bearer—*arma,* arms, *gerēre,* to bear.]

armilla *ar-mil'a, n.* bracelet (*archaeol.*; also **ar'mil**): frill on a mushroom stalk (*bot*) —*adj.* **armill'ary** (or *ar'*).—**armillary sphere** a skeleton sphere made up of hoops to show the motions of the heavenly bodies. [L. *armilla,* an armlet, dim of *armus,* the upper arm, the shoulder.]

Arminian *ar-min'i-an, n* a follower of *Arminius* (1560-1609), who denied the Calvinistic doctrine of absolute predestination, as well as irresistible grace —Also *adj* —*n.* **Armin'ianism.**

armistice *ar'mi-stis, n.* a suspension of hostilities: a truce —**Armistice Day** 11th Nov. 1918, the day fighting ended in the 1st World War, kept since as an anniversary. from 1946 as Remembrance Sunday (q.v.). [Fr ,—L.L. *armistitium*—L *arma,* arms, *sistēre,* to stop]

armlet. See **arm¹.**

armour, (*U.S* **armor**), *ar'mar, n.* defensive dress: protective covering: armoured vehicles: heraldic insignia —*adj.* **armō'rial** of heraldic arms —*n.* a book of coats-of-arms —*ns* **ar'morist** one skilled in heraldry;

ar'mory heraldry: armoury (*U.S.*): drill hall and headquarters of an army unit (*U.S.*): arsenal (*U.S.*).—*adj.* ar'moured protected by armour.—*n.* ar'mourer a maker, repairer or custodian of arms and armour.—*adj.* ar'mourless.—*n.* ar'moury a collection of arms and armour: a place where arms are kept: armour collectively.—ar'mour-bearer one carrying another's armour, a squire.—*adj.* ar'mour-clad' clad in armour.—ar'mour-clad an armoured ship, ar'moured-car', -crui'ser, -train'; ar'mour-plate a defensive plate for a ship, tank, etc.—*adj.* ar'mour-plat'ed.—armorial bearings the design in a coat of arms. [O.Fr. *armure*—L. *armātūra*—*arma*, arms.]

army *arm'ı*, *n.* a large body of people armed for war and under military command: a body of people banded together in a special cause, whether mimicking military methods as the 'Salvation Army', or not, as the 'Blue Ribbon Army': a host: a great number.—army ant any of several kinds of stinging ants which move about in vast numbers, army corps (*kōr, kor*) a miniature army comprising all arms of the service, army list a list of all commissioned officers; army worm the larva of a small fly (*Sciara*) that collects in vast armies: the larva of an American moth (*Leucania*) with the same habit. [Fr. *armée*, pa.p. fem. of *armer*—L. *armāre, -ātum* to arm.]

arnica *ar'nı-kə*, *n.* a tincture of the flowers of a composite plant, *Arnica montana*, or mountain tobacco, applied to sprains and bruises (but not to open wounds)

arnotto *ar-not'ō*. See annatto.

arnut *ar'nət*. Same as earth-nut.

aroid. See Arum.

aroma *ə-rō'mə*, *n.* a spicy fragrance: flavour or peculiar charm (*fig.*).—*adj.* aromatic (*ar-ō-mat'ık*) fragrant: spicy: in chemistry, belonging to the closed-chain class of organic compounds, or benzene derivatives—opp. to *fatty* or *aliphatic.*—Also *n.* [L., from Gr *arōma, -atos*, spice.]

arose. See arise.

around *ə-rownd'*, *prep.* on all sides of: round, round about: somewhere near: in existence or circulation.—*adv.* on every side: in a circle: round about, astir.—get around to (*coll.*) to reach the point of (doing something); have been around (*coll.*) to be experienced, sophisticated. [Prep. a, and around.]

arouse *ə-rowz'*, *v.t.* and *v.i.* to rouse: to stimulate.—*n.* an arousing, alarm.—*ns.* arous'al; arous'er. [Pfx. *a-*, intensive, and rouse[1].]

arpeggio *ar-ped'j(y)ō*, (*mus.*) *n.* a chord of which the notes are performed, not simultaneously, but in rapid (normally upward) succession: the notes of a chord played or sung, esp. as an exercise, in rapid ascending or descending progression, according to a set pattern:—*pl.* arpegg'ios.—*v.t.* arpegg'iate (*-ji-āt*) to perform or write in arpeggios.—*n.* arpeggia'tion. [It. *arpeggiare*, to play the harp—*arpa*, harp.]

arquebus(e), harquebus (*h*)*ár'kwi-bus*, *ns.* an old-fashioned handgun.—*n.* arquebusier (*-bus-ēr'*) a soldier armed with an arquebus. [Fr. *arquebuse*—Du. *haakbus*—*haak*, hook, and *bus*, box, barrel of a gun.]

arrack *ar'ək*, *n.* an ardent spirit used in the East, procured from toddy, or the fermented juice of the coco and other palms, as well as from rice and jaggery sugar. [Ar. *'araq*, juice.]

arraign *ə-rān'*, *v.t.* to call to account: to put upon trial: to accuse publicly.—*ns.* arraign'er; arraign'ing; arraign'ment. [O.Fr. *aresnier*—L.L. *arrationāre*—L. *ad*, to, *ratiō, -ōnis*, reason.]

arrange *ə-rānj'*, *v.t.* to set in a rank or row: to put in order: to settle: to adapt for other instruments or voices (*mus.*).—*v.i.* to come to an agreement (with

to): to make plans (with *for*).—*n.* arrange'ment. [O Fr. *arangier*—*à* (L *ad*, to), and *rangier, rengier*; see range.]

arrant *ar'ənt*, *adj.* downright, unmitigated, out-and-out: notorious: rascally [A variant of errant.]

arras *ar'əs*, *n.* tapestry (made at *Arras* in France). a hanging screen of tapestry for a wall.

array *ə-rā'*, *n.* order: dress: equipage: an imposing, purposeful, or significant arrangement: an arrangement of terms in rows and columns, (esp. if square) a matrix (*math.*).—*v.t.* to put in order: to arrange to empanel (jurors) (*law*): to dress, adorn, or equip —*n.* array'ment act of arraying. [A.Fr *arai*, O.Fr. *aret*, array, equipage—L. *ad*, and the Gmc root found in Eng ready, Ger. *bereit*]

arrear *ə-rēr'*, *n.* that which is in the rear or behind: (usu. in *pl*) that which remains unpaid or undone: (in *sing.* or *pl*) condition of being behind-hand.—in arrears behind-hand. esp. in the payment of rent, etc. [O Fr. *arere, ariere* (Fr *arrière*)—L. *ad*, to, *retrō*, back, behind.]

arrest *ə-rest'*, *v t.* to bring to a standstill, check. to seize: to catch, fix (as the attention) to apprehend by legal authority· to seize by warrant —*n* stoppage: seizure by warrant.—*adj* arrest'able.—*ns.* arrestation (*ar-es-tā'shən*) the act of arresting. arrest, arrestee' a person prevented by arrestment from making payment or delivery to another until the arrester's claim upon that other is secured or satisfied, arrest'er one who, or that which, arrests: a lightning-arrester: one who makes an arrestment (also arrest'or)—*adj.* arrest'ive tending to arrest.—*n.* arrest'ment a checking detention of a person arrested till liberated on bail, or by security (*law*): process which prohibits a debtor from handing over to his creditor money or property until a debt due by that creditor to a third party, the arrester, is paid or secured (*Scots law*).—arrester gear shock-absorbing transverse cables on an aircraft-carrier's deck for the arrester hook of an alighting aircraft to catch on: arrester hook a hook put out from an aircraft alighting on an aircraft-carrier, to catch on the arrester gear —arrest of judgment a delay between conviction and sentence because of possible error; cardiac arrest a heart attack: heart failure; under arrest, having been apprehended by legal authority. [O.Fr. *arester*—L. *ad*, to, *restāre*, to stand still.]

arrhythmic, arhythmic *ā-rith'mık, -ridh'*, *adj.* having an irregular or interrupted rhythm.—*n.* arrhyth'mia, arhyth'mia (*med.*) irregularity of the heart-beat. [Gr. *a-*, priv]

arrière-pensée *ar-ē-er-pä-sā*, (Fr.) *n* a mental reservation. a subsidiary aim

arris *ar'ıs*, *n.* a sharp edge on stone, metal, etc. at the meeting of two surfaces —arris rail a wooden, etc. rail of triangular section. [See arête.]

arrive *ə-rīv'*, *v.ı* to reach any place: to attain to any object (with *at*): to achieve success or recognition: to happen —*n.* arriv'al the act of arriving: a person or thing that arrives. [O.Fr. *ariver*—L.L. *adrīpāre*—L. *ad*, to, *rīpa*, shore.]

arrivederci, a rivederci *ar-ē-vəd-er'chē*, (It.) goodbye until we meet again.

arriviste *a'rē-vēst*, *n.* a person 'on the make': a parvenu: a self-seeker.—*n.* a'rrivisme. [Fr.].

arrogate *ar'ə-gāt*, *v.t* to claim as one's own. to claim proudly or unduly: to ascribe, attribute, or assign (to another).—*ns.* arr'ogance, arr'ogancy undue assumption of importance.—*adj.* arr'ogant claiming too much: overbearing.—*adv.* arr'ogantly.—*n.* arroga'tion act of arrogating. undue assumption [L *arrogāre*—*ad*, to, *rogāre, -ātum*, to ask, to claim.]

arrondissement *a-rɔ̄-dēs'mä*, *n.* a subdivision of a

French department [Fr ,—*arrondir*, to make round.]

arrow ar'ō, *n.* a straight, pointed missile, made to be shot from a bow or blowpipe: any arrow-shaped mark or object: the chief shoot of a plant, esp the flowering stem of the sugar-cane: (in *pl.*) darts (*coll.*).—*adj.* **arr'owy** of or like arrows.—**arr'ow-head** the head or pointed part of an arrow.—*adj.* **arr'ow-headed** shaped like the head of an arrow.—**arr'owroot** a West Indian plant, *Maranta arundinacea* or other species: its rhizome, esteemed in S. America as an antidote to arrow-poison: a nutritious starch from the rhizome: extended to other plants and their starch (see **Portland**); **arr'ow-shot** the range of an arrow. [O.E. *arwe*.]

arroyo ə-roi'ō, *n.* a rocky ravine: dry watercourse:—*pl.* **arroy'os.** [Sp.]

arse ars (U.S. ass as), (now *vulg.*) *n* the buttocks —*n* **arse'hole** (U.S. **ass'hole**) the anus (*vulg*): a worthless, contemptible, etc person (*vulg. slang*) — **arse licker, arse'-licker** (*vulg. slang*) an extremely obsequious person; **arse'-licking.**—**arse around, about** (*vulg. slang*) to mess around, do nothing in particular. [O E. *ærs* (*ears*).]

arsenal àrs'(ı-)nl, *n.* a magazine or manufactory for naval and military weapons and ammunition: a storehouse (*fig.*). [It. *arzenale*, *arsenale* (Sp., Fr *arsenal*)—Ar. *där accinä'ah*, workshop—(*där*, house), *al*, the, *çinä'ah*, art.]

arsenic ars'(ə-)nik, *n* the chemical element (As) of at number 33: a poison, the trioxide of the element (As₂O₃; **white arsenic**).—*ns.* **ar'senate, arseniate** (-sē'ni-ät) a salt of arsenic acid.—*adjs.* **arsenic** (-sen'ik), **-al, arse'nious** composed of or containing arsenic.—*ns* **ar'senide** a compound of arsenic with a metal; **ar'senite** a salt of arsenious acid; **arsine** (är'sēn, -sin, -sīn) the poisonous gas, hydride of arsenic (AsH₃): a compound in which one or more hydrogen atoms of AsH₃ are replaced by an alkyl radical, etc. [Gr. *arsenikon*, yellow orpiment, fancifully associated with Gr. *arsēn*, male, and the alchemists' notion that metals have sex.]

arsis är'sis, (Gr. *pros.* and *mus.*) *n.* lit a lift, an upbeat: hence the weak position in a bar or foot· understood by the Romans as the strong position: used in English in both senses: elevation of the voice to higher pitch:—*pl.* **ar'sēs**:—opp. to *thesis.* [L ,—Gr *arsis—airein*, to lift.]

arson är'sn, *n.* the crime of feloniously burning houses, haystacks, or similar property—*n.* **ar'sonist.** [O.Fr. *arson*—L *arsiō*, *-ōnis—ardēre, arsum*, to burn.]

art¹ ärt, (*arch.* and *poet.*) used as 2nd pers sing pres indic. of the verb *to be.* [O.E. (W.S.) *eart*, (Mercian) *earth*, (Northumbrian) *arth*; from the root *es*-seen in **is, are.**]

art² ärt, *n.* practical skill, or its application, guided by principles: human skill and agency (opp to *nature*): application of skill to production of beauty (esp. visible beauty) and works of creative imagination, as in the fine arts: a branch of learning, esp. one of the *liberal* arts, as in *faculty of arts*, *master of arts*: skill or knowledge in a particular department: a skilled profession or trade, craft, or branch of activity· magic or occult knowledge or influence: a method of doing a thing: a knack: contrivance: address: cunning: artifice: crafty conduct.—*adj.* of, for, concerned with, painting, sculpture, etc. (as *art gallery, art historian*): intended to be decorative: produced with studied artistry, not arising spontaneously by chance.—*adj.* **art'ful** cunning: produced by art.—*adv.* **art'fully.**—*n.* **art'fulness.**—*adj.* **art'less** simple· guileless, un-

affected —*adv.* **art'lessly.**—*n* **art'lessness.**—*adj.* **art'y** (*coll.*) aspiring to be artistic.—**art autre** (är-tō-tr') a post World War II movement in painting, including tachisme; **art deco** (ar dek'ō) the style of decorative art characteristic of the 1920s and 1930s, developing the curvilinearity of art nouveau into more streamlined geometrical forms; **art form** a set form or arrangement in poetry or music: an accepted medium of artistic expression; **art nouveau** (àr nōō-vō) a decorative form of art (*c.* 1890–1910) in which curvilinear forms are important and fundamentally unrelated images are often combined in a single design; **art paper** paper for illustrations, coated with a composition containing china clay; **arts student** a student in the faculty of arts; **art student** a student of painting, sculpture, etc ; **art'work** the illustrations and other decorative material in a publication.—*adj* **art'y-craft'y** self-consciously artistic—**art and part** originally (*law*) concerned in either by *art* in contriving or by *part* in actual execution, now loosely used in the sense of participating, sharing; **be a fine art** to be an operation or practice requiring nicety of craftsmanship; **get something down to a fine art** to become very skilled at something through practice, **the fine arts** painting, poetry, music, etc [L *ars*, *artis.*]

artefact, artifact ar'tı-fakt, *n.* (esp. *archaeol.*) a thing made by human workmanship [L. *arte*, by art (abl of *ars*), *factum*, made]

artery är'tər-ı, *n.* a tube or vessel that conveys blood from the heart: any main channel of communication —*adj.* **arterial** (-tē'ri-əl).—*n* **arterialisa'tion, -z-**.—*v t.* **arter'ialise, -ize** to make arterial.—*n* **arteriosclerō'sis** (Gr *sklērōsis*, hardening) hardening of the arteries —*adj* **arteriosclerotic** (-*ot'ik*). [L. *artēria* —Gr *artēriä*, windpipe, artery.]

Artesian ar-tē'zyən, -zh(y)ən, *adj* of Artois (L L. *Artesium*), in the north of France, or a type of well in early use there, in which water rises in a borehole by hydrostatic pressure from a basin whose outcrop is at a higher level Artesian well. See **art²**.

arthralgia ar-thral'j(ı-)ə, *n* pain in a joint.—*adj* **arthral'gic.**—*n.* **arthritis** (-thrī'tıs) inflammation of a joint: gout.—*adj* **arthritic** (-*thrit'ik*) of or near a joint· of, of the nature of, arthritis.—*n.* a gouty person: a person suffering from arthritis. [Gr *arthron*, a joint, *algos*, pain.]

arthropod ar'thrō-pod, *n* any member of the **Arthropoda** (ar-throp'od-ə), a great division of the animal kingdom, with segmented bodies and jointed appendages—crustacea, arachnids, millipedes, centipedes, insects, etc.—*adj* **arthrop'odal.** [Gr *arthron*, joint, and *pous, podos*, a foot]

arthrospore ar'thrō-spōr, -spor, *n.* a conidium: (inappropriately) a vegetative cell that has passed into a resting state [Gr *arthron*, joint, *sporä*, seed]

Arthurian àr-thū'rı-ən, *adj* relating to King *Arthur*, a ruler of the Britons, whose court is the centre of many legends, but who himself had perhaps real existence· pertaining to the legends

artic. See **articulated lorry** under **article.**

artichoke ar'tı-chōk, *n* a thistle-like perennial plant with large scaly heads and edible receptacles.—**Jerusalem artichoke** a totally different plant, a species of sunflower with edible tubers like potatoes, Jerusalem being a corr of It *girasole* (turn-sun). sunflower [North It *articiocco* (It *carciofo*)—Old Sp *alcarchofa*—Ar *al-kharshōfa, al-kharshūf*]

article ar'tı-kl, *n* a separate element, member, or part of anything· a particular object or commodity· an item a single clause or term: a distinct point in an agreement, or (in *pl.*) an agreement looked at as so made up, as in *articles of apprenticeship*, etc.: (in *pl.*) rules or conditions generally: a section, paragraph, or head: a literary composition in a newspaper, periodical, encyclopaedia, etc., treating of a subject distinctly and independently: the adjective *the* (*definite article*), *a* or *an* (*indefinite article*) or the equivalent in another language (*gram.*)—*v.t.* to bind by articles of apprenticeship: to set forth as a charge (that).—*adjs.* **ar'ticled** bound as apprentice; **artic'ũ-lable** that can be articulated; **artic'ũlar** belonging to the joints: at or near a joint—*adj.* **artic'ũlate** jointed: composed of distinct parts: composed of recognisably distinct sounds, as human speech: clear: able to express one's thoughts with ease.—*v.t.* to attach by a joint: to connect by joints: to form into distinct sounds, syllables, or words.—*v.i.* to form a joint (with; *lit.* and *fig.*): to speak distinctly.—*adj.* **artic'ũlated.**—*adv.* **artic'ũlately.**—*ns.* **artic'ũlateness**; **articũlã'tion** jointing: a joint: a segment: distinctness, or distinct utterance: a consonant; **artic'ũlãtor** one who articulates or speaks.—*adj.* **artic'ũlatory.**—**articulated lorry,** etc. a lorry, etc. made easier to manœuvre by having a detachable cab section, which, when attached, can move at an angle to the rest (*coll.* shortening **artic'** (or *ar'*)) —**articles of faith** binding statement of points of belief of a Church, etc.; **articles of war** code of regulations for the government and discipline of armed services; **Thirty-nine Articles** the articles of religious belief finally agreed upon by the bishops and clergy of the Church of England in 1562. [L. *articulus*, a little joint, *articulāre, -ātum*, to furnish with joints, to utter distinctly—*artus*, joint.]

artifact. See **artefact.**

artifice *ár'ti-fis, n.* skill: contrivance, or trickery: an ingenious expedient: a crafty trick.—*n.* **artif'icer** a mechanic (esp. *mil., navy*). one who creates skilfully: a craftsman: a contriver.—*adj.* **artificial** (*-fish'l,* or *ãr'*) contrived (opp. to *spontaneous*): made by man: synthetic (opp. to *natural*). fictitious, factitious, feigned, made in imitation (opp. to *real*): affected in manners.—*n.* **artificiality** (*-fish-i-al'i-ti*).—*adv.* **artific'ially.**—*n.* **artific'ialness.**—**artificial horizon** a gyroscopic device indicating an aircraft's altitude in relation to the horizontal, **artificial insemination** the injection of semen into the uterus otherwise than by sexual union; **artificial kidney** a kidney machine, **artificial language** an invented language functioning not as the native speech of its users but as a computer language or means of international communication; **artificial respiration** stimulation of respiration manually or mechanically by forcing air in and out of the lungs. [L. *artificium—artifex, -ficis,* an artificer—*ars, artis,* and *facĕre,* to make.]

artillery *ar-til'ər-i, n.* offensive weapons of war, formerly in general, now the heavier kinds—ancient ballistas, catapults, modern cannon, etc.. a branch of the military service using these: gunnery.—**artill'eryman** a soldier of the artillery. [O.Fr *artillerie—artiller,* to arm.]

artiodactyl *àr-ti-ō-dak'til, adj.* even-toed.—*n.* a member of the **Artiodac'tyla** or even-toed ungulates, in which the third and forth digit form a symmetrical pair and the hind-foot bears an even number of digits —cf **perissodactyl.** [Gr. *artios,* even in number, and *daktylos,* finger or toe.]

artisan *art-i-zan',* or *art',* n. a handicraftsman or mechanic, a skilled workman. [Fr. *artisan*—It. *artigiano,* ult. from L. *artitus,* skilled—*ars, artis,* art.]

artist *art'ist, n.* one who practises or is skilled in an art, now esp a fine art: one who has the qualities of imagination and taste required in art. a painter or draughtsman. a performer, esp. in music. a person

good at, or given to, a particular activity, as *booze artist* (esp. *Austr.* and *U.S. slang*).—*adjs.* **artist'ic, -al.**—*adv.* **artist'ically.**—*n.* **art'istry** artistic pursuits: artistic workmanship, quality, or ability.—**artistic temperament** the emotional and capricious temperament ascribed to artists. [Fr. *artiste*—L. *ars, artis,* art.]

artiste *ar-tēst', n.* a public performer: an adept in a manual art. [Fr.]

artless; arty. See **art.**

Arum *ã'rəm, n.* the cuckoo-pint or wakerobin genus: (without *cap*) any kindred plant.—*n.pl* **Arã'ceae** (*a-*) the family of spadicifloral monocotyledons to which it belongs.—*adjs.* **araceous** (*a-rã'shəs*), **aroid** (*ã'roid*) of the Araceae: like an arum.—*n.* **ã'roid** any plant of the family.—**arum lily** Zantedeschia. [L. *arum*—Gr. *aron.*]

arundinaceous *ə-run-di-nã'shəs, adj.* of or like a reed. [L. *arundināceus—arundō, -inis,* a reed.]

Aryan *a'ri-ən* or *à', adj.* Indo-Germanic, Indo-European: now generally of the Indian, or Indian and Iranian, branch of the Indo-European languages: speaking one of these languages: in Nazi politics, not Jewish.—*n.* the parent Indo-European language. a speaker of an Aryan language.—*v.t.* **Ar'yanise, -ize.** [Sans. *ārya,* noble.]

aryl *ar'il, n.* any aromatic univalent hydrocarbon radical. [**aromatic,** and Gr. *hylē,* matter.]

arytaenoid, arytenoid *ar-i-tē'noid, adj.* pitcher-shaped.—*n.* a cartilage or a muscle of the larynx. [Gr. *arytainoeidēs—arytaina,* a cup, *eidos,* form.]

as[1] *az, əz, adv.* in whatever degree, proportion, manner: to whatever extent: in that degree: to that extent. so. far. however: specifically: passing into *conj.* or almost *prep.,* for instance: in the manner, character, part, aspect, of: in so far as: whereas.— *conj.* because, since. while, when: as if.—*pron.* who, which, that (after *such, so, same,* or where a statement is treated as antecedent) —**as also** likewise; **as concerning, as for, as regards, as to,** for the matter of; **as from, as of** from (a specified time); **as how** that (with noun clause) (*illit.* or *dial.*); **as if, as though** as it would be if; **as it were** so to speak: in some sort; **as many as** all who; **as much the same:** just that, **as now,** **as then** just as at this, that, time, **as well** also: in addition. equally; **as yet** up to the moment, **as you were** a military order to return to the former position; **so as to** with the purpose or consequence specified; **when as** at what time (*arch.*) [O E. *all-swā* (*eall-swā*), all so, wholly so.]

as[2] *as, n.* a Roman unit of weight, a pound of 12 ounces a copper coin, originally a pound in weight, ultimately half an ounce:—*pl.* **ass'es.** [L. *ās, assis,* a unit.]

asafoetida *as-ə-fet'i-də,* or *-fēt', n.* an ill-smelling medicinal gum-resin, got from the root latex of some species of *Ferula*—also **asafetida, assafoetida, assafetida.** [Pers. *azā,* mastic, and L. *fētida* (*fem*) stinking.]

asana *ã'sə-nə, n.* any of the positions taught in yoga. [Sans. *āsana.*]

asbestos *az-bes'tos, n.* a fine fibrous amphibole capable of being woven into incombustible cloth: (commercially) chrysotile, a fibrous serpentine.— *adjs.* **asbes'tic, asbes'tiform, asbes'tine, asbes'tous** of or like asbestos.—*n.* **asbestō'sis** a lung disease caused by inhaling asbestos dust [Gr., (*lit.*) unquenchable —*a-,* priv , *sbestos,* extinguished.]

ascarid *as'kə-rid, n.* any nematode worm of the parasitic genus **As'caris** (family Ascar'idae), infesting the small intestines. [Gr *askaris,* pl. *askarides.*]

ascend *ə-send', a send', v.i.* to go up, mount, rise: to go back in time or ancestry.—*v.t.* to go up, mount, climb —ns. **ascend'ancy, -ency** dominating influence; **ascend'ant,** less commonly **ascend'ent,** (*astrol.*) the part of the ecliptic just risen or about to rise at any instant (a planet in this was supposed to influence a person born at the time): (from the phrase **in the ascendant**) a position of pre-eminence: an ancestor. one who rises or mounts: a rise, up-slope.—*adj* rising: just risen above the horizon: predominant.—*n* **ascend'er** one who ascends: (the upper part of) a letter such as b, d, h, k (*print.*, etc.).—*adjs* **ascend'ible** (also **-able**) scalable, **ascend'ing** rising: curving up from a prostrate to an erect position (*bot.*).—*n.* **ascension** (-sen'shən) ascent: an ascent to heaven, esp Christ's.—*n* **ascent'** a going up: advancement: a going back in time or ancestry: a way up: an up-slope —**Ascen'sion-day** (or Ascension Day) Holy Thursday, ten days before Whitsunday, commemorating Christ's Ascension —**ascend the throne** to become king or queen; **right ascension** (*astron*) a co-ordinate of the position of a heavenly body measured (usually in terms of time) eastwards along the celestial equator from the First Point of Aries, the other co-ordinate being the declination. [L *ascendĕre, ascēnsum*—*ad,* to, *scandĕre,* to climb]

ascertain *as-ər-tān',* *v.t.* to find out for certain: to insure, prove.—*adj.* **ascertain'able.**—*n.* **ascertain'ment.** [O Fr. *acertener—à,* to, *certain,* certain.]

ascesis *ə-sē'sis, n.* the practice of disciplining oneself: asceticism. [Gr *askēsis,* exercise, training.]

ascetic *a-* or *ə-set'ik, n.* one who rigidly denies himself ordinary bodily gratifications for conscience's sake: one who aims to compass holiness through mortification of the flesh: a strict hermit. one who lives a life of austerity.—*adjs* **ascet'ic, -al** rigorous in mortifying the flesh: of asceticism: recluse —*adv.* **ascet'ically.**—*n* **ascet'icism** (-sizm). [Gr *askētikos—askētēs,* one who is in training—*askeein,* to work, exercise, train.]

asci *pl.* of **ascus.**

ascidium *a-sid'i-əm, n.* a pitcher-shaped leaf or part of a leaf:—*pl.* **ascid'ia.**—*n.* **ascid'ian** a sea-squirt, or tunicate, shaped like a double-mouthed flask. [Gr. *askidion,* dim. of *askos,* a leathern bag, wine-skin.]

ascites *a-sī'tēz, n.* dropsy of the abdomen.—*adjs* **ascit'ic** (-sit'ik), **ascit'ical.** [Gr. *askītēs—askos,* belly.]

ascomycete, ascospore. See **ascus.**

ascorbic *ə-skör'bik, adj.* antiscorbutic—only in **ascorbic acid** vitamin C. [Gr *a-,* priv., and **scorbutic.**]

ascribe *ə-* or *ə-skrib', v.t.* to attribute, impute, or assign.—*adj.* **ascrib'able.**—*n.* **ascription** (-skrip'shən) act, expression, formula of ascribing or imputing, e.g that ascribing glory to God at the end of a sermon [L. *ascrībĕre—ad,* to, *scrībĕre, scrīptum,* to write.]

ascus *as'kəs,* (*bot.*) *n.* an enlarged cell, commonly elongated, in which usually eight spores are formed:—*pl.* **asci** (*as'ī*).—*ns.* **as'comycete** (*as'kō-mī-sēt*) any one of the **Ascomycetes** (-*sē'tēz*), one of the main divisions of the fungi, characterised by formation of asci; **as'cospore** a spore formed in an ascus [Gr *askos,* bag.]

Asdic *as'dik, n.* an apparatus for detecting and locating a submarine or other underwater object by means of ultrasonic waves echoed back from the submarine, etc. [Allied (or Anti-) Submarine Detection Investigation Committee.]

asepalous *a-, ā-,* or *ə-sep'ə-ləs, adj* without sepals. [Gr. *a-,* priv., and **sepal.**]

aseptic *a-, ā-,* or *ə-sep'tik, adj* not liable to, or preventing, decay or putrefaction: involving or accompanied by measures to exclude micro-organisms —*n.* an aseptic substance —*ns.* **asep'ticism** (-sizm) aseptic treatment, **asep'sis** freedom from sepsis or bloodpoisoning: the process of rendering, or condition of being, aseptic: exclusion of micro-organisms —*v t* **asep'ticise, -ize** (-ti-sīz) to make aseptic. to treat with aseptics. [Gr. *asēptos—a-,* priv., *sēpein,* to cause to decay]

asexual *a-, ā-,* or *ə-seks'ū-əl, adj* without sex: not involving sexual activity: vegetative —*n* **asexuality** (-al'i-ti).—*adv.* **asex'ually.** [Gr *a-,* priv., and **sexual.**]

ash [1] *ash, n* a well-known timber tree of the olive family. its wood, white, tough, and hard —*adj* **ash'en.** [O E. *æsc*]

ash [2] *ash, n.* (often in *pl*) the dust or remains of anything burnt: (also **volcanic ash(es)**) volcanic dust, or a rock composed of it: (in *pl*) remains of human body when burnt (in *pl*) a dead body (*fig*).—*adj* **ash'en** of the colour of ash: (of the face) very pale —*adj.* **ash'y.—ash'-bin, -bucket, -can** a receptacle for ashes and other household refuse —*adj* **ash-blond'** (of hair) of a pale, silvery blond colour: having hair of this colour.—*fem* (also *n.*) **ash-blonde'.—ash'-pan** a tray fitted underneath a grate to receive the ashes; **ash'-stand, ash'-tray** a small tray or saucer for tobacco ash; **Ash Wednesday** the first day of Lent, from the custom of sprinkling ashes on the head.—**the ashes** a term applied by the *Sporting Times* (in a mock 'In Memoriam' notice) to the loss of prestige in English cricket after the Australians' successful visit in 1882, after which English teams strove to 'bring back the ashes', or mortal remains [O.E *asce*]

ashamed *ə-shāmd', adj* affected with shame (with *of* action, person, *for,* meaning on behalf of, person, *to do; that*).—*adv.* **ashamed'ly** (or -id-li) —*n* **ashamed'ness** (or -id-nes) —*adj.* **asham'ing.** [Pfx. *a-,* intensive, and O E *sc(e)amian,* to shame.]

ashen, etc See **ash**[1,2].

ashet *ash'it,* (now only *Scot.*) *n* a large meat-plate [Fr. *assiette.*]

Ashkenazim *ash-kə-naz'im, n.pl.* the Polish and German Jews, as distinguished from the *Sephardim,* the Spanish and Portuguese Jews. [Heb *Ashkenaz,* a northern people (Gen x) by later Jews identified with Germany]

ashlar, ashler *ash'lər, n* a squared stone used in building or facing a wall: masonry of such stones.—Also *adj.*—*v t* to face with ashlar [O.Fr. *aiseler*—L *axillāris—axilla,* dim of *axis,* axle, plank.]

ashore *ə-shōr', -shor, adv* on, or on to, the shore or land (from the sea) [Prep **a,** and **shore**[1].]

ashram(a) *ash'ram(-ə) n.* usu in India, a hermitage, or a place of retreat for a religious group [Sans. *āśrama*]

Asian *ā'sh(i)ən, ā'shyən, -zh-,* **Asiatic** *-i-at'ik, adjs* belonging to *Asia* (esp. Asia Minor): (formerly) in literature or art, florid.—*n.* a native of Asia.—*adj* **Asianic** (-an'ik) Asian, esp of a group of non-Indo-European languages of Asia and Europe

aside *ə-sid', adv.* on or to one side: privately: apart.—*n.* words spoken in an undertone, so as not to be heard by some person present, words spoken by an actor which the other persons on the stage are supposed not to hear. an indirect effort of any kind —**aside from** apart from, **set aside** to quash (a judgment) [Prep **a,** and **side.**]

asinine *as'in-in, adj* of or like an ass.—*n.* **asininity** (-in'i-ti) [L *asininus—asinus,* ass]

ask *ask, v t* to seek to beg, request: to make a request of: to inquire to inquire of or invite to proclaim —*v t* to make a request (for): to inquire (*after* a person, his welfare, etc., *about* a matter, etc.) —*n* **ask'er.—asking price** price set by the seller of an article before bargaining has begun —**ask for it** (*coll.*) to behave in a way likely to bring trouble on oneself [O E *ascian, acsian.*]

askance *ə-skans', askant* *ə-skant', adv* sideways: awry:

obliquely.—eye, **look** or **view askance** to look (at) with disdain, disapprobation, envy, or (now usually) suspicion.

askari as'ka-rē, às-ka'rē, n. an East African soldier or policeman. [Ar. 'askarī, soldier.]

asker. See **ask**.

askesis. Same as **ascesis**.

askew ə-skū', adv. or adj. at or to an oblique angle: awry. [App. prep. **a**, and **skew**.]

aslant ə-slänt', adv. or adj. on the slant, slantwise.— prep. slantwise across, athwart. [Prep. **a**, and **slant**.]

asleep ə-slēp', adv or adj. in or to a sleeping state: dead: (of limbs) numbed, sometimes with tingling or prickly feeling [Prep. **a**, and **sleep**.]

asocial a-, ā-sō'shl, adj not social: antisocial. [Gr a-, priv., and **social**.]

asp asp, asp, n. a venomous snake of various kinds— *Vipera aspis* of Southern Europe, Cleopatra's asp (prob. the horned viper), the biblical asp (prob. the Egyptian juggler's snake, *Naja haje*), the cobra de capello. [L.,—Gr. *aspis*.]

Asparagus əs-par'ə-gəs, n. a genus of Liliaceae, with leaves reduced to scales: (without cap.) any of the members of this genus, some cultivated as ornamental plants, and one species (*A. officinalis*) for its young shoots as a table delicacy. [L.,—Gr. *asp(h)aragos*.]

aspect as'pekt, n. a look, a glance: a view: direction of facing: appearance presented: way of viewing: face: the situation of one planet with respect to another, as seen from the earth (*astron.*): in some languages, a verbal form expressing simple action, repetition, beginning, duration, etc. (*gram.*): attitude (*aircraft*). —adj. aspec'tual (*gram.* and *astron.*) of, relating to, aspect. [L. *aspectus*.]

aspen asp'ən, asp', -in, n. the trembling poplar [O.E. *æspe*.]

asper as'pər, adj. (*obs.*) rough, harsh.—n. **asperity** (-per') roughness: harshness: bitter coldness: (in pl.) excrescences, rough places. [L. *asper*.]

asperge as-pûrj', v.t. to sprinkle.—ns **asper'ges** a short service introductory to the mass; **aspergill** (as'pər-jil) a holy-water sprinkler.—Also **aspergillum** (-jil'əm):—pl. **aspergill'a, -ums; aspergillō'sis** a disease, fatal to birds and also occurring in domestic animals and man, caused by any of various moulds, esp. species of **Aspergillus; Aspergill'us** a genus of minute moulds occurring on decaying substances. [L. *aspergĕre*—ad, to, *spargĕre*, to sprinkle.]

asperity. See **asper**.

asperse as-pûrs', v.t. to slander or calumniate: to bespatter.—n. **asper'sion** calumny: slander.—adjs. **aspers'ive; aspers'ory** tending to asperse: defamatory.—n. **aspersō'rium** (-ri-əm) (L.) a holy-water vessel. [L. *aspergĕre, aspersum*—ad, to, *spargĕre*, to sprinkle.]

asphalt as'falt, n. a black or dark-brown, hard, bituminous substance, found native, and got as a residue in petroleum distillation, etc., anciently used as a cement: a mixture of this with rock chips or other material, used for paving, roofing, etc —v.t. **as'phalt** to lay, cover, or impregnate with asphalt.—adj **asphalt'ic**. [Gr. *asphaltos*, from an Eastern word.]

asphodel as'fə-del, -fo-, n. a plant of the lily family: applied to other plants, esp. **bog-asphodel**. [Gr. *asphodelos*; cf. **daffodil**.]

asphyxia as-fik'si-ə, n. cessation of the vital functions or suspended animation owing to any cause interfering with respiration.—Also **asphyx'y**.—n. and adj **asphyx'iant** (a chemical substance) producing asphyxia —v.t. **asphyx'iate** to produce asphyxia in.— adj. **asphyx'iated**.—ns **asphyxiā'tion; asphyx'iātor**.

[Gr. *asphyxiā*—a-, priv., *sphyxis*, pulse.]

aspic as'pik, n. a savoury meat-jelly containing fish, game, hard-boiled eggs, etc. [Perh. from *aspic*, asp, because it is 'cold as an aspic' (French proverb).]

Aspidistra as-pid-ist'rə, n. a genus of plants of the asparagus group of Liliaceae—often grown indoors: (without cap.) a plant of this genus. [Perh. Gr. *aspis*, a shield.]

aspire əs- or as-pīr', v.i. (with to, after, or an infinitive) to desire eagerly to aim at, or strive for, high things: to tower up.—n. **aspir'ant** (or as'pir-) one who aspires (with after, for): a candidate —adj. ambitious: mounting up (rare in both senses).—v.t. **aspirate** (as'pir-āt) to pronounce with a full breathing, i.e. the sound of h, as in house (phon): to follow (a stop) by an audible breath (phon.): to replace (a consonant) by another sound, normally a fricative, when there is a combination with the sound h or the letter h (gram., phon., etc.): to draw (gas, fluid, etc.) out of a cavity by suction: to inhale (med.).—Also v.i.—n. (-it, -ət) the sound represented by the letter h: a consonant sound, a stop followed by an audible breath: a mark of aspiration, the rough breathing (') in Greek: a letter representing an aspirate sound.—Also adj. —In French 'h aspirate', no longer sounded, still affects the junction with the preceding word.—ns. **aspirā'tion** eager desire: (usu. in pl.) lofty hopes or aims: pronunciation of a sound with a full breathing: an aspirated sound: drawing a gas, liquid or solid, in, out, or through; **as'pirātor** an apparatus for drawing air or other gases through bottles or other vessels: an instrument for removing fluids or solids from cavities of the body (med.).—adjs. **aspir'atory** (-ə-tə-ri or as'pir-) relating to breathing; **aspir'ing** desiring, aiming at, etc. —adv. **aspir'ingly**.—n. **aspir'ingness**. [L. *aspirāre, -ātum*—ad, to, *spirāre*, to breathe.]

aspirin as'pər-in, n a drug (acetyl-salicylic acid) used for relieving rheumatic pains, neuralgia, etc.

ass¹ as, äs, n a small, usually grey, long-eared animal of the horse genus: a dull, stupid fellow (fig.). [O.E. *assa*—L. *asinus*]

ass². See **arse**.

assafetida. Same as **asafoetida**.

assagai. Same as **assegai**.

assai às-sa'ē, (mus.) adv. very. [It.,—L. ad, to, satis, enough.]

assail ə-sāl', v.t. to attack.—adj. **assail'able**.—ns. **assail'ant** one who attacks; **assail'ment**. [O.Fr. asail-lir—L. assilīre—ad, upon, and salīre, to leap]

assassin ə- or a-sas'in, n. a follower of the Old Man of the Mountains, a member of his military and religious order in Persia and Syria (11th–13th cent), notorious for secret murders: one who, usually for a reward, or for political reasons, kills by surprise or secretly.— v t. **assass'inate** to murder by surprise or secret assault: to murder (especially a prominent person) violently, often publicly: to destroy by treacherous means, as a reputation (fig.).—ns. **assassinā'tion; assass'inātor**. [Through Fr. or It from Ar hash-shāshīn, hashish-eaters]

assault ə-solt', n. a sudden attack, a storming, as of a town: in Eng law, unlawful attempt to apply force to the person of another—when force is actually applied, the act amounts to battery: an attack of any sort by arguments, appeals, etc —v.t. to make an assault or attack upon.—adj. used in attack: preparing, or prepared, for attack —n. **assault'er.—assault course** a course laid out with obstacles that must be negotiated, used for training soldiers, etc. [O.Fr asaut—L ad, upon, saltus, a leap, salīre, to leap See **assail**.]

assay a- or ə-sā', v.t. to put to the proof to make trial of to test· to determine the proportion of a metal, or other component, in: to give as result —*v.t.* to adventure, make an attempt· to practise assaying (of ores, etc.)—*n.* (by some *as'ā*) a test, trial: a determination of proportion of metal: a specimen used for the purpose: experiment: experience.—*adj.* **assay'able.**—*ns* **assay'er** one who assays metals; **assay'ing.** [O.Fr *assayer*, n *assai*; see **essay.**]

assegai, assagai *as'ə-gī, n.* a slender spear of hard wood tipped with iron, some for hurling, some for thrusting with—used in South Africa.—*v.t.* to kill or wound with an assegai. [Through Fr. or Port from Ar. *az-zaghāyah*—*az* = *al,* the, *zaghāyah,* a Berber word.]

assemble *ə-sem'bl, v.t.* to call or bring together: to collect: to put together the parts of.—*v.t* to meet together.—*ns* **assem'blage** a collection of persons or things: the whole collection of remains found on an archaeological site: (also *a-sā-bläzh*), (putting together) a sculptural or other work of art consisting in whole or in part of selected objects, usu. objects made for another purpose; **assem'bler;** **assembly** the act of assembling: the putting together of parts: a company assembled: a formal ball or meeting for dancing and social intercourse: a reception or at-home· a meeting for religious worship: a deliberative or legislative body, esp. in some legislatures a lower house.—**assembly line** a serial arrangement of workers and apparatus for passing on work from stage to stage in assembling a product; **assem'blyman** a member of assembly or lower house; **assembly room** a public ballroom.—**General Assembly** in Scotland, Ireland and the United States, the highest court of the Presbyterian Church; **Legislative Assembly, House of Assembly** the lower or only house of some legislatures. [Fr. *assembler*—L.L. *assimulāre,* to bring together—*ad,* to, *similis,* like See **assimilate.**]

assemblé *ä-sä-blä, n.* a ballet dancer's leap with extended leg followed by crossing of legs. [Fr. *assembler,* to bring together.]

assent *a-* or *ə-sent', v.i.* to express agreement or acquiescence (with *to*).—*n.* an agreeing or acquiescence: compliance.—*n.* **assent'er.**—*adjs.* **assentient** (*ə-sen'shənt*). **assent'ive,**—*adv.* **assent'ingly.**—*ns* **assent'iveness; assent'or** one who subscribes a candidate's nomination paper in addition to proposer and seconder.—**royal assent** the sovereign's formal acquiescence in a measure which has passed the Houses of Parliament. [L. *assentārī,* to flatter, freq. of *assentīrī,* to assent, agree.]

assert *ə-sûrt', v.t.* to vindicate or defend by arguments or measures (now used only with cause as object, or reflexively): to declare positively: to lay claim to: to insist upon: to affirm.—*adj.* **assert'able.**—*ns.* **assert'er, assert'or** a champion: one who makes a positive statement; **asser'tion** (*-shən*).—*adj.* **assert'ive** asserting or confirming confidently: positive: dogmatic.—*adv.* **assert'ively.**—*n.* **assert'iveness.**—*adj.* **assert'ory** affirmative.—**assert oneself** to defend one's rights or opinions, sometimes with unnecessary zeal: to thrust oneself forward. [L. *asserĕre, assertum,* to lay hands on, claim—*ad,* to, and *serĕre,* to join.]

assess *ə-ses', v.t.* to fix the amount of, as a tax: to tax or fine: to fix the value or profits of, for taxation (with *at*): to estimate, judge—*adj* **assess'able.**—*ns* **assess'ment** act of assessing: a valuation for the purpose of taxation: a tax; **assess'or** a legal adviser who sits beside a magistrate: one appointed as an associate in office with another: one who assesses taxes, or value of property, income, etc., for taxation —*adj* **assessō'rial** (*as-*) —*n.* **assess'orship.**—**assessment centre** a place where young offenders are detained, to await a decision about their future. [L. *assīdēre,*

assessum, to sit by, esp. of judges in a court, from *ad,* to, at, *sedēre,* to sit.]

assets *as'ets, n pl* (*orig. sing*) the property of a deceased or insolvent person, considered as chargeable for all debts, etc.: the entire property of all sorts belonging to a merchant or to a trading association —*false sing* **ass'et** an item of property· something advantageous or well worth having.—**ass'et-stripping** (now usu. *derog.*) the practice of acquiring control of a company and selling off its assets; **ass'et-stripper.** [From the Anglo-Fr law phrase *aver assetz,* to have enough, O Fr *asez,* enough—L *ad,* to, *satis,* enough]

asseverate *ə-, a-sev'ər-āt, v.t.* to declare solemnly —*n.* **asseverā'tion.** [L. *asseverāre, -ātum*—*ad,* to, *sevērus,* serious; see **severe.**]

assiduity *as-id-ū'i-ti, n* persistent application or diligence: (in *pl.*) constant attentions —*adj* **assiduous** (*ə-sid'ū-əs*) constant or unwearied in application —*adv.* **assid'ūously** unremittingly.—*n.* **assid'ūousness.** [L. *assiduus*—*ad,* to, at, *sedēre,* to sit]

assign *ə-sīn', v.t* to allot· to designate, appoint: to put forward, adduce: to make over, transfer· to ascribe, refer: to specify: to fix, determine.—*n.* one to whom any property or right is made over.—*adj.* **assign'able.**—*ns.* **assignation** (*as-ig-nā'shən*) an appointment to meet, used chiefly of love trysts, and mostly in a bad sense: the making over of any right to another (*Scots law*); **assignee** (*as-in-ē'*) one to whom any right or property is assigned: a trustee of a sequestrated estate; **assignment** (*-sīn'*) act of assigning: anything assigned: the writing by which a transfer is made: a task allotted; **assignor** (*as-i-nōr'*) one who makes over (*law*). [Fr. *assigner*—L *assignāre,* to mark out—*ad,* to, *signum,* a mark or sign.]

assimilate *ə-sim'il-āt, v t* to make similar or like (with *to, with*)· to convert into a like substance, as food in the body: to take fully into the mind, experience effects of (e.g. knowledge): to receive and accept fully within a group, absorb: to modify (a speech sound), making it more like a neighbouring sound in a word or sentence —*v.i* to become like (with *to*): to be incorporated or absorbed (into) —*adj.* **assim'ilable.**—*n* **assimilā'tion.**—*adj.* **assim'ilative** having the power or tendency to assimilate. [L. *assimilāre, -ātum*—*ad,* to, *similis,* like.]

assist *ə-sist', v.t.* to help (*with* work, etc.; *in* a matter, etc.) —*v.i* to help (with *with, in*) —*n.* **assis'tance** help· relief.—*adj* **assis'tant** helping.—*n.* one who assists: a helper.—*adj.* **assis'ted** for which help (e.g financial aid, additional power) is supplied. [Fr. *assister*—L *assistĕre,* to stand by—*ad,* to, *sistĕre,* to set, take one's stand.]

assize *ə-sīz', v.t.* to set or fix the quantity or price of.—*n.* (in *pl.*) periodical sittings of judges on circuit through the English counties, with a jury (till 1972). [O.Fr. *assise,* assembly of judges, set rate—*asseoir*—L. *assidēre*—*ad,* to, *sedēre,* to sit.]

associate *ə-sō'shi-āt, -si-, v t* to join, connect, link: to connect in one's mind: to make a colleague or partner.—*v i.* to consort, keep company (with *with*): to combine or unite.—*adj.* (*-ət, -āt*) associated: connected: confederate: joined as colleague or junior colleague.—*n.* (*-ət, -āt*) one joined or connected with another: a colleague, companion, friend, partner, or ally: a person admitted to a society without full membership.—*n.* **associabil'ity.**—*adj.* **asso'ciable** (*-shi-ə-bl,* or *-shə-bl*) capable of being associated.—*ns.* **asso'ciateship; associā'tion** (*-si-,* or *-shi-*) act of associating· union or combination: a society of persons joined to promote some object: a set of species of plants or animals characteristic of a certain habitat (*biol.*): loose aggregation of molecules (*chem.*):

fāte; far, mē; hûr (her); *mīne, mōte, fōr; mūte, mōōn; fōōt; dhen* (then), *el'ə-mənt* (element) (*football*; also **association football,** *coll.* **soccer**) the game as formulated by the Football Association (formed 1863), with eleven players a side, opp. to *Rugby*: connection of thoughts, of feelings: (usu. in *pl.*) thought, feeling, memory, more or less permanently connected with e.g. a place, an occurrence, something said.—*adj.* **assō'ciātive** tending to association.—*n.* **associativity** (-ǝ-*tiv'*).—**association of ideas** mental linkage that facilitates recollection—by similarity, contiguity, repetition. [L. *associāre*, -*ātum*—*ad*, to, *socius*, a companion.]

assonance *as'ǝn-ǝns, n.* a correspondence in sound: vowel-rhyme, coincidence of vowels without regard to consonants, as in *mate* and *shape, feel* and *need*: extended to correspondence of consonants with different vowels: resemblance, correspondence.—*adjs.* **ass'onant; assonantal** (-*ant'ǝl*).—*v.i.* **ass'onate** to correspond in vowel sound: to practise assonance. [L. *assonāre*, -*ātum*—*ad*, to, *sonāre*, to sound.]

assort *ǝ-sort', v.t.* to distribute in classes, classify: to class.—*v.i.* to agree or be in accordance: to suit well.—*adjs.* **assort'ative** (-*ǝ-tiv*); **assort'ed** classified, arranged in sorts: made up of various sorts.—*ns.* **assort'edness; assort'er; assort'ment** act of assorting: a quantity or number of things assorted: variety. [Fr. *assortir*—L. *ad*, to, *sors, sortis*, a lot.]

assuage *ǝ-swāj', v.t.* to soften, mitigate, or allay.—*n.* **assuage'ment.**—*n.* and *adj.* **assuag'ing.**—*adj.* **assuā'sive** (-*siv*) soothing: mitigating. [O.Fr. *assouager*—L. *ad*, to, *suāvis*, mild.]

assume *ǝ-sūm', -sōōm', v.t.* to adopt, take in: to take up, take upon oneself: to take for granted: to arrogate: to pretend to possess.—*v.i* to make undue claims: to be arrogant.—*adj.* **assum'able.**—*adv.* **assum'ably.**—*adj.* **assumed'** appropriated, usurped: pretended: taken as the basis of argument.—*adv.* **assum'edly.**—*adj.* **assum'ing** haughty: arrogant.—*n.* assumption: arrogance: presumption.—*conj.* (often with *that*) if it can be taken for granted that.—*adv.* **assum'ingly.**—*n.* **assumption** (-*sum'*, -*sump'*) an act of assuming: taking upon oneself: arrogance: taking for granted: supposition: that which is taken for granted or supposed: the minor premise in a syllogism (*logic*): a taking up bodily into heaven.—Also *adj.*—*adj.* **assump'tive** of the nature of an assumption: gratuitously assumed: apt, or too apt, to assume. [L. *assūmĕre, assūmptum*—*ad*, to, *sūmĕre*, to take.]

assure *ǝ-shōōr', v.t.* to make sure or secure: to give confidence: to tell positively: to insure.—*adj.* **assur'able.**—*n.* **assur'ance** confidence: feeling of certainty: subjective certainty of one's salvation (*theol.*): self-confidence: unabashedness: audacity: positive declaration: insurance, now esp. life-insurance: security: the securing of a title to property: a promise; a surety, warrant.—*adj.* **assured'** secured: pledged: certain: confident: beyond doubt: insured: self-confident: over-bold: brazen-faced.—*n.* a person whose life or property is insured: the beneficiary of an insurance policy.—*adv.* **assur'edly** certainly, in truth, undoubtedly (also *interj.*).—*ns.* **assur'edness; assur'er** one who gives assurance: an insurer or underwriter: one who insures his life. [O.Fr. *aseurer* (Fr. *assurer*)—L.L. *adsēcūrāre*—*ad*, to, *sēcūrus*, safe; see **sure.**]

assurgent *ǝ-sûr'jǝnt, adj.* rising, ascending: rising in a curve to an erect position (*bot.*).—*n.* **assur'gency** the tendency to rise. [L. *ad*, to, *surgĕre*, to rise.]

Assyrian *a-*, or *ǝ-sir'i-ǝn, adj.* of Assyria.—*n.* an inhabitant or native of Assyria: the Semitic language of ancient Assyria.—*ns.* **Assyriol'ogist; Assyriol'ogy** the science of Assyrian antiquities. [Gr. *Assyrios—Assyriā*.]

astable *ā-stā'bl, adj.* not stable: oscillating between two states (*elect.*). [Gr. *a-*, priv. and **stable.**]

astarboard *ǝ-stär'bōrd, -bord, adv.* on or towards the starboard. [Prep. **a,** and **starboard.**]

astatic *a-stat'ik, adj.* having no tendency to stand in a fixed position: without polarity, as a pair of magnetic needles set in opposite directions.—*n.* **astatine** (*as'tǝ-tēn*) a radioactive chemical element (at. numb. 85; symbol At) of the halogen series. [Gr. *astatos*, unstable—*a-*, priv., *statos*, verb. adj. of *histanai*, to make to stand]

aster *as'tǝr, n.* a starlike figure, as in mitotic cell-division: (with *cap.*) a genus of Compositae, with showy radiated heads, white to lilac-blue or purple, flowering in late summer and autumn, hence often called Michaelmas daisies: a plant of this genus or a related form: extended to the kindred **China aster** (*Callistephus hortensis*) brought from China to France by a missionary in the 18th century.—*n.* **as'terisk** a star-shaped mark (*) used as a reference to a note, as a mark of omission, as a mark of a word or root inferred to have existed but not recorded, and for other purposes.—*v t.* to mark with an asterisk.—*adj.* **as'terisked.**—*ns.* **as'terism** a group of stars: three asterisks placed to direct attention to a passage: in some minerals the property of showing by reflected or transmitted light a star-shaped luminous figure due to inclusions or tubular cavities; **as'teroid** a minor planet.—*adj.* resembling a star, starfish, or aster.—*adj.* **asteroid'al.** [Gr. *astēr*, star.]

astern *ǝ-stûrn', adv.* in or towards the stern: behind. [Prep. **a,** and **stern.**]

asthenia *as-thē'ni-ǝ, -thi-nī'ǝ, n.* debility.—*adj.* **asthenic** (-*then'ik*) of, relating to, asthenia: lacking strength: of a slender type, narrow-chested, with slight muscular development (*anthrop.*): belonging to a type thought prone to schizophrenia, having a small, light trunk and disproportionately long limbs (*psych.*).—*n.* a person of asthenic type. [Gr. *astheneia—a-*, priv., *sthenos*, strength.]

asthma *as'mǝ*, also *asth', ast',* in U.S. usu. *az', n.* a chronic disorder of the organs of respiration, characterised by difficulty of breathing, wheezing, and a tightness in the chest.—*adjs.* **asthmatic** (-*mat'*), (*old*) **-al.**—*adv.* **asthmat'ically.** [Gr. *asthma, -atos—aazein*, to breathe with open mouth.]

astigmatism *ǝ-stig'mǝ-tizm, n.* a defect in an eye, lens, or mirror, by which rays from one point are not focused at one point.—Also **astig'mia** (-*mi-ǝ*).—*adj.* **astigmatic** (*a-stig-mat'ik*).—*adv.* **astigmat'ically.** [Gr. *a-*, priv., and *stigma, -atos*, a point.]

astir *ǝ-stûr', adv.* on the move: out of bed: in motion or excitement. [Prep. **a,** and **stir[1].**]

astonish *as-ton'ish, v.t.* to impress with sudden surprise or wonder: to amaze.—*adjs.* **aston'ished** amazed; **aston'ishing** very wonderful, amazing.—*adv* **aston'ishingly.**—*n.* **aston'ishment** amazement: wonder: a cause for astonishment. [Ultimately from L. *ex*, out, *tonāre*, to thunder.]

astound *as-townd', v.t.* to amaze, to strike dumb with astonishment.—*adjs.* **astound'ed** stunned: dazed: amazed; **astound'ing.**—*adv.* **astound'ingly.**—*n.* **astound'ment.** [From the pa.p. of old verb **astone,** to astonish.]

astraddle *ǝ-strad'l, adv.* with legs wide apart. [Prep. **a,** on, and **straddle.**]

astragal *as'trǝ-gǝl, n.* a small semicircular moulding round a column or elsewhere (*archit.*): one of the bars that hold the panes of a window (*archit.*). [Gr. *astragalos*, a vertebra, ankle-bone, moulding.]

astrakhan *as-trǝ-kan', n.* lamb-skin with a curled wool from the Middle East; a rough fabric made in imitation of it. [*Astrakhan* on the Caspian Sea.]

astral *as'trəl, adj.* belonging to the stars: starry: in theosophy, of a supersensible substance supposed to pervade all space and enter into all bodies —**astral body** an astral counterpart of the physical body: a ghost or wraith. [L. *astrālis—astrum*, a star.]

astray *ə-strā', adv* out of the right way: out of one's reckoning: in a lost state. [Prep. **a**, on, and **stray**.]

astride *ə-strīd', adv.* in a striding position with a leg on each side.—*prep.* astride of: on either side of [Prep. **a**, on, and **stride**.]

astringent *ə-strin'jənt adj.* binding contracting: drawing together: having power to contract organic tissues: styptic: (of e g. manner) sharp, austere, severe.—*n.* an astringent agent.—*n.* **astrin'gency**. —*adv* **astrin'gently** [L. *astringĕre, astrictum—ad,* to, *stringĕre*, to draw tight.]

astro- *as'trō-, -tro',* in composition, star.—*n.* **as'trodome** a small transparent observation dome on the top of the fuselage of an aeroplane: a sports centre covered by a huge translucent plastic dome, orig. one at Houston, Texas.—*n.* **as'trolabe** (*-lāb*) an old instrument for taking altitudes (from *lab-*, root of Gr *lambanein,* to take); **astrol'oger**—*adjs.* **astrolog'ic, -al**.—*adv.* **astrolog'ically**.—*ns.* **astrol'ogy** the once-supposed art or science of the influence of the stars on human and terrestrial affairs; (Gr. *logos,* discourse), **astronaut** *(as'trō-nöt;* Gr. *nautes,* a sailor) one engaged in space travel—*n.sing.* **astronaut'ics** the science of travel in space.—*ns.* **astronaviga'tion** the navigation of aircraft, spacecraft or sailing craft by means of observation of the stars; **astron'omer**.— *adjs.* **astronom'ic, -al** relating to astronomy prodigiously great, like the distance of the stars— (**astronomical unit** the earth's mean distance from the sun, about 92.9 million miles, used as a measure of distance within the solar system; **astronomical year** see **year**) —*adv.* **astronom'ically**.—*n.* **astron'omy** the science of the heavenly bodies (Gr. *nomos,* law) —*adj.* **astrophys'ical**.—*n.* **astrophys'icist**.—*n.sing* **astrophys'ics** the science of the chemical and physical condition of the heavenly bodies [Gr. *astron,* star]

astute *as-, əs-tūt',* in U.S *-tōōt', adj* shrewd sagacious: wily —*adv.* **astute'ly**.—*n.* **astute'ness**. [L. *astūtus—astus* (found in abl *astū*), craft]

asunder *ə-sun'dər, adv.* apart: into parts: separately. [Prep. **a**.]

asylum *ə-sī'ləm, n.* a place of refuge for debtors and for those accused of crime: an institution for the care or relief of the unfortunate as the blind or (*old-fashioned*) mentally ill: (any place of) refuge or protection:—*pl.* **asy'lums**.—**political asylum** protection given to a person by one country from arrest in another: refuge provided by a country to a person leaving his own without the permission of its government. [L. *asȳlum*—Gr. *asÿlon* (neut) inviolate— *a-,* priv., *sȳlon, sȳlē,* right of seizure]

asymmetry *a-sim'ə-tri, ā-, n.* want of symmetry —*adjs* **asymmetric** *(-et'rik),* **-al**.—*adv.* **asymmet'rically**. [Gr. *asymmetriā—a-,* priv., *symmetriā,* symmetry]

asymptote *a'sim-tōt, (math.) n.* a line that continually approaches a curve but never meets it.—*adjs* **asymptotic** *(-tot'ik),* **-al**.—*adv.* **asymptot'ically**. [Gr. *asymptōtos—a-,* priv , *syn,* together, *ptōtos,* apt to fall, *piptein,* to fall]

asynchronism *a-sing'krə-nizm, ā-, n.* want of synchronism or correspondence in time —Also **asyn'chrony**. —*adj.* **asyn'chronous**. [Gr *a-,* priv., *syn,* together, *chronos,* time.]

asyndeton *a-sin'də-ton, (rhet)* n a figure in which the conjunctions are omitted—*adj.* **asyndet'ic**. [Gr. *asyndeton—a-,* priv., *syndeton,* bound together— *syn,* together, *deein,* to bind.]

asynergia *a-sin-ûr'ji-ə, ā-, n* lack of coordination in action, as of muscles [Gr. *a-,* priv , *syn,* together, *ergon,* work.]

asystole *a-sis'to-lē, ā-, (med.)* n. inability of the heart to empty itself.—Also **asys'tolism**. [Gr *a-,* priv., *systolē,* contraction.]

at *at, ət, prep* denoting (precise) position in space or time, or some kindred relation, as amount, response, occupation, aim, activity —**at it** occupied in a particular way, doing a particular thing; **at that** see **that**; **where it's at** see **where**. [O.E. *æt*]

atabrin, atebrin *at'ə-brin, n* mepacrine

atactic. See **ataxia**.

ataman *at'a-man, n* a Cossack headman or general—a hetman:—*pl.* **atamans**. [Russ.,—Ger. *Hauptmann—Haupt,* head, *Mann,* man.]

ataraxia *at-ə-rak'si-ə,* **ataraxy** *at'ə-rak-si, ns.* calmness, the indifference aimed at by the Stoics.—*adjs.* and *ns* **atarac'tic, atarax'ic** tranquillising (drug) [Gr. *ataraxiā—a-,* priv., *tarassein,* to disturb.]

atavism *at'əv-izm, n* appearance of ancestral, but not parental, characteristics: reversion to an ancestral, or to a primitive, type —*adj* **atavist'ic**. [L. *atavus,* a great-great-great-grandfather, an ancestor—*avus,* a grandfather.]

ataxia *a-tak'si-ə,* **ataxy** *a-tak'si, at'aks-i, ns.* inability to co-ordinate voluntary movements (*med.,* see **locomotor ataxy** under **locomotive**): lack of order —*adjs.* **atact'ic, atax'ic**. [Gr. *ataxiā,* disorder—*a-,* priv , *taxis,* order.]

ate *et,* or *āt, pa.t* of **eat**.

atebrin. See **atabrin**.

atelier *at'əl-yā, n* a workshop, esp. an artist's studio [Fr.]

a tempo *ä tem'pō, (mus.)* in time, i e revert to the previous or original tempo. [It.]

à terre *a ter,* (Fr.) on the ground: with the foot (usu both feet) flat on the ground (*ballet*)

Athanasian *ath-ə-nā'sh(y)ən, -z(h)yən, adj* relating to *Athanasius* (c 296–373), or to the creed erroneously attributed to him.

atheism *ā'thi-izm, n.* disbelief in the existence of a god —*n* **a'theist**.—*adjs.* **atheist'ic, -al**.—*adv.* **atheist'ically**. [Gr *atheos—a-,* priv , and *theos,* god]

athematic *ath-i-mat'ik, adj* without a thematic vowel (*gram., linguistics*) not using themes as a basis (*mus.*) —*adv* **athemat'ically**. [Gr *a-,* priv , and **thematic**.]

Athene *a-thē'nē,* **Athena** *-nə, n* Greek goddess of wisdom, tutelary goddess of Athens —*n* **Athenaeum** *(ath-ə-nē'əm)* a temple of Athene: an ancient institution of learning, or literary university: a name sometimes taken by a literary institution, library, or periodical —*adj* **Athenian** *(a-thē'ni-ən)* of Athens. —*n* a native or citizen of Athens or Attica.

athermancy *ath-ûr'mən-si, n.* impermeability to radiant heat.—*adj* **ather'manous**. [Gr *a-,* priv , *thermainein,* to heat.]

atheroma *ath-ər-ō'mə, n* a cyst with porridge-like contents: a thickening of the inner coat of arteries.—*adj.* **atherōm'atous**.—*n* **atherosclero'sis** *(-ō'sis)* arteriosclerosis, or a form or stage of it [Gr *athērōma— athērē* or *athārē,* porridge]

athetesis *ath-i-tē'sis, n* rejection as spurious.—*n* **athetō'sis** involuntary movement of fingers and toes due to a lesion of the brain —*adj* **ath'etoid**.—*n* a spastic who has involuntary movements. [Gr. *athetos,* without position, set aside, *athetēsis,* rejection—*a-,* priv , and the root of *tithenai,* to set.]

athirst *ə-thûrst', adj* thirsty eager [O.E. *ofthyrst;* see **thirst**.]

athlete *ath'lēt, n.* a contender for victory in feats of strength, speed, endurance, or agility: one vigorous in body or mind —*adj* **athletic** *(-let'ik)* of a long-limbed, large-chested, muscular type of body (*anthrop.*): relating to athletics: strong, vigorous.— *adv.* **athlet'ically.**—*n* **athlet'icism** (-*i-sizm*) practice of, training in, or devotion to, athletics —*n.pl.* or *n. sing.* **athlet'ics** athletic sports —*n. sing.* the practice of athletic sports.—**athlete's foot** a contagious disease of the foot, caused by a fungus. [Gr. *athlētēs—athlos,* contest.]

at-home. See **home.**

athrob *ə-throb', adj.* and *adv.* with throbs, throbbing [Prep. **a.**]

athwart *ə-thwort', prep.* across.—*adv.* sidewise· transversely: awry: wrongly: perplexingly [Prep. **a.**]

atilt *ə-tilt', adv.* on tilt: as a tilter [Prep. **a,** and **tilt.**]

atingle *ə-ting'gl, adj.* and *adv.* in a tingle. [Prep. **a,** and tingle¹.]

Atlantic, etc See **Atlas.**

Atlas *at'las, n.* the Titan who bore the heavens on his shoulders, and whose figure used to appear on titlepages of atlases: the African mountain range into which he was transformed: (*pl.* **Atlantes** *at-lan'tēz*) a figure of a man serving as a column in a building: (the following without *cap.*; *pl.* **at'lases**) the vertebra supporting the skull: a book of maps, plates, or the like. —*adjs* **Atlantë'an** of Atlas: gigantic: of Atlantis; **Atlan'tic** of Atlas: of the Atlantic Ocean.—*n.* the Atlantic Ocean —**Atlantic Charter** an Anglo-American declaration during the Second World War of eight common principles of right in future peace. [Gr. *Atlas, Atlantos.*]

atlas. See under **Atlas.**

atman *ät'mən, n* in Hinduism, the divine within the self. [Sans. *ātman,* self, soul.]

atmolysis *at-mol'i-sis, n.* a method of separating mixed gases by their different rates of passage through a porous septum.—*v.t.* **at'molyse, -yze** (-*līz*) [Gr. *atmos,* vapour, *lysis,* loosing—*lyein,* to loose.]

atmosphere *at'məs-fēr, n.* the gaseous envelope that surrounds the earth or any of the heavenly bodies: any gaseous medium: a unit of atmospheric pressure equal to the pressure exerted by a column of mercury 760 millimetres in height at 0°C, practically the same as standard atmosphere (see **standard**): a feeling of space and distance in a picture: any surrounding influence or pervading feeling (*fig.*)—*adjs.* **atmospher'ic** (-*fer'ik*), **-al** of or depending on the atmosphere.—*adv* **atmospher'ically.**—*n.pl* **atmospher'ics** noises interfering with radio reception, due to electric disturbances in the ether. [Gr. *atmos,* vapour, *sphaira,* a sphere.]

atoll *at'ol,* or *ə-tol', n.* a coral island consisting of a circular belt of coral enclosing a central lagoon. [Name in Maldive Islands.]

atom *at'əm, n.* a particle of matter so small that, so far as the older chemistry goes, it cannot be cut or divided· anything very small.—*adjs* **atomic** (*ə-tom'ik*) pertaining to atoms: obtained by means of atomic fission, as **atomic power:** driven by atomic power: heated by atomic power, **atom'ical.**—*ns* **atomicity** (*at-əm-is'i-ti*) state or fact of being composed of atoms: number of atoms in a molecule. valency; **atomisā'tion, -z-.**—*v.t.* **at'omise, -ize** to reduce to atoms to reduce (a liquid or solid) to a fine spray or minute particles. to destroy by bombing.—*ns.* **atomi'ser, -z-** an instrument for discharging liquids in a fine spray —**atom(ic) bomb** a bomb in which the nuclei of uranium or plutonium atoms bombarded by neutrons split with explosive transformation of part of their mass into energy, **atomic clock** a clock in which, to achieve greater accuracy, the oscillations of a quartz crystal (see **quartz clock**) are regulated by the vibration of certain atoms as a caesium atom; **atomic energy** nuclear energy, **atomic number** the number of units of charge of posi-

tive electricity on the nucleus of an atom of an element; **atomic pile** a device for the controlled release of nuclear energy, e.g. a lattice of small rods of natural uranium embedded in a mass of pure graphite which serves to slow down neutrons; **atomic theory** the hypothesis that all atoms of the same element are alike and that a compound is formed by union of atoms of different elements in some simple ratio; **atomic warfare** warfare using atomic bombs; **atomic weight** the inferred weight of an atom of an element relatively to that of oxygen as 16 or, more recently, C-12 = 12; **a'tom-smasher** (*coll.*) an apparatus for breaking up the atom, any accelerator. [Gr. *atomos—a-,* priv., and *tomos,* verbal adj. of *temnein,* to cut.]

atonal, etc. See **atony.**

atone *ə-tōn', adv.* at one, at once, together.—*v.i.* originally to make *at one,* to reconcile: to give satisfaction or make reparation (with *for*): to make up for deficiencies.—*v.t* to appease, to expiate.—*ns.* **atone'ment** the act of atoning: reconciliation: expiation: reparations: in Christian theology, the reconciliation of God and man by means of the incarnation and death of Christ; **aton'er.**

atony *at'ən-i, n.* want of tone or energy or of stress: debility: relaxation.—*adj.* **atonal** (*ā-tō'nl, a-; mus.*) not referred to any scale or tonic.—*ns.* **atonality** (*at-ə-nal'i-ti*); **atō'nalism.**—*adj.* **atonic** (*a-ton'ik*) without tone (*pros.*): unaccented (*pros*): debilitated. —*n* **atonic'ity** (-*is'*) debility, weakness. [Gr. *atonia —a-,* priv., *tonos,* tone, strength.]

atop *ə-top', adv* on or at the top.—*prep.* on top of [Prep. **a,** and **top.**]

atrabilious *at-rə-bil'yəs,* (*arch*) *adj.* of a melancholy temperament: hypochondriac: splenetic, acrimonious. [L. *āter, ātra,* black, *bilis,* gall, bile.]

atrip *ə-trip', adv.* (of an anchor when it is just drawn out of the ground), in a perpendicular position: (of a sail) when it is hoisted from the cap, sheeted home and ready for trimming. [Prep **a.**]

atrium *ā', ä'tri-əm,* L *at'ri-ōōm, n* the entrance hall or chief apartment of a Roman house: a cavity or entrance (*zool.*): either of the two upper cavities of the heart into which blood passes from the veins.—*pl* **a'tria.**—*adj.* **a'trial.** [L *ātrium*]

atrocious *ə-trō'shəs, adj.* extremely cruel or wicked heinous: very grievous: execrable —*adv.* **atrō'ciously.**—*ns* **atrō'ciousness; atrocity** (*ə-tros'i-ti*) atrociousness: an atrocious act. [L. *ātrōx, ātrōx, -ōcis,* cruel.]

atrophy *at'rəf-i, n.* wasting away. degeneration: diminution of size and functional activity by disuse emaciation —*v.t.* and *v.i.* to (cause to) suffer atrophy. to starve, to waste away —*adj.* **at'rophied.** [Gr. *a-,* priv , and *trophē,* nourishment.]

Atropos *at'rō-pos, n.* the Fate that cuts the thread of life.—*ns.* **At'ropa** the deadly nightshade genus of the potato family; **at'ropin, atropine** (-*pēn, -pin, -pīn*) a poisonous alkaloid in deadly nightshade. [Gr. *Atropos.*]

attach *ə-tach', v.t* to bind or fasten: to seize. to gain over: to connect, associate: to join in action, function, or affection: to arrest.—*v i.* to adhere, to be fastened: to be attributable, incident (to) to come into effect (*rare*).—*adjs* **attach'able; attached'.**—*n.* **attach'-ment** act or means of fastening. a bond of fidelity or affection: seizure of goods or person by virtue of a legal process: a piece, etc. that is to be attached [O.Fr. *atachier,* from *a* (—L. *ad*), and perhaps the root of **tack.**]

attaché *ə-tash'ā, n.* a junior member of an ambassador's suite.—**atta'ché-case** a small rigid rectangular leather receptacle for documents, etc [Fr., attached.]

attack *ə-tak', v t.* to fall upon violently: to assault: to

assail: to begin to affect or act destructively upon.— *v.t.* to take the initiative in attempting to score (*sport*).—*v.t.* and *v.i.* (*mus.*) to begin (a phrase or piece).—*n.* an assault or onset: the offensive part in any contest: the beginning of active operations on anything, even dinner: severe criticism or calumny: an access of illness: a performer's approach to a piece, dance, etc. or mode of beginning with respect to crispness, verve, and precision (*mus., ballet,* etc): used collectively to designate the players in a team who are in attacking positions.—*adj.* **attack'- able.**—*n.* **attack'er.** [Fr *attaquer*; a doublet of **attach.**]

attain *ə-tān'*, *v t.* to reach or gain by effort. to arrive at.—*v.i.* to come or arrive —*adj.* **attain'able** that may be reached.—*ns.* **attainabil'ity, attain'ableness; attain'ment** act of attaining: the thing attained: ac- quisition. (*pl*) acquirements in learning. [O.Fr. *ataindre*—L. *attingĕre*—*ad,* to, *tangĕre,* to touch.]

attainder *ə-tān'dər, n.* act of attainting: loss of civil rights through conviction for high treason (*law*) —*v.t.* **attaint'** to convict. to deprive of rights by conviction for treason (*law*). to accuse: to dis- grace, stain (from a fancied connection with *taint*).—*n.* attainder: a stain, disgrace. [O.Fr *ataindre*—see **attain.**]

attar *at'ər, n.* a very fragrant essential oil made in Bulgaria and elsewhere, chiefly from the damask rose.—Also **ott'o, ott'ar.** [Pers *atar.*]

attemper *ə-tem'pər, v.t.* to mix in due proportion: to modify or moderate: to adapt —*adj.* **attem'pered.** [L. *attemperāre*—*ad,* to, *temperāre,* to regulate]

attempt *ə-temt', v.t.* to try, endeavour (to do, or with *n.* of action).—*v.i.* to make an attempt or trial —*n.* an effort: a personal assault: any act that can fairly be described as one of a series which, if uninterrup- ted and successful, would constitute a crime (*law*).—*n.* **attemptabil'ity.**—*adj.* **attempt'able.** [O.Fr *atempter*—L *attentāre*—*ad,* and *temptāre, tentāre,* to try—*tendĕre,* to stretch.]

attend *ə-tend', v.t.* to wait on: to accompany (*arch.*): to be present at: to go regularly to (a school, etc.).—*v.i.* to listen (to): to apply oneself, direct one's mind and efforts (with *to*): to act as an atten- dant or companion (with *on, upon, arch.*): to wait, be consequent (with *on, upon, arch.*).—*ns.* **attend'- ance** the act of attending: presence gathering of persons attending.—*adj.* **attend'ant** giving attend- ance: accompanying.—*n* one who attends or ac- companies: a servant.—*ns.* **attend'er; atten'tion** (*-shən*) act of attending: steady application of the mind: heed: civility, courtesy: (in *pl*) courtship: position of standing rigidly erect with hands by the sides and heels together —*interj.* (*mil.*) a cautionary word calling for an attitude of readiness to execute a command.—*adj.* **attent'ive** full of attention: court- eous, mindful.—*adv.* **attent'ively.**—*n.* **attent'ive- ness.**—**attendance allowance** a grant paid to an invalid who requires the constant attendance of a nurse; **attendance centre** a centre where a young offender may be required to attend regularly, instead of serving a prison sentence.—**draw (some- one's) attention to** to direct (someone's) notice to- wards. [L. *attendĕre, attentum; attentiō, -ōnis.*]

attenuate *ə-ten'ū-āt, v.t.* to make thin or lean to break down into finer parts. to reduce in density to reduce in strength or value.—*v.i* to become thin or fine: to grow less.—*n* **atten'uant** anything that attenuates —Also *adj* —*adjs* **atten'uate, atten'u- ated** thin: thinned: dilute, rarefied tapering —*n* **attenuā'tion** process of making slender reduction of intensity, density, force, or (of bacteria) virulence in homoeopathy, the reduction of the active prin-

ciples of medicines to minute doses: reduction in magnitude, amplitude, or intensity, arising from absorption or scattering (*nuc., telecomm.*); **atten'uator.** [L. *attenuāre, -ātum*—*ad,* to, *tenuis,* thin.]

attest *ə-test', v.t.* to testify or bear witness to: to affirm by signature or oath: to give proof of, to manifest —*v.t.* and *v.i.* to enrol for military service.—*v.i* to bear witness (to).—*adjs.* **attest'- able, attest'ative.**—*n.* **attestā'tion** (*at-*) act of attesting: administration of an oath —*adj.* **attest'ed** certified free from the tubercle bacillus.—*ns.* **attest'- er, attest'or.** [L. *attestārī*—*ad,* to, *testis,* witness.]

Attic *at'ik, adj.* of Attica or Athens chaste, refined, classical, in taste, language, etc., like the Athenians —**Attic salt** wit of a dry, delicate, and refined quality. [Gr. *Attikos*—*Attikē,* Attica.]

attic *at'ik, n.* in archit , a low storey or structure above the cornice of the main part of an elevation a room in the roof of a house [The structure was supposed to be in the Athenian manner; see foregoing.]

attire *ə-tīr', v.t.* to dress, array or adorn. to pre- pare —*n.* dress any kind of covering —*ns* **attire'- ment; attir'ing.** [O Fr *atirer,* put in order—*à tire,* in a row—*à* (L *ad*), to, and *tire, tiere,* order, dress, see **tier.**]

attitude *at'i-tūd, n* posture, or position a studied or affected posture: a position on one leg with the other leg extended behind (*ballet*): of an aircraft in flight, or on the ground, the angles made by its axes with the relative airflow, or with the ground, respec- tively: the tilt of a vehicle measured in relation to the surface of the earth as horizontal plane (*space flight*): any condition of things or relation of per- sons viewed as expressing some thought, feeling, etc.—*adj.* **attitud'inal.**—*v i.* **attitud'inise, -ize** to assume affected attitudes.—*ns* **attitud'iniser, -z-; attitud'inising, -z-.**—**strike an attitude** to assume a position or figure indicative of a feeling or emotion not really felt. [Fr. *attitude* or It *attitudine*—L. *aptitūdō, -inis*—*aptus,* fit]

atto- *pfx.* one million million millionth, 10^{-18}. [Dan , Norw *atten,* eighteen.]

attorn *ə-tûrn', (law) v t* to transfer to another.—*n.* **attorn'ey** (O Fr pa p. *atorné*) one legally authorised to act for another. one legally qualified to man- age cases in a court of law: a solicitor—*pl* **attor'neys.**—*n* **Attor'ney-Gen'eral** the chief law- officer for England, the Republic of Ireland, a dominion, colony, etc.. in the United States, the head of the Department of Justice also the legal ad- viser of a State governor.—**attorney at law or public attorney** a professional and duly qualified legal agent, **attorney in fact or private attorney** one duly appointed by power of attorney to act for another in matters of contract, money payments, and the like, **letter, warrant,** or **power of attorney** a formal instrument by which one person authorises another to perform certain acts for him [L L *attornāre,* to assign; see **turn.**]

attract *ə-trakt', v.t.* to cause to approach otherwise than by material bonds: to draw (a crowd, attention, etc.): to entice —*adj* **attract'able.**—*n* **attract'ant** something that attracts, esp. that effects communication in insects and animals —*adv* **attract'ingly.**—*n.* **attrac'tion** act of attracting: an attracting force: that which attracts —*adj.* **attract'- ive** having the power of attracting alluring.—*adv.* **attract'ively.**—*ns.* **attract'iveness; attract'or.** [L *attrahĕre, attractum*—*ad,* to, *trahĕre,* to draw.]

attribute *ə-trib'ūt, v t* to ascribe, assign, or consider as belonging.—*n.* (*at'*) that which is attributed: that which is inherent in, or inseparable from, anything: that which can be predicated of anything: a quality of property: an accessory: a conventional symbol: a word added to another to denote an attribute (*gram.*).—*adj.* **attrib'utable.**—*n.* **attribution** (*at-ri-bū'shən*) act of attributing: that which is attributed.—*adj.* **attrib'utive** expressing an attribute: (of an adjective) placed immediately before or immediately after the noun it qualifies (*gram.*).—*n.* a word added to another to denote an attribute (*gram.*).—*adv.* **attrib'utively.** [L. *attribuĕre, -tribūtum—ad,* to, *tribuĕre,* to give.]

attrite *ə-trīt',* adj. worn by rubbing or friction: repentant through fear of punishment, not yet from the love of God (*theol.*).—*n.* **attrition** (a- or *ə-trish'ən*) rubbing together: wearing down: a defective or imperfect sorrow for sin (*theol.*): the wearing down of an adversary, resistance, resources, etc. (*fig.*).—*adj.* **attrit'ional.** [L. *attrītus—atterĕre—ad,* to, and *terĕre, trītum,* to rub.]

attune *ə-tūn',* in U.S. *-tōōn, v.t.* to put in tune: to make to accord: to arrange fitly: to make musical.—*n.* **attune'ment.** [L. *ad,* to, and **tune.**]

atypical *a-, ā-tip'i-kl,* adj. not typical. [Gr. *a-,* priv. and **typical.**]

aubade *ō-bäd',* n. a musical announcement of dawn: a sunrise song. [Fr.,—*aube,* dawn—Prov. *alba,* dawn.]

auberge *ō-berzh',* n. an inn.—*n.* **aubergiste** (*ō-ber-zhēst'*) an inn-keeper. [Fr., of Gmc. origin; see **harbour.**]

aubergine *ō'ber-jēn, -zhēn,* n. the fruit of the eggplant, the brinjal: its purple colour.—*adj.* of this colour. [Fr. dim. of *auberge,* a kind of peach—Sp. *alberchigo*—Ar. *al,* the, Sp. *pérsigo*—L. *persicum,* a peach.]

Aubrietia *ō-brē', ō-bri-ē'sh(y)ə,* n. a purple-flowered Mediterranean genus of trailing cruciferous plants: (without *cap.*) a plant of this genus. [After Claude *Aubriet* (c. 1665–1742), naturalist-painter.]

auburn *ō'bûrn,* adj. orig. light yellow: reddish brown. [L L. *alburnus,* whitish—L. *albus,* white.]

au courant *ō kōō-rä,* (Fr.) well up in the facts or situation.

auction *ōk'shən,* n. a public sale at which goods are sold to the highest bidder: auction bridge.—*v.t.* to sell by auction.—*adj.* **auc'tionary.**—*n.* **auctioneer'** one who sells or is licensed to sell by auction.—*v.t.* to sell by auction.—**Dutch auction** a kind of auction at which the salesman starts at a high price, and comes down till he meets a bidder. [L. *auctiō, -ōnis,* an increasing—*augēre, auctum,* to increase.]

audacious *ō-dā'shəs,* adj. daring: bold: impudent.—*adv.* **audā'ciously.**—*ns.* **audā'ciousness, audacity** (*ò-das'i-ti*). [Fr. *audacieux*—L. *audāx—audēre,* to dare.]

audible *ōd'i-bl,* adj. able to be heard.—*ns.* **audibil'ity, aud'ibleness.**—*adv.* **aud'ibly.**—*n.* **aud'ience** the act of hearing: a judicial hearing: admittance to a hearing: a ceremonial interview: an assembly of hearers or spectators.—*adj.* **audible** (*ō'dil, -dîl*) pertaining to hearing.—*n.* one inclined to think in terms of sound.—**audio-** (*ō'di-ō*) in composition, pertaining to sound, esp. broadcast sound: pertaining to, using, or involving, audio-frequencies.—*n.* **aud'io** reproduction of recorded or broadcast sounds (also *adj.*): an acoustic device by which an airman returning to an aircraft-carrier knows when he is at a proper speed for landing: short for **audiotypist** or **audiotyping.**—*ns.* **aud'io-engineer'** one concerned with the transmission and reception of broadcast sound; **audio-frequency** (*ō'di-ō-frē'kwən-si*) a frequency of oscillation which,

when the oscillatory power is converted into a sound pressure, is perceptible by the ear; **aud'iogram** a tracing produced by an audiograph; **aud'iograph** a machine used to test a patient's hearing by transmitting soundwaves directly to his inner ear; **audio-loca'tion** echo location.—*ns.* **audiol'ogist; audiol'ogy** the science of hearing; **audiom'eter** instrument for measuring differences in hearing: one for measuring minimum intensities of sounds which, for specified frequencies, are perceivable by the ear.—*adj.* **audiomet'ric.**—*ns.* **audiometrician** (*-mi-trish'ən*); **aud'iotyping; aud'iotyp'ist** typist able to type directly material reproduced by a Dictaphone.—*adj.* **audiovis'ual** concerned simultaneously with seeing and hearing.—*n.* **aud'it** an examination of accounts by an authorised person or persons: a calling to account generally: a statement of account: a check or examination.—*v.t.* to examine and verify by reference to vouchers, etc.—*ns.* **audi'tion** (*ò-dish'ən*) the sense, or an act, of hearing: a trial performance by an applicant for an acting, etc., position (also *v.t.* and *v.i.* with *for*): mode of hearing.—*adj.* **aud'itive** of, or related to, hearing.—*ns.* **aud'itor** a hearer: one who audits accounts:—*fem.* **aud'itress; auditō'rium** in a theatre, or the like, the space allotted to the hearers: the reception-room of a monastery:—*pl.* **audito'riums** or **-ia; aud'itorship.**—*adj.* **aud'itory** relating to the sense of hearing.—*n.* an audience: a place where lectures, etc., are heard.—**audio-visual aids** material such as pictures, closed-circuit TV, teaching machines, used in the classroom. [L. *audīre,* to hear.]

au fait *ō fe,* (Fr.) well-acquainted with a matter: well-informed, expert (with *with*).

Aufklärung *owf-kle'rōōng,* (Ger.) *n.* enlightenment, esp. the 18th-century intellectual movement.

au fromage *ō fro-mäzh,* (Fr.) with cheese.

auger *ō'gər,* n. a carpenter's boring tool.—**au'ger-bit** an auger that fits into a carpenter's brace. [From *nauger* (*an auger* for *a nauger*)—O.E. *nafugār—nafu,* a nave of a wheel, *gār,* a piercer; see **nave², gore².**]

aught *öt,* n. a whit: ought: anything: a part. [O.E. *ā-wiht* contr. to *āht* (whence **ought**), and shortened to *aht* (whence **aught**); *ā-wiht* is from *ā, ō,* ever, and *wiht,* creature, whit, wight.]

augment *ōg-ment',* v.t. to increase: to make larger.—*v.i.* to grow larger.—*n.* **aug'ment** (*-mənt*) increase: the prefixed vowel or initial vowel-lengthening in some past tenses of the verb in Sanskrit and Greek: sometimes applied also to such inflectional prefixes as the *ge-* of the German perfect participle.—*adjs.* **augment'able; augment'ative** having the quality or power of augmenting: (of an affix or derivative) increasing the force of the original word (*gram.*; also *n.*).—*n.* **augmenta'tion** increase: addition: the repetition of a melody in notes of greater length than the original (*mus.*).—*adj.* **augment'ed.**—*ns.* **augment'er; augment'or** a nerve that increases the rate of activity of an organ.—**augmented interval** (*mus.*) one increased by a semitone. [L. *augēre,* increase.]

au gratin *ō gra-tɛ̃,* (Fr.) cooked covered with breadcrumbs or grated cheese, or with both.

augur *ō'gər,* n. among the Romans, one who sought knowledge of secret or future things by observing the flight and the cries of birds: a diviner: a soothsayer.—*v.t.* to foretell from signs.—*v.i.* to guess or conjecture: to forebode.—*adjs.* **au'gural** (*-ū-rəl; -yar-əl*).—*ns.* **au'gurship; au'gury** the art or practice of auguring; an omen.—**augur well, ill,** for to be an encouraging, discouraging, sign with respect to. [L.; prob. from *avis,* bird.]

august *o-gust',* adj. venerable: imposing: sublime: majestic.—*adv.* **august'ly.**—*n.* **august'ness.** [L. *augustus—augēre,* to increase, honour.]

August ŏ'gəst, *n*. the eighth month of the year. [After the Roman emperor *Augustus*.]

Augustan ŏ-gust'ən, *adj*. pertaining to the Emperor *Augustus*, or to the time in which he reigned (31 B C —A D 14)—the most brilliant age in Roman literature: hence pertaining to any similar age, as the reign of Anne in English, and that of Louis XIV in French, literature: classic: refined.

Augustine o'gəst-ın, o-gust'in, **Augustinian** -tın'ı-ən, *ns*. one of any order of monks or nuns whose rule is based on the writings of St. Augustine: one who holds the opinions of St Augustine, esp on predestination and irresistible grace (*theol.*) —*adj*. **Augustin'ian** of or relating to St. Augustine.—*n*. **Augustin'ianism.**—**Augustinian canons** or **Austin canons** see **canon; Augustinian** or **Austin friars** or **hermits** the fourth order of mendicant friars, wearing a black habit, but not to be confused with the Black Friars or Dominicans.

auk ŏk, *n*. a short-winged, heavy-bodied bird of the family *Alcidae*.—*n*. **auk'let** one of the smaller birds of the family.—**great auk** garefowl, extinct *c* 1844, **little auk** an auk (*Plautus alle*) of the North Atlantic and Arctic Oceans. [O.N. *âlka*.]

auld ŏld, (*Scot*.) *adj*. old.—**auld lang syne** lit old long since, long ago. [O.E. *ald*.]

aumbry om'brı, *n*. Same as **ambry**.

au naturel ŏ na-tü-rel, (Fr.) in the natural state cooked plainly.

aunt ant, *n*. a father's or mother's sister, or an uncle's wife or a great-aunt: a woman to whom one can turn for advice, sympathy, practical help, etc. (*fig.*).— dim **auntie, aunty.**—**Auntie** a facetious name for the British Broadcasting Corporation; **Aunt Sally** a pastime at fairs, in which sticks or balls are thrown to smash a pipe in the mouth of a wooden figure: a target for abuse (*fig.*). [O.Fr. *ante*—L. *amita*, a father's sister.]

au pair ŏ per, (Fr.) *adj* orig. by mutual service without payment: used of arrangement whereby girls perform light domestic duties in exchange for board and lodging and pocket-money.—*n*. an au pair girl.

aura o'rə, *n*. a supposed subtle emanation, esp. that essence which is claimed to emanate from all living things and to afford an atmosphere for occult phenomena: air, distinctive character (*fig.*): peculiar sensations that precede an attack in epilepsy, hysteria, and certain other ailments (*path.*):—*pl* **aur'ae** (*-ē*), **aur'as.**—*adj*. **aur'al.** [L. *aura*, a breeze.]

aural o'rəl, *adj*. pertaining to the ear.—*adv*. **aur'ally.** —*adj*. **aur'iform** ear-shaped.—*ns*. **aur'iscope** an instrument for examining the ear; **aur'ist** a specialist in diseases of the ear. [L. *auris*, ear.]

aureate ŏ'ri-ət, *adj*. gilded: golden: floridly rhetorical —*ns*. **aure'ity** the peculiar properties of gold; **aur-ē'ola, aureole** (ŏ'ri-ŏl) a crown, or an increment to the ordinary blessedness of heaven, gained by virgins, martyrs, and doctors (*theol.*): the gold or coloured disc or ring round the head in a picture, symbolising glory: a glorifying halo (*fig.*): a halo or corona around the sun or moon, or the clear space within it (*meteor.*): the coloured rings around the spectre of the Brocken (*meteor*): (apparently erroneously) a halo surrounding the whole figure: any halo-like appearance.—*n*. **aureomycin** (-*mi'sin*) an antibiotic used against typhus and other diseases, got from *Streptomyces aureo*faciens.—*adjs*. **au'ric** pertaining to gold: containing trivalent gold (*chem.*), **aurous** (ŏ'rəs) containing univalent gold. [L. *aurum*, gold.]

au revoir ŏ rə-vwar, (Fr) goodbye until we meet again

auric. See **aureate.**

auricle or'ı-kl, *n*. the external ear: an ear-like appendage to an atrium in the heart, or the atrium

itself: an earlike lobe of a leaf, etc.—*adj*. **aur'icled** having appendages like ears.—*adj*. **auric'ūlar** pertaining to the ear: known by hearing, or by report: told privately.—*adv*. **auric'ūlarly.**—*adjs*. **auric'ūlate** (*-lət*), **auric'ūlated** ear-shaped.—**auricular confession** confession to a priest [L. *auricula*, dim. of *auris*, the ear.]

auriferous or-if'ər-əs, *adj*. bearing or yielding gold. [L. *aurifer*—*aurum*, gold, *ferre*, to bear; *facĕre*, to make]

auriform. See under **aural.**

auriscope, aurist. See under **aural.**

aurochs or', owr'oks, *n* the extinct urus or wild ox. (erroneously) the European bison. [O.H.G. *ûr-ohso*—*ûr* (adopted into L. as *ûrus*, into Gr. as *ouros*), and *ohso*, ox]

Aurora o-rō'rə, *-ro'*, *n*. the dawn: the goddess of dawn. (without *cap*) a rich orange colour: a luminous meteoric phenomenon of electrical character seen in and towards the Polar regions, with a tremulous motion, and streamers of light:—*pl* **auro'ras, -rae.**—*adjs*. **auro'ral, auro'rean** pertaining to the dawn or the aurora: rosy: fresh and beautiful.—*adv*. **auro'rally.**—**aurora borealis** (bō-rı-â'lıs, -a'lıs or bo-) or **septentrionalis** (sep-ten-trı-on-â'lıs) the northern aurora or northern lights; **aurora australis** (os-trä'lıs) the southern lights, a similar phenomenon in the southern hemisphere. [L. *Aurôra*.]

aurous. See **aureate.**

auscultation os-kul-tā'shən, *n*. the art of discovering the condition of the lungs and heart by applying the ear or the stethoscope —*v t*. and *v.i* **aus'cultate** to examine by auscultation.—*n*. **aus'cultātor** one who practises auscultation: an instrument for the purpose —*adj*. **auscultatory** (*-kul'tə-tə-rı*) [L *auscultâre*, to listen.]

Auslese ows'lā-zə, (Ger) *n*. choice, selection: wine made from selected bunches of grapes

auspice os'pıs, *n*. an omen drawn from observing birds: augury: prognostic: (in *pl.*) patronage.—*v.t*. **auspicate** (os'pı-kât) to foreshow: to initiate or inaugurate with hopes of good luck.—*adj*. **auspicious** (-pısh'əs) having good auspices or omens of success: favourable: fortunate: propitious.—*adv*. **auspi'ciously.**—*n* **auspi'ciousness.** [Fr ,—L *auspicium*—*auspex*, *auspicis*, a bird-seer, from *avis*, bird, and *specĕre*, to look, to observe.]

Aussie oz'i, os'i, (*slang*) *n*. and *adj*. Australian.

austere os-tēr', *adj*. sour and astringent harsh· severe· stern: grave: severe in self-discipline: severely simple, without luxury.—*adv* **austere'ly.**—*ns* **austere'ness, austerity** (*-ter'*) quality of being austere: severity of manners or life· harshness. asceticism: severe simplicity of style, dress, or habits —*adj*. evincing or adopted in austerity [L. *austêrus* —Gr. *austêros*—*auein*, to dry.]

Austin. See **Augustine.**

Austral os'trəl, *adj*. southern —*adj* **Australasian** (-â'zhən) pertaining to Australasia, or the lands that lie south-east of Asia.—*n*. a native or colonist of one of these.—*n* **Australopithecus** (-*pith'ə-kəs* or *-pı-thê'kəs*) a genus of extinct primates, represented by skulls, etc., found in southern Africa —*adj*. and *n* **Australopithecine** (-*pıth'ə-sîn*) [L *austrâlis*—*Auster*, the south wind.]

Australian os-trā'lı-ən, *adj* of, or pertaining to, Australia, the largest island in the world and the smallest continent, an independent member of the Commonwealth (formerly a British colony) —*n*. a white native or resident, or an aboriginal native, of Australia.—*n* **Austrā'lianism** an Australian idiom: feeling for Australia —**Australia Day** the first Monday after 26 January, a public holiday kept in celebration of the landing of the British in 1788; **Australian crane** see **brolga; Australian rules (football)** an Australian mixture of association and rugby football played by eighteen a side with a rugby ball (familiarly **rules**) [L. *austrālis*, southern—*Auster*, south wind.]

Austrian *òs'tri-ən, adj.* of or pertaining to *Austria.*—*n.* a native or citizen of Austria.

aut-. See **auto-**.

autacoid *o'ta-koid, n.* an internal secretion that excites or inhibits action in various tissues. a hormone or chalone. [Gr *autos,* self, *akos,* drug.]

autarchy *ot'ar-ki, n.* absolute power.—*adjs.* **autar'- chic(al).**—*n.* **aut'archist.** [Gr. *autos,* self, and *archein,* to rule.]

autarky *òt'ar-ki, n.* self-sufficiency.—*adjs.* **autar'kic, -al.**—*n.* **aut'arkist.** [Gr. *autarkeiā—autos,* self, *arkeein,* to suffice]

authentic, -al *o-then'tik, -əl, adjs.* genuine: authoritative: true, entitled to acceptance, of established credibility: (of writing) trustworthy, as setting forth real facts: in existentialism, used to describe the way of living of one who takes full cognisance of the meaninglessness of the world yet deliberately follows a consistent course of action.—*adv.* **authent'ically.** —*v.t.* **authen'ticate** to make authentic: to prove genuine: to give legal validity to: to certify the authorship of.—*ns.* **authentica'tion; authen'ticator; authenticity** (*ō-thən-tis'i-ti*) quality of being authentic: state of being true or in accordance with fact: genuineness.—**authentic cadence** (*mus.*) a perfect cadence. [Gr. *authentikos,* warranted—*autos,* self.]

author *öth'ər, n.* one who brings anything into being: a beginner of any action or state of things: the original writer of a book, article, etc. (*fem.* **auth'oress**).— Also *v.t.*—*adjs.* **authorial** (*-thō', -tho'*), **auth'orish.** —*v.t.* **auth'orise, -ize** to give authority to: to sanction: to justify: to establish by authority.—*adj.* **authoris'able, -z.**—*ns.* **authorisa'tion, -z-; auth'orship.**—**Authorised Version** the English translation of the Bible completed in 1611. [Through Fr. from L. *auctor—augēre, auctum,* to increase, to produce.]

authority *öth-or'it-i, n.* legal power or right: power derived from office or character or prestige: weight of testimony: permission: a person or body holding power: an expert: a passage or book referred to in witness of a statement: the original bestower of a name (*biol.*).—*adj.* **authorita'rian** setting authority above liberty.—Also *n.*—*n.* **authorita'rianism.**— **authoritative** (*o-thor'it-āt-iv, ō-thor'it-ət-iv*) having the sanction or weight of authority: dictatorial.—*adv.* **author'itatively.**—*n.* **author'itativeness.** [L. *auct- ōritas, -ātis—auctor.*]

autism *öt'izm, n.* absorption in imaginative activity directed by the thinker's wishes, with loss of contact with reality: an abnormality of childhood development affecting language and social communication. —*adj.* **autis'tic.**—*adv.* **autis'tically.** [Gr. *autos,* self.]

auto-, aut- *ö-t(ō)-,* in composition, (1) self; (2) same; (3) self-caused; (4) automobile; (5) automatic. [Gr. *autos,* self.]

auto *ö'tō, n.* (chiefly *U.S.*) short for **automobile**—*pl.* **au'tos.**

Autobahn *ow'tō-bān,* (Ger) *n.* an arterial double road for motor traffic only

autobiography *ö-tō-bi-og'rə-fi, n.* a person's life written by himself.—*n.* **autobiog'rapher.**—*adjs* **autobiographic** (*-ō-graf'ik*), **-al.**—*adv.* **autobiograph'ically.** [Gr. *autos,* self, *bios,* life, *graphein,* to write.]

autobus, autocar, autocycle *ns.* motor-bus, -car, -cycle. [auto- (5).]

autocephalous *o-tō-sef'ə-ləs, adj.* having its own head: independent.—*n* **autoceph'aly** condition of being autocephalous [Gr *autos,* self, *kephalē,* head]

autochanger *o'tō-chān-jər, n* (a record-player having) a device by means of which records are dropped from a stack one at a time on to the turntable [auto- (5).]

autochthon *o-tok'thon, n.* one of the primitive inhabitants of a country: an aboriginal:—*pl.* **autoch'- thons** and **autoch'thonēs.**—*adj.* **autoch'thonous** (of flora, fauna) indigenous. formed in the region where found (*geol.*): found in the place of origin.— *ns.* **autoch'thonism, autoch'thony.** [Gr. *auto- chthōn,* sprung from the soil—*autos,* self, *chthōn, chthonos,* soil.]

autoclave *o'tō-klāv, n.* a strong, sealed vessel for carrying out chemical reactions under pressure and at high temperatures, or one in which super-heated steam under pressure is used for sterilising or cooking. [Fr., self-fastening apparatus—Gr. *autos,* self, perhaps L *clāvis,* key or *clāvus,* nail.]

autocrat *o'tō-krat, n.* one who rules by his own power: an absolute sovereign.—*n.* **autocracy** (*-tok'rə-si*) an absolute government by one man: despotism.—*adj.* **autocrat'ic.**—*adv.* **autocrat'ically.** [Gr *autokratēs —autos,* self, *kratos,* power.]

autocross *o-tō-kros', n* a motor race round a grass field. [auto- (4)]

autocue *o'tō-kū, n.* a device showing a television speaker the text of what he has arranged to say [auto- (5).]

auto-da-fē *o'tō-da-fā', n.* the public declaration of the judgment passed on heretics in Spain and Portugal by the Inquisition: the infliction of the punishment that immediately followed thereupon, esp. the public burning of the victims:—*pl.* **autos-da-fē.** [Port *auto da fē* (Sp. *auto de fe*), *auto*—L. *actum,* act; *da,* of the—L. *de,* of; and *fē*—L. *fidēs,* faith.]

autodidact *o'tō-di-dakt, n* a self-taught person.— *adj.* **autodidact'ic.** [Gr. *autodidaktos—autos,* self, *didaktos,* taught.]

autoerotic *ō-tō-e-rot'ik, adj* relating to sexual excitement or gratification gained from one's own body, with or without external stimulation.—*ns.* **auto- erot'icism, autoer'otism.** [auto- (1), and Gr. *erōti- kos,* amorous—*erōtaein,* to love.]

autogamy *ō-tog'ə-mi, n.* self-fertilisation.—*adjs.* **autog'amous, autogamic** (*ō-tō-gam'ik*). [Gr. *auto- gamos,* breeding alone—*autos,* self, *gamos,* marriage.]

autogenous *o-toj'ə-nəs, adj.* self-generated: independent.—*ns.* **autogen'esis, autog'eny** spontaneous generation. [Gr. *autogenēs—genos,* offspring.]

autogiro, autogyro *o-tō-jī'rō, n* a rotating-wing aircraft whose chief support in flight is derived from the reaction of the air upon freely-revolving rotors: —*pl.* **autogi'ros, -gy'ros.** [Orig. trademark; invented by Juan de la Cierva: Sp.,—Gr *autos,* self, *gyros,* circle.]

autograft *o'tō-graft, n.* a graft from one part to another of the same body.—Also *v t.* [auto- (2) and **graft[1]**.]

autograph *ö'tō-graf, n.* one's own handwriting: a signature: an original manuscript.—*v.t.* to write with one's hand.—*adj.* **autographic** (*-graf'*).—*adv.* **auto- graph'ically.**—*n.* **autography** (*o-tog'rəfi*) act of writing with one's own hand: reproduction of the outline of a writing or drawing by facsimile. [Gr. *auto- graphos,* written with one's own hand—*autos,* self, *graphein,* to write.]

autoharp *o'tō-harp, n* a kind of zither, with button-controlled dampers, which produces chords [auto- (5).]

auto-immunisation, -z-, *o'tō-im-ūn-īz-ā'shən, n.* production by a living body of antibodies which attack constituents of its own tissues, perhaps the cause of certain serious diseases (**auto-immune diseases**).—*n.* **auto-immun'ity.** [auto- (1).]

auto-intoxication *o'tō-in-toks-ı-kā'shən, n.* poisoning by substances produced within the body.—*n* and *adj.* **au'to-intox'icant.** [auto- (1).]

autolysis *o-tol'ıs-ıs, n.* the breaking down of dead tissue by the organism's own ferments —*v.t* and *v.ı* **aut'olyse, -yze** (-*līz*) to (cause to) undergo autolysis.—*adj* **autolyt'ic.** [Gr *autos,* self, *lysis,* loosening.]

automaton *o-tom'ə-tən, n.* a self-moving machine, or one that moves by concealed machinery: a living being regarded as without consciousness: one who acts by routine, without intelligence:—*pl.* **autom'-atons, autom'ata.**—*n.* **aut'omat** (or -*mat'*) a restaurant where dishes, hot or cold, are obtained from slot machines: a slot machine of this kind: an automaton.—*v.t.* **automate** (*o'tō-māt*) to apply automation to.—*adj.* **automatic** (-*tə-mat'ık*) working by itself without direct and continuing human operation· (of a firearm) reloading itself from an internal magazine, or able to continue firing as long as there is pressure on the trigger: of (the gears of) a motor vehicle, operated by automatic transmission: (of behaviour, reactions, etc) done, etc. without thinking, mechanical: occurring as a matter of course.—*n.* an automatic firearm, machine, etc.. the position of the switches, etc on a machine, etc. that allows it to operate automatically.—*adv.* **automat'ically.**—*ns.* **automaticity** (-*tıs'ı-tı*) **automā'tion** a high degree of mechanisation in manufacture, the handling of material between processes being automatic, and the whole automatically controlled; **autom'atism** automatic or involuntary action· power of self-moving: power of initiating vital processes from within the cell, organ, or organism, independently of any direct or immediate stimulus from without· the self-acting power of the muscular and nervous systems, by which movement is effected without intelligent determination: action without conscious volition: suspension of control by the conscious mind, so that ideas may be released from the unconscious—a technique of surrealism (*art*), **autom'atist** one who acts automatically.—**automatic pilot** a device which can be set to steer an aircraft or a ship on a chosen course (also **autopilot**); automatic transmission in a motor vehicle, power transmission by fluid drive, allowing gears to change automatically, **automatic writing** writing performed without the volition of the writer [Gr. *automatos,* self-moving—*autos,* self.]

automobile *o-tō-mō-bēl', n.* or *o'*, or -*mō', adj* self-moving.—*n.* a motor-car.—*ns.* **automō'bilism, automō'bilist.** [Gr. *autos,* self; L. *mōbilis,* mobile.]

automotive *o-tō-mō'tıv, adj.* self-propelling: pertaining to automobiles. pertaining to the motor-car trade. [Gr. *autos,* self, L L *motıvus,* causing to move.]

autonomy *o-ton'əm-ı, n* the power or right of self-government, esp partial self-government· the doctrine that the human will carries its guiding principle within itself (Kant's *philos.*) —*adjs.* **autonomic** *o-tō-nom'ık,* self-governing: pertaining to the autonomic nervous system: spontaneous (*bot , zool*); **autonom'ical.**—*n.sing* **autonom'ics** the study of self-regulating systems for process control.—*n* **auton'omist.**—*adj.* **auton'omous** (of a country, etc) (partially) self-governing: independent. (of the will) guided by its own principles (*philos*). autonomic (*bot., zool*)—**autonomic nervous system** system of nerve fibres, innervating muscles, glands, etc.,

whose actions are automatic. [Gr. *autonomos—nomos,* law.]

autopilot. See **automatic pilot** under **automaton.**

autopista *ow'tō-pēs-ta,* (Sp) *n.* a highway for motor traffic only: a motorway.

autoplasty *o'tō-plas-tı, n* grafting of healthy tissue from another part of the same body.—*adj* **autoplas'tic.** [Gr *autos,* self, *plastos,* formed.]

autopsy *o'top-sı,* or -*top', autop'sia ns.* personal inspection a post-mortem examination.—*v t.* **autopsy.**—*adjs* **autopt'ic, -al.**—*adv* **autopt'ically.** [Gr, *autos,* self, *opsis,* sight.]

autoradiograph *o-tō-rā'dı-ō-graf, n.* in tracer work, the record of a treated specimen on a photographic plate caused by radiations from the radioisotope used —*n.* **autoradiog'raphy** (-*og'raf-ı*) the production of autoradiographs. [auto- (1).]

autoroute *ō-tō-rōōt,* (Fr) *n* a highway for motor traffic only: a motorway.

autosome *o'tō-sōm, n.* a chromosome other than a sex-chromosome.—*adj.* **autosom'al.** [Gr *autos,* self, *sōma,* body.]

autostrada *a'ōō tō-stra-da,* (It) *n* a highway for motor traffic only: a motorway

auto-suggestion *ō'tō-su-jes'chən, n* a mental process similar to suggestion, but originating in a belief in the subject's own mind. [auto- (3).]

autotimer *o'tō-tīm-ər, n.* a device on a cooker, etc. that can be adjusted in advance to turn the apparatus on or off at a desired time [auto- (5)]

autotomy *o-tot'ə-mı, n* reflex separation of part of the body. [Gr *autos,* self, *tomē,* cut]

autotoxin *o-tō-tok'sın, n.* a poisonous substance formed within the organism against which it acts [Gr. *autos,* self, and **toxin.**]

autotrophic *o-tō-trof'ık, adj* capable of building up food materials from inorganic matter.—*n.* **au'totroph** an autotrophic organism [Gr. *autos,* self, *trophē,* food.]

autotype *o'tō-tıp, n.* a true impress or copy of the original: a process of printing from a photographic negative in a permanent pigment.—*v.t* to reproduce by such a process —*n* **autotypog'raphy** a process by which drawings made on gelatine are transferred to a plate from which impressions may be taken [auto- (2)]

autumn *o'təm, n* the third season of the year, when fruits are gathered in, generally (in the northern hemisphere) from August or September to October or November: astronomically, from the autumnal equinox to the winter solstice· a period of harvest or of maturity —*adj* **autum'nal** (*o-tum'nl*) pertaining to autumn. blooming in autumn: beyond the prime· withering or withered —*adv.* **autum'nally.**—**autumn crocus** a species of *Colchicum,* meadow-saffron [L *autumnus.*]

auxesis *ok-sē'sıs, n* increase in size: hyperbole growth of cell, etc.—*adj* **auxet'ic.**—*n.* something that promotes auxesis [Gr. *auxēsis,* increase.]

auxiliar *og-zıl'yər,* **auxiliary** -*ı, adjs* helping. subsidiary —*ns.* **auxil'iar** an auxiliary; **auxil'iary** a helper: a subordinate or assistant person or thing. a verb that helps to form the moods, tenses or voices of other verbs (*gram.*) (esp in *pl*) a soldier serving with another nation a naval vessel not used for combat. [L *auxiliāris—auxilium,* help—*augēre,* to increase]

auxin *oks'ın, n* any of a number of growth-promoting substances present in minute quantities in plants. [Gr. *auxein,* to increase]

avadavat. Same as **amadavat.**

avail *ə-vāl', v t* to be of value or service to to benefit (used reflexively with *of* in the sense of make use, take advantage).—*v.i.* to be of use: to answer the purpose.—*n.* effectual advantage (esp. in phrases such as *of, to no avail, of any avail*).—*n.* **availabil'ity** quality of being available: power of effecting or promoting an end: the possession of qualities, other than merit, which predispose a candidate to success in an election (esp. *U.S. polit.*).—*adj.* **avail'able** that one may avail oneself of: accessible: within reach: obtainable: to be had or drawn upon: valid (*law*).—*n.* **avail'ableness.**—*adv.* **avail'ably.** [L. *ad,* to, *valēre,* to be worth, to be strong; app. modelled on **vail.**]

avalanche *av'ə-länsh, -länch, -o-, n.* a hurtling mass of snow, with ice and rock, descending a mountain side: a snow-slip, as from a roof: an overwhelming influx: a shower of particles resulting from the collision of a high-energy particle with matter (*nuc.*).—*v.t.* and *v.i.* to carry or come down as or like an avalanche. [Fr. dial. *avaler,* to descend—*à* (L. *ad*), to, *val* (L. *vallis*), valley.]

avant-garde *av-ä-gärd', n.* those who create or support the newest ideas and techniques in an art, etc.—Also *adj.*—*ns.* **avant-gard'ism** avant-garde theory or practice, or support of these; **avant-gard'ist(e)** a member of the avant-garde. [Fr. *avant-garde,* vanguard.]

avanturine. See **aventurine.**

avarice *av'ər-is, n.* eager desire for wealth: covetousness.—*adj.* **avaricious** (-*ish'əs*) extremely covetous: greedy of gain.—*adv.* **avari'ciously.**—*n.* **avari'ciousness.** [Fr.,—L. *avāritia*—*avārus,* greedy —*avēre,* to pant after.]

avast *ə-väst', (naut.) interj.* hold fast! stop! [Prob. Du. *houd vast,* hold fast.]

avatar *a-və-tär', n.* the descent of a Hindu deity in a visible form: incarnation: supreme glorification of any principle (*fig.*). [Sans. *ava,* away, down, and root *tar-,* to pass over.]

ave *ä'vē, ä'vi,* or *ä'vā, interj.* be well and happy: hail.—*n.* an address or prayer to the Virgin Mary, in full, **ave Maria** (*ä'vä mə-rē'ə*) or **ave Mary,** the Hail Mary, or angelic salutation (Luke i. 28). [Imper. of L. *avēre,* to be well. See **angelus.**]

avenge *ə-venj', -venzh', v.t.* to vindicate: to take vengeance on someone on account of.—*adjs.* **avenge'ful; aveng'ing.**—*ns.* **avenge'ment; aveng'er.** [O.Fr. *avengier*—L. *ad,* to, *vindicāre,* to claim. See **vengeance.**]

avens *av'ənz, n.* any plant of the rosaceous genus *Geum* (**water avens** *Geum rivale*; **wood avens** herb-bennet): also the related sub-alpine **mountain avens** (*Dryas octopetala*). [O.Fr. *avence.*]

aventurine *a-ven'chū-rin,* **avanturine** *-van', ns.* a brown, spangled kind of Venetian glass: a kind of quartz enclosing spangles of mica or haematite (also **gold'stone**).—*adj.* shimmering or spangled, as kinds of feldspar or sealing-wax. [It. *avventura,* chance—because of the accidental discovery of the glass.]

avenue *av'ən-ū,* in U.S. *-ōō, n.* the principal approach to a country-house, usually bordered by trees: a double row of trees, with or without a road: a wide and handsome street, with or without trees: any passage or entrance into a place: means of access or attainment (*fig.*). [Fr.,—L. *ad,* to, *venīre,* to come.]

aver *ə-vûr', v.t.* to declare to be true: to affirm or declare positively: to prove or justify (*law*):—*pr.p.* **averr'ing;** *pa.p.* **averred'.**—*n.* **aver'ment** positive assertion: a formal offer to prove a plea (*law*): the proof offered (*law*). [Fr. *avérer*—L. *ad* and *vērus,* true.]

average *av'ər-ij, n.* orig. a customs duty or similar charge: any expense other than freight payable by the owner of shipped goods: expense or loss by damage of ship or cargo: equitable distribution of expense or loss: assessment of compensation in the same propor-

tion as amount insured bears to actual worth: arithmetical mean value of any quantities: estimation of such a mean: loosely, ordinary or prevailing value, common run.—*adj.* mean: prevailing, ordinary.—*v t.* to obtain the average of: to amount to on an average: to do on an average.—*v.t* and *v.i.* to even out to an average.—**average adjuster** an assessor employed by an insurance company in marine claims.—**law of averages** pop., a proposition stating that the mean of a situation is maintained by the averaging of its extremes. [Cf. Fr. *avarie,* It. *avaria,* duty on goods.]

averse *ə-vûrs', adj.* disinclined (with *to*; but some prefer *from*): reluctant: turned away or backward.— *adv.* **averse'ly.**—*ns* **averse'ness; aver'sion** turning aside: dislike: hatred: the object of dislike.—*adj.* **aver'sive** showing aversion. with purpose, or result, of averting.—*v.t.* **avert'** to turn aside: to prevent. to ward off.—*adj.* **avert'ed.**—*adv* **avert'edly.**—*adj.* **avert'ible,** *rarely* **avert'able,** capable of being averted —**aversion therapy** treatment of a person suffering from a perversion or a compulsive form of behaviour by associating his or her thoughts about it with something unpleasant such as the administration of an electric shock. [L. *āvertĕre, āversus—ab,* from, *vertĕre,* to turn.]

avert. See **averse.**

Aves *ä'vēz,* L. *a'väs, -wäs, n.pl.* birds as a class of vertebrates.—*adjs.* **ā'vian, avine** (*ā'vin*) of birds.— *ns.* **ā'viarist** one who keeps an aviary, **ā'viary** a large cage or the like for keeping birds; **a'viculture** bird-rearing: bird-fancying; **āvifau'na** the assemblage of birds found in a region.—*adj.* **ā'viform** bird-like in form or structure; **avine** avian. [L. *avis,* bird, *avicula,* little bird, *aviculārius,* bird-keeper]

Avesta *ə-ves'ta, n.* the Zoroastrian holy Scriptures.— *adjs.* **Aves'tan, Aves'tic** of the Avesta or its East Iranian language.—*ns.* the lanaguage of the Avesta, also called **Zend.** [Pehlevi *Avīstâk,* lore.]

avian, aviary etc See **Aves.**

aviate *ä'vi-āt, v t* to fly mechanically, navigate the air. —*ns.* **aviā'tion** the art or practice of mechanical flight; **ā'viātor** an airman, flying man; **aviatrix** (*ā-vi-ā'triks*) a female pilot.—*adj.* **āvion'ic.**—*n. sing.* **āvion'ics** science concerned with development and use of electronic and electrical devices for aircraft (*aviation electronics*). [L. *avis,* a bird]

avid *av'id, adj.* greedy: eagerly desirous.—*n.* **avid'ity.** —*adv.* **av'idly.** [L. *avidus.*]

aviform, avine. See **Aves.**

avion *a-vy-ɔ̃, (*Fr.*) n.* aeroplane.—**par avion** (*par av-y-ɔ̃*) by air: by airmail

avionic(s). See **aviate.**

avital *ə-vī'tl, av'i-tl, adj.* of a grandfather: ancestral. [L. *avītus—avus,* a grandfather]

avitaminosis *ä-vit-ə-min-ōs'is, n.* lack of vitamins or a condition due to this [Gr. *a-,* priv.]

avocado *a-vō-kä'dō, n.* a tropical lauraceous tree: (also **avocado pear** (*pär*)) its pear-shaped fruit (also **alligator pear**): the colour of the skin of the fruit, blackish-green: the colour of the flesh of the fruit, yellowish-green.—*pl.* **avoca'dos.**—Also *adj.* [Sp. *aguacate*—Aztec *ahuacatl.*].

avocation *av-ō-kä'shən, n.* properly, a diversion or distraction from one's regular employment: improperly used for **vocation,** business which calls for one's time and attention: the calling of a case to a higher court (*law*). [L. *āvocātiō, -ōnis,* a calling away—*ab,* from, *vocāre,* to call]

avocet, avoset *av'ō-set, n.* a wading bird (genus *Recurvirostra*) with webbed feet and long, slender, curved, elastic bill. [Fr. *avocette,* It. *avosetta.*]

Avogadro's constant, number *a-vō-gä'drōz kon'stant, num'bər,* the number of specified elementary units (e.g. molecules) in a mole of any substance. **Avogadro's law**, **rule**, **hypothesis** the law that at equal temperature and pressure equal volumes of gases contain the same number of molecules [A. *Avogadro* (1776–1856), Italian physicist.]

avoid ə-*void'*, *v.t* to evade: to shun.—*adj.* **avoid'able**.—*n.* **avoid'ance**. [A Fr. *avoider*, O Fr *esvuidier*—L. *ex*, out, and root of **void**.]

avoirdupois, av-ər-də-*poiz'*, or *av'*, or av-war-dŭ-pwa' *n.* a system of weights in which the lb equals 16 oz.. (esp. *facet*) weight: heaviness or stoutness —*adj* of the system of weights [O Fr *aveir de pes*, to have weight—L. *habēre*, to have, *dē*, from, *pēnsum*, that which is weighed]

avoset. See **avocet**.

avouch ə-*vowch'*, *v.t* to avow· to acknowledge· to vouch for: to assert positively: to maintain: to guarantee· to own to: to appeal to.—*v.t.* to give assurance.—*adj* **avouch'able**.—*n* **avouch'ment**. [O Fr *avochier*—L, *advocāre*, to call to one's aid]

avow ə-*vow'*, *v t.* to declare: to acknowledge· to maintain.—*v.t.* (*law*) to justify an act done.—*n* a solemn promise: a vow.—*adj* **avow'able**.—*ns.* **avow'ableness**; **avow'al** a positive declaration: an acknowledgment: a frank confession.—*adj.* **avowed'**.—*adv.* **avow'edly**. [O Fr *avouer*, orig to swear fealty to—L. *ad*, to, and L.L *vōtāre*—L. *vōtum*, a vow: with sense affected by L *advocāre*. See **vow**, **avouch**.]

avulse ə-*vuls'*, *v t.* to pluck or tear away —*n.* **avul'sion** ·forcible separation: sudden removal of land by change of a river's course, whereby it remains the property of the original owner (opp. to *alluvion*). [L. *āvellēre*, *āvulsum*]

avuncular ə-*vung'kŭ-lər*, *adj* of an uncle [L. *avunculus*, an uncle.]

await ə-*wāt'*, *v.t* to wait or look for: to be in store for: to attend. [O N.Fr. *awaiter*—ā, to; see **wait**.]

awake ə-*wāk'*, *v t.* to rouse from sleep: to rouse from inaction.—*v t.* to cease sleeping: to rouse oneself from sleep or indifference·—*pa t.* **awoke'**, **awaked'**; *pa.p* **awaked'** or **awoke'**, sometimes **awōk'en**.—*adj.* not asleep: vigilant· aware, cognisant (with *to*) —*v t* **awak'en** to awake: to rouse into interest or attention. to call to a sense of sin (*theol.*) —*v.t.* to awake: to spring into being —*adj* **awak'ening** becoming awake· rousing: revivifying, reanimating.—*n.* a becoming awake, aware, active: a throwing off of indifference or ignorance: a rousing —*n.* and *adj.* **awak'ing**.—**be awake to** to be fully aware of. [O E. *āwæcnan* (pa.t. *āwōc*, pa.p *āwæcen*), confused with *āwacian* (pa t. *āwacode*) See **wake**, **watch**.]

award ə-*word'*, *v.t.* to adjudge. to determine: to grant —*n.* judgment. final decision, esp. of arbitrators: that which is awarded: a prize. [O.Fr. *ewarder*, *eswarder*—L. *ex*, in sense of thoroughly, and the root of **ward**, **guard**.]

aware ə-*wār'*, *adj.* wary: informed, conscious (with *of*). —*n.* **aware'ness** state of being aware: consciousness, esp. a dim form. [O E *gewær–wær*, cautious. See **ware**.]

awash ə-*wosh'*, *adv.* on a level with the surface of the water: afloat at the mercy of the waves —*adj.* having the surface covered with water: full of (with *with*) [Prep. **a.**]

away ə-*wā'*, *adv.* onward: continuously: without hesitation, stop, or delay: forthwith: out of the place in question: not at home: on the opponents' ground (*sport*; also *adj*), at or to a distance: off: in or into an averted direction: out of existence, life, or consciousness: with effect of removal or elimination· far· about (with *here*, *there*, *where*; now *dial.*): with omission of verb = go or (with *with*) take away (usu *imper.*), to endure (with *with*).—*n.* in football pools, a match won

by a team playing on the opponents' ground.—*interj* **begone** get out.—**away from it all** in or into a place which is remote from the bustle of life; **do away with** to abolish; **explain away** to explain so as to make the thing explained seem not to exist; **fall away** to dwindle: to waste away: to lose zeal and drop off, as followers; **fire away** go on, proceed now without further delay; **make away with** to destroy: to murder: to steal. [O E *aweg*, *onweg*–*on*, on, *weg*, way]

awe *o*, *n.* reverential wonder or fear: dread.—*v t* to strike with or influence by awe or fear —*adjs* **awed** (*od*) awe-stricken· expressive of awe; **awe'less** without awe: fearless.—*n* **awe'lessness**.—*adj.* **awe'some**, **aw'some** awed: awe-inspiring (*Scot.*)· dreadful.—*adv* **awe'somely**.—*n.* **awe'someness**.—*adj.* **aw'ful** inspiring awe: filled with awe· very bad, tiresomely great, etc. (*coll.*) —*adv* very (*coll.*) —*adv.* **aw'fully** in an awe-inspiring or awe-stricken manner: with awe. very (*coll.*).—*n* **aw'fulness**.—**awe'-inspiring**; **awe's stricken**, **-struck** struck with awe. [O.N *agi*.]

a-weather ə-*wedh'ər*, (*naut*) *adv.* towards the weather or windward side—opp to **alee** [Prep. **a.**]

a-weigh ə-*wā'*, *adv* in the act of being weighed, as an anchor just raised from the bottom [Prep. **a**, and **weigh**[1].]

awhile ə-(h)*wīl'*, *adv* for some time· for a short time [O.E. *āne hwīle*, a while (dat.)]

awkward *ok'wərd*, *adj.* clumsy: ungraceful: embarrassed: difficult to deal with· embarrassing —*adj.* **awk'wardish**.—*adv.* **awk'wardly**.—*n.* **awk'wardness** clumsiness· embarrassing or inharmonious quality or condition [Prob O.N. *afug*, turned wrong way, and suff *-ward*]

awl *ol*, *n* a pointed instrument for boring small holes. [O E. *æl*]

awn *on*, *n.* the beard of barley, or similar bristly process —*adj* **awned** [O.N *ogn* or a lost O.E cognate]

awning *on'ing*, *n.* a covering to shelter from the sun or weather —*v t* awn to shelter with an awning

awoke ə-*wōk'*, *pa.t* of **awake**.

awry ə-*rī'*, *adj.* twisted to one side: distorted, crooked: wrong: perverse.—*adv.* askew: unevenly: perversely: erroneously —**look awry** to look askance at anything; **walk awry** to go wrong. [Prep **a.**]

axe, **ax** *aks*, *n.* a tool for hewing or chopping, with edge and handle in the same plane. a stone-dressing hammer· ruthless cutting down of expenditure (*fig.*): —*pl.* **ax'es** (see also **axis**).—*v t.* to hew or strike with an axe. to dismiss as superfluous: to cut down, reduce (*fig.*)· to dispense with (*fig.*) —**axe to grind** a private purpose to serve [O.E. *æx*]

axel *aks'l*, *n* in figure skating, a jump from one skate to the other, incorporating one and a half turns in the air. [*Axel* Paulsen (1855–1938), a Norwegian skater.]

axerophthol aks-ər-of'*thol*, *n.* vitamin A [Gr *a-*, priv , and *xerophthalmia.*]

axial, **axile**. See under **axis**.

axilla ak-*sil'ə*, *n*. the armpit (*anat.*): axil (*bot.*):—*pl.* **axillae** (-ē) —*n* **ax'il** the angle between leaf and stem.—*adjs* **ax'illar**, **ax'illary**. [L. *āxilla*, the armpit.]

axiology aks-i-ol'*ə-ji*, *n.* the science of the ultimate nature, reality, and significance of values —*adj.* **axiological** (-ə-*loj'i-kl*).—*n.* **axiologist** (-ol'ə-jist). [Gr *axios*, worthy, *logos*, discourse]

axiom aks'i-əm, *n* a self-evident truth. a universally received principle· a postulate, assumption.—*adjs* **axiomat'ic**, **axiomat'ical**.—*adv* **axiomat'ically**.—*n sing.* **axiomat'ics** the study of axioms and axiom systems [Gr *axiōma*, -*atos*—*axioein*, to think worth, to take for granted—*axios*, worthy.]

axis *ak'sis*, *n* a line about which a body rotates, or about which a figure is conceived to revolve: a straight line about which the parts of a figure, body or system are symmetrically or systematically arranged: a fixed line adopted for reference in co-ordinate geometry, curve-plotting, crystallography, etc.: the second vertebra of the neck (*zool.*): the main stem or root, or a branch in relation to its own branches and appendages (*bot.*): an alliance of powers, as if forming together an axis of rotation—esp of Germany and Italy (1936):—*pl.* **axes** (*ak'sēz*).—*adj.* **ax'ial** relating to, or of the nature of, an axis.—*adv.* **ax'ially.**—*adj.* **ax'ile** (*ak'sīl*, U.S. *ak'səl*) coinciding with an axis.—*n.* **ax'on** a process of the nerve cell or neuron which in most cases transmits impulses away from the cell.—**axis of incidence** the line passing through the point of incidence of a ray perpendicularly to the refracting surface; **axis of refraction** the continuation of the same line through the refracting medium; **axis of the equator** the polar diameter of the earth which is also the axis of rotation. [L. *axis.*]

axle *aks'l*, **axle-tree** *aks'l-trē*, *ns.* the pin or rod in the nave of a wheel on which the wheel turns: a pivot or support of any kind.—**ax'le-box** the box in which the axle end turns; **ax'le-guard** a pedestal or pillowblock. [More prob. O.N. *öxull* than a dim. from O.E. *eax.*]

Axminster *aks'min-stər*, *n.* a variety of cut-pile carpet.—Also *adj.* [*Axminster* in Devon, where it originated.]

axolotl *aks'ə-lot-l*, *n.* the larval form of Amblystoma, commonly retaining its larval character in life, though capable of breeding. [Aztec.]

axon. See **axis.**

ay[1], **aye** *ī*, *adv.* yea: yes: indeed.—*n.* **aye** (*ī*) a vote in the affirmative: one who votes in the affirmative. [Perh. a dial. form of **aye,** ever; perh. a variant of **yea.**]

ay[2]. See **aye**[1].

ayah *ī'ə*, *n.* an Indian or South African waiting-maid or nursemaid.—Also **aia.** [Hind *āyā*; from Port. *aia,* nurse.]

ayatollah *a-yə-tol'ə, -tō'*, *n.* (sometimes with *cap.*) a Muslim religious leader of the Shiah sect. [Ar. *ayatollah,* sign of God—*āya,* sign, *ollāh,* God.]

aye[1], **ay** *ā*, *adv.* ever: always: for ever.—**for aye, for ever and aye** for ever, to all eternity [O.N. *ei,* ever, O.E. *ā*; conn. with **age, ever.**]

aye[2]. See **ay**[1].

aye-aye *ī'ī*, *n.* an aberrant squirrel-like lemur of Madagascar. [Malagasy *aiay.*]

Aylesbury *ālz'bər-i*, *n.* a breed of ducks much valued for the table —Also *adj.* [*Aylesbury,* a market town in Bucks.]

ayrie. Same as **eyrie.**

Ayrshire *ār'shər*, *n.* a breed of reddish-brown and white cattle.—Also *adj.* [*Ayrshire,* a former Scottish county, where they originated]

Azalea *a-zā'li-ə*, *n.* a genus close akin to, or subgenus of, *Rhododendron,* shrubby plants, with five stamens and annual leaves: (without *cap.*) a plant of the genus. [Gr. *azaleos,* dry; reason for name uncertain.]

azan *a-zän'*, *n.* the Muslim call to public prayer made five times a day by a muezzin. [Ar. *'adhan,* invitation.]

azeotrope *ə-zē'ə-trōp*, *n* any liquid mixture which distils over without decomposition in a certain ratio, the boiling-point of the mixture differing from that of any constituent.—*adj.* **azeotrop'ic** (*-trop'*). [Gr. *a-*, priv., *zeein,* to boil, *tropos,* a turn.]

azimuth *az'im-əth*, *n.* the arc of the horizon between the meridian of a place and a vertical circle passing through any celestial body.—*adj.* **az'imuthal** (or *-mūdh', -mūth'*) pertaining to the azimuth. [Ar. *as-sumūt, as = al,* the, *sumūt,* pl. of *samt,* direction. See **zenith.**]

azo- *āz'ō-, az'-* in combination, nitrogen —*ns* **az'o-com'pound** a compound in which two nitrogen atoms are each attached to (usually) a carbon atom, as **az'oben'zene** $C_6H_5N{:}NC_6H_5$; **az'o-dye'** a dye of such composition. [*azote,* an old name for nitrogen.]

azoic *a-zō'ik*, *adj.* without life: before the existence of animal life: formed when there was no animal life on the globe, as rocks. [Gr. *a-,* priv, and *zōē,* life.]

azonal *a-zōn'əl, ā-*, *adj.* not arranged in zones or regions.—*adj.* **azonic** (*a-zon'ik*) not limited to a zone, not local. [Gr. *a-,* priv., *zōnē,* a belt]

Aztec *az'tek*, *n.* one of a people dominant in Mexico before the Spanish conquest: Nahuatl.—Also *adj.*

azure *azh'ər, āzh'ər*, or *ā'zhūr*, *adj.* of a faint blue: sky-coloured: blue (*her.*).—*n.* a delicate blue colour. the sky. [O.Fr. *azur*—L.L. *azura*—Ar. (*al*) *lazward,* Pers. *lājward,* lapis lazuli, blue colour.]

azygous *az'i-gəs*, *adj.* not yoked or joined with another: unpaired (*anat.*).—*n* **azygy** (*az'i-ji*) [Gr. *azygos*—*a-,* priv., and *zygon,* a yoke.]

azymous *az'i-məs*, *adj.* unfermented: unleavened.—*n.* **az'ym** (*-im*), **az'yme** (*-īm, -im*) unleavened bread. [Gr. *azymos*—*a-,* priv., *zȳmē,* leaven.]

For other sounds see detailed chart of pronunciation.

B

B, b *bē, n.* the second letter of our alphabet: in music, the seventh note of the scale of C major: the subsidiary series of paper sizes, ranging from B0 (1000 × 1414 mm.) to B10 (31 × 44 mm.): second class or order (as a road of secondary importance), or a class arbitrarily designated B; see **blood-group**: designating of less importance (as the *B-side* of a record, a *B-movie*).

baa *ba, n.* the cry of a sheep.—*v.i.* to bleat.—*n.* **baa'ing**. [Imit.]

baas *bäs,* (*S. Afr.*) *n.* master, overseer, sir.—*n.* **baas'-skap** condition in which one section of the population is treated as a master race: the theory used to justify this. [Afrik.—Du.]

Baathist, Ba'athist *ba'thist, n.* a member of the socialist or reformist party of various Arab countries, esp. Syria and Iraq.—Also *adj.*—*n.* **Baa'thism, Ba'a'thism**. [Ar. *baath*, renaissance.]

baba *ba'ba, n.* a small cake, with or without fruit, soaked in a rum syrup.—Also **rum baba** or **baba au rhum** (*ô rom*). [Fr.—Pol. *baba*, 'old woman']

babacoote *bab'ə-kōōt, n.* a large lemur, the indri or a closely related species. [Malagasy *babakoto*.]

Babbitt *bab'it, n.* a conventional middle-class business-man (or other person) who esteems success and has no use for art or intellectual pursuits.—*ns.* **Babb'ittry; Babb'ittism**. [Hero of novel by Sinclair Lewis.]

babbit *bab'it, v.t.* to fit with **Babbitt(t's) metal**, a soft anti-friction alloy (tin, with copper antimony, and usu. lead). [Isaac *Babbitt* (1799–1862), the Massachusetts inventor.]

babble *bab'l, v.i* to speak like a baby: to make a continuous murmuring sound like a brook, etc.: to talk incessantly: to tell secrets.—*v.t.* to utter confusedly or by rote: to divulge by foolish talk.—*n.* idle senseless talk: confused murmur, as of a stream.—*ns.* **babb'lement; babb'ler**.—*n.* and *adj.* **babb'ling**.—*adj.* **babb'ly**. [Prob. imit.]

babe *bāb, n.* a form of **baby**.

Babel *bā'bl, n.* a foolishly conceived lofty structure: a confused sound of voices: a scene of confusion.—*ns.* **bā'beldom; bā'belism**.—*adj.* **bā'belish**. [Heb. *Bābel*, prob. Assyr. *bāb-ili*, gate of God.]

Babi, Babee *ba'bē, n.* a member of a Persian sect, followers of *Bab-ed-Din* 'the Gate of Righteousness', who claimed to be a prophet bringing a new revelation.—Also **Ba'bist**.—*ns.* **Ba'bism, Ba'biism, Ba'beeism**.

babiroussa, -russa *ba-bi-rōō'sə, n.* a wild hog found in Celebes, etc , with great upturned tusks and the male. [Malay *bābi*, hog, and *rūsa*, deer.]

baboo. See babu.

baboon *bə-bōōn', n.* large monkey with long face, dog-like tusks and a tail: a clumsy, brutish person.—*adj.* **baboon'ish**. [Fr. *babouin*.]

babouche, babuche, baboosh *bə-bōōsh', n.* an Oriental heelless slipper. [Fr.,—Ar. *bābūsh*—Pers. *pā*, foot, *pūsh*, covering.]

babu, baboo *bä'bōō, n.* a title for Hindus in some parts of India corresponding to Mr: an Indian clerk: an Indian with a superficial English education (esp. *hist.*).—Also *adj.*—*ns.* **ba'budom; ba'buism**. [Hind. *bābū*]

babuche. See babouche.

babushka *bə-bōōsh'kə, n.* a triangular headscarf tied under the chin. [Russ. *bábushka*, grandmother.]

baby *bā'bi, n.* an infant, young child: a young animal: a

---

babyish person: a thing small of its kind: a girl (*coll.*): an inexperienced person: one's pet project, machine, etc.: one's own responsibility.—*v.t.* to treat as a baby—Also *adj.*—*n.* **ba'byhood**.—*adj.* **ba'byish**.—**ba'by-batt'erer** one who indulges in **ba'by-batt'ering** in instances of the **battered baby syndrome** (q.v. under **batter**); **ba'by-boun'cer, -jump'er** a harness or seat suspended from springs, elastic straps, etc. in which a young baby can disport itself; **Baby Buggy**® a light, collapsible push-chair for a baby or toddler; **ba'by-mind'er** a person who takes in infants to nurse for pay; **ba'by-ribb'on** a very narrow ribbon.—*v.i.* **ba'by-sit** to act as baby-sitter.—**ba'by-sitter** one who mounts guard over a baby to relieve the usual attendant; **ba'by-sitting; ba'by-snatcher** a person marrying some-one who is much younger: a person who steals a baby, e.g. from its pram; **ba'by-snatching**; **ba'by-talk** the speech of babies learning to talk, or an adult's imit-ation of it; **ba'by-walker** a wheeled frame with a canvas, etc. seat for supporting a baby learning to walk.—**be left holding the baby** to be left in the lurch with a responsibility; **throw out the baby with the bathwater** to get rid of the essential along with the superfluous. [Prob. imitative.]

Babylonian *bab-i-lōn'i-ən, adj.* of Babylon: hence huge, gigantic.—Also **Babylon'ish**.

baccalaureate *bak-ə-lo'ri-āt, n.* the university degree of bachelor—*adj.* **baccalau'rean**. [L.L. *baccalaureus*, altered from *baccalārius*. See **bachelor**.]

baccarat, baccara *bak'ə-ra, n* a French card game played by betters and a banker. [Fr]

Bacchus *bak'əs, n.* the god of wine.—*n* **bacchanal** (*bak'ə-nəl*) a worshipper, priest or priestess, of Bac-chus: a drunken reveller: a dance, song, or revel in honour of Bacchus.—*adj.* relating to drinking or drunken revels.—Also **bacchanalian** (-nā'li-ən).—*ns.pl.* **bacchanā'lia, bacch'anals** feasts in honour of Bacchus: drunken revels.—*n.* **bacchanā'lianism**.—*n.* and *adj.* **bacchant** (*bak'ant*) a priest or votary of Bac-chus: a reveller: a drunkard.—*n.* **bacchante** (*bə-kant', bak'ant,* or *ba-kant'i*) a priestess of Bacchus: a female bacchanal.—*adjs.* **Bacch'ian, Bacchic** (*bak'ik*) re-lating to Bacchus: jovial: drunken. [L. *Bacchus*, Gr. *Bakchos*.]

baccy, bacco *bak'i, -ō,* short forms of **tobacco**.

bach. See bachelor.

bachelor *bach'əl-ər, n.* an unmarried man: one who has taken his or her first degree at a university: a young unmated bull-seal or other male animal.—*n.* **bach** (*coll.*) a bachelor.—*v.i.* to live as a bachelor: to do for oneself.—Also *v.t.* with *it*—*ns.* **bach'elordom; bach'elorhood; bach'elorism** habit or condition of a bachelor; **bach'elorship** the degree of bachelor—**bach'elor-girl** a young unmarried woman who supports herself, **bach'elor's-butt'ons** a double-flowered yellow or white buttercup: also applied to other plants. [O.Fr. *bacheler*—L.L. *baccalārius*]

bacillus *bə-sil'əs, n.* (*cap.*) a genus of rod-shaped bacteria: a member of the genus: loosely, any rod-shaped bacterium: popularly, any disease-causing bacterium:—*pl.* **bacill'i**.—*adjs.* **bacill'ar, bacill'ary** (or *bas'*) of the shape or nature of a bacillus, rodlike.—*n.* **bacill'icide** that which destroys bacilli.—*adj.* **bacill'iform**. [L.L. *bacillus*, dim. of *baculus*, a rod] back *bak*, *n* the hinder part of the body in man, and the upper part in beasts. the hinder part, or the side remote from that presented or habitually seen: the under side of a leaf or of a violin: part of the upper surface of the tongue opposite the soft palate; the convex side of a book, opposite to the opening of the leaves· the thick edge of a knife or the like. the up- right hind part of a chair, bench, etc.. something added to the hinder side: in football, etc , one of the players behind the forwards—*full back* (who guards the goal), *half* and *three-quarter backs*.—*adj* rearward. remote: reversed: made by raising the back of the tongue (*phon*): belonging to the past.—*adv*. to or towards the back: to or towards the place from which one came: to a former state or condition. behind: behind in time: in return: again.—*v t*. to mount or ride: to help or support: to support (an opinion, etc.) by a wager or bet on. to countersign or endorse. to furnish with a back: to lie at the back of to form the back of: to cause to move backward or in the opposite direction: to provide a backing for.—*v.i* to move or go back or backwards: (of the wind) to change counter-clockwise.—*adj*. backed having a back.—*ns*. back'er; back'ing support at the back. mounting of a horse. the action of putting or going back: a body of helpers: anything used to form a back or line the back: counter-clockwise change of wind: support for an enterprise: musical accompaniment, esp. of a popular song.—*adj*. back'most farthest to the back.—*adj*. and *adv*. backward (*bak'wərd*) to- wards the back: on the back: towards the past: from a better to a worse state: in a direction opposite to the normal.—*adj*. keeping back: shy, bashful: unwilling: slow in development: late: dull or stupid.—*n*. back- warda'tion percentage paid by a seller of stock for keeping back its delivery till the following account.— *adv* back'wardly.—*n*. back'wardness.—*adv*. back'- wards backward.—back'ache pain in the back.—*adj* back'-bench of or sitting on the back benches, the seats in parliament occupied by members who do not hold office —back'bench'er.—*v t*. back'bite to speak evil of in absence (also *v.i.*).—back'biter; back'biting (also *adj.*).—back'-board a board fastened across the back to straighten the body; back'-bone the spinal column: a main support or axis: mainstay: firmness of character.—*adj*. back'-boneless.—back'breaker a very heavy job.—*adj*. back'breaking.—back'chat answering back, repartee.—Also *v.i.*—back'-cloth, back'drop the painted cloth at the back of the stage: the background to any situation, activity, etc.—*v i* and *v.t*. back'-comb to give (the hair) a puffed-out appearance by combing the underlying hairs towards the roots and smoothing the outer hairs over them.— back'-country remote, thinly-populated districts.— *v.t*. back'-date to put an earlier date on: to count as valid retrospectively from a certain date.—back door a door in the back part of a building.—*adj*. back'-door unworthily secret: clandestine.—backdown see back down below; back'-draught a backward current; backdrop see back-cloth; back'-end' the rear end: the later part of a season (*dial.*), back'fill the material used in backfilling.—*v.t*. and *v.i*. to refill (e.g. found- ations or an excavation) with earth or other material. —back'fire ignition of gas in an internal-combustion engine's cylinder at the wrong time.—*v i* (*bak-fir'*) to have a backfire: to go wrong (*coll.*) —back'-for- mä'tion the making of a word from one that is taken to be a derivative.—back'-garden, back'-green a gar- den, green, at the back of a house; back'ground ground at the back: a place of obscurity: the space behind the principal figures of a picture. that against which anything is, or ought to be, seen (*fig*): upbring- ing and previous history. environment.—*adj*. in the

background (*lit*. or *fig*.).—background radiation low-level radiation from substances present in the environment; back'hand handwriting with the letters sloping backwards: the part of the court to the left of a right-handed player, or the right of a left-handed (*tennis*): a stroke made with the hand turned back- wards.—Also *adj*.—*adj*. back'-hand'ed backhand: (of a compliment, etc.) indirect, dubious, sarcastic, insincere.—back'-hand'er a blow with the back of the hand: a bribe (*coll*.); back'lash the jarring or play of ill-fitting machinery in recoil: reaction or conse- quence, esp. if violent; back'log a reserve or accumu- lation of business, stock, work, etc., that will keep one going for some time (*coll*.); back'-numb'er a copy or issue of a newspaper or magazine of a bygone date: a person or thing out of date or past the useful stage (*fig*.); back'pack a pack carried on the back.— *v.i*. to carry a pack on the back esp. as a hiker.— back'packer; back'packing; back'pay pay that is overdue.—*v.i*. back'-ped'al to press the pedals back, as in slowing a fixed-wheel bicycle: to hold back. to reverse one's course of action.—back'-ped'alling.— *adj*. back'room (of persons) doing important work behind the scenes, esp. in secret (*coll*.).—*v.i*. back'- scratch.—back'scratcher a clawed instrument for scratching the back. one who practises backscratch- ing; back'scratching doing favours in return for favours, for advantage of both parties: servile flat- tery; back'side the back or hinder side or part of any- thing: the hinder part of an animal; back'sight in surveying, a sight taken backwards: the sight of a rifle nearer the stock; back'-slang slang in which every word is pronounced as if spelt backwards.—*v.i*. back'- slide to slide or fall back in faith or morals —back'- slider; back'sliding.—back'spin a rotary movement against the direction of travel of a ball (in golf, billiards, etc.) imparted to reduce its momentum on impact.—*adj*. and *adv*. back'stage' (*lit*. and *fig*.) behind the scenes, unobserved by the public.—back'- stairs servants' or private stairs of a house.—*adj*. secret or underhand.—back'stays ropes or stays ex- tending from the topmast-heads to the sides of a ship, and slanting a little backward. any stay or support at the back; back'stitch a method of sewing in which, for every new stitch, the needle enters behind, and comes out in front of, the end of the previous one; back'stop a screen, wall, etc. acting as a barrier in various sports or games, e.g. shooting, baseball, etc.: (the position of) a player, e.g. in baseball who stops the ball: some- thing providing additional support, protection, etc.; back streets the less fashionable and usu. poorer streets of a town away from its centre, back-stroke back-crawl: a swimming-stroke with circular move- ments of the arms and legs, performed on the back.— *v.i*. back'track to go back on one's course.—back'- tracking; back-up see back up below; back'wash a receding wave: a backward current· a reaction, reper- cussion or aftermath.—back'water water held back by a dam: a pool or belt of water connected with a river but not in the line of its present course or cur- rent: water thrown back by the turning of a water- wheel: a place unaffected by the movements of the day (*fig*.): a backward current of water: swell of the sea caused by a passing ship; back'woods the forest beyond the cleared country; backwoods'man.—back'- yard' a yard behind a house.—back down to abandon one's opinion or position (*n*. back'down); back of (*U.S*) behind, back out to move out backwards. to evade an obligation or undertaking, back-seat driver one free of responsibility but full of advice: one con- trolling from a position from which he ought not to control; back-street abortion an abortion performed by an unqualified person operating illicitly: back up

to give support to (*n* and *adj* **back'-up**); **backward
and forward** to and fro; **back water** to ply the oars or
turn the paddle-wheels backward; **bend, fall, lean
over backwards** (*coll*) to go even to the point of personal discomfort (to be accommodating or to please);
break the back of to overburden: to accomplish the
hardest part of; **get off someone's back** to stop pestering or bothering someone; **know backwards** to
have a thorough knowledge of; **on the back of** close
behind; **put one's back into** to do with might and
main, **set** or **put one's, someone's, back up** to show
resentment, arouse resentment in someone; **take a
back seat** to withdraw into obscurity or subordination; **talk through the back of one's neck** see neck.
[O.E *bæc*]

backgammon *bak-gam'ən*, or *bak'*, *n* a game played by
two persons on a board with dice and fifteen men or
pieces each: a triple game scored by bearing all one's
men before the other has brought all to his own table
—*v.t.* to defeat in such a way. [**back**, because the
pieces are sometimes taken up and obliged to go *back*
—that is, re-enter at the table, and M E *gamen*,
play.]

backsheesh, backshish. See **baksheesh.**

backward(s), etc See **back**[1].

baclava. See **baklava.**

bacon *bā'kn*, *n.* pig's flesh (now the back and sides)
salted or pickled and dried —**bring home the bacon**
(*coll.*) to achieve an object, successfully accomplish a
task: to provide material support; **save (some)one's
bacon** (to enable someone) to come off scatheless
with difficulty. [O Fr. *bacon*]

Baconian *bā-kō'ni-ən*, *adj* pertaining to Francis *Bacon*
(1561–1626), or to his inductive philosophy, or to
Roger *Bacon* (d *c.* 1292) or his teaching, or to the
theory that Francis Bacon wrote Shakespeare's plays
—Also *n.*

bacteria *bak-tē'ri-ə*, *n.pl.* a class of microscopic unicellular or filamentous plants, agents in putrefaction,
nitrogen fixation, etc., and the cause of many
diseases:—*sing* **bactē'rium** any member of the class,
esp. a rod-shaped one.—*adjs.* **bactē'rial; bactē'rian,
bacteric** (-*ter'ık*); **bacterici'dal.**—*ns* **bactē'ricide** a
substance that destroys bacteria —*adj* **bactēriolog'ical.**—*ns.* **bacteriol'ogist; bactēriol'ogy** the scientific study of bacteria; **bacterioly'sin** (or -*ol'ı*-) an
antibody that destroys bacteria; **bactēriol'ysis** destruction of bacteria by an antibody (Gr. *lysis*, dissolution).—*adj.* **bactēriolyt'ic.**—*ns.* **bacteriophage**
(*bak-tē'ri-ō-fāj*, *-fazh*) any of a large number of viruslike agents, present in the atmosphere, soil, water, living things, etc., whose function is to destroy bacteria (Gr. *phagein*, to eat); **bactērios'tasis** inhibition
of the growth of bacteria (Gr. *stasis*, standing),
bactē'riostat an agent that inhibits their growth —
adj. **bactēriostat'ic.** [Gr *baktērion*, dim. of
baktron, a stick]

Bactrian *bak'tri-ən*, *adj* belonging to *Bactria* (now
nearly corresponding to Balkh, a district of N
Afghanistan), esp applied to a two-humped camel.
—Also *n.*

bad *bad*, *adj* ill or evil. wicked: hurtful incorrect,
faulty· poor: unskilful· worthless· unfavourable
painful unwell: spurious. severe having serious
effects—*compar.* **worse;** *superl* **worst.**—*n* **badd'ie,
badd'y** (*coll*) a criminal person or villain, esp as
portrayed in films, television or radio shows —*adj*
badd'ish somewhat bad· not very good —*adv* **bad'ly**
in a faulty or unskilful way: unfavourably: severely
to a marked extent· very much —*n.* **bad'ness.**—**bad
blood** angry feeling, **bad debt** a debt that cannot be
recovered; **bad lands** wastes in South Dakota: (usu
bad'lands) any similar region, **bad language** swearing.

—*adj.* **bad'ly-off** poorly provided esp with money.—
bad'man (*U.S.*) an outlaw —*v.t* **bad'mouth** (*coll*) to
criticise, malign.—**bad shot** a wrong guess.—**go bad**
to decay; **go to the bad** to go to moral ruin; **in someone's bad books** in disfavour with someone; **to the bad**
in a bad condition: in deficit; **with a bad grace**
ungraciously. [M.E. *badde*]

bade *bad* (*poet. bād*), *pa.t* of **bid** (both verbs)

badge *baj*, *n.* a mark or emblem showing rank,
membership of a society, etc. any distinguishing
mark or symbol. [M.E *bage.*]

badger *baj'ər*, *n.* a burrowing, nocturnal, hibernating
animal of the otter and weasel family, extending to
other animals—hyrax, wombat, ratel: a painting, or
other, brush made of badger's hair —*v t* to pester or
worry.—**badg'er-bait'ing, -drawing** the sport of setting dogs to draw out a badger from a barrel; **badg'er-dog** the dachshund, a long-bodied and short-legged
dog used in drawing the badger [Prob. from **badge**
and the noun-forming suffix -*ard*, in reference to the
white mark borne like a badge on its forehead.]

badinage *bad'in-azh*, *n.* light playful talk: banter.
[Fr. *badinage—badin*, playful or bantering.]

badminton *bad'min-tən*, *n.* a cooling summer drink
compounded of claret, sugar, and soda-water: a
game played with shuttlecocks [*Badminton* in
Gloucester]

baff *baf*, *v.t.* to strike the ground with the sole of a
golf-club in playing, and so to send the ball up in the
air.—*n.* **baffy** (*baf'i*) a club like a brassy, but with a
somewhat shorter shaft and a more sloping face.

baffle *baf'l*, *v.t.* to frustrate, confound, impede perplexingly.—*n.* a plate or like device for regulating
or diverting the flow of liquid, gas, sound-waves,
etc. (also **baff'le-board, baff'le-plate, baff'ler**).—*n*
baff'ler.—*adj.* **baff'ling.**—*adv.* **baff'lingly.** [Perh
Scottish; but cf. Fr. *bafouer*, or earlier *beffler*, from
O.Fr *befe*, mockery.]

baft *bäft*, (*arch.*) *adv.* and *prep.* behind: abaft, astern
(*naut.*). [O.E. *beæftan—be*, by, and *æftan*, behind.]

bag *bag*, *n* a sack, pouch. a bagful measure of quantity for produce: a game-bag, hence the quantity of
fish or game secured, however great: an udder. an
unattractive, slovenly or immoral woman (*slang*)· a
person's line or vocation (*slang*) (in *pl*) trousers
(*coll.*)—*v t* to bulge, swell out —*v.t.* to put into a
bag, specially of game: hence to kill (game)· to seize,
secure or steal—*pr.p* **bagg'ing;** *pa p.* **bagged.**—*n*
bag'ful as much as a bag will hold:—*pl.* **bag'fuls.**—
adj. **bagged** (*bagd*) in a bag. bulged slackly —*adv.*
bagg'ily —*adj.* **bagg'y** loose like a bag: bulged —
bag'wash a laundry service by which rough unfinished
washing is done.—**bag and baggage** completely as *to
clear out bag and baggage*; **bag of bones** an emaciated
living being; **bag of tricks** the whole outfit; **bags (I)**
(*slang*) I lay claim to, **bags of** (*slang*) plenty of; **in the
bag** secured or as good as secured; **let the cat out of
the bag** to disclose a secret [M E *bagge*, perh
Scand]

bagasse *bə-gas'*, *n* dry refuse in sugar-making [Fr ;
Sp *bagazo*, husks of grapes or olives after pressing]

bagatelle *bag-ə-tel'*, *n* a trifle· a piece of music in a
light style. a game played on a board with nine balls
and a cue, etc , the object being to put the balls into
numbered holes or sections [Fr ,—It *bagatella*, a
conjuror's trick, a trifle.]

bagel *bā'gəl*, (*U S*) *n* a hard leavened roll in the shape
of a doughnut. [Yiddish *beygel*—Ger. *Beugel*.]

baggage *bag'ıj*, *n* the tents, provisions, and other
necessaries of an army: traveller's luggage a
worthless woman· a saucy woman.—*ns.* **bagg'age-animal; bagg'age-car** (*U.S*) a railway luggage-van,

bagg'age-train a train of baggage-animals, wagons, etc. [O.Fr. *bagage—baguer*, to bind up.]

bagnio *ban'yō, n.* an Oriental prison: a brothel:—*pl* **bagn'ios.** [It. *bagno*—L. *balneum*, a bath.]

bagpipe *bag'pīp, n.* a wind-instrument consisting of a *bag* fitted with *pipes* (often in *pl.*).—*ns.* **bag'piper; bag'piping.**

baguette *bag-et', n.* a small moulding like an astragal (*archit.*): a precious stone cut in the shape of a long rectangle: a long narrow French loaf of white bread with a thick crust. [Fr., rod, dim —L. *baculum*.]

bah *bä, interj.* expressing disgust or contempt. [Fr]

Bahai, Baha'i *ba-ha'ē,* or *bə-, n.* an adherent of an orig Persian religion following the teaching of Baha-Ullah, who claimed to be the bringer of a new revelation from God: the religion itself.—Also *adj.*—*ns* **Baha'ist; Baha'ism; Baha'ite.**

Bahasa Indonesia *bə-ha'zə in-də-nē'zi-ə, -zhi-ə, -zhyə.* See **Indonesian.**

baht *bat, n.* the monetary unit of Thailand. [Thai *bät*.]

baignoire, *ben-war', n.* a theatre box on a level with the stalls. [Fr., bath.]

bail¹ *bāl, n.* one who procures the release of an accused person by becoming security for his appearing in court the security given.—*v.t.* to set a person free by giving security for him: to release on the security of another: to deliver (goods) in trust upon a contract.—*adj.* **bail'-able.**—*ns.* **bailee'** one to whom goods are bailed; **bail'er** one who bails goods.—**bail'bond** a bond given by a prisoner and his surety upon being bailed; **bails'man** one who gives bail for another.—**accept, admit to, allow bail** are all said of the magistrate; the prisoner **offers, surrenders to his bail;** the one who provides it **goes, gives** or **stands bail; bail out** (*coll.*) to stand bail for (a prisoner): to assist out of (financial) difficulties. [O.Fr. *bail,* custody, handing over, *bailler,* to control, guard, hand over.]

bail², bayle *bāl, n.* a barrier· a pole separating horses in an open stable.—*v.t.* **bail** to confine. [O.Fr. *baile,* perh. from *baullier,* to enclose; or L. *baculum,* a stick.]

bail³ *bāl, n.* one of the cross pieces on the top of the wicket in cricket. [Prob. conn. with **bail².**]

bail⁴ *bāl, n.* on a typewriter, teleprinter, etc , a hinged bar that holds the paper against the platen. [Prob conn. with **bail².**]

bail⁵ (also **bale**) *bāl, n.* a bucket or other vessel for ladling out water from a boat.—*v.t.* to clear of water with bails: to ladle (often with *out*).—*n.* **bail'er.—bale** (**bail**) **out** to escape from an aeroplane by parachute: to escape from a potentially difficult situation. [Fr. *baille,* bucket.]

bail⁶ *bāl, n.* a hoop: a hoop-handle, as in a kettle. [Prob. O.N. *beygla,* hoop, from the Gmc root *bug-,* to bend.]

bailey *bāl'i, n.* the outer wall of a feudal castle. hence the outer court, or any court within the walls [Fr *baille,* palisade, enclosure.]

Bailey bridge *bā'li brij,* a prefabricated bridge constructed speedily for emergency use. [Designed during World War II by Sir Donald *Bailey.*]

baillie *bāl'i, n.* in Scotland, title of magistrate who presides in borough court—elected by town council from among the councillors (now mainly *hist.*).—*n.* **bail'ieship.**—Also **bailli'ie, baill'ieship.** [O Fr *bailli,* bailiff; see **bailiff.**]

bailiff *bāl'if, n* formerly any king's officer, e g sheriff, mayor, etc., surviving in certain cases as a formal title. the first civil officer in Jersey and in Guernsey a foreign magistrate: a sheriff's officer: an agent or landsteward.—*n.* **bail'iwick** the jurisdiction of a bailiff· jurisdiction in general. [O.Fr. *baillif.* See **bail¹.**]

bailie. See bailie.

Baily's beads *bā'liz bēds,* bright spots visible during the last seconds before a total eclipse of the sun [Detected in 1836 by the astronomer F. *Baily.*]

bain-marie *ban-ma-rē', bē-ma-rē, n.* a water-bath (*chem.*): in cooking, a vessel of hot or boiling water into which another vessel is placed to cook slowly or keep hot. [Fr. *bain-marie,* bath of Mary—L. *balneum Mariae*]

Bairam *bī'ram, bī-ram', n.* the name of two Muslim festivals—the *Lesser Bairam* lasting three days, after the feast of Ramadan, and the *Greater,* seventy days later, lasting four days [Pers]

bairn *bärn,* (*Scot.*) *n.* a child [O.E. *bearn—beran,* to bear.]

bait *bāt, n.* food put on a hook to allure fish or make them bite: any allurement or temptation: a range (*slang*).—*v t.* to set with food as a lure: to tempt: to set dogs on (a bear, bull, etc.): to persecute, harass: to exasperate, esp. with malice, tease.—*ns.* **bait'er; bait'ing.**—**bait'fish** fish used as bait: fish that may be caught with bait. [M.E. *beyten*—O.N. *beita,* to cause to bite—*bita,* to bite.]

baize *bāz, n.* a coarse woollen cloth with a long nap, used mainly for coverings, linings, etc.: a table cover.—*v.t.* to cover or line with baize. [Fr. *baies,* pl. (fem) of *bai.*—L. *badius,* bay-coloured.]

bajra, bajri, bajree *baj'rə,* or *-ra, baj'rē, ns.* a kind of Indian millet. [Hind.]

bake *bāk, v.t.* to dry, harden, or cook by the heat of the sun or fire: to make or cook in an oven.—*v.t.* to work as a baker. to become firm through heat: to be very hot (*coll.*) *pr.p.* **bāk'ing.**—*ns.* **bāk'er; bak'ery** a bakehouse· a baker's shop; **bāk'ing** the process by which bread is baked: the quantity baked at one time.—**bake'apple** (*Can*) the fruit of the cloudberry; **bake'house** a house or place used for baking in, **bake'meat** (*B.*) pastry, pies; **bake'stone** a flat stone or plate of iron on which cakes are baked in the oven, **bak'ing-pow'der** a mixture (e.g tartaric acid and sodium bicarbonate) giving off carbon dioxide, used as a substitute for yeast in baking; **bak'ing-so'da** sodium bicarbonate [O.E. *bacan.*]

Bakelite® *bā'kəl-īt,* a synthetic resin made by condensation of cresol or phenol with formaldehyde. [From its inventor, L. H. *Baekeland* (1863–1944)]

Bakewell pudding, tart *bāk'wel pōōd'ing, tart* a pastry base spread with jam and a filling made of eggs, sugar, butter and ground almonds. [*Bakewell,* Derbyshire.]

baklava, baclava *bak'lə-və, n.* a Turkish dessert made of pieces of flaky pastry, honey, nuts, etc. [Turk.]

baksheesh, bakhshish, backsheesh, backshish *bak'* or *buk'shēsh, n.* a gift of money in India, Turkey, etc., a gratuity or tip. [Pers *bakhshīsh.*]

Balaclava cap, helmet *bal-ə-klä'və kap, hel'mit,* a warm knitted hat covering the head and neck, with an opening for the face [*Balaklava* in Crimea.]

balalaika *ba-lə-lī'kə, n.* a Russian musical instrument, like a guitar, with triangular body and ordinarily three strings. [Russ.]

balance *bal'əns, n.* an instrument for weighing, usu. formed of two dishes or scales hanging from a beam supported in the middle: act of weighing two things. equilibrium: harmony among the parts of anything: equality or just proportion of weight or power the sum required to make the two sides of an account equal, hence the surplus, or the sum due on the account: what is needed to produce equilibrium, a counterpoise· a contrivance that regulates the speed of a clock or watch: remainder —*v.t* to weigh in a balance: to poise to set or keep in equilibrium: to counterpoise: to compare to settle, as an account. to examine and test so as to make the debtor or creditor sides of an account agree (*book-keeping*) —*v.i* to have equal weight or power, etc to be or come to be in equilibrium; to hesitate or fluctuate.—*adj* bal'anced poised so as to preserve equilibrium: well-arranged, stable.—*n.* bal'ancer.—bal'ance-sheet a summary and balance of accounts, bal'ance-wheel a wheel in a watch or chronometer which regulates the beat or rate.—balance of mind sanity; balance of payments the difference over a stated period between a nation's total receipts (in all forms) from foreign countries and its total payments to foreign countries; balance of power a state of equilibrium of forces in which no nation or group of nations has the resources to go to war with another or others with likelihood of success; balance of trade the difference in value between a country's imports and exports; in the balance unsettled: undecided; off balance unstable, esp. mentally or emotionally: in a state of unreadiness to respond to an attack, challenge, etc.; on balance having taken everything into consideration. [Fr.—L *bilanx*, having two scales—*bis*, double, *lanx, lancis*, a dish or scale]

balata *bal'ə-tə, n.* the gum of the bullet- or bully-tree of South America, used as a substitute for rubber and gutta-percha [Prob. Tupí.]

balboa *bal-bō'ə, n.* the monetary unit of Panama [Vasco Nuñez de *Balboa, c* 1475–1517.]

balcony *balk'ə-ni n* a stage or platform projecting from the wall of a building within or without, supported by pillars or consoles, and surrounded with a balustrade or railing. in theatres, usu. the gallery immediately above the dress circle (*U S.* the dress circle itself).—*adj.* bal'conied. [It *balcone—balco,* of Gmc. origin.]

bald *bold, adj* without hair, feathers, etc , on the head (or on other parts of the body): bare, unadorned: lacking in literary grace: paltry, trivial (*arch.*): undisguised.—*adjs.* bald'ing going bald; bald'ish somewhat bald.—*adv.* bald'ly plainly, without tactful circumlocution.—*n.* bald'ness.—bald'-eagle the American white-headed eagle, used as the national emblem.—*adj.* bald'-faced having white on the face, as a horse.—*adj.* bald'-headed having a bald head.— *adj.* and *adv. (slang)* bald'-head'ed without restraint: out and out.—bald as a coot see coot. [Perh. balled, rounded.]

baldachin, baldaquin *bōl'də-kin, n.* silk brocade: a canopy over a throne, pulpit, altar, etc.: in R.C. processions, a canopy borne over the priest who carries the host. [It. *baldacchino,* Fr. *baldaquin,* a canopy, from It. *Baldacco,* Baghdad, whence was brought the stuff of which they were made.]

balderdash *bōl'dər-dash, n.* idle senseless talk· anything jumbled together without judgment.

baldmoney *bold'mun-i, n.* spignel. a subalpine umbelliferous plant: gentian of various kinds.

baldric, also **baldrick,** *bóld'rik, n.* a warrior's belt or shoulder sash. [Cf. M.H.G. *balderich,* girdle.]

bale[1] *bāl, n.* a bundle, or package of goods.—*v.t.* to make into bales.—*n.* bal'er. [M.E. *bale.*]

bale[2]. See bail[5].

bale[3] *bāl, n.* evil, injury. mischief (*arch*): misery, woe (*arch.*)—*adj.* bale'ful malignant, hurtful: of evil influence: painful (*arch.*): sorrowful (*arch.*): lugubrious —*adv.* bale'fully.—*n.* bale'fulness. [O.E *bealu.*]

balection. Same as bolection.

baleen *bə-, ba-lēn', n.* horny plates growing from the palate of certain whales, the whalebone of commerce. —Also *adj.* [O.Fr. *baleine*—L *balaena,* whale.]

balista. See ballista.

balk, baulk *bo(l)k, n.* an unploughed ridge: part of a billiard table marked off by the balk-line: a forbidden

action of the pitcher in baseball: a squared timber· a tie-beam of a house, stretching from wall to wall, esp. when laid so as to form a loft (the balks): a rope to connect fishing-nets: a check, frustration: a disappointment: failure to take a jump or the like.—*v.t.* to ignore, pass over: to shirk: to decline· to avoid: to let slip: to put a stumbling-block in the way of: to thwart: to frustrate: to foil: to check.—*v.t.* to pull up or stop short at a difficulty: to jib: to refuse a jump, etc.. to refrain: to desist —*n* balk'er.—*n.* and *adj.* balk'ing, —*adv.* balk'ingly.—*adj.* balk'y apt to balk· perverse, refractory —balk'line a line drawn across a billiard table: a boundary line for the preliminary run in a jumping competition or the like [O.E. *balca,* ridge]

Balkanise, -ize (also without *cap.*) *bòl'kən-īz, v t.* to reduce to the condition of the *Balkan* peninsula which was divided in the late 19th and early 20th centuries into a number of mutually hostile territories.— *n.* Balk, balkanisā'tion, -z-.

ball[1] *bòl, n* anything spherical or nearly so: the orb of sovereignty. any rounded protuberant part of the body: a bullet, or solid missile thrown from an engine of war: a throw or delivery of the ball at cricket, etc.: a game played with a ball, esp. (*U.S.*) baseball or football· the eyeball: a bolus for a horse· (in *pl*) testicles (*vulg.*): (in *pl*) nonsense (also *interj.*; *vulg.*) —*v.t.* to form into a ball —*v t.* to gather into a ball.— *adj.* balled formed into a ball —*n.* ball'ing forming into a ball: snowballing.—ball'-bear'ing(s) a device for lessening friction by making a revolving part turn on loose steel balls: (in *sing.* only) one of the balls so used; ball'cock the stopcock of a cistern turned by a floating ball that rises and falls with the water; ball'-game any game played with a ball, esp. (*U.S.*) baseball or football: a situation, as in *a new ball-game* (*coll.*); ball lightning a slowly-moving luminous ball occasionally seen during a thunderstorm; ball park (*U.S.*) a baseball field: a sphere of activity (*coll.*); ball'-point (pen) a fountain-pen having a tiny ball rotating against an inking cartridge as its writing tip. —ballsed-up, balls-up see balls up below.—ball-and-claw see claw-and-ball under claw; ball and socket a joint formed of a ball partly enclosed in a cup; ball of fire a lively, dynamic person: a glass of brandy (*coll.*); balls up (*vulg.*) to make a muddle or mess of: to throw into confusion (*n.* balls'-up; *adj.* ballsed'-up); keep the ball rolling to keep things going; make a balls of (*vulg.*) to do badly, make a mess of; no ball (*cricket*) a delivery adjudged contrary to rule; on the ball properly in touch with the situation: on the alert; play ball see play; set, start the ball rolling to make the first move: to start things going; the ball at one's feet success in one's grasp; the ball's in your court the responsibility for the next move is yours [M.E. *bal* —O N. *bollr.*]

ball[2] *bol, n* an assembly for dancing.—ball'-dress; ball'-room.—Also *adj.*—have a ball to enjoy oneself very much (*coll.*). [O.Fr. *bal—baller,* to dance— L.L. *ballāre,* perh.—Gr *ballizein,* to dance.]

ballad *bal'əd n.* orig. a song accompanying a dance: a simple narrative poem in short stanzas (usu. of four lines, of eight and six syllables alternately): a popular song, often scurrilous, referring to contemporary persons or events (chiefly *hist.*): any slow, sentimental song [O.Fr. *ballade*—L.L. *ballāre,* to dance; see ball[2].]

ballade *ba-lad', n.* a poem of one or more triplets of stanzas, each of seven, eight, or ten lines, including refrain, followed by an envoy, the whole on three (or four) rhymes: sometimes loosely, any poem in stanzas of equal length. an ill-defined form of instrumental music, often in six-eight or six-four time. [An earlier spelling of **ballad**, with old pronunciation restored.]

ballast *bal'əst*, *n.* heavy material used to weigh down and steady a ship or balloon: broken stone or other material used as the bed of a road or railway: that which renders anything steady.—*v.t.* to load with ballast: to make or keep steady.—**in ballast** carrying ballast only. [Prob. Old Sw. *barlast—bar*, bare, and *last*, load.]

ballerina *bal-ə-rē'nə*, *n.* a female ballet-dancer:—*pl* **balleri'ne** (*-nā*), **balleri'nas.** [It.]

ballet *bal'ā*, *n.* a theatrical performance of dancing with set steps and pantomimic action: (a suite of) music for it: a troupe giving such performances: the art or activity of dancing in this way: (*bal'ət*) a form of madrigal.—*adj.* **balletic** (*bal-et'ik*) of the art of ballet.—*adv.* **ballet'ically.**—**ball'et-dancer; ball'et-dancing; ball'et-master.** [Fr., dim. of *bal*, a dance.]

ballista, balista *ba-lis'tə*, *n.* a Roman military engine in the form of a crossbow for heavy missiles.—*adj.* **ballis'tic** projectile: relating to projectiles.—*n.* sing **ballis'tics** the science of projectiles.—**ballistic missile** a guided missile that ends in a ballistic descent, guidance being over only part of its course [L.,—Gr *ballein*, to throw.]

ballocks. See **bollocks.**

ballon d'essai *ba-lõ de-sā*, (Fr.) an experimental balloon: a feeler or preliminary sounding of opinion.

balloon *bə-lōōn'*, *n.* an apparatus for travel in the air, or for carrying recording instruments, consisting of a gas-bag and a car: a toy consisting of an inflatable rubber bag: anything inflated, empty (*fig.*): an ornamental ball on a pillar, etc. (*archit*): a balloon-shaped drawing enclosing words spoken in a strip cartoon.—*v.t.* to inflate: to send high in the air.—*v.i.* to ascend or travel in, or as if in, a balloon: to puff out like a balloon.—*ns.* **balloon'ing; balloon'ist.**—*adj.* **balloon'-back** (of a dining-room chair) having a circular or oval-shaped back-support.—**when the balloon goes up** when the trouble starts: when proceedings begin. [It. *ballone*, augmentative of *balla*, ball.]

ballot *bal'ət*, *n.* a little ball or ticket or paper used in voting: a secret vote or method of voting by putting a ball or ticket or paper into an urn or box: in U.S. extended to open voting.—*v.i.* to vote by ballot: to draw lots:—*pr.p.* **ball'oting;** *pa.t.* and *pa.p.* **ball'oted.**—**ball'ot-box** a box to receive ballots; **ball'ot-paper** a paper on which a ballot vote is recorded. [It. *ballotta*, dim. of *balla*, ball. See **ball**.]

bally *bal'i*, (*slang*) *adj.* a euphemism for **bloody**, but almost meaningless.

ballyhoo *bal-i-hōō'*, (*slang*) *n.* noisy propaganda.

ballyrag *bal'i-rag*, *v.t.* to bullyrag (q.v.).

balm *bäm*, *n.* an aromatic substance: a fragrant and healing ointment: aromatic fragrance: anything that heals or soothes pain: a tree yielding balm: a plant, with an aroma similar to that of lemon: extended to other garden herbs.—*n.* **balm'iness.**—*adj.* **balm'y** fragrant: mild and soothing: bearing balm: a variant of **barmy.**—**balm,** or **balsam, of Gilead** the resinous exudation of certain trees: the balsam fir [O Fr *basme*—L. *balsamum*. See **balsam**.]

balmoral *bal-mor'əl*, *n.* a flat Scottish bonnet: a figured woollen petticoat: a kind of boot lacing in front. [**Balmoral**, royal residence in Aberdeenshire.]

balneal *bal'ni-əl*, *adj* of baths or bathing.—*n* **bal'neary** a bath: a bathing-place: a medicinal spring.—*adj.* of or for bathing.—*ns.* **balnea'tion** bathing; **balneol'ogist; balneol'ogy** the scientific study of bathing and mineral springs; **balneother'apy** treatment of

disease by baths. [L. *balneum*—Gr. *balaneion*, bath.]

baloney, boloney *ba-*, *bə-lō'ni*, (*slang*) *n.* deceptive talk: nonsense. [Thought to be from **Bologna** (sausage).]

balsa *bol'sə*, *bàl'sə*, *n.* a raft or float: corkwood, a tropical American tree, with very light wood. [Sp., raft.]

balsam *bol'səm*, *n.* a plant of the genus *Impatiens*: a liquid resin or resinous oily substance, esp. balm of Gilead: any healing agent (*fig.*).—*adjs.* **balsamic** (*-sam'ik*); **balsamif'erous** producing balsam.—*adj.* **bal'samy** fragrant —**balsam fir** an American fir (*Abies balsamea*); **balsam of Peru, of Tolu** see **Peru, Tolu; Canada balsam** a turpentine from the balsam fir. [L. *balsamum*—Gr. *balsamon*.]

Balt *bolt*, *n.* an inhabitant of the Baltic provinces or states.—*adj.* **Balt'ic** of the sea separating Scandinavia from Germany and Russia: of the western division of the Baltoslavs.—*n.* **Balt'oslav'.**—*adjs.* **Balt'oslav, -ic, -on'ic** of a family of Indo-European languages including the Slavonic languages with Lettish, Lithuanian, and (extinct) Old Prussian. [From the *Baltic Sea*—L. *Baltia*, Scandinavia]

balthazar, balthasar *bal'thə-zar*, *n* a very large winebottle, in capacity usu. taken to equal 16 ordinary bottles (12·80 litres or 2·75 gallons).—Also **belshazzar** (*bel-shaz'ər*) [Coined in reference to Dan. v. 1.]

Baltimore *bol'tim-ōr*, *-or*, *n.* a common orange and black North American bird of the hang-nest family, called also *Baltimore oriole, fire-bird*, etc. [From Lord *Baltimore*, whose livery was orange and black.]

balu. See **baloo.**

baluster *bal'əs-tər*, *n.* a small pillar supporting a stair rail or a parapet coping, often circular in section and curvaceous in outline.—*adj.* (of a vessel, its stem or handle) like a baluster in shape.—*adj.* **bal'ustered.**—*n.* **bal'ustrade** a row of balusters joined by a rail or coping. [Fr. *balustre*—L.L. *balaustium*—Gr. *balaustion*, pomegranate flower; from its form.]

bambino *bam-bē'nō*, *n.* a child:—*pl.* **bambi'nos, -i'ni** (*-nē*). [It.]

bamboo *bam-bōō'*, *n.* a gigantic tropical and subtropical grass with hollow-jointed woody stem. [Perh. Malay *bambu.*]

bamboozle *bam-bōō'zl*, *v.t.* to deceive: to confound or mystify.—*n.* **bamboo'zlement.**

ban *ban*, *n.* sentence of banishment: anathematisation: a denunciation. a curse: a prohibition: a vague condemnation.—*v.i.* to anathematise: to forbid or prohibit. [O.E. *gebann*, proclamation, *bannan*, to summon cf **banns**.]

banal *bən-al'*, *bän'əl*, *ban'əl*, *adj.* commonplace, trivial, flat.—*n.* **banal'ity** triviality.—*adv.* **banal'ly.** [Fr.]

banana *bə-*, *ba-na'nə*, *n.* a gigantic tree-like herbaceous plant or its nutritious fruit.—**banana republic** (*derog.*) any of the small republics in the tropics depending on exports of fruit and on foreign investment: hence any small country dependent on foreign capital; **banana split** a dish composed of a banana halved lengthways, ice-cream, and other ingredients.—**be, go bananas** (*slang*) to be, go crazy [Sp. or Port., from the native name in Guinea.]

Banbury cake *ban'bər-i kāk*, a kind of mince-pie made in *Banbury*, Oxfordshire.

banc *bangk*, *n.* the judges' bench.—**in banc, in banco** in full court [Fr.]

band[1] *band*, *n.* that by which loose things are held together: a tie or connecting piece: (*pl.*) shackles, bonds, fetters —**band'-stone** a stone set transversely in a wall to bind the structure. [M.E. *band, bond*—O N *band*]

band² *band, n.* a flat strip (of cloth, rubber, metal, etc) to bind round anything: a stripe crossing a surface distinguished by its colour or appearance: a flat strip between mouldings, or dividing a wall surface: the neck-band or collar of a shirt: a belt, for driving machinery: (*pl.*) the pair of linen strips hanging down in front from the collar, worn by some Protestant clergymen and by barristers and advocates. a group or range of frequencies or wavelengths between two specified limits (*radio, electronics*): in sound reproduction, a separately recorded section of a record or tape· a group of close-set lines esp. in a molecular spectrum (*phys.*): a particular range, between an upper and lower limit, of e.g. intelligence, wealth, etc —*n.* **band'age** a strip of cloth for winding round an injured part of the body: an adhesive plaster for protecting a wound or cut: a piece of cloth used to blindfold the eyes.—*v.t.* to bind with a bandage.—*adj* **band'ed** fastened as with a band: striped with bands.— *n.* **band'ing** the division of children in the final year of primary school into three groups according to ability, in order to obtain an even spread in the mixed-ability classes usual in comprehensive schools.—**band'-box** (or *ban'boks*) a light kind of box for holding caps, millinery, etc., **band'brake, band'-clutch** a brake, clutch in the form of a flexible band that can be tightened about a wheel or drum; **band'-saw** an endless saw, a toothed steel belt; **band'-wheel** a wheel on which a strap or band runs. [M.E. *bande*—O Fr. *bande*, of Gmc. origin.]

band³ *band, n.* a number of persons bound together for any common purpose: a body of musicians, esp. performers on wind and percussion instruments: a herd or flock (*U.S.*).—*v.t.* to bind together.—*v.i.* to associate, assemble, confederate.—**band'master** the conductor of a band; **bands'man** a member of a band of musicians; **band'stand** a structure for accommodating a band of musicians; **band'wagon** the car that carries the band in a circus procession: a fashionable movement.—**Band of Hope** an association of young persons pledged to lifelong abstinence from alcoholic drinks; **beat the band** to be specially good or remarkable; **jump, leap on the bandwagon** to join in any popular and currently successful movement in the hope of gaining advantage from it; **then the band played** that was the end of it. [Fr. *bande*, of Gmc. origin, with changed sense; cf. **band¹·²**, **bend, bind.**]

bandage. See under **band²**.

bandana, bandanna *ban-dan'ə, n.* a silk or cotton coloured handkerchief, with spots or diamond prints, originally from India. [Hind. *bādhnū*, a mode of dyeing.]

bandeau *ban'dō, ban-dō', n.* a band to bind the hair· a band within a hat: a bandage for the eyes.—*pl* **bandeaux** (*ban'dōz, -dōz'*). [Fr]

bandelier *ban-də-lēr', n.* A form of **bandoleer.**

banderilla *ban-, ban-dā-rēl'ya, n.* a dart with a streamer, stuck by bullfighters in the bull's neck.—*n.* **banderillero** (*ban-, ban-dā-rēl-yā'rō*) a bullfighter who uses banderillas:—*pl.* **banderille'ros.**

banderol, banderole *ban'də-rōl,* **bandrol** *ban'drōl.* **bannerol** *ban'ə-rōl ns.* a small banner or streamer: a flat band with an inscription (*archit.*). [Fr]

bandicoot *ban'di-kōōt, n.* the largest species of rat, found in India and Sri Lanka, called also *Malabar-rat* and *pig-rat:* a member of the genus *Perameles* of small marsupials. [Telugu *pandikokku*, pig-rat.]

bandit *ban'dit, n.* an outlaw: a brigand: in airman's slang, an enemy plane:—*pl.* **ban'dits, banditti** (*ban-dit'ē*).—*n.* **ban'ditry.**—**one-armed bandit** a fruit-machine, so called from the similarity to an arm of the lever pulled to operate it, and the heavy odds against the user. [It. *bandito,* pl. *banditi*]

bandoleer, bandolier *ban-dō-lēr', n.* a shoulder belt, esp for ammunition [O Fr *bandouillere*—It *bandoliera—banda,* a band]

bandrol *band'rōl, n.* Same as **banderol.**

bandwagon. See **band³**.

bandy¹ *ban'di, v.t.* to beat to and fro: to toss from one to another (as words *with* any one): to pass from mouth to mouth (with *about*): to give and take (blows or reproaches):—*pr.p.* **ban'dying;** *pa.t.* and *pa.p* **ban'died.**—*n.* **ban'dying.**

bandy² *ban'di, adj.* bent wide apart at the knee: having bandy or crooked legs —*adj.* **ban'dy-legged'.** [Poss. **bandy¹.**]

bane *bān, n.* destruction: death: mischief: poison: source or cause of evil.—*v.t* to harm (*arch.*):—*adj* **bane'ful** destructive: pernicious: poisonous.—*adv* **bane'fully.**—*n.* **bane'fulness.** [O.E. *bana,* a murderer, O.N. *bani,* death.]

bang¹ *bang, n* a heavy blow· a sudden loud noise: an explosion: *fig.* meanings as thrill, burst of activity, sudden success: an act of sexual intercourse (*slang*).— *v.t.* to beat: to strike violently: to slam, as a door. to beat or surpass: to have sexual intercourse with (*slang*).—*v t.* to make a loud noise: to slam. to bounce (*dial*).—*adv* with a bang: abruptly: absolutely (as in *bang up-to-date*) —*n.* **bang'er** something that bangs: an explosive firework· a decrepit old car (*coll.*): a sausage (*slang*).—*adj.* **bang'ing** dealing blows: overwhelming, very great (*coll*).—**bang goes** (*coll.*) that's the end of; **bang on** (*coll.*) right on the mark; **bang off** (*coll.*) immediately; **Big Bang** see **big; go with a bang** to go well, be a success [O.N. *banga,* to hammer]

bang² *bang, n* hair cut square across the brow (often in *pl.*)—*v.t.* to cut square across.—*adj* **banged** wearing the hair in such a way.—**bang'-tail** a tail with the end tuft squared: a beast whose tail hair is banged [An Americanism, poss. from the phrase *bang off*]

bang³. Same as **bhang.**

bangle *bang'gl, n* a ring for arm or leg.—*adj* **ban'gled** wearing bangles [Hind *bangrī, bangli.*]

bania *ban'yə,* **banian, banyan,** *ban'yən, -yan, ns* an Indian fig-tree with vast rooting branches a loose jacket, gown, or under-garment worn in India. [Port *banian,* perh. through Ar *banyān,* from Hind. *baniyā—*Sans *vānija—vanij,* a merchant.]

banish *ban'ish, v.t.* to condemn to exile: to drive away: to expel.—*n* **ban'ishment** exile. [Fr. *bannir, baniss-*—L L *bannīre,* to proclaim.]

banister *ban'is-tər, η.* a stair-rail with its supports (often in *pl.*). [**baluster.**]

banjax *ban-jaks', ban', (slang) v.t* to ruin, destroy. [Anglo-Irish: poss. combination of *bang* and *smash.*]

banjo *ban'jō, ban-jō', n* a musical instrument played with the fingers or with a plectrum—having a long neck, a circular body of stretched parchment like a drum, and usu. five strings of catgut and wire: applied to various tools or devices shaped like a banjo:—*pl* **ban'jos, ban'joes.**—*n.* **ban'joist** (*-ist*) [Negro pronunciation of *bandore,* an Elizabethan stringed instrument]

bank¹ *bangk, n.* a mound or ridge. an acclivity: the margin of a river, lake, etc : the raised border of a road, railway cutting, etc.: the surface at a pit-mouth: the coal-face in a mine: a shoal or shallow: a bed of shellfish: a mass of cloud or mist: the tilt of an aeroplane.—*v.t* to enclose with a bank: to deposit or pile up. to cover (a fire) so as to lessen the rate of combustion—*v.t* and *v t* (of aircraft) to tilt in turning. [M E *banke,* prob. Scand]

bank² *bangk, n.* a bench in a gallery: the bench on which judges sat· a tier or rank, e g. of oars, keys on a typewriter, etc.: a range of apparatus or equipment: a working table in various crafts [O.Fr. *banc.*]

bank³ *bangk, n.* a bench, office, or institution for the keeping, lending, etc , of money: a money-box for savings: a stock of money, fund, or capital: in games of hazard, the money that the proprietor or other, who plays against all, has before him: a pool to draw cards from: any store of material or information — *v.t* to deposit in a bank.—*v.t.* to have a bank account. to count, rely (on) (*coll.*).—*adj.* **bank'able.**—*ns.* **bank'er** one who keeps a bank: one employed in banking business; **bank'ing** the business of the banker.—*adj.* pertaining to a bank —**bank'-bill** a bill drawn by one bank upon another; **bank'-book** a book in which record is kept of money deposited in or withdrawn from a bank; **banker's card** a card issued by a bank guaranteeing the honouring of any cheque up to a specified value; **banker's order** a standing order (q.v.); **bank'-hol'iday** a day on which banks are legally closed—in England observed as a general holiday, **bank'-man'ager; bank'-note** a note issued by a bank, which passes as money, being payable to bearer on demand; **bank'-rate** until 1972 the rate at which the Bank of England was prepared to discount bills (see **minimum lending rate** under **minim**); **bank'roll** money resources.—**break the bank** in gambling, to win from the management the sum fixed as the limit it is willing to lose on any one day; **clearing bank** a bank which is a member of the London Clearing-house; **joint-stock bank** one whose capital is subscribed by a large number of shareholders; **merchant bank** one whose functions include financing transit of goods and providing financial and commercial advice. [Fr *banque*—It. *banca*.]

banket *bang-ket', (S. Afr.) n.* an auriferous pebbly conglomerate. [Du. *banketje*, almond rock.]

bankrupt *bangk'rupt, n.* one who breaks or fails in business: an insolvent person.—*adj.* insolvent· destitute (with *of*) —*v.t.* to make bankrupt: to have (a person) declared bankrupt: to ruin, impoverish (*fig*).—*n.* **bank'ruptcy** (-*si*). [Fr. *banque-route*, It *banca rotta*—*banca*, bank, and *rotto*, *-a*—L. *ruptus*, broken.]

banner *ban'ər, n.* strictly, a square flag charged with a coat of arms: a military standard: a flag bearing some device, often carried on two poles, or hanging from a cross-piece, used in processions, etc —*adj.* **bann'ered** furnished with banners.—**banner headline** a large-type headline running right across a newspaper page. [O.Fr. *banere*—L.L. *bandum, bannum*.]

bannerol. See banderol.

bannock *ban'ək, (chiefly Scot.) n.* a flat home-made cake of oatmeal, barley, or pease-meal, usually baked on a griddle. [O.E. *bannuc.*]

banns *banz, n.pl.* a proclamation of intended marriage.—**forbid the banns** to make formal objection to a projected marriage. [**ban.**]

banquet *bangk'wit, n.* a feast.—*v.t* to give a feast to. —*v.t.* to fare sumptuously·—*pr.p.* **banq'ueting;** *pa.t* and *pa.p.* **banq'ueted.**—*ns.* **banq'ueter; banqueteer'; banq'ueting**—**banq'ueting-hall,** **-house.** [Fr.,—*banc*, bench.]

banquette *bang-ket', n.* a raised way inside a parapet· a built-in wall-sofa used instead of individual seats, e g. in a restaurant. [Fr., It. *banchetta*, dim. of *banca*, seat.]

banshee *ban'shē, n.* a female fairy in Ireland and elsewhere who wails and shrieks before a death in the family to which she is attached. [Ir. *bean sídhe*, Old Ir. *ben síde*, woman of the fairies.]

bantam *ban'təm, n.* a small variety of the common domestic fowl: a small man, esp a soldier —*adj.* of bantam breed little and combative —**ban'tam-weight,** a boxer over 8 st. and not over 8 st. 6 lb. (amateur 7 lb). [Prob *Bantam* in Java.]

banter *ban'tər, v.t.* to assail with good-humoured raillery: to joke or jest at: to impose upon, trick (*arch.*).—*n.* humorous raillery· jesting.—*n.* **bant'erer.**—*n.* and *adj.* **bant'ering.**—*adv.* **bant'eringly.**

Bantu *ban'tŏŏ, n.* a name given to a large group of African languages and the peoples speaking them in South and Central Africa· official name for African peoples of South Africa —Also *adj* —*n* **Ban'tustan** the coined name for a semi-independent region of South Africa populated and administered by Bantus. a region of similar status elsewhere

banyan. See banian.

banzai *ban'za-ē, interj.* a Japanese battle-cry and salute to the emperor· a Japanese exclamation of joy uttered on happy occasions [Jap. *banzai*, 10000 years, forever.]

baobab *bā'ō-bab, n.* a gigantic tropical Western African tree. [Prob. African]

bap *bap, (Scot.) n.* a large, flat and elliptical breakfast roll.

baptise, -ize *bapt-īz', v t.* to administer baptism to: to christen, give a name to. to name at launching and break a bottle of wine on the bow of —*n.* **bapt'ism** (*-izm*) immersion in or sprinkling with water as a religious ceremony: an experience regarded as initiating one into a society, group, etc —*adj.* **baptis'-mal.**—*adv* **baptis'mally.**—*ns.* **bapt'ist** one who baptises: (with *cap.*) one of a body who approve only of baptising by immersion, and that only of persons who profess their faith in Christ; **bap'tistery, bap'tistry** a place for administration of baptism, whether a separate building or part of a church —**baptism of fire** any trying ordeal, as a first experience of being under fire (*fig*); **clinical baptism** baptism administered to the sick, **conditional (or hypothetical) baptism** baptism administered conditionally when it is doubtful whether the person was previously baptised validly or at all; **private baptism** baptism elsewhere than in church. [Gr *baptizein*—*baptein*, to dip]

bapu *ba'pŏŏ, n.* spiritual father [Hindi]

bar¹ *bar, n* a rod, strip or oblong block of any solid substance· a pound, sovereign (*slang*)· a strong rod or long piece used as a lever. door fastening, barrier, part of a gate or grate, etc : a bolt a barrier· an obstruction or impediment: that which completely puts an end to an action or claim a bank or shoal as at the mouth of a river or harbour: a counter across which liquor or food is served a public-house: a rail or the like marking off a space. as in a house of parliament, or that at which prisoners are arraigned barristers or advocates collectively: a ballet-dancer's exercise rail (usu **barre**): an addition to a medal, a strip of metal below the clasp: a ridge a stripe, esp transverse: a horizontal band across a shield (*her.*) a vertical line across the staff marking off a measure (see also **double-bar;** *mus.*): the measure itself. a counter at which one particular article of food, clothing, etc , is sold, or one particular service is given.—*v t* to fasten, secure, shut (out, in), furnish or mark with a bar or bars· to hinder to obstruct· to exclude the possibility or validity of· to preclude to divide into bars:—*pr.p.* **barr'ing;** *pa.t* and *pa.p.* **barred.**—*prep* except, but for —*n* **barr'ing.**—*prep* except for: leaving out of consideration—**bar'-bell** a bar weighted at the ends for gymnastic exercises; **bar'-chart, bar'-graph** a graph showing comparative quantities by means of darkened oblong sections produced to the appropriate length; **bar code** an arrangement, readable by computer, of thick and thin parallel lines, e.g. printed on, and giving coded details of, goods in a supermarket, etc., **bar'keeper** keeper of a refreshment bar or toll-bar; **bar'-magnet** a permanent magnet in the form of a straight bar; **bar'maid, bar'man, bar'person** a woman, man, who serves at a public-house bar; **bar'-par'lour** a small room adjoining a bar in a public-house; **bar'-room** a room in which there is a bar, taproom; **bar'tender** a barman.—**at the bar** in court: in practice as a barrister or advocate; **bar none** (*coll.*) with no exceptions; **behind bars** in prison; **called to the bar** admitted as barrister or advocate; **called within the bar** made king's (or queen's) counsel. [O.Fr. *barre*—L.L. *barra*.]

bar² *bar, n.* a unit used in expressing atmospheric pressure (millibar equals a thousand dynes per square centimetre) (*meteor.*). [Gr. *baros*, weight.]

barathea *bar-ə-thē'ə, n.* a soft fabric of worsted, or of worsted and silk, etc.

barb¹ *barb, n.* the beard-like jag near the point of an arrow, fish-hook, etc : one of the thread-like structures forming a feather's web: a sting (*fig.*): a wounding or wittily-pointed remark.—*v.t.* to arm with barbs. —*adjs.* **barb'ate** bearing a hairy tuft; **barb'ated** barbed: bearded.—*n.* **barb'el** a freshwater fish of the carp family with beard-like appendages at its mouth: such an appendage.—*ns.* **barb'et** a tropical bird with bristly beak: a kind of poodle; **barbicel** (*bar'bi-sel*) a tiny hooked process on the barbule of a feather, **barb'ule** a small barb: a fish's barbel: a process on the barb of a feather. [L. *barba,* a beard.]

barb² *barb, n.* a swift kind of horse: a dark-coloured fancy pigeon [From *Barbary,* whence the breeds came.]

Barbadian, *bar-bā'di-ən, adj.* of the West Indian island of *Barbados.*—Also *n.*

barbarous *bar'bər-əs, adj.* falling short of the standard of correctness, classical purity, and good taste: unscholarly: corrupt or ungrammatical or unidiomatic: uncultured: uncivilised: brutal: harsh.—*n.* **barbār'ian** orig one who was not a Greek, later neither a Greek nor a Roman: one without taste or refinement: a somewhat uncivilised man.—Also *adj.*—*adj.* **barbar'ic** (*-bar'ik*) uncivilised, characteristic of barbarians: rude. tastelessly ornate and ostentatious: wild and harsh.—*n.* **barbarisation, -z-** (*-bər-i-zā'shən*).—*v.t.* **bar'barise, -ize** to make barbarous: to corrupt, as a language.—*ns.* **bar'barism** savage life: rudeness of manners: a form of speech offensive to scholarly taste; **barbar'ity** (*-bar'i-ti*) savageness: cruelty.—*adv* **bar'barously.**—*n.* **bar'barousness.** [Gr. *barbaros,* foreign, lit. stammering, from the unfamiliar sound of foreign tongues.]

Barbary *bar'bər-i, n.* the country of the *Berbers,* in North Africa.—**Barbary ape** a type of macaque, the only European monkey; **Barbary sheep** a North African wild sheep. [Berber.]

barbecue *bar'bi-kū, v.t.* to roast whole: to cure on a barbecue.—*n* a framework for drying and roasting meat: an animal roasted whole: a large social entertainment, esp. in the open air, at which food is cooked over a charcoal fire: food so cooked, esp. with a highly seasoned sauce. [Sp. *barbacoa*—Haitian *barbacòa,* a framework of sticks set upon posts.]

barbel. See **barb¹.**

barber *bar'bər, n.* one who shaves beards and dresses hair.—*v.t.* to shave or cut the hair of.—**bar'ber-shop** a type of music originating in the U.S., played, or esp. sung, in close harmony, usu. in quartets, orig. sung by men waiting to have their hair cut.—Also *adj.*—**barber's pole** the barber's sign, a pole striped spirally, generally red and white. [O.Fr. *barbour*—L *barba,* a beard.]

barberry *bar'bər-i, n.* a thorny shrub (*Berberis*) with yellow flowers and red berries, common in hedges [L L *berberis.*]

barbet. See **barb¹.**

barbette *bar-bet', n.* an earthen terrace inside the parapet of a rampart, serving as a platform for heavy guns: an armoured turret in a warship. [Fr.]

barbican *bar'bi-kən, n.* a projecting watch-tower over the gate of a castle or fortified town: esp. the outwork intended to defend the drawbridge. [O.Fr. *barbacane.*]

barbicel. See **barb¹.**

barbituric *bar-it-ū'rik,* (*chem.*) *adj.* applied to an acid, source of important sedatives.—*ns.* **barb'itone** (also **barb'ital**) a derivative of barbituric acid; **barbit'urate** (or *-tūr'*) a salt or ester of barbituric acid. [From the lichen Usnea *barbata* and *uric* acid.]

barbola (work) *bar-bō'lə, n.* ornamentation with small flowers, fruits, etc. made of plastic paste coloured. [Orig. proprietary term from Fr. **barbotine,** a fine clay.]

barbs *barbz,* (*slang*) *n pl.* short for **barbiturates.**

barbule. See **barb¹.**

barcarol(l)e *bar'kə-rōl, -rōl', -rol', n.* a gondolier's song: a musical composition of a similar character. [It. *barcarola,* a boat-song—*barca,* a boat.]

barchan(e). See **barkhan.**

bard¹ *bard, n.* a Celtic poet and singer: a strolling minstrel: a poet: a poet whose work has won a competition at the Eisteddfod.—*adj.* **bard'ic.** [Gael. and Ir *bard.*]

bard² *bard, n.* piece of bacon or pork fat used to cover meat or game during cooking to prevent drying-out.— *v.t.* to cover a piece of meat or game with bacon or pork fat. [Fr. *barde*—Sp. *albarda,* pack-saddle.]

bare *bār, adj.* uncovered. naked: open to view: bareheaded: unsheathed: unarmed, threadbare, worn: unprovided or scantily provided: poor: scanty: mere: unadorned: empty.—*v.t.* to strip or uncover.—*adv.* **bare'ly** nakedly: plainly: explicitly: openly: hardly, scarcely: just and no more: not quite.—*n.* **bare'ness.**— *adj.* **bār'ish** somewhat bare.—*adj.* and *adv.* **bare'back** without saddle.—*adjs.* **bare'backed** with bare back: unsaddled, **bare'faced** with the face uncovered: beardless: impudent —*adv* **barefacedly** (*-fāst'li, -fās'id-li*).—**bare'facedness.**—*adjs., adv.* **bare'foot, -ed** having the feet bare; **barehead'ed; bare'legged.**— **barefoot doctor** orig. in China, an agricultural worker trained in the basic principles of health, hygiene and first-aid. [O.E *bær.*]

barege, barège *ba-rezh', n.* a light, mixed dress-stuff. [*Barèges* in Hautes-Pyrénées.]

bargain *bar'gən, n.* a contract or agreement: a favourable transaction: an advantageous purchase.—*v.t.* to make a contract or agreement: to chaffer: to count (*on*), make allowance (*for* a possibility).—*v.t.* to lose by bad bargaining (with *away*) —*n* **bar'gainer.**— **bar'gain-basement, -counter** places in a shop where bargains are promised, **bar'gain-hunter** one who goes shopping in quest of bargains.—**into the bargain** over and above, **make the best of a bad bargain** to do one's best in an adverse situation; **strike a bargain** to come to terms. [O.Fr. *bargaine.*]

barge *barj, n.* a flat-bottomed freight boat used on rivers and canals: a lighter: a large pleasure or state boat.—*v.t.* to move clumsily: to bump (*into*): to push one's way rudely.—*n.* **barg'ee** a bargeman.— **barge'man** manager of a barge; **barge'master** proprietor of a barge; **barge'pole** a pole for propelling a barge.—**barge in** to intrude: to interfere; **not touch with a bargepole** to refuse to have anything to do with. [O Fr. *barge*—L.L. *barga.*]

barge-board *barj'bōrd, -bord, n* a board along the edge of a gable.—*n.pl* **barge'-stones** those making up the sloping edge of a gable. [Perh L L. *bargus,* a gallows.]

baric. See **barium.**

barilla *bar-il'ə, n.* an impure sodium carbonate got by burning certain seaside plants. [Sp.]

barite. See under **barium, baryta.**

baritone, rarely **barytone,** *bar'i-tōn, n.* a deep-toned male voice between bass and tenor: a singer with such a voice.—*adj.* of the pitch and compass of a baritone. [Gk *barytonos,* deep-sounding.]

barium *bā'ri-əm, n.* a metallic element (at. numb 56; symbol Ba) present in baryta.—*adj.* **bā'ric.**—*n* **bā'rite** *(rare)* barytes.—**barium meal** a mixture of barium sulphate administered to render the alimentary canal opaque to X-rays [See **baryta.**]

bark¹ *bärk, n.* the abrupt cry of a dog, wolf, etc.: report of a gun.—*v.i.* to utter a bark: to advertise wares noisily.—*v t.·* to utter abruptly and peremptorily: to make by barking —*n.* **bark'er** a barking dog: a tout advertising wares, a show, etc. in a loud voice to attract custom.—**bark up the wrong tree** to follow a false scent; **his bark is worse than his bite** his angry words are worse than his actual deeds. [O.E. *beorcan.*]

bark², barque *bärk, n.* formerly, any small sailing ship: a ship of small size, square-sterned, without headrails: technically, a three-masted vessel whose mizzenmast is fore-and-aft-rigged (instead of being square-rigged like the fore and main masts): any boat or sailing ship *(poet.).*—*n* **bark'entine, barqu'entine** (-*ən-tēn*) a three-masted vessel, with the fore-mast square-rigged, and the main-mast and mizzen-mast fore-and-aft-rigged. [Fr. *barque*—L.L. *barca.*]

bark³ *bärk, n.* the rind or covering of the trunk and branches of a tree: that used in tanning or dyeing: that used in medicine (cinchona): an outer covering or skin.—*v.t* to strip or peel bark or skin from: to encrust.—*v.i.* to form a bark.—*adjs.* **bark'less; bark'y.**—**bark'-beet'le** any beetle of the family *Scolytidae,* tunnellers in and under bark.—*adj* **bark'-bound** compressed by failure to shed the bark. [O.N. *börkr.*]

barkhan, barkan, barchan(e) *bär-kän', n.* a crescent-shaped sand-dune, of the type found in the Turkestan deserts. [Native word in Turkestan.]

barley *bar'li, n.* a hardy grass *(Hordeum vulgare* and other species): its grain used for food, and for making malt liquors and spirits.—**bar'leycorn** (personified as *John Barleycorn)* the grain from which malt is made: a single grain of barley; **barley sugar** sugar candied by melting and cooling (formerly by boiling with a decoction of barley); **barley water** a decoction of pearl barley.—**pearl barley** the grain stripped of husk and pellicle, and completely rounded by grinding; **pot barley** the grain deprived by milling of its outer husk, used in making broth, etc. [O.E. *bærlic,* of barley.]

barm *bärm, n.* froth of fermenting liquor: yeast.—*adj.* **barm'y** frothy: fermenting: mentally unsound *(slang;* also **balmy**).—*n.* **barm'iness.**—*adj.* **barm'y-brained.** [O.E. *beorma.*]

bar mitzvah, bar mizvah, bar mitsvah *bàr mits'və* (sometimes *caps.;* also hyphenated or as one word) in the Jewish religion, a boy attaining the age (usu. 13 years) of religious responsibility: the festivities held in recognition of this event. [Heb., son of the law.]

barn¹ *bàrn, n.* a building in which grain, hay, etc., are stored.—*v.t.* to store in a barn —**barn dance** an American dance like a schottische; **barn'-door** the door of a barn· humorously, any broad target; **barn owl** a species of owl, generally buff-coloured above and white below; **barn'-stormer** a strolling player (a type of ranting actor): a peripatetic public speaker — *v.i.* **barn'storm** to tour usu. country areas giving theatrical performances. to travel about speaking at meetings, usu. for election purposes.—*n.* **barn'yard**—also *adj.* as in **barnyard fowl.** [O.E. *bere-ern,* contracted *bern,* from *bere,* barley, *ern,* a house.]

barnacle¹ *bar'nə-kl, n.* a barnacle-goose: a cirripede

crustacean that adheres to rocks and ship bottoms: a companion not easily shaken off —**bar'nacle-goose** a wild goose once believed to develop from a barnacle (the **goose'-bar'nacle)** that attaches itself, esp to floating wood, by a thick stalk. [O.Fr. *bernaque*— L L. *bernaca.*]

barnacle² *bär'nə-kl, n* an instrument put on a restless horse's nose to keep him quiet. [O.Fr. *bernac.*]

barney *bar'ni, (coll.) n.* humbug: a prize-fight: a quarrel

barogram *bar'ō-gram, n.* a tracing produced by a barograph. [Gr. *baros,* weight, and **-gram.**]

barograph *bar'ō-graf, n* a recording barometer. [Gr. *baros,* weight, and **-graph.**]

barometer *bə-rom'i-tər, n.* an instrument for measuring atmospheric pressure: a weather-glass: an indicator of change *(e.g* in public opinion; *fig.).*—*adjs.* **barometric** *(bar-ō-met'rik),* **barometrical** *(-met'ri-kl).*—*adv.* **baromet'rically.**—*n.* **barometry** (*-rom'*). [Gr. *baros,* weight, *metron,* measure.]

baron *bar'ən, n.* a title of rank, the lowest in the peerage: a foreign noble of similar grade: the owner of a freehold estate, whether titled or not *(Scot. hist.):* the head of any organisation or institution who is regarded as wielding despotic power (as a *press baron):* formerly a peer or great lord of the realm generally—*ns.* **bar'onage** the whole body of barons: a list or book of barons; **bar'oness** a baron's wife, or a lady holding a baronial title in her own right.—*adj.* **baronial** *(bə-rō'ni-əl)* pertaining to a baron or barony: applied to a turreted style of architecture favoured by the Scottish land-holding class.—*n.* **bar'ony** the territory of a baron: in Ireland, a division of a county: in Scotland, a large freehold estate, or manor, even though not carrying with it a baron's title and rank: the rank of baron. [O.Fr. *barun, -on*—L.L. *barō, -ōnis,* man.]

baronet *bar'ən-et, n* the lowest British hereditary title. —*ns.* **bar'onetage** the whole body of baronets: a list or book of baronets; **bar'onetcy** the rank or title of baronet; **bar'oness** a woman who succeeds to a Scottish baronetcy —*adj* **baronet'ical.** [Dim of **baron.**]

baroque *bə-rok', -rōk', n.* a bold, vigorous, exuberant style in architecture, decoration, and art generally, that arose with the Counter-Reformation and prevailed in Louis XIV's time, degenerating into tasteless extravagance in ornament: comparable style in music, or literature —*adj.* in baroque style: whimsical: flamboyant: sometimes rococo [Fr. *baroque,* from Port. and Sp.; of architecture, from It]

baroscope *bar'ō-skōp, n.* an instrument for indicating changes in the density of the air [Gr. *baros,* weight, *skopeein,* to look at.]

barostat *bar'ō-stat, n.* an automatic device for regulating pressure, e g. in an aircraft. [Gr. *baros,* weight, and **-stat.**]

barouche *ba-* or *bə-rōō sh', n.* a double-seated four-wheeled carriage with a falling top. [Ger *Barutsche* —It. *baroccio*—L. *bis,* twice, *rota,* a wheel.]

barque, barquentine. See **bark².**

barrack¹ *bar'ək, n.* a building for soldiers, esp. in garrison (generally in *pl):* a huge plain, often bleak, building, esp. for housing many persons.—*v.t.* and *v.t.* to lodge in barracks.—**barrack-room lawyer** an argumentative soldier given to disputing military procedure: hence any insistent but unqualified giver of advice [Fr. *baraque*—It. *baracca,* or Sp. *barraca,* tent.]

barrack², *bar'ək, v.t* and *v i.* to make a hostile demonstration (against), esp by cheering ironically, at a cricket-match, etc.—*n* and *adj.* **barr'acking.**—*n.* **barr'acker.** [Aboriginal Austr *borak,* or perh. Northern Irish dialect, meaning 'to brag'.]

barracouta *bar-ə-kōō'tə, n.* a southern food-fish· (also

barracoo'ta, -cuda -də) a voracious West Indian fish akin to the grey mullets. [Sp. *baracuta*]

barrage *bar'ij*, or (*mil.*) *bar-azh'*, *bar'azh*, *n.* an artificial bar across a river the forming of such a bar. a barrier formed by continuous shower of projectiles along a fixed or a moving line (curtain-fire), or by captive balloons, or mines, or otherwise. a heavy or continuous fire, as of questions, criticisms, etc in sport, a heat or round to select contestants, or decide a dead-heat —**barr'age-balloon**. [Fr *barrage—barre*, bar.]

barramunda *bar-ə-mun'də*, **barramundi** *-mun'di*, *ns* an Australian river-fish. the Australian lung-fish. [Native name]

barre *bar*, *n.* a horizontal rail fixed to the wall at waist-level, which ballet-dancers use to balance themselves while exercising (sometimes **bar**). a capo on a guitar, lute, etc.—*adj.* **barré** (*ba-rā*) of a chord on a guitar, etc , played with the left forefinger laid across the strings [Fr.]

barrel *bar'əl*, *n.* a wooden vessel made of curved staves bound with hoops, its contents or its capacity: a revolving drum. a cylinder: a tube as of a gun: a button on a braided coat: the trunk of a horse, etc —*v.t* to put in barrels.—*ns.* **barr'elage; barr'elful** (*pl* **barr'elfuls**) as much as a barrel will hold.—*adj* **barr'elled** having a barrel or barrels. put in barrels.—*adj.* **barrel-chested** having a large, rounded, projecting ribcage.—**barr'el-house** a cheap saloon (*adj.* of jazz, crude and rough in style); **barr'el-or'gan** a mechanical instrument for playing tunes by means of a revolving drum set with pins turned by a handle; **barrel roll** in aerobatics, a complete revolution on the longitudinal axis, **barrel vault** a vault with a simple hemicylindrical roof (*adj.* **barr'el-vault'ed**) —**have someone over a barrel** to be in a position to get whatever one wants from someone. [Fr. *baril*.]

barren *bar'ən*, *adj.* incapable of bearing offspring not producing fruit, seed, crops, vegetation, etc : infertile: unproductive: unfruitful: arid: jejune —*n pl* (*cap.*), in North America, plateaux with small trees but no timber.—*n.* **barr'enness**. [O.Fr *barain*, *brahain*, *brehaing*]

barret *bar'it*, *n.* a flat cap: a biretta.—**barr'et-cap**. [Fr. *barette*; cf. **beret**, **biretta**.]

barrette *ba-ret'*, *n.* a bar-shaped hair-clip or hair ornament. [Dim. of Fr. *barre*, bar]

barricade *bar'ik-ād*, *n.* a temporary fortification raised to block a street: a barrier.—*v.t.* to block: to close or enclose with a barricade. [Fr. *barricade* or Sp *barricada*.]

barrier *bar'i-ər*, *n.* a defensive stockade or palisade· a fence or other structure to bar passage or prevent access: (in *pl.*) lists: a separating or restraining obstacle.—*v t* to shut by means of a barrier.—**barrier cream** a dressing for the skin used to prevent dirt from entering the pores and as a protection against oils and solvents; **barrier reef** a coral-reef fringing a coast with a navigable channel inside [O.Fr. *barrière*—L.L *barrâria—barra*]

barrio *bar'i-ō*, *n.* esp. in U S a Spanish-speaking, usu poor, community or district:—*pl* **barr'ios**. [Sp , district, quarter.]

barrister *bar'is-tər*, *n.* one who is qualified to plead at the bar in a law-court (in Scotland called *advocate*) —*adj.* **barristerial** (*-tē'ri-əl*).—*n.* **barr'istership**. [From L.L *barra*, bar (i.e orig. of the Inns of Court).]

barrow[1] *bar'ō*, *n.* a small usu. hand-propelled wheeled carriage used to convey a load —**barr'ow-boy** a street-trader with wares displayed on a barrow, **barr'ow-tram** the shaft of a barrow [O.E. *bearwe—beran*, to bear.]

barrow[2] *bar'ō*, *n.* a hill or hillock (*obs.* except in placenames) an ancient earth-built grave-mound, tumulus [O E. *beorg*]

barter *bar'tər*, *v t* to give in exchange (with *for*, *away*) —*v t.* to traffic by exchange of commodities.—*n* trade or traffic by direct exchange of goods.—*n* bar'terer. [Prob O.Fr *barat*]

Bartholin's glands *bar'tə-linz glandz*, a pair of mucus-secreting glands in the vagina [Discovered by Caspar *Bartholin* (1655–1738), a Danish anatomist]

bartisan, bartizan *bar'ti-zan*, *-zan'*, *n* a parapet or battlement: a projecting gallery on a wall-face· (erroneously) a corbelled corner turret.—*adj* **bar'tisaned** (or *-zand'*) [Apparently first used by Scott, who found a reading *bertisene*, for **bratticing**; see **brattice**.]

barycentric *bar-i-sen'trik*, *adj*. pertaining to the centre of gravity. [Gr *barys*, heavy, *kentron*, centre]

barye *bar'ē* Same as **microbar**.

baryon *bar'i-on*, *n* any one of the heavier class of subatomic particles, which includes protons and neutrons —opp to *lepton* [Gr. *barys*, heavy]

barysphere *bar'is-fēr*, *n.* the heavy core of the earth within the lithosphere [Gr. *barys*, heavy, *sphairā*, sphere]

baryta *bə-rī'tə*, *n* barium monoxide —*n* **bary'tes** (*-tēz*) heavy-spar, barium sulphate (also **barite** *bā'rīt*). (loosely) baryta.—*adj* **barytic** (*ba-rit'ik*) of or containing baryta or barium.—**baryta paper** paper coated on one side with an emulsion of barium sulphate and gelatine [Gr *barys*, heavy]

barytone. See baritone.

basal. See under **base[1]**.

basalt *bas'olt*, *bas-olt'*, *n.* a type of igneous rock —*adj* **basalt'ic**. [L. *basaltēs*—Gr *basanītēs* (*lithos*), touchstone.]

basbleu *ba-blø*, (Fr) *n* a bluestocking.

bascule *bas'kūl*, *n.* an apparatus of which one end rises as the other sinks —**bascule bridge** a bridge that rises when a counterpoise sinks in a pit [Fr. *bascule*, see-saw]

base[1] *bās*, *n.* that on which a thing rests: foot: bottom. foundation. support: the part, e.g. of an organ of a plant or animal, nearest the place of attachment: the foot of a pillar (*archit.*): the lower part of a shield (*her*): a number on which a system of numeration or of logarithms is founded: the chief ingredient: an ingredient of a mixture that plays a subsidiary but important part, such e g as giving bulk: in dyeing, a mordant, a starting-point: a standard against which comparisons can be made· a base-line· a fixed station in games such as baseball: a place from which operations are conducted or on which they depend. home or headquarters, a substance that reacts with an acid to form a salt, or dissolves in water forming hydroxyl ions (*chem*): that element in words to which suffixes and prefixes are added.—*v.t.* to found or place on a base.—*pr.p.* **bās'ing**; *pa p.* **based** (*bāst*).—*adj.* **bās'al** pertaining to or situated at the base: at the lowest level: (loosely) fundamental —*adj.* **base'less** without a base or foundation —*ns.* **base'lessness; base'ment** an underlying support· the lowest storey of a building beneath the principal one, esp. one below ground level.—*adj.* **bās'ic** belonging to or of the nature of a base· containing excess of a base· in geol., poor in silica—opp. to *acid.* fundamental.—*n.* (in *pl.*) fundamental principles —*adv* **bās'ically** with reference to what is basic fundamentally, essentially —*n* **bāsicity** (*-is'*) —*adj.* **basilar** (*bas'*) basal —**basal anaesthesia** anaesthesia acting as a basis for further and deeper anaesthesia; **basal metabolism** the level of metabolism occurring in an individual in a resting state, **base'ball** a development of rounders, played nine-a-side with bat and ball, the players on the batting side making a circuit of four bases: a ball for the game; **base'baller; base'-line** an accurately measured line used as a base for triangulation: a line at the end of the court (*lawn tennis*): a line joining bases (*baseball*); **base'plate** the foundation plate of a piece of heavy machinery; **base rate** the rate, determined by a bank, on which it bases its lending rates of interest; **basic process** a steel-making process with a furnace lined with material rich in metallic oxides; **basic slag** a by-product of the basic process rich in lime, used as manure.—**get to, make, first base** (*U.S. coll.*) to complete the first stage in a process, **off base** (*U.S. coll.*) wrong, mistaken [Fr. *base*—L. *basis*—Gr. *basis*—root of *bainein*, to go.]

base² *bās, adj.* low in place, value, estimation, or principle: mean. vile: worthless: debased: counterfeit: servile as opposed to *free* (*law*): humble.—*adv.* **base'ly.**—*n.* **base'ness.**—*adj.* **base'-born** low-born: illegitimate.—**base coin** spurious coin; **base metal** any metal other than the precious metals: a metal that alters on exposure to air—opp to *noble metal.*—*adjs* **base'-mind'ed** of a low mind or spirit: mean, **base'-spirited** mean-spirited [Fr. *bas*—L.L. *bassus*, thick, squat.]

baseball, basement. See under **base¹.**

basenji *bə-sen'jē, n.* a smallish erect-eared, curly-tailed African hunting dog that rarely barks. [Bantu, *pl.* of *mosenji, musengi,* native.]

bash *bash, v.t.* to beat, belabour. to smash: to attack maliciously, physically or verbally —*n.* a heavy blow: a dint.—*ns.* **bash'er** a person who, or thing that, bashes (*sometimes used as suffix*): a straw hat (*slang*), **bash'ing** (*often used as suffix,* as in *queer-bashing, union-bashing*) the activity of making malicious physical or verbal attacks on (members of) groups one dislikes.—**have a bash** (*coll.*), to have a try: to make an attempt (at); **on the bash** (*slang*), on the spree: on the streets as a prostitute. [Prob. Scand]

bashful *bash'fŏŏl, adj* easily confused: modest: shy, wanting confidence —*adv.* **bash'fully.**—*n.* **bash'fulness.**—*adj* **bash'-less** unashamed [See **abash.**]

bashi-bazouk *bash-ē-bə-zōŏk', n.* a Turkish irregular soldier [Turk *bashi-bozuq,* wild head]

basic. See **base¹.**

Basic, BASIC *bā'sik, n.* a computer language using a combination of simple English and algebra. [Acronym of *Beginners All-purpose Symbolic Instruction Code.*]

basidium *bas-id'i-əm, n.* a fungal fructification from which spores (usually four) are abstricted:—*pl.* **basid'ia.**—*adj* **basid'ial.**—*n pl* **Basidiomycetes** (*-ō-mī-sē'tēz*) one of the main groups of fungi, characterised by the possession of basidia, including the familiar toadstools as well as rusts and smuts [Gr. *basis,* basis, and dim. ending, *-idion*]

basil¹ *baz'il, n* an aromatic labiate plant (*Ocimum*): extended to calamint and other labiates [O.Fr. *basile*—L *basilisca,* representing Gr *basilikon,* lit royal, perh with reference to *basiliskos,* cobra. as a reputed cure for snakebite]

basil². See **bezel.**

basilica *bə-sil'i-kə, n* orig a royal palace. a large oblong hall, with double colonnades and commonly a semicircular apse, used for judicial and commercial purposes: a magnificent church formed out of such a hall, or built after its plan: a Roman Catholic church with honorific privileges —*adjs* **basil'ical** royal: **basil'ican** of a basilica [Gr *basilikos, -ē, -on,* royal —*basileus,* king]

basin *bā'sn, n.* wide open vessel or dish: a basinful any hollow place containing water, as a dock the area drained by a river and its tributaries —*n* **ba'sinful** as

much as will fill a basin:—*pl.* **ba'sinfuls.**—**have a basinful** (*coll.*) to have an excess of [O.Fr *bacin*—L L *bachinus,* perh from *bacca,* a vessel.]

basinet *bas'i-net,* **basnet** *bas'net, ns.* a light globular headpiece worn alone with a visor, or with the great helm over it. [Dim. of **basin.**]

basis *bās'is, n.* the foundation, or that on which a thing rests: the groundwork or first principle: the fundamental ingredient:—*pl* **bas'es** (*bās'ēz*) [See **base¹.**]

bask *bask, v.i.* to lie in the warmth or sunshine (often *fig.*) —**basking shark** a large but harmless shark that shows its great dorsal fin as it basks. [O N *bathask,* to bathe]

basket *bas'kit, n.* a receptacle of plaited or interwoven twigs, rushes, canes or other flexible materials: a basketful· a net used as goal at basketball: the back part of a stagecoach outside.—*ns.* **bas'ketful** as much as fills a basket:—*pl.* **bas'ketfuls; bas'ketry** basketwork.—**bas'ketball** a team game in which goals are scored by throwing a ball into a raised net (originally a basket); **bas'ket-chair** a wicker chair; **bas'ket-maker; bas'ket-making; bas'ket-stitch** in knitting, groups of plain and purl stitches alternating vertically and horizontally, resembling basketwork in effect, **bas'ket-weave** a form of weaving using two or more strands in the warp and weft; **bas'ketwork** articles made of interlaced twigs, canes, etc. the art of making these —**basket of currencies** (*econ.*) a name for the special monetary unit composed of various European currencies in fixed proportions, used as a standard against which to assess the value of any particular currency, or as a currency in its own right

bas mitzvah. See **bath mitzvah.**

basnet. See **basinet.**

Basque *bask, n.* a member of a people inhabiting the western Pyrenees, in Spain and France: their agglutinative language: (*without cap.*) a short-skirted jacket, or a continuation of a bodice a little below the waist.—*adj.* **Basque** of the Basques or their language or country [Fr]

bas-relief *bas'-ri-lēf',* or (It) **basso-rilievo** *bas'sō-rēl-yā'vō,* popularly **-relievo** *bas'ō-ri-lē'vō, n.* sculpture in which the figures do not stand far out from the ground on which they are formed [Fr and It See **base²,** and **relief.**]

bass¹ *bās, n* the low or grave part in music: a bass singer—often in Italian form **basso** (*bas'sō*), *pl.* **bas'sos, bas'si** (*-sī*): a bass instrument, esp. (*coll.*) a double-bass.—*adj.* (of a musical instrument or voice) low in pitch and compass —**bass'-bar** a strip of wood on the belly of a violin, etc , under the bass foot of the bridge, to distribute the vibrations; **bass clef** the F clef on the fourth line of the stave; **bass drum** the large drum of an orchestra or band; **bass fiddle** (*coll.*) a double-bass [See **base².**]

bass² *bas, n.* bast a container made of bast or the like, used for carrying fish. etc —**bass'wood** a lime-tree or its wood [See **bast.**]

bass³, basse *bas, n.* a European sea-fish of the seaperch family· extended to other sea and freshwater fishes [O E *bærs*]

basset *bas'it, n* a hound (**bass'et-hound**) like a badger-dog, but bigger an outcrop (*geol*) —*v i* to crop out —**basset horn** (It *corno di bassetto*) the richest and softest of all wind instruments, similar to a clarinet in tone and fingering, but with a twice-bent wooden tube [Fr ,—*bas,* low]

bassinet *bas'i-net, n* a kind of basket with a hood used as a cradle a similarly shaped perambulator a bed in hospital, with necessary equipment, for care of a baby. [Fr dim of *bassin,* a basin]

basso. See **bass¹.**

bassoon bə-sōōn', -zōō'n', n. a wood-wind instrument, its compass from B flat below the bass stave to C or F in the treble.—n. **bassoon'ist.** [It. bassone, augmentative of bassò, low.]

basso profondo ba'sō prŏ-fon'dō, (It.) a deep bass voice or singer.

basso-rilievo. See bas-relief.

basswood. See bass².

bast bast, n. phloem: inner bark, esp of lime: fibre: matting —Also **bass** (bas) See bass². [O E. bæst.]

bastard¹ bas'tərd, bäs', n. a child born of parents not married to each other: vulgarly, a recalcitrant person or thing, an unpleasant person, an unfortunate person, or almost meaninglessly, a chap.—adj. born out of wedlock: not genuine: resembling, but not identical with, the species bearing the name: of abnormal shape or size: false.—n. **bastardisa'tion**, -z-.—v.t. **bas'tardise**, **-ize** to reduce to a lower state or condition.—n. **bast'ardism** bastardy.—adj. **bas'tardly.**—n. **bas'tardy** the state of being a bastard.— **bastard file** file with teeth of a medium degree of coarseness; **bas'tard-wing** three, four, or five feathers on the first digit (homologue of the thumb) of a bird's wing. [O.F. bastard (Fr. bâtard), child of the pack-saddle (O.Fr. bast).]

bastard² bas'tərd, Afrık. **baster** bas'tər, (S. Afr.) ns. a person of mixed white and coloured parentage, whether legitimately born or not. [Du. bastaard, bastard.]

baste¹ bäst, v.i. to beat with a stick.—n. **bäst'ing.** [Prob. conn. with O.N. beysta, Dan. boste, to beat]

baste² bäst, v.t to drop fat or butter over, as in roasting.

baste³ bäst, v t. to tack in sewing. [O.Fr. bastir— O H.G. bestan, to sew.]

baster. See bastard².

bastille bas-tēl', n. a tower for the defence of a fortress (hist.): a movable tower used by besiegers. (with cap.) an old fortress and state prison in Paris, demolished in the Revolution (July 1789). [Fr.,—O.Fr, bastir (Fr. bätir), to build]

bastinado, bastinade bast-ın-äd'(ō), vs t to beat with a baton or stick, esp. on the soles of the feet (an Eastern punishment).—pr.p. **bastinäd'oing** or **bastinäd'ing**; pa p **bastinäd'oed** or **bastinäd'ed**.—ns **bastinade'; bastinäd'o:**—pl. **bastinä'does.** [Sp bastonada, Fr bastonnade—baston, baton, cf baton, batten.]

bastion bast'yən, n. a kind of tower at the angle of a fortification: a defence (fig.).—adj **bast'ioned.** [Fr ,—It bastione—bastıre, to build.]

Basuto ba-sōō'tō n. the Bantu people of Lesotho (form. Basutoland). a member thereof (pl. **Basu'tos**) their language (also **Sotho**) —Also **Basu'tu** (-tōō).

bat¹ bat, n. a heavy stick: a flattish club for striking the ball in cricket: a club for baseball. in tennis, etc., a racket (coll.): a batsman: a piece of brick' a blow: a sheet of batting (also **batt**): a layer of felt used in hat-making (also **batt**).—v.t. and v.ı. to hit with a bat in cricket, etc. to hit as with a bat:—pr.p. **batt'ing**; pa.t and pa p **batt'ed.**—ns. **batt'er; batt'ing** the management of a bat in playing games: cotton fibre prepared in sheets, for quilts, etc.—**bat'man** a man on an aerodrome or aircraft carrier who assists planes to taxi to position using a pair of lightweight bats (see also separate entry); **bats'man** one who wields the bat at cricket, etc.; **bats'manship.**—**off one's own bat** by one's own efforts (as a cricketer from his own hits): on one's own initiative. [Perh. from O.E. bat (a doubtful form), prob. Celt. bat, staff]

bat² bat, n. a flying mammal with wings attached mainly to its arms and hands, but extending along its sides to the hind-feet and tail —adjs **bats** (coll)

batty; bat'ty batlike: bat-infested: crazy (coll.).— batwing sleeve a sleeve that is very wide at the armhole and tight at the wrist.—**have, be bats in the belfry** (coll) to be crazy, slightly mad; **like a bat out of hell** (coll.) very quickly. [M.E. bakke, apparently from Scand.; cf Dan. aftenbakke, evening-bat.]

bat³ bat, v.t. to flutter, esp. an eyelid.—**not to bat an eye**(lid) not to sleep a wink: to show no surprise, no emotion. [Conn. obs. bate, to beat.]

batch bach, n the quantity of bread baked, or of anything made or got ready, at one time. a set.—v.t to collect into, or treat in, batches.—adj. **batch'ing.** [From the root of bake.]

bate¹ bāt, v.t. and v.ı. to abate: to lessen, diminish: to blunt.—**with bated breath** see breath. [Aphetic form of abate.]

bate². Same as bait, a rage (slang.).

bateau ba-tō', n. a light river-boat, esp. on Canadian rivers:—pl. **bateaux** (-tōz'). [Fr]

bateleur bat'lər, n. a short-tailed African eagle. [Fr , mountebank, app. from its characteristic movements.]

bath bath, n water for immersing the body. an act of bathing: a receptacle or a house for bathing. a place for undergoing medical treatment by means of bathing: the act of exposing the body to vapour, mud, sunlight, etc.: a liquid or other material (as sand), or a receptacle, in which anything is immersed for heating, washing, or steeping (chem.).—pl. **baths** (badhz, also bäths).—v.t. to give a bath to: to wash (oneself) in a bath.—v.i. to take a bath.—**bath'cube** bath-salts in the form of a solid cube, **bath'house**; **bath'robe** (U S.) dressing-gown; **bath'room**; **bath'salts** a usu sweet-smelling substance used in baths to soften and perfume the water; **bath'tub.**—**Order of the Bath** an English order of knighthood, so named from the bath before installation [O E. bæth.]

Bath bath, a famous city in Somerset, with Roman baths.—**Bath bun** a rich sweet bun, **Bath chair** (also without cap) a large wheeled chair for invalids, **Bath Oliver** a biscuit invented by Dr W Oliver of Bath.

bath-brick bath'brık, n a preparation used in cleaning knives [Traditionally named after the first maker, one Bath, or from its resemblance to a stone quarried at Bath.]

bathe bädh, v t. to wash as in a bath: to wash or moisten, with any liquid to moisten, suffuse, encompass. —v.ı to take a dip or swim. to bask —n the act of bathing. a swim or dip —n. **bäth'er**—**bäth'ing-box'**, **-hut'** a small structure for bathers to undress and dress in; **bäth'ing-cost'ume**, **-dress**, **-suit** a garb for bathing in; **bäth'ing-machine'** (hist.) a small carriage in which a bather may be carried out into water conveniently deep [O.E. bathian]

bathetic. See bathos.

bath mitzvah, bath mizvah, bath mitsvah bath mıts'və (also **bas** bas, **bat** bat, sometimes with caps.; also hyphenated or as one word) esp. in the U S., a girl of the Jewish religion attaining the age (usu 13 years) of religious responsibility the festivities held in recognition of this event [Heb , daughter of the law]

batholite bath'ō-lıt, n. a mass of igneous rock that has risen from a great depth.—Also **bath'olith**, **bath'ylite, bath'ylith.**—adjs. **batholit(h)ic, bathylit(h)ic** (-lıt', -luth') [Gr bathos, depth, bathys, deep, luthos, a stone.]

bathometer bath-om'ıt-ər, n. a bathymeter [Gr bathos, depth, metron, measure.]

bathos bā'thos, n a ludicrous descent from the elevated to the mean in writing or speech —adj bathos, depth. **bathetic** (bə-thet'ık). [Gr. bathos, depth.]

bathy- bath'ı-, -ı', in composition, deep.—adj. **bath'yal** (-ı-əl) of ocean depths of between 200 and

2000 metres.—*ns.* **bathymeter** (*-im'*; Gr *metron*, measure) a sounding instrument.—*adjs.* **bathymet'-ric, -al.**—*n* **bathym'etry** the science of sounding seas and lakes; **bath'ysphere** (Gr. *sphaira*, sphere) a submersible observation chamber (**bath'yscaph(e)**, **-scape**, later types). [Gr. *bathys*, deep]

batik *bat'ik*, *n* an Indonesian method of producing designs on cloth by covering with wax, for each successive dipping, those parts that are to be protected from the dye [Malay.]

batiste *ba-tēst'*, *n.* a fine fabric of linen, cotton, or wool. [Fr., cambric—*Baptiste*, the original maker; or from its use in wiping the heads of children after baptism]

batman *bat'mən*, *n* an officer's attendant.—See also under **bat¹**.—**bat'woman**. [Fr *bât*, pack-saddle.]

bat mitzvah. See **bath mitzvah**.

baton *bat'(ə)n* a staff of office, e.g that of a marshal: a policeman's truncheon: a short, stick passed on from one runner to the next in a relay-race: a light wand used by the conductor of an orchestra· a knobbed staff carried, tossed and twirled by a drum major, etc., at the head of a marching band, etc.—**baton gun** a gun which fires rubber bullets, used in riot-control; **bat'on-sin'ister** a heraldic indication of illegitimacy [Fr. *bâton*]

batsman. See **bat¹**.

batt. See **bat¹**.

battalia pie *bat-al'yə pī*, articles such as pin-cushions, embroidered by nuns in convents with scenes from the Bible· a pie containing sweetbreads, etc. [Fr *béatilles*, dim. from L *beātus*, blessed, and perh L. *pius*, pious.]

battalion *bə-tal'yən*, *n.* a body of soldiers consisting of several companies: a body of men drawn up in battle array [Fr. *batalhon*—It *battaglione*; see **battle**.]

battels *bat'lz*, *n.pl.* accounts for provisions received from college kitchens and butteries (*Oxford*): sums charged in college accounts generally.—*v i* **batt'el** to have such an account—*n* **batt'eler**. [Perh connected with O.N *bati*, improvement; see also **batten¹**.]

batten¹ *bat'n*, *v.i.* to thrive at the expense of (with *on*)· to grow fat· to feed abundantly (on, *lit.* and *fig.*) [O.N. *batna*, to grow better]

batten² *bat'n*, *n* a piece of sawn timber used for flooring, support of laths, etc a strip of wood fastened across parallel boards, or used to fasten down hatches aboard ship, etc : a row of electric lamps or a strip of wood carrying them.—*v t.* to fasten or furnish with battens —*n* **batt'ening** battens forming a structure [**baton**.]

Battenberg *bat'ən-bûrg*, *n.* a kind of cake usu made in pink and yellow squares and covered with marzipan [Perh. from *Battenberg*, a village in W. Germany.]

batter¹ *bat'ər*, *v.t.* to beat with successive blows: to wear with beating or by use: to attack with artillery.—*n.* ingredients beaten along with some liquid into a paste (*cook.*): paste for sticking.—*adj.* **batt'ered** suffering frequent violent assaults: covered, treated, with batter.—**batt'ering-ram** a large beam with a metal head like a ram's used for battering down walls.—**battered baby** (**or child**) **syndrome** a collection of symptoms found in a baby or young child, caused by violence on the part of the parent or other adult suffering from social and psychological disturbance. [O.Fr. *batre*—L.L. *battěre* (L. *ba(t)tuěre*), to beat.]

batter² *bat'ər*, *n* inward inclination from the perpendicular.—*v.i* to slope inward

batter³, *battered.* See **bat¹**.

battery *bat'ər-i*, *n.* the act of battering· a number of cannon with their equipment: the place on which

cannon are mounted: a unit of artillery or its personnel: a combination of Leyden jars, lenses, or other apparatus: a series of two or more electric cells arranged to produce, or store, electricity: à single voltaic or solar cell: an attack against a person, beating, wounding, or threatening by touching clothes or body (*law*): an arrangement of tiers of cages in which hens are kept: an arrangement of similarly restrictive compartments for rearing pigs or cattle intensively: an apparatus for preparing or serving meals.—**battery of tests** (*psych.*) a set of tests covering various factors relevant to some end purpose, e.g job selection

battle *bat'l*, *n.* a contest between opposing armies: a fight or encounter.—*v.i.* to fight: to struggle: to contend (with *against, with*).—*v.t.* to contest —*n* **batt'ler**.—**batt'le-axe, -ax** a kind of axe once used in battle. a formidable woman (*coll.*); **batt'le-cruiser** a large cruiser with battleship qualities; **batt'le-cry** a war-cry, slogan; **batt'ledress** a simplified military uniform, close-fitting at the waist, allowing freedom of movement: **battle fatigue** same as **combat fatigue; batt'lefield, batt'leground** the place on which a battle is or was fought; **battle royal** a general mêlée. —*adj* **batt'le-scarred** scarred in battle.—**batt'leship** a warship of the first class—**do battle** (often *fig.*) to fight; **half the battle** anything that brings one well on the way to success; **join battle** to engage in fighting. [Fr *bataille*—L. *battuālta*, fighting.]

battlement *bat'l-mənt*, *n.* a wall or parapet with embrasures [O Fr *batailler*, movable defences.]

battledore, battledoor *bat'l-dōr*, *-dor*, *n.* a wooden bat used for washing, etc.: a light bat for striking a ball or shuttlecock [Perhaps Sp. *batidor*, a beater, a washing beetle.]

battology *bat-ol'ə-ji*, *n.* futile repetition in speech or writing —*adj.* **battolog'ical**. [Gr *battologiâ*, stuttering.]

battue *ba-tōō'*, *ba-tū'*, *ba-tu*, *n.* a hunt in which animals are driven into some place for the convenience of the shooters· indiscriminate slaughter. [Fr.—*battre*, to beat]

batty. See **bat.**

bauble *bo'bl*, *n* a trifling piece of finery: a child's plaything: a jester's sceptre, a stick surmounted by a head with ass's ears: a piece of childish foolery [O.Fr. *babel*, *baubel*, toy, trinket.]

baud *bôd'*, (*teleg.*) *n.* a unit of signalling speed.

baudekin *bod'i-kin* Same as **baldachin**.

baudric, baudrick *bod'rik*. Same as **baldrick(k)**.

Bauhaus *bow'hows*, *n.* a German school of art and architecture (1919–33) having as its aim the integration of art and technology in design. [Lit. Building-house]

bauk, baulk. Same as **balk.**

bauxite, beauxite *bok'sīt*, *-zīt*, *bō'zīt*, *ns.* a clay compound containing aluminium.—*adj.* **bauxitic** (*-it'ik*). [From Les *Baux*, near Arles, and *-ite.*]

bavardage *bàv-ar-dazh'*, *n.* chattering, prattle. [Fr. *bavard*, garrulous—*bave*, drivel.]

bavin *bav'in*, *n* a fagot of brushwood.

bawble. Same as **bauble.**

bawd¹ *bod*, *n* a procuress (or till about 1700 procurer) of women for lewd purposes.—*adv.* **bawd'-ily.**—*ns.* **bawd'iness; bawd'ry** procuring: unchastity: bawdy talk —*adj.* **bawd'y** lewd.—*n.* bawdy talk. —**bawd'y-house** a brothel. [Prob M.E. *bawdstrot*, pander—O.Fr. *baldestrot*, prob.—*bald*, bold, gay, and the root of **strut.**]

bawdkin. Same as **baldachin.**

bawl *bôl*, *v t* and *v.i.* to shout or cry out very loudly. —*n* a loud cry or shout —*ns.* **bawl'er; bawl'ing.**— **bawl out** (*coll*) to reprimand bullyingly. [Perh.

L.L. *baulāre*, to bark, but cf. Icel. *baula*, to low like a
cow—O.N. *baula*, a cow.]

bay[1] *bā*, *adj.* reddish brown inclining to chestnut (of
horses, usu. with a black mane and tail).—*n.* a bay
horse. [Fr. *bai*—L. *badius*, chestnut-coloured.]

bay[2] *bā*, *n.* an inlet of the sea with a wider opening than
a gulf: an inward bend of the shore: a similar recess in
a land form, e.g. in a mountain range.—**bay salt**
coarse-grained salt, orig. from sea-water.—**the Bay
State** Massachusetts. [Fr. *baie*—L.L. *baia*, a harbour.]

bay[3] *bā*, *n.* the space between two columns, timbers,
walls, etc.: any recess or stall: a passing-place in a
military trench: a side-line in a railway station (also
bay'-line): a compartment (e.g. bomb bay) or section
of an aircraft.—**bay window** any window forming a
recess.—*adj.* **bay'-win'dowed.** [O.Fr. *baée*—*baer*,
to gape, be open; prob. conn **bay**.]

bay[4] *bā*, *n.* the laurel tree; extended to other trees and
shrubs, species of *Magnolia, Myrica*, etc.: (in *pl.*) an
honorary garland or crown of victory, originally of
laurel: hence, literary renown.—**bay'berry** the berry
of the bay tree, or of candle-berry: a tree (*Pimenta
acris*) akin to allspice; **bay leaf** dried leaf of laurel tree
(*Laurus nobilis*) used as flavouring agent in cooking;
bay rum an aromatic liquid prepared from the leaves
of *Pimenta acris* used medicinally and cosmetically
[O.Fr. *baie*, a berry—L. *bāca*.]

bay[5] *bā*, *n.* barking, baying (esp. of a dog in pursuit):
the combined cry of hounds in conflict with a hunted
animal: the last stand of a hunted animal when it faces
the hounds at close quarters.—*v.i.* to bark (esp. of
large dogs).—*v.t.* to bark at: to utter by baying: to
bring to bay.—**bay (at) the moon** to make a futile
gesture; **keep at bay** to prevent from coming closer;
stand, be, at bay to face the dogs at close quarters: to
face one's pursuers. [Partly O.Fr. *abai*, barking,
bayer, to bark, partly O.Fr. *bay*, open-mouthed
suspense—L.L *badāre*, to open the mouth.]

bayadère *bā-yä-der'*, *n.* a Hindu dancing-girl: a
horizontally-striped woven fabric. [Fr.,—Port.
bailadeira.]

bayle. Same as **bail**[2].

bayonet *bā'ə-nit*, *n.* a stabbing instrument of steel fixed
to the muzzle of a fire-arm: a type of fitting for a light
bulb, camera lens, etc.; in which prongs fit into slots
to hold it in place.—*v.t.* to stab with a bayonet: to
force at the point of the bayonet. [Fr. *baionnette*,
perh. from *Bayonne*, in France; or from O.Fr. *bayon*,
arrow.]

bayou *bī'ōō*, (*U.S.*) *n.* the marshy offshoot of a lake or
river. [Perh. Fr. *boyau*, gut, or Choctaw *bāyuk*,
little river.]

bazaar, bazar *bə-zär'*, *n.* an Eastern market-place or
exchange: a fancy fair in imitation of an Eastern
bazaar: sometimes, a big shop. [Pers. *bāzār*, a
market.]

bazooka *bə-zōō'kə*, *n.* an anti-tank gun for rocket-
driven projectiles: a rocket launcher situated on the
wing of an aeroplane. [Invented name.]

baz(z)azz. See **bez(z)azz.**

bdellium *del'i-əm*, *n.* a gum got from *Commiphora*
trees. [L.,—Gr. *bdellion*.]

be *bē*, *v.i. infin.* to live: to exist: to have the state or
quality mentioned:—*pr.p.* **be'ing**; *pa.p.* **been** (*bēn,
bin*); *pr.subj.* **be**; *arch.* and *dial. pr.indic.* **be** (see **am,
art, is, are**); for *pa.t.* see **was, wast, were, wert**.—*n.*
be'-all and end'-all the supreme aim, issue. [O.E.
bēon.]

be- *bi-*, *pfx.* used (1) to form verbs with the sense of
around, on all sides, in all directions, thoroughly; (2)
to form words from adjectives and nouns; (3)
formerly, to make intransitive verbs transitive, as

bespeak. [O E. *bi-*, weak form of *bī*.]

beach *bēch*, *n.* the shore of a sea or of a lake, esp. when
sandy or pebbly.—*v.t.* to drive or haul up on a beach.
—*adj.* **beached** having a beach: driven on a beach:
beach'y pebbly.—**beach'-ball** a large usu. inflatable,
colourful ball for playing games on a beach;
beach'comber (*-kōm-*) a long rolling wave: a loafer
about the wharfs in Pacific seaports: a settler on a
Pacific island who maintains himself by pearl-fishery,
or by gathering jetsam, etc. on beaches; **beach'-
combing; beach'head** an area held on an enemy's shore
for purpose of landing; **beach'-master** an officer
in charge of disembarking troops; **beach'-rescue** a
person employed to save beach bathers in difficulties. [Orig a dial. word for shingle.]

beacon *bē'kn*, *n.* a fire on an eminence used as a sign of
danger: a hill on which it could be lighted: an erection
with or without a light marking a rock or shoal in
navigable waters: a light to guide airmen: a sign marking a street crossing—e.g. a **Belisha** (*bə-lē'shə, -ish'*)
beacon named after the Minister of Transport 1934:
a wireless transmitter in which the radiation is concentrated in one or more narrow beams, so as to act
as a guide to shipping or aircraft: anything that
warns of danger.—*v.t* to act as a beacon to. to light
up. to mark by beacons [O.E. *bēacn*, a beacon, a
sign]

bead *bēd*, *n.* a little ball strung with others in a rosary,
for counting prayers: a similar ball or the like pierced
for stringing to form a necklace, etc.: a bead-like
drop: the front-sight of a gun: a narrow moulding of
semi-circular section, sometimes broken into bead-
like parts: the flange of a tyre.—*v t* to furnish with
beads or beading.—*v.t.* to form a bead or beads.—
adj. **bead'ed** having beads or a bead: in bead-like
form.—*n.* **bead'ing** bead moulding: work in beads —
adj. **bead'y** bead-like, small and bright (as eyes):
covered with beads or bubbles.—**draw a bead on**
(*U.S.*) to take aim at, **tell one's beads** to say one's
prayers [O.E. *gebed*, prayer, see **bid**[2].]

beadle *bēd'l*, *n.* a mace-bearer: a petty officer of a
church, college, etc.: a parish officer with the power
of punishing petty offenders: in Scotland, the church-
officer attending on the minister. [O.E. *bydel*—
bēodan, to proclaim, to bid; affected by O.Fr form
bedel.]

beady. See **bead.**

beagle *bē'gl*, *n.* a small hound: a spy a bailiff: a small
kind of shark.—*v t.* to hunt with beagles.—*ns*
bea'gler; bea'gling.

beak *bēk*, *n.* a bird's bill. a hard or sharp snout. a nose
(*jocular*) a pointed process or projection: in the
ancient galley a pointed iron projecting from the bow
for piercing the enemy's vessel: a magistrate, schoolmaster, or schoolmistress (*slang*).—*adj.* **beaked**
(*bēkt*).—**beak'-iron** same as **bick-iron.** [O.Fr. *bec*—
L. *beccus* (recorded by Suetonius), a cock's bill.]

beaker *bēk'ər*, *n.* a large drinking-bowl or cup, or its
contents: a deep glass or other vessel used by
chemists.—**Beaker Folk** a round-headed, heavy-
browed, square-jawed people that appeared in
Britain at the dawn of the Bronze Age, makers of
round barrows in which bell-shaped beakers are often
found. [O.N. *bikarr*.]

beam *bēm*, *n.* a large and straight piece of timber or
iron forming one of the main structural members of a
building, etc : any of the transverse pieces of framing
extending across a ship's hull: the greatest width of a
ship or boat. breadth: the part of a balance from
which the scales hang: the pole of a carriage: the
stem, or main part of an anchor, a plough: a cylinder
of wood in a loom: a shaft or ray of light or other
radiations: a gleam.—*v.t.* to send forth· to place on a

beam: to transmit by beam system —*v i.* to shine: to smile radiantly.—*n* **beam'er**.—*adv.* **beam'ily** radiantly.—*n.* **beam'iness** radiance breadth —*n.* and *adj.* **beam'ing**.—*adv.* **beam'ingly**.—*adjs* **beam'ish** radiant, **beam'less** without beams: emitting no rays, **beam'y** shining· radiant.—**beam'-ends** the ends of the transverse beams of a ship; **beam'-en'gine** a steam-engine with a beam connecting the piston-rod and the crank of the wheel-shaft; **off** or **on the beam** off or on the course shown by a radio beam: off or on the right track (*fig.*), **on her beam-ends** of a ship, so much inclined to one side that the beams become nearly vertical, **on one's beam-ends** in acute distress, destitute; **on the port, starboard, beam** applied to any distant point out at sea, at right angles to the keel, and on the left, or right, side. [O E *bēam*, tree, stock of a tree, ray of light.]

bean *bēn, n.* the name of several kinds of leguminous plants and their seeds, esp the common, or broad bean and the French kidney, or haricot bean: applied also to the seeds of other plants, from their bean-like form, as coffee: a coin (*coll*). head (*coll*).—*n* **bean'o** (*coll.*) a beanfeast, a disturbance, a jollification.—*pl* **bean'os**.—**bean'-bag** a small cloth bag containing dried beans, used in games, **bean'feast** an annual dinner given by employers to their workers at which beans used to be prominent· a jollification; **bean'pole** a supporting pole up which a bean plant climbs· a tall, very thin person (*coll*); **bean sprout** the young shoot of the mung bean or certain other beans, used as a vegetable esp. in Chinese cookery; **bean'stalk** the stem of a bean plant.—**full of beans** in high spirits; **give someone beans** to treat someone severely, **know how many beans make five** (*coll*) to be fully alert, know what's what; **old bean** see **old**. [O.E *bēan*]

bear[1] *bār, v.t.* to carry: to have. to convey: to remove from the board in the final stage of the game (*backgammon*): to sustain or support to thrust or drive. to endure: to admit of: to purport to afford: to behave or conduct (oneself). to bring forth, give birth to (*pa p.* **born** (*born*) in passive uses) —*v i* to suffer: to be patient: to have reference (with *on* or *upon*) to press (with *on* or *upon*): to lie in, or take, a direction· to be capable of sustaining weight to be productive —*pr p.* **bear'ing;***pa.t.* bore;*pa p.* **borne** (*born, bôrn*). —*adj.* **bear'able** that may be borne or endured.—*n* **bear'ableness**.—*adv.* **bear'ably**.—*ns* **bear'er** one who or that which bears: the actual holder of a cheque or the like: one who helps to carry a body to the grave: a carrier or messenger: in India a personal, household or hotel servant; **bear'ing** demeanour: direction: a supporting surface: relation: that which is borne upon an escutcheon: the part of a machine that bears friction, esp. a journal and its support (sometimes in *pl* see **ball-bearing**)—Also *adj* —**bearing rein** a fixed rein between the bit and the saddle, by which a horse's head is held up and its neck made to arch.— **bear a hand** see **hand**; **bear away** to sail away: to carry away; **bear down** to overthrow: to press downwards: (with *upon* or *towards*) to sail with the wind (towards): (with *upon*) to approach (someone or something) rapidly and purposefully, **bear hard, heavily upon** (*lit.* and *fig.*) to press heavily on: to oppress, afflict; **bear in mind** to remember (that). to think of, take into consideration, **bear in upon** (usu in *pass*) to impress upon, or to make realise, esp. by degrees, **bear out** to corroborate; **bear up** to keep up one's spirits; **bear with** to make allowance for; **bring to bear** to bring into operation (with *against, upon*); **find, lose one's bearings** to ascertain, or to become uncertain of, one's position or orientation. [O.E. *beran*]

bear[2] *bâr, n.* a heavy carnivorous animal with long shaggy hair and hooked claws: any rude, rough or ill-bred fellow: one who sells stocks for delivery at a future date, anticipating a fall in price—opp to *bull* —*v.t* to speculate for a fall —*adj* **bear'ish** like a bear in manners inclining towards, anticipating, a fall in prices (*Stock Exchange*) —*n* **bear'ishness**.—**bear'-baiting** the former sport of setting dogs to worry a bear; **bear garden** an enclosure for bear-baiting: a turbulent assembly, **bear'skin** the skin of a bear: a shaggy woollen cloth for overcoats the high fur cap worn by the Guards in England [O E *bera*.]

beard *bērd, n* the hair that grows on the chin and adjacent parts of a grown man's face. the tuft on the lower jaw of a goat, seal, etc.: a fish's barbel: an awn or threadlike spike as on the ears of barley (*bot*): a tuft of hairs: a barb of a hook, an arrow, etc.: the gills of an oyster, etc —*v t* to oppose to the face —*adjs* **beard'ed; beard'less**. [O.E *beard*]

béarnaise, Béarnaise (sauce) *bā-ar-nez* (*sos*), a sauce made from egg yolks, butter, shallots, tarragon, chervil and wine vinegar. [Fr. *béarnaise* (fem of *béarnais*) of Béarn, region of south-western France]

beast *bēst, n* an irrational animal, as opposed to man: a four-footed animal: a brutal person. anything beastly (*coll*) —*ns* **beast'ie** (orig. *Scot*) a dim. form of **beast**, the four-footed animal· an insect, spider, etc (*coll*), **beast'liness**.—*adjs* **beast'like** (also *adv.*); **beast'ly** like a beast in actions or behaviour: bestial. foul· sensual vile, disagreeable (*coll.*).—*adv* brutishly: abominably, frightfully (*coll.*).—**mark of the Beast** a stamp on the forehead or right hand of a worshipper of **the Beast** (Antichrist) of the Book of Revelation. a sign of whatever was considered to be of Antichrist or evil. [O Fr *beste*—L *bestia*]

beastings. Same as **beestings.**

beat *bēt, v.t.* to strike repeatedly· to batter: to whip up or switch: to flap· to strike (as bushes) in order to rouse game: to thrash: to defeat, to frustrate: to be too difficult for. to outdo, excel to spread flat and thin by beating with a tool (as gold): to mark (time)· with a baton, etc.—*v.i* to give strokes repeatedly: to pulsate· to impinge: to mark time in music:—*pr.p.* **beat'ing;***pa.t* **beat;** *pa.p.* **beat'en**, now rarely **beat.**— *n* a recurrent stroke, its sound, or its moment: accent: pulsation, esp that heard when two notes nearly in tune are sounded together: a round or course, as a policeman's: a place of resort.—*adj* weary. fatigued. relating to beatniks (*coll.*).—*adjs.* **beat'able; beat'en** made smooth or hard by beating or treading. trite: worn by use —*ns* **beat'er** one that beats or strikes one who rouses or beats up game: a crushing or mixing instrument; **beat'ing** —**beat music** popular music with a very pronounced rhythm; **beatnik** *bēt'nik*, a young person whose behaviour. dress, etc, are unconventional.—*adj* **beat'-up** dilapidated through excessive use —**beat a retreat** to retreat, originally to beat the drum as a signal for retreat (**beat the retreat** to perform the military ceremony (**beating the retreat**) consisting of marching and military music usu performed at dusk (originally marking the recall of troops to their quarters)); **beat down** of a buyer, to try to reduce (the price of goods), to persuade (the seller) to settle for less; **beat it** (*slang*) to make off hastily or furtively; **beat off** to drive back, **beat one's brains** to puzzle one's brains about something; **beat one's breast** (*fig.*) to show extravagant signs of grief; **beat out** to flatten or reduce in thickness by beating; **beat someone to it** to manage to do something before someone else can; **beat the bounds** to trace out boundaries in a perambulation, certain objects in the line of journey being formally struck, **beat the clock** to do or finish something within the time allowed; **beat up** to pound or whip into froth, paste, a mixture, etc.: to put up as by beating the bushes: to subject to a violent and brutal attack (*slang*): to disturb: to arouse: to go about in quest of anything: to make way against wind or tide, **take a beating** to suffer physical or verbal chastisement; **take some, a lot of, beating** (*coll.*) to be of very high quality, i.e. to be difficult to excel. [O.E. *bēatan*, pa.t. *bēot*.]

beatify *bi-at'i-fī*, *v.t.* to make blessed or happy; to declare to be in the enjoyment of eternal happiness in heaven.—*adjs.* **beatific** (*bē-ə-tif'ik*), **-al** making supremely happy.—*adv.* **beatif'ically.**—*n.* **beatifica'tion** the act of beatifying: in the R.C. church, a declaration by the Pope that a person is blessed in heaven, authorising a certain definite form of public reverence payable to him —the first step to canonisation. [L. *beātus*, blessed, and *facĕre*, to make.]

beatitude *bi-at'i-tūd*, *n.* happiness of the highest kind. a title given to patriarchs in the Orthodox Churches: (in *pl.*) sayings of Christ in Matt. v, declaring certain classes of person to be blessed. [L. *beātitūdō—beātus*, blessed.]

beatnik. See under **beat**.

beau[1] *bō*, *n.* a man attentive to dress or fashion: a fop or dandy: a lover:—*pl.* **beaux** (*bōz*):—*fem* **belle** (*bel*). [Fr. *beau*, *bel*—L *bellus*, fine, gay.]

beau[2] *bō*, (Fr.) *adj.* beautiful, handsome, fine; **beau geste** (*zhest*) gracious gesture; **beau monde** (*mɔ̃d*) the gay or fashionable world.

Beaufort *bō'fərt*, *adj.* devised by Sir Francis *Beaufort* (1774–1857), English admiral and hydrographer — **Beaufort scale** a scale of wind velocity, with 0 for calm, 12 for hurricane.

beauty *bū'ti*, *n.* the quality that gives pleasure to the sight, or aesthetic pleasure generally: a particular grace or excellence· a beautiful person (often *ironical*), esp. a woman; also applied collectively: a very fine specimen of its kind: (in *pl.*) beautiful passages or extracts.—*n.* **beaut** (*slang*) someone or something exceptionally beautiful or remarkable — *adj., interj.* (esp. *Austr.*) excellent, fine.—*adj* **beau'teous** (*-ti-əs*) a bookish word for beautiful.—*adv.* **beau'teously.**—*ns.* **beau'teousness; beautician** (*bū-tish'ən*) one engaged in women's hairdressing, facial make-up, manicuring, etc.; **beautifica'tion; beau'tifier** one who or that which beautifies or makes beautiful.—*adj.* **beau'tiful** fair: with qualities that give delight to the senses, esp. the eye and ear, or which awaken admiration in the mind.—*adv.* **beau'tifully.**—*v.t.* **beau'tify** to make beautiful: to grace: to adorn.—**beauty contest** a competition held for the selection of a beauty queen; **beauty parlour** an establishment for the hairdressing, manicuring, face-massaging, etc., of women; **beauty queen** a girl who is voted the most attractive or best-proportioned in a competition; **beauty sleep** the sleep before midnight, considered the most refreshing, **beauty spot** a patch placed on the face to heighten beauty: a birthmark resembling such a patch: a foil: a scene of outstanding beauty. [O.Fr. *biaute* (Fr *beauté*)—L L *bellitās*, *-ātis*—L. *bellus*.]

beaux arts *bō-zar*, (Fr.) fine arts

beauxite See **bauxite**.

beaver *bēv'ər*, *n.* an amphibious rodent (*Castor*): its valuable fur: a hat of beaver fur or a substitute: a glove of beaver fur: a heavy woollen cloth.—**beaver away** (*coll.*) to work very hard (at). [O.E. *befer*, *beofor*.]

bebop *bē'bop*, *n.* a variety of jazz music, from about 1940, which added new harmonies, melodic patterns, and rhythms to accepted jazz characteristics.—Also **bop.**—Also *v i.* [Imitative of two quavers in the rhythm.]

bebung *bā'boong*, (*mus.*) *n* a tremolo effect produced on the clavichord by fluctuating the pressure of the finger on the key. [Ger]

becalm *bi-kam'*, *v.t.* to make calm, still, or quiet.—*adj.* **becalmed'** motionless from want of wind. [**be-**(1).]

became *bi-kām'*, *pa.t.* of **become**.

because *bi-koz'*, *bi-koz'*, *adv* and *conj* for the reason that: on account (of). [**by, cause.**]

béchamel (sauce), bechamel *bā-sha-mel, besh'ə-mel, n* a white sauce with flavouring and/or cream. [Fr., from name of steward of Louis XIV]

bêche-de-mer *besh'də-mer, n* the trepang or sea-slug. much esteemed in China as a food delicacy [Fr.—Port *bicho do mar*, sea-slug]

beck[1] *bek, n.* a brook [O N. *bekkr*]

beck[2] *bek, n* a sign with the finger or head.—**at someone's beck (and call)** subject to someone's will. [A contr. of **beckon.**]

becket *bek'it*, (*naut.*) *n* a loop of rope having a knot at one end and an eye at the other: a large hook, or a wooden bracket used to keep loose tackle or spars in a convenient place. [Perh. Du. *bogt, bocht*, a bend of rope.]

beck-iron. Same as **bick-iron.**

beckon *bek'n*, *v.t.* and *v.i.* to nod or (now usu.) make a summoning sign (to). [O.E. *biecnan—bēacn*, a sign.]

become *bi-kum'*, *v i.* to come to be: to be the fate (followed by *of*).—*v t.* to suit or befit: to grace: to adorn fittingly: to look well in.—*pa.t* **became'**; *pa.p.* **become'.**—*adj.* **becom'ing.**—*adv.* **becom'ingly.**—*n.* **becom'ingness.** [O.E *becuman*; see **come.**]

bed *bed*, *n.* a couch or place to sleep on: a mattress: a bedstead: a garden plot: a layer of oysters, etc.: a place in which anything rests: conjugal union, sexual relationship, the marriage-bed, matrimonial rights and duties: the channel of a river· sea or lake bottom: a layer or stratum.—*v.t* to put to bed: to provide, or make, a bed for: to have sexual intercourse with: to plant in a bed: to lay in layers or on a surface: to embed.—*v i.* to go to bed: to cohabit:—*pr.p.* **bedd'ing;** *pa p.* **bedd'ed.**—*adj* **bedd'able** sexually attractive.—*ns.* **bedd'er** a plant suitable for a flower bed, **bedd'ing** mattress, bedclothes, etc.: litter for cattle. stratification (*geol*)—**bed'bug** the common bug; **bed'chamber** a bedroom, **bed'clothes** sheets, blankets, etc , for a bed; **bed'cover** an upper covering for a bed —**bed'fellow** a sharer of a bed: a colleague: something or someone that associates with another; **bed'-jacket** light jacket worn when sitting up in bed; **bed'-linen** sheets and pillow-cases, **bed'pan** a chamber utensil for use in sick-bed: a warming-pan; **bed'-plate** (*mech.*) the metal base to which the frame of a machine, engine, etc. is attached; **bed'post** a corner support of a bedstead —*adjs.* **bed'ridd(en)** confined to bed by age or sickness· worn out —**bed'rock** the solid rock underneath superficial formations: fundamental principles (*fig*): the lowest state.—*adj* bottom, lowest —**bed'-roll** a sleeping-bag or bedclothes rolled up so as to be easily carried by a camper, etc , **bed'room** a room with a bed: a sleeping apartment: room in bed, sleeping space; **bed'side** position by a bed.—Also *adj.*—**bedside book** one especially suitable for reading in bed; **bedside manner** that assumed by a doctor at a sickbed; **bed'-sitt'ing-room** a combined bedroom and sitting-room, e g. in lodgings (shortened to **bed'-sit', bed'-sitt'er**), **bed'socks** warm socks for wearing in bed, **bed'sore** an ulcer arising from long confinement to bed, esp over the bony prominences; **bed'spread** a coverlet put over a bed by day, **bed'stead** a frame for supporting a bed, **bed'straw** any plant of the genus *Galium*, esp (Our)

Lady's bedstraw; **bed'-table** a table for use by a person in bed; **bed'time** the hour for going to bed; **bed'-wetting** the accidental passing of urine in bed.—**bed and board** food and lodging: full connubial relations, **bed and breakfast** at a hotel, etc., overnight accommodation with breakfast (adj. **bed'-and-break'fast** of stock-exchange deals, in which shares standing at a loss are sold one day and rebought the next to establish a loss for tax purposes), **bed down** to (cause to) settle down, esp in a makeshift bed, for sleep; **bed of roses** any easy or comfortable place, **bed out** to plant out in a flower-bed, etc., **brought to bed** confined in childbirth (with of); **get out of bed on the wrong side** to start the day in a bad mood; **go to bed**, **put to bed** (of newspapers, magazines, etc.) to go to, send to, press; **keep one's bed** to remain in bed; **lie in the bed one has made** to have to accept the consequences of one's own acts; **make a bed** to put a bed in order; **take to one's bed** to go to bed because of illness, grief, age, etc. [O.E. bed(d).]

bedazzle bi-daz'l v.t. to dazzle or overpower by any strong light.—pa.p. **bedazz'led** stupefied, besotted. —n. **bedazz'lement.** [be- (1).]

beddable. See **bed.**

bedeck bi-dek', v.t. to deck or ornament. [be- (1).]

bedeguar bed'i-gar, n. a soft spongy gall found on the branches of sweet-brier and other roses, called also the sweet-brier sponge [Fr. bédeguar—Pers. and Ar. bādā-war, lit. wind-brought.]

bedel, bedell. Old spellings of **beadle,** still used at Oxford and Cambridge.

bedevil bi-dev'l, v.t. to throw into confusion: to play the devil with: to torment: to treat with devilish malignity: to possess as a devil.—pr.p. **bedev'illing;** pa.t. and pa p **bedev'illed.**—n. **bedev'ilment.** [be-(2).]

bedew bi-dū', v.t. to moisten gently, as with dew. [be- (2).]

bedizen bi-dīz'n, bi-diz'n, v.t. to dress gaudily.—adj. **bediz'ened.**—n **bediz'enment.** [be- (1).]

bedlam bed'ləm, n. an asylum for lunatics: a madhouse: a place of uproar.—adj. fit for a madhouse. [From the priory St Mary of Bethlehem, in London, afterwards a madhouse (Bethlehem Royal Hospital).]

Bedlington (terrier) bed'ling-tən (ter'i-ər), n. a long-bodied lightly-built terrier, swiftest of its kind. [Bedlington, near Morpeth, where it was first bred.]

bedouin, beduin bed'ōō-in, -ēn, -wēn, bed'win, n. a tent-dwelling nomad Arab'—pl. **bed'ouin, -ins.** [Fr. bédouin—Ar. badāwin, dwellers in the desert.]

bedraggle bi-drag'l, v.t. to soil by dragging in the wet or dirt.—adj. **bedragg'led.** [be- (1).]

beduin. Same as **bedouin.**

bee bē, n. a four-winged insect that makes honey: a gathering of persons to unite their labour for the benefit of one individual or family, or for some joint amusement, exercise or competition (as quilting-bee, husking-bee, spelling-bee: a busy person: (usu. in pl.) a lump of a type of yeast.—**bee'-bread** the pollen collected by bees as food for their young, **bee'-eat'er** any bird of a brightly-plumaged family allied to the kingfishers; **bee'-flower** a flower pollinated by bees; **bee'-glue** propolis; **bee'hive** a case or box in which bees are kept (adj. dome-shaped, like an old-fashioned beehive, as **beehive hairstyle, beehive tomb**); **bee'keeper; bee'keeping; bee'-kite** the honey-buzzard; **bee'-moth** a moth whose larvae are very destructive to young bees; **bee'-or'chis** an orchid whose flower resembles a bee; **bees'wax** the wax secreted by bees and used by them in constructing their cells.— v.t. to polish with beeswax.—**bees'wing** a filmy crust of tartar formed in port and some other wines after

long keeping.—**a bee in one's bonnet** a whimsical or crazy fancy on some point: an obsession, **make a beeline for** to take the most direct way towards (like the honey-laden bee's way home); **the bee's knees** (coll) someone, something, particularly good, admirable, etc [O E bēo]

Beeb beb, n. coll. for BBC—British Broadcasting Corporation.

beech bēch, n. a common forest tree of the genus Fagus with smooth grey bark: extended to the kindred genus Nothofagus and to many trees not related —**beech'e fern** a fern of the polypody family, **beech'-mar'ten** the stone-marten, **beech'-mast** the mast or nuts of the beech-tree, which yield a valuable oil, **beech'-oil; beech'-wood** a wood of beech-trees: beech timber. [O.E. boece, bēce.]

beef bēf, n. the flesh of the ox as food: extended to that of some other animals, as the horse: muscle: vigorous muscular force: a complaint. an argument, quarrel.— adj. of beef —v.i. to grumble.—adj. **beef'y** like beef: fleshy, muscular: stolid —**beef'burger** a round flat cake of finely chopped meat, usu. fried or grilled; **beef'cake** a picture of a muscle-man: brawn as distinct from brain; **beef'eater** an ox-bird: a consumer of beef: a yeoman of the guard: a warder of the Tower of London; **beef'-ham'; beef'steak** a thick slice of beef for broiling or frying; **beef'tea'** stimulating rather than nutritious food for invalids, juice of beef strained off, after simmering in water.—**beef up** (coll.) to add strength to, to reinforce. [O.Fr. boef (Fr. bœuf) —L. bōs, bovis.]

been bēn, sometimes bin, pa.p. of **be.**

beer bēr, n. an alcoholic beverage made by fermentation, in which the yeast settles to the bottom (cf. ale), from malted barley flavoured with hops: the generic name of malt liquor, including ale and porter: a glassful, etc., of this to drink.—adj. **beer'y** of, or affected by, beer.—n. **beer'iness.—beer'-barrel; beer'-bottle; beer'-engine, beer'-pump** a machine for drawing beer up from the casks to the bar; **beer'** gar'den a garden with tables where beer and other refreshments may be had; **beer'-money** money given in lieu of beer and spirits: a gratuity.—**beer and skittles** idle enjoyment; **bitter beer** pale ale, a highly hopped beer made from the very finest selected malt and hops (**mild or sweet ale** being of greater gravity or strength, and comparatively lightly hopped); **small beer** weak beer: something trifling or unimportant, esp. when compared with something else. [O.E. bēor.]

beestings bēst'ingz, n. the first milk drawn from a cow after calving. [O.E. bȳsting, bēost.]

beet bēt, n. a plant with a succulent root, used as food and as a source of sugar.—**beet'root** the root of the beet plant; **beet sugar.** [O.E. bēte—L. bēta.]

beetle¹ bē'tl, n. any insect of the Coleoptera, an order in which the fore-wings are reduced to hard and horny covers for the hind-wings: a game in which a drawing of a beetle is made up gradually of its component parts, body, head, etc., according to the throw of dice, the object being to produce a completed drawing: (esp. with cap.) a particular model of small Volkswagen car with rounded roof and bonnet, resembling a beetle (coll) —v.i. to jut: to overhang.— adj. (always applied to brows) overhanging, scowling. —adj. **beet'ling** jutting: prominent: overhanging.— adj. **beet'le-browed** with overhanging or prominent brows —**beet'le-crusher** (slang) a big heavy foot or boot: a policeman: an infantryman, **beetle drive** a progressive game of beetle.—**beetle off** to hurry away like a beetle (coll.): to fly (air-force jargon); **black beetle** the cockroach (properly not a beetle). [M.E. bityl—O E bitula, bitela—bitan, to bite.]

beetle[2] *bē'tl, n.* a heavy wooden mallet used for driving wedges, crushing or beating down paving-stones, or the like: a wooden pestle-shaped utensil for mashing potatoes, beating linen, clothes, etc [O.E *bīetl—bēatan,* to beat.]

beetroot. See beet.

beeves *bēvz, n.pl.* cattle, oxen [See beef.]

befall *bi-föl', v.t* (or *v.i.* with *dat.*) to fall or happen to: to occur to.—*v.i* to happen or come to pass: to fall in one's way:—*pr.p.* **befall'ing;** *pa.t.* **befell';** *pa.p.* **befall'en.** [O.E. *bef(e)allan;* see fall.]

befit *bi-fit', v t.* to be fitting, or suitable to: to beseem —*v.i.* to be right'—*pr.p.* **befitt'ing;** *pa.p.* **befitt'ed.**—*adj.* **befitt'ing.**—*adv.* **befitt'ingly.** [be-(1).]

before *bi-för', -for, prep.* in front of: ahead of: in presence or sight of: under the consideration or cognisance of: previous to: previous to the expiration of: in preference to: superior to.—*adv.* in front: sooner: earlier: in the past: formerly.—*conj.* previous to the time when (sometimes with *that*).—*adv.* **before'hand** before the time: in advance or anticipation: by way of preparation: in advance of one's needs.—*adj.* **before'-men'tioned.**—*adv.* **before'time** in former time.—**before Christ** (abbrev. B.C) before the date formerly assigned to the birth of Christ; **before the wind** in the direction in which the wind is blowing, and hence helped along by it. [O.E *beforan* See fore.]

befoul *bi-fowl', v.t.* to make foul: to soil. [be-(2)]

befriend *bi-frend', v.t.* to act as a friend to: to favour [be-(2).]

befuddle *bi-fud'l, v.t* to reduce to a fuddled condition. [be-(1).]

beg[1]. Same as bey.

beg[2] *beg, v.i.* to ask alms or charity, esp habitually· to sit up on the hind quarters, as a dog for a reward —*v.t.* to ask earnestly: to beseech: to pray: to take unwarrantedly for granted (esp. **to beg the question,** to fall into the fallacy of assuming what is to be proved as part of the would-be proof):—*pr.p.* **begg'ing;** *pa.t* and *pa p.* **begged** (*begd*).—*n* **beggar** (*beg'ər*) one who begs: one who lives by begging: (hyperbolically) one who is indigent: a mean fellow: a poor fellow: often used playfully and even affectionately. —*v.t.* to reduce to beggary: to exhaust or impoverish· to go beyond the resources of, as of description (*fig.*). —*n.* **begg'arliness.**—*adj* **begg'arly** poor· mean worthless.—*adv* meanly.—*n.* **begg'ary** extreme poverty.—*n.* and *adj.* **begg'ing.**—*adv* **begg'ingly.**—**begg'ar-man; begg'ar-my-neigh'bour** a game that goes on till one has gained all the others' cards; **begg'ing-bowl** a bowl carried by beggars, esp certain orders of monks, to receive food, money, etc., **begg'-ing-lett'er** a letter soliciting alms or subscriptions — **go (a-)begging** to be in want of a purchaser, occupant, etc. [Perh from **beghard** (q.v), the verb being a back-formation]

began *bi-gan', pa t.* of begin.

begat. See beget.

beget *bi-get', v.t* to produce or cause to generate (commonly of the father) to produce as an effect, to cause:—*pr.p.* **begett'ing;** *pa t* **begot'** (*arch* **begat'**), *pa.p.* **begott'en** (or **begot'**)—*n* **begett'er.** [O.E *begitan,* to acquire; see get.]

beggar. See beg[2].

beghard *beg'ard, n* a man living a monastic life without vows and with power to return to the world [Flem *beggaert.*]

begin *bi-gin', v.i.* to come into being· to take rise to perform the first act. to open· to have an opening — *v t.* to perform the first act of· to enter on to start'— *pr.p* **beginn'ing;** *pa t* **began'** (now rarely **begun'**), *pa p* **begun.**—*ns* **beginn'er** one who begins one who

is in the early stages of learning or doing anything; **beginn'ing** origin: a start· an entering upon action: an opening or first part: a rudiment —**to begin with** firstly· at first. [O.E. *beginnan* from pfx. *be-*, and *ginnan,* to begin.]

begird *bi-gûrd', v t.* to gird or bind with a girdle· to surround or encompass:—*pa.t.* and *pa.p* **begirt'** (or **begird'ed**) [O.E *begyrdan;* be-(1), and gird.]

begone *bi-gon', interj* be gone: be off: get away.

Begonia *bi-gō'ni-ə, n.* a genus of tropical, esp. American, plants cultivated in greenhouses: (without *cap*) a plant of the genus. [Named from Michel Bégon (1638–1710), patron of botany.]

begorra, begorrah *bi-gor'ə, interj* an Anglo-Irish modification of **by God.**

begot *bi-got',* **begotten** *bi-got'n* See beget.

begrime *bi-grīm', v t.* to soil with grime [be-(2).]

begrudge *bi-gruj', v t.* to grudge: to envy the possession of. [be-(1)]

beguile *bi-gīl', v.t.* to cheat or deceive: to pass with diversion of attention from anything tedious or painful: to wile into some course —*ns.* **beguile'ment;** **beguil'er.**—*adv* **beguil'ingly.** [be-(1), and obs. v.t *guile*]

béguine, beguine *bāg'ēn, beg'in, ns* a member of a sisterhood living as nuns but without vows, and with power to return to the world'—*masc.* **béguin, beguin** (*bāg-ɛ, beg'in*) a beghard —*n* **béguinage** (*bāg'ən-azh, beg'in-ij*) an establishment for béguines. [Fr *béguine.*]

beguine *bə-gēn', n.* a dance of French West Indian origin or its music, in bolero rhythm [Fr]

begum *bä'gəm, bē'gəm, n* a Muslim princess or lady of rank· a deferential title given to any Muslim lady [Urdu *begam;* cf **beg**[1], bey.]

begun *bi-gun', pa p* (sometimes *pa.t.*) of **begin.**

behalf *bi-haf', n.* favour or benefit. cause: sake, account. part.—**on** (*U S.* in) **behalf of, on** (*U.S.* in) **someone's behalf** speaking, acting, etc. for (someone ·else) [M.E. *behalve*—O E. *be healfe,* by the side. See half.]

behave, *bi-hāv', v t.* to bear or carry: to wield, manage, conduct (commonly with *self*) —*v.i* to conduct oneself (towards)· to conduct oneself well: to act· to function —*pa t , pa p* **behaved'.**—*n.* **behaviour** (*bi-hāv'yər*) conduct· manners or deportment, esp good manners· treatment of others: mode of action response to stimulus (*physiol.*) —*adj.* **behāv'ioural** of or relating to behaviour —*ns* **behāv'iourism** a psychological method which substitutes for the subjective element of consciousness, the objective one of observation of conduct in other beings under certain stimuli, **behāv'iourist** an upholder of behaviourism —**behavioural science** a science which studies the behaviour of human beings or other organisms (e g psychology, sociology); **behaviour therapy** treating a neurotic symptom (e.g a phobia) by desensitising the patient, *i e.* gradually conditioning him to react normally —**(up)on one's best behaviour** consciously trying to be as well-behaved as possible [be-(1), and **have.**]

behead *bi-hed', v t* to cut off the head of.—*ns* **behead'al** (*rare*), **behead'ing.** [be-(1), meaning off, away]

beheld *bi-held', pa t* and *pa p* of **behold.**

behest *bi-hest', n* command charge [O.E *behǣs,* a promise; see **hest.**]

behind *bi-hīnd', prep* at the back of (in place, or as support)· in the place or state left by· at the far side of· after (in time, rank, order)· in inferiority to, or less far advanced than —*adv* at the back, in the rear backward past· in arrears —*n* the hinder part. rump —*adj* **behind'-door'** surreptitious, clandestine

—*adj., adv.* **behind'-hand** being behind. tardy: ill-provided.—**behind someone's back** without someone knowing (when he might feel entitled to know); **put something behind one** to think of something (usu. unpleasant) as in the past, finished. [O.E. *behindan*; see **hind³**.]

behold *bi-hōld'*, *v.t.* to look upon: to contemplate: to view, see.—*v.i.* to look:—*pa.t.* and *pa.p.* **beheld'.**—*imper.* or *interj.* see: lo: observe.—*adj.* **behold'en** bound in gratitude (to): under an obligation (to).—*n.* **behold'er** one who beholds. an onlooker. [O.E. *behaldan* (W S. *behealdan*), to hold, observe—*be-* and *h(e)aldan*, to hold.]

behoof *bi-hōōf'*, *n.* benefit: convenience. [O.E. *behōf*.]

behove, behoove *bi-hōōv'* (unhistorically *bi-hōv'*), *v.t.* and *v.i.* to be fit, right, or necessary—now only used impersonally with *it*. [O E. *behōfian*, to be fit, to stand in need of.]

beige *bāzh*, *n.* a woollen fabric of undyed wool.—*adj.* greyish: recently, buff with a slight suffusion of pink. [Fr.]

beigel *bā'gəl*, *n.* an alternative spelling of **bagel.**

being *bē'ing*, *n* existence: substance: essence: any person or thing existing.—*adj.* existing, present.—*adj.* **bē'ingless.**—*n.* **bē'ingness.—the Supreme Being** God. [Verbal noun and *pr.p.* of **be.**]

bejabers *bi-jā'bərs*, *interj.* an Anglo-Irish modification of **by Jesus.**

bejewel *bi-jōō'əl*, *v.t.* to deck with jewels. [**be-** (2).]

bel *bel*, *n.* a measure for comparing intensity of noises, electric currents, etc., the number of bels being the logarithm to the base 10 of the ratio of one to the other. [From Graham *Bell* (1847–1922), telephone inventor.]

belabour *bi-lā'bər*, *v.t.* to beat soundly: to assail verbally. [**be-** (1).]

belate *bi-lāt'*, *v.t.* to make late. to retard.—*adj.* **belāt'ed** coming too late: out of date: benighted.—*n.* **belāt'edness.** [**be-** (2).]

belay *bi-lā'*, *v.t.* to set, overlay, with ornament: to beset: to besiege· to waylay: to make fast: to secure by a turn about a cleat, belaying pin, point of rock, etc.—*interj.* enough. hold.—*n.* a turn of a rope in belaying: that about which a belay is made.—**belaying pin** a pin for belaying ropes about. [O.E. *belecgan*.]

bel canto *bel kàn'tō*, (It.) a manner of operatic singing that cultivates beauty of tone.

belch *belch, belsh*, *v t.* and *v.i.* to void (wind) from the stomach by the mouth: to eject violently: to pour forth, as the smoke from a volcano, chimney, etc.—*n.* an eructation. [O.E. *bealcian*; Du. *balken*.]

beldam, beldame *bel'dam*, *n.* an old woman (formerly a term of address): a hag: a furious woman. [Formed from *dam*, mother, and *bel-*, used like *grand-*—Fr. *bel, belle*.]

beleaguer *bi-lēg'ər*, *v.t.* to lay siege to.—*n.* **beleag'uerment.** [Du. *belegeren*, to besiege—*be-*, and *leger*, camp.]

belemnite *bel'əm-nīt*, *n.* a fossil pointed like a dart, being the internal shell of a cephalopod. [Gr. *belemnitēs—belemnon*, a dart.]

bel esprit *be-les-prē*, (Fr.) a wit or genius:—*pl.* **beaux esprits.**

belfry *bel'fri*, *n.* the part of a steeple or tower in which bells are hung: a bell-tower, sometimes standing apart: a movable wooden tower, used in the Middle Ages in attacking a fortification.—*adj.* **bel'fried** having a belfry. [Orig. and properly a watch-tower, from O.Fr. *berfroi*—M.H.G. *berchfrit—bergan*, to protect, *frid, frit*, a tower.]

Belgian *bel'jən*, *adj.* of *Belgium*, a country of Europe.—*n.* a native or citizen of Belgium.—*adj.* **Bel'gic** of the *Belgae*, who anciently possessed Belgium, or of Belgium.—**Belgian hare** a hare-like breed of domestic rabbit. [L. *Belga, Belgicus*.]

belie *bi-lī'*, *v.t.* to give the lie to: to speak falsely of: to present in a false character: to counterfeit: to be false to: to falsify: to fail to fulfil or justify:—*pr.p.* **bely'ing**; *pa.t.* and *pa.p.* **belied'.** [**be-** (3).]

believe *bi-lēv'*, *v.t.* to regard as true: to accept as true what is said by: to suppose (followed by a noun clause).—*v.i.* to be firmly persuaded: to have faith (with *in, on*): to judge —*n.* **belief'** persuasion of the truth of anything: faith: the opinion or doctrine believed.—*adjs* **belief'less; believ'able.**—*n.* **believ'er** one who believes: one who professes Christianity, Islam, or whatever religion is relevant.—*adj.* **believ'ing** trustful: having belief.—*adv.* **believ'ingly.—be unable, hardly able, to believe one's eyes, ears** to receive with incredulity what one has just seen, heard; **I (don't) believe so I** (don't) think so; **make believe** see **make;** to **the best of my belief** as far as I know. [M.E. *bileven—bi-, be*, and *leven*.]

belike *bi-līk'*, (*arch.*) *adv.* probably: perhaps [O.E. pfx. *be-*, and **like.**]

Belisha beacon. See **beacon.**

belittle *bi-lit'l, v t.* to make small. to cause to appear small, to disparage.—*n.* **belitt'lement.**—*adj.* **belitt'ling.** [**be-** (2).]

bell *bel*, *n.* an instrument for giving a ringing sound, typically a hollow vessel of metal with flared mouth struck by a tongue or clapper, but taking many other forms: a corolla shaped like an ordinary bell. anything bell-shaped: the sound of a bell: a signal or intimation by bell: a stroke or double stroke of a bell to indicate the number of half-hours of the watch that have elapsed—'two bells', 'three bells', etc., meaning that there are two, three, etc. half-hours past (*naut.*).—*v.i.* to ring.—*v.t.* to furnish with a bell, esp in **bell the cat** to take the leading part in any hazardous movement, from the ancient fable of the mice who proposed to hang a warning bell round the cat's neck.—*adj.* **bell'-bird** any of various birds with bell-like notes.—*adj.* **bell's bottomed** (of trousers) widening towards the ankle.—**bell'-boy** (chiefly *U.S.*) a hotel porter or page; **bell's buoy** a buoy carrying a bell, rung by the waves; **bell's flower** a campanula; **bell'-founder** one who casts bells; **bell'-foundry; bell'-glass** a bell-shaped glass for sheltering flowers, etc.; **bell'-heather** heath; **bell'hop** a bell-boy; **bell'-jar** a bell-shaped glass cover, in laboratories placed over apparatus to confine gases, etc.; **bell'man** one who rings a bell, esp. on the streets, before making public announcements; **bell'-metal** the metal of which bells are made—an alloy of copper and tin; **bell'-pull** a cord or handle used in ringing a bell; **bell'push** a button used in ringing an electric or spring bell; **bell'-ringer** one who rings a bell on stated occasions: a performer with musical hand-bells; **bell's ringing; bell'-rope** the rope by which a bell is rung.—*adj.* **bell'-shaped.—bell'-tent** a bell-shaped tent; **bell'-tower** a tower built to contain one or more bells, a campanile; **bell'-turret** a turret containing a chamber for a bell, usually crowned with a spire; **bell'-wether** the leading sheep of a flock, on whose neck a bell is hung: any loud, turbulent fellow, a ringleader (*fig.*).—**bell, book, and candle** a phrase popularly used in reference to a form of excommunication ending, 'Do to (i.e. shut) the book, quench the candle, ring the bell'; **bells of Ireland** an annual plant, that has white flowers with green calyces, sometimes preserved for use in dried-flower arrangements; **bell the cat** see **bell** *v.t* above; **clear as a bell** (of a sound) distinct and pure in tone; **sound as a bell** in perfect condition, health, etc [O.E. *belle*]

belladonna *bel'ə-don'ə*, *n*. the deadly nightshade, all parts of which are narcotic and poisonous from the presence of atropine: the drug prepared from it — **belladonna lily** a pink-flowered South African Amaryllis [It. *bella donna*, fair lady, one property of belladonna is to enlarge the pupil of the eye]

bellarmine *bel'ar-mēn*, *n*. a greybeard, or large jug with a big belly, decorated with a bearded face, said to represent Cardinal *Bellarmine* (1542–1621), made in mockery by Dutch Protestants

belle¹ *bel*, *n* a handsome woman: the chief beauty of a place: a fair lady generally.—*n* **belle-de-nuit** (*-də-nwē*; Fr, night beauty) the marvel of Peru [Fr. *belle* (*fem*)—L. *bellus*, *-a*, *-um*]

belle² *bel*, (Fr.) *adj. fem* of **beau**.—**belle amie** (*be-la-mē*) a female friend, a mistress, **belle laide** (*bel led*) jolie laide; **belle vue** (*vü*) fine prospect.—**la belle époque** (*la-bel-ā-pok*; also with *caps*) 'the fine period', the time of security and gracious living for the well-to-do, ended by World War I

belles-lettres *bel-let'r'*, *n pl* polite or elegant literature, including poetry, fiction, criticism, aesthetics, etc.—*n*. **bellet(t)'rist.** [Fr , lit fine letters]

bellicose *bel'ik-ōs*, *adj*. contentious, war-like —*adv* **bell'icosely.**—*n*. **bellicosity** (*-kos'i-ti*) [L. *bellicōsus.*]

bellied. See **belly.**

belligerent *bel-ij'ər-ənt*, *adj* waging war. recognised legally as waging war: aggressive —*n* a party or person waging war: one recognised as so doing —*ns* **bellig'erence; bellig'erency.**—*adv*. **bellig'erently.** [L *belligerāre*, to wage war—*bellum*, war, *gerĕre*, to wage.]

bellow *bel'ō*, *v i* to roar like a bull: to make any violent outcry.—*v.t* to roar out.—*n*. the roar of a bull: any deep sound or cry —*n* **bell'ower.** [M E *belwen*; O.E. *bylgian*, to roar.]

bellows *bel'ōz*, *n.pl* or *n sing*. an instrument for producing a current of air to blow up a fire, or sound an organ, accordion, etc.. a contrivance for expanding a photographic camera or the like —**bell'ows-fish** the trumpet-fish. [Same as **belly.**]

belly *bel'i*, *n*. the part of the body between the breast and the thighs, containing the bowels the stomach, as the receptacle of the food: the bowels proper: the womb or uterus: the interior of anything: the bulging part of anything, as a bottle, or any concave or hollow surface, as of a sail: the front or under surface, as opposed to the *back*: in a violin or a leaf the upper surface: a sound-board.—*adj*. ventral, abdominal — *v.t.* to swell or bulge out (often with *out*):—*pa t* and *pa.p.* **bellied** (*bel'id*).—*adj* **bell'ied** with a belly, esp a big belly, pot-bellied: bulging: puffed out.—*n*. **bell'yful** a sufficiency: more than enough—*n* and *adj*. **bell'ying.**—**bell'y-ache** a pain in the belly: a persistent complaint, whine (*slang*)—*v.t.* (*slang*) to complain whiningly —**bell'y-band** a saddle-girth· a band fastened to the shafts of a vehicle, and passing under the belly of the horse drawing it; **bell'y-button** the navel (*coll.*); **bell'y-dance** a solo dance with very pronounced movement of abdominal muscles; **bell'y-dancer; bell'y-flop** an inexpert dive in which one lands face down, flat on the water· a belly-landing.— Also *v.t.*—**bell'y-landing** of an aircraft, a landing without using the landing-wheels, **bell'y-laugh** a deep unrestrained laugh. [M.E *bali*, *bely*—O E *bælig*, *belig*, *bælg*, *belg*, bag]

belong *bi-long'*, *v.i* (in all senses usu with *to*) to go along (with)· to pertain (to): to be the property (of) to be part or appendage (of), or in any way connected (with): to be specially the business (of) to be a native or inhabitant, or member (of) —*n pl* **belong'ings** matters connected with any person· possessions

accessories. [M.E *bi-*, *be-longen*, intens *of longen*, to belong, pertain.]

Belorussian, Byelorussian, *byel'ə-rush'ən*, *adj*. White Russian, of a region to the west of Moscow· of its language or people —Also *n*. [Russ *Belorossiya—beliy*, white.]

belove *bi-luv'*, *v.t* (*obs* except in *pa p* **beloved** *bi-luvd'*) to love —*adj* **beloved** (*bi-luv'id*) much loved, very dear—often compounded with *well-, best-*, etc —*n* (*bi-luv'id*) one who is much loved [**be-** (1).]

below *bi-lō'*, *prep* beneath in place, rank or quality· underneath: not worthy of —*adv*. in a lower place downstairs· on earth, or in hell (*fig.*) [**be-** (2).]

belshazzar. See **balthasar.**

belt *belt*, *n*. a girdle, zone, or band. a band of leather or other material worn around the waist: a band of flexible material used to transmit motion in machinery· a broad stripe of anything, different in colour or material: that which confines or restrains: a zone of country, a district (*geog.*)· a strait: a band for the waist awarded in recognition of a specific (grade of) achievement (see **black, Lonsdale**).—*v.t.* to surround with a belt, or to invest formally with one, as in conferring knighthood: to encircle: to thrash with a belt —*v i* (*slang*) to hurry —*adj*. **belt'ed** wearing, marked with, having a belt.—*n*. **belt'ing** belts collectively: material for making belts: a beating —**belt out** (*coll*) to sing, play or send out vigorously or with great enthusiasm, **belt up** (*slang*) to be quiet, **hit**, etc , **below the belt** to hit, etc., an opponent's body lower than the waist (forbidden in some sports)· (*fig*) to attack unfairly; **hold the belt** to hold the championship in wrestling, boxing, or the like; **tighten one's belt** to reduce one's demands or expenditure, **under one's belt** (*fig*) firmly and irrevocably secured or in one's possession [O E. *belt*—L. *balteus*]

Beltane *bel'tān*, *n* an ancient Celtic festival, held in the beginning of May· the first day of May (O.S.)— one of the four old quarter-days of Scotland.—Also *adj* [Gael *bealltainn, beiltene*, apparently bright fire]

beluga *bi-lōō'gə*, *n* the white whale, one of the dolphin family, found in Arctic seas: a great Russian sturgeon [Russ *beliy*, white.]

belvedere *bel'vi-dēr*, *n* a pavilion or raised turret or lantern on the top of a house, open for the view, or to admit the breeze: a summer-house on an eminence [It. *belvedere—bel*, beautiful, *vedere*, to see]

belying. See **belie.**

bema *bē'mə*, *n* the apse or chancel of a basilica [Gr. *bēma*, a step]

bemoan *bi-mōn'*, *v.t* to lament, bewail, to pity —*v.i* to grieve —*ns* **bemoan'er; bemoan'ing.** [**be-** (1)]

bemuse *bi-mūz'*, *v t* to put in confusion: to stupefy [**be-** (1).]

ben¹ *ben*, *n* a mountain peak [Gael *beinn*, oblique case of *beann*]

ben² *ben*, (*Scot*) *prep* and *adv* in or toward the inner or better, or (vaguely) another, apartment (of) —*n*. the inner or better apartment of a house, as opposed to the *but* or kitchen through which formerly one had generally to pass first —a **but and ben** a two-roomed house [M E *binne*—O E *binnan*, within]

ben³ *ben*, *n* the winged seed of the horseradish tree — **ben'-nut; ben'-oil.** [Ar *bān*, the ben-tree]

bench *bench, bensh*, *n* a long seat or form with or without a back a seat in a boat a work-table or working-place a judge's seat the body or assembly of judges a tribunal· an official seat· a level ledge in the slope of masonry or earthwork a terrace in a greenhouse or conservatory, a raised bed or a platform with sides for holding potted plants —*v t* to place on or furnish with benches: to put plants in greenhouse benches: to show (dogs).—*ns.* **bench'er** a senior member of an inn of court; **bench'ership.—bench'-mark** a surveyor's mark cut on a rock, etc. indicating a point of reference in levelling (from its horizontal line forming a bench for a levelling instrument): anything taken or used as a point of reference or comparison; **bench'-warr'ant** one issued by a judge rather than a justice or magistrate.—**on the bench** holding the office of a judge or bishop: officiating as judge; **raise to the bench** to make a judge or bishop. [O.E. *benc.*]

bend *bend, v.t.* to constrain: to subject to tension: to brace: to string: to nerve: to force into (or out of) a curved or angled form: to curve: to bow, turn downwards: to dispose, incline: to aim: to direct: to deflect: to subdue: to fasten (*naut.*).—*v.i.* to curve: to stoop: to bow: to give way, yield: to turn: to incline:—*pa.t.* and *pa.p.* **bent**; also **bend'ed.**—*n.* a knot by which a line is tied to another, or to itself after passing through a ring, etc.: a band, strip: an ordinary bounded by two parallel lines crossing the shield from dexter chief to sinister base (**bend'-sin'ister** from sinister chief to dexter base), occupying a fifth of the shield, or a third if charged (*her.*): an act of bending: state of being bent: a bent thing: a place of bending: a bow or stoop: (in *pl.*) caisson disease: (in *pl.*) aeroembolism.—*adj.* **bend'ed.**—*n.* **bend'er** one who, or that which bends: a thing very large or fine of its kind (*slang*): a (drunken) spree (*slang*).—*n.* and *adj.* **bend'ing.**—*adv.* **bend'ingly.**—*n.* **bend'let** (*her.*) a half-width bend.—*adv.* **bend'wise** (*her.*) diagonally. —*adj.* **bend'y** (*her.*) divided into bends.—*n.* and *adj.* **bent see bent.—bent'wood** wood artificially curved for chair-making, etc.—Also *adj.*—**bend over backwards** see **back; round the bend** (*coll.*) crazy, mad. [O.E. *bendan*, to constrain, bind, fetter, string (as a bow), *bend*, bond, fetter.]

beneath *bi-nēth', adv.* and *prep.* below: in a lower position so as to have overhead, or nearly so, or to be covered: inside, behind, at the back (of): at a lower level relatively to.—*prep.* in a manner unworthy the dignity of, unbecoming to. [O.E. *beneothan.*]

benedict *ben'i-dikt, (obs.) adj.* blessed: benign.—*n.* **benedic'tion** (*-shən*) a blessing: a solemn invocation of the divine blessing on men or things: a blessing pronounced at the end of a religious service: a brief and popular service in the Roman Catholic Church: grace before or after a meal: blessedness.—*adjs.* **benedic'tional; benedict'ive; benedict'ory.**—*n.* **Benedict'us** the canticle of Zacharias (Luke, i. 68–79), used in the Roman and Anglican services. [L. *benedicĕre, -dictum—bene*, well, *dicĕre*, to say, speak.]

Benedictine *ben-i-dik'tin, -tīn, adj.* pertaining to St *Benedict* of Nursia (480–543), or his monastic rule.— *n.* a monk or nun of the order founded by him at Monte Cassino: (*-tēn*) a cordial or liqueur resembling Chartreuse, distilled at Fécamp in Normandy—once distilled by Benedictine monks.

benefaction *ben-i-fak'shən, n.* the act of doing good: a good deed done or benefit conferred: a grant of endowment.—*n.* **ben'efactor** (or *-fak'*) one who confers a benefit: one who aids financially e.g. an institution, a patron:—*fem.* **ben'efactress** (or *-fak'*).—*adj.* **benefac'tory.** [L *benefactiō, -ōnis.*]

benefic *bi-nef'ik, adj.* kindly: benign: beneficent: favourable (*astrol.*).—*n.* **benefice** (*ben'i-fis*) a church living, esp. with cure of souls: a fief (*hist.*).—*adj.* **ben'eficed** possessed of a benefice.—*n.* **beneficence** (*bi-nef'i-səns*) active goodness: kindness: charity: a beneficent gift.—*adjs.* **benef'icent; beneficential** (*-sen'shl*).—*adv.* **benef'icently.**—*adj.* **beneficial** (*ben-i-fish'l*) useful: advantageous: enjoying the usufruct of property (*law*).—*adv* **benefic'ially.**—*ns.*

benefic'ialness; benefic'iary a holder of a benefice or a fief: one who receives a gift or advantage: one who enjoys, or has the prospect of enjoying, any interest or estate held in trust by others. [L. *beneficus*, kindly, beneficent, *beneficium*, a service, benefit—*bene*, well, *facĕre*, to do.]

beneficiate *be-ni-fish'i-āt, v.t.* to treat ores, etc. to get rid of impurities.—*v.i.* to receive profit from working a mine.—*n.* **beneficia'tion.** [Sp. *beneficiar*, to benefit—L. *beneficium*, a service, benefit.]

benefit *ben'i-fit, n.* a kindness: a favour: any advantage, natural or other: a performance, match, etc., whose proceeds go to one of the company, a player, or other particular person or object (also *adj.*): a right in the form of money or services enjoyed under social security or insurance schemes.—*v.t.* to do good to.— *v.i.* to gain advantage (with *from* or *by*):—*pr.p.* **ben'efiting**; *pa.t.* and *pa.p.* **ben'efited.—benefit of the doubt** favourable judgment when culpability is uncertain; **benefit society** a friendly society. [M.E. *benfet*—A.Fr. *benfet*—L. *benefactum.*]

Benelux *ben'ə-luks, n.* a name for Belgium, the Netherlands and Luxembourg.

benet *ben'it, n.* an exorcist, the third of the four lesser orders in the Roman Catholic church. [O.Fr. *beneit* —L. *benedictus*, blessed.]

benevolence *bi-nev'ə-ləns, n.* disposition to do good: an act of kindness: generosity: a gift of money, esp. for support of the poor: a kind of forced loan or contribution, levied by kings without legal authority (*Eng. hist.*).—*adj.* **benev'olent** charitable, generous, well disposed.—*adv.* **benev'olently.** [O.Fr. *benivolence* and L. *benevolentia.*]

Bengali *ben-gò'lē, adj.* of or belonging to *Bengal.*—*n.* a native of Bengal: the language of Bengal.

beni, beniseed. See **benne.**

benight *bi-nīt, v.t.* to involve in darkness: to cloud with disappointment.—*adj.* **benight'ed** overtaken by night: involved in darkness, intellectual or moral: ignorant. [Pfx. **be-** (2) and **night.**]

benign *bi-nīn', adj.* favourable, esp. in astrology, as opposed to *malign*: gracious: kindly: of a mild type, as opposed to *malignant* (*med.*): salubrious.—*n.* **benignancy** (*bi-nig'nan-si*).—*adj.* **benig'nant** kind: gracious: beneficial.—*adv.* **benig'nantly.**—*n.* **benig'nity** goodness of disposition: kindness: graciousness: favourable circumstances—of climate, weather, disease, planets —*adv.* **benign'ly** (*-nīn'*). [O.Fr. *benigne*—L. *benīgnus.*]

benison *ben'i-zn, -sn, n.* a benediction, blessing, esp. blessing of God. [O.Fr. *beneiçun*—L. *benedictiō, -ōnis.*]

Benjamin *ben'jə-min, n.* a youngest son: a favourite child. [As in Genesis xlii.]

benjamin *ben'jə-min, n.* gum benzoin (also **gum benjamin**).—**ben'jamin-tree** Styrax: the American spice-bush: a kind of fig-tree. [**benzoin.**]

benne *ben'ē, benni, beni ben'i, ns.* sesame.—**benn'e-seed, benn'i-seed, ben'iseed** sesame seed [From Malay *bene.*]

bennet *ben'it.* See **herb-bennet** at **herb.**

bent[1] *bent, pa.t.* and *pa.p.* of **bend.**—*adj.* curved: having a bend: intent, set (on or upon doing something): morally crooked, or criminal (*coll.*): homosexual, or otherwise sexually deviant (*slang*): stolen (*slang*).—*n.* curvature: curved part: tendency: trend: inclination: direction: leaning or bias: natural inclination of the mind: the extent to which a bow may be bent: degree of tension: capacity of endurance. [**bend.**]

bent[2] *bent, n.* any stiff or wiry grass: the old dried stalks of grasses: a genus of grasses, slender and delicate in appearance, some useful as pasture-grasses and for hay: a place covered with bents, a heath· a hillside.—Also **bent'-grass**. [O E. *beonet*]

Benthamism *ben'thəm-izm, n.* the social and political teaching of Jeremy *Bentham* (1748–1832), whose leading principle is summed up in Hutcheson's phrase, 'the greatest happiness of the greatest number'.

benthos *ben'thos, n.* the flora and fauna of the sea-bottom.—*adj.* **ben'thic** —*n.* **ben'thoscope** (*-thō-*) a submersible sphere from which to study deep-sea life. [Gr *benthos*, depth.]

bentonite *ben'tən-īt, n* a valuable clay, consisting mainly of montmorillonite, widely used in industry as a bond, filler, etc. [Fort *Benton*, Montana, where it was found.]

ben trovato *ben trō-va'tō*, (It.) aptly invented; **ben venuto** (*ven-ōō t'ō*) welcome.

bentwood. See **bend.**

benumb *bi-num', v.t* to make insensible or powerless: to stupefy (now chiefly of *cold*): to deaden the feelings of: to paralyse generally.—*adj.* **benumbed'.**—*ns.* **benumbed'ness; benumb'ment.** [Pfx **be-** (2)]

Benzedrine® *ben'zi-drēn, n* amphetamine.

benzene *ben'zēn, n.* simplest of the aromatic series of hydrocarbons, its molecule consisting of a ring or closed chain of six carbon atoms each with a hydrogen atom attached.—*ns.* **ben'zal** or **benzyl'idine** a radical whose oxide is **benzal'dehyde** or oil of bitter almonds; **benzine** (*ben'zēn*) a mixture of hydrocarbons got by destructive distillation of petroleum, used as a solvent, motor fuel, etc.: improperly, benzene; **benzocaine** (*ben-zō-kā'in, ben'zō-kān*) a drug used as a local anaesthetic and in the treatment of gastritis (**benzine** and **cocaine**); **benzodiazepine** (*ben-zō-dī-az'ə-pēn, -pin, -pīn*) one of a group of non-addictive tranquillising drugs.—*ns.* **ben'zol(e)** crude benzene, used as a motor-spirit: improperly, benzene; **ben'zoline** benzine: impure benzene; **benzylidine** see **benzal** above.—**benzene hexachloride** (known as BHC) a chlorinated hydrocarbon, a very toxic insecticide. [From **benzoin.**]

benzoin *ben'zō-in,* or *-zoin, n.* gum benjamin, the aromatic and resinous juice of *Styrax benzoin*, a tree of Java and Sumatra, used in perfumery, in pastilles, for incense and court-plaster, and friar's balsam — *adj.* **benzo'ic.** [In the 16th century, **benjoin,** most prob. through It. from Ar. *lubân jâwî,* frankincense of Jawa (i.e. Sumatra)]

bequeath *bi-kwēdh, v t.* to leave by will to another (strictly of personal property): to transmit to posterity, to leave behind: to commit or entrust to anyone.—*adj.* **bequeath'able.**—*ns.* **bequeath'al; bequeath'ment.** [O.E. *becwethan*—pfx. *bi-, be-,* and *cwethan,* to say; see **quoth.**]

bequest *bi-kwest', n.* act of bequeathing: that which is bequeathed, a legacy. [M.E. *biqueste*—O.E. pfx. *bi-, be-, cwethan,* to say; see **quoth.**]

berate *bi-rāt', v.t.* to scold or chide vigorously. [Pfx **be-** (1).]

Berber *bûr'bər, n.* a member of one of the Hamitic peoples of Barbary: the language of the Berbers.— Also *adj.* [Ar *barbar.*]

Berberis *bûr'bər-is, n* the barberry genus· (without *cap*) any shrub of this genus. [Latinised from Ar , see **barberry.**]

berceuse *ber-søz', n* a cradle song: a musical composition in similar rhythm. [Fr]

bereave *bi-rēv', v t* to rob of anything valued: to deprive: to widow, orphan, or deprive by death of some dear relative or friend to snatch away—*pa t.* and *pa p* **bereaved'** (usu. by death), **bereft'** (usu in general sense); *arch pa.p* **bereav'en.**—*adj* **bereaved'.**—*n* **bereave'ment** loss by death of a rela-tive or friend. [O E *berēafian,* to plunder; see **reave.**]

beret *ber'i,* **berret** *ber'et, ns* a flat, round, woollen cap worn by Basques and others [Fr *béret.*]

berg *bûrg, n.* a hill or mountain. short for **iceberg.**— **berg'-add'er** a venomous South African viper, **bergfall** (*berhh'fal, bûrg'fol*; Ger.) fall of mountain-rock, **bergmehl** (*berhh'mâl,* or *bûrg'*) a powdery deposit of diatom frustules (Ger , mountain flour), **bergschrund** (*berhh'shrōōnt*) a crevasse formed where a glacier or snowfield starts away from a mountain wall (Ger , mountain cleft); **berg wind** in South Africa, a hot, dry wind from the north, blowing in the coastal regions [Ger. *Berg*, Du., Sw. *berg,* hill.]

bergamot¹ *bûr'gə-mot, n.* a kind of citron or orange, whose aromatic rind yields oil of bergamot, used in perfumery: the essence so extracted: a mint of similar smell [Said to be from *Bergamo* in Italy; or *Bergama* (Pergamum) in Asia Minor; or as next word.]

bergamot² *bûr'gə-mot, n* a fine pear. [Fr ,—It.,— Turk. *begarmudi,* prince of pears.]

bergylt *bûr'gilt, n.* a red northern sea-fish. [Norw. *berggylta,* rock-pig.]

beribboned *bi-rib'ənd, participial adj.* decorated with ribbons [Pfx **be-** (2).]

beriberi *ber'i-ber-i, n.* an Eastern disease due to lack of vitamin B. [Sinh *beri,* weakness.]

berk, burk *bûrk,* (*slang*) *n.* a fool. [Short for Cockney rhyming slang *Berkeley Hunt,* for *cunt.*]

Berkeleian *bark'lē'ən, bârk'li-ən,* in *U.S. bûrk'-, adj.* pertaining to Bishop *Berkeley* (1685–1753), who maintained that the world we see depends for its actuality on being perceived.—*n.* a follower of Berkeley.—*n* **Berkelei'anism** (or *bark'*).

berkelium *bar-kē'li-əm* (earlier *bûrk'li-əm*), *n.* an element (at. numb. 97; symbol Bk), prepared in a cyclotron at *Berkeley,* California.

berlin *bûr'lin, bər-lên', -lin', n.* an old four-wheeled covered carriage, with a seat behind covered with a hood (also **ber'line**)· a closed motor-car with the driver's seat partitioned off [From the city of *Berlin.*]

berm *bûrm, n* a ledge: the area of level ground between the raised mound of a barrow or other earthwork and the ditch surrounding it (*archaeol*). [Fr. *berme.*]

Bermuda shorts *bər-mû'də,* shorts, for men or women, reaching to just above the knee.—Also **Bermudas;** **Bermuda Triangle** the area between Florida, the Bahamas, and Cuba where ships and aeroplanes mysteriously disappear.

berret. See **beret.**

berry *ber'i, n.* any small succulent fruit: a simple fruit with pericarp succulent throughout (thus excluding strawberry, raspberry, blackberry, which are aggregate fruits) (*bot.*): a coffee-bean: a cereal grain: a lobster's or crayfish's egg: a knob on a swan's bill.— *v.i.* to gather berries.—*adj.* **berr'ied** bearing berries: of lobsters, etc., having eggs.—*n.* **berr'ying.** [O.E. *berie.*]

bersaglieri *ber-sal-yā'rē, n.pl.* the riflemen or sharpshooters of the Italian army. [It , pl. of *bersagliere*—*bersaglio,* a mark.]

berserk, berserker *ber-sûrk'(ər),-zûrk'(ər),ns* a Norse warrior whom the sight of the field of battle would fill with a frenzied and resistless fury.—*adj* **berserk'** violently frenzied or angry —*advs* **berserk'** in a violent frenzy; **berserk'ly.** [O N *berserkr,* probably bear-sark]

berth *bûrth, n* sea-room a ship's station at anchor or at a wharf a room or sleeping-place in a ship, sleeping-carriage, etc any allotted or assigned place· a situation or place of employment, usually a comfortable one.—*v.t.* and *v.i.* to moor.—*v.t.* to furnish with a berth.—**give a wide berth to** to keep well away from generally.

bertha *bûr'thə*, *n.* a woman's falling collar (also **berthe**). [Woman's name.]

Berufsverbot *bə-rōōfs'fər-bōt*, (Ger) *n.* in Germany, the policy of excluding political extremists from public service.

beryl *ber'il*, *n.* a precious stone of which emerald and aquamarine are varieties, a silicate of beryllium and aluminium crystallising in the hexagonal system, green, colourless, yellow or blue, once esteemed as a magic crystal.—*adj.* pale greenish.—*ns.* **beryllium** a metallic element (at numb. 4; symbol Be), used as a moderator in nuclear reactors, and industrially to harden alloys, etc.; **beryl'ia** its oxide. [O.Fr. *beryl*—L. *bēryllus*—Gr. *bēryllos*.]

beseech *bi-sēch'* , *v.t.* to entreat, to implore: to ask or pray earnestly: to solicit:—*pa.t.* and *pa.p* **besought** (*bi-sōt'*) also **beseeched'**.—*n* **beseech'er**. —*n* and *adj.* **beseech'ing**.—*adv.* **beseech'ingly**.—*n.* **beseech'ingness**. [Pfx. be- (1), and M.E. *sechen*; see **seek**.]

beseem *bi-sēm'*, *v.i.* to be fitting or becoming.—*v.t.* to be seemly for: to become: to be fit for or worthy of.—*n.* and *adj.* **beseem'ing**.—*adv.* **beseem'ingly**.— *n.* **beseem'ingness**. [Pfx. be- (1).]

beset *bi-set'*, *v.t.* to surround or set round with anything (now only in *pa.p.*): to surround with hostile intentions, to besiege: to occupy so as to allow none to go out or in: to assail, perplex, endanger, as by temptations, obstacles, etc.:—*pr.p.* **beset'ting**; *pa.t* and *pa.p.* **beset'**.—*ns.* **beset'ment**; **besett'er**.—*adj.* **besett'ing** constantly assailing: dominant: obsessive. [O.E. *besettan*—*settan*, to set.]

beside *bi-sīd'*, *prep.* by the side of, near: over and above, besides (*rare*): outside of: away from: distinct from: apart from, not falling within, as of a question, resolution, etc.—*adv.* near by: besides: apart: to the side.—*adv.* **besides'** in addition: moreover: otherwise, else.—*prep.* over and above: else than.—**beside oneself** having lost self-possession; **beside the mark, point, question** irrelevant. [O.E. *besīdan*, by the side (dat.); the *s* is of the adverbial gen.]

besiege *bi-sēj'*, *v.t.* to lay siege to: to beset with armed forces: to throng round: to importune: to pester.—*ns.* **besiege'ment**; **besieg'er**.—*n.* and *adj.* **besieg'ing**.—*adv.* **besieg'ingly** (*rare*) urgently. [Pfx. be- (1).]

beslobber *bi-slob'ər*, *v.t.* to besmear with the spittle running from one's mouth: to cover with drivelling kisses: to flatter fulsomely. [Pfx. be- (1).]

besmear *bi-smēr'*, *v.t.* to smear over: to bedaub: to pollute. [Pfx. be- (1).]

besmirch *bi-smûrch'*, *v.t.* to soil, as with smoke or soot: to sully. [Pfx. be- (1).]

besognio *bi-zōn'yō*, *n.* a beggar:—*pl.* **besogn'ios**. [It.]

besoin *bə-zwē*, (Fr.) *n.* need, want, desire.

besom[1] *bē'zəm*, *bez'əm*, *n.* a bunch of twigs for sweeping: (*Scot.*, pron. *biz'əm*, *buz'əm*) a broom: any cleansing or purifying agent (*fig.*).—**jump the besom** see **broom**. [O.E. *besema*.]

besom[2] *biz'əm*, *bē'zəm*, (Scot. and *dial.*) *n* a term of reproach for a woman, implying generally slatternliness, laziness, impudence, or unscrupulous energy. [Perh. the same word as the preceding; perh. connected with O.E *bysn*, *bisn*, example, or O.N *býsn*, wonder.]

besot *bi-sot'*, *v t* to make sottish, dull, or stupid: to make a sot of: to cause to dote: to infatuate:—*pr.p.* **besott'ing**; *pa.p.* **besott'ed**.—*adj.* **besott'ed** infatuated.—*adv.* **besott'edly**.—*n.* **besott'edness**. [Pfx. be- (2).]

besought *bi-sōt'*, *pa.t.* and *pa.p.* of **beseech**.

bespangle *bi-spang'gl*, *v.t.* to adorn with spangles, or with anything sparkling or shining. [Pfx. be- (1).]

bespatter *bi-spat'ər*, *v.t.* to spatter or sprinkle with dirt or anything moist: to defame. [Pfx be- (1).]

bespeak *bi-spēk'*, *v.t.* to speak for or engage beforehand, to order or apply for: to stipulate or ask for: to betoken:—*pa.t* **bespoke'**, *arch.* **bespake'**; *pa.p.* **bespōk'en**, also **bespoke'** (see also **bespoke, bespoken** below).—*n.* an actor's benefit, so called because his friends and patrons choose the piece to be performed: an application in advance. [Pfx. be- (3).]

bespeckle *bi-spek'l*, *v.t* to mark with speckles or spots. [Pfx be- (1).]

bespectacled *bi-spek'tə-kld*, *adj.* having spectacles on. [Pfx. be- (2).]

bespoke *bi-spōk'*, **bespoken** *be-spōk'n*, *pa p.* of **bespeak**, ordered to be made, as clothes: (of a tailor, etc.) making clothes, etc. to order. [Pfx. be- (3).]

besprinkle *bi-spring'kl*, *v.t.* to sprinkle over [Pfx. be- (1).]

Bessemer *bes'əm-ər*, *adj.* pertaining to the steelmaking process invented by Sir Henry *Bessemer* (1813–98).—**Bessemer iron**, **pig** pig-iron suitable for making Bessemer steel.

best *best*, *adj.* (serving as *superl.* of **good**) good in the highest degree: first: highest: most excellent.— *n.* one's utmost endeavour: the highest perfection: the best share, part, success, or lot (as the *best of the bargain*, *the best of three*—tosses, games, etc.). —*adv.* (as *superl.* of **well**) in the highest degree: in the best manner.—*v.t.* (*coll.*) to get the better of. —**best boy, girl** (*coll*) a favourite associate of the opposite sex; **best man, best maid** (*Scot*) groomsman and bridesmaid at a wedding; **best part** greater part; **best'seller** a book that has had one of the biggest sales of the season: the writer of such a book.—**at best** on the most favourable supposition; **for the best** with the best of intentions or outcome; **give somone best** to concede the victory; **have the best of it** to gain the advantage in a contest; **I had best, I were best** (for earlier *me were best*) it were best for me; **make the best of one's way** to go as well as one can; **put one's best foot foremost** see **foot**; **with the best** as successfully as anyone. [O.E. *betst*, *betest*; see **better**.]

bestead *bi-sted'*, *v.t.* to help, relieve: to be of use to, avail.—*v.i.* to profit, be advantageous:—*pa.t.* **bestead'ed**, *pa.p.* **bestead'**, **bested'**. [Pfx be- (1) and obs. v.t. **stead**]

bestial *best'i-əl*, *adj.* like a beast: rude: brutally sensual.—*v t.* **best'ialise**, **-ize** to make like a beast —*ns.* **best'ialism** irrationality; **bestiality** (*-al'i-ti*) beastliness: disgusting vice: copulation between an animal and a person. [L. *bestiālis*—*bestia*, beast.]

bestiary *best'i-ər-i*, *n.* a book of a class popular in the Middle Ages, describing animals, a mixture of natural and unnatural history allegorised for edification. [L.L. *bestiārium*, a menagerie—*bestia*, a beast.]

bestir *bi-stûr'*, *v.t.* to put into lively action: to arouse into activity. [Pfx. be- (1).]

bestow *bi-stō'*, *v t.* to stow, place, or put by: to give or confer: to accommodate with quarters: to apply (with *on* and *upon*).—*ns.* **bestow'al** act of bestowing: disposal; **bestow'er**; **bestow'ment**. [Pfx be- ( )]

bestraddle *bi-strad'l*, *v t* to bestride [Pfx be- (3).]

For other sounds see detailed chart of pronunciation.

bestrew bi-strōō', v.t. to cover loosely with something strewn or scattered over:—pa.p. **bestrewed'**, **bestrown** (-strōn'), **bestrewn'** (with). [Pfx. **be-** (1).]

bestride bi-strīd', v.t. to stride over: to sit or stand across: to defend, protect, from the sense of standing over a fallen man to defend him:—pa.t. **bestrid'**, **bestrode'**; pa.p. **bestrid'**, **bestridd'en**.—adj. **bestrid'able**. [Pfx be- (3).]

bet bet, n. a wager: something staked to be lost or won on the result of a doubtful issue.—v t and v.i. to lay or stake, as a bet:—pr.p. **bett'ing**; pa.t. and pa.p **bet** or **bett'ed**.—ns. **bett'er** one who bets—also **bett'or**; **bett'ing.—an even bet** an equal chance; **you bet** (slang) certainly. [Poss. shortened from noun **abet**.]

beta bē'ta, n. the second letter (B, β) of the Greek alphabet· in classification, the second or one of the second grade; the grade below alpha: in a constellation, that second in brightness.—n. **be'tatron** (Gr -tron, agent suffix) a type of particle accelerator.— **be'ta-block'er** a drug that reduces heart-rate, used to treat e.g. high blood-pressure and angina, **beta rays** streams of **beta particles** or electrons, given off by radium and other radioactive substances. [Gr. bēta; see **B**.]

betake bi-tāk', v.t. to take (oneself) to, to go (with self), to apply or have recourse to.—pa t **betook'**; pa.p **betāk'en**. [Pfx. be- (1).]

bête, bet, (Fr.) n. a brute, a stupid person.—n. **bêtise** (bet-ēz) stupidity: a blunder.—**bête noire** (nwar) a black beast: a bugbear: a person or thing that one especially dislikes.

betel bē'tl, n. the leaf of the **be'tel-pepp'er** (Piper betle) which is chewed in the East along with the areca-nut and lime —**be'tel-nut** the areca-nut. [Through Port from Malayalam vettila.]

Beth Din bāt dēn, a Jewish court, in London presided over by the Chief Rabbi [Heb bēth, house, dīn, judgment.]

bethink bi-thingk', v.t. to think on or call to mind: to recollect (generally followed by a reflexive pronoun and of): to propose to oneself —v i. to consider:— pa.t. and pa.p. **bethought** (bi-thōt'). [O.E. bithencan. See **think**.]

betide bi-tīd', v.t. to befall, happen to (orig. dat. and formerly sometimes followed by to, unto): (erroneous and rare) to betoken:—pa.t. **beti'ded**, betid (-tid'), pa.p. **betid'**. [Pfx. be- (1), tide, to happen]

betimes bi-tīmz', adv. in good time: early: seasonably: speedily. [Pfx. be- (1), and **time**, with adverbial gen -s.]

bêtise. See **bête**.

betoken bi-tō'kn, v.t. to show by a sign: to foreshow: to mean: to symbolise (arch) [Pfx. be- (1).]

béton bā'tɔ̄, n. lime concrete: concrete. [Fr.]

betony bet'ən-i, n. a common labiate plant growing in woods, of great repute in ancient and mediaeval medicine: extended to various plants. [Fr. bétoine—L. betonica, vettonica.]

betook bi-tŏŏk', pa.t. of **betake**.

betray bi-trā', v.t. to give up treacherously: to disclose in breach of trust: to let go basely or weakly to deceive (the innocent and trustful), to seduce. to discover or show: to show signs of.—ns. **betray'al** act of betraying; **betray'er** a traitor· the seducer of a trustful girl [Pfx be- (1) and O.Fr trair (Fr. trahir)—L. tradère, to deliver up.]

betroth bi-trōdh', or -trōth', v.t. to contract, or promise, to marry (a woman): to affiance —ns. **betroth'al**, **betroth'ment** an engagement to marry· ceremonious declaration of such an engagement.— adj. and n. **betrothed'**. [Pfx be- (2), and **troth** or **truth**.]

better bet'ər, adj (serves as compar. of **good**) good in a greater degree: preferable: improved: more suitable: larger: kinder: stronger in health: completely recovered (Scot.).—adv. (compar. of **well**) well in a greater degree: more fully or completely: over or more: with greater advantage.—n. superior (esp. in pl.).—v.t. to make better: to surpass.—adjs. **bett'ered**; **bett'ering**.—ns. **bett'ering** amelioration: improvement; **bett'erment** improvement, esp. in standard of life or value of property.—n. **bett'erness**.—**better half** a jocose term for a wife; **be better than one's word** to do more than one had promised; **better off** in superior circumstances: more fortunate: richer; **for better** (or) **for worse** whatever the result may be; **get the better of** to gain the advantage over, overcome, **had better** see **have; have seen, known better days** to be worse off or in worse condition now than formerly; **the better part of** more than half of; **think better of** to revise one's decision about, esp. to decide not to do: to have a higher opinion of. [O.E. bet (adv.), betera (adj.) better.]

between bi-twēn', prep. in, to, through, or across the space that separates: intermediate to: on the part of in reciprocal relation: by combined action or influence of: from one to another of. in joint possession of (generally of two).—adv in or to an intermediate place: at intervals.—n. **between'ness** state of being between.—**between'-decks** the space between any two decks of a ship (also adv.)—advs. **between'time(s)**, **between'whiles** at intervals.—**between ourselves**, **between you and me** (slang and the cat or post or bedpost, etc) in confidence; **between the devil and the deep sea** in a desperate dilemma, **go between** to act as a mediator (n go'-between). [O.E. betwēonum, and betwēon—be, by, and twēgen, twā, twain, two.]

betwixt bi-twikst', prep. and adv. between.—**betwixt and between** in a middling position. [O.E betweox —twā, two, and the suffix -ix, -ish, with added -t, as in against, and amidst.]

beurré bœ-rā, n. a soft pear of various kinds [Fr., buttery.]

bevel bev'l, n. a slant or inclination of a surface: an instrument opening like a pair of compasses, and adjustable for measuring angles.—adj. having the form of a bevel: slanting.—v t. to form with a bevel or slant:—pr.p **bev'elling**; pa.t. and pa p. **bev'elled.**— adj. **bev'elled** cut to an oblique angle, sloped off —ns. **bev'eller**; **bev'elling**; **bev'elment.—bev'el-gear**, **bev'el-wheels** (mech.) wheels working on each other in different planes, the cogs of the wheels being bevelled or at oblique angles to the shafts [From the older form of Fr. beveau, bevel (instrument).]

beverage bev'ər-ij, n. any liquid for drinking, esp. tea, coffee, milk, etc —adj **bevv'ied** (slang) drunk —n. **bev**(v)**'y** (coll.) (an) alcoholic drink. [O Fr bevrage, beivre—L. bibère, to drink.]

bevy bev'i, n. a company or flock of larks, quails, swans, roes, or ladies

bewail bi-wāl', v.t to lament· to mourn loudly over (esp. the dead) —v.i. to utter lamentations.—adj. **bewailed'**.—n and adj **bewail'ing**. [Pfx. be- (1).]

beware bi-wār', v i (usu with of, or with that, lest) to be on one's guard.—v t. to be on one's guard against: to take care (with infin. or clause) (arch.) Used normally only in infinitive and imperative. [**be**, **ware**.]

bewig bi-wig', v.t. to cover with a wig.—adj **bewigged'**. [Pfx. be- (2).]

bewilder bi-wil'dər, v t. to lead astray (arch): to perplex, confuse.—adjs. **bewil'dered** lost (arch.). confused; **bewil'dering**.—adv **bewil'deringly**.—n **bewil'derment**. [Pfx be- (1) and obs Eng wildern— O E wilddēoren, wilderness—wild, wild, dēor, beast.]

bewitch bi-wich', v t to affect by witchcraft (mostly

malignantly): to fascinate or charm.—*n.* **bewitch'ery.** —*adj.* **bewitch'ing** charming: enchanting.—*adv.* **bewitch'ingly.**—*n.* **bewitch'ment.** [Pfx. **be-** (1).]

bewray *bi-rā'*, (*arch.*) *v.t.* to reveal: to divulge: to reveal the existence, presence, or whereabouts, of. [M.E. *bewreien—be-*, and O.E. *wrēgan*, to accuse.]

bey *bā*, *n.* a Turkish governor. [Turk.]

beyond *bi-yond'*, *prep.* on the farther side of: farther onward in comparison with: out of reach of: above, superior to: apart from.—*adv.* farther away.—*n.* the unknown: the hereafter.—**beyond measure** excessively; **beyond one** more than one is able to do: past one's comprehension; **go beyond** to surpass: to circumvent; **the back of beyond** a place of extreme remoteness; **the (Great) Beyond** the afterlife. [O.E. *begeondan*—pfx. *be-*, and *geond*, across, beyond; see **yon.**]

bezazz. See **bez(z)azz.**

bezel *bez'l*, *n.* the part of the setting of a precious stone which encloses it: the oblique side or face of a cut gem: the grooved rim in which a watch-glass is set, etc.: a sloped cutting edge (usually **basil** *baz'l*): an indicator light on a car dashboard. [From an O.Fr. word represented by mod. Fr. *biseau;* ult. origin uncertain.]

bezique *bi-sēk'*, *n.* a game at cards for two, three, or four, played with two to four packs, from which cards below the seven have been removed: the combination of the knave of diamonds and queen of spades. [Fr. *besigue.*]

bezoar *bē'zōr, -zor*, *n.* a stony concretion found in the stomachs of goats, antelopes, llamas, etc., formerly esteemed an antidote to all poisons.—*adj.* **bezoardic** (*bez-ō-ärd'ik*). [Through Sp. *bezoar* and Ar. *bāzahr*—Pers. *pādzahr*, antidote—*zahr*, poison.]

bez(z)azz, baz(z)azz, biz(z)azz *bə-zaz'*, (*coll.*) *n.* Variants of **piz(z)azz.**

bhang *bang*, *n.* a narcotic and intoxicant, leaves and shoots of hemp. [Hind. *bhāg.*]

bharal *bur'əl*, *n.* the blue sheep of the Himalaya.— Also **burrel, burrell, burrhel, burhel.** [Hind.]

bi-, *bī*, *pfx.* twice, double. [L. *bis*, twice, *bīnī*, two by two, for *duis, duinī.*]

biannual *bī-an'ū-əl*, *adj.* two-yearly: also half-yearly. [L. *bi-*, twice, *annus*, year.]

bias *bī'əs*, *n.* an obliquity: an oblique line: a bulge or greater weight on one side of a bowl (in the game of bowling), making it turn to one side: a turning to one side: a one-sided inclination of the mind: a prejudice: any special influence that sways the mind.—*adj.* biased: cut slantwise.—*adv.* slantwise.—*v.t.* to cause to turn to one side: to prejudice, or prepossess: to cut obliquely:—*pr.p.* **bi'asing** (by some **bi'assing**); *pa.t.* and *pa.p.* **bi'ased** (**bi'assed**).—*n.* **bi'asing** a bias or inclination to one side.—**bias binding** a long narrow folded piece of material cut slantwise and used for finishing hems, seams etc., in sewing. [Fr. *biais*, slant; of unknown origin.]

biathlon *bī-ath'lon*, *n.* an international competition in skiing and shooting. [L. *bi-*, twice, Gr. *athlon*, a contest.]

biaxial *bī-aks'i-əl*, *adj.* having two (optic, etc.) axes.— Also **biax'al.** [L. *bi-*, and **axial.**]

bib *bib*, *n.* a cloth or plastic shield put under a child's chin: of an apron, overalls, etc., the front part above the waist: a fish of the cod and haddock genus with a large chin barbel.—*v.t.* and *v.i.* to drink, to tipple.— *n.* **bibb'er** a tippler: chiefly used in composition as (*B.*) *wine-bibber.*—**best bib and tucker** best clothes. [Prob. from L. *bibere*, to drink; perh. partly imit.]

bibelot *bēb'lō*, *n.* a knick-knack. [Fr.]

Bible *bī'bl*, *n.* the Scriptures of the Old and New Testaments: (also **bible**) a big or authoritative book:

(without *cap.*) the third stomach of a ruminant, with many folds like the leaves of a book.—*adj.* **biblical** (*bib'li-kl*) of, like or relating to the Bible.—*adv.* **bib'lically.**—*ns.* **bib'licism** (*-sizm*) biblical doctrine, learning, or literature: literal acceptance of the Bible; **bib'licist, bib'list** one versed in biblical learning: one who makes the Bible the sole rule of faith: one who adheres to its letter.—**Bible belt** those areas of the Southern U.S.A. of predominantly fundamentalist and puritanical religion; **Bible paper** very thin strong paper for printing; **Bi'ble-thump'er** a vigorous and aggressive preacher. [Fr.,—L.L. *biblia*, fem. sing., earlier neut. pl., from Gr. *biblia*, books, esp. the canonical books.]

bibli- *bib'li-*, in composition, book.—*n.* **bibliographer** (*-og'rə-fər*).—*adjs.* **bibliographic** (*-ō-graf'ik*), **-al.**— *ns.* **bibliog'raphy** study, description or knowledge of books, in regard to their outward form, authors, subjects, editions, and history: a descriptive list of books: a book containing such a list; **bib'liophil(e)** (*-fil, -fīl*; Gr. *philos*, friend) a lover or collector of books.—Also *adj.*—*ns.* **biblioph'ilism; biblioph'ily; bibliophō'bia** (Gr. *phobeein*, to fear) hatred of books. [Gr. *biblion*, book; cf. **Bible.**]

bibulous *bib'ū'ləs*, *adj.* addicted to strong drink. [L. *bibulus—bibere*, to drink.]

bicameral *bī-kam'ər-əl*, *adj.* having two chambers.—*n.* **bicam'eralist** an advocate of the bicameral parliamentary system. [L. *bi*, twice, and *camera*, chamber.]

bicarbonate *bī-kär'bən-āt*, *n.* an acid salt of carbonic acid: sodium bicarbonate, used in baking-powder or as an antacid (*coll.* contraction **bicarb'**). [L. *bi-*, twice, and **carbonate.**]

bice *bīs*, *n.* a pale blue or green paint. [Fr. *bis.*]

bicentenary *bī-sen-tēn'ər-i*, or *-ten'*, or *-sen'*, *adj.* pertaining to two hundred (years).—*n.* a bicentennial. [L. *bi-*, twice, *centēnārius*, pertaining to a hundred— *centum*, a hundred.]

bicentennial *bī-sen-ten'yəl*, *adj.* pertaining to two hundred years.—*n.* a two hundredth anniversary. [L. *bi*, twice, *centum*, a hundred, *annus*, a year.]

biceps *bī'seps*, *n.* a two-headed muscle: esp. one in front of the upper arm or one on the back of the thigh. —*adj.* **bicipital** (*-sip'*) two-headed. [L. *biceps*, two-headed—*bis*, twice, and *caput*, head.]

bicker[1] *bik'ər*, *v.i.* to contend in a petty way.—*n.* a fight, a quarrel. [Poss. a freq. conn. with **beak.**]

bicker[2] *bik'ər*, *n.* a bowl, esp. of wood, for holding liquor: a vessel of wooden staves for porridge. [Scot. form of **beaker.**]

bick-iron *bik'i-ərn*, *n.* a small anvil with one horn: the tapered end of an anvil. [From earlier *bickern*, a two-horned anvil—Fr. *bigorne*—L. *bicornis*, two-horned.]

biconcave *bī-kon'kāv*, *adj.* concave on both sides. [L. *bi-*, twice, and **concave.**]

biconvex *bī-kon'veks*, *adj.* convex on both sides. [L. *bi-*, twice, and **convex.**]

bicuspid *bī-kus'pid*, *adj.* having two cusps.—*n.* a premolar tooth.—*adj.* **bicusp'idate.** [L. *bi-*, twice, and **cusp.**]

bicycle *bī'si-kl*, *n.* a vehicle with two wheels, one before the other, driven by pedals or a motor.—*v.i.* to ride a bicycle.—*n.* **bi'cyclist.**—**bicycle chain** the chain transmitting motion from the pedals to the wheels of a bicycle; **bicycle clip** a metal clip for holding a cyclist's trousers closely to his leg; **bicycle pump** a hand pump for inflating bicycle tyres. [L. *bi-*, twice, Gr. *kyklos*, a circle, wheel.]

bid[1] *bid*, *v.t.* to offer: to propose: to proclaim, as the banns of marriage: to command: to invite (*arch.*): to offer to pay at an auction: to call (in card games).—

v.i. to make an offer or venture:—*pr.p* **bidd'ing;** *pa.t.* **bade** (*bad*; also, as in the poets, *bād*), **bid;** *pa p* **bidd'en, bid.**—*n.* an offer of a price· a venturesome attempt or proposal: a call (at cards).—*adj.* **bidd'able** tractable.—*ns.* **bidd'er; bidd'ing** offer: command calling.—**bid fair** to seem likely; **bid in** (of owner or his agent), in an auction, to overbid the highest offer. [O.E. *bēodan.*]

bid² *bid*, *v.t.* to ask for (*arch.*): to invite· to command to pray (*obs.*): hence to salute with, say as a greeting· —Tenses are as in the preceding verb, with which it has been confused [O.E *biddan.*]

biddy *bid'i*, *n.* an old woman (*slang, derog*) [Poss the woman's name *Biddy* for *Bridget.*]

bide *bīd*, *v.i* (*arch.* and *Scot.*) to wait: to dwell: to remain.—*v.t.* to await (*obs.* except in sense of *bide one's time*, to await a favourable moment): to endure —*pa.t.* **bid'ed, bode,** (*Shak*) **bid,** (*Scot.*) **bade** (*bād*), *pa.p* **bid'ed,** (*obs.* and *Scot.*) **bidd'en.** [O.E. *bīdan*, but sometimes for **abide.**]

bidet *bē-dā*, *bi-det'*, *n* a bestridable basin on a low pedestal, for washing the genital and anal areas, etc [Fr., pony.]

bien *byē*, (Fr.) *adv.* well.—**bien-aimé** (*byē-ne-mā*) well-beloved; **bien élevé** (*-nā-lav-ā*) well brought up, well mannered; **bien-être** (*-netr*) a sense of well-being; **bien pensant** (*pā-sā*) right-thinking: orthodox; **bienséance** (*sā-ās*) propriety: (in *pl*) the proprieties.

biennial *bī-en'i-al*, *-en'yal*, *adj.* lasting two years: happening or appearing once in two years —*n.* a plant that flowers and fructifies only in its second year, then dies.—*adv.* **bienn'ially.** [L. *biennium*, two years—*bi-*, twice, and *annus*, a year]

bier *bēr*, *n.* a carriage or frame of wood for bearing the dead to the grave [O.E. *bēr.*]

bierkeller *bēr'kel-ər*, *n* a German bar, selling beer. [Ger., beer cellar]

biestings. Same as **beestings.**

bifacial *bī-fā'shl*, *adj.* two-faced. having two unlike sides. [L. *bi-*, twice, and **facial.**]

biff *bif*, (*coll.*) *n.* a blow —*v.t* to strike hard.

bifid *buf'id*, *bī'fid*, *adj.* cleft in two [L *bifidus—bi-*, twice, and *findēre*, to cleave or split]

bifocal *bī-fō'kəl*, *adj* composed of parts of different focal lengths.—*n.pl.* **bifo'cals** spectacles with bifocal lenses, for far and for near vision. [L *bi-*, twice, and **focal.**]

bifoliate *bī-fō'li-āt*, *adj.* having two leaves or leaflets —*adj.* **bifo'liolate** having two leaflets [L. *bi-*, twice, *folium*, leaf.]

bifurcate *bī'fūr-kāt*, or *-fūr'*, *adj.* two-forked, having two prongs or branches —*v i.* to divide into two branches —*n.* **bifurca'tion** a forking or division into two branches —*adj* **bi'furcated.** [L *bifurcus—bi-*, *bis*, twice, *furca*, a fork.]

big *big*, *adj.* (*compar.* **bigg'er;** *superl.* **bigg'est**) large or great: pregnant. grown up: older (as in *big sister*)· magnanimous: great in air, mien, or spirit: loud: pompous: very important, as the *Big Three, Big Four*, etc., leaders. countries. organisations. etc.—*adv* (*coll.*) boastfully or ambitiously, as in *talk big* greatly or impressively —*adj* **bigg'ish.**—*ns* **bigg'y, bigg'ie** (*coll*) a large or important person or thing; **big'ness** bulk, size.—**Big Bang** the explosion of a small dense mass which some scientists believe to have been the origin of the universe, **Big Brother** a dictator, as in George Orwell's *Nineteen Eighty-four* (1949): a powerful leader or organisation, perceived as ubiquitous and sinister; **big'-bud'** a swelling of currant buds owing to a gall-mite; **big business** large business enterprises and organisations, esp collectively, **big deal** (*coll*) used as a scornful response to an offer, boast, etc., **big dipper** a switchback at a fair (*orig*

U.S.): (with *caps.*) the constellation Great Bear (*U.S.*); **big end** in an internal-combustion engine, the larger end of the connecting rod; **big guns** (*coll.*) the important persons in an organisation, etc.; **big'-head** (*coll.*) a swelled-headed person: conceit.—*adj* **big'-headed.**—**big'horn** the Rocky Mountain goat or sheep; **big money** money in very large sums; **big mouth** (*slang*) a talkative and boastful person.—*adj* **big'-mouthed'.**—**big name** (*coll.*) a celebrity; **big noise** (*coll.*) an important person, **big shot** see **bigwig** below; **big stick** (*coll.*) a display of power; **big'-time** the top level in any pursuit:—*adj* at the top level· important —**big toe** see **toe; big top** a large circular tent used for circus performances; **big wheel** a Ferris wheel, **big'wig, big shot** (*coll*) a leading man, a person of some importance —**go over big** (**with**) (*coll*) to have a great effect (on)· to impress greatly, **in a big way** vigorously, enthusiastically; **that's big of him** etc. (usu. *iron.*) that action, etc. is generous on his, etc. part; **too big for one's boots** conceited, self-important [M E *big.*]

bigamy *big'ə-mi*, *n.* the custom, crime, or fact of having two legal, or supposed, wives or husbands at once: a second marriage (*eccl. law*) —*n* **big'amist** one who has committed bigamy.—*adj* **big'amous.**—*adv* **big'amously.** [L. *bi-*, twice; Gr. *gamos*, marriage.]

bight *bīt*, *n* wide bay· a bend or coil. [O.E. *byht.*]

Bignonia *big-nō'ni-ə*, *n.* a genus of tropical plants with trumpet-shaped flowers. [Named after the Abbé *Bignon*, Louis XIV's librarian]

bigot *big'ət*, *n* one blindly and obstinately devoted to a particular creed or party.—*adj.* **big'oted** having the qualities of a bigot.—*n.* **big'otry** blind or excessive zeal, esp. in religious matters [O.Fr.]

bijou *bē'zhōō*, *n.* a trinket: a jewel: a little box:—*pl* **bijoux** (*bē'zhōōz*) —*adj.* small and elegant —*n.* **bijouterie** (*bē-zhōōt'ər-ē*) jewellery, esp. trinkets [Fr.]

bike *bik*, *n.* and *v.i.* coll. for **bicycle.**.

bikini *bē-kē'nē*, *n.* a much reduced bathing-dress, in two parts [Said to be from *Bikini*, an atoll of the Marshall Islands, scene of atom-bomb experiments.]

bilabial *bī-lā'bi-əl*, *adj.* two-lipped· produced by contact or approximation of the two lips, as the sound of b, w, (*phon.*) —*n.* a bilabial consonant.—*adj.* **bilā'biate** two-lipped, as some corollas [L. *bi-*, twice, and *labium*, a lip]

bilateral *bī-lat'ər-əl*, *adj* having or involving two sides: affecting two parties or participants reciprocally.—*n.* **bilat'eralism** two-sidedness: equality in value of trade between two countries.—*adv* **bilat'erally.**

bilberry *bil'bər-i*, *n* a whortleberry or blaeberry shrub· its dark blue berry. [Cf. Dan *bollebær.*]

bile *bīl*, *n.* a thick bitter fluid secreted by the liver: derangement of its secretion: ill-humour (*fig.*) — *adjs.* **biliary** (*bil'yər-i*), of the bile, the bile ducts or the gall-bladder; **bilious** (*bil'yəs*) pertaining to or affected by bile —*adv* **bil'iously.**—*n.* **bil'iousness.**—**bile'-ducts** the ducts that convey the bile to the small intestine [Fr ,—L *bilis.*]

bilge *bilj*, *n* the bulging part of a cask the broadest part of a ship's bottom: filth such as collects there: piffle (*slang*).—*v.i* to spring a leak by a fracture in the bilge, as a ship —*adj* **bilg'y** having the appearance and disagreeable smell of bilge-water —**bilge's keel** a ridge along the turn of the bilge of a ship to check rolling; **bilge'-pump; bilge'-wat'er.** [Perh **bulge.**]

Bilharzia *bil-har'zi-ə*, *-tsi-ə*, *n.* a genus of trematode worms parasitic in human and other blood with two larval stages, first in water-snails and then in man.—

ns. **bilharz'ia, bilharzi'asis, bilharziö'sis** a disease caused by it, common in tropical countries, esp. Egypt and other parts of Africa (also known as schistosomiasis). [From the helminthologist, Theodor *Bilharz* (1825–62).]

biliary. See **bile.**

bilingual bī-ling'gwəl, *adj.* expressed in two languages: speaking two languages, esp. native or habitual languages.—*ns.* **biling'ualism; biling'uist.** [L. *bilinguis* —*bi-*, twice, *lingua*, tongue.]

bilious. See **bile.**

bilk *bilk, v.t.* to elude: to cheat.—*n.* **bilk'er.** [Perh. a form of **balk**; at first a term in cribbage]

bill[1] *bil, n.* a concave battle-axe with a long wooden handle: a kind of hatchet with a long blade and wooden handle in the same line with it, often with a hooked point, used in pruning.—**bill'hook** a bill or hatchet with curved point. [O.E. *bil.*]

bill[2] *bil, n.* the beak of a bird, or anything like it: a sharp promontory: the point of an anchor fluke.—*v.t.* to join bills as doves: to caress fondly.—*adj.* **billed** having a bill.—*n.* and *adj.* **bill'ing.—bill'board** a board used to protect the planking from injury by the bill when the anchor is weighed. [O.E. *bile*, prob. same as **bill[1]**.]

bill[3] *bil, n.* an account of money: a draft of a proposed law: a written engagement to pay a sum of money at a fixed date: a bank-note (*U.S.*): a placard: a slip of paper serving as an advertisement: a list of performers, etc. in order of importance: a programme of entertainment: any written statement of particulars· a written accusation of serious crime (*Eng. criminal law*).—*v.t.* to announce or advertise by bill: to send an invoice (to).—*adj.* **billed** (*bild*) named in a list or advertisement.—*n.* **bill'ing** the making out or sending of bills or invoices: total amount of money received from customers or clients: advertising· naming in an announcement or poster.—**bill'board** a board on which placards are posted; **bill'-fold** (*U.S.*) a note-case; **bill'head** a form used for business accounts, with name and address printed at the top; **bill'poster, bill'sticker** one who sticks or posts up bills or placards.—**bill of costs** an account of a solicitor's charges and disbursements in the conduct of his client's business; **bill of exceptions** a statement of objections, by way of appeal against the ruling of a judge who is trying a case with a jury in the Court of Session; **bill of exchange** a document purporting to be an instrument of pecuniary obligation for value received, employed for the purpose of settling a debt in a manner convenient to the parties concerned; **bill of fare** a list of dishes or articles of food; **bill of health** an official certificate of the state of health on board ship before sailing (**clean bill of health** a certificate stating that there is no illness on board: proof that a person is healthy: proof that an organisation, etc. is in a good condition (*fig.*)); **bill of indictment** a statement of a charge made against a person; **bill of lading** a paper signed by the master of a ship, by which he makes himself responsible for the safe delivery of the goods specified therein: a certificate stating that specified goods are aboard a vessel, **bill of rights** see **right**; **bill of sale** in English law, a formal deed assigning personal property; **double, triple bill** a programme of entertainment consisting of two, three main items. [L.L. *billa*—L. *bulla*, a knob, a seal, hence a document bearing a seal, etc.; cf. **bull[2]**.]

billabong *bil'ə-bong, (Austr.) n.* a cut-off loop of a river, replenished only by floods: an effluent from a river (strictly one that does not rejoin) [Native words *bulla*, river, *bung*, dead.]

billboard. See **bill[2,3]**.

billet[1], *bil'it, n.* a little note or paper: a ticket assigning

quarters to soldiers or others· quarters requisitioned: a destined resting-place: a post or occupation.—*v t.* to quarter or lodge, as soldiers:—*pr.p* **bill'eting;** *pa.t.* and *pa.p.* **bill'eted.** [O.Fr. *billette*, dim. of *bille*, see **bill[3]**.]

billet[2] *bil'it, n.* a small log of wood: a bar of metal· an ornament in Norman architecture in the form of short cylinders with spaces between [Fr. *billette*—*bille*, the young stock of a tree.]

billet-doux bil-i-dōō', *n.* a love-letter·—*pl.* **billets-doux'** (same pron. as *sing.*). [Fr. *billet*, letter, *doux*, sweet.]

billiards bil'yərdz, *n. sing.* a game played with a cue and balls on a table with pockets at the sides and corners.—*adj.* **bill'iard.—bill'iard-ball; bill'iard-cloth** a green cloth for covering a billiard-table; **bill'iard-table.** [Fr *billard—bille*, a stick, hence a cue]

billie. See **billy.**

Billings method bil'ingz meth'əd, a rhythm method of contraception involving the examination of the discharge from the cervix. [Dr Evelyn *Billings*, an Australian physician]

billion bil'yən, *n.* in Britain, France (since 1948), etc , a million millions (unit and twelve ciphers): in U.S., often now in Britain, one thousand millions (unit and nine ciphers) or milliard.—*n.* **billionaire'.—**adj , *n.* **bill'ionth.** [**bi-, million.**]

billon bil'ən, *n.* base metal: esp. an alloy of silver with copper, tin, or the like. [Fr., from same root as **billet[2]**.]

billow bil'ō, *n* a great wave: a wave, the sea (*poet*) — *v.t.* to roll or swell in great waves: to bulge flowingly.—*adjs.* **bill'owed; bill'owing; bill'owy.** [App. O.N *bylgja*; Sw. *bolja*, Dan. *bölge*, wave.]

billy, billie bil'i, *n.* an Australian bushman's (or other's) boiling-pan or tea-pot (also **bill'y-can;** poss. for *bouilli can*):—*pl* **bill'ies.—bill'y-goat** a he-goat. [Prob. from *Bull*, a familiar abbrev. of William]

billycock bil'i-kok, *n.* a hard felt hat. [Poss. from *William Coke*, nephew of Earl (1837) of Leicester, or from 19th-cent. Cornish hatter *William Cock*.]

billy-o(h) bil'i-ō, *n* in phrase **like billy-o(h)** vigorously, fiercely.

bilobar bī-lō'bər, **bilobate** bī-lō'bāt, **bilobed** bī'lōbd, *adjs.* having two lobes—*adj.* **bilobular** (bī-lob'ū-lər) having two lobules [L *bi-*, twice, and **lobe, lobule.**]

biltong bil'tong (*S Afr*) *n* sun-dried lean meat. [Du. *bil*, buttock, *tong*, tongue]

bimbashi bim-ba'shē, *n.* a military officer (in Turkey or Egypt). [Turk. *bin*, thousand, *bash*, head.]

bimetallic bī-mi-tal'ik, *adj* composed of, or using, two metals: of a monetary system, in which gold and silver are on precisely the same footing as regards mintage and legal tender —*n* **bimetallism** (bī-met'əl-izm) such a system —*n* and *adj.* **bimet'allist.—bimetallic** strip a strip, formed by bonding two metals one of which expands more than the other, which bends with change of temperature

bimonthly bī-munth'li, *adj.* once in two months· also twice a month. [L *bi-*, two, and **month.**]

bin *bin, n.* a receptacle for storing e.g. corn: a receptacle for rubbish: a stand or case with compartments in which to store bottled wine in a wine-cellar· the wine contained therein: a lunatic asylum (*slang*) — *v.t.* to put (bottled wine) into a bin:—*pr.p.* **binn'ing;** *pa.t* and *pa.p.* **binned.** [O.E *binn*, a manger]

binary bī'nər-i, *adj* composed of two· twofold.—*n* binary system, star.—**binary fission** (*biol.*) division of an organism or cell into two parts; **binary operation** in math , combining two elements in a collection of elements in such a way as to give another element from the same collection (as addition or multiplication in the ordinary number system); **binary scale** the scale of notation whose base is 2 (instead of 10); **binary system** two stars revolving about their centre of gravity (also **binary star**): system using the binary scale of notation: system in which numbers are expressed by using two digits only, viz. 1 and 0 [L. *binārius—bīnī*, two by two, *bis*, twice.]

binaural *bin-ö′rəl, adj.* having, employing, or relating to two ears: of reproduction of sound, using two sound channels.—*adv.* **binaur′ally.** [L. *bīnī*, two by two, *auris*, ear.]

bind *bīnd, v.t.* to tie or fasten together with a band: to encircle round: to restrain: to fix: to make fast: to sew a border on: to tie up or bandage: to fasten together and put a cover on (a book): to impose an obligation upon: to oblige by oath or promise: to indenture: to hold or cement firmly: to cause (dry ingredients) to cohere by adding a small amount of liquid (*cook.*): to render hard: to constipate.—*v.i.* to become bound: to complain (*slang*):—*pa.t.* and *pa.p.* **bound** (*bownd*).— *n.* in music, the tie for indicating that a note is to be held on, not repeated (of the same form as the slur or legato mark): a difficult or annoying situation, a bore (*slang*) —*ns.* **bind′er** one who binds (books, sheaves, etc.): anything that binds, as a rope, a bandage, a cementing agent, a tie-beam, a header in masonry, a case for binding loose papers: an attachment to a reaping-machine for tying the bundles of grain cut and thrown off: a reaping-machine provided with one; **bind′ery** a bookbinder's establishment.—*adj.* **bind′ing** restraining: obligatory.—*n.* the act of one who binds: anything that binds: the covering of a book.—**bind′weed** convolvulus: also (**black bindweed**) a species of *Polygonum.*—**be bound up in** to be wholly devoted to: **bind over** to subject to legal obligation; **I dare** or **will be bound** I will be responsible for the statement. See also **bound¹** and **bounden.** [O.E. *bindan.*]

bine *bīn, n.* the slender stem of a climbing plant: a flexible shoot. [Orig. dial. form of **bind.**]

binge *binj, binzh, n* a spree (*coll.*): a banquet, feast (*facet*): a bout of indulgence esp. in overeating (*coll.*).

bingo *bing′gō, n* a form of lotto in which, usu., the numbers in all the lines must be covered.—*interj.* the exclamation made by the first player to finish in this game: an exclamation expressing suddenness, unexpectedness, etc.:—*pl.* **bing′os.**

binnacle *bin′ə-kl, (naut.) n.* the box in which a ship's compass is kept. [Formerly *bittacle*—Port. *bitácola* —L. *habitāculum*, a dwelling-place—*habitāre*, to dwell.]

binocle *bin′o-kl, -ə-kl, n.* a telescope for use with both eyes at once.—*adj.* **binocular** (*bī-, bi-nok′ū-lər*) with two eyes. suitable for use with two eyes: stereoscopic. —*n.* a binocular telescope (usu. in *pl.*) or microscope. [L. *bīnī*, two by two, *oculus*, an eye.]

binomial *bī-nōm′i-əl, adj (alg.)* consisting of two terms, as *a + b —n.* a binomial expression. [L. *bi-*, twice, and *nōmen*, a name, a term.]

bint *bint, n.* a girl, woman (with various shades of meaning). [Ar., daughter.]

bio- *bī-ō-*, in composition, life: living organisms: living tissue—as in, e.g. the following.—*n sing* **bio-astronaut′ics** science dealing with the effects of travel in space on living organisms.—*adj.* **biochem′ical.**— *ns.* **biochem′ist; biochem′istry** the chemistry of living things, physiological chemistry.—*adj.* **biodegrad′able** (of substances) able to be broken down by bacteria — *n.* **biodegradā′tion** (also **biodeteriorā′tion**).—*adjs* **biodestruct′ible** biodegradable, **biodynam′ic** dealing with activities of living organisms (of system of land cultivation) fertilising with organic materials only —

n. sing **biodynam′ics.**—*ns.* **bioecol′ogy** the branch of ecology dealing with the interrelationship of plant and animal life; **bioengineer′ing** see **biological engineering** at end of article.—*n.sing.* **bioeth′ics** study of the ethical problems produced by medical and scientific research, etc —*ns* **biofeed′back** the clinical control of body functions in response to monitoring by electronic instruments such as an electrocardiograph; **bi′ogas** domestic or commercial gas obtained by treating naturally-occurring materials; **biogen′esis** (Gr *genesis*, production) the derivation of living things from living things only: biogeny.—*adjs* **biogenet′ic, biogen′ic** relating to biogeny, or to biogenesis; **biogenous** (*-oj′*) parasitic.—*ns.* **biog′eny** the course of organic evolution or development of the individual or the race; **biog′rapher** one who writes biography.—*adjs.* **biograph′ic, -al.**—*adv.* **biograph′-ically.**—*ns.* **biog′raphy** a written account or history of the life of an individual: the art of writing such accounts.—*adj.* **biological** (-*loj′*) of, pertaining to, biology: physiological: produced by physiological means: effected by living organisms or by enzymes —*adv.* **biolog′ically.**—*ns.* **biol′ogist; biol′ogy** the science of living things: sometimes restricted to ecology; **bioluminesc′ence** the emission of light by living organisms; **bi′omass** the quantity or weight of living material (animals, plants, etc.) in a unit of area.— *n.sing.* **biomechan′ics** the mechanics of movements in living creatures.—*adj.* **biomed′ical** of or pertaining to both biology and medicine: applied to the study of, the effects of stress, esp. space travel, on living organisms.—*n.* **biomed′icine.**—*adj.* **biomet′ric** (Gr. *metron*, measure).—*ns.* **biometrician** ′(-trish′ən); **biom′etry** the statistical or quantitative study of biology (also *n.sing.* **biomet′rics**); **bi′omorph** (Gr. *morphē*, form), a representation of a living thing in decoration.—*adjs.* **biomorph′ic; bion′ic** relating to, using, etc , bionics: superhuman (*coll.*).—*n.sing.* **bion′ics** the study of methods of working of living creatures and the application of the principles observed to design of computers, etc.: (*loosely*) the replacement of parts of the body with electronic or mechanical devices, such as power-controlled limbs, heart-valves, etc.—*adj.* **bionom′ic.**—*n.sing.* **bionom′ics** (Gr. *nomos*, law) the study of the relations between the organism and its environment: ecology.—*n.* **bi′opsy** a removal of tissue or fluid from a living body for diagnostic examination: such examination.—*n.pl.* **bi′orhythms** physiological, emotional and intellectual rhythms or cycles, supposed to cause variations in mood or performance.—*ns.* **bi′oscope** (Gr. *skopeein*, to look at) a cinematographic apparatus or theatre or, (*S.Afr.*), cinema; **bi′osphere** the part of the earth and its atmosphere in which living things are found.—*n.* **biosyn′thesis** the production of chemical substances by a living organism.— *adj.* **biosynthet′ic.**—*ns.* **bio′ta** flora and fauna of a region; **biotechnol′ogy** ergonomics; now usu. the application of biological organisms (such as bacteria) and biological processes to manufacturing and service industries.—*adj* **biotic** (*bī-ot′ik*) pertaining to life,— **biological clock** an inherent mechanism which regulates the physiological rhythms and cycles of living organisms; **biological control** a method of reducing the numbers of a pest—plant, animal or parasite—by introducing or fostering one of its enemies; **biological engineering** provision of aids (electronic, electrical, etc.) to functioning of the body, as hearing aids, aids to movement, etc. (also **bioengineering**). engineering required for methods of biosynthesis of animal and plant products, e.g. for fermentation processes (also **bioengineering**)· manipulating living cells so as to promote their growth in a desired way; **bio-**

logical warfare methods of fighting involving the use of disease bacteria. [Gr. *bios*, life.]

bio *bī'ō* (*pl.* **bi'os**), **blog** *bī'og*, *-og'*, *ns.* short for **biography.**

biont *bī'ont*, *n.* a living organism.—*adj.* **bion'tic.**—**-biont** in composition, an organism belonging to a particular habitat or environment.— **-bion'tic** adjective combining form. [Gr. *bios*, life, *ōn* (stem *ont-*) from *einai*, to be.]

biopic *bī'ō-pik*, *n.* a film, usu. an uncritically admiring one, telling the life-story of a celebrity. [*Bio*graphical *pic*ture.]

-biosis *-bi-ō'sis*, in composition, a specific way of living.— **-biotic** (*-ot'*) adjective combining form. [Gr. *biōsis*, way of life; adj. *biōtikos*.]

biotin *bī'ō-tin*, *n.* one of the members of the vitamin B complex (also known as vitamin H). [Gr. *biotos*, means of living.]

bipartite *bī-pärt'īt*, *adj.* divided into two parts: having two corresponding parts, as a document: affecting two parties, as an agreement.—*adj.* **bipart'isan** (*-i-zan*) pertaining to, supported by, or consisting of members of, two parties.—*n.* **bipartition** (*-tish'ən*) division into two parts. [L. *bi-*, *bis*, twice, *partītus*, divided—*partīre*, *-īrī*, to divide.]

biped *bī'ped*, *n.* an animal with two feet.—*adjs.* **bī'ped**, **bī'pedal** having two feet: using two feet for walking.—*n.* **biped'alism.** [L. *bipēs*, *-pedis*—*bi-*, twice, *pēs*, *pedis*, foot.]

bipinnate *bī-pin'āt*, *adj.* pinnate with each pinna itself pinnate. [L. *bi-*, twice, and **pinnate.**]

biplane *bī'plān*, *n.* an aeroplane or glider with two sets of wings, one above the other. [L. *bi-*, twice, and **plane²**.]

bipolar *bī-pō'lər*, *adj.* having two poles or extremities (*lit.* and *fig.*).—*n.* **bipolar'ity.** [L. *bi-*, twice, and **polar.**]

birch *bûrch*, *n.* a hardy forest-tree (*Betula*), with smooth white bark and very durable wood: a rod for punishment, consisting of a birch twig or twigs.—*v.t.* to flog.—*adjs.* **birch, birch'en** made of birch.—**birch rod** a birch for punishment. [O.E. *berc*, *bierce*.]

bird *bûrd*, *n.* a general name for a feathered animal (orig. applied to the young): a person (*slang*): an object of admiration (*slang*): a prison sentence (*slang*): a girl or woman (*arch.*, *dial.*; later *slang*).—*v.i.* to shoot at, seek to catch or snare birds.—*ns.* **bird'ie** (*dim.*) a little bird: the achievement of a hole in golf in one stroke less than par; **bird'ing.**—**bird'bath** a basin set up for birds to bathe in.—*adj.* **bird'-brained** (*coll.*) flighty, silly.—**bird'cage** a cage of wire or wicker for holding birds; **bird'call** a bird-catcher's instrument for imitating birds' notes; **bird'-catcher** a professional catcher of birds.—*n.* and *adj.* **bird'-catching** (**bird-catching spider** see **bird-spider**).—**bird'-cherry** a small wild cherry tree: its astringent fruit; **bird'dog** one trained to find or retrieve birds for hunters; **bird'-fancier** one who breeds birds, or keeps them for sale.—*adj.* **bird'-hipped** (of dinosaurs) having a pelvis slightly similar to a bird's, the pubis extending backwards to lie parallel with the upper pelvis, ornithischian.—**bird impact** bird strike; **bird'-lime** a sticky substance for catching birds; **bird'-of-par'adise** see **paradise**; **bird-of-paradise flower** Strelitzia; **bird'seed** seed (hemp, etc.) for cage-birds: a thing trifling in amount, chicken feed (*slang*); **bird's'eye** a kind of primrose, of speedwell, or of tobacco.—*adj.* such as might be seen by a flying bird: having markings like birds' eyes.—**bird'shot** pellets suitable for shooting birds; **bird's'-nest** the nest in which a bird lays and hatches her eggs: a name given to several plants from their appearance, esp. *Monotropa* and *Neottia* (bird's-nest orchis); **bird's'-nesting,**

bird'-nesting seeking and robbing birds' nests; **bird'-spider** a large spider that preys on small birds, found in Brazil: extended to others; **bird strike** collision of a bird with an aircraft resulting in aircraft damage; **bird'-table** a table, inaccessible to cats, for wild birds to feed on; **bird'watcher**; **bird'-watching** observation of birds in their natural habitat.—**a bird in the hand is worth two in the bush** a certainty is not to be thrown away for a poor chance of something better; **a little bird told me** I heard in a way I will not reveal; **bird's-eye view** a general view from above: a general view of a subject; **birds of a feather** see **feather**; **do bird** (*slang*) to serve a prison sentence; (**strictly**) **for the birds** (*slang*) not to be taken seriously, of little value; **get the bird** (i.e. the goose) in stage slang, to be hissed, hence dismissed. [O.E *brid*, the young of a bird, a bird.]

birefringent *bi-rə-frin'jənt*, *adj.* doubly refracting, as Iceland spar.—*n.* **birefrin'gence.** [L. *bi-*, twice, and **refringent.**]

bireme *bī'rēm*, *n.* an ancient vessel with two banks of oars. [L *birēmis*—*bi-*, twice, and *rēmus*, an oar.]

biretta *bir-et'ə*, *n.* a square cap worn by clergy—by priests, black; bishops, purple; cardinals, red. [It. *berretta*—L.L. *birretum*, cap.]

bir(i)yani *bir-ya'ni*, *bi-ri-ya'ni*, *ns.* a spicy rice dish. [From Urdu]

Biro® *bī'rō*, *n.* a kind of ball-point pen.—*pl.* **Bi'ros.** [L. *Biró*, Hungarian inventor.]

birth¹ *bûrth*, *n.* a ship's station at anchor. [Same as **berth.**]

birth² *bûrth*, *n.* the act of bearing or bringing forth: coming into the world: the offspring born: dignity of family: origin.—**birth control** the control of reproduction by contraceptives; **birth'day** the day on which one is born, or (usually) its anniversary, or a day officially held instead.—*adj.* relating to the day of one's birth.—**birth'day-book** a book for (autograph) records of friends' birthdays; **birthday honours** titles, etc., conferred on the king's (or queen regnant's) official birthday, **birth'day-suit** the naked skin; **birth'mark** a mark, e.g. a pigmented area or spot, on one's body at birth: a distinguishing quality (*fig.*); **birth'night** the night on which one is born, or the anniversary of that night; **birth pill** a contraceptive pill; **birth'place** the place of one's birth; **birth'-rate** proportion of births to population; **birth'right** the right or privilege to which one is entitled by birth: native rights. [Prob O.N. *byrthr*.]

biryani. See **bir(i)yani.**

bis *bis*, *adv.* twice: a direction for repetition (*mus.*). [L.]

biscacha. Same as **viscacha.**

biscuit *bis'kit*, *n.* a small, thin, crisp cake made of unleavened dough: a soft round cake (*U.S.*): pottery that has been fired but not yet glazed: a square mattress (*mil. slang*).—*adj.* pale brown in colour.—**take the biscuit** to surpass everything else (*iron.*). [O.Fr. *bescoit* (mod. *biscuit*)—L. *bis*, twice, *coquère*, *coctum*, to cook or bake]

bise *bēz*, *n.* a cold north or north-east wind prevalent at certain seasons in and near Switzerland. [Fr.]

bisect *bī-sekt'*, *v.t.* and *v i.* to divide into two (usu. equal) parts.—*ns.* **bisec'tion; bisec'tor** a line that divides an angle, etc., into two equal parts. [L. *bi-*, twice, and *secāre*, *sectum*, to cut.]

bisexual *bī-seks'ū-əl*, *adj.* hermaphrodite: attracted sexually to both sexes. [L. *bi-*, twice, **sexual.**]

bish *bish*, (*coll.*) *n.* a blunder, mistake.

bishop *bish'əp*, *n.* in the Western and Eastern Churches and in the Anglican communion, a clergyman consecrated for the spiritual direction of a diocese, usu. under an archbishop, and over the priests or presbyters and deacons: a spiritual overseer in the early Christian Church, whether of a local church or of a number of churches: a chessman whose move is in a diagonal line, its upper part carved into the shape of a bishop's mitre (formerly the *archer*): a wholesome hot drink compounded of red wine (claret, Burgundy, etc.) poured warm or cold upon ripe bitter oranges, sugared and spiced to taste: any of several kinds of weaver-bird (**bish'op-bird**) —*n* **bish'opric** the office and jurisdiction of a bishop: sometimes a diocese.—**bishop's cap** a genus (*Mitella*) of the saxifrage family, with one-sided inflorescences; **bishop's court** the court of a diocesan bishop, **bishop sleeve** a full sleeve drawn in tightly at the wrist [O E. biscop—L. episcopus—Gr. episkopos, overseer]

bisk. See **bisque¹**

bismuth bis' or biz'məth, n. a brittle reddish-white element (at. numb 83; symbol Bi) [Ger. Bismuth, Wissmuth (now Wismut), origin unknown.]

bison bi'sn, -zn, n. a large wild ox with shaggy hair and a fatty hump—the European bison, almost extinct except in parks, and the American, commonly called buffalo in America. [From L bisōn, -ontis, prob. of Gmc. origin; cf. O.H.G. wisunt, O E wesend.]

bisque¹, **bisk** bisk, n. a rich soup, esp. crayfish soup. [Fr.]

bisque² bisk, n a kind of unglazed white porcelain pottery that has undergone the first firing before being glazed [See biscuit.]

bisque³ bisk, n. a term at tennis, golf, etc., for the handicap whereby a player allows a weaker opponent (at latter's choice of time) to score a point in a set, or deduct a stroke at a hole, to take an extra turn in croquet, etc [Fr]

bistable bi'stā-bl, adj. (of a valve or transistor circuit) having two stable states.

bistort bis'tört, n. adderwort or snakeweed, a plant of the dock family with twisted rootstock [L. bistorta —bis, twice, tortus, -a, -um, twisted.]

bistoury bis'tər-i, n. a narrow surgical knife for making incisions. [Fr. bistouri.]

bistre, bister bis'tər, n. a pigment of a warm brown colour made from the soot of wood, esp. beech-wood.—*adj.* **bis'tred.** [Fr. bistre; origin unknown.]

bistro bē'strō, n a small bar or restaurant:—*pl.* **bis'tros.** [Fr slang.]

bisulphate bi-sul'fāt, n. an acid sulphate —*n.* **bisulph'ide** a disulphide.

bit¹ bit, n. a bite, a morsel: a small piece: a coin: 12½ cents (*U.S.*) (used only in **two, four, six bits**): the smallest degree: a brief space of time: a small boring tool (see **brace**): the boring part of a drilling machine: the part of the bridle that the horse holds in his mouth: the part of a key that engages the lever of the lock: a girl, young woman (*slang*).—*v.t.* to put the bit in the mouth of: to curb or restrain:—*pr.p.* **bitt'ing**; *pa.p* **bitt'ed**.—*adj* **bitt'y** scrappy. disjointed, made up of odds and ends: not forming an artistic whole.—**bit'(-part)** a small part in acting; **bit player** an actor who plays bit-parts.—**a bit (of)** somewhat, rather, as in *a bit of a fool, a bit stupid*; **a bit of all right** (*slang*) a person or thing highly approved of; **a bit off** (*coll.*) in bad taste; **bit by bit** piecemeal: gradually; **do one's bit** to do one's due share; **take, get, the bit in, between, one's teeth** to throw off control. [From **bite**.]

bit² bit, the smallest unit of information in computers and communications theory. [Contracted **b**inary dig**it**.]

bitch bich, n the female of the dog, wolf, and fox:

(abusively) a woman, very rarely a man: a malicious or arrogant woman. an act of grumbling (*slang*).—*v.t* (*slang*) to complain —*v t* (*slang*) to mess up, spoil (often *bitch up*) —*n*. **bitch'iness.**—*adj* **bitch'y.** [O.E bicce.]

bite bit, v.t and v i. to seize or tear with the teeth· to puncture with the mouth-parts, as an insect: to cut or penetrate· to eat into chemically: to take effect to grip: to deceive. to take in (now only in passive). to accept something offered as bait (also *fig*):—*pa t.* **bit;** *pa p.* **bit** or **bitt'en.**—*n* a grasp by the teeth manner in which the teeth come together: a puncture by an insect: the wound or sore caused thereby· a nibble at the bait· something bitten off: a mouthful· biting quality: grip: pungency: corroding action —*ns* **bit'er** one who bites: an animal with a habit of biting. a fish apt to take the bait: a cheat (*obs.*, except in the **biter bit**, the cheater cheated· the wrongdoer paid back), **bit'ing.**—*adj* which bites: sharp, cold· sarcastic —**bite in** (*etching*) to eat out the lines of with acid; **bite off more than one can chew** to over-estimate one's capacities· to undertake that which one cannot achieve; **bite (on) the bullet** to submit bravely to something unpleasant: to face up to an unpalatable fact or situation; **bite someone's head off** to speak to someone unnecessarily angrily; **bite the dust** to fall, to die; **what's biting you?** what is the matter with you? [O E. bītan.]

bitonal bī-ton'əl, adj using two musical keys simultaneously.—*n* **bitonal'ity.**

bitt bit, (naut.) n. a post for fastening cables (usu. in *pl*).—*v.t.* to fasten round the bitts.—*n.* **bitt'er** the turn of cable round the bitts, hence perhaps **the bitter end**, the end of the rope that remains aboard, and so the last extremity (but perhaps from **bitter** *adj*). [Perh. O N bitt, a cross-beam.]

bitter bit'ər, adj. having a taste like that of quinine or hops. sharp: painful: acrimonious.—*n.* any substance having a bitter taste, esp a type of ale.—*adj.* **bitt'erish**—*adv.* **bitt'erly.**—*n.* **bitt'erness.**—*n.pl.* **bitt'ers** a liquid prepared from bitter herbs or roots, and used as a stomachic.—**bitt'er-app'le** colocynth; **bitt'ersweet'** the woody nightshade, whose stems when chewed taste first bitter, then sweet: a mixture of sweet and bitter (also *fig*).—**a bitter pill to swallow** something which is difficult or unpleasant to accept, as an unwelcome fact, etc ; **the bitter end** see **bitt.** [O.E. biter—bītan, to bite.]

bittern bit'ərn. n a marsh bird of the heron family. [M.E. bittour, botor—O.Fr butor.]

bitty. See **bit.**

bitumen bit'ū-mən, or bi-tū', n. name applied to various inflammable mineral substances, as naphtha, petroleum, asphalt.—*v.t.* **bitū'minate** to mix with or make into bitumen—also **bitū'minise, -ize.**—*n.* **bituminisa'tion, -z-.**—*adj.* **bitū'minous** impregnated with bitumen—**bituminous coal** coal that flames in burning, from richness in volatile hydrocarbons. [L btūmen, -inis.]

bivalent bi-vā'lənt or biv'ə-lənt, adj. having a valency of two (*chem.*): pertaining to one of a pair of homologous chromosomes (also *n.*).—*ns.* **bivalence, bivalency.** [L. bi-, twice, and **-valent.**]

bivalve bi'valv, n. an animal having a shell in two valves or parts, like the oyster: a seed vessel of like kind —*adj.* having two valves. [L. bi-, twice, valva, a door-leaf.]

bivouac biv'ōō-ak, n. the resting at night of soldiers (or others) in the open air. instead of under cover in camp. —*v.i.* to pass the night in the open air:—*pr.p.* **biv'ouacking;** *pa p* **biv'ouacked.**—Also (*slang*) *n.* and *v* **bivv'y.** [Fr ,—Ger. Beiwacht, additional watch.]

bi-weekly *bī-wēk'li, adj.* occurring or appearing once in two weeks or twice a week.—Also *adv.—n.* a periodical issued twice a week

biz *biz.* Slang for **business.**

bizarre *bi-zär', adj.* odd: fantastic: extravagant. [Fr., —Sp. *bizarro,* gallant, brave.]

bizcacha. See **viscacha.**

biz(z)azz. See **bez(z)azz.**

blab *blab, v.i.* to talk much: to tell tales.—*v.t.* to let out (a secret):—*pr.p.* **blabb'ing;** *pa.p.* **blabbed.**—*n.* a tattler: tattling.—*ns.* **blabb'er,** **blabber'mouth.**—*n.* and *adj.* **blabb'ing.** [M E. *blabbe.*]

black *blak, adj.* of the darkest colour: reflecting no light: obscure: dismal: sullen: horrible: dusky: foul, dirty: malignant: dark-haired: wearing dark armour or clothes: illicit: under trade-union ban: Negro, of African, West Indian descent (often *offensive*: acceptable in the U.S., S. Africa): coloured, of mixed descent (esp. *S.Afr.*): (of an area or state) inhabited or controlled by a Negro population.—*n.* black colour or absence of colour: a Negro, a person of African, West Indian, etc , descent (often *offensive*: acceptable in U.S. and S. Africa): a black pigment: a smut: smut fungus: black clothes.—*v.t.* to make black: to soil or stain: to put under trade-union ban. —*v.t.* **black'en** to make black: to defame.—*v.i.* to become black.—*n.* **black'ing** a substance used for blacking leather, etc.—*adj.* **black'ish**—*n.* **black'ness.** —*adj.* **black'-and-blue'** livid in colour because of bruising.—**Black'-and-Tan'** an auxiliary policeman in Ireland, about 1920 (from his khaki uniform with black cap and armlet).—*adj.* **black'-and-white'** partly black, partly white: drawing or drawn in black on a white ground: not in colour (*TV*): consisting of extremes, not admitting any middle ground.—**black art** magic.—*v.t.* **black'ball** to vote against by putting a black ball into a ballot-box: to ostracise: to vote against, veto.—**black'balling; black'-bee'tle** a cockroach; **black belt** a belt showing the highest grade of proficiency in judo; **black'bird** a black species of thrush: a grackle or other bird of the *Icteridae* (*U.S.*): a Negro or Polynesian recruited or kidnapped for labour; **black'birder** a person or ship engaged in slave-trading; **black'board** a board painted black, for writing on.—**black body** one that absorbs all incident radiation, reflecting none; **black book** a book recording the names of persons deserving punishment; **black bottom** an American dance of late 1920s; **black box** a type of seismograph for registering underground explosions: a unit of electronic equipment in package form which records all the flight details in an aircraft: a closed experimental unit which can only be studied by comparing input with output; **black bread** rye-bread.—*adj.* **black'-browed'** sullen.—**black'buck** the common Indian antelope; **black'cap** a warbler with a black crown; **black cap** the cap put on by English judges to pronounce sentence of death (*hist.*); **black'cock** the male of the **black'-grouse** or **black'game,** a species of grouse, common in the north of England and in Scotland:—*fem.* **grey's hen; black coffee** coffee without milk or cream; **black comedy** a play in which, under fantasy and grotesque humour, the hopeless world of reality is clearly seen: also a comedy about dreadful events; **Black Country** the industrial Midland counties of England; **black'curr'ant** the small black berry of a garden shrub of the gooseberry genus; **black death** (also with *caps.*) a deadly epidemic of bubonic plague that swept over Asia and Europe, reaching England in 1348; **black diamond** same as **carbonado:** (in *pl.*) coal; **black economy** unofficial economic activity involving black money (q.v.) or payment in kind; **black eye** an eye of which the iris is dark: a discoloration around the eye

due to a blow or fall.—*adj.* **black'-faced.**—**black'-fellow** an Australian aboriginal; **black flag** the flag of a irate: that waved to call a driver in from a racing circuit; **black fly** an aphid that infests beans, etc : any of several black-bodied insects; **Black'foot** a member of a tribe of Algonquin American Indians.—*pl.* **-foot** or **-feet.**—Also *adj* —**black'-fox'** the pekan; **Black Friar** (also without *caps.*) a Dominican, from his black mantle (over a white woollen habit); **black Friday** Good Friday: an unlucky Friday (*orig. hist.*); **black'game, blackgrouse** see **blackcock; black gold** (*coll.*) oil; **blackguard** (*blag'ärd*) originally applied to the lowest menials about a court, who took charge of the pots, kettles, etc.: a contemptible scoundrel.— Also *adj.—v.t.* to vituperate.—*adj* and *adv.* **black'-guardly.**—**black'head** a comedo.—*adj.* **black'-headed** having a black head.—*adj.* **black-heart'ed** of an evil disposition.—**black hole** a field of such strong gravitational pull that matter and energy cannot escape from it, presumed to exist wherever a star has collapsed (*astron.*); **black ice** a thin layer of transparent ice on a road; **black'jack** vingt-et-un, or a game like it; **black'lead** a black mineral (plumbago, not lead) used in making pencils, etc.; **black'leg** a worker continuing to work during a strike or one taking a striker's place.—*v.i.* to work as a blackleg.— **black letter** the Old English (also called Gothic) type (𝔅𝔩𝔞𝔠𝔨-𝔩𝔢𝔱𝔱𝔢𝔯); **black light** invisible infrared or ultraviolet light, **black'list** a list of defaulters or persons against whom a warning is necessary, or who are liable to loss of employment or lack of full recognition because of their (usu. political) views.—*v.t.* **black'list** to put on a blacklist.—**black'list'ing; black lung** a lung disease of miners, pneumoconiosis: **black'mail** hush-money extorted under threat of, exposure, often baseless.—*v.t.* to extort money from (a person): to force by threats (into doing something).—**black'mailer; black Maria** a prison van; **black market** surreptitious trade in rationed goods: buying and selling that is against the law or official regulations (e.g. illegal traffic in drugs); **black'-marketeer'; black mass** a travesty of the mass in diabolism or devil-worship; **black money** income not reported for tax purposes, **Black Monk** a Benedictine (also without *caps.*); **black nationalism** a movement aimed at increasing Negro self-determination and reducing White influence in all areas with a Negro population; **black nationalist; black'out** total extinction or concealment of lights: sudden loss of consciousness, or failure of the mind to work: a complete stoppage or suppression (of news, communications, etc.).—*adj.* for blacking out with.—**black paper** an unofficial document similar in form to a government white paper, criticising official policy; **Black Pope** (*disparagingly*) the head of the Jesuits; **Black Power** (also without *caps.*) a militant movement to increase Negro influence, esp. in predominantly white countries; **black'-pudd'ing** a blood-pudding (q v.); **Black Rod** the usher of the chapter of the Garter and of the House of Lords; **black sheep** a disreputable member of a family or group; **Black'shirt** a member of a Fascist organisation, esp. in the Nazi SS and in Italy during World War II; **black'smith** a smith who works in iron; **black spot** name given to disease of various plants, e.g. roses· a small area which has bad conditions or a bad record; **black swan** a swan with black plumage and red beak native to Australia; **black'thorn** a dark-coloured thorn bearing sloes; **black velvet** champagne and stout; **Black Watch** see **watch; black widow** a very venomous American and Far Eastern spider, the female with a black body and the habit of eating her mate.—**black in the face** purple through strangulation, passion, or effort; **black out** to obliterate with black: to extinguish or cover all lights: suddenly to lose consciousness: to suppress (news or radio communication), **in black and white** in writing or in print: in art, etc. in no colours but black and white. **in someone's black books,** having incurred someone's displeasure; **in the black** solvent, out of debt: making a profit. [O.E. *blæc*, black.]

bladder *blad'ər*, *n.* a thin distended or distensible bag. any such bag in the animal body, esp. the receptacle for urine.—*adjs.* **bladd'ered, bladd'ery**—**bladd'er-worm** the asexual state of a tapeworm or cestode; **bladd'er-wrack** a common brown seaweed with bladders. [O E *blǣdre*—*blāwan*, to blow.]

blade *blād*, *n.* the flat or expanded part of a leaf or petal, esp. a leaf of grass or corn: the cutting part of a knife, sword, etc.: the flat part of an oar: the paddle-like part of a propeller: the free outer part of the tongue· a dashing fellow.—*adj.* **blad'ed**—**blade'bone** the flat bone at the back of the shoulder, the scapula. [O.E. *blæd*.]

blah *bla*, (*slang*) *n* bunkum. pretentious nonsense.—Also **blah'-blah'**.—*adj.* **blah** (*slang*) dull, insipid.

blain *blān*, *n* a boil or blister. [O.E. *blegen*.]

blame *blām*, *v.t.* to find fault with: to censure: to impute fault to: to charge with being cause.—*n.* imputation of a fault: culpability: responsibility for what is amiss.—*adj.* **blā'mable, blame'able**.—*n.* **blā'mableness, blame'ableness**—*adv.* **blā'mably, blame'ably**—*adjs.* **blamed** (*U.S. slang*) damned, confounded (also *adv.*); **blame'ful** meriting blame.—*adv.* **blame'fully**.—*n.* **blame'fulness**.—*adj.* **blame'less** without blame: guiltless: innocent.—*adv.* **blame'lessly**.—*adj.* **blame'worthy** worthy of blame: culpable.—**be to blame** to be blameworthy as being the cause. [Fr. *blâmer*, O.Fr. *blasmer*—Gr. *blasphēmeein*, to speak ill; see **blaspheme**.]

blanch *blänch, blansh, v.t.* to whiten: to immerse (fruit, vegetables, etc.) briefly in boiling water (*cook.*).—*v.i.* to grow white. [Fr. *blanchir*—*blanc*, white.]

blancmange *blə-mäzh'*, -*monzh'*, *n.* a milk dessert thickened with cornflour or gelatine and set in a mould. [Fr. *blancmanger*—*blanc*, white, *manger*, food.]

blanco *blangk'ō*, (*mil.*) *n.* an opaque white, khaki, etc. substance for treating uniform belts, etc.—*v.t.* to treat with blanco. [*Blanco*, a trademark—Fr *blanc*, white.]

bland *bland*, *adj.* smooth: gentle: mild: polite, suave: ironical.—*adv.* **bland'ly**.—*n.* **bland'ness**. [L. *blandus*.]

blandish *bland'ish*, *v.t.* to flatter and coax, to cajole —*n.* **bland'ishment**. [Fr. *blandir, blandiss*-, from L *blandīri*.]

blank *blangk*, *adj.* without writing or marks, as white paper: empty: featureless: expressionless: nonplussed: sheer: unrhymed.—*n* a paper without writing: a lottery-ticket that brings no prize: an empty space, a void or vacancy: the white mark in the centre of a target (*archery*): a form of document having blank spaces to be filled up (*arch.* except in *U.S.*): a roughly shaped piece to be fashioned into a manufactured article: a dash in place of an omitted word: a blank cartridge.—*v.t.* to make blank: to make pale —*adv.* **blank'ly**.—*n.* **blank'ness**.—**blank cartridge** one without a bullet; **blank cheque** a signed cheque in which the sum is not filled in: complete freedom to act as one thinks best (*fig.*); **blank verse** unrhymed verse esp. of five feet. [Fr. *blanc*.]

blanket *blangk'it*, *n.* a covering, generally woollen, for a bed, etc.: a covering generally: fertile material put round a nuclear reactor core to breed new fuel.—*v.t.* to cover, obstruct, or extinguish with, or as with, a

blanket (as a ship by taking the wind out of her sails, gun-fire by getting in the way).—*adj.* applying generally or covering all cases.—*n.* **blank'eting** cloth for blankets.—**blanket bath** the washing of a sick person in bed; **blanket stitch** a stitch used for the edge of a blanket —**on the wrong side of the blanket** illegitimately; **wet blanket** a damper of spirits: a killjoy. [O.Fr. *blankete*, dim. of *blanc*, white.]

blanquette *blä-ket*, (Fr.) *n.* a ragout made with a white sauce.

blare *blār*, *v* i. to roar: to sound loudly, usu. harshly, as a trumpet —*n.* roar: noise. [M.E. *blaren*.]

blarney *blär'ni*, *n.* flattery or cajoling talk.—*v.t.* to cajole. [*Blarney* Castle, near Cork, where a stone difficult to reach confers the gift of persuasive talk on those who kiss it.]

blasé *bla'zā*, *adj.* dulled to pleasures: surfeited with enjoyments. [Fr. *pa.p.* of *blaser*, to cloy.]

blaspheme *blas-fēm'*, *v.t.* to speak impiously of —*v.i* to speak profanely or impiously: to curse and swear. —*n.* **blasphem'er**.—*adj.* **blasphemous** (*blas'fi-məs*). —*adv.* **blas'phemously**.—*n.* **blas'phemy** impious or profane speaking: contempt or indignity offered to God. [Gr. *blasphēmiā*; see **blame**.]

blast *blast*, *n.* a blowing or gust of wind: a forcible stream of air: a sound of a wind instrument: an explosion or detonation: any scorching, withering or pernicious influence: a blight.—*v.i.* to emit blasts, blow: to use explosives: to curse.—*v.t.* to blow up: to rend asunder with an explosive: to blow into: to strike with a blast: to blight, wither, scorch: to strike with a curse.—*adj.* **blast'ed**.—*n.* **blast'er**.—*n.* and *adj.* **blast'ing**—**blast'-furnace** a smelting furnace into which hot air is blown; **blast'-furnaceman; blast'-off** the (moment of) launching of a rocket-propelled missile or space capsule (*v.t.* and *v.i.* **blast off**).—**in, at, full blast** in a state of maximum activity. [O.E *blǣst*.]

blasto- *blas'tō-*, in composition, sprout, bud, germ.—*ns.* **blas'tocyst** the blastula in mammals.—*ns.* **blas'-tomere** (Gr. *meros*, part) a cell formed in an early stage of the cleavage of a fertilised ovum, **blas'tosphere** (Gr. *sphaira*, a sphere) a blastula; **blas'tūla** a hollow sphere of cells, one cell thick, formed in the cleavage of a fertilised ovum.—*adj.* **blast'ūlar**. —*n.* **blastula'tion**. [Gr. *blastos*, a sprout.]

blatant *blā'tənt*, *adj.* clamorous: calumniously clamorous: egregiously vulgar: (loosely) flagrant.—*adv.* **blat'antly**. [Prob. a coinage of Spenser.]

blather. See blether.

blaubok *blow'bok*, *Afrik.* **bloubok** *blō'bok*, *n.* a small South African antelope: also a large extinct species. [Du. *blauw*, blue, *bok*, goat.]

blaze¹ *blāz*, *n.* a rush of light or of flame: an area of brilliant light or colour: a bursting out or active display.—*v.i.* to burn with a strong flame: to throw out a brilliant light: to be furious (*coll.*).—*n.* **blaz'er** a light sporting jacket, originally bright-coloured.—*n.pl.* **blaz'es** the fires of hell, in imprecations like to **blazes;** also like **blazes** with fury.—**blaze away** to fire a rapid and repeated stream of bullets: to work very hard (*coll.*); **blaze up** to burst into flames: to become furious (*coll.*). [O.E. *blæse*, torch.]

blaze² *blāz*, *n.* a white mark on a beast's face: a mark on a tree made by chipping the bark or otherwise.—*v.t.* to mark (a tree or a track) with a blaze.—**blaze the trail** to show the way as a pioneer. [Perh. Du. *bles* or O.N. *blesi*; or **blaze¹**.]

blaze³ *blāz*, *v.t.* to proclaim, to spread abroad. [Connected with O.N. *blāsa*, to blow, confused with **blazon**.]

blazer. See blaze¹.

blazon *blā'zn*, *v.t* to make public: to display

ostentatiously: to depict or to explain in heraldic terms (her.).—n. a coat-of-arms, heraldic bearings (also fig.): the science or rules of coats-of-arms —ns. **blaz'oner** one who blazons: a herald: a slanderer; **blaz'onry** the art of drawing or of deciphering coats-of-arms: heraldry. [Fr. blason, a shield, confused with **blaze**³.]

bleach blēch, v.t. to make pale or white: to whiten, as textile fabrics.—v.i. to grow white.—n. a process or act of bleaching: a bleaching agent.—n. **bleach'er**.—n. and adj. **bleach'ing.—bleaching powder** a compound of calcium, chlorine, and oxygen (CaOCl₂). [O.E. blǣcan.]

bleak¹ blēk, adj. colourless: dull and cheerless: cold, unsheltered.—adv. **bleak'ly.**—n. **bleak'ness.** [Apparently O.N. bleikr, answering to O.E. blǣc, blāc, pale, shining, black; cf. **bleach**.]

bleak² blēk, n. a small white river-fish. [O.N. bleikja, or a lost equivalent O.E. word]

blear blēr, adj. dim, watery: blurred as with inflammation.—v.t. to dim: to blur: to dim the sight of: to hoodwink.—adj. **bleared.**—n. **blear'iness.**—adj. **blear'y.**—adj. **blear'eyed, blear'y-eyed.** [Cf. Ger. Blerr, soreness of the eyes.]

bleat blēt, v.i. to cry like a sheep: to complain, grumble: to talk nonsense —n a sheep's cry or similar quavering sound: a complaint, grumble.—n. and adj. **bleat'ing.** [O.E. blǣan; imit.]

bleb bleb, n. a transparent blister of the cuticle: a bubble, as in water. [Prob. imit.]

bled bled, pa.t. and pa.p. of **bleed**.

bleed blēd, v.i. to lose blood or sap: to issue forth or drop as blood. to have money, etc., extorted from one: to feel great pity (fig.).—v.t. to draw blood from, esp. surgically: to draw sap from: to extort from: (in bookbinding) to trim so as to encroach on letterpress or illustrations: to draw off (air) from a hydraulic braking system, or (liquid or gas) from other closed system or holder:—pa.t. and pa.p. **bled**. —ns. **bleed'er** one who bleeds: a (nasty) person (slang); **bleed'ing** a discharge of blood or sap: letting blood: diffusion or running of colouring matter.— adj. full of compassion: emitting sap: bloody (Shak., coll.).—**bleeding heart** a name given to various plants of the genera Dicentra, Colocasia, etc.: a contemptuous name for a do-gooder.—**bleed like a pig** to bleed copiously. [O.E. blēdan. See **blood**.]

bleep blēp, v i. to give out a high sound or radio signal. —n. such a sound or signal: a bleeper—n. **bleep'er** a detecting device that bleeps on receiving a certain radio or other signal: such a device, carried on the person by e.g. a doctor, policeman, etc., by which he can be contacted. [Imit.]

blemish blem'ish, n. a stain or defect. reproach.—v t to mark with any deformity: to tarnish: to defame [O.Fr. blesmir, blemir, to stain, of dubious origin]

blench blench, blensh, v.i. to shrink or start back: to flinch. [O.E. blencan.]

blend blend, v.t. to mix together, esp. intimately or harmoniously.—v i. to be mingled: to harmonise: to shade off.—n. a mixture.—ns. **blend'er; blend'ing**. [M.E. blenden; cf. O.E. blandan, O.N. blanda.]

blende blend, n. a mineral, zinc sulphide [Ger. Blende—blenden, to deceive, from its resemblance to galena.]

blenny blen'i, n. member of the genus Blennius of fishes, usually slimy. [Gr. blennos, mucus]

blepharism blef'ər-izm, n spasm of the eyelid —n **blephari'tis** inflammation of the eyelid. [Gr. blepharon, eyelid.]

blesbok bles'bok, n. a South African antelope with a blazed forehead [Du bles, blaze, bok, goat.]

bless bles, v.t. to consecrate. to make the sign of the

cross over: to extol as holy, to pronounce holy or happy: to invoke divine favour upon: to wish happiness to: to make joyous, happy, or prosperous: to glorify: to approve officially.—pa.p. **blessed** (blest), or **blest.**—adj. **bless'ed, blest** happy: prosperous: in heaven: beatified: (euphemistically) accursed, confounded.—adv. **bless'edly.**—ns. **bless'edness; bless'ing** a wish or prayer for happiness or success: any means or cause of happiness: a gift or present (B.): a form of invoking the favour of God at a meal: official approval.—**blessed sacrament** the consecrated Host.—**be blessed with** to have the good fortune to possess; a **blessing in disguise** something proving unexpectedly advantageous. [O.E. blēdsian, blētsian, bletsian, to bless, prob. from blōd, blood.]

blest blest, pa.p. of **bless**.—Also adj.

blether (Scot.) bledh'ər, **blather** (U.S. and dial.) bladh'ər, vs.i. to talk garrulous nonsense.—n. one who blethers: (often in pl.) fluent, garrulous nonsense.—n. and adj. **bleth'ering.** [M.E. blather— O.N. blathra, talk, foolishly, blathr, nonsense.]

blew blōō, pa.t. of **blow**.

blewits blū'its, n. a kind of edible mushroom, bluish in part. [Perh. from **blue**.]

blight blīt, n. a disease in plants which blasts or withers them: a cause of blight: anything that injures, destroys, depresses, or frustrates: a damp, depression, decay, set-back, check.—v.t. to affect with blight: to blast: to frustrate.—adj. **blight'ed** affected with blight: of a (usu. urban) area, becoming a slum.—n. **blight'er** a cause of blighting: a term of (usu. playful) abuse, scamp, beggar, wretch (slang).—n. and adj. **blight'ing.—planning blight** a fall in value, and consequent neglect, of property in an area, caused by uncertainty about its planned future.

blighty blī'ti, (mil. slang) n. home: the home country: a wound necessitating return home. [Hind. bilāyati, foreign, European—Ar. wilāyat province, country.]

blimey, blimy blī'mi, interj. a Cockney vulgarism for God blind me.

blimp blimp, n a small type of airship for scouting, advertising, etc.. an incurably conservative elderly military officer, as Colonel Blimp of the cartoonist David Low (1891–1963), or any other person of similar views: soundproof housing for sound-film camera. —adj. **blimp'ish** like Colonel Blimp

blimy. See **blimey**.

blind blīnd, adj without sight: dark: obscure: invisible: concealed: not directed, or affording no possibility of direction, by sight or by foresight: ignorant or undiscerning: unobserving: voluntarily overlooking: without an opening: in flying, using instruments only, without seeing course or receiving radio directions· drunk (coll.).—n. something intended to blind one to the facts: a window-screen: a shade: a stake put up without seeing one's cards (poker).—v.t. to make blind: to darken, obscure, or deceive: to dazzle: to render matt.—v.i. to curse, swear (slang). —adj. **blind'ed** deprived of sight without intellectual discernment —n. **blind'er** one who or that which blinds. a horse's blinker.—n. and adj. **blind'ing.**— adv. **blind'ly.**—n **blind'ness.—blind'-all'ey** a cul-de-sac. a situation, job, etc., which does not offer any prospect of improvement or advancement (also adj.), **blind'-coal** anthracite (as burning without flame): coal partly carbonised by an igneous intrusion; **blind date** an appointment with someone one has not seen: the partner, etc , so chosen —adj. **blind'-drunk'** so drunk as to be like a blind man.—adj **blind'fold** having the eyes bandaged so as not to see.—Also n and adv —v t. to cover the eyes of —**blind'-gut** the caecum; **blind'man's-buff'** a game in which a blindfold player tries to catch the others; **blind-side** the side on which a person is blind to danger: weak point: (*usu.* **blind side**) the part of the field between the scrum, etc. and the touch-line nearer it (*rugby*); **blind spot** the spot on the retina where the optic nerve joins and where there are no visual cells: a region of understanding in which one's intuition and judgment always fail; **blind'worm** a slow-worm.—**not a blind bit** of (*coll.*) not any; **the blind leading the blind** the ignorant trying to instruct the ignorant. [O.E. *blind.*]

blink *blingk*, *v.i.* to glance, twinkle, or wink: to see obscurely: to look with the eyes half-closed: to shine unsteadily.—*v.t.* to shut out of sight: to ignore or evade.—*n.* a glimpse, glance, or wink: a gleam, esp momentary —*n.* **blink'er** a leather flap to prevent a horse from seeing sidewise.—*v.t.* to obscure or limit the vision of (*lit.* and *fig.*).—*adj.* or intensive *adv* **blink'ing** (*slang*) used to add force or emphasis, prob as a substitute for bloody.—**on the blink** (of electrical or electronic device) (going) out of order. [Cf blench.]

blintz(e) *blints*, **blin(i)** *blin, blin'i*, *ns.* a thin filled pancake. [Yiddish *blintse*—Russ. *blin*, pancake.]

blip *blip*, *n.* the image of an object on a radar screen, usu. a bright spot or sudden sharp peak on a line: the small, high sound made by a radar instrument —*v.i.* to produce a blip.

bliss *blis*, *n.* the highest happiness: the special happiness of heaven.—*adj.* **bliss'ful**.—*adv.* **bliss'fully**.—*n.* **bliss'fulness**. [O E. *bliths—blithe*, blithe.]

blister *blis'tər*, *n.* a thin bubble or bladder on the skin, often containing watery matter: a similar spot elsewhere, as on a leaf, metal, paint.—*v.t* to raise a blister or blisters on: to burn with scathing words (*fig.*).—*v.i.* to develop blisters.—*adjs.* **blis'tery** **blis'tering** of criticism, virulent, cruel (*fig.*): painfully intense or strenuous: of the weather, very hot — **blister card, pack** a bubble pack [M.E.; most prob O.Fr. *blestre*, conn. with O N. *blástr, blása,* to blow, Ger. *Blase.*]

blithe *blīdh,* *adj.* jocund: cheerful: gay: sprightly.— *adv.* **blithe'ly**.—*n.* **blithe'ness**.—*adv.* **blithe'some** joyous. [O.E. *blithe*, joyful. See **bliss**.]

blither *blīdh'ər*, *v.i.* another form of **blather, blether**. —*adj.* **blith'ering** (used as an expression of contempt).

blitz *blits*, *n* an attack or bombing from the air: any sudden, overwhelming attack (also **blitzkrieg** *blits'krēg*).—*v.t.* to attack or damage by air-raid. [Ger *Blitzkrieg*, lightning war, the German method in 1939—*Blitz*, lightning, *Krieg*, war.]

blizzard *bliz'ərd*, *n.* a blinding storm of wind and snow [A modern coinage.]

bloat *blōt*, *v.t.* to swell or puff out.—*v.t.* to swell or dilate: to grow turgid.—*n.* hoove (also **bloat'ing**) **bloatedness**: a drunkard.—*adj.* **bloat'ed** having been bloated: swollen (often as a result of gluttony): swollen with riches (*fig.*).—*n.* **bloat'er** a herring partially dried in smoke, esp. at Yarmouth [Cf. O.N. *blautr*, soft.]

blob *blob*, *n.* a drop or globule: anything soft and round, as a gooseberry: a round spot: zero [limit.]

bloc *blok*, *n.* a combination of parties, nations, or other units to achieve a common purpose [Fr.]

block *blok*, *n.* a mass of wood or stone, etc, usu flat-sided: a piece of wood or other material used as a support, or as a mould, or for printing from or as a toy: (in *pl.*) starting-blocks: a pulley with its framework or the framework alone: a compact mass, group or set: a group of buildings forming a square-shaped mass, bounded by intersecting streets. an

obstruction: a head· a blockhead. an impassive person: a psychological barrier preventing intellectual development, progress, etc.: an instance of, or a cause of, blockage or blocking: a bloc —*adj.* in a block or lump: comprising a number grouped and dealt with together.—*v.t* to enclose or shut up: to restrict: to obstruct:·to make inactive· to shape as on a block, or to sketch out roughly (often with *in* or *out*): to stop (a ball) with bat resting upright on the ground: to print (usu a fabric) from a block.—*n* **blockade'** cutting a place off by surrounding it with troops or by ships. obstruction.—*v.t* to block up by troops or ships —*ns* **block'age** act or instance of obstructing, or state of being obstructed; **block'er** (*med*) a substance, used as a drug, that prevents the production, or the operation, of some other substance in the body, **block'ing** interruption of a train of thought, esp. by unpleasant thoughts rising in the mind.— **block'board** board made up of plywood veneer enclosing thin strips of wood; **block'buster** a bomb or explosive charge able to destroy a number of buildings simultaneously: a thing or person notably forceful, effective and overwhelming (also *adj.*), **block'busting**.—Also *adj.*—**block capital** a capital letter written in imitation of type; **block grant** a fixed general grant made by the central government to a local authority for all its services; **block'head** a dolt; **block'house** a small temporary fort, **block letter** a block capital: block type; **block release** release from employment for a period in order to complete a course of study; **block type** a heavy-letter type, without serifs; **block vote** a vote by a delegate at a conference, counted as the number of people he represents —**on the block** up for auction [Fr. *bloc,* probably Gmc]

bloke *blōk*, *n.* a man (*slang*): the commander (*naut.*).

blond (*fem* **blonde**) *blond*, *n.* a person of fair complexion and light-coloured hair—opp. to *brunet(te)*.—*adj.* (of hair) between golden and light chestnut in colour: of a fair complexion: fair. [Fr.]

blood *blud*, *n.* the oxygenating fluid (red in the higher animals) circulating in the body: descent, good birth: relationship, kindred: (elliptically) a blood-horse, one of good pedigree· a swaggering dandy about town: the blood-royal (as in *princes of the blood*): temperament: bloodshed or murder: the supposed seat of passion—hence temper, anger (as *his blood is up*), etc.—*v.i.* to bleed: to smear with blood: to initiate into blood sports or to war (also *fig.*) —*adj.* **blood'ed** having blood: of pure blood, pedigreed: initiated.—*adj.* **blood'ily**.—*adj.* **blood'less** without blood: dead: anaemic: without bloodshed.—*n* **blood'lessness**.—*adj.* **blood'y** of the nature of blood: stained with blood: murderous, cruel.—as an *adj* emphasising anger or the like, or almost meaningless, as an *adv.* employed as an intensive (*coll.*) —*v.t.* to make bloody.—**blood agar** agar-agar for growing bacteria, to which blood has been added before the jelly set —*adj.* **blood'-and-thund'er** sensational, melodramatic.—**blood bank** a supply of blood plasma, or the place where it is kept; **blood'-bath** a massacre (also *fig.*); **blood'-brother** a brother by blood: among primitive peoples, one who has entered a close and binding friendship with another by ceremonies involving the mixing of blood; **blood count** the number of red or white corpuscles in the blood.—*adj* **blood'curdling** exciting horror with a physical feeling as if the blood had curdled.—**blood donor** one who gives blood for use in transfusion; **blood'-group** any one of the four types of human blood (designated O, A, B, AB); **blood'heat** the temperature of human blood (37°C, about 98°F); **blood'- horse** a horse of the purest and most highly prized blood, origin, or stock; **blood'hound** a large, keen-scented (sleuth) hound, noted for its powers of tracing: a detective (*fig.*); **blood'letting** bleeding by opening a vein: bloodshed; **blood'lust** desire for bloodshed; **blood'-money** money earned by laying or supporting a capital charge against anyone, esp. if the charge be false or made by an accomplice: money paid to a hired assassin: compensation formerly paid to the next of kin of a victim slain; **blood orange** a variety of orange with red or red-streaked pulp; **blood'-plate** a platelet; **blood'-poisoning** a name popularly, but loosely, used of pyaemia and allied diseases; **blood pressure** the pressure of the blood on the walls of the blood-vessels, varying with age and physical condition; **blood'-pudding** a pudding made with blood and other materials; **blood'-rela'tion** one related by common ancestry; **blood-roy'al** royal descent; **blood'shed** the shedding of blood: slaughter.—*adjs.* **blood'shot** (of the eye) red or inflamed with blood.— **blood'-spav'in** a disease of horses consisting of the swelling of a vein on the inside of the hock, from a checking of the blood; **blood sports** those involving the killing of animals—fox-hunting and the like; **blood'stain.**—*adj.* **blood'stained** stained with blood: guilty of murder.—**blood'stock** pedigree horses collectively; **blood'stone** a green chalcedony with blood-like spots of red jasper: haematite; **blood'stream** the blood flowing through the body: something playing a similarly vital part (*fig.*); **blood'sucker** an animal that sucks blood, esp. a leech: an extortioner: one who sponges upon another; **blood test** an examination of a small specimen of blood, **blood'thirstiness** eager desire to shed blood.—*adj.* **blood'thirsty.**—**blood transfusion** transfer of blood taken from the veins of one person to those of another; **blood'-vessel** a vein or artery; **bloody Mary** a cocktail consisting of vodka, tomato juice and seasoning.—*adj.* **blood'y-mind'ed** liking bloodshed, cruel: in a mood of, or inclined to show, aggressive obstinacy.—**blood'y-mind'edness.**—**after, out for (someone's) blood** having murderous intentions (towards someone) (*lit.* and *fig.*); **first blood** the first drawing of blood in a fight (also *fig.*); **fresh** or **new blood** new members in any association of people, to add liveliness; **in hot** or **cold blood** under or free from excitement or sudden passion; **in one's blood** in one's character, inborn; **make someone's blood boil** to arouse someone's fury. [O.E. *blōd.*]

bloom[1] *blōōm, n.* a blossom or flower (also collectively): the state of being in flower: the prime or highest perfection of anything: the first freshness of beauty of anything: rosy colour: the glow on the cheek: a powdery, waxy, or cloudy surface or appearance: an efflorescence.—*v.t.* to put forth blossoms: to flower: to be in a state of beauty or vigour: to flourish.—*v.t.* to give a bloom to.—*n.* **bloom'er** an absurd and embarrassing blunder (*slang*).—*adj.* **bloom'ing** flowering: flourishing: fresh and youthful: bright: euphemistically for bloody (*slang*). [O.N. *blóm*]

bloom[2] *blōōm, n.* a mass or bar of iron or steel in an intermediate stage of manufacture. [O.E. *blōma.*]

bloomer *blōōm'ər, n.* and *adj.* a dress for women, devised by Mrs *Bloomer* of New York about 1849, with a skirt falling a little below the knee, and Turkish trousers: (in *pl.*) bloomer trousers: (in *pl.*) a loose undergarment similar to knickers, but fuller

blossom *blos'əm, n.* a flower or bloom, esp. one that precedes edible fruit: the state of being in flower, literally or figuratively.—*v.t.* (often with *out*) to put forth blossoms or flowers: to flourish and prosper.— *n.* **bloss'oming.**—*adj.* **bloss'omy** covered with flowers, flowery. [O.E *blōstm, blōstma*]

blot[1] *blot, n.* a spot, as of a drop of ink: an obliteration·

a stain in reputation: a blemish.—*v.t.* to obliterate, destroy (with *out*): to spot or smudge: to disgrace: to blemish: to dry with blotting-paper:—*pr.p.* **blott'ing;** *pa.t.* and *pa.p.* **blott'ed.**—*ns.* **blott'er** one who blots: a sheet, pad, or book of blotting-paper.—Also *adj.*— *n.* **blott'ing.**—*adjs.* **blott'o** (*slang*) helplessly drunk; **blott'y** blotted: smudged —**blott'ing-paper** unsized paper, used for absorbing ink —**blot one's copybook** to blemish one's record, esp by an indiscretion

blot[2] *blot, n.* a piece liable to be taken at backgammon: exposure of a piece: a weak place in anything. [Cf. Dan. *blot,* Du. *bloot,* naked, exposed.]

blotch *bloch, n.* an irregular discoloration: a pustule: any plant disease characterised by blotching.—*v.t* to mark or cover with blotches —*adj* **blotched.**—*n.* **blotch'iness.**—*n.* and *adj.* **blotch'ing.**—*adj.* **blotch'y.** [Prob formed on **blot**[1].]

bloubok. See **blaubok.**

blouse *blowz, n* a loose sack-like, belted outer garment, like the smock-frock: a woman's usu. loose-fitting garment for the upper part of the body —*v.t.* to arrange in loose folds. [Fr.]

blouson *blōō'zon, n* a loose outer garment fastened at the waist by a belt, drawstring, etc. [Fr.]

blow[1] *blō, n* a stroke or knock. a sudden misfortune or calamity.—*adj.* **blow'-by-blow** of a story or description, very detailed.—**at a blow** by a single action, suddenly, **come to blows** (of people quarrelling) to start fighting [Found from the 15th century; perh. from **blow**[2] or conn. with Ger. *blàuen,* to beat.]

blow[2] *blō, v.i.* to produce a current of air: to move, as air or wind (often *impers.*): to breathe hard: to spout, as whales: to boast: (of insects) to deposit eggs: of an electric fuse, to melt (also *v.t.*).—*v.t.* to drive air upon or into: to drive by a current of air: to sound, as a wind-instrument: to destroy or force by explosive: to spread by report: to inform upon: to fan or kindle: (of insects) to deposit eggs on: to curse: to squander (*slang*):—*pa.t.* **blew** (*blōō*); *pa p.* **blown** (*blōn*), in imprecations **blowed** (*blōd*).—*n.* a blast. an insect egg.—*n.* **blow'er** one who blows: a machine for driving a blast of air: a speaking-tube, telephone, or similar means of sending messages (*coll.*): a communication system (*coll.*).—*adjs.* **blown** out of breath, tired: swelled: stale, worthless; **blow'y** windy: gusty.—**blow'down** an accident in a nuclear reactor.—*v.t.* **blow'-dry** to arrange (hair) by simultaneously brushing and drying it with a hand-held hair-drier.—Also *n.*—**blow'fly** a flesh-fly (*Sarcophaga*)· a bluebottle (*Calliphora*); **blow'hole** a whale's nostril· a hole in ice to which seals, etc., come to breathe: a vent for escape of gas, etc.: a natural vent from the roof of a cave up to the ground surface, through which air and water are forced by rising tides; **blow'lamp** a portable lamp producing heat by a blast; **blow'-mould'ing** a process used in fabricating plastic objects, the molten thermoplastic being blown against the sides of the mould; **blow'-out** a feast (*slang*): a tyre burst (*coll.*): a violent escape of oil and gas from an oilwell; **blow'pipe** a pipe through which air is blown on a flame, to increase its heat, used in *blowpipe analysis,* etc.: a long straight tube from which an arrow, pellet, etc., is blown by the breath: a glass-blower's tube; **blow'torch** a blowlamp; **blow'-up** an explosion: an enlargement of (part of) a photograph, illustration, etc.—**blow hot and cold** to be favourable and unfavourable by turns, to be irresolute; **blow in** to turn up casually, **blow it** (*slang*) to lose one's chance of success; **blow off** (steam, etc) to allow to escape, to escape forcibly, **blow one's, someone's, mind** (*slang*) to go, cause to go, into a state of ecstasy under the influence of a drug or of an exhilarating experience; **blow one's top** (*coll*) to explode in

anger, **blow out** to extinguish by blowing: to force
outwards by an explosion of a tyre, to burst (*coll*).
of an oilwell, to emit an uncontrolled jet of oil and
gas, **blow over** to pass away, as a storm, a danger or a
scandal, **blow someone's cover** (*slang*) to reveal someone's identity, **blow the whistle on** (*slang*) to inform
on (a person), **blow up** to destroy by explosion: to
explode to finish in disaster: to inflate: to scold, to
lose one's temper to enlarge, as an illustration
[O E *blāwan*]

blowze, blowse *blowz*, *n*. a ruddy, fat-faced wench —
adjs **blowzed, blowz'y, blowsed, blowsy** fat and
ruddy, or flushed with exercise, dishevelled: coarse,
rowdy [Perh. related to **blush** or **blow**, or of cant
origin.]

blub *blub*, (*coll*) *v i* to weep:—*pr p.* **blubb'ing**; *pa.t*
and *pa p* **blubbed**. [Short for **blubber**.]

blubber *blub'ər*, *n* the fat of whales and other sea
animals excessive fat: a bout of weeping.—*v.t.* to
weep effusively. [M E *blober, bluber*; prob imit.]

bludgeon *bluj'n*, *n.* a short stick with a heavy striking
end —*v t* to beat with a bludgeon. to assail heavily
to coerce (*coll.*)

blue [1] *blōō*, *adj* of the colour of the unclouded sky
livid, greyish dismal depressed. learned, pedantic
indecent or obscene dressed in blue symbolised by
blue —*n* one of the colours of the rainbow: the sky
the sea. a blue pigment. (also **wash'ing-blue**) a blue
powder or liquid (indigo, Prussian blue, etc) used in
laundries a present or past representative of Oxford
or Harrow (dark), Cambridge or Eton (light blue) in
sports a similar representative of any university the
badge awarded to him or her, or the honour of wearing it a butterfly of the family *Lycaenidae*: (in *pl*)
depression: (in *pl.*) slow, sad song orig. American
Negro folksong. characteristically with three four-bar
lines and blue notes, or any similar composition.—
v t to make blue to treat with blue.—*v.t.* to turn
blue —*n* **blu'ish.**—**blue baby** a baby with congenital
cyanosis, **blue'bell** in S. England the wood-hyacinth
(*blōō'bel'*) in Scotland and N. England the harebell,
blue'berry the fruit of *Vaccinium vacillans* and other
American species, **blue'bird** a small American bird
akin to the warblers, **blue blood** aristocratic blood
(Sp. *sangre azul*), **blue book** a report or other paper
printed by parliament (from its blue paper wrapper),
bluebreast see **bluethroat**; **blue'bottle** the blue cornflower. a large fly (*Calliphora*) with metallic blue
abdomen, a blowfly. a policeman or beadle (*slang*),
blue'buck the blaubok, **blue'-cheese** blue-veined
cheese, **blue'-chip'** a term applied to the most reliable
industrial shares, or to anything of high value or pres
tige, **blue'coat** a pupil of Christ's Hospital or other
Bluecoat school, whose garb is a blue coat.—Also
adj.—*adj.* **blue'-coll'ar** relating to manual work or
workers.—**Blue Ensign** a blue flag with the Union
Jack in canton, flown by the Naval Reserve and
certain yachts and merchant vessels; **blue film, blue
movie** a pornographic film, **blue fox** an arctic fox; **blue
funk** (*slang*) great terror; **blue'grass** a slightly glaucous permanent grass (*Poa pratensis*, etc) of Europe
and North America, esp. Kentucky: a simple style of
country music, originating in Kentucky and popular
in the Southern U.S.—**blue ground** a greyish-blue decomposed agglomerate in which diamonds are got.
blue gum species of Eucalyptus, esp *E. globulus,*
blue hare the mountain hare, **blue'jacket** a seaman in
the navy; **blue jay** an American jay (*Cyanocitta
cristata*); **blue John** ornamental fluorspar; **Blue
Mantle** one of the pursuivants of the English Heralds'
College, **blue moon** a very long but quite indeterminate time, **blue mould** a fungus that turns bread,
cheese, etc., blue, **blue movie** see **blue film; blue mur-**

der (*coll.*) extreme activity or commotion; **blue note** a
flattened note, usu third or seventh, characteristic of
the blues —*v t.* **blue-pen'cil** to correct, edit, or
censor (as if) with a blue pencil, the colour traditionally used.—**Blue Peter** a blue flag with a white
rectangle hoisted when a ship is about to sail a call for
trumps in whist; **blue'print** a photographic print,
white upon blue, on paper sensitised with a ferric salt
and potassium ferricyanide from a photographic
negative or a drawing on transparent paper: a preliminary sketch or plan of work to be done, or a guide
or model provided by agreed principles or rules or by
conclusions from earlier experiment.— Also *v.t.*—
blue ribbon, riband the ribbon of the Order of the
Garter. any very high distinction or prize; **blue sheep**
the bharal; **blue'stocking** a learned lady, esp one inclining to pedantry, **blue'throat** or **blue'breast** a bird
akin to the nightingale, **blue tit** a small bird with blue
wings and tail and a blue-topped head; **blue water**
open sea; **blue whale** Sibbald's rorqual, the biggest
living animal.—**blue-eyed boy** a favourite who can do
no wrong; **blue-sky laws** (*U S.*) laws to prevent fraud
in the sale of stocks (against capitalising of the blue
skies); **out of the blue** from the cloudless sky: hence,
entirely unexpectedly: **the Blues** the Royal Horse
Guards, **true blue** a person unswervingly faithful,
esp. to political party of blue persuasion (*adj.* **true'=**
blue) [M E. *blew*—O Fr *bleu*, of Gmc. origin]

blue [2] *blōō*, *v.t* to squander [Prob. for **blow**.]

bluff [1] *bluf*, *adj*. steep or upright in front rough and
hearty in a good-natured way outspoken (of the
shape of a body) such that, when it moves through air
or other fluid, it leaves behind it a large disorderly
wake and experiences a large drag—opp. of *streamlined.—n* a high steep bank.—*adv* **bluff'ly.**—*n.*
bluff'ness. [Perh. Du *blaf* (*obs.*), broad, flat; or
M L.G *blaff*, even, smooth.]

bluff [2] *bluf*, *v.t* or *v i.* to deceive or seek to deceive by
concealment of weakness or show of self-confidence
or threats (orig. in poker to conceal poor cards) —*n*
a bluffing act or behaviour; a horse's blinker —*n*
bluff'er.—call someone's bluff to expose or challenge
someone's bluff [Perh. Du *bluffen*, to brag,
boast.]

blunder *blun'dər*, *v i.* to make a gross mistake: to
flounder about—*v t.* to utter thoughtlessly: to
mismanage, bungle: to achieve, put, render, by
blundering.—*n.* a gross mistake.—*n.* **blun'derer.—n**
and *adj* **blundering.—*adv.* **blun'deringly.** [M.E.
blondren; prob. conn. with **blend**.]

blunderbuss *blun'dər-bus*, *n.* a short hand-gun with a
wide bore. [Du. *donderbus—donder*, thunder, *bus*,
a box, gun-barrel, gun]

blunge *blunj*, (*pottery*) *v.t.* to mix (clay or the like)
with water.—*n.* **blung'er.** [From **blend** and **plunge**.]

blunt *blunt*, *adj.* having a dull edge or point: rough'
outspoken: dull.—*v.t.* to dull.—*v.i.* to become dull.
—*adj.* **blunt'ish.**—*adv.* **blunt'ly.**—*n.* **blunt'ness.**

blur *blûr*, *n.* an ill-defined spot or smear: a confused
impression —*v.t.* to blot: to render indistinct in
outline: to blemish.—*v.i.* to make blurs:—*pr.p.*
blurr'ing; *pa t.* and *pa.p.* **blurred.** [Perh. a variety
of **blear**.]

blurb *blûrb*, *n* a publisher's commendatory description of a book, commonly printed on the jacket: any
brief commendatory advertisement. [Attributed to
Gelett Burgess, American author.]

blurt *blûrt*, *v.t.* to utter suddenly or unadvisedly (with
out).—*n* an abrupt outburst.—*adv.* with a blurt —*n.*
and *adj.* **blurt'ing.** [Prob. imit.]

blush *blush*, *n.* a red glow on the skin caused by shame,
modesty, etc . any reddish colour or suffusion.—*adj.*
pinkish.—*v.t.* to show shame or confusion by growing

red: to grow red.—*ns.* **blush'er** one who blushes: a cosmetic, usu. pinkish, applied to the cheeks to add colour to them.—*n. and adj.* **blush'ing.**—*adv.* **blush'ingly.**—**at the first blush** at the first glance or sight: offhand. [Cf. O.E. *blyscan,* to shine.]

bluster *blus'tər, v.i.* to blow boisterously: to storm, rage: to bully or swagger.—*v.t.* to utter stormily: to drive by storming.—*n.* a blast or roaring as of the wind: bullying or boasting language: a storm of anger —*n. and adj.* **blus'tering.**—*adv.* **blus'teringly.**—*adjs.* **blus'terous** noisy: boastful; **blus'tery** stormy: swaggering. [Cf. E. Frisian *blustern,* to bluster.]

blutwurst *blōōt'vŏōrst, n.* blood-pudding. [Ger.]

bo¹ (*pl.* **bos**), **boh** *bō,* **boo** *bōō, interjs.* an exclamation used to drive geese, or, in fun, to startle someone.—**not be able to say bo(o) to a goose** to be inarticulate from extreme meekness.

bo². See **bo tree.**

Boa *bō'ə, n* a genus, mainly South American, of large snakes that kill their prey by pressure: (without *cap.*) popularly any large constricting snake: long, serpentlike coil of fur, feathers, or the like worn round the neck by ladies.—**boa constrictor** properly the name of one species; popularly any boa, python, or similar snake. [L. *bóa,* a kind of snake.]

boar *bōr, bor, n.* the male swine. [O.E. *bār.*]

board *bōrd, bord, n.* a broad and thin strip of timber: a table: supply of food: provision of meals (with or without lodging): a council-table: a council or authorised body: a slab prepared for playing a game (as a chessboard) or other special purpose (as a notice-board, blackboard, knife-board): (in *pl.*) the stage: a kind of thick stiff paper or sheets of paper pasted together: a rectangular piece forming the side of a book-binding.—*v.t.* to cover with boards; to supply with food (and bed) at fixed terms: to enter (a ship or orig. U.S., a train, bus, etc.).—*v.t.* to receive food (and lodging).—*ns.* **board'er** one who receives board: one who boards a ship; **board'ing** the act of covering with boards: a structure or collection of boards: act of boarding a ship.—**board'-game** a game, e.g. chess, snakes-and-ladders, which is played with pieces, counters, etc. on a specially designed board; **board'ing-house** a house where boarders are kept, **boarding pass** a card allowing one to board an aircraft, ship, etc.; **board'ing-pike** a pike used in boarding a ship, or in defending it when attacked; **board'ing-school** a school in which board and lodging are provided for pupils; **board'room** a room for meetings of a board of directors; **board'walk** a footpath made of boards.—**above board** openly; **go by the board** to go over the side of a ship: to be discarded or ignored: to meet disaster; **on board** aboard; **sweep the board** to take all the cards: to win everything; **take on board** to receive, accept (new notions, additional responsibilities, etc.). [O.E. *bord,* board, the side of a ship.]

boart. See **bort.**

boast *bōst, v.i* to talk vaingloriously: to brag (with *of*).—*v.t.* to brag of: to speak proudly or confidently of, esp. justifiably: to possess with pride.—*n.* an expression of pride: a brag: the cause of boasting.—**boast'er.**—*adj.* **boast'ful** given to bragging —*adv* **boast'fully.**—*ns.* **boast'fulness; boast'ing.** [M.E *bōst.*]

boat *bōt, n.* a small open craft usually moved by oars: a ship· a boat-shaped utensil (as *sauce-boat*).—*v.i.* to sail about in a boat.—*v.t.* to put or convey in a boat: to ship (as oars): (with *it*) to go in a boát.—*ns.* **boat'er** one who boats: a straw hat; **boat'ing.**—**boat'-builder; boat'-deck** a ship's top deck, on which the small boats are carried; **boat'-hook** a hook fixed to a pole used for pulling or pushing off a boat, **boat'house** a house or shed for a boat; **boat'-load; boat'man** a man who has charge of a boat· a rower; **boat people** refugees, esp. from Vietnam, who set off in boats to find a country that will admit them; **boat'race** a race of rowingboats; **boat'-racing; boat'-song** a song sung by a boatman; **boat'-train** a train run in connection with a ship.—**in the same boat** (of persons) in the same unfavourable circumstances; **push the boat out** (*coll.*) to entertain, celebrate, etc , lavishly; **take to the boats** to escape to lifeboats from a sinking ship (also *fig.*). [O.E. *bāt.*]

boatel. See **botel.**

boatswain (often **bosun,** **bo'sun,** **bo's'n,** **bos'n**) *bō'sn, n.* the foreman of a crew (warrant-officer in the navy) who looks after a ship's boats, rigging, flags, etc.—**boatswain's call, pipe, whistle** see **whistle; boatswain's chair** a wooden seat slung from ropes, for a man working on a ship's side, rigging, etc.; **boatswain's mate** boatswain's assistant. [**boat, swain.**]

bob¹ *bob, v.i.* to move quickly up and down: to curtsey: to ride a bobsled: to fish with a bob.—*v.t.* to move in a short jerking manner: to execute with a bob: to cut (hair) square across: to dock, to bobtail: (*pr.p.* **bobb'ing;** *pa.t.* and *pa.p.* **bobbed**).—*n.* a short jerking motion: a curtsey: anything that moves with a bob or swing. the weight of a pendulum, plumb-line, or the like: a knot of hair: bobbed or docked hair: any small roundish body: a short line at or near the end of the stanza: a bobsled: a term in bell-ringing for certain changes.—*n.* **bobb'le** the movement of water in commotion: a woolly ball for trimming dresses, hats, etc.—**bob'cat** a kind of lynx; **bob'sled, -sleigh** a short sledge: a sleigh made up of two of these, sometimes with common seat; a racing sledge for two or more people, with a continuous seat, steering mechanism, and brakes; **bob'tail** a short or cut tail: an animal with a bobbed tail (also *adj.*): a word applied in contempt to the rabble, as in *rag-tag and bobtail.*—Also *v.t.*— *adj.* **bob'tailed** with tail cut short.—**bob up** to appear suddenly. [Poss. Gael. *baban, babag.*]

bob² *bob,* (*slang*) *n.* a shilling or 5 pence:—*pl.* **bob.** [Prob. not O.Fr. *bobe* = 1½d.]

bobbin *bob'in, n.* a reel or spool for winding yarn, wire, etc.—**bobb'in-lace** lace made on a pillow with bobbins; **bobb'in-net'** or **bobb'inet** a fine machinemade netted lace. [Fr. *bobine.*]

bobble. See **bob¹.**

bobby *bob'i,* (*slang*) *n* a policeman. [Familiar form of *Robert,* from Sir Robert Peel, Home Secretary at the passing of the Metropolitan Police Act, 1828; cf. **peeler.**]

bobby calf *bob'i kaf,* a calf slaughtered before it has been weaned.

bobby-dazzler *bob'i-daz-lər, n.* (*dial.*) anything overwhelmingly excellent, striking, or showy, esp. a woman, a young girl who sets out to make an impression.

bobby-pin *bob'i-pin, n.* a hairgrip

bobbysock *bob'i-sok,* (*slang*) *n.* an ankle-sock.—*n.* **bobb'ysoxer** an adolescent girl, teenager.

bobolink *bob'ō-lingk, n.* a North American singing bird. [At first *Bob Lincoln,* from its note.]

bobsled, bobsleigh. See **bob¹.**

bobstays *bob'stāz,* (*naut.*) *n.pl.* ropes or stays used to hold the bowsprit down to the stem or cut-water, and counteract the strain of the foremast-stays

bob-white *bob'(h)wīt', n.* an American quail. [Imit.]

bocage. Same as **boscage.**

boche, bosche *bosh, n.* abusive French slang for a German

bock *bok,* (Fr., from Ger.) *n.* a strong German beer— from *Einbocker bier, Eimbockbier*—beer from Einbeck (Eimbeck): now often a glass or mug of beer (quarter of a litre).

bod *bod*, (*orig. service slang*) *n.* a person [Contraction of **body** (*coll*).]

bode¹ *bōd*, *v.t.* to portend: to foreshow: to augur: to have a presentiment of.—*v.i.* to augur. [O.E. *bodian*, to announce—(*ge*)*bod*, a message; allied to **bid**.]

bode² *bōd*. See **bide**.

bodega *bo-dē′gə*, *n.* a wine-shop. [Sp.]

Bodhisattva *bō-dɪ-sat′wə*, (*Buddhism*) *n.* one who postpones entry into nirvana in order to help others: a future Buddha. [Sans.—*bodhi*, enlightenment, *sattva*, existence.]

bodhi tree. See **bo tree.**

bodice *bod′ɪs*, *n.* a stiffened inner garment (*orig. pl* of **body**) (*arch.*): a woman's outer garment covering the waist and bust: the close-fitting waist or body of a woman's gown.—**bod′ice-ripp′er** a romantic (historical) novel involving violence.

bodkin *bod′kɪn*, *n.* a small dagger: a small instrument for pricking holes, for dressing the hair, for correcting type, etc.: a large blunt needle. [Poss conn. with W. *bidog*, dagger.]

body *bod′ɪ*, *n.* the whole frame of a man or lower animal: the main part of an animal, as distinguished from the limbs: the main part of anything: the part of a vehicle which carries the load or passengers: a garment or part of a garment covering the trunk: a corpse: matter, as opposed to spirit: substance or substantial quality: fullness, as of flavour in a wine solidity: opacity of a paint or pigment· a mass: a person (*coll.*): a number of persons united by some common tie:—*pl.* **bod′ies.**—*v.t.* to give form to: to embody—*pr.p.* **bod′ying;** *pa.t.* and *pa.p.* **bod′ied.**—*adj.* **bod′ily** of the body, esp. as opposed to the mind —*adv.* in the flesh: as a whole.—**body blow** in boxing, a blow to the body: a serious setback; **bod′y-builder** a maker of vehicle bodies: an apparatus for exercising muscles: a nutritious food.—*n.* and *adj.* **bod′y-building.**—**body-cavity** the coelom, or cavity in which the viscera of the higher animals lie; **bod′yguard** a guard to protect the person, esp. of a sovereign; **body language** communication of information by means of conscious or unconscious gestures, attitudes, facial expressions, etc.; **body politic** the collective body of the people in its political capacity; **bod′yshell** bodywork; **bod′y-snatcher** one who secretly disinters the bodies of the dead for the purposes of dissection; **body stocking** a one-piece, skin-tight undergarment for women; **bod′y-warmer** a type of sleeveless padded jacket; **bod′ywork** the metal outer frame of a motor vehicle.—**body and soul** one's entire self; **body-line bowling** in cricket, fast bowling delivered at the batsman's body; **in a body** (acting) all together [O.E. *bodig*.]

Boer *bōōr*, (chiefly *hist.*) *n.* a S. African of Dutch descent, esp. one engaged in farming —Also *adj* [Du., see **boor, bower.**]

boffin *bof′ɪn*, (*orig. service slang*) *n.* research scientist, esp one employed by armed forces or government.

Bofors gun *bō′förz*, or -*fors, gun,* a single- or double-barrelled, quick-firing anti-aircraft gun. [From *Bofors*, Sweden, where orig made.]

bog *bog*, *n.* spongy, usu. peaty, ground: a marsh: a latrine, lavatory (*slang*) —*n.* **bogg′iness.**—*adj* **bogg′y.**—**bog′-as′phodel** a yellow-flowered bog-plant, **bog′bean** buckbean; **bog-iron** see **bog-ore; bog′-land; bog′-moss′** sphagnum, **bog′-myr′tle** sweetgale, a bog plant; **bog′oak′** trunks of oak embedded in bogs and preserved from decay, **bog′-ore, bog′-iron** an iron ore found in boggy land; **bog′-spav′in** in distension of the capsule of the hock-joint of the horse,

bog′trotter (*derog*) an Irishman —**bog down** to encumber with an overwhelming amount of work, a difficult task, etc. [Ir. and Gael *bogach; bog,* soft]

bogey¹ *bō′gɪ, n* in golf, the score, for a given hole or for the whole course, of an imaginary good player, Colonel *Bogey,* fixed as a standard—now usu a score of one stroke above the par for any hole [Perh. **bogy.**]

bogey². See **bogie, bogy.**

boggle *bog′l, v.i.* to stop or hesitate to start with fright. (of one's mind, esp. in *the mind boggles*) to be unable to imagine or grasp something, to be astounded by something (*coll.*) —*n.* **bogg′ler.** [**bogle.**]

bogie, bogey *bō′gɪ, n* a low heavy truck, a trolley· a railway coach: a pivoted undercarriage, as in a locomotive engine

bogle *bō′gl, n* a spectre or goblin: a scarecrow (*tatt′ie-bo′gle*): a bugbear, or source of terror [Scot ; possibly connected with **bug¹.**]

bogong. See **bugong.**

bogus *bō′gəs, adj.* counterfeit, spurious [An American cant word.]

bogy, bogey *bō′gɪ, n.* a goblin: a bugbear or special object of dread the devil: a policeman (*slang*) —*pl.* **bō′gies, bō′geys.**—*n.* **bō′g(e)yism.**—**bo′g(e)y-man** the Devil or other dreadful being with whom to threaten children [Perhaps a form of **bogle.**]

boh. See **bo¹.**

bohea *bō-hē′, n* the lowest quality of black tea· black tea generally. [From the *Wu-ɪ* hills in China.]

Bohemian *bō-hē′mɪ-ən, n* a native or inhabitant of Bohemia: a gypsy: an artist or man of letters, or indeed anyone, who sets social conventions aside.— Also *adj* —*n.* **Bohē′mianism.** [Fr *bohémien,* a gypsy, from the belief that these wanderers came from *Bohemia.*]

boil¹ *boil, v.i* to pass rapidly from liquid into vapour with violent evolution of bubbles: to bubble up as if from the action of heat· to be heated in boiling liquid: to be hot· to be excited or angry.—*v.i.* to heat to a boiling state: to cook, dress, clean or otherwise treat by boiling.—*n* act or condition of boiling —*ns.* **boil′er** one who boils: that in which anything is boiled. a vessel in which steam is generated· a vessel for heating water for baths, etc ; **boil′ing.**—*adj.* at boiling-point. very hot: bubbling. swelling with heat or passion —**boil′ing-point** the temperature at which a liquid, esp water, boils; **boiler suit** a workman's overall garment.—**boil down** to reduce in bulk by boiling to extract the substance of; **boil down to** (*fig.*) to mean. to signify when reduced to essentials, **boil over** to bubble over the sides of the containing vessel; to break out into unrestrained indignation, **come to the boil** to arrive at boiling-point: to arrive at a critical state. [O Fr *boillir*—L *bullīre*—*bulla,* a bubble.]

boil² *boil, n.* an inflamed swelling [O E *bȳl.*]

boisterous *bois′tər-əs, adj* wild· noisy and exuberant: turbulent stormy —*adv* **bois′terously.**—*n* **bois′terousness.** [M E *boistous*]

boko *bō′kō, (slang) n.* the nose —*pl* **bō′kos.**

bolas *bō′las, n.* (properly *pl*) a South American missile, consisting of two or more balls or stones strung together, swung round the head and hurled so as to entangle an animal [Sp . balls]

bold *bōld, adj.* daring forward or impudent presumptuous. executed with spirit striking to the sense, well marked —*adv.* **bold′ly.**—*n* **bold′ness.**—*adj* **bold′-faced** impudent of type, having a heavy face — **bold as brass** utterly unabashed, **make bold, be so bold as** to to venture, take the liberty [O E *bald*]

bole¹ *bōl n* the trunk of a tree [O.N *bolr*]

bole² *bōl n* a friable earthy clay. usually red [Gr *bolos· a* clod]

bolection, balection *bō-, bə-lek'shən, n* a moulding around a panel, projecting beyond the surface of the framing.

bolero *bə-lā'rō, n.* Spanish national dance: a tune to which it may be danced: (usu. *bol'ə-rō*) a jacket-like bodice, coming barely to the waist:—*pl.* **boleros.** [Sp.]

bolide *bō'līd, n.* a large meteor, esp. one that bursts: a fireball. [Fr.,—L. *bolis, -idis*]

bolivar *bol-ē'vär, n.* the standard monetary unit of Venezuela. [From Simón *Bolívar* (1783–1830).]

boliviano *bol-ē-vi-a'nō, n.* a Bolivian dollar (100 centavos):—*pl.* **bolivia'nos.**

bolix. Same as **bollocks.**

boll *bōl, n.* a swelling: a knob: a round capsule, as in cotton, flax, poppy, etc.—*v.i.* to swell, to form bolls.
—*adj.* **bolled** (*bōld*) swollen, podded.—**boll'-weevil** a weevil whose larvae infest cotton-bolls; **boll'-worm** a moth caterpillar that destroys cotton-bolls, etc. [A form of **bowl**—O.E. *bolla.*]

bollard *bol'ərd, n.* a short post on a wharf or ship, etc., round which ropes are secured: one of a line of short posts barring passage of motor vehicles [Prob. **bole.**]

bolletrie *bol'ə-trē.* Same as **bully-tree.**

bollocks *bol'əks,* **ballocks** *bol',* also *bal', n.pl.* testicles.—*n.sing.* (*slang*) nonsense: a muddle, mess.—*v.t.* to make a botch of. [O.E. *beallucas,* testicles.]

Bologna *bol-ōn'yä, adj.* of the town of *Bologna* in Italy.—*adj.* and *n.* **Bologn'ese** (or *-ēz'*).—**Bologna sausage.** [L. *Bonōnia.*]

bolometer *bō-lom'ι-tər, n.* an instrument for measuring radiant energy.—*adj.* **bolomet'ric.**—*n.* **bolom'etry.** [Gr. *bolē,* stroke, ray, *metron,* a measure.]

boloney. See **baloney.**

Bolshevik (or **bol-**) *bol'shə-vik, n.* a member of the Russian Majority (or Extreme) Socialist party (*hist.*): a violent revolutionary Marxian communist: anarchist, agitator, causer of trouble (used loosely as a term of disapprobation).—Also *adj.*—coll. contracted **bol'shie, bol'shy.**—*ns.* **bol'shevism; bol'shevist.** —Also *adj.* [Russ.—*bolshe,* greater, *-vik,* agent suffix.]

bolster *bōl'stər, n.* a long, sometimes cylindrical, pillow or cushion: a pad: anything resembling it in form or use, esp. any piece of mechanism affording a support against pressure; a form of cold chisel.—*v.t.* (also with *up*) to support: to hold up.—*adj.* **bol'stered** supported: swelled out.—*n.* and *adj.* **bol'stering.** [O.E. *bolster.*]

bolt¹ *bōlt, n.* a bar used to fasten a door, etc.: a stout pin with a head: an arrow, esp. for a crossbow: a thunderbolt: a roll of a definite measure (of cloth, etc.).—*v.t.* to fasten with a bolt: to swallow hastily.— *v.i.* to spring, dart: to rush away: to take flight: to run away: to start up: of a plant, to flower and run to seed.—*n.* **bolt'er.**—**bolt'head** the head of a bolt; **bolt'hole** a hole to receive a bolt: a secret passage or way of escape: a refuge from danger: a secluded, private place; **bolt'-rope** a rope sewed all round the edge of a sail to prevent it from tearing.—**bolt from the blue** an unexpected event; **bolt upright** upright and straight as an arrow; **have shot one's bolt** to be unable to do more than one has done. [O.E. *bolt.*]

bolt². See **boult.**

bolus *bō'ləs, n.* a rounded mass: a large pill. [L *bōlus* —Gr. *bōlos,* a lump.]

bomb *bom, n.* a hollow case containing explosive, incendiary, smoke-producing, poisonous, or other offensive material: (also **volcanic bomb**) a rounded mass of lava thrown out by a volcano.—*v.i.* to throw, discharge, or drop bombs: to be a flop, fail (*slang*) — *v.t.* to attack, injure, or destroy with bombs.—*n*

bombard (*bom'bard*) an early cannon an old form of bassoon.—*v.t* **bombard'** to attack with artillery: to batter or pelt: to subject to a succession of blows or impingements: to assail, as with questions (*fig*): to subject, as the atom, to a stream of particles at high speed (*phys.*).—*ns* **bombardier**(*bom-, bum-bər-dēr'*) the lowest non-commissioned officer in the British artillery; **bombardment** (*bom-bärd'mənt*); **bombar'don** (or *bom'*) the bass tuba; **bomber** (*bom'ər*) one who bombs: a bombing aeroplane.—Also *adj* — **bombardier beetle** a beetle that discharges an acrid volatile fluid; **bomb'-dispos'al** the act of removing and detonating unexploded bombs; **bomber jacket** a short jacket with zipped front and elasticated waist. —*adj.* **bomb'proof** proof or secure against the force of bombs.—**bomb'shell** a bomb: now only *fig* , a sudden and surprising piece of news; **bomb'site** an area which has been laid waste by air-raid(s).—**go like a bomb** to go very well or very quickly; **make a bomb** (*coll.*) to make or earn a great deal of money. [Fr *bombe,* prob —L. *bombus*—Gr *bombos,* humming sound.]

bombasine, bombazine *bom'bə-zēn,* or *-zēn', n.* a twilled or corded fabric of silk and worsted, or of cotton and worsted. [Fr *bombasin.*]

bombast *bom'bast, n.* high-sounding language.—*adj.* **bombas'tic** high-sounding: inflated.—*adv* **bombas'tically.** [L.L. *bombax,* cotton—Gr. *bombyx,* silk.]

Bombay duck *bom'bā duk,* a fish, the bummalo.

bombe *bom, bɔ̃b, n.* a dessert, usually ice-cream frozen in a round or melon-shaped mould. [Fr.]

bombé *bom'bā, bɔ̃-bā, adj.* of furniture, having a rounded, convex front. [Fr., bulging, convex.]

bombilate, bombinate *bom'bιl-āt, -bin-āt, v.t.* to hum, buzz, drone, boom.—*ns.* **bombilā'tion, bombinā'tion.** [L. *bombilāre, bombināre.*]

bon *bɔ̃,* (Fr.) *adj.* good.—**bon appetit** (*bo-na-pə-tē*) good appetite, said politely to those who are (about to start) eating; **bon goût** (*gōō*) good taste; **bonjour** (*-zhōō'r*) good day: good morning; **bon mot** (*pl.* **bons mots**) (*mō*) a witty saying; **bonsoir** (*-swär*) good evening; **bon ton** (*tɔ̃*) the height of fashion; **bon vivant** (*vē-vä*) a jovial companion: one who lives well, esp who enjoys fine food; **bon viveur** (*vē-vœr;* not used in Fr.) a bon vivant, esp. a man-about-town; **bon voyage** (*vwä-yäzh*) a good journey to you.

bona fide *bō'nə fīd, fī'da, -dι, bo'na fi'dā,* (L.) (*abl.*) in good faith—(used as *adj.*) genuine; **bona fides** (*fī'dēz, fīd'ās*) good faith: genuineness.

bonanza *bon-an'zə, n.* a rich mass of gold: any mine of wealth or stroke of luck. [Sp., good weather.]

bonbon *bon'bon, bɔ̃-bɔ̃, n.* a sweetmeat.—*n.* **bonbonnière** (*bɔ̃-bon-yer'*) a fancy box for holding sweets [Fr., redup. of *bon,* good.]

bonce *bons, n.* a large marble: the head (*coll.*).

bond¹ *bond, n* that which binds: link or connection or union: a writing of obligation to pay a sum or to perform a contract: a debenture: a mortgage (*Scots law*): any constraining or cementing force: in building, the overlapping connection of one stone or brick with another: (in *pl.*) imprisonment, captivity: the condition of goods retained in a warehouse, called a **bonded warehouse** or **bonded store,** until duties are paid.— *v.t.* to connect, secure, or bind with a bond. to put in a condition of bond: to cause to adhere (to) —*adj.* **bond'ed** secured by bond.—*ns.* **bond'er** a bondstone or header; **bond'ing** act of bonding: the forming of the attachment between a mother and her newborn child (*psych.*).—**bond'-holder** one who holds bonds of a private person or public company; **bond paper** a superior kind of paper; **bonds'man** a surety; **bond'stone** a stone that reaches a considerable distance into or entirely through a wall for the purpose of binding it together [A variant of **band**—O E *bindan*, to bind.]

bond² *bond, adj.* in a state of servitude.—*ns.* **bond'age** captivity: slavery.—**bond'maid**, **bond'-woman**, **bonds'woman** a woman-slave; **bond'man**, **bonds'man** a man-slave; **bond'manship**; **bond'servant** a slave; **bond'-service** the condition of a bondservant: slavery, **bond'-slave** a slave. [O.E *bonda*, a boor, a householder.]

bondsman. See bond¹,².

bone *bōn, n.* a hard substance forming the skeleton of the higher animals: a separate piece of the skeleton: a piece of whalebone: (in *pl.*) the skeleton or anything analogous: (in *pl*) mortal remains.—*v.t* to take the bones out of, as meat: to furnish with bones.—*adjs* **boned** having bones. having the bones removed, **bone'less** wanting bones· spineless (*fig.*).—**bō'niness** **bō'ner** (*U.S. slang*) a howler.—*adj.* **bō'ny** full of, or consisting of, or like bones: thin —**bone'-ash, bone'-earth** the remains of bones burned in an open furnace; **bone china** china in the making of which calcium phosphate, as in bone ash, is used.—*adj.* **bone'-dry** as dry as a bone.—**bone'-dust** ground or pulverised bones, used in agriculture; **bone'head** a blockhead.—*adj* **bone'-i'dle** utterly idle, idle to the bone —**bone'-lace** lace woven with bobbins, which were often made of bones, **bone'-meal** ground bones used as fertiliser and as animal feed; **bone'-oil'** a liquid got in dry distillation of bones; **bone'setter** one who treats broken or dislocated bones without being a duly qualified surgeon; **bone'shaker** a familiar name for earlier forms of bicycle: any crazy vehicle, **bone'-spav'in** a bony excrescence or hard swelling on the inside of the hock of a horse; **bone'-tur'quoise** blue fossil bone or tooth used as turquoise.—*adj.* **bone'-weary** utterly exhausted.—**bony fishes** the Teleostei, an order of fishes including most of the living forms.—**bare bones** the essentials (of a subject); **bone of contention** something that causes strife; **bone to pick** a difference to be cleared up (with somebody); **bone up on** (*slang*) to study or collect information about (a subject), **feel in one's bones** to know instinctively, without proof: **make no bones of, about** to have no scruples about: to make no fuss, difficulty, about; **near the bone** mean: on the verge of the indecent or offensively pointed, (never) **make old bones** (not) to live to old age, **to the bone** to the inmost part: to the minimum, **work one's fingers to the bone** to work until one is exhausted. [O E. *bān.*]

bonfire *bon'fīr, n.* a large fire in the open air on occasions of public rejoicing, for consuming garden refuse, etc.—originally a fire in which bones were burnt.—**Bonfire night** 5th November, Guy Fawkes night (see guy) [**bone**, and **fire.**]

bongo (drum) *bong'gō (drum), n.* a small Cuban drum played with the fingers—generally used in pairs:—*pl.* **bon'gos, bongo drums.** [Amer. Sp. *bongó.*]

bonhom(m)ie, *bon'o-mē, n.* easy good nature —*adj* **bon'homous.** [Fr.]

bonism *bon'izm, n.* the doctrine that the world is good, but could be perfected —*n.* **bon'ist.** [L *bonus.* good.]

bonito *bo-nē'tō, n* any of several large fish of the mackerel family.—*pl* **boni'tos.** [Sp]

bonkers *bong'kərz, (slang) adj.* slightly drunk: crazy

bonne *bon, fem. of* **bon,** (Fr) *adj* good.—*n* a French maid or nursemaid —**bonne chance** (*shās*) good luck, **bonne compagnie** (*kɔ̃-pa-nyē*) good society, **bonne foi** (*fwa*) good faith; **bonne grace** (*gras*) good grace, gracefulness: (in *pl*) favour, **bonne mine** (*mēn*) good appearance, pleasant looks

bonnet *bon'it, n* a woman's head-covering, tied on by

strings: a soft cap: the velvet cap within a coronet: an additional part laced to the foot of jibs, or other fore-and-aft sails, to gather more wind (*naut.*): a wire-cowl over a chimney-top: the cover of a motor-car engine, or of various parts of machinery, etc.: the second stomach of a ruminant.—*v.t.* to put a bonnet on.—*adj* **bonn'eted.**—**bonn'et-monkey** an Indian macaque (from the appearance of the head); **bonnet-rouge** (Fr *bon-ā-rōo zh*) the red cap of liberty of the French Revolution, in the form of a Phrygian cap. [O.Fr., —L.L. *bonnetum,* orig the name of a stuff.]

bonny, bonnie *bon'i, adj.* comely, pretty: plump: healthy-looking as a general term expressing appreciation, considerable, etc., often ironically. —Also *adv.*—*adv.* **bonn'ily** beautifully: gaily.—*n.* **bonn'iness** handsomeness: gaiety.

bonsai *bon'sī, bōn', n.* a dwarf tree growing in a pot, produced by special methods of cultivation (*pl.* **bon'sai**). the art of growing such trees. [Jap. *bon,* tray, bowl, *sai,* cultivation.]

bonspiel *bon'spēl, n* a great match, now only a curling match. [App. from some Du. compound of *spel,* play.]

bontebok *bon'tə-bok, n.* a South African antelope [Du. *bont,* particoloured, *bok,* goat.]

bonus *bō'nəs, n.* a premium beyond the usual interest for a loan: an extra dividend to shareholders: a policy-holder's share of profits: an extra payment to workmen or others: a douceur or bribe.—**bonus issue** an issue of additional shares to a company's share-holders, representing a capitalisation of reserves. [L. *bonus,* good.]

bonze *bonz, n.* a Buddhist priest. [Jap. *bonzō* or *bonzi,* a priest.]

bonzer *bon'zər, (slang; Austr.) adj.* very good.

boo¹, booh *bōō, interj* expressive of disapprobation or contempt.—*v.t.* and *v.i* to hoot.—**boo'-hoo'** (*hōō*) the sound of noisy weeping.—*v.i.* to weep noisily.

boo². See **bo'.**

boob¹ *bōōb, (coll.) v.t.* to bungle.—*v.i.* to blunder.— *n.* a blunder (also **booboo bōō 'bōō**). [**booby.**]

boob² *bōō b, (slang) n.* a female breast (usu. in *pl.*).— **boob'-tube** (*slang*) a woman's clinging garment covering the torso from waist to armpit: television.

booboo. See **boob¹.**

booby *bōō 'bi, n.* a stupid fellow: a sea-bird of the gannet tribe.—**boo'by-prize** a prize for the worst score or the lowest marks; **boo'by-trap** a form of practical joke, by which something is made to fall upon someone entering a door, or the like: a harmless-looking object which on being touched sets off an explosion. —*v.t.* to set up a booby-trap in or on. [Perh. Sp., *bobo,* a dolt.]

boodle *bōō d'l, n.* a crowd: pack: stock-in-trade, capital: counterfeit money: money got by political or official corruption: spoil. [Perh. Du. *boedel,* property.]

boogie-woogie *bōō g'i-wōō g'i, n.* a jazz rhythm in which the piano has an ostinato figure in the bass.—Also **boog'ie.** [From U.S. slang *boogie,* a Negro performer, and *woogie,* invented to rhyme]

booh. See **boo'.**

book *bōōk, n.* sheets of paper, etc., bound together or made into a roll, either printed, written on, or blank: a large-scale literary composition· a division of a volume or composition: (with **the**) the Bible. a record of bets made with different people· any source of instruction (*fig.*). a libretto: a structure resembling a book. (*pl.*). formal accounts of transactions —*v.t.* to write or enter in a book to engage in advance· of police, to take the name of, for an alleged offence. hence, to arrest: of a referee, to enter a player's name in a notebook for an offence (*football*) —*v i* to make a reservation in advance.—*adj.* **book'able.**—*n.* **book'ie** (*coll.*) a bookmaker.—*n.* **book'ing** a reservation of e.g. a room in a hotel, a theatre seat, a seat on a plane, train, etc.—*adj.* **book'ish** fond of books: acquainted only with books. savouring of books.—*n.* **book'ishness.**—*n.* **book'let** a small book.—**book'-binder** one who binds books; **book'binding; book'case** a case with shelves for books; **book club** a society that buys, circulates on loan, or prints books for its members.—*adjs.* **booked'-out, booked'-up** full up: unable to accept further reservations, bookings or appointments.—**book'-end** a prop for the end of a row of books; **book'ing-clerk'** one who sells tickets; **book'ing-hall; book'ing-off'ice** an office where names are booked or tickets sold; **book'keeper; book'keeping** the art of keeping accounts in a regular and systematic manner; **book'-learning** learning got from books, as opposed to practical knowledge; **book'louse** a wingless insect found among books and papers:—*pl.* **book'lice; book'maker** one who makes a living by betting at race-courses; **book'mark(er)** a (decorative) strip of leather, fabric, paper, etc., or other object, for placing between the pages of a book to mark a particular opening; **book'plate** a label usually pasted inside the cover of a book, bearing the owner's name, crest, coat-of-arms, or peculiar device; **book'-post** arrangement in the Post Office for the transmission of books; **book price, value** the officially-recorded value, not necessarily the market value, of a commodity; **book'rest** a support for a book, a bookstand; **book'seller** one who sells books: formerly a publisher; **book'selling; book'shelf** a shelf for books; **book'shop** a shop where books are sold; **book'stall** a stall or stand, generally in the open air, where books are sold; **book'stand** a bookstall: a stand or support for holding up a book in reading; **book'store** (*U.S.*) a bookshop; **book'-token** a paper to be exchanged for books of a stated price, sent as a gift; **book value** see **book price; book'work** study from books, theoretical as opposed to practical work; **book'worm** a grub that eats holes in books: a hard reader.—**be upon the books** to have one's name in an official list; **book in** to reserve a place or room (at): to register at a hotel; **book of words** directions for use; **bring to book** to bring to account; **closed book** a subject completely unknown or uncomprehended; **get one's books** to be dismissed; **in someone's good (bad) books** favourably (unfavourably) regarded by someone; **read like a book** to understand thoroughly (usu. a person's character or motives); **suit one's book** to be agreeable to or favourable to one; **take a leaf out of another's book** to profit by his example; **throw the book at** (*coll.*) to administer a lengthy and detailed reproof to. [O.E. *bōc,* book.]

Boolean algebra *boo'lē-ən al'ji-brə,* an algebra closely related to logic in which the symbols used do not represent arithmetical quantities. [Named after George Boole (1815–1864).]

boom[1] *boom, n.* a pole by which a sail is stretched: a chain or bar stretched across a harbour: a barrier of floating logs: an inflatable barrier used to contain oil from spillages, etc.: a long beam. [Du. *boom,* beam, tree.]

boom[2] *boom, v.t.* to make a hollow sound or roar.—*n.* a hollow roar. [From a L.G. root; like **bomb,** of imit. origin.]

boom[3] *boom, v.i.* to go on with a rush: to become suddenly prosperous: to increase sharply in value.—*n.* a sudden increase of activity in business, or the like: sudden rise in price or value.—*n.* and *adj.* **boom'ing.** —**boom town** one which has expanded rapidly and prospered because of e.g. the arrival of a valuable new industry. [Prob. from **boom**[2].]

boomerang *boom'ə-rang, n.* a bent missile used by the natives of Australia, sometimes so balanced that it returns towards the thrower: an act that recoils upon the agent (*fig.*).—*v i.* to recoil thus (*fig.*). [Australian.]

boon[1] *boon, n.* a gift, favour. [O.N *bōn,* prayer.]

boon[2] *boon, adj.* gay, merry, or kind (as a *boon companion*). [Fr. *bon*—L. *bonus,* good.]

boondocks *boon'doks, (U.S.) n.pl.* wild or remote country. [Tagálog *bundok,* mountain.]

boong *boong, (offensive) n.* a New Guinea native: an aborigine. [Aborigine word.]

boor *boor, n.* a Dutch colonist in South Africa: a coarse person.—*adj.* **boor'ish** like a boor: awkward or rude. —*adv.* **boor'ishly.**—*n* **boor'ishness.** [Du. *boer;* perh. partly O.E. *būr, gebūr,* farmer.]

boost *boost, v.t.* to push up: to raise, as price, morale: to advertise or promote: to supplement voltage of: to increase supply of air to, or pressure of: to push (a spacecraft) into orbit by means of a booster.—Also *n.* —*n.* **boost'er** a person or thing which boosts: an auxiliary motor in a rocket: any device to increase effect of another mechanism: an additional dose of a vaccine to increase or renew the effect of the original dose.

boot[1] *boot, n.* a covering for the foot and lower part of the leg, generally made of leather: an instrument of torture for the leg: a compartment in a motor car for luggage, etc.—*v.t.* to put boots on: to kick: to turn out, dismiss (with *out*).—*adj.* **boot'ed** having boots on, equipped for riding.—*ns.* **bootee** (*boo'tē, -tē'*) a lady's short boot: an infant's knitted boot; **boots** a hotel servant who cleans boots, runs messages, etc.— **boot'black** a shoeblack; **boot boy** same as **bovver boy.** —*adj.* **boot'-faced** with an unsmiling, expressionless face.—**boot'lace** a lace for fastening boots; **boot'last, boot'tree** the last or foot-like mould on which boots or shoes are made or stretched to keep their shape; **boot'leg** the leg of a high boot.—*v.t.* to smuggle (liquor): to make, or deal in (illicit goods).—Also *v.i.*— **boot'legger; boot'legging.**—*adj.* **boot'less** without boots.—**boot'licker** a toady (*U.S.* **boot'lick;** also *v.t.*); **boot'licking; boot'maker; boot'making.**—**bet one's boots** to be quite certain; **die in one's boots** to die a sudden death, not in bed; **get the boot** (*slang*) to be dismissed; **have one's heart in one's boots** to have lost courage; **lick someone's boots** to try to ingratiate oneself with someone by obsequious behaviour; **like old boots** (*slang*) vigorously; **pull oneself up by one's bootstraps** to get on by one's own efforts; **put the boot in** (*slang*) to resort to physical or verbal bullying; **the boot is on the other leg,** foot responsibility (now) lies the other way. [O.Fr. *bote*—L.L. *botta, bota.*]

boot[2] *boot, v.t.* to profit or advantage.—*adj.* **boot'less** without boot or profit: useless.—*adv.* **boot'lessly.**— *n.* **boot'lessness.**—**to boot** in addition. [O.E. *bōt,* compensation, amends.]

booth *boodh, booth, n.* a hut or small shop of simple construction: a covered stall at a fair or market: a partly-enclosed compartment, as one in which to vote, telephone, or eat in a restaurant. [O.N. *būth,* or a cognate word.]

booty *boo'ti, n.* spoil taken in war or by force. [O.N. *bȳti,* share—*bȳta,* to divide.]

booze *booz, (coll.) v.i.* to drink deeply or excessively.— *n.* intoxicating liquor: a drinking bout.—*adj.* **boozed.** —*n.* **booz'er** one who boozes: a public house (*slang*). —*adv.* **booz'ily.**—*adjs.* **booz'ing** drinking: for drinking; **booz'y, booz'ey** inclined to booze: drunken. —**booze'-up** a drinking bout.

bop[1] *bop.* Short for **bebop,** of which it was a development in the 1950s.—*n.* **bopp'er** a devotee of bebop.

bop[2] *bop, (slang) n.* a blow.—*v.t.* to strike. [Imit.]

For other sounds see detailed chart of pronunciation.

bora *bō'ra, bo'*, *n* a strong north-east wind in the upper Adriatic. [Venetian variant of It *borea*—L. *boreas*; or Slav., cf. Serbian *bura*]

boracic. See **borax.**

borage *bur'ij, bor'ij, n.* a blue-flowered bristly plant. [L.L. *borrāgō.*]

borane. See **boron.**

borax *bō'raks, bo', n* a mineral, hydrated sodium tetraborate, found on alkaline lake shores.—*adjs.* **bo'ric, boracic** (*bo-ras'ik*) of or relating to borax or boron—*n.* **bo'rate** a salt of boric acid.—**boric** or **boracic** or **orthoborac'ic acid** an acid (H₃BO₃) obtained by dissolving borax, and also found native in mineral springs in Italy [Fr. and L.L *borax*—Ar *būraq.*]

borazon. See **boron.**

borborygmus *bor-ba-rig'mas, n.* sound of flatulence in the intestines.—*adj.* **borboryg'mic.** [Gr. *borborygmos.*]

Bordeaux *bor-dō', n* claret, wine of *Bordeaux.*—**Bordeaux mixture** a mixture of lime and copper sulphate, used to kill fungus and insect parasites on plants.

bordel *bor'dal,* (*arch.*) *n.* a house for prostitution. [O Fr. *bordel*, a cabin—L L. *borda*]

border *bord'ar, n.* the edge or margin of anything. the boundary of a country, etc., esp. (*cap.*—also in *pl.*) that between England and Scotland: a flower-bed in a garden. a piece of ornamental edging or trimming.—*adj.* of or on the border.—*v.t.* to come near or to be adjacent (with *on, upon, with*).—*v.t.* to furnish with a border: to bound.—*adj.* **bord'ered.**—*n.* **bord'erer** one who dwells or was born on the border of a country.—*adj.* **bord'erless**—**bord'erland** a border region.—*adj.* belonging to the undefined margin between two things.—*adj.* **bord'erline** marginal, hardly or doubtfully coming within the definition.— Also *n.*—**Border terrier** a small rough-haired terrier, originally from the Borders. [O Fr. *bordure*; from root of **board.**]

bordure *bor'dūr, -joor, n.* (*her.*) a border surrounding a shield. [See **border.**]

bore¹ *bōr, bor, v.t.* to pierce so as to form a hole. to weary or annoy with tediousness (perh a different word) —*v.t.* to form a hole or borehole by drilling or piercing.—*n.* a hole made by boring. the size of the cavity of a tube: a person, thing, or activity that wearies: something that causes annoyance, a nuisance (*coll.*).—*ns.* **bore'dom** tedium; **bor'er.**—*adj* **bor'ing.** —*n.* the act of making a hole in anything: a hole made by boring: (in *pl.*) the chips produced by boring.— **bore'hole** a bore in the earth's crust for investigation or for water, oil, etc. [O.E *borian.*]

bore² *bōr, bor, pa.t.* of **bear.**

bore³ *bōr, bór, n.* a tidal flood that rushes with great violence up the estuaries of certain rivers, also called eagre. [O.N *bāra*, a wave or swell.]

Boreas *bor', bōr', bor'i-as, n.* the North Wind.—*adj.* **bo'real** of North Wind or North: (with *cap.*) of the northern and mountainous parts of the Northern hemisphere: (with *cap.*) of a post-glacial period when the climate of Europe and North America resembled that of the present Boreal region [L., Gr. *Boréas*]

borecole *bōr'kōl, bor', n* kale [Du. *boerenkool*, lit. peasant's cabbage.]

boric. Same as **boracic.** [See **borax.**]

born *born.* See **bear¹.**—**born again** having received new spiritual life, **born fool, mimic** etc., one whose folly, mimic ability, etc., is innate; **born to be** destined to be, **in (all) one's born days** in one's whole lifetime; **not born yesterday** not young in experience

borne *bōrn, born, pa p.* of **bear** to carry.

borné *bor'nā, adj.* limited, narrow-minded [Fr

pa.p. of *borner*, to limit.]

Bornholm disease *born'hōm diz-ēz', n.* epidemic pleurodynia, a rare infectious disease caused by a virus, named from the Baltic island *Bornholm*, where it was first described.

boron *bō'ron, bo', n.* a non-metallic element (at numb. 5; symbol B), present in borax and boric acid. —*ns.* **borane** (*bōr'ān, bor'*) any boron hydride, efficient as high-energy fuel; **borazon** (*bōr'a-zon, bor'*) a man-made compound of boron and nitrogen, hard as diamond, **boride** (*bōr'id, bor'*) any of a class of substances made by combining boron chemically with a metal [See **borax.**]

borough *bur'a, n.* a town with a corporation and special privileges granted by royal charter: a town that sends representatives to parliament.—**borough court** formerly an inferior court dealing with minor offences, etc , presided over by local magistrates: in Scotland, an inferior court of summary jurisdiction presided over by a bailie, **close** or **pocket borough** a borough whose representation was in the nomination of some person—common before 1832; **county borough** a borough (by Acts of 1888, 1926, 1958, respectively above 50000, 75000, 100000, inhabitants) with some of the characters of a county—abolished 1974, **rotten borough** one which still returned members to parliament although the constituency had disappeared—all abolished in 1832.—The Scottish terms are grouped under **burgh.** [O.E *burg, burh*, a city, from *beorgan*, Ger. *bergen*, to protect.]

borrow *bor'ō, n.* a slope on a green (*golf*).—*v.t.* and *v.i* to obtain on loan or trust: to adopt from a foreign source: to derive from another (with *from, of*).—*v.t.* to allow for slope or wind, esp. by putting the ball uphill of the hole (*golf*) —*adj.* **borr'owed** taken on loan. counterfeit: assumed —*n.* **borr'ower.**—*n* and *adj.* **borr'owing.**—**borrowed time** an unexpected extension of life, or of the time allowed for some activity. [O.E *borgian—borg, borh*, a pledge, security.]

borsch(t) *borsh(t), ns.* a Russian soup with beetroot, etc.—Also **bortsch** (*borch*), etc. [Russ. *borshch.*]

borstal, borstall *bor'stal, n* an establishment for the detention of young adult delinquents, named from the first reformatory of the kind at Borstal, a suburb of Rochester, Kent [O.E *beorh*, a hill, and *stīgel*, a stile, or *borg*, security, *steall*, place.]

bort, boart *bort, n.* diamond fragments or dust. a coarse diamond or semicrystallic form of carbon. [Fr.]

bortsch(t). See **borsch(t).**

borzoi *bor'zoi, n.* a dog like a huge greyhound, but with a soft coat about the length of a deer-hound's [Russ. *borzu*, swift]

bosbok. See **bush¹.**

boscage *bosk'ij, n.* thick foliage: woodland. [Fr. *boscage, bocage*—L L. *boscus*, conn. with Eng **bush.**]

boschbok, boschveld. See **bush¹.**

bosche. See **boche.**

bosh *bosh, n* nonsense. foolish talk.—Also *interj* [Turk. *bosh*, worthless]

bosk *bosk, n* a thicket. a little wood —*ns* **bosk'et** a thicket· a plantation; **bosk'iness.**—*adj.* **bosk'y** woody or bushy: shady. [Cf **bush, boscage.**]

bo's'n, bos'n. See **boatswain.**

bosom *booz'am, n* the breast of a human being: the part of the dress that covers it. (sometimes in *pl*) a woman's breasts. the imagined seat of the passions and feelings. the heart any close or secret receptacle —attributively, confidential intimate —*adjs* **bos'omed; bos'omy** of a woman, having large breasts —**Abraham's bosom** the abode of the blessed dead [O E *bōsm*]

boson *bō′son, n.* any of a class of subatomic particles whose behaviour is governed by Bose-Einstein statistics, according to which, under certain conditions, particles of the same kind will accumulate in each low-energy quantum mechanical state. [S. N. *Bose* (1894–1974), Indian physicist.]

boss[1] *bos, n.* a knob or stud: a raised ornament.—*v.t.* to ornament with bosses.—*adjs.* **bossed** embossed; **boss′y** having bosses [O.Fr. *boce* (Fr. *bosse*).]

boss[2] *bos, (coll.) n.* a chief or leader: a master, manager, or foreman: the person who pulls the wires in political intrigues.—*adj.* chief: excellent.—*v.t.* to manage or control: to domineer over (sometimes with *about* or *around*).—*n.* **boss′iness.**—*adj.* **boss′y.** [New York Dutch *baas*, master.]

boss[3] *bos: boss′-eyed adj.* with one good eye: squinteyed: out of true.

bossa nova *bos′ə nō′və,* a style of dancing originating in Brazil, or the music for it. [Port. *bossa*, trend, tendency, *nova*, new.]

boston *bost′ən, n.* a game of cards, somewhat similar to whist: a kind of waltz.—**Boston terrier** a breed of dog arising from a cross between a bulldog and a bullterrier. [From *Boston*, U.S.A.]

bosun, bo′sun. See **boatswain.**

bot, bott *bot, n.* the maggot of a botfly, parasitic in the intestines of the horse and other animals: (in *pl.*) the diseased condition thereby caused: colic.—**bot′fly** a name for various flies that lay their eggs on horses, etc.

botany *bot′ən-i, n.* the science of plants: the plants of an area: fine wool, orig. from Botany Bay, Australia (sometimes *cap.*; also *adj.*).—*adjs.* **botan′ic; botan′ical** (also *n.*, a vegetable drug).—*adv.* **botan′ically.**—*n.* **bot′anist** one skilled in botany. [Gr. *botanē*, grass, fodder.]

botargo *bot-är′gō, n.* a relish made of mullet or tunny roe:—*pl.* **botar′gos, -goes.** [It.,—Ar. *butarkhah.*]

botch *boch, n.* a clumsy patch: ill-finished work.—*v.t.* to patch or mend clumsily: to put together unsuitably or unskilfully: to bungle (often with *up*).—*v.i.* to do repairs: to bungle.—*ns.* **botch′er** a repairer: a bungler; **botch′ery.**—*n.* and *adj.* **botch′ing.**—*adj.* **botch′y** marked with or full of botches. [Partly O.N.Fr. *boche*, ulcer; partly perh. some other root.]

botel, boatel *bō-tel′,* (orig. *U.S.*) *n.* a waterside hotel catering especially for boat-owners: a boat or ship which functions as a hotel. [From *boat* and *hotel.*]

botfly. See **bot.**

both *bōth, adj.* and *pron.* the two: the one and the other.—*adv.* or *conj.* as well (sometimes of more than two). [O.N. *bāthar.*]

bothan *bo′han, n.* a booth, hut: an illegal drinking den. [Gael.]

bother *bodh′ər, v.t.* to perplex or tease: to worry or concern: to fluster: to pester.—*v.i.* to stir oneself: to worry or be concerned (about).—*n.* petty trouble, difficulty, or perplexity.—*interj.* expressing irritation.—*n.* **botherā′tion** (*coll.*).—*adj.* **both′ersome.**— I, they, etc. **cannot be bothered** I, they, etc. consider it too much trouble (to do something): I, they, etc. find (someone or something) annoying (with *with*). [First found in 18th-cent. Irish-born writers; poss. Anglo-Irish for **pother.**]

bothy, bothie *both′i, n.* a humble cottage or hut: a one-roomed hut or temporary dwelling: in Scotland, a barely furnished dwelling for farm-servants. [Cf. **booth.**]

bo tree, bodhi tree *bō trē, bōd′i,* in India and Sri Lanka the pipal, holy tree of the Buddhists, under which Buddha found enlightenment. [Sinh. *bo*, from Pali *bodhi*, perfect knowledge.]

bott. See **bot.**

bottine *bot-ēn′, n.* a high boot: a half-boot: a lady's boot: a small boot. [Fr., dim. of *botte*, boot.]

bottle *bot′l, n.* a narrow-necked hollow vessel for holding liquids: the contents of such a vessel: liquor or drinking: courage, firmness of resolve (*slang*).— *v.t.* to enclose in bottles: to preserve in bottles or jars: to block the entrance of (fig.).—*adj.* **bott′led** enclosed in bottles: preserved in bottles or jars: shaped or protuberant like a bottle: kept in restraint: drunk (*slang*).—*ns.* **bott′leful** as much as fills a bottle:—*pl.* **bott′lefuls; bott′ler** a person or machine that bottles.—**bottle bank** a purpose-built skip in which empty glass bottles, jars, etc. may be deposited for collection for recycling; **bott′le-brush** a brush for cleaning bottles, with bristles standing out from a central axis: a name given to various plants of like appearance.—*v.t.* **bott′le-feed** to feed milk to from a bottle rather than the breast.— **bott′le-gas, bottled gas** liquefied butane or propane gas in containers for use in lighting, cooking, heating, etc.; **bott′le-glass** a coarse green glass used in the making of bottles.—*adj.* and *n.* **bott′le-green** dark green, like bottle-glass.—**bott′le-neck** a narrow place in a road where traffic is apt to be congested (often fig.); **bott′le-nose** a bottle-nosed toothed whale (Hyperoodon); **bott′le-opener; bott′le-party** a more or less improvised drinking party where each brings a bottle; **bott′le-washer** one whose business it is to wash out bottles: a factotum generally.—**bottle off** to draw from the cask and put into bottles; **bottle up** to enclose as in a bottle: to hold back. [O.Fr. *bouteille*, dim. of *botte*, a vessel for liquids—L.L. *butis*, a vessel.]

bottom *bot′əm, n.* the lowest part or surface of anything: that on which anything rests or is founded: the sitting part of the body: the bed of the sea, a river, etc.: the part that supports the contents of a vessel: the seat of a chair: the less dignified end: the foot of a page, hill, etc.: low land, as by a river: the lower part of a ship: groundwork: fundamental character or ingredient: staying power: financial resources.—*adj.* undermost.—*v.t.* to ground or base.—*v.i.* to find bottom: to found, rest.—*adjs.* **bott′omed; bott′omless** having no bottom: very deep: limitless; **bott′ommost** (*-mōst, -məst*) nearest the bottom.—**bottom drawer** a supposed receptacle for possessions hoarded by a young woman against marriage; **bott′om-fish** a fish that feeds on the bed of the sea, a lake, etc. (also collectively).—**at bottom** fundamentally; **at the bottom of** the real origin of; **bet one's bottom dollar** to bet all one has; **bottom out** of prices, etc., to reach and settle at the lowest level, esp. just before a rise; **from the bottom of the heart** with heartfelt sincerity; **get to the bottom of** to investigate exhaustively; **the bottom has fallen out of the market** there has been a sudden reduction in the market demand (for something); **touch, hit,** etc. **bottom** to reach the lowest point. [O.E. *botm.*]

botulism *bot′ū-lizm, n.* sausage-poisoning, or poisoning by tinned or other food infected with *Bacillus botulinus* (or *Clostridium botulinum*) [L. *botulus*, sausage.]

bouclé *bōō′klä, n.* a yarn having the threads looped to give a bulky effect: a fabric made of such a yarn.— Also *adj.* [Fr., curled, looped.]

boudoir *bōō′d′war, n.* a lady's private room. [Fr., *bouder*, to pout, to be sulky.]

bouffant *bōō-fä,* (Fr.) *adj.* puffed out, full, bulging.

Bougainvillaea *bōō-g-ən-vil′t-ə,* or *-vil-ē′ə, n.* a Neotropical genus of Nyctaginaceae, frequently trained over trellises, its triplets of flowers almost concealed by rosy or purple bracts (also **Bougainvil′ia**): (without *cap.*) any member of the genus. [From the first

French circumnavigator of the globe, Louis Antoine de *Bougainville* (1729–1811).]

bough *bow, n.* a branch of a tree　[O E *bôg, bôh,* an arm, the shoulder]

bought. See **buy.**

bougie *boō´zhē, n.* a wax candle. an instrument (orig of waxed linen) for distending contracted mucous canals　[Fr ,—*Bougie* in Algeria.]

bouillabaisse *boō-ya-bes´, n.* a Provençal kind of fish chowder　[Fr]

bouilli *boō-yē, n.* boiled or stewed meat —*n* **bouillon** (*boō´y*ȳ) a strong broth　[Fr , see **boil.**]

boulder *bōld´ər, n.* a large stone rounded by the action of water. a mass of rock transported by natural agencies from its native bed (*geol.*).—*adj* containing boulders.—**bould´er-clay** a stiff stony mass of finely ground rock, usually containing boulders and pebbles, formed as a ground moraine under land-ice.

boule. Same as **buhl.**

boules *boōl, n.pl* a French form of bowls, pétanque. [Fr]

boulevard *boōl´(ə-)var(d), n.* a broad road, walk, or promenade bordered with trees, originally applied to those formed upon the demolished fortifications of a town. a broad main road　[Fr ,—Ger *Bollwerk,* see **bulwark.**]

boulle. See **buhl.**

boult, bolt *bōlt, v t.* to sift through coarse cloth. to examine by sifting —*ns* **bo(u)lt´er** a sieve. a machine for separating bran from flour, **bo(u)lt´ing.**—**bo(u)lting cloth** a firm silk or nylon fabric with various mesh sizes used for boulting meal or flour. for embroidery. or for photographic enlargements.　[O.Fr. *bulter—buleter,* app. from *bure*—L L. *burra,* a coarse reddish-brown cloth—Gr. *pyrrhos,* reddish.]

bounce *bowns, v.i* to jump or spring suddenly: to bound like a ball, to throw oneself about: to burst (into or out of a room, etc.): to come back to one, as a cheque that cannot be cashed.—*v.t* to cause to rebound. to turn out, eject, dismiss.—*n.* a thud a leap or spring.—*adv.* and *interj* expressing sudden or bouncing movement.—*n.* **bounc´er** one who, or that which, bounces· a cheque that bounces. in cricket. a ball bowled so as to bounce and rise sharply off the ground. one employed to eject undesirable people from a club, dance-hall, etc —*adv* **boun´cily.**—*n.* **boun´ciness.**—*adjs* **bounc´ing** large and heavy. lusty swaggering, **bounc´y** given to bouncing, cocky　[Du *bonzen,* to strike, from *bons,* a blow]

bound¹ *bownd, pa.t* and *pa p* of **bind.**—in composition, restricted to, or by, as *housebound, stormbound*—**bound to** obliged to (a person, etc.) certain to (do something) (perh partly from **bound⁴**).

bound² *bownd, n.* a limit: (in *pl*) the limit of that which is reasonable or permitted. (in *pl*) a borderland. land generally within certain understood limits. the district —*v t* to set bounds to to limit, restrain, or surround —*n* **bound´ary** a limit a border termination a hit to the limit of the ground (*cricket*). a score for such a hit —*adjs.* **bound´ed** restricted, cramped, **bound´less** having no limit vast —*n* **bound´lessness.** —**bound´ary-rider** (*Austr*) one who rides around a station and repairs fences —**out of bounds** not to be visited. entered, etc . in such a prohibited place [O Fr *bonne*—L L *bodina*]

bound³ *bownd, v.t* to spring or leap —*n* a spring or leap —*n* **bound´er** one who bounds an obtrusively ill-bred man one whose moral conduct is objectionable —*adj* **bound´ing** moving forward with a bound leaping —**by leaps and bounds** by startlingly rapid stages　[Fr *bondir,* to spring, in O Fr to resound— L *bombitāre*]

bound⁴ *bownd, adj* ready to start (for) on the way to

(with *for,* or following an *adv.,* e g *homeward bound,* also in composition, as *southbound*).—See also **bound¹.**　[O.N *būinn,* pa p. of *būa,* to prepare.]

bounden *bownd´n, adj.* obligatory.　[Archaic pa p. of **bind.**]

bounty *bown´ti, n* liberality in bestowing gifts: the gift bestowed: money offered as an inducement to enter the army, or as a premium.—*adjs* **boun´teous, boun´-** tiful liberal in giving. generous —*advs.* **boun´teously,** **boun´tifully.**—*ns.* **boun´teousness, boun´tifulness.**— **Lady Bountiful** the charitable great lady of a district. [O Fr *bontet* (*bonté*), goodness—L *bonitās, -ātis—bonus,* good.]

bouquet *boōk´ā,* or *-ā´, n* a bunch of flowers: a nosegay· the perfume exhaled by wine. a compliment, praise.—**bouquet garni** (*boō´kā gar-nē*) a bunch or sachet of herbs used as flavouring, removed before serving (Fr., garnished bouquet).　[Fr. *bouquet,* dim of *bois,* a wood; cf It *bosco;* see **boscage, bush.**]

bourbon *bûr´bən,* maize whisky (orig. made in *Bourbon* County, Kentucky).—**Bourbon biscuit** (*boōr´-bon*) two chocolate-flavoured pieces of biscuit with chocolate cream between.　[From the *Bourbon* family, which long reigned in France and Spain.]

bourdon *boōr´dən, n* the refrain of a song: a drone bass. a bass stop in an organ or harmonium.　[See **burden.**]

bourg *boōrg, n.* a town, esp beside a castle: a market-town.　[Fr.]

bourgeois *boōrzh´wa, n.* a citizen. a member of the middle class. a merchant or shopkeeper.—*adj.* middle class: conventional: humdrum. conservative. materialistic.—*n.* **bourgeoisie** (*boōr´zhwa-zē, -zē´*) the middle class of citizens.　[Fr. *bourgeois,* a citizen]

bourgeon. See **burgeon.**

bourkha. Same as **burk(h)a.**

bourn¹, bourne *boōrn, bôrn, born, n.* a boundary, limit, or goal　[Fr. *borne,* a limit.]

bourn², bourne. Same as **burn¹.**

bourree *boōr´ā, -ā´, n.* a brisk dance in duple time. originating in Auvergne or in the Basque provinces. a musical composition in the same rhythm, often introduced in old suites　[Fr.]

bourse *boōrs, n.* an exchange where merchants meet for business. a stock exchange, esp. (*cap.*) that in Paris　[Fr *bourse,* see **purse.**]

bouse, bowse *bows, v t* and *v i.* to haul with tackle.

boustrophedon *boō-* or *bow-strof-ē´don, adj.* and *adv.* (of ancient writing) ploughwise, alternately from right to left and from left to right　[Gr. *boustrophēdon—bous,* ox, *strophē,* a turning]

bout *bowt, n.* a turn, round a spell: a trial. in boxing or wrestling, a contest a fit　[Obs *bought,* conn **bight.**]

boutique *boō-tēk´, n* a shop a department in a shop: a tradesman's stock· about 1960, used esp. for a small, expensive, exclusive dress shop for women now, a small shop, or a department in a shop. selling fashionable clothes, etc　[Fr]

bouton *boō-tô, n.* an enlargement of the end of a nerve fibre in contact with part of another nerve fibre.—*n.* **boutonnière** (*-to-nyer*) a flower for the buttonhole, etc　[Fr , button.]

bouzouki *boō-zoō´ki, n* a plucked metal-stringed instrument, used esp. in Greece　[Mod. Gr.]

bovine *bō´vin, adj* pertaining to cattle· stupid, dull [L *bōs, bovis,* an ox or cow.]

bovver boy *bov´ər boi,* a member of a gang of hooligans in the habit of engaging in street fights using heavy, hobnailed boots (**bovver boots**) to kick their opponents a troublemaker, esp one who uses rough methods　[Prob Cockney pron of **bother.**]

bow¹ *bow, v t* to bend to bend the neck or body in

saluting, acknowledging a compliment, etc.: to submit (to).—*v.t.* to bend or incline downwards: to crush down: to usher with a bow: to express by a bow. —*n.* a bending of the neck or body in salutation.— *adj.* **bowed** (*bowd*) bent forward, esp. in the back.— **bow out** to withdraw or retire from a place, situation, etc.; **make one's bow** to retire ceremoniously: to leave the stage; **take a bow** to acknowledge applause or recognition. [O.E. *būgan*, to bend.]

bow² *bō, n.* a piece of elastic wood or other material for shooting arrows, bent by means of a string stretched between its ends: anything of a bent or curved shape, as the rainbow: a rod strung with horsehair, by which the strings of a violin, etc., are sounded: a ring of metal forming a handle: a knot with one or two loops: a looped knot of ribbons: a necktie or the like, so tied (also **bow tie**): a single movement (up or down) or stroke of the bow in playing an instrument.—*v.i.* to handle the bow in playing.—*v.t.* to play with a bow: to distribute between up-bows and down-bows: to mark such distribution.—*n.pl.* **bow'-compasses** a small pair of compasses, often with a bow-shaped spring instead of a hinge.—*adj.* **bow'-fron'ted** having a convex front.—**bow'-leg** a bandy leg like a bow.— *adj.* **bow'-legged** (*-legd* or *-leg-id*).—**bow'man** an archer; **bow'-saw** a saw with a narrow blade stretched like a bowstring in a narrow bow-shaped frame (also **log'-saw**): a saw with a narrow blade stretched in an H-shaped frame and held taut by tightening a cord at the opposite end of the frame; **bow'shot** the distance to which an arrow can be shot from a bow; **bow'string** the string by which a bow is drawn: a horizontal tie on a bridge or girder.—*adj.* of, for, having, a bowstring. —**bow tie** see bow; **bow'-win'dow** a window projecting in a curve.—**two strings to one's bow** an alternative in reserve. [O.E. *boga*.]

bow³ *bow, n.* the forepart of a ship—often used in *pl.*, the ship being considered to have starboard and port bows, meeting at the stem.—*ns.* **bow'er, bow'er-anch'or** an anchor at the bow or forepart of a ship; **bow'-oar** the oar nearest the bow.—**on the bow** within 45° of the point right ahead. [From a L.G., Du. or Scand. word for shoulder; see **bough**.]

bowdlerise, -ize *bowd'lər-īz, v.t.* to expurgate a book or writing, by removing whatever might raise a blush, esp to do so unnecessarily.—*ns.* **bowdlerisā'tion, -z-**; **bowd'leriser, -z-**; **bowd'lerism.** [From Dr T. *Bowdler* (1754–1825), who published an expurgated Shakespeare in ten volumes in 1818.]

bowel *bow'əl, n.* an interior part of the body: (in *pl.*) the entrails, intestines: (in *pl.*) the interior part of anything. [O.Fr. *boel*—L. *botellus*, a sausage, an intestine.]

bower¹ *bow'ər, n.* a shady enclosure or recess in a garden, an arbour.—**bow'er-bird** an Australian bird that makes a bower adorned with gay feathers, shells, etc. [O.E. *būr*, a chamber; root of *būan*, to dwell.]

bower², bower-anchor. See **bow³**.

bowie knife *bō'i*, in U.S. *bōō'i, nīf*, a strong, one-edged dagger-knife with a blade about twelve inches long. [From Colonel *Bowie*, its inventor, died 1836.]

bowl¹ *bōl, n.* a heavy wooden ball with a bias: (in *pl.*) a game played by rolling such balls on a green towards a jack: (in *pl.*) sometimes the game of skittles (ninepins) or American bowls (tenpins): (in *pl.*) the game of marbles.—*v.i.* to play at bowls: to roll or trundle: to travel swiftly and smoothly in a wheeled vehicle: to pitch the ball to the batsman at the wicket (*cricket*): to be bowler.—*v.t.* to roll or trundle: to deliver by bowling (*cricket*): to put out by hitting the wicket with a bowled ball (also with *out*; *fig.* to overcome).—*ns.* **bowl'er** one who plays at bowls or bowls in cricket; **bowl'ing.**—**bowl'ing-alley** a long narrow covered place for ninepin- or tenpin-bowling; **bowl'ing-crease** see **crease; bowl'ing-green** a smooth grassy plot for bowls.—**bowl over** to knock down: to overwhelm. [Fr. *boule*—L. *bulla*.]

bowl² *bōl, n.* a vessel, characteristically of approximately hemispherical shape, for domestic use: a round drinking-cup, rather wide than deep: the round hollow part of anything. [O.E. *bolla*.]

bowler *bō'lər, n.* a stiff felt hat with a roundish brim.— Also **bow'ler-hat'.** [Said to be name of a hatter who made it in 1850.]

bowline *bō'lin, n.* a rope from the weather side of the square sails to the larboard or starboard bow, to keep the sail close to the wind.—**bowline (knot)** a simple knot making a loop at the end of a rope which will not slip. [M.L.G. *bôline*, M.Du. *boechlyne*.]

bowse. Same as **bouse.**

bowser *bow'zər, n.* an early form of petrol pump: a light tanker used for refuelling aircraft on an airfield (also with *cap.*): a petrol pump (*Austr.* and *N.Z.*) [Orig. trade name.]

bowsprit *bō'sprit, n.* a strong spar projecting over the bows of a ship. [M.L.G. *bôgsprêt*, M Du. *boech-spriet.*]

bowwow *bow'wow', n.* a dog's bark: a dog (*childish* or *facet.*). [Imit.]

box¹ *boks, n.* an evergreen shrub or small tree with hard smooth yellowish wood, often used to border garden-walks and flower-beds (also **box'-tree, box'wood**): its wood (also **box'wood**): extended to various other plants, esp the Eucalyptus. [O.E. *box*—L. *buxus*—Gr. *pyxos*, the box-tree.]

box² *boks, n.* a case or receptacle for holding anything: the contents of a box: a fund: a (Christmas) present: a compartment: a ruled-off space: a pitcher's standing-place (*baseball*): a small house or lodge, as a *shooting-box*, etc.: in a theatre, a small enclosure with several seats: an old square pew or similar enclosure, as a *sentry-box, signal-box, bathing-box, witness-box*, etc.: the driver's seat on a carriage: the case of a ship's compass: a light, padded shield covering the genitals (*cricket*): part of a page enclosed within lines, etc.— *v.t.* to put into or furnish with boxes: to enclose, confine (often with *in*).—*n.* box'ful as much as a box will hold:—*pl.* box'fuls.—box-cam'era a simple box-shaped camera; box'car (*U.S.*) a box-wagon; box'-gird'er a hollow, square or rectangular, girder; Boxing Day the first working day after Christmas, when boxes or presents were traditionally given to employees, etc.; box junction an area at a cross-roads or other road-junction, marked with yellow criss-crossed lines, into which a vehicle may not move unless its exit is clear; box'-kite a kite composed of open-ended boxes; box number a number to which replies to advertisements may be sent, box'-office in a theatre, etc., the office at which seats may be booked: receipts from a play, etc.: ability to draw an audience: an attraction as judged by the box-office.—Also *adj.*— box'-pleat a type of double pleat formed by folding the cloth into two pleats facing opposite directions; box'room a room in which boxes, etc., are stored; box'-seat a driver's seat; box'-wag'on a closed railway wagon.—**box the compass** to name the 32 points in their order in either or both directions: hence to make a complete roundabout in any opinion; **the box** the television set: television (*facet.*). [O.E. *box*—L. *buxem*, acc. of *buxis*—Gr. *pyxis*, a box.]

box³ *boks, n* a blow on the head or ear with the hand. —*v.t.* to strike with the hand or fist.—*v.i.* to fight with the fists —*ns.* box'er one who boxes or is skilled in boxing: a medium-sized, smooth-haired dog of a breed, with bulldog blood, developed in Germany (with *cap.*) a member of a Chinese society hostile to foreigners; **box'ing.—box'ing-glove** a padded glove worn in boxing. [Possibly connected with Gr. *pyx*, with the fist.]

box-calf *boks'-kaf, n.* a tanned calfskin with rectangular markings made by rolling. [Said to be named after one Joseph *Box*, shoemaker.]

boy *boi, n.* a male child: a lad: a son: a young man generally: (Ireland and elsewhere) a man: in some countries a native or coloured servant or labourer (as a form of address, offensive in S. Africa): a slave: (in *pl*) a group of men with whom a man is friendly or familiar (*coll.*): a man with a particular function, skill, etc., as in *backroom boy.—n.* **boy'hood.—***adj.* **boy'ish.—** *adv.* **boy'ishly.—***n.* **boy'ishness.—boy'friend** a girl's favourite boy for the time being; **Boys' Brigade** an organisation of boys for the promotion of habits of obedience, reverence, discipline, and self-respect; (**Boy**) **Scout** a member of the (orig. Boy) Scouts Association, whose aim is to develop alertness and strong character.—**boys will be boys** one must expect and put up with foolish or childish behaviour; (**oh**) **boy** an expression of pleasure, enthusiasm, etc [M E. *boi,* boy.]

boyar *bo-yar', boi'ar, n.* a member of the old Russian aristocracy next in rank to the ruling princes, before the reforms of Peter the Great. [Russ *boyarin.*]

boycott *boi'kot, v.t.* to shut out from all social and commercial intercourse: to refuse to take part in, deal with, handle by way of trade, etc.—*n.* an act of boycotting. [From Captain *Boycott* of County Mayo, who was so treated by his neighbours in Dec. 1880.]

Boyle's law. See **law.**

bra *brà, n.* short for **brassière.—***adj.* **bra'less** not wearing a brassière.

brace *bràs, n.* anything that draws together and holds tightly. an instrument of wood or iron used by carpenters and metal-workers for turning boring tools: a mark ({ or }) connecting words, lines, staves of music, indicating that they are taken together, and also used as a bracket in algebra: a pair or couple (esp. of game shot): (in *pl.*) a combination of straps for supporting the trousers: (in *pl.*) ropes for squaring or traversing horizontally the yards of a ship: a piece of wire fitted over the teeth to straighten them.—*v.t.* to tighten or strengthen, to give firmness to: to tone up.—*n.* **brac'er.—***adj.* **brac'ing** giving strength or tone [O.Fr. *brace* (Fr. *bras*), the arm, power—L. *brāchium, bracchium,* Gr. *brāchiōn.*]

bracelet *bràs'lit, n* an ornament for the wrist: a handcuff (*coll.*). [Fr. dim ,—L. *brāchiāle—brāchium*; see **brace.**]

brachial *bràk'* or *brak'i-əl, adj.* of the arm.—*n* **brachi-a'tion** the use of arms as a supplementary means of locomotion. [L. *brāchium*; see **brace.**]

brachiopod *brak'i-ō-pod, n.* a member of a class **Brachiopoda** (*-op'o-də*) of shelled animals allied to worms and Polyzoa, having usually two long arm-like processes serving to waft food particles to the mouth. [Gr. *brāchiōn,* an arm, and *pous, podos,* a foot]

Brachiosaurus *brak-i-ō-so'rəs, n* a genus of huge lizard-hipped plant-eating dinosaurs, unusual in that their front legs were longer than their back legs: (without *cap.*) a member of the genus. [Gr *brāchiōn,* an arm, *sauros,* a lizard.]

brachy- *brak'i-, -i'-,* in composition, short.—*adjs.* **brachycephalic** (*-si-fal'ik*), **brachycephalous** (*-sef'-ə-les*), short-headed, having a skull whose breadth is 80 (or 78) per cent or more of its length.—*n.* **brachyceph'aly** short-headedness. [Gr. *brachys,* short.]

bracken *brak'ən, n.* the commonest British fern, abundant on hillsides, etc

bracket *brak'it, n* a projecting support a small shelf

fastened to a wall: a gas-pipe projecting from a wall. in printing, one of the marks used to enclose words or mathematical symbols: one of the side pieces of a gun-carriage, supporting the trunnions: the space intervening between overestimated and underestimated shots at a target in straddling (*artillery*): a bracketed group.—*v.t* to support by brackets: to enclose by brackets. to group, as in an honour list, implying equality· to straddle (*artillery*) —**bracket clock** a rectangular clock with an internal pendulum, usu. with one or two handles and often an arched top, designed to stand on a table or wall-bracket. [Fr *braguette*— Sp. *bragueta*—L. *brāca,* sing. of *brācae,* breeches]

brackish *brak'ish, adj.* saltish, rather salt.—*n* **brack'ishness.** [Du *brak,* brackish.]

bract *brakt, n.* a leaf (often modified) that bears a flower in its axil —*adj.* **bract'eal.—***n.* **bract'eate** (*archaeology*) a thin-beaten plate of gold or silver —*adj.* of metal beaten thin: having bracts.—*adj.* **bract'eolate** having bracteoles.—*n.* **bract'eole** a small leaf on the axis of a flower.—*adj.* **bract'less.—***n.* **bract'let** a bracteole. [L. *bractea,* a thin plate of metal, gold-leaf.]

brad *brad, n.* a small nail with a side projection instead of a head —**brad'awl** a small boring tool. [O N. *broddr,* spike.]

Bradshaw *brad'sho, n.* a noted railway-guide, 1839–1961, first issed by George *Bradshaw.*

brady- *brad'i,* in composition, slow.—*n.* **bradycard'ia** (Gr. *kardiā,* heart) slowness of heart-beat. [Gr *bradys,* slow]

brae *brā* (*Scot.*) *n.* the slope bounding a riverside plain a hill-slope [O.N. *brā,* eyelid, cf **brow.**]

brag *brag, v i* and *v.t.* to boast or bluster:—*pr p.* **brag'ging;** *pa.t.* and *pa.p.***bragged.—***n.* a boast or boasting: a thing one boasts of or is proud of· a card game like poker —*adv.* **bragg'ingly.**

braggadocio *brag-ə-dō'shi-ō, -chiō, n.* a braggart or boaster (often with *cap.*): empty boasting:— *pl.* **braggado'cios.** [From *Braggadochio* (prob. *-dok'yō*) in Spenser's *Faerie Queene.*]

braggart *brag'ərt, adj.* boastful.—*n* a vain boaster [Fr *bragard,* vain, bragging.]

Brahma[1] *brä'mə, n* a fowl of Chinese breed, modified in Europe and America.—Also *adj.* [*Brahmaputra,* whence it is said to have been brought.]

Brahma[2] *brä'mə* (*bra-ma'*), *n.* the supreme post-Vedic Hindu deity —*n* **Brah'man** (*-mən*), **Brah'min** one of the highest or priestly caste among the Hindus: (-**min**; *derog.*) a highly cultured person.—*adjs.* **Brahmanic** (*-man'*), **-al, Brahmin'ic, -al, Brah'minee** appropriated to the Brahmans.—*ns* **Brah'manism,** or **-min-,** one of the religions of India, worship of Brahma —**brahmin** (in U S. **Brahman**) **bull** or **cow** zebu, or zebu cross.

braid *brād, v.t.* to plait, intertwine: to arrange in plaits· to thread, wind about through· to trim, bind, or outline with braid —*n* a plait, especially of hair: a band for the hair. a fabric woven in a narrow band: an interweaving, plaiting: embroidery —*adj.* **braid'ed** plaited: entwined, trimmed with braid —*n* **braid'ing** plaiting· manufacture of braid: work in braid· embroidery· braids collectively. [O.E. *bregdan,* to move quickly, flash, change colour, plait, weave]

brail *brāl, n.* one of the ropes used to truss up a sail (*naut*)—*v.t* to haul in, as a sail, by pulling upon the brails. [O.Fr. *brail*—L. *brācāle,* a waist-belt— *brācae,* breeches.]

Braille *brāl, n* a kind of type in relief for the blind, having arbitrary signs consisting of varying combinations of six points arranged thus (⁝⁝) —Also *adj* [From Louis *Braille* (1809–52), the inventor.]

brain *brān, n* (sometimes in *pl*) in vertebrates, that part of the central nervous system that is contained within the skull: in invertebrates, the nervous ganglia near the head end of the body: the seat of the intellect and of sensation: the intellect: (in *pl.*) intelligence, common sense: a person of exceptional intelligence (*coll.*).—*v.t.* to dash out the brains of. —*adjs.* **brained** having brains; **brain'less** without brains or understanding: silly; **brain'y** (*coll.*) well endowed with brains: intellectual.—*n.* **brain'iness.**— **brain'case** the cranium; **brain'child** an original thought or work; **brain coral** a coral with brain-like convolutions.—*adj.* **brain'-dead'.**—**brain death** the cessation of function of the brain, thought by some doctors to be the true indication of death, rather than the cessation of the heartbeat.—Also **cerebral death; brain drain** the continuing loss of citizens of high intelligence and creativity through emigration, **brain'pan** braincase.—**brain stem** the stemlike part of the brain connecting the spinal cord with the cerebral hemispheres, and controlling certain major functions, e.g. the operation of the heart and lungs and the ability to be conscious; **brain'storm** a sudden disturbance of the mind: a sudden inspiration; **brains trust** a committee of experts. a number of reputedly well-informed persons chosen to answer questions of general interest in public and without preparation; **brain'-teaser** a difficult puzzle or problem, **brain'wash, -ing** the subjection of a person to systematic indoctrination or mental pressure with a view to getting him to change his views or to confess to a crime.—*v.t.* **brain'wash.**—**brain'-wave** a sudden bright idea: an access of cleverness.—**on the brain** as an obsession; **pick someone's brains** see **pick.** [O.E. *brægen*.]

braise *brāz, v.t.* to stew in a closed vessel. [Fr *braiser*.]

brake¹ *brāk, n.* a thicket.

brake² *brāk, n.* an instrument for breaking flax or hemp· a harrow: a contrivance for retarding by friction: a kind of vehicle (see **break²**).—*v.t* to slow down or stop with, or as if with, a brake —*v.t.* to apply or operate a brake, esp. on a vehicle: to be slowed down or stopped by a brake.—*adj.* **brake'less** without a brake.—**brake'-block** a block pressed against a wheel as brake; **brake'-shoe** the rubbing part of a brake; **brakes'-man** the man whose business it is to manage the brake of a railway train; **brake'-van** the carriage wherein the brake is worked, **brake'-wheel** the wheel to which a brake is applied. [From root of **break**, cf. Du. *braak*, a flax-brake.]

bramble *bram'bl, n.* the blackberry bush, a wild prickly shrub of the raspberry genus: any rough prickly shrub: a blackberry (*Scot.*).—*n.* **bram'bling** a bird nearly allied to the chaffinch.—*adj.* **bram'bly.** —**bram'ble-bush** blackberry bush or thicket, **bram'ble-finch** the brambling. [O.E. *brēmel.*]

bran *bran, n.* the refuse of grain: the inner husks of corn sifted from the flour: the coarser part of anything.—*adj.* **brann'y.**—**bran'-mash; bran'-pie'**, **bran'-tub** a tub of bran from which Christmas presents, etc., are drawn. [O.Fr. *bran*, bran, perh Celt.]

branch *branch, bransh, n.* a shoot or arm-like limb of a tree: anything like a limb of a tree: any offshoot from a main trunk, as a minor road, railway line, etc. (also *adj.*): a subdivision, a section or department of a subject: any subordinate division of a business, subsidiary shop, office, etc. (also *adj.*).— *v.t.* to divide into branches.—*v.i.* to spread out as a branch (with *out*, *off*, *from*), or in branches.— *adj.* **branched.**—*n.* and *adj.* **branch'ing.**—*adj.* **branch'less** without branches.—*adj.* **branch'y.** [Fr *branche*—L.L. *branca*, a beast's paw.]

branchia *brangk'i-ə, n.* a gill.—*pl* **branch'iae** (*-ē*).— *adjs* **branch'ial; branch'iate** having branchiae. [L. *branchia*—Gr. *branchion* (pl *-a*).]

brand *brand, n* a piece of wood burning or partly burned. an instrument for branding· a mark burned into anything with a hot iron: a trademark, made by burning or otherwise, as on casks: a particular class of goods (as if distinguished by a trademark): a mark of infamy. a general name for the fungoid diseases or blights of grain crops (*bunt, mildew, rust,* and *smut*) —*v.t.* to burn or mark with a hot iron, or otherwise to fix a mark of infamy upon (sometimes with *as*).— *adj.* **brand'ed.**—**brand'ing-iron; brand'-iron** a gridiron an iron to brand with· a trivet or tripod to set a pot or kettle upon; **brand'-name** a trade-name identifying a particular manufacturer's products — *adj.* **brand'-new** quite new (as if newly from the fire). [O E. *brand, brond,* O.N *brandr*, from root of **burn²**.]

brandish *brand'ish, v.t* to wave or flourish as a brand or weapon.—*n* a waving or flourish. [Fr. *brandir, brandiss-* from root of **brand.**]

brandy *brand'i, n.* an ardent spirit distilled from wine: a glass of this.—*adj* **bran'died** heartened or strengthened with brandy —**brand'y-ball** a kind of sweet; **bran'dy-glass** a stemmed drinking-glass with a globular bowl, **brand'y-snap** a thin crisp biscuit flavoured with ginger and orig brandy [Formerly *brand-wine*—Du *brandewijn—branden,* to burn, to distil, and *wijn,* wine]

brant-goose. See **brent-goose.**

brash¹ *brash, n* angular fragments of rock, which occasionally form the basement bed of alluvial deposits: fragments of crushed ice. clippings of hedges or trees.—*adj.* **brash'y.** [Prob. Fr. *brèche*]

brash² *brash, n* an eructation or belching of acid water from the stomach—water-brash. [Prob. onomatopoeic.]

brash³ *brash, adj.* reckless, impetuous (*U.S.*)· forward, bumptious: bold of wood, brittle (*U.S.*).

brasier. Same as **brazier.**

brass *bras, n* an alloy of copper and zinc: effrontery (*slang*): money (*slang*): an article or fixture of brass· a monumental plate of brass, commonly with effigy: (*collectively*) the brass wind-instruments or their players in an orchestra or band —*adj* of brass — *adv.* **brass'ily.**—*ns.* **brass'iness; brass'y** (a stroke with) a brass-soled wooden golf-club (also **brass'ie;** also *adj.*).—*adj* like brass. brazen-faced.—**brass band** a band of players of (mainly) brass wind instruments: a small military band; **brass farthing** a whit; **brass'founder** one who casts objects in brass; **brass hat** (*mil. slang*) a staff officer (with gold braid on his hat); **brass neck** (*coll*) effrontery; **brass'-rubbing** the process of copying the design on a brass plate, etc , on to paper by laying the paper over the brass and rubbing it with coloured wax, chalk, etc.: the copy so obtained; **brass tacks** details of practical business.—**brassed off** (*slang*) dissatisfied or bored; **top brass** brass hats: those in authority at the top (also **the brass**) [O.E. *bræs.*]

brassard *bras'ard, n.* a piece of armour for the arm (also **brassart** *bras'ert,* **brass'et**). an armband or armlet: a symbolic band for the arm. [Fr.—*bras,* arm.]

brasserie *bras'(ə-)rē, n.* a beer garden or restaurant. [Fr., brewery.]

Brassica *bras'i-kə, n.* the turnip and cabbage genus of Cruciferae: (without *cap.*) a plant of this genus. [L., cabbage.]

brassière *bras'i-er,* in U.S sometimes *brə-zēr', n.* a woman's undergarment supporting the breasts. [Fr]

brat *brat, n.* a contemptuous name for a child: an annoying child. [O.E. *bratt,* prob. Old Ir. *brat,* plaid, Gael. *brat,* apron]

brattice *brat'is, ns.* in mediaeval siege operations, a fixed tower of wood: a covered gallery on a castle wall, commanding the wall-face below: a wooden partition: a wooden lining: a partition to control ventilation in a mine. [O.Fr. *breteshe*—L.L. *bretachia;* cf. **bartisan.**]

bratwurst *brat'vöorst, n.* a type of German sausage. [Ger.]

bravado *brav-a'dö, n.* a display of bravery: a boastful threat:—*pl.* **brava'do(e)s.** [Sp. *bravada.*]

brave *bräv, adj.* daring, courageous: noble: making a fine appearance: excellent.—*v.t.* to meet boldly: to defy: to face (out).—*n.* a brave soldier, esp. among the North American Indians.—*adv.* **brave'ly.**—*n.* **brav'ery** courage: heroism: finery, showy dress.— **brave new world** a desirable or perfect future society (from Shak., *Tempest* V, i, 183), usu. used sardonically, specif. by Aldous Huxley as the title of his novel (1932) portraying a society where scientific, etc., progress has produced a repressive, totalitarian régime rather than a utopia. [Fr. *brave;* It. and Sp *bravo.*]

bravo *bra'vö, bra'vö', interj.* well done excellent:—*pl* **bravos, -voes.** [Sp. and It.]

bravura *bra-voo'ra, n.* spirit and dash in execution (*mus.*): a florid air with difficult and rapid passages (*mus.*): brilliant or daring display.—Also *adj.* [It.]

braw *bro, adj.* fine: attired in finery. [Scots form of **brave.**]

brawl *bröl, n.* a noisy quarrel.—*v.i.* to quarrel noisily: to make a disturbance: to murmur or gurgle.—*n.* **brawl'er.**—*n.* and *adj.* **brawl'ing.** [M.E. *bralle.*]

brawn *bron, n.* muscle, esp. of the arm or calf of the leg: thick flesh: muscular strength: a boar: a preparation of meat made from pig's head and ox-feet, cut up, boiled, and pickled.—*n.* **brawn'iness.**—*adj* **brawn'y** fleshy: muscular: strong. [O.Fr. *braon,* flesh (for roasting); of Gmc. origin.]

bray [1] *brä, v.t.* to break, pound, or grind small, as in a mortar.—*n.* **bray'er** an instrument for grinding or spreading ink in printing. [O.Fr. *breier* (Fr. *broyer*).]

bray [2] *brä, n.* the cry of the ass: any harsh grating sound.—*v.i.* to cry like an ass: to give forth harsh sounds. [O.Fr. *brai, brait; braire*—L.L. *bragíre.*]

braze [1] *bräz, v.t.* to cover with, or make like, brass.— *adj.* **brä'zen** of or belonging to brass: impudent.—*v.t.* to face (out) with impudence.—*adv.* **brä'zenly.**—*ns.* **brä'zenness, brä'zenry** effrontery; **brazier** (*bräz'yar, brázh'(y)ər*) a worker in brass.—**bra'zen-face** one remarkable for effrontery.—*adj.* **bra'zen-faced.** [**brass.**]

braze [2] *bräz, v.t.* to join with hard solder.—*n.* **brazier** (*bräz'yar, brázh'(y)ər*) a vessel or tray for hot coals. [O.Fr. *braser,* to burn; perh. influenced by **brass.**]

brazier. See **braze** [1,2].

brazil *bra-zil', n.* usually **brazil'-wood,** the hard reddish wood of the East Indian sappan tree or other species of *Caesalpinia,* used in dyeing: also that of *Guaiacum.*—*n.* **Brazil'ian** a native or citizen of Brazil, in South America.—*adj.* of Brazil.—**Brazil nut** the edible seed of a large Brazilian tree. [O.Fr. *bresil* (Sp. *brasil,* It. *brasile*)—L.L. *brasilium,* a red dye-wood brought from the East. When a similar wood was discovered in South America the country became known as *terra de brasil,* land of red dyewood.]

breach *brěch, n.* a break: an act of breaking: an opening, or discontinuity: a breaking of law, con-

tract, covenant, promise, etc.: a quarrel: a broken condition or part of anything: a gap made in a fortification: surf.—*v.t.* to make a breach or opening in.— **breach of promise** often used simply for breach of promise of marriage; **breach of the peace** a violation of the public peace by riot or the like. [O.E. *bryce, brice,* related to **break.**]

bread *bred, n.* food made of a baked paste of flour or meal: food: livelihood: money (*slang*).—*v.t.* to cover (a cutlet, etc.) with breadcrumbs before cooking.— *adj.* **bread'ed.**—**bread'-and-butt'er** bread sliced and buttered: livelihood.—*adj.* connected with making a living or with the consumption of bread-and-butter: materialistic, practical: descriptive of a letter of thanks for hospitality.—**bread'-basket** a basket for holding bread: the stomach (*slang*); **bread'-board** a board on which bread is cut; **bread'-crumb** (usu. in *pl.*) bread crumbled down e.g. as a dressing (when commercially produced usu. coloured orange) for fish, etc.—*v.t.* to cover with bread-crumbs.— **bread'fruit** the fruit of a tree of the South Sea Islands, which when roasted forms a good substitute for bread; **bread sauce** a thick milk-based sauce made with bread(-crumbs); **bread'-stick** a long, thin stick of bread dough baked until crisp; **bread'winner** one who earns a living for a family.—**bread and circuses** food and amusements at public expense; **bread buttered on both sides** very fortunate circumstances; **know which side one's bread is buttered on** to know how to act from self-interest, **on the breadline,** at subsistence level, with just enough to make ends meet (from **breadline,** a queue of poor or derelict people waiting for free food, esp. from government sources); **take the bread out of someone's mouth** to deprive someone of the means of living. [O.E. *brēad.*]

breadth *bredth, n.* extent from side to side: width: liberality of mind: in art, subordination of details to the harmony of the whole.—*adv.* **breadth'ways, -wise** in the direction of breadth: broadside on. [O.E. *brēdu.*]

break [1] *brāk, v.t.* to divide, part, or sever, wholly or partially, by applying a strain: to rupture: to shatter: to crush: to make by breaking: to destroy the continuity or integrity of: to interrupt (a fall, journey, etc.): to bruise or penetrate the surface of: to break a bone in, or separate the bones of: to subject, overcome, or wear out: to tame or habituate to obedience (also with *in*): to crush the spirit of: to cure (of a habit): to violate (as a law, promise, bounds, prison): to set aside (as a will): to unfurl: to impart (esp. with delicacy): to make bankrupt: to degrade or cashier.— *v.i.* to separate: to come apart, or go to pieces, esp with suddenness: to give way: to start away: to burst forth: to force a passage: to pass suddenly into a condition or action (as into laughter, revolt, sweat, spots): to become variegated or striped: to open or come into view (as day, hope, a scene): (of news) suddenly to become generally known: to become bankrupt: to crack (as the voice): to collapse: to burst into foam: to sever a connection: to fall out (with a friend): to change direction (as a cricket-ball on pitching). to break the balls (see below):—*pa.t.* broke; *pa.p.* brö'ken, less usu **broke.**—*n* an act of breaking: the state of being broken: an opening: a discontinuity: a pause, interval, or interruption: a pause for rest or refreshment: a consecutive series of successful strokes (*billiards, croquet*): the number of points so scored at billiards: a continuous run of anything: the deviation of a ball on striking the pitch (*cricket*): an instance of breaking service (*tennis*): the dawn (*break of day*): onset (of the monsoon): a chance (as in *an even break,* a fair or equal chance): a good chance.—*adj.* **break'able.**—Also *n.,* in *pl.*—*ns* break'ableness; break'age act of breaking or its consequences: a broken place; break'er a person or machine that breaks: a wave broken on rocks or shore.—n. and adj. break'ing.—break'away revolt: secession:—adj. having seceded.—break'down a stoppage through accident: collapse: disintegration: an analysis.—adj. assisting after a breakdown, etc.— n. and adj. break-even see break even.—break'-in an illegal (and sometimes violent) entering of a building; break'ing-point the point at which a person, relationship, situation, etc. breaks down under stress.— adj. break'neck headlong: very fast, usu. dangerously so.—break-out see break out; break point (tennis) a point giving one the opportunity to break service; break'through a forcible passage through a barrier: solving of a problem, esp. scientific, after much effort, opening the way to further developments: any comparable success; break'-up dissolution; break'water a barrier against force of waves.—break a record see record; break a strike see strike; break away to go away, escape, abruptly: to sever connection forcibly or abruptly; break camp to dismantle and pack one's tents, etc.; break cover to burst forth from concealment, as a fox; break down to demolish: to crush: to collapse: to fail completely: to analyse; break even to avoid loss but fail to gain (n. and adj. break'-e'ven); break forth to burst out, issue; break ground to begin working untouched ground: to lead in new work: break in to make (shoes, etc.) less stiff by use (and see break v.t. above); break in, in upon or into to enter violently: to interpose abruptly; breaking and entering house-breaking; break loose to extricate oneself forcibly: to break through all restraint; break off to detach by breaking: to put an abrupt end to: to leave off abruptly, break out to appear suddenly: to break through all restraint: to escape (n. break'-out): to come into sudden activity: to become covered with (a rash, etc.; with in); break service, break someone's serve to win a game in which one's opponent is serving (tennis, etc.); break someone's heart to crush someone with grief; break the balls (or simply break) to open the game by striking the red ball or giving a miss, or to continue the game thus when a similar position occurs (billiards): to open the game by striking one of the red balls (snooker); break the ice (fig.) to get through first difficulties, esp. restraint on first meeting; break through to force a passage through (a barrier); break up to break open: to break in pieces: to go to pieces: to put an end to: to disperse: to dig or plough up: to decay in health or faculties; break wind to void wind; break with to cease relations with, esp. to quarrel with: to cease adherence to (tradition, a habit). [O.E. brecan.]

break², brake brāk, n. a long wagonette: a carriage frame all wheels and no body, used in breaking in horses: an estate car. [break, v.t.]

breaker. See break¹.

breakfast brek'fast, n. a break or breaking of fast· the first meal of the day (also adj.).—v.i. to take breakfast.

bream¹ brēm, n. a freshwater fish of the carp family, with high-arched back: extended to other fishes. [O.Fr. bresme (Fr. brême)—O.H.G. brahsema.]

bream² brēm, v.t. to clean, as a ship's bottom, by burning off seaweed, shells, etc. [Prob. conn. with broom, Du. brem.]

breast brest, n. the forepart of the human body between the neck and the belly: one of the two mammary glands in women (or rudimentary in men), forming soft protuberances on the chest: the corresponding part of any animal: a swelling slope: the part of a jacket, etc. which covers the breast.—v.t. to op-

pose the breast to: to oppose manfully: to mount.— adj. (usu. in composition) breast'ed having (a certain type of) breast(s).—n. breast'bone the sternum, the bone running down the middle of the breast, to which the first seven ribs are attached.—v.t. breast'-feed to give milk to from the breasts rather than from a bottle.—breast'-feeding.—adv. breast'-high' high as the breast; breast'plate a plate or piece of armour for the breast; breast'stroke a swimming-stroke performed on the breast, with circling movements of the arms and legs; breastsummer, bressummer (bres'ə-mər) a summer or beam supporting the whole, or a great part, of the front of a building in the manner of a lintel, breast'work a hastily constructed earthwork.—double-, single-breasted see double, single; make a clean breast to make a full confession. [O.E. brēost.]

breath breth, n. the air drawn into and then expelled from the lungs: power of breathing: life: a single act of breathing: breathing without vibrating the vocal cords (phon.): the time occupied by one breathing: a very slight breeze.—breath'alyze (in Britain, usu. breath'alyse) to test with a breathalyzer. —n. breathalyzer (in Britain, usu. breathalyser) (breth'ə-lī-zər) a device which indicates amount of alcohol in a person's breath, by means of a chemical reaction whose extent is indicated by a moving pointer: a simpler device also using a chemical reaction.—adj. breath'less out of breath: with the breath held or taken away, from excitement, interest, etc.: breezeless.—adv. breath'lessly.—n. breath'lessness.—adj. breath'y of a speaking voice, accompanied by much unvocalised breath: of a singer or instrument-player, without proper breath control, causing impure sound.—adv. breath'ily.—n. breath'iness.—adj. breath'taking astounding.— breath'-test one carried out on a person's breath, by breathalyser or other device, to determine how much alcohol he has consumed.—below, under, one's breath in a low voice; catch one's breath to stop breathing for an instant; out of breath having difficulty in breathing: panting from exertion, etc.; waste one's breath to talk to no avail, profitlessly; take someone's breath away to render someone breathless through astonishment, delight, etc; with bated breath with breath restrained from reverence or fear. [O.E. brǣth.]

breathe brēdh, v.i. to draw in or expel breath or air to or from the lungs or other respiratory organs: to respire: to take breath, to rest or pause: to live.—v.t. to draw into or expel from the lungs: to infuse: to give out as breath: to utter by breath: to utter softly, whisper.—ns. breath'er one who breathes or lives: a spell of exercise: a rest to recover breath; breath'ing the act of breathing: aspiration, secret prayer: respite: one or other of two signs used in Greek to signify presence ('rough breathing') or absence ('smooth breathing') of the aspirate.—breath'ing-space time to breathe or rest: a brief respite.— breathe again to be relieved from an anxiety; breathe down someone's neck to keep too insistently close to someone, esp. by way of supervision; breathe freely to be at ease; breathe one's last to die. [From breath.]

breccia brech'yə, n. a rock composed of angular fragments.—adj. brecciated (brech'i-ā-tid) reduced to or composed of breccia. [It.]

bred bred, pa.t. and pa.p. of breed.

breech brēch, n. (almost always in pl., breeches brich'iz; in Amer. also britches) a garment worn by men on the lower parts of the body—strictly, as distinguished from trousers, coming just below the knee, but often used generally for trousers: the hinder part of anything, esp. of a gun (*pl.* in these senses pron. *brĕch'iz*) —*n.* **breeching** (*brich'ing*) a part of a horse's harness attached to the saddle, coming round the breech and hooked to the shafts: a strong rope attached to the breech of a gun to secure it to a ship's side —**breech birth, breech delivery** one in which the buttocks come first; **breech'es-buoy** a life-saving apparatus enclosing the person like a pair of breeches; **breech'-loader** a firearm loaded by introducing the charge at the breech instead of the muzzle —*adj.* **breech'-loading.—wear the breeches** (said of a wife) to be master [O.E. *brēc, pl* of *brōc.*]

breed *brēd, v.t.* to generate or bring forth: to cause or promote the generation of, or the production of breeds of: to train or bring up: to cause or occasion —*v.i.* to be with young: to produce offspring: to be produced or brought forth:—*pa.t* and *pa.p.* **bred.**—*n.* that which is bred, progeny or offspring: a strain, variety or race: a kind.—*ns* **breed'er; breed'ing** act of producing: education: manners.—Also *adj.*— **breeder reactor** a nuclear reactor capable of creating more fissile material than it consumes in maintaining the chain reaction; **breed'ing-ground** a place where animals, etc. go to breed: an attitude, environment, etc. which fosters or creates (esp something considered undesirable) (*fig.*). [O.E *brēdan,* to cherish, keep warm.]

breeks *brēks, n.pl* Scots form of **breeches,** trousers

breeze[1] *brēz, n* a light wind —*v i.* to blow as a breeze to go briskly (*slang*): to do, achieve, etc something with ease (with *through*).—*adj.* **breeze'less.**—*adv* **breez'ily.**—*n.* **breez'iness.**—*adj* **breez'y** fanned with or subject to breezes: bright, lively, exhilarating [Old Sp. *briz,* north-east wind.]

breeze[2] *brēz, n.* furnace refuse used in making **breeze brick, breeze blocks, breeze concrete** for building. [Perh. O Fr. *brese*]

bregma *breg'ma, n* the part of the skull where the frontal and the two parietal bones join—sometimes divided into the right and left bregmata:—*pl* **breg'-mata.** [Gr]

breloque *bra-lok', n* an ornament attached to a watch-chain. [Fr.]

bremsstrahlung *bremz'shtra-lŏŏng, n.* electromagnetic radiation produced when an electron collides with, or is deflected by, a positively charged nucleus [Ger *bremsen,* to brake, *Strahlung,* radiation.]

Bren (gun), bren *bren (gun), n* a light machine-gun [*Brno,* in Czechoslovakia, and *En*field, in England]

brent-goose *brent'gŏŏs, n* a small wild goose, having the head, neck, long wing feathers, and tail black, the belly white, the rest slaty-grey, often confounded with the barnacle goose —Also **brant'-goose** or **brent barnacle.** [Prob *branded,* brindled]

brer *brûr, brâr, n.* (southern *U.S dial*) brother

bressummer. Same as **breastsummer.**

brethren *bredh'ran, pl of* **brother.**

Breton *bret'an, n.* a native of Brittany (*Bretagne*), France: the Celtic tongue of Brittany (also without *cap.*; also **Breton hat**) a hat with a rounded crown and turned-up brim —*adj* of Brittany: Armoric

breve *brēv, n* the mark of a short vowel (as in *ĕ*), opp to **macron:** an obsolescent note. ‖ O ‖, twice as long as the longest now used (the semibreve), but half (or in 'perfect' time one-third) as long as the obsolete long (*mus*) [L *brevis,* short.]

brevet *brev'it, n* a military commission entitling an officer to take rank above that for which he receives pay —*v t* to confer such rank on —*pr p* **brev'eting;** *pa t* and *pa p* **brev'eted** (those who pronounce *bri-vet'* write **brevett'ing, brevett'ed**) [Fr .—L *brevis,* short]

breviary *brēv'i-ar-i, n* a book containing the daily

service of the R C Church. [L *brēviārium—brevis,* short.]

brevity *brev'it-i, n.* shortness. conciseness. [Poss A Fr. *breveté,* shortness, influenced by L. *brevitās, brevitātis,*—L. *brevis,* short.]

brew *brŏŏ, v.t.* to prepare by infusion, boiling and fermentation, as beer from malt and other materials, or by infusion, mixing, or boiling, without fermentation, as tea, punch: to contrive or plot —*v i.* to perform the operation of brewing ale or beer: to be gathering or forming —*n.* a brewing: a brewage: a variety of making of a brewed beverage: a variety.—*ns* **brew'age** something brewed: mixed liquor, **brew'er** one who brews; **brew'ery** a place for brewing, **brew'ing** the act of making liquor from malt: the quantity brewed at once.—**brewers' yeast, brewer's yeast** a yeast used in brewing, esp. *Saccharomyces cerevisiae,* also used medically as a source of the vitamin B complex vitamins. [Ó E. *brēowan.*]

briar. See **brier**[1,2].

Briard *brē-ar(d), n.* a large, heavy, hairy dog of a French breed [*Brie,* district in N.E. France.]

bribe *brib, n.* something offered to influence the judgment unduly or corrupt the conduct.—*v.t.* to influence by a bribe: to gain over.—*v.i.* to practise bribery.—*ns* **brib'er; brib'ery** the act of giving or taking bribes. [O Fr *bribe,* a lump of bread]

bric-à-brac, bricabrac *brik'a-brak, n.* old curiosities, knick-knacks, or other treasured odds and ends. [Fr]

brick *brik, n.* baked or 'burned' clay. a shaped block of burned clay, generally rectangular: a brick-shaped block of other material, often compressed: a child's building block of wood, etc : a loaf or a bun more or less in the shape of a brick: a good, kind person (*coll.*) —*adj.* made of brick(s).—*v t* (with *in, up,* etc) to fill with brick: to cover with brick or an appearance of brick: to wall in with brick —*n.* **brick'ing** brickwork: imitation brickwork —*adj* **brick'y** like or of brick —**brick'bat** a piece of brick, esp as a missile: a critical remark (*fig.*), **brick'-kiln** a kiln in which bricks are made, **brick'layer** one who builds with bricks; **brick'laying; brick'maker; brick'making.**—*adjs* **brick'-red** of the colour of an ordinary red brick, **brick'shaped** of the shape of a standard brick.—**brick'-tea'** tea pressed into cakes; **brick'work** work constructed in brick: bricklaying: (in *pl*) a factory for bricks.—**drop a brick** to say or do something horrifyingly tactless or indiscreet, **like a ton of bricks** heavily and promptly, **like banging, knocking one's head against a brick wall** said of a laborious but unrewarding attempt, e g to persuade, inform, etc ; **make bricks without straw** to try to do a piece of work without the materials necessary for it. to make something that will not last [Fr *brique,* from the root of **break.**]

bridal *brid'al, adj* belonging to a bride or a wedding: nuptial [O E *brydealo,* lit bride-ale; **bride and ale** (feast)]

bride *brid, n* a woman about to be married or newly married —**bride'cake, bride's'-cake** a cake distributed at a wedding, **bride'groom** a man about to be married or newly married, **brides'maid, brides'man** young unmarried people who attend the bride and bridegroom at a wedding [O E *bryd*]

bridge[1] *brij, n* a structure spanning a river, road, etc giving communication across it: the narrow raised platform whence the captain of a ship gives directions: a thin upright piece of wood supporting the strings in a violin or similar instrument the bony part of the nose. a support for a billiard cue: a bridge-like structure by which false teeth are borne by natural teeth or roots: in the theatre. a platform that rises above the stage· anything that connects across a gap —*v.t.* to be or to build a bridge over: to connect the extremities of (a gap) (*fig.*): to make an electrical connection between.—*n.* **bridg'ing** the process of making, or the construction forming, a bridge: a brace or braces fixed between joists to strengthen them: provision of credit necessary for a business transaction: a method of keeping balance on overhanging rock —Also *adj.*—**bridge'-builder** one who builds bridges· one who tries to reconcile hostile parties, etc., esp. in diplomacy; **bridge'head** a fortification covering the end of a bridge nearest to the enemy's position: a place suitable for such fortification: any advanced position seized in enemy territory, **bridging loan** a short-term loan, usu. for a fairly large sum and at a relatively high rate of interest, providing bridging for a business transaction, esp house purchase.—**cross a bridge when one comes to it** not to bother about a future problem until it affects one. [O.E. *bryg*]

bridge² *brij, n.* a modification of whist in which the dealer or his partner chooses the trump-suit, or notrumps, and the dealer plays his partner's hand as a dummy, with peculiarities in scoring—superseded by, and now usu. used to refer to, *auction bridge* and *contract bridge*. [Earlier known as *bridge whist, biruch.*]

bridie *brī'di, (Scot.) n.* a meat turnover

bridle *brīd'l, n.* the apparatus on a horse's head by which it is controlled: any curb or restraint: a movement expressing resentment, scorn, or vanity—a throwing back of the head with a forward tilt, like a horse pulled up by the bridle.—*v.t.* to put a bridle on· to manage by a bridle: to check or restrain.—*v.i.* to make the movement described (often with *up; at* the thing taken amiss) —*adj.* **bri'dled.—bri'dle-path, -road** a path or way for those riding or leading horses. [O.E *brīdel.*]

Brie *brē, n* a white, soft cheese made in *Brie,* N.E France

brief *brēf, n.* a summary of a client's case for the instruction of counsel: a writ: a short statement of any kind: instructions: (in *pl.*) close-fitting legless pants —*adj.* short. concise: insubstantial, barely adequate. —*v.t* to issue instructions to.—*n.* **brief'ing** action, or an instance, of making or giving a brief: instructions. —*adj.* **brief'less.—***adv.* **brief'ly.—***n.* **brief'ness.— brief'-bag, -case** a small case for carrying briefs, or for other papers, etc.—**hold a brief** to be retained as counsel: to assume the attitude of advocate rather than judge, **hold no brief for** not to support or advocate; **in brief** in few words; **papal brief** a papal document issued without some of the solemnities proper to bulls; **take a brief** to undertake a case, **to be brief** in order to speak in few words [Fr. *bref*—L. *brevis,* short]

brier¹, briar *brīr, brī'ər, n.* a prickly shrub: a wild rose bush.—**sweet brier** eglantine, a wild rose with scented leaves. [O.E (Anglian) *brēr* (W.S *brǣr*).]

brier², briar *brī'ər, n* the white heath, a shrub grown in Algeria· a tobacco-pipe made of its root. [Fr *bruyère,* heath.]

brig *brig, n* a two-masted, square-rigged vessel a place of detention on board ship (*U.S navy*): a prison (*U S slang*). [Shortened from **brigantine.**]

brigade *brig-ād', n* a body of troops consisting of a group of regiments, battalions, or batteries commanded by a general officer· a band of people more or less organised.—*v.t.* **brigadier** (*brig-ə-dēr'*) formerly **brig'adier-gen'eral** a general officer of the lowest grade, who has command of a brigade. [Fr. *brigade* —It *brigata*—L L *briga,* strife.]

brigand *brig'ənd, n.* a bandit or freebooter —*ns.*

brig'andage, brig'andry. [Fr ,—It *brigante*—L L *briga,* strife.]

brigantine *brig'ən-tēn, n* a two-masted vessel, with the main mast of a schooner and the foremast of a brig [Fr *brigantin*—It *brigantino,* pirate ship]

bright *brīt, adj* shining full of light: vivid: clear· cheerful. vivacious: clever: illustrious —*adv.* brightly clearly.—*v.t.* and *v.t.* **bright'en** to make or grow bright or brighter to clear up —*adv.* **bright'ly.** —*n.* **bright'ness.—bright and early** very early. in good time; **the bright lights** the places of entertainment in a city centre [O E. *byrht, beorht*]

brill *bril, n.* a fish akin to the turbot, spotted with white

brilliant *bril'yənt, adj.* sparkling· glittering: splendid superlatively bright, having a dazzling hard lustre· of outstanding or conspicuous ability. showily, strikingly, or superficially clever: performing or performed in a hard or showy manner or with great display of technical skill. brilliant-cut —*n.* a diamond or other gem cut in a many-faceted form resembling two truncated cones base to base —*ns.* **brill'iance, brill'iancy; brill'iantine** (*-tēn*) a dressing for making the hair glossy.—*adv.* **brill'iantly.—***n.* **brill'iantness.—***adj.* **brill'iant-cut** of gems, cut in a 58-faceted form. [Fr. *brillant,* pr.p. of *briller,* to shine.]

brim *brim, n.* the upper edge of a vessel or of a similarly-shaped cavity: the rim of a hat.—*v.i.* to be or become full to the brim.—*pr.p.* **brimm'ing;** *pa.t* and *pa.p* **brimmed.—***adj.* **brim'-full** full to the brim· brimming with tears.—*adjs.* **brim'less** without a brim; **brimmed** brim-full: having a brim (used also in composition).—*adv.* and *adj.* **brimm'ing.** [M.E *brymme.*]

brimstone *brim'stən, n.* sulphur: a virago (*fig.*): (in full, **brimstone butterfly**) a common yellow butterfly. [Lit burning stone, from O.E. *brȳne,* a burning—*byrnan,* to burn, and **stone;** cf Ger. *Bernstein.*]

brinded *brin'did,* **brindled** *brin'dld,* **brindle** *brin'dl, adjs.* marked with spots or streaks.—*n* **brin'dle** the state of being brindled. [See **brand.**]

brine *brin, n* very salt water —*adjs* **brin'ish** like brine· somewhat salt; **brin'y** pertaining to brine or to the sea. salt —**brine'-pan, -pit** a pan or pit in which brine is evaporated to obtain salt: a salt spring —**the briny** (*coll.*) the sea [O.E. *brȳne,* a burning.]

bring *bring, v t.* to fetch: to cause to come: to persuade. to adduce or institute (as an argument, charge, action):—*pa.t* and *pa p.* **brought** (*brot*).—*ns.* **bring'er; bring'ing.—bring about** to bring to pass, effect: to turn round; **bring down** to humble: to shoot: to overthrow: to lower; **bring down the house** to call forth a general burst of applause; **bring forth** to give birth to, produce; **bring forward** to advance. in bookkeeping (used in *pa.p.*), to transfer (a partial sum) to the head of the next column; **bring home** to prove: to impress; **bring in** to introduce: to yield. to pronounce (a verdict), **bring off** to bring away, as by a boat from a ship: to rescue· to achieve, **bring on** to induce to cause to advance· to advance the growth of (plants), **bring oneself to** to persuade or steel oneself to (do something unacceptable); **bring out** to make clear, or prominent: to put before the public, as a book, a play, a singer; **bring round** to restore from illness or unconsciousness: to win over, **bring to** to restore to consciousness: to bring to a standstill (*naut.*), **bring up** to rear or educate: to introduce to notice to make prominent: to vomit, **bring up the rear** to come last [O.E *bringan,* to carry, bring.]

brinjal *brin'jal, -jol, n* in India, the egg-plant, or its fruit [Sans *vātingana,* through Pers., Ar and Port]

For other sounds see detailed chart of pronunciation

brink *bringk*, *n* the edge or border of a steep place or of a river (often *fig*) —**brink'manship**, the action or art of going to the very edge of, but not into, war or other disaster in pursuit of a policy.—**on the brink of** (*fig.*) on the point of, very near. [Prob. Dan. *brink*, declivity.]

brio *brē'ō*, *n*. liveliness, vivacity, spirit. [It.]

brioche *brē-osh'*, *n*. a type of light, soft loaf or roll rich with butter and eggs. [Fr.]

briquette, briquet *bri-ket'*, *n*. a brick-shaped block made of coal-dust: a small brick-shaped slab. [Fr *briquette*, dim. of *brique*, brick.]

brisk *brisk*, *adj.* full of life and spirit: lively promptly active: sharp —*adv* **brisk'ly**.—*n* **brisk'ness**. [First found in Shakespeare's time; poss. Welsh *brysg*, brisk of foot; perh. Fr. *brusque*.]

brisket *bris'kit*, *n*. the breast (*Scot.*): the breast of an animal, esp. the part next to the ribs: meat from this part of an animal. [Perh. conn. with Fr. *brechet*, *brichet*.]

brisling *bris'ling*, *n* a Norwegian sprat. [Norw , sprat]

bristle *bris'l*, *n*. a short stiff hair.—*v.i.* to stand erect, as bristles: to be set as with bristles: to be copiously furnished, be full (with *with*; *fig.*): to have or set bristles erect: to show rage or resistance (*fig.*).—*v.t.* to cover, as with bristles: to make bristly: to erect (as bristles):—*pr.p.* **brist'ling**; *pa.t* and *pa p.* **brist'led**.—*adj.* **brist'led** furnished with bristles.—*n*. **brist'liness**. —*adj.* **brist'ly** set with bristles: rough —**brist'le-tail** any insect of the Thysanura; **brist'le-worm** a chaetopod. [Conn with O.E. *byrst*.]

Bristol *bris'tl*, *n*. a city in the county of Avon.—*n.pl.* **bris'tols** breasts (see **titty**; Cockney rhyming slang from *Bristol city*) —**Bristol fashion** in good order.

Brit *brit*, *n*. (*coll.* shortening of **British**) a Briton.

Britannic *brit-an'ik*, *adj.* pertaining to Britannia or Britain (*arch.*, surviving officially in *Britannic majesty*).—**Britann'ia** a seated female figure with a trident and helmet, representing Britain or the British Commonwealth.—**Britannia metal** an alloy, mainly tin with copper, antimony, lead or zinc or a mixture of these, similar to pewter. [L *Britannia*, *Brittan(n)ia*, Great Britain or the British Islands.]

britches. See **breech.**

British *brit'ish*, *adj.* pertaining to Britain, to its former or present inhabitants or citizens, or to the empire or commonwealth of nations of which it is the nucleus. —*n*. the language of the ancient Britons: the British people.—*ns.* **Brit'ishism, Brit'icism** (*-sizm*) an expression characteristic of the English spoken in Britain.—**Brit'isher** (orig. *U.S.*) a native or citizen of Britain.—**British disease** extreme militancy in industrial relations, esp. excessive use of strikes; **British thermal unit** see **heat unit** under **heat.** [O.E. *Brettisc—Bret*, a Briton, Welshman.]

Briton *brit'ən*, *n*. one of the Brythonic inhabitants of Britain before the coming of the English, or one of their present representatives the Welsh: a native or citizen of Great Britain or of any of the associated states. [L. *Britto*, *-ōnis*, or *-ōnis*; see **Brythonic.**]

brittle *brit'l*, *adj.* apt to break: easily broken: frail.— *n* **britt'leness**.—**britt'le-star** an ophiuroid or sandstar. [O E. *brēotan*, to break.]

broach *brōch*, *n.* a tapering, pointed instrument, used chiefly for boring or rounding holes: a spit: (also **broach'-spire**) a church spire without parapets, consisting of a tall octagonal and a low square pyramid interpenetrating each other: a visible corner of the square pyramid in such a spire.—*v.t.* to pierce as a cask, to tap: to open up or begin: to utter.—*n*. **broach'er.** [Fr. *broche*; cf. **brooch.**]

broad *brōd*, *adj* wide large, free or open outspoken:

coarse, indelicate: liberal minded: widely diffused: covering a wide range, spectrum, etc : giving prominence to main elements, or harmony of the whole, without insisting on detail: slow and full-toned: strongly marked in pronunciation or dialect.—*n* the broad part· (in East Anglia) a lake-like expansion of a river: a broadpiece: a woman (*slang*)· sometimes, a prostitute (*slang*).—*advs.* **broad; broad'ly**.—*v.t.* and *v.i.* **broad'en** to make or grow broad or broader.—*n*. **broad'ness**.—**broad'-arr'ow** a mark (↑) on government property.—*adj.* **broad'-based** including a wide range of opinions, subjects, political groups, etc.— **broad'-bean** the common bean.—*adj* **broad'cast** scattered or sown over the general surface: dispersed widely: communicated generally, by word of mouth, pamphlets, radio, TV, or any other means: by means of broadcast.—*adv.* in all directions —*n*. sowing by broadcasting· general dissemination: the sending forth of material by radio or TV for reception by the public.—*v.t* and *v.i.* to scatter, broadcast or disseminate freely by any means, esp by radio or TV transmission:—*pa t.* and *pa.p.* **broad'cast**, by some **broad'casted**.—*ns.* **broad'caster; broad'casting.**— **Broad Church** a party within the Church of England favouring a broad and liberal interpretation of dogmatic definitions and creed subscription; **broad'cloth** a fine woollen fulled black cloth; **broad day(light)** fully diffused daylight —*adj* **broad'-gauge** see **gauge.** —**broad jump** (*U S*) long jump.—*adjs.* **broad'-leaf** having broad leaves, not needles; **broad'loom** (of carpet) woven on a wide loom; **broad'-mind'ed** liberal: tolerant.—**Broad Scots** (also **Scotch**) older, or dialect, Scottish forms of English, **broad'sheet** a sheet of paper printed usu on one side only a newspaper of large format, measuring approx. 40 × 60 centimetres (about 16 × 24 inches); **broad'side** all the guns on one side of a ship of war: their simultaneous discharge: a critical attack (*fig.*) —*adj* **broad'-spectrum** widespectrum.—**broad'sword** a cutting sword with a broad blade.—**broad'tail** fur prepared from the skin of very young Karakul lambs.—*advs.* **broad'ways, -wise** breadthwise.—**as broad as it is long** six of one and half-a-dozen of the other [O E. *brād*.]

brocade *brōk-ād'*, *n.* a silk stuff on which figures are wrought.—*adj.* **brocad'ed** woven or worked in the manner of brocade: dressed in brocade. [It. *broccato*, Fr. *brocart*, from It *broccare*, Fr. *brocher*, to prick, stitch; from root of **broach.**]

broccoli *brok'ə-li*, *n.* a hardy variety of cauliflower: (also **sprouting broccoli**) a variety of which the purple or green floret buds, and their stalks, are eaten as a vegetable [It.; pl. of *broccolo*, a sprout, dim. of *brocco*, a skewer, a shoot]

broch *brohh*, *n.* a dry-built circular tower of the late Iron Age with galleries in the thickness of the wall, common in the north of Scotland, very rare in the south: a luminous ring around the moon.—Also **brogh** and **brough.** [Scots—O.N. *borg*.]

brochure *brō'shoor*, *-shoō r'*, *bro'*, *n.* a pamphlet. [Fr ,—*brocher*, to stitch—*broche*, a needle. See **broach.**]

brock *brok*, *n.* a badger. [O.E. *brocc*—Celt (as Gael. *broc*).]

brocket *brok'it*, *n.* a stag in its second year, with its first, dagger-shaped, horns. [Fr. *brocard—broque*, a spike]

broderie anglaise *brod-rē ā-glez*, *brō'də-ri ā'glāz*, open-work embroidery [Fr., English embroidery.]

brogh. See **broch.**

brogue *brōg*, *n.* a stout shoe (also **brō'gan**): an accent, esp. Irish (perh a different word) [Ir. *brōg*, dim *brōgan* and Gael *brōg*, a shoe.]

broil *broil*, *n* a noisy quarrel: a confused disturbance.

—*n.* **broil'er** one who stirs up broils. [Fr. *broullier*, to trouble.]

broil[2] *broil, v.t* to cook over hot coals: to grill.—*v.i.* to be greatly heated.—*n.* **broil'er** a very hot day: a quickly-reared young chicken sold ready for broiling (also *adj.*).

brokage. See **broker.**

broke *brōk, pa.t.* and old *pa.p.* of **break** surviving as *pa.p.* chiefly in the sense of hard up.—*pa.p.* **brōk'en.** —*adj.* **brōk'en** rent: infirm: humbled or crushed: thrown into disorder: dispersed, routed: altered in direction: shattered in health, spirit, estate or position: bankrupt: trained to saddle or bridle: infringed: variegated: with surface interrupted: incomplete, fragmentary: interrupted: uncertain: of a language, ill spoken, as by a foreigner.—*adv.* **brōk'enly.**—*n.* **brōk'enness.**—*adjs.* **brok'en-backed'** having the back dislocated: of a ship, so loosened in her frame as to droop at both ends; **brok'en-down** disintegrated: decayed: ruined in character or strength; **brok'en-heart'ed** crushed with grief: greatly depressed in spirit.—**broken home** the home of children whose parents are divorced or have separated; **broken man** one whose life is completely shattered.—*adj.* **brok'en-wind'ed** having short breath or disordered respiration, as a horse.

broker *brōk'ər, n.* one employed to buy and sell for others: a secondhand dealer: a go-between.—*v.i* **broke** to bargain, negotiate.—*ns.* **brōk'erage, brōk'age,** the business of a broker: commission for transacting business for others. [M.E. *brocour*— A.Fr. *brocour.* The original meaning seems to be tapster; cf. **broach.**]

brolly *brol'i,* (*coll.*; a clipped form) *n.* an umbrella.

brome-grass *brōm'-gräs, n.* a grass (*Bromus*) strongly resembling oats. [Gr. *bromos,* a kind of oats.]

bromine *brō'mēn, -min, -min, n.* a non-metallic chemical element (at. numb. 35; symbol Br), a red liquid giving off an irritating, poisonous brown vapour.—*n.* **brō'mate** a salt of bromic acid.—*adj* **brō'mic.**—*n.* **brō'mide** a salt of hydrobromic acid. a platitudinous person (from the use of bromides as sedatives): a platitude: a type of monochrome photographic print, loosely applied to other types.—*adj.* **brōmid'ic** conventionally commonplace.—**bromide paper** in photography, a paper with a sensitive surface containing silver bromide, used in printing from a negative. [Gr. *bromos,* stink.]

broncho. See **bronco.**

bronchus *brong'kəs, n.* either of the main forks of the windpipe:—*pl.* **bronch'i** (-*i*).—*n.pl.* **bronch'ia** the ramifications of the bronchi.—*adj.* **bronch'ial** pertaining to the bronchi, or the bronchia.—*n.* **bronch'iole** (-*ōl*) any of the minute branches of the bronchi.—*adj.* **bronchitic** (-*it'ik*) pertaining to bronchitis. —*n.* one suffering from bronchitis.—*n.* **bronchitis** (-*i'tis*) inflammation of the lining of the bronchial tubes.—**bron'cho-** (-*kō-*) in composition, relating to the bronchi.—*ns.* **bron'cho-dila'tor** any drug that causes the bronchi to expand; **bronch'oscope** an instrument which, when passed down into the bronchi, allows their examination, the removal of foreign bodies, etc.—*adjs.* **bronchoscop'ic, -al.**—*adv.* **bronchoscop'ically.**—*n.* **bronchos'copy.** [Gr. *bronchos,* windpipe; *bronchia,* bronchia.]

bronco, broncho *brong'kō, (U.S.) n.* a half-tamed horse:—*pl.* **bron'cos, bron'chos.**—**bronc'o-buster** one who breaks in broncos: a cowboy. [Sp. *bronco,* rough, sturdy.]

Brontosaurus *bron-tō-sör'əs, n.* a popular (and former) name for Apatosaurus, a genus of lizard-hipped, quadripedal, herbivorous dinosaurs, found fossil in Wyoming and Colorado: (without *cap.*) a member of this genus (also **bront'osaur**). [Gr. *brontē,* thunder, *sauros,* lizard.]

Bronx cheer *brongks chēr, (U.S.)* a vulgar sound of disapproval, a raspberry. [From the *Bronx* borough of New York City.]

bronze *bronz, n.* an alloy of copper and tin: a copper alloy without tin: anything cast in bronze: the colour of bronze: a bronze medal.—*adj.* made of bronze: coloured like bronze.—*v.t.* and *v.i.* to make or become bronze-like.—*adj.* **bronzed** coated with bronze: bronze-coloured, sunburned.—*n.* **bronz'ing** the process of giving or assuming the appearance of bronze.—*adj.* **bronz'y** having the appearance of bronze.—**Bronze Age** a prehistoric condition or stage of culture marked by the use of bronze as the material for tools and weapons—coming between the Stone Age and the Iron Age; **bronze medal** in athletics competitions, etc. the medal awarded as third prize [Fr ,—It. *bronzo, bronzino*—perh. from L. (*aes*) *Brundusīnum,* (brass) from Brindisi; or perh. from Pers. *birinj, pirinj,* copper.]

brooch *brōch, n.* an ornamental clasp with a joined pin fitting into a hook. [Fr. *broche,* a spit; see **broach.**]

brood *brōōd, n.* something bred: offspring, children, or family: a race, kind: the number hatched, produced, or cherished at once: condition of breeding or brooding.—*adj.* for breeding (as in *brood-mare,* etc.).—*v.t.* to sit upon or cover in order to breed or hatch: to hatch: to cover, as with wings: to mature or foster with care: to meditate moodily upon.—*v.i.* to sit as a hen on eggs: to hang envelopingly: to think anxiously for some time: to meditate silently (with *on, over*).—*ns.* **brood'er; brood'ness.**—*adv.* **brood'ingly.**—*adj.* **brood'y** inclined to sit or incubate: apt to brood or to breed. [O.E. *brōd;* Du. *broed;* cf. **breed.**]

brook[1] *brōōk, n.* a small stream. [O.E. *brōc,* water breaking forth.]

brook[2] *brōōk, v.t.* to enjoy: to bear or endure. [O.E. *brūcan,* to use, enjoy.]

brooklime *brōōk'līm, n.* a speedwell that grows in brooks and ditches. [**brook,** and O.E. *hleomoc,* brooklime.]

broom *brōōm, n.* a papilionaceous shrub, *Cytisus scoparius,* or kindred kind: a besom made of its twigs or of anything else: a long-handled domestic sweeping brush.—*v.t.* to sweep with a broom.— **broom'staff, broom'stick** the handle of a broom.— **marry over the broomstick** or **jump the besom** or **broomstick** to go through an irregular form of marriage in which both jump over a broomstick; **new brooms sweep clean** people newly appointed to a position work very conscientiously, or try to sweep away abuses, old attitudes, old methods, etc. [O.E *brōm.*]

brose *brōz, n.* a food made by pouring boiling water or milk on oatmeal or peasemeal, seasoned with salt and butter [Scot.]

broth *broth, n.* an infusion or decoction of vegetable and animal substances in water, used as soup or (often with other substances added) as a medium for culture of bacteria. [O.E. *broth*—*brēowan,* to brew, see **brew.**]

brothel *broth'l, n.* a house of prostitution [M.E. *brothel,* worthless person—O.E. *brothen,* ruined; influenced in meaning by **bordel.**]

brother *brudh'ər, n.* a male in relation to another of either sex born of the same parents or parent (*half-brother*)· any one closely united with or resembling another associated in common interests, occupation, etc . a fellow-member of a religious order, a guild, etc.: a fellow-creature· a fellow-citizen a co-religionist. a kinsman (*B*):—*pl* **broth'ers** and **breth'ren,** the latter esp. used in the sense of fellow-members and in the names of certain bodies —*adj* associated in any relation (also in composition as **brother-man'**) —*n* **broth'erhood** the state of being a brother: an association of men for any purpose.—*adj* **broth'erlike**. —*n*. **broth'erliness**.—*adj*. **broth'erly** like a brother: kind: affectionate.—**broth'er-in-law** the brother of a husband or wife: a sister's husband: a husband's or wife's sister's husband:—*pl*. **broth'ers-in-law**. [O.E. *brōthor*, pl. *brēther*.]

brough. See broch.

brought *brot*, *pa.t* and *pa.p*. of **bring**.

brouhaha, *broō-ha'ha*, *broō'ha-hä*, *n* fuss, excitement, clamour, or an instance of this. [Fr.; perh. from Heb.]

brow *brow*, *n*. the eyebrow: the ridge over the eyes: the forehead: the edge of a hill: a gallery in a coal-mine running across the face of the coal: a ship's gangway (*navy*): a pit-head: aspect, appearance (*fig*).—*v t* **brow'beat** to bear down with stern looks or speech: to bully [O E *brū*]

brown *brown*, *adj*. of a dark or dusky colour, inclining to red or yellow: dark-complexioned: sunburnt —*n* a dark-reddish colour. a close-flying number of game-birds, usu. in **fire into the brown** to shoot into a mass without aiming at a particular bird —*v t*. to give a brown colour to: to roast brown —*v t*. to become brown.—*ns*. **brown'le** a drudging domestic goblin (*folklore*): (with *cap*.; in full **Brownie Guide**) a member of the junior section of the Girl Guides, in brown garb: a (square piece of) a kind of rich, chewy chocolate cake containing nuts (*U S*.): a kind of currant bread (*Austr*. and *N.Z*.); **brown'ing** the process of making or becoming brown: a preparation for the purpose.—*adj*. **brown'ish**.—*n*. **brown'ness**.—*adj* **brown'y** of a brownish colour.—**brown algae, brown seaweeds** one of the main divisions of the algae; **brown bear** the common bear of Europe and Asia; **brown bread** any dark-coloured bread, esp that made of unbolted flour, **brown coal** lignite; **brown dwarf** see **dwarf**; **brown fat** heat-producing fat cells of a brownish colour, found in various parts of the body, e g between the shoulder-blades, thought to be activated by over-eating and thus to have a bearing on weight-gain; **brown owl** the tawny owl (with *caps*, correctly **Brownie Guider**) a woman who has charge of a group of Brownies; **brown paper** coarse and strong paper used chiefly for wrapping; **brown rice** rice hulled but not polished, **Brown'shirt** a member of Hitler's organisation of storm-troopers: a Nazi, **brown spar** a brownish variety of dolomite; **brown stout** a kind of porter; **brown study** reverie: absent-mindedness; **brown sugar** unrefined or partially refined sugar; **brown trout** a kind of trout common in Europe, dark-coloured on the back and lighter underneath.—**browned off** (*slang*) fed up: bored: dejected; **do brown** (*slang*) to do thoroughly, to deceive or take in completely. [O E *brūn*.]

Brownian *brown'i-ən*, *adj*. pertaining to Robert *Brown* (1773–1858), who drew attention to **Brownian movement**, an agitation of particles in a colloid solution caused by impact of molecules in the surrounding medium

browse *browz*, *v.t*. to feed on rough shoots of plants to read desultorily.—*v t*. to browse on.—*n*. a browsing.—*n*. **brows'ing** the action of the verb browse [O.Fr. *brouster* (Fr. *brouter*)—*broust*, a sprout]

brucellosis *broō-sel-ō'sis*, *n* a disease of animals, also called **contagious abortion** (see **abortion**), communicable to man as Malta, or undulant, fever [Sir David *Bruce*, bacteriologist, and *-ella*, *-osis*]

brucine *broō'sēn*, *n* an alkaloid got from nux vomica, wrongly thought to come from the genus *Brucea*.

named after James *Bruce* (1730–94), Scottish African traveller

bruhaha. A spelling of **brouhaha**.

bruise *broōz*, *v t*. to crush by beating or pounding without breaking the surface: to pound: to pulverise by pounding to mark and discolour part of the surface of, e g skin of person, fruit, etc.: to hurt by unkind words.—*v t* to be injured physically or in feelings — *n* an injury with discoloration of the human skin made by anything blunt and heavy: a similar injury to fruit or plants —*n*. **bruis'er** one who bruises: a prize-fighter.—*n*. and *adj*. **bruis'ing**. [O E *brȳsan*, to crush, combined with O.Fr *brisier*, *bruiser*, *bruser*, to break]

bruit *broōt*, *n* something noised abroad: a rumour or report· a murmur heard in auscultation —*v.t*. to noise abroad to report· to make famous [Fr *bruit*.]

brûlé *bru-lā*, (Fr.) *adj* cooked with brown sugar. compromised

Brum *brum*, *n*, Birmingham —*n* **Brumm'ie** (*coll*) a person from Birmingham.

brumby *brum'bi*, (*Austr*) *n* a wild horse [Aboriginal name.]

brume *broōm*, *n*. fog [L. *brūma*, winter, contr. from *brevima*, the shortest day]

brunch *brunch*, *brunsh*, *n* a compromise between breakfast and lunch [Portmanteau word]

brunette *broōn-et'*, *n*. a woman with brown or dark hair and complexion. [Fr dim of *brun*, brown.]

brunt *brunt*, *n*. the shock of an onset or contest· the force of a blow· the chief stress or crisis of anything.

brush *brush*, *n* an instrument set with bristles or the like for cleansing or for applying friction or a coating of some material: a painter's hair pencil: a manner of painting: a tuft: a bushy tail: a bundle of wires, strips, or the like, making electrical contact between surfaces in relative motion. any brushlike appearance· an application of a brush: a grazing contact: a skirmish: lopped or broken twigs: an assemblage of shrubs and small trees an area covered with thickets. the backwoods —*v t*. to pass a brush over: to touch or rub as if with a brush· to remove by a sweeping motion (with off, or away).—*v.t*. to use a brush: to pass with light contact —*adj*. **brushed** smoothed, rubbed, straightened, etc with a brush: of cloth, with the surface roughened or raised.—*ns*. **brush'er**; **brush'ing**.—*adj* **brush'y** like a brush: covered with brush —**brush'-fire** a fire of dry bushes, etc., which usually spreads quickly and dangerously; **brush'-off** (*coll*.) a curt or discourteous setting aside or ignoring: a rebuff; **brush'wheel** a revolving brush: a friction wheel with bristles on the rubbing surface; **brush'wood** loppings and broken branches: underwood or stunted wood; **brush'work** work done with a brush: a painter's manner of using the brush —**brush aside, brush off** to ignore, dismiss; **brush up** to freshen one's appearance to clean and tidy: to renew one's knowledge of (a subject; sometimes with *on*) (*n*. **brush'-up**). [O Fr *brosse*, brushwood; prob. connected with **bristle**.]

brusque *broōsk*, *brusk*, *adj* blunt and abrupt in manner.—*adv* **brusque'ly**.—*ns*. **brusque'ness**; **brusquerie** (*broō s'kə-rē*) [Fr]

Brussels *brus'əlz*, *n* the capital of Belgium —**Brussels lace** a fine lace with sprigs applied on a net ground; **Brussels sprouts** a variety of the common cabbage with sprouts like miniature cabbages

brut *broōt*, (Fr) *adj* of wines, raw, unsweetened

brute *broōt*, *adj* belonging to the lower animals· irrational· stupid· rude· crude.—*n* one of the lower animals, esp the larger mammals: a brutal man — *adj* **brut'al** like a brute· unfeeling· inhuman: stupidly cruel or sensual —*n.* **brutalisā'tion,** **-z-**.—*v t* **brut'alise, -ize** to make like a brute, to degrade: to treat with brutality —*v.i.* to live like a brute.—*n* **brutal'ity.**—*adv.* **brut'ally.**—*n.* **brute'ness** brutelike state: brutality.—*adj.* **brut'ish** brutal.—*adv.* **brut'-ishly.**—*n.* **brut'ishness.**—**brute force** sheer physical strength. [Fr. *brut*—L. *brūtus,* dull, irrational.]

bruxism *bruks'izm, n.* habitual grinding of the teeth [Gr. *brychein,* to gnash.]

bryology *brī-ol'ə-ji, n.* the study of mosses. [Gr. *bryon,* moss, liverwort, and *logos,* discourse.]

bryony *brī'ə-ni, n.* a wild climbing plant (*Bryonia dioica,* **white bryony**) of the gourd family, common in English hedgerows —**black bryony** a climbing plant (*Tamus communis*) of the yam family, similar to bryony in habit and disposition. [L. *bryōnia*—Late Gr. *bryōniā.*]

bryophyte *brī'ō-fīt, n.* a member of, one of the main groups of the vegetable kingdom, mosses and liverworts. [Gr. *bryon,* a moss, a liverwort, *phyton,* plant.]

Brython *brith'on, n.* a Celt of the group to which Welsh, Cornish, and Bretons belong —*adj* **Bryth-on'ic.** [Welsh *Brython,* Briton—introduced in philological use by Sir John Rhys (1840–1915).]

bub *bub,* **bubby** *bub'i,* (*U.S.*) *ns.* boy (in addressing). [Cf. Ger. *Bube,* boy.]

buba *bōō'ba, n.* another name for **yaws.**

bubble *bub'l, n.* a bladder of liquid or solidified liquid blown out with gas: anything empty: an unsound or fraudulent scheme.—*adj.* unsubstantial: deceptive: fleeting, transient.—*v.i.* to rise in bubbles: to give off bubbles: to make sounds as of rising and bursting bubbles: (with *with*) to show (great joy, rage, etc.).—*adj.* **bubb'ly.**—*n.* (*coll.*) champagne.—**bubb'le-and-squeak'** left-over potato, meat and cabbage fried together; **bubble bath** a cosmetic preparation that makes foam in bath-water; **bubb'le-car** a midget motor-car resembling a bubble in its rounded line and windowed top; **bubb'le-chamber** a device for showing the path of a charged particle by the string of bubbles left in its track—a variant of the cloud-chamber; **bubb'le-gum** a kind of chewing-gum that can be blown into large bubbles; **bubble memory** (*comput.*) a memory composed of minute moving pockets of magnetism that represent, by their presence or absence in relation to fixed points, bits (q.v.) of digital information; **bubble pack** a type of packaging in which goods are enclosed in a transparent bubble of plastic, etc. backed by card.—**bubble over** to show uncontrolled anger, mirth, etc. [Cf Sw. *bubbla,* Du *bobbel*]

bubo *bū'bō, n.* an inflammatory swelling of the lymph nodes, esp. in the groin or armpit:—*pl.* **bū'boes.**—*adj* **bubonic** (*-bon'*) relating to, characterised by, buboes.—*n.* **bubonocele** (*bū-bon'ō-sēl*; Gr. *kēlē,* tumour) an inguinal hernia.—**bubonic plague** a form of plague characterised by buboes [L *bŭbō*—Gr. *boubōn,* the groin, a bubo.]

buccal *buk'əl, adj.* pertaining to the cheek: pertaining to the mouth, oral. [L. *bucca,* cheek.]

buccaneer, buccanier *buk-ən-ēr', n.* one of the piratical adventurers in the West Indies during the 17th century, who plundered the Spaniards chiefly —*v.i.* to act as a buccaneer.—*n* **buccaneer'ing.**—*adj* **buccaneer'-ish.** [Fr. *boucanier*—*boucan,* a Carib wooden gridiron (used by French settlers in the West Indies).]

Buchmanism *bōō'kh'mən-izm, n.* the Oxford Group movement —*adj.* and *n.* **Buch'manite** (*-īt*) [See **Oxford.**]

buck¹ *buk, n.* the body of a cart —**buck'board** a board or rail projecting over cart-wheels a plank on four

wheels, with a light seat to hold two persons (*U.S.*); **buck'cart** a buckboard: a cart with boards projecting over the wheels. [O.E *būc,* body.]

buck² *buk, n.* the male of the deer, goat, hare, and rabbit (cf. *doe*): a male fallow-deer. a bok (q v.): a dashing fellow: a male Negro or American Indian (*offensive*): a counter (*cards*): a dollar (*U.S.*): an act of bucking —*v t* (of a horse or mule) to attempt to throw by rapid jumps into the air, coming down with the back arched, head down, and forelegs stiff.—*v.t.* to throw by bucking: to resist: to cheer, invigorate, tone up (*slang*).—*n.* **buck'er** an animal that bucks.—*adj* **buck'ish** lively, frisky: dandified: goatish.—**buck'-eye** the American horse-chestnut; **buck'horn, buck's'-horn** the material of a buck's horn; **buck'-hound** a small kind of staghound used for hunting bucks; **buck-passing** see **pass the buck** below; **buck'-rabb'it** a male rabbit: a Welsh rabbit with poached egg; **buck'saw** a large saw consisting of a blade set in an H-shaped frame tightened by a cord, used with a saw-buck; **buck'shot** a large kind of shot, used in shooting deer; **buck'skin** a soft leather made of deerskin or sheepskin: a strong twilled woollen cloth, cropped of nap: (in *pl.*) breeches or suit of buckskin.—*adj.* made of or like the skin of a buck.—**buck'thorn** a genus (*Rhamnus*) of shrubs whose berry supplies the sap-green used by painters; **buck'tooth** a projecting tooth.—**buck up** (*slang*) to bestir oneself: to cheer up: to improve: to stimulate; **make a fast buck** (*coll.*) to earn some money quickly or easily but not necessarily honestly; **pass the buck** (*coll.*) to shift the responsibility to someone else (as one passes a marker to the next dealer in forms of poker) (*n.* **buck'-passing**); **the buck stops here** the final responsibility rests here. [O.E. *buc, bucca.*]

buckaroo *buk'ə-rōō,* or *-rōō', (U S.) n.* a cowboy. [Sp *vaquero.*]

buckbean *buk'bēn, n* a marsh plant (*Menyanthes trifoliata*) of the gentian family.—Also **bog'bean.** [Flem. *bocks boonen,* goat's beans.]

bucket *buk'it, n.* a vessel for drawing or holding water, etc.: one of the compartments on the circumference of a water-wheel: one of the scoops of a dredging-machine: a waste-paper bin (*coll.*): the pitcher in some orchids a bucketful.—*v.t.* to lift in a bucket.—*v.t.* and *v.i.* to drive or ride very hard or bumpily: to push forward mercilessly —*v.i.* (of rain) to pour heavily (*coll.*).—*ns.* **buck'etful** as much as a bucket will hold:—*pl.* **buck'etfuls; buck'eting.**—**bucket seat** a round-backed, often forward-tipping, seat for one in a motor-car, aeroplane, etc.; **bucket shop** (*coll.*) the office of an outside broker—a mere agent for bets on the rise or fall of prices of stock, etc.: thus, any agency operating along similar lines, e.g. one dealing for unsold airline tickets; **buck'et-wheel** a contrivance for raising water by means of buckets attached to the circumference of a wheel.—**kick the bucket** (*slang*) to die. [Prob. conn with O E. *būc,* a pitcher, or O.Fr. *buket,* a pail.]

buckle *buk'l, n.* fastening for a strap or band, consisting of a rim and a tongue: a crisped, curled, or warped condition.—*v.t.* and *v t* to connect with a buckle: to prepare for action: to join closely as in fight or marriage. to bend or warp.—*n.* **buck'ler** a small shield used in parrying.—**buckle down** to apply oneself zealously (to); **buckle to** to buckle down, **buckle under** to give in, collapse, under strain. [Fr. *boucle,* the boss of a shield, a ring—L L *buccula,* dim. of *bucca,* a cheek.]

Buckley's (chance) *buk'liz (chans), (Austr. coll)* no chance at all.

bucko *buk'ō, n* a swaggerer, domineering bully (orig naut slang): young lad, chap (*chiefly Irish*) —*pl* **buck'oes** [. . .]

buckram *buk'rəm, n.* a coarse open-woven fabric of jute, cotton, or linen made very stiff with size. stiffness in manners and appearance.—*adj* made of buckram: stiff: precise. [O.Fr *boquerant.*]

buckshish *buk'shēsh.* Same as **baksheesh.**—*n* **buck'-shee'** (*mil. slang*) spoil, a windfall.—*adj.* free, gratuitous. [See **baksheesh.**]

buckthorn. See **buck²**.

buckwheat *buk'(h)wēt, n.* a cereal used in Europe for feeding horses, cattle and poultry, in America made into cakes for the breakfast table. [Prob Du. *boekweit*, or Ger. *Buchweizen*, beech-wheat, from the shape of the seeds.]

bucolic, -al *bū-kol'ik, -əl, adjs* pertaining to the tending of cattle: pastoral: rustic, countrified.—*n.* **bucol'ic** a pastoral poem or poet: a rustic. [L *būcolicus*—Gr. *boukolikos—boukolos*, a herdsman.]

bud¹ *bud, n.* a rudimentary shoot of a plant. a protuberance that develops asexually into a new individual (*biol.*): a young person (as a term of endearment) —*v.t.* to put forth as buds: to graft by inserting a bud under the bark of another tree —*v.i.* to put forth buds. to come as a bud: to be in or issue from the bud:—*pr.p.* **budd'ing;** *pa.t.* and *pa.p.* **budd'ed.**—*n* **budd'ing.**—*adj.* in bud: beginning to develop, show talent in a particular way (as *a budding poet*).—**in bud** putting forth buds; **nip in the bud** to destroy at its very beginning. [M.E. *budde.*]

bud². See **buddy.**

Buddha *bōōd'ə, n* a title applied to Sakyamuni or Gautama, the founder of a religion of spiritual purity: a general name for any one of a series of teachers of whom he is one —*ns.* **Budd'hism** the religion founded by the Buddha; **Budd'hist** a believer in Buddhism.—*adjs.* **Budd'hist, Buddhist'ic.** [Sans *buddha*, wise, from *bodhati*, he understands.]

Buddleia *bud'li-ə, bud-lē'ə, n* a genus of shrubs and trees with showy clusters of purple or orange flowers. (without *cap*) a plant of the genus. [Named in honour of Adam *Buddle* (d. 1715), botanist.]

buddy *bud'i, n* brother (*U S.*). a pal, one's most constant companion.—Also (esp in U S. as form of address) **bud.** [Prob. from same root as *butty*]

budge *buj, v.i.* and *v t.* to move or stir —*n* **budg'er.** [Fr *bouger*—L *bullīre*, to bubble]

budgerigar *buj'ər-i-gar, -gar', n* a cage and aviary bird, an Australian parrakeet.—*fam.* **budgie** *buj'i* [Australian native *budgeri*, good, *gar*, cockatoo]

budget *buj'it, n.* a financial statement and programme put before parliament by the Chancellor of the Exchequer: a plan of domestic expenditure or the like —*v i.* to prepare a budget —*v t.* to provide for in a budget:—*pr.p.* **budg'eting;** *pa.t.* and *pa.p* **budg'eted.** —*adj.* **bud'getary.**—**budget account** a special bank account, into which money is paid regularly by the bank from a customer's main account and from which payment of previously agreed recurring expenses, e.g. fuel bills, T.V. licence, is made: an account with a shop, into which the customer makes regular payments to cover purchases at the shop —**budget for** to allow for, when planning one's expenditure [Fr *bougette*, dim. of *bouge*, a pouch—L *bulga*]

budgie. See **budgerigar.**

buff¹ *buf, n.* originally buffalo-hide: now white leather from which the grain surface has been removed, used for army accoutrements: a military coat: the colour of buff, a light yellow: the bare skin: a buff-stick or buff-wheel: (in *pl.*) certain regiments in the British army, from their former buff-coloured facings. an enthusiast, fan (*coll.*)—Also *adj*—*v.t* to polish with a buff.—*n.* **buff'er** one who buffs or polishes —*ns* **buff'-leather; buff'-stick, buff'-wheel** a stick or wheel covered with buff-leather or the like, and charged with an abrasive for polishing —**in the buff** naked [Fr. *buffle*, a buffalo.]

buff² *buf, n* a dull blow or its sound —*v t.* to strike, esp. with a dull sound: to burst out.—*n.* **buff'er** a mechanical apparatus for deadening the force of a concussion, as in railway carriages: a ship's fender: a fellow, esp a dull or ineffectual fellow (as in *old buffer*): in chemistry, a substance or mixture which opposes change of hydrogen-ion concentration in a solution.—*v.t.* to treat with a buffer —*v.t* to use, or be used as, a buffer —*adj* **buff'ered.—buffer state, zone** a neutral country or zone lying between two others whose relations are or may become strained; **buffer stock** stock held in reserve to minimise the effect of price fluctuations [O.Fr *buffe*, a blow]

buffalo *buf'ə-lō, n* a name for certain large animals of the ox kind: the American bison (*U.S.*): a bison —*pl.* **buff'aloes.**—*v.t* to bewilder. to overawe [It. *buffalo*, through L from Gr *boubalos*]

buffet¹ *buf'it, n* a blow with the fist: a slap: a stroke, esp heavy and repeated, as of the wind, fortune, etc. —*v t* to strike with the hand or fist to struggle against, beat back —*v.i.* to deal heavy blows.—*n* **buff'eting** a striking with the hand, boxing: contention: repeated blows: irregular oscillation of any part of an aircraft, caused and maintained by an eddying wake from some other part. [O Fr *buffet—buffe*, a blow, esp on the cheek.]

buffet² *buf'it, n.* a sideboard: (usu *bōōf'ā*) a refreshment counter or bar: a meal set out on table, etc, from which the diner serves himself —Also *adj* — **buffet car** (*bōōf'ā kar*) a railway coach with light meal or snack service. [Fr. *buffet*]

buffoon *buf-ōōn', n.* one who sets himself to amuse by jests, grimaces, etc: a low, vulgar, or indecent jester.—*n.* **buffoon'ery** [Fr *bouffon*—It *buffone, buffare*, to jest]

bug¹ *bug, n.* (obs.) an object of terror —*n.* **bug'aboo** a bogy, or object of terror: a cause of anxiety — **bug'bear** an object of terror, dislike, or annoyance [M E. *bugge*, prob W *bwg*, a hobgoblin.]

bug² *bug, n.* a name applied loosely to certain insects, and specifically to one that infests houses and beds: any insect or small animal (*U.S*): a disease-germ: a viral disease (*coll.*): a craze, obsession: an enthusiast: a snag, a defect: a hidden microphone: a light vehicle stripped of everything inessential: lunar excursion module (see **module**)—*v.t* to plant a concealed listening device in: to annoy, irritate (*slang*) —*adj* **bugged.**—*n* and *adj.* **bugg'ing.** [Perh O E *budda*, beetle, perh same as **bug¹**.]

bug³ *bug,* (*U S.*) *v i.* to start or bulge:—*pr p.* **bugg'ing;** *pa.t* and *pa.p* **bugged.**—*adj.* **bug'-eyed'** with eyes protruding in astonishment, etc

bug⁴ *bug,* (*U S*) *v i* to leave —**bug out** to desert, esp in panic [Perh from **bugger** (**off**).]

bugger *bug'ər, n* one guilty of bestiality and unnatural sexual intercourse a term of abuse, often quite colourless or even kindly (*vulg coll.*): a rogue, scamp —applied inoffensively to child or animal (*U.S*): a difficult or unpleasant task, etc. (*vulg coll.*) —*v t* to have unnatural sexual, esp anal, intercourse with: (the following all *vulg coll*) to exhaust: to frustrate, ruin the plans of: to spoil, prevent success in (also with *up*) —*v.i* (with *off; vulg coll*) to go away quickly —*interj* (*vulg coll.*) used to express annoyance —*n* **bug'ery** (*law*) bestiality, unnatural sexual, esp anal, intercourse —**bugger about** (*vulg coll*) to potter about; **bugger all** (*vulg coll.*) none, nothing [Fr *bougre*—L *Bulgarus*, Bulgarian]

Buggins' turn *bug'inz tûrn,* turn for promotion, etc , in accordance with seniority, by rotation, etc

buggy *bug'i*, *n.* a light carriage or gig of several kinds —in America, a one-horse, four-wheeled vehicle with one seat; in England, two-wheeled; in India, hooded: a child's push-chair.

bugle *bū'gl*, *n.* (also **bū'gle-horn**) a horn used as a drinking vessel or hunting-horn: a treble instrument with or without keys, usu. made of copper, like the trumpet, but having the bell less expanded and the tube shorter and more conical, used more for signalling than music.—*v.i.* to sound a bugle —*ns.* **bū'gler** one who sounds the bugle; **bū'glet** a small bugle —**bū'gle-band; bū'gle-call.** [O.Fr. *bugle*—L. *būculus*, dim. of *bōs*, an ox.]

bugloss *bū'glos*, *n.* a name for several plants of the borage family. [Fr. *buglosse*—L. *būglōssa*—Gr. *bouglōssos*—*bous*, ox, *glōssa*, tongue.]

bugong *bōō'gong*, *n.* a noctuid moth eaten by Australian aborigines. [Native name.]

buhl *bōōl*, *n.* a complicated form of inlay, gold, silver, or brass and pewter, ivory and mother-of-pearl in tortoiseshell, etc., forming panels for furniture decoration: furniture thus decorated.—Also **boulle, boule.** [From Charles André *Boulle* (1642–1732), a cabinetmaker in the service of Louis XIV.]

build *bild*, *v.t.* to erect, as a house or bridge: to construct, as a railway, etc.: to establish (*fig.*): to base, as hopes (on): to form (combinations) (*cards*).—*v.i.* to depend (with *on, upon*):—*pa.t.* and *pa.p.* **built,** *arch.* **build'ed.**—*n.* form: make.—*ns.*build'er one who builds, or controls the work of building; **build'ing** the art or process of erecting houses, etc.: a substantial structure for giving shelter, e.g. a house, office-block.—*adj.* **built** formed or shaped.— **builders' merchant** a person whose job is to arrange deliveries and supplies of building materials to building-sites; **build'ing-block** a hollow or solid block made of concrete or other material, larger than a brick, **building society** a society that advances money to its members towards providing them with dwelling-houses; **build'-up** a building up, increasing, strengthening: the amount of this: a working up of favourable publicity: preliminaries leading up to a climax in a story, speech, etc.—*adjs.* **built'-in'** formed as part of a main structure, esp. if recessed: present as part of one's genetic inheritance: included (as part of a deal, etc.): very firmly fixed; **built'-up** of an area, covered with buildings.—**build in** to enclose or fix by building, **build up** to close up by building, as a door: to cover with buildings: to create, or be created, or to increase, gradually (as a concentration of troops, a reputation, voltage, tension): to put together from parts already made: to edify spiritually. [O.E. *gebyld*, pa.p. of an assumed *byldan*, to build—*bold*, a dwelling.]

bulb *bulb*, *n.* a subterranean bud with swollen leaf-bases in which reserve materials are stored: a protuberance or swelling: the medulla oblongata: a dilatation or expansion of a glass tube: the glass of an electric light.—*v.i.* to form bulbs: to bulge out or swell.—*adjs.* **bulb'ar; bulbed; bulbif'erous** of a plant, producing bulbs.—*adj.*bulb'ous bulging: swollen. [L. *bulbus*—Gr. *bolbos*, an onion.]

bulbul *bōōl'bōōl*, *n.* properly, a Persian nightingale: in India, extended to another genus of birds: a sweet singer. [Ar.]

Bulgarian *bul-gā'ri-ən*, *adj.* of *Bulgaria* or its language.—*n.* a native or citizen of Bulgaria: the Bulgarian language (Slavonic).—*n* **Bul'gar** (*-gar*) a member of an ancient Finnic or Ugrian tribe that moved from the Volga towards Bulgaria.—*adj.* **Bulgaric** (*-gar'ik*).—*n* the ancient language of the Bulgars.

bulge *bulj*, *n* a protuberance, swelling: temporary increase.—*v.i.* and *v.t.* to swell out.—*adjs.* **bul'ging** swelling out: over-full; **bul'gy.** [O.Fr. *boulge*, prob. L. *bulga*, a leather knapsack: a Gallic word; cf. **bilge.**]

bulimia *bū-lim'i-ə*, *n.* morbid hunger (also *fig.*). [Gr. *boulimiā*—*bous*, ox, *līmos*, hunger.]

bulk *bulk*, *n.* a cargo: the belly, trunk, or body: a hull or hold: volume or size: great size: the greater part: any huge body or structure: mass.—*v.i.* to be in bulk: to be of weight or importance.—*v.t.* to put or hold in bulk: (often with *out*; also with *up*) to cause to swell, make greater in size.—*adv.* **bulk'ily.**—*n.* **bulk'iness.**—*adj.* **bulk'y** having bulk: filling much space: unwieldy.—**bulk buying** large-scale purchase of a commodity, esp. on preferential terms and by a single buyer on behalf of a body of consumers: guaranteed purchase by one country of all or most of another's output of a commodity; **bulk carrier** vessel carrying cargo, such as grain, that is not in the form of separate packages.—**load in bulk** to put cargo in loose; **sell in bulk** to sell cargo as it is in the hold: to sell in large quantities. [Prob. (hypothetical) O.N. *bulki*, heap or cargo, confused with O.E. *buc*, belly.]

bulkhead *bulk'hed*, *n.* any of the partitions separating one part of a ship's interior from another: a protecting barrier or structure. [**bulk.**]

bull *bōōl*, *n.* an uncastrated male of the ox kind: a male whale, walrus, elephant, moose, etc.: (with *cap.*) Taurus (*astron.*): one who seeks to raise the price of stocks, and speculates on a rise (opp. to *bear*): a bull's-eye (*musketry*): nonsense (*slang*): spit and polish (*mil. slang*).—*adj* male: massive: favourable to the bulls, rising (*Stock Exchange*).—*v.t.* to try to raise the price of.—*adj.* **bull'ish** like a bull: obstinate: inclining towards rising prices (*Stock Exchange*).—*adv.* **bull'ishly.**—*ns.* **bull'ishness; bull'ock** an ox or castrated bull.—**bull ant** short for bull-dog ant; **bull'-calf** a male calf: a stupid fellow, a lout; **bull'dog** a breed of dogs of great courage, formerly used for baiting bulls: hence a person of obstinate courage.—*v.t.* to assail like a bulldog: to wrestle with and throw (a steer, etc.) (*U.S.*).— **bulldog ant** a black or red Australian ant with a vicious sting; **bulldog clip** a clip with a spring, used for holding papers, etc. together or to a board; **bull'fight** a popular spectacle in Spain, Portugal, Southern France, and Latin America, in which a bull is goaded to fury by mounted *picadores* armed with lances, and despatched by a specially skilful *espada* or swordsman; **bull'fighter; bull'fighting; bull'finch** a plump red-breasted finch: (perh. for *bull-fence*) a kind of high, thick hedge hard to jump, **bull'frog** a large frog; **bull'head** the miller's thumb, a small river fish with large, flat head: extended to various similar fishes, as the pogge (*armed bullhead*).— *adj.* **bull'-head'ed** impetuous and obstinate.—**bull's horn** a megaphone; **bull'-mastiff** a cross between the bulldog and the mastiff, the mastiff strain predominating.—*adjs.* **bull'-necked** thick-necked; **bull'-nosed** with a blunt nose, like a bull's.—**bull's pen** a pen for a bull: a similar enclosure for prisoners (*U.S.*): a part of the ground where pitchers warm up (*baseball*); **bull'-ring** the enclosure for bull-fighting or bull-baiting: a ring for a bull's nose; **bull'-roar'er** an oblong slip of wood, whirled at the end of a string to give a loud whirring noise; **bull's'-eye** the central boss formed in making a sheet of spun glass: a thick lens, or round piece of glass, as in a lantern: a round opening or window: the centre of a target: a shot that hits it: a big round hard peppermint sweet; **bull'shit** (*slang*) nonsense: deceptive humbug.—*v.i.* and *v.t.* to talk nonsense (to), often with the intention of deceiving.—**bull'-terr'ier** a breed of dog with a smooth, short-haired coat, orig a cross between bulldog and terrier.—**a bull in a china shop** one who lacks the delicacy that the situation calls for; **bull into** to plunge hastily into; **take the bull by the horns** to grapple boldly with a danger or difficulty [M.E. *bole*, prob. O.N. *bole, boli;* most prob. related to **bellow**.]

bull² *bōōl, n.* an edict of the pope with his seal affixed. [L *bulla*, a knob, a leaden seal.]

bulla *bōōl'ə, n.* a seal attached to a document —*adj* **bull'ate** blistered or puckered· bubble-like: knobbed: inflated. [L. *bulla.*]

bullace *bōōl'is, n* a shrub closely allied to the sloe. [Cf. O.Fr. *beloce.*]

bulldoze *bōōl'dōz, v t* to intimidate: to bully· to level and clear by bulldozer: to demolish as if by bulldozer: to force or push through against opposition (*fig*).—*n.* **bull'dozer** one who bulldozes: a tractor machine for levelling and clearing land.

bullet *bōōl'it, n.* a projectile, now esp. one (round or conical) discharged from any kind of small-arm: a plumb or sinker in fishing.—**bull'et-head** a round head: an obstinate fellow (*U.S.*).—*adjs.* **bull'et-head'ed; bull'et-proof** proof against bullets [Fr *boulette*, dim. of *boule*, a ball—L. *bulla*]

bulletin *bōōl'i-tin, n.* an official report of public news, or of a patient's progress. [Fr.,—It. *bullettino.*]

bullet-tree, bulletrie. Same as **bully-tree.**

bullion *bōōl'yən, n* gold and silver in the mass and uncoined: occasionally, precious metal, coined and uncoined. [Perh. conn. with L L *bulliō, -ōnis*, a boiling]

bullock. See bull¹.

bully¹ *bōōl'i, n.* a cruel oppressor of the weak: a blustering, noisy, overbearing fellow.—*adj.* excellent.—*v.t.* to oppress cruelly: to threaten in a noisy way:—*pr.p.* **bull'ying;** *pa.t.* and *pa.p.* **bull'ied.**—*interj.* good —**bull'y-boy** a ruffian hired to beat or intimidate someone.—**bully for you, him,** etc. (often *iron.*) good for you, him, etc. [Perh. Du. *boel*, a lover.]

bully² *bōōl'i, n.* a scrimmage (*football*): in hockey, the opening (or reopening) of the game—two opposing players each striking the ground on his own side of the ball and his opponent's stick alternately, three times, and then trying to strike the ball (also **bull'y-off'**).—*v.t.* and *v.i.* **bull'y (-off')**

bully³ *bōōl'i*, **bully-beef** *bōōl'i-bēf, ns.* canned or pickled beef. [Prob. Fr *bouilli*, boiled beef, influenced by **bull¹**.]

ballyrag *bōōl'i-rag,* **ballyrag** *bal'i-rag, vs.t* to assail with abusive language or horseplay: to badger

bully-tree *bōōl'i-trē, n.* a name for several West Indian sapotaceous trees yielding good timber, edible fruits, and balata.—Also **bull'et-tree, bull'etrie, boll'etrie.** [Perh. from **bullace;** perh. from **balata.**]

bulrush *bōōl'rush, n* a name given to two distinct tall marsh or water plants—the reed-mace or cat's-tail, and clubrush, a plant of the sedge family. [Perh. **bole¹** or **bull¹** in sense of massive or coarse, and **rush²**.]

bulwark *bōōl'wərk, n.* a fortification or rampart: a breakwater or sea-wall: the side of a ship projecting above the deck: any means of defence or security.—*v.t.* to defend: to fortify [Cf Ger *Bollwerk.*]

bum¹ *bum, n.* (*coll.*) the buttocks.—**bum'freezer** (*slang*) an Eton jacket: a waist-length jacket. [Cf **bump** in sense of swelling.]

bum² *bum, v.i.* to hum or make a murmuring sound, as a bee:—*pr p.* **bum'ming;** *pa.t.* and *pa.p.* **bummed.**—*n* a humming sound.—*n.* **bumm'er** a person or thing that bums. [Imit.]

bum³ *bum,* (*U.S. slang*) *n.* a spree: a dissolute fellow: a sponger.—*adj.* worthless: despicable: dud —*v.i.* to loaf: to sponge: to live dissolutely.—*n.* **bumm'er** a

plundering straggler or camp-follower (during the American Civil War): a dissolute fellow: a loafer. a sponger· a dismal failure (*coll.*).—**bum steer** (*slang*) something misleading, false or worthless, a dud.—**give someone the bum's rush** (*slang*) to eject someone by force: to dismiss someone summarily, esp from one's employment.

bumble, bummle *bum'(b)l, v t.* to bungle· to utter indistinctly: to bustle about blunderingly —*n.* confusion: indistinct utterance: a bungler· an idler —**bum'ble-bee'** a large wild loud-humming bee, a humble bee. [Freq of **bum²**.]

bum-boat *bum'bōt, n.* orig. a Thames scavenger's boat. a boat bringing vegetables, etc , for sale to ships

bumf, bumph *bumf*, (*coll.*) *n.* lavatory paper: papers, official papers, documents (*disparagingly*). [Short for *bum-fodder*, **bum¹** and **fodder**.]

bummalo *bum'ə-lō, n* the Bombay duck, a small Indian fish dried and eaten as a relish:—*pl.* **bum(m)'alo.** [Marathi *bombil*.]

bummer. See bum²,³.

bummle. See bumble.

bump *bump, v t.* to make a heavy or loud noise: to knock dully: to jolt: to move joltingly: (of a cricket-ball) to bound high on striking the pitch.—*v.t.* to strike with a dull sound: to strike against· in boat-racing, to overtake and impinge upon—the bumper consequently taking the place of the bumped in rank.—*n* a dull heavy blow: a thump: a high rebound of a cricket-ball: a jolt· a lump or swelling: a protuberance on the head confidently associated by phrenologists with qualities or propensities of mind: hence (*coll.*) faculty. —*n.* **bump'er** anything or person that bumps: a bar on a motor-car to lessen the shock of collision: a railway buffer (*U.S*): a bumping race: a cup or glass filled to the brim for drinking a toast: anything large or generous in measure: a crowded house at a theatre or concert —*adj* full to overflowing —*v.i.* to drink bumpers.—*n.* **bump'iness.**—*adj* **bump'y.**—**bumping race** a boat-race in which the boats seek to bump, not to pass.—**bump into** to happen to meet (someone); **bump off** (*slang*) to kill, murder; **bump start** (*n* **bump'-start**) same as **jump start**; **bump up** (*coll.*) to raise (prices): to increase size of [Imit]

bumph. See bumf.

bumpkin *bump'kin, n.* an awkward, clumsy rustic: a clown.—*adj* **bump'kinish.** [Prob. Du. *boomken*, a log.]

bumptious *bump'shəs, adj* offensively self-important. —*adv.* **bump'tiously.**—*n* **bump'tiousness.** [Prob. formed from **bump.**]

bun¹ *bun, n* a kind of sweet cake: a rounded mass of hair.—**bun'-fight** (*coll.*) a tea-party· a noisy occasion or assembly. [Perh. from O.Fr. *bugne*, a swelling.]

bun² *bun, n.* a playful name for a rabbit or a squirrel.

buna *bōō'na, n.* an artificial rubber made by the polymerisation of butadiene [Orig. trademark.]

bunch *bunch, bunsh, n.* a lump: a lumpish gathering: a number of things aggregated or fastened together: a cluster: a handful as of flowers: something in the form of a tuft or knot —*v.i.* to swell out in a bunch· to cluster.—*v.t.* to make a bunch of: to concentrate. —*adj.* **bunched** humped, protuberant: lumpy.—*ns* **bunch'iness; bunch'ing** the act of drawing together into a bunch. over-close grouping together of cars on a motorway, etc. (esp after a long gap), of ships arriving in port, etc.—*adj.* **bunch'y** growing in bunches or like a bunch. bulging.—**bunch of fives see five.**

bunco. See bunko.

buncombe. See bunkum.

bundle *bun'dl, n* a number of things loosely bound together: a bunch: a loose parcel, esp. one contained in a cloth: a strand of conducting vessels, fibres, etc (*biol.*): a definite measure or quantity, as two reams of paper, twenty hanks of linen yarn, etc.—*v.t.* to make into bundles: to put hastily or unceremoniously: to hustle.—*v.i.* to pack up one's things for a journey: to go hurriedly or in confusion (with *away, off, out*).—**go a bundle on** (*slang*) to like or be enthusiastic about. [Conn. with **bind** and **bond**.]

bung[1] *bung, n.* the stopper of the hole in a barrel: a large cork.—*v.t.* to stop up or enclose with a bung (also *fig.*) —**bung'-hole** a hole for a bung; **bung'-vent** a small hole in a bung to let gases escape, etc.

bung[2] *bung,* (*slang*) *v.t.* to throw or shove carelessly and hurriedly.

bungalow *bung'gə-lō, n.* a lightly-built house, properly with a veranda and one storey: now loosely, a one-storey house. [Hindi *baṅglā,* (house) in the style of Bengal, house.]

bungle *bung'gl, n.* anything clumsily done: a gross mismanagement.—*v.i.* to act in a clumsy manner.—*v.t.* to make or mend clumsily: to mismanage grossly: to make a failure of by want of skill.—*n.* **bung'ler.**—*adj.* **bung'ling** clumsy, awkward: unskilfully or ill done.— Also *n.*—*adv.* **bung'lingly.** [Ety. dub.; prob. onomatopoeic; cf. Sw. dial. *bangla,* to work ineffectually; Hindes Groome suggests Gypsy *bongo,* left, awkward.]

bunion *bun'yən, n.* a lump or inflamed swelling on the first joint of the great toe. [Ety. unknown; poss. It. *bugnone,* a botch.]

bunk[1] *bungk, n.* a box or recess in a ship's cabin, a sleeping-berth anywhere: one of a pair of narrow beds one above the other (also **bunk bed**).—*v.i.* to occupy a bunk.—*n.* **bunk'er** a large bin or chest, esp. for coals (*Scot.*): a slab beside a sink (*Scot.*): a compartment for fuel on shipboard: the fuel-oil carried by a ship for its own use: a sand-pit or sandy gap in turf, esp. as a hazard in a golf course.—*v.t.* to fuel: to play into a bunker.— *v.t.* to fuel.—*adj.* **bunk'ered** in a bunker: in difficulties. [Cf. O.N. *bunki,* Scand. *bunke,* heap.]

bunk[2] *bungk,* (*slang*) *n.* flight (esp. in phrase **to do a bunk**).—*v.i.* to flee.

bunk[3]. See **bunkum.**

bunker[1] *bung'kər, n.* an underground bombproof shelter. [Ger.]

bunker[2]. See **bunk**[1].

bunko, bunco *bung'kō,* (*U.S.*) *n.* a form of confidence-trick by which a simple fellow is swindled or taken somewhere and robbed:—*pl.* **bunk'os, bunc'os.**—*v t.* to rob or swindle in such a way.

bunkum *bung'kəm, n.* bombastic speechmaking intended for the newspapers rather than to persuade the audience: humbug: claptrap.—Also **bun'combe, bunk.** [From *Buncombe,* a county in North Carolina, whose member is said to have gone on talking in Congress, explaining apologetically that he was 'only talking for Buncombe'.]

bunny *bun'i, n.* a pet name for a rabbit.—**bunn'y-girl** (sometimes with *caps.*) a night-club hostess provocatively dressed in a brief, close-fitting costume with a white fluffy tail, and wearing rabbit-like ears.

Bunsen (burner) *bun'sən* or *bōōn'sən* (*bûrn'ər*), *n.* a gas-burner in which a plentiful supply of air is caused to mingle with the gas before ignition, so that a smokeless flame of low luminosity but great heating power is the result [From the inventor R. W. *Bunsen* (1811-99), a German chemist.]

bunt[1] *bunt, n.* stink-brand, a disease of wheat: the fungus (*Tilletia*) that causes it —*adjs* **bunt'ed; bunt'y.**

bunt[2] *bunt, n.* the bagging part of a fishing-net, a sail, etc.—*v.t.* to belly, as a sail.—**bunt'line** a rope passing from the foot-rope of a square sail to prevent bellying in furling

bunt[3] *bunt, v.i.* to push with the horns, butt: to spring, rear: to block a ball with the bat (*baseball*; also *v.t.* and *n.*).—*n.* a push.—*n.* **bunt'ing** pushing.

bunting[1] *bunt'ing, n.* a thin worsted stuff for ships' colours: flags, cloth decorations.

bunting[2] *bunt'ing, n.* any of a family of small finch-like birds.

bunting[3]. See **bunt**[3].

buoy *boi* (in U.S. often *bōō'ē* and in derivatives below, *bōō'y*-), *n.* a floating secured mark, serving (by its shape, colour, light, sound, etc.) as a guide or as a warning.—*v.t.* to furnish or mark with buoys or marks: to keep afloat, bear up, or sustain (usu. with *up*): to raise, lift (usu. with *up*).—*v.t.* to rise.—*ns.* **buoy'age** a series of buoys or floating beacons to mark the course for vessels: the provision, or system, of buoys, **buoy'ancy** capacity for floating lightly on water or in the air: loss of weight owing to immersion in a fluid: lightness of spirit, cheerfulness (*fig.*).—*adj.* **buoy'ant** tending to float or to buoy up: light, cheerful, and elastic: of share prices, sales, etc., tending to rise.— *n.* **buoy'antness.** [Du. *boei,* buoy, fetter, through Romance forms (Norman *boie*), from L L. *boia,* a collar of leather.]

bur. See **burr**[1,2].

Burberry *bûr'bər-i, n.* a kind of waterproof cloth: a raincoat made of this cloth. [From *Burberrys,* trademark of Burberrys Ltd., the manufacturers.]

burble *bûrb'l, n.* a murmur.—*v.t.* and *v.i.* to murmur: to gurgle: to talk excitedly and rather incoherently (*coll.*).—*n.* **burb'ling.** [Prob. onomatopoeic.]

burbot *bûr'bət, n.* a fresh-water fish, like the ling, with a longish barbel on its lower jaw. [Fr. *bourbotte, barbotte*—L.L. *borba,* mud, or L. *barba,* a beard]

burden[1] *bûr'dən* (*arch* **burthen** *-dhən*), *n.* a load: weight: cargo: a ship's carrying capacity (still often **burthen**): that which is grievous, oppressive, or difficult to bear: an obligation: any restriction, limitation, or encumbrance affecting person or property (*Scots law*): (in *pl.*) a boat's floorboards.—*v.t.* to load: to oppress: to encumber.—*adjs.* **bur'denous, bur'densome** heavy: oppressive.—**burden of proof** the obligation to prove one's contention. [O.E. *byrthen*—*beran,* to bear.]

burden[2] *bûr'dən,* (*arch.* **burthen** *-dhən*), *n.* bourdon or bass: part of a song repeated at the end of every stanza, refrain: the leading idea of anything. [Fr. *bourdon,* a humming tone in music—L.L. *burdō,* a drone bee; confused with **burden**[1].]

burdock. See **burr**[1].

bureau *bū'rō, bū-rō', bu-rō', n.* a writing-table combined with chest of drawers: a room or office where such a table is used: a department or office for the transacting of business, such as collecting and supplying information: a government department:— *pl.* **bureaux, bureaus** (*-ōz*). [Fr. *bureau*—O.Fr. *burel,* russet cloth—L. *burrus,* red]

bureaucracy *bū-rok'rə-si,* or *-rōk', n.* a system of government by officials, responsible only to their departmental chiefs.—*ns.* **bur'eaucrat, bureau'crat** one who practises or favours bureaucracy —*adj.* **bureaucrat'ic.**—*adv.* **bureaucrat'ically.**—*n.* **bureaucratisā'tion,** *-z-.*—*v.t* **bureauc'ratise, -ize** to form into a bureaucracy: to make bureaucratic. [**bureau,** and Gr *kratos,* power.]

bureau de change *bu-rō də shäzh,* (Fr.) an office where currency can be exchanged.

burette *bū-ret', n.* a graduated glass tube with a tap, for measuring liquids run off an altar-cruet. [Fr.]

burg *bōō rg, bûrg, n.* a fortress or a walled town (*hist*): a town (*U S coll* ; *bûrg*). [West Gmc *burg,* O E *burh*]

burgee *bûr'jē, n* a swallow-tailed flag or pennant

burgeon, bourgeon *bûr'jən*, *v.i.* to put forth sprouts or buds: to grow [Fr *bourgeon*, a bud, shoot]

burger *bûr'gər*, (*coll.*) *n.* short for **hamburger, cheeseburger**, etc —**-burger** used as a compounding element as in *beefburger, cheeseburger*, to denote (a bread roll containing) a fried cake of meat, etc., made of, or accompanied by, the particular food mentioned

burgess *bûr'jis*, *n* a freeman or citizen of a borough: a member of a privileged class in a town: a member of parliament for a borough (*hist*): a borough magistrate or town councillor (*hist.*). [O Fr. *burgeis*].

burgh *bûr'ə*, spelling of **borough**, used for Scottish burghs, otherwise archaic.—*adj.* **burghal** (*bûrg'l*) — *n* **burgher** (*bûrg'ər*) a freeman or citizen of a borough (burgh): a townsman· a citizen of one of the South African Boer republics (*hist*) —**parliamentary burgh** one whose boundaries, as first fixed in 1832 for parliamentary representation, were adopted later for municipal purposes: a burgh which by itself or in combination elects a member of parliament: often applied to one that has ceased to do so; **royal burgh** a corporate body deriving its existence, constitution, and rights from a royal charter, actual or presumed to have existed [See **borough**.]

burglar *bûrg'lər*, *n*. one who enters a building as a trespasser (before 1969, by night) to commit a felony, e.g. to steal —*v.t.* **burg'larise, -ize** (U S. *coll*).—*n.* **burg'lary.**—*v.t.* **burgle** (*bûr'gl*; a back-formation from **burglar**) to commit burglary.—*v.t* to enter as a burglar.

burgomaster *bûr'gō-mäs-tər*, *n.* the chief magistrate of an Austrian, Dutch, Flemish or German town. [Du. *burgemeester*, Ger *Bürgermeister*, lit boroughmaster.]

burgoo *bûr-gōō'*, *bûr'gōō*, *n* a sailor's dish of boiled oatmeal with salt, butter, and sugar· a stew or thick soup for American picnics

burgundy *bûr'gən-di*, *n* a French wine (generally red), made in *Burgundy*· a similar wine made elsewhere — **Burgundy mixture** a fungicide composed of copper sulphate, sodium carbonate, and water

burhel. Same as **bharal.**

burial *ber'i-əl*, *n.* the act of burying.—**bur'ial-ground** a ground set apart for burials; **bur'ial-place** a burialground: the place where anyone is buried. [O E *byrgels*, a tomb; see **bury**.]

burin *bûr'in*, *n*. a kind of chisel of tempered steel, used in copper engraving· the distinctive style of an engraver: a palaeolithic flint tool.—*n* **bur'inist** an engraver. [Fr.; from root of **bore**.]

burk. See **berk.**

burk(h)a *boor'kə*, *n.* a loose garment, with veiled eyeholes, covering the whole body [Urdu *burga'*—Ar.]

burl *bûrl*, *n.* a small knot in thread: a knot in wood.

burlap *bûr'lap*, *n.* a coarse canvas for wrappings, wallcoverings, etc —usually in *pl*

burlesque *bûr-lesk'*, *n* ludicrous imitation· a piece of literature, of acting, or other performance that mocks its original by grotesque exaggeration or by combining the dignified with the low or the familiar· an entertainment combining often coarse jokes, strip-tease, songs, and dancing (*U.S.*). a playful or jocular composition (*mus.*).—*adj.* of the nature of burlesque: practising burlesque.—*v.t.* to mock by burlesque to make a burlesque of [It *burlesco*, prob from L L *burra*, a flock of wool, a trifle]

burly *bûr'li*, *adj* big and sturdy.—*n* **bur'liness.** [M.E. *borlich*]

Burmese *bûr'mēz, -mēz'*, *adj* relating to *Burma* or its people or language —*n* a native of Burma. the language of Burma.—Also **Bur'man.**—**Burmese cat** a short-haired domestic cat, dark brown in colour, with golden eyes.

burn¹ *bûrn*, (now chiefly *Scot*) *n.* a small stream or brook [O E *burna*, brook, spring]

burn² *bûrn*, *v.t.* to consume or injure by fire or great heat· to produce an effect of heat upon (as to bake pottery, calcine lime, scorch food, wither grass): to oxidise· to use (up), e g. uranium, in a nuclear reactor (usu with *up*) to corrode: to make by fire or analogous means —*v.i* to be burnt· to be on fire· to give out heat or light. to glow: to feel excess of heat· to be inflamed with passion:—*pa.t* and *pa.p* **burnt** or **burned.**—*n.* a hurt or mark due to burning: the firing of a rocket engine in order to impart thrust· a very fast ride, etc. on a motor-cycle, in a speed-boat, etc —*ns.* **burn'er** one who burns· a fixture or part of a lamp or gas-jet from which a flame comes; **burn'ing** act of consuming by fire: conflagration: inflammation: a quantity burned at one time: controlled expenditure of rocket propellant for course adjustment purposes —*adj* very hot: scorching· ardent: excessive.—Also *adv* —**burn'ing-glass** a convex lens concentrating the sun's rays at its focus; **burn'ing-mirr'or** a concave mirror for producing heat by concentrating the sun's rays; **burning question, issue** one keenly discussed; **burnt almonds** almonds in burnt sugar; **burnt'-cork** charred cork used for blacking the face; **burnt'-off'ering** something offered and burned upon an altar as a sacrifice, **burnt'-sienn'a** see **sienna**; **burn'-up** the using up of fuel in a nuclear reactor.—**burn a hole in one's pocket** said of money when one is eager to spend it; **burn down** to burn to the ground, **burned out** ineffective, exhausted; **burned up** (*U.S slang*) angry, **burn in** to fix and render durable by intense heat: to imprint indelibly, **burn one's boats** to cut oneself off from all chance of retreat: to stake everything on success; **burn one's fingers, get one's fingers** burnt to suffer as a result of interfering, embarking in speculations, etc ; **burn out** to destroy or drive out by burning· to burn till the fire dies down from want of fuel. to (cause to) become ineffective through overwork, exhaustion, etc. (*n.* **burn'-out**), **burn the candle at both ends** see **candle**; **burn the midnight oil** to study late into the night; **burn up** to consume completely by fire: to be burned completely: to increase in activity of burning: to make short or easy work of. to become or make angry (*U S slang*); **(money) to burn** (money) in great abundance [O E the transitive weak verb *bærnan, bærnde, bærned*, has been confused with the intransitive strong verb *beornan, byrnan, barn, bornen*; cf Ger. *brennen*, to burn]

burnet *bûr'nit*, the name of two closely related rosaceous plants, the great burnet, a meadow-plant, and common or salad burnet found on the chalk and sometimes used in salads, etc , both with close aggregates of brownish-purple flowers —**burnet moth** (or **burnet**) a moth of the Zygaenidae, esp. of the genus *Arthrocera*, with red-spotted or redstreaked fore-wings [O Fr *burnete, brunette*; see **brunette.**]

burnish *bûrn'ish*, *v t* to polish: to make bright by rubbing —*n* polish: lustre —*ns.* **burn'isher; burn'ishing; burn'ishment.** [Fr *brunir, bruniss-*, to burnish—*brun*, brown]

burnous *bûr-nōōs'*, **burnouse** *-nōōz'*, *ns.* a mantle with a hood much worn by the Arabs [Fr ,—Ar *burnus*]

burnt *pa t.* and *pa p.* of **burn²**.—Also *adj*

burp *bûrp*, *v t* to belch (*coll*) —Also *n* —*v t* to rub or pat a baby's back after feeding to cause it to belch [Imit]

burqa *bûr'kə* Same as **burk(h)a**.

burr[1], **bur** *bûr, n.* the prickly seed-case or head of certain plants, which sticks to clothes or animals: any impediment or inconvenient adherent: any lump, ridge, etc., more or less sharp, an excrescence on a tree, or markings representing it in wood: a knot in thread: a knob at the base of a deer's horn: the rough edge to a line made by an engraving tool, which, when the plate is inked, gives a further quality to the line: waste raw silk: the sweetbread or pancreas: the name for various tools and appliances, as the triangular chisel for clearing the corners of mortises, etc : the blank driven out of a piece of sheet-metal by a punch: a partly vitrified brick.—*adj.* **burr'y.**—**bur'dock** a composite plant with hooked involucral bracts and docklike leaves: any species of *Xanthium.*—**burr in the throat** something seeming to stick in the throat, producing a choking sensation. [Cog. with Dan *borre,* a bur.]

burr[2], **bur** *bûr, n.* the rough sound of *r* pronounced in the throat, as by many Northumberland people.—*v.i.* to whisper hoarsely, to murmur. [Usually associated with **burr**[1] but perh. imit.]

burrel, burrell, burrhel. Same as **bharal.**

burro *boo͞o'ō, n.* a donkey:—*pl.* **burr'os.** [Sp.]

burrow *bur'ō, n.* a hole in the ground dug esp. by certain animals for shelter or defence: a passage, hole, or gallery dug or eaten through wood, stone, etc.: a refuge.—*v.i.* to make holes underground as rabbits: to work one's way through earth, etc.: to dwell in a concealed place.—*v.t.* to make a burrow in: to make by burrowing. [Prob. a variant of **borough** —O.E. *beorgan,* to protect.]

bursa *bûr'sə, n.* a pouch or sac, esp. one containing viscid lubricating fluid at points of friction (*zool.*):—*pl.* **bur'sae** (*-sē*).—*adj.* **bur'sal** relating to a bursa: fiscal.—*n.* **bur'sar** one who keeps the purse, a treasurer: in Scotland, a student or pupil maintained at a university or school by funds derived from endowment.—*adj.* **bursarial** (*-sā'ri-əl*).—*ns.* **bur'sar-ship** the office of a bursar; **bur'sary** the treasury of a college or monastery: in Scotland, a scholarship.— *n.* **burs'ītis** inflammation of a bursa. [L.L. *bursa,* a purse—Gr. *byrsa,* skin or leather.]

burst *bûrst, v.t.* to break into pieces: to break open or cause to give way suddenly or by violence: to make by bursting.—*v.i.* to fly open or in pieces, esp. owing to a force from within: to give way suddenly: to break forth or away: to force a way: to break suddenly into being, or into some condition, activity, or expression of feeling:—*pa.t.* and *pa.p.* **burst.**—*n.* an act, occasion, or result of bursting: a sudden outbreak: a hard gallop: a spurt: a drunken bout.—**burst'-up** a complete break: disruption: commotion: collapse: failure. [O.E. *berstan;* see also **bust**[2].]

burthen *bûr'dhan, n.* and *v.t.* See **burden**[1,2].

Burton *bûr'tn, n.* a town of Staffordshire famous for its beer: a drink.—**gone for a Burton** (*airmen's slang*) drowned, dead: absent: missing: no longer in existence.

bury *ber'i, bûr'i, v.t.* to hide in the ground: to cover: to consign to the grave, the sea, etc., as a dead body: to hide or blot out of remembrance:—*pr.p.* **bur'ying;** *pa.t., pa.p.* **bur'ied.**—**bur'ying-beetle** a beetle that buries small animals as food for its larvae; **bur'ying-ground** ground set apart for burying the dead: a graveyard; **bur'ying-place.**—**bury the hatchet** to renounce enmity. [O.E. *byrgan,* to bury.]

bus *bus, n.* an omnibus: car, aeroplane, etc. (*slang*): a number of conductors forming a circuit or route along which data or power may be transmitted (also **high-way** or **trunk;** *comput.*):—*pl.* **bus'es, buss'es.**—*v.t.* to transport by bus.—*v.i.* to go by bus.—*ns.* **bus'ing, buss'ing** the transporting by bus of people from one district to another, esp. children to school, to achieve a more even racial, etc. balance.—**bus'-fare; bus'man** the driver or conductor of a bus; **bus'-stop** a halting-place for a bus, for passengers to board it or alight: the post or sign usu. marking such a place.—**busman's holiday** a holiday spent in activities similar to one's work; **miss the bus** to lose an opportunity. [Short for **omnibus.**]

busby *buz'bi, n.* a fur hat with a bag hanging on its right side, worn esp. by hussars. [Prob. Hung.]

bush[1] *boosh, n.* a woody plant in size between a tree and an undershrub: a shrub thick with branches: anything of bushy tuft-like shape: forest: wild uncultivated country (even though treeless): such country covered with bushes: the wild.—*adj.* **bushed** (*slang*) bewildered: tired.—*n.* **bush'iness.**—*adj.* **bush'y** full of or like bushes: thick and spreading.—**bush'-baby** a small South African lemur; **bush'-buck** a small S. African antelope, or any other of the same genus (Tragelaphus).—Also (Du.) **boschbok** (*bos'bok*), (Afrik.) **bosbok** (*bos'bok*); **bush'-cat** the serval; **bush'-fruit** a fruit growing on a bush, as gooseberry, raspberry; **bush'man** a settler, or traveller, in uncleared land: a woodsman: (with *cap.*) one of a now almost extinct nomadic, short-statured, yellowish-brown, aboriginal race of huntsmen in S. Africa.— Also *adj.*—**bush'master** a venomous South American snake; **bush pilot** an air-line pilot operating over uninhabited country; **bush'ranger** in Australia, a lawless person, often an escaped criminal, who takes to the bush and lives by robbery; **bush shirt, jacket** a cotton, etc., garment with four patch pockets and a belt; **bush telegraph** (*facet.*) the rapid transmission of news among primitive communities by drum-beating, etc.: gossip, rumour; **bush'veld, bosch'veld** (*bos'*) veld made up largely of woodland.—*v.i.* **bush'whack** to range through the bush: to fight in guerrilla warfare: to travel through woods, esp. by clearing a way to do so.—*v.t.* to ambush.—**bush'whacker** a guerrilla fighter: a sniper; **bush'whacking.—beat about the bush** to go round about anything, to evade coming to the point. [M.E. *busk, busch*—O.N. *buskr.* Some uses are from the corresponding Du. *bosch.*]

bush[2] *boosh, n.* the metal box or lining of any cylinder in which an axle works.—*v.t.* to furnish with a bush. —**bush'-met'al** hard brass, gunmetal, a composition of copper and tin, used for journals, bearings, etc. [Du. *bus*—L. *buxus,* box-tree.]

bushel *boosh'əl, n.* a dry measure of 8 gallons, no longer official, for grain, fruit, etc. (*imperial bushel,* 2219·36 cub. in.): a container for this quantity.—**hide one's light under a bushel** to keep quiet about or conceal one's talents or abilities. [O.Fr. *boissiel*—root of **box**[2].]

bushido *boo͞o'shi-dō, n.* a Japanese code of chivalry. [Jap. *bushi,* warrior, *dō,* doctrine.]

business *biz'nis, n.* employment: trade, profession, or occupation: a task or errand incumbent or undertaken: matter requiring attention: dealings, commercial activity: a commercial or industrial concern: one's concerns or affairs: a matter or affair: action as distinguished from dialogue (*theat.*): a thing, used quite indefinitely (*coll.*): (*biz'i-nis,* also written **busyness**) state of being busy.—Also *adj.* (*biz'nis*).— *adj.* **bus'iness-like** methodical, systematic, practical. —**business card** a card carried by business people, with their name and designation, and the name, address, telephone number and description, etc. of their firm; **business end** (*coll.*) the end or part of something that actually functions or does the work (as *business end of a fork*); **bus'inessman** one engaged in commercial transactions.—**like nobody's business** (*coll.*) keenly, energetically; **make it one's business** to undertake to accomplish something or see it done; **mean business** to be in earnest; **mind one's own business** to confine oneself to one's own affairs; **send someone about his business** to dismiss someone unceremoniously. [busy.]

busk *busk*, *v.i.* to play as a wandering musician or actor.—*ns.* **busk'er** a wandering musician or actor. **busk'ing**. [Prob Sp *buscar*, to seek.]

buskin *busk'in*, *n* a high thick-soled boot worn in ancient times by actors in tragedy [Ety. uncertain; cf. O.Fr. *brousequin*; Du *broosken*; Sp *borcegui*.]

buss *bus*, *n*. a rude or playful kiss, a smack.—*v t*. to kiss, esp in a rude or playful manner. [Cf Ger dial. *buss*, W. and Gael. *bus*, L. *bāsium*.]

bust *bust*, *n* a sculpture representing the head and breast of a person: the upper front part of the human body, esp. a woman's.—*adjs*. **bust'ed** breasted adorned with busts; **bust'y** (*coll*) of a woman, having a large bust [Fr. *buste*; It. and Sp. *busto*]

bust *bust*, (*coll*.) *v.t.* and *v.t.* to break, shatter: to make or become bankrupt—*v.t.* to arrest—*pa.t.* and *pa.p.* **bust'ed**, **bust**.—*n*. a drinking bout.—*adj* ruined, penniless.—*n*. **bust'er** (*coll*.) something large: a frolic· a roisterer: a horsebreaker: a form of address to a man or boy a strong south wind (*Austr*) someone or something that destroys or shatters, esp in combination, as *blockbuster*.—**busted flush** see **flush**[4]; **bust'-up** a quarrel or disruption: a disturbance or brawl—**go bust** to become bankrupt [Orig. a coll. form of **burst**.]

bustard *bust'ard*, *n*. any bird of the genus *Otis*, usually ranked with cranes. [Fr *bistard*—L *avis tarda*, slow bird (a misnomer).]

bustle *bus'l*, *v.i* to busy oneself noisily or fussily· to be full of or busy with (with *with*).—*n*. hurried activity: stir: tumult.—*n*. **bust'ler**. [M.E *bustelen*]

bustle *bus'l*, *n*. a frame or pad for causing a skirt to hang back from the hips; a car boot (*coll*.)

busy *biz'i*, *adj*. fully employed: active: diligent: meddling: fussily active: (of a telephone line) engaged: (of picture or design) unrestful because having too much detail.—*n* (*slang*) a detective —*v t* to make busy: to occupy:—*pr.p* **bus'ying**; *pa.t.* and *pa p.* **bus'ied**.—*adv.* **bus'ily**.—*n*. **bus'yness** state of being busy (see **business**)—**bus'ybody** one who meddles in others' affairs: mirror(s) at a window arranged to show passers-by; **busy Lizzie** a plant of the *Impatiens* genus. [O E. *bysig*.]

but *but*, *prep*. without (*obs*): except —*conj* on the other hand: in contrast: nevertheless, unless, if not: otherwise than (that): introducing emphasis, as in *nobody, but nobody, must go*: except that (merging in *prep*.): that not (developing into a negative *rel pron*.).—*adv.* only.—*n* an objection (as in 'But me no buts').—Also *adj*.—**anything but** certainly not; **but and ben** see ben[2]; **but for, but that** were it not for, or that. [O.E. *be-ūtan, būtan*, without—*be*, by, and *ūtan*, out—near, and yet outside.]

but *but*, *n*. Another spelling of **butt**[2,3,4].

butadiene *bū-tə-dī'ēn*, *n*. (L. *dis*, twice) a hydrocarbon, C_4H_6, used in making synthetic rubber —*n*. **bu'tane** a hydrocarbon of the methane series, C_4H_{10}, widely used as a fuel (see **bottle-gas**). [butyl.]

butch *bŏŏch*, *n*. an aggressively tough man (*slang*)· the 'male' partner in a lesbian relationship (*slang*).—*adj*. tough: aggressively masculine. [Amer boy's nickname.]

butcher *bŏŏch'ər*, *n*. one whose business is to slaughter animals for food, or who deals in their flesh: one who delights in bloody deeds.—*v.t.* to slaughter and prepare (animals) for sale as food· to put to a bloody death, to kill cruelly: to spoil, as a bad actor or the like (*fig*.).—*ns.* **butch'ering, butch'ing** (back-forma-

tion).—*ns.* **butch'er's** (orig. **butcher's hook**; *Cockney rhyming slang*) a look; **butch'ery** great or cruel slaughter: a slaughterhouse or shambles.—**butch'er-bird** a shrike. [O Fr *bochier, bouchier*, one who kills he-goats—*boc*, a he-goat; **buck**.]

but-end. Same as **butt-end** under **butt**[4].

butler *but'lər*, *n* a servant who has charge of liquors, plate, etc.: an officer in a royal household —*v i*. to act as butler —Also **butt'le** (back-formation) —*n* **but'lery** the butler's pantry. [Norm. Fr *butuiller*—L L *buticulārius*. See **bottle**.]

butment. Same as **abutment**.

butt *but*, *v t* to strike with the head, as a goat, etc.—*v t*. to strike with the head (also with *at, against*) to go or drive head first —*n* a push or blow with the head.—*n* **butt'er** an animal that butts —**butt in** to interfere, thrust oneself in [O Fr *boter*, to push, strike]

butt *but*, *n*. a large cask· a wine butt = 126 gallons, a beer and sherry butt = 108 gallons [Cf Fr *botte*, Sp *bota*, L.L *butta*]

butt *but*, *n* a mark or mound for archery practice: a mound behind targets. one who is made an object of ridicule· a hiding place for grouse-shooters. [Fr. *but*, goal]

butt *but*, *n* the thick and heavy end· the stump· a tree-trunk: the hinder part of a hide: thick leather: the fag-end of a cigar or cigarette: the buttocks (*U.S coll*): the wooden, etc. handle or steadying shoulder-part of a pistol or rifle. a remnant: the square end of a plank meeting another —*v.t* to abut: to meet end to end —**butted joint** a joint formed between the squared ends of the two jointing pieces, which come together but do not overlap; **butt'-end; butt welding** welding the seam formed by joining two butt-ends [Ety dub ; prob connected with **butt**[3] and **abut**.]

butter *but'ər*, *n* an oily substance obtained from cream by churning· extended to various substances resembling or containing it: flattery —*v t* to spread over with butter, mortar, or other soft substance: to flatter (usu with *up*) —*adj*. **butt'ery** like butter: smeared with butter or the like.—**butt'er-bean'** an American bean akin to the French bean, **butt'er-cloth'**, **-mus'lin** a loose-woven cloth suitable for wrapping butter; **butt'ercup** a crowfoot (*Ranunculus*), esp of one of those species that have golden-yellow cup-shaped flowers; **butt'er-dish**, **-plate** a dish or plate for holding butter at table; **butt'er-fat'** the fat contained in butter, chiefly glycerides of palmitic and oleic acids —*adj*. **butt'er-fingered** prone to let things slip—**butt'er-fingers** (*sing*) one who lets a ball, etc , he ought to catch slip through his fingers; **butt'erfly** a general name for any of the daylight Lepidoptera, roughly distinguished from moths by their clubbed antennae a gay, flighty person (*fig*.): butterfly breast-stroke:—*pl* **butt'erflies**.—*adj*. light, flighty, like a butterfly—**butterfly (breast-) stroke** a swimming-stroke performed on the breast, the arms working simultaneously with an over-arm action; **butt'erfly-screw'**, **-nut'** a screw or nut, turned by winged finger-grips; **butterfly valve** a disc-shaped valve in a carburettor, etc : a valve consisting of two hinged plates, **butt'er-knife** a blunt knife for taking butter from a butter dish; **butt'er-milk** the milk that remains after the butter has been separated from the cream by churning; **butter-muslin** see **butter-cloth** above; **butt'ernut** the oily nut of the North American white walnut: the tree itself: its light-coloured close-grained wood: the souari-nut of Guiana; **butt'er-pat** a pat of butter· a wooden instrument for working butter into shape; **butt'erscotch** a kind of toffee containing much butter —**butterflies in the stomach** nervous tremors in the stomach; **butter**

up to flatter. [O.E. *butere*; Ger. *Butter*; both from L. *būtyrum*—Gr. *boutyron*, app.—*bous*. ox, *tyros*, cheese.]

butter². See **butt¹.**

buttery¹ *but'ər-i, n* a storeroom, often in a college, for provisions, esp. liquors.—**butt'ery-bar'** the ledge for holding tankards in the buttery; **butt'ery-hatch'** a half-door over which provisions are handed from the buttery. [Fr *bouteillerie*, lit place for bottles; *butler, bottle*.]

buttery². See **butter¹.**

buttle. See **butler.**

buttock *but'ək, n.* the rump or protuberant part of the body behind: in wrestling, a throw by use of the buttock —*v t.* to throw in this way [Dim. of **butt⁴**.]

button *but'n, n* a knob or disc, used as a fastening, ornament, or badge. a knob, e g. that at the end of a foil, that for winding a watch, that to which a violin tailpiece is looped: a bud: the head of an unexpanded mushroom: a pimple: the knob of an electric bell, etc · anything of small value —*adj.* like a button, used e g. of small varieties of vegetables, blooms, etc of a compact, globular shape.—*v.t.* to fasten by means of buttons: to close up tightly.—*v.t* to admit of fastening with buttons.—*n sing* **butt'ons** a page in a hotel, etc —*adj* **butt'ony** set with buttons· like a button.—*adj.* **butt'oned-up** (*slang*) uncommunicative —**butt'on-hole** the slit through which a button is passed: a flower or flowers for wearing in the button-hole of a lapel.— *v.t.* to make button-holes in. to work with a stitch suitable for defence of edges (*button-hole-stitch*): to detain in talk (orig **butt'onhold**) —**butt'on-hook** a hook for pulling buttons through button-holes ' in boots, gloves, etc.—**buttoned up** (*slang*) successfully fixed up: safe in hand: ready for action [Fr *bouton*, any small projection, from *bouter*, to push.]

buttress *but'rəs, n.* a projecting support built on to the outside of a wall: any support or prop.—*v.t* to prop or support, as by a buttress. [App O Fr *bouterez*— *bouter*, to push, bear against.]

butty *but'i,* (*dial.*) *n* a sandwich, snack.

butyric *bū-tir'ik, adj.* pertaining to or derived from butter —*n.* **bū'tyrate** a salt of butyric acid.—**butyric acid** a volatile fatty acid (C_3H_7·COOH), smelling like rancid butter. [See **butter¹**.]

buxom *buks'əm, adj.* yielding, elastic: gay, lively, jolly: plump and comely —*n.* **bux'omness.** [M.E. *buhsum*, pliable, obedient—O.E *būgan*, to bow, yield, suff. *-some*.]

buy *bī, v.t* to purchase for money: to bribe: to obtain in exchange for something: to accept, believe (*slang*):— *pr p.* **buy'ing;** *pa.t.* and *pa.p.* **bought** (*bot*).—*n.* something purchased.—*adj.* **buy'able.**—*n.* **buy'er** one who buys: one employed to buy goods.—**buyers' market** one in which buyers rule the price, supply exceeding demand.—**a good buy** (*coll*) a wise purchase, a bargain; **buy in** to collect a stock of by buying: to buy back for the owner at an auction (*n.* **buy'-in**); **buy into** to pay for a share or interest in; **buy off** to buy exemption or release for: to get rid of by paying; **buy out** to dispossess entirely by payment (*n.* **buy'-out**): to buy off; **buy over** to win over by payment: to bribe; **buy up** to purchase the whole stock of; **have bought it** (*slang*) to have been killed; **I'll buy that** I don't know, I give it up, tell me: I'll accept that explanation though it seems surprising. [O.E. *bycgan, bohte, boht*; Goth. *bugjan*.]

buzz *buz, v.i.* to make a noise like that of insects' wings: to murmur: to move quickly (*slang*).—*v.t.* to utter with a buzzing sound. to whisper or spread secretly· to transmit by Morse over a telephone wire by means of a key: to make a telephone call to. to throw (*slang*) to fly very low over or very close to: to interfere with in

flight by flying very near to (*aero.*) —*n* the noise of bees and flies. a humming sound· a voiced hiss: a whispered report: a telephone call: a pleasant feeling (*coll.*) —*n.* **buzz'er** one who buzzes. an apparatus that makes a buzzing sound.—*n.* and *adj* **buzz'ing.**—*adv* **buzz'ingly.**—*adj* **buzz'y.**—**buzz bomb** a flying bomb, **buzz'-saw** (*U.S.*) a circular saw; **buzz word** (*coll.*) a well-established term in the jargon of a particular subject, science, etc , its use conveying the impression of specialised knowledge —**buzz off** (*slang*) to go away. [From the sound]

buzzard *buz'ard, n.* a large bird of prey of the genus *Buteo*: extended to some others, as the *honey-buzzard, turkey-buzzard.* [Fr. *busard*.]

bwana *bwa'na, n.* master sir [Swahili]

by *bī, prep* at the side of. near to· along a route passing through, via: past in oaths, in the presence of, or with the witness of. through (denoting the agent, cause, means, etc.): to the extent of: in quantity measurable in terms of· in accordance with in respect of· of time, not after. during (day, night, etc) multiplied into, or combined with another dimension of: in succession to: (of horses, etc) sired by —*adv.* near aside· away past: in reserve.—*n* and *adj.* see **bye¹**.—*adv* **by'-and-by'** at some future time· before long —**by'-blow** a side blow, **by'-election** a parliamentary election for a seat during the sitting of parliament; **by'-end** a subsidiary aim, **by'-form** a subsidiary form. a form varying from the usual one, **by'going** the action of passing by (esp. in **in the by-going,** in passing) —*adj* **by'gone** (*-gon*) —*n.pl.* **by'gones** past happenings or grievances. ornaments, household articles, etc., of former times which are not fine enough, or not old enough, to be valued as antiques (also in *sing*) —**by'-lane** a side lane or passage out of the common road, **bylaw, bye-law** see separate entry; **by'line** a line at the head of a newspaper or magazine article telling by whom it is written, **by'-name** a nickname.—**by'pass** a road, route or passage for carrying traffic, fluids, electricity, etc , round an obstruction, congested place, etc.—*v.t* to supply with a bypass: to direct (e g fluid) along a bypass: to go round and beyond by a bypass (also *fig* to ignore, leave out): to evade.—**by'-passage** a side passage.—**by'path** a secluded or indirect path, **by'-play** action subordinate to and apart from the main action of a play, **by'-plot** a subsidiary plot, **by'-product** a product formed in the process of making something else; **by'road** a retired side road; **by'stander** one who stands by or near one: a looker-on; **by'-street** an obscure street, **by'way** a private, secluded, or obscure way; **by'word** a common saying, proverb. an object of scorn: a person noted for a specified characteristic.—**by and by** presently: in the course of time; **by and large** whether close-hauled or before the wind (*naut*): speaking generally: on the whole, **by oneself** alone; **by the by(e),** by the way in passing, incidentally; **let bygones be bygones** let past quarrels be ignored [O E *bī, bi, big*; Ger *bei*, L *ambi-* See **bye¹**.]

by². See **bye¹**.

bye¹ *bī, n.* anything of minor importance, a side issue, a thing not directly aimed at· in games, the state of one who has not drawn an opponent, and passes without contest to the next round· in golf, the holes remaining after the match is decided, played as a subsidiary game: in cricket, a run made from a ball bowled but not struck or touched by the batsman — *adj.* subsidiary. part. indirect See also **by¹**.

bye² *bī, n.* **bye-bye** *bī'bī, bə-bī',* coll forms of **good-bye.**

bye-law. See **bylaw.**

Byelorussian. See **Belorussian.**

bygoing, bygones. See **by¹.**

bylaw, bye-law *bī'lo, n* the law of a local authority or private corporation: a supplementary law or an inferred regulation. [O.N. *bӯjar-log*; from O.N. *būa*, to dwell.]

byline, bypass, bypath, byplace. See by[1].

byre *bīr*, (mainly *Scot.*) *n.* a cowhouse.—**byre'man, byre'woman** a farm-servant with care of cows. [O.E. *bӯre.*]

byroad, bystander, byway, etc. See by[1].

Byronic *bī-ron'ik*, *adj.* possessing the characteristics of Lord Byron (1788–1824), or of his poetry, overstrained in sentiment or passion, cynical and libertine.

byssus *bis'əs*, *n.* a fine yellowish flax: linen made from it (the 'fine linen' of the Bible): the bundle of fila-ments by which some shellfish attach themselves. [L.,—Gr. *byssos*, a fine flaxen substance.]

byte *bīt*, (*comput.*) *n.* a set of usu. eight binary digits (bits) considered as a unit [Poss. from binary digit eight, or from bit[2] and bite.]

Byzantine *biz-an'tīn*, or *bīz-an'tīn*, or *-tin*, or *biz'ən-*, *adj.* relating to *Byzantium* (Constantinople, now Istanbul): rigidly hierarchic: intricate, tortuous.—*n.* an inhabitant of Byzantium.—*n.* **Byzan'tinist** a person who studies, or is expert in, Byzantine history, affairs, etc.—**Byzantine Church** the Eastern or Greek Church; **Byzantine Empire** the Eastern or Greek Empire from A.D. 395 to 1453. [Gr. *Bӯzantion.*]

fāte; far; mē; hûr (her); *mīne; mōte; for; mūte; mōōn; fŏŏt; dhen* (then); *el'ə-mənt* (element)

C

C, C *sē, n* the third letter of our alphabet, a rounded form of the Greek *gamma* (see G), one of the notes of the musical gamut, the sound on which the system is founded—the keynote of the natural scale, C major, having neither flats nor sharps: as a Roman numeral, C = 100 —**c-spring** see **cee-spring.**

ca' *ko* (*Scot*) *v.t* and *v.t* to call, to drive, to propel, to knock (with *down, off, over,* etc.) —**ca' canny** to go easy, deliberately to restrict output or effort [**call.**]

cab *kab, n.* a public carriage, orig. horse-drawn now usu. motor-driven a taxi-cab: the driver's shelter on a locomotive, motor-lorry, etc.—*n.* **cabb'y, cabb'ie** a familiar dim. of **cab'man,** one who drives a horse cab, or of **cab'-driver,** a taxi-driver —**cab'-rank, cab's stand** a place where cabs stand for hire. [**cabriolet.**]

cabal *kə-bal', n.* a small party united for some secret design, the plot itself: a name given to five unpopular ministers of Charles II (1672), whose initials happened to make up the word.—*v.t* to form a party for a secret purpose, to intrigue:—*pr.p* **caball'ing;** *pa.t.* and *pa.p* **caballed'.**—*n.* **caball'er.** [Fr *cabale,* from Heb *qabbalah,* see **cabbala.**]

cabala, etc See **cabbala.**

caballero *kab-al-yār'ō, n.* a Spanish gentleman.—*pl.* **caballer'os.** [Sp ,—L *caballārius,* horseman—*caballus,* horse.]

cabana *kə-ban'(y)ə, (U S.) n* a small tentlike cabin on the beach or by a swimming-pool [Sp *cabaña.*]

cabaret *kab'ə-rā, n.* a restaurant with variety turns: the kind of entertainment there given [Fr , tavern.]

cabbage *kab'ij, n.* a vegetable (*Brassica oleracea*) of the Cruciferae the edible terminal bud of various palms. a dull, inactive person.—*adj.* **cabb'agy.**—**cabb'age butt'erfly, cabb'age-white** a large white butterfly (*Pieris*) whose larvae injure the leaves of cabbage and kindred plants, **cabb'age-fly** a fly whose maggots injure cabbage roots, **cabb'age-lett'uce** a lettuce with cabbage-like head, **cabb'age-moth** a moth whose larva feeds on the cabbage, **cabb'age-palm, cabb'age-tree** *Oreodoxa oleracea* or other palm with an edible cabbage, **cabb'age-rose** a rose of bunchy cabbage-like form, **cabb'age-worm** the larva of the cabbage-butterfly or of the cabbage-moth [Fr *caboche,* head—L *caput*]

cabbala, cabala *kab'ə-lə* or *kə-ba'lə, n* a secret traditional lore of Jewish rabbis, who read hidden meanings into the Bible —*ns.* **cab(b)'alism** the science of the cabbala, **cab(b)'alist** one versed in the cabbala —*adjs.* **cab(b)alist'ic, -al** relating to the cabbala. having a hidden meaning. [Heb. *qabbālāh,* tradition, *qibbēl,* to receive]

cabbie, cabby. See **cab.**

caber *kāb'ər, n.* a pole, generally the stem of a young tree, poised and tossed by athletes [Gael. *cabar.*]

cabin *kab'in, n.* a hut or cottage. a small room, esp in a ship, for officers or passengers a compartment for passengers in an aircraft —*v.t* to shut up in a cabin or in a cramped space —**cab'in-boy** a boy who waits on the officers or cabin passengers of a ship. **cabin class** the class between tourist and first class, **cabin crew** members of aircraft crew who look after passengers, **cabin cruiser** a power-driven boat with full provision for living on board, **cabin passenger** a passenger having cabin accommodation [Fr *cabane*—L L *capanna*]

cabinet *kab'(i-)nit, n* a small room, closet, or private apartment: a case for storing or displaying articles of value: a cupboard or drawer for storage. (usu. *cap.*) a select inner group of the ministers who govern a country—**cab'inetmaker** a maker of cabinets and other fine furniture; **cab'inetmaking** the occupation or art of the cabinetmaker; **cabinet minister** a member of a cabinet; **cab'inet-pudd'ing** a cake-like pudding. [Dim of **cabin.**]

cable *kā'bl, n.* a strong rope or chain for hauling or tying anything, esp a ship's anchor: a cable-length: a line of submarine telegraph wires: a bundle of insulated wires laid underground: a cabled message —Also *adj.*—*v t* and *v t* to provide with a cable, to tie up. to telegraph or send by cable.—*n.* **cā'bling** a bead or moulding like a thick rope.—**câ'ble-car** a car suspended from a moving cable, used as a method of transport up mountains, across valleys, etc ; **cā'blegram** a telegram sent by cable, **câ'ble-length, câ'ble's-length** a tenth of a nautical mile, approximately 200 yards or 100 fathoms; **câ'ble-mould'ing** a bead or moulding carved in imitation of a thick rope; **câ'ble-stitch** (a series of stitches producing) a pattern suggestive of cables; **cable television** the transmission of television programmes by cable to individual subscribers; **câ'ble-tram'way, -rail'way** one along which cars or carriages are drawn by an endless cable; **câ'bleway** a structure for transport of material in cars suspended from a cable [Fr ,—L.L. *caplum,* a halter—L *capēre,* to hold.]

cabochon *ka-bō-shɔ̃, n.* a precious stone polished but uncut, or cut **en** (*ā*) **cabochon,** i.e. rounded on top and flat on back, without facets.—Also *adj.* [Fr , *caboche*—L *caput,* head.]

caboodle *kə-bōō'dl, (slang) n* crowd. collection.

caboose *kə-bōō's', n.* a ship's kitchen: a car on a train for the train crew or workmen (*U S.*): a hut. [Du *kombuis*]

cabotage *kab'o-tij, n* coastal trading: restriction of this within a country's territory [Fr]

cabriole *kab'ri-ōl, n.—adj.* of furniture legs, curved, often like an animal's paw.—*n.* **cabriolet** (*-lā'*) a light carriage with two wheels: a cab: a motor-car with folding top: a small armchair of curved design (18th century). [Fr.,—L *capra,* a goat]

cacao *kə-ka'ō, kə-kā'ō, n.* tropical American tree *Theobroma cacao* or its seeds from which cocoa and chocolate are made. [Mex. *cacauatl,* cacao tree.]

cachaemia *ka-kē'mi-ə, n.* a morbid state of the blood.—*adj* **cachae'mic.** [Gr *kakos,* bad, *haima,* blood.]

cachalot *kash'ə-lot, -lō, n.* the sperm-whale [Fr.]

cache *kash, n.* a hiding-place for treasure, provisions, ammunition, etc stores so hidden —*v.t.* to hide. [Fr *cacher,* to hide.]

cachet *kash'ā, n* a seal any distinctive stamp (*fig.*), esp. something showing or conferring prestige: a capsule enclosing a medicine [Fr]

cachexy, cachexia *ka-kek'si, -ə, ns.* a bad state of body or depraved habit of mind —*adjs.* **cachec'tic, -al.** [L , —Gr *kachexiā*—*kakos,* bad, *hexis,* condition]

cachinnate *kak'in-āt, v.t* to laugh loudly.—*n* **cachinna'tion.**—*adj* **cachinn'atory** (or *kak'*) [L. *cachinnāre,* to laugh loudly]

cacholot. Same as **cachalot.**

cachou *ka-shōō', n* a pill or lozenge of extract of liquo-

---

fāte, fär, mē, hûr (her), *mīne, mōte, for, mūte, mōōn: fŏŏt, dhen* (then): *el'ə-mənt* (element) rice, cashew-nut, or the like, used by some smokers in the hope of sweetening the breath. [Fr]

cachucha *kə-chōō'chə*, *n*. a lively Spanish dance in 3–4 time, like the bolero. [Sp.]

cacique *ka-sēk'*, *n*. a West Indian chief· in Spain or Latin America, a political boss —Also *cazique'*. [Haitian]

cack-handed *kak'-hand'id*, (*slang*) *adj* left-handed: clumsy.—Also **kack'-hand'ed.** [Dial. *cack*, excrement, from L. *cacāre*, to defecate.]

cackle *kak'l*, *n*. the sound made by a hen or goose: talk or laughter of similar sound or value.—*v.t.* to make such a sound.—Also *v.t.*—*n.* **cack'ler.**—**cut the cackle** (*slang*) to stop the useless talk. [M.E. *cakelen*; cog. with Du *kakelen*.]

cacodaemon, cacodemon *kak-ō-dē'mən*, *n*. an evil spirit. [Gr. *kakos*, bad, *daimōn*, spirit]

cacodyl *kak'ō-dil*, *n* a colourless stinking liquid, composed of arsenic, carbon, and hydrogen. [Gr. *kakōdēs*, stinking, *hȳlē*, matter.]

cacoepy *kak-ō'ə-pi*, *n*. bad or wrong pronunciation. [Gr. *kakos*, bad, *epos*, word.]

cacoethes *kak-ō-ē'thēz*, *n*. a bad habit or itch:—**cacoethes loquendi** (or *ka-ko-ûth'ās*) *lō-kwen'dī* (or *lo-kwen'dē*), (L.) an itch for speaking; **cacoethes scribendi** *skrī-ben'dī* (or *skrē-ben'dē*) an itch for scribbling. [Gr. *kakoëthēs*, *-ēs*, ill-disposed—*kakos*, bad, *ēthos*, habit.]

cacography *kak-og'rə-fi*, *n*. bad handwriting or spelling.—*n.* **cacog'rapher.**—*adjs.* **cacographic, -al** (*-ō-graf'ik*, *-əl*). [Gr. *kakos*, bad, and *graphē*, writing.]

cacology *ka-kol'ə-ji*, *n*. faulty vocabulary or pronunciation. [Gr. *kakos*, bad, *logos*, speech.]

cacomistle, cacomixl *ka'kə-mi(k)s-əl*, *ns*. a small carnivore found in south-west U.S. and Mexico [Mex. Sp.,—Nahuatl *tlaco*, half, *ruiztli*, cougar.]

cacophony *ka-kof'ə-ni*, *n*. a disagreeable sound: discord of sounds.—*adjs.* **cacoph'onous, cacophonic** (*-ō-fon'ik*), **-al, cacophonious** (*-fō'ni-əs*) harsh-sounding. [Gr. *kakos*, bad, *phōnē*, sound.]

cacotopia *kak-ō-tō'pi-ə*, *n*. a state in which everything is as bad as possible—opp of *Utopia*.—*adj.* **cacotō'pian.** [Gr. *kakos*, bad. *topos*, a place.]

cactus *kak'tus*, *-təs*, *n*. a plant of any part of the American family **Cactā'ceae** whose stems store water and do the work of leaves, which are generally reduced to spines: (also **cactus dahlia**) a type of double-flowered dahlia:—*pl.* **cac'ti** or **cac'tuses.**—*adjs.* **cactā'ceous; cac'tiform.** [L.,—Gr. *kaktos*, a prickly plant found in Sicily.]

cacumen *ka-kū'men*, *n*. a top or point.—*adjs.* **cacū'minal** pertaining to the top: produced by turning the tip of the tongue up and back (*phon.*); **cacū'minous** with pointed or pyramidal top. [L. *cacūmen*, *-inis*.]

cad *kad*, *n*. a low vulgarian: one who lacks the instincts of a gentleman —*adj.* **cadd'ish.**—*n.* **cadd'ishness.** [Short for **cadet.**]

cadastral *ka-das'trəl*, *adj.* pertaining to a **cadastre** (*ka-das'tər*) or public register of the lands of a country for fiscal purposes: applied also to a survey on a large scale [Fr ,—L L *capitastrum*, register for a poll-tax.—L. *caput*, the head]

cadaverous *kə-dav'ə-rəs*, *adj* corpselike sickly-looking: gaunt, haggard —*n* **cadăv'er** (or *-dav'*) a corpse.—*adj.* **cadăv'eric.**—*n.* **cadav'erousness.** [L. *cadăver*, a dead body—*cadēre*, to fall (dead)]

caddice. See **caddis.**

caddie, caddy *kad'i*, *n*. one who attends a golfer at play, carrying the clubs.—*v.i.* to carry clubs.—**caddie car** or **caddy car** a device for taking a bag of golf clubs round the course—also **caddie** (or **caddy**) **cart.** [See **cadet.**]

caddis, caddice *kad'is*, *n* the larva of the **cadd'is-fly** which lives in water in a **cadd'is-case**, a silken sheath covered with fragments of wood, stone, etc.—Also **cadd'is-worm.**

caddy[1] *kad'i*, *n*. a small box for holding tea [Malay *kati*, the weight of a small packet of tea.]

caddy[2]. See **caddie.**

cade[1] *kād*, *n*. a barrel or cask [Fr —L. *cadus*, a cask.]

cade[2] *kād*, *n*. a lamb or colt brought up by hand, a pet lamb.—Also *adj.*

cadence *kā'dəns*, *n*. the fall of the voice: rise and fall of sound, modulation: rhythm: a succession of chords closing a musical period.—*adj* **cā'denced** rhythmical. —*n.* **cā'dency** rhythm —*adj.* **cadential** (*kə-den'shəl*) [Fr.—L. *cadĕre*, to fall.]

cadenza *ka-dent'sa*, *kə-den'zə*, *n* an outstanding virtuoso passage or flourish given by a solo voice or instrument towards the end of a movement.—*adj.* **cadential** (*kə-den'shəl*) [It. *cadenza*—L. *cadĕre*, to fall.]

cadet *kə-*, *ka-det'*, *n* a younger son: a member of the younger branch of a family: one undergoing training for one of the armed forces: in New Zealand, a newcomer gaining experience.—*n.* **cadet'ship.**—**cadet corps** an organised body undergoing military training. [Fr. *cadet*, formerly *capdet*—dim of L. *caput*, the head.]

cadge *kaj*, *v.t.* and *v.i.* to bet or go about begging: to sponge (money, etc.) —*n* **cadg'er.** [Prob. conn. with **catch.**]

cadi *ka'di*, *kā'di*, *n* a magistrate in Muslim countries. [Ar. *qādī*, a judge.]

Cadmean *kad-mē'ən*, *adj* —**Cadmean victory** one very costly to both sides (Cadmus sowed a dragon's teeth from which sprang soldiers who fought each other until only five were left)

cadmium *kad'mi-əm*, *n*. an element (at numb. 51; symbol Cd), a white metal, occurring in zinc ores.—**cadmium yellow** cadmium sulphide used as pigment [Gr *kadmiā*, *kadmeiā* (*gē*), Cadmean (earth), calamine.]

cadre *kad'r*, *kad'ri*, *kad'ər*, *kād'*, *n*. a framework, esp the permanent skeleton of a military unit: any nucleus of key persons: (prob from Fr. through Russ.) a cell of trained Communist leaders: a member of such a cell. [Fr]

caduceus *ka-dū'si-us*, (*myth*) *n*. the rod of Hermes, messenger of the gods—a wand surmounted with two wings and entwined by two serpents.—*pl* **cadū'cei.**—*adj* **cadū'cean.** [L. *cādūceus*, akin to Gr. *kērȳkeion*, a herald's wand—*kēryx*, *-ykos*, a herald]

caducous *ka-dū'kəs*, *adj* falling early, as leaves or flowers [L. *cadūcus*—*cadēre*, to fall.]

Caecilia *sē-sil'i-ə*, *n*. a genus of legless burrowing Amphibia with hidden eyes —*adj* **caecil'ian.**—*n* any member of the class to which Caecilia belongs [L *caecus*, blind]

caecum *sē'kəm*, in U S. **cecum**, *n* a blind sac: a sac or bag having only one opening, connected with the intestine of an animal.—*pl* **cae'ca.**—*adj* **cae'cal.** [L., neut of *caecus*, blind]

Caenozoic *sē-nō-zō'ik* Same as **Cainozoic.**

caerulean. Same as **cerulean.**

Caesalpinia *ses-*, *sēz-al-pin'i-ə*, *n* a genus giving name to a family **Caesalpinia'ceae** of leguminous plants — *adj* **caesalpinia'ceous.** [Andrea *Cesalpino* (1519–1603), Italian botanist]

Caesar *sē'zər*, *n*. an absolute monarch, an autocrat, from the Roman dictator Gaius Julius *Caesar* (100–44 B C): (also without *cap.*) a Caesarean operation (*coll*).—*adj* **Caesarean, -ian** (*-ā'ri-ən*) relating to Julius Caesar. —*n*. an adherent of Caesar, an imperialist —*ns* **Cae'sarism; Cae'sarist; Cae'sar-**

ship.—**Caesarean operation, section** delivery of a child by cutting through walls of abdomen (perh. *Lex Caesarea*, perh *caedĕre*, to cut—Pliny connects with first bearer of cognomen *Caesar*).

caesium *sēz'ı-əm, n.* an element (at. numb. 55; symbol Cs), a silver-white, soft alkaline metal; used in form of compounds or alloys in photoelectric cells, etc [L. *caesius*, bluish grey]

caesura, cesura *si-zū'rə, (pros.) n.* division of a foot between two words: a pause in a line of verse (generally near the middle).—*adj.* **caesū'ral.** [L *caesūra—caedĕre, caesum,* to cut off.]

cafard, *ka-far', n* depression, the blues [Fr]

café, cafe *kaf'ā, ka'fi, n* a coffee-house, a restaurant.—**café au lait** (*ō le*) coffee made with hot milk. coffee with milk added; **café noir** (*nwar*) black coffee (i.e without milk)

cafeteria *ka-fi-tē'ri-ə, n* a restaurant with a counter for self-service [Cuban Sp , a tent in which coffee is sold.]

caff. Slang term for **café,** coffee-house.

caffeine *kaf'ēn,* or *kaf-ē'in, n.* theine, an alkaloid present in coffee and tea.—*n.* **caff'e(in)ism** a morbid state caused by caffeine [Fr. *caféine*; see **coffee.**]

caftan *kaf'tən, kaf-tan', n.* a long-sleeved Persian or Turkish garment, reaching to the ankles and often tied with a sash. [Turk. *qaftān.*]

cage *kāj, n* a box or compartment wholly or partly of open work for captive animals: a prison: a frame with a platform or platforms used in hoisting in a vertical shaft. a wire guard: any structure resembling a bird's cage: a structure to protect garden fruit and vegetables from birds.—*v t* to imprison in a cage—*pr.p.* **cag'ing;** *pa t.* and *pa p* **caged.**—*adj* **caged** confined.—*n.* **cage'ling** a bird that is or has been kept in a cage.—**cage'bird** a bird of a kind habitually kept in a cage; **cage'work** open work like the bars of a cage.—**cage in** to imprison (usu. *fig*). [Fr.,—L. *cavea,* a hollow place]

cagey, cagy *kāj'ı, (coll) adj.* artfully shy, wary, chary: not frank, secretive —*adv.* **cag'ily.**—*n.* **cag'iness, cag'(e)yness.** [Perh. conn with **cadgy.**]

cagoul(e), kagool, kagoul(e) *kə-gōōl', n.* a lightweight, weather-proof anorak, often knee-length [Fr *cagoule,* a monk's hood.]

cagy. See **cagey.**

cahoot *kə-hōōt, n. (U S.)*—**in cahoots** in collusion (with)

caiman. Same as **cayman.**

Cain *kān, n.* Adam's son, murderer of Abel (Gen. iv.), hence allusively a murderer —**raise Cain** to make a determined or angry fuss.

Cainozoic *kī-nō-zō'ık, (geol.) adj.* and *n.* Tertiary [Gr *kainos,* new, *zōē,* life]

caique, caïque *ka-ēk', n.* a light skiff used on the Bosporus. [Fr.,—Turk. *kaik,* a boat.]

cairn *kārn, n.* a heap of stones, esp. one raised over a grave, or as a landmark on a mountain-top or path: a small variety of Scottish terrier (**cairn terrier**).—*n* **cairngorm'** (-stone) brown or yellow quartz found among the Cairngorm Mountains. [Gael. *càrn.*]

caisson *kā'sən, kə-sōōn', n.* ammunition wagon: a strong case for keeping out the water while the foundations of a bridge are being built: an apparatus for lifting a vessel out of the water for repairs or inspection: the pontoon or floating gate used to close a dry-dock.—**caisson disease** bends, a disease affecting divers, caisson-workers, etc , who are too suddenly subjected to decreased air pressure, it is due to formation of nitrogen bubbles in the body as nitrogen comes rapidly out of solu-

tion [Fr , from *caisse,* a case or chest (See **case[1].**)]

caitiff *kā'tıf, n.* a mean despicable fellow.—*adj.* mean, base. [O.Fr. *caitif*]—*L. captīvus,* a captive.]

cajole *kə-jōl', v t* to coax (into): to cheat by flattery (into, out of).—*ns.* **cajole'ment** coaxing for the purpose of deluding: wheedling: flattery; **cajol'er;** **cajol'ery.** [Fr. *cajoler,* to chatter; ety. dub.]

Cajun *kā'jən, n.* a descendant of the French-speaking Acadians deported to Louisiana in 1755: the language of the Cajuns —Also *adj.* [**Acadian.**]

cake *kāk, n.* a piece of dough that is baked: a small loaf of fine bread: any flattened mass baked, as *oatcake,* or formed by pressure or drying, as of soap, clay, snow, blood: a breadlike composition enriched with additions such as sugar, spices, currants, peel, etc : a separately made mass of such composition.—*v.t.* and *v.i.* to form into a cake or hard mass —*n.* and *adj.* **cāk'ing**—*adj.* **cāk'y.**—**cake hole** (*slang*) mouth; **cake'walk** a prancing movement once performed by American Negroes in competition for a *cake:* a dance developed therefrom: something accomplished with supreme ease. —**a piece of cake** (*coll.*) a thing easy to do; **cakes and ale** vaguely, all the goods things of life; **have one's cake and eat it, eat one's cake and have it** to have the advantage of both alternatives; **his cake is dough** his hope has failed; **take the cake** (*slang*) to carry off the honours, rank first (ironically). [O.N. *kaka.*]

calabash *kal'ə-bash, n.* a gourd, or its shell used as a vessel, tobacco-pipe, etc.: the fruit of the calabash tree or its shell similarly used [Fr *calebasse*—Sp. *calabaza*—Pers *kharbuz,* melon.]

calaboose *kal'ə-bōōs, -bōōs', (U.S.) n* a prison [Sp. *calabozo.*]

calabrese *kal-ə-brā'zā, n.* a kind of green sprouting broccoli. [It., Calabrian.]

calamander *kal-ə-man'dər, n.* a hard and valuable cabinet-wood of the ebony genus, brownish with black stripes, brought from India and Sri Lanka. [Prob. Sinh.]

calamary *kal'ə-mər-ı, n.* any of various species of squid. [L. *calamārius—calamus*—Gr *kalamos,* pen, from their internal shell.]

calamine *kal'ə-mīn, -mın, n.* a mineral, zinc carbonate.—**calamine lotion, ointment** a soothing lotion or ointment for the skin, containing zinc carbonate or oxide. [Fr.—L.L *calamīna,* prob —L. *cadmia;* see **cadmium.**]

calamint *kal'ə-mınt, n.* a genus of plants allied to mint and thyme [Fr.—Gr. *kalaminthē.*]

calamity *kə-lam'ı-tı, n.* a great misfortune: affliction. —*adj* **calam'itous** making wretched, disastrous.— *adv.* **calam'itously.**—*n.* **calam'itousness.** [Fr. *calamité*—L. *calamitās, -ātis*]

calamus *kal'ə-məs, n* the reed pen used by the ancients in writing: a quill (*zool.*): a genus of palms whose stems make canes or rattans:—*pl.* **cal'ami.** [L.—Gr. *kalamos,* reed, cane, pen.]

calando *kà-làn'dō, (mus)* *adj* and *adv.* gradually slower with diminishing volume of tone [It , falling off]

calandria *kal-an'drı-ə, n* a sealed vessel used in the core of certain types of nuclear reactor

calash *kə-lash', n* a light low-wheeled carriage with a folding top. a hood with hoops formerly worn by ladies over the cap [Fr *calèche;* of Slav origin.]

calcaneum *kal-kā'ni-əm, n* the heel-bone —*adjs.* **calca'neal, calca'nean.** [L. *calcāneum,* the heel—*calx,* the heel.]

calcar *kal'kar, n.* a spur-like projection. esp. from

the base of a petal (*bot.*) a bird's spur (*zool*) —*adjs*
cal'carate; calcar'iform; cal'carine. [L , a spur—
calx, the heel]

calcareous *kal-kā'ri-əs, adj* chalky limy. [L *calc-
ārius*, from *calx*, lime.]

calced *kalst, adj* shod, wearing shoes.—*v.t* **cal'ceate**
to shoe —*adjs* **cal'ceate, -d** shod; **cal'cēiform,
cal'ceolate** slipper-shaped. [L L *calceus*, a shoe—
calx, the heel.]

Calceolaria *kal-si-ō-lā'ri-ə, n.* a South American genus
largely cultivated for the beauty of the slipper-like
flowers. (without *cap.*) any plant of the genus,
slipperwort. [L *calceolus*, dim. of *calceus*, a shoe.]

calcium *kal'si-əm, n.* the metal (at. numb. 20, symbol
Ca) present in lime, chalk, gypsum, etc —*adjs.* **cal'cic**
containing calcium, **cal'cicole, calcic'olous** growing
on limestone or limy soils —*n* **calcif'erol** vitamin D_2
—*adjs.* **calcif'erous** containing lime; **cal'cific**
calcifying or calcified.—*n.* **calcification** the process of
calcifying, a changing into lime.—*adjs.* **cal'cifuge**
(*-fūj*), **calcif'ugous** (*-ū-gəs*) avoiding limestone.—
v.t. and *v.i.* **cal'cify** to make or become limy,
by secretion, deposition, or substitution.—*adjs*
calcigerous (*-sij'ə-rəs*) containing lime, **cal'cinable.**—
n. **calcinā'tion.**—*v.t* **cal'cine** (or *-sin'*) to reduce to a
calx by the action of heat to subject to prolonged
heating, esp so as to oxidise, or so as to drive off
water and carbon dioxide —*v i.* to become calx or
powder by heat.—*ns.* **cal'cite, calcspar** (*kalk'spar*) a
mineral, calcium carbonate crystallised in the hexagonal system; **calc'-sin'ter, calc'-tuff** a porous
deposit from springs charged with calcium carbonate.
[L. *calx, calcis,* lime, limestone]

calculate *kal'kū-lāt, v.t.* to count or reckon: to think
out, esp mathematically —*v.i.* to make a calculation. to estimate —*adj* **cal'culable.**—*adv*
cal'culably.—*adjs* **cal'culated** thought out: reckoned: computed, fitted, likely, of such a nature as
probably, **cal'culating** given to forethought: deliberately selfish and scheming —*n.* **calculā'tion** the art
or process of calculating estimate: forecast —*adjs*
calculā'tional, cal'culative relating to calculation.—
n. **cal'culātor** one who calculates a book, table, or
machine for obtaining arithmetical results.—
calculated risk a possibility of failure, the degree of
which has been estimated and taken into account
before a venture is undertaken, **calculating machine** a
machine for obtaining arithmetical results without
calculation. [L *calculāre, -ātum,* to reckon by help
of little stones—*calculus,* dim. of *calx,* a stone]

calculus *kal'kū-ləs, n.* a stone-like concretion which
forms in certain parts of the body (*pl* **cal'culi**) a
system of computation used in the higher branches of
mathematics (*pl.* **cal'culuses**) —*adjs* **cal'cular** pertaining to the mathematical calculus; **cal'culary,
cal'culose, cal'culous** pertaining to or affected with
stone or with gravel —**differential calculus** a method
of treating the values of ratios of differentials or the
increments of quantities continually varying, **integral
calculus** the summation of an infinite series of differentials [L., see foregoing]

caldera *kal-dā'rə, (geol)* n a volcanic crater of great
size [Sp , cauldron]

caldron. Same as **cauldron.**

Caledonian *kal-i-dō'ni-ən, adj* pertaining to ancient
Caledonia, to the Highlands of Scotland, Scotland
generally, or (*geol.*) to a mountain-forming movement, well developed in Scotland —*n.* a Scot [L
Cālēdōnia]

calefaction *kal-i-fak'shən, n.* the act of heating the
state of being heated —*adj.* **calefacient** (*-fā'shənt*)
warming.—*n* anything that warms a blister or superficial stimulant —*adj* **calefac'tory** warming —*n* a

room in which monks warmed themselves. [L.
calefacēre—calēre, to grow hot, *facēre, factum,* to
make]

calendar *kal'ən-dər, n.* the mode of adjusting the
natural divisions of time with respect to each other for
the purposes of civil life· an almanac or table of
months, days, and seasons, or of special facts, etc. a
list of events, appointments, etc —*v t.* to place in a
list. to analyse and index —*ns.* **cal'endarer, cal'en-
darist.**—**cal'endar-line** the date-line. [O.Fr
calandier—L. *calendārium,* an account-book, *kalendae,* calends]

calender *kal'ən-dər, n.* a machine with bowls or rollers
for finishing the surface of cloth, paper, etc , by
combined moisture, heat, and pressure: a person who
calenders (properly a calendrer) —*v.t.* to dress in a
calender —*ns* **cal'endering; cal'endrer; cal'endry** a
place where calendering is done [Fr *calandre*—L
cylindrus—Gr *kylindros,* roller.]

calends *kal'əndz, n.pl* among the Romans, the first
day of each month [L *kalendae—calāre,* Gr.
kaleein, to call (because the beginning of the month
was proclaimed).]

Calendula *ka-len'dū-lə, n.* the marigold genus: (without *cap.*) any plant of the genus [L *kalendae,*
calends (but the connection is not obvious).]

calenture *kal'ən-chər, n* a fever or delirium occurring
on board ship in hot climates [Fr —Sp *calentura*—
L. *calēns, -entis—calēre,* to be hot.]

calf [1] *kaf, n.* the young of the cow, elephant, whale,
and certain other mammals. calfskin leather: an
iceberg in relation to its parent glacier:—*pl.* **calves**
(*kavz*) —*v t.* and *v.i.* **calve** (*kav*) to bring forth a calf·
to detach (an iceberg).—*adj* **calf'-bound** bound in
calfskin.—**calf'-country, -ground** the home of one's
youth, **calf'dozer** a small bulldozer, **calf'-lick** a
cowlick, **calf'-love** a boy's or girl's transient amorous
attachment, **calf's'-foot, calves''-foot** the foot of the
calf, used in making a jelly, **calf'skin** the skin of the
calf, making a good leather for bookbinding and
shoes, **calf'-time** youth —**golden calf** wealth as an
object of worship, **half'-calf** a bookbinding in which
the back and corners are in calfskin; **in, with, calf** (of
cows) pregnant [O E (Anglian) *cælf.*]

calf [2] *kaf, n* the thick fleshy part at the back of the leg
below the knee.—*pl* **calves** (*kavz*). [O N *kálfi.*]

Caliban *kal'i-ban, n* a man of beastly nature, from the
monster of that name in Shakespeare's *Tempest*

calibre, caliber *kal'i-bər, n* the size of the bore of a
tube: diameter character, capacity (*fig.*).—*v.t.*
cal'ibrate to determine the calibre of, or the true
values answering to the graduations of.—*ns* **calib-
rā'tion; cal'ibrātor.**—*adj.* **cal'ibred, cal'ibered.**
[Fr *calibre,* the bore of a gun]

caliche *ka-lē'chā, n* Chile saltpetre [Sp]

calico *kal'i-kō, n* a cotton cloth first brought from
Calicut in India: plain white unprinted cotton cloth,
bleached or unbleached coarse printed cotton cloth.
—*pl.* **cal'icos, cal'icoes.**—*adj* made of calico
spotted

calid *kal'id, adj* warm —*n.* **calid'ity.** [L *calidus,*
hot.]

calif. See **caliph.**

californium *kal-i-for'ni-əm, n.* an element (at. numb.
98, symbol Cf) [Produced at the University of
California.]

calipash *kal'i-pash, n* the part of a turtle close to the
upper shell, a dull greenish fatty gelatinous
substance.—*n.* **cal'ipee** the light-yellowish portion of
flesh from the turtle's belly. [Prob from West Ind
words.]

calipers. See **callipers.**

caliph *kal'if,* or *kā'lif, n* a successor of Mohammed·

the spiritual leader of Islam.—Also **calif, khalif.**—*n* **cal'iphate** the office, rank, government or empire of a caliph. [Fr. *calife*—Ar *khalīfah*, a successor]

calisthenics. See callisthenics.

calk[1]. Same as caulk.

calk[2] *kok, n.* a pointed piece on a horseshoe to prevent slipping—also **calk'in, calk'er, caulk'er.**—*v t* to provide with a calk. [O E *calc*, shoe—L *calx*, a heel.]

calk[3], **calque** *kok, kalk, v t* to copy by rubbing the back with colouring matter and then tracing with a blunt point.—*n* (usu **calque**; *kalk*) a loan-translation (q v) [L *calcāre*, to tread, *calx*, the heel]

calker, calkin. See calk[2].

call *kol, v.i.* to cry aloud (often with *out*): to make a short visit (with *upon, for, at*): to make a telephone call: in poker, to demand a show of hands after repeated raising of stakes —*v t.* and *v.i* in card games, to declare (trump suit, etc)—*v t* to name: to summon: to rouse: to appoint or proclaim: to designate or reckon: to select for a special office, as to the bar: to telephone: to read out the names in (a roll): to demand the repayment of (a debt, loan, redeemable bonds, etc.): to apply (offensive name) to (*coll*)—*n* a summons or invitation (to the witness-box, the telephone, before the curtain, etc.): a sense of vocation: a demand: a short visit: a signal by trumpet, bell, etc : a telephone connection or conversation, or a request for one: in card games, a declaration or undertaking, or the right to make it in turn: a cry, esp. of a bird: an invitation to the pastorate of a congregation on the stock exchange, an option of buying within a certain time certain securities or commodities at a stipulated rice (also **call option**): occasion, cause (*coll*)—*ns.* **call'er; call'ing** vocation.—**call'-bird** a bird trained to allure others into snares, **call'-box** a public telephonebox, **call'-boy** a boy who waits upon the prompter in a theatre, and calls the actors when wanted on the stage; **call'-girl** a prostitute on call by telephone; **calling card** a visiting card, **call sign, signal** in communications, a combination of letters and numbers, identifying a particular ship, aircraft, transmitter, etc ; **call'-up** an act of calling up, esp. conscription into the armed forces —**at call** readily available; **boatswain's call** see under whistle; **call attention to** to point out; **call away** to divert the mind; **call back** to recall: to visit again: to telephone again; **call by** (*coll.*) to visit in passing; **call cousins** to claim kindred; **call for** to come for and take away with one to ask loudly for. to demand: to require (**called'-for** required, necessary; **not called for** uncalled-for); **call forth** to evoke; **call in** to bring in from public use old currency notes, etc.: to demand repayment of (a debt, etc.): to call to one's help (as a doctor, the police); **call in(to) question** to challenge, throw doubt on; **call off** to summon away; to withdraw or back out: to cancel or abandon; **call of nature** (*euph.*) the need to urinate, etc ; **call on** or **upon** to invoke, appeal to. to make a short visit to; **call out** to challenge to fight a duel: to summon to service, bring into operation: to instruct (members of a trade union) to come out on strike, **call over** to read aloud (a list); **call the shots** (*U S.*) to call the tune; **call the tune** to say what is to happen, to order, **call to mind** to recollect, or cause to recollect; **call to order** to call upon to observe the rules of debate; **call up** to summon, to a tribunal, to the colours, to memory; **on call** at call: ready to answer summons; **within call** within calling distance [O E (W.S.) *ceallian*; O N *kalla*]

Calla *kal'ə, n* a marsh plant of the arum family erroneously (often **calla lily**) the lily of the Nile

caller *kal'ər, kol'ər,* (*Scot*)*adj* fresh: cool [Prob the same as **calver.**]

callid *kal'id, adj* shrewd.—*n* **callid'ity** shrewdness

[L *callidus,* expert]

calligraphy *kə-lig'rə-fi, n.* fine penmanship: a characteristic style of writing.—*n* **callig'rapher.**—*adjs.* **calligraphic** (*kal-i-graf'ik*), **-al.**—*ns* **callig'raphist; call'igram(me)** a design using the letters of a word [Gr *kallos,* beauty. *graphein,* to write]

Calliope *kə-lī'ə-pi, kal-ī'o-pē, n* the muse of epic poetry: (without *cap*) a set of steam-whistles played by a keyboard [Gr *Kalliopē*]

callipers, calipers *kal'i-pərz, n pl.* compasses with legs suitable for measuring the inside or outside diameter of bodies —*adj* **call'iper.**—**calliper** (**splint**) a splint fitted to the leg. so that the patient may walk without any pressure on the foot [calibre.]

callisthenics *kal-is-then'iks, n.pl* exercises for cultivating gracefulness and strength —*adj* **callisthen'ic.**—Also **calisthen'ics, -ic.** [Gr *kallos,* beauty, *sthenos,* strength]

callous *kal'əs, adj.* hardened: unfeeling, cruel —*n.* **callos'ity** a thickening of the skin: callousness —*adv* **call'ously.**—*n.* **call'ousness** lack of feeling, brutality [L *callōsus—callus,* hard skin.]

callow *kal'ō, adj* not covered with feathers: unfledged, unbearded: inexperienced [O E. *calu;* Ger *kahl,* bald.]

callus *kal'əs, n* a thickening of the skin: new material by which fractured bones are consolidated (*path.*): soft tissue that forms over a cut surface (*bot.*) [L]

calm *kam, adj.* still or quiet: (of person, action) serene, tranquil, assured: cool, impudent (*coll*) —*n* absence of wind—also in *pl* : repose: serenity of feelings or actions.—*v t.* and *v i.* (also **calm down**) to make or become calm: to quiet —*v t.* to becalm —*ns* and*adjs* (*med*) **calmant, calmative** (both *kal'* or *ka'*) —*adj.* **calmed** (*kamd*).—*adv* **calm'ly.**—*n* **calm'ness.** [Fr. *calme* (It *calma*), from L L. *cauma*—Gr. *kauma,* noonday heat—*kaiein,* to burn.]

calomel *kal'ō-mel, n.* mercurous chloride, used in medicine. [Fr. *calomel,* apparently from Gr *kalos,* beautiful, *melās,* black.]

calorie *kaloar-i, n.* the amount of heat needed to raise a gram of water 1° centigrade in temperature (*small* or *gram-calorie*): (sometimes with *cap*) the amount of heat needed to raise a kilogram of water 1° centigrade in temperature (*great, large, kilogram-calorie, kilocalorie;* = 1000 small calories) (used in expressing the heat- or energy-producing value of foods).—*adj* **calorif'ic** causing heat: heating.—*ns* **calorificā'tion; calorim'eter** an instrument for measuring heat (not temperature) or thermal constants; **calorim'etry.**—**calor gas**® (sometimes with *caps.*) a type of gas for cooking, heating, etc usually sold in large metal containers for use where there is no permanent supply of gas; **calorific value** of a food or fuel, the number of heat units got by complete combustion of unit mass [L *calor,* heat]

calotte *kal-ot', n.* a plain skull-cap or coif worn by R C clergy [Fr]

calotype *kal'ō-tīp, n* an early kind of photography —*n* **cal'otypist.** [Gr *kalos,* beautiful, *typos,* an image]

calque. See calk[3]

caltrop *kal', kol'trop, n* an instrument armed with four spikes. so arranged that one always stands upright, used to obstruct an enemy: a name for several plants with fruits so shaped, e.g (esp in *pl*) water chestnut. —Also **cal'trap, cal'throp.** [O E *coltetræppe, calcatrippe*—L *calx,* heel, and the root of **trap**[1].]

calumet *kal'ū-met, n.* the peace-pipe of the North American Indians, a tobacco-pipe smoked in token of peace [Norman Fr *calumet,* shepherd's pipe (Fr *chalumet*)—L *calamus,* reed]

calumny *kal'əm-ni, n* false accusation: slander —*v t*

calumniate (*ka-lum'ni-āt*) to accuse falsely: to slander
—*v.i.* to spread evil reports.—*ns.* **calumnia'tion;**
calum'niator.—*adjs.* **calum'niatory, calum'nious** of
the nature of calumny: slanderous.—*adv.* **calum'niously.** [L. *calumnia*, prob. conn. with *calvī*, to
deceive.]

Calvados *kal'va-dos*, or *-dos'*, *n.* a liqueur made from
cider or apple-pulp, esp. in the Calvados department
of Normandy.

Calvary *kal'va-ri, n* the name of the place where Jesus
was crucified: a representation of Christ's crucifixion,
or a series of scenes connected with it.—**Calvary cross**
a Latin cross on three steps [L. *calvāria, skull*]

calve, calves. See **calf.**

calver *kal'var, v t.* to prepare (salmon or other fish)
when alive or freshly caught.—*adj.* **cal'vered.** [Cf.
caller.]

Calvinism *kal'vin-izm, n.* the doctrines of the great
Genevan religious reformer, John *Calvin*
(1509–1564), as these are given in his *Institutio*, esp. on
particular election, predestination, the incapacity for
true faith and repentance of the natural man, efficacious grace, and final perseverance (continuance
of the saints in a state of grace until the final state of
glory).—*n* **Cal'vinist.**—*adjs* **Calvinist'ic, -al.**

calvities *kal-vish'i-ēz, n.* baldness. [L. *calvitiēs—
calvus*, bald.]

calx *kalks, n.* the substance of a metal or mineral that
remains after strong heating:—*pl.* **calxes** (*kalk'siz*) or
calces (*kal'sēz*). [L. *calx, calcis*, lime.]

Calycanthus, etc. See under **calyx.**

calypso *ka-lip'sō, n.* a West-Indian folk-song, usually
dealing with current events, usually made up as the
singer goes along:—*pl.* **calyp'sos.**

calyx *kā'liks, kal'iks, n.* the outer covering of a flower,
its separate leaves termed sepals (*bot.*). applied to
various cup-like structures, as the cup of a coral (*zool.*;
by confusion with L. *calix*, cup).—*pl.* **ca'lyces** (*-sēz*) or
ca'lyxes.—*ns.* **calycantheny** (*kal-ik-an'thi-mi*) the
condition of having the calyx like a corolla, **Calyc-
an'thus** a small North American genus of shrubs,
Carolina allspice or strawberry shrub: (without *cap.*) a
shrub of the genus.—*adjs.* **calyciform** (*kal-is'*) having
the form of a calyx; **calyc'inal, calycine** (*kal'i-sīn*)
pertaining to a calyx; **cal'ycoid, calycoi'deous** like a
calyx. [Gr. *kalyx*, a covering—*kalyptein*, to cover.]

cam *kam, (mech.) n.* an eccentric projection on a revolving shaft, shaped so as to give some desired linear
motion to another part.—**cam'shaft, cam'-wheel** a
shaft, wheel, bearing a cam or cams. [Du. *kam*, cam,
comb.]

camaraderie *kam-a-rád'a-rē, n.* good fellowship: the
intimacy of comradeship. [Fr.]

camarilla *kam-a-ril'a, n.* a body of secret intriguers. a
small room. [Sp. dim. of *cámara*, a chamber.]

camber *kam'bar, n.* a slight convexity upon an upper
surface (as on a road, a beam, the deck of a ship, etc.)—
v.t. and *v.i.* to arch slightly [Fr. *cambre*—L.
camerāre, to vault.]

Camberwell beauty *kam'bar-wal bū'ti*, a large and
beautiful butterfly, first recorded in 1748 at
Camberwell.

cambist *kam'bist, n* one skilled in the science of financial exchange.—*ns.* **cam'bism, cam'bistry.** [It.
cambista—L. *cambīre*, to exchange.]

cambium *kam'bi-am, (bot) n.* a layer or cylinder of
meristem by whose differentiation into xylem and
phloem new wood and bast are formed—*adjs.* **cam'-
bial; cam'biform.** [L.L—L *cambīre*, to change]

Cambrian *kam'bri-an, adj.* pertaining to *Cambria* or
Wales: the geol. system (well represented in
Wales) next above the Archaean.—*n* an inhabitant of
Cambria, or Wales: the Cambrian system. [Lat-

inised from W *Cymry*, Welshmen. *Cymru*, Wales.]

cambric *kām'brik, n* a fine white linen, originally
manufactured at *Kamerijk* (Cambrai) in French Flanders. a cotton imitation.

came *kām, pa t* of **come.**

camel *kam'al, n.* an animal of Asia and Africa with one
or two humps on its back, used as a beast of burden and
for riding: a watertight structure for raising a vessel in
shallow water· a humped type of aeroplane.—*ns*
cam'eleer one who drives or rides a camel; **cam'eline** a
material made from camel's hair —*adj.* of the nature of
a camel.—*adjs.* **cam'elish** like a camel, obstinate,
cam'eloid of the camel family.—Also *n —n.*
cam'elry.—**cam'elback** an inferior grade of rubber.—
adj. **cam'el-backed** hump-backed.—**cam'el-corps**
troops mounted on camels; **camel('s) hair** the hair of
the camel: the hair of the squirrel's tail used for paint-
brushes. [L. *camēlus*—Gr. *kamēlos*—Phoenician or
Heb. *gāmāl.*]

Camellia *ka-mēl'ya, -mel', n.* a genus of evergreen
shrubs close akin to tea, natives of eastern Asia,
grown for the singular beauty of their flowers: (without *cap.*) any shrub of the genus. [Named from
Camellus, a Jesuit, who collected plants in the Philippine Islands.]

camelopard *kam-el'ō-pard*, or *kam'al-ō-pard, n.* the
giraffe [L. *camēlopardus*—Gr. *kamēlos*, the camel,
and *pardālis*, the panther.]

Camembert *kam'am-ber, Fr kam-ā-ber, n.* a soft rich
cheese made near *Camembert*, in Normandy.

cameo *kam'i-ō, n.* a gem with figure carved in relief, esp
one in which a differently coloured lower layer serves
as ground a short literary piece: a small rôle in a play or
film:—*pl.* **cam'eos.**—*adj.* miniature, small and perfect of its kind.—**cam'eo-part, -rôle; cameo ware** pottery with relief figures against a different colour. [It
cammeo—L.L. *cammaeus*]

camera *kam'ar-a, n.* a vaulted room: a judge's private
chamber: the photographer's apparatus, in which the
outside image is recorded on a light-sensitive plate or
film. the apparatus that receives the image of the
scene and converts it into electrical impulses for
transmission (*TV*):—*pl.* **cam'eras.**—*adjs.* **cam'eral;**
cam'erāted chambered: vaulted.—*n.* **camerā'tion.**—
cam'eraman a photographer, esp. for press, television, or cinema; **camera obscura** (*ob-skūr'a;* L .
dark chamber) dark chamber in which an image of
outside objects is thrown upon a screen —*adj*
cam'era-shy (*coll*) not liking to be photographed
—**in camera** in a (judge's private) room: in secret;
on camera in front of a camera, being filmed. [L
camera, Gr. *kamarā*, vault]

camerlengo *kam-ar-leng'gō*, **camerlingo** *-ling'gō, ns* a
papal treasurer:—*pls* **camerleng'os, -ling'os.** [It.]

camiknickers. See under **camisole.**

camion *kam'i-an, n.* a heavy lorry, wagon. [Fr]

camisole *kam'i-sōl, n* a sleeved jacket, a woman's loose
morning gown or jacket: a loose underbodice with or
without sleeves.—*n.pl* **cam'iknick'ers** combined
camisole and knickers [Sp and Prov. *camisa*, shirt
—L. *camisia.*]

camlet *kam'lit, n* a cloth perhaps originally of camel's
hair, but now chiefly of wool and goat's hair [Fr
L L *camelotum*—L. *camēlus*; or perh Ar. *khamlat*,
nap]

camomile, chamomile *kam'ō-mīl, n* a name for several
plants akin to chrysanthemum, or their dried flowers,
used in medicine, affording a bitter stomachic and
tonic —**c(h)amomile tea** medicinal tea made with
dried camomile flowers. [Gr *chamaimēlon*, lit
earth-apple. from the apple-like smell of its
blossoms]

camouflage *kam'ōō-flazh, n* any device or means (esp

visual) for disguising, or for deceiving an adversary: the use of such a device or means.—*v.t.* and *v.i.* to deceive, to counterfeit, to disguise. [Fr. *camouflet*, a whiff of smoke intentionally blown in the face, an affront, a camouflet.]

camp¹ *kamp*, *n* a place on which a tent or tents or the like are pitched: a collection of temporary dwellings, or their inhabitants collectively: temporary quarters of an army, tribe, travellers, holiday-makers, or others: an old fortified site: a permanent military station: a party or side —*v.i.* to encamp, or pitch tents: to lodge in a camp (often with *out*, i.e. in the open).—*n.* **camp'er** one who camps: a motor vehicle purpose-built, or which can be converted, for use as temporary living accommodation.—**camp'-bed**, **-chair**, **-stool** a portable folding bed, etc.; **camp'a fe'ver** typhus, typhoid, or other fever apt to occur in camps: **camp'-fire** the fire of an encampment: a re-union, lodge, or section, of certain organisations; **camp'-foll'ower** a non-combatant who follows in the train of an army, as sutler, servant, etc.: a person associated with a (political, etc.) group without actually being a member; **camp'-meet'ing** a religious gathering in the open air or in a temporary encampment; **camp'-preach'er** one who preaches at such meetings; **camp'site** ground suitable, or specially laid out, for camping.—**camp out** to live temporarily in a tent or in the open air: to stay temporarily in improvised accommodation. [L. *campus*, a plain.]

camp² *kamp*, *adj.* theatrical, affected, exaggerated: homosexual: characteristic of homosexuals.—*n.* absurd extravagance in manner, deliberate (**high camp**) or without full awareness of the effect.—Also *v.i.*—*adj.* **camp'y.**—**camp up** to make exaggerated, etc.; **camp it up** to show camp qualities ostentatiously.

campaign *kam-pān'*, *n.* the time during which an army keeps the field: the operations of that time: an excursion into the country: an organised series of operations in the advocacy of some cause or object.—*v.i.* to serve in or conduct a campaign.—*n.* **campaign'er.** [Fr. *campagne*—L *campania*—*campus*, a field.]

campana *kam-pā'nə*, *n.* a bell-shaped object.—*n* **campanist** (*kam'pən-ist*) one versed in bells.—*adjs* **campaniform** (*-pan'*) bell-shaped; **campanolog'ical.** —*ns.* **campanol'ogist; campanol'ogy** the subject or science of bells or bell-ringing; **Campan'üla** a genus (giving name to a family **Campanulä'ceae**) commonly known as bell-flowers or bells, the best-known being the harebell or Scottish bluebell.— *adjs.* **campanülä'ceous; campan'ülar.**—*adj.* **campan'ülate** bell-shaped. [It. *campana*, a bell.]

campanile *kam-pan-ē'lā*, *n.* a bell-tower, esp. a tall one detached from the church [It., from *campana*, a bell.]

campanology, etc. See under **campana.**

campeachy-wood *kam-pēch'ı-wŏŏd*, *n.* logwood, first exported from Campeachy (*Campeche*, in Mexico).

camphor *kam'fər*, *n.* a solid essential oil, got from the camphor laurel (a species of cinnamon-tree) of Taiwan, etc., or synthetically manufactured, having a peculiar aromatic taste and smell: any similar compound.—*adj.* **camphorä'ceous** like camphor.—*v.t.* **cam'phorate** to impregnate with camphor.—*adj.* **camphoric** (*-for'ik*) pertaining to camphor. [Fr. *camphre*—L.L. *camphora*—Ar. *kāfūr.*]

campion *kam'pi-ən*, *n.* any plant of the genera *Lychnis* (or *Melandryum*) and *Silene.*

camp-sheathing, **-shedding,** **-sheeting,** **-shot** *kamp'shē'dhing,* **-shed'ing,** **-shet'ing,** **-shot,** *ns* piles and boarding protecting a river bank or the like

campus *kam'pəs*, *n.* college grounds (and buildings), or college, or self-contained division of a university: a

university: the academic world [L., field]

camus *kam'əs*, *adj.* flat-nosed. [Prob Fr. *camus*]

cam-wood *kam'wŏŏd*, *n.* the wood of a West African tree, at first white, turning red on exposure to air, used as a red dye. [Perh from African name *kambi.*]

can¹ *kan*, *v t.* (*obs.* in *infin* except in Scots) to be able to have sufficient power: to have skill in:—*3rd pers* **can**, *2nd sing.* **canst**; *pa.t.* **could.** [O.E. *cunnan*, to know (how to do a thing), to be able, pres indic. *can* See **con²**, **ken**, **know**; also **cannot**, **can't**.]

can² *kan*, *n.* a vessel for holding or carrying liquids, generally of tinned iron, with a handle over the top: a tin, vessel of tin-plate in which meat, fruit, etc , are sealed up: a container for various things, as ashes, rubbish (*U.S.*), or film in quantity: a jacket in which a fuel rod is sealed in an atomic reactor: (with *the*) jail (*slang*): a lavatory (*slang*): (in *pl.*) headphones (*slang*).—*v.t.* to put up for preservation in tins: to store in containers:—*pr.p.* **cann'ing;** *pa p.* and *pa t* **canned.**—*adj.* **canned** packed in tins: drunk (*slang*): (of music) recorded for reproduction by e.g. gramophone.—*ns* **can'ful** as much as a can will hold:—*pl.* **can'fuls; cann'er; cann'ery** a place where provisions are tinned.—**can'-opener** a tin-opener.—**can it!** (*slang*) stop talking about, doing, etc., that!; **can of worms** an unpredictable and potentially difficult situation or problem; **carry the can** (*slang*) to take the blame. [O.E. *canne.*]

Canadian *kə-nā'di-ən*, *adj.* pertaining to *Canada* —*n.* a native or citizen of Canada.

canaille *kan-āy'*, *kan-ī'*, *kən-āl'*, *n* the mob, the vulgar rabble. [Fr.,—L *canis*, a dog.]

canakin. See **cannikin.**

canal *kə-nal'*, *n.* an artificial watercourse, esp. for navigation: a duct that conveys fluids (*biol*)· a groove.—*adjs.* **canalicular** (*kan-ə-lik'ū-lər*) like or pertaining to a canaliculus; **canalic'ulate,** **-d** channelled, grooved.—*ns.* **canalic'ulus** (*anat.*) a small furrow or channel:—*pl* **canalic'uli; canalisation,** **-z-** (*kan-əl-ī-zā'shən*) the construction of canals. formation of an artificial channel: conversion into a canal: direction into a fixed channel (*lit.* and *fig*)—*v t* **can'alise,** **-ize** to make a canal through: to convert into a canal: to direct into a fixed channel (*lit* and *fig*).—**canal'-boat** a boat for canal traffic, **canal'-rays** (*phys*) positive rays, a stream of positively electrified particles through a perforation in the cathode of a vacuum-tube. [L *canālis*, a water-pipe]

canapé *ka'nə-pi*, *ka-na-pā*, *ns.* a small biscuit or piece of pastry or bread, etc., with a savoury filling or spread, usu. served with drinks: a sofa. [Fr.]

canard *ka-nar(d')*, *n.* a false rumour· an early duck-like type of aeroplane. [Fr , lit. duck.]

canary *kə-nā'ri*, *n.* a light sweet wine from the *Canary* Islands: a song-bird (finch) found in the Canary Islands, bright yellow in domestic breeds —*adj* canary-coloured, bright yellow.—*v.t.* to dance the canary: to prance about —**canā'ry-grass** a grass whose seed (**canä'ry-seed**) is used to feed canaries

canasta *kə-nas'tə*, *n* a card game of the rummy type, originating in South America [Sp., basket]

canaster *kə-nas'tər*, *n.* a kind of tobacco, so called from the rush basket in which it was originally brought from Spanish America [Sp. *canastra*—Gr *kanastron.*]

cancan *kaŋ'kan*, *n* a stage dance of French origin, orig. considered particularly indecorous [Fr. *cancan*, chatter, scandal, the cancan.]

cancel *kan'sl*, *v.t* to cross out· to annul or suppress: to abolish or wipe out: to counterbalance or compensate for: (often with *out*) to remove as balancing each other, e.g. like quantities from opposite sides of an equation, like factors from numerator and denominator of a fraction.—*v.i.* (with *out*) to neutralise each other:—*pr.p.* **can'celling;** *pa.t.* and *pa.p.* **can'celled.** —*n.* the suppression of a printed leaf or sheet: the part so cancelled, or (usually) the new one substituted.—*adjs.* **can'cellate, -d** marked latticewise, reticulated.—*n.* **cancellā'tion** cancelling: crosswise marking. [L. *cancellāre*, to cross out.]

cancellarial, -ian *kan-səl-ār'i-əl, -i-ən, adjs.* relating to a chancellor.—*n.* **cancellā'riate** chancellorship. [L. *cancellārius;* see **chancellor.**]

Cancer *kan'sər, n.* the genus to which the edible crab belongs: a constellation (the Crab) between Gemini and Leo, and a sign of the zodiac (once coincident with it) (**cancer**) loosely any malignant new growth or tumour: properly a carcinoma or disorderly growth of cells which invade a adjacent tissue and spread to other parts of the body: any corroding evil (*fig.*).— *v.i.* **can'cerate** to become cancerous.—*n.* **cancerā'tion.**—*adj.* **can'cerous** of, like, affected with, cancer. —*adjs.* **cancriform** (*kang'kri-form*) crab-shaped: like cancer; **cancroid** (*kang'kroid*) crab-like cancer-like. —Also *n.* [L., *crab*.]

candela *kan-del'ə, -dē'lə, n.* a unit of luminous intensity [**candle.**]

candelabrum *kan-di-lä'brəm,* or *-la', n.* a branched and ornamented candlestick or lampstand:—*pl.* **candela'bra**—also used as a false sing. with *pl.* **candela'bras.—candelabrum tree** any of several African trees with branches arranged like a candelabrum. [L. *candēlābrum—candēla,* candle.]

candent *kan'dənt, adj.* glowing: white-hot.—*n.* **candescence** (*kan-des'əns*) white heat.—*adj.* **candesc'ent.** [L. *candēre,* to glow (inceptive *candēscēre*).]

candid *kan'did, adj.* shining, clear: frank, ingenuous: free from prejudice. fair, impartial.—*adv.* **can'didly.** —*n.* **can'didness.—candid camera** a type of camera used for taking unposed photographs or films of people engaged in the normal occupations of their daily life: this style of photography. [L. *candidus,* white.]

candidate *kan'di-dāt, n.* one who offers himself for any office or honour, so called because, at Rome, the applicant used to dress in white: an examinee.—*ns* **can'didature, can'didateship, can'didacy** (*-də-si*). [L. *candidātus—candidus,* white.]

candie. See **candy².**

candied. See **candy¹.**

candle *kan'dl, n.* a cylinder of wax, tallow, or the like surrounding a wick: a candle-shaped object: a jet in a gas-stove· a photometric unit: (or **new candle**) **candela: (international candle** or **standard candle)** a former unit of luminous intensity.—*v.t.* to test (as an egg) by holding up before a candle or other light.— **can'dle-berry** wax-myrtle or bayberry of the spurge family, or its fruit; **can'dle-dipp'ing** the method of making candles by dipping instead of moulding, can'dle-end the end-piece of a burnt-out candle, **can'dle-holder** one who holds a candle to another while working—hence one who abets or connives; **can'dle-light** the light of a candle: illumination by candles; **can'dle-lighter** one whose business is to light the candles: a spill; **can'dle-power** illuminating power in terms of a standard candle—a name applied to various units of photometry; **can'dle-snuffer** a snuffer, instrument or person (see **snuff²;** also *fig*); **can'dlestick** a portable stand for a candle, originally a stick or piece of wood; **can'dle-waster** one who studies late, **can'dlewick** the wick of a candle. a cotton tufted material used for bedspreads, etc , **can'dle-wood** the wood of various West Indian and Mexican resinous trees —**burn the candle at both ends** to exhaust oneself by attempting to do too much,

usu. by going to bed late and getting up early for work; **do a candle** of a parachute, to fail to inflate; **not fit to hold a candle to** not be be compared with; **the game is not worth the candle** the thing is not worth the labour or expense of it. [O.E. *candel*—L. *candēla,* from *candēre,* to glow.]

Candlemas *kan'dl-məs, n.* the R.C. festival of the purification of the Virgin Mary, on 2nd February, when candles are blessed. [**candle, mass.**]

candour, in U.S. **candor,** *kan'dər, n.* sincerity: frankness. [Fr. *candeur*—L. *candor,* whiteness, from *candēre,* to shine.]

candy¹ *kan'di, n.* a sweetmeat of sugar boiled and crystallised (also **su'gar-can'dy**): any form of confectionery (*U.S.*).—*v.t.* to preserve or dress with sugar: to crystallise as sugar or the like: to encrust.—*v.i.* to crystallise: to become encrusted.—*adj.* **can'died** encrusted with candy or sugar: sugared, flattering (*fig.*). —**candy floss** a fluffy ball of spun coloured and flavoured sugar sold on the end of a stick: something insubstantial or ephemeral.—Also *adj.*—**candy stripe** a textile fabric pattern, consisting of narrow coloured stripes on a white background. [Fr. *candi,* from Ar. *qandah,* candy.]

candy² *kan'di, n.* a South Indian weight, about 500 pounds English.—Also **can'die** and **kan'dy.** [Tamil.]

candytuft *kan'di-tuft, n.* a cruciferous plant with flowers in tufts, the outer petals larger than the inner. [*Candia* (Crete), whence a species was brought, and **tuft.**]

cane *kān, n.* the stem of one of the small palms (as calamus or rattan) or the larger grasses (as bamboo, sugar-cane), or raspberry or the like: a slender rod for beating: a walking-stick.—*v.t.* to beat with a cane: to make or weave with canes, e.g. chairs.—*n.* **can'ing** a thrashing with a cane.—*adj.* **can'y** like, made of, or abounding in cane.—*adj.* **cane'-bottomed** having a seat of interwoven cane strips.—**cane's brake** a thicket of canes; **cane'-chair** chair made of rattan; **cane'fruit** fruit borne upon canes, as raspberries, blackberries; **cane'-mill** a mill for crushing sugarcane; **cane'-sugar** sucrose, esp. that obtained from the sugar-cane. [Fr *canne*—L. *canna*—Gr. *kannē,* a reed.]

canescent *ka-nes'ənt, adj.* tending to white: hoary.—*n.* **canesc'ence.** [L. *cānēscēns—cānēre—cānus,* hoary.]

cangue, cang *kang, n.* a Chinese portable pillory borne on the shoulders by petty offenders. [Fr. *cangue*— Port. *cango,* a yoke.]

canikin. See **cannikin.**

canine *kan'īn, kān'īn, adj.* like or pertaining to the dog.—*n.* any animal of the dog tribe: a canine tooth —*ns.* **caninity** (*kə-* or *kā-nin'i-ti*); **Ca'nis** the dog genus, typical of the family **Can'idae.—canine appetite** a huge appetite· **canine tooth** a sharp-pointed tooth between the incisors and the pre-molars. [L. *canīnus—canis,* a dog.]

canister *kan'is-tər, n.* a box or case, for holding tea, shot, etc.—*vs.t* **can'ister, can'isterise, -ize** to put into, pack in, canister(s).—*n.* **canisterisā'tion, -z-.** [L. *canistrum,* a wicker-basket; Gr. *kanastron— kannē,* a reed.]

canities *ka-nish'i-ēz, n.* whiteness of the hair. [L.]

canker *kang'kər, n.* an eating sore: a gangrene: a fungus disease in trees: inflammation in horses' feet: eczema of dogs' ears: an abscess or ulcer in birds: anything that corrupts, consumes, irritates or decays a canker-worm —*v t.* to eat into, corrupt, or destroy. to infect or pollute. to make sour and ill-conditioned —*v i.* to grow corrupt: to decay —*adj.* **cank'ered** malignant, soured, crabbed.—*adv.* **cank'eredly.**—*n.* **cank'eredness.**—*adjs.* **cank'erous** corroding like a canker; cank'ery affected with canker.—**cank'er-worm** a larva that cankers or eats into plants [L. *cancer*, a crab, gangrene.]

cann. Same as con³.

canna. See cannot.

cannabic *kan'ab-ik*, or *-ab'*, *adj.* pertaining to hemp.—*ns.* **cann'abin** a resin obtained from the dried leaves and flowers of the hemp plant, containing the active principle of the drug cannabis; **Cann'abis** the hemp (q.v.) genus: (without *cap.*) a narcotic drug obtained esp from *Cannabis sativa* (common hemp) or *C. indica* (Indian hemp).—**cannabis resin** cannabin. [Gr. *kannabis.*]

cannel *kan'l*, *n.* a bituminous coal that burns with a bright flame, used for making oils and gas.—Also **cann'el-coal.** [Prob. form of **candle.**]

cannelloni *kan-ə-lō'nē*, *n.* hollow tubelike pieces of pasta like macaroni, stuffed with cheese or meat. [It.]

cannelure *kan'i-lūr*, *n.* a groove or a fluting: a groove round the cylindrical part of a bullet. [Fr.]

cannibal *kan'i-bl*, *n.* an eater of the flesh of his own species.—*adj.* relating to or practising cannibalism.—*v.t* **cann'ibalise, -ize** to repair (a vehicle, aircraft, etc.) with parts taken from other vehicles, etc.: to take (parts), or take parts from (aircraft), for such repairs.—*n.* **cann'ibalism** the practice of eating one's own kind.—*adj* **cannibalist'ic.** [Sp. *Canibal, Caribal,* Carib.]

cannikin *kan'i-kin*, *n.* a small can.—Also **can'akin, can'ikin.** [Dim. of **can.**]

cannon *kan'ən*, *n.* a great gun (*pl.* **cann'ons** or **cann'on**): a rapid-firing, large-calibre gun fitted to an aeroplane or helicopter gunship (*pl.* **cann'ons** or **cann'on**): a cannon bone: a cannon bit: a stroke in billiards in which the cue-ball hits both the red and the opponent's ball (perh. for **carom**).—*v.i.* to cannonade: to make a cannon at billiards: to strike on the rebound: to collide.—*v.t.* to collide with.—*n.* **cannonade'** an attack with cannon.—*v.t.* to attack or batter with cannon.—*ns.* **cannoneer', cannonier'** one who manages cannon; **cann'onry** cannonading: artillery.—**cann'onball** a ball to be shot from a cannon; **cannon bit** a smooth round bit, **cann'on-fodder** men regarded merely as material to be consumed in war; **cann'on-met'al** gun-metal.—*adj.* **cann'on-proof** proof against cannon-shot.—**cann'on-shot** a cannonball: the distance to which a cannon will throw a ball. [Fr. *canon*—L. *canna*, a reed.]

cannot *kan'ət*, *vb.* can not (contracted **can't** *kànt*, Scots **canna** *kan'ä, kan'ə*). [**can, not.**]

cannula *kan'ū-lə*, *n.* a surgical tube, or the breathing-tube inserted in the windpipe after tracheotomy:—*pl.* **cann'ulae** (*-ū-lē*) or **cann'ulas.**—*adj.* **cann'ulate.** [Dim. of *canna*, a reed.]

canny *kan'i*, *adj.* (*Scot.* and *Northern*) knowing: skilful: shrewd: sparing in money matters: gentle: innocent, harmless (sometimes euphemistically): sly or pawky.—Also *adv.*—*adv.* **cann'ily.**—*n.* **cann'iness.** [App. conn. with **can¹.**]

canoe *kə-nōō'*, *n.* a boat made of the hollowed trunk of a tree, or of bark or skins: a skiff driven by paddling.—*v.i.* to paddle a canoe.—*ns.* **canoe'ing**; **canoe'ist.** [Sp. *canoa*—Haitian *canoa.*]

cañon, canyon *kan'yən*, *n.* a deep gorge or ravine. [Sp. *cañón*, a hollow, from root of **cannon.**]

canon¹ *kan'ən*, *n.* a law or rule, esp in ecclesiastical matters: a general rule or principle: standard or criterion: the books of the Bible accepted as the standard or rule of faith by the Jewish or Christian faiths: works forming any similar standard: the recognised genuine works of any author: a species of musical composition constructed according to a rule, one part

following another in imitation: a list of saints canonised.—*adjs.* **canonic** (*kə-non'ik*) **-al** of the nature of, according to, or included in a canon: regular: ecclesiastical.—*adv.* **canon'ically.**—*n.pl.* **canon'icals** the official dress of the clergy, regulated by the church canons.—*ns.* **canonicity** (*kan-ən-is'i-ti*) the state of belonging to the canon; **canonisa'tion, -z-.**—*v.t.* **can'onise, -ize** to enrol in the canon or list of saints.—*n.* **can'onist** one versed in canon law.—*adj.* **canonist'ic.**—**canonical hours** set hours for prayer; **canon law** a digest of the formal decrees of councils, and of patriarchal decision as to doctrine and discipline. [Gr. *kanōn*, a straight rod—*kannē*, a reed.]

canon² *kan'ən*, *n.* a member of a body of clergymen serving a cathedral or other church and living under a rule: a clerical dignitary belonging especially to a cathedral, enjoying special emoluments, and obliged to reside there part of the year.—*ns.* **can'oness** a member of a community of women living under a rule: a woman holding a prebend or canonry, often living in the world; **can'onry** the benefice of a canon. [O E. *canonic*—L. *canonicus*—*canōn*; see previous article.]

canoodle *kə-nōō'dl*, (*slang*) *v.t.* to embrace amorously. [Origin obscure.]

canopy *kan'ə-pi*, *n.* a covering hung over a throne or bed: a covering of state held over the head: any overhanging covering, as the sky: the topmost layer of branches in a forest: a rooflike projection over a tomb, stall, etc.: the transparent cover of the cockpit of an aircraft: the overhead fabric part of a parachute.—*v.t* to cover with a canopy:—*pr.p* **can'opying**; *pa.t.* and *pa.p* **can'opied.** [Gr. *kōnōpion*, a couch with a mosquito curtain—*kōnōps*, a mosquito.]

canst. See **can.**

cant¹ *kant*, *v.i.* to use the language of thieves, etc.: to talk in an affectedly solemn or hypocritical way.—*n.* a hypocritical or affected or perfunctory style of speech or thought: the language peculiar to a sect: odd or peculiar talk of any kind: slang: affected use of religious phrases or sentiments.—Also *adj.*—*n.* **cant'er.**—*adj.* **cant'ing** whining, pretending to piety. [L. *cantäre*, freq. of *canere*, to sing.]

cant² *kant*, *n.* an inclination from the level: a toss or jerk: a sloping or tilted position or face: a ship's timber lying obliquely to the line of the keel.—*v.t.* and *v.i.* to turn on the edge or corner: to tilt or toss suddenly.—*n.* **cant'ing** tilting.—**cant'-board** a sloping board; **cant'dog, -hook** a metal hook on a long handle, for rolling logs; **cant'-rail** a timber supporting the roof of a railway carriage. [Prob. conn. with Du. *kant*; Ger *Kante*, corner.]

can't *kànt*, a colloquial contraction for **cannot.**

Cantab *kan'tab*, for **Cantabrigian** *kan-tə-brij'i-ən*, *adj.* of or pertaining to Cambridge (Latinised *Cantabrigia*).—Also *n.*

cantabile *kan-ta'bē-lā*, *adj.* easy and flowing. [It]

cantaloup(e) *kan'tə-lōōp*, *n.* a small, ribbed muskmelon: in U.S. extended to other varieties. [Fr.,—It. *Cantalupo*, near Rome, where it was first grown in Europe.]

cantankerous *kən-tang'kər-əs*, *adj.* cross-grained: perverse in temper.—*adv.* **cantan'kerously.**—*n.* **cantan'-kerousness.** [M.E. *contek*, strife.]

cantata *kan-ta'tə*, *n.* a choral work, a short oratorio or opera intended for concert performance only.—*n.* **cantatrice** (*kan-ta-trē'chā* or *kan'tə-trēs*) a female singer. [It.,—L. *cantäre*, freq. of *canere*, to sing.]

cantate *kan-tä'tä, kan-tä'tē*, *n.* the 98th Psalm, from its opening words in Latin, 'Cantate Domino'.

canteen *kan-tēn'*, *n.* a vessel used by soldiers, etc., for holding liquids: a box of cooking utensils or of knives, forks and spoons: a barrack-tavern, or refreshment house for soldiers: a restaurant attached to an office, works, or the like —**wet, dry, canteen** one in which alcoholic liquors are, are not, sold. [Fr *cantine*—It *cantina,* a cellar]

canter *kan'tər, n* an easy gallop.—*v.t.* to move at an easy gallop —*v.t.* to make to canter [Orig *Canterbury-gallop,* from the easy pace at which the pilgrims rode to Canterbury]

canterbury *kan'tər-bər-ɪ, n* a stand with divisions in it for holding books, music, etc —**Canterbury bells, bell** *Campanula medium* with large blue, white, or pink bells

canthus *kan'thəs, n* the angle at the junction of the eyelids —*pl* **can'thi.** [Gr *kanthos*]

canticle *kan'tɪ-kl, n* a song a non-metrical hymn, esp one used in church service as the *Benedicite* a short canto (in *pl.*) the Song of Solomon —*n* **can'ticum** a canticle. a part-song in an ancient play [L *canticum,* dim *canticulum*]

cantilena *kan-tɪ-lē'nə, n* a ballad or light song a vocal or instrumental melody a singing exercise [L *cantilēna*]

cantilever *kan'tɪ-lēv-ər,* or -*lēv', n* a large bracket for supporting cornices, balconies, and even stairs — **cantilever bridge** one composed of arms projecting from the piers and connected together in the middle of the span [Perh **cant,** angle, and **lever.**]

cantillate *kan'tɪ-lāt, v.t* and *v t* to chant, intone —*n* **cantillā'tion.**—*adj* **can'tillatory.**

cantina *kan-tē'nə, n* a bar, saloon a wine-shop [Sp and It.]

cantle *kan'tl, n.* a corner, edge or slice of anything. the raised hind part of a saddle.—*v.t* to cut a piece from to divide —*n* **cant'let** a fragment [**cant, edge.**]

canto *kau'tō, n* a division of a long poem. the part that carries the melody (*mus.*) —*pl.* **can'tos.** [It ,—L *cantus—canēre,* to sing]

canton *kan'tən, kan-ton', n* a division of territory, constituting in Switzerland a separate government, in France a subdivision of an arrondissement —*v t* to divide into cantons (mil pron *kən-tōōn'*) to allot quarters to.—*adj* **can'tonal** pertaining to or divided into cantons —*n.* **canton'ment** (mil pron *kən-tōōn'mənt*) the temporary quarters of troops taking part in manoeuvres or active operations [O Fr *canton,* It *cantone,* corner, district—*canto,* a corner cf **cant².**]

Cantonese *kan-ton-ēz', adj* belonging to or typical of *Canton,* a city in S China esp of a style of cooking originating there —*n* a native of Canton the dialect of Canton —*pl* **Cantonese'.**

cantor *kan'tor, n* .the leader of the singing in a church, a precentor in a synagogue, the person who chants the liturgy and leads the congregation in prayer [L , singer, *canēre,* to sing]

cantrip *kan'trɪp* (*Scot*) *n* a freak or wilful piece of trickery· a witch's spell

canuck *kə-nuk'*, (*coll , often derog*) *n* a French-Canadian (*Can*) a small horse.

canvas *kan'vəs, n* a coarse cloth made of hemp or other material, now esp cotton, used for sails, tents, etc , and for painting on the sails of a ship. a piece of stretched canvas, painted or to be painted material for covering the ends of a racing-boat (whence a **canvas-length, win by a canvas**).—*v t* to cover with canvas —**can'vas-stretch'er** a wooden frame on which canvas is stretched for oil-painting, **can'vas-work** embroidery upon canvas, or upon cloth over which canvas has been laid to guide the stitches — **under canvas** having the sails unfurled, under sail living in tents [O Fr *canevas*—L *cannabis*—Gr *kannabis,* hemp]

canvass *kan'vəs, v t* to examine to discuss to solicit votes, orders, contributions, etc , from —*v.t.* to solicit votes, etc (with *for*).—*n.* close examination a seeking or solicitation —*n* **can'vasser.** [**canvas.**]

cany. See **cane.**

canyon. Same as **cañon.**

canzone *kant-sō'nā,* **canzona** *kan-zō'nə, ns* a song or air resembling a madrigal but less strict —*pls* **canzo'ni** (-*nē*), -**nas.**—*ns* (dim) **canzonet** (*kan-zō-net'*), **canzonetta** (*kan-tsō-net'ə,* pl. **canzonet'te** -*tā*) [It , a song, L *cantiō, -ōnis—canēre,* to sing]

caoutchouc *kow'chōōk, n* india-rubber, gum-elastic the latex of rubber trees [Fr ,—Carib *cahuchu.*]

cap *kap, n* a woman's light head-dress, brimless covering for the head: an official or symbolic head-dress or one appropriated to a special class or use, academic, athletic, etc membership of a team symbolised by a cap a caplike covering of any kind. the top of a toadstool the uppermost or terminal part of anything: (or Dutch cap) a contraceptive diaphragm.— *v t* to cover the end or top of: to touch with a cap in conferring a degree. to admit to membership of a team. to outdo or surpass by following with a better *v.t.* and *v.t* to salute by raising the cap.—*pr.p* **capp'ing;** *pa p* and *pa t* **capped** (*kapt*).—*ns* **capp'er; capp'ing** a covering. a graduation ceremony —**cap'-paper** a kind of wrapping paper. a size of writing paper, **cap rock** a stratum of (usu impervious) rock overlying oil- or gas-bearing strata; **cap sleeve** a short sleeve, just covering the shoulder; **cap'stone** a coping stone. —**cap and bells** the marks of a professional jester, **cap in hand** submissively. supplicatingly, **cap of liberty,** the conical cap given to a Roman slave on enfranchisement, now the symbol of republicanism, **cap verses** to quote verses in turn, according to rule, **college cap** a mortar-board or trencher-cap, **set one's cap at** of a woman, to set oneself to captivate (a man), **the cap fits** the allusion is felt to apply, **throw up one's cap** to make this gesture (*lit.* or *fig*) in token of immoderate joy, **to cap it all** as a (usu unpleasant) climax. [O.E *cæppe*—L.L *cappa,* a cape or cope.]

capable *kā'pə-bl, adj.* having practical ability able (often with *of*). qualified —*ns* **capabil'ity** quality or state of being capable (usu. in *pl*) a feature capable of being used or developed. ability for the action indicated, because provision and preparation have been made: manufacturing facilities, as factories, plant, **cā'pableness.**—**capable** of able, good, wellmade, etc , enough to, or bad, foolish, etc , enough to (fol by verbal noun or other action noun) susceptible of [Fr ,—L L *capābilis*—L *capēre,* to hold, take.]

capacity *kə-pas'ɪ-tɪ, n.* power of holding, containing, absorbing, or grasping room: volume. ability power of mind character in which one does something. legal competence maximum possible output or performance. capacitance· possession of industrial plant, technology, etc , with resulting ability to produce goods —*adj* attaining the full capacity —*adj* **capacious** (*kə-pā'shəs*) including much. roomy wide: extensive —*adv.* **capā'ciously.**—*ns* **capā'ciousness; capac'itance** the property that allows a system or body to store an electric charge the value of this expressed in farads (q v) —*v t* **capac'itate** to make capable. to qualify —*ns* **capacitā'tion; capac'itor** an electrical device having large capacitance.—**capacity for heat** power of absorbing heat, **legal capacity** the power to alter one's rights or duties by the exercise of free will, or responsibility for one's acts, **to capacity** to the utmost capacity, the fullest extent possible [Fr *capacité*—L *capâx, -âcis,* able to receive— *capère,* to hold]

cap-à-pie *kap-ə-pē, adv.* from head to foot, referring to arming, as a knight. [O.Fr. *cap a pie* —L. *caput, head, ad,* to, *pēs,* foot.]

caparison *kə-par'ı-sən, n* the covering of a horse: a rich cloth laid over a warhorse: dress and ornaments generally.—*v t.* to cover with a cloth, as a horse: to dress very richly —*adj.* **capar'isoned.** [Fr. *caparaçon*—L.L. *cappa.*]

cape[1] *kāp, n* a covering for the shoulders attached to a coat or cloak: a sleeveless cloak. [O.Fr. *cape*—L.L. *cappa.*]

cape[2] *kāp, n* a head or point of land running into the sea or a lake —*v i.* (*naut.*) to keep a course.—**Cape Coloured** (*S. Afr*) a person of mixed race, mainly in the W. Cape area; **Cape doctor** a south-east wind in the Cape; **Cape Dutch** former name for *Afrikaans* (*q.v.*); **Cape gooseberry** a S. American solanaceous plant with bladdery calyx: its edible fruit; **Cape nightingale** a frog; **Cape smoke** (*slang*) S. African brandy.—**the Cape** Cape of Good Hope: Cape Province, Capetown, and Cape Peninsula. [Fr. *cap*—L. *caput,* the head.]

capelin *kap'ə-lin, n* a small fish of the smelt family, abundant off Newfoundland, much used as bait.—Also **cap'lin.** [Fr. *capelan.*]

caper[1] *kā'pər, n.* the pickled flower-bud of a bush grown in Sicily —**cā'per-bush; cā'per-sauce** a sauce for boiled mutton, etc., made with capers. [L. *capparis*—Gr. *kapparis.*]

caper[2] *kā'pər, v i.* to leap or skip like a goat: to dance in a frolicsome manner.—*n.* a leap: a frisk: an escapade any activity or pursuit (*coll.*): an illegal or questionable act (*slang*).—*n.* **cā'perer.**—**cut a caper** to execute a frisk. [See **capriole.**]

capercailzie, -llie *cap-ər-kā'l(y)ı, n.* a species of grouse weighing up to 12 pounds. [Gael. *capull coille,* horse of the wood.]

capias *kā'pı-as, ka', (law) n* a writ which authorises the arrest of the person named in it. [L., you should seize, 2nd sing. pres subj. of *capěre,* to take.]

capillaceous *kap-ı-lā'shəs, adj.* hairlike.—*n.* **capillarity** (*-lar'ı-tı*) capillary quality: capillary attraction. —*adj.* **capillary** (*kə-pıl'ə-rı,* sometimes *kap'*) having to do with hair: hairlike: of very small bore: relating to capillary attraction.—*n.* a fine-bored tube: a minute vessel such as those that connect arteries with veins.—*n.* **capillitium** (*kap-ı-lish'ı-əm*) a mass of threads.—**capillary attraction** the force that causes liquids to rise in capillary tubes and wicks, to spread through blotting-paper, etc [L. *capillus,* hair]

capita. See **caput.**

capital[1] *kap'ıt-l, adj.* relating to the head: involving the death penalty: placed at the head: principal excellent: relating to capital.—*n* the chief or most important thing: the chief town or seat of government: a large letter at the beginning of a sentence, etc.: the property and equipment and/or money used for carrying on a business —*interj* excellent.—*n* **capitalisā'tion, -z-.**—*v t.* **cap'italise, -ize** to furnish with capital: to convert into capital or money: to turn to account: to print or write with capital letters —*v ı* to turn to one's advantage (with *on*) —*ns* **cap'italism** the condition of possessing capital: the economic system which generates and gives power to capitalists, **cap'italist** one who derives income and power from capital —Also *adj* —*adj.* **capitalist'ic.**—*adv.* **cap'itally** chiefly principally. excellently (*coll*): by capital punishment —**capital assets** fixed capital (see below); **capital expenditure** spending on capital assets: expenditure from which benefits may be expected in the long term, **capital gains** profits from the sale of bonds or other assets; **capital goods** goods to be used in production, not for consumption, **capital**

murder a murder involving the death penalty; **capital sin** deadly sin —**capital transfer tax** a tax payable on gifts of money or property over a certain value, made either during the lifetime of the giver or after his death, **circulating** or **floating capital** that which constantly changes hands, as wages paid to workmen, raw material used; **fixed capital** buildings, machines, tools, etc , **make capital (out) of** to turn to advantage; **working capital** capital needed to carry on a business: assets after debts have been paid [O.Fr *capitel*—L. *capitālis*—*caput,* the head.]

capital[2] *kap'ıt-l, n.* the head or top part of a column, etc.: a chapter of a book. [L *capitellum,* dim of *caput,* head.]

capitate *kap'ıt-āt, adj* having a head, knob, or capitulum —*n.* **capitā'tion** numbering of heads or individuals: a poll-tax —**capitation allowance, grant** an allowance, grant of so much a head. [L. *capitātus,* headed, *capitātiō, -ōnıs,* poll-tax—*caput,* head.]

capitellum. See **capitulum.**

Capitol *kap'ıt-ol, -əl, n* the temple of Jupiter at Rome, built on the *Capitoline* hill: the house where Congress or a state legislature meets (*U.S.*).—*adjs.* **capitō'lian, capit'oline.** [L *Capitōlium*—*caput,* the head.]

capitular *kə-pıt'ūl'ər, n.* a statute passed in a chapter or ecclesiastical court. a member of a chapter.—*adj.* relating or belonging to a chapter in a cathedral —*adj.* **capit'ularly.**—*n.* **capit'ulary** a collection of ordinances. [See **chapter.**]

capitulate *kə-pıt'ūl-āt, v.i.* to yield or surrender on certain conditions or heads.—*ns* **capit'ulant** one who capitulates; **capitulā'tion.**—*adj.* **capit'ulatory.** [L.L. *capitulātus,* pa.p. of *capitulāre,* to arrange under heads—*capitulum,* a chapter]

capitulum *kə-pıt'ū-ləm, n* a close head of sessile flowers:—*pl.* **capit'ula.**—*adjs.* **capit'ular; capit'ulate.** [L., dim. of *caput,* head.]

caplin. See **capelin.**

capo; capodastro. See **capotasto.**

capon *kā'pn, n* a castrated cock.—*v.t* **cā'ponise, -ize.** [O E *capun*]

capot *kə-pot', n* the winning of all the tricks at the game of piquet, and scoring forty —*v.t.* to score capot against. [Fr.]

capotasto *kap'ō-tas-tō,* **capodastro** *kap'ō-das-trō, ns* a movable bridge secured over the fingerboard and strings of a lute or guitar, to alter the pitch of all the strings together—*pls* **cap'otastos, -dastros.**—Also **cap'o** —*pl.* **cap'os.** [It *capo tasto, dastro,* head stop]

capote *kə-pōt', n* a long kind of cloak or mantle. [Fı dim. of *cape,* a cloak, see **cape.**]

cappuccino *kap-pōō̄t-chē'nō, ka-pōō̄-, n* black coffee with a little milk: white coffee, esp from a machine, topped with froth:—*pl.* **cappuccin'os.** [It , Capuchin]

capric *kap'rık,* **caproic** *kap-rō'ik,* **caprylic** *kap-rıl'ık, adjs* applied to three fatty acids obtained from butter, etc , with goat-like smell —*ns* **cap'rate, cap'roate, cap'rylate** salts respectively of these, **caprolactam** (*kap-rō-lak'tam*) a crystalline amide used in the production of nylon [L. *caper,* a goat]

caprice *kə-prēs', n* a change of humour or opinion without reason a freak changeableness a capriccio (*mus*).—*n* **capriccio** (*ka-prē'chō*) a sportive motion a species of free composition, not subject to rule as to form or figure (*mus.*) —*pl.* **capri'ccios, capricci** (*-prē'chē*) —*adv* **capriccioso** (*-chō'sō*) in a free style (*mus*) —*adj* **capricious** (*kə-prish'əs*) full of caprice: changeable —*adv* **capri'ciously.**—*n* **capri'ciousness.** [Fr *caprice* and It *capriccio,* perh from L *caper* (m), *capra* (f), a goat]

Capricorn *kap'rı-korn, n* a constellation and a sign of

the zodiac represented as a horned goat or monster.
—See also **tropic**. [L. *capricornus*—*caper*, a goat,
cornū, a horn.]

capriform *kap'ri-förm*, *adj.* goatlike. [L *caper*,
goat, *förma*, form.]

caprify. See **caprifig.**

caprine *kap'rin*, *adj.* goat-like. [L. *caprinus*—*caper*,
a goat.]

capriole *kap'ri-ōl*, *n.* a caper a leap without advancing.—*v.i.* to leap: caper [O.Fr. *capriole*—It.
capriola—L *caper* (m.), *capra* (f.), a goat.]

caproic, caprolactam, caprylic, etc. See **capric.**

caps *kaps*, (*coll.*) *n.pl.* for **capitals,** capital letters.

Capsicum *kap'si-kəm*, *n* a tropical shrubby genus of
the potato family, yielding a fleshy, many-seeded
fruit· (without *cap.*) the fruit of one species, eaten as
a vegetable (also called *green* or *red pepper*). (without
cap.) the dried seeds of other species, yielding paprika and cayenne pepper. [Perh. L *capsa*, a case.]

capsid *kap'sid*, *n.* the outer protein shell of some
viruses. [L. *capsa*, case.]

capsid (bug) *kap'sid* (*bug*), *n.* any of several small active plant pests. [Gr. *kapsis*, gulping—*kaptein*, to
gulp down.]

capsize *kap-siz'*, *v.t.* to upset.—*v i.* to be upset.—*n.* an
overturning.—*adj.* **capsiz'able.**—*n.* **capsiz'al.**

capstan *kap'stən*, *n.* an upright machine turned by bars
or otherwise so as to wind a cable upon it: the revolving shaft which controls the spin of a tape in a tape-
recorder, etc.—**capstan lathe** a lathe with a revolving
turret holding several tools which can be used in succession: **capstan table** a round-topped, often revolving table [Fr. *cabestan, capestan*, through L L.
forms from L. *capere*, to take, hold.]

capsule *kap'sūl*, *n.* a dry dehiscent fruit of more than
one carpel (*bot.*); a fibrous or membranous covering
(*zool.*): a gelatine case for holding a dose of medicine. a small dish· a metallic or other container: a
self-contained spacecraft or a part of one: a similar
craft used on or under water.—*adjs.* **cap'sular** in the
form of, resembling, a capsule· brief, condensed,
cap'sulary; cap'sulate.—*v.t.* **cap'sulise,** **-ize** to condense. [Fr ,—L. *capsula*, dim. of *capsa*, a case—
capēre, to hold.]

captain *kap'tin*, *n.* a head or chief officer: the commander of a troop of horse, a company of infantry, a
ship, or a portion of a ship's company: in the navy, an
officer ranking with a colonel: in the army, an officer
ranking with a naval lieutenant. the senior pilot of a
civil aircraft. the leader of a team or club. the head-
boy of a school.—*v t.* to lead or act as captain.—*ns.*
cap'taincy the rank or commission of a captain,
cap'tainship the rank or condition of a captain: skill in
commanding.—**cap'tain-gen'eral** the commander of
an army; **captain's chair** a wooden armchair with back
and arms in one semicircular piece supported on
vertical spindles.—**captain of industry** a great industrial employer. [O.Fr. *capitaine*—L.L. *capitāneus*,
chief—L *caput*, head]

caption *kap'shən*, *n.* the act of taking: an arrest: a
heading, legend, or accompanying wording of an
article, chapter, illustration, or cinematograph picture, etc.—*v.t.* to give a caption (heading, etc.) to.—
adj. **cap'tious** ready to catch at faults or take offence·
peevish.—*adv.* **cap'tiously.**—*n.* **cap'tiousness.** [L
captiō, *-ōnis*—*capere*, to take.]

captive *kap'tiv*, *n.* a prisoner: a person or animal kept
in confinement.—*adj.* confined: kept in bondage. restrained by a line (as a balloon)· charmed or subdued
by anything (*fig*): pertaining to captivity: that
cannot refuse what is offered (as a *captive audience,
market*, etc.).—*v t* **cap'tivate** to charm. to engage
the affections of.—*adj.* **cap'tivating.**—*ns*

captiv'ity; cap'tor one who takes a captive or a prize;
cap'ture the act of taking: the thing taken: an arrest.
—*v t* to take as a prize: to take by force: to succeed in
representing (something intangible or elusive) in a
fixed or permanent form: of an atomic or nuclear
system, to acquire an additional particle (*phys.*).—
captive bolt (pistol) a gunlike device which fires a rod,
used in slaughtering animals. [L. *captivus, captor,
captūra*—*capēre, captum*, to take.]

capuche *kə-pōōsh'*, *-pōōch'*, *n.* a hood, esp. that worn
by the *Capuchins*.—*n* **Capuchin** (*kap'ū-chin* or *kap-
ōō-shēn'*) a friar of a branch of the Franciscan order so
called from the hood he wears: (without *cap.*) a cloak
like a Capuchin's: (without *cap.*) a capuchin monkey
—**capuchin monkey** a South American monkey with
hair like a cowl. [Fr. cowl—L.L. *cappa*.]

caput *kap'ut*, *-ət*, *n.* a head: a knob:—*pl.* **cap'ita.** · [L.]

capybara *kap-i-ba'rə*, *n.* the largest living rodent, a
native of South America, allied to the guinea-pig.
[Port. from Tupi.]

car *kar*, *n.* a vehicle moved on wheels, applied to very
various forms—a large and splendid vehicle, as a
triumphal car, a funeral car, a motor-car: a street
tramway carriage: in America, applied to all vehicles
for railway travelling, in Britain, to certain forms of
railway carriage: the part of a balloon, cable-car, or
airship that carries passengers and load.—**car'-coat** a
short coat designed for wearing in a car; **car'man** a
man who drives a car or cart: a carter; **car'park** an
open space or a building for parking cars; **car pool** an
arrangement by which several car owners take turns
in giving lifts to each other; **car'port** a covered parking space, esp. a space under a roof projecting from a
building —*adj* **car'-sick** affected with nausea by the
movement of a car.—**car'-wash** a place specially
equipped for the automatic washing of cars. [O.Fr.
carre—L L *carra*, a Celt. word, seen in Ir. *carr*, Bret
karr.]

carabine. See **carbine.**

caracal *kar'ə-kal*, *n.* the Persian lynx. [Fr.]

carack. See **carrack.**

caracol, caracole *kar'ə-kōl*, *n.* a half-turn or wheel
made by a horseman.—*v.i.* to turn half-round. [Fr.
caracole—It. *caracollo*—Sp. *caracol*, a spiral snail
shell.]

caracul. See **karakul.**

carafe *kə-raf'*, *n.* a water-bottle or wine-flask for the
table: the amount contained in a carafe. [Fr. *carafe*,
prob. from. Ar. *gharafa*, to draw water.]

carambole *ka'ram-bōl.* See **carom.**

caramel *kar'ə-mel*, *n.* a dark-brown substance produced from sugar by loss of water on heating, used in
colouring puddings, whisky, wines, etc.: a tenacious
sweetmeat made with sugar, butter, etc.—*adj.* made
of or containing caramel: of the colour of caramel.—
n. **caramelisa'tion,** *-z-.*—*vs.t.* and *vs.i.* **car'amel,
car'amelise, -ize.** [Fr.,—Sp. *caramelo*.]

Carapa *kar'ə-pə*, *kə-rap'ə*, *n.* a genus of tropical trees
of the mahogany family yielding **car'ap** (or **carap'**,
also **crab'**)-**nuts, -oil, -wood.**—*n.* **car'ap** any tree
of the Carapa genus. [*caraipi*, the native Guiana
name]

carapace *kar'ə-pās*, *n* the shell of the crab, tortoise,
etc.—*adj.* **carapā'cial** (*-shl*). [Fr.,—Sp *carapacho*.]

carat *kar'ət*, *n* a unit of weight (metric carat = 200
milligrams) used for gems. (also **karat**) a unit used in
expressing fineness of gold, 24-carat gold being pure
gold. [Fr.—Ar *qīrāt*, perh. from Gr. *keration*, a
carob-seed used as a weight.]

caravan *kar'ə-van*, *-van'*, a company travelling together for security, esp. in crossing the deserts: a
company of people: a fleet with convoy: a covered
van. a house on wheels.—*v.i.* to travel in a caravan:—

pr p. **car'avaning** or **caravann'ing;** *pa.p.* and *pa.t* **car'avaned, caravanned'.**—*ns.* **caravaneer'** the leader of a caravan; **caravan(n)'er** a caravaneer: one who stays in a caravan. esp. for holidays; **caravanette'** a motorised mobile home; **caravanserai** (*-van'sə-rī*) a kind of unfurnished inn or extensive enclosed court where caravans stop.—Also **caravansarai, -sary.—caravan site, park** an open space laid out for caravans. [Pers. *kārwān*, caravan; *kārwānsarāī* (*sarāī*, inn).]

caravel *kar'ə-vel, n.* a light Mediterranean sailing-ship. [Fr. *caravelle*]

caraway *kar'ə-wā, n.* an umbelliferous plant with aromatic fruits (**caraway seeds**) used as a tonic and condiment. [Prob. Sp. *alcaravea* (*carvi*), Ar. *kar-wiyā*—Gr. *karon.*]

carbide *kar'bīd, n.* a compound of carbon with another element, esp. calcium carbide. [**carbon.**]

carbine *kar'bīn,* **carabin(e)** *kar'ə-bin, -bīn, ns.* a short light rifle.—*ns.* **car(a)bineer', -ier** a soldier armed with a carbine. [Fr. *carabine.*]

carbohydrate *kar-bō-hī'drāt, n.* a compound of carbon, hydrogen, and oxygen, the last two being in the same proportion as in water: extended to kindred compounds. [See **carbon, hydrate.**]

carbolic *kar-bol'ik, n.* (in full **carbolic acid**) phenol [L *carbō*, coal, *oleum*, oil.]

carbon *kar'bən, n.* a non-metallic element (at. numb. 6; symbol C), widely diffused, occurring uncombined as diamond and graphite: a piece of carbon (esp. an electrode or a lamp-filament), or of carbon paper: a carbon copy: a carbonado diamond.—Also *adj.—adj.* **carbonā'ceous** coaly: containing much carbon: like carbon.—*n.* **car'bonate** a salt of carbonic acid.—*v.t.* to combine or impregnate with carbon dioxide: to carbonise.—*n.* **carbonā'tion.**—*adjs.* **carbonic** (*-bon'ik*) pertaining to carbon; **carbonif'erous** producing carbon or coal: (with *cap.*; *geol.*) belonging to the Carboniferous system.—*n.* **carbonisā'tion, -z-.**—*v.t.* **car'bonise, -ize** to reduce to carbon: to char or coke: to cover with carbon.—*v.t.* to become carbonised.—**carbon-14** a radioactive isotope of carbon used, e.g. as a tracer element in biological studies or in dating archaeological material; **carbon arc** an arc between two carbon electrodes, used for high-intensity lighting; **carbon black** a form of finely divided carbon produced by partial combustion of hydrocarbons; **carbon copy** a duplicate of writing or typed matter made by interleaving **carbon paper,** a paper coated with lampblack: any exact duplicate.—**carbon dating** estimating the date of death of prehistoric organic material from the amount of carbon-14 still present in it; **carbon dioxide** an oxide of carbon (CO_2) a colourless, odourless, incombustible gas, present in the atmosphere, which in solution in water forms **carbonic acid** (H_2CO_3), a weak acid; **carbon fibres** very fine filaments of carbon used in bundles, bound together by resins, to increase the strength of e.g. plastics; **carbon monoxide** (CO) a colourless, odourless, very poisonous gas which burns with a blue flame to form carbon dioxide; **carbon steel** steel containing carbon, with different properties according to the quantity of carbon used, **carbon tetrachloride** (CCl_4) a solvent, etc.; **the Carboniferous (System)** one of the main divisions of the Palaeozoic rocks, overlying the Devonian or Old Red Sandstone, underlying the Permian. [Fr. *carbone*—L. *carbō, -ōnis,* coal, charcoal.]

carbonado *kar-bən-ā'dō, n* a variety of crystalline carbon, black, opaque, harder than diamond, used in drilling, etc.—Also called **black diamond, carbon.** [Port , carbonated.]

Carborundum® *kar-bər-un'dum, n.* a silicon carbide, used as a substitute for corundum. [**carbon** and **corundum;** a trademark in some countries.]

carboxyl *kär-boks'il, n* the radical COOH. [**carbon,** oxygen, Gr *hȳlē,* matter.]

carboy *kar'boi, n.* a large glass bottle, with basketwork or other casing, for dangerous chemicals. [Pers. *qarābah.*]

carbuncle *kar'bung-kl, n.* a mythical self-luminous gem. a fiery-red precious stone: a pimple on the nose: a local inflammation of the skin and subcutaneous tissues, caused by bacterial infection.—*adjs.* **car'buncled** set with the gem carbuncle: afflicted with carbuncles; **carbun'cular** belonging to or like a carbuncle: red: inflamed. [L. *carbunculus,* dim. of *carbō,* a coal.]

carburet *kar'bū-ret,* or *-ret', n.* a carbide (*obs.*).—*vs.t.* **carburet, car'burate, car'burise, -ize** to combine with carbon: to charge with carbon compounds.—*ns* **carburā'tion, carburetion** (*-rāsh'ən, -resh'ən*), **carburisā'tion, -z-.**—*adj.* **car'buretted** (or *-ret'*).—*n.* **car'burettor, -er,** *U.S.* **carburetor, -er** (or *-ret'*) an apparatus for charging a gas with carbon compounds, esp. part of an internal-combustion engine in which air is mixed with volatile fuel in the desired proportion [Fr. *carbure*—L. *carbō,* coal.]

carcajou *kar'kə-jōō, n.* the glutton or wolverene. [Canadian Fr., prob. from an Indian name.]

carcase, carcass *kar'kəs, n.* a dead body, no longer used of a human corpse: (*disrespectfully*) a live human body: the framework of anything: a ruin.—**carcase meat, carcass meat** raw meat as prepared for the butcher's shop, not tinned. [O.Fr. *carquois* (mod. *carcasse*), a skeleton.]

carcinogen, -ic. See **carcinoma.**

carcinoma *kar-si-nō'mə, n.* a cancer:—*pl.* **carcinō'mata, -nō'mas.**—*adj.* **carcinō'matous.**—*ns.* **carcin'ogen** (*-jen*) a substance that encourages the growth of cancer; **carcinogen'esis.**—*adj.* **carcinogen'ic.**—*ns.* **carcinogenic'ity; carcinō'sis, carcinōmatō'sis** spread of cancer in the body. [Gr. *karkinōma—karkinos,* crab.]

card¹ *kard,* a small piece of pasteboard: one with figures for playing a game, with a person's name and address, with a greeting, invitation, message, programme, etc.: a perforated plate used as a guide in weaving: the programme of races at a race-meeting: a person (*slang*): a wag or eccentric: (in *pl.*) a game played with cards.—*v.t.* to return on a scoring-card (*golf*): to enter in a card index —**card'board** a stiff, finely finished pasteboard.—*adj.* made of cardboard: flimsy, insubstantial.—*adj.* **card'-carrying** openly expressing membership of or support for a party or group.—**card'castle** an erection of playing cards in storeys: any flimsy or precarious structure; **card catalogue** a card index; **card'-game** a game played with playing-cards; **card'-holder** one who has a membership card; **card index** one with entries on separate cards.—*v.t.* **card'-in'dex.—card'punch** (*comput*) a machine which perforates cards to record data; **card'-sharp(er)** one who cheats at cards; **card'-table** a table for playing cards on; **card'-vote** a voting system that gives each delegate's vote a value in proportion to the number he represents.—**cards on the table** one's resources and moves freely laid open; **card up one's sleeve** an advantageous factor or argument kept in reserve; **get one's cards** to be dismissed; **house of cards** a card-castle; **on the cards** not improbable; **play one's cards well, badly** to make, not to make, the best of one's chances; **show one's cards** to expose one's secrets or designs; **the cards are stacked against (someone, something)** the circumstances, facts, are ranged (against a person, an argument, etc.); **throw up (or in) the cards** to give in: to confess defeat. [Fr *carte*—L. *c(h)arta*—Gr. *chartēs,* paper; cf **carte.**]

card² *kard, n* an instrument for combing wool or flax.—

v.t. to comb (wool, etc.) —*n.* **card'er.** [Fr. *carde*— L *carduus*, a thistle]

cardamom *kàr'də-məm, n.* the capsules of several tropical plants of the ginger family, which form an aromatic, pungent spice —Also **card'amon.** [L *cardamômum*—Gr. *kardamômon.*]

cardi, cardy *kar'di, n.* Coll. for cardigan.

cardiac *kar'di-ak, adj.* belonging to the heart or to the upper end of the stomach —*n* a cordial or heart stimulant: a person with cardiac disease.—*adj* **cardinal** (-*di'ə-kl*) cardiac.—*ns.* **cardialgia** (-*di-al'ji-ə*), **car'dialgy** heartburn, **car'diogram** a tracing obtained from a cardiograph, **car'diograph** an instrument for recording movements of the heart; **cardiog'rapher** one who uses a cardiograph, **cardiog'raphy.**—*ns.* **cardiol'ogist; cardiology** (-*ol'ə-ji*) the science that deals with the structure, function, and diseases of the heart.—*adj* **cardiovascular** (-*vas'kū-*) pertaining to , involving, heart and blood-vessels — *n.* **cardi'tis** inflammation of the heart.—**cardiac arrest** stopping of the heart-beat; **cardiac failure** heart-failure. [Gr *kardiā*, heart, the upper end of the stomach]

cardigan *kar'di-gən, n* a knitted woollen jacket, named after Lord *Cardigan* (1797–1868).

cardinal *kàr'di-nl, adj.* pertaining to a hinge: on which a thing hinges: of fundamental importance: of a deep scarlet colour, like a cardinal's cassock or hat —*n.* one of the princes of the church constituting the sacred college at Rome, to whom pertains the right of electing a new pope —*ns.* **car'dinalate, car'dinalship** the office or dignity of cardinal.—*adv* **car'dinally** fundamentally. **car'dinal-bishop, car'dinal-priest, car'dinal-deacon** the three orders of cardinal in the sacred college, **cardinal numbers** numbers expressing how many (1, 2, 3, distinguished from *ordinals*); **cardinal points** north, south, east, and west, **cardinal virtues** justice, prudence, temperance, fortitude [L *cardinālis*—*cardō, cardinis,* a hinge.]

cardiograph, cardiovascular, carditis, etc See **cardiac.**

cardoon *kar-dōōn', n* a Mediterranean plant close akin to the true artichoke, its leafstalks and ribs eaten like celery [Obs Fr *cardon*—L *carduus,* a thistle.]

cardy. See **cardi.**

care *kàr, n.* affliction: anxiety heedfulness: heed. charge, oversight: medical or social welfare services. an object of anxiety or watchfulness.—*v.i* to be anxious: to be inclined: to be concerned: to mind: to have liking or fondness: to provide, look after, watch over (with *for*).—*adj.* **care'ful** full of care heedful.—*adv.* **care'fully.**—*n.* **care'fulness.**—*adj* **care'less** without care. heedless, unconcerned.— *adv.* **care'lessly.**—*n.* **care'lessness.**—*adj.* **car'ing** compassionate: concerned professionally with social, medical, etc , welfare (as the *caring professions,* i.e. social workers, nurses, etc.) —*adj* **care'free** void of anxiety.—**care label** a label on a garment, giving washing, etc., instructions; **care'taker** one put in charge of anything, esp a building.—*adj.* exercising temporary supervision or control, as *caretaker government.*—*adj.* **care'worn** worn or vexed with care.—**care of** to be delivered to the custody of, or at the address of; **for all I,** etc **care** it is a matter of indifference to me, etc ; **have a care** to take care; **I,** etc. **couldn't care less I,** etc do not care in the least; **in care** (of a child) in the guardianship of a local authority or other official organisation: (of an elderly person) in an old people's home or geriatric ward, **take care** to be careful or cautious, **take care of** to look after with care: to make the

necessary arrangements regarding (*coll*) [O.E. *caru.*]

careen *kə-rēn', v.t* to turn over on the side, esp for repairing or cleaning—Also *v.i* —*n* a heeling position —*n.* **careen'age** a place where ships are careened. the cost of careening [L *carīna,* keel.]

career *kə-rēr', n.* a rush: progress through life. (advancement in) profession or occupation —*adj.* having a career. dedicated to a career —*v.i.* to gallop: to move or run rapidly.—*ns* **career'ism;** **career'ist** one intent on his own advancement — Also *adj.*—**careers** master, **mistress** a schoolteacher who advises pupils on their choice of career, **career woman** a woman who is very interested in her job, in promotion, etc [Fr *carrière,* a racecourse—L L *carrāria,* carriage-road—*carrus,* wagon]

carème *ka-rem,* (Fr) *n* Lent

caress *kə-res', v t.* to touch endearingly: to fondle — *n.* an endearing touch.—*n* and *adj.* **caress'ing.**— *adv.* **caress'ingly.** [Fr *caresser*—It *carezza,* an endearment—L *cârus,* dear.]

caret *kar'ət, n.* a mark, ∧, to show where to insert something omitted. [L , 'there is wanting']

carfuffle, curfuffle *kər-fuf'l, n* commotion, agitation.—Other present-day spellings include **kefuffle.** [Gael. pfx. *car-,* Scot *fuffle,* to disorder]

cargo *kar'gō, n* the goods carried by a ship or aeroplane:—*pl* **-oes.**—*v t.* to load, weigh down (with *with*)—**cargo cult** a type of religion in certain South Pacific islands based on the belief that ancestors or supernatural beings will return bringing products of modern civilisation and thus make the islanders rich and independent. [Sp ,—root of **car.**]

cariacou *kar'i-ə-kōō,* **carjacou** *kar'jə-kōō, ns.* any deer of the American genus or subgenus *Cariacus,* including the Virginian deer. [Tupi, *cariacu*]

Carib *kar'ib,* one of a race inhabiting parts of Central America and northern South America: their language.—Also *adj* —*n.* and *adj* **Caribbē'an** of, pertaining to, the West Indies, their inhabitants (not all of Carib origin), or their culture [Cf **cannibal.**]

caribou *kar-i-bōō', kar', n.* the American reindeer. [Can Fr]

caricature *kar'i-kə-tūr,* or *-tūr',* or *-chōōr,* or *-chōōr', n.* a likeness of anything so exaggerated or distorted as to appear ridiculous (formerly **caricatū'ra**) —*v.t.* to turn into ridicule by distorting a likeness: to burlesque —*adj.* **caricatūr'al.**—*n* **caricatūr'ist.** [It. *caricatura*—*caricare,* to load, from root of **car.**]

caries *kā'ri-ēz, n.* decay, esp of teeth [L. *cariēs.*]

carillon *kə-ril'yən, kar'il-yən, n* a set of bells for playing tunes. a mechanism for playing them: a melody played on them.—*ns.* **carill'on(n)eur** (or *-nûr'*), **carill'onist** (or *kar'*) [Fr.,—L L *quadriliō. -ōnis,* a quaternary, as formerly rung on four bells]

carina *kə-rī'nə,* (*biol*) *n* a keel or keel-like ridge — *adj.* **carinate** (*kar'i-nāt*) keeled [L. *carīna,* a keel.]

carioca *kar-ē-ō'kə, n.* a Brazilian dance or its tune, a maxixe or variety thereof. [Port.]

cariole, carriole *kar'i-ōl, n.* a small open carriage: a light cart. [Fr *carriole*—root of **car.**]

carjacou. See **cariacou.**

carl *karl, n.* a churl (*arch.*).—*adj.* **carl'ish** (*arch.*) churlish clownish. [O N *karl,* a man, a male; see **churl.**]

carline *kar'lin, n.* any plant of a genus (*Carlina* **Carline thistle**) closely allied to the true thistles [From *Carolus, Karl,* or Charlemagne.]

Carlovingian. Same as **Carolingian.**

Carmelite *kar'mi-līt, n* a White Friar, or friar of the order of Our Lady of Mount *Carmel,* in Palestine (now Israel), founded there *c.* 1156, made a mendicant order in 1247

carminative *kar'min-ə-tıv*, or *-mın'*, *adj.* expelling flatulence.—*n.* a medicine with that effect. [L. *cârminâre*, to card, comb out—*cârmen*, a card for wool.]

carmine *kar'min*, *-mın*, *n* the red colouring matter of the cochineal insect: its colour.—*adj.* of that colour. [Fr. *carmin—same root as* crimson.]

carnage *kar'nıj*, *n* slaughter. [Fr.,—It *carnaggio*, carnage—L *carô, carnis*, flesh.]

carnahuba. See carnauba.

carnal *kar'nl*, *adj.* fleshly: sensual: unspiritual: bodily. sexual.—*v t.* car'nalise, -ize to sensualise.— *ns.* car'nalism; car'nalist a sensualist; carnality (*-nal'ı-tı*) the state of being carnal.—*adv.* car'nally. —*adj.* carnass'ial adapted for flesh-eating.—*n.* a carnivore's scissor-tooth, usually long and large, used for tearing flesh.—*adjs.* car'neous, car'nose fleshy: of or like flesh.—*n* carnos'ity a fleshy excrescence growing in and obstructing any part of the body —carnal knowledge (*law*) sexual intercourse.—*adj.* car'nal-mind'ed worldly-minded. [L. *carô, carnıs*, flesh.]

carnassial. See carnal.

carnation *kar-nā'shən*, *n* a colour ranging from light pink to deep crimson: a florists' double-flowering variety of the clove pink.—*adj.* of the colour carnation.—*adj* carnā'tioned ruddy [L. *carnâtiô*, *-ônis*, fleshiness.]

carnauba, carnahuba *kar-na-ōō'bə*, or *-now'*, *n.* a Brazilian palm: its yellowish wax. [Braz.]

carneous. See carnal.

carnet *kar'nā*, *n.* a customs or other permit: a book of tickets, vouchers, or the like. [Fr.]

carnival *kar'ni-vl*, *n.* a feast observed by Roman Catholics just before the fast of Lent: any season of revelry or indulgence. riotous feasting, merriment, or amusement: a fair-like entertainment. [It. *carnevale*, apparently from L. *carnem levâre*, to put away flesh.]

Carnivora *kar-nıv'ə-rə*, *n.pl.* an order of flesh-eating mammals.—*n* car'nivore (*-vôr*, *-vor*) a carnivorous animal.—*adj.* carniv'orous flesh-eating.—*adj.* carniv'orously.—*n.* carniv'orousness. [L. *carô, carnıs*, flesh, *vorâre*, to devour.]

carnose, carnosity. See carnal.

carob *kar'ob*, *-əb*, *n.* a caesalpiniaceous Mediterranean tree: its fruit: a substitute for chocolate prepared from the fruit. [Fr *carobe*—Ar *kharrûbah*]

carol *kar'əl*, *n.* a song of joy or praise: Christmas song or hymn —*v.i.* to dance or sing a carol: to sing or warble.—*v.t.* to praise or celebrate in song:— *pr.p.* car'olling; *pa p* and *pa.t.* car'olled.—*n* car'oller. [O.Fr. *carole*.]

Carolingian *kar-ə-lın'jı-ən*, **Carlovingian** *kar-lō-vin'jı-ən*, *adjs.* relating to a dynasty of Frankish kings, so called from *Karl* (L. *Carolus*) the Great or Charlemagne (742–814).—**Carolingian** (or **Caroline**) **minuscule** a script developed in France at the time of Charlemagne.

Carolus *kar'ə-las*, *n.* a gold coin of the time of Charles I.—*adjs.* **Carolean** (*kar-ō-lē'ən*) belonging to the time of Charles I or II; **Car'oline** belonging to the time of Charles I or II, or Charlemagne, or any other Charles.—**Caroline minuscule** see **Carolingian**. [L. *Carolus*, Charles.]

carom *kar'əm*, *n.* and *v.t.* a shortened form of **carambole** (*kar'əm-bôl*), the same as **cannon** in billiards.

carotene *kar'ō-tēn*, **carotin** *-tin*, *ns.* any of a number of reddish-yellow pigments widely distributed in plants, precursors of vitamin A —*n* **carotenoid**, **carotinoid** (*kar-ot'in-oid*) any of a group of pigments similar to carotenes, some of which are pre-

cursors of vitamin A.

carotid *kə-rot'id*, *adj.* relating to the two great arteries of the neck. [Gr. *karôtidēs* (pl.)—*karos*, sleep, the ancients supposing that deep sleep was caused by compression of them.]

carouse *kə-rowz'*, *n.* a drinking-bout: a noisy revel.— *v.ı.* to hold a drinking-bout: to drink freely and noisily.—*ns.* carous'al a carouse: a feast; carous'er. —*adv* carous'ingly. [Ger *gar aus*, quite out, that is, empty the glass.]

carousel, in U.S **carrousel**, *kar-ōō-zel'*, *-ə-sel'*, *n.* a tilting match or tournament: a merry-go-round (*U.S*) a rotating conveyor, e.g for luggage. [Fr. *carrousel*.]

carp¹ *karp*, *v t.* to catch at small faults or errors (with *at*) —*n.* carp'er.—*n.* and *adj.* carp'ing cavilling: fault-finding.—*adv.* carp'ingly. [Most prob. Scand., O N *karpa*, to boast, modified in meaning through likeness to L. *carpēre*, to pluck, deride.]

carp² *karp*, *n* a fresh-water fish common in ponds. [O.Fr *carpe*—L.L. *carpa*; poss. Gmc]

carpal. See carpus.

carpel *kar'pl*, *n* a modified leaf forming the whole or part of the female parts of a flower.—*adj.* **car'pellary**. [Gr. *karpos*, fruit]

carpenter *kar'pınt-ər*, *n* a worker in timber. as used in building houses, etc.—*v t.* to do the work of a carpenter.—*v.t.* to make by carpentry. —*n* car'pentry the trade or work of a carpenter.—car'penter-bee', -ant' a bee or ant that excavates its nest in wood. [O.Fr. *carpentier*, from root of **car.**]

carpet *kàr'pıt*, *n* the woven, felted or tufted covering of floors, stairs, etc.: a smooth, or thin, surface or covering —*v.t* to cover with or as if with a carpet: to have up for reprimand:—*pr.p.* car'peting; *pa.p* and *pa.t* car'peted.—*n.* car'peting material of which carpets are made: carpet, or carpets.— car'pet-bag' a travelling-bag made of carpeting; car'petbagger one who comes to a place for political or other ends (as if he carried his whole property qualification for citizenship with him in his carpet-bag); car'pet-beating the removing of dust from carpets by beating; car'pet-bomb'ing systematic bombing of a whole area; car'pet-rod one of the rods used to keep a stair carpet in its place; carpet shark a shark with a spotted back like a patterned carpet; car'pet-slipper a slipper whose upper was orig. made of carpeting; car'pet-snake a variegated python of Australia; car'pet-sweeper an apparatus with a revolving brush and a dust-pan, for sweeping carpets; carpet tiles small squares of carpeting which are laid together in such a way as to form an area of carpet.—on the carpet under discussion: up before someone in authority for reprimand; sweep under the carpet to hide from notice, put out of mind (unpleasant problems or facts). [O.Fr. *carpite*—L.L. *carpeta*, *-pıta*, coarse fabric made from rags pulled to pieces—L. *carpēre*, to pluck.]

carpus *kar'pəs*, *n.* the wrist, or corresponding part of the fore-limb.—*adj.* car'pal pertaining to the carpus.—*n* a bone of the carpus. [Latinised from Gr *karpos*, wrist.]

carr *kar*, *n.* (a copse in) boggy ground. [O.N. *kjarr*]

carrack *kar'ək*, (*hist*) *n.* a large ship of burden, which was also fitted for fighting.—Also car'ack, carr'act, carr'ect. [O.Fr. *carraque*—L.L. *carraca*.]

carrag(h)een *kar-ə-gēn'*, *n.* a purplish-red North Atlantic seaweed used for making soap and a kind of blancmange, as well as for size—also called *Irish moss*—*n.* carragee'nan, carrag(h)ee'nin a colloid prepared from red algae, used in food processing, pharmaceuticals, etc. [Prob. Ir. *carraigín*, little rock.]

carrect. See **carrack.**

carrel(l) *kar'əl, n.* a carol (*hist.*): a desk or alcove in a library for private study. [See **carol.**]

carriage *kar'ij, n.* the act or cost of carrying: a vehicle for carrying: a wheeled support of a gun: the structures on which an aeroplane lands: a carrying part of a machine: behaviour (*arch.*): bearing.—*adj.* **carr'iageable** that may be conveyed in carriages.—**carriage clock** a small portable clock, usu. with a case; **carr'iage-drive** a road for carriages through parks, etc —*advs.* **carr'iage-free'** without charge for transport; **carr'iage-for'ward** without prepayment of carriage.—**carriage horse** a horse that draws a carriage.—*adv.* **carr'iage-paid'** with prepayment of carriage.—**carriage trade** trade from the wealthy; **carr'iageway** a road, or part of a road, used by vehicles. [See **carry.**]

carrick bend *kar'ik bend'* (*naut.*) a knot for joining two ropes. [Perh. conn **carrack**, and root of **bind.**]

carrier. See **carry.**

carriole. See **cariole.**

carrion *kar'ı-ən, n.* the dead and putrid body or flesh of any animal: anything vile.—*adj.* relating to, or feeding on, putrid flesh.—**carr'ion-crow'** the common crow. [Fr. *charogne*—L.L. *carōnia*—L *carō, carnis,* flesh.]

carronade *kar-ən-ād', n.* (*hist.*) a short cannon of large bore. [*Carron,* town in Scotland with ironworks.]

carrot *kar'ət, n.* a plant having a tapering root of a reddish or yellowish colour: the root itself, which is edible and sweet: an incentive, enticement.—*adj.* **carr'oty** carrot-coloured, applied to the hair.—**carrot and stick** incentive and punishment, as alternative methods of persuasion. [Fr. *carotte*—L. *carōta.*]

carrousel. U.S. spelling of **carousel.**

carry *kar'i, v.t.* to convey: to bear: to lead or transport: to take by force: to effect: to gain: to behave or demean: (of money) to be sufficient for: to pass, by a majority: to add to another column (*arith.*): (of a newspaper) to publish (e.g. an item of news), or to publish as a regular feature: to do the work of, cover up the deficiencies of (another).—*v.i.* (of a voice, a gun, etc.) to reach, indicating its range:—*pr.p.* **carr'ying;** *pa.p.* and *pa.t.* **carr'ied.**—*n.* the distance a golf ball goes when struck till it touches the ground: range: an act of carrying: the portage of a boat: land across which a boat has to be carried between one navigable stream or stretch and another.—*n.* **carr'ier** one who carries, esp. for hire. anything that carries: an instrument for carrying: a passenger aircraft: a basket, framework, or the like, for carrying luggage, as on a bicycle: one who transmits disease (without suffering from it) by harbouring germs, virus, etc.: a vehicle for communicating a signal in cases where the medium cannot convey the actual signal (as speech, etc., in radio transmission): non-active material mixed with, and chemically identical to, a radioactive compound (*nuc.*): a carrier-pigeon: a carrier bag.—**carrier bag** a strong paper or plastic bag for carrying shopping, etc.; **carr'ier-pig'eon** a pigeon with homing instincts, used for carrying messages; **carrier rocket** a rocket used to carry, e.g. a satellite into orbit; **carr'ycot** a small portable cot for a baby.—**carry all before one** to bear down all obstacles; **carry away** to carry off: to deprive of self-control by exciting the feelings: to transport; **carry forward** to transfer written or printed matter to the next page, or figures to the next column; **carry off** to cause the death of: to kidnap, abduct: to gain, to win, as a prize: to cause to pass muster; **carry on** to manage: to continue: to proceed: to complain or behave unrestrainedly (*ns.* **carr'y-on', carry'ing-on'**): to flirt (with); carry one's point to overrule objections to one's plan or view; **carry out** to accomplish; **carry over** to bring into the other (political, etc.) party: to take to a new page, as an account, etc.: to postpone to next occasion; **carry the day** to be successful: to win the day; **carry through** to support through difficulties: to accomplish; **carry too far** to continue beyond reasonable limits; **carry weight** to possess authority: to have force. [O.Fr. *carier*—L.L. *carricāre,* to cart—L. *carrus,* a car.]

carse *kars,* (*Scot.*), *n* an alluvial river-side plain. [Perh. **carr.**]

cart *kärt, n.* a vehicle used for farm purposes, or for conveying heavy loads: a light two-wheeled vehicle with springs.—*v.t.* to convey in a cart: to carry, esp. with difficulty (often with *around*).—*ns.* **cart'age** the act or cost of carting; **cart'er.**—**cart'-horse** a horse suitable for drawing a cart; **cart'-house** a shed for keeping carts; **cart'load** as much as a cart can carry; **cart'road, cart'-track, cart'way** a road or way by which carts may pass; **cart'wheel** the wheel of a cart: a sideways somersault, or Catherine-wheel.—*v.t.* to make a sideways somersault.—**cart'wright** a carpenter who makes carts.—**cart off** (*coll.*) to remove; **put the cart before the horse** to reverse the natural or sensible order of things.]

carte *kärt, n.* a bill of fare: a *carte-de-visite.*—**carte's blanche'** (*-bläsh*) freedom of action; **carte-de-visite** (*-də-vē-zēt'*) a small photographic portrait pasted on a card [Fr.,—L *c(h)arta;* see **card.**]

cartel *kar'tal, n* a political condition or bloc: (also *kar-tel'*) a combination of firms for certain purposes.—*n.* **cartelisā'tion, -z-.**—*v t.* and *v.i.* **car'telise, -ize.** [Fr.,—L. *c(h)arta;* see **card.**]

Cartesian *kar-tē'zi-ən,* or *-zhyən, adj.* relating to the French philosopher René *Descartes* (1596–1650), or his philosophy, or mathematical methods.—*n.* a follower of Descartes.—*n.* **Cartes'ianism.**—**Cartesian co-ordinates** co-ordinates of a point which have reference to two fixed lines that cross each other in a plane, or to three meeting surfaces; **Cartesian devil, diver,** or **bottle-imp** a scientific toy named after Descartes, a glass container with a floating figure that sinks when the top of the container is pressed.

Carthusian *kar-thū'zi-ən,* or *-thōō', n.* a monk or (since 1229) a nun of an order founded by St Bruno in 1086, noted for its strictness: a scholar of the Charterhouse School.—*adj* of or pertaining to the order or the school. [L. *Cartusiānus,* Chatrousse, near which their first monastery was founded.]

cartilage *kar'tı-lij, n.* gristle, a firm pearly white substance, often (*temporary cartilage*) converted later into bone.—*adj.* **cartilaginous** (*-laj'*). [Fr.,—L. *cartilāgō, -inis.*]

cartography *kar-tog'rə-fi, n.* map-making.—*n.* **cartog'rapher.**—*adjs.* **cartographic** (*-tō-graf'ik*), **-al.**—*ns.* **car'togram** a map presenting statistical information in diagrammatic form; **cartol'ogy** the science of maps and charts.—*adj.* **cartolog'ical.** [L. *c(h)arta*—Gr. *chartēs,* a sheet of paper, and Gr. *graphein,* to write.]

cartomancy *kar'tō-mən-si, n.* divination by playing-cards. [L.L. *carta,* a card, Gr. *manteiā,* divination.]

carton *kàr'tən, n.* a thin pasteboard: a box made from it. [Fr.; see **cartoon.**]

cartoon *kar-tōōn', n.* a preparatory drawing: any large sketch or design on paper: a comic or satirical drawing: a cinematograph film made by photographing a succession of drawings —*v.t.* [Fr. *carton* or It. *cartone,* augm of *carta.*]

cartouche *kar-tōōsh', n.* a case for cartridges or formerly for mortar bullets: a scroll-like ornament with rolled ends (*archit.*): an ancient Egyptian oval figure enclosing royal or divine names.—Also **cartouch'**. [Fr.,—It. *cartoccio*—L. *c(h)arta*—Gr *chartēs*, paper.]

cartridge *kär'trij*, *n*. a case containing the charge for a gun (**blank'-car'tridge** with powder only; **ball'-car'tridge** with a bullet as well): a small container holding e.g. film for a camera, ink for a pen: a cassette.—**car'tridge-belt** a belt having pockets for cartridges; **car'tridge-pa'per** a light-coloured, strong paper. [**cartouche**.]

caruncle *ka-*, *kə-rung'kl*, *n*. a small fleshy excrescence —*adjs*. **carun'cular**, **carun'culate**, **carun'-culous**. [Fr —L. *caruncula*.]

carve *kärv*, *v.t.* to cut into forms, devices, etc.: to make or shape by cutting: to cut up (meat) into slices or pieces: to apportion or distribute.—*v.i.* to exercise the art or perform the act of carving.—*adj.* **carv'en** carved.—*ns.* **carv'er**; **carv'ing** the act or art of sculpture esp. in wood or ivory: a carved device or figure: the act or art of cutting up meat at table. —**carv'ing-knife** a large knife for carving meat.— **carve out** to hew out: to gain by one's exertions; **carve up** (*slang*) to divide: to injure a person, esp. by slashing with a razor (*n*. **carve'-up**); **cut and carve** to refine. [O.E. *ceorfan*, to cut.]

carvel *kär'vəl*, *n*. an older form of **caravel**.—*adj.* **car'vel-built** built without overlap of planks.

caryatid *kar-i-at'id*, *n*. a female figure used instead of a column to support an entablature:—*pl* **caryat'ids**, **caryat'ides** (*-i-dēz*).—*adjs.* **caryat'ic**; **caryat'idal**; **caryatide'an**; **caryatid'ic**. [Gr. *Kary-ātis*, a priestess of Artemis at *Karyai* (*Caryae*), pl. *Karyātidēs*.]

Casanova *kas-ə-nō'və*, *n*. a person conspicuous for his amorous adventures, as was Giovanni Jacopo *Casanova* de Seingalt (1725–1798).

casbah. Same as **kasba(h)**.

cascade *kas-kād'*, *n*. a waterfall: a trimming of lace or other material in a loose wavy fall: apparatus connected in series, each piece operating the next one in turn or acting on the output of the preceding one.—*v.i.* to fall in cascades. [Fr.,—It. *cascata*—L. *cadēre*, to fall.]

cascara *kas-kä'rə* or *-kä'* or *kas'kə-rə*, *n*. a Californian buckthorn: the bark of the cascara, used as a tonic aperient. [Sp. *cáscara*, bark.]

case[1] *kās*, *n*. a covering, box, or sheath: a set: the boards and back of a book.—*v.t.* to enclose in a case: to skin.—*n*. **cās'ing** the act of putting on a case, or of skinning: an outside covering of any kind, as of boards, plaster, etc.—*adj.* **case'-bound** (of a book) with a hard cover.—*v.t* **case'-hard'en** to harden on the surface: to make callous or insensitive (*fig.*).—**case'-hard'ening**; **case'-knife** a large knife kept in a sheath; **case'maker** one who makes covers for books; **case'man** a compositor; **case'-worm** caddis-worm. [O N.Fr. *casse* (mod Fr. *châsse* and *caisse*)—L. *capsa—capēre*, to take.]

case[2] *kās*, *n*. that which falls or happens, event state or condition: subject of question or inquiry. an instance of disease: (records relating to) a person under medical treatment or being dealt with by a social worker, etc.. an odd character (*slang*): a legal statement of facts: a lawsuit. a plausible contention, something to be said for a position or action the grammatical relation of a noun, pronoun, or (in some languages) adjective to another word in the sentence, or its variation in form to express that relation —*v t.* (*slang*) to reconnoitre or examine. usu with a view to burglary —**case'book** a book recording medical, legal, etc , cases which are valuable as examples for reference; **case history** a record of ancestry, environment, personal history,

etc., for use in diagnosis and treatment, or for some other purpose; **case'-law** law as decided in previous cases; **case'-load** the number of cases a doctor, social worker, etc. has to deal with at a particular time; **case'-study** a study based on the analysis of one or more cases or case histories, **case'-work** the study of maladjusted individuals or families, their environment and history, often together with supervision and guidance; **case'-worker**.—**case in point** an example of what is under discussion; **in any case** at all events: at any rate; **in case** in the event that: lest; **make out one's case** to give good reasons for one's statements or position; **the case** the fact, the reality. [O.Fr. *cas*—L. *cāsus—cadēre*, to fall.]

caseation, **casein**. See **caseous**.

casemate *kās'māt*, *n*. any bomb-proof vaulted chamber: orig. a loopholed gallery.—*adj.* **case'mated**.

casement *kās'mənt*, *n* the case or frame of a window: a window that opens on vertical hinges: a hollow moulding —*adj.* **case'mented** having casements. [For **encasement** or L.L. *casamentum*, house-frame, or from **case**[1].]

caseous *kā'si-əs*, *adj* cheeselike. [L. *cāseus*, cheese.]

cash *kash*, *n*. coin or money. ready money.—*v.t.* to turn into or exchange for money.—*n*. **cashier'** one who has charge of the receiving and paying of money.—**cash'-account'** an account to which nothing is carried but cash.—**cash'-book** a book in which an account is kept of the receipts and disbursements of money; **cash crop** a crop intended for sale, not for consumption by the producer, **cash desk** a table, etc. with a till where money is taken for goods purchased; **cash dispenser** a machine which dispenses money on the insertion of a special voucher; **cash flow** the movement of money in and out of a business, **cash'-keeper** cashier, **cash point** the place in a shop, supermarket, etc. where money is taken for goods purchased; **cash'-reg'ister** a till that automatically and visibly records the amount put in.—**cash and carry** sale for cash, with delivery up to the buyer: a usu. large shop which trades in this way; **cash down** with payment at the time of purchase; **cash in** to seize an advantage; **cash in on** to turn to one's advantage; **cash in (one's checks)** to exchange counters for money on leaving the gaming-table: to die (*slang*); **cash up** to count the money taken in a shop, etc.; **out of cash**, **in cash** without, or with, money [O.Fr. *casse*, a box.]

cashew *kə-shōō'*, *kash'ōō*, *n*. a spreading tropical American tree with kidney-shaped nuts (**cash'ew-nuts**) whose kernels and fleshy stalks (**cash'ew-app'les**) are used as food. [Tupi *caju*.]

cashier[1] *kash-ēr'*, *v.t.* to dismiss from a post in disgrace: to discard or put away: to annul —*ns.* **cashier'er**; **cashier'ing**; **cashier'ment** dismissal [Du. *casseren*, to cashier—L. *cassus*, void, empty.]

cashier[2]. See **cash**.

cashmere *kash'mēr*, *n* (a shawl or fabric made from) fine soft *Kashmir* goats' hair. any similar product.— Also *adj*

casino *kə-sē'nō*, *n* a room for public dancing: a building with public dance halls, gaming tables, etc· a card-game:—*pl.* **casi'nos**. [It.]

cask *kask*, *n*. a hollow round vessel for holding liquor, made of staves bound with hoops. a measure of capacity—*v.t.* to put in a cask.—**cask'-stand**. [Sp *casco*, skull, helmet, cask.]

casket *kask'it*, *n* a little cask or case: a small case for holding jewels, etc.

casque *kask*, *n* a helmet [**cask**.]

Cassandra *kəs-an'drə*, *n* a daughter of Priam, king of Troy, beloved by Apollo, who gave her the gift of prophecy, but not of being believed—hence any one who expresses gloomy views of the political or social future and is not listened to.

cassation *ka-sā'shən*, *n.* annulment. [L.L. *cassātiō*, *-ōnis—cassāre*, to bring to nought.]

cassava *kə-sä'və*, *n.* manioc: tapioca [From a Taino (language of extinct West Indian tribe) name.]

casserole *kas'ə-rōl*, *n.* a stew-pan: a vessel in which food is both cooked and served —*v.t* to cook in a casserole. [Fr.]

cassette *kas-et'*, *n.* a small casket: a light-tight container for an X-ray film, or one for film that facilitates loading in a camera, etc.: a holder with reel of magnetic tape [Fr. dim. of *casse*, case.]

cassia *kas(h)'yə*, *n.* a coarser kind of cinnamon (**cass'la-bark'**): the tree that yields it: a genus of shrubs yielding senna. [L. *casia*—Gr. *kasiā* (also *kassiā*)— Heb *qetsī'āh.*]

cassis *ka-sēs'*, *n.* a syrupy blackcurrant drink or flavouring. [Fr.]

cassiterite *ka-sit'ə-rīt*, *n* a brown native tin dioxide. [Gr. *kassiteros*, tin.]

cassock *kas'ək*, *n.* a long robe or outer coat worn by clergy and choristers: a shorter garment worn by Scottish ministers —*adj.* **cass'ocked**. [Fr. *casaque*— It. *casacca*.]

cassoulet *ka-soo̅-le*, (Fr.) *n* a stew consisting of beans and various kinds of meat.

cassowary *kas'ə-wər-i*, *n* any member of a genus of flightless birds, found esp. in New Guinea, closely related to the emu [Malay *kasuārī* or *kasavārī*.]

cast *kast*, *v.t.* to throw or fling: to throw off, shed, drop: to drop prematurely: to throw down: to throw up: to reckon: to add: to project: to mould or shape: to appoint as actor (*for* a part): to assign as his part (*to* an actor).—*v.i.* to warp—*pa.t.* and *pa.p.* **cast.**—*n.* the act of casting: a throw of anything, as the sounding-lead, a fishing-line· the thing thrown, esp. in angling: the distance thrown: a motion, turn, or squint, as of the eye: matter ejected by a bird, earthworm, etc.: a throw or turn of fortune, a chance: a mould: a rigid casing for holding a broken bone in place while it sets: form, manner, stamp, or quality: the assignment of the various parts of a play, etc. to the several actors, etc.: the company of actors, etc. playing rôles.—*adj.* moulded: rejected, cast off —*n.* **cast'ing** the act of casting or moulding: that which is cast: a mould —**cast'away** one shipwrecked in a desolate place: an outcast—*adj.* worthless, rejected.— **casting couch** (*facet.*) a couch on which girls are said to be seduced with the promise of a part in a film, play, etc ; **cast'ing-net** a species of net for fishing; **cast'ing-vote'** a chairman's deciding vote in case of equality; **cast'-i'ron** an iron-carbon alloy distinguished from steel by its containing substantial amounts of cementite or graphite, which make it unsuitable for working.—*adj.* hard, rigid; unassailable.—*adj.* **cast'-off** rejected, laid aside, given away, no longer wanted, etc.—*n.* anything, esp. clothing, given or thrown away, no longer wanted, etc.: the act or result of casting off copy.—**cast'-steel'** steel that has been cast, not shaped by mechanical working.— **cast about** to contrive, to look about, to search for, as game or in one's mind; **cast a horoscope**, **nativity** to make an astrological calculation; **cast an eye**, **a glance** to look; **cast a spell upon** to put under an enchantment; **cast a vote** to record or make a vote; **cast away** to wreck: to waste; **cast back** to revert; **cast down** to deject or depress in mind· to turn downward; **cast loose** to set loose or adrift; **cast off** to reject: to unmoor. in knitting, etc , to eliminate stitches: to estimate amount of printed matter that copy will make; **cast on** in knitting, etc., to make stitches; **cast**

up to throw up: to bring up as a reproach. [O.N. *kasta*, to throw.]

castanets *kas'tə-nets, -nets'*, *n pl.* two hollow shells of ivory or hard wood, struck by the finger to produce a clicking sound—an accompaniment to dances and guitars. [Sp. *castañeta*—L. *castanea*, a chestnut.]

caste *kast*, *n.* a social class in India: an exclusive social class.—**caste'-mark** an indication of caste worn on the forehead (also *fig.*).—**lose caste** to descend in social rank. [Port. *casta*, breed, race—L. *castus*, pure, unmixed.]

castellan, castellated, castellum. See **castle.**

caster. Same as **castor¹.**

castigate *kas'tig-āt*, *v.t.* to chastise: to criticise severely: to emend —*ns.* **castigā'tion; cas'tigātor.**— *adj.* **cas'tigatory** (*-ə-tər-i*). [L. *castigāre, -ātum.*]

Castilian *kas-til'yən*, *adj* of Castile.—*n* a native of Castile: the language thereof, standard Spanish. [Sp. *Castellano.*]

castle *käs'l*, *n.* a fortified house or fortress: the residence of a prince or nobleman, or a large country mansion generally· a rook in chess.—*v.t.* to enclose or fortify with a castle.—*v.i.* (*chess*) to move the king two squares towards the castle and place the castle on the square the king has passed over.—*n.* **castellan** (*kas'təl-an*) the governor or captain of a castle.—*adj.* **castellated** (*kas'tel-āt-id*) having turrets and battlements like a castle —*n.* **castell'um** a small Roman fort: a mile-castle —*adj.* **cas'tled** furnished with castles.—**cas'tle-guard** the guard for the defence of a castle.—**castles in the air** or **in Spain** groundless or visionary projects. [O.E. *castel*—L. *castellum*, dim. of *castrum*, a fortified place.]

castor¹, caster *käst'ər*, *n.* a small solid swivelled wheel on a leg of furniture: a vessel with perforated top for sprinkling.—**castor sugar, caster sugar** white granulated sugar finely crushed. [**cast.**]

castor² *kås'tər*, *n.* the beaver.—*n.* **castoreum** (*-tō'ri-əm, -to*) strong-smelling substance got from the beaver, once used in medicine and perfumery [L. *castōr, -ōris*— Gr. *kastōr, -oros*, beaver.]

castor-oil *kas'tər-oil'*, *n* a medicinal and lubricating oil obtained from the seeds of a tropical African plant, *Ricinus communis.* [Perh. from use as substitute for **castor(eum).**]

castral *kas'trəl*, *adj* belonging to the camp. [L. *castra.*]

castrate *kas-trāt'*, *v.t.* to remove the testicles from: to take from or render imperfect.—*adj.* **castrat'ed** gelded: expurgated.—*ns.* **castrā'tion; castrato** (*kas-trä'tō*; It.) a male singer castrated in boyhood so as to preserve a soprano or alto voice:—*pl.* **castra'ti** (*-tē*). [L. *castrāre, -ātum.*]

casual *kaz(h)'ū-əl*, *adj.* accidental: unforeseen: occasional: off-hand: negligent: unceremonious: (of a worker) employed only for a short time, without fixed employment.—*n.* a chance or occasional visitor, labourer, etc.—*v.t.* **cas'ualise, -ize** to turn (regular workers) into casual labourers.—*ns* **casualisa'tion, -z-**; **cas'ualism** belief that chance governs all things— *adv* **cas'ually.**—*n.* **cas'ualness.**—*n.pl.* **cas'uals** slip-on flat-heeled shoes: loose-fitting comfortable and informal clothing.—*n.* **cas'ualty** an accident: a misfortune: loss by wounds, death, desertion, etc (*mil.*): a person injured or killed· a thing damaged or done for —**casual clothes** informal clothing; **casual labour** workers without fixed employment; **casual labourer; casualty department, ward** a hospital department, ward, in which accidents are treated. [L. *cāsuālis— cāsus*; see **case.**]

Casuarina *kas-ū-ə-rī'nə*, *n.* genus of trees, mainly Australian, perhaps akin to birch. [Named from its resemblance to *Cassowary* plumage.]

casuist *kaz'ū-ıst, n.* one who studies and resolves cases of conscience: often, one who argues sophistically in such cases.—*adjs.* **casuist'ic, -al.**—*adv.* **casuist'ically.**—*n.* **cas'ūistry** the science or doctrine of cases of conscience: the reasoning which enables a man to decide in a particular case between apparently conflicting duties—often with a suggestion of sophistry [Fr. *casuiste*—L *cāsus*, see **case.**]

casus belli *kā'səs be'lī, ka'zōōs be'lē,* whatever involves or justifies war. [L.]

cat *kat, n.* a carnivore of genus Felis, esp the domesticated kind or any of the smaller wild species: a spiteful woman: short for the **cat-o'-nine'-tails,** a whip with nine knotted tails or lashes, once used in the army and navy. a man, fellow (*slang*).—*v.t.* to raise the anchor to the cathead.—*ns* **cat'hood** the state of being a cat or having the nature of a cat, **cat'kin** a crowded spike or tuft of small flowers, as in the willow, hazel, etc.—*adj* **cat'-like** like a cat noiseless, stealthy —*ns.* **cat'ling** a little cat, a kitten; **catt'ery** a place where cats are bred, or cared for in their owners' absence.—*adjs.* **catt'ish, catt'y** like a cat: spiteful. back-biting.—**catamoun'tain** a leopard, panther, or ocelot. a wild mountaineer —*adj* ferocious, savage —*adjs.* **cat'-and-dog'** constantly quarrelling, **cat'-and-mouse'** consisting of harassing or toying with an opponent, victim, etc before finally killing, defeating or otherwise disposing of him: consisting of waiting and watching for the right moment to attack and dispose of one's opponent.—**cat'bird** an American bird of the thrush family with a mewing note: an Australian bower-bird; **cat'-burglar** a burglar who performs nimble climbing feats: **cat'call** a shrill whistle or cry expressing disapprobation.—*v.t.* to sound a catcall.—*v.t.* to assail with one.—*adj.* **cat'-eyed** having eyes like a cat. able to see in the dark.—**cat'fish** a fish with cat-like features; **cat'gut** a kind of cord made from the intestines of sheep and other animals used for violin strings, surgical ligatures, etc.—*adj.* **cat'-hammed** with thin hams like a cat's —**cat'head** one of two strong beams projecting from the bow of a ship through which the tackle passes by which the anchor is raised; **cat'house** a brothel (*slang*). **cat'-lap** any thin or despised drink, **cat'mint, cat'nep, cat'nip** a mint-like plant of which cats are fond; **cat'nap** a brief sleep, in a chair, etc.; CAT scanner see **computer-assisted** or **computed axial tomography scanner** under **compute; cat's'-cra'dle** a pastime in which a string looped about the fingers and passed from player to player is transformed from one symmetrical figure to another, **cat's'-eye** name for various minerals ® a reflector set in a frame fixed in a road surface; **cat's'-foot** ground-ivy, **cat'-sil'ver** a variety of silvery mica, **cat'skin; cat's'-paw** a light breeze (*naut.*). one who is made the tool of another; **cat's'-tail** a catkin the bulrush; **cat'suit** a type of one-piece trouser suit; **cat's walk** a narrow footway, as on a bridge.—**catted and fished** (of an anchor) raised to the cathead and secured to the ship's side, **care killed the (or a) cat** worry killed the cat even with his proverbial nine lives; **Cheshire cat** (*chesh'ər kat, chesh'ēr*) one proverbially notable for grinning, like the Cheshire cat in Lewis Carroll's *Alice's Adventures in Wonderland;* **enough to make a cat laugh** ı e. even the least inclined; **like a cat on hot bricks** (*coll.*) uneasy· nervous, **like something the cat brought in** bedraggled, slovenly in dress, etc., **not have a cat in hell's chance** (*slang*) to have no chance at all, **play cat-and-mouse with** to deal with in a cat-and-mouse way, **put the cat among the pigeons** to stir up trouble, **rain cats and dogs** to pour down heavily, **room to swing a cat** a minimum of space, **see which way the cat jumps** to

watch how things are going to turn before committing oneself; **the big cats** lions, tigers, leopards, etc., **the cat's pyjamas, the cat's whiskers** (*slang*) the very thing that is wanted: anything very good. [O.E. *cat.*]

catachresis *kat-ə-krē'sis, (rhet.) n.* misapplication of a word.—*adjs.* **catachrestic** (*-kres'tik,* or *-krēs'tik*), **-al.**—*adv.* **catachres'tically.** [Gr. *katachrēsis,* misuse.]

cataclasm *kat'ə-klazm, n.* a disruption, breaking down —*adj* **cataclas'mic.** [Gr. *kataklasma—kata,* down, *klaein,* to break.]

cataclysm *kat'ə-klızm, n.* a flood of water: a debacle: a great revolution —*adj.* **cataclys'mic**—*adv.* **cataclys'mically.** [Gr. *kataklysmos—kata,* downward, *klyzein,* to wash.]

catacomb *kat'ə-kōm,* or *-kōōm, n* a subterranean excavation used as a burial-place, esp near Rome, where many of the early Christian victims of persecution were buried· any place built with crypt-like recesses —*adj.* **catacumbal** (*-kum'bl*) [It. *catacomba—* L.L. *Catacumbas.*]

catadromous *kət-ad'rəm-əs, adj.* of fishes, descending periodically for spawning to the lower parts of a river or to the sea (opp. to *anadromous*). [Gr. *kata,* down, *dromos,* a run]

catafalque *kat'ə-falk, n.* a temporary tomb-like structure used in funeral ceremonies. a funeral car.—Also **catafal'co:**—*pl* **catafal'coes.** [Fr.,—It. *catafalco.*]

Catalan *kat'ə-lan, adj* of or belonging to *Catalonia:* of or concerning Catalan.—*n* a native of Catalonia: the language spoken in Catalonia.

catalectic *kat-ə-lek'tik, adj.* incomplete: wanting one syllable in the last foot (*pros.*).—*n* **catalex'is.** [Gr. *katalēktikos,* incomplete—*katalēgein,* to stop.]

catalepsy *kat'ə-lep-sı, n.* a state of more or less complete insensibility, with bodily rigidity: cataplexy in animals.—*adj* and *n.* **catalep'tic.** [Gr. *katalēp-sis,* seizure, catalepsy—*kata,* down, *lēpsis,* taking, seizure.]

catalexis. See **catalectic.**

catalo. Same as **cattalo.**

catalogue *kat'ə-log,* in U.S. often **catalog,** *n.* a systematic list of names, books, pictures, etc.—*v.t* to put in a catalogue: to make a catalogue of.—*n.* **cat'aloguer,** in U S often **cat'aloger.**—*v.t.* **cat'aloguise, -ize,** in U S often **cat'alogize.** [Gr *katalogos,* from *kata,* in order, *legein,* to reckon.]

Catalpa *kət-al'pə, n.* genus of low trees with profuse blossoms and long cigar-like pods: (*without cap*) a tree of the genus. [American Indian (Creek) *kutuhlpa.*]

catalysis *kə-tal'ı-sıs, n.* the chemical influence of a substance not itself permanently changed—*v.t.* **cat'alyse, -yze** (*-līz*) to subject to catalysis —*ns* **cat'alyser** (or *-z-*), **cat'alyst** (*-list*) a catalysing agent. —*adjs.* **catalytic** (*-lit'ik*), **-al.**—*adv* **catalyt'ically.** [Gr *katalysis—kata,* down, *lyein,* to loosen]

catamaran *kat'ə-mə-ran',* or *kat-am'ə-ran, n* a raft of logs lashed together: a boat with two hulls [Tamil, *kaṭṭu-maram,* tied wood]

catamite *kat'ə-mīt, n* a boy kept for homosexual purposes [L *catamītus*—Gr *Ganymēdēs,* Ganymede.]

catamountain. See **cat.**

cataplasm *kat'ə-plazm, n* a plaster or poultice [Gr *kataplasma.*]

cataplexy *kat'ə-plek-sı, n* a condition of immobility induced by emotion: in animals the state called shamming death —*adj.* **cataplec'tic.** [Gr. *kataplēxis,* amazement—*kata,* down, *plēssein,* to strike.]

catapult *kat'ə-pult, n* anciently, an engine of war for throwing stones, arrows, etc a small forked stick having an elastic string fixed to the two prongs, used by boys for throwing small stones: any similar device, as for launching aeroplanes —*v.t.* and *v.i.* to shoot out from, or as if from, a catapult.—*adj.* **catapul'tic.** —*n.* **catapultier** (-*tēr'*).—**catapult fruit** one that shoots out its seeds [L. *catapulta*—Gr. *katapeltēs*]

cataract *kat'ə-rakt*, *n.* a water-spout, etc.; a waterfall: an opaque condition of the lens of the eye, painless, unaccompanied by inflammation. [L. *cataracta*— Gr. *kataraktēs*, portcullis, waterfall.]

catarrh *kat-ar'*, *n.* a discharge of fluid from the inflammation of a mucous membrane, esp. of the nose, esp. when chronic: a cold in the head —*adjs.* **catarrh'al, catarrh'ous.** [L. *catarrhus*—Gr. *katarrhous*—*kata*, down, *rheein*, to flow]

catastrophe *kə-tas'trə-fi*, *n.* an overturning: a final event: the climax of the action of the plot in play or novel: an unfortunate conclusion: a sudden calamity a sudden and violent upheaval in some part of the surface of the Earth.—*adj.* **catastrophic** (*kat-ə-strof'ik*)—*adv* **catastroph'ically.**—*ns.* **catas'trophism** the old theory of geological change by vast catastrophes and new creations: **catas'trophist.** [Gr. *kata*, down, *strophē*, a turning]

catatonia *kat-ə-tō'ni-ə*, **catatony** *kət-at'ə-ni*, *ns.* a type of schizophrenia characterised by periodic states of stupor.—*adj.* and *n.* **catatonic** (-*ton'*). [Gr. *kata*, down, *tonos*, stretching, straining.]

catawba *kə-tö'bə*, *n.* an American grape (*Vitis labrusca*): a wine made from it. [*Catawba* River in Carolina.]

catcall. See cat.

catch *kach*, *v.t.* to take hold of, esp. of a thing in motion: to gather (the ball) after the batsman has hit it and before it touches the ground (*cricket*): to dismiss (a batsman) thus: to apprehend or understand: to seize after pursuit: to trap or ensnare: to come upon: to be in time for: to strike: to take (a disease) by infection. to take (fire): to take up by sympathy or imitation.—*v.i* to be contagious: to be entangled or fastened.—*n.* seizure: an act of catching, esp. the ball at cricket, etc.: a clasp, or anything that seizes or holds: that which is caught or is worth catching: a sudden advantage taken: a concealed difficulty or disadvantage: a round for three or more voices, later seeking comic effect by the interweaving of the words.—*adj.* **catch'able** that may be caught.—*ns.* **catch'er; catch'ing.**—*adj.* infectious: captivating, attractive.—*n.* **catch'ment** river drainage —*adj.* **catch'y** attractive: deceptive· readily taking hold of the mind, as a tune, etc.: fitful.—*adj.* **catch'-all** covering or dealing with a number of instances, eventualities or problems, esp. ones not covered or dealt with by other provisions.—**catch'-as-catch'-can'** a style of wrestling in which any hold is allowed.—Also *adj.* and *adv.*—**catch'-basin, -pit** a trap for dirt in a drain; **catch'-crop** a secondary crop grown before, after, or at the same time as, and on the same piece of ground as, one's main crop; **catch'-drain** a drain on a hillside to catch the surface-water; **catch'fly** a name for a species of campion and several of bladder-campion with sticky stems; **catchment area** the area from which a river or reservoir is fed (also **catchment basin**): the area from which are drawn those served by some public facility such as a school, a library or a hospital; **catch'penny** a worthless thing made only to sell.—Also *adj.*—**catch'-phrase** a phrase that becomes popular and is much repeated: a slogan.— *adj.* **Catch 22** (title of novel by J. Heller, 1961) denoting an absurd situation in which one can never win, being constantly balked by a clause, rule, etc which itself can change to block any change in one's course of action, or being faced with a choice of courses of action, both or all of which would have

undesirable consequences —*n* such a situation; **catch'weed** goosegrass or cleavers; **catch'word** an actor's cue: the word at the head of the page in a dictionary or encyclopaedia: the first word of a page given at the bottom of the preceding page: any word or phrase taken up and repeated esp. as the watchword or symbol of a party —**catch at** to snatch at; **catch fire** to become ignited· to become inspired by passion or zeal; **catch hold of** to seize; **catch it** to get a scolding or the like; **catch me, him,** etc , an emphatic colloquial phrase implying that there is not the remotest possibility of my or his doing something suggested; **catch on** to comprehend· to catch the popular fancy; **catch out** to detect in error or deceit; **catch sight of** to get a glimpse of; **catch up** to draw level and sometimes overtake; **catch up** or **away** to snatch or seize hastily [From O.Fr *cachier*—L.L *captāre* from *captāre*, intens. of *capĕre*, to take; see **chase.**]

catchup, catsup. See ketchup.

cat-cracker *kat'krak-ər*, *n.* (in full, **catalytic cracker**), a plant in which the cracking of petroleum is speeded up by the use of a catalyst.—*n.* **cat'-cracking.**

catechise, -ize *kat'i-kīz*, *v t.* to instruct by question and answer: to question as to belief: to examine systematically by questioning.—*adjs* **catechetic** (-*ket'ik*), **-al** relating to catechism or oral instruction in the first principles, esp. of Christianity.—*adv.* **catechet'ically.**—*ns* **cat'echiser, -z-;** **cat'echising, -z-;** **cat'echism** any compendious system of teaching drawn up in form of question and answer: a set of questions: an examination by questions, **cat'echist** one who catechises: a teacher of catechumens: a native teacher in a mission church.—*adjs* **catechis'tic, -al, catechis'mal** pertaining to a catechist or catechism. [L. *catēchismus*, formed from Gr *katēchizein, katēcheein*, to din into the ears—*kata*, back, *echē*, a sound.]

catechu *kat'i-chōō, -shōō*, *n.* a dark extract of Indian plants (acacia, betel-nut, etc.) rich in tannin [Cf Malay, *cachu.*]

catechumen *kat-i-kū'mən*, *n.* one who is being taught the rudiments of Christianity.—*n.* **catechū'menate.**— *adj.* **catechūmen'ical.**—*adv* **catechūmen'ically.**—*ns.* **catechū'menism, catechū'menship.** [Gr. *katēchoumenos*, being taught, pr.p. pass. of *katēcheein*, to teach; cf. **catechise.**]

category *kat'i-gər-i, n* a class or order: (in *pl.*) the highest classes under which objects of philosophy can be systematically arranged, understood as an attempt at a comprehensive classification of all that exists (*phil.*).—*adjs.* **categorematic** (-*gor-i-mat'ik*) capable of being used by itself as a term; **categorial** (*ka-tə-gör'i-əl, -gör'*) of or pertaining to a category.— *adv.* **categor'ially.**—*adj.* **categorical** (-*gor'*) positive: absolute: without exception—*adv.* **categor'ically** absolutely: without qualification: expressly.—*n.* **categor'icalness** the quality of being absolute and unqualified.—*v.t* **cat'egorise, -ize** to place in a category or list: to class.—*n.* **cat'egorist** one who categorises —**categorical imperative** in the ethics of Kant, the absolute unconditional command of the moral law. [Gr. *katēgoriā*, assertion, predication, accusation.]

catena *kə-tē'nə, n* a chain or connected series:—*pl.* **cate'nae** (-*nē*), **cate'nas.**—*adj.* **catenarian** (*kat-i-nā'ri-ən*) of, or of the nature of, a chain or a catenary. —*n.* **cate'nary** (*U.S. kat'*) the curve formed by a flexible cord hanging freely between two points of support.—*adj* relating to, like, a chain.—*v.t.* **catenate** (*kat'i-nāt*) to connect as in·or by a chain.— *adj.* linked as in a chain.—*n.* **catena'tion.** [L *catēna*, chain.]

For other sounds see detailed chart of pronunciation.

cater *kā'tər, v.i.* to provide food, entertainment, etc. (for).—*ns.* **ca'terer; ca'teress; ca'tering.** [Ultimately from L. *captāre,* to seize.]

caterpillar *kat'ər-pil-ər, n.* a butterfly or moth grub: extended to other insect larvae: (from **Caterpillar®**) a tractor or other vehicle running on endless articulated tracks consisting of flat metal plates. [Prob. O.Fr. *chatepelose,* hairy cat; see **cat, pile.**]

caterwaul *kat'ər-wöl, n.* the shriek or cry emitted by the cat when in heat.—*v.i.* to make such a noise: to make any discordant noise: to behave lasciviously: to quarrel like cats.—*n.* **cat'erwauling.** [**cat;** the second part prob. imit.]

catgut. See **cat.**

cathartic, -al *kath-art'ik, -l, adjs.* cleansing, purifying: having the power of cleansing the bowels: purgative: causing emotional or psychological catharsis.—*n.* **cathart'ic** a purgative medicine.—*v.t.* **cath'arise, -ize** to render absolutely clean.—*n.* **cathar'sis** purification: evacuation of the bowels: purification of the emotions, as by the drama according to Aristotle: the purging of the effects of a pent-up emotion and repressed thoughts, by bringing them to the surface of consciousness (*psych.*). [Gr. *kathartikos,* fit for cleansing, *katharos,* clean.]

cathead. See **cat.**

cathectic. See **cathexis.**

cathedral *kə-thē'drəl, n.* the principal church of a diocese, containing the bishop's throne.—*adj.* belonging to a seat of authority or a cathedral: having a cathedral.—*n.* **cathedra** (*-thē'drə, -thed'rə*) a bishop's seat. [L. *cathēdra,* *cathēdra*—Gr. *kathēdrā,* a seat.]

Catherine-wheel *kath'(ə-)rin-(h)wēl, n.* a rose-window (*archit.*): a rotating firework: a sidewise somersault. [From St *Catherine* of Alexandria (4th cent.), who miraculously escaped torture on a wheel.]

catheter *kath'i-tər, n.* a tube for admitting or removing gases or liquids through channels of the body, especially for removing urine from the bladder.—*ns.* **cath'eterism** the use of the catheter; **cathetom'eter** an instrument for measuring small differences of level of different liquids in tubes. [Gr. *kathetos,* perpendicular, *kathetēr,* a catheter.]

cathexis *kə-thek'sis,* (*psych.*) *n.* a charge of mental energy attached to any particular idea or object—*pl.* **cathex'es.**—*adj.* **cathec'tic.** [Gr. *kathexis,* holding.]

cathode *kath'ōd, n.* the negative terminal of an electrolytic cell at which positively charged ions are discharged into the exterior electric circuit: in valves and tubes, the source of electrons (opposed to *anode*).—*adjs.* **cath'odal; cathöd'ic.**—*ns.* **cathod'o-graph** a photograph by X-rays; **cathodog'rapher; cathodog'raphy.**—**cathode-ray oscillograph** complete equipment for registering transient waveforms on a photographic plate within the vacuum of a cathode-ray tube; **cathode-ray oscilloscope** complete equipment for observing repeated and transient wave-forms of current or voltage, which present a display on a phosphor; **cathode rays** streams of negatively charged particles, electrons, proceeding from the cathode of a vacuum tube; **cathode-ray tube** a device in which a narrow beam of electrons, which can be deflected by magnetic and/or electrostatic fields, impinges on a fluorescent screen or photographic surface—used in television, etc. [Gr. *kathodos,* a going down—*kata,* down, *hodos,* a way.]

catholic *kath'ə-lik, adj.* universal: general, embracing the whole body of Christians: orthodox, as opposed to *heterodox* and *sectarian:* liberal, the opposite of exclusive: (with *cap.*) belonging to the Christian Church before the great schism between East and West, or to any church claiming to be in historic continuity with it, esp. after the schism the Western

church, after the Reformation the Church of Rome (Roman Catholic), but applied also, e.g., to Anglicans: (with *cap.*) relating to the Roman Catholics.—*n.* (with *cap.*) an adherent of the R.C. Church.—*v.t.* and *v.i.* **cathol'icise, -ize** (also with *cap.*) to make or become Catholic —*ns.* **Cathol'icism** the tenets of the R.C. Church; **catholicity** (*-is'i-ti*) universality: liberality or breadth of view; **cathol'icon** (*-kon*) a panacea; **cathol'icos** the Patriarch of Armenia.—**Catholic emancipation** the relief of the Roman Catholics from certain vexatious penal regulations and restrictions, granted in 1829. [Gr. *katholikos,* universal—*kata,* throughout, *holos,* the whole.]

cation, kation *kat'ī-ən, n.* an ion that travels towards the cathode: a positively-charged ion. [Gr. *kata,* down, *iōn,* neut.—pr.p. of *ienai,* to go.]

catkin, catling, catmint. See **cat.**

catoptric *kat-op'trik, adj.* relating to reflection.—*n. sing.* **catop'trics** the part of optics which treats of reflected light. [Gr. *katoptron,* a mirror.]

CAT scanner. Short for **computer-assisted** or **computed axial tomography scanner** (qq.v. under **compute**).

cattalo *kat'ə-lō, n.* a cross between the bison ('buffalo') and the domestic cow:—*pl.* **catt'alo(e)s.** [From *cattle* and buff*alo.*]

cattle *kat'l, n.pl.* beasts of pasture, esp. oxen, bulls, and cows.—**cattle cake** a concentrated, processed food for cattle, in the form of blocks or cakes; **cattle grid,** in U.S. **cattle guard,** a frame of spaced bars covering a trench or depression in a road where it passes through a fence, crossable by motor vehicles or pedestrians but deterring hoofed animals; **catt'le-lift'er** a stealer of cattle; **catt'le-lift'ing; catt'leman** one who tends cattle, or who rears them on a ranch; **cattle show** an exhibition of cattle or other domestic animals in competition for prizes. [O.Fr. *catel, chatel*—L.L. *captāle,* L. *capitāle*—*caput,* the head.]

Caucasian *kö-kā'z(h)i-ən, n.* a person belonging to that one of the main ethnological divisions of mankind which is native to Europe, North Africa and western and central Asia: a member of the white race: a white person: a native of the *Caucasus* or the country around it.—*adj.* of or pertaining to a Caucasian or Caucasians in any of the above senses: pertaining to the Caucasus or the country around it.

caucus *ko'kəs, n.* any small group which acts as a body within a larger group or organisation, esp. (*opprobriously*) one which is excessively influential.—*v.i.* to hold a caucus: to control by means of a caucus.

caudal *ko'dl, adj.* pertaining to the tail.—*adjs.* **cau'date, -d** tailed. [L. *cauda,* tail.]

caudex *ko'deks,* (*bot.*) *n.* the stem of a tree, esp. of a palm or tree-fern:—*pl.* **caud'ices** (*-i-sēz*), **caud'exes.** [L.]

caudillo *kow-dēl'yō, n.* in Spanish-speaking countries, a leader: the head of the state:—*pl.* **caudil'los.** [Sp.]

caudle *ko'dl, n.* a warm drink, sweetened and spiced, given to the sick, esp. women in childbed.—*v.t.* to give a caudle to: to mix. [O.N.Fr. *caudel*—L. *calidus,* hot.]

caught *kot, pa.t.* and *pa.p.* of **catch.**

caul *kol, n.* a net or covering for the head: the membrane covering the head of some infants at their birth. [O.Fr *cale,* a little cap, prob. Celt.]

cauldron, caldron *kol'drən, n.* a large kettle for boiling or heating liquids [O.Fr. *caudron*—L. *caldārium*—*calidus,* hot—*calēre,* to be hot.]

cauliflower *ko', ko'li-flowr, n.* a variety of cabbage whose white flower-head is eaten —**cauliflower ear** an ear permanently thickened by injury, esp from boxing. [L *caulis,* cabbage, see **flower.**]

caulk, calk *kök, v.t.* to render watertight by pressing oakum, etc. into the seams.—*ns.* **caulk'er; caulk'ing.** —**caulk'ing-i'ron** an instrument like a chisel used for pressing oakum into the seams of ships. [O.Fr *cauquer*, to press—L. *calcāre*, to tread—*calx*, heel.]

caulker. See **calk²**.

cause *koz, n.* that which produces an effect: that by or through which anything happens: a motive: an inducement: a legal action between contending parties: that side of a question which is taken up by an individual or party.—*v.t.* to produce: to make to exist: to bring about.—*conj.* (*dial* or *coll*) because (usu. **'cause**).—*adj.* **caus'al** being the cause, that causes: relating to a cause or causes.—*n.* **causal'ity** the relation of cause and effect: the working of a cause.—*adv.* **caus'ally.**—*ns* **causā'tion** the act of causing· the bringing about of an effect, the relation of cause and effect: **causā'tionism** the principle of universal causation; **causā'tionist.**—*adj.* **caus'ative** causal: of the nature of, or expressing, causation.—*n* a form of verb expressing causation.— *adv.* **caus'atively.**—*adj.* **cause'less** without cause: without just cause.—*adv.* **cause'lessly.**—*ns.* **cause'lessness; caus'er.**—**first cause** the original cause or creator of all; **have** or **show cause** to have to give reasons for a certain line of action; **make common cause** (often with *with*) to unite for a common object, secondary causes such as are derived from a primary or first cause. [Fr.,—L. *causa*.]

cause célèbre *köz sā-lebr'*, (Fr.) a very notable or famous trial

causerie *köz'ər-ē, n.* a talk or gossip: a paragraph of chat about literature or art. [Fr.]

causeway *köz'wā,* **causey** *köz'i, ns.* a raised way through a marsh or water: a pathway raised and paved with stone: a paved or cobblestoned road —*vs t.* to pave.—*p.adjs.* **cause'wayed, caus'eyed.** [M.E *causee*—O.Fr. *caucie*—L.L. (*via*) *calciāta,* a trodden way.]

caustic *kös'tik, adj.* burning· corroding: pertaining to, or of the shape of, a caustic (*math., phys.*): bitter, severe, cutting (*fig.*).—*n.* a substance that exerts a corroding or disintegrating action on the skin and flesh: an envelope of rays proceeding from a fixed point and reflected or refracted by a curve (*math.*): a caustic curve or caustic surface (*phys.*).—*adv.* **caus'tically.**—*n.* **causticity** (*-tis'i-ti*) quality of being caustic.—**caustic ammonia** ammonia as a gas, or in solution; **caustic curve** a curve in the shape of a caustic, the form of a plane section through a caustic surface (*phys.*); **caustic lime** quicklime; **caustic potash** potassium hydroxide; **caustic soda** sodium hydroxide. **caustic surface** a caustic-shaped surface, the envelope of rays of light reflected or refracted by a curved surface (*phys.*). [L. *causticus*—Gr *kaustikos*—*kaiein,* to burn]

cauterise, -ize *kö'tər-īz, v.t.* to burn or destroy with a caustic, a hot iron, etc · to sear (*fig.*).—*ns* **cau'ter, cau'tery** burning or destroying with caustics, a hot iron, etc.: a burning iron, caustic, etc for burning or destroying tissue.—*ns.* **cau'terant** a cauterising substance; **cauterisā'tion, -z-.**—*adj.* **cauterising, -z-.** —*n.* **cau'terism.** [Fr *cautériser*—L.L. *cautērizāre* —Gr. *kautēr,* a hot iron—*kaiein,* to burn]

caution *ko'shən, n* heedfulness: a warning: a warning that what a person says may be used as evidence (*law*): an alarming, amusing, or astonishing person or thing (*coll.*).—*v.t.* to warn to take care: to give (someone) a caution (*law*).—*adj* **cau'tionary** containing caution or cautions: given as a pledge.—*n* **cau'tioner.**—*adj.* **cautious** (*kö'shəs*) possessing or using caution: watchful: prudent.—*adv.* **cau'tiously.** —*n* **cau'tiousness.**—**caution money** money paid in

advance as security for good behaviour. [Fr.,—L. *cautiō, -ōnis*—*cavēre,* to beware.]

cavalcade *kav-əl-kād', kav', n* a train of persons on horseback: a parade —*v i.* to go in a cavalcade [Fr., through It. and L.L.—L. *caballus,* a horse.]

cavalier *kav-əl-ēr', n.* a knight: (with *cap*) a Royalist in the great Civil War· a swaggering fellow. a gallant or gentleman in attendance upon a lady.—*adj* like a cavalier: gay: war-like: haughty, supercilious, free-and-easy, off-hand.—*adj* **cavalier'ish** like, characteristic of, a cavalier—*n.* **cavalier'ism.**—*adv.* **cavalier'ly** off-hand: with supercilious disregard or curtness —*adj* cavalierish [Fr ,—It *cavallo;* see **cavalcade.**]

cavalry *kav'əl-ri, n.* horse-soldiers· a troop of horse or horsemen.—*n.* **cav'alryman.**—**cavalry twill** see **twill.** [Fr. *cavallerie*—It. *cavalleria*—L. *caballārius,* horseman—*caballus,* horse]

cavatina *kav-at-ē'nə, n* a melody with no second part or da capo: loosely, a short operatic air, of a smooth and melodious character, often part of a grand scena. [It.]

cave¹ *kāv, n.* a hollow place in a rock: a small faction of seceders from a political party (from the Cave of Adullam, 1 Sam xxii, 1–2).—*v t.* to hollow out.—*v i.* to lodge in a cave.—*n.* **cav'ing (in)** falling into a hollow: yielding.—**cave'-bear** a Pleistocene bear found fossil in caves; **cave'-dweller** one who lives in a cave, esp. one of the Stone Age of prehistoric times; **cave'-earth'** a fine deposit on cave floors; **cave'man** a cave-dweller: a modern male of primitive ways (*coll*).— **cave in** to slip, to subside, to fall into a hollow (*n.* **cave'-in**)· to yield to outside pressure, to give way, collapse [Fr. *cave*—L *cavus,* hollow.]

cave² *kav'i, kāv'i, v.i.* or *interj.* (*schoolboy slang*) beware.—*n* **caveat** (*kā'vi-at*) a notice or warning. [L. *cāvē,* imper. sing., *cāvēat,* 3rd sing pres. subj., of *cāvēre,* to take care.]

caveat actor *kā'vi-at* (*ka've-at, -we-*) *ak'tör,* (L.) let the doer beware; **caveat emptor** (*emp'tör*) it is the buyer's look-out.

cavendish *kav'ən-dish, n.* tobacco moistened and pressed into quadrangular cakes. [Possibly from the name of the original manufacturer]

cavern *kav'ərn, n* a deep hollow place in rocks.—*v t* to put in a cavern: to hollow out —*adjs.* **cav'erned** full of caverns: dwelling in a cavern; **cav'ernous** hollow: full of caverns —*adv* **cav'ernously.** [L. *caverna*—*cavus,* hollow.]

cavesson *kav'əs-ən, n.* a nose-band for a horse. [Fr. *caveçon*—It *cavezzone*—L. *capitia, capitium,* a head-covering.]

cavetto *ka-vet'ō, n.* a hollowed moulding whose curvature is the quarter of a circle, used chiefly in cornices. —*pl.* **cavett'i** (*-ī*) [It ; dim of *cavo*—L. *cavus,* hollow.]

caviare, caviar *kav'i-ar, kav-i-ar',* also *kav-yar', ns* salted roe of the sturgeon, etc.: something whose flavour is too fine for the vulgar taste (*fig*). [Prob the 16th-cent. It. *caviale*]

cavil *kav'il, v i* to make empty, trifling objections (with *at* or *about*): to use false arguments:—*pr p.* **cav'illing;** *pa.t.* and *pa.p.* **cav'illed.**—*n.* a frivolous objection.—*ns* **cavillā'tion, cav'illing; cav'iller.** [O Fr *caviller*—L. *cavillārī,* to practise jesting]

cavity *kav'it-i, n.* a hollow· a hollow place: hollowness. a decayed hollow in a tooth —*n* **cavitā'tion** the formation of cavities in a structure, or of gas bubbles in a liquid, or of a vacuum, or of a partial vacuum as between a body moving in a fluid and the fluid: a cavity —*adj* **cav'itied.**—**cavity wall** a wall consisting of two layers with a space between [L. *cavitās*— *cavus,* hollow]

cavort *kə-vort'*, *v.i.* to frolic, bound [Explained as a corr of **curvet.**]

cavy *kāv't*, *n.* a member of the guinea-pig genus (*Cavia*) of rodents [*Cabiai*, native name in French Guiana]

caw *kö*, *v.i.* to cry as a crow —*n.* the cry of a crow.—*n.* **caw'ing.** [From the sound]

cawker. Same as **calker.**

cay *kā*, *n.* a low islet, the same as **key²**. [Sp *cayo*]

cayenne *kā-en'*, *n.* a very pungent red pepper (**cay'enne-pepp'er**) made from several species of Capsicum — *adj.* **cayenned'** seasoned with cayenne. [Usually referred to *Cayenne* in French Guiana; but prob. from Tupí.]

cayman *kā'mən*, *n.* any of the Central and South American crocodilian animals of the genus *Caiman* and related genera, similar to alligators:—*pl.* **cay'mans.**—Also **cai'man.** [Sp. *caimán*, most prob Carib]

cayuse *kī-ūs'*, (*U.S*) *n.* an Indian pony: a small or poor horse. [Amer Indian.]

cazique. A form of **cacique.**

CB radio. See **Citizens' Band radio.**

cease *sēs*, *v.i.* and *v.i.* to give over: to stop: to end.—*n.* an end: a cessation —*adj.* **cease'less** without ceasing. incessant.—*adv* **cease'lessly.**—*n* **ceas'ing.**—**cease'-fire'** an order to cease firing: an agreed cessation of active hostilities. [Fr *cesser*—L *cessāre*, to give over—*cēdĕre*, to yield.]

cebadilla. See **sabadilla.**

cecils *ses'*, *sĕs'ilz*, *n.pl.* minced meat, bread-crumbs, onions, etc., made into balls and fried.

cecity *sē'si-ti*, *n.* blindness.—*n.* **cecutiency** (*si-kū'shyən-si*) a tendency to blindness [L. *caecus*, blind.]

cedar *sē'dər*, *n.* a large evergreen coniferous tree (*Cedrus*), remarkable for the durability and fragrance of its wood; applied also to many more or less similar trees.—*adj.* made of cedar.—*adjs* **cē'dared** covered with cedars; **cē'drine** belonging to the cedar-tree.—**ce'darwood** (also *adj.*). [L *cedrus*—Gr. *kedros.*]

cede *sēd*, *v.t.* to yield or give up to another.—*v.i.* to give way [L. *cēdĕre*, *cēssum*, to yield, to give up.]

cedilla *se-dil'ə*, *n.* a mark, originally a subscript Z, placed under the letter c (thus ç), formerly used in Spanish to indicate that the letter had the sound of (Spanish) *z* where that of *k* would be expected, still used esp in French and Portuguese to indicate an *s*-sound as before *a, o, u,* and in other languages to denote other sounds, e.g. Turkish ş (*sh*) and ç (*ch*). [Sp. (Fr. *cédille*, It. *zediglia*), all dims. from *zēta*, the Greek name of *z*; see z.]

cedrate *sē'drāt*, *n.* citron. [Fr *cédrat*—L. *citrus.*]

cedrine. See **cedar.**

cee *cē*, *n.* the third letter of the alphabet (C, c): anything shaped like it.—**cee-spring**, **c-spring** (*sē'spring*) a spring in the shape of a C to support the frame of a carriage.

Ceefax® *sē'faks*, *n.* the teletext (q.v.) service of the British Broadcasting Corporation. [See, facts.]

cell *sēl*, *v.t.* to provide with a ceiling.—*n* **ceil'ing** the inner roof of a room: the highest altitude at which an aircraft can fly: an upper limit.—*adj* **ceil'inged** having a ceiling. [Prob. conn. with Fr *ciel*, It. *cielo*, L L *caelum*, a canopy.]

ceilidh *kā'li*, *n* in Scotland and Ireland, an informal evening of song, story and dancing. [Gael , a visit]

celandine *sel'ən-dīn*, *n.* (*Chelidonium majus*); **greater celandine**) a plant of the poppy family, supposed to flower when the swallows came, and to perish when they went. also *Ranunculus ficaria*, **lesser celandine** [O.Fr *celidoine*—Gr *chelidonion*—*chelidôn*, a swallow]

celebrate *sel'i-brāt*, *v t* to make famous to distinguish

by solemn ceremonies, as a festival or an event: to perform with proper rites and ceremonies, as mass, marriage, etc : to publish the praises of.—*v i.* to do something enjoyable because of a feeling of pleasure at some event, achievement, etc.—*n.* **cel'ebrant** one who celebrates: the principal officiant at a rite.—*adj.* **cel'ebrated** distinguished: famous —*ns.* **celebrā'tion; cel'ebrātor; celebrity** (*si-leb'ri-ti*) the condition of being celebrated: fame: notoriety: a person of distinction or fame [L *celebrāre*, -*ātum*—*celeber*, frequented.]

celerity *si-ler'i-ti*, *n.* quickness: rapidity of motion. [Fr. *célérité*—L *celeritās*—*celer*, quick.]

celery *sel'ər-i*, *n.* an umbelliferous plant whose blanched leaf-stalks are eaten cooked or uncooked.—*n.* **celeriac** (*si-ler'i-ak*) a turnip-rooted variety of celery. [Fr *céleri*—Gr. *selinon*, parsley]

celesta *si-les'tə*, **celeste** *si-lest'*, *ns* a keyboard instrument in which the hammers strike steel plates over wooden resonators. [Fr. *céleste*, heavenly.]

celeste *si-lest'*, *adj.* sky-blue —*n* voix céleste: a kind of soft pedal on a piano. [Fr. *céleste.*]

celestial *si-lest'yəl*, *adj.* heavenly: dwelling in heaven: in the visible heavens.—*n.* an inhabitant of heaven.— *adv* **celest'ially.** [Through French from L. *caelestis*—*caelum*, heaven.]

celiac. Same as **coeliac.**

celibacy *sel'i-bəs-i*, *n.* the unmarried state, esp. under a vow.—*adjs.* **celibatā'rian** favouring celibacy; **cel'ibate** (*-it*) living single.—*n.* one who is unmarried, or bound not to marry. [L. *caelebs*, single.]

cell *sel*, *n.* a small room in a prison, monastery, etc.: a monastery or nunnery dependent on another: a hermit's one-roomed dwelling: a small cavity: one compartment of a comb in a hive: a vessel with electrodes and an electrolyte, for electrolysis or for generating an electric current by chemical action: a unit-mass of living matter, whether walled or unwalled, by itself or associated with others in a higher unity: a unit group, esp. of communist propagandists or other political activists: the unit of storage in computing.— *n* **cell'a** the inner chamber of a temple—*pl.* **cell'ae** (*-ē*).—*adjs.* **celled** having cells, cellular; **cellif'erous** having or producing cells; **cell'ular** consisting of, characterised by or containing cells or compartments: porous: of open texture; **cell'ūlated.**—*n* **cell'ule** a little cell.—*adj.* **cellūlif'erous** having or producing little cells.—*ns.* **cell'ūlite** deposits of fat, not responsive to dieting or exercise, which give the skin a dimpled, pitted appearance, **cellūli'tis** spreading infection of subcutaneous tissue with pyogenic bacteria; **cell'ūloid** (® with *cap.* in U.S.) a thermoplastic, which is elastic and very strong: a sheet of this material.—*adj.* **cell'ūlose** containing cells.—*n.* a carbohydrate forming the chief component of cell-walls of plants and of wood.—*adj.* **cellūlōs'ic** containing, or derived from cellulose.—*n* a compound or substance containing cellulose —**cell'-division** (*biol.*) the process in which cells each split into two new cells, so increasing in number during growth or reproduction [O Fr *celle*—L. *cella*, conn with *celāre*, to cover.]

cella. See **cell.**

cellar *sel'ər*, *n.* any underground room or vault: a room for storing wine, beer, coal, etc.: a stock of wine.—*v.t* to store in a cellar —*ns* **cell'arage** cellars: a charge for storing in cellars, **cell'arer, cell'arist** one who has charge of the cellar. an officer in a monastery who looks after the provisions, **cell'aret** a case for holding bottles —**cell'ar-book** a record of wines kept in a cellar, **cell'ar-flap** a plate covering an entrance to a cellar, **cell'arman** one who has the care of a cellar [O.Fr. *celier*—L *cellarium*—*cella*]

cello chel'ō, n. a shortened form of **violoncello** (sometimes written **'cello**):—pl. **cell'os.**—n. **cell'ist, 'cell'ist** for **violoncellist.**

cellophane® sel'ō-fān, n. a tough, transparent, paperlike wrapping material made from viscose. [*cellulose* and Gr. *phainein*, to show.]

cellulite, celluloid, cellulose. See **cell.**

celom. See **coelom(e).**

Celsius sel'si-əs. See **centigrade.**

Celt kelt, selt, n. a Gaul (*hist.*): extended to include members of other Celtic-speaking or recently Celtic-speaking peoples—also **Kelt.**—adjs. **Celt'ic, Kelt'ic** pertaining to the Celts: of a branch of the Indo-European family of languages including Breton, Welsh, Cornish, Irish, Gaelic, Manx.—ns. **Celt'icism, Kelt'-icism** a Celtic idiom or custom; **Celtomā'nia, Keltomā'nia.**—**Celtic cross** a Latin cross with a broad circle around the point of intersection of the crossbar and the upright. [L. *Celtae*; Gr. *Keltoi* or *Keltai*]

cembalo chem'ba-lō, n. a musical instrument with strings struck by hammers, a dulcimer: a harpsichord or pianoforte·—pl. **cem'balos.**—n. **cem'balist.** [It , see **cymbal.**]

cement si-ment', n. anything that makes two bodies stick together: mortar. a bond of union. the bony substance forming the outer layer of the root of a tooth.—v.t. to unite with cement: to join firmly.—ns. **cementation** (sem-ən-tā'shən) the act of cementing: the process of impregnating the surface of one substance with another by surrounding it with powder and heating, as in steel-making; **cement'ite** an iron carbide, Fe₃C.—adjs. **cement'atory, cementi'tious** having the quality of cementing or uniting firmly. [O.Fr. *ciment* —L. *caementum*, chip of stone used to fill up in building a wall, *caedimentum*—*caedēre*, to cut.]

cemetery sem'i-tri, n. a burying-ground. [L L. *coem-ētērium*—Gr. *koimētērion*, sleeping-place.]

cenesthesis. Same as **coenaesthesis.**

cenobite. Same as **coenobite.**

cenotaph sen'ō-täf, n. an empty tomb: a sepulchral monument in honour of one or more people buried elsewhere. [Gr. *kenotaphion*—*kenos*, empty, and *taphos*, a tomb.]

Cenozoic sē-nō-zō'ik. Same as **Cainozoic.**

cense sens, v.t. to burn incense before. [**incense²**.]

censer sens'ər, n. a pan in which incense is burned. [O.Fr. *censier, encensier* (mod. *encensoir*)—L.L. *incēnsorium*—L. *incendēre, incēnsum*, to burn.]

censor sen'sor, or -sər, n. a magistrate who kept account of the property of Roman citizens, imposed taxes, and watched over their morals (*hist.*): an official with analogous functions elsewhere: an official who examines books, papers, telegrams, letters, films, etc., with powers to delete material, or to forbid publication, delivery, or showing: an unconscious inhibitive mechanism in the mind, that prevents what is painful to conscious aims from emerging into consciousness (*psych.*): one who censures or blames.—v.t to subject to censorial examination or condemnation.—adjs. **censorial** (-ô'ri-əl, -o') belonging to a censor, or to the correction of public morals; **censo'rian** censorial; **censo'rious** expressing censure: fault-finding.—adv. **censo'riously.**—ns. **censo'riousness; cen'sorship** the office of censor: the time during which he holds office: a policy, programme or act of censoring. [L. *cēnsor, -ōris.*]

censure sen'shər, n. an opinion or judgment (formerly general, now unfavourable only): blame: reproof.—v.t. to form or give an opinion or judgment (now unfavourable) of. to blame.—adj. **cen'surable** deserving of censure· blamable.—n. **cen'surableness.**—adv. **cen'surably.** [L. *cēnsūra—cēnsēre*, to estimate]

census sen'səs, n an official enumeration of inhabitants

with statistics relating to them. [L. *cēnsus, -ūs*, a register.]

cent sent, n. a hundredth part, esp. of a dollar: a coin of that value.—ns. **cent'age** rate by the hundred; **cent'al** a weight of 100 lb.—**per cent** by the hundred. [L. *centum*, a hundred.]

centaur sen'tor, n. a mythical monster, half man, half horse.—adj. **centau'rian.** [Gr *kentauros.*]

centaury sen'to-ri, n. a name applied to plants of the genera Erythraea and Chlora, and to the composite genus **Centaurea** (knapweed, etc) [The *centaur* Chiron is said to have healed a wound with *kentaurion*, one of these plants.]

centavo sen-ta'vō, n. a Spanish American coin and money of account:—pl. **centa'vos.** [Sp.]

centenary sen-tēn'ər-i (also -tēn' or sen'), n. a hundred: a century or hundred years: a centennial.—adj. pertaining to a hundred or to a centennial —n. **centenā'rian** one who is a hundred years old or more. [L. *centēnārius—centēnī*, a hundred each—*centum*.]

centennial sen-ten'yəl, adj. happening once in a hundred years: having lasted a hundred years.—n. a hundredth anniversary. [L. *centum*, a hundred, *annus*, a year]

center. The American spelling of **centre.**

centering, centreing, centring sen'tər-ing, (*archit.*) n the framework upon which an arch or vault of stone, brick, or iron is supported during its construction.

centesimal sen-tes'i-məl, adj hundredth: designating a centigrade thermometer.—adv **centes'imally.** [L. *centēsimus—centum*.]

centi- sen-ti-, in composition, 1/100 of the unit named. [L. *centum*, a hundred.]

centiare sen'ti-ar, n. the hundredth part of an are, 1·196 sq. yards. [L. *centum*, a hundred, *area*, area.]

centigrade sen'ti-grād, adj. having a hundred degrees: divided into a hundred degrees, as the centigrade thermometer constructed by Celsius (1701–44), in which freezing-point of water is zero and boiling-point is 100°. [L. *centum*, a hundred, and *gradus*, a step, a degree.]

centigram(me) sen'ti-gram, n. the hundredth part of a gram(me). [Fr.,—L. *centum*, a hundred, and **gram(me).**]

centilitre sen'ti-lē-tər, n. the hundredth part of a litre, 10 cubic centimetres. [Fr.,—L. *centum*, a hundred, and **litre.**]

centime sā'tēm, sä-tēm', n a French coin, 1/100 of a franc. [Fr.,—L. *centesimum*, a hundredth.]

centimetre, (*U.S.*) **centimeter,** sen'ti-mē-tər, n. a lineal measure, the hundredth part of a metre. [Fr.,—L. *centum*, a hundred, and **metre²**.]

centipede sen'ti-pēd, n any myriapod of the class Chilopoda, carnivorous flattened animals with many joints, most of which bear one pair of legs. [L. *centum*, a hundred, and *pēs, pedis*, a foot.]

centner sent'nər, n. a hundredweight, usually of 50 kg. [Ger.,—L. *centēnārius*; cf. **centenary.**]

cento sen'tō, n. a poem manufactured by putting together verses or passages of one author, or of several authors a composition formed by joining scraps from other authors:—pl. usually **cen'tos.**—adj. **cen'tonate** (*bot*) blotched.—ns. **cen'toist, cen'tonist.** [L. *centō, -ōnis*, Gr. *kentrōn*, patchwork.]

central, etc. See **centre.**

centre (*U.S.* **center**), sen'tər, n. the middle point of anything, esp a circle or sphere: the middle: a fixed point of reference: the point toward which all things move or are drawn: a nucleus: a resort: a meeting place: a player in a central position: a centre-forward: politicians of moderate political opinions —v.t. to place on or collect to a centre.—v t to be placed in the middle: to have a centre. to lie or move in relation to a centre (often with (up)on, (a)round):—pr.p. cen'tring, cen'tering; pa.t. and pa.p. cen'tred, cen'tered.—adj. cen'tral belonging to, in, or near, the centre: principal, dominant.—ns. centralisā'tion, -z-, cen'tralism the tendency to administer by the sovereign or central government matters which would be otherwise under local management; cen'-tralist (also adj.).—v.t. cen'tralise, -ize to draw to or concentrate at a centre.—n. centrality (-tral'i-ti) central position.—adv. cen'trally.—n. cen'treing see separate article centering.—adj. cen'tric relating to, placed in, or containing the centre.— -cen'tric in composition, having a specific centre.—adj. cen'trical.—adv. cen'trically.—ns. cen'tricalness; centricity (-tris'i-ti); cen'tring see separate article centering.—adj. and n. cen'trist (a person) having moderate, non-extreme political opinions.—ns. cen'trism; cen'trum the body of a vertebra.—central forces forces causing an acceleration towards or from a fixed point, the centre of force; central heating a system of heating a building by water, steam or warm air conducted throughout the building from one point; cen'tre-bit a joiner's tool, turning on a centre, for boring circular holes; cen'tre-board a movable plate, fitted to drop below the keel of a racing yacht; cen'trefold, centre spread the two facing centre pages of a newspaper, magazine, etc.: an article or set of photographs printed on these; cen'tre-for'ward in association football and hockey, the central player among the forwards; cen'tre-half'(-back) the central player among the half-backs; cen'tre-piece an ornament for the middle of a table, ceiling, etc.—central nervous system (zool.) the main ganglia of the nervous system with their associated nerve cords; Central Powers in and before the war of 1914-18, the German Empire and Austria-Hungary; central processor, central processing unit the part of a computer which performs the logical and arithmetical operations on the data and which controls other units of the computer system; central to important for the understanding or working of; centre of attraction the point to which bodies tend by the force of gravity or the like; centre of gravity the point at which the weight of a body may be supposed to act. [Fr.,—L. centrum—Gr. kentron, a sharp point.]

centri- sen-tri', sen'tri-, centro- sen'tro-, in composition, centre.—adj. centrifugal (sen-trif'ū-gal, sen',-fū') tending away from a centre: using, or produced by centrifugal force.—v.t. centrif'ugalise, -ize (or sen',-fū') to subject to centrifugal force.—adv. centrifugally.—n. cen'trifuge (-fūj) a machine which, by rapid rotation, separates substances of different densities—used in industry, biochemistry, etc.—v.t. to subject to such rotation.—ns. centrifugation (-fūgā'shən), centrifugence (-trif'ū-jəns, sen',-fū') centrifugal tendency or force.—adj. centrip'etal tending towards a centre.—n. centrip'etalism.—centrifugal force the resistance of a revolving body, by virtue of its inertia, to an acceleration towards the centre, equal and opposite to the constraining force; centrifugal machine a centrifuge. [Gr. kentron and L. centrum (from Gr.) a sharp point.]

centric, etc. See centre.

centrifugal, centripetal, etc. See centri-.

centuple sen'tū-pl, adj. hundredfold.—v.t. to multiply or increase a hundred times.—n. centuplicā'tion.—adj. centū'plicate.—n. one of a hundred like things or copies.—v.t. to centuple. [L. centuplus and centuplex—centum, plicāre, to fold.]

century sen'tū-ri, n. a set or series of a hundred, as Roman soldiers, runs at cricket, or miles ridden, or consecutive years (esp. reckoned from the conventionally accepted date of Christ's birth).—adj.

centūrial.—ns. centuriā'tion division into hundreds; centū'rion in the Roman army, the commander of a century: one who has scored or achieved a hundred in any way. [L. centuria, a century—centum, a hundred.]

cep sep, n. a type of edible mushroom of the Boletus genus. [Fr. cèpe,—L. cippus, a stake.]

cephal- sef'al-, si-fal', kef'al-, ki-fal' in composition, head.—adjs. ceph'alate having a head; cephal'ic of, belonging to, the head: for curing pains in the head.—n. a remedy for head-pains.— -cephal'ic, -ceph'alous adjective combining forms.—adj. ceph'alous having a head.—ns cephalag'ra gout in the head; cephalal'gia headache.—adj. cephalal'gic.—ns. cephali'tis inflammation of the brain, ceph'alopod (-pod) a member of the Cephalopoda (-op'od-ə), the highest class of molluscs, usu. large animals, exclusively marine, with the foot modified into arms surrounding the mouth—cuttle-fish, etc.—cephalic index the ratio of the breadth to the length of the skull expressed as a percentage; cephalic presentation the usual position of a child in the womb just before birth, head downwards. [Gr. kephalē, head.]

ceramic, keramic se- or ke-ram'ik, adjs pertaining to a ceramic or to ceramics: made of a ceramic.—n. ceram'ic any product that is first shaped and then hardened by means of heat, or the material from which it is formed.—n. sing. ceram'ics the potter's art —ns. ceram'ist, ceram'icist one who makes a scientific study of clays and other ceramic materials, or who puts them to practical use.—cer'amet a cermet; cer'met a combination of ceramic particles and a metal matrix. [Gr. keramos, potter's earth.]

cerastes se-ras'tēz, n. the North African horned viper, with a horny process over each eye:—pl. ceras'tes. [Gr. kerastēs—keras, a horn.]

cerate. See cere.

ceratitis. Same as keratitis.

ceratoid ser'ə-toid, adj. horny. [Gr. keratoeidēs—keras, horn. eidos, form.]

cercus sûr'kəs, a tail-like appendage.—adj. cer'cal pertaining to a tail. [Gr. kerkos, tail.]

cere sēr, v.t. to cover with wax.—n. the bare waxlike patch at the base of the upper part of a bird's beak.—adj. cērā'ceous waxy.—n. cēr'ate a paste or stiff ointment containing wax.—adj. cēr'eous waxy.—cere'-cloth, cerement (sēr'mənt) a cloth dipped in melted wax to wrap a dead body in. [L. cēra, wax.]

cereal. See Ceres.

cerebrum ser'i-brəm, n. the front and larger part of the brain.—adjs. cerebell'ar, cerebell'ous pertaining to the cerebellum.—n. cerebell'um the hinder and lower part of the brain.—adj. cer'ebral (also sə-rē'brəl) pertaining to the brain or the cerebrum: intellectual, as opposed to practical: cacuminal (phon.).—v.i. cer'ebrate to show brain action.—n. cerebrā'tion action of the brain, esp. unconscious.—adjs. cer'ebric (or sər-eb'rik) cerebral; cereb'riform brain-shaped.—cerebri'tis inflammation of the cerebrum.—adjs. cer'ebrospin'al relating to the brain and spinal cord together; cer'ebrovas'cular relating to the cerebrum and its blood vessels.—cerebral death see brain death under brain; cerebral haemorrhage haemorrhage of the blood-vessels in the brain; cerebral hemispheres the two great divisions of the cerebrum; cerebral palsy a form of congenital paralysis marked by lack of muscular coordination, etc.; cerebrospinal fever meningitis; cerebrovascular accident a paralytic stroke. [L. cerebrum, the brain; prob. cog. with Gr. karā, the head, krānion, the cranium.]

cerement, cereous. See cere.

ceremony ser'i-mə-ni, n. a rite: a formal act: the outward form, religious or other: any empty form without inwardness: pomp or state.—*adj.* **ceremonial** (*-mō'ni-ǝl*) relating to ceremony.—*n.* outward form: a system of ceremonies.—*n.* **ceremō'nialism** adherence to outward form.—*adv* **ceremō'nially.**— *adj.* **ceremō'nious** full of ceremony: particular in observing forms: precise.—*adv.* **ceremō'niously.**—*n.* **ceremō'niousness.**—**master of ceremonies** the person who directs the form and order of the ceremonies to be observed on some public occasion: a compère; **stand on ceremony** to be punctilious about forms; **without ceremony** informally: without formalities. [L. *caerimōnia*, sanctity.]

Ceres *sē'rēz, n.* the Roman goddess of tillage and corn —*adj.* **cereal** (*sē'ri-ǝl*) relating to edible grain.—*n* a grain used as food, such as wheat, barley, etc : a food prepared from such grain, esp a breakfast food easily got ready. [L. *Cěrēs, -eris*, prob. from root of *creāre*, to create.]

ceresin, ceresine *ser'ǝ-sin, -sēn, n.* a kind of hard, whitish wax prepared from ozokerite. [L. *cera*, wax.]

cerge *sûrj, n.* a large wax-candle burned before the altar. [O.Fr.,—L. *cěreus—cēra*, wax.]

ceria. See **cerium.**

cerise *sǝr-ēz', also -ēs', n.* and *adj.* light and clear red [Fr., cherry.]

cerium *sē'ri-ǝm, n.* a metallic element (at numb. 58; symbol Ce). [Named from the planet *Ceres* discovered about the same time.]

cermet. See under **ceramic.**

cerograph *sē'rō-gräf, n.* a writing on wax: engraving by means of a plate spread with wax.—*adjs* **cērograph-ic** (*-graf'ik*), **-al.**—*ns.* **cērographist** (*-rog'rǝ-fist*); **cērog'raphy.** [Gr. *kēros*, wax, *graphein*, to write.]

ceroplastic *sē-rō-plas'tik, adj.* pertaining to wax-modelling.—*n. sing.* **ceroplas'tics** the art of wax-modelling. [Gr. *kēros*, wax, *plastikos*, plastic— *plassein*, to mould]

cert. See **certain.**

certain *sûr'tn, adj.* sure: not to be doubted: resolved: fixed: determinate: regular: inevitable: some: one.— *adv.* **cer'tainly** without doubt, undoubtedly: in a resolved, fixed, etc. manner.—*interj.* yes, of course. —*ns.* **cer'tainty** (*slang* **cert**, sometimes in the phrase **dead cert**); **cer'titude.**—**a certain person** implying some degree of contempt; **for certain** assuredly; **in a certain condition** a euphemism for pregnant. [O.Fr.,—L. *certus—cernĕre*, to decide.]

certes *sûr'tiz, adv.* certainly: in sooth. [Fr.]

certificate *sǝr-tif'i-kāt, -kǝt, n.* a written declaration, official or formal, of some fact: a statement of qualification(s) or recognised professional status.—*v.t.* to give a certificate to.—*adj.* **cer'tifiable** (*-fi-ǝ-bl*) capable of being certified (esp. as insane).—*adv.* **cer'tifiably.**—*adj.* **certif'icated** (of e.g. a teacher) holding a certificate of training and fitness.—*ns* **certifica'tion; certif'icatory** a certificate.—Also *adj.* —*n.* **cer'tifier.**.—*v.t.* **cer'tify** to make known as certain: to inform: to declare in writing: to certify as insane:—*pr.p.* **cer'tifying;** *pa.p.* **cer'tified.** [Fr *certificat*—L. *certificāre, certus*, certain, and *facĕre*, to make.]

certiorari *sûr-shi-ō-rā'rī, n.* a writ by which causes are removed from inferior courts into the High Court of Justice. [L.L. *certiōrārī*, to be informed of—*certior*, compar. of *certus*, certain]

certitude. See **certain.**

cerulean, caerulean *si-rōō'li-ǝn, adj.* sky-blue: dark-blue: sea-green—*adj.* **cerū'leous.** [L. *caerŭleus*, dark blue or green.]

cerumen *si-rōō'men, n.* ear wax.—*adj.* **ceru'minous.** [L. *cēra*, wax.]

ceruse *sē'rōōs*, or *si-rōōs', n.* white lead.—*n* **cē'rus(s)ite** native lead carbonate [Fr.,—L. *cěrussa*, conn. with *cēra*, Gr *kēros*, wax.]

cervelat *ser've-la, n.* a kind of smoked sausage, made of pork. [Fr.—It. *cervellata*.]

cervix *sûr'viks, n.* the neck of an organ, esp. the uterus. —*adj.* **cervical** (*sûr'vi-kl, sǝr-vī'kl*).—**cervical smear** the collection of a sample of cells from the neck of the womb and the examination of these cells under a microscope, as a test for early cancer. [L. *cervix, cervicis*, neck.]

cervine *sûr'vīn, adj.* relating to deer: like deer: fawn-coloured [L. *cervīnus—cervus*, a stag]

Cesarean. Esp U S spelling of **Caesarean.**

cesarevitch, -witch, cesarevna. See **tsar.**

cesium. U.S spelling of **caesium.**

cessation *ses-ā'shan, n.* a ceasing or stopping: a rest: a pause. [L *cessātiō, -ōnis* See **cease.**]

cession *sesh'ǝn, n.* a yielding up.—*n.* **cess'ionary** one to whom an assignment has been legally made. [L. *cěssiō, -ōnis*; see **cede.**]

cesspit *ses'pit*, **cesspool** *-pōōl, ns.* a pit or pool for collecting filthy water.

cestode *ses'tōd, n.* a tapeworm or bladder-worm —*n.* **ces'toid** a cestode —Also *adj.*—*n* and *adj.* **cestoid'ean.** [Gr *kestos*, a girdle, a strap, and *eidos*, form.]

cestus *ses'tas, n.* an ancient boxing-glove loaded with metal. [L. *caestus*]

cesura. See **caesura.**

Cetacea *si-tā'shi-ǝ, -shyǝ, n.pl.* an order of mammals of aquatic habit and fish-like form including the toothed whales (sperm whales, bottle-noses, dolphins, etc.) and the baleen whales (right whale, hump-backs, rorquals) —*n.* and *adj.* **cetā'cean.**—*adj.* **cetā'ceous.**—*n.* **cetol'ogy** the study of whales. [Gr. *kētos*, a sea-monster]

cetane *sē'tān, n.* a paraffin hydrocarbon found in petroleum —**cetane number** a measure of the ignition quality of diesel engine fuel; **cetyl alcohol** a waxy crystalline solid used in detergents and pharmaceuticals, so called because compounds of it occur in spermaceti [Gr *kētos*, a sea-monster.]

ceteris paribus *set'ǝr-is par'i-bus, kā'te-rēs pa'ri-bōōs,* (L.) other things being equal.

cetology. See **Cetacea.**

cetyl. See **cetane.**

cevadilla. See **sabadilla.**

cha *cha, n.* tea: rolled tea [Chin. *ch'a.*]

Chablis *shab'lē, n* a very dry white Burgundy wine made at *Chablis*, department of Yonne, in France

chabouk *chǝ'bōōk, n.* a horsewhip. [Pers. *chābuk.*]

cha-cha (*-cha*) *cha'-cha' (-cha'), n* a West Indian dance, a later form of the mambo.

chaconne *sha', sha-kon', n.* an old dance, with slow movement: its music, a series of variations on a ground bass, in triple time [Fr ,—Sp *chacona*— Basque *chucun*, pretty]

chadar, chaddar, chador, chuddah, chuddar *chud'ǝ(r), ns* the large veil worn by Muslim and Hindu women, covering head and body: a cloth spread over a Muslim tomb. [Pers *chaddar*, Hindi *caddar*, a square cloth.]

chaeta *kē'tǝ, n.* a chitinous bristle on the body of the earthworm and other invertebrates'-—*pl* **chaetae** (*kē'tē*) —*n* **chaetopod** (*kē'tō-pod*) a worm (as earthworm) of the class **Chaetop'oda**, that crawls with the help of bristles. [Gr *chaitē*, hair.]

chafe *châf, v.t.* to heat, fret, or wear by rubbing: to cause to fret or rage —*v.i* to fret or rage (with *against, at*) —*n.* heat caused by rubbing: rage: passion.—**chaf'ing-dish** a vessel for heating by hot coals, etc a dish for cooking on the table [Fr *chauffer*—L. *calefacĕre*—*calĕre*, to be hot, and *facĕre*, to make.]

chafer *chāf'ər, n.* a beetle, esp. of the Scarabaeidae. [O.E. *cefer*; Du. *kever*; Ger. *Kafer*.]

chaff *chäf, chaf, n.* husks of corn as threshed or winnowed: cut hay and straw: refuse, or worthless matter: light banter, badinage (perh. a different word).—*v.t.* to banter.—*n.* and *adj.* **chaff'ing.**—*adv.* **chaff'ingly.**—*adjs.* **chaff'less; chaff'y.** [O.E. *ceaf.*]

chaffer *chaf'ər, v.t.* to bargain: to haggle about price. —*ns.* **chaff'erer; chaff'ery** buying and selling. [M.E. *chapfare*, a bargain, from O.E. *cēap*, price, *faru*, way.]

chaffinch *chaf'inch, -insh, n.* a little song-bird of the finch family. [Said to delight in *chaff*; see **finch.**]

chagrin *shag'rin, shə-grēn', n.* that which wears or gnaws the mind: vexation: annoyance.—*v.t.* to vex or annoy.—*p.adj.* **chagrined'.** [Fr. *chagrin*, shagreen, rough skin, ill-humour.]

chain *chān, n.* a series of links or rings passing through one another: a linked series: a mountain range: a string of islands: something that binds: a connected course or train of events: a measure of 100 links, or 66 feet: a succession of cigars or cigarettes smoked without intermission: a series of shops, hotels, restaurants, etc. under the same management: a number of atoms linked in succession (*chem.*): (in *pl.*) fetters, bonds, confinement generally: (in *pl.*) a circular apparatus of metal links fitted to the wheels of a car in icy conditions to prevent skidding.—*v.t.* to fasten (also **chain up, down**): to fetter: to restrain.—*p.adj.* **chained** bound or fastened, as with a chain: fitted with a chain.—*adj.* **chain'less** without chains: unfettered. —*n.* **chain'let** a small chain.—**chain'-arm'our** chainmail; **chain'-bridge** a suspension-bridge; **chain'-cable** a cable composed of iron links; **chain'-drive** transmission of power by chain-gear.—*adj.* **chain'-driven.**— **chain'-gang** a gang of convicts chained together; **chain'-gear, -gearing** gearing consisting of an endless chain and (generally) sprocket-wheels; **chain'-letter** a letter soliciting (among other things) the sending, by the recipient, of similar letters with or without a limit to other people; **chain'-light'ning** forked or zigzag lightning; **chain'-mail** armour of connected links, much used in Europe in the 12th and 13th centuries; **chain'-pier** a pier supported by chains like a chainbridge; **chain reaction** a process in which each reaction is in turn the stimulus of a similar reaction; **chain'saw** a power saw with teeth linked in an endless chain.— *v.t.* and *v.i.* **chain'-smoke'** to smoke (cigarettes, etc.) non-stop.—**chain'-smok'er; chain'stitch** a stitch resembling the links of a chain; **chain'-store** one of a series of shops, esp. department stores, under the same management. [O.Fr. *chaeine*—L. *catēna.*]

chair *chār, n.* a movable seat for one, with a back to it: a vehicle, wheeled or carried, for one person (*hist.*): the seat or office of one in authority, as a judge, a bishop, or the person presiding over any meeting: the chairman: a professorship: the instrument or the punishment of electrocution.—*v.t.* to place in a seat of authority: to carry publicly in triumph: to conduct as chairman, etc. (a meeting).—**chair'-bed** a chair capable of being turned into a bed.—**chair'lift** a set of seats suspended from cables used to take skiers uphill; **chair'man** one who takes the chair, or presides at an assembly or meeting (also **chair'person**); *fem.* **chair'woman**); **chair'manship** [Fr. *chaire*—L.—Gr. *kathedrā.*]

chaise *shāz, n.* a light open carriage for one or more persons.—**chaise'-longue'** (*-l5g'*) a couch with back at one end and short armrest. [Fr., a form of *chaire*; see **chair.**]

chalaza *ka-lā'za, n.* in a bird's egg, the string that holds the yolk-sac in position (*zool.*): the base of the ovule (*bot.*). [Gr. *chalaza*, hail, lump.]

chalcedony *kal-sed'ə-ni*, or *kal', n.* a beautiful mineral composed of silica, usually banded, translucent, of waxy lustre, generally white or bluish-white, consisting of crystalline fibres.—*adj.* **chalcedonic** (*-si-don'ik*). [Gr. *chalkēdōn*, possibly from *Chalcedon*, in Asia Minor.]

chalcography *kal-kog'ra-fi, n.* the art of engraving on copper or brass.—*ns.* **chalcog'rapher, chalcog'raphist.** [Gr. *chalkos*, copper, *graphein*, to write.]

chalcopyrite *kal-kō-pī'rīt, n.* copper pyrites. [Gr. *chalkos*, copper, and **pyrite.**]

chaldron *chöl'drən, n.* an old coal-measure, holding 36 heaped bushels (= 25½ cwt.). [Fr. *chaudron*; see **cauldron.**]

chalet *shal'ā, n.* a summer hut used by Swiss herdsmen in the Alps: a wooden villa: a small house, usu. of wood, built for use by holidaymakers, etc. [Fr.]

chalice *chal'is, n.* a cup or bowl: a communion-cup. [O.Fr. *chalice*—L. *calix, calicis.*]

chalk *chök, n.* white soft rock, composed of calcium carbonate: a substitute for this used for writing, etc. —*v.t.* to write, rub, mark, or manure, with chalk.— *n.* **chalk'iness.**—*adj.* **chalk'y.**—**chalk'board** a blackboard; **chalk'pit** a pit in which chalk is dug; **chalk'stone** a stone or piece of chalk: (in *pl.*) the white concretions formed round the joints in chronic gout.—**as like, as different, as chalk and cheese** completely unalike; **by a long chalk** by a considerable distance or degree, orig. referring to the habit of scoring with chalk; **chalk out** to trace out, as with chalk, to plan; **chalk up** to make a special note of: to record (a score, etc.): to charge or ascribe (to e.g. a person); **not to know chalk from cheese** to know nothing about the matter; **the Chalk** (*geol.*) the uppermost part of the Cretaceous system in England. [O.E. *cealc*—L. *calx*, limestone.]

challenge *chal'inj, v.t.* to call on to settle a matter by fighting or by any kind of contest: to claim as one's own: to accuse: to object to.—*n.* a summons to a contest of any kind, but esp. a duel: a calling of anyone or anything in question: exception to a juror: the demand of a sentry: an accusation: a claim: a difficulty which stimulates interest or effort: a task, undertaking, etc. to test one's powers and capabilities to the full.—*adj.* **chall'engeable** that may be challenged.—*n.* **chall'enger.**—*adj.* **chall'enging.**—*adv.* **chall'engingly.** [O.Fr. *chalenge*, a dispute, claim —L. *calumnia*, a false accusation—*calvī* or *calvĕre*, to deceive.]

challis, shalli *chal'is, shal'is, shal'ι, n.* a soft glossless silk and worsted fabric, later of other materials.

chalone *kāl', kal'ōn, n.* an internal secretion which inhibits action as a hormone excites it.—*adj.* **chalon'ic.** [Gr. *chalaein*, to relax.]

chalumeau *shal-ū-mō', shal-u-mō', n.* an early reed instrument that developed into the clarinet: the lowest register of the clarinet:—*pl.* **chalumeaux** (*-mōz'*). [Fr.—O.Fr. *chalemel*—L.L. *calamellus*, dim. of *calamus*, a pipe, a reed.]

Chalybean *kal-ib-ē'ən*, or *ka-lib'i-ən, adj.* well tempered.—*adj.* **chalyb'eate** containing iron.—*n.* a water or other liquid containing iron. [Gr. *chalyps, chalybos*, steel, or *Chalyps*, one of the *Chalybēs*, a nation famous for steel.]

chamaeleon. See **chameleon.**

chamber *chām'bər, n.* a room: the place where an assembly meets: a house of a legislature, esp the French Chamber of Deputies: an assembly or body of men met for some purpose, as a chamber of commerce: a hall of justice: a compartment: a cavity: the back end of the bore of a gun: (in *pl.*) a suite of rooms in a house occupied separately, esp. by lawyers: (in *pl*) a judge's room for hearing cases not taken into court.—*v.t* to put in a chamber: to confine.—*adj* **cham'bered** confined: having rooms or room, or (of a shell) parts separated by a succession of walls.—**chamber concert** a concert of chamber music; **cham'bermaid** a female servant who has the care of bedrooms in hotels, etc.; **chamber music** music, performed by a small group such as a quartet, suitable for a room rather than a theatre or a large hall; **chamber of commerce** (sometimes with *caps.*) a group of businessmen working together to promote local trade, **cham'berpot** a bedroom vessel for urine [Fr. *chambre*—L. *camera*—Gr *kamarā*, a vault, a room.]

chamberlain *châm'bər-lin, n* an officer appointed by a king or nobleman, or by a corporation, to perform domestic and ceremonial duties or to act as factor or steward —*n.* **cham'berlainship.**—**Lord Chamberlain** an officer of high standing in the royal household [O.Fr. *chambrelenc*; O.H G. *chamerling*—L. *camera*, a chamber, and affix *-ling* or *-lenc* = Eng. *-ling* in *hireling.*]

chambré *shā-brā*, (Fr) *p. adj* of wine, at room temperature.

chameleon, chamaeleon *kə-mēl'yən, n* a small lizard famous for changing its colour: an inconstant person (*fig.*).—*adjs.* **chameleonic** (*-i-on'ik*); **chamel'eonlike.** [L. *chamaeleón*—Gr. *chamaileón*—*chamai*, on the ground (i.e. dwarf) and *león*, a lion.]

chamfer *cham'fər, n.* a bevel or slope made by paring off the edge of anything originally right-angled: a groove, channel, or furrow —*v.t.* to cut or grind off bevel-wise, as a corner: to channel or make furrows upon: to flute, as a column.—*adj.* **cham'fered.** [Fr *chanfrein*—O.Fr *chanfraindre*, apparently—L. *cantum frangēre*, to break the edge or side]

chamlet *cham'* or *kam'let, n* Same as **camlet.**

chamois *sham'wa, n.* a goat-like antelope inhabiting high mountains in southern and central Europe (*pl* **chamois** *sham'wa*): (*sham'i*) a soft kind of leather originally made from its skin (in this sense also **shammy**). [Fr.]

chamomile. See **camomile.**

champ¹ *champ, v.i.* to make a snapping noise with the jaws in chewing.—*v.t.* to bite or chew: to munch. to crush: to mash.—*n.* a champing.—**champ at the bit** to show signs of impatience while waiting for something (*fig*) [Cf. **jam²**.]

champ² *champ, n.* slang shortening of **champion.**

champagne *sham-pān', n.* a white sparkling wine, strictly from *Champagne* in France. the amber-like colour of white champagne

champaign *cham'pān', also sham-pān', n* an open level country. [Doublet of **campaign**.]

champers *sham'pərz, (coll)* n. champagne.

champerty *cham'pər-ti, n.* an illegal bargain whereby the one party is to assist the other in a suit, and is to share in the proceeds. [Norm Fr —L *campī pars*, part of the field]

champignon *sham'pin-yō, n* a mushroom or other edible fungus, esp the fairy-ring champignon

champion *cham'pi-ən, n.* one who fights in single combat for himself or for another one who defends a cause: a successful combatant in sports, one who has excelled all others. a hero.—*adj* acting or ranking as champion, first. excellent (*coll.*).—*v.t* to defend: to support.—*ns* **cham'pioness; cham'pionship** a contest held to decide who is the champion: the position of honour gained by being champion: the act of championing [Fr ,—L L *campiō*, *-ōnis*—L. *campus*, a plain, a place for games.]

champlevé *shā-lə-vā, n.* enamel work done with vitre-

ous powders in channels cut in a metal base —Also *adj.* [Fr]

chance *chans, n.* that which falls out or happens fortuitously, or without assignable cause: fortune. an unexpected event: risk: opportunity. possibility of something happening· (sometimes in *pl*) probability —*v.t* to risk.—*v.i* to happen· (with (*up*)*on*) to happen to find or meet —*adj* happening by chance.—*adjs.* **chance'ful** full of chance(s); **chance'less** without an opportunity —*n.* **chanc'er** (*coll*) a person prepared to take risks for his own advancement —*adj* **chanc'y** risky, uncertain.—**by chance** accidentally; **chance one's arm** to take a chance, often recklessly; **chance upon** to find by chance; **even chance** equal probability for or against; **stand a good chance** to have a reasonable expectation; **take one's chance** to accept what happens· to risk an undertaking; **an eye to the main chance** thought for self-enrichment [O Fr. *cheance*—L L *cadentia*—L. *cadēre*, to fall.]

chancel *chan'sl, n.* the eastern part of a church, originally separated from the nave by a screen of latticework. [O.Fr.,—L. *cancellī*, lattices]

chancellor *chan'səl-ər, n.* a chief minister: the president, or a judge, of a court of chancery or other court· the titular head of a university.—*ns* **chan'cellorship; chan'cellery**, *-ory* the position, department, etc , of a chancellor.—**Chancellor of the Exchequer** the chief minister of finance in the British government; **Lord Chancellor, Lord High Chancellor** the Speaker of the House of Lords, presiding judge of the Chancery Division, keeper of the great seal. [Fr *chancelier*—L.L *cancellārius*, orig an officer that had 'charge of records, and stood near the *cancelli* (L), cross-bars surrounding the judgment seat]

chance-medley *chans-med'li, n.* unintentional homicide in which the killer is not entirely without blame: action with an element of chance [O.Fr *chance medlée*, mingled chance]

Chancery *chän'sər-i, n.* a division of the High Court of Justice: a court of record generally: the office of a chancellor.—**in chancery** (of an estate, etc) in litigation in an awkward predicament (*slang*) [Fr. *chancellerie.*]

chancre *shang'kər, n* the hard swelling that constitutes the primary lesion in syphilis —*n.* **chanc'roid** a non-syphilitic ulceration of the genital organs due to venereally contracted infection —*adjs* **chanc'roid;** **chanc'rous.** [Fr ; a form of **canker**.]

chancy. See **chance.**

chandelier *shan-di-lēr', n* a frame with branches for holding lights —*ns* **chandler** (*chand'lər*) a candle-maker: a dealer in candles, oil, soap, etc , a dealer generally (as in *corn-chandler, ship-chandler*); **chand'lering**,—*adj* **chand'lerly.**—*n* **chand'lery** goods sold by a chandler [Fr ,—L.L *candēlārius*, a candle-maker, *candēlāria*, a candlestick—L *candēla*, a candle]

change *chānj, v t.* to alter or make different: to put or give for another: to make to pass from one state to another: to exchange —*v i* to suffer change to change one's clothes or vehicle —*n.* the act of changing alteration or variation of any kind a shift. variety money given for money of a different kind, or in adjustment of a payment small coin· satisfaction (*coll*) —*ns* **changeabil'ity, change'ableness** fickleness the power of being changed —*adj* **change'able** subject or prone to change fickle inconstant admitting possibility of change —*adv* **change'ably.**—*adj* **change'ful** full of change: changeable —*adv* **change'fully.**—*n* **change'fulness.**—*adj* **change'less** without change constant.—

ns. **change'ling** a surreptitious substitute: a child substituted for another, esp. one supposed to be left by the fairies; **chǎng'er.—change'-over** transition to a new system or condition; **change-ringing** see **ring the changes** below.—**change colour** to blush or turn pale; **change of life** the menopause; **change one's mind** to form a different opinion; **change one's tune** to change from joy to sorrow: to change one's manner of speaking; **put the change on** to delude, trick; **ring the changes** to go through all the possible permutations in ringing a peal of bells (*n.* **change'-ringing**): to do, use, etc. a limited number of things repeatedly in varying ways, order, etc.; **small change** small coin: a petty thing. [Fr. *changer*—L. *cambīre*, to barter.]

channel *chan'l, n.* the bed of a stream of water. a strait or narrow sea: a navigable passage: a passage for conveying a liquid: a groove or furrow: a gutter: means of passing or conveying: (in *pl.*) means of communication: a one-way path for a signal: a path for information in a computer: a narrow range of frequencies, part of a frequency band, for the transmission of radio and television signals without interference from other channels.—*v.t.* to make a channel: to furrow: to convey (through): to direct (into a particular course; *lit.* and *fig.*):—*pr.p.* **chann'elling**; *pa.t.* and *pa.p.* **chann'elled.**—*adj.* **chann'elled.—the Channel** the English Channel. [O.Fr. *chanel, canel*—L *canālis*, a canal.]

chanoyu *chǎ'no-ū, n.* a Japanese tea ceremony. [Jap. lit. *tea of hot water.*]

chanson *shā'sɔ̃; n.* a song.—**chanson de geste** (*də zhest*) an old French epic poem. [Fr.]

chant *chant, v.t.* to sing: to celebrate in song: to recite in a singing manner: to intone.—*n.* song: melody: a kind of church music, in which prose is sung.—*ns.* **chant'er, chant'or** a singer: a precentor: in a bagpipe, the pipe with fingerholes, on which the melody is played; **chant'ress; chant'ry** an endowment, or chapel, for the chanting of masses; **chanty** see **shanty**[2]. [Fr. *chanter*—L. *cantāre*, to sing.]

chanterelle[1] *shan-, shā-tər-el', n.* the highest string of a musical instrument. [Fr.—L. *cantāre*, to sing.]

chanterelle[2] *chan-tər-el', n.* a yellowish edible fungus. [Fr., dim. from Gr. *kantharos*, cup.]

chanteuse *shan'tōōs* or *-tōōz, shā-tøz, n.* a female nightclub singer. [Fr.]

chantey. See **shanty**[2].

chanticleer *chant'ı-klēr, -klẽr', n.* a cock. [From the name of the cock in the old beast-epic of *Reynard the Fox*—O.Fr. *chanter*, to sing, *cler*, clear.]

chantie. See **shanty**[2].

Chantilly *shan-ti'li, shā-tē-yē, n.* a silk or linen lace of delicate pattern.—Also **Chantilly lace** (*lās*).—*adj* of cream, sweetened and whipped. [*Chantilly*, France, where the lace was first made.]

chantor, chantress, chantry. See **chant.**

chanty. See **shanty**[2].

chaos *kā'os, n.* the shape of matter before it was reduced to order: disorder: shapeless mass.—*adj* **chaot'ic** confused.—*adv.* **chaot'ically.** [Gr.]

chap[1] *chap, v.i.* to crack.—*v.t.* to fissure.—*n.* a crack: an open fissure in the skin, caused by exposure to cold.—*adjs.* **chap'less; chapped** cracked, of a heavy soil in dry weather, or of the skin in cold weather; **chapp'y.** [M.E. *chappen*.]

chap[2] *chap, n.* a fellow (*coll.*).—*n.* **chapp'ie** a familiar dim. of **chap.—chap'book** a book or pamphlet of a popular type such as was hawked by chapmen; **chap'man** an itinerant dealer: a pedlar. [O.E. *cēap*, trade, *cēapman*, trader.]

chap[3] *chap, n.* a chop or jaw: a cheek.—*adj.* **chap'-fall'en** same as **chopfallen.** [Cf. **chop**[3].]

chaparajos *shap-ə-rā'ōs, chà-pa-rá'hhos,* **chaparejos**

-rā', -rē', ns.pl. cowboy's leather riding leggings (short form **chaps**). [Mex. Sp]

chaparral *shap-ə-ral', chap-a-ral', n.* dense tangled brushwood.—**chaparral cock** a ground-cuckoo of the Californian and Mexican chaparral [Sp ,—*chaparro*, evergreen oak, one of its constituents]

chapati, chapatti *chəp-ät't, n.* a thin flat loaf of unleavened bread [Hind *capatı.*]

chapel *chap'l, n.* a place of worship inferior or subordinate to a regular church, or attached to a house or institution: a cell of a church containing its own altar: a place of worship of Nonconformists in England, Roman Catholics or Episcopalians in Scotland, etc.: a chapel service· a printing office, or an association or trade union of workmen therein.—*n.* **chap'elry** the jurisdiction of a chapel—**chap'el-master** a music-director; **chapel royal** the oratory of a royal palace.—**chapel of ease** a chapel for worshippers at some distance from the parish church; **father of the chapel** the president of a printing office or chairman of a printers' association or trade union branch; **proprietary chapel** one that is private property. [O.Fr. *capele*—L L *cappella*, dim of *cappa*, a cloak or cope, orig. from the cloak of St Martin]

chaperon (now often **chaperone**) *shap'ə-rōn, n.* a kind of hood or cap: one (esp. an older woman) who accompanies a girl for protection, restraint, or appearance's sake—*v t.* to attend in such a capacity —*n.* **chap'eronage.** [Fr., a large hood—*chape,* a hooded cloak—L.L *cappa;* see **cape**[1].]

chaplain *chap'lin, n.* a clergyman attached to an institution, establishment, organisation, or family.—*ns* **chap'laincy, chap'lainry, chap'lainship.** [O.Fr *chapelain*—L.L. *cappellānus*—*cappella*, see **chapel**.]

chaplet *chap'lıt, n.* a garland or wreath for the head: a circlet of gold, etc.: a string of beads used in counting prayers, one-third of a rosary in length: anything in a string: a metal support of a cylindrical pipe.—*adj* **chap'leted.** [O.Fr. *chapelet*—*chape,* a head-dress.]

chapman, chapple. See **chap**[2].

chaps. See **chaparajos.**

chapter *chap'tər, n* a main division of a book, or of anything· a subject or category generally: a division of the Acts of Parliament of a session: an assembly of the canons of a cathedral or collegiate church, or the members of a religious or military order (from the custom of reading a chapter of the rule or of the Bible): its members collectively: an organised branch of a society or fraternity—*v.t.* to put into chapters.—**chap'ter-house** a building used for meetings of a cathedral, church, etc chapter.—**chapter and verse** the exact reference to the passage of the authority of one's statements. [O.Fr. *chapıtre*—L. *capitulum,* dim of *caput,* the head.]

char[1], **charr** *char, n.* a small fish (*Salvelinus*) of the salmon kind, found in mountain lakes and rivers. [Prob. Celt.; cf. Gael. *ceara,* red, blood-coloured.]

char[2] *char, v.t.* to reduce to carbon.—*v.t.* and *v.i.* to scorch:—*pr.p.* **charr'ing;** *pa.t.* and *pa.p.* **charred.**

char[3] *char, n.* an occasional piece of work, an odd job: a charwoman.—*v.i.* to do odd jobs of work: to do house-cleaning:—*pr.p.* **charr'ing;** *pa.t.* and *pa.p.* **charred.**—**char'woman, char'lady** a woman hired to do rough cleaning. [O E *cerran, cierran,* to turn.]

char[4] *char, n.* (*slang*) tea. [Cockney spelling of **cha.**]

charabanc *shar'ə-bang, -bã, n.* formerly, a long open vehicle with rows of transverse seats: more recently, a tourist coach. [Fr. *char à bancs,* carriage with benches.]

character *kar'ək-tər n.* a letter, sign, figure, stamp, or distinctive mark. a mark of any kind, a symbol in writing, etc.: writing generally, handwriting: one of a set of symbols, e.g letters of the alphabet, numbers, punctuation marks, that can be arranged in groups to represent data for processing (*comput.*): any essential feature or peculiarity: a quality: nature: the aggregate of peculiar qualities which constitutes personal or national individuality: esp. moral qualities. the reputation of possessing these: a formal statement of the qualities of a person who has been in one's service or employment a person noted for eccentricity or well-marked personality. a personality as created in a play or novel or appearing in history: a person (*slang*).—*n.* **characterisā'tion, -z-**.—*v t.* **char'acterise, -ize** to describe by peculiar qualities: to be a distinguishing mark or quality of.—*ns.* **char'acterism** a characteristic: a characterisation, **characteris'tic** that which marks or constitutes the character: the integral part of a logarithm.—*adjs* **characteris'tic,-al**.—*adv.* **characteris'-tically**.—*adj.* **char'acterless** without character or distinctive qualities.—**character actor** one who plays character parts, **character assassination** the destruction of a person's reputation by slander, rumour, etc., **characteristic radiation** the wavelength of radiation that characterises a particular substance; **character part** a stage or film rôle portraying an unusual or eccentric personality type; **character sketch** a short description of the main traits in a person's character.—**in character** in harmony with the part assumed, appropriate: in keeping with the person's usual conduct or attitudes: dressed for the part; **out of character** not in character. [Fr. *caractère*—L. *charactēr*—Gr. *charaktēr*, from *charassein*, to cut, engrave.]

charade *shə-räd'*, in U.S. usu. *-rād'*, *n.* an acted riddle in which the syllables and the whole are uttered or represented in successive scenes: a piece of ridiculous pretence. [Fr , perh.—Prov. *charrada*, chatter, or Sp *charrada*, clownishness]

charcoal *char'kōl, n.* charred wood, or coal made by charring wood: the carbonaceous residue of substances that have undergone smothered combustion.—*n.* and *adj.* (also **charcoal grey**) (of) a dark grey colour [**char², coal**.]

chard *chard, n.* the edible leafstalk of cardoon, artichoke, or a variety (*Swiss chard*) of white beet. [L. *carduus*, thistle.]

charge *charj, v.t.* to load, to put something into, to fill: to load heavily, burden: to fill completely: to cause to accumulate electricity: to lay a task upon, to enjoin, command: to accuse: to place a bearing upon (with *with*; *her.*): to exact or demand from, to ask as the price: to set down as a liability against: to attack at a rush: to advance in accusation (that).—*v.t.* to make an attack.—*n.* that which is laid on: cost or price: the load of powder, fuel, etc., for a gun, furnace, etc.: an attack or onset: care, custody: the object of care: an accumulation of electricity. a command: an exhortation: an accusation (*law*): a device borne on a shield (*her.*): (in *pl.*) expenses.—*adj.* **charge'able** liable to be charged, imputable: blamable —*n.* **charge'ableness**.—*adv.* **charge'ably**.—*adj.* **charge'less**.—*n.* **char'ger** a flat dish capable of holding a large joint, a platter. a warhorse.—**charge account** an account in which goods obtained are entered to be paid for later; **charge'-hand, -man** the leader of a group of workmen; **charge'-nurse** a nurse in charge of a ward; **charge'-sheet** a police list of accused and the charges against them.—**bring a charge** to accuse (with *against, law*); **give in charge** to hand over to the police; **in charge** in control or authority, responsible (often with *of*); **take charge of** to assume the care of. [Fr. *charger*—L.L *carricāre*, to load—L. *carrus*, a wagon, see **car, cargo**.]

chargé-d'affaires *shar'zhā-da-fer', n.* a diplomatic agent of lesser rank:—*pl.* **chargés-d'affaires** (*shar'-zhā-*). [Fr.]

charily, chariness. See **chary**.

chariot *char'i-ət, n.* a pleasure or state car: a god's car: a car used in ancient warfare or racing.—*n.* **charioteer'** one who drives a chariot. [Fr., dim. of *char*, a car.]

Charis *kar'is*, any one of the three **Char'ites** (*-tēz*), the Graces, Greek goddesses of whatever imparts graciousness to life.—*ns.* **char'ism, charis'ma** a spiritual power given by God: personal quality or gift that enables an individual to impress and influence many of his fellows.—*adj.* **charismat'ic** of, pertaining to, or having a charism or charisma —**charismatic movement** a non-denominational religious movement based on a belief in the divinely-inspired gifts of speaking in tongues, healing, prophecy, etc. [Gr. *charis, -itos*, grace.]

charity *char'i-ti, n.* universal love (*N.T.*): the disposition to think favourably of others, and do them good: almsgiving: a usu. non-profit-making foundation, institution, or cause, devoted to caring for those in need of help, etc.—*adj.* **char'itable** of or relating to, showing, inspired by charity: (of an institution, etc.) having the status of, being in the nature of, a charity.— *n.* **char'itableness**.—*adv.* **char'itably**. [Fr. *charité*— L. *cāritās, -ātis—cārus*, dear.]

charivari *shar-i-var' i, n.* a cacophonous mock serenade, rough music. [Fr.,—L.L *caribaria*, a headache.]

charlatan *shar'lə-tan, n.* a mere talking pretender, esp. one who claims to have medical knowledge: a quack.— *adjs.* **charlatanic** (*-tan'ik*), **-al**.—*ns.* **char'latanism; char'latanry**. [Fr.,—It. *ciarlatano—ciarlare*, to chatter; imit]

Charles's wain *charlz'iz wān*, the Plough. [O.E. *Carles wægn*, Carl being Charlemagne.]

Charley, Charlie (also without *cap.*), *char'li, n.* an inefficient, forceless person, a fool (often in the phrase *a proper Charlie*) [From the name *Charles*]

charlock *char'lək, n* wild mustard, a common yellow-flowered cornfield weed. [O E. *cerlic*.]

charlotte *shar'lət, n* a dish of cooked apple or the like, covered with crumbs a kind of tart containing fruit.— **charlotte russe** (*rus*) a custard or cream enclosed in a kind of sponge-cake [From the name.]

charm *charm, n.* a spell: something thought to possess occult power, as an amulet, a metrical form of words, etc · an amulet, etc : a trinket: power of fascination: attractiveness. (in *pl.*) personal attractions: that which can please irresistibly: in particle physics, the quantum number used to account for the unusual behaviour of certain elementary particles.—*v.t* to influence by a charm: to subdue by secret influence: to enchant: to delight: to allure.—*adj.* **charmed** bewitched: delighted protected as by a special charm.—*n.* **charm'er**.—*adjs.* **charm'ful** abounding in charms; **charm'ing** highly pleasing: delightful: fascinating —*adv.* **charm'ingly**.—*adj* **charm'less**.—*adv.* **charm'lessly**. [Fr. *charme*—L. *carmen*, a song]

Charon *kā'rən, n.* in Greek mythology, the ferryman who rowed the shades of the dead across the river Styx.

charqui *char'kē, n.* beef cut into long strips and dried in the sun—jerked beef. [Quechua]

charr. Same as **char¹**.

chart *chart, n.* a marine map, exhibiting part of a sea or other water, with the islands, coasts, soundings, currents, etc . an outline-map, curve, or a tabular statement giving information of any kind: (usu. in *pl.*) the lists of the ten, twenty, etc most popular records, i e. those which have sold the most copies, each week.— *v.t.* to map.—*ns.* **chart'ist** one who makes and/or studies charts of past performances, esp. of stocks and shares, with a view to forecasting future trends; **chart'ism**.—*adj* **chart'less**.—**chart'house, chart'-room** the room in a ship where charts are kept. [O.Fr. *charte*—L *ch*(*a*)*rta*, a paper—Gr. *chartēs*.]

charter *chart'ər, n.* any formal writing in evidence of a grant, contract, or other transactions, conferring or confirming titles, rights, or privileges, or the like: the formal deed by which a sovereign guarantees the rights and privileges of his subjects: a document creating a borough or other corporation: a patent: grant.—*v.t.* to establish by charter: to let or hire, as a ship, on contract.—*adj.* hired, as *charter plane*: made in a hired aeroplane, as *charter flight.*—*n.* chart'erer.—*adj.* chart'ered granted or protected by a charter: privileged: licensed: hired by contract.—chartered accountant, engineer, surveyor, etc. one qualified under the regulations of the relevant institute or professional body which has a royal charter; chartered company a trading company acting under a charter from the crown. [O.Fr. *chartre*—L. *cartula*, *c(h)arta* —Gr. *chartēs*, a sheet of paper]

Charterhouse *chart'ar-hows*, *n.* a Carthusian monastery. the famous hospital and school instituted in London in 1611, on the site of a Carthusian monastery.—*n.* Chartreuse (*shar-trœz'*) a Carthusian monastery, esp. the original one, La Grande Chartreuse near Grenoble in France: a famous liqueur, usu. green, or yellow, long manufactured there by the monks from aromatic herbs and brandy. [See Carthusian.]

Chartism *chart'izm*, *n.* a movement in Great Britain for the extension of political power to the working-classes.—*n.* Chart'ist.—Also *adj.* [See charta.]

chartist, chartism. See Chart.

chartography *kàr-tog'ra-fi*. Same as cartography.

Chartreuse. See Charterhouse.

chartulary *kär'tū-lar-i*. Same as cartulary.

chary *chā'ri*, *adj.* cautious: wary (of doing, saying, giving, etc.).—*adv.* chār'ily.—*n.* chār'iness. [O.E. *cearig—cearu*, care.]

Charybdis *ka-rib'dis*, *n.* in the Odyssey a dangerous monster that dwelt under a rock, later a whirlpool on the Sicilian side of the Straits of Messina—with Scylla providing a proverbial alternative of evil or disaster.

chase[1] *chās*, *v.t.* to pursue: to hunt: to seek: to drive away: to put to flight.—*v.i.* (*coll.*) to hurry (about, around, after).—*n.* pursuit: a hunting.—*n.* chas'er a pursuer: a hunter: a horse for steeplechasing: a cooling drink after spirits.—beasts of chase wild beasts that are hunted generally; give chase to set off in pursuit, go and chase yourself (*slang*) go away, clear out; wild-goose chase any foolish or profitless pursuit of the unattainable. [O.Fr. *chacier*, *chasser*—L. *captāre*, freq. of *capēre*, to take.]

chase[2] *chās*, *v.t* to enchase, to decorate by engraving.—*ns.* chas'er; chas'ing the art of engraving on the outside of raised metal work: the art of cutting the threads of screws. [Short for enchase.]

Chasid, Chasidic, etc. See Hasid.

chasm *kaz'am*, *n.* a yawning or gaping hollow: a gap or opening.—*adjs.* chas'med; chasmic (*kaz'mik*), chas'my. [Gr. *chasma*, from *chainein*, to gape; cf. chaos.]

chasse *shas*, *n.* a dram or liqueur taken after coffee.— Also chasse-café'. [Fr. *chasser*, to chase.]

chassé *shas'ā*, *n.* a gliding step in dancing.—*v.i.* to make such a step. [Fr.]

chasseur *shas-œr'*, *n.* a hunter or huntsman: one of a select body of French light infantry or cavalry: a liveried attendant. [Fr.,—*chasser*, to hunt; see chase[1].]

Chassid, Chassidic, etc. See Hasid.

chassis *shas'ē*, *-i*, *n.* the frame, wheels, and machinery of a motor-car: an aeroplane's landing-carriage:—*pl.* chassis (*shas'ēz*, *-iz*). [Fr. *chassis*, frame.]

chaste *chāst*, *adj.* sexually virtuous: modest: refined and pure in taste and style.—*adv.* chaste'ly.—*v.t.* chasten (*chās'n*) to free from faults by punishing: hence, to punish: to purify or refine: to restrain or

moderate.—*p adj* chas'tened purified: modest: tempered.—*ns.* chas'tener; chaste'ness; chas'tenment.—*v.t.* chastise (*chas-tīz'*) to inflict punishment upon for the purpose of correction: to reduce to order or to obedience.—*adj.* chastis'able.—*ns.* chastisement (*chas'tiz-mant*); chastity (*chas'ti-ti*) sexual purity: virginity—chastity belt a device said to have been worn by e g. wives of absent crusaders, to prevent their having sexual intercourse. a device made in modern times according to its supposed design.—Also fig [O Fr *chaste*—L. *castus*, pure.]

chasuble *chaz'* or *chas'ū-bl*, *n.* a sleeveless vestment worn by the priest while celebrating mass [Fr.— L.L *casubula*—L. *casula*, dim. of L. *casa*, a hut.]

chat[1] *chat*, *v.i.* to talk easily or familiarly.—*v.t* (often with *up*) to talk to informally but with a purpose, e.g. in order to cajole:—*pr.p.* chatt'ing; *pa.t.* and *pa.p.* chatt'ed.—*n.* familiar, easy talk.—*n.* chatt'iness.—*adj* chatt'y given or inclined to chat: of the nature of chat.—chat'-show (*coll.*) a radio or television programme in which invited personalities talk informally with their host.—Also talk'-show. [From chatter.]

chat[2] *chat*, *n.* a genus of small birds in the thrush family, including the stonechat. [From the sound of their voice.]

château *shā'tō*, *n.* a castle: a great country-seat, esp in France: a vineyard estate around a castle, esp. in Bordeaux:—*pl.* chât'eaux (*-tōz*)—*ns.* châtelain (*shat'a-lē*) a castellan; chât'elaine (*-len*) a female castellan: an ornamental bunch of short chains bearing keys, scissors, etc., attached to the waist-belt: a similar thing in miniature attached to the watch-chain [Fr (O.Fr. *chastel*)—L. *castellum*, dim. of *castrum*, a fort.]

chattel *chat'l*, *n.* any kind of property which is not freehold.—goods and chattels all corporeal movables [O.Fr *chatel*—L.L. *captāle*—L *capitāle*, etc., property, goods.]

chatter *chat'ar*, *v.i.* to talk idly or rapidly: (of birds) to utter a succession of rapid short notes: to sound as the teeth when one shivers.—*n.* noise like that made by a magpie, or by the striking together of the teeth: idle talk.—*ns.* chatt'erer; chatt'ering.—chatt'erbox one who talks or chatters incessantly [From the sound.]

chatty. See chat[1].

Chaucerian *cho-sē'ri-an*, *adj.* like or pertaining to *Chaucer*—*n.* a student or follower of Chaucer.—*n.* Chau'cerism anything characteristic of Chaucer.

chaudfroid *shō-frwa*, *n.* a jellied sauce, or a dish, e.g. of chicken, including it. [Fr , (*lit.*) hot-cold]

chauffeur *shō'far*, *-fœr'*, *n.* one employed to drive a motor-car:—*fem.* chauffeuse (*-fœz'*). [Fr., stoker.]

chauvinism *shō'vin-izm*, *n.* an absurdly extravagant pride in one's country, with a corresponding contempt for foreign nations: extravagant attachment to any group, place, cause, etc —*ns.* chau'vin; chau'vinist.—*adjs* chau'vinist; chauvinist'ic. [From Nicolas *Chauvin*, an ardent veteran of Napoleon's.]

cheap *chēp*, low in price: charging low prices: of a low price in relation to the value: easily obtained: of small value, or so reckoned: paltry: inferior: vulgar.—Also *adv.*—*v.t.* cheap'en to make cheap, to lower the price of: to lower the reputation of: to beat down the price of.—*n.* cheap'ener.—*adv.* cheap'ly.—*n* cheap'ness. —cheap'-jack a travelling hawker who professes to give great bargains—*adj.* inferior, of bad quality — cheap labour labour paid at a poor rate, cheap'skate (*slang*) a miserly or despicable person.—cheap and nasty offensively inferior and of low value; dirt cheap ridiculously cheap; feel cheap to have a sense of inferiority and humiliation; on the cheap cheap or cheaply. [O.E. *cēap*, price, a bargain, *ceapian*; Ó N. *kaupa*, Ger *kaufen*, to buy.]

cheat *chēt, n.* a fraud: a deception: a card-game in which deception is allowed: one who cheats.—*v.t.* to deceive, defraud, impose upon.—*v.t.* to practise deceit.—*ns.* **cheat'er**; **cheat'ery** (*coll.*) cheating. [escheat.]

check *chek, v.t.* to bring to a stop: to restrain or hinder: to rebuke: to control by comparison: to verify: to punch (as a ticket): to nip, pinch, crush, as by biting or shutting to deposit or receive in exchange for a check: to place in check at chess: to mark with a pattern of crossing lines.—*v.t.* to come to a stop: to make investigations.—*n.* a position in chess when one party obliges the other either to move or guard his king: anything that checks: a sudden stop, repulse, or rebuff: restraint: control: a rebuke: a mark put against items in a list: an order for money (usually written **cheque** except in U.S.): a means of verification or testing: a restaurant bill: a counter used in games at cards (hence *pass in one's checks* = to die): a pattern of cross lines forming small squares, as in a chessboard: any fabric woven with such a pattern.—*adj.* divided into small squares by crossing lines.—*n.* **check'er** one who hinders, rebukes, or scrutinises: (in *pl.*; *U.S.*) the game of draughts.—**check digit** (*comput.*) a digit carried in computer processes to discover errors, check accuracy, etc.; **check'er-board** a checked board on which checkers or draughts is played; **check'list** a list for verification purposes: a comprehensive list: an inventory; **check'mate** in chess, a check given to the adversary's king when in a position in which it can neither be protected nor moved out of check, so that the game is finished: defeat.—*v.t.* in chess, to put in checkmate: to defeat. —**check'-out** the cash-desk where one pays for goods bought in a supermarket, etc.: the act of checking out (see below); **check'point** a place where an official check of documents, etc. is made; **check'-rein** a strap hindering a horse from lowering its head; **check'-up** a testing scrutiny: one of a series of regular medical examinations; **check'-weigh'er, -weigh'man** one who on the part of the men checks the weight of coal sent up to the pit-mouth.—**check in, out** to record one's arrival or departure from work: to perform the necessary business at a hotel office, airport, etc., on arriving, or leaving (*ns.* **check'-in, check'-out**); **check out** (*coll.*) to test, examine, investigate (*n.* **check'-out**); **check up** to investigate: to examine and test (often with *on*).—**hold, keep, in check** to restrain, keep back. [O.Fr. *eschec, eschac,* through Ar. from Pers *shāh,* king, checkmate being O.Fr. *eschec mat*—Ar. *shāh māt(a),* the king is dead.]

checker. See check; also under cheque.

Cheddar *ched'ər, n.* a kind of cheese first made at *Cheddar* in Somerset.

cheek *chēk, n.* the side of the face below the eye, the fleshy lateral wall of the mouth: effrontery, impudence (*coll.*): a side-post of a door, window, etc.: (*coll.*) a buttock.—*v.t.* (*coll.*) to address insolently.—*adv.* **cheek'ily.**—*adj.* **cheek'y** (*coll.*) rude: saucy.—**cheek'-bone** the bone above the cheek; **cheek'-pouch** a dilatation of the cheek, forming a bag, as in monkeys, etc.; **cheek'-tooth** a molar tooth.— **cheek by jowl** side by side. [O.E. *cēce, cēace,* cheek, jaw.]

cheep *chēp, v.t.* to chirp, as a young bird.—*n.* a sound of cheeping. [Imit.]

cheer *chēr, n.* disposition, frame of mind (with *good,* etc.): joy: a shout of approval or welcome: entertainment: fare, food.—*v.t.* to comfort: to encourage: to applaud.—*v.i.* to shout encouragement or applause. —*n.* **cheer'er.**—*adj.* **cheer'ful** in, of, promoting, or accompanied by good spirits.—*adv.* **cheer'fully.**—*n.* **cheer'fulness.**—*adv.* **cheer'ily.**—*n.* **cheer'iness.**—

interjs. **cheerio', cheer'o** a bright informal goodbye: —*adj.* **cheer'less** comfortless.—*interj.* **cheers!** (*coll.*) good health! (used when drinking a toast): thank you!: cheerio, goodbye!—*adj.* **cheer'y** cheerful: promoting cheerfulness.—**cheer'-leader** (esp. *U.S.*) one who directs organised cheering, as at team games.— **cheer up** (*coll.*) to make, or become, more cheerful. [O.Fr *chiere,* face—L.L. *cara,* the face.]

cheese[1] *chēz, n.* a wholesome article of food, made from the curd of milk coagulated by rennet, separated from the whey, and pressed into a solid mass: a compressed cake of various nature: the flattened cheese-shaped bowl used in skittles.—*n.* **chees'iness.** —*adj.* **chees'y** having the nature of cheese.—**cheese's board** a flat wooden board on which cheese is served; **cheese'burger** a hamburger cooked with cheese on top of it; **cheese'cake** a kind of cake having a base of pastry or biscuit crumbs, with a filling of cream cheese, sugar, eggs, flavouring, etc.: female shapely charms (*slang*); **cheese'cloth** a loose-woven cloth suitable for pressing cheeses: a stronger type of loosely-woven cotton cloth used for making shirts, etc.; **cheese'-monger** a dealer in cheese; **cheese'-paring** a very thin man: parsimony.—*adj.* mean and parsimonious.—**cheese'-press** a machine in which curds for cheese are pressed; **cheese straw** a long thin biscuit flavoured with cheese; **cheese'-wring** a cheese-press. —**green cheese** cheese not yet dried; **hard cheese** (*slang*) hard luck. [O.E. *cēse, cȳse,* curdled milk— L. *cāseus.*]

cheese[2] *chēz, n.* anything of excellent quality.—**big cheese** (*slang*) a person of importance. [Prob. Pers. and Hindi *chīz,* thing.]

cheese[3] *chēz, v.t.* (*slang*) in the phrases **cheese it** to stop, have done, run off; **cheesed off** (also **cheesed**) fed up.

cheetah *chē'tə, n.* an Eastern animal like the leopard, used in hunting. [Hindi *cītā*—Sans. *citraka, citrakāya,* having a speckled body.]

chef *shef, n.* a usu. male cook, esp. a head-cook (in full **chef de cuisine** (*də kwē-zēn*) the head of a kitchen).— **chef d'œuvre** (*shā-dœ-vr'*), a masterpiece:—*pl.* **chefs d'œuvre** (*shā-*). [Fr. head, chief; see **chief.**]

cheiro- *kī'rō-, kī-ro'-,* (see also **chiro-**) in composition, hand.—*ns.* **cheirog'nomy, chirog'nomy** palmistry; **ch(e)irog'raphy** handwriting, penmanship; **ch(e)i'romancy** (*-man-si*) fortune-telling by the hand; **ch(e)irop'teran** a member of the **Ch(e)irop'tera,** the order of bats. [Gr. *cheir,* hand.]

chela[1] *kē'lə, n.* the prehensile claw of an arthropod:— *pl.* **chē'lae** (*-ē*).—*adj.* **chē'late.**—*n.* a co-ordination compound (e.g. haemoglobin) in which a central metallic ion is attached to an organic molecule at two or more positions.—*v.i.* to form a chelate.—*ns.* **chēlā'tion; chēlā'tor.**—*adj.* **chēlif'erous** having a chela or chelae.—**chelation therapy** the treatment of heavy metal (e.g. lead) poisoning or certain other diseases by substances (**chelating agents**) which combine chemically with the toxic substances and render them harmless. [Latinised from Gr. *chēlē.*]

chela[2] *chā'lə, n.* a novice in Buddhism: a disciple of a religious teacher or leader.—*n.* **che'laship.** [Hindi *celā,* servant, disciple.]

chelicera *kē-lis'ə-rə, n.* a biting appendage in Arachnida:—*pl* **chēlic'erae** (*-rē*). [Gr *chēlē,* a crab's claw, *keras,* horn.]

cheliferous. See **chela.**

cheloid. See **keloid.**

Chelonia *ki-lō'ni-ə, n.* an order of reptiles with horny shell and horny beak, tortoises and turtles.—*adj.* and *n.* **chelō'nian.** [Gr. *chelōnē,* a tortoise.]

Chelsea *chel'sē, n.* a district of London.—**Chelsea bun** a rolled bun filled with currants and raisins; **Chelsea**

pensioner an elderly, often disabled, ex-soldier, connected with the Chelsea Royal Hospital.

chemic, etc. See under **chemistry.**

chemin de fer *shə-mē-də-fer',* *n* a variety of baccarat [Fr railway]

chemise *shə-mēz',* *n* a woman's shirt, a smock or straight dress. [Fr. *chemise*—L.L *camisia,* a nightgown, surplice]

chemistry *kem'is-tri,* *n.* the science of the properties of substances elementary and compound, and the laws of their combination and action one upon another.— *adjs* **chemiat'ric** iatrochemical; **chem'ic** chemical.— *v t.* to treat with bleaching powder:—*pr.p.* **chem'icking;** *pa t.* and *pa.p.* **chem'icked.**—*adj.* **chem'ical** relating to chemistry: versed in or studying chemistry.—*n.* a substance obtained by chemical means or used in chemical operations.—*adv.* **chem'ically.**—*ns* **chem'ism** chemical action; **chem'ist** one skilled in chemistry: a manufacturer of or dealer in chemicals and drugs: a pharmacist, (the following words in **chemo-** also *kē-,* esp. in US.) **chemōpsychi'atry** treatment of mental illness by drugs; **chemōrecep'tor** a sensory nerve-ending, receiving a chemical stimulus, **chemōsyn'thesis** (*bot.*) the formation of organic material by some bacteria by means of energy derived from chemical changes; **chemōtherapeu'tics** (*n. sing.*), **chemōther'apy** treatment of a disease by means of a chemical compound. **chemical closet, toilet** a kind of toilet containing deodorising and liquefying chemicals, used when running water is not available; **chemical engineering** design, construction, and operation of chemical plant and works, esp. in industrial chemistry; **chemical warfare** warfare involving the use of irritating or asphyxiating gases, oil flames, etc [See **alchemy.**]

chenille *shə-nēl',* *n.* a thick, velvety cord of silk or wool resembling a woolly caterpillar: a velvet-like material used for table-covers, etc. [Fr. *chenille,* caterpillar —L. *canicula,* a hairy little dog, *canis,* a dog.]

cheong-sam *chong'sam',* *n.* a tight-fitting high-necked dress with slits at the sides. [Chin.]

cheque, in U.S. **check,** *chek,* *n.* a money order on a banker —*n.* **cheq'uer** alternation of colours, as on a chess-board (see also **checker**)—*v.t.* to mark in squares of different colours: to variegate: to interrupt —*adjs.* **cheq'uered, check'ered** variegated, like a chessboard: varying in character: eventful, with alternations of good and bad fortune.—*adv.* **cheq'uerwise.** —**cheque'-book** a book of cheque forms; **cheque card** a card issued by a bank to a client, undertaking payment of cheques up to a certain limit; **chequered flag** the black and white flag shown to the winner and subsequent finishers in a motor race; **cheq'uer-work** any pattern having alternating squares of different colours.—**blank cheque** a cheque signed by the drawer without having the amount indicated· concession of power without limit (*fig.*); **cheque-book journalism** news, articles, etc., based on information bought, usu at a high price; **crossed cheque** an ordinary cheque with two transverse lines drawn across it, which have the effect of making it payable only through a bank account. [See **check.**]

cherish *cher'ish,* *v.t.* to protect and treat with affection: to nurture, nurse: to entertain in the mind.—*n.* **cher'ishment.** [Fr *chérir, chérissant—cher,* dear— L. *cārus.*]

chernozem *chûr'nō-zem,* *n.* a very fertile soil of subhumid steppe, consisting of a dark topsoil over a lighter calcareous layer. [Russ., black earth]

Cherokee *cher'ə-kē,* *n.* (a member of) a tribe of Iroquoian Indians: the language of the Cherokee

cheroot *shə-rōōt',* *n* a cigar not pointed at either end. [Fr. *cheroute,* Tamil *shuruttu,* a roll.]

cherry *cher'i,* *n.* a small stone-fruit: the tree that bears it: extended to many fruits resembling it in some way. —*adj.* like a cherry in colour: ruddy.—**cherr'y-bob'** in children's games, two cherries joined by the stalks; **cherry brandy** a liqueur made by steeping Morello cherries in brandy; **cherr'y-lau'rel** a species of cherry with evergreen laurel-like leaves; **cherr'y-pie'** a pie made of cherries. the common heliotrope; **cherr'y-plum** a plum of flavour approaching a cherry; **cherr'y-stone** the hard endocarp of the cherry.—**have or take two bites or a second bite at the cherry** (*coll.*) to have a second chance, opportunity [O.E. *ciris*—L. *cerasus*—Gr. *kerasos,* a cherry-tree.]

chert *chûrt,* *n.* a compact flinty chalcedony.

cherub *cher'əb,* *n.* a winged creature with human face, represented as associated with Jehovah· a celestial spirit: a chubby-faced person, esp. a child:—*pl.* **cher'ubs, cher'ubim** (*-ə, -ū, -bim*), **cher'ubims**—*adjs.* **cherubic** (*-ōō'bik*), **-al, cherubim'ic** angelic.—*adv.* **cheru'bically.** [Heb. *k'rub,* pl. *k'rubim.*]

chervil *chûr'vil,* *n.* an umbelliferous plant (*Anthriscus cerefolium*) cultivated as ·a pot-herb: also other species of Anthriscus (*common, wild,* and *rough cher- vil*): extended to sweet cicely (*sweet chervil*). [O.E. *cerfille*—L. *caerefolium*—Gr. *chairephyllon.*]

chess *ches,* *n.* a game of skill for two, played with figures or men of different kinds which are moved on a chequered board.—**chess'board** the board on which chess is played: a chequered design; **chess'man.** [O.Fr. *eschès*—Pers. *shāh,* a king.]

chessel *ches'l,* *n.* a cheese mould. [**cheese**[1].]

chest *chest,* *n.* a large strong box: the part of the body between the neck and the abdomen, the thorax: a treasury: a chestful.—*adj.* **chest'ed** having a chest: placed in a chest.—*n.* **chest'ful** enough to fill a chest. —*adj* **chest'y** of the quality of the chest-voice: suggestive of disease of the chest (*coll.*): self-important (*slang*) —**chest'-note** in singing or speaking, a deep note; **chest'-protec'tor** a covering to keep the chest warm; **chest'-register, -tone, -voice** the lowest register of the voice—**chest of drawers** a case in which drawers slide; **off one's chest** (*coll.*) off one's mind: admitted, stated, declared openly. [O E. *cyst*—L. *cista*—Gr. *kistē.*]

chesterfield *chest'ər-fēld,* *n.* a long overcoat: a heavily padded sofa. [Lord *Chesterfield.*]

chestnut *ches'nut,* *n.* a tree of genus Castanea, esp. the *Spanish* or *Sweet Chestnut*: its edible nut, encased (three together) in a prickly husk: its hard timber: the **horse-chestnut** (*Aesculus hippocastanum*), its fruit or nut: a chestnut horse: a stale joke or cliché (*slang*).— *adj* of chestnut colour, reddish-brown.—**pull the chestnuts out of the fire** to take control and rescue someone from a difficult situation. [O.Fr. *chastaigne* —L. *castanea*—perh. from *Castana,* in Thessaly.]

chevalet *shə-va'lā, she',* *n.* the bridge of a stringed instrument (*mus.*). [Fr. dim. of *cheval,* a horse.]

cheval-glass *shə-val'glas,* *n.* a large glass or mirror supported on a frame [Fr. *cheval,* horse, stand.]

chevalier *shev-ə-lēr',* *n.* a cavalier: a knight: a gallant. [Fr.,—L.L. *cabqllārius*—L. *caballus,* a horse.]

cheven *chev'ən,* *n.* the chub.—Also **chev'in.** [Fr. *chevin, chevanne.*]

cheverel, -il *chev'ər-əl,* *n.* a kid: soft, flexible kidskin leather.—*adj.* like kid leather, pliable. [Fr. *chevreau, chevrette,* a kid—*chèvre*; L. *capra,* a she-goat.]

chevin. See **cheven.**

Cheviot *chē'vi-ət* (or *chev'i-ət*), *n.* a hardy breed of short-woolled sheep reared on the *Cheviot* Hills: a cloth made from their wool.

chevron *shev'rən,* *n.* a rafter: the representation of two rafters of a house meeting at the top (*her.*): a V-shaped band on the sleeve, a mark of non-commissioned rank or (in army and R A F , inverted) of long service and good conduct —*adj.* **chev'roned.**— **chevron board** a road sign consisting of a line of horizontal V-shapes, used to indicate a sharp change in direction. [Fr. *chevron*, rafter—L. *capreolus*, dim. of *caper*, a goat]

chevrotain *shev'rō-tān*, or *-tan*, *n.* a mouse-deer, any member of an Old World tropical family of small deerlike animals. [Fr., dim. of *chèvre*—L *capra*, she-goat.]

chevy *chev'ı*, **chiv(v)y** *chiv'ı*, *ns.* a hunting cry. a pursuit.—*v.t* to chase. (very often **chivv'y**) to harass [Perh from the Border ballad of battle, *Chevy Chase*.]

chew *choō*, *v t.* to bruise and grind with the teeth: to masticate to meditate, reflect (*fig*).—*n.* the action of chewing. a quid of tobacco.—*adj.* **chew'y** soft, able to be chewed, like toffee —**chew'ing-gum** a preparation made from chicle gum, produced by the sapodilla plum tree, sweetened and flavoured.— **chew the cud** of cows, etc , to masticate a second time food that has already been swallowed and passed into the first stomach: to ruminate in thought (*fig* , also **chew over**); **chew the rag, the fat** (*slang*) to keep on arguing the point. [O.E. *cēowan*; cf. **jaw.**]

chez *shā*, *prep* at the home or establishment of. [Fr.]
chi *kī, hhē, n* the twenty-second letter (X, χ) of the Greek alphabet, representing an aspirated *k* sound. [Gr. *chei, chī*.]

Chianti *kē-an'tı, -an', It. kyan'tē, n* a red (or white) wine of Tuscany. [*Chianti* Mountains.]

chiaroscuro *kyar-ō-skoō'rō, n* management of light and shade in a picture. a monochrome painting· the effect of light and shade (also *fig.*).—pl **chiaroscu'ros.**

chiasm *kī'azm*, (*anat*) *n.* a decussation or intersection, esp that of the optic nerves —Also **chias'ma.**—*n* **chias'mus** (*rhet*) contrast by parallelism in reverse order, as *Do not live to eat, but eat to live.*—*adj* **chias'tic.** [Gr. *chiasma*, a cross-shaped mark, *chiastos*, laid crosswise, like the Greek letter X (*chi, chei*)]

chibouk, chibouque *chi-boōk', n.* a long straight-stemmed Turkish pipe. [Turk *chibūk*.]

chic *shēk, n* style, elegance· artistic skill —*adj* having chic: smart and fashionable —*adv* **chic'ly.** [Fr.]

chicane *shi-kān', n* a trick or artifice a barrier or obstacle in motor-racing, etc —*ns* **chica'nery** trickery or artifice, esp in legal proceedings quibbling; **chica'ning** quibbling [Fr. *chicane*, sharp practice at law.]

chicano *chi-ka'nō, shi-, n* (*U.S* , sometimes considered *derog.*, also with *cap*) an American of Mexican descent —*pl* **chica'nos.**—Also *adj.* [Sp *mejicano*, Mexican]

chichi, chi-chi *shē'shē, chē'chē, adj.* pretentious: fussy, precious, affected· stylish, chic, self-consciously fashionable.—*n.* something that is, or quality of being, chichi [Fr.]

chick *chik, n* the young of fowls, esp of the hen. a child, as a term of endearment· a girl or young woman (*slang*).—*n.* **chick'en** the young of birds, esp. of the domestic fowl the flesh of a fowl a youthful person, esp a girl· a faint-hearted person (*coll*) a type of sometimes competitive game in which one dares to perform some physically dangerous activity (*coll*) — *adj* (*coll.*) cowardly, frightened —*v.i* (*coll*) to show fear —*n* **chick'ling** a little chicken —**chick'-a- biddy, chick'-a-didd'le** terms of endearment addressed to children; **chick'en-feed** poultry food small change (*coll.*) something of little value (*coll*) —*adj.* **chick'en-heart'ed,** -liv'ered timid, cowardly — **chick'en-pox** a contagious febrile disease, chiefly of children, not unlike a mild form of smallpox.

chick'en-run a run for hens, **chick'en-wire** wire-netting, **chick'-pea** see **chickling'; chick'weed** one of the commonest of weeds, much relished by fowls and cagebirds.—**chicken-and-egg situation** one in which it is impossible to tell which is the cause and which the effect; **chicken out** (*coll* ; often with *of*) to desert, quit, through cowardice. [O E. *cicen*]

chickadee *chik-ə-dē', n* an American titmouse [From its note]

chickling' *chick'ling, n.* a species of pea (also **chickling vetch**) —**chick'-pea** gram, a plant of the pea family its edible seed [Fr. *chiche*—L. *cicer*, chick-pea.]

chickling². See **chick.**

chicle *chik'l, chik'li, n* the gum of the sapodilla tree, chewing-gum [Sp ,—Mex.]

chicly. See chic.

chicory *chik'ə-rı, n* a blue-flowered composite: its carrot-like root (ground to mix with coffee). [Fr. *chicorée*—L *cichorēum*—Gr. *kichorion*.]

chide *chīd, v.t* to scold, rebuke, reprove by words.— *v.t* to make a snarling, murmuring sound, as a dog or trumpet:—*pr.p* **chid'ing;** *pa.t.* **chid,** sometimes **chid'ed;** *pa.p.* **chid, chidd'en,** sometimes **chid'ed.**—*n.* **chid'ing** scolding. [O.E. *cidan*.]

chief *chēf, adj.* head. principal, highest, first: outstanding, important (with *compar.* **chief'er,** *superl* **chief'est**).—*adv.* chiefly.—*n.* a head or principal person. a leader. the principal part or top of anything: the greater part: the upper part, generally one-third of the area of the shield (*her.*).—*ns.* **chief'dom, chief'ship** state of being chief: sovereignty; **chief'ess** a female chief —*adj.* **chief'less** without a chief or leader —*n* **chief'ling.**—*adv* **chief'ly** in the first place· principally for the most part —*ns* **chief'- tain** the head of a clan: a leader or commander:— *fem.* **chief'tainess; chief'taincy, chief'tainry; chief'tainship.**—**Chief Constable** (in Britain) an officer commanding the police force in an administrative area.— **-in-chief** in composition, at the head, as *commander-in-chief*.—**chief of staff** (*mil.*) a senior staff officer (with *cap.*) the senior officer of each of the armed forces, in chief borne in the upper part of the shield (*her.*)· of a tenure, held directly from the sovereign most importantly [Fr *chef*—L *caput*, the head.]

chiff-chaff *chif'-chaf, n* a small warbler. [Imit]
chiffon *shif'on, shē'fš, n* (in *pl.*) trimmings, or other adornments: a thin fine clothing fabric of silk, nylon, etc —*n.* **chiffonier** (*shif-ən-ēr'*) an ornamental cabinet. [Fr , rag, adornment—*chiffe*, rag]

chignon *shē'nyš, n* a fold or roll of hair worn on the back of the head and neck [Fr]

chigoe *chig'ō*, **chigre, chigger** *chig'ər, ns.* a West Indian and South American flea which buries itself, esp. beneath the toe-nails: the larva of an American harvestmite that burrows in the skin.—Also **jigg'er.** [W Indian name]

chihuahua *chi-wa'wa, n* a very small dog (2 lb or so) with big eyes and pointed ears [*Chihuahua* in Mexico]

chilblain *chil'blān, n* a painful red swelling, esp on hands and feet in cold weather. [chill and **blain.**]

child *chīld, n.* a very young person (up to the age of sixteen for the purpose of some acts of parliament, under fourteen in criminal law) a son or daughter one standing in a relationship of adoption or origin (to a person, place, etc) disciple· (in *pl*) offspring. (in *pl*) descendants (in *pl*) inhabitants:—*pl* **children** (*chil'drən*)—*n* **child'hood** the state of being a child. the time of being a child —*adj* **child'ish** of or like a child silly· trifling —*adv* **child'ishly.**—*n* **child'ishness** what is natural to a child puerility — *adjs* **child'less** without children; **child'like** like a

child: becoming a child· docile· innocent.—
child'bearing the act of bringing forth children, **child benefit** an allowance granted by the government to parents for children; **child'birth** the giving birth to a child, **child'minder** a person, usu with little training, officially recognised as being fit to look after children —*adjs* **child'-proof, -resis'tant** not able to be damaged, opened, worked, etc , by a child — **child's play** something very easy to do; **child'-study** the psychology and physiology of children; **child welfare** health and well-being of young children as an object of systematic social work —**second childhood** the childishness of old age, **with child** pregnant [O E *cild*, pl *cild*, later, *cildru, -ra*]

Childermas *chil'dər-məs, n* Innocents' Day, a festival (Dec 28) to commemorate the slaying of the children by Herod [O E *cildra*, gen pl of *cild*, child, *mæsse*, mass]

Chile *chil'i, adj* of Chile —*n* and *adj* **Chil'ean** (*obs* **Chil'ian**).—**Chile(an)** pine the monkey-puzzle; **Chile saltpetre** sodium nitrate.

chili, chile *chil'i* Variant forms of **chilli.**

chiliad *kil'i-ad, n.* the number 1000: 1000 of anything (e g years) —*ns* **chiliarch** (*kil'i-ark*) a leader or commander of a thousand men; **chil'iarchy** the position of chiliarch, **chil'iasm** the doctrine that Christ will reign bodily upon the earth for 1000 years; **chil'iast** one who holds this opinion· one who believes in a coming happier time on earth —*adj* **chilias'tic.** [Gr *chilias, -ados—chilioi*, 1000.]

chill *chil, n* coldness· a cold that causes shivering anything that damps or disheartens —*adj* shivering with cold· slightly cold· opposite of *cordial* —*v i.* to grow cold —*v.t.* to make chill or cold. to cool: to preserve by cold to injure with cold —*adj* **chilled** made cold· preserved by cold, as beef —*adv* **chill'ily.—***n.* **chill'iness.—***n.* and *adj.* **chill'ing.—***n* **chill'ness.—***adj.* **chill'y** cold: chilling: sensitive to cold —**chill factor** the degree by which weather conditions, e.g. wind, increase the effect of low temperatures —**take the chill off** to warm slightly. [O E *cele, ciele*, cold; see **cold, cool.**]

chilli *chil'i, n* the pod of the capsicum, extremely pungent and stimulant, used in sauces, pickles, etc , and dried and ground to form Cayenne pepper —Also **chili, chile.—chilli con carne** (*kon kar'në*) a dish of minced meat, beans and chillis, originating in Mexico [Nahuatl]

chimb. See chime[2]

chime[1] *chim, n* a set of bells tuned in a scale: (often in *pl*) the ringing of such bells in succession a definite sequence of bell-like notes sounded as by a clock. the harmonious sound of bells or other musical instruments· agreement of sound or of relation: harmony rhyme· jingle —*v i* to sound a chime or in chime· to accord or agree· to jingle: to rhyme· to say words over mechanically —*v t* to strike, or cause to sound in chime: to indicate by chiming.—**chime in** to join in, in agreement [M.E *chimbe*, prob O Fr *cymbale—* L *cymbalum*, a cymbal.]

chime[2], chimb *chim, n.* the rim formed by the ends of the staves of a cask [Cog. with Ger *Kimme*, edge]

chimera, chimaera *ki-, ki-më'rə, n* (often with *cap*) a fabulous, fire-spouting monster, with a lion's head, a serpent's tail, and a goat's body· any idle or wild fancy: a picture of an animal having its parts made up of various animals· an organism made up of two genetically distinct tissues.—*adjs.* **chimeric** (*-mer'ik*), **-al** of the nature of a chimaera wild· fanciful —*adv* **chimer'ically.** [L ,—Gr *chimaira*, a she-goat]

chimney *chim'ni, n.* a passage for the escape of fumes, smoke, or heated air from a fireplace or furnace· a glass tube surrounding a lamp flame· a volcanic vent

a cleft in a rock-face just large enough for a mountaineer to enter and climb —**chim'ney-breast** the part of a wall that projects into a room and contains the fireplace and chimney; **chim'ney-can** a chimney-pot, **chim'ney-cor'ner, -nook** in old chimneys, the space between the fire and the side-wall of the fireplace: fireside, commonly spoken of as the place for the aged and infirm, **chim'ney-piece** a shelf over the fireplace, **chim'ney-pot** a cylindrical pipe at the top of a chimney; **chim'ney-stack** a group of chimneys carried up together, **chim'ney-stalk** a very tall chimney, **chim'ney-sweep, chim'ney-sweeper** one who sweeps or cleans chimneys; **chim'ney-top** the top of a chimney [Fr *cheminée—*L *caminus*, a furnace]

chimpanzee *chim-pən-zë', n* one of the African anthropoid apes:—often shortened to **chimp.** [West African]

chin *chin, n.* the jutting part of the face below the mouth —*adj* **chin'less** having a receding chin: upperclass and not very clever, esp in *chinless wonder* (*facet*) —**chin'strap** the strap on a helmet, etc that goes under the chin —*n* and *v i* **chin'wag** (*slang*) talk —(**keep one's) chin up!** (to) keep cheerful in a difficult situation. [O E *cin*]

china *chi'nə, n.* (orig **Chi'na-ware**) articles of porcelain brought from China in 16th cent. Chinese porcelain or, esp , Western imitation or version of it (*Cockney rhyming slang*) mate (from *china plate*) —*adj* of china: (*cap*) of, from, etc , China.—**china clay** fine white clay used in making porcelain, etc ; **Chi'naman** a Chinese (*derog*); **China tea** a kind of tea grown in China and smoke-cured; **Chi'natown** a Chinese quarter in a town —*n.* **Chinese** *chi-nēz'*, a native or citizen of China (*pl* **Chinese'**): the language of China —*adj.* (in names of commodities, sometimes without capital) of, concerning or relating, etc to China, its language or its people.—**Chinese checkers** a board game similar to draughts, **Chinese gooseberry** subtropical vine with edible fruit; **Chinese lantern** a paper lantern; **Chinese leaves** Chinese cabbage; **Chinese puzzle** a very difficult puzzle or problem [Prob. from the *Ch'in* dynasty, third cent B C]

chinch *chinch, n.* the bed-bug in America. [Sp *chinche—*L *cimex.*]

chincherinchee, chinkerinchee *ching'kə-rin-chē', chin-kə-rin'chē, n* a white-flowered S African plant of the star-of-Bethlehem genus —Also (*coll.*) **chinks.** [Said to be imitative of the flower-stalks rubbing together in the wind.]

chinchilla *chin-chil'ə, n* a small rodent of South America valued for its soft grey fur: the fur itself (with *cap*) a breed of rabbits, or of cats, with soft grey fur [Sp]

chin-chin *chin'chin', (coll) interj* hello or good-bye: good health[1] (as a toast) [Anglo-Chin —Chin *ts'ing ts'ing*]

chindit *chin'dit, n* a member of General Wingate's commando force in Burma during World War II [Burmese *chinthey*, a griffin, the force's badge]

chine[1] *chin, n* a piece of the backbone and adjoining parts (esp. of a pig) for cooking: a ridge crest —*v t.* to break the back of [O Fr *eschine*, prob from O H G *scina*, pin, thorn]

chine[2] *chin, n* a ravine [O E *cinu*, a cleft]

chiné *shē-nā', adj* mottled, with the pattern printed on the warp [Fr , dyed in a (supposedly) Chinese way]

Chinee, Chinese. See China.

chink[1] *chingk, n.* a cleft, a narrow opening.—*v.t.* to crack —*v.t* to fill up cracks —*adj.* **chink'y** full of chinks [Apparently formed upon M E. *chine*, a crack—O E *cinu*, a cleft]

chink² *chingk, n.* the clink, as of coins: money (*slang*).
—*v.t.* to give forth a sharp sound.—*v.t.* to clink together. [Imit.]

Chink *chingk,* **Chinkie, Chinky** *chingk'i,* (*coll. offensive*) *n.* and *adj.* Chinese. [China.]

chinkerinchee, chinks. See **chincherinchee.**

chino *chē'nō,* (*U.S.*) *n.* strong khaki-like twilled cotton: (in *pl.*) trousers made of it:—*pl.* **chi'nos.** [Amer.—Sp.]

chinoiserie *shē-nwa-z(ə)rē,* (Fr.) *n.* Chinese objects, decoration, behaviour, etc.

Chinook *chin-ōōk',* *n.* a warm dry wind blowing down the eastern side of the Rocky Mts, making winter grazing possible: also a warm moist wind from the Pacific.

chintz *chints, n.* a cotton printed generally in several colours on a white or light ground.—*adj.* **chintz'y** covered with, or like, chintz: cheap, gaudy. [Orig. pl.—Hindi *chīt,* spotted cotton-cloth.]

chip *chip, v.t.* to strike with small sharp cutting blows: to strike small pieces off the surface of (also with *at*): to remove by chipping (often with *away* or *off*): to slice or pare: to cut as with an adze: to chaff, tease (*coll.*) —*v.i.* to become chipped: to play a chip-shot: —*pr.p.* **chipp'ing;** *pa.t.* and *pa.p.* **chipped.**—*n.* an act of chipping: a piece chipped off, esp. a flattish fragment: a surface flaw: a thin slice of fruit, etc.: a potato-chip: a thin strip of wood, used for making boxes, baskets, etc.: a chip-basket: a small, flat piece of wood, plastic, etc. used to represent money in certain games: a minute piece of silicon or other semiconducting material on which one or more microcircuits can be printed (also **microchip, silicon chip**): in sport, a hit or kick which sends a ball high into the air over a short distance.—*adj.* **chipp'y** abounding in chips: dry as a chip.—*n.* **chips** (*slang*) a carpenter (also **chipp'y**). money.—*n.pl.* fried potato-chips (*coll.*).—**chip'-basket** a fruit basket of interwoven chips: a metal basket in which potato-chips are placed for frying; **chip'board** reconstructed wood made by consolidation of chips from woodland trimmings, workshop waste, etc., with added resin; **chip'-shot** (*golf*) a short lofted approach.—**chip in** to enter the game by putting chips on the table: to interpose: to pay part of the cost of something (*coll.*); **chip off** (orig. **of**) **the old block** one with the characteristics of his father; **chip on one's shoulder** a defiant manner, as if daring anyone to knock it off: readiness to take offence: bitterness, grievance; **have had one's chips** to have died· to have had one's chance; **when the chips are down** at a critical moment when it is too late to alter the situation. [M.E. *chippen;* M.L.G., M.Du. *kippen,* to hatch by chipping shell.]

chipmunk *chip'mungk, n.* a North American squirrel. [From Indian name.]

chipolata *chip-ə-lä'tə, n.* a small sausage, used as a garnish, etc. [Fr ,—It. *cipolla,* onion.]

Chippendale *chip'ən-dāl, adj.* applied to a style of furniture, after the name of a well-known cabinetmaker of the 18th century: also applied to a style of bookplates.

chipper *chip'ər, adj.* brisk and cheerful. [Perh. same word as Northern dial. *kipper,* lively.]

chirk *chûrk, v.i.* to chirp or squeak. [O.E. *cearcian,* to creak.]

chiro-. See **cheiro-.**

chiropodist *ki-rop'ə-dist,* older *ki-,* also *shi-, n.* one who treats minor ailments of the feet, e.g. corns, verrucas.—*adj.* **chiropō'dial.**—*n.* **chirop'ody.** [App. Gr. *chēir,* hand, and *pous, podos,* foot; but *cheiropodēs* means having chapped feet.]

chiropractic *ki-rə-prak'tik, n.* a method of healing concerned with disorders of the locomotor system, which relies upon the removal of nerve interference by manual adjustment of the spinal column: a chiropractor.—*n.* **chiroprac'tor** one who practises chiropractic. [Gr. *cheir,* hand, *prāktikos,* concerned with action—*prattein,* to do.]

chirp *chûrp, n.* the sharp thin sound of certain birds and insects.—*v.i.* to make such a sound: to talk in a cheerful and lively strain.—*v.t.* to urge by chirping. —*n.* **chirp'er** a little bird.—*adv.* **chirp'ily.**—*n.* **chirp'iness.**—*adjs.* **chirp'ing; chirp'y** lively: merry. [Imit.]

chirr *chûr, v.i.* to chirp like a cricket or grasshopper. [Imit.]

chirrup *chir'əp, v.i.* to chirp: to make a sound with the mouth to urge on a horse: to cheer up.—*adj.* **chirr'upy** cheerful. [Lengthened form of **chirp,** associated with **cheer up.**]

chisel *chiz'l, n.* a tool with the end bevelled to a cutting edge, in literature esp. the tool of the sculptor.—*v.t.* to cut, carve, etc. with a chisel: to cheat (*slang*):—*pr.p.* **chis'elling.** *pa.t.* and *pa.p.* **chis'elled.**—*adj.* **chis'elled** cut with a chisel: having sharp outlines, as cut by a chisel (*fig.*).—*n.* **chis'elling.** [O.Fr. *cisel*—L. *caedēre,* to cut.]

chit¹ *chit, n.* a short informal letter: a bill which one signs and pays at a later date, esp. in a club, service mess, etc.: an order or pass: testimonial.—Also **chitt'y.** [Hindi *citthī.*]

chit² *chit, n.* a child: a girl (*slightingly*).—*adjs.* **chitt'y; chitt'y-faced.** [Same as *kit,* a kitten.]

chitchat *chit'chat, n.* chatting or idle talk: prattle: gossip. [A reduplication of **chat¹.**]

chitin *ki'tin, n.* the substance which forms most of the hard parts of arthropods.—*adj.* **chi'tinous.** [Fr. *chitine*—Gr. *chitōn,* a tunic.]

chiton *ki'ton, n.* the ancient Greek tunic: (with *cap.*) a genus of marine molluscs with shell of movable plates. [Gr. *chitōn,* a tunic.]

chitterling *chit'ər-ling, n.* (also in *pl.*) the smaller intestines of a pig or other edible animal.

chiv *chiv, shiv,* (*slang*) *n.* and *v.t.* knife.—Also **shiv.** [From older *chive,* knife (*thieves' slang*) or perh. Romany *chiv,* blade.]

chivalry *shiv'əl-ri, n.* the usages and qualifications of chevaliers or knights: bravery and courtesy: the system of knighthood in feudal times and its social code.—*adjs.* **chivalric** (*-al'*), **chiv'alrous** pertaining to chivalry: bold: gallant.—*adv.* **chiv'alrously.**—*n.* **chiv'alrousness.** [Fr *chevalerie*—*cheval*—L.L. *caballus,* a horse.]

chive *chiv, n.* a herb like the leek and onion, with tufts of leaves (used in cooking) and clustered bulbs. [Fr. *cive*—L. *cēpa,* an onion.]

chivy, chivvy *chiv'i, n.* and *v.* See **chevy.**

chlamys *klam'is, n.* a short cloak for men: a purple cope:—*pl.* **chlam'ydes** (*-i-dēz*).—*adjs.* **chlam'ydate** (*zool.*) having a mantle; **chlamyd'eous** (*bot.*) having a perianth.—*ns.* **Chlamydōmō'nas** a genus of freshwater algae; **chlam'ydospore** a thick-walled spore. [Gr. *chlamys,* pl. *chlamydēs.*]

chloasma *klō-az'mə, n.* a skin disease marked by yellowish-brown patches. [Gr. *chloasma,* greenness, yellowness—*chloē,* verdure.]

chloracne *klōr-ak'ni, n.* a type of disfiguring skin disease resembling acne in appearance.

chlorine *klō', klō'rēn, -rin, -rīn, n.* a yellowish-green gas (Cl) with a peculiar and suffocating odour, used in bleaching, disinfecting, and poison gas warfare.—*ns.* **chlor'al** (or *-al'*) a limpid, colourless, oily liquid ($CCl_3 \cdot CHO$), of penetrating odour, formed when anhydrous alcohol is acted on by dry chlorine gas: loosely **chloral hydrate,** a white crystalline substance used as a hypnotic, **chlo'ralism** the habit, or the morbid effects, of using chloral hydrate; **chlo'rate** a salt of chloric acid.—*adjs.* **chlo'ric, chlo'rous** of or from chlorine.—**chloric acid** (HClO₃), a syrupy liquid, a vigorous oxidising agent.—*n.* **chlo'ride** a compound of chlorine with another element or radical: bleaching powder (*chloride of lime*), not a true chloride.—*v.t* **chlo'ridise, -ize** to convert into a chloride: to cover with chloride of silver (*phot.*).— Also **chlo'ridate.**—*v.t.* **chlor'inate** to treat with chlorine (as in sterilisation of water, extraction of gold from ore).—*n.* **chlorinā'tion.**—*v.t.* **chlo'rinise, -ize** to chlorinate.—*n.* **chlo'rite** a salt of chlorous acid (*chem.*): a general name for a group of minerals, hydrated silicates of magnesia, iron, and alumina.— *adj.* **chlorit'ic** pertaining to, of the nature of, or containing, the mineral chlorite.—*n.* **chloroform** (*klor'ō-form* or *klō'rō-form*) a limpid, mobile, colourless, volatile liquid (CHCl₃) with a characteristic odour and a strong sweetish taste, used to induce insensibility.—*v.t.* to administer chloroform to.—*ns.* **chlor'oformer, -ist; Chloromy'cetin®** (or *-mī-sēt'in*) a drug used against typhoid, cerebrospinal meningitis, etc., **chlorophyll, -phyl** (*klor'ō-fil,* or *klō'rō-fil*) the ordinary green colouring matter of vegetation; **chlo'roplast** a chlorophyll-bearing plastid, **chlorō'sis** properly *green sickness,* a form of anaemia affecting young women: blanching of the green parts of a plant, esp. for want of iron (*bot.*).—*adj.* **chlorot'ic** pertaining to or affected by chlorosis. [Gr. *chlōros,* pale green.]

choc *chok, (coll.) n.* and *adj.* a short form of **chocolate.** —**choc'-ice, choc'-bar** an ice-cream with a chocolate covering.

chock *chok, v.t.* to fasten as with a block or wedge.—*n.* a wedge to prevent movement: a log.—*adjs.* **chock's a-block', chock'-full', choke'-full'** quite full.—*adj.* **chock'-tight** very tight. [See **choke.**]

chocolate *chok'(ə-)lit, n.* a paste made of the ground seeds of *Theobroma cacao* (cocoa), with sugar and flour or similar material: a sweetmeat made of, or covered with, the paste: beverage made by dissolving the paste, or a powder prepared from it, in hot water or milk.—*adj.* chocolate-coloured, dark reddish-brown: made of or flavoured with chocolate.—*adj.* **choc'olate-box** pretty-pretty or over-sentimental, esp. of a painting. [Sp. *chocolate;* from Nahuatl, *chocólatl,* a mixture containing chocolate.]

Choctaw *chok'tò, n.* an American Indian of a tribe formerly chiefly in Mississippi: the tribe, or its language: (sometimes without *cap.*) a skating movement, forward on the edge of one foot, then backward on the opposite edge of the other (cf. **Mohawk**). [Choctaw *Chahta.*]

choice *chois, n.* the act or power of choosing· the thing chosen: an alternative: a preference: the preferable or best part: variety from which to choose.—*adj.* worthy of being chosen: select: appropriate.—*adv.* **choice'ly** with discrimination or care.—*n.* **choice'ness** particular value: excellence: nicety.—**by, for, from choice** by preference; **Hobson's choice** the choice of a thing offered or nothing, from *Hobson,* a Cambridge horsekeeper, who lent out the horse nearest the stable door, or none at all; **make choice of** to select; **take one's choice** to take what one wishes. [Fr. *choix* —*choisir;* cf. **choose.**]

choir *kwir, n.* a chorus or band of singers, esp those belonging to a church: the part of a church appropriated to the singers.—**choir'boy, choir'-girl, choir's man** a boy, girl or man who sings in a choir; **choir's master** the director of a choir; **choir school** a school usu. maintained by a cathedral to educate boys who also sing in the choir, **choir'-screen** a screen of latticework, separating the choir from the nave —*n pl*

choir'-stalls fixed seats in the choir of a church, generally of carved wood. [Fr. *chœur*—L. *chorus*—Gr. *choros;* see **chorus.**]

choke *chōk, v.t.* to stop or interfere with the breathing of (whether by compression, blocking, fumes, emotion, or otherwise): to injure or suppress by obstruction, overshadowing, or deprivation of air, etc : to constrict: to block: to clog: to obstruct.—*v.i.* to be choked.—*n.* a complete or partial stoppage of breath: the sound of choking: a constriction: a device to prevent the passage of too much petrol, oil, gas, electric current, etc.—*adj.* choked (*coll.*) angry: upset.—*ns.* **chōk'er** that which or one who chokes: a large neck-cloth: a very high collar: a close-fitting necklace or jewelled collar; **chokey** see separate entry **choky.**—*adj.* **chōk'y** tending to, or inclined to, choke. —**choke'damp** carbon dioxide or other suffocating gas in mines.—*adj.* **choke-full** see **chock-full.**—**chok'- ing-coil** a coil of thick wire, used to limit the supply of electric light.—**choke back, down** to repress as if by a choking action; **choke off** to get rid of; **choke up** to fill completely: to block up.

choky, chokey *chō'ki, n.* a prison: a toll-station [Hindi *caukī.*]

cholangiography *kol-an-ji-og'rə-fi, n.* the examination by X-ray of the gall-bladder and bile-ducts. [Gr *cholē,* bile, *angeion,* case, vessel.]

cholecyst *kō'li-sist, n.* the gall-bladder.—*ns.* **cholecys-ti'tis** inflammation of the gall-bladder; **cholecystos'tomy, cholecystot'omy** surgical opening of the gall-bladder; **cholecystec'tomy** excision of the gall-bladder. [Gr. *cholē,* bile, *kystis,* a bladder.]

choler *kol'ər, n.* the bile: anger, irascibility.—*adj.* **chol'eric** full of choler: passionate.—*adv.* **chol'erically** (also *-er'*). [Gr. *cholerā—cholē,* bile, partly through Fr.]

cholera *kol'ər-ə, n.* a high infectious and deadly disease characterised by bilious vomiting and purging.—*adj.* **choleraic** (*kol-ər-ā'ik*).—**cholera belt** a waist-band of flannel or other material worn as a precaution against disease. See **choler.** [Gr. *cholerā—cholē,* bile.]

choleric. See **choler.**

cholesterol *ko-les'tər-ol, n.* an alcohol (C₂₇H₄₅OH), occurring abundantly in gall-stones, nerves, bloodstream, etc., a white crystalline solid, thought to be a cause of arteriosclerosis—formerly **choles'terin**—*adj.* **cholester'ic.** [Gr. *cholē,* bile, *stereos,* solid]

choli *chō'lē, n.* a short, short-sleeved blouse often worn under a sari. [Hindi *colī.*]

cholic *kol'ik, kōl'ik, adj.* pertaining to bile, as **cholic acid** (C₂₄H₄₀O) got from bile.—*n* **chol'ine** (*kō'lin, -lēn*) an alcohol (C₅H₁₅NO₂) discovered in bile. [Gr. *cholē,* bile.]

chomp *chomp, (coll.) v.t.* and *v.i.* to munch with noisy enjoyment. [Variant of **champ**[1].]

chondrus *kon'drəs, n.* a cartilage: a chondrule:—*pl.* **chon'dri.**—*adj.* **chon'dral.**—*ns.* **chondre** (*kon'dər*) a chondrule; **chondrifica'tion** formation of chondrin or development of or change into cartilage —*v.t.* and *v.i.* **chon'drify** to change into cartilage.—*ns.* **chon'- drin** a firm elastic, translucent, bluish-white gelatinous substance, the ground-substance of cartilage; **chon'drite** a meteorite containing chondrules.—*adj.* **chondrit'ic.**—*adj.* **chon'droid** like cartilage.—*n.* **chon'drule** a rounded granule found in meteorites and in deep-sea deposits. [Gr. *chondros,* a grain, grit, cartilage]

choo-choo *chōō'chōō, n.* a child's word for a railway train. [Imit.]

chook *chōōk, (coll.,* esp *Austr.) n.* a hen, chicken.— Also **chook'ie** (also *Scot*). [Imit.]

choose *chōōz, v.t.* to take or pick out in preference to another thing: to select: to will or determine: to think fit.—*v.i* to make a choice (between, from, etc.):—*pa.t.* **chose** *chōz*, *pa.p.* **chos'en**.—*n.* **choos'er**.—*adj.* **choos'(e)y** (*coll.*) difficult to please, fastidious.—**not much to choose between** each about equally good or bad; **pick and choose** to select with care or at leisure; **the chosen people** the Israelites (1 Chron. xvi 13). [O.E. *cēosan*, Du. *kiesen*.]

chop[1] *chop*, *v.t.* to cut with a sudden blow (away, down, off, etc.): to cut into small pieces.—*v.i.* to hack: to crack or fissure: to take a direction (running into **chop**[2]):—*pr.p.* **chopp'ing**; *pa.t.* and *pa.p.* **chopped**.—*n.* an act of chopping: chopped food: a piece cut off: a slice of mutton or pork, containing a rib: a crack: a sharp downward blow.—*n.* **chopp'er** one who or that which chops: a cleaver: a helicopter (*slang*): (in *pl.*) teeth (*slang*).—*n.* and *adj.* **chopp'ing**.—*adj* **chopp'y** full of chops or cracks: (of the sea, etc) running in irregular waves (also **chopp'ing**).—**chop'-house** a house where mutton-chops and beefsteaks are served: an eating-house; **chopp'ing-block**, **-board** one on which material to be chopped is placed; **chopp'ing-knife** a knife for chopping or mincing meat. —**chop at** to aim a blow at; **chop in** to break in, interrupt; **chop up** to cut into small pieces; **for the chop** (*slang*) about to get the chop; **get the chop** (*slang*) to be dismissed from one's job, etc : to be killed. [A form of **chap**[1].]

chop[2] *chop*, *v.t.* and *v.i.* to change direction (running into **chop**[1]):—*pr.p.* **chopp'ing**; *pa.t.* and *pa.p.* **chopped**.—*n.* an exchange: a change.—**chop'-log'ic** chopping of logic: one who chops logic.—**chop and change** to buy and sell: to change about; **chop logic** to argue contentiously; **chops and changes** vicissitudes. [Connection with **chop**[1] and with **chap**[2] is not clear.]

chop[3] *chop*, *n.* the chap or jaw —*adj.* **chop'fallen** lit having the chop or lower jaw fallen down cast-down: dejected. [See **chap**[3].]

chop[4] *chop*, *n.* in China and India, a seal: a brand: a sealed document.—**first chop** best quality; **no chop** no good [Hindi *chāp*, seal, impression.]

chop-chop *chop'chop'*, *adv.* promptly [Pidgin English.]

chop-stick *chop'stik*, *n.* (usu. in *pl.*) either of two small sticks used by the Chinese instead of a fork. [**chop-chop**, and **stick**[2].]

chop-suey *chop-sōō'ı*, *n.* a miscellaneous Chinese dish, fried in sesame-oil. [Chin., mixed bits.]

choral, chorale. See **chorus**.

chord[1] *kord*, (*mus.*) *n.* the simultaneous union of sounds of a different pitch.—*adj.* **chord'al.** [From **accord**.]

chord[2] *kord*, *n.* a string of a musical instrument (*poet.*): a sensitive area of the emotions (*fig.*): a straight line joining any two points on a curve (*geom.*): a cord (see **spinal**, **vocal**): the straight line joining the leading and the trailing edges of an aerofoil section (*aero.*).—*adj.* **chord'al.**—*n.pl.* **Chordat'a** the highest phylum of the animal kingdom, including the vertebrates—animals possessing a notochord.—*n.* **chor'date** a member of the Chordata.—Also *adj.*—*n.* **chordophone** (*kòr'dō-fōn*; *mus.*) a stringed instrument.—*adj.* **chordophonic** (*-fon'ik*).—**strike a chord** to prompt a feeling of recognition, familiarity, etc. [Gr. *chordē*, a string, intestine.]

chore *chōr*, *chòr*, *n.* a household task: an unenjoyable task. [Form (orig. *U.S.*) of **char**[3].]

chorea *ko-rē'ə*, *n.* St Vitus's dance, a nervous disease, causing irregular involuntary movements of the limbs or face. [L.,—Gr. *choreiā*, a dance.]

choreography, choreographer, etc. See **chorus**.

choriamb *kor'ı-amb*, *n.* a foot of four syllables, the

first and last long, the others short —*adj.* and *n.* **choriam'bic**. [Gr. *choriambos—choreios*, a trochee, *iambos*, iambus.]

choric, **chorine**. See **chorus**.

chorion *kō'ri-on*, *kō'*, *n.* the outer foetal envelope:—*pl.* **cho'ria**.—*adjs.* **cho'rioid**; **cho'roid**. [Gr. *chorion*.]

chorist, etc. See **chorus**.

chorography *kō-rog'rə-fı*, *ko-*, *n* geography topography.—*adjs.* **chorographic** (*-ro-graf'ik*), **-al**; **chorolog'ical**.—*ns.* **chorol'ogist**; **chorol'ogy** the science of geographical distribution. [Gr *chōrā*, region, country.]

choroid. See **chorion**.

chortle *chōrt'l*, *v.i.* to chuckle: to utter a low, deep laugh.—Also *n.* [Coined by Lewis Carroll in 1872.]

chorus *kō'ras*, *ko'*, *n.* a band of singers and dancers: in Greek plays, a number of persons who between the episodes danced, and chanted comment and counsel: a person who performs similar functions by himself: a company of singers: that which is sung by a chorus: the combination of voices in one simultaneous utterance: a refrain, in which the company may join. —*v.t.* to sing or say together:—*pr p.* **cho'rusing**; *pa.t.* and *pa.p.* **cho'rused**.—*adj.* **chor'al** pertaining to a chorus or a choir.—*n.* (*ko-ral'*; often altered to **chorale'**) a simple harmonised composition with slow rhythm: a psalm or hymn tune.—*adv* **chor'ally** in the manner of a chorus: suitable for a choir.—*adj* **choric** (*kor'ik*, *kō'rık*).—*ns.* **chorist** (*kor'ıst*, *kō'rist*), **chor'ister** a member of a choir.—*v t.* **chor'eograph** to arrange (a dance, dances, etc.).—*v.i.* to practise choreography.—*ns.* **chor'eograph**, **choreographer** (*kor-i-og'rə-fər*).—*adj.* **choreograph'ic** (*-graf'ik*).—*ns.* **choreog'raphy**, **choreg'raphy** the art, or the notation, of dancing, esp. ballet-dancing: the art of arranging dances, esp. ballets: the arrangement of a ballet; **choreol'ogist**; **choreol'ogy** the study of ballets and their history.—**chor'us-girl** a woman employed to sing or dance in a chorus on the stage. [L.,—Gr. *choros*, dance; see also **choir**.]

chose, **chosen**. See **choose**.

chou *shōō*, *n.* a cabbage: a soft rosette: a cream bun: dear, pet:—*pl.* **choux** (*shōō*).—**choux pastry** very light, rich pastry. [Fr.]

chough *chuf*, *n.* the red-legged crow, or any bird of the genus *Fregilus* or *Pyrrhocorax*. [Perh. from its cry.]

chough[2]. See **chuff**.

choux. See **chou**.

chow-chow *chow'chow*, shortened as **chow**, *n.* food: a Chinese mixed condiment: a mixed fruit preserve: a dog of a Chinese breed —*adj.* mixed, miscellaneous —*n.* **Chow** a Chinese (*arch. slang*). [Pidgin Eng., food.]

chowder *chow'dər*, *n.* a stew or thick soup made of fish with meat and vegetables. [Fr. *chaudière*, a pot.]

chow-mein *chow'mēn'*, *-mân'*, *n.* fried noodles: a dish of seasoned shredded meat and vegetables, served with fried noodles. [Chin., fried noodles.]

chrematist *krē'ma-tist*, *n.* a political economist.—*adj.* **chrematis'tic** pertaining to finance, money-making, or political economy.—*n sing.* **chrematis'tics** the science of wealth. [Gr. *chrēmatistēs*, a money-getter.]

chrestomathy *kres-tom'ə-thı*, *n.* a book of selections esp. in a foreign language, usu for beginners —*adjs.* **chrestomathic** (*-tō-math'ik*), **-al**. [Gr. *chrēstos*, useful, *mathein*, (aorist) to know]

chrism *krızm*, *n.* consecrated or holy oil: unction: chrisom —*adj* **chris'mal** pertaining to chrism —*n* a case for containing chrism a veil used in christening —*ns.* **chris'om**, **christ'om**, **chris'om-cloth** a white cloth or robe put on a child newly anointed with chrism after its baptism. [O.Fr *chresme* (Fr *chrême*)—Gr. *chrisma*—*chriein*, to anoint.]

Christ *krīst, n.* the Anointed, a name given to Jesus: a Messiah.—*v.t* **christen** (*krīs'n*) to baptise in the name of Christ: to give a name to.—*ns.* **Christendom** (*krīs'n-dəm*) that part of the world in which Christianity is the received religion· the whole body of Christians, **christening** (*krīs'ning*) the ceremony of baptism; **Christian** (*krīs'chən*) a believer in the religion of Christ or one so classified. a follower of Christ· one whose behaviour is considered becoming to a follower of Christ· often a vague term of approbation, a decent, respectable —*adj.* relating to Christ or his religion: in the spirit of Christ.—*n* **christianisâ'tion, -z-**.—*v.t.* **christ'ianise, -ize** to make Christian: to convert to Christianity.—*ns* **Christ'ianism; Christianity** (*kris-ti-an'ı-tı*) the religion of Christ: the spirit of this religion.—*adjs.* **Christ'ian-like; Christ'ianly**.—*ns.* **Christ'ianness; christ'ingle** a Christmas symbol for children, usu. consisting of an orange containing a candle, with fruit and nuts and red paper or ribbon, representing Christ as the light of the world, its creation and his passion; **Christ'liness**.—*adjs.* **Christ'like; Christ'ly** like Christ.—**Christian era** the era counted from the date formerly assigned to the birth of Christ; **Christian name** the name given at christening: the personal name as distinguished from the surname; **Christian Science** a religion which includes spiritual or divine healing, founded in 1866 by Mrs Eddy; **Christian Scientist.** [O E. *Crist*—Gr. *Christos*—*chriein*, to anoint.]

Christadelphian *kris-tə-del'fi-ən, n.* a member of a small religious body believing in conditional immortality. [Gr. *Christos*, Christ, *adelphos*, brother.]

Christiania *kris-ti-an'i-ə*, **Chris'tie, -ty** (also without *caps.*), *ns.* a turn with skis parallel executed when descending at speed. [Former name of Oslo.]

christingle. See under Christ.

Christmas *krıs'məs, n.* an annual festival, orig a mass, in memory of the birth of Christ, held on the 25th of December: the season at which it occurs.—Also *adj* —*adj.* **Christ'mas(s)y** savouring of Christmas.— **Christmas box** a box containing Christmas presents: a Christmas gift, often of money to tradesmen, etc , **Christmas cake** a rich fruit-cake. usu. iced, made for Christmas; **Christmas card** a card sent to one's friends at Christmas; **Christmas daisy** the aster; **Christmas eve** Dec 24; **Christmas pudding** a rich, spicy fruit-pudding, eaten at Christmas; **Christ'mas-tide, -time** the season of Christmas; **Christmas tree** a tree, usu. fir, set up in a room or public place, and loaded with Christmas gifts and/or gauds [**Christ** and **mass²**.]

Christology *kris-tol'ə-ji, n.* that branch of theology which treats of the nature and person of Christ — *adj.* **Christological** (*-to-loj'i-kl*) —*n* **Christol'ogist.** [Gr. *Christos*, and *logos*, discourse.]

christom *krız'əm* Same as **chrisom.**

christophany *kris-tof'ə-nı, n.* an appearance of Christ to men [Gr. *Christos*, and *phainesthai*, to appear.]

Christy. See **Christiania.**

chroma *krō'mə, n.* quality of colour· a hue —*n.* **chrō'mate** a salt of chromic acid —*adj.* **chrō'mat'ic** pertaining to, or consisting of, colours. coloured: relating to notes in a melodic progression, which are raised or lowered by accidentals, without changing the key of the passage, and also to chords in which such notes occur (*mus*).—*adv* **chrōmat'ically**.—*ns.* **chrōmaticity** (*-tıs'*) the colour quality of light depending on hue and saturation; **chrōmat'ics** the science of colours —*n* **chrō'matin** a readily stained substance in the nucleus of a cell —*adj* **chrōmatograph'ic**.—*ns* **chrōmatog'raphy** methods of separating substances

in a mixture which depend on selective adsorption, partition between non-mixing solvents, etc., using a **chrōmat'ograph,** and which present the substances as a **chrōmat'ogram**, such as a series of visible bands in a vertical tube; **chrome** chromium or a chromium compound.—Also *adj.*—*ns* **chrō'mite** a mineral, a double oxide of chromium and iron, **chrō'mium** a metallic element (at. numb 24, symbol Cr) remarkable for the beautiful colour of its compounds; **chrō'mosome** a rod-like portion of the chromatin of a cell-nucleus, performing an important part in mitotic cell-division, and in the transmission of hereditary characters.—*adj.* **chrōmosō'mal**.—**chromatic aberration** a lack of focus of colours after refraction, **chromatic scale** (*mus.*) a scale proceeding by semitones; **chrome'-plat'ing** electroplating with chromium, **chrome'-steel'** an alloy steel containing chromium; **chrome'-yell'ow** a pigment of lead chromate; **chromic acid** an acid of chromium (H_2CrO_4), of an orange-red colour, much used in dyeing and bleaching. [Gr *chrōma, -atos*, colour]

chron-, chrono- *kron', -ō-, -ə-, krən-, kron-o'*, in composition, time.—*adj.* **chron'ic** lasting a long time: of a disease, deep seated or long continued, as opp. to *acute*: deplorable (*slang*) —*n* a chronic invalid.— *adj.* **chron'ical** chronic —*adv.* **chron'ically**.—*ns* **chronic'ity; chron'icle** a bare record of events in order of time. a history. a story, account: (in *pl.*, with *cap.*) the name of two of the O.T books.—*v t.* to record as in a chronicle.—*ns.* **chron'icler** a writer of a chronicle, **chron'ograph** an instrument for taking exact measurements of time, or for recording graphically the moment or duration of an event; **chronog'rapher** a chronicler; **chronog'raphy** chronology; **chronol'oger**.—*adjs.* **chronolog'ic, -al**.—*adv.* **chronolog'ically**.—*ns.* **chronol'ogist; chronol'ogy** the science of computing time: a scheme of time: order of time, **chronom'eter** an instrument for accurate measurement of time —*adjs.* **chronomet'ric, -al**.— *ns* **chronom'etry** the art of measuring time by means of instruments· measurement of time; **chrō'mon** (*phys*) a unit of time—that required for a photon to travel the diameter of an electron, **chron'oscope** an instrument used for measuring extremely short intervals of time, especially in determining the velocity of projectiles.—**chronological age** age in years, etc , opp e.g to *mental age* [Gr *chronos*, time.]

chrys- *kris-*, **chryso-** *kris'ō-, -ə-, kris-ō'*, in composition, gold —*ns.* **chrys'alid, chrys'alis** orig a golden-coloured butterfly pupa· a pupa generally: a pupa case·—*pls* **chrysalides** (*kris-al'ı-dēz*), **chrys'alises, chrys'alids; Chrysan'themum** (*kris-* or *krız-*) a genus of composite plants to which belong the corn marigold and ox-eye daisy· (without *cap.*) any plant of the genus· (without *cap*) any of several cultivated plants of the genus, with colourful double flower-heads (often shortened to **chrysanth'**) —*adj* **chryselephant'ine** made of gold and ivory —*ns.* **chrysober'yl** a mineral, beryllium aluminate, of various shades of greenish-yellow or gold colour, **chrys'olite** olivine, esp yellow or green precious olivine; **chrys'oprase** (*-prāz*) a green chalcedony [Gr. *chrȳsos*, gold.]

chthonian *thō'nı-ən, adj* pertaining to the underworld and the deities inhabiting it· ghostly —Also **chthonic** (*thon'ık*) [Gr *chthōn, chthōnos*, the ground]

chub *chub, n* a small fat river-fish of the carp family.— *adjs.* **chubbed, chubb'y** short and thick, plump —*n* **chubb'iness.**

chuck¹ *chuk, n* the call of a hen a chicken (dim **chuck'ie**) a word of endearment —*v ı* to call, as a hen [A variant of **cluck.**]

chuck² *chuk n* a gentle blow under the chin· a toss or

throw, hence dismissal (*coll.*).—*v.t.* to tap under the chin: to toss: to pitch: to abandon or dismiss.— **chuck'er-out** (*coll.*) one who expels undesirable people.—**chuck it** (*coll.*; sometimes with *in*) to stop, give over; **chuck out** (*coll.*) to expel (a person): to throw away, get rid of; **chuck up** (*coll.*) to give up. to give in. [Fr *choquer*, to jolt; allied to **shock**.]

chuck³ *chuk, n.* a lump or chunk: an instrument for holding an object so that it can be rotated, as upon a lathe: food (*slang*).—**chuck'-wagon** a wagon carrying food, cooking apparatus, etc.

chuckle¹ *chuk'l, n.* a quiet laugh: the cry of a hen.—*v.t* to call, as a hen does her chickens —*v.t.* to laugh in a quiet, suppressed manner, in derision or enjoyment. —*n* **chuck'ling.** [Cf. **chuck¹**.]

chuckle² *chuk'l, adj.* clumsy.—**chuck'le-head** a loutish fellow [Prob **chock**, a log.]

chuddah, chuddar. Variants of **chadar**.

chuff, chough *chuf, n.* a clown: a surly fellow.—*n.* **chuff'iness** boorishness.—*adjs.* **chuffed** disgruntled; **chuff'y** coarse and surly. [M.E. *chuffe, choffe,* a boor.]

chuffed *chuft,* (*coll.*) *adj.* very pleased [Dial. *chuff,* chubby.]

chug *chug, n.* a rapid explosive noise, as of an internal-combustion engine.—*adj.* **chugg'ing.**—*v.t.* **chug** to make a chugging noise: of a vehicle, to move while making such a noise. [Imit.]

chukker, chukka *chuk'ər, -ə, ns.* a period of play in polo [Hindi *cakkar,* a round.]

chum *chum, n.* a friend or associate.—*v.t.* to share a room: to be or become a chum.—*v.t.* to be or become a chum to: to accompany.—*adj.* **chumm'y** sociable. —**chum up** with to become intimate with. [Perh. a mutilation of **chamber-fellow**.]

chump *chump, n.* an end lump of wood, mutton, etc.: a thick lump: a blockhead: the head.—**off one's chump** out of one's mind. [Perh. related to **chunk**.]

chunder *chun'dər,* (*Austr. slang*) *v.i.* to vomit.

chunk *chungk, n.* a thick piece of anything, as wood, bread, etc.—*adj.* **chunk'y** in chunks: short and broad: of sweaters, etc., thick and heavy. [Perh related to **chuck**.]

Chunnel *chun'l, n.* (also without *cap.*) the proposed tunnel underneath the English Channel, connecting England and France. [*Channel tunnel*]

chunter *chun'tər,* (*dial.*) *v.i.* (often with *on*) to mutter: to grumble [Imit.]

chupati, chupatti. Same as **chapati, chapatti**.

church *chûrch, n.* a house set apart for public worship, esp. that of a parish, and esp. that of an established or once established form of religion: a church service: the whole body of Christians: the clergy: any particular sect or denomination of Christians: any body professing a common creed —*adj.* of the church: ecclesiastical.—*v.t.* to perform a service in church with (e.g. a woman after childbirth) —*adjs.* **church'less** not belonging to a church; **church'ly** concerned with the church: ecclesiastical.—*adv* **church'ward(s),**—*adj.* **church'y** obtrusively devoted to the church: savouring of church.—**Church Army** an organisation of the Church of England, resembling the Salvation Army; **church'-goer** one on the way to, or who habitually goes to church; **church'-going** act or habit of going to church; **church'man** a clergyman or ecclesiastic: a member or upholder of the established church; **church'-off'icer** a church attendant or beadle; **church'-parade** a uniformed parade of a military or other body for the purpose of church-going; **church'-ser'vice** a religious service in a church: the form followed: a book containing it; **church'-war'den** an officer who represents the interests of a parish or church, **church'woman** a female member or upholder

of a church, esp. the Anglican Church, **church'yard** a burial-ground round a church. [O.E. *cirice, circe*— Gr. *kȳriakon,* belonging to the Lord—*kȳrios,* lord.]

churinga *chōō-ring'gə, n.* a stone amulet. [Austr.]

churl *chûrl, n.* a rustic, labourer: an ill-bred, surly fellow.—*adj.* **churl'ish** rude: surly: ungracious.— *adv.* **churl'ishly.**—*n.* **churl'ishness.** [O.E. *ceorl,* a countryman.]

churn *chûrn, n.* an apparatus used for the production of butter from cream or from whole milk: a large milk-can suggestive of an upright churn.—*v.t.* to agitate so as to obtain butter: to stir, agitate, violently (often with *up*): to turn over persistently (ideas in the mind).—*v.i.* to perform the act of churning: to move restlessly and with violence.—*n.* **churn'ing** the act of making butter. the quantity of butter made at once —**churn out** to produce continuously with effort. [O.E. *cyrin.*]

churr *chûr, n.* a low sound made by certain birds and insects.—*v.i* to make this sound. [Prob. imit.]

chut *chut, interj.* an expression of impatience.

chute¹, shoot *shōō t, n.* a waterfall, rapid: a passage or sloping trough for sending down goods, water, logs, rubbish, etc.: a slide in a park, etc. [Fr. *chute,* fall, combined with **shoot**.]

chute² *shōō t,* abbrev. for **parachute**.

chutney *chut'ni, n.* an East Indian condiment, of mangoes, chillies, etc.: an imitation made with home materials, as apples. [Hindi *catni.*]

chutzpah *hhōōt'spə, n.* effrontery, nerve. [Yiddish.]

chyle *kil, n.* a white fluid, mainly lymph mixed with fats derived from food in the body. [Gr. *chȳlos,* juice—*chein,* to pour.]

chyme *kīm, n.* the pulp to which food is reduced in the stomach.—*n.* **chymifica'tion** the act of being formed into chyme.—*v.t.* **chym'ify** to form into chyme.—*adj.* **chym'ous.** [Gr. *chȳmos,* chyme, juice—*chein,* to pour.]

chypre *shē'pr`, n.* a scent from Cyprus. [Fr., Cyprus.]

ciao *chow, interj.* an informal greeting used on meeting or parting.

ciborium *si-bō'ri-əm, -bo',* *n.* a vessel closely resembling a chalice: a canopy supported on four pillars over the high altar:—*pl.* **cibo'ria.** [L., a drinking-cup—Gr. *kibōrion,* the seed-vessel of the Egyptian water-lily.]

cicada *si-ka'də, -kä'də,* **cicala** *-ka'lə, ns.* a homopterous insect remarkable for its loud chirping sound. [L *cicāda;* It. *cicala.*]

cicatrice *sik'ə-tris, n.* a scar over a healed wound: scar in the bark of a tree: the mark left where a leaf, etc., has been attached:—*pl.* **cicatri'ces.**—Also **cicatrix** (*sik-ā'-triks, sik'ə-triks*):—*pl.* **cic'atrixes.**—*n.* **cicatrisa'tion,** *-z-,* the process of healing over.—*v.t.* **cic'at-rise,** *-ize* to help the formation of a cicatrix on: to scar. —*v i.* to heal. [L. *cicātrīx, -icis,* a scar.]

cicely *sis'ə-li, n.* a name for several umbelliferous plants allied to chervil, esp. *Myrrhis odorata* (**sweet cicely**). [L and Gr. *seseli.*]

Cicero *sis'ə-rō n.* a famous Roman orator.—*n.* **cicerone** (*chich-ə-rō'ni,* also *sis-ə-rō-ni*) one who shows strangers the curiosities of a place: a guide:—*pl.* **cicerō'ni** (*-nē*).—*adjs.* **Cicerō'nian** (*sis-*), **Ciceronic** (*-ron'ik*).—*n.* **Cicerō'nianism** the character of Cicero's Latin style. [L. *Cicerō, -ōnis;* It. *Cicerone.*]

cichlid *sik'lid, n.* any fish of the family **Cich'lidae,** to which the angel-fish of the Amazon belongs.—*adj.* **cich'loid.** [Gr. *kichlē,* a kind of wrasse.]

-cide *-sīd,* in composition, (1) killing, murder; (2) killer, murderer.—**-ci'dal** adjective combining form. [L. *caedere,* to kill.]

cider (sometimes **cyder**) *sī'dər, n.* an alcoholic drink made from apples.—*adj.* **ci'dery.**—**ci'der-and** a mixture of cider and spirits; **ci'der-cup** a drink of sweetened cider, with other ingredients; **ci'der-press** an apparatus for pressing the juice from apples. [Fr. *cidre*—L. *sīcera*—Gr. *sikera*, strong drink—Heb *shēkār*.]

ci-devant *sē-də-vä*, (Fr.) *adj.* and *adv.* before this, former, formerly.

cigar *si-gar'*, *n.* a roll of tobacco-leaves with a pointed end for smoking.—*ns.* **cigarette** (*sig-ə-ret'*) finely-cut tobacco rolled in thin paper (*coll.* shortened forms **cig, cigg'ie, cigg'y**); **cigarillo** (*sig-ə-ril'ō*) a small cigar: —*pl.* **cigarill'os**.—**cigarette'-card** a picture card formerly given away with a packet of cigarettes; **cigarette'-end, cigarette'-butt** the unsmoked remnant of a cigarette; **cigarette'-holder, cigar'-holder** a mouthpiece for a cigarette or cigar; **cigarette'-lighter** a mechanical contrivance for lighting cigarettes; **cigarette'-paper** paper for making cigarettes. [Sp. *cigarro*.]

cilice *sil'is*, *n.* haircloth: a penitential garment made of haircloth.—*adj.* **cilicious** (*-ish'əs*). [L.,—Gr. *kilikion*, a cloth made of Cilician goat's hair.]

cilium *sil'i-əm*, *n.* a hair-like lash borne by a cell: a flagellum:—*pl.* **cil'ia**.—*adj.* **cil'iary**.—*adjs.* **cil'iate, -d** bearing a cilium or cilia: fringed with hairs. [L. *cilium*, eyelash.]

cill *sil*, (*building*) *n.* an old variant of **sill**, now usual in the trade.

Cimmerian *sim-ē'ri-ən*, *adj.* relating to the Cimmerii, a tribe fabled to have lived in perpetual darkness.

cinch *sinch*, *n* a saddle-girth (*U.S.*): a secure hold (*coll.*): a certainty (*coll.*): something easy (*coll.*).— *v.t.* to tighten the cinch.—*v.t.* to bind firmly, esp. with a belt around the waist: to make sure of (*coll.*). [Sp. *cincha*—L *cingula*.]

Cinchona *sing-kō'nə*, a genus of trees, yielding the bark from which quinine and its congeners are obtained— also called *Peruvian bark*.—*adjs* **cinchonaceous** (*-kən-ā'shəs*), **cinchonic** (*-kon'ik*).—*n.* **cinch'onine** an alkaloid obtained from cinchona bark. [Said to be so named from the Countess of *Chinchón*, who was cured of a fever by it in 1638.]

cincture *singk'chər*, *n.* a girdle or belt: a moulding round a column.—*v t.* to gird, encompass.—*adjs.* **cinct** surrounded; **cinc'tured** having a cincture. [L. *cinctūra*—*cingēre, cinctum*, to gird.]

cinder *sin'dər*, *n.* the refuse of burned coals: an ember: anything charred by fire: a fragment of lava.—*n.* **Cinderell'a** a scullery-maid: the despised and neglected one of a set.—Also *adj.*—*adj.* **cin'dery**.— **cin'der-cone** a hill of loose volcanic materials; **Cinderell'a-dance** a dancing-party ending at midnight —from the nursery tale; **cin'der-path, -track** a path, racing-track, laid with cinders. [O E. *sinder*, slag.]

cine-, ciné- *sin'i-*, in composition, cinematograph — **cin'e-cam'era, cin'é-** a camera for taking moving photographs; **cin'e-project'or, ciné-; Cinerama**® (*-ə-ra'mə*) a method of film projection on a wide curved screen to give a three-dimensional effect; the picture is photographed with three **cineramic** cameras.—**ciné vérité** cinéma vérité.

cinéaste, cineast(e) *sin'ē-ast*, *n.* one who takes an artistic interest in, or who makes, motion pictures [Fr.]

cinema *sin'ə-mə, -ma*, *n.* a cinematograph: a building in which motion pictures are shown: (with *the*) motion pictures collectively, or as an art.—*adj.* **cinemat'ic** pertaining to, suitable for, or savouring of, the cinema.—**cin'ema-or'gan** an organ with showier effects than a church organ; **Cin'emaScope**® name of one of the methods of film projection on a wide curved screen to give a three-dimensional effect—the picture is photographed with a special type of lens;

cinéma vérité realism in films sought by photographing scenes of real life. [**cinematograph**.]

cinematograph *sin-ə-mat'ə-gräf*, *n.* apparatus for projecting a series of instantaneous photographs so as to give a moving representation of a scene, with or without reproduction of sound: an exhibition of such photographs.—*n.* **cinematog'rapher**.—*adjs.* **cinematograph'ic, cinematograph'ical.**—*ns.* **cinematog'raphist; cinematog'raphy** the art of making motion pictures. [Fr. *cinématographe*—Gr *kīnēma, -atos*, motion, *graphein*, to write, represent.]

cineraria *sin-ə-rā'ri-ə*, *n.* a brightly-flowered variety of plants with ashy down on the leaves: see **cinerarium**. [L *cinerārius*, ashy—*cinis, cineris*, ash.]

cinerary *sin'ə-rə-ri*, *adj.* pertaining to ashes: for containing ashes of the dead.—*ns.* **cinera'rium** a place for depositing the ashes of the dead:—*pl.* **cinera'ria; cinera'tion; cinera'tor; cine'rea** grey nerve matter.— *adjs.* **cine'real** ashy: cinerary; **cine'reous** ashy-grey: ashy; **cineri'tious** ashy-grey: pertaining to grey nerve matter. [L. *cinereus*, ashy—*cinis, cineris*, ash.]

cingulum *sing'gū-ləm*, *n.* a girdle: a girdle-like structure. [L. *cingēre*, to gird.]

cinnabar *sin'ə-bär*, *n* a mineral, sulphide of mercury, called vermilion when used as a pigment.—*adj.* vermilion-coloured.—*adjs.* **cinnabaric** (*-bär'ik*); **cinn'abarine** (*-bə-rēn*). [Gr. *kinnabari*, from Persian.]

cinnamon *sin'ə-mən*, *n.* the spicy bark of a lauraceous tree of Sri Lanka: the tree: a light yellowish brown.— Also *adj.* [Gr. *kinnamōmon*, later *kinnamon*— Heb *qinnāmōn*.]

cinque *singk*, *n.* the number five as on dice.—**cinque's foil** a flower with five petals (*her.*): a similar figure formed by cusps in circular window or the head of a pointed arch (*archit.*): species of the genus Potentilla (*bot.*): the five-bladed clover (*bot.*).—**Cinque Ports** the five ancient ports on the south of England lying opposite to France—Sandwich, Dover, Hythe, Romney, and Hastings (later associated with Winchelsea, Rye, and a number of subordinate ports). [Fr.]

cinquecento *ching'kwe-chen-tō*, *n.* the 16th century— the art and architecture of the Renaissance period. [It., five hundred, *mil*, one thousand, being understood.]

cipher (*sometimes* **cypher**) *sī'fər*, *n.* the character 0 (*arith.*): any of the Arabic numerals: any person or thing of little value: a nonentity: an interweaving of the initials of a name: a secret code.—*v.t.* to write in cipher: to calculate.—*n.* **ci'phering**.—**ci'pher-key** a key to a cipher or piece of secret writing. [O.Fr. *cyfre*, Fr. *chiffre*—Ar. *çifr*, zero, empty.]

cipollino *chē-pol-lē'nō*, *n.* a marble with green bands: —*pl.* **cipolli'nos**.—Also **cipolin** (*sip'ō-lin*). [It. *cipolla*, an onion.]

circa *sûr'kə*, *prep.* and *adv.* about, around. [L.]

circadian *sûr-kā'di-ən, adj.*, esp. in *circadian rhythm*, pertaining to any biological cycle (e g. of varying intensity of metabolic or physiological process, or of some feature of behaviour) which is repeated, usu. approx. every 24 hours. {From L. *circa*, about, *di(em)*, day, and suff *-an*.]

circinate *sûr'sin-āt*, *adj.* ring-shaped: rolled inwards (*bot.*). [L. *circināre, -ātum*, make round.]

circiter *sûr'si-tər*, *prep.* (with dates) about, around. [L.]

circle *sûr'kl*, *n.* a plane figure bounded by one line every point of which is equally distant from a fixed point called the centre: the circumference of the figure so defined: a circular object: a ring: a planet's orbit: a series ending where it began. a group of things in a circle: a company surrounding or associating with the principal person: those of a certain class or group.

—*v.i.* to move round: to encompass: to draw a circle around.—*v.i.* (often with (*a*)*round*) to move in a circle: to stand in a circle.—*adj.* cir'cled circular: encircled.—*ns.* cir'cler; cir'clet a little circle: a little circular band or hoop, esp. a metal headband.—*n.* and *adj.* cir'cling moving in a circle.—**come full circle** to return to the beginning: to regain or turn out to be in a former state; **go round in circles** to get no results in spite of effort: not to get anywhere; **great, small, circle** a circle on the surface of a sphere whose centre is, is not, the centre of the sphere; **reasoning in a circle** assuming what is to be proved as the basis of the argument; **run round in circles** to act in too frenzied a way to achieve anything useful. [O.E. *circul*—L. *circulus*, dim. of *circus*; allied to O.E. *hring*, a ring.]
circs *sûrks*, (*slang*) *n.pl.* a shortened form of **circumstances**.

circuit *sûr'kit*, *n.* a journey round: a way round: perimeter: a roundabout way: an area enclosed: the path, complete or partial, of an electric current: a round made in the exercise of a calling, esp. by judges: the judges making the round: a district in which such a round is made, as by Methodist preachers, commercial travellers: a group of theatres, cinemas, etc., under common control, through which an entertainment circulates: the venues visited in turn and regularly by sports competitors, performers, etc.—*v.i.* to go round—*adj.* circuitous (-*kū'i-təs*) roundabout.—*adv.* circū'itously.—*ns.* circū'itousness; circuitry (*sûr'kit-ri*) the detailed plan of a circuit, as in radio or television, or its components, circū'ity motion in a circle: an indirect course.—cir'cuit-breaker a switch or other device for interrupting an electric circuit; **circuit judge** a judge in a county or crown court. [Fr.,—L *circuitus*—*circuire* —*circum*, round, *ire*, to go.]

circular *sûr'kū-lər*, *adj.* of or pertaining to a circle: in the form of a circle: round: ending in itself: recurring in a cycle: addressed to a circle of persons.—*n.* an intimation sent to a number of persons.—*v.i.* cir'cularise, -**ize** to make circular: to send circulars to—*n.* circularity (-*lar'i-ti*).—*adv.* cir'cularly.— **circular letter** a letter of which copies are sent to several persons; **circular saw** a power-driven saw in the shape of a flat disc with a serrated edge. [L. *circulāris*.]

circulate *sûr'kū-lāt*, *v.t.* to make to go round as in a circle: to spread.—*v.i.* to move round: to be spread about: to repeat in definite order (of decimals).—*adj.* cir'culable capable of being circulated.—*n.* and *adj.* cir'culating.—*n.* circula'tion the act of moving in a circle or in a closed path (as the blood): spreading or moving about: dissemination: the sale of a periodical: the money in use at any time in a country.—*adjs.* cir'culative, cir'culatory circulating.—*n.* cir'culator.— **circulating library** one from which books are circulated among subscribers; **in, out of, circulation** in, out of, general use, activity, etc. [L. *circulāre*, -*ātum*.]

circum-*sûr'kəm-, sər-kum'-, sûr-kəm-*, in composition, around. [L. *circum*.]

circumambient *sûr-kəm-am'bi-ənt*, *adj.* going round about, encompassing.—*ns.* circumam'bience, circumam'biency. [L. *ambire*, to go round.]

circumambulate *sûr-kəm-am'bū-lāt*, *v.i.* to walk round about.—*n.* circumambula'tion. [L *circum*, around, *ambulāre*, -*ātum*, to walk.]

circumcentre *sûr'kem-sen-tər*, *n.* the centre of the circumscribed circle or sphere. [circum-.]

circumcise *sûr'kəm-sīz*, *v.t.* to cut or cut off all or part of the foreskin (male) or (*rare*) all or part of the clitoris (female), often as a religious rite: to purify (*fig.*). —*ns.* cir'cumciser; circumcision (-*sizh'n*) the act of

circumcising: the state of being circumcised. [L. *circumcīdĕre*, -*cīsum*—*caedĕre*, to cut.]

circumference *ser-kum'fər-əns*, *n.* the boundary-line, esp. of a circle: compass: distance round.—*adj.* circumferential (-*en'shl*).—*n.* circum'ferentor (-*en-tər*) an instrument for measuring horizontal angles, consisting of a graduated circle, sights, and a magnetic needle: a graduated wheel for measuring the circumference of wheels. [L. *circum*, around, *ferre*, to carry.]

circumflect *sûr-kəm-flekt'*, *v.t.* to bend round: to mark with a circumflex.—*ns.* cir'cumflex an accent (^) originally denoting a rising and falling of the voice on a vowel or syllable—also *adj.*; circumflexion (-*flek-shən*) a bending round. [L. *circum*, around, *flectĕre*, *flexum*, to bend.]

circumfluence *sər-kum'floo-əns*, *n.* a flowing round: the engulfing of food by surrounding it (as by protozoa, etc).—*adjs* circum'fluent, circumflu'ous. [L. *circum*, around, *fluĕre*, to flow.]

circumfuse *sûr-kəm-fūz'*, *v.t.* to pour around.—*p.adj.* circumfused'.—*adj.* circumfus'ile molten.—*n.* circumfusion (-*fū'zhən*). [L. *circum*, around, *fundĕre*, *fūsum*, to pour.]

circumjacent *sûr-kəm-jā'sənt*, *adj.* lying round: bordering on every side —*n* circumjā'cency. [L. *circum*, around, *jacēns*, -*entis*, lying—*jacēre*, to lie.]

circumlittoral *sûr-kəm-lit'ə-rəl*, *adj.* adjacent to the shore-line. [L. *circum*, around, *litus*, for *litus*, -*oris*, shore.]

circumlocution *sûr'kəm-lō-kū'shən*, *n.* expressing an idea in more words than are necessary: an instance of this: evasive talk.—*v.i.* circumlocute' to use circumlocution —*n.* circumloch'tionist one who does this — *adj.* circumlocutory (-*lok'ū-tər-i*). [L. *circum*, around, *loquī*, *locūtus*, to speak.]

circumlunar *sûr'kəm-loo'nər*, -*lū'*, *adj* situated or moving round the moon. [L. *circum*, around, *lūna*, the moon.]

circumnavigate *sûr-kəm-nav'i-gāt*, *v.t.* to sail round.—*adj.* circumnav'igable.—*ns.* circumnaviga'tion; circumnav'igator. [circum-.]

circumpose *sûr-kəm-pōz'*, *v.t.* to place round.—*n.* circumposi'tion the act of placing round. [L. *circumpōnĕre*, by analogy with *impose*, etc.]

circumscribe *sûr-kəm-skrīb'*, *v.t.* to draw a line round: to describe a curve or figure touching externally: to enclose within certain limits, to curtail, abridge.— *adj.* circumscrib'able able to be circumscribed.—*ns.* circumscrib'er one who circumscribes; circumscription (-*skrip'shən*) limitation: the line that limits: the act of circumscribing: an inscription running round: a defined district.—*adj.* circumscrip'tive marking the external form or outline. [L. *circum*, around, *scrībĕre*, *scrīptum*, to write.]

circumsolar *sûr'kəm-sō'lər*, *adj.* situated or moving round the sun. [L. *circum*, around, *sōl*, the sun.]

circumspect *sûr'kəm-spekt*, *adj.* looking round on all sides watchfully: cautious: prudent.—*n.* circumspec'tion watchfulness: caution: examining.—*adj.* circumspec'tive looking around: wary.—*adv.* cir'cumspectly.—*n.* cir'cumspectness. [L. *circum*, around, *specēre*, *spicēre*, *spectum*, to look.]

circumstance *sûr'kəm-stəns*, *n* the logical surroundings of an action: an attendant fact: an accident or event: ceremony: detail: (in *pl.*) the state of one's affairs.— *v.t.* to place in particular circumstances.—*adj.* circumstantial (-*stan'shl*) consisting of details: minute —*n.* circumstantiality (-*stan-shi-al'i-ti*) the quality of being circumstantial: minuteness in details: a detail.—*adv.* circumstan'tially.—*n.pl.* circumstan'tials incidentals: details.—*v.t* circumstan'tiate to prove by circumstances: to describe exactly —

circumstantial evidence evidence which is not positive nor direct, but which is gathered inferentially from the circumstances in the case; **in good** or **bad circumstances** prosperous or unprosperous; **in, under, no circumstances** never; **in, under, the circumstances** conditions being what they are. [L. *circum*, around, *stāns, stantis*, standing—*stāre*, to stand.]

circumterrestrial *sûr-kəm-tı-res'trı-əl, adj* situated or moving round the earth. [L. *circum*, around, *terrestris,—terra*, the earth]

circumvent *sûr-kəm-vent'*, *v.t* to go round: to encompass: to surround so as to intercept or capture: to get round, or to outwit.—*n*. **circumven'tion.**—*adj.* **circumvent'ive** deceiving by artifices [L. *circum*, around *venīre, ventum* to come.]

circumvolve *sûr-kəm-volv'*, *v t.* to roll round.—*v.i.* to revolve —*n*. **circumvolution** (*-lōō', -lū'*) a turning or rolling round: anything winding or sinuous [L. *circum*, around, *volvěre, volūtum*, to roll]

circus *sûr'kəs, n*. a circular building for the exhibition of games: a place, building, or tent for the exhibition of feats of horsemanship and other performances: a show of this kind or the company of performers (also *fig.*): a group of houses arranged in the form of a circle: an open place at a street junction· a natural amphitheatre: a group of people who travel around putting on a display (as *flying circus*), often in the form of a competition (as *tennis circus*)· a noisy entertainment or scene.—*adj.* **cir'cus(s)y.**—*n.* **cirque** (*sûrk*, from Fr) a circus: a deep round hollow, a natural amphitheatre (*geog.*). [L. *circus*—Gr *kırkos*.]

ciré *sē'rā, n*. (a fabric with) a highly glazed finish [Fr. pa p. of *cirer*, to wax.]

cire perdue *sēr per-du*, (Fr.) lit. 'lost wax', a method of casting in metal, the mould being formed round a wax model which is then melted away.

cirl *sûrl, n*. a species of bunting (usu. **cirl bunting**). [It *cirlo*.]

cirque. See under **circus.**

cirrate, cirriform, etc. See **cirrus.**

cirrhosis *sı-rō'sıs, n*. a wasting of the proper tissue of an organ, accompanied by abnormal growth of connective tissue [Gr *kirrhos*, tawny—from the colour of the liver so diseased.]

cirripede *sır'ı-pēd, n*. one of the **Cirripē'dia,** a degenerate class of Crustacea, the barnacles and acornshells.—Also **cirr'iped** (*-ped*) [L. *cirrus*, a curl, *pēs, pedis*, foot.]

cirrus *sir'əs, n* the highest form of clouds, consisting of curling fibres: a tendril (*bot.*): any curled filament (*zool.*):—*pl. cirri*—*adjs.* **cirr'ate, cirr'iform** like a cirrus, **cirr'igrade** moving by cirri; **cirr'ose** with tendrils; **cirr'ous** having a cirrus —**cirr'o-cū'mulus** a cloud of small white flakes or ripples; **cirr'o-strā'tus** a high thin sheet of haze-like cloud [L., a curl, tuft]

Cisalpine *sıs-alp'in, -īn, adj* on this (i.e. the Roman) side of the Alps —*adjs.* **Cisatlan'tic; cislu'nar** on this side of the moon, i.e between the moon and the earth; **Cispadane** (*-pā'dān, sıs'pa-dān*) on this (Roman) side of the Po; **cispon'tine** on this side of the bridges, viz. in London, north of the Thames. [L *cıs* on this side]

ciselure *sēz'lōō r, n*. the art or operation of chasing: the chasing upon a piece of metalwork —*n* **cis'eleur** (*-lər*), a chaser [Fr.]

cissy *sis'i, (slang) n* an effeminate person.—Also *adj* [Partly from the name *Cecily*, partly from **sister;** cf **sis.**]

cist *sıst, n* a tomb consisting of a stone chest covered with stone slabs —*adjs* **cist'ed** containing cists, **cist'ic** like a cist [See **chest.**]

Cistercian *sıs-tûr'shən, n* a member of the order of monks established in 1098 in the forest of Cîteaux, (*Cistercium*), in France—an offshoot of the Benedictines —Also *adj.*

cistern *sis'tarn, n*. an artificial reservoir or tank for holding water or other liquid: a natural reservoir. [L. *cisterna—cista*, a chest]

cistic. See **cist.**

Cistus *sis'təs, n*. the rock-rose genus of shrubby plants: (without *cap.*) any plant of the genus:—*pl.* **cis'tuses.** [Gr. *kistos*, rock-rose.]

citadel *sit'ə-dəl, n* a fortress in or near a city [It. *cittadella*, dim. of *città*, a city; see **city.**]

cite *sīt, v.t.* to call or summon· to summon to appear in court: to quote: to name: to adduce as proof.—*adj.* **cit'able** that can be cited.—*ns.* **cit'al** summons to appear; **cita'tion** (*sīt-, sit-*) an official summons to appear· a document containing the summons: the act of quoting: the passage or name quoted: mention in dispatches: offical recognition of achievement.—*adj.* **cit'atory** having to do with citation: addicted to citation. [L. *cıtāre, -ātum*, to call, intens. of *ciēre, cīre*, to make to go]

cithara *sith'ə-rə, n*. an ancient Greek musical instrument differing from the lyre in its flat shallow soundchest.—*n*. **cith'arist** a player on it.—*adj.* **citharist'ic.** —*ns.* **cith'er, cith'ern, citt'ern** an early modern metal-stringed musical instrument, played with a plectrum: the Tirolese zither. [L.,—Gr. *kitharā*; cf. **guitar, zither.**]

citizen *sit'i-z(ə)n, n*. an inhabitant of a city: a member of a state: a townsman: a freeman:—*fem.* **cit'izeness.** —*v.t.* **cit'izenise, -ize** to make a citizen of—*ns.* **cit'izenry** the general body of citizens; **cit'izenship** the state of being or of having rights and duties of a citizen. conduct in relation to these duties.—**citizen's arrest** an arrest, legally allowable, made by a member of the public; **Citizens' Band** (orig. *U.S.*) a band of radio frequencies on which the public are permitted to broadcast personal messages, etc.; **Citizens' Band radio** (also **CB radio**). [M.E. *citesein*—O.Fr. *citeain*; see **city.**]

citron *sit'rən, n*. the fruit of the citron tree, resembling a lemon· the tree that bears it, considered to be the parent of the lemon and lime-fruit —*ns.* **cit'range** (*-rənj*) a hybrid between citron and orange; **cit'rate** a salt of citric acid.—*adj.* **cit'ric** derived from the citron (**citric acid** the acid to which lemon and lime juice owe their sourness, $C_6H_8O_7$).—*n.* **cit'rin** the watersoluble vitamin P, found in citrus fruits, etc.—*adj.* **cit'rous.**—*n. cit'rus* a citron tree: (with *cap.*) a genus of Rutaceae including the citron, lemon, orange, etc. —**citron tree;** **citrus fruits** citrons, lemons, limes, oranges, grapefruit [L *citrus*, from which comes also Gr. *kitron*, a citron]

cittern. Same as **cither.** [See under **cithara.**]

city *sit't, n* a large town: an incorporated town that has or had a cathedral: in various countries a municipality of higher rank, variously defined· the business centre or original area of a large town: (often with *cap*) the centre of British financial affairs, most banks, etc. being in the City of London.—**city editor** the financial editor; **city fathers** the magistrates. the town or city council; **city hall** a town hall; **cit'yscape** a view or picture of a city (following *landscape*); **cit'y-slick'er** a sophisticated city-dweller nattily dressed, **city state** a sovereign state consisting of a city with a small surrounding territory —**city of God, heavenly city,** etc , the ideal of the Church of Christ in glory; **Eternal City** Rome, **Holy City** Jerusalem. [Fr. *cité*, a city— L *civitās, -ātis*, the state—*civis*, a citizen.]

civet *siv'it, n* a perfume obtained from the **civet** or **civet cat,** a small cat-like carnivore of Africa, India, etc [Fr *civette*—Ar *zabād*]

civic *siv'ik*, *adj.* pertaining to a city or citizen.—*adv.*
civ'ically.—*n. sing.* **civ'ics** the science of citizenship.
—**civic centre** a place in which the chief public buildings of a town are grouped. [L *civicus—civis*, citizen.]

civil *siv'il*, *adj* pertaining to the community. polite (in any degree short of discourtesy) pertaining to ordinary life, not military: pertaining to the individual citizen. relating to private relations amongst citizens, and such suits as arise out of these, as opposed to *criminal (law).*—*n.* **civil'ian** one engaged in civil as distinguished from military and naval pursuits.—Also *adj* —*n.* **civil'ity** politeness· polite attentions.—*adv.* **civ'illy.**—*n.* **civv'y** (*slang*) civilian. (in *pl* civv'ies) civilian clothes —Also *adj.*—**civil aviation** non-military flying, esp. commercial airlines and their operation; **civil defence** a civilian service for the wartime protection of the civilian population against the effects of enemy attack by air, etc.; **civil disobedience** refusal to obey laws and regulations, pay taxes, etc., used as non-violent means of forcing concessions from government, **civil engineer** one who plans and builds railways, docks, etc.; **civil law** as opposed to criminal law, the law laid down by a state regarding the rights of the inhabitants, esp. that founded on Roman law; **civil liberty** (often in *pl.*) personal freedom of thought, word, action, etc.; **civil list** the expenses of the sovereign's household (**civil list pensions** those granted by royal favour); **civil rights** (often with *caps.*) the rights of a citizen to personal freedom, i.e. political, racial, legal, social, etc. —Also *adj.*—**civil servant**; **civil service** the paid service of the state, in so far as it is not military or naval; **civil war** a war between citizens of the same state, **civvy street** (*coll*) civilian life after the Services. [L. *civilis—civis*, citizen.]

civilise, -ize *siv'il-īz*, *v.t.* to reclaim from barbarism: to instruct in arts and refinements.—*adj.* **civilis'able, -z-.**—*n.* **civilisation, -z-** the state of being civilised culture: cultural condition or complex.—*adj* **civ'ilised, -z-** (having) advanced beyond the primitive savage state. refined in interests and tastes: sophisticated, self-controlled and fair-spoken.—*n.* **civ'iliser, -z-.** [See civil.]

civvies. See civil.

clack *klak*, *v.t.* to make a noise as of a flat thing flapping: to chatter. to cackle —*n.* a noise of this kind: an instrument making it: sound of voices: the tongue (*coll.*) —*n.* **clack'er.** [Prob. from the sound.]

clad *klad*, *pa t.* and *pa.p.* of **clothe.**—*adj.* clothed, or covered.—*v.t.* to cover one material with another, e.g. one metal with another (as in nuclear reactor), or brick or stonework with a different material (in building) —*n* **cladd'ing.**

cladode *klad'ōd*, (*bot.*) *n.* a branch with the appearance and functions of a leaf. [Gr. *klados*, a shoot.]

claim *klām*, *v t.* to call for. to demand as a right: to maintain or assert —*v.i.* to make a claim (on one's insurance policy, etc.).—*n* a demand for something supposed due: a right or ground for demanding: the thing claimed, esp a piece of land appropriated by a miner or other a call, shout.—*adj.* **claim'able** that can be claimed.—*ns.* **claim'ant**, **claim'er** one who makes a claim —**claim'-jumper** one who takes possession of another's mining claim; **claims assessor** an assessor employed by an insurance company, usu. in motor accident claims.—**lay claim to** to assert a right to [O.Fr. *claimer*—L *clāmāre*, to call out.]

clairaudience *klār-od't-əns*, *n.* the alleged power of hearing things not present to the senses.—*n.* and *adj* **clairaud'ient.** [Fr. *clair*—L *clārus*, clear, and *audience.*]

clairvoyance *klār-voi'əns*, *n* the alleged power of see-

ing things not present to the senses.—*n.* and *adj.*
clairvoy'ant. [Fr *clair*—L. *clārus*, clear, and Fr. *voir*—L *vidēre*, to see.]

clam¹ *klam*, *n.* a gripping instrument: a very reticent person (*coll.*): a scallop or scallop-shell: in America an edible shellfish of various kinds.—*v.t.* to gather clams —*pr.p.* **clamm'ing**; *pa.t.* and *pa.p.* **clammed.**—**clam'bake** a baking of clams on hot stones, with potatoes, etc., popular at picnic parties in U.S.: such a party, **clam-chow'der** chowder made with clams; **clam'-shell.**—**clam up** (*coll.*) to be silent. [O.E. *clam*, fetter.]

clam² *klam*, *n.* dampness (*dial.*).—*adv.* **clamm'ily.**—*n.* **clamm'iness.**—*adj.* **clamm'y** sticky: moist and adhesive. [O E. *clæman*, to anoint: cf. Du., Dan. *klam*, damp.]

clamant *klam'ənt*, *klām'ənt*, *adj.* calling aloud or earnestly.—*n.* **clam'ancy** urgency. [L *clāmāre*, to cry out.]

clamber *klam'bər*, *v.i.* to climb with difficulty, grasping with hands and feet —*n.* the act of clambering. [From the root of **climb.**]

clamour, in U.S. **clamor**, *klam'ər*, *n.* a loud continuous outcry: uproar: any loud noise: persistent expression of dissatisfaction —*v.i.* to cry aloud in demand (often with *for*): to make a loud continuous outcry.—*adj* **clam'orous** noisy, boisterous.—*adv.* **clam'orously.**—*ns.* **clam'orousness; clam'ourer.** [L. *clāmor, -ōris*.]

clamp¹ *klamp*, *n.* a piece of timber, iron, etc., used to fasten things together or to strengthen any framework: any instrument for holding.—*v.t.* to bind with a clamp to grasp or press firmly: to put (on) authoritatively, impose.—**clamp down on** to suppress, or suppress the activities of, firmly (*n* **clamp'down**). [From a root seen in O.E. *clam*, fetter.]

clamp² *klamp*, *n* a heavy tread.—*v.i.* to tread heavily. [Prob. from the sound.]

clan *klan*, *n.* a tribe or collection of families subject to a single chieftain, commonly bearing the same surname, and supposed to have a common ancestor: a clique, sect: a collective name for a number of persons or things.—*adj.* **clann'ish** closely united and holding aloof from others, like the members of a clan. —*adv* **clann'ishly.**—*ns.* **clann'ishness; clan'ship** association of families under a chieftain: feeling of loyalty to a clan.—**clans'man**, **clans'woman** a member of a clan [Gael. *clann*, offspring, tribe— L *planta*, a shoot.]

clandestine *klan-des'tin*, *adj.* concealed or hidden: private: sly.—*adv.* **clandes'tinely.**—*ns.* **clandes'-tineness, clandestin'ity.** [L *clandestīnus—clam*, secretly]

clang *klang*, *v.i.* to produce a loud deep ringing sound —*v.t.* to cause to clang.—*n.* a ringing sound, like that made by striking large pieces of metal.—*n.* **clang'er** a singularly ill-timed remark or comment: a stupid mistake.—*n.* and *adj.* **clang'ing.**—*adj.* **clangorous** (*klang'gar-əs*).—*adv.* **clang'orously.**—*n.* **clang'our**, in U.S. **clang'or**, a clang: a loud ringing noise —*v.i.* to make a clangour.—**drop a clanger** (*coll.*) to say something tactless. to make a stupid blunder. [L *clangēre*, to sound; *clangor*, noise of birds or wind instruments.]

clank *klangk*, *n.* a metallic sound, less prolonged than a clang, such as is made by chains hitting together.— *v.i.* or *v.t* to make or cause to make a clank.—*n.* **clank'ing.** [Prob. formed under the influence of **clink¹** and **clang¹**.]

clap¹ *klap*, *n.* a sudden blow or stroke (*lit* or *fig.*): a slap. a pat (*Scot.*): the noise made by the sudden striking together of two things, as the hands: a burst of sound, esp. thunder —*v.t* to strike together so as to make a noise: to thrust or drive together suddenly: to fasten promptly: to pat (*Scot*): to applaud with the hands· to bang: to put suddenly (e.g. in prison).—*v i.* to strike the hands together: to strike or slam with noise: to applaud:—*pr.p.* **clapp'ing;** *pa.t* and *pa.p.* **clapped.**—*n.* **clapp'er** one who claps: that which claps, as the tongue of a bell: an instrument for making a noise, as a rattle: the tongue (*slang*) —*v i.* to make a noise like a clapper.—*v t.* to ring by pulling on a clapper.—*n.* and *adj* **clapp'ering**—*n* **clapp'ing** noise of striking: applause.—**clap'board** a thin board used in covering wooden houses (U.S.).—*adj.* **clapped'-out'** (*coll.*) tired, exhausted· finished, of no more use — **clapp'erboard(s)** (a set of) hinged boards clapped together in front of camera before or after shooting a piece of film to help to synchronise sound and vision; **clapp'erboy** the person who works the clapperboards; **clap'trap** flashy display: empty words.—Also *adj.*—**claptrapp'ery.**—**clap eyes on** to catch sight of; **clap hands** to applaud with the hands; **clap hold of** to seize roughly; **like the clappers** (*coll.*) at top speed. [O N. *klappa,* to pat; Du and Ger. *klappen.*]

clap¹ *klap,* (*slang*) *n.* gonorrhoea.—*v.t.* to infect with gonorrhoea. [Cf. Du. *klapoor.*]

claque *klak, n.* an institution for securing the success of a performance, by pre-concerted applause: a body of hired applauders.—*n.* **claqueur** (*kla-kûr'*) a member of a claque. [Fr.—*claquer,* to clap.]

claret *klar'ət, n.* originally applied to wines of a light-red colour, but now used in Britain for the dark-red wines of Bordeaux: a dark red colour (also *adj*).— **clar'et-cup** a drink made up of iced claret, brandy, sugar, etc.; **clar'et-jug** a fancy jug for holding claret. [Fr. *clairet*—*clair*—L. *clārus,* clear.]

clarify *klar'i-fī, v.t.* to make clear or pure, esp butter, etc : to make clear, easily understood.—*v i.* to become clear:—*pr.p.* **clar'ifying;** *pa.t.* and *pa.p.* **clar'ified.**—*ns.* **clarificá'tion;** **clar'ifier.** [L. *clārus,* clear, and *facĕre,* to make.]

clarinet, *klar-in-et', klar', n.* a wind instrument, usually of wood, in which the sound is produced by a single thin reed, the compass being approximately that of the violin.—*n.* **clarinett'ist.**—**bass clarinet** one pitched an octave lower than the ordinary clarinet [Fr.,—L. *clārus,* clear.]

clarion *klar'i-ən, n.* a kind of trumpet whose note is clear and shrill: the sound of a trumpet, or a sound resembling that of a trumpet —**clarion call** (*fig.*) a stirring summons (to duty, etc). [Fr. *clairon*—*clair*—L. *clārus,* clear.]

clarity *klar'i-ti, n.* clearness. [M.E. *clarte*—L. *clāritās, -ātis.*]

clarsach *klar'sahh, n.* the old Celtic harp strung with wire. [Gael. *clàrsach* and Ir. *cláirsach,* a harp.]

clary *klā'ri, n.* a plant of the sage genus with pale-blue flowers and large coloured bracts: extended to others of the genus. [L.L. *sclarea.*]

clash *klash, n.* a loud noise, such as is caused by the striking together of sheets of metal: opposition: contradiction: an outbreak of fighting —*v.i.* to dash noisily together: to meet in opposition: to act in a contrary direction: to disagree: of events, to coincide disturbingly.—*v.t.* to strike noisily against: to bang, slam (*dial.*).—*n.* **clash'ing.** [Imit.]

clasp *klasp, n.* a fastening: a bar on the ribbon of a medal: an embrace: a grasp.—*v t.* to fasten with a clasp: to enclose and hold in the hand or arms: to embrace.—*ns.* **clas'per** that which clasps: the tendril of a plant: a clasping organ (*zool*); **clasp'ing.**—**clasp'-knife** a knife whose blade folds into the handle. [M.E *clapse.*]

class *klás, n.* a rank or order of persons or things: high rank or social standing: the system or situation in any community in which there is division of people into different social ranks: a number of students or scholars who are taught together, or are in the same year of their course: a scientific division or arrangement in biological classification· a grade, as of merit in examination, accommodation in a ship or railway train: style, quality (*coll*).—*v t* to form into a class or classes: to arrange methodically—*v.i.* to take rank.—*adj.* (*slang*) of high class.—*adjs.* **class'able, class'ible** capable of being classed; **classed.**—*n.* **classic** (*klas'ik*) any great writer, composer, or work, esp. in Greek and Latin literature. a standard work: (in *pl.*) Greek and Latin studies —*adjs.* **class'ic, -al** of the highest class or rank, esp in literature and music: originally and chiefly used of the best Greek and Roman writers· (as opposed to *romantic*) like in style to the authors of Greece and Rome or the old masters in music· chaste, refined, restrained, in keeping with classical art: having literary or historical associations: traditionally accepted, long established: excellent, standard (*slang*)· of clothes, made in simple tailored style that does not soon go out of fashion.—Also *n.*—*n.* **classical'ity**—*adv* **class'ically.**—*ns.* **class'icalness; class'icism** (*-sizm*) a classical idiom: in literature, music, etc , a principle, character, or tendency such as is seen in Greek classical literature, marked by beauty of form, good taste, restraint, and clarity—opposed to *romanticism;* **class'icist** one versed in the classics, or devoted to their being used in education· one who is for classicism rather than romanticism —*adjs.* **class'less** having no class distinctions: not belonging obviously to any social class: not confined to any particular category; **class'y** (*coll*) of or characteristic of high or upper class.—**class'-book** a book used in class teaching.—*adj* **class'-con'scious** clearly or acutely conscious of membership of a social class.—**class-con'sciousness; class-distinc'tion; class'-fellow,** **class'mate** a pupil in the same class at school or college; **classic races** the five chief annual horse-races—the Two Thousand Guineas, One Thousand, Derby, Oaks, and St Leger; **class'room** a room in which a class is held; **class'-war'** hostility or hostilities between different social ranks or classes, esp. between the proletariat and the combined middle and upper classes.— **in a class of, on,** its own so good as to be without an equal. [L. *classis,* a division of the Roman people.]

classify *klas'i-fī, v.t* to arrange in classes: to make secret for security reasons:—*pr.p.* **class'ifying;** *pa p.* **class'ified.**—*adjs.* **class'ifiable** (or *-fī'*) capable of being classified; **classif'ic** denoting classes.—*n.* **classificá'tion** the act or a system of arranging in classes.—*adjs.* **classificá'tory; class'ified** arranged in classes: of a road, in a class entitled to receive a government grant.—*n.* **class'ifier.**—**classified advertisements** advertisements in a newspaper or periodical grouped according to the goods or services offered. [L. *classis,* and *facĕre,* to make.]

classis *klas'is, n.* a group. [L]

clastic *klas'tik, (geol.) adj.* composed of fragments, fragmental. [Gr. *klastos—klaein,* to break.]

clathrate *klath'rit, -rāt, adj.* lattice-shaped (*biol.*): of a molecular compound, having one component enclosed in the cavities of the crystals of another component (*chem.*). [L *clāthrāre,* to furnish with a lattice]

clatter *klat'ər, n.* a repeated rattling noise: a repetition of abrupt, sharp sounds: noisy talk.—*v.i.* to make rattling sounds: to chatter —*v.t* to cause to rattle.— *n.* **clatt'erer.**—*adv.* **clatt'eringly.** [O.E. *clatrung,* clattering (verbal noun).]

claudication *klō-di-kā'shən, n.* a limp. [L *claudi-cātio, -ōnis—claudus,* lame.]

clause *klōz, n.* a sentence· part of a sentence with

subject and predicate: an article or part of a contract, will, act of parliament, etc.—*adjs.* **claus'al; claus'ular** pertaining to, or consisting of, a clause or clauses.—**dependent clause** a part of a sentence which cannot stand in isolation as a sentence in itself (opp. to **independent clause**). [Fr. *clause*—L. *claudĕre*, to shut.]

claustral *klōs'trəl, adj.* cloistral, secluded: pertaining to a claustrum: narrow-minded (*fig.*).—*ns.* **claustrā'tion** the act of shutting in a cloister; **claus'trum** a thin layer of grey matter in the brain hemispheres:—*pl.* **claus'tra; claustrophō'bia** a morbid dread of confined places.—*adj.* **claustrophō'bic** (or *-fob'*). [L. *claustrum*, an enclosed place.]

clavate, -d *klā'vāt, klav'āt, -id, adjs.* (*biol.*) club-shaped. [L. *clāva*, a club.]

clave¹ *klāv, pa.t.* of **cleave²**.

clave² *klā'vä, n.* one of a pair of small wooden cylinders held in the hands and struck together to mark S. American dance rhythm. [Sp., key to code, etc., clef—L. *clāvis*, key.]

clavicembalo *klav-i-chem'bə-lō, n.* a harpsichord:—*pl.* **clavicem'balos**. [It.,—L. *clāvis*, key, and **cembalo**]

clavichord *klav'i-körd, n.* an old keyboard stringed instrument in which the tangent striking the string and producing the sound also determines the vibrating length. [L. *clāvis*, a key, *chorda*, a string.]

clavicle *klav'i-kl, n.* the collar-bone.—Also **clavic'ula**. —*adj.* **clavic'ular**. [Fr. *clavicule*—L. *clāvicula*, dim. of *clāvis*, a key.]

clavier *klä-vēr', n.* the keyboard of a musical instrument: a stringed keyboard instrument, esp. the clavichord or the pianoforte. [Fr., (or Ger. *Klavier*,—Fr.),—L. *clāvis*, a key.]

clavis *klā'vis, n.* a key, hence a clue or aid for solving problems, interpreting a cipher, etc.:—*pl.* **clā'ves** (*-vēz*).—*n.* **claviger** (*klav'i-jər*) one who keeps a key, a custodian.—*adj.* **clavig'erous** keeping keys. [L. *clāvis*, a key.]

claw *klō, n.* the hooked nail of a beast or bird, or the creature's foot with a number of such nails: the leg of a crab, insect, etc., or its pointed end or pincer: anything like a claw.—*v.t.* to scratch: to tear: to scrape: to seize.—*adjs.* **clawed** having claws; **claw'less.**—*adj.* **claw-and-ball'** of furniture, having feet carved to represent an animal's claw holding a ball (also **ball'-and-claw'**).—**claw'back** a toady, flatterer: an arrangement by which financial benefit is partially recouped in extra taxation: extended to other situations; **claw'-hammer** a hammer with one part of the head divided into two claws, for drawing nails.—**claw me and I'll claw thee** favour me and I shall do you good in return. [O.E. *clawu*; akin to **cleave²**.]

clay *klā, n.* earth in very fine particles, tenacious and impervious (*agri.*): a tenacious ductile earthy material, hydrated aluminium silicates more or less impure (*chem.* and *min.*): earth in general: the human body: (in full **clay'-pipe'**) a tobacco-pipe of baked clay.—*adjs.* **clay'ey** made of clay: covered with clay: like clay; **clay'ish** of the nature of clay.—**clay'-court** a type of hard-surfaced tennis-court; **clay pigeon** a disc thrown from a trap and shot at as a substitute for a pigeon; **clay'-pit** a pit from which clay is dug.—**feet of clay** (*fig.*) faults and weaknesses of character not at first suspected. [O.E. *clæg*.]

claymore *klā-mōr', -mōr', n.* a large sword formerly used by the Scottish Highlanders. [Gael. *claidheamhmór*—Gael. and Ir. *claidheamh*, sword, *mór*, great.]

clean *klēn, adj.* neat: free from dirt, stain, or whatever defiles: pure: guiltless: honest, without corruption: having nothing of an incriminating nature on one's person (*slang*): (of a driving licence) without any

endorsements for motoring offences: complete: free of radioactive fall-out: of a design that causes little turbulent wake (*aerodynamics*).—*adv.* quite: entirely: smoothly: without mishap.—*v.t.* to make clean, or free from dirt.—*n.* act or instance of cleaning.—*n.* **clean'er.**—*n.* and *adj.* **clean'ing** (the act of) making clean.—*n.* **cleanliness** (*klen'li-nis*) habitual cleanness or purity.—*adj.* **cleanly** (*klen'li*) clean in habits and person: pure: neat.—*adv.* (*klēn'li*) in a clean manner.—*n.* **cleanness** (*klēn'nis*).—*adj.* **clean'-cut'** neat, well-shaped: with a neat, respectable appearance.—**clean hands** freedom from guilt or corruption.—*adjs.* **clean'-limb'ed** with shapely limbs: trim; **clean'-liv'ing** morally upright: respectable; **clean'-shav'en** with all facial hair shaved off.—**clean up** an act of thorough cleaning: the stamping out of an evil (see also **clean up** below).—**a clean sheet, slate** a fresh start; **a clean sweep** a complete change: the winning or gaining of all the prizes, votes, etc. (usu with *of*); **clean as a whistle** completely emptied; **clean out** to clean the inside of: to take away all someone's money from (someone) (*coll.*); **clean up** to make clean: to free from vice, corruption, etc.: to make (large profits) (*n* **clean'-up**); **come clean** (*slang*) to confess, to divulge, everything; **make a clean break** to sever a relationship, etc. completely; **show a clean pair of heels** to escape by running; **take (someone) to the cleaners** (*slang*) to take all, or a great deal of, a person's money, etc.: to beat or criticise (someone) severely. [O.E. *clǣne*.]

cleanse *klenz, v.t.* to make clean or pure.—*adj.* **cleans'able.**—*ns.* **cleans'er** one who, or that which, cleanses: cleansing-cream or the like; **cleans'ing** purification.—**cleans'ing-cream** a type of cream used to remove make-up from the face; **cleansing department** the section of local administration that deals with the collecting and disposing of refuse and the cleaning of streets. [O.E. *clǣnsian*.]

clear *klēr, adj.* pure, bright, undimmed, unclouded, undulled: free from obstruction, difficulty, complication, contents, blame, or accusation: disengaged: plain: distinct: obvious: without blemish, defect, drawback, or diminution: perspicuous: transparent: not coded.—*adv.* in a clear manner: plainly: wholly: quite: out of the way (of).—*v.t.* to make clear: to empty: to free from obscurity, obstruction, or guilt: to free, acquit, or vindicate: to leap, or pass by or over: to make as profit: to settle, as a bill: to decode: to unscramble: to declare free from security, etc., restrictions: of a cheque, etc., to pass through a clearing-bank: to pass through (customs, etc.).—*v.i.* to become clear: to grow free, bright, transparent.—*ns.* **clear'age** a piece of land cleared; **clear'ance** the act of clearing: general removal or emptying: eviction from lands: removal of hindrances: intervening space: play between parts, as of a machine: a declaration of freedom from restrictions; **clear'er; clear'ing** the act of making clear: the tract of land cleared of wood, etc., for cultivation: the method by which bankers change cheques and drafts, and arrange the differences.—*adv.* **clear'ly** in a clear manner: distinctly.—*n.* **clear'ness.**—**clearance sale** a sale of goods at reduced prices in order to make room for new stock.—*adjs.* **clear'-cut'** sharp in outline: free from obscurity; **clear'-eyed** clear-sighted, discerning; **clear'head'ed** having a clear understanding.—**clear'ing-bank** a bank that is a member of the London Bankers' Clearing House, through which it makes credit and cheque transfers to and from other banks; **clear'ing-house** an office where financial clearing business is done; a central source or pool of information, etc. (*fig.*).—*adj.* **clear'-sight'ed** having clearness of sight: discerning.—**clear'-sight'edness; clear'-story** see clerestory; clear'way a stretch of road on which motorists are not allowed to stop.—clear off to get rid of, dispose of: to go away, esp. in order to avoid something (coll.); clear one's throat to give a slight cough; clear out to get rid of: to empty: of a ship, to clear and leave port: to take oneself off; clear the air to simplify the situation and relieve tension; clear the way to make the way open; clear up to make or to become clear: to explain (a mystery, misunderstanding, etc.); in the clear free of suspicion: out of a difficulty: solvent. [Fr. clair—L. clārus, clear.]

clearcole klēr'kōl, n. a priming coat consisting of size or glue with whiting. [Fr. claire colle, clear glue.]

cleat klēt, n. a wedge: a piece of wood, etc., nailed across anything to keep it in its place or give it an additional strength: a piece attached to parts of a ship for fastening ropes.—v.t. to strengthen with a cleat: to fasten to or by a cleat   [From a supposed O.E. clēat.]

cleave[1] klēv, v t. to divide, to split: to separate with violence: to go through: to pierce.—v.t. to part asunder: to crack:—pr.p. cleav'ing; pa.t clōve or cleft; pa.p. clōv'en or cleft.—adj. cleav'able capable of being cleft.—ns. cleav'ableness; cleav'age a split: a tendency to split, esp. (in rocks and minerals) in certain directions: mitotic cell-division: the hollow between a woman's breasts, esp. as shown by a low-cut dress; cleav'er one who or that which cleaves· a butcher's chopper.—adj. cleav'ing splitting.—n. a cleft.—in a cleft stick (fig.) in a difficult situation: in a dilemma. [O.E. clēofan.]

cleave[2] klēv, v.i. to stick or adhere: to unite:—pa t. cleaved or clāve; pa.p cleaved.—ns. cleav'ers, clivers (kliv'ərz) goose-grass which cleaves to fur or clothes by its hooks, cleav'ing the act of adhering.—Also adj. [O.E. clifian.]

clef klef, n. a character placed on the stave by which the absolute pitch of the notes is fixed. [Fr clef, key —L. clāvis.]

cleft[1] kleft, pa.t. and pa.p. of cleave[1].

cleft[2] kleft, n. an opening made by cleaving or splitting: a crack, fissure, or chink. [Cf. Ger. Kluft, Dan. klyft, a hole.]

cleg kleg, n. a gadfly, horse-fly. [O.N. kleggi.]

cleistogamy, clistogamy klīs-tog'ə-mi, (bot.) n. production of small flowers, often simplified and inconspicuous, which do not open, and in which self-pollination occurs.—adjs. cleistogamic (-tə-gam'ik), cleistog'amous. [Gr. kleistos, closed, gamos, marriage.]

Clematis klem'ə-tis, klə-mā'tis, n. a genus of Ranunculaceae, including virgin's-bower or traveller's-joy: (without cap.) a plant of the genus. [L.,—Gr. klēmatis, a plant, prob. periwinkle—klēma, a twig.]

clement klem'ənt, adj. mild: gentle: kind: merciful.— n. clem'ency the quality of being clement: mildness: readiness to forgive.—adv. clem'ently. [Fr.,—L. clēmēns, -entis.]

clementine klem'ən-tēn, -tīn, n. a type of orange.

clench klench, klensh, v.t. to close tightly: to grasp: to clinch.   [Same as clinch.]

clepsydra klep'si-drə, n. an instrument for measuring time by the trickling of water, a water-clock. [L.,— Gr. klepsydrā—kleptein, to steal, hydōr, water.]

clerestory, clear-story clēr'stō-ri, -stō-, n. an upper storey or part with its own row of windows—esp. the storey above the triforium in a church. [clear, prob. in sense of lighted, and storey.]

clergy klûr'ji, n. the ministers of the Christian or other religion.—adjs. cleric, -al (kler'ik, -əl) belonging to the clergy: pertaining to a clerk or scribe.—ns. cler'ic a clergyman; cler'icalism undue influence of the clergy: sacerdotalism; cler'icalist.—n.pl. cler'icals

clerical garb.—ns. cler'icate clerical position; clericity (klar-is'-ti) the state of being a clergyman; clerisy (kler'i-si) the class of learned men, scholars.— cler'gyman one of the clergy, a regularly ordained minister; cler'gy-woman a woman who is a minister of religion; clerical collar the white collar worn by many Christian clergy, fastening behind the neck. [Fr. clergé—L. clēricus—Gr. klērikos, from klēros, a lot, a heritage, then the clergy]

cleric, etc.   See clergy, clerk.

clerihew kler'i-hū, n. a jingle in two short couplets purporting to quintessentialise the life and character of some notable person. [Started by E. Clerihew (Bentley) in his Biography for Beginners (1905).]

clerisy.   See clergy.

clerk klärk (U S. klûrk), n a clergyman or priest: a scholar: in common use, one employed as a writer, assistant, copyist, account-keeper, or correspondent in an office.—v.i. to act as clerk.—adj. cler'ical of, done by, etc., clerks (see also under clergy).—ns. clerk'dom; clerk'ess a female clerk.—adj. clerk'ish like a clerk, clerk'less ignorant; clerk'-like scholarly.—n. clerk'ling a young clerk.—adj. clerk'ly scholarly.—adv in a scholar-like or learned manner.—n. clerk'ship.—clerk of the course in horse- or motor-racing, an official in charge of administration; clerk of works one who superintends the erection and maintenance of a building, etc. [O E. clerc, a priest—L.L clēricus; see clergy.]

clever klev'ər, adj. able or dexterous: ingenious: skilful.—n clev'erness.—adj. clev'erish somewhat clever.—adv. clev'erly.—clever dick (slang) a person who thinks himself clever

clevis klev'is, n. a U-shaped piece of metal through which tackle may pass, fixed at the end of a beam. [Ety. dub.]

clew, clue klōō, n. a thread that guides through a labyrinth: the corner of a sail.—v.t. to coil up into a clew or ball: to tie up to the yards (usu. with up): to fix up (fig.) —n.pl clew'-lines ropes on the smaller square sails by which they are clewed up for furling. [O.E. cliwen.]

Clianthus kli-an'thəs, n. an Australian genus of shrub or vine with hanging red flowers: (without cap.) any plant of the genus. [L.,—G. kleos, glory, anthos, flower.]

cliché klē'shā, n. an electrotype or stereotype plate: a stereotyped phrase, or literary tag: something hackneyed as idea, plot, situation.—adjs. cli'ché-ridden, cli'ché(')d filled with clichés. [Fr.]

click klik, n. a short, sharp ticking sound: anything that makes such a sound, a clucking sound characteristic of certain South African native languages: a latch for a gate.—v.i. to make a light, sharp sound: to fit into place opportunely or successfully, esp. to succeed in coming into relations of sociability with a person of the other sex (slang).—ns. click'er; click'ing the action of the verb.—click'-clack a persistent clicking noise.—click'ety-click', -clack' a continuous, usu. regular, clicking sound. [Dim. of clack.]

client kli'ənt, n a vassal, dependant, or hanger-on: one who employs a lawyer or other professional adviser: a customer.—n. cli'entage the whole number of one's clients: the client's relation to the patron.—adj. cliental (-ent'l).—ns. clientèle (klē-ā-tel'), clientele (kli'ən-tēl), a following: the whole connection of a lawyer, shopkeeper, etc.; cli'entship. [L. cliēns, -entis, a dependant upon a patrōnus.]

cliff klif, n. a high steep rock: the steep side of a mountain.—adjs. cliffed, cliff'y having cliffs: craggy.— cliff'-face' the sheer or steep front of a cliff; cliff'-hanger a tense, exciting adventure or contest: an ending line of an episode of a serial, etc. that leaves one in suspense: a serial, film, etc. that keeps one in suspense.—*v.i.* **cliff'hang.**—*n.*, *adj.* **cliff'hanging.** [O.E. *clif;* Du. *clif;* O.N. *klif.*]

climacteric *klī-mak'tər-ık* or *klī-mak-ter'ik*, *n.* a critical period in human life, in which some great bodily change takes place: a critical time.—*adj.* pertaining to such a period: critical.—*adj.* **climacter'ical.** [Gr. *klīmaktēr—klīmax*, a ladder.]

climactic, -al. See **climax.**

climate *klī'mıt, -māt, n.* the condition of a country or place with regard to temperature, moisture, etc. (also *fig.*): the character of something (*fig.*).—*adjs.* **cli'matal; climatic** (*-mat'ik*), **-al.**—*v.t.* **cli'matise, -ize** see **acclimatise.**—*adj.* **climatograph'ical.**—*n.* **climatog'raphy** a description of climates.—*adj.* **climatolog'ical.**—*ns.* **climatol'ogist; climatol'ogy** the science of climates, or an investigation of the causes on which the climate of a place depends.—**climate of opinion** the critical atmosphere or complex of opinions prevalent at a particular time or in a particular place. [Fr. *climat*—L. *clima*—Gr. *klima, -atos,* slope—*klīnein,* to slope.]

climax *klī'maks, n.* the arranging of discourse in order of increasing strength (*rhet.*): loosely, the last term of the rhetorical arrangement: hence, a culmination: of a story, play, piece of music, etc., the most interesting and important or exciting part: the relatively stable culmination of a series of plant and animal communities developing in an area (also **climax community**): sexual orgasm.—*v.i.* to ascend in a climax: to culminate (in).—*adjs.* **climact'ic, -al** pertaining to a climax.—*adv.* **climact'ically.** [Gr. *klīmax, -akos,* a ladder—*klīnein,* to slope.]

climb *klīm, v.t.* or *v.t.* to ascend or mount by clutching with the hands and feet: to ascend with difficulty: to mount: of plants, to ascend by means of tendrils; or otherwise: extended to similar downward movement:—*pa.t.* and *pa.p.* **climbed.**—*n.* an act of climbing: an ascent.—*adjs.* **climb'able.**—*n.* **climb'er.**—*n.* and *adj* **climb'ing.**—**climb down** to become more humble: to abandon a firmly stated opinion or resolve, or an excessive or overweening demand, position or attitude (*n.* **climb'-down**).—**climb'ing-frame** a wooden or metal structure on or through which children can climb. [O.E. *climban;* cf. Ger. *klimmen;* **clamber, cleave**[2].]

clime *klīm, n.* a country, region, tract. [**climate.**]

clinch *klinch, klinsh, v.t.* to fasten or rivet a nail by bending and beating down the point: to drive home (an argument; *fig.*): to settle or confirm (*fig.*).—*v.t.* to grapple.—*n.* something set firmly: the fastening of a nail by beating it back: an embrace (*coll.*): a pun.—*n.* **clinch'er** one that clinches: a decisive argument.—*adj.* **clinch'er-built** same as **clinker-built.** [Same as **clench;** causal form of **clink**[3].]

cline *klīn,* (*biol.*) *n.* a gradation of differences of form, etc., seen, e.g. within one species over a specified area of the world. [See **clino-.**]

cling *kling, v.i.* to stick close by adhesive surface or by clasp: to adhere in interest or affection: to remain by an opinion:—*pa.t.* and *pa.p.* **clung.**—*n.* adherence.—*adjs.* **cling, cling'stone** (of peaches, *etc.*) having the pulp adhering firmly to the stone.—*n.* **cling'iness.**—*adj.* **cling'y** sticky.—**cling film** a type of transparent plastic film used to seal food containers, etc. [O E. *clingan.*]

clinic *klin'ik, n.* the instruction of medicine or surgery at the bedside of hospital patients: a session of such instruction: a private hospital or nursing-home: an institution, or a department of one, or a group of doctors, for treating patients or for diagnosis or giving advice: any group meeting for instruction, often remedial, in a particular field.—Also *adj.*—*adj.*

clin'ical hospital-like: concerned with, based on, observation: strictly objective: plain, functional in appearance.—*adv.* **clin'ically.**—*n.* **clinician** (*-ish'ən*) a doctor, etc. who works directly with patients: a doctor, etc. who runs, or works in, a clinic.—**clinical death** a state of the body in which the brain has entirely ceased to function, though artificial means can be used to maintain the action of the heart, lungs, etc.; **clinical medicine** or **surgery** medicine or surgery as taught by clinics; **clinical lecture** one to students at the bedside of the sick; **clinical thermometer** one for taking the temperature of patients. [Gr. *klinikos—klīnē,* a bed.]

clink[1] *klingk, n.* a ringing sound made by striking metal, glass, etc.—*v.t* to cause to make a ringing sound.—*v.t.* to ring: to go with a clink.—*n.* **clink'er** a hard brick (also **klink'er** as Dutch): the incombustible residue of fused ash raked out of furnaces: furnace slag. the cindery crust of some lava-flows. [A form of **click** and **clank.**]

clink[2] *klingk, n.* (*slang*) prison. [Appar. orig. one in Southwark.]

clink[3] *klingk, v.t.* to clinch: to rivet.—*n.* **clink'er** a nail used as a protective stud in footwear: anything worthy of warm admiration (*slang*): a blunder (*slang*).—*adj.* (*slang*) **clink'ing.**—*adj.* **clink'er-built** made of planks which overlap those below and fastened with clinched nails. [Northern form of **clinch.**]

clinker. See **clink**[1,3].

clino- *klī'nō-,* in composition, oblique.—*n* **clinometer** (*klin-, klin-om'ı-tər*) any of various instruments for measuring slope, elevation, or inclination.—*adj.* **clinomet'ric.**—*n.* **clinom'etry.** [Gr. *klīnein,* to lean]

Clio *klī'ō, n.* the muse of history. [Gr. *Kleiō,* proclaimer.]

cliometrics *klī-ō-met'riks, n. sing.* the application of econometrics in economic history. [**Clio,** econometrics.]

clip[1] *klıp, v.t.* to cut with shears: to cut off: to trim or cut off the hair, twigs, ends, edges, etc. of: to reduce or curtail: to shorten in indistinct utterance: to punch a piece from: to hit sharply.—*v.t.* to go at a good speed:—*pr.p.* **clipp'ing;** *pa.p.* **clipped, clipt.**—*n.* an act of clipping: the thing removed by clipping: yield of wool: a smart blow: high speed: a piece taken from a film for separate showing.—*adj.* **clipped, clipt.**—*ns.* **clipp'er** one who clips: a clipping instrument: a swift mover: a fast sailing-vessel; **clipp'ing** the act of clipping, esp. the edges of coins: a small piece clipped off, shred, paring: a newspaper cutting.—*adj.* superb: fast-going.—**clip'-joint** a place of entertainment, e.g. a night-club, where customers are overcharged or cheated.—**clip the wings** to cut the feathers of a bird's wings to prevent it from flying: to restrain ambition (*fig.*): to deprive of the means of rising. [Prob. from O.N. *klıppa,* to cut.]

clip[2] *klıp, v.t.* to encircle: to hold firmly.—*n.* a device for gripping, clasping, fastening, or holding things together: a container for ammunition which is clipped on to a rifle, etc.—**clip'board** a firm board to which papers can be clipped in order to take notes easily; **clip'-fas'tener** a name for a press-stud. [O.E. *clyppan,* to embrace.]

clip-clop. See **clop.**

clipt. See **clip**[1].

clique *klēk, n* an exclusive group of persons: a faction: a coterie—used generally in a bad sense.—*adjs.* **cliqu'(e)y, cliqu'ish** relating to a clique: exclusive.—*ns.* **cliqu'iness; cliqu'ishness; cliqu'ism** the tendency to form cliques. [Fr , prob. conn. with **click.**]

clistogamy. See **cleistogamy.**

clitoris *kli', klī'tə-ris, n.* a homologue of the penis in the female.—*adj.* **clit'oral**. [Gr. *kleitoris.*]

clivers. Same as **cleavers.**

cloaca *klō-ā'kə, n.* a sewer: a privy: a cavity in birds and reptiles, in which the intestinal and urinary ducts terminate:—*pl.* **cloacae** (*klō-ā'sē*).—*adjs.* **cloā'cal, cloā'calin(e), cloacinal** (*klō-ə-sī'nl*). [L. *cloaca—cluēre,* to purge.]

cloak *klōk, n.* a loose outer garment: a covering: that which conceals: a disguise, pretext.—*v.t.* to clothe with a cloak: to cover: to conceal (usu with *with* or *in*).—*adjs.* **cloak'-and-dagg'er** concerned with plot and intrigue esp espionage; **cloak'-and-sword'** concerned with fighting and romance.—**cloak'room** a room for keeping coats and hats: a lavatory. [O.Fr *cloke, cloque*—L.L. *cloca,* a bell, horseman's bell-shaped cape; see **clock**[1].]

clobber[1] *klob'ər,* (*slang*), *n.* clothing, gear.

clobber[2] *klob'ər* (*slang*) *v.t.* to strike very hard: to attack, cause to suffer (*fig.*): to defeat overwhelmingly.

cloche *klosh, n.* a glass under which plants are forced: a lady's close-fitting hat. [Fr.; see **clock**[1].]

clock[1] *klok, n.* a machine for measuring time, strictly one with a bell: a speedometer (*coll.*).—*v.t.* to time by a clock or stop-watch: to achieve (a certain officially attested time for a race): to hit (*slang*).—*v.i.* to register a time by a recording clock.—*adv.* **clock'-wise** in the manner or direction of the hands of a clock.—**clock'maker; clock'-ra'dio** an electronic apparatus combining the functions of alarm-clock and radio, esp. for bedside use.—Also **alarm'-ra'dio; clock tower** a usu. a square tower having a clock at the top with a face on each exterior wall; **clock'work** the works or machinery of a clock: machinery steady and regular like that of a clock.—*adj.* automatic.—**against the clock** with effort to overcome shortage of time or achieve the shortest time, **beat the clock** to finish a job, etc., before the time limit runs out; **clock in, out, on, off** to register time of coming or going, in, out, on, off; **clock up** (*coll.*) to reach (a certain speed, score, etc.); **like clockwork** as smoothly as if driven by clockwork (*fig.*); **o'clock,** for earlier *of the clock,* as reckoned or shown by the clock· in a direction corresponding to that which would be taken by the hour-hand of a horizontal clock relative to a person at the centre and facing twelve; **put back the clock, put the clock back** to return to earlier time and its conditions; **round the clock** for the whole of the twenty-four hours; **watch the clock** to wait eagerly for one's worktime to finish, i.e. to skimp one's work, do no more than is necessary (*ns.* **clock'-watcher; clock' watching**). [M.E. *clokke,* prob. through O.Fr. from L.L. *cloca, clocca,* a bell.]

clock[2] *klok, n.* an ornament on the side of a stocking.—*adj.* **clocked** ornamented with such clocks.

clod *klod, n.* a thick round mass or lump, that sticks together, esp of earth or turf: a concreted mass: the ground: a stupid fellow.—*adj.* **clodd'ish.**—*n* **clodd'-ishness.**—*adj.* **clodd'y** abounding in clods: earthy.—*adv.* **clod'ly.**—**clod'hopper** a countryman: a peasant: a dolt: a heavy, clumsy shoe (*slang*).—*adj.* **clod'hop-ping** boorish—**clod'pate, clod'pole, clod'poll** a stupid fellow.—*adj* **clod'pated.** [A later form of **clot.**]

clog *klog, n.* a block of wood· an obstruction: a wooden shoe: a shoe with a wooden sole—*v.t.* to fasten a piece of wood to: to choke up with an accumulation (often with *up*): to obstruct.—*adj.* **clogged** encumbered.—*ns.* **clogg'er** one who makes clogs; **clogg'-iness.**—*adj.* **clogg'y** lumpy, sticky.—**clog'dance** a dance performed with clogs, the clatter keeping time to the music.

cloison *klwä-zō, kloi'zn, n.* a partition, dividing fillet or band.—*adj.* **cloisonné** (*klwäz-on-ā, kloi-zon'ā,* or *-ā'*) decorated in enamel, in compartments formed by small fillets of metal.—*n.* work of this kind. [Fr.]

cloister *klois'tər, n.* a covered arcade forming part of a monastic or collegiate establishment: a place of religious retirement, a monastery or nunnery: an enclosed place: monastic life.—*v.t.* to confine in a cloister: to confine within walls.—*adj.* **clois'tered** dwelling in or enclosed by cloisters: sheltered from reality and the full experience of life.—*n.* **clois'terer** one belonging to a cloister.—*adj.* **clois'tral** claustral, pertaining or confined to a cloister: secluded. [O.Fr. *cloistre* (O.E. *clauster*)—L. *claustrum—claudĕre, clausum,* to shut.]

clone *klōn,* (*biol.*) *n.* the whole stock of individuals derived asexually from one sexually produced: any of such individuals.—*v.t.* to reproduce as a clone: to produce a clone or clones of.—*adj.* **clō'nal.** [Gr. *klōn,* shoot.]

clonic. See **clonus.**

clonk *klongk, n.* the sound of something heavy falling on to a surface.—*v.i.* to make or go with such a sound. —*v.t.* to hit. [Imit.]

clonus *klō'nəs, n.* a spasm of alternate contractions and relaxations of the muscles.—*adj.* **clonic** (*klon'ik*). [Latinised from Gr. *klōnos,* tumult.]

clop *klop, n.* the sound of a horse's hoof-tread.—*adv.* with a clop.—*v.i.* to make, or go with, such a sound. —Also **clip'-clop', clop'-clop'.** [Imit.]

cloqué *klo-kā', n.* an embossed material.—Also *adj.* [Fr.]

close[1] *klōs, adj.* shut up: with no opening: confined, unventilated: stifling: narrow: stingy: near, in time or place (often with *to* or *by*): intimate: compact: crowded: hidden: reserved: private: secret: thorough, in detail.—*adv.* in a close manner: tightly: nearly: densely: secretly.—*n.* an enclosed place: a narrow passage off a street, esp. leading to a tenement stairway or courtyard: the precinct of a cathedral.—*adv.* **close'ly.**—*n.* **close'ness.**—*adjs.* **close'-band'ed** closely united; **close'-barred** firmly closed; **close'-bod'ied** fitting close to the body.—**close call** a narrow escape; **close company** a firm controlled by five, or fewer, people; **close corporation** a corporation which fills up its own vacancies, without outside interference; **close encounter** a direct personal confrontation with an extra-terrestrial being (also *fig.*).—*adjs.* **close'-fist'ed, close'-hand'ed** penurious, covetous; **close'-fitt'ing** of clothes, designed to fit tightly; **close'-grained** with the particles, fibres, etc., close together, compact.—**close harmony** harmony in which the notes of chords lie close together.—*adjs.* **close'-knit'** of communities, etc., closely connected, bound together; **close'-lipped', -mouthed'** reticent, saying little.—**close season, time** a time of the year when it is illegal to kill certain game or fish—the breeding season: a prohibited or inactive period; **close shave, thing** a close call, **close'-up'** a photograph or film taken near at hand and thus detailed and big in scale: a close scrutiny.—**close to the chest** without revealing one's intentions. [Fr. *clos,* shut—L. *claudĕre, clausum,* to close, shut up.]

close[2] *klōz, v.t.* to make close: to draw together and unite: to end.—*v.i.* to come together: to grapple: to come to an end: to agree (with).—*n.* the manner or time of closing: a pause or stop: a cadence: the end.—*adj.* **closed** shut: blocked: not open to traffic: with permanent sides and top: with lid, etc.: exclusive, having few contacts outside itself (e.g. *a closed community*): continuous and finishing where it began.—*ns.* **clos'er; clos'ing** enclosing: ending: agreement; **clos'ure** the act of closing: the end.—**closed book**

(*fig.*) a mystery: something about which one knows nothing.—*adj.* **closed'-chain'** (*chem.*) having a molecule in which the atoms are linked ringwise, like a chain with the ends united.—**closed circuit** (*television*) a system in which the showing is for restricted not general viewing; **closed shop** an establishment in which only members of a trade union, or of a particular trade union, will be employed: the principle or policy implied in such a regulation; **closed syllable** one ending in a consonant; **closing price** the value of shares on the stock-market when business stops for the day; **closing-time** the time at which business stops, esp. in public houses.—**close a bargain** to make an agreement; **close down** to come to a standstill or stoppage of work: to give up business (*n.* **close'-down**); **close in upon** to surround and draw near to; **close one's eyes** to ignore purposely; **close ranks** (of soldiers drawn up in line) to stand closer together in order to present a more solid front to the enemy: to unite, make a show of solidarity in the face of a common danger; **close with** to accede to: to grapple with; **with closed doors** in private, the public being excluded, as in special cases in court, etc. (*adj.* **closed'-door'**). [Fr *clore*, *clos*—L. *claudēre*, *clausum*.]

closet *kloz'it*, *n.* a small private room: a recess off a room: a privy: the private chamber of a sovereign.—*v.t.* to shut up in or take into a closet: to conceal:—*pr.p.* **clos'eting**; *pa.t.* and *pa.p.* **clos'eted**.—**clos'et-play**, **-drama** a play to be read rather than acted; **closet queen** (*slang*) a homosexual who does not openly admit his homosexuality; **clos'et-strat'egist** a mere theorist in strategy. [O.Fr. *closet*, dim. of *clos*, an enclosure; see **close**.]

closure. See **close²**.

clot *klot*, *n.* a mass of soft or fluid matter concreted, as blood: a fool.—*v.t.* and *v.i.* to form into clots:—*pr.p* **clott'ing**; *pa.t.* and *pa.p.* **clott'ed**.—*v.t.* **clott'er** to coagulate.—*ns.* **clott'iness**; **clott'ing** coagulation.—*adj.* **clott'y**.—**clotted** (also **clouted**) **cream** a famous Devonshire dainty, prepared by scalding milk. [O.E. *clott*, a clod of earth.]

cloth *kloth*, *klòth*, *n.* woven material from which garments or coverings are made: a piece of this material: clothing: the usual dress of a trade or profession, esp. the clerical: a table-cloth: sails:—*pl.* **cloths** (*kloths*, *klòdhz*).—*v.t.* **clothe** (*klōdh*) to cover with a garment: to provide with clothes: to invest as with a garment (*fig.*): to cover:—*pr.p.* **clothing** (*klōdh'ing*); *pa.t.* and *pa.p.* **clothed** (*klōdhd*) or **clad**.—*n.pl.* **clothes** (*klōdhz*; *coll.* *klōz*) garments or articles of dress: blankets, sheets and cover for a bed.—*ns* **clothier** (*klō'dhi-ər*) one who makes or sells cloth or clothes; **clothing** (*klō'dhing*) clothes, garments: covering.—**cloth cap** a flat cap.—*adjs.* **cloth'-cap'** symbolic of the working-class; **cloth'-eared** (*slang*) deaf, usu. because inattentive.—**clothes'-brush** a brush for clothes.—*adj.* **clothes'-conscious** concerned about one's clothes and appearance.—**clothes'-horse**, **clothes'-screen** a frame for hanging clothes on to dry, **clothes'-line** a rope or wire for hanging clothes on to dry; **clothes'-peg**, **-pin** a forked piece of wood or a wooden or plastic clamp to secure clothes on a line; **clothes'-pole** a pole from which clothes-lines are hung; **clothes'-press** a place for holding clothes: an apparatus for pressing clothes; **clothes'-prop** a movable notched pole for raising or supporting a clothes-line; **clothes'-sense** dress-sense.—**clothe in words** to express in words; **cloth of gold** a tissue of threads of gold and silk or wool; **the cloth** the clerical profession: the clergy. [O.E. *clāth*, cloth.]

cloture *klō'chər*, Fr. *klô-tur*, *n.* closure: the limitation of a debate in a legislative assembly, usu. by calling

for an immediate vote (*U.S.*).—Also *v.t.* [Fr. *clôture*; see **closure**.]

cloud *klowd*, *n.* a mass of fog, consisting of minute particles of water, often in a frozen state, floating in the atmosphere: anything unsubstantial (*fig.*): a great number of anything: anything that obscures, as a cloud: a dullness: a dark or dull spot: a great volume of dust or smoke: anything gloomy, overhanging or bodeful.—*v.t.* to overspread with clouds: to darken: to defame: to stain with dark spots or streaks: to dull.—*v.i.* to become clouded or darkened.—*n.* **cloud'age.**—*adj.* **cloud'ed** hidden by clouds: darkened, indistinct, dull (*fig.*): variegated with spots.—*adv.* **cloud'ily.**—*ns.* **cloud'iness**; **cloud'ing** a cloudy appearance.—*adj.* growing dim.—*adj.* **cloud'-less** unclouded, clear.—*adv.* **cloud'lessly.**—*n.* **cloud'-let** a little cloud.—*adj.* **cloud'y** darkened with, or consisting of, clouds: obscure: gloomy: stained with dark spots.—**cloud base** the under-surface of cloud(s): the height of this above sea-level; **cloud'-berry** a low plant related to the bramble: with an orange-red berry; **cloud'burst** a sudden flood of rain over a small area; **cloud'-cuck'oo-land** an imaginary situation or land; **cloud'-chamber** an apparatus in which the path of charged particles is made visible by means of water-drops condensed on gas ions; **cloud'-seeding** the induction of rainfall by scattering particles, e.g. dry ice, silver iodide, on clouds from aircraft.—**on cloud nine** (*coll.*) intensely happy; **under a cloud** in trouble, disgrace, or disfavour; **with one's head in the clouds** in a dreamy impractical way. [O.E. *clūd*, a hill, then a cloud.]

clough *kluf*, or *klow*, *n.* a ravine: a valley. [O.E. would be *clōh*.]

clout *klowt*, *n.* a piece of cloth, esp. used for mending: a patch: a protective plate or nail: a blow or cuff: influence, power (*coll.*).—*v.t.* to mend with a patch: to protect with a plate or with nails: to cover with a cloth: to cuff. [O.E. *clūt*.]

clouted *klowt'id*, *adj.* clotted. [See **clot**.]

clove¹ *klōv*, *pa.t.* of **cleave¹**.—**clove'-hitch'** a kind of hitch knot.

clove² *klōv*, *n.* a division of a bulb, as in garlic. [O.E. *clufu*; cf. **cleave¹**.]

clove³ *klōv*, *n.* the flower-bud of the **clove'-tree** dried as a spice, and yielding an essential oil: (in *pl.*) a cordial got therefrom.—**clove'-gill'yflower**, **clove'-pink** a variety of pink, smelling of cloves. [Fr. *clou*, nail, from its shape—L. *clāvus*, a nail.]

cloven *klōv'n*, *p.adj.* split: divided.—*adjs.* **clov'en-foot'ed**, **clov'en-hoofed'** having the hoof divided, as the ox or sheep.—**the cloven hoof** applied to any indication of devilish agency or temptation, from the early representation of the devil with cloven hoofs. [*Pa.p.* of **cleave**, to divide.]

clover *klō'vər*, *n.* a genus (Trifolium) of papilionaceous plants, with heads of small flowers and trifoliate leaves, affording rich pasturage.—*adj.* **clov'ered** covered with clover.—*adj.* **clov'ery** abounding in clover.—**clov'er-grass** clover; **clov'erleaf** a traffic arrangement in which one road passes over the top of another and the roads connecting the two are in the pattern of a four-leafed clover.—**live in clover** to live luxuriously or in abundance [O.E. *clāfre* (usu. *clæfre*).]

clown *klown*, *n.* a rustic or country-fellow: an ill-bred fellow: a fool or buffoon, esp. of the circus: a stupid person (*coll*).—*v.i.* to play the clown.—*ns.* **clown'-ery** a clown's performance; **clown'ing.**—*adj.* **clown'-ish** of or like a clown: coarse and awkward. rustic.—*adv.* **clown'ishly.**—*ns.* **clown'ishness**; **clown'ship.** [Perh.—L. Ger., cf. Fris. *klonne*, *klünne*]

cloy *kloi*, *v t.* to overcharge with food, to satiate, esp with sweetness: to disgust, weary.—*v.i* to cause distaste, become distasteful from excess.—*adjs.* **cloyed; cloy'ing.** [Aphetised from *accloy*—O.Fr. *encloyer.*—L.L. *inclāvāre*, to drive in a nail.]

cloze *klōz*, (*education*) *adj.* denoting a type of exercise in which the reader is required to supply words that have been deleted from a text, as a test of comprehension in reading. [Formed from **closure**.]

club *klub, n* a heavy tapering stick, knobby or massy at one end, used to strike with: a cudgel: a bat used in certain games: an instrument for playing golf, with a wooden, iron, or aluminium head, or a wooden head with brass sole: a bunch: a card of one of the four suits: a combination: a clique, set: an association of persons for social, political, athletic, or other ends: an association of persons who possess a building as a common resort for the members: a club-house, or the house occupied by a club.—*v.t.* to beat with a club: to gather into a bunch: to combine: to use as as a club: to throw into confusion (*mil.*).—*v.i.* to join together for some common end: to combine together: to share in a common expense.—*adjs.* **club'(b)able** sociable; **clubbed** enlarged at the end like a club.—*n.* **clubb'ing** beating: combination: a thickening, as of finger-ends. —**club'-face** the face of a golf-club; **club'-foot'** a deformed foot.—*adj.* **club'-foot'ed.**—**club'-head** the head of a golf-club; **club'house** a house for the accommodation of a club; **club'-line** a short line at the end of a paragraph; **club'man** one who carries a club: a member of a club: a frequenter of clubs, man-about-town; **club'room** the room in which a club meets; **club'root** a fungal disease which attacks the roots of plants of the Cruciferae; **club'-rush** any sedge of the genus Scirpus; **club sandwich** a sandwich of toast, usu. three slices, containing chicken or turkey, bacon or ham, lettuce, tomato, and mayonnaise; **club soda** soda water; **club'woman.—in the (pudding) club** (*slang*) pregnant; **join the club** (*coll.*) we are all in the same position: me too. [O.N. and Sw. *klubba*; same root as **clump**.]

cluck *kluk, n.* the call of a hen to her chickens: any similar sound.—*v.i.* to make such a sound. [Imit.]

clue[1] *klōō, n.* anything that points to the solution of a mystery.—*adj.* **clue'less** without a trace: trackless: ignorant: stupid.—*adj.* **clued'-up'** (*coll.*) (well-)informed.—**clue in** (*coll.*) to inform; **not have a clue** to have no information; **to have no idea, no notion at all.** [See **clew**.]

clue[2]. See **clew**.

clump *klump, n.* a thick, short, shapeless piece of anything: a cluster: a clot: a thick additional sole: a blow. —*v.i.* to walk heavily: to clot: to cluster.—*v.t.* to put in a clump: to beat.—*n.* **clump'iness.**—*adj.* **clump'ing** (*coll.*) clumsy.—*adj.* **clump'y** abounding in clumps: heavy. [Prob. Scand.]

clumsy *klum'zi, adj.* shapeless: ill-made: unwieldy: awkward: ungainly.—*adv.* **clum'sily.**—*n.* **clum'siness.** [M.E. *clumsen*, to be stiff or benumbed.]

clung *klung, pa.t.* and *pa.p.* of **cling.**

clunk *klungk, n.* a thump.—*v.i.* to fall with a thumping sound. [Imit.]

cluster *klus'tər, n.* a number of things of the same kind growing or joined together: a bunch: a mass: a crowd. —*v.i.* to grow in or gather into clusters.—*v.t.* to collect into clusters: to cover with clusters.—*adjs* **clus'tered** grouped; **clus'tering; clus'tery.—clus'ter-bomb** a bomb that opens on impact to throw out a number of small bombs; **clust'er-pine** the pinaster (*Pinus pinaster*), a pine with clustered cones. [O.E. *clyster.*]

clutch[1] *kluch, v.t.* to close the hand upon: to hold firmly: to seize or grasp.—*v.i.* to make a snatching movement (with *at*).—*n.* a hand (often in *pl.*): a device by which two shafts or rotating members may be connected or disconnected either while at rest or in relative motion: grasp: a snatching movement: (in *pl.*) power, control.—**clutch bag** a kind of handbag without strap or handle, carried in the hand or under the arm. [O.E. *clyccan*, to clench.]

clutch[2] *kluch, n.* a brood of chickens: a sitting of eggs: (*loosely*) a number, group.—*v.t.* to hatch. [O.N. *klekia.*]

clutter *klut'ər, n.* a clotted or confused mass: a disorderly accumulation: confusion: irregular interference on radar screen from echoes, rain, buildings, etc.—*v.i.* to crowd together.—*v.t.* to litter, clog with superfluous objects, material, etc. (often with *up*). [From **clot**; influenced by **cluster** and **clatter**.]

Clydesdale *klīdz'dāl, adj.* (of a breed of cart-horses) originating in *Clydesdale* in southern Scotland.—*n.* a Clydesdale horse.

clypeus *klip'i-əs, n.* the shield-like part of an insect's head.—*adjs.* **clyp'eal** of the clypeus; **clyp'eate, clyp'eiform** buckler-shaped. [L. *clipeus* (*clypeus*), a round shield.]

clyster *klis'tər, n.* a liquid injected into the intestines. [Gr. *klystēr*, a clyster-pipe—*klyzein*, to wash out.]

co-. See **com-.**

co. *kō.* An abbreviation for **company.**

coacervate *kō-as'ər-vāt* (or -*ər'*), *v.t.* to heap: to cause to mass together.—Also *adj.*—*n.* (*also* **coacerva'-tion**) a reversible aggregation of particles into liquid droplets before flocculation. [L. *coacervāre, -ātum —acervus,* heap.]

coach *kōch, n.* formerly, a private carriage: a large, close, four-wheeled carriage, esp. one for state occasions or one plying for conveyance of passengers: a railway carriage: a bus for tourists and sightseers: a ship's cabin near the stern: a private tutor: a professional trainer in athletics.—*v.t.* to tutor, instruct, prepare for an examination, boat-race, etc.—*v.i.* to go by coach.—*ns.* **coach'er** one who coaches: a coach-horse; **coach'ing** travelling by coach: tutoring: instruction.—**coach'builder** a person who builds the bodies of cars, lorries, railway carriages, etc.; **coach's building.**—*adj.* **coach'-built** of prams, of solid construction and upholstered.—**coach'dog** a Dalmatian; **coach'-horse** a horse used for drawing a coach; **coach's house** a house to keep a coach in; **coach'man** the driver of a coach: a servant employed to drive a carriage; **coach'work** the fine work of a motor-car body. [Fr. *coche*—Hung. *kocsi*, from *Kocs*, in Hungary.]

coact[1] *kō-akt', v.i.* to act together.—*n.* **coaction** (*kō-ak'shən*) mutual relations.—*adj.* **coac'tive** acting together.—*n.* **coactiv'ity.** [Pfx. **co-** and **act**.]

coact[2] *kō-akt', v.t.* to compel.—*n.* **coaction** (*kō-ak'shən*) compulsion.—*adj.* **coac'tive** compulsory. [L. *cōgĕre, cōāctum,* to compel.]

coadjacent *kō-ə-jās'ənt, adj.* contiguous.—*n.* **coadja'cency.**

coadjutant *kō-aj'ə-tənt, adj.* mutually helping.—*n.* one who helps another.—*ns.* **coadj'utor** a helper, assistant, esp. of a bishop: an associate.—*fem.* **coadj'utress, coadj'utrix; coadj'utorship.** [L. *adjūtor,* a helper—*ad,* to , *juvāre,* to help.]

co-agent *kō-ā'jənt, n* a joint agent.—*n.* **co-a'gency.**

coagulate *kō-ag'ū-lāt, v.t.* to make to curdle, clot, or set by a chemical reaction.—*v.i.* to curdle, clot, or set irreversibly.—*adj.* curdled.—*n.* **coagulabil'ity.**—*adj.* **coag'ulable.**—*ns.* **coag'ulant** a substance that causes coagulation; **coagula'tion.**—*adj.* **coag'ulative.**—*n.* **coag'ulator.**—*adj.* **coag'ulatory.**—*n.* **coag'ulum** what is coagulated. [L. *coāgulāre, -ātum—agĕre,* to drive.]

coal *kōl, n.* a piece of charcoal, esp. glowing: a firm, brittle, generally black combustible carbonaceous rock derived from vegetable matter: a piece of this rock: a cinder: an ember.—*v.i.* to take in coal.—*v.t.* to supply with coal.—*adj.* **coal'y** of or like coal: covered with coal.—**coal'-bed** a stratum of coal.—*adj.* **coal'-black** black as coal, very black —**coal'-box** a box for holding coal; **coal'-bunker** a box, recess, or compartment for holding coal; **coal'-cellar** a cellar or similar place for storing coal; **coal'-cutter** a machine for undercutting a coal-bed; **coal'-dust** coal in fine powder; **coal'-face'** the exposed surface of coal in a mine: **coal'field** a district containing coal strata.—*adj.* **coal'-fired** burning or fuelled by coal.—**coal'fish** a dusky fish of the cod family, with a green back; **coal'-gas** the mixture of gases produced by the distillation of coal, used for lighting and heating; **coal'-hole** a small coal-cellar: a hole in the pavement for filling a coal-cellar; **coaling station** a port at which steamships take in coal; **coal'man** one who has to do with coals; **Coal Measures** (*geol.*) the uppermost division of the Carboniferous; **coal'-merchant; coal'-mine, -pit** a pit or mine from which coal is dug; **coal'-miner; coal-mouse** see **coal-tit; coal'-scuttle** a fireside vessel for holding coal; **coal'-tar** gas-tar, a thick, black, opaque liquid formed when coal is distilled; **coal'-tit, coal'-tit'mouse, coal'-mouse** (also **cole-**) a dark species of tit.—**carry coals to Newcastle** to take a thing where it is already most abundant; **haul or call over the coals** to reprimand; **heap coals of fire on someone's head** to excite someone's remorse and repentance by returning good for evil (Rom. xii. 20) [O.E. *col.*]

coalesce *kō-ə-les'*, *v.i.* to grow together or unite into one body.—*n.* **coalesc'ence** growing into each other: fusion.—*adj.* **coalesc'ent.**—*v.t.* and *v.i.* **coalise, -ize** (*kō'ə-līz*) to bring or come into coalition.—*n.* **coalition** (*-lish'ən*) combination or alliance short of union, esp. of states or political parties.—*adj.* **coali'tional.** —*ns.* **coali'tioner; coali'tionism; coali'tionist.**—**coalition government** government by a coalition of parties. [L. *coalēscēre*—*alēscēre,* to grow up.]

coaming *kōm'ing* (*naut.*) *n.* (usu. in *pl.*) raised work about the edges of the hatches of a ship to keep water out.

coapt *kō-apt'*, *v.t.* to adjust.—*n.* **coapta'tion.** [L. *co-aptāre*—*aptāre,* to fit.]

coarse *kōrs, kôrs,* *adj.* common, base, inferior: rough: rude: uncivil: harsh: gross: large in grain, fibre, or mesh, etc.: without refinement: roughly approximate.—*adv.* **coarse'ly.**—*v.t.* and *v.i.* **coars'en** to make or become coarse.—*n.* **coarse'ness.**—*adj.* **coars'ish** somewhat coarse.—**coarse fish** freshwater fish other than those of the salmon family; **coarse fishing.**—*adj.* **coarse'-grained** large in grain: coarse in nature (*fig.*): gross. [From phrase 'in course', hence *ordinary.*]

coast *kōst, n.* the border of land next to the sea: the seashore: an act or spell of coasting.—*v.i.* to sail along or near a coast: to travel downhill on a sledge, on a cycle without pedalling or in a motor-car out of gear: to glide: to succeed or proceed without effort.—*v.t.* to sail by or near to.—*adj.* **coast'al.**—*n.* **coast'er** a vessel that sails along the coast: a container or mat for a decanter or glasses on a table.—*adj.* **coast'ing** keeping near the coast: trading between ports in the same country.—*ns.* the act of sailing, or of trading, along the coast: sliding downhill.—*advs.* **coast'ward, -s** toward the coast; **coast'wise** along the coast.—*adj* carried on along the coast.—**coast'guard** a body of men, and now also women, organised to watch along the coast for prevention of smuggling, for life-saving, defence, etc.: a member thereof; **coast'line** the line or boundary of a coast: shoreline.—**the coast is clear**

there is no obstacle or danger in the way. [O.Fr. *coste* (Fr. *côte*)—L. *costa,* rib, side.]

coat *kōt, n.* an outer garment with sleeves: an overcoat: the hair or wool of a beast: vesture or habit: any covering: a membrane or layer, as of paint, etc.: a coat of arms (see below).—*v.t.* to clothe: to cover with a coat or layer.—*ns.* **coat'ee** a short close-fitting coat, **coat'ing** a covering, layer: cloth for coats.—**coat'-card** a card bearing the representation of a coated figure, the king, queen, or knave—now, less correctly, called *court-card*; **coat'-hanger** a curved piece of wood, etc., with a hook, by which clothes may be hung and kept in shape; **coat'rack, coat'stand** a rack or stand with pegs for hanging coats on; **coat tails** the long back-pieces of a tail-coat.—**coat of arms** the family insignia embroidered on the surcoat worn over the hauberk, or coat of mail: the heraldic bearings of a gentleman; **coat of mail** a piece of armour for the upper part of the body, made of metal scales or rings linked one with another; **turn one's coat** to change one's principles, or to turn from one party to another. [O.Fr. *cote* (Fr. *cotte*)—L.L. *cottus, cotta,* a tunic.]

coati *kō-ä'tē* or *-ti,* or *kə-wä'tē, n.* an American carnivorous mammal allied to the raccoons.—Also **coati-mun'di, -mon'di.** [Tupi.]

co-author *kō-o'thər, n.* a joint author.

coax *kōks, v.t.* to persuade by fondling or flattery: to humour or soothe: to pet.—*ns.* **coax, coax'er** one who coaxes.—*adv.* **coax'ingly.** [**cokes**, a simpleton.]

coaxial *kō-ak'si-əl, adj.* having the same axis.—*adv.* **coax'ially.**—**coaxial cable** a cable consisting of one or more **coaxial pairs,** each a central conductor within an outer tubular conductor.

cob¹ *kob, n.* a short-legged strong horse: a male swan (also **cob'-swan**): a lump: a rounded object: a cobloaf: a corncob: a cobnut.—**cob'loaf** a rounded, round-headed or misshappen loaf; **cob'nut** a large hazelnut. [Perh. conn. with **cop¹.**]

cob² *kob, n.* a kind of composition of clay and straw for building.—**cob'-wall.**

cobalt *kō'bölt, n.* a metallic element (at. numb. 27; symbol Co): a blue pigment prepared from it—also **cō'balt-blue'.**—*adj.* of this deep-blue colour.—**cobalt-60** a radioactive isotope of cobalt used in the gamma-ray treatment of cancer.—*adjs.* **cobalt'ic; cobaltif'erous.**—*n.* **cō'baltite** a mineral containing cobalt, arsenic, and sulphur (also **cobalt glance).**—**cobalt bomb** a suggested bomb consisting of a hydrogen bomb encased in cobalt—made more dangerous than ever by the cobalt-60 dust released. [Ger. *Kobalt,* from *Kobold,* a demon, a nickname given by the German miners.]

cobber *kob'ər,* (*Austr.*; *coll.*) *n.* mate, chum, buddy.

cobble¹ *kob'l,* **cobblestone** *-stōn, ns.* a rounded stone, esp. used in paving.—*v.t.* to pave with cobblestones.

cobble² *kob'l, v.t.* to mend shoes: to patch up, put together, or mend coarsely (often with *together* or *up*).—*ns* **cobb'ler** one who cobbles or mends shoes: an iced drink made up of wine or spirits, sugar, lemon, etc : (a (usu. fruit) pie with) a thick pastry crust: (in *pl.*; *slang*) nonsense; **cobb'lery; cobb'ling.**

co-belligerent *kō-bi-lij'ə-rent, adj.* co-operating in warfare.—Also *n.*

Cobol *kō'böl, -bol, n.* a computer programming language, for commercial use, which uses English words. [*Common business oriented language.*]

cobra *kō'brə, kob'rə, n.* a poisonous snake, found in India and Africa, which dilates its neck so as to resemble a hood.—*adjs* **cob'ric; cob'riform** like or akin to the cobra. [Port., snake.]

cobweb *kob'web, n.* a spider's web or net: any snare or device intended to entrap: anything flimsy or easily

broken: anything that obscures.—*adj.* **cob'webby.**
[From obs. *attercop*, spider, and **web**.]

coca *kō'kə, n.* a Peruvian shrub whose leaves furnish an important narcotic and stimulant.—*ns* **cocaine** (*ko-kān'*) an alkaloid obtained from coca-leaves, used as a local anaesthetic and as an intoxicant; **co-cain'ism** a morbid condition induced by addiction to cocaine; **cocain'ist.** [Sp.—Quechua *coca*]

Coca-Cola® *kō'kə-kō'lə, n* a carbonated soft drink (often shortened to **Coke**).

coccid, etc See **coccus.**

coccus *kok'əs, n* a one-seeded portion of a dry fruit that breaks up (*bot.*): a spherical bacterium: (with *cap*) a genus of insects in the Hemiptera, type of a family **Coccidae** (*kok'si-dē*):—*pl.* **cocci** (*kok'sī*).—*adj.* **coccal** (*kok'əl*) —*n.* **coccid** (*kok'sid*) any of the Coccidae —Also *adj.*—*ns.* **coccidium** (*kok-sid'i-əm*) a protozoan parasite of the order **Coccid'ia:**—*pl.* **-ia;** **coccidiosis** (*kok-sid-i-ōs'is*) a contagious infection of birds and animals by coccidia   [L ,—Gr. *kokkos,* a berry.]

coccyx *kok'siks* (*anat*) *n.* the terminal triangular bone of the vertebral column:—*pl* **coccyges** (*kok-sī'jēz*) —*adjs.* **coccygeal** (*kok-sij'i-əl*), **coccyg'ian.** [Gr *kokkyx, -ȳgos,* cuckoo, coccyx (as resembling its bill)]

cochineal *koch'i-nēl, -nēl', n.* a scarlet dye-stuff consisting of the dried bodies of a Coccus insect gathered from a cactus in Mexico. the West Indies, etc.: the insect itself   [Sp. *cochinilla,* dim of L. *coccinus,* scarlet—*coccum,* a berry]

cochlea *kok'li-ə, n.* anything spiral-shaped, esp. a snail-shell, a winding stair: the spiral cavity of the ear (*anat.*) —*adj* **coch'lear** (*-li-ər*) pertaining to the cochlea of the ear: spoon-shaped.—*ns.* **coch'lear,** **cochleâr'e** (L.) a spoon.—*adjs.* **coch'leate, coch'le-ated** twisted spirally: spoon-like [L. *coc(h)lea,* a shell, screw, and *coc(h)leare,* a spoon—Gr *kochlias,* a snail.]

cock¹ *kok, n* a male bird, esp. of the domestic fowl (often compounded, as **cock'bird,** **cock-rob'in,** **cock-sparr'ow**): a male crab, lobster or salmon: a weathercock: a plucky chap, a term of familiarity (*slang*): anything set erect: a tap: part of the lock of a gun, held back by a spring, which, when released by the trigger, produces the discharge: a penis (*vulg.*).—*v.t.* to set erect or upright (often with *up*): to set up the brim of: to draw back, as the cock of a gun: to turn up or to one side: to tilt up knowingly, inquiringly, or scornfully.—*v i.* to strut: to swagger.—*adj.* **cocked** set erect: turned up or to one side.—*ns* **cock'er** one who follows cock-fighting: a small spaniel employed in pheasant and woodcock shooting; **cock'erel** a young cock.—*adv.* **cock'ily.**—*ns.* **cock'iness;** **cocks'iness,** **cox'iness.**—*adj.* **cocks'y,** **cox'y** self-important, bumptious; **cock'y** pert.—**cock'-a-dood'le(-doo')** the crow of a cock.—*v.t.* to crow.—*adj.* **cock-a-hoop'** in exultant spirits.—*adj.* **cock'-and-bull'** (of a story) fabricated and incredible.—**cock'-chafer** a large greyish brown beetle most destructive to vegetation; **cock'-crow, -ing** early morning, when cocks crow; **cocked hat** an old-fashioned three-cornered hat; **cocker spaniel** a cocker; **cock'eye** a squinting eye.—*adj.* **cock'eyed** having a cockeye: off the straight, awry (*coll.*): tipsy (*coll.*).—**cock'-fight, -ing** a fight or contest between game-cocks. a fight; **cockhorse'** a child's imaginary or toy horse — *adv.* properly **a-cockhorse'** (*i.e.* on cockhorse) on horseback: exultingly.—**cock'pit** a pit or enclosed space where game-cocks fought: a frequent battleground: part of a ship-of-war's lower regions used for the wounded in action: a sheltered depression in the deck of a yacht or small ship: in aircraft, a

compartment in the fuselage for pilot or passenger: the driver's seat in a racing car; **cock's'-comb, cocks'comb** the comb or crest on a cock's head: a jester's cap: a name for various plants: a coxcomb; **cock'-sparr'ow** a male sparrow: a small, lively person: **cock'spur** a spur on the leg of a cock —*adj.* **cock'sure'** quite sure, self-confident, esp. offensively.— **cock'tail** a concoction of spirituous or other liquors, used as an appetiser: a non-alcoholic appetiser consisting e g. of sea-food with a sauce.—Also *adj.*— **cocktail bar, lounge** a superior kind of bar, e.g. in a hotel; **cocktail dress** one for semi-formal wear; **cocktail shaker, mixer** a container for mixing cocktails; **cocktail stick** a small wooden or plastic stick for a cherry, olive, small sausage, etc. when eaten with drinks; **cock'-up** (*coll.*) a muddle, mess, confusion —**cock of the walk** the chief of a set: a person who (thinks he) is the most important in a group; **go off at half cock** (*coll.*) to begin too soon, when not properly prepared; **knock into a cocked hat** to give a profound beating. [O.E. *coc*]

cock² *kok, n.* a small pile of hay, dung, etc.—*adj.* **cocked** heaped up in cocks. [Cf O N *kókkr,* a lump.]

cockade *kok-ād', n.* a rosette worn on the hat as a badge. [Fr. *cocarde—coq,* cock.]

cockatoo *kok ə-tōō', n.* a large crested parrot of the Australian region.—*n.* **.cockatiel, cockateel** (*-tēl'*) a small crested parrot of Australia. [Malay *kakatua.*]

cockatrice *kok'ə-trīs, -tris, n.* a fabulous monster like a serpent: a cock-like monster with a dragon's tail (*her.*). [O.Fr. *cocatris.*]

cockboat *kok'bōt, n.* a ship's small boat: a small frail boat. [Obs. *cock,* a boat.]

cockchafer. See **cock¹.**

cocker¹ *kok'ər, v t.* to pamper: to fondle: to indulge

cocker², cockerel. See **cock¹.**

cockeye(d), cockhorse. See **cock¹.**

cockle¹ *kok'l, n.* a cornfield weed, esp. now the corncockle. [O.E. *coccel.*]

cockle² *kok'l, n* a large bivalve mollusc with thick, ribbed, heart-shaped, equal-valved shell: its shell: a bivalve shell generally.—*adj.* **cock'led** shell like a cockle.—**cock'leshell** the shell of a cockle: a frail boat.—**cockles of the heart** the heart itself. [Fr. *coquille*—Gr. *konchylion—konchē,* a cockle.]

cockle³ *kok'l, n.* a pucker.—*v.i.* to pucker.—*v.t.* to cause to pucker. [Perh. Fr. *coquiller,* to blister—*coquille;* see **cockle².**]

cockney *kok'ni, n.* an egg, esp. a small misshapen egg (*obs.* or *dial.*): (often with *cap.*) one born in London, strictly, within hearing of Bow Bells: London dialect. —*adj.* (often with *cap.*) characteristic of a Cockney. —*ns* **cock'neydom** the domain of Cockneys; **cock'neyism** a Cockney idiom or characteristic. [M.E. *coken-ey,* cock's egg; others would connect with Fr. *coquin,* a rogue—L. *coquus,* a cook.]

cockroach *kok'rōch, n.* an orthopterous insect, the so-called black beetle [Sp *cucaracha,* woodlouse, cockroach.]

cockscomb, cocktail, etc. See **cock¹.**

cocky. See **cock¹.**

coco *kō'kō, n.* a tropical seaside palm-tree (*Cocos nucifera*), with curving stem (also **co'co-palm, co'conut-palm, co'co-tree**) producing the coconut:— *pl.* **cō'cos.**—**co'conut,** a large edible nut, yielding **co'conut-butt'er** or **co'conut-oil'**, and **co'conut-milk'**; **co'conut-matt'ing** matting made from the husk of the coconut; **co'conut-shy** a fairground throwing game with coconuts as targets or as prizes [Port. and Sp. *coco,* a bugbear; applied to the nut from the three marks at the end of it, which form a grotesque face.]

cocoa *kō'kō, n* the seed of the cacao or chocolate tree:

a powder made from the seeds: a drink made from the powder.—**co'coa-beans** the seeds, esp. when dried and fermented; **co'coa-butt'er, co'coa-fat'** a fat got from the seeds (different from *coconut*-butter). [**cacao.**]

cocoon *ko-kōōn'*, *n.* the silken sheath spun by many insect larvae in passing into the pupa stage and by spiders for their eggs: the capsule in which earthworms and leeches lay their eggs: a preservative covering for military and other equipment.—*v.t.* to wrap carefully as in a cocoon.—*n.* **cocoon'ery** a place for keeping silkworms when feeding and spinning cocoons. [Fr. *cocon*, from *coque*, a shell—L. *concha*, a shell.]

cocotte *ko-kot'*, *n.* a small fireproof dish, usu. for an individual portion.

cod¹ *kod*, **codfish** *kod'fish*, *n.* a food fish (*Gadus morrhua*) of northern seas: any fish of the genus Gadus or the family Gadidae.—*n.* **cod'ling** a small cod.—**cod'-fisher; cod'-fish'ery; cod'-fishing.—cod'-liver oil'** a medicinal oil extracted from the fresh liver of the common cod or related fish.

cod² *kod*, (*obs.*) *n.* a bag: a pod: the scrotum.—**cod'-piece** a baggy appendage once worn in front of tight hose. [O.E. *codd*, a small bag.]

cod³ *kod*, (*slang*) *n.* a jest: a hoax.—*adj.* mock: done, intended, etc. as a joke or take-off.—*v.t.* to hoax: to poke fun at:—*pr.p.* **codd'ing;** *pa t.* and *pa.p.* **codd'ed.**

coda *kō'da*, *n.* a passage forming the completion of a piece, rounding it off to a satisfactory conclusion (*mus.*): any similar passage or piece in a story, dance sequence, etc. [It.,—L. *cauda*, a tail.]

coddle *kod'l*, *v.t.* to pamper: to fondle: to parboil.

code *kōd*, *n.* a collection or digest of laws: a system of rules and regulations (*specif.* regarding education): established principles or standards (of art, moral conduct, etc.): a system of signals: a system of words, letters, or symbols which represent sentences or other words, to ensure economy or secrecy in transmission: a cipher.—*v.t.* to codify: to express in code.—*ns.* **codifica'tion** (*kod-, kōd-*); **codifier** (*kod', kōd'*), **cod'ist** one who codifies.—*v.t.* **codify** (*kod', kōd'*) to put into the form of a code: to digest: to systematise. —*pr.p.* **cod'ifying;** *pa.t.* and *pa.p.* **cod'ified.—code'-breaker** a person who tries to interpret secret codes, **code'-breaking; code'-name, -number** a name or number used for convenience, economy, secrecy, etc —*adj.* **code'-named.—code of conduct, practice** an established method or set of rules for dealing with, behaving in, etc. a particular situation. [Fr. *code*, see **codex.**]

codeine *kō'dēn, -di-in, n.* an alkaloid, obtained from opium, used as an analgesic and sedative. [Gr. *kōdeia*, poppy-head.]

codex *kō'deks, n.* a manuscript volume:—*pl.* **codices** (*kōd'i-sēz*).—*n.* **cōdicol'ogy** the study of manuscript volumes.—*adj.* **cōdicolog'ical.** [L. *cōdex* or *caudex, -icis,* trunk of a tree, set of tablets, a book.]

codger *koj'ər, n.* a mean fellow: an old person: a chap. [Prob. a variant of **cadger.**]

codicil *kod'i-sil, n.* a supplement to a will.—*adj* **codicill'ary.** [L *cōdicillus,* dim. of *cōdex.*]

codicology. See **codex.**

codification, etc. See **code.**

codling¹ *kod'ling,* **codlin** *kod'lin, n.* an elongated apple.

codling². See **cod¹.**

codon *kō'don, n.* a triplet of bases in the messenger-RNA molecule, which determines a particular amino-acid in protein synthesis.

cod's(-)wallop, codswallop *kodz'wol-əp, n.* (*coll*) nonsense, rubbish

coeducation *kō-ed-ū-kā'shən, n* education of the sexes together.—*n.* **co'ed'** (usu. *U.S.*) a girl or woman educated at a coeducational institution.—*adjs.* **co'ed; coeduca'tional.**

coefficient *kō-if-ish'ənt, n.* that which acts together with another thing: a numerical or literal expression for a factor of a quantity in an algebraic term (*math.*): a numerical constant used as a multiplier to a variable quantity, in calculating the magnitude of a physical property (*phys.*).

coelacanth *sē'la-kanth, n.* any of a group of fishes of very great antiquity. [From Gr. *koilos,* hollow, *akantha,* spine.]

Coelenterata *sə-len-tər-ā'tə, sē-, n.pl.* a phylum of many-celled animals, radially symmetrical, with a single body-cavity, the enteron.—*adj.* and *n.* **coelen'terate.** [Gr. *koilos,* hollow, *enteron,* intestine.]

coeliac, celiac *sē'li-ak, adj.* relating to the belly.—**coeliac disease** a disease of the intestines by which fat cannot be properly digested. [Gr. *koiliakos—koiliā,* the belly.]

coelom(e), celom *sē'lōm, -lom, n.* the body-cavity, or space between the intestines and the body-wall in animals above the Coelenterates.—*n.pl.* **Coelō'mata** animals possessing a coelom.—*adj.* **coe'lomate** having a coelom.—*n.* a coelomate animal.—*adjs.* **coelomat'ic, coelom'ic.** [Gr. *koilōma, -atos,* a cavity.]

coenobite, cenobite *sēn'o-bīt, n.* a monk who lives in a community.—*adjs.* **coenobitic** (*-bit'ik*), **-al.**—*ns.* **coen'obitism; coenō'bium** a religious community: a colony of unicellular organisms (*biol.*):—*pl.* **coenō'bia.** [Gr. *koinóbion—koinos,* common, *bios,* life.]

coequal *kō-ē'kwəl, adj.* equal with another of the same rank or dignity.—*n.* one of the same rank.—*n.* **cō-equality** (*-i-kwol'*).—*adv.* **coe'qually.**

coerce *kō-ûrs', v.t.* to restrain by force: to compel.—*adj.* **cōer'cible.**—*adv.* **cōer'cibly.**—*ns.* **cōer'cion** restraint: government by force; **cōer'cionist.**—*adj.* **cōer'cive** having power to coerce: compelling: tending to or intended to coerce.—*adv.* **cōer'cively.**—*n.* **cōer'civeness.** [L. *coercēre—arcēre,* to shut in.]

coetaneous *kō-i-tā'ni-əs, adj.* of the same age: contemporary. [L. *aetās, aetātis,* age.]

coeval *kō-ē'vəl, adj.* of the same age.—*n.* one of the same age: a contemporary. [L. *coaevus—aevum,* age.]

co-exist *kō-igz-ist', -egz-, v.i.* to exist at the same time or together.—*n.* **co-exist'ence.**—*adj.* **co-exist'ent.—peaceful co-existence** a living side by side in mutual toleration.

co-extend *kō-iks-tend', -eks-, v.i.* to extend equally.—*n.* **co-exten'sion.**—*adj.* **co-exten'sive.**

coffee *kof'i, n.* a powder made by roasting and grinding the seeds of a tree (*Coffea arabica, robusta,* etc.) of the madder family: a drink made from the powder.—**coffee bar, shop** a small restaurant where coffee, tea, cakes, etc. are served; **coff'ee-bean** the seed of the coffee-tree, **coffee break** a break for coffee during the working day; **coff'ee-cup** a cup for coffee; **coffee grounds** the sediment left after coffee has been infused; **coff'ee-house** a house where coffee and other refreshments are sold, **coff'ee-mill** a machine for grinding coffee-beans; **coffee morning** a morning social gathering at which coffee is drunk; **coff'ee-pot** a pot in which coffee is prepared and served; **coffee service, set** a set of utensils for serving and drinking coffee; **coff'ee-table** a small low table; **coff'ee-tree.—coffee-table book** a large, expensive and profusely illustrated book of the kind one would set out on a coffee-table for visitors to admire, **white, black coffee** coffee respectively with and without milk. [Turk *kahveh*—Ar. *qahwah,* orig meaning wine.]

coffer kof'ər, n. a chest for holding money or treasure. a deep panel in a ceiling.—v.t. to hoard up —adj **coff'ered.**—**coff'er-dam** a watertight structure allowing underwater foundations to be built dry [O.Fr cofre, a chest—L. cophinus, a basket—Gr kophinos, a basket]

coffin kof'in, n. a chest for a dead body.—v.t. to place in a coffin —**coff'in-bone** a bone enclosed in a horse's hoof; **coff'in-nail** (slang) a cigarette.—**drive a nail in one's coffin** to do something-tending to hasten death or ruin [O.Fr cofin—L. cophinus—Gr. kophinos, a basket.]

coffle kof'l, n a gang, esp. of slaves. [Ar qāfilah, a caravan]

cog[1] kog, v.t. to cheat or deceive.—n. cogg'er. [Thieves' slang.]

cog[2] kog, n. a catch or tooth as on a wheel: an unimportant person in a large organisation (fig).—v t. to furnish with cogs: to stop (a wheel) by putting a block before it—pr p. cogg'ing; pa t. and pa.p. cogged.— **cog'-wheel** a toothed wheel. [M E. cogge.]

cogent kō'jənt, adj. powerful: convincing.—ns. **cō'gence, cō'gency** convincing power.—adv. **cō'gently.** [L. cōgēns, -entis, pr.p. of cōgĕre co-agĕre, to drive.]

cogitate koj'i-tāt, v.i to turn a thing over in one's mind· to meditate: to ponder.—adj. **cog'itable** capable of being thought —n. **cogita'tion** deep thought: meditation.—adj **cog'itative** having the power of thinking: given to cogitating. [L. cōgitāre, -ātum, to think deeply—co-, agitāre, to put in motion.]

Cognac kon'yak, n. a French brandy made near Cognac, in Charente.

cognate kog'nāt, adj. of the same family, kind, or nature: derived from the same ancestor, root, or other original: related or allied.—n. one related by blood, a kinsman —ns. **cog'nateness; cogna'tion.**— **cognatic succession** the succession to the throne of the eldest child, irrespective of sex. [L. cognātus—co-, (g)nāscī, to be born]

cognition kog-nish'ən, n. a knowledge: apprehension. knowing, in the widest sense, including sensation, perception, etc. (psychol.).—adj. **cognisable, -z-** (kog'niz-ə-bl; also kon'iz-) that may be known or understood: that may be judicially investigated.— adv. **cog'nisably, -z-.**—ns. **cog'nisance, -z-** (or kon'iz-) knowledge or notice, judicial or private: observation: jurisdiction: that by which one is known, a badge.—adj. **cog'nisant, -z-** (or kon'iz-) having cognisance or knowledge of.—v t **cognise', -ize'** to become conscious of.—adjs. **cognit'ional; cog'nitive** capable of, or pertaining to, cognition.—adv **cog'nitively.**—n. **cognitiv'ity.**—**take cognisance of** to recognise, take into consideration. [L. cognitiō, -ōnis— cognōscĕre, cognitum—co-, (g)nōscĕre, to know.]

cognomen kog-nō'mən, n. a surname: a nickname: a name: the last of the three names of a Roman, indicating the house or family to which he belonged [L. cognōmen, -inis—co-, (g)nōmen, a name.]

cognoscente ko-nyō-shent'ā, n. one professing a critical knowledge of works of art, music, literature, etc.: a connoisseur—pl **cognoscent'i (-ē).** [It. (mod. conoscente)—L. cognōscĕre, to know.]

cognovit kog-nō'vit, (law) n. an acknowledgment by a defendant that the plaintiff's cause is just [L. cognōvit actiōnem, (he) has confessed the action.]

cohabit kō-hab'it, v.t. to dwell together as husband and wife, or as if husband and wife.—ns. **cohab'itant** one dwelling with others; **cohabita'tion; cohabitee'.** [L. cohabitāre—co-, habitāre, to dwell.]

co-heir kō-ār', n. a joint heir:—fem. **co-heir'ess.**—n. **coheritor** (kō-her'it-ər)—a co-heir

cohere kō-hēr', v i to stick together: to be consistent

—ns. **coher'ence** a sticking together: consistency; co-hēr'ency.—adj. **coher'ent** sticking together: connected: consistent in thought or speech: (of a system of units) such that one unit multiplied or divided by another gives a third unit in the system exactly: (of beam of radiation) showing definite, not random, relationships between points in a cross-section —adv. **coher'ently.**—n. **coher'er** an apparatus for detection of electric waves by reduced resistance of imperfect contact, as if by cohesion.—adj. **cohesible (-hēz')** capable of cohesion.—n. **cohē'sion (-zhən)** the act of sticking together: a form of attraction by which particles of bodies stick together: concrescence of like parts (bot.): logical connection.—adj. **cohē'sive (-siv, -ziv)** having the power of cohering: tending to unite into a mass —adv. **cohe'sively.**—ns. **cohe'siveness; cohesibil'ity (-hēz-)** [L cohaerēre, -haesum—co-, haerēre, stick.]

coheritor. See co-heir.

coho, cohoe kō'hō, n a Pacific salmon:—pl. **co'ho(e)s.**

cohog. Same as quahog.

cohort kō'hört, n. a tenth part of a Roman legion: any band of warriors: a group of individuals: (popularly) a companion or follower. [L. cohors, -tis, an enclosed place, a multitude enclosed, a company of soldiers.]

coif koif, n. a covering for the head, esp. worn by women.—v.t. to provide with a coif: to dress (the hair).—ns. **coiffeur (kwä-fœr')** a hairdresser:—fem. **coiffeuse (-œz');** **coiffure (kwa-fur')** ε style of hairdressing: a head-dress.—Also v.t. [Fr. coiffe— L.L. cofia, a cap.]

coign, coigne koin.—**coign(e) of vantage** an advantageous salient corner: hence, a good position generally.

coil[1] koil, v.t. to wind in rings: to enclose in twists — v.i. to wind.—n. a coiled object: one of the rings into which anything is coiled: a wire wound spirally to conduct electricity: a contraceptive device consisting of a metal or plastic coil fitted in the uterus. [O.Fr. coillir (Fr. cueillir)—L. colligĕre—col-, together, legĕre, to gather; cf. cull, collect.]

coil[2] koil, n. tumult: hubbub: noise: fuss.—**mortal coil** (Hamlet III. i. 68) the toil and trouble of human life.

coin koin, n. a piece of metal legally stamped and current as money: money —v.t. to convert into money: to stamp: to invent, fabricate, esp. a new word.—ns. **coin'age** the act of coining money: the currency: the pieces of metal coined: the invention, or fabrication, of something new, esp. a word or phrase: what is invented; **coin'er** one who coins money: a maker of counterfeit coins: an inventor; **coin'ing** minting: invention.—**coin'-box** a telephone which one operates by putting coins in a slot.—adjs. **coin'-op'erated, coin'-op'** of a machine, operated by inserting a coin in a slot.—**coin a phrase** to use a new phrase or expression (usu. iron., i.e. to repeat a cliché); **coin money** to make money rapidly; **pay a man in his own coin** to give tit for tat: to give as good as one got. [Fr. coin, a wedge (see quoin), also the die to stamp money—L. cuneus, a wedge.]

coincide kō-in-sīd', v i to occupy the same place or time: to agree: to correspond: to be identical.—ns. **coincidence (kō-in'si-dəns)** fact, event, or condition of coinciding: the occurrence of events simultaneously or consecutively in a striking manner but without any causal connection between them; **coin'cidency.**— adjs. **coin'cident, coincidental (-dent'l)**—advs. **coincident'ally; coin'cidently.** [L. co-, incidĕre—in, in, cadĕre, to fall.]

co-insurance kō'in-shoō'rəns, n. insurance jointly with another, esp. when the insurer bears part of the risk

coir koir, n. the strong fibre of coconut husk. [From Tamil or Malayalam.]

coition kō-ish'ən, cō'itus ko'it-əs, ns sexual inter-

coke

188

collate

course.—*adj.* **cō'ital.—coitus interruptus** coitus intentionally interrupted by withdrawal before semen is ejaculated; **coitus reservātus** coitus in which ejaculation is avoided. [L. *coitiō*, *-ōnis—co-*, together, *īre*, *ītum*, to go.]

coke[1] *kōk, n.* a form of fuel obtained by the heating of coal in confined space whereby its more volatile constituents are driven off: the residue when any substance (e.g. petrol) is carbonised.—*v.t.* and *v.i.* to make into, or become, coke.

coke[2] *kōk, n.* cocaine (*slang*): (®; with *cap.*) Coca-Cola.

col *kol, n.* a depression or pass in a mountain-range (*geog.*): a region between two anticyclones giving a similar figure when represented in contour (*meteor.*). [Fr.,—L. *collum*, a neck.]

col-. See **com-.**

cola, kola *kō'lə, n.* (with *cap*) a genus of West African trees producing nuts used in drugs and for flavouring soft drinks: a soft drink so flavoured. [African name.]

colander *kul'ən-dər, n.* a perforated vessel used as a strainer in cookery.—*adj.* **cō'liform** like a sieve. [L. *cōlāre*, to strain.]

colatitude *kō-lat'i-tūd, n.* the complement of the latitude. [**complement, latitude.**]

Colchicum *kol'ki-kəm, n.* a genus of *Liliaceae* including meadow saffron: (without *cap.*) its corm and seeds, used for gout and rheumatism and yielding **col'chicine** (*-chi-* or *-ki-sēn*), an alkaloid used in plant breeding: (without *cap.*) a plant of the genus. [L.,— Gr. *kolchikon*, meadow saffron.]

cold *kōld, adj.* giving or feeling a sensation that is felt to be the opposite of hot: chilly: low in temperature: without passion or zeal: spiritless: unfriendly: indifferent: reserved: suggesting cold rather than heat, as blue or grey (*paint.*): without application of heat: used of operations formerly requiring heat, e.g. **cold's cast'ing, -forg'ing, -mould'ing, -weld'ing.**—*n.* a relative want of heat: the feeling or sensation caused by the absence of heat: coldness: a spell of cold weather: a catarrhal inflammation of the mucous membrane of the respiratory organs, caused by a virus, usually accompanied by hoarseness and coughing: catarrh: chillness.—*adj.* **cold'ish** somewhat cold.—*adv.* **cold'ly.**—*n.* **cold'ness.**—*adj.* **cold-blood'ed** having body-temperature depending upon environment, as fishes: without feeling: (of persons or actions) hardhearted.—*adv.* **cold'-blood'edly.—cold'-blood'ed-ness; cold cathode** (*elect.*) an electrode from which electron emission results from high-potential gradient at the surface at normal temperatures; **cold'-chis'el** a strong and finely-tempered chisel for cutting cold metal; **cold'-cream-** a creamy ointment used to remove make-up or as a cooling dressing for the skin; **cold cuts** slices of cold cooked meat; **cold feet** loss of nerve: cooling off of courage or ardour; **cold fish** a person with no emotion; **cold'-frame', cold'house** a plant frame, greenhouse, without artificial heat; **cold front** the surface of an advancing mass of cold air where it meets a retreating mass of warmer air.—*adj.* **cold'-heart'ed** wanting feeling: indifferent.—*v.t* **cold'-should'er** to give the cold shoulder to (see below).—**cold snap** a sudden spell of cold weather, **cold sore** a blister or group of blisters on or near the mouth, caused by a viral infection (*herpes simplex*); **cold steel** cutting or stabbing weapons, opp. to bullets; **cold storage** storage and preservation of goods in refrigerating chambers: abeyance (*fig.*); **cold turkey** sudden withdrawal of narcotics; **cold water** water at its natural temperature in ordinary conditions.—*v.t.* **cold'-work** to shape (metals) at or near atmospheric temperature by rolling, pressing, etc.—

catch cold to contract a cold; **cold as charity** a proverbial phrase expressing ironically great coldness or indifference; **give, show, the cold shoulder** to show studied indifference: to give a rebuff; **in a cold sweat** (as if) sweating with fear; **in cold blood** with deliberate intent, not under the influence of passion; **leave one cold** to fail to impress; **leave out in the cold** to neglect, ignore; **throw cold water on** to discourage. [O.E. (Anglian) *cald* (W.S. *ceald*).]

cole *kōl, n.* a general name for all sorts of cabbage.— **cole'-seed** the seed of rape: rape; **cole'-slaw** cabbage salad; **cole'-wort** cole. [O E. *cawel*; from L. *cōlis, caulis*, a stem, esp. of cabbage.]

cole-mouse. See under **coal.**

Coleoptera *kol-i-op'tər-ə, n.pl.* an order of insects having the fore-wings hard or horny, serving as wing-cases for the functional wings—the beetles.—*adjs.* **coleop'teral, coleop'terous.—n. coleop'terist** a student of beetles. [Gr. *koleos*, a sheath, and *pteron*, a wing.]

cole-slaw. See **cole.**

cole-tit, cole-titmouse. See under **coal.**

Coleus *kō'li-əs, n.* a genus of plants with variegated coloured leaves often used for indoor decoration: (without *cap.*) a plant of the genus. [Gr. *koleos*, a sheath.]

coley *kō'li, n.* the coalfish.

colic, colicky. See **colon**[2].

coliform. See **colander.**

coliseum. See **colosseum** under **colossus.**

colitis. See **colon**[2].

collaborate *kəl-ab'ər-āt, v.i.* to work in association (sometimes invidiously, with an enemy).—*n.* **collaborā'tion.—adj. collab'orative.—ns. collab'-orātor; collabo'rationist** (in invidious sense). [L. *collabōrāre, -ātum—labōrāre*, to work.]

collage *kol-azh', n.* a picture made from scraps of paper and other odds and ends pasted out: any work put together from assembled fragments. [Fr., pasting.]

collagen *kol'ə-jen, n.* a protein in fibrous connective tissue, readily turned into gelatine. [Gr. *kolla*, glue, and *gen-*, the root of *gignesthai*, to become.]

collapse *kəl-aps', n.* a falling away or breaking down: any sudden or complete breakdown or prostration.— *v.i.* to cave in: to close or fold up: to break down: to go to ruin: to lose heart.—*n.* **collapsibil'ity, -abil'ity.** —*adj.* **collaps'ible, -able** capable of collapsing. [L. *collāpsus—col-*, together, and *lābī, lāpsus*, to slide or fall.]

collar *kol'ər, n.* something worn round the neck by man, horse, dog, etc.: the part of a garment at the neck: the part of an animal's skin or coat, or a bird's feathers, round the neck: a ring: a surrounding band: the junction of root and stem in a plant: a piece of meat rolled up and tied.—*v.t.* to seize by the collar: to put a collar on: to seize (*slang*).—*n.* **collarette'** a small collar.—**coll'ar-beam** a horizontal piece of timber connecting or bracing two opposite rafters, to prevent sagging; **coll'ar-bone** the clavicle, a bone connecting the shoulder-blade and breast-bone; **coll'ar-stud** a stud for fastening a collar. [O.Fr. *colier—*L. *collāre—collum*, the neck.]

collard *kol'ərd, n.* cole-wort [**cole-wort.**]

collate *kol-āt', v.t.* to bring together for comparison: to examine and compare, as books, and esp. old manuscripts: (to place in order, as sheets of a book for binding, and) to examine with respect to completeness and sequence of sheets, etc.—*adj.* **colla'table.—ns colla'tion** the act of collating: a bringing together for examination and comparison; **colla'tor.** [L *collātum*, used as supine of *conferre—pfx col-* and *lātum* (*ferre*, to bring).]

For other sounds see detailed chart of pronunciation.

collateral *kol-at'ər-l, adj.* side by side: running parallel or together: corresponding: descended from the same ancestor, but not in direct line.—*n.* a collateral relation: a contemporary: a rival: collateral security.—*adv.* **collat'erally.**—**collateral security** an additional and separate security for repayment of money borrowed. [L. *col-, latus, lateris,* a side.]

colleague *kol'ēg, n.* one associated with another in some employment.—*n.* **coll'eagueship.** [Fr. *collègue*—L. *collēga—col-, legēre,* to choose.]

collect *kəl-, kol-ekt', v.t.* to assemble or bring together: to put (one's thoughts) in order: to receive payment of: to call for and remove.—*v.i.* to run together: to accumulate.—*n.* **collect** (*kol'*) a short prayer.—*adj.* and *adv.* (-*ekt'; U.S.*) of a telephone call, telegram, etc., paid for by the recipient.—*adj.* **collect'able, -ible.**—*adj.* **collect'ed** gathered together: (of a poet's or other writer's works) assembled in one volume, one set of volumes, etc.: having unscattered wits: cool: firm.—*adv.* **collect'edly.**—*n.* **collect'edness** self-possession: coolness.—*n.* and *adj.* **collect'ing.**—*n.* **collec'tion** the act of collecting: the gathering of contributions, esp. of money: the money collected: money intended for collection in church: an assemblage: a book of selections: composure.—*adj.* **collect'ive** considered as forming one mass or sum: congregated: common: expressing a number or multitude (*gram.*).—*n.* a gathering, assemblage: a unit of organisation in a collectivist system: (*loosely*) a group of people who run a business, etc. for their mutual benefit, often with no specifically designated jobs.—*adv.* **collect'ively.**—*v.t.* **collect'ivise, -ize** to give a collectivist organisation to.—*ns.* **collect'ivism** the economic theory that industry should be carried on with a collective capital—a form of socialism: a system embodying this; **collect'ivist.**—Also *adj.*—*ns.* **collectiv'ity; collect'or** that which, or one who, collects: one who sets himself to acquire and set together examples or specimens; **collect'orate, collect'orship.**—**collect'ing-box** a field-naturalist's box for specimens: a box for receiving money contributions; **collective bargaining** negotiation on conditions of service between an organised body of workers on one side and an employer or association of employers on the other; **collective farm** a state-controlled farm consisting of a number of small-holdings operated on a co-operative basis; **collective unconscious** (*psych.*) the part of the unconscious mind that originates in ancestral experience. [L. *colligĕre, collēctum—legĕre,* to gather.]

colleen *kol'ēn, kol-ēn', n.* a girl. [Irish *cailín.*]

college *kol'ij, n.* an incorporation, company, or society of persons joined together generally for literary or scientific purposes, and often possessing peculiar or exclusive privileges: a body or society that is a member of a university or is co-extensive with a university: a seminary of learning: a literary, political, or religious institution: the edifice appropriated to a college.—*n.* **coll'eger** a member of a college: one of the foundationers at Eton College.—*adj.* **collegial** (*kə-lē'ji-əl*) pertaining to a college or university, or to a collegium.—*ns.* **collegial'ity** sharing by bishops in papal decision-making; **collē'gian** a member or inhabitant of a college.—*adj.* **collē'giate** pertaining to or resembling a college: containing a college, as a town: instituted like a college: corporate.—**college pudding** a kind of steamed dried fruit pudding; **collegiate church, collegial church** a church having a college or chapter, consisting of a dean or provost and canons, attached to it: in Scotland, a church occupied by two or more pastors of equal rank (also **collegiate charge**).—**college of cardinals** the whole body of cardinals, electors of the pope; **college of education** a college for training teachers. [Fr. *collège*—L. *collēgium,* from *col-,* and *legĕre,* to gather.]

collegium *ko-lē'ji-əm, n.* college of cardinals: an administrative board. [L. *collēgium;* see **college.**]

collenchyma *kol-eng'ki-mə, (bot.) n.* the strengthening tissue of thick-cornered cells. [Gr. *kolla,* glue, *en,* in, *chyma,* that which is poured.]

collet *kol'it, n.* a ring or collar: the collar of a plant: the part of a ring which contains the stone. [Fr.,—L. *collum.*]

collide *kə-līd', v.i.* to dash together: to clash.—*n.* **collision** (*-lizh'n*) the state of being struck together: a violent impact, a crash: conflict: opposition: clashing.—**collision course** a course which, if persisted in, will result in a collision (*lit.* and *fig.*).—**elastic collision** a collision in which both kinetic energy and momentum are conserved (*phys.*): a collision in which the bombarding particle does not excite or break up the struck nucleus, and is simply scattered (**elastic scattering**) (*nuc.*); **inelastic collision** a collision in which momentum, but not kinetic energy, is conserved (*phys.*): a collision in which there is a change in the total energies of the particles involved, the resultant scattering being termed **inelastic scattering** (*nuc.*). [L. *collīdĕre, collīsum—col-, laedĕre,* to strike.]

collie, colly *kol'i, n.* a long-haired, intelligent breed of sheep-dog, originating in Scotland.

collier *kol'yar, n.* a coal-miner: a ship that carries coal: a sailor in such a ship.—*n.* **coll'iery** a coal-mine. [coal.]

colligate *kol'i-gāt, v.t.* to bind together.—*n.* **colliga'tion** conjunction: bringing together under a general principle or conception. [L. *colligāre, -ātum—col-, ligāre,* to bind.]

collimate *kol'i-māt, v.t.* to make parallel: to adjust accurately parts of (an optical instrument, as a surveying telescope).—*ns.* **collima'tion; coll'imator** a device for obtaining a beam of parallel rays of light or a beam of particles moving in parallel paths: a subsidiary telescope for collimating other instruments. [*collimāre,* a wrong reading for L. *collīneāre,* to bring into line with—*col-,* together, *līnea,* a line.]

collinear *ko-lin'i-ər, adj.* in the same straight line.

collision. See **collide.**

collocate *kol'ō-kāt, v.t.* to place together: to set: to arrange.—*n.* **colloca'tion.** [L. *collocāre, -ātum,—col-, locāre,* to place.]

collocutor, collocutory. See **colloquy.**

collodion *kol-ō'di-ən, n.* a gluey solution of nitrated cotton (or cellulose nitrates) in alcohol and ether, used in surgery and photography. [Gr. *kollōdēs—kolla,* glue, *eidos,* form, appearance.]

collogue *kə-lōg', v.i.* to converse confidentially with. [Prob. from L. *colloquī,* to speak together.]

colloid *kol'oid, n.* a substance in a state in which, though apparently dissolved, it cannot pass through a membrane: a substance that readily assumes this state: a colloidal system.—*adj.* **colloid'al.**—**colloidal system** a dispersed substance plus the material in which it is dispersed. [Gr. *kolla,* glue, *eidos,* form.]

collop *kol'əp, n.* a slice of meat (*dial.*).

colloquy *kol'ə-kwi, n.* a speaking together: mutual discourse: conversation.—*n.* **collocutor** (*kol-ok'ū-tər*).—*adjs.* **colloc'utory; colloquial** (*kə-lō'kwi-əl*) pertaining to or used in common conversation.—*ns.* **collō'quialism** a form of expression used in familiar talk; **collō'quialist.**—*adv.* **collō'quially.**—*n.* **collō'quium** a conference: a meeting for discussion: a seminar:—*pl.* **collō'quia, -iums.** [L. *colloquium—col-, loquī,* to speak.]

collotype *kol'ō-tīp, n.* a form of gelatine process in

book illustration and advertising. [Gr *kolla*, glue, and type.]

collude *kol-ūd'*, *-ōōd'*, *v.i.* to play into each other's hands: to act in concert, esp in a fraud.—*ns.* **collud'er; collu'sion** the act of colluding: a secret agreement to deceive: deceit.—*adj.* **collu'sive** fraudulently concerted: deceitful.—*adv* **collu'sively.** [L. *collūdĕre*, *collūsum*, from *col-*, and *lūdĕre*, to play.]

colly. See collie.

collywobbles *kol'i-wob-lz*, *n.* (*facet.*) abdominal pain or disorder [Prob. **colic** and **wobble.**]

Colobus *kol'ō-bəs*, *n.* an African genus of monkeys, almost thumbless: (without *cap.*) any of several monkeys of the genus:—*pl.* **col'obi** (*-bī*, *-bē*). [Gr *kolobos*, maimed.]

colocynth *kol'o-sinth*, *n.* a kind of cucumber: a cathartic drug got from it. [Gr. *kolokynthis*.]

colon¹ *kō'lən*, *n.* the punctuation mark (:), used to indicate a distinct member or clause of a sentence, or to introduce a list, spoken or reported words, etc. [Gr. *kōlon*, a limb, member.]

colon² *kō'lən*, *n* the large intestine from the caecum to the rectum.—*n.* **colic** (*kol'ik*) a disease attended with severe pain and flatulent distention of the abdomen, without diarrhoea—*adjs.* **col'ic; col'icky** like, suffering or causing colic.—*n.* **colitis** (*kō-*, *ko-lī'tis*) inflammation of the colon.—*adj.* **colon'ic** of the colon.—*n.* **colos'tomy** (*kə-*) the making of an artificial anus by surgical means. [Gr. *kōlon*, the large intestine.]

colonel *kûr'nəl*, *n.* an officer who has command of a regiment, or one of equivalent rank.—*ns.* **col'onelcy** (*-si*) the office or rank of colonel; **col'onelship** colonelcy: the quality of being a colonel.—**col'onel-in-chief** an honorary colonel. [Older Fr. and Sp. *coronel*—It. *colonello*, the leader of a *colonna*, or column—L. *columna*.]

colonic. See colon².

colonnade *kol-ən-ād'*, *n.* a range of columns placed at regular intervals: a similar row, as of trees.—*adj* **colonnad'ed.** [Fr.,—L *columna*]

colony *kol'ən-i*, *n.* a name vaguely applied to a state's dependencies overseas or abroad (distinguished from a *dominion*): a body of persons settled in a foreign country, or forming a separate group in any way (as by common occupation), or organised for purposes of support, labour, treatment, etc.: the settlement so formed: the place they inhabit: a number of organisms, esp. of one kind, living together as a community (*biol.*).—*adj.* **colonial** (*kə-lō'ni-əl*) pertaining to, of the nature of, or dating from the time when a territory was, a colony.—*n.* an inhabitant, citizen, or member of a colony, a colonist.—*ns.* **colō'nialism** a trait of colonial life or speech: the colonial system (see below): policy of obtaining, or maintaining hold over, colonies, esp. with the purpose of exploiting them.—*adj.* and *n.* **colōn'ialist.**—*adv.* **colōn'ially.**—*n.* **colonisā'tion, -z-** the act or practice of colonising: state of being colonised—*v.t.* **col'onise, -ize** to plant or establish a colony in: to form into a colony—*v t* to settle.—*n.* **col'onist** an inhabitant of a colony: a voter set up for election purposes: a weed of cultivated ground (*bot.*)—**colonial animals** organisms consisting of numerous individuals in bodily union; **colonial system** the theory that the settlements abroad should be treated as proprietary domains exploited for the benefit of the mother country [L *colōnia*—*colōnus*, a husbandman—*colĕre*, to till.]

colophon *kol'ə-fon*, *-fən*, *n* an inscription at the end of a book, often naming the author and scribe or printer, with place and date of execution, etc.: a publisher's imprint or device, with name, date, etc. [L. *colophōn*—Gr. *kolophōn*, summit, finishing touch.]

colophony *kol-of'ə-ni*, or *kol'*, *n.* rosin. [Gr. *kolophōnia* from *Kolophōn*, Colophon, in Asia Minor.]

coloquintida *kol-o-kwin'ti-də*. Same as **colocynth.**

color. U.S. spelling of **colour.**

Colorado beetle *kol-ər-ä'dō bē'tl*, an American beetle, yellow with black stripes, a potato pest. [State of *Colorado*.]

coloration. See under **colour.**

coloratura *kol-or-ət-ōō'rə*, (*mus.*) *n.* florid vocal passages.—*adj.* florid.—**coloratura soprano** a high and flexible soprano voice, capable of singing coloratura passages: a singer with such a voice [It., colouring]

colorific, etc. See under **colour.**

colossus *kəl-os'əs*, *n.* a gigantic statue, esp. that of Apollo at (but not astride of) the entrance of the harbour of Rhodes: a person or organisation of gigantic power and influence (*fig.*).—*adj.* **coloss'al** like a colossus: gigantic.—*ns.* **colosse'um, colisē'um** a large place of entertainment, from Vespasian's amphitheatre at Rome, which was the largest in the world. [L.,—Gr. *kolossos*.]

colostomy. See **colon².**

colostrum *ko-los'trəm*, *n.* a mammal's first milk after parturition. [L.]

colour, also, esp. in U.S., **color,** *kul'ər*, *n.* a sensation of light induced in the eye by electromagnetic waves of a certain frequency—the colour being determined by the frequency: a property whereby bodies have different appearances to the eye through surface reflection or absorption of rays: hue, one of the constituents into which white light can be decomposed: appearance of blood in the face: race or race-mixture other than Caucasian: appearance: plausibility: reason, pretext: tint: shade: paint: vividness: timbre (*mus.*): variety: (in *sing.* or *pl.*) a flag, ensign, or standard: (in *pl.*) a symbol of membership of a party, club, college, team, etc.—*v.t.* to put colour on: to stain: to paint: to set in a fair light: to exaggerate: to disguise: to misrepresent.—*v.i.* to take on colour: to blush.—*ns.* **col'orant** (also **col'ourant**) a substance used for colouring; **colora'tion** (also **coloura'tion**) colouring: mode of colouring: disposition of colours. —*adj.* **colorif'ic** (*kol-*, *kul-*) producing colours.—*ns.* **colorim'eter** (*kol-*, *kul-*) an instrument for comparison of colours; **colorim'etry.**—*adjs.* **col'oured** having colour: of the complexion, other than white: (*loosely*; often *derog.*) belonging to a dark-skinned race: (usu. with *cap.*) in South Africa, of mixed racial descent—partly Caucasian, partly of darker race: (also with *cap.*) in South Africa, of one of the official racial groups, neither white nor African: not of Caucasian race.—*n.* (usu. with *cap.*) in South Africa, a person of mixed racial descent: (also with *cap.*) in South Africa, a member of one of the official racial groups, one who is neither white nor African.—*adj.* **col'ourful** full of colour: vivid.—*ns.* **col'ouring** any substance used to give colour: the actual colours of anything, and their arrangement: manner of applying colours: appearance, esp. a person's hair and skin colour: tone; **col'ourist** one who colours or paints: one who excels in colouring—*adjs.* **col'ourless** without colour: transparent: pale: neutral: lacking distinctive character; **col'oury** having much colour.—**colour bar** social discrimination between whites and other races.—*adj.* **col'our-blind** unable to distinguish some colours from others, or to see them at all.—**colour blindness; colour code** a system of identification e.g. of electrical wires by different colours.—*v.t.* to mark with different colours for identification—*adj.* **col'our-fast** of material, etc., with colours that will not run when washed.—**colour film** a film for making colour photographs; **col'ourman** one who prepares or sells paints; **colour scheme** general conception of combination of colours in a design; **col'our-sergeant** the sergeant who guards the colours of a regiment; **colour supplement** an illustrated magazine printed in colour and published as a usu. weekly part of a newspaper.—*adj.* of a style often pictured in such a magazine, i.e. expensive and rather exclusive.—*n.pl.* **col'our-ways** combinations of colours.—**colour in** to fill in an area on a piece of paper, etc. with colour, **colour up** to blush, flush, **come off with flying colours** to do something with éclat, **come out in one's true colours** to appear in one's real character; **false colours** a false pretence; **fear no colours** to fear no enemy; **give colour** to give plausibility; **high colour** ruddiness of complexion; **in one's true colours** as one really is; **join the colours** to enlist; **lose colour** to lose one's good looks: to become pale. to appear less probable (*fig.*); **nail one's colours to the mast** to commit oneself to some party or plan of action; **off colour** faded: indisposed: past one's best: slightly indecent; **see the colour of a person's money** to be sure that a person has money to pay for an article about to be bought. [O.Fr. *color*—L. *color, -ōris*; akin to *cēlāre*, to cover, to conceal.]

colposcope kol'pō-skōp, *n.* an instrument for examining the neck of the uterus, used esp. for early detection of cancer.—*adj.* **colposcop'ical.**—*adv.* **colposcop'ically.**—*n.* **colpos'copy** examination using a colposcope. [Gr. *kolpos*, the womb, *skopeein*, to see.]

colt kōlt, *n.* a young horse: an awkward fellow: an inexperienced youth: in sports and games, a young, inexperienced player.—*adj.* **colt'ish** like a colt. frisky: wanton.—**colts'foot** a composite plant with shaggy stalk and large soft leaves; **colt's tooth** wantonness [O.E *colt.*]

Colt kōlt, *n.* a pistol invented by Samuel *Colt* (1814–62)

colter. Same as **coulter.**

Coluber kol'ū-bər, *n* an extensive genus of non-venomous snakes. (without *cap.*) any snake of the genus.—*adj* **col'übrine** snakelike. [L. *coluber*, a snake.]

columbine kol'əm-bīn, *adj.* of or like a dove: dove-coloured.—*n.* any plant of the ranunculaceous genus Aquilegia, with coloured sepals and spurred petals, giving the appearance of a bunch of pigeons —*ns* **columbā'rium** a dovecot: a niche for a sepulchral urn; **col'umbary** a dovecot. [L. *columba*, a dove.]

column kol'əm, *n* a long round body, used as support or adornment: any upright body or mass like a column: a body of troops with narrow front: a perpendicular row of figures, etc.: a perpendicular section of a page or of a table a special section in a newspaper: a bundle of nerve-fibres: the central part of an orchid —*adjs.* **columnal** (kə-lum'nl), **colum'nar** pertaining to columns: like a column: formed in columns.—*n* **columnist** (kol'əm-ist, -nist) one who conducts a column in a newspaper. [L. *columna*, akin to *celsus*, high; Gr. *kolōnē*, a hill; see **hill.**]

colure kō-lūr', kōl', kol'yər, *n* a great circle of the celestial sphere passing through the poles of the equator and either the solstitial or the equinoctial points [Gr *kolouros—kolos*, docked, *ourā*, tail]

colza kol'zə, *n* cole-seed, yielding **col'za-oil.** [Du. *koolzaad*, cabbage-seed.]

com— kom-, con- kon-, co- ko-, kō-, also, by assimilation, **col**- kol-, **cor**- kor-, *pfxs.* together, with: similar: used as intensive. [L *com*, old form of *cum*, with.]

coma¹ kō'mə, *n.* deep sleep: stupor.—*adj.* **com'atose** affected with coma. drowsy [Gr *kōma, -atos*]

coma² kō'mə, *n.* a tuft (*bot*): the head of a tree: the nebulous envelope of the head of a comet (*astron.*). —*adjs.* **cō'mal, cō'mate, cō'mose, cō'mous.** [Gr *kōmē*, hair of head.]

comate. See **coma².**

comatose. See **coma¹.**

comb¹ kōm, *n.* a toothed instrument for separating and cleaning hair, wool, flax, etc.: anything of similar form: the fleshy crest of some birds: the top or crest of a wave, of a roof, or of a hill: an aggregation of cells for honey.—*v.t.* to separate, to arrange, or clean by means of a comb or as if with a comb: to dress with a comb: to search thoroughly.—*v.i.* to break with a white foam, as the top of a wave.—*adj.* **combed.**—*n.* **comb'er** one who or that which combs wool, etc.: a long foaming wave.—*n.pl.* **comb'ings** hairs combed off —*adjs.* **comb'less; comb'y.**—*adv.* **comb'wise.**—**comb out** to arrange hair by combing after rollers, etc. have been removed: to remove (tangles, etc.) from hair by combing: to search for and remove. [O.E. *camb.*]

comb², combe. See **coomb.**

combat kom'bət, *v t.* to contend or struggle.—*v.t.* to beat against: to contest: to oppose: to debate:—*pr.p.* **com'bating;** *pa.t.* and *pa.p.* **com'bated.**—*n.* a struggle: a fight —*adjs.* **com'batable; com'batant** disposed to combat: taking part or liable to take part in action.—*n.* one who takes part in a combat.—*adj.* **com'bative** inclined to quarrel.—*n.* **com'bativeness.** —**combat fatigue** mental disturbance in a fighting soldier, formerly called shell-shock. [Fr. *combattre*, to fight—L. pfx. *com*-, mutual, and *bātuēre*, to strike.]

comber¹ kom'bər, *n.* the gaper (a sea-perch): a species of wrasse.

comber². See under **comb¹.**

combine kəm-bīn', *v.t.* to join together: to unite intimately (with).—*v.i.* to come into close union (with): to co-operate: to unite and form a new compound (*chem.*).—*n* (kom'bīn) a syndicate, a trust, an association of trading companies: a combine harvester.—*adj.* **combinate** (kom'bin-āt) combined. —*n.* **combinā'tion** the act of combining: union of individual things: a motor-cycle with sidecar: persons united for a purpose: in mathematics, a possible set of a given number of things selected from a given number: the series of letters or numbers that must be dialled to move the mechanism of a combination lock and so open it.—*n.pl.* **combinā'tions** (*coll.* shortened form **com(b)s** (komz)) an under-garment comprising vest and drawers.—*adjs.* **com'binative; combinato'rial** concerned with arrangement (*math.*); **combined'; combin'ing.**—*n.* **combo** (kom'bō) a small jazz or dance band: any combination (*coll.*):—*pl.* **com'bos.**—**combination lock** a lock used on safes, etc., with numbered dials which must be turned in a special order a certain number of times to open it; **combine harvester** a combined harvesting and threshing machine [L. *combīnāre*, to join—*com*-, *bīnī*, two and two.]

combs komz Short for **combinations.**

combust kom-bust', *v t* to burn up.—*n.* **combustibil'ity.**—*adj.* **combust'ible** liable to take fire and burn: excitable.—*n* anything that will take fire and burn —*ns* **combust'ibleness** quality of being combustible; **combust'ion** (-yən) a burning: the action of fire on combustible substances: oxidation or analogous process with evolution of heat.—**spontaneous combustion** burning caused by heat generated in the substance itself. [L. *combūrěre, combūstum*, to consume—*com*-, intens., *ūrěre*, to burn]

come kum, *v i.* to move toward the place that is the point of view (the opposite of *go*): to draw near: to arrive at a certain state or condition. to issue· to happen: to become: to turn out: to amount (to): to reach: to begin to be in some condition: to achieve a sexual orgasm (*slang*). (only *3rd pers sing.*; esp. in *subj.*) when (a certain time) comes (as in *Come five o'clock, I shall be exhausted*).—*v t.* (*coll.*) to act the part of, assume the behaviour of, as in *Don't come the innocent with me*: (with *it*) to try to impress, assert one's authority over, etc.:—*pr.p* **com'ing**;*pa.t* **came** *kām; pa.p.* **come.**—*interj* (or *imper.*) expressive of encouragement, protest, or reproof (often in phrases **come come, come now**).—*n* **com'er; com'ing** arrival or approach: (esp. with *cap.*) the Advent, or the hoped-for return (also **Second Coming**) of Christ.—*interj.* or *pr p.*, used as a promise of attention.—*adj* future: of future importance.—*adj* **come-at'-able** accessible.—**come'-back** a return, esp. to a former good, popular, successful, etc. state: a revival: a retort: cause or ability to complain; **come'down** a descent: a disappointment: a degradation; **come-hith'er** an invitation to approach: allure.—*adj.* of a look, manner, etc., inviting.—**come'-on** encouragement, esp. sexual: persuasion, **come(-)up(p)'ance** (*coll.*) deserved rebuke or punishment.—**all comers** anyone that likes; **as they come** as they are made, as they are to be had, as they turn up; **come about** to happen; **come again?** (*slang*) what did you say?: pardon?; **come and go** to fluctuate: to have freedom of action; **come at** to reach: to attack; **come away** to become detached; **come back** to return to popularity, office, etc.: to retort; **come by** to come near: to pass: to obtain: to come in; **come down** to descend: to be reduced: to lose esp. financial status; **come down upon** to be severe with; **come down with** to pay down: to become ill with (a disease); **come for** to arrive in order to collect: to attack; **come forward** to identify oneself (to the police, etc.), **come home** to return to one's house: to touch one's interest or feelings closely (with *to*); **come in** to enter: to reply to a radio signal or call; **come in for** to receive as, or as if as, one's share: to receive incidentally; **come into** to fall heir to; **come it strong** (*coll.*) to do or say much, go to great lengths, exaggerate; **come of** to descend from: to be the consequence of, arise from: to become of, **come of age** to reach full legal age; **come off** to come away: to become detached: to turn out: to escape: to desist from: to prove successful, **come off it!** (*coll.*) don't be ridiculous!; **come on** to advance: to thrive: to proceed· to begin: often in *imper.* as a challenge or invitation to attack; **come on stream** of oil-wells, to start regular pumping (also *fig.*); **come out** to result: to be published: to become known or evident. to enter society: to declare openly one's homosexuality (*slang*); **come out with** to utter: to exclaim; **come over** to befall: to come into the mind of· to experience a certain feeling (*coll.*); **come round** to come by a circuitous path: to happen in due course: to veer: to become favourable: to recover from a faint, etc.; **come short** to fail; **come short of** to fail to attain; **come to** to obtain: to amount to: to recover consciousness; **come to grief** to meet with disaster; **come to oneself** to return to normal state of mind; **come to pass** to happen; **come to stay** to become permanent; **come true** to be fulfilled; **come under** to be included under, **come undone, unfastened,** etc. to become detached, loose, etc., **come up** to present itself in discussion, etc., **come up against** to encounter (an obstacle, difficulty); **come upon** to attack: to meet; **come up with** to overtake: to suggest, **give someone the come-on** to invite or entice, esp sexually, **have it coming (to one)** (*coll.*) to have no chance of avoiding one's just deserts, **how come?** how does it happen that .. ?, **to come** future [O.E cuman.]

Comecon *kom'i-kon, n.* a Communist organisation, the Council for Mutual *Economic* Aid, or Assistance.

comedo *kom'i-dō, n.* a blackhead:—*pl.* **com'edos.** [L. *comedō, -ōnis,* glutton—*comedēre,* to eat up, from its wormlike appearance.]

comedy *kom'i-di, n.* a dramatic piece of a pleasant or humorous character: a story with a happy ending: an incident suggesting comic treatment.—*ns.* **comedian** (*kə-mē'di-ən*) one who acts or writes comedies: an entertainer who tells jokes, etc.—*fem.* **comédienne** (*ko-me-, -mē-, -di-en'*).—**comedy of manners** satirical comedy dealing with the manners or fashions of a social class. [Fr. *comédie*—L. *cōmoedia*—Gr. *kōmōidiā*—*kōmos,* revel, or *kōmē,* village, *ōidē,* song.]

comely *kum'li, adj.* pleasing: graceful: handsome.—*adv.* in a comely manner.—*n.* **come'liness.** [Conn O.E. *cymlic*—*cyme,* suitable, *lic,* like.]

comestible *kom-est'ibl, adj.* eatable.—*n.* (usu. in *pl.*) food. [Fr.,—L. *comedēre,* to eat up.]

comet *kom'it, n.* a heavenly body with a very eccentric orbit, having a definite nucleus, a nebulous light surrounding the nucleus, and commonly a luminous tail turned away from the sun [Gr. *komētēs,* long-haired—*komē,* hair.]

comfit *kum'fit, n.* a sweetmeat: a sugar-coated seed or almond. [A doublet of **confect.**]

comfort *kum'fərt v.t.* to relieve from pain or distress: to soothe, cheer.—*n.* relief: encouragement: ease: quiet enjoyment: freedom from annoyance: whatever gives ease, enjoyment, etc.: a subject of satisfaction.—*adj.* **com'fortable** imparting or enjoying comfort: easy (*fig.*): having enough money to live well.—*adv.* **com'fortably.**—*n.* **com'forter** one who administers comfort: a long narrow woollen scarf: a dummy teat —*adj.* **com'fortless.**—*n.* **com'fortlessness.**—*adj.* **com'fy** (*coll.*) comfortable.—**cold comfort** little, if any, comfort. [O.Fr. *conforter*—L. *con-,* intens., and *fortis,* strong]

comfrey *kum'fri, n.* a rough plant related to borage. [O.Fr. *confirie.*]

comic *kom'ik, adj.* relating to comedy: raising mirth: droll.—*n.* the quality or element that arouses mirth: an actor of droll parts: a humorous entertainer on stage, in clubs, on TV, etc.: an amusing person (*coll.*): a paper or magazine, esp. for children, with illustrated stories, strip cartoons, etc (orig. comic, later also serious, even horrific; also **comic book**).—*adj.* **com'ical** funny.—*ns.* **comical'ity, com'icalness.**—*adv.* **com'ically.**—**comic strip** a strip cartoon. [See **comedy.**]

comity *kom'i-ti, n.* courteousness: civility.—**comity of nations** the international courtesy by which effect is given (within limits) to the laws of one state within the territory of another state. [L. *cōmitās, -ātis*—*cōmis,* courteous.]

comma *kom'ə, n.* a phrase (*rhet.*): in punctuation, the point (,) that marks the smallest division of a sentence: the smallest interval, break, discontinuity.—**comma bacillus** the micro-organism that causes cholera; **inverted commas** a set of double or single superscript commas used to introduce and close a quotation, the introductory one(s) being inverted (" .'',`.'.') [L.—Gr. *komma,* a section of a sentence, from *koptein,* to cut off]

command *kəm-ànd', v.t.* to order: to bid: to exercise supreme authority over: to demand: to have within sight, range, influence, or control.—*v.i.* to have chief authority: to govern.—*n.* an order: authority· control· power to overlook, influence or use: the thing commanded· a military division under separate control ability or understanding· a signal activating a mechanism or setting in motion a sequence of operations by instruments.—*ns.* **commandant** (*kom-ən-dant'*) an officer who has the command of a place or of a body of troops; **commandant'ship.**—*v.t.* **commandeer'** to compel to military service, or seize for military use: to take arbitrarily.—*ns.* **command'er** one who commands: an officer in the navy next in rank under a captain: a high-ranking police officer in charge of a district: a member of a higher class in an order of knighthood; **command'ership** religious military orders.—*adj.* **command'ing** fitted to impress or control: strategic.—*adv.* **command'ingly.**—*ns.* **command'ment** a command: a precept; **command'o** a unit of a special service raiding brigade equivalent to a battalion (*mil.*): one serving in such a unit:—*pl.* **command'os.**—**command'er-in-chief'** the officer in supreme command of an army, or of the entire forces of the state; **command module** the part of a spacecraft from which operations are directed; **command performance** a performance by royal command; **command post** a military unit's (temporary) headquarters.—**at command** available for use. [Fr. *commander*—L.L. *commandāre* (L. *commendāre*)—L. *mandāre*, to entrust.]

commedia dell'arte *ko-mā'dē-a de-lär'te*, Italian Renaissance comedy, with stock characters.

comme il faut *ko-mēl-fō*, (Fr.) as it should be: correct: approved by the fashionable world: genteel.

commemorate *kəm-em'ə-rāt*, *v.t.* to call to remembrance by a solemn or public act: to celebrate: to preserve the memory of.—*adj.* **commem'orable.**—*n.* **commemorā'tion** preserving the memory of some person or thing, esp. by a solemn ceremony: the specification of individual saints in the prayers for the dead. —*adjs.* **commem'orative, commem'oratory** tending or serving to commemorate.—*n.* **commem'orātor.** [L. *commemorāre*, *-ātum*, to remember—*com-*, intens., and *memor*, mindful.]

commence *kəm-ens'*, *v.i.* to begin: to originate: to take rise.—*v.t.* to begin: to originate: to enter upon.— *n.* **commence'ment** the beginning. [O.Fr. *com(m)encier*—L. *com-*, intens., and *initiāre*, to begin—*in*, into, and *īre*, to go.]

commend *kəm-end'*, *v.t.* to commit as a charge: to recommend as worthy: to praise.—*adj.* **commend'able.**—*n.* **commend'ableness.**—*adv.* **commend'ably.** —*n.* **commendation** (*kom-ən-dā'shən*) the act of commending: praise: declaration of esteem.—*adj.* **commend'atory** commending: containing praise or commendation: presenting to favourable notice or reception. [L. *commendāre*—*com-*, intens., and *mandāre*, to trust.]

commensal *kə-men'səl*, *adj.* eating at the same table: living together for mutual benefit (*biol.*).—*n.* a messmate: an organism living in partnership (not parasitism) with another.—*ns.* **commen'salism;** **commensal'ity.**—*adv.* **commen'sally.** [L. *com-*, together, *mēnsa*, a table.]

commensurable *kəm-en'shə-rə-bl*, *-sū-*, *adj.* having a common measure: capable of being measured exactly by the same unit: in due proportion.—*ns.* **commensurabil'ity; commen'surableness.**—*adv.* **commen'surably.**—*adj.* **commen'surate** equal in measure or extent: in due proportion.—*adv.* **commen'surately.** —*ns.* **commen'surateness; commensurā'tion.** [L. *com-*, *mēnsūra*, a measure—*mētīrī*, *mēnsus*, to measure.]

comment *kom'ənt*, *-ent*, *n.* a note conveying illustration or explanation: a remark, observation, criticism. —*v.i.* (or *kəm-ent'*) to make critical or explanatory notes (on): to annotate.—*v.t.* to say in comment.—*n.* **comm'entary** a comment: a remark: a series or book of comments or notes: a continuous description of a sport, etc. broadcast (also **running commentary**).—

v.i. **comm'entate** to give a running commentary.—*ns.* **commentā'tion** annotation; **comm'entātor** one who comments: the writer of a commentary: a broadcaster of a running commentary.—*adj.* **commentātō'rial** (or *-to'*) pertaining to the making of commentaries.—*n.* **comm'enter**, **-or** (or *-ment'*).—**no comment** (*coll.*) I have nothing to say (usu. to a newspaper or television reporter). [L. *commentārī*, to devise, contrive—*com-* and L. *mēns*, *mentis*, the mind.]

commerce *kom'ûrs*, *n.* interchange of merchandise on a large scale between nations or individuals: extended trade or traffic: intercourse.—*adj.* **commer'cial** (*-shl*) pertaining to commerce: mercantile: having profit as the main aim: commercially viable.—*n.* a commercially-sponsored advertisement on radio or TV.—*n.* **commercialese'** business jargon.—*v.t.* **commer'cialise, -ize** to reduce to a branch of commerce: to subject to the commercial spirit: to turn (something) into a source of profit (often *derog.*).—*ns.* **commer'cialism** the commercial spirit: an expression characteristic of commercial language; **commer'cialist;** **commerciality** (*-shi-al'i-ti*).—*adv.* **commer'cially.**—**commercial traveller** an accredited travelling representative of a trading house. [Fr.,—L. *commercium* —*com-*, mutual, *merx*, *mercis*, merchandise.]

commie *kom'i*, (*coll.*) *n.* and *adj.* a contraction for **communist.**

comminate *kom'in-āt*, *v.t.* to threaten.—*n.* **comminā'tion** threatening, denunciation: a recital of God's threatenings.—*adjs.* **comm'inative, comm'inatory** threatening punishment. [L. *comminārī*, *-ātum*—*com-*, intens., and *minārī*, to threaten.]

commingle *kəm-ing'gl*, *v.t.* and *v.i.* to mingle or mix together.—*adj.* **comming'led.**

comminute *kom'in-ūt*, *v.t.* to reduce to minute particles: to pulverise.—*n.* **comminū'tion.** [L. *comminuēre*, *-ūtum*, to break into pieces.]

commis *ko'mē*, *n.* an agent, deputy: an apprentice waiter, steward or chef. [Fr.]

commiserate *kəm-iz'ər-āt*, *v.t.* to feel or express compassion for: to pity: to condole with.—Also *v.i.* (often with *with*).—*n.* **commiserā'tion** pity. [L. *com-*, with, *miserāri*, to deplore—*miser*, wretched.]

commissary *kom'is-ər-i*, *n.* one to whom any charge is committed: a deputy: an officer representing a bishop: an officer who furnishes provisions, etc., to an army.—*n.* **commissar'** a commissary: in the Soviet Union, a head of a government department (since 1946 called **minister**).—*adj.* **commissā'rial** pertaining to a commissary.—*ns.* **commissā'riat** the department charged with the furnishing of provisions, as for an army: the supply of provisions: the office of a commissary or of a commissar: a body of commissars; **comm'issaryship.** [L.L. *commissārius*—*committēre, commissum.*]

commission *kəm-ish'ən*, *n.* the act of committing: the state of being commissioned or committed: that which is committed: an instrument conferring authority, or the authority itself, esp. that of a military, naval, or air officer, or a justice of the peace: a percentage paid to an agent: a body of persons appointed to perform certain duties: an order for a piece of work, esp. of art: (of a warship, etc.) the state of being manned, equipped, and ready for service.—*v.t.* to give a commission to or for: to empower: to appoint: to put in commission.—*v.i.* to be put in commission —*n.* **commissionaire** (*-ār'*) a messenger or door-keeper in uniform.—*adj.* **commiss'ioned.**—*ns.* **commiss'ioner; commiss'ionership.**—**commissioned officer** one appointed by commission.—**High Commission** the embassy representing one country that is a member of the British Commonwealth in another such country; **High Commissioner** the chief representative in a High Commission; **in, out of, commission** (of warships) prepared, unprepared for service: in, not in, usable or working condition. [See **commit.**]

commit kə-mit', v.t. to give in charge or trust: to consign: to become guilty of, perpetrate: to compromise or involve: to pledge:—pr.p. **committ'ing**; pa.t. and pa.p. **committ'ed.**—ns. **commit'ment** the act of committing: an order for sending to prison: imprisonment: an obligation undertaken: declared attachment to a doctrine or cause; **committ'al** commitment. (the ceremony of) the placing of a coffin in a grave, crematorium furnace or the sea: a pledge, actual or implied.—adj. **committ'ed** having entered into a commitment: (of literature) written from, (of author) writing from, a fixed standpoint or with a fixed purpose, religious, political, or other.—ns. **committ'ee** a portion selected from a more numerous body (or the whole body) to which some special business is committed: (kom-i-tē') a person to whom something is committed: one charged with the care of a lunatic or imbecile (law); **committ'eeship.**—**commit oneself** to make a definite decision or judgment (on): to make a definite agreement; **commit to memory** to learn by heart. [L. committēre—com-, with, mittēre, to send.]

commix kə-miks', v.t. to mix together.—v.i. to mix.—ns. **commix'tion** (-chən), **commix'ture** the act of mixing together: the state of being mixed: the compound formed by mixing.

commodious kə-mō'dyəs, adj. roomy, spacious: comfortable.—n. **commode'** a small sideboard: an ornamental chest of drawers: a chair containing a chamberpot.—adv. **commo'diously.**—ns. **commo'diousness; commodity** (-mod') an article of traffic: (in pl.) goods, produce. [L. commodus—com-, together, modus, measure.]

commodore kom'ə-dōr, -dōr, n. an officer intermediate between an admiral and a captain: the senior captain in a fleet of merchantmen: the president of a yacht-club: a commodore's ship. [Perh. from Du. kommandeur.]

common kom'ən, adj. belonging equally to more than one: public: general: usual: frequent: ordinary: easy to be had: of little value: vulgar: of low degree.—n. a tract of open land, used in common by the inhabitants of a town, parish, etc.—adj. **comm'onable** held in common.—ns. **comm'onage** right of pasturing on a common: the right of using anything in common: a common; **commonal'ity** frequency, widespreadness; **comm'onalty** the general body of the people: the common people; **comm'oner** one who is not a noble.—adv. **comm'only** in a common manner: meanly, vulgarly: ordinarily: usually: generally.—n. **comm'onness.**—n.pl. **comm'ons** the common people: (with cap.) their representatives—i.e. the lower House of Parliament or House of Commons: common land: food in general, rations.—**common gender** the gender of a noun or pronoun having one form for male and female, as L. bōs, bull, cow, Eng. student; **common ground** a common subject of interest, argument, etc.; **common market** an association of countries as a single economic unit with internal free trade and common external tariffs; **common noun** a name that can be applied to all the members of a class—opp. to proper noun.—adj. **comm'on-or-gar'den** ordinary.—**comm'onplace** a platitude.—adj. lacking distinction: hackneyed.—**commonplace book** a note or memorandum book; **common room** in schools, colleges, etc., a room to which the members have common access; **common sense** average understanding: good sense or practical sagacity.—adjs. **comm'onsense'; commonsens'ical.**—**common stair** an

interior stair giving access to several independent flats or dwellings; **common time** (mus.) four-beat or two-beat rhythm.—**common law husband, wife** in England, a husband or wife legally recognised as such by long association and repute, not by a marriage contract; **in common** together (with): shared or possessed equally; **make common cause with** to cast in one's lot with: to have the same interest and aims with; **short commons** scant fare; **the common** that which is common or usual; **the common good** the interest of the community at large; **the common people** the people in general. [Fr. commun—L. commūnis, prob. from com-, together, and mūnis, serving, obliging.]

commonweal kom'ən-wēl, n. the common good, welfare of the community.—n. **comm'onwealth** (-welth) the public or whole body of the people: a form of government in which the power rests with the people: a state or dominion: a group of states united by a strong but elastic link as the British Commonwealth. [See **wealth.**]

commotion. See **commove.**

commove kə-mōōv', (arch.) v.t. to put in motion: to agitate: to disturb, excite.—n. **commotion** (-mō'shən) a violent motion or moving: excited or tumultuous action, physical or mental: agitation: tumult. [L. com-, intens., and movēre, mōtum, to move.]

commune[1] kom'ūn, n. a corporation: in France, etc , a small territorial division: in some communist countries, an agricultural community: a group of people living communally.—adj. **communal** (kom'ū-nl, kə-mū') pertaining to a commune or a community: owned in common, shared.—ns. **communalisa'tion**, -z-.—v.t. **commu'nalise, -ize** (or kom') to make communal.—ns. **comm'unalism; comm'unalist.**—adv. **comm'unally.** [Fr. commune; see **common.**]

commune[2] kə-mūn', kom'ūn, v.i. to converse or talk together: to have intercourse, esp. spiritual: to receive Holy Communion.—n. **comm'une** converse.—n. and adj. **commun'ing.** [O.Fr. communer, to share.]

communicate kə-mū'ni-kāt, v.t. to give a share of, impart: to reveal: to bestow.—v.i. to have something in common with another: to have communication: to have means of passage: to have intercourse: to partake of Holy Communion: to succeed in conveying one's meaning to others.—adj. **commu'nicable** that may be communicated (esp. of a disease).—adv. **commu'nicably.**—ns. **commu'nicant** one who partakes of Holy Communion; **communica'tion** an act of communicating: that which is communicated: intercourse: correspondence: a means of communicating, a connecting passage or channel: (in pl.) means of giving information, as the press, cinema, radio, and television: a means of transporting, esp. troops and supplies.—adj. **commu'nicative** inclined to communicate or give information.—adv. **commu'nicatively.**—n. **commu'nicator.**—adj. **commu'nicatory** imparting knowledge.—**communique, communiqué** (kom-ū'ni-kā) an official announcement.—**communicating door** a door which gives access from one room, etc. to another; **communication cord** a cord in the wall or ceiling of a railway train which can be pulled in an emergency to stop the train; **communications satellite** an artificial satellite in orbit around the earth, used to relay radio, television and telephone signals; **communication(s) theory** the theory of the transmitting of information, esp. to, from, or between machines. [L commūnicāre, -ātum—commūnis, common.]

communion kəm-ūn'yən, n. act of communing: spiritual intercourse: fellowship: union in religious service: the body of people who so unite: (Holy Communion)

sacrament commemorating the Last Supper.—
commun'ion-cloth, -cup, -table those used at a service
of Holy Communion. [L. *commūniō, -ōnis,* from
commūnis, common.]
communique, communiqué. See **communicate.**
communism *kom'ūn-izm, n.* a theory or condition of
things according to which private property should be
abolished, and all things held in common: (often with
cap.) Marxian socialism as understood in Russia.—*n.*
comm'ūnist a believer in communism.—*adjs.*
comm'ūnist, commūnist'ic, of, or pertaining to,
communism: believing in or favouring communism:
(**commūnistic**) of or favouring communal living and
ownership.
community *kəm-ūn'i-ti, n.* common possession or
enjoyment: agreement: communion: people having
common rights, etc.: the public in general: a body of
persons in the same locality: a body of persons leading a common life, or under socialistic or similar
organisation: a monastic body —*adj.* of, for, or by a
local community.—*n.* **communitā'rian** a member of a
community.—**community centre** a place where
members of a community may meet for social and
other activities; **community work** a form of social
work based on the needs of local communities; **community worker.** [O.Fr. *communité*—L. *commūni-
tās, -ātis*—*commūnis,* common.]
commute *kə-mūt', v.t.* to exchange: to exchange for
a punishment less severe: to compound for (by a
single payment, a simple or more convenient method,
etc.): to change (electric current) from alternating to
direct or vice versa.—*v.i.* to travel regularly, esp.
between suburban home and town office.—*n.*
commūtabil'ity.—*adj.* **commūt'able** that may be
commuted or exchanged.—*v.t.* **commūtate** (*kom';*
elect.) to commute.—*n.* **commūtā'tion** the act of
commuting: change or exchange of one thing for
another: the change to a lighter penalty, simpler or
easier mode of payment, etc.—*adj.* **commū'tative** (or
kom'ū-tā-tiv) relating to exchange: interchangeable:
such that *x* * *y* = *y* * *x*—where * denotes a binary
operation (*math.*).—*adv.* **commūtatively.**—*ns.*
commū'tātor an apparatus for reversing electric currents; **commūt'er** one who commutes. [L. *commū-
tāre*—*com-,* with, *mūtāre,* to change.]
comose, comous. See **coma².**
comp *komp, n.* contracted form of **compositor.**
compact¹ *kəm-pakt', adj* closely placed or fitted together: composed or framed: firm: close: brief.—*n.*
compact (*kom'*) a compacted body or structure, a
combination: a small case containing face-powder for
carrying in the handbag (**powder compact**).—*v.t.*
(*-pakt'*) to press closely together: to consolidate.—
adj. **compact'ed.**—*adv.* **compact'edly.**—*n.* **compact'-
edness.**—*adv.* **compact'ly.**—*ns.* **compac'tion** act of
compacting, or state of being compacted: sediments
compacted by pressure from above (*geol.*): an area
formed by dumping rock waste, etc., pressing it together by means of heavy machines, and causing or
allowing grass to grow over the whole; **compact'ness;
compact'or** a machine which crushes solid waste into
the ground.—**compact disc** a disc, smaller than the
standard seven-inch record, the sound recorded on
which is read for reproduction by means of a laser
beam. [L. *compāctus, pa.p.* of *compingēre*—*com-,*
pangēre, to fix.]
compact² *kom'pakt, n.* a mutual bargain or agreement:
a league, treaty, or union.—*adj.* (*kom-pakt'*) united:
leagued. [L. *compactum*—*compacīscī,* from *com-,*
with *pacīscī,* to bargain.]
companion¹ *kəm-pan'yən, n.* one who keeps company
or frequently associates with another: a member of an
order, esp. in a lower grade: one of a pair or set of

things: an often pocket-sized book on a particular
subject.—*adj.* of the nature of a companion. accompanying.—*adj.* **compan'ionable** fit to be a
companion: agreeable.—*adv.* **compan'ionably.**—
adjs **compan'ionate** shared in companionship;
compan'ioned having a companion.—*n* **compan'ion-
hood.**—*adj.* **compan'ionless.**—*n.* **compan'ionship**
state of being a companion: company fellowship: a
body of companions. [Fr. *compagnon,* from L L
compānium, a mess—L. *com-,* with, and *pānis,*
bread]
companion² *kəm-pan'yən,* (*naut.*) *n.* the skylight or
window-frame through which light passes to a lower
deck or cabin: companion-ladder.—**compan'ion-
hatch** the covering of an opening in a deck,
compan'ion-ladd'er the ladder or stair leading from
the deck to a cabin or to the quarter-deck;
compan'ion-way a staircase from the deck to a cabin.
[Cf. Du. *kompanje;* O.Fr. *compagne;* It. *compagna,*
store-room.]
company *kum'pə-ni, n.* a person or persons associating
with one: any assembly of persons, or of beasts and
birds: persons associated for trade, etc : a society: a
sub-division of a regiment: the crew of a ship: state of
being a companion: presence in association· fellowship: social intercourse.—*adj.* belonging to, relating to, or associated with, a commercial company
—**good, bad, company** having, lacking companionable qualities; **in company** in the presence of other
people; **keep company** to associate (with): to court;
know a man by his company to determine his character by the quality of his friends; **part company** to
separate, go different ways [Fr. *compagnie;* same
root as **companion¹.**]
compare *kəm-pār', v.t.* to set together so as to ascertain
how far things agree or disagree (often with *with*): to
liken or represent as similar (with *to*): to give the
degrees of comparison of (*gram.*).—*v.i* to make
comparison: to stand in comparison: to vie.—*n.*
comparabil'ity.—*adj.* **comparable** (*kom'pər-ə-bl*).—
n. com'parableness.—*adv.* com'parably.—*adv.* com-
parative (*kəm-par'ə-tiv*) pertaining to or making
comparison: estimated by comparing with something
else: not positive or absolute: expressing more
(*gram.*).—*adv.* **compar'atively.**—*ns.* **compar'ator**
any device for comparing accurately, so as e.g. to
detect deviations from a standard or to confirm
identity; **comparison** (*-par'i-sən*) the act of
comparing: capacity of being compared· a comparative estimate: a simile or figure by which two things
are compared: the inflection of an adjective or adverb
to express different relative degrees of its quality
(*gram.*). —**comparability** study a comparison of
wages, conditions, etc. in different jobs, or the same
job in different areas, usu. in order to determine level
of wages.—**beyond compare** without any rival or like;
compare notes to share or exchange one's ideas. [L.
comparāre, to match, from *com-, parāre,* to make or
esteem equal.—*par,* equal.]
compartment *kəm-pärt'mənt, n.* a partitioned-off or
marked-off division of an enclosed space or area. a
division of a railway carriage: a division of anything
—*n.* compartmentalisā'tion, -z-.—*v t.* compartment'alise, -ize to divide into categories or into units,
esp units with little intercommunication.—*adv.*
compartment'ally. [Fr. *compartiment*—L. *com-,*
intens., *partīrī,* to divide—*pars, partis,* a part.]
compass *kum'pəs, n.* a circuit or circle· space: limit:
range of pitch of a voice or instrument: circumference: girth: an instrument consisting of a magnetised needle, used to find directions: (*pl*) a pair of
jointed legs, for describing circles, etc —*v.t.* to pass
or go round: to surround or enclose: to besiege: to

grasp, comprehend. to bring about, accomplish, achieve, or obtain.—*adj.* com'passable capable of being compassed.—*n.* com'passing contrivance, design.—com'pass-card the circular card of a compass, compass rose the circular arrangement showing the principal directions on a map or chart; com'pass-saw one for cutting in curves, com'pass-win'dow a semicircular bay-window.—fetch a compass to go round in a circuit. [Fr. *compas*, a circle, prob from L L. *compassus*—L. *com*-, intens., *passus*, a step.]

compassion *kəm-pash'ən, n.* fellow-feeling, or sorrow for the sufferings of another: pity.—*adjs.* compass'ionable pitiable, compass'ionate inclined to pity or mercy: merciful.—*adv.* compass'ionately.—compassionate leave, discharge, etc leave, discharge, etc in exceptional circumstances for personal reasons [Fr ,—L.L. *compassiō, -ōnis*—*com*-, with, *patī*, *passus*, to suffer.]

compatible *kəm-pat'i-bl, adj.* consistent (with), congruous capable of co-existence: admissible in combination.—*ns.* compatibil'ity congruity. ability to co-exist; compat'ibleness.—*adv* compat'ibly. [Fr ,— L. *com*-, with, *patī*, to suffer.]

compatriot *kəm-pāt'ri-ət,* or *-pat', n.* a fellow-countryman.—Also *adj* —*adj.* compatriotic (-*ot'ik*) [Fr *compatriote*—L. *compatriōta*; see patriot.]

compeer *kəm-pēr', kom'pēr, n.* an equal: a companion. [L. *compār*—*com*-, intens., *pār*, equal.]

compel *kəm-pel', v.t.* to drive or urge on forcibly (to): to oblige: to force.—*pr.p.* compell'ing; *pa t.* and *pa.p.* compelled'.—*adjs.* compell'able; compell'ing forcing attention. [L. *com*-, intens , *pellēre, pulsum*, to drive.]

compendium *kəm-pen'di-əm, n.* a shortening or abridgement: an abstract: a collection of boardgames in one box: —*pl.* -diums, -dia.—*adj.* compen'dious short: concise, comprehensive.—*adv.* compen'diously.—*n.* compen'diousness. [L.*compendium*, what is weighed together, or saved—*com*-, together, *pendēre*, to weigh; see compulse.]

compensate *kom'pən-sāt*, or *kəm-pen'sāt, v.t.* to make amends (for), or to recompense. to counterbalance.— *v.i.* to make up (for).—*n.* compensa'tion (*kom*-) act of compensating: amends, esp. financial, for loss, injury, etc. sustained: the neutralisation of opposing forces (*phys.*): process of compensating for sense of failure or inadequacy by concentrating on achievement or superiority, real or fancied, in some other sphere: the defence mechanism involved in this (*psych*).—*adjs.* compensa'tional, com'pensative (or *kəm-pen'sə-tiv*), compen'satory giving compensation.—*n.* com'pensător. [L *com*-, intens., and *pensāre*, freq. of *pendēre*, to weigh.]

compère *kō-per, kom'per, n.* one who introduces and interlinks items of an entertainment.—*v.t.* to act as compère to. [Fr., god-father.]

compete *kəm-pēt', v.i.* to seek or strive for something in opposition to others: to contend for a prize.—*n.* competition (*kom-pi-tish'ən*) the act of competing: rivalry in striving for the same object: a match or trial of ability.—*adj.* competitive (*kəm-pet'i-tiv*) pertaining to or characterised by competition: (of e.g. price) such as to give a chance of successful result in conditions of rivalry.—*ns.* compet'itiveness; compet'itor one who competes: a rival or opponent.— in competition competing (with). [L. *competēre*, to strive together—*com*-, *petēre*, to seek, strive after.]

competent *kom'pi-tənt, adj.* suitable: sufficient: fit: efficient: belonging: legally qualified: legitimate.— *ns.* com'petence, com'petency fitness: efficiency: capacity: sufficiency: legal power or capacity.—*adv.* com'petently. [L. *competēre*, to come together, be convenient—*com*-, *petēre*, to seek.]

compile *kəm-pīl', v.t.* to write or compose by collecting the materials from other books: to draw up or collect: to compose.—*ns.* compilā'tion (-*pil*- or -*pīl*-) the act of compiling: the thing compiled; com'pilător one who compiles.—*adj.* compi'latory.—*ns.* compile'ment a compilation; compil'er one who compiles: a complex program which translates instructions in a programlanguage into machine code (*comput.*) (cf. interpreter). [Fr. *compiler*, prob. from L. *compīlāre*—*com*-, together, *pīlāre*, to plunder, or *pīlāre*, to pound down.]

complacent *kəm-plā'sənt, adj.* showing satisfaction: self-satisfied, usu with insufficient regard to problems, dangers, etc.: pleased.—*ns.* complā'cence, complā'cency pleasure: (self-) satisfaction: complaisance.—*adv.* complā'cently. [L. *complacēre*—*com*-, intens., *placēre*, to please]

complain *kəm-plān', v.i.* to express grief, pain, censure (at, about): to murmur or express a sense of injury: to accuse: to make a mournful sound: to indicate that one has an illness (with *of*).—*v.t.* to deplore: to utter as a complaint.—*ns.* complain'ant one who complains: one who raises a suit, a plaintiff (*law*); complain'er a murmurer: complainant.—*n.* and *adj.* complain'ing.—*adv.* complain'ingly.—*n.* complaint' a complaining: an expression of grief and dissatisfaction: a representation of pains or injuries: a finding fault: the thing complained of: a grievance: a disease: an ailment. [Fr. *complaindre*—L.L. *complangēre*—L. *com*-, intens., *plangēre*, bewail.]

complaisant *kəm-plā'zənt, adj.* desirous of pleasing: obliging: facile, ready to condone.—*n.* complais'ance care or desire to please, esp. in excess: an obliging civility.—*adv.* complaisantly. [Fr., *complaire*—L. *complacēre*.]

complement *kom'pli-mənt, n.* that which completes or fills up: that by which an angle or arc falls short of a right angle or quadrant: that which is added to certain verbs to make a complete predicate: one of two colours which together give white: full number or quantity: all members of a set not included in a given subset (*math.*).—*v.t.* complement (-*ment*' or *kom'pli-mənt*) to be the complement of.—*adj.* complement'al completing.—*adv.* complement'arily.—*n.* complementar'ity a concept, which accepts the existence of superficially inconsistent views of an object or phenomenon.—*adj.* complement'ary completing: together making up a whole, right angle, white. [L. *complēmentum*—*com*-, intens., and *plēre*, to fill.]

complete *kəm-plēt', adj.* free from deficiency: perfect: finished: entire: fully equipped: consummate.—*v.t.* to finish: to make perfect or entire: to accomplish.— *adjs.* complet'able; complet'ed.—*adv.* complete'ly.— *ns.* complete'ness; comple'tion. [L. *complēre, -ētum*, to fill up—*com*-, intens., and *plēre*, to fill.]

complex *kom'pleks, adj.* composed of more than one, or of many parts: not simple: intricate: difficult.—*n.* a complex whole: a group of (repressed and forgotten) ideas or impressions to which are ascribed abnormal mental conditions and abnormal bodily conditions due to mental causes (*psychology*): loosely applied to the mental condition itself: a complex chemical substance: a collection of interrelated buildings, units, etc., forming a whole, as a *sports complex*.—*ns.* complex'edness, com'plexness, complex'ity state of being complex: complication.—complex number the sum of a real and an imaginary number; complex sentence one consisting of a principal clause and one or more subordinate clauses. [L. *complex*—*com*-, together, and root of *plicāre*, to fold.]

complexion *kəm-plek'shən, n.* disposition: colour: quality: colour or look of the skin, esp. of the face: general appearance, temperament, or texture: general character or nature (*fig.*).—*adjs.* **complex'ioned** having a certain complexion, or temperament; **complex'ionless** colourless. pale [Fr ,—L *complexiō, -ōnis*, a combination, physical structure of body—*com-*, and *plectěre*, to plait.]

compliance *kəm-plī'əns, n.* a yielding: agreement. complaisance: assent: submission (in bad sense).— *adj.* **compli'ant** yielding: pliant civil —*adv* **compli'antly**. [See **comply**.]

complicate *kom'pli-kāt, v.t* to twist or plait together: to render complex: to entangle —*adj* complex: involved folded together —*adj.* **com'plicated** intricate, confused.—*n.* **complica'tion** an intricate blending or entanglement: (usu in *pl*.) disease or illness starting during treatment of or recovery from an existing medical condition: something which causes or adds to difficulty or confusion —**complicated fracture** a fracture where there is some other injury (e.g. a dislocation). [L. *com-*, together, and *plicāre*, *-ātum*, to fold.]

complicity *kəm-plis'i-ti, n.* the state or condition of being an accomplice.

compliment *kom'pli-mənt, n.* an expression of regard or praise: delicate flattery: an expression of formal respect or civility: a present.—*v.t.* **compliment** (*-ment* or *kom'pli-mənt*) to pay a compliment to· to express respect for· to praise: to flatter: to congratulate: to present in compliment.—*adj.* **compliment'ary** conveying, or expressive of, civility or praise: using compliments: bestowed in compliment, given free —*n.* **compliment'er**.—**compliments of the season** compliments appropriate to special times, as Christmas, etc., **left-handed compliment** a saying intended to seem a compliment, but in reality the reverse, **pay or present one's compliments** to give one's respects or greeting. [Fr. *compliment*—L. *complimentum*; see **comply**.]

complin, compline *kom'plin, n.* the 7th and last service of the day, at 9 p.m , completing the canonical hours [O Fr *complie*—L. *complēta (hōra)*]

comply *kəm-plī', v i.* to yield to the wishes of another: to agree or consent to (with *with*) —*n.* **compli'er**.— *p adj* **comply'ing** compliant [It *complire*, to fulfil, to suit, to offer courtesies—L *complēre*, to fulfil, see **complete**.]

compo[1] *kom'pō, n.* a mortar of cement a mixture of whiting, resin, and glue for ornamenting walls·—*pl.* **com'pos**.—**compo ration** (*mil.*) ration for use in the field when no fresh food is available. [**composition**.]

compo[2] *kom'pō, (coll.) n.* compensation for industrial injuries:—*pl.* **com'pos**. [**compensation**.]

component *kəm-pō'nənt, adj* making up: forming one of the elements or parts.—*n* one of the parts or elements of which anything is made up, or into which it may be resolved —**componential** (*-nen'shəl*) [L *compōněre*]

comport *kəm-pōrt', -port', v.i* to agree, suit (with *with*) —*v.t.* (*refl*) to bear: to behave —*n.* manner of acting —*n* **comport'ment** behaviour [L *comportāre*—*com-*, with, *portāre*, to carry]

compose *kəm-pōz', v t.* to form by putting together or being together: to set in order or at rest: to settle or soothe. to dispose artistically. to set up for printing. to create (esp in literature and music) —*v i* to write (esp.) music· to set type —*p.adj.* **composed'** settled quiet calm —*adv* **compos'edly**.—*ns* **compos'edness; compōs'er** a writer or author, esp of music, **composure** (*kəm-pōzh'(y)ər*) calmness self-possession [Fr *composer*—L *com-*, with, *pausāre*, to cease, rest; confused and blended in meaning with words from *pōněre, positum*, to place]

composite *kom'pəz-it*, formerly *-pōz'*, *adj* made up of distinct parts or elements: in bot , belonging to the **Compositae** (*kəm-poz'i-tē*), a great family akin to the bell-flowers but having small flowers crowded together in heads on a common receptacle surrounded by bracts so as to resemble single flowers.—*ns.* **com'posite** a composite thing: something made up of distinct parts or diverse elements: a plant of the Compositae; **com'positeness; compos'i'tion** the act or art of composing: the nature or proportion of the ingredients of anything: a thing composed: a work of art, esp. in music: an exercise in writing prose or verse. disposition of parts: congruity: combination: an artificial mixture, esp. one used as a substitute: mental or moral make-up: a compromise: a picture, photograph formed from several images.—*adjs.* **composi'tional; compositive** (*-poz'*).—*ns* **compos'itor** one who sets up type; **compost** (*kom'post*) a mixture: a manure consisting of a mixture of decomposed organic substances.—*v.t.* to treat with compost: to convert into compost.—**composite portrait** a blend of several portraits: a photograph printed from several negatives representing different persons or the same person at different times; **com'post-heap** a pile of plant refuse, soil, and often chemical fertiliser, which decomposes to form compost. [L. *compositus, compositus*—*com-*, together, *pōněre*, to place.]

compos mentis *kom'pos men'tis*, (L.) of sound mind, sane.

compost. See **composite**.

composure. See **compose**.

compot, compote *kom'pōt*, or *kom'pōt, n.* fruit preserved in syrup: stewed fruit. [Fr. *compote*.]

compound[1] *kəm-pownd', v.t.* to make up: to combine: to settle or adjust by agreement: to agree for a consideration not to prosecute (a felony): to intensify, make worse or greater.—*v.i.* to agree, or come to terms.—*adj.* (*kom'*) mixed or composed of a number of parts: in chem., so united that the whole has properties of its own which are not necessarily those of its constituents: in arith., not simple, dealing with numbers of various denominations of quantity, etc., or with processes more complex than the simple process.—*n* a mass made up of a number of parts: a word made up of two or more words: a compound substance (*chem.*).—*n.* **compound'er**.—**compound animals** same as **colonial animals; compound eye** in insects, etc., an eye made up of many separate units; **compound interest** interest added to the principal at the end of each period (usu. a year) to form a new principal for the next period; **compound leaf** one divided into leaflets by divisions reaching the mid-rib; **compound sentence** (*gram.*) one containing more than one principal clause; **compound time** (*mus.*) time in which each bar is made up of two or more simple measures [O.Fr. *compundre* from L. *compōněre*—*com-*, together, *pōněre*, to place]

compound[2] *kom'pownd, n.* an enclosure round a house or factory (in India), or for housing labourers (S. Africa). [Malay *kampong, kampung*, enclosure.]

comprehend *kom-pra-hend', v.t* to seize or take up with the mind, to understand: to comprise or include. —*ns* **comprehensibil'ity; comprehen'sibleness.**—*adj.* **comprehen'sible** capable of being understood.—*adv.* **comprehen'sibly**.—*n.* **comprehen'sion** power of the mind to understand: the inclusion of Nonconformists within the Church of England —*adj.* **comprehen'sive** having the quality or power of comprehending or containing much: inclusive: compendious.—*n* a comprehensive school —*adv* **comprehen'sively**.—*n.* **comprehen'siveness**.—*n.* **comprehensivisā'tion, -z-** the act of converting schools to comprehensives.— *v t* **comprehen'sivise, -ize**.—**comprehensive school** a secondary school, serving a particular area, that provides education for pupils of all levels and types [L *comprehendĕre, -hēnsum—com-, prehendĕre,* to seize.]

compress *kəm-pres', v.t.* to press together: to force into a narrower space: to condense or concentrate.—*n.* (*kom';surg.*) a pad used to apply pressure to any part: a folded cloth applied to the skin.—*adj.* **compressed'** pressed together: compacted: laterally flattened or narrowed (*biol.*).—*n.* **compressibil'ity.**—*adj.* **compress'ible** that may be compressed.—*ns* **compress'ibleness; compression** (*kəm-presh'ən*) the act of compressing: state of being compressed: condensation: flattening: deformation by pressure: the stroke that compresses the gases in an internal-combustion engine.—*adjs.* **compress'ional; compress'ive** able to compress.—*ns.* **compress'or; compressure** (*-presh'ər*).—**compressed air** air at more than atmospheric pressure. [L. *compressāre, com-,* together, and *pressāre,* to press—*premĕre, pressum,* to press.]

comprise *kəm-prīz', v.t.* to contain, include: to consist of.—*adj.* **compris'able.**—*n.* **compris'al** the act, condition, or fact of comprising. [Fr. *compris,* pa.p. of *comprendre*—L. *comprehendĕre;* see **comprehend.**]

compromise *kom'prə-mīz, n.* a settlement of differences by mutual concession: anything of intermediate or mixed kind, neither one thing nor another.—*v.t.* to settle by mutual concession: to involve or bring into question: to expose to risk of injury, suspicion, censure, or scandal.—*v.i* to make a compromise. [Fr. *compromis*—L. *comprōmittĕre, -missum—com-,* together, *prōmittĕre,* to promise.]

comptroll, comptroller. See under **control.**

compulsion *kəm-pul'shən, n.* the act of compelling: force: a strong irrational impulse.—*adj.* **compul'sive** with power to compel: pertaining to compulsion: (of person) driven by, (of action) caused by, a specific constant and irresistible impulse: irresistible.—*advs.* **compul'sively; compul'sorily.**—*adj.* **compul'sory** compelled: obligatory: compelling.—*n.* an exercise comprising specified compulsory figures, movements, or dances, e.g. in ice-skating.—**compulsory purchase** enforced purchase by a public authority of property needed for public purposes. [L. *compulsāre,* freq. of *compellere;* see **compel.**]

compunction *kəm-pungk'shən, n.* remorse tinged with pity.—*adj.* **compunc'tious.** [O.Fr.,—L. *compunctiō, -ōnis—com-,* intens., and *pungĕre, punctum,* to prick.]

compute *kəm-pūt', v.t.* to calculate: to number: to estimate.—*adj.* **computable** (*kom'* or *-pūt'*) calculable.—*ns.* **com'putant, com'putātor, com'putist** a calculator; **comput'er** a calculator: a machine or apparatus, mechanical, electric or electronic, for carrying out, esp. complex, calculations, dealing with numerical data or with stored items of other information; also used for controlling manufacturing processes, or co-ordinating parts of a large organisation; **computā'tion** the act of computing: reckoning: estimate: arithmetic.—*adjs.* **computā'tional** involving calculation; **com'putative** (or *-pūt'*) given to computation.—*v.t.* **comput'erise, -ize** to bring computer(s) into use to control (operation, system of operations): to process (data) by computer.—*n.* **computerisā'tion, -z-.—computer-assisted** or **computed axial tomography scanner** a machine which produces X-ray pictures of sections of the body with the assistance of a computer (shortened to CAT scanner); **computer language** a system of alphabetical or numerical signs used for feeding information into a computer; **computer science** the sciences connected with computers, e.g. computer design, programming, data processing, etc.; **computer scientist; computer typesetting** the use of electronic equipment to process an unjustified input of keyed material into an output

of justified and hyphenated, etc., lines, the output being either a new tape to be used on a typesetting or filmsetting machine or, in some systems, the final product. [L. *computāre—com-,* intens., *putāre,* to reckon.]

comrade *kom'rid, kum'rid , n.* a close companion: an intimate associate: in some socialist and communist circles used as a term of address, or prefixed to a name: a communist (*slang; derog.*).—*n.* **com'radeship.**—*adj.* and *adv.* **com'radely.** [Sp. *camarada,* a roomful, a room-mate—L. *camera,* a room—Gr. *kamarā.*]

coms. See **combinations** under **combine.**

comsat. Abbrev. for *communications satellite.*

con[1] *kon, adv.* and *n.* a contraction of L. *contrā,* against, as in **pro** and **con,** for and against.

con[2] *kon, v.t.* to study carefully, scan, pore over: to commit to memory.—*ns.* **conn'er; conn'ing.** [O.E. *cunnan,* to know; perh. partly *cunnian,* to seek to know, examine.]

con[3], **conn** *kun, kon, (naut.) v.t.* to direct the steering of.—Also *v.i.*—*n.* the act or station of conning.—*ns.* **conner** (*kun'ər, kon'ər*); **conn'ing.—conn'ing-tower** the pilot-house of a warship or submarine. [Older forms *cond, condue,* etc., apparently—Fr. *conduire* —L. *condūcĕre;* see **conduct.**]

con[4] *kon, (slang) adj.* short for **confidence,** as in **con game, con trick** a swindle, **con man** a swindler, esp. one with a persuasive way of talking.—*v.t.* **con** to swindle: to trick: to persuade by dishonest means.— *n.* a trick, swindle.

con[5] *kon, (slang) n.* a prisoner. [Abbrev. of **convict.**]

con-. See **com-.**

con amore *kon am-ör'e, -o're,* (It.) with love: very earnestly.

conatus *kō-nā'təs, n.* an effort: an impulse: a tendency, nisus:—*pl.* **conā'tus.**—*n.* **conā'tion** the active aspect of mind, including desire and volition.—*adj.* **conative** (*kon', kon'ə-tiv*). [L. *cōnātus, -ūs,* effort.]

con brio *kon brē'ō,* (It.) with spirit.

concatenate *kən-kat'ə-nāt, v.t.* to chain or link together: to connect in a series.—*n.* **concatenā'tion** a series of links united: a series of things depending on each other. [L. *con-, catēna,* a chain.]

concave *kon'kāv, kon-kāv', adj.* curved inwards (opp. to *convex*).—*v.t.* and *v.i.* to make or become hollow —*adv.* **con'cavely** (or *-kāv'*).—*n.* **concavity** (*kən-kav'i-ti*) the quality of being concave: a hollow.— *adjs.* **concā'vo-con'cave** or **doub'le-con'cave** concave on both sides; **concā'vo-con'vex** concave on one side, and convex on the other. [L. *concavus,* from *con-,* intens., and *cavus,* hollow; see **cave**[1].]

conceal *kən-sēl', v.t.* to hide completely or carefully: to keep secret: to disguise: to keep from telling.—*n.* **conceal'ment.** [O.Fr. *conceler*—L. *concēlāre,* from *con-,* intens., and *cēlāre,* to hide.]

concede *kən-sēd', v.t.* to yield or give up: to admit, allow.—*v.t.* to make concession.—*n.* **conced'er.** [L. *concēdĕre, -cēssum—con-,* wholly, and *cēdĕre,* to yield.]

conceit *kən-sēt', n.* overweening self-esteem: fancy: wit: a witty thought, esp. far-fetched, affected or over-ingenious: estimate.—*adj.* **conceit'ed** egotistical.—*adv.* **conceit'edly.**—*n.* **conceit'edness.—out of conceit with** displeased with. [From **conceive** on the analogy of **deceive, deceit.**]

conceive *kən-sēv'. v.t.* to receive into or form in the womb: to form in the mind: to imagine or think: to understand. to grasp as a concept: to express —*v i.* to become pregnant: to think.—*ns.* **conceivabil'ity,** **conceiv'ableness.**—*adj.* **conceiv'able.**—*adj* **conceiv'-ably.** [O.Fr. *concever*—L. *concipĕre, conceptum,* from *con-,* together, and *capĕre,* to take]

For other sounds see detailed chart of pronunciation.

concelebrate *kon-sel'ə-brāt, v.t.* of two or more priests, to celebrate (mass) jointly.—*ns.* **concel'ebrant** a priest taking part in a concelebrated mass; **concelebrā'tion.** [L. *con-*, together, and **celebrate**.]

concentrate *kon'sən-trāt, v.t.* to bring towards a common centre: to focus: to direct with exclusive attention upon the matter in hand: to condense, to increase the quantity in unit space.—*v.i.* to draw towards a common centre: to direct one's thoughts or efforts towards one object.—*n.* a product of concentration.—*adj.* concentrated.—*n.* something concentrated, as animal feed.—*n.* **concentrā'tion** the act of concentrating: condensation: the proportion of molecules or ions to unit volume: the keeping of the mind fixed on something.—**concentration camp** a settlement for persons in the way of, or obnoxious to, the authorities. [A lengthened form of **concentre**.]

concentre *kən-sent'ər, v.i* to tend to or meet in a common centre: to be concentric.—*v.t.* to bring or direct to a common centre or point.—*adjs.* **concen'tric, -al** having a common centre.—*adv.* **concen'trically.**—*n.* **concentricity** *(kon-sən-tris'i-ti).* [Fr. *concentrer*—L. *con-*, *centrum*—Gr. *kentron*, point.]

concept *kon'sept, n.* a thing conceived, a general notion: an idea, invention.—*n* **concep'tion** the act of conceiving: the fertilisation of an ovum: the formation, or power of forming in the mind, of a concept, plan, thought, etc.: a concept: a notion.—*adjs.* **concept'ive** capable of conceiving; **concep'tual** pertaining to conception or concepts.—*n.* **conceptualisā'tion, -z-.**—*v.t.* **concep'tualise, -ize** to form a concept of.—*v.i.* to form concepts: to think abstractly.—*ns.* **conceptualism** the doctrine in philosophy that universals exist only in the mind; **concep'tualist.**—*adj.* **conceptualis'tic.** [L. *concipēre, -ceptum,* to conceive.]

concern *kən-sûrn', v.t.* to relate or belong to: to affect or interest: to involve by interest, occupation or duty: to trouble.—*n.* that which concerns or belongs to one: affair: business: interest: regard: anxiety: a business establishment.—*adj.* **concerned'** interested: involved: taking an active interest in current social, etc., problems: troubled.—*adv.* **concern'edly.**—*n.* **concern'edness.**—*prep.* **concern'ing** regarding: about.—*n.* **concern'ment** concern: importance.—**as concerns** as regards. [L. *concernēre,* to distinguish, later to have respect to.]

concert *kon'sərt, n.* union or agreement in any undertaking: harmony: musical harmony: a musical entertainment.—*v.t. (kən-sûrt')* to frame or devise together: to arrange, adjust.—*adj.* **concerted** *(-sûrt')* mutually planned: arranged in parts *(mus.).*—*n.* **concertina** *(kon-sər-tē'nə)* a musical instrument consisting of a pair of bellows, usually hexagonal, the sounds produced by free vibrating reeds of metal, as in the accordion.—*v.i.* to collapse or fold up like a concertina.—*n.* **concerto** *(kon-chûr'tō)* a composition for solo instrument(s) and orchestra in sonata form:—*pl.* **concer'tos.**—**con'cert-goer** a habitual attender of concerts; **con'cert-grand** a grand piano suitable for concerts; **con'cert-hall;** **con'cert-master** the leader of an orchestra.—**in concert** working or conspiring together: performing at a concert. [It. *concertare,* to sing in concert, perh.—L. *con-, certāre,* to strive.]

concession *kən-sesh'ən, n.* the act of conceding: the thing conceded: a grant: the right, granted under government licence, to drill for oil or gas in a particular area.—*n.* **concession(n)aire'** one who has obtained a concession.—*adj.* **concess'ionary, -adj** **concess'ive** implying concession. [See **concede**.]

conch *kongk, konch, n.* the name for various marine gasteropods and their shells: a shell used as a trumpet: a concha.—*n.* **conch'a** in archit, the semidome of an apse: the apse itself: the outer ear, or its

cavity.—*adjs.* **conch'ate, conch'iform** shaped like a shell, esp. one valve of a bivalve shell; **concholog'ical.**—*ns.* **conchol'ogist; conchol'ogy** the study of molluscs and their shells. [L. *concha*—Gr. *konchē,* a cockle or mussel.]

conchy, conchie *kon'shi,* (slang) *n.* a conscientious objector.

concierge *kɔ̃-si-erzh', n.* a warden: a janitor: a porter or a portress. [Fr.]

conciliar *kən-sil'i-ər, adj.* pertaining to an ecclesiastical council.—Also **concil'iary.** [L. *concilium,* council.]

conciliate *kən-sil'i-āt, v.t.* to gain, or win over: to reconcile, bring together (esp. opposing sides in an industrial dispute).—*v.i.* to make friends.—*n.* **concilia'tion** the act of conciliating.—*adj.* **concil'iative** (or *-ā-tiv*).—*n.* **concil'iātor.**—*adj.* **concil'iatory.** [L. *conciliāre, -ātum—concilium,* council.]

concise *kən-sīs', adj.* cut short: brief.—*adv.* **concise'ly.**—*ns.* **concise'ness** the quality of being concise: terseness; **concision** *(-sizh'ən)* mutilation: conciseness [L. *concīsus,* pa.p. of *concīdēre—con-,* intens., *caedēre,* to cut.]

conclave *kon'klāv, n.* the room in which cardinals meet to elect a pope: the body of cardinals: any close assembly. [L. *conclāve—con-,* with, *clāvis,* a key.]

conclude *kən-klōōd', v.t.* to close: to end: to decide: to settle or arrange finally: to infer.—*v.i.* to end: to form a final judgment.—*p.adj.* **conclud'ed** finished: settled.—*adj.* **conclud'ing** final, closing.—*n.* **conclu'sion** *(-zhən)* the act of concluding: the end, close, or last part: inference: judgment.—*adjs.* **conclusive** *(-klōō'siv),* **conclu'sory** final: convincing.—*adv.* **conclus'ively.**—*n.* **conclus'iveness.**—**in conclusion** finally; **try conclusions** to experiment: to engage in a contest (with). [L. *conclūdēre, conclūsum—con-,* intens., *claudēre,* to shut.]

concoct *kən-kokt', v.t.* to digest: to prepare or mature: to plan, devise: to fabricate.—*ns.* **concoct'er, concoct'or; concoc'tion** the action of concocting: ripening: preparation of a medical prescription, etc.: a made-up story. [L. *concoquēre, concoctum—con-,* together, and *coquēre,* to cook, to boil.]

concomitant *kən-kom'i-tənt, adj.* accompanying: conjoined: occurring along with, because of, or in proportion to, (something else).—*n.* one who or that which accompanies.—*adv.* **concom'itantly.** [L. *con-,* intens., *comitāns, -antis,* pr.p. of *comitārī,* to accompany—*comes,* a companion.]

concord *kon'kōrd, or kong'-, n.* the state of being of the same heart or mind: harmony: agreement: a combination of sounds satisfying to the ear.—*v.i.* **concord'** *(kən-)* to agree: to harmonise.—*n.* **concord'ance** agreement: an index of the words or passages of a book or author.—*adj.* **concord'ant** harmonious, united.—*adv.* **concord'antly.**—*n.* **concord'at** an agreement, esp. between the pope and a secular government. [Fr. *concorde*—L. *concordia—concors,* of the same heart, from *con-, cor, cordis,* the heart.]

concourse *kon'kōrs, kong', -kōrs, n.* the assembly of persons or things running or drawn together: a large hall: an open space, esp. in a railway station, airport, etc. [Fr. *concours*—L *concursus—con-, currēre,* to run.]

concrescence *kən-kres'əns, n* a coalescence or growing together.—*adj.* **concresc'ent.** [L. *concrēscentia—con-, crēscēre,* to grow.]

concrete *kon'krēt (or kən-krēt'), adj.* formed into one mass: the opposite of *abstract,* and denoting a particular thing: *(kon')* made of concrete.—*n. (kon')* a mass formed by parts growing or sticking together: a mixture of sand, gravel, etc., and cement, used in building —*v.t. (-krēt')* to form into a solid mass: *(kon')* tō cover with concrete.—*v.i. (-krēt')* to harden —*adv.* **concrete'ly** (or *kon'*) —*ns.* **concrete'- ness** (or *kon'*); **concretion** (-*krē'shən*) a mass concreted: a nodule or lump formed within a rock (*geol.*): a solid mass formed within an animal or plant body — *adj* **concre'tionary**.—*n* **con'cretism** regarding, representing, abstract things as concrete.—*n., adj* **con'cretist.—concrete** mixer a machine with a large revolving drum for mixing concrete, **concrete music** see **musique concrète; concrete poetry** an art form which seeks to introduce a new element into poetry by means of visual effects such as the arrangement of letters on the printed page [L. *concrētus—con-*, together, and *crēscēre, crētum* to grow.]

concubine *kong'kū-bīn, n* one (esp a woman) who cohabits without being married —*n.* **concubinage** (*kon-kū'bin-āj*) the state of living together as man and wife without being married —*adj.* **concu'binary.** [Fr ,—L *concubīna—con-*, together, *cubāre*, to lie down.]

concupiscence *kən-kū'pis-əns, n.* a violent desire: sexual appetite lust —*adj* **concu'piscent.** [L. *concupīscentia—concupīscēre—con-*, intens., *cupēre*, to desire.]

concur *kən-kûr', v ı* to run together: to meet in one point: to coincide. to act together to agree. to assent: —*pr p.* **concurr'ing;** *pa p.* **concurred'.**—*n* **concurrence** (-*kur'*) the meeting of lines in one point coincidence: joint action assent.—*adj.* **concurr'ent** meeting in the same point running, coming, acting, or existing together coinciding. accompanying.—*adv* **concurr'ently.**—*adj* **concurr'ing** agreeing [L *concurrēre—con-, currēre*, to run.]

concuss *kən-kus', v ı* to disturb to shake —*n.* **concussion** (-*kush'*) the state of being shaken: a violent shock caused by the sudden contact of two bodies: a violent blow, esp on the head: the resulting injury to the brain, causing temporary loss of consciousness. [L *concussus*, pa.p of *concutēre—con-*, together, *quatēre*, to shake.]

condemn *kən-dem', v.t* to pronounce guilty: to censure or blame: to sentence: to give up to some fate to pronounce unfit for use to reject —*n* **condemnation** (*kon-dəm-nā'shən*) the state of being condemned.—*adj.* **condem'natory** expressing or implying condemnation —*p.adj* **condemned'** pronounced to be wrong, guilty, or useless belonging or relating to one who is sentenced to punishment (e.g. *condemned cell*): declared dangerous or unfit. [L. *condemnāre*, from *con-*, intens , and *damnāre*, to hurt.]

condense *kən-dens', v.t* to reduce to smaller compass: to render more dense or more intense: to subject to condensation (*chem.*).—*v ı.* to become condensed.— *v.t* and *v.i.* **condens'ate** to condense —*n.* a product of condensation —*ns.* **condensā'tion** (*kon-*) the act of condensing: the union of two or more molecules of the same or different compounds with the elimination of water, alcohol, or other simple substances (*chem.*): loosely applied to almost any reaction in which a product of higher molecular weight than the reactant is obtained; **condens'er** an apparatus for reducing vapours to a liquid form: a mirror or lens for focusing light: a capacitor —**condensation trail** see **contrail; condensed milk** milk reduced by evaporation, and sugared. [L *condēnsāre—con-*, intens., and *dēnsus*, dense.]

condescend *kon-di-send', v ı* to descend willingly from a superior position: to act graciously to inferiors: to deign: to stoop to what is unworthy.—*adj* **condescend'ing** gracious to inferiors offensively patronising.—*adv.* **condescend'ingly.**—*n.* **condescen'sion.** [L *con-*, intens., and *dēscendēre*, to descend.]

condign *kən-dīn', adj* well merited (usu. of punishment) [L *condignus—con-*, intens., *dignus,*

worthy.]

condiment *kon'di-mənt, n.* a seasoning. [L. *condīmentum—condīre*, to preserve, to pickle.]

condition *kən-dish'ən, n.* the state in which things exist: a good or fit state: a particular manner of being: quality: prerequisite: a term of a contract: (in *pl.*) circumstances: that which must precede the operation of a cause (*logic*) a provision upon which an obligation depends (*law*).—*v ı.* to agree upon: to restrict, limit: to determine: to put into the required state: to prepare, train (person, animal) for a certain activity or for certain conditions of living: to secure by training (a certain behavioural response to a stimulus).—*adj.* **condi'tional** depending on conditions: expressing condition.—*n.* **conditional'ity.**—*adv.* **condi'tionally.**—*adj.* **condi'tioned** having a certain condition, state, or quality: circumstanced: depending: relative—the opposite of *absolute*: subject to condition.—*ns.* **condi'tioner** a person, substance, or apparatus that brings into good or required condition; **condi'tioning.—conditioned reflex, response** a reflex response to a stimulus which depends upon the former experience of the individual.—**in, out of, condition** in good, bad, condition: physically fit, unfit [L. *condiciō* (wrongly *conditiō*), *-ōnis*, a compact—*condicēre,—con-*, together, *dīcēre*, to say.]

condole *kən-dōl', v.i.* to grieve with another: to express sympathy in sorrow.—*adj.* **condol'atory** expressing condolence.—*n.* **condol'ence** an expression of sympathy with another's sorrow. [L. *con-*, with, *dolēre*, to grieve.]

condom *kon'dom* or *-dəm', n* a contraceptive rubber sheath. [Perh. from name of inventor.]

condominium *kon-do-min't-əm, n.* joint sovereignty: a country whose government is controlled by two or more other countries: a block of flats in which each flat is separately owned (*U.S.*): such a flat (*U.S.*) [L *con-*, together, *dominum*, lordship.]

condone *kən-dōn', v.t.* to forgive: to pass over without blame, overlook: to excuse, atone for.—*n.* **condona'tion** (*kon-*). [L. *con-*, intens., *dōnāre*, to give; see **donation**.]

condor *kon'dor, -dər, n.* a large South American vulture. [Sp. *cóndor*—Quechua *cuntur*.]

conduce *kən-dūs', v.t.* to help to bring about, contribute (towards a result).—*adj.* **conduc'ive** leading or tending. favourable to or helping towards something.—**conducive to** helping towards or encouraging. [L. *con-*, together, *dūcēre*, to lead.]

conduct *kən-dukt', v.t.* to lead or guide: to convey (water, blood, sap, etc.): to direct: to manage: to behave: to carry or transmit (*elect.*): to beat time for and co-ordinate (*mus.*):—*n.* (*kon'dukt*), the act or method of leading or managing: guidance: escort: guide: management: behaviour.—*ns.* **conduct'ance** a conductor's power of conducting electricity, the reciprocal of the resistance; **conductibil'ity.**—*adj.* **conduct'ible** capable of conducting heat, etc.: capable of being conducted or transmitted.—*n.* **conduc'tion** act or property of conducting or transmitting: transmission by a conductor, as heat.—*adj.* **conduct'ive** having the quality or power of conducting or transmitting.— *ns.* **conductiv'ity** the power of transmitting heat, electricity, stimuli: a substance's specific power of conducting electricity; **conduct'or** the person or thing that conducts: a leader: a manager: a director of an orchestra or choir: one in charge of a bus, etc.: a railway guard (*U.S.*): that which has the property of transmitting electricity, heat, etc.:—*fem.* **conduct'ress; conduct'orship** the office of conductor. [L. *conductus—condūcēre.* See **conduce.**]

conduit *kon'dit*, or *kun', n.* a channel or pipe conveying water or other fluid, or covering electric wires, etc. [Fr. *conduit*—L. *conductus*—*condūcĕre*, to lead.]

condyle *kon'dil, n.* a protuberance at the end of a bone serving for articulation with another bone.—*adjs.* **con'dylar, con'dyloid.** [Gr. *kondylos*, knuckle.]

cone *kōn, n.* a solid figure with a point and a base in the shape of a circle or elipse: anything shaped like a cone· a volcanic hill· the typical flower (or fruit) or inflorescence of the Coniferae, more or less conical: an ice-cream cornet —*v.t.* to shape like a cone.—*v t.* to bear cones.—*adjs.* **conic** (*kon'ik*), **-al** having the form of or pertaining to a cone.—*n.* a conic section.—*adv.* **con'ically.**—*n. sing.* **con'ics** the geometry of the cone and its sections.—*adj* **cō'niform** in the form of a cone.—**conic section** a figure made by the section of a cone by a plane. [Gr. *kōnos*]

coney. See cony.

confabulate *kən-fab'ū-lāt, v t.* to chat (*coll* **confab'**): to imagine experiences to compensate for loss of memory (*psych.*).—*adjs.* **confab'ular; confab'ulatory.**—*ns.* **confabula'tion** (*coll.* **confab'** or *kon'*); **confab'ulator.** [L. *cōnfābulārī—con-, fābulārī*, to talk.]

confect *kən-fekt', v.t.* to prepare: to preserve.—*n.* **confec'tion** composition, compound: a sweetmeat: a ready-made article of dress for women's wear.—*v.t* to make (into a confection).—*n.* **confec'tionary** a sweetmeat: a place where confections are made or kept.—*adj.* pertaining to or of the nature of confectionery.—*ns.* **confec'tioner** one who makes or sells sweets; **confec'tionery** confectioners' work or art: sweetmeats in general. [L. *cōnficĕre, cōnfectum*, to make up together—*con-, facĕre*, to make.]

confederate *kən-fed'ər-āt, adj.* leagued together: allied (esp. the seceding American states of the Civil War). —*n.* one united in a league: an ally: an accomplice.—*v.t.* and *v.t.* to league together or join in a league.—*n.* **confed'eracy** a league or mutual engagement: persons or states united by a league: a conspiracy.—*n.* **confedera'tion** a league: alliance, esp. of princes, states, etc.: an association of more or less autonomous states united permanently by a treaty. [L. *cōnfoederāre, -ātum—con-, foedus, foedĕris*, a league.]

confer *kən-fûr', v.t.* to give or bestow: to compare (*obs.*)—in use as abbrev. **cf.**—*v.t.* to talk or consult together:—*pr.p.* **conferr'ing;** *pa.t.* and *pa p.* **conferred'.**—*ns.* **conference** (*kon'*) the act of conferring: an appointed meeting for instruction or discussion; **confer'ment** bestowal: a thing bestowed.—**in conference** attending a meeting: engaged. [L. *cōnferre* —*con-*, together, *ferre*, to bring.]

confess *kən-fes', v.t.* to acknowledge fully (esp something wrong): to own or admit: to make known, as sins to a priest: to hear a confession from, as a priest. —*v.t* to make confession.—*ns.* **confession** (*kən-fesh'ən*) acknowledgment of a crime or fault: avowal: the thing confessed: a statement of religious belief: acknowledgment of sin to a priest; **confess'ional** the seat or enclosed recess where a priest hears confessions: the institution of confession.—*adj.* pertaining to confession.—*ns* **confess'or** a priest who hears confessions and grants absolution: one who makes avowal, esp. of religious faith:—*fem.* **confess'oress; confess'orship.**—*adjs.* **confessed', confest'** admitted: avowed. evident. —*advs.* **confess'edly, confest'ly.**—**confess to** to admit, acknowledge. [Fr *confesser*—L *cōnfitērī, cōnfessus—con-*, sig. completeness, and *fatērī*, to confess—*fārī*, to speak]

confetti *kən-fet'i, n.pl.* bits of coloured paper flung at brides and bridegrooms [It.]

confide *kən-fīd', v.i.* to trust wholly or have faith (with *in*): to impart secrets to someone with trust (with *in*) —*v t* to entrust: to impart with reliance upon

secrecy.—*ns.* **confidant** (*kon-fi-dant'*) one confided in or entrusted with secrets, esp. in love affairs: a bosom friend:—*fem.* **confidante'; confidence** (*kon'fidəns*) firm trust or belief: faith: trust in secrecy: self-reliance: firmness: boldness: presumption: admission to knowledge of secrets or private affairs: a confidential communication.—*adj* **con'fident** trusting firmly: having full belief: assured: bold.—*adj.* **confidential** (*-den'shl*) given in confidence: admitted to confidence: private.—*n.* **confidential'ity.**—*advs.* **confiden'tially; con'fidently.**—*n.* **confid'er.**—*adj.* **confid'ing** trustful.—*adv* **confid'ingly.**—**confidence trick** a swindler's trick, whereby a person is induced to hand over money as a mark of confidence in the swindler. [L. *cōnfidĕre—con-*, sig. completeness, and *fidĕre*, to trust.]

configuration *kən-fig-ū-rā'shən, n.* external figure or shape: outline: relative position or aspect, as of planets: spatial arrangements of atoms in a molecule (*chem.*): Gestalt, the organised whole (*psych.*).—*adj* **configura'tional.** [L. *cōnfigūrāre*, to form.]

confine *kon'fin, n.* a border, boundary, or limit—generally in *pl.*—*v.t* **confine'** to limit, enclose: to imprison —*adjs.* **confin'able; confined'** limited: imprisoned: narrow —*n.* **confine'ment** the state of being shut up: restraint: imprisonment.—*adj.* **confin'ing** bordering: limiting.—**be confined** to be limited: to be restrained to bed or indoors in childbirth. [L. *cōnfīnis*, bordering—*con-*, together, *fīnis*, the end.]

confirm *kən-fûrm', v.t.* to strengthen: to fix or establish: to ratify: to verify: to assure· to admit to full communion.—*adj.* **confirm'able.**—*ns* **con'firmand** a candidate for confirmation; **confirma'tion** a making firm or sure: convincing proof: the rite by which persons are admitted to full communion in many churches.—*adj.* **confirm'ative** tending to confirm —*n.* **con'firmator.**—*adjs.* **confirm'atory** giving additional strength to: confirming; **confirmed'** settled: inveterate.—*ns.* **confirmee'** one to whom a confirmation is made; **confirm'er; confirm'ing; confirm'or.** [O.Fr. *confermer*—L. *cōnfirmāre—con-*, intens., and *firmāre—firmus*, firm.]

confiscate *kon'fis-kāt, v.t.* to appropriate to the state, as a penalty: to take possession of by authority.—*adj.* forfeited.—*adjs.* **con'fiscable** (or *-fis'*); **confiscatory** (*kon'fis-kā-tər-i* or *kən-fis'kə-tər-i*) of the nature of confiscation.—*ns.* **confisca'tion** the act of confiscating; **con'fiscator.** [L. *cōnfiscāre, -ātum—con-*, together, *fiscus*, a basket, purse, treasury.]

conflagrate *kon'flə-grāt, v.t.* and *v.i.* to burn up.—*n.* **conflagra'tion** a great burning or fire. [L. *cōnflagrāre—con-*, intens., and *flagrāre*, to burn; see **flagrant.**]

conflate *kən-flāt', v.t.* to fuse: to combine (two variant readings of a text) into one —*n.* **confla'tion.** [L. *cōnflāre, -ātum*, to blow together.]

conflict *kon'flikt, n.* violent collision: a struggle or contest.—*v.i.* (*kən-flikt'*) to fight: contend: to be in opposition: to clash.—*adj.* **conflict'ing** clashing: contradictory —*n.* **conflic'tion.**—**in conflict** incompatible, or irreconcilable (with) [L. *cōnflīgĕre, -flīctum—con-*, together, and *flīgĕre*, to strike.]

confluence *kon'floo-əns, n.* a flowing together: a meeting-place, as of rivers: a concourse: the act of meeting together.—*adj.* **con'fluent** flowing together: running into one: uniting.—*n.* a stream uniting and flowing with another —*adv.* **con'fluently.**—*n* **con'flux** (*-fluks*) a flowing together. [L. *cōnfluĕre—con-*, together, *fluĕre, fluxum*, to flow.]

conform *kən-form', v.t.* to make like or of the same form: to adapt.—*v.i.* to be or become of the same form: to comply: to obey —*adj* **conform'able** corresponding in form. suitable compliant. in unbroken

continuity of bedding (*geol*).—*adv.* **conform'ably.**—
adj. **conform'al** of a map, representing small areas in
their true shape.—*ns.* **conformā'tion** particular form,
shape, or structure: adaptation; **conform'er, conform'ist** one who conforms; **conform'ity** likeness:
compliance. consistency.—**in conformity with** in
accordance with. [L. *cōnfōrmāre—con-, fōrmāre—
fōrma,* form.]

confound *kən-fownd',* *v.t.* to overthrow, defeat: to
confuse, fail to distinguish: to throw into disorder to
perplex: to astonish: used in the imperative as a mild
curse.—*adj.* **confound'ed** confused: astonished: consummate, egregious (at term of disapprobation;
coll.). [O.Fr. *confondre*—L. *cōnfundēre, -fūsum*—
con-, together, *fundēre,* to pour.]

confraternity *kon-frə-tûr'ni-ti,* *n.* a brotherhood clan
brotherly friendship. [L *con-, frāter,* brother.]

confrère *k5-frer,* *n.* a colleague: a fellow-member or
associate.—*n.* **confrérie** (*k5-frā-rē*) a brotherhood
[Fr.,—L. *con-,* together, *frāter,* a brother.]

confront *kən-frunt',* *v t.* to come or be face to face
with: to face in opposition: to bring face to face: to
compare.—*n.* **confrontā'tion** (*kon-*) the bringing of
people face to face: continued hostile attitude, with
hostile acts but without declaration of war.—*adj*
confrontā'tional involving, causing, etc confrontation.—*n.* **confrontā'tionism** the favouring of confrontation as a political means. [Fr. *confronter*—L.
con-, together, and *frōns, frontis,* forehead; see
front.]

confuse *kən-fūz',* *v.t.* to pour or mix together so that
things cannot be distinguished: to throw into disorder: to perplex: to fail to distinguish—*adj.* **confused'** perplexed: disordered.—*adv.* **confus'edly** in a
confused manner: disorderly.—*ns.* **confus'edness**
state of being confused; **confū'sion** (*-zhən*) the state
of being confused: disorder: perplexity: embarrassment: turmoil. [See **confound.**]

confute *kən-fūt',* *v.t.* to prove to be false: to refute: to
bring to naught.—*adj.* **confūt'able.**—*n.* **confūtā'tion**
(*kon-*). [L. *cōnfūtāre.*]

conga *kong'gə,* *n.* a Cuban dance in single file. music
for it.—Also *v.i.*—**conga drum** a narrow drum beaten
with the hands. [Amer. Sp., Congo.]

congé *k5-zhā,* **congee** *kon'ji, ns.* a bow: dismissal: leave
to depart [Fr. *congé*—L. *commeātus,* leave of
absence—*com-,* together, *meāre,* to go.]

congeal *kən-jēl',* *v.t.* to freeze: to change from fluid to
solid by cold: to solidify, as by cold.—*v.t.* to pass from
fluid to solid, as by cold: to stiffen: to coagulate.—
adj. **congeal'able.**—*ns.* **congeal'ment, congelation**
(*kon-ji-lā'shən*) the act or process of congealing: anything congealed. [L *congelāre,* from *con-,* intens ,
and *gelū,* frost.]

congee. See **congé.**

congener *kon'ji-nər,* *n.* a person or thing of the same
kind or nature: a member of the same genus.—*adj.*
akin.—*adjs.* **congeneric** (*-ner'ik*), **-al** of the same
genus, origin, or nature. [L. *con-,* with, and *genus,
generis,* kind.]

congenial *kən-jē'ni-əl, adj.* of the same genius, spirit, or
tastes: kindred, sympathetic: to one's taste: suitable
—*n.* **congēniality** (*-al'i-ti*).—*adv.* **congē'nially.** [L.
con, with, and *geniālis,* see **genial.**]

congenital *kən-jen'i-təl, adj.* begotten or born with one
—said of diseases or deformities dating from birth:
innate —*adv.* **congen'itally.** [L. *congenitus,* from
con-, together, and *genitum,* to beget.]

conger *kong'gər, n.* a large sea-fish of the eel family—
also **con'ger-eel'.** [L.—Gr *gongros.*]

congeries *kon-jer'i-ēz, -jēr', n* an aggregation.—*pl*
conger'ies. [L. *congeries—con-,* together, *gerěre,
gestum,* to bring.]

congest *kən-jest', v.t* to bring together, or heap up: to
accumulate. to cause congestion in —*adjs* **congest'ed**
overcrowded: packed closely: clogged; **congest'ible.**
—*n.* **congestion** (*-jes'chən*) an accumulation of blood
in any part of the body: fullness: an overcrowded
condition.—*adj* **congest'ive** indicating or tending to
congestion [L *congerēre, congestum—con-,* together, and *gěrere, gestum,* to bring.]

conglomerate *kən-glom'ər-it, adj.* gathered into a clew
or mass: bunched: composed of pebbles cemented
together (*geol.*).—*v.t.* and *v i.* (*-āt*) to gather into a
ball.—*n* (*-it*) a conglomerate rock (*geol*): a miscellaneous mass or collection: an industrial group made
up of companies which often have diverse and
unrelated interests.—*n.* **conglomerā'tion** the state of
being conglomerated: a collection or jumble of
things [L. *conglomerāre, -ātum—con-,* together,
and *glomus, glomeris,* a clew, akin to *globus.*]

congratulate *kən-grat'ū-lāt, v.t.* to express pleasure in
sympathy with: to felicitate: to pronounce or deem
happy (esp. *refl.*).—*adjs.* **congrat'ūlable; congrat'ūlant** expressing congratulation.—*n.* a con-
gratulator.—*ns* **congratūlā'tion; congrat'ūlator.**—
adjs. **congrat'ūlative, congrat'ūlatory** (or *lā'*)
expressing congratulation. [L *congrātulāri, -ātus—
con-,* intens , *grātulāri—grātus,* pleasing.]

congregate *kong'grə-gāt, v.t.* to gather together: to
assemble.—*v.i.* to flock together —*p.adj.* **con'-
gregated** assembled: aggregated.—*ns.* **con'gregant** a
member of a congregation, esp. of a Jewish congregation; **congrega'tion** the act of congregating. an assemblage of persons or things: a body of people actually
or habitually attending a particular church: a board
charged with some department of administration in
the Roman Catholic Church: a name given to certain
religious orders without solemn vows: an academic
assembly.—*adj.* **congregā'tional** pertaining to a congregation: (with *cap.*) pertaining to the Independent
Church.—*ns.* **Congregā'tionalism** a form of church
government in which each congregation is independent in the management of its own affairs—also
called *Independency*; **Congregā'tionalist** an Independent —**Congregation for the Doctrine of the Faith** see
Inquisition. [L. *congregāre, -ātum—con-,* together,
and *grex, gregis,* a flock.]

congress *kong'gres, n.* the act of meeting together.
intercourse: an assembly of delegates, ambassadors,
etc.: (with *cap.*) the federal legislature of the United
States.—*v.i.* to meet in congress.—*adj.* **congressional**
(*-gresh'*).—*n.* **Con'gressman** a member of Congress,
esp of the House of Representatives:—*fem.* **Con'-
gresswoman.** [L. *con-,* together, and *gradi, gressus,*
to step, to go]

congruence *kong'grōō-əns, n.* the quality of being congruent: agreement: suitableness.—*adj.* **con'gruent**
agreeing: suitable: congruous —*n.* **congru'ity** agreement, between things: consistency: fitness.—*adj.*
con'gruous suitable: fit: consistent.—*adv.* **con'gru-
ously.**—*n* **con'gruousness.** [L *congruěre,* to run
together.]

conia. See **coniine.**

conic, -al. See **cone.**

conidium *kon-id'i-əm, n.* a spore produced by abstric-
tion, not in a sporangium:—*pl.* **conid'ia.**—*adj.*
conid'ial. [Gr. *konis,* dust.]

conifer *kon'* or *kōn'i-fər, n* a member of the **Conif'-
erae,** including yews, pines, firs, etc., which typically
bear cones.—*adj.* **conif'erous** cone-bearing: of the
Coniferae [L. *cōnus,* a cone, *ferre,* to bear.]

coniform See **cone.**

coniine *kō'ni-ēn, n* a liquid, highly poisonous alkaloid
(C$_8$H$_{17}$N) found in hemlock (*Conium*).—Also
cō'nia, cō'nine. [Gr *kōneion,* hemlock.]

conjecture kən-jek'chər, n. a forecast: an opinion formed on slight or defective evidence or none: an opinion without proof: a guess: an idea.—v.t. to make conjectures regarding.—v.i. to guess.—adjs. **conject'urable** that may be conjectured; **conject'ural** involving conjecture: given to conjecture.—adv. **conject'urally**. [L. conjicĕre, conjectum, to throw together—con-, jacĕre, to throw.]

conjoin kən-join', v.t. to join together: to combine.—v.i. to unite.—adjs. **conjoined'** united: in conjunction; **conjoint'** joined together: united.—adv. **conjoint'ly**. [Fr. conjoindre—L. con-, jungĕre, junctum, to join; see **join**.]

conjugal kon'jōō-gəl, adj. pertaining to marriage.—n. **conjugality** (-gal'i-ti).—adv. **con'jugally**.—**conjugal rights** the right of sexual relations with a spouse [L. conjugālis—conjux, a husband or wife—con-, together, and jugum, a yoke.]

conjugate kon'jōō-gāt, v.t. to give the various inflections or parts of (a verb) (gram.): to unite (biochemistry).—v.i. to unite.—adj. joined: connected: coupled: occurring in pairs (bot.): reciprocally related.—n. a word agreeing in derivation with another word: anything conjugate with another—joined, or from same root, or reciprocally related.—adjs. **con'jugated** conjugate: (of atoms, groups, bonds, or the compounds in which they occur) showing a special type of mutual influence, esp. characterised by an arrangement of alternate single and double bonds between carbon atoms (chem.); **conjuga'tional**, **con'jugative** conjugate.—n. and adj. **con'jugating**.—n. **conjuga'tion** the act of joining: union: a connected view or statement of the inflectional forms of a verb (gram.): a class of verbs similarly inflected (gram.). [L. conjugāre, -ātum—con-, together, and jugāre—jugum, a yoke.]

conjunct kən-junkt', or kon', adj. conjoined: joint.—n. **conjunc'tion** connection, union: combination: a word that connects sentences, clauses, and words (gram.): one of the aspects of the planets, when two bodies have the same celestial longitude or the same right ascension (formerly when they were in the same sign).—adj. **conjunc'tional** relating to a conjunction.—adv. **conjunc'tionally**.—n. **conjunctiva** (kon-jungkt-ī'və) the modified epidermis of the front of the eye.—adjs. **conjuncti'val** of the conjunctiva; **conjunc'tive** closely united: serving to unite: connective.—adv. **conjunc'tively**.—ns. **conjunc'tiveness**; **conjunctivitis** (-iv-ī'tis) inflammation of the conjunctiva.—adv. **conjunct'ly** conjointly: in union.—n. **conjunc'ture** combination of circumstances: important occasion, crisis. [L. conjunctiō, -ōnis—conjungĕre; see **conjoin**.]

conjure kun'jər, v.i. to practise magical arts.—v.t. (usu. kən-jōōr') to call on or summon by a sacred name or in a solemn manner: to implore: to implore earnestly: (kun'jər) to compel (a spirit) by incantations: to put a spell upon: to call before the imagination (often with up): to render, effect, cause to be or become, by magic or jugglery.—ns. **conjura'tion** conspiracy: act of summoning by a sacred name or solemnly: enchantment; **conjurer**, **-or** (kun', kon') one who practises magic: one who produces magical effects by sleight-of-hand, etc.; **con'juring** magic-working: the production of effects apparently miraculous by natural means.—**to conjure with** meriting being regarded as influential, powerful or important. [Fr. conjurer—L. conjūrāre, to swear together—con-, and jūrāre, to swear.]

conk[1] kongk, n. the nose (slang).—ns. **conk'er** a strung snail-shell or horse chestnut used in the game of **conkers**, in which each seeks to break his opponent's: a horse chestnut. [**conch**.]

conk[2] kongk, (slang) v.i. to get out of order, fail, break down (often with out): to fall asleep, collapse from exhaustion (with out).

conk[3] kongk, (slang) n. the head: a blow on the head.—v.t. to strike (a person) on the head.

conn. See **con**[3].

connascent kən-ās'ənt, adj. born or produced at the same time.—ns. **connasc'ence**; **connasc'ency**.—adj. **connate** (kon'āt) inborn: innate: allied: congenital: united in growth.—n. **conna'tion** (biol.) union, esp of like parts.—adj. **connatural** (kon-ach'ər-əl) of the same nature as another.—adv. **connat'urally**. [L. con-, nāscī, nātus, to be born.]

connect kən-ekt', v.t. to tie or fasten together: to establish a relation between: to associate.—v.i. to be, or become, joined: to be significant (coll.): to hit (a target) with a blow, a kick, etc. (coll.).—adj. **connect'able**, **-ible** capable of being connected.—p.adj. **connect'ed** joined: linked: coherent. related.—adv. **connect'edly** in a connected manner.—ns. **connect'er**, **-or**; **connection**, **connexion** (-ek'shən) the act of connecting: that which connects: a body or society held together by a bond: coherence: intercourse: context: relation: opportunity of change of trains, buses, etc.: a relative: (in pl.) the owner of a racehorse and the owner's associates.—adj. **connect'ive** binding together.—n. a word that connects sentences and words.—adv. **connect'ively**.—**connective tissue** an animal tissue including a great variety—e.g. bone, cartilage, ligaments.—adj. **well-connect'ed** related to people of good social standing. [L. con-, and nectĕre, nexum, to tie.]

conner[1]. See **con**[2,3].

conner[2] kun'ər, n. an inspector or tester [O E. cunnere—cunnian, to learn, seek to know.]

connexion. See **connect**.

conning-tower. See **con**[3].

connive kən-īv', v.i. to wink (usu. fig., as at a fault): to take no notice: to have a private understanding.—ns. **conniv'ance**, **conniv'er**. [L. connīvēre, cōnīvēre, to wink.]

connoisseur kon-əs-ûr', kon', n. a well-informed judge in the arts, etc. [Fr. (now connaisseur),—connoître (connaître)—L. cognōscĕre, to know.]

connote kon-ōt', v.t. to signify secondarily: to imply an inherent attributes: to include.—v.t. **connotate** (kon'ō-tāt) to connote.—n. **connota'tion** the implication of something more than the denotation of an object: an attribute, or the aggregation of attributes, connoted by a term.—adjs. **conn'otative** (or -nō'tə-tiv), **connō'tive**. [L. con-, with, notāre, to mark.]

connubial kən-ū'bi-əl, adj. pertaining to marriage.—n. **connubiality** (-al'i-ti).—adv. **connū'bially**. [L. con-, nūbĕre, to marry.]

conoid kōn'oid, n. anything like a cone in form: a solid generated by the revolution of a conic section about its axis.—adjs. **cōn'oid**, **cōnoid'al**, **cōnoid'ic**, **-al**. [Gr. kōnos, a cone, eidos, form.]

conquer kong'kər, v.t. to gain by force or with an effort: to overcome or vanquish.—v.i. to be victor.—adj. **con'querable**.—n. **con'querableness**.—adj. **con'quering**.—adv. **con'queringly**.—ns. **con'queror** one who conquers: a victor.—fem. **con'queress**; **conquest** (kong'kwest) the act of conquering: that which is conquered or acquired by physical or moral force: the act of gaining the affections of another: the person whose affections have been gained [O.Fr. conquerre—L. conquīrĕre, conquaerĕre—con-, intens., quaerĕre, to seek.]

conquistador kong'kĕs-ta-dôr', -dor or -kwis', n. a conqueror, applied to the conquerors of Mexico and Peru:—pl. **-dors**, **-dores** (-dôr'es, -dor'es) [Sp.,—

L. *conquīrĕre*.]

consanguine *kon-sang'gwin, adj.* related by blood: of the same family or descent—also **consanguin'eous**.—*n.* **consanguin'ity** relationship by blood as opposed to affinity or relationship by marriage. [L. *cōnsanguineus*—*con-*, with, *sanguis*, or *sanguĭs*, blood.]

conscience *kon'shans, n.* moral sense: scrupulousness, conscientiousness.—*adjs.* **con'scient** aware: conscious; **conscientious** (*-shi-en'shas*) regulated by a regard to conscience: scrupulous.—*adv.* **conscien'tiously.**—*n.* **conscien'tiousness.**—*adj.* **con'scionable** (*-shan-a-bl*) governed or regulated by conscience.— **conscience clause** a clause in a law to relieve persons of conscientious scruples, esp. against religious instruction; **conscience money** money given to relieve the conscience, by discharging a claim previously evaded; **conscientious objector** one who objects on grounds of conscience, esp. to military service — **freedom of conscience** the right to hold religious or other beliefs without persecution; **good** or **bad conscience** an approving or reproving conscience; **in all conscience** certainly: by all that is right and fair (*coll.*); **on one's conscience** causing feelings of guilt; **prisoner of conscience** a person imprisoned on account of his or her political beliefs. [Fr.,—L. *cōnscientia*, knowledge—*cōnscīre*, to know well, in one's own mind—*con-*, intens., *scīre*, to know.]

conscious *kon'shas, adj.* having the feeling or knowledge of something: aware: having consciousness.— *n.* the conscious mind.— **-conscious** in composition, being very aware of and concerned about, as *clothes-conscious, cost-conscious*.—*adv.* **con'sciously.**—*n.* **con'sciousness** the waking state of the mind: the knowledge which the mind has of anything: awareness: thought.—**con'sciousness-rais'ing** development of awareness of one's identity and potential.—Also *adj.* [L. *cōnscius*—*cōnscīre*, to know; see **conscience**.]

conscribe *kan-skrīb', v.t.* to enlist by conscription — *adj.* **conscript** (*kon'skript*) enrolled, registered, esp. compulsorily.—*n.* one enrolled and liable to serve compulsorily.—*v.t.* (*kan-skrīpt'*) to enlist compulsorily.—*n.* **conscrip'tion** a compulsory enrolment for service: the obtaining of recruits by compulsion. [L. *cōnscrībĕre*, to enrol—*con-*, together, *scrībĕre, scrīptum*, to write.]

consecrate *kon'si-krāt, v.t.* to set apart for a holy use: to render holy or venerable: to devote.—*adj.* **consecrated:** devoted: sanctified.—*ns.* **con'secratedness;** **consecra'tion** the act of devoting to a sacred use; **con'secrator.**—*adj.* **consecratory** (*-krā'tar-i*) making sacred. [L. *cōnsecrāre, -ātum*, to make wholly sacred.]

consecution *kon-si-kū'shan, n.* a train of consequences or deductions: a series of things that follow one another.—*adj* **consecutive** (*kan-sek'ū-tiv*) following in regular order or one after another; expressing consequence (*gram.*)—*adv.* **consec'utively.**—*n* **consec'utiveness.** [L. *cōnsequī*—*con-*, intens., *sequī, secūtus*, to follow.]

consensus *kan-sen'sas, n* agreement of various parts: agreement in opinion· unanimity: (*loosely*) trend of opinion.—*adj.* **consen'sual** relating to consent: involving voluntary and involuntary action in correlation.—*adv.* **consen'sually.** [L. *cōnsēnsus—cōnsentīre*; see next word.]

consent *kan-sent', v.i* to be of the same mind· to agree to give assent: to yield· to comply —*v t.* to agree —*n* agreement —*adj.* **consentaneous** (*kon-san-tā'ni-as*) agreeable or accordant: consistent —*n* **consentience** (*kan-sen'shans*) agreement: power of unifying impressions below the level of consciousness· imperfect consciousness.—*adj.* **consen'tient** agreeing having con-

sentience.—**age of consent** the age at which a person is legally competent to give consent to certain acts, esp. marriage, sexual intercourse; **with one consent** unanimously. [L. *cōnsentīre—con-, sentīre*, to feel, to think.]

consequence *kon'si-kwans, n.* that which follows or comes after as a result or inference: effect: the relation of an effect to its cause: importance: social standing: consequentiality: (in *pl.*) a game describing the meeting of a lady and gentleman and its consequences, each player writing a part of the story, not knowing what the others have written.—*adj.* **con'sequent** following, esp. as a natural effect or deduction. —*n.* that which follows: the natural effect of a cause. —*adj.* **consequential** (*-kwen'shl*) following as a result, esp. an indirect result: self-important.—*advs.* **consequen'tially; con'sequently.**—**of no consequence** trivial, unimportant; **take the consequences** to accept the results of one's actions. [Fr.,—L. *cōnsequī—con-*, intens., *sequī*, to follow.]

conserve *kan-sûrv', v.t.* to keep entire: to retain: to preserve.—*n.* (also *kon'*) something preserved, as fruits in sugar.—*adj.* **conser'vable.**—*n.* **conser'vancy** a court or board having authority to preserve fisheries, etc., of a river: the act of preserving: esp. official care of a river, forest, etc.—*p.adj.* **conser'vant.**—*n.* **conserva'tion** (*kon-*) the act of conserving (as old buildings, flora and fauna, environment): the keeping entire.—*adj.* **conserva'tional.**—*ns.* **conserva'tionist; conser'vatism** the opinions and principles of a Conservative: dislike of innovations.—*adj.* **conser'vative** tending or having power to conserve: averse to change: (*loosely*) moderately estimated or understated: (with *cap.*) belonging, or pertaining, to the Conservative party.—*n.* one averse to change: (with *cap.*) one belonging to or supporting the political party which favours the preservation of existing institutions and seeks to promote free enterprise.—*ns.* **conser'vativeness; conservatoire** (*kō-ser-va-twär, kan-sûr-va-twär'*), **conservato'rium** a school of music; **con'servator** (or *kan-sûr'va-tar*) one who preserves from injury or violation:'a guardian, custodian:—*fem* **conserva'trix; conser'vatory** a storehouse: a greenhouse or place in which exotic plants are kept: a school of music.—*n.* **conser'ver.**—**conservation area** an area designated as being of special architectural or historic interest, and therefore protected from any alterations which would destroy its character; **conservation of energy** the principle that the total amount of energy in an isolated system is constant; **conservation of matter** the principle of the indestructibility of matter [L. *cōnservāre—con-, servāre*, to keep.]

consider *kan-sid'ar, v.t.* to look at attentively or carefully: to think or deliberate on: to take into account: to attend to: to regard as: to think, hold the opinion (that): to reward.—*v.i* to think seriously or carefully: to deliberate.—*adj.* **consid'erable** worthy of being considered: of some importance: more than a little —*n.* **consid'erableness.**—*adv.* **consid'erably.**—*adj.* **consid'erate** (*-it*) thoughtful for the feelings and interests of others.—*adv.* **consid'erately.**—*ns.* **consid'erateness** thoughtfulness for others; **considera'tion** considerateness: careful thought: importance: motive or reason: recompense, payment.—*n.* and *adj.* **consid'ering** —*prep.* in view of.—*conj* seeing that —*adv.* everything considered —**in consideration of** as payment for, **take into consideration** to allow for, **under consideration** being considered or dealt with. [L. *cōnsīderāre*.]

consign *kan-sīn', v t* to sign or seal: to devote: to transfer to entrust to commit: to transmit —*adj.* **consign'able.**—*adj* **consigned'** given in trust —*ns* **consignee**

(kon-sīn-ē') one to whom anything is consigned or entrusted; **consign′er, consign′or; consign′ment** the act of consigning· the thing consigned. a set of things consigned together. [L. *cōnsignāre*, to attest.]

consist *kən-sıst′ v.i.* to be composed (of): to agree.—*ns.* **consist′ence** substance, **consist′ency** consistence: degree of density or thickness: agreement: self-consistency.—*adj.* **consist′ent** fixed: not fluid· agreeing together, compatible. free from self-contradiction: true to principles.—*adv* **consist′ently.**—*adjs.* **consistō′rial; consistō′rian.**—*n.* **con′sistory** (or -*sıst′*) an assembly or council· a spiritual or ecclesiastical court —**consist in** to have as essence: to be composed of, **consist of** to be made up of. [L. *cōnsistere*—*con*-, together, *sistēre*, to set, stand.]

console¹ *kən-sōl′, v.t.* to give solace or comfort to: to cheer in distress.—*adj.* **consōl′able.**—*n.* **consolā′tion** solace: alleviation of misery: a comforting circumstance.—*adj.* **consolatory** (*kən-sol′ə-tər-i*, or -*sōl′*) comforting.—*ns* **console′ment; consol′er.**—**consolā′tion-match, -prize, -race,** etc , a match, prize, race, etc., for the otherwise unsuccessful. [L. *cōnsōlāri*—*con*-, intens., *sōlāri*, to comfort.]

console² *kon′sōl, n* the key-desk of an organ: a panel or cabinet with dials, switches, etc., control unit of an electrical, electronic, or mechanical system. [Fr.]

consolidate *kən-sol′i-dāt, v.t.* to make solid: to form into a compact mass: to unite into one: to merge: to rearrange and strengthen (*mil.*).—*v.i.* to grow solid or firm: to unite.—*adj.* made firm or solid: united.—*p adj.* **consol′idated.**—*n.* **consolidā′tion.**—*adj.* **consol′idative** tending to consolidate: having the quality of healing.—*n.* **consol′idator.** [L. *cōnsolidāre*, -*ātum*—*con*-, intens., and *solidus*, solid.]

consommé *kɔ-som-ā, kən-som′ā, n.* a soup made from meat by slow boiling: a clear soup. [Fr.]

consonant *kon′sən-ənt, adj.* consistent (with). suitable· harmonious.—*n.* any speech sound other than a vowel: a letter of the alphabet representing such a sound.—*ns.* **con′sonance** a state of agreement: agreement or unison of sounds; **con′sonancy** harmony.—*adj.* **consonantal** (-*ant′l*)—*adv.* **con′sonantly.** [L *cōnsonāns, -antis,* pr.p. of *cōnsonāre,* to harmonise —*con*-, *sonāre,* to sound.]

consort *kon′sort, -sərt, n.* a pàrtner: a companion: a wife or husband: an accompanying ship.—*v.t.* **consort′** to accompany: to associate.—*v.i.* to associate or keep company: to agree.—*adj.* **consort′ed** associated. —*ns.* **consort′er** one who consorts; **con′sortism** symbiosis; **consortium** (*kon-sōr′ti-əm, -shəm, -shi-əm*) fellowship: association: a combination of several banks, business concerns, or other bodies:—*pl.* **consor′tia.**— **in consort** in company: in harmony [L. *cōnsors, -sortis*—*con*-, *sors,* a lot.]

conspectus *kən-spek′təs, n.* a comprehensive view or survey: a synopsis. [L. *cōnspectus*—*cōnspicēre,* to look at.]

conspicuous *kən-spık′ū-əs, adj.* catching the eye· prominent.—*ns.* **conspicū′ity** (*kon*-), **conspic′uousness.**—*adv* **conspic′uously.** [L *cōnspicuus*— *cōnspicēre*—*con*-, intens., *specēre,* to look.]

conspire *kən-spīr′, v.i.* to plot or scheme together: to devise: to act together to one end.—*v.t.* to plan, devise.—*n.* **conspiracy** (*-spir′ə-si*) the act of conspiring: a banding together for a purpose, often secret, usu. unlawful: a plot: joint action, concurrence.—*adj.* **conspir′ant** conspiring.—*ns.* **conspirā′tion** conspiracy, **conspir′ātor** one who conspires:— *fem.* **conspir′atress.**—*adj.* **conspiratō′rial.**—*adv.* **conspir′ingly.**—**conspiracy of silence** an agreement not to talk about a particular matter. [L. *cōnspīrāre* —*con*-, together, *spīrāre,* to breathe.]

constable *kun′stə-bl,* or **kon′,** *n.* formerly a state-

officer of the highest rank: the warden of a castle: a peace-officer: a policeman of the lowest rank.—*n.* **constabulary** (*kən-stab′ū-lər-ı*) an organised body of constables: a police force.—*adj.* of or pertaining to constables, or peace-officers.—**special constable** a person sworn in by the justices to preserve the peace, or to execute warrants on special occasions. [O.Fr. *conestable.*—L. *comes stabulī,* count or companion of the stable.]

constant *kon′stənt, adj.* fixed: unchangeable: firm: continual: faithful.—*n.* (*math.*) a fixed quantity.—*n.* **con′stancy** fixedness: unchangeableness: faithfulness.—*adv.* **con′stantly.** [L. *cōnstāns, -stantis,* from *cōnstāre,* to stand firm—*con*-, intens., *stāre,* to stand.]

constatation *kon-stə-tā′shən, n.* a statement, assertion; ascertaining, verification. [Fr. *constater.*]

constellate *kon′stəl-āt,* or *kən-stel′āt, v.t.* to cluster: to compel or affect by stellar influence.—*v.i.* to cluster together.—*n.* **constellā′tion** a group of stars: any grouping of persons, ideas, factors in a situation, etc.: in astrol., a particular disposition of the planets, supposed to influence the course of human life or character —*adj.* **constell′atory.** [L. *cōnstellātus,* studded with stars—*con*-, *stellāre*—*stella,* a star.]

consternate *kon′stər-nāt, v.t.* to fill with dismay.—*n.* **consternā′tion** terror that throws into confusion: dismay. [L. *cōnsternāre, -ātum,* from *con-*, wholly, *sternēre,* to strew.]

constipate *kon′stip-āt, v.t.* to cause an irregular and insufficient action of the bowels of: to deprive of vigour (*fig.*).—*adj.* **con′stipated.**—*n.* **constipā′tion.** [L. *cōnstīpāre, -ātum,* to press together—*con*-, *stīpāre,* to pack.]

constitute *kon′stit-ūt, v.t.* to set up: to establish: to form or make up: to appoint: to give being to.—*n.* **constituency** (*kən-stit′ū-ən-sı*) the whole body of voters, or a district, or population, represented by a member of parliament or the like: a set of people supporting, patronising, or forming a power-base for, a business organisation, pressure group, etc.—*adj.* **constit′uent** constituting or forming: essential: elemental: component: electing: constitution-making.—*n.* an essential or elemental part: one of those who elect a representative, esp. in parliament: an inhabitant of one's constituency.—*n.* **constitū′tion** (*kon*-) the act of constituting: the natural condition of body or mind: disposition: a system of laws and customs established by the sovereign power of a state for its own guidance: an established form of government: a particular law or usage: in chem., molecular structure, taking into account not only the kinds and numbers of atoms but the way in which they are linked.—*adj.* **constitū′tional** inherent in the natural frame: natural: agreeable to the constitution or frame of government: essential: legal: reigning subject to fixed laws: supporting the existing constitution.—*n.* a walk for the sake of one's health.—*v.t.* **constitū′-tionalise, -ize** to make constitutional.—*ns.* **constitū′-tionalism** adherence to the principles of the constitution; **constitū′tion(al)ist** one who favours or studies a constitution or the constitution; **constitutional′ity.**— *adv.* **constitū′tionally.**—*adj.* **con′stitutive** that constitutes or establishes: having power to constitute: essential: component. [L. *cōnstituēre, cōnstitūtum* —*con*-, intens., *statuēre,* to make to stand, to place.]

constrain *kən-strān′, v.t.* to force, compel: to confine: to restrict by a condition.—*adj.* **constrain′able.**— *p.adj.* **constrained** forced, compelled: lacking ease and spontaneity of manner.—*adv.* **constrain′edly.**— *n.* **constraint** compulsion: confinement: a restricting condition. [O.Fr. *constraindre*—L. *cōnstringēre*— *con*-, *stringēre,* to press.]

constrict kən-strikt', v.t. to press together: to contract: to cramp: to narrow locally.—*p.adj.* **constrict'ed.**—*n.* **constric'tion** a pressing together: contraction: tightness: a narrow place.—*adj.* **constrict'ive.**—*n.* **constrict'or** that which constricts or draws together: a muscle that compresses an organ or structure· a snake that crushes its prey in its folds. [L *cōnstringĕre, -strictum;* see preceding.]

construct kən-strukt', v t. to build up: to compile: to put together the parts of: to make: to compose: to put in grammatical relation.—*adj.* **constructed.**—*n* (kon'strukt) a thing constructed, esp. in the mind· an image or object of thought constructed from a number of sense-impressions or images (*psych.*).—*adjs.* **construct'able, construct'ible** able to be constructed.—*ns.* **construct'er, construct'or;** **construc'tion** the act of constructing: anything piled together: building· a stage structure: manner of forming: the syntactic relations of words in a sentence (*gram.*): interpretation: meaning.—*adj.* **construc'tional** pertaining to construction: used for structures: making use of structures.—*n.* **construc'tionism** use of structures: principle of using structures or of following structure.—*adj.* **construct'ive** capable of, tending towards, or concerned in, constructing: embodying positive advice—opp to *destructive.*—*adv.* **construct'ively.**—*ns.* **construct'iveness;** **construct'ivism** constructionism: a non-representational style of art using man-made industrial materials and processes such as twisting, welding. [L. *cōnstruĕre, -structum* —*con-, struĕre,* to build.]

construe kən-strōō', kon'strōō, v.t. to exhibit in another language the grammatical structure and literal meaning of: to translate: to explain: to interpret: to construct grammatically: to infer.—*v.i.* to admit of grammatical analysis. [L. *cōnstruĕre, constructum,* to pile together.]

consubstantial kon-sub-stan'shl, adj. of the same substance, nature, or essence, esp. of the Trinity.—*v.t.* and *v.i.* **consubstan'tiate** (-shi-āt) to unite in one common substance or nature.—*adj.* so united.—*ns* **consubstantia'tion** the doctrine of the actual, substantial presence of the body and blood of Christ coexisting in and with the bread and wine used at the Lord's Supper (cf. **transubstantiation**); **consubstantia'tionist.** [L. *con-,* with, and **substantial,** etc.]

consuetude kon'swi-tūd, n custom: familiarity.—*adj.* **consuetu'dinary** customary. [L. *cōnsuētūdō, -inis,* custom.]

consul kon'səl, n. one of the two chief magistrates in the Roman republic: an agent for a foreign government appointed to attend to the interests of its citizens and commerce.—*adj.* **con'sular** (-sū-lər) pertaining to a consul.—*ns.* **con'sulate** (-sūl-, or -səl-) the office, residence, jurisdiction, government, or time of a consul or consuls; **con'sulship** the office, or term of office, of a consul. [L. *cōnsul.*]

consult kən-sult', v.t. to ask advice of: to look up for information or advice.—*v.i.* to consider jointly: to take counsel.—*ns.* **consult'ancy** the post of consultant: an agency which provides professional advice; **consultant** (kən-sult'ənt) one who seeks advice or information: one who gives professional advice or takes part in consultation.—Also *adj* —*n.* **consulta'tion** (konsəl-, -sul-) deliberation, or a meeting for deliberation, esp. of physicians or lawyers.—*adjs* **consult'ative** of or pertaining to consultation, esp of bodies without vote on the decision; **consult'atory** of the nature of consultation.—*ns.* **consultee'** the person consulted; **consult'er** one who consults.—*adjs* **consult'ing** of a physician, lawyer, etc , prepared to give professional advice to others in the same field; **consult'ive** consultative.—*n.* **consult'or.**—*adj* **consult'-**

ory consultatory.—**consult'ing-room** the room in which a doctor sees a patient. [L. *cōnsultāre,* intens. of *cōnsulĕre,* to consult.]

consume kən-sūm', -sōōm', v.t. to destroy by wasting, fire, evaporation, etc.: to use up: to devour: to waste or spend: to exhaust.—*v.i.* to waste away.—*adj* **consum'able.**—*n.* something that can be consumed.—*ns* **consum'er** one who consumes: one who uses an article produced (opp. to *producer*); **consum'erism** (the promotion of) the protection of the interests of buyers of goods and services against defective or dangerous goods, etc.; **consum'erist.**—*n* and *adj.* **consum'ing** wasting or destroying: engrossing.—**consumer durables** goods for domestic use needing infrequent replacement; **consumer research** the study of the needs and preferences of consumers. [L. *cōnsūmĕre, -sūmptum,* to destroy—*con-,* sig. completeness, *sūmĕre,* to take.]

consummate kon'sum-āt, or -səm-, v.t. to raise to the highest point· to perfect or finish: to make (marriage) legally complete by sexual intercourse.—*adj.* (kən-sum'āt, -it), complete, supreme, perfect of its kind.— *adv.* **consumm'ately** perfectly.—*n.* **consumma'tion** the act of completing: perfection: the subsequent intercourse which makes a marriage legally valid.— [L. *cōnsummāre, -ātum,* to perfect—*con-,* intens., *summus,* highest, perfect, *summa,* a sum.]

consumption kən-sum(p)'shən, n. the act or process of consuming or using up: the quantity consumed: wasting of the body: pulmonary tuberculosis.—*adj.* **consump'tive** wasting away: inclined to the disease consumption —*n.* one affected by consumption —*adv.* **consump'tively.**—*ns* **consump'tiveness, consump'tivity** (kon-) a tendency to consumption. [See **consume.**]

contact kon'takt, n. touch: meeting: meeting in a point without intersection (*math.*): close approximation allowing passage of electric current or communication of disease: a place or part where electric current may be allowed to pass: association: means or occasion of communication: a person who has been exposed to contagion: a person through whom one can get in touch (esp secretly) with an individual or group, esp with shady person(s).—*adj.* involving contact: caused or made active by contact.—*v.t* and *v.i.* (also *kon-takt'*) to bring or to come into contact: to get in touch with, or establish a connection with.—**contact lens** a lens, usu. of plastic material, worn in contact with the eyeball instead of spectacles; **contact man** (*coll.*) an intermediary in transactions, esp. shady ones. [L. *contingĕre, contactum,* to touch—*con-,* wholly, *tangĕre,* to touch]

contagion kən-tā'jən, n. transmission of a disease by direct contact with an infected person or object: a disease or poison so transmitted: the means of transmission· a hurtful influence.—*adj.* **contā'gious** communicable by contact. carrying disease or other contagion: spreading easily (*fig.*; *coll.*).—*adv.* **contā'giously.**—*n.* **contā'giousness.** [L *contāgiō, -ōnis* —*con-, tangĕre,* to touch]

contain kən-tān', v.t to have within, enclose, to comprise, include: to restrain: to keep fixed: to hold back: to keep in check —*adj.* **contain'able.**—*ns.* **contain'er** that which contains: that in which goods are enclosed for transport; **containerisā'tion, -z-.**—*v.t.* **contain'erise, -ize** to put (freight) into standard sealed containers· to use such containers for (e g. a transport operation) —*n.* **contain'ment** the act of containing: the act or policy of preventing the spread beyond certain limits of a power or influence regarded as hostile, by means other than war· the successful result of this —**container port** a terminal port equipped to handle large containers; **container ship** a ship designed for the most efficient stowing and transport of such containers. [O.Fr. (Fr.) *contenir*—L. *continēre*—*con*-, *tenēre*, to hold.]

contaminate *kən-tam'i-nāt*, *v.t.* to defile by touching or mixing with: to pollute, esp. by radioactivity: to corrupt: to infect.—*adj.* **contam'inable.**—*ns.* **contam'inant; contaminā'tion** pollution. [L. *contamināre*, *-ātum*—*contāmen*, pollution.]

contango *kən-tang'gō*, *n.* a percentage paid by the buyer to the seller of stock for keeping back its delivery to the next settling-day:—*pl.* **contang'os.** [Arbitrarily from **continue.**]

contemn *kən-tem'*, *v.t.* to despise. [L. *contemnēre*, *-temptum*, to value little.]

contemplate *kon'tem-plāt*, *v.t.* to consider or look at attentively: to meditate on or study: to intend.—*v.t.* to think seriously: to meditate (on, upon).—*n.* **contemplā'tion** meditation: a meditative condition of mind: attentive viewing or consideration: matter for thought: purpose.—*adj.* and *n.* **con'templātive** (or *kən-tem'plə-*) given to contemplation.—*adv.* **con'templatively** (or *-tem'*).—*ns.* **con'templativeness** (or *-tem'*); **con'templātor** one who contemplates: a student.—**contemplative life** (*theol.*) life devoted to meditation (opposed to the *active life*). [L. *contemplārī*, *-ātus*, to mark out carefully a *templum* or place for auguries—*con*-, sig. completeness, and *templum.*]

contemporaneous *kən-tem-pə-rā'nyəs*, *adj.* living, happening, or being at the same time.—*n.* **contemporaneity** (*-ə-nē'i-ti*).—*adv.* **contempora'neously.**—*ns.* **contempora'neousness; contem'porariness.**—*adj.* **contem'porary** belonging to the same time (with): of the same age: present-day (an inaccurate use), esp. up-to-date, fashionable.—*n.* one who lives at the same time.—*v.t.* **contem'porise, -ize** to make contemporary in mind.. [L. *con*-, *tempus*, *-oris*, time.]

contempt *kən-tempt'*, *n.* scorn (with *for*): disgrace: disregard of the rule, or an offence against the dignity, of a court, etc., as in *contempt of court*, *contempt of Parliament.*—*ns.* **contemptibil'ity, contempt'ibleness.**—*adj.* **contempt'ible** despicable.—*adv.* **contempt'ibly.**—*adj.* **contempt'uous** haughty, scornful.—*adv.* **contempt'uously.**—*n.* **contempt'uousness.** [See **contemn.**]

contend *kən-tend'*, *v.i.* to strive: to struggle in emulation or in opposition: to dispute or debate (with *against*, *for*, *with*, *about*).—*v.t.* to maintain in dispute (that).—*n.* **contend'er.**—*n.* and *adj.* **contend'ing** striving.—*n.* **conten'tion** a violent straining after any object: strife: debate: a position argued for.—*adj.* **conten'tious** quarrelsome: given to dispute: in, or relating to, dispute.—*adv.* **conten'tiously.**—*n.* **conten'tiousness.** [L. *contendēre*, *-tentum*—*con*-, *tendēre*, to stretch.]

content[1] *kon'tent*, *n.* that which is contained: capacity: the substance: (in *pl.*) the things contained: (in *pl.*) list of chapters, etc., in a book. [See **contain.**]

content[2] *kən-tent'*, *adj.* having the desire limited by present enjoyment: satisfied: quietly happy.—*n.* satisfaction.—*v.t.* to make content.—*adj.* **content'ed** content.—*adv.* **content'edly.**—*ns.* **content'edness; content'ment.** [Fr.,—L. *contentus*, contained, hence, satisfied—*con*-, and *tenēre*, to hold.]

conterminous *kən-tûr'min-əs*, *adj.* adjacent, meeting along a common boundary: meeting end to end. [L. *conterminus*, neighbouring—*con*-, *terminus*, a boundary.]

contest *kən-test'*, *v.t.* to call in question or make the subject of dispute: to strive to gain.—*v.t.* to contend —*n.* (*kon'*) a struggle for victory: a competition: strife: a debate, dispute, argument.—*adj.* **contest'able.**—*ns.* **contest'ant** one who contests; **contestā'tion** the act of contesting: contest, strife: emulation.

—*p.adjs.* **contest'ed; contest'ing.** [Fr. *contester*—L. *contestārī*, to call to witness.]

context *kon'tekst*, *n.* the parts of a discourse or treatise which precede and follow a special passage and may fix its true meaning: associated surroundings, setting. —*adj.* **context'ual.**—*n.* **contextualisā'tion, -z-.**—*v.t.* **context'ualise, -ize** to place in context: to study (words, etc.) in their context.—*adv.* **context'ually.** —*n.* **context'ure** structure: fabric. [L. *contextus*, *contexēre*—*con*-, *texēre*, *textum*, to weave.]

contiguous *kən-tig'ū-əs*, *adj.* touching, adjoining: near. —*ns.* **contigū'ity; contig'uousness.**—*adv.* **contig'uously.** [L. *contiguus*—*contingēre*, to touch on all sides—*con*-, wholly, *tangēre*, to touch.]

continent *kon'ti-nənt*, *n.* a great extent of land not broken up by seas: one of the great divisions of the land surface of the globe: the mainland portion of one of these: (usu. with *cap.*) the mainland of Europe.— *adj.* restraining within due bounds, or absolutely abstaining from, the indulgence of pleasure, esp. sexual: able to control one's evacuations: temperate: virtuous.—*ns.* **con'tinence, con'tinency** self-restraint or abstinence, esp. sexual: chastity: ability to control one's evacuations.—*adj.* **continental** (*-ent'l*) of, characteristic of, or of the nature of, a continent.—*n.* a native or inhabitant of a continent.—*adv.* **con'tinently** in a continent manner.—**continental breakfast** a light breakfast of rolls and coffee; **continental drift** hypothetical slow drifting apart of land masses, as e.g. in A. L. Wegener's theory of the formation of world continents from one original land mass; **continental quilt** a duvet; **continental shelf** a gently sloping zone, under relatively shallow seas, offshore from a continent or island. [L. *continēns*, *-entis*—*continēre*, to contain—*con*-, *tenēre*, to hold.]

contingent *kən-tin'jənt*, *adj.* dependent on something else: liable but not certain to happen: accidental.—*n.* an event liable but not certain to occur: a share, quota, or group, esp. of soldiers.—*n.* **contin'gency** the quality or state of being contingent: close connection: uncertainty: chance: a chance happening or concurrence of events: a possible future event: something dependent on such (also *adj.*): an incidental.— *adv.* **contin'gently.**—**contingency plans** plans or arrangements made in case a particular situation should arise. [L. *contingēns*, *-entis*—*con*-, mutually, *tangēre*, to touch.]

continue *kən-tin'ū*, *v.t.* to draw out or prolong: to extend: to maintain: to go on with: to resume: to adjourn: to be a prolongation of.—*v.i.* to remain in the same place or state: to last or endure: to persevere.—*adjs.* **contin'uable; contin'ual** without interruption: unceasing: persistent.—*adv.* **contin'ually.**— *n.* **contin'uance** duration: uninterrupted succession: stay.—*adj.* **contin'uant** continuing: capable of continuing.—*n.* **continuā'tion** going on: persistence: constant succession: extension: resumption: a further instalment.—*adj.* **contin'ued** uninterrupted: unceasing: extended: resumed: in instalments.—*adv.* **contin'uedly.**—*ns.* **contin'uedness; contin'uer; continū'ity** the state of being continuous: uninterrupted connection: a complete scenario of a motion-picture: the person who writes it (in full **continuity writer**): the ordering or arrangement of film or television shots and scenes, or of parts of a radio broadcast, in a correct or consistent way.—*adj.* **contin'uous** joined together without interruption.—*adv.* **contin'uously.** —*ns.* **contin'uousness; contin'ūum** that which is continuous: that which must be regarded as continuous and the same and which can be described only relatively:—*pl.* **contin'ua.**—**continuous creation** the notion of creation as going on always, not as a single act at one particular time (*philos.*). [L. *continuāre*—

continuus, joined, connected, from *continēre*, to hold together.]

contort *kən-tort'*, *v.t.* to twist or turn violently: to writhe.—*adj.* **contort'ed** twisted.—*n.* **contor'tion** a violent twisting: deformation.—*adjs.* **contor'tional, contor'tionate.**—*ns.* **contor'tionism; contor'tionist** a gymnast who practises contorted postures: one who twists words and phrases.—*adj.* **contort'ive.** [L. *con-*, intens., and *torquēre, tortum*, to twist.]

contour *kon'tōōr*, *n.* outline: general character or aspect: a contour line.—*v.t.* to mark with contour lines: to follow the contour lines of.—*adj.* **con'toured** of chairs, etc., shaped to fit the lines of the human body.—**contour cultivation, farming, ploughing** the ploughing (and planting) of sloping land along the contour lines to counter erosion; **contour line** a line on the ground whose points are all at the same height above sea-level: representation of such a line on a map. [Fr. *contour*.—It.—L. *con-, tornāre*, to turn in a lathe.]

contra- *kon'tra, -trə,* *pfx.* against: contrary. [L. *contrā*.]

contra *kon'tra, -trə, adv.* and *prep.* against.—*n.* an argument against: the other side.

contraband *kon'trə-band, adj.* excluded by law: prohibited.—*n.* illegal traffic: smuggled or prohibited goods. [Sp. *contrabanda*—It. *contrabbando*—L. *contrā*, L.L. *bandum*, ban.]

contrabass *kon'trə-bās, n.* the double-bass, playing an octave below the 'cello. [It. *contra(b)basso*—pfx. *contra-* indicating an octave lower, and *basso*, bass.]

contrabassoon *kon'trə-bas-ōōn', n.* the double bassoon. [*contra-* (see **contrabass** above), and **bassoon.**]

contraception *kon-trə-sep'shən, n.* prevention of conception.—*n.* **contracep'tive** a drug, device or other means of contraception.—Also *adj.* [L. *contrā*, against, and **(con)ception.**]

contract *kən-trakt', v.t.* to draw together: to lessen: to shorten: to effect by agreement: to come into, become the subject of: to incur, catch (a disease): to bargain for: to betroth.—*v.i.* to shrink: to become less: to become shorter: to make a contract (with *or* for).—*n.* (*kon'trakt*), an agreement on fixed terms: a bond: a betrothal: the writing containing an agreement: an undertaking: in criminal circles, an undertaking to kill a particular person, esp. for an agreed sum of money (*slang*).—*n.* **contractabil'ity.**—*adjs.* **contract'able** (*kən-*) able to be contracted, esp. of a disease or habit; **contract'ed** drawn together· shortened: narrow: mean: affianced.—*adv.* **contract'edly.**—*ns.* **contract'edness; contractibil'ity.**—*adjs.* **contract'ible** capable of being contracted; **contract'ile** tending or having power to contract or to draw in.—*ns.* **contractil'ity** (*kon-*); **contrac'tion** (*kən-*) the act of contracting: a word shortened in speech or spelling: a symbol for shortening: a tightening of the muscles or muscle fibres —*adjs* **contrac'tional, contrac'tionary** having the effect of contracting; **contract'ive** tending to contract.—*n.* **contract'or** one of the parties to a bargain or agreement: one who engages to execute work or furnish supplies at a stated rate —*adj.* **contract'ûal.**—**contract bridge** a development of auction bridge, in which tricks beyond the number bid for count only like honours, **contract in** to agree to participate on certain conditions; **contract out** to arrange that certain conditions shall not apply: to withdraw from an obligation, agreement, etc : to decide not to participate in a pension scheme, etc. [L. *contractus*—*con-*, together, *trahēre, tractum*, to draw.]

contradict *kon-trə-dikt', v.t.* to deny what is affirmed by, to assert the contrary of: to deny· to be contrary to in character.—*adj.* **contradict'able.**—*n.* **contradic'-**tion act of contradicting: a speaking against: denial: inconsistency.—*adj.* **contradict'ive** contradicting.—*adv.* **contradict'ively.**—*n.* **contradict'or.**—*adv.* **contradict'orily.**—*n.* **contradict'oriness** the quality of being contradictory.—*adj.* **contradict'ory** affirming the contrary: inconsistent.—*n.* a word, principle, that contradicts another: either of two propositions such that both cannot be true, or both cannot be false (*log.*).—**contradiction in terms** a group of words containing a contradiction. [L. *contrādicĕre, -dictum*—*contrā-*, against, *dicĕre*, to say.]

contradistinction *kon-trə-dis-tingk'shən, n.* distinction by contrast.—*adj.* **contradistinct'ive** distinguishing by opposite qualities.—*v.t.* **contradistin'guish** to contrast and mark the difference between. [L. *contrā*, against, and **distinction.**]

contrail *kon'trāl, n.* a trail of condensed vapours left by a high-flying aircraft. [**con(densation)** and **trail.**]

contraindicate *kon'trə-in'di-kāt, v.t.* to point to (a particular treatment or procedure) as unsuitable (*med.*): to show or give as reason for not being, doing or having, etc.: to forbid.—*ns.* **contrain'dicant; con'traindica'tion.**—*adj.* **contraindic'ative.** [L. *contrā*, against, and **indicate.**]

contralto *kən-tral'tō* or *-träl', n.* the lowest musical voice in women: a singer with such a voice: a part for such a voice:—*pl.* **contral'ti** (*-tē*), **-tos.**—Also *adj.* [It., *contra-*, and **alto.**]

contraption *kən-trap'shən, n.* a contrivance. [Perh. *contrivance* adaption.]

contrapuntal, contrapuntist. See **counterpoint.**

contrary *kon'trə-ri, adj.* opposite: contradictory: (usu. *kən-trā'ri*) perverse.—*n.* an extreme opposite: a proposition so related to another that both cannot be true though both may be false (*log.*).—*n.* **contrariety** (*-rī'i-ti*) opposition: inconsistency.—*adv.* **contrarily** (*kon'* or *-trā'*).—*n.* **contrariness** (*kon'* or *-trā'*).—*adv.* **con'trariwise** (or *-trā'* or *-tra'*) in the contrary way: on the other side: on the other hand.—**on the contrary** far otherwise; **to the contrary** to the opposite effect. [L. *contrārius*—*contrā*, against.]

contrast *kən-träst', v.i.* to stand in opposition.—*v.t.* to set in opposition to, in order to show difference.—*n.* (*kon'träst*) opposition or unlikeness in things compared: exhibition of differences: the (degree of) difference in tone between the light and dark parts of a photograph or a television picture.—*adj.* **contrast'ive.** [Fr. *contraster*—L. *contrā*, opposite to, *stāre*, to stand.]

contrate *kon'trāt, adj.* of wheels (esp. in watchmaking), having cogs parallel to the axis. [L. *contrā*, opposite.]

contravene *kon-trə-vēn', v.t.* to oppose: to infringe.—*n.* **contraven'tion.** [L. *contrā*, against, *venīre, ventum*, to come.]

contretemps *kɔ̃-tr'-tä, n.* something happening inopportunely or at the wrong time, anything embarrassing, a hitch. [Fr. *contre*, against, *temps*, time.]

contribute *kən-trib'ūt* (*dial. kon'*), *v.t.* to give along with others: to give for a common purpose: to add towards a common result, to a fund, etc.: to write and send for publication with others.—*v.i.* to give or bear a part: to be a contributor.—*adj.* **contrib'utable** payable: subject to contribution.—*n.* **contribu'tion** (*kon-*) the act of contributing: something contributed: a levy or charge imposed upon a number of persons: anything furnished to a common stock or done towards a common end: a written composition supplied to a periodical, etc.—*adjs.* **contrib'utive, contrib'utory** giving a share. helping.—*n.* **contrib'utor.** [L. *con-, tribĕre, -ūtum*, to give.]

contrite *kon'trīt*, or *kən-trīt', adj.* brokenhearted for sin penitent —*adv* **contritely.**—*ns.* **contriteness;**

contrition (kon-trish'ən) deep sorrow for sin: remorse. [L. *contrītus—conterēre—con-*, wholly, *terēre*, to bruise.]

contrive *kən-trīv'*, *v.t.* to plan: to invent: to bring about or effect: to manage, arrange: to plot.—*adj.* **contriv'able** that may be contrived.—*n.* **contriv'ance.**—*adj.* **contrived'** laboured, artificially intricate. [O.Fr. *controver—con-*, intens., *trover*, to find.]

control *kən-trōl'*, *n.* restraint: authority: command: regulation: a check: a means of operating, regulating, directing or testing: a station for doing so: an experiment performed to afford, to provide, or (any of) the subjects providing, a standard of comparison for other experiments (also **control experiment**): a disembodied spirit or other agency supposed to direct a spiritualistic medium.—*adj.* pertaining to control. —*v.t.* to check: to restrain: to govern:—*pr.p.* **contrōll'ing**; *pa.t.* and *pa.p.* **controlled'.**—Formerly **comptroll'.**—*n.* **controllabil'ity.**—*adj.* **controll'able** capable of, or subject to, control.—*ns.* **controll'er** one who checks the accounts of others by a counter-roll (also **comptroll'er**): an official authorised to control some activity or department: an instrument for regulating; **control'ership.**—**control panel, board** a panel or board containing dials, switches and gauges for operating and monitoring electrical or other apparatus; **control room** a room in which control instruments are placed, e.g. in a broadcasting station, **control tower** a building at an aerodrome from which take-off and landing instructions are given. [Fr *contrôle*, from *contre-rôle*, a duplicate register—L *contrā*, against, *rotulus*, a roll.]

controvert *kon'trə-vûrt*, *v.t.* to oppose: to argue against: to dispute.—*adj.* **controver'sial** (*-shl*) relating to controversy.—*n.* **controver'sialist** one given to controversy.—*adv.* **controver'sially.**—*n.* **con'troversy** (also *kən-tro'*) a debate: contention: dispute a war of opinions, in books, pamphlets, etc.—*adj* **controvert'ible.**—*adv.* **controvert'ibly.** [L. *contrā*, against, and *vertěre*, to turn.]

contumacious *kon-tū-mā'shəs*, *adj.* opposing lawful authority with contempt: obstinate: stubborn.—*adv.* **contumā'ciously.**—*ns.* **contumā'ciousness; con'-tumacy** (*-məs-i*) obstinate disobedience or resistance [L. *contumāx, -ācis*, insolent.]

contumely *kon'tūm-li*, *n.* scornful insolence.—*adj.* **contumē'lious** haughtily insolent. [L. *contumēlia*, prob. from the same source as *contumāx*.]

contuse *kən-tūz'*, *v.t.* to beat or bruise: to crush.—*n.* **contusion** (*-tū-zhən*) the act of bruising: the state of being bruised: a bruise.—*adj.* **contū'sive** apt to bruise. [L. *contunděre, contūsum—con-*, intens., *tunděre*, to bruise.]

conundrum *kən-un'drəm*, *n.* a riddle turning on some odd or fanciful resemblance between things quite unlike: any puzzling question.

conurbation *kon-ûr-bā'shən*, *n.* an aggregation of towns. [L. *con-*, together, *urbs*, city.]

convalesce *kon-vəl-es'*, *v.i.* to regain health.—*ns.* **convales'ence** gradual recovery of health and strength. —*adj.* **convalesc'ent** gradually recovering health.—*n.* one recovering health. [L. *con-*, intens., *valēscěre—valěre*, to be strong.]

convection *kən-vek'shən*, *n.* a transmission, esp. that of heat or electricity through liquids or gases by means of currents: vertical movement, esp upwards, of air or atmospheric conditions (*meteor.*).—*adjs.* **convec'tion; convec'tional; convec'tive.**—*n.* **convec'tor** apparatus for heating by convection. [L. *convectiō, -ōnis*, bringing together—*con-*, and *vehěre*, to carry.]

convene *kən-vēn'*, *v.i.* to come together: to assemble. —*v.t.* to call together.—*adj.* **convēn'able.**—*n* **convēn'er, convēn'or** one who convenes a meeting: the chairman of a committee. [Fr. *convenir—L. convenīre—con-*, together, and *venīre*, to come.]

convenient *kən-vēn'yənt*, *adj.* suitable: handy: commodious.—*n.* **convēn'ience** suitability: an advantage: any means or device for promoting (esp. domestic) ease or comfort: a lavatory or water-closet, esp (**public convenience**) a building containing several for use by the public.—*adv.* **convēn'iently.**—**convenience food** food (partly) prepared before sale so as to be ready, or almost ready, for the table.—**at one's (earliest) convenience** (on the first occasion or at the earliest time) when it is suitable or opportune [L. *convenīre.*]

convent *kon'vənt*, *n.* an association of persons secluded from the world and devoted to a religious life: the house in which they live, a monastery or (now usu.) nunnery.—*adj.* **convent'ual** belonging to a convent. —*n.* a monk or nun. [Though Fr. from L. *conventum, convenīre*, to come together.]

conventicle *kən-vent'i-kl*, *n.* a secret, illegal, or forbidden religious meeting. [L. *conventiculum*, a secret meeting of monks.]

convention *kən-ven'shən*, *n.* the act of convening: an assembly, esp. of representatives or delegates for some common object: a meeting of political party delegates for nominating a candidate for the presidency or other purpose (*U.S.*): any temporary treaty: an agreement: established usage: fashion: in card games, a mode of play in accordance with a recognised code of signals —*adj.* **conven'tional** formed or adopted by convention: bound or influenced by convention: growing out of tacit agreement or custom: customary. arbitrary.—*v.t.* **conven'tionalise, -ize** to make conventional: to delineate according to a convention rather than nature.—*ns.* **conven'tionalism** that which is established by tacit agreement, as a mode of speech, etc., **conven'tionalist** one who adheres to a convention, or is swayed by conventionalism; **conventional'ity** state of being conventional: that which is established by use or custom. —*adv.* **conven'tionally.**—**conventional weapons** weapons that are not nuclear. [L. *conventiō, -ōnis*; see convene.]

converge *kən-vûrj'*, *v.i.* to tend towards or meet in one point or value: to acquire like character independently.—*n.* **conver'gence** the act or point of converging (also **conver'gency**). the property of having a limit, for infinite series, sequences, products, etc (*math.*).—*adjs* **conver'gent** converging: due to or characterised by convergence; **conver'ging** meeting in a point: coming nearer together: with gradually approaching tips (*bot.*). [L. *con-*, *vergěre*, to bend, to incline.]

converse *kən-vûrs'*, *v.i.* to have social intercourse: to talk familiarly: to commune.—*adj.* **convers'ant** (also *kon'*) acquainted by study: familiar: concerned or occupied.—*n.* **conversā'tion** intercourse: talk: familiar discourse.—*adj.* **conversā'tional.**—*ns.* **conversā'-tionalist, conversā'tionist** one who excels in conversation.—**conversation piece** a painting of a number of persons: an object that arouses comment by its novelty. [Fr. *converser—L. conversārī*, to turn about, go about, associate, dwell—*con-*, intens., and *versāre*, to keep turning—*vertěre*, to turn.]

convert *kən-vûrt'*, *v.t.* to change or turn from one thing, condition, opinion, party or religion to another: to change from an irreligious to a holy life: to change into the converse: to alter into something else: to exchange for an equivalent.—*n.* (*kon'*) one who is converted.—*adj.* **con'verse** reversed in order or relation —*n.* that which is the opposite of another: a proposition in which the subject and predicate have changed places (*log*): a proposition in which that which is given and that which is to be proved in another proposition are interchanged (*math.*).—*adv.* **con-verse'ly.**—*ns.* **conver'sion** a change from one condition, use, opinion, party, religion or spiritual state to another: appropriation to a special purpose; **convert'er; convertibil'ity.**—*adj.* **convert'ible** that may be converted: convertible *paper*, that may be converted into gold (or dollars) at a fixed price: equivalent.—*n.* anything convertible: a car with a folding top.—*adv.* **convert'ibly.** [L. *convertĕre, conversum—con-, vertĕre,* to turn.]

convex *kon'veks,* also *kon-veks',* adj. rising into a round form on the outside, the reverse of concave.—*n* a convex figure, surface, body, or part.—*ns.* **convex'ity** roundness of form on the outside: a convex part or figure; **con'vexness** (or *-veks'*).—*adv.* **con'vexly** (or *-veks'*).—*adjs.* **convex'o-con'cave** (or *-kăv'*) convex on one side, and concave on the other; **convex'o-con'vex** (or *-veks'*) convex on both sides. [L *convexus—con-vehĕre—con-, vehĕre,* to carry.]

convey *kan-vā',* v.t. to carry: to transmit: to impart: to steal: to communicate, as ideas: to make over in law.—adj. **convey'able.**—*ns.* **convey'al; convey'ance** act or means of conveying: a vehicle of any kind: the act of transferring property (*law*); **convey'ancer** one who prepares deeds for the transference of property; **convey'ancing; convey'er, convey'or** a person or thing that conveys in any sense: a mechanism for continuous transport of materials, packages, goods in process of manufacture, etc. (also **convey'or-belt**). [O.Fr. *conveier*—L. *con-, via,* a way.]

convict *kan-vikt',* v.t to prove guilty: to pronounce guilty.—*n.* (*kon'*) one convicted or found guilty of crime: one who has been condemned to penal servitude.—*n.* **convic'tion** act of convincing: strong belief: a proving guilty.—**carry conviction** to bear irresistibly the stamp or proof of truth. [Root as **convince.**]

convince *kan-vins',* v.t. to subdue the mind of by evidence: to satisfy as to truth or error.—*adjs.* **convinc'ible; convinc'ing** producing conviction: certain, positive, beyond doubt: by a large or significant margin.—*adv* **convinc'ingly.** [L. *convincĕre, con-,* sig. completeness, and *vincĕre, victum,* to conquer.]

convivial *kan-viv'ī-al,* adj. feasting or drinking in company: relating to a feast: social: jovial.—*ns.* **conviv'ialist** a convivial fellow: convivial'ity.—*adv.* **conviv'ially.** [L. *convīvium,* a living together, a feast—*con-,* together, *vīvĕre,* to live.]

convoke *kan-vōk',* v.t. to call together: to assemble (also **convocate** (*kon'vō-kăt*)).—*n.* **convocā'tion** the act of convoking: a provincial synod of clergy.—*adj.* **convocā'tional.**—*n.* **convocā'tionist.** [L. *convocāre—con-,* together, and *vocāre, -ātum,* to call.]

convolve *kan-volv',* v.t. to roll together, or one part on another.—*adjs.* **convolute** (*kon'va-lōō t, -lūt*), *-d* rolled together, or one part on another: coiled laterally with one margin within, one without (*bot.*): of a flowerbud, contorted (*bot.*): of a shell, having the inner whorls concealed or overlapped by the outer (*zool.*).—*n.* **convolution** (*-lōō', -lū'*) twisting: a fold or sinuosity, esp. of the brain surface. [L. *con-,* together, *volvĕre, -ūtum,* to roll.]

Convolvulus *kan-vol'vū-las, n.* the bindweed genus of twining or trailing plants: (without *cap.*) a plant of the genus. [L. *convolvĕre;* see above.]

convoy *kon-voi',* v.t. to accompany for protection.—*n.* (*kon'*) the act of convoying: protection: a ship or ships of war guarding a fleet of merchant-vessels: the ships so protected: an escort: a supply of stores, etc , under escort. [Fr. *convoyer;* see **convey.**]

convulse *kan-vuls',* v.t. to agitate violently: to affect by spasms.—*n.* **convul'sion** any involuntary contraction

of the voluntary muscles of the body, esp. such seizures in which the body is thrown into violent spasmodic contractions: any violent disturbance: (in *pl.*) fits of immoderate laughter (*coll*).—*adj.* **convuls'ive** attended with convulsions: spasmodic.—*adv.* **convuls'ively.**—*n.* **convuls'iveness.** [L. *con-,* intens., and *vellĕre, vulsum,* to pluck, to pull]

cony, coney *kō'ni, kun'ı, n.* a rabbit: rabbit-skin. [Prob. through O.Fr. *conil,* from L. *cunĭculus,* a rabbit.]

coo[1] *kōō, v.t.* to make a sound as a dove: to converse fondly.—*v.t.* to murmur softly or ingratiatingly: to effect as by cooing.—*n.* the sound emitted by doves.—*n.* and *adj.* **coo'ing.**—*adv.* **coo'ingly.** [Imit.]

coo[2] *kōō,* (*slang*) *interj.* expressive of surprise.

cooee, cooey *kōō 'ē, n.* a call to attract attention.—*v.i.* to utter the call.—*interj.* attracting attention.

cook *kōōk, v.t.* to prepare as food by heat: to manipulate for any purpose, or falsify, as accounts, etc.: to concoct (often with **up**).—*v.i.* to practise cookery: to undergo cooking.—*n.* one who undertakes or is skilled in cooking: a process of heating.—*ns.* **cook'er** a stove, special vessel, or other apparatus for cooking: a variety (e.g. of apple) suitable for cooking; **cook'ery** the art or practice of cooking food.—**cook'ery-book** a book of recipes for cooking dishes; **cook'house** a building or room for cooking in; **cook'ing-apple,** etc., an apple, etc., specially suitable for cooking; **cook'ing-range** a stove adapted for cooking several things at once.—**cook someone's goose** (*slang*) to finish off, to kill, to ruin, to spoil someone's plans; **cook the books** (*coll.*) to falsify accounts, etc.; **what's cooking?** (*coll.*) what is afoot? [O E. *cōc,* a cook—L. *coquus.*]

cookie *kōōk'i, n* a bun: a small sweet biscuit or cake.—**that's how, the way, the cookie crumbles** that's what the situation is: that's just what one would expect to happen. [Du. *koekje,* a cake.]

cool *kōōl, adj.* slightly cold: free from excitement: calm: not zealous, ardent or cordial: indifferent: impudent: a slang term of approval: unemotional and relaxed: excellent and up to date: pleasing, satisfying.—*v.t.* to make cool: to allay or moderate, as heat, excitement, passion, etc.—*v.i.* to grow cool.—*n.* that which is cool: coolness: coolness, self-possession.—*ns.* **cool'ant** a cooling agent; **cool'er** anything that cools: a vessel in which something is cooled: jail (*slang*).—*adj.* **cool'ish** somewhat cool.—*adv.* **cool'ly** in a cool manner: indifferently: impudently.—*n.* **cool'ness** moderate cold: indifference: diminution of friendship: want of zeal: lack of agitation: self-possession.—*adj.* **cool'head'ed** not easily excited: capable of acting with composure.—**cool it** to calm down, act in a relaxed fashion (*slang*); **cool off** to become less angry and more amenable to reason (*n.* and *adj.* **cooling-off'**): to grow less passionate (*n.* and *adj.* **cool'ing-off'**); **cool one's heels** to be kept waiting; **keep one's cool** (*coll.*) to remain calm, keep one's head; **lose one's cool** to become flustered. [O.E. *cōl.*]

coolabah *kōōl'a-bä, n.* any of several species of Australian eucalypt. [Native word.]

coolie, cooly *kōōl'i, n.* a hired native labourer in India and China (*derog.*): in South Africa, an Indian (*offensive*). [Prob. *Kolī,* a tribe of W. India; or Tamil, *kūli,* hire.]

coomb, comb(e) *kōōm, n.* a deep little wooded valley: a hollow in a hillside. [O.E. *cumb,* a hollow.]

coon *kōōn, n.* the raccoon: a sly fellow: a Negro (*derog.*) [U.S.; for **raccoon.**]

coop *kōōp, n.* a wicker basket: a box or cage for fowls or small animals: a prison: a confined, narrow place.—*v.t.* (often with **up**) to confine in a coop or elsewhere.

co-op *kō-op', kō'op,* (*coll.*) short for **co-operative society** or **store.**

cooper *kōōp'ǝr*, *n.* one who makes tubs, casks, etc.—*v.t.* to repair (tubs, etc.): to prepare, patch up —*ns.* **coop'erage** the work or workshop of a cooper: the sum paid for a cooper's work; **coop'ering.** [Also L.G.,—L.L. *cūpārius—cūpa*, cask; cf. **coop.**]

co-operate (also **coop-** in all words) *kō-op'ǝr-āt*, *v.i.* to work together.—*n.* **co-opera'tion** joint operation: combination in co-operative societies:—*adjs.* **co-op'erative** (also *n.*); **co-op'erant** working together.—*n.* **co-op'erator** one who co-operates. a member of a co-operative society —**co-operative society** an association for supplying goods or for carrying on some branch of industry, the profits going to the members; **co-operative store** the shop of a co-operative society [Pfx. **co-**, together, and **operate.**]

co-opt *kō-opt'*, *v.t.* to elect into any body by the votes of its members.—*ns.* **co-opta'tion, co-op'tion.**—*adjs* **co-op'tative, co-op'tive.** [L. *cooptāre, -ātum—co-*, together, *optāre*, to choose.]

co-ordinate (also **coor-** in all words) *kō-or'di-nāt*, *adj.* of the same order or rank: pertaining to or involving co-ordination or co-ordinates.—*v.t.* to place or classify in the same order or rank: to adjust the relations or movements of. to combine or integrate harmoniously: to harmonise.—*n.* an element of the same order as another: each of a system of two or more magnitudes used to define the position of a point, line, or surface by reference to a fixed system of lines, points, etc.· (in *pl.*) outer garments in harmonising colour, material and pattern (cf. **separates**).—*n.* **co-or'dinance** a joint ordinance.—*adv.* **co-or'dinately.**—*ns.* **co-or'dinateness; co-ordina'tion.**—*adj.* **co-or'dinative** co-ordinating: co-ordinated, indicating co-ordination.

coot *kōōt*, *n.* a short-tailed water-fowl, with a characteristic white spot on the forehead: a foolish person (*coll.*). [M.E. *cote.*]

cop¹ *kop*, *n.* a top or head of anything: a conical ball of thread on a spindle.—Also **cop'in.**—*adj.* **copped** rising to a cop or head. [O E. *cop, copp.*]

cop² *kop*, (*slang*) *v.t.* to capture. to catch: to acquire, get.—*n.* a policeman: a capture.—*n.* **copp'er** (*slang*) a policeman.—**cop'-shop** (*slang*) police station.—**cop out** (*slang*) not to take responsibility for, to refuse to participate in (*n* **cop'-out**). [Perh. Fr. *caper*, to seize—L. *capĕre, captum*, to take; cf. Du. *kapen*, to steal.]

copaiba, copaiva *kō-pī'bä, -vä*, or *-pä'*, *ns.* a balsam obtained from S. American caesalpiniaceous trees (*Copaifera*) much used in medicine. [Sp. and Port. from Tupí.]

copal *kō'pǝl*, *n.* a hard resin got from many tropical trees, and also fossil. [Sp.,—Nahuatl *copalli*, resin.]

copartner *kō-pärt'nǝr*, *n.* a joint partner.—*ns.* **copart'nership; copart'nery.**

cope¹ *kōp*, *n.* a covering: a cap or hood: anything spread overhead: a coping: a semicircular, sleeveless hooded vestment worn over the alb or surplice.—*v.t.* to cover as with a cope.—*n.* **cop'ing** the covering course of masonry of a wall.—**cope'-stone, cop'ing-stone** a stone that copes or tops a wall; **cop'ing-saw** a narrow saw for cutting curves. [M.E. *cape*—hypothetical O.E. *cāpe*—L.L. *cāpa*; cf. **cap.**]

cope² *kōp*, *v.i.* (esp. with *with*) to contend: to deal (with) successfully. [Fr. *couper*—L. *colaphus* (Gr. *kolaphos*), a buffet.]

copeck. Same as **kopeck.**

copepod *kō'pe-pod*, *n.* a member of the **Copep'oda,** a class of Crustacea, minute animals with oarlike swimming feet. [Gr. *kōpē*, handle, oar, *pous, podos*, foot.]

Copernican *ko-pûr'ni-kǝn*, *adj.* relating to *Copernicus*,

the famous Polish astronomer (1473–1543), or to his system, in which the earth revolves about the sun.

copier. See **copy.**

coping. See **cope¹.**

co-pilot, copilot *kō'pī-lǝt*, *n.* a fellow pilot.

copious *kō'pi-ǝs*, *adj.* plentiful: overflowing: abounding.—*adv.* **cō'piously.**—*ns.* **cō'piousness.** [L. *cōpiōsus—cōpia*, plenty—*co-*, intens., *ops, opis*, wealth.]

copita *ko-pē't'ǝ*, *n.* a tulip-shaped sherry glass [Sp.]

co-polymer *kō-pol'i-mǝr*, *n.* a substance polymerised along with another, the result being a chemical compound, not a mixture.—*v.t.* **co-pol'ymerise, -ize.** —*n.* **co-polymerisā'tion, -z-.**

copper¹ *kop'ǝr*, *n.* a reddish moderately hard metallic element (at. numb. 29; symbol Cu for L. *cuprum*), perhaps the first metal used by man: money, or a coin, made orig. of copper: a copper vessel: a boiler (orig. of copper) for clothes, or soap, etc.—*adj.* made of copper: copper-coloured.—*v t.* to cover with copper. —*n* **copp'ering** the act of sheathing with copper: a covering of copper.—*adjs.* **copp'erish** somewhat like copper; **copp'ery** like copper.—**copp'er-beech'** a variety of the common beech with purplish, copper-coloured leaves.—*v.t.* **copp'er-bott'om** to cover the bottom of with copper.—*adj* **copp'er-bott'omed** having the bottom covered with copper: sound, reliable, esp. financially.—**copp'erhead** a venomous United States snake akin to the rattlesnake; **copp'er-plate** a plate of polished copper on which something has been engraved: an impression taken from the plate: faultless handwriting; **copp'er-pyri'tes** a yellow double sulphide of copper and iron; **copp'ersmith** a smith who works in copper; **copp'er-work** work in copper: (also *n. sing.* **-works**) a place where copper is wrought or manufactured. [O.E. *copor*—L.L. *cuper*—L. *cuprum*, a form of *cyprium* (*aes*), Cyprian (brass), because found in *Cyprus*.]

copper². See **cop².**

copperas *kop'ǝr-ǝs*, *n.* ferrous sulphate. [Fr. *couperose*, perh.—L *cuprī rosa*, rose of copper, or *aqua cuprōsa*, copper water.]

coppice *kop'is*, **copse** *kops*, *ns.* a wood of small growth for periodical cutting: a wood of sprouts from cut stumps.—*v.t.* to make into coppice: to cover with coppice.—*adj.* **cop'sy.—copse'wood.** [O.Fr. *copeiz*, wood, newly cut—L.L. *colpare*, to cut—L. *colaphus*—Gr. *kolaphos*, a buffet.]

coppin. See **cop¹.**

copra *kop'rǝ*, *n.* the dried kernel of the coconut, yielding coconut oil. [Port., from Malayalam.]

co-presence, copresence *kō-prez'ǝns*, *n.* presence together.—*adj* **co'pres'ent.**

copro-, in composition, dung —*n.* **coprol'ogy** the unclean in literature and art.—*adj.* **coproph'agous** (*-gǝs*).—*ns.* **coproph'agy** (*-ji*); **coprophil'ia** morbid pleasure in dung or filth.—*adj.* **coproph'ilous** delighting in dung or filth: growing on or in dung. [Gr. *kopros*, dung.]

copse, copsewood, copsy. See **coppice.**

Copt *kopt*, *n.* a Christian descendant of the ancient Egyptians.—*adj.* **Copt'ic.**—*n.* the language of the Copts. [Gr. *Aigyptios*, Egyptian.]

copula *kop'ū-lǝ*, *n.* that which joins together: the word joining the subject and predicate (*log.* or *linguistics*). —*adj.* **cop'ular.**—*v.t.* **cop'ulate** to unite.—*v.i.* to unite in sexual intercourse.—*n.* **copulā'tion.**—*adj.* **cop'ulatory.** [L. *cōpula—co-*, *apĕre*, to join.]

copy *kop'i*, *n.* an imitation: a transcript: a reproduction: that which is imitated or reproduced: matter (e.g. a newspaper article) for printing: something newsworthy.—*v.t.* to write, paint, etc. in the manner of: to imitate closely: to transcribe: to reproduce or duplicate.—*v.i.* to make a copy: to follow:—*pr.p.*

cop'ying; *pa.t.* and *pa.p.* cop'ied.—*ns.* cop'ier one who or that which copies: an imitator; cop'yist one whose business is to copy documents. a mere copier.—cop'y-book a writing or drawing book of models printed for imitation: a collection of copies of documents.—*adj.* conventional, commonplace: (of example, operation, etc.) perfect, or carried out flawlessly.—cop'y-cat (*slang*) a term applied in resentful derision to an imitator.—*v t.* and *v.i.* to imitate.—cop'yholder an assistant who reads copy aloud to a proof-reader; cop'y-right the sole right to reproduce a literary, dramatic, musical, or artistic work—also to perform, translate, film, or record such a work —*adj.* protected by copyright —*v.t.* to secure the copyright of.—*adj.* cop'y-rightable.—cop'y-typing; cop'y-typist a typist who copies written, printed, etc matter, not working from shorthand or recorded sound; cop'ywriter a writer of copy (esp. advertisements) for the press. [Fr. *copie,* from L. *cōpia,* plenty; in L.L. a transcript]

coquet, coquette *ko-, kō-ket', v i.* to flirt. to dally:—*pr.p.* coquett'ing; *pa.p.* and *pa.t.* coquett'ed.—*ns.* cō'-quetry (-*kit-ri*) the act of coquetting: the attempt to attract admiration, without serious affection: deceit in love: any artful prettiness; coquette' a woman (rarely a man) who seeks admiration from mere vanity: a flirt —Also *adj.*—*adj.* coquett'ish practising coquetry: befitting a coquette.—*adv.* coquett'ishly.—*n.* coquett'ishness. [Fr. *coqueter—coquet,* dim. of *coq,* a cock.]

cor *kor,* (*coll.*) *interj.* an expression of surprise.—cor blimey a form of gorblim(e)y. [Vulg. form of God.]

cor-. See com-.

coracle *kor'ə-kl, n.* a small oval rowing-boat used in Wales. [Conn. W. *corwg,* anything round.]

coral *kor'əl, n.* a hard substance of various colours deposited on the bottom of the sea, skeleton, mostly calcareous, of Anthozoa and of some Hydrozoa: the animal or colony that produces it. (in *pl.*) a necklace of coral: a deep orange-pink colour.—*adj.* made of or like coral, esp. red coral.—*adjs.* corallá'ceous like, or having the qualities of, coral, corallif'erous containing coral; coralliform (-*al'*) having the form of coral. corallig'enous producing coral, cor'alline of, like, or containing coral —*n.* cor'allite the cup of a simple coral or of one polyp: a fossil coral.—*adjs.* cor'alloid, coralloid'al in the form of coral: resembling coral.—cor'al-fish a tropical, spiny-finned fish of many kinds abundant about coral reefs, cor'al-is'land; cor'al-reef' a reef or bank formed by the growth and deposit of coral, cor'al-rock' a limestone composed of coral [L. *corallum*—Gr *korallion*]

cor anglais *kòr ā-glā',* an oboe set a fifth lower than the ordinary oboe. [Fr., English horn.]

corbel *kor'bl,* (*archit.*) *n.* a projection from the face of a wall, supporting a weight.—*adj.* cor'belled.—*n* cor'belling.—cor'bel-ta'ble a row of corbels and the parapet or cornice they support. [O.Fr *corbel*—L.L *corvellus,* dim of *corvus,* a raven.]

corbicula *kor-bik'ū-lə, n.* the pollen basket of bees, consisting of the dilated posterior tibia with its fringe of long hairs:—*pl.* corbic'ulae (-*lē*).—*adj.* corbic'-ulate. [L. dim. of *corbis,* a basket.]

corbie *kòr'bi,* (*Scot.*) *n* a raven: a crow.—cor'bie-steps crow-steps. [O.Fr. *corbin*—L *corvus,* a crow.]

cord *kord, n.* a small rope or thick string: something resembling a cord (as spinal cord, umbilical cord), anything that binds or restrains: a measure of cut wood (128 cubic feet), orig. determined by use of a cord or string: a raised rib on cloth: ribbed cloth, esp. corduroy (also *adj.*): (in *pl.*) corduroy trousers a flex for an electrical apparatus.—*v.t.* to supply with a cord· to bind with a cord.—*n.* cord'age a quantity of cords or ropes, as the rigging of a ship, etc —*adj.* cord'ed

fastened with cords: ribbed: piled in cords.—*ns.* cord'ing the act of binding: cordage; cord'ite a cord-like smokeless explosive.—*adj.* cord'less (of an electrical device) operating without a flex, battery-powered.—*n.* cordot'omy cutting in certain parts of the spinal cord to relieve great pain. [Fr. *corde*—L. *chorda;* see chord.]

cordate *kor'dāt, adj.* heart-shaped: having the base indented next the petiole (*bot.*).—*adj.* cord'iform heart-shaped [L *cor, cordis,* the heart.]

cordial *kor'di-əl, adj.* hearty: with warmth of heart: sincere. affectionate: reviving the heart or spirits.—*n.* anything which revives or comforts the heart: a medicine or drink for refreshing the spirits: a beverage containing alcohol or sugar or stimulating drugs —*v.i.* cor'dialise, -ize to become cordial, to fraternise—*ns.* cordiality (-*al'i-ti*); cor'dialness.—*adv.* cor'dially. [Fr.,—L. *cor, cordis,* the heart.]

cordiform. See cordate.

cordillera *kor-dil-yā'rə, n.* a chain of mountains, as the Andes and Rocky Mountains. [Sp.,—Old Sp. *cordilla*—L. *chorda,* cord—Gr. *chordē.*]

cordiner *kór'di-nər.* See cordovan.

cordite. See cord.

cordon *kor'don, -dən, n.* a cord or ribbon bestowed as a badge of honour: a row of stones along the line of a rampart (*fort.*): a line of police, soldiers, etc., or a system of road-blocks, encircling an area so as to prevent or control passage into or out of it: a single-stemmed fruit-tree·—*v.t.* to close (off) an area with a cordon of men, ring of barriers, etc. [Fr.]

cordon bleu *kor-dõ blø,* (Fr.) blue ribbon: a cook of the highest excellence.—*adj.* (of a cook or cookery) of a very high standard.

cordon sanitaire *kor-dõ sa-nē-ter,* (Fr.) a line of sentries posted to restrict passage into and out of an area and so keep contagious disease within that area: neutral states keeping hostile states apart: a barrier (*lit.* or *fig.*) isolating a state, etc.

cordotomy. See cord.

cordovan *kor'do-vən,* cordwain *kord'wän, n.* goatskin leather, originally from *Cordova* (*Córdoba*) in Spain. —*ns.* cord'wainer, cord'iner a worker in cordovan or cordwain: a shoemaker; cord'wainery.

corduroy *kor-də-roi', or kor', n.* a ribbed cotton stuff made after the fashion of velvet. (in *pl.*) corduroy trousers.—*adj* of corduroy. [Perh Fr *corde du roi,* king's cord.]

core *kor, kor, n* in an apple, pear, etc the central casing containing the seeds. the innermost or most essential part of something· the central part of the earth (*geol.*). a cylindrical sample of rock, soil, etc. extracted by drill: the lump of stone or flint remaining after flakes have been struck off it (*archaeol*): the part of a nuclear reactor containing the fissile material (*phys.*): (also magnetic core) a small ferromagnetic ring which, charged or uncharged by electric current, can thus assume two states corresponding to the binary digits 0 and 1; used for computer memory.—*v t.* to take out the core of (an apple, etc.).—*adj.* cored having the core removed. cast by means of a core: having a core.—*n* cor'er an instrument for removing the core. [Poss L. *cor,* the heart, or Fr. *cor,* horn, corn (on the foot), or *corps,* body.]

co-relation, co-relative. See correlate.

co-religionist *kō-rə-lij'ən-ist, n.* one of the same religion as another.

co-respondent *kō-rə-spond'ənt,* (law) *n.* a man or woman charged with adultery, and proceeded against along with the wife or husband who is the *respondent*

corf *korf, n.* a coal-miner's basket, now usu. a tub or trolley a cage for fish or lobsters —*pl* corves (*korvz*) [Du ,—L. *corbis,* basket.]

corgi *kör'gi, n.* a Welsh breed of dog, having a fox-like head and short legs. [Welsh *corr*, dwarf, *ci*, dog.]

coriaceous. See **corium**.

coriander *kor-i-an'dər, n.* an umbelliferous plant whose seeds are used as spice, etc. [Fr. *coriandre*—L. *coriandrum*—Gr. *koriannon*.]

Corinthian *kor-inth'i-ən, adj.* of *Corinth* in Greece: of an ornate style of Greek architecture, with acanthus capitals: profligate.—*n.* a profligate: an amateur sportsman.

Coriolis effect *kor-i-ō'lis i-fekt', (phys., meteor.)* the deflection (to the right in the Northern, left in the Southern, hemisphere) and acceleration of bodies, etc. moving relative to the earth's surface, caused by the earth's rotation. [First studied by G. B. *Coriolis*, (1792–1843).]

corium *kö'ri-əm, kö', n.* the true skin, under the epidermis *(anat.)*.—*adjs.* **coria'ceous**, **co'rious** leathery [L. *corium*—Gr. *chorion*, skin, leather.]

cork *körk, n.* the outer bark of the cork-tree, an oak found in S. Europe, N. Africa, etc.: a stopper made of cork: any stopper: a tissue of close-fitting, thick-walled cells, almost airtight and watertight, forming bark or covering the surfaces of wounds *(bot.)*: a piece of cork: a float of cork.—*adj.* made of cork.—*v.t.* to stop with a cork: to bottle up, repress (with *up*; *fig.*).—*n.* **cork'age** corking or uncorking of bottles: a charge made by hotel-keepers for uncorking of bottles when the liquor has not been supplied from the house.—*adj.* **corked** stopped as by a cork: tainted as if by the cork, as wine.—*ns.* **cork'er** something conclusive, a finisher *(slang)*: a person or thing that surpasses *(slang)*: a person or device that inserts corks; **cork'iness**.—*adjs.* **cork'ing** *(slang)* surpassing; **cork'y** of, or resembling, cork.—**cork'-oak** a species of oak (*Quercus suber*) which supplies the cork of commerce in Spain and Portugal; **cork'-screw** a screw for drawing corks from bottles.—*adj.* like a cork-screw in shape.—*v.i.* to move in a spiral manner.—**cork'-tree** the cork-oak: applied to various trees with corky bark or very light wood; **cork'wood** very light wood: applied to many trees with light wood, e.g. balsa. [Perh. from Sp. *alcorque*, cork slipper, which may be from L. *quercus*, oak, with the Arabic article *al*.]

corm *körm, n.* a short, bulbous, subterranean stem as in the crocus. [Gr. *kormos*, the lopped trunk of a tree.]

cormorant *kör'mə-rənt, n.* a member of a genus of web-footed sea-birds, of great voracity: a glutton. [Fr. *cormoran*, from L. *corvus marīnus*, sea crow.]

corn *körn, n.* a grain, hard particle: a kernel, small hard seed: collectively seeds of cereal plants, or the plants themselves—esp. (in England) wheat, (in Scotland and Ireland) oats, (in North America) maize: something old-fashioned or hackneyed.—*adj.* of, for, pertaining to, made from, growing among, feeding upon, corn: granular.—*v.t.* to make granular: to salt.—*v.i.* to form seed.—*p.adj.* **corned** granulated: salted (e.g. **corned beef**—also **corn'-beef**).—*adj.* **corn'y** like corn: produced from corn: old-fashioned, uninteresting from frequent use, dull *(slang)*.—**corn'-bor'er** a European moth whose larvae have become a maize pest in America; **corn'-bran'dy** spirits made from grain: whisky; **corn'brash** *(geol.)* a clayey limestone giving good corn soils; **corn'-bread**, **-cake** *(U.S.)* bread, a cake, made of maize meal; **corn'-chandler** a retailer of grain; **corn'-chandlery**; **corn'-cob** the woody axis of a maize ear; **corn'crake** a rail with characteristic cry, inhabiting cornfields; **corn'-dealer**, **-factor**, **-merchant** one who buys and sells corn; **corn-dollie** see **kirn**; **corn'-exchange** a mart for trade in corn.—*adj.* **corn'-fed** fed on corn: well fed.—**corn'field** a field in which corn is growing; **corn'-flag** a

gladiolus: **corn'flakes** toasted flakes of maize, eaten esp. as a breakfast cereal; **corn'flour** finely ground maize, rice, or other grain: a pudding made of it; **corn'flower** a beautiful blue-flowered cornfield weed of the Compositae; **corn'land** ground suitable for growing grain; **corn'-law** a law regulating trade in grain, esp. (in *pl.*) laws that restricted importation to Britain by a duty, repealed 1846; **corn'loft** a granary; **corn'-pone** *(U.S.)* maize-bread: a maize loaf; **corn'-rent** rent paid in corn, not money; **corn'-shuck** *(U.S.)* the leaves enclosing a maize ear; **corn'-shucking** the removal of corn-shucks: an assembly for the purpose; **corn'starch** maize starch or flour, for puddings; **corn'-thrips** a minute insect that sucks the sap of grain; **corn'-weevil** a small weevil destructive in granaries; **corn'-whisky** an American whisky made from maize. —**corn-cob pipe** a tobacco-pipe with the bowl made of a maize cob; **corn on the cob** a cob of maize with grains still attached, boiled whole and eaten as a vegetable. [O.E. *corn*; akin to L. *grānum*.]

corn[2] *körn, n.* a small hard growth chiefly on the toe or foot, resulting from an increase of thickness of cuticle, caused by pressure or friction.—*adj.* **corn'eous** horny. —*ns.* **corn'icle**, **cornic'ulum** a little horn: a hornlike process.—*adjs.* **cornic'ulate** horned: horn-shaped; **corn'y** of or pertaining to horns or corns: having corns: horny.—**corn'-cure** a remedy for corns; **corn plaster** a remedial plaster for corns.—**tread on someone's corns** to hurt someone's feelings. [L. *cornū*, a horn.]

cornea *kör'ni-ə, n.* the transparent horny membrane that forms the front covering of the eye.—*adj.* **cor'neal**.—**corneal lens** a contact lens covering the transparent part of the eye only. [L. *cornea* (*tēla*), horny (tissue).]

cornel *kör'nəl, n.* the so-called cornelian-cherry or cornelian-tree, a small tree (*Cornus mas*) of middle and southern Europe. [L.L. *cornolium*—L. *cornus*, cornel.]

cornelian *kör'nē'li-ən, n.* a fine chalcedony, generally translucent red. [Fr. *cornaline*—L. *cornū*, a horn, or *cornum*, cornelian-cherry.]

corneous. See **corn**[2].

corner *kör'nər, n.* the point where two lines or several planes meet: an angular projection or recess: a secret or confined place: an embarrassing position, difficulty: a free shot, taken from the corner of the field, given to the opposite side when a player in football or hockey e.g. plays the ball over his own goal-line: an operation by which the whole of a stock or commodity is bought up so that the buyers may resell at their own price.—*v.t.* to supply with corners: to put in a corner: to put in a fix or difficulty: to form a corner against: to get control of by forming a corner.—*v.i.* to turn a corner.—*adj.* **corn'ered** having corners: put in a difficult position.—*adv.* **corn'erwise** with the corner in front: diagonally.—**corn'er-stone** a stone that unites the two walls of a building at a corner: the principal stone, esp. the corner of the foundation of a building: something of prime importance *(fig.)*.—**turn the corner** to go round the corner: to get past a difficulty or danger, begin to pick up; **within the four corners of** contained in. [O.Fr. *corniere*—L. *cornū*, horn.]

cornet *kör'nit n.* a treble brass valve instrument, more tapering than the trumpet: a cornet-player: any funnel-shaped object, as a piece of gold for assaying, a shopkeeper's screwed paper bag, an ice-cream-filled wafer cone, a cream-filled pastry.—*n.* **cor'netist**, **cornett'ist**, a cornet-player. [Fr. *cornet*, dim. of *corne*—L. *cornū*, horn.]

cornice *kör'nis, n.* the uppermost member of the entablature, surmounting the frieze *(classical archit.)*: a projecting moulding along the top of a building, window, etc.: a plaster moulding round a ceiling: a moulded ridge for supporting picture-hooks.—*v.t.* to furnish with a cornice.—*adj.* **cor'niced.** [Fr ,—It., poss. Gr. *korōnis*, a curved line, cf. L. *corōna*.]

corniche *kor-nēsh*, (Fr.) *n.* a coast road built along a cliff-face.

cornicle, corniculate etc. See **corn²**.

Cornish *kŏr'nish*, *adj.* pertaining to Cornwall.—*n.* the Celtic language of Cornwall, dead since the later 18th cent.—**Cornish pasty** a pasty (**pasty²**) with meat and vegetables.

cornucopia *kŏr-nū-kō'pi-ə*, *n.* the horn of plenty—according to one fable, the horn of the goat that suckled Jupiter, placed among the stars as an emblem of plenty: an ornament consisting of a horn overflowing with fruits: an abundant source of supply.—*adj.* **cornucō'pian.** [L. *cornū cōpiae*—*cornū*, horn, *cōpia*, plenty.]

corny. See **corn¹,².**

corolla *kor-ol'ə*, *-ōl'ə*, *n.* the inner circle or whorl of the floral envelopes.—*adj.* **corolla'ceous.** [L. *corolla*, dim. of *corōna*, a crown.]

corollary *kər-ol'ə-ri* *n.* an easy inference: a consequence or result: a supplement, surplus, or supernumerary. [L. *corollārium*, a garland, money for a garland, a tip—*corolla*.]

corona *ko-rō'nə*, *kə-*, *n.* the large, flat, projecting member of a cornice crowning the entablature (*archit.*): the trumpet of a daffodil, etc.: a coloured ring round the sun or moon, distinguished from halo by having red outermost: a round pendent chandelier:—*pl.* **corō'nas, corō'nae** (*-ē*).—*n.* **cor'onal** (*-ə-nl*) a circlet, small crown or garland.—*adjs.* **corō'nal** pertaining to a crown, a corona, or to the top of the head: like a crown; **cor'onary** (*-ən-ə-ri*) coronal: surrounding a part (**coronary arteries** those that supply the muscle of the heart-wall with blood; so **coronary circulation**).—*n.* a coronary thrombosis.—*adjs.* **cor'onate, -d** crowned: applied to shells with a row of projections round the apex.—*n.* **coronā'tion** the ceremony of crowning.—**coronary thrombosis** stoppage of a branch of a coronary artery by a clot of blood. [L. *corōna*, a crown.]

coronal, coronary, etc. See **corona**.

coroner *kor'ə-nər*, *n.* an officer whose chief duty is to enquire into the causes of accidental or suspicious deaths. [O.Fr. *corouner*—L. *corōna*, crown.]

coronet *kor'ə-nit*, *n.* a small crown worn by the nobility: an ornamental head-dress: the part of a horse's pastern just above the coffin.—*adj.* **cor'oneted.** [O.Fr. *coronete*, dim. of *corone*, crown—L. *corōna*.]

corozo *kor-ō'sō*, *n.* a South American short-stemmed palm whose seed (**corozo nut**) gives vegetable ivory:—*pl.* **corō'zos.** [Sp. from an Indian language.]

corpora. See **corpus**.

corporal¹ *kŏr'pə-rəl*, *n.* a non-commissioned officer next under a sergeant.—*n.* **cor'poralship.** [Fr. *caporal*—It. *caporale*—*capo*, the head—L. *caput*, the head.]

corporal² *kŏr'pə-rəl*, *adj.* belonging or relating to the body: having a body: material: not spiritual.—*n.* in Catholic and episcopal churches, the cloth on which the bread and wine of the Eucharist are laid out and with which the remains are covered.—*n.* **corporality** (*-al'i-ti*).—*adv.* **cor'porally.**—*adj.* **cor'porate** legally united into a body so as to act as an individual: belonging or pertaining to a corporation: united.—*adv* **cor'porately.**—*ns.* **cor'porateness; corporā'tion** a body or society authorised by law to act as one individual: a town council: a company: a belly, esp. a pot-belly (*coll.*); **cor'poratism** (the policy of) control of a country's economy through the combined power of the trade unions, large businesses, etc.—*n.* and

adj. **cor'poratist.**—*adj.* **corporeal** (*kor-pō'ri-əl -po'*) having a body or substance: material.—*ns.* **corpō'realism** materialism; **corpō'realist; corpōreality** (*-al'i-ti*).—*adv.* **corpō'really.**—**corporal punishment** punishment inflicted on the body, as flogging, etc ; **corporation aggregate** a corporation consisting of several persons; **corporation sole** a corporation which consists of one person and his successors; **corporation tax** a tax levied on the income of companies. [L. *corpus, corpŏris*, the body.]

corps *kŏr*, *kor*, *n.* a division of an army forming a tactical unit: a branch or department of an army: a set of people working more or less together:—*pl.* **corps** (*kŏrz, korz*). [Fr.,—L. *corpus*, body.]

corps de ballet *kor də ba-le*, (Fr.) the company of ballet dancers at a theatre; **corps d'élite** (*kor dā-lēt*) (Fr.) a small number of people picked out as being the best in any group; **corps diplomatique** (*dē-plō-ma-tēk*) (Fr.) the whole diplomatic staff at a particular capital.

corpse *kŏrps*, or *kòrs*, *n.* a dead human body. [M.E. *corps*, earlier *cors*—O.Fr. *cors*—L. *corpus*, the body]

corpus *kŏr'pəs*, *n.* a body, esp. a dead body: any special structure in the body: a body of literature, law, etc.:—*pl.* **cor'pora** (*-pə-rə*).—*ns.* **cor'pulence, cor'pulency** fleshiness of body: excessive fatness.—*adj.* **cor'pulent.**—*adv.* **cor'pulently.**—*n.* **cor'puscle** (*-pus-l*; sometimes *-pus'l*) a cell or other minute body suspended in fluid, esp. a red or white cell in the blood: a minute particle (also **corpus'cule**).—*adj.* **corpus'cular.**—**Corpus Christi** (*kris'tē, -tī*) the festival in honour of the Eucharist, held on the Thursday after the festival of the Trinity; **corpus delicti** (*di-lik'tī, de-lik'tē; law*) the essential facts of the crime charged, e.g. in a murder trial, that somebody is actually dead and has been murdered; **corpus luteum** (*lōō'ti-əm*) a mass of yellow tissue that develops in a Graafian follicle after the discharge of an ovum and secretes progesterone:—*pl.* **cor'pora lu'tea; corpus vile** (*vī'lē, vē'le, wē-*) a person or thing considered so expendable as to be a fit object for experimentation regardless of consequences:—*pl.* **cor'pora vi'lia** [L. *corpus*, the body.]

corrade *kə-rād'*, *kor-*, (*geol.*) *v.t.* to wear away through the action of loose solid material, e.g. pebbles in a stream or wind-borne sand.—*n.* **corrasion** (*-rā'zhən*) [L. *corrādēre*, to scrape together—*con-*, together *rādēre, rāsum*, to scratch.]

corral *kə-* or *ko-ral'*, *n.* a pen for cattle: an enclosure to drive hunted animals into: a defensive ring of wagons —*v.t.* to pen: to form into a corral. [Sp.]

correct *kə-* or *ko-rekt'*, *v.t.* to make right or supposedly right: to remove or mark faults or supposed faults from or in: to do this and evaluate: to set (a person right: to punish: to counterbalance: to bring into a normal state: to reduce to a standard.—*adj.* right according to standard: free from faults.—*adjs* **correct'able, correct'ible.**—*adv.* **correct'ly.**—*n* **correc'tion** emendation or would-be emendation amendment: punishment: reduction: compensation quantity to be added to bring to a standard or balance an error: bodily chastisement.—*adj.* **correc'tional.**—*n.* **correct'itude** correctness of conduct or behaviour —*adj.* **correct'ive** of the nature of, by way of, correction: tending to correct: correcting.—*n.* that which corrects.—*ns.* **correct'ness; correct'or** he who, or that which, corrects: a director or governor: a proof reader.—*adj.* **correct'ory** corrective. [L. *corrigĕre corrĕctum*—*cor-*, intens., *regĕre*, to rule.]

correlate *kor'i-lāt*, *v.i.* to be related to one another.—*v.t.* to bring into relation with each other: to establish relation or correspondence between.—*n.* either of two things so related that one implies the other or is complementary to it.—*adj.* **correla'table.**—*n.* **correla'tion** the state or act of correlating: mutual relation, esp. of phenomena regularly occurring together: interdependence, or the degree of it.—*adj* **correlative** (-*el'ə-tiv*).—*n.* a person or thing correspondingly related to another person or thing.—*adv* **correl'atively.**—*ns.* **correl'ativeness, correlativ'ity.** [L *cor-*, with, and **relate.**]

correspond *kor-i-spond'*, *v i.* to answer, suit, agree (with *to*, *with*): to hold intercourse, esp. by letter — *ns* **correspond'ence, correspond'ency** suitability: harmony: relation of agreement, part to part, or one to one: communication by letter: a body of letters — *adj.* **correspond'ent** answering: agreeing: suitable.— *n* one with whom intercourse is kept up by letters: one who contributes letters, or is employed to send special reports (e.g. *foreign correspondent, war correspondent*) to a periodical.—*adv.* **correspond'ently.** —*adj.* **correspond'ing** correspondent: answering: similar, comparable, matching· suiting: carrying on correspondence by letters.—*adv.* **correspond'ingly.** —*adj.* **correspon'sive** corresponding· answering.— **correspondence course, school,** etc., one conducted by postal correspondence. [L *cor-*, with, and *respondēre.*]

corrida (de toros) *kō-rē'dha* (*dā tō'rōs*) (Sp) a bullfight.

corridor *kor'i-dor*, *n.* a passageway or gallery communicating with separate rooms or dwellings in a building or compartments in a railway train: a strip of territory by which a country has access to a port, etc. —**corridors of power** (*fig.*) the higher reaches of government administration. [Fr.,—It. *corridore*— It. *correre*, to run—L. *currēre.*]

corrie *kor'i*, *n.* a semicircular mountain recess or cirque. [Gael. *coire*, a cauldron.]

corrigendum *kor-i-jen'dəm*, *n.* that which requires correction:—*pl.* **corrigen'da**, esp. corrections to be made in a book. [L., gerundive of *corrigĕre*, to correct.]

corrigent *kor'i-jənt*, *adj.* and *n.* corrective.—*adj.* **corr'igible** that may be corrected: open to correction. —*n.* **corrigibil'ity.** [L. *corrigĕre*, to correct; see **correct.**]

corroborate *kər-ob'ə-rāt*, *v.t.* to confirm: to make more certain.—*adjs.* **corrob'orable; corrob'orant; corrob'orative** tending to confirm.—*n.* that which corroborates.—*ns.* **corrobora'tion** confirmation; **corrob'orator.**—*adj.* **corrob'oratory** corroborative [L. *cor-*, intens., and *rōborāre*, *-ātum*, to make strong; see **robust.**]

corroboree *kə-rob'ə-rē*, *n.* a dance of Australian aborigines: a song for such a dance: a festive gathering —*v.i.* to hold a corroboree. [Native word.]

corrode *kər-ōd'*, *v.t.* to eat away by degrees, esp. chemically: to rust.—*v.i.* to be eaten away.—*adj.* **corrod'ent** having the power of corroding.—*n.* that which corrodes —*n.* **corrōsibil'ity.**—*adj.* **corrōs'ible** (also **corrōd'ible**).—*n.* **corrosion** (*-rō'zhən*) the act or process of eating or wasting away.—*adj.* **corrōs'ive** having the quality of eating away.—*n.* that which has the power of corroding.—*adv.* **corrōs'ively.**—*n.* **corrōs'iveness.** [L. *cor-*, intens., *rōdĕre*, *rōsum*, to gnaw.]

corrugate *kor'ə-* or *kor'oo-gāt*, *v.t.* to wrinkle or draw into folds.—*n.* **corruga'tion** the act of wrinkling or state of being wrinkled: a wrinkle.—**corrugated iron** sheet iron bent by ridged rollers into a wavy form for the sake of strength, **corrugated paper** a wrinkled paper used as wrapping material. [L. *cor-*, intens., *rūgāre*, *-ātum*, to wrinkle—*rūga*, a wrinkle.]

corrupt *kər-upt'*, *v.t.* to make putrid: to taint: to debase: to spoil: to destroy the purity of: to pervert: to bribe.—*v.i* to rot: to lose purity.—*adj.* putrid: depraved. defiled: not genuine: much vitiated or debased in transcription: bribed: dishonest, venal: of the nature of, or involving, bribery.—*ns.* **corrupt'er; corruptibil'ity.**—*adj.* **corrupt'ible** liable to be corrupted —*n* **corrupt'ibleness.**—*adv.* **corrupt'ibly.**—*ns.* **corrup'tion** rottenness: putrid matter: impurity: bribery, **corrup'tionist** one who defends or who practises corruption.—*adj.* **corrupt'ive** having the quality of corrupting —*adv.* **corrupt'ly.**—*n* **corrupt'ness.** [L *cor-*, intens., and *rumpĕre*, *ruptum*, to break.]

corsage *kor-sazh'*, *n.* the bodice or waist of a woman's dress: a bouquet to be worn there or elsewhere. [O.Fr.,—*cors*—L. *corpus*, the body.]

corsair *kor'sār*, *n.* a privateer (esp. of Barbary): a privateering ship: a pirate [Fr *corsaire*, one who courses or ranges—L *cursus*, a running—*currĕre.*]

corselet, corselette. See **corslet.**

corset *kor'sit*, *n.* a close-fitting stiff inner bodice: stays: a stiff belt coming down over the hips: a term for the controls imposed by the Bank of England to restrict banks' capacity to lend money.—*v.t.* to furnish with a corset:—*pr.p.* **cor'seting;** *pa.t* and *pa.p.* **cor'seted.**— *n* **corsetier** (*kor-sə-tyā*, also *-tēr'*), *fem.* **corsetière** (*kor-sə-tyer*, also *-tēr'*) a maker or seller of corsets. [Dim. of O.Fr. *cors*—L. *corpus*, the body.]

corslet, corselet *kors'lit*, *n.* a cuirass, a protective bodycovering of leather, or steel, etc.: a modified corset, or combined belt and brassière.—Also **corselette'.**—*adj.* **cors'leted.** [Fr. *corselet*, dim. of O.Fr. *cors*—L *corpus*, the body.]

cortège *kor-tezh'*, *n.* a train of attendants: a procession, a funeral procession [Fr.,—It. *corte*, court.]

cortex *kor'teks*, *n.* the bark or skin of a plant between the epidermis and the vascular bundles (*bot.*): the outer layer of an organ, esp. of the brain (*zool.*):—*pl* **cortices** (*kor'ti-sēz*), sometimes **cor'texes**—*adjs.* **cor'tical** pertaining to the cortex: external; **cor'ticāte**, **-d** furnished with bark.—*ns.* **cor'ticoster'oid, cor'ticoid** any of the steroids, e.g. cortisone, extracted from the adrenal cortex. [L *cortex*, *corticis*, bark.]

cortisone *kor'ti-zōn*, *-sōn*, *n.* 'compound E', a steroid isolated from the adrenal cortex, or prepared from ox bile, etc., an anti-inflammatory agent.

corundum *kə-run'dəm*, *n.* a mineral consisting of alumina, second in hardness only to the diamond —including sapphire, ruby, emery. [Tamil *kurundam.*]

coruscate *kor'əs-kāt*, *v.i.* to sparkle: to throw off flashes of light.—*adj.* **coruscant** (*-rus'*) flashing.—*n.* **corusca'tion** a glittering: sudden flash of light. [L. *coruscāre*, *-ātum*, to vibrate, glitter.]

corvée *kor-vā'*, *n.* the obligation to perform gratuitous labour (such as the maintenance of roads) for the sovereign or feudal lord. [Fr.,—L.L. *corrogāta*—L. *corrogāre*—*cor-*, together, *rogāre*, to ask.]

corves. See **corf.**

corvette *kor-vet'*, *n.* formerly a flush-decked vessel, with one tier of guns: now an escort vessel specially designed for protecting convoys against submarine attack. [Fr.,—Sp *corbeta*—L. *corbīta*, a slow-sailing ship—*corbis*, a basket.]

Corvus *kor'vəs*, *n.* the crow genus, typical of the family **Cor'vidae** and subfamily **Corvi'nae.**—*n.* **cor'vid** (*zool.*) a member of the Corvidae.—*adj.* **cor'vine** (*-vīn*). [L. *corvus*, a raven.]

corybant *kor'ə-bant*, *n.* a priest of Cybele, whose rites were accompanied with noisy music and wild dances. —*adj.* **coryban'tic** wildly excited.—*n.* **cor'ybantism.** [Gr. *korybās*, *korybantos.*]

corymb *kor'imb*, (*bot.*) *n.* a flattish-topped raceme.— *adj.* **cor'ymbose** (or *-imb'*). [L. *corymbus*—Gr. *korymbos*, a cluster.]

coryphene kor'i-fēn, n. a fish of the genus Coryphaena, called the dolphin. [Gr. koryphaina.]

coryza ko-rī'zə, n. a cold in the head: nasal catarrh. [L.,—Gr. koryza.]

cos[1] kos, n. a long-leaved lettuce.—Also **cos lettuce**. [Introduced from the Aegean island of Cos (Gr. Kōs).]

cos[2]. See **cosine**.

'cos koz, kəz, (coll.) adv. and conj. because.

Cosa Nostra kō'zə nos'trə, the Mafia organisation, esp. in U.S. [It., 'our thing'.]

cosecant kō-sek'ənt, -sēk', n. the secant of the complement of an angle—abbrev. **cosec** (kō'sek).—n. **cosech** (kōsh-ek') for hyperbolic cosecant.

coseismal kō-sīz'məl, adj. experiencing an earthquake shock simultaneously.—Also **coseis'mic**. [L. co-, together, Gr. seismos, earthquake.]

cosh[1] kosh, (slang) n. a bludgeon, truncheon, leadpipe, piece of flexible tubing filled with metal, or the like, used as a weapon.—Also v.t.

cosh[2]. See **cosine**.

co-signatory kō-sig'nə-tə-ri, adj. uniting with others in signing.—n. one who does so.

cosine kō'sīn, n. the sine of the complement of an angle—abbrev. **cos** (kos).—n. **cosh** (kosh or kos-āch') a conventional abbreviation for hyperbolic cosine.

cosmetic koz-met'ik, adj. purporting to improve beauty, esp. that of the complexion: correcting defects of the face, etc., or supplying deficiencies (as cosmetic surgery, hands): involving or producing an apparent or superficial concession, improvement, etc. without any real substance to it.—n. (usu. in pl) a preparation for the improvement of beauty, etc., sometimes including shampoo, deodorant, toothpaste, etc.—n. cosmē'sis cosmetic surgery or treatment.—adj. cosmet'ical.—adv. cosmet'ically.—n cosmetic'ian one who produces, sells, or is skilled in the use of, cosmetics (sometimes fig.).—v.t. cosmet'icise, -ize.—ns. cosmet'icism; cosmetol'ogy the art or profession of applying cosmetics, or of carrying out plastic surgery. [Gr. kosmētikos—kosmeein, to adorn—kosmos, order.]

Cosmos koz'mos, n. an American plant genus of composites akin to the dahlia: (without cap.) any plant of the genus. [Gr. kosmos, ornament.]

cosmos koz'mos, n. the world or universe as an orderly or systematic whole—opp. to chaos: order—adjs cos'mic relating to the cosmos: universal: orderly; cos'mical cosmic: happening at sunrise (astron.): rising with the sun (astron.).—adv. cos'mically.—adjs. cosmogon'ic, -al relating to cosmogony.—ns. cosmog'onist one who speculates on the origin of the universe; cosmog'ony a theory or a myth of the origin of the universe, esp. of the stars, nebulae, etc.; cosmog'rapher.—adjs. cosmograph'ic, -al.—n. cosmog'raphy a description of the world: the science of the constitution of the universe.—adj. cosmolog'ical.—ns. cosmol'ogist; cosmol'ogy the science of the universe as a whole: a treatise on the structure and parts of the system of creation; cos'monaut an astronaut.—n. cosmonau'tics.—n. cosmopol'itan a citizen of the world: one free from local or national prejudices: a communist sympathetic towards or tolerant of non-communism in other countries.—adj. belonging to all parts of the world: unprejudiced.—n. cosmopol'itanism.—n. and adj. cosmopolite (koz-mop'ə-līt)—cosmical constant a number, at present of the order of 10[78], believed to be fundamental to the structure of the universe; cosmic rays the shortest electro-magnetic waves known, thought to come from interstellar space; cosmological principle according to the cosmology of general re-

lativity, the principle that, at a given time, the universe would look the same to observers in other nebulae as it looks to us [Gr kosmos, order, world, universe.]

Cossack kos'ak, n. one of a people in south-eastern Russia, formerly serving as cavalry—**Cossack hat** a brimless hat of fur or similar material. [Turk quzzāq, freebooter]

cosset kos'it, n. a hand-reared lamb: a pet—v.t. to fondle: to pamper:—pr.p. coss'eting; pa.t and pa.p. coss'eted. [Perh. O E. cot-sæta, cot-setla, cotdweller.]

cost kost, v.t. or v.i to be obtainable at a price of: to involve an expenditure of: to require to be laid out or suffered or lost:—pa.t. and pa.p. cost.—v.t to estimate the cost of production of:—pa.t. and pa.p. costed.—n. what is or would have to be laid out or suffered or lost to obtain anything: (in pl.) expenses of a law-suit.—n. cost'liness.—adj. cost'ly highpriced: valuable.—cost'-account'ant one who analyses and classifies elements of cost, as material, labour, etc., or who devises systems of doing this; cost'-account'ing (v.t. cost'-account').—adj cost'-effec'tive giving adequate return for outlay.—cost'-effec'tiveness, cost efficiency.—adj cost'-free' free of charge.—Also adv.—cost plus a work contract where payment is based on the actual production cost plus an agreed percentage of that cost as profit.—adj. cost'-plus'.—cost price the price the merchant pays for goods bought; cost push (econ.) inflation due to rising production costs—Also cost-push inflation.—at all costs no matter what the cost or consequences may be; cost of living the total cost of goods ordinarily required in order to live up to one's usual standard; cost of living index an official number showing the cost of living at a certain date compared with that at another date taken as a standard; prime cost the price of production, without regard to profit or overhead expenses. [O Fr. couster (Fr. coûter)—L. cōnstāre, to stand at.]

costa kos'tə, n. a rib: a rib-like structure, vein, ridge:—pl. cos'tae (-ē)—adj. cos'tal of or near the ribs or the side of the body.—adjs. cos'tāte, -d having or resembling ribs. [L. costa, a rib.]

co-star kō'stär, n. a cinema, etc star appearing with other stars.—v.i. to appear with other stars:—pr.p. co'-starr'ing; pa.t. and pa.p. co'-starred'.

costard kos'tərd, n. a large kind of apple.—ns. cos'tardmonger, cos'termonger, cos'ter a seller of apples and other fruit: a seller of fruit and other wares from a barrow. [Perh. L costa, a rib.]

costate, -d. See **costa**.

costive kos'tiv, adj. constipated.—adv. cos'tively.—n. cos'tiveness. [Fr. constipé; see **constipate**.]

costmary kost'mār-i, n. a composite of southern Europe, grown in gardens for its fragrant leaves. [L. costum—Gr. kostos, costus, and Maria, the Virgin Mary.]

costume kos'tūm, n. a manner of dressing: dress, garb. a woman's outer dress as a unit: fancy dress: (a piece of) clothing for a particular purpose, as in swimmingcostume.—v.t. (kos-tūm'), to dress.—adj. costumed'.—ns. costum'er, costum'ier one who makes or deals in costumes.—costume drama, piece, play one in which the actors wear the costumes of an earlier era; costume jewellery jewellery worn as an adornment only, without pretence of being genuine gems. [Fr.,—It. costume—L. cōnsuētūdō, -inis, custom.]

Costus kos'təs, n a genus of plants of the ginger family: (without cap.) an aromatic root wrongly assigned to it. [Latinised from Gr. kostos.]

cosy, kō'zi, adj. snug: comfortable.—n. a covering

used for a teapot, to keep the tea warm (also **tea'**= **cosy**): a similar covering for a boiled egg.—*adv.* **cō'sily.**—*n.* **cō'siness.**

cot¹ *kot,* (*poet.*) *n.* a small dwelling, a cottage. [O.E. *cot.*]

cot² *kot, n.* a small bed, esp. one with high sides for a young child: a swinging bed of canvas (for officers, sick, etc.) (*naut.*): a hospital bed —**cot death** the sudden, unexplained death in sleep of an apparently healthy baby.—Also **sudden infant death syndrome.** [Anglo-Ind.,—Hindi *khāt.*]

cot³. See **cotangent.**

cotangent *kō-tan'jənt, n.* the tangent of the complement of an angle—*abbrev.* **cot** (*kot*).—*n.* **coth** (*koth*) for hyperbolic *cotangent.*

cote *kōt, n.* a cot: a place for animals, as *dovecote* or *dovecot, sheep-cote.* [O.E. *cote;* cf. **cot¹**.]

coterie *kō'tə-ri, n.* a social, literary, or other exclusive circle. [Fr ; orig. a number of peasants holding land jointly from a lord—L.L. *cota,* a cot.]

coth. See **cotangent.**

co-tidal *kō-tīd'l, adj.* having high tide at the same time.

cotillion *ko-til'yən,* **cotillon** *ko-tē'yɔ̄, ns.* a sort of country dance. [Fr., petticoat—*cotte,* a coat—L.L. *cotta,* a tunic; see **coat.**]

Cotinga *kō-ting'gə, n.* a tropical American genus of bright plumaged passerine birds: (without *cap.*) any bird of its fam., **Cotingidae** (-*tin'ji-dē*). [Of Tupí origin.]

Cotoneaster *ko-tō-ni-as'tər, n.* a genus of shrubs or small trees akin to hawthorn: (without *cap.*) a plant of this genus. [L. *cotōnea,* quince.]

cotta *kot'ə, n* a surplice. [L.L. *cotta.*]

cottage *kot'ij, n.* a small dwelling-house: a country residence.—*adj.* **cott'aged** covered with cottages.— *n.* **cott'ager** one who dwells in a cottage, esp. of labourers.—**cottage cheese** soft white loose cheese made from skim-milk curds; **cottage hospital** a small, rural hospital without resident doctors: one housed in a cottage or cottages; **cottage industry** one in which the work is done wholly or largely by people in their own homes; **cottage loaf** a loaf consisting of a smaller lump on the top of a bigger one; **cottage piano** a small upright piano; **cottage pie** shepherd's pie. [L.L *cottagium*—O.E. *cot;* see **cot¹**.]

cottar, cotter *kot'ər, n.* one of a class of mediaeval villeins: a peasant occupying a cot or cottage for which he has to give labour (*Scot.*). [**cot¹**.]

cotter *kot'ər, n.* a pin or wedge for fastening and tightening.—*n.* **cott'er-pin** a pin for keeping a cotter in place.

cotton *kot'n, n.* a soft substance like fine wool, the long hairs covering the seeds of the cotton-plant: the plant itself, individually or collectively: yarn or cloth made of cotton.—*adj.* made of cotton.—*v.i* to agree (the connection of the intransitive meaning is unknown)—*adj.* **cott'ony** like cotton: soft: downy.— **cott'on-boll** the pod of the cotton-plant; **cotton cake** cakes or pellets of compressed cotton-seed, used as an animal feed, **cotton candy** (*U.S.*) candy floss; **cott'on-gin** a machine for separating the seeds from the fibre of cotton; **cott'on-mill** a factory where cotton is spun or woven.—*adj.* **cott'on-pick'ing** (*U.S slang;* sometimes *facet.*) used as a relatively mild pejorative.—**cott'on-plant** one of various species of Gossypium yielding cotton; **cott'on-press** a press for compressing cotton into bales; **cott'onseed** the seed of the cotton-plant, yielding a valuable oil, **cott'on-spinner** one who spins cotton, or employs those who do, **cott'ontail** any of several species of rabbits of the genus *Sylvilagus,* the ordinary United States rabbit; **cott'on-waste** refuse from cotton mills, used for cleaning machinery. etc.; **cott'on-wood** any one of

several American species of poplar; **cott'on-wool'** cotton in its raw or woolly state: loose cotton pressed in a sheet as an absorbent or protective agent, for stuffing, etc.—**cotton on to** (*slang*) to take to: to understand. [Fr. *coton*—Ar. *qutun.*]

cotyledon *kot-i-lē'dən, n.* a seed-leaf (*bot.*): (with *cap.*) a genus of S Afr, plants: a plant of this genus.—*adjs.* **cotyle'donary; cotyle'donous** pertaining to or having cotyledons. [Gr. *kotylēdōn—kotylē,* a cup.]

coucal *kōō'kal, n.* any member of a genus (*Centropus*) of common bush-birds in Africa, India and Australia, the lark-heeled cuckoos [Imit]

couch¹ *kowch, v.t.* to lay down: to lower to cause to lie close: to spread: to level: to arrange in language, to express to depress or remove (a cataract in the eye). —*v.i.* to lie down for the purpose of sleep, concealment, etc.: to bend or stoop.—*n.* any place for rest or sleep: a bed: a kind of sofa with half back and one raised end.—*adj.* **couch'ant** couching or lying down: lying down with head up (*her.*).—*n.* **couch'ing** embroidery in which the surface is covered with threads and these are secured by stitches forming a pattern [Fr. *coucher,* to lay down—L. *collocāre,* to place— *col-,* together, *locus,* a place]

couch², **couch-grass** *kowch', kōōch' (gras), ns.* a grass akin to wheat, a troublesome weed owing to its creeping rootstocks. [A variant of **quitch.**]

couchette *kōō-shet', n.* a sleeping-berth on a continental train or a cross-channel boat, convertible from and into ordinary seating. [Fr.]

coudé *kōō-dā', adj.* bent like an elbow: (of a reflecting telescope) in which one or more plane mirrors reflect the light down the polar axis. [Fr.]

cougar *kōō'gär, -gər,* **couguar** *-gwär, ns.* a puma. [Fr. *couguar*—Port. *cucuarana,* adapted from a Tupí-Guaraní name.]

cough *kof, v.t.* to expel air with a sudden opening of the glottis and a characteristic sound.—*v t.* to expel by coughing.—*n.* the act or the sound of coughing: an ailment of which coughing is a symptom.—*ns.* **cough'er; cough'ing.—cough'-drop** a cough-lozenge: a person of spicy character; **cough'-lozenge** a medicated lozenge to allay coughing; **cough'-mixture.—cough up** (*slang*) to pay out, hand over, under compulsion. [M.E. *coughen.*]

could *kōōd, pa.t.* of **can¹**. [M.E *coude, couth*—O.E. *cūthe* for *cunthe,* was able; *l* is inserted from the influence of *would* and *should.*]

coulée *kōō-lā', n.* a lava-flow: a ravine (*U.S.* and *Can.*) [Fr *couler,* to flow]

coulisse *kōō-lēs', n* a piece of grooved wood, as the slides in which the side-scenes of a theatre run— hence (in *pl.*) the wings [Fr. *couler,* to glide, to flow—L *côlāre,* to strain]

couloir *kōōl-war', n.* a gully. [Fr., passage.]

coulomb *kōō-lom', n.* the MKSA and SI unit of electric charge (static or as a current), furnished by one ampere flowing for one second.—*n.* **coulom'eter** a voltameter —Also **coulomb'meter.**—*adj* **coulomet'ric.** [From the French physicist, C. A. de Coulomb (1736–1806)]

coulter, colter *kōl'tər, n.* the iron cutter in front of a ploughshare [O E *culter*—L. *culter,* knife.]

coumarin, cumarin *kōō'mə-rin, n* a crystalline compound ($C_9H_6O_2$) obtained from Tonka beans, woodruff, melilot, etc.—*adjs.* **coumaric** (-*mar'*), **coumaril'ic.** [Tupí *cumarú,* Tonka bean.]

council *kown'sl, -sil, n* an assembly called together for deliberation, advice, administration or legislation: the persons constituting such an assembly. the body directing the affairs of a town, county, parish, etc.: an assembly of ecclesiastics met to regulate doctrine or discipline a governing body in a university a committee that arranges the business of a society.—Also *adj.*—*n.* **coun'cillor,** a member of a council.— **coun'cil-cham'ber** the room where a council is held; **council estate** an area set apart for council-houses; **coun'cil-house'** a house in which a council meets: a house erected by a municipal council.—**Council of Ministers** in the EEC, the decision-making body comprising ministers of the member countries; **council of war** a conference of officers called to consult with the commander (also *fig.*); **in council** in the council-chamber: in consultation; **legislative council** a council to assist a governor, with power to make laws. [Fr. *concile*—L. *concilium*.]

counsel *kown'sl, n.* consultation: deliberation: advice: plan: purpose: one who gives counsel, a barrister or advocate.—*v.t.* to advise: to warn:—*pr.p.* **coun'selling;** *pa.t.* and *pa.p.* **coun'selled.**—*adj.* **couns'ellable** that may be counselled.—*n.* **coun'selling** (a service consisting of) giving advice on miscellaneous problems to, e.g. citizens, children in a school.—Also *adj.* —*ns.* **coun'sellor** one who counsels: a barrister; **coun'sellorship.**—**counsel of perfection** a commendation of something beyond the binding minimum, something not absolutely imperative, but commended as the means of reaching greater 'perfection'; **keep counsel** to keep a secret; **King's, Queen's Counsel** (K.C., Q.C.) a barrister or advocate appointed by letters-patent—the office is honorary, but gives the right of precedence in all the courts. [Fr. *conseil*—L. *consilium,* advice—*consulĕre,* to consult.]

count¹ *kownt, n.* on the Continent, a noble equal in rank to an earl.—*n.* **count'ess** a lady of the same rank as a count or earl: the wife of a count or earl.—*ns.* **count'ship** a count's dignity or domain (also used as a title); **coun'ty** a portion of a country separated for administrative, parliamentary or other purposes, a shire.—*adj.* of a, or the, county: of county family.— **county council** a council for managing the public affairs of a county; **county councillor; county court** the highest court of law within a county; **county cricket** cricket played in matches between clubs representing counties; **county family** a family of nobility or gentry (**coun'ty-people**) with estates and a seat in the county; **county town** the town in which the public business of the county is transacted. [O.Fr. *conte*—L. *comes, comitis,* a companion, *con-,* with, *ire,* to go.]

count², *kownt, v.t.* to number, sum up: to name the numerals up to: to take into account, reckon as significant or to be recognised: to ascribe: to reckon, esteem, consider.—*v.i.* to number: to be numbered: to be of account: to be recognised in reckoning: to have a certain value: to reckon: to name the numerals in order.—*n.* the act of numbering: reckoning: the number counted: the counting of the seconds in which a fallen man may rise and resume (also **count'-out**) (*boxing*): esteem, consideration, account: a particular charge in an indictment.—*adj.* specifying a noun which, since it denotes an entity of which there can be one or more than one, is able to form a plural. —*adjs.* **count'able** capable of being counted: to be counted: accountable: of a noun, count; **count'ed** accounted, reckoned.—*n.* **count'er** he who or that which counts: that which indicates a number: a disc or the like, used in reckoning or, in games, as a substitute for a coin or a marker of one's position on a board: a table on which money is counted or goods laid.—*adj.* **count'less** that cannot be counted: innumerable.—**count'-down** a descending count or counted check to a moment of happening regarded as zero, as in the firing of a rocket; **count'ing-house, count'ing-room** a room in which a merchant keeps his

accounts and transacts business; **count-out see count** above.—**count out** of a meeting (esp. of the House of Commons), to bring to an end by pointing out that a quorum is not present: in children's games, to eliminate players by counting while repeating a rhyme (**counting-out rhyme**): in boxing, etc., to adjudge defeated by counting seconds; **keep count** to keep an accurate numerical record (of); **lose count** to fail to keep count (of); **out for the count** (*fig.*) unconscious, or completely exhausted; **under the counter** hidden from customers' sight (*adj.* **un'der-the-count'er** reserved for the favoured: secret, furtive). [O.Fr. *cunter* (Fr. *compter*)—L. *computāre.*]

countenance *kown'tən-əns, n.* the face: the expression of the face: appearance: demeanour shown towards a person: favour: approbation: acquiescence.—*v.t.* to favour or approve. [O.Fr. *contenance*—L. *continentia,* restraint, demeanour—*continēre,* to contain.]

counter¹ *kown'tər, adv.* the opposite way: in opposition.—*adj.* contrary: opposing: opposite.—*n.* that which is counter or opposite: the part of a horse's breast between the shoulders and under the neck: the part of a ship's stern from the lower moulding to the water-line (*naut.*).—*v.t.* to encounter: to contradict: to meet or answer by a stroke or move: to strike while receiving or parrying a blow (*boxing*).—**run counter to** to move in the opposite direction (to): to act, happen, in a way contrary (to instructions, expectations, etc.). [Partly aphetic for **encounter,** partly directly from A.Fr. *countre,* O.Fr. (Fr.) *contre*—L. *contrā,* against.]

counter². See **count².**

counter- *kown'tər-,* in composition, against.—*v.t.* **counteract'** to act counter or in opposition to: to hinder or defeat: to neutralise.—**counterac'tion.**— *adj.* **counteract'ive** tending to counteract.—*n.* one who or that which counteracts.—*adv.* **counteract'ively.**—**coun'ter-attack** an attack in reply to an attack.—Also *v.t.* and *v.i.*—**coun'ter-attrac'tion** attraction in an opposite direction: a rival show.—*v.t.* **counterbal'ance** to balance by weight on the opposite side: to act against with equal weight, power, or influence.—**coun'terbalance** an equal weight, power, or agency working in opposition; **coun'terblast** a defiant pronouncement or denunciation; **coun'terblow** a return blow; **coun'tercharge** a charge brought forward in opposition to another charge.—*v.t.* **countercheck'** to check by some obstacle: to rebuke. —**coun'tercheck** a check in opposition to another: a rebuke; **coun'ter-claim** (esp. *law*) a claim brought forward as a partial or complete set-off against another claim.—*adv.* **coun'ter-clock'wise** in a direction contrary to that of the hands of a clock.— **coun'ter-current** a current flowing in an opposite direction; **coun'ter-esp'ionage** spying in opposition, espionage directed against the enemy's spy system; **coun'terfoil** the corresponding part of a bank cheque, postal order, ticket, etc., retained by the giver (see **foil²**); **coun'ter-force** an opposing force; **coun'ter-in'fluence** an opposing influence; **coun'ter-intell'igence** activities, as censorship, camouflage, use of codes, etc., aimed at preventing an enemy from obtaining information, or the organisation that carries these out; **coun'ter-irr'itant** an irritant used to relieve another irritation.—*v.i.* **coun'termarch** to march back or in a direction contrary to a former one. —*n.* a marching back or in a direction different from a former one.—**coun'termeasure** an action intended to counteract the effect of another action or happening; **coun'ter-move, -move'ment** a contrary move, movement; **coun'ter-offen'sive** counter-attack: an attack by the defenders; **coun'terpart** the part that answers to another part: that which fits into or completes another, having the qualities which another lacks, and so an opposite: a duplicate: a double.—*v.t.* **coun'ter-plot'** to plot against in order to frustrate another plot.—*n.* a plot or stratagem opposed to another plot.—*v.t.* **coun'terpoise** to poise or weigh against or on the opposite side: to act in opposition to with equal effect.—*n.* an equally heavy weight in the other scale.—*adj.* **coun'ter-produc'tive** acting against productivity, efficiency, or usefulness. —**coun'ter-proposal** one which proposes an alternative to a proposal already made; **Coun'ter-Reform-a'tion** (*hist.*) a reform movement within the Roman Catholic Church, following and counteracting the Reformation; **coun'ter-revolu'tion** a subsequent revolution counteracting the effect of a previous.—*n.* and *adj.* **coun'ter-revolu'tionary** (a person) opposing a particular revolution or opposed to revolutions.— **coun'terscarp** (*fort.*) the side of the ditch nearest to the besiegers and opposite to the scarp; **coun'tershaft** an intermediate shaft driven by the main shaft.—*v.t.* **countersign'** to sign on the opposite side of a writing: to sign in addition to the signature of a superior, to attest the authenticity of a writing.—*n.* (*kownt'*) a military private sign or word, which must be given in order to pass a sentry.—**coun'ter-sig'nature** a name countersigned to a writing.—*v.t.* **coun'tersink** to bevel the edge of (a hole), as for the head of a screwnail: to set the head or top of on a level with, or below, the surface of the surrounding material.— **coun'ter-ten'or** the highest alto male voice (so called because a contrast to tenor).—*v.t.* **countervail'** to be of avail against: to act against with equal effect: to be of equal value to: to compensate.—**coun'ter-weight** weight in an opposite scale: a counterbalancing influence or force. [A.Fr. *countre*, O.Fr. *contre*— L. *contrā*, against.]

counterfeit *kown'tər-fit*, *-fēt*, *v.t.* to imitate: to copy without authority: to forge.—*n.* something false or copied, or that pretends to be true and original.—*adj.* pretended: made in imitation: forged: false.—*n.* **coun'terfeiter** one who counterfeits.—*adv.* **coun'terfeitly** in a counterfeit manner: falsely. [O.Fr. *contrefet*, from *contrefaire*, to imitate—L. *contrā*, against, *facĕre*, to do.]

countermand *kown-tər-mānd'*, *v.t.* to give a command in opposition to one already given: to revoke.—*n.* (*kownt'*) a revocation to a former order.—*adj.* **countermand'able**. [O.Fr. *contremander*—L. *contrā*, against, and *mandāre*, to order.]

counterpane *kown'tər-pān*, *n.* a coverlet for a bed. [O.Fr. *contrepoint*—*coultepointe*—L. *culcita puncta*, a stitched pillow; see **quilt**.]

counterpoint *kown'tər-point*, *n.* the art of combining melodies (*mus.*): a melody added to another (*mus.*): an opposite point.—*adj.* **contrapunt'al**.—*n.* **contrapunt'ist** a composer skilled in counterpoint. [Fr. *contrepoint* and It. *contrappunto*—L. *contrā*, against, *punctum*, a point, from the pricks, points or notes placed against those of the melody; in some senses **counter-** and **point**.]

country *kun'tri*, *n.* a region: a state: a nation: rural districts as distinct from town: the land of one's birth or citizenship.—*adj.* belonging to the country: rural: rustic: rude.—*adj.* **coun'trified**, **coun'tryfied** like or suitable for the country in style: like a person from the country in style or manner.—*n.* **coun'tryside** a district or part of the country: rural districts in general.—*adj.* **countrywide'** all over the country.— **coun'try-and-west'ern** a popularised form of music deriving from the rural folk-music of the United States.—Also *adj* —**country** cousin a relative from the country, unaccustomed to town sights or man-

ners; **coun'try-dance'** a dance as practised by country people: a type of dance in which either an indefinite number of couples in a circle or two lines, or groups of fixed numbers of couples in two lines, can take part, tracing a precise and sometimes complex pattern of movements; **coun'try-dan'cing; coun'try-folk** fellow-countrymen: rural people; **country gentleman** a landed proprietor who resides on his estate in the country; **coun'try-house'**, **-seat'** the residence of a country gentleman; **coun'tryman** one who lives in the country: a farmer: one belonging to the same country, fellow-countryman; **country music** the folk-music of the rural areas of the United States: country-and-western music: both of these taken together. **country town** a small town in a rural district; **coun'trywoman** a woman who dwells in the country: a woman of the same country.—**go to the country** to appeal to the community by a general election. [O.Fr. *contrée*—L.L. *contrāta*, *contrāda*, an extension of L. *contrā*, over against.]

county. See **count**[1].

coup *kōō*, *n.* a blow, stroke: a clever and successful stroke in a board or card game: a masterstroke, clever and successful stratagem (*fig.*): a coup d'état.—**coup d'essai** (*de-sā*) an experimental work: a first attempt; **coup de foudre** (*də fōō-dr'*) a sudden and astonishing happening: love at first sight; **coup de grâce** (*də grās*) a finishing blow to put out of pain: a finishing stroke generally; **coup de main** (*də mē*) a sudden overpowering attack; **coup d'état** (*dā-tä*) a violent or subversive stroke of state policy; **coup de théâtre** (*də tä-atr'*) a sudden and sensational turn as in a play; **coup d'oeil** (*dœy*) a general view at a glance. [Fr.— L.L. *colpus*—L. *colaphus*—Gr. *kolaphos*, a blow.]

coupe[1] *kōō p*, (Fr.). *n.* a dessert, usu. made with ice-cream and often fruit, served in a glass bowl: a glass container for serving such a dessert, usu. with a shallow bowl and a short stem.

coupe[2] *kōō p*, (U.S.). n. a coupé (motor-car).

coupé *kōō-pā'*, *n.* a four-wheeled carriage seated for two inside, with a separate seat for the driver: a two-door motor-car with a roof sloping towards the back. [Fr., pa.p. of *couper*, to cut.]

couple *kup'l*, *n.* that which joins two things together: two of a kind joined together, or connected: two: a pair: a pair of equal forces acting on the same body in opposite and parallel directions (*statics*).—*v.t.* to join together.—*v.i.* to pair sexually.—*ns.* **coup'lement** union: a couple; **coup'ler** one who or that which couples or unites: an organ mechanism by which stops of one manual can be played from another or from the pedals; **coup'let** a pair, couple: a twin: two successive lines of verse that rhyme with each other; **coup'ling** that which connects: an appliance for transmitting motion in machinery, or for connecting vehicles as in a railway train.—**a couple of** (loosely) two or three: a few. [O.Fr. *cople*—L. *cōpula*.]

coupon *kōō'pon*, *-pən*, *-pō*, *-pong*, *n.* a billet, check, or other slip of paper cut off from its counterpart: a separate ticket or part of a ticket: a voucher that payments will be made, services performed, goods sold, or the like: a piece cut from an advertisement entitling one to some privilege: a printed betting form on which to enter forecasts of sports results. [Fr. *couper*, to cut off.]

courage *kur'ij*, *n.* the quality that enables people to meet danger without giving way to fear: bravery: spirit.—*interj.* take courage.—*adjs.* **cour'ageful**; **courageous** (*kə-rā'jəs*) full of courage: brave.— *adv.* **courageously.**—*n.* **coura'geousness.**—**Dutch courage** a factitious courage induced by drinking; **pluck up courage**, **take one's courage in both hands** to nerve oneself: to gather boldness; **the courage of one's**

convictions courage to act up to, or consistently with, one's opinions. [O Fr. *corage* (Fr. *courage*), from L. *cor*, the heart.]

courant *kōō-rant'*, (*her.*) *adj.* in a running attitude.— *ns.* **courante, courant** (*kōō-rant'*) an old dance with a kind of gliding step: music for it. [Fr., pr.p. of *co-urir*, to run; see **current.**]

courgette *kōōr'zhet, n.* a small marrow. [Fr. *courge*, gourd.]

courier *kōō'ri-ər, n.* a runner: a messenger: a state messenger: an official guide who travels with tourists: a frequent title of newspapers. [Fr.,—L. *currēre*, to run.]

course *kōrs, kors, n.* a run (*arch*): the path in which anything moves: the ground over which a race is run, golf is played, or the like: a channel for water: the direction pursued: a voyage: a race: regular progress from point to point: a habitual method of procedure: a prescribed series, sequence, process, or treatment, as of lectures, training, pills, etc.: each of the successive divisions of a meal—soup, fish, etc : conduct: a range of bricks or stones on the same level in building. —*v.t.* to run, chase, or hunt after: to use in coursing —*v.i.* to run: to move with speed, as in a race or hunt. —*ns* **coers'er** a runner: a swift horse: one who courses or hunts: a swift running bird; **cours'ing** hunting of esp. hares with greyhounds, by sight rather than by scent.—**in course** in regular order; **in due course** eventually: at a suitable later time; **in the course of** during: in the process of: undergoing (something); **in the course of time** eventually: with the passing of time; **of course** by natural consequence: indisputably (often a mere apology for making a statement): it must be remembered (often used to introduce a comment on a preceding statement); **run or take its or their course** to proceed or develop freely and naturally, usu. to a point of completion or cessation. [Fr. *cours*—L. *cursus*, from *currēre. cursum*, to run.]

court *kōrt, kort, n.* space enclosed: space surrounded by houses: a piece of ground or floor on which certain games are played: a division marked off by lines on such a place: the palace of a sovereign: the body of persons who form his suite or council: an assembly of courtiers: a hall of justice (*law*): the judges and officials who preside there: any body of persons assembled to decide causes: a sitting of such a body.— *v.t.* to pay attentions to: to woo: to solicit: to seek.— *ns.* **court'ler** one who frequents courts or palaces: one who courts or flatters; **court'ing** paying addresses, wooing: **court'liness.**—*adj.* **court'ly** having manners like those of, or befitting, a court: politely stately: fair and flattering.—*n.* **court'ship** courtly behaviour: wooing.—**court'-card** see **coat-card;** **court'-day** a day on which a judicial court sits; **court'-dress** the special regulation costume worn on state or ceremonious occasions; **court'-house** a building where the law-courts are held; **courtly love** a conception and tradition of love, originating in late mediaeval European literature, in which the knight sublimates his love for his lady in submission, service, and devotion; **court'-mar'tial** a court held by officers of the army, navy or air force for the trial of offences against service laws (one improvised in time of war round an upturned drum for summary judgment was a **drumhead court-martial**):—*pl.* **courts'-mar'tial**, (*coll.*) **court'-mar'tials.**—*v.t.* to try before a court-martial:—*pr.p.* **court'-mar'tialling**; *pa.t.* and *pa.p.* **court'-mar'tialled.**—**court order** a direction or command of a justiciary court —**court'-plas'ter** sticking-plaster made of silk, originally applied as patches on the face by ladies at court; **court'room** a room in a court-house in which lawsuits and criminal cases are heard; **court**

shoe a light high-heeled dress shoe; **court'yard** a court or enclosed ground attached to a house.—**go to court** to institute legal proceedings against someone; **hold court** to preside over admiring followers, etc.; **out of court** without a trial in a law-court. [O.Fr. *cort* (Fr *cour*)—L.L. *cortis*, a courtyard—L. *cors, cohors, -tis*, an enclosure.]

court bouillon *kōōrbōō -yō', a* seasoned stock made with water, vegetables and wine or vinegar, in which fish is boiled. [Fr. *court*, short—L. *curtus*; and **bouillon.**]

Courtelle® *kōōr-tel', n* a synthetic acrylic wool-like fibre.

courteous *kûrt'yəs, kort'yəs, adj.* polite, considerate or respectful in manner and action: obliging.—*adv.* **court'eously.**—*ns.* **court'eousness; courtesy** (*kûrt', or kört'ə-si*) courteous behaviour: an act of civility or respect.—**courtesy light** a small light in a motor vehicle usu. operated by the opening and closing of the doors; **courtesy title** a title really invalid, but allowed by the usage of society—as to children of peers. [Ó.Fr. *corteis, cortois*; see **court.**]

courtesan, -zan *kört', kûrt'i-zan,* or *-zan', n.* a court mistress: a whore. [Fr. *courtisane*—It. *cortigiana,* orig a woman of the court.]

couscous, kouskous *kōōs'kōōs, n.* granulated wheat flour: a N. African dish of steamed couscous with meat, vegetables, etc. [Fr ,—Ar. *kuskus—kaskasa,* to pound.]

cousin *kuz'n, n.* formerly a kinsman generally: now, the son or daughter of an uncle or aunt: a term used by a sovereign in addressing another, or to one of his own nobles: a person belonging to a group related by common ancestry, interests, etc.: something kindred or related to another.—*ns.* **cousinage; cous'inhood; cous'inship.**—*adj.* **cous'inly** like, or having the relation of, a cousin.—*n.* **cous'inry** cousins collectively. —**cous'in-ger'man** a first cousin: something closely related.—**cross'-cous'in** the son or daughter of one's father's sister or mother's brother; **first cousin** the child of one's aunt or uncle, a full cousin; **first cousin once removed** the son or daughter of a cousin-german —sometimes loosely called *second cousin*, **forty-second cousin** vaguely, a distant relative; **second cousin** the child of one's parent's first cousin: (*loosely*) a first cousin once removed. [Fr.,—L. *consōbrīnus—con-*, sig. connection, and *sobrīnus,* applied to the children of sisters from the root of *soror,* a sister.]

couture *kōō-tür, n.* dressmaking or dress designing.— *n.* **couturier** (*kōō-tür'yä* fem. **couturière** (*-yer'*) a dressmaker or dress designer. [Fr.]

couvade *kōō-väd', n.* a custom among primitive peoples in many parts of the world for the father to take to his bed at the birth of a child, and submit to certain restrictions of food, etc.

covalency *kō-vā'lən-si, n.* the union of two atoms by the sharing of a pair of electrons, one from each atom —cf. **electrovalency.**—*adj.* **cova'lent.** [L. *co-*, together, and **valency.**]

cove¹ *kōv, n.* a small inlet of the sea: a bay: a cavern or rocky recess: the moulding covering the junction of wall and ceiling (also **cō'ving**).—*v.t.* to overarch. [O E. *cofa,* a room.]

cove² *kōv,* (*slang*) *n* a fellow, a customer

coven *kuv'in,* or *-ən, n.* a gathering of witches: a gang of thirteen witches. [See **covin.**]

covenant *kuv'ə-nənt, n.* a mutual agreement: the writing containing the agreement: an engagement entered into between God and a person or a people— a dispensation, testament.—*v.t* to enter into an agreement.—*v.t.* to agree to: to stipulate.—*adj.* **cov'-enanted** agreed to by covenant: bound by covenant. holding a position under a covenant or contract —*ns*

covenantee' the person to whom a covenant is made; **cov'enanter** (usually in Scotland *kuv-ə-nant'ər*) one who signed or adhered to the *Scottish National Covenant* of 1638 (the *Solemn League and Covenant* of 1643 was in effect an international treaty between Scotland and England for securing civil and religious liberty); **cov'enantor** that party to a covenant who subjects himself to the penalty of its breach.—**covenant of grace, redemption** in Christian theology, that by which life is freely offered to sinners on condition of faith in Christ. [O.Fr.,—L. *con-*, together, and *venīre*, to come.]

Coventry *kov'*, *kuv'ənt-ri*, *n.* a city in the West Midlands of England.—**send to Coventry** to exclude from social intercourse.

cover *kuv'ər*, *v.t.* to put or spread something on, over or about: to come or be on, over or about: to hide: to clothe: to protect: to screen: to brood or sit on: to suffice for: to provide for or against: to comprise: to traverse: to take as field of operations: to play a higher card upon: to table upon a coin of equal value in wagering: to set as for a meal: to copulate with—esp. of a stallion: to command with a weapon: to report.—*v.i.* to put one's hat on.—*n.* that which covers or is intended to cover: a bedcover: a lid: the binding of a book: an envelope: an envelope with a stamp and postmark, as *first-day cover*: undergrowth, thicket, concealing game, etc.: a pretext: a disguise: an apparently genuine identity, job, etc. used as a front, esp. by spies: a confederate: a cover version: a cover point.—*adj.* intended to conceal the true nature or identity of a person, organisation, etc.—Also in composition.—*n.* **cov'erage** the area or (*fig.*) amount covered or included: the group or section of the community reached by an advertising medium: the protection provided by an insurance: the amount available to cover liabilities: the (extent of) reporting of a topic, event, etc. on television, in the press, etc. —*adj.* **cov'ered** having a cover: sheltered, concealed: roofed over: with a hat on.—*n.* **cov'ering** anything that covers.—*adj.* **cov'ert** covered: concealed: secret. —*n.* a feather covering the quill-bases of wings and tail: (usu. pron. *kuv'ər*) a cover for game: a shelter.— *adv.* **cov'ertly** in a covered or concealed manner.—*n.* **cov'erture** covering, shelter: disguise.—**cov'erall** a boiler suit (*U.S.*; *often in pl.*): a one-piece garment for babies, covering arms, legs and body.—*adj.* **covering** or including everything.—**cover charge** a charge per person made by a restaurant, in addition to charge for food; **cover drive** (*cricket*) a drive past cover point; **covered wagon** a large wagon with bonnet-shaped canvas hood, esp. that used by pioneers to the American West; **cover girl** a girl pictured on a magazine cover; **covering letter** a letter to explain documents enclosed with it; **cover note** (*insurance*) a note certifying that the holder has a current insurance policy: a note issued to an insured person certifying that he has insurance coverage while his policy is being prepared; **cover point** in cricket, etc., the player who supports point and stands to his right: the position of such a player; **cov'erslip** a loose cover for a duvet; **cover version** a recording of a song, etc. which has been recorded by someone else, usu. very similar to the original.—**cover for** to act in the place of (one who is absent, etc.); **cover in** to fill in: to complete the covering of, esp. of roof of building; **cover up** to cover completely: to conceal, withhold information (*coll.*; *n.* **cov'er-up**). [Fr. *couvrir* (L. *coprīre*)—L. *cooperīre*—*co-*, and *operīre*, to cover.] **coverlet** *kuv'ər-lit*, *n.* a bedcover.—Also **cov'erlid**. [Fr. *couvrir*, to cover, *lit* (L. *lectum*), a bed.] **covert, covertly, coverture.** See cover.

covet *kuv'it*, *v.t.* to desire or wish for eagerly: to wish for wrongfully:—*pr.p.* **cov'eting**; *pa.t.* and *pa.p.* **cov'eted.**—*adjs.* **cov'etable**; **cov'eted.**—*adv.* **cov'etingly.** —*adj.* **cov'etous** inordinately desirous: avaricious — *adv.* **cov'etously.**—*n.* **cov'etousness.** [O.Fr. *coveit(i)er* (Fr. *convoiter*)—L. *cupiditās*, *-ātis*—*cupěre*, to desire.]

covey *kuv'i*, *n.* a brood or hatch of partridges: a small flock of game birds: a party, a set. [O.Fr. *covée*—L. *cubāre*, to lie down.]

covin *kŏv'in*, *kuv'in*, *n.* a conspiracy: a coven. [O.Fr. *covin*—L.L. *convenium*—*con-*, together, *venīre*, to come.]

coving *kō'ving*, *n.* See cove¹.

cow¹ *kow*, *n.* the female of the bovine animals: the female of certain other animals, as the elk, elephant, whale, etc.: an ugly, ungainly, slovenly, or objectionable woman (*vulg.*).—**cow'bell** a bell for a cow's neck; **cow'berry** the red whortleberry; **cow'bird, cow blackbird** an American bird that accompanies cattle, and drops its eggs into other birds' nests; **cow'boy** a boy who has the care of cows: a man who has the charge of cattle on a ranch (*U.S.*): any rather rough male character in stories, etc. of the old American West, such as a gun-fighter or a man involved in fighting Indians: a rodeo performer (*U.S.*): a young inexperienced lorry-driver, or anyone who drives an unsafe or overloaded lorry (*slang*): a person who behaves wildly or irresponsibly (*slang*): a derogatory term for an often inadequately qualified person providing inferior services (*coll.*).—Also *adj.*—**cow'-calf** a female calf; **cow'catcher** (*U.S.*) an apparatus on the front of a railway engine to throw off obstacles; **cow'-cher'vil, -pars'ley, -weed** wild chervil; **cow'-dung; cow'girl** a young woman who dresses like and does the work of a cowboy; **cow'grass** perennial red clover: zigzag clover; **cow'hand** a cowboy (*U.S.*); **cow'heel** an oxfoot stewed to a jelly; **cow'herd** one who herds cows; **cow'hide** the hide of a cow: the hide of a cow made into leather: a coarse whip made of twisted strips of cowhide.—*v.t.* to whip with a cowhide.— **cow'house** a building in which cows are stalled, a byre; **cow'lick** a tuft of turned-up hair on the forehead; **cow'man** one who tends cows: one who owns a cattle ranch (*U.S.*); **cow-parsley** see cow-chervil; **cow'-pars'nip** an umbelliferous plant, hogweed used as fodder; **cow'pat** a roundish lump of cow-dung; **cow'poke** (*U.S. coll.*) a cowboy; **cow'pox** a disease that appears in pimples on the teats of the cow, the matter thereof used for vaccination; **cow'puncher** (*U.S. coll.*) a cowboy: a driver of cows; **cow'shed** a cowhouse; **cow-weed** see cow-chervil.—**till the cows come home** for a long time of unforeseeable duration. [O.E. *cū*.]

cow² *kow*, *v.t.* to subdue the spirit of: to keep under.— *adj.* **cowed** abjectly depressed or intimidated. [Perh. from O.N. *kūga*; Dan. *kue*, to subdue.]

coward *kow'ərd*, *n.* a reprehensibly faint-hearted person: one without courage: often applied to one who, whether courageous or not, brutally takes advantage of the weak.—*ns.* **cow'ardice** (*-is*) want of courage: timidity; **cow'ardliness.**—*adj.* **cow'ardly** having the character of a coward: befitting a coward: characteristic of a coward.—*adv.* like a coward: with cowardice. [O.Fr. *couard* (It. *codardo*)—L. *cauda*, a tail.]

cower *kow'ər*, *v.i.* to sink down through fear, etc.: to crouch shrinkingly.—*adv.* **cow'eringly.** [Cf. O.N. *kūra*, Dan. *kure*, to lie quiet.]

cowhage, cowage, cowitch *kow'ij*, *-ich*, *ns.* a tropical leguminous climber: the stinging hairs on its pod, used as a vermifuge: its pods. [Hindi *kavāc*.]

cowl *kowl*, *n.* a cap or hood: a monk's hood: the badge of monkhood: a monk: a cover for a chimney: an engine bonnet: a cowling.—*v.t.*,to make a monk of: to cover like a cowl.—*adj.* **cowled** wearing a cowl.—*n.* **cowl'ing** the casing of an aeroplane engine. [O.E. *cugele*; akin to L. *cucullus*, hood.]

co-worker *kō-wûr'kər, n.* an associate: one who works (on a project, etc.) with another. [**co-**.]

cowrie, cowry *kow'ri, n.* a mollusc of a large genus (Cypraea) of gasteropods the shells of which are used in certain primitive societies as money and magical objects: a shell of the mollusc. [Hindi *kaurī*.]

cowslip *kow'slip,—n.* a species of primrose, with flowers in umbels, common in pastures. [O.E. *cūslyppe—cū*, cow, *slyppe*, slime, i.e. cow-dung.]

cox *koks.* A shortened form of **coxswain.**

coxa *koks'ə, n.* the hip: the proximal joint of an arthropod's leg:—*pl.* **cox'ae** (-*ē*).—*adj* **cox'al.**—*n.* **coxal'gia** (*ji-ə*) pain in the hip. [L.]

coxcomb *koks'kōm, n.* a strip of red cloth notched like a cock's comb, which professional fools used to wear: a fool: a fop.—*adjs.* **coxcombic** (-*kōm'*, -*kom'*), **-al**, **coxcom'ical** foppish: vain.—*n.* **coxcombical'ity.**—*adv.* **coxcomb'ically.**—*n.* **cox'combry** the manner of a coxcomb. [**cock's comb.**]

coxiness. See **cock[1].**

coxswain, cockswain *kok'sn,* or *kok'swān, n.* one who steers a boat: a petty officer in charge of a boat and crew.—*v.t.* and *v.t.* to act as coxswain (for).—Often contr. **cox.** [**cock,** a boat, and **swain.**]

coxy. See **cock[1].**

coy *koi, adj.* bashful: affectedly shy.—*adj.* **coy'ish.**—*adv.* **coy'ishly.**—*n.* **coy'ishness.**—*adv.* **coy'ly.**—*n.* **coy'ness.** [Fr. *coi*—L. *quiētus,* quiet.]

coyote *kot'ōt, koi-ōt'(i), kī-ōt'i, kī'ōt, n.* a prairie-wolf, a small wolf of N. America:—*pl.* **coyo'tes** or **coyo'te.** [Mex. *coyotl.*]

coypu *koi'pōō,* or *-pōō',* or *-pū, n.* a large South American aquatic rodent yielding nutria fur. [Native name.]

cozen *kuz'n, v.t.* to cheat.—*ns.* **coz'enage** deceit; **coz'ener.** [Perh. Fr. *cousiner,* to claim kindred; see **cousin.**]

crab[1] *krab, n.* any of the Brachyura or short-tailed decapod crustaceans: Cancer (sign of the zodiac and constellation): a portable winch: a crab-louse.—*v.i.* to fish for crabs.—*adjs.* and *advs.* **crab'like; crab'wise.—crab'-louse** a crab-shaped louse infesting the hair of the pubis, etc.; **Crab Nebula** the expanding cloud of gas in the constellation of Taurus, being the remains of a supernova observed in 1054 AD; **crab's yaws** framboesia tumours on the soles and palms.—**catch a crab** to sink the oar too deeply (or not enough) in the water and fall back in consequence. [O.E. *crabba.*]

crab[2] *krab, n.* a wild bitter apple: a sour-tempered person.—*ns.* **crab'-apple; crab'stick; crab'-tree.**

crabbed *krab'id, adj.* ill-natured: harsh: undecipherable: cramped.—*adv.* **crabb'edly.**—*n.* **crabb'edness.** —*adj.* **crabb'y.** [**crab[1]** intermixed in meaning with **crab[2].**]

crab-nut, -oil, -wood. See **Carapa.**

crack *krak, v.t.* and *v.i.* to make or cause to make a sharp sudden sound: to split: to break partially or suddenly: to fracture, the parts remaining in contact: to (cause to) give way under strain, torture, etc.: (of the voice) to change tone or register suddenly: (of petroleum, etc.) to break into simpler molecules.—*v.t.* to break open (a safe, etc.): to solve the mystery of (a code, etc.).—*n.* a sudden sharp splitting sound: a partial fracture: a flaw: a blow: break (of day): an expert: a quip, gibe: a try (*slang*).—*adj.* (*coll.*) excellent: expert.—*adj.* **cracked** rent: damaged: crazy.—*n.* **crack'er** one who or that which cracks: a

thin crisp biscuit: a colourful tubular package that comes apart with a bang, when the ends are pulled, to reveal a small gift, motto, etc.: a small, noisy firework: the apparatus used in cracking petroleum: something exceptionally good or fine of its type (*coll.*).—*adjs.* **crack'ers** crazy: unbalanced; **crack'ing** (*coll.*) of speed, etc., very fast: very good.—**crack'er-jack** a person or thing of highest excellence.—Also *adj.*—*adj.* **crack'jaw** hard to pronounce.—**crack'pot** a crazy person.—Also *adj.*—**crack a bottle, can,** etc. to open or drink a bottle, can, etc.; **crack a joke** to utter a joke with some effect; **crack down on** to take firm action against (*n.* **crack'down**); **crack the whip** to assert authority suddenly or forcibly; **crack up** to praise: to fail suddenly, to go to pieces; **fair crack of the whip** a fair opportunity; **get cracking** to get moving quickly. [O.E. *cracian,* to crack.]

crackle *krak'l, v.i.* to give out slight but frequent cracks.—*n.* the giving out of slight cracks: a kind of china-ware, purposely cracked in the kiln as an ornament.—*n.* **crack'ling** the rind of roast pork.—*adj.* **crack'ly** brittle.—*n.* **crack'nel** a light, brittle biscuit: (in *pl.*) pieces of fat pork fried crisp. [Freq. of **crack.**]

-cracy *-krə-si, suffix* used to indicate rule, government (by a particular group, etc.) as in *democracy, mobocracy.*—*suffix* **-crat** (-*krat*) person supporting, or partaking in, government (by a particular group, etc.).—*adj.* suffixes **-cratic, -cratical.** [Gr. *-kratia,* from *kratos,* power.]

cradle *krā'dl, n.* a bed or crib in which a child is rocked: infancy (*fig.*): one's place of origin or nurture: a stand, rest or holder for supporting something: a suspended platform or trolley which can be raised and lowered and from which work can be carried out on the side of a ship, building, etc.: a framework, esp. one for keeping bedclothes from pressing on a patient, or one under a ship for launching: a rocking box for gold-washing.—*v.t.* to lay or rock in a cradle: to nurture.—*n.* **cra'dling** (*archit.*) a wooden or iron framework within a ceiling.—**from the cradle to the grave** throughout one's life. [O.E. *cradol.*]

craft *kräft, n.* cunning: dexterity: art: skilled trade: occupation: a ship or ships: aircraft, spacecraft.—*v.t.* to make or construct, esp. with careful skill.—*adv.* **craft'ily.**—*n.* **craft'iness.**—*adjs.* **craft'less** free from craft: unskilled in any craft; **craf'ty** cunning: wily.—**craft'-broth'er** a person engaged in the same trade as another; **craft'-guild** an association of people engaged in the same trade; **craft shop** a shop in which materials and tools for creative activities such as embroidery, basketry, model-making, etc. are sold; **crafts'man** one engaged in a craft; **crafts'manship.** [O.E. *cræft.*]

crag[1] *krag, n.* a rough steep rock or point, a cliff.—*adj.* **cragg'ed** craggy.—*ns.* **cragg'edness, cragg'iness.**—*adj.* **cragg'y** full of crags or broken rocks: rough: rugged.—**crag'-and-tail'** (*geol.*) a hill-form with steep declivity at one end and a gentle slope at the other.—**crags'man** one skilled in rock-climbing. [App. conn. with Gael. *creag, carraig.*]

crag[2] *krag, n.* neck: throat. [Cf. Du. *kraag,* Ger. *Kragen,* the neck.]

crake *krāk,* (*dial.*) *n.* a crow, raven: corncrake: the cry of the corncrake. [Cf. **corncrake, croak.**]

cram *kram, v.t.* to press close: to stuff: to fill to superfluity: to overfeed: to feed with a view to fattening: to teach, or prepare, hastily for a certain occasion (as an examination, a lawsuit), to the extent required for the occasion.—*v.t.* to eat greedily: to prepare for an examination, etc. by cramming:—*pr.p.* **cramm'ing;** *pa t.* and *pa.p.* **crammed.**—*n.* a crush: information that has been crammed: the system of cramming.—

adjs. **cramm'able; crammed.**—*n.* **cramm'er** a person or machine that crams poultry: one who, or an establishment that, crams pupils or a subject.—*adj.* **cram'-full'.** [O.E. *crammian.*]

crambo *kram'bō, n.* a game in which one gives a word to which another finds a rhyme: rhyme:—*pl.* **cram'boes.** [Prob. from L. *crambē repetīta,* cabbage served up again.]

cramp *kramp, n.* an involuntary and painful contraction of a voluntary muscle or group of muscles: restraint: a cramp-iron: a contrivance with a movable part that can be screwed tight so as to press things together.—*v.t.* to affect with spasms: to confine: to hamper: to fasten with a cramp-iron.—*adj.* **cramped** of handwriting, small and closely written: compressed: restricted, without enough room, confined.—*n.* **cramp'on** a grappling-iron: a spiked contrivance attached to the boots for climbing mountains or telegraph poles or walking on ice.—*adj.* **cramp'y** affected or diseased with cramp: producing cramp.— **cramp'-iron** a piece of metal bent at both ends for binding things together.—**bather's cramp** paralysis attacking a bather; **writer's cramp** a common disease affecting those in the habit of constant writing, the muscles refusing to obey only when an attempt to write is made.—**cramp someone's style** to restrict someone's movements or actions. [O.Fr. *crampe.*]

crampon. See **cramp.**

cran *kran, n.* a measure of capacity for herrings just landed in port—37½ gallons. [Prob. from Gael. *crann,* a measure.]

cranberry *kran'bər·i, n.* the red acid berry of a small evergreen shrub growing in peaty bogs and marshy grounds or the larger berry of an American species, both made into jellies, sauces, etc.: the shrub itself.

crane¹ *krān, n.* any bird of the *Gruidae,* large wading birds with long legs, neck, and bill: a machine for raising heavy weights, usu. having a rotating boom from the end of which the lifting gear is hung: a travelling platform for a film camera.—*v.t.* to raise with a crane: to stretch as a crane does its neck.—*v.i.* to stretch out the neck.—**crane'-fly** a fly with very long legs—the daddy-long-legs.—*adj.* **crane'-necked.** —**cranes'bill, crane's'-bill** any wild species of Geranium, from the beaked fruit. [O.E. *cran.*]

crane². Same as **cranium.**

cranium *krā'ni·əm, n.* the skull: the bones enclosing the brain:—*pl.* **crā'nia.**—*adj.* **crā'nial.**—*ns.* **crāni-ol'ogist; craniol'ogy** the study of skulls: phrenology; **crānio'meter** an instrument for measuring the skull; **crāniom'etry; cranios'copist** a phrenologist; **crānios'copy** phrenology; **crāniot'omy** the act of crushing the skull of a foetus in obstructed deliveries (*obstetrics*): incision of the skull esp. for the purpose of neurosurgery.—**cranial index** the breadth of a skull as a percentage of the length. [L.L. *cranium*—Gr. *krānion,* the skull.]

crank¹ *krangk, n.* a crook or bend: a conceit in speech: a faddist: an arm on a shaft for communicating motion to or from the shaft (*mach.*).—*v.i.* to move in a zigzag manner: to turn a crank (often with *up*).—*v.t.* to shape like a crank: to provide with a crank: to move or seek to move by turning a crank.—*adj.* crooked: crabbed: loose or slack.—*adv.* **crank'ily.**—*n.* **crank'-iness.**—*adj.* **crank'y** crooked: infirm: full of whims: cross.—**crank'case** a box-like casing for the crankshaft and connecting-rods of some types of reciprocating-engine; **crank'shaft** the main shaft of an engine or other machine, which carries a crank or cranks for the attachment of connecting rods. [O.E. *cranc,* cf. Ger. *krank,* ill.]

crank⁴ *krangk,* **crank-sided** *krangk-sī'did,* (*naut.*) *adjs.* liable to be upset.

crannog *kran'og, n.* in Scotland and Ireland a fortified island (partly natural and partly artificial) in a lake: a lake-dwelling. [Gael. *crann,* a tree.]

cranny *kran'i, n.* a rent: a chink: a secret place.—*adj.* **crann'ied** having crannies, rents, or fissures. [Fr. *cran,* a notch.]

crap *krap, n.* excrement (*vulg.*): rubbish (*slang*): nonsense (*slang*).—*v.i.* to defecate (*vulg.*). [M.E. *crappe,* chaff—M.Du. *krappe,* prob. from *krappen,* to tear off.]

crape *krāp, n.* a thin silk fabric, tightly twisted, without removing the natural gum—usually dyed black, used for mournings.—*adj.* made of crape. [O.Fr. *crespe* (Fr. *crêpe*)—L. *crispus,* crisp.]

craps *kraps, n. sing.,* a gambling game in which a player rolls two dice.—**shooting craps** playing this game.

crapulence *krap'ū-ləns, n.* sickness caused by excessive drinking: intemperance.—*adjs.* **crap'ulent; crap'-ulous.**—*n.* **crapulos'ity.** [Fr. *crapule*—L. *crāpula,* intoxication.]

craquelure *krak'ə-lūr, -lōōr, n.* the fine cracking that occurs in the varnish or pigment of old paintings. [Fr.]

crases. See **crasis.**

crash¹ *krash, n.* a noise as of things breaking or being crushed by falling: the shock of two bodies meeting: a collision between vehicles, etc.: the failure of a commercial undertaking: economic collapse: a fall or rush to destruction.—*adj.* intended to lessen effects of a crash: planned to meet an emergency quickly: involving suddenness, or speed, great effort.—*v.t.* and *v.i.* to dash, or fall, to pieces with a loud noise: to move with a harsh noise: to (cause a vehicle to) collide with another vehicle, etc.: to (cause an aircraft to) fall violently to earth or into the sea, usu. with extensive damage: to gatecrash (*coll.*).—*v.i.* to come to grief, fail disastrously.—*adj.* **crash'ing** (*coll.*) extreme, overwhelming, esp. in *a crashing bore.*— **crash barrier** a protective barrier usu. of steel placed e.g. along the edge of a road or the central reservation of a motorway; **crash course** a short-lasting but intensive programme of instruction; **crash'-helmet** a padded safety head-dress for motor-cyclists, racing motorists, etc.—*v.i.* and *v.t.* **crash'-land** in an emergency, to land (an aircraft) abruptly, with resultant damage.—**crash'-land'ing; crash'pad** padding inside a motor vehicle to protect the occupants in case of accident: a place providing temporary accommodation (*slang*).—*adj.* **crash'-proof.** [Imit.]

crash² *krash, n.* a coarse strong linen. [Perh. from Russ. *krashenina,* coloured linen.]

crasis *krā'sis, n.* the mingling or contraction of two vowels into one long vowel, or into a diphthong (*gram.*):—*pl.* **crā'sēs** (*-sēz*). [Gr. *krāsis,* mixture.]

crass *kras, adj.* gross: thick: dense: stupid: tactless, insensitive.—*adv.* **crass'ly.**—*n.* **crass'ness.** [L. *crassus.*]

-crat, -cratic(-al). See **-cracy.**

cratch *krach, n.* a crib to hold hay for cattle, a manger. [Fr. *crèche,* manger.]

crate *krāt, n.* a wicker-work case for packing crockery in, or for carrying fruit: a packing-case: an open frame-work of spars: a decrepit aeroplane or car (*coll.*).—*v.t.* to pack in a crate. [L. *crātis,* a hurdle.]

crater *krāt'ər, n.* the mouth of a volcano: a hole in the ground where a meteor has fallen, or a shell, mine, or bomb exploded.—**crater lake** one formed in the crater of an extinct volcano. [L.,—Gr. *krāter,* a mixing bowl.]

cravat *krə-vat', n.* a neckcloth worn chiefly by men — *v.t.* to dress in a cravat. [Fr. *cravate*—introduced in 1636 from the *Cravates* or Croatians.]

For other sounds see detailed chart of pronunciation.

crave *krāv*, *v.t.* to beg earnestly: to beseech: to require: to long for.—*ns.* **crav′er** one who craves: a beggar: **crav′ing** a longing. [O.E. *crafian*, to crave.]

craven *krāv′n*, *n.* a coward: a spiritless fellow.—*adj.* cowardly: spiritless.—*adv.* **crav′enly.**—*n.* **crav′enness.**

craw *krö*, *n.* the crop, throat, or first stomach of fowls: the stomach of animals generally. [M.E. *crawe.*]

crawfish. See **crayfish.**

crawl *kröl*, *v.i.* to move slowly with the body on or close to the ground: to move on hands and knees: to creep: to move slowly or stealthily: to behave abjectly: to be covered with crawling things: to swim using the crawl stroke.—*n.* the act of crawling: a slow pace: an alternate overhand swimming stroke.—*n.* **crawl′er** one who or that which crawls: an abject person: a sluggish person: a creeping thing: a caterpillar tractor: a baby's overall, a romper-suit.—*n.* **crawl′ing.**—*adj.* creeping: lousy, verminous.—*adj.* **craw′ly** (*coll.*) with, or like the feeling of, something crawling over one: creepy. [Scand.]

crayfish *krā′fish*, **crawfish** *krö′fish*, *ns.* a large fresh-water crustacea. [M.E. *crevice*—O.Fr. *crevice* (Fr. *écrevisse*, a crayfish)—O.H.G. *krebiz*, a crab.]

crayon *krā′an*, *n.* a pencil made of chalk, wax or pipe-clay, variously coloured, used for drawing: a drawing done with crayons.—*v.t.* and *v.i.* to draw with a crayon. [Fr. *crayon—craie*, chalk, from L. *crēta*, chalk.]

craze *krāz*, *v.t.* to crack: to cover with fine cracks (as pottery): to weaken: to impair: to derange (of the intellect).—*v.i.* to develop fine cracks: to become mad.—*n.* a crack, flaw: a finely cracked condition: insanity: fashion, fad: a small structural defect in plastic.—*adj.* **crazed.**—*adv.* **crāz′ily.**—*n.* **crāz′iness.** —*adj.* **crāz′y** frail: cracked: insane: demented: fantastically composed of irregular pieces (as a quilt or pavement): extravagantly enthusiastic or passionate (about) (*coll.*).

creak *krēk*, *v.i.* to make a sharp, grating sound, as of a hinge, etc.—*n.* a grating noise.—*adv.* **creak′ily.**— *adj.* **creak′y.** [From the sound.]

cream *krēm*, *n.* the oily substance that rises on milk, yielding butter when churned: that which rises to the top: the best part of anything: the pick of a group of things or people: a food largely made of, or like, cream, as *ice-cream*: a cream-like substance, as *cold-cream* for skin.—*v.t.* to take off the cream from: to select (the best) from a group, etc. (with *off*) (fig.): to treat with cream: to make creamy (e.g. a mixture of sugar and butter in cake-making).—*v.i.* to gather or form as or like cream.—*adj.* of the colour of cream: prepared with cream: of sherry, sweet.—*ns.* **cream′er** a device for separating cream from milk: a small jug for cream; **cream′ery** an establishment where butter and cheese are made from the milk supplied by a number of producers: a shop for milk, butter, etc.; **cream′iness.**—*adj.* **cream′y** full of cream, or like cream in appearance, consistency, etc.—**cream′-bun, -cake** a kind of bun, cake, filled with cream or creamy material, etc; **cream′-cheese′** cheese made with cream.—*adj.* **cream′-coloured** of the colour of cream, light yellow.—**cream cracker** a crisp, unsweetened type of biscuit.—*adj.* **cream′-laid** of paper, of a cream colour or white with a laid water-mark.—**cream′-nut** the Brazil nut; **cream puff** a confection of puff pastry filled with cream; **cream′-slice** a wooden blade for skimming cream from milk; **cream soda** (chiefly *U.S.*) a vanilla-flavoured fizzy drink.—*adj.* **cream′-wove** of paper, of a cream colour or white, and wove —**cream of chicken**, etc. **soup** chicken, mushroom, etc. soup made with milk or cream; **cream of tartar** a white crystalline compound, potassium hydrogen tar-

trate. [O.Fr. *cresme*, *creme*—L. *chrisma*—Gr. *chrīsma*, unction.]

crease *krēs*, *n.* a mark made by folding or doubling anything: such a mark pressed centrally and longitudinally into a trouser-leg: a regulative line, of three kinds—*bowling crease*, *popping-crease*, *return crease* (cricket).—*v.t.* to make creases in.—*v.i.* to become creased—*v.t.* and *v.i* (*coll.*) to double up with laughter (often with *up.*).—*adj.* **creas′y** full of creases.— *adj.* **crease-resist′ant**, **-resist′ing** of a fabric, not becoming creased in normal wear.

create *krē-āt′*, *v.t.* to bring into being or form out of nothing: to bring into being by force of imagination: to make, produce, or form: to design: to invest with a new form, office, or character: to institute.—*v.i.* (slang) to make a fuss.—*n.* **creation** (*krē-ā′-shən*) the act of creating, esp. the universe: that which is created: the world, the universe: a specially designed, or particularly striking, garment.—*adj.* **creā′tional.** —*ns.* **creā′tionism** the theory that everything that exists had its origin in special acts of creation by God (opp. to *evolutionism*); **creā′tionist.**—*adj.* **creā′tive** having power to create: that creates. showing, pertaining to, imagination, originality.—*adv.* **creā′tively.**—*ns.* **creā′tiveness**; **creativity** (*krē-ə-tiv′*) state or quality of being creative: ability to create; **creā′tor** one who creates: a maker:—*fem.* **creā′trix**, **creā′tress**; **creā′torship.**—*adjs.* **creatural** (*krē′chər-əl*), **crea′turely** pertaining to a creature or thing created.—*ns.* **creature** (*krē′chər*) anything that has been created, animate or inanimate, esp. an animated being, an animal, a man: a term of contempt or of endearment: a dependent, instrument, or puppet: (*coll.*—usu. with *the*) alcoholic liquor, **crea′tureship.**—**creature comforts** material comforts, food, etc.: liquor, esp. whisky; **the Creator** the Supreme being, God. [L. *creāre*, *-ātum*, to create, *creātūra*, a thing created.]

creatine *krē′ə-tin*, *-tēn*, *n.* a constant and characteristic constituent of the striped muscle of vertebrates ($C_4H_9N_3O_2$). [Gr. *kreas*, *kreatos*, flesh.]

creative, creator, creature. See **create.**

crèche *kresh*, *n.* a public nursery for children: a model representing the scene of Christ's nativity. [Fr. *crèche*, manger.]

credal. See **creed.**

credence *krē′dəns*, *n.* belief: trust: the small table beside the altar on which the bread and wine are placed before being consecrated.—Also **credence table**, **shelf** and **credenza.**—*adjs.* **crē′dent** credible: credulous: believing; **credential** (*kri-den′shl*) giving a title to belief or credit.—*n.* that which entitles to credit or confidence: (in *pl.*) esp. the letters by which one claims confidence or authority among strangers. —*n.* **credibil′ity** (*kred-*) the quality of being worthy of belief or trust: the capacity for believing or trusting. —*adj.* **cred′ible** that may be believed: seemingly worthy of belief or of confidence: reliable: of a nuclear weapon, in whose use and effectiveness one can believe—*n.* **cred′ibleness.**—*adv.* **cred′ibly.**—*n.* **cred′it** belief: esteem: reputation: honour: distinction: good character: acknowledgment. sale on trust: time allowed for payment: a balance in a person's favour in an account: an entry in an account making acknowledgment of a payment: the side of an account on which such entries are made: a sum placed at a person's disposal in a bank up to which he may draw: in American schools and colleges, certified completion of a course of study counting towards a final pass: (in *pl.*) credit titles: (in *pl.*) a list of acknowledgments in a book, etc.—*v.t.* to believe: to trust: to sell or lend to on trust: to enter on the credit side of an account: to set to the credit of (with *to* or *with*): to mention in the credit titles.—*adj.* **cred'itable** trustworthy: bringing credit or honour: praiseworthy.—*n.* **cred'itableness.**—*adv.* **cred'itably.**—*ns.* **cred'itor** one to whom a debt is due; **cre'dō** the Apostles' Creed or the Nicene Creed, or a musical setting of either of these for church services: a belief or set of beliefs:—*pl.* **cre'dōs**; **credulity** (*kri-dū'li-ti*) credulousness: disposition to believe on insufficient evidence.—*adj.* **credulous** (*kred'*) easy of belief: apt to believe without sufficient evidence: unsuspecting.—*adv.* **cred'ulously.**—*n.* **cred'ulousness.**—**credence shelf, table** see **credence** above; **credibility gap** (*politics*, etc.) the discrepancy between what is claimed or stated and what actually is, or seems likely to be, the case; **credit card** a card obtainable from a credit card company which, in places where the card is recognised, enables the holder to have purchases, services, etc. debited to an account kept by the company: a similar card issued by other organisations, or by certain banks (to be used with cheque-book); **credit rating** (an assessment of) the level of a person's or business's creditworthiness; **credit titles** acknowledgments of the work of participants shown at the beginning or end of a cinema film, television programme, etc; **cred'itworthiness** entitlement to credit as judged from earning capacity, promptness in debt-paying, etc.—*adj.* **cred'itworthy.**—**be a credit to someone**, etc. to be proof of time, trouble, etc. well-invested in one by someone, etc. [L. *crēdĕre, crēditum*, to believe.]

credenza. See **credence.**

credit, etc., **credulity,** etc. See **credence.**

creed *krēd, n.* a summary of articles of religious belief: any system of belief.—*adjs.* **creed'al;** **creed'al.**—**the Creed** the Apostles' Creed or the Nicene Creed. [O.E. *crēda*—L. *crēdō,* I believe.]

creek *krēk, n.* a small inlet or bay, or the tidal estuary of a river: any turn or winding: in America and Australia, a small river or brook.—**up the creek** (*slang*) in dire difficulties. [Prob. Scand., O.N. *kriki,* a nook.]

creel *krēl, n.* a basket, esp. a fish basket.

creep *krēp, v.i.* to move with the belly on or near the ground: to move or advance slowly or stealthily: to slip or encroach very gradually: to grow along the ground or on supports, as a vine: to fawn or cringe: to have the physical sensation of something creeping over or under the skin: to shudder: to undergo creep (*metallurgy*):—*pa.t.* and *pa.p.* **crept.**—*n.* a crawl: a slow slipping or yielding to stress: crystallisation or rise of a precipitate on the side of a vessel above the surface of a liquid: gradual alteration of shape under stress (*metallurgy*): a narrow passage: an enclosure in which young farm animals may feed, with an approach too narrow to admit the mother: a silent, boring, or unpleasant person (*slang*).—*ns.* **creep'er** anything that creeps: a creeping plant: a small bird that runs up trees: an endless chain or conveyor: a crêpe-soled, or other soft-soled, shoe (*coll.*).—*adj.* **creep'ing.**—*adv.* **creep'ingly.**—*adj.* **creep'y.**—*n.* **creep'y-crawl'y** a creeping insect (also *adj.*).—**creeping Jesus** (*slang*) a slinking person.—**the creeps** a feeling of horror or revulsion. [O.E. *crēopan;* Du. *kruipen.*]

cremate *kri-māt', v.t.* to burn (esp. a dead body).—*ns.* **crema'tion; crema'tionist** one who advocates cremation; **cremāt'or** one who cremates: a furnace for cremation: an incinerator.—*adj.* **cremātorial** (*krem-ə-tō'ri-əl, -tō'*).—*n.* **cremātō'rium** a place for cremating dead bodies.—*adj.* **crem'atory** (*-ə-tər-i*).—*n.* a crematorium. [L. *cremāre, -ātum,* to burn.]

crème, crème *krem,* (Fr.) *n.* cream—applied to various creamy substances.—**crème caramel** (*kar-a-mel*) an egg custard baked in a dish lined with caramel; **crème de menthe** (*də māt*) a peppermint-flavoured liqueur.

crème de la crème *krem də la krem,* (Fr.) cream of the cream, the very best.

crenate, -d *krēn'āt, kren'āt, kren-āt', -id,* (*bot.*) *adjs.* having rounded teeth between sharp notches.—*ns.* **cre'na** a notch or tooth; **crenā'tion; crenature** (*krē', kren'*).—*adjs.* **crēn'ulate, -d** finely notched or crenate. [From an inferred L *crēna,* a notch.]

crenel *kren'l,* (*archit.*) *n.* a notch in a parapet.—*v.t.* to indent with crenels.—*v.t.* **cren'ellate,** to embattle.—*adjs.* **cren'ellate, -d** embattled: indented.—*n.* **crenellā'tion.**—*adj.* **cren'elled.** [O.Fr. *crenel*—inferred L. *crēna,* a notch.]

crenulate. See **crenate.**

creole *krē'ōl, krē-ōl', adj.* and *n.* strictly applied in the former Spanish, French, and Portuguese colonies of America, Africa and the East Indies to natives of pure European blood (in opposition to immigrants born in Europe or to coloured natives): native, but not aboriginal or indigenous: (*loosely*) native, but of mixed blood: applied to the native French or Spanish stock in Louisiana (*U.S.*): a colonial patois (French, Spanish, etc.).—*n.* (also **creolised, creolized, language**) a language formerly a pidgin which has developed and become the accepted language of a region. [Fr. *créole*—Sp. *criollo,* dim. of *criado,* nursling—*criar,* lit. to create, hence to bring up, nurse—L. *creāre.*]

creosote *krē'ə-sōt, n.* an oily liquid obtained by destructive distillation of wood-tar: a somewhat similar liquid got from coal-tar (**creosote oil** or **coal-tar creosote**).—*v.t.* to treat with creosote. [Gr. *kreas,* flesh, *sōtēr,* saviour—*sōzein,* to save.]

crêpe *krāp, krep, n.* a crape-like fabric: rubber rolled in thin crinkly sheets (**crêpe rubber**): a pancake.—*v.t.* to frizz, as hair.—**crêpe-de-chine** (*də shēn*) a crape-like fabric, originally of silk; **crêpe paper** thin crinkled paper.—*adj.* **crêpe'-soled** soled with crêpe rubber.—**crêpe suzette** (*su-zet*) a thin pancake in a hot orange- or lemon-flavoured sauce, usu. flambéed:—*pl.* **crêpes suzettes.** [See **crape.**]

crepitate *krep'i-tāt, v.i.* to crackle, snap: to rattle: (of beetles) to discharge an offensive fluid.—*adj.* **crep'itant** crackling.—*n.* **crepitā'tion** the act of crepitating: crackle: a sound detected in the lungs in certain diseases.—*adj.* **crep'itative.**—*n.* **crep'itus.** [L. *crepitāre, -ātum,* freq. of *crepāre,* to crack, rattle.]

crept *krept, pa.t.* and *pa.p.* of **creep.**

crepuscular *kri-pus'kū-lər, adj.* of or pertaining to twilight. [L. *crepusculum*—*creper,* dusky, obscure.]

crescendo *kresh-en'dō,* (*mus.*) *adj.* and *adv.* gradually increasing in loudness.—*n.* increase of loudness: a passage of increasing loudness: a high point, a climax (*fig.*):—*pl.* **crescen'dos.** [It., increasing.]

crescent *kres'ənt, krez', adj.* increasing: shaped like the waxing moon.—*n.* the waxing moon: a figure like the crescent moon: the Turkish standard or emblem: the Turkish power: the Muslim faith: a curved range of buildings (sometimes applied at random): a crescent-shape roll or bun. [L. *crēscĕre,* to grow, pr.p. *crēscēns, -entis.*]

cresol *krēs'ol, n* a product of distillation of coal-tar resembling phenol—C_7H_8O. [From *creosote* and alcohol.]

cress *kres, n.* a name for many pungent-leaved cruciferous plants of various genera.—*adj.* **cress'y** abounding in cresses. [O.E. *cresse, cerse.*]

cresset *kres'it, n.* an iron basket, or the like, for combustibles, placed on a beacon, lighthouse, wharf, etc.: a torch generally. [O.Fr. *cresset, crasset* (Fr. *creuset*)—Old Du. *kruysel,* a hanging lamp.]

crest *krest, n.* the comb or tuft on the head of a cock or other bird. the summit of anything, as a roof-ridge,

to bite off in eating: to raise crops on: to cut the hair of.—*v.i.* to yield a crop: to come to the surface (with *up* or *out*): hence, to come (up) casually, as in conversation:—*pr.p.* cropp'ing; *pa.t.* and *pa.p.* cropped.—*ns.* cropp'er one who or that which crops: a plant that yields a crop: one who raises a crop for a share of it: a fall (*coll.*): a failure (*coll.*); cropp'ing the act of cutting off: the raising of crops; crop'dusting the spraying of crops with fungicides or insecticides from the air; crop'-duster one who does this; crop'-ear a person, horse, dog, etc., with cropped ears.—*adj.* crop'-eared having ears cropped, or hair cropped to show the ears.—crop'-marks (*archaeol.*) variations in the depth or colour of a crop growing in a field, which, viewed from the air, can show the presence of a structure beneath the soil.—come a cropper (*coll.*) to have a fall, perhaps from the phrase *neck and crop*. [O.E. *crop*, the top shoot of a plant, the crop of a bird.]

croquet *krō′kā*, *n.* a game in which wooden balls are driven by means of long-handled mallets, through a series of hoops.—*v.t.* to drive away by striking another ball in contact. [North Fr. *croquet*, a dial. form of *crochet*, dim. of *croc*, *croche*, a crook.]

croquette *krŏ-ket′*, *n.* a ball or round cake, usu. of minced meat, fish, or potato, seasoned and fried. [Fr.,—*croquer*, to crunch.]

crosier, crozier *krō′z(h)yar*, *n.* the pastoral staff or crook of a bishop or abbot: erroneously, an archbishop's cross.—*adj.* cro′siered. [M.E. *crose* or *croce*—Late L. *crocia*, a crook.]

cross *kros*, *n.* a gibbet on which the Romans exposed malefactors, typically consisting of two pieces of timber, one placed tranversely to the other: the particular one on which Christ suffered: the symbol of the Christian religion, or of the crusades: a representation of Christ's cross: any object, figure, or mark formed by two parts or lines transverse to each other, with or without elaboration: such a mark used instead of a signature by an illiterate person: such a mark used to symbolise a kiss in a letter: a monument not always in the form of a cross, where proclamations are made, etc.: a place in a town or village where such a monument stands or stood: a cross-shaped pendant or medal: a crossing or crossway: anything that crosses or thwarts: adversity or affliction in general, or a burden or cause of suffering, as in *bear one's cross*: mixing of breeds: a hybrid: something intermediate in character between two other things: a transverse pass, esp. towards the opposing team's goal (*football*).—*adj.* lying across or crosswise: transverse: oblique: adverse: interchanged: peevish: angry, displeased (with): hybrid: balancing, neutralising.—*adv.* and *prep.* across.—*v.t.* to mark with a cross: to make the sign of the cross over: to set something, or draw a line, across: to place crosswise: to cancel by drawing cross lines: to pass from one side to the other of: to pass transversely, esp. in the direction of the opposing team's goal (*football*): to extend across: to interbreed: to draw two lines across (a cheque), thereby restricting it to payment through a bank: to obstruct: to thwart: to annoy: to bestride.—*v.i.* to lie or pass across: to meet and pass: to interbreed.—*adj.* crossed.—*n.* cross′ing the act of making the sign of the cross: the act of going across: a place where a roadway, etc., may be crossed; intersection: act of thwarting: cross-breeding.—*adv.* cross′ly.—*n.* cross′ness.—*adv.* cross′wise across.—cross′bar a transverse bar: a kind of lever.—*adj.* cross′barred.—cross′beam a large beam stretching across a building and serving to hold its sides together; cross′bench a bench laid crosswise: a bench on which independent members of parliament sometimes sit.—*adj.* independent: impartial.—cross′bencher; cross′bill a

finch of the genus Loxia with mandibles crossing near the points; cross′bones a figure of two thigh-bones laid across each other—forming with the skull a conventional emblem of death or piracy; cross′bow a weapon for shooting arrows, formed of a bow placed crosswise on a stock; cross′bower, -bowman one who uses a crossbow.—*adj.* cross′bred.—cross′breed a breed produced by crossing: the offspring of a cross; cross′breed′ing; cross′-butt′ock a particular throw over the hip in wrestling.—*v.t.* cross′-check′ to test the accuracy of e.g. a statement by consulting various sources of information.—Also *v.i.* and *n.*—cross′s claim a claim made by the defendant against the plaintiff.—*adj.* and *adv.* cross′-coun′try through fields, woods, over hills, etc., rather than by road, esp. (of running, skiing, etc.) over a long distance.—*ns.* cross′-current in the air, sea, or a river, a current flowing across the main current; cross′cut a crosswise cutting: a short way across from one point to another.—*v.t.* (-*kut′*) to cut across.—crosscut saw a large saw worked by two men, one at each end, for cutting beams crosswise; cross′cutting (*cinema*, *TV*) cutting and fitting together film sequences so that in the finished picture the action moves from one scene to another and back again, thus increasing dramatic tension; cross′-examina′tion.—*v.t.* cross′-exam′ine to question minutely, or with a view to checking evidence already given: to subject to examination by the other side.—*adj.* cross′-eyed squinting.—*v.t.* cross′-fade (*television*, *radio*) to cause (a sound source or picture) to fade away while gradually introducing another (also *v.i.*).—cross′-fertilisa′tion the fecundation of a plant by pollen from another: fruitful interaction of ideas from e.g. different cultures; cross′fire (*mil.*) the crossing of lines of fire from two or more points (also *fig.*).—*adj.* cross′-grained having the grain or fibres crossed or intertwined: perverse: contrary: intractable.—*adv.* across the grain: perversely.—cross′-hatch′ing in drawing, etc. shading by intersecting sets of parallel lines; cross-infec′tion infection of an already ill or injured person with germs unrelated to his own complaint, liable to occur e.g. in hospitals where a variety of diseases are being treated; cross-lat′eral a person affected with crosslaterality.—Also *adj.*—cross-lateral′ity a mixture of physical one-sidedness, as the combination of a dominant left eye with a dominant right hand.—*adjs.* cross′-leaved having leaves in four rows, set crosswise; cross′-legged having the legs crossed.—Also *adv.*—*v.t.* cross′-match′ to test (blood samples from a donor and a recipient) for compatibility.—cross′over a road passing over the top of another: a place or point at which a crossing or transfer is made; cross′patch an ill-natured person; cross′piece a piece of material of any kind crossing another; cross′-ply tyre tyre in which the plies of fabric in the carcass are wrapped so as to cross each other diagonally; cross′s pollina′tion transfer of pollen from one flower to the stigma of another; cross′-pur′pose a contrary purpose: (in *pl.*) a game in which answers to questions are transferred to other questions: (in *pl.*) confusion in conversation or action by misunderstanding.—*v.t.* cross′-ques′tion to cross-examine.—cross′-ref′erence a reference in a book to another title or passage.—*v.t.* and *v.t.* cross-refer′.—cross′-rib an arch supporting a vault; cross′road a road crossing the principal road, a bypath: a road joining main roads: (often *pl.*) a place where roads cross (in *pl.*) a stage at which an important decision has to be made.—*adj.* cross′roads.—cross′-ruff′ alternate ruffing by partners, each leading a suit that the other lacks; cross′-sec′tion a transverse section: a comprehensive representation.—*v.t.* to make a cross-section of —*adj.* cross-sec′tional.—

cross'-staff a surveying instrument consisting of a staff surmounted with a frame carrying two pairs of sights at right angles; **cross'-stitch** a stitch in the form of a cross; needlework of such stitches; **cross'-talk** interference of one telephone conversation with another: backchat: repartee; **cross'way** a way that crosses another or links others; **cross'wind** a wind blowing across the path of, e.g. an aeroplane; **cross'word (puzzle)** a type of puzzle invented in America in 1913, in which a square with blank spaces is to be filled with letters which, read across or down, will give words corresponding to clues given.—**cross one's fingers, keep one's fingers crossed** to place one finger across another to ensure good luck; **cross one's heart** to emphasise that one is being truthful by making the sign of a cross over one's heart: **cross someone's mind** to flash across someone's mind; **cross someone's palm** to put a coin in someone's hand; **cross someone's path** to come in someone's way: to thwart someone; **cross swords** to enter into a dispute (with); **on the cross** diagonally. [O.E. *cros*—O.N. *kross*—L. *crux*, *crucis*.]

crosse *kros*, *n*. the stick with which the game of lacrosse is played, having at its top end a network of leather thongs enclosed in a triangular frame. [Fr.]

crotch *kroch*, *n*. a fork, as of a tree: the bifurcation of the human body.—*adj.* **crotched.**

crotchet *kroch'it*, *n*. a hook: a note in music, equal to half a minim.; : a crooked or perverse fancy: a whim, or conceit.—*adjs.* **crotch'eted, crotch'ety** having crotchets or peculiarities: whimsical: short-tempered. [Fr. *crochet*, dim. of *croche*, a hook; see **crochet.**]

Croton *krō'tən*, *n*. a genus of tropical plants of the spurge family: (without *cap.*) any plant of the genus. —**croton oil** a powerful purgative got from the seeds of *Croton tiglium*. [Gr. *krótōn*, a sheep-tick, which the seed resembles.]

crouch *krowch*, *v.i.* to squat or lie close to the ground, as an animal preparing to spring: to bend low with legs doubled: to cringe: to fawn.—*v.t.* to bend.—*n.* act or position of crouching. [Possibly connected with **crook.**]

croup[1] *krō͞op*, *n.* inflammation of the larynx and trachea in children, associated with difficulty in breathing and a peculiar ringing cough: a burr.—*v.i.* to croak or speak hoarsely.—*n.* **croup'iness.**—*adjs.* **croup'ous; croup'y.** [From the sound made.]

croup[2], **croupe** *krō͞op*, *n.* the rump of a horse: the place behind the saddle. [Fr. *croupe*, a protuberance; allied to **crop.**]

croupier *krō͞o'pi-ər*, or *-pi-ā*, *n.* one who officiates at a gaming-table, collecting the stakes and paying the winners. [Fr., one who rides on the croup.]

croupous, croupy. See **croup**[1].

croûte *krō͞ot*, *n.* a thick slice of fried bread for serving entrées.—*n.* **croûton** (*-tō, -ton'*) a small piece of fried bread. [Fr. *croûte*, crust.]

crow *krō*, *n.* any of several large black birds of the genus Corvus esp. *C. corone* (the so-called *carrion crow*): extended to other birds of this genus, esp. the rook: the defiant or triumphant cry of a cock: a child's inarticulate cry of joy.—*v.i.* to croak: to utter a crow: to boast, swagger, triumph (often with *over*):—*pa.t.* **crew** (*krō͞o*), or **crowed.**—**crow'-bar** a large iron bar mostly bent at the end, to be used as a lever; **crow'foot** a buttercup, sometimes extended to other plants (*pl.* in this sense **crow'foots**): crow's-foot; **crow's'-foot** one of the wrinkles produced by age, spreading out from the corners of the eyes; **crow's'-nest** (*naut.*) an elevated shelter for a man on the lookout.—*n.pl.* **crow'-steps** steps on a gable.—**as the crow flies** in a straight line; **eat crow, eat boiled crow** to be forced to do something very disagreeable,

humiliate oneself; **stone the crows** (*slang*) an expression of amazement, horror, etc. [O.E. *crāwe*, a crow, *crāwan*, to crow.]

crowd *krowd*, *n.* a number of persons or things closely pressed together, without order: the rabble: multitude: a set.—*v.t.* to gather into a lump or crowd: to fill by pressing or driving together: to compress: to thrust, put pressure on.—*v.i.* to press on: to press together in numbers: to swarm.—*adj.* **crowd'ed.** [O.E. *crūdan*, to press.]

crowdie *krowd'i*, (*Scot.*) *n.* a mixture of meal and water: brose: a cheese-like preparation of milk.

crown *krown*, *n.* a circular head ornament, esp. as a mark of honour: the diadem or state-cap of royalty: kingship: the sovereign: governing power in a monarchy: honour: the top of anything, as a head, hat, tree, arch: the visible part of a tooth: a substitute for this, made of gold or synthetic material, etc., fitted over a broken or bad tooth: in gem-cutting, the upper of the two conical surfaces of a brilliant: the junction of root and stem: a short rootstock: a clasping metal cap for a bottle: chief ornament: completion or consummation: a coin originally stamped with a crown, esp. a 5s. piece: used to translate various coin names, as krone.—*v.t.* to cover or invest with a crown: to cap: to invest with royal dignity: in draughts, to convert into a king or crowned man by the placing of another draught on the top: to adorn: to dignify: to complete happily: to hit on the head (*slang*).—*adj.* **crowned.**—*n.* **crown'ing.**—*adj.* **crown'less.**—*n.* **crown'let** a small crown.—**crown agent** a solicitor in Scotland who prepares criminal prosecutions: (with *caps.*) one of a British body of business agents operating internationally, appointed by the Ministry for Overseas Development; **crown'-cap** a lined metal cap for a bottle; **crown colony** colony administered directly by the home government; **crown courts** the system of courts replacing assize courts and quarter sessions; **crown Derby** a late 18th-century porcelain made at Derby, marked with a crown; **crowned head** a monarch; **crown'-glass** alkali-lime glass: window-glass formed in circular plates or discs; **crown'-green** a bowling-green with a crown or arched surface; **crown'-jew'el** a jewel pertaining to the crown or sovereign; **crown'-land** land belonging to the crown or sovereign; **Crown Office** the office for the business of the crown side of the King's Bench: the office in which the great seal is affixed; **crown-of-thorns** starfish a starfish that eats living coral; **crown prince** the heir apparent to the crown; **crown princess** the female heir to a throne: the wife of a crown prince; **crown'-wheel** a wheel with teeth set at right angles to its plane; **crown witness** a witness for the crown in a criminal prosecution instituted by it. [O. Fr. *corone* —L. *corōna*; cf. Gr. *koronos*, curved.]

crozier. See **crosier.**

cru *krü*, (Fr.) *n.* a vineyard or group of vineyards.

cruces, crucial, cruciate. See **crux.**

crucian, crusian *krō͞o'shən*, *n.* the German carp, without barbels. [L.G. *karusse* (Ger. *Karausche*)—L. *coracīnus*—Gr. *korakīnos*, a black perch-like fish— *korax*, raven.]

crucible *krō͞o'si-bl*, *n.* an earthen pot for melting ores, metals, etc. [L.L. *crucibulum*.]

crucifer *krō͞o'si-fər*, *n.* a cross-bearer in a procession: a member of the Cruciferae.—*n.pl.* **Crucif'erae** a family of archichlamydeous dicotyledons, with cross-shaped flowers, including cabbage, turnip, cress, wallflower.—*adj.* **crucif'erous** bearing or marked with a cross: with four petals placed crosswise: of the Cruciferae. [L. *crux*, *crucis*, a cross, *ferre*, to bear.]

cruciform, crucigerous. See **crux.**

crucify krōō´si-fī, v.t. to expose or put to death on a cross: to fasten to a wheel or the like, as a military field punishment: to subdue completely: to mortify: to torment: to treat harshly or cruelly: to hold up to scorn or ridicule:—pr.p. cru´cifying: pa.t. and pa.p. cru´cified.—ns. cru´cifier one who crucifies; cru´cifix a figure or picture of Christ fixed to the cross; crucifixion (-fik´shən). [O.Fr. crucifier—L. crucifigĕre, crucifixum—crux, cross, and figĕre, to fix]

crud krud, krōōd, n. dirt, filth, esp. if sticky (slang): a contemptible person (slang).—adj. crudd´y dirty (slang): contemptible (slang).

crude krōōd, adj. raw, unprepared: not reduced to order or form: unfinished: undigested: immature: unrefined: coarse, vulgar, rude: inartistic.—crude oil.—adv. crude´ly.—ns. crude´ness; crud´ity rawness: unripeness: that which is crude.—crude oil petroleum in its unrefined state. [L. crūdus, raw.]

crudités krü-dē-tá, (Fr.) n.pl. fresh fruit and vegetables.

cruel krōō´əl, adj. disposed to inflict pain, or pleased at suffering: void of pity, merciless, savage: severe.—adj. cru´elly.—n. cru´elty.—adj. cru´el-heart´ed delighting in cruelty. [Fr. cruel—L. crūdēlis.]

cruet krōō´it, n. a small jar or phial for sauces and condiments for the table: a vessel for wine, oil, or water for religious ceremonies.—cru´et-stand a stand or frame for holding cruets. [A.Fr., dim. of O.Fr. cruye, jar, from root of crock¹.]

cruise krōōz, v.i. to sail to and fro: (of a vehicle, aircraft, etc.) to progress smoothly at a speed economical in fuel, etc.: to wander about seeking something (with about, etc.; coll.).—n. a sailing to and fro: a wandering voyage in search of an enemy or for the protection of vessels or for pleasure or health: a land journey of similar character.—ns. cruis´er one who or that which cruises: a speedy warship, specially for cruising: a privateer: a cruising yacht: a cruiser-weight boxer.—cruise missile a type of subsonic guided missile using the air for support; cruis´er-weight a boxer between middle and heavy, a light-heavyweight; cruise´way a canal for exclusively recreational use. [Du. kruisen, to cross.]

crumb krum, n. a small bit or morsel of bread: a small particle of anything: the soft part of bread.—v.t. to break into crumbs: to put crumbs in or on: to remove crumbs from.—v.i. to crumble.—adjs. crumb´y in crumbs: soft; crum´my crumby: not good, worthless, inferior, unpleasant, out of sorts, etc. (coll.). [O.E. cruma.]

crumble krum´bl, v.t. to break into crumbs.—v.i. to fall into small pieces: to decay.—n. a crumb: that which crumbles easily: a sweet dish consisting of a layer of stewed fruit covered with a crumbled mixture of flour, butter and sugar.—adj. crum´bly. [Orig. dim. of crumb.]

crumbs krumz, (schoolchildren's slang) interj. expressive of surprise, dismay, etc. [Euphemism for Christ.]

crumhorn. See krummhorn.

crummock, crummack krum´ək, n. a crook, stick with curved head. [Gael. cromag, hook, crook.]

crummy. See crumb.

crump¹ krump, (mil. slang) n. (the sound of) an exploding bomb, etc. [Imit.]

crump² krump, adj. crooked: wrinkled: crisp, friable (Scot.).—n. crump´et a soft, unsweetened griddle cake: the head (slang): a girl (slang). [O.E. crump—crumb, crooked.]

crumple krump´l, v.t. to crush into irregular wrinkles: to wrinkle: to cause to collapse.—v.i. to wrinkle: to collapse.—adj. crump´led.—n. crump´ling.—crumple zones the front and rear portions of a motor car designed to crumple and absorb the impact in a collision while the passenger area remains intact. [crump².]

crunch krunch, v.t. to crush with harsh noise, with the teeth, under foot, or otherwise: to chew anything hard, and so make a noise.—v.i. to make such a noise: to chew with, or as with, such a noise.—n. the act or sound or crunching: (with the) the real testing or critical moment, trial of strength, time or cause of difficulty, etc. (coll.): a crisis, emergency (coll.).—n. crunch´iness.—adj. crunch´y.

crupper krup´ər, n. a strap of leather fastened to the saddle and passing under the horse's tail to keep the saddle in its place: the hind part of a horse. [O.Fr. cropiere—crope, the croup.]

crural krōō´rəl, adj. belonging to or like a leg. [L. crūrālis, from, crūs, crūris, the leg.]

crusade krōō-sād´, n. a military expedition under the banner of the cross to recover the Holy Land from the Turks: any daring or romantic undertaking: concerted action to further a cause.—v.i. to go on a crusade.—n. crusad´er one engaged in a crusade. [Fr. croisade—Prov. crozada—croz—L. crux, a cross.]

cruse krōōz, also krōōs, n. an earthen pot: a small cup or bottle. [Cf. O.N. krūs; Ger. Krause.]

crush krush, v.t. to break or bruise: to squeeze together: to beat down or overwhelm: to subdue: to ruin.—v.i. to become broken or crumpled under pressure.—n. a violent squeezing: a close crowd of persons or things: a drink made from fruit juice; a narrowing passage for cattle: an infatuation (with on), or its object (slang).—adjs. crush´able; crushed.—n. crush´er.—adj. crush´ing.—adv. crush´ingly.—crush´-barrier a barrier erected to restrain a crowd; crush´-hat an opera-hat; crush´-room a room where an audience may promenade during the intervals of the entertainment. [O.Fr. croissir.]

crusian. See crucian.

crust krust, n. the hard rind or outside coating of anything: the outer part of bread: a dried-up scrap of bread: hence, a livelihood (slang): the covering of a pie, etc.: the solid exterior of the earth.—v.t. to cover with a crust or hard case.—v.i. to gather into a hard crust.—adjs. crust´al pertaining to a crust esp. the earth's; crust´ate, crustat´ed covered with a crust.—n. crustā´tion an adherent crust.—adv. crust´ily.—n. crust´iness.—adjs. crust´less; crust´y of the nature of or having a crust, as port or other wine: having a hard or harsh exterior: hard: snappy: surly. [L. crusta, rind.]

Crustacea krus-tā´sh(y)ə, -shi-ə, n.pl. a large class of arthropod animals with hard shells, almost all aquatic —crabs, lobsters, shrimps, sand-hoppers, wood-lice, water-fleas, barnacles, etc.—adj. and n. crustā´cean.—adj. crustā´ceous crusty. [L. crusta, shell.]

crutch kruch, n. a staff with a cross-piece at the head to place under the arm of a lame person: any support of like form: a bifurcation, crotch: a small figure inserted to show the number to be carried (arith.).—v.t. to support: to prop: to clip wool from the hindquarters of (a sheep) (Austr.).—v.i. to go on crutches. [O.E. crycc.]

crux kruks, n. a cross: something that occasions difficulty or perplexity (fig.): that on which a decision turns: the essential point, as of a problem:—pl. crux´es, cruces (krōō´sēz).—adjs. crucial (krōō´shəl) crosslike: of the nature of a crux· testing or decisive: essential or very important; cruciate (krōō´shi-āt) cross-shaped.—v.t. to torment.—adjs. cruciform (krōō´si-förm) cross-shaped; crucigerous (krōō-sij´ər-əs) bearing a cross. [L. crux, crucis, a cross.]

cruzeiro krōō-zā´rō, n. the monetary unit of Brazil:—pl. cruzei´ros. [Port. cruz, cross.]

cry krī, v.i. to utter a shrill loud sound, esp. one of pain or grief: to lament: to weep: to bawl: to call (Scot.).—

v.t. to utter loudly: to exclaim: to proclaim or make public: to offer for sale by crying: to call (*Scot.*):—*3rd pers. sing.* **cries**; *pr.p.* **cry'ing**; *pa.t.* and *pa.p.* **cried** (*krīd*).—*n.* any loud sound, esp. of grief or pain: a call or shout: a fit of weeping: a particular sound uttered by an animal: bawling: lamentation: prayer: clamour: a general utterance: a watchword, battle-cry, or slogan: a street call of wares for sale or services offered:—*pl.* **cries**.—*ns.* **cri'er** one who cries, esp. an official maker of proclamations; **cry'ing** the act of calling loudly: weeping.—*adj.* calling loudly: claiming notice and usu. redress, as in *a crying shame.* —**cry'-baby** one who cries childishly.—**a far cry** a great distance; **cry against** to protest against; **cry down** to decry; **cry for the moon** to beg, or sigh, for something unattainable; **crying in the wilderness** voicing opinions or making suggestions that are not (likely to be) heeded; **cry off** to withdraw from an agreement; **cry one's eyes, heart, out** to weep copiously or bitterly; **cry out** to give a shout or shriek, e.g. of alarm, pain, etc.; **cry out for** to be in urgent or obvious need of; **cry out to be (done, used,** etc.) to be someone or something that very much ought to be (done, used, etc.); **cry over spilt milk** to waste time in bemoaning what is irreparable; **cry quits** to declare a thing even; **cry stinking fish** to decry one's own goods; **cry up** to praise; **for crying out loud** (*slang*) an expression of frustration, impatience, etc.; **great cry and little wool** much ado about nothing; **in full cry** in full pursuit; **within cry of** within hearing distance. [Fr. *crier*—L. *quirītāre*, to scream.]

cryo- *krī'ō-, krī-o'-*, in composition, frost, ice.—*n.* **cryobiol'ogy** the biology of organisms below their normal temperature.—*adj.* **cryobiolog'ical.**—*ns.* **cryobiol'ogist; cry'ogen** (*-jen*) a substance used for obtaining low temperatures, a freezing mixture.— *adj.* **cryogen'ic** pertaining to the science of cryogenics, or to work done, apparatus used, or substances kept, at low temperatures.—*n. sing.* **cryogen'ics** the branch of physics concerned with phenomena at very low temperatures.—*ns.* **cryogeny** (*-oj'ə-ni*) refrigeration: cryogenics; **cry'olite** an-ice-stone or Greenland spar, sodium aluminium fluoride, earliest source of aluminium; **cryom'eter** (Gr. *metron*, measure) a thermometer for low temperatures.—*adj.* **cryomet'ric.**—*n. sing.* **cryon'ics** the practice of preserving human corpses by freezing them, with the idea that advances in science may enable them to be revived at some future time.—**cry'o-stat** apparatus for achieving or demonstrating cooling by evaporation: any apparatus for maintaining a low temperature; **cryosur'gery** surgery using instruments at very low temperatures; **cryother'apy** medical treatment using extreme cold. [Gr. *kryos*, frost.]

crypt *kript*, *n.* an underground cell or chapel.—*adjs.* **cryp'tal** pertaining to, or of the nature of, a crypt; **cryp'tic, -al** hidden: secret: unseen: mysteriously obscure.—*adv.* **cryp'tically.** [L. *crypta*—Gr. *kryptē* —*kryptein*, to hide; cf. **grot.**]

crypt-, crypto- *kript-, -ō-, -o-*, in composition, hidden. —*ns.* **cryptanal'ysis** the art of deciphering codes, etc.; **cryptanal'yst; cryp'to-Chris'tian; cryp'to-comm'unist.**—*adj.* **cryptocryst'alline** with crystalline structure visible only under the microscope.—*n.* **cryp'togam** any member of the class of flowerless plants, so named by Linnaeus in the expectation that sexual reproduction would one day be discovered in them.—*adjs.* **cryptoga'mian; cryptogamic** (*-gam'ik*); **cryptog'amous.**—*ns.* **cryptog'amist; cryptog'amy.**— *ns.* **cryp'togram, cryp'tograph** anything written in cipher.—*ns.* **cryptog'rapher, -ist.**—*adj.* **cryptograph'ic.**—*n.* **cryptog'raphy.**—*adj.* **cryptolog'ical.**—*ns.* **cryptol'ogist; cryptol'ogy** secret language: the sci-entific study of codes; **cryp'tonym** a secret name.— *adj.* **crypton'ymous.** [Gr. *kryptos*, hidden.]

crypto *krip'tō, n.* a secret member of a party, sect, organisation, etc., esp. a crypto-communist:—*pl.* **cryp'tos.** [See **crypt-, crypto-**.]

crystal *kris'tl, n.* rock-crystal, a clear quartz, like ice: a body, generally solid, whose atoms are arranged in a definite pattern, outwardly expressed by geometrical form with plane faces: a crystalline element, of piezoelectric or semiconductor material, functioning as e.g. a transducer, oscillator, etc. in an electronic device: a globe of rock-crystal or the like in which one may see visions: anything bright and clear: a superior glass of various kinds: cut glass.—*adj.* composed of or like crystal.—*adj.* **crys'talline** (*-īn, -in*) like crystal or a crystal: composed of crystal, crystals, or parts of crystals: having the structure of a crystal.—*n.* a crystalline substance.—*n.* **crystallin'ity.**—*adj.* **crystalli'sable, -z-.**—*n.* **crystallisa'tion, -z-.**—*v.t.* and *v.i.* **crys'tallise, -ize** to form into crystals: to make or become definite or concrete: of fruit, to coat with sugar crystals.—*ns.* **crys'tallite** a small, imperfectly formed or incipient crystal: a minute body in glassy igneous rocks; **crystallog'rapher.**—*adj.* **crystallograph'ic.**—*ns.* **crystallog'raphy** the science of the structure, forms, and properties of crystals; **crys'talloid** a substance in a state in which it dissolves to form a true solution which will pass through a membrane: a minute crystalline particle of protein (*bot.*). —*adj.* like a crystal: of the nature of a crystalloid.— *adj.* **crys'tal-clear'** very, completely clear.—**crys'tal-gazer; crys'tal-gazing** gazing in a crystal or the like to obtain visual images, whether in divination or to objectify hidden contents of the mind; **crystalline lens** the transparent refractive body of the eye; **crystal rectifier** rectifier that depends on differential conduction in semiconductor crystals suitably doped; **crystal set** a simple wireless receiving apparatus in which a crystal and a cat's-whisker rectify the current. [O.Fr. *cristal*—L. *crystallum*—Gr. *krystallos*, ice— *kryos*, frost.]

csárdás *chär'däsh, n.* a Hungarian dance, or its music, in two movements, one slow and the other fast.— Also (wrongly) **czar'das.** [Hung.]

c-spring. See **cee-spring.**

ctene *tēn, n.* a comb-like swimming organ in the Ctenophora.—*adjs.* **cteniform** (*tēn'*, or *ten'*), **cten'oid** comb-shaped.—*n.pl.* **Ctenoph'ora** a class of Coelenterates—beautifully delicate, free-swimming marine organisms, moving by means of comb-like plates.— *n., adj.* **ctenoph'oran.**—*n.* **cten'ophore** any member of the Ctenophora. [Gr. *kteis, ktenos,* comb.]

cub[1] *kub, n.* the young of certain animals, as foxes, etc.: a whelp: a young boy or girl (playful or contemptuous, esp. of the ill-conditioned, unmannerly, raw, or conceited): (in full **Cub Scout**) an embryo Scout: a beginner, novice, apprentice: a young or inexperienced reporter.—*v.t.* and *v.i.* to bring forth: —*pr.p.* **cubb'ing**; *pa.t.* and *pa.p.* **cubbed.**

cub[2] *kub, n.* a cattle-pen: a chest.—*ns.* **cubb'y, cubb'y-hole** a snug enclosed place. [Prob. from L.G.]

Cuban *kū'bən, adj.* pertaining to *Cuba* or its people.— *n.* a native of Cuba.—**Cuban heel** on footwear, a medium high heel without curves.

cubby-hole. See **cub[2].**

cube *kūb, n.* a solid body having six equal square faces, a solid square: the third power of a quantity.—*v.t.* to raise to the third power: to cut into cubes: to calculate the amount or contents of in cubic units.—*adjs.* **cū'bic, -al** pertaining to a cube: of or involving the third power or degree: solid.—*adv.* **cū'bically.**—*n.* **cū'bicalness.**—*adj.* **cū'biform.**—*n.* **cū'bism** a modern movement in painting, which seeks to represent several aspects of an object seen from different standpoints arbitrarily grouped in one composition, making use of cubes and other solid geometrical figures.—*n.* and *adj.* **cū'bist**.—*n.* **cū'boid** a rectangular parallelepiped esp. one whose faces are not all equal.—*adjs.* **cū'boid, cū'boidal** resembling a cube in shape.—**cube root** the quantity of which the given quantity is the cube. [Fr.,—L. *cubus*—Gr *kybos*, a die.]

cubeb *kū'beb*, *n.* the dried berry of *Piper cubeba*, a Sumatran climbing pepper shrub—used in medicine. [Fr. *cubèbe*—Ar. *kabābah*.]

cubic. See **cube.**

cubicle *kū'bi-kl*, *n.* a bedroom: part of a dormitory or other large room which is partitioned off: a cell or compartment. [L. *cubiculum*—*cubāre*, to lie down.]

cubic zirconia. See under **zircon.**

cubism, etc. See **cube.**

cubit *kū'bit*, *n.* an old measure, the length of the arm from the elbow to the tip of the middle finger. [L. *cubitum*, the elbow; cf. L. *cubāre*, to lie down.]

cuboid, etc. See **cube.**

cucking-stool *kuk'ing-stōōl*, *n.* a stool in which scolds and other culprits were placed, usually before their own door, to be pelted by the mob. [Mentioned in the Domesday Book as in use in Chester, and called *cathedra stercoris*; from an obs. word *cuck*, to defecate; cf. O.N. *kūka.*]

cuckold *kuk'əld*, *n.* a man whose wife has proved unfaithful.—*v.t.* to make cuckold.—*ns.* **cuck'oldom, cuck'oldry** the state of a cuckold: the act of making a cuckold. [O.Fr. *cucuault*—*cucu*, cuckoo.]

cuckoo *kōō'kōō*, *n.* a bird, *Cuculus canorus*, that cries *cuckoo*, remarkable for depositing its eggs in the nests of other birds: any bird of this or related genera: a silly person.—*adj.* (*coll.*) silly.—**cuck'oo-clock** a clock in which the hours are told by a cuckoo-call; **cuck'oo-flower** a species of Cardamine—lady's-smock: ragged robin; **cuck'oo-pint** (*-pint, -pint*) the wake-robin, *Arum maculatum*; **cuck'oo-spit, -spitt'le** a froth secreted by frog-hoppers on plants, surrounding the larvae and pupae. [Imit.]

cucullate, -d *kū'kul-āt*, or *-kul'*, *-id*, *adjs.* hooded: shaped like a hood. [L. *cucullatus*—*cucullus.*]

cucumber *kū'kum-bər*, *-kəm-*, *n.* a creeping plant with bristly lobed leaves and tendrils: its large oblong fruit, used as a salad and pickle. [L. *cucumis, -eris.*]

cucurbit *kū-kûr'bit*, *n.* a chemical vessel used in distillation, originally shaped like a gourd: a cucurbitaceous plant.—*adjs.* **curcur'bital, cucurbità'-ceous** pertaining to the *Curcurbitā'ceæ*, a family of sympetalous dicotyledons, including gourd, melon, etc.: gourd-like. [L. *cucurbita*, a gourd.]

cud *kud*, *n.* food brought back from first stomach of a ruminating animal to be chewed again.—**cud'weed** a woolly composite plant of the genus Gnaphalium: extended to kindred plants.—**chew the cud** (*coll.*) to meditate, to reflect. [O.E. *cwidu.*]

cuddle. See **cuddy**[2].

cuddle *kud'l*, *v.t.* to hug: to embrace: to fondle.—*v.i.* to lie close and snug together.—*n.* a close embrace.—*adjs* **cudd'lesome, cudd'ly** pleasant to cuddle, being e.g. attractively plump, soft, etc.: suggestive of, conducive to, cuddling.

cuddy[1] *kud'i*, *n.* a small cabin or cookroom, in the fore-part of a boat or lighter: in large vessels, the officers' cabin under the poop-deck.

cuddy[2], **cuddie** *kud'i*, (*Scot.* and *dial.*) *n.* a donkey: a horse: a stupid person. [Perh. *Cuthbert.*]

cudgel *kuj'l*, *n.* a heavy staff: a club.—*v.t.* to beat

with a cudgel:—*pr.p.* **cudg'elling;** *pa.t.* and *pa.p.* **cudg'elled.**—*ns.* **cudg'eller; cudg'elling.**—**take up the cudgels** to join in defence. [O.E. *cycgel.*]

cue[1] *kū*, *n.* the seventeenth letter of the alphabet (Q, q).

cue[2] *kū*, *n.* the last words of an actor's speech serving as a hint to the next speaker: any hint: the part one has to play.—*v.t.* to give a cue to: to insert (e.g. a film sequence, sound effect, etc.) into a script:—*pr.p.* **cue'ing, cū'ing;** *pa.t.* and *pa.p.* **cued.**—**cue someone in** to inform (someone); **on cue** just at the right moment. [Acc. to some from Fr. *queue*, tail (see next word); in 17th cent. written Q, and derived from L. *quando*, when, i.e. when the actor was to begin.]

cue[3] *kū*, *n.* a twist of hair at the back of the head: a rod used in playing billiards, etc.—*v.t.* to form a cue in (hair): to hit (a ball) with a cue (also *v.i.*):—*pr.p.* **cue'ing, cū'ing;** *pa.t.* and *pa.p.* **cued.**—*n.* **cue'ist** a billiard-player.—**cue-ball** the ball struck by the cue. [Fr. *queue*—L. *cauda*, a tail.]

cuesta *kwes'tə*, *n.* a hill ridge having a steep scarp on one side and a gradual slope on the other, caused by denudation of gently dipping hard rock strata. [Sp.]

cuff[1] *kuf*, *n.* a stroke with the open hand.—*v.t.* to strike with the open hand: to beat.

cuff[2] *kuf*, *n.* the end of the sleeve near the wrist: a covering for the wrist: a handcuff: a turned-up fold at the bottom of a trouser leg (*U.S.*).—**cuff'-link** either of a pair of usu. decorative fasteners, orig. consisting of two buttons linked together, now usu. one button-like object attached to a pivoting bar, used for fastening a shirt cuff.—**off the cuff** unofficially and offhand. [Prob. cog. with **coif.**]

cui bono? *kī', kwē', bō'nō, kōō'ē bo'nō*, (L.) for whose benefit is it?: who is the gainer?

cuirass *kwi-ras'* (or *kū'*), *n.* a defensive breastplate and backplate fastened together: a breastplate alone.—*v.t.* to furnish with a cuirass.—*n.* **cuirassier** (*-ēr'*) a horse-soldier wearing a cuirass. [Fr. *cuirasse*—*cuir*, leather—L. *corium*, skin, leather.]

Cuisenaire rods *kwē-zə-nār' rodz*, a set of small wooden rods, of significant related sizes and colours, used in teaching arithmetic. [Georges *Cuisenaire*, a Belgian educationalist.]

cuish. See **cuisse.**

cuisine *kwē-zēn'*, *n.* a kitchen or cooking department: cookery.—*n.* **cuisin'ier** (*-yā*) a cook. [Fr.,—L. *coquīna*—*coquĕre*, to cook.]

cuisse *kwis*, **cuish** *kwish*, *ns.* thigh armour. [Fr. *cuisse*—L. *coxa*, hip.]

cul-de-sac *kōōl'də-sak, kul'*, *n.* a street, etc., closed at one end: a blind-alley. [Fr. *cul*, bottom—L. *cūlus*; Fr. *de*, of, *sac*, sack.]

Culex *kū'leks*, *n.* the typical genus of **Culic'idæ** or gnats: (without *cap.*) an insect of this genus:—*pl.* **culices** (*kū'li-sēz*).—*adjs.* **culiciform** (*-lis'*); **cu'licine.**—*n.* **cu'licid.** [L. *culex, -icis.*]

culinary *ku'lin-ər-i, kū'*, *adj.* pertaining to the kitchen or to cookery: used in the kitchen. [L. *culinārius*—*culīna*, a kitchen.]

cull *kul*, *v t* to gather: to select: to pick out and destroy, as inferior or superfluous members of a group, e.g. of seals, deer.—*n.* an act of culling: an unsuitable animal eliminated from a flock or herd.—*ns.* **cull'er; cull'ing.** [Fr. *cueillir*, to gather—L. *colligĕre*—*col-*, together, *legĕre*, to gather.]

cullet *kul'it*, *n.* waste glass, melted up again with new material. [Fr. *collet*—L. *collum*, neck.]

cullis *kul'is*, *n.* a roof gutter or groove. [Fr *coulisse.*]

culm[1] *kulm*, *n.* a grass or sedge stem.—*v.i.* to form a

culm.—*adj.* **culmif'erous** having a culm. [L. *culmus*, a stalk.]

culm² *kulm, n.* coal-dust: anthracite dust: in some parts of England, anthracite.—*adj.* **culmif'erous** producing culm.

culmen *kul'men, n.* the highest point: the top ridge of a bird's bill. [L.; see **culminate.**]

culmiferous. See **culm¹,².**

culminate *kul'min-āt, v.i.* to be on, or come to, the meridian, and thus the highest (or lowest) point of altitude (*astron.*): to reach the highest point (with *in*).—*v.t.* to bring to the highest point.—*adj.* **cul'minant** at its highest point.—*n.* **culmina'tion** the act of culminating: the top: the highest point: transit of a body across the meridian (*astron.*). [L.L. *culmināre, -ātum—culmen,* or *columen, -inis,* a summit.]

culottes *kū-lot', kōō-, n.pl.* a divided skirt.—Also in *sing.* **culotte'.** [Fr. *culotte*, breeches.]

culpable *kul'pə-bl, adj.* faulty: criminal.—*ns.* **culpabil'ity, cul'pableness** liability to blame.—*adv.* **cul'pably.**—*adj.* **cul'patory** expressive of blame. [L. *culpa,* a fault.]

culprit *kul'prit, n.* one in fault: a criminal. [From the fusion in legal phraseology of *cul. (culpable, culpābilis),* and *prit, prist* (O.Fr. *prest*), ready.]

cult *kult, n.* a system of religious belief: formal worship: a sect: an unorthodox or false religion: a great, often excessive, admiration for a person or idea: (with *of*) a fad.—Also **cult'us.**—*adjs.* **cult; cult'ic.** [L. *cultus—colĕre,* to worship.]

cultigen. See under **cultivate.**

cultivate *kul'ti-vāt, v.t.* to fill or produce by tillage: to prepare for crops: to devote attention to: to civilise or refine.—*n.* **cultigen** (*kul'ti-jen*) a cultivated type of plant of uncertain origin.—*adjs.* **cul'tivable, cultivat'able** capable of being cultivated.—*ns.* **cultivar** (*kul'ti-vär*) a plant variety produced from a naturally occurring species, that has been developed and maintained by cultivation (*cultivated variety*); **cultiva'tion** the art or practice of cultivating: civilisation: refinement; **cul'tivator** one who cultivates: an agricultural implement—a grubber.—**cultivate someone's friendship** to seek to gain or foster it. [L.L. *cultivāre, -ātum*—L. *colĕre,* to till, to worship.]

culture *kul'chər, n.* cultivation: the state of being cultivated: refinement: the result of cultivation: a type of civilisation: a crop of experimentally-grown bacteria or the like.—*v.t.* to cultivate: to improve.—*adjs.* **cul'turable; cul'tural.**—*adv.* **cul'turally.**—*adj.* **cul'tured** cultivated: well educated: refined.—*adj.* **cul'tureless.**—*n.* **cul'turist** a devotee of culture.—**cultured pearl** a pearl grown round a small foreign body deliberately introduced into an oyster's shell; **culture vulture** derogatory term for one who has an extravagant interest in the arts. [L. *cultūra—colĕre.*]

cultus. See **cult.**

culvert *kul'vərt, n.* an arched channel for carrying water beneath a road, railway, etc. [Perh. from Fr. *couler,* to flow—L. *colāre.*]

cum *kum, prep.* combined with: with the addition of: used in combination to indicate dual function, nature; etc., as in *kitchen-cum-dining-room.* [L.]

cumarin. See **coumarin.**

cumbent *kum'bənt, adj.* lying down: reclining. [L. *cumbēns, -entis,* pr.p. of *cumbĕre,* to lie down.]

cumber *kum'bər, v.t.* to trouble or hinder with something useless: to get in the way of: to occupy obstructively.—*n.* encumbrance: cumbering.—*adj.* **cum'bered** hampered: obstructed.—*n.* **cum'berer.**—*adj.* **cum'berless** unencumbered.—*n.* **cum'berment.**—*adj.* **cum'bersome** unwieldy.—*n.* **cum'brance** encumbrance —*adj.* **cum'brous** hindering: obstructing:

unwieldy. [Apparently O.Fr. *combrer,* to hinder— L.L. *cumbrus,* a heap—L. *cumulus,* a heap.]

cumec *kū'mek,* (*eng.*) *n.* short for cubic metre per second, a unit for measuring volumetric rate of flow.

cum grano salis *kum grä'nō sā'lis, kŏōm grä'nō sa'lis,* (L.) with a grain of salt.

cumin, cummin *kum'in, n.* an umbelliferous plant of the Mediterranean region, with seeds like caraway, valuable as carminatives. [O.E. *cymen*—L. *cumīnum*—Gr. *kymīnon,* cog. with Heb. *kammon.*]

cummerbund *kum'ər-bund, n.* a waist-belt, a sash. [Pers. *kamarband,* a loin-band.]

cummin. See **cumin.**

cumquat. Same as **kumquat.**

cumulate *kūm'ū-lāt, v.t.* and *v.i.* to heap together: to accumulate.—*adjs.* **cum'ulate, -d** heaped up.—*n.* **cumula'tion** accumulation.—*adj.* **cum'ulative** increasing by successive additions.—*adv.* **cum'ulatively.**—**cumulative vote** a system by which a voter may distribute a number of votes at will among the candidates, giving more than one to a candidate if he chooses. [L. *cumulāre, -ātum—cumulus,* a heap.]

cumulus *kū'mū-ləs, n.* a heap: a kind of cloud consisting of rounded heaps with a darker horizontal base:— *pl.* **cū'muli.**—*adjs.* **cū'muliform; cū'mulose.**— **cū'mulo-cirr'us** a delicate cirrus-like cumulus; **cū'mulo-nim'bus** a cumulus discharging showers. [L. *cumulus,* a heap.]

cunctator *kungk-tā'tər, n.* one who delays or puts off. [L. *cunctātor—cunctāri,* to delay.]

cuneal *kū'ni-əl,* **cuneate** *kū'ni-āt, adjs.* wedge-shaped. —*adjs.* **cuneat'ic** cuneiform; **cuneiform** (*kū-nē'i-förm, kū'ni(i-)förm*) wedge-shaped—specially applied to the old Hittite, Babylonian, Assyrian and Persian writing, of which the characters were impressed by the wedge-shaped facets of a stylus.—*n.* cuneiform writing. [L. *cuneus,* a wedge.]

cunjevoi *kun'ji-voi,* (*Austr.*) *n.* a marine animal: a large-leaved araceous plant. [Native word.]

cunnilingus *kun-i-ling'gəs, n.* oral stimulation of the female genitalia. [L. *cunnus,* vulva, *lingĕre,* to lick.]

cunning *kun'ing, adj.* knowing: skilful: artful: crafty. —*n.* knowledge: skill: faculty of using stratagem to accomplish a purpose: craftiness.—*adv.* **cunn'ingly.** —*n.* **cunn'ingness** the quality of being cunning: artfulness, slyness. [O.E. *cunnan,* to know.]

cunt *kunt, n.* the female genitalia: a term of abuse (*vulg.*). [M.E. *cunte.*]

cup *kup, n.* a drinking-vessel, usu. roughly hemispherical: an ornamental vessel offered as a prize: a hollow: a cup-shaped structure: either of the two cup-shaped supports for the breasts in a brassière: a cupful: half a pint (*U.S.*): the liquid contained in a cup: a mixed beverage made with wine (as *claret-cup*): that which we must receive or undergo.—*v.t.* to form into a cup: to lodge in or as if in a cup: to extract blood from by means of cupping-glasses.—*v.t.* to become cup-shaped:—*pr.p.* **cupp'ing;** *pa.t.* and *pa.p.* **cupped.** —*ns.* **cup'ful** as much as fills a cup:—*pl.* **cup'fuls; cup'pa** (*coll.*) a cup of tea; **cupp'ing** the application of cups from which the air has been exhausted in order to draw blood.—**cup'-and-ball'** a ball and socket joint: the game of catching a tethered ball in a cup on the end of a stick; **cup'-and-ring'(mark)** a cup-mark surrounded by one or more incised rings; **cup'bearer** one who attends at a feast to fill and hand out wine cups; **cupboard** (*kub'ərd*) a place for keeping victuals, dishes, etc.—*v.t.* to store.—**cup'board-love, faith** love or faith with a material end; **cup'-mark** a cup-shaped hollow made by prehistoric man on rocks, standing-stones, etc.; **cupp'ing-glass** a glass used in cupping; **cup'-tie** one of a series of games to determine the winners of a cup.—**in his cups** under the influence of liquor; **there's many a slip 'twixt the cup and the lip** failure is possible at the last moment. [O.E. *cuppe*—L. *cūpa, cuppa*, a tub.]

cupel *kū'pəl, n.* a small vessel used by goldsmiths in assaying precious metals.—*v.t.* to assay in a cupel:—*pr.p.* **cū'pelling;** *pa.t.* and *pa.p.* **cū'pelled.**—*n.* **cūpellā'tion** recovery of precious metal in assaying. [L. *cūpella*, dim. of *cūpa*; see **cup.**]

Cupid *kū'pid, n.* the Roman love-god, identified with Greek Eros: (without *cap.*) a winged figure of a young boy representing the love-god (*art*, etc.).—*adj.* **cūpid'inous** full of desire, esp. amorous.—*n.* **cūpid'ity** covetousness. [L. *Cupīdo, -inis—cupĕre*, to desire.]

cupola *kū'pə-lə, n.* a spherical vault, or concave ceiling, on the top of a building: the internal part of a dome: a dome: a lantern on the top of a dome: an armoured dome or turret to protect a gun: a furnace used in iron-foundries.—*v.t.* to furnish with a cupola.—*adjs.* **cū'pola'd** (or **cū'polaed**); **cū'polar; cū'polated**. [It.,—L. *cūpula*, dim. of *cūpa*, a cask.]

cuppa. See **cup.**

cupreous *kū'pri-əs, adj.* of, containing, or like copper.—*adjs.* **cū'pric** of or containing bivalent copper; **cū'priferous** yielding copper; **cū'prous** of or containing univalent copper.—*n.* **cū'pro-nick'el** an alloy of copper and nickel. [L. *cupreus—cuprum*; see **copper.**]

cupule *kū'pūl, n.* a small cup in a liverwort containing gemmae: a cup-shaped envelope on the fruit of some trees, e.g. oak, beech, chestnut.—*adjs.* **cū'pūlar, cū'pūlate** cup-like: pertaining to a cupule; **cūpūlif'erous** bearing cupules. [L. *cūpula*, dim. of *cūpa*, tub.]

cur *kûr, n.* a worthless dog, of low breed: a contemptible scoundrel.—*adj.* **curr'ish.**—*adv.* **curr'ishly.**—*n.* **curr'ishness.** [M.E. *curre*; cf. O.N. *kurra*, to grumble.]

curaçao, curaçoa, *kōō-rä-sä'ō, kū'rə-sō, kū-rə-sō', ns.* a liqueur flavoured with bitter orange peel. [*Curaçao*, island in West Indies, where first made.]

curacy. See **curate.**

curare, curari *kū-* or *kōō-rä'ri, n.* a paralysing poison extracted from wourali root (*Strychnos toxifera*), etc., by South American Indians for arrows—now a source of valuable drugs.—*n.* **cura'rine** a highly poisonous alkaloid therefrom, used, in surgery, as a muscle relaxant. [Port. from carib *kurari.*]

curassow *kū'rə-sō, kū-räs'ō, n.* a large turkey-like S. American bird. [From the island of *Curaçao.*]

curate *kûr'it, n.* one who has the cure of souls: a clergyman in the Church of England, assisting a rector or vicar.—*ns.* **cur'acy** (*-ə-si*), **cur'ateship** the office, employment, or benefice of a curate.—**curate's egg** anything of which parts are excellent. [L.L *cūrātus*, L. *cūra*, care.]

curative. See **cure.**

curator *kûr-ā'tər, n.* one who has the charge of anything: a superintendent, esp. of a museum:—*fem.* **cura'trix.**—*n.* **cura'torship.** [L. *cūrātor.*]

curatory. See **cure.**

curb *kûrb, n.* a chain or strap attached to the bit for restraining a horse: another spelling for **kerb** (chiefly *U.S.*): a check or restraint.—*v.t.* to furnish with or guide by a curb: to restrain or check. [Fr. *courbe*—L. *curvus*, bent.]

Curcuma *kûr-kū'ma, n.* a genus of the ginger family yielding turmeric: (without *cap.*) any plant of the genus.—*n.* **cur'cumine** the colouring matter of turmeric. [Ar. *kurkum*, saffron.]

curd *kûrd, n.* milk thickened or coagulated by acid: the cheese part of milk, as distinguished from the whey: any similar substance: the flowering head of cauli-

flower, broccoli, etc.—*n.* **curd'iness.**—*v.t.* and *v.i.* **curd'le** to turn into curd: to coagulate: to thicken.—*adj.* **curd'y** like or full of curd. [Prob. Celt.; Gael. *gruth*, Ir. *cruth.*]

cure *kûr, n.* care of souls or spiritual charge: care of the sick: an act of healing: that which heals: a remedy, or course of remedial treatment: a means of improving a situation: a course or method of preserving or arresting decomposition: the total quantity cured: treatment by which a product is finished or made ready for use.—*v.t.* to heal or make better: to preserve as by drying, salting, etc.: to finish by means of chemical change, e.g., to vulcanise (a rubber), or to use heat or chemicals in the last stage of preparing (a thermosetting plastic).—*v.i.* to undergo a process or course of curing.—*adj.* **cūr'able;**—*ns.* **cūr'ableness; cūrabil'ity.**—*adjs.* **cūr'ative, cūr'atory** tending to cure.—*adj.* **cūre'less** that cannot be cured.—*n.* **cūr'er.**—**cūre'-all** a panacea. [O.Fr. *cure*—L. *cūra*, care.]

curé *kū'rā, n.* a parish priest in France. [Fr.; see **curate.**]

curettage *kū-ret'ij, n.* scraping of a body cavity by means of a surgeon's instrument known as a **curette'**. [Fr. *curer*, to clean, clear.]

curfew *kûr'fū, n.* in feudal times the ringing of a bell as a signal to put out all fires and lights: the ringing of a bell at a certain hour continued as a traditional custom. a signal for the imposition of restrictions of other kinds, e.g. from being abroad in the streets at night: the time of curfew: the bell itself: a regulation obliging persons to be indoors within certain hours.—**cur'few-bell.** [O.Fr. *covrefeu; couvrir*, to cover, *feu*, fire—L. *focus.*]

curfuffle. See **carfuffle.**

curia *kū'ri-ə, n.* one of the ten divisions of a Roman tribe: a building in which the senate met: a provincial senate: a court, legislative or judicial: the court of the papal see. [L. *cūria.*]

curie *kū-rē', kū'rē, n.* orig., the quantity of radon in radioactive equilibrium with a gram of radium: now, the quantity of a radioactive substance that undergoes $3 \cdot 70 \times 10^{10}$ radioactive transformations per second.—*n.* **curium** (*kū'*) a chemical element (at. numb. 96; symbol Cm). [After Marie and Pierre *Curie*, discoverers of radium.]

curio *kū'ri-ō, n.* any article of virtu or bric-à-brac, or anything considered rare and curious:—*pl.* **cū'rios.** [For **curiosity.**]

curious *kū'ri-əs, adj.* anxious to learn: inquisitive: singular: rare: odd.—*n.* **curiosity** (*-os'i-ti*) state or quality of being curious: inquisitiveness: that which is curious: anything rare or unusual.—*adv.* **cū'riously.**—*n.* **cū'riousness.** [Fr. *curieux*—L. *cūriōsus—cūra.*]

curium. See **curie.**

curl *kûrl, v.t.* to twist into ringlets: to coil: to cause to move in a curve: to ripple.—*v.i.* to shrink into ringlets: to move in curves: to writhe: to ripple: to eddy: to play at the game of curling.—*n.* a ringlet of hair, or what is like it: a wave, bending, or twist: an eddy: a plant disease in which leaves curl: a curled condition.—*adj.* **curled.**—*ns.* **curl'er** one who, or that which, curls: a player at the game of curling; **curl'iness; curl'ing** a game common in Scotland, consisting in sliding heavy smooth stones along a sheet of ice.—*adj.* **curl'y** having curls: full of curls.—**curl'ing-irons, curl'ing-tongs** an instrument used for curling the hair; **curl'ing-pond** a pond on which curling is played; **curl'ing-stone** a heavy stone with a handle, used in playing curling; **curl'-pap'er** a paper twisted into the hair to give it curl; **curl'y-greens** kale.—*adj.* **curl'y-head'ed.** [M.E. *crull.*]

curlew *kûr'lōō*, *-lū*, *n.* a moorland bird of the woodcock family with long curved bill and long legs, and plaintive whistling cry. [O.Fr. *corlieu*; prob. from its cry.]

curlicue *kûr'lǝ-kū*, *n.* a fantastic curl: a fancy twist. [curly, and cue².]

curmudgeon *kǝr-muj'ǝn*, *n.* an avaricious, ill-natured churlish fellow: a miser.—*adj.* and *adv.* **curmud'geonly.**

curmurring *kǝr-mûr'ing*, *n.* a rumbling sound, esp. that made in the bowels by flatulence. [Imit.]

curnaptious. See carnaptious.

currach, -agh *kur'ǝ(hh)*, *n.* a long-shaped boat of similar construction to a coracle. [Ir. *curach*.]

currajong. See kurrajong.

currant *kur'ǝnt*, *n.* a small black raisin or dried seedless grape (imported from eastern Mediterranean countries): extended to several species of Ribes (*black, red, white, flowering currant*), and to various other plants, and their fruits.—*adj.* **curr'anty** full of currants.—**curr'ant-bread'** a sweetened bread with some (grape) currants in it; **curr'ant-bun, curr'ant-loaf'** a dark spiced cake full of currants; **curr'ant-cake'** a cake with currants in it; **curr'ant-jell'y** a jelly made from red or black currants; **curr'ant-wine'.** [Corinth.]

currawong *kur'ǝ-wong*, *n.* any of several Australian birds of the genus *Strepera*. [Native name.]

current *kur'ǝnt*, *adj.* running or flowing: passing from person to person: generally or widely received: now passing: present: belonging to the period of time now passing.—*n.* a running or flowing: a stream: a portion of water or air moving in a certain direction: a flow of electricity: course.—*n.* **curr'ency** circulation: that which circulates, esp. the money of a country: general estimation.—*adv.* **curr'ently.**—*n.* **curr'entness.**—**current account** a bank account from which money may be withdrawn by cheque.—**pass current** to be received as genuine. [L. *currēns, -entis*—pr.p. of *currĕre*, to run.]

curricle *kur'i-kl*, *n.* a two-wheeled open chaise, drawn by two horses abreast. [L. *curriculum*, course, race, racing chariot—*currĕre*, to run.]

curriculum *kǝ-rik'ū-lǝm*, *n.* a course, esp. the course of study at a university, etc.:—*pl.* **curric'ula** or **-ums.**—*adj.* **curric'ular** of or relating to a curriculum or to courses of study.—**curriculum vitae** (*kǝ-rik'ūl-ǝm vī'tē, kōōr-ik'ōō-lōōm vē'tī, wē'tī*) (a biographical sketch of) the course of one's life. [L.; see curricle.]

currish, currishly, etc. See cur.

curry¹ *kur'i*, *n.* a meat or other dish prepared with turmeric and mixed spices.—*v.t.* to make a curry of. —**curr'y-leaf** an Indian tree whose leaves are an ingredient in curry-powder; **curr'y-pow'der** ground spices and turmeric. [Tamil *kari*, sauce.]

curry² *kur'i*, *v.t.* to dress (leather): to rub down and dress (a horse): to beat: to scratch:—*pr.p.* **curr'ying;** *pa.t.* and *pa.p.* **curr'ied.**—*ns.* **curr'ier** one who curries or dresses tanned leather; **curr'ying.**—**curr'y-comb** an iron instrument or comb used for currying or cleaning horses.—**curry favour** to seek to ingratiate oneself. [O.Fr. *correier* (Fr. *corroyer*), *conrei*, outfit, from L. *con-*, with, and the root seen in array.]

curse *kûrs*, *v.t.* to invoke or wish evil upon: to blaspheme: to afflict with: to utter doom or damnation against: to excommunicate.—*v.i.* to utter imprecations: to swear. —*n.* an invocation or wishing of evil or harm: evil invoked on another: excommunication sentence: an imprecation: any great evil: (with *the*) menstrual period (*coll.*).—*adj.* **curs'ed** under a curse: hateful.—*adv.* **curs'edly.**—*ns.* **curs'edness; curs'er; curs'ing.**—*adj.* **curst** cursed. [O.E. *cursian—curs*, a curse.]

cursive *kûr'siv*, *adj.* (of handwriting) written with a running hand: flowing.—*adv.* **cur'sively.** [L.L. *cursīvus*—L. *currĕre*, to run.]

cursor *kûr'sǝr*, *n.* a sliding part of a measuring instrument: one of several (usu. flashing) devices appearing on a VDU screen used to indicate position, e.g. of the next input character, of a correction, etc.—*adj.* **cur-so'rial** adapted for running.—*adv.* **cur'sorily** (*-sǝr-*).—*n.* **cur'soriness.**—*adj.* **cur'sory** running quickly over: hasty: superficial. [L. *cursor*, pl. *cursōrēs*, a runner—*currĕre, cursum*, to run.]

curst. See curse.

curt *kûrt*, *adj.* short: concise: discourteously brief or summary.—*adv.* **curt'ly.**—*n.* **curt'ness.** [L. *curtus*, shortened.]

curtail *kǝr-tāl'*, *v.t.* to cut short: to cut off a part of: to abridge.—*n.* **curtail'ment.** [Old spelling *curtal*, O.Fr. *courtault*—L. *curtus*, shortened.]

curtain *kûr'tǝn*, *n.* hanging drapery at a window, around a bed, etc.: the part of a rampart between two bastions: a curtain wall: a screen of cloth or metal concealing the stage, or restricting the spread of fire (*theat.*): the fall of the curtain, close of a scene or act (*theat.*): a protective barrier in general.—*v.t.* to enclose or furnish with curtains.—**curtain call** a summons from the audience to appear at the end of a scene; **cur'tain-raiser** a short play preceding the main performance: an event which precedes and foreshadows a more important event; **curtain speech** a speech made before a theatre curtain; **curtain wall** a wall that is not load-bearing, e.g. does not support a roof.—**be curtains (for)** to be the end or death (of) (*coll.*); **behind the curtain** away from public view; **draw the curtain** to draw it aside, so as to show what is behind, or to draw it in front of anything so as to hide it. [O.Fr. *cortine*—L.L. *cortīna*; prob. L. *cors, cōrtis*, a court.]

curtana *kûr-tä'nǝ, -tā'nǝ, n.* a sword without a point, symbolic of mercy, carried at coronations. [L. *curtus*, short.]

curtilage *kûr'til-ij, n.* a court or area of land attached to and including a dwelling-house, etc. [O.Fr. *courtillage*; see court.]

curtsy, curtsey *kûrt'si, n.* an obeisance, esp. by women, made by bending the knees.—*v.i.* to make or 'drop' a curtsy. [See courtesy.]

curvaceous, curvate, etc. See curve.

curve *kûrv, n.* anything bent: a line that is not straight: a line (including a straight line) answering to an equation: a graph: a curved surace: an arch: (in *pl.*) the rounded contours of a woman's body (*coll.*).—*v.t.* to bend: to form into a curve.—*v.i.* to bend: to move in a curve.—*adjs.* **curvaceous, curvacious** (*kûr-vā'shǝs; coll.*) (of a woman) having shapely curves; **cur'vate, -d** curved or bent in a regular form.—*n.* **curvā'tion.**—*adj.* **cur'vative** (*-vǝ-tiv*).—*n.* **cur'vature** (*-vǝ-chǝr*) a curving or bending: the continual bending, or the amount of bending, from a straight line: the reciprocal of the radius at any point.—*adjs.* **curved; curve'-some** curvaceous; **curvicau'date** having a crooked tail; **curvicos'tate** having curved ribs; **curvifo'liate** having curved leaves; **cur'viform; curvilin'eal, cur-vilin'ear** bounded by curved lines.—*n.* **cur-vilinear'ity.**—*adjs.* **cur'ving; curv'y.** [L. *curvus*, crooked.]

curvet *kûr'vet, kǝr-vet', n.* a light leap of a horse in which he raises his forelegs together, next the hindlegs with a spring before the forelegs touch the ground: a leap, frolic.—*v.i.* (*kǝr-vet', kûr'vet*), to leap in curvets: to frisk:—*pr.p.* **curvett'ing, cur'-veting;** *pa.t.* and *pa.p.* **curvett'ed, cur'veted.** [It. *corvetta*, dim. of *corvo*—L. *curvus*.]

curvicaudate, curvilineal, etc. See curve.

cusec *kū'sek*, (*eng.*) *n.* short for cubic feet per second, a unit for measuring volumetric rate of flow.

cush. See **cushion.**

cushat *kush'ət*, (*Scot*) *n.* the ringdove or wood-pigeon. [O.E. *cúscute*, perh. from its note, and *scēotan*, to shoot.]

cushion *kŏŏsh'ən*, *n.* a case filled with some soft, elastic stuff, e.g. feathers, foam rubber, for resting on: a pillow: a pad: the elastic lining of the inner side of a billiard-table (*coll.* **cush**): a body of steam remaining in the cylinder of a steam-engine, acting as a buffer to the piston: anything that serves to a deaden a blow.— *v.t.* to seat on, or furnish with, a cushion: to serve as a cushion for or against: to suppress (complaints) by ignoring.—*adj.* **cush'ioned** furnished with a cushion, padded: having cushion-tyres.—*n.* **cush'ionet** a little cushion.—*adj.* **cush'iony** like a cushion, soft.— **cush'ion-tyre, -tire** a cycle tyre of rubber tubing, with rubber stuffing. [O.Fr. *coissin*—L. *coxīnum, coxa,* hip, or perh.   L. *culcita*, mattress, cushion.]

Cushite, Kushite *kŏŏsh'īt, n.* a group of languages of eastern Africa: a (member of a) race speaking any of these languages.—*adj.* of or relating to the languages or the race.—Also **Cushitic, Kushitic** (*-it'*). [*Cush,* an ancient kingdom in the Nile valley, and **-ite.**]

cushy *kŏŏsh'i,* (*slang*) *adj.* easy and comfortable: not dangerous. [Perh. Hind. *khush,* pleasant, *khushī,* happiness.]

cusp *kusp, n.* a point: the point or horn of the moon, etc.: a tooth-like meeting of two branches of a curve, with sudden change of direction: a tooth-like ornament common in Gothic tracery (*archit.*): a prominence on a tooth: a division between signs of the zodiac (*astrol.*).—*adjs.* **cus'pate; cusped; cus'pid; cus'pidal; cus'pidate, -d** (*biol.*) having a rigid point. [L. *cuspis, -idis,* a point.]

cuspidor(e) *kus'pi-dôr* or *-dor,* (*U.S.*) *n.* a spittoon. [Port.,—L. *conspuĕre,* to spit upon.]

cuss *kus,* (*slang*) *n.* a curse: a fellow.—*v.t.* and *v.i.* to curse.—*adj.* **cuss'ed** cursed: obstinate.—*n.* **cuss'edness** contrariness.—**cuss'-word.** [*curse;* prob. sometimes associated with **customer.**]

custard *kus'tərd, n.* a baked mixture of milk, eggs, etc., sweetened or seasoned (now usu. **egg custard**): a cooked mixture of similar composition, thickened with cornflour.—**cus'tard-apple** the fruit of a W. Indian tree with eatable pulp, like a custard; **custard-pie (comedy)** slapstick, esp. of early U.S. films in which comedians threw custard pies at each other; **custard powder** a flavoured preparation containing cornflour, sugar, etc. for using with milk to make custard. [Earlier *custade,* a corr. of *crustade,* a pie with a crust; see **crust.**]

custody *kus'tə-di, n.* a watching or guarding: care: security: imprisonment.—*adj.* **custo'dial.**—*ns.* **custo'dian,** **cus'tode, custo'dier, cus'tos** one who has care, esp. of some public building, **custo'dianship.** [L. *custōdia,* guard, *custōs, -ōdis,* a keeper.]

custom *kus'təm, n.* what one is wont to do: what is usually done by others: usage: frequent repetition of the same act: regular trade or business: any of the distinctive practices and conventions of a people or locality: a tax on goods: (in *pl.*) duties on imports and exports. (in *pl.*) the collecting authorities.—*adj* (esp *U.S*) made to order.—*adv* **cus'tomarily.**—*n* **cus'tomariness.**—*adj.* **cus'tomary** according to use and wont: usual: holding or held by custom: copyhold —*n.* **cus'tomer** one accustomed to a frequent a certain place of business: a buyer: a person (*slang*).— *v.t* **cus'tomise, -ize** to make in such a way as to suit specified individual requirements —*adj.* **cus'tomized, -z-.**—*adjs* **cus'tom-built', cus'tom-made'** built (as e g a motor-car) or made to a customer's order.—

cus'tom-house the place, esp. at a port, where customs or duties on exports and imports are collected.—**customs union** a territory treated as if one state for purposes of custom duties. [O.Fr. *custume, costume*—L. *cōnsuētūdō, -inis—cōnsuēscĕre,* to accustom.]

customary. See **custom.**

cut *kut, v.t.* to penetrate with a sharp edge: to make an incision in: to cleave or pass through: to divide: to carve, hew, or make or fashion by cutting: to sever: to reap: to excise; to intersect: to divide (a pack of cards) by lifting the upper portion at random: to expose (a card or suit) in this way: in tennis, golf, etc., to strike obliquely, imparting spin to: to reduce or lessen: to abridge: to trim: to wound or hurt: to affect deeply: to shorten: to pass intentionally without greeting: to renounce, give up: to stay away from: to make (a sound recording, e.g. a disc): to grow (teeth) through the gums.—*v.i.* to make an incision: to intersect: to strike obliquely: to be cut: to dash, go quickly: to run away, to be off (*slang*): in film-making, to cease photographing: (of a film) to change rapidly to another scene:—*pr.p.* **cutt'ing;** *pa.t.* and *pa.p.* **cut.**— *n.* a cleaving or dividing: an excavation for a road, railway, etc.: a cross passage: a stroke or blow: in various games, a particular stroke, generally implying obliquity and spin: in cricket, a stroke to the off side with horizontal bat: a reduction or diminution: an act of unkindness: the result of fashioning by cutting, carving, etc. (e.g. clothes, hair, gem stones): the act, or outcome, of cutting a pack of cards: an incision or wound: an excision: a piece cut off: total quantity cut: a varying unit of length for cloth and yarn: an engraved block or the picture from it: manner of cutting, or fashion: a rake-off or share (*slang*): in films, the action of cutting or its result.—*adj.* (*slang*) of a drug, adulterated or diluted.—*ns.* **cutt'er** a person or thing that cuts: a tailor who measures and cuts out the cloth: a small vessel with one mast, a mainsail, a forestay-sail, and a jib set to bowsprit-end; **cutt'ing** a dividing or lopping off: an incision: a piece cut from a newspaper: a piece of a plant cut off for propagation: an open excavation for road, railway, etc.: editing of film or recording.—*adj.* of a remark, etc., intended to be cruel or hurtful: of wind, penetrating.—**cut'away** a coat with the skirt cut away in a curve in front.—Also *adj.*—**cut'back** a going back in a plot to earlier happenings: a reduction or decrease, esp. in expenditure, workforce, production, etc.; **cut glass** flint glass shaped by cutting or grinding; **cut'-in'** the act of cutting in; **cut'-off** that which cuts off or shortens, e.g. a straighter road: a device for shutting off steam, water, light, etc.: the point at which something ceases to operate or apply (also *adj.*); **cut'-out** the act of cutting out: something which has been cut out: a safety device, e.g. for breaking an electric circuit.— *adj.* **cut'-price** at a reduced rate.—**cut'purse** a pickpocket; **cut'-throat** an assassin: a ruffian: an open razor.—*adj.* murderous: ruinous.—**cut'-water** the forepart of a ship's prow.—a **cut above** something distinctly better; **cut a dash** or **figure** to have a striking appearance; **cut and cover** a method of forming a tunnel by making an open cutting, arching it over, and covering in; **cut and dry** or **cut and dried** ready made, fixed beforehand—from the state of herbs in the shop instead of the field; **cut and run** to be off quickly; **cut and thrust** in fencing, the use of the edges and the point of the weapon: swift, shrewd, and cleverly-calculated action or reaction, argument, etc. (*adj* **cut'-and-thrust'**); **cut back** to prune close to the stem: to revert to a previous scene: to reduce; **cut both ways** of a decision, action, situation, etc , to have or result in both advantages and disadvantages, **cut corners** to turn corners by the quickest way, not keeping close to the edge of the road: to do something (e.g. a piece of work) with the minimum of effort and expenditure and therefore often imperfectly; **cut dead** to refuse to recognise; **cut down** to take down by cutting the rope on which one has been hanged: to bring down by cutting: to reduce, curtail; **cut down to size** to cause (a person) to feel less important or to be less conceited; **cut in** to interpose: to deprive someone of a dancing partner: to eavesdrop by telephone: to take one's place in a line of traffic in front of an overtaken vehicle, etc., esp. when meeting others: to come into a game by cutting a card: to give a share; **cut it fine** to take risks by calculating too narrowly; **cut it out** (coll.) to make an end of it, leave off; **cut off** to sever: to isolate: put to an untimely death: to intercept: to stop: of an electrical device, to stop working, usu. automatically, esp. as a safety measure: to disinherit; **cut off with a shilling** to bequeath only a shilling: to disinherit; **cut one's coat according to one's cloth** to adapt oneself to circumstances; **cut one's losses** to have done with an unprofitable matter; **cut one's teeth (on)** (coll.) to gain experience (by means of): to practise (on); **cut out** to shape: to contrive: to debar: to supplant: to separate from a herd: to pass out of a game on cutting a card: to pass out of a line of traffic in order to overtake: of an engine, suddenly to stop functioning; **cut out for** naturally fitted for; **cut short** to abridge: to make short by cutting: to silence by interruption; **cut teeth** to have teeth grow through the gums, as an infant; **cut up** to cut into pieces: to criticise severely: to turn out (well or ill) when divided into parts: (in pass.) to be deeply afflicted; **cut up rough** to take something amiss.

cutaneous. See cutis.

cute kūt, adj. an aphetic form of **acute:** daintily or quaintly pleasing.—n. **cū'tie, cūt'ey** a smart girl.

cuticle, etc. See cutis.

cutis kū'tis, n. the skin: the true skin, as distinguished from the cuticle.—adj. **cūtān'eous** belonging to the skin.—n. **cū'ticle** the outermost or thin skin: the dead skin at the edge of finger- and toenails: the waxy or corky layer on the epidermis in plants (bot.).—adj. **cūtic'ular.** [L.]

cutlass kut'las, n. a short, broad sword, with one cutting edge, formerly used in the navy. [Fr. coutelas, augmentative from L. cultellus, dim. of culter, a ploughshare, a knife.]

cutler kut'lər, n. one who makes or sells knives.—n. **cut'lery** the business of a cutler: edged or cutting instruments in general: implements for eating food. [Fr. coutelier—O.Fr. coutel—L. culter, knife.]

cutlet kut'lit, n. rib and the meat belonging to it or similar piece of mutton, veal, etc.: other food made up in the shape of a cutlet. [Fr. côtelette, dim. of côte, from L. costa, a rib.]

cuttle kut'l, n. a cephalopod mollusc remarkable for its power of ejecting a black, inky liquid (also **cutt'lefish**): extended to other cephalopods.—**cutt'le-bone** the internal shell of the cuttlefish, used for making tooth-powder, for polishing metals and for cage-birds to sharpen their beaks on. [O.E. cudele.]

cutto, cuttoe kut'ō, n. a large knife:—pl. **cutt'oes.** [Fr. couteau.]

cutty kut'i, (Scot.) adj. short, curtailed.—**cutt'y-sark'** a short shift, or its wearer; **cutt'y-stool** the stool of repentance in old Scottish church discipline. [cut.]

cuvée kü-vā, kōō-vā', n. a vat of blended wine of uniform quality. [Fr.]

cwm. Welsh form of coomb.

cyanogen sī-an'ō-jən, n. a compound of carbon and nitrogen $(CN)_2$ forming a colourless, poisonous gas

with a characteristic odour—an essential ingredient of Prussian blue.—ns. **cy'an** a greenish blue: printers' blue ink; **cyanate** (sī'ən-āt) a salt of cyanic acid.—adj. **cyan'ic** of or belonging to cyanogen.—n. **cy'anide** a direct compound of cyanogen with a metal.—v.t. to treat with a cyanide.—ns. **cy'aniding** extraction of gold or silver from ore by means of potassium cyanide; **cy'anin** a plant pigment, blue in cornflower, but red in the rose because of its reaction with acids; **cy'anine** any of a group of dyes used as sensitisers in photography.—v.t. **cy'anise, -ize** to turn into cyanide. —ns. **cyanocobal'amin** vitamin B_{12}, which has a large and complicated molecule, in one form including a cyanide group, in all forms including a cobalt atom; **cyanom'eter** an instrument for measuring the blueness of the sky or ocean.—**cyanic acid** an acid composed of cyanogen, oxgen and hydrogen (HCNO). [Gr. kyanos, blue.]

cybernetics sī-bər-net'iks, n. sing. the comparative study of automatic communication and control in functions of living bodies and in mechanical electronic systems (such as in computers).—adj. **cybernet'ic.** — n. **cybernet'icist** (-sist). [Gr. kybernētēs, a steersman.]

cycad sī'kad, n. one of an order of gymnospermous plants, more or less akin to conifers but superficially resembling ferns and palms.—adj. **cycadā'ceous.** [Formed from supposed Gr. kykas, a misreading of koīkas, accus. pl. of koïx, doum-palm.]

cycl-. See cycl(o)-.

cyclamate sik'lə-māt, sīk', n. any of a number of very sweet substances derived from petrochemicals, formerly used as sweetening agents in food, soft drinks, etc.

Cyclamen sik'lə-mən, n. a S. European genus of Primulaceae, with nodding flowers and bent-back petals: (without cap.) a plant of the genus. [Gr. kyklaminos.]

cycle sī'kl, n. a period of time in which events happen in a certain order, and which constantly repeats itself: a recurring series of changes: an age: an imaginary circle or orbit in the heavens: a series of poems, romances, etc., centring in a figure or event: a group of songs with related subjects: a bicycle or tricycle: complete series of changes in a periodically varying quantity, e.g. an alternating current, during one period: sequence of computer operations which continues until a criterion for stoppage is reached, or the time of this.—v.t. to cause to pass through a cycle of operations or events: to transport or accompany on a cycle.—adjs. **cy'clic, -al** pertaining to or containing a cycle: recurring in cycles: arranged in a ring or rings. —n. **cyclical'ity.**—adv. **cy'clically.**—ns. **cy'clicism; cyclic'ity; cy'clist** one who rides on a cycle; **cy'cloid** a figure like a circle: a curve traced by a point on the circumference of a circle which rolls along a straight line.—adj. nearly circular: cyclothymic: characterised by swings of mood (psych.).—adj. **cycloid'al.** —ns. **cyclom'eter** an instrument for measuring circular arcs: an apparatus attached to the wheel of a cycle for registering the distance traversed; **cyclo'sis** circulation.—**cy'cle-car** a small light motor-car; **cy'cleway** a track or path, often running alongside a road, constructed and reserved for cyclists; **cyclic compound** a closed-chain or ring compound in which the ring consists of carbon atoms only (carbocyclic compound) or of carbon atoms linked with one or more other atoms (heterocyclic compound); **cy'clocross** a pedal-bicycle race over rough country in the course of which bicycles have to be carried over natural obstacles.—**cycle per second** see hertz. [Gr. kyklos, circle.]

cycl(o)- sīk-l(ō)-, in composition, cycle: ring: circle:

cyclic compound. See cycle, and also entries below. [Gr. *kyklos*, circle.]

cyclo sī'klō, (*coll.*) *n.* a trishaw:—*pl.* cy'clos. [cycle.]

cycloid. See cycle.

cyclone sī'klōn, *n.* a system of winds blowing spirally inwards towards a centre of low barometric pressure: loosely, a wind-storm: a separating apparatus, a kind of centrifuge.—*adj.* cyclon'ic. [Gr. *kyklōn*, contr pr.p. of *kykloein*, to whirl round.]

cyclopaedia, cyclopedia sī-klō-pē'di-ə, *n.* a shortened form of encyclopaedia.—*adj.* cyclopae'dic, cyclo-pe'dic.

cyclopropane sī-klō-prō'pān, *n.* a cyclic hydrocarbon C_3H_6, a general anaesthetic. [Gr. *kyklos*, circle, and propane.]

Cyclops sī'klops, *n.* one of a fabled race of giants who lived chiefly in Sicily, with one eye in the middle of the forehead (*pl.* Cy'clops, Cyclō'pes, or Cy'clopses): (without *cap.*) a one-eyed monster (*pl.* cyclō'pes). [Gr. *kyklōps*, pl. *kyklōpēs*—*kyklos*, a circle, and *ōps*, an eye.]

cyclorama sī-klō-rä'mə, *n.* a circular panorama: a curved background in stage and cinematograph sets, used to give impression of sky distance, and for lighting effects. —*adj.* cycloram'ic. [Gr. *kyklos*, circle, *horāma*, view.]

cyclospermous sī-klō-spûr'məs, (*bot.*) *adj.* with embryo bent round the endosperm. [Gr. *kyklos*, circle, *sperma*, seed.]

Cyclostomata sī-klō-stō'mə-tə, *n.pl.* a class of animals with fixed open mouth, including the lampreys.—*n.* cy'clostome a member of the class.—*adj.* cyclostom-ous (*-klos'to-məs*). [Gr. *kyklos*, wheel, *stōma*, mouth.]

cyclostyle sī'klō-stīl, *n.* an apparatus for multiplying copies of a writing by use of a pen with a small puncturing wheel. [Gr. *kyklos*, circle, and style.]

cyclothymia sī-klō-thī'mi-ə, *n.* a temperament inclined to alternation of high and low spirits.—*n.* cy'clothyme a person having such a temperament.—*adj.* cyclothy'mic. [Gr. *kyklos*, circle, *thymos*, spirit.]

cyder. Same as cider.

cyesis sī-ēs'is, *n.* pregnancy. [Gk. *kyēsis*.]

cygnet sig'nit, *n.* a young swan. [Dim. from L. *cygnus*, directly or through Fr. *cygne*, which seems to be a reshaping of *cisne*—L.L. *cicinus*, L. *cycnus*—Gr. *kyknos*, a swan.]

cylinder sil'in-dər, *n.* a solid figure of uniform cross-section generated by a straight line remaining parallel to a fixed axis and moving round a closed curve—ordinarily in a circle perpendicular to the axis (giving a *right circular cylinder*): a roller-shaped object: a cylindrical part, solid or hollow, as a rotating part of a printing press, the tubular chamber in which a piston works (*mech.*).—*adjs.* cylin'dric, -al.—*adv.* cylin'-drically.—*n.* cylindricity (*-dris'i-ti*).—*adj.* cylin'-driform in the form of a cylinder.—*ns.* cylin'drite a mineral of cylindrical habit, compound of tin, lead, antimony, and sulphur; cyl'indroid a body like a cylinder.—Also *adj.*—cyl'inder-block a casing in which the cylinders of an internal-combustion engine are contained; cyl'inder-head the closed end of the cylinder of an internal-combustion engine; cylinder lock a type of lock comprising a movable cylinder which can be rotated inside a fixed cylinder only when the correct key is inserted.—firing, working, etc. on all cylinders working at full strength or perfectly: in good condition. [Gr. *kylindros*, roller, *kylindein*, to roll.]

cymbal sim'bəl, *n.* a hollow brass plate-like musical instrument, beaten with a stick, etc. or against another of a pair —*ns* cym'balist a cymbal-player; cym'balo the dulcimer:—*pl.* cym'baloes, -os.—*adj.*

cym'biform boat-shaped. [L. *cymbalum*—Gr. *kymbalon*—*kymbē*, the hollow of a vessel.]

cyme sīm, (*bot.*) *n.* a young shoot: any sympodial inflorescence, the main shoot ending in a flower, the subsequent flowers growing on successive lateral branches.—*adj.* cym'oid, cym'ose, cym'ous. [L. *cyma*, *cīma*—Gr. *kyma*, a sprout.]

Cymric *kum'rik, kum'*, or *sim'*, *adj.* Welsh.—*n* Cym'ry the Welsh. [W. *Cymru*, Wales.]

cynic, -al *sin'ik, -əl*, *adjs.* dog-like: surly: snarling: disinclined to recognise or believe in goodness or selflessness.—*ns.* Cyn'ic one of a sect of philosophers founded by Antisthenes of Athens (born c. 444 B.C.), characterised by an ostentatious contempt for riches, arts, science, and amusements—so called from their morose manners: (without *cap.*) a morose man: (without *cap.*) a snarler: (without *cap.*) one who takes a pessimistic view of human motives and actions; cyn'icism (*-i-sizm*) surliness: contempt for and suspicion of human nature: heartlessness, misanthropy: a cynical remark —*adv.* cyn'ically.—*n.* cyn'icalness. [Gr. *kynikos*, dog-like—*kyōn, kynos*, dog.]

cynosure *sin'* or *sīn'ō-shōōr*, *n.* the dog's tail, or Lesser Bear (*Ursa Minor*), the constellation containing the North Star: the North Star itself: hence anything that strongly attracts attention or admiration. [Gr. *kyōn, kynos*, a dog, *ourā*, a tail.]

cypher. Same as cipher.

cypress sī'prəs, *-pris*, *n.* a coniferous tree (Cupressus), whose branches used to be carried at funerals: hence a symbol of death: extended to various other trees, esp. in America to the swamp-growing deciduous conifer *Taxodium distichum.*—cy'press-swamp'. [O.Fr. *ciprès* (Fr. *cyprès*)—L. *cupressus*—Gr. *kyparissos.*]

Cyprian sip'ri-ən, *adj.* of the island of Cyprus.—*n.* a Cypriot.—*n.* Cyp'riot(e) a native of Cyprus.

Cyprinus si-prī'nəs, *n.* the carp genus of fishes, giving name to the fam. Cyprinidae (*si-prin'i-dē*).—*adjs.* cyprine (*sip'rin*), cyp'rinoid (*-rin-oid*). [L.—Gr. *kyprinos*, a kind of carp.]

Cypriot(e). See Cyprian.

Cypripedium *sip-ri-pē'di-əm*, *n.* a genus of orchids: (without *cap.*) a plant of the genus, lady's slipper:—*pl.* cypripē'dia. [Gr. *Kypris*, Aphrodite, *podion*, a little foot, modified by L. *pēs*, foot.]

Cyrillic *sir-il'ik*, *adj.* pertaining to the alphabet attributed to St Cyril (9th cent.), distinguished from the other Slavonic alphabet, the Glagolitic.

cyst *sist*, *n.* (*biol.*) a bladder or bag-like structure, whether normal or containing morbid matter: a membrane enclosing an organism in a resting stage.—*adjs.* cyst'ic, cyst'iform.—*ns.* cysti'tis inflammation of the bladder; cys'tocele hernia of the bladder; cyst'oscope an instrument for examining the inside of the bladder; cystos'copy; cystot'omy the operation of cutting into the bladder.—cystic fibrosis (*fī-brō'sis*) a hereditary disease, appearing in infancy or childhood, characterised by too great production of mucus and of fibrous tissue, and the presence of cysts, conditions which interfere with digestion, breathing, etc. [L.L. *cystis*—Gr. *kystis*, a bladder.]

cyte *sīt*, *n.* (*biol.*; *rare*) a cell.—*ns.* cyt'ase an enzyme that breaks down cellulose; cyt'ochrome any of a group of substances in living cells, of great importance in cell oxidation; cyt'ode a protoplasm body without nucleus; cytodiagnos'is medical diagnosis following the close examination of the cells of the body tissues or fluids, e.g. the smear test for cervical cancer; cytogen'esis cell formation.—*n. sing* cytogenet'ics genetics in relation to cytology.—*adj.* cyt'oid cell-like.—*n.* cytokin'in any of numerous substances which regulate plant growth by inducing cell division.—*adj.* **cytolog'ical.**—*ns.* **cytol'ogist; cytol'ogy** that part of biology that deals with cells; **cytol'ysis** (Gr. *lysis*, loosening) dissolution of cells; **cyt'oplasm** the protoplasm of a cell apart from that of the nucleus.—*adj.* **cytotox'ic.**—*ns.* **cytotoxic'ity; cytotox'in** a substance poisonous to cells. [Gr. *kȳtos*, vessel, hollow.]

cyto- *sī-tō-*, in composition, cell; see **cyte.**
cytochrome, etc., **cytology,** etc. **cytotoxin.** See **cyte.**

czar, czarina, etc. See **tsar,** etc.
czardas. A faulty spelling of **csárdás.**
Czech *chek, n.* a member of a westerly branch of the Slavs, the Bohemians, and sometimes also the Moravians: a Czechoslovak: the language of the Czechs, Bohemian, closely allied to Polish.—Also *adj.*—*n.* **Czechoslo'vak** a native or citizen of *Czechoslovakia*: a member of the Slavic people including the Czechs and the Slovaks.—Also *adj.*—*adj.* **Czechoslovak'ian.** [Polish.]

For other sounds see detailed chart of pronunciation.

D

D, d dē, n. the fourth letter in our alphabet: the second note in the natural scale (*mus.*): as a Roman numeral, D = 500.—**D-day** (dē'dā) the opening day (6th June 1944) of the Allied invasion of Europe in World War II: any critical day of action; **D'-mark** Deutsche mark (see **mark**[2]); **D'-notice** a notice officially sent to newspapers, etc., asking them not to publish certain information.

'd d, a shortened form of **had, would**.

dab[1] dab, v.t. to strike gently with something soft or moist: to peck: to smear:—*pr.p.* **dabb'ing;** *pa.t.* and *pa.p.* **dabbed.**—*n.* a gentle blow: a small lump of anything soft or moist: (usu. in *pl.*) a fingerprint (*slang*): a species of flatfish.—**dab'chick** the little grebe. [Cf. early Mod. Du. *dabben*, to pinch; confused with **daub** and **tap**.]

dab[2] dab, n. an expert person.—Also *adj.*—**a dab hand** at an expert at.

dabble dab'l, v.t. to shake about in liquid: to spatter with moisture.—*v.i.* to play in liquid with hands or feet: to do anything in a trifling or small way.—*n.* the act of dabbling.—*n.* **dabb'ler.**—*n.* and *adj.* **dabb'-ling.**—*adv.* **dabb'lingly.** [Freq. of **dab**.]

da capo dä kä'pō, (*mus.*) an indication in music that the performer must return to the beginning of the piece and conclude at the double bar marked *Fine*: abbrev. **D.C.** [It., from the head or beginning.]

dace dās, **dart** därt, ns. a small river fish of the carp family and chub genus. [M.E. *darce*—O.Fr. *dars*—L.L. *dardus*, a dart.]

dacha dä'chə, n. a country house in Russia. [Russ.]

dachshund däks'hoõnt, daks'hoõnd, n. a dog of German origin, with long body and very short legs. [Ger. *Dachs*, badger, *Hund*, dog.]

dacoit, dakoit dä-koit', n. one of a gang of robbers in Indian and Burma.—*ns.* **dacoit'y, dakoit'i, dacoit'age** robbery by gang-robbers, brigandage. [Hind. *dākait, dakait*, a robber.]

dactyl dak'til, n. a foot of three syllables, one long followed by two short, like the joints of a finger (*pros.*).—*adj.* **dactyl'ic.**—*adv.* **dactyl'ically.** [Gr. *daktylos*, a finger.]

dad, dad **daddy** dad'i, (*childish* and *coll.*) ns. father.—**dadd'y-long'-legs** the crane-fly.

Dada, Dadaism dä'dä(-izm), ns. a short-lived (from 1916—c. 1920) movement in art and literature which sought to abandon all form and throw off all tradition.—*n.* **Da'daist.**—*adj.* **Dadais'tic.** [Fr., *dada*, hobby-horse.]

daddy. See **dad**.

dado dä'dō, n. the cubic block forming the body of a pedestal (*classical archit.*): a skirting of wood along the lower part of the walls of a room, often merely represented by wall-paper, painting, etc.:—*pl.* **dä'dos, dä'does.** [It.; see **die**[2].]

daedal dē'dəl, **Daedalian** dē-dä'li-ən, adjs. formed with art: displaying artistic or inventive skill: intricate, varied.—*adj.* **daedal'ic.**—Also **dē'dal, dē-dä'lian.** [From Gr. *Daidalos*, the mythical artist who constructed the Cretan labyrinth]

daemon dē'mən, n a spirit holding a middle place between gods and men, a good genius.—*adj* **daemonic** (-mon'ik) supernatural: inspired [Gr *daimōn, -ōnos*, a spirit, a genius; see **demon**.]

daff, daffy. Short for **daffodil**.

daffodil daf'ə-dil, often *coll.* **daff, daff'y,** ns. a yellow-flowered narcissus.—*adj.* pale yellow. [M.E. *affodille*—O.Fr. *asphodile*—Gr. *asphodelos*, asphodel; the d is unexplained.]

daffy[1] daf'i, (*coll.*) adj. daft, crazy.

daffy[2]. Short for **daffodil**.

daft däft, (*coll.*) adj. silly: weak-minded: insane: unreasonably merry.—*n.* **daft'ie.**—*adv.* **daft'ly.**—*n.* **daft'ness.** [M.E. *daffte*, mild, meek. See **deft**.]

dag dag, n. a tag, scallop, or laciniation (*obs.*): a dirt-clotted tuft of wool on a sheep (also **dag'lock**).—*v.t.* to cut off a sheep's dags.

dagga dag'ə, duhh'ə, n Indian hemp (called true dagga): in U.S., marijuana: an African labiate plant *Leonotis leonurus* or other species (Cape or red dagga) smoked as a narcotic, called the love-drug. [Hottentot *dachab*.]

dagger dag'ər, n. a knife or short sword for stabbing at close quarters: an obelus, a mark of reference † (*print.*).—**at daggers drawn** in a state of hostility; **double dagger** diesis ‡; **look daggers** to look in a hostile manner. [M.E. *dagger*; cf. Fr. *dague*.]

daglock. See **dag**.

dago dä'gō, (*offensive*) n. a man of Spanish, Portuguese, or Italian origin:—*pl.* **dä'goes.** [Prob. Sp. *Diego*.]

daguerreotype də-ger'ō-tīp, n. a method of photography by mercury vapour development of silver iodide exposed on a copper plate: a photograph so taken.—*v.t.* to photograph by that process. [Fr., from Louis *Daguerre* (1789–1851).]

dagwood. Same as **dogwood** (see under **dog**).

dahl. See **dal**.

Dahlia dāl'yə, in U.S. däl'yə, n. a Mexican genus of garden composites with large brightly-coloured flowers: (without *cap.*) any plant of this genus. [From *Dahl*, an 18th-cent. Swedish botanist.]

Dáil (Eireann) doil (ār'ən), n. the lower house of the legislature of the Republic of Ireland. [Ir., 'assembly (of Ireland)'.]

daily dä'li, adj. and *adv.* every day.—*n.* a daily paper: a non-resident servant.—**daily dozen** physical exercises done regularly, usu. every morning (*coll.*). [**day**.]

daimio dī'myō, n. a Japanese territorial noble under the old feudal system:—*pl.* **dai'mios.** [Jap.]

dainty dän'ti, adj. pleasant to the palate: delicate: tasteful: fastidious: choicely or fastidiously neat.—*n.* that which is dainty, a delicacy, esp. a small cake.—*adv.* **dain'tily.**—*n.* **dain'tiness.** [M.E. *deintee*, anything worthy or costly.—L. *dignus*, worthy.]

daiquiri dī'kə-ri, dak'ə-ri, n. a cocktail containing rum and lime-juice. [*Daiquirí*, Cuban place name.]

dairy dä'ri, n. a place where milk is kept, and butter and cheese made: a shop where milk and other dairy produce is sold.—*n.* **dai'rying.**—**dairy cattle** cattle reared mainly for the production of milk, as distinct from *beef* cattle, reared primarily for their meat products; **dai'ry-farm; dai'rymaid; dai'ryman; dairy** products milk and its derivatives, butter, cheese, etc [M.E. *deye*—O.E. *dæge*, a dairymaid.]

dais dās (dä'is is only a guess from the spelling), n. a raised floor at the upper end of the dining-hall where the high table stood: a raised floor, usually with a seat and perhaps a canopy: the canopy over an altar, etc. [O.Fr. *deis*—L.L. *discus*, a table.—Gr. *diskos*, a disc.]

daisy *dā'zi, n.* a composite plant growing in pastures and meadows: extended to other plants, as the *Ox-eye daisy*, which is a chrysanthemum: a general term of admiration, often ironical.—**dai'sy-chain** a succession of daisies strung one upon another; **dai'sy-cutter** a fast-going horse that does not lift its feet high (*arch.*): a cricket-ball skimmed along the ground; **dai'sy-wheel** a flat, horizontal, wheel-shaped device with printing characters at the end of the spokes. [O.E. *dæges ēage*, day's eye.]

dakoit. See **dacoit.**

dal *dal, n.* the pigeon-pea, a pea-like plant cultivated in India and the tropics: pulse: a purée of pulse.—Also **dahl, dhal, dholl.** [Hind. *dal*, to split.]

dalai lama *da'lī lam'ə,* the head of the Tibetan Buddhist hierarchy. [Mongolian, *dalai*, ocean, Tibetan, *lama*, high-priest.]

dale *dāl, n.* the low ground between hills: the valley through which a river flows.—**dales'man** specifically, a man of the dales of Yorkshire. [O.E. *dæl*, reinforced by O.N. *dalr*.]

Dalek *da'lek, n.* a mobile mechanical being. [From a children's television series.]

dali *da'li, n.* a tropical American tree akin to nutmeg yielding staves, etc , and wax seeds. [Native name.]

dally *dal'i, v.t.* to lose time by idleness or trifling: to play (with): to exchange caresses:—*pr.p.* **dall'ying;** *pa.t* and *pa.p.* **dall'ied.**—*ns.* **dall'iance** dallying, toying, or trifling: interchange of embraces: delay; **dall'ier** a trifler. [O.Fr. *dalier*, to chat.]

Dalmatian *dal-mā'shən, adj.* belonging to *Dalmatia* (now a part of Yugoslavia): denoting a Dalmatian (dog).—**Dalmatian (dog)** the spotted coach-dog, like the pointer in shape.

dalmatic *dal-mat'ik, n.* a loose-fitting, wide-sleeved ecclesiastical vestment, worn specially by deacons in the R.C. Church, also sometimes by bishops. [L.L. *dalmatica*, a robe worn by persons of rank.]

dal segno *dal sān'yō,* an indication in music that the performer must return to the sign ( ) —abbrev. D.S. [It. *dal segno*, from the sign.]

Daltonism² *dol'tən-izm, n.* colour-blindness: inability to distinguish red from green.—*adj.* **Daltō'nian.** [John *Dalton* (1766–1844), who described his own case.]

Daltonism² *dol'tən-izm, n.* a school method (the Dalton plan) by which each pupil pursues separately a course suited to himself, in monthly instalments. [First tried in 1920 at *Dalton,* Massachusetts.]

dam¹ *dam, n.* an embankment to restrain water: the water thus confined; a restraint (*fig.*).—*v.t.* to keep back by a bank:—*pr.p.* **damm'ing;** *pa.t.* and *pa.p* **dammed.** [Gmc.; Du. *dam,* Ger. *Damm,* etc.]

dam² *dam, n.* a mother, usu. of cattle, horses, etc., or contemptuous. [A form of **dame.**]

dam³ *dam,* a coll. form of **damn, damned.**—*adj.* **dam'fool'** stupid, ridiculous:—*interj.* **damm'it** damn it.—**as near as dammit** see **near.**

damage *dam'ij, n.* hurt, injury, loss: the value of what is lost: cost (*coll.*): (*pl.*) the financial reparation due for loss or injury sustained by one person through the fault or negligence of another.—*v.t.* to harm.—*v.i.* to be injured.—*adj.* **dam'ageable.** [O.Fr. *damage* (Fr. *dommage*)—L *damnum,* loss.]

damascene *dam'ə-sēn, dam-ə-sēn', n.* a Damascus or damascened sword: inlay of metal (esp. gold) or other materials on steel, etc.: the structure or surface appearance of Damascus steel.—*v.t.* to decorate (esp. steel) by inlaying or encrusting: to ornament with the watered or wavy appearance of Damascus steel, or in

imitation of it.—**Damascus blade** a Damascus sword, the surface marked by wavy pattern. [From *Damascus,* famous for its steel and (see **damask**) silk work.]

damask *dam'əsk, n.* figured material, originally of silk, now usually of linen, the figure woven not printed: Damascus steel or its surface appearance: the red colour of the damask rose.—*v.t.* to flower or variegate (cloth): to damascene.—*adj.* red, like a damask rose. —**damask plum** the damson; **damask rose** a bluish-red variety of rose; **dam'ask-steel** Damascus steel. [From *Damascus* (see **damascene**).]

dame *dām, n.* the mistress of a house, a matron (now usu. jocular or patronising): a mother: a woman (*slang*): the comic vulgar old woman of the pantomime, usually played by a male actor: a noble lady: (title of) a lady of the same rank as a knight: a baronet's or knight's wife (as a formal title prefixed to the lady's name) (*obs.*).—**dame'-school** (*hist.*) a school for young children usually kept by a woman. [Fr. *dame* —L *domina,* a lady.]

damfool. See **dam³.**

dammar *dam'ər, n.* a copal used for making varnish, obtained from various conifers.—Also **damm'er.** [Malay *damar*]

dammit. See **dam³.**

damn *dam, v.t.* to censure: to sentence to eternal punishment: to doom: to curse or swear at.—*n.* an interjection expressing annoyance, disgust or impatience (*coll.*): something of little value (*coll.*): a curse.—*adj.* **damnable** (*dam'nə-bl*) deserving or tending to damnation: hateful: pernicious.—*ns.* **dam'nableness, damnabil'ity.**—*adv.* **dam'nably.**—*n.* **damnation** (*-nā'shən*) condemnation: the punishment of the impenitent in the future state (*theol.*): eternal punishment.—*adjs.* **dam'natory** (*-nə-tər-i*) consigning to damnation; **damned** (*damd*; poet. *dam'nid*) sentenced to everlasting punishment (**the damned** *damd,* those so sentenced): hateful: very surprised (as in *I'll be damned!*).—*adv.* very, exceedingly.—*n.* **damnification** (*dam-ni-fi-kā'shən*) infliction of injury or loss. —*v.t.* **dam'nify** to cause loss to.—*adj.* **damning** (*dam'ing, -ning*) exposing to condemnation.—**damn all** (*coll.*) nothing at all, **damn with faint praise** to condemn in effect by expressing too cool approval; **do one's damnedest** (*damd'əst; coll.*) to do one's very best. [Fr. *damner*—L. *damnāre,* to condemn— *damnum,* loss.]

damo(i)sel, damozel *dam'ō-zel, n.* Same as **damsel.**

damp *damp, n.* vapour, mist: moist air: in mines, etc., any gas other than air. a gloom: discouragement.—*v.t* to wet slightly. to discourage. to check: to make dull: to slow down the rate of burning (of a fire) (often with *down*).—*adj* moist.—*v.t.* and *v.i.* **damp'en** to make or become damp or moist: to stifle (*fig.*).—*ns.* **damp'er** one who or that which damps: a depressive influence: a door or shutter for shutting off or regulating a draught: a device for diminishing the amplitude of vibrations or cycles: a mute (*mus.*): in a piano, harpsichord, etc., the pad which silences a note after it has been played: a kind of unfermented bread (orig. *Austr.*).—*adj.* **damp'ish.**—*n.* **damp'ishness.**—*adv.* **damp'ly.**—*n.* **damp'ness.**—**damp'-course** a layer of moisture-proof material in a masonry wall.—*adj* **damp'-proof** impervious to moisture. [M E. *dampen.*]

damsel *dam'zl, n.* a young unmarried woman: a girl. [O.Fr. *dameisele*—L.L. *domicella,* dim. of L. *domina,* lady.]

damson *dam'zn, n.* a rather small oval dark purple plum —**damson cheese** damsons pressed into a solid cake [Shortened from *Damascene*—*Damascus.*]

dan *dan, n.* in Japanese combative sports, a level of proficiency (usu. 1st rising to 10th): a person who has gained such a level. [Jap.]

dance *dåns*, *v.i.* to move with measured steps, esp. to music: to spring.—*v.t.* to make to dance or jump: to perform, execute, as a dance.—*n.* a movement of one or more persons with measured steps: the tune to which dancing is performed: the musical form of a dance-tune: a meeting for dancing.—*ns.* **danc'er**; **danc'ing**.—**danc'-band**; **dance'-hall** a public hall for dancing; **dance'-music**; **dance'-tune**; **danc'ing-girl**; **danc'ing-master**.—**dance attendance** to wait assiduously (on); **dance of death** a series of allegorical paintings symbolising the universal power of death, represented as a skeleton; **lead one a (merry) dance** to keep one involved unnecessarily in a series of perplexities and vexations. [O.Fr. *danser*, from Gmc.]

dandelion *dan'di-lī-ən*, *n.* a common yellow-flowered composite with jagged-toothed leaves. [Fr. *dent de lion*, lion-tooth.]

dander *dan'dər*, *n.* a form of **dandruff**: anger: passion. —**get someone's, one's dander up** or **raise someone's, one's dander** to make or become angry.

Dandie Dinmont *dan'di din'mənt*, a short-legged rough-coated terrier of Scottish Border breed. [From *Dandie Dinmont* in Scott's *Guy Mannering*.]

dandify, etc. See **dandy**[1].

dandle *dan'dl*, *v.t.* to play with: to fondle, toss in the arms or dance lightly on the knee (a baby).

dandruff, **dandriff** *dand'rəf*, *n.* a scaly scurf on the skin under the hair.

dandy *dan'di*, *n.* a foppish, silly fellow: one who pays much attention to dress: a dandy-cock: a dandy-roll. —*adj.* (*coll.*) smart, fine—a word of general commendation.—*adj.* **dand'ified** inclined to be a dandy.—*v.t.* **dan'dify** to dress up.—*adv.* **dan'dily**.— *adj.* **dan'dyish**.—*n.* **dan'dyism**.—**dan'dy-brush** a hard horse brush of whalebone bristles; **dan'dy-roll** a wire-gauze cylinder that impresses the ribs and water-mark on paper.

Dane *dån*, *n.* a native or citizen of Denmark: a Northman: a very large dog (great Dane).—*adj.* **Danish** (*dān'ish*) belonging to Denmark.—*n.* the language of the Danes.—**Danish blue** a kind of blue-veined, strongly-flavoured cheese; **Danish pastry** a flaky confection of sweetened dough, containing jam or other fillings and often iced. [Dan. *Daner* (pl.).]

danegeld, **danegelt** *dān'geld*, *-gelt*, *ns.* a tax imposed in the 10th cent., to buy off the Danes or to defend the country against them. [O.E. *Dene*, Danes, *geld*, payment.]

Danelaw, **Danelagh** *dān'lō*, *n.* that part of England, N.E. of Watling Street, occupied (9th–11th cent.) by the Danes: (without *cap.*) the Danish law which prevailed there. [O.E. *Dena lagu*, Danes' law.]

danger *dān'jər*, *n.* peril, hazard, or risk: insecurity.— *adj.* **dan'gerous** full of danger: unsafe: insecure.— *adv.* **dan'gerously**.—*n.* **dan'gerousness**.—**danger money** extra money paid for doing a more than usually perilous job; **dangerous drugs** certain specific drugs, including morphine, cocaine, heroin, etc., to the dispensing of which stringent regulations apply.— **in danger of** liable to, on the point of; **on the danger list** in a hospital, etc., categorised as being dangerously ill (also *fig.*). [O.Fr. *dangier*, absolute power, hence power to hurt.—L.L. *dominium*, feudal authority.]

dangle *dang'gl*, *v.i.* to hang loosely or with a swinging motion.—*v.t.* to make to dangle (often with intent to entice or encourage).—*n.* **dang'ler**.—*n.* and *adj.* **dang'ling**. [Cf. Dan. *dangle*—O.N. *dingla*.]

Daniel *dan'yəl*, *n.* a wise judge. [From Daniel in the Apocryphal *Book of Susannah*.]

Danish. See **Dane**.

dank *dangk*, *adj.* unpleasantly moist, wet.—*n.* (*Milt.*) a wet place.—*adj.* **dank'ish**.—*n.* **dank'ness**.

danse macabre *dās ma-kābr'*, (Fr.) dance of death (q.v.).

danseur *dā-sœr*, *n.* a male ballet dancer.—*n.* **danseuse** (*dā-sœz*) a female dancer: a ballet dancer [Fr.]

Dantean *dan'ti-ən*, **Dantesque** *dan-tesk'*, *adjs.* like the poet *Dante*: sublime: austere.

dap *dap*, *v.i.* to bounce: to drop bait gently into the water.

Daphne *daf'ni*, *n.* a genus of shrubs, including spurge-laurel: (without *cap.*) any plant of this genus [Gr. *daphnē*, sweet bay.]

dapper *dap'ər*, *adj.* little and active: neat: spruce.—*n.* **dapp'erness**. [Du. *dapper*, brave; cf. Ger. *tapfer*, quick, brave.]

dapple *dap'l*, *adj.* marked with spots.—*v.t.* to variegate with spots.—*adj.* **dapp'led**.—*adj.* and *n.* **dapp'le-grey'** (an animal, esp. a horse) of a pale grey colour with darker spots.

darbies *dār'biz*, (*slang*) *n.pl.* handcuffs. [App. from the personal name *Darby*.]

Darby and Joan *dār'bi-ənd-jōn'*, a devoted elderly married couple. [Poss. from characters in an 18th-cent. song.]

dare *dār*, *v.t.* and *v.t.* to be bold enough (to): to venture:—*3rd pers. sing.* **dare(s)**; *p.t.* **durst** (now rare, used esp. in subjunctive sense), **dared**; *pa.p.* **dared**.— *v.t.* to challenge: to defy: to face:—*3rd pers. sing.* **dares**; *pa.t.* and *pa.p.* **dared**.—*n.* an act of daring or a challenge to perform it.—*adj.* **dar'ing** bold: courageous: fearless.—*n.* boldness.—*adv.* **dar'ingly**.—**dare'-devil** a rash, venturesome fellow.—*adj.* unreasonably rash and reckless.—**dare'-dev'ilry**; **dar'ing-do** same as derring-do.—**I dare say, I daresay** I suppose. [O.E. *durran*.]

dari. See **durra**.

dariole *da'ri-ōl*, *dar'yōl*, *n.* a shell of pastry, etc., or small round mould: a dish comprising such a shell and its filling. [Fr.]

dark *dārk*, *adj.* without light: black, or somewhat blackish: (of hair and skin colouring) not of a fair or light hue: gloomy: difficult to understand: unenlightened: secret: sinister.—*n.* absence of light: nightfall: a state of ignorance.—*v.t.* **dark'en** to make dark or darker: to render ignorant: to sully.—*v.i.* to grow dark or darker.—*n.* **dar'kle** a darky.—*adj.* **dark'ish**. —*adv.* and *adj.* **dark'ling** dark: in the dark.—*adv.* **dark'ly**.—*adj.* **dark'some** dark: gloomy (*poet.*).—*ns.* **dark'(e)y** a Negro (*offensive, old-fashioned*); **dark'ness.—Dark Ages** the period of intellectual darkness in Europe, from the 5th to the 9th or 12th (or 15th) century; **Dark Continent** Africa; **dark horse** in racing, a horse whose capabilities are not known; also *fig.* of a person (usu. implying undisclosed ability): a candidate not brought forward till the last moment (esp. *U.S.*) **dark'-lant'ern** a lantern whose light can be covered; **dark'room** a room for developing and printing photographs free from such light as would affect photographic plates; **dark star** a star that emits no visible light, and can be detected only by its radiowaves, gravitational effect, etc.— **darken someone's door** (often with negative, often implying unwelcomeness) to appear as a visitor; **in the dark** ignorant, unaware; **keep it dark** to conceal it; **prince of darkness** Satan. [O.E. *deorc*.]

darling *dār'ling*, *n.* and *adj.* (one) dearly beloved (often *voc.*): (a) favourite. [O.E. *dēorling*; see **dear**.]

darn[1] *dārn*, *v.t.* to mend by interwoven stitches.—*n.* a darned place.—*ns.* **darn'er**; **darn'ing.—darn'ing-needle**.

darn[2], **darned** *dārn(d)*, minced forms of **damn**, **damned**.

darnel *dār'nl*, *n.* a species of rye-grass: perh. the tares of the Bible. [Poss. conn. with O.Fr. *darne*, stupid, from its supposed narcotic properties.]

darshan *dār'shən*, *n.* a blessing conferred by seeing or touching a great or holy person. [Hindi.]

dart[1] *därt*, *n.* a pointed weapon or toy for throwing with the hand: anything that pierces: a tapering fold sown on the reverse of material in order to shape it: (in *pl.*) a game in which darts are thrown at a board: in some snails, a calcareous needle supposed to be used as a sexual stimulus: a sudden forward movement.— *v.t.* to hurl suddenly: to send or shoot forth.—*v.i.* to move, start or shoot forth rapidly.—*n.* **dar'ter** one who or that which darts: a fresh-water diving bird allied to cormorants: an archer-fish: applied also to various small American fishes akin to perch.—*adj.* **dart'ing.**—*adv.* **dart'ingly.**—**dart'-board** the target used in the game of darts. [O.Fr. *dart*; cf. O.E. *daroth*.]

dart[2]. See **dace.**

dartre *där'tər*, *n.* herpes. [Fr.]

Darwinism *där'win-izm*, *n.* the theory of the origin of species propounded by Charles *Darwin* (1809–82).— *adj.* and *n.* **Darwin'ian.**

darzi *där'zē*, *dûr'zē*, *n.* a tailor. [Hind. *darzī*.]

dash *dash*, *v.t.* to throw, thrust, or drive violently: to break by throwing together: to bespatter: to frustrate: to confound: to modify by dilution or admixture.—*v.i.* to rush with violence.—*n.* a violent striking: a rush: a violent onset: a blow: a splash: a splash of colour: a stroke of the pen or similar mark: a mark (—) at a break in a sentence or elsewhere: a euphemism for damn (sometimes represented by this sign): a staccato mark: an acute accent used in algebra and in lettering of diagrams as a discriminating mark: a long element in the Morse code: verve: ostentation: a slight admixture: a dashboard.—*n.* **dash'er.**—*adj.* **dash'ing** spirited: showy: fashionable.—*adv.* **dash'ingly.**—**dash'board** a board, screen or partition in front of a driver, on a horse-vehicle to keep off splashes of mud, in a motor-car or aeroplane to carry instruments; **dash'-pot** a device for damping vibration by a piston moving in a cylinder containing liquid.— **dash off** to throw off or produce hastily: to leave abruptly; **dash out** to knock out by striking against something. [M.E. *daschen*, *dassen*, to rush, or strike with violence.]

dassie *das'i*, (*S. Afr.*) *n.* the hyrax. [Du. *dasje*, *dim.* of *das*, badger.]

dastard *däs'tərd*, *n.* a cowardly fellow: loosely, one who does a brutal act without giving his victim a chance.—*adj.* shrinking from danger: cowardly.— *adj.* **das'tardly.**—*n.* **das'tardliness.** [Prob. conn. with **dazed.**]

dasyphyllous *das-i-fil'əs*, *adj.* having crowded, thick, or woolly leaves. [Gr. *dasys*, bushy, *phyllon*, leaf.]

dasyure *das'i-ûr*, *n.* any marsupial of the flesh-eating genus **Dasyu'rus** (called native cat) or the fam. **Dasyu'ridae** (Tasmanian devil, Tasmanian wolf, etc.). [Gr. *dasys*, shaggy, *ourā*, tail.]

data *dā'tə*, (in U.S. and technical Eng. *dä'tə*), *n.pl.* (commonly treated as *sing.*) facts given, from which others may be inferred:—*sing.* **da'tum** q.v.—*n.* **data-ma'tion** shortened term for **automatic data processing.**—**da'tabank**, **da'tabase** a body of information stored in a computer, from which particular pieces of information can be retrieved when required; **data highway** connecting link between computers at different places rendering all information stored available at each place; **data processing** see **process.**— **(direct) data capture** the putting of information, esp. concerning (cash) sales, into a form that can be fed directly into a computer. [L. *dāta*, things given.]

date[1] *dāt*, *n.* a statement of time, or time and place, of writing, sending, executing, as on a letter, book, document, etc.: a particular day of the month: the time of an event: an appointment or engagement (*coll.*): the person dated (in the last sense of the *v.t.*). —*v.t.* to affix a date to: to ascertain the date of: to suggest the date of: to make an appointment with (*coll.*): to go out with (a member of the opposite sex), esp. regularly (*coll.*).—*v.i.* to reckon: to take beginning: to savour of a particular time: hence, to become old-fashioned.—*adjs.* **dāt'able, dāt'eable; dat'ed** old-fashioned, out of date; **date'less** without date or fixed limit: free from engagements.—*n.* **dāt'er.**—**date'-coding** marking in code on the container a date after which food should not be used; **date line** short for International Date Line; **date'-line** a line giving the date, as on a newspaper.—**out of date** see **out; to date** until now; **up to date** abreast of the times: adapted or corrected to the present time: modern. [O.Fr. *date* —L. *dātum*, given.]

date[2] *dāt*, *n.* the fruit of the date-palm.—**date'-palm**, a palm of N. Africa and S.W. Asia; **date'-su'gar.** [Fr. *datte*—Gr. *daktylos*, a finger, a date.]

dative *dāt'iv*, *adj.* expressing an indirect object (*gram.*).—*n.* the dative case: a word in the dative.— *adj.* **datival** (*də-ti'vəl*). [L. *dātīvus*—*dāre*, to give.]

datum *dā'təm*. See **data.**—**dā'tum-line, -level, -plane** the horizontal base-line from which heights and depths are measured. [L. *dātum*, given—*dāre*, to give.]

Datura *də-tū'rə*, *n.* the thorn-apple genus of the potato family, with strongly narcotic properties: (without *cap.*) any plant of this genus: (without *cap.*) the poison got from these plants. [Hind. *dhatūrā*.]

daub *döb*, *v.t.* to smear: to paint coarsely.—*n.* a coarse painting.—*ns.* **daub'er; daub'ing.**—*adj.* **daub'y** sticky. [O.Fr. *dauber*, to plaster—L. *dealbāre*, to whitewash.]

daube *dōb*, (Fr.) *n.* a meat stew.

daughter *dö'tər*, *n.* a female in relation to her parent: a female descendant: woman (generally).—*adj.* (*biol.*) derived from another: of a nuclide, formed by the radioactive decay of another (*phys.*).—*n.* **daugh'ter-liness.**—*adj.* **daugh'terly** like or becoming a daughter.—**daugh'ter-in-law** a son's wife:—*pl.* **daugh'ters-in-law.** [O.E. *dohtor*.]

daunt *dönt*, or *dänt*, *v.t.* to frighten: to discourage: to subdue.—*adj.* **daunt'less** not to be daunted.—*adv.* **daunt'lessly.**—*n.* **daunt'lessness.** [O.Fr. *danter* — L. *domitāre*.]

dauphin *dö'fin*, *n.* the eldest son of the king of France (1349–1830).—*ns.* **dau'phiness, dauphine** (*dō-fēn'*) his wife. [O.Fr. *dauphin*—*Delphinus*, family name of the lords of the Viennois—hence Dauphiné for their province (ceded to the king, 1349).]

davenport *dav'n-pört, -pôrt*, *n.* a small ornamental writing-desk—also **dev'onport:** a large sofa. [Prob. from the maker.]

Davis apparatus *dā'vis ap-ər-ā'təs*, a device making possible escape from a crippled submarine. [From the inventor.]

davit *dav'it*, *dā'vit*, *n.* one of a pair of erections on a ship for lowering or hoisting a boat. [App. from the name *David*.]

Davy *dā'vi*, **Davy-lamp** *-lamp*, *ns.* the safety-lamp used in coalmines invented by Sir Humphry *Davy* (1778–1829).

Davy Jones *dā'vi jōnz*, a sailor's familiar name for the (malignant) spirit of the sea, the devil.—**Davy Jones's locker** the sea, as the grave of men drowned at sea.

daw *dö*, *n.* a bird of the crow kind, a jackdaw. [M.E. *dawe*.]

dawdle *dö'dl*, *v.i.* to waste time by trifling: to act or move slowly.—*n.* **daw'dler.**—*adv.* **daw'dlingly.**

dawn *dön, v.i.* to become day: to begin to grow light: to begin to appear.—*n.* daybreak: beginning.—Also **dawn'ing.**—**dawn chorus** the singing of birds at dawn. —**dawn on** to begin to become evident to or be understood by. [Appears first as **dawning,** prob. from O.N.; cf. Sw. and Dan. *dagning.*]

day *dā, n.* the time of light, from sunrise to sunset, morning till night: twenty-four hours, from midnight to midnight: the time the earth takes to make a revolution on its axis: morning and afternoon, as opp. to evening and night: the hours devoted to work (*working-day*): a day set apart for a purpose, as for receiving visitors: lifetime: time of existence, vogue, or influence: a time: daylight.—**day'-bed** a kind of couch or sofa; **day'-book** a book for entering the transactions of each day; **day'-boy, -girl** see **day scholar** below; **day'break** dawn; **day care** daytime supervision and help given by trained nursing and other staff to a group of pre-school children, or elderly or handicapped people; **day (care) centre** a centre which provides social amenities and/or supervision for elderly or handicapped people, vagrants, alcoholics, petty offenders, etc.; **day'dream** a dreaming or musing while awake.—Also *v.i.*—**day'dreamer; day'-la'bour** labour paid by the day; **day'-la'bourer; day'light** the light of day: a clear space; **day'light-sav'ing** reduction of loss of daylight, for work or play, by advancing the clock; **day'-lil'y** a liliaceous plant whose blossoms last only for a day.—*adj.* **day'long** during the whole day. —*adj.* **day'-old** one day old,—**day'-release'** a system by which workers are freed from employment during the day so as to attend an educational course.—Also *adj.*—**day'-return'** a usu. reduced rail or bus fare for a journey to a place and back on the same day: a ticket for this type of journey; **day room** a room used as a communal living-room in a school, hospital, hostel, etc.; **day'-scholar** a pupil who attends a boarding-school during the school-hours, but boards at home (also **day'-boy, day'-girl**); **day'-school** a school held during the day, as opposed both to a night-school and to a boarding-school; **day'-shift** a group of workers that takes its turn during the day: the daytime period of work; **day'spring** dawn; **day'star** the morning star; **day'time** the time of daylight: day, as opp. to evening and night.—Also *adj.*—*adj.* **day'-to-day'** daily, routine.—**day trip** a trip made to somewhere and back within one day; **day'-tripper.**—**at the end of the day** (*fig.*) when all is said and done; **call it a day** to announce a decision to leave off; **day about** on alternate days; **day by day** daily; **day in, day out** for an indefinite succession of days; **day off** a day's holiday; **day out** a servant's free day: a day spent away from home for pleasure, as a holiday, etc.; **days of grace** three days allowed for payment of bills, etc., beyond the day named; **from day to day** concerned only with the present; **in this day and age** at the present time; **knock, beat the (living) daylights out of** (*coll.*) to beat severely; **one of these days** some indefinite time in the near future; **scare the (living) daylights out of** (*coll.*) to terrify; **see daylight** to arrive at some comprehension, illumination, prospect of a solution; **that will be the day** (*coll.*) that is very unlikely; **the day** the time spoken of or expected; **the other day** not long ago; **the time of day** the hour of the clock: a greeting; **win the day** to gain the victory. [O.E. *dæg;* Ger. *Tag.*]

daze *dāz, v.t.* to stun, to stupefy.—*n.* (a state of) bewilderment.—*adj.* **dazed** (*dāzd*).—*adv.* **dazedly** (*dāz'id-li*).—**in a daze** stunned. [O.N. *dasa-sk* (refl.), to be breathless.]

dazzle *daz'l, v.t.* to daze or overpower with strong light: to confound by brilliancy, beauty, or cleverness.—*v.i.* to be dazzled.—*n.* the act of dazzling: that which dazzles; **dazz'ler; dazz'ling** (also

adj.).—*adv.* **dazz'lingly.**—**dazz'le-paint'ing** fantastic painting for camouflage. [Freq. of **daze.**]

DDT. dichlorodiphenyltrichloroethane.

de- *dē-, di-, pfx.* (1) meaning down from, away: (2) indicating a reversal of process, or deprivation: (3) used intensively. [L., or Fr.—L.]

deacon *dē'kn, n.* in Episcopal churches, a member of the order of clergy under priests: in some Presbyterian churches, an officer, man or woman, distinct from the elders, who attends to the secular affairs of the church: in Congregational and some other churches, an officer who advises the pastor, distributes the elements at communion, and dispenses charity.—*n.* **dea'coness** a female servant of the Christian society in the time of the apostles: one of an order of women in some Protestant churches whose duties are pastoral, educational, social and evangelical.—See also **diaconate.** [L. *diāconus*—Gr. *diākonos,* a servant.]

deactivate *dē-ak'tiv-āt, v.t.* to diminish or remove the activity of.—*n.* **deactivā'tion.** [Pfx. **de-** (2).]

dead *ded, adj.* no longer alive: inanimate: deathlike: of a ball, at rest, out of play: of a golf-ball, within a certain putt, or into the hole: out of use: obsolete: inactive: cold and cheerless: dull: numb: insensitive: as good as dead: inelastic: without vegetation: utter: unerring.—*adv.* in a dead manner: absolutely: utterly: directly: exactly (*coll.*).—*n.* the time of greatest stillness, as *the dead* of night.—*v.t.* **dead'en** to make dead: to deprive partly of vigour, sensibility, or sensation: to blunt: to lessen: to make soundproof. —*ns.* **dead'ener; dead'ening** (also *adj.*); **dead'liness.** —*adj.* **dead'ly** causing death: fatal: implacable: very great (*coll.*).—*adv.* in a manner resembling death: extremely (*coll.*).—*n.* **dead'ness.**—*adj.* **dead'-and-alive'** dull, inactive.—**dead'-beat** (*coll.*) a down-and-out.—*adj.* **dead'-beat** (*coll.*) quite overcome, exhausted.—**dead'-bolt', -lock** one moved by turning key, knob, without intervention of a spring.—*adj.* **dead'-drunk'** completely drunk.—**dead duck** (*coll.*) a plan, idea, person, etc., that has no chance of success or survival; **dead'-end'** a pipe, passage, etc., closed at one end: a blind alley (*lit.* and *fig.*).—*adj.* leading nowhere (*lit.* and *fig.*).—**dead'-eye** (*naut.*) a round, flattish wooden block with a rope or iron band passing around it, and pierced with three holes for a lanyard; **dead'-fall** a trap with a weight that falls when its support is removed; **dead'-hand** mortmain; **dead's-head** one who enjoys privileges without paying, as in a theatre, etc.—*v.t.* to remove the withered heads of flowers, in order to encourage further growth.— **dead'-heat'** (the result of) a heat or race in which two or more competitors are equal.—Also *v.t.*—**dead language** one no longer spoken; **dead'-lett'er** a letter undelivered and unclaimed at the post-office: a law or ordinance made but not enforced.—*n.pl.* **dead'-lights** storm-shutters for a cabin window.—**dead'line** closing date, last possible minute; **dead'lock** the case when matters have become so complicated that all is at a complete standstill: see also **dead'-bolt'.**—*v.t.* and *v.t.* to reach or bring to a standstill because of difficulties, etc.—**dead loss** a complete loss: a useless ally (*fig.*); **dead'ly-night'shade** belladonna; **deadly sin** a mortal sin (see **seven**); **dead'-march'** a piece of solemn music played at funeral processions, esp. of soldiers.—*n.pl.* **dead'-men** (*coll.*) empty bottles after a carouse.—**dead'-nett'le** labiate plant superficially like the nettle but stingless.—*adj.* **dead'pan** expressionless: emotionless: dead serious or mock serious.— **dead'-reck'oning** an estimation of a ship's place simply by the log-book; **dead ringer** (*slang*) a person who, or a thing which, looks exactly like someone or something else; **dead'-set'** a complete standstill, as of a setting dog: a determined and prolonged onslaught, esp. with a view to captivation; **dead's part** (*Scots law*) the part of a man's moveable property which he may bequeath by will, and which is not due to wife and children. **dead'-weight** unrelieved weight: heavy and oppressive burden: difference in a ship's displacement loaded and light; **dead'-wood** useless material.—**dead as a dodo, door-nail, herring** absolutely dead; **dead man's handle** a device, e.g. on an electric train, which allows current to pass only so long as there is pressure on it; **dead man's pedal** a foot-operated safety device on the same principle, used esp. on diesel trains; **dead set** see **set; dead (set) against** utterly opposed to; **dead spit** exact image; **dead to the world** very soundly asleep: unconscious. [O.E. *dēad*; from root of **die.**]

deaf *def, adj.* dull of hearing: unable to hear at all: not willing to hear: inattentive.—*v.t.* **deaf'en** to make deaf: to stun.—*adj.* **deaf'ening** making deaf (with noise): very loud.—*adv.* **deaf'ly.**—*n.* **deaf'ness.**—**deaf'-aid** a hearing-aid; **deaf'-mute'** one who is both deaf and dumb.—**deaf-and-dumb alphabet (language)** digital and manual signs used to express letters (and words and phrases) visually; **turn a deaf ear** to pretend not to have heard: to ignore. [O.E. *dēaf.*]

deal[1] *dēl, n.* a portion: an indefinite quantity: a large quantity: the act of dividing cards: a business transaction (esp. a favourable one): treatment.—*v.t.* to divide, to distribute: to throw about: to deliver.—*v.i.* to transact business (in): to act: to distribute cards:—*pa.t.* and *pa.p.* **dealt** (*delt*).—*ns.* **deal'er** one who deals or whose turn it is to deal, or who has dealt the hand in play: a trader; **deal'ership; deal'ing** (often in *pl.*) manner of acting towards others: intercourse of trade.—**deal with** to have to do with, to treat of: to take action in regard to. [O.E. *dǣlan—dǣl*, a part; Ger. *teilen—Teil*, a part or division; cf. **dole**[1].]

deal[2] *dēl, n.* a fir or pine board of a standard size: soft wood.—*adj.* of deal. [M.L.G. *dele.*]

dealt. See **deal**[1].

dean[1], **dene** *dēn, n.* a small valley. [O.E. *denu,* a valley; cf. **den.**]

dean[2] *dēn, n.* a dignitary in cathedral and collegiate churches who presides over the canons: the president of a faculty in a college or of the Faculty of Advocates: a resident fellow of a college who has administrative and disciplinary functions: the senior member of a corps or body.—*ns.* **dean'ery** the office of a dean: a group of parishes presided over by a dean: a dean's house.—**rural dean** one who, under the bishop, has the special care and inspection of the clergy in certain parishes. [O.Fr. *deien*—L.L. *decānus* or Gr. *dekānos,* a chief of ten.]

dear *dēr, adj.* high in price: costly: characterised by high prices: scarce: highly valued: beloved: a conventional form of address used in letter-writing.—*n.* one who is dear or beloved.—*adv.* at a high price: dearly.—*interj.* indicating surprise, pity, or other emotion.—*adv.* **dear'ly.**—*ns.* **dear'ness; dear'ie, dear'y** (*coll.*) one who is dear.—**dear(y) me** an expression of various emotions; **dear knows** an expression of ignorance. [O.E. *dēore, dȳre.*]

dearth, *dûrth, n.* dearness, high price: scarcity: want: famine: barrenness. [**dear.**]

death *deth, n.* state of being dead: extinction or cessation of life: manner of dying: mortality: a deadly plague: cause of death: spiritual lifelessness: the killing of the animal in hunting.—*adj.* **death'less** never dying: everlasting.—*n.* **death'lessness.**—*adj.* **death'like** deadly: like death.—*n.* **death'liness.**—*adj.* **death'ly** deadly: deathlike.—**death'-add'er** a poisonous Australian snake; **death'-ag'ony** the struggle often preceding death; **death angel** death-cap; **death'-bed** the bed on which one dies: the last

illness; **death'-blow** a blow that causes death; **death'-cap, -cup** a very poisonous toadstool (*Amanita phalloides*) often mistaken for an edible mushroom; **death'-cell** a prison cell for condemned prisoners awaiting execution; **death certificate** a legal certificate on which a doctor states the fact and usu. cause of a person's death.—*adj.* **death'-dealing.**—**death'-duty** (often in *pl.*) duty paid on inheritance of property; **death'-knell** the ringing of a bell to announce a death: something that announces the end of one's hopes, ambitions, etc. (*fig.*).—**death'-mask** a plaster-cast taken from the face after death; **death'-rate** the proportion of deaths to the population; **death'-ratt'le** a rattling in the throat that sometimes precedes death; **death'-ray** an imaginary ray that could destroy all life; **death'-roll** a list of the dead; **death's'-head** the skull of a human skeleton, or a figure of it; **death'-throe** the dying agony; **death'-trap** an unsafe structure or place that exposes one to great danger of death; **death'-warrant** an order from the authorities for the execution of a criminal; **death'-watch** a watch by a dying person: a beetle that produces a ticking noise, (also **death's-watch beetle**); **death wish** (*psych.*) a wish, conscious or unconscious, for death for oneself or another.—**at death's door** very near to death; **catch one's death (of cold)** (*coll.*) to catch a very bad cold; **death's-head moth** a hawk-moth with pale markings on the back of the thorax somewhat like a skull; **death on** fatal to, fond of, good at; **do or put to death** to kill: to cause to be killed; **gates or jaws of death** the point of death; **in at the death** up on the animal before the dogs have killed it: present at the finish, crux, climax, etc. of anything (*fig.*); **like grim death** tenaciously; **the death penalty** capital punishment; **to death** (until) dead: to a state of exhaustion; **to the death** to the uttermost. [O.E. *dēath.*]

deb. Coll. form of **débutante.**

debacle, débâcle *di-bak'l, dā-bāk'l', n.* a breaking up of ice on a river: a sudden flood of water leaving its path strewed with debris (*geol.*): a complete break-up or collapse: a stampede. [Fr. *débâcle; dé-, des-,* and *bâcler,* to bar—L. *baculus,* a stick.]

de-bag *di-bag',* (*coll.*) *v.t.* to remove the trousers of, as a prank or punishment.—*n.* **de-bagg'ing.** [Pfx. **de-**(2), **bags.**]

debar *di-bär', v.t.* to bar out: to exclude: to hinder:—*pr.p.* **debarr'ing;** *pa.t.* and *pa.p.* **debarred'.**—*n.* **debar'ment.** [Pfx. **de-**(3).]

debark *di-bärk', v.t.* or *v.i.* to disembark.—*n.* **debarka'tion, débarca'tion.** [Fr. *débarquer—des*(—L. *dis-*), away, and Fr. *barque,* a ship.]

debase *di-bās', v.t.* to lower: to make mean or of less value: to adulterate.—*adj.* **debased'** degraded.—*ns.* **debas'edness; debase'ment** degradation; **debâs'er.**—*adj.* **debâs'ing.**—*adv.* **debâs'ingly.** [Pfx. **de-**(1).]

debate *di-bāt', n.* a contention in words or argument: a (parliamentary) discussion.—*v.t.* to contend for in argument: to argue about.—*v.i.* to deliberate: to consider: to join in debate.—*adj.* **debat'able,** also **debate'able,** liable to be disputed: open to argument: contentious.—*n.* **debat'er.** [O.Fr. *debatre*—L. *dē,* and *batuēre,* to beat.]

debauch *di-böch', v.t.* to lead away from duty or allegiance: to corrupt with lewdness: to seduce: to vitiate.—*v.i.* to over-indulge.—*n.* a fit or period of intemperance or debauchery.—*adj.* **debauched'** corrupt: profligate.—*adv.* **debauch'edly.**—*ns.* **debauch'edness; debauchee** (*di-boch-ē', -bösh-ē'*) a libertine; **debauch'er; debauch'ery** excessive intemperance: habitual lewdness; **debauch'ment.** [O.Fr. *desbaucher* to corrupt—*des-,* and *baucher,* to hew.]

debenture *di-ben'chər, n.* a written acknowledgment of

a debt: a security issued by a company for money borrowed on the company's property, having a fixed rate of interest and usually fixed redemption rates: a certificate entitling an exporter of imported goods to a repayment of the duty paid on their importation.—*adj.* **deben'tured** entitled to drawback or debenture, as goods. [L. *dēbentur*, there are due—the first word of the receipt.]

debilitate *di-bil'i-tāt, v.t.* to make weak: to impair the strength of.—*n.* **debilitā'tion.**—*adj.* **debil'itative.**—*n.* **debil'ity** weakness and languor. [L. *dēbilitāre, -ātum—dēbilis,* weak—*dē,* from, *habilis,* able.]

debit *deb'it, n.* a debt or something due: an entry on the debtor side of an account, recording a sum owing (*book-k.*).—*v.t.* to charge with debt: to enter on the debtor side of an account. [L. *dēbitum,* what is due, from *dēbēre,* to owe.]

debonair *deb-ə-nār', adj.* of good appearance and manners: elegant: courteous: gay.—*adv.* **debonair'ly.**—*n.* **debonair'ness.** [Fr. *de,* of, *bon,* good, and the old word *aire* (*masc.*), manner, origin.]

debouch *di-bowch', di-bōōsh', v.i.* to issue, emerge, to march or flow out from a narrow pass or confined place.—*n.* **debouch'ment** an act or place of debouching. [Fr. *déboucher—de,* from, *bouche,* mouth— L. *bucca,* cheek.]

Debrett *di-bret', n.* a peerage edited from 1784 until his death by John Field *Debrett,* still in publication.

debrief *dē-brēf', v.t.* to gather information from a soldier, astronaut, etc., on his return from a mission. [Pfx. **de-** (2).]

debris, débris *deb'rē, dəb-rē',* or *dāb'rē, n.* wreckage: ruins: rubbish: a mass of rocky fragments. [Fr., from *briser,* akin to **bruise.**]

debt *det, n.* what one owes to another: what one becomes liable to do or suffer: a state of obligation or indebtedness: a duty: a sin (*B.*).—*n.* **debt'or** one who owes a debt.—**bad debt** a debt of which there is no prospect of payment; **debt of honour** a debt not recognised by law, but binding in honour—esp. a gambling or betting debt; **debt of nature** death; **floating debt** miscellaneous public debt, like exchequer and treasury bills; **in someone's debt** under an obligation (not necessarily pecuniary) to someone; **national debt** see **nation.** [O.Fr. *dette—*L. *dēbitum, dēbēre,* to owe.]

debug *dē-bug', v.t.* to remove concealed listening devices from: to find faults or errors in and remove them from (something mechanical): to remove insects from (*coll.*). [L. *dē,* from, and **bug.**]

debunk *dē-bungk', v.t.* (*slang*) to clear of bunk or humbug: to remove the whitewash from (a reputation): to show up (e.g. a theory) as false. [Pfx. **de-** (2).]

début *dā-bū', n.* a beginning or first attempt: a first appearance before the public, or in society.—*n.* **débutante** (*dā'bū-tāt, deb'ū-tənt; coll.* shortening **deb**) a young woman making her début in society. [Fr. *début,* a first stroke—*de,* from, *but,* aim, mark.]

deca- *dek-ə-,* prefix signifying ten. [Gr. *deka.*]

decade *dek'ād, dek-ād', n.* a series of ten years: any group or series of ten.—*adj.* **dec'adal.** [Gr. *dekas, -ados—deka,* ten.]

decadence *dek'ə-dəns, dec'adency ns.* state of decay: a decline from a superior state, standard or time.—*adj.* **dec'adent** decaying, declining: lacking in moral, physical or artistic vigour.—*n.* one who is degenerate.—*adv.* **decadently.** [Fr.,—L.L. *dēca- dentia,* from L. *dē,* down, *cadēre,* to fall.]

decaffeinate *dē-kaf'i-nāt, v.t.* to extract (most of) the caffeine from coffee. [Pfx. **de-** (2).]

decagon *dek'ə-gon, n.* a plane figure of ten angles and sides.—*adj.* **decagonal** (*-ag'ən-əl*). [Gr. *deka,* and *gōniā,* an angle.]

decagramme, decagram *dek'ə-gram, n.* a weight of ten

grammes. [Fr. *décagramme—*Gr. *deka,* ten, and **gramme.**]

decahedron *dek-ə-hē'drən, n.* a solid figure having ten faces.—*adj.* **decahē'dral.** [Gr. *deka,* and *hedrā,* a seat.]

decal *dē'kal, dek'al, n.* a transfer (picture or design). [From Fr. *décalquer,* to trace, copy.]

decalcify *dē-kal'si-fī, v.t.* to deprive of lime.—*n.* **decalcificā'tion.** [Pfx. **de-** (2).]

decalitre *dek'ə-lēt-ər, n.* ten litres, about 2·2 imperial gallons. [Fr. *décalitre—*Gr. *deka,* ten, and *lītrā,* a pound.]

decalogue *dek'ə-log, n.* the ten commandments. [Gr. *deka,* ten, *logos,* a discourse.]

decametre *dek'ə-mēt-ər, n.* ten metres. [Fr. *décamètre —*Gr. *deka,* ten, *metron,* a measure.]

decamp *di-kamp', v.i.* to make off, esp. secretly: to break camp.—*n.* **decamp'ment.** [Fr. *décamper.*]

decanal *dek-ān'əl, adj.* pertaining to a dean or deanery: **decani.**—*adj.* **decān'i** dean's, i.e. south (of the side of a choir where the dean sits, opposed to **cantoris**): used (*mus.*) in antiphonal singing. [L.L. *decānus, -i.*]

decani. See **decanal.**

decant *di-kant', v.t.* to pour off, leaving sediment: to pour from one vessel into another: to move (people) to another area, etc.—*n.* **decant'er** an ornamental stoppered bottle for holding decanted liquor. [Fr. *décanter—*L. *dē,* from, *canthus,* beak of a vessel.]

decapitate *di-kap'i-tāt, v.t.* to behead.—*n.* **decapitā'tion.** [L.L. *dēcapitāre—*L. *dē,* from, and *caput,* the head.]

Decapoda *di-kap'ə-də, n.pl.* an order of higher crustaceans with ten feet (including pincers)—crabs, lobsters, shrimps, prawns, etc.: an order of cephalopods with ten arms.—*n.* **dec'apod** a member of either of these orders.—Also *adj.—adjs.* **decap'odal, decap'odan, decap'odous.** [Gr. *deka,* ten, and *pous, podos,* a foot.]

decarbonise, -ize *dē-kär'bən-īz, v.t.* to remove carbon or carbon dioxide from (also **decar'burise, -ize**; *decar'bonate*).—*ns.* **decarbonā'tion; decarbonisā'tion, -z-; decarburisā'tion, -z-.**—See also **decarb** under **decoke.** [Pfx. **de-** (2).]

decasyllable *dek-ə-sil'ə-bl, n.* a verse-line, or a word, of ten syllables.—*adj.* **decasyllabic** (*-ab'ik*). [Gr. *deka,* ten, *syllabē,* a syllable; see **syllable.**]

decathlon *dek-ath'lon, n.* a two-day contest of ten events held at the modern Olympic Games since 1912. —*n.* **decath'lete.** [Gr. *deka,* ten, *athlon,* a contest.]

decay *di-kā', v.i.* to fall away from a state of health or excellence: to waste away: to rot.—*v.t.* to cause to waste away: to impair.—*n.* a falling into a worse or less perfect state: a wearing away: rotting: bad or rotten matter (e.g. in a tooth): loss of fortune: disintegration of a radioactive substance.—*adj.* **decayed'** rotten: reduced in circumstances, impoverished. [O.Fr. *decair—*L. *dē,* from, *cadēre,* to fall.]

decease *di-sēs', n.* death.—*v.i.* to die.—*adj.* **deceased'** dead: lately dead.—*n.* the dead person in question. [O.Fr. *deces—*L. *dēcessus,* departure, death.]

decedent *di-sē'dant, n* (*U.S. law*) a deceased person. [L. *dēcēdēns, -entis,* pr.p. of *dēcēdēre,* to depart.]

deceit *di-sēt', n.* act of deceiving: anything intended to mislead another: fraud: falseness.—*adj.* **deceit'ful** full of deceit: disposed or tending to deceive: insincere.— *adj.* **deceit'fully.**—*n.* **deceit'fulness.** [O.Fr. *deceite —*L. *dēcipěre, dēceptum,* to deceive.]

deceive *di-sēv', v.t.* to mislead or cause to err: to cheat: to disappoint (*arch.*).—*adj.* **deceiv'able** that may be deceived: exposed to imposture.—*ns.* **deceiv'ableness, deceivabil'ity.**—*adj.* **deceiv'ably.**—*n.* **deceiv'er.** [Fr. *décevoir—*L. *dēcipěre, dēceptum,* to deceive.]

decelerate dē-sel'ər-āt, v.t. and v.i. to retard.—ns. **decelerā'tion; decel'erator; decelerom'eter** an instrument for measuring deceleration. [L. dē, down, celer, swift.]

December di-sem'bər, n. formerly the tenth, now the twelfth month of the year. [L. December—decem, ten.]

decemvir dı-sem'vər, n. a member of a body of ten men: esp. of those who drew up the Laws of the Twelve Tables at Rome (451–450 B.C.):—pl. **decem'virs** or **decem'virī** (L. dek'em-wi-rē).—adj. **decem'viral.**—n. **decem'virāte** a body of ten men in office: the term of office of decemvirs. [L. decem, ten, and vir, a man.]

decency. See decent.

decennary dı-sen'ər-i, n. a period of ten years—also **decenn'ium.**—adj. **decenn'ial** consisting of, or happening every, ten years. [L. decem, ten, and annus, a year.]

decent dē'sənt, adj. becoming: seemly: proper: modest: moderate: fairly good: passable: showing tolerant or kindly moderation (coll.): nice, pleasant (coll.).—n. **dē'cency** becomingness: modesty: considerateness, sense of what may be fitly expected of one (coll.): (in pl.) the conventions of respectable behaviour.—adv. **dē'cently.** [L. decēns, -entis, pr.p. of decēre, to be becoming.]

decentralise, -ize dē-sen'trəl-īz, v.t to withdraw from the centre: to transform by transferring functions from a central government, organisation or head to local centres.—n. **decentralisā'tion, -z-.** [Pfx. de- (2).]

deception di-sep'shən, n. act of deceiving: state of being deceived: means of deceiving or misleading: trick: illusion.—adjs. **decep'tive** tending to deceive: misleading.—adv. **decep'tively.**—n. **decep'tiveness.** [O.Fr.,—L.L. dēceptiō, -ōnis—dēcipēre, to deceive.]

deci- des'i-, prefix signifying one-tenth. [L. decimus, tenth.]

decibel des'ı-bel, n. the tenth part of a bel—unit more commonly used than bel (q.v.). [L. deci-, and **bel.**]

decide dı-sīd', v.t. to determine: to end: to settle: to resolve.—v.i. to make up one's mind.—adjs. **decid'able** capable of being decided; **decid'ed** determined: clear, unmistakable: resolute.—adv. **decid'edly.**—n. **decid'er** one who, or that which, decides: an action, etc., that proves decisive, as the winning goal in a match (coll.). [O.Fr. decider—L. dēcīdēre—dē, away, caedēre, to cut.]

deciduous dı-sıd'ū-əs, adj. liable to be shed at a certain period: transitory, not permanent: shedding all the leaves together (opp. to evergreen) (bot.): shedding wings (as some insects).—n. **decid'uousness.** [L. dēciduus—dēcīdēre—dē, from, cadēre, to fall.]

decilitre des'ı-lē-tər, n. a tenth part of a litre.

decillion di-sil'yən, n. a million raised to the tenth power: in American notation, a thousand raised to the eleventh power.—adj. and n. **decill'ionth.** [L. decem, ten, and **million.**]

decimal des'i-məl, adj. numbered or proceeding by tens.—n. a decimal fraction.—v.t. **dec'imalise, -ize** to convert to a decimal system, esp. the metric system. —n. **decimalisā'tion, -z-.**—adv. **dec'imally.**—**decimal currency** one in which the basic unit is divided into ten, or a multiple of ten, parts; **decimal fraction** a fraction expressed by continuing ordinary decimal notation into negative powers of ten, a point being placed after the unit figure; **decimal notation** a system of writing numbers based on ten and powers of ten, our ordinary system; **decimal places** the number of figures written after the point (**decimal point**) which separates the unit and the decimal fraction; **decimal system** a system in which each unit is ten times the

next below it, esp. the metric system of weights and measures. [L. decima (pars), a tenth (part).]

decimate des'i-māt, v.t. to take the tenth part of: to punish by killing every tenth man: (loosely) to reduce very heavily.—ns. **decimā'tion; dec'imātor.** [L. decimāre, -ātum—decimus, tenth—decem, ten]

decimetre des'i-mē-tər, n. a tenth of a metre.

decipher di-sī'fər, v.t. to uncipher: to read or transliterate or interpret from secret, unknown, or difficult writing: to make out.—n. **decipherabil'ity.**—adj. **deci'pherable.**—ns. **deci'pherer; deci'pherment.** [Pfx. de- (2).]

decision di-sizh'ən, n. the act or product of deciding: settlement: judgment: the quality of being decided in character.—adj. **decisive** (-sīs'ıv) having the power of deciding: showing decision: final: positive.—adv. **decī'sively.**—n. **decī'siveness.**—adj. **decī'sory** decisive. [See **decide.**]

deck dek, v.t. to clothe: to adorn: to furnish with a deck.—n. a horizontal platform extending from one side of a vessel to the other, thereby joining them together, and forming both a floor and a covering (naut.): a floor, platform, or tier as in a bus, bridge, etc.: the ground (slang): a pile of things laid flat: a pack of cards: the part of a pack used in a particular game, or the undealt part: the turntable of a record-player: that part of a tape-recorder or computer in which the magnetic tapes are placed, and the mechanism for running them: a set of punched cards.—adj. **decked** (dekt) adorned, decorated.—ns. **deck'er** the person or thing that decks: a vessel, vehicle, or other structure that has a deck or decks (used only in composition, as three-decker); **deck'ing** adornment: a platform.—**deck'chair** a chair, usually folding and made of canvas, such as passengers sit or lie on deck in; **deck'-hand** a person employed on deck: an ordinary sailor; **deck'-house** a house, room, or box on deck; **deck'-passage** a passage securing only the right of being on deck, without cabin accommodation; **deck'-pass'enger; deck'-quoits** quoits as played on a ship's deck, with rope rings; **deck'-tenn'is** lawn-tennis modified for playing on board ship.—**clear the decks** to tidy up, remove encumbrances, esp. in preparation for action (orig. naval action, now often fig.); **hit the deck** (slang) to lie, fall, or be pushed down quickly. [Verbal meanings—Du. dekken, to cover; substantive meanings—M.Du. dec, roof, covering.]

deckle dek'l, n. in paper-making a contrivance for fixing width of sheet: a deckle-edge.—adj. **deckled** (dek'ld) deckle-edged.—**deck'le-edge** the raw or ragged edge of handmade paper or an imitation of it. [Ger. Deckel, lid.]

decko. See **dekko.**

declaim di-klām', v.i. to make a set or rhetorical speech: to harangue: to recite.—v.t. to utter, repeat, or recite declamatorily.—ns. **declaim'ant, declaim'er.**—n. and adj. **declaim'ing.**—n. **declamation** (dek-lə-mā'shən) act of declaiming: a set speech in public: display in speaking.—adv. **declamatorily** (di-klam'ə-tə-ri-li).—adj. **declam'atory** of the nature of declamation: appealing to the passions: noisy and rhetorical [L. dēclāmāre—de-, intens., clāmāre, to cry out.]

declare di-klār', v.t. to make known: to announce: to assert: to make a full statement of, as of goods at a custom-house: to expose and claim a score (as at bezique, etc.): to announce one's choice of trump-suit or no trumps (bridge).—v.i. to make a statement: to announce one's decision or sympathies: to show cards in order to score: to end an innings voluntarily before ten wickets have fallen (cricket).—adj. **declar'able** capable of being declared, exhibited, or proved.—ns. **declar'ant** one who makes a declaration; **declaration**

(dek-lə-rā'shən) act of declaring: that which is declared: a written affirmation: a formal announcement (e.g. of war): in common law, the pleading in which the plaintiff in an action at law sets forth his case against the defendant.—*adjs.* **declarative** (*di-klar'ə-tiv*), **declăr'atory.**—*advs.* **declăr'atively,** **declăr'atorily.**—*adj.* **declăred'** avowed.—*n.* **declăr'er.**—*adv.* **declă'redly** avowedly.—(**well**) **I declare!** *interj.* expressing surprise. [L. *dēclārāre* (*partly through Fr. déclarer*).]

declass dē-klās', *v.t.* to remove or degrade from one's class.—*adj.* **déclassé,** *fem.* **déclassée** (*dā-klā-sā;* Fr.) having lost caste or social standing. [Fr. *déclasser*.]

declassify dē-klas'i-fī, *v.t.* to take off the security list. [Pfx. **de-** (2).]

declension di-klen'shən, *n.* a falling off: decay: descent: system of cases and case-endings (*gram.*): a class of words similarly declined: a statement in order of the cases of a word.—*adj.* **declen'sional.** [See **decline.**]

decline di-klīn', *v.i.* to bend or turn away: to deviate: to refuse: to bend or slope down: to fail or decay e.g. in health, fortune: to stoop or condescend: to draw to an end.—*v.t.* to bend down: to turn away from: to refuse: to give the various cases of (*gram.*).—*n.* a falling off: deviation: decay: a gradual sinking of the bodily faculties, consumption (*arch.*): a down-slope.—*adj.* **declin'able** having inflection for case.—*ns.* **declinā'tion** act of declining (*U.S.*): a sloping or binding downwards: deviation: angular distance from the celestial equator (*astron.*); **declinom'eter** an instrument for measuring the **declination of the compass**— i.e. the deviation of the magnetic needle from the true north.—**on the decline** in the process of becoming less, deteriorating. [L. *dēclīnāre*—(partly through Fr. *décliner*).]

declivity di-kliv'i-ti, *n.* a place that declines, or slopes downward, opposite of *acclivity:* inclination downwards.—*adj.* **decliv'itous.** [L. *dēclīvitās, -ātis* —dē, downward, *clīvus,* sloping.]

declutch dē-kluch', *v.i.* to release the clutch. [Pfx. **de-** (2).]

decoct di-kokt', *v.t.* to extract the substance of by boiling.—*n.* **decoc'tion** an extract of anything got by boiling. [L. *dēcoquĕre, dēcoctum—dē,* down, *coquĕre,* to cook.]

decode dē-kōd', *v.t.* to translate from a code.—*n.* **decō'der.** [Pfx. **de-** (2).]

decoke dē-kōk', earlier **decarb** dē-kärb', (*coll.*) *vs.t.* to decarbonise (an internal combustion engine). [Pfx. **de-** (2).]

decollate dē-kol'āt, *v.t.* to behead. [L. *dēcollāre—dē,* from, *collum,* the neck.]

décolleté dā-kol-tā, *adj.* with neck uncovered: of dress, low cut.—*n.* **décolletage** (*dā-kol-täzh'*) (a dress with) a low-cut neckline. [Fr., pa.p. of *décolleter,* to bare the neck and shoulders—*collet,* collar.]

decolonise, -ize dē-kol'ə-nīz, *v.t.* to release from being a colony, grant independence to.—*n.* **decolonisā'tion,** -z-. [Pfx. **de-** (2).]

decolour, decolor dē-kul'ər, *v.t.* to deprive of colour— also **decol'o(u)rise, -ize.** [L. *dēcolōrāre—dē,* from, *color,* colour.]

decompose dē-kom-pōz', *v.t.* to separate the component parts of: to resolve into elements.—*v.i.* to decay, rot—*n.* **decompŏsabil'ity.**—*adj.* **decompŏs'able.**—*n.* **decompŏs'er.** [Fr. *décomposer*—pfx. *dé-* (L. *dis-,* apart), and *composer;* see **compose.**]

decomposition di-kom-pə-zish'ən, *n.* act or state of decomposing: decay. [Fr. pfx. *dé-* (L. *dis-*), apart, and **composition.**]

decompress dē-kəm-pres', *v.t.* to release from pressure. —*n.* **decompression** (-*presh'ən*) the act or process of releasing from pressure: the gradual release of air pressure on persons (as divers, construction workers, etc.) on returning to normal atmospheric conditions: any operation to relieve excessive pressure (*surg.*).— *adj.* **decompress'ive.**—*n.* **decompress'or.**—**decompression chamber** a chamber in which excessive pressure can be reduced gradually to atmospheric pressure, or in which a person can be subjected gradually to decreased atmospheric pressure; **decompression sickness** same as **caisson disease.** [Pfx. **de-** (2).]

decongest dē-kən-jest', *v.t.* to relieve or end the congestion of.—*ns.* **deconges'tant** (*med.*) an agent that relieves congestion; **decongest'ion** (-*yən*).—*adj.* **deconges'tive.** [Pfx. **de-** (2).]

deconsecrate dē-kon'si-krāt, *v.t.* to deprive of the character given by consecration: to secularise.—*n.* **deconsecrā'tion.** [Pfx. **de-** (2).]

decontaminate dē-kən-tam'in-āt, *v.t.* to free from contamination.—*ns.* **decontam'inant; decontaminā'tion.**—*adj.* **decontam'inative.**—*n.* **decontam'inātor.** [Pfx. **de-** (2).]

decontrol dē-kən-trōl', *v.t.* to remove (esp. official) control from.—*n.* removal of control. [Pfx. **de-** (2).]

décor dā'kōr, *n.* scenery and stage embellishments: ornament: general decorative effect (colour-scheme, furnishings, etc) of a room. [Fr., decoration.]

decorate dek'ə-rāt, *v.t.* to ornament, to beautify: to paint, put wallpaper on (a house, etc.): to honour with a badge or medal.—*adj.* **dec'orated.**—*n.* **decorā'tion** ornament: the applied paint and wallpaper in e.g. a house: badge of an order: (in *pl.*) flags, bunting, paper chains, etc., put out or hung at a time of rejoicing.— *adj.* **dec'orative** (-*rə-tiv*) ornamental.—*adv.* **dec'oratively.**—*n.* **dec'orativeness; dec'orātor** one who decorates, esp. houses.—**Decorated style** (*archit.*) a style of Gothic architecture, elaborate and richly decorated, which prevailed till near the end of the 14th century. [L. *decorāre, -ātum—decēre,* to be becoming.]

decorous de'kə-rəs, *adj.* becoming: suitable: proper: decent.—*adv.* **dec'orously.**—*ns.* **dec'orousness; deco'rum** that which is becoming in outward appearance: propriety of conduct: decency. [L. *decōrus,* becoming; L. *decēre,* to be becoming.]

decoupage dā-kōō-pāzh', *n.* the craft, originating in the 18th century, of applying decorative paper cut-outs to e.g. wood surfaces. [Fr. *découper,* to cut out.]

decoy di-koi', *v.t.* to allure: to entrap: to lure into a trap. —*n.* (*dē'koi*) anything intended to lure into a snare (also *fig.*): apparatus of hoops and network for trapping wild-ducks: one employed to allure others into a snare. [Perh. Du. *de,* the, *kooi,* a cage.]

decrease di-krēs', *v.i.* to become less.—*v.t.* to make less.—*n.* (*dē'krēs*) a growing less: loss.—*adv.* **decreas'ingly.** [O.Fr. *decrois,* a decrease—L. *dēcrēscĕre* —dē, from, *crēscĕre,* to grow.]

decree di-krē', *n.* an order by one in authority: an edict or law: a judicial decision: a predetermined purpose (*theol.*).—*v.t.* to decide or determine by sentence in law: to appoint.—*v.i.* to make a decree:—*pr.p.* **decree'ing;** *pa.t.* and *pa.p.* **decreed'.**—*adj.* **decrē'tal** pertaining to a decree.—*n.* decree, esp. of the pope: (in *pl.*; often with *cap.*) the second part of the canon law, the decrees of various popes determining points of ecclesiastical law.—**decree nisi** (*nī'sī;* L. *nisi,* unless) a decree that becomes a **decree absolute** unless cause be shown to the contrary—granted esp. in divorce cases. [O.Fr. *decret* and L. *dēcrētālis*—L. *dēcrētum—dēcernĕre,* to decide.]

decrement dek'ri-mənt, *n.* the act or state of decreasing: the quantity lost by decrease: the decrease in value of a variable (*math.*): the ratio of successive amplitudes in an oscillator (*phys.*). [L. *dēcrēmentum.*]

decrepit di-krep'it, *adj.* worn out by the infirmities of old age: in the last stage of decay.—ns. **decrep'itness; decrep'itude** state of being decrepit or worn out with age. [L. *dēcrepitus*, noiseless, very old—*dē*, from, *crepitus*, a noise.]

decrepitate *di-krep'i-tāt*, *v.i.* to crackle, as salts when heated.—*v.t.* to roast so as to cause a continual crackling, to calcine.—*n.* **decrepita'tion**. [L. *dē*-, intens., *crepitāre*, to rattle.]

decrescent *di-kres'ənt*, *adj.* becoming gradually less.— *n.*, *adj.* and *adv.* **decrescendo** (*dā-kre-shen'dō*; *mus.*; It.) diminuendo:—*pl.* **decrescend'os**. [L. *dē*, *crēscĕre*.]

decretal, etc. See **decree**.

decriminalise, -ize *dē-krim'in-əl-īz*, *v.t.* to make a practice, etc., no longer a criminal offence in law.—*n.* **decriminalisa'tion, -z-**. [Pfx. de- (2).]

decrufitment *dē-kroot'mənt*, *n.* an esp. U.S. term for making, or being made, redundant.—*v.t.* **decruit'**. [Pfx. de- (2), and **recruit**.]

decry *di-krī'*, *v.t.* to cry down: to condemn: to censure as worthless: to blame:—*pr.p.* **decry'ing;** *pa.t.* and *pa.p.* **decried'**.—*ns.* **decri'al; decri'er**. [Fr. *dé-*, *des-* (L. *dis-*), and *crier*, to cry; see **cry**.]

decrypt *dē-kript'*, *v.t.* to decode.—*n.* **decryp'tion**. [de- (2) and **crypt-**.]

decuman *dek'ū-mən*, *adj.* principal, large—of waves, etc.: connected with the principal gate of a Roman camp (near which the 10th cohort of the legion was stationed).—*n.* a great wave, as every tenth wave was supposed to be. [L. *decumānus—decem*, ten.]

decumbent *di-kum'bənt*, *adj.* lying down: lying flat with rising tip (*bot.*).—*ns.* **decum'bence, decum'bency**. [L. *dē*, down, and -*cumbĕre* (in compounds only), to lie.]

decuple *dek'ū-pl*, *adj.* tenfold.—*n.* a number ten times repeated.—*v.t.* to make tenfold. [Fr. *décuple*—L. *decuplus*.]

decussate *di-kus'āt*, *v.t.* to divide in the form of an X.— *v.i.* to cross in such a form: to intersect.—*adjs.* **decuss'ate, -d** crossed: arranged in pairs which cross each other, like some leaves.—*adv.* **decuss'ately**.—*n.* **decussa'tion** (*dek-*). [L. *decussis*, a coin of ten asses (*decem asses*) marked with X, ten.]

dedal, dedalian. See **daedal**.

dedans *də-dā*, *n.* an open gallery at the end of the service side of a (real) tennis-court: spectators at a court tennis match. [Fr.]

dedicate *ded'i-kāt*, *v.t.* to set apart and consecrate to some sacred purpose: to devote wholly or chiefly: to inscribe to anyone: to inaugurate or open (*U.S.*).— *adj.* devoted.—*adj.* **ded'icated** consecrated: giving one's whole interest and work to a particular cause or belief: single-minded: manufactured or set aside for a specific purpose, as a *dedicated calculator*.—*ns.* **dedicatee** (*ded-i-kā-tē'*) one to whom a thing is dedicated; **dedica'tion** the act of dedicating: an address to a patron, prefixed to a book; **ded'icator**.— *adjs.* **dedica'tional; ded'icatory** (*-kə-* or -*kā-*), **ded'icative**. [L. *dēdicāre, -ātum—dē*, down, *dicāre*, to declare.]

deduce *di-dūs'*, *v.t.* to derive: to infer from what precedes or from premises.—*n.* **deduce'ment** what is deduced.—*adj.* **deduc'ible** that may be deduced or inferred.—*ns.* **deducibil'ity, deduc'ibleness** the quality of being deducible.—*v.t.* **deduct** (*-dukt'*) to take away: to separate: to subtract.—*adj.* **deduct'ible**.—*ns.* **deductibil'ity; deduc'tion** the act of deducing: that which is deduced: the drawing of a particular truth from a general, antecedently known, as distinguished from *induction*, rising from particular truths to a general: the act of deducting: that which is deducted: abatement.—*adj.* **deduct'ive** concerned with deduction from premises or accepted principles.—*adv.*

deduct'ively. [L. *dēdūcĕre, dēductum—dē*, from, *dūcĕre*, to lead.]

dee *dē*, *n.* the fourth letter of the alphabet (D, d): anything shaped like it.—*n.* a substitute for **damn**.

deed *dēd*, *n.* something done: an act: an exploit: a legal transaction, esp. involving the transference of property: the written evidence of it, signed, sealed and delivered.—*v.t.* to transfer (property).—*adv.* **deed'ily**.—*adj.* **deed'y** industrious, active.—**deed poll** a deed executed by one party, esp. one by which a person changes his/her name, originally having the edge **polled** or cut even, not indented.—**in deed** in reality. [O.E. *dǣd—dōn*, to do; Ger. *Tat*.]

dee-jay, deejay *dē'jā*, or -*jā'*, (*coll.*) *n.* a phonetic representation of the initials **D.J.**, abbrev. of **disc-jockey**.

deem *dēm*, *v.t.* or *v.i.* to judge: to think: to believe.—*ns.* **deem'ster** a judge—now only in the Isle of Man; **dempster** (*dem'stər*) formerly in Scotland an officer who repeated the sentence after the judge. [O.E. *dēman*, to form a judgment—*dōm*, judgment.]

deep *dēp*, *adj.* extending or placed far down or far from the outside: far recessed: far involved: engrossed (in): difficult to understand: secret: wise and penetrating: cunning: profound: intense: excessive: heartfelt: sunk low: low in pitch: in the out-field, not close to the wickets (*cricket*).—*adv.* in a deep manner.—*n.* that which is deep: the sea: a deep place: anything profound or incomprehensible.—*v.t.* **deep'en** to make deeper in any sense: to increase.—*v.i.* to become deeper.—*adv.* **deep'ly**.—*n.* **deep'ness**.—*adjs.* **deep'-dyed** thoroughgoing, extreme—in a bad sense; **deep'felt**.—**deep field** fielding position deep behind the bowler; **deep'-freeze'** storage of foodstuffs, or other perishable substances, at very low temperature: the container in which the material is stored.—Also *v.t.*—*v.t.* **deep'-fry'** to fry food completely submerged in fat.—*adj.* **deep'-laid**.—**deep litter** a method of keeping hens in a henhouse with a peat material on the floor.—*adjs.* **deep-root'ed; deep'-sea** pertaining to the deeper parts of the sea; **deep'-seat'ed** not superficial.—**Deep South** region of the United States roughly Georgia, Alabama, Mississippi and Louisiana; **deep space** the area of space beyond the moon's orbit; **deep structure** (*linguistics*) the basic grammatical concepts of a sentence from which its **surface structure** (q.v.) derives; **deep therapy** the treatment of disease by deep X-rays or gamma rays.—*adj.* **deep'-toned** having a deep tone. —**go, dive or be thrown in at the deep end** to plunge, or be plunged, straight into an activity, job, etc., with little or no experience; **go off the deep end** to express strong feelings with abandonment; **in deep water** in difficulties; **two deep, three deep**, etc., in two, three, etc., layers or rows. [O.E. *dēop*.]

deer *dēr*, *n.* any kind of animal (as in *small deer*; *obs.*): any animal of the Cervidae, a family of even-toed ungulates characterised by the possession of antlers by the males at least—including stag, reindeer, etc.:—*pl.* **deer**.—**deer'-fence** a very high fence that deer cannot jump over; **deer'-forest** wild tract reserved for deer; **deer'(-)horn** a deer's antler or its material: a freshwater mussel (*U.S.*); **deer'-hound** a large roughcoated greyhound; **deer'-lick** a spot of salt ground whither deer come to lick the earth; **deer'-park**; **deer'skin** skin of the deer, or leather therefrom; **deer'-stalker** one who stalks deer: a sportsman's helmetshaped cap; **deer'stalking**. [O.E. *dēor*.]

deface *di-fās'*, *v.t.* to destroy or mar the face or external appearance of, to disfigure.—*ns.* **deface'ment**; **defā'cer**.—*adv.* **defa'cingly**. [O.Fr. *desfacer*—L. *dis-*, away, *faciès*, face.]

de facto *dē, dā fak'tō*, (L.) actual, if not rightful (e.g. *the de facto ruler*): in fact, actually.

defalcate *dē'fal-kāt*, *v.i.* to embezzle money held on trust.—*ns.* **defalca'tion; de'falcator** [L. *dē*, from *falcāre*, to cut—*falx, falcis*, a sickle.]

defame *di-fām'*, *v.t.* to take away or destroy the good fame or reputation of: to speak evil of.—*n.* **defamation** (*def-ə-mā'shən*) the act of defaming: calumny: slander.—*adv.* **defamatorily** (*di-fam'ə-tər-i-li*).—*adj.* **defam'atory**. [O.Fr. *diffamer*—L. *diffāmāre*—*dis-*, away, *fāma*, report.]

default *di-fölt'*, *n.* a fault, failing, or failure: defect: neglect to do what duty or law requires: failure to fulfil a financial obligation.—*v.i.* to fail through neglect of duty: to fail to appear in court when called upon: to fail to fulfil a financial obligation (with *on* or *in*).—*n.* **default'er** one who defaults: a military offender.—**judgment by default** judgment given against a person because he fails to plead or make an appearance in court; **in default of** in the absence of: for lack of. [O.Fr. *defaute* (noun) and *default* (3rd sing. of *defaillir*)—L. pfx. *dē-* and *fallēre*; see **fault**.]

defeasance *di-fēz'əns*, *n.* a rendering null or void (*law*).—*adj.* **defeas'ible** that may be annulled.—*ns.* **defeasibil'ity; defeas'ibleness**. [O.Fr. *defesance*—*desfaire*; see **defeat**.]

defeat *di-fēt'*, *v.t.* to win a victory over: to get the better of: to ruin: to frustrate.—*n.* a frustration of plans: ruin: overthrow, as of an army in battle: loss of a game, race, etc.—*ns.* **defeat'ism** disposition to accept defeat; **defeat'ist**.—Also *adj.* [O.Fr. *defait*—*desfaire*, to undo—L. *dis-*, neg., *facēre*, to do.]

defecate *def'*, *def'i-kāt*, *v.t.* to clear of dregs or impurities: to purify from extraneous matter.—*v.i.* to void excrement.—*ns.* **defeca'tion; def'ecator**. [L. *dē-faecāre, -ātum*, to cleanse—*dē*, from, *faex, faecis*, dregs.]

defect *di-fekt'*, *dē'fekt*, *n.* a deficiency: a want: imperfection: blemish: fault.—*v.i.* (*di-fekt'*) to desert one's country, a cause, transferring one's allegiance (to another).—*n.* **defec'tion** desertion: a failure, a falling away from duty: revolt.—*adj.* **defect'ive** having defect: wanting in some necessary quality: imperfect: faulty: insufficient: incomplete in inflexions or forms (*gram.*).—*n.* a person deficient in physical or mental powers.—*adv.* **defect'ively**.—*ns.* **defect'iveness; defect'or** one who deserts his country, etc.—**the defects of one's qualities** virtues carried to excess, the faults apt to accompany or flow from good qualities. [L. *dēficēre, dēfectum*, to fail—*dē*, down, and *facēre*, to do.]

defence, in U.S. **defense**, *di-fens'*, *n.* a defending: capability or means of resisting an attack: protection: vindication: a defendant's plea (*law*): the defending party in legal proceedings: the members of a (football, hockey, etc.) team who are in defending positions, e.g. halves, backs, goalkeeper.—*adv.* **defence'lessly**.—*n.* **defence'lessness**.—*v.t.* **defend** (*di-fend'*) to keep off anything hurtful from: to guard or protect: to maintain against attack: to represent or vindicate in court (*law*).—*v.i.* to have the responsibility for preventing scoring (*sport*).—*adj.* **defend'able**.—*n.* **defend'ant** a person accused or sued (*law*).—*ns.* **defend'er** one who defends: a player who defends the goal: the holder of a championship, etc., who seeks to maintain his title: a person sued or accused (*Scots law*); **defensibil'ity**.—*adj.* **defens'ible** that may be defended.—*adv.* **defens'ibly**.—*adj.* **defens'ive** serving to defend: in a state or posture of defence.—*n.* posture of defence.—*adv.* **defens'ively**. —**defence mechanism** an unconscious mental process by which an individual excludes ideas painful to him (*psych.*): a response by the body in reaction to harmful organisms (*med.*).—**defender of the faith** a title borne by the sovereigns of England since Henry VIII, on whom it was conferred in 1521 for his book

against Luther; **stand, be, on the defensive** to be in the attitude of self-defence. [L. *dēfendēre, dēfēnsum*, to ward off—*dē*, off, and *fendēre*, to strike (found in compounds).]

defenestration *dē-fen-is-trā'shən*, *n.* a flinging out of a window. [L. *dē*, from, *fenestra*, window.]

defense. See **defence**.

defer[1] *di-fûr'*, *v.t.* to put off to another time: to delay: —*pr.p.* **deferr'ing**; *pa.t.* and *pa.p.* **deferred'**.—*adj.* **defer(r)'able**.—*ns.* **defer'ment; deferr'al; deferr'er**. —**deferred payment** payment by instalments; **deferred shares** shares not entitling the holder to a full share of profits. [L. *differre*—*dis-*, asunder, *ferre*, to bear, carry; cf. **differ**.]

defer[2] *di-fûr'*, *v.i.* to yield (to the wishes or opinions of another, or to authority).—*v.t.* to submit to or lay before somebody:—*pr.p.* **deferr'ing**; *pa.t.* and *pa.p.* **deferred'**.—*n.* **deference** (*def'ər-əns*) a deferring or yielding: respectful compliance: submission.—*adj.* **def'erent** deferential.—*adj.* **deferential** (*-en'shl*) showing deference.—*adv.* **deferen'tially**. [L. *dē-ferre*—*dē*, down, and *ferre*, to bear.]

defiance *di-fī'əns*, *n.* the act of defying: a challenge to combat: aggressiveness: contempt of opposition.— *adj.* **defi'ant** full of defiance, insolently bold.—*adv.* **defi'antly**. [**defy**.]

defibrillator *dē-fib'ri-lā-tər* or *-fib'*, (*med.*) *n.* a machine which applies an electric current to the chest or heart to stop fibrillation of the heart. [Pfx. **de-**(2).]

deficient *di-fish'ənt*, *adj.* wanting (in): less than complete: defective.—*n.* **defic'iency** defect: shortage: the amount which is lacking for completeness.—*adv.* **defic'iently**.—*n.* **deficit** (*def'i-sit*, or *-fis'*) deficiency, esp. of revenue, as compared with expenditure: amount of the deficiency.—**deficiency disease** a disease due to lack of necessary substances (as vitamins) in the diet, such as rickets, scurvy, beriberi, pellagra. [L. *dēficēre*; see **defect**.]

defied, defier, etc. See **defy**.

defilade. See **defile**[1].

defile[1] *di-fīl'*, *v.i.* to march in file.—*n.* (*dē'fīl, di-fīl'*) a long narrow pass or way, in which troops can march only in file: a gorge.—*v.t.* **defilade** (*def-i-lād'*) to plan a fortification so as to protect it from enfilading fire.—Also *n.* [Fr. *défiler*—L. *dis-*, and *filum*, a thread.]

defile[2] *di-fīl'*, *v.t.* to befoul: to pollute or corrupt: to violate.—*ns.* **defile'ment** act of defiling: foulness; **defil'er**. [L. *dē*, and O.E. *fȳlan*—*fūl*, foul; confused with O.Fr. *defouler*, to trample, violate.]

defilement. See **defile**[1,2].

define *di-fīn'*, *v.t.* to fix the bounds or limits of: to determine with precision: to describe accurately: to fix the meaning of.—*n.* **definabil'ity**.—*adj.* **defin'able**.—*adv.* **defin'ably**.—*adj.* **definite** (*def'i-nit*) defined: having distinct limits: fixed: exact: clear: referring to a particular person or thing (*gram.*; see also **article**).—*adv.* **def'initely** in a definite manner: yes indeed (*coll.*).—*ns.* **def'initeness; defini'tion** a defining: a description of a thing by its properties: an explanation of the exact meaning of a word, term, or phrase: sharpness of outline.—*adj.* **definitive** (*di-fin'i-tiv*) defining or limiting: positive: final.—*n.* (*gram.*) an adjective used to limit the extent of signification of a noun.—*adv.* **defin'itively**.—*ns.* **defin'itiveness**. [L. *dēfinīre, -itum*, to set bounds to— *dē, finis*, a limit.]

deflagrate *def'lə-grāt*, *v.i.*, *v.t.* to burn suddenly, generally with flame and crackling noise.—*n.* **deflagra'tion**. [L. *dēflagrāre*—*dē*, down, *flagrāre*, to burn.]

deflate *dē-flāt'*, *v.t.* to reduce from a state of inflation. —*v.i.* to become deflated.—*n.* **defla'tion** the act or process of deflating: the state of being deflated: a financial condition in which there is an undue decrease in the amount of money available relative to its buying power—the converse of **inflation** (econ.). removal of loose material by the wind.—adj. **defla'tionary.**—n. **defla'tionist** one who favours deflation of currency.—Also adj —ns. **defla'ter; defla'tor.** [L. dē, from, flāre, to blow.]

deflect di-flekt', v.t. or v.t. to turn aside: to swerve or deviate from a right line or proper course.—ns. **deflec'tion, deflex'ion** (L. dēflexiō) bending: turning: deviation.—adj **deflec'tive** causing deflection.—n **deflec'tor** a device for deflecting a flame, electric arc, etc. [L. dē, from, down, and flectēre, flexum, to bend, turn.]

deflower di-flowr', v.t. to deprive of flowers: to deprive of grace and beauty, or of virginity: to ravish.—n. **deflower'er.** [O.Fr. desflorer—L. dē, from, flōs, flōris, a flower.]

defoliate di-fō'li-āt, v.t. to deprive of leaves —ns. **defō'liant** a chemical preparation used to remove leaves; **defōlia'tion; defō'liator.** [L.L. dēfoliāre, -ātum—dē, off, folium, a leaf.]

deforest dē-for'ist, v.t. to deprive of forests.—n. **deforestā'tion.** [Pfx. de- (2).]

deform di-förm', v.t. to alter or injure the form of: to disfigure: to change the shape of without breach of continuity.—adj. **deform'able.**—ns. **deformabil'ity; dēforma'tion.**—adj. **deformed'** misshapen.—adv. **deform'edly.**—ns. **deformed'ness; deform'er; deform'ity** state of being deformed: want of proper form: ugliness: disfigurement: anything that destroys beauty: an ugly feature or characteristic. [L. dēfōrmis, ugly—dē, from, fōrma, beauty.]

defraud di-fröd', v.t. to deprive by fraud (of): to cheat or deceive.—n. **defraud'er.** [L. dēfraudāre—dē, from, fraus, fraudis, fraud.]

defray di-frā', v.t. to pay—pr.p. **defray'ing;** pa.t. and pa.p. **defrayed'.**—adj. **defray'able.**—ns. **defray'al, defray'ment; defray'er.** [O.Fr. desfrayer—des- = L. dis-, and frais, expenses.]

defreeze dē-frēz', v.t. to thaw out, esp. frozen foods. [Pfx. de- (2).]

defrock. Same as **unfrock.**

defrost dē'frost', v.t. to remove frost or ice from: to thaw out.—Also v.i.—n. **de'frost'er** a device for defrosting esp. a windscreen. [Pfx. de- (2).]

deft deft, adj. handy, clever, esp. in movement.—adv. **deft'ly.**—n. **deft'ness.** [O.E. gedæfte, meek—dæftan, gedæftan, prepare, make fit.]

defunct di-fungkt', adj. having finished the course of life, dead: finished, no longer working (fig.). [L. dēfungī, dēfunctus, to finish.]

defuse, defuze dē-fūz', v.t. to remove the fuse of (a bomb, etc.), so making it harmless.—Also fig.

defy di-fī', v.t. to challenge: to brave, dare: to flout, or to resist (e.g. convention, order, person)—pr.p. **defy'ing;** pa.t. and pa.p. **defied';** 3rd pers. pres. ind. **defies'.**—n. **defi'er.** [O.Fr. defier—L.L. diffīdāre, to renounce faith or allegiance.]

dégagé dā-gā-zhā, (Fr.) adj. unembarrassed, unconstrained, easy: uninvolved. [Pa.p. of Fr. dégager, to disentangle.]

degarnish. Same as **disgarnish.**

degauss dē-gows', v.t. to protect against magnetic mines by equipment for neutralising a ship's magnetic field: to remove the magnetic field from. [Pfx. de- (2), **gauss.**]

degenerate di-jen'ər-it, adj. having departed from the high qualities of race or kind, become base.—n. one who is degenerate.—v.i. (-āt) to fall from a nobler state to be or to grow worse.—ns. **degen'eracy, degenera'tion** the act or process of becoming de-

generate: the state of being degenerate.—adv. **degen'erately.**—n. **degen'erateness.**—adj. **degen'erative** tending or causing to degenerate. [L. dēgenerāre, -ātum, to depart from its kind—dē, from, down, genus, genĕris, kind.]

degrade di-grād', v.t. to lower in grade or rank: to deprive of office or dignity. to lower in character, value, or position, or in complexity: to disgrace: to wear down (geol.): to decompose (chem.).—v.i. to decompose (chem.).—adj. **degrad'able** able to decompose chemically or biologically (also **biodegradable**).—n. **degradation** (deg-rə-dā'shən) degrading: disgrace: degeneration: abortive structural development: a lowering in dignity: decomposition (chem.). —adjs. **degrad'ed** reduced in rank: base: low; **degrad'ing** debasing: disgraceful. [O.Fr. degrader— L. dē, down, and gradus, a step. See **grade.**]

degrease dē-grēs', v.t. to deprive of, or cleanse from, grease.—n. **degreas'ant** a substance which removes grease. [Pfx. de- (2).]

degree di-grē', n. a grade or step (arch.): a gradation on a scale, or that which it measures: a unit of temperature: one of a series of advances or steps: relative position: rank: extent: a mark of distinction conferred by universities, whether earned by examination or granted as a mark of honour: the 360th part of a revolution: 60 geographical miles: nearness of relationship: comparative amount of criminality, severity, etc.: one of the three stages (positive, comparative, superlative) in the comparison of an adjective or adverb: the highest sum of exponents in any term (alg.): the number of points in which a curve may be met by a straight line.—**by degrees** by little and little, gradually; **degree of freedom** any one of the independent variables defining the state of a system (e.g. temperature, pressure, concentration): a capability of variation (e.g. a system having two variables one of which is dependent on the other has one degree of freedom); **first, second, third degree burn** (med.) the three categories of seriousness of a burn, third degree being most serious; **first, second, third degree murder** (U.S.) the three categories of criminality of a murder, first degree being most serious; **forbidden degrees** the degrees of consanguinity within which marriage is not allowed; **third degree** an American police method of extracting a confession by bullying or torture: any ruthless interrogation, **to a degree** to a certain degree: to a great degree, to an extreme. [Fr. degré—L. dē, down, gradus, a step.]

dehisce di-his', v.i. to gape, burst open (bot., etc.).—n. **dehisc'ence.**—adj. **dehisc'ent.** pr.p. of dēhiscēre—dē, intens., and hiscēre, inceptive of hiāre, to gape.]

dehorn dē-hörn', v.t. to dishorn: to prune (a tree).—n. **dehorn'er.** [Pfx. de- (2).]

dehumanise, -ize dē-hū'mən-īz, v.t. to deprive of specifically human qualities. [L. dē, from, down, and **humanise.**]

dehydrate dē-hī'drāt, v.t. to deprive of water chemically: to remove moisture from, dry: to deprive of strength, interest, etc. (fig.).—v.i. to lose water.— ns. **dehydra'tion** loss or withdrawal of moisture: excessive loss of water from the tissues of the body (med.); **dehy'drator, dehy'drater.** [L. dē, from, Gr. hydōr, water.]

de-ice dē'īs', v.t. to dislodge ice from (aircraft surfaces, etc.), or to treat them so as to prevent its formation. —n. **dē'-ic'er** any means of doing this, whether a fluid, a paste, or a mechanical or pneumatic device. [Pfx. de- (2).]

deictic. See **deixis.**

deify dē'i-fī, v t. to exalt to the rank of a god: to worship as a deity: to make godlike:—*pr.p.* **de'ifying;** *pa.t.* and *pa.p.* **de'ified.**—*adjs.* **deif'ic, -al** making godlike or divine.—*ns.* **deifica'tion; de'ifier.** [Fr. *déifier*—L. *deificāre*—*deus*, a god, and *facĕre*, to make.]

deign *dān, v.i.* to condescend.—*v.t.* to condescend to give. [Fr. *daigner*—L. *dignārī*, to think worthy— *dignus*, worthy.]

dei gratia *dē'i grā'shi-ə, dā'ē gra'ti-a,* (L.) by the grace of God.

deindustrialise, -ize *dē-in-dus'tri-əl-īz, v.t.* to disperse or reduce the industrial organisation and potential of a nation, area, etc.—*n.* **deindustrialisa'tion, -z-.** [Pfx. **de-** (2).]

deipnosophist *dīp-nos'ə-fist, n.* one who converses learnedly at dinner, a table-philosopher—from Athenaeus's work, *Deipnosophistai* (end of 2nd century). [Gr. *deipnon*, dinner, *sophos*, wise.]

deist *dē'ist, n.* one who believes in the existence of God, but not in a revealed religion—*n.* **de'ism.**— *adjs.* **deist'ic, -al.** [L. *deus*, a god.]

deity *dē'i-ti, n.* godhood: divinity: godhead: a god or goddess: (*cap.*; with **the**) the Supreme Being. [Fr *déité*—L.L. *deitās*—L. *deus*, god; Sans. *deva.*]

deixis *dīk'sis,* (gram.) *n.* the use of words relating to the time and place of utterance, e.g. personal pronouns, demonstrative adverbs, adjectives and pronouns.—*adj.* **deictic** *(dīk'tik)* designating words relating to the time and place of utterance (also *n.*): proving directly.—*adv.* **deic'tically.** [Gr *deiknynai*, to show.]

déjà vu *dā-zhä vü,* in any of the arts, unoriginal material, old stuff: an illusion of having experienced before something that is really being experienced for the first time, a form of paramnesia (*psych.*). [Fr., already seen.]

deject *di-jekt', v.t.* to cast down the spirits of.—*adj.* **deject'ed** cast down: dispirited.—*adv.* **deject'edly.**— *ns.* **deject'edness; dejec'tion.** [L. *dējicĕre, -jectum* —*dē*, down, *jacĕre*, to cast.]

de jure *dē jōō're, dā zhōō're,* (L.) by right: rightful.

dekko, decko *dek'ō,* (slang) *n.* a look:—*pl.* **dekk'os, deckos.**—*v.i.* to look.—**have, take, a dekko** to have a (quick) look. [Hind. *dekho*, imp. of *dekhnā*, to see.]

delaminate *di-lam'i-nāt, v.i.* to split into layers.—*n.* **delamina'tion.** [L. *dēlamināre*—*dē*, *lāmina*, a layer.]

delay *di-lā', v.t.* to put off to another time: to defer: to hinder or retard.—*v.i.* to pause, linger, or put off time:—*pr.p.* **delay'ing;** *pa.t.* and *pa.p.* **delayed.**—*n.* a putting off or deferring: the time during which something is put off: a lingering: hindrance.—*n.* **delay'er.**—**delayed action** a method of operating a switch, detonating explosive, etc., some time after the mechanism has been set; **delayed drop** (aero.) a live parachute descent in which the parachutist deliberately delays pulling the ripcord. [O.Fr. *delaier.*]

dele *dē'lē, v.t.* delete, a direction in proof-reading to remove a letter or word, indicated by *of* or other sign [L. *dēlē*, imper. of *dēlēre*, to delete.]

delectable *di-lekt'ə-bl, adj.* delightful: pleasing.—*ns* **delect'ableness; delectabil'ity.**—*adv.* **delect'ably.**— *n. delecta'tion* (*dē*-) delight. [Fr.,—L. *dēlectābilis* —*dēlectāre*, to delight.]

delegate *del'i-gāt, v.t.* to send as a legate or representative: to entrust or commit.—*n* one who is delegated: a deputy or representative: a person elected to represent a Territory in Congress, as distinguished from the representatives of the States (*U.S.*).—*adj* delegated, deputed.—*adj* **del'egable.**—*ns.* **del'egacy** act or system of delegating. a delegate's

appointment or authority: a body of delegates; **delega'tion** a delegating: a deputation: a body of delegates (*U.S.*). [L. *dē*, away, and *lēgāre, -ātum,* to send as ambassador.]

delete *di-lēt', v.t.* to blot out: to erase: to destroy.—*n.* **dele'tion.** [L. *dēlēre, dēlētum,* to blot out.]

deleterious *del-i-tē'ri-əs, adj.* hurtful or destructive: poisonous.—*adv.* **delete'riously.**—*n.* **delete'riousness.** [Gr. *dēlētērios*, hurtful—*dēleesthai*, to hurt.]

delf, delph *delf,* **delft** *delft, ns.* (in full **Delft'ware**), a kind of earthenware originally made at Delft, Holland.

deli. Short for **delicatessen.**

deliberate *di-lib'ər-āt, v.t.* to weigh well in one's mind.—*v.i.* to consider the reasons for and against anything: to reflect: to consider: to take counsel: to debate.—*adj.* (*-it*) well considered: not impulsive: intentional: considering carefully: slow in determining: cautious.—*adv.* **delib'erately** in a deliberate manner: (*loosely*) quietly, without fuss or haste.— *ns.* **delib'erateness; delibera'tion** the act of deliberating: mature reflection: calmness: coolness.— *adj.* **delib'erative** proceeding or acting by deliberation.—*adv.* **delib'eratively.**—*ns.* **delib'erativeness; delib'erātor.** [L. *dēlīberāre, -ātum*—*dē-,* intens., and *lībrāre,* to weigh—*lībra,* a balance.]

delicate *del'i-kit, adj.* pleasing to the senses, esp. the taste: dainty: nicely discriminating or perceptive: fastidious: of a fine, slight texture or constitution: tender: not robust: pale: requiring nice handling: refined in manners: not immodest: gentle, polite: luxurious.—*n.* **del'icacy** (*-kə-si*) state or quality of being delicate: refinement: nicety: tenderness, weakness: luxuriousness: anything delicate or dainty, esp. to eat.—*adv.* **del'icately.**—*n.* **del'icateness.** [L. *dēlicātus,* prob. conn. with *dēliciae,* allurements, luxury.]

delicatessen *del-i-ka-tes'n, n.pl.* or *sing.* prepared foods, esp cooked meats, pâtés, and unusual or foreign foods: (*sing.*; coll. short form **deli'**) a shop selling these. [Ger. pl. of Fr. *délicatesse,* delicacy.]

delicious *di-lish'əs, adj.* pleasing to the senses, esp. taste: affording exquisite pleasure.—*adv.* **deli'ciously** in a delicious manner.—*n.* **deli'ciousness.** [L. *dēliciōsus*—*dēliciae,* or *dēlicium,* delight.]

delight *di-līt', v.t.* to please highly.—*v.i.* to have or take great pleasure: to be greatly pleased.—*n.* a high degree of pleasure: extreme satisfaction: that which gives great pleasure.—*adj.* **delight'ed** greatly pleased.—*adv.* **delight'edly.**—*n.* **delight'edness.**— *adj.* **delight'ful,** causing, or full of delight.—*adv.* **delight'fully.**—*n.* **delight'fulness.** [O.Fr. *deliter*—L. *dēlectāre.*]

Delilah *di-lī'la, n.* the Philistine woman who befooled Samson: a courtesan: a temptress: an alluring object.

delimit *di-lim'it,* **delimitate** *di-lim'i-tāt, vs.t.* to fix or mark the limit of.—*n.* **delimita'tion.**—*adj.* **delim'itative.** [L. *dēlīmitāre*—*dē,* intens., *līmitāre;* see **limit.**]

delineate *di-lin'i-āt, v.t.* to mark out with lines: to represent by a sketch or picture: to draw: to describe.—*adj.* **delin'eable.**—*n.* **delinea'tion** the act of delineating: a sketch, representation, or description.—*adj.* **delin'eative.**—*n.* **delin'eātor.** [L. *dēlīneāre, -ātum*—*dē,* down, and *līnea,* a line.]

delinquent *di-ling'kwənt, adj.* failing in duty.—*n.* one who fails in his duty: an offender: a person lacking in moral and social sense.—*n.* **delin'quency** failure in or omission of duty: a fault: crime.—*adv.* **delin'quently.** [L. *dēlinquēns, -entis,* pr.p. of *dēlinquĕre* —*dē-,* intens., and *linquĕre, lictum,* to leave.]

deliquesce *del-i-kwes', v i.* to melt and become liquid by absorbing moisture, as certain salts, etc.—*n.* **deli-quesc'ence.**—*adj.* **deliquesc'ent.** [L. *dēliquēscēre—dē-*, intens., *liquēscēre*, to become fluid.]

delirious *di-lir'i-əs*, *adj.* wandering in mind: light-headed: insane.—*adv.* **delir'iously.**—*ns.* **delir'iousness; delir'ium** state of being delirious: strong excitement: wild enthusiasm.—**delirium tremens** (*trē'menz; coll. abbrev.* **DT's**) a delirious disorder of the brain produced by over-absorption of alcohol, often marked by convulsive or trembling symptoms and hallucination. [L. *dēlīrus*, crazy—*dēlīrāre*, lit. to turn aside—*dē*, from, and *līra*, a furrow; *tremēns*, the pr.p. of *tremĕre*, to tremble.]

deliver *di-liv'ər*, *v.t.* to liberate or set free from restraint or danger: to rescue from evil or fear: to give up: to hand over, distribute: to communicate: to pronounce: to give forth, as a blow, a ball, etc.: to discharge: to assist (a mother) at the birth (of).—*adj.* nimble.—*adj.* **deliv'erable.**—*ns.* **deliv'erance** liberation: release: the utterance of a judgment or authoritative opinion; **deliv'erer; deliv'ery** the act of delivering: a giving up: the act or manner of speaking in public, of discharging a shot, of throwing a cricket-ball, etc.: a distribution: a round of distribution: the act of giving birth.—**be delivered of** (*arch.*) to give birth to; **deliver the goods** (*slang*) to carry out what is required or promised. [Fr. *délivrer*—L. *dē*, from, *līberāre*, to set free—*līber*, free.]

dell *del*, *n.* a deep hollow or small valley, usually covered with trees. [O.E. *dell;* cf. **dale.**]

delouse *dē-lows'*, *v.t.* to free from lice, or (*fig.*) from land-mines, etc. [Pfx. **de-** (2).]

delph. See **delf.**

Delphic *del'fik*, *adj.* relating to *Delphi*, a town of ancient Greece, or to its famous oracle: oracular.—Also **Del'phian.** [Gr. *Delphikos—Delphoi.*]

Delphinium *del-fin'i-əm*, *n.* a genus of Ranunculaceae, comprising the larkspurs and stavesacre: (without *cap.*) any plant of the genus:—*pl.* **delphin'iums, delphin'ia.** [Latinised from Gr. *delphinion*, larkspur, dim. of *delphīs*, dolphin, from the appearance of the flowers.]

delta *del'tə*, *n.* the fourth letter (Δ δ) of the Greek alphabet, answering to *d*: an alluvial deposit at the mouth of a stream, Δ-shaped in the case of the Nile: in classification, the fourth or one of the fourth grade, the grade below gamma.—*adjs.* **delta'ic** belonging to a delta; **del'toid** of the form of the Greek Δ: triangular.—**del'ta-wing** (*aeroplane*) a jet aeroplane with triangular wings; **deltoid muscle** the large triangular muscle of the shoulder. [Gr.,—Heb. *daleth*, a tent-door.]

deltiology *del-ti-ol'ə-ji*, *n.* the study and collection of picture postcards.—*n.* **deltiol'ogist.** [Gr. *deltion*, small writing-tablet.]

delude *di-lōōd', di-lūd'*, *v.t.* to deceive, cause to accept what is false as true.—*adjs.* **delud'able; delud'ed.**—*n.* **delud'er.** [L. *dēlūdĕre*, to play false—*dē*, down, *lūdĕre*, *lūsum*, to play.]

deluge *del'ūj*, *n.* a great overflow of water: a flood, esp. Noah's: an overwhelming flow (*fig.*).—*v.t.* to inundate: to overwhelm as with water. [Fr. *déluge* —L. *dīluvium—dīluĕre—dis-*, away, *luĕre*, to wash.]

delusion *di-lōō'zhən, di-lū'zhən*, *n.* the act of deluding: the state of being deluded: a hallucination: a false belief (esp. *psych.*): error.—*adj.* **delu'sional** pertaining to delusions, afflicted with such.—*n.* **delu'sionist.**—*adjs.* **delu'sive** (*-siv*), **delu'sory** apt or tending to delude: deceptive.—*adv.* **delu'sively.**—*n.* **delu'siveness.** [See **delude.**]

de luxe *də lūks', di lŏŏks', luks'*, sumptuous, luxurious: having refinements or superior qualities. [Fr., of luxury.]

delve *delv*, *v.t.* and *v.i.* to dig, esp. with a spade: to make deep research (*fig.*).—*n.* **delv'er.** [O.E. *delfan*, to dig; conn. with **dale, delf, dell.**]

demagnetise, -ize *dē-mag'nit-īz*, *v.t.* to deprive of magnetic properties.—*ns.* **demagnetisā'tion, -z-; demag'netiser, -z-.** [Pfx. **de-** (2).]

demagogue *dem'ə-gog*, *n.* a leader of the people: a popular and factious orator.—*adjs.* **demagogic, -al** (*-gog'* or *-goj'*).—*ns.* **demagogism, demagoguism** (*dem'ə-gog ism*); **dem'agoguery** (*-gog-*); **dem'agogy** (*-goj-*). [Gr. *dēmagōgos—dēmos*, people, *agōgos*, leading—*agein*, to lead.]

demand *di-mänd'*, *v.t.* to claim: to ask peremptorily or authoritatively for: to require.—*n.* the asking for what is due: peremptory asking for something: a claim: desire shown by consumers: the amount of any article, commodity, etc., that consumers will buy.—*adj.* **demand'able** that may be demanded.—*ns.* **demand'ant** one who demands: a plaintiff; **demand'er.**—*adj.* **demand'ing** requiring much attention, effort, etc.—**demand feeding** the practice of feeding a baby when it wants food, rather than at set times.—**in (great) demand** much sought after; **on demand** whenever required. [Fr. *demander*—L. *dē-*, intens., and *mandāre*, to put into one's charge.]

demarcation, demarkation *dē-märk-ā'shən*, *n.* the act of marking off or setting bounds: separation: a fixed limit: in trade unionism, the strict marking off of the field of one craft from that of another.—*v.t.* **dē'marcate** to mark off or limit. [Sp. *demarcación—de*, from, *marcar*, to mark.]

démarche *dā-märsh*, (Fr.) *n.* a step or measure (esp. diplomatic).

dematerialise, -ize *dē-mə-tē-ri-əl-īz*, *v.t.* to deprive of material qualities or character.—*v.i.* to become immaterial.—*n.* **dematerialisā'tion, -z-.** [Pfx. **de-** (2).]

deme *dēm*, *n.* a subdivision of ancient Attica and of modern Greece, a township: a group of plants or animals that are closely related and live in a single distinct locality (*biol.*). [Gr. *dēmos*, people.]

demean[1] *di-mēn'*, *v.t.* to bear, behave, conduct (*refl.*). —*n.* **demeanour,** *U.S.* **demean'or,** (*di-mēn'ər*) behaviour: bearing towards another. [O.Fr. *demener—de-*, intens., and *mener*, to lead—L. *mināre*, to drive—*minārī*, to threaten.]

demean[2] *di-mēn'*, *v.t.* to lower in status, reputation, or (often *refl.*) dignity. [Prob. on the analogy of *debase*, pfx. **de-** (1) and **mean.**]

dement *di-ment'*, (*rare*) *v.t.* to drive crazy, render insane.—*n.* a demented person.—*adj.* **dement'ed** out of one's mind: insane: suffering from dementia.—*adv.* **dement'edly.**—*ns.* **dement'edness; dementia** (*di-men'shi-ə*) (*psychol.*) any form of insanity characterised by the failure or loss of mental powers: the organic deterioration of intelligence, memory, and orientation.—**dementia praecox, precox** (*prē'koks*) schizophrenia. [L. *dēmēns, dēmentis*, out of one's mind—*dē*, from, and *mēns*, the mind.]

démenti *dā-mä-tē*, *n.* a contradiction, denial. [Fr. *dé-mentir*, to give the lie to.]

demerara *dem-ə-rä'rə, -rā'*, *n.* brown sugar in large crystals: a type of rum. [*Demerara* in Guyana.]

demerit *dē-, di-mer'it*, *n.* ill-desert: fault: a mark given for a fault or offence, esp. in schools or the army, etc. (*U.S.*). [L. *dēmerēt, dēmeritum*, to deserve fully, later understood as to deserve ill.]

demersal *di-mûrs'əl*, *adj.* subaqueous: found on or near the bottom. [L. *dē*, down, *mergĕre, mersum*, to plunge.]

demesne *di-mān', -mēn'*, *n.* a manor-house with lands adjacent to it not let out to tenants: any estate in land. [Form of **domain.**]

demi- *dem'i*, in composition, half, half-sized.—*ns.*

dem'igod a half-god: one whose nature is partly divine, esp. a hero fabled to be the offspring of a god and a mortal:—*fem.* **dem'igoddess**; **demi-monde** (*dem'i-mond*) a class of women in an equivocal social position, the kept mistresses of society men: the shady section of a profession or group; **demi-mondaine** (*-en'*) a woman member of the demi-monde.— Also *adj.*—*ns.* **demi-pension** (*dem'i-pā'sy5*) hotel accommodation providing bed and breakfast and one main meal a day; **dem'irep** (for *demi-reputable*) a person, esp. a woman, of dubious reputation; **demirep'dom**; **demi-semiquaver** (*dem-i-sem'i-kwā-vər, mus.*) a note equal in time to the half of a semiquaver. [Fr. *demi*—L. *dimidium*—*di-*, apart, *medius*, the middle.]

demijohn *dem'i-jon, n.* a glass bottle with a full body and narrow neck often enclosed in wickerwork. [Fr. *dame-jeanne*, Dame Jane.]

demilitarise, -ize *dē-mil'i-tər-īz, v.t.* to release from military control.—*n.* **demilitarisā'tion, -z-**. [Pfx. **de-** (2).]

demirep. See demi-.

demise *di-mīz', n.* a transferring: death, esp. of a sovereign or a distinguished person: a transfer of the crown or of an estate to a successor.—*v.t.* to send down to a successor: to bequeath by will.—*adj.* **demi'sable**. [O.Fr. *demise*, pa.p. of *desmettre*, to lay down.—L. *dis-*, aside, *mittěre, missum*, to send.]

demist *dē-mist', v.t.* to clear (e.g. a car windscreen) of condensation.—Also *v.i.*—*n.* **demist'er** a mechanical device which does this, usu. by blowing hot air. [Pfx. **de-** (2).]

demit *di-mit'* (esp. *Scot.*) *v.t.* to dismiss: to relinquish: to resign. [Fr. *démettre*—L. *dimittěre*—*dis-*, apart, *mittěre*, to send.]

demitasse *dem'i-tas, n.* a small cup of, or for, (esp. black) coffee. [Fr., half-cup.]

demiurge *dem'i-ûrj, n.* the maker of the world: among the Gnostics, the creator of the world and man, subordinate to God the supreme.—*adjs.* **demiur'gic** (*-jik*), **-al**. [Gr. *dēmiourgos*—*dēmos*, the people, and *ergon*, a work.]

demo. See **demonstration** under **demonstrate**.

demobilise, -ize *di-mōb'il-īz, v.t.* to take out of mobilisation: to disband: to discharge from the army (*coll.*).—*n.* **demobilisā'tion, -z-**.—*n.* and *v.t.* **demob'** (*pr.p.* **demobb'ing**; *pa.p.* **demobbed'**) coll. shortening of *demobilisation, demobilise*.—Also *adj.* [Pfx. **de-** (2).]

democracy *di-mok'rə-si, n.* a form of government in which the supreme power is vested in the people collectively, and is administered by them or by officers appointed by them: the common people: a state of society characterised by recognition of equality of rights and privileges: political, social or legal equality: (usu. with *cap.*) in the U.S., the Democratic party.—*n.* **democrat** (*dem'ō-krat*) one who adheres to or promotes democracy as a principle: a member of the Democratic party in the United States, the party generally inclining to look to the rights of States against centralisation of government.—*adjs.* **democrat'ic, -al** relating to democracy: insisting on equal rights and privileges for all.—*adv.* **democrat'ically.**—*v.t.* **democratise, -ize** (*di-mok'*) to render democratic. —*ns.* **democratisā'tion, -z-**. [Fr. *démocratie*—Gr. *dēmokratiā*—*dēmos*, the people, *kratos*, strength.]

démodé *dā-mō-dā*, (Fr.) *adj.* out of fashion.

demoded *dē'mōd'id, adj.* (disparagingly) no longer in fashion. [Pfx. **de-** (2).]

demography *dē-mog'rə-fī, n.* the study of population. —*n.* **demog'rapher**.—*adj.* **demographic** (*-ō-graf'ik*). [Gr. *dēmos*, the people, *graphein*, to write.]

demoiselle *dəm-wä-zel', n.* a young lady (*arch.* or playful): a graceful kind of crane (*Anthropoides*

virgo): a dragonfly: a fish akin to the wrasses. [Fr.; see **damsel**.]

demolish *di-mol'ish, v.t.* to lay in ruins: to destroy, put an end to.—*n.* **demoli'tion** (*dem-ō-*) act of pulling down: ruin; **demoli'tionist**. [Fr. *démolir*—L. *dēmōliri*, to throw down.]

demon *dē'mən, n.* an evil spirit, a devil: sometimes like **daemon**, a friendly spirit or good genius: a person of great energy or enthusiasm (*fig.*):—*fem.* **dē'moness**. —*adj.* **demoniac** (*di-mōn'i-ak*).—*n.* one possessed by a demon or evil spirit.—*adj.* **demoniacal** (*dē-mə-nī'ə-kl*) pertaining to or like demons or evil spirits: influenced by demons.—*adv.* **demoni'acally**. —*adj.* **demonic** (*dē-mon'ik*) same as **daemonic**.—*ns.* **dē'monism** a belief in demons; **dē'monist**; **dēmonol'atry** the worship of demons; **dēmonol'ater**; **dēmonol'ogy** an account of, or the study of, demons and their agency.—*adjs.* **dēmonolog'ic, -al**.—*ns.* **dēmonol'ogist**. [L. *daemōn*—Gr. *daimōn*, a spirit, genius; in N.T. and Late Greek, a devil; see **daemon**.]

demonetise, -ize *dē-mon'i-tīz*, or *-mun', v.t.* to divest of value as money.—*n.* **demonetisā'tion, -z-**. [Pfx. **de-** (2).]

demonstrate *dem'ən-strāt* (or *di-mon'strāt*), *v.t.* to make manifest: to give proof of: to prove with certainty: to teach, expound, explain, or exhibit by practical means.—*v.i.* to exhibit one's feelings: to act as demonstrator.—*adj.* **demon'strable** (or *dem'ən-*) that may be demonstrated.—*ns.* **demon'strableness, -strabil'ity**.—*adv.* **demon'strably** (or *dem'*).—*n.* **demonstrā'tion** a pointing out: proof beyond doubt: expression of the feelings by outward signs: a public expression of feelings, as by a mass-meeting, a procession, etc. (*coll.* shortening **dem'ō**:—*pl.* **dem'ōs**): show: a movement to exhibit military intention, or to deceive an enemy: a practical lesson or exhibition.— *adj.* **demon'strative** pointing out (as a *demonstrative adjective*): making evident: proving with certainty: of the nature of proof: given to the manifestation of one's feelings.—*adv.* **demon'stratively.**—*ns.* **demon'strativeness; dem'onstrātor** one who proves beyond doubt: a teacher or assistant who helps students with practical work: one who goes about exhibiting the uses and merits of a commodity: one who takes part in a public demonstration. [L. *dēmōnstrāre, -ātum*—*dē-*, intens., and *mōnstrāre*, to show.]

demoralise, -ize *dē-mor'əl-īz, v.t.* to corrupt in morals: to lower the morale of—that is, to deprive of spirit and confidence: to throw into confusion.—*n.* **demoralisā'tion, -z-**. [Pfx. **de-** (2).]

demos *dē'mos, n.* the people (esp. contemptuously).— *adj.* **demot'ic** pertaining to the people: popular: of a simplified kind of writing distinguished from the hieratic, or priestly, and from hieroglyphics (*Egypt ant.*).—*ns.* **demot'icist, demot'ist** a student of demotic script. [Gr. *dēmos.*]

demote *dē-mōt', v.t.* to reduce in rank.—*n.* **demō'tion**. [On the analogy of *promote*; de- (2).]

demount *dē-mownt', v.t.* to take down from a support, etc.: to take (e.g. a building) to pieces in such a way that it can be reassembled.—*adj.* **demount'able**. [Pfx. **de-** (2), **mount**, to set in position.]

dempster. Same as **deemster**. [See under **deem**.]

demulcent *di-mul'sənt, adj.* soothing.—*n.* a medicine that allays irritation. [L. *dēmulcēns, -entis*—*dē*, down, *mulcēre*, to stroke, to soothe.]

demur *di-mûr', v.i.* to hesitate from uncertainty or before difficulty: to object:—*pr.p.* **demurr'ing**; *pa.t.* and *pa.p.* **demurred'**.—Also *n.* (also **demurr'al**).— *adj.* **demurr'able**.—*ns.* **demurr'age** undue delay or detention of a vessel, railway wagon, etc.: compensation for such detention; **demurr'er** one who demurs. an objection: a plea in law that, even if the opponent's facts are as he says, they yet do not support his case (*law*). [Fr. *demeurer*—L. *dēmorārī*, to loiter, linger—*de-*, intens., and *morārī*, to delay—*mora*, delay.]

demure *di-mūr′*, *adj.* sober: staid: modest: affectedly modest: making a show of gravity.—*adv.* **demure′ly.** —*n.* **demure′ness.** [O.Fr. *meur* (Fr. *mûr*)—L. *matūrus*, ripe; pfx. unexplained.]

demy *di-mī′*, *n.* before metrication a size of printing and writing paper—approximating to A2: a holder of certain scholarships in Magdalen College, Oxford:— *pl.* **demies′.**—*n.* **demy′ship.** [Fr. *demi*—L. *dīmidium*, half—*dis-*, apart, *medius*, the middle.]

demythologise, -ize *dē-mith-ol′ə-jīz*, *v.t.* to remove mythology from, esp. the Bible, in order to arrive at the basic meaning. [Pfx. **de-** (2).]

den *den*, *n.* the hollow lair of a wild beast: a pit, cave: a haunt of vice or misery: a private retreat for work or pleasure (*coll.*). [O.E. *denn*, a cave, lair; akin to *denu*, a valley.]

denary *dēn′ər-i*, *adj.* containing or depending on the number ten: ten.—*n.* the number ten: a group of ten. —*n.* **denarius** (*di-nā′ri-əs*) the chief Roman silver coin under the Republic, divided into ten asses. [L. *dēnārius*—*dēnī*, ten by ten—*decem*, ten.]

denationalise, -ize *dē-nash′ən-əl-īz*, *v.t.* to deprive of national rights or character: to return from state to private ownership.—*n.* **denationalisa′tion, -z-.** [Pfx. **de-** (2).]

denaturalise, -ize *dē-nach′ər-əl-īz*, *v.t.* to make unnatural: to deprive of naturalisation.—*n.* **denaturalisa′tion, -z-.** [Pfx. **de-** (2).]

denature *dē-nā′chər*, **denaturise, -ize** *dē-nā′chər-īz*, *vs.t.* to change the nature or properties of, as a protein by heat or other treatment: of alcohol, etc., to render unfit for consumption: to add (non-radioactive material) to radioactive material, in order to prevent its being used in an atomic bomb (*nuc.*).—*n.* **dena′turant** a substance used to denature another. [Pfx. **de-** (2).]

dendrite *den′drīt*, *n.* a branching process of a nerve-cell: a tree-like crystalline aggregate or skeleton crystal.—*adj.* **dendrit′ic.**—*n.* **dendrochronology** (*den-drō-kron-ol′ə-ji*) fixing of dates in the past by comparative study of the annual growth rings in ancient trees.—*adj.* **den′droid, -al** tree-like.—*n.* **dendrol′atry** (Gr. *latreiā*, worship) the worship of trees.—*adj.* **dendrolog′ical.**—*ns.* **dendrol′ogist**; **dendrol′ogy** a treatise on trees: the natural history of trees. [Gr. *dendron*, tree.]

dene¹ *dēn*, *n.* a small valley. [See **dean¹**.]

dene² *dēn*, *n.* a sandy tract, a dune.

denegation *den-i-gā′shən*, *n.* a denial. [L. *dēnegāre*, *-ātum*, to deny—*dē-*, intens., and *negāre*, to deny.]

dengue *deng′gā*, *n.* an acute tropical epidemic fever, seldom fatal—also **breakbone fever.** [Apparently Swahili, *dinga*.]

deniable, denial, denier, etc. See **deny**.

denier *də-nēr′*, *n.* a copper coin of the value of ½ sou—hence a very trifling sum: a unit of silk, rayon, and nylon yarn weight (usu. *den′i-ər*). [Fr.—L. *dēnārius*.]

denigrate *den′i-grāt*, *v.t.* to blacken (esp. a reputation).—*adj.* blackened.—*ns.* **denigra′tion; den′i-grator.** [L. *dē-*, intens., *nigrāre*, to blacken, *niger*, black.]

denim *den′im*, *n.* coloured twilled cotton fabric for overalls, etc.: (in *pl.*) a garment made of denim. [Fr. *de*, of, and *Nîmes*.]

denitrate *dē-nī′trāt*, *v.t.* to free from nitric acid or other nitrogen compounds.—*ns.* **denitra′tion; denitrifica′tion,** removal of nitrogen or its compounds; **deni′trificator.**—*v.t.* **deni′trify.** [Pfx. **de-** (2).]

denizen *den′i-zn*, *n.* an inhabitant (human or animal): one admitted to the rights of a citizen: a wild plant, probably foreign, that keeps its footing: a naturalised foreign word, etc. [O.Fr. *deinzein*—*deinz*, *dens* (Fr. *dans*), within.]

denominate *di-nom′in-āt*, *v.t.* to give a name to: to call.—*n.* **denomina′tion** the act of naming: a name or title: a class or group, esp. of units in weights, money, etc: a collection of individuals called by the same name: a sect.—*adj.* **denomina′tional** belonging to a denomination or sect.—*adv.* **denomina′tionally.**— *adj.* **denom′inative** giving or having a title.—*adv.* **denom′inatively.**—*n.* **denom′inator** the lower number in a vulgar fraction, which names the parts into which the integer is divided (*arith.*).—**common denominator** a number that is a multiple of each of the denominators of a set of fractions, esp. the least: something that makes comparison, communication, agreement, etc., possible. [L. *dē-*, intens., *nōmināre*, to name—*nōmen*, name.]

denote *di-nōt′*, *v.t.* to note or mark off: to indicate by a sign: to signify or mean.—*n.* **dēnotā′tion.**—*adj.* **denō′tative** (or *dē′*).—*adv.* **denō′tatively** (or *dē′*). [Fr. *dénoter*—L. *dēnotāre*, *-ātum*—*dē*, intens., and *notāre*.]

dénouement *dā-nōō′-mā*, *n.* the unravelling of a plot or story: the issue, event, or outcome. [Fr.,—L. *dis-*, *nodāre*, to tie—*nodus*, a knot.]

denounce *di-nowns′*, *v.t.* to inform against or accuse publicly: to inveigh against: to notify formally termination of (treaties, etc.).—*ns.* **denounce′ment** denunciation; **denounc′er.** [Fr. *dénoncer*—L. *dēnuntiāre* —*dē-*, intens., and *nuntiāre*, to announce.]

de novo *dē nō′vō*, *dā nō′wō*, (L.) anew.

dense *dens*, *adj.* thick, close, compact: impenetrably stupid.—*adv.* **dense′ly.**—*ns.* **dense′ness; dens′ity** the quality of being dense: the proportion of a mass to bulk or volume: the quantity of matter per unit of bulk; **densim′eter** an instrument for measuring the relative density or the closeness of grain of a substance.—*adj.* **densimet′ric.**—*ns.* **densim′etry; densitom′eter** any instrument for measuring the optical transmission or reflecting properties of a material.—*adj.* **densitomet′ric.**—*n.* **densitom′etry.** [L. *dēnsus*, thick, dense.]

dent *dent*, *n.* a hollow in a surface, caused by a blow.— *v.t.* to make such a hollow in.—Also *fig.* [variant of **dint.**]

dental *dent′əl*, *adj.* pertaining to or concerned with the teeth or dentistry: produced by the aid of the teeth.— *n.* a sound pronounced by applying the tongue to the teeth or (loosely) the gums.—*ns.* **Denta′lium** a genus of scaphopod molluscs with shell like an elephant's tusk—tooth-shell or tusk-shell: (without *cap.*) any mollusc or shell of the genus:—*pl.* **denta′liums** or **-la.** —*adjs.* **dent′ate, -d** toothed: notched: set as with teeth.—*n.* **dent′icle** a small tooth-like structure: a dentil.—*adjs.* **dentic′ulate, -d** notched: having dentils.—*n.* **denticula′tion.**—*adj.* **dent′iform** having the form of a tooth or of teeth.—*ns.* **dent′ifrice** (L. *fricāre*, to rub) a substance used in rubbing or cleaning the teeth—toothpaste or tooth-powder; **dent′il** a denticle: one of a series of square blocks or projections as in the bed-moulding of a cornice of columns. —*adj.* **dentilin′gual** (L. *lingua*, tongue) formed between the teeth and the tongue, as *th* in *thin*, *this*. —*n.* a consonant so formed.—*ns.* **dent′ine** (*-ēn*), **den′tin** the substance of which teeth are mainly composed.—*ns.* **dent′ist** one qualified to treat diseases and malformations of, and injuries to, teeth; **dent′istry** the art or work of a dentist; **dent′ition** the cutting or growing of teeth: the conformation, number, and arrangement of the teeth.—*n.* **dent′ure**

a set of (esp. artificial) teeth.—**dental floss** see **floss.** [L.L. *dentālis*—L. *dēns, dentis,* a tooth; dim. *denticulus.*]

denude *di-nūd', v.t.* to make nude or naked: to lay bare.—*n.* **denudation** (*den-ū-dā'shən*) a making nude or bare: the wearing away of rocks whereby the underlying rocks are laid bare (*geol.*). [L. *dēnūdāre* —*dē-,* intens., *nūdāre, -ātum,* to make naked.]

denumerable *dı-nū'mər-əbl,* (*math.*) *adj.* able to be put in a one-to-one correspondence with the positive integers.—*adv.* **denu'merably.** [Pfx. de- (3).]

denunciate *di-nun's(h)i-āt, v.t* to denounce.—*n.* **denuncia'tion** any formal declaration: act of denouncing; **denun'ciator** one who denounces.—*adj.* **denun'ciatory** containing a denunciation. [L *dēnunciāre* or *dēnuntiāre;* see **denounce.**]

deny *di-nī', v.t.* to gainsay or declare not to be true: to reject: to refuse: to refuse to admit: to refuse a visitor access to: to disown:—*pr.p.* **deny'ing;** *pa.t.* and *pa.p.* **denied'.**—*n.* **denial** (*di-nī'əl*) the act of denying: refusal: rejection.—*adj.* **deni'able.**—*adv.* **deni'ably.**— *n.* **deni'er.**—**deny oneself** to refuse to allow oneself gratification: to exercise self-denial. [Fr. *dénier*— L. *dēnegāre*—*dē-,* intens., and *negāre,* to say no.]

Deo *dē'ō, dā'ō,* (L.) to, for, with God.—**Deo gratias** *grā'shi-əs, grá'tē-ās,* thanks to God; **Deo volente** (abbrev. **D.V.**) *vo-len'tē, wo-len'tā,* God willing.

deoch-an-doruis *dohh'ən dō'ris, dō', n.* a stirrup-cup, a parting cup. [Gael. *deoch,* drink, *an,* the, *doruis,* gen. of *dorus,* door.]

deodand *dē'ō-dand, n.* in old English law, a personal chattel which had been the immediate accidental cause of the death of a human being, forfeited to the crown for pious uses. [L. *deō,* to God, *dandum,* that must be given—*dāre,* to give.]

deodar *dē'ō-där, n.* a cedar (*Cedrus deodara*) of the Himalayas, much praised by Indian poets. [Sans. *deva-dāru,* divine tree.]

deodorise, -ize *dē-ō'dər-īz, v.t.* to take the odour or smell from.—Also *fig.*—*ns.* **deō'dorant, deō'doriser,** **-z-** a substance that destroys or conceals unpleasant smells; **deō'dorisa'tion, -z-.** [Pfx. de- (2).]

deontology *dē-on-tol'ə-ji, n.* the science of duty, ethics —Also *n. sing.* **deon'tics.**—*adjs.* **deon'tic; deontological** (*-tə-loj'*).—*n.* **deontol'ogist.** [Gr. *deon,* *-ontos,* neut. pr.p. of *deein,* to be necessary, to behave, *logos,* discourse.]

deoxidate *dē-oks'i-dāt, v.t.* to take oxygen from, or reduce.—Also **deox'idise, -ize.**—*ns.* **deoxidā'tion; deoxidisa'tion, -z-; deox'idiser, -z-** a substance that deoxidises.—*v.t.* **deoxygenate** (*dē-oks'ij-ən-āt*) to deprive of oxygen.—Also **deox'ygenise, -ize.**—*pfxs.* **deoxy-, desoxy-** containing less oxygen.—**deoxyribonucleic acids** (*dē-oks-i-rī'bō-nū-klē'ik*) nucleic acids present in chromosomes of all plant and animal cells, and carrying instructions for passing on hereditary characteristics—abbrev. **DNA.** [Pfx. de- (2).]

depart *di-pärt', v.i.* to go away: to quit or leave: to die. —*ns.* **depart'er; depart'ure** act of departing: a going away from a place: deviation: the distance in nautical miles made good by a ship due east or west: death.—**a new departure** a change of purpose or method, a new course of procedure; **the departed** the deceased. [Fr. *départir*—L. *dis-,* apart, and *partīre* (*partīrī*), to part, to divide.]

department *di-pärt'mənt, n.* a special or allotted function, sphere of activity, duty, or competence: a section of an administration, university, office or other organisation: a division of a country, esp. of France.—*adj.* **departmental** (*dē-pärt-ment'l*).—*v.t* **department'alise, -ize** to form into separate departments: to deal with by allotting a specific share to different departments.—*n.* **department'alism** too

strict division of work among departments with little intercommunication.—*adv.* **department'ally.**— **department store** (orig. *U.S.*) a big shop selling a variety of goods in different departments. [Fr. *département*—*départir.*]

depend *di-pend', v.i.* to be sustained by or connected with anything: to rely (on): to rest (on).—*adj.* **depend'able** that may be depended on: reliable.—*adv* **depend'ably.**—*n.* **depend'ant** one who depends on another for support or otherwise: a hanger-on—*adj.* **depend'ent** depending, relying, contingent, relative: awaiting settlement.—*ns.* **depend'ence** state of being dependent: reliance, trust: that on which one depends: **depend'ency** that which depends: a foreign territory dependent on a country, a kind of subordinate colony without self-government. [Fr. *dépendre* —L. *dēpendēre*—*dē,* from, and *pendēre,* to hang.]

depersonalise, -ize *dē-pûr'sən-əl-īz, v.t.* to take away the characteristics or personality of.—*n.* **depersonalisā'tion, -z-.** [Pfx. de- (2).]

depict *di-pikt', v.t.* to paint carefully: to make a likeness of: to describe minutely.—*ns.* **depict'er, -or; depic'tion.**—*adj.* **depict'ive.** [L. *dēpingĕre, dēpictum* —*dē-,* intens., *pingĕre,* to paint.]

depilate *dep'i-lāt, v.t.* to remove the hair from.—*ns.* **depilā'tion** removal or loss of hair; **dep'illātor; depilatory** (*di-pil'ə-tər-i*) an application for removing superfluous hairs.—*adj.* possessing this quality. [L. *dēpilāre, -ātum*—*dē,* out, *pilus,* hair.]

deplete *di-plēt', v.t.* to empty, reduce, exhaust.—*n.* **deple'tion.** [L. *dēplēre, dēplētum* to empty, *dē-,* neg., *plēre,* to fill.]

deplore *di-plōr', -plór', v.t.* to feel or express deep grief for: to disapprove strongly of:—*adj.* **deplor'able** lamentable: hopelessly bad.—*ns.* **deplor'ableness, deplorabil'ity.**—*adv.* **deplor'ably.** [L. *dēplōrāre* —*dē-,* intens., *plōrāre,* to weep.]

deploy *di-ploi', v.t.* to open out or extend: to spread out and place strategically (any forces).—*v.i.* to open from column into line, as a body of troops.—*ns.* **deploy', deploy'ment.** [Fr. *déployer*—L. *dis-,* apart, and *plicāre,* to fold.]

deplume *di-plōōm', v.t.* to take the plumes or feathers from. [Pfx. de- (2).]

depolarise, -ize *dē-pō'lar-īz, v.t.* to deprive of polarity. —*n.* **depolarisā'tion, -z-.** [Pfx. de- (2).]

depoliticise, -ize *dē-po-lit'i-sīz, v.t.* to remove the political nature or awareness from. [Pfx. de- (2).]

deponent *dipō'nənt,* (*gram.*) *adj.* having a passive form but active signification.—*n.* a deponent verb: one who makes a deposition, esp. under oath, or whose written testimony is used as evidence in a court of justice. [L. pr.p. *dēpōnēns, -entıs*—*dē,* down, *pōnēre,* to place, lay.]

depopulate *dē-, di-pop'ū-lāt, v.t.* to deprive of population, to dispeople.—*v.i.* to become dispeopled.—*n.* **depopulā'tion.** [L *dēpopulārī, -ātus,* to swarm over a country, said of hostile people (L. *populus*)—hence to ravage, later understood as to deprive of people.]

deport [1] *di-, dē-pōrt', -port', v.t.* to expel (e.g. as an undesirable alien).—*ns.* **deportā'tion; deportee'.** [Fr *déporter*—L. *dēportāre*—*dē-,* away, and *portāre,* to carry.]

deport [2] *di-pōrt', -port', v.t.* to behave (*refl.*).—*n.* **deport'ment** behaviour: bearing: manners. [O.Fr. *deporter*—L. *dē-,* intens., *portāre,* to carry.]

depose *di-pōz', v.t.* to remove from a high station: to degrade —*v.i.* to bear witness.—*adj.* **depōs'able.**—*n.* **depōs'er.** [Fr *déposer*—L. *dē,* from, *pausāre,* to pause, (late) to place.]

deposit *di-poz'it, v.t.* to put or set down: to place: to lay: to lay up or past: to entrust: to lodge as a pledge: to lay down as a coating, bed, vein or the like.—*n* that which is deposited or put down: a sum of money paid to secure an article, service, etc., the remainder of the cost being paid later: an accumulation by sedimentation, precipitation, sublimation, or other natural means: something entrusted to another's care, esp. money put in a bank: a pledge: the state of being deposited.—*n.* **depos'itary** a person with whom anything is left for safe keeping: a guardian—sometimes **depos'itory**—*ns.* **depos'itor**; **depos'itory** a place where anything is deposited—sometimes **depos'itary.**—**deposit account** a bank account in which money is deposited to gain interest, and for which cheques are not used. [L. *dēpŏsitum*, placed.]

deposition *dēp-ə-zish'ən, n.* act of deposing: declaration, testimony taken authoritatively, to be used as a substitute for the production of the witness in open court: removal: act of depositing. [**deposit;** blended with root of **depose.**]

depot *dep'ō, n.* a place of deposit: a storehouse: a military station where stores are kept and recruits trained: the headquarters of a regiment: the portion of a regiment left at home: a place where buses or tram-cars are kept. [Fr. *dépôt*—L. *dēpōnĕre* to put down.]

deprave *di-prāv', v.t.* to make morally bad or worse: to corrupt.—*n.* **depravation** (*dep-rə-vā'shən*).—*adj.* **depraved'** corrupt.—*n.* **depravity** (*di-prav'i-ti*) corrupt state of moral character: extreme wickedness: the hereditary tendency of man toward sin (*theol.*). [L. *dēprāvāre*—dē-, intens., *prāvus,* bad.]

deprecate *dep'ri-kāt, v.t* to desire earnestly the prevention or removal of: to regret deeply: to argue or protest against.—*n.* **depreca'tion.**—*adjs.* **dep'recative, dep'recatory.**—*n.* **dep'recator.** [L. *dēprecāri, -ātus*—*dē,* away, and *precāri,* to pray.]

depreciate *di-prē'shi-āt, v.t.* to lower the worth of: to undervalue: to disparage.—*v.i.* to fall in value.—*n.* **depreciation** (*-s(h)i-ā'shən*) the falling of value: disparagement.—*adjs.* **depre'ciative, depre'ciatory** tending to depreciate or lower.—*n.* **depre'ciator.** [L. *dēpretiāre, -ātum*—dē, down, and *pretium,* price.]

depredation *dep'ri-dā'shən, n.* act of plundering: state of being ravaged; **dep'redator.** [L. *dēpraedāri, -ātus*—dē-, intens., and *praedāri*—*praeda,* plunder.]

depress *di-pres', v.t.* to press down: to lower: to cause to sink: to dispirit or cast a gloom over.—*n.* **depress'ant** that which lowers activity or spirits: a sedative.— Also *adj.*—*adjs.* **depressed'** pressed down: lowered: flattened or slightly hollowed: dejected; **depress'ing** tending to depress.—*n.* **depression** (*di-presh'ən*) a sinking: a lowering: a region of low barometric pressure: a hollow: dejection: a reduced condition of trade and prosperity.—*adj.* **depress'ive** tending to depress: suffering from periods of depression.—*n.* one suffering from these.—*n.* **depress'or** that which lowers activity: a muscle that draws down: a surgical instrument for pressing down.—**depressed area** a region suffering from depression of trade: a region of specially heavy unemployment. [L. *dēprimĕre, -pressum*—dē, down, *premĕre,* to press.]

depressurise, -ize *dē-presh'ər-īz, v.t.* to release, e.g. an aircraft cabin, from controlled air-pressure.—*n.* **depressurisa'tion, -z-.** [Pfx. de- (2).]

deprive *di-prīv', v.t.* to dispossess: to keep out of enjoyment: to degrade (esp. a clergyman) from office: to bereave.—*adj.* **depriv'able.**—*ns.* **depriv'al, depriva'tion** (*dep-ri-* or *dē-prī-*) the act of depriving: the state of being deprived: degradation from office: loss: bereavement.—*adj.* **deprived'** having been dispossessed (of): suffering from hardship, esp. the lack of good educational, social, medical, etc., facilities. [L.L. *dēprīvāre,* to degrade—L. *dē,* from, and *prīvāre,* to deprive.]

de profundis *dē prə-fun'dis, dā pro-fŏŏn'dēs,* (L.) out of the depths—Psalm cxxx.

depth *depth, n.* deepness: the measure of deepness down or inwards: a deep place: intensity: the innermost or intensest part, as *depth of winter:* abstruseness: extent of sagacity and penetration.— *adj.* **depth'less** having no depth: bottomless.— **depth'-bomb, -charge** a powerful bomb that explodes under water (dropped over or near submarines); **depth psychology** the psychology of the unconscious; **depth psychologist.**—**in depth** (of defence) consisting of several successive lines: extensive(ly) and thorough(ly) (*adj.* **in'-depth** see in); **out of one's depth** in water where one cannot touch bottom: beyond one's understanding; **the depths** the lowest pitch of humiliation and misery. [Not in O.E.; possibly O.N. *dýpth;* or formed from **deep,** on analogy of **length,** etc.]

depute *di-pūt', v.t.* to appoint or send as a substitute or agent: to send with a special commission: to make over (one's authority).—*adj.* (*dep'ūt*) in Scotland, appointed deputy (as in *sheriff-depute*).—*n.* **deputation** (*dep-ū-tā'shən*) act of deputing: the person or persons deputed or appointed to transact business for another: a body of persons sent to state a case.—*v.t.* **dep'utise, -ize** to appoint as deputy.—*v.i.* to act as deputy.—*n.* **dep'uty** one deputed or appointed to act for another: a delegate or representative, or substitute: a legislator, member of a chamber of deputies: one who attends to protective arrangements in a coal-mine. [L. *dēputāre,* to prune, (later) to select.]

deracinate *dē-ras'i-nāt, v.t.* to root up.—*n.* **deracina'tion.** [Fr. *déraciner*—L. *dē,* from. L.L. *rādicīna,* dim. of L. *rādix,* a root.]

derail *di-rāl', v.t.* to cause to leave the rails.—*v.i.* to go off the rails.—*n.* **derail'ment.** [Pfx. de- (2).]

dérailleur (gear), *dā-ra-yœr (gēr), də-rāl'yər, n.* a variable bicycle-gear depending on a mechanism by means of which the chain can be transferred from one sprocket wheel to another of different size. [Fr. *dérailler,* to derail.]

derange *di-rānj', v.t.* to put out of place or order: to disorder: to make insane.—*adj.* **deranged'** disordered: insane.—*n.* **derange'ment** disorder: insanity. [Fr. *déranger*—dé- (L. *dis-*), asunder, *ranger,* to rank.]

derate *dē-rāt', v.t.* to relieve (wholly or partially) from local rates.—*n.* **derat'ing** relief from rates (also *adj.*). [Pfx. de- (2).]

deration *dē-ra'shən, v.t.* to free from rationing. [Pfx. de- (2).]

Derby *där'bi, n.* a horse-race held annually on Epsom Downs (instituted by Earl of *Derby,* 1780): (often without *cap.*) any race attracting much interest, or a keen sporting contest, esp. one of local importance: (*där'bi; U.S.*; often without *cap.*) a bowler hat: (sometimes without *cap.*) a strong type of boot.

derelict *der'i-likt, adj.* forsaken: abandoned, falling in ruins: neglectful of duty (chiefly *U.S.*).—*n.* anything (esp. a ship) forsaken or abandoned: a person abandoned by society, a down-and-out.—*n.* **derelic'tion** act of forsaking, unfaithfulness or remissness: state of being abandoned: land gained from the water by a change of water-line. [L. *dērelinquĕre, -lictum*—dē, intens., *re-,* behind, and *linquĕre,* to leave.]

deride *di-rīd', v.t.* to laugh at: to mock.—*n.* **derid'er.** —*adj.* **derisible** (*-riz'*).—*n.* **derision** (*di-rizh'-ən*) act of deriding: mockery: a laughing-stock.—*adjs.* **derisive** (*di-rīs'iv,* or *riz'*) scoffing; **deris'ory** scoffing: ridiculous.—*adv.* **deris'ively** (or *-riz'*).—*n.* **deris'iveness** (or *-riz'*). [L. *dērīdēre, -rīsum*—dē, intens., and *rīdēre,* to laugh.]

de rigueur *də rē-gœr*, (Fr.) required by strict etiquette, or by fashion, etc.

derision, derisive, etc. See **deride**.

derive *di-rīv'*, *v.t.* to conduct, draw, take, obtain, or receive (from a source or origin): to infer: to trace to an origin.—*v.i.* to descend or issue.—*adj.* **deriv'able**. —*n.* **deriva'tion** act of deriving: the tracing of a word to its root: source: that which is derived: descent or evolution: a sequence of statements showing how a certain result must follow from other statements already accepted, as in a mathematical formula, logical progression, etc.—*adj.* **deriva'tional**.—*adj.* **derivative** (*di-riv'ə-tiv*) derived or taken from something else: not radical or original.—*n.* that which is derived: a word formed from another word: a differential coefficient (*math.*).—*adv.* **deriv'atively**. [Fr. *dériver*—L. *dērivāre*—*dē*, down, from, *rīvus*, a river.]

derm *dûrm*, *n.* the true skin—also **der'ma**, **der'mis**.— *adjs.* **der'mal**, **der'mic** pertaining to the skin: consisting of skin.—*n.* **dermati'tis** inflammation of the skin —*adj.* **dermatolog'ical**.—*ns.* **dermatol'ogist**; **dermatol'ogy** the branch of science that treats of the skin. [Gr. *derma*, *-atos*, the skin.]

dernier *der-nyā*, (Fr.) *adj.* last.

dernier cri *der-nyā krē*, (Fr.) the last word (lit. cry), the latest fashion.

derogate *der'ō-gāt*, *v.i.* to lessen by taking away: to detract.—*n.* **deroga'tion** a taking from: detraction: depreciation: the allowed breaking of a rule.—*adj.* **derog'ative**.—*advs.* **derog'atively**; **derogatorily** (*di-rog'ə-tər-i-li*).—*n.* **derog'atoriness**.—*adj.* **derog'atory** detracting: injurious. [L. *dērogāre*, *-ātum*, to repeal part of a law—*dē*, down, from, and *rogāre*, to propose a law.]

derrick *der'ik*, *n.* an arrangement for hoisting materials, by a boom stayed from a central post: a framework or tower over a borehole or the like. [From *Derrick*, a 17th-century hangman.]

derrière *der-yer*, *der'i-er*, (Fr.) *n.* the behind, buttocks.

derring-do, *der'ing-dōō*, (*false archaic*) *n.* daring action. [Spenser mistook Lydgate's *dorryng do*, i.e. daring (to) do) (misprinted *derrynge do*) for a noun.]

derringer *der'in-jər*, *n.* a short American pistol. [Inventor's name.]

Derris *der'is*, *n.* a tropical genus of papilionaceous plants whose roots yield an insecticide powder: (without *cap.*) any plant of the genus. [Gr. *derris*, a leather coat.]

derv *dûrv*, *n.* diesel engine fuel oil. [From *diesel* engined road vehicle.]

dervish *dûr'vish*, *n.* a member of one of numerous Muslim fraternities, professing poverty and leading an austere life. [Turkish *dervīsh*—Pers. *darvīsh*, a dervish—lit., a poor man.]

desalinate *dē-sal'in-āt*, *v.t.* to remove salt from (esp. sea water).—*ns.* **desalina'tion**; **desal'inātor**. [Pfx. **de-** (2).]

descant *des'kant*, *n.* an accompaniment above and harmonising with the air: a discourse or disquisition under several heads.—*adj.* (of a musical instrument) with a higher register and pitch than most others of the same family.—*v.i.* **descant'** to sing a descant: to discourse at length: to comment. [O.N.Fr. *descant*—L. *dis-*, apart, and *cantus*, a song.]

descend *di-send'*, *v.i.* to climb down: to pass from a higher to a lower place or condition: to pass from general to particulars: to make an invasion: to be derived (from): (of the testes) to move from the abdominal cavity into the scrotum.—*v.t.* to go down upon, to traverse downwards.—*n.* **descend'ant** one who descends, as offspring from an ancestor.—*adjs.* **descend'ed** derived by descent; **descend'ent** going down: proceeding from an ancestor.—*n.* **descend'er**

the part of a letter such as *j, p*, etc. that comes below the line of type (*print.*).—*adjs.* **descend'ible** (also **-able**) that may descend or be descended: capable of transmission by inheritance, heritable.—*n.* **descent'** act of descending: transmission by succession: motion or progress downward: slope: a raid or invasion: derivation from an ancestor: a generation, a degree in genealogy: descendants collectively. [Fr. *descendre*—L. *descendere*—*dē*, down, *scandĕre*, to climb.]

describe *di-skrīb'*, *v.t.* to trace out or delineate: to give an account of.—*adj.* **describ'able**.—*ns.* **describ'er**; **description** (*di-skrip'shən*) act of describing: an account of anything in words: (loosely) sort, class, or kind.—*adj.* **descrip'tive** containing description.— *adv.* **descrip'tively**.—*ns.* **descrip'tiveness**; **descrip'-tivism** the use of, or belief in, descriptive linguistics (see below): a theory of ethics by which only empirical statements are acceptable.—**descriptive linguistics** the study of the description of a language structure as it occurred individually at a particular time, i.e. with no reference to its history, any other language, etc. [L. *describĕre*—*dē*, down, *scrībĕre*, *scrīptum*, to write.]

descry *di-skrī'*, *v.t.* to discover by the eye: to espy:— *pr.p.* **descry'ing**; *pa.t.* and *pa.p.* **descried'**. [App. two words: O.Fr. *descrire* for *descrivre*—L. *dēscrībĕre*, and O.Fr. *descrier*, *decryer*, proclaim, announce.]

desecrate *des'i-krāt*, *v.t.* to divert from a sacred purpose: to profane.—*ns.* **des'ecrater**, **-or**; **desecrā'tion** act of desecrating: profanation. [Coined on the analogy of *consecrate*—L. *dē*, from.]

desegregate *dē-seg'ri-gāt*, *v.t.* to abolish racial segregation in (e.g. a university).—*n.* **desegregā'tion**.—*n.* and *adj.* **desegregā'tionist**. [Pfx. **de-** (2).]

deselection *dē-si-lek'shən*, *n.* the non-reselection of a sitting M.P., etc. as candidate in a forthcoming election.—*v.t.* **deselect'**. [Pfx. **de-** (2) and **select**.]

desensitise, -ize *dē-sen'sit-īz*, *v.t.* and *v.i.* to make or become less sensitive. [Pfx. **de-** (2).]

desert[1] *di-zûrt'*, *n.* that which is deserved: claim to reward: merit.—*adj.* **desert'less** without merit. [O.Fr., pa.p. of *deservir*; see **deserve**.]

desert[2] *di-zûrt'*, *v.t.* to leave: to forsake.—*v.i.* to run away: to quit a service, as the army, without permission.—*ns.* **desert'er** one who deserts or quits a service without permission; **deser'tion** act of deserting: state of being deserted: wilful abandonment of a legal or moral obligation. [L. *dēserĕre*, *dēsertum*—*dē-*, neg., and *serĕre*, to bind.]

desert[3] *dez'ərt*, *adj.* uninhabited: uncultivated.—*n.* a desolate or barren tract: a waste: a solitude.—*ns.* **desertifica'tion**, **desertisā'tion**, **-z-** the deterioration or reversion of land to desert conditions, owing to overgrazing, erosion, etc.—**desert pea** an Australian pea with purple-spotted scarlet flower; **desert rat** (from the divisional sign, a jerboa) a soldier of the British 7th Armoured Division with service in North Africa in 1941–42. [O.Fr. *desert*—L. *desertum*—*dēserĕre*, to desert, unbind.]

deserve *di-zûrv'*, *v.t.* to be entitled to by merit: to merit. —*v.i.* to be worthy of reward.—*adj.* **deserved'**.—*adv.* **deserv'edly**.—*adj.* **deserv'ing** worthy.—*adv.* **deserv'-ingly** according to desert: justly. [O.Fr. *deservir*—L. *dēservīre*—*dē*, intens., *servīre*, to serve.]

déshabillé. Same as **dishabille**.

desiccate *des'i-kāt*, *v.t.* to dry up: to preserve by drying. —*v.i.* to grow dry.—*adjs.* **des'iccant**, **desiccative** (*di-sik'ə-tiv*) drying: having the power of drying.—*ns.* a drying agent.—*ns.* **desiccā'tion** the act or process of drying up: state of being dried up; **des'iccātor** apparatus for drying. [L. *dēsiccāre*, *-ātum*, to dry up —*dē-*, intens, *siccus*, dry.]

desiderate *di-sid'ər-āt*, *v.t.* to long for or earnestly desire: to want or miss.—*n.* **desiderā'tion**.—*adj.*

desid'erative implying desire (as in *desiderative verb*).—*n.* **desidera'tum** (or *ä'*) something desired or much wanted:—*pl.* **desidera'ta.** [L. *dēsīderāre, -ātum,* to long for; *dēsīdērium,* longing. A doublet of **desire.**]

design *di-zīn', v.t.* to draw: to form a plan of: to contrive: to intend: to set apart or destine.—*n.* a drawing or sketch: a plan in outline: a plan or scheme formed in the mind: plot: intention.—*adj.* **design'able.**—*v.t.* **designate** (*dez'ig-nāt*) to mark out so as to make known: to show: to name: to be a name for: to appoint or nominate.—*adj.* nominated to but not yet in possession of an office (used after the *n.*, as in *chairman designate*).—*n.* **designa'tion** a showing or pointing out: a name: a title: an appellation descriptive of occupation, standing, etc.: nomination to office.—*n.* **des'ignator.**—*adv.* **designedly** (*di-zīn'id-li*) by design: intentionally.—*n.* **design'er** one who furnishes designs or patterns: a draughtsman: a plotter.—*adj.* designed by and bearing the name of a known fashion designer.—*adj.* **design'ing** artful: scheming.—*n.* the art of making designs or patterns.—**design engineer** a designer in engineering.—**by design** intentionally. [Fr. *désigner*—L. *dēsignāre, -ātum*—*dē-*, off, and *signum*, a mark.]

desire *di-zīr', v.t.* to long for: to wish for: to ask.—*v.i.* to be in a state of desire.—*n.* an earnest longing or wish: a prayer or request: the object desired: lust.—*adj.* **desir'able** worthy of desire: to be approved of: pleasing: agreeable.—*n.* a desirable person or thing.—*ns.* **desir'ableness, desirabil'ity.**—*adv.* **desir'ably.**—*adj.* **desir'ous** (usu. with *of*) full of desire: wishful: eager. [Fr. *désirer*—L. *dēsīderāre.*]

desist *di-zist', -sist', v.i.* to leave off. [L. *dēsistēre*—*dē*-, away from, and *sistēre,* to cause to stand.]

desk *desk, n.* a sloping or flat table for writing or reading, often fitted with drawers, etc.: a shut-up writing-box: a pulpit or lectern: a counter in a public place for information, registration, etc.: a department of a newspaper office, e.g. *the news desk*: a music-stand: in an orchestra, esp. among strings, (players in) a seating position determined by rank (e.g. *the first desk*).—**desk'-work** work done at a desk, as by a clerk or author. [M.E. *deske*—L. *discus*—Gr. *diskos.*]

desman *des'man, n.* a Russian aquatic insectivore with long snout and musk-glands: a kindred Pyrenean species. [Sw. *desman,* musk.]

desolate *des'ō-lāt, v.t.* to make lonely or forlorn: to make joyless: to deprive of inhabitants: to lay waste.—*adj.* (*-lit*) comfortless: dreary: forlorn: lonely: destitute of inhabitants: laid waste.—*adv.* **des'olately.**—*ns.* **des'olateness; des'olater,** -**or; desola'tion.** [L. *dēsōlāre, -ātum*—*dē-,* intens., and *sōlāre,* to make alone—*sōlus,* alone.]

desorb. See **desorption.**

desorption *dē-sörp'shan, n.* release from an adsorbed state.—*v.t.* **desorb'.** [Pfx. **de-** (2).]

despair *di-spār', v.i.* to be without hope (of).—*n.* hopelessness: that which causes despair.—*adj.* **despair'ing** apt to despair: full of despair.—*adv.* **despair'ingly.** [O.Fr. *desperer*—L. *dē-,* neg., and *spērāre,* to hope.]

despatch. Same as **dispatch.**

desperado *des-par-ä'dō, -ā'dō, n.* a desperate fellow: one reckless of danger: a wild ruffian:—*pl.* **despera'dos, -oes.** [Old Sp.—L. *dēspērātus.*]

desperate *des'par-it, adj.* in a state of despair: hopeless: beyond hope: despairingly reckless: extremely bad.—*adv.* **des'perately.**—*ns.* **des'perateness; despera'tion** state of despair: despairing: disregard of danger. [See **despair.**]

despicable *des'pik-a-bl, dis-pik', adj.* deserving to be despised: contemptible: worthless.—*ns.* **despicabil'-**

ity, des'picableness (or *-pik'*).—*adv.* **despic'ably** (or *des'*). [See **despise.**]

despise *di-spīz', v.t.* to look down upon with contempt.—*n.* **despis'er.** [O.Fr. *despire* (*despis-*)—L. *despicēre—dē,* down, *specēre,* to look.]

despite *di-spīt', n.* violent malice or hatred.—*prep.* in spite of: notwithstanding. [O.Fr. *despit* (mod. *dépit*)—L. *dēspectus—dēspicēre;* see **despise.**]

despoil *di-spoil', v.t.* to plunder completely: to strip: to bereave: to rob.—*ns.* **despoil'er; despoil'ment.** [O.Fr. *despoiller* (mod. *dépouiller;* see next).]

despoliation *di-spōl-i-ā'shan, n.* despoiling. [L. *dēspoliāre—dē-,* intens., and *spolium,* spoil.]

despond *di-spond', v.i.* to be wanting in hope, to be dejected.—*n.* (Bunyan) despondency.—*n.* **despond'ency.**—*adj.* **despond'ent.**—*adv.* **despond'ently.** [L. *dēspondēre,* to resign—*dē,* away, and *spondēre,* to promise.]

despot *des'pot, -pat, n.* one invested with absolute power: a tyrant.—*adj.* **despotic** (*dis-pot'ik*) pertaining to or like a despot: having absolute power: tyrannical.—*adv.* **despot'ically.**—*n.* **des'potism** absolute power: a state governed by a despot. [O.Fr. *despot*—Gr. *despotēs,* a master.]

dessert *diz-ûrt', n.* a final course of a meal, pudding or other sweet item: fruit, sweetmeats, etc. served at the end of a meal.—**dessert'spoon** a spoon smaller than a tablespoon and larger than a teaspoon; **dessert'spoon'ful.** [O.Fr. *dessert, desservir,* to clear the table.]

destabilise, -ize *dē-stā'bil-īz, v.t.* to make unstable or less stable (*lit.* and *fig.*). [Pfx. **de-** (2).]

destine *des'tin, v.t.* to ordain or appoint to a certain use or state: to intend: to fix: to doom.—*ns.* **destina'tion** the purpose or end to which anything is destined or appointed: place to which one is going; **des'tiny** the purpose or end to which any person or thing is appointed: unavoidable fate: necessity. [Fr. *destiner*—L. *dē-,* intens., and root of *stāre,* to stand.]

destitute *des'ti-tūt, adj.* in utter want: entirely lacking in (with *of*).—*n.* **destitu'tion** the state of being destitute: poverty. [L. *dēstitu ere, -ūtum—dē-,* away, and *statuēre,* to place.]

destrier *des'tri-ar, des-trēr', (arch.) n.* a warhorse. [Fr.,—L. *dextrārius,* led by the (squire's) right hand.]

destroy *di-stroi', v.t.* to pull down: to overturn: to ruin: to put an end to:—*pr.p.* **destroy'ing;** *pa.t.* and *pa.p.* **destroyed'.**—*adj.* **destroy'able.**—*n.* **destroy'er** a person or thing that destroys: a small, fast-moving warship. [O.Fr. *destruire* (Fr. *détruire*)—L. *dē-,* down, and *struēre,* to build.]

destruction *di-struk'shan, n.* act or process of destroying: overthrow: physical or moral ruin: death: a cause of destruction.—*v.t.* **destruct'** to destroy a rocket or missile in flight.—Also *v.i.*—*adj.* **destruc'tible** liable to be destroyed.—*ns.* **destructibil'ity, destruc'tibleness.**—*adj.* **destruc'tive** causing or concerned with destruction: mischievous.—*adv.* **destruc'tively.**—*ns.* **destruc'tiveness; destruc'tor** (*di-*) a furnace for burning up refuse.—**destructive distillation** the distillation of solid substances accompanied by their decomposition. [L. *dēstruēre, -structum;* see **destroy.**]

desuetude *di-sū'i-tūd, des'wi-tūd, n.* disuse: discontinuance. [L. *dēsuētūdō—dēsuētum, dēsuēscēre—dē,* neg., and *suēscēre,* to become used.]

desultory *des'al-tar-i, adj.* jumping from one thing to another: without rational or logical connection: rambling.—*adv.* **des'ultorily.**—*n.* **des'ultoriness.** [L. *dēsultōrius—dēsultor,* a vaulter—*dē,* from, and *salīre,* to jump.]

detach *di-tach', v.t.* to unfasten: to take away or separate: to withdraw: to send off on special service.—*v.i.*

to separate.—*adj.* **detach'able.**—*adj.* **detached'** unconnected: separate: aloof: free from care, passion, ambition, and worldly bonds.—*adv.* **detach'edly.**—*ns.* **detach'edness; detach'ment** the state of being detached: the act of detaching: that which is detached, as a body of troops. [Fr. *détacher*—O.Fr. pfx. *des-* (L. *dis-*), apart, and root of **attach.**]

detail *di-tāl'*, *v.t.* to relate minutely: to enumerate: to set apart for a particular service.—*v.i.* to give details about anything.—*n.* (*dē'tāl*, also *di-tāl'*) a small part: an item: a particular account: (chiefly *mil.*) a small body set apart for special duty.—*adj.* **detailed'** giving full particulars: exhaustive.—**go into detail** to study, discuss, etc , a matter deeply, considering the particulars; **in detail** circumstantially, point by point: piecemeal. [Fr. *détailler*—*de-*, intens., and *tailler*, to cut.]

detain *di-tān'*, *v.t.* to hold back: to withhold: to stop: to keep: to keep in custody —*ns.* **detain'ee** a person kept in custody; **detain'er** the holding of what belongs to another (*law*): a warrant to a sheriff to keep in custody a person already in confinement; **detain'ment** detention. [O.Fr. *detenir*—L. *dētinēre*; see **detent.**]

detect *di-tekt'*, *v.t.* to discover: to discern: to find out (esp. something elusive or secret).—*adjs.* **detect'able, -ible.**—*n.* **detec'tion** discovery of something hidden or not easily observed: state of being found out.—*adj.* **detect'ive** employed in or concerned with detection.—*n.* a policeman, usually not in uniform, or other person (*private detective*) who investigates cases of crime or watches behaviour of suspected persons.—*n.* **detec'tor** an apparatus for detecting something, as smoke, tampering with a lock, pressure of electric currents, of electric waves.—**detective story** one in which clues to the detection of a criminal are set forth and unravelled. [L. *dētegĕre, -tēctum—dē-*, neg., *tegĕre*, to cover.]

detent *di-tent'*, *n.* a catch, esp. for regulating the striking of a clock.—*n.* **deten'tion** act of detaining: state of being detained: confinement, or restriction of liberty, esp. of an offender —**detention centre** a place of confinement for young offenders. [L. *dētinēre, dētentum—dē*, from, *tenēre*, to hold.]

détente *dā-tāt*, (Fr.) *n.* relaxation of strained relations (esp. between countries).

deter *di-tûr'*, *v.t.* to frighten from: to hinder or prevent:—*pr.p.* **deterr'ing;** *pa.t.* and *pa.p.* **deterred'.**—*ns.* **deter'ment; deterrence** (*di-ter'əns*).—*adj.* **deterrent** (*di-ter'ənt*) serving to deter.—*n.* anything that deters: *specif.*, a nuclear weapon. [L. *dēterrēre—dē*, from, *terrēre*, to frighten.]

deterge *di-tûrj'*, *v.t.* to cleanse (as a wound).—*n.* **deterg'ent** that which cleanses: a cleansing agent esp (commonly) a soapless cleanser.—*adj.* (also **deters'ive**) cleansing: purging. [L. *dētergēre, dētersum—dē*, off, and *tergēre*, to wipe.]

deteriorate *di-tē'ri-ə-rāt*, *v.t.* to make worse.—*v.i.* to grow worse.—*n.* **deteriora'tion** the act of making worse: the process of growing worse. [L. *dēteriorāre, -ātum*, to make worse—*dēterior*, worse.]

determine *dē-tûr'min*, *v.t.* to limit: to fix or settle: to define: to decide: to resolve: to cause to resolve: to put an end to.—*v.i.* to come to a decision: to come to an end.—*adj.* **deter'minable.**—*n.* **deter'minacy** (*-ə-si*).—*adj.* **deter'minant** serving to determine.—*n.* that which serves to determine: the sum of all the products got by taking one from each row and column of a square block of quantities, each product being reckoned positive or negative according as an even or an odd number of transpositions reduces it to the order of the rows (or of the columns)—used for the solution of equations and other purposes (*math.*).—

adj. **deter'minate** determined or limited: fixed: decisive: cymose (*bot.*).—*n.* **determina'tion** the act of determining: condition of being determined: that which is determined or resolved on: end: direction to a certain end: resolution: fixedness of purpose: decision of character.—*adj.* **deter'minative** that determines, limits, or defines.—*adj.* **deter'mined** ascertained: fixed: firm in purpose: resolute.—*adv.* **deter'minedly.**—*ns.* **deter'miner** one who, or that which, determines: a limiting adjective or modifying word such as *each, my*, etc. (*gram.*); **deter'minism** the doctrine that all things, including the will, are determined by causes—the converse of free-will.—*n.* **deter'minist.** [L. *dētermināre, -ātum—dē*, intens., and *terminus*, a boundary.]

deterrent. See **deter.**

detest *di-test'*, *v.t.* to hate intensely.—*adj.* **detest'able** extremely hateful: abominable.—*ns.* **detestabil'ity, detest'ableness.**—*adv.* **detest'ably.**—*n.* **detestā'tion.** [Fr.,—L. *dētestāri—dē*, intens., and *testāri*, to execrate.]

dethrone *di-thrōn'*, *v.t.* to remove from a throne.—*ns.* **dethrone'ment; dethrōn'er; dethrōn'ing.** [Pfx. de- (2).]

detonate *det'ō-nāt* or *dēt'ō-nāt*, *v.t.* and *v.i.* to explode or cause to explode rapidly and loudly: in an internal-combustion engine, to explode by spontaneous combustion with a hammering sound (pinking or knock).—*ns.* **detona'tion** an explosion with report: knock; **det'onātor** a substance that detonates: a substance or contrivance whose explosion initiates that of another explosive. [L. *dētonāre, -ātum—dē*, down, and *tonāre*, to thunder.]

detour *dē'*, *dā'tōōr, di-tōōr'*, *n.* a winding: a circuitous way.—Also *v.t.* and *v.i.* [Fr. *dé-* (L. *dis-*) asunder, and *tour*, turning.]

detoxicate *dē-toks'i-kāt*, **detox'ify** *-i-fī*, *vs.t.* to rid of poison or the effects of it.—*n.* **detox'icant** a substance that detoxicates.—Also *adj.*—*ns.* **detoxica'tion, detoxifica'tion—detoxification centre** a centre for the cure of alcoholism. [Pfx. de- (2).]

detract *di-trakt'* *v.t.* to take away, abate: to defame.—*v.i.* to take away (with *from*): to reduce in degree: to diminish.—*ns.* **detract'or; detrac'tion** depreciation: slander.—*adj.* **detract'ive** tending to detract: derogatory. [L. *dētrahĕre—dē*, from, *trahĕre, tractum*, to draw.]

detrain *dē-trān'*, *v.t.* to set down out of a railway train.—*v.i.* to alight from a train.—*n.* **detrain'ment.** [Pfx. de- (2).]

detriment *det'ri-mənt*, *n.* diminution: damage: loss.—*adj.* **detrimental** (*-ment'l*).—*adv.* **detriment'ally.** [L. *dētrīmentum—dē*, off, and *terĕre, trītum*, to rub.]

detritus *di-trī'tas*, *n.* a mass of substance gradually worn off solid bodies: an aggregate of loosened fragments, esp. of rock.—*adj.* **detri'tal.**—*ns.* **detrition** (*di-trish'ən*) wearing away. [L. *dētrītus*, worn—*dē*, off, and *terĕre, trītum*, to rub.]

de trop *də trō*, (Fr.) superfluous: in the way.

detumescence *dē-tū-mes'əns*, *n.* diminution of swelling —opp. to **intumescence.** [Pfx. de- (2).]

deuce[1] *dūs, n.* a card or die with two spots: a situation ('forty all') in which one side must gain two successive points to win the game, or ('five all', 'games all') two successive games to win the set (*lawn-tennis*). [F. *deux*, two—L. *duōs*, accus. of *duo*, two.]

deuce[2] *dūs, n.* the devil—in exclamatory phrases.—*adj.* **deuced** (*dū'sid*, or *dūst*) devilish: excessive.—*adv.* confoundedly.—Also **deuc'edly.** [Prob. from the deuce (see foregoing), the lowest throw at dice.]

deus *dē'əs, dā'ōōs*, (L.) *n.* god.—**Deus avertat** (*a-vûr'tat, a-wer'tat*) God forbid; **deus ex machina** (usu. *eks mak'in-a*, sometimes *mə-shē'nə*) a god brought on the stage by a mechanical device: a contrived and inartistic solution of a difficulty in a plot.

deuter(o)- *dū-tər(-ō)-*, in composition, second, secondary.—*v.t.* **deu'terate** to add deuterium to, or to replace hydrogen by deuterium in (molecules).—*ns.* **deuterā'tion; deuterium** (*-tē'ri-əm*) heavy hydrogen, an isotope of hydrogen of double mass.—**deu'teron** the nucleus of heavy hydrogen, of mass 2, carrying unit positive charge; **Deuteronomy** (*-on'ə-mi*, or *dū'*; Gr. *nomos*, law) the fifth book of the Pentateuch, containing a repetition of the decalogue and laws given in Exodus.—**deuterium oxide** heavy water. [Gr. *deuteros*, second.]

Deutschmark *doich'mark*, *n.* (also **Deutsche Mark** *doich'ə mark*) the standard monetary unit of West Germany. [Ger.]

Deutzia *dūt'si-ə* or *doit'si-ə*, *n.* a genus of saxifragaceous plants with panicles of white flowers, introduced from China and Japan. [After Jan *Deutz*, 18th-cent. Dutch naturalist.]

devalue *dē-val'ū*, *v.t.* to reduce the value of.—Also *v.i.* (esp. of currency).—*n.* **devaluā'tion.**—*v.t.* **de-val'uate.** [Pfx. de- (2).]

devanagari *dā-və-nä'gə-ri*, *n.* the character in which Sanskrit is usually written and printed.—Also with *cap.* [Sans. *devanāgari*, town-script of the gods; see **nagari.**]

devastate *dev'əs-tāt*, *v.t.* to lay waste, plunder.—*adj.* **dev'astating** ravaging: (*coll.*) overpoweringly effective.—*adv.* **dev'astatingly.**—*n.* **devastā'tion** act of devastating: state of being devastated: havoc.—*n.* **dev'astātor.** [L. *dēvastāre*, *-ātum—dē-*, intens., *vastāre*, to lay waste.]

develop *di-vel'əp*, *v.t.* to bring out what is latent or potential in: to bring to a more advanced or more highly organised state: to work out the potentialities of: to elaborate: to cause to grow or advance: to evolve: to contract (a disease): to make more available: to exploit the natural resources of (a region): to build on or prepare for building on (land): to bring into a position useful in attack (*chess*): to disclose: to express in expanded form (*math.*): to unroll into a plane surface (*geom.*): to render visible the image on a negative by the use of chemicals (*phot.*).—*v.i.* to open out: to evolve: to advance through successive stages to a higher, more complex, or more fully grown state:—*pr.p.* **devel'oping;** *pa.t.* and *pa.p.* **devel'oped.**—*adjs.* **devel'opable; devel'oped.**—*ns.* **devel'oper** one who develops: a reagent for developing photographs; **develop'ment** the act or process of developing: state of being developed: a gradual unfolding or growth: evolution: the expression of a function in the form of a series (*math.*): elaboration of a theme, or that part of a movement in which this occurs (*mus.*): new situations that emerge.—*adj.* **development'al** pertaining to development.—*adv.* **development'ally.**—**development area** a region of heavy unemployment where new industry is given official encouragement. [Fr. *développer*, opposite to *envelopper*, of obscure origin.]

deviate *dē'vi-āt*, *v.i.* to go from the way: to turn aside from a certain course: to diverge, differ, from a standard, mean value, etc.: to err.—*n.* (*dē'vi-ət*; *psych.*) one who deviates much from the normal.—*ns.* **dē'viance, dē'viancy.**—*adj.* **dē'viant** which deviates from the norm, esp. sexually.—Also *n.*—*n.* **dēvi-ā'tion; dē'viātor.**—*adj.* **deviā'tory.**—**deviation of the compass** departure of the mariner's compass from the magnetic meridian, owing to the ship's magnetism or other local causes; **standard deviation** the square root of the variance of a number of observations. [L. *dēviāre*, *-ātum—dē*, from, *via*, a way.]

device *di-vīs'*, *n.* that which is devised or designed

contrivance: an emblem: a motto.—**leave someone to his own devices** to leave someone alone, not distracting or interfering with him. [O.Fr. *devise*; see **devise.**]

devil *dev'l*, *-il*, *n.* an evil spirit: (*cap.*) the supreme spirit of evil: wicked person: reckless, lively person: (usu. pitying) a fellow: an animal, thing, problem, difficult to deal with: one who excels or exceeds in anything: a printer's devil: a drudge (esp. legal or literary): a dust-storm: fighting spirit: a plumber's portable furnace: a machine of various kinds, esp. for tearing: used as a mild oath.—*v.t.* to season highly and broil.—*v.i.* to perform another person's drudgery: to do very menial work:—*pr.p.* **dev'illing;** *pa.t.* and *pa.p.* **dev'illed.**—*adj.* **dev'ilish** fiendish, malignant: very bad.—*adv.* (*coll.*) very, exceedingly. —*adv.* **dev'ilishly.**—*ns.* **dev'ilment** frolicsome mischief; **dev'ilry; dev'il-fish** the fishing-frog or angler: the giant ray of the United States: the octopus.—*adj.* **dev'il-may-care'** reckless, audacious.—**devil's advocate** advocatus diaboli, the Promoter of the Faith, an advocate at the papal court whose duty it is to propose objections against a canonisation: a person who states the case against a proposal, course of action, etc., usu. for the sake of argument; **dev'il's-bit** a species of scabious (*Succisa pratensis*) with rootstock as if bitten off.—**between the devil and the deep (blue) sea** in a desperate dilemma; **devil a bit, a one, a thing** etc., not at all, not one, etc.; **devil's coach-horse** a large dark-coloured beetle (*Ocypus olens*); **devil's food cake** (chiefly *U.S.*) a kind of chocolate cake; **dev'ils-on-horse'back** same as **angels-on-horseback; devil take the hindmost** each man for himself; **go to the devil** to become ruined: (*interj.*) go away!; **play the devil** to make havoc (with); **printer's devil** the youngest apprentice in a printing-office: a printer's errand-boy; **talk of the devil** here comes the person we were talking of; **the devil and all** much ado: turmoil; **the devil to pay** serious trouble (as a consequence of an action, etc.). [O.E. *dēofol*, *dēoful*—L. *diabolus*—Gr. *diabolos*, from *diaballein*, to throw across, to slander.]

devious *dē'vi-əs*, *adj.* remote: out of the way: roundabout: winding: erring: tortuous of mind: deceitful.—*adv.* **dē'viously.**—*n.* **dē'viousness.** [L. *dēvius*; see **deviate.**]

devise *di-vīz'*, *v.t.* to imagine: to compose: to scheme: to contrive: to bequeath.—*v.i.* to consider: to scheme.—*n.* act of bequeathing: a will: property bequeathed by will.—*adj.* **devis'able.**—*ns.* **devis'al; devisee** (*dev-ī-zē'*) one to whom real estate is bequeathed; **devi'ser** one who contrives; **devis'or** one who bequeaths. [O.Fr. *deviser*, *devise*—L.L. *dīvīsa*, a division of goods, a mark, a device.]

devitalise, -ize *dē-vī'tə-līz*, *v.t.* to deprive of vitality or life-giving qualities.—*n.* **devitalisā'tion, -z-.** [Pfx. de- (2).]

devoid *di-void'*, *adj.* (with *of*) destitute, free: empty. [O.Fr. *desvoidier*—L. *dis-*, away, *viduāre*, deprive.]

devoir *dev'wär*, *n.* (often in *pl.*) what is due, duty: service: an act of civility. [Fr.,—L. *dēbēre*, to owe.]

devolution *dēv-*, *dev-ə-lōō'shən*, *-lū'*, *n.* a passing from one person to another: a handing over of powers: a modified home rule, the delegation of certain powers to regional governments by a central government. —*adj.* **devolu'tionary.**—*n.* **devolu'tionist.** [See **devolve.**]

devolve *di-volv'*, *v.t.* to roll down: to hand down: to deliver over, esp. powers to regional governments by a central government.—*v.i.* to roll down: to fall or pass over in succession (with *on*).—*n.* **devolve'ment.** [L. *dēvolvĕre*, *-volūtum—dē*, down, *volvĕre*, to roll.]

Devonian *di-vō'ni-ən*, *adj.* belonging to *Devonshire*:

belonging to a system above the Silurian and below the Carboniferous (*geol.*).—*n.* a native of Devonshire: the Devonian system.—**Devonshire cream** clotted cream.

devote *di-vōt'*, *v.t.* to set apart or dedicate by a vow or solemn act: to give up wholly.—*adj.* **devōt'ed** given up, as by a vow: doomed: strongly attached (to): zealous.—*adv.* **devōt'edly**.—*ns.* **devōt'edness; devotee** (*dev-ə-tē'*, or *dev'*) one wholly or superstitiously devoted, esp. to religion: a votary: one strongly and consistently interested in something (with *of*); **devō'tion** the act of devoting: state of being devoted: consecration: giving up of the mind to the worship of God: piety: prayer: strong affection or attachment: ardour: faithful service: (in *pl.*) prayers.—*adj.* **devō'tional**.—*adv.* **devō'tionally**. [L. *dēvovēre, dēvōtum* —*dē*, away, and *vovēre*, to vow.]

devour *di-vowr'*, *v.t.* to swallow greedily: to eat up: to consume or waste with violence or wantonness: to take in eagerly by the senses or mind.—*n.* **devour'er**. —*adj.* **devour'ing**.—*adv.* **devour'ingly**.—*n.* **devour'ment**. [O.Fr. *devorer*—L. *dēvorāre*—*dē*, intens., and *vorāre*, to swallow.]

devout *di-vowt'*, *adj.* given up to religious thoughts and exercises: pious: solemn: earnest.—*adv.* **devout'ly**.—*n.* **devout'ness**. [O.Fr. *devot*—L. *dēvōtus*; see **devote**.]

dew *dū*, *n.* moisture deposited from the air on cooling, esp. at night, in minute specks upon the surface of objects: a similar deposit or exudation of other kinds: early freshness.—*v.t.* to wet with dew: to moisten.— *adv.* **dew'ily**.—*n.* **dew'iness**.—*adj.* **dew'y.—dew'berry** a kind of bramble or blackberry having a bluish, dew-like bloom on the fruit; **dew'-claw** a rudimentary inner toe, esp. on a dog's leg; **dew'-drop**; **dew'-fall** the deposition, or time of deposition, of dew; **dew'point** the temperature at which a given sample of moist air becomes saturated and forms dew; **dew'-pond** a hollow supplied with water by mist.—*adj.* **dew'y-eyed** fresh, innocent (often *iron.*).—**mountain dew** (*coll.*) whisky. [O.E. *dēaw*; cf. O.N. *dögg*, Ger. *Tau*, dew.]

dewan, diwan *dē-wän'*, *n.* in India, a financial minister: a state prime minister. [Pers. *dīwān*; see **divan**.]

Dewar-flask *dū'ar-fläsk*, *n.* a type of vacuum flask. [From Sir James *Dewar* (1842–1923), its inventor.]

dewlap *dū'lap*, *n.* the pendulous skin under the throat of oxen, dogs, etc.: the fleshy wattle of the turkey. [Prob. **dew** and O.E. *læppa*, a loose hanging piece.]

dexter *deks'tar*, *adj.* on the right-hand side: right: of that side of the shield on the right-hand side of the bearer, the spectator's left (*her.*).—*n.* **dexterity** (-*ter'i-ti*) skill of manipulation, or generally: adroitness.—*adj.* **dex'terous, dex'trous** adroit: subtle.— *adv.* **dex't(e)rously**.—*n.* **dex't(e)rousness**.—*adj.* **dex'tral** right: right-handed: turning to the right: of flatfish, lying right-side-up: of a spiral shell, turning in the normal manner.—*n.* **dextral'ity**.—*adv.* **dex'trally**.—*ns.* **dex'tran** a carbohydrate formed in sugar solutions, a substitute for blood plasma in transfusion; **dex'trin, dex'trine** British gum, a gummy mixture got from starch by heating or otherwise.—**dextro-** in composition, pertaining to, or towards, the right.—*ns.* **dextrocar'dia** (Gr. *kardia*, heart) a condition in which the heart lies in the right side of the chest, not the left.—*adj.* **dextrorō'tatory** rotating to the right (clockwise).—*ns.* **dextrorotā'tion; dex'trōse** glucose. [L. *dexter*; Gr. *dexios*, Sans. *dakṣiṇa*, on the right, on the south.]

dextral, dextro-, etc. See **dexter**.

dextrorse *deks-trörs'*, or *deks'*, (*biol.*) *adj.* rising spirally and turning to the left, i.e. crossing an outside observer's field of view from left to right upwards

(like a screw-nail). [L. *dextrōrsus*, towards the right —*dexter*, and *vertĕre*, to turn.]

dey *dā*, *n.* the pasha or governor of Algiers before the French conquest. [Turk. *dāi*.]

dhal. Same as **dal.**

dharma *dûr'mà*, *n.* the righteousness that underlies the law: the law. [Sans.]

dhobi *dō'bi*, *n.* an Indian washerman. [Hindi *dhobī*]

dholl. Same as **dal.**

dhoti *dō'ti*, **dhooti** *dōō'tī*, *ns.* the Hindu loin-cloth: a cotton fabric used for this. [Hindi *dhotī*.]

dhow, better **dow**, *dow, n.* an Arab lateen-sailed vessel of the Indian Ocean. [Origin unknown; cf. Ar. *dāw*, Marathi *dāw*.]

dhurra. Same as **durra.**

di- *dī*, *pfx.* two, twice, double. [Gr. *dis*, twice.]

dia- *dī'a-*, *-ə-*, *pfx.* through: across: during: composed of. [Gr.]

diabetes *dī-ə-bē'tēz*, *n.* a disease marked by a morbid and excessive discharge of urine—**diabetes insip'idus** caused by a disorder of the pituitary gland leading to malfunction of the kidney, **diabetes melli'tus** (L., honied) caused by insulin deficiency or, rarely, an excess of insulin, with excess of sugar in the blood and urine.—*adj.* **diabetic** (-*bēt'* or *-bet'*), relating to, or suffering from, diabetes: for the use of diabetics.—*n.* one suffering from diabetes. [Gr. *diabētēs*, a siphon, *dia*, through, and *bainein*, to go.]

diablerie, *dē-äb'lə-rē*, *n.* magic: the black art: sorcery: mischief. [Fr. *diable*; see **devil**.]

diabolic, -al *dī-ə-bol'ik, -əl*, *adjs.* devilish: (usu. **-al**) extremely unpleasant, very bad (*coll.*).—*adv.* **diabol'ically**.. [Gr. *diabolikos—diabolos*; see **devil**.]

diabolo *di-a'bol-ō*, or *dī-, n.* a game in which a two-headed top is spun, tossed, and caught on a string attached to two sticks, held one in each hand. [Gr. *diaballō*, I throw over, toss.]

diachronic *dī-ə-kron'ik*, *adj.* of the study of a subject (esp. a language) through its historical development —opp. of *synchronic*.—*adv.* **diachron'ically**.—*n.* **diachronism** (*dī-ak'*).—*adjs.* **diachronist'ic; diach'ronous**. [Pfx. **dia-**, and Gr. *chronos*, time.]

diacid *dī-as'id*, *adj.* having two replaceable hydrogen atoms: capable of replacing two hydrogen atoms of an acid. [Pfx. **di-**.]

diaconate *dī-ak'ə-nāt*, *n.* the office of a deacon.—*adj.* **diac'onal** pertaining to a deacon. [See **deacon**.]

diacritic, -al *dī-ə-krit'ik, -əl*, *adjs.* distinguishing— used of marks (e.g. accents, cedillas, etc.) attached to letters to indicate modified sound, value, etc.—*n.* **diacrit'ic** such a mark. [Gr. *diakritikos—dia*, between, and *kritikos*; see **critic**.]

diadem *dī'ə-dem*, *n.* a crown, head-band, or the like. [O.Fr. *diademe*—Gr. *dia*, round, and *deein*, to bind.]

diaeresis, dieresis *dī-ēr'i-sis, -er'*, *n.* a mark ( ) placed over a vowel-letter, esp. the second of two adjacent ones to show that it is to be pronounced separately, as *naif*:—*pl.* **diaer'eses, dier'eses** (-*ēz*). [Gr. *diairesis*, separation—*dia*, apart, *haireein*, to take.]

diagnosis *dī-əg-nō'sis*, *n.* the identification of a disease by means of its symptoms: a formal determining description:—*pl.* **diagnō'ses** (-*ēz*).—*v.t.* **diagnose** (-*nōz'*, *-nōs'*) to ascertain from symptoms, as a disease.—*adj.* **diagnōs'tic** distinguishing: different-iating.—*n.* that by which anything is known: a symptom.—*n. sing.* **diagnos'tics** diagnosis as a branch of medicine.—*n.* **diagnostic'ian** (-*nos-tish'ən*) one skilled in diagnosis. [Gr., *dia*, between, *gnōsis*, knowing.]

diagonal *dī-ag'ə-nəl*, *adj.* through the corners, or joining two vertices that are not adjacent, of a polygon: (of a plane) passing through two edges, not adjacent, of a polyhedron: slantwise.—*n.* a straight line or

diagram 263 **diarchy**

plane so drawn.—*adv.* **diag'onally.** [L. *diagōnālis*, from Gr. *dia*, through, and *gōnia*, a corner.]

diagram *dī'ə-gram, n.* a figure or plan intended to explain rather than represent actual appearance: an outline figure or scheme: a curve symbolising a set of facts: a record traced by an automatic indicator.—*adj.* **diagrammatic** (*-grə-mat'ik*).—*adv.* **diagrammat'ically.** [Gr. *diagramma—dia*, round, *graphein*, to write.]

diagrid *dī'ə-grid, n.* a structure of diagonally intersecting beams, used for support. [*diagonal grid*.]

dial *dī'əl, n.* an instrument for showing the time of day by the sun's shadow (as in *sundial*): the face of a watch or clock: graduated plate on which a movable index shows the value of some quantity measured, or can be set to make an adjustment (as in getting a telephone connection, tuning a radio): a face (*slang*).—*v.t.* to measure or indicate or get into communication with by dial.—*v.i.* to use a telephone dial:—*pr.p.* **di'alling;** *pa.t.* and *pa.p.* **di'alled.**—*ns.* **di'aller; di'alling** the art of constructing sundials: the science which explains the measuring of time by the sundial: surveying by dial.—**dialling code** a group of numbers dialled to obtain the desired exchange in an automatic dialling system; **dialling tone** the continuous sound heard on picking up a telephone receiver which indicates that one may begin dialling. [L.L. *diālis*, daily—L. *diēs*, a day.]

dialect *dī'ə-lekt, n.* a variety or form of a language peculiar to a district or class, esp. but not necessarily other than a literary or standard form: a peculiar manner of speaking.—*adj.* **dialect'al.**—*adv.* **dialect'ally.**—*ns.* **dialectol'ogist; dialectol'ogy.** [Through Fr. and L. from Gr. *dialektos*, speech, manner of speech, peculiarity of speech—*dia*, between, *legein*, to speak.]

dialectic, -al *dī-ə-lek'tik, -əl, adjs.* pertaining to discourse or to dialectics: logical.—*n.* **dialec'tic,** or *n. sing* **dialec'tics,** the art of discussing: that branch of logic which teaches the rules and modes of reasoning.—*adv.* **dialec'tically.**—*n.* **dialecti'cian** one skilled in dialectics, a logician. [Gr. *dialektikos*.]

dialogue, *U.S.* **dialog,** *dī'ə-log, n.* conversation between two or more persons, esp. of a formal or imaginary nature: an exchange of views in the hope of ultimately reaching agreement.—*adjs.* **dialog'ic** (*-loj'*), **dialogist'ic, -al.** [Fr.,—L. *dialogus*—Gr. *dialogos*, a conversation—*dialegesthai*, to discourse.]

dialysis *dī-al'i-sis,* (*chem.*) *n.* the separation of substances by diffusion through a membranous septum or partition: separation: removal of impurities from the blood by a kidney machine (q.v.) (*med.*):—*pl.* **dial'yses** (*-sēz*).—*adj.* **dialysable, -z-** (*dī-ə-līz'ə-bl*).—*v.t.* **dialyse,** (*U.S.*) **-yze** (*dī'ə-līz*) to separate by dialysis.—*v.i.* to use a kidney machine.—*n.* **di'alyser, -z-.**—*adj.* **dialytic** (*-lit'ik*). [Gr. *dialysis—dia*, asunder, *lyein*, to loose.]

diamagnetic *dī-ə-mag-net'ik, adj.* cross-magnetic: applied to any substance of which a rod suspended between the poles of a magnet arranges itself across the lines of force.—*n.* **diamag'net** a diamagnetic substance.—*adv.* **diamagnet'ically.**—*n.* **diamag'netism.** [Pfx. **dia-, magnetic.**]

diamanté *dē-a-mā-tā, dī-ə-man'ti, n.* a decoration, e.g. on a dress, consisting of glittering particles: a fabric so decorated.—Also *adj.*—*adj.* **diamantine** (*dī-ə-man'tīn*) of, or resembling, diamonds. [Fr., *diamant*, diamond.]

diameter *dī-am'i-tər, n.* the measure through or across: a straight line passing through the centre of a circle or other figure, terminated at both ends by the circumference.—*adjs.* **diam'etral, diametric** (*dī-ə-met'rik*),

-al in the direction of a diameter: pertaining to the diameter: as of opposite ends of a diameter (as in *diametrical opposition*).—*advs.* **diam'etrally; diamet'rically.** [Through Fr. and L. from Gr. *diametros—dia*, through, across, and *metron*, a measure.]

diamond *dī'ə-mənd, n.* a highly prized gem stone, and the hardest of all minerals, carbon crystallised in the cubic system: a rhombus: a card of a suit distinguished by pips of that form: a baseball field, or the part between bases.—*adj.* resembling diamonds: made of diamonds: marked with diamonds: lozenge-shaped, rhombic.—*adj.* **di'amonded** furnished with diamonds.—**di'amond-drill** a borer whose bit is set with bort; **diamond jubilee** a sixtieth anniversary (of marriage, **di'amond-wedd'ing**); **diamond snake** a carpet snake with diamond-shaped markings.—**black diamonds** (*fig.*) coal; **diamond cut diamond** an encounter between two very sharp persons; **rough diamond** an uncut diamond: a person possibly of great worth, but of rude exterior and unpolished manners. [M.E. *diamaunt*—O.Fr. *diamant*—L.L. *diamas, -antis*—Gr. *adamas, -antos*; see **adamant.**]

Diana *dī-an'ə, n.* Roman goddess of light, the moon-goddess, representative of chastity and hunting—identified with the Greek Artemis: a huntress. [L. *Diāna.*]

diandrous *dī-an'drəs, adj.* having two stamens. [Gr. *dis*, twice, *anēr, andros*, a man, male.]

dianetics® *dī-ə-net'iks, n. sing.* a method of diagnosing and treating psychosomatic ills (held to be caused by pre-natal experiences). [Gr. *dianoētikos—dia*, through, *noeein*, to think.]

Dianthus *dī-an'thəs, n.* the genus of herbaceous flowers to which carnations and pinks belong: (without *cap.*) any plant or flower of the genus. [Poss. Gr. *Dios anthos*, Zeus's flower; or *dianthēs* flowering in succession.]

diapason *dī-ə-pā'zn, -sn, n.* a whole octave: a full volume of various sounds in concord: the whole range or compass of tones: a standard of pitch: a foundation-stop of an organ (*open* or *stopped diapason*) extending through its whole compass. [Gr. *dia pasōn chordōn symphōniā*, concord through all the notes.]

diapause *dī'ə-pöz, n.* in insects, a period of suspended animation and growth. [Gr. *diapausis*, pause—*dia-pauein*, to pause—*dia*, between, *pauein*, to stop.]

diaper *dī'ə-pər, n.* linen or cotton cloth with a square or diamond pattern, used chiefly for table linen and towels: esp. in U.S., a baby's napkin: a diamond pattern for ornamentation. [O.Fr. *diaspre, diapre*—Gr. *dia*, through, *aspros*, white.]

diaphanous *dī-af'ə-nəs, adj.* transparent: translucent: light, delicate.—*adv.* **diaph'anously.**—*n.* **diaph'-anousness.** [Gr. *diaphanēs—dia*, through, and *phainein*, to show, shine.]

diaphoresis *dī-ə-for-ē'sis, n.* sweat, esp. artificially induced.—*adj.* **diaphoretic** (*-et'ik*) promoting sweating.—*n.* a sudorific. [Gr. *diaphorēsis*, sweating—*dia*, through, *pherein*, to carry.]

diaphragm *dī'ə-fram, -frəm, n.* a thin partition or dividing membrane: the midriff, a structure separating the chest from the abdomen: a metal plate with a central hole, for cutting off side-rays in optical instruments: a strengthening or stiffening plate (*engineering*): in a telephone, a thin vibrating disc that converts electrical signals into sound waves and vice versa: a contraceptive device, a thin rubber or plastic cap placed over the mouth of the cervix.—*adj.* **diaphragmatic** (*-frag-mat'*). [Gr. *diaphragma*, partition, midriff—*dia*, across, *phragma*, a fence.]

diapositive *dī-ə-poz'i-tiv, n.* a transparent photographic positive. [Pfx. **dia-, positive.**]

diarchy *dī'är-ki, n.* a form of government in which two persons, states, or bodies are jointly vested with supreme power.—*adjs.* **diarch′al, diarch′ic.** [Gr. *di-*, twice, *archein*, to rule.]

diarrhoea, (*U.S.*) **diarrhea,** *dī-ə-rē′ə*, *n.* a persistent purging or looseness of the bowels: an excessive flow of anything (*fig.*; *coll.*).—*adjs.* **diarrhoe′al, diarrhoe′ic** (also *U.S.* **-rhē′al,** etc.). [Gr. *diarroia—dia*, through, *rhoiā*, a flow.]

diary *dī′ə-ri*, *n.* a daily record: a book for making daily records, noting engagements, etc. [L. *diārium—diēs*, day.]

diaspora *dī-as′por-ə*, *n.* (with *cap.*) dispersion, used collectively for the dispersed Jews after the Babylonian captivity, and also in the apostolic age for the Jews living outside of Palestine, now, for Jews outside Israel: a similar dispersion or migration of other peoples or communities.—Also *adj.* [Gr. *diasporā—dia*, through, *speirein*, to scatter.]

diastase *dī′ə-stās*, *n.* an enzyme that converts starch into sugar, produced in germinating seeds and in pancreatic juice.—*adjs.* **diastā′sic; diastatic** (*-stat′ik*). [Gr. *diastasis*, division—*dia*, apart, *stasis*, setting.]

diastole *dī-as′ta-lē*, *n.* dilatation of the heart, auricles, and arteries—opp. to *systole*, or contraction.—*adj.* **diastolic** (*dī-ə-stol′ik*). [Gr. *diastolē—dia*, asunder, and *stellein*, to place.]

diatessaron *dī-ə-tes′ə-ron*, *-rən*, *n.* a harmony of the four gospels. [Gr. *dia tessarōn*, through, or composed of, four.]

diathermic *dī-ə-thûr′mik*, *adj.* permeable by radiant heat.—Also **diather′mal, diather′manous, diather′mous.**—*ns.* **diather′macy, diather′mancy, diatherman′ity** permeability by radiant heat; **di′athermy** heating of internal parts of the body by electric currents. [Gr. *dia*, through, *thermē*, heat.]

diathesis *dī-ath′i-sis*, *n.* a particular condition or habit of body, esp. one predisposing to certain diseases.—*adj.* **diathetic** (*dī-ə-thet′ik*). [Gr. *diathesis—dia*, asunder, *tithenai* to place.]

diatom *dī′ə-təm*, *n.* one of a class of microscopic unicellular algae with flinty shells in two halves, fitting like box and lid.—*adj.* **diatomā′ceous.**—*n.* **diatomite** (*dī-at′əm-īt*, or *dī′ət-*) diatomaceous earth, a powdery siliceous deposit of diatom frustules. [Gr. *diatomos*, cut through—*dia*, through, *temnein*, to cut.]

diatomic *dī-ə-tom′ik*, *adj.* consisting of two atoms: having two replaceable atoms or groups: bivalent. [Pfx. **di-, atom.**]

diatonic *dī-ə-ton′ik*, *adj.* proceeding by the tones and intervals of the natural scale in music.—*adv.* **diaton′ically.** [Gr. *diatonikos—dia*, through, *tonos*, tone.]

diatribe *dī′ə-trīb*, *n.* a continued discourse or disputation: an invective harangue. [Gr. *diatribē*, a spending of time—*dia*, through, *tribein*, to rub, wear away.]

diazo *di-az′ō*, *adj.* of compounds containing two nitrogen atoms and a hydrocarbon radical: of a photocopying process using a diazo compound decomposed by exposure to light (also **dye′line**).—*n.* a copy made by the diazo method:—*pl.* **diaz′os** or **diaz′oes.** [Pfx. **di-,** and **azo-.**]

dib¹ *dib*, *v.i.* to dip, as in angling:—*pr.p.* **dibb′ing;** *pa.t.* and *pa.p.* **dibbed.** [Prob. a form of **dab.**]

dib² *dib*, *n.* one of the small bones of a sheep's leg: (*pl.*) a children's game, played by throwing up such small bones or stones (**dib′-stones**) from the palm and catching them on the back of the hand—also *jacks*, in Scots *chuckie-stanes*, or *chucks:* (*pl.*) money (*slang*). **dibasic** *dī-bā′sik*, *adj.* capable of reacting with two equivalents of an acid: (of acids) having two replaceable hydrogen atoms. [Pfx. **di-, basic.**]

dibber. See **dibble.**

dibble *dib′l*, *n.* a pointed tool used for making holes for seeds or plants—also **dibb′er.**—*v.t.* **dibb′le** to plant

with a dibble.—*v.i.* to make holes: to dip, as in angling.—*n.* **dibb′ler.** [Prob. connected with **dab.**]

dicast, dikast *dik′ast*, *n.* one of the 6000 Athenians annually chosen to act as judges.—*n.* **dicas′tery** their court. [Gr. *dikastēs—dikē*, justice.]

dice¹, dicey, dicing. See **die².**

dice² *dīs*, *v.t.* (*Austr. coll.*) to reject.

dicephalous *di-sef′ə-las*, *adj.* two-headed. [Gr. *di-kephalos—di-*, double, *kephalē*, a head.]

dichlorodiphenyltrichloroethane *dī-klō′rō-dī-phē′nīl-trī-klō′rō-ēth′ān*, *n.* known as DDT, a white powder orig. used to kill lice and thus prevent the spread of typhus; effective also against other insects, but having long-term disadvantages.

dichotomy *dik-* or *dīk-ot′ə-mi*, *n.* a division into two strongly contrasted groups or classes: repeated branching.—*v.t.* and *v.i.* **dichot′omise, -ize.**—*n.* **dichot′omist.**—*adj.* **dichot′omous.**—*adv.* **dichot′o-mously.** [Gr. *dichotomiā—dicha*, in two, *tomē*, a cut—*temnein*, to cut.]

dichroism *dī′krō-izm*, *n.* the property of showing different colours exhibited by doubly refracting crystals when viewed in different directions by transmitted light.—*adjs.* **dichro′ic, dichroit′ic.** [Gr. *dichroos*, two-coloured—*di-*, twice, *chroā*, colour.]

dichromate *dī-krō′māt*, a salt of **dichro′mic acid** ($H_2Cr_2O_7$) containing two chromium atoms.—Also **bichro′mate.** [Pfx. **di-, chromate.**]

dichromatic *dī-krō-mat′ik*, *adj.* having two colours, esp. in different individuals of the same species: able to see two colours and two only, as in red-green colour-blind persons who see only blue and yellow.—*n.* a person of dichromatic vision.—*n.* **dichro′matism.**—*adj.* **dichro′mic** dichroic: dichromatic. [Gr. *di-*, twice, *chrōma, -atos*, colour.]

dichromic. See (1) **dichromate**; (2) **dichromatic.**

Dick (also without *cap.*) *dik*, (*slang*) *n.* a man: detective: (without *cap.*) a penis (*vulg.*).—**clever Dick** one who thinks himself to be cleverer than he is. [*Dick*, for Richard.]

dickens *dik′ənz*, *n.* the deuce, the devil, as in *what the dickens, play the dickens.* [App. *Dickon*, Richard, as a substitute for **devil.**]

Dickensian *dik-en′zi-ən*, *adj.* pertaining to Charles *Dickens* (1812–70), the novelist: pertaining to conditions, esp. squalid social or working conditions, like those described in his novels.

dicker *dik′ər*, (*U.S.*) *n.* haggling, bargaining: petty trade by barter, etc.—*v.i.* to haggle: to hesitate, dither. [Prob. the obs. *dicker*, the number ten, esp. of hides or skins.—L. *decuria*.]

dickey, dicky *dik′i*, *n.* a leathern apron for a gig, etc.: the driver's seat in a carriage: a seat at the back of a carriage: a folding seat at the back of a motor-car: a false shirt-front. [perh. from *dick*, a dial. Eng. word for a leathern apron; perh. Du. *dek*, a cover.]

dicky-bird *dik′i-bûrd*, *n.* a small bird (*childish*): a word (*rhyming slang*). [*Dick*, for Richard.]

dicky *dik′i*, (*coll.*) *adj.* shaky: not in good condition.

diclinous *dī′kli-nəs*, or *-klī′*, *adj.* having the stamens and pistils in separate flowers, whether on the same or on different plants.—*n.* **di′clinism.** [Gr. *di-*, twice, double, *klīnē*, a bed.]

dicotyledon *dī-kot-i-lē′dən*, *n.* a plant having embryos with two cotyledons.—*adj.* **dicotylē′donous.** [Gr. *di-*, twice, and **cotyledon.**]

dicrotic *dī-krot′ik*, *adj.* of the pulse, having two beats to one beat of the heart.—Also **dī′crotous.**—*n.* **dī′crotism.** [Gr. *di-*, twice, double, and *krotos*, beat.]

dicta. See **dictum.**

Dictaphone® *dik′tə-fōn*, *n.* a recording apparatus for dictating letters, etc. [L. *dictāre*, to dictate, Gr. *phōnē*, sound.]

dictate *dik-tāt'*, formerly *dik'tāt*, *v.t.* to say or read for another to write: to lay down with authority: to command.—*v.i.* to give orders: to behave dictatorially.—*n.* (*dik'tāt*) an order, rule, direction: impulse. —*ns.* **dicta'tion** act, art, or practice of dictating: speaking or reading of words for a pupil, amanuensis, etc., to write: overbearing command; **dicta'tor** one invested with absolute authority—originally an extraordinary Roman magistrate: one who, or that which, dictates.—*adj.* **dictatorial** (*dik-tə-tō'ri-əl*, *-tō'*) like a dictator: absolute: overbearing.—*adv.* **dictato'rially.** —*n.* **dicta'torship.**—*adj.* **dic'tatory.** [L. *dictāre*, *-ātum*, freq. of *dīcĕre*, to say.]

diction *dik'shən*, *n.* a saying or speaking· manner of speaking or expressing: choice of words: style: (*U.S.*) enunciation. [L *dictio*, *-ōnis*—*dīcĕre*, *dictum*, to say.]

dictionary *dik'shən-ə-ri*,*n* book containing the words of a language alphabetically arranged, with their meanings, etymology, etc.. a lexicon: a work containing information on any department of knowledge, alphabetically arrañged. [L.L. *dictiōnārium.*]

Dictograph® *dik'tō-graf*, *n.* a telephone for transmitting speech from room to room, with or without the speaker's knowledge. [L. *dictum*, thing said, Gr. *graphein*, to write.]

dictum *dik'təm*, *n.* something said: a saying: an authoritative saying:—*pl* **dic'ta.** [L.]

did did, *pa.t.* of **do.**

didactic, -al *di-dak'tik*, *-əl*, *dī-*, *adjs.* fitted or intended to teach: instructive: preceptive.—*adv* **didac'tically.** —*n.* **didac'ticism** (*-sizm*).—*n. sing.* **didactics** the art or science of teaching. [Gr. *didaktikos*—*didaskein*, to teach; akin to L. *docēre*, *discĕre*.]

didapper *dī'dap-ər*, *n.* the dabchick or little grebe: one who disappears and bobs up again. [dive and dapper, a variant of **dipper**; cf. O.E. *dūfedoppa*, pelican.]

didascalic *did-as-kal'ik*, *adj.* didactic. [Gr. *didask-alikos*—*didaskalos*, teacher.]

didder *did'ər*, (*dial.*) *v.i.* to shake. [See **dither.**]

did(d)icoy, -coi *did'i-koi*, *n.* an itinerant tinker or scrap-dealer, not a true gypsy. [Romany.]

diddle *did'l*, *v.t.* to cajole, swindle.—*n.* **didd'ler.**

didgeridoo *did'jər-i-dōō'*, *n.* an Australian aboriginal musical instrument, consisting of a very long tube.

dido *dī'dō*, (*slang*) *n.* an antic, caper: a frivolous or mischievous act:—*pl.* **di'does, di'dos.** [Origin unknown.]

didymium *di-* or *dī-dim'i-əm*, *n.* a supposed element discovered in 1841, later resolved into neodymium and praseodymium. [Gr. *didymos*, twin, from its constant association with *lanthanum.*]

didymous *did'i-məs*, *adj.* twin: twinned: growing in pairs:- composed of two parts slightly connected [Gr. *didymos*, twin.]

die¹ *dī*, *v.i.* (or *v.t.* with object *death*) to lose life: to perish: to wither: hyperbolically, to languish, suffer, or long, be very eager: to become insensible: to merge: —*pr.p.* **dy'ing;** *pa.t.* and *pa.p.* **died** *dīd*.—*adj.* **die'-away** languishing.—**die'-hard** an irreconcilable conservative.—**die away** to disappear by degrees, become gradually inaudible; **die back** (*bot.*) to die by degrees from the tip backwards (*n* **die'back**); **die down** to subside: to die above ground, leaving only roots or rootstocks; **die game** to keep up one's spirit to the last; **die hard** to struggle hard against death, to be long in dying: to be difficult to suppress or eradicate; **die off** to die quickly or in large numbers; **die out** to become extinct, to disappear; **die the death** (*theat slang*) to arouse no response from one's audience; **never say die** never give up.—See also **dying.** [Prob from a lost O.E. (Anglian) *dēgan*, but commonly referred to a Scand. root seen in O.N *deyja, doyja*]

die² *dī*, *n.* (*also* **dice** *dīs*) a small cube with faces numbered or otherwise distinguished, thrown in gaming, etc.: (*also* **dice**) a small cubical piece: (*also* **dice**) hazard: a stamp for impressing coin, etc.: applied to various tools for shaping things by stamping or cutting: —*pl.* (gaming, cookery, and the like) **dice;** (stamping and shaping) **dies** (*dīz*).—*v.i.* **dice** to play with dice.— *v.t.* to cut into dice: to chequer:—*pr.p.* **dic'ing;** *pa.t.* and *pa.p.* **diced.**—*adj* **dic'ey** (*coll.*) risky: tricky: uncertain in result.—*v.t.* **die'-cast** to shape (metal or plastic) by casting in a metal mould.—*ns.* **die'-casting;** **die'-sink'er; die'-sink'ing** the engraving of dies for embossing, etc.—**no dice** no answer, or a negative answer: no success; **straight as a die** (i.e. a gaming die; *fig.*) completely honest; **the die is cast** an irrevocable step has been taken: there is no turning back now. [O.F.L. *de*, pl. *dez*, from L.L. *dadus* = L. *datus*, given or cast.]

dielectric *dī-i-lek'trik*, *adj.* non-conducting: transmitting electric effects without conducting.—*n* a substance, solid, liquid or gas, capable of supporting an electric stress, and hence an insulator.—**dielectric constant** relative permittivity (see **permit**); **dielectric heating** the heating of a non-conducting substance as a result of loss of power in dielectric. [Gr. *dia*, through, and **electric.**]

dieresis. Same as **diaeresis.**

dies *dī'ēz*, *dē'ās*, (L.) *n.* day:—*pl.* **dies.**—**dies irae** (*īr'ē*, *ēr'ī*) the day of wrath: the day of judgment (from a Latin hymn); **dies non** (*non, nōn*) a day on which judges do not sit, or one on which normal business is not transacted.

diesel *dēz'l*, *n.* a diesel engine: a locomotive, train, etc., driven by a diesel engine: diesel oil.—**diesel engine** a compression-ignition engine in which the oil fuel is introduced into the heated compressed-air charge as a jet of liquid under high pressure; **diesel oil** heavy fuel oil used in diesel engines. [Rudolph *Diesel* (1858–1913), German engineer.]

diesis *dī'i-sis*, *n.* the difference between a major and a minor semitone (*mus.*): the double-dagger (‡) (*print.*):—*pl.* **dieses** (*-sēz*) [Gr. *diesis*, a quarter-tone.]

diet¹ *dī'ət*, *n.* mode of living, now only with especial reference to food: planned or prescribed selection of food.—*v.t.* to prescribe a diet for, put on a diet.—*v.i.* to take food according to rule.—*adj.* **di'etary** pertaining to diet or the rules of diet.—*n.* course of diet: allowance of food, esp. in large institutions.—*n.* **di'eter.**—*adjs.* **dietet'ic, -al** pertaining to diet.—*adv.* **dietet'ically.**—*n. sing.* **dietet'ics** the study of, or rules for regulating, diet.—*n.* **dietitian, -cian** (*-ish'ən*) an authority on diet. [Fr. *diète*—L.L. *diaeta*—Gr. *diaita*, mode of living, diet.]

diet² *dī'ət*, *n.* a national, federal, or provincial assembly, council, or parliament: a conference: the proceedings under a criminal libel (*Scots law*). [O.Fr. *diete*— L.L. *diēta*—Gr. *diaita*; or from L. *diēs*, a (set) day.]

differ *dif'ər*, *v.i.* to be unlike, distinct, or various (used by itself, or followed by *from*): to disagree (with *with*, sometimes *from*).—*ns.* **diff'erence** dissimilarity: the quality distinguishing one thing from another: a contention or quarrel: the excess of one quantity or number over another: differentia: a distinguishing mark: a modification to distinguish the arms of a branch from those of the main line (*her.*).—*adj.* **diff'erent** distinct: separate: unlike: not the same (with *from*, also *to*): out of the ordinary (*slang*): novel. —*n.* **differentia** (*-en'shi-ə*; L.) in logic, that property which distinguishes a species from others:—*pl.* **differen'tiae** (*-ē*).—*adj.* **differen'tial** (*-shəl*) constituting or pertaining to a difference or differentia: discriminating: pertaining to infinitesimal differences (*math.*).—*n.* an infinitesimal difference: a differential gear: a price or wage difference.—*adv.* **differen'tially.**—*v.t.* **differentiate** (*-en'shi-āt*) to make different, cause to develop difference(s): to classify as different: to constitute a difference between: to obtain the differential coefficient of (*math.*).—*v.i.* become different by specialisation: to distinguish (*from, between*).—*ns.* **differentia'tion** the act of distinguishing: description of a thing by giving its differentia: a change by which what was generalised or homogeneous became specialised or heterogeneous: the act or process of differentiating, or determining the ratio of the rates of change of two quantities one of which is a function of the other (*math.*); **differen'tiator.**—*adv.* **diff'erently; differential calculus** see **calculus; differential coefficient** the ratio of the rate of change of a function to that of its independent variable; **differential equation** one involving total or partial differential coefficients; **differential gear** a gear permitting relative rotation of two shafts driven by a third; **differential motion** a mechanical movement in which the velocity of a driven part is equal to the difference of the velocities of two parts connected to it. [L. *differre—dif-* (for *dis-*), apart, *ferre*, to bear.]

difficult *dif'i-kəlt, adj.* not easy: hard to be done: requiring labour and pains: hard to please: not easily persuaded: unmanageable.—*adv.* **diff'icultly** (mainly *chem.*).—*n.* **diff'iculty** quality or fact of being difficult: laboriousness: obstacle: objection: that which cannot be easily understood or believed: embarrassment of affairs: a quarrel.—**make difficulties** to be hard to please: to make objections. [The adj. was formed from *difficulty*—L. *difficultās—dif-ficilis—dis-*, neg., and *facilis*, easy.]

diffident *dif'i-dənt, adj.* distrusting: wanting in self-confidence.—*n.* **diff'idence.**—*adv.* **diff'idently.** [L. *diffīdere*, to distrust—*dis-*, neg., *fīdere*, to trust.]

diffract *di-frakt', v.t.* to break up: to subject to diffraction.—*n.* **diffrac'tion** the spreading of light or other rays passing through a narrow opening or by the edge of an opaque body or reflected by a grating, etc , with interference phenomena, coloured and other.—*adj.* **diffrac'tive.**—*ns.* **diffractom'eter** an instrument used in examination of the atomic structure of matter by means of diffraction of X-rays, electrons, or neutrons. [L. *diffringěre, diffráctum—dis-*, asunder, *frangěre*, to break.]

diffuse *di-fūz', v.t.* to pour out all round: to send out in all directions: to scatter: to circulate: to publish.—*v.i.* to spread.—*ns.* **diffus'er; diffusibil'ity.**—*adj* **diffus'ible.**—*ns.* **diffu'sion** a spreading or scattering abroad: extension: distribution: mixture through each other of gases or liquids in contact: spread of cultural elements from one region or community to another (*anthrop.*).—*adj.* **diffu'sive** (*-siv*).—*adv.* **diffu'sively.**—*ns.* **diffu'siveness; diffusiv'ity.**—**diffused lighting** lighting that, being evenly distributed, produces no glare. [L. *diffunděre, diffūsum—dif-* (*dis-*), asunder, *funděre*, to pour out.]

diffuse *di-fūs', adj.* diffused: widely spread: wordy: not concise.—*adv.* **diffuse'ly.**—*n.* **diffuse'ness.** [Root as above]

dig *dig, v.t.* to excavate: to turn up with a spade or otherwise. to get or put by digging: to poke or thrust: to understand, approve (*slang*).—*v.i.* to use a spade. to seek (for) by digging (*lit.* and *fig.*): to burrow: to mine: to lodge (*slang*): to study hard (*U.S. slang*):—*pr.p.* **digg'ing;** *pa t.* and *pa.p.* **dug.**—*n.* an act or course of digging: an archaeological excavating expedition: an excavation made by archaeologists: a poke: a taunt.—*adj.* **digg'able.**—*ns.* **digg'er** a person or animal that digs: a miner, esp. a gold-miner: an

Australian or New Zealander (*slang*): a machine for digging.—*n.pl.* **digg'ings** places where mining is carried on, esp. for gold: lodgings, rooms (abbrev **digs;** *slang*.).—**digg'er-wasp** a burrowing wasp of various kinds.—**dig in** to cover over by digging to work hard: to begin eating (*coll.*); **dig oneself in** to entrench oneself: to establish oneself in a position; **dig one's heels in** to refuse to be moved or persuaded; **dig out** to unearth (*lit.* or *fig.*); **dig up** to remove from the ground by digging: to excavate: to obtain by seeking (*coll*). [Prob. O.Fr. *diguer*, to dig; of Gmc. origin]

digamma *dī-gam'ə, n* vau, the obsolete sixth letter (F, C. later ç) of the Greek alphabet with the sound of our *w.* [Gr. *di-*, twice, and *gamma*, from its form like one capital Γ over another.]

digastric *dī-gas'trik, adj* fleshy at each end, as one of the muscles of the lower jaw. [Gr *di-*, double, *gastēr*, the belly.]

digest *di-jest'* (also *dī-*), *v.t* to dissolve in the stomach: to soften by heat and moisture: to distribute and arrange: to prepare or classify in the mind: to think over, to take in gradually, the meaning and implications of.—*v.i.* to be dissolved in the stomach. to be softened by heat and moisture.—*ns.* **digest'er** a vessel in which strong extracts are made from animal and vegetable substances; **digestibil'ity.**—*adj.* **digest'ible** that may be digested.—*n.* **digestion** (*di-jest'yən*) the dissolving of the food in the stomach: orderly arrangement: exposing to slow heat, etc.—*adj.* **digest'ive** pertaining to digestion: promoting digestion.—*n.* something which promotes digestion: (also **digestive biscuit**) a round, semi-sweet biscuit, the basic ingredient of which is meal.—*adv.* **digest'ively.** [L. *digerěre, digestum*, to carry asunder or dissolve.]

digest *dī'jest, n.* a body of laws collected and arranged, esp. the Justinian code of civil laws: a synopsis: an abstract: a periodical abstract of news or current literature [L. *digesta*, neut. pl. of *digestus*, pa.p. of *dīgerěre*, to carry apart, to arrange.]

dight *dīt, v.t.* to adorn (*arch.*).—*adj.* disposed: adorned [O.E. *dihtan*, to arrange, prescribe, from L. *dictāre*, to dictate (whence Ger. *dichten*, to write poetry).]

digit *dij'it, n.* a finger or toe: a finger's breadth or ¾ inch: a figure used in arithmetic to represent a number.—*adj.* **dig'ital** pertaining to the fingers, or to arithmetical digits: showing numerical information by a set of digits to be read off, instead of by a pointer on a dial, etc.: of continuous data (e.g. sound signals), separated into discrete units to facilitate transmission, processing, etc.—*ns.* **digitalin** (*dij-i-tā'lin*) a glucoside or mixture of glucosides got from foxglove; **Digita'lis** the foxglove genus: dried foxglove leaves used as a drug.—*adjs.* **dig'itate, -d** consisting of several finger-like sections.—*adv.* **dig'itately.**—*n.* **digita'tion** finger-like arrangement: a finger-like division.—*adjs.* **digit'iform** formed like fingers; **dig'itigrade** walking on the toes.—*n.* an animal that walks on its toes.—*v.t.* **dig'itise, -ize** to put (data) into digital form, e.g. for use in a digital computer.—*n.* **dig'itiser, -z-.**—**digital clock, watch** a clock, watch, without a conventional face, on which the time is indicated directly by numbers; **digital computer** an electronic calculating machine using arithmetical digits, generally binary or decimal notation; **digital disc, tape** a gramophone record or length of magnetic tape recorded from a digital sound signal. [L. *digitus*, finger, toe.]

diglot *dī'glot, adj.* bilingual.—*n.* a bilingual person or book. [Gr. *diglōttos—di-*, double, *glōtta*, tongue.]

dignify *dig'ni-fī, v.t.* to invest with honour: to exalt: to lend an air of dignity to:—*pr p.* **dig'nifying;** *pa.t.* and *pa.p.* **dig'nified.**—*adj.* **dig'nified** marked or consistent with dignity: exalted: noble: grave. [L.L *dignificāre*—*dignus*, worthy, *facĕre*, to make.]

dignity *dig'ni-ti*, *n.* the state of being dignified: elevation of mind or character: grandeur of mien: elevation in rank, place, etc.: degree of excellence: preferment: high office.—*n.* **dig'nitary** one in a high position or rank, esp. in the church.—**beneath one's dignity** degrading, at least in one's own estimation; **stand on one's dignity** to assume a manner that asserts a claim to deference. [Fr. *dignité*—L. *dignitās, -ātis*—*dignus*, worthy.]

digraph *dī'gräf*, *n.* two letters expressing but one sound, as *ph* in digraph. [Gr. *di-*, twice, *graphē*, a mark, a character—*graphein*, to write.]

digress *di-gres', dī-gres', v.i.* to depart from the main subject: to introduce irrelevant matter.—*n.* **digression** (-*gresh'ən*) a going from the main point: a part of a discourse not upon the main subject.—*adjs.* **digress'ional, digress'ive.** [L. *dīgredī, dīgressus*—*dī-* (*dis-*), aside, *gradī*, to step.]

dihedral *dī-hē'drəl, adj.* bounded by two planes, or two plane faces.—*n.* a dihedral angle.—*n.* **dihē'dron** the limiting case of a double pyramid when the vertices coincide.—**dihedral angle** the angle made by the wing of an aeroplane with the horizontal axis. [Gr. *di-*, twice, *hedrā*, a seat.]

dihydric *dī-hī'drik, adj.* having two hydroxyl groups. [Pfx. **di-**.]

dikast. See dicast.

dik-dik *dik'dik, n.* a name for several very small E. African antelopes, species of *Madoqua*, etc. [Said to be a name in Ethiopia.]

dike¹, dyke *dīk, n.* a trench, or the earth dug out and thrown up: a ditch: a mound raised to prevent inundation: in Scotland, a wall: an igneous mass injected into a fissure in rocks, sometimes weathered out into wall-like forms (*geol.*): a lavatory (*slang*).—*v.t.* to provide with a dike.—*v.i.* to make a dike.—*n.* **dik'er.** [O.E. *dīc;* Du. *dijk,* Ger. *Teich,* a pond; see **dig, ditch.**]

dike², dyke *dīk,* (*slang*) *n.* a lesbian.—*adj.* **dik'ey, dyk'ey.**

diktat *dik-tàt', n.* a harsh settlement forced on the defeated or powerless: an order or statement admitting of no opposition. [Ger., something dictated.]

dilapidate *di-lap'i-dāt, v.t.* to pull down, stone from stone: to waste: to suffer to go to ruin.—*adj.* **dilap'idated** in ruins.—*ns.* **dilapida'tion** the state of ruin: (*pl.*) damage done to a building during tenancy: (*pl.*) money paid at the end of an incumbency by the incumbent for putting the parsonage, etc., in good repair; **dilap'idator.** [L. *dīlapidāre*—*dī-*, asunder, *lapis, lapidis,* a stone.]

dilate *dī-lāt', di-lāt', v.t.* to spread out in all directions: to enlarge.—*v.i.* to widen: to swell out: to speak at length.—*n.* **dilatabil'ity.**—*adj.* **dilat'able** that may be dilated or expanded.—*ns.* **dilatation** (-*lə-tā'shən*) or **dila'tion** expansion: a transformation which produces a figure similar to, but not congruent with, the original (*math.*); **dil'atator** an instrument or a muscle that expands.—*adj.* **dilat'ed** expanded and flattened.—*n.* **dilator** a dilatator: one who dilates (also **dilat'er**).—*adj.* **dilat'ive.** [L. *dīlātus* (used as pa.p. of *differre*), from *dī-* (*dis-*), apart, and *lātus,* wide.]

dilatory *dil'ə-tə-ri, adj.* slow: given to procrastination: loitering: tending to delay.—*adv.* **dil'atorily.**—*n.* **dil'atoriness.** [L. *dīlātōrius.* See **dilate.**]

dildo *dil'dō, n.* an object serving as an erect penis substitute (also **dil'doe;** *slang*):—*pl.* **dil'dos, dildoes.**

dilemma *di-, dī-lem'ə, n.* a form of argument in which the maintainer of a certain proposition is committed to accept one of two propositions each of which contradicts his original contention: a position where each of two alternative courses (or of all the feasible courses) is eminently undesirable. The argument was called a 'horned syllogism', hence the **horns of a dilemma.**—*adj.* **dilemmat'ic.** [L.,—Gr *dilēmma*—*di-*, twice, double, *lēmma,* an assumption—*lambanein,* to take.]

dilettante *dil-et-an'ti, n.* one who loves the fine arts but in a superficial way and without serious purpose: a dabbler in art, science, or literature·—*pl.* **dilettan'ti** (-*tē*).—*adj* **dilettan'tish.**—*ns.* **dilettan'tism, dilettan'teism.** [It., pr.p. of *dilettare*—L. *dēlectāre,* to delight.]

diligent *dil'i-jənt, adj.* steady and earnest in application: industrious.—*n.* **dil'igence** steady application: industry: a French or continental stage-coach (also pronounced *dē-lē-zhäs*).—*adv.* **dil'igently.** [Fr.,—*dīligēns, -entis,* pr.p. of L. *dīligēre,* to choose.]

dill *dil, n.* an umbelliferous annual akin to parsnip, the fruits or 'seeds' used as condiment and carminative.—**dill pickle** pickled cucumber flavoured with dill; **dill'water** a medicinal drink prepared from the seeds. [O.E. *dile.*]

dilly-dally *dil'i-dal'i, v t.* to loiter, trifle. [Reduplication of **dally;** cf. **shilly-shally.**]

dilute *dī-lūt' v.t.* to make thinner or more liquid: to diminish the concentration of, by mixing, esp. with water: of labour, to increase the proportion of unskilled to skilled in.—*v.i.* to become mixed.—*adj.* diminished in concentration by mixing.—*adj.* **diluent** (*dil'ū-ənt*) diluting.—*n.* that which dilutes.—*ns.* **dilut'ee** an unskilled worker introduced into a skilled occupation; **dilute'ness; dilut'er, dilut'or; dilu'tion.** [L. *dīluĕre, dīlūtum*—*dī-*, away, *luĕre,* to wash.]

diluvium *dil-ū'vi-əm, dil-ōō', n.* an inundation or flood.—*adjs.* **dilu'vial, dilu'vian** pertaining to a flood, esp. Noah's: caused by a deluge.—*n.* **dilu'vialist** one who explains geological phenomena by the flood. [L. *dīluvium,* a deluge—*dīluĕre,* to wash away.]

dim *dim, adj.* not bright or distinct: obscure: not seeing clearly: mentally dull, stupid (*coll.*).—*v.t.* to make dark: to obscure.—*v.i.* to become dim:—*pr.p.* **dimm'ing;** *pa.t.* and *pa.p.* **dimmed.**—*adv.* **dim'ly.**—*n.* **dimm'er** an arrangement for regulating the supply of light.—*adj.* **dimm'ish** somewhat dim.—*n.* **dim'ness.**—**dim'wit** (*coll.*) a stupid person.—**a dim view** (*coll.*) an unfavourable view; **dim out** to reduce the lighting (of) gradually (*n.* **dim'-out**). [O.E. *dimm;* akin to O.N. *dimmr,* dark, and Ger. *Dämmerung,* twilight.]

dime *dīm, n.* the tenth part of an American dollar, 10 cents.—**dime novel** a cheap novel, usually sensational.—**a dime a dozen** cheap, commonplace. [Fr., orig. *disme,* from L. *decima* (*pars*), a tenth (part).]

dimension *dī-* or *di-men'shən, n.* measure in length, breadth, or thickness (the three dimensions of space): scope, extent (also *fig.*): size: the sum of the indices in a term (*alg.*).—*v.t.* to give the dimensions of: to make to specified dimensions.—*adjs.* **dimen'sional** concerning dimension: in composition, of so many dimensions; **dimen'sionless.**—**dimension** work masonry in stones of specified size.—**fourth dimension** an additional dimension attributed to space: in relativity theory etc., time; **new dimension** (*fig.*) a fresh aspect; **third dimension** depth, thickness: a rounding out, completeness, given by added detail, etc. (*fig.*). [Fr.,—L *dīmēnsiō, -ōnis*—*dīmētīrī, dīmēnsus*—*dī-* (*dis-*), apart, *mētīrī,* to measure.]

dimer *dī'mər, n.* a compound whose molecule has twice as many atoms as another compound of the same empirical formula (the *monomer*)—*adj.* **dimeric**

(-*mer'ık*).—*n.* **dimerisā'tion, -z-.**—*v.t* **di'merise, -ize.** [Pfx. **di-**, and monomer.]

dimerous *dim'ə-ras*, *adj.* consisting of two parts: with two members in each whorl (*bot.*): having two-jointed tarsi (*entom.*).—*adj.* **dimeric** (*di-mer'ik*) bilaterally symmetrical: dimerous.—*n* **dimerism** (*dim'ər-ızm*). [Gr. *di-*, double, twice, and *meros*, a part.]

dimeter *dim'ı-tər*, *adj.* containing two measures.—*n.* a verse of two measures. [L.,—Gr. *dimetros—di-*, twice, *metron*, a measure.]

dimidiate *di-mid'ı-āt, adj.* divided into halves.—*n* **dimidiātion.** [L. *dīmidiāre, -ātum*, to halve—*dīmidius.*]

diminish *di-min'ısh, v.t* to make less: to take a part from: to degrade —*v.i.* to grow or appear less: to subside.—*adjs.* **dimin'ishable; dimin'ished** made smaller· humbled: of a semitone less than perfect or minor (*mus.*).—*n.* and *adj.* **dimin'ishing.**—*adv.* **dimin'ishingly.**—*n* **dimin'ishment.**—**diminished responsibility** limitation in law of criminal responsibility on ground of mental weakness or abnormality, not merely of actual insanity.—**law of diminishing returns** the fact that there is a point beyond which any additional amount of work, expenditure, taxation, etc results in progressively smaller output, profits, yields, etc. [Coined from **minish**, in imitation of L. *dīmunuēre*, to break in pieces—*minuēre*, to make less.]

diminuendo *di-min-ū-en'dō*, (*mus.*) *adj* and *adv* letting the sound die away.—Also *n.*—*pl.* **-o(e)s.** [It., —L **dēminuendus**, ger. of *dēminuēre, dēminūtum*, to lessen.]

diminution *dim-in-ū'shən*, *n.* a lessening: degradation —*adj.* **dimin'utive** of a diminished size: very small: contracted.—*n.* (*gram*) a word formed from another to express a little one of the kind.—*adv.* **dimin'utively.**—*n.* **dimin'utiveness.** [**diminish**.]

dimissory *dim'is-ə-ri, di-mis'ə-ri, adj* sending away or giving leave to depart to another jurisdiction. [L. *dīmissōrius—dīmittēre, dīmissum—dis-*, apart, *mittēre*, to send]

dimity *dim'ı-ti*, *n.* a stout white cotton, striped or figured in the loom by weaving with two threads [Gr *dimitos—di-*, twice, *mitos*, a thread.]

dimmer, dimming. See **dim.**

dimorphism *di-mor'fizm*, *n.* the occurrence of two forms in the same species (*biol.*): the property of crystallising in two forms (*chem.*).—*adjs.* **dimor'phic, dimor'phous.** [Gr. *di-*, twice, *morphē*, form.]

dimple *dim'pl*, *n.* a small hollow, esp. on the surface of the body.—*v.i* to form dimples.—*adjs.* **dim'pled; dim'ply.** [Apparently cogn with Ger. *Tumpel*, pool.]

dim sum *dim sum*, a Chinese appetiser consisting of steamed dumplings with various fillings. [Chin.]

din *din*, *n.* a loud continued noise.—*v.t.* to assail (the ears) with noise.—*pr.p.* **dinn'ing;** *pa.t.* and *pa.p.* **dinned.**—**din into** (*coll.*) to instil knowledge into (a person) by forceful repetition. [O.E. *dynn, dyne*; cf. O.N *dynr*, Dan. *don*, noise.]

dinar *dē-när'*, *n.* an ancient Arab gold coin of 65 grains' weight. the monetary unit of Yugoslavia, and of Algeria, Tunisia, Iraq, and other Arab countries. [L. *dēnārius.*]

dine *dīn, v.ı.* to take dinner.—*v.t.* to furnish with a dinner.—*ns.* **din'er** one who dines: a dining-car: a small, cheap restaurant (esp. *U.S.*); **dinette'** an alcove or other part of a room or kitchen set apart for meals —**din'er-out** one who goes much to dinner-parties; **din'ing-car** a railway carriage in which meals are served; **din'ing-hall; din'ing-room; din'ing-table.** —**dine off, on** to have as one's dinner; **dine out** to dine

elsewhere than at home, **dine out on** to be invited to dinner, or, loosely, to enjoy social success, on the strength of one's possession of e.g interesting information. [O.Fr. *disner* prob.—L. *dis-*, expressing undoing, and *jējūnus*, fasting.]

ding *ding*, *v.i.* to ring, keep sounding.—*v.t.* to reiterate to a wearisome degree.—**ding'-dong'** the sound of bells ringing: monotony: sameness: an argument or fight.—*adj.* and *adv.* like a bell ringing: keenly contested.—*v.t.* and *v.i* to ring: to nag. [Imit.]

dingbat *ding'bat*, (*U.S. slang*) *n.* something whose name one has forgotten, or does not want to use: a foolish person: a tramp: money. [Perh. **ding**, to beat, and **bat**[1].]

dinge. See **dingy.**

dinges *ding'əs*, *n.* an indefinite name for any person or thing whose name one cannot or will not remember —Also **ding'us.** [Du.,—Afrik. *ding*, thing.]

dinghy *ding'gı*, *n.* a small rowing-boat or ship's tender: an airman's collapsible rubber boat. [Hind *dingī*, a small boat.]

dingle *ding'gl*, *n.* a dell.

dingo *ding'gō*, *n.* the native dog of Australia·—*pl* **ding'oes.** [Name in obs. native dialect.]

dingus. See **dinges.**

dingy *din'jı*, *adj.* of a dim or dark colour: dull: soiled —*n* **dinge** dinginess —*v t* to make dingy.—*n.* **din'giness.**

dinkum *ding'kəm*, (*Austr slang*) *adj.* real, genuine. square, honest.—Also *adv* —Also **dink'y-di(e).** [Perh. from E. dial. *dinkum*, a fair share of work]

dinky *ding'kı*, (*coll.*) *adj.* neat: dainty. trivial, insignificant (*U S.*). [Scot. *dink*, neat.]

dinner *din'ər, n.* the chief meal of the day: a feast.—*v.i.* to dine.—**dinn'er-dance** a dance following a dinner, **dinn'er-gown** a less formal evening dress; **dinn'er-hour;** **dinn'er-jacket** a tailless dress-coat; **dinn'er-service, -set** a complete set of plates and dishes for a company at dinner; **dinn'er-table; dinn'er-time;** **dinn'er-wagon** orig. a shelved trolley for a dining-room: a sideboard in two tiers [O.Fr *disner*, prop. breakfast; see **dine.**]

dinosaur *di'nō-sor, n* any extinct (Mesozoic) reptile of the order **Dinosaur'ia** in length from two to eighty feet: a chance survivor of a type characteristic of a bygone era (*fig.*) [Gr *deinos*, terrible, *sauros*, lizard.]

dint *dint*, *n.* a blow or stroke: the mark of a blow (often **dent**): force (as in *by dint of*).—*v t.* to make a dint in. [O.E. *dynt*, a blow.]

diocese *di'ə-sis, -sēs, n.* the circuit or extent of a bishop's jurisdiction.—*adj.* **diocesan** (*di-os'i-sn, -zn*) pertaining to a diocese.—*n.* a bishop in relation to his diocese· one of the clergy in the diocese. [Through Fr and L from Gr *dioikēsis—dioikeein*, to keep house.]

diode *di'ōd*, *n.* the simplest electron tube with heated cathode and anode: a two-electrode semiconductor device evolved from primitive crystal rectifiers [Gr. *di-*, twice, *hodos*, way.]

dioecious *di-ē'shas, adj.* having the sexes separate: having male or female flowers on different plants.— *n.* **dioe'cism** (*-sizm*) [Gr. *di-*, twice, *oikos*, a house.]

Dionysia *di-ə-niz'ı-ə*, or *-nis'*, *n.pl.* dramatic and orgiastic festivals in honour of *Dionÿsos* (Bacchus), god of wine.—*adjs* **Dionys'iac; Dionys'ian.**

Diophantine *di-ə-fan'tin, adj.* pertaining to the Alexandrian mathematician *Diophantos* (*c.* A D 275).—**Diophantine equations** (*math*) indeterminate equations for which integral or rational solutions are required.

dioptric, -al *di-op'trık, -əl, adjs.* pertaining to dioptrics

or a diopter.—*n.* **diop'ter** (also **diop'tre**) a unit of
measurement of the power of a lens, the reciprocal of
the focal distances in metres, negative for a divergent
lens.—*n. sing.* **diop'trics** the part of optics that treats
of refraction [Gr *dioptrā*, a levelling instrument,
dioptron, a spyglass.]

diorama *dī-ə-rä'mə*, *n.* an exhibition of translucent pictures seen through an opening with lighting effects: a
miniature three-dimensional scene with figures: a display of e.g. a stuffed animal in a naturalistic setting: a
miniature film or television set —*adj.* **dioram'ic**.
[Gr. *dia*, through, *horāma*, a sight.]

diorite *dī'ə-rīt*, *n.* a crystalline granular igneous rock
composed of plagioclase and hornblende.—*adj.*
diorit'ic. [Gr. *diorizein*, to distinguish—*dia*,
through, *horos*, a boundary.]

dioxide *dī-ok'sīd*, *n.* an oxide with two atoms of oxygen
in the molecule. [Pfx. **di-**, **oxide**.]

dioxin *dī-ok'sin*, *n.* an extremely toxic poison found in
certain weedkillers which causes cancer, skin, liver,
and kidney disease, and birth defects.

dip *dip*, *v.t.* to immerse for a time: to lower: to lower
and raise again (as a flag): to baptise by immersion: to
lift by dipping (usu. with *up*): to dye or clean by dipping: to involve in money difficulties (*coll.*): to mortgage: to pawn.—*v.i.* to plunge and emerge: to sink: to
reach down into something: to enter slightly: to look
cursorily: to incline downwards:—*pr.p.* **dipp'ing**;
pa t. and *pa.p.* **dipped**.—*n.* the act of dipping: a hol-
low· a sag: that which is taken by dipping: inclination
downwards: a sloping: the angle a stratum of rock
makes with a horizontal plane (*geol.*): a bath: a short
swim: a liquid in which anything is dipped (as sheep,
garments, etc.): a creamy mixture into which bread,
biscuits, etc., are dipped: a candle made by dipping a
wick in tallow: a pickpocket (*slang*).—*n.* **dipp'er** one
that dips: a ladle: a bucket or scoop of a dredge or
excavator: a contrivance for directing motor-car
headlights upwards or downwards (also **dip'-switch**):
a dipping bird, the water-ouzel: a nickname for a
Baptist —**dip'-circle** or **dipp'ing-needle** an instrument for determining magnetic dip: **dip'-net** a long-
handled net for dipping up fish; **dip'-stick** a rod for
measuring depth of liquid in a sump, etc.; **dip'-switch**
see **dipper**.—**dip in** to take a share; **dip into** to put
one's hand into to remove something: to read cursorily in; **dip of the horizon** the angle of the visible
horizon below the level of the eye; **dip of the needle**
the angle a balanced magnetic needle makes with the
horizontal plane. [O.E. *dyppan*, causal of *dȳpan*, to
plunge in—*dēop*, deep; cf Dan. *dyppe*; Ger. *taufen*,
to immerse.]

diphtheria *dif-thē'ri-ə*, *n.* an infectious throat disease
in which the air-passages become covered with a
leathery membrane.—*adjs.* **diphtheric** (*-ther'ik*),
diphtheritic (*-thər-it'ik*); **diph'theroid**. [Gr.
diphtherā, leather.]

diphthong *dif'thong*, *n.* two vowel-sounds pronounced
as one syllable (as in *out*, *mind*):(loosely) a digraph:
the ligature *æ* or *œ*.—*adj.* **diphthongal** (*-thong'gəl*).—
adv. **diphthong'ally**.—*v.t.* **diph'thongise**, **-ize** (*-gīz*)
[Gr. *diphthongos*—*di-*, twice, *phthongos*, sound,
vowel.]

dipl(o)- *dip-l(ō, o)*, in composition, double.—*n.*
Diplod'ocus (Gr. *dokos*, beam, bar, from its appearance), a gigantic, quadrupedal, herbivorous dinosaur
of the sauropod group, remains of which have been
found in the Jurassic rocks of the Rocky Mountains.
—*adj* **dip'loid** (Gr *eidos*, form; *biol.*) having the full
or unreduced number of chromosomes characteristic
of the species, as in body cells: opp to *haploid*.—*n*
diploid'y. [Gr. *diploos*, double.]

diploma *di-plō'mə*, *n.* a document conferring some

honour or privilege, as a university degree, etc.—*v t.*
to furnish with a diploma.—*ns.* **diplomacy** (*di-
plō'mə-si*, or *-plo'*) the art of negotiation, esp. in relations between states: tact in management of persons
concerned in any affair; **diplomat** (*dip'lə-mat*) one
employed or skilled in diplomacy; **diplomate**
(*dip'lə-māt*) one who holds a diploma.—*n. sing.* **diplomat'ics** the science of deciphering ancient writings,
as charters, etc.—palaeography.—*adj.* **diplomat'ic**
pertaining to diplomacy: tactful and skilful in
negotiation.—*adv.* **diplomat'ically**.—*v.i.* **diplo'-
matise**, **-ize** to practice diplomacy.—*ns.* **diplo'matist**
a diplomat; **diplomatol'ogy** the study or science of
diplomatics, charters, decrees, etc.—**diplomatic bag**
a bag used for sending documents, etc., to and from
embassies, free of customs control: the contents of
such a bag; **diplomatic corps** the whole body of
foreign diplomatists resident in any capital; **diplomatic immunity** immunity from local laws and taxation enjoyed by diplomats abroad; **diplomatic relations** formal relations between states marked by the
presence of diplomats in each other's country. [L.,
—Gr. *diplōma*, a letter folded double—*diploos*,
double.]

dipolar *dī-pō'lər*, *adj.* having two poles.—*n.* **di'pole**
two equal and opposite electric charges or magnetic
poles of opposite sign a small distance apart: a body
or system having such: a type of aerial. [Pfx. **di-**.]

dippy *dip'i*, (*coll.*) *adj.* crazy: insane.

dipsomania *dip-sō-mā'ni-ə*, *n.* an intermittent morbid
craving for alcoholic stimulants.—*n.* **dipsomá'niac**
one who suffers from dipsomania.—Coll. **dip'sō**:—
pl. **dip'sos**. [Gr. *dipsa*, thirst, *maniā*, madness.]

Diptera *dip'tər-ə*, *n.pl.* two-winged insects or flies.—
adj. **dip'teral** two-winged: with double peristyle.—
ns. **dip'teran** a dipterous insect; **dip'terist** a student of
flies.—*adj.* **dip'terous** with two wings or winglike expansions. [Gr. *dipteros*, two-winged, *di-*, twice,
pteron, a wing.]

diptych *dip'tik*, *n.* a double-folding writing-tablet: a
pair of pictures as folding-tablets [Gr. *diptychos*—
di-, and *ptychē*, a tablet, a fold.]

dire *dīr*, *adj.* dreadful: calamitous in a high degree.—
adj. (poet) **dire'ful**.—*adv.* **dire'fully**.—*n.* **dire'fulness**. [L. *dirus*.]

direct *di-rekt'*, *dī'rekt*, *adj.* straight: straightforward:
by the shortest way: forward, not backward or
oblique: at right angles: immediate: without intervening agency or interposed stages: (of a dye) fixing
itself without a mordant: in the line of descent: outspoken: sincere: unambiguous: unsophisticated in
manner.—*n.* (*mus.*) an indication of the first note or
chord of next page or line.—*adv.* straight: by the
shortest way: without deviation, intervening agency
or interposed stages.—*v.t.* to keep or lay straight: to
point or aim: to point out the proper course to: to
guide: to order: to address, mark with the name and
residence of a person: to plan and superintend (the
production of a film or play).—*v.i.* to act as director:
to direct letters, etc.—*n.* **direc'tion** aim at a certain
point: the line or course in which anything moves or
on which any point lies: guidance: command: the
body of persons who guide or manage a matter: the
address, or written name and residence of a person.—
adjs. **direc'tional** relating to direction in space;
direct'ive having power or tendency to direct.—*n.* a
general instruction.—*n* **directiv'ity** the property of
being directional.—*adv* **direct'ly** in a direct manner:
without intermediary· immediately (in time and
otherwise).—*conj.* (often with *that; coll*) as soon as.
—*ns.* **direct'ness**; **direct'or** one who directs: one who
directs the shooting of a motion picture: a manager or
governor· a member of a board conducting the affairs

of a company: a counsellor: part of a machine or instrument which guides the motion:—*fem.* **direct'-ress.**—*ns.* **direct'orate** the office of director: a body of directors.—*adjs.* **directorial** (*-tô'*, *-to'*); **direct'ory** containing directions: guiding.—*n.* a body of directions: a guide: a book with the names and residences of the inhabitants of a place: a body of directors: (with *cap.*) the *Directoire*, or French Republican government of 1795–99.—*ns.* **direc'torship; direct'-rix** a line serving to describe a conic section, which is the locus of a point whose distances from focus and directrix have a constant ratio:—*pl.* **directrices** (*-trī'sēz*).—**direct access** same as **random access; direct action** coercive methods of attaining industrial or political ends as opposed to pacific, parliamentary, or political action; **direct current** an electric current flowing in one direction only; **direct debiting** an arrangement by which a creditor can claim payment direct from the payer's account; **direct drilling** the ploughing and sowing of a field in one operation; **directional aerial** one that can receive or transmit radio waves in one direction only; **direc'tion-finder** a wireless receiver that determines the direction of arrival of incoming waves; **direct labour** labour employed directly, not through a contractor; **direct method** a method of teaching a foreign language through speaking it, without translation, and without formal instruction in grammar; **direct object** word or group of words denoting that upon which the action of a transitive verb is directed; **direct'or-gen'eral** a chief administrator of a usu. non-commercial organisation; **direct speech** speech reported as spoken, in the very words of the speaker (L. *ōrātiō rēcta*); **direct tax** one levied directly from those on whom its burden falls.—**direct-grant school** until 1979, a fee-paying school which received a state grant on condition that it took a specified number of non-fee-paying pupils. [L. *dīrigĕre, dīrēctum—dī-*, apart, *regĕre,* to rule.]

Directoire dē-rek-twär, *n.* the French Directorate of 1795–99.—*adj.* after the fashion in dress or furniture then prevailing: of knickers, knee-length, with elastic at waist and knee. [Fr.; see **direct.**]

dirge dûrj, *n.* a funeral song or hymn: a slow and mournful piece of music. [Contracted from *dirige* (imper. of L. *dīrigĕre,* to direct), the first word of an antiphon sung in the office for the dead.]

dirham dûr-ham', *də-ram', dē'ram, n.* the monetary unit of Morocco: a coin equal to this in value: a coin used in several N. African and Middle Eastern countries, with varying value. [Ar., Pers., and Turk. forms of the Greek *drachmē,* a drachma or dram.]

dirigible dir'i-ji-bl, *-rij', adj.* that can be directed.—*n.* a navigable balloon or airship.—*adj.* **dir'igent** directing. [See **direct.**]

dirigism(e) dē-rēzh-ēzm', *n.* control by the State in economic and social spheres.—*adj.* **dirigiste** (*-ēst'*). [Fr.,—It *dirigismo.*]

diriment dir'i-mənt, *adj.* nullifying. [L. *dirimĕre.*]

dirk dûrk, *n.* a Highland dagger: a side-arm worn by midshipmen and naval cadets (*hist.*).

dirndl dûrn'dl, *n.* an Alpine peasant woman's dress with close-fitting bodice and full skirt: an imitation of this, esp. a full skirt with a tight, often elasticated, waistband. [Ger. dial., dim. of *dirne,* girl.]

dirt dûrt, *n.* any filthy substance, such as dung, mud, etc.: foreign matter adhering to anything: loose earth: rubbish: obscenity: spiteful gossip.—*adv.* **dirt'ily.**—*n.* **dirt'iness.**—*adj.* **dirt'y** foul, filthy: stormy: obscene: unclean in thought or conversation: despicable: mean: sordid: dishonest, treacherous.—*v.t.* to soil with dirt: to sully:—*pr.p.* **dirt'ying;** *pa t* and *pa.p.* **dirt'ied.**—*adj.* **dirt'-cheap'** cheap as dirt, very cheap.—**dirt'-road** (*U.S.*) a soft road, unpaved

and unmacadamised; **dirt'-track** a motor-cycling racing-track, with earthy or cindery surface; **dirty bomb** one that produces a large amount of radioactive contamination, **dirty dog** (*slang*) a dishonest or contemptible person; **dirty look** (*coll*) a threatening or malevolent look, **dirty money** money earned by base means: in dock labour, extra pay for unloading offensive cargo: extra pay for any unpleasant, dirty, etc task; **dirty trick** a dishonest or despicable act; **dirty word** an obscene word· a word for something, as a feeling, principle, or belief, that is regarded with disfavour at the present time; **dirty work** work that dirties the hands or clothes: dishonourable practices, esp. undertaken on behalf of another: foul play.—**dirty old man** (*coll.*) a man whose sexual aspirations and actions are considered appropriate only to a younger man; **do the dirty on** to play a low trick on, cheat; **eat dirt** submissively to acquiesce in a humiliation; **throw dirt** to besmirch a reputation. [M.E. *drit,* prob. O.N. *drit,* excrement.]

dis-, di-, *dis-, di-, pfx.* (1) meaning in two, asunder, apart: (2) meaning 'not' or a reversal: (3) indicating a removal or deprivation: (4) used intensively. [L. *dis-, dī-.*]

disable dis-ā'bl, *v.t.* to deprive of power: to weaken: to cripple, incapacitate: to disqualify.—*adj.* **disā'bled.**—*ns.* **disā'blement; disābil'ity** want of power: want of legal qualification: a disqualification: a handicap, esp. physical. [Pfx **dis-** (2).]

disabuse dis-ə-būz', *v.t.* to undeceive or set right. [Pfx. **dis-** (2).]

disaccord dis-ə-kord', to be at discord. [Pfx. **dis-** (2).]

disadvantage dis-əd-vant'ij, *n* unfavourable circumstance or condition: loss: damage.—*adj.* **disadvan'-taged** deprived of the resources and privileges, usu social, enjoyed by the majority of people: in unfavourable conditions relative to other (specified) people; **disadvantageous** (*dis-ad-vant-ā'jəs*) attended with disadvantage: unfavourable.—*adv.* **disadvantā'geously.**—*n.* **disadvantā'geousness.** [Pfx. **dis-** (2).]

disaffect dis-ə-fekt', *v.t.* to take away the affection of: to make discontented or unfriendly:—*pa.p.* and *adj.* **disaffect'ed** ill-disposed: tending to break away.—*adv.* **disaffect'edly.**—*ns.* **disaffect'edness; disaffec'-tion** the state of being disaffected: want of affection or friendliness: alienation: ill-will: political discontent or disloyalty. [Pfx. **dis-** (3).]

disaffiliate dis-ə-fil'i-āt, *v.t.* and *v.t.* to end an affiliation (to): to separate oneself (from).—*n.* **disaffiliā'-tion.** [Pfx. **dis-** (2).]

disaffirm dis-ə-fûrm', *v.t.* to contradict: to repudiate. —*n.* **disaffirmā'tion** (*dis-a-*). [Pfx. **dis-** (2).]

disafforest dis-ə-for'ist, *v.t.* to bring out of the operation of forest laws: to clear of forest, disforest —*ns.* **disafforestā'tion, disaffor'estment.** [L. *dis-,* reversal, and L.L. *afforestāre,* to make into a forest.]

disagree dis-ə-grē', *v.i.* to differ or be at variance: to dissent: to quarrel: to prove unsuitable or a source of annoyance, as of food disagreeing with the stomach. —*adj.* **disagree'able** not amicable: unpleasant: offensive.—*ns.* **disagree'ableness, disagreeabil'ity.**—*n.pl.* **disagree'ables** annoyances.—*adv* **disagree'ably.**—*n.* **disagree'ment** want of agreement: difference: unsuitableness: dispute. [Pfx. **dis-** (2).]

disallow dis-ə-low', *v.t.* not to allow: to refuse to sanction: to deny the authority, validity, or truth of: to reject, to forbid.—*adj.* **disallow'able.**—*n.* **disallow'ance.** [Pfx. **dis-** (2).]

disappear dis-ə-pēr', *v.i.* to vanish from sight.—*n.* **disappear'ance** a ceasing to be in sight: removal from sight, flight, secret withdrawal. [Pfx. **dis-** (3).]

disappoint dis-ə-point', *v.t.* to frustrate the hopes or expectations of: to defeat the fulfilment of.—*v.i.* to cause disappointment.—*adjs.* **disappoint'ed** balked: frustrated; **disappoint'ing** causing disappointment.— *n.* **disappoint'ment** the defeat of one's hopes or expectations: frustration: the vexation accompanying failure. [O.Fr. *desapointer, des-* (L. *dis-*), away, and *apointer*, to appoint.]

disapprobation *dis-ap-rō-bā'shən, n.* disapproval.— *adjs.* **disapp'robative, disapp'robatory.** [Pfx. **dis-** (2).]

disapprove *dis-ə-prōō'v', v.t.* and *v.i.* to give or have an unfavourable opinion (of): to reject.—*n.* **disapprov'al.**—*adv.* **disapprov'ingly.** [Pfx. **dis-** (2).]

disarm *dis-arm', v.t* to deprive of arms: to strip of armour: to render defenceless: to deprive of the power of hurt: to conciliate (*fig.*): to deprive of suspicion or hostility: to reduce to a peace footing.— *v.i.* to disband troops, reduce national armaments.— *n.* **disarm'ament.**—*adj.* **disarm'ing** charming. [Pfx. **dis-** (3).]

disarrange *dis-ə-rānj', v.t.* to undo the arrangement of: to disorder: to derange.—*n.* **disarrange'ment.** [Pfx. **dis-** (2).]

disarray *dis-ə-rā', v.t.* to break the array of: to throw into disorder.—*n.* want of array or order. [Pfx. **dis-** (2), (3).]

disarticulate *dis-är-tik'ūl-āt, v.t.* to separate the joints of.—*v.i.* to separate at a joint.—*n.* **disarticulā'tion.** [Pfx. **dis-** (1).]

disassemble *dis-ə-sem'bl, v.t.* to take apart.—*n.* **dis-assem'bly.** [Pfx. **dis-** (1).]

disassociate *dis-ə-sō'shi-āt, v.t.* (with *from*) to disconnect: to dissociate.—*n.* **disassociā'tion.** [Pfx. **dis-** (2).]

disaster *diz-às'tər, n.* an adverse or unfortunate event: a great and sudden misfortune: calamity.—*adj.* **disas'trous** calamitous, ruinous: gloomy, foreboding disaster.—*adv.* **disas'trously.—disaster area** an area in which there has been a disaster (e.g. flood, explosion), requiring special official aid: loosely, any place where a misfortune has happened: anything which is untidy, ugly, disadvantageous, etc. (*coll.*). [O.Fr. *desastre*—L *dis-*, with evil sense, *astrum*, star.]

disattune *dis-ə-tūn', v.t.* to put out of harmony. [Pfx. **dis-** (2).]

disavow *dis-ə-vow', v.t.* to disclaim knowledge of, or connection with: to disown: to deny.—*n.* **disavow'al.** [O.Fr. *desavouer, des-*, away, *avouer,* to avow.]

disband *dis-band', v t* to disperse, break up, esp. of troops.—*v.i.* to break up —*n* **disband'ment.** [O.Fr. *desbander,* to unbind, *des-*, reversal, *bander,* to tie]

disbar *dis-bär', v.t.* to expel from the bar.—*n.* **disbar'-ment.** [Pfx. **dis-** (3).]

disbelieve *dis-bə-lēv', v.t* to believe to be false: to refuse belief or credit to.—*v.i.* to have no faith (*in*).— *ns.* **disbelief'; disbeliev'er.** [Pfx. **dis-** (2).]

disbench *dis-bench', -bensh', v.t.* to deprive of the privilege of a bencher (e.g. in the Inns of Court). [Pfx. **dis-** (3).]

disbud *dis-bud', v.t.* to remove buds from. [Pfx. **dis-** (3).]

disburden *dis-bûr'dn, vs t.* to rid of a burden: to free. to unload, discharge. [Pfx. **dis-** (3).]

disburse *dis-bûrs', v t.* to pay out.—*ns.* **disburs'al, disburse'ment** a paying out: that which is paid. [O.Fr. *desbourser, des-* (L *dis-*), apart, and *bourse,* a purse.]

disc, disk *disk, n.* a quoit thrown by ancient Greek athletes: any flat thin circular body or structure: a circular figure, as that presented by the sun, moon, and planets: the enlarged torus of a flower a layer of

fibrocartilage between vertebrae, the slipping of which (*slipped disc*) causes pressure on spinal nerves and hence pains: a gramophone record: a disc file (*comput.*).—*adjs.* **disc'oid, discoid'al.**—*ns* **discog'-raphy** collection, description, etc , of gramophone records: the history or description of musical recording: a list of recordings by one composer or performer; **discog'rapher; disc'ophile** (*-ō-fīl*) one who makes a study of and collects gramophone records; **diskette** (*dis-ket'*) (*comput.*) a storage device in the form of a small disc.—**disc brake** one in which the friction is obtained by pads hydraulically forced against a disc on the wheel; **disc file, store** (*comput.*) a random access device consisting of discs coated with magnetisable material, on which data is stored in tracks; **disc'-harr'ow, -plough** a harrow, or plough, in which the soil is cut by inclined discs; **disc'-jockey** a person who introduces and plays records (esp. of popular music) on a radio or television programme, etc.; **disc parking** a system according to which the motorist himself is responsible for affixing to his car special disc(s) showing his time of arrival and the time when permitted parking ends; **disc player** a machine for playing videodiscs. [Gr. *diskos.*]

discalced *dis-kalst', adj.* without shoes, bare-footed, as a branch of the Carmelite order.—*n.* and *adj.* **discal'ceate.** [L. *discalceātus—dis-*, neg., and *calceus,* a shoe.]

discapacitate *dis-kə-pas'i-tāt, v.t.* to incapacitate. [Pfx. **dis-** (2).]

discard *dis-kärd', v.t.* and *v.i.* to throw away, as not needed or not allowed by the game, said of cards: in whist, etc., to throw down a (useless) card of another suit when one cannot follow suit and cannot or will not trump: to reject.—*n.* (also *dis'*) the act of discarding: the card or cards thrown out of the hand: abandonment: a cast-off, anything discarded. [Pfx. **dis-** (3)]

discern *di-sûrn', -zûrn', v.t.* to make out: to distinguish by the eye or understanding.—*n.* **discern'er.**—*adj.* **discern'ible.**—*adv.* **discern'ibly.**—*adj.* **discern'ing** discriminating, acute.—*n.* **discern'ment** power or faculty of discriminating: judgment: acuteness. [L. *discernēre—dis-*, thoroughly, and *cernēre,* to sift, perceive.]

discharge *dis-chärj', v t.* to free from or relieve of a charge of any kind (burden, explosive, electricity, liability, accusation, etc.): to set free: to acquit: to dismiss: to fire (as a gun): to eject: to pour out: to emit or let out: to perform: to pay: to give account for: to distribute (as weight).—*v.i.* to unload: to become released from a charged state: to allow escape of contents: to flow away or out.—*n.* (also *dis'*) the act of discharging: release from a charge of any kind: unloading: liberation: acquittal: dismissal: outflow: rate of flow: emission: payment: performance: that which is discharged.—*ns* **discharg'er** one who discharges: an apparatus for discharging, esp. electricity: apparatus for firing an explosive.—**dis-charge'-tube** a tube in which an electric discharge takes place in a vacuum or in a gas at low pressure. [O.Fr. *descharger—des-*, apart, *charger;* see **charge.**]

disciple *dis-ī'pl, n.* one who professes to receive instruction from another: one who follows or believes in the doctrine of another: a follower, esp. one of the twelve apostles of Christ.—*n.* **disci'pleship.** [Fr.,— L *discipulus,* from *discēre,* to learn: akin to *docēre,* to teach]

discipline *dis'i-plin, n.* instruction: a branch of learning, or field of study: a branch of sport· training, or mode of life in accordance with rules: subjection to control: severe training: mortification: punishment —*v t* to subject to discipline· to train: to educate, to bring under control: to chastise.—*adjs.* **disc'iplinable; disc'iplinal** (or *-plī'*).—*n.* **disciplinā'rian** one who enforces strict discipline.—*adj.* **disc'iplinary** of the nature of discipline.—*n.* **disc'ipliner.** [L. *disciplina,* from *discipulus*]

disclaim *dis-klām',* *v.t.* to renounce all claim to: to refuse to acknowledge or be responsible for: to repudiate: to reject: to cry out against the claim of.—*v.i* to make a disclaimer.—*n.* **disclaim'er** a denial, disavowal, or renunciation. [O Fr. *disclaimer*—L. *dis-,* apart, *clāmāre,* to cry out.]

disclose *dis-klōz',* *v.t.* to lay open: to bring to light. to reveal.—*n.* **disclō'sure** (*-zhər*) act of disclosing: that which is disclosed or revealed. [O.Fr. *desclos*—L. *dis-,* apart, *claudēre, clausum,* to shut]

disco *dis'kō, n.* short for **discothèque:**—*pl.* **dis'cos.**— *adj.* suitable, or specially produced, for discothèques, as **disco dancing, disco dress, disco music.**

discobolus *dis-kob'ə-ləs, n.* a disc-thrower: the name of a famous statue ascribed to Myron. [L.,—Gr. *diskobolos*—*diskos,* a quoit, *ballein,* to throw.]

discographer, -graphy, discoid, -al, etc. See **disc.**

discolour *dis-kul'ər, v t.* to take away colour from: to change or to spoil the natural colour of: to mark with other colours, to stain: to dirty, disfigure.—*v.i.* to become discoloured.—*n.* **discolo(u)rā'tion.**—*adj.* **discol'oured.** [O.Fr. *descolorer*—L. *dis-,* apart, and *colōrāre*—*color,* colour]

discombobulate *dis-kəm-bob'-ū-lāt, (U.S. slang) v.t.* to disconcert, upset

discomfit *dis-kum'fit, v.t.* to disconcert, to balk: to defeat or rout:—*pr.p.* **discom'fiting;** *pa.t.* and *pa.p.* **discom'fited.**—*n.* **discom'fiture.** [O.Fr. *desconfit*—L. *dis-,* neg., *conficēre,* to prepare.]

discomfort *dis-kum'fərt, n.* want of comfort: uneasiness.—*v.t.* to deprive of comfort: to make uneasy. [O Fr *desconforter*—*des-,* priv., *conforter,* to comfort; see **comfort.**]

discommode *dis-kə-mōd', (arch.) v.t.* to incommode.— *adj* **discommō'dious.**—*adv.* **discommō'diously.** [Pfx. **dis-** (2), obs. vb. *commode,* to suit.]

discompose *dis-kəm-pōz', v.t.* to deprive of composure, disturb, agitate: to disarrange, disorder. —*n.* **discompō'sure** (*-zhər, -zhyər*) [Pfx. **dis-** (2).]

disconcert *dis-kən-sûrt', v.t.* to throw into confusion: to disturb: to frustrate: to put out of countenance.— *ns* **disconcer'tion** confusion; **disconcert'ment.** [Obs. Fr *disconcerter, des-,* apart, and *concerter,* to concert.]

disconformable *dis-kən-form'ə-bl, adj.* not conformable.—*n.* **disconform'ity** want of conformity: unconformity (*geol.*). [Pfx. **dis-** (2).]

disconnect *dis-kən-ekt', v.t.* to separate or disjoin (from).—*adj.* **disconnect'ed** separated: loosely united, as of a discourse.—*adv.* **disconnect'edly.**—*ns.* **disconnec'tion, disconnex'ion.** [Pfx. **dis-** (1).]

disconsolate *dis-kon'sə-lit, adj.* without consolation or comfort.—*adv.* **discon'solately.**—*n.* **discon'solateness.** [L. *dis-,* neg., and *consōlāri, consōlātus,* to console.]

discontent *dis-kən-tent', n.* want of contentment: dissatisfaction.—*v.t.* to deprive of content: to stir up to ill-will.—*adj* **discontent'ed** dissatisfied.—*adv.* **discontent'edly.**—*ns.* **discontent'edness; discontent'ment.** [Pfx. **dis-** (2), (3)]

discontinue *dis-kən-tin'ū, v t.* to cease to continue: to put an end to: to leave off: to stop.—*v.i* to cease. to be separated.—*ns* **discontin'uance, discontinuā'tion** a breaking off or ceasing, **discontinu'ity** (*-kon-*).— *adj.* **discontin'uous** not continuous. broken off: separated. interrupted by intervening spaces —*adv.* **discontin'uously.** [O Fr *discontinuer*—L *dis-,* reversal, and *continuāre,* to continue]

discophile. See **disc.**

discord *dis'kord, n.* opposite of *concord:* disagreement, strife: difference or contrariety of qualities: a combination of inharmonious sounds: uproarious noise: a dissonance, esp. unprepared.—*v.i.* **discord'** to disagree.—*ns.* **discord'ance, discord'ancy.**—*adj.* **discord'ant** without concord or agreement: inconsistent: contradictory: harsh: jarring.—*adv.* **discord'antly.** [O.Fr. *descord*—L. *discordia*—*dis-,* apart, and *cor, cordis,* the heart.]

discothèque, -theque *dis'kə-tek, n* a club or party where music for dancing is provided by records: the equipment and records used to provide such music.— Coll. **dis'co** (q.v.) [Fr., a record-library—Gr. *diskos,* disc, *thēkē,* case, library.]

discount *dis'kownt, n.* a sum taken from the reckoning: a sum returned to the payer of an account: the rate or percentage of the deduction granted: a 'deduction made for interest in advancing money on a bill: the amount by which the price of a share or stock unit is below the par value.—*v.t.* **discount'** to allow as discount: to allow discount on: to pay (rarely to receive) beforehand the present worth of: to put a reduced value on, as in an extravagant statement or fabulous story or an event foreseen: to ignore.—*v.i.* to practise discounting.—*adj.* **discount'able.**—*n.* **discount'er.**— **discount house** a company trading in bills of exchange, etc.: (also **discount store**) a shop where goods are sold at less than the usual retail price; **discount rate** the rate at which a discount is granted: the rate at which banks can borrow funds using bills as security: in U.S., bank rate.—**at a discount** below par: not sought after: superfluous: depreciated in value. [O Fr *descompter, des-,* away, *compter,* to count.]

discountenance *dis-kown'tən-əns, v.t.* to put out of countenance: to abash: to refuse support to: to discourage.—*n.* disapprobation. [O.Fr. *descontenancer*—*des-,* reversal, *contenance,* countenance.]

discourage *dis-kur'ij, v.t.* to take away the courage of: dishearten: to oppose by showing disfavour.—*n* **discour'agement** act of discouraging: that which discourages: dejection.—*n.* and *adj.* **discour'aging** disheartening, depressing.—*adv.* **discour'agingly.** [O.Fr *descourager.* See **courage.**]

discourse *dis-kōrs', -körs',* or *dis', n.* speech or language generally: conversation: the reasoning faculty: a treatise: a speech: a sermon.—*v.i.* to talk or converse: to reason: to treat formally.—*v.t.* to utter or give forth. [Fr. *discours*—L. *discursus*—*dis-,* away, *currēre,* to run.]

discourteous *dis-kûrt'yəs adj.* wanting in courtesy: uncivil.—*adv.* **discourt'eously.**—*ns.* **discourt'eousness, discourt'esy.** [Pfx. **dis-** (2)]

discover *dis-kuv'ər, v.t.* to lay open or expose: to reveal· to make known: to find out: to espy.—*adj.* **discov'erable.**—*ns.* **discov'erer** one who makes a discovery, esp. of something never before known; **discov'ery** the act of finding out: the thing discovered: gaining knowledge of the unknown: the unravelling of a plot: exploration or reconnaissance (**voyage of discovery**). [O Fr *descouvrir, des-* (L. *dis-*), away, *couvrir,* to cover; see **cover.**]

discredit *dis-kred'it, n.* want of credit: bad credit: illrepute: disgrace.—*v.t* to refuse credit to, or belief in: to deprive of credibility: to deprive of credit: to disgrace.—*adj.* **discred'itable** not creditable: disgraceful.—*adv.* **discred'itably.** [Pfx. **dis-** (2), (3).]

discreet *dis-krēt', adj.* having discernment: wary: circumspect: prudent.—*adv* **discreet'ly.**—*n.* **discreet'ness.** [O Fr *discret*—L. *discrētus*—*discernēre,* to separate, to perceive.]

discrepancy *dis-krep'ən-si,* or *dis', n.* disagreement, variance of facts or sentiments.—*n* **discrep'ance** (or *dis'*).—*adj.* **discrep'ant** (or *dis'*) contrary, disagreeing. [L. *discrepāns, -antis,* different—*dis-,* asunder, and *crepāns,* pr.p. of *crepāre,* to sound.]

discrete *dis'krēt, dis-krēt', adj.* separate: discontinuous: consisting of distinct parts: referring to distinct objects.—*adv.* **discrete'ly.**—*n.* **discrete'ness.** [L *discrētus;* cf. **discreet.**]

discretion *dis-kresh'ən, n.* quality of being discreet. prudence: liberty to act at pleasure.—*adjs.* **discre'tional, discre'tionary** left to discretion: unrestricted —*advs.* **discre'tionally, discre'tionarily.**—**age, years, of discretion,** mature years; **at discretion** according to one's own judgment; **be at someone's discretion** to be under someone's power or control. [O Fr. *discrecion*—L. *dscrētiō, -ōnis—discernĕre, -crētum*]

discriminate *dis-krim'i-nāt, v.t.* to note the difference of or between: to distinguish: to select from others.—*v.i.* to make or note a difference or distinction: to distinguish: to treat differently because of prejudice (with *against*).—*adj.* (*-nit*) discriminated: discriminating.— *n.* a special function of the roots of an equation, expressible in terms of the coefficients—zero value of the function showing that at least two of the roots are equal.—*adv.* **discrim'inately.**—*adj.* **discrim'inating** noting distinctions: gifted with judgment and penetration.—*adv* **discrim'inatingly.**—*n.* **discrimină'tion** the act or process of discriminating: judgment: good taste: the selection of a signal having a particular characteristic (frequency, amplitude, etc.) by the elimination of all the other input signals (*telecomm.*).—*adj.* **discrim'inative** that marks a difference: characteristic. observing distinctions.— *adv* **discrim'inatively.**—*n.* **discrim'inātor,** a person who, or thing which, discriminates: a device which affects the routing and/or determines the fee units for a call originating at a satellite exchange (*telecomm.*) —*adj.* **discrim'inatory** discriminative: favouring some, not treating, or falling on, all alike.—**positive discrimination** discrimination in favour of those who were formerly discriminated against. [L. *discriminăre, -ātum—discrīmen,* that which separates.]

discumber *dis-kum'bər, v.t.* to discumber. [Pfx. **dis-** (2).]

discursive *dis-kûr'siv, adj.* running from one thing to another. roving, desultory. proceeding regularly from premises to conclusion: intellectual, rational.—*adv.* **discur'sively.**—*n.* **discur'siveness.** [See **discourse.**]

discus *dis'kəs, n.* a disc, flat circular image or object: a heavy wooden disc, thickening towards the centre, thrown for distance in athletic contests. [L.,—Gr *diskos.*]

discuss *dis-kus', v.t.* to examine in detail, or by disputation: to debate' to sift: to consume, as a bottle of wine (*facet.*).—*adj* **discuss'able, -ible.**—*n.* **discussion** (*dis-kush'ən*) debate: the dispersion of a tumour (*surg.*). [L. *discutĕre, discussum—dis-,* asunder, *quatĕre,* to shake.]

disdain *dis-dān', v.t.* to think unworthy: to scorn.—*n.* a feeling of contempt, generally tinged with superiority: haughtiness.—*adj.* **disdain'ful.**—*adv.* **disdain'fully.** —*n.* **disdain'fulness.** [O.Fr. *desdaigner* with *des-* (L. *dis-*) for L. *dē* in L. *dēdīgnārī—dīgnus,* worthy.]

disease *diz-ēz', n.* a disorder or want of health in mind or body: an ailment: cause of pain.—*adj.* **diseased'** affected with disease.—*n.* **diseas'edness.** [O.Fr. *desaise—des-* (L. *dis-,* not), *aise,* ease; see **ease.**]

diseconomy *dis-ə-kon'ə-mi, n.* (an instance of) something which is economically wasteful or unprofitable [Pfx. **dis-** (2).]

disembark *dis-im-bark', v.t.* to set ashore: to take out of a ship.—*v.i.* to quit a ship: to land.—*n.* **disembarkă'tion.** [O.Fr. *desembarquer—des-* (L. *dis-*), *embarquer*]

disembarrass *dis-im-bar'əs, v.t.* to free from embarrassment, an encumbrance or perplexity.—*n.* **disembarr'assment.** [Pfx. **dis-** (2).]

disembody *dis-im-bod'i, v.t* to take away from or out of the body (esp. of spirits): to discharge from military embodiment.—*adj.* **disembod'ied.**—*n.* **disembod'iment.** [Pfx. **dis-** (3).]

disembogue *dis-im-bōg', v.t.* and *v.i.* to discharge at the mouth, as a stream.—*n.* **disembogue'ment.** [Sp. *desembocar*—L. *dis-, in,* into, *bucca,* mouth.]

disembowel *dis-im-bow'əl, v.t.* to take out the bowels of: to tear out the inside of.—*n.* **disembow'elment.** [Pfx. **dis-** (3).]

disembroil *dis-im-broil', v.t.* to free from broil or confusion. [Pfx. **dis-** (2).]

disenchant *dis-in-chänt', v.t.* to free from enchantment, to disillusion.—*n* **disenchant'ment.** [Pfx. **dis-** (2).]

disencumber *dis-in-kum'bər, v.t.* to free from encumbrance: to disburden.—*n.* **disencum'brance.** [Pfx. **dis-** (2).]

disendow *dis-in-dow', v.t.* to take away the endowments of (esp. of an established church)—*adj.* **disendowed'.**—*n.* **disendow'ment.** [Pfx. **dis-** (3).]

disenfranchise *dis-in-fran'chīz, -shīz, (rare) v.t.* to disfranchise: to deprive of suffrage.—*n.* **disenfran'chisement** (*-chiz-, -shis-*). [Pfx. **dis-** (2).]

disengage *dis-in-gāj', v.t.* to separate or free from being engaged: to separate: to set free: to release.—*v.i.* to come loose.—*adj.* **disengaged'** at leisure, without engagement.—*n.* **disengage'ment.** [O.Fr. *desengager—des-* (L. *dis-,* neg.), *engager,* to engage.]

disentail *dis-in-tāl', v.t.* to break the entail of (an estate): to divest.—*n.* the act of disentailing. [Pfx. **dis-** (2).]

disentangle *dis-in-tang'gl, v.t.* to free from entanglement or disorder: to unravel: to disengage or set free. —*n.* **disentang'lement.** [Pfx. **dis-** (2).]

disenthral, disenthrall *dis-in-thröl', v t.* to free from enthralment.—*n.* **disenthral(l)'ment.** [Pfx **dis-** (2).]

disentitle *dis-in-tī'tl, v.t.* to deprive of title or right. [Pfx. **dis-** (2).]

disentomb *dis-in-tōōm', v.t.* to take out from a tomb. [Pfx. **dis-** (2).]

disenviron *dis-in-vī'rən, v.t.* to deprive of environment. [Pfx. **dis-** (3).]

disequilibrium *dis-ek-wi-lib'ri-əm, n.* want of balance, esp. in economic affairs.—*pl.* **disequilib'ria.** [Pfx. **dis-** (2).]

disestablish *dis-is-tab'lish, v.t.* to undo the establishment of: to deprive (a church) of established status.— *n.* **disestab'lishment.** [Pfx. **dis-** (2).]

disesteem *dis-is-tēm', n.* want of esteem: disregard.— *v.t.* to disapprove: to dislike. [Pfx. **dis-** (2).]

diseuse *dē-zœz,* masc. **diseur** *dē-zœr,* (Fr.) *ns.* a reciter or entertainer

disfavour *U.S.* **disfavor** *dis-fā'vər, n.* want of favour: displeasure: dislike.—*v.t.* to withhold favour from: to disapprove: to oppose. [Pfx **dis-** (2).]

disfigure *dis-fig'ər, v.t.* to spoil the figure of: to change to a worse form: to spoil the beauty of: to deform.—*n.* **disfig'urement.** [O Fr. *desfigurer*—L. *dis-,* neg., *figūrāre,* to figure.]

disforest *dis-for'ist, v.t.* to strip of trees: to disafforest. [Pfx. **dis-** (2).]

disfranchise *dis-fran'chīz, -shīz, v.t.* to deprive of a franchise, or of rights and privileges, esp. that of voting for an M.P —*n* **disfran'chisement.** [Pfx **dis-** (2).]

disfrock *dis-frok', v t* to unfrock, deprive of clerical garb or character. [Pfx. **dis-** (3).]

disgorge *dis-gorj', v.t.* to discharge from the throat: to vomit: to throw out with violence: to give up: to remove sediment from (champagne) after fermentation in the bottle.—*n.* **disgorge'ment.** [O.Fr. *desgorger, des,* away, *gorge,* throat. See **gorge.**]

disgown *dis-gown', v.t.* or *v.i.* to strip of a gown: to deprive of or to renounce orders or a degree. [Pfx. **dis-** (3).]

disgrace *dis-grās', n* the state of being out of grace or favour, or of being dishonoured: a cause of shame: dishonour: disfigurement: ugliness: defect of grace.— *v.t.* to put out of favour: to bring disgrace or shame upon.—*adj.* **disgrace'ful** bringing disgrace: causing shame: dishonourable.—*adv.* **disgrace'fully.**—*ns.* **disgrace'fulness; disgra'cer.** [Fr. *disgrâce*—L. *dis-,* not, and *grātia,* favour, grace.]

disgruntle *dis-grun'tl, (coll.) v.t.* to disappoint, disgust. —*adj.* **disgrun'tled** out of humour [Pfx. **dis-** (4), and **gruntle,** freq. of **grunt.**]

disguise *dis-gīz', v.t.* to change the guise or appearance of: to conceal the identity of, e.g. by a dress intended to deceive, or by a counterfeit manner and appearance —*n.* a dress intended to disguise the wearer: a false appearance —*adj.* **disguised'.**—*ns* **disguise'ment; disguis'er.** [O.Fr. *desguiser—des-* (L *dis-,* reversal), *guise,* manner; see **guise.**]

disgust *dis-gust', n.* (formerly) distaste, disfavour, displeasure: (now) loathing, extreme distaste, extreme annoyance.—*v.t.* to cause disgust in.—*adj.* **disgust'ed.** —*adv.* **disgust'edly.**—*adj.* **disgust'ing.**—*adv.* **disgust'ingly.**—*n.* **disgust'ingness.** [O.Fr. *desgouster—des-* (L. *dis-*), and *gouster*—L. *gustāre,* to taste.]

dish *dish, n.* a vessel, esp. one that is flat, or shallow, or not circular, or one for food at table: a dishful: the food in a dish: a cup (of tea, coffee, etc.) (*arch.*): a particular kind of food: a hollow: concavity of form, as in a wheel, a chair-back: a concave reflector used for directive radiation and reception, esp. for radar or radio telescopes: a good-looking person, esp. of the opposite sex (*coll.*).—*v.t.* to put in a dish, for serving at table: to make concave: to outwit, circumvent (*coll.*): to ruin (*coll.*).—*adj.* **dished** having a concavity: of a pair of wheels on a car, etc , sloping in towards each other at the top: completely frustrated (*coll.*).—*n.* **dish'ful.**— *adj.* **dish'y** (*coll.*) good-looking, attractive.—**dish aerial** a dish-shaped aerial used esp. in satellite communications; **dish'-cloth, dish'-clout** a cloth for washing, drying, or wiping dishes; **dish'-cover** a cover for a dish to keep it hot; **dish'-rag** a dish-cloth; **dish'-towel** a tea-towel; **dish'-washer** a machine which washes dishes, cutlery, etc.; **dish'-water** water in which dishes have been washed: a liquid deficient in strength or cleanliness.—**dish out** to serve out: to share (food) among several people: to give out (*fig.; coll.; usu. disparagingly*); **dish up** to serve up, esp. figuratively of old materials cooked up anew. [O.E. *disc,* a plate, a dish, a table—L. *discus*—Gr. *diskos; cf.* **disc, desk;** Ger. *Tisch,* table]

déshabillé *dis-ə-bēl', n.* a negligent toilet: undress: an undress garment.—Also **déshabillé** (*dā-zā-bē-yā*). [Fr. *déshabillé,* pa.p. of *déshabiller,* to undress—*des-* (L. *dis-*), apart, *habiller,* to dress.]

disharmony *dis-här'mə-ni, n.* lack of harmony: discord: incongruity.—*adjs.* **disharmonic** (*-mon'*) out of harmony: discordant: incongruous; **disharmonious** (*-mō'*).—*adv.* **disharmo'niously.** [Pfx. **dis-** (2).]

dishearten *dis-härt'n, v.t.* to deprive of heart, courage, or spirits: to discourage: to depress.—*adjs.* **disheart'ened; disheart'ening.**—*adv.* **disheart'eningly.** [Pfx. **dis-** (2).]

dishevel *di-shev'l, v.t.* to disorder, as hair: to cause to hang loose: to ruffle.—*pr.p.* **dishev'elling;** *pa.t.* and *pa.p.* **dishev'elled.**—*n.* **dishev'elment.** [O.Fr. *discheveler*—L. *dis-,* in different directions, *capillus,* the hair.]

dishonest *dis-on'ist, adj.* not honest: wanting integrity: disposed to cheat: insincere.—*adv* **dishon'estly.**—*n.* **dishon'esty.** [O. Fr. *deshoneste.*]'

dishonour U.S. **dishonor** *dis-on'ər, n* want of honour: disgrace: shame: reproach.—*v.t* to deprive of honour: to disgrace: to cause shame to: to seduce: to degrade: to refuse the payment of, as a cheque — *adj.* **dishon'ourable** not in accordance with a sense of honour: disgraceful.—*n.* **dishon'ourableness.** —*adv.* **dishon'ourably.**—*n.* **dishon'ourer.** [O Fr. *deshonneur.*]

dishorn *dis-hörn', v t.* to deprive of horns. [Pfx **dis-** (3).]

disillusion *dis-i-lōō'zhən, -lū' n.* a freeing from illusion: state of being disillusioned.—*v.t.* to free from illusion, disenchant.—*adj.* **disillu'sioned** freed from illusion: often, bereft of comfortable beliefs whether they were false or true —*v.t.* **disillu'sionise, -ize.**—*n* **disillu'sionment.** [Pfx. **dis-** (3).]

disincentive *dis-in-sen'tiv, n* a discouragement to effort.—Also *adj.* [Pfx. **dis-** (2)]

disinclination *dis-in-kli-nā'shən, n.* want of inclination: unwillingness —*v.t.* **disincline** (*-klīn'*) to turn away inclination from: to excite the dislike or aversion of.— *adj.* **disinclined'** not inclined: averse. [Pfx. **dis-** (2)]

disincorporate *dis-in-kör'pə-rāt, v.t* to deprive of corporate rights.—*n* **disincorpora'tion.** [Pfx **dis-** (2).]

disindividualise, -ize *dis-in-di-vid'ū-əl-īz, v t.* to deprive of individuality. [Pfx **dis-** (2)]

disinfect *dis-in-fekt', v.t.* to free from infection: to purify from infectious germs.—*n.* **disinfect'ant** anything that destroys the causes of infection —Also *adj.* —*ns.* **disinfec'tion; disinfect'or.** [Pfx. **dis-** (2).]

disinfest *dis-in-fest', v.t.* to free from infesting animals. —*n.* **disinfesta'tion.** [Pfx **dis-** (2)]

disinflation *dis'in-flā-shən, n.* return to the normal condition after inflation —*adj* **disinfla'tionary.** [Pfx. **dis-** (2).]

disinformation *dis-in-fər-mā'shən, n.* deliberate leakage of misleading information. [Pfx. **dis-** (2).]

disingenuous *dis-in-jen'ū-əs, adj.* not ingenuous: not frank or open: crafty.—*n* **disingenu'ity** (*rare*).—*adv.* **disingen'uously.**—*n.* **disingen'uousness.** [Pfx **dis-** (2).]

disinherit *dis-in-her'it, v.t.* to cut off from hereditary rights: to deprive of an inheritance.—*n.* **disinher'itance.** [Pfx **dis-** (3)]

disintegrate *dis-in'ti-grāt, v.t.* and *v.i.* to separate into parts: to break up: to crumble —*ns.* **disintegra'tion** the act or state of disintegrating: a process in which a nucleus ejects one or more particles, esp. in spontaneous radioactive decay (*nuc.*); **disin'tegrator** a machine for crushing or pulverising. [Pfx. **dis-** (1).]

disinter *dis-in-tûr', v t.* to take out of the earth, from a grave, or from obscurity.—*n.* **disinter'ment.** [Pfx. **dis-** (2).]

disinterest *dis-in'tər-ist, n.* disinterestedness: lack of interest.—*v.t.* to free from interest.—*adj.* **disin'terested** not influenced by private feelings or considerations: not deriving personal advantage: impartial: unselfish, generous: (revived from obsolescence) uninterested.—*adv.* **disin'terestedly.**—*n.* **disin'terestedness.** [Pfx. **dis-** (2).]

disinvest *dis-in-vest', v.t.* to remove investment (from; with *in*).—*n.* **disinvest'ment.** [Pfx. **dis-** (2).]

disjoin *dis-join', v.t.* to separate after having been joined.—*v.t* **disjoint'** to put out of joint: to separate united parts of: to break the natural order or relations of: to make incoherent.—*adj* **disjoint'ed** incoherent, esp. of discourse: badly assorted.—*adv* **disjoint'edly.** —*n* **disjoint'edness.** [O.Fr. *desjoindre*—L. *disjungĕre*—*dis-,* apart, *jungĕre,* to join.]

disjunct dis-jungkt', also dis', adj disjoined — n **disjunc'tion** the act of disjoining: disunion. separation —adj. **disjunct'ive** disjoining. tending to separate. uniting sentences but disjoining the sense. or rather marking an adverse sense (gram.) —n a word which disjoins —adv **disjunct'ively**. —n. **disjunct'ure**. [O.Fr desjoinct, desjoindre See above]

dislike dis-lik', v.t to be displeased with· to disapprove of to have an aversion to.—n (dis-lik', sometimes dis') disinclination· aversion· distaste: disapproval —adjs **dislike'able, dislik'able**. [Pfx **dis-** (2) and **like²**; the genuine Eng word is mislike]

dislocate dis'lō-kāt, v t. to displace· to put out of joint —adv **dis'locatedly**.—n **disloca'tion** a dislocated joint: displacement: disorganisation derangement (of traffic, plans, etc) a fault (geol.) [L L. dislocāre, -ātum—L. dis-, apart, locāre, to place]

dislodge dis-loj', v t to drive from a lodgment or place of rest: to drive from a place of hiding or of defence —v i. to go away —n **dislodg(e)'ment**. [O Fr desloger—des- (L dis-). apart, loger, to lodge]

disloyal dis-loi'əl, adj not loyal unfaithful —adv **disloy'ally**.—n **disloy'alty**. [O Fr desloyal—L dis-, neg , légalis, legal.]

dismal diz'məl, adj gloomy: dreary: sorrowful: depressing —n (in pl) the dumps (obs.).—adv **dis'mally**.—ns **dis'malness**.—**dismal** Jimmy a confirmed pessimist [O Fr dismal—L dies mali, evil, unlucky days]

dismantle dis-man'tl, v t to strip: to deprive of furniture, fittings, etc., so as to render useless to raze the fortifications of to take to bits, pull down [O.Fr desmanteller—des- away, mantel, a mantle]

dismast dis-mast', v t to deprive of a mast or masts — n **dismast'ment**. [Pfx **dis-** (3)]

dismay dis-, diz-mā', v.t. to appal to discourage —n. the loss of strength and courage through fear [App through O.Fr —L dis-, neg . and O H G magan, to have might or power.]

dismember dis-mem'bər, v t to divide member from member: to separate a limb from. to disjoint· to tear to pieces —n **dismem'berment**. [O Fr desmembrer]

dismiss dis-mis', v.t to send away: to dispatch: to discard: to remove from office or employment: to reject, to put out of court, to discharge (law)· in cricket, to put out (batsman, -men): (imper) as a military command, to fall out —ns **dismiss'al, dismission** (-mish'ən) —adjs **dismiss'ible; dismiss'ive, dismiss'ory**. [Pfx **dis-** (3), and L mittĕre, missum, to send, L. dimissus.]

dismount dis-mownt', v i. to come down. to come off a horse, bicycle, etc.—v.t. to throw or bring down from any elevated place· to unhorse, to remove from a stand, framework, setting, carriage, or the like [O Fr. desmonter.]

disobedient dis-ō-bēd'yənt, adj neglecting or refusing to obey —n. **disobed'ience**.—adv **disobed'iently**. [Pfx. **dis-** (2)]

disobey dis-ō-bā', dis-ə-bā', dis', v t. and v i to neglect or refuse to obey. [O Fr desobeir—des- (L dis-). neg., and obeir, to obey.]

disoblige dis-ō-blīj', -ə-blīj', v t to refuse or fail to oblige or grant a favour to to offend or injure thereby.—n **disobligement** (-blīj').—adj **disobliging** not obliging. not careful to attend to the wishes of others: unaccommodating: unkind —adv. **disoblig'ingly**.—n **disoblig'ingness**. [Pfx **dis-** (2)]

disoperation dis-op-ər-ā'shən, (ecology) n a mutually harmful relationship between two organisms in a community [Pfx **dis-** (2).]

disorder dis-or'dər, n want of order. confusion· disturbance: breach of the peace· disease.—v t. to throw out of order. to disarrange· to disturb: to produce disease in —adj **disor'dered** confused, deranged — n. **disor'derliness**.—adj **disor'derly** out of order: in confusion. irregular lawless: defying the restraints of decency —**disorderly conduct** (legal) any of several minor infringements of the law likely to cause a breach of the peace, **disorderly house** a brothel: a gaming-house [O Fr desordre—des- (L. dis-), neg , ordre, order]

disorganise, -ize dis-or'gən-īz, v t. to destroy the organic structure of· to disorder.—adj. **disorganic** (-gan').—n. **disorganisā'tion, -z-**. [Pfx. **dis-** (2).]

disorient dis-ō'ri-ənt, -o', v t to turn from the east: to confuse as to direction to throw out of one's reckoning —Also **diso'rientate**.—n **disorientā'tion**. [Pfx **dis-** (2)]

disown dis-ōn' v.t to refuse to own or acknowledge as belonging to oneself: to deny: to repudiate, cast off. —n **disown'ment**. [Pfx **dis-** (2)]

disparage dis-par'ij, v t to lower in rank or estimation: to talk slightingly of —ns **dispar'agement; dispar'ager**.—adv **dispar'agingly**. [O Fr desparager—des- (L dis-), neg , and parage; see **parage**.]

disparate dis'pər-it, -āt, adj. unequal. incapable of being compared —adv. **dis'parately**.—n **dis'parateness**.—n.pl. **dis'parates** things or characters of different species. [L disparātus—dis-, not, and parāre, make ready; influenced by dispar, unequal]

disparity dis-par'i-ti, n. inequality· unlikeness so great as to render comparison difficult and union unsuitable [L dispar, unequal—dis-, neg., par, equal.]

dispark dis-park', v.t to throw open, deprive of the character of a park· to remove from a park [Pfx. **dis-** (2, 3).]

dispart dis-part', v t. to divide, to separate —n the difference between the thickness of metal at the breech and the mouth of a gun [Pfx **dis-** (1)]

dispassion dis-pash'ən, n freedom from passion: a calm state of mind.—adj **dispass'ionate** (-it) free from passion: unmoved by feelings: cool· impartial. —adv **dispass'ionately**. [Pfx. **dis-** (2).]

dispatch, despatch dis-pach', v t to send away hastily. to send out of the world: to put to death: to dispose of: to perform speedily —n. a sending away in haste: dismissal: rapid performance: haste· the taking of life: the sending off of the mails: that which is dispatched, as a message, esp. telegraphic: (in pl.) statepapers or other official papers (diplomatic, military, etc.) —n. **dispatch'er; dispatch'-box, -case** a box or case for holding dispatches or valuable papers; **dispatch'-rider** a carrier of dispatches, on horse-back or motor-cycle —**mentioned in dispatches** as a distinction, commended in official military dispatches for bravery, etc [It. dispacciare or Sp. despachar—L. dis-, apart, and root of pangĕre, pactum, to fasten.]

dispel dis-pel', v t to drive away and scatter: to make disappear.—v i. to scatter or melt away.—pr.p **dispell'ing**; pa.t and pa.p. **dispelled'**. [L. dispellĕre —dis-, away, pellĕre, to drive]

dispensary. See **dispensation**.

dispensation dis-pən-sā'shən, n. the act of dispensing or dealing out: administration: a dealing of Providence, or of God, or nature: a method or stage of God's dealing with man licence or permission to neglect a rule, esp. of church law in the R C church: ground of exemption —adj **dispens'able** that may be dispensed, or dispensed with —ns **dispensabil'ity, dispens'ableness**.—adv **dispens'ably**.—n. **dispens'ary** a place where medicines are dispensed (esp form gratis)· an out-patient department of a hospital.—adjs **dispensā'tional; dispens'atory** granting dispensation.—n a book containing medical prescriptions.

—*v.t.* **dispense'** to deal out: to distribute: to administer: to make up for distributing or administering.—*n.* **dispens'er** one who dispenses, esp. a pharmacist who dispenses medicines: a container, or machine that gives out in prearranged quantities.—**dispense with** to permit the want of: to do without. [Fr. *dispenser*—L. *dis-, pēnsāre*, to weigh.]

dispeople *dis-pē'pl*, *v.t.* to empty of inhabitants [Pfx. **dis-** (2).]

disperse *dis-pûrs'*, *v t.* to scatter in all directions: to spread: to diffuse: to drive asunder: to cause to vanish: to put in a colloidal state.'—*v.i.* to separate: to spread abroad: to vanish.—*ns.* **dispers'al** dispersion· distribution: the spread of a species to new areas, **dispers'ant** a substance causing dispersion —*adv.* **dispers'edly.**—*ns.* **dispers'edness; dispers'er; dispersion** (*dis-pûr'shən*) a scattering, or state of being scattered: the removal of inflammation (*med*), the spreading out of rays owing to different refrangibility (*phys.*): the scattering of values of a variable from the average (*statistics*): the state of a finely divided colloid: a substance in that state: the diaspora.—*adj.* **dispers'ive** tending or serving to disperse. [L. *dispergĕre, dispersum—dī-*, asunder, apart, *spargĕre*, to scatter.]

dispirit *dis-pir'it*, *v.t.* to dishearten: to discourage.—*adj.* **dispir'ited** dejected: feeble, spiritless.—*adv* **dispir'itedly.**—*n.* **dispir'itedness.**—*adj.* **dispir'iting** disheartening.—*adv.* **dispir'itingly.**—*n.* **dispir'itment.** [Pfx. **dis-** (2).]

displace *dis-plās'*, *v.t.* to put out of place: to disarrange: to remove from a state, office, or dignity: to supplant: to substitute something for.—*adj.* **displace'able.**—*n.* **displace'ment** a putting or being out of place: the difference between the position of a body at a given time and that occupied at first: the quantity of water displaced by a ship afloat or an immersed body: the disguising of emotional feelings by unconscious transference from one object to another (*psychol.*).—**displaced person** one removed from his country as a prisoner or as slave labour· a refugee or stateless person. [O.Fr. *desplacer—des-* (L. *dis-*), neg., and *place*, place.]

display *dis-plā'*, *v.t.* to unfold or spread out: to exhibit to set out ostentatiously: to make prominent by large type, wide spacing, etc. (*print.*).—*n.* a displaying or unfolding: exhibition: ostentatious show: an animal's or bird's behaviour when courting, threatening intruders, etc., in which the crest is raised, feathers spread, etc.: the 'picture' on a cathode-ray tube screen making the information visible (*electronics*). —*adj.* **displayed'.**—*n.* **display'er.** [O.Fr. *despleier —des-* (L. *dis-*), neg., and *plier, ploier*—L *plicāre*, to fold; doublet **deploy**; see **ply**¹.]

displease *dis-plēz'*, *v.t.* to offend: to make angry in a slight degree: to be disagreeable to.—*v.i.* to raise aversion.—*adj.* **displeased'** vexed, annoyed; **displeas'ing** causing displeasure: giving offence.—*adv.* **displeas'ingly.**—*ns.* **displeas'ingness; displeasure** (*dis-plezh'ər*) the feeling of one who is offended: anger: a cause of irritation. [O.Fr. *desplaisir—des-* (L. *dis-*), reversal, *plaisir*, to please.]

dispone *dis-pōn'*, *v.t.* to set in order, dispose (*arch.*): to make over to another (*Scots law*): to convey legally [L. *dispōnĕre*, to arrange.]

disport *dis-pôrt'*, *-port'*, *v t.* (usu. *refl.*) and *v i.* to divert, amuse: to move in gaiety.—*n.* **disport'ment.** [O.Fr. *se desporter*, to carry (oneself) away from one's work, to amuse (oneself)—L *dis-, portāre*, to carry.]

dispose *dis-pōz'*, *v.t.* to arrange: to distribute to place to apply to a particular purpose: to make over by sale, gift, etc.: to bestow: to incline.—*v.i.* to settle things.

to ordain what is to be: to make a disposition.—*n.* disposal, management: behaviour, disposition.—*adj.* **dispōs'able** able to be disposed of: intended to be thrown away or destroyed after use.—*n.* **dispōs'al** the act of disposing: order. arrangement: management: right of bestowing: availability for use, control, service, etc.—*adj.* **disposed'** inclined: of a certain disposition (with *well, ill*, etc. *towards*).—*adv.* **dispōs'edly** in good order with measured steps.—*n.* **dispōs'er.**—*n.* and *adj.* **dispōs'ing.**—*adv.* **dispōs'ingly.**—**disposable income** one's net income after tax has been paid, available for spending, saving, investing, etc.—**dispose of** to settle what is to be done with: to make an end of: to have done with: to part with: to get rid of: to sell. [Fr. *disposer—dis-* (L. *dis-*), asunder, *poser*, to place—L. *pausāre*, to pause, (late) to place]

disposition *dis-pə-zish'ən*, *n* an arrangement: distribution. a plan for disposing of one's property, etc.: natural tendency: temper: a giving over to another, conveyance or assignment.—*adjs.* **disposi'tional; disposi'tioned.** [Fr ,—L., from *dis-*, apart, *pōnĕre, positum*, to place.]

dispossess *dis-pə-zes'*, *v t.* to put out of possession.—*adj* **dispossessed'** deprived of possessions, property, etc : deprived of one's home or country: deprived of rights, hopes, expectations, etc —*ns.* **dispossession** (*dis-pə-zesh'ən*), **dispossess'or.** [Pfx dis- (2).]

dispraise *dis-prāz'*, *n.* the expression of an unfavourable opinion· blame: reproach —*v.t* to blame· to censure —*adv.* **disprais'ingly.** [O.Fr *despreisier—des-* (L *dis-*), reversal, *preisier*, to praise.]

disproof *dis-prōōf'*, *n.* a disproving· refutation. [Pfx. dis- (2).]

disproportion *dis-prə-pōr'shən, -por'*, *n.* want of suitable proportion —*v.t* to make unsuitable in form or size, etc.—*adj.* **dispropor'tional.**—*adv* **dispropor'tionally.**—*adj* **dispropor'tionate.**—*adv* **dispropor'tionately.**—*adv* **dispropor'tionateness.** [Pfx dis- (2).]

disprove *dis-prōōv'*, *v.t* to prove to be false or wrong: —*pa.p* **disproved'**,**disproven**(*-prōv'·;-prōōv'*) —*adj.* **disprov'able.**—*n* **disprov'al.** [O.Fr *desprover*, see **prove.**]

dispute *dis-pūt'*, *v.t.* to make a subject of argument: to contend for: to oppose by argument to call in question.—*v.i.* to argue: to debate —*n* a contest with words: an argument: a debate: a quarrel —*adj* **dis'putable** (also *-pūt'*) that may be disputed: of doubtful certainty.—*ns.* **disputabil'ity, dis'putableness.**—*adv.* **dis'putably.**—*n* and *adj.* **dis'putant.**—*ns* **disput'er; disputa'tion** a contest in argument· an exercise in debate —*adjs.* **disputa'tious, dis'putative** inclined to dispute, cavil, or controvert.—*advs.* **disputa'tiously, disput'atively.**—*ns.* **disputa'tiousness, disput'ativeness.**—**beyond** or **without dispute** indubitably, certainly [O.Fr. *desputer*—L *disputāre—dis-*, apart, and *putāre*, to think.]

disqualify *dis-kwol'i-fī*, *v t* to deprive of the qualities or qualifications necessary for any purpose: to make unfit. to disable. to debar to declare to be disqualified —*adj.* **disqualifi'able.**—*ns* **disqualifica'tion** state of being disqualified· anything that disqualifies or incapacitates, **disqual'ifier.** [Pfx. dis- (3).]

disquiet *dis-kwī'ət*, *n* want of quiet: uneasiness, restlessness: anxiety —*v t.* to render unquiet: to make uneasy: to disturb —Also **disqui'eten.**—*adj.* **disqui'eting**—*adv* **disqui'etingly.**—*n.* **disqui'etude.** [Pfx. dis- (2).]

disquisition *dis-kwi-zish'ən*, *n* a careful inquiry into any matter by arguments, etc : an essay —*adjs* **disquisi'tional, disquisi'tionary** pertaining to or of the nature of a disquisition [L *disquisītiŏ, -ōnis—dis-, intens., quaerēre,* to seek.]

disrate *dis-rāt'. (naut.) v.t* to reduce to a lower rating or rank, as a petty officer. [Pfx **dis-** (3).]

disregard *dis-ri-gärd', v.t.* to pay no attention to.—*n* want of attention: neglect: slight —*adj.* **disregard'ful.**—*adv.* **disregard'fully.** [Pfx. dis- (2)]

disrelish *dis-rel'ish, v.t.* not to relish: to dislike the taste of: to dislike.—*n.* distaste. dislike: disgust.—*adj* **disrel'ishing** offensive [Pfx **dis-** (2).]

disremember *dis-ri-mem'bǝr, (dial. or U.S. coll.) v.t* not to remember, to forget. [Pfx. **dis-** (2).]

disrepair *dis-ri-pār', n.* the state of being out of repair [Pfx. **dis-** (2).]

disrepute *dis-ri-pūt', n* bad repute. discredit.—*adj.* **disrep'utable** in bad repute: disgraceful: not respectable: disordered and shabby —*ns.* **disrep'utableness, disreputabil'ity** *(rare).*—*adv.* **disrep'utably.** [Pfx. dis- (2).]

disrespect *dis-ri-spekt', n* want of respect: discourtesy. incivility.—*v.t.* (arch.) not to respect.—*adj* **disrespect'ful** showing disrespect: irreverent: uncivil.—*adv.* **disrespect'fully.**—*n.* **disrespect'fulness.** [Pfx. **dis-** (2).]

disrobe *dis-rōb', v.t.* and *v.i.* to undress. to uncover: to divest of robes. [Pfx- **dis-** (2), (3).]

disrupt *dis-rupt', v.t.* and *v.i.* to burst asunder, to break up: to interrupt (growth, progress, etc.).—*ns* **disrupt'er, disrupt'or; disrup'tion** the act of breaking asunder: the act of bursting and rending: breach: (with *cap.*) in Scottish ecclesiastical history, the separation of the Free Church from the Established Church for the sake of spiritual independence (1843). —*adj.* **disrup'tive** causing, or accompanied by, disruption.—*adv.* **disrupt'ively.** [L. *disruptus, dīruptus—dīrumpĕre—dis-,* asunder, *rumpĕre,* to break.]

diss *dis, n.* an Algerian reedy grass (*Ampelodesma tenax*) used for cordage, etc. [Ar. *dīs*]

dissatisfactory *dis-sat-is-fak'tǝr-i, adj.* causing dissatisfaction.—*n.* **dissatisfac'tion** state of being dissatisfied: discontent: uneasiness. [Pfx **dis-** (2).]

dissatisfy *dis-sat'is-fī, v.t.* to fail to satisfy: to make discontented: to displease.—*adj.* **dissat'isfied** discontented: not pleased. [Pfx. **dis-** (2).]

dissect *di-sekt', v.t.* to cut asunder: to cut into parts for the purpose of minute examination: to divide and examine: to analyse and criticise.—*adjs.* **dissect'ed** deeply cut into narrow segments (*bot.*): cut up by valleys (*geol.*), **dissect'ible.**—*n.* **dissec'tion** the act or the art of cutting in pieces a plant or animal in order to ascertain the structure of its parts —*adj.* **dissect'ive** tending to dissect —*n* **dissect'or.**—**dissecting microscope** a form of microscope that allows dissection of the object under examination. **dissecting room, table** a room in, table on, which anatomical dissection is practised. [L. *dissecāre, dissectum—dis-,* asunder, *secāre,* to cut.]

disseise, disseize *dis-sēz', v.t.* to deprive of possession of an estate of freehold: to dispossess wrongfully.— *ns.* **disseis'in, disseiz'in; disseis'or, disseiz'or.** [Pfx **dis-** (3).]

dissemble *di-sem'bl, v.t* to disguise. to mask.—*v.i.* to assume a false appearance· to play the hypocrite: to dissimulate.—*ns.* **dissem'blance.** [L. *dissimulāre—dissimilis,* unlike—*dis-,* neg , and *similis,* like; perh remodelled on *resemble*]

disseminate *di-sem'i-nāt, v.t.* to sow or scatter abroad: to propagate: to diffuse.—*adj.* scattered —*n.* **disseminā'tion.**—*n.* **dissem'inātor.**—**disseminated sclerosis** a chronic progressive disease in which patches of thickening appear throughout the central nervous system, resulting in various forms of paralysis. [L.

dissēminare, -ātum—dis-, asunder, *sēminare,* to sow.]

dissent *di-sent', v.i.* to think differently: to disagree in opinion: to differ (with *from*).—*n.* the act of dissenting: difference of opinion: a protest by a minority: a differing or separation from an established church.— *ns.* **dissen'sion** disagreement in opinion: discord: strife; **Dissent'er** one (esp. a Protestant) who is separate from an established church: a nonconformist: (without *cap.*) a dissentient.—*adj.* **dissen'tient** (*-shǝnt*) declaring dissent: disagreeing.—*n* one who disagrees: one who declares his dissent.—*adj.* **dissent'ing.**—*adv* **dissent'ingly.** [L. *dissentire, dissēnsum—dis-,* apart, *sentīre,* to think.]

dissepiment *di-sep'i-mǝnt, n* a partition in an ovary (*bot*): a partition partly cutting off the bottom of a coral cup (*zool.*).—*adj.* **dissepimental** (*-ment'l*) [L. *dissaepimentum,* a partition—L. *dissaepīre—dis-,* apart, *saepīre,* to hedge in, to fence.]

dissertate *dis'ǝr-tāt, v.i.* to discourse.—*n.* **dissertā'tion** a formal discourse: a treatise.—*adjs.* **dissertā'tional, diss'ertātive.**—*n.* **diss'ertātor.** [L. *dissertāre,* intens. of *disserēre,* to discuss—*dis-, serēre,* to put together.]

disserve *dis-sûrv', (arch.) v* t to do an ill turn to: to clear (a table) —*n.* **disserv'ice** injury: mischief: an ill turn. [O.Fr. *desservir—*L. *dis-,* neg., *servīre,* to serve.]

dissever *di-sev'ǝr, v.t.* to sever: to part in two: to separate: to disunite.—*ns.* **dissev'erance, disseverā'tion, dissev'erment** a dissevering or parting.—*adj.* **dissev'ered** disunited. [O.Fr. *dessevrer—*L. *dis-,* apart, *sēparāre,* to separate.]

dissident *dis'i-dǝnt, adj.* dissenting.—*n.* a dissenter, esp. one who disagrees with the aims and procedures of the government.—*n.* **diss'idence** disagreement. [L. *dissidēns, -entis,* pr.p. of *dissidēre—dis-,* apart, *sedēre,* to sit.]

dissimilar *di-sim'ilǝr, adj.* unlike.—*n.* **dissimilarity** (*-ar'*) unlikeness.—*adv.* **dissim'ilarly.**—*v.t.* **dissim'ilate** to make unlike.—*ns.* **dissimilā'tion** the act of rendering dissimilar: katabolism; **dissimil'itude.** [Pfx. dis- (2).]

dissimulate *di-sim'ū-lāt, v.t.* to pretend the contrary of: to conceal or disguise: to dissemble.—*v.i.* to practise dissimulation, play the hypocrite.—*n.* **dissimulā'tion** the act of dissembling: a hiding under a false appearance: false pretension: hypocrisy —*adj.* **dissim'ulative.**—*n.* **dissim'ulātor.** [L. *dissimulāre, -ātum,* to dissimulate—*dis-,* neg., *similis,* like.]

dissipate *dis'i-pāt, v.t.* to scatter: to squander: to waste: to dispel.—*v.i.* to separate and disappear: to waste away.—*adjs.* **diss'ipable** that may be dissipated; **diss'ipated** dissolute, esp. addicted to drinking.—*adv.* **diss'ipatedly.**—*n.* **dissipā'tion** dispersion: state of being dispersed: scattered attention: a course of frivolous amusement or of dissolute life.—*adj.* **diss'ipative** tending to dissipate or disperse. [L *dissipāre, -ātum—dis-,* asunder, and (archaic) *supāre,* to throw]

dissociate *di-sō'shi-āt, v.t.* and *v.i.* to separate from society or from association of any kind: to separate: to subject to or suffer dissociation —*adj.* separated —*n.* **dissociā'tion** (*-sō-shi-* or *-sō-si-*) act of dissociating: state of being dissociated: separation into simpler constituents, esp. a reversible separation caused by heat, or separation into ions (*chem.*): splitting of personality (*psych.*): splitting off from consciousness of certain ideas and their accompanying emotions· breaking of associations.—*adj.* **dissō'ciative.** [L. *dissociāre, -ātum—dis-,* asunder, *sociāre,* to associate.]

dissoluble *dis-ol'ū-bl* or *dis'ǝl-ū-bl, -ŏō-bl, adj.* capable of being dissolved.—*ns.* **dissolūbil′ity, dissol′ūbleness.**—*adj.* **diss′olute** (-*lōō̄t* or -*lūt*) loose, esp. in morals, debauched.—*n.* a dissolute person.—*adv.* **diss′olutely.**—*ns.* **diss′oluteness; dissolution** (-*lōō̄′* or -*lū′*) the breaking up of an assembly: loosening: melting: break-up: death.—*ns.* **dissolvabil′ity** (*diz-*); **dissolv′ableness.**—*adj.* **dissolv′able** capable of being dissolved.—*v.t.* **dissolve** (*di-zolv′*) to undo: to separate or break up: to put an end to (as a parliament): to melt in solution (formerly also in fusion): to disperse. —*v.i.* to go into solution: to break up: to waste away: to fade away: in films and television, to fade out one scene gradually while replacing it with another (also *n.*): to melt.—*n.* **dissolv′ent** (*rare*) a solvent.—*adj.* having power to melt. [L. *dissolvĕre, dissolūtum—dis-,* asunder, *solvĕre, -ūtum,* to loose.]

dissonant *dis′ə-nənt, adj.* not agreeing or harmonising in sound: without concord or harmony: disagreeing. —*n.* **diss′onance** disagreement of sound: want of harmony: discord: disagreement: *specif.,* a combination of musical sounds that calls for resolution (also **diss′onancy**).—*adv.* **diss′onantly.** [L. *dissonāns, -antis—dis-,* apart, *sonāre,* to sound.]

dissuade *di-swād′, v.t.* to divert by advice (from).—*ns.* **dissua′der; dissua′sion** (-*zhən*).—*adj.* **dissua′sive** (-*siv*) tending to dissuade.—*n.* that which tends to dissuade.—*adv.* **dissua′sively..** [L. *dissuādēre—dis-,* apart, *suādēre, suāsum,* to advise.]

dissyllable. A variant of **disyllable.**

dissymmetry *dis-sim′i-tri, n.* want of symmetry: enantiomorphy—the symmetry of right and left hand, object and mirror-image.—*adjs.* **dissymmetric, -al** (-*et′*).—*adv.* **dissymmet′rically.** [Pfx. **dis-** (2).]

distaff *dis′täf, n.* the stick that holds the bunch of flax, tow, or wool in spinning.—**distaff side** the female part, line, side, or branch of a family or descent. [O.E. *distæf,* from the root found in L.G. *diesse,* the bunch of flax on the staff; and *stæf,* staff.]

distal *dis′təl,* (*biol.*) *adj.* far apart, widely spaced: pertaining to or situated at the outer end: farthest from the point of attachment—opp. to *proximal.*—*adv* **dis′tally.** [Formed from **distance** on the analogy of *central*]

distance *dis′təns, n.* measure of interval between: remoteness: a remote place or region: the remote part of the field of view or the part of a picture representing it: degree of remoteness: opposition: standoffishness or aloofness of manner: the scheduled duration of a boxing match, etc.: in horse-racing, the space measured back from the winning-post which a horse, in heat-races, must reach when the winner has covered the whole course, in order to run in the final heat —*adj.* in athletics, of races, over a long distance —*v.t.* to place at a distance: to leave at a distance behind.—**go the distance** to complete what one has started (*coll.*): to endure to the end of a (boxing, etc) bout; **keep someone at a distance** to treat someone with aloofness; **keep one's distance** to abstain from familiarity (with): to keep aloof (from). [See **distant.**]

distant *dis′tənt, adj.* at a certain distance: at a great distance: remote, in time, place, resemblance, or connection: indistinct: reserved or aloof in manner.— *adv.* **dis′tantly.**—*n* **dis′tantness.**—**dis′tant-signal** on a railway, a signal farther from the destination than the home-signal. [Fr.,—L. *distāns, -antis—dī-,* apart, *stāns, stantis,* pr.p. of *stāre,* to stand.]

distaste *dis-tàst′, n* disrelish (for): dislike (for) —*adj* **distaste′ful** unpleasant to the taste: unpleasant.— *adv.* **distaste′fully.**—*n.* **distaste′fulness.** [Pfx. **dis-** (2).]

distemper[1] *dis-temp′ər, n.* a mode of painting in size, water-glass, or other watery vehicle giving body to

the pigment: paint of this kind—for indoor walls, scenery, etc.—*v.t.* to paint in distemper. [L. *dis-,* reversal, *temperāre,* to regulate, mix in proportion; cf. next word.]

distemper[2] *dis-temp′ər, n.* a morbid or disorderly state of body or mind (*arch.*): disease, esp. of animals: specifically a disease of the dog and ferret families caused by a virus. [O.Fr. *destemprer,* to derange— L. *dis-, temperāre,* to regulate.]

distend *dis-tend′, v.t.* to stretch forth or apart: to stretch in three dimensions: to swell: to exaggerate. —*v.i.* to swell.—*n.* **distensibil′ity** capacity for distension.—*adjs.* **disten′sible** that may be stretched.— *n.* **disten′sion** act of distending or stretching: state of being stretched. [L *distendĕre—dis-,* asunder, *tendĕre, tēnsum* or *tentum,* to stretch.]

distich *dis′tik, n.* a couple of lines or verses, making complete sense: a couplet.—*adj.* having two rows.— *adjs.* **dis′tichal; dis′tichous** in or having two rows: (esp. *bot.*) arranged in, having, two opposite vertical rows. [Gr. *distichos—di-,* twice, *stichos,* a line.]

distil *dis-til′, v.i.* to fall in drops: to flow gently: to use a still.—*v.t.* to let or cause to fall in drops: to convert from liquid into vapour by heat, and then to condense again: to extract by evaporation and condensation:— *pr.p.* **distill′ing;** *pa.t.* and *pa.p.* **distilled′.**—*adj.* **distill′able.**—*ns.* **dis′tilland** that which is to be, or is being, distilled; **dis′tillate** the product of distillation; **distilla′tion** the act of distilling.—*adj.* **distill′atory** or for distilling.—*ns.* **distill′er; distill′ery** a place where distilling, esp. of alcoholic spirits, is carried on. —**destructive distillation** the collection of volatile matters released when a substance is destroyed by heat in a close vessel (as coal in making gas); **fractional distillation** the separation by distilling of liquids having different boiling-points, the heat being gradually increased and the receiver changed; **vacuum distillation** distillation under reduced pressure (effecting a lowering of the boiling point). [O.Fr. *distiller,* with substitution of prefix—L. *dēstillāre, -ātum—dē,* down, *stillāre,* to drop—*stilla,* a drop.]

distinct *dis-tingkt′, adj.* separate: different: well-defined: clear.—*n* **distinction** (*dis-tingk′shən*) separation or division: discrimination: a distinguishing mark or character: difference: a mark or honorific recognition of excellence: an honour: discriminating favour: noticeable eminence: outstanding merit: impressive and meritorious individuality. —*adj.* **distinc′tive** marking or expressing difference: characteristic.—*adv.* **distinct′ively.**—*n* **distinct′iveness.**—*adv.* **distinct′ly.**—*ns.* **distinct′ness.** [See **distinguish.**]

distingué *dē-stē-gā,* (Fr) *adj.* distinguished: striking:— *fem.* **distinguée.**

distinguish *dis-ting′gwish, v.t.* to mark off, set apart (often with *from*): to recognise by characteristic qualities: to make out: to separate by a mark of honour: to make eminent or known.—*v i.* to make or show distinctions or differences, to recognise a difference (often with *between*).—*adj* **disting′uishable** capable of being distinguished—*adv.* **disting′uishably.**—*adj.* **disting′uished** illustrious—*n* **disting′uisher.**—*adj.* **disting′uishing** peculiar [L. *distinguĕre, distinctum—dī-,* asunder, *stinguĕre,* orig. to prick.]

distort *dis-tort′, v.t* to twist aside: to put out of shape without breach of continuity: to turn aside from the true meaning: to pervert: to misrepresent.—*adj.* **distort′ed.**—*n.* **distortion** (-*tor′shən*) a twisting awry deformation without breaking: change of wave-form in course of transmission: crookedness: perversion [L *dis-,* asunder, *torquēre, tortum,* to twist]

distract *dis-trakt'*, *v.t.* to draw aside, apart, or in different directions—esp of the mind or attention: to confuse: to harass: to render crazy.—*adj.* **distract'ed.** —*adv.* **distract'edly.**—*ns.* **distract'edness; distractibil'ity.**—*adjs.* **distract'ible; distract'ing.**—*adv.* **distract'ingly.**—*n.* **distrac'tion** state of being distracted: that which distracts: perplexity: agitation: madness: recreation, relaxation. [L. *distrahĕre, -tractum—dis-*, apart, *trahĕre*, to draw.]

distrain *dis-trān'*, *v.t.* to seize (esp. goods for debt, esp. for non-payment of rent or rates).—*v.t.* to seize the goods of a debtor —*adj.* **distrain'able.**—*ns.* **distrainee'** a person whose property has been distrained; **distrain'er; distrain'ment; distrain'or** (*law*); **distraint'** seizure of goods. [O.Fr. *destraindre—*L. *dī-*, asunder, *stringĕre*, to draw tight.]

distrait *dĕs-tre*, (Fr.) *adj.* absent-minded:—*fem.* **distraite** (*dĕs-tret*).

distraught *dis-trot'*, *adj.* distracted: mad: perplexed. [**distract**, modified by association with words like **caught, taught.**]

distress *dis-tres'*, *n.* extreme pain or suffering: that which causes suffering: calamity: misfortune: acute poverty: exhaustion: peril: difficulty: act of distraining goods.—*v.t.* to afflict with pain or suffering: to harass: to grieve: to distrain.—*adj.* **distressed'.**— *adj.* **distress'ful.**—*adv.* **distress'fully.**—*n.* **distress'- fulness.**—*adj.* **distress'ing.**—*adv.* **distress'ingly.**— **distressed area** a region of unusually severe unemployment; **in distress** (of a ship or aircraft) in danger, needing help. [O.Fr. *destresse—*L. *distringĕre*.]

distribute *dis-trib'ūt*, or *dis'*, *v.t.* to divide amongst several: to deal out or allot: to classify: to disperse about a space: to spread out: to separate and put back in compartments (*print.*): to use with full extension, including every individual to which the term is applicable (*log.*).—*adjs.* **distrib'utable** that may be divided; **distrib'utary** distributing.—*n.* a branch of a distributing system: an off-flow from a river that does not return to it.—*ns.* **distrib'utor, distrib'uter** a device in a petrol engine whereby high tension current is transmitted in correct sequence to the sparking plugs; **distribu'tion** the act or process of distributing: dispersal: division: range: allotment: classification: the application of a general term to all the objects denoted by it: the manner in which the products of industry are shared among the people (*econ.*).—*adjs.* **distribu'tional; distrib'utive** that distributes, separates, or divides: giving to each his own.—*n.* a word, like *each* or *every*, that indicates the several individuals of a number taken separately.—*adv.* **distrib'u- tively.**—*n.* **distrib'utiveness.** [L. *distribuĕre—dis-*, asunder, *tribuĕre, tribūtum*, to allot.]

district *dis'trikt*, *n.* a portion of territory defined for political, judicial, educational, or other purposes (as a registration district, a militia district, the District of Columbia): a region: the smaller of the two local-government administrative units in Scotland (cf. **region**): a constituency (*U.S.*).—*v.t.* to divide into districts.—**district attorney** (*U.S.*) a public prosecutor for a district; **district council** the council of an urban or rural district: the council elected to govern a Scottish district; **district heating** the distribution of heat from a central source to buildings in the surrounding area; **district nurse** a nurse appointed to attend to cases in their own homes; **district visitor** a church worker who visits parishioners in a district. [Fr.,— L.L. *districtus*, jurisdiction—*distringĕre*; see **distrain.**]

distringas *dis-tring'gas*, *n.* an old writ directing a sheriff or other officer to distrain [Second pers sing. pres. subj. of L. *distringĕre*]

distrust *dis-trust'*, *n.* want of trust: want of faith or confidence: doubt.—*v.t.* to have no trust in: to disbelieve. to doubt —*adj* **distrust'ful** full of distrust: apt to distrust: suspicious.—*adv.* **distrust'fully.** —*n.* **distrust'fulness.** [Pfx. **dis-** (2), (3).]

disturb *dis-tûrb'*, *v.t.* to throw into confusion: to agitate. to disquiet: to interrupt: to inconvenience.— *n.* disturbance.—*n.* **disturb'ance** agitation: tumult: interruption: perplexity —*adj.* **disturbed'** worried: confused, esp. emotionally.—*n.* **disturb'er.** [O.Fr. *destourber—*L. *dis-*, asunder, *turbāre*, to agitate]

disulphide *dī-sulf'id*, *n.* a sulphide containing two atoms of sulphur to the molecule. [Pfx **di-**.]

disunion *dis-ūn'yan*, *n.* want of union: breaking up of union or concord: separation.—*v.t.* **disunite'** to separate from union: to sever or sunder.—*v i.* to fall asunder: to part.—*n.* **disu'nity** state of disunion. [Pfx. **dis-** (2), (1).]

disuse *dis-ūs'*, or *dis'ūs*, *n.* the state of being out of use.' —*v.t.* (*dis-ūz'*) to cease to use or practise: to leave out of use. [Pfx **dis-** (2), (3).]

disyllable *dis-il'a-bl*, *n.* a word of two syllables.—*adj.* **disyllabic** (*-ab'ik*). [Gr. *di-*, twice, *syllabē*, a syllable.]

dit *dē*, (Fr.) *adj* named: reputed.

ditch *dich*, *n.* a trench dug in the ground: any long narrow depression carrying water: the border of a bowling-green.—*v.t.* to make, repair or clean a ditch or ditches: of an aircraft, to come down in the sea (*coll.*).—*v.t.* to dig a ditch in or around: to drain by ditches: to throw, or drive, into a ditch: to abandon, or get rid of (*slang*): to escape from or leave in the lurch (a person) (*slang*): to bring (an aircraft) down in the sea (*coll.*).—*n.* **ditch'er** a man or machine that makes, cleans or repairs ditches.—**ditch'-water** stagnant foul water such as is found in ditches, proverbially dull. (O.E. *dic*, whence also *dike*.]

ditheism *dī'thē-izm*, *n.* the doctrine of the existence of a two supreme gods.—*n.* **di'theist.**—*adjs.* **ditheist'ic, -al.** [Gr. *di-*, twice, and *theos*, a god.]

dither *didh'ar*, *v.i.* to tremble, shiver, quake: to waver. —*v.t.* to perturb, confuse.—*n.* a trembling condition: a quaking fit: tremulous excitement: perturbation. —*n* **dith'erer.**—**all of a dither** nervous, agitated. [Prob. imit.]

dithyramb *dith'i-ram(b)*, *n* an ancient Greek hymn sung in honour of Bacchus: a short poem of a like character.—*adj.* **dithyram'bic** of or like a dithyramb: rapturous: wild and boisterous.—*adv.* **dithyram'- bically.**—*n.* **dithyram'bist.** [Gr. *dithyrambos*.]

dittany *dit'a-ni*, *n.* an aromatic plant (*Dictamnus albus*), secreting much volatile oil. [O.Fr. *dictame* —Gr. *diktamnos*, prob. from Mt. *Diktē* in Crete.]

ditto *dit'ō*, contracted **do.,** *n.* that which has been said: the same thing.—*adv.* as before, or aforesaid: in like manner.—*v.t.* to duplicate. [It. *ditto—*L. *dictum*, said, *pa.p.* of *dicĕre*, to say.]

dittography *di-tog'ra-fi*, *n.* unintentional repetition of letters or words in copying a manuscript. [Gr. *dittos*, double, *graphein*, to write.]

ditty *dit'i*, *n.* a song: a little poem to be sung.—*v.t.* to set to music. [O.Fr. *ditte—*L. *dictātum*, neut perf part. (pass.) of *dictāre*, to dictate.]

ditty-bag *dit'i-bag*, *n.* a sailor's bag for personal belongings.—Also **ditt'y-box.**

diuretic *dī-ū-ret'ik*, *adj.* promoting the discharge of urine.—*n.* a medicine causing this discharge.—*n.* **diure'sis** discharge of urine, esp in excess. [Gr. *diourētikos—dia*, through, *ouron*, urine.]

diurnal *dī-ûr'nal*, *adj* daily: relating to or performed in or lasting a day: (of animals) having one period of rest and one of activity in twenty-four hours (*biol*): belonging to the daytime —*n.* a service-book containing the day hours, except matins (a night-office): a diary, journal.—*adv.* **diur'nally.** [L. *diurnālis—diēs,* a day; see **journal.**]

diva *dē'va, n.* a popular female singer· a prima donna [It.,—L. *dīva,* fem. of *dīvus,* divine.]

divagate *dī'və-gāt, v.t* to wander about: to digress.—*n.* **divaga'tion.** [L. *dīvagārī,* to wander.]

divalent *dī-vā'lənt* or *div'əl-ənt, n.* a chemical element or atom capable of uniting with two atoms of hydrogen or their equivalent —*adj.* having two combining equivalents.—Also **bivalent.** [Gr. *di-,* twice, L *valēre,* to be worth.]

divan *di-van', n.* a collection of poems: a council of state: a court of justice· poetically, any council or assembly: a council-chamber with cushioned seats: an Eastern couch: a couch of similar type (without back or sides) often used as couch and bed (**divan'-bed'**): a smoking-room: a dewan [Ar and Pers. *dīwān,* a long seat.]

divaricate *dī-var'ı-kāt, v.t.* to part into two branches, to fork: to diverge —*v.t* to divide into two branches —*adj.* widely divergent, spreading apart.—*n.* **divarica'tion.** [L. *dīvaricāre, -ātum—* dis-, asunder, *varicāre,* to spread the legs—*varus,* bent apart.]

dive *div, v.i.* to dip or plunge into or down through water or down through the air: to go headlong into a recess, etc.: to plunge or go deeply into any matter.—*v.t.* to plunge, dip.—*n.* a plunge: a swoop: a headlong descent: a refuge: a resort, generally disreputable, often underground (*slang*): a subway.—*n.* **div'er** one who dives or can dive: one who dives for pearls: one who works from a diving-bell or in a diving-suit beneath water: a bird expert at diving, esp. the loon, loosely applied to auks, grebes, penguins, etc : a pickpocket (*slang*).—*n.* and *adj.* **div'ing.**—*v.t.* and *v.i.* **div'e-bomb** to attack with, or as if with, a dive-bomber: to discharge bombs while diving; **dive's bomber** an aeroplane that discharges a bomb while in a steep dive; **dive'-bombing; div'ing-bell** a hollow vessel or chamber, originally bell-shaped, open at the bottom and supplied with air by a tube from above, in which one may descend into and work under water; **div'ing-board** a board for diving from; **div'ing-suit,** a water-tight costume for a diver, with special provision for receiving air, etc. [O E *dȳfan, dūfan—*O.N. *dȳfa.*]

diverge *di-* or *dī-vûrj', v.i.* to incline or turn apart: to tend from a common point in different directions: to vary from the standard.—*ns.* **diverg'ence, diverg'ency.**—*adj.* **diverg'ent.**—*adv.* **diverg'ently.**—*adj.* **diverg'ing.**—*adv.* **diverg'ingly.** [L. *dī-,* asunder, *vergēre,* to incline.]

divers *dī'vərz, adj.* sundry: several: more than one — *adj.* **diverse** (*dī'vərs, dī-vûrs'*) different: unlike: multiform: various.—*adv.* **di'versely** or **diverse'ly.**—*adjs.* **diversifi'able; diver'sified.**—*n.* **diversifica'tion.**—*v.t.* **divers'ify** to give variety to: to make (investments) in securities of different types so as to lessen risk of loss: to engage in production of a variety of (manufactures, crops).—Also *v i.:—pr.p.* **diver'sifying;** *pa.t., pa.p.* **diver'sified.**—*n.* **diver'sion** act of diverting or turning aside: that which diverts: amusement, recreation· something done to turn the attention of an opponent: a detour round part of a road which is temporarily closed.—*adj.* **diver'sionary** of the nature of a diversion, designed to distract the attention of an opponent.—*ns.* **diver'sionist** a deviationist; **diver'sity** state of being diverse: difference: unlikeness: variety. —*adv.* **di'versly** in divers ways.—*v.t.* **divert** (*di-vûrt', dī-*) to turn aside (also *arch., v.t.*): to change the direction of: to turn from business or study: to amuse —*adj.* **divert'ible.**—*ns.* **divertibil'ity; divertimen'to** (the following meanings all *mus*) a piece in several

movements. a pot-pourri a light piece of music: a ballet-interlude (*pl.* **-ti** *-tē*).—*adj.* **divert'ing.**—*adv* **divert'ingly.**—*n.* **divertissement** (Fr.; *dē-ver-tēs'mä*) a divertimento —*adj* **divert'ive.** [Fr ,—L. *dīvertēre, dīversum—dī-,* aside, *vertēre,* to turn.]

diverticulum *dī-vər-tik'ū-ləm, (anat.) n* a blind tubular branch.—*adjs.* **divertic'ular, divertic'ulate, -d.**—*ns* **diverticuli'tis** inflammation of the diverticula, **diverticulō'sis** the presence of several diverticula in the intestines. [L. *dīverticulum,* a byway, retreat]

divertimento, divertissement. See **divert.**

Dives *dī'vēz, n.* the rich man at whose gate Lazarus lay (Luke xvi. 19) a rich and luxurious person. [L *dives,* rich (man), understood as a proper name.]

divest *dī-* or *di-vest', v.t.* to strip or deprive of anything —*adj.* **divest'ible.**—*n.* **divest'iture.** [O.Fr. *desvestir,* with change of prefix (*dis-* for *dē-*) from L. *dēvestīre—dē,* away from, *vestīre,* to clothe—*vestis,* a garment.]

divi. See **divvy.**

divide *di-vīd', v.t* to break up, or mark off, into parts, actually or in imagination: to separate or distinguish the parts of: to classify· to share: to allot: to deal out: to ascertain how many times a quantity is contained in (*math*) to be a boundary or a subject of difference between: to keep apart: to cause to vote for and against a motion: to sever.—*v t* to separate: to fall apart: to branch: to vote for and against a motion: to admit of or be susceptible of division —*n.* the act of dividing (*coll*): a watershed: something that divides or separates, a gap —*adjs.* **divid'able** (or *div'id-*) **divisible** —*n.* **divid'er** one who or that which divides: (in *pl*) a kind of compasses for measuring —**divided highway** (*U S.*) a dual carriageway. [L. *dīvidēre, dīvīsum—dis-,* asunder, root *vid,* to separate.]

dividend *div'i-dend, n.* that which is to be divided: the share of a sum divided that falls to each individual, by way of interest or otherwise —**dividend stripping** a method of evading tax on dividends by a contrived arrangement between a company liable to tax and another in a position to claim repayment of tax, **div'idend-warr'ant** a certificate entitling to payment of dividend.—**declare a dividend** to announce the sum per cent a trading concern is prepared to pay its shareholders [L *dīvidendum,* to be divided, *dīvidēre*]

dividivi *div'i-div-i, n.* the curved pods of *Caesalpinia coriaria,* imported for tanning and dyeing. [Carib name.]

divine *di-vīn', adj.* belonging to or proceeding from a god: holy· excellent in the highest degree.—*n.* one skilled in divine things: a minister of the gospel: a theologian —*v t* to foresee or foretell as if divinely inspired: to guess or make out: to prognosticate: to search for (underground water, etc.), esp. with a divining-rod.—*v.t.* to profess or practice divination: to have forebodings —*ns.* **divina'tion** the act or practice of divining: seeking to know the future or hidden things by magical means: instinctive prevision: prediction· conjecture; **divin'er** one who divines or professes divination· a conjecturer —*adj.* **divin'atory** relating to divination, conjectural —*adv* **divine'ly.**—*n* **divine'ness.**—**divin'ing-rod** a rod, usually of hazel, used by those professing to discover water or metals under ground [O.Fr *devin,* soothsayer, and L *dīvīnus—dīvus, deus,* a god]

diving. See **dive.**

divinity *di-vin'i-ti, n.* godhead· the nature or essence of a god· a celestial being. a god: the science of divine things: theology [O Fr *devinite—*L *dīvīnitās, -tātis,* see **divine.**]

division *di-vizh'ən, n* act of dividing· state of being divided: that which divides: a partition· a barrier· a portion or section· the taking of a vote: an army unit (usually half an army corps) containing almost all branches of the service: separation: difference in opinion, etc.: disunion: the process of finding how many times one quantity is contained in another (*math*).—*n.* **divisibil'ity** (-*viz*-).—*adj.* **divis'ible** capable of being divided or separated. capable of being divided without remainder.—*adv.* **divis'ibly.**—*adjs* **divisional** (-*vizh'*), **divis'ionary** pertaining to or marking a division or separation; **divisive** (-*viz'*) forming division or separation. creating discord —*ns* **divis'iveness; divis'or** (*math.*) the number which divides the dividend.—*division-lobby* see **lobby.** [L *divisio*, -*onis*, *divisor*, -*oris*—*dividere*, to divide]

divorce *di-vors'*, -*vors'*, *n.* the legal dissolution of marriage· separation (*fig.*).—*v t* to dissolve the marriage of· to put away by divorce. to separate.—*v i.* to obtain a divorce.—*adj.* **divorce'able.**—*ns.* **divorcee'** a divorced person, **divor'cer.**—*adj.* **divor'cive** having power to divorce [Fr ,—L *divortium*—*divortere*, another form of *divertere*, see **divert.**]

divot *div'ət*, (*Scot.*) *n.* a thin sod, cut for roofing, etc., or accidentally by golfers when hitting the ball

divulge *di-* or *di-vulj'*, *v.t.* to spread abroad among the people to make public: to reveal.—*v.t.* **divul'gate** (-*gåt*) to publish.—*n.* **divulga'tion.** [L. *divulgare*—*di-*, abroad, *vulgare*, to publish—*vulgus*, the common people]

divvy, divi *div'i*, (*slang*) *n.* a dividend.—*v t* and *v i.* to divide. to go shares.—Also **divvy up.** [Abbrev of **divide, dividend.**]

Diwali *di-wa'le, n* the Hindu or Sikh festival of lamps held in October or November. [Hindi *diwali.*]

diwan. Same as **dewan.**

dixie, dixy *diks'i, n.* a military cooking-pail or camp-kettle. [Perh. Hindi *degci*—Pers. *degcha*, dim of *dig*, large metallic cooking utensil.]

Dixieland *dik'si-land, n.* an early style of jazz in New Orleans, played by small combinations of instruments [*Dixie*, name given to southern states of U.S.]

DIY *dee'i-wi', n.* and *adj.* abbrev. of **do-it-yourself.**

dizzy *diz'i, adj.* giddy: confused: causing giddiness· silly (*coll.*): extreme (*coll.*).—*v.t.* to make dizzy: to confuse —*adv.* **dizz'ily.**—*n.* **dizz'iness.**—*adj.* **dizz'y**-ing making dizzy. [O.E. *dysig,* foolish]

djellaba, djellabah *jə-lä'bə, n.* a cloak with a hood and wide sleeves.—Also **jellab'a.** [Ar. *jallabah, jallâb.*]

djinn, djinni. See **jinn.**

DNA *dē-en-ā, n.* deoxyribonucleic acid (q.v.).

do¹ *dōō, v.t* to put in some condition: to render: to confer: to bestow: to perform: to accomplish: to finish: to exhaust: to work at: to perform work upon: to beat up, thrash (*slang*): to prepare, set in order: to cook: to cheat, or overreach (*slang*)· to raid, rob (*slang*): to treat: to make the round of, see the sights of. to spend in prison —*v.i.* to act, be active: to behave: to fare: to thrive: to suffice: to be good enough to pass:—*2nd sing.* **do'est, dost** *dust, 3rd* **does** *duz*, also **do'eth, doth** *duth; pa.t.* **did;** *pr.p.* **do'ing;** *pa.p.* **done** *dun* —*Do* serves as a substitute for a verb that has just been used. It is used as an auxiliary verb (where there is no other auxiliary) with an infinitive in negative, interrogative, emphatic, and rhetorically inverted sentences, in some dialects merely periphrastically, and in verse sometimes to gain a syllable or postpone the accent; but these uses are limited with the verbs *have* and *do.*—*n.* a feast, celebration: a swindle, hoax (*slang*):—*pl.* **do's** or **dos**.—*adj* **do'able** that can be done.—*n.* **do'er** one who does, or habitually does, anything· an agent.—*adj* **do'ing** active (as in *up and doing*).—*n.* (*coll*) a scolding· thrashing severe treatment. (in *pl*) activities, behaviour (in *pl*) fancy dishes or adjuncts: (in *pl*) what's-its-name

(*slang*).—**done** *pa.p.* of **do.**—*adj* utterly exhausted: socially acceptable —*interj.* agreed.—*n.* (*cook.*) **done'ness** the state of being, or degree to which something is, cooked.—**do'-good'er** a slighting name for one who tries to benefit others by social reforms etc., implying that his, her, efforts are unwelcome or ineffectual, **do'-good'ery** (*slang*); **do'-good'ism.**—*adj* **do'-it-yourself** designed to be built, constructed, etc by an amateur rather than by someone specially trained.—Also *n* —**do'-noth'ing** a lazy or idle person; **do'-noth'ingism;** **do'-noth'ingness.**—*all done* completely finished, used up, **be done** to be at an end, **be, have done with** to finish with, end contact or dealings with; **do away with** to abolish, destroy; **do by** to act towards; **do down** to cheat, get the better of (*slang*); **do for** to suit: to provide for. to ruin: to kill (*coll*)· to do domestic work for (*coll*), **do in** to exhaust: to ruin. to murder; **do or die** to make a final desperate attempt to do, achieve, etc. something, no matter what the cost or consequences (*adj.* **do'-or-die'**); **do's and don'ts** advice or rules for action, esp. in particular circumstances; **do over** to cover over, as with paint: to beat up (*slang*); **do someone proud** (*coll.*) to make someone feel flattered. to treat lavishly; **do to death** to murder: to repeat too often; **do up** to fasten up: to put up, make tidy, arrange, tie up. to redecorate: to apply cosmetics: to dress: to fatigue utterly; **do well** to be justified: to prosper; **do without** not to be dependent on, to dispense with; **have done** to desist: to stop it: to have no more dealings; **have to do with** to have any sort of connection with; **have you done?** are you finished?; **how do you do?** a conventional phrase used on greeting; **nothing doing** no; **that's done it** it is completed: (*interj.* indicating dismay) it is spoiled, ruined. [O.E. *dōn, dyde, gedōn*; Du. *doen,* Ger. *tun*; conn with Gr. *tithenai*, to put, place]

do² *dō,* (*mus.*) *n* a syllable representing the first note of the scale—anglicised as **doh:**—*pl.* **dos** or **do's** [Perh. from G.B. *Doni* (1593–1647), who is said to have substituted it for the Aretinian syllable *ut* (see **gamut**).]

doat. Same as **dote.**

dobbin *dob'in, n.* a workhorse [An altered dim. of *Robert*]

Doberman(n) pinscher *dōb'ər-mən pin'shər,* a breed of terrier—large, smooth-coated, with long forelegs. [*Dobermann*, the first breeder, and Ger. *Pinscher*, terrier.]·

doc *dok, n.* a familiar contraction of **doctor.**

Docetism *dō-sē'tizm, n* a 2nd-century heresy, that Christ's body was only a semblance, or else of ethereal substance.—*n.* **Doce'tist**—*adj* **Docetic** (-*sēt'*, -*set'*). [Gr. *dokēsis*, phantom, semblance—*dokeein*, to seem.]

dochmius *dok'mi-əs, n.* a foot of five syllables, typically with first and fourth short, the rest long.—*adj.* **doch'miac.** [L —Gr. *dochmios.*]

docile *dō'sil adj.* teachable· ready to learn: easily managed.—*n.* **docil'ity.** [Fr.,—L *docilis*—*docere,* to teach]

dock¹ *dok, n* a weed with large leaves and a long root. [O.E *docce*]

dock² *dok, v t* to cut short to curtail: to cut off: to clip: to deprive of pay —*n.* the part of a tail left after clipping [M.E *dok*, prob.—O.N. *dokkr*, stumpy tail]

dock³ *dok, n.* (often used in *pl.*) an artificial basin for the reception of vessels and cargo: the waterway between two wharves or two piers a wharf or pier· the enclosure in court for the accused: in a railway station, the place of arrival and departure of a train —*v t* to place in a dock. to bring into dock· to equip with docks: to join (space-craft) together in space — Also *v.i.*—*v.i.* to enter a dock.—*ns.* **dock'age** accommodation in docks for ships: dock-dues; **dock'er** one who works in the docks; **dock'ing.**— **dock'-dues** payments for use of a dock; **dock'land** a district about docks; **dock'-master** the person superintending a dock; **dock'yard** a naval establishment with docks, building-slips, stores, etc.—**in the dock** (*lit.* and *fig.*) accused of, charged with some misdemeanour. [Origin obscure, cf O Du *dokke*]

docket *dok'it, n* a summary of a larger writing: a bill or ticket affixed to anything indicating its contents a label: a list or register of cases in court, or of legal judgments, or (*U.S.*) business to be transacted· a customhouse certificate of payment.—*v t* to make a summary of the heads of a writing: to enter in a book to mark the contents of papers on the back.—*pr.p.* **dock'eting;** *pa.t.* and *pa.p.* **dock'eted.** [Perh a dim of **dock,** to curtail]

doctor *dok'tər, n.* a teacher (*arch.*). a learned father of the church: a cleric especially skilled in theology or ecclesiastical law: one who has received the highest degree in any faculty: a physician or medical practitioner, whatever be his degree in medicine· a mender: a ship's cook: a name for various contrivances for removing defects in manufacture· an angler's fly.— *v.t.* to treat, as a doctor does. to patch up, repair: to sophisticate, tamper with, falsify: to address as doctor: to confer a doctor's degree upon.—*v.t* to practise medicine —*adj.* **doc'toral.**—*v t.* **doc'torate** to confer the degree of doctor upon —*n.* an academic degree of doctor.—*adjs.* **doctorial** (-*tō'ri-əl, -to'ri-əl*); **doc'torly.**—*n.* **doc'torship.**—**doc'tor-fish** a sea-surgeon; **Doctors' Commons** before the establishment of the Divorce Court and Probate Court in 1857, the college of the doctors of civil law in London, incorporated by royal charter in 1768 —**what the doctor ordered** (*coll.*) the very thing that's needed. [L , a teacher—*docēre,* to teach]

doctrinaire *dok-tri-nār', n.* an unpractical theorist, disposed to carry principles to logical but unworkable extremes.—*adj.* theoretical [Fr.,—L.L *doctrīnārius*]

doctrine *dok'trin, n.* a thing taught. a principle of belief.—*adj.* **doc'trinal** (or *-trī'nəl*).—*adv* **doc'trinally** (or *-trī'*). [L. *doctrīna—docēre,* to teach.]

document *dok'ū-mənt, n* a paper or other material thing affording information, proof, or evidence of anything —*v.t.* (also *-ment'*) to furnish with documents to support or prove by documents —*adjs.* **documental** (*-ment'*), **document'ary** relating to or found in documents: aiming at presentation of reality.—*ns.* **document'alist** one who specialises in documentation: one who collects and classifies documents; **document'ary** a motion-picture presenting an activity or occupation of real life without fictional colouring or professional actors; **documenta'tion** preparation, setting forth, or use of documentary evidence and authorities: in fiction, realistic reproduction of records, real or supposed [Fr ,—L. *documentum—docēre,* to teach.]

dodder *dod'ər, n.* a leafless, twining, pale parasitic plant of or akin to the convolvulus family. [M.E *doder;* cf. Ger. *Dotter.*]

dodder *dod'ər, v.i.* to shake: to tremble to totter: to be decrepit in mind or body.—*n.* **dodd'erer.**—*adjs* **dodd'ering; dodd'ery.** [Perh. conn. with **doddered.**]

doddered, doddard *dod'ərd, adj.* orig. perh. pollard: decayed with loss of branches

dodeca- *dō-dek-ə-,* in composition, twelve.—*ns* **dodec'agon** (Gr. *gōniā,* an angle) a plane figure with twelve angles and sides; **dodecahe'dron** (*-hē'dron,* Gr.; *hedrā,* a seat) a solid figure, having twelve faces

—*adjs* **dodecahē'dral; dodecaphon'ic** (*mus.*; Gr *phōnē,* voice) twelve-tone —*n* **dodecasyll'able** (*pros.*) a line of twelve syllables.—*adj.* **dodecasyllab'ic.** [Gr *dōdeka,* twelve]

dodge *doj, v.t* to start aside or shift about: to evade or use mean tricks. to shuffle or quibble.—*v.t.* to evade by a sudden shift of place: to evade: to trick.—*n.* an evasion· a trick· a quibble —*n.* **dodg'er** one who dodges ·a screen on a ship's bridge for shelter in rough weather: an advertising leaflet (*U S*).—*adj* **dodg'y** artful, tricky: difficult to do or carry out· risky — **dodge the column** (*slang*) to evade one's duties

Dodgem(s)® *doj'əm(z), n.* (also without *cap.*) an amusement in which drivers of small electric cars within an enclosure strive to bump others without being bumped.

dodo *dō'dō, n* a clumsy flightless bird, about the size of a turkey, a native of Mauritius, extinct about the end of the 17th century:—*pl* **do'do(e)s.** [Port *doudo,* silly]

doe *dō, n.* the female of the fallow-deer or buck: extended to the female of other deer, of antelope, rabbit, hare, and sometimes other animals —*adj.* **doe'-eyed** having large, dark eyes like those of a deer, **doe'-skin** the skin of a doe: a smooth, close-woven, woollen cloth. [O.E. *dā,* Dan *daa,* deer.]

doer, does etc. See **do[1]**.

doff *dof, v.t* to take off: to put off: to remove [**do[1]**, **off.**]

dog *dog, n.* a wild or domestic animal of the same genus as the wolf· a male of the species: a mean scoundrel: a term of contempt: a fellow: either of the two constellations, the Greater and the Lesser Dog: an andiron: a hook for holding logs: a gripping appliance of various kinds: a cock, as of a gun: a dogfish: a prairie dog: heavy ostentation (*slang*): (in *pl.*) greyhound races (*coll.*).—*adj. (and in composition)* of dogs: male (opposed to *bitch*): spurious, base, inferior.—*adv. (esp. in composition)* utterly.—*v.t.* to follow as a dog: to track and watch constantly: to worry, plague, infest:—*pr p.* **dogg'ing;** *pa.t.* and *pa.p.* **dogged.**—*adj.* **dogg'ed** dog-like: sullen: pertinacious.—*adv.* **dogg'edly.**—*ns* **dogg'edness; dogg'iness.**—*adj.* **dogg'ish** doglike: characteristic of dogs: churlish: brutal —*adv.* **dogg'ishly.**—*n.* **dogg'ishness.**—*adj.* **dogg'y** fond of dogs: doglike; **dog'berry** the fruit of the wild cornel or dogwood; **dog'-bis'cuit** a biscuit for feeding dogs, **dog'cart** a two-wheeled horse-vehicle with seats back to back, originally used to carry sporting dogs; **dog'-collar** a collar for a dog: a clerical collar fastened behind; **dog'days** the period when the Dogstar rises and sets with the sun (generally reckoned July 3rd to August 11th).—*adj.* **dog'-eared** of pages of a book, turned down like the ears of a dog: hence, shabby, scruffy.—**dog'-eat-dog'** a ruthless pursuit of one's own interests, savage self-concern.— Also *adj.*—**dog'-end** (*slang*) a cigarette-end; **dog's fancier** a breeder or seller of dogs; **dog'fight** a fight between dogs: a confused fight or mêlée: a fight between fighter aircraft, esp. at close quarters, **dog'fish** a small shark of various kinds; **dog'gy-bag** a bag used by diners to carry home leftover food from a restaurant (for their pets); **dog'gy-paddle, dog'-paddle** a crude swimming stroke used by humans in imitation of a dog; **dog'-house** a dog-kennel· a place of disgrace (*fig*); **dog'-Lat'in** barbarous Latin.—*adj* **dog'-leg(ged)** bent like a dog's hind leg; **dog'-rose** species of wild rose; **dog's'-body** (orig. *naut. slang*) junior naval (or other) officer: (usu. without hyphen) a general drudge; **dog'shores** pieces of timber used to shore up a vessel before launching; **dog'skin** leather made of or in imitation of dog's skin; **dog's'-meat** scraps and refuse sold as food for dogs; **dog's'-nose** gin and beer, or similar mixture; **dog's'-tail-grass'** a common British pasture grass; **Dog' star** Sirius, in the constellation of the Greater Dog, brightest star in the heavens and giving name to the dogdays; **dog's'-tongue** hound's-tongue; **dog's'-tooth** a broken-check pattern used extensively in the weaving of tweeds.—*adj.* **dog'-tired** tired as a dog, completely worn out —**dog'tooth** a moulding in later Norman architecture, consisting of a series of ornamental square pyramids; **dog'-vi'olet** a scentless wild violet; **dog'-watch** (*naut.*) on shipboard, a watch 4–6 p.m. or 6–8 p.m., consisting of two hours only, instead of four; **dog'wood** the wild cornel, a small tree with white flowers and purple berries, the shoots and leaves turning red in autumn.—**dog in the manger** one who will not let others enjoy what he has himself no use for; **dog's age** (*coll.*) a long time; **dog's breakfast, dinner** anything very untidy; **dog's chance** a bare chance; **dog's life** a wretched, miserable life; **dogs of war** (*fig.*) troops, aggressors, mercenaries, warlike people; **go to the dogs** to be ruined; **hot dog** a roll containing a hot sausage; **like a dog's dinner** (*slang*) very smart, dressed up flamboyantly. [Late O.E. *docga.*]

doggone(d) *dog-gon(d')*, *interj.* expressing, vexation—Also *adj.*

doge *dōj*, or *dō'jā*, *n.* the chief magistrate in republican Venice and Genoa. [It. (Venetian dial.) for *duce*, duke—L. *dux*, a leader.]

dogger[1] *dog'ər*, *n.* a two-masted Dutch fishing-vessel.—**dogg'erman**. [Du.]

dogger[2] *dog'ər*, *n.* a concretion, esp. of ironstone: a sandy ironstone or ferruginous sandstone: part of the Middle Jurassic.

doggerel *dog'ər-əl*, *n.* irregular measures in burlesque poetry, so named in contempt: worthless verses.—*adj* irregular in rhythm, mean.—Also **dogg'rel**.

doggo *dog'ō*, (*coll.*) *adj.* hidden. [Poss. from **dog**[1].]

dogie, dogy *dō'gi*, (*U.S.*) *n.* a motherless calf.

dogma *dog'mə*, *n.* a settled opinion: a principle or tenet: a doctrine laid down with authority.—*adjs.* **dogmatic** (*-mat'ik*) **-al** pertaining to a dogma: asserting a thing as if it were a dogma: asserting positively: overbearing.—*adv.* **dogmat'ically**.—*n. sing.* **dogmat'ics** (*theol.*) the statement of Christian doctrines, systematic theology.—*v.i.* **dog'matise, -ize** (*-mə-tīz*) to state one's opinion dogmatically or arrogantly.—**dog'matiser, -z-; dog'matism** dogmatic or positive assertion of opinion; **dog'matist** one who makes positive assertions; **dogmatol'ogy** the science of dogma. [Gr. *dogma, -atos*, an opinion—*dokein*, to think, seem.]

doh. See **do**[2].

doily *doi'li*, *n.* a small lace or lacy paper, etc. ornamented napkin, often laid on or under dishes.—Also **doy'ley**. [From *Doily* or *Doyley*, a famous haberdasher.]

doit *doit*, *n.* a small Dutch coin worth about half a farthing: a thing of little or no value. [Du. *duit*.]

Dolby® *dol'bi*, *n.* an electronic device which reduces the amount of extraneous noise on recorded or broadcast sound. [*Dolby*, its inventor.]

dolce *dol'chā*, *adj.* sweet, esp. of music.—*n.* a soft-toned organ-stop.—**dolce far niente** (*fär nē-en'tā*) sweet doing-nothing, pleasant idleness; **dolce vita** (*vē'ta*; It., sweet life) a life of wealth, pleasure and self-indulgence. [It.,—L. *dulcis*.]

doldrums *dol'drəmz*, *n. pl.* those parts of the ocean about the equator where calms and baffling winds prevail: low spirits. [Prob. conn. with obs. *dold*, stupid, or *dol*, dull.]

dole[1] *dōl*, *n.* a share: a dealing out: something given in charity: (usu. contemptuously) state pay to unemployed.—*v.t.* to deal out in small portions. [O.E. *dāl*; cf. **deal**[1].]

dole[2] *dōl*, *n.* pain· grief: heaviness at heart (*arch.* and *poet.*) —*adj.* **dole'ful** full of dole or grief: melancholy.—*adv.* **dole'fully**.—*n.* **dole'fulness**. [O.Fr. *doel* (Fr. *deuil*), grief—L. *dolēre*, to feel pain.]

dolerite *dol'ər-it*, *n.* a basic igneous rock like basalt in composition but coarser grained.—*adj.* **dolerit'ic**. [Fr. *dolérite*—Gr *doleros*, deceptive.]

dolia. See **dolium**.

dolicho- *dol-i-kō-*, in composition, long.—*adj.* **dolichocephalic** (*-sif-al'ik*; Gr. *kephalē*, the head) long-headed—having a breadth of skull (from side to side) less than 75 (or 78) per cent. of the length (front to back)—opp. to *brachycephalic*.—Also **dolichoceph'alous**.—*ns.* **dolichoceph'aly, dolichoceph'alism**. [Gr. *dolichos*, long.]

doll *dol*, *n.* a puppet: a toy in human form: an insipid woman, esp. one who is over-dressed and silly: a young woman (*slang*).—*v.i.* and *v.t.* to dress (often with *up*).—*adj.* **doll'ish**.—*ns.* **doll'ishness; doll'y** dim. of **doll**, an attractive young girl (also **dolly girl** or **bird**): formerly, a dolly-mop: a slow, easy catch (*cricket*) or shot.—Also *adj.*—**doll's'-house; doll'y-shop** a marine store—a low pawn-shop—often having a black doll as sign. [Prob. from *Dolly*, familiar dim. of *Dorothy*.]

dollar *dol'ər*, *n.* a silver coin (= 100 cents) of U.S.A., Canada, Australia, New Zealand, Mexico, Hong-Kong, etc.: a thaler: five shillings (*old slang*).—*n.* **dollaroc'racy**.—**dollar area** those countries as a whole whose currencies are linked to the U.S. dollar; **dollar diplomacy** diplomacy dictated by financial interests: diplomacy that employs financial weapons to increase political power; **dollar gap** the excess of imports from a dollar country over exports to it, necessitating settlement by dollar exchange or in gold. [Ger. *T(h)aler* (L. G. *daler*), short for *Joachimsthaler* because first coined at the silver-mines in Joachimsthal (Joachim's dale) in Bohemia.]

dollop *dol'əp*, *n.* a lump. [Prob. conn. with Norw. dial. *dolp*, a lump.]

dolly[1]. See **doll**.

dolly[2] *dol'i*, *n.* a wooden shaft attached to a disc with projecting arms, used for beating and stirring clothes in a washing-tub: somewhat similar apparatus in mining, pile-driving, etc.: a tool for holding the head of a rivet: a trolley, truck, or platform on wheels or roller.—*v.t.* to operate upon, yield, or obtain, with a dolly.—**dolly camera** a camera moving on a dolly; **doll'y-shop** see **doll**; **dolly shot** a shot taken with a dolly camera; **dolly switch** a switch, for an electric light, etc., pushed up and down vertically; **doll'y-tub** a tub for washing clothes or ores with a dolly. [Prob. from *Dolly*, the familiar form of *Dorothy*.]

Dolly Varden *dol'i var'dən*, a flowered muslin dress for women: a large hat, one side bent downwards, abundantly trimmed with flowers: a large American fish of the char genus. [Named from a character in Dickens's *Barnaby Rudge*.]

dolman *dol'mən*, *n.* a Turkish robe with slight sleeves and open in front: a hussar's jacket, worn like a cloak, with one or both sleeves hanging loose: a woman's mantle.—**dolman sleeve** a kind of sleeve which tapers from a very wide armhole to a tight wrist. [Turk. *dōlāmān*.]

dolmen *dol'mən*, *n.* a stone table: a prehistoric sepulchral chamber of erect unhewn stones, supporting a flattish stone. [Fr. *dolmen*; usually explained as—Bret. *dol, taol*, table, *men*, stone; but *tolmēn* in Cornish meant hole of stone.]

dolomite *dol'ə-mīt*, *n.* a mineral, double carbonate of calcium and magnesium: a rock composed of that mineral, magnesian limestone.—*adj.* **dolomitic** (*-mit'ik*). [After the French geologist D. Guy de *Dolomieu* (1750–1801).]

dolour *dol'ər, döl'ər, n.* pain: grief: anguish.—*adjs.* **doloriferous, dolori'fic** causing or conveying dolour, pain, or grief.—*adv.* **doloro'so** (It.; *mus.*), in a soft and pathetic manner.—*adj.* **dol'orous** full of dolour, pain, or grief: doleful.—*adv.* **dol'orously.**—*n.* **dol'orousness.** [O.Fr.,—L. *dolēre,* to grieve.]

dolphin *dol'fin, n.*-any of a group of animals of the whale kind, about 8 to 10 feet long, with a beak-like snout: sometimes used loosely in the U.S. to include the porpoise: a fish about 5 feet in length noted for the brilliancy of its colours when dying (also **dol'phinfish**): a buoy or pile for mooring.—*ns.* **dolphinarium** (-*á'ri-əm*) an aquarium for dolphins:—*pl.* **-á'riums, -á'ria** (*-ə*). [O.Fr. *daulphin*—L. *delphinus*—Gr. *delphīs, -phīnos.*]

dolt *dölt, n.* a dull or stupid fellow.—*adj.* **dolt'ish** dull: stupid.—*adv.* **dolt'ishly.**—*n.* **dolt'ishness.** [For **dulled** or blunted.]

Dom *dom, n.* the Portuguese form of *Don:* also a title given to certain Catholic dignitaries and members of some monastic orders, esp. the Benedictine. [L. *dominus,* lord.]

-dom *-dom, dəm, suff.* forming nouns, denoting dominion, power, state, act. [O.E. *dōm,* judgment; Ger. *-tum.*]

domain *dō-mān', n.* what one is master of or has dominion over: an estate: territory: ownership of land: the scope or range of any subject or sphere of knowledge: an aggregate to which a variable belongs (*math.*).—*adjs.* **domain'al, domā'nial.** [Fr. *domaine*—L. *dominicum*—*dominus,* a master.]

dome *dōm, n.* a structure, usually hemispherical, raised above a large building: a large cupola: a building, esp. a great or stately building (*poet.*): anything approaching the form of a hemispherical vault, esp. a head, the cover of a reverberatory furnace, the steam-chamber on a locomotive boiler, a clip-fastener that fits into a hold.—*v.t.* to furnish with a dome: to form into a dome.—*v.i.* to swell or rise as a dome. [L. *domus,* a house.]

Domesday-, Doomsday-book *dōōmz'dā-bŏŏk n.* a book compiled by order of William the Conqueror, containing a survey of all the lands in England, their value, owners, etc.—so called from its authority in judgment (O.E. *dōm*) on the matters contained in it.

domestic *dō-, də-mes'tik, adj.* belonging to the house: remaining much at home: private: tame: not foreign. —*n.* a servant in the house.—*adj.* **domes'ticable.**— *adv.* **domes'tically.**—*v.t.* **domes'ticate** to make domestic or familiar: to tame.—*adj.* **domes'ticated** adapted to or content with home life and activities: tamed.—*ns.* **domestica'tion; domes'ticator.**—*n.* **domesticity** (*dō-, do-mis-tis'*) domestic or domesticated state: home life: (in *pl.*) home conditions and arrangements.—**domestic architecture** the architecture of mansions, dwelling-houses, cottages, etc.; **domestic economy** the principles of efficient ordering of a household; **domestic science** the household arts. [L. *domesticus*—*domus,* a house.]

domicile *dom'i-sīl, -sil, dom'icīl -sil, ns.* a dwelling-place, abode: one's legally recognised place of residence.—*v t.* (**domicile**) to establish in a fixed residence —*adjs.* **dom'iciled; domiciliary** (*-sil'*) pertaining to the domicile: dealing with, or available to, people in their own homes —**domiciliary visit** a visit, under authority, to a private house for the purpose of searching it: a visit made by a doctor, etc. to a patient's or client's home. [Fr ,—L. *domicilium*— *domus,* a house.]

dominant *dom'in ənt, adj.* prevailing: predominant overtopping of an ancestral character, appearing in the first generation of cross-bred offspring to the exclusion of the alternative character in the other parent, which may yet be transmitted to later generations (*genetics*).—*n.* the fifth above the tonic (*mus.*): a dominant Mendelian character: one of the prevailing species in a plant community.—*ns.* **dom'inance, dom'inancy** ascendency: the state of being dominant.—*adv.* **dom'inantly.** [L. *dominans, -antis,* pr.p. of *dominārī,* to be master.]

dominate *dom'in-āt, v.t.* to be lord over: to govern: to prevail over: to tower over: to command a view of: to be the controlling position of: to be predominant in: to project one's personality, influence, etc. strongly over.—Also *v.i.*—*n.* the Roman Empire in its later more avowedly absolute form.—*n.* **domina'tion** government; absolute authority: tyranny.—*n.* **dom'inator.** [L. *dominārī, -ātus,* to be master— *dominus,* master—*domāre,* to tame.]

domineer *dom-in-ēr', v.i.* (often with *over*) to rule arbitrarily: to command haughtily: to be overbearing.— *adj.* **domineer'ing** overbearing. [Prob. through Du. from O.Fr. *dominer*—L. *dominārī.*]

dominical *do-min'i-kl, adj.* belonging to the Lord, as the Lord's Prayer, the Lord's Day.—**dominical letter** one of the first seven letters of the alphabet, used in calendars to mark the Sundays throughout the year. [L.L. *dominicālis*—*dominus,* lord, master.]

Dominican *do-min'i-kən, adj.* belonging to St. *Dominic* or to the Dominicans.—*n.* a friar or monk of the order of St. Dominic—*Fratres Predicatores,* founded in 1215, or *Black Friars,* from their black mantle.

dominie *dom'i-ni, n.* a schoolmaster, a tutor. [L. *domine,* voc. of *dominus,* master.]

dominion *də-min'yən, n.* lordship: sovereignty: a domain or territory with one ruler, owner or government: a completely self-governing colony, not subordinate to but freely associated with the mother-country: control. [L.L. *dominiō, -ōnis—dominus,* master.]

domino *dom'i-nō, n.* a long cloak of black silk with a hood, used at masked balls, or its wearer: a mask: one of the oblong pieces with which the game of **dom'inoes** (*-nōz*) is played, usually twenty-eight in number, divided into two compartments, each of which is a blank or marked with from one to six spots —**domino theory** the theory that one event (orig. the fall of one S.E. Asian country to Communism) sets off a series of similar events (i.e. the neighbouring countries following suit), thus exhibiting the **domino effect,** the fall of one domino standing on end causing the whole row to fall in turn. [Apparently Sp. *dominó, dómino,* in some way conn. with L. *dominus,* master.]

don[1] *don, n.* (with *cap.*) a Spanish title, corresponding to English Sir, Mr (*fem.* **Doña** (*dón'ya*) (Italian form **Don'na**): a Spanish nobleman, a Spaniard: a fellow of a college, a college authority —*adj* **donn'ish** pertaining to a don: with the airs of a don.—**Don Juan** (*hwàn, jōō'ən*) a libertine of Spanish legend: an attractive profligate. [Sp.,—L. *dominus.*]

don[2] *don, v.t.* to do or put on: to assume:—*pr.p* **donn'ing;** *pa.t.* and *pa.p.* **donned.** [do, on.]

donation *dō nā'shən, n.* an act of giving: that which is given, a gift of money or goods: the act by which a person freely transfers his title to anything to another (*law*).—*v.t.* **dōnate'** (a back-formation from **donation**) to give as gift: to contribute, esp. to charity —*n.* **dōnative** (or *don'*), a gift: a gratuity. a benefice presented by the founder or patron without reference to the bishop —*adj.* vested or vesting by donation —*ns* **dōnā'tor** one who makes a gift, a donor, **dōnee'** the person to whom a gift is made, **dō'nor** a giver a benefactor: a person who (or animal which) provides blood, semen, or tissue or organs for use in transplant surgery.—**donor card** a card carried by a person willing to have parts of his body (usu. kidneys) used in transplant surgery in the event of his death. [Fr.—L. *dōnāre, -ātum—dōnum*, a gift—*dāre*, to give.]

done. See **do¹.**

dong *dong, n.* a deep ringing sound, as that of a large bell.—Also *v.i.* [Imit.]

donga *dong'gə,* (orig. *S. Afr.) n.* a gully. [Zulu, bank, side of a gully.]

donjon *dun'jən, n.* a strong central tower in ancient castles, to which the garrison retreated when hard pressed. [A doublet of **dungeon.**]

donkey *dong'ki, n.* an ass: a stupid person:—*pl.* **don'keys.**—**don'key-en'gine** a small auxiliary engine; **donkey jacket** a strong jacket, with shoulders of leather or (usu.) a substitute, and patch pockets; **don'key-work** drudgery.—**argue, talk, the hindleg(s) off a donkey** to do so with invincible pertinacity; **donkey's years** a long time (a pun on *ears*). [Still regarded as slang in 1823; perh. a double dim. of *dun,* from its colour; or from *Duncan.*]

Donna. See **don¹.**

donnard, donnart. See **donnered.**

donné(e) *do'nā, n.* a datum: basic assumption(s), as e.g. a given situation, on which a work of literature is founded: the main fact or condition determining the character and timing of an action:—*pl.* **donn'é(e)s** (*-ā(z)*). [Fr.]

donnered, donnerd, donnert, donnard, donnart *don'ərd, -ərt,* (*Scot.) adjs.* stupid: dull-witted.

Donnerwetter *don'ər-vet-ər,* (Ger.) *n.* thunderstorm (used as an interjection of annoyance, etc.).

Donnybrook *don'i-brŏŏk, n.* a riotous assembly. [From the fair at *Donnybrook,* Dublin.]

donor. See **donation.**

don't *dōnt,* for **do not.**—*n.* something one must not do. —**don't-know** (the answer given by) one whose mind is not made up with regard to some, esp. political, issue.

donut. Same as **doughnut.**

doodad *dōō'dad, n.* a small ornament or trinket: a gadget.—*n.* **doodah** (*dōō'dā*) a state of agitation, in phrase **all of a doodah.** [Both coined from **do¹.**]

doodle *dōō d'l, v.i.* to scrawl, scribble, meaninglessly.— *n.* something doodled.—*n.* **dood'ler.**

doodlebug *dōō d'l-bug, n.* the larva of an ant-lion or other insect (used in divination in America; *U.S.*): any instrument, scientific or unscientific, used by prospectors to indicate the presence of minerals: a flying bomb (*war slang*).

doom *dōōm, n.* judgment: condemnation: destiny: ruin: catastrophe: death: final judgment.—*v.t.* to pronounce judgment on: to condemn: to destine:—*pr.p.* **doom'ing;** *pa.t.* and *pa.p.* **doomed.**—**dooms'day** the day of doom, the last judgment; **doom'watch** pessimism about the contemporary situation and about the future, esp. of the environment: observation of the environment to prevent its destruction by pollution, over-population, etc.—Also *adj.* and *v.i.*—**doom'-watcher; doom'watching.**—**Doomsday-book** see **Domesday-book.**—**crack of doom** the last trump; **till doomsday** forever. [O.E. *dōm,* judgment.]

door *dōr, dör, n.* the usual entrance into a house, room, or passage: a frame for closing up the entrance: a house, etc., as in *three doors away:* a means of approach or access.—**door'bell; door'-keeper; door'-knob; door'-knocker; door(s)'-man** a porter, doorkeeper; **door'mat** a mat for wiping shoes or other purpose at a door: a person whom others trample upon (*coll.*); **door'nail** a stud for a door, proverbially dead, **door'post** the jamb or side-piece of a door; **door'step** a step at a door: a thick slice of bread (*coll*).—*v.t.* to go from door to door round (an area), e.g. canvassing in

an election:—*pr.p.* **door'stepping;** *pa.t.* and *pa.p.* **door'stepped.**—**door'stepper**—*adj.* **door'-to-door'** calling at each house in an area for purposes of selling, canvassing, etc.—**door'way** an opening where there is or might be a door.—**close, open the door to** to make impossible, possible; **doorstep selling** going from house to house to (try to) sell goods or services; **leave the door open** to preserve a situation in which something remains possible; **next door (to)** in the next house: near, bordering upon; **on one's doorstep** close to one's house, etc.; **out of doors see out; show someone the door** to turn someone out of the house. [O.E. *duru* (fem.) and *dor* (neut.).]

dop *dop, n.* Cape brandy made from grape-skins. [Du. *dop,* shell, husk.]

dopa *dō'pə, n.* a naturally-occurring amino-acid, a form of which, **L-dopa,** is used in the treatment of Parkinson's disease. [From *dioxyphenylalanine,* a former name for the compound.]

dope *dōp, n.* a thick liquid, semi-liquid, or pasty material: lubricating grease: aeroplane varnish: a substance added to improve the efficiency or modify the properties of anything: opium: a drug, esp. one administered to a racehorse or taken by an addict: drugtaking: confidential or fraudulent information in advance (*coll.*): information in general (*coll.*): anything supplied to dull, blind, or blunt the conscience or insight: a fool (*coll.*).—*v.t.* to give or apply dope to: to drug: to add impurities to.—*v.i.* to take dope.—*ns.* **dōp'ant** (*electronics*) a substance used in doping; **dōp'er.**—*adj.* **dope'y, dōp'y** stupefied: stupid.—*n.* **dōp'ing** the addition of known impurities to a semiconductor, to achieve the desired properties in diodes and transistors (*electronics*).—**dope'-fiend** a drug addict. [Du. *doop,* a dipping, sauce; *doopen,* to dip.]

doppel-gänger *dop'l-geng'ər, n.* a double: a wraith. [Ger., lit. double-goer.]

dopplerite *dop'lər-ıt, n.* a black elastic substance (calcium salts of humus acids) found in peat beds.— **Doppler('s) principle** the law of change of wavelength when a source of vibrations is moving towards or from the observer; **Doppler effect** this observed change, used in e.g. Doppler radar to determine velocities of observed objects. [From Christian *Doppler* (1803–53), an Austrian physicist, who announced the principle in 1842.]

dorado *də-rä'dō, n.* the coryphene, so called from its beautiful colour when dying:—*pl.* **dora'dos.** [Sp. from *dorar,* to gild—L. *deaurāre, -ātum.*]

Dorian *dō'ri-ən, dō', adj.* belonging to *Doris* in Greece or to the Dorians.—*n.* a native of Doris: a member of one of the main divisions of the ancient Greeks who arrived about 1100 B.C. and made their home in Doris, S.E. Peloponnese, Crete, Rhodes, etc.—**Dorian mode** a mode of ancient Greek music, traditionally of a stirring, solemn, simple and martial quality: an authentic mode of old church music, extending from d to d with d as its final. [L. *Dōrius*—Gr. *Dōrios—Dōris.*]

Doric *dor'ik, adj.* belonging to *Doris* in Greece, or the Dorians, or their dialect: denoting one of the Greek orders of architecture, distinguished by its simplicity and massive strength.—*n.* a Greek dialect: any dialect imagined to resemble it, esp. Scottish. [L. *Dōricus*—Gr *Dōrikos—Dōris.*]

Dorking *dörk'ing, n.* a square-bodied breed of poultry, variously coloured, and with five claws on each foot—so named from *Dorking* in Surrey.

dorm *dörm,* (*coll.*) *n.* short for **dormitory.**

dormant *dör'mənt, adj.* sleeping: with suspended animation or development: torpid: at rest: not used, in abeyance (as a title).—*n.* **dor'mancy.** [O.Fr. *dormant,* pr.p. of *dormir*—L. *dormīre,* to sleep.]

dormer *dör'mər, n.* a dormer-window —**dor'mer-**

win'dow a small window with a gable, projecting from a sloping roof (orig a dormitory window). [O Fr *dormeor*—L *dormītōrium*—*dormīre*, to sleep.]

dormie. See **dormy**.

dormitory *dor'mı-tar-ı, n* a large sleeping-room with many beds, whether in separate cubicles or not: a college hostel (*U.S.*): a small town or a suburb (also **dormitory town, suburb**), the majority of whose residents work elsewhere. [L *dormītōrium*—*dormīre*, to sleep.]

dormouse *dor'mows, n.* any member of a family of rodents akin to mice but somewhat squirrel-like in form and habit—*pl* **dor'mice.** [Perh connected with L. *dôrmīre*, to sleep (from their hibernation); prob **mouse.**]

dormy, dormie *dor'mı, adj.* in golf, as many holes up or ahead as there are yet to play. [Conjecturally connected with L. *dormīre*, to sleep; the player who is *dormy* cannot lose though he go to sleep.]

Dorothy bag *dor'ə-thı bag,* a type of ladies' handbag closed by draw-strings at the top and hung from the wrist.

dorp *dorp, n.* a Dutch or S. African village or small town: sometimes with a derog. sense in S. Africa (*coll.*). [Du., Afrik., *dorp,* O E. *thorp.*]

dorsal *dor'sl, adj.* pertaining or belonging to the back —*n.* a dorsal fin: a dorsal vertebra.—*adv.* **dor'sally.** —*n.* **dorsiflex'ion** a bending backwards: a bending of the back, a bow.—*adj* **dor'sigrade** walking on the back of the toes [L. *dorsum,* the back.]

dorter, dortour *dor'tar,* (*arch.*) *n.* a dormitory, esp monastic. [O.Fr. *dortour*—L. *dormītōrium.*]

dory[1] *dō'rı, do', n.* a golden-yellow fish (*Zeus faber*) of the mackerel family.—Also **John Dory.** [Fr. *dorée,* from *dorer* to, gild—L. *deaurâre,* to gild—*dē-,* in the sense of over, *aurum,* gold.]

dory[2] *dō'rı, do',* (*esp. Amer.*) *n.* a small boat, with flat bottom, sharp bow and stern, especially suited for surf-riding. [Origin uncertain.]

dos-à-dos *dō-za-dō', adv.* (*arch.*) back to back —*n.* a square-dance figure in which dancers pass either back to back [*dō-sē-dō'*; also **dosi-do':**—*pl.* **dosi-dos'.**) [Fr.]

dose *dōs, n.* the quantity of medicine, electric current, X-rays, etc., administered at one time: a portion, esp a measured portion, of something given or added anything disagreeable or medicinal to be taken: a bout.—*v.t.* to give doses to.—*ns* **dōs'age** the practice, act, or method of dosing: the regulation of dose the proper size of dose; **dōsim'eter** an instrument for measuring radiation; **dōsim'etry.** [Fr ,—Gr. *dósıs,* a giving—*dıdonaı,* to give.]

dosi-do. See **dos-à-dos.**

doss *dos (slang) n.* a bed, sleeping-place: a sleep.—*v.t.* to sleep: to go to bed.—*n.* **doss'er** one who lodges in a doss-house, or wherever he can.—**doss'-house** a very cheap lodging-house. [Perh. from *doss,* a dial. Eng name for a hassock.]

dossal *dos'əl, n.* a cloth hanging for the back of an altar, sides of a church chancel, etc. [L.L. *dossâle,* *dorsâle*—L. *dorsum,* back.]

dossier *do'sı-ā, do-syâ', dos'ı-ər, n.* a bundle of documents relating to a person or case: a brief. [Fr .— *dos*—L *dorsum,* back.]

dost *dust,* 2nd pers sing pres indic of **do.**

dot[1] *dot, n.* a very small spot: a short element in the Morse code —*v t.* to mark with a dot or dots: to scatter with objects: to hit to place, stand, etc. at irregular spaced intervals:—*pr.p.* **dott'ing;** *pa t.* and *pa.p* **dott'ed.**—*n.* **dott'iness.**—*adj.* **dott'y** crazed (*coll.*).— **dotted line** a line composed of dots or dashes that (on printed forms, etc.) one is instructed to sign on, tear along, etc , **dotted note, rest** (*mus.*) one whose length

is increased by one half by a dot placed after it; **dotted rhythm** one characterised by dotted notes.—**dot and carry** (*arith*) to set down the units and carry over the tens to the next column, **dot one's i's and cross one's t's** to pay great attention to detail; **on the dot (of)** exactly (at) (a given time); **the year dot** (*coll*) the very beginning of time [O.E. has *dott,* head of a boil; Du. *dot,* tuft, knot.]

dot[2] *dot, n.* a marriage portion —*adj* **dôt'al** pertaining to dowry or to dower [Fr ,—L. *dôs, dôtıs*]

dote, doat *dōt, v ı.* to be foolish (*arch.*): to be weakly affectionate: to show excessive love (with *upon, on*) —*ns.* **dôt'age** the childishness of old age; **dôt'ard** one showing the weakness of old age. [Cf. Old Du *doten,* to be silly.]

doth *duth,* 3rd pers. sing. pres. indic of **do.**

dotterel *dot'-ə-rəl, n* a kind of plover, named from its apparent stupidity in allowing itself to be approached and caught: a stupid fellow, a dupe [**dote.**]

douane *dōō-an', dwan, n* a custom-house.—*n* **douanier** (*dwa-nyâ'*), a custom-house officer [Fr , —Ar. *dîwân*]

Douay *dōō-â,* among Catholics often *dow'ı, n.* the town of *Douaı* in France, famous for its Catholic colleges. —**Douay Bible** an English Roman Catholic translation of the Bible done at Douaı in 1609–10

double *dub'l, adj* twofold twice as much: of about twice the weight, size, or quality two of a sort together: in pairs: paired: for two people folded once: sounding an octave lower. having stamens in the form of petals.—*adv.* to twice the extent: twice over: two together: deceitfully —*v t.* to multiply by two: to make twofold: to make twice as much or as many: to be the double of: in acting, to play by doubling: to be a substitute for or counterpart of: in bridge, to double the scoring value of: to sound in another octave: to line (*her.*): to fold: to clench: to pass (esp sail) round or by.—*v.i.* to increase to twice the quantity: to turn sharply back on one's course: to act as substitute: in acting, to play two different parts in the same piece: in bridge, to make a double (bid).—*n.* a quantity twice as much: a score of twice the amount shown, as in the outer ring of a dartboard: a combination of two things of the same kind (as a binary star): (in *pl*) in tennis, etc., a game with two players on each side: in tennis, two faults in succession: in bridge, a bid which, if successful, would double one's score for the hand: a win, or a defeat, in two events on the same programme a combined bet on two races, stake and winnings from the first being bet on the second: a duplicate: an actor's substitute: a quick pace (short for **double-quick**): one's wraith or apparition: an exact counterpart:—*ns.* **doub'leness** the state of being double: duplicity; **doub'leton** (the possession of) two cards of a suit in a hand.—*adv.* **doub'ly.**—*adj* **doub'le-act'ing** applying power in two directions producing a double result.—**doub'le-a'gent** one secretly acting simultaneously for two opposing powers, **doub'le-axe'** a religious symbol of Minoan Crete and the Aegean, a double-headed axe.—*adj* **doub'le-banked'** having two men at each oar, or having two tiers of oars one above the other, as in ancient galleys.—*adj* **doub'le-barr'elled** having two barrels: of a surname, hyphened: of a compliment, ambiguous —*adj* **doub'le-bass'** a stringed instrument— contrabass or *violone;* **double bill** see under **bill**[3].— *adjs.* **doub'le-blind'** denoting a comparative experiment, trial, etc. in which the identities of the control group are known neither to the subjects nor to the experimenters —**doub'le-bott'om (lorry)** an articulated lorry pulling a second trailer —Also **drawbar outfit.**—*adj* **doub'le-breast'ed** of a coat, having two breasts, one to be folded over the other —*v t.* and *v.ı*

doub'le-check' to check a second time —Also *n* — **doub'le-chin'** a chin with a fold of flesh; **double cream** a cream with a higher fat-content than single cream; **doub'le-cross** a betrayal or deceiving of someone for whom one was supposed to be betraying or deceiving someone else —*v.t.* to betray by double-cross — **doub'le-cross'er; doub'le-dagg'er** a diesis (‡); **doub'le-deal'er** a deceitful person; **doub'le-deal'ing** duplicity. —*adj* **doubl'le-decked** having two decks.—**doub'le-deck'er** a double-decked ship: a bus, tram-car, etc., in two stories or tiers.—*v.i* **doub'le-declutch'** (*motoring*) to change into a different gear by first changing to neutral, increasing the engine speed, then engaging the chosen gear, disengaging the clutch at both stages —**doub'le-decomposi'tion** a chemical action in which two compounds exchange some of their constituents, **double door(s)** a door consisting of two parts hung on opposite posts, **double-dotted note, rest** (*mus.*) one whose length is increased by three-quarters by two dots placed after it; **double-dotted rhythm** one characterised by double-dotted notes; **doub'le-Dutch** incomprehensible talk —*adj.* **doub'le-dyed** twice-dyed: deeply imbued.—**doub'le-eagle** (*U S*) a gold coin worth $20· a heraldic representation of an eagle with two heads, as in the old arms of Russia and Austria.—*adj* **doub'le-edged'** having two edges: cutting or working both ways.—**doub'le-en'try** (*book-k*) a method by which two entries are made of each transaction.—**double fault** (*tennis*, etc.) two faults served in succession, causing the loss of a point.—*v.t.* **doub'le-fault'**.—**double feature** a cinema programme involving two full-length films.—*adj.* **doub'le-fig'ure.**— **double figures** a score, total, etc. of any number equal to or greater than 10 but less than 100; **doub'le-first** a university degree with first-class honours in two different subjects. one who has such a degree; **doub'le-glaz'ing** a double layer of glass in a window with an air-space between the layers to act as insulation —*adj* **doub'le-glazed'**.—**double Gloucester,** (*glos'tər*) a Gloucestershire cheese of extra richness; **double helix** the DNA molecule; **double jeopardy** second trial for the same offence —*adjs.* **doub'le-joint'ed** having joints admitting some degree of movement backward, **doub'le-locked** locked with two locks or bolts: locked by two turns of the key; **doub'le-mean'ing** ambiguous. —Also *n* —**doubl'e-mind'edness; double negative** a construction consisting of two negatives, esp. when only one is logically required.—*v.t.* and *v.i.* **doub'le-park'** to park (a car, etc.) alongside vehicles already parked at the kerb —*adj.* and *adv.* **doub'le-quick'** at a pace approaching a run —*n.* the double-quick pace.— **double salt** a salt whose crystals dissolve to give two different salts in solution; **double standard** a principle, etc. applied in such a way as to allow different standards of behaviour to different people, groups, etc.: (in *pl.*) the practice of advocating (for others) certain moral, etc. standards not followed by oneself, **doub'le-stopp'ing** playing on two stopped strings of an instrument at once; **doub'le-take'** a second look impelled by surprise or admiration: delayed reaction; **doub'le-talk** talk that sounds to the purpose but amounts to nothing. ambiguous, deceptive talk, **doub'le-think** the faculty of simultaneously harbouring two conflicting beliefs—coined by George Orwell in his *Nineteen Eighty-Four* (1949) —*adj* **doub'le-tongued'** deceitful —**double-u** (*dub'l-ū*) the twenty-third letter of the alphabet (W, w) —**double back** to go back in the direction one has just come, usu. not by the same path, **double or quits** in gambling, the alternative, left to chance, of doubling or cancelling payment (*adj* **double'-or-quits'**); **double up** to fold double: to bend over (as with laughter). to share with another. [O Fr *doble*—L *duplus*, double]

double entendre *dōō-blä-tä'dr'*, (the use of) a word or phrase with two meanings, one usually more or less indecent. [Fr. of 17th century, superseded now by (*mot*) *à double entente.*]

doublet *dub'lit*, *n.* a close-fitting garment for the upper part of the body—with *hose*, the typical masculine dress in the 14th–17th c . a thing that is repeated or duplicated: one of a pair, esp one of two words orig. the same but varying in spelling and meaning, *e.g balm, balsam.* [O Fr , dim. of *double.*]

doubletree *dub'l-trē*, *n.* the horizontal bar on a vehicle to which the whippletree (with harnessed animals) is attached.

doubloon *dub-lōōn'*, *n* an obsolete Spanish gold coin [Sp. *doblón*, aug of *doble*, double.]

doubt *dowt*, *v.i* to be undecided in opinion.—*v.t.* to hold in doubt: to hesitate or scruple: to incline to believe with fear or hesitation: to distrust: to incline to think (esp *Scot.*): to suspect (*arch.*; also *refl.*).—*n* uncertainty of opinion: a suspicion: a thing doubtful or questioned.—*adj.* **doubt'able.**—*n.* **doubt'er.**—*adj* **doubt'ful** full of doubt: subject to doubt: not clear: insecure: not confident. not likely or not certain to participate, co-operate, etc.—*n.* a doubtful person or thing.—*adv.* **doubt'fully.**—*n.* **doubt'fulness.**—*n.* and *adj* **doubt'ing.**—*adv.* **doubt'ingly.**—*adv.* **doubt'less.** without doubt: certainly. no doubt (often a mere concession of possibility).—*adv* **doubt'lessly.**—**doubting Thomas** a doubter or sceptic: one who needs proof before believing something (from the doubting of *Thomas,* in John, xx, 25).—**beyond (a shadow of) doubt** certain(ly); **in doubt** not certain, undecided; **no doubt** see no. [O.Fr. *douter*—L. *dubitāre*]

douce *dōōs*, *adj.* sober, peaceable, sedate (*Scot.*).— *adv* **douce'ly.**—*ns.* **douce'ness; douceur** (*dōō-sûr'*) a conciliatory present, bribe, or tip [Fr *doux, douce,* mild—L. *dulcis,* sweet.]

douche *dōōsh,* *n.* a jet of water directed upon or into the body from a pipe an apparatus for throwing it.—*v.t* to turn a douche upon [Fr.,—It *doccia,* a water-pipe—L. *dūcĕre,* to lead.]

dough *dō,* *n.* a mass of flour or meal moistened and kneaded, but not baked: money (*slang*).—*n* **dough'iness.**—*adj.* **dough'y** like dough: soft: of complexion, pallid, pasty (*coll.*) —**dough'-boy** boiled flour dumpling (also **dough'-ball**): an American infantryman (*mil. slang*); **dough'nut** sweetened dough fried in fat· an accelerating tube in the form of a toroid (*nuc.*). a toroidal assembly of enriched fissile material for increasing locally the neutron intensity in a reactor (*nuc*) [O E. *dāh*; dough.]

doughty *dow'ti,* *adj* able, strong: brave —*adv.* **dough'tily.**—*n* **dough'tiness.** [O E *dyhtig,* later *dohtig,* valiant—*dugan,* to be strong.]

Douglas fir *dug'las fûr,* a tall western American coniferous timber tree. [David *Douglas* (1798–1834), who introduced it to Britain.]

Doukhobor. See **Dukhobor.**

douleia. See **dulia.**

doum-palm *dowm', dōōm'-pam, n.* an African palm (*Hyphaene*), with a branched stem, and a fruit with the taste of gingerbread. [Ar *daum, dūm*]

dour *dōōr,* (*Scot*) *adj.* obstinate: sullen: grim —*n* **dour'ness.** [Apparently L. *dūrus,* hard.]

doura. See **durra.**

douroucouli *dōō-rōō-kōō'lē, n.* a night-ape, any monkey of the S American genus *Nyctipithecus* [S Amer name.]

douse¹, dowse *dows, v t.* to plunge into water —*v i* to fall suddenly into water

douse², dowse *dows, v.t* to strike: to strike or lower (a sail) —*n* a heavy blow [Prob. related to Old Du *dossen,* to beat.]

douse³, dowse *dows, v.t.* to put out, extinguish (esp. in the *slang* **douse the glim**, to put out the light).—*n.* **dous'er** a shutter for cutting off light in a cinema projector. [Perh. connected with **dout** or with **douse²**.]

dout *dowt, v.t.* to put out, extinguish.—*n.* **dout'er**. [**do out**.]

dove *duv, n.* a pigeon (esp. in comp., as *ring-dove, turtle-dove*, etc.): a word of endearment: an emblem of innocence, gentleness, also of the Holy Spirit (Matt. iii. 16): in politics, industrial relations, etc., a person who seeks peace and conciliation rather than confrontation or war (opp. to *hawk*).—**dove'-colour** a greyish, bluish, pinkish colour, **dove'cot, -cote** a small cot or box in which pigeons breed: a pigeon-house; **dove'tail** a tenon shaped like a dove's spread tail, for fastening boards: a joint of alternate tenons and mortises of that shape.—*v.t.* and *v.i.* to fit by, or as if by one or more dovetails.—**dove'tailing**. [O.E. *dūfe*, found only in the compound *dūfe-doppa*, a diving bird; Ger. *Taube*.]

dovekie *duv'ki, n.* the little auk or rotch: the black guillemot. [Dim. of **dove**.]

Dover's powder *dō'vərz pow'dər,* a sudorific compounded of ipecacuanha root, opium and potassium sulphate (or, in the U.S.A., lactose). [First prescribed by Dr. Thomas *Dover* (1660–1742).]

dow. See **dhow**.

dowager *dow'ə-jər, n.* a widow with a dower or jointure: a title given to a widow to distinguish her from the wife of her husband's heir (also *adj.*): an elderly woman of imposing appearance. [O.Fr. *douagere*—L. *dōtāre*, to endow.]

dowdy *dowd'i, n.* a woman who wears dull-looking, clumsy, ill-shaped clothes.—*adv.* **dowd'ily**.—*n.* **dowd'iness**.—*adjs.* **dowd'y; dowd'yish**.

dowel *dow'əl, n.* a pin for fastening things together by fitting into a hole in each.—*v.t.* to fasten by means of dowels. [Prob. related to Ger. *Döbel, Dübel*, a plug.]

dower *dow'ər, n.* a jointure: a dowry: an endowment.—*v.t.* to bestow a dowry upon: to endow.—*adj.* **dow'erless**.—**dow'er-house** the house set apart for the widow. [O.Fr. *douaire*—L. *dōtāre*, to endow.]

Dow-Jones average, index *dow'jōnz' av'ər-ij, in'deks,* (*U.S.*) an indicator of the relative prices of stocks and shares on the New York Stock exchange. [Charles H. *Dow* (1851–1902), and Edward D. *Jones* (1856–1920), American economists.]

dowlas *dow'las, n.* a coarse linen cloth. [From *Daoulas* or *Doulas*, near Brest, in Brittany.]

down¹ *down, n.* soft feathers: a soft covering of fluffy hair. *ns.* **Down'ie®** a duvet; **down'iness**.—*adj.* **down'y** covered with or made of down: like down. [O.N *dūnn;* Ger. *Daune,* L.G. *dune.*]

down² *down, n.* a treeless upland: (in *pl.*) an undulating upland tract of pasture-land, esp. in S.E England (the Downs).—*n.* **down'land**. [O.E. *dūn,* a hill—Celt. *dun.*]

down³ *down, adv.* (passing into *adj.* in predicative use), to a lower position, level or state: away from a centre (capital, great town, university, etc.): southward: to leeward: in a low or lowered position or state· below: on or to the ground· downstairs: under the surface: from earlier to later times: to a further stage in a series· from greater to less: to a standstill, exhaustion, or conclusion: to a final state of subjection, silence, etc in a fallen state· in adversity: at a disadvantage ill· behindhand: in writing or record, in black and white: on the spot, in cash: in watchful opposition or hostility (with *on, upon*).— Also elliptically, passing into an interjection or verb by omission of *go, come, put,* etc , often followed by *with* —*adj.* going, reaching, or directed towards a lower position or level: depressed: low: broken, not operational (*comput.*).—*prep.* in a descent along, through, or by: to or in a lower position on or in: along in the direction of the current: along.—*n.* a descent: a low place: a reverse of fortune: an act of throwing or putting down: a tendency to be down on one.—*v.t.* to knock, throw or set down: to put down, overthrow: to dispirit.—*n.* **down'er** (*slang*) a depressant drug: any depressing experience, etc.—*advs.* **down'ward, down'wards** (*-wərd(z)*), from higher to lower: from source to outlet: from more ancient to modern: in the lower part.—*adj.* **down'ward**.—*adv.* **down'wardly**.—*n* **down'wardness** a sinking tendency: a state of being low.—*adj.* **down'-and-out'** at the end of one's resources.—*ns.* **down'-and-out'(er)**.—*adj.* **down'-at-heel'** having the back of the shoe trodden down: generally shabby.—**down'-beat** a downward movement of the conductor's baton: an accented beat.—*adj.* (*coll.*) relaxed, unworried: unemphatic: depressed: gloomy: depressing; **down'cast** dejected.—*n.* a current of air into a mine: a shaft carrying it.—**down'-draught** a current of air downwards; **down'fall** fall, failure, humiliation, ruin: a falling down, as of rain; **down'grade** a downward slope or course.—*adj.* and *adv.* downhill. —*v.t.* to reduce in status, etc.: to belittle, underrate.—*adjs.* **down'-heart'ed** dejected; **down'hill** descending, sloping.—*adv.* **downhill'**.—**down'-line** the line of a railway leading from the capital, or other important centre, to the provinces.—*adj.* **down'-mar'ket** of (buying, selling or using) commodities relatively low in price, quality or prestige.—Also *adv.*—*adv.* and *adj.* **down'most** superlative of *down*.—**down payment** a deposit on an article, service, etc.; **down'pipe** a drainpipe which takes rainwater from the gutter of a roof; **down'pour** a heavy fall of rain, etc.—*adv.* **down'right** in plain terms: utterly.—*adj.* plain-spoken: brusque: utter, out-and-out (as in *downright madness*).— **down'rightness; down'rush** a rushing down (as of gas, hot air, etc.).—*advs.* **down'stage'** towards the footlights (also *adj.*); **downstairs'** in, or towards, a lower storey.—*n.* a lower storey, usu. the ground floor.— *adj* **down'stair(s)**.—*adv.* **downstream'** with the current.—*adj.* **down'stream** further down the stream: going with the current.—**down'stroke** a downward line made by the pen in writing; **down'swing** a downward trend in volume of trade, etc : the part of the swing where the club is moving down towards the ball (*golf*).—*adj.* **down'-to-earth'** sensible: practical: realistic.—*adj.* and *adv* **down'-town'** in or towards the lower part or (esp. *U.S.*) the business and shopping centre of the town.—*n.* this part of a town.— **down'-train** a railway train proceeding from the chief terminus.—*adj.* **down'-trodden** trampled on: tyrannised over.—**down'turn** a downward trend, decline —*adj.* and *adv* **down'wind'** in the direction in which the wind is blowing: in or to a position (relative to someone or something) in this direction (often with *of*).—**down in the mouth** in low spirits; **down on one's luck** in ill-luck; **down tools** to stop work, strike; **down to the ground** (*coll*) completely, **down town** in or towards the centre of a town, **down with** put down· swallow· (as *interj.*) depose, get rid of, abolish, **go down** (often with *with*) to be received (well or badly) (by): (often with *with*) to be acceptable (to): (with *with*) to contract (illness), **go downhill** to deteriorate (in health, prosperity, morality): **up and down** often merely to and fro [M E. *a-down, adun*—O E. *of dūne,* from the hill]

Downie®. See **down¹**.

Down's syndrome *downz' sin'drōm,* Mongolism

dowry *dow'ri, n* the property which a woman brings to

her husband at marriage—sometimes used for dower: sometimes a gift given to or for a wife at marriage: a natural endowment. [See **dower.**]

dowse[1] *dows*, *v.t.* and *v.i.* See **douse**[1,2,3].

dowse[2] *dowz*, *v.i.* to use the divining-rod.—*n.* **dows'er** a water-diviner.

doxographer *doks-og'rə-fər*, *n.* a compiler of opinions of philosophers.—*ns.* **doxog'raphy; doxol'ogy** a hymn or liturgical formula ascribing glory to God. [Gr. *doxa*, opinion, reputation, glory, *graphein*, write, *logos*, discourse.]

doxy *dok'si*, *n.* a woman of loose character.

doyen *doi'ən*, *dwä-yā*, *n.* a dean, senior member (of an academy, diplomatic corps, class, profession, etc.):—*fem.* **doyenne** (*doi-en'*, *dwà-yen*). [Fr.—L. *decānus*.]

doyley. See **doily.**

doze *dōz*, *v.i.* to sleep lightly, or to be half-asleep: to be in a dull or stupefied state.—*v.t.* to spend in drowsiness (with *away*).—*n.* a short light sleep.—*ns.* **dō'zer; dō'ziness.**—*adj.* **dō'zy** drowsy. [Cf. O.N. *dūsa*, Dan. *döse.*]

dozen *duz'n*, *n.* a set of twelve: also used, esp. in *pl.*, for a less exact number:—*pl.* **doz'en** when preceded by a numeral, otherwise **doz'ens.**—*adj.* and *n.* **doz'enth.**—**baker's, devil's, long, dozen** thirteen; **daily dozen** see **daily; half'-a-doz'en** six: approximately six; **round dozen** full dozen. [O.Fr. *dozeine*—L. *duodecim.*]

dozer. Coll. for **bulldozer.**

drab[1] *drab*, *n.* a low, sluttish woman: a whore. [Poss. Gael. *drabag*; Ir. *drabog*, slut.]

drab[2] *drab*, *n.* a grey or dull-brown colour, perh. from the muddy colour of undyed wool: uninteresting unvaried dullness.—*adj.* of the colour of drab: dull and monotonous.—*adv.* **drab'ly.**—*n.* **drab'ness.** [Perh. Fr. *drap*, cloth—L.L. *drappus.*]

drabble *drab'l*, *v.t.* to besmear, bedraggle. [L. Ger. *drabbeln*, to wade about.]

drachm *dram*, *n.* a drachma: a dram.

drachma *drak'mə*, *n.* an ancient Greek weight, and a silver coin of different values: the standard unit of modern Greek currency. [Gr. *drachmē*—*drassesthai*, to grasp with the hand.]

Draconian *drə-* or *drā-kō'ni-ən*, **Draconic** (*-on'ik*), *adj.* extremely severe, as the laws of *Draco* (Gr. *Drakōn*), archon at Athens 621 B.C.

draff *dräf*, *n.* dregs: the refuse of malt after brewing. [Prob. related to Du. *draf.*]

draft *dräft*, *n.* anything drawn: the selecting of a smaller body (of men, animals, things) from a larger: the body so selected (esp. *mil.*): conscription (*U.S.*): an order for the payment of money: a demand (upon resources, credulity, patience, etc.): a plan: a preliminary sketch: (occasional and *U.S.*) a draught (in various senses).—*v.t.* to draw an outline of: to draw up in preliminary form: to draw off: to detach.—*ns.* **draftee** a conscript; **draft'er, draught'er** one who drafts: a draught-horse.—**draft'-dodger** (*U.S. coll.*) one who avoids conscription.—**draft'-horse, draft'-ox, drafts, drafts'man, drafts'manship** see **draught.** [**draught.**]

drag *drag*, *v.t.* to draw by force: to draw slowly: to pull roughly and violently: to trail: to explore with a drag-net or hook: to apply a drag to.—*v.i.* to hang so as to trail on the ground: to be forcibly drawn along: to move slowly and heavily: to lag: to give the feeling of being unduly slow or tedious:—*pr.p.* **dragg'ing;** *pa.t.* *pa.p.* **dragged.**—*n.* anything dragged: an act of dragging: a dragging effect: the component of the aerodynamic force on a body travelling through a fluid (esp. a vehicle travelling through air) that lies along the longitudinal axis (*aero.*): a net or hook for

dragging along to catch things under water: a heavy harrow: a long open carriage, with transverse or side seats: a contrivance for retarding a wheel, esp. an iron shoe that drags on the ground: any obstacle to progress: a tedious, dreary occupation or experience (*slang*): a trail of scent left by an animal, or a trail of broken undergrowth caused by an animal dragging off its prey: an artificial scent dragged on the ground for foxhounds to follow: a short 'draw' on a cigarette (*slang*): (the wearing of) transvestite clothing, now usu. women's dress worn by a man (*slang*; also *adj.*):—*n.* **drag'ster** a car for drag-racing.—**drag'hound** a foxhound trained to follow a drag; **drag'line** an excavating machine, crane-like in appearance, moving on articulated tracks, and drawing towards itse!f a bucket suspended from a long jib; **drag'-net** a net to be dragged along the bottom of water or the ground: a systematic police search for a wanted person; **drag race** a contest in acceleration, with standing start and quarter-mile course.—**drag one's feet, heels** to hang back deliberately in doing something; **drag out of** to get (information, etc.) from (someone) with difficulty; **drag up** (*coll.*) to mention, quote inappropriately or unnecessarily. [North.—O.E. *dragan* or O.N. *draga.*]

dragée *dra'zhā*, *n.* a sweetmeat enclosing a drug, or a nut or fruit, etc.: a chocolate drop: a small silvered ball for decorating a cake. [Fr.]

draggle *drag'l*, *v.t.* or *v.i.* to make or become wet and dirty, as by dragging along the ground: to trail.—**dragg'le-tail** a slut.—*adj.* **dragg'le-tailed.** [Freq. of **drag,** and a doublet of **drawl.**]

dragoman *drag'ō-mən*, *n.* an interpreter or guide in Eastern countries:—*pl.* **drag'omans.** [Fr., from Ar. *tarjumān*—*tarjama*, to interpret.]

dragon *drag'ən*, *n.* a fabulous winged scaly-armoured fire-breathing monster, often a guardian of treasure, ravaging a country when its hoard is rifled: a fierce, intimidating, or watchful person: a paper kite: a dragon lizard: applied to various plants.—*n.* **drag'onet** a spiny fish; **drag'onfly** a predaceous long-bodied often brilliantly-coloured insect; **drag'on's-blood** a red resinous exudation from the dragon-tree and many other trees, used for colouring varnishes, etc.; **drag'on-tree'** a great tree of the Canary Islands, remarkable for its resin (a variety of dragon's blood), its growth in thickness like a dicotyledon, and the great age it attains. [Fr.,—L. *dracō, -ōnis*—Gr. *drakōn, -ontos*, perh.—*derkesthai*, to see clearly.]

dragonnade *drag-ən-ād'*, *n.* the persecution of French Protestants under Louis XIV by means of dragoons: any persecution by military means (usu. in *pl.*). [Fr., from *dragon*, dragoon.]

dragoon *drə-gōōn'*, *n.* a heavy cavalryman, as opp. to hussars and lancers—surviving in the names of certain regiments.—*v t.* to compel by military bullying: to coerce. [Fr *dragon*, dragon, dragoon.]

drail *drāl*, *n.* a piece of lead round the shank of the hook in fishing.—*v.t.* to draggle. [Prob. a combination of **draggle** and **trail.**]

drain *drān*, *v.t.* to draw off by degrees: to filter. to draw off water, sewage, or other liquid from: to furnish means of withdrawal of liquid from: to make dry: to drink dry: to exhaust.—*v.i.* to flow off gradually: to part with liquid by flowing, trickling or dripping: to discharge.—*n.* a water-course: a channel for escape of liquid: a ditch: a sewer: a drink (*slang*): exhausting expenditure.—*adj.* **drain'able.**—*ns.* **drain'age** act, process, method, or means of draining: mode of discharge of water: the system of drains in a town; **drain'er** a device on which articles are placed to drain. —**drain'age-basin** the area of land that drains into one river; **drain'ing-board** a sloping surface beside a sink, where dishes, etc. are placed to drain when washed; **drain'-pipe** a pipe to carry away waste water or rainwater: (in *pl.*; *coll.*) very narrow trousers.— **down the drain** (*slang*) gone for good: wasted. [O.E. *drēahnian.*]

drake *drāk, n.* the male of the duck. [Ety obscure; cf. provincial Ger. *draak*; O.H.G *antrahho*, Ger. *Enterich*, the first element usually explained as *eend, end, anut,* duck.]

dram *dram, n.* a contraction of **drachm:** 674th of an ounce avoirdupois: formerly, with apothecaries, ⅛th of an ounce: a small drink of alcoholic liquor: a tipple. [Through Fr. and L., from Gr. *drachmē*; see **drachma.**]

drama *dràm'ə, n.* a story of life and action for representation by actors: a composition intended to be represented on the stage: dramatic literature: theatrical entertainment: a dramatic situation, or series of absorbing events.—*adj.* **dramat'ic** (*drə-mat'ık*) belonging to the drama: appropriate to or in the form of drama: with the force and vividness of the drama: impressive or important because of speed, size, suddenness, etc.—*adv.* **dramat'ically.**—*n.* (usu. *sing.*) **dramat'ics** the acting, production, study of plays: a show of excessive, exaggerated emotion (*coll.*).—*adj.* **dramatis'able** (*dram-*), -z-.—*n.* **dramatisa'tion,** -z- the act of dramatising: the dramatised version of a novel or story.—*v.t.* **dram'atise, -ize** to compose in, or turn into, the form of a drama or play: to exaggerate the importance or emotional nature of.—*n.* **dram'atist** a writer of plays—**drama documentary** see **faction; dramatic irony** a situation, etc. in a play, the irony of which is clear to the audience but not to the characters; **dram'atis persō'nae** (*-ē*) the characters of a drama or play. [L.,—Gr. *dráma, drāmatos—drāein,* to do.]

dramaturgy *dram'ə-tûr-ji, n.* the principles of dramatic composition: theatrical art.—*ns.* **dram'aturge, dram'aturgist** a playwright.—*adjs.* **dramatur'gic(al).** [Through Fr from Gr. *drāmatourgiā, drāmatourgos,* playwright—*dráma,* and *ergon,* a work.]

drank *drangk, pa.t.* of **drink.**

drape *drāp, v.t.* to cover as with cloth: to hang cloth in folds about: (*refl.*) to assume a casual and graceful pose.—*n.* a hanging or curtain (*U.S.* and *theatre*) —*n.* **drāp'er** a dealer in cloth and cloth goods.—*n.* **drāp'ery** cloth goods: hangings: the draper's business: the representation of clothes and hanging folds of cloth (*art*):—*pl.* **drāp'eries.** [O.Fr. *draper,* to weave, drape, *drapier,* draper—*drap,* cloth, prob. Gmc.]

drastic *dras'tik, adj.* forcible, powerful in action: violent: unsparing.—*n.* a severe purgative —*adv.* **dras'tically.** [Gr. *drastikos—drāein,* to act, to do.]

drat *drat, interj.* a minced oath used to express vexation, (sometimes with an object).—*adj.* **dratt'ed.** [Aphetic from **God rot.**]

draught *dràft, n.* drawing or pulling: the thing or quantity drawn: readiness for drawing from the cask: the act of drinking: the quantity drunk in one breath: a dose of liquor or medicine: the outline of a picture, or a preliminary sketch or plan (usu. **draft**): that which is taken in a net by drawing: a chosen detachment of men (usu. **draft**): a current of air: the depth to which a ship sinks in the water: a thick disc used in the game of draughts: (in *pl.*) a game played by two persons moving draughtmen alternately on a chequered board.—*adj.* on draught.—*v.t.* to sketch out, make a preliminary plan of or attempt at (also **draft**): occasionally for **draft** in sense of draw off, set apart from a larger body.—*n.* **draught'iness.**—*adj* **draught'y** full of draughts or currents of air.— **draught'-animal, -horse,** -ox, etc., one used for

drawing heavy loads; **draught'board** a chessboard used for playing draughts; **draught'-en'gine** the engine over the shaft of a coal-pit.—**draughts'man** a piece used in playing draughts; one skilled or employed in drawing: one who draughts or draws up documents (in this sense usually **draftsman**).—**feel the draught** (*fig.*) to be unpleasantly conscious of difficult conditions, esp economic; **on draught** of liquor, sold from the cask. [O.E. *draht—dragan,* to draw; see **drag, draw.**]

Dravidian *drə-vid'i-ən, adj.* belonging to a dark, long-headed, wavy-haired race of the Deccan: belonging to a group of languages in Southern India, including Tamil, Malayalam, Kannada, Telugu, etc.—Also *n.* [Sans *Drāviḍa,* an ancient province of Southern India]

draw *dro, v t.* to pull: to drag. to pull along: to bring forcibly towards or after one: to pull into position: to pull back: to pull back the string of: to take at random from a number: to entice, attract: to coax into giving information: to stimulate to self-expression (usu. **draw out**): to inhale to take out: to unsheathe: to withdraw: to cause to flow out: to extract by pulling: to extract the essence of: to eviscerate: to deduce: to lengthen: to receive or take from a source or store: to demand by a draft: to get by lot: to trace: to construct in linear form: to make a picture of, by lines drawn: to describe: to put into shape, frame: to write out (as a cheque): to require as depth of water for floating: to finish without winning or losing: to glance (*cricket*): to hit (the ball) too much to the left (if right-handed) (*golf*). to deliver (a bowl) so that it draws (*bowls*): to force one's opponents to play (all their cards of a suit, esp. trumps) by continually leading cards of that suit (*bridge,* etc.): to hit (the cue ball) so that it recoils after striking another ball (*billiards,* etc.).—*v.i.* to pull: to practise drawing: to move: to make one's way, betake oneself: to allow a free current: to act as drawer: to draw a card, a sword, lots: to infuse: to end a game without winning or losing: to move in a curve to the point aimed for (*bowls*):—*pa.t.* **drew** (*drōō*); *pa.p.* **drawn.**—*n.* the act of drawing: assignment by lot, as of prizes, opponents in a game: anything drawn: a drawn or undecided game: an attraction.— *adj.* **draw'able.**—*ns.* **drawee'** the person on whom a bill of exchange is drawn; **draw'er** he or that which draws: (*drōr*) a thing drawn out, as the sliding box in a **chest of drawers:** (in *pl.*) a close undergarment for the lower part of the body and the legs; **draw'ing** the art of representing objects or forms by lines drawn, shading, etc.: a picture in lines: an assigning by lot: the act of pulling, etc.—*adj.* **drawn** pulled together: neither won nor lost: unsheathed: eviscerated: strained, tense.—**draw'back** a disadvantage: a receiving back some part of the duty on goods on their exportation; **draw'-bar** a sliding bar: a bar used in coupling railway vehicles; **drawbar outfit** a double-bottom lorry; **draw'bridge** a bridge that can be drawn up or let down at pleasure; **draw'ing-board** a slab on which paper can be pinned for drawing on: the planning stage of a project, etc. (*fig.*); **draw'ing-master; draw'ing-paper; draw'ing-pen; draw'ing-pencil; draw'ing-pin** a short broad-headed pin; **draw'ing-room** see separate article; **drawn'-(thread') work** ornamental work done by pulling out some of the threads of a fabric; **draw'-sheet** a hospital sheet that can be drawn out from under a patient; **draw'-string** a string, cord, etc., in a casing in, or threaded through, material, by which the material may be drawn or gathered up—**at daggers drawn** openly hostile; **draw a blank** to get a lottery ticket that wins no prize: to get no result; **draw back** to recoil: to withdraw; **draw, hang, and quarter** see **hang; draw in** to reduce, contract: to become shorter; **draw near** to approach; **draw off** to cause to flow from a barrel, etc.: to withdraw; **draw on** to approach: to pull on; **draw on, upon** to make a draught upon: to make a demand upon (patience, resources): to draw one's sword, pistol, against; **draw out** to leave the place (of an army, etc.): to lengthen: to entice into talk and self-expression; **draw rein** to slacken speed, to stop; **draw stumps** to end play in cricket by removing the wickets; **draw the line** to fix a limit; **draw the teeth of** to render harmless; **draw up** to form in regular order: to compose, put into shape: to stop; **out of the top drawer** of top grade, esp socially. [O.E. *dragan*; cf. **drag**.]

Drawcansir *drò-kan'sər*, *n.* a blustering bully. [*Drawcansir* who 'kills 'em all on both sides' in Buckingham's *Rehearsal* (performed 1671).]

drawing-room *drò'ing-rōōm*, *n.* a room to which the company withdraws after dinner, a sitting-room.— *adj.* suitable for the drawing-room. [Orig. **withdrawing-room**.]

drawl *dröl*, *v.i.* to speak in a slow lengthened tone — *v.t.* to utter in a slow and sleepy manner.—*n.* a slow, lengthened utterance.—*n.* **drawl'er**. [Connected with **draw**.]

drawn *drön*, *pa.p.* of **draw**, and *adj.*

dray[1] *drā*, *n.* a low strong cart for heavy goods: a timber sledge.—**dray'-horse**; **dray'man**. [Cf. O.E. *drǣge*, drag-net—*dragan*, to draw; see **drag, draw**.]

dray[2]. Same as **drey**.

dread *dred*, *n.* great fear: awe: an object of fear or awe. —*adj.* dreaded: inspiring great fear or awe.—*v.t.* to fear greatly: to reverence.—*adj.* **dread'ful** producing great fear or awe: terrible: very bad, unpleasant (*coll.*).—*adv.* **dread'fully** in a dreadful way: very (much) (*coll.*).—*n.* **dread'fulness.**—**dread locks, dread'locks** the long-plaited hairstyle adopted by Rastafarians; **dread'nought** a thick cloth or garment thereof: a powerful type of battleship or battlecruiser (dating from 1905–6).—**penny dreadful** a cheap sensational serial or tale. [M.E. *dreden*— O.E. *ondrǣdan*, to fear.]

dream *drēm*, *n.* a train of thoughts and fancies during sleep, a vision: something only imaginary: a distant hope or ideal, probably unattainable.—*v.i.* to fancy things during sleep: to think idly (with *of*): to think (of) as possible, contemplate as imaginably possible. —*v.t.* to see or imagine in, or as in, a dream:—*pa.t.* and *pa.p.* **dreamed** or **dreamt** (*dremt*).—*ns.* **dream'er**.—*adv.* **dream'ily.**—*n.* **dream'iness.**—*adj.* **dream'less.**—*adv.* **dream'lessly.**—*n.* **dream'lessness.**—*adj.* **dream'y** full of dreams: given to dreaming: appropriate to dreams: dream-like: lovely (*coll.*). —**dream'boat** (*slang*) someone wonderful and desirable—usu. of the opposite sex; **dream'-land** the land of dreams, reverie, or imagination; **dream's world** a world of illusions.—**dream up** to plan in the mind, often unrealistically. [M.E. *dream, drēm.*]

dreary *drēr'i*, *adj.* gloomy: cheerless.—*adj.* **drear** dreary.—*n.* **drear'iness.**—*adv.* **drear'ily.** [O.E. *drēorig*, mournful, bloody—*drēor*, gore.]

dredge[1] *drej*, *n.* a bag-net for dragging along the bottom to take oysters, biological specimens, mud, etc.: a machine for deepening a harbour, canal, river, etc., for excavating under water or on land, or for raising alluvial deposits and washing them for minerals.—*v.t.* and *v.i.* to gather, explore, or deepen with a dredge.—*n.* **dredg'er** one who dredges: a machine for dredging: a boat, ship, or raft equipped for dredging. [Conn. with **drag, draw**.]

dredge[2] *drej*, *v.t.* to sprinkle.—*n.* **dredg'er** a vessel with perforated lid for dredging. [O.Fr. *dragie*, sugar-plum—Gr. *tragēmata*, dessert.]

dregs *dregz*, *n.pl.* impurities in liquor that fall to the bottom, the grounds: dross: the vilest part of anything.—*n.* **dregg'iness.**—*adj.* **dregg'y** containing dregs: muddy: foul. [O.N. *dregg.*]

drench *drench, drensh*, *v.t.* to wet thoroughly: to soak: to force an animal to take medicine —*n* a dose of physic forced down the throat. [O.E. *drencan*, to cause to drink.]

Dresden (**china, porcelain, ware**) *drez'dən* (*chī'nə, pörs'lin, wār*), fine decorated china made in Saxony (Royal Saxon porcelain factory established at Meissen, 1710).

dress *dres*, *v.t.* to set in order: to prepare: to draw (fowl): to manure: to add seasoning to (food): to finish or trim: to treat: to tend: to apply suitable materials to: to clothe: to adorn: to tie (a fly) (*angling*).— *v.t.* to come into line: to put on clothes: to put on finer, more elaborate, or more formal clothes:—*pa.t.* and *pa.p.* **dressed.**—*n.* the covering or ornament of the body: a lady's gown: manner of clothing: ceremonial or formal clothing.—*adj.* pertaining to evening dress.—*ns.* **dress'er** one who dresses: a medical student who dresses wounds: a person who assists an actor to dress in a theatre: a tool or machine for dressing: a sideboard: a chest of drawers or dressing-table (*U.S.*); **dress'ing** dress or clothes: material applied to land, a wound, manufactured goods, etc.: matter used to give stiffness and gloss to cloth: sauce, stuffing, etc., used in preparing a dish for the table, etc —*adj.* **dress'y** fond of dress: showy: indicating care in dressing.—**dress'-cir'cle** the first gallery of a theatre; **dress'-coat** a fine black coat with narrow or cut-away skirts, worn in full dress; **dress'ing-case** a case of toilet requisites; **dress'ing-down** a severe scolding: a thrashing; **dress'ing-gown** a loose garment used in dressing, or in dishabille; **dress'ing-room**; **dress'ing-station** a place where wounded are collected and tended by members of a field-ambulance; **dress'ing-table**; **dress'-length** enough to make a dress; **dress'maker** one who makes clothes: one who makes clothes for women and children as a living; **dress'making**; **dress'-rehears'al** a full rehearsal in costume with everything as for the performance.— Also *fig.*—**dress sense** sense of style in dress, knowledge of what suits one; **dress'-shield** a device to protect the armpit of a dress against sweat; **dress'-shirt'**, **dress'-suit'**, **dress'-tie'** one for formal evening dress; **dress uniform** a formal, ceremonial uniform.—**dress down** to handle with severity: to reprimand: to thrash: to dress deliberately informally; **dress up** to dress elaborately: to dress for a part: to masquerade: to treat so as to make appear better, more interesting, etc., than it really is; **evening dress, full dress** the costume prescribed by fashion for evening receptions, dinners, balls, etc.—**get dressed** to put one's clothes on. [O.Fr. *dresser*, to prepare—an inferred L.L. *directiāre*, to straighten; see **direct**.]

dressage *dres'äzh*, *n.* training of a horse in deportment and response to controls. [Fr.]

drew *drōō*, *pa.t.* of **draw**.

drey, dray *drā*, *n.* a squirrel's nest. [Ety. dub.]

drib *drib*, *n.* a drop: a trickle: a small quantity.—*ns.* **dribb'let, drib'let** a drop: a trickle: a small quantity. —**dribs and drabs** small quantities at a time. [Akin to **drip**.]

dribble *drib'l*, *v.i.* to fall in small drops: to trickle: to slaver, as a child.—*v t.* to let fall in drops: to give out in small portions: to move the ball forward little by little, tricking opponents (*football, hockey,* etc.).— Also *n.*—*n.* **dribb'ler.**—*adj.* **dribb'ly.** [Freq. of **drib**.]

dried, drier, dries, driest. See **dry**.

drift *drift*, *n.* a driving: a heap of matter driven together, as snow: floating materials driven by water: a streaming movement: the direction in which a thing is driven· a slow current caused by the wind: passive travel with the current, wind, etc.: abandonment to external influences: tendency. a drift-net: the meaning of words used: loose superficial deposits, esp. glacial or fluvio-glacial (*geol.*): a horizontal or oblique excavation or passage (*mining*) —*v.t.* to carry by drift: to cause or allow to drift: to pierce or tunnel —*v.i* to be floated along· to be driven into heaps: to leave things to circumstances· to wander around, or live, without any definite aim —*ns* **drift'age; drift'er** one who or that which drifts an aimless shiftless person: a fishing-boat that uses a drift-net --**drift'-ice** floating masses of ice drifting before the wind; **drift'-net** a net which is allowed to drift with the tide, **drift'-wood** wood drifted by water [M.E , O.N. *drift*, snowdrift; root as **drive.**]

drill[1] *dril*, *v.t* to bore, pierce· to make with a drill. to exercise (soldiers, pupils, etc) by repeated practice to sow in rows.—*n.* an instrument for boring stone, metal, teeth, or other hard substances, actuated by a kind of bow, by a brace, or otherwise: a large boring instrument used in mining: a type of shellfish which bores into the shells of oysters: training exercise: a spell of it· a ridge with seed or growing plants on it (turnips, potatoes, etc.): the plants in such a row: the machine for sowing the seed: correct procedure or routine (*coll*).—**drill'-sergeant** a sergeant who drills soldiers [Prob borrowed from Du. *drillen*, to bore.]

drill[2] *dril*, *n.* a W. African baboon, smaller than the mandrill. [Perh. a W. African word.]

drill[3] *dril*, *n.* a stout twilled linen or cotton cloth [Ger. *Drillich*, ticking—L. *trilix*, three-threaded; *trēs*, *tria*, three, *licium*, thread]

drily. See under **dry.**

drink *dringk*, *v.t.* to swallow as a liquid: to empty, as a glass, bowl, etc.. to absorb: to take in through the senses —*v i* to swallow a liquid: to take intoxicating liquors to excess:—*pr.p.* **drink'ing;** *pa.t.* **drank;** *pa.p* **drunk.**—*n.* an act of drinking: a quantity drunk: something to be drunk: a beverage: intoxicating liquor.—*adj.* **drink'able.**—*ns.* **drink'ableness;** **drink'er** one who drinks: a tippler; **drink'ing.**—*adj.* fit to drink: for drinking.—**drinking-fountain; drink's mon'ey** a gratuity.—**drink in** to absorb (rain, etc.), as dry land does: to take in eagerly (something seen, said, etc.), **drink off** to quaff wholly and at a gulp; **drink the others under the table** to continue drinking and remain (comparatively) sober after the others have completely collapsed; **drink to, drink (to) the health of** to drink wine, etc., with good wishes for the health, prosperity, etc. of; **drink up** to exhaust by drinking, **in drink** (while) intoxicated; **strong drink** alcoholic liquor; **the drink** (*slang*) the sea.—See also **drunk.** [O.E. *drincan*; Ger. *trinken.*]

drip *drip*, *v.i.* to fall in drops: to let fall drops.—*v.t.* to let fall in drops·—*pr.p.* **dripp'ing;** *pa.t.* and *pa.p.* **dripped.**—*n.* a falling in drops: that which falls in drops: the edge of a roof: a device for passing a fluid slowly and continuously, esp. into a vein of the body (also **drip'-feed**)· the material so passed: a forceless person (*coll.*): drivel, esp sentimental (*slang*).—*n.* **dripp'ing** that which falls in drops, as fat from meat in roasting.—*adj.* **drip'-dry** (of a material or garment) which, when allowed to dry by dripping, requires no, or little, ironing.—Also *v.i.*, *v.t.*—**drip'-feed** a drip (see above).—*v.t.* to treat (a patient, etc.) with a drip.—**drip'-stone** a projecting moulding over doorways, etc , serving to throw off the rain [O.E *dryppan—drēopan.*]

drive *drīv*, *v t* to urge along: to hurry on· to control or guide the movements or operations of: to convey or carry in a vehicle: to force in. to push. to furnish motive power to. to urge, as a point of argument. to carry through, as a bargain: to compel: to send away with force, as a ball, esp. in golf, to play from the tee or with a driver, in cricket to hit strongly down the pitch, in tennis, to return forcibly underarm: to chase: to excavate (e.g. tunnel).—*v.i* to control an engine, vehicle, draught-animal, etc.. to press forward with violence: to be forced along, as a ship before the wind: to be driven: to go in a vehicle· to aim or tend towards a point (with *at*)· to strike with a sword, the fist, etc. (with *at*) —*pr.p.* **driv'ing;** *pa t.* **drōve;** *pa.p.* **driv'en.**—*n.* an excursion in a vehicle: a road for driving on, esp. the approach to a house within its own grounds. a driving stroke in games: impulsive force power of getting things done: the chasing of game towards the shooters: pushing sales by reducing prices: an organised campaign to attain any end: a meeting in order to play certain games, e.g whist: apparatus for driving.—*n* **driv'er** one who or that which drives, in all senses: a club used in golf to propel the ball from the teeing-ground.—**drive'-in** a refreshment halt, store, cinema, etc., where patrons are catered for while still remaining in their motor-cars. —Also *adj* —**driving licence** an official licence to drive a motor vehicle; **driv'ing-mirror** a small mirror in which a driver can see what is behind his vehicle; **driving test** a test of ability to drive safely, esp. an official and obligatory test, **driv'ing-wheel** a main wheel that communicates motion to other wheels: one of the main wheels in a locomotive.—**drive a coach and horses through** (*coll.*) to demolish (an argument, etc.) by demonstrating the obvious faults in it to brush aside, ignore completely; **drive home** to force (e.g. a nail) completely in: to make completely understood or accepted [O E. *drīfan*, to drive; Ger. *treiben*, to push.]

drivel *driv'l*, *v.i* to slaver like a child. to be foolish: to speak like an idiot:—*pr.p.* **driv'elling;** *pa.t.* and *pa.p.* **driv'elled.**—*n.* slaver· nonsense.—*n.* **driv'eller.** [M E *drevelen*, *dravelen*; O.E. *dreflian*]

driven. See **drive.**

drizzle *driz'l*, *v.i* to rain in small drops.—*v.t.* to shed in small drops.—*n.* a small, light rain —*adj.* **drizz'ly.** [Freq. of M.E. *dresen*—O.E. *drēosan*, to fall; Goth. *driusan.*]

drogue *drōg*, *n* the drag of boards, attached to the end of a harpoon-line: a conical canvas sleeve open at both ends, used as one form of sea-anchor, or to check the way of an aircraft, etc.· a parachute used to reduce speed of a falling object: a funnel device on the end of the hose of a tanker aircraft: a wind-sock: an air target of similar shape.

droit *drwa* (before a vowel *drwat*; Eng *droit*), *n.* right, legal claim. [Fr.]

droll *drōl*, *adj.* odd: amusing: laughable.—*n.* **droll'-ery** drollness: a jest —*n* **droll'ness.**—*adv.* **drolly** (*drōl'li*). [Fr. *drôle*, prob. from Du. *drollig*, odd—*trold*, a hobgoblin, cf. Ger. *Droll*, a short thick person.]

drome *drōm*, (*coll.*) *n.* an aerodrome.

dromedary *drum'i-dər-i*, *drom'*, *n.* a thoroughbred camel: a one-humped Arabian camel. [L.L. *dromedārius*—Gr. *dromas*, *dromados*, running.]

dromond *drom'*, *drum'ənd*, *n.* a swift mediaeval ship of war. [O.Fr.,—L.L. *dromō*, *-ōnis*—Byzantine Gr. *dromōn—dromos*, a running, *dramein* (aor.) to run.]

drone *drōn*, *n.* the male of the honey-bee: one who lives on the labour of others: a lazy, idle fellow: a deep humming sound: a bass-pipe of a bagpipe: its note: a monotonous speaker or speech. an aircraft piloted by remote control.—*v.i.* to emit a monotonous humming sound —*v t.* to utter with such a tone.—**drone'-pipe** a pipe producing a droning sound. [O.E. *drān*, bee, but the quantity of the *a* is doubtful, and relations obscure: perh —Old Saxon.]

drongo *drong'gō, n.* any member of the family *Dicruridae*, glossy-black fork-tailed insect-catching birds of the Old World tropics: a nitwit (*Austr. slang*):—*pl* **drong'o(e)s.** [From Malagasy.]

drool *drōōl, v.i.* to slaver: to drivel: to show effusive or lascivious pleasure (with *over*).—*n. drivel.* [drivel.]

droop *drōōp, v.i.* to hang down: to grow weak or faint: to decline.—*v.t.* to let hang down.—*n.* a drooping position.—*adv.* **droop'ily,**—*n.* **droop'iness.**—*adj.* **droop'y.** [O.N. *drūpa,* to droop.]

drop *drop, n.* a small rounded blob of liquid that hangs or falls at one time: a very small quantity of liquid: anything hanging like a drop: a pendant: a round sweetmeat: a curtain dropped between acts (also **drop'-cur'tain**): (in *pl.*) a medicine taken in drops: a fall: a vertical descent, difference of level: a landing by parachute: an instance of dropping anything: a trap in the gallows scaffold, the fall of which allows the criminal to drop: a device for lowering goods into a ship's hold.—*v.i.* to fall in drops: to let drops fall: to fall suddenly, steeply or sheer: to let oneself fall gently: to sink: to lapse: to diminish: to subside into a condition, come gradually to be.—*v.t.* to let fall in drops: to let fall: to let go, relinquish, abandon: to omit: to lower: to lay: to give birth to: to spot, bespatter, sprinkle: to utter casually: to write and send (a note) in an offhand manner: to set down, part with: to cause to fall, e.g. by shooting: to hole, etc. (a ball): to score (a goal) with a drop-kick: to set down from a vehicle, a ship: to cease to associate with: to lose (a sum of money, a game as part of a contest): to take one more (shot, stroke) than par (*golf*): to cause to fall: to bring down by a shot:—*pr.p.* **dropp'ing;** *pa.t.* and *pa.p.* **dropped.**—*ns.* **drop'let** a little drop; **dropp'er** one who or that which drops: a tube or contrivance for making liquid issue in drops; **dropp'ing** that which is dropped: (usu. in *pl.*) dung, excrement; **drop'-forging** the process of shaping metal parts by forging between two dies, one fixed to the hammer and the other to the anvil of a steam or mechanical hammer; **drop'-goal** (*Rugby*) a goal secured by a drop-kick; **drop'-hamm'er, drop'-press** a swaging, stamping, or forging machine; **drop'-kick** a kick made when the ball rebounds from the ground after dropping from the hand (*Rugby football*; also *v.t.*), **drop-out** see drop out below; **drop'-scene** a drop-curtain; **drop(ped)'-scone** a scone made like a pancake; **drop'-shot** (*tennis*, etc.) a ball made to drop close to the net, **drop'-wort** a species of spiraea with bead-like root tubercles.—**a drop in the ocean** a quantity infinitesimal in proportion; **at the drop of a hat** immediately: on the smallest provocation; **drop a brick** see brick; **drop a curtsy** to curtsy; **drop away, off** to depart, disappear; **drop in** to come, fall, set, etc. in casually, unintentionally, or one by one; **drop off** to fall asleep: to become less, to diminish; **drop out** to disappear from one's place: to make a drop-kick (*Rugby football*): to withdraw, esp. from an academic course or from conventional life in society (*n.* and *adj.* **drop'-out**); **let drop** to disclose inadvertently, or seemingly so [O E *dropa,* a drop, *dropian, droppian,* to drop; Du *drop,* Ger *Tropfe.*]

dropsy *drop'si, n.* a morbid accumulation of watery fluid in any part of the body —*adj* **drop'sical.** [Aphetic for *hydropsy.*]

droshky *drosh'ki, n* a low four-wheeled open carriage used in Russia [Russ *drozhki.*]

Drosophila *dros-of'i-la, n.* a genus of small yellow flies —fruit-flies—which breed in fermenting fruit juices

and are utilised in experiments in heredity: (without *cap*) any fly of the genus. [Gr. *drosos,* dew, moisture, *phileein,* to love.]

dross *dros, n.* the scum of melting metals: waste matter: small or waste coal: refuse.—*n.* **dross'iness.**—*adj.* **dross'y.** [O.E. *drōs.*]

drought *drowt,* **drouth** *drowth, ns.* dryness: want of rain or of water: a condition of atmosphere favourable to drying: thirst.—*n.* **drought'iness.**—*adjs.* **drought'y, drouth'y.** [O.E. *drūgath,* dryness— *drūgian,* to dry.]

drouth, etc. See **drought.**

drove *drōv, pa.t* of **drive.**—*n.* a number of cattle, or other animals, driven: a crowd, horde, moving together.—*n.* **drov'er** one whose occupation is to drive cattle.—**drove'-road** an old generally grassy track used or once used by droves of cattle. [O.E. *drāf, drīfan,* to drive.]

drown *drown, v.i.* to die of suffocation in liquid.—*v.t.* to kill by suffocation in liquid: to submerge: to flood: to extinguish: to make indistinguishable or imperceptible. [M.E. *drounen.*]

drowse *drowz, v.i.* to be heavy with sleep.—*v.t.* to make heavy with sleep: to pass in a half-sleeping state.—*adv.* **drows'ily.**—*n.* **drows'iness.**—*adj.* **drows'y** sleepy: heavy: dull: inducing sleep. [Apparently O.E. *drūsian,* to be sluggish.]

drub *drub, v.t.* to beat or thrash:—*pr.p.* **drubb'ing;** *pa.t.* and *pa.p.* **drubbed.**—*n.* **drubb'ing** a cudgelling: in games, a thorough defeat. [Ar. *daraba,* to beat, *bastinado*—*darb,* a beating, has been suggested.]

drudge *druj, v.i.* to do dull, laborious or very mean work.—*n.* one who does heavy monotonous work: a slave: a menial servant: dull task-work.—*n.* **drudg'ery** the work of a drudge: uninteresting toil: hard or humble labour. [Ety. unknown; perh. from root of O.E. *drēogan,* to perform, undergo.]

drug *drug, n.* any substance used in the composition of medicine: a substance used to stupefy or poison or for self-indulgence: an article that cannot be sold, generally owing to overproduction.—*v.t.* to mix or season with drugs: to administer a drug to: to poison or stupefy with drugs.—*v.i.* to administer drugs or medicines: to take drugs, esp. narcotics, habitually: —*pr.p.* **drugg'ing;** *pa.t.* and *pa.p.* **drugged.**—*n.* **drugg'ist** one who deals in drugs: a pharmacist (*U.S.*).—**drug'-add'ict, drug'-fiend** a habitual taker of drugs; **drug'-store** (*U.S.*) a chemist's shop (usually in America selling a variety of goods, including refreshments) [O.Fr. *drogue*]

drugget *drug'it, n.* a woven and felted coarse woollen fabric: a protective covering, made of such fabric, for a floor or carpet. [O.Fr. *droguet.*]

Druid *drōō'id, n.* a priest among the ancient Celts of Britain, Gaul and Germany: an Eisteddfod official.— *adjs.* **druid'ic, -al.**—*n.* **dru'idism** the doctrines which the Druids taught: the ceremonies they practised. [L. pl *druidae,* from a Celtic stem *druid-.*]

drum[1] *drum, n.* an instrument of percussion, a skin stretched on a frame: anything shaped like a drum: the tympanum of the ear: the upright part of a cupola (*archit.*): a cylinder, esp. a revolving cylinder: a magnetic drum (*comput.*; see under **magnet**): a cylindrical barrel.—*v.t.* to beat a drum: to beat rhythmically.— *v.t* to expel by beat of drum (with *out*; also *fig.*): to summon (with *up*): to impress by iteration:—*pr.p.* **drumm'ing;** *pa t.* and *pa.p.* **drummed.**—*n.* **drumm'er** one who drums: a commercial traveller —**drum'beat;** **drum brake** a type of brake in which two shoes grip the inside of the brake drum; **drum'head** the head or skin of a drum: the top part of a capstan —*adj.* (*mil*) improvised in the field (see **court-martial**).—**drum'- ma'jor** the marching leader of a military band; **drum**

majorette a girl who heads a marching band, usu twirling a baton, in a parade, etc.: a majorette; **drum'stick** the stick with which a drum is beaten: the tibia of a dressed fowl.—**beat, bang the drum** to indulge in publicity. [From a Gmc. root found in Du. *trom,* Ger. *Trommel,* a drum; prob. imit.]

drum[2] *drum, n.* a ridge.—*n.* **drum'lin** *(geol.)* a ridge formed under the ice-sheet of the Glacial Period (also **drum**). [Ir. and Gael. *druim,* back.]

drumlin. See **drum**[2].

drunk *drungk, pa.p* of **drink.**—*adj.* intoxicated (also *fig.*).—*n* a drunk person.—*n.* **drunk'ard** one who frequently drinks to excess: a habitual drinker.—*adj.* **drunk'en** given to excessive drinking: resulting from intoxication: drunk.—*adv.* **drunk'enly.**—*n.* **drunk'enness.**

drupe *droop, n.* a fleshy fruit with a stone.—*adj.* **drupā'ceous**—*ns.* **drup'el, drupe'let** a little drupe, forming part of a fruit, as in the raspberry. [L. *drūpa*—Gr. *dryppā,* an olive.]

druse *drooz, n.* a rock cavity lined with crystals, a geode. [Ger. *Druse*—Czech. *druza,* a piece of crystallised ore.]

Druz, Druze, Druse *drooz, n.* one of a people inhabiting chiefly a mountainous district in the south of Syria, whose religion contains elements found in the Koran, the Bible, Gnosticism, etc. [Perh. from *Darazi,* an early exponent of the religion.]

dry *drī, adj.* without water or liquid, contained or adhering: free from, or deficient in, moisture, sap, rain: thirsty: out of water: failing to yield water, or milk, or other liquid: of a fruit, not fleshy: not green: unbuttered: not drawing blood: of wines, etc., free from sweetness and fruity flavour: legally forbidding the liquor trade: enforcing or subjected to prohibition: uninteresting: frigid, precise, formal: of humour, quiet, restrained, and unobtrusive: of manner, distantly unsympathetic:—*compar.* **dri'er;** *superl.* **dri'est.**—*v.t.* to free from or exhaust of water or moisture (often with *off*).—*v.i.* to become dry (often with *off*): to evaporate entirely:—*pr.p.* **dry'ing;** *pa.t.* and *pa.p.* **dried;** *3rd pers. sing. pr.t.* **dries.**—*n.* **dri'er, dry'er** one who or that which dries: a machine for extracting moisture from cloth, grain, etc.: a drying agent for oils, paint, etc.—*adv.* **dri'ly, dry'ly** in a dry manner.—*adj.* **dry'ish.**—*n.* **dry'ness.** —**dry battery** *(elect.)* a battery composed of drycells; **dry'-cell** an electric cell in which the electrolyte is not a liquid but a paste.—*vs.t.* **dry'-clean** to clean (clothes, etc.) using e.g. a petroleum-based solvent rather than water; **dry'-cure** to cure by drying.—**dry dock** a dock that can be emptied of water in order to effect repairs to the underside of a ship.—*v.t.* **(dry'-dock)** to put in dry dock.—*adj.* **dry'-eyed** tearless.— *adj.* **dry'-fly** (of fishing) without sinking the fly in the water.—*n.pl.* **dry'-goods** drapery and the like distinguished from groceries, hardware, etc.—**dry ice** see **ice; dry land** land as opposed to sea; **dry measure** a system of measure by bulk, used for grain, etc.; **dry's plate** a sensitised photographic plate, with which a picture may be made without the preliminary use of a bath; **dry'-point** a sharp needle by which fine lines are drawn in copper-plate engraving; a plate or impression produced with it, **dry'-rot** a decay of timber caused by *Merulius lacrymans* and other fungi which reduce it ultimately to a dry brittle mass. A concealed decay or degeneration *(fig.),* **dry run** a practice exercise *(mil.):* a rehearsal.—*v.t.* **dry'-salt** to cure (meat) by salting and drying.—*n.* **dry'salter** a dealer in gums, dyes, etc.; **dry'saltery.**—*adj.* and *adv.* **dry'-shod** without wetting the shoes or feet.—**dry ski** an adaptation of a ski with which one can practise skiing on a dry surface; **dry skiing.**—*adj* **dry'-stone** built of stone

without mortar, as some walls.—**dry'-wall'er** one who builds walls without mortar.—**cut and dried** see cut; **dry out** *(coll.)* to take or give a course of treatment to cure oneself or another person of alcoholism; **dry up** to dry thoroughly or completely: to cease to produce liquid (water, milk, etc.): to forget one's lines or part (as an actor, etc ; *coll.):* to stop talking *(slang);* **go dry** to adopt liquor prohibition; **high and dry** see **high.** [O E. *drȳge;* cf. Du. *droog,* Ger. *trocken.]*

dryad *drī'ad, -əd, n.* a wood nymph: a forest-tree. [Gr. *drȳas, -ados,* from *drȳs,* oak tree.]

dual *dū'əl, adj.* two-fold: consisting of two: expressing or representing two things *(gram.).*—*n.* a grammatical form indicating duality: a word in the dual number.—*n.* **dū'alism** *(philos.)* that view which seeks to explain the world by the assumption of two radically independent and absolute elements—e.g. (1) the doctrine of the entire separation of spirit and matter, thus being opposed both to *idealism* and to *materialism;* (2) the doctrine of two distinct principles of good and evil, or of two divine beings of these characters; **dū'alist.**—*adj.* **dūalis'tic.**—*adv.* **dūalis'- tically.**—*n.* **duality** *(dū-al'i-ti)* doubleness: state of being double.—*adv.* **dū'ally.**—**dual carriageway** a road consisting of two separated parts, each for use of traffic in one direction only; **dual control** joint control or jurisdiction.—*adj.* **du'al-control** able to be operated by either or both of two persons.—**dual personality** a condition in which the same individual shows at different times two very different characters.—*adj.* **du'al-pur'pose** serving or intended to serve two purposes. [L. *duālis*—*duo,* two.]

dub[1] *dub, v.t.* to confer knighthood upon, from the ceremony of striking the shoulders with the flat of a sword: to confer any name or dignity upon: to rub a softening and waterproof mixture into (leather): to dress (a fly) for fishing:—*pr.p.* **dubb'ing;** *pa.p.* **dubbed.**—*n.* **dubb'ing** (also **dubb'in)** a preparation of grease for softening leather. [O.E. *dubbian,* to dub knight.]

dub[2] *dub, v.t.* to give (a film) a new sound-track, e.g one in a different language: to add sound effects or music: to transfer (recorded music, etc.) to a new disc or tape: to combine so as to make one record (music, etc., from more than one source, e.g. a live performance and a recording. [Abbrev. of **double.**]

dubbin. See **dub**[1].

dubious *dū'bi-əs, adj.* doubtful, causing doubt: uncertain: of uncertain event or issue: arousing suspicion or disapproval: hesitating (about).—*n* **dūbiety** *(-bī'i-ti)* doubt.—*adv.* **dū'biously.**—*n.* **dū'biousness.** [L. *dubius.*]

ducal *dū'kəl, adj.* pertaining to a duke.—*adv.* **dū'cally.** [Fr.,—L.L. *ducālis*—L. *dux,* leader.]

ducat *duk'ət, n.* a gold or silver coin of varying values, formerly much used on the Continent. [O.Fr. *ducat* —It. *ducato*—L.L. *ducātus,* a duchy.]

duce *doo'chā, n.* the title assumed by the Italian dictator Mussolini. [It.,.leader—L *dux*]

duchess, duchesse. See **duchy.**

duchy *duch'i, n.* the territory of a duke, a dukedom.— *ns* **duch'ess** the consort or widow of a duke: a woman of the same rank as a duke in her own right, **duchesse** *(duch'es, du-shes',* Fr., duchess) a table-cover or centre-piece—**duchesse lace** Flemish pillow lace with designs in cord outline, **duchesse potatoes** piped shapes of mashed potato, butter, milk and egg-yolk baked until light brown. [O.Fr. *duché*—L L. *ducātus;* Fr. *duchesse*—L L. *ducissa*]

duck[1] *duk, n.* a kind of coarse cotton, linen, etc. cloth for small sails, sacking, etc . (in *pl*) garments made of duck. [Du *doek,* linen cloth; Ger *Tuch*]

duck[2] *duk, v t.* to dip for a moment in water: to avoid (*coll.*).—*v.i.* to dip or dive: to lower the head suddenly to cringe, yield.—*n.* a quick plunge, dip: a quick lowering of the head or body, a jerky bow.— *n.* **duck'er; duck'ing.—duck out of** to shirk, avoid (responsibilities, etc.). [M.E. *douken* from an assumed O.E. *dûcan,* to duck, dive.]

duck[3] *duk, n.* any bird of the family *Anatidae,* the prominent marks of which are short webbed feet, with a small hind-toe not reaching the ground, the netted scales in front of the lower leg, and the long bill· the female duck as distinguished from the male *drake:* in cricket (originally *duck's egg*), the zero (O), which records in a scoring-sheet that a player made no runs: a darling, sweetheart (*coll.*) —*ns.* **duck'ling** young duck; **ducks, duck'y** (*coll.*) a term of endearment.—*adj.* **duck'y.—duck'bill** an aquatic burrowing and egg-laying Australian monotreme, with broadly webbed feet, and duck-like bill.—*adj.* **duck'-billed. —duck'-board** planking for swampy ground, trenches, etc.; **duck'-hawk** moor-buzzard or marsh-harrier: (*U.S*) peregrine falcon; **duck'-pond; duck's arse** a hairstyle in which the hair is swept back to a point on the neck resembling a duck's tail; **duck'weed** any plant of the family Lemnaceae, monocotyledons most of which consist of a small flat green floating plate —**Bombay duck** bummalo; **break one's duck** (*cricket*) to make one's first run (see above); **lame duck** a defaulter; a bankrupt: anything disabled: an inefficient or helpless person or organisation; **like a dying duck** languishing; **make, play, ducks and drakes** to make flat stones skip on the surface of water: to use recklessly: to squander, waste (with *of, with*); **sitting duck** an easy target, helpless victim; **wild'-duck** the mallard, esp. the hen-bird. [O.E. *dûce* (or *duce*?), a duck.]

duck[4] *duk, n.* a kind of amphibious military transport vehicle or landing craft. [From manufacturers' code initials, DUKW.]

duct *dukt, n.* a tube conveying fluids in animal bodies or plants: a pipe for an electric cable: an air-passage. —*adj.* **duct'less.—ductless glands** masses of glandular tissue that lack ducts and discharge their products directly into the blood. [L. *ductus—dūcĕre,* to lead.]

ductile *duk'tīl, -til, adj.* easily led: yielding: capable of being drawn out into threads.—*ns* **ductility** (*-til'*), **duc'tileness** capacity of being drawn out without breaking. [Fr.,—L. *ductilis—dūcere,* to lead]

dud *dud, (coll)* *n* a bomb or projectile that fails to go off: a dishonoured cheque: a counterfeit: any person or thing useless or ineffective: a failure.—Also *adj.*

dude *dūd, dōod, (orig. U.S. slang) n.* a fop or dandy: a townsman.—*adj.* **du'dish.—n.** **du'dism.—dude ranch** ranch run as a holiday resort or for training in ranching.

dudeen *dōo-dēn', -dhēn', n.* a short clay tobacco-pipe [Ir *dúidín,* dim of *dûd,* pipe.]

dudgeon *duj'ən, n.* resentment: offended indignation, as in in high dudgeon.

due *dū, adj.* owed: that ought to be paid or done to another: proper· appointed, under engagement, to be ready, arrive, etc.—*adv.* exactly, directly —*n* that which is owed: what one has a right to, has earned fee, toll, charge, or tribute: (in *pl*) subscription to a club or society —**due to** caused by: (wrongly) owing to, because of; **give someone his/her due** to be fair to someone; **give the devil his due** to give a fair hearing to one of notorious character; **in due course** in the ordinary way when the time comes [O.Fr. *deu,* pa p of *devoir*—L *debēre,* to owe.]

duel *dū'əl, n.* a combat between two persons, prearranged and fought under fixed conditions, gen-

erally on an affair of honour: single combat to decide a quarrel: any fight or struggle between two parties. —*v.i.* to fight in a duel:—*pr.p.* **dū'elling;** *pa t.* and *pa.p.* **dū'elled.—ns.** **dū'eller; dū'elling; dū'ellist.** [It. *duello*—L. *duellum,* the original form of *bellum —duo,* two.]

duenna *dū-en'ə, n.* a lady who acts the part of governess or chaperons a younger. [Sp. *dueña*—L. *domina,* fem. of *dominus,* lord.]

duet *dū-et', n* a composition in music for two performers: the performance of such: the performers of such any action involving two parties.—*ns.* **duett'ist.** [It. *duetto,* dim of *duo—due,* two—L. *duo.*]

duff[1] *duf, n.* dough: a stiff flour pudding boiled in a bag. [A form of **dough.**]

duff[2] *duf, v.t.* to make to look new: to alter brands on (stolen cattle): to steal cattle —**duff up, over** (*slang*) to beat up. [Perh. a back-formation from **duffer.**]

duff[3] *duf, v.t.* to play amiss by hitting the ground behind the ball (*golf*): to bungle. [Back-formation from **duffer**[1].]

duff[4] *duf, (coll.) adj.* no good: broken, not working. [Prob. **duff**[3].]

duffel *duf'l, n.* a thick, coarse woollen cloth, with a thick nap—also **duff'le.—duffel bag** a canvas bag, cylindrical in shape, orig. used for a sailor's kit; **duffel coat** a jacket or coat, usu. hooded, made of duffel. [Du., from *Duffel,* a town near Antwerp.]

duffer *duf'ər, n.* an unskilful person: one who fakes up sham articles or duffs cattle.

duffle. See duffel.

dug[1] *dug, n.* a nipple or udder of a cow or other beast. [Cf. Sw. *dægga,* Dan. *dægge,* to suckle.]

dug[2] *dug, pa.t.* and *pa.p.* of **dig.—dug'out** a boat made by hollowing out the trunk of a tree: a rough dwelling or shelter dug out of a slope or bank or in a trench: a superannuated person brought back to employment (*slang*)

dugong *dōo'gong, n.* a herbivorous marine mammal of the order Sirenia—the supposed original of the mermaid [Malayan *dúyong.*]

duiker, duyker *dī'kər, n.* a small S. African antelope: a cormorant (*S. Afr.*). [Du., diver, from plunging into the bush, or into the sea.]

duke *dūk, n* a sovereign prince of a small state: a nobleman of the highest order: (*dōok; slang*) the fist —*n.* **duke'dom.** [O.Fr. *duc*—L. *dux, ducis,* a leader —*dūcere,* to lead.]

Dukhobor, Doukhobor *dōo'hhō-bor, dōo'kō-bor, n.* a member of a Russian sect who trust to an inner light, reject the doctrine of the Trinity, and refuse military service, many of them settled in Canada since 1899. [Russ. *Dukhoborets—dukh,* spirit, *borets,* fighter.]

DUKW. See duck[4].

dulcet *duls'it, adj* sweet: melodious, harmonious.—*n.* **dulcifica'tion.—v.t.** **dul'cify** (*rare*) to make sweet.— *ns.* **Dul'citone®** a keyboard instrument in which graduated tuning-forks are struck by hammers [L *dulcis,* sweet]

dulcimer *dul'si-mər, n.* a musical instrument like a flat box, with sounding-board and wires stretched across bridges. [Sp. *dulcemele*—L. *dulce melos,* a sweet song.]

Dulcinea *dul-sin-ē'ə, dul-sin'i-ə, n.* a sweetheart [From *Dulcinea* del Toboso, the name given by Don Quixote to the mistress of his imagination.]

dulcify. See dulcet.

dulia, douleia *dū-, dōo-lī'ə, (R C Church) n.* the inferior veneration accorded to saints and angels, as opposed to **hyperdulia,** that accorded to the Virgin Mary, and **latria,** that accorded to God alone. [Gr. *douleiā,* servitude—*doulos,* a slave.]

dull *dul, adj* slow of learning, or of understanding:

wanting in keenness of hearing or other sense: insensible: without life or spirit: uninteresting: slow of motion: drowsy: downcast: lacking brightness or clearness: cloudy: muffled: obtuse: blunt —*v.t.* to make dull.—*v.t.* to become dull.—*n.* **dull'ard** a dull and stupid person—*adj.* **dull'ish.**—*ns.* **dull'ness, dul'ness.**—*adv.* **dully** (*dul'li*). [Related to O.E. *dol.*, foolish, and *dwellan*, to err.]

dulse *duls*, *n* an edible red seaweed, esp. *Rhodymenia palmata.* [Gael *duileasg.*]

duly *dū'li*, *adv* properly: fitly: at the proper time. [See **due¹**.]

duma *doo̅'mə*, *n* an elected council, esp. the Russian parliament of 1906-17.—*n.* **dum'aist** a duma member [Russ *duma*, of Gmc. origin.]

dumb *dum*, *adj.* without the power of speech: silent: soundless: stupid (*U.S.* after Ger. or Du.) —*adv.* **dumb'ly.**—*ns.* **dumb'ness; dumm'y** one who is dumb. a mere tool, man of straw. a block or lay-figure: a sham or counterfeit article taking the place of a real one: an unprinted model of a book: a rubber teat: an exposed hand of cards: the imaginary player of such a game or hand: a feint of passing or playing the ball (*Rugby football*, etc.).—*v.t.* and *v.t.* to sell the dummy (to; see below).—*adj.* silent: sham.—**dumb'-bell** a double-headed weight swung in the hands to develop the muscles: any object or figure of the same shape; **dumb'-cluck** a fool.—*vs.t* **dum(b)found'**,*-er* to strike dumb: to confuse greatly: to astonish —**dumb'-pla'no** a soundless keyboard for piano practice; **dumb'-show'** gesture without words. pantomime.—*adj.* **dumb'struck** silent with astonishment.—**dumb'-wait'er** a movable platform used for conveying food, dishes, etc., at meals: a stand with revolving top for holding dessert, etc.: a small lift for food and dishes; **dummy run** an experimental run: a try-out or testing. —**sell the dummy** (*Rugby football*, etc.) to deceive an opponent by a feint of passing or playing the ball (also *fig.*); **strike dumb** to silence with astonishment. [O.E. *dumb*; Ger *dumm*, stupid, Du. *dom*.]

dumdum *dum'dum*, *n.* a soft-nosed expanding bullet, first made at *Dum Dum* near Calcutta.

dummy. See **dumb.**

dump¹ *dump*, *v.t* to set down heavily or with a thump: to unload: to land and sell at prices below cost of production in the exporting country—or (according to some) in the importing country (*econ.*): to tip (esp rubbish): to get rid of.—*n* a place for the discharge of loads, or for rubbish: a deposit: store (*mil.*): a dirty, dilapidated place.—**dump bin** in a shop, a container for e.g. bargain items; **dump(er) truck** a lorry which can be emptied by raising the front of the carrier to allow the contents to slide out the back (also **dump'er**). [Cf. Dan *dumpe*, Norw. *dumpa*, to fall plump.]

dump² *dump*, *n.* dullness or gloominess of mind, ill-humour, low spirits—now only used in the pl.—**(down) in the dumps** (*coll.*) depressed. [Prob. related to O Du. *domp*, mist; or Ger. *dumpf*, gloomy]

dumper. See **dump¹.**

dumpling *dump'ling*, *n* a kind of thick pudding or mass of paste: a dumpling-shaped person or animal.

dumpy *dump'i*, *adj.* short and thick.—*n.* a dumpy person or animal, esp. one of a breed of very short-legged fowls.—*n.* **dump'iness.** [18th cent.; perh. from **dumpling.**]

dun¹ *dun*, *adj* greyish brown. mouse-coloured: dingy. dusky.—*n.* a dun colour: a horse of dun colour — **dun'-bird** the pochard, esp. the hen-bird; **dun'-div'er** the merganser. [O.E *dun*, prob. not Celt.]

dun² *dun*, *v.t.* to importune for payment:—*pr.p* **dunn'ing;***pa.t.* and*pa p.* **dunned.**—*n.* one who duns a demand for payment [Perh allied to **din.**]

dun³ *dun*, *n.* a hill: a fortified mound. [Celt.; in many place-names; adopted in O.E. as *dūn*; see **down²**.]

dunce *duns*, *n.* one slow at learning: a stupid person.— **dunce's cap** a tall conical hat, formerly worn at school to indicate stupidity [*Duns* Scotus (died 1308), leader of the schoolmen, from him called *Dunses*, who opposed classical studies on the revival of learning-- hence any opposer of learning, a blockhead.]

dunder *dun'dər*, *n.* lees, dregs of sugar-cane juice. [Sp. *redundar*, to overflow.]

dunderhead *dun'dər-hed*, *n.* a stupid person.—*adj.* **dun'derheaded.**

Dundreary *dun-drēr'i*, *adj.* denoting a style of long side-whiskers like Lord *Dundreary's*, in Tom Taylor's *Our American Cousin*

dune *dūn*, *n.*, a low hill of sand, esp. on the seashore.— **dune'-bugg'y** (orig. *U S.*) a usu. small car with large tyres, used for driving on beaches [Fr.,—O.Du. *duna:* cf. **down².**]

dung¹ *dung*, *n.* excrement. manure.—*v.t.* to manure with dung.—*v.t.* to void excrement.—**dung'-bee'tle, dung'-fly** one developing or breeding on dung; **dung'-fork** a fork used for moving stable manure; **dung'-heap, dung'-hill** a heap of dung: any mean situation. [O.E. *dung.*]

dungaree *dung-gə-rē'*, or *dung'*, *n.* a coarse Indian calico: (in *pl.*) overalls, esp. ones including trousers, made of it: (in *pl.*) a similar garment for casual wear. [Hindi *dūgrī.*]

dungeon *dun'jən*, *n.* ong. the principal tower of a castle: a close, dark prison: a cell under ground. [O.Fr. *donjon*—L.L. *domniō, -ōnis*—L. *dominus*, a lord.]

dunk *dungk*, *v t.* and *v.t.* to dip cake, etc., that one is eating in one's coffee or other beverage. [Ger. *tunken*, to dip]

dunlin *dun'lin*, *n* the red-backed sandpiper. [Dim. of **dun¹.**]

dunnage *dun'ij*, *n.* loose wood of any kind laid in the bottom of the hold to keep the cargo out of the bilge-water, or wedged between parts of the cargo to keep them steady: sailor's baggage.

dunno *də-nō'*. Coll. contr. of (I) don't know.

dunnock *dun'ək*, *n.* the hedge-sparrow. [Dim. of **dun¹.**]

dunny *dun'i*, (*coll* or *dial.*) *n.* a lavatory (esp *Austr.* and *New Zealand*): an outside lavatory (esp. *Scot.*)

duo *doo̅'ō*, *dū'ō*, *n* a duet: two persons, etc., associated in some way, e.g. a pair of musicians or variety artists: —*pl.* **dū'os.** [It.—L. *duo*, two.]

duodecennial *dū-ō-di-sen'yəl*, *adj.* occurring every twelve years. [L. *duodecim*, twelve. *annus*, year.]

duodecimal *dū-ō-des'i-ml*, *adj.* computed by twelves: twelfth. [L. *duodecim*, twelve—*duo*, two, and *decem*, ten.]

duodecimo *dū-ō-des'i-mō*, *adj.* formed of sheets folded so as to make twelve leaves.—*n.* a book of such sheets —usually written 12mo. [L. in *duodecimō*, in twelfth —*duo*, two, *decem*, ten.]

duodenary *dū-ō-dē'nə-ri*, *adj.* relating to twelve, twelvefold. [L. *duodēnārius.*]

duodenum *dū-ō-dē'nəm*, *n.* the first portion of the small intestine, so called because about twelve fingers'-breadth in length:—*pl.* **duodē'na.**—*adj.* **duode'nal.**—*ns.* **duodenec'tomy** excision of the duodenum; **duodēni'tis** inflammation of the duodenum. [Formed from L. *duodēnī*, twelve each.]

duologue *dū'ō-log*, *n.* a piece spoken between two [L. *duo* (or Gr. *dyo*), two, Gr *logos*, discourse.]

duomo *dwō'mō*, *n.* a cathedral:—*pl.* **duō'mos, duō'mi** (-*ē*). [It. See **dome¹.**]

duopoly *dū-op'ə-li*, *n* a situation in which two companies, etc. monopolise trading in a commodity. [L. *duo* (or Gr. *dyo*), two, and mono*poly.*]

duotone *dū'ō-tōn, n.* and *adj.* (a drawing, print, etc.) done in two tones or colours. [L. *duo*, two, and **tone.**]

dupe *dūp, n.* one who is cheated.—*v.t.* to deceive: to trick.—*n.* **dūpabil'ity.**—*adj.* **dū'pable.**—*ns.* **dū'per; dū'pery** the art of deceiving others. [Fr *dupe*; of uncertain origin.]

dupion *dū'pi-ən, -on, n.* a double cocoon, made by two silk-worms spinning together: a kind of coarse silk made from these cocoons. [Fr. *doupion*, from It. *doppione*, double.]

duple *dū'pl, adj.* double, twofold: having two beats in the bar (*mus*). [L *duplus*; cf. **double.**]

duplex *dū'pleks, adj.* twofold, double: having some part doubled: allowing communication, transmission, in both directions simultaneously (*comput., teleg.,* etc.)—*n.* **duplicity** (*dū-plis'i-ti*) doubleness, esp. in conduct and intention: insincerity: double-dealing.—*adj.* **duplic'itous.**—**duplex (apartment)** a flat on two floors; **duplex (house)** (*U.S.*) a house, divided either horizontally or vertically, providing accommodation for two families. [L. *duplex, -icis.*]

duplicate *dū'pli-kit, adj.* double: twofold: like, equivalent or alternative.—*n.* another (esp. subsidiary or spare) thing of the same kind: a copy or transcript. condition of being in two copies—*v.t.* (-*kāt*) to double: to copy: repeat.—*n.* **dūplicā'tion.**—*adj.* **dū'plicative.**—*n.* **dū'plicātor** a copying apparatus—**in duplicate** in two copies, or original accompanied by a copy. [L. *duplicāre, -ātum, duo,* two, *plicāre,* to fold.]

duplicity. See **duplex.**

dupondius *dū-pon'di-əs,* (*hist.*) *n.* an ancient Roman coin. [L.]

duppy *dup'i, n.* a ghost. [West Indian Negro word.]

dura. Same as **durra.**

durable *dūr'ə-bl, adj.* able to last or endure: hardy: permanent.—*n.* something that will endure, esp. (*pl.*) goods that do not need replacing frequently.—*ns.* **durabil'ity, dur'ableness.**—*adv.* **dur'ably.**—*ns.* **dur'ance** continuance (*obs.*): imprisonment (*arch.*); **durā'tion** continuance in time: time indefinitely: power of continuance: length of time.—*adj.* **durā'tional.**—**for the duration** (*coll.*) as long as the war (or the situation under discussion) continues. [L *dūrāre,* to harden, endure, last.]

Duralumin® *dūr-al'ū-min, n.* a strong, light, aluminium alloy containing copper. [L. *dūrus,* hard, and *aluminium.*]

dura mater *dū'rə mā'tər,* L. *dōō'ra ma'ter,* the exterior membrane of the brain and spinal column. [L. *dūra māter,* hard mother, a translation of the Ar. name.]

duramen *dū-rā'mən, n.* heartwood. [L. *dūrāmen,* hardness—*dūrus,* hard.]

durance, duration. See **durable.**

durbar *dûr'bär, n.* a reception or levee: an Indian court. [Pers. *darbār,* a prince's court, lit. a door of admittance.]

duress *dûr-es', dūr'es, n* constraint: imprisonment: constraint illegally exercised [O Fr. *duresse*—L. *dūritia*—*dūrus,* hard.]

durian *dōō'ri-ən,* or *dū', n.* a lofty Indian and Malayan fruit-tree, with leaves like a cherry's: its large fruit, with hard rind and pulp of foul smell but fine flavour [Malay *dūrī,* thorn.]

during *dū'ring, prep.* throughout the time of· in the course of. [Orig. *pr.p.* of obs. *dure,* to last.]

durmast *dûr'mäst, n.* a variety of sessile-fruited oak with leaves downy below. [Origin unknown: perhaps a blunder for *dun mast*]

durra *doo'rə, n.* Indian millet, a grass (*Sorghum vulgare*) akin to sugar-cane, much cultivated for grain in Asia and Africa, or other species of the genus.—

Also **dou'ra, dhu'rra, du'ra** and **dari** (*dur'i*). [Ar. *dhurah.*]

durst *dûrst, pa.t.* of **dare,** to venture. [O.E. *dorste,* pa.t. of *durran,* to dare.]

durum (wheat) *dū'rəm* ((*h*)*wēt*), *n.* a kind of spring wheat grown esp. in Russia, North Africa and North America, whose flour is used in making spaghetti, etc. [L. *triticum dūrum,* hard wheat.]

dusk *dusk, adj.* darkish: of a dark colour.—*n.* twilight: partial darkness: darkness of colour—*v.t.* and *v.t.* to make or become dusky.—*adv.* **dusk'ly.**—*n.* **dusk'iness.**—*adj.* **dusk'y** partially dark or obscure; dark-coloured: gloomy. [Apparently connected with O.E. *dox,* dark.]

dust *dust, n* fine particles of solid matter: a cloud of powdery matter· powder: earth: the grave: a mean condition: a disturbance, a brawl.—*v.t.* to free from dust (also *v.t.*): to sprinkle.—*n.* **dust'er** a cloth or brush for removing dust: a sprinkler.—*adv.* **dust'ily.** —*n* **dust'iness.**—*adjs.* **dust'less; dust'y,** covered or sprinkled with dust; like dust; contemptible, bad (in phrase *not so dusty; slang*).—**dust'-bath** the action of birds in rubbing dust into their feathers, prob. to get rid of parasites; **dust'bin,** a receptacle for household rubbish: a repository for anything unwanted, unimportant, etc. (*fig.*); **dust'-bowl** a drought area subject to dust-storms; **dust'-cart** a cart for taking away household rubbish; **dust'-coat** an overall: a light overcoat; **dust'-cover** the jacket of a book; **dusting powder** fine powder, esp. talcum powder; **dust'-jacket** dust-cover; **dust'man** one who removes household rubbish; **dust'-pan** a pan or shovel for removing dust swept from the floor.—*adj.* **dust'proof** impervious or inaccessible to dust.—**dust'-sheet** a cloth for protecting furniture from dust; **dust'-shot** the smallest size of shot; **dust-storm** a small storm in which a whirling column of dust or sand travels across a dry country; **dust'-up** a quarrel, a brawl; **dusty answer** an unsatisfying, unfruitful, or sordid response (*fig.*); **dust'y-mill'er** the auricula, from the white dust upon its leaves and flowers.—**bite the dust** see **bite; kick up, raise a dust** see **kick; throw dust in someone's eyes** to deceive someone. [O.E. *dūst;* cf. Ger. *Dunst,* vapour.]

Dutch *duch, adj.* pertaining to the Netherlands, its people, or language.—*n.* the language of the Netherlands: (*pl.*) the people of the Netherlands.—**Dutch'-man** a native or citizen of the Netherlands:—*pl.* **Dutch'men;** *fem.* **Dutch'woman;**—*pl.* **Dutch'women.** —**Dutch auction** see **auction; Dutch barn** a storage barn consisting of a roof on a steel framework; **Dutch cap** see **cap; Dutch cheese** a small round cheese made on the Continent from skim-milk; **Dutch comfort** 'Thank God it's no worse'; **Dutch courage** see **courage; Dutch doll** a wooden doll with jointed legs; **Dutch hoe** a hoe with blade attached as in a spade; **Dutch oven** a cooking-pot used by burying in coals; **Dutch treat** one at which each brings or pays for his own share.—**double Dutch** any unknown or unintelligible language; **Dutch elm disease** a fungal, often fatal, disease of elm trees, spread by bark beetles, causing a gradual withering; **go Dutch** (*coll.*) to pay each for himself; **talk like a Dutch uncle** to utter a rebuke [Ger. *deutsch,* (lit) belonging to the people—O.H.G. *diutisc,* cf. O.E. *thēod,* Goth. *thiuda,* nation; see **Teutonic.**]

dutch *duch,* (*costermonger's slang*) *n.* a wife. [**duchess.**]

duty *dū'ti, n.* that which is due: what one is bound by any (esp. moral) obligation to do: one's proper business· service: attendance: supervision of pupils out of school hours: performance of function or service: the work done by a machine under given conditions, or for a specified amount of energy supplied: respect:

tax on goods, etc.—*adj.* **du'teous** devoted to duty: obedient.—*adv.* **du'teously.**—*n* **du'teousness.**—*adjs.* **du'tiable** subject to custom duty; **du'tied** subjected to duties and customs; **du'tiful** attentive to duty: respectful: expressive of a sense of duty —*adv.* **du'tifully.**—*n.* **du'tifulness.**—*adjs.* **du'ty-bound'** obliged by one's feeling of duty: honour-bound, **du'ty-free'** free from tax or duty.—**duty officer** the officer on duty at any particular time.—*adj.* **du'ty-paid'** on which duty has been paid.—**do duty for** to serve as, to act as substitute for; **on duty** performing one's duties, or liable to be called upon to do so, during a specified period of time (*opp.* **off duty**). [Anglo-Fr. *dueté*; see **due**[1].]

duumvir *dōō-*, *dū-um'vir*, *-vər*, *n.* one of two associated in the same office:—*pl.* **duum'virs, duum'viri** (*-ī*; L. *dōō-ōō m-wir'ē*).—*adj.* **duum'viral.**—*n.* **duum'virate** an association of two men in one office: a government by duumvirs. [L. *duumvirī*, for *duovirī*—*duo*, two, and *vir*, a man.]

duvet *dōō'vā*, (Fr *du-vä*), *n.* a quilt stuffed with eiderdown, swan's-down or man-made fibres, used on a bed in place of blankets, etc. [Fr.]

dux *duks*, *n.* the top academic prize-winner in a school or class. [L., a leader.]

duyker. See **dulker.**

dwale *dwäl*, *n.* deadly nightshade (*bot.*). [O.N. *dvöl*, *dvali*, delay, sleep.]

dwarf *dwörf*, *n.* a diminutive person: a small manlike mythological being, esp. a metal-worker: an animal or plant much below the ordinary height: anything very small of its kind: a small star of high density and low luminosity (**white, red, brown dwarf**, etc. according to colour).—*adj.* **dwarfed**: very small.—*v.t.* to hinder from growing: to make to appear small.—*v.i.* to become dwarfed.—*adjs.* **dwarfed; dwarf'ish** like a dwarf: very small.—*adv.* **dwarf'ishly.**—*ns.* **dwarf'ishness; dwarf'ism** condition of being a dwarf.—**dwarfed tree** bonsai. [O.E. *dweorg*.]

dwell *dwel*, *v.i.* to abide: to reside: to remain: to rest attention (on):—*pr.p.* **dwell'ing**; *pa.t.* and *pa.p.* **dwelt** or **dwelled.**—*n.* a pause, hesitation in the working of a machine (*eng.*): a part of a cam shaped so as to allow a pause in operation at the point of maximum lift (*eng.*);—*ns.* **dwell'er; dwell'ing** the place where one dwells: a house: habitation: continuance.—**dwell'ing-house** a house used as a dwelling, in distinction from a place of business or other building; **dwell'ing-place.** [O.E. *dwellan*, to go astray, delay, tarry.]

dwindle *dwind'l*, *v.i.* to grow less: to waste away: to grow feeble: to become degenerate. [O.E. *dwīnan*, to fade.]

dyad *dī'ad*, *n.* a pair of units treated as one: a bivalent atom, radical, or element (*chem.*).—*adj.* **dyad'ic.** [Gr. *dyas, -ados*—*dyo*, two.]

dybbuk *dib'ək*, (Jewish folklore) *n.* evil spirit, or soul of dead person, that enters the body of a living person and controls his actions. [Heb. *dibbūq*.]

dye *dī*, *v.t.* to stain: to give a new colour to:—*pr.p.* **dye'ing**; *pa.t.* and *pa.p.* **dyed.**—*n.* colour: tinge: stain: a colouring liquid.—*adjs.* **dy(e)'able; dyed.**—*ns.* **dye'ing; dy'er** one whose trade is to dye cloth, etc.—**dye-line** (*dī'līn*) see **diazo; dye'stuff** a material used in dyeing; **dye'-wood** any wood from which material is obtained for dyeing; **dye'-work(s)** an establishment for dyeing.—**dye in the wool** to dye (the wool) before spinning, to give a more permanent result (*adj.* **dyed-in-the-wool** (*fig.*) (too) fixed in one's opinions or attitudes). [O.E. *dēagian*, to dye, from *dēag, dēah*, colour.]

dying *dī'ing*, *pr.p.* of **die**[1].—*adj.* destined for death: mortal: declining: occurring immediately before death, as **dying words**: pertaining to death: last, final.—**dying declaration** (*law*) declaration made by a dying person who does not survive through the trial of the accused. [See **die**[1].]

dyke, dykey. See **dike**[1,2].

dynamic *dīn-am'ik*, or *din-*, *adj.* relating to force: relating to dynamics: relating to the effects of forces in nature: relating to activity or things in movement: relating to dynamism: causal: forceful, very energetic.—*n.* a moving force: any driving force instrumental in growth or change (esp *social*) —*adj.* **dynam'ical.**—*n.* **dynam'ically.**—*n.* **dynam'icist** a person who studies dynamics.—*n.sing* **dynam'ics** the science of matter and motion, mechanics, sometimes restricted to kinetics: (often *n.pl.*) (signs indicating) varying levels of loudness (*mus.*); **dyn'amism** a theory which explains the phenomena of the universe by some immanent energy: operation of force: dynamic quality: quality of restless energy; **dyn'amist.**—*adj.* **dynamis'tic.** [Gr. *dýnamikos*—*dýnamis*, power—*dýnasthai*, to be able.]

dynamite *dīn'ə-mīt*, *n.* explosive consisting of absorbent matter, as porous silica, saturated with nitroglycerine: something highly dangerous to deal with.—*v.t.* to blow up with dynamite.—*n.* **dyn'amiter.** [Gr. *dýnamus*, power.]

dynamo *dīn'ə-mō*, *n.* contraction for **dynamo-electric machine**, a machine for generating electric currents by means of the relative movement of conductors and magnets:—*pl.* **dyn'amos.**—*adjs.* **dyn'amo-elec'tric, -al.**—*n.* **dynamom'eter** an instrument for measuring force, or power.—*adjs.* **dynamomet'ric, -al.**—*ns.* **dynamom'etry; dyn'amotor** an electrical machine with two armature windings, one acting as a motor and the other as a generator, and a single magnetic field, for converting direct current into alternating current; **dyn'atron** (*electronics*) a four-electrode thermionic valve used to generate continuous oscillation. [Gr. *dýnamis*, power.]

dynast *din'ast*, *-əst*, also *dīn'*, *n.* a ruler.—*adjs.* **dynas'tic, -al** relating to a dynasty.—*adv.* **dynast'ically.**—*n.* **dyn'asty** (*-əs-ti*) a succession of kings of the same family, or of members of any powerful family or connected group. [Fr. *dynastie*, or L.L. *dynastīa*—Gr. *dýnasteia*, power, dominion—*dýnasthai*, to be able.]

dyne *dīn*, *n.* the C.G.S. unit of force—the force which, acting on a mass of one gramme, produces an acceleration of one centimetre per second per second, equal to 10^{-5} of a newton. [Gr. *dýnamis*, force.]

dys- *dis-*, *pfx.* ill, bad, abnormal. [Gr.]

dysentery *dis'ən-tər-i*, *-tri*, *n.* a term formerly applied to any condition in which inflammation of the colon was associated with the frequent passage of bloody stools: now confined to **amoebic dysentery** and to **bacillary dysentery.**—*adj.* **dysenteric** (*-ter'ik*). [Gr. *dysenteria*—*dys-*, amiss, *enteron*, intestine.]

dysfunction *dis-fung(k)'shən*, *n.* impairment or abnormality of the functioning of an organ.—*adj.* **dysfunc'tional.** [Pfx. dys-.]

dysgenic *dis-jen'ik*, *adj.* unfavourable to race-improvement. [Pfx. dys-, and the root of *gennaein*, to beget.]

dysgraphia *dis-graf'i-ə*, *n.* inability to write, arising from brain damage or other cause.—*adj.* **dysgraph'ic.** [Pfx. dys-, and Gr. *graphein*, to write.]

dyslexia *dis-leks'i-ə*, *n.* word-blindness, great difficulty in learning to read or spell, of which the cause (not lack of intelligence) has not been established.—*adjs* and *ns.* **dyslec'tic, dyslex'ic.** [Pfx. dys-, and Gr. *lexis*, word]

dyslogistic *dis-lə-jis'tik*, *adj.* conveying censure, opprobrious.—*adv.* **dyslogis'tically.** [Pfx. dys-, and Gr. *logos*, discourse.]

dysmenorrhoea, -rhea *dis-men-ō-rē'ə, n.* difficult or painful menstruation.—*adjs* **dysmenorrh(o)e'al, dysmenorrh(o)e'ic.** [Pfx. dys-, and Gr *mēn,* month, *rhoiā,* flow.]

dyspepsia *dis-pep'si-ə, n.* indigestion.—*n.* **dyspep'tic** a person afflicted with dyspepsia.—*adjs* **dyspep'tic** afflicted with, pertaining to, or arising from, indigestion: bad-tempered.—*adv* **dyspep'tically.** [Gr *dyspepsiā*—*dys-,* ill, *pepsis,* digestion—*peptein,* to digest.]

dysphagia *dis-fā'ji-ə, n.* difficulty in swallowing —*adj* **dysphagic** (*-faj'ik*). [Pfx **dys-,** and Gr. *phagein* (aorist), to eat.]

dysphasia *dis-fāz'i-ə, -fā'zhə, n.* difficulty in expressing or understanding thought in spoken or written words, caused by brain damage. [Pfx. **dys-,** and Gr *phasis,* speech.]

dysphemism *dis'fə-mizm, n.* the replacing of a mild or inoffensive word or phrase by an offensive one: the offensive word or phrase substituted.—*adj.* **dysphemis'tic.** [From pfx. **dys-,** and **euphemism.**]

dysphoria *dis-fō'ri-ə, -fö', n.* impatience under affliction: morbid restlessness: uneasiness: want of feeling of wellbeing.—*adj.* **dysphōr'ic.** [Gr. *dysphōriā,* affliction, pain—*dys-,* ill. and the root of *pherein,* to bear]

dyspnoea *disp-nē'ə, n* difficulty of breathing —*adjs* **dyspnoe'al, dyspnoe'ic.**—Also **dyspnea,** etc [Gr *dyspnoia*—*dys-,* ill, *pnoē,* breathing]

dysprosium *dis-prōz'i-əm, n.* a metal of the rare earths, the element of atomic number 66 (symbol Dy). [Gr *dysprositos,* difficult to reach—*dys-,* ill, difficult, *pros,* to, *ienai,* to go]

dysthymia *dis-thī'mi-ə, n* morbid anxiety and despondency.—*n* **dysthym'iac** one who suffers from dysthymia.—*adj.* **dysthym'ic.** [Pfx. **dys-,** and Gr *thymiā,* despair.]

dystopia *dis-tō'pi-ə, n* a place thought of as the opposite to Utopia, i e. where everything is as bad as possible. —*adj.* **dysto'pian.** [From pfx **dys-,** and **utopia.**]

dystrophy *dis'trə-fi,* (*biol.*) *n* imperfect nutrition. any of several disorders in which there is wasting of muscle tissue, etc.—*adj.* **dystrophic** (*-tro'fik*).—**muscular dystrophy** see **muscle.** [Pfx **dys-,** and Gr. *trophē,* nourishment.]

dysuria *dis-ū'ri-ə, n.* a difficulty or pain in passing urine —*adj.* **dysū'ric.** [Gr *dysouriā*—*dys-,* ill, *ouron,* urine.]

dziggetai *dzig'ə-tī, n.* a Central Asian wild ass, rather like a mule [Mongolian, *tchikhtei.*]

For other sounds see detailed chart of pronunciation

E

E, e *ē, n.* the fifth letter in our own and cognate alphabets· in music the third note or sound of the natural diatonic scale, the major third above the tonic C: as a mediaeval Roman numeral E = 250.—**E'·boat** (enemy *boat*), a fast German motor torpedo-boat; **E. coli** see **Escherichia coli**.

each *ēch, adj.* and *pron.* every one separately considered.—**each other** a compound reciprocal pronoun, one another, by some restricted in application to two; **each way** in betting, for a win and for a place. [O.E. *ælc—ā,* ever, *gelic,* alike]

eager[1] *ē'gər, adj* excited by desire· ardent to do or obtain: keen, severe —*adv.* **ea'gerly.**—*n.* **ea'gerness.** —**eager beaver** an enthusiast: a zealous person: one over-eager for work [O.Fr. *aigre*—L. *ācer, ācris,* sharp.]

eager[2]. Same as **eagre.**

eagle *ē'gl, n* a name given to many large birds of prey: a military standard carrying the figure of an eagle: a lectern in the form of an eagle: the badge of certain orders: a gold coin of the United States, worth ten dollars: a hole at golf played in two strokes less than par —*n.* **ea'glet** a young or small eagle —*adjs.* **ea'gle-eyed, ea'gle-sight'ed** having a piercing eye· discerning; **ea'gle-owl** any of a number of large horned owls of the genus Bubo [O.Fr. *aigle*—L. *aquila.*]

eagre *ā'gər, ē'gər, n.* a bore or sudden rise of the tide in a river.

ealdorman. See **alderman** (first meaning and derivation)

ear[1] *ēr, n.* a spike, as of corn.—*v.i.* to put forth ears — *adj.* **eared** of corn, having ears. [O E *ēar,* Ger *Ahre.*]

ear[2] *ēr, n.* the organ of hearing, or the external part merely: the sense or power of hearing: the faculty of distinguishing sounds esp. of a different pitch: attention: anything projecting or shaped like an ear, as the auricle of a leaf, lug of a vessel, a projecting part for support, attachment, etc —*adj.* **eared.**—*ns* **ear'ful** (*coll.*) rough or scolding words, a reprimand; **ear'ing** (*naut.*) one of a number of small ropes to fasten the upper corner of a sail to the yard.—*adj* **ear'less.**— **ear'ache** pain in the ear —*v.t* **ear'bash** to talk incessantly (*Austr slang*) —**ear'drop** an ornamental pendant hanging from the ear; **ear'drum** the drum or middle cavity of the ear, tympanum; **ear'flap** one of two coverings for the ears, attached to a cap, to protect them from cold or injury; **ear'-hole** the aperture of the ear; **ear'mark** an owner's mark on an animal's ear· a distinctive mark —*v t.* to put an earmark on: to set aside for a particular purpose —**ear'muffs** a pair of ear coverings joined by a band of material across the head; **ear'phone** a headphone; **ear'piece** the part of a telephone, etc. that is placed next to the ear — *adj.* **ear'-pierc'ing** shrill, screaming —*n.* the piercing of the lobe of the ear (in order to insert earrings) — **ear'plug** a plug of soft material inserted into the outer ear to exclude unwanted sound, water, etc , **earring** (*ēr'ing*) a piece of jewellery hung from, or fixed on or in, the ear; **ear'-shot** the distance at which a sound can be heard —*adj* **ear'-splitt'ing** ear-piercing —**ear'· trum'pet** a tube to aid in hearing, **ear'wax** a waxy substance secreted by the glands of the ear, **ear'wig** (O E *ēarwicga, ēare,* ear, *wicga,* insect, beetle) a

long-bodied insect with an abdomen terminating in pincers, once supposed to creep into the ear: a flatterer.—**about one's ears** said of something falling about one (e.g house), or assailing one al. around (also *fig.*); **be all ears** to give every attention; **fall on deaf ears** of a remark, request, etc., to be ignored; **give ear** to attend (to); **go in (at) one ear and out (at) the other** to make no permanent impression; **have someone's ear** to be secure of someone's favourable attention; **have, keep, one's ear to the ground** to keep oneself well informed about what is going on around one; **lend an ear** to listen (to); **make a pig's ear of** see **pig; make someone's ears burn** to discuss someone in his absence; **out on one's ear** (*coll.*) turned out, dismissed; **pin back one's ears** to listen attentively; **set by the ears** to set at strife; **turn a deaf ear** to refuse to listen (to); **up to one's ears** in deeply involved in; **walls have ears** there may be listeners. [O.E *ēare;* cf. Ger. *Ohr,* L. *auris.*]

earl *ûrl, n.* a British nobleman ranking between a marquis and a viscount:—*fem.* **count'ess.**—*n.* **earl'dom** the dominion or dignity of an earl.—**Earl Marshal** an English officer of state, president of the Heralds' College. [O.E. *eorl,* a warrior, hero]

early *ûr'li, adv.* near the beginning (of a time, period, series): soon: in good time: before appointed time:— *compar* **ear'lier;** *superl.* **ear'liest.**—*adj.* belonging to or happening in the first part of time, period, or series: belonging to or happening in the first stages of development: beforehand: ready, advanced, astir, or on the spot in good time: happening in the remote past or near future —*n* **ear'liness.**—**early bird** the proverbial catcher of the (early) worm: an early riser: (with *caps.*) a name given to a type of communications satellite; **early closing** observance of a weekly half-holiday; **Early English** the form of Gothic architecture in which the pointed arch was first employed in Britain.—**early and late** at all times; **earlier on** previously, **early on** before much time has elapsed; **early warning system** a system of advance notice, esp of nuclear attack, (**it's**) **early days** (*coll.*) (it's) too soon to know, have a result, etc.; **keep early hours** to rise and go to bed early. [O.E. *ǣrlice* (adv.)—*ǣr,* before.]

earn *ûrn, v t.* to gain by labour: to acquire· to deserve. —*n* **earn'er.**—*n.pl* **earn'ings** what one has earned: money saved. [O.E *earnian,* to earn.]

earnest[1] *ûr'nist, adj.* intent: sincere. serious.—*n.* seriousness: reality —*adv* **ear'nestly.**—*n* **ear'nestness.** [O E *eornost,* seriousness]

earnest[2] *ûr'nist, n.* payment given in token of a bargain made: a pledge first-fruits.

earth *ûrth, n.* the third planet in order from the sun (often with *cap.*): the matter on the surface of the globe: soil, a mixture of disintegrated rock and organic material in which plants are rooted: dry land, as opposed to sea: the world the inhabitants of the world· dirt: a burrow· an electrical connection with the earth an old name for certain oxides of metals (see **rare earth** —*v.t.* to hide or cause to hide in the earth, or in a hole· to connect to earth electrically to clog, cover, smear, or partially cover with earth (often with *up*) —*v t* to burrow· to hide —*adj.* **earth'en** made of earth or clay.—*ns* **earth'iness;**

earth'liness; earth'ling a dweller on the earth: a worldly-minded person.—*adj* **earth'ly** belonging to the earth: vile: worldly: conceivably possible on earth.—*n* (*coll.*) chance (for *earthly chance*)—*adv.* **earth'ward** —*adj.* **earth'y** consisting of, relating to, or resembling earth: inhabiting the earth: gross: unrefined —*adjs.* **earth'born** born from or on the earth, **earth'bound** bound to earth.—**earth'-closet** a closet in which earth is used for the deodorisation of faecal matters; **earth'enware** crockery· coarse pottery; **earth'-house** an underground stone-lined gallery associated with the Iron Age, which may have functioned as a storehouse or possibly dwelling; **earth's hunger** passion for acquiring land; **earth-light** see **earth-shine; earth mother** the earth personified as a goddess· a woman, typically fertile and of generous proportions, who seems to symbolise motherhood; **earth'-move'ment** elevation, subsidence, or folding of the earth's crust; **earth'-nut** the edible root-tuber of *Conopodium flexuosum*, a woodland umbelliferous plant: the peanut; **earth'quake** a quaking or shaking of the earth: a heaving of the ground; **earth science** any of the sciences dealing with the earth, e.g. geography, geology; **earth'-shine, earth'-light** the faint light visible on the part of the moon not illuminated by the sun; **earth'-tremor** a slight earthquake; **earth'work** a fortification of earth: an embankment· work of excavation and embanking; **earth'worm** the common worm.—**cost the earth** (*coll*) to be very expensive; **down, back to earth** back to reality; **go to earth** to seek a hole or hiding-place (also *fig*); **on earth** used for emphasis in phrases such as *how on earth, why on earth*, etc ; the **Earthshaker** (*myth*) Poseidon, the god responsible for causing earthquakes [O.E *eorthe*; cf. Du *aarde*, Ger. *Erde.*]

ease *ēz, n.* freedom from pain or disturbance: rest from work. quiet: freedom from difficulty· naturalness: unconstrained manner.—*v t* to free from pain, trouble, or anxiety: to relieve: to calm: to move gently.—*v.i* to become less great or severe (often *ease off, up*): to move very gradually· to become less in demand.—*adj.* **ease'ful** ease-giving: quiet, fit for rest —*n.* **ease'ment** gratification (*obs.*): legally, the right to use something (esp. land) not one's own or to prevent its owner from making an inconvenient use of it —*adv* **eas'ily.**—*n.* **eas'iness.**—*adj.* **eas'y** at ease: free from pain· tranquil: unconstrained: giving ease: not difficult: convenient· yielding· not straitened (in circumstances): not tight. not strict: in plentiful supply: (*of market*) not showing unusually great activity —*adv* —*interj.* command to lower, to go gently, to stop rowing, etc —*adj.* **eas'y-care'** esp of materials, easy to look after, clean, etc.—**eas'y-chair** an arm-chair for ease or rest —*adj.* **eas'y-go'ing** (*coll.*) indolent placid —**easy money** money made without much exertion or difficulty; **easy street** (*coll.*) a situation of comfort or affluence; **easy terms** hire purchase; **easy touch** see **touch.—be easy** to be quite willing to fall in with one arrangement or another; **chapel of ease** see **chapel; ease off** to slacken gradually: to make or become less intense; **easy does it!** take your time, do (it) slowly, carefully; **easy on the eye** (*coll.*) good to look at, **go easy on** to be lenient with: to use sparingly; **ill at ease** uncomfortable; **stand at ease** used of soldiers, when freed from attention; **stand easy** used of a still easier position; **take it easy** to avoid exertion: to be in no hurry; **take one's ease** to make oneself comfortable. [O Fr *aise*; cog with It *agio*, Prov. *ais*, Port. *azo*]

easel *ēz'l, n* the frame for supporting a picture during painting. [Du *ezel*, or Ger *Esel*, an ass]

east *ēst, n.* that part of the heavens where the sun rises

at the equinox: one of the four cardinal points of the compass: the east part of a region: the east wind.—*adj* and *adv* toward the rising of the sun: (blowing) from the east.—*adjs.* **east'ern** toward the east: connected with the east: dwelling in the east; **east'erly** situated in the east: coming from the eastward: looking toward the east —*adv* on the east: toward the east.—*n.* an east wind.—*n.* **east'erner** a native or inhabitant of the east —*adj.* **east'ernmost** situated furthest east.—*advs.* **east'ward, east'wards** toward the east.—*adj.* **east'ward.—east'-by-north' (south)** 11½ degrees north (south) from due east; **East End** the eastern part of London or other town, often an area inhabited by people of the poorer classes; **East's end'er; Eastern Church** the Greek Church; **East-Ind'laman** a vessel used in the East Indian trade; **east'-north-(south)-east'** 22½ degrees north (south) from the east.—**the East** the countries between the Balkans and China (see also **Near East, Middle East, Far East**). [O.E. *ēast*; Ger. *Ost*; akin to Gr. *ēŏs*, the dawn.]

Easter *ēst'ər, n.* a Christian festival commemorating the resurrection of Christ, held on the Sunday after Good Friday.—**Easter Day** Easter Sunday; **Easter dues, offerings** customary sums paid to the parson by his people at Easter; **Easter egg** a painted, decorated, stained or artificial (esp. made of chocolate) egg, given as a present at Easter; **East'ertide, East'ertime** either Easter week or the fifty days from Easter to Whitsuntide [O.E. *ēastre*; Bede derives the word from *Eostre* (*Eastre*), a goddess whose festival was held at the spring equinox.]

easy. See **ease.**

eat *ēt, v t.* to take into the body by the mouth as food: to consume: to corrode.—*v.i.* to take food:—*pr.p.* **eat'ing;** *pa t.* **ate** (*et* or *āt*); *pa.p.* **eaten** (*ētn*) or, *obs.,* **eat** (*et.*)—*n.* (in *pl.*, *coll.*) food —*adj.* **eat'able.**—*n.* anything used as food (chiefly in *pl.*; *coll.*).—*ns* **eat'er** one who, or that which, eats: variety suitable for eating uncooked; **eat'ery** (*slang*) a restaurant. — **eat'ing-apple** etc , one suitable for eating uncooked; **eat'ing-house** a restaurant.—**eat away** to destroy gradually: to gnaw; **eat dirt, humble pie** see **dirt, humbles; eat one's hat** an undertaking promised on conditions one thinks very improbable; **eat one's head off** to cost more for food than one is worth; **eat one's heart out** to pine away, brooding over misfortune; **eat one's terms** to study for the bar, with allusion to the number of times in a term that a student must dine in the hall of an Inn of Court; **eat one's words** to take back what one has said; **eat up** to devour entirely: to consume, absorb; **what's eating you?** (*coll.*) what is irking you? [O.E. *etan*; cf. Ger. *essen*, O.N. *eta*, L. *edĕre*, Gr. *edein.*]

eau *ō, n.* the French word for water, used in English in various combinations.—**eau de Javelle** see **Javel water; eau de Nil** a pale-green colour, Nile green; **eau de vie** (*da vē*) brandy.

eaves *ēvz, n.pl.* the projecting edge of the roof: anything projecting.—*v.i.* **eaves'drop** to stand under the eaves or near the windows of a house to listen: to listen for secrets —Also *v.t.*—**eaves'dropper; eaves'dropping.** [O.E *efes*, the clipped edge of thatch, cf. Icel. *ups.*]

ebb *eb, n.* the going back or retiring of the tide: a decline.—*v.i.* to flow back· to sink: to decline.—*adj.* **ebb'less.—ebb'tide** the ebbing tide.—**at a low ebb** (*fig.*) in a low or weak state. [O.E. *ebba.*]

ebony *eb'ən-ı, (poet.* **ebon** *eb'ən), n.* a kind of wood (family **Ebena'ceae**) almost as heavy and hard as stone, usually black, admitting of a fine polish: a tree yielding it —*adj* made of ebony: black as ebony.— *v t.* and *v.i* **eb'onise, -ize** to make or become like ebony.—*n.* **eb'onite** black vulcanised rubber, vulcanite. [L. (*h*)*ebenus*—Gr *ebenos*, cf. Heb *hobnīm*, pl. of *hobnī, obnī*—*eben*, a stone.]

ebullient *ɪ-bul'yant, adj.* boiling: enthusiastic.—*ns* **ebull'ience, ebull'iency** a boiling over: cheerful enthusiasm.—*n.* **ebullition** (*eb-ə-lɪsh'ən*) the act of boiling: an outbreak. [L. *ēbulliēns, -entis*—*ēbullīre* —*ē*, out, and *bullīre*, to boil.]

eburnean *eb-ûr'nɪ-ən, adj.* of or like ivory [L. *eburneus*—*ebur*, ivory.]

ecad *ek'ad,* (*bot.*) *n.* a plant form which is assumed to have adapted to its environment [*ecology*, and suff. *-ad*.]

écarté *ā-kar'tā, n.* a game in which cards may be discarded for others. [Fr., discarded—L *ē*, out of, from, Fr. *carte*, a card.]

écarté *ā-kar'tā, n.* in ballet, a position in which the arm and leg are extended to the side. [Fr., spread, separated.]

ecce *ek'ā, ech'ā,* (L.) *interj* behold.—**ecce homo** (*hō'mō, hom'ō;* L , man) behold the man (John xix. 5): a portrayal of Christ crowned with thorns (*art*).

eccentric *ek-sen'trɪk, adj.* departing from the centre: not having the same centre as another, said of circles: out of the usual course: not conforming to common rules: odd.—*n.* a circle not having the same centre as another: a contrivance for taking an alternating rectilinear motion from a revolving shaft (*mech.*). an eccentric person.—*adv.* **eccen'trically.—*n.* **eccentricity** (*-san-tris'*) the condition of being eccentric: in a conic section, the constant ratio of the distance of a point in the curve from the focus to its distance from the directrix: singularity of conduct. oddness. [Gr. *ek*, out of, *kentron*, centre.]

Eccles cake *ek'lz kāk,* a cake like a Banbury cake. [*Eccles* in Lancashire.]

ecclesia *ɪ-klē'zɪ-ə, n.* a popular assembly, esp of Athens, where the people exercised full sovereignty. applied to the Jewish commonwealth, and to the Christian Church.—*ns.* **Ecclesias'tes** one of the books of the Old Testament, traditionally ascribed to Solomon; **ecclesias'tic** one consecrated to the church, a priest, a clergyman.—*adjs.* **ecclesias'tic, -al** relating to the church.—*adv.* **ecclesias'tically.—*n.* **Ecclesias'ticus** one of the books of the Apocrypha.—*adj.* **ecclesiólóg'ical.—*ns.* **ecclesiól'ogist; ecclesiól'ogy** the science of church forms and traditions, of building and decorating churches.—**ecclesiastical year** see **year.** [L.L.,—Gr. *ekklēsia*, an assembly called out of the world, the church—*ek*, out of, and *kaleein*, to call.]

eccrinology *ek-ri-nol'ə-ji, n.* the branch of physiology that relates to the secretions.—*adj.* **eccrine** (*ek'rīn*) of a gland, esp. the sweat glands, secreting externally [Gr *ek*, out of, *krīnein*, to separate, secrete.]

ecdysis *ek'dɪ-sis, n* the act of casting off an integument, sloughing.—*n.* **ecdysiast** (*-dɪz', facet.*) a stripteaser [Gr *ekdysis*—*ek*, out of, *dyein*, to put on.]

échappé *ā-sha-pā,* (Fr.) *n.* in ballet, a leap with change of foot position.

echelon *esh'ə-lon, n.* a stepwise arrangement of troops, ships, planes, etc.: a group of persons of one grade in an organisation [Fr *échelon*—*échelle*, ladder, stair.]

Echidna *ek-ɪd'nə, n.* a genus of Australian toothless, spiny, egg-laying, burrowing monotremes: (without *cap*) any member of the genus.—*n.* **echid'nine** snake-poison. [Gr. *echidna*, viper.]

echinus *e-kī'nəs, n.* a sea-urchin: the convex projecting moulding (of eccentric curve in Greek examples) supporting the abacus of the Doric capital (*archit.*).—*n* **echi'noderm** any one of a phylum of radially sym-

metrical marine animals, having the body-wall strengthened by calcareous plates, and moving usually by tube-feet—starfishes, sea-urchins, brittle-stars, sea-cucumbers, and sea-lilies —*adjs.* **echino-der'mal; echinoder'matous; echi'noid** like a sea-urchin —*n.* a sea-urchin. [Gr *echīnos*, a hedge-hog]

echo *ek'ō, n.* the sending back or reflection of sound or other waves: the repetition of sound by reflection. a reflected sound: repetition: imitation: an imitator: conventional play to indicate what cards one holds.—*pl* **echoes** (*ek'ōz*).—*v i.* to reflect sound to be sounded back. to resound· to play a card as echo —. *v.t* to send back (sound or other waves): to send back the sound of. to repeat: to imitate: to follow slavishly: —*pr.p* **ech'oing;** *pa t* and *pa.p* **ech'oed** (*-ōd*).—*n.* **ech'öer.**—*adj* **echō'ic** of the nature of an echo: ono-matopoeic (*philol.*).—*n.* **ech'öism** the formation of imitative words —*ns.* **ech'ogram** the record produced in echo-sounding, **echolalia** (*ek-ō-lā'li-ə;* Gr. *lalia*, talk) senseless repetition of words heard, occurring in disease of the brain or in insanity —**echo chamber** a room in which sound can be echoed, for recording or radio effects, or when measuring acoustics; **echo location** determining (as a bat does) the position of objects by means of supersonic vibrations echoed from them; **ech'o-sounding** a method of measuring depth of water, locating shoals of fish, etc., by noting time for return of echo from the bottom, or bottom and shoal, etc ; **echo virus** any of a group of viruses which can cause respiratory and intestinal diseases, and meningitis (enteric cytopathogenic *h*uman orphan virus).—**cheer to the echo** to applaud most heartily. [L.,—Gr. *ēchō*, a sound.]

echt *ehht,* (Ger.) *adj.* genuine, authentic.

éclair *ā-kler',* or *-klâr', n.* a cake, long in shape but short in duration, with cream filling and chocolate or other icing. [Fr. *éclair*, lightning.]

éclaircissement *ā-kler-sēs'mā, n* the act of clearing up anything explanation. [Fr. *éclaircir*—L. *ex*, out, *clārus*, clear.]

eclampsia *ɪ-klamp'sɪ-ə, n.* a condition resembling epilepsy: now confined to acute toxaemia with convulsive fits about the time of childbirth.—*adj.* **eclamp'tic.** [Gr. *eklampsis*—*eklampein*, to flash forth violently (as a fever)—*ek*, out of, *lampein*, to shine]

éclat *ā-kla, n.* a striking effect. showy splendour: distinction. applause. [Fr. *éclat*, from O.Fr. *esclater*, to break, to shine]

eclectic *ek-lek'tɪk, adj.* selecting or borrowing: choosing the best out of everything. broad, the opposite of exclusive —*n.* one who selects opinions from different systems, esp in philosophy.—*adv* **eclec'tically.—*n.* **eclec'ticism** (*-sɪzm*). [Gr. *eklektikos*—*ek*, from, *legein*, to choose.]

eclipse *i-klips', n.* the total or partial disappearance of a heavenly body by the interposition of another between it and the spectator, or by passing into its shadow· a throwing into the shade· loss of brilliancy. darkness.—*v.t* to hide wholly or in part. to darken to throw into the shade, to cut out, surpass.—*n.* **eclip'tic** the great circle in which the plane containing the centres of the earth and sun cuts the celestial sphere: hence, the apparent path of the sun's annual motion among the fixed stars —*adj* pertaining to an eclipse or the ecliptic. [O.Fr.—Gr. *ekleipsis,* failure—*ek,* out of, *leipein*, to leave]

eclogue *ek'log, n.* a short pastoral poem like Virgil's *Bucolics.* [L. *ecloga* -Gr. *eklogē*, a selection.]

eclosion *ɪ-klō'zhən, n* emergence, esp of insect from pupal case or larva from egg -*v t.* **eclose'.** [Fr *éclosion*—L. *(* *ex* *, claudere*, to shut.]

eco-, *ēk'*, *ek'ō-*, in composition, concerned with habitat and environment in relation to living organisms, as in **ecology**.—*ns.* **ec'ocide** the destruction of the aspects of the environment which enable it to support life; **ec'osphere** the parts of the universe, or esp. the earth, in which life is possible; **ec'osystem** a unit consisting of a community of organisms and their environment.

ecology *ē-kol'ə-ji*, *ek-ol'*, *ik-*, *n.* a study of plants, or of animals, or of peoples and institutions, in relation to environment.—*adjs.* **ecologic** (*-ko-loj'ik*), **-al**.—*adv.* **ecolog'ically**.—*n.* **ecol'ogist**.—Also **oecology**, etc. [Gr. *oikos*, house, *logos*, discourse.]

economy *i-*, *e-*, *ē-kon'ə-mi*, *n.* the administration of the material resources of an individual, community, or country: the state of these resources: a frugal and judicious expenditure of money: thrift: the efficient use of something, e.g. speech, effort, etc.: an organised system: regular operations, as of nature.—*adj.* pertaining to a cheaper class of air or sea travel: (of goods) of a larger size, so costing less than several small sizes (of packets, etc.).—*adj.* **economet'ric**.—*n.* **econometrician** (*-mə-trish'ən*).—*n. sing.* **economet'rics** statistical analysis of economic data and their interrelations—*n.* **economet'rist**.—*adjs.* **economic** (*ē-*, *e-kən-om'ik*) pertaining or having reference to economy or to economics: relating to industry or business: operated at, or capable of yielding, a profit: economical: **econom'ical** conducive to thrift: frugal: careful: economic.—*adv.* **econom'ically**.—*n. sing.* or *n.pl.* **econom'ics** (see also **home economics** under **home**): pecuniary position and management: financial or economic aspects.—*n.sing.* political economy.—*n.* **economisa'tion**, **-z-** the act of economising.—*v.i.* **econ'omise**, **-ize** to manage with economy: to spend money carefully: to save.—*v.t.* to use prudently: to spend with frugality.—*ns.* **econ'omiser**, **-z-** one who is economical: a device for saving heat, fuel, etc.; **econ'omism** a (sometimes too great) belief that economic causes and theories are of primary importance; **econ'omist** one who studies or is an expert on political economy: an economiser. [L. *oeconomia*—Gr. *oikonomiā*—*oikos*, a house, *nomos*, a law.]

écossaise *ā-ko-sez'*, *n.* originally a dance or dance-tune of Scottish origin in 3-4 or 2-4 time: later a lively country-dance or its music in 2-4 time. [Fr., fem. of *écossais*, Scottish.]

ecru *e-*, *ā-krōō'*, *-krü'*, *n.* unbleached linen: its colour. —*adj.* like unbleached linen. [Fr. *écru*—L. *ex*, intensive, *crūdus*, raw.]

ecstasy *ek'stə-si*, *n.* a state of temporary mental alienation and altered or diminished consciousness: excessive joy: enthusiasm, or any exalted feeling.—*v.t.* to fill with joy.—*adj.* **ecstat'ic** causing ecstasy: amounting to ecstasy: rapturous.—*n.* one given to ecstasy.—*adv.* **ecstat'ically**. [Gr. *ekstasis*—*ek*, from, and root of *histanai*, to make to stand.]

ecto- *ek-tō-*, in composition, outside, often opp. to **endo-**, **ento-**. See also **exo-**.—*n.* **ec'toblast** (Gr. *blastos*, a shoot, bud) the outer cell-layer of a gastrula, the epiblast.—*adj.* **ectoblas'tic**.—*n.* **ec'toderm** (Gr. *derma*, skin) the external germinal layer on epiblast of the embryo, or any part of the mature animal derived from it.—*adjs.* **ectoderm'al**; **ectoderm'ic**.—*n.* **ec'tomorph** (Gr. *morphē*, form) a person of light and delicate build.—*adj.* **ectomorph'ic**.—*ns.* **ec'tomorphy**; **ectopar'asite** an external parasite; **ec'toplasm** (Gr. *plasma*, mould) the outer layer of cytoplasm of a cell (*biol.*): an emanation of bodily appearance believed by some spiritualists to come from a medium.—*adjs.* **ectoplas'mic**; **ectoplas'tic**.—*n.* and *adj.* **ectozō'an**.—*adj* **ectozō'ic**.—*adj.* **ecto-**

zō'on (Gr. *zōion*, animal) an animal ectoparasite:— *pl.* **ectozō'a**. [Gr. *ektos*, outside.]

ectogenesis *ek-tō-jen'i-sis*, *n.* development outside the body: variation in response to outside conditions.— *adjs.* **ectogenetic** (*-jən-et'ik*) produced by or pertaining to ectogenesis; **ectogen'ic** of external origin: ectogenous; **ectogenous** (*ek-toj'ə-nəs*) capable of living independently, or outside the body of the host (as some parasites). [Gr. *ektos*, outside, *genesis*, generation.]

ectomorph, etc., **ectoparasite**. See **ecto-**.

ectophyte *ek'tō-fīt*, *n.* a vegetable ectoparasite.—*adj.* **ectophytic** (*-fīt'ik*). [Gr. *ektos*, outside, *phyton*, a plant.]

ectopia *ek-tō-pi-ə*, **ectopy** *ek'to-pi*, (*path.*) *ns.* morbid displacement of parts: a condition in which the foetus is outside the womb.—*adj.* **ectop'ic**. [Gr. *ek*, from, *topos*, place.]

ectoplasm ... to ... **ectozoon**. See **ecto-**.

ecumenic, **-al** *ēk-*, or *ek-ū-men'ik*, *-əl*, *adjs.* general, universal, belonging to the entire Christian Church: of or relating to the ecumenical movement.—*adv.* **ecumen'ically**.—*ns.* **ecumen'icalism**, **ecumen'icism** (*-is-izm*), **ecumen'ism** doctrines and practice of the Christian ecumenical movement —*n. sing.* **ecumen'ics** the study of ecumenical awareness and the ecumenical movement in the Christian church.— Also **oecumenic**, etc.—**ecumenical movement** a movement within the Christian church towards unity on all fundamental issues of belief, worship, etc. [L. *oecumenicus*—Gr. *oikoumenikos*—*oikoumenē* (*gē*), inhabited (world).]

eczema *ek'si-mə*, *n.* a skin disease, in which part of the skin is red, with numerous small papules that turn into vesicles.—*adj.* **eczematous** (*-sem'*, or *-zem'ət-əs*). [Gr. *ekzeein*—*ek*, out of, *zeein*, to boil.]

edacious *i-*, *ē-*, *e-dā'shəs*, *adj.* given to eating: gluttonous.—*adv.* **edā'ciously**.—*ns.* **edā'ciousness**; **edacity** (*i-dās'i-ti*). [L. *edāx*, *edācis*—*edĕre*, to eat.]

Edam *ē'dam*, *n.* a type of mild Dutch cheese, shaped into globes with a red outer skin. [After *Edam* near Amsterdam.]

edaphic *i-daf'ik*, *adj.* pertaining to the soil.—*n.* **edaphology** (*ed-əf-ol'ə-ji*). [Gr. *edaphos*, ground.]

Edda *ed'ə*, *n.* the name of two Scandinavian books— the *Elder Edda*, a collection of mythological songs; and the *Younger* or *Prose Edda*, mythological stories, poetics, and prosody.—*adjs.* **Edda'ic**; **Edd'ic**. [O.N. apparently akin to *ōdr*, mad, *ōthr*, spirit, mind, poetry.]

eddy *ed'i*, *n.* a current running back, contrary to the main stream, thus causing a circular motion: a whirlpool: a whirlwind.—*v.i.* to move round and round:—*pr.p.* **edd'ying**; *pa.t.* and *pa.p.* **edd'ied**.— **eddy current** an electric current caused by varying electromotive forces which are due to varying magnetic fields, and causing heating in motors, transformers, etc.—Also **Foucault current** (*fōō-kō'*). [Cf. O.N. *itha*; prob. conn. with O.E. pfx. *ed-*, back.]

edelweiss *ā'dəl-vīs*, *n.* a small white composite (*Leontopodium alpinum*), with woolly heads, found in damp places on the Alps [Ger. *edel*, noble, *weiss*, white.]

edema, **edematose**, **-ous**. See **oedema**.

Eden *ē'dn*, *n.* the garden of Adam and Eve: a paradise. —*adj.* **Edenic** (*-den'*). [Heb. *ēden*, delight, pleasure]

edentate *ē-den'tāt*, *adj.* without teeth: wanting front teeth.—*n.* a member of the **Edentā'ta**, a New World order of mammals having no front teeth or no teeth at all—sloths, ant-eaters, armadillos. [L. *ēdentātus*, toothless—*ē*, out of, *dēns*, *dentis*, a tooth.]

edge *ej*, *n.* the border of anything: a rim: the brink: the intersection of the faces of a solid figure: a ridge or crest· the cutting edge of an instrument: something that wounds or cuts: keenness: sharpness of mind or appetite: irritability· advantage (*coll.*).—*v.t.* to put an edge on. to place a border on· to border: to move gradually: to thrust edgewise: to strike with the edge —*v.t.* to move sideways: to move gradually.—*advs* **edge'ways, edge'wise** in the direction of the edge: sideways.—*ns.* **edg'iness** angularity, over-sharpness of outline: the state of being on edge; **edg'ing** any border or fringe round a garment: a border of box, etc., round a flower-bed.—*adj* **edg'y** with edges: sharp, hard in outline: irritable, on edge.—**edge tool, edged tool** a tool with a sharp edge.—**edge in a word, get a word in edgeways** to get a word in with difficulty; **edge out** to remove or get rid of gradually: to defeat by a small margin (*U.S.*); **go, be over the edge** (*coll.*) to go, have gone, beyond what can be endured: to have, have had, a nervous breakdown; **have the, an, edge on, against** to have the, an, advantage over; **on edge** in a state of expectant irritability: nervous, tense: all agog; **set one's teeth on edge** to cause a strange grating feeling in the teeth: to give a feeling of abhorrent discomfort. [O.E. *ecg;* cf. Ger. *Ecke,* L. *aciēs.*]

edh. See eth.

edible *ed'i-bl, adj.* fit to be eaten.—*n.* something for food.—*ns.* **edibil'ity, ed'ibleness.** [L. *edibilis*—*edēre,* to eat.]

edict *ē'dikt, n.* something proclaimed by authority: an order issued by a king or lawgiver.—*adj.* **edict'al.**—*adv.* **edict'ally.** [L *ēdictum*—*ē,* out of, *dīcĕre, dictum,* to say.]

edifice *ed'i-fis, n.* a building: a large building or house. [Fr. *édifice*—L *aedificium*—*aedificāre.*]

edify *ed'if-ī, v.t.* to strengthen spiritually: to improve the mind of:—*pr.p.* **ed'ifying;** *pa.t.* and *pa.p.* **ed'ified.** —*n.* **edificā'tion** instruction: progress in knowledge or in goodness.—*adj.* **edif'icatory** (or *ed'*) tending to edification.—*n.* **ed'ifier** one who edifies.—*adj.* **ed'ifying** instructive: improving.—*adv.* **ed'ifyingly.** [L. *aedificāre*—*aedēs,* a temple, house, *facĕre,* to make.]

edile. Same as aedile.

edit *ed'it, v.t.* to prepare for publication. broadcasting, etc.: to superintend the publication of: to compile: to garble, cook up: to revise: to censor, bowdlerise: to make up the final version of a motion picture by selection, rearrangement, etc., of material photographed previously.—*ns.* **edi'tion** one of the different forms in which a book is published. the form given to a text by its editor: the number of copies of a book printed at a time, or at different times without alteration: number of identical articles, as e.g. copies of a work of art, issued at one time: reproduction; **ed'itor** one who edits books, etc.: one who conducts a newspaper, periodical, etc., or a section of it:—*fem.* **ed'itress.**—*adj.* **edito'rial** (or *-tó'*) of or belonging to an editor.—*n.* an article in a newspaper written by an editor or leader writer.—*v.i.* **edito'rialise, -ize** to introduce opinions or bias into reporting.—*n.* **editorialisā'tion, -z-.**—*adv.* **edito'rially.**—*n.* **ed'itorship.**—**edit out** to remove (a piece of film, tape, etc) during editing [L. *ēdĕre, ēditum*—*ē,* from, *dāre,* to give.]

editio princeps *i-dish'i-ō prin'seps, ā-dit'i-ō prin'keps,* (L) original edition (esp. of a work till then known only in MS).

educate *ed'ū-kāt, v.t.* to bring up and instruct· to teach: to train.—*adj.* **ed'ucable.**—*ns.* **educabil'ity; educātabil'ity; educā'tion** bringing up or training, as of a child: instruction: strengthening of the powers of body or mind. culture.—*adj* **educā'tional.**—*adv* **educā'tionally.**—*ns* **educā'tion(al)ist** one skilled in

methods of educating or teaching: one who promotes education.—*adj.* **ed'ucātive** of or pertaining to education. tending to teach.—*n.* **ed'ucātor.**—*adj.* **educatory** (*ed'* or *-kā'ta-ri*). [L *ēducāre, -ātum,* to rear—*ēdūcĕre*—*ē,* from, *dūcĕre,* to lead.]

educe *i-* or *ē-dūs', v.t.* to draw out: to extract: to cause to appear, elicit.—*n.* **educe'ment.**—*adj.* **educ'ible.**—*n* **eduction** (*ē-duk'shən*) [L *ēdūcĕre, ēductum*—*ē,* from, and *dūcĕre,* to lead.]

edulcorate *i-dul'ka-rāt, v.t.* to free from soluble particles by washing —*adj.* **edul'corant.**—*n.* **edulcorā'tion.**—*adj.* **edul'corātive.**—*n.* **edul'corātor.** [L *ē-,* intens., *dulcōrāre,* to sweeten—*dulcis,* sweet.]

Edwardian *ed-wörd'i-ən, adj.* belonging to or characteristic of the reign of (any) King *Edward,* esp. Edward VII.—Also *n.*

eel *ēl, n.* any fish of the *Anguillidae, Muraenidae,* or other family of *Apodes,* fishes with long smooth cylindrical or ribbon-shaped bodies, scaleless or nearly, without pelvic fins: extended to various other fishes of similar form, as the **sand eel** (or launce), **electric eel.**—**eel'grass, eel'wrack** grasswrack a grasslike flowering plant of the pondweed family, growing in sea-water; **eel'pout** (*-powt;* O.E. *ǣlepūte*) the burbot: the viviparous blenny; **eel'worm** a nematode. [O E. *ǣl;* Ger. *Aal,* Du. *aal.*]

e'en *ēn.* A contraction of **even.**

e'er *ār.* A contraction of **ever.**

eerie, eery *ē'ri, adj.* exciting fear: weird: affected with fear, timorous (*dial.*).—*adv.* **ee'rily.**—*n.* **ee'riness.** [Scot.; M.E. *arh, eri*—O E. *ǣrg* (*earg*), timid.]

eff *ef, euph.* for **fuck,** esp. in *adj.* **eff'ing** and *v.i.* **eff off.**

efface *i-, e-fās', v.t.* to destroy the surface of: to rub out· to obliterate, wear away.—*adj.* **efface'able.**—*n.* **efface'ment.**—**efface oneself** to avoid notice. [Fr. *effacer*—L *ex,* out, *faciēs,* face.]

effect *i-fekt', n.* the result of an action: the impression produced: purport: reality: (in *pl.*) goods, property: (in *pl.*) sound, and also lighting, devices contributing to the illusion of the place and circumstance in which the action is carried on (*theatre, cinema,* etc.).—*v.t* to produce: to accomplish, bring about.—*n.* **effec'ter.**—*adjs* **effec'tible; effec'tive** having power to effect· causing something: successful in producing a result or effect: powerful: serviceable: actual: in force.—*n.* a soldier, or a body of soldiers, ready for service —*adv* **effec'tively.**—*n.* **effec'tiveness.**—*n.* **effec'tor** (*biol.*) an organ or substance that effects a response to stimulus —*adj.* **effec'tual** successful in producing the desired effect.—*ns.* **effectual'ity; effec'tualness.**—*adv.* **effec'tually.**—*v t.* **effec'tuate** to accomplish.—*n.* **effectuā'tion.**—**for effect** so as to make a telling impression; **give effect to** to carry out, perform; **in effect** in truth, really· substantially; **take effect** to begin to operate: to come into force [O.Fr.,—L. *effectus*—*ex,* out, *facĕre,* to make.]

effeminate *e-, i-fem'in-at, adj.* womanish: unmanly: weak: soft.—*n.* an effeminate person —*v.t.* (*-āt, arch*) to make womanish: to weaken, unman.—Also *v.i.* (*-āt; arch.*) —*n.* **effem'inacy** (*-ə-si*).—*adv.* **effem'inately.**—*n.* **effem'inateness.** [L. *effēmināre,* to make womanish—*ex,* out, and *fēmina,* a woman.]

effendi *e-fen'di, n* a title for civil officials and educated persons generally (abolished in Turkey in 1934) [Turk., from Gr *authentēs,* an absolute master.]

efferent *ef'ə-rənt, adj.* conveying outward or away, as (*zool.*) **efferent nerve,** a nerve carrying impulses away from the central nervous system.—*n.* **eff'erence.** [L. *ē,* from, *ferēns, -entis,* pr p of *ferre,* to carry.]

effervesce *ef-ər-ves', v.i* to boil up to bubble and hiss to froth up.—*ns* **effervesc'ence; effervesc'ency.**—

*adj*s **effervesc'ent** boiling or bubbling from the disengagement of gas [L *effervescĕre—ex*, intens , and *fervēre*, to boil.]

effete *e-fēt'*, *adj*. exhausted. degenerate, decadent.—*adv*. **effete'ly.**—*n*. **effete'ness.** [L *effētus*, weakened by having brought forth young—*ex*, out, *fētus*, a bringing forth young.]

efficacious *ef-ı-kā'shəs*, *adj* able to produce the result intended.—*adv* **effica'ciously.**—*ns* **effica'ciousness; efficacity** (*-kas'ı-tı*), **eff'icacy** (*-kə-sı*) the power of producing an effect: effectiveness [L *efficāx*, *-ācis* *—efficĕre*; see **efficient.**]

efficient *ı-fish'ənt*, *adj* capable of doing what may be required· effective —*n* **effi'ciency** power to produce the result intended, adequate fitness: ratio of a machine's output of energy to input.—*adv*. **effi'ciently.** [Fr ,—L *efficiēns*, *-entis*, pr p of *efficĕre—ex*, out, *facĕre*, to make.]

effigy *ef'ı-jı*, *n*. a likeness or figure of a person: the head or impression on a coin —**burn, hang, in effigy** to burn or hang a figure of a person, as an expression of dislike. [L *effigiēs—effingĕre—ex*, intens., *fingĕre*, to form]

effing. See **eff.**

effleurage *ef-lə-razh'*, *n*. a stroking movement in massage —Also *v* t. and *v.t.* [Fr , glancing, grazing]

effloresce *ef-lo-res'*, *v.ı.* to blossom forth: to become covered with a powdery crust (*chem.*)· to form such a crust.—*n* **efflores'ence** production of flowers: the time of flowering: a redness of the skin: a powdery surface crust: the formation of such a crust: giving up of water of crystallisation to the atmosphere.—*adj*. **effloresc'ent.** [L. *efflōrēscĕre—ex*, out, *flōrēscĕre*, to blossom—*flōs*, *flōris*, a flower.]

effluent *ef'loō-ənt*, *adj*. flowing out —*n* a stream that flows out of another stream or lake: liquid industrial waste: outflow from sewage during purification.—*n*. **eff'luence.** [L. *effluēns*, *-entis*, pr p. of *effluēre—ex*, out, *fluĕre*, to flow.]

effluvium *e-floō'vı-əm*, *n*. minute particles that flow out from bodies: disagreeable vapours rising from decaying matter:—*pl* **efflu'via.**—*adj*. **efflu'vial.** [L L.,—L *effluēre*.]

efflux *ef'luks*, *n*. the act of flowing out. that which flows out.—Also **effluxion** (*e-fluk'shən*). [L *effluēre—ex*, out, *fluĕre*, *fluxum*, to flow]

efforce *e-förs'*, *-fors'*, (*obs*) *v* t. to compel to force· to force open. to do violence to: to put forward with force. [Fr., *efforcer—*L.L. *exfortiāre—ex*, out, *fortis*, strong.]

effort *ef'ərt*, *n*. a putting forth of strength. attempt: struggle: a piece of work produced by way of attempt. anything done or produced (*coll.*).—*adj* **eff'ortless** making no effort, passive: easy, showing no sign of effort. [Fr.,—L. *ex*, out, *fortis*, strong.]

effrontery *ı-*, *e-frunt'ər-ı*, *n*. shamelessness: impudence: insolence. [Fr. *effronterie—*L. *ex*, out, without, *frōns*, *frontis*; forehead.]

effulge *ı-*, *e-fulj'*, *v* ı. to shine forth.—*n* **efful'gence** great lustre or brightness: a flood of light.—*adj*. **efful'gent.**—*adv* **efful'gently.** [L *effulgĕre,—ex*, out, *fulgēre*, to shine.]

effuse *e-fūz'*, *v.t* to pour forth (as words).—*adj* (*e-fūs'*) loosely spreading (*bot*): (of shells) with the lips separated by a groove.—*n*. **effusion** (*e-fū'zhən*) pouring or streaming out: shedding (as of blood): an outpouring, esp. in poetic form.—*adj*. **effusive** (*e-fū'zıv*) poured out abundantly: gushing: poured out at the surface in a state of fusion, volcanic (*geol.*): expressing emotion in a copious and demonstrative manner.—*adv*. **effus'ively.**—*n*. **effus'iveness.** [L *effundĕre—ex*, out, *fundĕre*, to pour.]

eft *eft*, *n*. a newt [O E. *efeta*, see **newt.**]

egad *ı-gad'*, *interj*. a minced oath. [Perh orig. **ah! God!**]

egalitarian *ı-gal-ı-tā'rı-ən*, *adj* and *n*. equalitarian —*n*. **egalitā'rianism.** [O Fr *egal—*L *aequālis—aequus*, equal]

Egeria *ē-jē'rı-ə*, *e-*, *n*. a female adviser. [L *Ēgērıa*, or *Aegērıa*, the nymph who instructed Numa Pompilius]

egg¹ *egg*, *n* an oval body laid by birds and certain other animals from which the young is hatched. an ovum or female gamete (also **egg'-cell**): a zygote —*ns* **egg'er** any moth of the family *Lasiocampidae*, whose cocoons are egg-shaped (also **egg'ar**) —*adj*. **egg'y** savouring of, or marked with, eggs —**egg'-and-anch'or, egg'-and-dart', egg'-and-tongue'** ornaments on mouldings in the form of eggs alternating with anchors, darts or tongues, **egg'-beater** an egg-whisk. a helicopter (*slang*), **egg'-cosy** a cover for keeping a boiled egg hot; **egg'cup** a cup for holding a boiled egg at table; **egg custard** see **custard; egg'-flip** a drink made of ale, wine, spirits, or milk, with eggs, sugar, spice, etc , **egg'head** (*coll*) an intellectual.—Also *adj* —**egg'nog** a drink of eggs and hot beer, spirits, etc ; **egg'-plant** the aubergine or brinjal, an East Indian annual plant with edible egg-shaped fruit, **egg'-plum** a yellowish egg-shaped plum; **egg'shell** the calcareous covering of a bird's egg: a very thin kind of porcelain.—*adj*. thin and delicate: (of paint, etc.) having a slight gloss —**egg'-slice** a utensil for lifting fried eggs out of a pan; **egg'-spoon** a small spoon used in eating boiled eggs from the shell; **egg'-tim'er** a small sand-glass for timing the boiling of eggs, **egg'-tooth** a hard point on the beak by which an unhatched bird or reptile breaks the eggshell, **egg'-whisk** an instrument for beating raw eggs —**a bad egg** (*coll*.) a worthless person; **egg-and-spoon race** a race in which each competitor carries an egg in a spoon; **good egg!** (*coll*.) an exclamation of approval; **have, put, all one's eggs into one basket** to risk all on one enterprise; **have, get, egg on one's face** (*slang*) to be left looking foolish; **teach your grandmother to suck eggs** spoken contemptuously to one who would teach those older and wiser than himself [O.N *egg*, cf. O E *æg*, Ger. *Ei*, perh L. *ōvum*, Gr *ōon*.]

egg² *eg*, *v* t. (now with *on*) to incite, urge on [O.N *eggja—egg*, an edge.]

eggar, egger, eggy. See **egg¹.**

eglantine *eg'lən-tın*, *n*. the sweet-brier [Fr ,—O Fr *aiglent*, as if from a L. *aculentus*, prickly.]

ego *e'gō*, *ē'gō*, *n*. the 'I' or self—that which is conscious and thinks· an image of oneself: self-confidence: egotism.—*adj*. **egocen'tric** self-centred· regarding or regarded from the point of view of the ego.—*ns* **egocentri'city; e'goism** the doctrine that we have proof of nothing but our own existence (*philos.*): the theory of self-interest as the principle of morality (*ethics*): selfishness: egotism; **e'goist** one who holds the doctrine of egoism one who thinks and speaks too much of himself or of things as they affect himself: an egotist —*adj*. **egoist'ic, -al.**—*adv*. **egʒis'tically.**—*ns*. **egomā'nia** morbid egotism, **egomā'niac.**—*adj*. **egomān'iacal.**—*n* **e'gotheism** (or *-thē'*) the deification of self. identification of oneself with God.—*v* ı. **e'gotise, -ize** to talk much of oneself.—*ns*. **e'gotism** a frequent use of the pronoun I: thinking or speaking too much of oneself: self-exaltation; **e'gotist.**—*adjs*. **egotis'tic, -al.**—*adv*. **egotist'ically.**—**e'go-trip** (*slang*) an action or experience which inflates one's good opinion of oneself [L *ego*, *egō*, and Gr. *egō*, I]

egregious *ı-grē'jəs*, *adj* outrageous: notorious.—*adv* **egrē'giously.**—*n* **egrē'giousness.** [L *ēgregius*, chosen out of the flock—*ē*, out of, *grex*, *gregis*, a flock.]

egress *ē'gres*, *n* the act of going out· departure: the way out: the power or right to depart.—*n.* **egression** (*i-, ē-gresh'ən*) the act of going out: departure. [L. *ēgredī, ēgressus—ē,* out of, *gradī, to go.*]

egret *ē'gret, n.* a white heron of several species: an aigrette. [See **aigrette.**]

Egypt, *ē'jipt, n.* a country of N E Africa —*adj.* **Egyptian** (*ē-jip'shən*) belonging to Egypt —*n.* a native or citizen of Egypt.—*adj.* **Egyptolog'ical.**—*ns.* **Egyptol'ogist; Egyptol'ogy** the science of Egyptian antiquities.

eh *ā, interj.* expressing inquiry, failure to hear, or slight surprise.

eider *ī'dər, n.* the **ei'der-duck'**, a northern sea-duck, sought after for its fine down.—**ei'derdown'** the soft down of the eider-duck, used for stuffing quilts. a quilt. [Prob through Sw. from O.N. *æthar,* gen. of *æthr,* an eider-duck.]

eidetic *ī-det'ik, adj.* vividly clear: reproducing, or able to reproduce, a vividly clear visual image of what has been previously seen.—*n.* a person with this ability —*adv.* **eidet'ically.** [Gr. *eidētikos,* belonging to an image—*eidos,* form.]

eidolon *ī-dō'lon, n.* an image: a phantom or apparition: a confusing reflection or reflected image —*pl.* **eidō'la.** [Gr ; see **idol.**]

eigen-i-gən-, in composition, proper, own.—*ns.* **ei'genfre'quency** one of the frequencies with which a particular system may vibrate; **ei'gentone'** a tone characteristic of a particular vibrating system; **ei'genval'ue** any of the possible values for a parameter of an equation for which the solutions will be compatible with the boundary conditions. [Ger]

eight *āt, n.* the cardinal number one above seven: a symbol (8, viii, etc.) representing that number· a set of eight things or persons (syllables, leaves, oarsmen, etc.): an eight-oar boat: a card with eight pips: a shoe or other article of a size denoted by 8: the eighth hour after midday or midnight.—*adj.* of the number eight· eight years old.—*adj.* **eighth** (*ātth*) last of eight: next after the seventh: equal to one of eight equal parts.— *n.* an eighth part: a person or thing in eighth position: an octave (*mus.*).—*adv.* **eighthly** (*ātth'li*).—*n* **eight'some** a group of eight: eight together a Scottish reel for eight dancers (also *adj.*) —**figure of eight** a figure shaped like an 8 made in skating, etc.; **one over the eight** (*coll*) one drink too many; **piece of eight** an old Spanish coin worth eight reals; **the eights** annual boat-races between the various Oxford colleges [O.E. (Anglian) *æhta* (W.S. *eahta*); Ger *acht,* L *octō,* Gr. *oktō.*]

eighteen *ā-tēn', ā' tēn, n.* and *adj.* eight and ten.—*adj* and *n.* **eighteen'mo** octodecimo·—*pl.* **eighteen'mos.** —*adj.* **eigh'teenth** (or *-tēnth'*) last of eighteen: next after the seventeenth: equal to one of eighteen equal parts —*n.* an eighteenth part: a person or thing in eighteenth position.—*adv.* **eighteenth'ly.**—*adj* **eigh'teen-hole** having eighteen golf-holes. [O.E. (Mercian) *æhtatēne* (W.S. *eahtatiene*).]

eighty *ā'ti, n.* and *adj.* eight times ten.—*n.pl.* **eight'ies** the numbers eighty to eighty-nine: the years so numbered in life or any century: a range of temperatures from eighty to just less than ninety degrees —*adj.* **eigh'tieth** last of eighty: next after the seventy-ninth: equal to one of eighty equal parts —*n.* an eightieth part: a person or thing in eightieth position. [O.E. *æhtatig* (W.S. *eahtatig,* or *hundeahtatig*)]

eikon. Same as **icon.**

einsteinium *īn-stīn'i-əm, n.* the element (symbol Es) of atomic number 99, artificially produced and named after Albert *Einstein* (1879–1955)

eirenicon, irenicon *ī-rē'ni-kon,* a proposition or scheme for peace: a peace-making message —*adj* **eirē'nic** same as **irenic.** [A partly Latinised spelling of Gr

eirēnikon, neut. of *eirēnikos,* peaceful, peaceable— *eirēnē,* peace.]

eisteddfod *īs-tedh'vod, U S. ās-, n.* orig. a competitive congress of Welsh bards and musicians, now any of several gatherings in Wales for competitions in music, poetry, drama, etc., esp. (with *cap.*) the Royal National Eisteddfod—*pl* **-fodau** (*-vo-dī*), **-fods.** [W., lit. session—*eistedd,* to sit.]

either *ī'dhər, ē'dhər, adj.* or *pron.* the one or the other- one of two: each of two.—*conj.* correlative to *or.*— *adv* (used with a neg.) also, likewise (not), as in *He isn't hungry and she isn't either:* (after a neg) more-over, besides. [O.E. *ægther,* contraction of *æghwæthər—ā,* aye, pfx *ge-,* and *hwæther,* whether.]]

ejaculate *i-jak'ū-lāt, v.t.* to eject: to utter with suddenness —*v.i* to utter or make an ejaculation: to emit semen —*n.* **ejaculā'tion** —*adjs.* **ejac'ulātive** (or *-lā-*), **ejac'ulātory** (or *-lā-*). [L. *ē,* from, and *jaculārī, -ātus—jacēre,* to throw.]

eject *ē-jekt', i-, v.t.* to cast out· to dismiss· to turn out: to expel.—*v i* to cause oneself to be ejected as from an aircraft or spacecraft —*n.* **ejec'tion** discharge: expulsion: the state of being ejected: vomiting: that which is ejected —*adj.* **ejec'tive.**—*ns.* **eject'ment** expulsion: dispossession· an action for the recovery of the possession of land (*law*), **eject'or** one who ejects or dispossesses another of his land: any mechanical apparatus for ejecting or discharging.—**eject'or-seat,** (*U.S.*) **ejection seat,** a seat that can be shot clear with its occupant in an emergency. [L *ējectāre,* freq. of *ējicēre, ējectum—ē,* from, *jacēre,* to throw.]

eke[1] *ēk, v t.* to add to, increase: to lengthen: to supplement, make up to the required measure (often with *out*). [O.E. *ēcan* (W.S *īecan*); L *augēre;* Gr. *auxanein*]

eke[2] *ēk, adv* in addition: likewise. [O E *ēac;* Ger *auch,* perh from root of **eke**[1].]

ekistics *ek-is'tiks, n.sing.* the science or study of human settlements.—*adj.* **ekis'tic.**—*n.* **ekistician** (*-tish'ən*) [From Mod. Gr. *oikistikē*—Gr. *oikistikos,* of or relating to settlement—*oikos,* a house]

ekka *ek'ə, n.* a small one-horse carriage [Hindi— *ekkā,* one—Sans *eka*]

el *el,* (*U S coll*) *n* an *el*evated railroad

elaborate *i-lab'ər-āt, v.t.* to produce by labour to work out in detail: to build up from raw or comparatively simple materials: to add detail to.—*v.i* to become elaborate.—*adj.* (*i-lab'ər-it*) wrought· with labour: done with fullness and exactness: highly detailed· complicated.—*adv* **elab'orately.**—*ns.* **elab'orateness; elabora'tion.**—*adj.* **elab'orātive** (or *-rā-*).—*n* **elab'orātor.** [L. *elabōrāre, -ātum—ē,* from, *labōrāre—labor,* labour.]

élan *ā-lan', ā-lā, n.* impetuosity, dash [Fr]

eland *ē'lənd, n.* a S African antelope, resembling the elk in having a protuberance on the larynx [Du.,— Ger *Elend* (now *Elen*)—Lith. *élnis,* elk]

elapse *i-laps', v.t.* to slip or glide away: to pass silently, as time [L *ēlāpsus, ēlābī—ē,* from, *lābī, lāpsus,* to slide]

elasmobranch *i-laz'mō-brangk,* or *-las',* *n.* any member of the **Elasmobranch'ii,** a class of fishes including sharks and skates, having a cartilaginous skeleton and plate-like gills. [Gr *elasmos,* a beaten-metal plate, *branchia,* gills.]

elastic *i-las'tik,* or *-las', adj.* having a tendency to recover the original form or size: springy: able to recover quickly a former state or condition after a shock (*fig*): flexible: capable of stretching to include much (*lit.* and *fig.*)· made of elastic.—*n* a string or ribbon with rubber strands —*adv.* **elas'tically.**—*v t.* **elas'ticate** to make elastic·—*p.adj* **elas'ticated.**—*v t.* **elas'ticise, -ize** (*-ti-sīz*) to make elastic.—*ns* **elasticity**

(*el-* or *ēl-əs-tis'*) power of returning to original form or size: springiness: power to recover from depression, **elas'ticness; elas'tin** a protein, chief constituent of elastic tissue; **elas'tomer** any rubber-like substance —*adj.* **elastomeric** (*-mer'*).—**elastic band** a loop of thin rubber; **elastic collision, scattering** see under **collide**. [Late Gr. *elastikos—elaunein*, to drive]
Elastoplast® *i-last'ō-plast, -plast, n.* a dressing for a wound, consisting of gauze on a backing of adhesive tape
elate *i-lāt', v.t.* to make exultant or proud —*adv* **elāt'edly.—***ns* **elāt'edness; elā'tion** pride resulting from success: exaltation, high spirits. [L. *ēlātus,* used as pa p of *efferre—ē,* from, *lātus,* carried]
elbow *el'bō, n* the joint where the arm bends· the corresponding joint in vertebrates: the part of a sleeve which covers the elbow: any sharp turn or bend —*v.t.* to push with the elbow, to jostle.—**el'bow-grease** (*humorously*) vigorous rubbing: hard work; **el'bow-room** room to extend the elbows: space enough for moving or acting: freedom and scope —at **one's elbow** close at hand; **bend** or **lift the elbow** to drink alcoholic liquor, esp. too much; **out at elbow** with coat ragged at the elbows; **up to the elbows** completely engrossed. [O E. *elnboga;* see **ell,** and **bow**[1] *n* and *v.t.*]
eld *eld,* (*arch.*) *n.* age: old age, senility: former times, antiquity [O.E *eldo*]
elder[1] *eld'ər, n* a shrub or tree (Sambucus) of the Caprifoliaceae, with small flowers and three-seeded fruits.—**eld'erberry** the purple-black fruit of the elder; **eld'erberry wine.** [O E. *ellærn*]
elder[2] *eld'ər, adj* older: having lived a longer time: prior in origin.—*n* one who is older: an ancestor: one advanced to office on account of age: one of a class of office-bearers in the Presbyterian Church (*presbyter* of the New Testament).—*n.* **eld'erliness.—***adj.* **eld'erly** somewhat old: bordering on old age —*n.* (with *the*) elderly people.—*adj.* **eld'est** oldest —**elder** or **eldest hand** the player on the dealer's left, who leads in card-playing; **Elder Statesman** a retired statesman consulted by the government: any administrator of age and experience. [O.E *eldra* (W.S *ieldra, yldra*), compar., *eldesta* (*ieldesta*), superl of *ald* (*eald*), old.]
El Dorado, Eldorado *el-də-rä'dō,* the golden land (or city) imagined by the Spanish conquerors of America: any place where wealth is easily to be made. [Sp. *el,* the, *dorado,* pa.p of *dorar,* to gild—the gilded king of the legendary city of Manoa; afterwards transferred to the city itself.]
eldritch *el'(d)rich,* (*Scot.*) *adj.* weird: uncanny [Perh connected with **elf.**]
elecampane *el-i-kam-pān', n.* a composite plant (*Inula helenium*) formerly much cultivated for its medicinal root: a sweetmeat flavoured with an extract from the root. [L. *enula campāna,* field, or Campanian, inula.]
elect *i-lekt', v t.* to choose (in preference): to select for any office or purpose: to select by vote.—*adj.* taken by preference from among others: chosen for an office but not yet in it (almost always after the noun): chosen by God for salvation (*theol.*).—*n.* one chosen or set apart —*n.* **elec'tion** (*-shən*) the act of electing or choosing: the public choice of a person for office, usually by the votes of a constituent body: freewill: the exercise of God's will in the predetermination of certain persons to salvation (*theol.*).—*v.t.* **electioneer'** to labour to secure the election of a candidate.—*n.* **electioneer'er.—***n.* and *adj.* **electioneer'ing.—***adj.* **elect'ive** pertaining to, dependent on, or exerting the power of choice.—*adv.* **elect'ively.** —*ns.* **electiv'ity** (*ē-, e-*); **elect'or** one who elects· one

who has a vote at an election: the title formerly belonging to those princes and archbishops of the German empire who had the right to elect the Emperor: —*fem* **elect'ress.—***adj.* **elect'oral** pertaining to elections or to electors· consisting of electors.—*ns* **elect'orate** the dignity or the territory of an elector: the body of electors: **elect'orship.—electoral college** in U.S , the body of people who elect the President and Vice-President, themselves elected by popular vote: any body of electors with a similar function. [L. *ēligēre, ēlectum—ē,* from, *legēre,* to choose.]
Electra complex *i-lek'trə kom'pleks,* (*psych.*) the attachment of a daughter to her father, with hostility to her mother. [Greek story of *Electra,* who helped to avenge her mother's murder of her father.]
electret *i-lek'trit,* (*elect*) *n.* a permanently polarised (piece of) dielectric material [*Electri*city and *magnet*]
electric *i-lek'trik, adj* pertaining to electricity: charged with or capable of being charged with electricity: producing or produced by, conveying, operated by, or making use of electricity: thrilling (*fig.*): producing a sudden startling effect.—*adj.* **elec'trical.—***adv.* **elec'trically.—***ns.* **electrician** (*el-ik-trish'ən*) one who makes, instals, or repairs electrical apparatus; **electricity** (*el-ik-tris'i-ti*) the attractive power of amber and other substances when rubbed: the manifestation of a form of energy associated with separation or movement of charged particles, as electrons and protons: the science that deals with this: a feeling of excitement.—*adj* **elec'trifiable.—***n.* **electrifica'tion.—***v.t.* **elec'trify** to communicate electricity to: to excite suddenly: to astonish: to adapt to electricity as the motive power:—*pr.p.* **elec'trifying;** *pa.t.* and *pa.p* **elec'trified.—electric arc** a luminous space between electrodes when a current passes across; **electric battery** a group of cells connected in series or in parallel for generating an electric current by chemical action; **electric blanket** a blanket heated by electric current; **electric blue** a steely blue colour; **electric chair** the seat on which a condemned criminal is put to death by electricity; **electric eel** a S. American eel-shaped fish capable of delivering a powerful electric shock from an organ in the tail region; **electric eye** a photo-electric cell: a miniature cathode ray tube; **electric fence** a wire fence electrically charged; **electric guitar** one with an electrical amplifying device; **electric organ** an organ in which the sound is produced by electrical devices instead of wind (*mus.*): in certain fishes, a structure that generates, stores and discharges electricity (*zool.*); **electric ray** the fish Torpedo; **electric storm** a violent disturbance in the electric condition of the atmosphere [L. *ēlectrum—*Gr *ēlektron,* amber, in which electricity was first observed.]
electrify. See electric.
electro- *i-lek'trō, el-ik-tro',* in composition, electric.—*ns.* **elec'tro** (*coll.*) short for **electroplate** and **electrotype.—***ns.* **elec'trobiol'ogist; elec'trobio'logy** the science of the electrical phenomena in living organisms; **elec'trocar'diogram** a photographic record of the electrical variations that occur during contraction of the muscle of the heart; **elec'trocar'diograph** a galvanometer used for making such records; **elec'trocardiog'raphy.—***adj.* **elec'trochem'ical.—***ns.* **elec'trochem'ist; elec'trochem'istry** the study of the relation between electricity and chemical change.—*adj.* **elec'tro-convuls've** (**electro-convulsive therapy** shock-therapy—abbrev. **ECT**).—*v.t.* **elec'trocute** to inflict a death penalty by means of electricity: to kill by electricity.—*ns.* **electrocu'tion; elec'trode** (Gr. *hodos,* way) a conductor by which a current of electricity enters or leaves an electrolytic

cell, gas discharge tube, or thermionic valve; **elec'-trodeposi'tion** deposition of a layer of metal by electrolysis.—*n. sing.* **elec'trodynam'ics** the study of electricity in motion, or of the interaction of currents and currents, or currents and magnets.—*ns.* **elec'tro-dynamom'eter** an instrument for measuring currents by the attraction or repulsion between current-bearing coils; **elec'troenceph'alogram** (*-sef'*, *-kef'*) a record made by an **elec'troenceph'alograph**, an instrument recording small electrical impulses produced by the brain; **elec'troencephalog'raphy**; **electrolier** (*-lēr'*) an electric-light fixture resembling a chandelier.—*v.t.* **elec'trolyse, -lyze** (*-līz*) to break up by electric means: to subject to electrolysis.—*ns.* **electrolysis** (*-trol'i-sis*; Gr. *lysis*, loosing) decomposition by electric current, with migration of ions shown by changes at the electrodes: term used for the removal of hair by applying an electrically charged needle to the follicle; **elec'trolyte** (*-līt*) a substance that admits of electrolysis.—*adj.* **electrolytic** (*-lit'ik*). —*adv.* **electrolyt'ically.**—*n.* **elec'tromag'net** a piece of soft iron, etc., rendered magnetic by a current of electricity passing through a coil of wire wound round it.—*adj.* **elec'tromagnet'ic** (**electromagnetic theory** Clerk Maxwell's theory explaining light in terms of electromagnetic waves; **electromagnetic wave** a travelling disturbance in space produced by the acceleration of an electric charge, comprising an electric field and a magnetic field at right angles to each other, both moving at the same velocity in a direction normal to the plane of the two fields).—*ns.* **elec'tro-mag'netism** a branch of science which treats of the relation of electricity to magnetism; **electrōm'eter** an instrument for measuring difference of electric potential.—*adjs.* **electromet'ric, -al.**—*n.* **electrom'-etry** the science of electrical measurements.—*adjs.* **electromō'tive** pertaining to the motion of electricity or the laws governing it (**electromotive force** difference of potential).—*ns.* **electromō'tor** an apparatus for applying electricity as a motive power; **electrophorē'sis** (Gr. *phoreein*, to bear) migration of suspended particles, as protein macromolecules, under the influence of an electric field.—*adj.* **electro-phoretic** (*-et'ik*) pertaining to electrophoresis.—*n.* **electrōph'orus** an instrument for obtaining statical electricity by means of induction.—*v.t.* **elec'troplate** to plate or cover, esp. with silver, by electrolysis —*n* electroplated ware.—*n.* **elec'troscope** an instrument for detecting the presence of electricity in a body and the nature of it.—*adj.* **electroscop'ic.**—*ns.* **elec'tro-shock** an electric shock.—*adj.* **elec'trostat'ic.**—*ns sing.* **elec'trostat'ics** the branch of science which treats of electricity at rest; **elec'trotech'nics** (also **elec'trotechnol'ogy**) electric technology; **electro-therapeu'tics** (also **electrother'apy**) treatment of disease by electricity.—*ns.* **elec'trotype** a printing plate made by electrolytically coating a mould with copper; **elec'trotyper**; **elec'trovalency** union within a chemical compound achieved by transfer of electrons, the resulting ions being held together by electrostatic attraction.—*adj.* **elec'trovalent.** [Gr. *ēlektro-*, combining form of *ēlektron*; see **electron.**] **electron** *i-lek'tron, n.* a natural alloy of gold and silver used by the ancients (also Latinised as **elec'trum**): a minute particle charged with electricity, or a unit charge having inertia, normally forming part of an atom but capable of isolation as in cathode rays.— *adj.* **electronic** (*el-, il-, ēl-ik-tron'ik*) of or pertaining to electronics: worked or produced by devices made according to the principles of electronics. concerned with, or working with, such devices —*adv.* **electron'-ically.**—*n.sing.* **electron'ics** the science and technology of the conduction of electricity in a vacuum, a

gas, or a semiconductor, and devices based thereon. —**electron camera** any device that converts an optical image into a corresponding electric current directly by electronic means; **electron gun** the assembly of electrodes in a cathode ray tube which produces the electron beam; **electronic brain** any electronic computer; **electronic flash** an extremely intense and brief flash for high-speed photography produced by passing an electric charge through a gas-filled tube, or the apparatus for producing it; **electronic music** music made by arranging sounds previously generated in the laboratory and recorded on tape; **electronic piano** a kind of synthesiser; **electron microscope** a microscope that makes use of a beam of electrons instead of light; **electron telescope** an optical instrument with electronic image converter used with a normal telescope, **electron tube** an electronic device in which the electron conduction is in a vacuum or gas inside a gas-tight enclosure—including a thermionic valve; **elec'tron-volt** a unit of energy equal to that acquired by an electron when accelerated by a potential of one volt. [Gr. *ēlektron*, amber]

electronic, etc. See **electron.**

electrophoresis ... to ... electrovalent. See **electro-.**

electrum. See **electron.**

electuary *i-lek'tū-ər-i, n.* a medicine mixed with honey or the like. [L.L. *ēlectuārium*, perh.—Gr. *eklei-chein*, to lick up.]

eleemosynary *el-ē, el-i-ē-moz'i-nər-i,* or *-mos', adj.* relating to charity or almsgiving: dependent on charity: of the nature of alms. [Gr. *eleēmosynē*, alms— *eleos*, pity; see **alms.**]

elegant *el'i-gənt, adj.* pleasing to good or fastidious taste: very careful or ornate in dress: graceful in form and movement: refined and luxurious: (of style) polished: (of apparatus or work in science or mathematics) simple and effective.—*ns* **el'egance, el'-egancy.**—*adv.* **el'egantly.** [Fr.,—L. *ēlegāns, -antis —ē,* from, and root of *legēre,* to choose.]

elegy *el'i-ji, n.* a song of mourning: a funeral-song: a poem of serious, pensive, or reflective mood: a poem written in elegiac metre.—*adj.* **elegi'ac** belonging to elegy: mournful: used in elegies, esp. applied to classical verse in couplets of hexameter and pentameter lines (**elegiac couplets**), or two stanzas of four iambic pentameters rhyming *abab* (**elegiac stanzas**). —*n.* elegiac verse.—*adj.* **elegi'acal.**—*n.* **el'egist** a writer of elegies.—*v i.* **el'egise, -ize** to write elegiac-ally.—*v.t.* to write an elegy on. [L. *elegīa*—Gr. *elegeia—elegos,* a lament.]

element *el'ə-mənt, n.* a first principle: one of the essential parts of anything: an ingredient: the proper medium, habitat or sphere of any thing or being: any one of the four substances, fire, air, earth, and water, supposed by the ancients to be the foundation of everything: (in *pl.*) the rudiments of learning. (usu. *pl.*) the bread and wine used in the Eucharist. a substance that cannot be resolved by chemical means into simpler substances (*chem.*): a member or unit of a structure: a resistance wire in an electric heater: an electrode. a determining fact or condition in a problem: (in *pl'*) the weather, the powers of nature.—*adj* **elemental** (*-ment'l*) pertaining to the elements: be longing to or produced by or inhabiting the elements. —*n* an elemental spirit: a nature spirit. a disembodied spirit.—*adj.* **element'ary** of a single element: primary: rudimentary: simple: uncompounded. pertaining to the elements: treating of first principles— **elemental spirits** beings in mediaeval belief who presided over the four elements, living in and ruling them, **elementary particle** any of a number of particles, e g electron, proton, neutron, neutrino, kaon, or pion, so-called because supposed indivisible.—in one's **element** in the surroundings most natural or pleasing to one. [L. *elementum*, pl. *elementa*, first principles.]

elemi *el'im-i, n.* a fragrant resinous substance obtained from various tropical trees, esp. a species of *Canarium.* [Perh. Ar.]

elenchus *i-lengk'əs (pl.* **elench'i**) *n.* refutation: a sophism.—*adj.* **elenc'tic.** [L.,—Gr. *elenchein,* refute.]

elephant *el'i-fənt, n.* a Proboscidean (*Elephas*) of several fossil and two surviving species, the largest living land mammal, having a very thick skin, a trunk, and ivory tusks: a size of paper before metrication.— *n.* **elephantī'asis** (Gr. *elephantīāsis*) a disease chiefly of tropical climates, consisting of an overgrowth of the skin and connective tissue usually of the legs and scrotum.—*adjs.* **elephant'ine** pertaining to an elephant: like an elephant: very large or ungainly; **elephant'oid** elephant-like.—**elephant seal** the largest of the seals, the male measuring about 20 feet in length; **el'ephant's-ears'** or **-ear'** begonia.—**pink elephants** hallucinations caused by over-indulgence in alcoholic drink; **white elephant** anything that gives more trouble than it is worth—a (so-called) white elephant being an honourable but onerous gift of the kings of Siam to a courtier they wished to ruin: an unwanted possession, often given away to a jumble sale: something which proves to be useless. [M.E. *olifaunt*—Gr. *elephās, -antos.*]

Eleusinian *el-ū-sin'i-ən, adj.* relating to *Eleusis* in Attica.—**Eleusinian mysteries** the mysteries of Demeter celebrated there.

elevate *el'i-vāt, v.t.* to raise to a higher position: to raise in mind and feelings: to exhilarate.—*adjs.* **el'evate, -d** raised: lofty: exhilarated, esp by liquor. —*ns.* **eleva'tion** the act of elevating or raising, or the state of being raised: exaltation: an elevated place: height: a representation of the flat side of a building, drawn with mathematical accuracy, but without any attention to effect (*archit.*): angular height above the horizon: an angle made by a line with the plane of the horizon: a leap with apparent suspension in the air (*ballet*); **el'evator** a person or thing that lifts up: a lift or machine for raising grain, etc., to a higher floor: a lift (*U.S.*): a storehouse for grain: movable control surface or surfaces at the tail of an aeroplane by which it is made to climb or dive.—*adj.* **el'evatory.**—*n.* **elevon** (*el'ə-vən*) a wing flap on delta-wing or tailless aircraft acting both as an *elev*ator and as an aile*ron.*— **elevated (railroad)** a railway borne on pillars or trestles over a roadway, as in some American towns (familiarly **el,** or **L**). [L. *ēlevāre, -ātum—ē,* from, *levāre,* to raise—*levis,* light; see **light**[2].]

eleven *i-lev'n, n.* the cardinal number next above ten: a team of eleven (cricket, association football, etc.): the eleventh hour after noon or midnight.—*adj.* of the number eleven.—*n.* (usu. *n.pl.,* sometimes *n.sing.*) **elev'enses** (*coll.*) an eleven o'clock snack: morning coffee or the like.—*adj.* **elev'enth** next after the tenth: equal to one of eleven equal parts.—*n.* an eleventh part: an octave and a fourth (*mus.*).—*adv* **elev'enthly.**—**eleventh hour** the very last moment, referring to Matt. xx. 6, 9 (*adj.* **elev'enth-hour'**).— **eleven-plus (examination)** (*formerly*) a school examination taken by pupils about the age of eleven to determine to which type of secondary education (academic, non-academic, or technical) they were to proceed. [O.E. *en(d)le(o)fan;* perh. (ten and) *one left,* from the root of L. *linquĕre,* Gr. *leipein,* to leave.]

elevon. See **elevate.**

elf *elf, n.* in European folklore, a supernatural being, generally of human form but diminutive size, some-

times more malignant than a fairy: a tricky or fairylike being:—*pl.* **elves** (*elvz*).—*adj.* **elf'in** small, with delicate frame: small, mischievous and charming.—*adjs.* **elf'ish, elv'ish.—elf'-child** a changeling, or a child supposed to have been left by elves in place of one stolen by them; **elf'land; elf'-locks** locks of hair clotted together, supposedly by elves.—**elf'-shot** a prehistoric flint or stone arrowhead. [O.E. *ælf;* cf. O.N. *ālfr,* Sw. *elf.*]

elicit *i-, ē-, e-lis'it, v.t.* to draw forth: to evoke.—*ns.* **elicita'tion; elic'itor.** [L. *ēlicēre, ēlicitum.*]

elide *ē-, i-līd', v.t.* to cut off, as a syllable: to suppress, abridge.—*n.* **elision** (*i-lizh'ən*). [L. *ēlīdĕre, ēlīsum* —*ē,* from, *laedĕre,* to strike.]

eligible *el'i-ji-bl, adj.* fit or worthy to be chosen: legally qualified for election or appointment: desirable.—*n.* **eligibil'ity.**—*adv.* **el'igibly.** [Fr.,—L. *ēligĕre;* see **elect**.]

eliminate *i-, ē-, e-lim'in-āt, v.t.* to remove, cancel, get rid of: to expel waste matter.—*adjs.* **elim'inable; elim'inant** (*med.*) causing elimination of waste or morbid matter.—*n.* an eliminating agent.—*n.* **elimina'tion.**—*adj.* **elim'inative.**—*n.* **elim'inator** one who or that which eliminates; esp. a device for substituting an electric main for a battery in a wireless receiving set.—*adj.* **elim'inatory.** [L. *ēlimināre, -ātum—ē,* from, *līmen, -inis,* a threshold.]

elision. See **elide.**

élite *i-, ā-lēt', n.* a chosen or select part, the pick or flower of anything: a size of typewriter type allowing twelve letters to the inch.—Also *adj.*—*n.* **élit'ism** (belief in) government by an élite: consciousness of belonging to an élite: the favouring or creation of an élite.—*adj.* **élit'ist.**—Also *n.* [Fr. *élite*—L. *ēlecta* (*pars,* a part, understood); see **elect**.]

elixir *i-, ē-, e-liks'ər, n.* a liquor once supposed to have the power of indefinitely prolonging life (**elixir of life**), or of transmuting metals: the quintessence of anything: a panacea: a strong tincture. [L.L.,—Ar. *al-iksīr,* the philosopher's stone, from *al-,* the, *iksīr,* prob. from Late Gr. *xērion,* a desiccative powder for wounds—Gr. *xēros,* dry.]

Elizabethan *i-, e-liz-ə-bē'thən, adj.* pertaining to a Queen *Elizabeth* or her reign, esp. to the first Queen Elizabeth (1533–1603) or her reign (1558–1603)—of dress, manners, literature, etc.—*n.* a person, esp. poet or dramatist, of that age.

elk *elk, n.* a deer of northern Europe and Asia, identical or close akin with the moose of N. America, the largest of all living deer: the wapiti (*U.S.* and *Can.*).—**elk'hound** a large strong Norwegian breed of dog with thick coat and curled tail.—**Irish elk** a giant deer now extinct, known from remains found in Ireland. [Poss. O.E. *elh* (W.S. *eolh*).]

ell *el, n.* a varying measure of length originally taken from the arm: a cloth measure equal to 1¼ yd (*obs.*). [O.E. *eln,* Du. *el,* Ger. *Elle,* L *ulna,* Gr. *ōlenē,* elbow.]

ellipse *i-, e-lips', (geom*) *n.* a figure produced by the section of one branch of a right circular cone by a plane passing obliquely and failing to meet the other branch.—*ns.* **ellip'sis** a figure of syntax by which a word or words are left out and implied (*gram.*): mark(s) indicating ellipsis (*print.*):—*pl.* **ellip'sēs; ellip'soid** (*geom.*) a surface (or the enclosed solid) of which every plane section is an ellipse or a circle.— *adjs.* **ellipsoi'dal; ellip'tic, -al** pertaining to an ellipse: oval: pertaining to ellipsis. having a part understood —*adv* **ellip'tically.**—*n.* **ellipticity** (*el-ip-tis'i-ti*) [L. *ellipsis*—Gr. *elleipsis*—*elleipein,* to fall short— *en,* in, *leipein,* to leave.]

elm *elm, n.* a tree (Ulmus) with serrated leaves unequal at the base, and small flowers in clusters ap-

pearing before the leaves: its timber (also **elm'wood**)
—*adj* of elm. [O.E. *elm;* Ger. *Ulme,* L *ulmus*]

elocution *el-ə-kū'shən, n.* the art of effective speaking,
more esp. of public speaking, regarding solely the
utterance or delivery.—*adj.* **elocū'tionary.**—*n.* **eloc-
ū'tionist.** [L. *ēlocūtiō, -ōnis, ēloquī, -cūtus—ē,*
from *loquī,* to speak.]

éloge *ā-lōzh', n.* a funeral oration. [Fr. *éloge,* and its
source L. *ēlogium,* an inscription on a tomb.]

Elohim *e-lō'him, n.* a Hebrew name for God —*n* **Elō'-
hist** the writer or writers of the passages of the Old
Testament in which the name Elohim is used instead
of Yahweh (Jehovah). [Heb pl. of *Eloah*—
explained as a plural of intensity.]

elongate *ē'long-gāt, i-long', v.t* to make longer: to
extend.—*v.i.* to grow longer.—*adjs.* **elongate, -d.**—
n. **elongā'tion** the act of lengthening out: the moon's
or a planet's angular distance from the sun. [L.L
ēlongāre, -ātum—ē, from, *longus,* long.]

elope *e-, i-lōp', v.i.* to escape privately, esp with a
lover (usu. with marital intentions): to run away,
bolt.—*ns.* **elope'ment; elō'per.** [Cf. O.Du. *ont-
löpen,* Ger. *entlaufen,* to run away.]

eloquent *el'ə-kwənt, adj.* having eloquence: persuasive: strongly expressive.—*n.* **el'oquence** the power,
art, or practice of uttering strong emotion in correct,
appropriate, expressive, and fluent language: the art
of such language: persuasive speech.—*adv.* **el'o-
quently.** [L. *ēloquēns, -entis,* pr.p. of *ēloquī.*]

else *els, adj.* (or *adv.*) other (in addition or instead).—
adv. otherwise: besides: except that mentioned.—
advs. **elsewhere'** in or to another place. [O.E *elles,*
otherwise, orig. gen. of *el,* other.]

eluant, eluate. See **elution.**

elucidate *ē-, i-lū'si-dāt,* or *-lōō', v.t.* to make lucid or
clear: to throw light upon —*n.* **elucidā'tion.**—*adjs.*
elu'cidative, elu'cidatory.—*n.* **elu'cidator.** [L.L.
ēlūcidāre, -ātum—ē, intens., and *lūcidus,* clear.]

elude *ē-, i-lūd'* or *-lōōd', v.t.* to escape by stratagem: to
baffle: (of a fact, etc.) to fail to be discovered,
remembered, etc.—*adj.* **elu'dible.**—*n.* **elu'sion**
(*-zhən*) act of eluding: evasion.—*adj.* **elu'sive**
(*-ziv, -siv*).—*adv.* **elu'sively.**—*n.* **elu'soriness.**—*adj.*
elu'sory. [L. *ēlūdĕre, ēlūsum—ē,* from, *lūdĕre,* to
play.]

elution *ē-, i-lōō'shən, -lū', (chem.) n.* purification or
separation by washing.—*ns.* **el'uant** a liquid used for
elution; **el'uate** liquid obtained by eluting.—*v.t*
elute'. [L. *ēlūtiō, -ōnis,* washing—*ē,* from, *luĕre,* to
wash.]

elutriate *ē-, i-lōō'tri-āt, -lū', v.t.* to separate by
washing into coarser and finer portions.—*ns.* **elutri-
ā'tion; elu'triator** an apparatus for elutriating [L
ēlutriāre, to wash out—*ē,* from, *luĕre,* to wash]

elver *el'vər, n.* a young eel.

elves, elvish. See under **elf.**

Elysium *ē-, i-, e-liz(h)'i-əm, n.* among the Greeks, the
abode of the blessed dead (*myth*): any delightful
place.—*adj.* **Elys'ian.** [L.,—Gr. *elysion (pedion),*
the Elysian (plain).]

elytrum *el'it-rəm, n.* a beetle's forewing modified to
form a case for the hind-wing.—Also **el'ytron:**—*pl.*
el'ytra. [Latinised from Gr. *elytron,* a sheath.]

Elzevir *el'zi-vēr, -vər, adj.* published by the *Elzevirs,* a
family of printers in Holland, whose small neat editions were chiefly published between 1592 and 1681.

em *em, n.* the unit of measurement (12-point lower-
case 'm') used in spacing material and in estimating
dimensions of pages (*print.*)

em- *em-, pfx.* a form of **en-** used before *b, m* or *p*

'em *əm, pron.* them: for. [Orig the unstressed
form of *hem,* dat. and accus pl of *he;* now used coll.
as if an abbreviation of **them.**]

emaciate *i-mā'shi-āt, -si, v t.* to make meagre or lean:
to deprive of flesh. to waste.—*n.* **emāciā'tion.** [L
ēmaciāre—ē-, intens, *maciāre,* to make lean.]

emanate *em'ə-nāt, v i.* to flow out of or from anything:
to proceed from some source: to arise.—*adj.* **em'an-
ant** flowing out —*n* **emanā'tion** a flowing out from a
source: that which issues or proceeds from some
source· a radioactive gas given off by radium, thorium
and actinium—radon.—*adjs.* **em'anative, em'ana-
tory, emanā'tional.** [L *ēmānāre, -ātum—ē,* out
from, *mānāre,* to flow.]

emancipate *e-, i-man'si-pāt, v.t.* to set free from restraint or bondage or disability of any kind.—*ns.*
emancipā'tion the act of setting free from bondage or
disability of any kind: the state of being set free:
emancipā'tionist; eman'cipātor; eman'cipist (*hist.*) a
convict who has served his time of punishment in a
penal colony. [L. *ēmancipāre—ē,* away from, *man-
cipāre,* to transfer property.]

emasculate *i-, ē-mas'kū-lāt, v.t.* to deprive of the
properties of a male: to castrate: to deprive of masculine vigour: to render effeminate: to lessen or take
away the power, force or effectiveness of (*fig.*).—*ns.*
emasculā'tion; emas'culātor.—*adj.* **emas'culatory**
(*-lə-tər-i*). [L.L. *ēmasculāre—ē,* from, *masculus,*
dim. of *mās,* a male.]

embalm *im-, em-bäm', v t.* to preserve from decay by
aromatic drugs, as a dead body: to preserve with fragrance: to preserve unchanged but lifeless: to
impregnate with balm, perfume.—*ns.* **embalm'er;
embalm'ing, embalm'ment.** [Fr. *embaumer,* from
em-, in, and *baume,* see **balm.**]

embank *im-, em-bangk', v.t.* to enclose or defend with
a bank or dike.—*n.* **embank'ment** a bank or mound
made to keep water within certain limits: a mound
constructed so as to carry a level road or railway over
a low-lying place. [Pfx. **em-** (**en-** (1a))]

embarcation. Same as **embarkation.**

embargo *em-bär'gō, n.* a temporary order from the
Admiralty to prevent the arrival or departure of
ships: a stoppage of trade for a short time by
authority: a prohibition, ban:—*pl.* **embar'goes.**—*v.t.*
to lay an embargo on: to seize:—*pr.p.* **embar'gōing;**
pa.t and *pa.p.* **embar'goed** (*-gōd*). [Sp.,—
embargar, to impede, to restrain—Sp. pfx. *em-,* in,
L.L. (and Sp.) *barra,* a bar.]

embark *im-, em-bärk', v.t.* to put on board ship: to
engage, invest, in any affair.—*v.i.* to go on board
ship: to engage in (with *on, in*).—*n.* **embarkā'tion**
(*em-*) a putting or going on board. [Fr. *embarquer,*
from *em-,* in, *barque,* bark.]

embarras de (du) choix *ä-ba-ra-rə (du) shwa,* (Fr.)
embarrassment in choice, a perplexing number of
things to choose from; **embarras de(s) richesses** (*də
(dä) rē-shes*) a perplexing amount of wealth or of
abundance of any kind

embarrass *im-, em-bar'əs, v.t.* to encumber: to involve
in difficulty, esp. in money matters: to put out of
countenance, disconcert: to perplex.—*adj.*
embarr'assed.—*n.* **embarr'assment** the state of feeling embarrassed: something which causes one to feel
embarrassed· difficulties in money matters: a perplexing amount (see **embarras de choix,** etc). [Fr
embarrasser—em-, in, *barre,* L.L. *barra,* bar.]

embassy *em'bə-si, n.* the charge or function of an
ambassador: the person or body of persons sent on
an undertaking· an ambassador's residence. [See
ambassador.]

embattle[1] *im-bat'l, v t.* to furnish with battlements.—
adj. **embatt'led** furnished with battlements: having
the outline like a battlement (*her*) [Pfx **en-** (1c)
and O Fr *batailler,* to embattle.]

embattle[2] *im-bat'l, v.t* to range in order of battle.—

adj **embatt'led** arranged for battle: involved in battle (also *fig.*). [O Fr. *embataillier*—*em*-, in, *bataille*, battle.]

embay *im-bā'* *v.t.* to enclose in a bay: to land-lock.—*n* **embay'ment** a bay. [Pfx **en**- (1a).]

embed, imbed *im-bed'*, *v t.* to place in a mass of matter (also *fig.*) —*n* **embed'ment** the act of embedding: the state of being embedded [Pfx. **en**- (1a).]

embellish *im-bel'ish*, *v.t.* to make beautiful with ornaments: to decorate: to illustrate pictorially, as a book: to add interesting and possibly untruthful details to (an account, narrative, etc).—*n.* **embell'isher.**—*adv* **embell'ishingly.**—*n.* **embell'ishment** the act of embellishing or adorning: a decoration: ornament [Fr *embellir*, *embellissant*—*em*-, in, *bel* (*beau*) beautiful.]

ember *em'bər*, *n* a piece of live coal or wood: (the following definitions chiefly in *pl*) red-hot ashes: smouldering remains of a fire, or (*fig.*) of love, passion, etc. [O E. *æmerge*; O.N. *eimyrja*.]

Ember-days *em'bər-dāz*, *n.pl.* the three Fast-days (Wednesday, Friday, Saturday) in each quarter, following the first Sunday in Lent, Whitsunday, Holy Cross Day (Sept 14th), and St Lucia's Day (Dec. 13th). [O.E *ymbryne*, a circuit—*ymb* round, and *ryne*, a running, from *rinnan*, to run.]

ember-goose *em'bər-gōōs*, *n.* the great northern diver. [Norw. *emmer*; Ger. *Imber.*]

embezzle *im-bez'l*, *v.t.* to appropriate fraudulently (now only what has been entrusted).—*ns.* **embezz'lement; embezz'ler.** [Anglo-Fr. *embesiler*, to make away with]

embitter *im-bit'ər*, *v.t.* to make bitter or more bitter: to make more bitterly hostile —*n.* **embitt'erment.** [Pfx. **em**- (**en**- (1b)).]

emblazon *im-blā'zn*, *v.t.* in heraldry, to adorn with figures: to depict heraldically: to celebrate.—*ns.* **emblā'zoner; emblā'zonment.** [Pfx. **em**- (**en**- (1c)).]

emblem *em'bləm*, *n.* a picture representing to the mind something different from itself: a symbolic device or badge: a type or symbol.—*adjs.* **emblemat'ic, -al** pertaining to or containing emblems: symbolical: representing (with *of*).—*adv.* **emblemat'ically.**—*vs.t.* **emblematise, -ize** (*-blem'ə-tīz*), **em'blemise, -ize** to represent by an emblem. [L.—Gr. *emblēma*, *-atos*, a thing inserted—*en*, in, and the root of *ballein*, to throw.]

emblements *em'bli-mənts*, *n.pl.* crops raised by the labour of the cultivator, but not tree-fruits or grass. [O.Fr. *emblaer*, to sow with corn—L.L. *imbladāre*—*in*, in, *bladum*, wheat.]

embody *im-bod'i*, *v.t.* to form into a body: to make corporeal: to make tangible: to express (in words, in tangible form, etc.): to make part of a body, to incorporate: to organise:—*pr.p.* **embod'ying;** *pa.t.* and *pa p.* **embod'ied.**—*adj.* **embod'ied.**—*n.* **embod'iment** the act of embodying: the state of being embodied: that in which something is embodied. [Pfx. **em**- (**en**- (1a)).]

embolden *im-bōld'n*, *v.t.* to make bold or courageous: to give the necessary courage for some action.—*n* **embold'ener.** [Pfx **em**- (**en**- (1b)).]

embolism *em'bol-izm*, *-bəl-*, *n* an intercalation of days in the calendar to correct error: the presence of one or more obstructing clots, etc. in the blood vessel —*n* **em'bolus** a clot obstructing a blood-vessel.—**embolismic year** see **year.** [Late Gr. *embolismos*, intercalation, Gr. *embolē*, insertion, ramming—*emballein*, to throw in.]

embonpoint *ā-bɔ̃-pwē'*, *adj.* stout, plump, full in figure: well-fed.—*n.* stoutness, plumpness, well-fed condition. [Fr.,—*en bon point*, in good form.]

embosom *im-bōōz'əm*, *v.t.* to take into the bosom: to

enclose or surround. [Pfx. **en**- (1a).]

emboss *im-bos'*, *v.t.* to raise in relief: to ornament with raised work —*adj.* **embossed'** raised, standing out in relief: having a protuberance in the centre (*bot.*).—*ns.* **emboss'er; emboss'ment.** [Pfx. **em**- (**en**- (1a)).]

embouchure *ā-bōō-shur'*, *n.* the mouth of a river: the mouthpiece of a wind instrument: the disposition of the mouth in playing a wind instrument. [Fr.,—*emboucher*, to put to the mouth, to discharge—*en*, in, *bouche*, a mouth.]

embower *im-bow'ər*, *v.t* to place in a bower: to shelter, as with trees. [Pfx **en**- (1a).]

embrace *im-brās'*, *v.t.* to take in the arms: to press to the bosom with affection: to take eagerly or willingly: to comprise: to admit, adopt, or receive.—*v.i* to join in an embrace:—*pr.p.* **embrac'ing;** *pa.t.* and *pa.p* **embraced'.**—*n.* an embracing. fond pressure in the arms. (in *pl*; *arch.*) sexual intercourse.—*ns.* **embrace'ment; embrac'er.** [O.Fr. *embracer*—L. *in*, in, into, *brā(c)chium*, an arm.]

embranchment *im-branch'mənt*, *-sh-*, *n.* a branching off, as an arm of a river, a spur of a mountain, etc [Fr. *embranchement.*]

embrangle *im-brang'gl*, *v.t.* to confuse, perplex.—*n.* **embran'glement.** [Pfx **en**- (1a).]

embrasure *im-brā'zhər*, (*archit.*) *n.* an internally splayed recess of a door or window: the slant of such a recess. an opening in a wall for cannon.—Also **embrā'zure.** [Fr.,—O.Fr. *embraser*, to slope the sides of a window—*em*- (—L. *in*), *braser*, to skew.]

embrocate *em'brō-kāt*, *v.t.* to moisten and rub, as with a lotion.—*n.* **embrōcā'tion** the act of embrocating: the lotion used. [L.L. *embrocāre*, *-ātum*, from Gr *embrochē*, a lotion—*en*-, in, into, *brechein*, to wet.]

embroglio. See **imbroglio.**

embroider *im-broid'ər*, *v.t.* to ornament with designs in needlework: to add ornament or fictitious detail to.—*ns.* **embroid'erer; embroid'ery** the art of producing ornamental designs in needlework on textile fabrics, etc.: ornamental needlework: embellishment: exaggeration or invented detail. [M.E. *embrouderie*—O.Fr. *embroder*; confused with or influenced by O.E. *bregdan*, to weave, braid.]

embroil *im-broil'*, *v.t.* to involve in a broil, or in perplexity (with): to entangle: to distract: to throw into confusion.—*n* **embroil'ment.** [Fr. *embrouiller*—pfx. *em*-, and *brouiller*, to break out.]

embrown *im-brown'*, *v.t.* to make brown: to darken, obscure.—*adj.* **embrown'ing.** [Pfx. **en**- (1b).]

embrue. Same as **imbrue.**

embryo *em'bri-ō*, *n.* a young animal or plant in its earliest stages of development: the beginning of anything:—*pl.* **em'bryos.**—Also *adj.*—*ns.* **embryogen'esis, embryogeny** (*-oj'i-ni*) the formation and development of the embryo.—*adjs.* **embryolog'ic, -al.**—*ns.* **embryol'ogist; embryol'ogy** the science of the formation and development of the embryo.—*adjs.* **em'bryonal, embryon'ic** of or relating to anything in an imperfect or incomplete state: rudimentary. [L L.,—Gr. *embryon*—*en*, in, *bryein*, to swell.]

embus *im-bus'*, *v.t* to put (esp. troops) into a bus.—*v.i.* to mount a bus:—*pr.p.* **embuss'ing;** *pa.t.* and *pa.p.* **embussed'.** [Pfx. **en**- (1a).]

emcee *em'sē*, (*coll*) *n.* a master of ceremonies, a phonetic representation of the abbrev. MC.—*v.t.* and *v.t.* to act as a master of ceremonies (for).

emend *ē-mend'*, *v.t.* to make alterations in with a view to improving (a text).—*adj* **ēmend'able.**—*ns* **ēmendā'tion** the removal of an error or fault: correction, ê'mendător.—*adj* **ēmen'datory.** [L. *ēmendāre*, *-ātum*—*ē*, from, *mendum*, a fault.]

emerald *em'ər-əld*, *n.* a gem-stone, a beautiful velvety green variety of beryl: (also **emerald green**) its colour. —**Emerald Isle** Ireland, from its greenness. [O.Fr. *esmeralde*—Gr. *smaragdos*.]

emerge *i-, ē-mûrj'*, *v.i.* to rise out of anything: to issue or come forth: to reappear after being concealed: to come into view: to come into being in the course of evolution: to crop up —*ns.* **emer'gence** the act of emerging: a sudden appearance; **emer'gency** an unexpected occurrence, requiring immediate action: pressing necessity.—Also *adj*—*adj* **emer'gent** suddenly appearing: coming into being in the course of evolution: (of a state) having recently become independent.—*n* **emer'sion** (*-shən*) the act of emerging: the reappearance of a heavenly body after eclipse or occultation (*astron.*).—**state of emergency** a situation in which a government suspends the normal constitution in order to deal with an emergency such as a natural disaster or civil disorder. [L *ēmergĕre, ēmersum—ē*, out of, *mergĕre*, to plunge]

emeritus *i-, ē-mer'i-tas, adj*. (often following a noun) honourably discharged from the performance of public duty, esp. denoting a retired professor. [L. *ēmeritus*, having served one's time—*ē-*, sig completeness, and *merērī*, to deserve.]

emersion. See **emerge**.

emery *em'ər-i, n* a very hard mineral, a variety of corundum, used as powder for polishing, etc —*v t*. to rub or coat with emery.—**em'ery-board** a small flat strip of wood or card coated with emery-powder, used in manicure; **em'ery-cloth, -paper** cloth, paper, covered with emery-power for polishing. [O.Fr. *esmeril, emeril*—L.L. *smericulum*—Gr. *smēris, smŷris.*]

emetic *i-met'ik, adj*. causing vomiting.—*n* a medicine that causes vomiting —*n* **emesis** (*em'i-sis*) vomiting —*adj*. **emet'ical.**—*adv*. **emet'ically**. [Gr. *emetikos* —*emeein*, to vomit.]

émeute *ā-møt'*. sometimes *i-mūt'*, *n* a popular rising or uproar. [Fr]

emigrate *em'i-grāt, v.i.* and *v.t.* to remove from one country (or state) to another as a place of abode.— *adj.* **em'igrant** emigrating or having emigrated —*n* one who emigrates.—*n.* **emigrā'tion.**—*adj.* **em'igratory.**—*n.* **émigré** (*ā-mē-grā'*) an (esp. political) emigrant [L. *ēmigrāre, ēmigrāre, -ātum—ē*, from, *migrāre*, to remove.]

éminence grise *ā-mē-nās grēz*, (Fr.) one exercising power in the background, as Cardinal Richelieu's private secretary Père Joseph, nicknamed *l'Éminence Grise*.

eminent *em'i-nənt, adj*. rising above others: conspicuous: distinguished: exalted in rank or office.—*ns.* **em'inence** a part eminent or rising above the rest: a rising ground: a ridge or knob: height: distinction: a title given in 1631 to cardinals, till then styled Most Illustrious; **em'inency.**—*adv.* **em'inently.**—**eminent domain** the right by which the supreme authority in a state may compel a proprietor to part with what is his own for the public use. [L. *ēminēns, -entis*, pr.p. of *ēminēre—ē*, from, *minēre*, to project.]

emir *ā-mēr' n.* a title given in the East and in N Africa to all independent chieftains, and also (perh. improperly) to all the supposed descendants of Mohammed through his daughter Fatima.—*n.* **emir'ate** the office, jurisdiction, or state of an emir. [Ar *amīr*, ruler]

Emi-Scanner® *em'i-skan-ər, n.* a machine which produces X-ray pictures of the head or body with the assistance of a computer. [EMI—see List of Abbreviations.]

emit *i-, ē-mit', v.t* to send out: to throw or give out: to issue: to utter (a declaration):—*pr.p* **emitt'ing;** *pa t* and *pa.p*. **emitt'ed.**—*n.* **emissary** (*em'is-ər-i*) one sent out on a mission, esp an underhand or secret mission

—*n.* **emission** (*-mish'ən*) the act of emitting: that which is issued at one time: the discharge of semen. the release of electrons from parent atoms on absorption of energy exceeding the average.—*adj.* **emiss'ive.**—*n.* **emissiv'ity** (*ē-*) the property or power of emitting or radiating. [L. *ēmittēre, ēmissum—ē*, out of, *mittēre*, to send.]

Emmanuel, Immanuel *i-man'ū-əl, -el, n.* the symbolical name of the child announced by Isaiah (Isa. vii. 14), and applied to Jesus as the Messiah in Matt i 23. [Gr *Emmanouēl*—Heb *'Immānūēl—'im*, with, *ānū*, us, *ēl*, God.]

Emmental, -thal *em'ən-tal, ns.* applied to a Swiss cheese, like Gruyère

emmer *em'ər, n.* a species of wheat, *Triticum dicoccum.* [Ger dial.]

emmet *em'it*, (*arch.* and *dial.*) *n* the ant. [O.E. *æmete.*]

Emmy *em'i, n* a television trophy, corresponding to the cinema Oscar, awarded by the American Academy of Television Arts and Sciences:—*pl.* **Em'mys, Em'mies.**

emollient *i-mol'yənt, adj.* softening: making supple — *n.* a softening application, as poultices, fomentations, etc. (*med.*). [L. *ēmollīre—ē*, intens., *mollīre*, to soften.]

emolument *i-mol'ū-mənt, n.* (often in *pl*) profit arising from employment, as salary or fees —*adjs.* **emolumen'tal; emolumen'tary.** [L. *ēmolimentum*, prob. from *ēmōlēre*, to grind out—*ē-*, and *mōlēre*, to grind.]

emotion *i-mō'shən, n* a moving of the feelings: agitation of mind: one of the three groups of the phenomena of the mind—feeling, distinguished from cognition and will (*phil.*) —*v.i.* **emote** (*i-mōt'*) to show or express exaggerated emotion.—*adj.* **emō'tional.**—*n.* **emō'tionalism** a tendency to emotional excitement: the habit of working on the emotions: the indulgence of superficial emotion.— *adv.* **emō'tionally.**—*adj.* **emō'tive** (*-tiv*) tending to arouse emotion. [L *ēmōtiō, -ōnis—ēmovēre, -mōtum*, to stir up]

empanel *im-pan'əl, v.t.* to enter on a panel:—*pr.p* **empan'elling;** *pa.t.* and *pa p* **empan'elled.**—*n.* **empan'elment.**—Also **impanel.** [Pfx. **en-** (1a)]

empathy *em'pə-thi, n.* the power of entering into another's personality and imaginatively experiencing his experiences: the power of entering into the feeling or spirit of something (esp. a work of art) and so appreciating it fully.—*adjs.* **empathet'ic; empath'ic.** —*v.i.* **em'pathise, -ize.** [Gr. *en*, in, *pathos*, feeling.]

empennage *em-pen'ij, ā-pen-äzh', n.* an aeroplane's tail as a unit, including elevator, rudder, and fin [Fr., feathering of an arrow—L *penna*, feather, wing]

emperor *em'pər-ər, n.* the head of an empire: a high title of sovereignty: before metrication, a paper size (48 × 72 in.):—*fem.* **em'press.—emperor moth** except the death's-head, the largest British moth, its expanse of wings being about three inches; **emperor penguin** the largest of the penguins. [O Fr. *emperere*—L. *imperātor*, a commander (fem *imperātrix*)—*imperāre*, to command.]

emphasis *em'fə-sis, n.* forcible or impressive expression an insistent or vigorous way of attributing importance or thrusting upon attention: stress: accent: prominence:—*pl.* **em'phases** (*-sēz*).—*v.t.* **em'phasise, -ize** to make emphatic: to lay stress on.—*adj.* **emphat'ic** (*im-, em-fat'ik*), expressed or expressing with emphasis: stressed forcibly: impressive: strongly marked.—*adv* **emphat'ically.** [Gr. *emphasis*, implied meaning—*en*, in, *phainein*, to show.]

emphysema *em-fis-ē'mə, (med.) n* an unnatural distension of a part of the body with air distension of the lung, with breathing difficulties, etc.—*adj.* **emphyse'matous.** [Gr. *emphȳsēma—emphȳsaein*, to inflate.]

empire *em'pīr, n.* (*loosely*) a widespreading dominion, or group of states, etc., under the same sovereign power—not always an emperor: supreme control or dominion: the government or office of an emperor: the time of its duration: a large industrial organisation embracing many firms: a country whose sovereign owes no allegiance to another (*hist.*).—*adj.* (usu. with *cap.*) relating to or in the style of, esp. of dress or furniture, the first French Empire (1804–14). —**em'pire-building** the practice or policy of increasing one's power or authority.—Also *adj.*—**Empire Day** formerly, a public holiday celebrated on (or near) 24th May (Queen Victoria's birthday). [Fr., —L. *imperium*.]

empiric *em-pir'ik, adj.* empirical.—*n.* one who makes trials or experiments: a quack.—*adj.* **empir'ical** resting on trial or experiment: known or knowing only by experience.—*adv.* **empir'ically.—***ns.* **empir'icism** (*-sizm*) the system which, rejecting all *a priori* knowledge, rests solely on experience and induction (*phil.*): the practice of medicine without a regular education: quackery; **empir'icist** (*-sist*).—**empirical formula** (*chem.*) a formula showing in simplest form the ratio of atoms in a molecule, not the absolute number. [Fr.,—L. *empīricus*—Gr. *empeirikos—en*, in, *peira*, a trial.]

emplacement *im-plās'mənt, n.* the act of placing: a gun-platform (*mil.*).—*v.t.* **emplace'** (back-formation) to put in or provide with an emplacement. [Fr. *emplacement.*]

emplane *im-plān', v.t.* to put or take on an aeroplane. —*v.i.* to mount an aeroplane. [Pfx. em- (en- (1a)) and plane².]

employ *im-ploi', v.t.* to occupy the time or attention of: to use as a means or agent: to give work to.—*n.* employment.—*adj.* **employ'able** fit, able, to be employed.—*adj.* **employed'** having employment, in a job.—*ns.* **employ'ee** (or *em-ploi-ē'*) a person employed: **employ'er;** **employ'ment** the act of employing: that which engages or occupies: occupation.—**employment agency** an agency which finds work for the unemployed and employees for vacant positions; **Employment Service Agency** a government agency run by the Department of Employment, which finds work for the unemployed, pays out unemployment benefit, etc. [Fr. *employer*—L. *implicāre*, to enfold—*in*, in, and *plicāre*, to fold; cf. **imply**, **implicate**.]

empolder. See **impolder.**

emporium *em-pō'ri-əm, -po', n.* a commercial or trading centre or mart: a big shop:—*pl.* **empō'ria**, **empō'riums.** [L.,—Gr. *empŏrion*, a trading station —*empŏros*, a wayfarer, trader, *en*, in, *poros*, a way.]

empower *im-pow'ər, v.t.* to authorise. [Pfx. en- (1a).]

empress. See **emperor.**

empressement *ä-pres-mä*, (Fr.) *n.* demonstrative warmth of manner.—*adj.* **empressé** (*-pres-ā*; Fr.) eager, enthusiastic

emprise *em-prīz', (arch.) n.* an enterprise. [O.Fr.— L. *in*, in *praehendĕre*, take.]

empty *emp'ti, adj.* having nothing within: unoccupied unfurnished without effect· unsatisfactory. wanting substance: meaningless: empty-headed: hungry (*coll.*): devoid (of).—*v.t.* to make empty: to deprive of contents: to remove from a receptacle —*v i.* to become empty: to discharge:—*pr.p.* **emp'tying;** *pa t* and *pa p.* **emp'tied.—***n.* an empty bottle, box, sack, etc.:—*pl.* **emp'ties.—***n* **emp'tiness—***adjs* **emp'ty-head'ed** bringing or taking away nothing or no gift, **emp'ty-head'ed** frivolous. [O E. *æmetig—æmetta,*

leisure, rest; the *p* is excrescent.]

empyema *em-pī-ē'mə,* or *-pi-, n.* a collection of pus in any cavity, esp. the pleura. [Gr. *empyēma, empȳēsis—en,* in, *pyon,* pus.]

empyreal *em-pir-ē'al, adj.* formed of pure fire or light: pertaining to the highest and purest region of heaven: sublime.—*adj.* **empyre'an** empyreal.—*n.* the highest heaven, where the pure element of fire was supposed to subsist: the heavens. [Gr. *empyros,* fiery—*en,* in, *pȳr,* fire.]

empyreuma *em-pir-ū'mə, n.* the burned smell and acrid taste that come when vegetable or animal substances are burned:—*pl.* **empyreu'mata.** [Gr. *empȳreuma, -atos,* embers—*en,* in *pȳr,* fire.]

emu *ē'mū, n.* an Australian running bird of the Ratitae, akin to the cassowary, largest of living birds after the ostrich. [Port. *ema,* an ostrich.]

emulate *em'ū-lāt, v.t.* to strive to equal or excel: to rival successfully: (*loosely*) to imitate.—*n.* **em'ulation.—***adj.* **em'ulative.—***n.* **em'ulator.—***adj.* **em'ulous** eager to emulate: desirous of like excellence with another: engaged in competition or rivalry.—*adv.* **em'ulously.—***n.* **em'ulousness.** [L. *aemulāri, -ātus —aemulus,* emulous.]

emulsion *i-mul'shən, n.* a colloidal suspension of one liquid in another: a light-sensitive coating on photographic plates: a liquid mixture containing globules of fat (as milk), or of resinous or bituminous material.— *ns.* **emulsifica'tion;** **emul'sifier** apparatus for preparing emulsions.—*vs.t.* **emul'sify; emul'sionise, -ize.** —*adj.* **emul'sive.—emulsifying agent** a substance whose presence in small quantities stabilises an emulsion; **emulsion paint** a water-thinnable paint made from a pigmented emulsion of a resin in water. [L. *ēmulgēre, ēmulsum,* to milk out—*ē,* from, and *mulgēre,* to milk.]

en *en, n.* half of an em (*print.*; see also **quadrat**).

en- *en-, in-, pfx.* (1) in words derived from L. through Fr., (a) used to form verbs with the sense of *in, into, upon;* (b) used to form verbs with the sense *cause to be;* (c) used intensively or almost meaninglessly; (2) in words derived from Gr. used to form verbs with the sense of *in.*

enable *in-ā'bl, v.t.* to make able: to give power, strength, or authority to: to make possible.—**enabling act, bill, resolution** one giving or proposing to give power to act. [Pfx. en- (1b).]

enact *in-akt', v.t.* to perform: to act the part of: to establish by law.—*adj.* **enact'ive.—***ns.* **enac'tion** (*-shən*), **enact'ment** the passing of a bill into law: that which is enacted· a law; **enact'or.** [Pfx. en- (1b), **act.**]

enamel *in-am'əl, n.* vitrified coating applied to a metal or other surface and fired: any glossy enamel-like surface or coating, esp that of the teeth: a work of art in enamel: a paint giving an enamel-like finish.—*v.t.* to coat with or paint in enamel: to form a glossy surface on, like enamel:—*pr.p.* **enam'elling;** *pa.t.* and *pa.p.* **enam'elled.—***ns* **enam'eller, enam'ellist.** [O.Fr. *enameler—en,* in, *esmail,* enamel.]

enamour, in U.S. **enamor,** *in-am'ər, v.t* to inflame with love: to charm.—**enamoured of** in love with. keen on. [O.Fr. *enamourer*—pfx. *en-, amour*—L. *amor, -ōris,* love.]

enantiomorph *en-an'ti-ō-morf, n* a shape or object (as a crystal, a molecule) exactly similar to another except that right and left are interchanged, each being a mirror-image of the other —*adjs* **enantiomorph'ic; enantiomorph'ous.—***ns* **enantiomorph'ism; enantiomorph'y.** [Gr *enantios,* opposite, *morphē,* shape]

enarthrosis *en-ar-thrō'sis,* (*anat.*) *n.* a ball-and-socket joint [Gr *enarthrōsis—en,* in, *arthron,* a joint]

en attendant ä-na-tä-dä, (Fr) in the meantime, while waiting.

en avant ä-na-vä, (Fr.) forward

en bloc ä blok, (Fr.) as one unit, wholesale.

en brosse ä bros, (of hair) cut short and standing up stiffly. [Fr., like a brush.]

en cabochon. See cabochon.

encaenia en-sē′ni-ə, n. the annual commemoration of founders and benefactors at Oxford, held in June [L..,—Gr enkainia (pl.), a feast of dedication—en, in, kainos, new.]

encage in-kāj′, v.t. to shut up in a cage [Pfx. en- (1a).]

encamp in-kamp′, v.t. to form into a camp: to lodge in a camp.—v.i. to pitch tents: to make, or stay in, a camp.—n. **encamp′ment** the act of encamping: the place where a camper or company is encamped: a camp. [Pfx. en- (1b).]

encapsulate in-kap′sūl-āt, v.t. to enclose in a capsule: to capture the essence of, to describe succinctly but sufficiently.—n. **encapsula′tion** [Pfx. en- (1a).]

encase in-kās′, v t. to enclose in a case: to surround, cover: to line.—n. **encase′ment** [Pfx en- (1a).]

encash in-kash′, v.t. to convert into cash.—n. **encash′ment**. [Pfx. en- (1b).]

encaustic en-kōs′tik, adj. having the colours burned in: of or pertaining to encaustic.—n. an ancient method of painting in melted wax.—**encaustic tile** a decorative glazed and fired tile, having patterns of different coloured clays inlaid in it and burnt with it. [Gr. enkaustikos—enkaiein, to burn in—en, in, kaiein, to burn.]

enceinte[1] ä-sēt′, (fort.) n. an enclosure, generally the whole area of a fortified place. [Fr.,—enceindre, to surround—L. in, in, cingère, cinctum, to gird.]

enceinte[2] ä-sēt′, adj. pregnant, with child. [Fr.,—L incincta, girt about or ungirt.]

encephalon en-sef′əl-on, or -kef′, n. the brain.—adj. **encephalic** (-al′ik) belonging to the head or brain.—n. **encephalin(e)** (-sef′ə-lin) a rarer spelling of enkephalin(e) (q.v.).—adj. **encephalit′ic** pertaining to encephalitis.—ns **encephali′tis** inflammation of the brain; **enceph′alogram, enceph′alograph** an X-ray photograph of the brain; **encephalog′raphy** radiography of the brain, its cavities having been filled with air or dye injected into the space around the spinal cord —adj. **enceph′alous** cephalous.—**encephalitis leth-ar′gica** (-ji-kə) an acute disease marked by profound physical and mental lethargy—popularly called sleeping-sickness. [Gr. enkephalos—en, in, kephalē, head.]

enchain in-chān′, v.t. to put in chains to hold fast (fig.).—n. **enchain′ment**. [Fr. enchaîner—en, in, chaîne, chain—L. catēna.]

enchant in-chänt′, v.t. to act on by songs or rhymed formulas of sorcery: to cast a spell upon: to compel by enchantment: to charm: to delight in a high degree.— adj. **enchant′ed** under the power of enchantment: delighted: possessed by witches or spirits.—n **enchant′er;**—fem. **enchant′ress.**—n. **enchant′ment.** —**enchanter's nightshade** a plant of the evening-prim-rose family, growing in shady places—the name transferred apparently from another plant (perhaps mandrake). [Fr. enchanter—L. incantāre, to sing a magic formula over—in, on, cantāre, to sing.]

encharm in-chärm′, (obs.) v.t. to cast a spell on: to charm. [Pfx. en- (1c).]

enchase in-chās′, v.t. to fix in a border or setting: to insert, let in: to set with jewels: to engrave: to adorn with raised, or embossed work. [Fr. enchâsser—en, in, châsse, shrine, setting—L. capsa, a case.]

enchilada en-chi-lad′ə, n. a Mexican dish consisting of a fried stuffed tortilla with chilli sauce. [Amer. Sp.—

Sp. enchilar, to season with chilli.]

enchiridion en(g)-kī-rid′i-on, n a book to be carried in the hand for reference: a manual. [Gr encheiridion —en, in, cheir, hand.]

encipher in-sī′fər, v.t. to put into cipher. [Pfx. en- (1a).]

encircle in-sûrk′l, v t. to enclose in a circle· to pass round —ns. **encir′cling; encir′clement.** [Pfx. en- (1a).]

en clair ä kler, (Fr) not in cipher.

enclasp in-klasp′, v.t. to clasp. [Pfx. en- (1c).]

enclave en′klāv, also en-klāv′, or ä-klāv′, n. a piece of territory entirely enclosed within foreign territory: an enclosure.—v.t. to surround. [Fr.,—L.L. inclāvāre —L. in, and clāvis, a key.]

enclitic en-klit′ik, adj. (of a word, esp. a particle) with-out accent, behaving as if not a separate word or, in ancient Greek, transferring its accent to the pre-ceding word (gram.).—n. (gram) a word or particle which always follows another word and which is enclitic to it.—adv. **enclit′ically**. [Gr enklitikos— en, in, klinein, to lean.]

enclose, inclose in-klōz′, v.t to close or shut in: to confine: to surround. to put within, esp of something sent within a letter or within its envelope: to seclude: to fence, esp. used of waste land.—ns. **enclosure, inclosure** (-klō′zhər) the act of enclosing: the state of being enclosed: that which is enclosed, esp. in a let-ter: a space fenced off.—**enclosed order** a religious order leading an entirely contemplative life, not going out into the world to work [Pfx. en- (1a) and close[2].]

encode in-kōd′, v t. to encipher: to record in a form other than plain written or printed text. [Pfx en- (1a).]

encomium en-kō′mi-əm, also encō′mion (-on) ns. high commendation: a eulogy:—pl. **encō′miums, encō′mia.**—n. **encō′miast** one who utters or writes encomiums: a praiser.—adjs. **encomias′tic, -al** bestowing praise.—adv **encomias′tically**. [L.,— Gr enkōmion, a song of praise—en, in, kōmos, festivity.]

encompass in-kum′pəs, v t to surround or enclose: to go round (obs.): to bring about.—n **encom′pass-ment.** [Pfx. en- (1a).]

encore ä-, ong-kör′, -kör′, interj. calling for repetition of a performance, or an additional item.—n. a call of encore: an item given in response to such a call.—v t. to call encore to. [Fr , again, still.]

encounter in-kown′tər, v.t. to meet face to face, esp. unexpectedly: to meet in a contest: to oppose.—n. a meeting unexpectedly: an interview: a fight.— **encounter group** a group which meets with a view to establishing greater self-awareness and greater understanding of others by indulging in unrestrained verbal and physical confrontation and contact. [O.Fr. encontrer—L. in, in, contrā, against.]

encourage en-kur′ij, v.t. to put courage in: to inspire with spirit or hope: to incite: to patronise: to cherish. —ns. **encour′agement** the act of encouraging: that which encourages; **encour′ager**.—n. and adj. **encour′-aging.**—adv. **encour′agingly.** [O.Fr. encoragier (Fr encourager)—pfx. en-, corage, courage.]

encrinite en(g)′kri-nīt, n a fossil crinoid: a crinoid [Gr. en, in, krinon, a lily]

encroach in-krōch′, v.i. to seize on the rights of others: to intrude beyond boundaries: to extend into the territory, sphere, etc., of others.—n. **encroach′er.**— n. **encroach′ment.** [O.Fr. encrocher, to seize—en-and croc, a hook.]

encrust, incrust in-krust′, v.t. to cover with a crust or hard coating: to form a crust on the surface of.—v.i. to form a crust.—ns **encrust′ment; encrusta′tion**

(en-, usu **incrustâ'tion** ın-) [L. *ıncrustâre, -âtum*— ın, on, *crusta,* crust.]

encumber ın-*kum'bər, v.t* to impede the motion of: to hamper: to embarrass: to burden. to load with debts —*ns.* **encum'berment; encum'brance** that which encumbers or hinders: a legal claim on an estate: one dependent on another, esp. a child. [O Fr. *encombrer,* from en-, and *combrer;* see **cumber.**]

encyclical en-*sīk'lık-l,* or *-sik', adj.* sent round to many persons or places.—*n.* a letter addressed to the Pope to all his bishops.—Also **encyc'lic.** [Gr *enkyklios*— en, ın, *kyklos,* a circle.]

encyclopaedia, encyclopedia en-*sī-klō-pē'dı-ə, n* a work containing information on every department, or on a particular department, of knowledge, generally alphabetically arranged.—*adjs.* **encyclopae'dic, -al** pertaining to an encyclopaedia: all-comprehensive full of information.—*ns.* **encyclopae'dism** comprehensive knowledge; **encyclopae'dist** the compiler, or one who assists in the compilation, of an encyclopaedia. [False Gr *enkyklopaideıâ,* a wrong reading for *enkyklios paideiâ,* general education—en, ın, *kyklos,* circle; *paıdeıâ,* education—*paıs, paidos,* a child.]

encyst en-*sist', v.t* or *v.i.* to enclose or become enclosed in a cyst or vesicle —*ns* **encystâ'tion; en-cyst'ment.**—*adj.* **encyst'ed.** [Pfx. en- (1a).]

end *end, n.* the last point or portion· termination or close: death: consequence: an object aimed at: a fragment, odd piece: part of a game played from one end (of the bowling-green, archery-ground, etc)—*v.t.* to bring to an end: to destroy.—*v.i.* to come to an end: to cease.—*adj* **end'ed** brought to an end: having ends.—*n.* **end'ing** a termination: a conclusion. that which is at the end: the terminal syllable or portion of a word, esp an inflection (*gram.*).—*adj.* **end'less** without end: returning upon itself: everlasting: incessant.—*adv.* **end'lessly.**—*n* **end'lessness.**—*adj* **end'most** farthest.—*advs.* **end'ways, end'wise** on end: with the end forward.—**end'game** the final stage of a game of chess or certain other games· one's manner of playing the endgame; **endless chain** a chain whose ends are joined; **endless gearing, screw, worm an** arrangement for producing slow motion ın machinery, consisting of a screw whose thread gears ınto a wheel with skew teeth.—*adv* and *adj.* **end'-on'** ın the direction in which the end points.—**end organ a** specialised sensory or motor structure at a nerve-end; **end'-paper** a paper at the beginning or end of a book, pasted to the binding and leaving an additional fly-leaf; **end'-product** the final product of a series of operations; **end result** the final result or outcome.—*adj.* **end'-stopped** having a pause at the end of each line (of verse).—**end use** the final use to which a manufactured article is put.—*n* and *adj.* **end'-user.**—**all ends up** completely: convincingly, **at a loose end** with nothing to do; **at an end** terminated: discontinued: exhausted; **at one's wit's end** see **wit²;** at **the end of one's tether** without further resource, **be the end of** to cause the death of (often a coll. exaggeration); **end up** to arrive or find oneself eventually or finally: to finish (with, by): to become in the end; **get hold of the wrong end of the stick** to misunderstand blunderingly; **in the end** after all· at last; **keep one's end up** to maintain one's part; **loose end** (often in *pl.*) an unsettled matter, **make both ends meet** to live within one's income (both ends meaning both ends of the year), **no end** (*coll*) very much; **on end** erect. at a stretch, **the end the last straw**· the limit; **the end of the road** the point beyond which one can no longer continue or survive. [O.E. *ende*]

endamoeba. See **entamoeba.**

endanger in-*dān'jər, v t.* to place in danger· to expose

to loss or injury.—*ns* **endan'gerer; endan'germent** hazard, peril. [Pfx **en-** (1b)]

endear in-*dēr', v.t.* to make dear or more dear.—*adj.* **endear'ing** arousing affection —*adv.* **endear'ingly.**—*n.* **endear'ment** a caress or utterance of love. [Pfx. **en-** (1b).]

endeavour ın-*dev'ər, v.i.* to strive. to attempt.—*n.* an attempt or trial [From such phrases as to *put oneself in devoir* do what one can,—Fr *en,* ın, *devoir,* duty.]

endemic en-*dem'ık, adj* prevalent or regularly found in a people or a district confined to a particular area (*biol.*).—*n.* a disease constantly or generally present ın a place.—*adv.* **endem'ically.**—*ns.* **endemicity** (*-is't-ti*), **en'demism** the state of being endemic; **endemiol'ogy** (*-dem-,* or *-dēm-*) the scientific study of endemic diseases [Gr. *endēmios*—en, in, and *dēmos,* a people, a district.]

endermic en-*dûrm'ik, adj.* through or applied directly to the skin. [Gr *en,* ın, *derma,* şkın.]

endive *en'div, -dīv, n.* a salad plant (*Cichorium endıvıa*) of the chicory genus: loosely, chicory. [Fr., —L. *intubus.*]

endo- en'*dō-, en-do'-,* in composition, inside, often interchanging with **endo-** and opp. to **ecto-, exo-.**—*n* **en'doblast** (Gr. *blastos,* a shoot, bud) the inner cell-layer of a gastrula, the hypoblast.—*adjs.* **endocar'-diac, endocar'dial** within the heart.—*ns.* **endocar-di'tis** inflammation of the endocardium, esp. over the valves; **endocar'dium** (Gr *kardiâ,* heart) the lining membrane of the heart; **en'docarp** (Gr. *karpos,* fruit; *bot.*) a differentiated innermost layer of the pericarp, usu. hard, as a plum stone.—*adjs.* **endocrī'nal; en'do-crine** (or *-krın;* Gr. *krīnein,* to separate; *physıol.*) secreting internally: applied esp. to certain glands that pour secretions ınto the blood (also *n.*); **endocri-nic** (*-krin'ık*).—*ns.* **endocrinol'ogy** the science of the discharge of ductless glands; **en'doderm** (Gr *derma,* skın) the inner layer of cells in a gastrula: the tissues derived from that layer.—*adjs.* **endoderm'al, endo-derm'ic.**—*ns.* **endoderm'is** a close-set sheath, one cell thick, enclosing the central cylinder in plants.—*adjs.* **endogamic** (*-gam'ık*), **endogamous** (*-dog'ə-məs*).—*ns.* **endogamy** (en-*dog'əm-i;* Gr. *gamos,* marriage) the custom forbidding marriage outside one's own group: inbreeding: pollination between two flowers on the same plant: the union of female gametes; **en'dogen** (*-jen;* Gr. *genēs,* born; *obs.*) any plant, including the monocotyledons, regarded as growing from within.—*adjs.* **endogen'ic** pertaining to the processes of change within the earth; **endogenous** (en-*doj'i-nəs*) increası.,g by internal growth: formed within: (of depression) with no external cause.—*ns.* **endog'eny; en'dolymph** the fluid within the membranous labyrinth of the ear. —*adj.* **endomēt'rial.**—*ns* **endometri'tis** inflammation of the endometrium; **endomētrió'sis** (a condition caused by) the presence of active endometrial tissue where it should not be, esp when affecting other organs of the pelvic cavity, **endomēt'rium** (Gr. *mētra,* womb) the mucous membrane lining the cavity of the uterus; **en'domorph** (Gr. *morphē,* form) a mineral enclosed within another mineral, the latter being termed a perimorph: a person of rounded build.—*adj.* **endomorph'ic.**—*ns.* **endomorph'y; endopar'asite** an internal parasite —*n* **endophyte** (*en'dō-fīt;* Gr. *phyton,* a plant) a plant living within another, whether parasitically or not.—*adj.* **endophytic** (*-fit'ik*).—*n.* en'doplasm the inner portion of the cytoplasm of a cell.—*adjs.* **endoplas'mic, endoplas'-tic.**—*n.* **endoradiosonde'** an electronic device put within the body to send out information about a bodily function such as, e g. digestion —*ns* en'do-**sarc** (Gr. *sarx, sarkos,* flesh) endoplasm, en'doscope

(Gr. *skopeein*, to look) an instrument for viewing the cavities of internal organs.—*adj.* **endoscopic** (-*skop'ik*).—*n.* **endoscopy** (*en-dos'kə-pı*)—*adj* **endoskel'etal.**—*ns.* **endoskel'eton** the internal skeleton or framework of the body; **en'dosperm** (Gr *sperma*, seed) in a seed, nutritive tissue formed from the embryo-sac.—*adj.* **endosper'mic.**—*n.* **en'dospore** (Gr *sporos*, seed) the innermost layer of a sporewall: a spore formed within a mother-cell —*adj* **endotherm'ic** (Gr. *thermē*, heat) accompanied by, characterised by, or formed with absorption of heat [Gr. *endon*, or *endō*, within]

endorphin *en-dor'fin*, *n* any of a group of opiate-like substances produced by the brain and the pituitary gland with pain-killing, etc properties similar to morphine. [**endo-** and **morphine.**]

endorse, indorse *in-dörs'*, *v.t.* to write on the back of (esp one's signature, a note of contents, a record of an offence): to assign by writing on the back of· to give one's sanction to: to express approbation of to do so as a form of advertising, usu in return for money —*adj* **endors'able.**—*ns* **endorsee'** (*en*-) the person to whom a bill, etc , is assigned by endorsement; **endorse'ment** the act of endorsing: that which is written on the back: a sanction: a record of a motoring offence on a driving licence: an additional clause on a policy altering the coverage in some way (*insurance*); **endors'er.** [M E. *endosse*—O Fr. *endosser*; changed under the influence of L L *in-dorsāre*—*in*, on, *dorsum*, the back.]

endosarc .. to .. **endothermic.** See **endo-**.

endow *in-dow'*, *v.t.* to give a dowry or marriage portion to: to settle a permanent provision on: to provide permanent means of support for: to enrich with any gift or faculty: to present.—*adj* **endowed'** having (a gift, faculty, etc.) (with *with*).—*ns.* **endow'er; endow'ment** the act of endowing: that which is settled on any person or institution: a quality or faculty bestowed on anyone.—**endowment assurance, insurance** a form of insurance providing for the payment of a certain sum at a certain date or at death if earlier. [Fr *en* (—L *in*), *douer*, to endow—L *dōtāre*—*dōs, dōtis*, a dowry.]

endue, indue *in-dū'*, *v.t.* to invest with: to supply [O.Fr. *enduire*—L. *indūcĕre*—*in*, into, *dūcĕre*, to lead, influenced by *induĕre*, to put on.]

endure *in-dūr'*, *v.t.* to remain firm under. to bear without sinking: to tolerate.—*v.i.* to remain firm: to last.—*adj.* **endur'able.**—*ns.* **endur'ableness.**—*adv.* **endur'ably.**—*ns.* **endur'ance** the state or power of enduring or bearing: a suffering patiently without sinking: patience: lasting quality: maximum performance under given conditions; **endur'er.**—*adj* **endur'ing** lasting.—*adv.* **endur'ingly.** [O.Fr. *endurer*—L *indūrāre*—*in*, in, *dūrus*, hard.]

en effet *ā-ne-fe*, (Fr.) in effect: in fact.

enema *en'i-mə*, *n.* a fluid injected into the rectum: the process of injecting such a fluid:—*pl.* **en'emas, ene'mata.** [Gr. *enēma, -atos—enienai*, to send in]

enemy *en'i-mi*, *n.* one who hates or dislikes, or who is hated or disliked: a foe· a hostile force· something which is harmful to or which acts against (*fig*).—*adj* hostile —**how goes the enemy?** (*coll.*) what time is it?, **the enemy, the old enemy** the Devil. [O.Fr *enemi* (Fr. *ennemi*)—L *inimícus—in-*, neg., *amícus*, a friend.]

energumen *en-ər-gū'mən*, *n* one possessed· a demoniac. [L.L. *energūmenus*—Gr *en*, in, *ergon*, work]

energy *en'ər-ji*, *n.* the power of doing work: the power exerted: vigorous activity. vigour. forcefulness. the capacity of a material body or of radiation to do work (*phys.*).—*adjs* **energet'ic, -al** having, requiring, or showing energy: active: forcible· effective —*adv*

energet'ically.—*v t* **en'ergise, -ize** to give strength or active force to: to stimulate to activity.—*v t* to act with force.—**energy gap** the amount by which energy requirements exceed the energy supply. [Gr *energeia—en*, in, *ergon*, work]

enervate *en'ər-vāt*, *v t* to deprive of nerve, strength, or courage: to weaken.—*adj.* weakened. spiritless — *adjs* **en'ervating, en'ervative.**—*n* **enervā'tion.** [L. *ēnervāre, -ātum—ē*, out of, *nervus*, a nerve.]

en face *ā fas*, (Fr.) in front. opposite straight in the face: facing forward

en famille *ā fa-mē-y'*, (Fr) amongst the family, as at a family gathering, at home, without ceremony

enfant *ā-fā*, (Fr), *n.* a child.—**enfant gâté** (*ga-tä*) a spoilt child (fem **gâtée**); **enfant terrible** (*te-rē-bl'*) a precocious child whose sayings embarrass his elders· a person whose behaviour, etc is indiscreet, embarrassing to his associates, or (*loosely*) unconventional

enfeeble *in-fē'bl*, *v t* to make feeble· to weaken —*n* **enfee'blement** weakening. weakness [Pfx. **en-** (1b).]

enfeoff *in-fef'*, *en-fēf'*, *v t* to invest with a possession in fee: to surrender —*n* **enfeoff'ment** the act of enfeoffing: the deed which invests with the fee of an estate [O Fr *enfeffer—en-*, and *fief*]

en fête *ā fet*, (Fr) in festivity· keeping, dressed for, etc. a holiday

enfilade *en-fi-lād'*, *n* a fire that rakes a line or position from end to end (*mil*).—*v t.* to rake with shot through the whole length of a line. [Fr. *enfiler—en* (L *in*), and *fil*—L *fílum*, a thread.]

enfold, infold *in-fōld'*, *v.t.* to wrap up: to encompass. —*n* **enfold'ment.** [Pfx **en-** (1a).]

enforce *in-förs'*, *-fors'*, *v t.* to put in force: to give effect to: to urge· to compel.—*adj.* **enforce'able.**—*adv.* **enforce'dly.**—*n.* **enforce'ment.**—**enforcement notice** (*law*) an order served on one who has breached town-planning regulations; **enforcement officer; enforcement work.** [O.Fr *enforcer—en* (L. *in*), and *force*.]

enfranchise, -ize *in-fran'chīz, -shīz*, *v t* to set free: to give a franchise or political privileges to.—*n.* **enfran'chisement** (*-chiz-, -shiz-*) [O Fr *enfranchir—en*, and *franc*, free, see **franchise.**]

engage *in-gāj'*, *v t* to bind by a gage or pledge· to secure for service· to enlist: to win over, attract: to betroth· to bespeak, reserve: to hold or occupy: to enter into contest: to fasten (*archit.*): to interlock — *v.i.* to pledge one's word: to become bound: to take part: to occupy or busy oneself: to enter into conflict —*adj.* **engaged'** pledged: promised, esp. in marriage: taken, booked, or bespoke. occupied: partly built or sunk into, or so appearing (*archit.*)· geared together, interlocked: of literature or writer, committed (cf **engagé**).—*ns.* **engage'ment** the act of engaging the state of being engaged· that which engages: betrothal· promise: appointment: employment: a fight or battle: commitment (cf. **engagé**).—*adj.* **engag'ing** winning. attractive —*adv.* **engag'ingly.**—*n.* **engag'ingness.—engage'ment-ring** a ring given in token of betrothal, esp. by the man to the woman —**engage for** to answer for. [Fr *engager—en gage*, in pledge, see **gage.**]

engagé *ā-ga-zhā'*, *adj* committed to a point of view, or to social or political action.—*n* **engagement** (*ā-gazh-mā*; sometimes *in-gāj'mənt*) commitment [Fr]

en garçon *ā gar-sɔ̃*, (Fr) like a bachelor: in bachelor style

en garde *ā gard*, (Fr) in fencing, a warning to assume a defensive position in readiness for an attack

engender *in-jen'dər*, *v t* to beget: to bear to breed· to sow the seeds of to produce —*v t* to be caused or produced. [Fr. *engendrer*—L. *ingenerāre*—*in*, and *generāre*, to generate.]

engine *en'jin*, *n.* a mechanical contrivance, esp. a complex piece of machinery in which power is applied to do work: a locomotive: a military machine: a device, contrivance: a person used as a tool (*arch.*).—*v.t.* to equip with an engine or engines.—*n.* **engineer'** one who designs or makes, or puts to practical use, engines or machinery of any type, including electrical: one who designs or constructs public works, such as roads, railways, sewers, bridges, harbours, canals, etc.: one who constructs or manages military fortifications, etc. (*hist.*): a soldier of a division of an army called Engineers, concerned with entrenching, road-making, etc.: an officer who manages a ship's engines: an engine-driver (esp. *U.S.*): one who contrives to bring about (with *of*).—*v.i.* to act as engineer.—*v t.* to arrange, contrive: to manoeuvre, guide.—*ns.* **engineer'ing** the art or profession of an engineer; **enginery** (*en'jin-ri*) the art of managing engines: engines collectively: machinery.—**en'gine-driver** a workman who controls an engine, esp. a railway locomotive; **en'gine-room** the room in a vessel in which the engines are; **en'gine-turning** a kind of ornament made by a rose-engine, as on the backs of watches, etc. [O.Fr. *engin*—L. *ingenium*, skill; see **ingenious**.]

engird *in-gûrd'*, *v.t.* to gird round: to encircle: *pa.p.* and *pa.t.* **engirt'.**—*v.t.* **engir'dle.** [Pfx. en- (1a).]

English *ing'glish*, *adj.* belonging to England or its inhabitants: of or relating to English.—*n.* the English people (as *pl.*): a Germanic language spoken in the British Isles, U.S.A., most parts of the British Commonwealth, etc.: 14-point type.—*v.t.* to translate into English.—*ns.* **Eng'lander** an Englishman; **Englishism** (esp. *U.S.*) an expression or idiom originating in or found only in the English of England or Britain: a custom or practice peculiar to England; **Eng'lishman** a native or naturalised inhabitant of England:—*fem.* **Eng'lishwoman.**—**Early English** often means Early Middle English: (*archit.*), see **early**; **English breakfast** a cooked breakfast, usu. consisting of several dishes or courses (cf. *continental breakfast*); **English flute** the recorder; **English horn** the cor anglais; **little Englander** an opponent of British imperialism and empire-building; **Middle English** from about 1100 or 1150 A.D. till about 1500; **Modern English** from about 1500 onwards; **Old English** a kind of type—black-letter: the English language down to about 1100 or 1150 A.D. (formerly, and still popularly, *Anglo-Saxon*).—**in plain English** in clear, simple language. [O.E. *Englisc*—*Engle*, Angles.]

engorge *in-görj'*, *v.t.* to glut.—*adj.* **engorged'** filled to excess (with blood, etc.).—*n.* **engorge'ment.** [Pfx. en- (1c).]

engraft *in-gräft'*, *v.t.* to graft: to insert: to join on (to something already existing): to fix deeply.—*ns.* **engrafta'tion** (*en-*); **engraft'ment.** [Pfx. en- (1a).]

engrail *in-grāl'*, *v.t.* to border with fine semicircular indents (*her.*).—*n.* **engrail'ment.** [O.Fr. *engresler* (Fr. *engrêler*)—*gresle*, slender—L. *gracilis*.]

engrain, ingrain *in-grān'*, *v.t.* to dye of a fast or lasting colour: to dye in the raw state: to infix deeply.—*adj.* **engrained'**, more often **ingrained'** (or *in'*), dyed in grain: deeply coloured or permeated: inveterate (e.g. *engrained laziness*): thorough-going (*fig.*).—*n.* **engrain'er.** [Orig. to dye in grain, i.e , with grain; see **grain**.]

engram *en'gram*, less often **engramma** *en-gram'ə*, *ns.* a permanent impression made by a stimulus or experience: a stimulus impression supposed to be inheritable: a memory trace.—*adj.* **engrammat'ic.** [Ger.

Engramm—Gr. *en*, in, *gramma*, that which is written.]

engrave *in-grāv'*, *v.t.* to cut with a graver on wood, steel, etc.: to cut into: to impress deeply: to form or represent by engraving:—*pa.p.* **engraved', engrav'en.**—*ns.* **engrav'er; engrav'ing** the act or art of cutting or incising designs on metal, wood, etc., for the purpose of printing impressions from them—in metal, the lines to be printed are sunk or incised; in wood, the lines to be printed appear in relief, the wood between them being cut away: an impression taken from an engraved plate: a print. [Pfx. en- (1a) and **grave¹**.]

engross *in-grōs'*, *v.t.* to monopolise: to take wholly to oneself: to absorb the whole attention or powers of: to copy in a large hand or in distinct characters: to write in legal form.—*adj.* **engrossed'.**—*n.* **engross'er.**—*adj.* **engross'ing** monopolising: absorbing.—*n.* **engross'ment** buying up wholesale: that which has been engrossed: a fair copy.—**engrossing a deed** writing it out in full and regular form for signature. [Fr. *en gros*—L. *in*, in, *grossus*, large; see **gross**.]

engulf *in-gulf'*, *v.t.* to swallow up wholly, as in a gulf: to cause to be swallowed in a gulf.—*n.* **engulf'ment.** [Pfx. en- (1a).]

enhance *in-häns'*, *v.t.* to raise in value: to heighten: to intensify: to add to, increase: to make more important.—*v.i.* to increase: to rise in value.—*n.* **enhance'ment.**—*adj.* **enhanc'ive.**—**enhanced radiation weapon** a neutron bomb. [A.Fr. *enhauncer*, prob. from O.Fr. *enhaucer*—L. *in*, and *altus*, high; cf. **hance**.]

enharmonic, -al *en-här-mon'ik, -l*, *adjs.* pertaining to music constructed on a scale containing intervals less than a semitone: pertaining to that scale of music current among the Greeks in which an interval of 2¼ tones was divided into two quarter tones and a major third: distinguishing between those tones that are identified in equal temperament.—*adv.* **enharmon'ically.** [Gr. *enharmonikos*—*en*, in, *harmoniā*, harmony.]

enhydros *en-hī'dros*, *n.* a chalcedony nodule with water or other liquid in a cavity.—*n.* **enhy'drite** a mineral with fluid inclusions.—*adjs.* **enhydrit'ic,** **enhy'drous.** [Gr. *enydros*, containing water—*en*, in, *hydōr*, water.]

enigma *in-ig'mə*, *n.* a statement with a hidden meaning to be guessed: anything very obscure: a mysterious person or situation: a riddle.—*adjs.* **enigmat'ic, -al** (*en-*) relating to, containing, or resembling an enigma: obscure: puzzling.—*adv.* **enigmat'ically.**—*v.t.* **enig'matise, -ize** to express enigmatically or symbolically.—*ns.* **enig'matist** one who concocts or deals in riddles. [L. *aenigma*—Gr. *ainigma—ainissesthai*, to speak darkly—*ainos*, a fable.]

enisle, inisle *in-īl'*, *v t* to put on, or make into, an island: to isolate. [Pfx. en- (1a, b).]

enjambment, enjambement *in-jam(b)'mənt, ā-zhäb-mä'*, *n.* in verse, the continuation of the sense without a pause beyond the end of the line.—*v.t.* and *v.i.* **enjamb** (*in-jam'*). [Fr. *enjambement—enjamber*, to stride, encroach—*en*, in, *jambe*, leg.]

enjoin *in-join'*, *v t.* to lay upon, as an order: to order or direct with authority or urgency: (*law* and *U.S.*) to forbid, to prohibit by *injunction*.—*ns.* **enjoin'er;** **enjoin'ment.** [Fr. *enjoindre*—L. *injungēre*—*in*, and *jungēre*, to join.]

enjoy *in-joi'*, *v.t.* to joy or delight in: to feel or perceive with pleasure: to possess or use with satisfaction or delight: to have the use of: (usu. of a man) to have sexual intercourse with (*arch.*).—*adj.* **enjoy'able** capable of being enjoyed: giving pleasure, delightful.—*n* **enjoy'ableness.**—*adv.* **enjoy'ably.**—*ns.* **enjoy'er; enjoy'ment** the state or condition of enjoying: the satisfactory possession or use of anything: pleasure: happiness.—**enjoy oneself** to feel pleasure, have a pleasant time. [O.Fr. *enjoier*, to give joy to—*en* (L. *in*), *joie*, joy; or O.Fr *enjoir*, to enjoy—*en*, and *joir*—L. *gaudēre*, to rejoice.]

enkephalin(e) *en-kef'ə-lin, n.* a chemical found in small quantities in the brain, which relieves pain and can now be produced synthetically. [Gr. *en*, in, *kephalē*, head.]

enkindle *in-kin'dl, v.t.* to kindle or set on fire: to inflame: to rouse.—*adj.* **enkin'dled.** [Pfx. en- (1c).]

enlace *in-lās', v.t.* to encircle: to embrace: to entwine. —*n* **enlace'ment.** [Pfx. en- (1c).]

enlarge *in-larj' v.t.* to increase in size or quantity: to expand: to amplify: to reproduce on a larger scale (esp. of a photograph).—*v.i.* to grow large or larger: to be diffuse in speaking or writing: to expatiate —*adj.* **enlarged'.**—*adv.* **enlar'gedly.**—*ns.* **enlar'gedness; enlarge'ment** increase: extension: a photograph reproduced on a larger scale; **enlarg'er.** [O.Fr. *enlarger*—*en* (L. *in*), *large*, large.]

enlighten *in-līt'n, v.t.* to impart knowledge or information to: to elevate by knowledge or religion: to free from prejudice and superstition.—*n.* **enlight'enment** the act of enlightening: the state of being enlightened: (usu. with *cap.*) the spirit of the French philosophers of the 18th century, with a belief in reason and human progress and a questioning of tradition and authority. [O.E. *inlīhtan*—*in*, in, *līhtan*, to light; or independently formed later.]

enlist *in-list', v.t.* to enrol: to engage as a soldier, etc : to employ in advancing an object.—*v.i* to engage in public service, esp. as a soldier: to enter heartily into a cause.—*n.* **enlist'ment.**—**enlisted man** (*U S.*) a member of the armed forces below the rank of warrant officer, other than a cadet or midshipman. [Pfx. en- (1a).]

enliven *in-līv'n, v.t.* to put life into: to excite or make active: to make sprightly or cheerful: to animate.— *ns.* **enliv'ener; enliv'enment.** [Pfx. en- (1b).]

en masse *ä mas,* (Fr.) in a body: all together

enmesh *in-mesh', v.t.* to catch in a mesh or net: to entangle. [Pfx. en- (1a).]

enmity *en'mi-ti, n* the quality of being an enemy: unfriendliness: ill-will: hostility. [O.Fr. *enemistié*—L. *inimīcus*; see **enemy**.]

ennea- *en'i-ə-,* in composition, nine.—*n.* **ennead** (*en'i-ad;* Gr. *enneas, -ados*) the number nine: a set of nine things.—*adj.* **ennead'ic.**—*n.* **enn'eagon** (*-ə-gon;* Gr. *gōniä,* angle) a polygon with nine angles.—*adj.* **enneagonal** (*-ag'ən-l*). [Gr. *ennea,* nine.]

ennoble *i-nō'bl, v.t.* to make noble: to elevate, distinguish: to raise to nobility.—*n.* **enno'blement** the act of making noble: that which ennobles. [Fr. *ennoblir* —Fr. *en* (L. *in*), and *noble.*]

ennui *ä-nwē', on'wē, on-wē', n.* a feeling of weariness or languor: boredom: the occasion of ennui —*v.t.* (found mostly as *pa.p.*) to weary: to bore:—*pr.p* **ennuying;** *pa.t.* and *pa.p.* **ennuied, ennuyed.**—*adj* **ennuyé** (Fr.; *-yä*), bored. [Fr., distress—O.Fr. *anoi* —L. *in odiō,* as *in odiō habeō,* I hold in hatred, i e I am tired of; see **annoy.**]

enormous *i-nor'məs, adj.* immense: huge.—*n.* **enor'mity** a great crime: great wickedness: outrage: hugeness.—*adv.* **enor'mously.**—*n.* **enor'mousness.** [L. *ēnormis—ē,* out of, *norma,* rule.]

enosis *en'ō-sis, en-ō'sis, n.* union, the aim and rallying-cry of the Greek Cypriot movement for union with Greece [Gr. (anc. and mod.) *henosis—heis, henos,* one.]

enough *i-nuf', adj.* as much as need be: sufficient: giving content: satisfying want.—*adv.* sufficiently: quite: fairly: tolerably: used in phrases which stress or

admit the state of something, as in *oddly enough, fair enough* —*n* as much as satisfies desire or want: a sufficient degree or extent. [O.E. *genōh* (nom., neut. accus., and adv., for earlier *genōg*).]

enow *i-now', (arch.) adj* and *adv.* enough: formerly used as plural of enough. [O.E *genōg* (*genōh*), with *g* preserved in inflective forms; cf. **enough.**]

en papillote *ä pa-pē-yot,* (Fr.) (of food) cooked and served in an envelope of oiled paper or foil.

en passant *ä-pa-sä,* (Fr) in passing: by the way: applied in chess to the taking of a pawn that has just passed two squares as if it had moved only one.

en pension *ä-pä-syō,* (Fr.) at a fixed rate for board and lodging.

en plein air *ä ple-ner,* (Fr.) in the open air.

en plein jour *ä plē zhōōr,* (Fr.) in broad daylight.

en poste *ä post,* (Fr) of a diplomat, resident at a place in an official capacity.

en principe *ä prē-sēp,* (Fr.) in principle.

enprint *en'print, n.* an enlarged photographic print, e.g. $5 \times 3\frac{1}{2}$ in.

en prise *ä prēz,* (Fr.) (of a pawn in chess) exposed to capture.

enquire. See **inquire.**

enrage *in-rāj', v t.* to make angry.—*adj.* **enraged'** angered: furious.—*n.* **enrage'ment.** [O.Fr *enrager*—*en* (L. *in*), and *rage,* rage.]

en rappel *ä ra-pel,* (Fr.) of a method of descent in mountaineering using a rope which is easily pulled free after descent. [Fr.,—*rappel,* recall.]

en rapport *ä ra-pòr,* (Fr.) in direct relation: in close touch or sympathy.

enrapture *in-rap'char, v.t.* to put in rapture or ecstasy: to transport with pleasure or delight.—*adjs.* **enrap'tured, enrapt'** in ecstasy. [Pfx en- (1a).]

en règle *ä re-gl',* (Fr.) in due order: according to rule.

en retraite *ä ra-tret,* (Fr.) in retirement: on half-pay.

en revanche *ä ra-väsh,* (Fr.) in return or requital.

enrich *in-rich', v.t* to make rich: to fertilise: to adorn: to enhance: to increase the proportion of some valuable substance in: to increase the proportion of one or more particular isotopes in a mixture of the isotopes of an element, e g. to raise the proportion of fissile nuclei above that for natural uranium in reactor fuel. —*n.* **enrich'ment.** [Pfx. en- (1b).]

enrobe *in-rōb', v.t.* to dress, clothe, or invest. [Pfx. en- (1c).]

enrol, enroll *in-rōl', v.t.* to insert in a roll, list or register: to enter in a list as pupil, member, etc.: to enlist: to record.—*v.i.* to enrol oneself:—*pr p.* **enroll'ing;** *pa.t.* and *pa.p.* **enrolled'.**—*ns.* **enroll'er; enrol(l)'ment.** [O.Fr. *enroller* (Fr. *enrôler*)—*en,* and *rolle,* roll.]

en route *ä rōōt,* (Fr.) on the road, on the way: let us go: march.

ens *enz, n* an entity, as opp. to an attribute:—*pl.* **entia** (*en'shi-ə*). [L.L. *ēns,* pr p. from L *esse,* to be]

ensample *en-säm'pl, (arch.) n.* example —*v.t.* to give an example of. [O.Fr. *essample;* see **example.**]

ensanguine *in-sang'gwin, v t.* to stain or cover with blood.—*adjs.* **ensan'guinated** (esp *facet.*), **ensan'-guined** bloody. [Fr pfx. *en-,* in, L *sanguis, -inis,* blood.]

ensate *en'sāt, adj.* sword-shaped [L. *ēnsis,* sword]

ensconce *in-skons', v t.* to hide safely: to settle comfortably. [Pfx. en- (1a).]

ensemble *ä-sä-bl', n.* all parts of a thing taken together: the union of performers in a concerted number (*mus.*): the group of musicians so combining: the combined effect of the performance: a costume consisting of several (matching) garments: a group of supporting dancers, corps de ballet —Also *adj* —**tout ensemble** (*tōō-tä-*) general appearance or effect.

[Fr. *ensemble*, together—L. *in*, in, *simul*, at the same time.]

enshrine *en-shrīn'*, *v.t.* to enclose in or as in a shrine. [Pfx. **en-** (1a).]

enshroud *en-shrowd'*, *v.t.* to cover up: to cover with a shroud. [Pfx. **en-** (1a).]

ensiform *en'si-form*, *adj.* sword-shaped. [L. *ēnsis*, a sword, *fōrma*, form.]

ensign *en'sīn*, *-sīn*, *n.* a badge, sign, or mark: a sign or flag, distinguishing a nation or a regiment (see also under **blue, red, white**): one who carries the colours: until 1871, the officer of lowest commissioned rank in the British infantry: an officer of lowest commissioned rank (*U.S. navy*). [O.Fr. *enseigne*—L. *īnsignia*, pl. of *īnsigne*, a distinctive mark—*in*, and *signum*, a mark.]

ensilage *en'sil-ij*, *n.* the storing of green fodder in pits or silos.—*vs.t.* **ensile** (*en-sīl'*, or *en'sīl*), **en'silage** to store by ensilage. [Fr.,—Sp. *en*, in, and *silo*—Gr. *siros*, pit for corn.]

enslave *in-slāv'*, *v.t.* to reduce to slavery: to subject to a dominating influence.—*adj.* **enslaved'**.—*ns.* **enslave'ment** act of enslaving: state of being enslaved: slavery: bondage; **enslav'er**. [Pfx. **en-** (1b).]

ensnare *in-snār'*, *v.t.* to catch in a snare: to entrap: to entangle. [Pfx. **en-** (1a).]

ensoul *in-sōl'*, *v.t.* to animate as a soul. [Pfx. **en-** (1b).]

ensphere *in-sfēr'*, *v.t.* to enclose or place in a sphere: to give a spherical form to. [Pfx. **en-** (1a).]

ensue *in-sū'*, *v.i.* to follow, to come after: to result (with *from*):—*pr.p.* **ensū'ing;** *pa.t.* and *pa.p.* **ensūed'**. [O.Fr. *ensuir* (Fr. *ensuivre*)—L. *in*, after—L. *sequī*, to follow.]

en suite *ä swēt*, (Fr.) in succession or connected series: forming a unit, or a set (not in Fr.).

ensure *in-shōōr'*, *v.t.* to make sure. to make safe. [See **insure**.]

enswathe *in-swādh'*, *v.t.* to wrap.—*n.* **enswathe'ment**. [Pfx. **en-** (1c).]

entablature *en-tab'lə-chər*, *n.* in classic architecture, that part which surmounts the columns and rests upon the capitals: an engine framework upon columns. [It. *intavolatura—in*, in, *tavola*—L. *tabula*, a table.]

entablement *in-tā'bl-mənt*, *n.* a platform above the dado on a pedestal, on which a statue rests: an entablature. [Fr.]

entail *in-tāl'*, *v.t.* to settle on a series of heirs, so that the immediate possessor may not dispose of the estate: to bring on as an inevitable consequence.—*n.* the settlement of an entailed estate: an estate entailed: the transmission, or the rule of descent, of an estate.—*ns.* **entail'er; entail'ment** the act of entailing: the state of being entailed. [Pfx. **en-** (1a), and **tail²**.]

entamoeba *en-tə-mē'bə*, *n.* any amoeba of the genus *Entamoeba*, one of the species of which causes amoebic dysentery in man.—Also **endamoe'ba**. [**ento-, endo-** and **amoeba**.]

entangle *in-tang'gl*, *v.t.* to twist into a tangle, or so as not to be easily separated: to involve in complications or in an embarrassing or a compromising situation: to perplex: to ensnare.—*n* **entang'lement** a confused state: perplexity. a tangled obstacle: a tangle: an entangling connection. [Pfx. **en-** (1c).]

entasis *en'tə-sis*, (*archit.*) *n.* the slightly swelling outline of the shaft of a column or the like. [Gr. *entasis* —*en*, in, *tasis*, a stretch.]

entelechy *en-tel'ə-ki*, (*philos.*) *n.* actuality· distinctness of realised existence: a vital principle supposed by vitalists to direct processes in an organism towards realisation of a certain end. [Gr. *entelecheia—en*,

in, telos, perfection, end, *echein*, to have.]

entellus *en-tel'əs*, *n.* the hanuman monkey of India. [App. from *Entellus* the old Sicilian in *Aeneid*, book V, from its old-mannish look.]

entente *ä-tāt*, *n.* an understanding: a friendly agreement or relationship between states—as the **entente cordiale** (*kör-dē-äl'*) between Britain and France (1904). [Fr.]

enter *en'tər*, *v i* to go or come in: to penetrate: to come upon the stage: to take possession: to become a member: to put down one's name (as competitor, candidate, etc.): to become a party or participator.— *v.t.* to come or go into: to penetrate: to join or engage in: to begin: to put into: to enrol or record: to admit: to inscribe or cause to be inscribed: to register (as a vessel leaving a port, a horse for a race, a pupil for a school, etc.): to insert a record of: to initiate: to become a member of: to take possession of.—*adj.* **en'terable.**—*n.* **en'terer.**—*n.* and *adj.* **en'tering.**— **enter into** to become a party to: to be interested in: to participate actively or heartily in: to understand sympathetically: to take up the discussion of: to be part of; **enter on, upon** to begin: to engage in. [Fr. *entrer* —L. *intrāre*, to go into, related to *inter*, between.]

enter(o)- *en'tər(-ō)-*, in composition, intestine.—*adjs.* **en'teral** pertaining to, within, or by way of, the intestine; **en'terate** having an alimentary canal.—*n.* **enterec'tomy** (Gr. *ektomē*, a cutting out) surgical removal of part of the bowel.—*adj.* **enteric** (*en-ter'ik*) pertaining to the intestines: possessing an alimentary canal.—*n.* enteric fever (**enteric fever** typhoid fever, an infectious disease due to a bacillus, characterised by fever, rose-red rash, enlargement of the spleen and ulceration of the intestines).—*ns.* **enteri'tis** inflammation of the intestines, esp. the small intestine; **en'teron** in coelenterates, the body-cavity: in higher animals, the gut or alimentary canal: —*pl.* **en'tera; enteros'tomy** (Gr. *stoma*, mouth) surgical formation of an opening in the intestine; **enterot'omy** incision of the intestinal wall; **entero-vi'rus** any of several viruses occurring in and infecting the intestine. [Gr. *enteron*, gut.]

enterprise *en'tər-prīz*, *n.* an undertaking: a bold or dangerous undertaking: readiness, initiative, and daring in undertaking: a business concern.—*v.t.* to undertake.—*n.* **en'terpriser** an entrepreneur.—*adj.* **en'terprising** forward in undertaking: adventurous: full of initiative.—*adj.* **en'terprisingly.** [O.Fr. *entreprise*, pa.p. of *entreprendre—entre*, between (L. *inter*), and *prendre*—L. *praehendēre*, to seize.]

entertain *en-tər-tān'*, *v.t.* to provide lodging or refreshment for: to treat hospitably: to hold the attention or thoughts of: to hold the attention of pleasurably: to amuse: to receive and take into consideration: to keep or hold in the mind.—*n.* **entertain'er** one who gives or offers entertainment in any sense: one who gives amusing performances professionally.—*adj.* **entertain'ing** affording entertainment: amusing.— Also *n.*—*adv.* **entertain'ingly.**—*n.* **entertain'ment** the act of entertaining: the reception of and provision for guests: hospitality at table: that which entertains: amusement· a performance or show intended to give pleasure. [Fr. *entretenir*—L. *inter*, among, *tenēre*, to hold.]

entêté *ä-te-tā*, (Fr.) *adj.* infatuated: opinionative:— *fem.* **entêtée.**

enthalpy *en-thal'pi*, *en'thəl-pi*, *n.* the heat content of a substance per unit mass. [Gr. *enthalpein*, to warm in]

enthetic *en-thet'ik*, *adj.* (of diseases, etc) introduced from without. [Gr *enthetikos—entithenai*, to put in]

enthrall, enthral *in-throl'*, *v.t.* to bring into thraldom

or bondage· to hold in thrall: to hold spellbound:—
pr.p. **enthrall'ing;** *pa.t.* and *pa.p* **enthralled'.—***n.*
[Pfx. **en-** (1a).]
enthrone *in-thrōn'*, *v t* to place on a throne: to exalt to
the seat of royalty: to install as bishop: to exalt.—*ns*
enthrone'ment, enthronisā'tion, -z- the act of
enthroning or of being enthroned.—*v.t.* **enthrō'nise,
-ize** (or *en'*) to enthrone, as a bishop: to exalt. [Pfx
en- (1a)]
enthusiasm *in-, en-thū'zi-azm*, or *-thōō'*, *n* intense interest: passionate zeal.—*v.t* and *v.i.* **enthuse'** (back-
formation) to make, be, become, or appear enthusiastic.—*n.* **enthu'siast** one filled with enthusiasm.—
adjs. **enthusias'tic, -al** filled with enthusiasm. zealous: ardent.—*adv.* **enthusias'tically.** [Gr *enth-
ousiasmos*, a god-inspired zeal—*enthousiazein*, to be
inspired by a god—*en*, in, *theos*, a god.]
enthymeme *en'thi-mēm*, *n.* an argument of probability
only (*rhet.*): a syllogism in which one premise is
suppressed (*logic*).—*adj.* **enthymemat'ical.** [Gr.
enthȳmēma, a consideration—*enthȳmeesthai*, to consider—*en*, in, *thȳmos*, the mind.]
entia. See ens.
entice *in-tīs'*, *v.t.* to induce by exciting hope or desire.
to tempt: to lead astray.—*adj.* **entice'able.—***ns.*
entice'ment the act of enticing: that which entices or
tempts: allurement; **entic'er.—***n.* and *adj.* **entic'ing.**
—*adv.* **entic'ingly.** [O.Fr. *enticier*, provoke; prob.
related to L. *titiō*, a brand.]
entire *in-tīr'*, *adj.* whole: complete: unmingled. intact:
unimpaired: not castrated (esp of a horse): with
untoothed and unlobed margin (*biol.*).—*n.* the
whole: completeness: a stallion: porter or stout as
delivered from the brewery—*adv.* **entire'ly.—***n.*
entire'ness, enti'rety completeness: the whole.—**in
its entirety** in its completeness: (considered, taken,
etc.) as a whole. [O.Fr. *entier*—L. *integer*, whole,
from *in-*, not, and root of *tangĕre*, to touch.]
entitle *en-tī'tl*, *v t.* to give a title to: to style: to give a
right or claim to —*n.* **enti'tlement.** [O Fr *entiteler*
—L.L. *intitulāre*—*in*, in, *titulus*, title.]
entity *en'ti-ti*, *n* being, existence: something with
objective reality: an abstraction or archetypal conception. [L.L. *entitās*, *-ātis*—*ēns*; see **ens.**]
ento- *en'tō-, en-to', ent- ent-*, in composition, inside,
often interchanging with **endo-** and opp. to **ecto-,
exo-.—***n* **en'toblast** endoderm: a cell nucleolus;
en'toderm endoderm.—*adj.* **entophytal** (*-fī'tl*).—*n.*
en'tophyte (*-fīt*) an endophyte.—*adjs.* **entophytic**
(*-fit'ik*), **entophytous** (*en-tof'i-təs* or *en-tō-fī'təs*),
entop'ic developed, etc., in the usual place; **entopt'ic**
(Gr. *ōps, ōpos*, eye) within the eyeball; **ento'tic** (Gr
ous, ōtos, ear) of the interior of the ear [Gr. *entos*,
within.]
entomb *in-tōōm'*, *v t.* to place in a tomb: to bury.—*n*
entomb'ment burial [O.Fr. *entoumber*—*en*, in,
tombe, a tomb.]
entomic *en-tom'ik*, *adj* pertaining to insects.—*adj.*
entomolog'ical.—*adv* **entomolog'ically.—***v.i* **entomol'ogise, -ize.—***ns.* **entomol'ogist** one learned in
entomology; **entomol'ogy** the science of insects.—
adj. **entomoph'agous** (Gr. *phagein*, to eat—aorist) insectivorous.—*n* **entomoph'agy** the practice of eating
insects.—*adj.* **entomoph'ilous** (Gr. *phileein*, to love)
specially adapted for pollination by insects.—*n.* **entomoph'ily** pollination by insects. adaptation to pollination by insects. [Gr. *entoma*, insects—*entomos*,
cut up—*en*, in, *tomē*, a cut.]
entophyte. to . **entotic.** See **ento-.**
entourage *ä-tōō-razh'*, *n.* surroundings: followers,
attendants. [Fr.;—*entourer*, to surround—*en*, in,
tour, a circuit]
en tout cas *ä-tōō-ka'*, a parasol that can be used as an

umbrella —**En-Tout-Cas®** a hard tennis court that
can be used in all weathers [Fr , in any case.]
entr'acte *ä-trakt'*, *n.* the interval between acts in a
play a piece of music or other performance between
acts [Fr ,—*entre*, between, *acte*, act.]
entrails *en'trālz*, *n.pl* the internal parts of an animal's
body, the bowels: the inside of anything. [O.Fr. *en-
traille*—L L. *intrālia—inter*, within.]
entrain[1] *in-trān'*, *v.t.* to put into a railway train, esp
used by troops.—*v.i* to get into a train: to take a
train.—*n* **entrain'ment.** [Pfx. **en-** (1a)] ·
entrain[2] *in-trān'*, *v.t* to transport one substance, e.g
small liquid particles, in another, e g. a vapour: to
suspend bubbles or particles in a moving fluid.—*n.*
entrain'ment. [Fr *entraîner.*]
entrain[3] *ä-trē*, (Fr) *n* liveliness, spirit.—*n.* **entraine-
ment** (*ä-tren-mä*) enthusiasm
en train *ä trē*, (Fr.) in progress.
entrammel *in-tram'l*, *v t* to trammel, fetter [Pfx
en- (1c)]
entrance[1] *en'trəns*, *n.* an act of entering a coming upon
the stage: the power or right to enter: a place of enter-
ing· a door —*n* **en'trant** one who, or that which,
enters —**entrance fee** the money paid on entering a
society, club, etc [Fr. *entrer*—L. *intrāre*, to enter.]
entrance[2] *in-, en-trans'*, *v.t* to put into a trance: to fill
with rapturous delight —*n.* **entrance'ment** a state of
trance or of excessive joy —*adj.* **entranc'ing**
charming, transporting. [Pfx **en-** (1a).]
entrap *in-trap'*, *v.t.* to catch, as in a trap: to ensnare: to
entangle —*ns.* **entrap'ment** the act of entrapping the
state of being entrapped· the act of luring a person
into the commission of a crime so that he may be
arrested and prosecuted; **entrapp'er.** [O.Fr. *en-
traper*—*en*, in, *trappe*, a trap]
entreat *in-trēt'*, *v.t* to ask earnestly to beseech: to beg
for —*v.i.* to beseech, ask —*ns* **entreat'y** the act of
entreating: earnest prayer. [O Fr *entraiter*—*en*,
and *traiter*, to treat]
entrechat *ä-tr'-sha'*, (*ballet*) *n* a leap during which a
dancer beats his heels together [Fr.,—It *intrec-
ciata*, plaited, complicated (caper).]
entrecôte *ä'tr'-kōt*, *n* a steak cut from between two
ribs.—Also *adj* [Fr]
entrée *ä', on'trä*, *n* entry, freedom of access, admit-
tance· a dish served at dinner between the chief
courses or as a substitute: an introduction or prelude
(*mus.*): the act of entering, a formal entrance, or
music for it —**entrée dish** a dish, usually silver, with a
cover, suitable for an entrée [Fr.]
entremets *ä'trə-mä, -me*, *n* any dainty served at table
between the chief courses. [O Fr. *entremes*—*entre*,
between, *mes* (Fr. *mets*), dish.]
entrench, intrench *in-trench', -trensh', v.t.* to dig a
trench around: to fortify with a ditch and parapet· to
establish in a strong position —*v.t* to encroach.—*n*
entrench'ment, intrench'ment a defensive earthwork
of trenches and parapets: any protection [Pfx **en-**
(1c).]
entre nous *ä-tr' nōō*, (Fr.) between ourselves
entrepot, entrepôt *ä'trə-pō*, *n* a storehouse: a bonded
warehouse: a seaport through which exports and
imports pass. [Fr.]
entrepreneur *ä-trə-prə-nœr'*, *n* one who undertakes an
enterprise esp. a commercial one, often at personal
financial risk a contractor or employer: an organiser
of musical or other entertainments:—*fem.* **entre-
preneuse** (*-nœz'*) —*adj* **entrepreneur'ial** (*-nœr'i-əl,
-nū', -nōō'*) —*n* **entrepreneur'ship.** [Fr]
entresol *en'tər-sol*, or *ä'tr'-sol*, *n* a low storey between
two main storeys of a building. generally between the
ground floor and the first floor [Fr.,—*entre*,
between, *sol*, the ground]

fāte; far, mē; hûr (her); *mīne, mōte, for; mūte; mōōn; fōōt, dhen* (then); *el'ə-mənt* (element)

entrism, etc. See **entryism** under **entry.**

entropy *en'trə-pi, (phys.) n.* a measure of unavailable energy, energy still existing but lost for purpose of doing work because it exists as the internal motion of molecules: a measure of the disorder of a system: a measure of heat content, regarded as increased in a reversible change by the ratio of heat taken in to absolute temperature. [Gr. *en,* in, *tropē,* turning, intended to represent 'transformation content'.]

entrust, intrust *in-trust', v.t.* to give in trust: to commit as a trust: to charge trustingly.—*n.* **entrust'ment.** [Pfx. **en-** (1c).]

entry *en'tri, n.* the act of entering in any sense: a coming upon the stage: the coming in of an instrument or performer: entrance: a narrow lane between houses *(dial.):* a lobby or vestibule: the act of committing to writing in a record: the thing so written: a list of competitors: a taking possession *(law).*—*ns.* **en'tryism, en'trism** the practice of joining a political body in sufficient numbers to swing its policy, specif. of Trotskyists, etc. in branches of the Labour Party.—*ns.* and *adjs.* **en'tryist, en'trist.**—*entry* fee entrance fee.—**card of entry** *(bridge,* etc.) a card to bring in one's hand with; **port of entry** see **port³.** [Fr. *entrée—entrer—*L. *intrāre,* to go into.]

Entryphone® *en'tri-fōn, n.* a telephonic device at the entrance to e.g. a block of flats, etc. allowing communication between individual occupiers and visitors.

entwine *in-twīn', v.t.* to interlace: to weave. [Pfx. **en-** (1c).]

entwist *in-twist', v.t.* to twist round. [Pfx. **en-** (1c).]

enucleate *in-ū'kli-āt, v.t.* to extract, e.g. a tumour, swelling, etc. *(surg.).*—*adj.* without a nucleus.—*n.* **enuclea'tion.** [L. *ēnucleāre—ē,* from, *nucleus,* a kernel.]

enumerate *i-nū'mər-āt, v.t.* to count the number of: to name over.—*n.* **enūmerā'tion** the act of numbering: a detailed account.—*adj.* **enū'merative.**—*n.* **enū'merātor** one who enumerates. [L. *ē,* from, *numerāre, -ātum,* to number.]

enunciate *i-nun's(h)i-āt, v.t.* to state formally: to pronounce distinctly: to utter.—*adj.* **enun'ciable** (*-shi-* or *-si-*)—*n.* **enunciation** (*i-nun-si-ā'shən*) the act of enunciating: the manner of uttering or pronouncing: a distinct statement or declaration: the words in which a proposition is expressed.—*adjs.* **enun'ciative** (*-si-ā-, -syā-, -sh(y)ā-,* or *-shə-*) **enun'ciatory** containing enunciation or utterance: declarative.—*n.* **enun'ciātor** one who enunciates. [L. *ēnuntiāre, -ātum—ē,* from, *nuntiāre,* to tell—*nuntius,* a messenger.]

enuresis *en-ū-rē'sis, n.* incontinence of urine.—*adj.* and *n.* **enūret'ic.** [Gr. *en,* in, *ourēsis,* urination.]

envelop *in-vel'əp, en-, v.t.* to cover by wrapping: to surround entirely: to hide.—*n.* **envelope** (*en'vəl-ōp*) that which envelops, wraps, or covers: a cover for a letter (in this sense sometimes but quite unnecessarily pronounced *on', ä'* in imitation of French): one of the coverings of a flower—calyx or corolla *(bot.):* the gas-bag of a balloon or airship: the locus of ultimate intersections of a series of curves *(math.).*—*n.* **envel'opment** a wrapping or covering on all sides. [O.Fr. *enveloper;* origin obscure.]

envenom *in-ven'əm, v.t.* to put venom into: to poison: to taint with bitterness or malice. [O.Fr. *envenimer—en,* and *venim,* venom.]

en vérité *ä vä-rē-tä,* (Fr.) in truth.

envermeil *en-vûr'mil, (Milt.) v.t.* to dye red, to give a red colour to. [O.Fr. *envermeiller—en,* in, *vermeil,* red, vermilion.]

environ *in-vī'rən, v.t.* to surround: to encircle.—*n.* **envi'ronment** a surrounding: external conditions

influencing development or growth of people, animals or plants: living or working conditions.—*adj.* **environment'al.**—*ns.* **environment'alism** the belief that environment rather than heredity is the main influence on a person's behaviour and development *(psych.):* concern about the environment and its preservation from the effects of pollution, etc ; **environment'alist** one who advocates environmentalism *(psych.):* one who is concerned with the protection of the environment, esp. from pollution.—*n. sing.* **environics** (*en-vī-ron'iks*) the study of methods of influencing behaviour by controlling environmental factors—*n.pl.* **environs** (*in-vī'rənz,* or *en'vi-*) the places that environ: the outskirts of a city: neighbourhood [Fr. *environner—environ,* around—*virer,* to turn round.]

envisage *in-viz'ij, v.t* to consider: to present to view or to mental view: to visualise.—*n.* **envis'agement.** [Fr. *envisager—en,* and *visage,* the face.]

envision *in-vizh'ən, v.t.* to see as in a vision: to visualise: to envisage [Pfx. **en-** (1c).]

envoy¹ *en'voi, n.* a messenger, esp one sent to transact business with a foreign government: a diplomatic minister of the second order—*n.* **en'voyship.** [Fr. *envoyé—*pa.p. of *envoyer,* to send.]

envoy², envoi *en'voi, n.* the concluding part of a poem or a book· the author's final words, esp. now the short stanza concluding a poem written in certain archaic metrical forms. [O.Fr *envoye—envoiier,* to send—*en voie,* on the way—L. *in,* on, *via,* a way.]

envy *en'vi, n.* a feeling of chagrin at the good looks, qualities, fortune, etc., of another: an object or person contemplated with grudging or emulous feeling. —*v.t.* to feel envy towards, or on account of: to desire with emulation or rivalry:—*pr.p.* **en'vying;** *pa.t.* and *pa.p.* **en'vied.**—*adj.* **en'viable** that is to be envied.— *n.* **en'viableness.**—*adv.* **en'viably.**—*n.* **en'vier** one who envies.—*adj.* **en'vious** feeling envy: directed by envy.—*adv.* **en'viously.**—*n.* **en'viousness.** [Fr. *envie—*L. *invidia—invidēre,* to look askance at, to envy—*in,* on, *vidēre,* to look.]

enwind *in-wīnd', v.t.* to wind about, enwrap. [Pfx. **en-** (1a).]

enwrap *in-rap', v.t.* to cover by wrapping: to enfold: to engross. [Pfx **en-** (1a).]

enwreathe *in-rēdh', v.t.* to wreathe: to envelop: to encircle, as with a wreath [Pfx. **en-** (1a).]

Enzed *en-zed', (Austr. coll.) n.* New Zealand: (also **Enzedd'er**) a New Zealander. [The abbrev NZ phonetically represented.]

enzootic *en-zō-ot'ik, adj.* of animal diseases, prevalent in a particular district or at a particular season.—*n.* a disease of this character. [Gr. *en,* in, *zōion,* animal, in imitation of *endemic.*]

enzyme *en'zīm, n* any one of a large class of protein substances produced by living cells which act as catalysts.—*adjs.* **enzymat'ic, enzym'ic.**—*ns.* **enzymol'ogist; enzymol'ogy** the scientific study of enzymes. [Gr. *en,* in, *zȳmē,* leaven.]

Eocene *ē'ō-sēn, (geol.) adj.* belonging to the oldest division of the Tertiary formation.—*n.* the Eocene system, period, or strata. [Gr. *ēōs,* daybreak, *kainos,* new—from the very small proportion of living species of molluscs among its fossils.]

Eohippus *ē'ō-hip-əs, n* the oldest known horselike animal, an Eocene fossil [Gr *ēōs,* dawn, *hippos,* horse.]

eolith *ē'ō-lith, n.* a very early roughly-broken stone implement, or one naturally formed but assumed to have been used by man.—*adj* **eolith'ic.** [Gr. *ēōs,* dawn, *lithos,* stone.]

eon. See **aeon.**

eonism *ē'ə-nizm, (psychiatry) n* adoption by a male of

female dress and manner. [Chevalier d'Éon, Fr diplomat (d. 1810), who chose female dress as a disguise.]

eosin *e'ō-sin, n.* a red dyestuff.—*adj.* **eosin'ophil** readily staining with eosin.—*n.* a type of white blood cell, so called because it is easily stained by eosin. [Gr. *ēōs*, dawn.]

Epacris *ep-ak'ris, ep'ə-kris, n.* a chiefly Australian genus of heath-like plants [Gr *epi*, upon, *akris*, a summit.]

epact *ē'pakt, n* the moon's age at the beginning of the year: the excess of the calendar month or solar year over the lunar [Fr. *épacte*—Gr. *epaktos*, brought on—*epi*, on, *agein*, to bring]

eparch *ep'ark, n.* the governor of a modern Greek province a metropolitan.—*ns* **ep'archate**, **ep'archy** the province, territory or diocese of an eparch. [Gr *eparchos*—*epi*, upon, *archē*, dominion.]

épatant *ā-pa-tā,* (Fr) *adj* wonderful, marvellous.

epaule *e-pol', n* the shoulder of a bastion —*n.* **epaule'-ment** a side-work of a battery or earthwork to protect it from a flanking fire a particular placing of a dancer's shoulders, one forward, one back (*ballet*) [Fr *épaule*, shoulder—L *spatula.*]

epaulet, epaulette *ep'əl-et, n* a shoulder-piece a badge of a military or naval officer (now disused in the British army): an ornament on the shoulder of a lady's dress. [Fr *épaulette*—*épaule*, the shoulder.]

epaxial *ep-aks'i-əl, adj.* above the axis. [Gr *epi*, on, over, and *axis*.]

épée *ā-pā', n.* a sharp-pointed, narrow-bladed sword, without a cutting edge, used for duelling, and, with a button on the point, for fencing practice [Fr.]

Epeira *ep-īr'ə, n.* a genus of spiders, the type of the **Epeir'idae**, including the common garden spider: (without *cap.*) a spider of this genus.—*n.* **epeir'id** a member of the family. [Perh Gr. *epi*, on, *eirein*, to string.]

epeirogenesis *ep-ī-rō-jen'i-sis,* (geol.) *n.* continent-building.—Also **epeirogeny** (*-roj'i-ni*).—*adjs.* **epeirogen'ic, epeirogenetic** (*-jin-et'ik*) [Gr *ēpeiros*, mainland, *genesis*, formation.]

epenthesis *e-pen'thə-sis, n.* the insertion of a sound within a word.—*adj* **epenthetic** (*-thet'ik*). [Gr.]

epergne *i-pûrn', n.* a branched ornamental centre-piece for the table. [Fr *épargne* (saving), as used in phrases *taille* or *gravure d'épargne*, metal or etching with parts left in relief.]

epexegesis *ep-eks-i-jē'sis, n* the addition of words to make the sense more clear.—*adjs.* **epexeget'ic** (*-jet'ik*), **-al.**—*adv.* **epexeget'ically.** [Gr. *epexēgēsis*—*epi*, in addition, *exēgeesthai*, to explain.]

epha, ephah *ē'fə, n.* a Hebrew measure for dry goods [Heb.; prob. of Egyptian origin.]

ephebe *ef-ēb', n.* in ancient Greece, a young male citizen from 18 to 20 years of age.—*adj.* **epheb'ic** pertaining to an ephebe: pertaining to the adult period in the life-history of an individual (*biol.*) —*n.* **ephebophilia** (*-fil'*) sexual desire for youths or adolescents. [Gr. *ephēbos*—*epi*, upon, *hēbē*, early manhood.]

Ephedra *ef'ed-ra, ef-ēd'ra, ef-ed'rə, n.* sea-grape, a genus of jointed, all but leafless desert plants of the Gnetaceae: (without *cap.*) a plant of this genus.—*n* **eph'edrine** (or *ef-ed'rin*) an alkaloid got from Ephedra or produced synthetically, used in treating hay fever, asthma, etc. [Gr. *ephedrā*, horsetail.]

Ephemera *ef-em'ər-ə,* or *-ēm', n.* a genus of insects whose adult life is very short, the mayflies: (without *cap.*) an insect of this genus: (without *cap*) that which lasts a short time (but see also **ephemeron** below):—*pl.* **ephem'eras** or **ephem'erae.**—*adj.* **ephem'eral** existing only for a day. short-lived: fleeting —*n.* anything very short-lived —*ns* **ephemeral'ity; ephem'-**

erid an insect of the mayfly family, **Ephemer'idae** (*-mer'i-dē*) —*ns.* **ephem'eris** an astronomical almanac tabulating the daily positions of the sun, moon, planets and certain stars, etc.:—*pl.* **ephemerides** (*ef-e-mer'i-dēz*); **ephem'erist** one who studies the daily motions of the planets: a student or collector of ephemera, **ephem'eron** an insect that lives only for a day: (usu. in *pl*) an object of limited worth or usefulness, having no lasting value: anything ephemeral:—*pl.* **ephem'era.** [Gr. *ephēmeros*, living a day—*epi*, for, *hēmerā*, a day]

Ephesian *ef-ē'zi-ən, -ē'zhən, adj.* of or pertaining to *Ephesus* —*n.* an inhabitant of Ephesus.

ephod *ef'od, n.* a kind of linen surplice worn by the Jewish priests. a surplice, generally [Heb. *ēphōd*—*āphad*, to put on]

ephor *ef'or, ef'ər, n* a class of magistrates whose office apparently originated at Sparta, being peculiar to the Doric states —*n* **eph'oralty.** [Gr *epi*, upon, and root of *horaein*, to see.]

epi- *ep-i-* (or **ep-** *ep-* before a vowel or *h*), *pfx.* above, over, upon, on, as *epidermis*: in addition, after, as *epiphenomenon* [Gr *epi*, on, over.]

epiblast *ep'i-blast. n.* the outer germinal layer of an embryo —*adj.* **epiblast'ic.** [Gr *epi*, upon, *blastos*, a germ, shoot.]

epic *ep'ik, adj* applied to a long narrative poem that relates heroic events in an elevated style: characteristic of an epic poem impressive large-scale.—*n.* an epic poem epic poetry as a genre. a story comparable to that of an epic poem. esp. a long adventure novel or film —*adj* **ep'ical.**—*adv.* **ep'ically.** [Gr. *epikos* —*epos*, a word]

epicalyx *ep-i-kāl'iks,* or *-kal', n.* an apparent accessory calyx outside of the true calyx, composed of bracts or of fused stipules of sepals [Gr. *epi*, on, and **calyx.**]

epicanthus *ep-i-kan'thəs, n.* a fold of skin over the inner canthus of the eye, characteristic of the Mongolian race.—*adj* **epican'thic.** [Gr *epi*, on, and **canthus.**]

epicarp *ep'i-karp,* (*bot.*) *n* the outermost layer of the pericarp or fruit. [Gr *epi*, upon, *karpos*, fruit.]

epicede *ep'i-sēd,* **epicedium** *ep-i-sē'di-əm* or *-dī', ns.* a funeral ode:—*pls.* **ep'icedes, epicē'dia.**—*adjs.* **epicē'dial, epicē'dian** elegiac. [L. *epicēdium*—Gr. *epikēdeion*—*epi*, upon, *kēdos*, care.]

epicene *ep'i-sēn, adj.* common to both sexes: having characteristics of both sexes, or neither: effeminate: of common gender (*gram.*) sometimes restricted to those words that have one grammatical gender though used for both sexes.—Also *n* [Gr. *epi*, upon, *koinos*, common.]

epicentre *ep'i-sen-tər, n.* that point on the earth's surface directly over the point of origin of an earthquake.—Also *fig* —*adj* **epicen'tral.** [Gr. *epi*, upon, over, *kentron*, a point.]

epiclesis *ep-i-klē'sis, n* in the Eastern church, an invocation of the Holy Spirit at the consecration of the elements (bread and wine). [Gr *epiklēsis*, invocation—*epikalein*, to summon.]

epicotyl *ep-i-kot'il, n.* the stem of an embryo plant or seedling between the cotyledons and the next leaf [Gr *epi*, over, and **cotyledon.**]

epicritic *ep-i-krit'ik,'adj.* (of certain sensory nerve fibres in the skin) able to discriminate accurately between small degrees of sensation. [Gr. *epikritikos*, determining—*epi*, on, *krinein*, to judge.]

epicure *ep'i-kūr, n.* a person of refined and fastidious taste, esp in food, wine, etc.—*adj* **Epicur'ean** pertaining to *Epicurus* (341–270 B.C), the Greek philosopher, who taught an atomic materialism in physics and hedonism in ethics, misrepresented by opponents as brutish sensuality: (without *cap.*) given to luxury, esp. refined luxury.—*n*. a follower of Epicurus: (without *cap*.) a hedonist, an epicure.—*n* **Epicur-ē'anism** the doctrines of Epicurus: attachment to these doctrines: epicurism.—*n*. **ep'icurism** pursuit of pleasure: fastidiousness in luxury. [L. *Epicūrus*—Gr. *Epikouros*.]

epicycle *ep'i-sī-kl, n*. a circle whose centre is carried round the circumference of another circle.—*adj*. **epi-cy'clic**.—*n*. **epicy'cloid** a curve described by a point on the circumference of a circle rolling on the outside of the circumference of another circle.—*adj*. **epicyc-loi'dal**. [Gr. *epi*, upon, *kyklos*, a circle.]

epideictic, -al *ep-i-dīk'tik, -al, adjs*. done for show or display. [Gr. *epi*, upon, *deiknynai*, to show.]

epidemic *ep-i-dem'ik, adj*. affecting a community at a certain time: prevalent.—*n*. a disease that attacks great numbers in one place, at one time, and itself travels from place to place: a widespread outbreak.—*adj*. **epidem'ical**.—*adv*. **epidem'ically**.—*adj*. **epidēm-iolog'ical** pertaining to epidemiology.—*ns* **epidēm-iol'ogy** the science of epidemics; **epidēmiol'ogist**. [Gr. *epidēmos*, general—*epi*, among, *dēmos*, the people.]

epidermis *ep-i-dûr'mis, n*. cuticle, forming an external covering of a protective nature for the true skin or corium (*zool*.): an outer sheath of close-set cells, usually one deep (*bot*.).—*adjs*. **epider'mal; epider'-mic; epiderm'oid**. [Gr. *epidermis*—*epi*, upon, *derma*, the skin.]

epidiascope *ep-i-dī'ə-skōp, n*. a lantern for projecting images of objects whether opaque or transparent. [Gr. *epi*, upon, *dia*, through, *skopeein*, to look at.]

epididymis *ep-i-did'i-mis, n*. a mass of sperm-carrying tubes at the back of the testis:—*pl* **epidid'ymides** (*-mi-dēz*). [Gr.—*epi*, upon, *didymis*, testicle.]

epidural *ep-i-dūr'əl, adj*. situated on, or administered outside, the lowest portion of the spinal canal.—*n*. short for **epidural anaesthetic**, the epidural injection of an anaesthetic, esp. in childbirth.—**epidural anaesthesia** loss of painful sensation in the lower part of the body produced by injecting an anaesthetic into the lowest portion of the spinal canal. [Gr. *epi*, upon, and **dura (mater)**.]

epifocal *ep-i-fō'kl, adj*. epicentral.

epigastrium *ep-i-gas'tri-əm, n*. the part of the abdomen extending from the sternum towards the navel—the pit of the stomach —*adj*. **epigas'tric**. [Gr. *epi*, upon, *gastēr*, the stomach.]

epigeal *ep-i-jē'əl*, **epigc'ous** *-əs*, **epige'an** *-ən, adjs*. grow-ing or living close to the ground: with cotyledons above ground. [Gr. *epigaios*—*epi*, on, *gaia, gē*, earth.]

epigene *ep'i-jēn*, (*geol*.) *adj*. acting or taking place at the earth's surface. [Fr. *épigène*—Gr. *epigenēs*, born after.]

epiglottis *ep-i-glot'is, n*. a cartilaginous flap over the glottis.—*adj*. **epiglott'ic**. [Gr. *epiglōttis*—*epi*, over, *glōttis*, glottis.]

epigon *ep'i-gon*, **epigone** *ep'i-gōn, ns*. one of a later generation:—*pls*. **ep'igons, ep'igones** (*-gōnz*), (often with *cap*.) **epig'oni** sons or successors: undistinguish-ed descendants of the great. [Gr *epi*, after, *gonē*, birth.]

epigram *ep'i-gram, n*. any concise and pointed or sarcastic saying: a short poem expressing an ingenious thought with point, usually satirical.—*adjs* **epigram-matic** (*-grəm-at'ik*), **-al** relating to or dealing in epi-grams: like an epigram: concise and pointed.—*adv* **epigrammat'ically**.—*v.t*. **epigramm'atise, -ize** to make an epigram on.—*n*. **epigramm'atist** one who writes epigrams. [Through Fr. and L , from Gr. *epi-gramma*—*epi*, upon, *gramma*, a writing—*graphein*, to write.]

epigraph *ep'i-graf, n*. an inscription, esp on a building: a citation or motto at the beginning of a book or its part —*v t*. to provide with an epigraph.—*ns*. **epi-grapher** (*ep-ig'rə-fər*), **epig'raphist**.—*adj*. **epigraph-ic** (*-graf'ik*).—*n*. **epig'raphy**. [Gr *epigraphē*—*epi*, upon, *graphein*, to write.]

epilate *ep'i-lāt, v.t*. to remove (hair) by any means —*ns* **epila'tion; ep'ilator**. [Fr. *épiler*—L *ex*, from, *pilus*, hair]

epilepsy *ep'i-lep-si, n*. a chronic functional disease of the nervous system, manifested by recurring attacks of sudden insensibility or impairment of conscious-ness, commonly accompanied by peculiar convulsive seizures.—*n*. **epilep'tic** an epileptic patient —*adj*. **epilep'tic**. [Gr. *epilēpsiā*—*epi*, upon, and root of *lambanein*, to seize]

epilimnion *ep-i-lim'ni-ən, n* the upper, warm layer of water in a lake [Gr *epi*, upon, *limnion*, dim of *limnē*, a lake.]

epilogue *ep'i-log, n*. the concluding section of a book, etc.: a short poem or speech at the end of a play. the speaker thereof: the conclusion of a radio or TV pro-gramme.—*adj*. **epilogic** (*-loj'ik*).—*n*. **epil'ogist**. [Fr.,—L. *epilogus*—Gr. *epilogos*, conclusion—*epi*, upon, *legein*, to speak.]

epimer *ep'i-mər, n*. an isomeric compound, differing from its corresponding isomer only in the relative positions of an attached hydrogen and hydroxyl.—*adj*. **epimeric** (*-mer'ik*) having the characteristics or relationship of epimers. [*epi-* and isomer.]

epinasty *ep'i-nas-ti*, (*bot*.) *n*. down-curving of an organ, caused by a more active growth on its upper side.—opp. to *hyponasty*.—*adj* **epinas'tic**.—*adv*. **epinas'tically**. [Gr *epi*, upon, *nastos*, pressed close]

epinephrine *ep-i-nef'rin, -rēn, n*. adrenaline. [Gr *epi*, upon, *nephros*, kidney.]

Epiphany *e-pif'ə-ni, n*. a church festival celebrated on 6th Jan., in commemoration of the manifestation of Christ to the wise men of the East: the manifestation of a god: a usu. sudden revelation or insight into the nature, essence or meaning of something.—*adj*. **epi-phanic** (*-fan'*). [Gr. *epiphaneia*, appearance—*epi*, to, *phainein*, to show.]

epiphenomenon *ep-i-fin-om'ən-ən, n*. an accompany-ing phenomenon, a fortuitous, less important, or irrelevant, by-product: something appearing after, a secondary symptom of a disease (*path*.):—*pl*. **epi-phenom'ena**.—*n*. **epiphenom'enalism** interpretation of mind as an epiphenomenon upon the physical.—*n*. and *adj*. **epiphenom'enalist**. [Gr. *epi*, after, *phaino-menon*, neut. pr.p. pass. of *phainein*, to show.]

epiphragm *ep'i-fram, n*. the disc with which certain molluscs close the aperture of their shell. [Gr. *epi-phragma*, covering—*epiphrassein*, to obstruct.]

epiphysis *ep-if'i-sis, n*. any portion of a bone having its own centre of ossification: the pineal gland (*epiphysis cerebri*):—*pl*. **epiph'yses**. [Gr., excrescence.]

epiphyte *ep'i-fīt, n* a plant growing on another plant, without being parasitic: a vegetable parasite on the surface of an animal (*path*.).—*adjs*. **epiphyt'al, epi-phytic** (*-fit'ik*), **-al**.—*n*. **ep'iphytism** (or *-fīt'*) the con-dition of being epiphytic: a similar relation among animals. [Gr. *epi*, upon, *phyton*, a plant.]

epirrhema *ep-i-rē'mə, n*. in Greek comedy the address of the Coryphaeus to the audience after the para-basis.—*adj* **epirrhēmat'ic**. [Gr.—*epi*, on, after, *rhēma*, word.]

episcopacy *e-pis'kə-pas-i, n*. church government by bishops. the office of a bishop: a bishop's period of office: the bishops, as a class.—*adj*. **epis'copal** governed by bishops: belonging to or vested in bish-ops —*adj*. **episcopā'lian** belonging to bishops, or

government by bishops, or to an episcopal church.—
n. one who belongs to an episcopal (especially Anglican) church.—*ns.* **episcopa'lianism, epis'-copalism** episcopalian government and doctrine.—*adv.* **epis'copally.**—*n.* **epis'copate** a bishopric: the office of a bishop: a bishop's period of office: the order of bishops. [Gr. *episkopos*, an overseer.]

episcope *ep'i-skōp, n.* a lantern for projecting images of opaque objects. [Gr. *epi*, on, over, *skopeein*, to look.]

episemon *ep-i-sē'mon, n.* a badge or characteristic device: one of three obsolete Greek letters.—*adj.* **episēmat'ic** (*zool.*) serving for recognition. [Gr. *episēmon*, a badge—*epi*, on, *sēma*, a sign.]

episiotomy *ep-iz-i-ot'ə-mi, n.* an incision made in the perinaeum to facilitate delivery of a foetus. [Gr. *epision*, pubic region, and *-tomy.*]

episode *ep'i-sōd, n.* a story introduced into a narrative or poem to give variety: an interesting incident: a passage affording relief from the principal subject (*mus.*): an incident or period detachable from a novel, play, etc.: a part of a radio or television serial which is broadcast at one time.—*adjs.* **episodic** (*-sod'*), **episōd'ical** pertaining to or contained in an episode: brought in as a digression: abounding in episodes.—*adv.* **episōd'ically** by way of episode: incidentally. [Gr. *epeisodion*—*epi*, upon, *eisodos*, a coming in.]

epistaxis *ep-i-stak'sis, n.* bleeding from the nose. [Gr. *epistazein*, to shed in drops.]

epistemology *ep-is-tə-mol'ə-ji, n.* the theory of knowledge.—Also *n.sing.* **epistemics** (*ep-i-stēm'iks*).—*adjs.* **epistemological** (*-ə-loj'*), **epistēm'ic.**—*n.* **epistemol'ogist.** [Gr. *epistēmē*, knowledge, *logos*, discourse.]

epistle *i-pis'l, n.* a writing sent to one, a letter: esp. a letter to an individual or church from an apostle, as the Epistles of Paul: the extract from one of the apostolical epistles read as part of the communion service: a verse composition in letter form.—**epistoler** (*i-pist'ə-lər*) one who reads the liturgical epistle in the communion service.—*adjs.* **epis'tolary, epis'tolatory, epistolic** (*ep-is-tol'ik*) pertaining to or consisting of epistles or letters: suitable to an epistle: contained in letters. [O.Fr.,—L. *epistola*—Gr. *epistolē*—*epi*, on the occasion of, *stellein*, to send.]

epistrophe *e-pis'trə-fē, n.* ending of successive clauses with the same word: a refrain in music. [Gr. *epistrophē*, a return—*epi*, upon, *strephein*, to turn.]

epistyle *ep'i-stīl, n.* an architrave. [Gr. *epi*, upon, *stylos*, a pillar.]

epitaph *ep'i-täf, n.* a tombstone inscription: a composition in the form of a tombstone inscription.—*n.* **ep'i-taphist** a composer of epitaphs.—*adj.* **epitaph'ic.** [Gr. *epitaphion*—*epi*, upon, *taphos*, a tomb.]

epitaxy *ep'i-tak-si, n* the growth of a thin layer of crystals on another crystal so that they have the same structure.—*adj.* **epitax'ial.** [Gr. *epi*, on, *taxis*, arrangement.]

epithalamium, epithalamion *ep-i-thə-lā'mi-əm, -on, ns.* a song or poem in celebration of a marriage:—*pl.* **epithalā'mia.**—*adj.* **epithalām'ic.** [L. *epithalamium*, Gr. *epithalamion*—*epi*, upon, *thalamos*, a bride-chamber.]

epithelium *ep-i-thē'li-əm, n.* the cell-tissue that invests the outer surface of the body and the mucous membranes connected with it, and also the closed cavities of the body.—*adj.* **epithē'lial.**—*n.* **epithēlio'ma** carcinoma of the skin.—*adj.* **epithēlio'matous.** [Mod. L.,—Gr., *epi*, upon, *thēlē*, nipple.]

epithet *ep'i-thet, n.* an adjective expressing some real quality of the thing to which it is applied: a descriptive term.—*adj.* **epithet'ic** pertaining to an epithet:

abounding with epithets. [Gr. *epitheton*, neut. of *epithetos*, added—*epi*, on, *tithenai*, to place.]

epitome *i-pit'ə-mē, n.* an abridgment or short summary of anything, as of a book: an embodiment in little: a typical example: a personification.—*adjs* **epitomic** (*ep-i-tom'ik*), **-al.**—*v.t.* **epit'omise, -ize** to make an epitome of: to shorten: to condense: to typify: to personify.—*ns.* **epit'omiser, -z-, epit'omist** one who abridges.—**in epitome** on a small scale. [Gr. *epi*, upon, *tomē*, a cut.]

epitrite *ep'i-trīt, (pros.) n.* a foot made up of three long syllables and one short. [Gr. *epitritos*—*epi*, in addition to, *tritos*, third.]

epizoon *ep-i-zō'on, n.* an animal that lives on the surface of another animal, whether parasitically or commensally:—*pl.* **epizō'a.**—*adj.* and *n.* **epizō'an.**—*adjs.* **epizō'ic** dwelling upon an animal: having seeds dispersed by animals; **epizootic** (*ep-i-zō-ot'ik*) pertaining to epizoa: affecting animals as an epidemic does mankind.—*n.* an epizootic disease.—*n.sing.* **epizoöt'ics** the science or study of epidemic animal diseases. [Gr. *epi*, upon, *zōion*, an animal.]

epoch *ēp'ok, ēp'ohh, ep'ok, n.* a point of time fixed or made remarkable by some great event from which dates are reckoned: the particular time, used as a point of reference, at which the data had the values in question (*astron.*): a planet's heliocentric longitude at the epoch (*astron.*): a precise date: a time from which a new state of things dates: an age, geological, historical, or other.—*adj.* **epochal** (*ep'ok-l*).—**ep'och-mâking** important enough to be considered as beginning a new age; **ep'och-marking.** [Gr. *epochē*—*epechein*, to stop, take up a position—*epi*, upon, *echein*, to hold.]

epode *ep'ōd, n.* a kind of lyric poem in which a longer verse is followed by a shorter one: the last part of a lyric ode.—*adj.* **epodic** (*-od'ik*). [Gr. *epōidos*—*epi*, on, *ōidē*, an ode.]

eponychium *ep-o-nik'i-əm, n.* a narrow band of cuticle over the base of a nail. [Gr. *epi*, on, *onyx, onychos*, nail.]

eponym *ep'ə-nim, n.* one who gives his name to something: a hero invented to account for the name of a place or people: a character who gives a play, etc., its title.—*adj.* **eponymous** (*i-pon'i-məs*). [Gr. *epōnymos*, eponymous—*epi*, upon, to, *onyma, onoma*, a name.]

epopee *ep'o-pē, n.* epic poetry: an epic poem. [Gr. *epopoiiā*—*epos*, a word, an epic poem, *poieein*, to make.]

epos *ep'os, n.* the elementary stage of epic poetry: an epic poem: a series of events such as are treated in epic poetry:—*pl.* **ep'oses.** [Gr. *epos*, a word.]

epoxy *e-pok'si, adj.* containing oxygen bound to two other atoms, often carbon, which are already attached in some way.—*n.* an epoxy resin.—*n.* **ep-ox'ide** an epoxy compound.—**epoxy** (or **epoxide**) **resins** synthetic polymers used as structural plastics, surface coatings, adhesives and for encapsulating and embedding electronic components.

épris, *fem.* **éprise,** *ā-prē, -prēz,* (Fr.) *adj.* captivated, smitten.

epsilon *ep-sī'lən, ep'si-lon, n.* fifth letter (E, ε) of the Greek alphabet, short e. [Gr. *e psilon*, bare or mere e.]

epsomite *ep'səm-īt, n.* a mineral, hydrated magnesium sulphate.—**Ep'som salt(s)'** a purgative medicine of like composition, originally got from the springs at Epsom, in Surrey—used also in dyeing, etc.

epyllion *e-pil'i-ən, n.* a poem with some resemblance to an epic but shorter. [Gr.; dim. of *epos*, word.]

equable *ek'wə-bl, adj.* even, uniform: smooth: without great variations or extremes: of even temper.—*ns.*

equabil'ity, e'quableness.—*adv.* **e'quably.** [L *ae-quâbilis—aequâre—aequus,* equal.]

equal *ē'kwəl, adj.* identical in quantity of the same value: adequate: in just proportion: fit: equable: uniform: equitable: evenly balanced: just: equally developed on each side (*bot.*)—*n* one of the same age, rank, etc.—*v.t.* to be, or to make, equal to: to reach the same level as (*bot*)—*pr.p.* **e'qualling;** *pa.t.* and *pa p.* **e'qualled.**—*n.* **equalisā'tion, -z-** the act of making equal: the state of being equalised—*v.t.* **e'qualise, -ize** to make equal or uniform.—*v i* to become equal. to make one's score equal to one's opponent's.—*n.* **equall'ser, -z-** a person or thing that equalises: a score that makes both sides alike.—*adj* **equalitār'ian** (*-kwol-*) of or pertaining to the equality of mankind.—*n.* one who believes in or favours political and social equality of mankind.—*ns.* **equalita'rianism; equality** (*ē-kwol'i-ti*) the condition of being equal: sameness: evenness.—*adv.* **equally** (*ē'kwə-li*).—*v.t.* **e'qualness** equality: equability.—*v.t.* **equāte'** to reduce to an average or to a common standard of comparison: to state as equal: to regard as equal.—*v.i.* to be, or be regarded, treated, etc. as, equal.—*n.* **equā'tion** the act of making equal: a statement of the equality of two quantities: reduction to a common standard: correction to compensate for an error, irregularity, or discrepancy: the quantity added for this purpose: a formula expressing a chemical action and the proportions of the substances involved.—**equal opportunities** in employment, etc , the avoidance of any discrimination between applicants, etc. on the grounds of sex, race, etc.; **equal(s) sign** the symbol =, which indicates that two (numerical) values are equal; **equal temperament** see **temperament.—equal to the occasion** fit or able for an emergency; **personal equation** a correction to be applied to the reading of an instrument on account of the observer's tendency to read too high, too low, etc.; any tendency to error or prejudice due to personal characteristics for which allowance must be made. [L. *aequālis,* equal, *aequâre, -âtum,* to make equal—*aequus,* equal.]

equanimity *e-kwə-nim'i-ti, ē-, n* evenness of mind or temper.—*adj.* **equanimous** (*i-kwan'i-məs*)—*adv* **equan'imously.** [L. *aequanimitās—aequus,* equal, *animus,* the mind.]

equate, equation. See **equal.**

equator *i-kwā'tər, n.* an imaginary great circle passing round the middle of the globe and equidistant from N. and S. poles: the corresponding great circle of another body: the imaginary great circle in which the plane of the earth's equator intersects the celestial sphere (so called because day and night are equal when the sun reaches it): the middle belt or line of any globular or nearly globular body that has some sort of polarity—*adj* **equatorial** (*ek-wə-tō'ri-əl, -to',* or *ēk-*) of, pertaining to, of the nature of, or in the neighbourhood of, an equator.—*n.* a telescope mounted on an axis, capable of moving parallel to the equator and so following a star in any part of its diurnal course.—*adv.* **equato'rially** so as to have motion or direction parallel to the equator. [See **equal.**]

equerry *ek'wə-ri, ik-wer'i, n* an official in attendance upon a prince or personage. [Fr *écurie*—L.L *scūria,* a stable.]

equestrian *i-kwes'tri-ən, adj.* pertaining to horsemanship, or to the Roman order of *equitēs* or knights: on horseback.—*n.* a horseman· a performer on horseback:—*fem.* (sham Fr.) **equestrienne'.**—*n.* **eques'trianism** horsemanship [L *equester, equestris—eques* a horseman—*equus,* a horse.]

equi- *ē-kwi-,* a prefix meaning equal, from L *aequus.*—*adj.* **equian'gular** having equal angles.—*n.* **equi-angular'ity.**—*n.* **equidis'tance.**—*adj.* **equidis'tant** equally distant.—*adv.* **equidis'tantly.**—*adjs.* **equi-lat'eral** (L. *latus, -eris,* side) having all sides equal; **equipoten'tial** of equal power, capability, potential, or potentiality.

Equidae *ek'wi-dē, n.pl* a family of ungulate mammals consisting of the genus **Eq'uus** (horse, ass, zebra) and various fossil forms. [L. *equus,* horse.]

equidistant ... to .. **equilateral.** See **equi-.**

equilibrium *ēk-, ek-wi-lib'ri-əm, n.* balance: the state of even balance: a state in which opposing forces or tendencies neutralise each other.—*v.t.* and *v.i.* **equilibrate** (*ēk-wi-līb'rāt,* or *-lib'rāt,* or *-kwil'*) to balance: to counterpoise.—*ns.* **equilibrā'tion; equil'ibrator** (or *-līb'*) a balancing or stability device, esp. an aeroplane fin; **equil'ibrist** (or *lib',* or *-līb'*) one who does balancing tricks; **equilib'rity.** [L. *ae-quilibrium—aequus,* equal, *lībra,* balance.]

equine *e', ē'kwīn,* **equinal** *e-, ē-kwīn'əl, adjs.* pertaining to, or of the nature of, a horse or horses. [L. *equīnus—equus,* a horse.]

equinox *ek', ēk'wi-noks, n.* the time when the sun crosses the equator, making the night equal in length to the day, about 21st March and 23rd Sept.: an equinoctial point.—*adj.* **equinoc'tial** pertaining to the equinoxes, the time of the equinoxes, or to the regions about the equator.—*n.* the celestial equator or **equinoctial line.**—*adv.* **equinoc'tially** in the direction of the equinox.—**equinoctial gales** high gales popularly supposed to prevail about the times of the equinoxes—the belief is unsupported by observation; **equinoctial point** either of the two points in the heavens where the equinoctial line cuts the ecliptic; **equinoctial year** see **year.** [L. *aequus,* equal, *nox, noctis,* night]

equip *i-kwip', v.t.* to fit out: to furnish with everything needed:—*pr.p.* **equipp'ing;** *pa.t.* and *pa.p.* **equipped'.**—*n* **equipage** (*ek'wi-pāj*) a carriage and attendants: retinue.—*n* **equip'ment** the act of equipping: the state of being equipped: things used in equipping or furnishing: outfit. [Fr. *équiper,* prob.—O.N. *skipa,* to set in order, *skip,* a ship; partly influenced by confusion with L. *equus,* horse]

équipe *ā-kēp,* (Fr.) *n.* in motor-racing and other sport, a team.

equipoise *ek'wi-poiz, n.* a state of balance: a counterpoise.—*v.t.* to balance: to counterpoise. [L. *aequus,* equal, and **poise.**]

equipollent *ē-, e-kwi-pol'ənt, adj.* having equal power or force: equivalent.—*n.* an equivalent.—*ns.* **equipoll'ence, equipoll'ency.** [L. *aequus,* equal, *pollēns, pollentis,* pr.p. of *pollēre,* to be strong, able.]

equiponderate *ē-, e-kwi-pon'dər-āt, v.t.* to be equal in weight: to balance.—*adj.* equal in weight. —*n.* **equipon'derance.**—*adj.* **equipon'derant.** [L. *aequus,* equal, *pondus, ponderis,* weight.]

equipotential. See **equi-.**

Equisetum *ek-wi-sē'təm, n.* the only surviving genus of the family **Equisetā'ceae,** stiff herbaceous plants with almost leafless articulated and whorled stems and branches: (without *cap.*) a plant of this genus—also **horsetail.** [L *equus,* a horse, *sēta,* a bristle.]

equitation *ek-wi-tā'shən, n.* the art of riding on horseback. [L. *equitāre,* to ride—*equus,* a horse.]

equity *ek'wi-ti, n.* right as founded on the laws of nature: moral justice, of which laws are the imperfect expression: the spirit of justice which enables us to interpret laws rightly: fairness: an equitable right: the value of property in excess of any charges upon it (*U.S.*): (in *pl*) ordinary shares: (with *cap.*) British actors' trade union.—*adj.* **eq'uitable** possessing or showing or in accordance with equity: held or exercised in equity.—*n.* **eq'uitableness.**—*adv.* **eq'uitably.** [O.Fr. *equité*—L. *aequitās, -ātis*—*aequus*, equal.]

equivalent *i-kwiv'ə-lənt, adj.* equal in value, power, meaning, etc.: interchangeable: of like combining value (*chem.*).—*n* a thing equivalent: an equivalent weight (*chem.*).—*ns.* **equiv'alence, equiv'alency.**—*adv.* **equiv'alently.**—**equivalent weight** (*chem.*) that weight which displaces or combines with or otherwise represents a standard unit—atomic weight, or atomic weight divided by valence. [Fr.,—L. *aequus*, equal, *valēns, valentis*, pr.p. of *valēre*, to be worth.]

equivocal *i-kwiv'ə-kl, adj.* capable of meaning two or more things: of doubtful meaning: capable of a double explanation: suspicious: questionable.—*adv.* **equiv'ocally.**—*n.* **equiv'ocalness.**—*v.i.* **equiv'ocate** to use equivocal or doubtful words in order to mislead. —*ns.* **equivoca'tion; equiv'ocator.**—*adj.* **equiv'ocatory** containing or characterised by equivocation.—*n.* **equivoke, equivoque** (*ek'wi-vōk*) a quibble: a pun. [L. *aequus*, equal, and *vōx, vōcis*, the voice, a word] **Equus.** See **Equidae.**

er *ûr, interj.* expressing hesitation.

-er¹ *-ər, suff.* marks the agent (person or thing), designating persons according to occupation (e.g. writ*er*), or place of abode (e.g. London*er*) (O.E. *-ere*); some similar words, e.g. groc*er*, offic*er*, are from Fr. *-ier* (L. *-arius*).

-er² *-ər, suff.* marks the comparative degree of adjectives (long*er*) and some adverbs (fast*er*). [O.E. *-ra* (*adj.*), *-or* (*adv.*).]

era *ē'rə, n.* a series of years reckoned from a particular point, or that point itself: an important date: an age: a main division of geological time. [L.L. *aera*, a number, orig. counters, pieces of copper used in counting, pl. of *aes*, copper.]

eradiate *i-, ē-rā'di-āt, v.t.* and *v.i.* to shoot out like a ray of light.—*n.* **eradia'tion.** [L. *ē-*, from, *radius*, a ray.]

eradicate *i-rad'i-kāt, v.t.* to pull up by the roots: to root out: to extirpate.—*adj.* **erad'icable.**—*n.* **eradica'tion.**—*adj.* **erad'icative.**—*n.* **erad'icator.** [L. *ērādīcāre, -ātum*, to root out—*ē*, from, *rādīx, -īcis*, a root.]

erase *i-rāz', v.t.* to rub or scrape out: to efface: to destroy: to replace the data of a storage area with characters representing zero (*comput.*).—*adj.* **erā'sable.**—*ns.* **erā'ser** one who, or that which, erases, as *ink-eraser*; **era'sure** (*-zhər*) the act of erasing: a rubbing out: scraping away: the place where something written has been rubbed out. [L. *ērādēre*—*ē*, from, *rādēre, rāsum*, to scrape.]

Erastian *e-ras'ti-ən, -tyən, n.* a follower of Thomas *Erastus* (1524–83), a Swiss physician, who denied the church the right to inflict excommunication and disciplinary penalties: one who would subordinate the church jurisdiction to the state—a position not held by Erastus at all.—*adj.* relating to the Erastians or their doctrines.—*n.* **Eras'tianism** control of the church by the state.

Erato *er'ə-tō, n.* the Muse of amatory lyric poetry. [Gr. *Eratō*.]

erbium *ûr'bi-əm, n.* a rare metal (at numb. 68, symbol Er), found in gadolinite, at Ytt*erby*, near Stockholm

ere¹ *ār, adv., prep.* and *conj.* before.—**ere long** before long: soon; **ere now** before this time. [O.E. *ǣr*; cf. Du. *eer.*]

erect *i-rekt', adj.* upright: directed upward: right end up, not inverted: not decumbent (*bot.*): turgid and raised (*zool.*).—*v.t.* to set upright: to set erect: to set at right angles: to raise: to build.—*ns.* **erect'er, erect'or** one who, or that which, erects or raises: a muscle which assists in erecting a part or an organ: an attachment to a compound microscope for making the image erect instead of inverted.—*adj.* **erect'ile** (*-īl*) that may be erected.—*ns.* **erectility** (*e-, ē-rek-til'i-ti*); **erec'tion** the act of erecting: the state of being erected: anything erected: a building of any kind: an enlarging and hardening of the penis usu. in response to sexual stimulation.—*adj.* **erect'ive** tending to erect.—*adv.* **erect'ly.**—*n.* **erect'ness.** [L. *ērigĕre, ērēctum*, to set upright—*ē*, from, *regĕre*, to direct.]

eremite *er'i-mīt, n.* a recluse who lives apart, esp. from religious motives: a hermit.—*adjs.* **eremitic** (*-mit'ik*), **-al.**—*n.* **er'emitism.** [L.L. *erēmīta*—Gr. *erēmītēs*—*erēmos*, desert.]

erepsin *e-rep'sin, n.* an enzyme of the small intestine, acting upon casein, gelatine, etc. [L. *ēripĕre, ērep-tum*—*ē*, from, *rapĕre*, to snatch.]

erethism *er'e-thizm, n.* excitement or stimulation of an organ: abnormal irritability.—*adjs.* **erethis'mic; erethis'tic; erethit'ic.** [Gr. *erethismos*.]

erf *ûrf, (S. Afr.) n.* a garden plot or small piece of ground:—*pl.* **er'ven.** [Du.; cf. O.E. *erfe*, inheritance.]

erg *ûrg, n.* the unit of work in the centimetre-gramme-second system—that is, the quantity of work done when the point of operation of a force of one dyne is allowed to move one centimetre in the direction of the force.—*adj.* **ergonom'ic.**—*n.sing.* **ergonom'ics** the study of man in relation to his working environment: the adaptation of machines and general conditions to fit the individual so that he may work at maximum efficiency.—*n.* **ergon'omist.** [Gr. *ergon*, work.]

ergo *ûr'gō (log.) adv.* therefore, used to introduce the conclusion of a syllogism. [L. *ergō*, therefore.]

ergonomics, etc. See **erg.**

ergosterol. See **ergot.**

ergot *ûr'got, n.* a disease of grasses (esp. rye) and sedges: a seed so diseased.—*n.* **ergos'terol** an unsaturated sterol got from ergot.—*n.* **er'gotism** poisoning caused by eating bread made of rye diseased with ergot. [Fr.]

Erica *er'i-kə, n.* the heath genus: (without *cap.*) a member of the genus.—*adjs.* **ericaceous** (*er-i-kā'shəs*) belonging to plants of the genus Erica, or its family **Erica'ceae:** heathlike. [L.,—Gr. *ereikē*, heath.]

Erigeron *e-rij'ə-ron, n.* the flea-bane genus of composites: (without *cap.*) a member of the genus. [Gr. *ērigerōn*, groundsel—*ēri*, early, *gerōn*, old.]

Erinys *e-ri'nis, n.* a Fury:—*pl.* **Erinyes** (*e-rin'i-ēz*). [Gr. *Erinȳs*, pl. *Erinȳes*.]

erio- *er-i-ō-, -o-*, in composition, wool, fibre.—*ns.* **Eriocaulon** (*-ō-ko'lon*; Gr. *kaulos*, stalk) the pipewort genus; **Eriöden'dron** (Gr. *dendron*, tree) the silk-cotton genus of trees; **Eriophorum** (*-of'ər-əm*; Gr. *phoros*, carrying) the cotton-grass or cotton-sedge genus: (without *cap.*) a member of the genus. [Gr. *erion*, wool.]

eristic, -al *er-is'tik, -l, adjs.* of or pertaining to controversy or disputatious reasoning. [Gr. *eristikos*—*eris*, strife.]

erk *ûrk, (airmen's slang) n.* an aircraftsman [From *airk*, for aircraftsman.]

erl-king *ûrl'-king, n.* for German *Erlkönig*, which was a mistranslation (alder-king) of the Danish *eller-konge* (from *elverkonge*, king of the elves).

ermine *ûr'min, n.* the stoat a white fur, the stoat's winter coat in northern lands, used for the robes of judges and magistrates with the black tail-tip (or an imitation) attached. [O.Fr. *ermine* (Fr. *hermine*), perh. from L. (*mūs*) *Armēnius*, lit. (mouse) of Armenia.]

erne, ern *ûrn, n.* the eagle. [O.E. *earn*]

Ernie *ûr'ni, n.* the electronic machine which picks, by methods that allow full scope for chance, numbers to be used as winning numbers on premium bonds. [Abbreviation of *e*lectronic *r*andom *n*umber *i*ndicator equipment.]

erode *i-*, *e-rōd'*, *v.t.* to eat away, wear away: to form by wearing away.—*adj.* and *n.* **erō'dent** caustic.—*n.* **erosion** (*-rō'zhən*) eating away, wearing down: the denuding action of weathering, water, ice, wind, etc. (*geol.*).—*adj.* **erosive** (*-rō'ziv*). [L. *ē*, from, *rōdĕre*, *rōsum*, to gnaw.]

Erodium *e-rō'di-əm*, *n.* the stork's-bill genus of the geranium family: (without *cap.*) a plant of the genus [Gr. *erōdios*, a heron.]

erogenic, erogenous. See Eros.

Eros *ēr'os* (prop. in Gr. *er-ōs*), *er'os*, *n.* the Greek love-god, identified by the Romans with Cupid: a minor planet discovered in 1898, notable for its near approach to the earth.—*adjs* **erotic** (*e-rot'ik*), pertaining to sexual love: amatory: amorous.—*n pl.* **erot'ica** erotic literature.—*ns.* **erot'icism** (*-sizm*) amorous temperament or habit: erotism; **erot'icist**; **er'otism** sexual desire: the manifestations of sex in its widest application.—*adjs.* **erotogenic** (*er-ət-ō-jen'ik*), **erotogenous** (*-oj'*), less correctly **erogen'ic, erog'enous**, productive of erotic desire or gratification.—*ns.* **erōtomā'nia** morbid sexual passion; **erōtomā'niac**. [Gr. *Erōs, -ōtos.*]

erosion, erosive. See erode.

erotic, erotism, erotogenic, etc. See Eros.

err *ûr*, *v.i* to miss the mark: to be inaccurate: to make a mistake: to sin:—*pr.p.* **erring** (*ûr'ing* or *er'ing*); *pa.t.* and *pa.p.* **erred** (*ûrd*).—*adj.* **errant** (*er'ənt*) wandering: roving: quixotic: erring.—*n.* **err'antry** an errant or wandering state: a rambling about like a knight-errant.—*adj.* **erra'tic** wandering: having no certain course: not stationary: irregular, capricious, irregular or unpredictable in behaviour.—*n.* an erratic block or boulder.—*adv.* **errat'ically**.—*n.* **errā'tum** an error in writing or printing, esp. one noted in a list in a book (*pl.* **errā'ta**).—*adj.* **erroneous** (*i-rō'ni-əs*) erring: full of error: wrong: mistaken.—*adv.* **errō'neously**.—*ns.* **errō'neousness; error** (*er'ər*) mistaken opinion: difference between a quantity obtained by observation and the true value: a blunder or mistake: wrong-doing.—**erratic block** a mass of rock transported by ice and deposited at a distance. [L. *errāre*, to stray; cog. with Ger. *irren*, and *irre*, astray.]

errand *er'ənd*, *n.* a mission, purpose: a commission to say or do something usually involving a short journey —**err'and-boy, -girl—a fool's errand** a futile journey; **run errands** to be sent to convey messages or perform small pieces of business. [O E. *ærende*; O.N. *eyrindi*.]

errant, erratic, erratum. See under err.

erroneous, error. See under err.

ersatz *er'zats*, *ûr'-*, *er-zats'*, *n.* a substitute.—*adj.* substitute: fake. [Ger.]

Erse *ers, ûrs, n.* the name given by Lowland Scots to the language of the people of the West Highlands, as being of Irish origin: now sometimes used for Irish Gaelic, as opposed to Scottish Gaelic. [Variant of **Irish**.]

erst *ûrst, adv.* at first: formerly.—*adv.* **erst'while, erstwhile'** formerly.—*adj.* former. [O.E. *ærest*, superl. of *ǣ*; see **ere**.]

erubescent *er-ōō-bes'ənt, adj.* growing red: blushing.—*ns.* **erubesc'ence, erubesc'ency** [L. *ērubēscĕre*, to grow red.]

Eruca *i-rōō'kə, n.* a genus of herbs of the family Cruciferae. [L. *ērūca*, rocket (see **rocket**[2]).]

eruciform *e-rōō'si-form, adj.* like a caterpillar [L. *ērūca*, caterpillar, *fōrma*, form.]

eruct *i-rukt'*, **eructate** *-āt, vs.t.* to belch out, as wind from the stomach ame the final stage of a game (also

v.t.; also *fig.*): of a volcano, to emit (fumes and ash or lava).—*n.* **eructā'tion** (*ē-*). [L. *ēructāre, -ātum—ē*, from, *ructāre*, to belch forth.]

erudite *er'ōō-dīt, -ū-, adj.* learned.—*n.* a learned person.—*adv* **er'uditely**.—*n.* **erudi'tion** the state of being learned: knowledge gained by study: learning, esp. in literature. [L. *ēruditus—ērudīre, ērudītum*, to free from rudeness—*ē*, from, *rudis*, rude.]

erupt *i-rupt', v.i.* to break out or through, as a volcano, a tooth from the gum, a rash on the skin.—*n.* **erup'tion** a breaking or bursting forth: that which bursts forth: a breaking out of spots on the skin: the action of a volcano.—*adj.* **erupt'ive**.—*n.* **erupt'iveness**. [L *ērumpĕre, ēruptum—ē*, from, *rumpĕre*, to break.]

erven. See erf.

eryngo *e-ring'gō, n.* the candied root of sea-holly: the plant itself, a superficially thistle-like umbellifer:—*pl* **eryn'gos, -goes**.—*n.* **Eryn'gium** (*-ji-əm*) a genus of bristly plants including the sea-holly (fam. Umbelliferae): (without *cap.*) a plant of the genus. [Gr. *ēryngos*.]

erysipelas *er-i-sip'i-ləs, n.* an inflammatory disease, generally in the face, marked by a bright redness of the skin. [Gr; prob.—root of *erythros*, red, *pella*, skin.]

erythema *er-i-thē'mə, n.* redness of the skin.—*adjs.* **erythemal** (*er-ith'*); **erythemat'ic; erythem'atous**. [Gr. *erythēma—erythainein*, to redden—*erythros*, red.]

erythr(o)- *er-ith-r(ō)-*, in composition, red.—*ns.* **eryth'roblast** (*-blast*; Gr *blastos*, a sprout) a cell in bone marrow that develops into an erythrocyte; **eryth'rocyte** (Gr *kytos*, case) a red blood corpuscle; **erythromycin** (*-mī'sin*; Gr. *mykēs*, fungus) an antibiotic similar to penicillin. [Gr. *erythros*, red.]

escadrille *es-kə-dril', n.* a French squadron of aircraft: a flotilla. [Fr., flotilla.]

escalade *es-kə-lād', n.* the scaling of the walls of a fortress by means of ladders.—*v.t.* to scale: to mount and enter by means of ladders.—*v.i.* **es'calate** to increase rapidly in scale or intensity.—Also *v.t.*—*n.* **escalā'tion**.—*n.* **es'calator** a moving staircase —*adj.* **es'calatory.**—**escalator clause** a clause in an agreement allowing for adjustment up or down according to change in circumstances, as in cost of material in a work contract or in cost of living in a wage agreement. [Fr.,—Sp. *escalada—escala*, a ladder—L. *scāla*.]

Escallonia *es-kal-ōn'i-ə, n.* a South American genus of shrubs of the Saxifrage family: (without *cap.*) a plant of this genus. [Discovered by *Escallon*, an 18th-cent. Spanish traveller.]

escallop *is-kal'əp, n.* a variant of **scallop**.—*adj.* **escall'oped** (*her.*) covered with scallop-shells.

escalope *es'ka-lop, n.* a boneless slice of meat, cut thin and often beaten out still thinner. [Fr.]

escape *is-kāp', v.t.* to free oneself from: to pass out of danger from: to evade, elude.—*v i.* to come off or come through in safety: to emerge into or gain freedom: to flee: to slip out: to issue: to leak.—*n.* act of escaping, a means of escaping: flight: flight from reality: an outlet: a leakage: an accidental or inadvertent emission: an outburst: a sally: a person or thing that has escaped, esp. a garden plant maintaining itself wild.—*adj.* of literature, providing escape from reality: of a clause in an agreement, defining the conditions under which a party is relieved of obligation.—*adj.* **escap'able**.—*ns.* **escapade** (*es-kə-pād'*): a mischievous adventure; **escapee'** one who has-escaped, e.g. from prison.—*ns.* **escape'ment** part of a timepiece connecting the wheelwork with the pendulum or balance, and allowing a tooth to escape at each vibration: the clearance in a pianoforte between the string and the hammer after it has struck the string, while the key is held down; **escáp'er; escáp'ism; escáp'ist** one who seeks escape, esp. from reality.—Also *adj.*—*ns.* **escapol'ogist; escapol'ogy** the study of methods of escape from any sort of constraint or confinement and the putting into practice of these methods.—**escape hatch** an emergency means of escape from ship, submarine, etc.; **escape mechanism** (*psych.*) a mental process by which one evades the unpleasant; **escape road** a short track leading off a road on a steep hill, sharp bend, etc., for vehicles going out of control; **escape valve** a valve to let steam, etc., escape when wanted; **escape velocity** (*phys.*) the minimum velocity needed to escape from the gravitation field of a body; **escape wheel** the wheel that the pallets act upon in a clock. [O.Fr. *escaper* (Fr. *échapper*)—L.L. *ex cappâ*, (lit.) out of one's cape or cloak.]

escargot *es-kar-gõ*, (Fr.) *n.* an edible snail.

escarp *is-karp'*, the side of the ditch next the rampart (*fort.*).—*n.* **escarp'ment** the precipitous side of a hill or rock: escarp. [Fr. *escarper*, to cut down steep, from root of **scarp.**]

eschatology *es-kə-tol'ə-ji*, (*theol.*) *n.* the doctrine of the last or final things, as death, judgment, the state after death.—*adjs.* **eschatolog'ic, -al.**—*n.* **eschatol'ogist.** [Gr. *eschatos*, last, *logos*, a discourse.]

escheat *is-chēt'*, *n.* property that falls to the feudal lord or to the state for want of an heir, or by forfeiture.—*v.t.* to confiscate.—*v.i.* to fall to the lord of the manor or the state.—*adj.* **escheat'able.**—*ns.* **escheat'age; escheat'ment; escheat'or** an official who watched over escheats. [O.Fr. *eschete—escheoir* (Fr. *échoir*)—L. *ex*, from, *cadēre*, to fall.]

Escherichia *esh-ə-rik'i-ə*, *n.* a genus of rod-shaped, gram-negative bacteria.—**Escherichia coli** the type species of this genus, occurring naturally in the intestines of vertebrates, and sometimes pathogenic [T. *Escherich* (d. 1911), Ger. physician.]

eschew *is-chōō'*, *v.t.* to shun: to abstain from. [O.Fr. *eschever*.]

Eschscholtzia *e-sholt'si-ə*, *n.* a genus of Papaveraceae, including the Californian poppy, a showy garden annual: (without *cap.*) a plant of the genus. [J. F. von *Eschscholtz*, a member of the expedition that discovered the poppy in 1821.]

escort *es'kõrt*, *n.* a person or persons, ship or ships, etc., accompanying another or others for protection, guidance, or merely courtesy: an armed guard: a police officer accompanying a person under arrest to prevent escape: a man who accompanies a woman on an evening out: a person, usu. of the opposite sex, hired to accompany one to entertainments, etc.: attendance.—Also used as *adj.*—*v.t.* **escort'** to attend as escort.—**escort agency** one which provides people to act as hired escorts. [Fr. *escorte*—It. *scorta—scorgere*, to guide—L. *ex*, out, *corrigere*, to set right.]

escribe *ē-skrīb'*, *v.t.* to describe (e.g. a triangle) so as to touch one side externally, the others (produced) internally. [L. *ē*, out, *scribere*, write.]

escritoire *es-krē-twär'*, *n.* a writing-desk.—*adj.* **escritó'rial** (or *-ōr*). [Fr. *escritoire*—L.L. *scrīptōrium*—L. *scribēre*, *scriptum*, to write.]

escrow *es-krō'*, *n.* a deed in the hands of a third party, to take effect when a condition is fulfilled [A.Fr. *escroele, escroe*; see **scroll.**]

escudo *es-kōō'dõ*, *n.* the Portuguese unit of currency: a coin representing this: form., a coin or currency unit of various values in other countries:—*pl.* **escu'dos.** [Port. and Sp , shield.]

esculent *es'kū-lənt*, *adj.* eatable: fit to be used for food by man.—*n.* something that is eatable. [L. *es-*

culentus, eatable—*esca*, food—*edēre*, to eat.]

escutcheon *es-kuch'ən*, *n.* a shield on which a coat of arms is represented: a family shield.—**a blot on the escutcheon** a stain on one's good name. [O.Fr. *escuchon*—L. *scūtum*, a shield.]

-ese *-ēz*, *suff.* denoting a relationship with a country or region, as in *Japanese, Maltese*, or the literary style, jargon, etc. of a particular group, as in *journalese, officialese*.

esker, eskar *esk'ər*, (*geol.*) *n.* a kame, or ridge of gravel and sand laid down by a subglacial stream or one which issues from a retreating glacier. [Ir. *eiscir*, a ridge.]

Eskimo *es'ki-mõ*, *n.* and *adj.* one of a people inhabiting arctic America with its islands, Greenland, and the nearest Asiatic coast: their language:—*pl.* **Es'kimo, -s.**—**Eskimo dog** one of a breed of powerful dogs, with a double coat of hair, widely distributed in the Arctic regions, and indispensable for drawing sledges. [Prob. from an Indian word meaning eaters of raw flesh.]

esophagus. U.S. spelling of **oesophagus.**

esoteric *es-ō-ter'ik*, *adj.* inner: secret: mysterious: taught to a select few—opp. to *exoteric* (*philos.*).—*n.pl.* **esoter'ica** esoteric objects, etc.—*adv.* **esoter'ically.**—*ns.* **esoter'icism** (*-i-sizm*) the holding of esoteric opinions. [Gr. *esōterikos—esōterō*, compar. of *esō, eisō*, within.]

espadrille *es-pə-dril'*, *n.* a rope-soled shoe. [Fr.,—Prov. *espardillo—espart*, esparto.]

espalier *es-pal'yər*, *n.* a lattice-work of wood to train trees on: a fruit-tree trained on stakes.—*v.t.* to train as an espalier. [Fr.,—It. *spalliera*, a support for the shoulders.]

esparto *es-pär'tō*, *n.* a strong grass (*Stipa tenacissima*, and others) grown in Spain, N. Africa, etc., and used for making paper, baskets, cordage, etc.:—*pl.* **espar'tos.** [Sp.,—L. *spartum*—Gr. *sparton*, a kind of rope.]

especial *is-pesh'l*, *adj.* special: particular: principal: distinguished.—*adv.* **espec'ially.** [O.Fr.,—L. *speciālis—speciēs*, species.]

Esperanto *es-pər-an'tō*, *n.* an international language devised by Dr Zamenhof, published 1887.—Also *adj.*—*n.* **Esperan'tist** a speaker of Esperanto. [Inventor's pseudonym, the hoping one.]

espial. See **espy.**

espionage *es-pyon-äzh'*, *es'pi-ə-nij*, *n.* spying: use of spies. [Fr. *espionner—espion*, spy.]

esplanade *es-plə-nād'*, *n.* a level space between a citadel and the first houses of the town: any level space for walking or driving in, esp. by the sea. [Fr.,—Sp. *esplanada*—L. *explānāre—ex*, out, *plānus*, flat.]

espouse *is-powz'*, *v.t.* to give or take in marriage or betrothal: to take upon oneself or embrace, as a cause.—*ns.* **espous'al** the taking upon oneself, as a cause: (usu. *pl.*; *arch.*) a wedding: a formal betrothal; **espous'er.** [O.Fr. *espouser* (Fr. *épouser*)—L. *spōnsāre*, to betroth—*spondēre, spōnsum*, to vow.]

espresso *es-pres'ō*, *n.* a form of coffee-making machine giving high extraction under pressure: coffee so made:—*pl.* **espress'os.**—Also *adj.*, esp. of a type of coffee bar or the coffee. [It., pressed.]

esprit *es-prē*, (Fr.) *n.* wit, liveliness.—**esprit de corps** (*es-prē də kor*) regard for the honour of the body to which one belongs: loyalty of a member to the whole; **esprit de l'escalier** (*də-les-kal-yā*) thinking of an apt or witty retort after the opportunity of making it is past. [Fr. *esprit*, spirit, *de*, of, *corps*, body, *escalier*, staircase.]

espy *es-pī'*, *v.t.* to see at a distance: to catch sight of: to observe:—*pr.p.* **espy'ing;** *pa.t.* and *pa.p* **espied';** *3rd* *pers. sing.* **espies'.**—*n.* **espi'al** the act of espying: observation. [O.Fr. *espier;* see **spy.**]

-esque *-esk, suff.* in the style or manner of, similar to, as *Kiplingesque.*

Esquimau *es'ki-mō,* a French spelling of **Eskimo:**—*pl.* **Esquimaux** (*es'ki-mōz*).

esquire *es-kwīr',* Sometimes *es', n.* orig. a squire or shield-bearer: a landed proprietor: a title of dignity next below a knight: a general title of respect in addressing letters (usu. abbrev. **esq.**). [O.Fr. *esquier* (Fr. *écuyer*)—L. *scūtārius—scūtum,* a shield.]

essay *es'ā, n.* an attempt: a tentative effort: a written composition less elaborate than a treatise.—*v t.* **essay'** to try: to attempt:—*pr.p.* **essay'ing;** *pa.t.* and *pa.p.* **essayed'.**—*ns.* **essay'er; ess'ayist** one who essays: a writer of essays. [O.Fr. *essai*—L. *exagium,* weighing—*exagĕre,* to try, examine.]

essence *es'əns, n.* the inner distinctive nature of anything: the qualities which make any object what it is: a being: an alcoholic solution of a volatile or essential oil: a perfume of such composition: the extracted virtues of any drug: a liquid having the properties of the substance from which it is got.—*adj.* **essential** (*is-, es-en'shl*) relating to, constituting, or containing the essence: necessary to the existence of a thing: indispensable or important in the highest degree: highly rectified: pure: of e.g. disease, having no known cause.—*n.* something necessary: a leading principle. —*ns.* **essen'tialism:** a philosophical doctrine that distinguishes between the essence of material objects and their existence or appearance; **essen'tialist; essentiality** (*is-en-shi-al'i-ti*) the quality of being essential; an essential quality or element.—*adv.* **essen'tially.**—*n.* **essen'tialness.**—**essential oils** oils forming the odorous principles of plants, also called *ethereal oils, volatile oils.*—**in essence** basically, fundamentally; **of the essence** of the utmost importance. [Fr.,—L. *essentia—essēns, -entis,* assumed pr.p. of *esse,* to be.]

Essene *es-ēn', es'ēn, n.* one of a small religious fraternity among the ancient Jews leading retired ascetic lives and holding property in common.—*n.* **Ess'enism.** [Gr. *essēnos;* origin doubtful.]

-est *-əst, suff.* marks the superlative degree of adjectives (long*est*) and some adverbs (fast*est*). [O.E. *-est, -ost.*]

establish *is-, es-tab'lish, v.t.* to settle or fix: to set up: to place in fixed position, possession, or power: to make good: to prove: to ordain: to found: to set up in business: to institute by law as the recognised state church, and to recognise officially.—*adj.* **estab'lished** fixed: ratified: instituted by law and backed by the state.—*ns.* **estab'lisher; estab'lishment** the act of establishing: a fixed state: that which is established: a permanent civil or military force: permanent staff: one's residence, household, and style of living: a business: a settlement: the church established by law: (with *cap.; derog.*) the class in a community, or in a field of activity, who hold power, usu. because they are linked socially, and who are usu. considered to have conservative opinions and conventional values. —*adj.* **establishmentār'ian** maintaining the principle of church establishment: favouring or upholding the Establishment.—Also *n.* [O.Fr. *establir,* pr.p. *establissant*—L. *stabilīre—stabilis,* firm—*stāre,* to stand.]

estaminet *es-tam'ē-nā, n.* a small bar or café. [Fr.]

estate *is-, es-tāt', n.* rank: worldly condition: total possessions: property, esp. landed: a landed property, esp. of some size: a piece of land built over either privately or by a local authority, with dwelling-houses (**housing estate**) or factories (**trading** or **industrial estate**): a piece of land given over to the cultivation of a particular crop: an order or class of men in the body politic—**estate agent** the manager of landed property: an intermediary in the sale of landed property; **estate car** a car designed to carry passengers and goods, usu. with a large area behind the seats for luggage, etc., and a rear door; **estate duty** death duty. —**man's estate** the state of manhood; **personal estate** see **person; real estate** see **real¹; the estates of the realm** are three—Lords Spiritual, Lords Temporal, and Commons; **the fourth estate** (*coll.*) the press. [O.Fr. *estat* (Fr. *état*)→L. *status,* a state.]

esteem *is-, es-tēm', v.t.* to set a high estimate or value on: to regard with respect or friendship: to consider or think.—*n.* high estimation or value: favourable regard: estimation of worth.—*adjs.* **esteemed'** respected: in commercial correspondence, a colourless complimentary word; **es'timable** that can be estimated or valued: worthy of esteem: deserving our good opinion.—*adv.* **es'timably.**—*v.t.* **estimate** (*es'ti-māt*) to judge of the worth of: to ascertain how much is present of: to calculate.—*n.* (*-mit*) a valuing in the mind: judgment or opinion of the worth or size of anything: a rough calculation: a preliminary statement of the probable cost of a proposed undertaking: estimation.—*n.* **estimā'tion** an act of estimating: a reckoning of value: esteem, honour: conjecture.— *adj.* **es'timative.**—*n.* **es'timator.**—**hold in estimation** to esteem highly; **the estimates** accounts laid before parliament, etc., showing the probable expenditure for the year. [Fr. *estimer*—L. *aestimāre.*]

ester *es'tər, n.* a compound formed by the condensation of an alcohol and an acid, with elimination of water. —*n.* **esterifica'tion** (*-ter-*).—*v.t.* **ester'ify** (or *es'*). [Named by Leopold Gmelin (1788–1853), prob.— Essig, vinegar, Äther, ether.]

esthesia, esthesiogen, etc. U.S. spellings of **aesthesia,** etc.

Est(h)onian *es-t(h)ō'ni-ən, adj.* pertaining to *Est(h)onia,* a Baltic republic, till 1918 a province of Russia, incorporated in 1940 as a republic of the U.S.S.R.—*n.* a native or citizen thereof: its language.

estimate, estimation. See **esteem.**

estipulate, estipule. See **exstipulate.**

estival, etc. U.S. spelling of **aestival,** etc.

Estonian. See **Est(h)onian.**

estop *es-top', v.t.* to hinder, preclude (*law*):—*pr.p.* **estopp'ing;** *pa.t.* and *pa.p.* **estopped'.**—*ns.* **estopp'age** the state of being estopped; **estopp'el** a conclusive admission, which cannot be denied by the party whom it affects. [O.Fr. *estoper—estoupe*—L. *stuppa,* flax; see **stop, stuff.**]

estover *es-tō'vər, n.* a right to necessaries allowed by law, as wood to a tenant for necessary repairs, etc.— **common of estovers** the right of taking necessary wood from another's estate for household use and the making of implements of industry. [O.Fr. *estover,* to be necessary, necessaries.]

estrange *is-trānj', v.t.* to cut off, remove: to alienate, esp. from friendship: to divert from original use or possessor.—*adj.* **estranged'** alienated: disaffected.— *ns.* **estrang'edness; estrange'ment; estrang'er.** [O.Fr. *estranger* (Fr. *étranger*)—L. *extrāneāre—extrāneus;* see **strange.**]

estreat *es-trēt', (law) n.* a true copy of some original record, esp. of fines to be levied.—*v.t.* to extract from the records of a court, as a forfeited recognisance: to levy, exact. [O.Fr. *estraite*—L. *extra-hēre—ex,* from, *trahēre* to draw; see **extract.**]

estrogen, estrum, etc. U.S. spellings of **oestrogen, oestrum,** etc.

estuary *es'tū-ər-i, n.* the wide lower tidal part of a river. —*adjs.* **estuarial** (*-ā'ri-əl*); **estuā'rian; es'tuarine**

(-ə-rĭn). [L. *aestuārium—aestus,* burning, boiling, commotion, tide.]

esurient *es-ū'ri-ənt, adj.* hungry: rapacious.—*n.* **esū'rience, esū'riency** greedy hunger: needy rapacity [L. *ēsuriēns, -entis,* pr.p. of *ēsurīre,* to be hungry— desiderative of *edĕre,* to eat.]

eta *ē'tə, ā'tə, n.* the seventh letter of the Greek alphabet, long e (H, η). [Gr. *ēta.*]

eta *ā'tə, n.* (also with *cap.*) esp. form., a member of the lowest Japanese class, which did work considered menial or degrading. [Jap.]

etaerio *et-ē'ri-ō, (bot.) n.* an aggregated fruit, a group of achenes or drupels:—*pl.* **etae'rios.** [Fr. *étairion* —Gr. *hetaireiā,* association.]

et alia (alii) *et ā'li-ə, a'li-a (ā'li-ī, a'li-ē),* (L.) and other things (people); abbrev. **et al.**

etalon *ǎr'ǎl-on, n.* an interferometer consisting of an air film enclosed between half-silvered plane-parallel glass or quartz plates. [Fr.,—M.Fr. *estalon,* standard of weights and measures—O.Fr. *estal,* place.]

état *ā-ta,* (Fr.) *n.* state, rank.—*n.* **étatisme** (*ā-ta-tēzm'*) extreme state control over the individual citizen.

et cetera *et set'ər-ə,* usually written etc. or &c., a Latin phrase meaning 'and the rest': and so on.—*n.* something in addition, which can easily be understood.

etch *ech, v.t.* and *v.i.* to design on metal, glass, etc. by eating out the lines with an acid.—*ns.* **etch'ant** an acid or corrosive used in etching; **etch'er; etch'ing** the act or art of etching or engraving: the impression from an etched plate. [Ger. *ätzen,* to corrode by acid; from same root as Ger. *essen;* see **eat.**]

eternal *i-, ē-tûr'nl, adj.* without beginning or end of existence: everlasting: ceaseless: unchangeable: seemingly endless, occurring again and again (*coll.*). —*v.t.* **eter'nalise, -ize, eter'nise, -ize** (or *ē'tər-nīz*) to make eternal: to immortalise with fame.—*adv.* **eter'nally.**—*n.* **eter'nity** eternal duration: the state or time after death.—**eternal triangle** a sexual relationship, full of tension and conflict, between two men and a woman or two women and a man; **eternity ring** a ring set all round with stones, emblematic of everlasting continuity.—**The Eternal** an appellation of God; **the Eternal City** Rome; **the eternities** the eternal reality or truth. [Fr. *éternel*—L *aeternus* —*aevum,* an age.]

etesian *e-tē'zh(y)ən, -zyən, adj.* blowing at stated seasons, as certain winds, esp. the north-west winds of summer in the Aegean. [Gr. *etēsios,* annual— *etos,* a year.]

eth, edh *edh, n.* a letter (D ð), a barred D, used in Old English, without distinction from thorn, for voiced or voiceless th, in Icelandic and by phoneticians set apart for the voiced sound, thorn standing for the voiceless.

ethane *eth'ān, ēth', n.* a colourless, odourless hydrocarbon of the methane series.—*n.* **eth'anol** ethyl alcohol. [**ether.**]

ethene. See under **ethyl.**

ether *ē'thər, n.* the clear, upper air: a medium, not matter, assumed in 19th cent. to fill all space and transmit electromagnetic waves—(in these senses also **aether**): a colourless transparent, volatile liquid of great mobility and high refractive power, used as a solvent or anaesthetic: extended to the class of compounds in which two alkyl groups are united with an oxygen atom.—*adj.* **ethe'real, ethe'rial** consisting of ether: heavenly: airy: spirit-like.—*n.* **ethērealisa'tion, -z-.**—*v.t.* **ethe'realise, -ize** to convert into ether, or the fluid ether: to render spiritlike.—*n.* **ethēreal'ity.**—*adv.* **ethe'really.**—*n.* **ethērisa'tion, -z-.**—*v.t.* **e'thērise, -ize** to convert into

ether: to stupefy with ether.—**ethereal oils** essential oils. [L *aethĕr*—Gr. *aithĕr,* the heavens—*aithein,* to light up.]

ethic *eth'ik,* (now *rare*) *adj.* ethical.—*n.* (more commonly *n.sing.* **eth'ics**) the science of morals, that branch of philosophy which is concerned with human character and conduct: a system of morals, rules of behaviour: a treatise on morals.—*adj.* **eth'ical** relating to morals, the science of ethics, professional standards of conduct: relating to, or in accord with, approved moral behaviour: denoting a proprietary pharmaceutical not advertised to the general public. —*adj.* **eth'ically.**—*v.t.* **eth'icise, -ize** (-*sīz*) to make ethical: to treat as ethical.—*ns.* **eth'icism** the tendency to moralise or ethicise: great interest in ethics or passion for ethical ideals; **eth'icist** one versed in ethics: one who detaches ethics from religion.— **eth'ico-** in composition, ethical or of ethics.—**ethical,** or **ethic, dative** a dative implying an indirect interest in the matter, used to give a livelier tone to the sentence (e.g. *He could swear me as fluently as any bargee*). [Gr. *ēthikos—ēthos,* custom, character.]

Ethiopian *ē-thi-ō'pi-ən, adj.* pertaining to Ethiopia or its natives: Negro (*arch.*).—*n.* a native of Ethiopia: a Negro (*arch.*).—*adj.* **Ēthiōp'ic** belonging to Ethiopia, to the Ethiopian church, or to a group of Semitic languages. [Gr. *Aithiops—aithein,* to burn, *ops, ōps,* face.]

ethmoid *eth'moid, adj.* like a sieve.—*adj.* **ethmoid'al.** —**ethmoid bone** one of the bones forming the anterior part of the brain-case. [Gr. *ēthmos,* a sieve, and *eidos,* form.]

ethnic, -al *eth'nik, -əl, adjs.* concerning nations or races: pertaining to gentiles or the heathen: pertaining to the customs, dress, food, etc. of a particular racial group or cult: belonging to a particular racial group: foreign: exotic.—*ns.* **eth'narch** (*-närk*; Gr. *archos,* leader) a ruler or governor of a people; **eth'narchy; eth'nic** a member of a racial or cultural minority group.—*adv.* **eth'nically.**—*n.* **ethni'city** (*-si-ti*).—*adj.* **ethnocen'tric.**—*ns.* **ethnocen'trism** belief in the superiority of one's own cultural group or society and corresponding dislike or misunderstanding of other such groups; **eth'nocide** (*-sīd;* L. *caedĕre,* to kill) the extermination of a racial or cultural group; **ethnog'rapher.**—*adjs.* **ethnograph'ic, -al** pertaining to ethnography: of objects useful in the study of ethnography.—*n.pl.* **ethnograph'ica** (a collection of) ethnographic objects: (loosely) exotica.—*n.* **ethnog'raphy** the scientific description of the races of the earth.—*n.sing* **ethnolinguist'ics** the study of the relationship between language and cultural behaviour.—*adj.* **ethnolog'ical.**—*adv.* **ethnolog'ically.**—*ns.* **ethnol'ogist; ethnol'ogy** the science that treats of the varieties of the human race: cultural anthropology; **ethnomusicol'ogist** one who makes a study of the music and/or musical instruments of primitive peoples in relation to their cultures; **ethnomusicol'ogy.** [Gr. *ethnos,* a nation.]

ethos *ē'thos, n.* habitual character and disposition of individual, group, race, etc.: moral significance.— *adjs.* **etholog'ic, -al.**—*ns.* **ethol'ogist; ethol'ogy** the science of character: bionomics: the scientific study of the function and evolution of animal behaviour patterns. [Gr. *ēthos,* custom, character.]

ethyl *eth'il, ēth'il, n.* the base (C_2H_5) of common alcohol, ether, etc.—*n.* **eth'ylene** (also **eth'ene**) olefiant gas, heavy carburetted hydrogen.—**ethyl alcohol** ordinary alcohol; **ethylene glycol** a thick liquid alcohol used as an antifreeze. [**ether,** and Gr. *hylē,* matter.]

etiolate *ē'ti-o-lāt, v.t.* to cause to grow pale small

yellow leaves for want of light, to blanch (*bot.*): to make pale.—*v.i.* to become pale.—*n.* etiola'tion. [Fr. *étioler* to become pale, to grow into stubble, *éteule*, stubble—L. *stipula*, a stalk, straw.]
etiology. U.S. spelling of aetiology.

etiquette *et'i-ket*, or *-ket'*, *n.* forms of ceremony or decorum: ceremony: the conventional laws of courtesy observed between members of the same profession, players, etc. [Fr. *étiquette*; see ticket.]

Eton *ē'tn*, *n.* a town opposite Windsor with an old public school.—*n.* Etonian (*ē-tōn'i-ən*) one educated at *Eton* College.—Also *adj.*—Eton collar a boy's broad starched turned-down collar: a like-shaped collar to a woman's jumper, etc.; Eton crop a fashion of cutting ladies' hair short and sleeking it; Eton jacket a boy's black dress-coat, untailed.

étrier *ā-trē-yā'*, *n.* a small rope ladder of 1–4 rungs used as a climbing aid by mountaineers. [Fr., stirrup.]

Etruria *i-trōō'ri-ə*, *n.* an ancient state of Italy north of the Tiber.—*n.* and *adj.* Etru'rian.—*adj.* Etruscan (*i-trus'kən*) Etrurian.—*n.* a native of Etruria: the language of the Etruscans. [L. *Etrūria, Etrūscus.*]

et sequens *et sē'kwənz, se-kwäns'*, (L.) and that which follows; et sequentes (*si-kwen'tēz, se-kwen'tās*), *neut.* et sequentia (*si-kwen'shi-ə, se-kwen'ti-a*), and those that follow.

étude *ā-tūd'*, (*mus.*) *n.* a composition intended either to train or to test the player's technical skill. [Fr., study.]

étui, etwee *ā-twē'*, *et-wē'*, *ns.* a small case for holding small articles, [Fr. *étui*, a case, sheath.]

etymon *et'i-mon*, *n.* the true origin of a word: an original root:—*pl.* et'yma, et'ymons.—*adj.* etymolog'ical.—*adv.* etymolog'ically.—*v.i.* etymol'ogise, -ize to inquire into or discuss etymology.—*v.t.* to trace or propound an etymology for.—*ns.* etymol'ogist; etymol'ogy the science or investigation of the derivation and original signification of words: an etymon. [Neut. of Gr. *etymos*, true.]

Eucalyptus *ū-kə-lip'təs*, *n.* a large characteristically Australian genus of the myrtle family, with leathery often glaucous leaves turned edgewise to the sun and flower-buds opening lid-wise, yielding timber, oils, and gum: (without *cap.*) a tree or shrub of this genus: (without *cap.*) eucalyptus oil:—*pl.* eucalyp'tuses, eucalyp'ti.—*n.* eu'calypt a eucalyptus. [Latinised from Gr. *eu*, well, *kalyptos*, covered.]

eucaryon, eucaryot(e), -otic. Same as eukaryon, etc.
Eucharist *ū'kə-rist*, *n.* the sacrament of the Lord's Supper: the elements of the sacrament.—*adjs.* Eucharist'ic, -al. [Gr. *eucharistiā*, thanksgiving —*eu*, well, and *charizesthai*, to show favour—*charis*, grace, thanks.]

euchre *ū'kər*, *n.* an American card game for two, three, or four persons, with the 32, 28, or 24 highest cards of the pack—if a player fails to make three tricks he is *euchred*, and his adversary scores against him.—*v.t.* to score over, as above: to outwit.

euclase *ū'klās*, *n.* a hydrated beryllium aluminium silicate occurring in pale-green transparent crystals. [Fr.,—Gr. *eu*, well, *klasis*, breaking.]

Euclidean *ū-klid'i-ən*, *ū-kli-dē'ən*, *adj.* pertaining to Euclid, a geometrician of Alexandria c. 300 B.C., or to space according to his assumptions.—Euclidean geometry a geometry based on the postulates of Euclid.

eudaemonism, eudemonism *ū-dē'mən-izm*, *n.* a system of ethics that makes happiness the test of rectitude— whether *egoistic*, as Hobbes's, or *altruistic*, as Mill's. —*adj.* eud(a)emon'ic conducive to happiness.—*n. sing.* eud(a)emon'ics.—*ns.* eud(a)e'monist; eud(a)e'mony, eud(a)emō'nia happiness, well-being: in Aristotelian philosophy, a full, active life governed by reason. [Gr. *eudaimoniā*, happiness—*eu*, well,

daimōn, a spirit.]
eudiometer *ū-di-om'i-tər*, *n.* an apparatus for gas analysis, a graduated tube holding the gas over mercury, usually with wires for sparking—early used for testing the air at different times. [Gr. *eudios*, clear, fine (as weather), *metron*, measure.]

Eugenia *ū-jē'ni-ə*, *n.* the clove genus of the myrtle family.—*n* eugenol (*ū'jin-ol*) the chief constituent of oil of cloves—also eugenic (*-jen'*) acid. [Named after Prince *Eugene* of Savoy (1663–1736).]

eugenic[1] *ū-jen'ik*, *adj.* pertaining to race improvement by judicious mating and helping the better stock to prevail.—*adv.* eugen'ically.—*n. sing.* eugen'ics the science of race improvement.—*ns.* eu'genism (*-jin-*); eu'genist; eugen'ecist, eugen'icist. [Gr. *eugenēs*, of good stock.]

eugenic[2]. See eugenol under Eugenia.
euharmonic *ū-här-mon'ik*, *adj.* in just intonation. [Gr. *eu*, well, *harmoniā*, harmony.]

Euhemerism *ū-hē'mə-rizm*, *n.* the system which explains mythology as growing out of real history, its deities as merely magnified men.—*v.t.* and *v.i.* euhē'merise, -ize.—*n.* and *adj.* euhē'merist.—*adj.* euhemeris'tic.—*adv.* euhemeris'tically. [From *Euhēmerus*, Gr. *Euēmeros*, a 4th-cent. (B.C.) Sicilian philosopher.]

eukaryon *ū-kar'i-ən*, (*biol.*) *n.* the highly organised cell nucleus, surrounded by a membrane, characteristic of higher organisms (cf. *prokaryon*).—*n.* eukar'yot(e) (*-ōt, -ət*) an organism whose cells have such nuclei.— Also *adj.*—*adj.* eukaryōt'ic.—Also eucaryon, etc. [Gr. *eu*, well, *karyon*, kernel.]

eulogium *ū-lō'ji-əm*, eulogy *ū'lə-ji*, *ns.* praise: a speech or writing in praise: a funeral oration:—*pls.* eulō'gia, -iums, eu'logies.—*v.t.* eu'logise, -ize to extol.—*n.* eu'logist one who extols another.—*adj.* eulogist'ic full of praise.—*adv.* eulogist'ically. [L.L. *eulogium* —Gr. *eu*, well, *logos*, a speaking.]

Eumenides *ū-men'i-dēz*, *n.pl.* euphemistic name for the Erinyes or Furies. [Gr. *Eumenidēs*, gracious ones—*eu*, well, *menos*, disposition.]

eunuch *ū'nək*, *n.* a castrated man, esp. one in charge of a harem, or a high-voiced singer: an ineffectual person (*fig.*).—*ns.* eu'nuchism the condition of being a eunuch; eu'nuchoidism a condition in which there is some deficiency of sexual development and in which certain female sex characteristics, e.g. high voice, are often present.—*n.* and *adj.* eu'nuchoid. [Gr. *eunouchos—eunē*, bed, *echein*, to have (charge of).]

Euonymus *ū-on'i-məs*, *n.* the spindle-tree and burning bush genus of Celastraceae: (without *cap.*) a plant of this genus. [Gr. *euōnymos*, spindle-tree.]

eupatrid *ū-pat'rid*, *n.* a member of the aristocracy in ancient Greek states. [Gr. *eupatridēs—eu*, well, *patēr*, father.]

eupepsy *ū-pep'si*, eupepsia *-ə*, *ns.* good digestion—opp. to *dyspepsia*.—*adj.* eupep'tic pertaining to good digestion: cheerful (*fig.*).—*n.* eupepticity (*-tis'i-ti*). [Gr. *eupepsiā*, digestibility—*eu*, well, *pepsis*, digestion—*peptein*, to digest.]

euphemism *ū'fim-izm*, *n.* a figure of rhetoric by which an unpleasant or offensive thing is designated by a milder term: such a term.—*v.t.* eu'phemise, -ize to express by a euphemism.—*v.i.* to use euphemistic terms.—*adj.* euphemist'ic.—*adv.* euphemist'ically. [Gr. *euphēmismos—euphēmizein*, to speak words of good omen—*eu*, well, *phanai*, to speak.]

euphony *ū'fə-ni*, *n.* an agreeable sound: a pleasing, easy pronunciation.—*adjs.* euphonic (*-fon'*), -al, euphō'nious agreeable in sound.—*adv.* euphō'niously.—*v.t.* eu'phonise, -ize to make euphonious.—*n.* euphō'nium the bass saxhorn. [Gr. *euphōniā— eu*, well, *phōnē*, sound.]

Euphorbia ū-for'bi-ə, n. the spurge genus of plants: (without cap.) a plant of this genus. [*Euphorbos*, Greek physician to Juba, king of Mauritania.]

euphoria ū-fō'ri-ə, fö', n. an exaggerated feeling of well-being, esp. irrational or groundless.—adj. **euphor'iant** inducing euphoria.—n. a drug which does this.—adj. **euphoric** (-for'). [Gr. *euphŏriă*.]

euphrasy ū'frə-si, -zi, (bot.) n. eyebright (*Euphrasia*) once thought good for disorders of the eyes. [Gr. *euphrăsiă*, delight—*euphrainein*, to cheer—*eu*, well, *phrēn*, the mind.]

euphroe ū'frō, (naut.) n. the wooden block through which the lines of a crowfoot are rove.—Also **ū'phroe**. [Du. *juffrouw—jong*, young, *vrouw*, woman.]

Euphrosyne ū-froz'i-nē, or -fros', n. one of the three Charites or Graces. [Gr. *Euphrosynē—euphrŏn*, cheerful.]

Euphuism ū'fū-izm, n. the affected and bombastic literary style brought into vogue by John Lyly's romance *Euphues* (1579–80): (without cap.) a high-flown expression in this style.—v.i. **eu'phuise, -ize**.—n. **eu'phuist**.—adj. **euphuist'ic**.—adv. **euphuist'ically**. [Gr. *euphyēs*, graceful, goodly.]

Eur(o)- ū'r(ō)-, in composition, European (and): of or pertaining to the European Common Market: of or pertaining to Europe.—adj. **Euraf'rican** pertaining to Europe and Africa, or Europe and North Africa, jointly: of a human race common to Europe and North Africa, the Mediterranean race: of mixed European and African parentage or descent.—n. a person of Eurafrican race in either sense.—adj. **Eurá'sian** of mixed European and Asian parentage or descent: of, or pertaining to, Europe and Asia (*Eurasia*) taken as one continent.—n. a person of mixed European and Asian parentage.—ns. **Eurat'om** the European Atomic Energy Community (1958), an association for joint peaceful development of nuclear energy; **Eu'ro-Amer'ican**; **Eu'robond** a borrowing in Eurocurrency by a company from subscribers, which may or may not be marketable and for which the rate and life may be either fixed or variable.—adj **Eurocent'ric** Europocentric.—ns. **Eurocomm'unism** the theory of communism professed by Communist parties in Western Europe, more pragmatic than the Soviet theory and asserting independence of it; **Eurocomm'unist**; **Eu'rocrat** an official concerned with the administration of any organisation within the Common Market; **Eurocracy** (ū-rok'rə-si).—adj. **Eurocrat'ic**.—ns. **Eu'rocurrency** the currency of any of the countries of the Common Market; **Eu'rodoll'ars** U.S. dollars deposited in European banks to facilitate financing of trade; **Eu'romarket, Eu'romart** the European Common Market, one of the West European stock exchanges; **Eu'ro-MP** a member of the European Parliament; **Eu'ronet** an information network linking various European databanks; **Eu'rovision** the European television network.

eureka, ū-rē'kə, interj. announcing a discovery.—n. a brilliant discovery [Gr. *heurēka*, I have found, perf. tense of *heuriskein*, to find, the cry of Archimedes when he thought of a method of detecting the adulteration of the gold for Hiero's crown.]

eurhythmy, eurythmy ū-rith'mi, or -ridh', n. rhythmical movement or order harmony of proportion.—adj. **eurhyth'mic**.—n. sing. **eurhyth'mics** the art or system of rhythmic movement expounded by E. Jaques-Dalcroze (1865–1950) [Gr. *eurythmiă—eu*, well, *rhythmos*, rhythm.]

euro ū'rō, n. a wallaroo:—pl **eu'ros**. [Native name.]

Euro-. See **Eur-**.

European ū-rō-pē'ən, adj. belonging to Europe.—n. a native of Europe: a member of the white race of man

characteristic of Europe: a Europeanist.—v.t. **europe'anise, -ize** to assimilate to European character or ways: to integrate into the Common Market.—ns. **Europe'anism; Europe'anist** one who favours the Common Market and seeks to uphold or develop it.—**European Commission** a body composed of members from all the Common Market countries, which develops and submits policy proposals to the European Parliament; **European (Economic) Community** the (European) Common Market (see **common**); **European Parliament** the legislative assembly of the Common Market; **European plan** (*U.S.*) in hotels, the system of charging for lodgings and service without including meals. [Gr. *Eurōpē*.]

europium ū-rō'pi-əm, n. a metal of the rare earths (at. numb. 63; symbol Eu), discovered spectroscopically by Demarçay in 1896. [**Europe**.]

Europocentric ū-rōp-ō-sent'rik, **Eurocentric** ū-rō-sent'-rik, adjs. centred, or concentrating, on Europe or its civilisation. [**Europe**, and **centric** (see **centre**).]

Eurus ū'rəs, n. the south-east wind. [L.,—Gr. *Euros*.]

Eustachian ū-stā'ki-ən, adj. pertaining to the Italian physician Bartolommeo *Eustachio* (died 1574).—**Eustachian tube** the tube leading from the middle ear to the pharynx; **Eustachian valve** the rudimentary valve at the entrance of the inferior vena cava in the heart.

eustacy, eustasy ū'stə-si, n. changes in world shore-line level, prob. caused by rise or fall of the sea-level and not by subsidence or elevation of the land.—adj. **eustat'ic** [Gr. *eu*, well, *stasis*, standing, *statikos*, causing to stand.]

eutectic, eutectoid. See eutexia.

Euterpe ū-tûr'pē, n. the Muse of music and lyric poetry: a genus of palms.—adj. **Euter'pean** pertaining to Euterpe, or to music. [Gr. *Euterpē—eu*, well, *terpein*, to delight.]

eutexia ū-tek'si-ə, n. the property of being easily melted.—n. **eutec'tic** a mixture in such proportions that the melting-point (or freezing-point) is a minimum, the constituents melting (or freezing) simultaneously.—adj. of maximum fusibility: pertaining to a eutectic.—n. **eutec'toid** an alloy similar to a eutectic but involving formation of two or three constituents from another solid constituent.—Also adj.—**eutectic point** the temperature at which a eutectic melts or freezes. [Gr. *eutēktos*, easily melted—*eu*, well, *tēkein*, to melt.]

euthanasia ū-thən-ā'zi-ə, n. an easy mode of death: the act or practice of putting painlessly to death, esp. in cases of incurable suffering.—Also **euthanasy** (-thən'ə-si). [Gr. *euthanasiă—eu*, well, *thanatos*, death.]

euthenics ū-then'iks, n. sing. the science concerned with the improvement of living conditions.—n. **euthen'ist**. [Gr. *euthēneein*, to flourish.]

eutrapelia ū-trə-pē'li-ə, n. wit, ease and urbanity of conversation. [Gr. *eutrapelos*, pleasant in conversation.]

eutrophy ū'trə-fi, n. healthy nutrition: the state (of a body of water) of being eutrophic.—adj. **eutrophic** (ū-trof'ik) pertaining to healthy nutrition: (of a body of water) over-rich in nutrients either naturally or as a result of artificial pollutants, and hence having a too-abundant growth of water-plants and animals.—n. **eutrophica'tion**. [Gr. *eutrophiă*.]

evacuate i-, ē-vak'ū-āt, v.t. to throw out the contents of: to discharge: to withdraw. to remove, as from a place of danger: to clear out troops, inhabitants, etc., from: to nullify (*law*).—v.i. to move away (from a place of danger): to void excrement.—adj. and n. **evac'uant** purgative.—n. **evacua'tion** an act of evacuating: withdrawal, removal: that which is discharged.

—*adj.* **evac'uative.**—*ns.* **evac'uator;** **evac'üee** a person removed in an evacuation. [L. *ē*, from, *vacuāre*, *-ātum*, to empty—*vacuus*, empty.]

evade *i-*, *ē-vād'*, *v.t.* to escape or avoid artfully: to shirk: to baffle, elude.—*adj.* **evā'dable.** [L. *ēvādēre* —*ē*, from *vādēre*, to go.]

evaginate *i-*, *ē-vaj'i-nāt*, *v.t.* to turn outside in: to evert.—*n.* **evagina'tion.** [L. *ēvāgināre*, *-ātum*, to unsheathe—*ē*, from, *vāgina*, a sheath.]

evaluate *i-*, *ē-val'ū-āt*, *v.t.* to determine the value of.— *n.* **evaluā'tion.**—*adj.* **eval'uative** tending, serving, to evaluate. [Fr. *évaluer.*]

evanescent *ev-ən-es'ənt*, *adj.* fleeting: vanishing.—*v.i.* **evanesce'** to fade away.—*n.* **evanesc'ence.**—*adv.* **evanesc'ently.** [L. *ēvānēscēns*, *-entis—ē*, *vānēscēre*, to vanish—*vānus*, empty.]

evangel *i-van'jəl*, *n.* good news (*poet.*): gospel: a doctrine set up as a saving principle, esp. in morals or politics.—*adjs.* **evangelic** (*ev-* or *ēv-ən-jel'ik*), **-al** of or pertaining to the Gospel: relating to the four Gospels: according to the doctrine of the Gospel: maintaining the teaching of the Gospel: Protestant: of the school that insists especially on the total depravity of unregenerate human nature, the justification of the sinner by faith alone, the free offer of the Gospel to all, and the plenary inspiration and exclusive authority of the Bible.—*ns.* **evangel'ical** one who belongs to the evangelical school; **evangel'icalism.**—*adv.* **evangel'ically.**—*ns.* **evangel'icalness;** **evangelisā'tion,** *-z-* (*i-van-jəl-*) the act of proclaiming the Gospel: Christianisation.—*v.t.* **evan'gelise, -ize** to make acquainted with the Gospel: to Christianise.—*v.i.* to preach the Gospel from place to place.—*ns.* **evan'gelism** evangelising: evangelicalism; **evan'gelist** one who evangelises: (with *cap.*) an author of a Gospel, especially one of the canonical Gospels: an assistant of the apostles: one who is authorised to preach but who is without a fixed charge: an itinerant preacher: a lay missionary in the Catholic Apostolic Church.—*adj.* **evangelis'tic** tending or intended to evangelise. [L. *evangelicus* —Gr. *euangelikos—eu*, well, *angellein*, to bring news.]

evanish *i-van'ish*, *v.i.* to vanish: to die away.—*ns.* **evan'ishment.** [O.Fr. *evanir, evaniss-* —L. *ex*, from, *vānus*, empty.]

evaporate *i-vap'ər-āt*, *v.i.* to fly off in vapour: to pass into an invisible state: to depart, vanish.—*v.t.* to convert into vapour: to dry by evaporation: to sublimate (a metal) in order to deposit as a film.—*adj.* **evap'orable** able to be evaporated or converted into vapour. —*n.* **evaporā'tion** the act of evaporating or passing off in steam or gas: the process by which a substance changes into the state of vapour.—*adj.* **evap'orative.**—*n.* **evap'orātor.**—*evaporated milk* milk thickened by evaporation, unsweetened. [L. *ē*, from, *vapōrāre*, *-ātum—vapor*, vapour.]

evasion *i-vā'zhən*, *n.* the act of evading or eluding: an attempt to escape the force of an argument or accusation: an excuse.—*adj.* **evā'sive** (*-siv*) that evades or seeks to evade: elusive: not straightforward: shuffling.—*adv.* **evā'sively.**—*n.* **evā'siveness.**—*take evasive action* to move or act in such a way as to avoid an object or consequence. [L. *ēvādēre, ēvāsum*; see **evade**.]

eve. See **even²**.

evection *i-*, *ē-vek'shən*, (*astron.*) *n.* a lunar inequality, the combined effect of the irregularity of the motion of the perigee and alternate increase and decrease of the eccentricity of the moon's orbit [L. *ēvectiō*, *-ōnis—ē*, from, *vehēre, vectum*, to carry.]

even¹ *ēv'n*, *ēvn*, *adj.* flat: level: smooth: uniform: in a straight line or plane. balanced: equal: on an equality: exact: divisible by 2 without a remainder: denoted by such a number.—*v.t.* to make even or smooth: to put on an equality: to liken: to equal.— *v.i.* to become even.—*adv.* exactly: nearly: indeed: so much as: still: extreme as the case may be, nevertheless.—*adv.* **ev'enly.**—*ns.* **ev'enness; ev'ens** even money.—*adj.*, *adv.* quits.—**even chance** an equal probability (of success or failure, etc.); **even date** the same date.—*adjs.* **ev'en-hand'ed** impartial: just; **ev'en-mind'ed** having an even or calm mind: equable; **ev'en-tem'pered** of an equable temperament, calm.— **even money** an equal sum bet on each side.—**be even with** to be revenged on (also **get even with**): to be quits with; **even now** a very little while ago (*arch.*): after all that has happened; **even out** to become even; **even so** nevertheless; **even up on** to requite, come square with; **on an even keel** balanced, not tilting to one side or the other (also *fig.*). [O.E. *efen;* Du. *even*, Ger. *eben.*]

even² *ēv'n*, *n.* evening (*poet.*).—*ns.* **eve** (*ēv*) evening (*poet.*): the night, or the whole day, before a festival: the time just preceding an event; **evening** (*ēv'ning*) the close of the daytime: the decline or end of life: an evening party, gathering or entertainment.—*adv.* **eve'nings** (*U.S.*) in the evening.—**evening class** a class held in the evenings, usu. for those who work during the day; **eve'ning-dress** the dress conventionally appropriated to social functions in the evening; **evening primrose** a N. American plant (Oenothera) with pale yellow flowers that open in the evening; **eve'ning-star** a planet, usu. Venus or Mercury, seen in the west setting soon after the sun; **ev'ensong** evening prayer, the Anglican form appointed to be said or sung at evening: the time proper for such; **ev'entide** the time of evening, evening; **eventide home** a home for old people. [O.E. *ǣfen, ǣfnung.*]

event *i-vent'*, *n.* that which happens: result: any incident or occurrence: contingency: an item in a programme of sports: a horse-riding competition, often over three days (**three-day event**), consisting of three sections— dressage, cross-country riding and show-jumping.—*n.* **event'er** a horse trained to take part in events: the rider of such a horse, as *three-day eventer*.—*adj.* **event'ful** full of events: momentous.—*n.* **event'ing** taking part in riding events.—*adj.* **event'ual** happening as a consequence: final.—*n.* **eventual'ity** a contingency.—*adv.* **event'ually** finally: at length.—*v.i.* **event'uate** to turn out.—**at all events, in any event** no matter what happens; **in the event** as things turn(ed) out; **in the event of, that** in the case of: if. [L. *ēventus—ēvenīre*, to come out, happen—*ē*, from, *venīre*, to come.]

ever *ev'ər*, *adv.* always: eternally: at all times: continually: at any time: on record (as *the biggest ever*, the biggest that ever was or happened): in any degree: at all: in the world: very, extremely (*slang*, orig. *U.S.*; used as part of an interjection or statement, as *was I ever hungry*, I was very hungry).—As a suffix, giving complete generality to relative adverbs and pronouns. —*adj.* **ev'ergreen** in leaf throughout the year: always fresh and green: unfading: never failing, retaining one's, or its, vigour, freshness, popularity, interest, etc. for ever.—*n.* a tree or shrub that is green throughout the year.—*adj.* **everlast'ing** endless: perpetual: unceasing: eternal: wearisomely long-continued.—*n.* eternity: a flower (of *Helichrysum, Antennaria*, or other genus) that may be kept for years without much change of appearance: a very durable cloth.—*adv.* **everlast'ingly.**—*n.* **everlast'ingness.**— *adv.* **evermore'** (or *ev'*) for all time to come (also **for evermore**): ever: unceasingly.—**ever and anon** from time to time; **ever so** to any extent: to a very great extent; **ever such a** (*coll.*) a very; **for ever** to all eternity: for a long time (*coll.*). [O.E. *ǣfre.*]

Everest ev'ə-rəst, *n.* the name of the highest mountain in the world, in the Himalayas: anything difficult to accomplish, the height of ambition (*fig.*).

everglade ev'ər-glād, *n.* a large shallow lake or marsh: (with *cap.*; chiefly in *pl.*) such a marsh in southern Florida, enclosing thousands of islets covered with dense thickets. [Perh. **ever,** and **glade.**]

evert ē-, or ι-vûrt', *v.t.* to turn inside out: to turn outwards.—*adj.* **ever'sible.**—*n.* **ever'sion.** [L. *ēvertēre* -ē, from, *vertēre, versum,* to turn.]

every ev'ri, *adj.* each of a number: all taken separately. —*prons.* **ev'erybody, ev'eryone** every person.—*adj.* **ev'eryday** of or belonging to every day, daily: common, usual: pertaining to weekdays, not Sunday. —*ns.* **ev'erydayness; Ev'eryman** the hero of an old morality play, representing mankind, everybody, anybody.—*adv.* **ev'eryplace** (*U.S.*) everywhere.— *pron.* **ev'erything** all things taken singly: all.—*advs.* **ev'eryway** in every way or respect, **ev'erywhere** in every place.—**every bit, whit** the whole: quite; every **last** every; **every man Jack, every mother's son** every one without exception; **every now and then,** or **again,** at intervals; **every other** every second or alternate; **every so often** at intervals; **every which way** (*U.S.*) every way: in disorder; **have everything** (*coll.*) to be well endowed with possessions, attractiveness, etc. [O.E. *æfre,* ever, and *ǣlc,* each.]

evict i-, ē-vikt', *v.t.* to dispossess by law: to expel.—*ns.* **evic'tion** the act of evicting from house or lands: the dispossession of one person by another having a better title of property in land; **evic'tor.** [L. *ēvictus,* pa.p. of *ēvincēre,* to overcome.]

evident ev'i-dənt, *adj.* that can be seen: clear to the mind: obvious.—*n.* that which serves as evidence.— *n.* **ev'idence** that which makes evident: means of proving an unknown or disputed fact: support for a belief: indication: information in a law case: testimony: a witness or witnesses collectively.—*v.t.* to render evident: to attest, prove: to indicate.—*adjs.* **evidential** (*-den'shəl*), **eviden'tiary** furnishing evidence: tending to prove.—*advs.* **eviden'tially; ev'idently** obviously: manifestly.—**in evidence** received by the court as competent evidence: plainly visible, conspicuous, **turn King's (Queen's) evidence,** (*U.S.*) **turn State's evidence** to give evidence against an accomplice in a crime. [L. *ēvidēns, -entis*—ē, from, *vidēre,* to see.]

evil ē'v(i)l, *adj.* wicked: bad: mischievous: disagreeable: unfortunate.—*adv.* in an evil manner: badly.— *n.* that which produces unhappiness or calamity: harm: wickedness: depravity: sin.—*adv.* **evilly** (*ē'vil-ι*) in an evil manner: not well.—*n.* **e'vilness** the state of being evil: wickedness.—**e'vil-doer** one who does evil; **evil eye** a supposed power to cause harm by a look.—*adj.* **e'vil-fa'voured** having a repulsive appearance: ugly.—**e'vil-fa'vouredness** ugliness: deformity.—*adjs.* **e'vil-mind'ed** inclined to evil: malicious: wicked; **e'vil-tem'pered** bad-tempered, unpleasant, spiteful.—**the evil one** the devil; **speak evil of** to slander. [O.E. *yfel.*]

evince i-vins', *v.t.* to prove beyond doubt: to show clearly: to make evident: to give indication of.—*n.* **evince'ment.**—*adj.* **evinc'ible.**—*adv.* **evinc'ibly.**— *adj.* **evinc'ive** tending to evince, prove, or demonstrate. [L. *ēvincēre,* to vanquish—ē-, intens , *vincēre,* to overcome.]

eviscerate ē- or i-vis'ər-āt, *v.t.* to tear out the viscera or bowels of: to gut.—*n.* **evisceră'tion.** [L. *ē,* from, *viscera,* the bowels.]

evocation, etc. See **evoke.**

evoke i-vōk', *v.t.* to call out: to draw out or bring forth to call up or awaken in the mind.—*n.* **evocă'tion.**— *adjs.* **evocative** (*i-vok'ə-tiv*) **evoc'atory.**—*n* **evoc'ativeness.** [L. *ēvocāre*—ē, from, and *vocāre,* to call]

évolué ā-vol-ü-ā', *n.* a member of a primitive group of people who has been educated to the standards of a more advanced civilisation.—Also *adj.* [Fr., developed.]

evolution ēv-, ev-ə-lōō'shən, *n.* the act of unrolling or unfolding: gradual working out or development: a series of things unfolded: the doctrine according to which higher forms of life have gradually arisen out of lower. the extraction of roots (*math.*): (usu. in *pl.*) orderly movements as of a body of troops, flock of birds, etc.—*n.* **ev'olute** (*math.*) an original curve from which another curve (the *involute*) is described by the end of a thread gradually unwound from the former. —*adj.* rolled back.—*v.t.* and *v.i.* to develop by evolution.—*adjs.* **evolu'tional, evolu'tionary** of or pertaining to evolution.—*ns.* **evolu'tionism** the doctrine of evolution; **evolu'tionist.**—*adj.* **ev'olutive.** [L. *ēvolūtiō, -ōnis,*—*ēvolvēre;* see **evolve.**]

evolve i-, or ē-volv', *v.t.* to unroll: to disclose: to develop: to unravel.—*v.i.* to disclose itself: to result. —*adj.* **evolv'able** that can be drawn out.—*n.* **evolve'ment.**—*adj.* **evolv'ent.** [L. *ēvolvēre*—ē-, from, *volvēre, volūtum,* to roll.]

evzone ev'zōn, *n.* a soldier in an élite Greek infantry regiment. [Mod. Gr. *euzōnos*—Gr., girt for action —*eu,* well, *zōnē,* girdle.]

ewe ū, *n.* a female sheep.—**ewe'-lamb** a female lamb. a poor man's one possession, one's dearest possession. [O.E. *ēowu;* cf. L. *ovis,* Gr. *ois,* Sans. *avi,* a sheep.]

ewer ū'ər, *n.* a large water jug with a wide spout. [Through Fr. from L. *aquārium* (neut. of *aquārius,* of water)—*aqua,* water.]

Ewigkeit ā'vihh-kīt, *n.* eternity. [Ger.]

ex eks, (*L.*) *prep.* from, out of: direct from, as *ex works, ex warehouse* (*commerce*).

ex- eks-, *pfx.* former but surviving, as **ex-emperor** formerly employed, etc. by.—*prep.* without, as *ex dividend,* without the next dividend.—*n.* **ex** (*coll.*) one who is no longer what he or she was, esp. a person's former husband or wife:—*pl.* **ex's, exes.**

exacerbate iks-, or igz-as'ər-bāt, *v.t.* to embitter: to provoke: to render more violent or severe, as a disease.—*n* **exacerbā'tion** increase of irritation or violence, esp. the increase of a fever or disease: embitterment. [L. *exacerbāre, -ātum*—*ex,* and *acerbāre,* from *acerbus,* bitter]

exact igz-akt', *v.t.* to force out: to compel payment of: to demand and obtain: to extort: to require as indispensable.—*adj.* precise: rigorous: accurate: absolutely correct: finished: consummate: strict.—*adj.* **exact'ing** compelling full payment: unreasonable in making demands: demanding much.—*ns.* **exac'tion** the act of exacting or demanding strictly: an oppressive demand: that which is exacted, as excessive work or tribute; **exact'itude** exactness: correctness.—*adv.* **exact'ly.**—*ns.* **exact'ment; exact'ness** the quality of being exact: accuracy; **exact'or, -er** one who exacts: an extortioner: one who claims rights, often too strictly.—**exact sciences** the mathematical sciences, whose results are precise or quantitative.—**not exactly** not altogether: not at all (*coll., iron.*). [L. *exigēre, exāctum,* to demand, to weigh strictly—*ex,* from, *agēre,* to drive.]

exaggerate igz-aj'ər-āt, *v.t.* to magnify unduly: to overstate: to represent too strongly to intensify.— *v.i.* to speak hyperbolically, to overstate the case.— *n.* **exaggerā'tion** extravagant representation: a statement in excess of the truth.—*adjs* **exagg'erative,** **exagg'eratory** containing exaggeration or tending to exaggerate.—*n.* **exagg'erător.** [L. *exaggerāre, -ātum*—*ex-,* aggerāre, to heap up—*agger,* a heap.]

exalt igz-ölt', *v.t.* to set aloft: to elate or fill with the joy of success: to extol—*n.* **exaltā'tion** (*egz-ol-*)

exam 335 **exchange**

elevation in rank or dignity: high estate: elation: a planet's position of greatest influence (*astrol*.): a flight (of larks) (*arch*.).—*adj.* **exalt'ed** elevated: lofty: dignified.—*n* **exalt'edness.** [L. *exaltāre—ex-, altus,* high.]

exam. Short for **examination.**

examine *igz-am'in, v.t.* to test: to inquire into: to question: to look closely into: to inspect.—*adj* **exam'in-able.**—*ns.* **examinā'tion** careful search or inquiry: close inspection: trial: a test of capacity and knowledge, familiarly contracted to **exam'**: formal interrogation in court of a witness or accused person (*law*); **examinee'** one under examination; **exam'iner** one who examines.—*adj.* **exam'ining.—examinā'tion-in-chief** (*law*) questioning of one's own witness (cf. **cross-examination**).—*v.t.* **exam'ine-in-chief.** [Fr. *examiner—*L. *exāmināre—exāmen,* the tongue of a balance.]

example *igz-am'pl, n.* a specimen: an illustration: a copy of a book: a person or thing to be imitated or not to be imitated: a pattern: a warning: an instance.—*v.t.* (*rare*) to exemplify. to instance.—**for example** for instance: as an illustration; **make an example of** to punish severely as a warning to others. [O Fr.,—L. *exemplum—eximĕre,* to take out—*ex,* out of, *emĕre, emptum,* to take.]

exanimate *egz-, igz-an'i-mât, adj.* lifeless: spiritless: depressed.—*n.* **exanimā'tion.** [L. *exanimātus—ex,* from, *anima,* breath.]

exanthem *eks-an'thəm,* **exanthema** *eks-an-thē'mə, ns.* a skin eruption, esp. accompanied by fever: a disease so characterised:—*pl.* **exan'thems, exanthē'mata.** —*adjs.* **exanthēmat'ic; exanthē'matous.** [Gr. *exanthēma, -atos—ex-,* out, *antheein,* to blossom.]

exarch *eks'ark, n.* a Byzantine provincial governor, esp. of Italy: a metropolitan (*Orthodox Church*): a bishop of rank between a patriarch and a metropolitan (*Orthodox Church*): the head of the Bulgarian church: an ecclesiastical inspector: a legate —*ns.* **exarch'ate** (or *eks'*), **ex'archy** the office, jurisdiction or province of an exarch. [Gr. *exarchos,* leader.]

exasperate *igz-as'pər-āt, v.t.* to make more grievous or painful: to make very angry: to irritate in a high degree.—*adj.* **exas'perating.**—*ns.* **exasperā'tion; exas'-perātor.** [L. *ex-,* intens., *asperāre,* to make rough—*asper,* rough.]

Excalibur *eks-kal'ib-ər, n.* the name of King Arthur's sword. [O.Fr. *Escalibor* for Caliburn; cf. *Caladbolg,* a famous sword in Irish legend.]

ex cathedra *eks kə-thē'drə,* or *eks kath'ə-dra,* (L.L.) from the chair of office, esp. the Pope's throne in the Consistory, or a professor's chair: hence authoritatively, judicially.

excavate *eks'kə-vāt, v.t.* to hollow or scoop out: to dig out: to lay bare by digging.—*ns.* **excavā'tion** the act of excavating: a hollow or cavity made by excavating: an archaeological site, a dig; **ex'cavātor** one who excavates: a machine used for excavating. [L. *excavāre—ex-,* out, *cavus,* hollow.]

exceed *ik-sēd', v.t.* to go beyond the limit or measure of: to surpass or excel.—*adj.* **exceed'ing** surpassing: excessive.—Also *adv.* (*arch*.) exceedingly.—*adv.* **exceed'ingly** very much: greatly. [L. *ex-,* beyond, *cēdĕre, cēssum,* to go.]

excel *ik-sel', v t.* to be superior to: to surpass.—*v.t.* to have good qualities in a high degree: to perform very meritorious actions: to be superior:—*pr p.* **excell'ing;** *pa.t.* and *pa.p.* **excelled'.—*ns.* excellence** (*eks'ə-ləns*), **exc'ellency** great merit: any excellent quality: worth-greatness: (usu. **Exc'ellency**) a title of honour given to persons high in rank or office.—*adj.* **exc'ellent** surpassing others in some good quality: of great

virtue, worth, etc.: good in a high degree.—*adv.* **exc'ellently.—*interj.* excel'sior** (L. *compar. adj.,* taller, loftier) higher still.—*n.* (sometimes with *cap.;* orig. *U.S*) a trade name for wood shavings for packing. [L. *excellĕre—ex-,* out, up, *celsus,* high.]

excellence *ek-se-lās,* (Fr.) *n.* excellence.—**par excellence** eminently, by way of ideal.

excentric. Same as **eccentric.**

except *ik-sept', v.t.* to take out, or leave out: to exclude.—*prep.* leaving out: excluding: but.—*conj.* (*arch*.) unless.—*prep.* **except'ing** with the exception of, except.—*n.* **excep'tion** the act of excepting: that which is excepted: exclusion: objection: offence.—*adj.* **excep'tionable** objectionable.—*adv.* **excep'-tionably.**—*adj.* **excep'tional** unusual (esp in a good sense).—*adv.* **excep'tionally.—take exception** to object (to); **the exception proves the rule** the making of an exception proves that the rule holds in cases not excepted. [L. *excipĕre, exceptum—ex,* from, *capĕre,* to take.]

exceptis excipiendis *ik-sep'tis ik-sip-i-en'dis, eks-kep'-tēs eks-ki-pi-en'dēs,* (L.L.) excepting what is to be excepted: with proper exceptions.

excerpt *ek'sûrpt,* or *ek-sûrpt'; n.* a passage selected from a book, opera, etc., an extract.—*v.t.* **excerpt'** to select: to extract.—*ns.* **excerpt'ing; excerp'tion; excerp'tor.** [L *excerptum,* pa.p. of *excerpĕre—ex,* from, *carpĕre,* to pick.]

excerpta *ik-sûrp'ta, eks-kerp'ta,* (L.; *pl. of* **excerp'tum** *-təm, -tōōm*), *n.pl.* extracts, selections.

excess *ik-ses', n.* a going beyond what is usual or proper: intemperance: that which exceeds: the degree or amount by which one thing exceeds another.—*adj.* in excess.—*adj.* **excess'ive** beyond what is usual or right: immoderate: extreme.—*adv.* excessively.—*adv.* **excess'ively.**—*n.* **excess'iveness.—excess fare** payment for distance travelled beyond, or in a class superior to, that allowed by the ticket; **excess baggage, luggage** luggage above the weight allowed free; **excess postage** payment due when insufficient stamps have been put on a letter or packet.—**carry to excess** to do too much; **excess profits tax** a tax on profits in excess of those for a specified base period or over a rate adopted as a reasonable return on capital; **in excess of** more than. [L. *excēssus—excēdĕre, excēssum,* to go beyond.]

exchange *iks-chānj', v.t.* to give or give up in return for something else: to give and take mutually: to barter. —*v.i.* to pass by exchange of office with another.—*n.* the giving and taking of one thing for another: barter: the thing exchanged: process by which accounts between distant parties are settled by bills instead of money: money-changing business: exchanging currency of one country for that of another: the difference between the value of money in different places. a stock exchange: the building where merchants, etc., meet for business: a central office where telephone lines are connected: in chess, the taking by both players of a piece in consecutive moves.—*n.* **exchangeabil'ity.**—*adj.* **exchange'able** that may be exchanged.—*n.* **exchan'ger** one who exchanges or practises exchange.—**exchange control** the official control of a country's foreign exchange settlements so as to conserve its holding of foreign currency; **exchange rate** (or **rate of exchange**) the ratio at which one currency can be exchanged for another; **exchange student, teacher** a student or teacher spending some time at a school in a foreign country while one from that country attends his school —**exchange words,** blows to quarrel verbally or physically; **force the exchange** in chess, to play so as to force one's opponent to take one piece for another; **win** (or **lose**) **the exchange** in chess, to gain (or lose) a superior piece in

For other sounds see detailed chart of pronunciation

exchange for an inferior. [O.Fr. *eschangier* (Fr. *échanger*)—L.L. *excambiāre*—L. *ex*, from, L.L. *cambiāre*, to barter.]

exchequer *iks-chek'ər*, *n.* a department of state having charge of revenue, so named from the chequered cloth which covered the table, and on which the accounts were reckoned: the Court of Exchequer: a national treasury: one's funds, finances, purse.—*v.t.* to proceed against in the Court of Exchequer.—**exchequer bill** a bill issued at the Exchequer, as security for money advanced to the government.—**Chancellor of the Exchequer** see chancellor; **Court of Exchequer** in England originally a revenue court developed out of the judicial branch of the Exchequer, acquired a general common-law jurisdiction by a legal fiction, became a division of the High Court of Justice in 1875, and is now merged in the King's (Queen's) Bench Division: in Scotland a revenue court, abolished in 1886, its jurisdiction transferred to the Court of Session. [See chequer, check, chess.]

excise[1] *ek'sīz* or *-sīz'*, *n.* a tax on certain home commodities, and on licences for certain trades: the department in the civil administration concerned with this tax.—Also *adj.*—*v.t.* to subject to excise duty.—*adj.* **excis'able** liable to excise duty.—**ex'ciseman** (or *-sīz'*) an officer charged with collecting the excise. [M.Du. *excijs*—O.Fr. *acceis*, tax—L.L. *accensāre*, to tax—*ad*, to, and *census*, a tax.]

excise[2] *ek-sīz'*, *v.t.* to cut off or out.—*n.* **excision** (*ek-sizh'ən*) a cutting out or off of any kind: extirpation. [L. *excīdĕre*, to cut out—*ex*, from, *caedĕre*, to cut.]

excite *ik-sīt'*, *v.t.* to call into activity: to stir up: to rouse: to energise: to produce electric or magnetic activity in: to sensitise: to stir emotionally: to raise (a nucleus, atom, molecule, etc.) to an excited state.—*n.* **excitabil'ity**.—*adj.* **excit'able** capable of being excited: responsive to stimulus: easily excited.—*ns.* **excit'ableness**; **excitancy** (*ek'si-tən-si*), excitant property; **excitant** (*ek'si-* or *ek-sī'*) that which excites or rouses the vital activity of the body: a stimulant: the electrolyte in an electric cell.—*adj.* exciting: stimulating.—*n.* **excita'tion** (*ek-si-*) the act of exciting: means of excitement: a state of excitement.—*adjs.* **excit'ative**, **excit'atory** tending to excite.—*adj.* **excit'ed** agitated: roused emotionally: in a state of great activity: having energy higher than that of the ground, or normal, state.—*ns.* **excite'ment** agitation: that which excites; **excit'er** one who or that which excites: an auxiliary machine supplying current for another machine: a sparking apparatus for producing electric waves.—*adj.* **excit'ing** tending to excite: stirring, thrilling.—*ns.* **excit'on** (or *ek'si-ton*) a bound pair comprising an electron and a hole; **exci'tor** exciter: an afferent nerve stimulating a part. [Fr. *exciter*—L. *excitāre*, *-ātum*—*excīēre*—*ex-*, out, *cīēre*, to set in motion.]

exclaim *iks-klām'*, *v.t.* and *v.i.* to cry out: to utter or speak vehemently.—*n.* an exclamation, outcry.—*n.* **exclamation** (*eks-klə-mā'shən*) vehement utterance: outcry: an uttered expression of surprise and the like: the mark expressing this (!) (also **exclamation mark**): an interjection.—*adj.* **exclam'atory** containing or expressing exclamation. [Fr. *exclamer*—L. *exclāmāre*, *-ātum*—*ex-*, out, *clāmāre*, to shout.]

exclave *eks'klāv*, *n.* a part of a country, province etc., disjoined from the main part, being enclosed in foreign territory. [See enclave.]

exclosure *eks-klō'zhər*, *n.* an area shut off from intrusion. [L. *ex-*, from, and close[1].]

exclude *iks-klōōd'*, *v.t.* to shut out: to thrust out: to hinder from entrance: to omit: to hinder from participation: to except.—*n.* **exclu'sion** (*-zhən*) a shutting or putting out: ejection: exception.—*adj.* **exclu'sive**

(*-siv*) able or tending to exclude: incompatible: debarring from participation: of the nature of monopoly: socially inaccessible or aloof: sole: not to be had elsewhere or from another: select, fashionable: without taking into account: not included.—*n.* an exclusive product: a newspaper story published by one paper only.—*adv.* **exclu'sively**.—*ns.* **exclu'siveness**.—*adj.* **exclu'sory** exclusive.—**exclusion order** an order prohibiting the presence in, or entry to, Britain of any person known to be concerned in acts of terrorism; **exclusion principle** a fundamental law of quantum mechanics that no two particles of a group called fermions can exist in identical quantum states; **Exclusive Brethren** see Close Brethren.—**law of excluded middle** (*log.*) that everything is either A or not-A; **to the exclusion of** so as to exclude. [L. *ex-clūdĕre*, *-clūsum*—*ex-*, out, *claudĕre*, to shut.]

excogitate *eks-koj'i-tāt*, *v.t.* to discover by thinking: to think out earnestly or laboriously.—*n.* **excogita'tion** laborious thinking: invention: contrivance.—*adj.* **excog'itative**. [L. *excōgitāre*, *-ātum*—*ex-*, out, *cōgitāre*, to think.]

excommunicate *eks-kəm-ūn'i-kāt*, *v.t.* to put out of or expel from the communion of the church: to deprive of church privileges.—*adjs.* **excommun'icable**; **excommun'icate** (*-kit*, *-kāt*) excommunicated.—Also *n.*—*n.* **excommunica'tion** the act of expelling from the communion of a church.—*adj.* **excommun'icatory** of or pertaining to excommunication. [From L.L. *excommūnicāre*—L. *ex*, *commūnis*, common.]

excoriate *eks-kō'ri-āt*, *-kō'ri-*, *v.t.* to strip the skin from: to criticise severely (*fig.*).—*n.* **excoria'tion**. [L. *excoriāre*, *-ātum*—*ex*, from, *corium*, the skin.]

excrement *eks'kri-mənt*, *n.* useless matter discharged from the animal alimentary, etc. system, now esp. dung.—*adjs.* **excremental** (*-ment'l*), **excrementi'tious**. [L. *excrēmentum*—*excernĕre*—*ex-*, out, *cernĕre*, to sift.]

excrementa *eks-kri-men'tə*, *-kre-men'ta* (L.; *pl.* of **excrementum** *-təm*, *-tōōm*), *n.pl.* refuse matter.

excrescence *iks-kres'əns*, *n.* an outgrowth or projection, esp. abnormal, grotesque, or offensive: a wart or tumour: a superfluous part: an outbreak.—*n.* **excresc'ency** the state of being excrescent: excrescence.—*adjs.* **excresc'ent** growing out: superfluous: of a sound or letter, added to a word for euphony, etc., without etymological justification; **excrescential** (*eks-kri-sen'shl*). [L. *excrēscĕre*—*ex-*, out, *crēscĕre*, to grow.]

excrete *eks-krēt'*, *v.t.* to separate and discharge: to eject.—*n.pl.* **excre'ta** matters discharged from the animal body.—*n.* **excre'tion** the excreting of matter from an organism: that which is excreted.—*adjs.* **excre'tive** able to excrete: concerned with excretion; **excre'tory** (or *eks'kri-tər-i*) having the quality of excreting. [L. *ex*, from, *cernĕre*, *crētum*, to separate.]

excruciate *iks-krōō'shi-āt*, *v.t.* to torture: to rack: to inflict severe pain: to irritate greatly.—*adj.* **excru'ciating** extremely painful: racking: torturing: agonising: intensely irritating.—*adv.* **excru'ciatingly**.—*n.* **excrucia'tion** torture: vexation. [L. *ex-*, out, *cruciāre*, *-ātum*, to crucify—*crux*, *crucis*, a cross.]

excudit *eks-kū'dit*, *-kōō'*, (L.) (he, she) struck, hammered, forged, printed (this).

exculpate *eks'kul-pāt*, also *-kul'*, *v.t.* to clear from the charge of a fault or crime: to absolve: to vindicate.—*adj.* **excul'pable**.—*n.* **exculpa'tion**.—*adj.* **exculpatory** tending to free from the charge of fault or crime. [L. *ex*, from, *culpa*, a fault.]

excursion *iks-kûr'shən*, *n.* a going forth: a deviation: a pleasure trip: a company or collection of people on a pleasure outing: a digression.—*n.* **excur'sionist** one who goes on a pleasure trip.—*adj.* **excur'sive** rambling: deviating.—*adv.* **excur'sively.**—*ns.* **excur'-siveness**; **excur'sus** a dissertation on some particular matter appended to a book or chapter:—*pl.* **excur'-suses.**—**excursion fare** a special cheap fare allowed on certain journeys by public transport; **excursion ticket**; **excursion train** a special train, usually with reduced fares, for persons making an excursion. [L. *ex-*, out, *currĕre*, *cursum*, to run.]

excuse *iks-kūz'*, *v.t.* to free from blame or guilt: to exonerate: to pass over, overlook: to pardon or condone (in small matters): to free from an obligation: to release, dispense with: to allow to absent oneself: to seek to extenuate or justify: to make an apology or ask pardon for.—*n.* (*iks-kūs'*) a plea offered in extenuation: indulgence.—*adj.* **excūsable** (*iks-kūz'ə-bl*).—*n.* **excūs'ableness.**—*adv.* **excūs'ably.**—*adj.* **excūs'atory.**—**be excused** (*euphemism*) to go to the lavatory to relieve oneself; **excuse** (*iks-kūs'*) **for a** very poor example of; **excuse me** an expression used as an apology for any slight or apparent impropriety, or for controverting a statement that has been made; **excuse-me** (**dance**) a dance during which one may change partners; **excuse oneself** to ask permission and then leave: to explain and seek pardon (*for* a misdeed). [L. *excūsāre—ex*, from, *causa*, a cause, accusation.]

ex-directory *eks-dī-rek'tə-ri*, *-di-*, *adj.* of a telephone number, not listed in a directory: of a person, having such a number. [ex, **directory** (see **direct**).]

exeat *eks'i-at*, *n.* formal leave of absence, esp. for a student to be out of college for more than one night. [L., let him go out: 3rd pers. sing. pres. subj. of *exīre*.]

execrate *eks'i-krāt*, *v.t.* to curse: to denounce evil against: to denounce: to detest.—*adj.* **ex'ecrable** deserving execration: detestable: accursed: very bad, of low quality.—*adv.* **ex'ecrably.**—*n.* **execrā'tion** the act of execrating: a curse pronounced: that which is execrated.—*adj.* **ex'ecrative** of or belonging to execration.—*adv.* **ex'ecratively.**—*adj.* **ex'ecratory.** [L. *exsecrārī*, *-ātus*, to curse—*ex*, from, *sacer*, sacred.]

execute *eks'i-kūt*, *v.t.* to perform: to give effect to: to carry into effect: to put to use, bring into action: to put to death by law: to run through (a program, etc.) using computer language (*comput.*).—*adj.* **execūt-able** (*eks'i-kūt-ə-bl*, *ek-sek'ūt-ə-bl*) that can be executed.—*ns.* **execūtant** (*eg-zek'*) one who executes or performs: a technically accomplished performer of music; **execūter** (*eks'*); **execū'tion** the act of, or skill in, executing or performing: accomplishment: completion: carrying into effect the sentence of a court of law. the warrant for so doing: the infliction of capital punishment; **execū'tioner** one who executes, esp. one who inflicts capital punishment.—*adj.* **executive** (*eg-zek'ū-tiv*) designed or fitted to execute or perform: concerned with performance, administration, or management: active: qualifying for or pertaining to the execution of the law: administrative: for the use of business executives: hence (*loosely*) expensive, sophisticated.—*n.* the power or authority in government that carries the laws into effect: the persons who administer the government or an organisation: a person in an executive position in government or business: the head of an executive, as president, governor, mayor, etc.—*adv.* **exec'ūtively.**—*n.* **execūtor** (*eg-zek'*) one who executes or performs: a person appointed to see a will carried into effect:—*fem.* **exec'ūtrix** (*pl.* **-trixes** or **executri'cēs**).—*adj.* **execūtō'rial.**—*n.* **exec'ūtorship.**—*adj.* **exec'ū-tory** executing official duties: designed to be carried into effect.—**executive program** (*comput.*) a program which controls the use of a computer and of other programs; **executive session** (*U.S.*) a meeting of the Senate for executive business, usu. held in private: hence, any meeting in private. [[L. *exsequī*, *exsecūtus—ex*, out, *sequī*, to follow.]

exegesis *eks-i-jē'sis*, *n.* interpretation, esp. Biblical.—*ns.* **ex'egète**, **exegēt'ist** one who interprets or expounds.—*adjs.* **exegetic** (*-jet'ik*), **-al**, pertaining to exegesis: explanatory.—*adv.* **exegēt'ically.**—*n. sing.* **exegēt'ics** the science of exegesis. [Gr. *exēgēsis—exēgeesthai*, to explain—*ex-*, out, *hēgeesthai*, to guide.]

exempla. See **exemplum.**

exemplar *egz-em'plər*, *-plär*, *n.* a person or thing to be imitated: the ideal model of an artist: a type: an example: a copy of a book.—*adv.* **exem'plarily.**—*ns.* **exem'plariness**; **exemplarity** (*-plar'*) exemplariness: exemplary conduct.—*adj.* **exem'plary** worthy of imitation or notice: serving as model, specimen, illustration, or warning.—**exemplary damages** (*law*) damages in excess of the value needed to compensate the plaintiff. [L. *exemplar—exemplum*, example.]

exemplify *igz-em'pli-fī*, *v.t.* to illustrate by example: to make an attested copy of: to prove by an attested copy:—*pr.p.* **exem'plifying;** *pa.t.* and *pa.p.* **exem'plified.**—*adj.* **exem'plifiable.**—*n.* **exemplificā'tion** the act of exemplifying: that which exemplifies: an attested copy or transcript. [L. *exemplum*, example, *facĕre*, to make.]

exempli gratia *ig-zem'plī grä'shi-ə*, *eks-em'plē grä'ti-ä*, (L.) by way of example, for instance—often abbreviated **e.g.**

exemplum *ig-zem'pləm*, *n.* an example: a short story, or anecdote pointing a moral:—*pl.* **exem'pla** (*-plə*). [L., example.]

exempt *igz-empt'*, *-emt'*, *v.t.* to free, or grant immunity (from).—*adj.* taken out: not liable: of goods and services, carrying no value-added tax, but on which tax charged by suppliers, etc. cannot be reclaimed.—*n.* **exemp'tion** the act of exempting: the state of being exempt: freedom from any service, duty, burden, etc.: immunity. [Fr.,—L. *eximĕre*, *exemptum—ex*, from, *emĕre*, to buy.]

exequatur *eks-i-kwā'tər*, *n.* an official recognition of a consul or commercial agent given by the government of the country in which he is to be. [L. *exequātur*, let him execute—the opening word.]

exequy *eks'i-kwi* (usu. in *pl.* **exequies** *-kwiz*), *n.* a funeral procession: funeral rites.—*adj.* **exequial** (*eks-ē'kwi-əl*). [L. *exequiae—ex*, from, *sequī*, to follow.]

exercise *eks'ər-sīz*, *n.* a putting in practice: exertion of the body for health or amusement or acquisition of skill: a similar exertion of the mind: a task designed or prescribed for these purposes: a written school task: a study in music: a set of problems, passages for translation, etc., in a text-book: an academical disputation: (in *pl.*) military drill or manoeuvres: a ceremony or formal proceeding (*U.S.*): an act of worship or devotion.—*v.t.* to train by use: to improve by practice: to give exercise to: to trouble: to put in practice: to use: to wield.—*v.i.* to take exercise: to drill.—*adj.* **ex'ercisable.**—*n.* **ex'erciser** one who or that which exercises: a device, usu. with elasticated cords, to help in exercising the muscles.—**ex'ercise-book** a book for writing school exercises in.—**the object of the exercise** the purpose of a particular operation or activity. [O.Fr. *exercice—*L. *exercitium—*L. *exercēre*, *-citum*, pfx. *ex-*, and *arcēre*, to shut up, restrain.]

exercitation *egz-ûr-sit-ā'shən*, *n.* putting into practice: employment: exercise: a discourse. [L. *exercitātiō*, *-ōnis—exercēre*, to exercise.]

exergue *eks'* or *eks-ûrg'*, *n.* a part on the reverse of a coin, below the main device, often filled up by the date, etc.—*adj.* **exer'gual.** [Fr.,—Gr. *ex*, out of, *ergon*, work.]

exert *igz-ûrt'*, *v.t.* to bring into active operation.—*n.* **exer'tion** a bringing into active operation: striving: activity.—*adj.* **exert'ive** having the power or tendency to exert: using exertion. [L. *exserĕre, exsertum*—*ex*, from, *serĕre*, to put together.]

exes *eks'əz*, *n.pl.* a slang abbreviation of **expenses**: see also **ex** under **ex-**.

exeunt *eks'i-unt*, *-ōŏnt*, (L.) (they) go out, leave the stage.—**exeunt omnes** (*om'nēz*, *-nās*) all go out. [See **exit**.]

exfoliate *eks-fō'li-āt*, *v.t.* to shed in flakes: to remove in flakes.—*v.i.* to come off in flakes: to separate into layers.—*n.* **exfolia'tion**.—*adj.* **exfō'liative**. [L. *exfoliāre, -ātum*, to strip of leaves—*ex*, from, *folium*, a leaf.]

ex gratia *eks grā'shi-ə, grā'ti-ā*, (L.) as an act of grace: as a favour, not out of obligation, and with no acceptance of liability (as *ex gratia payment*).

exhale *eks-hāl'*, *egz-āl'*, *v.t.* to breathe forth: to emit or send out as vapour, smell, etc.—*v.i.* to breathe out: to rise or come off as a vapour, smell, emanation. —*adj.* **exhāl'able**.—*n.* **exhalation** (*eks-, egz-ə-lā'shən*) the act or process of exhaling: that which is exhaled, vapour, emanation. [L. *exhālāre*—*ex*, from, *hālāre, -ātum*, to breathe.]

exhaust *igz-öst'*, *v.t.* to draw off: to use the whole strength of: to use up: to empty: to wear or tire out: to treat of or develop completely.—*n.* the exit of used working fluid from the cylinder of an engine: the period of discharge of the fluid: the fluid so escaping (**exhaust'-gas, -steam**).—*adj.* **exhaust'ible**.—*n.* **exhaustion** (*-öst'yən*) the act of exhausting or consuming: the state of being exhausted: extreme fatigue.—*adj.* **exhaust'ive** tending to exhaust: investigating all parts or possibilities.—**exhaust'-pipe'**, **-valve'** the pipe, valve, through which exhaust gases pass out. [L. *exhaurīre, exhaustum*—*ex*, from, *haurīre*, to draw.]

exhibit *igz-ib'it*, *v.t.* to hold forth or present to view: to present formally or publicly: to show.—*n.* a document or object produced in court to be used as evidence (*law*): something exhibited: an article at an exhibition.—*ns.* **exhib'iter; exhibition** (*eks-i-bish'ən*) presentation to view: display: showing off: a public show, esp. of works of art, manufactures, etc.: that which is exhibited: an allowance towards support, esp. to scholars in a university; **exhibi'tioner** one who enjoys an exhibition at a university; **exhibi'tionism** extravagant behaviour aimed at drawing attention to self: perversion involving public exposure of one's sexual organs (*psychiatry*); **exhibi'tionist**.—*adj.* **exhibitionis'tic**.—*adv.* **-ist'ically**.—*n.* **exhibitor** (*igz-ib'i-tər*).—*adj.* **exhib'itory**.—**make an exhibition of oneself** to behave foolishly, exciting ridicule. [L. *exhibēre, -itum*—*ex*, out, *habēre, -itum*, to have.]

exhilarate *igz-il'ə-rāt*, *v.t.* to raise the spirits of: to enliven: to cheer.—*adjs.* **exhil'arant** exhilarating; **exhil'arating** cheering: gladdening.—*adv.* **exhil'aratingly**.—*n.* **exhilarā'tion** the state of being exhilarated: joyousness.—*adjs.* **exhil'arative, exhil'aratory**. [L. *exhilarāre, -ātum*—*ex-*, intens., *hilaris*, cheerful.]

exhort *ig-zört'*, *v.t.* to urge strongly and earnestly: to counsel.—*n.* **exhortā'tion** (*eks-* or *egz-*) the act of exhorting: language intended to exhort: counsel: a religious discourse.—*adjs.* **exhort'atory** (*igz-*) tending to exhort or advise.—*n.* **exhort'er**. [L. *exhortārī, -ātus*—*ex-* intens., *hortārī*, to urge.]

exhume *esk-hūm'*, *ig-zūm'*, *v.t.* to take out of the ground or place of burial: to disinter: to bring to light. —*ns.* **exhumā'tion** (*eks-*); **exhum'er**. [L. *ex*, out of, *humus*, the ground.]

ex hypothesi *eks hī-poth'ə-sī*, (L.L.) from the hypothesis.

exigent *eks'i-jənt*, *adj.* pressing: urgent: exacting: demanding immediate attention or action.—*ns.* **ex'igence, ex'igency** (or *-ij'*) pressing necessity: emergency: distress. [L. *exigēns, -entis*—pr.p. of *exigĕre*—pfx. *ex-, agĕre*, to drive.]

exigible *eks'i-jib-l*, *adj.* liable to be exacted. [See **exact**.]

exiguous *egz-, eks-ig'ū-əs*, *adj.* scanty: slender —*ns.* **exigū'ity** (*eks-*); **exig'uousness**. [L. *exiguus*—*exigĕre*, to weight strictly; see **exact**.]

exile *eks'*, or *egz'īl*, *n.* enforced or regretted absence from one's country or home: banishment: (with *cap.*) the captivity of the Jews in Babylon (in these senses formerly *egz-īl'*): one who is in exile: a banished person.—*v.t.* (formerly *egz-īl'*) to expel from one's country, to banish.—*adj.* **exilic** (*egz-il'ik*, or *eks-*) pertaining to exile, esp. that of the Jews in Babylon. [O.Fr. *exil*—L. *exsilium*, banishment—*ex*, out of, and root of *salīre*, to leap.]

exist *igz-ist'*, *v.i.* to have an actual being: to live: to occur: to continue to live, esp. in unfavourable circumstances.—*n.* **exist'ence** the state of existing or being: livelihood: life: anything that exists: being.—*adjs.* **exist'ent** having being: at present existing; **existential** (*eks-is-ten'shəl*).—*ns.* **existen'tialism** a term covering a number of related doctrines denying objective universal values and holding that a person must create values for himself through action and by living each moment to the full; **existen'tialist**. [L. *existĕre, exsistĕre*, to stand forth—*ex-*, out, *sistĕre*, to stand.]

exit *ek'sit, eg'zit*, *n.* the departure of a player from the stage: any departure: a passage out: a way of departure: death: a place on a motorway where vehicles can leave by a slip road: the last instruction of a subroutine (*comput.*):—*pl.* **ex'its**.—*v.i.* to make an exit: to die: to lose the lead deliberately (*cards*):—*pa.p.* and *pa.t.* **ex'ited**. [Partly from the L. stage direction *exit*, goes out; partly—L. *exitus*, a way out.]

ex-libris *eks-lī'bris, -li'*, *n.* a book plate. [L *ex lībris*, from the books (of so-and-so).]

ex nihilo *eks nī'hi-lō, ni'*, (L.) out of nothing, as *creation ex nihilo*.

exo- *eks'ō-, eks-ō'*, in composition, outside, often opp. to **endo-, ento-**. (See also **ecto-**.)—*ns.* **exobiol'ogy** the study of (possible) extra-terrestrial life; **exobiol'ogist; ex'ocarp** (Gr. *karpos*, fruit) the epicarp of a fruit—*adj.* **ex'ocrine** (Gr. *krīnein*, to separate; *physiol.*) of glands, secreting through a duct.—*n.* an exocrine gland.—*n.* **ex'oderm** exodermis: ectoderm.—*adj.* **exoderm'al**.—*ns.* **exoder'mis** (Gr. *dermis*, skin) the outer cortex layer of a root; **exog'amy** (Gr. *gamos*, marriage) the practice of marrying only outside of one's own group: union of gametes not closely related (*biol.*).—*adjs.* **exogam'ic**; **exog'amous**.—*n.* **ex'ogen** (*obs.*) a dicotyledon—so called because its stem thickens by layers growing on the outside of the wood.—*adj.* **exog'enous** growing by successive additions to the outside: developing externally: having an external origin.—*ns.* **ex'oplasm** ectoplasm; **exoskel'eton** a hard supporting or protective structure secreted externally to the ectoderm.—*adj.* **exoskel'etal**.—*n.* **ex'osphere** (Gr. *sphaira*, sphere) the outermost layer of the earth's atmosphere: the boundary of the earth's atmosphere and interplanetary space.—*adjs.* **exospher'ic, -al**.—*adjs.* **exother'mal, exother'mic** (Gr. *thermē*, heat; *chem.*) involving evolution of heat.—*n.* **exothermi'city**. [Gr. *exō*, outside.]

Exocet® *eks'a-set*, *n.* a French-built surface-skimming missile able to be launched from surface or air. [Fr. *exocet*, flying fish.]

exodus *eks'ə-dəs*, *n.* a going out, esp that of the

Israelites from Egypt: (with *cap.*) the second book of the Old Testament. [L.,—Gr. *exodos*—*ex*-, out, *hodos*, a way.]

ex officio eks o-fish'i-ō, -fik', (L.) by virtue of his office.

exon eks'on, *n.* an officer of the Yeomen of the Guard. [App. intended to express the pronunciation of Fr. *exempt*; see **exempt**.]

exonerate igz-on'ər-āt, *v.t.* to free from the burden of blame or obligation: to acquit.—*n.* **exonera'tion** the act of exonerating.—*adj.* **exon'erative** freeing from a burden or obligation. [L. *exonerāre*, *-ātum*,—*ex*, from, *onus*, *oneris*, burden.]

exophthalmia, *-mos*, *-mus* eks-of-thal'mi-ə, *-məs*, *n.* a protrusion of the eyeballs.—*adj.* **exophthal'mic**. [Gr. *ex*, out, *ophthalmos*, eye.]

exorbitant igz-ör'bi-tənt, *adj.* going beyond the usual limits: excessive.—*ns.* **exor'bitance**, **exor'bitancy** great excess.—*adv.* **exor'bitantly**. [L. *exorbitāre*—*ex*, out of, *orbita*, a track—*orbis*, a circle.]

exorcise, **-ize** eks'ör-sīz, *v.t.* to adjure by some holy name: to call forth or drive away, as a spirit: to deliver from the influence of an evil spirit.—*ns.* **ex'orcism** (-*sizm*) the act of exorcising or expelling evil spirits by certain ceremonies: a formula for exorcising; **ex'orcist** one who exorcises or pretends to expel evil spirits by adjuration (also **ex'orciser**, *-z*-). [L.L. from Gr. *exorkizein*—*ex*-, out, *horkos*, an oath.]

exordium egz-ör'di-əm, *n.* the introductory part of a discourse or composition:—*pl.* **exor'diums**, **-ia**.—*adj.* **exor'dial**. [L.,—*ex*, out of, *ordīrī*, to begin.]

exoteric eks-ō-ter'ik, *adj.* external: fit to be communicated to the public or multitude—opp. to *esoteric*.—*adj.* **exoter'ical**.—*adv.* **exoter'ically**.—*n.* **exoter'icism** (*-sizm*). [Gr. *exōterikos*—*exōterō*, comp. of *exō*, outside.]

exotic igz-ot'ik, *adj.* introduced from a foreign country: alien: foreign-looking: outlandish: romantically strange, or rich and showy, or glamorous: pertaining to strip-tease.—*n.* anything of foreign origin: something not native to a country, as a plant, a word, a custom.—*n.pl.* **exot'ica** exotic objects: theatrical or musical items with an unusual theme or with a foreign flavour.—*n.* **exot'icism** (*-sizm*). [Gr. *exōtikos*—*exō*, outside.]

expand iks-pand', *v.t.* to spread out: to lay open: to enlarge in bulk or surface: to develop, or bring out in fuller detail: to express at length.—*v.i.* to become opened: to increase in volume: to enlarge: to spread: to become communicative (*fig.*): to speak or write more fully (on).—*ns.* **expand'er**, **-or** an electronic device which increases the range of amplitude variations in a transmission system; **expanse** (*-pans'*) a wide extent: a stretch: the amount of spread or stretch; **expansibil'ity**.—*adj.* **expans'ible** capable of being expanded.—*adv.* **expans'ibly**.—*adj.* **expans'ile** (*-īl*) capable of expansion.—*n.* **expan'sion** enlargement: that which is expanded: amount of expanding: territorial extension: extension—*adj.* **expan'sionary** tending to expansion.—*ns.* **expan'sionism**; **expan'sionist** one who favours territorial or currency expansion.—Also *adj.*—*adj.* **expans'ive** widely extended: causing expansion: worked by expansion: effusive: talkative, communicative: marked by excessive feeling of well-being and delusions of self-importance (*psychiatry*).—*adv.* **expans'ively**.—*ns.* **expans'iveness**; **expansiv'ity** (*eks*-).—**expanded metal** steel, etc., stretched to form a mesh, used for reinforcing concrete, etc.; **expanded plastic** foam plastic; **expanding universe** (*astron.*) the theory that the whole universe is constantly expanding and the galaxies moving away from each other. [L. *expandēre*—*ex*-,

out, *pandēre*, *pānsum*, to spread.]

ex parte eks pär'tē, pär'te, *adj.* on one side only: partial: prejudiced. [L. *ex*, from, *parte*, abl. of *pars*, *partis*, party, side.]

expatiate eks-pā'shi-āt, *v.i.* to range at large (usu. *fig.*): to enlarge in discourse, argument, or writing.—*n.* **expatia'tion**.—*adjs.* **expā'tiative**, **expā'tiatory** expansive.—*n.* **expā'tiator**. [L. *exspatiārī*, *-ātus*—*ex*, out of, *spatiārī*, to roam—*spatium*, space.]

expatriate eks-pā'tri-āt, *v.t.* to send out of one's country: to banish, exile (oneself or another): to deprive of citizenship.—Also *n.* and *adj.* (*-tri-ət*).—*n.* **expatria'tion**. [L.L. *expatriāre*, *-ātum*—*ex*, out of, *patria*, fatherland.]

expect iks-pekt', *v.t.* to look forward to as likely to come or happen, or as due: to suppose.—*ns.* **expect'ance**, **expect'ancy** the act or state of expecting: that which is expected: hope.—*adj.* **expect'ant** looking or waiting for something: in expectation: not yet but expecting to be: pregnant.—*n.* one who expects: one who is looking or waiting for some benefit or office.—*adv.* **expect'antly**.—*ns.* **expecta'tion** (*eks*-) the act or state of expecting: the prospect of future good: that which is or may fairly be expected: the degree of probability: the value of something expected: (in *pl.*) prospect of fortune or profit by a will.—**be expecting** (*coll.*) to be pregnant; **life expectancy**, **expectation of life** the average length of time that one may expect to live. [L. *expectāre*, *-ātum*—*ex*, out, *spectāre*, to look, freq. of *specēre*, to see.]

expectorate eks-pek'tə-rāt, *v.t.* to expel from the breast or lungs by coughing, etc.: to spit forth.—*v.i.* to discharge or eject phlegm from the throat: to spit.—*adj.* **expec'torant** tending to promote expectoration.—*n.* a medicine that promotes expectoration.—*n.* **expectora'tion** the act of expectorating: that which is expectorated: spittle.—*adj.* **expec'torative** having the quality of promoting expectoration. [L. *expectorāre*, *-ātum*—*ex*, from, *pectus*, *pectoris*, breast.]

expedient iks-pē'di-ənt, *adj.* suitable: advisable.—*n.* that which serves to promote: means suitable to an end: contrivance, shift.—*ns.* **expē'dience**; **expē'diency** fitness: desirableness: conduciveness to the need of the moment: that which is opportune: self-interest.—*adv.* **expē'diently**. [L. *expediēns*, *-entis*, pr.p. of *expedīre*; see **expedite**.]

expedite eks'pi-dīt, *v.t.* to free from impediments: to hasten: to send forth: to despatch.—*n.* **expedition** (*-di'shən*) speed: promptness: an organised journey to attain some object, as hunting, warfare, exploration, etc.: the party undertaking such a journey.—*adjs.* **expedi'tionary** belonging to an expedition: of the nature of an expedition; **expedi'tious** characterised by expedition or rapidity: speedy: prompt.—*adv.* **expedi'tiously**.—*n.* **expedi'tiousness**. [L. *expedīre*, *-ītum*—*ex*, from, *pēs*, *pedis*, a foot.]

expel iks-pel', *v.t.* to drive out: to eject: to discharge in disgrace (from school, etc.): to banish:—*pr.p.* **expell'ing**; *pa.t.* and *pa.p.* **expelled'**.—*adj.* and *n.* **expell'ant**, **-ent**.—*n.* **expellee'** one who is expelled. [L. *expellēre*, *expulsum*—*ex*, from, *pellēre*, to drive.]

expend iks-pend', *v.t.* to lay out: to employ or consume in any way: to spend.—*adj.* **expend'able** that may be expended, esp. that may be sacrificed to achieve some end.—Also *n.*—*ns.* **expendabil'ity**; **expen'der**; **expend'iture** the act of expending or laying out: that which is expended: the process of using up: money spent; **expense** (*-pens'*) expenditure: outlay: cost: (in *pl.*) money out of pocket, or an allowance therefor.—*adj.* **expens'ive** causing or requiring much expense: costly: lavish.—*adv.* **expens'ively**.—*n.* **expens'iveness**.—**expense(s) account** a statement of outlay incurred in carrying out a business commission.—**at the**

For other sounds see detailed chart of pronunciation.

expense of to the cost, detriment of (often **at some-one's**, etc. **expense**): with the loss or sacrifice of. [L. *expendēre—ex-*, out, *pendēre, pēnsum*, to weigh.]

experience *iks-pē'ri-əns, n.* practical acquaintance with any matter gained by trial: long and varied observation, personal or general: wisdom derived from the changes and trials of life: the passing through any event or course of events by which one is affected: an event so passed through: anything received by the mind, as sensation, perception, or knowledge.—*v.t* to have practical acquaintance with: to prove or know by use: to have experience of: to feel, suffer, undergo.—*adj.* **expe'rienced.**—*adj.* **expèrien'tial** (*-en'shl*) pertaining to or derived from experience.—*ns.* **expèrien'tialism** the doctrine that all knowledge comes from experience; **expèrien'tialist.** [Fr. *ex-périence* and L. *experientia*, from *experīrī—ex-*, intens., and old verb *perīrī*, to try.]

experiment *iks-per'i-mənt, n.* a trial: something done to test a theory, or to discover something unknown.—*v.i.* (also *-ment'*) to make experiment or trial: to search by trial.—*adj.* **experiment'al** pertaining to experiment: based on or proceeding by experiment. trying out new styles or techniques: tentative.—*v i.* **experiment'alise, -ize.**—*ns.* **experiment'alism** reliance on experiment; **experiment'alist; experi'menter** (or *-ment'*).—*adv.* **experiment'ally.**—*n.* **experimentā'tion,** from *experīrī*, to try thoroughly; see **experience.**

expert *eks'pûrt, adj.* taught by practice: having a familiar knowledge: having a facility of performance (with *at* or *in*): skilful, adroit (with *at* or *in*).—*ns.* **ex'pert** one who is skilled in any art or science: a specialist: a scientific or professional witness; **expertise** (*-ēz'*) expert knowledge. expertness: expert appraisal.—*adv.* **ex'pertly.**—*n.* **ex'pertness.** [Fr.,—L. *expertus—experīrī*, to try thoroughly; see **experience.**]

expiate *eks'pi-āt, v.t.* to make complete atonement for: to make satisfaction or reparation for.—*adj.* **ex'piable** capable of being expiated, atoned for, or done away.—*ns.* **expiā'tion** the act of expiating: the means by which atonement is made: atonement, **ex'piator.**—*adj.* **ex'piatory** (*-ə-*, or *-ā-tər-i*). [L. *expiāre, -ātum—ex-*, intens., *piāre*, to appease, atone for.]

expire *iks-, eks-pīr', v.t.* to breathe out.—*v.i.* to breathe out: to die: to come to an end: to lapse: to become invalid by lapse of time.—*n.* **expirā'tion** (*eks-pi-* or *-pī-*) the act of breathing out.—*adj.* **expi'ratory.**—*n.* **expi'ry** the end or termination, esp by lapse of time: expiration. [Fr. *expirer—L. ex,* from; *spīrāre, -ātum,* to breathe.]

explain *iks-plān', v.t.* to make plain or intelligible: to unfold and illustrate the meaning of: to expound: to account for.—*v.i.* to give an explanation.—*adj.* **explain'able.**—*ns.* **explain'er; explanā'tion** (*eks-plə-nā'shən*) the act of explaining or clearing from obscurity: that which explains or clears up: the meaning or sense given to anything: a mutual clearing up of matters.—*adv.* **explan'atorily** (*iks-plan'ə-tər-i-li*).—*adj.* **explan'atory** serving to explain or clear up: containing explanations.—**explain away** to modify the force of by explanation, generally in a bad sense. [L. *explānāre—ex-,* out, *plānāre,* to level—*plānus,* flat, plain.]

explantation *eks-plän-tā'shən, n.* the culture in an artificial medium of a part or organ removed from a living individual.—*n.* and *v.t.* **explant'.** [L. *explantāre—ex-,* out, *plantāre,* to plant.]

expletive *eks-, iks-plē'tiv,* or *eks'pli-tiv, adj* filling out: added merely to fill up.—*n.* a word or anything present merely to fill a gap: a meaningless oath: a

swear-word of any kind.—*adj.* **explè'tory** (also *eks'pli-*) serving to fill up· expletive: supplementary. [L *explētivus—ex,* out, *plēre,* to fill]

explicate *eks'pli-kāt, v.t.* to unfold, develop: to lay open or explain the meaning of —*adj.* **explic'able** (older *eks'*) capable of being explicated or explained. —*n.* **explicā'tion** explanation.—*adjs.* **explic'ative, explic'atory** (older *eks'*) serving to explicate or explain.—*n.* **ex'plicātor.** [L. *explicāre—ex,* out, *plicāre,* to fold.]

explicit *iks-plis'it, adj.* not implied merely, but distinctly stated: plain in language: outspoken: clear unreserved.—*adv.* **explic'itly.**—*n.* **explic'itness.** [See **explicate.**]

explode *iks-plōd', v.t.* to bring into disrepute, and reject: to cause to blow up.—*v t.* to burst with a loud report: to burst out, break forth suddenly.—*adj.* **explō'ded** blown up: (of a theory, etc.) rejected because proved false: (of a drawing or diagram of a machine, building, organism, etc.) showing the internal structure and separate parts and their relationship.—*ns.* **explō'der; explō'sion** (*-zhən*) the act of exploding: a sudden violent burst with a loud report: an outburst: breaking out of feelings, etc : a great and rapid increase or expansion, as *population explosion.* —*adj.* **explō'sive** (*-siv, -ziv*) liable to or causing explosion: worked, set in place, etc., by an explosion: bursting out with violence and noise.—*n.* something that will explode.—*adv.* **explō'sively.**—*n.* **explō'siveness.—exploding star** a star that flares up, such as a nova or supernova; **explosion welding** welding metals with very different melting points by means of pressure produced by an explosion. [L *explōdēre, explōsum—ex,* from, *plaudēre,* to clap the hands.]

exploit *eks'ploit, n.* a deed or achievement, esp. an heroic one: a feat.—*v.t.* (*iks-ploit'*) to work, make available: to turn to use: to make gain out of or at the expense of.—*adj.* **exploit'able.**—*ns.* **exploit'age; exploitā'tion** (*eks-*) the act of successfully applying industry to any object, as the working of mines, etc.: the setting-up and getting into production of an oilfield, mine, etc.: the act of using for selfish purposes, **exploit'er.**—*adjs.* **exploit'ive; exploit'ative.** [O Fr *exploit—L. explicitum,* unfolded; see **explicate.**]

explore *iks-plōr',* or *-plôr', v.t.* and *v.i.* to search or travel through for the purpose of discovery: to examine thoroughly.—*n.* **explorā'tion** (*eks-*) the act of searching, or searching for (something), thoroughly: travel for the sake of discovery.—*adjs* **explor'ative, explor'atory.**—*n.* **explor'er.** [Fr.,—L. *explōrāre, -ātum,* to search out.]

explosion. See **explode.**

expo *eks'pō, n.* an exhibition or public showing:—*pl.* **ex'pos.** [*exposition.*]

exponent *eks-pō'nənt, adj.* setting forth: expounding. —*n.* an expounder (of): an interpreter of an art by performance: an example, illustration, type (of): a symbol showing what power a quantity is raised to, an index (*math.*).—*adj.* **exponential** (*eks-pō-nen'shl*) pertaining to or involving exponents.—*n.* an exponential function.—*adv.* **exponen'tially.—exponential curve** a curve expressed by an exponential equation; **exponential equation** one in which the variable occurs in the exponent of one or more terms; **exponential function** a quantity with a variable exponent, esp. e^x, where *e* is the base of natural logarithms. [L. *expōnēns, -entis,* setting forth—*ex-,* out, *pōnēre,* to place.]

export *eks-pōrt', -pôrt', v.t.* to carry or send out of a country, as goods in commerce.—*n.* **ex'port** the act of exporting: that which is exported: a commodity which is or may be sent from one country to another in traffic: a type of strong brown beer.—*adj.* **export'-**

able.—*ns.* exportabil'ity; exportā'tion; export'er.— export reject a manufactured article that is flawed in some way and so not passed for export, often sold at a reduced price on the home market.—invisible exports such items in a national trade balance as money spent by tourists from abroad, etc.—opp. to visible exports goods sold abroad by traders. [L. *exortāre, -ātum* —*ex*-, out of, *portāre*, to carry.]

expose *iks-pōz'*, *v.t.* to lay forth to view: to deprive of cover, protection, or shelter: to make bare: to abandon (an infant): to submit (to an influence, as light, weather): to put up (for sale): to disclose: to show up. —*ns.* expōs'al exposure: exposition; exposé (*eks-pō'zā*) an exposing: a shameful showing up: an article or programme exposing crime, scandal, etc. to public notice: a formal statement or exposition; exposure (*-pō'zhər, -zhyər*) the act of laying open or bare: subjection to an influence: the act of allowing access of light (*phot.*): duration of such access: the act of showing up an evil: a state of being laid bare: openness to danger: a shelterless state: position with regard to the sun, influence of climate, etc.: appearance in public, esp. on television.—exposure meter (*phot.*) an instrument, now often incorporated in the camera, for measuring the light falling on or reflected from a subject.—expose oneself to expose one's sexual organs in public. [Fr. *exposer*—L. *ex*-, out, and *pausāre*, to rest, confused with *expōnĕre*, to expose.]

exposition *eks-pō-zish'ən, n.* the act of exposing: a setting out to public view: a public exhibition: explanation: commentary: the enunciation of themes in a composition: that part of a sonata, fugue, etc., in which themes are presented.—*adj.* expositive (*-poz'*). —*n.* expos'itor one who, or that which, expounds. —*adj.* expos'itory serving to explain: explanatory. [L. *expositiō, -ōnis, expositor, -ōris—expōnĕre, expositum*, to expose, set forth; see expound.]

ex post facto *eks pōst fak'tō*, (L.; *lit.* from what is done or enacted after) retrospective: retrospectively.

expostulate *iks-post'ū-lāt*, *v.i.* to remonstrate: to discuss (*Shak.*): to claim (*Milt.*).—*n.* expostulā'tion. —*adjs.* expost'ūlative (or *-ə-tiv*), expost'ūlatory (*-ā-* or *-ə-tər-i*) containing expostulation.—*n.* expost'-ūlator. [L. *expostulāre, -ātum—ex*, intens., *postulāre*, to demand.]

exposure. See expose.

expound *iks-pownd'*, *v.t.* to expose, or lay open the meaning of: to explain: to interpret: to explain in a certain way.—*n.* expound'er. [O.Fr. *espondre*—L. *expōnĕre—ex*-, out, *pōnĕre*, to place.]

express *iks-pres'*, *v.t.* to press or force out: to represent or make known by a likeness, words, signs, symbols, etc.: to put into words: to symbolise: to state explicitly: to reveal: to designate: to despatch.—*adj.* clearly brought out: exactly representing: directly stated: explicit: clear: intended or sent for a particular purpose: expeditious.—*adv.* with haste: specially: by express train or messenger: by express. —*n.* a regular and quick conveyance: a system for the speedy transmission of messages or goods: an express train: an express messenger.—*n.* express'age the system of carrying by express: the charge for doing so. —*adj.* express'ible.—*ns.* expression (*-presh'ən*) the act of forcing out by pressure: the act, or mode, or power, of representing or giving utterance: representation or revelation by language, art, the features, etc.: the manner in which anything is expressed: a word, phrase: a symbol: intonation: due indication of feeling in performance of music.—*n.* express'ionism in literature and painting, a revolt against impressionism, turning away from the outer life to the inner —*n.* and *adj.* express'ionist.—*adjs.* expressionis'tic;

express'ionless; express'ive serving to express or indicate: full of expression: vividly representing (with *of*): emphatic: significant.—*adv.* express'ively.—*ns.* express'iveness; expressiv'ity the quality of being able to express: the extent to which a gene produces an effect (*biol.*).—*adv.* express'ly explicitly: for the express purpose: definitely.—express delivery immediate delivery by special messenger: delivery by express agency; expression mark a direction written on a piece of music (usu. in Italian); expression stop a stop in a harmonium by which the performer can regulate the air to produce expression; express letter, packet, parcel one sent by special messenger; express messenger a special messenger; express rifle a rifle for big game at short range, with heavy charge of powder and light bullet; express train a railway-train which travels at high speed and with few stops; express'way a road for fast motor traffic, with dual-carriageway and no crossings on the same level.—express oneself to give expression to one's thoughts, ideas and opinions. [L. *exprimĕre, expressum—ex*, from, *premĕre, pressum*, to press; partly through Fr. *exprès*, etc.]

expressis verbis *eks-pre'sis vûr'bis, eks-pre'sēs wer'-bēs*, (L.) in express terms.

expropriate *iks-prō'pri-āt*, *v.t.* to dispossess.—*adj.* exprō'priable.—*ns.* expropriā'tion; exprō'priator. [L. *expropriāre, -ātum—ex*, from, *proprium*, property.]

expulsion *iks-pul'shən n.* the act of expelling: banishment.—*adj.* expul'sive able or serving to expel. [L. *expulsāre*, freq. of *expellĕre*; see expel.]

expunge *iks-punj'*, *v.t.* to wipe out: to efface: to mark for deletion.—*ns.* expunc'tion (*-pungk'shən*); expun'-ger. [L. *expungĕre*, to mark for deletion by a row of dots.]

expurgate *eks'pûr-gāt*, also *-pûr'*, *v.t.* to purge out or render pure: to purify from anything supposed to be offensive, noxious, or erroneous.—*ns.* expurgā'tion the act of expurgating or purifying: bowdlerising; expurgator (*eks'pûr-gā-tər*, or *eks-pûr'gə-tər*).—*adjs.* expurgato'rial (*-gə-tō'ri-əl, -to'*), expur'gatory. [L. *expurgāre, -ātum—ex*, out, *purgāre*, to purge.]

exquisite *eks'kwiz-it*, also *-kwiz'*, *adj.* delicious: of consummate excellence: compelling the highest admiration: of delicate perception or close discrimination: fastidious: exceeding, extreme, as pain or pleasure.—*n.* one exquisitely nice or fastidious in dress: a fop.—*adv.* ex'quisitely.—*n.* ex'quisiteness. [L. *exquisītus—ex*, out, *quaerĕre*, to seek.]

exscind *ik-sind'*, *v.t.* to cut off. [L. *ex*, from, *scindĕre*, to cut.]

exsert *ik-sûrt'*, *v.t.* to protrude.—*n.* exser'tion. [L. *exserĕre, -sertum*; see exert.]

ex-service *eks-sûr'vis, adj.* formerly in one of the fighting services.—*n.* ex-ser'viceman.

exsiccate *ek'si-kāt*, *v.t.* to dry up. [L. *exsiccare—ex*-, *siccus*, dry.]

extant *iks-tant', eks'tənt, adj.* still standing or existing. [L. *extāns, -antis—ex*-, out, *stāre*, to stand.]

extempore *iks-tem'pə-ri, adv.* on the spur of the moment: without preparation: suddenly.—*adj.* sudden: rising at the moment: without help of manuscript: composed and delivered or performed impromptu.—*n.* an impromptu.—*adj.* extem'poral. —*n.* extemporaneity (*-ə-nē'i-ti*).—*adj.* extempora'neous.—*adv.* extempora'neously.—*n.* extempora'neousness.—*adv.* extem'porarily.—*n.* extem'-porariness.—*adj.* extem'porary done on the spur of the moment: hastily prepared: speaking extempore: done without preparation.—*n.* extemporisā'tion, *-z-*. —*v.t* extem'porise, *-ize* to speak, or compose and play, extempore or without previous preparation: to discourse without notes. [L. *ex*, out of, and *tempore*, abl. of *tempus*, time.]

extend *iks-tend'*, *v.t.* to stretch out: to prolong in any direction: to enlarge: to expand: to widen: to unfold: to straighten out: to hold out: to offer, accord: to exert to the full.—*v.i.* to stretch, reach: to be continued in length or breadth.—*n.* **extendabil'ity**.—*adj.* **extend'able**.—*n.* **extendibil'ity**.—*adj.* **extend'ible**.—*n.* **extensibil'ity**.—*adjs.* **extens'ible**, **extensile** (*eks-ten'sil*, *-sil*) that may be extended.—*n.* **extension** (*iks-*, *eks-ten'shən*) an act of extending: the condition of being extended: an added piece: a wing or annex of a house: the property of occupying space: the extent of the application of a term or the number of objects included under it—opp. to *intension* (*logic*): a word or words added to subject, predicate, or object (*gram.*): an additional telephone using the same line as the main one.—*adj.* **exten'sional**.—*adv.* **exten'sionally**.—*n.* **extensional'ity**.—*adj.* **extens'ive** large: widespread: comprehensive: (*eks-*) pertaining to extension: seeking or deriving a comparatively small crop cheaply from a wide area—opp. to *intensive*.—*adv.* **extens'ively**.—*ns.* **extens'iveness**; **extensom'eter**, **extensim'eter** (*eks-*) an instrument for measuring small strains in metal; **exten'sor** a muscle that extends or straightens any part of the body; **extent'** the space or degree to which a thing is extended: bulk: compass: scope: degree or amount (as *to some extent*): a stretch or extended space.—**extended family** a social unit comprising not only a couple and their children but other relatives, e.g. aunts, uncles, grandparents; **extended play** of a gramophone record, giving longer reproduction because of a closer groove and the use of a larger part of its surface area.—**university extension** the enlargement of the aim of a university, in providing instruction for those unable to become regular students. [L. *extendēre*, *extentum*, or *extensum*—*ex-*, out, *tendēre*, to stretch.]

extenuate *iks-ten'ū-āt*, *v.t.* to lessen: to underrate: to weaken the force of: to palliate.—*n.* and *adj.* **exten'ūating** palliating.—*adv.* **exten'ūatingly**.—*n.* **extenūā'tion** the act of representing anything as less wrong or criminal than it seems: palliation: mitigation.—*adjs.* **exten'ūative**, **exten'ūatory** tending to extenuate: palliative.—*n.* **exten'ūator**. [L. *extenuāre*, *-ātum*—*ex-*, intens., *tenuis*, thin.]

exterior *eks-tē'ri-ər*, *adj.* outer: outward, external: on or from the outside: foreign.—*n.* the outside, outer surface: a representation of an outdoor scene: an outer part (esp. in *pl.*).—*v.t.* **extēr'iorise**, **-ize** to externalise: to bring an internal part temporarily outside the body (*surg.*).—*ns.* **exteriorisā'tion**, **-z-**; **extēriority** (*-or'i-ti*).—*adv.* **extē'riorly** outwardly.—**exterior angle** (*math.*) the angle between any side produced and the adjacent side (not produced) of a polygon. [L. *exterior*, compar. of *exter*, *exterus*, outward—*ex*, from.]

exterminate *iks-tûr'mi-nāt*, *v.t.* to destroy utterly: to put an end to: to root out.—*adj.* **exter'minable**.—*n.* **exterminā'tion**.—*adjs.* **exter'minative**, **exter'minatory**.—*n.* **exter'minātor**. [L. *ex*, out of, *terminus*, boundary.]

external *eks-tûr'nəl*, *adj.* exterior: lying outside: outward: belonging to the world of outward things: that may be seen: not innate or intrinsic: accidental: foreign.—*n.* exterior: (in *pl.*) the outward parts: (in *pl.*) outward or non-essential forms and ceremonies: (in *pl.*) outward circumstances or appearances.—*n.* **externalisā'tion**, **-z-**.—*v.t.* **exter'nalise**, **-ize** to give form or apparent reality to: to give external expression to: to extravert (one's personality): to ascribe to causes outside oneself: to regard as consisting of externals only.—*ns.* **exter'nalism** undue regard to mere

externals or non-essential outward forms, esp. of religion; **exter'nalist**; **externality** (*-nal'i-ti*).—*adv.* **exter'nally**.—**external examiner** an examiner from another seat of learning who has had no part in teaching the examinees; **external student** one examined by a university in which he has not studied. [L. *externus*, outward—*exter*, outside.]

exteroceptor *eks'tar-ō-sep-tar*, (*zool.*) *n.* a sensory organ, e.g. the eye, receiving impressions from outside the body. [L. *exterus*, exterior, and *receptor*.]

exterritorial *eks-ter-i-tō'ri-əl*, *-tō'*. Same as **extraterritorial**.

extinct *iks-tingkt'*, *adj.* no longer existing: dead.—*n.* **extinc'tion** extinguishing, quenching or wiping out: destruction: the absorbing by the earth's atmosphere of a planet's or star's light (*astron.*).—*adj.* **extinct'ive**. [L. *ex*(*s*)*tinctum*; see **extinguish**.]

extinguish *iks-ting'gwish*, *v.t.* to quench, put out: to render extinct: to put an end to: to destroy, annihilate: to obscure by superior splendour: to pay off (a debt) (*law*).—*v.i.* to die out.—*adj.* **exting'uishable**.—*ns.* **exting'uisher** one who, or that which, extinguishes: a small hollow conical instrument for putting out a candle, etc.: a device for putting out fire: a conical structure resembling a candle extinguisher; **exting'uishment**. [L. *ex*(*s*)*tinguēre*, *ex*(*s*)*tinctum*—*ex-*, out, *stinguēre*, to quench.]

extirpate *eks'tar-pāt*, *v.t.* to root out: to destroy totally: to remove surgically: to exterminate.—*adj.* **extirpable** (*eks-tûrp'ə-bl*).—*ns.* **extirpā'tion** extermination: total destruction; **ex'tirpātor** one who extirpates: an implement for weeding.—*adjs.* **ex'tirpative**; **extirpatory** (*ekstûrp'ə-tər-i*). [L. *exstirpāre*, *-ātum*—*ex*, out, and *stirps*, a stock, root.]

extol *iks-tōl'*, *-tol'*, *v.t.* to praise highly:—*pr.p.* **extoll'ing**; *pa.t.* and *pa.p.* **extolled**'.—*n.* **extol'ment**. [L. *extollēre*—*ex-*, up, *tollēre*, to lift or raise.]

extort *iks-tört'*, *v.t.* to wring out: to gain or draw out by compulsion or violence.—*n.* **extortion** (*-tör'shən*) illegal or oppressive exaction: that which is extorted.—*adjs.* **extor'tionary** pertaining to or implying extortion; **extor'tionate** oppressive: exacting, demanding too much.—*adv.* **extor'tionately**.—*ns.* **extor'tioner**, **extor'tionist** one who practises extortion. [L. *extorquēre*, *extortum*—*ex-*, out, *torquēre*, to twist.]

extra[1] *eks'trə*, *adj.* beyond or more than the usual or the necessary: extraordinary: additional.—*adv.* unusually.—*n.* what is extra or additional: a special edition of a newspaper containing later news: a run scored at cricket from a bye, leg-bye, wide, or no-ball (not hit): a film actor temporarily engaged for a minor part, as to be one of a crowd.—**extra cover** in cricket, a fielding position between cover point and mid off, or the player in this position.—*adjs.* **extracurric'ular** of a subject or activity, outside and additional to the regular academic course; **ext'raspec'ial** much out of the way.—**extra time** additional time allowed at the end of a match because of time lost through injury, or for other reason. [Prob. contracted from **extraordinary**.]

extra- *eks'tra-*, *-trə-*, *pfx.* outside.—*adjs.* **ex'tracorpor'eal** outside the body; **ex'tragalac'tic** outside the Milky Way; **ex'trajudi'cial** not made in court, beyond the usual course of legal proceeding.—*adv.* **ex'trajudi'cially**.—*adjs.* **ex'tramar'ital** (of relations, etc.) outside marriage, though properly confined to marriage; **ex'tramun'dane** beyond the material world; **ex'tramu'ral** without or beyond the walls: connected with a university but not under its direct control; **ex'tra-phys'ical** not subject to physical laws; **extrasensory** outside the ordinary senses as in clairvoyant and telepathic perception (**extra-sensory perception** the ability to perceive without the normal senses (cf.

sixth sense)); **ex'tra-terres'trial** outside, or from outside, the earth; **ex'tra-territo'rial** outside a territory or territorial jurisdiction—also **exterritor'ial**. —*n.* **ex'traterritorial'ity** the privilege of being outside the jurisdiction of the country one is in.—Also **exterritorial'ity.**—*adj.* **ex'travehic'ūlar** situated, used, or happening, outside a spacecraft. [L. *extrā,* outside.]

extract *iks-, eks-trakt',* *v.t.* to draw out by force or otherwise: to choose out or select: to find out: to extort: to copy passages from: to publish passages from: to withdraw by chemical or physical means from containing or combined matter: to exhaust or treat by extraction.—*n.* **extract** (*eks'*) anything drawn from a substance by heat, distillation, solvents, etc., as an essence: a passage taken from a book or writing.—*adjs.* **extract'able** (also **extract'ible**).—*ns.* **extractabil'ity; extrac'tion** the act of extracting: derivation from a stock or family: birth: lineage: that which is extracted.—*adj.* **extract'ive** tending or serving to extract: of the nature of an extract (**extractive matter** the soluble portions of any drug).—*n.* an extract.—*n.* **extract'or** he who, or that which, extracts.—**extractor fan** an electric fan which extracts air, gas, etc., from a room or building.—**extract the root of a quantity** to find its root by a mathematical process. [L. *extrahēre, extractum—ex,* from, *trahēre,* to draw.]

extradition *eks-tra-dish'ən, n.* a delivering up of accused persons by one government to another.—*adj.* **extraditable** (*-dīt'əbl*).—*v.t.* **ex'tradite** to hand over for trial or punishment to a foreign government. [L. *ex,* from, *trāditiō, -ōnis—trādēre, trāditum,* to deliver up.]

extrados *eks-trā'dos, n.* the convex surface of an arch: the external curve of the voussoirs. [Fr.,—L. *extrā,* outside, Fr. *dos,* back.]

extraneous *eks-trān'yəs, adj.* external: foreign: not belonging to or dependent on a thing: not essential.—*ns.* **extraneity** (*-tra-nē'i-ti*), **extrān'eousness.**—*adv.* **extrān'eously.** [L. *extrāneus,* external, *extrā,* outside.]

extraordinary *eks-trōrd'(i)nər-i,* or *eks-tra-ōrd',* or *iks-trōrd', adj.* beyond ordinary: not usual or regular: remarkable, wonderful: special or supernumerary, as 'physician extraordinary' in a royal household, being inferior to the ordinary official.—*adv.* **extraord'inarily.**—*n.* **extraord'inariness.** [L. *extraordinārius—extrā,* outside, *ordō, -inis,* order.]

extrapolate *iks-trap'ō-lāt, -ə-lāt, eks', v.t.* to estimate from observed tendencies the value of (any variable) outside the limits between which values are known: to infer, conjecture from what is known: to project into a new area of experience or activity.—Also *v.i.*—*n.* **extrapola'tion.**—*adjs.* **extrap'olative, extrap'olatory.**—*n.* **extrap'olātor.** [L. *extrā,* and **interpolate.**]

extravagant *iks-trav'ə-gənt, adj.* irregular: unrestrained: excessive: profuse in expenses: wasteful.—*ns.* **extrav'agance** excess: lavish expenditure.—*adv.* **extrav'agantly.** [L. *extrā,* beyond, *vagāns, -antis,* pr.p. of *vagārī,* to wander.]

extravaganza *iks-trav-ə-gan'zə, n.* an extravagant or eccentric musical, dramatic, or literary production: extravagant conduct or speech. [It. *(e)stravaganza.*]

extravasate *iks-trav'ə-sāt, v.t.* to let, or force (blood) out of the proper vessels: to pour out (lava).—*n.* **extravasā'tion.** [L. *extrā,* out of, *vās,* a vessel.]

extravert, extrovert *eks'tra-* or *-trō-vûrt, vs.t.* to turn outward or outside in. to make manifest.—*n.* (*eks'*) a person interested mainly in the world external to himself—opp. to **introvert**.—Also *adj.*—*ns.* **extraver'sion, extrover'sion.** [L *extrā,* outside, *vertēre,* to turn; the **extro-** forms by analogy with **introvert**.]

extreme *iks-trēm'* (*arch. eks'*), *adj.* outermost: most remote: last: highest in degree: greatest: most violent: of opinions, etc., not moderate, going to great lengths: stringent.—*n.* the utmost point or verge: end: utmost or the highest limit or degree.—*adv.* **extrēme'ly.**—*ns.* **extrē'mism; extrē'mist** one ready to go to extremes: a holder of extreme opinions: an advocate of extreme action; **extremity** (*-trem'i-ti*) the utmost limit: the highest degree: greatest necessity or distress: extreme condition: an end: hand or foot.—**extreme unction** see **unction.**—**extremely high frequency** see **frequency; go to extremes** to go too far: to use extreme measures; **in the extreme** in the last, highest degree: extremely; **the last extremity** the utmost pitch of misfortune: death. [O.Fr. *extreme* —L. *extrēmus,* superl. of *exter, exterus,* on the outside.]

extricate *eks'tri-kāt, v.t.* to free from entanglements or perplexities: to disentangle: to set free.—*adj.* **ex'tricable.**—*n.* **extrica'tion** disentanglement: the act of setting free. [L. *extricāre, -ātum—ex,* from, *trīcae,* hindrances.]

extrinsic *iks-trin'sik, adj.* external: not contained in or belonging to a body: foreign: not essential: of a muscle, running from the trunk to limb or girdle—opp. to **intrinsic**.—*adj.* **extrin'sical.**—*n.* **extrinsical'ity.**—*adv.* **extrin'sically.** [Fr. *extrinsèque*—L. *extrīnsecus—exter,* outside, suff. *-in, secus,* beside.]

extrovert, extroversion. Same as **extravert,** etc.

extrude *iks-trōōd', v.t.* to force or urge out: to protrude: to make rods, tubes, etc. by extrusion (*metallurgy*).—*v.i.* to protrude.—*ns.* **extrud'er; extrusion** (*-trōō'zhən*) the act of extruding, thrusting, or throwing out: expulsion: rocks formed by the cooling of magma or lava.—*adjs.* **extrusive** (*-trōō'siv*); **extru'sory** (*-sər-i*). [L. *extrūdēre, extrūsum—ex-,* out, *trūdēre,* to thrust.]

exuberant *eg-, ig-zū'bər-ənt, -zōō', adj.* luxuriant: overflowing: abounding: in high spirits: lavish.—*ns.* **exu'berance, exu'berancy** the quality of being exuberant: luxuriance, an overflowing quantity: redundancy: outburst.—*adv.* **exu'berantly.** [L. *exūberāns, -antis,* pr.p. of *exūberāre—ex-,* intens., *ūber,* rich.]

exude *igz-, iks-ūd', v.t.* to discharge by sweating: to discharge through pores or incisions.—*v.i.* to flow out of a body through the pores: to ooze out.—*ns.* **exudate** (*eks'*) exuded matter; **exudā'tion** (*eks-*) the act of exuding or discharging through pores: that which is exuded.—*adj.* **exūd'ative.** [L. *exūdāre—ex,* from, *sūdāre,* to sweat.]

exult *igz-ult', v.i.* to rejoice exceedingly: to triumph.—*ns.* **exult'ance, exult'ancy** exultation: triumph.—*adj.* **exult'ant** exulting: triumphant.—*adv.* **exult'antly.**—*n.* **exulta'tion** (*egz-*) triumphant delight: transport.—*adv.* **exult'ingly.** [L. *ex(s)ultāre, -ātum,* from *ex(s)ilīre—ex-,* out or up, *salīre,* to leap.]

exurbia *eks-ûr'bi-ə,* (*U.S.*) *n.* the residential areas outside the suburbs of a town.—*adj.* **exur'ban.**—*n.* and *adj.* **exur'banite.** [L. *ex-,* outside, and **suburbia.**]

exuviae *igz-, iks-ū'vi-ē, n.pl.* cast-off skins, shells, or other coverings of animals: fossil remains of animals (*geol.*).—*adj.* **exū'vial.**—*v.i.* **exū'viate** to shed, cast off, for a new covering or condition.—*n.* **exuvia'tion** the act of exuviating [L., *exuēre,* to draw off.]

ex voto *eks vō'tō, wō',* (L.) according to one's prayer, by reason of a vow: votive.—*n.* a votive offering.

eyas *ī'as, n.* an unfledged hawk [*An eyas* for *a nyas*—Fr. *niais*—L. *nīdus,* nest.]

eye *ī, n.* the organ of sight or vision: more narrowly the globe or movable part of it: the power of seeing: sight. regard: aim: keenness of perception: anything resembling an eye, as an eye-spot: a central spot· the hole of a needle: a round aperture: a wire loop or ring for a hook: the seed-bud of a potato: the central calm area of a cyclone: (in *pl.*) the foremost part of a ship's bows, the hawse-holes:—*pl.* eyes.—*v.t.* to look on: to observe narrowly:—*pr.p.* ey'ing or eye'ing; *pa.t.* and *pa.p.* eyed (*īd*).—*n.* eye'ful as much as the eye can take in: something worth looking at, a fascinating sight or an attractive woman (*slang*).—*adj.* eye'less deprived of eyes: blind.—*n.* eyelet see separate entry. —eye'ball the ball or globe of the eye.—*v.t.* (*coll.*) to face someone eyeball to eyeball, to confront: to examine closely.—eye bank see bank³; eye'-bath a cup that can be held in the orbit to bathe the eye; eye'bolt a bolt, with an eye instead of the normal head, used for lifting purposes on heavy machines, etc.; eye'bright a little plant of the genus Euphrasia formerly used as a remedy for eye diseases; eye'brow the hairy arch above the eye.—*adj.* eye'-catching striking.—eye'-drops medicinal drops for the eye; eye'glass a glass to assist the sight, esp. one held on the bridge of the nose by a spring; eye'-hole an eyelet; eye'lash the row, or one, of the hairs that edge the eyelid.—*adj.* eye-leg'ible (of headings, etc. on microfilm or microprint) able to be read by the naked eye. —eye'lid the lid or cover of the eye: the portion of movable skin by means of which the eye is opened or closed; eye'liner a kind of cosmetic used for drawing a line along the edge of the eyelid in order to emphasise the eye; eye'-opener something that opens the eyes literally or figuratively, a startling enlightenment; eye'-piece the lens or combination of lenses at the eye end of an optical instrument; eye'-rhyme a would-be rhyme between words that are spelt as if they rhymed but do not; eye'shade a piece of stiff, usu. tinted transparent, material, worn like the peak of a cap to protect the eyes from the sun or other bright light; eye'-shadow a coloured cosmetic for the eyelids; eye'-shot the reach or range of sight of the eye: a glance; eye'sight power of seeing: view: observation; eye socket either of the two recesses in the skull in which the eyeballs are situated, the orbit; eye'sore anything that is offensive to look at.—eye'stalk a stalk on the dorsal surface of the head of many Crustacea, bearing an eye; eye'strain tiredness or irritation of the eyes;

eye'-tooth a canine tooth, esp. in the upper jaw, below the eye; eye'-wash a lotion for the eye: humbug: deception; eye'-wit'ness one who sees a thing done.—all my eye (*slang*) humbug; be all eyes to give all attention; clap, lay, set, eyes on (*coll.*) to see; cry one's eyes out see cry; eyeball to eyeball (of discussion, confrontation, diplomacy) at close quarters, dealing with matters very frankly and firmly; electric eye see electric; eye for eye *lex talionis* (Exod. xxi. 24); eye of day the sun; eyes down the start of a bingo game, or of any non-physical contest; give an eye to to attend to; glad, green eye see glad, green¹; have an eye to to contemplate: to have regard to: to incline towards; in one's mind's eye in imagination; in the eyes of in the estimation, opinion, of; in the wind's eye against the wind; keep one's (or an) eye on to observe closely: to watch; keep one's eye(s) skinned, peeled (for) to be keenly watchful; make eyes at to look at in an amorous way, to ogle; my eye! a mild asseveration; naked eye see naked; one in the eye a rebuff; open a person's eyes to show him something of which he is ignorant; pipe, or put a finger in, the eye to weep; private eye see private; put a person's eye out to blind him: to supplant him in favour; raise an eyebrow to be mildly surprised, shocked or doubtful; see eye to eye from Isa. lii. 8, but used in the sense of to think alike; make, sheep's eyes at to ogle; turn a blind eye on to feign not to see; under the eye of under the observation of; up to the eyes deeply involved (in); with, having, an eye to considering. [O.E. *ēage*.]

eyelet *ī'lit, n.* a small eye or hole to receive a lace or cord, as in garments, sails, etc.: a small hole for seeing through (also eye'let-hole): a little eye. [O.Fr. *oillet*—L. *oculus*, influenced by eye.]

Eyeti, Eyetie, Eytie *ī'tī,* (*slang*) *n.* an Italian.

eyra *ī'rə, n.* a South American wild cat. [Guaraní.]

eyre *ār,* (*hist.*) *n.* a journey or circuit: a court of itinerant justices in the late 12th. and 13th. cent. [O.Fr. *eire,* journey, from L. *iter,* a way, a journey—*ire, itum,* to go.]

eyrie, eyry (also aerie, aery, ayrie) *ā'ri, ē'ri, ī'ri, ns.* the nest of a bird of prey, esp. an eagle: a house or stronghold perched on some high or steep place. [O.Fr. *aire;* origin unknown.]

F

F, f *ef*, *n*. the sixth letter in the English and Latin alphabets: the fourth note of the natural diatonic scale of C (*mus.*): F is used as a contraction for Fahrenheit; F_1, F_2 (Mendelism) first and second filial generations.—**F′-clef** a clef marking F, the fourth line in the bass, the bass-clef; **f′-number** (*phot.*) the ratio of the focal length to the true diameter of a lens.

fa *fä*, *n*. the fourth note in the sol-fa notation—also anglicised in spelling as **fah**. [See **Aretinian**.]

fab *fab*, (*slang*) *adj*. excellent, marvellous. [Contr. of **fabulous**.]

Fabian *fā′bi-ən*, *adj*. delaying, avoiding battle, cautious: favouring the gradual introduction and spread of Socialism.—*n*. a member or supporter of the *Fabian Society* (founded 1884) for this purpose.—*ns*. **Fā′bianism; Fā′bianist**. [From Q. *Fabius* Maximus, surnamed Cunctator (delayer), from the masterly tactics with which he wore out the strength of Hannibal.]

fable *fā′bl*, *n*. a narrative in which things irrational, and sometimes inanimate, are, for the purpose of moral instruction, made to act and speak with human interests and passions: any tale in literary form intended to instruct or amuse: a fiction or myth: a ridiculous story, an old wives' tale: a falsehood: subject of common talk.—*v.i.* to tell fictitious tales.—*v.t.* to feign: to invent: to relate as if true.—*adj*. **fā′bled** mythical: renowned in story: feigned.—*n*. **fā′bler**.—*n*. and *adj*. **fā′bling**.—*ns*. **fab′ulist** one who invents fables; **fabulos′ity**.—*adj*. **fab′ulous** feigned, false: related in fable: celebrated in story: immense, amazing: excellent (*coll.*).—*adv*. **fab′ulously**.—*n*. **fab′ulousness**. [Fr. *fable*, and L. *fābula*,—*fārī*, to speak.]

fabric *fab′rik*, *n*. texture: anything framed by art and labour: a building: buildings, stonework, etc.: manufactured cloth: any system of connected parts: framework (also *fig.*).—*v.t.* **fab′ricate** to put together by art and labour: to manufacture: to produce: to devise falsely.—*n*. **fabrica′tion** construction: manufacture: that which is fabricated or invented: a story: a falsehood.—*adj*. **fab′ricative**.—*n*. **fab′ricātor**. [L. *fābrica*, fabric—*fāber*, a worker in hard materials: partly through Fr. *fabrique*.]

fabulist, fabulous, etc. See **fable**.

façade *fa-säd′*, *n*. the exterior front or face of a building: the appearance presented to the world, esp. if showy and with little behind it (*fig.*). [Fr.,—*face*, after It. *facciata*, the front of a building—*faccia*, the face.]

face *fäs*, *n*. the front part of the head, including forehead and chin: the outside form or appearance: front or surface: a flat surface of a solid geometrical figure, crystal, etc.: the striking surface of a golf-club, etc.: the edge of a cutting-tool, etc.: the front or upper surface, or that usually presented: the exposed surface in a cliff, mine, or quarry: the dial of a watch, etc.: the printed surface of a playing card: special appearance or expression: aspect, look, configuration: command of facial expression and bearing: boldness, effrontery: a grimace: presence: anger or favour (*B.*).—*v.t.* to meet in the face or in front: to stand opposite to or looking towards: to confront: to stand up to: to brave: to resist: to put an additional face or surface on: to cover in front: to trim.—*v.i.* (often with *on*, *to*, *towards*) to direct or turn the face: to take or have a direction.—*adjs*. **faced** having a face: having the outer surface dressed: with the front covered with another material; **face′less** without a face: (of person(s) concerned in some action) with identity concealed: robot-like, esp. of bureaucratic officials who allow no degree of personality to intrude on their decision-making processes.—*n*. **fac′er** one who faces something: a severe blow on the face (*slang*): an affront (*coll.*): anything that staggers one (*coll.*).—*adj*. **facial** (*fā′shl*) of or relating to the face: for the face.—*n*. a beauty. treatment to the face (*coll.*).—*adv*. **fa′cially**.—*n*. **fac′ing** a covering in front for ornament or protection.—**face′-card** a playing-card bearing a face (king, queen or knave); **face′-cloth** a cloth used in washing the face; **face′-lift** renovating process, esp. one applied to the outside of a building (also *fig.*): face-lifting; **face′-lifting** an operation aiming at smoothing and firming the face; **face′man, face′worker** a miner who works at the coal-face; **face′-off** in ice-hockey, etc., the dropping of the puck between two players to start the game: a confrontation (*fig.*); **face pack** a creamy cosmetic mixture put on to the face for a certain time; **face′s powder** a cosmetic powder for the face; **face′-saver** a course of action that saves one's face (see below); **face′-saving**.—Also *adj*.—**face value** the value as stated on the face of a coin, etc.: the apparent value of anything, which may not be the same as its real value.—**face down** to abash by stern looks: to confront and make concede; **face out** to carry off by bold looks; **face the music** (*slang*) to accept the unpleasant consequences at their worst: to brave a trying situation, hostile reception, etc.; **face to face** opposite: in actual presence: in confrontation (*adj*. **face′-to-face′**); **face up to** to face, stand up to: to recognise (fact, facts) and prepare to endure or act bravely; **fly in the face of** to set oneself directly against; **in the face of** in defiance of, despite; **lose face** to lose prestige; **loss of face** humiliation, loss of dignity; **make, pull, faces at** to distort one's face into exaggerated expressions in order to amuse, annoy, etc.; **on the face of it** on its own showing: as is palpably plain: at first glance; **pull a long face** to look dismal; **put a good, brave face on (it)** to assume a bold or contented bearing (as regards something); **save one's face** to avoid humiliation or appearance of climbing down; **set one's face against** to oppose strenuously; **show one's face** to appear; **to one's face** in one's presence, openly. [Fr. *face*—L. *faciēs*, form, face; perh. from *facēre*, to make.]

facet *fas′it*, *n*. a small surface, as of a crystal: an aspect or view.—*adj*. **fac′eted** having or formed into facets. [Fr. *facette*, dim. of *face*, face.]

facetious *fə-sē′shəs*, *adj*. witty, humorous, jocose: waggish: would-be-funny.—*adv*. **facē′tiously**.—*n*. **facē′tiousness**. [L. *facētia*—*facētus*, merry, witty.]

facia. Same as **fascia**.

facies *fā′shi-ēz*, *n*. general aspect, esp. of plant, animal or geological species or formations. [L. *faciēs*, face.]

facile *fas′il*, or -*il*, *adj*. easily persuaded. yielding: easy of accomplishment: easy: working with ease: fluent (usu. depreciatory) —*adv.* **fac'ilely.**—*n.* **fac'ileness.**—*v.t.* **facilitāte** (*fə-sil'*) to make easy or easier —*n* **facilitā'tion.**—*adj.* **facil'itātive.**—*ns.* **facil'itātor; facil'ity** ease in performance or action: fluency. easiness to be persuaded· pliancy: (esp in *pl.* **facil'ities**) means or opportunities that render anything readily possible: anything specially arranged or constructed to provide recreation, a service, etc : an agreed amount of money made available for borrowing (*econ.*). [Fr.,—L. *facilis,* easy—*facĕre,* to do.]

facsimile *fak-sim'i-li, n* an exact copy, as of handwriting, a coin, etc : accurate reproduction:—*pl* **facsim'iles.**—*adj.* exactly corresponding —*v.t.* to make a facsimile of, to reproduce:—*pr.p.* **facsim'ileing;** *pa.t.* and *pa.p.* **facsim'iled.**—*n* **facsim'ilist.**—**facsimile edition** an edition of a book, etc., that is an exact reproduction of an earlier edition. [L. *fac,* imper of *facĕre,* to make, *simile,* neut. of *similis,* like.]

fact *fakt, n.* a truth: truth: reality, or a real state of things, as distinguished from a mere statement or belief: an assertion of fact: a crime committed (*obs.* except in **after, before the fact**).—*adj.* **fact'ual** pertaining to facts: actual.—*ns.* **factual'ity; fact'ualness.**—*adj.* **fact'-finding** appointed to ascertain, directed towards ascertaining, all the facts of a situation —**as a matter of fact** in reality; **facts of life** the details of reproduction, esp. human reproduction: the realities of a situation; **in fact, in point of fact** indeed; **the fact of the matter** the plain truth about the subject in question. [L. *factum,* neut. pa.p. of *facĕre,* to do.]

faction¹ *fak'shən, n.* a company of persons associated or acting together, mostly used in a bad sense: a contentious party in a state or society: dissension.—*adj.* **fac'tional.**—*ns.* **fac'tionalism; fac'tionalist.**—*adj* **fac'tious** turbulent: given to faction: proceeding from party spirit: seditious. [L. *factiō, -ōnis—facĕre,* to do.]

faction² *fak'shən, n.* a play, programme, piece of writing, etc., that is a mixture of fact and fiction— also called **drama documentary, news fiction.** [*fact,* fiction.]

factitious *fak-tish'əs, adj.* artificial: made: produced by artificial conditions.—*adv.* **facti'tiously.**—*n.* **facti'tiousness.**—*adjs.* **fac'titive** causative; **fac'tive** making. [L. *facticius, factitivus—facĕre,* to make.]

factor *fak'tər, n.* a doer or transactor of business for another: one who buys and sells goods for others, on commission: an agent managing heritable estates for another (*Scot.*): in math., one of two or more quantities which, when multiplied together, result in the given quantity—e.g. 6 and 4 are factors of 24: an element in the composition of anything, or in bringing about a certain result: a fact, etc. which has to be taken into account or which affects the course of events.—*v.i.* to work, act, etc. as a factor.—*adj.* **factō'rial** of or pertaining to a factor.—*n.* the product of all whole numbers from a given number down to one.—*n.* **fac'toring** the work of a factor: the business of buying up trade debts, or lending money on the security of these.—*v.t.* **fac'torise, -ize** to resolve into factors.—*ns.* **factorisā'tion, -z-; fac'torship; fac'tory** a place where goods are manufactured: a trading settlement in another country.—**factory farm** one carrying out **factory farming,** farming by methods of feeding and housing animals in which everything is subordinated to achieving maximum production, rapid growth, and qualities in demand on the market; **fac'tory-ship** a whaling-ship on which whales are processed.—**safety factor** see **safe.** [L. *facĕre,* to do.]

factotum *fak-tō'təm, n.* a person employed to do all kinds of work for another:—*pl.* **facto'tums.** [L.L , —L. *fac,* imper of *facĕre,* to do, *tōtum,* all.]

faculty *fak'əl-ti, n* facility or power to act: any particular ability or aptitude. an original power of the mind: any physical capability or function: personal quality or endowment. right, authority, or privilege to act: licence. a department of learning at a university, or the professors and lecturers constituting it: the members of a profession: executive ability —*adj.* **fac'ultative** optional: incidental· of or pertaining to a faculty: conferring privilege, permission or authority. able to live under different conditions (*zool.*).— *adv* **fac'ultatively.** [Fr. *faculté*—L. *facultās, -ātis— facilis,* easy.]

fad *fad, n.* a weak or transient hobby, crotchet, or craze: any unimportant belief or practice intemperately urged.—*n.* **fadd'iness.**—*adj.* **fadd'ish.**— *ns.* **fadd'ishness, fadd'ism; fadd'ist.**—*adj.* **fadd'y.**

fade *fād, v.i.* to lose strength, freshness, loudness, brightness, or colour gradually: to die away: to disappear.—*v.t.* to cause to fade· to cause to change gradually in distinctness (as *fade out, fade in*): to impart a fade to (*golf*).—*n.* a fading: a slight, delayed (often deliberate) slice (*golf*).—*adv.* **fā'dedly.**—*n.* **fā'dedness.**—*n.* and *adj.* **fād'ing.**—**fade down** (of sound or light) to fade out (*n.* **fade'-down**); **fade in** in films, radio, television, etc., to introduce (sound, a picture) gradually, bringing it up to full volume or clarity (*n.* **fade'-in**); **fade out** in films, radio, television, etc., to cause (sound, a picture) to disappear gradually (*n.* **fade'-out**); **fade up** (of sound or light) to fade in (*n.* **fade'-up**). [O Fr. *fader—fade*—L. *vapidum,* acc. to Gaston Paris.]

faeces *fē'sēz, n.pl.* sediment after infusion or distillation: dregs: excrement.—*adj.* **faecal** (*fē'kl*). [L , pl. of *faex, faecis,* dregs, grounds.]

faerie, faery *fā'(ə)ri,* (*arch.*) *n.* the world of fairies, fairyland: a fairy.—Also *adj.* [A variant of **fairy.**]

faff *faf,* (*coll.*) *v i.* to dither, fumble (usu. with *about*).

fag¹ *fag, v.i.* to become weary or tired out: to work hard: to be a fag.—*v.t.* to weary: to use as a fag:— *pr.p.* **fagg'ing;** *pa.t* and *pa.p.* **fagged.**—*n.* a schoolboy forced to do menial offices for another: a tiresome piece of work: drudgery: orig. an inferior cigarette (for *fag-end; slang*): hence any cigarette (*slang*).—*n.* **fagg'ery** drudgery: fagging.—*n.* and *adj.* **fagg'ing.**—**fag'-end'** the end of a web of cloth that hangs loose: the untwisted end of a rope: the end, refuse or meaner part of a thing: the stump of a cigar or cigarette (*slang*) [Ety. dub.; perh. a corr. of **flag¹,** to droop (q.v.).]

fag². See **faggot.**

faggot, fagot *fag'ət, n.* a bundle of sticks for fuel, fascines, etc : a stick: anything like a faggot: a bundle of pieces of iron or steel cut off into suitable lengths for welding: a roll of internal organs, etc., of a pig mixed with bread and savoury herbs: derogatory term for an old woman: a male homosexual (also **fag;** *slang,* orig. *U.S.*).—*v.t.* to tie together.—*n.* **fagg'oting, fag'oting** a kind of embroidery in which some of the crossthreads are drawn together in the middle. [Fr. *fagot,* a bundle of sticks.]

fah. See **fa.**

Fahrenheit *fa', fä'rən-hīt, adj.,* of a thermometer or thermometer scale, having the freezing-point of water marked at 32, and the boiling-point at 212, degrees. [Named from the inventor, Gabriel D *Fahrenheit* (1686-1736).]

faience, faïence *fā-yäs, n.* glazed coloured earthenware. [Fr ; prob. from *Faenza* in Italy]

fail *fāl, v.i.* to fall short or be wanting (with *in*): to fall away: to decay: to prove deficient under trial, examination, pressure, etc.: to miss achievement: to be disappointed or baffled: to become insolvent or bankrupt.—*v.t* not to be sufficient for· to leave undone, omit. to disappoint or desert: to declare deficient after examination —*n.* failure, esp in an examination —*adj* **failed** that has failed: decayed, worn out: bankrupt.—*n* **fail'ing** a fault, weakness: a foible: failure —*adj.* that fails.—*prep* in default of —*n* **fail'ure** a falling short, or cessation: lack of success: omission: decay bankruptcy: an unsuccessful person.—*adj.* **fail'-safe** pertaining to a mechanism incorporated in a system to ensure that there will be no accident if the system does not operate properly —Also *fig* —**without fail** for certain. [O.Fr *faillir*—L. *fallĕre*, to deceive.]

faille *fāl, fīl, fā-y*`, *n.* a soft, closely-woven silk or rayon fabric with transverse ribs. [Fr]

fain *fān,* (*arch.* and *poet.*) *adj.* glad or joyful· eager (with *to*).—*adv.* gladly. [O.E. *fægen*, joyful]

faint *fānt, adj.* wanting in strength (*arch.*): dim: lacking distinctness: not bright or forcible: weak in spirit (*arch.*): lacking courage (*arch*): done in a feeble way: inclined to faint —*v i* to swoon: to fade or decay (*arch.*): to lose courage or spirit (*arch.*).—*n* .a swoon. —*n.* and *adj* **faint'ing**.—*adv.* **faint'ly**.—*n.* **faint'ness** want of strength: feebleness of colour, light, etc.: dejection.—*adjs.* **faint'-heart** (also *n.*), **faint'-heart'ed** spiritless: timorous —*adv.* **faint'-heart'edly**.— **faint'-heart'edness**. [O Fr. *feint*, feigned—L. *fingĕre*, to feign.]

fair[1] *fār, adj.* bright· clear: clean: free from blemish: pure: pleasing to the eye: beautiful: of a light hue: free from rain, fine, dry: unobstructed: open: smoothly curving: prosperous: impartial: just: good, pleasing: plausible: civil: specious. reasonable: likely: favourable: pretty good: passable.—*v.i.* to clear up, as the weather from rain.—*adv.* in a fair manner (in all senses): full, square, directly (e.g. *hit fair in the centre*): quite (*dial.*).—*n.* **fair'ing** adjustment or testing of curves in ship-building: means of reducing head-resistance in an aeroplane.—*adv.* **fair'ly** justly: reasonably: plainly: fully, quite. tolerably.—*n.* **fair'ness**.—*adj.* **fair'-and-square'** honest (also *adv.*).—**fair** copy a clean copy after correction; **fair'-deal'ing; fair game** an object for justifiable attack or ridicule.—*adj.* **fair'-haired** having light-coloured hair —**Fair Isle** type of design used in knitwear, named from a Shetland island.— *adj.* **fair'-minded** judging fairly.—**fair play** honest dealing: justice.—*adj.* **fair-spok'en** bland and civil in language and address.—**fair'way** the navigable channel or usual course of vessels in a river, etc.: in golf, the smooth turf between tee and putting-green, distinguished from the uncut rough and from hazards.— *adj.* **fair'-weath'er** suitable only for, or found only in, fair weather or (esp. of friends or supporters) favourable circumstances.—**bid fair** see **bid; fair do's** (*dōōz* —*pl.* of **do;** *coll.*) an expression appealing for, or agreeing to, fair play, strict honesty, etc.; **fair enough** expressing acceptance, though not necessarily full agreement; **in all fairness** being scrupulously fair; **stand fair with** to be in the good graces of; **the fair sex** the female sex. [O.E. *fæger.*]

fair[2] *fār, n.* a great periodical market, with or without amusements: often reduced to a collection of shows, swing-boats, etc.: charity bazaar: trade show.—*n.* **fair'ing** a present given at or from a fair: any complimentary gift.—**fair'-ground.—a day after the fair, behind the fair** too late. [O.Fr *feire*—L *fēria*, holiday.]

fairy *fār'i, n.* an imaginary being, generally of diminutive and graceful human form, capable of kindly or unkindly acts towards man: an enchantress· a male homosexual.—*adj.* like a fairy, fanciful, whimsical, delicate —*adj.* and *adv.* **fair'ylike** like fairies or like something in fairyland: very delicate and charming —

fai'ry-cy'cle a child's bicycle; **fair'y-god'mother** a benefactress such as Cinderella had; **fair'yland** the country of the fairies, **fairy light** (usu. in *pl.*) a tiny coloured light used as decoration; **fair'y-ring** a ring of darker-coloured grass due to outward spread of a fungus, attributed to the dancing of fairies; **fairy tale** a story about fairies or other supernatural beings: a folk-tale: a romantic tale: an incredible tale: euphemistically, a lie: a marvel —*adj.* **fair'y-tale** beautiful, fortunate, etc., as in a fairy tale. [O.Fr. *faerie*, enchantment—*fae* (mod. *fée*); see **faerie, fay**[1].]

fait accompli *fe-ta-kɔ̄-plē,* (Fr.) an accomplished fact, a thing already done.

faith *fāth, n.* trust or confidence: belief in the statement of another: belief in the truth of revealed religion: confidence and trust in God: the living reception of religious belief: that which is believed: any system of religious belief, esp. the religion one considers true: fidelity to promises: honesty: word or honour pledged: faithfulness.—*interj.* (*arch.*) by my faith: indeed.—*adj* **faith'ful** believing: firm in adherence to promises, duty, friendship, love, etc.· worthy of belief: true: exact —*adv.* **faith'fully** with confidence with fidelity: with sincerity: with scrupulous exactitude: solemnly (*coll.*).—*n.* **faith'fulness**.—*adj.* **faith'less** without faith or belief: not believing, esp. in God or Christianity: not adhering to promises, duty, etc.: inconstant: adulterous: untrustworthy: delusive.—*adv.* **faith'lessly**.— *n.* **faith'lessness.—faith'-heal'er; faith'-heal'ing** or **-cure** a system of belief that sickness may be cured without medical advice or appliances, if the prayer of Christians be accompanied in the sufferer by true faith: cure by suggestion.—**bad faith** treachery· the breaking of a promise; **in good faith** with honesty and sincerity: acting honestly; **keep faith** to act honestly, according to one's promise (with); **the Faithful** believers, esp. Muslims: (without *cap.*) adherents, supporters, etc. (*coll.*). [M.E. *feith, feyth*—O.Fr. *feid*—L. *fidēs*—*fidĕre*, to trust.]

fake[1] *fāk, v.t.* to fold, coil.—*n.* a coil or rope, etc.

fake[2] *fāk, v t.* to doctor, cook, or counterfeit.—*n.* a swindle, dodge, sham: a faked article.—*adj.* false, counterfeit.—*n.* **fak'er.** [Prob. the earlier *feak, feague*, Ger. *fegen*, to furbish up.]

fakir *fā-kēr'*, or *fā'kɔr, n.* religious (esp. Muslim) mendicant, ascetic, or wonder-worker in India, etc.—*n.* **fakir'ism** (or *fā'*). [Ar. *faqīr*, a poor man.]

Falange *fā-läng'hhä* (Sp.), also *fɔ-lanj', fā', n.* a Spanish fascist group.—*ns.* **Falangism** (*fɔ-lan'jizm*) (also without *cap.*); **Falan'gist** (also without *cap.*). [Sp., —Gr. *phalanx*, phalanx (q.v.).]

falbala *fal'bɔ-lɔ, n.* a trimming or flounce: a furbelow. [Ety. dub.; cf. **furbelow**.]

falcate, -d *fal'kāt, -id, adjs.* bent like a sickle.—*adjs.* **falciform** (*fal'si-förm*) sickle-shaped; **fal'culate**. [L. *falx, falcis,* a sickle.]

falciform. See **falcate.**

falcon *föl'kɔn, fo'kɔn, n.* a bird of prey of a kind trained to the pursuit of game: by falconers confined to the female (cf. **tercel**): any of the long-winged birds of prey of the genus *Falco* or its kindred.—*ns.* **fal'coner** one who sports with, or who breeds and trains, falcons or hawks for taking wild-fowl.—*n.* **fal'conry** the art or practice of training, or hunting with, falcons. [O.Fr. *faucon*—L.L. *falcō, -ōnis.*]

falderal *fal'dɔr-al', n.* a meaningless refrain in songs: any kind of flimsy trifle—also **folderol** (*fol'dɔr-ol'*).

faldstool *fold'stōōl, n.* a folding or camp stool: a coronation stool: a bishop's armless seat: a small desk in churches in England, at which the litany is to be sung or said. [L.L. *faldistolium, faldistorium*—

O.H.G. *faldstuol—faldan* (Ger. *falten*), to fold, *stuol* (Ger. *Stuhl*), stool.]

fall[1] *föl*, *v.i.* to descend, esp. to descend freely and involuntarily by force of gravity: to drop: to drop prostrate: to throw oneself down: to be dropped in birth: to collapse: to become lower literally or figuratively: to die away: to subside: to ebb: to decline: to sink: (of the face) to relax into an expression of dismay: to flow downwards: to slope or incline down: to hang, dangle, or trail down: to be cast or shed: to drop dead or as if dead, esp. in fight: to be overthrown: to come to ruin: to lose power, station, virtue or repute: to be degraded: to be taken or captured: to become a victim: to yield to temptation: to pass into any state or action (as *fall asleep*): to rush: to become involved: to betake oneself: to come to be: to befall: to come about: to come by chance or as if by chance: to come in due course: to occur: to chance, light: to issue: to come forth: to appertain: to be apportioned, assigned: to come as one's share, lot, duty, etc.: to take position or arrangement: to find place: to be disposed: to impinge: to lapse: to terminate: to revert:—*pr.p.* **fall′ing**; *pa.t.* **fell**; *pa.p* **fallen** *(fö′lən)*.—*n.* the act, manner, occasion, or time of falling or of felling: descent by gravity, a dropping down: that which falls: as much as comes down at one time: onset: overthrow: descent from a better to a worse position: slope or declivity: descent of water: a cascade: length of drop, amount of descent: decrease in value: a sinking of the voice: a cadence: autumn (chiefly *U.S.*): a bout of wrestling: the passing of a city or stronghold to the enemy: a lapse into sin, esp. that of Adam and Eve—'the Fall (of Man)'· a falling band, a hanging fringe, flap, or ornament: a lowering or hoisting rope.—*adj.* **fall′en** having fallen: killed, esp. in battle: overthrown: seduced: in a degraded state, ruined.—*n.* **fall′ing**.—*adj.* **fall′-back** used as a retreat, or second alternative.—Also *n.*—**fall-in** see **fall in** below; **fall′ing-off** decline; **falling star** a meteor; **fall′-out** by-product, side benefit (*coll.*): a deposit of radioactive dust from a nuclear explosion or plant: the aftermath of any explosive occurrence or situation (*fig.*): see **fall out** below.—**fall about** to laugh hysterically, to collapse (with laughter); **fall across** (*arch.*) to meet by chance; **fall among** to find oneself in the midst of; **fall away** to decline gradually: to languish: to grow lean: to revolt or apostatise; **fall back** to retreat, give way; **fall back upon** to have recourse to as an expedient or resource in reserve; **fall behind** to lag: to be outstripped: to get in arrears; **fall between two stools** to be neither one thing nor the other: to succeed in neither of two alternatives; **fall down on** (*coll.*) to fail in; **fall flat** to fail completely, have no effect; **fall for** (*coll.*) to become enamoured of: to be taken in by (a trick, etc.); **fall foul of** see **foul**; **fall in** to (cause to) take places in ranks (*mil.*; *n.* **fall′-in′**): to become hollowed: to revert; **fall in with** to concur or agree with: to comply with: to meet by chance; **fall off** to become detached and drop: to deteriorate: to die away, to perish: to revolt or apostatise: to draw back; **fall on** to begin eagerly: to make an attack; **fall on one's feet** to come well out of a difficulty: to gain any unexpected good fortune; **fall out** to quarrel: to happen or befall: to (cause to) quit ranks (*mil.*); **fall over backwards** see **backwards** under **back**; **fall over oneself** (*coll.*) to put oneself about, to be in great haste or eagerness (to do something); **fall short** to turn out to be short or insufficient: to become used up: to fail to attain or reach what is aimed at (with *of*); **fall through** to fail, come to nothing; **fall to** to begin hastily and eagerly: to apply oneself to: to begin to eat; **fall upon** to attack: to rush against: to devolve upon: to chance upon

[O.E. *fallan*.]
fall[2] *föl*, *n.* a trap.—**fall′-guy**, **fall guy** a dupe, easy victim: a scapegoat. [O.E. *fealle—feallan*, to fall.]
fallacy *fal′ə-si*, *n.* something fallacious: deceptive appearance: an apparently genuine but really illogical argument: a wrong but prevalent notion.—*adj.* **fallacious** *(fə-lā′shəs)* of the nature of fallacy: deceptive: misleading: not well founded: causing disappointment: delusive.—*adv.* **falla′ciously**.—*n.* **falla′ciousness**. [L. *fallācia—fallāx*, deceptive—*fallĕre*, to deceive.]
fallible *fal′i-bl*, *adj.* liable to error or mistake.—*n.* **fallibil′ity** liability to err.—*adv.* **fall′ibly**. [L.L. *fallibilis—fallĕre*, to deceive.]
Fallopian *fə-lō′pi-ən*, *adj.* relating to the Italian anatomist Gabriele *Fallopio* (1523–62).—**Fallopian tubes** two tubes or ducts through which the ova pass from the ovary to the uterus, perhaps discovered by him.
fallow[1] *fal′ō*, *adj.* left untilled or unsown for a time. —*n.* land that has lain a year or more untilled or unsown after having been ploughed.—*v.t.* to plough with- out seeding.—*n.* **fall′owness**. [O.E. *fealgian*, to fallow; *fealh*, fallow land.]
fallow[2] *fal′ō*, *adj.* brownish-yellow.—**fallow deer** a yellowish-brownish deer smaller than the red deer, with broad flat antlers. [O E. *falu (fealu)*.]
false *fols*, *adj.* wrong: deceptive or deceiving: untruthful: unfaithful: untrue: not genuine or real: improperly so called: artificial, as opposed to natural, of teeth, etc.: incorrect, not according to rule: out of tune.—*adv.* incorrectly: untruly: dishonestly: faithlessly.—*n.* **false′hood** the state or quality of being false: want of truth: an untrue statement: the act of lying: a lie.—*adv.* **false′ly**.—*ns.* **false′ness**; **fal′sie(s)** pad(s) of rubber or other material inserted into a brassière to enlarge or improve the shape of the breasts: **fals′ity** quality of being false: a false assertion.—**false acacia** Robinia; **false alarm** a warning without danger; **false bottom** a partition cutting off a space between it and the true bottom; **false card** the card played to deceive; **false dawn** deceptive appearance simulating dawn; **false face** a mask. —*adj.* **false′-heart′ed** treacherous, deceitful.—**false imprisonment** illegal detention by force or influence; **false leg** a proleg, **false pregnancy** a psychosomatic condition marked by many of the symptoms of pregnancy; **false pretences** deception; **false rib** one that does not reach the breastbone; **false teeth** artificial teeth, dentures.—**play someone false** to act falsely or treacherously to a person; **put in a false position** to bring any one into a position in which he must be misunderstood. [O.Fr. *fals* (mod. *faux*)—L. *falsus*, pa.p. of *fallĕre*, to deceive.]
falsetto *fol-set′ō*, *n.* usu. in a man, forced voice of range or register above the natural: one who uses such a voice: false or strained sentiment:—*pl.* **falsett′os**.—*adj.* and *adv.* in falsetto. [It. *falsetto*, dim. of *falso*, false.]
falsify *föls′i-fī*, *v.t.* to forge or counterfeit: to tamper with: to misrepresent: to prove or declare to be false:—*pr.p.* **fals′ifying**; *pa.t.* and *pa.p.* **fals′ified**.— *adj.* **fals′ifiable**.—*n.* **falsifiabil′ity** **falsifica′tion**; **fals′ifier**. [Fr. *falsifier*—L.L. *falsificāre*—L *falsus*, false, *facĕre*, to make.]
falsity. See **false**.
falter *fol′tər*, *v.i.* to stumble· to go unsteadily: to hesitate in speech as if taken aback: to flinch: to waver: to flag: to fail.—*v t.* to utter falteringly.—*n* unsteadiness.—*n.* and *adj.* **fal′tering**.—*adv.* **fal′teringly**. [Prob a freq. of M E. *falden*, to fold]
fame *fām*, *n.* renown or celebrity, chiefly in a good sense.—*adj.* **famed** renowned.—**house of ill fame** a

brothel. [Fr.,—L. *fāma*, report, rumour, fame.]

familial. See **family**.

familiar *fə-mil'yər*, *adj.* well acquainted or intimate: in the manner of an intimate: free: unceremonious: having a thorough knowledge: well known or understood: private, domestic: common, everyday.—*n.* one well or long acquainted: a spirit or demon supposed to attend a person at call.—*v.t.* **famil′iarise**, **-ize** to make thoroughly acquainted with: to make easy by practice or study.—*n.* **familiarity** (*-i-ar′i-ti*) intimate acquaintanceship: freedom from constraint: any unusual or unwarrantable freedom in act or speech toward another, act of licence—usu. in *pl.*—*adv.* **famil′iarly.** [O.Fr. *familier*—L. *familiāris*, from *familia*, a family.]

family *fam′i-li*, *n.* the household, or all those who live in one house (as parents, children, servants): parents and their children: the children alone: the descendants of one common progenitor: race: honourable or noble descent: a group of people related to one another, or otherwise connected: a group of animals, plants, languages, etc., more comprehensive than a genus: a collection of curves in the equations of which different values are given to the parameter(s) (*math.*).—*adj.* of or concerning the family: belonging to or specially for a family.—*adjs.* **famil′ial** (*fəm-*) characteristic of a family; **famil′iar** see above.—**family allowance** an allowance formerly paid by the state for the support of children, now replaced by child benefit; **family Bible** a large Bible for family worship, with a page for recording family events; **family circle** the members of the family taken collectively: one of the galleries in a theatre; **family doctor** a general practitioner; **family man** a man with a family: a domesticated man: a man dedicated to, and who enjoys sharing activities with, his wife and children; **family name** surname; **family planning** regulating the number and spacing of children, e.g. by using contraceptives; **family tree** a diagram showing the branching of a family.—**family income supplement** a payment by the state to a family whose income from employment is below a certain level; **in the family way** pregnant. [L. *familia*—*famulus*, a servant.]

famine *fam′in*, *n.* extreme general scarcity of food: scarcity of anything: hunger: starvation. [Fr.,—L. *famēs*, hunger.]

famish *fam′ish*: be **famished**, **famishing** to feel very hungry. [Obs. *fame*, to starve—L. *famēs*, hunger.]

famous *fā′məs*, *adj.* renowned: noted: excellent (*coll.*).—*adv.* **fā′mously.**—*n.* **fā′mousness.** [O.Fr., —L. *fāmōsus*—*fāma*, fame.]

fan[1] *fan*, *n.* a basket formerly used for winnowing corn by throwing it in the wind: a broad, flat instrument esp. used by women to cool themselves—typically in or spreading into the shape of a sector of a circle: any fan-shaped structure, as a deposit of alluvium: anything spreading in a fan shape, e.g. a bird's wing or tail: a propeller screw or propeller blade: a rotating ventilating or blowing apparatus.—*v.t.* to move by a fan or the like: to direct a current of air upon: to cool or to kindle with, or as with, a fan.—*v.i.* to move like a fan: to spread out like a fan:—*pr.p.* **fann′ing**; *pa.t.* and *pa.p.* **fanned.**—*n.* **fann′er.**—**fan dance** a solo dance in the nude (or nearly so) in which the performer attempts concealment (or nearly so) by tantalising manipulation of a fan or fans or bunch of ostrich plumes; **fan′-jet′** (a plane with) an engine in which air is taken in through a fan and some of it, bypassing compressors, combustion chamber and turbines, mixes with the jet formed by the rest; **fan′light** a window resembling in form an open fan.—*adj.* **fan′-shaped** forming a sector of a circle.—**fan′tail**

a tail shaped like a fan: a variety of domestic pigeon with tail feathers spread out like a fan: a member of various other classes of fantailed birds: an artificially bred goldfish with double anal and caudal fins.—Also *adj.*—**fan wheel** a wheel with fans on its rim for producing a current of air.—**fan out** to fan, spread as a fan from a centre. [O.E. *fann*, from L. *vannus*, a basket for winnowing.]

fan[2] *fan*, *n.* a devotee or enthusiastic follower of some sport or hobby or public favourite.—**fan club** a group united by devotion to a celebrity; **fan mail** letters from devotees to a celebrity. [From **fanatic**.]

fanatic *fə-nat′ik*, *adj.* extravagantly or unreasonably zealous, esp. in religion: excessively enthusiastic.—*n.* a person frantically or excessively enthusiastic, esp. on religious subjects.—*adj.* **fanat′ical.**—*adv.* **fanat′ically.**—*v.t.* **fanat′icise**, **-ize** (*-i-sīz*) to make fanatical.—*v.i.* to act as a fanatic.—*n.* **fanat′icism** (*-sizm*). [L. *fānāticus*, belonging to a temple, inspired by a god, *fānum*, a temple.]

fancy *fan′si*, *n.* that faculty of the mind by which it recalls, represents, or makes to appear past images or impressions—imagination, esp. of a lower, passive, or more trivial kind: an image or representation thus formed in the mind: an unreasonable lightly-formed or capricious opinion: a whim: capricious inclination or liking: taste.—*adj.* pleasing to, or guided by, or originating in fancy or caprice: fantastic: capriciously departing from the ordinary, the simple, or the plain: ornate: parti-coloured (of flowers).—*v.t.* to picture in the mind: to imagine: to be inclined to believe: to have a liking for: to be pleased with: to breed or cultivate, with a view to development of conventionally accepted points:—*pr.p.* **fan′cying**; *pa.t.* and *pa.p.* **fan′cied.**—*interj.* (also **fancy that!**) exclamation of surprise.—*adj.* **fan′cied** formed or conceived by the fancy: imagined: favoured.—*n.* **fan′cier** one who fancies: one who has a liking for anything and is supposed to be a judge of it: a breeder for points.—*adj.* **fan′ciful** guided or created by fancy: imaginative: whimsical: wild: unreal.—*adv.* **fan′cifully.**—*n.* **fan′cifulness.**—**fancy dress** dress arranged according to the wearer's fancy, to represent some character; **fancy dress ball.**—*adj.* **fan′cy-free′** free from the power of love.—**fancy goods** fabrics of variegated rather than simple pattern, applied generally to articles of show and ornament.—**fancy man** a woman's lover (*derog.*): a pimp; **fancy woman** a mistress: a prostitute; **fan′cywork** ornamental needlework.—**fancy oneself** to be conceited; **the fancy** sporting characters generally, esp. pugilists: pugilism; **tickle, take someone's fancy** to attract someone mildly in some way. [Contracted from **fantasy**.]

fandangle *fan-dang′gl*, *n.* elaborate ornament: nonsense. [Perh. from **fandango**.]

fandango *fan-dang′gō*, *n.* an old Spanish dance for two or its music in 3-4 time:—*pl.* **fandang′os.** [Sp.]

fanfare *fan′fār*, *n.* a flourish of trumpets or bugles. [Fr., perh. from the sound.]

fang *fang*, *n.* the tooth of a wolf, dog, etc.: the venom-tooth of a serpent: the embedded part of a tooth, etc.: a tang (of a tool): a prong.—*adjs.* **fanged** having fangs or anything resembling them; **fang′less.** [O.E. *fang*, from the same root as *fōn*, to seize.)

fank *fangk*, (*Scot.*) *n.* a coil: a noose: a tangle.—*v.t.* **fank′le** to entangle.—*n.* a tangle, muddle. [Conn. with **fang**.]

fanny *fan′i*, (*slang*) *n.* buttocks (chiefly *U.S.*): the female genitals (*vulg.*).

Fanny Adams *fan′i ad′əmz*, (*slang*) tinned mutton.—**sweet Fanny Adams, sweet FA** (*slang*, in Services a euphemism) nothing at all. [From a girl murdered and cut up *c.* 1812.]

fantasia *fan-tä'zi-ə, -ta', -zhə,* or *-tə-zē'ə, n.* a musical or other composition not governed by the ordinary rules of form. [It ,—Gr. *phantasiā*; see **fantasy**.]

fantasy, phantasy *fan'tə-si, -zi, n.* fancy: imagination: mental image: caprice: fantasia: a story, film, etc., not based on realistic characters or setting: preoccupation with thoughts associated with unobtainable desires.—*v.t* and *v i.* **fan'tasise, -ize.**—*ns.* **fan'tasist** a person who creates or indulges in fantasies; **fan'tasm** same as **phantasm.**—*adj.* **fantasque** (*-task'*) fantastic.—*n.* fantasy.—*adjs.* **fantas'tic, -al** fanciful: not real: capricious: whimsical: wild: (not **-al**) incredible: (not **-al**) excellent (*slang*).—*adv.* **fantas'tically.**—*ns.* **fantas'ticism** (*-sizm*); **fan'tastry.** [O.Fr. *fantasie* —through L. from Gr *phantasiā*—*phantazein,* to make visible; cf. **fancy, fantasia.**]

far *fär, adj.* remote: more distant of two.—*adv.* to, at, or over a great distance or advanced stage: remotely: in a great degree: very much.—*adv.* **far'most** most distant or remote.—*n.* **far'ness** the state of being far: remoteness, distance.—*adj.* **far'away** distant: abstracted, absent-minded.—**far cry** a long distance; **Far East** China, Korea, Japan, etc.: often also the countries from Burma to Indonesia and the Philippines and, as used by some, the countries of the Indian subcontinent.—*adjs.* **far'-fetched'** forced, unnatural; **far'-flung** thrown far and wide: extensive. —**Far North** the Arctic regions.—*adj.* and *adv* **far's off** in the distance.—*adjs.* **far'-out'** of jazz or its addicts, more up to date than 'cool': intellectual: satisfying; **far'-reach'ing** having wide validity, scope, or influence; **far'-sight'ed** seeing far: having defective eyesight for near objects: prescient.—**Far South** the Antarctic regions; **Far West** (esp. formerly) the Great Plains, Rocky Mountains and Pacific side of North America: (now usu.) the area between the Rockies and the Pacific.—**as far as** to the extent that: up to (a particular place); **by far** in a very great degree; **far and away** by a great deal; **far and near, far and wide** everywhere, all about; **far between** at wide intervals: rare; **far be it** God forbid; **far from it** on the contrary; **go too far** to go beyond reasonable limits, esp. of tact or behaviour; **I'll see you far** (or **farther**) **first** I will not do it by any means; **in so far as** to the extent that.—See also **farther.** [O.E. *feor(r)*.]

farad *far'əd, n.* a unit of electrical capacitance, the capacitance of a capacitor between the plates of which appears a difference of potential of one volt when it is charged by one coulomb of electricity.—*n.* **far'aday** a unit used in electrolysis, equal to 96 500 coulombs.—*adj.* **faradic** (*-ad'ik*) pertaining to Faraday, esp. in connection with induced currents. [From Michael *Faraday* (1791–1867).]

farce *färs, v.t.* to cram: to stuff, fill with stuffing.—*n.* stuffing, force-meat: comedy of extravagant humour, buffoonery, and improbability: ridiculous or empty show: a hollow formality.—*n.* **farceur** (*fär-sœr'*; Fr.) a joker, buffoon: one who writes or acts in farces:—*fem.* **farceuse** (*-sœz'*).—*adjs.* **farci** (*fär-sē;* Fr.) stuffed; **far'cical'ity** farcical quality.—*adv.* **far'cically.** [Fr. *farce,* stuffing, from L. *farcīre,* to stuff.]

farcy *fär'si, n.* chronic glanders. [Fr. *farcin*—L.L. *farcīminum.*]

fard *färd, n.* white paint for the face.—*v.t.* to paint with fard: to gloss over: to trick out. [Fr., of Gmc. origin.]

fardel *fär'dl, n.* a pack: anything cumbersome or irksome: the manyplies or omasum. [O.Fr. *fardel* (Fr. *fardeau*), dim. of *farde,* a burden, possibly—Ar. *fardah,* a package.]

fare *fär, v.i.* to travel: to get on or succeed: to happen well or ill to: to be in any particular state, to be, to go

on: to be fed.—*n* a course or passage: the price of passage: a passenger (or passengers): food or provisions for the table.—*interj.* **farewell'** may you fare well[1], a parting wish for safety or success: good-bye. —*n* well-wishing at parting: the act of departure.— *adj.* (*fär'wel*) parting: valedictory: final. [O.E. *faran.*]

farina *fə-rī'nə, fə-rē'nə, n.* ground corn: meal: starch: pollen: a mealy powder.—*adjs.* **farinaceous** (*far-i-nā'shəs*) mealy: consisting of cereals; **far'inose** (*-i-nōs*) yielding farina. [L. *farīna*—*fär,* corn.]

farm *färm, n.* a tract of land (originally one leased or rented) used for cultivation and pasturage, along with a house and other necessary buildings: farmhouse: farmstead: a piece of land or water used for breeding animals (as *fox-, oyster-farm*): a place for treatment and disposal (*sewage-farm*): a place where e.g. children are handed over to be taken care of.—*v.t.* to grant or receive the revenues of for a fixed sum: to rent to or from another: to cultivate: to use as farm: to arrange for maintenance of at fixed price.—*v.i.* to practise the business of farmer.—*n.* **farm'er** one who farms land: the tenant of a farm: one who receives taxes, etc., for fixed payment; **farm'ing** business of cultivating land —**farmer general** one of those who, in France before the Revolution, leased the public revenues; **farm'house** the farmer's house attached to a farm; **farm'-hand, -labourer** one who works on a farm.—*n.pl.* **farm'-offices** outbuildings on a farm.— **farm'stead, farm steading** farmhouse with buildings belonging to it; **farm'yard** yard or enclosure surrounded by farm buildings.—**farm out** to board out for fixed payment: to give, e.g. work for which one has made oneself responsible, to others to carry out. [L.L. *firma,* a fixed payment—L. *firmus,* firm.]

farmost. See **far.**

faro *fär'ō, n.* a game of chance played by betting on the order of appearance of certain cards. [Perh. from *Pharaoh;* reason unknown.]

farouche *fə-rōōsh', fa-, adj.* shy, ill at ease: sullen and unsociable: socially inexperienced and lacking polish. [Fr , wild, shy, savage.]

farrago *fə-rä'gō, fä-ra'gō, n.* a disordered mixture:— *pl.* **farrag'oes.** [L *farrāgō, -inis,* mixed fodder— *fär,* grain.]

farrier *far'i-ər, n.* one who shoes horses: one who cures horses' diseases: one in charge of cavalry horses.—*n.* **farr'iery** the farrier's art: veterinary surgery. [O.Fr. *ferrier*—L. *ferrum,* iron.]

farrow[1] *far'ō, n.* a litter of pigs.—*v.i.* or *v.t.* to bring forth (pigs). [O.E. *fearh,* a pig.]

farrow[2] *far'ō, adj.* not with calf for the time being. [Ety. dub.; with *farrow cow* cf Flem. *verwekoe, varwekoe.*]

fart *färt,* (*vulg.*) *v.i.* to break wind from the anus.— Also *n.* [O.E (assumed) *feortan.*]

farther *fär'dhər,* **far'thermore, far'thermost, far'thest.** Same as **further,** etc , and sometimes preferred where the notion of distance is more prominent. [A variant (M.E. *ferther*) of **further**[1] that came to be thought a compar. of **far.**]

farthing *fär'dhing, n.* the fourth of a pre-1971 penny (from Jan. 1961, not legal tender): anything very small: the Gr. *assarion* (L *as*) and also *kodrantēs* (L. *quadrāns*), fourth of an as (*B.*) [O.E. *fēorthing,* a fourth part—*fēortha,* fourth, and suff. *-ing.*]

farthingale *fär'dhing-gāl, n.* a kind of crinoline of whalebone for distending women's dress. [O.Fr. *verdugale*—Sp. *verdugado,* hooped, *verdugo,* rod.]

fasces *fas'ēz, n.pl.* the bundle of rods, with or without an axe, borne before an ancient Roman magistrate of high grade. [L. *fascēs,* pl. of *fascis,* bundle.]

fascia *fas(h)'i-ə, n.* a broad flat band, as in an architrave, or over a shop-front (*archit.*): a board in like position, commonly bearing the shopkeeper's name: (also **fasc'ia-board**) the instrument-board of a motor-car: any bandlike structure, esp. of connective tissue ensheathing a muscle (*zool.*).—*adjs.* **fasc'ial; fasc'i-ate, fasc'iated.**—*ns.* **fascia'tion** (*bot.*) union of a number of parts side by side in a flat plate; **fasciola** (*fə-si'ō-la*), **fasciole** (*fas'i-ōl*) a band of colour. [L. *fascia*, band, bandage.]

fascicle *fas'i-kl*, *n.* a bundle or bunch, esp. a bunched tuft of branches, roots, fibres, etc.: a part of a book issued in parts.—Also **fasc'icûle**, **fascic'ûlus**—*pl.* **fascic'ûli**.—*adjs.* **fasc'icled**, **fascic'ûlar**, **fascic'ûlate, -d.** [L. *fasciculus*, dim. of *fascis*, bundle.]

fascinate *fas'i-nāt*, *v.t.* to control by the eye like a snake: to entangle the attention of: to charm: to captivate.—*adj.* **fasc'inating** charming, delightful: binding the attention.—*n.* **fascina'tion** the act of charming: power to harm, control, allure, or render helpless by looks or spells: state of being fascinated: **fasc'inator** one who fascinates: a woman's light, soft head-covering. [L. *fascināre, -ātum.*]

fascine *fas-ēn'*, *n.* a brushwood faggot, used to fill ditches, protect a shore, etc. [Fr.,—L. *fascina—fascis*, a bundle.]

Fascism *fash'izm*, It. **Fascismo** *fa-shēz'mō*, *ns.* the authoritarian form of government in Italy from 1922–1943, characterised by extreme nationalism, militarism, anti-communism and restrictions on individual freedom: (also without *cap.*) the methods, doctrines, etc. of fascists or the Fascists; **Fasc'ist** (It. **Fascista** *fā-shēs'tə*) a member of the ruling party in Italy from 1922–1943, or a similar party elsewhere: (also without *cap.*) an exponent or supporter of Fascism, or (loosely) anyone with extreme right-wing, nationalistic, etc. views or methods:—*pl.* **Fasc'ists** (It. **Fasc'sti** *-tē*).—*adjs.* **fasc'ist, fascis'tic.** [It. *fascio*, bundle, group, with a hint of **fasces** (q.v.).]

fasciole. See **fascia**.

fashion *fash'n*, *n.* the make or cut of a thing: form or pattern: vogue: prevailing mode or shape of dress or that imposed by those whose lead is accepted: a prevailing custom: manner: genteel society: appearance.—*v.t.* to make: to mould according to a pattern: to suit or adapt.—*adj.* **fash'ionable** according to prevailing fashion: prevailing or in use at any period: observant of the fashion in dress or living: moving in high society: patronised by people of fashion.—*n.* a person of fashion.—*n.* **fash'ionableness.**—*adv.* **fash'ionably.**—*ns.* **fash'ioner; fash'ionist.—fashion house** an establishment in which fashionable clothes are designed, made and sold.—**after** or **in a fashion** in a way: to a certain extent; **in the fashion** in accordance with the prevailing style of dress, etc. [O.Fr. *fachon* —L. *factiō, -ōnis—facēre*, to make.]

fast[1] *fäst*, *adj.* firm: fixed: steadfast: fortified: (of sleep) sound: (of colours) not liable to fade or run.—*adv.* firmly, unflinchingly: soundly or sound (asleep): close: near.—*n.* **fast'ness** fixedness: a stronghold, fortress, castle.—**play fast and loose** to be unreliable, shifty: to behave without sense of moral obligation. [O.E. *fæst*.]

fast[2] *fäst*, *adj.* quick: rapid: before time (as a clock): promoting fast play: for fast-moving traffic, as in *fast lane*: seeking excitement: rash: dissolute.—*adv.* swiftly: in rapid succession: extravagantly.—*adj.* **fast'ish.**—*n.* **fast'ness.—fast food(s)** kinds of food, e.g. hamburgers, chips, etc., which can be prepared and served quickly; **fast neutron** a neutron of very high energy; **fast reactor** a nuclear reactor using fast neutrons, and little or no moderator.—**a fast buck** (*slang*) money quickly and easily obtained; **fast and furious** rapidly and vigorously; **fast-breeder reactor** a

nuclear reactor using fast neutrons which produces at least as much fissionable material as it uses; **pull a fast one** to gain an advantage by trickery. [A special use of **fast**[1] derived from Scand. sense of urgent.]

fast[3] *fäst*, *v.i.* to keep from food: to go hungry: to abstain from food in whole or part, as a religious duty. —*n.* abstinence from food: special abstinence enjoined by the church: the day or time of fasting.— *ns.* **fast'er; fast'ing.—fast'-day.** [O.E. *fæstan*, to fast.]

fasten *fäs'n*, *v.t.* to make fast or firm: to fix securely: to attach.—*v.i.* to admit of being fastened.—*ns.* **fastener** (*fäs'nər*) a clip, catch, or other means of fastening; **fas'tening** (*fäs'ning*) that which fastens.— **fasten on** to direct (one's eyes) on: to seize on, e.g. a fact: to fix the blame, responsibility for, on (a person) (*slang*). [**fast**[1].]

fastidious *fas-tid'i-əs*, *adj.* affecting superior taste: over-nice: difficult to please: exacting in taste: nicely critical.—*adv.* **fastid'iously.**—*n.* **fastid'iousness.** [L. *fastīdiōsus—fastīdium*, loathing.]

fastigiate *fas-tij'i-āt*, *adj.* pointed, sloping to a point or edge: with branches more or less erect and parallel (*bot.*): conical.—*adj.* **fastig'iated.** [L. *fastīgium*, a gable-end, roof.]

fat *fat*, *adj.* plump, fleshy: well-filled out: thick, full-bodied (as of printing types): corpulent: obese: having much, or of the nature of, adipose tissue or the substance it contains: oily: fruitful or profitable: rich in some important constituent: gross: fulsome:—*compar.* **fatt'er;** *superl.* **fatt'est.**—*n.* a substance found in adipose tissue: solid animal or vegetable oil: any member of a group of naturally occurring substances consisting of the glycerides of higher fatty acids, e.g. palmitic acid, stearic acid, oleic acid (*chem.*): the richest part of anything: inclination to corpulency.—*adv.* in golf, striking the ground before the ball.—*v.t.* to make fat:—*pr.p.* **fatt'ing;** *pa.t.* and *pa.p.* **fatt'ed.**—*n.* **fat'ness** quality or state of being fat: fullness of flesh: richness: fertility: that which makes fertile.—*adj.* **fatt'ed (fatted calf** the not always approved fare for the returned prodigal— Luke xv. 23, etc.).—*v.t.* to grow fat.—*ns.* **fatt'ener; fatt'ening** (also *adj.*); **fatt'iness.**—*adj.* **fatty** containing fat: having qualities of fat.—*n.* a fat person. —**fat cat** (*U.S. slang*) a wealthy, prosperous person; **fat'-head** a dullard.—*adj.* **fat'-head'ed.—fat stock** livestock fattened for market; **fatty acids** acids which with glycerine form fats.—**a fat lot** (*slang*) not much; **the fat is in the fire** a critical act has precipitated the trouble. [O.E. *fætt*, fatted.]

fatal, fatalism, etc. See **fate**.

fate *fāt*, *n.* inevitable destiny or necessity: appointed lot: destined term of life: ill-fortune: doom: final issue: (in *pl.*; with *cap.*) the three goddesses of fate, Clotho, Lachesis, and Atropos, who determine the birth, life, and death of men.—*adj.* **fat'al** belonging to or appointed by fate: announcing fate: causing ruin or death: mortal: calamitous.—*ns.* **fat'alism** the doctrine that all events are subject to fate, and happen by unavoidable necessity: acceptance of this doctrine: lack of effort in the face of threatened difficulty or disaster; **fat'alist.**—*adj.* **fatalist'ic.**—*n.* **fatality** (*fə-tal'i-ti*) the state of being fatal or unavoidable: the decree of fate: fixed tendency to disaster or death: mortality: a fatal occurrence: a person who has been killed, esp. in an accident, etc.—*adv.* **fat'ally.**—*adjs.* **fat'ed** doomed: destined; **fate'ful** charged with fate. —*adv.* **fate'fully.**—*n.* **fate'fulness.** [L. *fātum*, a prediction—*fātus*, spoken—*fārī*, to speak.]

father *fa'dhər*, *n.* a male parent: an ancestor or forefather: a fatherly protector: a contriver or originator:

a title of respect applied to a venerable man, to confessors, monks, priests, etc.: a member of certain fraternities: (usu. in *pl.*) a member of a ruling body, as *conscript fathers, city fathers:* the oldest member, or member of longest standing, of a profession or body: one of a group of ecclesiastical writers of the early centuries, usually ending with Ambrose, Jerome, and Augustine: (with *cap.*) the first person of the Trinity.—*v.t.* to adopt: to ascribe to one as his offspring or production—*n* **fa'therhood** state or fact of being a father.—*adj.* **fa'therless** destitute of a living father: without a known author.—*ns* **fa'therlessness; fa'therliness.**—*adj.* **fa'therly** like a father: paternal.—**Father Christmas** same as **Santa Claus; fa'ther-figure** a senior person of experience and authority looked on as a trusted leader or protector, **fa'ther-in-law** the father of one's husband or wife:—*pl.* **fa'thers-in-law; fa'therland** native land, esp Germany (*Vaterland*): the country of one's ancestors; **Father's Day** a day on which fathers are honoured, the third Sunday in June.—**Holy Father** the Pope; **the father and mother of** see under **mother.** [O.E. *fæder.*]

fathom *fadh'əm, n.* a nautical measure, six feet: penetration of mind—*pl.* **fath'om, fath'oms.**—*v.t.* to try the depth of: to comprehend or get to the bottom of.—*adjs.* **fath'omable; fath'omless.**—*n.* **fathom'eter** a sonic depth measurer.—**fath'om-line** a sailor's line and lead for taking soundings. [O.E. *fæthm.*]

fatigue *fə-tēg', n.* weariness from labour of body or of mind: toil: lessened power of response to stimulus, resulting from activity: failure under repeated stress as in metal: fatigue-duty (sometimes allotted as a punishment): (in *pl.*) military overalls.—*v.t.* to reduce to weariness: to exhaust the strength or power of recovery of:—*pr.p.* **fatigu'ing;** *pa.t.* and *pa.p.* **fatigued'.**—*adv.* **fatigu'ingly.**—**fatigue'-dress** working dress; **fatigue'-duty** the part of a soldier's work distinct from the use of arms; **fatigue'-party.** [Fr *fatigue*—L *fatīgāre*, to weary]

Fatimid *fat'i-mid, n.* a descendant of Mohammed's daughter, *Fatima,* and his cousin, Ali, esp one of a dynasty ruling parts of northern Africa from 909 to 1171.—Also *adj.*

fatso *fat'sō, (derog. slang) n.* a fat person:—*pl.* **fat'so(e)s.** [**fat¹.**]

fatuous *fat'ū-əs, adj.* silly: imbecile —*adj.* **fatū'itous.**—*ns.* **fatū'ity, fat'uousness** unconscious stupidity: imbecility. [L. *fatuus.*]

faubourg *fō-bōōr, (Fr.) n.* a suburb just beyond the walls or a district recently included within a city

fauces *fō'sēz, n.pl.* the upper part of the throat. [L *faucēs.*]

faucet *fō'sit, n.* a pipe inserted in a barrel to draw liquid: a tap (*U.S.*). [Fr. *fausset.*]

fault *fōlt, n.* a failing: error: blemish: imperfection: a slight offence: a dislocation of strata or veins (*geol*) a stroke in which the player fails to serve the ball properly or into the proper place (*tennis*)· culpability for that which has happened amiss.—*v.i.* to be faulty· to commit a fault.—*v.t.* to find fault with· to find flaw(s) in: to cause a fault in (*geol.*).—*adv.* **fault'ily.** —*n.* **fault'iness.**—*adj.* **fault'less** with- out fault or defect.—*adv.* **fault'lessly.**—*n.* **fault'less- ness.**—*adj.* **fault'y** imperfect, defective: guilty of a fault: blamable.—**fault'-finder; fault'-finding; fault plane** (*geol.*) a usu. uncurved surface of rock strata where a fault has occurred —**at fault** (of dogs) unable to find the scent: at a loss: to blame: guilty; **find fault to** carp, be critical: (with *with*) to censure for some defect; **to a fault** excessively [O Fr *faute, falte*—L *fallěre*, to deceive.]

fauna *fō'nə, n.* the assemblage of animals of a region or

period: a list or account thereof—*pl.* **faun'as, faun'ae** (*-ē*).—*n.* **faun** a Roman rural deity, protector of shepherds.—*adj.* **faun'al.** [L. *Fauna, Faunus,* tutelary deities of shepherds—*favēre, fautum,* to favour.]

fauteuil *fō-tœ-y', also fō'til, n* an armchair, esp a president's chair: a theatre stall [Fr.]

Fauve, Fauvist *fōv, fōv'ist, ns.* one of a group of painters at the beginning of the 20th century, including Matisse, who viewed a painting as essentially a two-dimensional decoration in colour, not necessarily imitative of nature.—*n* **Fauv'ism.** [Fr. *fauve,* wild beast]

faux *fō,* (Fr) *adj.* false —**faux ami** (*fōz a-mē*) a word in a foreign language that does not mean what it appears to, e.g. in Italian, *pretendere* does not mean 'to pretend'.—*n.* and *adj.* **faux-naïf** (*fō-na-ēf*) (a person) seeming or pretending to be simple and unsophisticated.—**faux pas** (*fō pa*) a false step: a mistake, blunder.

favour, or (esp. *U.S.*) **favor,** *fā'vər, n.* countenance: good-will a kind deed: an act of grace or lenity: indulgence: partiality: advantage : a concession of amorous indulgence: a knot of ribbons worn at a wedding, election, etc.: a thing given or worn as a token of favour.—*v.t.* to regard with goodwill: to be on the side of: to treat indulgently: to give support to: to afford advantage to: to resemble (*coll.*): to choose to wear, etc.—*adj.* **fā'vourable** friendly: propitious: conducive: advantageous: satisfactory, promising. —*n.* **fā'vourableness.**—*adv.* **fā'vourably.**—*adj.* **fā'voured** enjoying favour or preference: wearing favours: having a certain appearance, featured—as in *ill-favoured, well-favoured.*—*ns.* **fā'vouredness; fā'vourer; fā'vourite** (*-it*) a person or thing regarded with marked preference: one unduly loved and indulged, esp. by a king: one expected to win.—*adj.* esteemed, preferred.—*n.* **fā'vouritism** inclination to partiality: preference shown to favourites.—*adj.* **fā'vourless** without favour —**in favour of** for: on the side of: for the advantage of; **in (out of) favour** (not) approved of. [O.Fr.,—L *favor*—*favēre,* to favour, befriend.]

fawn¹ *fōn, n.* a young deer, esp. a fallow deer: its colour, light yellowish brown.—*adj.* resembling a fawn in colour.—*v.t.* and *v.i* to bring forth (a fawn). [O.Fr. *faon,* through L.L. from L. *fētus,* offspring.]

fawn² *fōn, v.i.* to cringe, to flatter in a servile way (with *upon*).—*n* **fawn'er** one who flatters to gain favour.—*n.* and *adj.* **fawn'ing.**—*adv.* **fawn'ingly.**—*n* **fawn'ingness.** [A variant of **fain¹**—O.E. *fægen,* glad.]

fax *faks,* abbrev. for **facsimile** in **fax machine,** a machine which scans a document, etc electronically and transfers the information to a receiving machine by a telephone line

fay¹ *fā, n* a fairy [O Fr. *fae*—L L. *fāta,* see **fate.**]

fay². Same as **fey.**

fayence. Same as **faience.**

faze *fāz* See **feeze.**

fealty *fē'əl-ti,* or **fēl'ti,** *n* the vassal's obligation of fidelity to his feudal lord (*hist*): loyalty [O.Fr *fealte*—L. *fidēlitās, -tātis,—fidēlis,* faithful—*fidēre,* to trust.]

fear *fēr, n.* a painful emotion excited by danger apprehension of danger or pain: alarm: solicitude· an object of alarm: that which causes alarm· reverence (*B.*): piety towards God: risk —*v t.* to regard with fear: to expect with alarm· to be regretfully inclined to think.—*v.i* to be afraid: to be in doubt —*adj* **fear'ful** timorous: exciting intense fear· terrible loosely, very great, very bad —*adv.* **fear'fully.**—*n* **fear'fulness.**—*adj* **fear'less** without fear· daring.

feasible   353   **feed**

brave.—*adv.* **fear'lessly**.—*n.* **fear'lessness**.—*adj.*
fear'some causing fear, frightful.—*adv.* **fear'somely**.
—**for fear** in case, lest; **no fear** (*interj*, *slang*) definitely not. [O.E. *fǣr*, fear, *fǣran*, to terrify.]
feasible *fē'zi-bl*, *adj.* practicable, possible: (loosely)
probable, likely.—*ns.* **feas'ibleness**, **feasibil'ity**.—
adv. **feas'ibly**.—**feasibility study** an investigation to
determine whether a particular project, system, etc. is
desirable, practicable, etc. [Fr. *faisable*, that can be
done—*faire*, *faisant*—L. *facēre*, to do.]
feast *fēst*, *n.* a day of unusual solemnity or joy: a festival
in commemoration of some event—*movable*, of
varying date, as Easter; *immovable*, at a fixed date, as
Christmas: a rich and abundant repast: rich enjoyment: festivity.—*v.i.* to hold a feast: to eat sumptuously (with *on*): to receive intense delight.—*v.t.* to
entertain sumptuously: to delight.—*n.* **feast'er**.—*adj.*
feast'ful festive, joyful, luxurious.—*n.* **feast'ing**.—
feast'-day. [O.Fr. *feste* (Fr. *fête*)—L. *fēstum*, a holiday, *fēstus*, solemn, festal.]
feat *fēt*, *n.* a deed manifesting extraordinary strength,
skill, or courage, an exploit, achievement. [Fr. *fait*
—L. *factum*—*facēre*, to do: cf. **fact**.]
feather *fedh'ər*, *n.* one of the growths that form the
covering of a bird: a featherlike appearance, ornament
or flaw: the feathered end of an arrow: plumage: condition: a projecting longitudinal rib or strip: a formation of hair, e.g. on the legs of certain breeds of dog or
horse: the act of feathering an oar.—*v.t.* to furnish or
adorn with a feather or feathers: to move edgewise (as
an oar, to lessen air-resistance), or to make a propeller-blade, etc., rotate in such a way as to lessen
resistance.—*v.i.* to take the appearance of a feather
—*adj.* **feath'ered** covered or fitted with feathers, or
anything featherlike.—*ns.* **feath'eriness**; **feath'ering**
plumage · the addition of a feather or feathers: a
featherlike appearance: an arrangement of small arcs
separated by cusps, within an arch (*archit.*).—*adj.*
feath'ery pertaining to, resembling, or covered with
feathers or appearance of feathers.—**feath'er-bed** a
mattress filled with feathers.—*v.t.* to pamper.—
feath'er-brain, **feath'er-head** a frivolous person,
feath'er-dust'er a brush of feathers, used for dusting;
feath'er-stitch one of a series of stitches making a
zigzag line; **feath'erweight** lightest weight that may be
carried by a racing-horse: boxer (over 8 st. 6 lb., amateur 7 lb., and not over 9 st.), wrestler, etc., below a
lightweight: anyone of small moment —**a feather in
one's cap** an achievement of which one can be proud;
birds of a feather persons of like character; **feather
one's nest** to accumulate wealth for oneself while serving others in a position of trust; **in full** or **high feather**
greatly elated or in high spirits; **make the feathers fly** to
throw into confusion by a sudden attack; **show the
white feather** to show signs of cowardice—a white
feather in a gamecock's tail being considered as a sign
of degeneracy. [O.E. *fether*.]
feature *fē'chər*, *n.* form, outward appearance: cast of
face: an element or prominent trait of anything: a
characteristic: a part of the body, esp. of the face: (*pl.*)
the face: a non-news article in a newspaper: anything
offered as a special attraction or distinctive characteristic.—Also *adj.*—*v.t.* to have features resembling
(*coll.*): to be a feature of: to make a feature of: to
present prominently.—*adjs.* **feat'ured** with features
well marked; **feat'ureless** destitute of distinct
features.—**feature film** a long cinematograph film
forming the basis of a programme. [O.Fr. *faiture*—
L. *factura*—*facēre*, to make.]
febrile *feb'*, *feb'rīl*, or *-ril*, *adj.* of or like fever: feverish.
—*adj.* **febrifugal** (*fi-brif'ū-gl*, *feb-ri-fū'gl*; L *fugāre*,
to drive off).—*ns.* **febrifuge** (*feb'* or *fēb'ri-fūj*) that
which drives off fever; **febril'ity**. [L. *febris*, fever]

February *feb'rōō-ər-i*, *n.* the second month of the year
[L. *Februārius* (*mēnsis*), the month of expiation, *februa*, the feast of expiation.]
feces, fecal. Same as **faeces**, **faecal**.
feck *fek*, (*Scot.*) *n* efficacy.—*adj* **feck'less** spiritless:
helpless: futile —*adv.* **feck'lessly**.—*n* **feck'lessness**.
[Aphetic for **effect**.]
fecula *fek'ū-lə*, *n.* starch got as a sediment: sediment,
dregs.—*ns.* **fec'ulence**, **fec'ulency**.—*adj.* **fec'ulent**
containing or consisting of faeces or sediment· foul:
turbid. [L. *faecula*, dim. of *faex*, dregs]
fecund *fek'und*, *fek'und*, *-ənd*, *adj.* fruitful: fertile: prolific.—*v.t.* **fec'undate** to make fruitful: to impregnate.
—*ns* **fecunda'tion**; **fecundity** (*fi-kund'i-ti*) fruitfulness: prolificness. [L. *fēcundus*, fruitful]
fed *fed*, *pa.t.* and *pa.p.* of **feed**[1].
Fed *fed*, (*slang*) *n.* a Federal (agent). i e an agent of the
Federal Bureau of Investigation —Also without *cap*
[Contr of **Federal**.]
fedayee *fə-dä'yē*, *n* Arab commando, esp. in the conflict against Israel.—*pl.* **feda'yeen**. [Ar *fidā'ī*.]
federal *fed'ər-əl*, *adj.* pertaining to or consisting of a
treaty or covenant: confederated, founded upon
mutual agreement: of a union or government in which
several states, while independent in home affairs,
combine for national or general purposes, as in the
United States (in the American Civil War, *Federal* was
the name applied to the states of the North which
defended the Union against the *Confederate* separatists of the South).—*n.* a supporter of federation: a
Unionist soldier in the American Civil War.—*ns.* **fed'-
eracy**; **federalisa'tion**, *-z-*.—*v.t* **fed'eralise**, **-ize**.—*ns.*
fed'eralism the principles or cause maintained by federalists; **fed'eralist** a supporter of a federal constitution or union.—*v.t* and *v.i.* **fed'erate** to join in league
or federation.—*adj.* united by league: confederated.
—*n.* **federa'tion** the act of uniting in league· a federal
union.—*adj.* **fed'erative** united in league.—**Federal
Bureau of Investigation** in the U.S., a bureau or
subdivision of the Department of Justice that investigates crimes, such as smuggling and espionage, that
are the concern of the federal government. [L.
foedus, *foederis*, a treaty, akin to *fidĕre*, to trust.]
fee *fē*, *n.* the price paid for services, as to a lawyer or
physician: recompense, wages: the sum exacted for
any special privilege: a grant of land for feudal service
(*hist*) · feudal tenure: fee simple.—*v.t* to pay a fee to·
to hire (*Scot*):—*pr.p* **fee'ing**; *pa.t.* and *pa.p.* **feed** or
fee'd.—**fee simple** unconditional inheritance; **fee tail**
an entailed estate, which may descend only to a certain
class of heirs [Partly O.E *feoh*, cattle, property;
partly A.Fr. *fee*, probably ultimately Gmc and of the
same origin.]
feeble *fē'bl*, *adj.* very weak. forceless· vacillating:
faint —*n.* **fee'bleness**.—*adv.* **fee'bly**.—*adj.* **fee'ble-
mind'ed** weak-minded to the extent of being unable
to compete with others or to manage one's affairs
with ordinary prudence: irresolute.—*adv.* **fee'ble-
mind'edly**.—**fee'ble-mind'edness**. [O.Fr *foible*, for
floible—L. *flēbilis*, lamentable, from *flēre*, to weep.]
feed[1] *fēd*, *v.t* to give, furnish, or administer food to: to
nourish: to furnish with necessary material. to foster:
to give as material to be used progressively. to furnish
(an actor) with cues or opportunities of achieving an
effect: in football, to pass the ball to.—*v.i.* to take
food: to nourish oneself by eating (with *on*):—*pa t*
and *pa.p.* **fed**.—*n.* an allowance of provender, esp. to
cattle: fodder: feeding: pasture: a plentiful meal:
material supplied progressively for any operation: the
means, channel, motion or rate of such supply: rate of
progress of a tool: a theatrical feeder —*n.* **feed'er** one
who feeds: an actor who feeds another· that which
supplies (water, electricity, ore, paper, etc.): a

For other sounds see detailed chart of pronunciation

tributary: an overhead or underground cable, of large current-carrying capacity, used to transmit electric power between generating stations, substations and feeding points: a feeding-bottle: a bib.—*adj.* secondary, subsidiary, tributary.—*n.* **feed'ing** act of eating: that which is eaten: pasture: the placing of the sheets of paper in position for a printing or ruling machine. —**feed'-back** return of part of the output of a system to the input as a means towards improved quality or self-correction of error; used also in speaking of biological, etc., self-adjusting systems: response or reaction providing useful information or guidelines for further development: in a public address system, etc., the returning of some of the sound output back to the microphone, producing a whistle or howl; **feed'ing-bottle** a bottle for supplying liquid food to an infant; **feed'-pipe** a pipe for supplying liquid, as water to a boiler or cistern; **feed'-pump** a force-pump for supplying a boiler with water, **feed'stock** raw material used in an industrial process; **feed'stuff** any type of food for animals, esp. cattle, pigs, sheep, etc.—**fed to the (back) teeth** (*slang*) fed up; **fed up** (*slang*) sated: jaded: nauseated: bored; **off one's feed** without appetite, disinclined to eat.　[O.E. *fēdan,* to feed.]

feed² *fēd, pa.t.* and *pa.p.* of **fee.**

feel *fēl, v.t.* to perceive by the touch: to try by touch: to be conscious of: to be keenly sensible of: to have an inward persuasion of: to experience.—*v.i.* to know by the touch: to have the emotions excited: to produce a certain sensation when touched, as to feel hard or hot:—*pr.p.* **feel'ing;** *pa.t.* and *pa.p.* **felt.**—*n.* the sensation of touch.—*ns.* **feel'er** a remark cautiously dropped, or any indirect stratagem, to sound the opinions of others: a tentacle: a jointed organ in the head of insects, etc., possessed of a delicate sense— an antenna; **feel'ing** the sense of touch. perception of objects by touch: consciousness of pleasure or pain: tenderness: emotion: sensibility, susceptibility, sentimentality: opinion as resulting from emotion: (in *pl.*) the affections or passions.—*adj.* expressive of great sensibility or tenderness: easily or strongly affected by emotion: sympathetic: compassionate: pitying: deeply felt.—*adj.* **feel'ingless**—*adv.* **feel'ingly.—bad feeling** animosity: ill-feeling; **feelings (are) running high** (there is) a general feeling of anger, emotion, etc.; **good feeling** kindly feeling: amicable relations.　[O.E. *fēlan,* to feel.]

feet *fēt, pl.* of **foot.**

feeze, pheese, pheeze, phese *fēz, v.t.* to worry, perturb, discompose.—Also (*U.S.*) **faze, phase** (*fāz*).　[O.E *fēsian,* to drive away.]

feign *fān, v.t.* to invent: to assume fictitiously: to make a show or pretence of, to counterfeit, simulate.—*adj.* **feigned** pretended: simulating: fictitious.—*adv.* **feign'edly.**—*ns.* **feign'edness; feign'ing.**　[Fr. *feindre,* pr.p. *feignant,* to feign—L. *fingĕre, fictum,* to form.]

feint¹ *fānt, n.* a false appearance: a pretence: a mock-assault: a deceptive movement in fencing, boxing, etc.—*v.i.* to make a feint.　[Fr. *feinte,* see above.]

feint² *fānt, adj.* a printers' or stationers' spelling of **faint.**

feisty *fī'sti,* (*coll.,* orig. *U.S.*) *adj.* excitable, irritable, touchy.　[From old U.S. dial. *fist,* a small aggressive dog—M.E. *fisten,* to break wind.]

feldspar *fel(d)'spär,* **felspar** *fel'spar, ns.* any member of the most important group of rock-forming minerals, anhydrous silicates of aluminium along with potassium (as *orthoclase, microcline*), sodium, calcium, or both (the *plagioclases*), or sodium and barium (*hyalo-　phane*).—*adj.* **fel(d)spathic** (-*spath'ik*).　[Swed. *feldtspat*—Sw. *feldt* or *falt,* field, *spat,* spar.]

felicity *fi-lis'i-ti, n.* happiness: delight· a blessing: a happy event: a happiness of expression.—*v.t.* **felic'itate** to express joy or pleasure to: to congratulate.—*n.* **felicitā'tion** the act of congratulating. —*adj.* **felic'itous** happy: prosperous: delightful: appropriate.—*adv.* **felic'itously.**　[O.Fr. *felicité*— L. *fēlicitās, -ātis,* from *fēlix, -icis,* happy.]

feline *fē'lin, adj.* pertaining to the cat or the cat kind: like a cat.—*n.* any animal of the cat tribe.—*ns.* **felinity** (*fi-lin'i-ti*); **Fe'lis** the cat genus.　[L. *fēlinus*— *fēlēs,* a cat.]

fell¹ *fel, n.* a hill: an upland tract of waste, pasture, or moorland.—**fell'-walking (-running)** the pastime (sport) of walking (running) over fells; **fell'-walker (-runner).**　[O.N. *fjall;* Dan. *fjeld.*]

fell² *fel, pa t.* of **fall.**

fell³ *fel, v.t.* to cause to fall: to knock down: to bring to the ground: to cut down: to prostrate (as by illness; *dial.*): to stitch down with an overturned edge.—*n.* a quantity felled at a time: a felled seam.—*adj.* **fell'able.**—*n* **fell'er.**　[O.E. *fælla(n), fella(n)* (W.S. *fiellan*), causative of *fallan* (*feallan*), to fall.]

fell⁴ *fel, n.* a skin: a membrane: covering of rough hair. —**fell'monger** one who prepares skins for the tanner. [O.E. *fell.*]

fell⁵ *fel, adj.* cruel: fierce: dire: ruthless: deadly: keen: doughty.—*adv.* in a fell manner.—*n.* **fell'ness.**—*adv.* **felly** (*fel'li*).　[O.Fr. *fel,* cruel—L.L. *fellō, -ōnis;* see **felon.**]

fella(h). See **fellow.**

fellah *fel'ə, n.* a peasant, esp. in Egypt:—*pl* **fell'ahs, fellahin** (-*hēn'*).　[Ar. *fellāh,* tiller.]

fellatio *fe-lā'shi-ō, n.* oral stimulation of the male genitalia.　[L.—*fellātus, pa.p.* of *fellāre,* to suck.]

feller. See **fell³, fellow.**

felloe. See **felly¹.**

fellow *fel'ō, n.* an associate: a companion and equal: one of a pair, a mate: a counterpart: the like: a member of a university who enjoys a fellowship: a member of a scientific or other society: a man generally: a worthless or contemptible person.—Also (*coll.*) **fella(h), feller.**—*n.* **fell'owship** the state of being a fellow or partner: friendly intercourse: communion: an association: an endowment in a college for the support of graduates called Fellows: the position and income of a fellow: reckoning of proportional division of profit and loss among partners.—**fell'ow-cit'izen** one belonging to the same city; **fell'ow-coun'tryman** a man of the same country; **fell'ow-crea'ture** a creature like oneself; **fell'ow-feel'ing** feeling of common interest: sympathy; **fell'ow-man** one who shares humanity with oneself; **fell'ow-mem'ber** a member of the same body; **fell'ow-trav'eller** one who travels in the same railway carriage, bus, etc., or along the same route: derogatory term for one who, though not a party member, takes the same political road, a sympathiser (trans. of Russ. word).　[M.E. *felawe*—O.N. *fēlagi,* a partner in goods, from *fē* (O.E. *feoh;* Ger. *Vieh*), cattle, property, and root *lag-,* a laying together, a law. Cf. **fee, law, lay.**]

felly¹ *fel'i,* **felloe** *fel'i, fel'ō, ns.* a curved piece in the circumference of a wheel: the circular rim of the wheel　[O.E *felg.*]

felly². See **fell⁵.**

felon¹ *fel'ən, n.* one guilty of felony.—*adj.* **felonious** (*fi-lō'ni-əs*) pertaining to felony.—*adv.* **felo'niously.** —*ns.* **felo'niousness; fel'ony** a grave crime.　[O.Fr., —L.L *fellō, -ōnis,* a traitor.]

felon² *fel'ən, n.* an inflamed sore　[Perh. **felon¹.**]

felspar. See **feldspar.**

felt¹ *felt, pa.t.* and *pa.p.* of **feel.**

felt² *felt, n.* a fabric formed without weaving, using the natural tendency of the fibres of wool and certain kinds of hair to interlace and cling together.—*v.t.* to make into felt: to cover with felt.—*v.i.* to become felted or matted.—*n.* **felt'ing** the art or process of making felt or of matting fibres together: the felt itself.—**felt-tip(ped) pen, felt pen** a pen with a nib of felt or similar fibrous substance. [O.E. *felt*.]

felucca *fe-luk'ə, n* a small merchant-vessel used in the Mediterranean, with two masts, lateen sails, and often a rudder at each end. [It. *feluca*; cf. Ar. *falūkah*.]

female *fē'māl, n.* a woman or girl (sometimes used derogatorily): any animal or plant of the same sex as a woman.—*adj.* of the sex that produces young or eggs, fructifications or seeds: for, belonging to, characteristic of, or fancifully attributed to that sex; of the sex characterised by relatively large gametes (*biol.*): of parts of mechanism, hollow and adapted to receive a counterpart (*mach.*).—*ns.* **fe'maleness, femality** (*fē-mal'i-ti*).—**female screw** a cylindrical hole with a thread or groove cut on the inward surface. [Fr. *femelle*—L. *fēmella*, a girl, dim. of *fēmina*, woman; the second syllable influenced by association with **male**.]

feminine *fem'in-in, adj.* female: characteristic of, peculiar or appropriate to, woman or the female sex: womanish: of that gender to which words denoting females, and in some languages various associated classes of words, belong (*gram.*).—*n.* the female sex or nature: a word of feminine gender.—*adv.* **fem'ininely.**—*ns.* **fem'inineness; fem'ininism** an idiom or expression characteristic of woman: addiction to feminine ways; **feminin'ity** the quality of being feminine.—*v.t.* and *v.i* **fem'inise, -ize** to make or become feminine.—*ns.* **fem'inism** advocacy of women's rights, of the movement for the advancement and emancipation of women; **fem'inist** an advocate or favourer of feminism: a student of women.—*adj.* **feminist'ic.**—**feminine ending** (*Fr. pros.*) ending of a line in mute *e* (the French feminine suffix): ending in one unstressed syllable; **feminine rhyme** a rhyme on a feminine ending. [L. *fēmina*, woman, dim. *fēminīna*.]

femme *fam,* (Fr.) *n.* a woman, wife.—**femme fatale** (*fa-tal*) an irresistibly attractive woman who brings difficulties or disaster on men: a siren.

femto- *fem'tō-, pfx.* a thousand million millionth (10^{-15}).

femur *fē'mər, n.* the thigh-bone: the third segment of an insect's leg:—*pl.* **fe'murs, fēmora** (*fem'ər-ə*).—*adj.* **femoral** (*fem'*) belonging to the thigh. [L. *fēmur, -ōris,* thigh.]

fen *fen, n.* low marshy land often, or partially, covered with water: a morass or bog.—*adjs.* **fenn'ish; fenn'y.**—**fen'land; fen'man** a dweller in fen country. [O.E. *fenn.*]

fence *fens, n.* a barrier, esp. of wood or of wood and wire for enclosing, bounding or protecting land: the art of fencing: defence: a receiver of stolen goods (*thieves' slang*).—*v.t.* to enclose with a fence: to fortify: to shield: to keep off.—*v.i.* to guard: to practise fencing: to be a receiver or purchaser of stolen goods: to answer or dispute evasively: to leap fences. —*adjs.* **fenced** enclosed with a fence; **fence'less** without fence or enclosure, open.—*n.* **fenc'er** one who makes or repairs fences: one who practises fencing with a sword, etc.—*n.* **fenc'ible** (*hist.*) a militiaman or volunteer enlisted at a crisis.—*adj.* **fenc'ing** defending or guarding.—*n.* the act of erecting a fence: material for fences: fences collectively: the leaping of fences: receiving stolen goods (*thieves' slang*): the act, art or sport of attack and defence with a sword, foil or the like.—**fenc'ing-master** one who teaches

fencing.—**mend one's fences** to improve or restore one's relations, reputation, or popularity, esp. in politics (*n.* and *adj.* **fence'-mending**); **sit on the fence** to avoid committing oneself: to remain neutral; **sunk fence** a ditch or water-course. [Aphetic from **defence.**]

fend *fend, v.t.* to ward off: to shut out: to defend.—*v.i.* to offer resistance: to provide. [Aphetic for **defend.**]

fender *fend'ər, n.* a guard before a hearth to confine the ashes: a protection for a ship's side against piers, etc., consisting of a bundle of rope, etc.: any structure serving as a guard against contact or impact [**fend.**]

fenestella *fen-is-tel'ə, n.* a niche containing the piscina. [L., dim. of *fenestra*, a window.]

fenestra *fi-nes'tra, n.* a window or other wall-opening: a perforation: a translucent spot.—*n.* **fenes'tral** a window with some translucent material instead of glass.—*adj.* of or like a window: perforated: with translucent spots.—*adjs.* **fenestrate** (*fen'is-trit, fi-nes'trit, -trāt*), **-d** having windows or appearance of windows: pierced: perforated having translucent spots.—*n.* **fenestra'tion** the arrangement of windows in a building: fact of being fenestrate: perforation: the operation of making an artificial fenestra when the fenestra ovalis has been clogged by growth of bone.—**fenestra ovalis, rotunda** the oval and round windows, two membrane-covered openings between the middle and the internal ear. [L]

Fenian *fē'nyən, n.* a member of an association of Irishmen founded in New York in 1857 for the overthrow of the English government in Ireland: a (esp. Irish) Catholic (*offensive*)—*adj.* belonging to the modern Fenians: Catholic (*offensive*).—*n.* **Fē'nianism.** [Old Ir. *Féne*, one of the names of the ancient population of Ireland, confused in modern times with *fiann*, the militia of Finn and other ancient Irish kings.]

fennec *fen'ək, n.* a little African fox with large ears [Ar. *fenek*.]

fennel *fen'əl, n.* a yellow-flowered umbelliferous plant of the genus *Foeniculum*, the seeds and leaves being used for seasoning.—**dwarf, Florence, French, sweet fennel** see **finocchio.** [O.E *finul*—L. *fēniculum, fēnuc(u)lum*, fennel—*fēnum*, hay]

fennish, fenny. See fen¹.

fent *fent, n* a slit, crack. [O Fr. *fente*—L. *findēre*, to cleave.]

fenugreek *fen'ū-grēk, n.* a plant (*Trigonella foenumgraecum*), allied to melilot. [L. *fēnum graecum*, Greek hay.]

feod, feodal. Same as **feud², feudal.**

feoff *fef, fēf, n.* a fief.—*v.t.* to grant possession of a fief or property in land.—*ns.* **feoffee'** the person invested with the fief; **feoff'er, feoff'or** he who grants the fief; **feoff'ment** the gift of a fief [O.Fr. *feoffer* or *fiefer* —O.Fr. *fief.* See **fee.**]

feral *fē'rəl, adj.* wild: untamed: uncultivated: run wild: brutish.—*adjs.* **fer'alised, -ized** run wild from domestication. [L. *fera*, a wild beast.]

fer-de-lance *fer'də-läs, n.* the lance-headed or yellow viper of tropical America. [Fr., lance-head (*lit* iron).]

feretory *fer'i-tər-i, n.* a shrine for relics carried in processions. [L. *feretrum*—Gr *pheretron*, bier, litter —*pherein*, to bear.]

ferial *fē'ri-əl, adj.* pertaining to holidays: belonging to any day of the week which is neither a fast nor a festival. [L. *fēria, a holiday.*]

ermata *fûr-mä'tə, (mus.) n.* a pause. [It.]

erment *fûr'mənt, n.* a substance that excites fermentation: internal motion amongst the parts of a fluid: agitation: tumult.—*v.t.* **ferment** (*-ment'*) to excite fermentation in: to work up, excite.—*v.i.* to rise and swell by the action of fermentation: to work, used of wine, etc.: to be in excited action: to work in the mind, as emotions.—*n.* **fermentabil'ity**.—*adj.* **fer'ment'able** capable of fermentation.—*n* **ferment-á'tion** the act or process of fermenting. a slow decomposition process of organic substances induced by micro-organisms, or by complex nitrogenous organic substances (*enzymes*) of vegetable or animal origin, usually accompanied by evolution of heat and gas, e.g. alcoholic fermentation of sugar and starch, and lactic fermentation: restless action of the mind or feelings —*adj.* **ferment'ative** causing or consisting in fermentation.—*n.* **ferment'ativeness**.—*adj.* **ferment'ed**. [Fr.,—L. *fermentum*, for *fervimentum*—*fervēre*, to boil.]

fermi *fûr'mi*, *n.* a unit equal to 10^{-5} angstrom or 10^{-15} m.—*ns.* **fer'mion** one of a group of subatomic particles obeying the exclusion principle; **fer'mium** the element (symbol Fm) of atomic number 100 [Italian physicist Enrico *Fermi* (1901–54).]

fern *fûrn*, *n.* one of the class of higher or vascular cryptogamous plants, *Filices*, plants with feather-like leaves.—*adj.* **fern'y**. [O.E. *fearn*.]

ferocious *fə-rō'shəs*, *adj.* savage, fierce: cruel.—*adv.* **ferō'ciously**.—*ns.* **ferō'ciousness; ferocity** (*-ros'i-ti*) savage cruelty of disposition: untamed fierceness. [L. *ferōx*, *ferōcis*, wild—*ferus*, wild.]

ferrate *fer'āt*, *n.* a salt of (hypothetical) ferric acid.—*adjs.* **ferr'eous** pertaining to, containing, or like iron; **ferr'ic** of iron; of trivalent iron (*chem.*); **ferrif'erous** bearing or yielding iron.—*n.* **ferr'ite** a form of pure iron: any of a number of new magnetic materials (generally mixtures of iron oxide with one or more other metals) which are also electric insulators.—*adjs.* **ferrit'ic** consisting mainly of ferrite; **ferr'ous** of bivalent iron: loosely, containing iron.—**ferr'o-all'oy** (or *-oi'*) an alloy of iron and some other metal, e.g. **ferr'o-nick'el; ferr'o-con'crete** reinforced concrete.—*adj* **ferroelec'tric** exhibiting electric polarisation; **ferromagnet'ic** strongly magnetic. [L. *ferrum*, iron.]

ferrel. See **ferrule.**

ferret *fer'it*, *n.* a half-tamed albino variety of the polecat, employed in unearthing rabbits.—*v.t* to drive out of a hiding-place: to search out persistently.—*v t.*, *v.i* to hunt with a ferret:—*pr.p.* **ferr'eting;** *pa p* **ferr'eted.**—*n* **ferr'eter** one who ferrets.—*adj.* **ferr'ety** like a ferret. [O.Fr. *furet*, a ferret, dim.—L.L. *fūrō*, *-ōnis*, ferret, robber—L. *fūr*, a thief.]

ferriage. See under **ferry.**

Ferris wheel *fe'ris* (h)*wēl*, (orig. *U.S.*) an amusement device, a large upright wheel having seats suspended on the circumference which remain horizontal while the wheel rotates [G W. G. *Ferris*, American engineer.]

ferro-alloy, etc See **ferrate.**

ferruginous *fe-*, *fə-rōō'jin-əs*, *adj.* of the colour of iron-rust: impregnated with iron.—Also **ferrugin'eous** (*fer-*). [L. *ferrūgō*, *-inis*, iron-rust—*ferrum*.]

ferrule *fer'ōōl*, *-əl*, *n.* a metal band, ring or cap on a stick, etc —Also **ferr'el**. [O.Fr *virole*—L *viriola*, a bracelet]

ferry *fer'i*, *v.t* to carry or convey (often over a water, etc , in a boat, ship or aircraft): to deliver (an aircraft coming from a factory) under its own power.—*v.i.* to cross by ferry:—*pr.p.* **ferr'ying;** *pa.t.* and *pa.p.* **ferr'ied.**—*n.* a place or route of carriage over water: the right of conveying passengers: a ferry-boat.—*n.* **ferr'iage** provision for ferrying: the fare paid for it.—**ferr'y-boat; ferr'y-house** a ferryman's house: a place of shelter or refreshment at a ferry; **ferr'yman**. [O.E. *ferian*, to convey, *faran*, to go.]

fertile *fûr'tīl*, *U.S.* *-təl*, *adj.* able to bear or produce abundantly: rich in resources: inventive: fertilising: capable of breeding, hatching, or germinating.—*adv.* **fer'tilely**.—*n.* **fertilisation**, **-z-** (*-ti-li-zā'shən*) the act or process of fertilising.—*v.t.* **fer'tilise, -ize** to make fertile or fruitful: to enrich: to impregnate: to pollinate —*ns.* **fer'tiliser, -z-** one who, or that which, fertilises; **fertility** (*-til'i-ti*) fruitfulness: richness: abundance.—**Fertile Crescent** a crescent-shaped region stretching from Armenia to Arabia, formerly fertile but now mainly desert, considered to be the cradle of civilisation; **fertility drug** a drug given to apparently infertile women to induce ovulation. [Fr.,—L. *fertilis*—*ferre*, to bear.]

ferule *fer'ōōl*, *n.* a cane or rod used for punishment. [L *ferula*, a giant fennel—*ferīre*, to strike.]

fervent *fûr'vənt*, *adj.* hot: ardent: zealous: warm in feeling.—*n.* **fer'vency** heat: eagerness: emotional warmth.—*adv.* **fer'vently.**—*adjs.* **fervescent** (*-ves'ənt*) growing hot; **fer'vid** very hot: having burning desire or emotion: glowing: zealous.—*n.* **fervid'ity.**—*adv.* **fer'vidly.**—*ns.* **fer'vidness; fer'vour** heat: heat of emotion. zeal. [L. *fervēre*, to boil, *fer-vēscēre*, *fervidus*.]

fescue *fes'kū*, *n.* any one of the grasses, nearly allied to the brome-grasses, of the genus *Festuca*, which includes many pasture and fodder grasses: a pointer used in teaching. [O.Fr. *festu*—L. *festūca*, a straw.]

fesse, fess *fes*, (*her.*) *n.* a horizontal band over the middle of an escutcheon, usually one-third of the whole. [Fr. *fasce*—L. *fascia*, a band.]

-fest *-fest*, *n.* in composition, a party or gathering, esp. for a particular activity, e.g. *songfest*. [Ger. *Fest*, festival.]

festal *fes'tl*, *adj.* pertaining to a feast or holiday: joyous: gay.—*n.* a festivity.—*adv.* **fes'tally.** [See **feast.**]

fester *fes'tər*, *v.i.* to become corrupt or malignant: to suppurate: to be idle (*coll.*).—*v.t.* to cause to fester or rankle —*n.* a wound discharging corrupt matter. [O.Fr. *festre*—L. *fistula*, an ulcer.]

festive *fes'tiv*, *adj.* festal: mirthful.—*n.* **fes'tival** a joyful or honorific celebration: a feast: a season or series of performances of music, plays, or the like.—*adv.* **fes'tively.**—*n.* **festiv'ity** social mirth: joyfulness: gaiety: (in *pl.*) joyful celebrations. [L. *fēstīvus*—*fēstus.*]

festoon *fes-tōōn'*, *n.* a garland suspended between two points: an ornament like a garland (*archit.*).—*v.t.* to adorn, hang, or connect with festoons —*v.i.* to hang in festoons [Fr. *feston*, app. conn. with L. *fēstum*, a festival.]

festschrift *fest'shrift*, *n.* a collection of learned papers or the like, presented by their authors and published in honour of some person. [Ger., festival writing.]

fetal. See **foetus.**

fetch *fech*, *v.t.* to bring: to go and get: to obtain as its price: to cause to come: to call forth: to recall from a swoon: to draw (as blood, breath): to achieve the gaining over of, to take: to derive: to strike: to perform, make, take, utter (as a leap, a sigh, a circuit): to achieve: to reach or attain.—*v.i.* to make one's way. to arrive: to be effective.—*n.* the act of bringing: the distance travelled by a wind or wave without obstruction: a stratagem.—*adj.* **fetch'ing** fascinating, charming.—**fetch and carry** to perform humble services for another; **fetch off** to bring out of danger or difficulty; **fetch out** to draw forth, develop; **fetch up** to recover: to come to a stop. [O.E. *feccan*, app. an altered form of *fetian*, to fetch.]

fête *fet*, *fât*, *n.* a festival: a holiday: the festival of the saint whose name one bears.—*v.t* to entertain at a feast: to honour with festivities.—**fête champêtre** (*shä-pe-tr'*) a rural festival, garden party. [Fr.]

feticide. See **foetus**.

fetid *fē'tid*, or *fet'id*, *adj*. stinking: having a strong offensive smell.—*ns.* **fe'tidness**, **fe'tor**.—Less justifiable spellings are **foetid**, **foetor**. [L. *fētidus*, *fetor—fētēre*, to stink.]

fetish *fe'tish*, *fē'tish*, *n*. an object believed to procure for its owner the services of a spirit lodged within it: something regarded with irrational reverence.—*ns.* **fet'ishism** the worship of a fetish: a belief in charms: pathological attachment of sexual interest to an inanimate object; **fet'ishist**.—*adjs.* **fetishist'ic**. [Fr. *fétiche*—Port. *feitiço*, magic, orig. artificial—L. *facticius—facēre*, to make.]

fetlock *fet'lok*, *n*. a tuft of hair that grows above a horse's hoof: the part where this hair grows.—*adj.* **fet'locked** having a fetlock: tied by the fetlock.

fetter *fet'ər*, *n*. (usu. in *pl*.) a chain or shackle for the feet: (usu. in *pl*.) anything that restrains.—*v.t.* to put fetters on: to restrain. [O.E. *feter*; conn. with *fōt*, foot.]

fettle *fet'l*, *v.t.* to make ready, set in order, arrange: to line (a furnace).—*v.i.* to potter fussily about.—*n*. condition, trim, form: lining for a furnace.—*ns.* **fett'-ler; fett'ling**. [Prob. O.E. *fetel*, a belt.]

fettuc(c)ine, fettucini *fet-ōō-chē'nä, -nē*, *n*. tagliatelle. [It.]

fetus. See **foetus**.

feu *fū*, (*Scot.*) *n*. a right to the use of land, houses, etc., in perpetuity, for a stipulated annual payment (**feu'-du'ty**): a piece of land held in feu.—*v.t.* to vest in one who undertakes to pay the feu-duty.—*adj.* **feud'al** pertaining to a feu. [O.Fr. *feu;* see **fee**.]

feud[1] *fūd*, *n*. a war waged by private individuals, families, or clans against one another on their own account: a bloody strife: a persistent state of private enmity.—Also *v.i.*—*n.* and *adj.* **feud'ing**. [O.Fr. *faide, feide*—L.L. *faida*—O.H.G. *fēhida;* see **foe**.]

feud[2], **feod** *fūd*, *n*. a fief or land held on condition of service.—*adj.* **feud'al**, **feod'al** pertaining to feuds or fiefs: belonging to feudalism.—*n.* **feudalisa'tion, -z-**.—*v.t.* **feud'alise, -ize**.—*ns.* **feud'alism** the feudal system or its principles: a class-conscious social or political system resembling the mediaeval feudal system; **feud'alist; feudal'ity** the state of being feudal: the feudal system.—*adv.* **feud'ally.**—**feudal system** the system by which vasals held lands from lords-superior on condition of military service. [L.L. *feudum;* see **fee**.]

feudal. See **feu** and **feud**[2].

fever *fē'vər*, *n*. disease (esp. infectious) marked by great bodily heat and quickening of pulse: extreme excitement of the passions, agitation: a painful degree of anxiety.—*v.t.* to put into a fever.—*v.i.* to become fevered.—*adjs.* **fe'vered** affected with fever: excited; **fe'verish** slightly fevered: indicating fever: restlessly excited: morbidly eager.—*adv.* **fe'verishly.** —*n.* **fe'ver-ishness**.—*adj* **fe'verous** feverish: marked by sudden changes: apt to cause fever.—**fe'verfew** a composite perennial closely allied to camomile, so called from its supposed power as a febrifuge; **fe'ver-heat** the heat of fever: an excessive degree of excitement; **fever pitch** a state of great excitement, agitation. [O.E. *fēfor*—L. *febris*.]

few *fū*, *adj.* small in number: not many.—*n* **few'ness** smallness of number.—**a few** a small number (of)—used as a noun, often without a compound adjective; also facetiously as an *adv.*, a little; **a good few, quite a few** (*coll*) a considerable number; **in few** briefly, some few an inconsiderable number; **the few** the minority. [O E. *fēa*, pl. *fēawe*.]

fey, fay, fie *fā*, *adj.* fated soon to die—imagined to be marked by extravagantly high spirits (chiefly *Scot*.): foreseeing the future, esp. calamity (chiefly *Scot*.): eccentric, slightly mad: supernatural: fairy-like: elfin. [M.E. *fay, fey*—O.E. *fǣge*, doomed.]

fez *fez*, *n*. a red brimless truncated conical cap of wool or felt, with black tassel, worn in Egypt:—*pl.* **fezz'es**, **fez'es**. [From *Fez* in Morocco.]

fiacre *fē-ak'r'*, *n.* a hackney-coach: a cab. [Fr , from the Hôtel de St *Fiacre* in Paris, where first used.]

fiancé, fem. fiancée, *fē-ä'sä*, *n.* one betrothed. [Fr.]

fianchetto *fyäng-ket'to*, (*chess*) *n.* the early movement of a knight's pawn to develop a bishop on a long diagonal:—*pl.* **fianchett'ti** (*-tē*).—Also *v.t.* [It.. dim. of *fianco*, flank.]

fiasco *fē-as'kō*, *n.* a flask, bottle: a failure in a musical performance: a complete failure of any kind:—*pl.* **fias'cos, fias'coes**. [It. *fiasco*, bottle.]

fiat *fī'at*, L. *fē'ät*, *n.* a formal or solemn command: a short order or warrant of a judge for making out or allowing processes, letters-patent, etc. [L. *fiat*, let it be done, 3rd pers. sing. (plur.) pres. subj. of *fiĕrī*, serving as passive of *facĕre*, to do.]

fib *fib*, *n.* something said falsely: a not very serious lie.—*v.i.* to tell a fib or lie: to speak falsely:—*pr.p.* **fibb'ing;** *pa.p.* **fibbed**.—*n.* **fibb'er** one who fibs. [Perh. **fable**.]

fiber. See **fibre**.

Fibonacci numbers, sequence, series *fē-bō-nä'chē num'bərz, sē'kwəns, sē'rēz*, a series of numbers in which each term is the sum of the preceding two terms. [Leonardo (*Fibonacci*) of Pisa (1170–1230).]

fibre, fiber *fī'bər*, *n.* any fine thread-like object, of animal, vegetable, or mineral origin, natural or synthetic: a structure or material composed of fibres: texture: stamina.—*adjs.* **fi'bred** having fibre; **fi'bre-less** without fibre, strength, or nerve.—*n.* **fi'bril** a small fibre: a root-hair: a minute thread-like structure.—*adjs.* **fi'brillar, fi'brillary, fi'brillate, -d** pertaining to, of the nature of, or having fibrils or fibrous structure.—*v.i.* **fi'brillate** to undergo fibrillation.—*n.* **fibrilla'tion** the production or formation of fibrils or fibres: a mass of fibrils: a twitching of muscle fibres: uncoordinated contraction of muscle-fibres in the heart (*med.*).—*adjs.* **fi'brillose** having, or covered with, small fibres or the appearance of small fibres; **fi'brillous** pertaining to or having small fibres.—*ns.* **fi'brin** an insoluble protein precipitated as a network of fibres when blood coagulates; **fibrinol'ysin** an enzyme in the blood which causes breakdown of fibrin in blood clots: a drug having the same effect.—*adj.* **fi'brinous** of or like fibrin.—*adj.* **fi'broid** of a fibrous character.—*n.* a fibrous tumour.—*ns.* **fi'bro-line** (*-lēn*) a yarn of flax, hemp, and jute waste, used with linen or cotton for backs of carpets, etc.; **fibrō'ma** a tumour composed of fibrous tissue:—*pl.* **fibrō'mata**.—*adj.* **fibrose** (*fī'brōs*) fibrous.—*ns.* **fibro'sis** a morbid growth of fibrous tissue; **fibrosi'tis** inflammation (esp. rheumatic) of fibrous tissue.—*adjs.* **fibrot'ic** pertaining to fibrosis; **fi'brous** composed of or like fibres.—**fi'breglass** a synthetic fibre made of extremely fine filaments of molten glass, used in textile manufacture, in heat and sound insulation, and in reinforced plastics; **fibre optics** technique using fibre optic(s) bundles (as *adj* usu. **fibre optic**).—**fibre optic(s) bundle** a bundle of extremely thin flexible glass fibres suitably coated, used in optical instruments to transmit maximum light, and images of maximum clarity, and designed, because of their flexibility, for seeing into otherwise inaccessible places. [Fr , —L. *fibra*, thread, fibre.]

fibula *fib'ū-lə*, *n* a brooch: the outer of the two bones from the knee to the ankle.—*adj.* **fib'ular**. [L. *fibula*, brooch]

fiche *fēsh, n.* a card or strip of film containing miniaturised data.—Also short for **microfiche**. [Fr., a slip of paper, etc.]

fichu *fi'shōō, fē-shu, n.* a three-cornered cape worn over the shoulders, the ends crossed upon the bosom: a triangular piece of muslin, etc., for the neck. [Fr.]

fickle *fik'l, adj.* inconstant: changeable.—*n.* **fick'le-ness.** [O E. *ficol; gefic,* fraud.]

fictile *fik'tīl, -til, adj.* used or fashioned by the potter: plastic. [L. *fictilis—fingĕre,* to form or fashion.]

fiction *fik'shən, n.* a feigned or false story: a falsehood: romance: the novel, story-telling as a branch of literature: a supposition of law that a thing is true, which is either certainly not true, or at least is as probably false as true.—*adj.* **fic'tional.**—*v.t.* **fic'tionalise, -ize** to give a fictional character to (a narrative dealing with real facts).—*adj.* **fic'tionalised, -z-.**—*adj.* **fictitious** (*-tish'əs*) of the nature of fiction: imaginary: not real: feigned.—*adv.* **ficti'tiously.**—*adj.* **fic'tive** fictitious, imaginative. [Fr.,—L. *fictiō, -ōnis—fictus,* pa.p. of *fingĕre,* to form, fashion.]

fid *fid, n.* a conical pin of hard wood, used by sailors to open the strands of rope in splicing: a square bar, with a shoulder, used to support the weight of the topmast or top-gallant mast.

fiddle *fid'l, n.* the violin (*coll.*): a similar instrument with raised bridge and fingerboard: extended to like instruments as *bass fiddle:* a violin-player: a device to keep dishes from sliding off a table at sea: a swindle, esp. petty (*slang*).—*v.t.* and *v.i.* to play on a fiddle.—*v.t.* to swindle: to falsify.—*v.i.* to be busy over trifles, to trifle.—*n.* **fidd'ler** one who fiddles: (also **fiddler crab**) a small crab of the genus *Uca* or *Gelasimus,* from the attitude of its enlarged claw).—*adjs.* **fidd'ling** trifling, busy about trifles; **fidd'ly** requiring much dexterity: time-consuming: awkward.—**fidd'le-back** the fiddle-shaped back of a chair.—*interj.* **fiddle-de-dee'** nonsense!.—*v.i.* **fidd'le-fadd'le** to trifle, to dally.—*n.* trifling talk or behaviour.—*adj.* fussy, trifling.—*interj.* nonsense!.—**fidd'lestick** a violin bow: derisively, a mere nothing or anything.—*interj.* **fidd'lestick(s)** nonsense!—**a face like a fiddle** a long or dismal face; **as fit as a fiddle** in the best of condition; **play first** or **second fiddle** to act as a first-violin or a second-violin player in an orchestra: to take a leading, or a subordinate, part in anything. [O.E. *fithele.*]

fidei defensor *fi'dē-ī di-fen'sór, fi-dā'ē dā-fēn'sor* defender of the faith.

fideism *fē'dā-izm, n.* the doctrine that knowledge depends on faith rather than reason. [L. *fidēre,* to trust.]

fidelity *fi-del'i-ti, n.* faithfulness: faithfulness to a husband or wife: honesty: firm adherence: exactitude in reproduction. [L. *fidēlitās, -ātis—fidēlis,* faithful—*fidēre,* to trust.]

fidget *fij'it, v.i.* to be unable to rest: to move about uneasily:—*pr.p.* **fidg'eting;** *pa.t.* and *pa.p.* **fidg'eted.** —*n.* one who fidgets: irregular motion: restlessness: (in *pl.*) general nervous restlessness with a desire of changing position.—*n.* **fidg'etiness.**—*adj.* **fidg'ety** restless: uneasy. [Perh. related to **fike.**]

fiducial *fi-dū'sh(y)əl, adj.* serving as a basis of reckoning: showing confidence or reliance: of the nature of trust.—*adv.* **fidū'cially.**—*adj.* **fidū'ciary** of the nature of a trust: depending upon public confidence: held in trust.—*n.* one who holds anything in trust. [L. *fidūcia,* confidence—*fidēre,* to trust.]

fie[1] *fi, interj.* denoting disapprobation or disgust, real or feigned. [Cf. Fr. *fi,* L. *fī;* O.N. *fȳ, fei;* Ger *pfui.*]

fie[2]. See **fey.**

fief *fēf, n.* land held in fee or on condition of military service. [Fr.,—L L. *feudum;* see **fee, feoff.**]

field *fēld, n.* country or open country in general: a piece of ground enclosed for tillage or pasture or sport: the range of any series of actions or energies: speciality: an area of knowledge, interest, etc.: a region of space in which forces are at work (*phys.*): the locality of a battle: the battle itself: a wide expanse: area visible to an observer at one time (e.g. in a microscope): one of the two interlaced sets of scanning lines making up the picture (*TV*): a region yielding a mineral etc.: the surface of a shield (*her.*): the background of a coin, flag, etc.: those taking part in a hunt: the entries collectively against which a contestant has to compete: all parties not individually excepted: disposition of fielders: a set of characters comprising a unit of information (*comput.*).—*v.t.* at cricket and baseball, to catch or stop and return to the fixed place. to handle skilfully (esp. questions): to put into the field for play, military action, or (*fig.*) other form of contest.—*v.t.* to stand in position for catching or stopping the ball in cricket.—*ns.* **field'er** one who fields; **field'ing** the acting in the field at cricket as distinguished from batting.—**field ambulance** a medical unit on the field of battle; **field artillery** mobile ordnance for active operations in the field; **field battery** a battery of field artillery; **field book** a book used in surveying fields, etc.; **field day** a day when troops are drawn out for instruction in field exercises: any day of unusual activity or success; **field event** an athletic event other than a race; **field'fare** a species of thrush; **field glass(es)** a binocular telescope for use in the field or open air; **field goal** (*U.S. football, basketball*) a goal scored from normal play; **field gun** a light cannon mounted on a carriage; **field hand** an outdoor farm labourer; **field hockey** (*U.S.*) hockey played on grass (as opposed to ice hockey); **field hospital** a temporary hospital near the scene of battle; **field ice** ice formed in the polar seas in large surfaces, distinguished from icebergs; **field kitchen** portable cooking equipment for troops, or the place where it is set up; **field marshal** an army officer of highest rank; **field meeting** a conventicle; **field'mouse** a name for various species of mouse and vole that live in the fields; **field naturalist** one who studies natural history out of doors.—*n.pl.* **field notes** data noted in the field, to be worked up later.—**field officer** a military officer above the rank of captain, and below that of general.—*adj.* **field'-sequen'tial** (*TV*) relating to the association of individual primary colours with successive fields.—**fields'man** a fielder.—*n.pl.* **field sports** sports of the field, as hunting, racing, etc.—**field trial** a test in practice, as distinct from one under laboratory conditions; **field trip** an expedition (esp. by students) to observe and study something at its location; **field'work** farm work in fields: work (scientific surveying, etc.) in the field, opposed to laboratory, office, etc.: (often in *pl.*) a temporary fortification thrown up by troops in the field, either for protection or to cover an attack upon a stronghold; **field'worker** a practical research worker.—**field of view, vision** what is visible at one moment, **keep the field** to keep the campaign open: to maintain one's ground; **take the field** to assemble on a playing-field: to begin warlike operations. [O.E. *feld.*]

fiend *fēnd, n.* a devil: one actuated by the most intense wickedness or hate: an addict: a devotee.—*adj.* **fiend'-ish** like a fiend: devilishly cruel.—*n.* **fiend'ishness.** [O.E. *fēond,* enemy, orig. pr.p. of *fēon,* to hate.]

fierce *fērs, adj.* savage: ferocious: violent.—*adv.* **fierce'ly.**—*n.* **fierce'ness.** [O.Fr. *fers* (Fr *fier*)—L. *ferus,* wild, savage.]

fiery *fīr'i, adj.* like or consisting of fire: ardent: impetuous: irritable: of ground in games, dry, hard, fast.—*adv.* **fier'ily.**—*n.* **fier'iness.**—**fiery cross** a charred cross dipped in blood, formerly carried round in the Scottish Highlands as a call to arms. [**fire.**]

fiesta *fē-es'tǝ, n.* saint's day: holiday: festivity [Sp.]

fife *fīf, n.* a smaller variety of the flute —*v.i.* to play on the fife —*n.* **fif'er** a fife-player. [Ger. *Pfeife,* pipe, or Fr. *fifre,* fifer, both—L. *pīpāre,* to cheep]

fifteen *fif'tēn,* or *fif-tēn', adj* and *n.* five and ten: a set, group, or team of fifteen (as formerly the Court of Session).—*adj.* **fifteenth'** (or *fif'*) last of fifteen: next after the fourteenth: equal to one of fifteen equal parts.—*n* a fifteenth part: a person or thing in fifteenth position: a double octave (*mus*): an organ stop sounding two octaves above the diapason [O.E. *fīftēne;* see **five, ten.**]

fifth *fifth, adj.* last of five: next after the fourth: equal to one of five equal parts —*n.* one of five equal parts: a person or thing in fifth position: an interval of four (conventionally called five) diatonic degrees (*mus.*): a tone at that interval from another: a combination of two tones separated by that interval.—*adv* **fifth'ly** in the fifth place.—**Fifth Amendment** an amendment to the U S. constitution which allows a person on trial not to testify against himself and forbids a second trial if a person has been acquitted in a first; **fifth column** sympathisers among the enemy, awaiting their time (expression used by a Spanish insurgent general when four columns were advancing upon Madrid); **fifth columnist** (*kol'ǝm-ist*) [O.E. *fīfta,* assimilated to other ordinals in *-th.*]

fifty *fif'ti, adj.* and *n.* five tens or five times ten.—*n.pl.* **fif'ties** the numbers fifty to fifty-nine: the years so numbered (of a life or century): a range of temperatures from fifty to just less than sixty degrees.—*adj.* **fif'tieth** last of fifty: next after the forty-ninth: equal to one of fifty equal parts.—*n.* a fiftieth part: a person or thing in fiftieth position.—*adj.* **fif'tyish** apparently about fifty years old.—*n.* and *adj.* and *adv.* **fif'ty-fif'ty** half-and-half: fifty per cent of each of two things: share and share alike. [O.E *fīftig—fīf,* five, and *-tig,* the suff. *-ty.*]

fig[1] *fig, n.* the fig-tree (Ficus, of the mulberry family), or its fruit, growing in warm climates: a thing of little or no consequence.—**fig'-leaf** the leaf of the fig-tree: a representation of such a leaf for veiling the private parts of a statue or picture: any scanty clothing (from Gen. iii. 7): any prudish evasion: a makeshift: something intended to conceal the reality of actions or motives, esp. political or international; **fig'-tree.** [Fr. *figue*—L *ficus,* a fig, fig-tree.]

fig[2] *fig, (coll.) n.* figure: dress: form.—**in full fig** in full dress, array. [Perh. **figure.**]

fight *fīt, v.i.* to strive: to contend in war or in single combat.—*v.t.* to engage in conflict with: to contend against: to maintain or contend for by combat, action at law, or otherwise: to manipulate in fight: to achieve by struggle: to cause to fight:—*pa.t.* and *pa.p.* **fought** (*fot*) —*n.* a struggle: a combat: a strong disagreement: a battle or engagement: fighting spirit: inclination to fight.—*n.* **fight'er** one who fights: a boxer: an aircraft engaged in war.—*adj.* **fight'ing** engaged in, eager for, or fit for war or strife.—*n.* the act of fighting or contending.—**fighting chance** a chance of success given supreme effort; **fighting cock** a gamecock: a pugnacious fellow; **fighting fish** a small freshwater fish of Thailand, kept for its extraordinary readiness for fighting, bets being laid on the issue — **fight back** to retaliate: to counterattack (*n.* **fight'(-)back)**; **fighting fit** in good condition; **fight it out** to struggle on until the end; **fight off** to resist, repel; **fight shy of** to avoid from mistrust; **fight to the finish, to the last ditch** to fight until completely exhausted; **live like fighting cocks** to get the best of meat and drink. [O.E. *feohtan.*]

figment *fig'mǝnt, n.* a fabrication or invention. [L. *figmentum—fingĕre,* to form]

figuline *fig'ū-lin, -lin, adj.* of earthenware: fictile.—*n.* an earthen vessel. [L. *figulinus—figulus,* potter.]

figure *fig'ǝr, (U S. and dial) -yǝr,* (old-fashioned) *fig'ūr, n* the form of anything in outline: appearance: a shape· a geometrical form· a diagram: a design: an illustration: bodily shape a human form or representation of it· a personality, personage, character: an impressive, noticeable, important, ludicrous, or grotesque person: a character denoting a number: amount: value or price. a deviation from the ordinary mode of expression (*rhet.*) a group of notes felt as a unit (*mus.*): a series of steps or movements in a dance or in skating: a type or emblem —*v.t.* to make an image of: to represent: to mark with figures or designs: to imagine: to reckon, to work out (often with *out*) to note by figures —*v.t.* to make figures: to appear in figures, make an appearance or show· to follow as a logical consequence, be expected (*coll.*). —*n.* **figurabil'ity** the quality of being figurable — *adjs.* **fig'urable; fig'ural** represented by figure.—*n.* **figurant, figurante** (*fig'ū-rant;* It. *fēg-ōō-rän'tä*) a ballet dancer, one of those who form a background for the solo dancers —*adj.* **fig'ūrate** of a certain determinate form: florid (*mus.*).—*n.* **figūrā'tion** act of giving figure or form: representation by or in figures or shapes, esp. significant, typical or emblematic, figures: a figure of this kind: ornamentation with a design: florid treatment (*mus.*) —*adj.* **fig'ūrative** representing by, containing, or abounding in figures of speech (*rhet.*): metaphorical: representing a figure: emblematic, symbolic.—*adv* **fig'ūratively.** —*n.* **fig'ūrativeness.**—*adj.* **fig'ured** (*-ǝrd*) having a figure: marked or adorned with figures: delineated in a figure: in the form of figures.—*n.* **fig'urine** (*-ēn, -ēn'*) a small carved or moulded figure.—**fig'urehead** the figure or bust under the bowsprit of a ship: a nominal head; **fig'ure-skating** skating in prescribed patterns on ice.—**cut a figure** to make a conspicuous appearance; **figure on** to count upon: to plan (*U.S.*). [Fr.,—L. *figūra—fingĕre,* to form.]

fike *fīk, (Scot.) v.i.* to fidget restlessly.—*n.* restlessness: any vexatious requirement or detail in work; a pernickety exacting person.—*n.* **fik'ery** fuss.—*adjs.* **fik'ish, fik'y.** [Prob. O N. *fīkja.*]

filabeg. See **filibeg.**

filaceous. See **file**[1].

filagree. Same as **filigree.**

filament *fil'ǝ-mǝnt, n.* a slender or threadlike object: a fibre: the stalk of a stamen (*bot.*): a chain of cells: a thread of high resistance in an incandescent lamp or thermionic valve (*elec.*).—*adjs.* **filamentary** (*-ment'-ǝ-ri*) like a filament; **filament'ous** threadlike. [L. *filum,* a thread.]

filar. See **file**[1].

Filaria *fi-lā'ri-ǝ, n.* a genus of nematode worms introduced into the blood by mosquitoes: (without *cap.*) any worm of the genus.—*adj.* **filā'rial.**—*n.* **filariasis** (*-lǝ-rī'ǝ-sis*) a disease due to the presence of filaria in the blood. [L. *filum,* thread.]

filature *fil'ǝ-chǝr, n.* the reeling of silk, or the place where it is done.—*n.* **fil'atory** a machine for forming or spinning threads [Fr.,—L. *filum,* a thread.]

filbert *fil'bǝrt, n.* the nut of the cultivated hazel. [Prob. from St *Philibert,* whose day fell in the nutting season, Aug. 22 (O.S.)]

filch *filch, v.t.* to steal: to pilfer.—*n.* **filch'er** a thief.— *n.* and *adj.* **filch'ing.**—*adv.* **filch'ingly.**

file[1] *fīl, n.* a line or wire on which papers are strung: any contrivance for keeping papers in order: a collection of papers arranged for reference: a line of soldiers, chessboard squares, etc., ranged one behind another: a small body of soldiers —*v.t.* to put upon a file: to arrange in an orderly way: to put on record: to bring before a court: to deposit, lodge.—*v.i.* to march in file.—*adjs.* **filaceous** (*fil-ā'shəs*) composed of threads; **filar** (*fī'lər*) having threads or wires; **filiform** (*fil'*) threadlike; **filose** (*fī'lōs*) threadlike: having a threadlike end.—**filing cabinet** a cabinet for storing files.—**file off** to wheel off at right angles to the first direction; **on file** on record, catalogued; **single file, Indian file** one behind another. [L. *filum*, a thread.]

file² *fil, n* an instrument with sharp-edged furrows for smoothing or rasping metals, etc.: a small metal or emery-paper instrument for smoothing fingernails: a shrewd, cunning person, a deep fellow.—*v.t.* to cut or smooth with, or as with, a file: to polish, improve, esp. of a literary style.—*adj.* **filed** polished, smooth.—*ns.* **fil'er;** (usu. in *pl*) **fil'ing** a particle rubbed off with a file. [O.E. *fȳl* (W.S. *fēol*).]

filet *fē-le* (Fr.) *n.* undercut of beef, tenderloin: a kind of lace consisting of embroidery on a square-mesh net.

filet mignon *fē-le mē-nyɔ̃,* (Fr.) a small cut of beef from the thick end of an undercut.

filial *fil'i-əl, adj.* pertaining to or becoming a son or daughter bearing the relation of a child.—*adv.* **fil'ially.** [Fr.,—L.L. *filiālis*—L. *filius,* a son.]

filiate, filiation. Same as **affiliate, affiliation.**

filibeg, filabeg, fillibeg, phil(l)abeg, phil(l)ibeg *fil'i-beg, n.* the kilt, the dress or petticoat reaching nearly to the knees, worn by the Highlanders of Scotland. [Gael. *feileadhbheag*—*feileadh,* plait, fold, *beag,* little.]

filibuster *fil'i-bus-tər, n.* a piratical adventurer, buccaneer: a military adventurer, one who makes unauthorised war: one who obstructs legislation by speeches, motions, etc.: obstruction in a legislative body.—*v.i* to act as a filibuster.—*ns.* **filibus'terer; filibus'tering; filibus'terism.**—*adj.* **filibus'terous.** [Sp. *filibustero,* through Fr. *flibustier, fribustier,* from Du. *vrijbuiter* (cf. Eng. **freebooter** (under **free**), Ger. *Freibeuter*), from *vrij,* free, *buit,* booty.]

filicide *fil'i-sid, n* the murder of one's own child: one who murders his child [L. *filius, filia,* son, daughter; *caedere,* to kill.]

filiform. See file¹.

filigree *fil'i-grē, n.* a kind of ornamental metallic lacework of gold and silver, twisted into convoluted forms, united and partly consolidated by soldering: a delicate structure resembling this (also **fil'agree**).—*adj.* **fil'igreed** ornamented with filigree. [Fr. *filigrane*—It. *filigrana*—L. *filum,* thread, *grānum,* a grain.]

filing. See file².

Filipino *fil-i-pē'nō, n.* a native of the *Philippine Islands:*—*pl* **Filipi'nos:**—*fem.* **Filipi'na.**—Also *adj.* [Sp.]

fill *fil, v.t.* to make full: to put into until all the space is occupied: to supply abundantly: to satisfy: to glut: to perform the duties of: to supply (a vacant office): to put amalgam, gold, etc. into (a cavity in a tooth): to fulfil, carry out (esp. *U.S.*): to make up (a prescription) (*U.S.*).—*v.i.* to become full: to become satiated.—*n.* as much as fills or satisfies: a full supply: the fullest extent: a single charge of anything: anything used to fill.—*ns.* **fill'er** he who, or that which, fills: a vessel for conveying a liquid into a bottle: a substance added to various materials to impart desired qualities; **fill'ing** anything used to fill up, stop a hole, to complete, etc., as amalgam, etc. into a tooth, the woof in weaving.—**filler cap** a device for closing the filling pipe of a petrol tank in a motor vehicle, **filling station** a roadside installation where petrol and oil are sold to motorists —**fill in** to occupy (time). to add

what is necessary to complete, e.g. a form: to act as a temporary substitute (for; *coll.*); **fill out** to make or become more substantial, larger, fuller; **fill someone in** (*coll.*) to give someone detailed information about a situation: to thrash, beat up someone (*slang*); **fill the bill** to be adequate; **fill up** to fill, or be filled, by addition of more. [O.E. *fyllan*—*full,* full.]

fillet *fil'ət, n.* a narrow piece of wood, metal, etc.: a band for the hair: meat or fish boned and rolled: a piece of meat without bone, esp. the fleshy part of the thigh or the undercut of the sirloin: a boned whole, or thick boneless slice of fish: a small space or band used along with mouldings (*archit.*).—*v.t.* to bind or adorn with a fillet: to make into fillets: to bone:—*pr.p.* **fill'eting;** *pa.t.* and *pa.p.* **fill'eted.** [Fr. *filet,* dim. of *fil,* from L. *filum,* a thread.]

fillibeg. See filibeg.

fillip *fil'ip, v.t.* to strike with the fingernail released from the ball of the thumb with a sudden jerk: to incite, stimulate:—*pr.p.* **fill'iping;** *pa.t.* and *pa.p.* **fill'iped.**—*n.* a jerk of the finger from the thumb: a stimulus. [A form of **flip.**]

fillister *fil'is-tər, n.* a kind of rabbeting plane.

filly *fil'i, n.* a young mare: a lively, wanton girl. [Dim. of **foal;** prob. from O.N.]

film *film, n.* a thin skin or membrane: a thin layer or coating: a pellicle: a very slender thread: a mistiness: a coating of a sensitive substance for taking a photograph: a sheet or ribbon of celluloid or the like prepared with such a coating for ordinary photographs or for instantaneous photographs for projection by cinematograph: a motion picture, or connected series of motion pictures setting forth a story, etc.: (in *pl.*) the cinema.—*v.t.* to cover with a film: to photograph, record on film: to make a motion picture of: to adapt and enact for the cinema.—*v.i.* to become covered with a film.—*adj.* **film'able** suitable for making a film of.—*ns.* **filmi'ness; filmog'raphy** a list of the films of a particular actor or director.—*adj.* **film'y** composed of or like a film: covered with a film: gauzy: clouded. —**film'goer; film noir** a bleak or pessimistic film; **film'setting** typesetting by exposing type on to film which is then transferred to printing plates; **film star** a favourite cinema performer. [O.E. *filmen,* conn. with *fell,* skin.]

filose. See file¹.

filoselle *fil-ō-sel', n.* coarse floss silk. [It. *filosello*—L.L. *folexellus,* cocoon; infl. by It. *filo,* thread.]

filter *fil'tər, n.* an apparatus for purifying a fluid of solid matter by pouring it through porous material: a device for wholly or partly eliminating undesirable frequencies from light or electric currents: at a road junction an auxiliary traffic light in the form of a green arrow which allows one lane of traffic to move while the main stream is held up.—*v.t.* to pass through a filter: to separate by a filter (esp. with *out*).—*v.i.* to pass through a filter: to percolate: to pass gradually and dispersedly through obstacles: to join gradually a stream of traffic: of a lane of traffic, to move in the direction specified by the filter: to become known gradually (*fig.*).—*adj.* **fil'terable, fil'trable** able to pass through a filter: capable of being filtered.—*n.* **filt(e)rabil'ity.**—*v.t.* and *v.i.* **fil'trate** to filter or percolate.—*n.* a filtered liquid.— *n.* **filtra'tion** act or process of filtering.—**fil'ter-bed** a bed of sand, gravel, clinker, etc., used for filtering water or sewage; **fil'ter-paper** porous paper for use in filtering; **fil'ter-tip** a cigarette with a filter at the mouth end. [O.Fr. *filtre*—L.L. *filtrum,* felt.]

filth *filth, n.* foul matter: anything that defiles, physically or morally: obscenity.—*adv.* **filth'ily.**—*n.* **filth'iness.**—*adj.* **filth'y** foul: unclean: impure. [O.E. *fȳlth*—*fūl,* foul.]

fimbria *fim'bri-ə, n.* a fringing filament.—*adj.* **fim'-briate** fringed: having a narrow border (*her.*).—*adj.* **fim'briated.**—*n.* **fimbria'tion.** [L. *fimbriae,* fibres, fringe.]

fin *fin, n.* an organ by which an aquatic animal steers, balances, or swims: a fixed vertical surface on the tail of an aeroplane: a portion of a mechanism like a fish's fin in shape or purpose: a thin projecting edge or plate: hand, arm (*slang*).—*adjs.* **fin'less; finned** having fins; **finn'y** finned.—**fin'back, fin'-whale** a rorqual. [O.E. *finn.*]

finable. See **fine²**.

finagle *fi-nā'gəl, v.t.* to wangle: to obtain by guile or swindling: to cheat (a person; usu. with *out of*).—Also *v.i.* [Eng. dial. *fainaigue,* cheat, shirk.]

final *fi'nl, adj.* last: decisive, conclusive: respecting the end or motive: of a judgment ready for execution.—*n.* the last of a series (as the letters of a word, games in a contest, examinations in a curriculum, etc.).—*v t.* **fi'nalise, -ize** to put the finishing touches to: to put an end to completely.—*ns* **fi'nalist** one who reaches the final stage in a competition; **finality** (*-al't-ti*) state of being final: completeness or conclusiveness: the principle of final cause: that which is final.—*adv.* **fi'nally.** [Fr.,—L. *finālis—finis,* an end.]

finale *fi-na'lā, -li, n.* the end: the last movement in a musical composition. the concluding number of an opera or the like. [It. *finale,* final—L *finālis.*]

finance *fi, fi', fi-nans', n.* money affairs or revenue, esp. of a ruler or state: public money: the art of managing or administering the public money: (in *pl.*) money resources.—*v.t.* to manage financially: to furnish with money.—*v.i.* to engage in money business.—*adj.* **finan'cial (-shəl)** pertaining to finance.—*n.* **finan'cialist** a financier.—*adv.* **finan'cially.**—*n.* **finan'-cier** (*-si-ər; U.S. fin-an-sēr'*) one skilled in finance, one who administers the public revenue.—*v t.* and *v.t.* (*sēr'*) to finance: to swindle.—**finance company, house** a company specialising in lending money against collateral, esp. to finance hire-purchase agreements; **financial year** any annual period for which accounts are made up: the annual period ending April 5th, functioning as the income-tax year [Fr ,—O.Fr. *finer,* to settle—L. *finis,* an end.]

finback. See **fin¹**.

finch *finch, -sh, n.* a name applied to many passerine birds, esp. to those of the genus *Fringilla*—bullfinch, chaffinch, goldfinch, etc. [O.E. *finc.*]

find *find, v.t.* to come upon or meet with: to discover or arrive at: to come to perceive: to experience: to supply: to determine after judicial inquiry: to succeed in getting.—*v t.* to come upon game:—*pr.p.* **find'ing;** *pa.t.* and *pa.p.* **found.**—*n.* an act of finding. something found, esp. of value or interest.—*ns.* **find'er** one who finds: a small telescope attached to a larger one, or a lens attached to a camera, to facilitate the directing of it upon the object required; **find'ing.**—**finders keepers** (*coll.*) those who find something are entitled to keep it; **find one's feet** to become able to stand, able to cope readily with new conditions, **find oneself** to feel, as regards health, happiness, etc.: to come to terms with oneself: to discover one's true vocation and interests, **find out** to discover, to detect [O.E. *findan.*]

fin de siècle *fē də sye-kl',* (Fr.) the end of the (19th) century, or of an era: characteristic of the ideas, etc , of that time: decadent.

fine¹ *fin, adj* excellent: beautiful: fair. not coarse or heavy: consisting of small particles. subtle. slender sharp. keen: exquisite: nice: delicate: sensitive. over-refined: showy splendid: striking or remarkable egregious: pure· refined: containing so many parts of pure metal out of twenty-four (as 22 carats, or ounces, fine, 22/24 gold or silver), or out of a thousand.—*v.t.* to make fine: to refine: to purify: to change by imperceptible degrees.—*adj.* and *adv.* at a more acute angle with the line of flight of the ball (as *fine leg*): (of a billiards, etc. stroke) making very slight contact.—*adv.* well, well enough (*coll.*): narrowly: with little to spare.—*adv.* **fine'ly.**—*ns.* **fine'-ness; fin'er** a refiner; **fin'ery** splendour: showy adornments: a place where anything is fined or refined: a furnace for making iron malleable.—*n.pl.* **fines** material (ore, coal, etc.) in a fine state of division separated out by screening; **fin'ing** process of refining or purifying: a clarifying agent (often in *pl.*).—**fine arts** see under **art**.—*v.t.* **fine'-draw** to draw or sew up so finely that no rent is seen: to draw out finely or too finely —*adj.* **fine'-drawn.**—*adjs.* **fine'-spoken** using fine phrases; **fine'-spun** finely spun out: over-subtle. —**fine-tooth(ed) comb, fine comb** a comb with slender teeth set close together.—*v.t.* **fine-tune'** to make delicate adjustments to.—**fine-tun'ing; fin'ing-pot** a vessel used in refining.—**cut it fine** to do something with little time, space to spare; **go over, through with a fine-tooth(ed) comb** to investigate very thoroughly. [Fr *fin,* prob. a back-formation from L. *finitus,* finished, pa.p. of *finire,* to finish—*finis,* an end.]

fine² *fin, n.* (*obs.* except in phrase *in fine*) end, conclusion: a fee paid on some particular occasion: a money penalty.—*v.t.* to impose a fine on: to punish by fine —*adj.* **fin'able** liable to a fine. [L. *finis,* an end]

fine³ *fēn, n.* ordinary French brandy.—**fine Champagne** (*shā-pany'*) brandy distilled from wine made from grapes grown in the Champagne area of France. [Fr.]

fines herbes *fēn-zerb,* (Fr) (*cook.*) a mixture of herbs used as a garnish or, chopped, as a seasoning.

finesse *fi-nes', n.* subtlety of contrivance: artifice: an endeavour by a player holding a higher card to take the trick with a lower, risking loss.—*v.t.* and *v.i.* to play in finesse.—*v.t* to use artifice.—*ns.* **finess'er; finess'ing.** [Fr.]

finger *fing'gər, n.* one of the five terminal parts of the hand, or of the four other than the thumb: anything shaped like a finger: the part of a glove that covers a finger: a finger-breadth: touch: share, interest: (in *pl*) grip, control.—*v t.* to handle or perform with the fingers: to pilfer: to toy or meddle with: to make or indicate choice of fingers in performing (*mus.*): to indicate, identify a guilty person (*slang*).—*v.t.* to use or move the fingers —*adj.* **fing'ered** having fingers, or anything like fingers, or indication of fingering.—*n.* **fing'ering** act or manner of touching with the fingers: the choice of fingers as in playing a musical instrument: the indication thereof —*adj.* **fing'erless.** —*n* **fing'erling** a very diminutive being or thing: a fish no bigger than a finger, esp. a salmon parr or young trout less than a year old.—**fing'erboard** the part of a violin, etc., against which the strings are stopped by the fingers, **fing'erbowl, -glass** a bowl for water to cleanse the fingers at table; **fing'er('s)-breadth** the breadth of a finger, a digit, ⅞ of an inch; **fin'gerhold** a grasp by the fingers: something by which the fingers can hold (also *fig*); **fin'gerhole** a hole in a wind instrument closed by the finger to modify the pitch, **fing'ermark** a mark, esp a soil, made by the finger, **fing'ernail; fing'er-paint** a somewhat thick gelatinous paint used esp. by children and applied with the hands and fingers rather than with a brush.—Also *v t.*—**fing'er-painting; fing'erplate** a plate to protect a door from dirty fingers; **fing'erprint** an impression of the ridges of the finger-tip.—*v.t.* to take the fingerprints of —**fin'gerprinting; fing'er-**

stall a covering for protecting the finger; **fing'ertip.—
a finger in the pie** a share in the doing of anything
(often said of vexatious meddling); **get, pull the** or
one's finger out (*coll.*) to start working hard or doing
one's job properly or efficiently; **have at one's finger-
tips** to be master of (a subject); **lay, put a finger on** to
touch; **not lift a finger** to take no action; **point the
finger at** to call attention to in reproof; **put, lay one's
finger on** to indicate, comprehend and express, or
recall, precisely; **to one's fingertips** completely: in all
respects; **twist someone round one's little finger** see
little. [O.E. *finger.*]

fingering *fing'gər-ing, n.* a woollen yarn of two or more
strands, used in hand-knitting, orig. esp. for stockings. [Perh. Fr. *fin grain,* fine grain]

finial *fin'i-əl, n.* the bunch of foliage, etc. on the top of
a pinnacle, gable, spire, etc. [L. *finis,* end.]

finical *fin'i-kl, adj.* affectedly or excessively precise in
trifles: nice: foppish.—*n.* **finicality** (*-kal'i-ti*) the
state of being finical: something finical.—*adv.* **fin'-
ically.—*ns.* **fin'icalness,** **fin'icking** fussiness and
fastidiousness.—*adjs.* **fin'icking,** **fin'icky,** **fin'ikin**
particular about trifles [Prob conn. with **fine'**.]

fining. See **fine'.**

finish *fin'ish, v.t.* to end: to complete the making of· to
perfect: to give the last touches to: to complete the
education of, esp. for life in society: to complete the
course of a race: to put an end to, to destroy.—Also
v.i. —*n.* that which finishes or completes: the end of a
race, hunt, etc.: the last touch, elaboration, polish:
the last coat of plaster or paint —*adj.* **fin'ished**
brought to an end or to completion: complete: consummate: perfect.—*n.* **fin'isher** one who finishes:
one who completes or perfects, esp. in crafts.—*n.* and
adj. **fin'ishing.—finishing school** an establishment
where some girls complete their education, with emphasis on social refinements, etc. rather than
academic achievement. [Fr. *finir, finissant—*L
finire, to end.]

finite *fi'nit, adj.* having an end or limit: subject to
limitations or conditions (opp. to *infinite*) —*adv.*
fi'nitely.—*ns.* **finiteness, **finitude** (*fin'i-tūd*).—**finite**
verb a verb limited by person, number, tense, mood,
opp. to infinitive, gerund, participle. [L. *finitus,*
pa.p. of *finire,* to limit.]

fink *fingk, (slang) n.* a strike-breaker: an informer: an
unpleasant person.—Also *v.i.* (often with *on*).

Finn *fin, n.* a member of a people dwelling in Finland
and adjacent regions: more generally, a member of
the group of peoples to which the Finns proper belong.—*ns.* **Fin'lander** a native or citizen of Finland;
Finlandisā'tion, -z- in relations with the Soviet
Union, a policy of accommodation rather than confrontation.—*adjs.* **Finn'ic** pertaining to the Finns or
the Finno-Ugrians; **Finn'ish** pertaining to the Finns,
or to Finland, or its language.—*n.* the Finno-Ugrian
language of Finland.—*adjs.* **Finno-Ugrian, Finno-
Ugric** (*fin'ō-ū'gri-ən, -ōō'gri-ən, -grik*) belonging to
the north-western group of Ural-Altaic languages
and peoples—Finnish, Estonian, Lapp, etc. [O.E.
finnas, Finns.]

finnan *fin'ən, n.* a kind of smoked haddock, probably
named from Findon, Kincardineshire.—Also
finn'an-hadd'ock.

fino *fē'nō, n.* a dry sherry:—*pl.* **fi'nos.** [Sp., fine,
excellent.]

finoc(c)hio, finnochio *fin-ok'i-ō, n.* a dwarf variety of
fennel.—Also called **dwarf, Florence, French** or **sweet
fennel.** [It., fennel.]

fiord, fjord *fyör(d), fyor(d), n.* a long, narrow, rock-
bound inlet. [Norw. *fjord.*]

fioritura *fyor-i-tōō'ra (mus.) n.* a florid embellishment·
—*pl.* **fioriture** (*-rā*). [It., flowering—L. *flōs, flōris.*]

fipple *fip'l, n.* an arrangement of a block, and a sharp
edge against which it directs the wind, in the recorder,
etc.—**fipp'le-flute'** a flute with a fipple, a recorder or
flageolet [Cf O.N *flipi,* a horse's lip.]

fir *fûr, n.* the name of several conifers, resinous trees,
valuable for their timber —*adj.* **firr'y** abounding in
firs: of fir.—**fir'-cone; fir'-tree; fir'-wood.** [O.E
fyrh]

fire *fir, n.* the heat and light of burning: a mass of
burning matter, as of fuel in a grate: flame or incandescence a conflagration. firing. fuel: a heating
apparatus. heat or light due to other causes than burn-
ing· volcanic or plutonic heat: great heat· the heat of
fever or inflammation: glowing appearance: a sparkle
of light· discharge of fire-arms (also *fig.*): enthusiasm:
ardour· spirited vigour or animation —*v.t.* to ignite: to
cause to explode: to expose to heat· to bake: to
cauterise: to fuel: to affect as if by fire: to discharge. to
drive out: to dismiss (from employment, etc.): to
inflame: to animate· to rouse to passion of any kind.—
v i. to take fire· to shoot with firearms: to become
inflamed: to break out in anger: of a car, engine, etc.,
to start —*adjs.* **fired** affected, or having the appearance of having been affected, with fire: baked: ignited:
kindled: discharged; **fire'less.—*ns.* **fir'er** one who
fires, in any sense, **fir'ing** ignition: discharge of guns,
etc : simultaneous ringing of a peal of bells: fuelling:
firewood: fuel: cautery. injury by overheating: subjection to heat.—**fire'-alarm** an apparatus for giving
warning of fire: a warning of fire; **fire'arm** a weapon
discharged by explosion (usu. in *pl.*); **fire'ball** a
bolide: ball-lightning: an incendiary or illuminating
projectile: the luminous sphere of hot gases at the
centre of a nuclear explosion; **fire'-bomb** an incendiary bomb; **fire'brand** a burning piece of wood: one
who foments strife; **fire'-break** a strip of land kept
clear to stop the spread of a fire (also *fig.*); **fire'brick** a
brick refractory to fire, used for furnace-linings, grates
etc.; **fire'-brigade** a body of firemen; **fire'-bucket** a
bucket containing sand or water for putting out fires,
fire'-clay a clay poor in lime and iron, suitable for
making refractory pottery and firebricks; **fire'-cracker**
a device for making a noise, a cylinder of paper or
cardboard containing an explosive and a fuse; **fire'-
crest** or **fire-crested wren** a bird close akin to the
goldcrest, a kinglet; **fire'damp** a combustible gas given
off by coal, etc , chiefly methane; **fire'dog** an andiron;
fire'-drill practice in putting out or escaping from fire;
fire'-eater a juggler who seems to eat fire: a seeker of
quarrels; **fire'-engine** an engine or pump for extinguishing fires; **fire'-escape** a fixed or movable way of
escape from a burning building; **fire'-extinguisher** a
contrivance for ejecting agents, e.g. water or a
chemical, to put out fires.—**fire'-fighter** a fireman;
fire'-fighting; fire'fly an insect, generally a beetle,
that emits light by night; **fire'guard** a protective wire-
frame or railing in front of a fireplace; **fire'-hose** a hose
for extinguishing fires; **fire'-insurance** insurance
against loss by fire; **fire'-irons** fireside implements—
poker, tongs, shovel—not necessarily of iron;
fire'light the light of a domestic fire; **fire'lighter** a
piece of readily inflammable material or other means
of lighting a fire; **fire'man** one whose function is to
assist in putting out fires and rescuing those in danger:
a stoker: a train driver's assistant (stoker on steam
engine): one who attends to conditions of safety in a
mine: one who explodes charges; **fire'-master** the head
of a fire brigade; **fire'-office** a fire insurance office;
fire'place the place in a house appropriated to the fire,
as the opening of a chimney into a room; **fire'-plug** a
hydrant for use against fires; **fire'-power** (*mil.*) the
weight of missiles that can be fired with effect in a given
time —*adj.* **fire'proof** proof against fire: incombus-

tible.—*v.t.* to render fireproof. —**fire'proofing; fire's raiser** an incendiary; **fire'-raising** arson.—*adjs.* **fire'-resist'ant, fire'-resist'ing** immune to effects of fire up to a required degree.—**fire'-risk; fire'screen** a screen for intercepting the heat of a fire; **fire'ship** a ship carrying combustibles sent among the enemy's ships, **fire'-shovel; fire'side** the side of the fireplace: the hearth: home.—*adj.* domestic: familiar.—**fire station** a place where fire-engines, firemen, etc. are kept in readiness to attend a fire; **fire'-stick** a primitive implement for getting fire by friction; **fire'stone** a rock, esp. a sandstone, that stands much heat without injury; **fire'-storm** a huge blaze (esp. a result of heavy bombing) which fans its own flames by creating its own draught (also *fig.*); **fire'-warden** (*U.S.*) an official charged with prevention and extinction of fires, **fire'-watcher** one who watches against fire; **fire's watching; fire'-water** ardent spirits; **fire'weed** the rose-bay willow-herb, which springs up after forest, etc., fires; **fire'wood** wood for fuel; **fire'work** a contrivance for producing sparks, jets, flares, or glowing pictorial designs in fire for amusement: (now only in *pl.*) a display of these: (in *pl.*) a florid technical display in music, talk, etc.: (in *pl.*) a display of temper; **fire'worm** a glow-worm: a firefly; **firing line** area or troops within range of the enemy for practical purposes; **firing party** a detachment told off to fire over a grave or shoot a condemned prisoner; **firing pin** a pin that strikes the detonator and explodes the cartridge in a rifle; **firing squad** a firing party, a detachment told off to shoot a condemned prisoner.—**catch, take fire** to become ignited: to become aroused about something; **fire away** (usu. *imper.*; *coll.*) to go ahead: to begin; **fire off** to discharge: to ask, utter in rapid succession; **fire up** to start a fire: to fly into a passion; **on fire** in a state of fiery combustion; **play with fire** to expose oneself to unnecessary risk: to treat lightly a situation which could prove dangerous; St **Anthony's fire** see **Anthony; St Elmo's fire** see **Saint; set on fire, set fire to** to ignite; **under fire** exposed to the enemy's fire: exposed to criticism. [O.E. *fȳr.*]

firkin *fûr'kin, n.* a measure equal to the fourth part of a barrel (*brewing*): 9 gallons (*brewing*): 56 lb. of butter. [With dim. suff. *-kin*, from Old Du. *vierde*, fourth.]

firm¹ *fûrm, adj.* fixed: compact: strong: not easily moved or disturbed: unshaken: resolute: decided: (of prices, commodities, markets, etc.) steady, stable (*com- merce*).—Also *adv.*—*v.t.* to make firm.—*v.i.* to be- come firm: to become stable or rise slightly (*commerce*).—*adv.* **firm'ly.**—*n.* **firm'ness.**—**firm down** to make (ground, etc.) firm or firmer; **firm up** (of prices, etc.) to firm (*commerce*): to make (a promise, etc.) firmer or firmer. [O.Fr. *ferme*—L. *firmus.*]

firm² *fûrm, n.* the title under which a company transacts business: a business house or partnership [It. *firma*, from L. *firmus*; see **farm.**]

firmament *fûr'mə-mənt, n.* the solid sphere in which the stars were thought to be fixed: the sky.—*adj.* **firmamental** (*-ment'l*). [L. *firmāmentum*—*firmus*, firm.]

firring. Same as **furring.**

first *fûrst, adj.* foremost: in front of or before all others: most eminent: chief: referring to the speaker or writer (*gram.*).—*n.* one who or that which is first or of the first class: a place in the first class: first gear.— *adv.* before anything or anyone else: for the first time.—*n.* **first'ling** the first produce or offspring, esp. of animals.—*adv.* **first'ly** in the first place.— **first'-aid'** treatment of a wounded or sick person before the doctor's arrival; **first'-aid'er.**—*adjs.* **first'- born** born first.—*n.* the eldest child.—*adj.* **first's class'** of the first class, rank, or quality.—**first floor** (*adj* **first'-floor**) see **floor; first'-foot'** (*Scot.*) the first person to enter a house after the beginning of the new year.—*v.t.* to visit as first-foot.—*v.i.* to go around making visits as first-foot —**first'-foot'er; first'-fruit(s)'** the fruits first gathered in a season: first products or effects of anything: payment to a superior.—*adj.* **first'-hand** obtained directly, or in order to obtain (information, etc) directly, without an intermediary.—*adv.* **first-hand'.**—**first lady** the wife of the chief executive of a city, state, or country, esp.of the president of the U.S A., or any woman chosen by him to carry out official duties as hostess, etc. (*U.S.*; often with *caps.*). a prominent or leading woman in any field, profession, etc.; **first lieutenant** in the Royal Navy, the executive officer, not necessarily a lieutenant, of a ship or naval establishment; **first light** the time when daylight first appears in the morning; **first name** Christian name, or the name that comes first in full name; **first'-night'** the first night of a performance; **first'-offend'er** one convicted for the first time.—*adjs.* **first'-past'-the-post'** denoting or relating to a system of voting in which each voter casts only one vote, the candidate receiving the most votes being declared the winner; **first'-rate** of highest rate or excellence: pre-eminent in quality, size, or estimation.—*adv.* **first-rate'** excellently.—**first school** a school catering for those aged five to eight, nine or ten.—*adj.* **first'-time** immediate.—**at first** at the beginning, in the early stages, etc.; **first-class mail, post** mail sent at a higher rate to obtain quicker delivery; **first-day cover** an envelope with stamps postmarked on their first day of issue; **not know the first thing about** to know nothing about; **(the) first thing** before doing anything else. [O.E. *fyrst*, superl.; cf *fore*, before.]

firth *fûrth, n.* an arm of the sea, esp. a river-mouth.— Also **frith** (*frith*). [O.N. *fiörthr*; Norw. *fjord.*]

fisc *fisk, n.* the state treasury: the public revenue: one's purse.—*adj.* **fisc'al** pertaining to the public treasury or revenue.—*n.* in Scotland, an officer who prosecutes in criminal cases in local and inferior courts—in full, **procurator-fiscal.**—**fiscal drag** the means by which the inland revenue automatically benefits from any increase in earned income without any actual increase in taxation rates; **fiscal year** (esp. *U.S.*) financial year. [L. *fiscus*, a basket, a purse.]

fisgig. See **fizgig.**

fish¹ *fish, n.* a vertebrate that lives in water and breathes through gills: loosely, any exclusively aquatic animal: fish flesh: a person, as in *queer fish*: a fish-dive:—*pl.* **fish** or **fish'es.**—*v.i.* to catch or try to catch or obtain fish, or anything that may be likened to a fish often with *for*): to serve the purpose of fishing.—*v.t.* to catch and bring out of water: to bring up or out from a deep or hidden place, obscurity or the like: to elicit (with *out*): to practice the fisher's craft in: to ransack.—*ns.* **fish'er** one who fishes for sport or gain; **fish'ery** the business of catching fish: a place for catching fish: right of fishing.—**fish'iness.**—*adj.* **fish'- ing** used in fishing.—*n.* the art or practice of catching fish.—*adj.* **fish'y** consisting of fish: like a fish: abounding in fish: dubious, as a story: equivocal, unsafe.—**fish'ball, -cake** a ball or cake of chopped fish and mashed potatoes, fried; **fish'-bone; fish's carv'er, fish'-trowel** a large flat implement for carving fish at table; **fish('-dive')** (*slang*) a ballerina's leap on to a partner's outstretched arms; **fish'erman** a fisher; **fish'eye lens** (*phot.*) an ultra-wide-angle lens covering up to 180°; **fish'-farm; fish'- farmer; fish'-farming** rearing fish in ponds or tanks; **fish'-fing'er** a fairly small oblong cake of fish coated in batter or breadcrumbs; **fish'-glue** isinglass, or any other glue made from the skins, air-bladders, etc. of fish; **fish'-hawk** osprey; **fish'-hook** a barbed hook for catching fish; **fish'ing-rod** a long slender rod to which a line is fastened for angling; **fish'ing-tack'le** tackle—nets, lines, etc.—used in fishing; **fish'-kett'le** a long oval dish for boiling fish, **fish'-ladd'er,** **fish'-way** an arrangement of steps and shelters for enabling a fish to ascend a fall, etc., **fish'-manure'** fish used as a fertiliser; **fish'-meal** dried fish ground to meal, **fish'-monger** a dealer in fish.—*adj.* **fish'-net** woven as a fine net —**fish'-pond** a pond in which fish are kept; **fish'-sauce** sauce proper to be eaten with fish; **fish'-skin** the skin of a fish: (also **fish'skin disease**) ichthyosis; **fish'-slice** a flat implement for carving fish at table: a broad, flat implement for turning fish, etc., in the frying-pan.—*adj.* **fish'-tail** shaped like the tail of a fish.—*v.i.* to swing the tail of an aircraft from side to side to reduce speed while gliding downward; **fish'-wife, fish'-woman** a woman who carries fish about for sale —**a fish out of water** a person in an unaccustomed, unsuitable situation which makes him ill at ease, **big fish** (*slang*) an important or leading person; **drink like a fish** to drink to excess; **fish in troubled waters** to take advantage of disturbed times to further one's own interests, **have other fish to fry** to have something else to do or attend to; **odd fish** or **queer fish** a person of odd habits, or of a nature with which one is not in sympathy, **pretty kettle of fish** see **kettle** [O E. *fisc.*]

fish² *fish, n.* a piece of wood placed alongside another to strengthen it (*naut*): a counter for games.—**fish'-plate** an iron plate used in pairs to join railway rails. [Prob. Fr. *fiche,* peg, mark.]

fishgig. See **fizgig.**

fissile *fis'il, -il, adj.* ready split: capable of nuclear fission.—*ns.* **fissility** (*-il'*) cleavableness; **fission** (*fish'ən*) a cleaving. reproduction by dividing: the splitting of the nucleus of an atom into two roughly equal parts accompanied by great release of energy. —*adjs* **fiss'ionable** capable of nuclear fission; **fiss'-ive.**—*n.* **fissure** (*fish'ər*) an act of cleaving. a narrow opening—chasm, cleft, groove: a sulcus, esp. one of the furrows on the surface of the brain, as the longitudinal fissure separating the hemispheres.—*v.t.* to crack, cleave, divide.—*adj.* **fiss'ured** cleft, divided.— *ns.* **fissip'arism** (L. *parĕre,* bring forth), **fissipar'ity.** —*adj.* **fissip'arous** reproducing by fission.—*adv* **fissip'arously.**—**fission bomb** a bomb deriving its energy from atomic fission; **fission reactor** a nuclear reactor in which nuclear fission takes place. [L *findĕre, fissum,* to cleave.]

fissure, fissured. See **fissile.**

fist *fist, n.* the closed or clenched hand: handwriting (*coll.*): an index (*print.*).—*v.t.* to strike or grip with the fist.—*n.* **fist'ful** a handful.—**fist'icuff** a blow with the fist: (*in pl.*) boxing: (in *pl*) a fight with fists [O E *fȳst.*]

fistula *fist'ū-la, n.* a narrow passage or duct: an artificially- made opening (*med.*). a long narrow pipe-like ulcer (*path.*).—*pl.* **fist'ulae** (*-lē*), **fist'ulas.**— *adjs.* **fist'ūlar, fist'ūlose, fist'ūlous.** [L *fistula,* a pipe.]

fit¹ *fit, adj* suitable: in suitable condition: meeting required standards· convenient· befitting: in good condition: in good health.—*n.* success in fitting: adjustment and correspondence in shape and size: a thing (esp. a garment) that fits.—*v.t.* to make suitable or able: to alter to make so as to be in adjustment. to adjust: to piece together: to be suitable or becoming for. to be of such size and shape as to adjust closely to: to be in agreement or correspondence with· to furnish, supply —*v.i* to be suitable or becoming: to go into place with accurate adjustment

to space: to be of such size and shape as to be able to do so.—*pr.p.* **fitt'ing;** *pa.t.* and *pa.p.* **fitt'ed.**—*adv.* **fit'ly** (*compar.* **fit'lier;** *superl.* **fit'liest**).—*ns.* **fit'-ment** an article of furniture or equipment: a fitting; **fit'ness.**—*adj.* **fitt'ed** (of a cover, clothing, etc.) made, cut, sewn, etc. to fit exactly: (of a cupboard, etc.) constructed to fit a particular space and attached to, or built into, the wall of a room: (of a room) fully furnished with (matching) fitted cupboards, etc.—*n.* **fitt'er** he who, or that which fits or makes fit: one who fits on clothes: one who assembles the parts of a machine, etc.—*adj.* **fitt'ing** fit: appropriate.—*n.* anything used in fitting up, esp., in *pl.,* equipment accessories: a fixture: the work of a fitter: the act or time of trying on an article of clothing so that it can be adjusted to fit the wearer.—*adv.* **fitt'ingly.**—**fit'-up** temporary, improvised stage and properties (*theat.*): a frame-up, esp. by the police (*slang*).—**fit in** to find enough room or time for someone or something: to be, or cause to be, in harmony (with); **fit on** to try on. to try on a garment upon; **fit out** to furnish, equip; **fit up** to provide with fittings: to frame (*slang*).

fit² *fit, n.* an attack of illness, esp. epilepsy: a convulsion or paroxysm. an access, temporary attack, or outburst of anything, as laughter: a sudden effort or motion: a mood or passing humour.—*adj* **fit'ful** marked by sudden impulses: capriciously intermittent. spasmodic.—*adv.* **fit'fully.**—*n.* **fit'fulness.**— **fits and starts** spasmodic and irregular bursts of activity. [O.E. *fitt,* a struggle.]

fitch *fich, n.* a polecat: polecat fur: a paint-brush of polecat-hair. a small hog's-hair brush.—*ns.* **fitch'et, fitchew** (*fich'ōō*) the polecat or its fur. [M.Du. *visse* and O.Fr. *fissle, fissau,* from the root of Du. *visse,* nasty.]

five *fiv, n.* four and one: a symbol (5, v, etc.) representing that number: a group of five: a score of five points, strokes, etc.: a card with five pips: an article of the size so numbered: the fifth hour after midnight or midday: the age of five years:—*adj.* of the number five: five years old.—*adj* and *adv.* **five'fold** in five divisions: five times as much: folded in five thicknesses.—*n.* **fiv'er** (*coll*) a five-pound note: a five-dollar note (*U.S.*).—**five'pence.**—*adj.* **five'-penny.**—**five'pins** a game with five 'pins', resembling ninepins and tenpins (*adj.* **five'pin** as in *fivepin bowling alley*).—**bunch of fives** (*slang*) the fist; **five-day week** a week, five days of which are working days; **five-o'clock shadow** (*coll*) the new growth of hair that becomes noticeable on a man's shaven face in the late afternoon. [O.E. *fīf.*]

fives *fivz, n.pl.* a ball game played with the (gloved) hand (or a bat) in a walled court.

fix *fiks, v.t* to make firm or fast: to establish: to drive in: to settle. to make or keep permanent, solid, rigid, steady, or motionless: to fasten or attach: to put to rights, mend: to arrange, attend to (a matter; sometimes by means of trickery): to prepare: to prevent from causing further trouble (*slang*). to get even with (*slang*): to chastise (*slang*).—*v.i.* to settle or remain permanently: to become firm, stable or permanent. —*n.* a difficulty (*coll*) a dilemma (*coll.*): the position of an aircraft as calculated from instrument readings: a shot of heroin or other drug (*slang*).—*adj.* **fix'able** capable of being fixed.—*ns.* **fixa'tion** the act of fixing, or state of being fixed: steadiness, firmness. state in which a body does not evaporate: conversion of atmospheric nitrogen into a combined form: emotional arrest of personality, instinctive forces maintaining their earlier channels of gratification: loosely, an abnormal attachment, or an obsession: **fix'ative** a fixing agent.—*adj* **fixed** settled: not apt to evaporate. steadily directed: fast, lasting, per-

manent· not varying or subject to alteration —*adv*.
fix'edly.—*ns* **fix'edness; fix'er; fix'ing** the act or process of making fixed: arrangement: (in *pl*.) adjuncts, trimmings· (in *pl*) equipment, **fix'ity** fixedness —*ns* **fix'ture** fixing: a movable that has become fastened to land or to a house. a fixed article of furniture: a thing or person permanently established in a place: a fixed or appointed time or event, as a horse-race —**fixed capital** see **capital; fixed idea** a monomania; **fixed odds** a betting method whereby a stated amount per unit stake is offered for a certain result or combination of results.—*adj*. **fixed'-pen'alty** of or relating to an offence, such as illegal parking, the penalty for which is invariable and obligatory, e g. a fine which may be imposed and paid without the offender appearing in court.—**fixed-wing aircraft** an aircraft in which the wings are attached to the fuselage, as opposed to e.g. a helicopter with rotating 'wings' or propellers; **fix on** to single out, decide for; **fix up** to arrange or make arrangements for: to settle: to put to rights, attend to [L. *figĕre, fixus,* to fix, prob. through L L *fixāre*]

fizgig, fisgig *fiz'gig, n.* a giddy girl: a firework of damp powder: a gimcrack, a crotchet: a harpoon (also **fish'-gig**). [**gig**.]

fizz, fiz *fiz, v.t.* to make a hissing or sputtering sound: —*pr.p.* **fizz'ing;** *pa.t.* and *pa.p.* **fizzed.**—*n.* a sputtering sound. a frothy drink, esp. champagne.—*n* **fizz'er** that which fizzes. anything excellent (*coll.*): a very fast ball.—*n.* and *adj.* **fizz'ing.**—*v t* **fizz'le** to hiss or sputter: to go out with a sputtering sound (often with *out*): to come to nothing. be a fiasco, fail (often with *out*) —*n.* an abortive effort.—*adj.* **fizz'y.** —**be fizzing** (*coll.*) to be very angry [Formed from the sound.]

fjord. Same as **fiord.**

flabbergast *flab'ər-gäst,* (*coll.*) *v.t.* to stun, confound. [Prob. conn. with **flabby** and **gast,** to astonish.]

flabby *flab'i, adj.* soft, yielding: hanging loose —*ns.* **flab** (*coll*) excess body fat; **flabb'iness.** [**flap**.]

flaccid *flak'sid, fla'sid, adj.* limp: flabby: lax· easily yielding to pressure: soft and weak: clammy.—*adv.* **flac'cidly.**—*ns.* **flac'cidness, flaccid'ity.** [L. *flaccidus—flaccus,* flabby.]

flag¹ *flag, v.i.* to droop: to flap feebly: to grow languid or spiritless:—*pr.p.* **flagg'ing;** *pa.t.* and *pa.p.* **flagged.**—*n.* **flagg'iness.** [Perh. O.Fr. *flac*—L. *flaccus;* prob. influenced by imit. forms as **flap**.]

flag² *flag, n.* a piece usually of bunting with a design, used as an emblem for military or naval purposes, signalling, decoration, display, propaganda, etc.: a conspicuous sign to mark a position, e.g. of a golfhole, or convey information: a flagship: a bushy tail —*v.t.* to indicate, inform by flag-signals.—*v.t* to decorate with flags: to inform by flag-signals —**flag'-cap'tain** the captain of a flagship; **flag'-day** a day on which collectors levy contributions to a fund in exchange for small flags as badges to secure immunity for the rest of the day; **flag'-lieuten'ant** an officer in a flagship, corresponding to an aide-de-camp in the army; **flag'-off'icer** a naval officer privileged to carry a flag denoting his rank—admiral, vice-admiral, rear-admiral, or commodore; **flag'ship** the ship carrying an admiral and flying his flag. anything of a similar level of importance or pre-eminence (*fig.*); **flag'pole, flag'staff, flag'stick** a pole, etc., for displaying a flag. —**dip the flag** to lower the flag and then hoist it—a token of respect; **flag down** to signal (e.g. a car) to stop; **flag of convenience** a foreign flag under which a shipping company registers its tonnage to avoid taxation or other burdens at home; **flag of distress** a flag displayed as a signal of distress—usually upside down or at half-mast; **flag of truce** a white flag displayed

during war when some pacific communication is desired; **show, carry, the flag** to put in an appearance, or otherwise ensure that one, or the nation, firm, etc.· one represents, is not overlooked; **strike or lower the flag** to pull down the flag as a token of relinquishment of command, respect, submission, or surrender.

flag³ *flag, n.* a stone that separates in slabs: a flat paving-stone —*v t.* to pave with flagstones.—*n.* **flagg'ing** flagstones: a pavement thereof.—*adj.* **flagg'y.**—**flag'stone.** [O.N. *flaga,* a slab.]

flagellum *flə-jel'əm, n.* a scourge. a long runner (*bot.*): a long cilium or whip-like appendage (*biol.*):—*pl.* **flagell'a.**—*v.t.* **flag'ellate** to scourge —*adj.* having a flagellum or flagella.—*adjs.* **flag'ellated; flag'ellant** scourging.—*n.* one who scourges, esp himself in religious discipline.—*ns.* **flag'ellantism; flagella'tion; flag'ellator.**—*adjs* **flag'ellatory; flagelli'ferous; flagell'iform.** [L. *flagellum,* dim. of *flagrum,* a whip.]

flageolet¹ *flaj-ō-let', flaj', n.* a small fipple-flute. [Fr , dim. of O.Fr. *flageol, flajol,* a pipe.]

flageolet² *flaj-ō-let', n.* a variety of kidney bean. [Corr of Fr. *fageolet;* L. *faseolus.*]

flagon *flag'ən, n.* a large, esp. wide, bottle: a liquorjug. [Fr. *flacon—flascon*—L L. *flascō, -ōnis;* see **flask.**]

flagrant *flā'grənt, adj.* notorious: outrageous, conspicuous.—*ns.* **flā'grance, flā'grancy.**—*adv.* **flā'grantly.** [L. *flagrāns, -antis,* pr.p. of *flagrāre,* to burn.]

flagrante delicto *flə-gran'tē di-lik'tō, fla-gran'te, dä-lik'tō,* (L.) in the very act (lit. 'while the crime is blazing')

flail *flāl, n.* an implement for threshing corn, consisting of a wooden bar (the *swingle*) hinged or tied to a handle: a mediaeval weapon with spiked iron swingle. —*v.t* to strike with, or as if with, a flail.—Also *v.t.* [O.E. *fligel,* influenced by O.Fr. *flaiel,* prob. from L. *flagellum,* a scourge.]

flair *flār, n.* intuitive discernment: faculty for nosing out: popularly and loosely, a natural aptitude. [Fr., sense of smell.]

flak *flak, n.* anti-aircraft protection, missiles, or fragments (*mil slang*): adverse criticism: heated disagreement, dissension.—**flak jacket** a heavy protective jacket reinforced with metal. [Initials of Ger. *Flieger-* (or *Flug-)abwehrkanone,* anti-aircraft cannon.]

flake¹ *flāk, n.* a small flat scale or layer: a very small loose mass, as of snow: a spark or detached flame.— *v t.* to form into flakes.—*v.i.* to come off in flakes.— *n.* **flak'iness.**—*adj.* **flak'y.**—**flake out** to collapse from weariness or illness. [Perh. conn. with O.N. *flöke,* flock of wool; O.H.G. *floccho.*]

flake² *flāk, n.* a frame or rack. [Cf. O.N. *flake;* Du. *vlaak.*]

flam *flam, n.* a whim (*arch.*): an idle fancy (*arch.*): a falsehood.—*v.t.* to deceive: to get, manage, etc. by deception. [Perh. **flim-flam** or **flamfew.**]

flambé *flam'bā, flä-bā, adj* (also **flambéed** *flām'bād*) in cookery, prepared or served with a dressing of flaming liquor, usu. brandy [Fr., pa.p. of *flamber,* to flame, singe.]

flambeau *flam'bō, n.* a flaming torch:—*pl.* **flam'beaux** or **-beaus** (*-bōz*). [Fr.,—O.Fr *flambe*—L. *flamma*]

flamboyant *flam-boi'ənt, adj.* gorgeously coloured: (of person, style, action, etc.) ostentatious, colourful.—*ns.* **flamboy'ance, flamboy'ancy.**—*adv.* **flamboy'antly.** [Fr., pr.p. of *flamboyer,* to blaze.]

flame *flām, n* a gaseous matter undergoing combustion: the gleam or blaze of a fire: rage: ardour of temper: vigour of thought: warmth of affection: love or its object.—*v.i.* to burn as flame: to break out in passion.—*v.t.* to set aflame.—*adj.* **flam'ing** brilliantly red: gaudy: violent: furious: flagrant: often used intensively or to express irritation, etc. (*coll.*) —*adv.* **flam'ingly.**—*n.* **flammabil'ity.**—*adjs.* **flamm'able** inflammable; **flam'y** pertaining to, or like, flame.—*adj.* **flame'-coloured** of the colour of flame, bright reddish-yellow.—**flame'-thrower** an apparatus for throwing jets of flame in warfare; **flame'-tree** a thick-stemmed Australian tree with glossy leaves and scarlet bell-shaped flowers. [O.Fr. *flambe*—L. *flamma.*]

flamenco *flä-meng'kō,* *n.* a type of gypsy song or dance from Andalusia:—*pl.* **flamen'cos.** [Sp., 'Flemish', flamingo, gypsy.]

flamfew *flam'fū, n.* a fantastic trifle. [Fr *fanfelue.*]

flamingo *flə-ming'gō, n.* a tropical or subtropical bird of a pink or bright-red colour, with long legs and neck:—*pl.* **flaming'o(e)s.** [Sp *flamengo* (now *flamenco*).]

flammability, flammable. See **flame.**

flan *flan,* *n.* a flat open tart. [O.Fr. *flaon*—L.L. *fladō, -ōnis*—O.H.G. *flado.*]

flanch *flanch, flanch, -sh,* **flaunch** *flonch, -sh, v.i.* to widen, esp. outwards or upwards, to flare (often with *out*) —*v.t.* to cause to slope in towards the top (often with *up*).—*n.* **fla(u)nch'ing** the action or state of the verb: (**flaunching**) a sloping piece of cement e.g round the base of a chimney-pot.

flange *flanj, n.* a projecting or raised edge or flank, as of a wheel or of a rail.—*v.i.* to widen out.—*v.t.* to put a flange on.—*adj.* **flanged.** [Perh. conn. with **flank.**]

flank *flangk, n.* the side of an animal from the ribs to the thigh: the side or wing of anything, esp. of an army or fleet: a body of soldiers on the right or left extremity.—*v.t.* to be on, pass round, attack, threaten, or protect the flank of.—*n.* **flank'er** a fortification that commands the flank of an assailing force: one of the two outside men of the second row of the scrum (also **flank forward, wing forward**; *Rugby football*). [Fr. *flanc.*]

flannel *flan'əl, n.* a light woollen textile used for clothing: the garment itself: a piece of this or other cloth used for washing or rubbing, now esp. a piece of towelling for washing the face, a face-cloth: flattery, soft-soap, words intended to hide one's ignorance, true opinions, etc. (*coll.*): (in *pl.*) trousers, esp. of flannel or a similar cloth.—*v.t.* to wrap in flannel: to rub with a flannel: to flatter, to soft-soap, to utter flannel (*coll.*).—*n.* **flannelette'** a cotton imitation of flannel.—*adjs.* **flann'elled; flann'elly.**—**flann'elboard, flann'elgraph** a board covered with flannel or felt, and letters, pictures, etc., backed with material which will stick when pressed against the board. [Poss. O.Fr. *flaine*, blanket, or Welsh *gwlanengwlan*, wool.]

flap *flap, n.* the blow or motion of a broad loose object: anything broad and flexible hanging loose, as material covering an opening: skin or flesh detached from the underlying part for covering and growing over the end of an amputated limb: a fluster, a panic (*coll.*): any surface attached to the wing of an aircraft which can be adjusted in flight to alter the lift as a whole: an 'r' sound produced by a single light tap of the tongue against the alveolar ridge or uvula (*phon.*).—*v.t.* to beat or move with a flap: to fluster. —*v.i.* to move, as wings: to hang like a flap: to get into a panic or fluster:—*pr.p.* **flapp'ing;** *pa.t.* and *pa.p.* **flapped.**—*n.* **flapp'er** one who or that which flaps: a flipper: a young wild duck or partridge: in the 1920s, a flighty young girl (*slang*).—**flap'doodle** gross flattery, etc.: nonsense; **flap'jack** a kind of broad,

flat pancake: a biscuit made with rolled oats and syrup: a flat face-powder compact. [Prob. imit.]

flare *flār, v.i.* to spread: to wave: to widen out bellwise: to burn with a glaring, unsteady light: to glitter, flash: to blaze up, lit. or in anger (with *up*).—*v.t.* to display glaringly: to dispose of (superfluous gas or oil) by means of a flare (with *off*; *chem. engineering*). —*n.* a widening out, as in the bell of a horn, a bowl, a skirt: an unsteady glare: an unshaded flame: a sudden blaze: a torch: a signalling light: (the flame or light produced by) a device composed of combustible material, activated to give warning, illumination, etc.: a device for the safe disposal of superfluous gas, oil, etc. by burning in the open (*chem. engineering*).— *adj.* **flar'ing.**—*adv.* **fla'ringly.**—*adj.* **fla'ry.**—**flare'path** a path lit up to enable an aircraft to land or take off when natural visibility is insufficient; **flare'-up.** [Poss. conn. with Norw. *flara,* to blaze.]

flash *flash, n.* a momentary gleam of light: (the momentary illumination from) a flash-bulb (*phot.*): a sudden burst, as of merriment: a moment, an instant: a sudden rush of water: a board for deepening or directing a stream of water: a bright garter or ribbon worn on the hose with knickerbockers or kilt, a small portion showing below the knee: a distinctive mark on a uniform: a sticker or overprinted label on a piece of merchandise advertising a reduction in price, etc.: a brief news dispatch by telegraph —*adj.* showy: vulgar.—*v.i.* to break forth, as a sudden light (*lit.* and *fig.*): to give forth flashes of light: to sparkle brilliantly: to blaze out: to break out into intellectual brilliancy: to burst out into violence: to move like a flash: to expose oneself indecently (*slang*).—*v.t.* to cause to flash: to send by some startling or sudden means: to show briefly.—*n.* **flash'er** one who or that which flashes: a device for turning off and on lights as advertising, warning, etc. signs: the signs themselves: on a vehicle, a direction indicator: a person given to indecent exposure (*slang*).—*adv.* **flash'ily.**—*ns.* **flash'iness; flash'ing** the act of blazing: a sudden burst, as of water: a strip put over a junction to make it watertight: the practice of indecently exposing oneself (*slang*).—*adj.* emitting flashes: sparkling.—*adj.* **flash'y** dazzling for a moment: showy but empty: gaudy: tawdry —**flash'-back, -forward** in a film, a scene of the past, future, inserted as comment or explanation; **flash'-bulb** an oxygen-filled electric bulb in which aluminium or other foil or filament may be fired to provide a brilliant flash, esp. for illuminating a photographic subject; **flash card** a card on which a word is printed or written, to be shown briefly to a child as an aid to learning; **flash'cube** a plastic cube containing four flash-bulbs; **flash'-gun** device holding and firing a flash-bulb; **flash'light** a light that flashes periodically: a sudden light used to take photographs: an electric torch; **flash'-point** the temperature at which a liquid gives off enough inflammable vapour to flash when a light is applied to it: a point in the development of a tense situation when violent action takes place: a place in the world where an outbreak of hostilities may occur at any time as a result of tension. —**flash in the pan** see **pan; news'flash** brief preliminary dispatch about news just becoming known [Prob imit.]

flask *flask, n.* a narrow-necked vessel for holding liquids: a bottle: a usu. flat pocket-bottle: a horn or metal vessel for carrying powder. [O.E. *flasce;* prob. from L L. *flascō*—L. *vasculum,* a flask.]

flat *flat, adj.* smooth: level: monotonous: uniform: fixed, unvarying: no longer brisk or sparkling: defeated: failing of effect: dejected: downright, out-and-out, sheer: (of feet) having little or no arch: (of shoes) not having a raised heel: relatively low (*mus*):

below the right pitch (*mus.*): having flats in the key-signature (*mus.*): (of a battery) dead, unable to generate.—*n.* a level part: a plain: a tract covered by shallow water: something broad: a story or floor of a house, esp. one, or part of one, used as a separate residence: the floor of a particular compartment (*naut.*): a flat piece of scenery slid or lowered on to the stage: an insipid passage: a simpleton, a dupe (*coll.*): a character (♭) that lowers a note a semitone (*mus.*): a note so lowered (*mus.*): a punctured tyre.— *adv.* in or to a flat position: evenly: too low in pitch: without qualification: exactly (used in giving time taken for e.g. a race) —*n.* **flat'let** a small flat of two or three rooms.—*adv.* **flat'ly.**—*n.* **flat'ness.**—*adj.* **flatt'ed** divided into flats.—*v.t.* **flatt'en** to make flat: to knock to the ground: to knock out: to amaze.—*v.i.* to become flat.—*adj.* **flatt'ish** somewhat flat.—*adj.* or *adv.* **flat'ways, flat'wise** with or on the flat side.— **flat'boat** large flat-bottomed boat for floating goods downstream.—*adj.* **flat broke** (*coll.*) having no money whatsoever.—**flat'fish** marine fish that habitually lies on one side, with unsymmetrical flat body —flounder, turbot, etc.—*adj.* **flat'-footed** having flat feet: ponderous: unimaginative: uninspired.—**flat's footedness; flat'iron** an iron for smoothing cloth; **flat'mate** a person with whom one shares a flat; **flat's race** a race over open or clear ground; **flat rate** a fixed uniform rate; **flat spin** rotation about a horizontal axis: confused excitement; **flat tyre** a punctured tyre; **flat'worm** a tapeworm or other member of the Platyhelminthes.—**flatten out** to bring an aeroplane into a horizontal position; **flat out** at full speed: using every effort; **that's flat** I tell you plainly; **the flat** the horse flat-racing season. [O.N. *flatr*, flat.]

flatter *flat'ǝr*, *v.t.* to treat with insincere praise and servile attentions: to please with false hopes or undue praise: to overpraise: to represent over-favourably: to coax: to please with belief: to gratify.—*n.* **flatt'-erer.**—*adj.* **flatt'ering.**—*adv.* **flatt'eringly.**—*n.* **flatt'ery** exaggerated or insincere praise. [Conn. with O.Fr. *flater*.]

flatus *flā'tǝs*, *n.* gas generated in the stomach or intestines.—*ns.* **flatulence** (*flat'ū-lǝns*), **flat'ülency** distension of stomach or bowels by gases formed during digestion: emptiness of utterance.—*adj.* **flat'ülent.**—*adv.* **flat'ülently.** [L. *flātus*, *-ūs*, a blowing—*flāre*, to blow.]

flaunch. A variant of **flanch.**

flaunt *flönt*, *v.i.* to move ostentatiously: to carry a gaudy or saucy appearance.—*v.t.* to display ostentatiously —*n.* **flaunt'er.**—*adjs.* **flaunt'ing, flaunt'y.**—*adv.* **flaunt'ingly.** [Prob. Scand.]

flautist *flöt'ist*, *n.* a flute player. [It *flautista*.]

flavour *flā'vǝr*, *n.* that quality of anything which affects the smell or taste: a smack or relish: characteristic quality or atmosphere (*fig*) —*v.t.* to impart flavour to.—*adj.* **flā'vorous.**—*n.* **flā'vouring** any substance used to give a flavour.—*adjs.* **flā'vourless; flā'voursome.** [O.Fr. *flaur*; prob influenced by *savour*.]

flaw *flo*, *n.* a break, a crack: a defect.—*v.t.* to crack or break.—*adjs.* **flawed; flaw'less.** [O N. *flaga*, a slab]

flax *flaks*, *n.* the fibres of the plant Linum, which are woven into linen cloth: the plant itself.—*adjs.* **flax'en** made of or resembling flax· light yellow; **flax'y** like flax: of a light colour.—**flax'-bush, flax'-lil'y** a New Zealand plant (Phormium) of the lily family, yielding a valuable fibre, **New Zealand flax; flax'-dresser** one who prepares flax for the spinner by the successive processes of rippling, retting, grassing, breaking, and scutching; **flax'-seed** linseed [O E *flæx* (W S *fleax*)]

flay *flā*, *v.t.* to strip off the skin from: to flog: to subject to savage criticism.—*n.* **flay'er.** [O.E. *flēan*.]

flea *flē*, *n.* any of an order of wingless, very agile, blood-sucking insects.—**flea'-bag** (*slang*) a sleeping-bag: a distasteful place, esp. used of lodgings; **flea's bane** a name for various composite plants (Erigeron, Pulicaria, etc.) whose strong smell is said to drive away fleas; **flea'-bite** the bite of a flea: a small mark caused by the bite: a trifle (*fig.*).—*adj.* **flea'-bitten** bitten by fleas: mean (*fig.*): having small reddish spots on a lighter ground, esp. of horses.—**flea's circus** a show of performing fleas; **flea market** (*coll.*) a shop, etc. selling second-hand goods, orig. esp. clothes; **flea'-pit** a public building, e.g a cinema, supposedly infested with vermin.—**a flea in one's ear** a stinging rebuff. [O.E. *flēah*.]

flèche *flesh*, *n.* a slender spire rising from the intersection of the nave and transepts in some large churches. [Fr., arrow.]

fleck *flek*, *n.* a spot or speckle: a little bit of a thing.— *adjs.* **flecked** spotted, dappled. [O.N. *flekkr*, a spot.]

fled *fled*, *pa.t.* and *pa.p.* of **flee.**

fledge *flej*, *v.t.* to furnish with feathers or wings.—*v.i.* to acquire feathers for flying.—*adj.* **fledged.**—*n.* **fledg'ling** (*rarely* **fledge'ling**) a bird just fledged: a very immature or inexperienced person. [M.E. *flugge, flegge*—an assumed O.E. (Kentish) *flecge*.]

flee *flē*, *v.i.* to run away, as from danger: to disappear. —*v t.* to keep at a distance from: to run away from, leave hurriedly:—*pr.p.* **flee'ing;** *pa.t* and *pa.p.* **fled.** —*n* **flé'er.** [O.E. *flēon*.]

fleece *flēs*, *n.* a sheep's coat of wool: the wool shorn from a sheep at one time: anything like a fleece.—*v.t.* to shear: to plunder: to charge (a person) exorbitantly: to cover, as with wool.—*adjs.* **fleeced** having a fleece; **fleece'less.**—*n.* **fleec'er** one who strips, plunders or charges exorbitantly.—*adj.* **fleec'y** woolly: like a fleece. [O.E. *flēos*.]

fleer *flēr*, *v.i.* to make wry faces in contempt: to leer.— *v.t.* to mock.—*n.* mockery. [Cf. Norw. *flira*, Sw. *flissa*, to titter.]

fleet[1] *flēt*, *n.* a number of ships (birds, aircraft, motor-cars, etc.) in company or otherwise associated: a navy: a division of a navy under an admiral. [O.E. *flēot*, a ship—*flēotan*, to float.]

fleet[2] *flēt*, *adj.* swift: nimble: transient.—*n.* **fleet'ness.** [Prob. O.N. *fliōtr*, swift; but ult. cog. with succeeding word.]

fleet[3] *flēt*, *v t.* to flit, pass swiftly.—*adj.* **fleet'ing** passing quickly: temporary.—*adv.* **fleet'ingly.** [O.E. *flēotan*, to float.]

Fleet Street *flēt strēt*, journalism or its ways and traditions, from the London street with many newspaper offices.

Flemish *flem'ish*, *adj.* of or belonging to the Flemings, or Flanders —*n.* the Flemings as a people: one of the two languages of Belgium, virtually identical with Dutch —*n.* **Flem'ing** a native of Flanders: a Flemish-speaking Belgian [Du *Vlaamsch*.]

flench *flench*, **flense** *flens*, **flinch** *flinch*, *vs.t.* to cut up the blubber of, as a whale: to flay. [Dan *flense*.]

flesh *flesh*, *n.* muscular tissue: all the living substance of the body of similar composition to muscle: the soft substance that covers the bones of animals: animal food: the bodies of beasts and (sometimes) birds, not fish: the body, not the soul: animals, or animal nature· human bodily nature: mankind: kindred: bodily appetites· the soft substance of fruit, esp. the part fit to be eaten —*v.t.* to train to an appetite for flesh, as dogs for hunting: to use upon flesh, as a sword to use for the first time —*adj* **fleshed** (*flesht*) having flesh.—*ns.* **flesh'er** an instrument for scraping hides: a butcher (esp. *Scot.*); **flesh'iness.**—*n.pl.* **flesh'ings** actors' flesh-coloured tights.—*adj.* **flesh'-less** without flesh: lean.—*n.* **flesh'liness.**—*adj.* **flesh'ly** corporeal: carnal: not spiritual.—Also *adv.*—*adj.* **flesh'y** fat: pulpy: plump.—**flesh'-brush** a brush used for rubbing the skin to excite circulation; **flesh'-colour** the normal colour of the skin of a European; **flesh'-fly** (esp. Sarcophaga) whose larvae feed on flesh; **flesh'-pot** a pot or vessel in which flesh is cooked: abundance of flesh: (usu. in *pl.*) high living; **flesh'-wound** a wound not reaching beyond the flesh. —**flesh and blood** bodily or human nature; **flesh out** to give substance to, elaborate on (an idea, etc.); **in the flesh** in bodily life, alive: incarnate: in person, actually present; **make someone's flesh creep** to arouse a feeling of horror in someone; **one flesh** united in marriage; **one's own flesh and blood** one's own kindred. [O.E. *flǣsc*.]

fletch *flech*, *v.t.* to feather.—*n.* **fletch'er** one who makes arrows. [Fr. *flèche*, an arrow, O.Fr. *flecher*, a fletcher.]

fleur-de-lis, -lys *flær-də-lē', -lēs'*, *n.* the iris: an ornament and heraldic bearing of disputed origin (an iris, three lilies, etc.), borne by the kings of France:—*pl.* **fleurs-de-lis, fleurs-de-lys** *(flær-)*. [Fr.; *lis*, being O.Fr. *liz*—L. *lilium*, lily.]

flew[1] *floō*, *pa.t.* of **fly**; coll. used for **fled** *(pa.t.)*.

flew[2] *floō*, *n.* a dog's pendulous chop (usu. in *pl.*).

flex *fleks*, *v.t.* and *v.i.* to bend.—*n.* a bending: a flexible cord or line, esp. of insulated wire.—*n.* **flexibil'ity.**—*adj.* **flex'ible** easily bent: pliant: docile. —*n.* **flex'ibleness.**—*adv.* **flex'ibly.**—*n.pl.* **flex'ihours** hours of working under flexitime.—*adj.* **flex'ile** *(-īl, -əl)* flexible.—*ns.* **flexion** *(flek'shən)* a bend: a fold: the action of a flexor muscle: inflexion *(gram.)*; **flexi'time, Flextime**® a system of flexible working hours in which an agreed total of hours may be worked at times to suit the worker, often with the proviso that each day certain hours **(core times)** are included; **flex'or** a muscle that bends a joint, as opposed to *extensor.*—*adjs.* **flex'uose, flex'uous** full of windings and turnings: undulating; **flexural** *(flek'shər-əl)*.—*n.* **flex'ure** a bend or turning: the curving of a line or surface *(math.)*: the bending of loaded beams.—**flexible disc** *(comput.)* a floppy disc. —**flex one's muscles** to cause the muscles of one's arms, shoulders, etc. to contract, in order to display them, test them as a preliminary to a trial of strength, etc. (often *fig.*). [L. *flectĕre, flexum,* to bend.]

flibbertigibbet *flib'ər-ti-jib'it*, *n.* a flighty person: an imp. [Poss. imit. of meaningless chatter.]

flick[1] *flik*, *v.t.* to strike lightly, as with a lash or a finger-nail.—*n.* a stroke of this kind.—**flick'-knife** a knife the blade of which springs out on pressure of a button in the handle.—**flick through** to turn the pages of (a book, etc.) idly, or in order to get a rough impression of it. [Echoic.]

flick[2] *flik*, *(slang) n.* a cinematograph film: *(pl.)* a cinematograph performance. [**flicker.**]

flicker *flik'ər*, *v.i.* to flutter and move the wings, as a bird: to burn unsteadily, as a flame.—*n.* an act of flickering, a flickering movement or light.—*adv.* **flick'eringly.** [O.E. *flicorian*; imit.]

flier, flies. See under **fly**.

flight[1] *flīt*, *n.* a passing through the air: a soaring: distance flown: a series of steps: a flock of birds flying together: the birds produced in the same season: a volley: the power of flying: the art or the act of flying with wings or in an aeroplane or other machine: a unit of the Air Force answering to a platoon in the army: a regular air journey, numbered and at a fixed time: a line of hurdles across a race-track.—*v.t.* to cause

(birds) to fly up: to shoot (wildfowl) in flight: to put a feather in (an arrow): to impart a deceptive trajectory to (a cricket ball).—*adv.* **flight'ily.**—*n.* **flight'iness.** —*adjs.* **flight'less** without power of flying; **flight'y** changeable: giddy-minded.—**flight crew** the members of an aircraft crew whose responsibility is operation and navigation; **flight'-deck** the deck of an aircraft-carrier where the planes take off or land: the compartment for the crew in an aircraft; **flight'-feather** a quill of a bird's wing; **flight'-lieuten'ant** an Air Force officer of rank corresponding to naval lieutenant or army captain; **flight path** the course (to be) taken by an aircraft, spacecraft, etc.; **flight plan** a statement of the proposed schedule of an aircraft flight; **flight'-recorder** a device which records on tape or wire information about the functioning of an aircraft and its systems.—**flight of fancy** an instance of rather free speculation or indulgence in imagination; **in the first, top, flight** in the highest class. [O.E. *flyht*—*flēogan*, to fly.]

flight[2] *flīt*, *n.* an act of fleeing.—**take (to) flight** to flee: to disappear quickly *(fig.)*. [Assumed O.E. *flyht*; cf. *flēon*, to flee.]

flim-flam *flim'flam*, *n.* a trick, deception: idle, meaningless talk. [Cf. **flam.**]

flimsy *flim'zi*, *adj.* thin: without solidity, strength, or reason: weak.—*n.* transfer-paper: a carbon copy on thin paper.—*adv.* **flim'sily** in a flimsy manner.—*n.* **flim'siness.** [First in 18th century; prob. suggested by **flim.**]

flinch[1] *flinch*, *-sh*, *v.i.* to shrink back, from pain, fear, etc.: to fail.—*n.* **flinch'er.**—*n.* and *adj.* **flinch'ing.**—*adv.* **flinch'ingly.** [Prob. conn. with M.E. *fleechen*, O.Fr. *flechir*, L. *flectĕre*, to bend.]

flinch[2]. Same as **flench.**

flinder *flin'dər*, *n.* a splinter or small fragment—usually in *pl.* [Norw. *flindra*, a splinter.]

fling *fling*, *v.t.* to throw, cast, toss: to send forth: to send suddenly: to cause to fall.—*v.i.* to throw the body about: to kick out: to dash or rush, throw oneself impetuously:—*pa.t.* and *pa.p.* **flung.**—*n.* a cast or throw: a try: a passing attack: a jibe: a taunt: complete freedom, full enjoyment of pleasure: a lively Scottish country-dance.—**full fling** at the utmost speed, recklessly. [Cf. O.N. *flengja*; Sw. *flänga*.]

flint *flint*, *n.* a hard mineral, a variety of quartz, from which fire is readily struck with steel: a concretion of silica: a piece of flint, esp. one used for striking fire, or one manufactured into an implement: anything proverbially hard.—*adj.* made of flint: hard.—*adv.* **flint'ily.**—*n.* **flint'iness.**—*adj.* **flint'y** consisting of, abounding in, or like flint: hard: cruel: obdurate.—**flint'-glass** a very fine and pure lead glass, originally made of calcined flints; **flint'lock** a gunlock or gun with a flint. [O.E. *flint*.]

flip *flip*, *v.t.* and *v.i.* to fillip: to flick: to flap.—*n.* a fillip: a flick: a hot drink of beer and spirits sweetened, or similar concoction: a trip in an aeroplane, a pleasure-flight *(coll.)*.—*adj.* flippant: pert, over-smart.—*n.* **flipp'er** a limb adapted for swimming: a rubber foot-covering imitating an animal's flipper, worn by swimmers, divers, etc.—*adj.* and *adv.* **flipp'ing** *(coll.)* nasty, unpleasant: often used intensively or meaninglessly.—*adv.* **flip'-flap, flip'-flop'** with repeated flapping.—**flip'flop** a form of somersault: orig., and still in U.S., a bistable pair of valves or transistors, two stable states being switched by pulses: in Britain, a similar circuit with one stable state temporarily achieved by pulse: a type of flimsy sandal, esp. one held on the foot by a thong between the toes; **flip'-side** the side of a gramophone record carrying the song, etc., of lesser importance, the reverse of the side on whose merits the record is expected to sell.—**flip one's lid** (*slang*) to go mad. [Cf. **fillip, flap.**]

flippant *flip'ənt, adj.* pert and frivolous of speech: showing disrespectful levity.—*ns.* **flipp'ancy, flipp'antness** pert fluency of speech: pertness: levity.—*adv.* **flipp'antly.** [Cf. **flip**, and O.N. *fleipa*, to prattle.]

flirt *flûrt, v.t.* to jerk: to move about quickly like a fan, to flick, rap.—*v.i.* to trifle with love: to play at courtship (with *with*): to move briskly about.—*n.* one who coquets for amusement, usually a woman.—*n.* **flirta'tion** the act of flirting: a light-hearted and short-lived amorous attachment.—*adj.* **flirta'tious** (*coll.*) given to flirting.—*n.* **flirt'ing.**—*adv.* **flirt'ingly.**—*adj.* **flirt'ish** betokening a flirt.—**flirt with** to treat (death, danger, etc.) lightly, by indulging in dare-devil behaviour, etc.: to entertain thoughts of adopting (an idea, etc.) or joining (a movement, etc.). [Origin obscure; perhaps conn. with Fr. *fleureter*, to talk sweet nothings.]

flit *flit, v.i.* to move about lightly: to fly silently or quickly: to be unsteady or easily moved: to change one's abode (*Scot.*): to do this stealthily in order to avoid creditors, etc.—*v.t.* to remove, transfer:—*pr.p.* **flitt'ing;** *pa.t.* and *pa.p.* **flitt'ed,** Spens. **flitt.**—*n.* **flitt'ing.** [O.N. *flytja*; Sw. *flytta.*]

flitch *flich, n.* the side of a hog salted and cured. [O.E. *flicce.*]

flitt. See **flit.**

flitter *flit'ər, v.i.* to flutter. [**flit.**]

float *flōt, v.t.* to be supported on or suspended in a fluid: to be buoyed up: to move lightly, supported by a fluid: to seem to move in such a way: to be free from the usual attachment: to drift about aimlessly: in weaving, to pass threads without interweaving with them: to use a float: (of a currency) to be free to fluctuate in value in international exchange (*econ.*).—*v.i.* to cause to float: to cover with liquid: to convey on floats: to levitate: to separate by flotation: to smooth: to pare off (as turf): to launch (e.g. scheme): to circulate (e.g. rumour): to offer for sale (stocks, etc.) to raise capital: to negotiate (a loan).—*n.* a contrivance for floating or for keeping something afloat: a blade in a paddle-wheel or water-wheel: a tool for smoothing: a plasterer's trowel: a low cart for carrying cattle, milk, etc., or decorated as an exhibit in a street parade, etc.: a footlight or the footlights collectively: money in hand for a purpose such as to give change to customers, to provide for expenses.—*adj.* **float'able.**—*ns.* **float'age, flō'tage** buoyancy· that which floats: the part of a ship above the water-line; **float'ant** an agent that causes something to float; **floata'tion** same as **flotation; floatel** see **flotel; float'er** one who or that which floats: a person who is a vagrant, or who drifts from job to job or allegiance to allegiance: a blunder (*slang*).—*adj.* **float'ing** that floats, in any sense: not fixed: fluctuating: circulating: not clearly committed to one side or the other (*politics*).—*n.* action of the verb: the spreading of plaster on the surface of walls.—*adv.* **float'ingly.**—*adj.* **float'y.**—**float glass** glass hardened floating on the surface of a liquid; **floating capital** goods, money, etc.: capital not permanently invested; **floating debt** unfunded debt, short-term government loan; **floating dock** a floating structure that can be sunk by admitting water to its air chambers, and raised again carrying a vessel to be repaired; **floating island** a floating aggregation of driftwood, or a mass of vegetation buoyed up from the bottom by marsh gas, or the like; **floating kidney** an abnormally mobile kidney; **floating policy** an insurance policy covering movable property irrespective of its location; **floating**

rib see **rib; floating vote** the votes of electors who are not permanently attached to any one political party; **floating voter.** [O.E. *flotian*, to float.]

floccus *flok'əs, n.* a tuft of woolly hair: a tuft, esp. at the end of a tail: the covering of unfledged birds:—*pl.* **flocci** *flok'sī.*—*adjs.* **flocc'ose** (or *-ōs'*) woolly; **flocc'ular; flocc'ulate.**—*v.t.* and *v.i.* **flocc'ulate** to aggregate in tufts, flakes or cloudy masses.—*ns.* **floccula'tion; flocc'ule** a flocculus; **flocc'ulence** flocculated condition.—*adj.* **flocc'ulent** woolly: flaky: flocculated.—*n.* **flocc'ulus** a small flock, tuft, or flake: a small outgrowth of the cerebellum: a light or dark patch on the sun's surface, usu. near sunspots, caused by calcium or hydrogen vapour:—*pl.* **flocculi** (*flok'ū-lī*). [L. *floccus*, a lock, a trifle; dim. *flocculus.*]

flock[1] *flok, n.* a company of animals, as sheep, birds, etc.: a company generally: a church congregation, considered as the charge of a minister.—*v.i.* to gather or go in flocks or in crowds.—**flock'-mas'ter** an owner or overseer of a flock. [O.E. *flocc*, a flock, a company.]

flock[2] *flok, n.* a lock of wool: a tuft: cloth refuse, waste wool (also in *pl.*): a woolly-looking precipitate (also in *pl.*): fine particles of wool or other fibre applied to cloth to give a raised velvety surface or pattern.—**flock'-bed** a bed stuffed with wool; **flock'-pa'per** a wallpaper dusted over with flock.]O.Fr. *floc*—L. *floccus*, a lock of wool.]

floe *flō, n.* a field of floating ice. [Prob. Norw. *flo*, layer—O.N. *flō.*]

flog *flog, v.t.* to beat or strike: to lash: to chastise with blows: to sell, sometimes illicitly (*slang*):—*pr.p.* **flogg'ing;** *pa.t.* and *pa.p.* **flogged.**—*n.* **flogg'ing.** [Late; prob. an abbrev. of **flagellate.**]

flong *flong, n.* papier-mâché for stereotyping. [Fr. *flan.*]

flood *flud, n.* a great flow of water: an inundation: a deluge: a condition of abnormally great flow in a river: a river or other water (*poet.*): the rise of the tide: any great inflow or outflow: a floodlight (*coll.*).—*v.t.* to overflow: to inundate: to supply in excessive quantity.—*v.i.* to overflow: to bleed profusely, as after parturition.—*adj.* **flood'ed.**—*n.* **flood'ing.**—**flood'gate** a gate for allowing or stopping the flow of water; **flood lamp** a floodlight; **flood'light** lighting of a large area or surface by illumination from lamps situated at some distance (also **floodlighting**): a floodlight lamp.—Also *v.t.*:—*pa.t.* and *pa.p.* **flood'-lighted, flood'lit.**—**flood'tide** the rising tide; **flood'-water; flood'way** an artificial passage for floodwater.—**the Flood** Noah's deluge. [O.E. *flōd.*]

floor *flōr, flôr, n.* the lower supporting surface of a room, etc.: a platform: rooms in a building on the same level: a bottom surface: that on which anything rests or any operation is performed: a levelled area: the ground (*coll.*): the part of a legislative assembly where members sit and speak: the (part of a hall, etc. accommodating) members of the public at a meeting, etc: the part of an exchange on which dealers operate: a lower limit of prices, etc.—*v.t.* to furnish with a floor: to throw or place on the floor: to vanquish, stump (*coll.*).—*adj.* **floored.**—*n.* **floor'ing** material for floors: a platform.—**floor'board** one of the narrow boards making up a floor; **floor'cloth** a cloth for washing floors, **floor plan** a diagram showing the layout of rooms, etc. on one storey of a building; **floor show** a performance on the floor of a ballroom, dining-room, etc., not on a platform; **floor'walker** supervisor of a section of a large store, who attends to customers' complaints, etc.—**first floor** the floor in a house above the ground floor, the second storey: in U.S. usu. the ground floor.—Also *adj.*—**cross the**

floor (of a member of parliament, etc.) to change one's allegiance from one party to another; **hold the floor** to dominate a meeting by much speaking: to speak boringly much; **take the floor** to rise to address a meeting, or to take part in a dance. [O.E. *flōr*.]

floosie flōō'zi, *n.* an attractive young woman esp. of loose morals: a prostitute, esp. a slovenly one.—Also **floosy, -zy, -zie.**

flop *flop, n.* a limp, heavy, flapping movement, fall, or sound: a collapse: a fiasco: a failure.—*adv* with a flop.—*v.t.* and *v.i.* to move with a flop: to drop heavily.—*v.t.* to collapse: to fail dismally.—*adv.* **flopp'ily.**—*n.* **flopp'iness.**—*adj.* **flopp'y.**—**floppy disc** (*comput.*) a storage device in the form of a thin, bendable disc. [A form of **flap.**]

flora flō'rə, flō', *n.* the assemblage of vegetable species of a region, or age. a list or descriptive enumeration of these:—*pl.* flo'ras, flo'rae.—*adj.* flo'ral pertaining to floras, or to flowers.—*adv.* flo'rally.—*n.* **florescence** (*flor-es'əns*) a bursting into flower: time of flowering (*bot.*).—*adj.* floresc'ent bursting into flowers.—*n.* **floret** (*flor'it*) a small flower: a single flower in a close-packed inflorescence.—*adjs.* **flo'riated, flo'reated** decorated with floral ornament—*n.* **floribunda** (*flor-, flōr-, flōr-i-bun'də*) a plant, esp. a rose, whose flowers grow in clusters.—*adj.* **flōr'id** flowery: bright in colour: flushed with red: characterised by flowers of rhetoric, melodic figures, or other ornament: overadorned: richly ornamental, **flōrid'ity.**—*adv.* **flōr'idly.**—*n.* **flōr'idness.**—*adjs.* **florif'erous** bearing or producing flowers; **flo'riform** flower-shaped.—*n.* **flōr'ist** a cultivator or seller of flowers: (*flō', flō'rist*) a student of flowers or of floras.—*adj.* **flōrist'ic.**—*adv.* **flōrist'ically.**—*n* **flōr'istry** the art of cultivating or selling flowers [L. *Flōra*, goddess of flowers; *flōs, flōris*, a flower.]

Florentine *flor'ən-tīn, adj.* pertaining to *Florence* in Tuscany.—*n.* a native or inhabitant thereof. [L. *Flōrentīnus—Flōrentia.*]

florescent, floret, florid, etc. See **flora.**

florin *flor'in, n.* orig. a Florentine gold coin with a lily stamped on one side: an English silver or cupro-nickel coin worth one-tenth of a pound first minted in 1849: in Holland, the gulden. [Fr., from It. *fiorino—fiore*, a lily—L. *flōs, flōris.*]

florist, etc. See **flora.**

floruit *flō'rū-it, flō'rōō-, flor'ū-, -ōō-, n.* period during which a person flourished or guiding date indicating when he or she was alive. [L., 3rd pers. sing. perf indic. of *flōrēre*, to flourish.]

floss *flos, n.* the rough outside of the silkworm's cocoon, and other waste of silk manufacture: fine silk in spun strands not twisted together, used in embroidery and tooth-cleaning: any loose downy or silky plant substance.—*adj.* **floss'y** made of, like, or pertaining to floss: showy, overdressed (*slang*). [Prob O.Fr. *flosche*, down: or from some Gmc. word cog. with fleece; cf. O.N. *flos*, nap.]

flote *flōt, n.* (*obs.*) a wave.—*n.* **flō'tage** see **floatage.**—*n.* **flota'tion** the act of floating: the science of floating bodies: the act of starting a business, esp. a limited liability company. [See **float.**]

flotel, floatel *flō-tel', n.* a platform or boat containing the sleeping accommodation, and eating, leisure, etc. facilities for workers on oil-rigs. [**float, hotel.**]

flotilla *flo-til'ə, n.* a fleet of small ships. [Sp., dim. of *flota*, a fleet.]

flotsam *flot'səm, n.* goods lost by shipwreck and found floating on the sea (see **jetsam**). [Anglo-Fr *floteson* (Fr. *flottaison*)—O.Fr. *floter*, to float.]

flounce¹ *flowns, v.i.* to move abruptly or impatiently. —*n.* an impatient fling, flop, or movement.—*adv.*

with a flounce. [Prob cog. with Norw. *flunsa*, to hurry, Sw. dial. *flunsa*, to plunge.]

flounce² *flowns, n.* a hanging strip sewn to the skirt of a dress by its upper edge.—*v.t.* to furnish with flounces.—*n.* **floun'cing** material for flounces. [Old word *frounce*, a plait or wrinkle.]

flounder¹ *flown'dər, v.i* to struggle with violent and awkward motion: to stumble helplessly in thinking or speaking.—*n.* an act of floundering [Prob. an onomatopoeic blending of the sound and sense of earlier words like **founder, blunder.**]

flounder² *flown'dər, n.* a name given to a number of species of flatfish. [Anglo-Fr. *floundre*, O.Fr. *flondre*, most prob. of Scand. origin.]

flour *flowr, n.* the finely-ground meal of wheat or other grain: the fine soft powder of any substance.—*v t.* to reduce into or sprinkle with flour.—*adj.* **flour'y** covered with flour: like flour. [Same word as **flower.**]

flourish *flur'ish, v.i.* to grow luxuriantly: to thrive: to be in full vigour: to be prosperous: to display ostentatiously: to play or sing ostentatious passages, or ostentatiously (*mus.*): to play a fanfare.—*v.t.* to adorn with flourishes or ornaments: to brandish in show or triumph or exuberance of spirits.—*n.* showy splendour: a figure made by a bold stroke of the pen: the waving of a weapon or other thing: a parade of words: a showy, fantastic, or highly ornamental passage of music.—*adjs.* **flour'ished** decorated with flourishes, **flour'ishing** thriving: prosperous: making a show.—*adv* **flour'ishingly.**—*adj.* **flour'ishy** abounding in flourishes.—**flourish of trumpets** a fanfare heralding great persons: any ostentatious introduction. [O.Fr. *florir, floriss-*—L. *flōs, flōris*, flower]

flout *flowt, v.t.* to jeer at: to mock: to treat with contempt: to reject, defy (orders, etc.).—*v.i.* to jeer.—*n.* a jeer.—*adv.* **flout'ingly.** [Prob. a specialised use of *floute*, M.E. form of **flute,** to play on the flute.]

flow *flō, v.i.* to run, as water: to move or change form like a fluid: to rise or come in, as the tide: to move in a stream: to glide smoothly: to abound, run over: to run in smooth lines: to stream or hang loose and waving.—*v.t.* to cover with water:—*pa.t.* and *pa.p.* **flowed.**—*n.* a stream or current: movement of, or like that of, a fluid: that which flows or has flowed: mode of flowing: the setting in of the tide: copious fluency.—*adj.* **flow'ing** moving, as a fluid: fluent: smooth and continuous: falling in folds or in waves. —**flow chart** a flow sheet: a chart pictorially representing the nature and sequence of operations to be carried out in a computer programme or any other activity; **flow'meter** a device for measuring, the rate of flow of a fluid in a pipe; **flow sheet** a chart showing the successive stages of an industrial process. [O.E. *flōwan.*]

flower *flow('ə)r, n.* a growth comprising the reproductive organs of seed plants: the blossom of a plant: the flowering state: a flowering plant, esp. one valued for its blossoms: the prime of life: the best of anything: the person or thing most distinguished: the embodiment of perfection: a figure of speech: ornament of style: (in *pl.*) a sublimate (as **flowers of sulphur**): (in *pl.*) applied to some fungous growths —*v.i.* to blossom: to flourish.—*ns.* **flower'er** a plant that flowers; **flower'iness.**—*n.* and *adj.* **flower'ing.** —*adjs.* **flower'less; flower'y** full of, or adorned with, flowers: highly embellished, florid.—**flower'-bed** a garden bed for flowers; **flower'-bud** a bud with the unopened flower; **flower'-garden; flower'-girl** a girl or woman who sells flowers in the street; **flower'-head** a close inflorescence in which all the florets are sessile on the receptacle; **flower'pot** a pot in which a plant is grown; **flower'-show** an exhibition of flowers; **flower'-stalk** the stem that supports the flower. [O.Fr. *flour* (Fr. *fleur*)—L. *flōs, flōris*, a flower.]

flown *flōn, pa.p.* of **fly**; old *pa.p.* of **flow**.

flu, flue *floo, n.* shortened form of **influenza**.

fluctuate *fluk'tū-āt, v.i.* to move like a wave: to go up and down or to and fro: to vary this way and that.—*v t.* to throw into fluctuation.—*adjs.* **fluc'tūant; fluc'tūāting.**—*n.* **fluctūā'tion** rise and fall: motion to and fro: wavelike motion: alternate variation. [L. *fluctuāre, -ātum—fluctus*, a wave—*fluěre*, to flow.]

flue *floo, n.* a pipe for conveying hot air, smoke, flame, etc.: a small chimney: a flue pipe (*mus.*): the opening by which the air escapes from the foot of a flue pipe. —**flue pipe** a pipe, esp. in an organ, in which the sound is produced by air impinging upon an edge.

fluent *floo'ənt, adj.* ready in the use of words: voluble: marked by copiousness: smooth, easy, graceful.—*ns.* **flu'ency, flu'entness.**—*adv.* **flu'ently.** [L. *fluēns, fluentis*, pr.p. of *fluěre*, to flow.]

fluff *fluf, n.* a soft down from cotton, etc.: anything downy: a fault in performing (a play, piece of music, etc.): a duffed stroke at golf, etc.—*v.t.* to make fluffy.—*v.t.* and *v i.* to bungle, in sport, musical performance, etc.—*n.* **fluff'iness.**—*adj.* **fluff'y.**

flügel, flugel *flü'hhəl, floo'gl, ns.* a grand piano.—**flü'gelhorn, flu'gelhorn** a hunting-horn, a kind of keyed bugle. [Ger., wing.]

fluid *floo'id, adj.* that flows: unsolidified: likely to, tending to change: easily changed.—*n.* a substance whose particles can move about with freedom—a liquid or gas.—*adjs.* **flu'idal; fluid'ic.**—*vs.t.* **fluid'ify; flu'idise, -ize** to make fluid: to cause (fine particles) to move as a fluid, e.g. by suspending them in a current of air or gas: to fill with a specified fluid. —*ns.* **fluidisā'tion, -z-; fluid'ity, flu'idness.—fluid drive** a system of transmitting power smoothly through the medium of the change in momentum of a fluid, usu. oil. [L. *fluidus*, fluid—*fluěre*, to flow.]

fluke[1] *flook, n.* a flounder: a trematode worm, esp. that which causes liver-rot in sheep, so called because like a miniature flounder (also **fluke'-worm**). [O.E. *flōc*, a plaice.]

fluke[2] *flook, n.* the barb of an anchor: a barb: a lobe of a whale's tail. [Prob. a transferred use of the foregoing.]

fluke[3] *flook, n.* an accidental success.—*v.t.* to make, score, etc. by a fluke.—*adj.* **fluk'(e)y.**

flume *floom, n.* an artificial channel for water: a ravine occupied by a torrent (*U.S.*). [O.Fr. *flum*—L. *flūmen*, a river—*fluěre*, to flow.]

flummery *flum'ər-i, n.* an acid jelly made from the husks of oats: blancmange: anything insipid: empty compliment, humbug, pretentiousness. [W. *llymru* —*llymrig*, harsh, raw—*llym*, sharp.]

flummox *flum'əks, (coll.) v.t.* to perplex

flump *flump, (coll.) v.t.* to throw down heavily.—*v.t.* to move with a flop or thud.—*n.* the dull sound so produced. [Imit.]

flung *flung, pa.t.* and *pa.p.* of **fling**.

flunk *flungk, (slang) v.i.* to fail in an examination: to be dismissed from college, etc. for such failure (with *out*).—Also *v.t.* and *n.* [Perh. combined **flinch[1], funk[1]**.]

flunkey *flung'ki, n.* a livery servant: a footman: a mean cringer. [Perh. orig. *flanker*, one who runs alongside.]

fluor *floo'ər, -ör, n.* fluorite.—*v.t.* **fluoresce** (-ər-es').— *n.* **fluoresc'ence** the property of some substances (e.g. fluor) of emitting, when exposed to radiation, rays of greater wavelength than those received.—*adjs.* **fluoresc'ent.**—*vs t.* **flu'oridate, -idise, -ize** to add a

fluoride to (a water or milk supply).—*ns.* **fluorid-ā'tion; flu'oride** a compound of fluorine with another element or radical; **flu'orine** (-*ēn*) an element (at. numb. 9; symbol F), a pale greenish-yellow gas; **fluorite** (*floo'ər-īt*) a mineral, calcium fluoride; **flu'orocarbon** any of a series of compounds of fluorine and carbon highly resistant to heat and chemical action.—**flu'oroscope** an instrument for X-ray examination by means of a fluorescent screen; **fluoros'copy; flu'orspar** fluorite.—**fluorescent lighting** brighter lighting obtained for the same consumption of electricity, by using fluorescent material to convert ultraviolet radiation in the electric lamp into visible light [L. *fluor*, flow, from its use as a flux.]

flurry *flur'i, n.* a sudden blast or gust: agitation: bustle: a fluttering assemblage of things, as snow-flakes.—*v.t.* to agitate, to confuse:—*pr.p.* **flurr'y-ing;** *pa.t., pa.p.* **flurr'ied.** [Prob. onomatopoeic, suggested by **flaw[1], hurry**, etc.]

flush[1] *flush, n.* a sudden flow: a flow of blood to the skin, causing redness: a suffusion of colour, esp. red: a sudden growth: a renewal of growth: a rush of feeling: bloom, freshness, vigour· abundance.—*v.i.* to glow: to beco· e red in the face: to flow swiftly, suddenly, or cu,piously.—*v.t.* to cleanse by a copious flow of water: to clear by a blast of air: to cause to glow: to elate, excite the spirits of.—*adj.* overflowing: abounding: well supplied, as with money: flushed.—*adj.* **flushed** suffused with ruddy colour: excited.—*ns.* **flush'er; flush'ing; flush'ness.**—*adj.* **flush'y** reddish [Prob. next word influenced by **flash, blush.**]

flush[2] *flush, v.i.* to start up like an alarmed bird.—*v.t.* to rouse and cause to start off: to force from concealment (with *out*).—*n.* the act of starting. [Prob. onomatopoeic; suggested by **fly, flutter, rush[1].**]

flush[3] *flush, v.t.* to make even: to fill up to the level of a surface (often with *up*).—*adj.* having the surface in one plane with the adjacent surface (with *with*).— Also *adv.* [Prob. related to **flush[1].**]

flush[4] *flush, n.* in card-playing, a hand in which all the cards or a specified number are of the same suit.— *adj.* in poker, consisting of cards all of the same suit. —**busted flush** in poker, a flush that is never completed: something that has to be abandoned as a failure (*fig.*); **straight flush** in poker, a sequence of five cards of the same suit (**royal flush**, if headed by ace). [Prob. Fr. *flux*—L. *fluxus*, flow; influenced by **flush[1].**]

fluster *flus'tər, n.* hurrying: flurry: confused agitation. —*v.t.* to make hot and flurried: to fuddle with drink: to confuse.—*v.i.* to bustle: to be agitated or fuddled. —*adj.* **flus'tery** confused. [O.N. *flaustr*, hurry.]

flute *floot, n.* either of two types of wind instrument consisting of a wooden or metal tube with holes stopped by the finger-tips or by keys, the one type blown from the end through a fipple, the other (also called **transverse flute**) held horizontally and played by directing the breath across a mouth-hole: in organ-building, a stop with stopped wooden pipes, having a flute-like tone: a longitudinal groove, as on a pillar: a tall and narrow wine-glass.—*v.i.* to play the flute: to make fluty sounds.—*v.t.* to play or sing in soft flute-like tones: to form flutes or grooves in.—*adj.* **flut'ed** ornamented with flutes, channels, or grooves.—*ns.* **flut'er; flut'ing** flute-playing or similar sounds: longitudinal furrowing; **flut'ist.**—*adj.* **flut'y** in tone like a flute. [O.Fr. *fleüte*.]

flutter *flut'ər, v.i.* to move about nervously, aimlessly, or with bustle: of a bird, to flap wings: of a flag, etc., to flap in the air: to vibrate, e.g. of a pulse, to beat irregularly: to be in agitation or in uncertainty.—*v.t.* to throw into disorder: to move in quick motions.—*n.*

quick, irregular motion: agitation: confusion: a gambling transaction (*coll.*): a small speculation (*coll.*): in wind-instrument playing, rapid movement of the tongue as for a rolled 'r' (also **flutt'er-tongu'ing**): in sound reproduction, undesirable variation in pitch or loudness: abnormal oscillation of a part of an aircraft. [O.E. *flotorian*, to float about.]

fluvial *flōō'vi-əl, adj.* of or belonging to rivers. [L. *fluviālis—fluvius*, a river, *fluĕre*, to flow.]

flux *fluks, n.* act of flowing: a flow of matter: a state of flow or continuous change: matter discharged: excrement: an easily fused substance, esp. one added to another to make it more fusible: the rate of flow of mass, volume, or energy (*phys.*).—*v.i.* to melt.—*v.i.* to flow: to fuse.—*n.* **fluxion** (*fluk'shən*) a flowing or discharge: excessive flow of blood or fluid to any organ (*med.*): a difference or variation: the rate of change of a continuously varying quantity (*math.*).—**in a state of flux** in an unsettled, undetermined state. [O.Fr.,—L. *fluxus—fluĕre*, to flow.]

fly *flī, v.i.* to move through the air, esp. on wings or in aircraft: to operate an aircraft: to move swiftly: to hurry: to pass quickly: to flee: to flutter.—*v.t.* to avoid, flee from: to cause to fly, as a kite, aircraft, etc.: to conduct or transport by air: to cross or pass by flying:—*pa.t.* **flew** (*flōō*); *pa.p.* **flown** (*flōn*); *3rd sing. pres. indic.* **flies.**—*n.* any insect of the *Diptera*: often so widely used, esp. in composition—e.g. *butterfly, dragonfly, mayfly*—as to be virtually equivalent to insect: a fish-hook dressed in imitation of a fly: a flight: a flap, esp. a tent-door: a flap of material covering, e.g. trouser opening: the trouser fastener, e.g. zip: the free end of a flag, or the like: a flywheel: (in *pl.*) the large space above the proscenium in a theatre, from which the scenes, etc., are controlled —*pl.* **flies.**—*adj.* (*slang*) wideawake, knowing: surreptitious, sly.—*ns.* **flier, flyer** (*flī'ər*) one who flies or flees: an airman: an object, e.g. train, moving at top speed: a financial speculation (*slang*): a rect-angular step in stairs: a flying leap (*coll.*).—*n.* **fly'ing.**—*adj.* that flies or can fly: moving, or passing, very rapidly: organised for speedy action or transfer to any location as the need arises: (of a visit) very brief.—**fly agaric** a poisonous type of toadstool, *Amanita muscaria*, used in the production of flypaper and having hallucinogenic properties; **fly'blow** the egg of a fly.—*adj.* **fly'-blown** tainted with flies' eggs or maggots (also *fig.*).—**fly'book** a case like a book for holding fishing-flies; **fly'-by** a flight, at low altitude or close range, past a place, or body in space, for observation; **fly'-by-night** one who gads about at night: an absconding debtor: an irresponsible person. —*adj.* irresponsible, esp. in business matters: unreliable: transitory.—**fly'catcher** name for various birds that catch flies on the wing; **fly'-dressing** fly-tying; **fly'-fisher** one who uses artificial flies as lure; **fly'-fishing; fly'-half** (*Rugby*) a stand-off half; **flying boat** a seaplane with boat body; **flying bomb** a bomb in the form of a jet-propelled aeroplane; **flying buttress** an arch-formed prop.—*n.pl.* **flying colours** flags unfurled: triumphant success.—**Flying Corps** the precursor (1912–18) of the Royal Air Force; **flying doctor** a doctor, esp. orig. in the remote parts of Australia, who can be called by radio, etc., and who flies to visit patients, **flying fish** a fish that can leap from the water and sustain itself in the air for a short time by its long pectoral fins, as if flying; **flying fox** a large frugivorous bat; **flying leap** one made from a running start; **flying lemur** an animal (not in fact a lemur) of the islands of SE Asia, whose fore and hind limbs are connected by a fold of skin; **flying lizard** a dragon lizard; **flying machine** a power-driven aircraft; **flying officer** an officer in the Air Force of rank answering to

sub-lieutenant in the navy and lieutenant in the army; **flying pickets** mobile pickets available for reinforcing the body of local pickets during a strike; **flying saucer** a disc-like flying object reported to have been seen by sundry persons; **flying squad** a body of police, etc. with special training, available for duty where the need arises, or one organised for fast action or movement; **flying squirrel** a name for several kinds of squirrels with a parachute of skin between the fore and hind legs: also applied to a flying phalanger; **flying start** in a race, a start given after the competitors are in motion (also *fig.*); **fly'-kick** a kick made while running; **fly'leaf** a blank leaf at the beginning or end of a book; **fly'-man** one who works the ropes in theatre flies; **fly'over** a processional flight of aircraft: a road or railway-line carried over the top of another one at an intersection; **fly'paper** a sticky or poisonous paper for destroying flies; **fly'-past** a ceremonial flight analogous to a march past; **flypost'-ing** the practice of affixing bills illegally; **fly'-sheet** a piece of canvas that can be fitted to the roof of a tent to give additional protection: a handbill; **fly'-spray** (an aerosol containing) an insecticide; **fly'trap** a trap to catch flies: a plant that traps flies (*bot.*); **fly'-tying** making artificial flies for angling; **fly'-under** a road or railway-line carried under another one at an intersection; **fly'weight** a boxer of eight stone or less; **fly'wheel** a large wheel with a heavy rim applied to machinery to equalise the effect of the driving effort. —**a fly in the ointment** some slight flaw which corrupts a thing of value (Eccles. x. 1): a minor disadvantage in otherwise favourable circumstances; a **fly on the wall** the invisible observer that one would like to be on certain occasions; **fly a kite** see **kite-flying; fly at, upon** to attack suddenly; **fly high** to aim high, be ambitious; **fly in the face of** to insult: to oppose, defy: to be at variance with; **fly off the handle** (*slang*) to lose one's temper; **fly open** to open suddenly or violently; **let fly** to attack: to throw or send off; **like flies** (dying, etc.) in vast numbers with as little resistance as insects; **make the feathers fly** see **feather; no flies on** no want of alertness in. [O.E. *flēogan*, to fly. pa.t. *flēah*; *flēoge*, fly, insect.]

foal *fōl, n.* the young of the horse family.—*v.i.* and *v.t.* to bring forth (a foal).—**in foal** (of a mare) pregnant. [O E. *fola*.]

foam *fōm, n.* bubbles on surface of liquor: a suspension of gas in a liquid: sea (*poet.*): frothy saliva or perspiration: any of many light, cellular materials, rigid or flexible, produced by aerating a liquid, then solidifying it.—*v.i.* to gather or produce foam: to come in foam.—*v.t.* to pour out in foam: to fill or cover with foam.—*n.* and *adj.* **foam'ing.**—*adv.* **foam'ingly.**—*adjs.* **foam'less; foam'y** frothy.—**foam at the mouth** to produce frothy saliva: to be extremely angry (*coll.*) [O.E. *fām.*]

fob *fob, v.t.* (*arch.* except with *off*) to cheat: to give as genuine: to put off: to foist, palm. [Cf. Ger. *foppen*, to jeer.]

fob² *fob, n.* a small watch pocket in the waistband of trousers: a chain with seals, etc., hanging from the fob.—*v.t.* to pocket. [Perh. conn. with L. Ger. *fobke*, little pocket, H.Ger. dial *fuppe*, pocket.]

focal. See **focus.**

fo'c's'le *fōk'sl,* contr. form of **forecastle.**

focus *fō'kəs, n* in geometry, a fixed point such that the distances of a point on a conic section from it and from the directrix have a constant ratio: in optics, a point in which rays converge after reflection or refraction, or from which (*virtual focus*) they seem to diverge: any central point: the point or region of greatest activity: the point of origin (as of an earthquake): the position, or condition, of sharp definition of an image:—*pl.* **foci** (*fō'sī*), **fo'cuses.**—*v.t.* to bring to a focus: to adjust to focus: to adjust so as to get a sharp image of: to concentrate:—*pr.p.* **fo'cusing;** *pa.t.* and *pa.p.* **fo'cused;** some double the *s.*—*adj.* **fo'cal** of or belonging to a focus.—*v.t.* **fo'calise, -ize** to focus.—**in focus** placed or adjusted so as to secure distinct vision, or a sharp, definite image. [L. *fōcus*, a hearth.]

fodder *fod'ər, n.* food supplied to cattle: food (*slang*). —*v.t.* to supply with fodder.—*ns.* **fodd'erer; fodd'-ering.** [O.E. *fōdor*; cf. **food, feed**[1].]

foe *fō, n.* an enemy:—*pl.* **foes.—foe'man** an enemy in war (*pl.* **foe'men**). [M.E. *foo*—O.E. *fāh, fā* (adj.) and *gefā* (noun).]

foehn. See **föhn.**

foetid, foetor. See **fetid, fetor.**

foetus, fetus *fē'tas, n.* the young animal in the egg or in the womb, after its parts are distinctly formed.—*adj.* **foe'tal, fe'tal.**—*n.* **foe'ticide, fe'ticide** destruction of a foetus.—*adj.* **foetici'dal, fe-.** [L. *fētus*, offspring.]

fog[1] *fog, n.* a thick mist: watery vapour condensed about dust particles in drops: cloudy obscurity: confusion, bewilderment: a blurred patch on a negative, print, or transparency (*phot.*).—*v.t.* to shroud in fog: to obscure: to confuse: to produce fog on (*phot.*).— *v.i.* to become coated, clouded, blurred, confused: to be affected by fog (*phot.*).—*adj.* **fogged** (*fogd*) clouded, obscured: bewildered.—*adv.* **fogg'ily.**—*n.* **fogg'iness.**—*adjs.* **fogg'y** misty: damp: fogged: clouded in mind: stupid; **fog'less** without fog, clear.— **fog'-bank** a dense mass of fog like a bank of land.— *adj.* **fog'bound** impeded by fog.—**fog'horn** a horn used as a warning signal by or to ships in foggy weather: a siren: a big bellowing voice; **fog'-lamp** a lamp, esp. on a vehicle, used to improve visibility in fog; **fog'-signal** a detonating cap or other audible warning used in fog.—**not have the foggiest** not to have the least idea. [Origin obscure; perh. conn. with Dan. *fog*, as in *snee-fog*, thick falling snow.]

fog[2] *fog, foggage fog'ij, ns.* grass that grows after the hay is cut.

fogey. See **fogy.**

fogy, fogey *fō'gi, n.* a dull old fellow: one with anti-quated notions. [Prob. from *foggy*, moss-grown.]

föhn, foehn *fœn, n.* a hot dry wind blowing down a mountain valley. [Ger.,—Romansch *favugn*—Lat. *Favōnius*, the west wind.]

foible *foi'bl, n.* a weakness: a penchant: a failing: a faible. [O.Fr. *foible*, weak; cf. **faible, feeble.**]

foie gras *fwä-grä,* (Fr.) fat liver (of goose) made into *'pâté de foie gras* (or *foies gras*) (*pä-tä də*).

foil[1] *foil, v.t.* to defeat: to baffle: to frustrate.—*n.* an incomplete fall in wrestling: a blunt fencing sword with a button on the point. [O.Fr. *fuler*, to stamp or crush—L. *fullō*, a fuller of cloth.]

foil[2] *foil, n.* a leaf or thin plate of metal, as tinfoil: a mercury coating on a mirror: metal-coated paper: a thin leaf of metal put under a precious stone to show it to advantage: anything that serves to set off something else: a small arc in tracery: an aerofoil or hydrofoil. [O.Fr. *foil* (Fr. *feuille*)—L. *folium*, a leaf.]

foist *foist, v.t.* to bring in by stealth: to insert wrongfully: to pass off (*in* or *into* the thing affected, *upon* the person).—*n.* **foist'er.** [Prob. Du. dial. *vuisten*, to take in hand; *vuist*, fist.]

fold[1] *fōld, n.* a doubling of anything upon itself: a crease: the concavity of anything folded: a part laid over on another.—*v.t.* to lay in folds, double over: to enclose in a fold or folds, to wrap up: to embrace.— *v.i.* to become folded: to be capable of folding: (of a business, etc.) to collapse, cease functioning (also with *up*; *coll.*).—*suff.* **-fold** (with numerals), times, as in **ten'-fold.**—*n.* **fold'er** the person or thing that

folds: a folding case for loose papers.—*adj.* **fold'ing** that folds, or that can be folded.—*n.* a fold or plait: the bending of strata, usu. as the result of compression (*geol.*).—**fold'ing-door'** a door consisting of two parts hung on opposite jambs.—*adj., n.* **fold'-out** (a large page, e.g. containing a diagram) folded to fit into a book, and to be unfolded for inspection (also **gate'fold**).—**fold in** to mix in carefully and gradually (*cook.*). [O.E. *faldan* (W.S. *fealdan*), to fold.]

fold[2] *fōld, n.* an enclosure for protecting domestic animals, esp. sheep: the Christian Church (*fig.*). [O.E. *falod, fald*, a fold, stall.]

folderol. See **falderal.**

foliage, foliate, etc. See **folium.**

folic acid *fō'lik* (*fo'lik*) *as'id,* an acid in the vitamin B complex, or a similar acid which cures some of the symptoms of pernicious anaemia (see **pterin**). [See **folium.**]

folie *fo-lē,* (Fr.) *n.* madness, insanity: folly.—**folie de grandeur** (*grä-dœr*) delusions of grandeur.

folio *fō'li-ō, n.* a leaf (two pages) of a book: a sheet of paper once folded: a book of such sheets: the size of such a book: one of several sizes of paper: a page in an account-book, or two opposite pages numbered as one (*book-k.*): a page number in a book (*print.*): a wrapper for loose papers:—*pl.* **fo'lios.**—*adj.* consisting of paper only once folded: of the size of a folio.— **in folio** in sheets folded once: in the form of a folio. [L. *in foliō*, on leaf (so-and-so), used in references; L. *folium*, a leaf, a sheet of paper.]

folium *fō'li-əm, n.* a leaf, lamina, or lamella:—*pl.* **fo'lia.**—*adj.* **foliaceous** (*-ā'shəs*) leaflike: like a foliage leaf: leaf-bearing: laminated.—*n.* **fo'liage** leaves collectively: a mass of leaves: plant forms in art.—*adjs.* **fo'liaged** having foliage: worked like foliage; **fo'liar** pertaining to leaves: resembling leaves.—*v.t.* **fo'liate** orig., to beat into a leaf: to cover with leaf-metal: to number the leaves (not pages) of. —*adj.* **fo'liated** beaten into a thin leaf: decorated with leaf ornaments or foils: consisting of layers or laminae.—*ns.* **folia'tion; fo'liature** foliation; **fo'liole** a leaflet of a compound leaf (*bot.*): a small leaflike structure.—**foliage plant** one grown for the beauty of its foliage. [L. *folium*, a leaf.]

folk *fōk, n.* people, collectively or distributively: a nation or people: those of one's own family, relations (*coll.*): now generally used as a pl. (either **folk** or **folks**) to mean people in general.—*adj.* handed down by tradition of the people.—*adj.* **folk'sy** (chiefly *U.S.*) everyday: friendly: sociable: of ordinary people: (artificially) traditional in style.—*n.* **folk'siness.**—**folk'-dance** a dance handed down by tradition of the people; **folk'-etymol'ogy** popular unscientific attempts at etymology.—**folk'lore** the study of ancient observances and customs, the notions, beliefs, traditions, superstitions, and prejudices of the common people.—*adj.* **folk'loric.**— **folk'lorist** one who studies folklore; **folk-mem'ory** a memory of an event that survives in a community through many generations; **folk'-song** any song or ballad originating among the people and traditionally handed down by them; **folk'-tale** a popular story handed down by oral tradition from a more or less remote antiquity; **folk'-weave** a loosely woven fabric. [O.E. *folc.*]

follicle *fol'i-kl, n.* a fruit formed from a single carpel containing several seeds, splitting along the ventral suture only (*bot.*): any small saclike structure, as the pit surrounding a hair-root (*zool.*).—*adjs.* **follic'ulated, follic'ular, follic'ulose, follic'ulous.** [L. *folliculus*, dim. of *follis*, a wind-bag.]

follow *fol'ō, v.t.* to go after or behind: to keep along the line of: to come after, succeed: to pursue: to attend: to imitate: to obey: to adopt, as an opinion: to keep the eye or mind fixed on: to grasp or understand the whole course or sequence of: to result from, as an effect from a cause.—*v.i.* to come after: to result: to be the logical conclusion.—*n.* a stroke that causes the ball to follow the one it has struck (*billiards*; commonly **follow-through'**).—*ns.* **foll'ower** one who comes after: a copier: a disciple: a retainer, ân attendant: a servant-girl's sweetheart: a part of a machine driven by another part; **foll'owing** a body of supporters.—*adj.* coming next after: to be next mentioned.—*prep.* after.—**follow-my-lead'er** a game in which all have to mimic whatever the leader does; **follow-on'**, **-through'** an act of following on or through.—**follow on** in cricket, to take a second innings immediately after the first, as compulsory result of being short in number of runs: to follow immediately (*coll.*): to start where another left off (*coll.*); **follow out** to carry out (e.g. instructions): to follow to the end or conclusion; **follow suit** in card-playing, to play a card of the same suit as the one which was led: to do what another has done; **follow through** to complete the swing of a stroke after hitting the ball; **follow up** to pursue an advantage closely: to pursue a question that has been started (*n.* **foll'ow-up**). [O.E. *folgian*, *fylgan*.]

folly *fol'i, n.* silliness or weakness of mind: a foolish thing: a monument of folly, as a great useless structure, or one left unfinished, having been begun without a reckoning of the cost. [O.Fr. *folie—fol*, foolish.]

foment *fō-ment', v.t.* to apply a warm lotion to: to foster (usu. evil).—*ns.* **fomenta'tion** the application of a warm lotion (extended sometimes to a dry or cold application): the lotion so applied: instigation; **fomen'ter**. [L. *fōmentum* for *fovimentum—fovēre*, to warm.]

fond *fond, adj.* weakly indulgent: prizing highly (with *of*): very affectionate: kindly disposed: foolish.—*v.t.* **fond'le** to handle with fondness: to caress.—*ns.* **fond'ler; fond'ling** a pet.—*adv.* **fond'ly.**—*n.* **fond'ness.** [Pa.p. of *fon*—M.E. *fonnen*, to act foolishly, *fon*, a fool.]

fondant *fon'dənt, n.* a soft sweetmeat that melts in the mouth. [Fr.,—*fondre*, to melt—L. *fundēre*.]

fondle, etc. See **fond.**

fondue *fon'dōō, f3-dü, n.* a sauce made from cheese and wine, etc., and which is eaten by dipping pieces of bread, etc., in the mixture: a dish consisting of small cubes of meat cooked at the table on forks in hot oil and served with piquant sauces: a soufflé with bread or biscuit crumbs. [Fr.,—fem. pa.p. of *fondre*, to melt.]

font[1] *font, n.* a vessel for baptismal water: a fount, fountain (*poet.*).—*adj.* **font'al** pertaining to a font or origin. [O.E. *font*—L. *fōns, fontis*, a fountain.]

font[2] *font.* See **fount**[1].

fontanelle, **fontanel** *fon-tə-nel', n.* a gap between the bones of the skull of a young animal: an opening for discharge. [Fr. dim.,—L *fōns, fontis*, fountain.]

food *food, n.* what one feeds on: that which, being digested, nourishes the body: whatever sustains or promotes growth (also *fig.*): substances elaborated by the plant from raw materials taken in (*bot.*).—**food chain** a series of organisms connected by the fact that each forms food for the next higher organism in the series; **food poisoning** gastrointestinal disorder caused by the ingestion of foods naturally toxic to the system or of foods made toxic by contamination with bacteria or chemicals; **food processor** an electrical appliance for cutting, blending, mincing, etc. food; **food'-stuff** a substance used as food; **food values** the relative nourishing power of foods. [O.E. *fōda*]

fool[1] *fool, n.* one wanting in wisdom, judgment or sense: a person of weak mind: a jester: a tool or victim, as of untoward circumstances, a dupe: one with a weakness for (with *for*).—*v.t.* to deceive: to make to appear foolish: to get by fooling.—*v.i.* to play the fool: to trifle.—*adj.* (*Scot.* and *U.S.*) foolish.—*ns.* **fool'ery; fool'ing.**—*adj.* **fool'ish** weak in intellect: wanting discretion: unwise: ridiculous: marked with folly: paltry.—*adv.* **fool'ishly.**—*n.* **fool'ishness.** —**fool'hard'iness.**—*adjs.* **fool'hardy** foolishly bold: rash or incautious; **fool'proof** not liable to sustain or inflict injury by wrong usage: infallible.—**fool's cap** a jester's head-dress, usu having a cockscomb hood with bells; **fool's errand** a silly or fruitless enterprise; **fool's gold** iron pyrites; **fool's mate** (*chess*) the simplest of the mates (in two moves each); **fool's paradise** a state of happiness based on fictitious hopes or expectations.—**fool around** to waste time: to trifle: to trifle with someone's affections; **fool with** to meddle with officiously; **make a fool of** to bring a person into ridicule: to disappoint; **nobody's fool** a sensible person; **play, act the fool** to behave as a fool: to sport. [O Fr. *fol* (Fr. *fou*)—L. *follis*, a wind-bag.]

fool[2] *fool, n.* a crushed fruit or the like scalded or stewed, mixed with cream and sugar, as *gooseberry fool.* [Prob. a use of preceding suggested by *trifle.*]

foolscap *fool'skap, n.* a long folio writing- or printing-paper, generally $17 \times 13\frac{1}{2}$ in., originally bearing the watermark of a *fool's cap* and bells.

foot *foot, n.* the part of its body on which an animal stands or walks: a muscular development of the ventral surface in molluscs: the part on which a thing stands: the base: the lower or less dignified end: a measure = 12 in., orig., the length of a man's foot: the corresponding square or cubic unit: foot-soldiers: a division of a line of poetry:—*pl.* **feet;** also, as a measure, **foot;** in some compounds and in sense of dregs, or footlights, **foots.**—*v.t.* and *v.i.* to dance: to walk.—*v.t.* to kick: to pay: to add a foot to: to grasp with the foot.—*n.* **foot'age** measurement or payment by the foot: an amount (i.e. length) of cinema film.—*adj.* **foot'ed** provided with a foot or feet.—*ns.* **foot'er** (*slang*) football; **-foot'er** (in *comp.*) something of a particular length in feet; **foot'ing** place for the foot to rest on: standing: terms: installation: an installation fee or treat: foundation: lower part: position: settlement: track: tread: dance: plain cotton lace.—**foot'-ball** a large ball for kicking about in sport: a game played with this ball: a bargaining-point, point of controversy, etc. (*fig.*); **foot'baller** a football player; **foot'bar** the bar controlled by the pilot's feet, for operating the rudder in aircraft; **foot'board** a support for the foot in a carriage or elsewhere: the footplate of a locomotive engine; **foot brake** a brake operated by the foot; **foot'bridge** a bridge for foot-passengers; **foot'fall** the sound of setting the foot down; **foot'-fault** (*lawn tennis*) an overstepping of the line in serving.—Also *v.t.* and *v.i.*—**foot'hill** a minor elevation below a higher mountain or range (usually in *pl.*); **foot'hold** a place to fix the foot in: a grip: a firm starting position; **foot'light** one of a row of lights along the front of the stage.—*adj.* **foot'loose** free, unhampered.—**foot'man** a servant or attendant in livery (*pl.* **foot'men**); **foot'mark** see **foot'print; foot'-note** a note of reference or comment at the foot of a page; **foot'pad** a highwayman on foot; **foot'path** a way for walkers only: a side pavement; **foot'plate** a platform for foot **platemen**, train driver and assistant (on steam locomotive, stoker); **foot'-pound**[1] the energy needed to raise a mass of one pound through the height of one foot; **foot'print** the mark left on the ground or floor by a person's or animal's foot (also **foot'mark**); **foot'-pump** a pump held or operated by the foot; **foot'-rest** a support for the foot; **foot'-rope** a rope under a ship's yard to stand on when furling the sails; **foot'rot** affection of the feet in sheep; **foot'rule** a rule or measure a foot in length or measured off in feet.—*v.i.* **foot'slog** to march, tramp.—**foot'slogger**; **foot'slogging**; **foot'-soldier** a soldier serving on foot. —*adj.* **foot'sore** having sore or tender feet, as by much walking.—**foot'stalk** (*bot.*) the stalk or petiole of a leaf; **foot'step** a tread: a footfall: a footprint: (in *pl.*, *fig.*) course, example; **foot'stool** a stool for placing one's feet on when sitting.—*adj.* **foot'stooled**. —**foot'-ton** a unit of work or energy equal to the work done in raising one ton one foot against normal gravity; **foot'-warmer** a contrivance for keeping the feet warm; **foot'way** a footpath; **foot'wear** boots and shoes; **foot'work** use or management of the feet, as in games.—*adj.* **foot'worn** worn by many feet: footsore. —**a foot in the door** a first step towards a usu. difficult desired end; **at the feet of** in submission, homage, supplication, or devotion to, under the spell of; **drag one's feet** see drag.—**foot-and-mouth disease** a contagious disease of cloven-footed animals, characterised by vesicular eruption, esp. in the mouth and in the clefts of the feet; **have one foot in the grave** to be not far from death, **have one's feet on the ground** to act habitually with practical good sense; **my foot!** *interj.* expressing disbelief, usu. contemptuous; **on foot** walking or running: in activity or being; **play footsie** (*coll.*) to rub one's foot or leg against another person's, usu. with amorous intentions; **put a, or one's, foot wrong** (usu. in *neg.*) to make a mistake, blunder; **put one's best foot forward** to make one's best effort; **put one's foot down** to take a firm decision, usu. against something; **put one's foot in it** to spoil anything by some indiscretion; **the ball is at his feet** he has nothing to do but seize his opportunity; **the wrong foot** disadvantageous position or circumstances, as **catch on the wrong foot** to catch unprepared, **get off on the wrong foot** to make a bad beginning. [O.E. *fōt*, pl. *fēt*.]

footle *fōōt'l*, *v.i.* to trifle, to show foolish incompetence, to bungle.—*n.* silly nonsense.—*n.* and *adj.* **foot'ling.**

foo yung, yong. See **fu yung.**

foozle *fōōz'l*, (*coll.*) *n.* a bungled stroke at golf, etc.— *v.i.* and *v.t.* to bungle. [Cf. Ger. dial. *fuseln*, to work badly, to potter.]

fop *fop*, *n.* an affected dandy.—*adj.* **fopp'ish** vain and showy in dress: affectedly refined in manners.—*adv.* **fopp'ishly.**—*n.* **fopp'ishness.** [Cf. Ger. *foppen*, to hoax.]

for *för*, *far*, *prep.* in the place of: in favour of: on account of: in the direction of: with respect to: in respect of: by reason of: appropriate or adapted to, or in reference to: beneficial to: in quest of: in spite of: in recompense of: during: in the character of: to the extent of.—*conj.* because.—**as for** as far as concerns; **for all (that)** notwithstanding; **nothing for it but (to)** no other possible course but (to); **to be (in) for it** to have something unpleasant impending. [O.E. *for.*]

for- *för-*, *far-*, *pfx.* (1) in words derived from O.E., used to form verbs with the senses: (a) away, off; (b) against; (c) thoroughly, utterly: intensive; (d) exhaustion; (e) destruction. (2) used in words derived from O.E. to form adjs. with superlative force. (3) a contraction of *fore-*. (4) in words derived from L. *foris*, outside, *forās*, forth, out. No longer a living prefix.

fora. See **forum.**

forage *for'ij*, *n.* fodder, or food for horses and cattle: provisions: the act of foraging.—*v.i.* to go about and forcibly carry off food for horses and cattle: to rummage about for what one wants.—*v.t.* to plunder.

—*n.* **for'ager.**—**for'age-cap** the undress cap worn by infantry soldiers. [Fr. *fourrage*, O.Fr. *feurre*, fodder, of Gmc. origin; cf. **fodder.**]

foramen *fō-rā'man*, *fo-*, *n.* a small opening:—*pl.* **foramina** *-ram'i-na.*—*adjs.* **foram'inal; foram'inated, foram'inous** pierced with small holes: porous. [L. *forāmen—forāre*, to pierce.]

forasmuch *för-*, *far-az-much'*, *conj.* because, since (with *as*).

foray *for'ā*, *n.* a raid: a venture, attempt.—*v.t.* and *v.i.* to raid: to forage.—*n.* **for'ayer.** [**forage.**]

forbad(e). See **forbid.**

forbear[1] *for-*, *far-bār'*, *v.i.* to keep oneself in check: to abstain.—*v.t.* to abstain from: to avoid voluntarily: to spare: to withhold:—*pa.t.* **forbore**'; *pa.p.* **forborne**'.—*n.* **forbear'ance** exercise of patience: command of temper: clemency.—*adjs.* **forbear'ant, forbear'ing** long-suffering: patient.—*adv.* **forbear'ingly.** [O.E. *forberan*, pa.t. *forbær*, pa.p. *forboren*; see pfx. **for-** (1a), and **bear.**]

forbear[2] *för'bār.* Same as **forebear.**

forbid *far-*, *for-bid'*, *v.t.* to prohibit: to command not to:—*pa.t.* **forbade** *-bad'*, by some *-bād'*, or **forbad'**; *pa.p.* **forbidd'en.**—*adj.* **forbidd'en** prohibited: unlawful: not permitted, esp. in certain scientific rules: (of a combination of symbols) not in an operating code, i.e., revealing a fault (*comput.*).—*n.* **forbidd'ing.**—*adj.* uninviting: sinister: unprepossessing: threatening or formidable in look.—*adv.* **forbidd'ingly.**—*n.* **forbidd'ingness.**—**forbidden degrees** see **degree**; **forbidden fruit** that forbidden to Adam (Gen. ii. 17): anything tempting and prohibited. [O.E. *forbēodan*, pa.t. *forbēad*, pa.p. *forboden*; see pfx. **for-** (1a), and **bid.**]

forbore, forborne. See **forbear**[1].

force[1] *förs*, *fôrs*, *n.* strength, power, energy: efficacy: validity: influence: vehemence: violence: coercion: a group of men assembled for collective action (as *police force*), (in *pl.*; sometimes with *cap.*) navy, army, air force: an armament: any cause which changes the direction or speed of the motion of a portion of matter. —*v.t.* to draw or push by main strength: to thrust: to compel: to overcome the resistance of by force: to do violence to: to achieve or bring about by force: to take by violence: to strain: to cause to grow or ripen rapidly (*hort.*): to work up to a high pitch: to induce to play in a particular way (*cards*): to cause the playing of (*cards*). —*adj.* **forced** accomplished by great effort, as a forced march: strained, excessive, unnatural: artificially produced.—*adv.* **forc'edly.**—*n.* **forc'edness** the state of being forced: constraint: unnatural or undue distortion.—*adj.* **force'ful** full of force or might: energetic: driven or acting with power.—*adv.* **force'fully.**—*adj.* **force'less** weak.—*n.* **forc'er** the person or thing that forces.—*adj.* **forc'ible** having force: done by force.— *ns.* **forc'ibleness, forcibil'ity.**—*adv.* **forc'ibly.**—*v.t.* **force'-feed** to feed (a person or animal) forcibly, usu. by the mouth:—*pa.t.*, *pa.p.* **force'-fed.**—**force's feed'ing.**—*v.i.* **force'-land** to make a forced landing.— **forced land'ing** (*aero.*) a landing at a place where no landing was orig. planned, necessary because of some mishap; **force'-pump, forc'ing-pump** a pump that delivers liquid under pressure greater than its suction pressure; **forc'ing-house** a hothouse for forcing plants, or a place for hastening the growth of animals; **force the pace** to bring and keep the speed up to a high pitch by emulation; **in force** operative, legally binding: in great numbers. [Fr.—L.L. *fortia*—L. *fortis*, strong.]

force[2] *förs*, *fors*, *foss* *fos*, *ns.* a waterfall. [O.N. *fors.*]

force[3] *förs*, *fors* (*cook.*) *v.t.* to stuff, as fowl.— **force'meat** meat chopped fine and highly seasoned, used as a stuffing or alone. [For **farce.**]

force majeure *fors ma-zhār*, (Fr.) superior power: unavoidable accident, act of God (*legal*).

forceps *for'seps*, *n*. a pincer-like instrument or organ for holding, lifting, or removing:—*pl.* **for'ceps** also **for'cepses**. [L.,—*formus*, hot, *capère*, to hold.]

forcible, etc. See **force[1]**.

ford *förd*, *förd*, *n*. a place where water may be crossed by wading —*v.t.* to wade across.—*adj.* **ford'able**. [O E. *ford-faran*, to go.]

fore *för*, *för*, *adj*. in front.—*adv.* at or towards the front: previously.—*n*. the front: the foremast.—*interj*. (*golf*) a warning cry to anybody in the way of the ball.—*adj.* **foremost** (*för'möst*, *för'*; double superl. —O.E. *forma*, first, superl. of *fore*, and superl. suffix *-st*) first in place: most advanced: first in rank and dignity.—*adj*. and *adv.* **fore'-and-aft'** lengthwise of a ship: without square sails.—**fore-and-aft sail** any sail not set on yards and lying fore-and-aft when untrimmed; **to the fore** at hand: (loosely) prominent [O E *fore*, radically the same as for, prep.]

fore- *för*, *för-*, *pfx.* before: beforehand: in front —*n*. **fore'arm** the part of the arm between the elbow and the wrist.—*v.t.* **forearm'** to arm or prepare beforehand.—*n*. **forebear**, **forbear** (*för'bär*, *for'*, *Scot.*) an ancestor (from **be** and **suff** *-er*).—*v t*. **forebode'** to prognosticate: to have a premonition of (esp of evil).—*n*. **forebod'ing** a boding or perception beforehand: apprehension of coming evil.—*adv.* **forebod'ingly**.—*ns*. **fore'-brain** the front part of the brain; **fore'cabin** a cabin in a ship's forepart.—*v.t.* **fore'cast** to contrive or reckon beforehand: to foresee: to predict.—*v.i* to form schemes beforehand:—*pa.t.* and *pa.p.* **fore'cast** sometimes **fore'casted**.—*n*. **fore'cast** a previous contrivance: foresight: a prediction: a weather forecast (q.v); **fore'caster**; **fore'castle**, **fo'c'sle** (*fŏk'sl*, sometimes *för'kas-l*, *for'*) a short raised deck at the fore-end of a vessel: the forepart of the ship under the maindeck, the quarters of the crew; **fore'cloth** a cloth that hangs over the front of an altar; **fore'course** a foresail; **fore'court** a court in front of a building: an outer court: the front area of a garage or filling-station, where the petrol pumps are situated.—*v.t.* **foredate'** to date before the true time —*n*. **fore'deck** the forepart of a deck or ship.—*v.t.* **foredoom'** to doom beforehand.—*ns.* **fore'-end**; **fore'-father** an ancestor; **fore'finger** the finger next the thumb; **fore'foot** one of the anterior feet of a quadruped:—*pl.* **fore'feet**; **fore'front** the front or foremost part.—*adj*. **fore'gone** (**foregone conclusion** a conclusion come to before examination of the evidence: an obvious or inevitable conclusion or result).—*ns*. **foregone'ness**; **fore'ground** the part of a picture or field of view nearest the observer's eye, as opp. to the **background** (also *fig*); **fore'gut** the front section of the digestive tract of an embryo or an invertebrate animal; **fore'hand** the front position or its occupant: the upper hand, advantage, preference: the part of a horse that is in front of its rider: the part of the court to the right of a right-handed player or to the left of a left-handed player (*tennis*): a stroke played forehand (*tennis*).—*adj*. done beforehand: with the palm in front—opp. to **backhand**—*adv.* with hand in forehand position —*adj* **fore'handed** forehand, as of payment for goods before delivery, or for services before rendered: seasonable.—*ns*. **forehead** (*for'id*, *-ed*, *för'hed*, *för'hed*) the forepart of the head above the eyes, the brow; **fore'-horse** the foremost horse of a team.—*v.t.* **forejudge'** to judge before hearing the facts and proof: see **forjudge**.—*n* **forejudg'(e)ment**.—*v.t.* **foreknow'** (*för-*, *för-*) to know beforehand: to foresee.—*n* **foreknowledge** (*-nol'y*).—*adj*. **foreknown'**.—*ns* **fore'land** a point of land running forward into the sea, a headland: a front

region; **fore'leg** a front leg; **fore'limb**; **fore'lock** the lock of hair on the forehead (**pull, touch, tug the forelock** to raise one's hand to the forehead in sign of respect, subservience, etc.; **fore'man** the first or chief man, one appointed to preside over, or act as spokesman for, others: an overseer:—*pl.* **fore'men**; **fore'-mast** the mast that is forward, or next the bow of a ship; **fore'mastman** any sailor below the rank of petty officer.—*adj*. **fore'men'tioned** mentioned before in a writing or discourse —*n*. **fore'name** the first or Christian name.—*adj*. **fore'named** mentioned before. —*n*. **forenoon** (*för-nōō'n*, *för-*, *för'nōōn*, *för'*; chiefly *Scot.* and *Ir*) the morning: the part of the day before midday, as opposed to early morning.—*adj* (*för'*, *för'*) pertaining to this time.—*v.t* **fore'ordain'** to arrange beforehand: to predestinate —*ns*. **foreordina'tion**; **fore'part** the front: the early part; **fore'paw** a front paw; **fore'pay'ment** payment beforehand; **fore'play** sexual stimulation before intercourse.—*v.t* **fore'run'** to run or come before: to precede.—*n*. **fore'runner** a runner or messenger sent before: a precursor: a prognostic.—*adj*. **fore'said** already mentioned (see also **foresay**).—*n*. **foresail** (*för'sl*, *för'*, *-säl*) the chief and lowest square sail on the foremast: a triangular sail on the forestay.—*v t* **foresay'** to predict or foretell.— *v t*. and *v.i*. **foresee'** to see or know beforehand:—*pa.t.* **foresaw'**; *pa.p.* **foreseen'**.—*adjs.* **foresee'able**; **fore'see'ing**.—*adv* **foresee'ingly**.—*v.t.* **foreshad'ow** to shadow or typify beforehand: to give, or have, some indication of in advance.—*n*. **fore'shore** the space between high and low water marks.—*v t*. **foreshort'en** to draw or cause to appear as if shortened, by perspective —*ns*. **foreshort'ening**; **fore'side** the front side; **fore'sight** or power of foreseeing: wise forethought, prudence: the sight on the muzzle of a gun: a forward reading of a levelling staff —*adjs.* **fore'sighted**; **fore'sightful**; **fore'sightless**.—*n* **fore'skin** the skin that covers the glans penis, the prepuce.—*v.t.* **forestall** (*för-stöl'*, *för-*: O E *foresteall*, ambush, lit a place taken beforehand—*steall*, stand, station) to buy up before reaching the market, so as to sell again at higher prices: to anticipate: to hinder by anticipating: to bar.—*ns* **forestall'er**; **forestall'ing**; **forestal'ment**; **fore'stay** a rope reaching from the foremast-head to the bowsprit end to support the mast —*v.t.* **foretaste'** to taste before possession: to anticipate: to taste before another.—*n*. **fore'taste** a taste beforehand: anticipation.—*v.t.* **foretell'** to tell before: to prophesy—*pa.t.* and *pa.p* **foretold'**.—*ns*. **fore'thought** thought or care for the future: anticipation: thinking beforehand; **fore'token** a token or sign beforehand — *v.t.* **foretō'ken** to signify beforehand —*n*. and *adj* **foretō'kening**.—*ns*. **fore'tooth** a tooth in the forepart of the mouth:—*pl* **fore'teeth**; **fore'top** the platform at the head of the foremast (*naut.*); **foretop'mast** the mast erected at the head of the foremast, at the top of which is the **fore'top-gall'ant-mast**.—*v.t* **forewarn'** to warn beforehand: to give previous notice.—*ns*. **forewarn'ing**; **fore'wing** either of an insect's front pair of wings; **fore'woman** a woman overseer, a headwoman, a spokeswoman for a group (e g. for a jury):—*pl* **fore'women**; **fore'word** a preface [O E. *fore*]

foreclose *för-klōz'*, *for-*, *v.t* to preclude: to prevent: to stop: to bar the right of redeeming.—*n*. **foreclosure** (*-klō'zhэr*) a foreclosing the process by which a mortgagor, failing to repay the money lent on the security of an estate, is compelled to forfeit his right to redeem the estate (*law*). [O Fr *forclos*, pa.p of *forclore*, to exclude—L *foris*, outside, and *claudёre*, *clausum*, to shut]

foregather. See **forgather**.

forego. See **forgo**.

foreign *for'in, adj.* belonging to another country: from abroad: alien: extraneous: not belonging: unconnected: not appropriate.—*ns.* **for'eigner** a native of another country; **for'eignness.**—**foreign correspondent** a newspaper correspondent in a foreign country in order to report its news, etc.; **foreign exchange** the exchange, conversion, etc. of foreign currencies, **foreign legion** an army unit consisting of aliens (*caps.*) a former French army unit, consisting of soldiers of all nationalities, serving outside France; **Foreign Office** government department dealing with foreign affairs. [O.Fr. *forain*—L L. *foràneus*—L *forâs*, out of doors]

forejudge¹. See **fore-.**

forejudge². See **forjudge.**

forensic *fə-ren'sik, adj.* belonging to courts of law, held by the Romans in the forum: loosely, of or pertaining to sciences or scientists connected with legal investigations.—**forensic medicine** medical jurisprudence, the application of medical knowledge to the elucidation of doubtful questions in a court of justice [L. *forènsis—forum*, market-place, forum]

forest *for'ist, n* a large uncultivated tract of land covered with trees and underwood: woody ground and rude pasture: a preserve for big game: a royal preserve for hunting.—*adj.* pertaining to a forest silvan: rustic —*v t.* to cover with trees.—*adj.* **for'estal, foresteal** (*fər-est'i-əl*).—*n.* **foresta'tion** afforestation.—*adj* **for'ested.**—*n.* **for'ester** one who has charge of a forest: one who has care of growing trees a member of the Ancient Order of Foresters or similar friendly society· an inhabitant of a forest.—*adj* **for'estine.**—*n.* **for'estry** the art of planting, tending, and managing forests; forest country: an extent of trees [O.Fr *forest* (Fr *forêt*)—L.L. *forestis* (*silva*), the outside wood, as opposed to the *parcus* (park) or walled-in wood—L. *foris*, out of doors.]

forever *fər-ev'ər, adv* for ever, for all time to come: eternally: everlastingly.—*adv.* **forev'ermore** for ever hereafter

forfeit *for'fit, n* that to which a right is lost a penalty for a crime, or breach of some condition: a fine: something deposited and redeemable by a sportive fine or penalty, esp in *pl.*, a game of this kind.—*adj.* **forfeited.**—*v.t.* to lose the right to by some fault or crime: to penalise by forfeiture. loosely, to give up voluntarily.—*adj.* **for'feitable.**—*n.* **for'feiture** act of forfeiting: state of being forfeited the thing forfeited. [O.Fr *forfait*—L.L. *forisfactum*—L *foris*, outside, *facère*, to make]

forgather, foregather *fər-gadh'ər, v t* to meet, esp by chance: to fraternise. [Pfx. **for-** (1c).]

forgave. See **forgive.**

forge¹ *förj, forj, n.* the workshop of a workman in iron, etc : a furnace, esp. one in which iron is heated: a smithy: a place where anything is shaped or made — *v.t.* to form by heating and hammering, by heating and pressure, or by pressure alone (in the last case, often **cold forge**): to form· to make falsely: to fabricate: to counterfeit for purposes of fraud: to form by great pressure, electricity, or explosion.—*v.t.* to commit forgery —*adj.* **forge'able.**—*ns* **forg'er** one who forges, **forg'ery** fraudulently making or altering anything, esp. a writing· that which is forged or counterfeited; **forg'ing** a piece of metal shaped by hammering: act of one who forges —**forge'man.** [O.Fr. *forge*—L *fabrica—faber*, a workman.]

forge² *förj, forj, v.t.* to move steadily on (usu with *ahead*).

forget *fər-get', v.t.* to lose or put away from the memory: to fail to remember or think of· to leave behind accidentally· to neglect:—*pr.p.* **forgett'ing;** *pa.t.* **forgot',** *pa.p* **forgott'en** (also in *U S.*, but

otherwise *arch.* **forgot'**).—*adj.* **forget'ful** apt to forget: inattentive.—*adv.* **forget'fully.**—*n.* **forget'fulness.**—*adj.* **forgett'able.**—*n.* **forgett'er.**—*n.* and *adj* **forgett'ing.**—*adj.* **forgott'en.**—*n.* **forgott'enness.**—**forget'-me-not** any plant of the genus Myosotis, regarded as an emblem of loving remembrance —**forget it** (*coll.*; esp in *imper.*) used to state that there is no need to offer apologies, thanks, etc , or to say or do anything further about a particular matter; **forget oneself** to lose one's self-control or dignity, to descend to words and deeds unworthy of oneself [O.E. *forgetan* (*forgietan*)—*pfx for-*, away, *getan* (*gietan*), to get.]

forgive *fər-giv', v t* to pardon: to overlook.—*v.t.* to be merciful or forgiving:—*pa.t.* **forgave',** *pa p.* **forgiv'en.**—*adj* **forgiv'able.**—*n.* **forgive'ness** pardon remission: a disposition to pardon.—*adj.* **forgiv'ing** ready to pardon: merciful: compassionate [O E. *forgiefan*—pfx. *for-*, away, *giefan*, to give.]

forgo, forego *för-, för-; får-gö', v.t.* to leave: to give up to relinquish: to do without: to forbear the use or advantage of.—*v.i* to go or pass away—*pr.p* **for(e)go'ing;** *pa.p.* **for(e)gone';** *pa.t* **for(e)went'.**— See also **forego.** [O E. *forgân*, to pass by, abstain from—pfx *for-*, away, *gân*, to go.]

forgot, forgotten. See **forget.**

forint *for'int, n* the monetary unit of Hungary since 1946

forjudge, forejudge *för-juj', for-,* (*law*) *v t.* to deprive of a right, object. etc. by a judgment. [O Fr *forjugier—fors*,—L. *foris*, out, and *jugier* (Fr *juger*), to judge.]

fork *fork, n.* a pronged instrument: anything that divides into prongs or branches: a branch or prong: the space or angle between branches, esp. on a tree or between the legs: a confluent, tributary, or branch of a river· one of the branches into which a road divides: a (place of) bifurcation: the part of a bicycle to which a wheel is attached: the appearance of a flash of lightning a simultaneous attack on two pieces by one piece (*chess*)—*v.i.* to branch: to follow a branch road.—*v.t.* to form as a fork: to move with a fork: to stab with a fork: to menace two pieces simultaneously (*chess*).—*adj.* **forked** shaped like a fork.—*adv.* **fork'edly.**—*ns.* **fork'edness; fork'er; fork'iness.**—*adj* **fork'y.**—**fork lunch(eon), supper,** etc., a buffettype meal eaten with a fork.—*adj.* **fork'-tailed.**—**fork-lift truck** a power-driven truck with an arrangement of steel prongs which can lift, raise up high, and carry heavy packages and stack them where required (often used with a pallet); **fork out, over, up** (*slang*) to hand or pay over, esp. unwillingly. [O.E. *forca*—L. *furca.*]

forlorn *fər-lorn', adj* quite lost: forsaken: neglected: wretched.—*adv.* **forlorn'ly.**—*n* **forlorn'ness.** [O E *forloren*, pa.p of *forlêosan*, to lose—pfx. *for-*, away, and *lêosan*, to lose]

forlorn hope *fər-lorn' höp'* a body of soldiers selected for some service of uncommon danger: a desperate enterprise of last resort· a vain or faint hope (from association with hope = expectation). [Du *verloren hoop*, lost troop.]

form *form, n* shape: a mould: something that holds, shapes: a species: a pattern: a mode of being: a mode of arrangement: order. regularity: system, as of government. style and arrangement· structural unity in music, literature, etc.: a prescribed set of words or course of action: ceremony: behaviour. condition of fitness or efficiency: a schedule to be filled in with details a specimen document for imitation· the inherent nature of an object (*phil.*). type from which an impression is to be taken arranged and secured in a chase—*U K* usu **forme** (*print.*) a long seat, a bench: a school class: the criminal record (*slang*): the condition of fitness of e.g. horse, athlete: (*coll.*; with *the*) the situation, position.—*v.t.* to give form or shape to: to bring into being: to make: to contrive: to conceive in the mind: to go to make up: to establish. —*v.i.* to assume a form.—*adj.* **form'al** according to form or established mode: relating to form ceremonious, punctilious, methodical: having the form only: having the power of making a thing what it is: essential: proper.—*n.* **formalisā'tion, -z-.**—*v.t* **form'alise, -ize** to make formal: to make official or valid: to make precise, give a clear statement of.—*v.i.* to be formal.—*ns.* **form'alism** excessive observance of form or conventional usage, esp. in religion: stiffness of manner, **form'alist** one having exaggerated regard to rules or established usages; **formal'ity** the precise observance of forms or ceremonies: a matter of form: a ceremonious observance: established order: sacrifice of substance to form.—*adv.* **form'ally.**—*n.* **form'ant** a component of a speech sound determining its quality.—*n.* **formā'tion** a making or producing: a structure: an arrangement of e.g. troops, aircraft, players: a stratigraphical group of strata (*geol.*).—*adj.* **form'ative** giving form, determining, moulding: capable of development: growing: serving to form words by derivation or inflection, not radical (*gram.*).—*n.* (*gram.*) a formative element: any grammatical element from which words and sentences are constructed.—*adj.* **formed.** —*ns.* **form'er; form'ing.**—*adj.* **form'less.**—*adv.* **form'lessly.**—*n.* **form'lessness.**—formal logic see **logic; formal verdict** (*law*) one in which the jury follows the judge's directions: in Scotland, in a fatal accident inquiry, a finding of death by misadventure with no apportioning of blame; **form horse** in horseracing the favourite, the expected winner (also *fig.*); **form master, mistress, teacher** esp. in a secondary school, the teacher who is responsible for the administration, welfare, etc. of a form.—**good** or **bad form** according to good or recognised social usage, or the opposite. [L. *fōrma*, shape.]

-form *fōrm*, in composition, having a specified form or number of forms. [L. *fōrma*, form.]

formaldehyde, formalin. See under **formic.**

format *fōr'mat*, *n.* of books, etc., the size, form, shape in which they are issued: the style, arrangement and contents of e.g. a radio or television programme: (the description of) the way data is, or is to be, arranged in a file, on a card, etc. (*comput.*). [Fr.]

forme (*print.*). See **form.**

former *form'ər*, *adj.* (*comp.* of **fore**) before in time: past: first mentioned (of two).—*adv.* **form'erly** in former times: heretofore [Formed late on analogy of M.E. *formest*, foremost, by adding comp. suff. *-er* to base of O.E *forma*, first, itself superlative.]

formic *fōr'mik*, *adj.* pertaining to ants.—*ns.* **formal'-dehyde** a formic aldehyde, formalin; **for'malin, for'mol** (*-mol*, *-mōl*) a formic aldehyde used as an antiseptic, germicide, or preservative.—*n.* **formica'-tion** a sensation like that of ants creeping on the skin —**formic acid** a fatty acid H·CO·OH. found in ants and nettles [L *formica*, an ant.]

Formica® *fōr-mī'kə*, *n.* any of a number of plastic laminates used to provide hard, heat-resistant, easily-cleaned surfaces.

formidable *fōr'mid-ə-bl*, by some *-mid'*, *adj.* causing fear: inspiring awe: redoubtable.—*ns.* **formid-abil'ity; for'midableness.**—*adv.* **for'midably.** [Fr . —L. *formīdābilis—formīdō*, fear.]

formol. See under **formic.**

formula *form'ū-lə*, *n.* a prescribed form: a formal statement of doctrines: a recipe: a milk mixture used as baby food: a statement of joint aims or principles

worked out for practical purposes by diplomats of divergent interests: a solution or answer worked out by different sides in a dispute, etc.: a technical specification governing cars entered for certain motor-racing events: a general expression for solving problems (*math.*): a set of symbols expressing the composition of a body (*chem.*): a list of ingredients of a patent medicine:—*pl.* **formulae** (*fōrm'ū-lē*), **form'ülas.**—*adjs.* **form'ūlar, formülaris'tic.**—*v.t.* **form'ülarise, -ize.**—*ns.* **formülarisā'tion, -z-, formülā'tion; form'ülary** a formula: a book of formulae or precedents.—*adj.* prescribed: ritual.— *vs.t* **form'ülate, form'ülise, -ize** to reduce to or express in a formula: to state or express in a clear or definite form. [L. *fōrmula*, dim. of *fōrma.*]

fornicate *fōr'ni-kāt*, *v.i.* to commit fornication.—*ns.* **fornica'tion** voluntary sexual intercourse of the unmarried, sometimes extended to cases where only one of the pair concerned is unmarried: adultery (*B.*), or idolatry (*fig.*); **for'nicātor; for'nicātress.** [L. *fornicārī, -ātus—fornix*, a vault, brothel.]

forsake *fər-sāk'*, *for-*, *v.t.* to desert: to abandon:— *pr.p.* **forsāk'ing;** *pa.t.* **forsook';** *pa.p* **forsāk'en.**— *adj.* **forsāk'en.**—*adv.* **forsāk'enly.**—*ns.* **forsāk'en-ness; forsāk'ing** abandonment. [O.E. *forsacan—for-*, away, *sacan*, to strive.]

forsooth *fər-sōōth'*, *fōr-*, *adv.* in truth: certainly (now only ironically). [**for sooth.**]

forswear *fər-swār'*, *fōr-*, *v.t.* to deny or renounce upon oath.—*v.i.* to swear falsely:—*pa.t.* **forswore';** *pa.p.* **forsworn'.**—*adj.* **forsworn'** perjured, having forsworn oneself.—*n.* **forsworn'ness.**—**forswear oneself** to swear falsely. [Pfx. **for-** (1b).]

Forsythia *fōr-sī'thi-ə*, *-sī'*, *n.* a genus of shrubs with flowers like jasmine: (without *cap.*) a plant of this genus. [After William *Forsyth* (1737–1804), botanist.]

fort *fōrt*, *fort*, *n.* a small fortress: (in N. America) an outlying trading-station.—*v.t.* to fortify.—**hold the fort** to take temporary charge. [Fr.,—L. *fortis*, strong.]

fortalice *fōrt'ə-lis*, *n.* a fortress: a small outwork of a fortification. [L.L. *fortalitia—L. fortis.*]

forte[1] *fōrt'i*, *n.* that in which one excels. [Fr. *fort*, strong.]

forte[2] *for'ti*, (*mus.*). *adj.* and *adv.* loud:—*superl.* **fortis'simo, double** *superl.* **fortissis'simo** as loud as possible.—*n.* a loud passage in music.—*adj.* and *adv.* **fortepia'no** loud with immediate relapse into softness. [It.]

forth *fōrth*, *forth*, *adv.* forward: onward: out: into the open: in continuation. abroad.—*adj.* **forth-com'ing** just coming forth: about to appear: approaching: at hand, ready to be produced: (of a person) friendly, communicative.—*adv.* **forth'right** (or *-rīt'*) straightforward: at once.—*adj.* straightforward: downright.—*adv.* **forth'rightly.**—*n.* **forth'-rightness.**—*adv.* **forthwith** (*-with'*, *-widh'*, or *fōrth'*) immediately.—**and so forth** and so on. [O.E. **forth—fore**, before.]

forties, fortieth. See **forty.**

fortify *for'ti-fī*, *v.t.* to strengthen with forts, etc., against attack: to invigorate: to confirm: to strengthen (esp. certain wines) by adding alcohol: to enrich (a food) by adding e.g. vitamins:—*pr.p.* **for'tifying;** *pa t.* and *pa.p.* **for'tified.**—*adj.* **for'tifiable.**—*ns.* **fortifica'tion** the art of strengthening a military position by means of defensive works: the work so constructed. that which fortifies; **for'tifier.** [Fr. *fortifier*—L.L. *fortificāre* —*fortis*, strong, *facĕre*, to make.]

fortis *for'tis*, (*phon.*) *adj.* of a consonant, articulated with relatively great muscular effort and pressure of breath (opp. to *lenis*).—Also *n*.:—*pl.* **fortes**. [L., strong.]

fortissimo. See forte.

fortitude *för'ti-tūd*, in *U.S.* -*tōō d*, *n.* courage in endurance. [L. *fortitūdō*, -*inis*—*fortis*, strong.]

fortnight *fört'nīt*, *n.* two weeks or fourteen days.— *adj.* and *adv.* **fort'nightly** once a fortnight.—*n.* a magazine, etc. appearing fortnightly. [O.E. *fēowertýne niht*, fourteen nights.]

Fortran *för'tran*, *n.* a computer language widely used in scientific work. [*Formula translation*.]

fortress *för'tras*, *för'*, *n.* a fortified place. [O.Fr. *forteresse*, another form of *fortelesce* (see **fortalice**).]

fortuitous *for-tū'i-tas*, in *U.S.* -*tōō'*, *adj.* happening by chance: fortunate.—*ns.* **fortū'itism** belief in evolution by fortuitous variation; **fortū'itist**.—*adv.* **fortū'itously**.—*ns.* **fortū'itousness**, **fortū'ity**. [L. *fortuītus*.]

fortune *för'chan*, *n.* whatever comes by lot or chance. luck: the arbitrary ordering of events: a prediction of one's future: success: a great accumulation of wealth: a large amount of money.—*adj.* **for'tunate** happening by good fortune: lucky: auspicious: felicitous. —*adv.* **for'tunately** in a fortunate way, by good luck: I'm glad to say, happy to report.—**fortune cookie** (*U.S.*) dough wrapped and cooked around a piece of paper which has a (supposed) fortune or a maxim on it, served esp. in Chinese homes and restaurants; **for'tune-hunter** one who hunts for a wealthy marriage; **for'tune-teller** one who professes to foretell one's fortune; **for'tune-telling.—a small fortune** quite a large fortune. [Fr.,—L. *fortūna*.]

forty *för'ti*, *adj.* and *n.* four times ten.—*n.pl.* **forties** the numbers forty to forty-nine: the fortieth or forty-ninth years (of life, a century): a range of temperature from forty to just less than fifty degrees: (*cap.* with *the*) the sea area lying between NE Scotland and SW Norway, with a minimum depth of 40 fathoms.—*adj.* **for'tieth** the last of forty, or in an equivalent position: equal to one of forty equal parts —*n.* one of forty equal parts; a person or thing in fortieth position.—*adj.* **for'tyish** apparently about forty years old.—**for'ty-five'** a record played at a speed of 45 revolutions per minute: (*cap.* with *the*) the Jacobite rebellion of 1745; **forty winks** a short nap, esp. after dinner.—**roaring forties** the tract of stormy west winds south of 40°S latitude (occasionally also in the Atlantic north of 40°N) [O.E. *fēowertig—fēower*, four, -*tig*, ten (as suffix).]

forum *fō'ram*, *fō'*, *n.* a market-place, esp. that in Rome where public business was transacted and justice dispensed: a meeting to discuss topics of public concern:—*pl.* **fo'rums**, **fo'ra**. [L. *forum*.]

forward *för'ward*, *adj.* near or at the forepart: in advance: well advanced: ready: too ready: presumptuous: officious: early ripe.—*v.t.* to help on: to send on.—*advs.* **for'ward**, **for'wards** towards what is in front: onward: progressively.—*adv.* **forward** (*för'ad*) towards, in, the front part of a ship.—*ns.* **for'ward** in football, etc., a player in the front line; **for'warder**; **for'warding** the act of sending forward merchandise, etc.—*adv.* **for'wardly**.—*n.* **for'wardness**.—*adj.* **for'ward-looking** having regard to the future: progressive. [O.E. *foreward* (W.S. *foreweard*)—*fore*, and -*ward* (-*weard*) sig. direction; the *s* of *forwards* is a gen. ending.]

forwent *far-*, *för-went'*. See **forgo**.

forzando, **forzato**. See **sforzando**.

foss[1], **fosse** *fos*, *n.* a ditch, moat, trench, or canal.— **foss(e) way** any of the British Roman roads having a fosse on either side. [Fr. *fosse*—L. *fossa*—*fodēre*, *fossum*, to dig.]

foss[2]. See **force**[2].

fossa *fos'a*, (*anat.*) *n.* a pit or depression. [L., a ditch.]

fossil *fos'l*, or -*il*, *n.* a relic or trace of a former living thing preserved in the rocks (*geol.*): an antiquated, out-of-date, or unchanging person or thing (*fig.*).— *adj.* dug out of the earth: in the condition of a fossil: antiquated.—*adj.* **fossilif'erous** bearing or containing fossils.—*n.* **fossilisā'tion**, -*z*-.—*v.t.* **foss'ilise**, -*ize* to convert into a fossil (also *fig.*).—*v.i.* to become fossil: to look for fossils (*coll.*).—**fossil fuel** coal, oil, etc., produced in the earth by process of fossilisation [Fr. *fossile*—L. *fossilis*—*fodēre*, to dig.]

fossorial *fos-ō'ri-al*, -*ō'*, (*zool.*) *adj.* adapted for digging. [L. *fossor*—*fodēre*, to dig.]

fossula, **fossulate**. See **fossa**[2].

foster *fos'tar*, *v.t.* to bring up or nurse, esp. a child not one's own: to put a child into the care of one not its parent: to treat, e.g. the elderly, in a similar fashion: to encourage: to promote: to cherish.—*v.i.* to care for a child or elderly person in a foster-home.—*adj.* of or concerned with fostering.—*ns.* **fos'terage** the act or custom of fostering or nursing: the condition or relation of foster-child: the care of a foster-child: the act of encouraging or cultivating; **fos'terer**; **fos'tering**; **fos'terling** a foster-child.—**fos'ter-brother** a male child nursed or brought up with a child or children of different parents; **fos'ter-child** a child nursed or brought up by one who is not its parent; **fos'ter-daughter**; **fos'ter-father** one who brings up a child in place of its father; **fos'ter-home**; **fos'ter-mother** one who brings up a child not her own: an apparatus for rearing chickens; **fos'ter-nurse**; **fos'ter-parent**; **fos'ter-sister**; **fos'ter-son**. [O.E. *fōstrian*, to nourish, *fōster*, food.]

fouetté *fwe'tā*, *n.* ballet-step in which the foot makes a whip-like movement. [Fr.]

fought *fot*, *pa.t.* and *pa.p.*, of **fight**.

foul *fowl*, *adj.* filthy: dirty: disfigured: untidy: loathsome: obscene: impure: shameful: gross: in bad condition: stormy: unfavourable: unfair: of little worth: choked up: entangled: bad (*coll.*).—*v.t.* to make foul: to collide with, come in accidental contact with: to obstruct.—*v.i.* to collide.—*n.* the act of fouling: any breach of the rules in games or contests.—*adv.* in a foul manner: unfairly.—*adv.* **foul'ly**.—*n.* **foul'ness**. —*adjs.* **foul'-mouthed**, **foul'-spok'en** addicted to the use of foul or profane language.—**foul'-mouth'edness**; **foul play** unfair action in any game or contest: dishonest dealing generally: violence or murder; **foul'-up** see **foul up**.—**claim a foul** to assert that a rule has been broken, and claim the penalty; **fall foul of** to come against: to clash with: to assail; **foul up** to befoul, make dirty: to (cause to) be or become blocked or entangled: to spoil (*coll.*): to cause to fail or break down (*coll.*): to bungle, make a mistake in (*coll.*) (*n.* **foul'-up**); **make foul water** (*naut.*) to come into such shallow water that the keel raises the mud. [O.E. *fūl.*]

foulard *fōō-lärd'*, -*lär'*, *n.* a soft untwilled silk fabric: a silk handkerchief. [Fr.]

foumart *fōō'mart*, -*mart*, *n.* a polecat. [M.E. *fulmard* —O.E. *fūl*, foul, *mearth*, a marten.]

found[1] *pa.t.* and *pa.p.* of **find**.—**found'ling** a little child found deserted.—**all found** see **all**; **found money** money gain got for nothing.

found[2] *fownd*, *v.t.* to lay the bottom or foundation of: to establish on a basis: to originate: to endow.—*v.i.* to rely (with *on*).—*ns.* **founda'tion** the act of founding: the base of a building: the groundwork or basis: a permanent fund for a benevolent purpose or for some special object: a cosmetic preparation used as a base for facial make-up: a priming substance applied to a canvas or board as a base for oil-painting; **founda'**-

tioner one supported from the funds or foundation of an institution; **found'er** one who founds, establishes or originates: an endower:—*fem.* **found'ress.**—**foundation garment** a woman's undergarment for supporting or controlling the figure; **founda'tion-stone** one of the stones forming the foundation of a building, esp. a stone laid with public ceremony; **found'er-member** one of those members of a society who were instrumental in its foundation; **founding father** one who forms or establishes an institution, organisation, etc. [Fr. *fonder*—L. *fundāre*, *-ātum*, to found—*fundus*, the bottom.]

found³ *fownd*, *v.t.* to make by melting and allowing to harden in a mould (esp. metals): to cast.—*ns.* **found'er; found'ry** the art of founding or casting: a place where founding is carried on: articles produced by founding. [Fr. *fondre*—L. *fundĕre*, *fūsum*, to pour.]

founder *fownd'ər*, *v.i.* (of a building) to subside: to collapse in ruins (also *fig.*): to go to the bottom: (of a ship) to fill with water and sink: to stumble: (of a lame: to stick in mud.—*v.t.* to cause to founder.—*n.* a collapse. [O.Fr. *fondrer*, to fall in—*fond*—L *fundus*, bottom.]

fount¹ *fownt*, *font*, (*print.*) *n.* a complete assortment of types of one sort, with all that is necessary for printing in that kind of letter.—Also (esp in U.S.) **font.** [Fr. *fonte*—*fondre*—L. *fundĕre*, to cast.]

fount² *fownt*, *n.* a spring of water: a source. [L. *fōns*, *fontis*.]

fountain *fownt'in*, *n.* a spring of water, a jet: a structure for supplying drinking water or other liquid: an ornamental structure with jets, spouts, and basins of water: a reservoir from which oil, ink, etc., flows, as in a lamp, a pen: the source.—**fount'ain-head** the head or source: the beginning; **fount'ain-pen'** a pen with a reservoir for ink. [Fr. *fontaine*—L.L. *fontāna*—L. *fōns*, *fontis*, a spring.]

four *fōr*, *fōr*, *n.* the cardinal number next above three: a symbol representing that number: a set of four things or persons (leaves, oarsmen, etc.): a four-oar boat: a four-cylinder engine or car: a shoe or other article of a size denoted by 4: a card with four pips: a score of four points, tricks, strokes, etc.: the fourth hour after midday or midnight: the age of four years.—*adj.* of the number four: four years old.—*adj.* and *adv.* **four'fold** in four divisions: four times as much.—*ns.* **four'foldness; four'some** a group of four: anything in which four act together, esp. a game of golf (two against two, partners playing the same ball) or a reel—also *adj.*—*adjs.* **four'-ball** (*golf*) played two against two with four balls, best ball counting; **four's figure** running into four figures: to four places of decimals; **four'-foot** measuring four feet; **four'-foot'ed** having four feet; **four'-hand'ed** having four hands: played by four players (*cards*).—**four'-in-hand** a coach drawn by four horses.—*adjs.* **four'-leaved, four'-leafed, four'-leaf; four'-legged'; four'-part, four-part'ed** in four parts.—**four'pence** the value of four pennies.—*adj.* **four'penny** sold or offered for fourpence; (**fourpenny one** (*slang*) a blow, punch).—**four'-post'er** a large bed with four curtain posts; **four'-pound'er** a gun that throws a four-pound shot.—*adj.* **four'score** eighty.—**four'-seat'er** a vehicle seated for four.—*adjs.* **four'-square'** (also *adv.*) square: presenting a firm bold front: frank, honest, forthright; **four'-wheel** acting on or by means of four wheels; **four'-wheeled.—four'-wheel'er** a cab or other vehicle with four wheels.—**four-letter word** any of a number of vulgar short words, esp. of four letters, referring to sex or excrement; **four-stroke cycle** in an internal-combustion engine, a recurring series of four strokes of the piston—an out-stroke

drawing the mixed gases into the cylinder. an in-stroke compressing them, an out-stroke impelled by their explosion and working the engine, and an in-stroke driving out the burnt gas; **on all fours** on four feet, or hands and feet or hands and knees: analogous, strictly comparable; **the four seas** see **sea.** [O.E. *fēower*.]

fourchette *fōō r-shet'*, *n.* a forked piece between glove fingers, uniting the front and back parts: the furcula, or wishbone, of a bird: an animal's web foot: part of the external female genitals, a membrane at the posterior junction of the labia minora. [Fr., dim. of *fourche*—L. *furca*, fork.]

fourteen *fōr-*, *fōr-tēn'*, or *fōr'*, *fōr'tēn*, *n.* and *adj.* four and ten.—*adj.* **four'teenth** (or *-tēnth'*) last of fourteen: next after the thirteenth: equal to one of fourteen equal parts.—*n.* a fourteenth part: a person or thing in fourteenth position.—*adv.* **fourteenth'ly.** [O.E. *fēowertēne* (*-tiene*); see **four** and **ten.**]

fourth *fōrth*, *fōrth*, *adj.* last of four: next after the third: equal to one of four equal parts.—*n.* one of four equal parts: a person or thing in fourth position: an interval of three (conventionally called four) diatonic degrees: a tone at that interval from another: a combination of two tones separated by that interval.—*adv.* **fourth'ly.—fourth dimension** that of time, as opposed to the three spatial dimensions: that which is beyond ordinary experience.—*adjs.* **fourth'-dimensional; fourth'-rate** of the fourth order: inferior.—**Fourth World** the poorest of the poor countries of the world. [O.E. *fēowertha*, *fēortha*.]

fovea *fō'vi-ə*, (*anat.*) *n.* a depression or pit:—*pl.* **fo'veae** (*-ē*).—*adjs.* **fo'veal; fo'veate** pitted. [L. *fovea*.]

fowl *fowl*, *n.* a bird: a bird of the poultry kind, a cock or hen: the flesh of fowl:—*pl.* **fowls, fowl.**—*v.i.* to kill or try to kill wildfowl.—*ns.* **fowl'er** one who takes wildfowl; **fowl'ing.—fowl'ing-net** a net for catching birds; **fowl'ing-piece** a light gun for small-shot, used in fowling; **fowl'-pest** an acute contagious virus disease of birds (**fowl'-plague**): another similar disease, Newcastle disease. [O.E. *fugol*.]

fox *foks*, *n.* an animal akin to the dog having upright ears and a long bushy tail:—*fem.* **vix'en:** extended to other animals, as flying-fox: anyone notorious for cunning.—*v.t.* (*coll.*) to baffle, deceive, cheat.—*v.i.* (*coll.*) to act cunningly: to cheat.—*v.i.* and *v.t.* (of paper) to discolour, showing brownish marks.—*adj.* **foxed** of books, discoloured: drunk: baffled.—*ns.* **fox'iness** craftiness: decay: a harsh, sour taste: spotted state as in books; **fox'ing** the act of one who foxes.—*adj.* **fox'y** of foxes: fox-like: cunning: reddish brown.—**fox'-bat** a flying-fox, a fruit-bat; **fox'-earth** a fox's burrow.—**fox'glove** a plant (Digitalis) with flowers like glove-fingers; **fox'hole** a fox's earth; a small entrenchment (*mil.*); **fox'hound** a hound used for chasing foxes; **fox'-hunt; fox'-hunter; fox'-hunting; fox'-tail** a fox's brush: a genus (Alopecurus) of grasses, with head like a fox's tail; **fox'-terr'ier** a kind of terrier trained to unearth foxes; **fox'-trot** a shuffling dance to syncopated music. [O.E. *fox.*]

foyer *foi'ā*, *foi'ər* (Fr. *fwä-yā*), *n.* in theatres, a public room opening on the lobby. [Fr.,—L. *focus*, hearth.]

fra *frà*, (It.) *n.* brother, friar.

frabjous *frab'jəs*, *adj.* perh. joyous: surpassing.—*adv.* **frab'jously.** [Invented by Lewis Carroll.]

fracas *frak'ä*, *fra-kä'*, *n.* uproar: a noisy quarrel:—*pl.* **fracas** (*-kaz*) [Fr.—It. *fracasso*—*fracassare*, to make an uproar.]

fraction *frak'shən*, *n.* a fragment or small piece: any part of a unit (*arith*.): a portion separated by fractionation: the breaking of the bread in the Eucharist.—

adj. **frac'tional** belonging to a fraction or fractions: of the nature of a fraction.—*n.* **fractionalisā'tion, -z-.**—*v.t.* **frac'tionalise, -ize** to break up into parts.—*ns.* **frac'tionalism** the state of consisting of discrete units: the action of forming a fraction within the Communist party; **frac'tionalist** a breaker-up of political unity.—*adv.* **frac'tionally.**—*adj.* **frac'tionary** fractional: fragmentary.—*v.t.* **frac'tionate** to break up into smaller units: to separate the components of by distillation or otherwise.—*ns.* **fractionā'tion; frac'tionātor** a plant for carrying out fractional distillation.—*n.* **fractionisā'tion, -z-.**—*v.t.* **frac'tionise, -ize** to break up into fractions.—*adj.* **frac'tious** ready to quarrel: cross.—*adv.* **frac'tiously.**—*ns.* **frac'tiousness; frac'ture** (*-char*) breaking: the breach or part broken: the surface of breaking, other than cleavage: the breaking of a bone.—*v.t.* and *v.i.* to break through: to crack.—**fractional distillation** a distillation process for the separation of the various constituents of liquid mixtures by means of their different boiling points.—**comminuted fracture** a fracture in which the bone is splintered; **compound fracture** the breaking of a bone, communicating with a co-existing skin wound; **greenstick fracture** a fracture where the bone is partly broken, partly bent, occurring esp. in limbs of children; **impacted fracture** a fracture in which the ends of bone are driven into each other; **simple fracture** a fracture of bone without wound in the skin. [L. *frangēre*, *frāctum*, to break (partly through Fr.).]

fraenum. Same as **frenum.**

fragile *fraj'īl*, in U.S. *-al, adj.* easily broken: frail: delicate.—*adv.* **fra'gilely.**—*ns.* **fragility** (*fra-jil'*), **fra'gileness.** [Fr.,—L. *fragilis*—*frangēre*, *frāctum.*]

fragment *frag'mant, n.* a piece broken off: a usu. small piece of something broken or smashed: an unfinished portion.—*v.t.* and *v.i.* (*frag-ment'*) to break into fragments.—*adj.* **fragmental** (*-ment'*; also *frag'-man-tal*) composed of fragments of older rocks: in fragments.—*adv.* **frag'mentally.**—*n.* **frag'-mentariness.**—*adjs.* **frag'mentary, fragment'ed** consisting of fragments: broken: in fragments: existing or operating in separate parts, not forming a harmonious unity.—*n.* **fragmentā'tion** division into fragments: cell division without mitosis (*biol.*).—**fragmentation bomb, grenade** one which shatters into small destructive fragments on explosion. [L. *fragmentum*—*frangēre, frāctum*, to break.]

fragrant *frā'grant, adj.* sweet-scented.—*ns.* **fra'grance, fra'grancy.**—*adv.* **fra'grantly.**—*n.* **fra'grantness.** [L. *frāgrāns, -antis*, pr.p. of *frāgrāre*, to smell.]

frail *frāl, adj.* very easily shattered: feeble and infirm (*esp. Scot.*): decrepit: morally weak.—*adv.* **frail'ly.**—*ns.* **frail'ness, frail'ty.** [O.Fr. *fraile*—L. *fragilis*, fragile.]

fraise *frāz, n.* a tool for enlarging a drillhole. [Fr.]

framboesia *fram-bē'zi-a, n.* yaws. [Fr. *framboise*, raspberry.]

frame *frām, v.t.* to form: to put together: to plan, adjust, or adapt: to contrive or concoct: to bring about: to articulate: 'to set about: to enclose in a frame or border: to make victim of a frame-up.—*n.* the body: a putting together of parts: a structure: a case made to enclose, border or support anything: the skeleton of anything: the rigid part of a bicycle: a structure on which embroidery is worked: a stocking-making machine: a structure for cultivation or sheltering of plants: state (of mind), mood: unit picture in cinema film: the total TV picture: a triangular support in which the balls are grouped for the break (*snooker*, etc.): the balls so grouped (*snooker*, etc.): in the jargon of certain games, a definite part of a

game, a game, or a definite number of games.—*ns.* **fram'er** one who forms or constructs: one who makes frames for pictures, etc.; one who devises: one who formulates (e.g. law); **fram'ing** the act of constructing: a frame or setting.—**frame'-maker** a maker of picture-frames; **frame'-saw** a thin saw stretched in a frame; **frame'-up** a trumped-up affair, esp. a false criminal charge against an innocent person; **frame'work** the work that forms the frame: the skeleton or outline of anything.—**frame of reference** a set of axes with reference to which the position of a point, etc., is described (*lit.*): the structure of standards, arising from the individual's experience, and continually developing, to which he refers, in all cases from the simplest to the most complicated, when judging or evaluating (*fig.*). [O.E. *framian*, to be helpful, *fram*, forward.]

franc *frangk, n.* a coin forming since 1795 the unit of the French monetary system: the unit also in Belgium, Switzerland, etc. [O.Fr. *franc*, from the legend *Francorum rex* on the first coins.]

franchise *fran'chīz, -shīz, n.* liberty: a privilege or exemption by prescription or grant: the right of voting, esp. for an M.P.: voting qualification: a commercial concession by which a retailer is granted by a company the exclusive right of retailing its goods in a specified area, or a similar concession granted by a public authority to a broadcasting company.—*n.* **fran'chiser** a voter: a firm, etc. which grants a commercial concession. [O.Fr.—*franc*, free.]

Franciscan *fran-sis'kan, adj.* belonging to the order of mendicant friars in the R.C. Church, founded by St Francis of Assisi (1182–1226).—*n.* a friar of this order. [L. *Franciscus*, Francis.]

francium *fran'si-am, n.* the chemical element of atomic number 87, symbol Fr, discovered by a French-woman, Mlle Perey. [France.]

Franco- *frangk'ō-*, in composition, French: French and, as **Fran'co-Ger'man, Fran'co-Russ'ian** etc.—*adj.* **Franc'ophone** (also without *cap.*) French-speaking (used e.g. of Africans for whom French is a second mother-tongue or French-speaking Canadians).

francolin *frang'kō-lin, n.* a (bird of the) genus (*Francolinus*) of partridges. [Fr.]

frangible *fran'ji-bl, adj.* easily broken.—*n.* **frangibil'ity.** [L. *frangēre*, to break; see **fract.**]

frangipani *fran-ji-pā'nē, n.* the red jasmine or other species of *Plumeria*, tropical American shrubs with scented flowers: a perfume from or in imitation of red jasmine: (also **frangipane** *fran'ji-pān*) a pastry-cake filled with cream, almonds, and sugar. [From the name of the inventor of the perfume *Frangipani.*]

Frank *frangk, n.* a German of a confederation in Franconia of which a branch conquered Gaul in the 5th century, and founded France: in the East, a Western European.—*adj.* **Frank'ish.** [See **frank.**]

frank *frangk, adj.* free, open: open or candid in expression.—*v.t.* to sign so as to ensure free carriage: to send thus signed: to mark by means of a **frank'ing-machine** to show that postage has been paid.—*n.* the signature of a person who had the right to frank a letter: a franked cover.—*adv.* **frank'ly** to be frank: in a frank manner.—*n.* **frank'ness.** [O.Fr. *franc*—L.L. *francus*; O.H.G. *Franko*, Frank, hence a free man.]

Frankenstein *frangk'an-stīn, n.* the hero of Mrs. Shelley's romance so named, who by his skill forms an animate creature like a man, only to his own torment: hence, by confusion, any creation that brings disaster to its author.

Frankfurter *frangk'fûr-tar, -fōōr-tar,* (often without *cap.*) *n.* a small smoked sausage. [Short for Ger. *Frankfurter Wurst*, Frankfurt sausage.]

frankincense *frangk'in-sens, n.* olibanum, a sweet-smelling resin from Arabia, used as incense: spruce resin. [O.Fr. *franc encens*, pure incense.]

franklin *frangk'lın*, (*hist.*) *n.* an English freeholder, free from feudal servitude to a subject-superior [L.L. *francus;* see **frank.**]

frantic *fran'tik*, *adj.* mad, furious: wild.—*adv* **fran'-tically.**—*n.* **fran'ticness.** [O.Fr. *frenetique*—L. *phreneticus*—Gr. *phrenētikos*, mad—*phrēn*, the mind; see **frenetic, frenzy.**]

frap *frap*, *v.t.* to secure by many turns of a lashing (*naut.*). [Fr. *frapper*, to strike.]

frappé *fra'pā*, *p. adj.* iced: artificially cooled:—*fem* **frap'pée.** [Fr.. *pa.p* of *frapper*, to strike.]

frass *fras*, *n.* excrement or other refuse of boring larvae [Ger.,—*fressen*, to eat; cf. **fret¹**.]

frate *fra'tā*, (It.) *n* a friar, a mendicant Franciscan:— *pl* **fra'ti** (*-tē*)

frater¹ *fra'tər*, *n* a refectory: sometimes applied in error to a monastic common-room or to a chapter-house.—Also **fra'ter-house, frā'try.** [O.Fr. *fraitur* for *refreitor*—L.L. *refectōrium*.]

frater² *fra'tər*, *n* a friar: a comrade.—*adj* **fraternal** (*fra-tûr'nl*) belonging to a brother or brethren. brotherly.—*adv* **frater'nally.**—*n* **fraternisā'tion, -z-** (*frat-*)—*v.t.* **frat'ernise, -ize** to associate as brothers: to seek brotherly fellowship. to come into friendly association (with).—*ns* **frat'erniser, -z-; frater'nity** the state of being brethren: a brotherhood: a society formed on a principle of brotherhood: an American college association: any set of people with something in common.—**fraternal twins** dizygotic twins. [L. *frāter*, a brother.]

fratricide *frat'rı-sīd*, or *frāt'*, *n* one who kills his brother: the murder of a brother.—*adj.* **fratrici'dal.** [Fr.,—L. *frāter, frātrıs, caedēre*, to kill.]

frau, Frau *frow*, *n.* a woman: a wife: Mrs.—*n.* **fräulein, Fräulein** (*froi'lın*) an unmarried woman: often applied to a German governess: Miss. [Ger]

fraud *frod*, *n.* deceit: imposture: a deceptive trick: a cheat, swindler (*coll.*): a fraudulent production.—*ns.* **fraud'ster** a swindler; **fraud'ulence, fraud'ulency.**—*adj.* **fraud'ulent** using fraud.—*adv* **fraud'ulently.** [O.Fr. *fraude*—L. *fraus*, fraud]

fraught *frôt*, *adj* filled (with): having or causing (esp something bad or undesirable e.g. danger; with *with*): feeling or making anxious or distressed. [Prob. Old Du. *vracht*. Cf. **freight.**]

fräulein. See **frau.**

fray¹ *frā*, *n.* an affray: a brawl.—*v.t.* to frighten [Aphetic from **affray.**]

fray² *frā*, *v.t.* to wear off by rubbing: to ravel out the end or edge of: to cause a strain on (e.g. nerves, temper, etc.).—*v.i.* to become frayed.—*n.* **fray'ing** the action of the verb: frayed-off material. [Fr. *frayer* —L. *frıcāre*, to rub.]

frazil *fraz'il*, *frā'zil*, *n.* ground-ice: ice in small spikes and plates in rapid streams. [Canadian Fr *frasil;* prob. Fr. *fraisil*, cinders.]

frazzle *fraz'l*, *v.t.* to fray, wear out.—*n* the state of being worn out: a shred.—**burnt, etc to a frazzle** completely burnt, etc.

freak *frēk*, *n.* a caprice· sport: an abnormal production of nature, a monstrosity: an eccentric. one who is wildly enthusiastic about something (usu. in composition, as in *film-freak*).—*adj.* capricious: unusual.— *ns.* **freak'iness, freak'ishness.**—*adjs.* **freak'ish, freak'ful, freak'y** apt to change the mind suddenly unusual, odd.—*adv.* **freak'ishly.**—**freak'-out** (*slang*) a (drug-induced) hallucinatory or (*loosely*) wildly exciting, unconventional experience or occurrence (*v.t.* **freak (out)).** [A late word; cf. O.E *frīcıan*, to dance]

freckle *frek'l*, *v.t.* to spot: to colour with spots.—*n.* a yellowish or brownish-yellow spot on the skin, esp. of fair-haired persons: any small spot.—*n.* **freck'ling** a little spot —*adjs.* **freck'ly, freck'led** full of freckles. [O.N. *freknur* (pl.), Dan. *fregne.*]

free *frē*, *adj.* not bound: not under arbitrary government: not strict, or bound by rules: not literal: unimpeded: unconstrained: readily cut, separated or wrought: ready (esp in phrase *free to confess*): frank lavish: uncombined: unattached: exempt (with *from*): having a franchise (with *of*): without payment. bold; indecent.—*compar* **freer** *frē'ər; superl* **freest** *frē'ist* —*adv.* freely: without payment· without obstruction —*v.t* to set at liberty: to deliver from what confines: to rid (with *from, of*).—*pr.p* **free'ing;** *pa.t* and *pa.p.* **freed.**—*in composition* free from, as in *trouble-free*—*n.* **free'bie** (esp *U.S. slang*) something supplied free of charge.—Also *adj.*—**free'dom** liberty: frankness: outspokenness: unhampered boldness separation: privileges connected with a city (often granted as an honour merely). improper familiarity: licence.—*adv* **free'ly.**—*ns.* **free'ness; freer** (*frē'ər*) a liberator.—**free agency** the state or power of acting freely, or without necessity or constraint upon the will; **free agent.**—*adj.* **free'-and-eas'y** informal in manners, without ceremonious restraint.— *adj.* **free'-arm** with unsupported arm.—**free association** a technique in psychoanalysis based either on the first association called forth by each of a series of words or on a train of thought suggested by a single word; **free'-board** the distance between water-line and deck. a strip of land outside a fence, or a right thereto; **free'booter** one who roves about freely in search of booty (Du. *vrijbuiter*).—*adj.* **free'born** born free.—**Free Church** in England, a Nonconformist church; **freed'man** a man who has been a slave and has been freed:—*pl.* **freed'men;** *fem.* **freed'woman;** *pl.* **freed'women; freedom fighter** one who fights in an armed movement for the liberation of a nation, etc. from a government considered unjust, tyrannical, etc.; **free enterprise** the conduct of business without interference from the state; **free'-fall** the motion of an unpropelled body in a gravitational field, as that of a spacecraft in orbit: the part of a parachute jump before the parachute opens; **free flight** a confused or promiscuous fight; **free flight** the flight of a rocket, etc. when its motor is no longer producing thrust; **free'-for-all'** a contest open to anybody: a free fight —Also *adj.*—*adj.* **free'-hand** executed by the unguided hand.—**free hand** complete freedom of action.—*adj.* **free'-hand'ed** open-handed: liberal.— **free'hold** a property held free of duty except to the monarch, **free'holder** one who possesses a freehold; **free house** a public-house that is not tied to a particular supplier; **free kick** (*football*) a kick allowed without interference, as a penalty against the opposing side for infringing the rules; **free'-lance** any one who works for himself, employed or paid by others only for particular, usu. short-term, assignments (also **free'lancer**)—Also *adj., adv* and *v.i.*—*v.t.* **free'load** (esp. *U.S., coll.*) to eat at someone else's expense: to sponge: to gain from others' efforts.— *n.* a free meal.—*n.* **free'loader.**—*n* and *adj* **free'loading.—free love** the claim to freedom in sexual relations, unshackled by marriage; **free'man** a man who is free or enjoys liberty: one who holds a particular franchise or privilege:—*pl.* **free'men;** *fem.* **free'-woman;** *pl.* **free'women; free'mā'son** a member of a secret fraternity, united in lodges for social enjoy- ment and mutual assistance.—*adj* **freemason'ic.—freemā'sonry** the institutions, practices, etc. of freemasons: instinctive understanding and sympathy; **free'-port** a port open on equal terms to all traders: a free-trade zone adjacent to a port.

allowing duty-free import and re-export of goods; **free radical** a group of atoms containing at least one unpaired electron existing briefly during certain chemical reactions.—*adj.* **free'-range'** (of poultry) allowed some freedom to move about: (of eggs) laid by free-range hens.—**free'-school** a school where no tuition fees are exacted; **free'sheet** a newspaper distributed free; **free skating** competitive figure-skating in which the skater selects movements from an officially approved list of jumps, spins, etc.; **free speech** the right to express one's opinions freely in public.—*adj.* **free'-spók'en** accustomed to speak without reserve.—**free'-spók'enness.**—*adj.* **free'-stand'ing** not supported by or attached to anything else.—**Free States** in America, before the Civil War of 1861–65, those of the United States in which slavery did not exist; **free'stone** any easily wrought building stone without tendency to split in layers: a freestone fruit. —*adj.* (of a type of peach, etc.) having a stone from which the pulp easily separates—opp. to *clingstone.* —*adjs.* **free'-style** of a (esp. swimming) race or competition, in which a competitor is free to choose which style or method to use: of wrestling, all-in: of a competitor, taking part in free-style competitions, etc.; **free'-swimm'ing** swimming about, not attached. —**free'thinker** one who rejects authority in religion: a rationalist.—*n.* and *adj.* **free'-thinking.**—**free's thought; free'-trade** free or unrestricted trade: free interchange of commodities without protective duties; **free'-trad'er** one who practises or advocates this: a smuggler: a smuggling vessel; **free verse** verse defying the usual conventions as to regularity of metre, rhyme, length of lines, etc.: rhythmic prose arranged as irregular verses; **free vote** a vote left to individual choice, free from party discipline; **freeway** (*U.S.*) a toll-free road for high-speed traffic; **free'-wheel** the mechanism of a bicycle by which the hind-wheel may be temporarily disconnected and set free from the driving-gear.—*v.i.* to cycle with wheel so disconnected: (of motor vehicle or its driver) to coast: to move, act, live, without restraint or concern (*fig.*). —**free'-wheel'ing; free'-will'** freedom of the will from restraint: liberty of choice: the power of self-determination.—*adj.* **free'-will** spontaneous: voluntary.—**Free World** the collective name used of themselves by non-communist countries.—**for free** (*coll.*) given without desire for payment or other return; **free on board (f.o.b.)** delivered on a vessel or other conveyance without charge; **make free with** to be familiar with, to take liberties with: to help oneself liberally to; **make so free as to** to venture to. [O.E. *frēo.*]

freebie. See under **free.**

Freesia *frē'zi-ə,* a South African genus of the iris family, scented greenhouse plants: (without *cap.*) a plant of this genus. [After F. H.T. *Freese,* German physician, or H. Th. *Frees,* German physician, or according to some, E. M. *Fries,* Swedish botanist.]

freeze *frēz, v.i.* to become ice: to become solid by fall of temperature: to be at a temperature at which water would freeze: to be very cold: to become motionless, stiff, attached, or stopped by, or as if by, cold.—*v.t.* to cause to freeze: to fix: to stabilise: to prevent the use of or dealings in: to stop at, not develop beyond, a particular state or stage: to stop (a moving film) at a particular frame: to preserve (esp. food) by freezing and storing below freezing-point: to anaesthetise (a part of the body):—*pr.p.* **freez'ing;** *pa.t.* **frōze;** *pa.p.* **frō'zen.**—*n.* a frost: a stoppage.—*adj.* **freez'able.**—*ns.* **freez'er** a freezing apparatus: anything that freezes: a special compartment in a refrigerator designed to freeze fresh foods: a deep-freeze; **freez'ing.** —*v.t.* **freeze'-dry'.**—**freeze'-dry'ing** evaporation to dryness in a vacuum for preservation or storage of a

substance, e g. an antibiotic; **freeze'-up** in U.S. and Canada, the period when ice forms on lakes, etc., at onset of winter; **freez'ing-down** lowering of the body temperature; **freez'ing-point** the temperature at which a liquid solidifies.—**freeze down** to lower the body temperature in preparation for heart and other operations; **freeze out** (*coll.*) to oblige to leave: to exclude. [O.E. *frēosan,* pa.p. *froren.*]

freight *frāt, n.* the lading or cargo, esp. of a ship: the charge for transporting goods by water or land.—*v.t.* to load (esp. a ship): to hire, let out.—*ns.* **freight'age** money paid for freight; **freight'er** one who freights a vessel: a cargo-carrying boat, etc.—**freight'-car** (*U.S.*) a luggage van: a goods van or wagon; **freight'-liner** a train having specially designed containers and rolling-stock and used for rapid transport of goods.— Also *adj.*—**freight'-train** a goods train. [Prob. Old Du. *vrecht,* a form of *vracht.*]

frena. See **frenum.**

French *french, -sh, adj.* belonging to *France* or its people: originating in France (sometimes without *cap.*).—*n.* the people of France: the language of France, also an official language in Belgium, Switzerland, Canada and other countries.—*n.* **French-ifica'tion.**—*v.t.* **French'ify** to make French or Frenchlike.—*n.* **French'y** a contemptuous name for a Frenchman.—**French bean** the common kidney-bean eaten, pods and all, as a table vegetable.—*adj.* **French'-Cana'dian** of the French-speaking part of Canada.—*n.* a French-Canadian person: the French language of Canada; **French chalk** soapstone; **French curve** a thin plate with the outlines of various curves on it, used for drawing curves; **French dressing** a salad dressing consisting of oil and vinegar or lemon juice, and usu. seasoning; **French fry** (*pl.* **French fries**), **French fried potato** a potato-chip; **French horn** the orchestral horn; **French kiss** a kiss in which the tongue is inserted into one's partner's mouth; **French letter** (*slang*) a condom; **French loaf** crusty bread baked in long narrow shape with tapered ends; **French'man:**— *pl.* **French'men;** *fem.* **French'woman:**—*pl.* **French'-women;** **French polish** a varnish for furniture, consisting chiefly of shellac dissolved in spirit.—*v.t.* **French'-pol'ish** to treat with French polish.—**French-pol'isher; French-pol'ishing; French sash, window** a doorlike window; **French seam** seam stitched on right side then on wrong side to cover raw edges; **French stick** a very narrow French loaf; **French toast** bread dipped in egg (and milk) and fried; **French window** see **French sash.**—**pardon, excuse my French** (*coll.*) pardon my bad language; **take French leave** to depart without notice or permission: to disappear suspiciously. [O.E. *Francisc*—L. *Francus*—O.H.G. *Franko.*]

frenetic, phrenetic *fri-net'ik, adj.* delirious: frantic: frenzied: mad: distracted.—*n.* a madman.—*adj.* **frenet'ical, phrenet'ical.**—*adv.* **frenet'ically, phrenet'ically.** [O.Fr. *frénétique*—L. *phreneticus* —late Gr. *phrenētikos*—Gr. *phrenītis,* delirium— *phrēn,* heart, mind; see **phrenesis.**]

frenum, fraenum *frē'nəm, n.* a ligament restraining the motion of a part of the body:—*pl.* **fr(a)e'na.** [L. *frēnum,* a bridle.]

frenzy *fren'zi, n.* a violent excitement: a paroxysm of madness.—*v.t.* to drive to frenzy.—*adjs.* **fren'zical, fren'zied.** [O.Fr. *frenesie*—L. and late Gr. *phrenēsis*—Gr. *phrenītis;* see **frenetic.**]

frequent *frē'kwənt, adj.* coming or occurring often: crowded.—*v t* (*fri-kwent'*), to visit often: to associate with: to resort to: to crowd.—*ns.* **frē'quence** frequency; **frē'quency** commonness of recurrence: the number of vibrations, cycles, or other recurrences in unit time (in ascending order, high, very high, ultra-high, extremely high, super-high frequency); **frĕquentā'tion** the act of visiting often.—*adj.* **frequentative** (fri-kwent'ə-tiv; *gram.*) denoting the frequent repetition of an action.—*n.* (*gram.*) a verb expressing this repetition.—*n.* **frequent'er.**—*adv.* **frĕ'quently.**—*n.* **frĕ'quentness.**—**frequency modulation** modulation in radio transmission by varying the frequency of the carrier wave, giving greater fidelity than amplitude modulation and almost freedom from atmospherics; **high frequency** a radio frequency of between 3 and 30 megahertz; **low frequency** a radio frequency of between 30 and 300 kilohertz. [L. *frequēns, frequentis*; conn. with *farcīre*, to stuff.]

frère *frer*, (Fr.) *n.* a brother.

fresco *fres'kō, n.* a mode of painting upon walls covered with damp plaster: a picture so painted:—*pl.* **fres'coes, fres'cos.**—*v.t.* to paint in fresco.—*adj.* **fres'coed** (-kōd).—*ns.* **frescoer** (*fres'kō-ər*); **fres'coing; fres'coist.** [It. *fresco*, fresh.]

fresh *fresh, adj.* in new condition: not stale, faded or soiled: new, recently added: raw, inexperienced: in youthful bloom: cool, invigorating: brisk: amorously over-free (*slang*): without salt: not preserved by pickling, drying, salting, etc.: cheeky, pert.—*adv.* **freshly:** afresh: newly.—*v.t.* **fresh'en** to make fresh: to take the saltness from.—*v.i.* to grow fresh—*v.t.* and *v.i.* to make (oneself) fresh by washing, etc. (often with *up*).—*ns.* **fresh'ener; fresh'er** a student in his or her first year, a freshman; **fresh'et** a stream of fresh water: a flood.—*adv.* **fresh'ly** with freshness: newly: anew.—*n.* **fresh'ness.**—*n.* **fresh'man** a newcomer: a student in his first year.—*adj.* **fresh'water** of or pertaining to water not salt: accustomed to sail only on fresh water. [O.E. *fersc*.]

fret[1] *fret, v.t.* to eat into: to corrode: to wear away by rubbing: to rub, chafe: to vex, to irritate.—*v.i.* to wear away: to vex oneself: to worry: to chafe—*pr.p.* **frett'ing;** *pa.t.* and *pa.p.* **frett'ed.**—*n.* irritation: worry: a worn or eroded spot: sea fret.—*adj.* **fret'ful** peevish.—*adv.* **fret'fully.**—*n.* **fret'fulness.**—*adj.* **frett'ing** vexing.—*n.* peevishness. [O.E. *fretan*, to gnaw—pfx. *for-*, intens., and *etan*, to eat.]

fret[2] *fret, v.t.* to ornament with interlaced work: to variegate:—*pr.p.* **frett'ing;** *pa.t.* and *pa.p.* **frett'ed.** —*n.* ornamental network: a type of decoration for a cornice, border, etc., consisting of lines meeting usu. at right angles, the pattern being repeated to form a continuous band (also called **grecque, (Greek) key (pattern), meander**).—*adjs.* **frett'ed, frett'y** ornamented with frets.—**fret'saw** a saw with a narrow blade and fine teeth, used for fretwork, scrollwork, etc.; **fret'work** ornamental work consisting of frets: perforated woodwork. [O.Fr. *freter*, to adorn with interlaced work, *frete*, trelliswork; prob. influenced by or confused with O.E. *frætwa*, ornament.]

fret[3] *fret, n.* any of the wooden or metal ridges on the fingerboard of a guitar or other instrument on to which the strings are pressed in producing the various notes.—*v.t.* to furnish with frets. [Prob. same as the above.]

Freudian *froid'i-ən, adj.* pertaining to Sigmund *Freud* (1856–1939), his theory of the libido, or his method of psychoanalysis.—*n.* a follower of Freud.—**Freudian slip** an error or unintentional action, esp. a slip of the tongue, supposed to reveal an unconscious thought.

friable *frī'ə-bl, adj.* apt to crumble: easily reduced to powder.—*ns.* **fri'ableness, friabil'ity.** [Fr.,—L. *friābilis—friāre, friātum*, to crumble.]

friar *frī'ər, n.* a member of one of the mendicant monastic orders in the R.C. Church—the Franciscans (*Friars Minor* or *Grey Friars*), Dominicans (*Friars Preachers*, or *Black Friars*), Carmelites (*White Friars*), Augustinians (*Austin Friars*), and others.— *n.* **fri'ary** a convent of friars.—**fri'arbird** an Australian honey-eater with featherless head; **friar's balsam** a tincture of benzoin, storax, tolu and aloes. [O.Fr. *frere*—L. *frāter*, a brother.]

fricandeau *frik-ən-dō', or frik', n.* a thick slice of veal, etc., larded:—*pl.* **fricandeaus** (-*dōz*). [Fr.]

fricassee *frik-ə-sē', n.* a dish of fowl, rabbit, etc. cut into pieces served in sauce.—*v.t.* to dress as a fricassee:—*pr.p.* **fricassee'ing;** *pa.t.* and *pa.p.* **fricassee'd'.** [Fr. *fricassée*; origin unknown.]

friction *frik'shən, n.* rubbing: a force acting in the tangent plane of two bodies, when one slides or rolls upon another, in direction opposite to that of the movement (*statics*): disagreement, jarring.—*adj.* **fric'ative** produced by friction: pertaining to, being, a fricative.—*n.* a consonant produced by the breath being forced through a narrow opening.—*adjs.* **fric'tional; fric'tionless.** [L. *fricāre, frictum*, to rub.]

Friday *frī'di, n.* the sixth day of the week.—**Black Friday** Good Friday, from the black vestments of the clergy and altar in the Western Church: any Friday marked by a great calamity; **Good Friday** the Friday before Easter, kept in commemoration of the Crucifixion; **Holy Friday** Friday in an Ember-week— also **Golden Friday** sometimes put for Good Friday itself. [O.E. *Frīgedæg*, day of (the goddess) Frig.]

fridge *frij, (coll.) n.* short for **refrigerator.**

fried. See **fry.**

friend *frend, n.* one loving or attached to another: an intimate acquaintance: a favourer, wellwisher, supporter: one of a society so named.—*adj.* **friend'less** without friends: destitute.—*n.* **friend'lessness.**—*adv.* **friend'lily.**—*n.* **friend'liness.**—*adj.* **friend'ly** like a friend: having the disposition of a friend: favourable: amicable: of a football match, etc., played for amusement rather than competitively (also *n.*): able to handle small variations in the input format and/or enabling the easy correction of input errors (*comput.*).—*n.* **friend'ship** attachment from mutual esteem: friendly assistance.—**friendly society** a benefit society, an association for relief in sickness, old age, widowhood, by provident insurance.—**be friends with** to be on good terms with, well disposed towards; **have a friend at court** to have a friend in a position where his influence is likely to prove useful; **Society of Friends** the proper designation of a sect of Christians better known as Quakers. [O.E. *frēond* (orig. a pr.p.; cf. *frēon*, to love).]

frier, fries. See **fry.**

Friesian. See **Frisian.**

frieze[1] *frēz, n.* a rough, heavy woollen cloth. [Fr. *frise*.]

frieze[2] *frēz, (archit.) n.* the part of the entablature between the architrave and cornice, often ornamented with figures: a decorated band along the top of a room wall. [O.Fr. *frise*; It. *fregio*; perh. L *Phrygium* (*opus*), Phrygian (work).]

frig[1] *frig, (vulg.) v.i.* and *v.t.* to masturbate: loosely, to have sexual intercourse with: (often with *about*) to potter about:—*pr.p.* **frigg'ing;** *pa.t.* and *pa.p.* **frigg'ed.**—*n.* masturbation.—*n.* **frigg'ing** masturbation: pottering about.—*adj.* and *adv.* as an intensive, to a great extent, very: often used as a colourless descriptive. [Late M.E. *friggen*—L. *fricāre*, to rub.]

frig[2] *frij, (coll.) n.* short for **refrigerator.**

frigate *frig'it, n.* formerly a vessel in the class next to ships of the line: now denoting an escort vessel.— **frigate bird** a large tropical sea-bird (*Fregata*) with very long wings. [O.Fr. *fregate*—It. *fregata*.]

fright *frīt, n.* sudden fear: terror: a figure of grotesque or ridiculous appearance (*coll*).—*v.s.t.* **fright** (now rare), **fright'en** to make afraid: to alarm: to drive by fear.—*adj.* **fright'ened.**—*n.pl.* **fright'eners** (*slang*) something intended to frighten, esp. for criminal purposes.—*adj.* **fright'ening.**—*adv.* **fright'eningly.**—*adj.* **fright'ful** terrible: horrible: unpleasant (*coll.*): great (*coll.*).—*adv.* **fright'fully** dreadfully: very (*coll.*).—*n.* **fright'fulness** the quality of being frightful: terrorism.—**put the frighteners on someone** (*slang*) to frighten someone into (not) doing something, esp. for criminal purposes; **take fright** to become afraid. [O.E. *fyrhto*.]

frigid *frij'id, adj.* frozen or stiffened with cold: cold: chillingly stiff: without spirit or feeling: unanimated: leaving the imagination untouched: of a woman, sexually unresponsive.—*n.* **frigid'ity** coldness: coldness of affection: want of animation: sexual unresponsiveness.—*adv.* **frig'idly.**—*n.* **frig'idness.**—**frigid zones** the parts of the earth's surface within the polar circles. [L. *frigidus—frigere*, to be cold—*frigus*, cold.]

frigorific *frig-ər-if'ik, adj.* causing cold: freezing. [L. *frigus, -oris*, cold, *facĕre*, to make.]

frijol, frijole *frē'hhōl, frē-hhōl'*, *n.* the kidney-bean, or any species of Phaseolus:—*pl.* **frijoles** (*-les*). [Sp. *frijol, frijol, fréjol*.]

frill *fril, n.* a ruffle: a ruffled or crimped edging: superfluous ornament: (in *pl.*) affected airs.—*v.t.* to furnish with a frill.—*n.pl.* **frill'ies** light and pretty women's underwear.—*n.* **frill'ing.**—*adj.* **frill'y.**—**frilled lizard** a large Australian lizard (*Chlamydosaurus*) with an erectile frill about its neck.—**without frills** (in a manner, form, etc. which is) straightforward, clear, without posturing, with no superfluous additions, etc.

fringe *frinj, n.* a border of loose threads: hair falling over the brow: a border: anything bordering on or additional to an activity.—*v.t.* to adorn with a fringe: to border.—*adj.* bordering, or just outside, the recognised or orthodox form, group, etc. as in *fringe medicine, fringe banks*: less important or popular, as in *fringe sports.*—*adjs.* **fringed; fringe'less; fring'y** ornamented with fringes.—**fringe benefit** something in addition to wages or salary that forms part of the regular remuneration from one's employment.—**lunatic fringe** any, usu. small, group of fanatics or extremists within a political party, pressure group, etc. [O.Fr. *frenge—*L. *fimbria*, threads, akin to *fibra*, a fibre.]

frippery *frip'ər-i, n.* tawdry finery: foppish triviality: useless trifles.—*adj.* useless: trifling. [O.Fr. *freperie—frepe*, a rag.]

Frisbee® *friz'bi, n.* a plastic saucer-shaped disc which can be made to skim through the air, used in various catching-games, etc.

Frisian *friz'i-ən, n.* a native of *Friesland*: the Low German language of Friesland.—*adj.* of Friesland, its people, or their language.—*adj.* **Friesian** (*frēz'*) Frisian, esp. of a heavy breed of dairy-cattle.—*n.* a Friesian bull or cow.

frisk *frisk, v.i.* to gambol: to leap playfully.—*v.t.* to search (a person or pockets) (*slang*): to search for radioactive radiation by contamination meter.—*n.* a frolicsome movement.—*n.* **frisk'er.**—*adv.* **frisk'ily.**—*n.* **frisk'iness.**—*adj.* **frisk'y** lively: jumping with gaiety: frolicsome. [O.Fr. *frisque*.]

frisket *frisk'it,* (*print.*) *n.* the light frame between the tympan and the forme, to hold in place the sheet to be printed. [Fr. *frisquette*.]

frisson *frē-sɔ̃, n.* a shiver: a thrill. [Fr.]

frit[1] *frit, n.* the mixed materials for making glass, pottery glazes, etc.—*v.t.* to fuse partially:—*pr.p.* **fritt'ing;** *pa.t.* and *pa.p.* **fritt'ed.** [Fr. *fritte*—It. *fritta*—L. *frigĕre, frictum*, to roast.]

frit[2] *frit, n.* a small fly destructive to wheat and other cereal crops.—Also **frit'fly.**

frith. See **firth[1]**.

fritillary *frit'il-ər-i,* or *-il', n.* a member of the genus (*Fritillaria*) of the lily family, the best-known species with chequered purple flowers: a name for several butterflies of similar pattern. [L. *fritillus*, a dice-box.]

fritter[1] *frit'ər, n.* a piece of fruit, etc., fried in batter. [O.Fr. *friture—*L. *frigĕre, frictum*, to fry.]

fritter[2] *frit'ər, n. v.t.* to squander piecemeal.—*n.* **fritt'erer** one who wastes time. [Perh. O.Fr. *freture—*L. *fractūra—frangĕre, frāctum*, to break.]

fritto misto *frē'tō mēs'tō,* (It.) a mixed dish of fried food.

frivolous *friv'ə-ləs, adj.* trifling: silly.—*n.* **frivolity** (*-ol'*) a trifling habit or nature: levity.—*adv.* **friv'olously.**—*n.* **friv'olousness.** [L. *frivolus*.]

frizz, friz *friz, v.t.* to curl tightly.—*n.* a curl: frizzed hair.—*adjs.* **frizzed** having the hair crisped into frizzes; **frizz'y.** [O.Fr. *friser*, to curl; perh. conn. with **frieze[1]**.]

frizzle[1] *friz'l, v.t.* to form in small short curls.—*v.i.* to go into curls.—*n.* a curl: frizzled hair.—*adj.* **frizz'ly.** [Related to **frizz** and **frieze[1]**.]

frizzle[2] *friz'l, v.t.* and *v.i.* to fry: to scorch. [Perhaps onomatopoeic adaptation of **fry**.]

fro *adv.* away, only in to and fro (see to). [O.N. *frá*.]

frock *frok, n.* a monk's wide-sleeved garment: a frock-coat: a smock-frock: a sailor's jersey: a woman's or child's dress: an undress regimental coat.—*adj.* **frocked** clothed in a frock.—*n.* **frock'ing** cloth suitable for frocks, coarse jean.—*adj.* **frock'less.**—**frock'-coat** a double-breasted full-skirted coat for men. [O.Fr. *froc*, a monk's frock.]

Froebelian *frœ-bēl'i-ən, adj.* pertaining to Friedrich *Froebel*, German educationist (1782–1852), or to his system of kindergarten schools.—*n.* **Froe'belism.**

frog[1] *frog, n.* a tailless web-footed amphibian, esp. one of the genus Rana, more like a toad: a swelling in the throat: (with *cap.*) a contemptuous name for a Frenchman: on a railway, a structure in the rails allowing passage across or to another track: a depression made in the face(s) of a brick: the block by which the hair is attached to the heel of a violin, etc. bow.—*n.*—*adj.* **frogg'y** froglike.—*n.* (with *cap.*) a contemptuous name for a Frenchman.—**frog'bit** a small aquatic plant with floating leaves; **frog'-fish** a name for various fishes, esp. the angler; **frog'-hopper** a froth-fly; **frog'man** an underwater swimmer fitted with webbed froglike feet.—*v.t.* **frog'-march** to carry face downwards between four men, each holding a limb: now usually, to seize from behind and force forwards while holding firmly by the arms or clothing: sometimes, to propel backwards between two people, each holding an arm.—*n.* the act or process of frog-marching.—**frog'-spit** cuckoo-spit.—**a frog in the, one's, throat** hoarseness. [O.E. *frogga*; also *frox*.]

frog[2] *frog, n.* a V-shaped band of horn on the underside of a horse's hoof. [Perh. same as **frog[1]**. Gr. *batrachos* means frog in both senses.]

frog[3] *frog, n.* an ornamental fastening or tasselled or braided button: an attachment to a belt for carrying a weapon.—*adj.* **frogged** having ornamental stripes or workings of braid or lace, mostly on the breast of a coat. [Perh. Port. *froco—*L. *floccus*, a flock, lock.]

frolic *frol'ik, n.* gaiety: a prank: a gambol: a merrymaking.—*v.i.* to play wild pranks or merry tricks: to gambol:—*pr.p.* **frol'icking;** *pa.t.* and *pa.p.* **frol'icked.**—*adj.* **frol'icsome** gay: sportive. [Du. *vrolijk*, merry.]

from *from, frəm, prep.* out of: away, to or at a greater

distance relatively to: springing out of: beginning at: apart relatively to: by reason of. [O.E. *fram, from.*]
fromenty. See **frumenty**.
frond *frond, n.* a leaf, esp. of a palm or fern: a leaflike thallus, or a leaflike organ of obscure morphological nature. [L. *frōns, frondis*, a leaf.]
front *frunt, n.* the face, appearance: the forepart of anything: the side presented to view: the face of a building, esp. the principal face: the part facing the sea or other water: a seaside promenade: the foremost line: the scene of hostilities: the direction in which troops are facing when lined up (*mil.*): a combined face presented against opponents: a group of people, organisations or parties having the same or broadly similar (esp. political or revolutionary) outlook and aims, who act together against opponents, as in *popular front* (q.v.): a set of false curls for the forehead: the breast of a man's shirt, a dickey: the middle part of the tongue: the auditorium of a theatre: the bounding surface between two masses of air of different density and temperature (*meteor.*): the apparent or nominal leader behind whom the really powerful man works anonymously (also *front man*): something acting as a cover or disguise for secret or disreputable activities: boldness: impudence.—*adj.* of, relating to, in, the front: articulated with the front of the tongue.—*v.t.* to stand in front of or opposite: to face towards: to meet, or to oppose, face to face: to add a front to: to serve as a front to: to change into or towards a front sound.—*v.i.* to face: to act as a front for someone else or as a cover for something secret or illicit.—*ns.* **front'age** the front part of a building: extent of front: ground in front; **front'ager** (*law*) a person who owns or occupies property along a road, river or shore.—*adj.* **front'al** (*frunt'l*, also *front'l*) of or belonging to the front, or the forehead.—*n.* the façade of a building: something worn on the forehead or face: a hanging of silk, satin, etc., embroidered for an altar—now usually covering only the top.—*adj.* **front'ed** formed with a front: changed into or towards a front sound.—*n.* **front'let** a band worn on the forehead.—*advs.* **front'ward(s)** towards the front; **front'ways, -wise** with face or front forward.—*adj.* **front'-bench** sitting on a front bench, as a minister, or an opposition member of like standing.—*ns.* **front'-bench'er; front door; front line** the battle positions closest to the enemy: the most active, exposed or dangerous position or rôle in any activity or situation, esp. a conflict (*fig.*).—*adj.* **front'-line** of or relating to the front line: of or relating to a state bordering on another state in which there is an armed conflict, and often involved in that conflict.— **front'man** the person who appears on television as presenter of an esp. documentary programme, **front man** see **front** *n.* above.—*adjs.* **front'-page** suitable for the front page of a newspaper: important; **front'-rank** of foremost importance.—**front'-ranker; front'-runner** in a race, one who runs best while leading the field or one who sets the pace for the rest of the runners: one who or that which is most popular, most likely to succeed, etc., esp. in some kind of competition.—**front of the house** in a theatre, the collective activities such as box-office and programme selling carried on in direct contact with the public (*adj.* **front'-of-house'**); **in front (of)** before. [L. *frōns, frontis*, the forehead.]
frontier *frunt'* or *front'ēr*, *-yar*, or *-ēr'*, *n.* the border of a country: the border of settled country, esp. in U.S. the advancing limit of the West pioneered in the 19th cent.: (in *pl.*) the extreme limit of knowledge and attainment in a particular discipline or line of inquiry.—*adj.* belonging to a frontier: bordering.—**front'-**
iersman (or *-tērz'*) a dweller on a frontier. [O.Fr.

frontier—L. *frōns, frontis.*]
frontispiece *frunt'is-pēs* (or *front'*), *n.* the principal face of a building (*archit.*): a figure or engraving at the front of a book. [Fr. *frontispice*—L.L. *frontispicium*—*frōns, frontis*, forehead, and *specēre, spicĕre*, to see.]
fronton *frun'ton*, (*archit.*) *n.* a pediment.—Also **fron-toon** (*-tōōn'*). [Fr.,—It. *frontone.*]
frost *frost, n.* a state of freezing: temperature at or below the freezing-point of water: frozen dew, or hoar-frost: coldness of manner or relations.—*v.t.* to affect with frost: to cover with hoar-frost: to make like hoar-frost.—*v.i.* to assume a frost-like appearance.—*adj.* **frost'ed** covered by frost: having a frost-like appearance: injured by frost.—*adv.* **frost'ily.**—*ns.* **frost'iness; frost'ing** coating with hoar-frost: material or treatment to give appearance of hoar-frost: icing (esp. *U.S.*).—*adjs.* **frost'less** free from frost; **frost'y** producing, attended with, covered with, frost: chill: frost-like.—**frost'bite** injury, sometimes ending in mortification, in a part of the body by exposure to cold.—*adjs.* **frost'bitten** bitten or affected by frost (also *fig.*); **frost'bound** bound or confined by frost.—**frost'work** tracery wrought by frost, as on windows: work resembling frost tracery, etc. [O.E. *frost, forst.*]
froth *froth, n.* foam: chatter (*fig.*): something frivolous or trivial.—*v.t.* to cause froth on.—*v.i.* to throw up froth.—*n.* **froth'ery** mere froth.—*adv.* **froth'ily.**—*n.* **froth'iness.**—*adjs.* **froth'less; froth'y** full of or like froth or foam: empty: unsubstantial.—**froth'-fly, froth'-hopper** a frog-hopper. [O.N. *frotha.*]
frottage *fro-tăzh', n.* rubbing: the use of rubbing(s) to obtain texture effect(s) in a work of art: a work of art made by this means. [Fr]
froward *frō'ard*, (*arch.*) *adj.* self-willed: perverse: unreasonable (opp. to *toward*).—*adv.* **fro'wardly.**—*n.* **fro'wardness.** [fro, and suffix. *-ward.*]
frown *frown, v.i.* to wrinkle the brow as in anger: to look angry, gloomy, threatening: to show disapprobation.—*v.t.* to express, send, or force by a frown. —*n.* a wrinkling or contraction of the brow in displeasure, etc.: a stern look.—*adj.* **frown'ing** gloomy: disapproving: threatening.—*adv.* **frown'ingly.**—**frown on, upon** to disapprove of. [From O.Fr. *froignier* (Fr. *refrogner*), to knit the brow.]
frowst *frowst, n.* hot stuffy fustiness.—*n.* **frowst'iness.** —*adj.* **frowst'y** fusty: close-smelling: ill-smelling.
frowzy, frowsy *frow'zi*, (*dial.*) *adj.* fusty: stuffy, offensive: unkempt.
frozen *frōz'n, pa.p.* of **freeze.**—*adj.* preserved by keeping at a low temperature: very cold: stiff and unfriendly.—**frozen shoulder** a shoulder joint which has become stiff owing to enforced immobilisation, or to injury to the joint or its surrounding tissue.
fructed *fruk'tid, adj.* (*her.*) bearing fruit.—*adj.* **fructif'erous** bearing fruit.—*n.* **fructifica'tion** fruit-production: a structure that contains spores or seeds (*bot.*).—*v.t.* **fruc'tify** to make fruitful: to fertilise.— *v.i.* to bear fruit.—*adj.* **fructiv'orous** (L. *vorāre*, to devour) frugivorous.—*ns.* **fruc'tose** fruit sugar or laevulose; **fruc'tuary** one enjoying the fruits of anything.—*v.i.* **fruc'tuate** to come to fruit: to fructify.— *n.* **fructua'tion** coming to fruit, bearing of fruit.—*adj.* **fruc'tuous** fruitful. [L. *frŭctus*, fruit.]
frugal *frōō'gl, adj.* economical in the use of means: sparing: spare: thrifty.—*ns.* **fru'galist** one who is frugal; **frugality** (*-gal'*) economy: thrift.—*adv.* **fru'gally.** [L. *frūgālis—frūx, frūgis*, fruit.]
frugiferous *frōō-jif'a-ras, adj.* (L. *ferre*, to bear) fruit-bearing.—*adj.* **frugiv'orous** (L. *vorāre*, to eat) feeding on fruits or seeds. [L. *frūx, frūgis*, fruit.]
fruit *frōōt, n.* the produce of the earth: an edible part of

a plant, generally sweet, acid, and juicy, esp. a part that contains the seed, but sometimes extended to include other parts (e.g. the leaf-stalk in rhubarb): in bot., a fructification, esp. the structure that develops from the ovary and its contents after fertilisation, sometimes including also structures formed from other parts of the flower or axis: the offspring of animals: (often in *pl.*) product, effect, advantage: a male homosexual (*slang*, esp. *U.S.*).—*v.i.* to produce fruit.—*adj.* **fruit'ed** having produced fruit.—*ns.* **fruit'er** a tree, etc. as a producer of fruit, as in *good fruiter*: a fruit-grower; **fruit'erer** one who deals in fruit:—*fem.* **fruit'eress**; **fruit'ery** a place for storing fruit.—*adj.* **fruit'ful** productive.—*adv.* **fruit'fully.**—*ns.* **fruit'fulness**; **fruit'ing.**—*adj.* **fruit'less** barren: without profit: useless: in vain.—*adv.* **fruit'lessly.**—*n.* **fruit'lessness.**—*adj.* **fruit'y** like, or tasting like, fruit: rich: crazy (*U.S. slang*): male homosexual (*slang*, *U.S.*).—**fruit'-bat** large fruit-eating bat of the Old World; **fruit'-cake** a cake containing raisins, etc.: a slightly mad person (*coll.*); **fruit cocktail** a fruit salad, esp. one of small, usu. diced, pieces of fruit; **fruit'-fly** an insect of genus Drosophila; **fruit'-knife** a knife with a blade of silver, etc., for cutting fruit; **fruit'-machine** a coin-operated gaming machine in which chance must bring pictures of different fruits, etc. together in a certain combination to give a win; **fruit salad** a mixture of pieces of fruit, fresh or preserved; **fruit'wood** the wood of a fruit-tree (also *adj.*).—**bush fruits** small fruits growing on woody bushes; **first-fruits** see **first, annat**; **small, soft fruit(s)** strawberries, currants, etc. [O.Fr. *fruit*, *fruict*—L. *frūctus*—*fruī*, *frūctus*, to enjoy.]

fruition *frōō-ish'ən*, *n.* enjoyment: use or possession, esp. accompanied with pleasure: now often used for fruiting (q.v. under **fruit**).—*adj.* **fru'itive.** [O.Fr. *fruition*—L. *fruī*, to enjoy.]

frumenty *frōō'mən-ti*, *n.* hulled wheat boiled in milk.—Also **fro'menty**, **fur'menty**, **fur'mety**, **fur'mity** (*fûr'*). [O.Fr. *frumentee*—*frument*—L. *frūmentum.*]

frump *frump*, *n.* a dowdy woman.—*adjs.* **frump'ish, frump'y** ill-dressed, dowdy.

frustule *frus'tūl*, *n.* the siliceous two-valved shell of a diatom, with its contents.—**frust'um** a slice of a solid body: the part of a cone or pyramid between the base and a parallel plane, or between two planes:—*pl.* **frust'ums** or **frust'a**. [L. *frustum*, a bit.]

frustrate *frus-trāt'*, *frus'trāt*, *v.t.* to make vain or of no effect: to bring to naught: to balk: to thwart.—*adj.* (*frus'*) vain, ineffectual: balked.—*adj.* **frustrated** thwarted: having a sense of discouragement and dissatisfaction.—*n.* **frustrā'tion.** [L. *frustrāri.*]

frutex *frōō'teks*, *n.* a shrub:—*pl.* **fru'tices** (*-ti-sēz*).—*adj.* **fru'ticose** shrubby. [L. *frutex*, *-icis*, shrub.]

fry[1] *frī*, *v.t.* to cook in oil or fat in a pan: to burn or scorch (often *fig.*).—*v.i.* to undergo frying:—*pr.p.* **fry'ing**; *pa.t.* and *pa.p.* **fried**; *3rd pers. pres. indic.* **fries.**—*n.* a dish of anything fried, esp. the offal of a pig, lamb, etc.—*n.* **fri'er** (or **fry'er**) one who fries (esp. fish): a vessel for frying: a fish suitable for frying.—*n.* and *adj.* **fry'ing.**—**fry'ing-pan** a flat pan for frying with; **fry'-up** (*coll.*) mixed fried foods, or the frying of these.—**fry in one's fat** suffer the consequences of one's behaviour; **out of the frying-pan into the fire** out of one evil into a greater. [Fr. *frire*—L. *frīgĕre.*]

fry[2] *frī*, *n.* young, collectively: a swarm of young, esp. of fishes just spawned.—**small fry** small things collectively, persons or things of little importance. [O.N. *friŏ*, seed.]

fuchsia *fū'shə*, *n.* any plant of a S. American genus (**Fuchsia**) of the evening primrose family, with long pendulous flowers.—*n.* **fuchsine** (*fōō'ks'ēn*) the dye-

stuff magenta, a green solid, purplish-red in solution (from its colour, similar to that of the flower). [Named after Leonard *Fuchs*, a German botanist, 1501–66.]

fuck *fuk* (all words, meanings, still *vulg.*) *v.t.* to have sexual intercourse: (with *about* or *around*) to play around, act foolishly: (with *off*) to go away.—*v.t.* to have sexual intercourse with (usu. of a male): (with *about* or *around*) to deal inconsiderately with: (with *up*) to botch, damage or break (*n.* **fuck'-up**).—*n.* an act of sexual intercourse: a person, esp. female, considered as a (good, poor, etc.) partner in sexual intercourse: used in various phrases expressing displeasure, emphasis, etc.—*interj.* an expression of displeasure, etc. (often with an object, as in *fuck him!*).—*p. adj.* **fucked** exhausted.—*ns.* **fuck'er** one who fucks: a term of abuse: a fellow; a person; **fuck'-ing** sexual intercourse.—*adj.* expressing scorn or disapprobation: as an intensive, to a great extent: often used as a meaningless qualification.—*adv.* very.—(sweet) **fuck all** nothing at all. [Ety. dub., perh. Ger *ficken*, to strike, to copulate with.]

fuddle *fud'l*, *v.t.* to stupefy, as with drink: to confuse.—*v.i.* to drink to excess or habitually.—*pr.p* **fudd'-ling**; *pa.t.* and *pa.p.* **fudd'led.**—*n.* intoxication: a drinking bout: confusion.—*n.* **fudd'ler** a drunkard.—*n.* and *adj.* **fudd'ling** tippling.

fuddy-duddy *fud'i-dud-i*, *n.* an old fogy, stick-in-the-mud: a carper.—*adj.* old-fogyish: old-fashioned: stuffy: prim: censorious.

fudge[1] *fuj*, *n.* nonsense: a soft sweetmeat.—*interj.* bosh.

fudge[2] *fuj*, *v.t.* to cheat: to fail: to dodge.—*v.t.* to patch up: to fake: to distort: to dodge: to obscure, cover up. [Variant of *fadge*, to succeed.]

Fuehrer. Same as **Führer**.

fuel *fū'əl*, *n.* material for a fire: something that maintains or intensifies emotion, etc. (*fig.*): food, as maintaining bodily processes: fissile material for a nuclear reactor.—*v.t.* to furnish with fuel: to incite, encourage or stimulate (esp. anger, hate, violence, etc.).—*v.i.* to take or get fuel:—*pr.p.* **fu'elling**; *pa.t.* and *pa.p.* **fu'elled.**—*n.* **fu'eller.**—**fu'el-cell'** a cell generating electricity as part of a chemical reaction between an electrolyte and a combustible gas or vapour.—*adj.* **fu'el-injec'ted** having **fu'el-injec'tion**, a system of operating an internal-combustion engine in which vaporised liquid fuel is introduced under pressure directly into the combustion chamber, so dispensing with a carburettor.—**add fuel to the fire(s)** to make an angry person angrier, a heated discussion more heated, etc. [O.Fr. *fowaille*—L.L. *focāle*—L. *focus*, a fireplace.]

fug *fug*, *n.* a very hot close, often smoky, state of atmosphere.—*adj.* **fugg'y.**

fugacious *fū-gā'shəs*, *adj.* apt to flee away: fleeting: readily shed.—*ns.* **fuga'ciousness, fugacity** (*-gas'*). [L. *fugāx*, *-ācis*—*fugĕre*, to flee.]

fugal, fugato. See **fugue**.

fugitive *fū'ji-tiv*, *adj.* apt to flee away: fleeing: fleeting: evanescent: occasional, written for some passing occasion.—*n.* one who flees or has fled: one hard to be caught: an exile.—*adv.* **fu'gitively.**—*n.* **fu'gitiveness.** [L. *fugitīvus*—*fugĕre*, to flee.]

fugue *fūg*, *n.* in mus. a form of composition in which the subject is given out by one part and immediately taken up by a second (in *answer*), during which the first part supplies an accompaniment or counter-subject, and so on: a form of amnesia which is a flight from reality.—*adj.* **fu'gal.**—*adv.* **fu'gally.**—*adj.* and *adv* **fugato** (*fū-gä'tō*, It. *fōō-gä'tō*) in the manner of a fugue without being strictly a fugue.—Also *n.*:—*pl.* **fuga'tos.** [Fr.,—It. *fuga*—L. *fuga*, flight.]

Führer *fü′rər*, Ger. *fü′rər*, n. the title taken by Hitler as dictator of Nazi Germany. [Ger., leader, guide.]

fulcrum *ful′krəm*, *fŏŏl′*, n. the prop or fixed point on which a lever moves (*mech.*): a support: a means to an end (*fig.*):—pl. **ful′crums**, **ful′cra**. [L. *fulcrum*, a prop—*fulcīre*, to prop.]

fulfil *fŏŏl-fil′*, v.t. to complete: to accomplish: to carry into effect: to bring to consummation: to develop and realise the potential of:—pr.p. **fulfill′ing**; pa.t. and pa.p **fulfilled′**,—ns. **fulfil′er**; **fulfill′ing**, **fulfil′ment** full performance: completion: accomplishment. [O.E. *fullfyllan*—*full*, *fyllan*, to fill.]

fulgent *ful′jənt*, adj. shining: bright.—n. **ful′gency**. [L. *fulgēns*, *-entis*, pr.p. of *fulgēre*, to shine.]

fuliginous *fū-lij′i-nəs*, adj. sooty: dusky.—n. **fuligos′ity**. [L. *fūligŏ*, *-inis*, soot.]

full *fŏŏl*, adj. holding all that can be contained: having no empty space: abundantly supplied or furnished: copious: filling: containing the whole matter: perfect: maximum: strong: clear: intense: swelled or rounded: protuberant: having excess of material: at the height of development or end of course: (with *of*) unable to think or talk of anything but: drunk (*coll.*):—compar. **full′er**; superl. **full′est**.—n. the completest extent, as of the moon: the highest degree: the whole: the time of full moon.—v.t. to make with gathers or puckers.—v.i. to become full.—adv. quite: thoroughly, veritably: directly.—n. **full′ness**, **ful′ness** the state of being full: the moment of fulfilment —adv. **full′y** completely: entirely: quite.—**full back** see **back**; **full blast** full operation.—adv. **full′-blast′** with maximum energy and fluency.—**full′-blood** an individual of pure blood.—adjs. **full′-blood′ed** having a full supply of blood: vigorous: thoroughbred, of unmixed descent: related through both parents; **full′-blown** fully expanded, as a flower: beyond the first freshness of youth: fully qualified or admitted: puffed out to fullness; **full′-bod′led** with much body or substance.—**full brother**, **sister** son, daughter, of the same parents.—adv. **full′-cir′cle** round in a complete revolution.—**full′-cock′** the position of a gun cock drawn fully back, or of a tap fully open.—adv. in that position.—adj. **full′-cocked′**.—**full cousin** the son or daughter of an uncle or aunt, first cousin.—adjs. **full′-cream′** (of milk) not skimmed: made with unskimmed milk; **full′-dress** in the dress (**full dress**) worn on occasions of state or ceremony; **full′-face**, **full′-faced** having a full or broad face; **full′-fash′ioned**, **full′y-fash′ioned** of garments, esp. stockings, conforming to the body contour; **full′-fledged′**, **full′y-fledged′** completely fledged: having attained full membership; **full′-front′al** of the front view of a completely naked man or woman: with no detail left unrevealed (*fig.*); **full′-grown** grown to full size.—**full hand** full house.—adj. **full′-heart′ed** full of heart or courage: fraught with emotion.—**full house** a performance at which every seat is taken (*theat.*): three cards of a kind and a pair (*poker*; also **full hand**).—adj. **full′-length′** extending the whole length.—n. a portrait showing the whole length.—adv. stretched to the full extent.—**full moon** the moon with its whole disc illuminated, when opposite the sun: the time when the moon is full.—adj. **full′-mouthed** loud: sonorous.—**full nelson** a nelson.—adjs. **full′-out** at full power: total; **full′-page** occupying a whole page.—advs. **full′-pelt′**, **full′-speed′**, **full′-split′**, **full-tilt′** with highest speed and impetus.—**full pitch** in cricket, a ball which does not or would not pitch before passing or hitting the batsman's wicket—also **full toss**.—adj. **full′-rigged′** having three or more masts square-rigged.—adv. **full′-sail′**.—adjs. **full′-sailed** having all sails set: having sails filled with wind: advancing with speed

and momentum; **full′-scale** of the same size as the original: involving full power or maximum effort.—**full sister** see **full brother**.—advs. **full-speed**, **full-split** see **full-pelt**.—**full stop** a point marking the end of a sentence: an end, a halt.—adjs. **full′-throat′ed**, **full′-voiced** singing with the whole power of the voice.—adv. **full-tilt** see **full-pelt**.—**full time** the end of a football, rugby, etc. match.—adj. **full′-time** occupied during or extending over the whole working day, week, etc.—**full′-tim′er**; **full toss** see **full pitch**.—adjs. **full-voiced** see **full-throated**; **full′y-fash′ioned** full-fashioned; **fully-fledged** full-fledged.—**full of oneself** having a (too) high opinion of one's own importance, etc. (also **full of one's own importance**), too much the subject of one's own conversation; **full of years** old, aged: at a good old age; **full up** full to the limit; sated, wearied (*slang*); **in full** without reduction; **in full cry** in chase together, giving tongue; **in full rig** with maximum number of masts and sails; **in full swing** at the height of activity; **in the fullness of time** at the due or destined time; **to the full** in full measure, completely. [O.E. *full*.]

full² *fŏŏl*, v.t. to scour and beat, as a means of finishing or cleansing woollens: to scour and thicken in a mill.—n. **full′er** one who fulls cloth.—**fuller's earth** an earthy hydrous aluminium silicate, capable of absorbing grease. [O.Fr. *fuler* (see **foil¹**) and O.E. *fullere*, fuller, both—L. *fullŏ*, a cloth-fuller.]

fulmar *fŏŏl′mär*, *-mər*, n. a gull-like bird of the petrel family. [Perh. O.N. *fūll*, foul, *mär*, gull.]

fulminate *ful′min-āt*, v.i. to thunder or make a loud noise: to detonate: to issue decrees with violence, or threats: to inveigh: to flash.—v.t. to cause to explode: to send forth, as a denunciation: to denounce.—adj. **ful′minant** fulminating. developing suddenly (*path.*).—adj. **ful′minating** detonating.—n. **fulmina′tion** an act of thundering, denouncing, or detonating: a denunciation.—adj. **ful′minatory**. [L. *fulmināre*, *-ātum*—*fulmen*, *-inis*, lightning—*fulgēre*, to shine.]

fulness See **full¹**.

fulsome *fŏŏl′səm*, adj. cloying or causing surfeit: nauseous: offensive· rank· disgustingly fawning.—adv. **ful′somely**.—n. **ful′someness**. [**full**, and affix *-some*.]

fulvous *ful′vəs*, adj. dull yellow: tawny.—adj. **ful′vid**. [L. *fulvus*, tawny.]

fumarole *fūm′ə-rōl*, n. a hole emitting gases in a volcano or volcanic region. [Fr. *fumerolle* or It. *fumaruola*—L. *fūmus*, smoke.]

fumble *fum′bl*, v.i. to grope about awkwardly: to make bungling or unsuccessful attempts.—v.t. to handle, manage, or effect awkwardly or bunglingly.—n. **fum′bler**.—adv. **fum′blingly**. [Cf. Du. *fommelen*, to fumble; Dan. *famle*; O.N. *fālma*, to grope about.]

fume *fūm*, n. smoke or vapour, often odorous (often in pl.): any volatile matter: heat of mind, rage, fretful excitement.—v.i. to smoke: to throw off vapour: to come off or pass in fumes: to be in a rage.—v.t. to treat with fumes: to give off: to offer incense to.—adjs. **fūm′ous**, **fūm′y**.—**fume′-cham′ber**, **-cup′board** a case for laboratory operations that give off fumes. [L. *fūmus*, smoke.]

fumigate *fūm′i-gāt*, v.t. to expose to fumes, esp. for purposes of disinfecting, or destroying pests.—ns. **fūm′igant** a source of fumes, esp. a substance used for fumigation; **fūmiga′tion**; **fūm′igator** a fumigating apparatus.—adj. **fūm′igatory**. [L. *fūmigāre*, *-ātum*.]

fumitory *fūm′i-tər-i*, n. a plant of the genus *Fumaria*. [O.Fr. *fume-terre*, lit. earth-smoke—L. *fūmus*, smoke, *terra*, earth; so called because its rapid growth was thought to resemble the dispersal of smoke.]

fun *fun, n.* merriment: sport: a source of merriment or amusement.—*v.i.* to make sport:—*pr.p.* **funn'ing.**—*adj.* providing amusement; enjoyable, full of fun.—**fun'fair** a fair with side-shows and other amusements; **fun fur** an artificial or inexpensive (sometimes dyed) fur, esp. for casual wear; **fun park** an outdoor place of entertainment with various amusements.—**in fun** as a joke, not seriously; **like fun** (*coll.*) rapidly: not at all; **make fun of, poke fun at** to ridicule. [Prob. a form of obs. *fon,* to befool.]

funambulist *fū-nam'bū-list, n.* a rope-walker or rope-dancer. [L. *fūnambulus,* a rope walker—*fūnis,* rope, *ambulāre,* to walk.]

function *fung(k)'shən, n.* the doing of a thing: an activity appropriate to any person or thing: duty peculiar to any office: faculty, exercise of faculty: the peculiar office of anything: a solemn service: a ceremony: a social gathering: in math., a variable so connected with another that for any value of the one there is a corresponding value for the other: a correspondence between two sets of variables such that each member of one set can be related to one particular member of the other set: an event, etc. dependent on some other factor or factors: the vital activity of an organ, tissue, or cell: the part played by a linguistic form in a construction (*linguistics*).—*v.i.* to perform a function: to act: to operate: to work.—*adj.* **func'tional** pertaining to or performed by functions: of disease, characterised by impairment of function, not of organs: designed with special regard to purpose and practical use: serving a function.—*ns.* **func'-tionalism** the theory or practice of adapting method, form, materials, etc., primarily with regard to the purpose in hand; **func'tionalist.**—*adv.* **func'tionally.** —*n.* **func'tionary** one who discharges any duty: one who holds an office.—*adj.* **func'tionless** having no function. [O.Fr.,—L. *functiō, -ōnis—fungī, functus,* to perform.]

fund *fund, n.* a sum of money on which some enterprise is founded or expense supported: a supply or source of money: a store laid up: a supply: (in *pl.*) permanent government debts paying interest: (in *pl.*) money available to an organisation, for a project, etc., or (*coll.:* usu. *facet.*) available to an individual.—*v.t* to form into a stock charged with interest: to place in a fund: to provide (an organisation, project, etc.) with money.—*adj.* **fund'ed** invested in public funds: existing in the form of bonds.—*n.* **fund'ing.**—*n.* and *adj.* **fund'-raising** (for the purpose of) the raising of money for an organisation, project, etc. [L. *fundus,* the bottom.]

fundamental *fun-də-men'tl, adj.* basal: serving as foundation: essential: primary: important.—*n.* that which serves as a groundwork: an essential: the root of a chord or of a system of harmonics (*mus.*).—*ns.* **fund'ament** (*-mənt*) the lower part or seat of the body; **fundamen'talism** belief in the literal truth of the Bible, against evolution, etc.; **fundamen'talist** one who professes this belief or (*fig.*) other, e.g. political, beliefs considered fundamental.—Also *adj.* —*n.* **fundamental'ity.**—*adv.* **fundamen'tally.**—**fundamental particle** same as **elementary particle; fundamental units** see **absolute units.** [L. *fundāmentum,* foundation, *fundāre,* to found.]

fundus *fun'dəs, n.* bottom: the rounded bottom of a hollow organ (*anat.*):—*pl.* **fun'di** (*-ī*). [L.]

funeral *fū'nər-əl, n.* disposal of the dead, with any ceremonies or observances connected therewith: a procession to the place of burial or cremation, etc.—*adj.* pertaining to the disposal of the dead.—*adjs.* **fūne'bral, fūne'brial** funereal; **fū'nerary** pertaining

to or suiting a funeral; **fūne'real** pertaining to a funeral: dismal: mournful.—**funeral director** an undertaker; **funeral home** (esp. *U.S.*), **funeral parlour** a room that can be hired for funeral ceremonies. —**your, my,** etc. **funeral** your, my, etc. affair, or look-out. [L.L. *fūnerālis* and L. *fūnerārius, fūnebris, fūnēreus*—L. *fūnus, fūnēris,* a funeral procession.]

fungibles *fun'ji-blz,* (*law*) *n.pl.* movable effects which are consumed by use, and which are estimated by weight, number, and measure. [L.L. *fungibilis*—L. *fungī,* to perform; see **function.**]

fungus *fung'gəs, n.* a plant of one of the lowest groups, including mushrooms, toadstools, mould, etc.: proud-flesh formed on wounds:—*pl.* **fungi** (*fun'jī, -jī, -gī*), **fung'uses.**—*adjs.* **fung'al** pertaining to fungus; **fungicid'al** fungi-destroying: pertaining to a fungicide.—*n.* **fungicide** (*fun'ji-sīd*) a substance which kills fungi.—*adj.* **fung'oid** (*-goid*), **-al** fungus-like: of the nature of a fungus.—*n.* **fungos'ity.**—*adj.* **fung'-ous** of or like fungus: soft: spongy: growing suddenly: ephemeral. [L. *fungus,* a mushroom.]

funicle *fū'ni-kl, n.* a small cord or ligature: a fibre: the stalk of an ovule (*bot.*).—*adjs.* **fūnic'ūlar; fūnic'-ūlate.**—**funicular railway** a cable-railway. [L. *fūniculus,* dim. of *fūnus,* a rope.]

funk[1] *fungk,* (*coll.*) *n.* a state of fear: panic: shrinking or shirking from loss of courage: one who funks.—*v.t.* to flinch: to draw back or hold back in fear.—*v.t.* to balk at or shirk from fear.—*n.* **funk'iness.**—*adj.* **funk'y.**—**funk'hole** (*slang, orig. mil.*) a place of refuge, dug-out: a place to which one can retreat for shelter, etc. (*fig.*): a job that enables one to avoid military service.—**blue funk** see **blue**[1]. [Poss. Flem. *fonck.*]

funk[2] *fungk, n.* a strong, unpleasant smell (*obs.* or *U.S. dial.*): tobacco smoke (*obs.* or *U.S. dial.*): funky music (*slang*)—*adj.* **funk'y** with a strong, musty, or bad smell (*U.S. dial.*): of jazz, pop music, etc., unsophisticated, earthy, and soulful, like early blues music in style, emotion, etc. (*slang*): in the latest fashion, with it (*slang*): kinky (*slang*): odd, quaint (*slang*).

funnel *fun'l, n.* a vessel, usually a cone ending in a tube, for pouring fluids into bottles, etc.: a passage for the escape of smoke, etc.—*v.t.* to pour, pass, transfer, etc. through, or as if through, a funnel.—*adj.* **funn'elled** with a funnel: funnel-shaped. [Prob. through Fr. or Port. from L. *infundibulum—fundēre,* to pour.]

funny *fun'i, adj.* full of fun: droll: amusing, mirth-provoking: queer, odd (*coll.*).—*n.* a joke (*coll.*): (in *pl.*) comic strips, or the comic section of a newspaper (*U.S.*).—*adv.* **funn'ily.**—*n.* **funn'iness.**—**funny bone** the bone at the elbow with the comparatively unprotected ulnar nerve which, when struck, shoots a tingling sensation down the forearm to the fingers (a punning translation of L. *humerus*); **funny business** tricks, deception (*slang*): amusing behaviour, joke-telling, etc. (*coll.*); **funny farm** (*slang*) a mental hospital or asylum; **funny man** (*coll.*) a comedian, **funny stuff** funny business. [**fun.**]

fur *fûr, n.* the thick, soft, fine hair of certain animals: the skin with this hair attached: a garment of fur: furred animals (opp. to *feather*): a coating on the tongue: a crust in boilers, etc.: a strengthening piece nailed to a rafter.—*v.t.* to clothe, cover, coat, trim or line with fur: to coat.—*v.i.* to become coated:—*pr.p.* **furr'ing;** *pa.t.* and *pa.p.* **furred.**—*adj.* **furred.**—*ns.* **furr'ier** a dealer or worker in furs; **furr'ing** fur trimmings: a coating on the tongue· (also **firr'ing**) strips of wood fastened to joists, etc.: a lining to a wall to carry lath, provide an air-space, etc.—*adj.* **furr'y** consisting of, like, covered with, or dressed in fur.—**fur'-seal** an eared seal with close fur under its long hairs. [O.Fr. *forrer*, to line, encase—*forre, fuerre*, sheath.]

furbelow *fûr'bi-lō, n.* a plaited border or flounce: a superfluous ornament.—*v.t.* to flounce. [Fr., It., and Sp. *falbala*; of unknown origin.]

furbish *fûr'bish, v.t.* to purify or polish: to rub up until bright: to renovate.—*n.* **fur'bisher.** [O.Fr. *fourbir, fourbiss-*, from O.H.G. *furban*, to purify.]

furcate, furcated *fûr'kāt, -kit, -kā-tid, adjs.* forked.—*adj.* **fur'cal.**—*n.* **furca'tion.**—*adj.* **furciferous** (-*sif'*) bearing a forked appendage: rascally (*facet.*; in allusion to the *furca* or yoke of criminals).—*n.* **fur'cula** the united clavicles of a bird—the wishbone.—*adj.* **fur'cular** furcate: shaped like a fork. [L. *furca*, fork.]

furfur *fûr'fûr, -fər, n.* dandruff, scurf.—*adj.* **furfuraceous** (*fûr-fū-rā'shəs*) branny: scaly: scurfy. [L. *furfur*, bran.]

furioso *fōō-ri-ō'sō, fū-, (mus.) adj.* and *adv.* with fury. [It.; cf. **furious**.]

furious. See **fury**.

furl *fûrl, v.t.* to roll up. [Perh. **fardel**.]

furlong *fûr'long, n.* 40 poles, one-eighth of a mile. [O.E. *furlang—furh*, furrow, *lang*, long.]

furlough *fûr'lō, n.* leave of absence.—*v.t.* to grant furlough to. [Du. *verlof*.]

furmenty, furmety, furmity. See **frumenty**.

furnace *fûr'nis, n.* an enclosed structure in which great heat is produced: a time or place of grievous affliction or torment. [O.Fr. *fornais—*L. *fornāx, -ācis—fornus*, an oven.]

furnish *fûr'nish, v.t.* to fit up or supply completely, or with what is necessary: to supply, provide: to equip.—*adj.* **fur'nished** equipped: stocked with furniture.—*n.* **fur'nisher.**—*n.pl.* **fur'nishings** fittings of any kind, esp. articles of furniture, etc., within a house.—*n.* **fur'nishment.** [O.Fr. *furnir, furniss-*; of Gmc. origin.]

furniture *fûr'ni-chər, n.* movables, either for use or ornament, with which a house is equipped: the trappings of a horse: the necessary appliances in some arts: accessories: metal fittings for doors and windows: the piece of wood or metal put round pages of type to make margins and fasten the matter in the chase (*print.*). [Fr. *fourniture*.]

furor *fū'rör, n.* fury: excitement, enthusiasm. [L.]

furore *fū'rör, -rör, fōō-rör'ā, n.* a craze: wild enthusiasm: wild excitement. [It.]

furrier, furring. See **fur**.

furrow *fur'ō, n.* the trench made by a plough: a groove: a wrinkle.—*v.t.* to form furrows in: to groove: to wrinkle.—*adj.* **furr'owy.** [O.E. *furh*.]

furry. See **fur**.

further[1] *fûr'dhər, adv.* at or to a greater distance or degree: in addition.—*adj.* more distant: additional.—*adv.* **fur'thermore** in addition to what has been said, moreover, besides.—*adj.* **fur'thermost** most remote. —*adv.* **fur'thest** at or to the greatest distance.—*adj.* most distant.—**further education** post-school education other than at university, polytechnic, etc.—**see someone further** to see someone hanged, or the like. [O.E. *furthor* (adv.), *furthra* (adj.)—*fore* or *forth* with compar. suffix *-ther*.]

further[2] *fûr'dhər, v.t.* to help forward, promote.—*ns.* **fur'therance** a helping forward; **fur'therer** a promoter, advancer. [O.E. *fyrthran*.]

furtive *fûr'tiv, adj.* stealthy: secret.—*adv.* **fur'tively.** —*n.* **fur'tiveness.** [L. *furtīvus—fûr*, a thief.]

furuncle *fū'rung-kl, n.* a boil.—*adjs.* **fūrun'cular, fūrun'culous.** [L. *fūrunculus*, lit. a little thief.]

fury *fū'ri, n.* rage: violent passion: madness: (with *cap.*; *myth.*) any one of the three goddesses of vengeance: hence a passionate, violent woman.—*adj.* **furious**

(*fū'ri-əs*) full of fury: violent.—*n.* **furios'ity** madness. —*adv.* **fū'riously.**—*n.* **fū'riousness.**—**fast and furious** see **fast**[2]; **like fury** (*coll.*) furiously. [Fr. *furie*—L. *furia—furēre*, to be angry.]

furze *fûrz, n.* whin or gorse. [O.E. *fyrs*.]

fusain *fū-zān', n.* an important constituent of coal, resembling charcoal (also *fū'zān*): artists' fine charcoal: a drawing done with this. [Fr., the spindletree, or charcoal made from it.]

fuse[1] *fūz, v.t.* to melt: to liquefy by heat: to join by, or as if by, melting together: to cause to fail by melting of a fuse (*elect*).—*v.i.* to be melted: to be reduced to a liquid: to melt together: to blend, unite: of electric appliance, to fail by melting of a fuse.—*n.* a bit of fusible metal, with its mounting, inserted as a safeguard in an electrical circuit.—*n.* **fusibil'ity** the degree of ease with which a substance can be fused.—*adj.* **fus'ible** able to be fused or easily fused.—*n.* **fu'sion** (-*zhən*) melting: the state of fluidity from heat: a close union of things, as if melted together: nuclear fusion (q.v.).—**fuse box** a box containing the switches and fuses for the leads of an electrical system; **fusion bomb** one deriving its energy from fusion of atomic nuclei, as the hydrogen bomb; **fusion reactor** a nuclear reactor operating by nuclear fusion. [L. *fundĕre, fūsum*, to melt.]

fuse[2] *fūz, n.* a train of combustible material in waterproof covering, used with a detonator to initiate an explosion.—Also, esp. *U.S.*, **fuze**. [It. *fuso*—L. *fūsus*, a spindle.]

fusee, fuzee *fū-zē', n.* the spindle in a watch or clock on which the chain is wound: a match with long, oval head for outdoor use: a fuse for firing explosives. [O.Fr. *fusée*, a spindleful—L. *fūsus*, a spindle.]

fuselage *fū'zil-ij*, or *fū-zə-läzh', n.* the body of an aeroplane. [Fr. *fuseler*, to shape like a spindle—L. *fūsus*, spindle.]

fusel-oil *fū'zl-oil, n.* a nauseous oil in spirits distilled from potatoes, grain, etc. [Ger. *Fusel*, bad spirits.]

fusil *fū'zil, n.* a flint-lock musket.—*ns.* **fusilier', fusileer'** formerly a soldier armed with a fusil, now simply a historical title borne by a few regiments; **fusilade** (-*ād'*) simultaneous or continuous discharge of firearms: anything assaulting one in similar way (*lit., fig.*). [O.Fr. *fuisil*, a flint-musket, same as It. *focile*—L.L. *focile*, steel (to strike fire with), dim. of L. *focus*, a fireplace.]

fusion. See **fuse**[1].

fuss *fus, n.* a bustle: flurry: commotion, esp. over trifles: petty ostentatious activity or attentions.—*v.i.* to be in a fuss, agitate about trifles.—*v.t.* to agitate, flurry.—*n.* **fuss'er.**—*adv.* **fuss'ily.**—*n.* **fuss'iness.**—*adj.* **fuss'y** given to making a fuss: finicky: requiring careful attention: overtrimmed.—**fuss'-pot** one who fusses.—**make a fuss of** to give much (genuinely or apparently) affectionate or amicable attention to.

fust *fust, n.* a mouldy or musty smell.—*n.* **fust'iness.**—*adj.* **fust'y** smelling of the cask: musty: stale: stuffy: wanting in freshness. [O.Fr. *fust* (Fr. *fût*), cask—L. *fūstis*, a cudgel.]

fustanella *fus-tə-nel'ə, n.* a white kilt worn by Greek and Albanian men. [Mod. Gr. *phoustanella*, dim. of *phoustani*, Albanian *fustan*—It. *fustagno*, fustian.]

fustet *fus'tet, n.* Venetian sumach, or its wood, source of the dye called young fustic. [Fr ,—Prov. *fustet*—Ar. *fustuq*; see **fustic**.]

fustian *fus'chən, n.* a kind of coarse, twilled cotton fabric including moleskin, velveteen, corduroy, etc.: a pompous and unnatural style of writing or speaking: bombast.—*adj.* made of fustian: bombastic. [O.Fr. *fustaigne*—It. *fustagno*—L.L. *fustāneum*, prob. from *El-Fustāt* (Old Cairo) where it may have been made.]

fustic *fus'tik, n.* formerly, fustet (now called **young**

fustic): now, the wood of a tropical American tree (*Chlorophora tinctoria*), yielding a yellow dye (also **old fustic**).—Also **fus'toc**. [Fr. *fustoc*—Sp. *fustoc* —Ar. *fustuq*—Gr. *pistakē*, pistachio.]

futhork, futhorc, futhark *fōō'thork, -thàrk, ns.* the Runic alphabet. [From the first six letters, *f, u, þ(th), o* or *a, r, k.*]

futile *fū'til, U S. -təl, adj.* ineffectual: trifling: tattling (*obs.*).—*adv.* **fu'tilely.**—*n.* **futil'ity** uselessness. [L. *fūtilis*, leaky, futile—*fundĕre*, to pour.]

futon *fōō'ton, n.* a Japanese floor-mattress used as a bed. [Jap.]

futtock *fut'ək, n.* one of the crooked timbers of a wooden ship. [Perh. for **foot-hook**.]

future *fū'chər, adj.* about to be: that is to come: expressive of time to come (*gram.*).—*n.* time to come: life, fate or condition in time to come: the future tense (*gram.*): (in *pl.*) goods bought and sold to be delivered at a future time.—*adj.* **fut'ureless** without prospects. —*ns.* **fut'urism** (*art*) a movement claiming to anticipate or point the way for the future, esp. a 20th-century revolt against tradition; **fut'urist** one whose chief interests are in what is to

come: a believer in futurism.—*adj.* **futurist'ic.**—*n.* **futurity** (*fū-tū'ri-ti*) time to come: an event, or state of being, yet to come.—*adj.* **futurolog'ical.**—*ns.* **futurol'ogist; futurol'ogy** the science and study of sociological and technological developments, values, and trends, with a view to planning for the future.—*adj.* **fu'ture-per'fect** (*gram.*) expressive of action viewed as past in reference to an assumed future time. —*n.* the future-perfect tense: a verb in that tense. [Fr. *futur*—L. *futūrus*, used as fut.p. of *esse*, to be.]

fu yung *fōō yōō ng,* a Chinese omelette-like dish with bean sprouts, onion, meat, etc.—Also **foo yung, foo yong** (*yong*). [Chin., hibiscus.]

fuze *fūz, n.* a device used to cause a bomb, shell, mine, rocket, etc., to detonate.—Often, esp. *U.K.*, **fuse**. [**fuse²**.]

fuzee. See fusee.

fuzz *fuz, n.* light fine particles or fibres, as dust: fluff: blurr: police (*slang*).—*adv.* **fuzz'ily.**—*n.* **fuzz'iness.** —*adj.* **fuzz'y** covered with fuzz: fluffy: with many small tight curls: blurred.

fy *fī, interj.* Same as **fie¹**.

fāte; fär; mē; hûr (her); *mīne; mōte; för; mūte; mōōn; fōōt; dhen* (then); *el'ə-mənt* (element)

G

G, g *jē, n.* the seventh letter of our alphabet, and of the Roman: the fifth note of the diatonic scale of C major —also *sol* (*mus.*): the scale or key having that note for its tonic (*mus.*): a symbol (*g*) for acceleration due to gravity (see **gravity**): a symbol (*G*) for the constant of gravitation (see **gravity**): symbol for general intelligence.—**G'-clef** a clef, the treble clef, on the second line of the treble stave, marking G; **G'-man** (*U.S.*) an agent of the Federal Bureau of Investigation (for Government-man); **G'-string** same as **gee-string**; **g'-suit** a close-fitting suit with cells that inflate to prevent flow of blood away from the head, worn by airmen as a defence against blackout due to high acceleration and resultant great increase in weight (*g* for acceleration of gravity).

gab *gab,* (*coll.*) *v.i.* to chatter, prate.—*n.* idle or fluent talk: the mouth.—*n.* **gabb'er** a chatterer.—*adj.* **gabb'y** garrulous.—**gab'fest** (*slang;* chiefly *U.S.*) a gathering characterised by much talk or gossip: a prolonged conversation, discussion, etc.—**gift of the gab** a talent (or propensity) for talking.

gabardine. See **gaberdine.**

gabble *gab'l, v.i.* to talk inarticulately: to chatter: to cackle like geese.—*ns.* **gabb'le** gabbling; **gabb'ler**; **gabb'ling, gabb'lement.** [Perh. freq. of **gab,** perh M.Du. *gabbelen*—imit.]

gabbro *gab'rō, n.* a coarsely crystalline igneous rock composed of labradorite or similar plagioclase and pyroxene, often with olivine and magnetite:—*pl.* **gabb'ros.**—*adjs.* **gabbro'ic, gabbroitic** (-*it'ik*); **gabb'-roid** resembling gabbro. [It.]

gaberdine, gabardine *gab'ər-dēn, n.* a closely woven twill fabric, esp. of cotton and wool: a coat of this material. [O.Fr. *gauvardine*; perh. M.H.G. *wallevart,* pilgrimage.]

gabfest. See **gab.**

gabion *gā'bi-ən, n.* a bottomless basket of earth, used in fortification and engineering (*fort.*).—*ns.* (*fort.*) **gā'bionade** a work formed of gabions; **gā'bionage** gabions collectively.—*adj.* **gā'bioned** furnished with gabions. [Fr.,—It. *gabbione,* a large cage—**gabbia** —L. *cavea,* a cage.]

gable *gā'bl,* (*archit.*) *n.* the triangular part of an exterior wall of a building between the top of the side-walls and the slopes on the roof.—*adj.* **gā'bled.**— **gā'ble-end** the end-wall of a building on the side where there is a gable; **gā'ble-win'dow** a window in a gable-end: a window with its upper part shaped like a gable. [Prob. through O.Fr. *gable,* from O.N *gafl.*]

gaby *gā'bi,* (*dial.*) *n.* a simpleton.

gad¹ *gad, interj.* a minced form of God.—*interj.* (*arch.*) **gad-zooks'** minced oath (app for *God's hooks*).

gad² *gad, v.i.* to rush here and there in a wayward uncontrolled manner (*obs.*): to wander about, often restlessly, idly or in pursuit of pleasure (often with *about*): to straggle:—*pr.p.* **gadd'ing;** *pa.t.* and *pa.p.* **gadd'ed.**—*n.* wandering, gadding about.—*n.* **gadd'er.**—**gad'about** one who wanders restlessly from place to place.

Gadarene *gad'ə-rēn, adj.* indicative of mass panic and headlong flight towards disaster. [From the swine of *Gadara,* Matt. viii. 28.]

gade. See **Gadus.**

gadfly *gad'flī, n.* a blood-sucking fly that distresses

cattle: sometimes applied to a botfly: a mischievous gadabout. [O.E. *gād* (see **goad**) and **fly.**]

gadget *gaj'it, n.* any small ingenious device: a what-d'ye-call-it.—*ns.* **gadgeteer'** one who delights in gadgets; **gad'getry** gadgets: the making of gadgets.

gadgie, gadje *gaj'i,* **gaudgie, gauje** *gö'ji,* (*dial.*; usu. *derog.*) *ns.* a fellow. [Orig. variants of **gorgio.**]

Gadhel *gad'əl, n.* a Gael, a Celt of the branch to which the Irish, the Scottish Highlanders, and the Manx belong.—*adj.* **Gadhelic** (-*el'ik,* -*ēl'ik,* or *gad'*).—*n.* the Q- Celtic language of this group.—See also **Gael, Goidel.** [Ir. *Gaedheal* (pl. *Gaedhil*).]

gadoid. See under **Gadus.**

gadolinite *gad'ə-lin-īt, n.* a silicate of yttrium, beryllium, and iron.—*n.* **gadolin'ium** a metal of the rare earths (symbol Gd; at. numb. 64). [From the Finnish chemist *Gadolin* (1760–1852).]

gadroon *gə-drōōn', n.* a boss-like ornament, used in series in plate, etc., to form a cable or bead.—*adj.* **gadrooned'.**—*n.* **gadroon'ing.** [Fr. *godron.*]

Gadus *gā'dəs, n.* the cod genus, typical of the family **Gadidae** (*gad'i-dē*).—*ns.* **gade, gad'oid** a fish of the family.—*adj.* **gad'oid** codlike. [Latinised from Gr. *gados,* the hake or similar fish.]

gadwall *gad'wöl, n.* a northern freshwater duck.

Gael *gāl, n.* one whose language is Gadhelic, esp. a Scottish Highlander.—*adj.* **Gaelic** (*gāl'ik, gal'ik*) pertaining to the Gaels.—*n.* Gadhelic, the language of Ireland and (now *esp.*) that of the Scottish Highlands.—*v.t.* **gael'icise, -ize** (-*sīz*).—*n.* **gael'icism** (-*sizm*).—See also **Goidel.** [Scottish Gael. *Gaidheal.*]

Gaeltacht *gāl'tähht, n.* the Irish-speaking districts of Ireland. [Ir. *gaedhealtacht.*]

gaff¹ *gaf, n.* a hook used esp. for landing large fish: the spar to which the head of a fore-and-aft sail is bent (*naut.*).—*v.t.* to hook or bind by means of a gaff.— *adj.* **gaff'-rigged** (of a vessel) having a gaff.—**gaff'-sail** a sail attached to the gaff. [Fr. *gaffe.*]

gaff², gaffe *gaf, n.* a blunder. [Fr. *gaffe.*]

gaff³ *gaf,* (*slang*) *n.* humbug, nonsense.—**blow the gaff** to disclose a secret, to blab. [Prob. connected with **gaff²**; cf. O.E. *gegaf-sprǣc,* scurrility.]

gaffe. See **gaff².**

gaffer *gaf'ər, n.* originally a word of respect applied to an old man, now familiar (*fem.* **gammer**): the foreman of a squad of workmen. [**grandfather,** or **godfather.**]

gag¹ *gag, v.t.* to stop the mouth of forcibly: to silence: to prevent free expression by (the press, etc.): to choke up.—*v.i.* to choke: to retch:—*pr.p.* **gagg'ing;** *pa.t.* and *pa.p.* **gagged.**—*n.* something put into the mouth or over it to enforce silence (also *fig.*), or to distend jaws during an operation: the closure applied in a debate.—*n.* **gagg'er** one who gags.—**gag'-bit** a powerful bit used in breaking horses. [Prob. imitative of sound made in gagging.]

gag² *gag,* (*coll.*) *n.* an actor's interpolation into his part: a joke: a hoax.—*v.i.* to introduce a gag: to joke. —*v.t.* to introduce a gag into.—*n.* **gag'ster** (*coll.*) one who tells jokes, a comedian. [Possibly **gag¹.**]

gaga *ga'gä,* (*slang*) *adj.* fatuous: in senile dotage. [Fr.]

fāte, far; mē; hûr (her); *mīne, mōte; fōr; mūte, mōōn; fōōt; dhen* (then), *el'ə-mənt* (element) resin, chiefly got from *Garcinia morella*, used as a pigment and in medicine.—*adjs.* **gambogian** (-bōj', -bōō̆j'), **gambogic** (-bōj'). [From *Cambodia*, whence it was brought about 1600.]

gambol *gam'bl*, *v.i.* to leap: to frisk in sport:—*pr.p.* **gam'bolling**; *pa.t.* and *pa.p.* **gam'bolled**.—*n.* a frisk: a frolic. [Formerly *gambold*—O.Fr. *gambade*—It. *gambata*, a kick—L.L. *gamba*, leg.]

gambrel *gam'brəl*, *n.* the hock of a horse: a crooked stick for hanging a carcass, etc.—**gambrel roof** a mansard roof. [O Fr *gamberel*.]

game[1] *gām*, *n.* sport of any kind: (in *pl.*) athletic sports: a contest for recreation: a competitive amusement according to a system of rules: the state of a game: manner of playing a game: form in playing: the requisite number of points to be gained to win a game: jest, sport, trick: any object of pursuit: scheme or method of seeking an end, or the policy that would be most likely to attain it: (usu. **the game**) prostitution (*slang*): the spoil of the chase: wild animals hunted by sportsmen: the flesh of such animals.—*adj.* of or belonging to animals hunted as game: having the spirit of a fighting cock (*coll.*): plucky, courageous (*coll.*): having the necessary spirit and willingness for some act (*coll.*).—*v.i.* to gamble.—*adv.* **game'ly**.—*n.* **game'ness**.—*adj.* **game'some** playful.—*ns.* **game'someness**; **game'ster** a gambler.—*adj.* **game'sy** keen on sports.—*n.* **gam'ing** gambling.—*adj.* **gā'my** having the flavour of game, esp. that kept till tainted: savouring of scandal, sensational: spirited, plucky (*coll.*).—**game'-bag** a bag for holding a sportsman's game; **game ball** see **game point**; **game'-bird** a bird hunted for sport; **game'-chick'en**, **game'-cock** a cock of a breed trained to fight; **game chips** thinly-cut (usu. disc-shaped) potato chips served with game; **game'-dealer**; **game fish** a fish (esp. a large and powerful one) that affords sport to anglers (opp. to *coarse fish*); **game'keeper** one who has the care of game; **game laws** laws relating to the protection of game; **game licence** a licence to kill, or to sell, game; **game plan** the strategy or tactics used by a football team, etc.: any carefully devised strategy; **game point**, **game ball** the stage at which the next point wins the game; **game preserve** a tract of land stocked with game preserved for sport or with protected wild animals; **games'manship** (*facet.—Stephen Potter*) the art of winning games by talk or conduct aimed at putting one's opponent off; **games theory** (*math.*) the theory concerned with analysing the choices and strategies available in a game or other conflict in order to choose the optimum course of action; **game warden** a person who looks after game, esp. in a game preserve; **gam'ing-house** a gambling-house; **gam'ing-ta'ble** a table used for gambling.—**big game** the larger animals hunted; **give the game away** to disclose a secret; **have a game with**, **make game of** to make sport of, to ridicule; **on the game** earning one's living as a prostitute; **play the game** to act in a fair, sportsmanlike, straightforward manner; **red game** grouse; **round game** a game, as at cards, in which the number of players is not fixed; **the game is up** the game is started: the scheme has failed. [O.E. *gamen*, play.]

game[2] *gām*, *adj.* lame.

gamelan *gam'ə-lan*, *n.* an instrument resembling a xylophone: an orchestra of S.E. Asia consisting of percussion (chiefly), wind, and stringed instruments. [Javanese.]

gamete *gam'ēt*, *gam-ēt'*, *n.* a sexual reproductive cell—an egg-cell or sperm-cell.—*adjs.* **gam'etal** (or -*ēt*), **gametic** (-*et'* or -*ēt'*).—*ns.* **gametangium** (*gam-it-an'ji-əm*) a cell or organ in which gametes are formed: —*pl.* **gametan'gia**; **gametogen'esis** the formation of gametes; **game'tophyte** (or *gam'*) in alternation of

generations, a plant of the sexual generation, producing gametes. [Gr *gametēs*, husband, *gametē*, wife—*gameein*, to marry.]

gamic *gam'ik*, *adj* sexual: sexually produced. [Gr. *gamikos*—*gamos*, marriage.]

gamin *gam'in*, *ga-mē*, *n.* a street urchin, a precocious and mischievous imp of the pavement:—*fem.* **gamine** (-*mēn*) a girl of a pert, boyish, impish appearance and disposition.—*adj.* boyish or impish. [Fr.]

gamma, *gam'ə*, *n.* the third letter of the Greek alphabet (Γ, γ = G, g): in classification, the third or one of the third grade: the grade below beta.—*ns.* **gammad'ion**, **gamma'tion** (-*ti-on*) a figure composed of capital gammas, esp a swastika.—**gamma rays** a penetrating radiation given off by radium and other radioactive substances. [Gr.]

gammer *gam'ər*, *n.* an old woman (*masc* **gaffer**). [grandmother, or godmother.]

gammon[1] *gam'ən*, *n.* a double game at backgammon, won by bearing all one's men before one's opponent bears any: patter, chatter: nonsense, humbug.—*v.t* to defeat by a gammon at backgammon: to hoax, impose upon.—*v.i.* to talk gammon: to feign.—*ns.* **gamm'oner**; **gamm'oning**. [Prob O.E. *gamen*, a game]

gammon[2] *gam'ən*, *n.* the ham of a hog, esp. when cured, now usually with the adjacent parts of the side [O.N Fr. *gambon*, *gambe*, leg.]

gammy *gam'i*, (*dial*) *adj.* lame: maimed. [Cf. **game**[2].]

gamo-. See **-gam-**.

gamp *gamp*, (*coll.*) *n.* a large, untidy umbrella: an umbrella.—*adj.* **gamp'ish** bulging. [From Mrs Sarah Gamp, in Dickens's *Martin Chuzzlewit.*]

gamut *gam'ət*, *n.* any recognised scale or range of notes: the whole compass of a voice or instrument: the full extent of anything. [From *gamma*, the Gr letter G, adopted when it was required to name a note added below the A with which the old scale began, and *ut*, the Aretinian (q.v.) syllable.]

gander *gan'dər*, *n.* the male of the goose: a simpleton —**take a gander at** (*slang*) to take a look at. [O.E *ganra*, *gandra*.]

gang[1] *gang*, *n.* a band of roughs or criminals: a number of persons or animals (esp. elk) associating together: a number of labourers working together: a set of boys who habitually play together: a set of tools, etc., used together.—*v.t.* and *v.i.* to associate in a gang or gangs.—*v.t.* to adjust in co-ordination.—*ns.* **ganger** (*gang'ər*) the foreman of a gang of labourers; **gang'ing**; **gang'ster** a member of a gang of roughs or criminals; **gang'sterism**.—**gang'-bang** (*slang*) successive sexual intercourse with one, usu. unwilling, female by a group of males; **gang'land**, **gang'sterland** the domain of gangsters, the world of (esp organised) crime; **gang mill** a sawmill with gang saws; **gang saw** a saw fitted in a frame with others; **gangs'man** the foreman of a gang.—**Gang of Four** a term applied to a group of four of Chairman Mao's leading advisers after their political downfall: (also without *caps.*; sometimes *facet.*) any similar group in politics, etc.; **gang punch** (*comput.*) to punch (the same information) in a number of cards, or (a number of cards) with the same information; **gang up on** to make a concerted attack on; **gang up with** to join in the (doubtful) activities of. [O.E. *gang—gangan*, to go.]

gang[2] *gang*, *v.i.* and *v.t.* (*Scot.*) to go.—**gang'board** (*naut.*) a gang-way, plank, or platform for walking on; **gang'plank** a long, narrow, portable platform providing access to and from a ship; **gang'way** a passage into, out of, or through any place, esp. a ship: a way between rows of seats, esp. the cross-passage about halfway down the House of Commons.—*interj.* make way: make room to pass [O.E. *gangan*, to go.]

gang'. See gangue.

gangling *gang'gling, adj.* loosely-built, lanky —Also **gangly** (*gang'gli*). [Orig Scot. and Eng. dialect; O.E. *gangan*, to go.]

ganglion *gang'gli-ən, n.* a tumour in a tendon sheath: a nerve-centre:—*pl.* **gang'lia, gang'lions.**—*adjs* **gang'liar, ganglionic** (*-on'ik*) pertaining to a ganglion; **gang'liate, -d** provided with ganglion or ganglia; **gang'liform.** [Gr.]

gangrene *gang'grēn, n.* death of part of the body: the first stage in mortification —*adj.* **gangrenous** (*gang'grin-əs*) mortified. [Gr. *gangraina*, gangrene.]

gangue, gang *gang, n* rock in which ores are embedded [Fr ,—Ger. *Gang* a vein.]

gangway. See gang².

ganister, gannister *gan'is-tər, n.* a hard, close-grained siliceous stone, found in N. England.

ganja *gan'jə, n.* an intoxicating preparation, the female flowering tops of Indian hemp, i e. marijuana. [Hind. *gājā.*]

gannet *gan'ət, n.* a large white sea-bird of the family Sulidae, with black-tipped wings: a greedy person (*coll.*).—*n.* **gann'etry** a breeding-place of gannets [O.E. *ganot*, a sea-fowl.]

gannister. See ganister.

ganoid *gan'oid, adj.* (of fish scales) having a glistening outer layer over bone: (of fishes) belonging to an order **Ganoid'ei** (*-i-ī*) having commonly such scales.— *n.* a ganoid fish —*n.* **ganoin** (*gan'ō-in*) a calcareous substance, forming an enamel-like layer on ganoid scales. [Gr. *ganos*, brightness, *eidos*, appearance.]

gantry *gan'tri, n.* a stand for barrels: the shelving, racks, etc. in which drinks are displayed in a bar: a platform or bridge for a travelling-crane, railway signals, etc —**gantry crane** a crane in bridge form with vertical members running on parallel tracks. [Perh. O Fr. *gantier*—L *cantērius,* a trellis—Gr. *kanthēlios*, a pack-ass.]

gaol, etc. See jail, etc

gap *gap, n.* an opening or breach: a cleft: a passage: a notch or pass in a mountain-ridge: a breach of continuity: an unfilled space, a lack· a divergence, disparity.—*v.t.* to notch: to make a gap in.—*adj.* **gapp'y** full of gaps.—*adj.* **gap'-toothed** with teeth set wide apart. [O.N. *gap*]

gape *gāp, v.i.* to open the mouth wide: to yawn: to stare with open mouth: to be wide open.—*n* act of gaping: the extent to which the mouth can be opened. the angle of the mouth. a wide opening, parting, fissure, chasm, or failure to meet: (in *pl.*) a yawning fit· (in *pl*) a disease of birds of which gaping is a symptom, caused by a thread-worm, *Syngamus,* or **gape'worm,** in the windpipe and bronchial tubes —*n.* **gā'per** one who gapes: a mollusc (Mya) with shell gaping at each end· a sea-perch (Serranus): an easy catch (*cricket*).—*n.* and *adj.* **gā'ping.**—*adv* **gā'pingly.** [O N. *gapa,* to open the mouth, Ger *gaffen,* to stare]

gar, See garfish.

garage *gar'azh, gə-razh', gar'ij, n.* a building where motor-vehicles are housed or tended —*v.t* to put into or keep in a garage —*n.* **gar'aging** accommodation for cars, etc —**garage sale** a sale of various items held on the seller's premises, esp in his garage [Fr.,—*garer,* to secure; cf. **ware.²**]

garam masala *gar'əm məs-a'lə,* a spice mixture used in making curry.

garb *garb, n* fashion of dress dress semblance, appearance (*fig.*).—*v t.* to clothe, array [It *garbo,*

grace; of Gmc. origin.]

garbage *gär'bij, n.* any worthless matter: household food and other refuse.—*ns.* **gar'bo** (*Austr. coll.*) a dustman:—*pl.* **gar'bos; garbol'ogist** (*usu. facet.*) a dustman.—**gar'bageman** (*U.S.*) a dustman; **garbage can** (*U.S.*) a bin for food-waste, etc.

garble *gär'bl, v.t.* to misrepresent or falsify by suppression and selection: to mangle, mutilate.—*ns.* **gar'bler; gar'bling.** [It. *garbellare*—Ar. *ghirbál,* a sieve, perh.—L.L *cribellum,* dim. of *cribrum,* a sieve]

garbo. See garbage.

garboard *gar'bōrd, -bôrd, n.* the first range of planks or plates laid on a ship's bottom next to the keel.— Also **garboard strake.** [Du. *gaarboord.*]

garbologist. See garbage.

garçon *gar-sɔ̃, n.* a boy: a male servant, esp. a waiter in a restaurant. [Fr.]

garda *gor'də, n.* an Irish policeman or guard:—*pl.* **gardai** (*gor'də-ē*) —**Garda Síochana** (*shē'hhə-nə*; lit. guard of peace.—Ir *síocháin,* peace) the Irish police force. [Ir. *gárda.*]

garden *gar'dn, n.* a piece of ground on which flowers, etc , are cultivated: a pleasant spot: a fertile region: (in *pl.*) used in street-names.—*adj.* of, used in, grown in, a garden or gardens.—*v t.* to cultivate or work in a garden —*ns.* **gar'dener** one who gardens, or is skilled in gardening: one employed to tend a garden; **gar'dening** the laying out and cultivation of gardens.— **garden centre** an establishment where plants, gardening equipment, etc. are sold; **garden city, suburb, village** a model town, suburb, village, laid out with broad roads, trees, and much garden ground between the houses, **gardener's garters** variegated garden ribbon-grass; **gar'den-glass** a bell-glass for covering plants; **garden party** a social gathering held in the garden of a house; **garden patch; garden path; garden stuff** garden produce for the table.—**everything in the garden is lovely** all is, or appears to be, well; **hanging garden** a garden formed in terraces rising one above another; **lead someone up the garden (path)** to draw someone on insensibly, to mislead someone; **market garden** a garden in which vegetables, fruits, etc., are raised for sale; **market gardener; philosophers of the garden** followers of Epicurus, who taught in a garden. [O.Fr. *gardin* (Fr *jardin*); from Gmc.]

Gardenia *gar-dē'ni-ə, n.* a genus of the madder family, trees and shrubs with fragrant, usu. white flowers of a waxy appearance· (without *cap.*) a member of the genus. [American botanist Dr Alex. 'Garden (c 1730–91).]

garfish *gar'fish, n.* a pike-like fish with long slender beaked head: the bony pike, an American ganoid river-fish an Australian half-beak —Also **gar, gar'-pike.** [O.E *gār,* spear.]

garganey *gar'gə-ni, n* a bird akin to the teal, the summer teal [It. *garganello.*]

Gargantuan *gar-gan'tū-ən, adj.* like or worthy of Rabelais's hero *Gargantua,* a giant of vast appetite: enormous, prodigious (without *cap*).—*ns.* **Gargan'tuism; Gargan'tuist.**

garget *gar'git, n.* inflammation of the throat or udder in cows, swine, etc · pokeweed (*U.S.*).

gargle *gar'gl, v.t* and *v.i* to wash (the throat) preventing the liquid from going down by expelling air against it.—*n.* a liquid for washing the throat. [O Fr *gargouiller*—*gargouille,* the throat]

gargoyle *gar'goil, n.* a projecting spout, usually grotesquely carved, from a roof-gutter: any grotesque figure or person [O Fr *gargouille*—L L *gurgulio,* throat]

garial. See gavial.

garibaldi *gar-i-bol'di, -bal'di, n.* a woman's loose

blouse, an imitation of the red shirts worn by followers of the Italian patriot *Garibaldi* (1807–1882).—**Garibaldi biscuit** a biscuit with a layer of currants.

garish gār'ish; *adj.* showy; gaudy: glaring.—*adv.* **gar'ishly.**—*n.* **gar'ishness.**

garland gār'lənd, *n.* a wreath of flowers or leaves: a book of selections in prose or poetry.—*v.t.* to deck with a garland.—*n.* **gar'landry** garlands collectively. [O.Fr. *garlande.*]

garlic gār'lik, *n.* a bulbous liliaceous plant (*Allium sativum*) having a pungent taste and very strong smell: extended to others of the genus, as **wild garlic** (ramsons).—*adj.* **gar'licky** like garlic. [O.E. *gārlēac*—*gār*, a spear, *lēac*, a leek.]

garment gār'mənt, *n.* any article of clothing.—*v.t.* to clothe as with a garment.—*adjs.* **gar'mented**; **gar'mentless.**—*n.* **gar'menture** clothing. [O.Fr. *garniment*—*garnir*, to furnish.]

garner gār'nər, *n.* a granary: a store of anything.—*v.t.* to store. [O.Fr. *gernier* (Fr. *grenier*)—L. *grānārium* (usu. in pl.), a granary.]

garnet gār'nit, *n.* a mineral, in some varieties a precious stone, generally red, crystallising in dodecahedra and icositetrahedra, an orthosilicate of a bivalent and a tervalent metal. [O.Fr. *grenat*—L.L. *grānātum*, pomegranate; or L.L. *grānum*, grain, cochineal, red dye.]

garni. See **garnish.**

garnish gār'nish, *v.t.* to adorn: to furnish: to add herbs, etc., to a dish for flavour or decoration: to garnishee. —*n.* a gift of money, esp. that formerly paid to fellow-prisoners on entering prison or sometimes by workmen on starting a new job: something placed round a principal dish at table, whether for embellishment or relish: decoration, embellishment.—*adj.* **garni** (*gār-nē*) garnished.—*n.* **gar'nishee** a person warned not to pay money owed to another, because the latter is indebted to the garnisher who gives the warning.—*v.t.* to attach in this way: to serve with a garnishment.—*ns.* **garnishee'ment**; **gar'nisher** one who garnishes; **gar'nishing**; **gar'nishment** that which garnishes or embellishes: ornament: a garnisheement; **gar'nishry** adornment; **gar'niture** that which garnishes or embellishes. [O.Fr. *garniss*-, stem of *garnir*, to furnish (old form *warnir*), from a Gmc. root.]

garotte. See **garrotte.**

garpike. See **garfish.**

garran. Same as **garron.**

garret gar'it, *n.* a room just under the roof of a house. —*adj.* **garr'eted** provided with garrets: lodged in a garret. [O.Fr. *garite*, a place of safety, *guarir*, *warir*, to preserve.]

garrison gar'i-sn, *n.* a supply of soldiers for guarding a fortress: a fortified place.—*v.t.* to furnish with troops: to defend by fortresses manned with troops. —**garrison town** a town in which a garrison is stationed. [O.Fr. *garison*—*garir*, *guerir*, to furnish; Gmc.]

garron, garran gar'ən, *n.* a small horse. [Ir. *gearran.*]

garrotte, garotte (*U.S.* **garrote**) gä-rot', gə-rot', *n.* a Spanish mode of putting criminals to death: the apparatus for the purpose—originally a string round the throat tightened by twisting a stick, later a brass collar tightened by a screw, whose point enters the spinal marrow.—*v.t.* to execute by the garrotte: suddenly to render insensible by semi-strangulation in order to rob:—*pr.p.* **garrott'ing**, **garott'ing**; *pa.t.* and *pa.p.* **garrott'ed, garott'ed.**—*ns.* **gar(r)ott'er**; **gar(r)ott'ing.** [Sp. *garotte*; cf. Fr. *garrot*, a stick.]

garrulous gar'ŏŏ-ləs, -ə-, -ū-, *adj.* talkative: loquacious. —*n.* **garrulity** (-ŏŏ'li-ti, or -ū') loquacity.—*adv.* **garr'-**ulously.—*n.* **garr'ulousness.** [L. *garrulus*—*garrīre*, to chatter.]

garryowen ga-ri-ō'ən, (*Rugby football*) *n.* a high kick forward together with a rush towards the landing-place of the ball. [*Garryowen* Rugby Club in Limerick.]

garter gär'tər, *n.* a band used to support a stocking: (with *cap.*) (the badge of) the highest order of knighthood in Great Britain.—*v.t.* to put a garter on: to support, bind, decorate, or surround with a garter.— **gar'ter-snake** in N. America, any snake of the genus Eutaenia, non-venomous, longitudinally striped; **gar'ter-stitch** a plain stitch in knitting: horizontally ribbed knitting made by using plain stitches only.— **Garter King-of-Arms** the chief herald of the Order of the Garter. [O.Fr. *gartier* (Fr. *jarretière*)—O.Fr. *garet* (Fr. *jarret*), ham of the leg, prob. Celt., as Bret. *gar*, shank of the leg.]

garth gärth, *n.* an enclosure or yard: a garden: a weir in a river for catching fish. [O.N. *garthr*, a court.]

gas gas, *n.* a substance in a condition in which it has no definite boundaries or fixed volume, but will fill any space: often restricted to such a substance above its critical temperature: a substance or mixture which is in this state in ordinary terrestrial conditions: esp. coal-gas, or other gas for lighting or heating, or one used for attack in warfare: gaslight: empty, boastful, frothy, garrulous, or pert talk (*coll.*): something delightful, impressive, exciting (*coll.*): short for gasoline (petrol) (*U.S.*):—*pl.* **gas'es.**—*v.t.* to supply, attack, poison, light, inflate, or treat with gas.—*v.i.* to emit gas:—*pr.p.* **gass'ing**; *pa.t.* and *pa.p.* **gassed.**— *ns.* **gasalier', gaselier', gasolier'** a hanging frame with branches for gas-jets (formed on false analogy after *chandelier*); **gasel'ity.**—*adj.* **gaseous** (gāz', gās', gas', gaz'i-əs, gā'shəs, gash'əs) in a state of gas: of gas.—*ns.* **gas'eousness**; **gasifica'tion** conversion into gas.—*adj.* **gas'iform.**—*v.t.* **gas'ify** to convert into gas.—*ns.* **gas'ifier**; **gas'ohol, gas'ahol** a mixture of 8 or 9 parts petrol and 1 or 2 parts alcohol, used as a fuel; **gas'olene, -oline** (-ə-lēn) a low-boiling petroleum distillate: the ordinary name for petrol (*U.S.*); **gasom'eter** a storage tank for gas.—*adjs.* **gasomet'ric, -al** pertaining to the measurement of gas.—*ns.* **gasom'etry**; **gass'ing** poisoning by gas: idle talking.— *adj.* **gass'y** full of gas: abounding in or emitting gas: gaseous: given to vain and boastful talk (*slang*).— **gas'-bag** a bag for holding gas, esp. in a balloon or airship: a talkative person (*coll.*); **gas'-bottle** a steel cylinder for holding compressed gas; **gas'-burn'er** the perforated part of a gas-fitting where the gas issues and is burned; **gas'-cen'trifuge** a centrifuge for separating gases; **gas chamber, oven** an enclosed place designed for killing by means of gas; **gas chromatography** a widely used form of chromatography in which a gas is passed down the column which contains the mixture to be separated and a solvent; **gas'-cook'er** a cooking-stove using gas as fuel.—*adj.* **gas'-cooled** cooled by a flow of gas.—**gas'-en'gine** an engine worked by the explosion of gas; **gas'-escape'** a leakage of gas; **gas'field** a region in which natural gas occurs.—*adj.* **gas'-filled** filled with gas.—**gas'-fire** a heating-stove in which gas is burned.—*adj.* **gas'-fired** fuelled, or heated, by gas(es).—**gas'-fitter** one who fits up the pipes, etc. for gas appliances.—*n.pl.* **gas'-fittings** gas-pipes, etc., for lighting and heating by gas.—**gas'-fur'nace** a furnace of which the fuel is gas; **gas gangrene** gangrene resulting from infection of a wound by certain bacteria which form gases in the flesh.—*adj.* **gas'-guzzling** (*coll.*; esp. *U.S.*) consuming large amounts of petrol.—**gas'-heat'er** any heating apparatus in which gas is used; **gas'-jar** a jar for collecting and holding a gas in chemical experiments;

gas'-jet a jet of gas: a gas-flame: a burner, **gas'-lamp** a lamp that burns gas; **gas'light** light produced by combustion of gas: a gas jet, burner, or lamp.—*adj.* of, concerned with, for use by, gaslight.—*adj.* **gas'lit** lighted by gas.—**gas'-main** a principle gas-pipe from the gas-works; **gas'man** a man employed in gas-making, in repairing or installing gas fittings, or in the reading of meters; **gas'-man'tle** a gauze covering, chemically prepared, enclosing a gas-jet, and becoming incandescent when heated; **gas'-mask** a respiratory device (covering nose, mouth, and eyes) as a protection against poisonous gases; **gas'-mē'ter** an instrument for measuring gas consumed; **gas'-mo'tor** a gas-engine; **gas oil** a petroleum distillate, intermediate between kerosine and lubricating oil, used as (esp. heating) fuel; **gas'-pipe** a pipe for conveying gas; **gas'-po'ker** a gas-jet that can be inserted among fuel to kindle a fire; **gas'-retort** a closed heated chamber in which gas is made; **gas'-ring** a hollow ring with perforations serving as gas-jets; **gas'-stove** an apparatus in which coal-gas is used for heating or cooking; **gas'-tank** a reservoir for coal-gas; **gas'-tap; gas'-tar** coal-tar.—*adj.* **gas'-tight** impervious to gas.—**gas'-trap** a trap in a drain to prevent escape of foul gas; **gas'-turbine** a machine consisting of a combustion chamber, to which air is supplied by a compressor and in which the air is heated at constant pressure, and a turbine driven by the hot expanding gases; **gas'-well** a boring from which natural gas issues; **gas'-works** a factory where gas is made.—**gas and gaiters** nonsense; **step on the gas** (i.e. gasoline) to press the accelerator pedal of a motor-car: to speed up. [A word invented by J. B. van Helmont (1577–1644); suggested by Gr. *chaos*.]

gasahol, gasaller, gaselty, gaseller, gaseous. See under **gas.**

gash *gash, v.t.* to cut deeply into.—*n.* a deep, open cut. [Formerly *garse*—O.Fr. *garser*, to scarify—L.L. *garsa*, scarification, possibly—Gr. *charassein*, to scratch.]

gasification, gasify, etc. See under **gas.**

gasket *gas'kit, n.* a canvas band used to bind the sails to the yards when furled (*naut.*): a strip of tow, etc., for packing a piston, etc.: a layer of packing material, esp. a flat sheet of asbestos compound, sometimes between thin copper sheets, used for making gas-tight joints between engine cylinders and heads, etc.

gasohol, gasolene, gasometer, etc. See under **gas.**

gasp *gäsp, v.i.* to gape for breath: to catch the breath: to desire eagerly.—*v.t.* to breathe: to utter with gasps.—*n.* the act of gasping.—*ns.* **gasp'er** one who gasps: a cheap cigarette (*slang*); **gasp'iness.**—*n.* and *adj.* **gasp'ing.**—*adv.* **gasp'ingly.**—*adj.* **gasp'y.**—**the last gasp** the point of death. [O.N. *geispa,* to yawn.]

Gastarbeiter *gast'ar-bī-tər, n.* a migrant worker, esp. one who does menial work. [Ger., lit. guest-worker.]

gastero-, gastro-, gastr- *gast-(ə)-rō, -ro-* in composition, belly.—*n.* **gas'teropod, gas'tropod** any member of the **Gast(e)rop'oda,** a class of asymmetrical molluscs in which the foot is broad and flat, the mantle undivided, the shell in one piece, usually conical—limpets, whelks, snails, slugs, etc.—*n.* **gastralgia** (*gas-tral'ji-ə;* Gr. *algos,* pain) pain in the stomach.—*adj.* **gastral'gic.**—*n.* **gastrectomy** (*gas-trek'tə-mi*) surgical removal of the stomach, or part of it.—*adj.* **gas'tric** belonging to the stomach.—*ns.* **gastri'tis** inflammation of the stomach; **gastrocnemius** (*gas-trok-nē'mi-əs*) the muscle that bulges the calf of the leg:—*pl.* **-mii.**—*adj.* **gastroenter'ic** gastrointestinal.—*ns.* **gastroenteri'tis** inflammation of the lining of the stomach and intestines; **gastroenterol'ogist; gastroenterol'ogy** (*med.*) the study of the stomach

and intestines.—*adj.* **gastrointest'inal** (or *-in'l*) of, relating to, consisting of, the stomach and intestines.—*n.* **gastrol'oger.**—*adj.* **gastrolog'ical.**—*ns.* **gastrol'ogy** cookery, good eating; **gastronome** (*gas'trə-nōm*), **gastronomer** (*-tron'ə-mər*) an epicure.—*adjs.* **gastronomic** (*-nom'ik*), **-al.**—*ns.* **gastron'omist; gastron'omy** the art or science of good eating; **gas'troscope** an instrument for inspecting the interior of the stomach; **gastrot'omy** the operation of cutting open the stomach or abdomen; **gastrula** (*gas'troō-lə*) an embryo at the stage in which it forms a two-layered cup by the invagination of its wall; **gastrula'tion** formation of a gastrula.—**gastric fever** typhoid; **gastric juice** the acid liquid secreted by the stomach for digestion. [Gr. *gastēr,* belly.]

gastr(o)-. See **gastero-.**

gat [1] *gat,* (*slang*) *n.* a gun, revolver. [**gatling-gun.**]

gat [2] *gat* (*B.*) *pa.t.* of **get.**

gate [1] *gāt, n.* a passage into a city, enclosure, or any large building: a narrow opening or defile: a frame for closing an entrance: an entrance, passage, or channel: an obstacle consisting of two posts, markers, etc. between which competitors in a slalom, etc. must pass: at an airport, any of the numbered exits from which to board an aircraft: the people who pay to see a game, hence, the number attending: the total amount of money paid for entrance (also **gate'-money**): electronic circuit which passes impressed signals when permitted by another independent source of similar signals: an H-shaped series of slots for controlling the movement of a gear-lever in a gear-box.—*v.t.* to supply with a gate: to punish (students or school-children) by imposing a curfew on or by confining to school precincts for a time.—*adjs.* **gāt'ed** having a gate or gates: punished by gating; **gate'less.**—*n.* **gāt'ing.**—*v.i.* and *v.t.* **gate'-crash** to enter without paying or invitation.—**gate'-crasher; gate'fold** an oversize folded leaf in a book, etc., a fold-out; **gate'-house** (*archit.*) a building over or at a gate; **gate'-keeper, gate'-man** one who watches over the opening and shutting of a gate.—*adjs.* **gate'-legged, gate'leg** of a table, having a hinged and framed leg that can swing in to let down a leaf.—**gate'-post** a post from which a gate is hung or against which it shuts; **gate'way** the way through a gate: a structure at a gate: any entrance. [O.E. *geat,* a way.]

gate [2] *gāt,* (*Scot.* and *North. dial.*) *n.* a way, path, street (often in street-names, as *Cowgate, Kirkgate*): manner of doing. [O.N. *gata.*]

gâteau *gat'ō, gä-tō, n.* a rich cake, filled with cream, decorated with icing, etc.:—*pl.* **gateaus** (*gat'ōz*), **gâteaux** (*gat'ōz, gä-tō*). [Fr.]

gather *gadh'ər, v.t.* to collect: to assemble: to amass: to cull: to pick up: to draw together: in sewing, to draw into puckers by passing a thread through: to learn by inference. to have increase in (e.g. speed).—*v.i.* to assemble or muster: to increase: to suppurate: to arrange signatures of a book in correct sequence for binding.—*n.* a plait or fold in cloth, made by drawing threads through: (*pl.*) that part of the dress which is gathered or drawn in.—*ns.* **gath'erer** one who collects, amasses, assembles, or culls; **gath'ering** the action of one who gathers: a crowd or assembly: a narrowing: the assembling of the sheets of a book: a suppurating swelling.—**gath'ering-coal, -peat** a coal, peat, put into a fire, to keep it alive till morning; **gath'ering-cry** a summons to assemble for war; **gath'ering-ground** catchment area.—**gather breath** to recover wind; **gather ground** to gain ground; **gather oneself together** to collect all one's powers, like one about to leap; **gather to a head** to ripen: to come into a state of preparation for action or effect. [O.E. *gaderian, gæderian*; *(tō)gædere*, together; *geador*, together, *gæd*, fellowship.]

gatling-gun *gat'ling-gun*, *n.* a machine-gun invented by R. J. *Gatling* about 1861.

gau *gow*, *n.* a district.—*n.* **gauleiter** (*gow'lī-tər*) a chief official of a district under the Nazi régime: an overbearing wielder of petty authority. [Ger. *Gau*, district, *Leiter*, leader.]

gauche *gōsh*, *adj.* clumsy: tactless.—*n.* **gaucherie** (*gōsh'ə-rē, -rē'*) clumsiness: (an instance of) social awkwardness. [Fr., left.]

gaucho *gow'chō*, *n.* a cowboy of the pampas, usually of mixed Spanish and Indian descent:—*pl.* **gau'chos**. [Sp.]

gaud *göd*, *n.* an ornament: a piece of finery: showy ceremony.—*n.* **gaud'ery** finery.—*adv.* **gaud'ily**.—*ns.* **gaud'iness**; **gaud'y** an entertainment or feast.—*adj.* showy: gay: vulgarly bright. [In part app.—O.Fr. *gaudir*—L. *gaudēre*, to be glad, *gaudium*, joy; in part directly from L.]

gauge, also **gage**, *gāj*, *n.* a measuring apparatus: a standard of measure: a means of limitation or adjustment to a standard: a measurement, as the diameter of a wire, calibre of a tube: the distance between a pair of wheels or rails: a means of estimate: relative position of a ship (in this sense usu. **gage;**).—*v.t.* to measure: to estimate: to adjust to a standard.—*v.i.* to measure the contents of casks.—*adj.* **gauge'able** capable of being gauged.—*ns.* **gaug'er** one who gauges: an excise man; **gaug'ing** the measuring of casks holding excisable liquors.—**gauge'-glass** a tube to show height of water; **gaug'ing-rod** an instrument for measuring the contents of casks.—*adjs.* **broad'-, narr'ow-gauge** in railroad construction greater or less than standard gauge, in Britain 56½ inches (1·435 metres). [O.Fr. *gauge* (Fr. *jauge*).]

gauje. See **gadgie**.

Gaul *göl*, *n.* a name of ancient France: an inhabitant of Gaul.—*adj.* **Gaul'ish**.—*n.* the Celtic language of the Gauls. [Fr. *Gaule*—L. *Gallia, Gallus*.]

gauleiter. See **gau**.

Gaullist *gōl'ist*, *n.* a follower of the French soldier and statesman General Charles A. J. M. de *Gaulle* (President of the Fifth Republic 1958–69).—*n.* **Gaull'ism** principles and policies of Gaullists.

Gaultheria *göl-thē'ri-ə*, *n.* a genus of evergreen aromatic plants of the heath family, including the American wintergreen and salal: (without *cap.*) a plant of this genus. [From the Swedish–Canadian botanist Hughes *Gaulthier*.]

gaunt *gönt*, *adj.* thin: of a pinched appearance: grim.—*adv.* **gaunt'ly**.—*n.* **gaunt'ness**.

gauntlet[1] *gönt'lit*, *n.* the iron glove of armour, formerly thrown down in challenge and taken up in acceptance: a long glove covering the wrist: an extension of a glove covering the wrist.—*adj.* **gaunt'leted** wearing a gauntlet or gauntlets.—**throw down, take up, the gauntlet** to give, to accept a challenge. [Fr. *gantelet*, dim. of *gant*, glove, of Gmc. origin.]

gauntlet[2] *gönt'lit*, *n.* the military (or naval) punishment of having to run through a lane of soldiers (or sailors) who strike one as one passes.—**run the gauntlet** to undergo the punishment of the gauntlet: to expose oneself to hostile treatment. [Sw. *gatlopp—gata*, lane (cf. **gate**[2]), *lopp*, course (cf. **leap**); confused with **gauntlet**[1].]

gaup, gawp *göp*, (*coll.*) *v.i.* to gape in astonishment.—*n.* **gaup'us, gawp'us** a silly person. [From obs. *galp*.]

gaur *gowr*, *n.* a species of ox inhabiting some of the mountain jungles of India. [Hindustani]

gauss *gows*, *n.* the C.G.S. unit of magnetic flux density.—*adj.* **Gauss'ian** (also without *cap.*) of or due

to Johann Karl Friedrich *Gauss* (1777–1855), German mathematician and physicist.

gauze *göz*, *n.* a thin, transparent fabric: material slight and open like gauze.—*n.* **gauz'iness**.—*adj.* **gauz'y**.—*adj.* **gauze'-winged** having gauzy wings. [Fr. *gaze*.]

gave *gāv*, *pa.t.* of **give**.

gavel *gav'l*, *n.* a mallet: a chairman's hammer.

gavial *gā'vi-əl*, **garial, gharial** *gur'i-əl*, *ns.* an Indian crocodile with very long slender muzzle. [Hindi *ghariyāl*, crocodile.]

gavotte *gā-vot'*, *n.* a dance, somewhat like a countrydance, originally a dance of the Gavots, people of the French Upper Alps: the music for such a dance in common time, often occurring in suites.

gawk *gök*, *n.* an awkward or ungainly person, esp. from tallness, shyness, or simplicity: one who stares and gapes.—*v.i.* to stare and gape.—*ns.* **gawk'ihood**; **gawk'iness**.—*adj.* **gawk'y** awkward: ungainly.—*n.* a tall awkward person: a gawk.

gawp. See **gaup**.

gay *gā*, *adj.* lively: bright: sportive, merry: dissipated: of loose life: showy: in modern use, homosexual:—*compar.* **gay'er;** *superl.* **gay'est**.—*n.* a homosexual.—*n.* **gai'ety** merriness.—*adv.* **gai'ly**.—*n.* **gay'ness**.—**gay liberation** the freeing of homosexuals from social disadvantages and prejudice. [O.Fr. *gai*—perh. O.H.G. *wāhi*, pretty.]

gaze *gāz*, *v.i.* to look fixedly.—*n.* a fixed look.—*n.* **ga'zer**. [Prob. cog. with obs. *gaw*, to stare.]

gazebo *gə-zē'bō*, *n.* a belvedere:—*pl.* **gazě'bos, gazě'boes**.

gazelle, gazel *gə-zel'*, *n.* a small antelope (*Gazella dorcas*) of N. Africa and S.W. Asia, with large eyes, or kindred species. [Fr.,—Ar. *ghazāl*, a wild-goat.]

gazette *gə-zet'*, *n.* a newspaper: (with *cap.*) an official newspaper containing lists of government appointments, legal notices, despatches, etc.—*v.t.* to publish or mention in a gazette:—*pr.p.* **gazett'ing;** *pa.t.* and *pa.p.* **gazett'ed**.—*n.* **gazetteer'** (*gaz-*) a geographical dictionary: orig., a writer for a gazette, an official journalist.—*v.t.* to describe in gazetteers. [Fr.,—It. *gazzetta*, a small coin; or from It. *gazzetta*, dim. of *gazza*, magpie.]

gazpacho *gas-pách'ō, gəz-*, *n.* a spicy Spanish vegetable soup, served cold:—*pl.* **gazpach'os**. [Sp.]

gazump *gə-zump'*, *v.t.* and *v.i.* to raise the price of property, etc., after accepting an offer from (a buyer), but before the contract has been signed. [Prob. Yiddish *gezumph*, to swindle.]

G-clef. See under **G**.

gean *gēn*, *n.* the European wild cherry. [O.Fr. *guigne*.]

geanticline *jē-an'ti-klīn*, *n.* an anticline on a great scale.—*adj.* **geanticli'nal**. [Gr. *gē*, earth, and **anticline**.]

gear *gēr*, *n.* equipment: accoutrements: tackle: clothes, esp. (*coll.*) young people's modern clothes: armour: harness: apparatus: a set of tools or a mechanism for some particular purpose: possessions: stuff: matter: any moving part or system of parts for transmitting motion, e.g. levers, gear-wheels: connection by means of such parts: the actual gear ratio in use, or the gear-wheels involved in transmitting that ratio, in an automobile gear-box, e.g. first gear (low gear), fourth gear (high gear): working connection: working order.—*v.t.* to harness: to put in gear, as machinery: to connect in gear: to make to work in accordance with requirements of (a project or a larger organisation; *fig.*; with *to*).—*v.i.* to be in gear.—*adj.* (*slang*) unusually good, or (later) very up to date.—*adj.* **geared**.—*n.* **gear'ing** harness: working implements: means of transmission of motion, esp. a train of toothed wheels and pinions: in a company's capital, the ratio of ordinary shares to shares with fixed interest (*econ*.).—*adj* **gear'less.**—**gear'box, gear'-box** the box containing the apparatus for changing gear; **gear'-lever, -shift, -stick** a device for selecting or engaging and disengaging gears; **gear'-ratio** the ratio of the driving to the driven members of a gear mechanism; **gear'-wheel** a wheel with teeth or cogs which impart or transmit motion by acting on a similar wheel or a chain.—*adjs.* **high'-gear, low'-gear** geared to give a high or a low number of revolutions of the driven part relatively to the driving part—also *ns.*—**change gear** to select a higher or lower gear; **gear down, up** to make the speed of the driven part lower, higher, than that of the driving part. [M.E. *gere*, prob. O.N. *gervi*.]

gecko *gek'ō, n.* any lizard of the genus **Gecko** or the subclass **Geckō'nēs**, mostly thick-bodied, dull-coloured animals with adhesive toes:—*pl.* **geck'os, geck'oes.** [Malay *gēkoq*; imit. of its cry.]

gee[1] *jē, v i.* of horses, to move to the right or to move on.—*n.* **gee'-gee** a child's word for a horse.—**gee up, gee hup** to proceed faster, chiefly used as a command to horses.

gee[2] *jē,* (*U.S.*) *interj.* expressing surprise, sarcasm, enthusiasm, etc.: sometimes used only for emphasis—**gee whiz** *interj.* expressing surprise, admiration, etc. [Perh **Jesus.**]

geebung *jē'bung, n.* an Australian tree (**Persoonia**) or its fruit. [Native name.]

geese, *pl.* of **goose.**

gee-string *jē'string, n.* a string or strip worn round the waist and between the legs.—Also **G-string.**

geezer *gēz'ər,* (*slang*) *n* a queer elderly person: a man. [**guiser.**]

gefilte, gefüllte fish *gə-fil'tə fish,* a cooked mixture of fish, eggs, breadcrumbs and seasoning served as balls or cakes or stuffed into a fish. [Yiddish, lit. filled fish.]

Gehenna *gi-hen'ə, n.* the valley of Hinnom, near Jerusalem, in which the Israelites sacrificed their children to Moloch, and to which, at a later time, the refuse of the city was conveyed to be slowly burned: hence hell (*N.T.*): a place of torment [Heb. *Ge-hinnōm,* valley of Hinnom.]

Geiger (-Müller) counter *gī'gər (mūl'ər) kown'tər,* an instrument for detecting and measuring radioactivity by registering electrical output pulses caused by ionisation of particles in a gas-filled tube. [*Geiger* and *Müller,* German physicists.]

geisha *gā'shə, n* a Japanese girl trained to provide entertainment (as conversation, performance of dances, etc.) for men.—*pl.* **gei'sha, gei'shas.** [Jap.]

Geissler tube *gīs'lər tūb,* (*chem.*) a gas-filled discharge-tube, characterised by a capillary section for concentrated illumination. [Heinrich *Geissler* (1814–1879), the inventor.]

geist *gīst, n.* spirit, any inspiring or dominating principle. [Ger.]

gel *jel, n.* a jelly-like apparently solid colloidal solution: a (sheet of) transparent substance used in theatre and photographic lighting to produce light of different colours (short for **gelatine**).—*v.i.* to form a gel: to come together, to begin to work, take shape (*coll.*; also **jell**):—*pr.p.* **gell'ing;** *pa.t.* and *pa.p.* **gelled.**—*n.* **gelā'tion** see separate article. [**gelatine.**]

gelatine, gelatin *jel'ə-tēn, -tin, ns.* colourless, odourless, and tasteless glue, prepared from albuminous substances, e.g. bones and hides, used for foodstuffs, photographic films, glues, etc.—*vs.t* **gelatinate** (*ji-lat'i-nāt*), **gelat'inise, -ize** to make into gelatine or jelly: to coat with gelatine or jelly.—*vs.t.* to be converted into gelatine or jelly.—*ns* **gelatinā'tion, gelatinisā'tion, -z; gelat'iniser, -z-;**

gelat'inoid a substance resembling gelatine.—Also *adj.*—*adj.* **gelat'inous** resembling or formed into jelly. [Fr.,—It. *gelatina, gelata,* jelly—L *gelāre,* to freeze.]

gelation *jel-ā'shən, n.* a solidification by cooling: formation of a gel from a sol. [Partly L. *gelātiō, -ōnis—gelāre,* to freeze, partly **gel.**]

geld *geld, v.t* to emasculate, castrate: to spay: to deprive of anything essential, to enfeeble, to deprive: to expurgate.—*ns.* **geld'er; geld'ing** act of castrating: a castrated animal, esp. a horse. [O.N. *gelda.*]

gelid *jel'id, adj.* icy cold: cold.—*adv.* **gel'idly.**—*ns.* **gel'idness, gelid'ity.** [L. *gelidus—gelū,* frost.]

gelignite *jel'ig-nīt, n.* a powerful explosive used in mining, made from nitroglycerine, nitrocotton, potassium nitrate, and wood-pulp. [**gelatine** and L *ignis,* fire.]

gem *jem, n.* any precious stone, esp. when cut: a person or thing regarded as extremely admirable or flawless.—*adj.* **gem(m)olog'ical.**—*ns.* **gem(m)ol'ogist** one with special knowledge of gems; **gem(m)ol'ogy** the science of gems.—*adj.* **gemm'y** full of gems: brilliant.—**gem'-cutting** the art of cutting and polishing precious stones; **gem'-engraving** the art of engraving figures on gems; **gem'stone.** [O.E. *gim*; O.H.G. *gimma*—L. *gemma,* a bud.]

Gemara *gə-ma'rə, n.* the second part of the Talmud, consisting of commentary and complement to the first part, the Mishnah. [Aramaic, completion.]

geminate *jem'in-āt, v.t.* to double.—*adj.* (*bot.*) in pairs —*n.* **geminā'tion** a doubling.—*n.pl.* **Gemini** (*jem'i-nī*) the twins, a constellation containing the two bright stars Castor and Pollux: the third sign of the zodiac.

gemma *jem'ə, n.* a plant bud, esp. a leaf-bud (*rare*): a small multicellular body produced vegetatively, capable of separating and becoming a new individual (*bot.*): a bud or protuberance from the body that becomes a new individual (*zool.*):—*pl.* **gemm'ae** (*-ē*).—*adjs* **gemmā'ceous** bud-like: relating to gemmae; **gemm'ate** having or reproducing by buds or gemmae. —*v.i.* to reproduce by gemmae.—*n.* **gemmā'tion** budding or gemma-formation.—*adjs.* **gemm'ative** pertaining to gemmation; **gemmif'erous** bearing gemmae, **gemmip'arous** reproducing by gemmae. [L. *gemma,* a bud.]

gemmate, gemmation, etc. See **gemma.**

gem(m)ologist, etc., **gemmy.** See **gem.**

gemsbok *gemz'bok, n.* (*Oryx gazella*) S. African antelope, about the size of a stag, with long straight horns. [Du , male chamois—Ger. *Gemsbock.*]

gemütlich *gə-müt'lēhh,* (Ger.) *adj.* amiable: comfortable: cosy.—*n.* **Gemütlichkeit** (*-kīt*) kindness: comfort: cosiness.

gen *jen,* (*slang*) *n.* general information: the low-down or inside information.—**gen up** to learn (with *on*):—*pa.t.* **genned.**

-gen *-jən,* **-gene** *-jēn,* in composition used to denote (1) producing or produced, as in *oxygen, phosgene* (*chem.*); (2) growth, as in *endogen* (*bot.*). [Gr. *-genēs,* born.]

gendarme *zhä'darm, n.* since the French Revolution one of a corps of French military police: a similar policeman elsewhere:—*pl.* **gen'darmes** occasionally **gens'darmes.**—*n.* **gendarm'erie** (*-ə-rē*) an armed police force a police station or barracks. [Fr. *gendarme,* sing. from pl. *gens d'armes,* men-at-arms—*gens,* people, *de,* of, *armes,* arms.]

gender *jen'dər, n* a distinction of words roughly answering to sex (*gram.*): loosely or jocularly, sex. [Fr. *genre*—L. *genus,* kind.]

gene *jēn,* (*biol*) *n.* one of the units of DNA, arranged in linear fashion on the chromosomes, responsible for passing on specific characteristics from parents to off-spring.—*adj.* **gen'ic** of or relating to a gene.—*ns* **genom(e)** (*jē'nōm*) the full set of chromosomes of an individual: the total number of genes in such a set, **gen'otype** genetic or factorial constitution of an individual: group of individuals all of which possess the same genetic constitution.—*adj.* **genotypic** (*-tip'ik*) —*adv.* **genotyp'ically**.—*n.* **genotypic'ity.—gene flow** the passing of genes to succeeding generations. [Gr. *genos*, a race.]

-gene. See **-gen**.

genealogy *jē-ni-al'ə-ji*, or *jen'i-*, *n.* history of the descent of families: the pedigree of a particular person or family. —*adjs.* **genealogical** (*-ə-loj'i-kl*), **genealog'ic**. —*adv.* **genealog'ically.**—*v.t.* **geneal'ogise, -ize** to investigate or treat of genealogy.—*n.* **geneal'ogist** one who studies or traces genealogies or descents —**genealogical tree** a table of descent in the form of a tree with branches. [Gr. *geneālogiā—geneā*, race, *logos*, discourse.]

genera, *pl.* of **genus**.

generable. See **generate**.

general *jen'ə-rəl, adj* relating to a genus or whole class. including various species: not special. not restricted or specialised: relating to the whole or to all or most universal: nearly universal: common: prevalent: wide-spread: public: vague. (after an official title, etc.) chief, of highest rank, at the head of a department (as *director-general, postmaster-general*).—*n.* the total. the most part, majority: an officer who is head over a whole department: a general officer: the chief commander of an army in service: one skilled in leadership. tactics, management.—*v.t.* to act as general of —*n* **generalisa'tion, -z-.**—*v t.* **gen'eralise, -ize** to make general: to include under a general term: to reduce to a general form: to comprehend as a particular case within a wider concept, proposition, definition, etc to represent or endow with the common characters of a group without the special characters of any one member: to bring to general use or knowledge: to infer inductively.—*v.t.* to make general statements: to form general concepts: to depict general character. to reason inductively.—*ns.* **generalis'imo** supreme commander of a great or combined force, **gen'eralist** one whose knowledge and skills are not restricted to one particular field: opp. of *specialist*, **general'ity.**—*adv* **gen'erally** in a general or collective manner or sense. in most cases: upon the whole.—*n.* **gen'eralship** the position of a military commander: the art of manipulating armies: tactical management and leadership — **general election** an election of all the members of a body at once, **general practice** the work of a general **practitioner** (abbrev. **G.P.**), a doctor who treats patients for most illnesses or complaints, referring other cases to specialists: **general principle** a principle to which there are no exceptions within its range of application.—*adj.* **gen'eral-purpose** generally useful, not restricted to a particular function.—**general staff** military officers who advise senior officers on policy, administration, etc —**General Certificate of Education** in secondary education in England and Wales, a certificate obtainable at ordinary, advanced, and scholarship levels for proficiency in one or more subjects; **general post office** the head post office of a town or district; **in general** as a generalisation: mostly. as a general rule. [O.Fr. —L *generālis—genus*]

generant. See **generate**.

generate *jen'ər-āt, v.t* to produce. to bring into life or being: to evolve: to originate: to trace out (*geom.*).— *adj.* **gen'erable** that may be generated or produced.— *ns.* **gen'erant** a line, point, or figure that traces out another figure by its motion (*geom.*); **genera'tion** production or originating: a single stage in natural

descent. the people of the same age or period: descendants removed by the same number of steps from a common ancestor· the ordinary time interval between the births of successive generations—usu. reckoned at 30 or 33 years. offspring, progeny, race: any of a series of files, each one an amended and updated version of the previous one (*comput.*).—*adj.* **gen'erative** having the power of, or concerned with, generating or producing —*n* **gen'erator** a begetter or producer: an apparatus for producing gases, etc.: an apparatus for turning mechanical into electrical energy —**generating station** a plant where electricity is generated, **generation gap** a lack of communication and understanding between one generation and the next; **generative grammar** (*linguistics*) a description of language as a finite set of grammatical rules able to generate an infinite number of grammatical sentences. [L *generāre, -ātum—genus*, a kind]

generic, -al, generically. See **genus**.

generous *jen'ə-rəs, adj.* of a noble nature. liberal· bountiful· ample.—*adv* **gen'erously**.—*ns.* **gen'erousness**, **generos'ity** nobleness or liberality of nature [L. *generōsus*, of noble birth—*genus*, birth]

genesis *jen'i-sis, n.* generation, creation, or production· (with *cap*) the first book of the Bible.—*pl.* **gen'esēs**. [Gr]

genet¹. See **jennet**.

genet², genette *jen'it, ji-net', ns.* a carnivorous animal (genus *Genetta*) allied to the civet. its fur. or an imitation. [Fr. *genette*—Sp. *gineta*—Ar. *jarnait*.]

genetic, -al *ji-net'ik, -əl, adjs* pertaining to origin or to genes —*adv* **genet'ically**,—*n* **genet'icist** (*-i-sist*) a student of genetics.—*n sing* **genet'ics** the branch of biology dealing with heredity and variation. inherited characteristics of an organism: origin. development. —**genetic code** the system by which genes pass on instructions that ensure transmission of hereditary characters; **genetic counselling** advice, given to prospective parents on possible heritable defects in their children, **genetic engineering** a biological science whose aims include the control of hereditary defects by the modification or elimination of certain genes, and the mass production of useful biological substances (e.g. insulin) by the transplanting of genes, **genetic manipulation** the alteration of natural genetic processes, usu for the purposes of research [**genesis**.]

genette. See **genet²**.

geneva *ji-nē'və, n* a spirit distilled from grain and flavoured with juniper berries, made chiefly in the Netherlands Also called *Hollands*, see **gin¹**. [O.Du. *genever*, O Fr *genevre*—L. *jūniperus*, juniper, confused with town of *Geneva*.]

Genevan *ji-nē'vən, adj.* pertaining to Geneva.—*n.* an inhabitant of Geneva an adherent of Genevan or Calvinistic theology.—**Geneva bands** the two strips of white linen hanging. down from the neck of some clerical robes, **Geneva Bible** a version of the Bible, long popular, produced by English exiles at Geneva in 1560, **Geneva Convention** an international agreement of 1865 providing for the neutrality of hospitals, and the security of sanitary officers. naval and military chaplains; **Geneva cross** a red cross on a white ground displayed for protection in war of persons serving in hospitals. etc

genial¹ *jē'ni-əl, adj* favouring growth. cheering. kindly: sympathetic: healthful —*v t.* **gē'nialise, -ize** to impart geniality to.—*ns.* **gēniality** (*-al't-ti*), **gē'nialness**.— *adv* **gē'nially.** [L *geniālis—genius*, the tutelary spirit.]

genial² *jə-nī'əl, adj* of or pertaining to the chin. [Gr *geneion*, chin—*genys*, under jaw]

genic. See **gene**.

genie *jē'ni, n.* a jinnee (see **jinn**). [Fr. *génie*—L.

genius, adopted because of its similarity to the Arabic word.]

genii. See **genius**.

Genista jə-nis'tə, *n.* a genus of shrubby, papilionaceous plants, with simple leaves and yellow flowers: (without *cap.*) a plant of this genus. [L. *genísta*, broom.]

genital jen'i-təl, *adj.* belonging to generation or the act of producing.—*n.pl.* **gen'itals** (also **genita'lia**) the organs of generation, esp. external.—*adj.* **genito-ūr'inary** pertaining to genital and urinary organs or functions. [L. *genitális—gignĕre, genitum*, to beget]

genitive jen'i-tiv, *adj* of or belonging to case expressing origin, possession, or similar relation (*gram.*).—*n.* (*gram.*) the genitive case: a word in the genitive case.—*adj.* **geniti'val**.—*advs.* **geniti'vally, gen'itively**. [L. *genitívus (—gignĕre, genitum*, to beget) for Gr *geniké (ptôsis)*, properly, generic (case)—*genos*, a class.]

genitor jen'i-tər, *n.* a father: a parent—*fem.* **gen'etrix, gen'itrix**.—*n.* **gen'iture** engendering: birth [L.]

genius jēn'yəs, or jē'ni-əs, *n.* the special inborn faculty of any individual: special taste or natural disposition: consummate intellectual, creative, or other power, more exalted than talent: one so endowed: a good or evil spirit, supposed to preside over every person, place, and thing, and esp. to preside over a man's destiny from his birth: a person who exerts a power, influence (whether good or bad) over another: prevailing spirit or tendency:—*pl.* **ge'niuses**; in sense of spirit, **genii** (jē'ni-ī). [L *genius—gignĕre, genitum*, to beget.]

gennet. See **jennet**.

genoa, Genoa jen'ō-ə, jə-nō'ə, (*naut.*) *n.* a large jib which overlaps the mainsail.—**Genoa cake** a rich cake containing fruit, with almonds on the top [Genoa in Italy.]

genocide jen'ō-sīd, *n.* deliberate extermination of a race or other group: one who exterminates, or approves extermination of, a race, etc —*adj.* **genoci'dal**. [Gr. *genos*, race, and L. *caedĕre*, to kill]

genom(e), genotype, etc See **gene**.

genre zhä-r', *n* kind: a literary or artistic type or style a style of painting scenes from familiar or rustic life —Also *adj.* [Fr.—L. *genus*.]

gent jent, *n.* short for **gentleman**:—*pl* **gents**.—*n.* **gents'** men's public lavatory.

genteel jen-tēl', *adj.* well-bred: graceful in manners or in form: fashionable: now used mainly with mocking reference to a standard of obsolete snobbery or false refinement.—*adv.* **genteel'ly**.—*n.* **genteel'ness**. [Fr. *gentil*—L *gentílis*; see **gentle**.]

gentian jen'shən, *n* any plant of the genus *Gentiana*, herbs, usually blue-flowered, abounding chiefly in alpine regions: the root and rhizome of the yellow gentian used as a tonic and stomachic.—**gentian violet** a mixture of three dyes, methyl rosaniline, methyl violet, and crystal violet, which is antiseptic and bactericidal. [L. *gentiána*.]

Gentile, gentile jen'tīl, *n.* anyone not a Jew (*B*), or not a Christian (now *rare*), or not a Mormon —*adjs.* **gentile** belonging to the Gentiles; **gen'tilish** heathenish. —*n.* **gen'tilism** (-*til-*, or -*til-*) paganism [L. *gentílis—gēns*, a nation, clan]

gentilesse, gentility etc. See **gentle**.

gentle jen'tl, *adj.* mild and refined in manners· mild in disposition or action: amiable: soothing: moderate gradual —*ns.* **gentilesse** (-*til-es'*) quality of being gentle, courtesy, **gentil'ity** good birth or extraction. good breeding: politeness of manners· genteel people: marks of gentility.—*n.* **gen'tleness**.—*adv* **gent'ly**.—*n.pl* **gen'tlefolk** people of good family.— *adj.* **gen'tle-heart'ed** having a gentle or kind disposi-

tion.—**gen'tleman** a man of good birth or high social standing: every man above the rank of yeoman, including the nobility (*hist.*): a man of refined manners: a well-to-do man of no occupation· a man of good feeling and instincts, courteous and honourable: a polite term used for man in general:—*pl* **gen'tlemen**—also a word of address, **gen'tleman-hood, gen'tlemanship** the condition or character of a gentleman.—*adjs.* **gen'tlemanlike** like or characteristic of a gentleman; **gen'tlemanly** befitting a gentleman: well-bred, refined, generous — **gen'tlemanliness**; **gen'tlewoman**—*pl* **gen'tle-women**.—*adj.* **gen'tlewomanly** like, or characteristic of, a refined and well-bred woman.—*n* **gen'tle-womanliness**.—**gentleman farmer** a landowner who lives on his estate superintending the cultivation of his own soil: a farmer who deputes the work of his farm to a farm manager and other staff; **gentleman's (-men's) agreement** an agreement resting on honour, not on formal contract; **gentleman's gentleman** a valet. [O Fr. (Fr.) *gentil*—L *gentílis*, belonging to the same *gens* or clan, later, well-bred; see **genteel**.]

gentoo jen-tōō', jen', *n* a Falkland Island penguin —Also *adj* [Port. *gentio*, a Gentile.]

gentry jen'tri, *n.* the class of people next below the rank of nobility: people of a particular, esp an inferior, stamp (*coll*).—*n.* **gentrifica'tion** the move of middle-class people into a formerly working-class area with the consequent change in the character of the area: the modernising of old, badly-equipped property, usu. with a view to increasing its value.— *v.t.* **gen'trify**. [O.Fr. *genterise, gentelise*, formed from adj *gentil, gentle*.]

genuflect jen'ū-flekt, *v.i.* to bend the knee in worship or respect.—*n.* **genūflex'ion** (also **genuflec'tion**). [L. *genū*, the knee, *flectĕre, flexum*, to bend.]

genuine jen'ū-in, *adj.* natural· native: not spurious. real. pure: sincere.—*adv.* **gen'uinely**.—*n.* **gen'uineness**. [L *genuínus—gignĕre*, to beget.]

genus jē'nəs, *n.* a taxonomic group of lower rank than a family, consisting of closely related species, in extreme cases of one species only (*biol*): a class of objects comprehending several subordinate species (*log.*):—*pl* **genera** (jen'ə-rə), **gē'nuses**—*adjs.* **generic, -al** (ji-ner'ik, -əl) general, applicable to any member of a group or class —*adv.* **gener'ically**.— **generic name** (*biol.*) the name of the genus, placed first in naming the species. [L. *gĕnus, genĕris*, birth; cog. with Gr. *genos*]

geo- jē'ō, in composition, of the earth [Gr *gē*, the earth.]

geocentric jē-ō-sen'trik, *adj.* having the earth for centre: as viewed or reckoned from the centre of the earth (*astron*): taking life on earth as the basis for evaluation —Also **geocen'trical**.—*adv.* **geocen'-trically**.—*n* **geocen'tricism** (-*sizm*) belief that the earth is the centre of the universe [Gr *gē*, the earth, *kentron*, point, centre.]

geochemistry jē-ō-kem'is-tri, *n* the chemistry of the crust of the earth.—*adj* **geochem'ical**.—*adv* **geochem'ically**.—*n.* **geochem'ist**. [geo-.]

geochronology jē-ō-kron-ol'ə-ji, *n.* the science of measuring geological time.—*adj.* **geochronolog'ical**.—*n.* **geochronol'ogist**. [geo-.]

geode jē'ōd, *n.* (a rock or stone having) a druse, i.e a cavity lined with crystals that have grown inwards (*geol*) —*adj.* **geöd'ic**. [Fr *géode*—Gr. *geôdēs*, earthy—*gē*, earth, *eidos*, form.]

geodesy jē-od'i-si, *n.* earth measurement on a large scale: surveying with allowance for the earth's curvature —Also *n. sing* **geodetics** (jē-ō-det'iks).—*adjs.* **geodesic** (jē-ō-des'ik, -dē'sik), **-al** pertaining to or determined by geodesy.—*n.* **geod'esist** one skilled in geodesy.—*adjs.* **geodet'ic, -al** geodesic.—*adv.* **geodet'ically.—geodesic dome** a light strong dome made by combining a grid of triangular or other straightline elements with a section of a sphere; **geodesic** or **geodetic (line)** the shortest line on a surface between two points on it; **geodetic surveying** geodesy, surveying large areas with allowance for the earth's curvature. [Gr. *geōdaisiā*—*gē*, the earth, *daisis*, division.]

geodynamics *jē-ō-dī-nam'iks, n.* the study of the dynamic processes and forces within the earth.—*adjs.* **geodynam'ic(al).** [geo-.]

geogony *jē-og'ə-ni, n.* the science or theory of the formation of the earth.—Also **geogeny** (*-oj'*).—*adj.* **geogonic** (*jē-ō-gon'ik*). [Gr. *gē*, the earth, *gonē*, generation.]

geography *jē-og'rə-fi, n.* the science of the surface of the earth and its inhabitants: a book containing a description of the earth.—*n.* **geog'rapher.**—*adjs.* **geographic** (*jē-ō-graf'ik*), **-al.**—*adv.* **geograph'ically.** [Gr. *geōgraphiā*—*gē*, earth, *graphein*, to write.]

geoid *jē'oid, n.* the figure of the earth's mean sea-level surface assumed to be continued across the land, approximately an oblate ellipsoid of revolution.—*adj.* **geoid'al.** [Gr. *geōdēs, geoeidēs,* earth-like—*gē*, earth, *eidos,* form.]

geology *jē-ol'ə-ji, n.* the science relating to the history and development of the earth's crust, with its successive floras and faunas.—*ns.* **geologian** (*jē-ə-lō'ji-ən*), **geol'ogist, geol'oger.**—*adjs.* **geologic** (*-loj'ik*), **-al.**—*adv.* **geolog'ically.**—*v.i.* **geol'ogise, -ize** to work at geology in the field.—*v.t.* to investigate the geology of.—**geological time** time before written history, divided into epochs each of which saw the formation of one of the great rock systems.—**dynamical geology** the study of the work of natural agents in shaping the earth's crust—wind, frost, rivers, volcanic action, etc.; **structural geology** the study of the arrangement and structure of rock masses. [Fr. *géologie*—Gr. *gē*, earth, *logos*, a discourse.]

geomagnetism *jē-ō-mag'nət-izm, n.* terrestrial magnetism: the study of this.—*adj.* **geomagnet'ic.** [geo-.]

geomedicine *jē-ō-med'sin, n.* the study of diseases as influenced by geographical environment.—*adj.* **geomed'ical.** [geo-.]

geometry *jē-om'i-tri, n.* that part of mathematics which treats the properties of points, lines, surfaces, and solids, either under classical Euclidean assumptions, or (in the case of *elliptic, hyperbolic,* etc., *geometry*) involving postulates not all of which are identical with Euclid's: any study of a mathematical system in which figures undergo transformations, concerned with discussion of those properties of the figures which remain constant: a textbook of geometry.—*ns.* **geom'eter** a geometrician: a geometrid; **geometrician** (*-me-trish'ən*) one skilled in geometry.—*adjs.* **geometric** (*-met'*), **-al** relating to or according to geometry: consisting of or using simple figures such as geometry deals with.—*adv.* **geomet'rically.**—*v.t.* and *v.i.* **geom'etrise, -ize** to work geometrically: to show in geometric form.—*n.* **geom'etrist.—geometrical progression** a series of quantities each of which has the same ratio to its predecessor. [Gr. *geōmetriā*—*gē*, earth, *metron,* a measure.]

geomorphology *jē-ō-mör-fol'ə-ji, n.* the morphology of land forms including those under the sea.—*adjs.* **geomorpholog'ic, -al.**—*adv.* **geomorpholog'ically.**—*n.* **geomorphol'ogist.** [geo-.]

geophilous *jē-of'il-əs, adj.* living in or on the ground: having a short stem with leaves at ground-level.—*adj.* **geophil'ic.** [Gr. *gē*, earth, *phileein,* to love.]

geophysics *gē-ō-fiz'iks, n. sing.* the physics of the earth.—*adj.* **geophys'ical.**—*n.* **geophys'icist** (*-i-sist*). [geo-.]

geopolitics *jē-ō-pol'it-iks, n. sing.* a science concerned with problems of states, such as frontiers, as affected by their geographical environment: the special combination of geographical and political considerations in a particular state.—*adj.* **geopolit'ical.**—*n.* **geopolit'ician.** [Ger. *Geopolitik;* see geo-.]

geoponic, -al *jē-ō-pon'ik, -əl, adjs.* agricultural.—*n. sing.* **geopon'ics** the science of agriculture. [Gr. *geōponikos*—*gē*, earth, *ponos,* labour.]

geordie *jör'di, n.* a coal-pitman: a collier-boat: (usu. with *cap.*) a native of Tyneside.—*adj.* pertaining to Tyneside.

George *jörj, n.* a jewelled figure of St *George* slaying the dragon, worn by Knights of the Garter: the automatic pilot of an aircraft.—**George Cross** an award for outstanding courage or heroism given in cases where a purely military honour is not applicable—instituted during World War II; **George Medal** an award for gallantry given to civilians and members of the armed forces.—**St George's cross** the Greek cross of England, red on a white ground.

Georgian *jör'ji-ən, adj.* relating to or contemporary with any of the various *Georges,* kings of Great Britain, or other of the name: belonging to *Georgia* in the Caucasus, its people, language, etc.: of or pertaining to the American State of *Georgia.*—Also *n.*

geosphere *jē'ō-sfēr, n.* the solid part of the earth, distinguished from *atmosphere* and *hydrosphere.* [Gr. *gē*, earth, *sphaira,* sphere.]

geostatic *jē-ō-stat'ik, adj.* capable of sustaining the pressure of earth from all sides.—*n. sing.* **geostat'ics** the statics of rigid bodies. [Gr. *gē*, the earth, *statikos,* causing to stand.]

geostationary *jē-ō-stā'shən-ə-ri, adj.* of a satellite, etc., orbiting the earth in time with the earth's own rotation, i.e. circling it once every 24 hours, so remaining above the same spot on the earth's surface. [geo-.]

geostrophic *jē-ō-strof'ik, adj.* of a virtual force used to account for the change in direction of the wind relative to the surface of the earth arising from the earth's rotation: of a wind whose direction and force are partly determined by the earth's rotation. [Gr. *gē*, earth, *strophē,* a turn.]

geosynchronous *jē-ō-sing'krə-nəs, adj.* of a satellite, etc., geostationary. [geo-.]

geosyncline *jē-ō-sin'klin, n.* a syncline on a great scale. —*adj.* **geosyncli'nal.** [geo-.]

geotaxis *jē-ō-taks'is, n.* response of an organism to the stimulus of gravity.—*adjs.* **geotact'ic, -al.**—*adv.* **geotact'ically.** [Gr. *gē*, earth, *taxis,* arrangement.]

geothermic *jē-ō-thûr'mik,* **geothermal** *-əl, adjs.* pertaining to the internal heat of the earth.—**geothermal energy** energy extracted from the earth's natural heat, i.e. from hot springs and certain kinds of rock. [Gr. *gē*, earth, *thermē,* heat.]

geotropism *jē-ot'rop-izm, (bot.) n.* geotaxis (positive downwards, negative upwards).—*adj.* **geotrop'ic.**—*adv.* **geotrop'ically.** [Gr. *gē*, earth, *tropos,* a turning.]

geranium *ji-rān'yəm, n.* a plant of the genus **Geranium** with seed-vessels like a crane's bill, typical of the family **Geraniaceae** (*-i-ā'si-ē*): loosely, any cultivated plant of the genus *Pelargonium.* [L.,—Gr. *geranion* —*geranos,* a crane.]

Gerbera *gûr'bə-rə, jûr', n.* a genus of composite plants of S. Africa, etc: (without *cap.*) a plant of this genus. [T. *Gerber,* German naturalist.]

gerbil *jûr'bil, n.* a small desert-dwelling rodent capable of causing great damage to crops but often kept as a pet.—Also **jerb'il** and **gerb'ille.** [Fr. *gerbille.*]

For other sounds see detailed chart of pronunciation.

gerfalcon, gyrfalcon, jerfalcon *jûr'fö(l)-kn, n.* a large northern falcon. [O.Fr. *gerfaucon*—L.L. *gyrofalcō*, most prob. O.H.G. *gîr*, a vulture; see falcon.]

geriatrics *jer-i-at'riks, n. sing.* medical care of the old.—*adj.* geriat'ric.—*n.* (*coll.*) an old person.—*ns.* geriatrician (*-ə-trish'ən*), geriatrist (*-at'rist*); geriatry (*jer-i'ə-tri*) care of the old, old people's welfare. [Gr. *gēras*, old age, *iātros*, physician.]

germ *jûrm, n.* a rudimentary form of a living thing, whether plant or animal: a shoot: that from which anything springs, the origin or beginning: a first principle: that from which a disease springs: a micro-organism, esp. a malign one.—*v.i.* to put forth buds, sprout.—*ns.* ger'men, ger'min a rudiment: a shoot; germ'icide that which kills germs.—*adjs.* germici'dal; germ'inable that can be germinated; germ'inal pertaining to a germ or rudiment: in germ, or (*fig.*) earliest stage of development: seminal (*fig.*); germ'inant sprouting: budding: capable of developing.—*v.i.* germ'inate to begin to grow (esp. of a seed or spore).—*v.t.* to cause to sprout.—*n.* germina'tion.—*adj.* germ'inative—germ'-cell a sperm or ovum, a gamete or cell from which it springs; germ'-plasm that part of the nuclear protoplasmic material which, according to early theories of inheritance, is the vehicle of heredity, and maintains its continuity from generation to generation; germ warfare warfare in which bacteria are used as weapons. [Partly through Fr. *germe*, from L. *germen*, *-inis*, a sprout, bud, germ *germināre*, *-ātum*, to sprout.]

german *jûr'mən, adj.* of the first degree: full (see brother, cousin): closely allied.—*n.* a full brother or sister: a near relative.—*adj.* germane (*-mān'*) nearly related (to): relevant, appropriate (to).—*adv.* germane'ly.—*n.* germane'ness. [O.Fr. *germain*—L. *germānus*.]

German *jûr'mən, n.* a native or citizen of Germany, or one of the same linguistic or ethnological stock (*pl.* Ger'mans): the German language, esp. High German.—*adj.* of or from Germany, or the Germans: German-speaking.—*adjs.* Germanesque' marked by German characteristics; Germanic (*-man'ik*) of Germany: of the linguistic family to which German, English, Norwegian, etc., belong—Teutonic.—*n.* an extinct Indo-European tongue which differentiated into East Germanic (Gothic and other extinct languages), North Germanic or Scandinavian (Norwegian, Danish, Swedish, Icelandic) and West Germanic (English, Frisian, Dutch, Low German, High German).—*adv.* German'ically.—*v.t.* Ger'manise, -ize to make German.—*v.i.* to become German: to adopt German ways.—*n.* Germanisa'tion, -z-.—*adj.* Ger'manish somewhat German.—*ns.* Ger'manism a German idiom: German ideas and ways; Ger'manist one learned in German philology or other matters relating to Germany.—*adj.* Germanis'tic pertaining to the study of German.—*ns.* German'ophil a lover of the Germans and things German, now usu. German'ophile; Germanophil'ia; German'ophobe one who fears or hates the Germans and things German.—German measles rubella.—High German the speech, originally of High or Southern Germany, the literary language throughout Germany; Low German Platt-Deutsch, the language of Low or Northern Germany: formerly applied to all the West Germanic dialects except High German. [L. *Germānus*, German.]

germander *jər-man'dər, n.* a labiate herb with aromatic, bitter, and stomachic properties. [L.L. *germandra*—Late Gr. *chamandrya*—Gr. *chamaidrȳs*—*chamai*, on the ground, *drȳs*, oak.]

germane. See german.

germanium *jər-mā'ni-əm, n.* a metallic element (Ge; atomic number 32), much used in diodes, transistors and rectifiers for its properties as a semiconductor. [Discovered in 1885 by a German.]

germen, germicide. See germ.

germin, germinal, germinate, etc. See germ.

gerontic *ger-* or *jer-on'tik,* (*biol.*) *adj.* pertaining to the senescent period in the life-history of an individual.—*n.* gerontoc'racy government by old men.—*adjs.* gerontocrat'ic; gerontolog'ical.—*ns.* gerontol'ogist; gerontol'ogy scientific study of the processes of growing old. [Gr. *gerōn*, *-ontos*, old man.]

Gerry. See Jerry.

gerrymander *jer'i-man-dər,* also *ger', v.t.* to rearrange (voting districts) in the interests of a particular party or candidate: to manipulate (facts, arguments, etc.) so as to reach undue conclusions.—*n.* an arrangement of the above nature. [Formed from the name of Governor Elbridge *Gerry* (1744–1814) and *sala-mander*, from the likeness to that animal of the gerry-mandered map of Massachusetts in 1811]

gerund *jer'ənd, n.* a part of a Latin verb with the value of a verbal noun, as *amandum*, loving: in English, a noun with the ending *-ing* formed from a verb and having some of the qualities of a verb, as the possibility of governing an object, etc.; often preceded by a possessive (e.g. *My leaving her was unwise*).—*adjs.* gerundial (*ji-rund'i-əl*), gerundival (*jer-ən-dī'vl*), gerundive (*ji-rund'iv*).—*n.* gerund'ive a Latin verbal adjective expressing necessity, as *amandus, -a, -um*, deserving or requiring to be loved. [L. *gerundium*—*gerĕre*, to bear.]

gesso *jes'ō, n.* plaster of Paris: a plaster surface prepared as a ground for painting:—*pl.* gess'oes. [It.,—L. *gypsum*; see gypsum.]

gestalt *gə-shtält', n.* form, shape, pattern: organised whole or unit.—Gestalt psychology revolt from the atomistic outlook of the orthodox school, starts with the organised whole as something more than the sum of the parts into which it can be logically analysed. [Ger.]

Gestapo *gə-stä'pō, n.* the Nazi secret police in Germany. [From Ger. *Geheime Staatspolizei*, secret state police.]

gestate *jes-tāt', v.t.* to carry in the womb during the period from conception to birth: to conceive and develop slowly in the mind.—*v.i.* to be in the process of gestating.—*n.* gestation (*jes-tā'shən*).—*adjs.* gestā'tional, gesta'tive of carriage, esp. in the womb. [L. *gestāre, -ātum*, to carry—*gerĕre*, to bear.]

gesticulate *jes-tik'ū-lāt, v.i.* to make vigorous gestures.—*ns.* gesticula'tion; gestic'ulator.—*adjs.* gestic'ula-tive, gestic'ulatory. [L. *gesticulāri, -ātus*—*gesticulus*, dim. of *gestus*, gesture—*gerĕre*, to carry, behave.]

gesture *jes'chər, n.* an action, esp. of the hands, expressive of sentiment or passion or intended to show inclination or disposition: the use of such movements: an action dictated by courtesy or diplomacy, or by a desire to impress.—*v.t.* to make a gesture or gestures.—*v.t.* to express by gesture(s).—*adj.* ges'tural. [L.L. *gestūra*—L. *gestus*, from L. *gerĕre*, to carry, behave.]

Gesundheit *gə-zōōnt'hīt,* (Ger.) *interj.* your health (said to someone who has just sneezed).

get *get, v.t.* to obtain: to acquire: to procure: to receive: to attain: to come to have: to catch: to grasp or take the meaning of: to learn: to commit to memory: to hit: to descry: to make out: to succeed in coming into touch or communication with (e.g. a wireless station): to worst, have the better of, gain a decisive advantage over: to baffle: to irritate: to grip emotionally, take, captivate, hit the taste of exactly: to induce: to cause to be, go, or become: to betake: to

beget.—*v.i.* to arrive, to bring or put oneself (in any place, position, or state): to become: to become richer: to clear out:—*pr.p.* **gett'ing;** *pa.t.* **got,** *obs.* **gat;** *pa.p.* **got,** *arch., Scot.,* and *U.S.* **gott'en.**—*n.* **gett'er** one who, or that which evacuates: a material used, when evaporated by high-frequency induction currents, for evacuation of gas left in vacuum valves after sealing during manufacture.—*v.t.* to evacuate (a valve) using a getter.—*v.i.* to use a getter.—*ns.* **gett'ering** evacuation using a getter; **gett'ing** a gaining: anything gained: procreation.—*adj.* **get-at'-able** easily accessible.—**get ahead** to make an escape: a start: breaking cover; **get'-out** (*coll.*) a way of escape or avoidance.—Also *adj.*—*adj.* **get'-rich'-quick'** (*coll.*) wanting, or leading to, easy prosperity.—**get's together** a social gathering: an informal conference; **get'-up** (style of) equipment, outfit, make-up; **get's up-and-go'** (*coll.*) energy.—**get about, around** to travel, go visiting: to be mobile and active; **get across** (*coll.*) communicate successfully; **get ahead** to make progress, advance; **get along** to get on (see below); **get at** to reach, attain: to poke fun at (*slang*): to mean: to attack verbally: to influence by underhand or unlawful means; **get away with (something)** to pull something off: to carry a thing through successfully or with impunity; **get back at** to have one's revenge on; **get by** to succeed in passing: to elude notice and come off with impunity: manage satisfactorily, be sufficiently good (*coll.*); **get down** to alight: to depress (*coll.*); **get down to** set to work on, tackle seriously; **get in on** (*coll.*) to join in, become a participant in; **get off** to escape: to learn: to gain the affection of someone of the opposite sex (with *with*; *coll.*); **get on** to proceed, advance: to prosper: to agree, consort harmoniously: to fare; **get one's own back** (*coll.*) to have one's revenge (on); **get out** to produce: to extricate oneself (with *of*): to take oneself off; **get over** to surmount: to recover from: to make an impression on an audience; **get (something) over with** to accomplish (an unpleasant task, etc.) as quickly as possible; **get round** to circumvent: to persuade, talk over; **get round to** to bring oneself to do (something); **get there** (*slang*) to achieve one's object, succeed; **get through** to finish: to reach a destination: to receive approval, or to obtain it for (something): to be put in telephonic communication: to communicate with, reach the comprehension of (with *to*); **get together** to meet for social intercourse or discussion; **get up** to arise: to ascend: to arrange: to prepare: to learn up for an occasion: to commit to memory; **have got** (*coll.*) to have; **tell someone where he gets off** (*coll.*) to deal summarily or dismissively with someone; **have got to** to be obliged to. [O.N. *geta*.]

geta *gā'ta, n.* a Japanese wooden sandal with a thong between the big toe and the other toes:—*pl.* **ge'ta** or **ge'tas.** [Jap.]

Geum *jē'əm, n.* the avens genus of the rose family: (without *cap.*) a plant of this genus. [L.]

gewgaw *gū'gö, n.* a toy: a bauble.—*adj.* showy without value.

geyser *gā', gē'* or *gī'zər, n.* a spring that spouts hot water into the air: (usu. *gē'*) apparatus for heating water as it is drawn.—*n.* **gey'serite** sinter. [*Geysir,* a geyser in Iceland—Icel. *geysa,* O.N. *gòysa,* to gush.]

Ghanaian *gā-nā'yən, -nä', adj.* of or pertaining to Ghana.—*n.* a native or citizen of Ghana.

gharial. Same as **gavial, garial.**

gharri, gharry *ga'ri, n.* in India, a wheeled vehicle, generally for hire. [Hind. *gārī,* a cart.]

ghastly *gäst'li, adj.* death-like: hideous: deplorable (*coll.*).—*n.* **ghast'liness.** [O.E. *gǣstan.*]

ghat, ghaut *got, n.* in India, a mountain-pass: a landing-stair. [Hindi *ghāt,* descent.]

ghazi *gā'zē, n.* a veteran Muslim warrior: a slayer of infidels: a high Turkish title. [Ar. *ghāzi,* fighting.]

ghee, ghi *gē, g'hē, n.* clarified butter, esp. buffalo butter. [Hind. *ghī.*]

gherkin *gûr'kin, n.* a small cucumber used for pickling. [From an earlier form of Du. *augurk(je),* a gherkin; app. from Slavonic.]

ghetto *get'ō, n.* the Jews' quarter in an Italian or other city, to which they used to be confined: a quarter esp. poor, inhabited by any racial group:—*pl.* **ghett'o(e)s.** [Poss. shortening of *borghetto,* dim. of of It. *borgo,* village, or from It. *getto,* foundry, one having previously occupied the site of the Venetian ghetto.]

ghi. See **ghee.**

ghigal. See **gilgie.**

ghillie. Same as **gillie.**

ghost *gōst, n.* a spirit: the soul of a man: a spirit appearing after death: one who does another's work for him, as writing speeches or the like: a faint or false appearance: a semblance: a duplicated image (*TV*).—*v.i.* and *v.t.* to do another's work, esp. to write (speeches, memoirs, etc.) for him.—*adj.* **ghost'-like.**—*n.* **ghost'liness.**—*adjs.* **ghost'ly** spiritual: religious: pertaining to apparitions: ghost-like: faint; **ghost'y.**—**ghost'-story** a story in which ghosts figure; **ghost town** one which once flourished owing to some natural resource in the vicinity but which is now deserted since the natural resource has been exhausted; **ghost'-word** a word that has originated in the blunder of a scribe or printer.—*v.i.* and *v.t.* **ghost'-write** to write for another as a ghost.—**ghost'-writer.**—**give up the ghost** (*B.*) to die; **Holy Ghost** the Holy Spirit, the third person in the Christian Trinity; **not to have a ghost (of a chance)** not to have the least chance of success. [O.E. *gāst.*]

ghoul *gōōl, n.* an Eastern demon that preys on the dead: a gruesome fiend: a person of gruesome or revolting habits or tastes.—*adj.* **ghoul'ish.**—*adv.* **ghoul'ishly.**—*n.* **ghoul'ishness.** [Ar. *ghūl.*]

ghyll *gil.* See **gill³.**

giant *jī'ənt, n.* a huge mythical being of more or less human form: a person of abnormally great stature: anything much above the usual size of its kind: a person of much greater powers than his fellows:—*fem.* **gi'antess.**—*adj.* gigantic.—*ns.* **gi'anthood** the quality or character of a giant: the race of giants; **gi'antism** the occurrence of giants: gigantism.—*adj.* **gi'antly** giant-like.—*ns.* **gi'antry** giants collectively: giant stories or mythology; **gi'antship.**—**gi'ant-killer** one who defeats a far superior opponent; **giant star** (*astron.*) a star of great brightness and low mean density; **giant('s) stride** a gymnastic apparatus enabling one to take great strides around a pole. [O.Fr. *geant* (Fr. *géant*)—L. *gigās*—Gr. *gigās, gigantos.*]

giaour *jowr, n.* an infidel, a term applied by the Turks to all who are not of their own religion. [Through Turk.—Pers. *gaur.*]

gib *jib, gib, n.* a wedge-shaped piece of metal holding another in place, etc.—*v.t.* to fasten with a gib.

gibber *jib'ər, v.i.* to utter senseless or inarticulate sounds. [Imit.]

Gibberella *jib-ər-el'ə, n.* a genus of fungi found esp. on grasses—e.g. wheat scab.—*n.* **gibberell'in** any of several plant-growth regulators produced by a fungus of the genus.

gibberish *gib'ər-ish,* or *jib', n.* rapid, gabbling talk: unmeaning words.—*adj.* unmeaning. [Imit.]

gibbet *jib'it, n.* a gallows, esp. one on which criminals were suspended after execution: the projecting beam of a crane.—*v.t.* to expose on, or as on, a gibbet [O.Fr. *gibet,* a stick.]

gibbon *gib'ən, n.* an E. Indian anthropoid ape (of several species) with very long arms.

gibbous *gib'ɔs, adj* hump-backed humped: unequally convex on two sides, as the moon between half and full.—Also **gibb'ose.**—*ns.* **gibbos'ity, gibb'ousness.** —*adv.* **gibb'ously.** [L. *gibbōsus—gibbus*, a hump.]

gibe, jibe *jīb, v.i.* to scoff: to flout —*v t.* to scoff at: to taunt —*n* a flout: a taunt.—*n* **gi'ber, ji'ber.**—*adv.* **gi'bingly.**

giblets *jib'lits, n.pl.* the internal eatable parts of a fowl, etc.: entrails. [O.Fr *gibelet*]

giddy *gid'i, adj.* unsteady, dizzy: causing giddiness. whirling: light-headed: flighty —Also *v.i.* and *v.t* — *adv.* **gidd'ily.**—*n.* **gidd'iness.**—**play the giddy goat** to act the fool. [O.E *gidig, gydig*, insane, possessed by a god]

gidgee, gidjee *gi'jē, (Austr)* n a small acacia tree with foul-smelling flowers. [Native word.]

gift *gift, n.* a thing given: a quality bestowed by nature: the act of giving: something easily obtained, understood, etc —*v t.* to endow, esp. with any power or faculty: to present —*adj* **gift'ed** highly endowed by nature with talents, abilities, etc : esp of a child, exceptionally clever —*adv* **gift'edly.**—*n* **gift'edness.**—**gift'-book** a book suitable for intended for presentation; **gift horse** a horse given as a present, **gift'-shop** a shop selling articles suitable for presents —*v t.* **gift'-wrap** to wrap (a present) in coloured paper, with ribbons, etc.—**look a gift horse in the mouth** to criticise a gift (orig. to look at a gift horse's teeth to tell its age). [See give.]

gig¹ *gig, n.* a light, two-wheeled carriage: a long, light boat: a machine for raising the nap on cloth (in full, **gig mill**): a fishgig (see under **fizgig**) [M E. *gigge*, a whirling thing.]

gig² *gig, (slang) n.* an engagement, esp. of a band or pop-group for one performance only —*v.t.* to play a gig:—*pa.t.* **gigged.**

giga- *gī'gɔ, gig'ɔ, jī'gɔ, jig'ɔ, pfx.* meaning ten to the ninth power (10⁹).—**gi'ga-elec'tron-volt** a unit equal to a thousand million electron-volts; **gi'gahertz; gi'gawatt.** [Gr. *gigas*, giant.]

gigantic *jī-gan'tik, adj.* of, like or characteristic of a giant: huge —Also **giganté'an.**—*adj* **gigantesque'** befitting or suggestive of a giant.—*adv* **gigan'tically.** —*ns.* **gigan'ticide** the act of killing a giant; **gigant'ism** hugeness, of a business concern, etc · excessive overgrowth, usually owing to overactivity of the pituitary gland. [L. *gigās, gigantis,* Gr. *gigās, -antos,* a giant.]

giggle *gig'l, v.i.* to laugh with short catches of the breath, or in a silly manner.—*n.* a laugh of this kind: something unimportant *(slang)* —*n.* **gigg'ler; gigg'ling.**—*adjs.* **gigg'lesome, gigg'ly.** [Echoic]

gigolo *jig'ō-lō, n.* a professional male dancing partner: a young man living at the expense of an older woman:—*pl.* **gig'olos.** [Fr]

gigot *jig'ɔt, n.* a leg of mutton, etc.: a leg-of-mutton sleeve. [Fr.]

gigue *zhēg, (mus.) n.* a lively dance-form in triple time, common in old suites. [Fr.; cf. **jig.**]

gila *hhē'lā* (in full **gila monster**) n either of the two *Heloderma* species, the only venomous lizards known. [*Gila* River, Arizona.]

gilbert *gil'bɔrt, n.* the C.G.S. unit of magnetomotive force. [From the English physician and physicist William *Gilbert* (1540–1603)]

gild¹ *gild, v t.* to cover or overlay with gold or with any goldlike substance: to furnish with gold: to gloss over, give a specious appearance to: to adorn with lustre:—*pr.p.* **gild'ing;** *pa.t.* and *pa.p* **gild'ed** or **gilt.**—*ns* **gild'er** one who coats articles with gold; **gild'ing** act or trade of a gilder: gold or imitation thereof laid on a surface.—**gilded youth** rich young people of fashion.—**gild the lily** to embellish to an unnecessary extent; **gild the pill** to make a

disagreeable thing seem less so [O E *gyldan*— *gold*; see **gold.**]

gild². See **guild.**

gilet *zhē-lā, n* a waistcoat· in a woman's dress, a front part shaped like a waistcoat: in ballet dress, a bodice shaped like a waistcoat. [Fr]

gilgie *gil'gi,* **g(h)ilgai** *-ī. (Austr.) ns* a saucer-shaped depression forming a natural reservoir [Native word]

gill¹ *gil, n* an organ for breathing in water: one of the radiating plates under a mushroom or toadstool cap: a projecting rib of a heating surface —*v t.* to gut (fish): to catch (fish) by the gills in a net —**gill cover** a fold of skin, usu with bony plates, protecting the gills; **gill net** a type of fishing-net in which fish are caught by their gills. [Cf. Dan *giælle;* Sw. *gal.*]

gill² *jil, n* a small measure, having various values; in recent times = ¼ pint. [O Fr *gelle*]

gill³, ghyll *gil, n.* a small ravine, a wooded glen· a brook. [O N. *gil.*]

gillie, ghillie, gilly *gil'i, n.* a Highland chief's attendant *(hist)·* an attendant on or guide of hunting and fishing sportsmen —*v.t.* to act as gillie. [Gael. *gille,* a lad]

gillion *jil'yɔn, gil', n.* in Britain, a thousand millions, 10⁹, equivalent of a U.S. billion. [**giga-** and **million.**]

gilly. See **gillie.**

gillyflower *jil'i-flowr, n.* a flower that smells like cloves, esp. **clove-gillyflower, stock-gillyflower.** [O.Fr *girofle*—Gr *karyophyllon,* the clove-tree— *karyon,* a nut, *phyllon,* a leaf]

gilt *gilt, pa t* and *pa.p.* of **gild¹.**—*adj.* gilded: goldcoloured.—*adj.* **gilt'-edged** having the edges gilt: of the highest quality (**gilt-edged securities** those stocks whose interest is considered perfectly safe) —*ns.* **gilt'-edged, gilts.**

gimcrack, jimcrack *jim'krak, n.* a trumpery knickknack: a paltry, ill-made, flimsy article: a trivial mechanism.—*adj* trumpery, shoddy.—*n.* **gimcrack'ery.**

gimlet *gim'lit, n.* a small tool for boring holes by turning it by hand: half a glass of whisky, gin, or vodka, and lime-juice.—*v.t.* to pierce as with a gimlet: to turn like a gimlet —*adj.* **gim'let-eyed'** very sharp-sighted. [O.Fr *guimbelet,* from Gmc.]

gimmal *jim'l, n.* a ring (also **gimmal ring**) that can be divided into two (or three) rings: a joint or part in a piece of mechanism (also **gimm'er**).

gimme *gi'mi, (slang)* contracted form of *give me.*

gimmer. See **gimmal.**

gimmick *gim'ik, n* a secret device for performing a trick· a device (often peculiar to the person adopting it) to catch attention, publicity· an ingenious mechanical device.—*n.* **gimm'ickry** gimmicks in quantity: use of gimmick(s) —*adj.* **gimm'icky** pertaining to a gimmick. loosely, of little worth, importance.

gimp *gimp, n.* a yarn with a hard core: a trimming thereof: a fishing-line bound with wire: a coarse thread in lace-making —*v t.* to make or furnish with gimp.—Also **guimp(e).** [Fr *guimpe,* app. from O.H.G. *wimpal*]

gin¹ *jin, n* geneva: a spirit distilled from grain or malt and flavoured with juniper berries or other aromatic substances, made chiefly in Britain and the U S — **gin'-fizz'** a drink of gin, lemon-juice, effervescing water, etc.; **gin'-palace** *(derog.)* a showily pretentious public house, **gin'shop; gin'-sling** a cold gin and water, sweetened and flavoured.—**gin and it** gin and Italian vermouth [Contr. from **geneva.**]

gin² *jin, n.* a snare or trap: a machine, esp. one for hoisting· a cotton- gin —*v t* to trap or snare: to clear of seeds by a cotton-gin:—*pr p.* **ginn'ing;** *pa.t.* and *pa.p.* **ginned.**—*ns* **ginn'er** one who gins cotton; **ginn'-**

ery, **gin'house** a place where cotton is ginned —**gin trap** a powerful spring trap fitted with teeth. [engine.]

gin³ *jin, n* Australian aborigine woman [Native word]

gin⁴ *jin, n* a type of rummy in which a player whose unmatched cards count ten or less may stop the game. —Also **gin rummy.**

gingelly. See **gingili.**

ginger *jin'jər, n* the root-stock of *Zingiber officinale,* or other species of the genus (family Zingiberaceae) with a hot taste, used as a condiment or stomachic ginger beer: stimulation. mettle.—*adj* sandy, red-dish.—*v.t* to put ginger into: to make spirited, to enliven (often with *up*).—*adj* **gin'gery** of or like ginger. sandy in colour.—**gingerade'**, **ginger ale** an aerated drink flavoured with ginger; **ginger beer** an effervescent drink made with fermenting ginger; **ginger cordial** a cordial made of ginger, lemon-peel, raisins, water, and sometimes spirits; **ginger group** a group within e.g. a political party seeking to inspire the rest with its own enthusiasm and activity; **ginger nut** a small thick gingersnap, **ginger pop** weak ginger beer (*coll.*), **gin'gersnap** a gingerbread biscuit; **ginger wine** liquor made by the fermentation of sugar and water, and flavoured with various spices, chiefly ginger —**ginger beer plant** a symbiotic association of a yeast and a bacterium, by which ginger beer can be prepared. [M.E. *gingivere*—O Fr. *gengibre*—L L *gingiber*—L. *zingiber*—Gr. *zingiberis*—Prākrit—Sans. *śrnga,* horn, *vera,* body, Malayalam *inchiver.*]

gingerbread *jin'jər-bred, n.* a cake flavoured with treacle and usually ginger.—*adj.* of ornamental work, cheap and tawdry.—**take the gilt off the gingerbread** to destroy the glamour [O.Fr *gingumbrat*—L.L. *gingiber;* see **ginger;** confused with **bread.**]

gingerly *jin'jər-li, adv.* with soft steps. with extreme wariness and delicate gentleness —Also *adj*

gingham *ging'əm, n.* a kind of cotton cloth, woven from coloured yarns into stripes or checks. [Fr. *guingan,* orig. from Malay *ginggang,* striped.]

gingili, gingelly, jinjili *jin'ji-li, n.* a species of sesame: an oil got from its seeds. [Hind. *jinjalī,* prob.—Ar. *juljulān.*]

gingival *jin-ji'vl, adj.* pertaining to the gums.—*n.* **gin-givi'tis** inflammation of the gums [L. *gingīva,* gum]

gingko. See **ginkgo.**

ginglymus *jing'gli-məs* (or *ging'-*), *n.* a joint that permits movement in one plane only:—*pl* \ **ging'-lynii.**—*adj* **ging'limoid.** [Latinised from Gr. *gunglymos.*]

gink *gingk,* (*slang*) *n* a fellow

ginkgo *gingk'gō, n* the maidenhair tree, holy in Japan, perhaps still wild in China, forming by itself an order (**Ginkgoa'les**) of Gymnosperms.—Also **ging'ko:**—*pl* **gink'goes, ging'koes.** [Jap. *ginkyo*—Chin. *yin,* silver, *hing,* apricot.]

ginn. See **jinn.**

ginseng *jin'seng, n.* a plant of the araliaceous genus Panax, cultivated esp. in the Far East: its root, believed to have important restorative and curative properties. [Chin. *jên-shên,* perh. image of man.]

giocoso *jok-ō'sō,* (*mus.*) *adj.* played in a lively or humorous manner. [It.]

gip *jip, n.* Same as **gyp².**

gippo, gyppo *jip'ō,* (*offensive*) *n.* an Egyptian, esp. a native Egyptian soldier:—*pl.* **gipp'os, gypp'os.**—Also **gipp'y, gypp'ie, gypp'y.**—**gippy** (or **gyppy**) **tummy** (*coll.*) diarrhoea, thought of as a hazard of holidaying in hot countries. [*Egypt.*]

gippy. See **gippo.**

gipsy. See **gypsy.**

giraffe *ji-raf', n* an African ruminant with remarkably long neck and forelegs —*adj.* **giraff'ine.** [Ar *zarāfah.*]

girandole *jir'ən-dōl,* **girandola** *-and' ə-lə, ns.* a branched chandelier or similar structure a pendant, etc . with small jewels attached around it: a rotating firework · a number of linked mines (*mil.*). [Fr.,—It. *girandola* —*girare*—L *gyrāre,* to turn round—*gyrus*—Gr. *gyros,* a circle]

girasol, girasole *jir'ə-sol, -sōl, ns.* a fire-opal or other stone that seems to send a firelike glow from within in certain lights [It ,—*girare* (see **girandole**) and *sole* —L *sōl,* the sun]

gird *gûrd, v t* to bind round: to make fast by a belt or girdle to encompass to surround· to clothe, furnish· —*pa.t.* and *pa.p.* **gird'ed** and **girt.**—*ns.* **gird'er** a great beam, simple or built up, of wood, iron, or steel, to take a lateral stress, e g to support a floor, wall, roadway of a bridge. **gird'ing** that which girds.— **girder bridge** a bridge whose load is sustained by girders resting on supports.—**gird oneself** to tuck up loose garments under the girdle: to brace the mind for any trial or effort: see also **loin.** [O.E *gyrdan.*]

girdle¹ *gûrd'l, n.* a waist-belt: a cord worn about the waist by a monk, etc . anything that encloses like a belt: a woman's lightweight, close-fitting undergarment, a form of corset, reaching from waist to thigh: a worm's clitellum: a ring-shaped cut around a tree: the rim of a brilliant-cut gem.—*v.t* to bind, as with a girdle: to enclose· to cut a ring round (a tree, etc): to cut a circular outline around (a gemstone) —*adj* **gird'led.** [O.E. *gyrdel*—*gyrdan,* to gird]

girdle². See **griddle.**

girl *gûrl, n* a female child: a daughter: a young unmarried woman a woman irrespective of age: a sweetheart (*coll*): a maid servant.—*n.* **girl'hood** the state or time of being a girl —*adj* **girl'ie, girl'y** (of magazines, photographs etc) showing nude or scantily clad young women.—Also *n.*—*adj* **girl'ish** or of like a girl —*adv* **girl'ishly.**—*n.* **girl'ishness.**—**Girl Friday** a young woman who acts as secretary or personal assistant in a business office; **girl'friend** sweetheart, or girl who is often one's companion: (**girl friend**) a girl's young female friend, **Girl Guide** a member of an organisation for girls, analogous to the (Boy) Scouts' Association (also **Guide**), **Girl Scout** a member of a similar American organisation.—**old girl** a female former pupil· a kindly disrespectful mode of address or reference to a female of any age or species.

giro *ji'rō, n.* (also with *cap*) a banking system by which money can be transferred direct from the account of one holder to that of another person (or to those of others):—*pl.* **gi'ros.** [Ger., transfer—Gr. *gyros,* ring.]

girt *gûrt, pa.p.* of **gird** in all senses —*v.t.* to gird: to girth —*v t.* to girth.

girth *gûrth, n* belly-band of a saddle: circumferential measure of thickness —*v.t* to put a girth on: to measure the girth of.—*v.t.* to measure in girth. [O.N *gjorth.*]

gism. See **jism.**

gismo, gizmo *giz'mō,* (*coll*) *n.* gadget, thingumajig: —*pl.* **gis'mos, giz'mos.**

gist *jist, n.* the main point or pith of a matter. [O.Fr. *gist* (Fr. *gît*)—O Fr. *gesir* (Fr. *gésir*), to lie—L. *jacēre.*]

git *git,* (*slang*) *n.* a person, used contemptuously: a fool. [*get,* offspring, brat.]

gittern *git'ərn, n.* a kind of guitar, a cithern.—*v.i.* to play on the gittern [O Fr *guiterne,* conn. Gr. *kitharā.*]

give *giv*, *v.t.* to bestow: to impart: to yield: to grant: to donate: to permit: to afford: to furnish: to pay or render, as thanks: to pronounce, as a decision: to show, as a result: to apply, as oneself: to allow or admit.—*v.i.* to yield to pressure: to begin to melt: to grow soft: to open, or give an opening or view, to lead (with *upon*, *on*, *into*):—*pr.p.* **giv'ing;** *pa.t.* **gāve;** *pa.p.* **given** (*giv'n*).—*n.* yielding: elasticity.—*adj.* **giv'en** bestowed: specified: addicted, disposed: granted: admitted.—*ns.* **giv'enness; giv'er; giv'ing** the act of bestowing: the thing given.—*adj.* that gives.— **give'away** a betrayal, revelation, esp. if unintentional: something given free with the aim of increasing sales; **given name** the name bestowed upon the individual, not that of the family—the first or Christian name, distinguished from the *surname.*— **give and take** reciprocity in concession: mutually compensatory variations: fair exchange of repartee; **give away** to give for nothing: to betray: to bestow ceremonially (as a bride); **give birth to** to bring forth: to originate; **give chase** to pursue; **give ear** to listen (to); **give forth** to emit; **give ground, place** to give way, yield; **give in** to to yield to; **give it to one** (*coll.*) to scold or beat anybody severely; **give line, head, rein** etc., to give more liberty or scope; **give me** I would choose if I had the choice; **give off** to emit (e.g. a smell); **give oneself away** to betray one's secret unawares; **give out** to report: to emit: to distribute to individuals; **give over** to transfer: to cease (*N. dial.*); **give the lie to** to charge openly with falsehood; **give tongue** to bark: to utter, expound (with *to*); **give up** to abandon: to surrender: to desist from; **give way** to fall back, to yield, to withdraw: to break, snap, collapse, under strain: to allow traffic in a direction crossing one's path to proceed first. [O.E. *gefan* (W.S. *giefan*).]

gizmo. See **gismo.**

gizzard *giz'ərd*, *n.* a muscular stomach, esp. the second stomach of a bird.—**stick in someone's gizzard** to be more than someone can accept or tolerate. [M.E. *giser*—O.Fr. *guiser*, supposed to be—L. *gigeria* (pl.), cooked entrails of poultry.]

glabella *glə-bel'ə*, *n.* the part of the forehead between the eyebrows and just above their level:—*pl.* **glabell'-ae** (*-bel'ē*).—*adj.* **glabell'ar.** [L. *glaber*, bald, smooth.]

glabrous *glā'brəs*, **glabrate** *glā'brāt*, *-brət*, *adjs.* hairless. [L. *glaber.*]

glacé *gla'sā*, *adj.* frozen, or with ice: iced with sugar: candied: glossy, lustrous, esp. of a thin silk material or kid leather.—*v.t.* to ice with sugar: to candy:—*pres.p.* **glac'éing;** *pa.t.* and *pa.p.* **glac'éed.** [Fr.]

glacial *glās'yəl*, *glā'si-əl*, or *-shəl*, *adj.* icy: frozen: readily or ordinarily solidified: pertaining to ice or its action.—*ns.* **glā'cialist, glaciol'ogist** one who studies the geological action of ice.—*v.t.* **glaciate** (*glās'*, *glāsh'*) to polish by ice action: to subject to the action of land-ice: to freeze.—*n.* **glacia'tion.**—*adj.* **gla-ciolog'ical.**—*n.* **glaciol'ogy** the study of the geological nature, distribution, and action of ice.—**Glacial Period** the Ice Age, or any ice age. [L. *glaciālis*, icy, *glaciāre*, *-ātum*, to freeze—*glaciēs*, ice.]

glacier *glas'yər* or *-i-ər*, *glās'yər* or *glā'shər*, *n.* a mass of ice, fed by snow on a mountain, slowly creeping downhill to where it melts or breaks up into icebergs [Fr.,—*glace*, ice—L. *glaciēs*, ice.]

glaciology. See **glacial.**

glacis *glās-ē*, *glas'is*, *glās'is*, *n.* a gentle slope, esp. in fortification:—*pl.* **glacis** (*glas-ē*, *glas'iz*, *glās'iz*), **glac'ises.** [Fr., orig. a slippery place—L. *glaciēs*, ice.]

glad *glad*, *adj.* pleased: cheerful: bright: giving pleasure.—*v.t.* **gladd'en** to make glad: to cheer.—

adv. **glad'ly.**—*n.* **glad'ness.**—*adj.* **glad'some** (*arch.*) glad: joyous: gay.—**glad eye** (*slang*) an ogle; **glad hand** (*U.S.*) the hand of welcome; **glad'-hand'er** (*U.S.*) one out to make up to all and sundry; **glad rags** (*coll.*) best clothes, dress clothes.—**glad of** glad to have: glad because of. [O.E. *glæd.*]

glade *glād*, *n.* an open space in a wood.

gladiole, gladiolus. See **gladius.**

gladius *glad'i-əs*, *glad'*, *n.* a cuttlefish pen.—*adj.* **gladiate** (*glad'*, *glād'*) sword-shaped.—*n.* **gladiator** (*glad'i-ā-tər*) in ancient Rome, a professional combatant with men or beasts in the arena.—*adj.* **gladiatorial** (*-ə-tō'ri-əl*).—*ns.* **glad'iole, gladiolus** (*glad-i-ō'ləs*) any plant of a genus (*Gladiolus*) of the Iris family, with sword-shaped leaves:—*pl.* **glad'i-oles, gladio'li, gladio'luses.** [L. *gladius*, sword, dim. *gladiŏlus; gladiātor*, a gladiator.]

Gladstonian *glad-stō'ni-ən*, *adj.* pertaining to W. E. Gladstone (1809–98), four times prime minister.—*n.* a follower of Gladstone.—**Gladstone bag** a travelling bag or small portmanteau, opening out flat, named in his honour.

Glagolitic *glag-ō-lit'ik*, *adj.* of or pertaining to Glagol, an ancient Slavonic alphabet, apparently derived from the cursive Greek of the 9th century. [Old Slav. *glagolu*, a word.]

glair *glār*, *n.* the clear part of an egg used as varnish: any viscous, transparent substance.—*v.t.* to varnish with white of eggs. [Fr. *glaire*, perh.—L.L. *clāra* (*ōvī*), white (of egg)—L. *clārus*, clear.]

glamour, in U.S. **glamor**, *glam'ər*, *n.* fascination: enchantment: groomed beauty and studied charm.—*v.t.* to enchant, betwitch, cast a spell over.—*adjs.* **glam** (*slang*) glamorous; **glam'orous** full of glamour: bewitching, alluring.—*n.* **glamorisa'tion**, *-z-.*—*v.t.* **glamor'ise**, *-ize* to make glamorous: to romanticise.—*adv.* **glam'orously.**—**glamour boy, girl** (*coll.*) a man or woman considered to be very glamorous (often *derog.*). [M.E. *gramery*, skill in grammar, hence magic.]

glance[1] *glāns*, *v.i.* to fly (off) obliquely on striking: to make a passing allusion, esp. unfavourable (with *at*): to dart a reflected ray: to flash: to snatch a momentary view (with *at*).—*v.t.* to cause to glance: to deflect.—*n.* an oblique impact or movement: a stroke by which the ball is allowed to glance off an upright bat to fine leg (*cricket*): a sudden shoot of reflected light: a darting of the eye: a momentary look.—*n.* and *adj.* **glanc'ing.**—*adv.* **glanc'ingly.**—**at a glance** immediately, at a first look.

glance[2] *glāns*, *n.* a black or grey mineral with metallic lustre. [Ger. *Glanz*, glance, lustre.]

gland[1] *gland*, *n.* a secreting structure in plant or animal.—*adjs.* **glandif'erous** bearing acorns or nuts; **gland'-iform** resembling a gland: acorn-shaped; **gland'ular**, **gland'ulous** containing, consisting of, or pertaining to glands.—*n.* **gland'ule** a small gland.—*adj.* **glandulif'erous.**—*n.* **glans** (*glanz*) an acorn or similar fruit: a glandular structure (**glans clitoris, penis** the extremity of the clitoris, penis):—*pl.* **gland'es** (*-ēz*).— **glandular fever** a disease characterised by slight fever, enlargement of glands, and increase in the white cells of the blood. [L. *glāns*, *glandis*, an acorn.]

gland[2] *gland*, *n.* a device for preventing leakage at a point where a rotating or reciprocating shaft emerges from a vessel containing fluid under pressure.

glanders *gland'ərz*, *n. sing.* a malignant, contagious, and fatal disease of the horse and ass (and man), showing itself esp. on the mucous membrane of the nose, upon the lungs, and on the lymphatic system —*adjs.* **gland'ered, gland'erous** affected with glanders. [O.Fr. *glandre*, a gland.]

glandiferous, glandular, etc., glans. See **gland**[1].

glare *glār*, *n.* an oppressive or unrelieved dazzling light (also *fig.*): cheap or showy brilliance: a fierce stare.—*v.i.* to emit a hard, fierce, dazzling light: to be obtrusively noticeable, to shine dazzingly: to stare fiercely.—*v.t.* to send forth or express with a glare.—*adj.* **glar'ing** bright, and dazzling: flagrant.—*adv.* **glar'ingly.**—*n.* **glar'ingness.** [M.E. *glāren*, to shine.]

glass *gläs*, *n.* a hard, amorphous, brittle substance, usually transparent, made by fusing together one or more of the oxides of silicon, boron, or phosphorus with certain basic oxides (e.g. sodium, magnesium, calcium, potassium), and cooling the product rapidly to prevent crystallisation: an article made of or with glass, esp. a drinking-vessel, a mirror, a lens, the cover of a watch-face, a weather-glass, a telescope, etc.: the quantity of liquid a glass holds: any fused substance like glass, with a vitreous fracture: (*pl.*) spectacles.—*adj.* made of glass.—*v.t.* to glaze: to polish highly: to put in, under, or behind glass: to furnish with glass: to reflect in glass.—*n.* **glass'ful** as much as a glass will hold:—*pl.* **glass'fuls.**—*v.t.* and *v.i.* **glass'ify** to (cause to) become (like) glass.—*adv.* **glass'ily.**—*ns.* **glassine** (*-ēn'*) a transparent paper, used for book-covers; **glass'iness.**—*adj.* **glass'y** like glass: of eyes, expressionless.—**glass'-blower; glass'-blowing** the process of making glassware by inflating a viscid mass; **glass's cloth** a cloth for drying glasses: a material woven from glass threads: a polishing cloth covered with powdered glass; **glass'-cutter** a tool for cutting sheets of glass: one who does cut-glass work; **glass'-cutting** the act or process of cutting, shaping, and ornamenting the surface of glass; **glass eye** an artificial eye made of glass; **glass fibre** glass melted and then drawn out into extremely fine fibres, which are later to be spun, woven, etc. (also **fibreglass**); **glass'house** a glass factory: a house made of glass or largely of glass, esp. a greenhouse: military detention barracks.—*adj.* **glass'like.**—**glass'-paper** paper coated with finely pounded glass, used like sand-paper; **glass'-snake** a legless lizard (*Ophisaurus*) with brittle tail; **glass'-soap** manganese dioxide or other substance used by glassmakers to remove colouring from glass; **glass'ware** articles made of glass; **glass wool** glass spun into woolly fibres; **glass'work** furnishings or articles made of glass: (usu. in *pl.*) a glass factory; **glass'worker.—live in a glass house** to be open to attack or retort; **water, or soluble, glass** sodium or potassium silicate. [O.E. *glæs.*]

Glaswegian *glas-, gläs-wēj'(y)ən, n.* a native or citizen of Glasgow.—Also *adj.* [Modelled on *Norwegian.*]

glauberite *glö'bər-īt, n.* a greyish-white mineral, sodium calcium sulphate, found chiefly in rock-salt, named after the German chemist Johann Rudolf *Glauber* (1604–68).—**Glauber('s) salt** (*glow'bər, glo'bər*) hydrated sodium sulphate, discovered by him.

glaucescence, etc. See **glaucous.**

glaucoma *glö-kō'mə, n.* an insidious disease of the eye, marked by increased tension within the eyeball and growing dimness of vision.—*adj.* **glaucomatous** (*-kōm'ə-təs, -kom'*). [Gr. *glaukōma*, cataract; see **glaucous.**]

glaucous *glö'kəs, adj.* sea-green: greyish-blue: covered with a fine greenish or bluish bloom (*bot.*).—*n.* **glaucescence** (*-ses'əns*).—*adj.* **glaucesc'ent** somewhat glaucous. [L. *glaucus*—Gr. *glaukos*, bluish-green or grey (orig. gleaming).]

glaze *glāz, v.t.* to furnish or set with glass: to cover with a thin surface of glass or something glassy: to give a glassy surface to.—*n.* the glassy coating put upon pottery: a thin coat of transparent colour: any shining exterior.—*v.i.* to become glassy.—*ns.* **glā'zer** a workman who glazes pottery, paper, etc.; **glā'zier** (*-zyər*) one who set glass in window-frames, etc ; **glā'zing** the

act or art of setting glass: the art of covering with a vitreous substance.—*adj.* **glā'zy.** [M.E. *glasen*—*glas*, glass; see **glass.**]

gleam *glēm, v.i.* to glow or shine, usu. not very brightly.—*v.t.* to flash.—*n.* a faint or moderate glow: a small stream of light: a beam: brightness: often used fig. as *a gleam of hope, a gleam of understanding.*—*n.* and *adj.* **gleam'ing.**—*adj.* **gleam'y** casting gleams or rays of light. [O.E. *glǣm*, gleam, brightness; see **glimmer**[1].]

glean *glēn, v.t.* to gather in handfuls after the reapers: to collect (what is thinly scattered, neglected, or overlooked): to learn by laboriously scraping together pieces of information.—*v.t.* to gather the corn left by a reaper or anything that has been left by others: to gather facts bit by bit.—*n.* that which is gleaned: the act of gleaning.—*ns.* **glean'er; glean'ing.** [O.Fr. *glener* (Fr. *glaner*), through L.L. *glenāre*; origin unknown.]

glebe *glēb, n.* the land attached to a parish church.—**glebe'-house** a manse. [L. *glēba*, a clod.]

glee *glē, n.* joy: mirth and gaiety: impish enjoyment: a song or catch in parts, strictly one without an accompaniment (*mus.*).—*adjs.* **glee'ful, glee'some** merry.—**glee club** (chiefly *U.S.*) a club for singing glees, part-songs etc. [O.E. *glēo, glīw*, mirth.]

gleet *glēt, n.* a viscous, transparent discharge from a mucous surface.—*v.t.* to discharge gleet.—*adj.* **gleet'y.** [O.Fr. *glette, glecte*, a flux.]

glei. See **gley**[2].

glen *glen, n.* a narrow valley with a stream, often with trees: a depression, usu. of some extent, between hills. [Gael. *gleann.*]

glengarry *glen-gar'i, n.* a Highlander's cap of thick-milled woollen, generally rising to a point in front, with ribbons hanging down behind. [*Glengarry* in Inverness-shire.]

glenoid, -al *glē'noid, -əl, adjs.* socket-shaped: slightly cupped.—Also *n.* [Gr. *glēnoeidēs—glēnē*, a socket.]

gley, glei *glā, n.* a bluish-grey sticky clay found under some types of very damp soil. [Russ. *gley*, clay.]

glia *glī'ə, glē'ə, n.* neuroglia.—*adj.* **gli'al.**—*ns.* **gli'adin, gli'adine** a protein in gluten.—*n.* **gliō'ma** a tumour of the neuroglia in the brain and spinal cord:—*pl.* **gliō'mata, gliō'mas.**—*adj.* **gliō'matous.**—*n.* **gliomatō'sis** diffuse overgrowth of neuroglia in the brain or spinal chord. [Gr. *gliā*, glue.]

glib *glib, adj.* easy: facile: fluent and plausible.—*adv.* **glib'ly.**—*n.* **glib'ness.** [Cf. Du. *glibberig*, slippery.]

glide *glīd, v.i.* to slide smoothly and easily: to flow gently: to pass smoothly or stealthily: to travel through the air without expenditure of power: to travel by glider: to play a glide stroke.—*n.* act of gliding: a transitional sound produced in passing from one position to another (*phon.*): a smooth and sliding dance-step: an inclined plane or slide: stretch of shallow gliding water.—*ns.* **glīd'er** one who, or that which, glides: an aircraft like an aeroplane without engine (a *powered glider* has a small engine): a hydroplane; **glīd'ing** the action of the verb in any sense: the sport of flying in a glider.—*adv.* **glīd'ingly.**—**glide slope, path** the slope along which aircraft are assumed to come in for landing, marked out, e.g. by a radio beam. [O.E. *glīdan*, to slip; Ger. *gleiten.*]

glim *glim, n.* a light (*slang*): an eye (*slang*). [Cf **gleam, glimmer;** and Ger *Glimm*, a spark.]

glimmer[1] *glim'ər, v.i.* to burn or appear faintly.—*ns.* a faint light: feeble rays of light: an inkling, faint perception; **glimm'ering** a glimmer: an inkling.—*adv* **glimm'eringly.**—*adj.* **glimm'ery.** [M E. *glemern*, freq. from root of **gleam.**]

glimmer[2] *glim'ər, n.* mica [Ger.]

glimpse _glimps_, _n._ a short gleam (_arch_). a passing appearance: a momentary view.—_v.t._ to get a glimpse of [M E. _glymsen_, to glimpse.]

glint _glint_, _v.i._ to flash with a glittering light.—_v.t._ to reflect.—_n._ a gleam. [Earlier _glent_; prob. Scand.]

glissade _glēs-ad'_, _v.i._ to slide or glide down.—_n._ act of sliding down a slope: a gliding movement in dancing. [Fr]

glissando _glēs-an'dō_, _n._ the effect produced by sliding the finger along keyboard or strings: a similar effect on the trombone, etc.:—_pl._ **glissandos.**—Also _adj._ and _adv._ [It., from Fr. _glissant_, sliding.]

glisten _glis'n_, _v.i._ to shine, as light reflected from a wet or oily surface.—_n._ gleam. [M.E. _glisnen_—O.E _glisnian_, to shine; cf. Du. _glinsteren_.]

glister _glis'tər_, (_arch._) _v.i._ to sparkle, glitter.—_adj._ **glis'tering.** [M.E. _glistren_; cf **glisten**, and Du. _glisteren_.]

glit _glit_, _n._ sticky, slimy or greasy material: gleet [gleet.]

glitch _glich_, _n._ an instance of imperfect functioning in a spacecraft, as, e g. a minute change in voltage on a line.

glitter _glit'ər_, _v.i._ to sparkle with light: to be splendid: to be showy.—_n._ sparkle: showiness.—_n._ and _adj._ **glitt'ering.**—_adv._ **glitt'eringly.**—_adj._ **glitt'ery.** [M.E. _gliteren_.]

glitzy _glits'i_, (_U.S. coll._) _adj._ showy, garish, gaudy: glittering.—_n._ **glitz** a back-formation. [Perh. from Ger. _glitzern_, to glitter.]

gloaming _glōm'ing_, _n._ twilight, dusk. [Apparently from a derivative of O.E. _glōmung—glōm_, twilight.]

gloat _glōt_, _v.i._ to eye with intense, usu. malicious, satisfaction (esp. with _over_): generally, to exult (over).—_n._ an act of gloating.—_adv._ **gloat'ingly.** [Perh. O.N. _glotta_, to grin.]

glob _glob_, (_coll._) _n._ a roundish drop, dollop, etc. of a (semi-)liquid substance.

globe _glōb_, _n._ a ball: a round body, a sphere: the earth: a sphere representing the earth (terrestrial globe), or one representing the heavens (celestial globe): an orb, emblem of sovereignty: a lamp glass: a nearly spherical glass vessel.—_v.t._, _v.i._ to form into a globe. —_adj._ **glōb'al** spherical: world-wide: affecting, or taking into consideration, the whole world or all peoples: comprehensive.—_ns._ **globalisa'tion, -z-.**— _v.t._ **glō'balise, -ize** to make global.—_adv._ **glōb'ally.**— _adjs._ **glōb'ate, -d** globe-shaped; **globed** globe-shaped: having a globe.—_n._ **glob'in** the protein constituent of haemoglobin, a histone.—_adjs._ **glōb'old, glōbose'** (or _glōb'_) globate.—_n._ **globos'ity** (something having) the quality of being globate.—_adjs._ **glōb'ous; globular** (_glob'ū-lər_) spherical.—_n._ **globularity** (_glob-ū-lar'i-ti_).—_adv._ **glōb'ularly.**—_ns._ **glōb'ūle** a little globe or round particle: a drop: a small pill; **glōb'ulet; glōb'ū-lin** any one of a class of proteins soluble in dilute salt solutions but not in pure water; **glōb'ulite** a minute spheroidal crystallite occurring esp. in glassy rocks.— _adjs._ **globulif'erous** producing or having globules; **glōb'ulous.**—**globe'-fish** any fish of the families _Diodontidae_ and _Tetrodontidae_, capable of blowing itself up into a globe; **globe'-flower** a plant (_Trollius_) with a globe of large showy sepals enclosing the small inconspicuous petals; **globe'-trotter** one who goes sightseeing about the world, **globe'-trotting.** [L. _globus._]

Globigerina _glob-i-jə-rī'nə_, _n._ a genus of Protozoa with calcareous shell of globose chambers in a spiral: (without _cap._) (the shell of) a member of this genus: —_pl._ **globigerinae** (_-i'nē_).—**globigerina ooze** a deep-sea deposit of globigerina shells. [L. _globus_, globe, _gerĕre_, to carry]

globin, globold, globule, etc. See **globe**.

glockenspiel _glok'ən-shpēl_, _n._ an orchestral instrument consisting of a set of bells or bars struck by hammers, with or (more usually) without a keyboard. [Ger _Glocke_, bell. _Spiel_, play.]

glomerate _glom'ər-āt_, _adj._ balled: clustered in heads —_n._ **glomerā'tion.**—_adj._ **glomer'ūlate** of a glomerule.—_n._ **glom'erule** (_-ōōl; bot._) a little ball of spores: a cluster of short-stalked flowers. [L. _glomerāre_, _-ātum—glomus_, _glomeris_, a clew of yarn.]

gloom _glōōm_, _n._ partial darkness: cloudiness: a dark place: heaviness of mind: hopelessness: sullenness.— _v.i._ to be or look sullen or dejected: to be or become cloudy, dark or obscure: to scowl.—_adj._ **gloom'ful.**— _adv._ **gloom'ily.**—_n._ **gloom'iness.**—_adj._ **gloom'y** dim or obscure: dimly lighted: depressed in spirits: dismal. [M.E. _gloumbe_; see **glum.**]

gloria¹ _glō'_, _glō'ri-ə_, _n._ an aureole: a halo. [L.]

gloria² _glō'ri-a_, _glō'ri-ə_, (L.) _n._ glory: any doxology beginning with the word "Gloria".—**gloria in excelsis** (_in ek-, ik-sel'sis, eks-chel'sis, eks-kel'sēs_) glory (to God) on high; **gloria Patri** (_pat'rī, 'ri, pät'rē_) glory (be) to the Father.

glorify _glō'_, _glō'ri-fī_, _v.t._ to make glorious: to cast glory upon: to honour: to exalt to glory or happiness: to ascribe honour to: to ascribe great charm, beauty, etc., to, usually to a markedly exaggerated extent: to worship:—_pr.p._ **glō'rifying;** _pa.t._ and _pa.p._ **glō'rified.**—_n._ **glorifica'tion** an act of glorifying: a doxology. [L. _glōria_, glory, _facĕre_, to make.]

glory _glō'_, _glō'ri_, _n._ renown: exalted or triumphant honour: the occasion of praise: an object of supreme pride: splendour, beauty: resplendent brightness: summit of attainment, prosperity or gratification: in religious symbolism, a combination of the nimbus and the aureola, but often erroneously used for the nimbus: the presence of God: the manifestation of God to the blessed in heaven: a representation of the heavens opened: heaven.—_v.i._ to exult proudly: to rejoice:—_pr.p._ **glō'rying;** _pa.t._ and _pa.p._ **glō'ried.**— _interj._ expressing surprise.—_adj._ **glō'rious** noble: splendid: conferring renown.—_adv._ **glō'riously.**—_n._ **glō'riousness.**—**glo'rybox** (_Austr._) a box in which a young woman keeps her trousseau, etc.—a bottom drawer.—**glory** be a devout ascription of Glory to God: hence, an ejaculation of exultation: an interj. expressing surprise; **Old Glory** the Stars and Stripes. [O.Fr. _glorie_ and L. _glōria_.]

glory-hole _glō'_, _glō'ri-hōl_, _n._ a glass-maker's supplementary furnace: a hole for viewing the inside of a furnace: a nook or receptacle for miscellaneous odds and ends: a steward's room on a ship: a hiding-place: an excavation. [Perh. M.E. _glory_, to defile, or _Scot._ _glaury_, miry, or **glory**, and **hole.**]

gloss¹ _glos_, _n._ brightness or lustre, as from a polished surface: external show.—_v.t._ to give a superficial lustre to: to render plausible: to palliate.—_n._ **gloss'er.**— _adv._ **gloss'ily.**—_n._ **gloss'iness.**—_adj._ **gloss'y** smooth and shining: highly polished.—_n._ (_coll._) a glossy magazine.—**gloss paint** paint containing varnish, giving a hard, shiny finish; **glossy magazine** a magazine printed on glossy paper, abounding in illustrations and advertisements.—**gloss over** to explain away, render more acceptable. [Cf. O.N. _glossi_, blaze, _glōa_, to glow; see **glass.**]

gloss² _glos_, _n._ a marginal or interlinear explanation, e.g. of an obscure or unusual word: an explanation: a collection of explanations of words.—_v.t._ to give a gloss on: to explain away.—_v.i._ to comment or make explanatory remarks.—_n._ **gloss'a** (_anat._) the tongue. —_adjs._ **gloss'al; gloss'arial** relating to a glossary: containing explanation.—_ns._ **gloss'arist** (_-ə-rist_) a writer of a gloss or of a glossary; **gloss'ary** a collection of glosses: a partial dictionary for a special purpose; **glossa'tor, gloss'er** a writer of glosses or comments, a commentator, **glossec'tomy** surgical removal of the tongue; **gloss'eme** (*linguistics*) a unit or feature of a language that in itself carries significance and cannot be further analysed into meaningful units, **glossi'tis** inflammation of the tongue; **glossog'rapher.**—*adj* **glossograph'ical.**—*ns* **glossog'raphy** the writing of glosses or comments; **glossola'lia** the 'gift of tongues', abnormal utterance under religious emotion —*adj* **glossolog'ical.**—*n.* **glossol'ogist.** [Gr. *glōssa, glōtta,* tongue, a word requiring explanation]

glottis *glot'is, n.* the opening of the larynx or entrance to the windpipe:—*pl.* **glott'ises, glott'ides** (*-ι-dēz*) — *adjs.* **glott'al** of the glottis, **glott'ic** pertaining to the glottis or to the tongue: linguistic.—**glottal stop** a consonant sound produced by closing and suddenly opening the glottis, occurring as a phoneme in some languages, e.g. Arabic, and as a feature of others, and sometimes heard as a substitute for *t* in English [Gr. *glōttis—glōtta,* the tongue.]

glove *gluv, n.* a covering for the hand, with a sheath for each finger: a boxing-glove.—*v.t.* to cover with, or as with, a glove.—*adj.* **gloved.**—*n.* **glov'er** one who makes or sells gloves —**glove box** a closed compartment in which radioactive or toxic material may be manipulated by the use of gloves attached to the walls; **glove compartment** a small compartment in the front of a car, usu. part of the dashboard, in which gloves, etc. can be kept; **glove puppet** a puppet worn on the hand like a glove and manipulated by the fingers.—**the gloves are off** (*coll.*) now the fight, argument, etc. is about to begin. [O.E *glōf.*]

glow *glō, v.i.* to shine with an intense heat: to burn without flame: to emit a steady light: to flush: to tingle with bodily warmth or with emotion: to be ardent.—*n.* a shining with heat: a luminous appearance: a feeling of warmth: brightness of colour: warmth of feeling.—*adj.* **glow'ing.**—*adv.* **glow'-ingly.**—**glow discharge** a luminous electrical discharge in gas at low pressure; **glow'-worm** a beetle, esp. *Lampyris noctiluca,* whose larvae and wingless females are luminous. [O.E. *glōwan,* to glow.]

glower *glow'ər, glowr, v.i.* to stare frowningly to scowl.—*n.* a fierce or threatening stare.

Gloxinia *glok-sin'ι-ə, n.* a tropical American genus of Gesneriaceae, with bright bell-shaped flowers. [*Gloxin,* a German botanist.]

glucagon *glōō'kə-gon, n.* a polypeptide hormone secreted by the pancreas which accelerates glycogen breakdown in the liver, so increasing blood glucose levels. [Gr *glykys,* sweet.]

glucoprotein. See **glycoprotein.**

glucose *glōō'kōs, n.* grape-sugar or dextrose.—*ns.* **glu'-coside** any of the vegetable products making up a large group of the glycosides, which, on treatment with acids or alkalis, yield glucose or kindred substance; **glucosū'ria** glycosuria.—*adj* **glucosū'ric.** [Gr. *glykys,* sweet.]

glue *glōō, n.* an impure gelatine got by boiling animal refuse, used as an adhesive: any of several synthetic substances used as adhesives.—*v t.* to join with, or as with, glue or other adhesive:—*pr.p.* **glu'ing;** *pa.t.* and *pa.p.* **glued.**—*n.* **glu'er** one who cements with glue.—*adj.* **glu'ey** containing glue: sticky: viscous.—*n.* **glu'eyness.**—**glue'-pot** a vessel for melting or holding glue: a sticky place; **glue'-sniffer** a person who inhales the fumes of certain types of glue to achieve hallucinatory effects, etc.; **glue'-sniffing** the practice, sometimes fatal, of doing this —**marine glue** not a glue, but a composition of rubber, shellac, and oil, that resists sea-water. [Fr. *glu*—L L. *glus, glūtis.*]

glug *glug, n* a word representing the sound of liquid being poured from a bottle, down one's throat, etc.— *v.i.* to flow making this sound:—*pr.p.* **glugg'ing;** *pa.t.* and *pa.p.* **glugged.** [Imit.]

glum *glum, adj.* sullen: gloomy.—*adv* **glum'ly.**—*n.* **glum'ness.** [M.E. *glombe, glome,* to frown.]

glume *glōōm, n.* an outer sterile bract which, alone or with others, encloses the spikelet in grasses and sedges.—*adj.* **glumā'ceous** like a glume, thin, brownish and papery. [L. *glūma,* husk—*glūbēre,* to peel.]

gluon *glōō'on, n* the name given to a hypothetical particle thought of as passing between quarks and so signifying the force that holds them together [glue.]

glut *glut, v.t.* to gorge: to feed to satiety: to saturate: —*pr p.* **glutt'ing;** *pa.t.* and *pa.p.* **glutt'ed.**—*n.* a glutting: a surfeit: an oversupply. [L. *gluttīre,* to swallow]

glutaeus, gluteus *glōō-tē'əs, n* any of three muscles of the buttock and hip —*pl.* **glutae'ι, glutē'ι.**—*adj* **glutae'al, glutē'al.** [Gr. *gloutos,* the rump.]

gluten *glōō'tən, n.* the nitrogenous part of the flour of wheat and other grains, insoluble in water.—*ns.* **glu'-tamate** a salt of glutamic acid; **glu'tamine** (*-min, -mīn*) an amino acid found in proteins —*adjs.* **glu'-tenous** containing, made from, etc. gluten; **glu'tinous** gluey: tenacious: sticky.—*adv* **glu'tinously.**—**glu-tam'ic** or **glutamin'ic acid** an important amino-acid, $HOOC \cdot CH_2 \cdot CH_2 \cdot CH(NH_2) \cdot COOH.$ [L. *glūten, -inis,* glue; cf. **glue.**]

glutton *glut'n, n* one who eats to excess: one who is extremely eager (for something, e.g. hard work).— *v.i.* **glutt'onise, -ize** to eat to excess.—*adjs.* **glutt'on-ous, glutt'onish** given to, or consisting in, gluttony.— *adv.* **glutt'onously.**—*n.* **glutt'ony** excess in eating.— **glutton for punishment** one who seems indefatigable in seeking and performing strenuous or unpleasant work, etc. [Fr. *glouton*—L *glūtō, -ōnis—glūtīre, gluttīre,* to devour]

glutton[2] *glut'n, n.* a N European carnivore (*Gulo gulo*), 2-3 ft. long, having dark, shaggy fur: a related animal (*Gulo luscus*) of N. America, the wolverine. [Trans. of Ger. *Vielfrass,* lit. large feeder.]

glycerine, glycerin *glis'ə-rēn, -ιn,* **glycerol** *-ol, ns.* a trihydric alcohol, a colourless, viscid, neutral inodorous fluid, of a sweet taste, soluble in water and alcohol.—*adj.* **glycer'ic.**—*ns.* **glyc'eride** an ester of glycerol; **gly'ceryl** a radical of which glycerine is the hydroxide. [Gr. *glykeros,* sweet—*glykys.*]

glycin, glycine *glis'in, glī'sιn, -sēn, -sēn', n.* amino-acetic acid or glycocoll, $CH_2(NH_2) \cdot COOH,$ a sweetish colourless crystalline solid first prepared from glue. [Gr. *glykys,* sweet.]

glycogen *glik'ō-jən,* or *glīk', n.* animal starch, a starch found in the liver, yielding glycose on hydrolysis.— *adj.* **glycogen'ic.** [Gr. *glykys,* sweet, and the root of *gennaein,* to produce.]

glycol *glik'ol, glīk'ol, n.* the type of a class of compounds with two hydroxyl groups on adjacent carbon atoms, and so intermediate between alcohol and glycerine. [From *glycerine* and *alcohol.*]

glycoprotein *glī-kō-prō'tēn,* **glucoprotein** *glōō-kō-, ns* any of the compounds formed by the conjugation of a protein with a substance containing a carbohydrate group other than a nucleic acid. [Gr. *glykys,* sweet, and **protein.**]

glycose *glī'kōs, n.* glucose.—*n.* **gly'coside** any of a group of compounds derived from monosaccharides, yielding, on hydrolysis, a sugar and usu. a non-carbohydrate.—*adj* **glycosid'ic.**—*n.* **glycosū'ria** the presence of sugar in the urine.—*adj.* **glycosū'ric.** [Gr. *glykys,* sweet]

glyph *glif, n* (*archit*) an ornamental channel or

fluting, usually vertical: a sculptured mark —*adj.* **glyph'ic** carved [Gr. *glyphē*—*glyphein*, to carve.]

glyptic *glip'tik*, *adj* pertaining to carving, esp gemcarving.—*n sing* **glyp'tics** the art of gemengraving.—*adj.* **glyptograph'ic.**—*n* **glyptog'raphy** the art of engraving on precious stones. [Gr *glyptos*, carved.]

gnar[1] *nar*, *v i.* to snarl or growl —Also **gnarr, knar, gnarl.** [Onomatopoeic]

gnar[2]. See **knar**[1].

gnarl[1], **knarl** *narl*, *n* a lump or knot in a tree —*adjs* **gnarled, gnarl'y** knotty contorted rugged, weatherbeaten [After Shakespeare's *gnarled* for **knurled.**]

gnarl[2], **gnarr.** See **gnar**[1]

gnash *nash*, *v.t.* and *v i.* to strike (the teeth) together in rage or pain: to bite with a snap or clash of the teeth —*n.* a snap of the teeth —*adv* **gnash'ingly.** [M E *gnasten*, prob from O N, ultimately onomatopoeic]

gnat *nat*, *n* any small fly of the family Culicidae, of which the females are commonly bloodsuckers: a mosquito: extended to other small insects.—**gnat'-catcher** any of the insectivorous American songbirds of the genus *Polioptila.* [O.E *gnæt*]

gnathic *nath'ik*, **gnathal** *nath'*, *nā'thəl*, *adjs* of the jaws. [Gr. *gnathos*, jaw]

gnaw *no*, *v i.* and *v i* (with *at*) to bite with a scraping or mumbling movement. to wear away to bite in agony or rage. to distress persistently (*fig*).—*pa t* **gnawed;** *pa p* **gnawed, gnawn.**—*n* **gnaw'er** one who gnaws a rodent. [O E *gnagan*]

gneiss *nīs*, *n* coarse-grained foliated metamorphic rock, usually composed of quartz, feldspar, and mica. —*adjs* **gneiss'ic, gneissit'ic** of the nature of gneiss, **gneiss'oid** like gneiss; **gneiss'ose** having the structure of gneiss. [Ger. *Gneis*]

gnocchi *no'kē*, *no'kē*, *nyok'kē*, *n* a dish of small dumplings made from flour, semolina, or potatoes, sometimes served with a sauce [It]

gnome[1] *nōm*, *nō'mē*, *n.* a pithy and sententious saying, generally in verse, embodying some moral sentiment or precept—*pl.* **gnomes** (*nōmz*, *nō'mēz*), **gnomae** (*nō'mē*) —*adj* **gnō'mic.** [Gr *gnōmē*, an opinion, maxim]

gnome[2] *nōm*, *n.* a sprite guarding the inner parts of the earth and its treasures· a dwarf or goblin —*adj* **gnōm'ish.—the gnomes** of Europe, Zurich etc , the big bankers [Paracelsus's Latin *gnomus.*]

gnomon *nō'mon*, *n.* the pin of a dial, whose shadow points to the hour· an upright rod for taking the sun's altitude by its shadow· an index or indicator: that which remains of a parallelogram when a similar parallelogram within one of its angles is taken away (*geom*) —*adjs.* **gnomonic, -al** (*-mon'*) pertaining to a gnomon or to the art of gnomonics —*adv* **gnomon'ically.**—*n sing.* **gnomon'ics** the art of measuring time by the sundial [Gr. *gnōmōn*, a gnomon, a carpenter's square—*gnōnai* (aorist), to know]

gnosis *nō'sis*, *n.* knowledge, esp spiritual —*pl* **gnō'sēs.**—*gnō'sis* (-(g)*nō'sis*) in composition, knowledge, recognition:—*pl.* **-gnō'sēs.**—adjective and adverb combining forms **-gnos'tic, -gnos'tically** —*ns* **gnōseol'ogy, gnōsiol'ogy** the philosophy of knowledge —*adj* **gnos'tic** (*-nos'*) having knowledge: (with *cap*) pertaining to Gnosticism —*n.* (with *cap*) an adherent of Gnosticism —*adj* **gnos'tical** having knowledge.—*adv.* **gnos'tically.**—*n* **Gnos'ticism** the eclectic doctrines of the Gnostics, whose philosophy, esp in early Christian times, taught the redemption of the spirit from matter by spiritual knowledge, and believed creation to be a process of emanation from the original essence or Godhead [Gr *gnōsis* knowledge, *adj gnōstikos*—*gignōskein*, to know]

gnu *nōō*, *nū*, *n* a large African antelope, superficially like a horse or buffalo —*pl* **gnu, gnus.** [From Hottentot]

go[1] *gō*, *v.i* to pass from one place to another: to be in motion: (of a path, etc.) to lead or give access (to): to proceed: to run (in words or notes): (of verse) to flow smoothly: to depart: to work, to be in operation: to sound (as a bell, gun): to take a direction: to extend· (with *to*) to attend habitually (school, church, etc.)· (of a rumour, etc) to be current: to be valid, hold true: to be reckoned, to be regarded (as)· to be known (*by* or *under* a name)· to be on the whole or ordinarily to tend, serve as a means· to be or continue in a particular state: to elapse: to be sold: to be spent, consumed: to move, act, in a way shown or specified· to be assigned or awarded (to). to harmonise (as colours): to die. (with *by*, (*up*)*on*) to be directed by, to act according to: (with *to*) to subject oneself (to expense, trouble, etc) to become, or become as if to happen in a particular way: to turn.out· to fare: to contribute (to, towards, a whole, purpose or result) to be contained to be able to pass: to give way —*v.t.* to stake, bet to call, bid, declare·—*pr p. gō'ing, pa.p* **gone** (*gon*) (see separate articles), *pa.t* **went** (supplied from *wend*) —*n.* a going· affair, matter (*coll*)· energy, activity (*coll*): a bargain, deal (*coll*): a spell, turn, bout (*coll*) a portion supplied at one time (*coll*)· an attempt (*coll.*)·—*pl.* **goes.**—*interj.* (called to start race, etc) begin!—*ns* **gō'er; gō'ing** see separate article.—*adj.* **gō'-ahead** dashing, energetic: enterprisingly progressive.—*n* permission to proceed.—*adj.* **gō'-as-you-please** not limited by rules· informal —**go'-between** an intermediary; **go'-by** any intentional disregard, as in *give (someone) the go-by*; **go'-cart** same as **go-kart**; **go'-gett'er** (*coll.*) forceful aggressive person who sets about getting what he wants.—*adj.* **go'-gett'ing** forcefully ambitious.—**go'-kart** a low racing vehicle consisting of a frame with wheels, engine, and steering gear (*no usu* **kart**).—**all systems go** everything in the spacecraft operating as it should· everything in readiness; **at one go** in a single attempt or effort, simultaneously; **from the word go** from the very beginning; **give it a go** (*coll*) to try, make an attempt at something, **go about** to pass from place to place· to busy oneself with: to seek, endeavour to (with *pr p*): (of rumour, etc) to circulate: (of a ship) to change course; **go about one's business** to attend to one's own affairs· to be off; **go abroad** to go to a foreign country or out of doors: (of rumour, etc) to circulate; **go against** to turn out unfavourably for· to be repugnant to· to be in conflict with, **go ahead** to proceed at once; **go along with** to agree with, support, go and (*coll*) to be so stupid or unfortunate as to (e g hurt oneself); **go at** to attack vigorously, **go back on** to betray, fail to keep (promise, etc); **go bail** to give security (for); **go down** to sink, decline: to be swallowed, believed, or accepted (esp with pleasure)· to fail to fulfil one's contract (*bridge*). to leave a university, **go down the drain** (*coll*) to be wasted· to become valueless; **go down with** (*coll*) to contract (an illness), **go far** to go a long way (*lit* and *fig*) to achieve success; **go for** to assail. to set out to secure· to go or get or fetch: to be attracted by· to be true of, **go for nothing** to have no value, **go halves** to share equally between two; **go hard with** to prove difficult or unfortunate for; **go in** to enter to assemble regularly (*coll.*): (of sun, moon) to become concealed behind cloud: to take the batting (*cricket*); **go in and out** to come and go freely, **go in for** to make a practice of: to take up as a career or special interest to take part in (a competition, etc), **go into** to enter. to examine thoroughly, investigate to adopt as a profession, etc , **go in with** to enter into partnership with: to join, combine with; **go it** to act in a striking or dashing manner—often in *imper.* by way of encouragement; **go it alone** to undertake a usu. difficult or dangerous task alone: to manage by oneself; **go native** to assimilate oneself to an alien culture or to the way of life of a foreign country (usu. less advanced than one's own); **go off** to leave: to explode: to deteriorate: to proceed to an expected conclusion: to cease to like or be fond of (a person, etc.) (*coll.*): to cease to operate; **go off with** to go away with: to remove, take away (*coll.*); **go on** to continue, to proceed: an exclamation expressing disbelief (*coll.*): to behave, conduct oneself (*coll.*): to talk at length (*coll.*): to be capable of being fitted on to: to appear on stage: to fare: to begin to function: to proceed from (as in *nothing to go on*); **go one better** to excel: to cap a performance; **go one's own way** to act independently; **go one's way to depart; go out** to become extinguished: to become unfashionable: to mingle in society; **go over** to pass in review: to recall: to revise; **go over to** to transfer allegiance to; **go places** to travel widely: to go far in personal advancement; **go round** to be enough for all; **go slow** (of workers) deliberately to restrict output or effort in order to obtain concessions from employers (*adj.* and *n.* **go'-slow'**); **go steady** to court (with *with*); **go through** to perform to the end, often perfunctorily: to examine in order: to undergo; **go through fire and water** to undertake any trouble or risks (from the usage in ancient ordeals); **go through with** to carry out; **go under** to become submerged, overwhelmed, or ruined; **go up** to ascend: to be erected: to be destroyed by fire or explosion: to increase (as e.g. price). to enter a university; **go with** to accompany: to agree with: accord with: to court; **go without** suffer the want of; **go without saying** to be self-evident; **have a go** to make an attempt: (of a member of the public) to tackle a criminal; **have something going for one** to enjoy the advantage of something; **I could go** (*coll.*) I should enjoy (usu. food or drink); **no go** not possible: futile: in vain; **no-go area** a part of a city, etc. to which normal access is prevented by the erection of barricades, esp. by local militants, a paramilitary group, etc.; **on the go** very active; **to be going on with** (*coll.*) for the moment, in the meantime. [O.E. *gān,* to go.]

go² *gō, n.* a Japanese game for two, played with black and white stones (or counters) on a board, the object being to capture opponent's stones and be in control of the larger part of the board. [Jap.]

goad *gōd, n.* a sharp-pointed stick, often tipped with iron, for driving oxen: a stimulus.—*v.t.* to drive with a goad: to urge forward: to incite.—*ns.* **goads'man, goad'ster** one who uses a goad. [O.E. *gād.*]

goal *gōl, n.* the finishing point of a race: the winning-post or a similar marker: a pillar marking the turning-point in a Roman chariot race: the structure or station into which the ball is driven in some games: the sending of the ball between the goalposts or over the crossbar: a score for doing so: an end or aim.—**goal'-keeper** a player charged with defence of the goal (*coll.* **goal'ie); goal'-kick** (*soccer*) a free kick awarded to a defending player when an opponent has sent the ball over the goal-line but not between the posts; **goal'-line** the boundary marking each end of the field, on which the goals are situated; **goal'mouth** the space between the goalposts and immediately in front of the goal; **goal'post** one of the upright posts at the goal; **goal'-tender** in ice-hockey, a goalkeeper; **goal'-tending.**

goanna *gō-an'a, n.* in Australia, any large monitor lizard. [Iguana.]

goat *gōt, n.* a ruminant (Capra) allied to the sheep: a

lecher: a foolish person: (in *pl.*) the wicked (*B.*): (with *cap.*) the zodiacal sign or the constellation Capricorn.—*adj.* **goat'ish** resembling a goat, esp. in smell: lustful: foolish.—*ns.* **goat'ishness; goat'ling** a young goat in its second year.—*adj.* **goat'y.**—**goat'-fig** the wild fig; **goat'-god** Pan; **goat'herd** one who tends goats; **goat's'-beard** a composite plant of the genus *Tragopogon,* John-go-to-bed-at-noon: a herbaceous perennial of the genus *Aruncus sylvester*; **goat's'-hair** cirrus clouds; **goat'skin** the skin of the goat: leather, or a wine-skin, made from it; **goat'-sucker** the nightjar, a bird akin to the swift falsely thought to suck goats.—**get one's goat** to enrage one. [O.E. *gāt.*]

goatee *gō-tē', n.* a tuft on the chin, resembling a goat's beard.—*adj.* **goateed'.** [goat and *-ee,* suff. of uncertain meaning.]

gob *gob, n.* the mouth (*slang*): a mouthful, lump.—**gob'-stop'per** a very large hard round sweet for prolonged sucking. [O.Fr. *gobe,* mouthful, lump; cf. Gael. *gob,* mouth.]

gobang *gō-bang', n.* a game played on a board of 256 squares, with fifty counters, the object being to get five in a row. [Jap. *goban.*]

gobbet *gob'it, n.* a mouthful: a lump to be swallowed: an extract, esp. for translation or comment. [O.Fr. *gobet,* dim. of *gobe;* see **gob.**]

gobble *gob'l, v.t.* to swallow in lumps: to swallow hastily (often with *up*).—*v.i.* to eat greedily: to make a noise in the throat, as a turkey-cock.—*n.* **gobb'ler** a turkey-cock. [O.Fr. *gober,* to devour.]

gobbledegook, gobbledygook *gob-əl-di-gōōk', n.* official jargon: rubbish, nonsense. [Imit. of pomposity.]

Gobelin, Gobelins *gōb'ə-lin, -linz, gob'(ə)-, go-blē, n.* a rich French tapestry.—Also *adj.* [From the *Gobelins,* a famous family of French dyers settled in Paris as early as the 15th century.]

goblet *gob'lit, n.* a large drinking-cup, properly one without a handle. [O.Fr. *gobelet,* dim. of *gobel,* of doubtful origin.]

goblin *gob'lin, n.* a frightful sprite: a bogy or bogle. [O.Fr. *gobelin*—L.L. *gobellīnus,* perh.—*cobālus*—Gr. *kobālos,* a mischievous spirit.]

gobo *gō'bō,* (chiefly *U.S.*) *n.* a device used to protect a camera lens from light: a device for preventing unwanted sound from reaching a microphone:—*pl.* **gō'boes, gō'bos.**

goby *gō'bi, n.* any fish of the family **Gobi'idae** small fishes with ventral fins forming a sucker. [L. *gōbius* —Gr. *kōbios,* a fish of the gudgeon kind.]

god *god, n.* a superhuman being, an object of worship: (with *cap.*) the Supreme Being of monotheist religions, the Creator: an idol: an object of excessive devotion: a man of outstandingly fine physique: (*pl.*) the gallery (*theat.*):—*fem.* **godd'ess.**—*ns.* **god'head** state of being a god: divine nature: (*cap.* with *the*) God; **god'hood** position or state of being divine.—*adj.* **god'less** without a god: living without God.—*adv.* **god'lessly.**—*n.* **god'lessness.**—*adj.* **god'like** like a god: divine.—*n.* **god'liness.**—*adj.* **god'ly** like God in character: pious: according to God's laws.—*adj.* and *adv.* **god'ward** towards God.—*adv.* **god'wards.**—*adj.* **god-aw'ful** (*coll.*) very bad: unpleasant, distasteful. —**god'child** a person to whom one is a godparent.— *adjs.* (*coll.*) **godd'am(n), god'damned** damned, accursed, hateful: utter, complete.—Also *adv.*—**god'-daughter** a female godchild; **god'father** a male godparent: the head of a criminal organisation, esp. the mafia (*coll.*).—*adjs.* **God'-fearing** reverencing God; **god'-forgotten, god'-forsaken** (or with *cap.*) remote, miserable, behind the times; **God'-gift'ed; God'-given.**—**god'mother** a female godparent; **god'parent**

one who at baptism, guarantees a child's religious education; **god'send** a very welcome piece of good fortune; **god'son** a male godchild; **god'speed** (also with *cap.*) a wish for good fortune, expressed at parting; **God's truth** an absolute truth—an emphatic asseveration.—**for God's sake** an expression of urgent entreaty: *interj.* expressing, e.g. annoyance, disgust; **God knows** God is my, his, etc., witness that: (*flippantly*) it is beyond human understanding; **God's** (**own**) **country** a particularly well-favoured (esp. scenically beautiful) region; **God willing** if circumstances permit; **household gods** among the Romans, the special gods presiding over the family. [O.E. *god.*]

Godetia gō-dē'sh(y)ə, gə-, *n.* an American genus closely akin to the evening primrose: (without *cap.*) a plant of this genus. [C. H. *Godet*, Swiss botanist.]

godown gō-down', *n.* a warehouse, or a storeroom, in the East. [Malay *gudang.*]

godwit god'wit, *n.* a bird (*Limosa*) of the plover family, with long slightly up-curved bill and long slender legs, with a great part of the tibia bare.

goffer gōf'ər, gof', gōf', *v.t.* to plait, crimp.—*n.* goff'-ering plaits or ruffles, or the process of making them: indented tooling on the edge of a book. [O.Fr. *gauffrer—goffre*, a wafer.]

goggle gog'l, *v.i.* to strain or roll the eyes: (of the eyes) to protrude.—*v.t.* to turn about (the eyes).—*adj.* (of the eyes) rolling: staring: prominent.—*n.* a stare or affected rolling of the eyes: (*pl.*) spectacles with projecting eye-tubes: (*pl.*) protective spectacles: (*pl.*) spectacles (*coll.*): the eyes (*coll.*).—*adj.* gogg'led wearing goggles.—*ns.* gogg'ler a person with goggle eyes (*coll.*): an eye (*slang*): an assiduous television-viewer (*coll.*); gogg'ling.—Also *adj.*—*adj.* gogg'ly. —gogg'le-box (*coll.*) a television-set.—*adj.* gogg'le-eyed having bulging, staring, or rolling eyes.—Also *adv.*

go-go, gogo gō'gō, used loosely as *adj.* active, alert to seize opportunities.—**go-go dancer, girl** a girl who gyrates to a musical accompaniment in night-clubs or discothèques. [à gogo influenced by English go.]

Goidel goi'dəl, *n.* a Gael in the general sense (**Gadhel** (q.v.) now has the same meaning).—*adj.* **Goidelic** (-*del*') Gadhelic. [O.Ir. *Góidel.*]

going[1] gō'ing, *n.* the act of moving: departure: condition of the ground for, e.g., walking, racing: progress. —*adj.* in motion or activity: about, to be had: in existence: current.—**going concern** a business in actual activity (esp. successfully); **going-o'ver** a thorough check, examination: a complete treatment: a beating; **go'ings-on'** behaviour, activities, now esp. if open to censure.—**be hard, heavy, tough**, etc. **going** to prove difficult to do, etc.; **going-away dress** etc., that worn by a bride when leaving on the honeymoon. [go[1].]

going[2] gō'ing, *pr.p.* of go[1], in any sense: about or intending (to).—**going on** (for) approaching (an age or time); **going strong** in full activity, flourishing.

goitre, goi'tər, *n.* morbid enlargement of the thyroid gland, producing a swelling in front of the throat, sometimes accompanied by exophthalmus.—*adjs.* goi'tred; goi'trous. [Fr. *goître*—L. *guttur*, the throat.]

go-kart. See under go[1].

Golconda gol-kon'də, *n.* a rich source of wealth. [Ruined city near Hyderabad, India, once famous for diamond-cutting.]

gold gōld, *n.* a heavy yellow element (Au; atomic number 79), one of the precious metals, used for coin, etc.: articles made of it: money in the form of gold coins: a standard of money value which varies with the price of the metal: the gold standard: riches: anything very precious: the centre of an archery target: a

gold medal: yellow, the colour of gold.—*adj.* made of or like gold.—*adj.* **gold'en** of gold: of the colour of gold: bright, shining like gold: most valuable: happy: most favourable: of outstanding excellence.—*adv.* **gold'enly.**—*adjs.* **gold'ish** somewhat golden; **gold'less**; **gold'y** somewhat like gold.—**gold'-beater** one whose trade is to beat gold into gold-leaf; **gold'-beating**; **gold'-brick'** a block of gold or (orig. *U.S. slang*) of pretended gold, hence a sham or swindle; **gold'-cloth'** cloth of gold; **gold'crest** a golden-crested bird of the genus *Regulus* (also **golden-crested wren**); **gold'-digger** one who digs for gold: a woman who treats a man chiefly as a source of material gain; **gold'-digging**; **gold'-dust** gold in fine particles, as found in some rivers; **golden age** an imaginary past time of innocence and happiness: any time of highest achievement, **golden boy, girl** a young man, woman, of outstanding talents, good looks, etc. likely to win renown; **Golden Delicious** a kind of sweet eating-apple; **gold(en) disc** a gold replica of a recording that has sold 1 million copies, presented to the composer, performer, etc.; **golden eagle** the common eagle, from a slight golden gleam about the head and neck; **golden fleece** in Greek mythology, the fleece of the ram Chrysomallus, the recovery of which was the object of the famous expedition of the Argonauts; **golden goose** the fabled layer of golden eggs, killed by its over-greedy owner: a source of profit (*fig.*; also **the goose that lays the golden eggs**); **golden handshake** a large sum given to an employee or member forced to leave a firm, etc.; **golden jubilee** a fiftieth anniversary; **golden mean** the middle way between extremes: moderation; **golden oldie** (*coll.*) a song, recording, motion picture, etc. issued some considerable time ago and still popular; **golden opportunity** a very favourable one; **golden pheasant** a golden-crested Chinese pheasant; **golden plover** a plover with yellow-speckled feathers; **gold'enrod** any plant of the composite genus *Solidago*, with rodlike stems and yellow heads crowded along the branches; **golden rule** the precept that one should do as one would be done by: a rule of the first importance, a guiding principle; **golden section** division of a line so that one segment is to the other as that to the whole; **golden thistle, tulip** top award respectively in film-making, advertising; **golden wattle** any of various kinds of yellow-flowered Australian acacia; **gold'-fe'ver** a mania for seeking gold; **gold'field** a gold-producing region; **gold'finch** a beautiful finch, black, red, yellow and white, fond of eating thistle seeds; **gold'fish** a Chinese and Japanese freshwater fish closely allied to the carp, golden or (*silverfish*) pale in its domesticated state, brownish when wild; **gold'-foil'** gold beaten into thin sheets, but not as thin as gold-leaf: **gold'ilocks** a golden-haired person; **gold'-lace'** lace made from gold-thread.—*adj.* **gold'-laced.** —**gold'-leaf'** gold beaten extremely thin; **gold medal** in athletics competitions, etc., the medal awarded as first prize; **gold'-mine** a mine producing gold: a source of great profit; **gold'-miner**; **gold'-plate'** vessels and utensils of gold collectively: metal esp. silver, plated with gold.—*v.t.* to coat (another metal) with gold.— **gold reserve** the gold held by a central bank, etc., to cover and support all its dealings; **gold'-rush** a rush of prospectors to a new goldfield; **gold'smith** a worker in gold and silver; **gold'smithy, -ery**; **gold standard** a monetary standard or system according to which the unit of currency has a precise value in gold; **gold'-thread'** gold-wire used in weaving: silk wound with gilded wire; **gold'-washer** one who obtains gold from sand and gravel by washing: a cradle or other implement for washing gold; **gold'-wasp** any wasp of a family (*Chrysididae*) with brilliant metallic colouring and telescopic abdomen, whose larvae feed on those of wasps and bees—cuckoo-fly or ruby-tail, ruby-wasp; **gold'-wire'** wire made of or covered with gold. **—as good as gold** behaving in an exemplary manner (usu. of children); **goldfish bowl** a glass aquarium for goldfish: a situation entirely lacking in privacy. [O.E. *gold*.]

golf *golf, n.* a game played with a club or set of clubs over a prepared stretch of land, the aim being to propel a small ball into a series of holes.—*v.i.* to play golf.—*ns.* **golf'er, golf'ing.—golf'-bag** a bag for carrying golf-clubs; **golf'-ball** a small ball used in golf: in certain typewriters, etc. a small detachable metal sphere or hemisphere with the type characters moulded on to its surface; **golf'-club** a club used in golf: a golfing society; **golf'-course, golf'-links** the ground on which golf is played.

Goliath *gō-lī'əth, gə-, n.* a giant. [From *Goliath*, the Philistine giant in 1 Sam. xvii.]

golliwog. Same as **gollywog.**

gollop *gol'əp, v.t.* and *v.i.* to gulp greedily or hastily. [Perh. **gulp.**]

golly[1] *gol'i, interj.* expressing surprise. [Thought to be orig. a Negro modification of **God.**]

golly[2]. A short form of **gollywog.**

gollywog, golliwog *gol'i-wog, n.* a fantastical doll with black face, staring eyes, and bristling hair: a person who has fuzzy hair or is in some way grotesque. [*Golliwogg*, a doll in certain U.S. children's books, the first of which was published in 1895.]

golosh. Same as **galosh.**

goluptious *gol-up'shəs, goloptious* *-op', (jocular) adjs.* delicious: voluptuous.

gomphosis *gom-fō'sis, n.* an immovable articulation, as of the teeth in the jaw. [Gr. *gomphōsis—gomphos*, a bolt.]

-gon *-gon, -gən,* in composition, having a certain number of angles as in *hexagon, polygon.* [Gr. *gōniā,* angle.]

gonad *gon'ad, (biol.) n.* an organ that produces sex-cells.—*adjs.* **gonadial** (*-ā'di-əl*), **gonadic** (*-ad'*); **gonadotrop(h)'ic** stimulating the gonads.—*n.* **gonadotrop(h)'in** a substance that does this, used as a drug to promote fertility. [Gr. *gonē,* generation.]

gondola *gon'də-lə, n.* a long, narrow boat used chiefly on the canals of Venice: the car of an airship: the car of a balloon: a car resembling this suspended from an earth-supported structure: a (free-standing) shelved unit for displaying goods in a supermarket, etc.—*n.* **gondolier** (*-lēr*) one who rows a gondola. [Venetian dialect.]

gone *gon, pa.p. of* **go**[1], in an advanced stage: lost, passed beyond help: departed: dead: weak, faint, feeling a sinking sensation: pregnant (with specified time, e.g. *six months gone*): wide of the mark, of an arrow: enamoured of (with *on; slang*): in an exalted state (*slang*).—*ns.* **gone'ness** a sinking sensation; **gon'er** (*slang*) one dead or ruined beyond recovery: a thing beyond hope of recovery.—**gone goose, gosling** (*coll.*) a hopeless case.—**gone under** ruined beyond recovery.

gonfalon *gon'fə-lon, n.* an ensign or standard with streamers.—*ns.* **gonfalonier** (*-ēr*) one who bears a gonfalon; **gon'fanon** a gonfalon: a pennon. [It. *gonfalone* and O.Fr. *gonfanon*—O.H.G. *gundfano—gund,* battle, *fano,* a flag.]

gong *gong, n.* a metal disc, usu. rimmed, that sounds when struck or rubbed with a drumstick: an instrument of call, esp. to meals: a steel spiral for striking in a clock: a flat bell sounded by a hammer: medal (*slang*).—*v.t.* to call upon to stop by sounding a gong. —*n.* **gong'ster** one who gongs.—**gong'-stick.** [Malay.]

gonidium *gon-id'i-əm, n.* an algal cell in a lichen:—*pl.* **gonid'ia.**—*adjs.* **gonid'ial, gonid'ic.** [Gr. *gonē,* generation, seed.]

goniometer *gōn-, gon-i-om'i-tər, n.* an instrument for measuring angles, esp. between crystal-faces: a direction-finding apparatus.—*adjs.* **goniometric** (*-ə-met'rik*), **-al.**—*adv.* **goniomet'rically.**—*n.* **goniom'etry.** [Gr. *gōniā,* an angle, *metron,* measure.]

gonk *gongk, n.* a cushion-like soft toy, usu. with arms and legs. [Nonsense word.]

gonna *gon'ə,* (esp. *U.S.*) a coll. contraction of **going to.**

gonococcus *gon-ō-kok'əs, n.* the bacterium that causes gonorrhoea:—*pl.* **gonococci** (*-kok'sī*).—*adjs.* **gonococc'al, gonococcic** (*-kok'sik*); **gonococc'oid.** [Gr. *gonos,* seed, *kokkos,* a berry.]

gonocyte *gon'ō-sīt, n.* an oocyte or spermatocyte. [Gr. *gonos,* seed.]

gonorrhoea *gon-ō-rē'ə, n.* a contagious infection of the mucous membrane of the genital tract.—*adjs.* **gonorrhoe'al, -ic.—U.S. gonorrhe'a, gonorrhe'al, -ic.** [Gr. *gonorroiā—gonos,* seed, *rheein,* to flow, from a mistaken notion of its nature.]

goo *gōō, (slang) n.* a sticky substance: sentimentality. —*adj.* **goo'ey.**

goober *gōō'bər, n.* (also **goober pea**) peanut. [African.]

good *gŏŏd, adj.* having suitable or desirable qualities: promoting health, welfare, or happiness: virtuous: pious: kind: benevolent: well-behaved: not troublesome: of repute: doughty: worthy: commendable: suitable: adequate: thorough: competent: sufficient: valid: sound: serviceable: beneficial: genuine: pleasing: favourable: ample, moderately estimated: considerable, as in *a good deal, a good mind:* to be counted on:—*compar.* **bett'er;** *superl.* **best.**—*n.* the end of ethics: that which is good: prosperity: welfare: advantage, temporal or spiritual: benefit: avail: virtue: (usu. in *pl.*) movable property, chattels, merchandise, freight.—*interj.* well: right: be it so.—*adv.* well.—*n.* **good'lness** weak, priggish, or canting goodness.—*adj.* **good'ish** pretty good, of fair quality or quantity.—*n.* **good'liness.**—*adj.* **good'ly** comely: good-looking: fine: excellent: ample:—*compar.* **good'lier;** *superl.* **good'liest.**—*ns.* **good'ness** virtue: excellence: benevolence: substituted for God in certain expressions, as *for goodness sake,* and as *interj;* **good'y** (usu. in *pl.*) a delicacy or sweetmeat: (usu. in *pl.*) something pleasant or desirable (usu. *facet.*): the hero of a book, motion picture, etc. (*coll.*): a goody-goody.—*interj.* expressing pleasure. —*adj.* **goody-goody.**—*adj.* **good'y-good'y** mawkishly weakly benevolent or pious.—Also *n.*—*n.* and *interj.* **good afternoon** a salutation on meeting or parting in the afternoon.—*n.* or *interj.* **good-bye'** for *God be with you:* farewell, a form of address at parting.— *ns.* or *interjs.* **good-day'** a common salutation at meeting or parting; **good-eve'ning** a salutation on meeting or parting in the evening.—**good'fell'ow** a jolly or boon companion: a reveller; **good'fell'owship** merry or pleasant company: conviviality; **good folk** good people.—*adj.* **good'-for-nothing** worthless, useless. —*n.* an idle or worthless person.—**good-hu'mour** cheerful, tolerant mood or disposition.—*adj.* **good-hu'moured.**—*adv.* **good-hu'mouredly.—good-hu'mouredness.**—*adj.* **good'-look'ing** handsome, attractive.—**good-look'er** (*coll.*); **good looks** attractive appearance.—*ns.* and *interjs.* **good-morn'ing** or (*arch.*) **good-morr'ow** a salutation at meeting or parting early in the day.—**good-na'ture** natural goodness and mildness of disposition.—*adj.* **good'-na'tured.**—*adv.* **good-na'turedly.—good-na'turedness.**—*n.* and *interj.* **good-night'** a common salutation on parting at night or well on in the day.—*interj.* **good'-o, good'-oh**

expressing pleasure.—**good offices** mediation; **good people, good folk** the fairies (euphemistically); **good sailor** a person not liable to seasickness; **goods'-engine** an engine used for drawing goods-trains; **good'-sense'** sound judgment.—*adj.* **good'-sized'** (fairly) large.—**goods'-train** a train of goods wagons.—*adjs.* **good'-tem'pered** possessing a good temper; **good'time** pleasure-seeking.—**good turn** something done for someone in a kind and helpful spirit or manner; **good'will'** benevolence: well-wishing: the established custom or popularity of any business or trade—often appearing as one of its assets, with a marketable money value.—*adj.* **good'will** well-wishing: expressive of good-will.—**as good as** the same as, no less than: virtually; **be as good as one's word** to fulfil one's promise; **for good (and all)** permanently: irrevocably; **good and** (*coll.*) very; **goodies and baddies** characters in a drama regarded respectively as definitely good and definitely bad; **good for anything** ready for any kind of work; **good for you** *interj.* expressing approval (*Austr. coll.* **good on you**); **in somone's good books** in favour with someone; **make good** to fulfil, perform: to compensate: to come to success, esp. unexpectedly: to do well, redeeming a false start: to repair: to justify; **no good** useless: unavailing: worthless; **not, hardly** etc., **good enough** not sufficiently good: mean, unfair, very different from what was expected or promised; **stand good** to be lastingly good: to remain, **the Good Book** the Bible; **the goods** (*slang*) the real thing: that which is required, promised, etc , **to the good** for the best: on the credit or advantage side [O.E. *gōd*.]

gooey. See goo.

goof *gōōf, n.* a stupid or awkward person.—*v.i* to make a blunder —*adv.* **goof'ily.**—*n.* **goof'iness.**—*adj.* **goof'y.**—**goof'ball** (*slang*) a barbiturate pill used as an exhilarant. [Perh. Fr. *goffe.*]

googly *gōōg'li,* (*cricket*) *n.* an off-breaking ball with an apparent leg-break action on the part of the bowler, or conversely.—Also *adj.*

gook *gōōk,* (*slang*) *n.* one of Asiatic race, esp. a Japanese, Korean or Vietnamese soldier. esp in Rhodesia, a guerrilla or terrorist.

gooly, gooley *gōō'li, n.* a small stone (*Austr. coll.*): (in *pl.*) testicles (*vulg.*). [Perh. Hind. *goli*, a bullet, ball.]

goon *gōōn, n.* a hired thug (*U.S. slang*): a stupid person

gooney(-bird) *gōō'ne, n.* an albatross. [Prob. dial., simpleton—obs. *gony.*]

goop *gōōp, n.* a fool: a fatuous person: a rude, ill-mannered person (*U.S.*).—*adj.* **goop'y.** [Cf. *goof.*]

goosander *gōōs-an'dər, n.* a large duck of the merganser genus. [Perh. goose, and O.N. *önd*, pl. *ander*, duck.]

goose *gōōs, n.* any one of a group of birds of the duck family, intermediate between ducks and swans: a domesticated member of the group, descended mainly from the grey-lag: the female of such a bird:— *masc.* **gander:** a tailor's smoothing-iron, from the likeness of the handle to the neck of a goose: a stupid, silly person:—*pl.* **geese,** *gēs,* or, of tailor's goose, **goos'es.**—*v.t.* (*slang*) to hiss off the stage: to prod (someone) between the buttocks.—*ns.* **goos'ery** 'a place for keeping geese: stupidity; **goos'(e)y** a goose: a blockhead.—*adj.* like a goose: affected with gooseflesh.—**goose'flesh** a condition of the skin, like that of a plucked goose or other fowl: the bristling feeling in the skin due to erection of hairs through cold, horror, etc.; **goose'foot** any plant of a genus (Chenopodium) of the beet family, from the shape of the leaf:—*pl.* **goose'foots; goosegog, goosegob** see under gooseberry; **goose'-grass** cleavers: silverweed; **goose'herd** one who herds geese; **goose'-neck** a hook,

bracket, pipe, etc., bent like a goose's neck; **goose'-pimples** goose-flesh; **goose'-quill** one of the quills or large wing-feathers of a goose, esp. one used as a pen; **goose'-skin** goose-flesh, horripilation; **goose'-step** (*mil.*) a method of marching (resembling a goose's walk) with knees stiff and soles brought flat on the ground.—Also *v.i.* [O.E. *gōs* (pl. *gēs*).]

gooseberry *gōōz'bə-ri, n.* the fruit of the **gooseberry-bush** (*Ribes grossularia*) a prickly shrub of the saxifrage family; an unwanted third person —**goose'gog, goose'gob** (*coll.* and *dial.*) a gooseberry.—**Chinese gooseberry** a sub-tropical vine, *Actinidia chinensis*, with brown, hairy, edible fruit. [Perh. goose and berry; or *goose* may be from M.H.G. *krus* (Gr. *kraus*, crisp, curled).]

gopak *gō'pak, n.* a folk-dance from the Ukraine. [From Russ.]

gopher *gō'fər, n.* a name in America applied to various burrowing animals—the pouched rat, the ground squirrel, the land tortoise of the Southern States, and a burrowing snake.—*v.i.* to burrow: to mine in a small way. [Perh. Fr. *gaufre*, honeycomb]

goramy, gourami, gurami *gō', gō', gōō'rə-mi,* or *-rā'mi, ns.* a large freshwater food-fish (*Osphromenus olfax*) of the Eastern Archipelago. [Malay *gurāmī*.]

gorblim(e)y *gō-blī'mi,* (*Cockney*) *interj.* for God blind me.

Gordian *gōrd'yən, adj.* pertaining to *Gordium* the capital, or *Gordius* the king, of ancient Phrygia, or to the intricate knot he tied: intricate: difficult.—**cut the Gordian knot** to overcome a difficulty by violent measures as Alexander cut the knot with his sword.

gore[1] *gōr, gor, n.* clotted blood: blood.—*adv.* **gor'ily.** —*adj.* **gor'y** like gore: covered with gore: bloody. [O.E. *gor,* filth, dung; O.N. *gor,* cud, slime.]

gore[2] *gōr, gōr, n.* a triangular piece of land: a triangular piece let into a garment to widen it: a sector of a curved surface.—*v.t* to shape like or furnish with gores: to pierce with anything pointed, as a spear or horns. [O.E. *gāra,* a pointed triangular piece of land, and *gār,* a spear.]

gorge *gōrj, n.* the throat: a ravine: the entrance to an outwork (*fort.*): a hawk's crop: the maw: the contents of the stomach: a gluttonous feed.—*v.t.* to swallow greedily: to glut.—*v.i.* to feed gluttonously.— *adj.* **gorged** having a gorge or throat: glutted.—*n.* **gorg'et** a piece of armour for the throat: a wimple: a neck ornament.—**have one's gorge rise** to be filled with loathing; **heave the gorge** to retch. [O.Fr.]

gorgeous *gor'jəs, adj.* showy: splendid: magnificent: loosely, pleasant, good, etc.—*adv.* **gor'geously.**—*n.* **gor'geousness.** [O.Fr. *gorgias,* gaudy.]

gorget. See gorge.

gorgio *gor'jō, gor'ji-ō, n.* one who is not a gipsy.—Also **gajo** *go'jō:—pls. -s.* [Romany.]

Gorgon *gôr'gən, n* one of three fabled female monsters (Stheno, Euryale, and Medusa), of horrible and petrifying aspect, winged, with hissing serpents for hair: (usu without *cap.*) anybody, esp. a woman, very ugly or formidable.—Also *adj.*—*v.t* **gor'gonise, -ize** to turn to stone. [Gr. *Gorgō,* pl. *-ōnēs—gorgos,* grim.]

Gorgonia *gör-gō'ni-ə, n.* a genus of sea-fans or horny corals.—*adj.* **gorgo'nian.**—*n.* a horny coral. [L. *gorgōnia,* coral—*Gorgō,* Gorgon (from hardening in the air).]

Gorgonzola *gòr-gən-zō'lə, n.* a blue cheese of cow's milk. [*Gorgonzola,* Italian town near Milan.]

gorilla *gor-il'ə, n.* a great African ape, the largest anthropoid: a thug (*slang*).—*adjs.* **gorill'ian, gorill'-ine.** [Gr. *Gorillai* (pl.), reported by Hanno the Carthaginian as a tribe of hairy women.] •

gormand *gor'mənd, n.* older form of **gourmand.**—*v.t.*
gor'mandise, -ize to eat hastily or voraciously —*n.*
gor'mandise gourmandise: gluttony: gormandising.
—*ns.* **gor'mandiser, -z-; gor'mandising, -z-; gor'mandism** gluttony. [See **gourmand.**]
gormless *gorm'lis,* (*coll*) *adj.* clumsy: stupid, witless. [O.N. *gaumr,* heed, attention.]
gorse *gors, n.* furze or whin, a prickly papilionaceous shrub (Ulex).—*adj.* **gors'y.** [O.E. *gorst.*]
gory. See **gore¹.**
gosh *gosh,* (*coll.*) *interj.* for **God.**
goshawk *gos'hok, n.* a short-winged hawk, once used for hunting wild-geese and other fowl. [O.E *gōshafoc—gōs,* goose, *hafoc,* hawk.]
gosling *goz'ling, n.* a young goose. [O.E *gōs,* goose, double dim. *-l-ing.*]
gospel *gos'pəl, n.* the teaching of Christ: a narrative of the life of Christ, esp. one of those included in the New Testament, Matthew, Mark, Luke, and John· the principles set forth therein: the stated portion of these read at service: any strongly advocated principle or system. absolute truth (*coll.*): a type of ardently religious jazz music (esp. songs) originating amongst the black population of the southern U S.—*n.* **gos'peller** a preacher: an evangelist: one who reads the gospel in church. [O.E. *godspel(l),* a translation of L. *evangelium—gōd,* good (with shortened vowel being understood as *God,* God) and *spel(l),* story.]
gossamer *gos'ə-mər, n.* very fine spider-threads that float in the air or form webs on bushes in fine weather: any very thin material.—*adj.* light, flimsy.—*adj.* **goss'amery** like gossamer: flimsy. [M.E. *gossomer.*]
gossip *gos'ip, n.* a sponsor at baptism (in relation to child, parent, or other sponsor) (*arch.*) a woman friend who comes at a birth (*arch.*): one who goes about telling and hearing news, or idle, malicious, and scandalous tales: idle talk: tittle-tattle: scandalous rumours: easy familiar writing.—*v.i.* to run about telling idle or malicious tales: to talk much: to chat:—*pa.t.* **goss'iped.**—*n* and *adj.* **goss'iping.**—*n.* **goss'ipry.**—*adj.* **goss'ipy.**—**gossip column** the newspaper column written by a gossip-writer; **gossip columnist; goss'ip-monger** a person who spreads gossip and rumours; **goss'ip-writer** a journalist who writes articles about the lives and loves of well-known people. [O.E. *godsibb,* godfather, one who is **sib in God,** spiritually related.]
got. See under **get.**
Goth *goth, n.* one of an ancient Germanic nation, originally settled on the southern coasts of the Baltic, later founding kingdoms in Italy, southern France, and Spain: a rude or uncivilised person, a barbarian —*adj.* **Goth'ic** of the Goths or their language: barbarous: romantic: denoting the 12th–16th-cent style of architecture in churches, etc., with high-pointed arches, clustered columns, etc.: generally, the style, related to this, favoured in all the fine arts during this time: black-letter (*print.*): orig. applied to 18th-cent: tales, novels, of mystery with gloomy sinister backgrounds, now denoting psychological horror-tales (also **Gothick**).—*n.* language of the Goths, an East Germanic tongue: Gothic architecture.—*n.* and *adj.* **Goth'ick** (denoting) a style of architecture, c. 1720–1840, in which the Gothic style of the middle ages was imitated: (of 18th-cent. and modern tales, etc.) Gothic. [The native names *Gutans* (sing. *Guta*) and *Gutōs* (sing. *Guts*), and *Gutthiuda,* people of the Goths; Latinised as *Gothī, Gotthī*; Gr. *Gothoi, Gotthoi*; O.E. *Gotan* (sing. *Gota*)]
Gothamite *gōt', got'əm-it, n.* a simpleton: a wiseacre: (*goth', gōth'*) a New Yorker (*U.S.*). [From **Gotham,** a village in Nottinghamshire, with which name are connected many simpleton stories.]
Gothic, Gothick, etc See **Goth.**
gotta *got'ə,* a coll contraction of **got to.**
gotten. See under **get.**
Götterdämmerung *gœ-tər-dem'ə-rŏŏng,* (*Ger. myth.*) *n.* lit. the twilight of the gods, the ultimate defeat of the gods by evil.
gouache *gŏŏ-ash, gŏŏ ', n.* watercolour painting with opaque colours, mixed with water, honey, and gum, presenting a matt surface: work painted according to this method. [Fr.]
Gouda *gow'də, n.* a kind of mild cheese from *Gouda* in the Netherlands.
gouge *gowj,* also *gŏŏj, n.* a chisel with a hollow blade for cutting grooves or holes.—*v.t.* to scoop out, as with a gouge: to force out, as the eye with the thumb. [O.Fr.—L.L *gubia,* a kind of chisel.]
goulash *gŏŏ'lash, n.* a stew of beef, vegetables, esp. onions, and paprika: a re-deal of cards, so many (as e.g. 5) cards at a time (*bridge*). [Hung. *gulyás (hús)* herdsman (meat).]
gourami. See **goramy.**
gourd *gŏŏrd, gōrd, gôrd, n.* a large hard-rinded fleshy fruit characteristic of the cucumber family: the rind of one used as a bottle, cup, etc.: a gourd-bearing plant. [O.Fr. *gourde,* contr. from *cougourde—L.* *cucurbita,* a gourd.]
gourmand *gŏŏr'mənd, -mä, n.* one who eats greedily: a glutton: a lover of good fare.—*adj.* voracious: gluttonous.—*n.* **gourmandise** (*gŏŏr'mən-dīz, gŏŏ r-mä-dēz*) skill, or indulgence, in good eating; **gour'mandism.** [Fr.; cf. **gormand.**]
gourmet *gŏŏr'mä, -me, n.* an epicure, originally one with a delicate taste in wines. [Fr., a wine-merchant's assistant.]
gout *gowt, n.* a drop, spot (*arch.*): a disease in which excess of uric acid in the blood is deposited as urates in the joints, etc., with swelling esp. of the great toe. —*n.* **gout'iness.**—*adj.* **gout'y** relating to gout: diseased with or subject to gout. [O Fr. *goutte*—L. *gutta,* a drop.]
gov. See **governor.**
govern *guv'ərn, v t.* to direct: to control: to rule with authority: to determine: to determine the case of (*gram.*): to require as the case of a noun or pronoun. —*v i.* to exercise authority: to administer the laws. —*adj.* **gov'ernable.**—*ns.* **gov'ernance** government: control: direction; **gov'erness** a lady who has charge of the instruction of the young at home or in school.—*adjs.* **gov'ernessy** like a governess, esp. prim; **gov'erning** having control.—*n.* **government** (*guv'ər(n)-mənt*) a ruling or managing: control: system of governing: the body of persons authorised to administer the laws, or to govern a state: tenure of office of one who governs: the power of one word in determining the case of another (*gram.*).—*adj.* of or pursued by government.—*adj.* **governmental** (*-ment'l*) pertaining to government.—*ns.* **gov'ernor** a real or titular ruler, esp. of a state, province, colony: the head of an institution or a member of its ruling body (usu. *guv'nər*) a father, chief, or master, applied more generally in kindly, usually ironically respectful, address (sometimes shortened to **gov** *guv*) (*slang*):a regulator, or contrivance for maintaining uniform velocity with a varying resistance (*mach.*), **gov'ernorship.**—**gov'ernor-gen'eral** orig. the supreme governor of a country, etc., with deputy governors under him: the representative of the British crown in Commonwealth countries which recognise the monarchy as head of state:—*pl.* **gov'ernors-gen'eral; gov'ernor-gen'eralship.** [O.Fr. *governer*—L. *gubernāre*—Gr. *kybernaein,* to steer.]

gown gown, *n.* a loose flowing outer garment: a woman's dress: an academic, clerical, or official robe: the members of a university as opposed to the townspeople (see under **town**).—*v.t.* and *v.i.* to dress in a gown.—*v.t.* to invest or furnish with a gown.—*adj.* **gowned.** [O.Fr. *goune*—L.L. *gunna*.]

goy goi, *n.* a non-Jew, Gentile:—*pl.* **goy'im.**—*adjs* **goy'ish, goyisch** (*goi'ish*). [Heb., nation.]

Graafian grä'fi-ən, *adj.* pertaining to the Dutch anatomist Regnier de *Graaf* (1641–73) who discovered the **Graafian follicles** in which the ova are contained in the ovary of higher vertebrates.

grab grab, *v.t.* to seize or grasp suddenly: to lay hands on· to impress or interest (*slang*) —*v.i.* to clutch:—*pr.p.* **grabb'ing;** *pa.t.* and *pa.p.* **grabbed.**—*n.* a sudden grasp or clutch: unscrupulous seizure: a double scoop hinged like a pair of jaws —*n.* **grabb'er** one who grabs: an avaricious person.—**grab'-bag** a bag or other receptacle for miscellaneous articles.—**how does that grab you?** (*slang*) what's your reaction to that?; **up for grabs** (*slang*) (ready) for the taking, for sale, etc. [Cf. Sw. *grabba*, to grasp.]

grace grās, *n.* easy elegance in form or manner: what adorns and commends to favour: favour: kindness: the undeserved mercy of God: divine influence: eternal life or salvation: a short prayer before or after a meal: a ceremonious title in addressing a duke, an archbishop, or formerly a king: a short period of time in hand before a deadline is reached.—*v.t.* to mark with favour: to adorn.—*adj.* **grace'ful** elegant and easy: marked by propriety or fitness, becoming: having or conferring grace, in any sense.—*adv.* **grace'fully.**—*n.* **grace'fulness.**—*adj.* **grace'less** wanting grace or excellence: indecorous.—*adv.* **grace'lessly.**—*n.* **grace'lessness.**—*n.* **graciosity** (*grä-shi-os'i-ti*) graciousness.—*adj.* **gracious** (*grä'shəs*) abounding in grace or kindness: acceptable: affable: becoming in demeanour.—*n.* used as substitute for God.—*adv.* **gra'ciously.**—*n.* **gra'ciousness.**—*adj.* **grace-and-favour** (of a residence) belonging to the British sovereign and granted rent-free to a person of importance.—**grace note** (*mus.*) a note introduced as an embellishment, not being essential to the harmony or melody; **gracious living** (living in) conditions of ease, plenty, and good taste —**days of grace** days allowed for the payment of a note or bill of exchange after it falls due; **fall from grace** to backslide, to lapse from the state of grace and salvation or from favour; **good gracious, gracious me** exclamations of surprise; **saving grace** divine grace so bestowed as to lead to salvation: a compensating virtue or quality; **with (a) good, bad, grace** in amiable, ungracious, fashion; **year of grace** year of Christian era, A.D. [Fr. *grâce*—L. *grätia*, favour—*grätus*, agreeable.]

grackle, grakle grak'l, *n.* a myna (hill myna) or kindred bird: an American 'blackbird' of the family Icteridae. [L. *grāculus*, jackdaw.]

grade grād, *n.* a degree or step in quality, rank, or dignity: a stage of advancement: rank: a yearly stage in education (*U.S.*): a pupil's mark of proficiency (*U.S.*): position in a scale: a class, or position in a class, according to value: gradient or slope: a class of animals produced by crossing a breed with one purer. —*v.t.* to arrange according to grade: to assign a grade to: to adjust the gradients of.—*v.i.* to shade off.—*adj.* of improved stock.—*adj.* **gra'dable** able to be graded.—*v.t.* and *v.i.* **gradate** (*grə-dāt'*) to shade off imperceptibly.—*n.* **grada'tion** a degree or step: a rising step by step: progress from one degree or state to another: position attained: state of being arranged in ranks: a gradual shading off: ablaut (*philol.*).—*adjs.* **grada'tional; grada'tioned** formed by gradations or stages: **gradatory** (*grad'ət-ə-ri*) proceeding

step by step: adapted for walking; **gradient** (*grä'di-ənt, -dyənt*) rising of falling by degrees: walking.—*n.* the degree of slope as compared with the horizontal: rate of change in any quantity with distance, e.g. in barometer readings: an incline.—*ns.* **gradin, gradine** (*grä'din, grə-dēn'*) a rising tier of seats, as in an amphitheatre: a raised step or ledge behind an altar.—*adj.* **gradual** (*grad'ū-əl*) advancing by grades or degrees: gentle and slow (of a slope).—*n* in the R C Church, the portion of the mass between the epistle and the gospel, formerly always sung from the steps of the altar: the book containing such anthems.—*ns.* **grad'ualism** the principle, policy, or phenomenon, of proceeding by degrees; **grad'ualist; gradual'ity.**—*adv.* **grad'ually.**—*n* **grad'uand** one about to receive a university degree.—*v.t.* **graduate** to divide into regular intervals: to mark with degrees: to proportion.—*v.i.* to pass by grades: to receive a university degree.—*n.* one who has obtained a university degree.—*adj.* **grad'uated** marked with degrees, as a thermometer.—*ns.* **grad'uateship; gradua'tion** division into proportionate or regular sections, for measurement, etc.: a mark or all the marks made for this purpose: the gaining of a university degree: the ceremony marking this; **grad'uator** an instrument for dividing lines at regular intervals.—**grade crossing** (*U.S*) a level crossing; **graded post** in British schools, a post with some special responsibility, and so extra payment; **grade school** (*U.S.*) elementary school.—**make the grade** orig. to succeed in climbing a steep hill· to overcome obstacles: to succeed: to be up to standard. [L. *gradus*, a step—*gradi*, to step.]

gradely grād'li, (*dial.*) *adj.* decent: proper: fit: fine.—*adv.* properly: readily: very.—Also **graith'ly.** [O.E. *geræde*, ready.]

gradient, etc., **gradin**, etc , **gradual**, etc., **graduate**, etc. See **grade**.

Graecise, -ize grē'sīz, *v.t.* to make Greek: to hellenise —*n.* **Grae'cism** a Greek idiom: the Greek spirit.—*adj.* **Graeco-Ro'man** (*grē'kō-*) of or pertaining to both Greece and Rome, esp. the art of Greece under Roman domination: applied to a mode of wrestling imagined to be that of the Greeks and Romans.—Also **Grecise, -ize** etc. [L. *Graecus*—Gr. *Graikos*, Greek; *graikizein*, to speak Greek.]

graffito gräf-fē'tō, *n.* a mural scribbling or drawing, as at Pompeii, Rome, and other ancient cities.—*n.pl.* or, *loosely*, *n sing.* **graffi'ti** (*tē*) scribblings or drawings, often indecent, found on public buildings, in lavatories, etc. [It.,—Gr *graphein*, to write.]

graft¹ gräft, *n.* a small piece of a plant or animal inserted in another individual or another part so as to come into organic union: the act of inserting a part in this way: the place of junction of stock and scion: the double plant composed of stock and scion.—*v.t.* to insert a graft in: to insert as a graft.—*v.i.* to insert grafts.—*ns.* **graft'er; graft'ing.** [From older **graff** —O.Fr. *graffe* (Fr *greffe*)—L. *graphium*—Gr. *graphion, grapheion*, a style, pencil—*graphein*, to write.]

graft² gräft, *n.* hard work (*slang*): a criminal's special branch of practice (*slang*): illicit profit by corrupt means, esp. in public life (*slang*): corruption in official life (*slang*).—*v.i.* to work hard (*slang*): to engage in graft or corrupt practices (*slang*).—*n.* **graft'er.**

grail grāl, *n.* (often **holy grail**; often with *caps.*) in mediaeval legend, the platter (sometimes supposed to be a cup) used by Christ at the Last Supper, in which Joseph of Arimathaea caught his blood, said to have been brought by Joseph to Glastonbury, and the object of quests by King Arthur's Knights: a cherished ambition or goal. [O.Fr *graal* or *grael*, a flat dish—L.L. *gradālis*, a flat dish, ultimately from Gr. *krātēr*, a bowl.]

grain *grān*, *n*. a single small hard seed: corn, in general: a hard particle: a very small quantity: the smallest British weight (the average weight of a seed of corn) = 1/7000 of a pound avoirdupois: the arrangement, size and direction of the particles, fibres, or plates of stone, wood, etc.: texture: a granular surface: dried bodies of kermes or of cochineal insects, once thought to be seeds: the red dye made from these: innate quality or character: the particles in a photographic emulsion which go to compose the photograph.—*v.t.* to form into grains, cause to granulate: to paint in imitation of grain' to dye in grain: in tanning, to take the hair off —*n.* **grain'age** duties on grain.—*adj.* **grained** granulated: subjected to graining: having a grain: rough: furrowed —*ns.* **grain'er** one who grains. a paint-brush for graining; **grain'ing** specif., painting to imitate the grain of wood: a process in tanning in which the grain of the leather is raised.—*adj.* **grain'y** having grains or kernels: having large grains, so indistinct (*phot*).— **grain alcohol** alcohol made by the fermentation of grain —**against the grain** against the fibre of the wood —hence against the natural temper or inclination; **in grain** in substance, in essence. [Fr. *grain*, collective *graine*—L. *grānum*, seed and *grāna*, orig. pl.; akin to **corn¹**.]

grakle. See **grackle.**

gralloch *gral'əhh*, *n.* a deer's entrails.—*v.t.* to disembowel (deer). [Gael. *grealach*.]

gram¹ *gram*, *n.* chick-pea: pulse generally [Port *grão* (sometimes *gram*)—L. *grānum*, a grain.]

gram², **gramme** *gram*, *n.* a unit of mass in the metric system—formerly that of a cubic centimetre of water at 4°C. now a thousandth part of the International Prototype Kilogram (see **kilogram**).—**gram'-at'om**, **gram'-atom'ic weight**, **gram'-mol'ecule**, **gram's molec'ular weight** the quantity of an element, a compound, whose mass in grams is equal to its atomic weight, molecular weight; **gram'-equiv'alent (weight)** the quantity of a substance whose mass in grams is equal to its equivalent weight [Fr. *gramme*—L *gramma*—Gr. *gramma*, a letter, a small weight.]

-gram *-gram*, in composition, something written or drawn to form a record. [Gr. *gramma*, letter.]

Gram's method *gramz meth'əd*, a technique used in classifying bacteria.—*adjs.* **Gram'-neg'ative** (also **gram-**) losing a stain of methyl violet and iodine on treatment with alcohol; **Gram'-pos'itive** (also **gram-**) retaining the stain. [H. J. C. *Gram*, deviser of the method.]

Gramineae *gra-*, *gra-*, *grā-min'i-ē*, *n.pl.* the grass family.—*adjs.* **graminā'ceous** (*grā-*, *gra-*), **gramin'eous; graminiv'orous** (*gra-*) feeding on grass, cereals, etc. [L. *grāmen*, *grāminis*, grass.]

grammalogue *gram'ə-log*, *n.* a word represented by a single sign: a sign for a word in shorthand [Gr. *gramma*, a letter, *logos*, a word.]

grammar *gram'ər*, *n.* the science of language, from the points of view of pronunciation, inflexion, syntax, and historic development: the art of the right use of language by grammatical rules: a book that teaches these subjects: any elementary work.—*n.* **grammā'rian** one versed in grammar, a teacher of or writer on grammar.—*adjs.* **grammat'ic**, **-al** belonging to, or according to the rules of, grammar.—*adv.* **grammat'ically.**—**grammar school** orig. a school in which grammar, esp Latin grammar, was taught: now a secondary school in which academic subjects predominate; **grammatical meaning** the functional significance of a word, etc. within the grammatical

framework of a particular sentence, etc [Gr. *gramma*, *-atos*, a letter; partly through O.Fr. *gramaire*]

gramme. See **gram².**

Grammy *gram'ı*, (*U* S.) *n.* an award, corresponding to the cinema Oscar, awarded by the National Academy of Recording Arts and Sciences [From *gram*ophone]

gramophone *gram'ə-fōn*, *n* an instrument (invented by E Berliner, 1887) for reproducing sounds by means of a needle moving along the grooves of a revolving disc, a record-player —*adj.* **gramophonic** (*-fon'ık*).— *adv* **gramophon'ically.** [Ill-formed from Gr. *gramma*, letter, record, *phōnē*, sound]

grampus *gram'pəs*, *n* a popular name for many whales, esp the killer: technically, Risso's dolphin (*Grampus griseus*). [O.Fr *graspeis*—L *crassus*, fat, *piscis*, fish, confused with Fr *grand*, big.]

gran¹ *gran*, (It) *adj* great.—**gran turismo** (*tōō-rēz'mō*) (a motor car) designed for touring in luxury and at high speed (term sometimes used loosely) — Abbrev **G.T.**

gran² *gran*, (coll) *n.* short for **granny.**

granadilla *gran-ə-dıl'ə*, **grenadilla** *gren'*, *ns.* the edible, oblong, fleshy fruit of *Passiflora quadrangularis*, a tropical American passion-flower the edible fruit of various other passion-flowers. [Sp]

granary *gran'ə-rı*, *n.* a storehouse for grain or threshed corn: a rich grain-growing region [L *grānārium*— *grānum*.]

grand¹ *grand*, *adj.* pre-eminent: supreme chief· main: exalted: magnificent: dignified: sublime. imposing: would-be-imposing: on a great scale. in complete form: in full proportions: very good (coll): (in composition) of the second degree of parentage or descent, as grandchild, granddaughter, grandfather, grandmother, grandson, etc.—*n.* a grand piano' a thousand dollars, pounds (slang) —*ns.* **grandee'** a noble in the kingdom of Castile, the members of the royal family being included: a man of high rank or station; **grandee'ship; grandeur** (*grand'yər*) vastness: splendour of appearance: loftiness of thought or deportment; **grandil'oquence**—*adj* **grandil'oquent** speaking, or expressed, bombastically.—*adv* **grandil'oquently.**—*adj* **gran'diose** grand or imposing: bombastic —*adv.* **gran'diosely.**—*n.* **grandios'ity.**— *adv.* **grand'ly.**—*n.* **grand'ness.**—**grand'(d)ad** old man: a grandfather; **grand'(d)addy** (coll) a grandfather: a person or thing considered the oldest, biggest, first, etc. of its kind; **gran'dam** (arch.) an old dame or woman: a grandmother; **grand'-aunt** a great-aunt; **grand'child** a son's or daughter's child, **grand'-daughter** a son's or daughter's daughter.—*adj.* **grand'-du'cal.**—**grand duke** a title of sovereignty over a **grand duchy**, first created by the Pope in 1569 for the rulers of Florence and Tuscany, assumed by certain German and Russian imperial princes (fem. **grand duchess); grand'father** a father's or mother's father.—*adj.* **grand'fatherly** like a grandfather, kindly.—**grandfather('s) clock** an old-fashioned clock (longcase clock) standing on the ground— larger than a **grandmother('s) clock; grand juror** member of a **grand jury**, a special jury in the U.S. which decides whether there is sufficient evidence to put an accused person on trial; **grand'mam(m)a**, **grand'ma** a grandmother; **grand'mas'ter** orig. the title given to a chess-player winning a great international tournament, now given generally to unusually skilled players: any such player; **grand'-mother** a father's or mother's mother; **Grand National** a steeplechase held annually at Aintree in Liverpool; **grand'-neph'ew** a great-nephew; **grand's niece** a great-niece, **grand'papa**, **grand'pa** a grandfather, **grand'parent** a grandfather or grandmother; **grand piano** a large harp-shaped piano, with horizontal strings, **grand'sire** a grandfather (*arch.*). any ancestor (*arch*); **grand slam** the winning of every trick at bridge. in sports such as tennis, golf, etc., the winning of all major championships in a season, **grand'son** a son's or daughter's son, **grand'stand** an elevated erection on a racecourse, etc , affording a good view, **grandstand finish** a close and rousing finish to a sporting contest. a supreme effort to win at the close of a sporting contest; **grand total** the sum of all subordinate sums, **grand'-un'cle** a great-uncle — **grand old man** (*coll*) a person commanding great respect and veneration. [Fr *grand*—L *grandis*, great.]

grand² *grā*, (Fr.) *adj* great —**grand cru** (*kru*) of a wine, from a famous vineyard or group of vineyards, **grand mal** (*mal*) a violently convulsive form of epilepsy (see **petit mal**); **grand merci** (*mer-sē*) many thanks, **grand prix** (*prē*) chief prize· (*cap.*) any of several international motor races —*pl.* **grands prix.**

grandad, grandam. See **grand¹.**

grande *grãd*, (Fr) *adj fem* of **grand².—grande dame** (*dam*) a great and aristocratic lady, or a socially important and very dignified one.

grandee, grandeur, grandiloquence, etc . **grandiose,** etc See **grand¹.**

grange *grānj, n* a farmhouse with its stables and other buildings.—*n.* **gran'ger** the keeper of a grange [O.Fr *grange*, barn—L L *grānea*—L *grānum*, grain]

granite *gran'it, n.* a coarse-grained igneous crystalline rock, composed of quartz, feldspar, and mica —*adj* of granite: hard like granite —*adj* **granit'ic** pertaining to, consisting of, or like granite —*n* **granitifica'tion.—***adj.* **granit'iform.—***n.* **granitisá'tion, -z-.**—*v t.* **gran'itise, -ize.**—*adj* **gran'itoid** of the form of or resembling granite —*adj.* **granolith'ic** composed of cement and granite chips —**graniteware** (*gran'it-wār*) a kind of speckled pottery resembling granite a type of enamelled ironware. [It *granito*, granite, lit. grained—L. *grānum*, grain]

granivorous *gran-iv'ar-as, adj* grain-eating: feeding on seeds —*n* **gran'ivore.** [L *grānum*, grain, *vorāre*, to devour]

granny, -ie *gran'i, n* a grandmother an old woman. an old-womanish person: a revolving cap on a chimney-pot —**granny flat, annexe** a self-contained flat, bungalow, etc., built on to, as part of, or close to, a house, for a grandmother or other elderly relative; **granny knot** a knot like a reef knot, but unsymmetrical, apt to slip or jam

grant *grant, v.t* to bestow: to admit as true: to concede —*n.* a bestowing. something bestowed, an allowance: a gift: conveyance of property by deed (*Eng law*) —*adj.* **grant'able.**—*pa.p.* or *conj* **grant'ed** (often with *that*) (it is) admitted, accepted —*ns.* **grantee'** (*law*) the person to whom a grant, gift, or conveyance is made; **grant'er, grant'or** (*law*) the person by whom a grant or conveyance is made.— **grant'-in-aid'** an official money grant for a particular purpose, esp from the government to a lesser department —**take for granted** to presuppose, assume, esp tacitly or unconsciously [O.Fr. *graanter, craanter, creanter,* to promise—L *crēdēre,* to believe]

Granth *grunt,* **Granth Sahib** *grunt sa'ib, n* the holy book of the Sikhs. [Hind.]

granule *gran'ūl, n.* a little grain. a fine particle.—*adjs* **gran'ūlar, gran'ūlose, gran'ūlous** consisting of or like grains or granules.—*n.* **granūlar'ity.—***adv.* **gran'-ūlarly.**—*v.t* **gran'ūlate** to form or break into grains or small masses: to make rough on the surface.—*v t* to be formed into grains —*adj.* granular: having the

surface covered with small elevations —*n.* **granūlá'tion** act of forming into grains, esp. of metals by pouring them through a sieve into water while hot.—*adj.* **gran'ūlative.—***ns.* **gran'ūlātor, -er.**—*adjs.* **granūlif'erous; gran'ūliform.—***n.* **gran'ūlocyte** a blood cell of the leucocyte division.—*adj* **granūlocÿt'ic.—** **granulated sugar** white sugar in fairly coarse grains [L *grānulum,* dim. of *grānum,* grain.]

grape *grāp, n.* the fruit of the grapevine —*adj.* **grape'less** without the flavour of the grape, said of wine —*n* **grā'pery** a place where grapes are grown — *adj* **grā'p(e)y** made of or like grapes.—**grape'fruit** a fine variety of the shaddock, the pompelmoose, with sometimes a slightly grapelike taste, **grape hyacinth** (Muscari) a near ally to the hyacinths, with clusters of small grapelike flowers; **grape'seed** the seed of the vine, **grape'seed-oil** an oil expressed from it; **grape'shot** shot that scatters, **grape'stone** the pip of the grape; **grape sugar** glucose or dextrose; **grape'vine** *Vitis vinifera* or other species of *Vitis.* the bush telegraph· rumour (from its far-stretching branches) —**sour grapes** things decried because they cannot be attained (from Aesop's fable of the fox and the grapes); **the grape** (*usu facet*) wine. [O.Fr *grape, grappe,* a cluster of grapes—*grape,* a hook, orig. Gmc]

graph *graf, n* a symbolic diagram a drawing depicting the relationship between two or more variables.—*v t.* to plot on a graph —**graph** is used as a terminal in many compounds to denote an agent that writes, records, etc , as *telegraph, seismograph,* or the thing written, as in *autograph,* etc —*n* **grapheme** (*graf'ēm*) a letter of an alphabet· all the letters or combinations of letters together that may be used to express one phoneme —*adj* **graphēm'ic.—***adv.* **graphēm'ically**—*n sing* **graphēm'ics** the study of systems of representing speech sounds in writing — *adjs.* **graphic** (*graf'ik*), **-al** pertaining to writing, describing, delineating, or diagrammatic representation· picturesquely described or describing: vivid.— *n* (**graph'ic**) a painting, print, or illustration or diagram.—*adv.* **graph'ically.—***n* **graph'icness.—***n. sing* **graph'ics** graphic means of presenting, or means of reproducing, informational material: the art or science of mathematical drawing, and of calculating stresses, etc , by geometrical methods —*n.* **graph'ite** a mineral, commonly called blacklead or plumbago, though composed of carbon—*adjs.* **graphit'ic; graph'itoid.**—*n* **graphitisá'tion, -z-.**—*v t.* **graph'-itise, -ize** to convert wholly or partly into graphite — *n* **graphol'ogy** the art of estimating character, etc , from handwriting —*adjs* **grapholog'ic, -al.—***n* **graphol'ogist.—graphic arts** painting, drawing, engraving, as opposed to music, sculpture, etc.; **graphic formula** a chemical formula in which the symbols for single atoms are joined by lines representing valency bonds; **graph paper** squared paper suitable for drawing graphs [Gr *graphē,* a writing—*graphein,* to write.]

grapnel *grap'nal, n.* a small anchor with several claws or arms: a grappling-iron· a hooking or grasping instrument. [Dim of O Fr *grapin*—*grape,* a hook.]

grappa *gra'pa, n.* a brandy, orig Italian, made from residue from a wine-press. [It., grape stalk.]

grapple *grap'l, n* an instrument for hooking or holding: a grasp, grip, hold, or clutch: a state of being held or clutched.—*v.t* to seize: to lay fast hold of.— *v.i.* to contend in close fight (also *fig.*) —**grapp'ling-i'ron, -hook** an instrument for grappling: a large grapnel for seizing hostile ships in naval engagements. [Cf. O.Fr. *grappil*—*grape,* a hook.]

graptolite *grap'ta-līt, n.* one of a group of fossil Hydrozoa—characteristic Silurian fossils like writing upon shales.—*adj.* **graptolit'ic.** [Gr. *graptos*, written—*graphein*, to write, *lithos*, stone.]

grasp grasp, *v t* to seize and hold: to take eagerly: to comprehend —*v t* to endeavour to seize (with *at*, *after*): to seize or accept eagerly (with *at*) —*n* grip: power of seizing: mental power of apprehension —*adj.* **grasp'able.**—*n* **grasp'er.**—*adj.* **grasp'ing** seizing: avaricious —*adj.* **grasp'ingly.**—*n* **grasp'-ingness.**—*adj.* **grasp'less** feeble, relaxed. [M E *graspen*, *grapsen*, from the root of *grāpian*, to grope]

grass gras, *n.* common herbage: any plant of the mono-cotyledonous family Gramineae, the most important to man in the vegetable kingdom, with long, narrow leaves and tubular stems, including wheat and other cereals, reeds (but not sedges), bamboo, sugar-cane: pasture grasses: pasturage: time of grass, spring or summer: an informer (*slang*) marijuana (*slang*) — *v t.* to cover with grass: to feed with grass: to bring to the grass or ground: to inform (on) (*slang*).—*v.t* to inform (on) (*slang*) —*ns* **grass'iness; grass'ing** bleaching by exposure on grass.—*adj* **grass'y** covered with or resembling grass, green —**grass'-box** a receptacle attached to some lawn-mowers to catch the grass cuttings; **grass court** a grass-covered tennis-court, **grass'-cutter** a mowing machine —*adjs.* **grass'-green** green green with grass: green as grass; **grass'-grown** grown over with grass.—**grass'hopper** a name for various saltatorial, orthopterous insects akin to locusts and crickets, that lurk among grass and chirp by rubbing their wing-covers, **grass'land** permanent pasture; **grass'-plot** a plot of grassy ground; **grass'-roots'** (orig. *U S.*) the rural areas of a country: the ordinary people, the rank and file in a country, political party, etc , thought of as voters foundation, basis, origin, primary aim or meaning.—Also *adj.*—**grass'-snake** the harmless common ringed snake, **grass'-tree** an Australian plant (*Xanthorrhoea*) of the lily family, with shrubby stems, tufts of long wiry foliage at the summit, and a tall flower-stalk, with a dense cylindrical spike of small flowers; **grass'-wid'ow** a wife temporarily separated from or deserted by her husband—*masc* **grass'-wid'ower; grass'-wrack** eelgrass.—**go, be put out, to grass** to be turned out to pasture, esp of a horse too old to work: to go into retirement, to rusticate, **hear the grass grow** to have exceptionally acute hearing: to be exceptionally alert; **let the grass grow under one's feet** to loiter, linger, and so lose opportunity [O E *gærs*, *græs*.]

grate¹ grāt, *n* a framework of bars with interstices, esp one for holding a fire or for looking through a door, etc : a cage: a grid.—*adj* **grāt'ed** having a grating.—*ns* **graticulation** (*gra-* or *gra-tik-ū-lā'shon*) the division of a design into squares for convenience in making an enlarged or diminished copy; **graticule** (*grat'i-kūl*) a ruled grating for identification of points in a map, the field of a telescope, etc., **grāt'ing** the bars of a grate a perforated cover for a drain or the like: a partition or frame of bars: a surface ruled closely with fine lines to give a diffraction spectrum [L L *grāta*, a grate—L *crātis*, a hurdle, see **crate.**]

grate² grāt, *v.t* to rub hard or wear away with anything rough: to grind (the teeth): to emit or utter jarringly. —*v i.* to make a harsh sound: to jar, rasp (on, against) to fret, irritate (usually with *on*, *upon*) —*n* **grāt'er** an instrument with a rough surface for rubbing down to small particles —*adj* **grāt'ing** rubbing harshly: harsh irritating —*adv* **grāt'ingly.** [O.Fr *grater*, through L L., from O H.G *chrazzon* (Ger. *kratzen*), to scratch]

grateful grāt'f(*ōō*)l, *adj* causing pleasure, acceptable thankful: having a due sense of benefits. expressing gratitude —*adv* **grate'fully.**—*ns* **grate'fulness; gratifica'tion** (*grat-*) a pleasing or indulging: that which gratifies: delight, feeling of satisfaction; **grat'i-fier.**—*v t* **grat'ify** to do what is agreeable to: to please: to satisfy: to indulge.—*pr.p* **grat'ifying**; *pa t.* and *pa.p* **grat'ified.**—*adj.* **grat'ifying**—*adv* **grat'ify-ingly.** [O.Fr. *grat*—L. *grātus*, pleasing, thankful]

graticule, etc. See **grate¹.**

gratin. See au **gratin.**

gratis grā', *gra'tis*, *adv.* for nothing: without payment or recompense [L. *grātis*, contr. of *grātiīs*, abl. pl of *grātia*, favour—*grātus.*]

gratitude grat'i-tūd, *n.* warm and friendly feeling towards a benefactor: thankfulness [Fr.,—L L. *grātitūdō*—L *grātus.*]

gratuity grə-tū'i-ti, *n.* a present: a tip: a payment to a soldier, etc , on discharge —*adj* **gratū'itous** done or given for nothing: voluntary: without reason, ground, or proof: uncalled for —*adv* **gratū'itously.** [Fr. *gratuité*—L L *grātuītās*, *-ātis*—L. *grātus.*]

gravamen grav-ā'men, *n* grievance: the substantial or chief ground of complaint or accusation:—*pl.* **gravā'-mina.** [L. *gravāmen*—*gravis*, heavy.]

grave¹ grāv, *v.t.* to engrave on hard substance: to fix deeply (e g. on the mind) —*v.i.* to engrave:—*pa.p.* **graved** or **grav'en.**—*n.* a pit dug out, esp. one to bury the dead in: any place of burial. death, destruction (*fig.*): a deadly place.—*ns.* **grāv'er** an engraver: a burin, **grāv'ing.**—*n pl.* **grave'-clothes** the clothes in which the dead are buried.—**grave'-digger; grave'stone** a stone placed as a memorial at a grave; **grave'yard** a burial-ground.—**with one foot in the grave** on the brink of death. [O.E. *grafan*, to dig, *græf*, a cave, grave, trench.]

grave² grāv, *adj.* of importance: serious: not gay or showy: sedate: solemn: weighty: calling for anxiety. low in pitch.—*n.* (also *grav*) grave accent.—*adv* **grave'ly.**—*n* **grave'ness.**—**grave accent** (*U K. grav*) a mark (`), originally indicating a pitch falling somewhat, or failing to rise, now used for various purposes [Fr.,—L *gravis.*]

gravel grav'l, *n.* an assemblage of small rounded stones: small collections of gravelly matter in the kidneys or bladder —*v t.* to cover with gravel: to puzzle, perplex to irritate (*coll.*):—*pr p* **grav'elling**; *pa t* and *pa p* **grav'elled.**—*adj* **grav'elly.**—**grav'el-pit** a pit from which gravel is dug —*adj.* **grav'el-voiced'** harsh-voiced [O Fr *gravele* (Fr *gravier*): prob Celt]

graven grāv'n, *pa.p.* of **grave¹.**—**graven image** an idol: a solemn person.

Graves grav, *n* a white, or red, table wine from the Graves district in the Gironde department of France

gravid grav'id, *adj.* pregnant —*n.* **gravid'ity.** [L *gravidus*—*gravis*, heavy]

gravimeter grə-vim'i-tər, *n* an instrument for measuring variations in gravity at points on the earth's surface.—*adjs.* **gravimetric** (*grav-i-met'rik*), **-al** pertaining to measurement by weight.—*n.* **gravim'etry.** —**gravimetric(al) analysis** the chemical analysis of materials by the separation of the constituents and their estimation by weight. [L. *gravis*, heavy, Gr *metron*, measure]

gravity grav'i-ti, *n* weightiness: gravitational attraction or acceleration: graveness: lowness of pitch —*n* **grav'itas** (*-as*) seriousness: weight, importance.—*v t* **grav'itāte** to be acted on by gravity: to tend towards the earth or other body: to be attracted, or move, by force of gravitation: to sink or settle down: to be strongly attracted or move (towards; *fig*) —*n.* **gravitā'tion** act of gravitating: the force of attraction between bodies.—*adj* **gravitā'tional.**—*adv.* **gravit-ā'tionally.**—*adj.* **grav'itātive.**—*n* **grav'iton** a hypothetical quantum of gravitational field energy — **acceleration due to gravity** (symbol *g*) the acceleration of a body falling freely under the action of gravity in a vacuum, about 32·174 feet or 9·8 metres per second per second. [L *gravitās*, *-ātis—gravis*, heavy.]

gravure *gra-vūr'*, *n*. any process of making an intaglio printing plate, including photogravure: the plate, or an impression from it [Fr , engraving.]

gravy *grāv'ı*, *n*. the juices from meat while cooking: money, profit, or pleasure, unexpected or in excess of what one might expect (*coll.*): graft (*slang*).—**grav'y-boat** a vessel for gravy; **gravy train** (*coll.*) a position in which one can have excessive profits or advantages in contrast to other people [Perh *gravé*, a copyist's mistake for O.Fr *grané—grain*, a cookery ingredient.]

gray. Same as **grey.**—*n*. **gray'ling** a silvery-grey fish (*Thymallus*) of the salmon family, with larger scales: a grey butterfly of the Satyridae.

graze[1] *grāz*, *v.t.* to eat or feed on (growing grass or pasture): to feed or supply with grass.—*v.t.* to eat grass: to supply grass.—*ns*. **grāz'er** an animal that grazes; **grāz'ier** one who pastures cattle and rears them for the market, **grāz'ing** the act of feeding on grass: the feeding or raising of cattle. [O.E. *grasian—græs*, grass.]

graze[2] *grāz*, *v.t.* to pass lightly along the surface of — *n*. a passing touch or scratch.

grease *grēs*, *n*. a soft thick animal fat oily matter of any kind: condition of fatness.—*v.t.* (in U.K. usu. pron. *grēz*) to smear with grease: to lubricate: to bribe (*slang*): to facilitate.—*n*. **greaser** (*grēz'ər*, or *grēs'ər*) one who greases: a ship's engineer. a Mexican or a Sp. American (*U.S.*; *offensive*).—*adv*. **greas'ily.**—*n*. **greas'iness.**—*adj*. **greas'y** (in U.K. usu. *grēz'ı*) of or like grease or oil: smeared with grease: having a slippery coating: fatty: oily: obscene: unctuous or ingratiating.—**grease cup** a lubricating device which stores grease and feeds it into a bearing; **grease'-gun** a lubricating pump; **grease'-mon'key** (*slang*) a mechanic; **grease paint** a tallowy composition used by actors in making up.—*adj*. **grease'-proof** resistant or impermeable to grease.—**grease the wheels** (*fig.*) to make things go smoothly. [O.Fr. *gresse*, fatness, *gras*, fat—L. *crassus*.]

great *grāt*, *adj*. big: large: of a high degree of magnitude of any kind: elevated in power, rank, station, etc : pre-eminent in genius· highly gifted: chief: sublime: weighty: outstanding: pregnant, teeming (*arch.*)· swelling with emotion: much addicted or given to, or excelling in the thing in question: favourite: habitual: in high favour or intimacy: in a high degree: on a large scale: excellent (*coll.*, often *ironic*): in composition indicating one degree more remote in the direct line of descent (as **great'-grand'father, great'-grand'son** and similarly **great'-great'-grandfather** and so indefinitely).—*n*. one who has achieved renown: used collectively for those who have achieved renown.—*adv*. (*coll.*) very well.—*v.t.* **great'en** to make great or greater.—*v.i.* to become great.—*adj*. great er compar. of great: (with geographical names) in an extended sense (as *Greater London*).—*adv*. **great'ly.**—*n*. **great'ness.**—*n.pl*. **Greats** the final honour School of Literae Humaniores (*Classical Greats*) or of Modern Philosophy (*Modern Greats*) at Oxford.—**great ape** any of the larger anthropoid apes—the chimpanzee, gibbon, gorilla, orang-utan; **great auk** a large, flightless auk once common in North Atlantic areas, now extinct; **great'-aunt** a grandparent's sister.—**Great Britain** England, Scotland and Wales; **great'coat** an overcoat; **Great Dane** a large close-haired dog; **great'-grand'child** the child of a grandchild; **great'-grand'father, -grand'-mother** the father (mother) of a grandparent; **great**

gross a unit of quantity equal to 12 gross.—*adj* **great'-hearted** having a great or noble heart: high-spirited: magnanimous.—**great'-heart'edness; great'-nephew, -niece** a brother's or sister's grandson. granddaughter; **great Scot(t)** exclamation of surprise. **Great Sea** the Mediterranean; **great tit** a kind of tit *Parus major*, with yellow, black and white markings, **great'-uncle** a grandparent's brother: **Great War** term applied esp. to war of 1914–18.—**Great White Way** a nickname for Broadway in New York: any brightly-lit street with theatres, etc., **the greatest** (*slang*) a wonderful, marvellous person or thing; **the great unwashed** a contemptuous term for the populace [O.E. *great.*]

greave *grēv*, *n*. armour for the leg below the knee. [O.Fr. *greve*, shin, greave.]

grebe *grēb*, *n*. a short-winged almost tailless freshwater diving bird (*Podiceps*). [Fr *grèbe.*]

Grecian *grēsh'(y)ən. adj*. Greek.—*n*. a Greek: one well versed in the Greek language and literature.—**Grecian nose** a straight nose which forms a continuous line with the forehead [L. *Graecia*, Greece—Gr. *Graikos*, Greek.]

Grecise, -ize, Grecism, Greco-Roman. See **Graecise, -ize**, etc.

greedy *grēd'ı, adj*. having a voracious appetite: inordinately desirous of increasing one's own share: covetous: eagerly desirous.—*n* **greed** an eager desire or longing: covetousness.—*adv*. **greed'ily.**—*n*. **greed'iness.**—**greedy guts** (*slang*) a glutton. [O E. *grēdıg.*]

greegree. See **grisgris.**

Greek *grēk, adj*. of Greece, its people, or its language. —*n*. a native or citizen of Greece, of a Greek state, or of a colony elsewhere of a Greek state: the language of Greece: any language of which one is ignorant, jargon, anything unintelligible.—*adjs*. **Greek'ish; Greek'less** without knowledge of Greek.—**Greek architecture** that developed in ancient Greece (Corinthian, Doric, Ionic); **Greek Church** the church that follows the ancient rite of the East and accepts the first seven councils, rejecting papal supremacy—(*Greek*) *Orthodox* or *Eastern* Church; **Greek cross** an upright cross with arms of equal length; **Greek gift** a treacherous gift (from Virgil's *Aeneid*, ii, 49); **Greek nose** a Grecian nose. [O.E. *Grēcas*, *Crēcas*, Greeks, or L *Graecus—Gr. Graikos*, Greek.]

green *grēn, adj*. of the colour usual in leaves, between blue and yellow in the spectrum· growing: vigorous: hale: new: young: unripe: fresh: undried: raw: incompletely prepared· immature: unseasoned: inexperienced: jealous: easily imposed on: relating to currency values expressing EEC farm prices, e.g. *green pound*, *green franc*, *green rate*, etc : concerned with care of the environment esp. as a political issue.—*n* the colour of green things: this colour as a symbol of the Irish republic: a grassy plot, esp. that common to a village or town, or for bowling, or bleaching, drying of clothes: a golf-course: the prepared ground (*putting-green*) round a golf-hole: a green pigment: (*pl.*) fresh leaves: (*pl.*) green vegetables for food, esp. of the cabbage kind.—*v.t.* and *v.i* to make or become green. —*ns* green'ery green plants or boughs. verdure; **green'ing** a becoming or making green: a kind of apple green when ripe.—*adj*. **green'ish.**—*adv*. **green'ly** immaturely, unskilfully.—*ns* **green'ness; greenth** greenness, verdure.—*adj*. **green'y.**—**green'back** an American note; **green ban** (*Austr.*) the refusal of trade unions to work on environmentally and socially objectionable projects; **green belt** a strip of open land surrounding a town; **Green Beret** (*coll.*) a British or American commando—*adj*. **green'-eyed** having green eyes: jealous (**the green-eyed monster** jealousy).—**greenfield site** a site, separate from existing developments, which is to be developed for the first time; **green'finch, green'linnet** a finch of a green colour, with some grey; **green'fingers** (or **thumb**) a knack of making plants grow well; **green'fly** a plant-louse or aphis; **green'grocer** a dealer in fresh vegetables; **green'hand** an inferior sailor; **green'heart** a S. American tree of the laurel family with very hard wood; **green'horn** a raw, inexperienced youth; **green'house** a glasshouse for plants, esp. one with little or no artificial heating: the cockpit of an aircraft—from the transparent sides (*airmen's slang*); **greenhouse effect** the progressive warming-up of the earth's surface due to the blanketing effect of man-made carbon dioxide in the atmosphere; **Green** or **Emerald Isle** Ireland; **green'keeper** one who has the care of a golf-course or bowling-green; **green light** permission to go ahead, **green manuring** growing one crop and digging it under to fertilise its successor; **green monkey** a West African long-tailed monkey, *Cercopithecus sabaeus* (**green monkey disease** a sometimes fatal virus disease with fever and haemorrhaging, orig. identified among technicians handling green monkeys in Marburg, Germany (also *Marburg disease*)); **green paper** a statement of proposed government policy, intended as a basis for parliamentary discussion; **green plover** the lapwing; **green pound** the agreed value of the pound used to express EEC farm prices in sterling; **green revolution** agricultural advances in developing countries; **green road, way** a grassy country track used by walkers; **green'room** the retiring-room of actors in a theatre, which originally had the walls coloured green; **green'shank** a large sandpiper with long, somewhat greenish legs; **green sickness** chlorosis; **greenstick fracture** see **fract**; **green'stone** nephrite: a vague name for any compost basic or intermediate igneous rock, **green'stuff** green vegetables, esp. of the cabbage kind; **green'sward** sward or turf green with grass; **green turtle** a tropical and sub-tropical sea turtle (*Chelonia mydas*) with a greenish shell.—**Green Cross Code** a code of road-safety rules for children issued in 1971; **something green in one's eye** a sign that one is gullible. [O E. *grēne*]

greengage *grēn'gāj'*, *n.* a green and very sweet variety of plum. [Said to be named from Sir W. *Gage* of Hengrave Hall, near Bury, before 1725]

Greenwich (Mean) Time *grin'ij, gren', -ıch (mēn) tīm* mean solar time for the meridian of *Greenwich*.

greet' *grēt, v.t.* to accost with salutation or kind wishes: to send kind wishes to: to meet, receive: to become evident to:—*pr.p* **greet'ing**; *pa.t.* and *pa.p.* **greet'ed**. —*n.* **greet'ing** expression of kindness or joy: salutation. [O.E *grētan*, to greet, to meet.]

greet² *grēt, (Scot.) v.ı* to weep.—*n.* weeping: a spell of weeping. [O.E. (Anglian) *grētan*.]

gregarious *gri-gā'rı-əs, adj.* associating in flocks and herds: growing together but not matted (*bot.*): fond of the company of others (*fig.*).—*adv.* **grega'riously.**—*n.* **grega'riousness.** [L. *gregārius—grex, gregis,* a flock.]

Gregorian *gri-gō'ri-ən, -go', adj.* belonging to or established by *Gregory*—as the Gregorian chant or tones, introduced by Pope Gregory I (6th cent), the calendar, reformed by Gregory XIII (1582), the reflecting telescope of James Gregory (1638–75).—*n* follower of any Gregory: member of an 18th-century English brotherhood

gremial *grē'mi-əl, adj.* pertaining to the lap or bosom.— *n.* a cloth laid on a bishop's knees to keep his vestments clean from oil at ordinations. [L. *gremium,* the lap.]

gremlin *grem'lin, n.* orig. a goblin accused of vexing airmen, causing mechanical trouble to aircraft. an imaginary mischievous agency.

grenade *gri-nād', n.* a small bomb thrown by the hand or

shot from a rifle: a glass projectile containing chemicals for putting out fires, testing drains, dispensing poison-gas or tear-gas, etc.—*ns.* **grenadier** (*gren-ə-dēr'*) orig. a soldier who threw grenades: then, a member of the first company of every battalion of foot: now used as the title (Grenadier Guards) of part of the Guards Division of infantry; **grenadine** (*-dēn'*) a pomegranate (or other) syrup: slices of veal or poultry fillets [Fr.,—Sp. *granada,* pomegranate—L. *grānātus,* full of seeds (*grāna*).]

grenadilla. Same as **granadilla.**

grenadier¹. See under **grenade.**

grenadine² *gren'ə-dēn, n.* a thin silk or mixed fabric. [Fr., perh. *Granada.*]

gressorial *gres-ō', -o'rı-əl, (zool)* adj. adapted for walking.—Also **gresso'rious.** [L. *gressus,* pa.p. of *gradī,* to walk.]

grew *grōō, pa.t.* of **grow.**

grey, gray *grā, adj* of a mixture of black and white with little or no hue: dull: dismal: neutral· anonymous: intermediate in character, condition, etc.: grey-haired, old, mature.—*n.* a grey colour: a grey or greyish animal, esp a horse.—*v.t.* to make grey or dull.— *v i.* to become grey or dull.—*adj.* **grey'ish** somewhat grey.—*adv.* **grey'ly.**—*n.* **grey'ness.**—**grey area** an area between two extremes, having (mingled) characteristics of both of them· a situation in which there are no clear-cut distinctions; **grey'beard** one whose beard is grey: an old man: a stoneware jar for liquor.—*adj.* **grey'-eyed.**—**Grey Friar** (also without *caps.*) a Franciscan; **grey'-goose** the common wild goose (*Anser anser*).—*adjs.* **grey'-haired, grey'-headed.**—**grey'hen** the female of the blackcock; **grey'-lag** the grey-goose (perhaps from its lateness in migrating)—also **grey-lag goose; grey matter** the ashen-grey active part of the brain and spinal cord; **grey squirrel** a N American squirrel naturalised in Britain; **grey wolf** the N. American timber wolf. [O.E. *grǣg.*]

greyhound *grā'hownd, n.* a tall and slender dog with great speed and keen sight. [O.E. *grīghund* (cf. O.N. *greyhundr—grey,* bitch), *hund, dog.*]

greywacke *grā-wak'ı, n.* an indurated sedimentary rock composed of grains (round or angular) and splinters of quartz, feldspar, slate, etc., in a hard matrix. [Ger. *Grauwacke,* partly translated, partly adopted.]

gribble *grıb'l, n* a small marine isopod (genus *Limnoria*) that bores into timber under water. [Perh.— *grub.*]

grid. See **gridiron.**

griddle *grid'l, n.* a flat iron plate for baking cakes.— Also (*Scot.*) **gird'le** (*gûr'dl, gir'dl*) [Anglo-Fr. *gridil,* from a dim. of L. *crātis,* a hurdle.]

gridiron *grid'ī-ərn, n.* a frame of iron bars for broiling over a fire: a frame to support a ship during repairs: a network: a football field (*U.S.*).—*v.t.* to cover with parallel bars or lines.—*n.* **grid** (back formation) a grating: a gridiron: a framework: a network· a network of power transmission lines: a network of lines for finding places on a map, or for other purpose: framework above a theatre stage from which scenery and lights may be suspended.—**grid'lock** (*U.S.*) a traffic jam. [M.E. *gredıre,* a griddle; from the same source as **griddle**, but the term. *-ıre* became confused with M.E. *ire,* iron.]

grief *grēf, n.* sorrow: distress: great mourning: affliction: cause of sorrow.—*adjs.* **grief'ful** full of grief; **grief'less.**—*adj.* **grief'-stricken** crushed with sorrow. —**come to grief** to meet with reverse, disaster, mishap. [O.Fr.,—L. *gravis,* heavy.]

grieve *grēv, v.t.* to cause grief or pain of mind to: to make sorrowful: to vex —*v i.* to feel grief· to mourn —*ns.* **griev'ance** cause or source of grief: ground of complaint· condition felt to be oppressive or

wrongful. distress: burden. hardship grief; **griev'er.**
—*adv.* **griev'ingly.**—*adj.* **griev'ous** causing grief:
burdensome: painful: severe: hurtful —*adv.* **griev'-
ously.**—*n* **griev'ousness.** [O Fr *grever*—L. *gravāre*
—*gravis*, heavy.]

griffin, griffon, gryfon, gryphon *grif'in, -ən, ns.* an
imaginary animal with lion's body and eagle's beak
and wings: a tip, a signal or warning.—*adj.* **griff'inish.**
—**griffon vulture** a European vulture, *Gyps fulvus*
[Fr. *griffon*—L *grȳphus*—Gr *gryps*, a bird, probably
the *lämmergeier*, a griffin—*grȳpos*, hook-nosed.]

griffon *grif'ən, n.* a dog like a coarse-haired terrier.—
Brussels griffon a toy dog with a rather snub nose.
[Prob. from **griffin.**]

grift *grift*, (*U.S.*) *v ι.* to swindle.—Also *n.*—*n.* **grif'ter**
a con man, swindler. [Perh from **graft**².]

grig *grig, n* a cricket: a grasshopper: a small lively eel,
the sand-eel.—**merry as a grig** very merry and lively.

gri(-)gri. See **grisgris.**

grill¹ *gril, v.t.* to broil on a gridiron, etc. by radiant
heat: to scallop: to torment: to cross-examine harass-
ingly.—*v.ι.* to undergo grilling.—*n.* a grating: a
gridiron: the part of a cooker on which meat, etc. is
grilled: a grill-room: a grilled dish: an act of grilling.
—*ns.* **grillade'** anything grilled.—*adj.* **grilled.**—*n.*
grill'ing.—**grill'-room** part of a restaurant where
beefsteaks, etc., are served grilled to order.—**mixed
grill** a dish of several grilled meats usu. with mushrooms, tomatoes, etc. [Fr. *griller*—*gril*, a gridiron,
from a dim. of L. *crātis*, a grate.]

grill², grille *gril, n.* a lattice, or grating, or screen, or
openwork of metal, generally used to enclose or protect a window, shrine, etc.: a grating in a convent or
jail door, etc. [Fr.; see **grill¹**.]

grilse *grils, n.* a young salmon on its first return from
salt water.

grim *grim, adj.* forbidding: ferocious: ghastly: sullen·
repellent. stern: unyielding: unpleasant.—*adv.*
grim'ly.—*n.* **grim'ness.** [O.E. *grim(m)*.]

grimace *gri-mās', n.* a distortion of the face, in jest,
etc.: a smirk.—*v.ι.* to make grimaces. [Fr.]

grimalkin *gri-mal'kin, -mol'kin, n.* an old cat: a cat
generally. [grey and **Malkin,** a dim. of *Maud.*]

grime *grīm, n* sooty or coaly dirt: ingrained dirt.—*v.t.*
to soil deeply.—*adv.* **grim'ily.**—*n* **grim'iness.**—*adj.*
grim'y. [Cf. Flem. *grijm.*]

grin *grin, v.ι.* to set the teeth together and withdraw
the lips in pain, derision, etc: to give a broad smile.—
v t. to express by grinning:—*pr.p.* **grinn'ing;** *pa.t.* and
pa.p. **grinned.**—*n.* act of grinning. [O.E. *grennian*;
allied to **groan.**]

grind *grīnd, v.t.* to reduce to powder by friction or
crushing: to wear down, sharpen, smooth or roughen
by friction: to rub together: to force (in, into; *lit.* and
fig.): to produce by great effort, or by working a
crank (with *out*): to oppress or harass: to work by a
crank.—*v.ι.* to be moved or rubbed together: to jar or
grate: to drudge at any tedious task: to read hard:—
pr.p. **grind'ing;** *pa.t.* and *pa.p* **ground** (*grownd.*)—*n.*
the act, sound, or jar of grinding: drudgery: laborious
study for a special examination, etc.—*ns.* **grind'er;**
grind'ery a place, where knives, etc., are ground;
grind'ing act or process of the verb to grind: reducing
to powder.—*adj.* for grinding: wearing down: very
severe: extortionate: (of sound) harsh: giving a harsh
sound.—**grind'stone** a circular revolving stone for
grinding or sharpening tools, **ground glass** glass
obscured by grinding, sandblast, or etching.—**grind
the face(s) of** to oppress as by taxation; **keep one's nose
to the grindstone** to subject one to severe continuous
toil or punishment. [O.E. *grindan.*]

gringo *gring'gō, n.* in Spanish-speaking America, one
whose language is not Spanish:—*pl.* **grin'gos.** [Sp.,

gibberish, prob.—*Griego,* Greek]

grip *grip, n.* a grasp or firm hold, esp. with the hand or
mind: strength of grasp: the handle or part by which
anything is grasped: a mode of grasping. a particular
mode of grasping hands for mutual recognition: a
gripsack, travelling bag (orig. *U.S*): a holding or
clutching device, e.g. a clasp for the hair: power:
pinch of distress: mastery: power of holding the mind
or commanding the emotions: gripe: grippe.—*v.t.* to
take or maintain fast hold of· to hold fast the attention or interest of: to command the emotions of.—
Also *v ι.*—*pr.p.* **gripp'ing;** *pa.t.* and *pa.p.* **gripped**
(*gript*).—*n.* **gripp'er** one who, that which, grips: a
clutch: a claw.—**grip'sack** a bag for travel.—**come,
get to grips (with)** to tackle at close quarters, or (*fig.*)
seriously and energetically. [O.E. *gripe,* grasp,
gripa, handful.]

gripe *grīp, v.t.* to grasp: to seize and hold fast: to
squeeze: to afflict: to oppress· to give pain to the
bowels of.—*v.ι.* to clutch. to keep on complaining
(*coll.*).—*n.* fast hold: grasp: forcible retention: a
grumble (*coll.*): pain: (esp. in *pl.*) severe spasmodic
pain in the intestines.—*n* **grip'er.**—*adj.* **grip'ing**
avaricious: of a pain, seizing acutely —*adv.* **grip'-
ingly.**—**gripe'-water** a carminative solution given
esp. to babies. [O.E. *gripan* (*grāp, gripen*).]

grippe *grēp, n.* influenza. [Fr.,—*gripper,* to seize.]

grisaille *grē-zāl', -za'ē, n.* a style of painting on walls or
ceilings, in greyish tints in imitation of bas-reliefs: a
similar style of painting on pottery, enamel, glass: a
work in this style.—Also *adj.* [Fr.,—*gris,* grey.]

Griselda *griz-el'də, n.* a woman of excessive meekness
and patience, from the heroine of an old tale.

griseofulvin *griz-i-ō-fōōl'vin,* (*med.*) *n.* oral antibiotic
used as treatment for fungus infections. [Isolated
from the fungus *Penicillium griseofulvin dierckx*; L.
griseus, grey, *fulvus,* reddish yellow.]

grisette *gri-zet', n.* a gay young working-class French-
woman. [Fr. *grisette,* a grey gown, which used to be
worn by that class—*gris,* grey.]

grisgris, grigri, greegree (also **gris-gris** etc.) *grē'grē, n.*
African charm, amulet, or spell [Fr.; prob. of
African origin.]

grisly *griz'li, adj.* frightful, ghastly.—*n.* **gris'liness.**
[O.E *grislic*]

grist *grist, n.* corn for grinding, or ground: corn for
grinding, or ground, at one time: malt for one
brewing: profit (*fig.*).—**grist'-mill** a mill for grinding
grain.—(**bring**) **grist to the mill** (to be) a source of
profit. [O.E *grīst;* cf. **grind.**]

gristle *gris'l, n.* cartilage.—*n.* **grist'liness.**—*adj.*
grist'ly. [O.E. *gristle.*]

grit *grit, n.* small hard particles of sand, stone, etc.:
small woody bodies in a pear: a coarse sandstone,
often with angular grains: texture of stone: firmness
of character, spirit.—*v.t.* and *v.i.* to grind: to grate: to
spread with grit.—*ns.* **gritt'er; gritt'iness.**— *adj.*
gritt'y having or containing hard particles: of the
nature of grit. grating: determined, plucky.—**grit
blasting** a process used in preparation for metal
spraying which cleans the surface and gives it the
roughness required to retain the sprayed metal particles; **grit'stone.** [O.E. *grēot.*]

grits *grits, n.pl.* coarsely ground grain, esp. oats: a
boiled dish of this. [O.E *grytta;* cf. **groats.**]

grizzle¹ *griz'l, n.* a grey colour —*adjs* **grizz'led** grey,
or mixed with grey, **grizz'ly** of a grey colour.—*n.* the
grizzly bear (*Ursus horribilis*) of the Rocky Mountains. [M.E. *grisel*—Fr. *gris,* grey.]

grizzle² *griz'l, v.ι.* to grumble to whimper: to fret.—*n.*
a bout of grizzling.—*n.* **grizz'ler.**

groan *grōn, v ι* to utter a deep rumbling or voiced
sound as in distress or disapprobation: to be afflicted

(fig.) —*n.* a deep moan: a grinding rumble.—*n.* and *adj* **groan'ing.**—**groaning board** a table weighed down with very generous supplies of food. [O.E *grānian.*]

groat *grōt, n* an English silver coin, worth fourpence. [O.L.G. *grote,* or Du *groot,* lit, great, i.e. thick.]

groats *grōts, n.pl.* the grain of oats deprived of the husks. [O.E. *grotan* (pl.).]

grocer *grōs'ər, n.* a dealer in staple foods, general household supplies.—*ns.* **gro'cery** the trade or business of a grocer: (usu in *pl*) articles sold by grocers; **grocetē'ria** a self-service grocery store. [Earlier *grosser,* a wholesale dealer; O.Fr. *grossier*—L L *grossārius*—*grossus,* cf. **gross.**]

grog *grog, n.* a mixture of spirits and water: (an) alcoholic drink, esp beer (*Austr. coll*).—*v.i* to drink grog —*ns* **grogg'ery** (*U.S.*) a low public-house; **grogg'iness** state of being groggy.—*adj.* **grogg'y** affected by grog, partially intoxicated (*arch.*): dazed, unsteady from illness or exhaustion: weak and staggering from blows (*boxing*). [From Old *Grog,* the nickname (apparently from his *grogram* cloak) of Admiral Vernon, who in 1740 ordered that rum (until 1970 officially issued to sailors) should be mixed with water]

grogram *grog'rəm, n.* a kind of coarse cloth of silk and mohair. [O.Fr. *gros grain,* coarse grain.]

groin[1] *groin, n.* the fold between the belly and the thigh: the line of intersection of two vaults, also a rib along the intersection (*archit.*).—*v.t.* to form into groins, to build in groins.—*adj.* **groined.**—*n.* **groin'ing.**—**groin'-cen'tring** the centring of timber during construction [Early forms *grind, grine,* perh.—O.E. *grynde,* abyss.]

groin[2]. U.S. spelling of **groyne** (q.v.).

gromet, grommet. Same as **grummet.**

groom *grōōm, grōōm, n.* one who has the charge of horses: a title of several household officers· a bridegroom.—*v.t.* to tend, esp. a horse: to smarten. to prepare for political office, stardom, or success in any sphere.—**grooms'man** the attendant on a bridegroom.

groove *grōōv, n.* a furrow, or long hollow, such as is cut with a tool: the track cut into the surface of a gramophone record along which the needle of the gramophone moves: a set routine: an exalted mood, one's highest form (*jazz slang*).—*v t.* to grave or cut a groove or furrow in.—*v.i.* (*slang*) to experience great pleasure. to be groovy.—*adj.* **groov'y** (also **in the groove;** *jazz slang*) in top form, or in perfect condition: up to date in style: generally, pleasant, delightful: following a set routine [Prob. Du. *groef, groeve,* a furrow.]

grope *grōp, v.i* to search, feel about, as if blind or in the dark.—*v t* to search by feeling (one's way) to fondle (someone) lasciviously (*coll.*).—*adv.* **grop'-ingly.** [O.E. *grāpian;* allied to **grab, gripe.**]

groper. Same as **grouper.**

grosbeak *grōs'bēk, n.* the hawfinch, or other finch, with thick, heavy, seed-crushing bill: now usu applied to various more or less related birds, as the cardinal and the rose-breasted grosbeak [Fr *grosbec*—*gros,* thick, *bec,* beak.]

groschen *grō'shən, n* an Austrian coin, a 100th part of a schilling· a ten-pfennig piece. [Ger.]

grosgrain *grō'grān, n.* a heavy corded silk used especially for ribbons and hat bands [Fr.]

gros point *grō point,* a large cross-stitch: embroidery composed of this stitch [Fr.]

gross *grōs, adj.* coarse rough dense· palpable· flagrant, glaring extreme. shameful whole coarse in mind: stupid· sensual· obscene total, including everything —*n* the main bulk· the whole taken to-

gether: twelve dozen:—*pl.* **gross.**—*v.t.* to make as total profit.—*adv* **gross'ly.**—*n.* **gross'ness.**—**great gross** a dozen gross; **gross domestic product** the gross national product less income from foreign investments; **gross national product** the total value of all goods and services produced by a country in a specified period (usu. annually); **gross up** to convert a net figure into a gross one for the purpose of tax calculation, etc.; **in gross** in bulk, wholesale. [Fr *gros*—L. *grossus,* thick.]

grotesque *grō-tesk', adj.* extravagantly formed: fantastic: ludicrous, absurd.—*n.* extravagant ornament, containing animals, plants, etc., in fantastic or incongruous forms (*art*): a bizarre figure or object.—*adv.* **grotesque'ly.**—*ns.* **grotesque'ness; grotesqu'ery, grotesqu'erie.** [Fr *grotesque*—It. *grottesca*—*grotta,* a grotto.]

grotto *grot'ō, n.* a cave: an imitation cave, usu. fantastic:—*pl.* **grott'oes, grott'os.** [It. *grotta* (Fr *grotte*) —L. *crypta*—Gr. *kryptē,* a crypt, vault.]

grotty *grot'i,* (*slang*) *adj* ugly, in bad condition, or useless. [**grotesque.**]

grouch *growch, v.i.* to grumble —*n.* a grumbling: sulks: a grumbler.—*adv.* **grouch'ily.**—*n.* **grouch'-iness.**—*adj.* **grouch'y.** [O.Fr. *groucher,* to grumble.]

ground[1]. See **grind.**

ground[2] *grownd, n* the solid land underlying an area of water (*naut.*): the solid surface of the earth: a portion of the earth's surface: land: soil: the floor, etc.: earth (*elect.*): position: field or place of action: that on which something is raised (*lit.* or *fig.*): foundation: sufficient reason: the surface on which the work is represented (*art*): surrounding rock (*mining*): the space within which the batsman must be in touch if he is not to be stumped or run out (*cricket*): (*pl.*) an area of land attached to or surrounding a building: (*pl.*) dregs or sediment: (*pl.*) basis of justification —*v.t.* to fix on a foundation or principle: to put or rest on the ground: to cause to run aground: to instruct in first principles: to cover with a layer of plaster, etc., as a basis for painting: to coat with a composition, as a surface to be etched: to put to earth (*elect.*): to keep on the ground, prevent from flying.—*v.i.* to come to the ground: to strike the bottom and remain fixed.— *n.* **ground'age** a charge on a ship in port.—*adj.* **ground'ed.**—*adv.* **ground'edly** on good grounds.— *ns* **ground'er** a ball that keeps low; **ground'ing** foundation: sound general knowledge of a subject: the background of embroidery, etc.: act or process of preparing or laying a ground: act of laying or of running aground.—*adj.* **ground'less** without ground, foundation, or reason.—*adv.* **ground'lessly.**—*ns.* **ground'lessness; ground'ling** a fish that keeps near the bottom of the water.—**ground'bait** bait dropped to the bottom to bring fish to the neighbourhood, **ground'-bass** a bass part constantly repeated with varying melody and harmony (*mus.*); **ground'burst** the explosion of a bomb on the ground (as opposed to in the air), **ground'-cherry** any of the European dwarf cherries· any of several plants of the genus Physalis. the fruit of these plants; **ground'-control** control, by information radioed from a ground installation, of aircraft observed by radar; **ground cover** low plants and shrubs growing among the trees in a forest: various low herbaceous plants used to cover an area instead of grass; **ground crew** see **ground staff;** **ground effect** the extra aerodynamic lift, exploited by hovercraft, etc. and affecting aircraft flying near the ground, caused by the cushion of trapped air beneath the vehicle; **ground'-feed'er** a fish that feeds at the bottom, **ground floor, storey** the floor on or near a level with the ground; **ground'-hog** the woodchuck·

the aardvark, **ground'-ivy** a British labiate creeping-plant (*Nepeta*) whose leaves when the edges curl become ivy-like, **ground'mass** the fine-grained part of an igneous rock, glassy or minutely crystalline, in which the larger crystals are embedded; **ground'-nut** the peanut or monkey-nut, **ground'-plan** plan of the horizontal section of the lowest or ground storey of a building. first plan, general outline, **ground'prox** a device, fitted to large passenger aircraft, which warns the pilot when altitude falls below a given level (*ground prox*imity warning system), **ground'-rent** rent paid to a landlord for the use of the ground for a specified term, usually in England ninety-nine years, **ground rule** a basic rule of procedure· a modifying (sports) rule for a particular place or circumstance, **ground'sheet** a waterproof sheet spread on the ground by campers, etc, **grounds'man, ground'man** a man charged with the care of a cricket-ground or a sports-field. an aerodrome mechanic; **ground'speed** (*aero*) speed of an aircraft relative to the ground, **ground'-squirr'el** the chipmunk or hackee; **ground staff** aircraft mechanics, etc , whose work is on the ground (also **ground crew**)· paid staff of players (*cricket*): people employed to look after a sports-field, **ground stroke** in tennis, a return played after the ball has bounced, **ground swell** a broad, deep undulation of the ocean caused by a distant gale or earthquake: a movement, as of public or political opinion or feeling, which is evident although the cause or leader is not known, **ground'work** that which forms the ground or foundation of anything. the basis: the essential part the first principle —**break ground** to take the first step in any project; **cut, take the ground from under someone, someone's feet** to anticipate someone's arguments or actions and destroy their force; **fall to the ground** to come to nothing, **gain ground** to advance: to become more widely influential: to spread, **give ground** to fall back, retreat (*lit.* and *fig*); **hold** or **stand one's ground** to stand firm, (**let in**) **on the ground floor** (to admit) on the same terms as the original promoters, or at the start (of a business venture, etc.); **lose ground** to fall back to decline in influence, etc ; **off the ground** started, under way; **on one's own ground** in circumstances with which one is familiar; **run to ground** to hunt out, track down, **shift one's ground** to change one's standpoint in a situation or argument; **to ground** into hiding [O.E. *grund*.]

groundsel grown(d)'sl, *n.* a very common yellow-flowered composite weed of waste ground (*Senecio vulgaris*). [O.E. *gundeswilge*, appar —*gund*, pus, *swelgan*, to swallow, from its use in poultices.]

group grōōp, *n.* a number of persons or things together a number of individual things related in some definite way differentiating them from others: a clique, school, section of a party: a scientific classification: a combination of figures forming a harmonious whole (*art*): a system of elements having a binary operation that is associative, an identity element for the operation, and an inverse for every element (*math.*): a division in the Scout organisation. a pop-group.—*v t* to form into a group or groups.—*v i.* to fall into harmonious combination.—*ns.* **group'age** the collection of objects or people into a group or groups, **group'ie, group'y** (*slang*) a (usu. female) fan who follows pop-groups, or other celebrities, wherever they appear, often in the hope of having sexual relations with them; **group'ing** the act of disposing and arranging figures in a group (*art*); **group'ist** an adherent of a group.—Also *adj.*—**group'-captain** an airforce officer answering to a colonel or naval captain; **group dynamics** the interaction of human behaviour within a small social group; **group insurance** insurance issued on a number of people under a single policy, **group practice** a medical practice in which several doctors work together as partners, **group sex** sexual activity in which several people take part simultaneously; **group theory** (*math*) the investigation of the properties of groups; **group therapy** therapy in which a small group of people with the same psychological or physical problems discuss their difficulties under the chairmanship of, e.g , a doctor. [Fr *groupe*—It *groppo*, a bunch, knot—Gmc.]

grouper grōōp'ər, **groper** grōp'ər, *ns* names given to many fishes, esp various kinds resembling bass [Port *garoupa*]

grouse¹ grows, *n.* the heathcock or moorfowl (*Lagopus scoticus*, the red grouse), a plump bird, found on Scottish moors and hills and in certain other parts of Britain: extended to other birds of the family Tetraonidae, incl the *black grouse* or *blackcock:—pl.* **grouse.**

grouse² grows, *v i* to grumble.—*n.* a grumble.—*n* **grous'er.** [Cf **grouch.**]

grout¹ growt, *n* the sediment of liquor a thin coarse mortar: a fine plaster for finishing ceilings —*v t* to fill and finish with grout —*n* **grout'ing** filling up or finishing with grout the material so used.

grout² growt, *v.t.* to root or grub with the snout. [Perh conn with O E *grēot*, grit]

grove grōv, *n.* a wood of small size, generally of a pleasant or ornamental character. an avenue of trees [O E *grāf*, possibly tamarisk]

grovelling gruv', grov'(ə)-ling, *adv* and *adj* prone face-down: later felt to be the pr p. or verbal noun of the new *v.t* **grov'el**, to crawl on the earth, esp in abject fear, etc to be base or abject:—*pa t* and *pa.p* **grov'elled.**—*n* **grov'eller.** [M E *groveling, grofling*, prone—O N. *grūfa*, and suff -*ling*.]

grow grō, *v.i* to have life to become enlarged by a natural process: to advance towards maturity to increase in size. to develop: to become greater in any way: to become.—*v.t* to cause or allow to grow: to produce. to cultivate: (in *pass.*) to cover with growth. —*pa t* **grew** (grōō), *pa p* **grown** (grōn) —*n.* **grow'er.** —*n* and *adj* **grow'ing.**—*n* **growth** a growing· gradual increase: progress, development: that which has grown: a morbid formation: increase in value (**growth-orientated** providing increased capital rather than high interest).—Also *adj* —**grow'-bag** , **grow'ing-bag** a large plastic bag containing compost in which seeds can be germinated and plants grown to full size; **grow'ing-pains'** neuralgic pains in young persons (also *fig*), **grow'ing-point** (*bot*.) the meristem at the apex of an axis, where active cell-division occurs and differentiation of tissues begins, **grown'-up** an adult.—Also *adj* —**grow on, upon** to gain a greater hold on to gain in the estimation of; **grow out of** to issue from, result from. to pass beyond in development: to become too big for, **grow together** to become united by growth; **grow up** to advance in growth. become full-grown, mature, or adult to spring up. [O E. *grōwan*]

growl growl *v.i.* to utter a deep rough murmuring sound like a dog: to grumble surlily —*v t* to utter or express by growling —*n.* a murmuring, snarling sound, as of an angry dog a surly grumble.—*ns.* **growl'er; growl'ery** a retreat for times of ill-humour, **growl'ing.**—*adv.* **growl'ingly.**—*adj* **growl'y.**

grown, growth. See **grow.**

groyne groin, *n* breakwater, of wood or other material. to check erosion and sand-drifting [Prob O Fr *groign*, snout—L *grunnire*, to grunt, but perh the same as **groin¹**.]

grub grub, *v.t.* to dig in the dirt to be occupied meanly —*v t* to dig or root out of the ground (generally followed by *up* or *out*) to dig up the surface of (ground) to clear it for agriculture, etc —*n* an insect larva, esp one thick and soft: food (*coll*) —*n* **grubb'er** he who, or that which, grubs an implement for grubbing or stirring the soil· a grub-kick.—*adj.* **grubb'y** dirty: infested with grubs —**grub'-kick** (*Rugby football*) a kick where the ball moves along the ground; **grub'-screw** a small headless screw; **grub'-stake** (*U.S.*) outfit, provisions, etc , given to a prospector for a share in finds —*v t.* to provide with.—**Grub Street** a former name of Milton Street, London, once inhabited by hacks and shabby writers generally: applied to any mean literary production [M.E. *grobe.*]

grudge *gruj, v t.* to look upon with envy to give or allow unwillingly (something to a person): to be loth (to do) —*n* secret enmity or envy· an old cause of quarrel —*n.* and *adj.* **grudg'ing.**—*adv.* **grudg'ingly.** [O Fr *groucher,* to grumble.]

gruel *groo'əl, n.* a thin food made by boiling oatmeal in water.—*v t.* to subject to severe or exhausting experience.—*n.* and *adj* **gru'elling.** [O Fr. *gruel* (Fr *gruau*), groats—L L. *grûtellum,* dim of *grûtum,* meal.]

gruesome *groo'səm, adj.* horrible· grisly: macabre.—*n* **grue'someness.** [Cf Du. *gruwzaam,* Ger. *grausam.*]

gruff *gruf, adj.* rough, or abrupt in manner or sound.—*adj.* **gruff'ish.**—*adv* **gruff'ly.**—*n.* **gruff'ness.** [Du. *grof.*]

grumble *grum'bl, v t.* to murmur with discontent· to express discontent· to mutter, mumble, murmur. to growl: to rumble.—*n.* the act of grumbling: an instance of grumbling: a cause of grumbling.—*n.* **grum'bler.**—*n.* and *adj* **grum'bling.**—*adv.* **grum'blingly.**—*adj.* **grum'bly** inclined to grumble [Cf Du *grommelen,* freq. of *grommen,* to mutter]

grume *groom, n.* a thick fluid a clot.—*adjs* **grum'ous, grum'ose** composed of grains [O.Fr *grume,* a bunch —L. *grûmus,* a little heap.]

grummet, grommet, gromet *grum'it, n* a ring of rope· a metal ring lining an eyelet: an eyelet: a washer.—**grumm'et-hole.** [Perh. 15th-cent. Fr. *gromette,* curb of a bridle]

grumose, -ous. See grume.

grumpy *grum'pi, adj.* surly —*adv* **grum'pily.**—*n.* **grump'iness.** [Obs. *grump,* snub, sulkiness.]

Grundyism *grun'di-izm, n.* conventional prudery, from Mrs *Grundy* in Morton's play, *Speed the Plough* (1798).

grunion *grun'yən, n.* a small Californian sea-fish which spawns on shore. [Prob. Sp. *gruñon,* grunter.]

grunt *grunt, v.i.* to make a sound like a pig.—*v.t.* to utter with a grunt.—*n.* a sound made by a pig: a similar sound: a fish of a family akin to the snappers, that grunts when taken from the sea.—*n.* **grunt'er** one who grunts: a pig: a grunting fish of various kinds.—*n.* and *adj* **grunt'ing.**—*adv.* **grunt'ingly.** [O E *grunnettan,* freq. of *grunian.*]

Gruyère *gru' or groo'yer,* or *-yer', n.* a whole-milk cheese, made at *Gruyère* (Switzerland) and elsewhere **gryfon, gryphon.** See griffin.

grysbok *gris'bok, n.* a small S. African antelope, ruddy chestnut with white hairs. [Du \ greybuck]

G-string. Same as gee-string.

g-suit. See under G.

guacamole *gwa-kə-mō'li, n.* a dish of mashed avocado with tomatoes, onions and seasoning. [Amer. Sp.— Nahuatl *ahuacamolli—ahuacatl,* avocado, *molli,* sauce.]

Guaiacum *gwi'ə-kəm, n.* a tropical American genus of trees, yielding lignum-vitae. (without *cap*) their greenish resin, used in medicine: (without *cap*) a tree of this genus. [Sp *guayaco,* from a Haitian word.]

guanaco *gwa-na'kō, n.* a wild llama.—Also **huana'co**

(*wa-*):—*pls* **guana'co(s), huana'co(s).** [Quechua *huanaco*]

guanin(e). See guano.

guano *gwa'nō, n.* the dung of sea-fowl, used as manure: artificially produced fertiliser, esp. made from fish—*pl* **gua'nos.**—*adj* **guanif'erous.**—*n* **gua'nin(e)** (*-nin, -nén*) a yellowish-white, amorphous substance, found in guano, liver, other organs of animals, germ cells of plants—a constituent of nucleic acids [Sp *guano, huano*—Peruv *huanu,* dung]

Guaraní *gwa-ra-nē', n* an Indian of a group of tribes of southern Brazil and Paraguay (*pl* **Guarani**)· their language, cognate with Tupí· **guarani** (*pl* **guaranies**) the monetary unit of Paraguay.—Also *adj.*

guarantee *gar-ən-tē', n* a person who makes a contract to see performed what another has undertaken: such a contract. surety or warrant: one responsible for the performance of some action, the truth of some statement, etc —*v.t.* to undertake as surety for another. to secure: to engage, undertake:—*pr p.* **guarantee'ing;** *pa.t.* and *pa.p* **guaranteed'.**—*ns* **guar'antor** (or *-tôr'*) one who makes a guaranty; **guar'anty** a securing, guaranteeing· a written undertaking to be responsible: a person who guarantees: a security.—*v.t.* to guarantee [Anglo-Fr *garantie—garant,* warrant and prob. Sp *garante;* see **warrant.**]

guard *gärd, v.t.* to ward, watch, or take care of. to protect from danger or attack: to escort· to protect the edge of, as by an ornamental border: to furnish with guards.—*v.i* to watch: to be wary.—*n.* ward, keeping: protection: watch: that which guards from danger: a man or body of men stationed to watch, protect, or keep in custody· one in charge of stage-coach or railway train state of caution: posture of defence: part of a sword hilt· a watch-chain· a cricketer's pad: (*pl*) household troops (Foot, Horse, and Life Guards).—*adjs.* **guard'able; guard'ant** (*her.*) having the face turned towards the beholder, **guard'ed** wary: cautious: uttered with caution —*adv.* **guard'edly.**—*ns.* **guard'edness; guard'ian** one who guards or takes care: one who has the care of a person, property, and rights of another (e g. a minor, law).—*adj.* protecting.—*n.* **guard'ianship.**—*adj* **guard'less** without a guard: defenceless —**guard dog** a watch-dog; **guard hair** one of the long coarse hairs which form the outer fur of certain mammals; **guard's house, guard'-room** a house or room for the accommodation of a guard of soldiers, where defaulters are confined; **guardian angel** an angel supposed to watch over a particular person: a person specially devoted to the interests of another; **guard'-rail** a rail acting as a safety barrier: an additional rail fitted to a railway track to improve a train's stability; **guard'-ring** a keeper, or finger-ring that serves to keep another from slipping off; **guards'man** a soldier of the guards, **guard's van** on a railway train, the van in which the guard travels —**mount guard** to go on guard; **on or off one's guard** on (or not on) the alert for possible danger: wary about what one says or does (or the reverse). [O Fr *garder*—O.H.G. *warten;* O E *weardian,* mod. Eng **ward.**]

guava *gwä'və, n.* a small tropical American tree (*Psidium*) its yellow, pear-shaped fruit, often made into jelly. [Sp. *guayaba,* guava fruit; of S Amer origin.]

guayule *gwà-ú'lâ, n.* a Mexican composite plant: the rubber yielded by it [Sp ; of Nahuatl origin.]

gubbins *gub'inz,* (*coll*) *n.sing.* a trivial object: a device, gadget.—*n sing* or *pl* rubbish [From obs. *gobbon,* portion. perh conn with **gobbet.**]

gubernator *gü'bər-nä-tər, n* a governor.—*n.* **gubernâ'tion** control, rule.—*adj.* **gubernatorial**

(-nə-tō'ri-əl, -to'). [L. gubernător, a steersman.]

gudgeon¹ guj'ən, n. an easily caught small carp-like freshwater fish (Gobio) a person easily cheated.— v.t. to impose on, cheat. [O.Fr. goujon—L. gōbiō, -ōnis, a kind of fish—Gr. kōbios; see goby.]

gudgeon² guj'ən, n· the bearing of a shaft, esp when made of a separate piece: a piece let into the end of a wooden shaft: a pin. [O.Fr goujon, pin of a pulley.]

guelder-rose gel'dər-rōz, n. a Viburnum with large white balls of flowers. [From Geldern or from Gelderland.]

guenon gen'ən, gə-nɔ̃, n. any species of the genus Cercopithecus, long-tailed African monkeys. [Fr.]

guerdon gûr'dən, n a reward or recompense.—v.t. to reward [O.Fr. guerdon.]

guéridon gā-rē-dɔ̃, ger'i-dən, n. a small ornate table or stand. [Fr.]

guernsey gûrn'zi, n. a close-fitting knitted upper garment, worn by sailors. (with cap.) one of a breed of dairy cattle from Guernsey, in the Channel Islands.

guerrilla, guerilla gər-il'ə, n. petty warfare: loosely, one who takes part in such warfare (properly **guer-rillero** -yā'ro, pl. **guerrilleros**).—Also adj.—**guerrilla strike** a sudden and brief industrial strike. [Sp. guerrilla, dim. of guerra, war.]

guess ges, v.t. to think, believe, suppose. to judge upon inadequate knowledge or none at all: to conjecture: to hit on or solve by conjecture.—v.i to make a conjecture or conjectures.—n. judgment or opinion without sufficient evidence or grounds: a random surmise.—adj. **guess'able**.—n. **guess'er**.—n. and adj. **guess'ing**.—adv. **guess'ingly**.—n. **guess'timate** an estimate based on very little knowledge.—**guess's work** the process or result of guessing—**anybody's guess** purely a matter of individual conjecture. [M.E. gessen.]

guest gest, n. a visitor received and entertained gratuitously or for payment: an animal inhabiting or breeding in another's nest.—adj. and n. (an artist, conductor, etc.) not a regular member of a company, etc., or not regularly appearing on a programme, but taking part on a special occasion.—v.i. to be a guest artist, etc.—**guest'-room** a room for the accommodation of a guest; **guest'-house** a hospice: a boarding-house; **guest'-night** a night when non-members of a society are entertained; **guest'-rope** a rope hanging over the side of a vessel to aid other vessels drawing alongside, etc. [O E. (Anglian) gest.]

guff guf, (slang) n. nonsense, humbug. [Perh. imit.]

guffaw guf-ö', v.i. to laugh loudly.—n. a loud laugh. [From the sound.]

guichet gē'shā, n. a small opening in a wall, door, etc., a ticket-office window. [Fr.; cf. wicket.]

guide gīd, v.t. to lead, conduct, or direct: to regulate: to influence.—n. he who, or that which, guides: one who conducts travellers, tourists, mountaineers, etc a Girl Guide (see **girl**): a guide-book: anything serving to direct, show the way, determine direction of motion or course of conduct.—adj. **guid'able**.—ns **guid'age** guidance, guid'ance direction: leadership, **guid'er** one who guides: a device for guiding: a captain or lieutenant in the Girl Guides.—adj **guide'less**.—n. **guide'ship**.—n and adj. **guid'ing**.—n. **guid'on** a pennant carried by a cavalry company or mounted battery: the officer bearing it —**guide'-book** a book of information for tourists, **guided missile** a jet- or rocket-propelled projectile carrying a warhead and electronically directed to its target for the whole or part of the way by remote control; **guide dog** a dog trained to lead blind persons, **guide'line** a line drawn, or a rope, etc., fixed, to act as a guide. an indication of course that should be followed, or of what future policy will be (fig), **guide'-post** a post to guide the

traveller; **guiding light, star** a person or thing adopted as a guide or model. [O.Fr. guider; prob. from a Gmc. root.]

guild, gild gild, n. an association for mutual aid: a corporation: a mediaeval association providing mutual support and protection (hist.).—**guild'hall** the hall of a guild: a town-hall. [O.E. gield, influenced by O.N. gildi.]

guilder, gilder gild'ər, n. an old Dutch and German gold coin: a modern Dutch gulden. [Du. gulden.]

guile gīl, n. wile, jugglery: cunning: deceit.—adjs. **guiled** armed with deceit: treacherous; **guile'ful** crafty deceitful.—adv. **guile'fully**.—n. **guile'fulness**.—adj **guile'less** without deceit: artless.—adv. **guile'lessly**.—n. **guile'lessness**. [O.Fr. guile, deceit, perh. Gmc.]

guillemot gil'i-mot, n a diving bird (Uria) of the auk family. [Fr., dim. of Guillaume, William, perh. suggested by Bret. gwelan, gull.]

guilloche gi-lōsh', n. an ornament formed of interlacing curved bands enclosing circles.—v.t. to decorate with intersecting curved lines. [Fr.]

guillotine gil'ə-tēn, -tēn', gē'yə-, n. an instrument for beheading by descent of a heavy oblique blade—adopted during the French Revolution, and named after Joseph Ignace Guillotin (1738–1814), a physician, who first proposed its adoption: a machine for cutting paper, straw, etc : a surgical instrument for cutting the tonsils: a specially drastic rule or closure for shortening discussion.—v.t. to behead, crop, or cut short by guillotine.

guilt gilt, n. the state of having done wrong: sin, sinfulness: the state of having broken a law: liability to a penalty.—adv. **guilt'ily**.—n. **guilt'iness**.—adj. **guilt'less** free from crime: innocent.—adv. **guilt'lessly**.—n. **guilt'lessness**.—adj. **guilt'y** justly chargeable: wicked: involving, indicating, burdened with, or pertaining to guilt.—**guilt complex** a mental preoccupation with one's (real or imagined) guilt; **guilty party** a person, organisation, etc. that is guilty.—**guilty of** having committed (evil or injudicious act). [Orig. a payment or fine for an offence; O.E. gylt.]

guimp, guimpe. See **gimp**.

guinea gin'i, n. an obsolete English gold coin first made of gold brought from Guinea, in Africa: its value, finally 21s.—adj. priced at a guinea.—**guin'ea-fowl** an African bird (Numida) of the pheasant family, dark-grey with white spots; **guin'ea-hen** a guinea-fowl: formerly, a turkey; **guin'ea-pig** a small S. American rodent, the cavy: a person used as the subject of an experiment—as the cavy commonly is in the laboratory.

guipure gē-poor', n. a kind of lace having no ground or mesh, the pattern sections fixed by interlacing threads: a species of gimp. [Fr. guipure—O.Fr guiper]

guise gīz, n manner, behaviour. custom: external appearance: dress.—v.t. to act as a guiser.—n. **guis'er** (chiefly Scot.) a person in disguise: a Christmas (or now usu Hallowe'en) mummer. [O.Fr. guise.]

guitar gi-tär', n. a fretted musical instrument, now six-stringed—like the lute, but flat-backed.—n. **guitar'ist**. [Fr guitare—L cithara—Gr kithara.]

gulag gōō'lag, n one of the system of esp. political prisons and forced labour camps in the Soviet Union (also fig.) [Russ. acronym, popularised by A Solzhenitsyn, Russ. author (1918–), in The Gulag Archipelago.]

gulch gulch, n. (U S) a ravine or narrow rocky valley, a gully

gulden gōōl'dən, n a gold or silver coin in Germany in the Middle Ages. a Dutch coin, the guilder or florin [Ger , lit golden.]

gules *gŭlz*, (*her.*) *n* a red colour. [O Fr. *gueules*, perh.—L. *gŭla*, the throat.]

gulf *gulf*, *n.* an indentation in the coast: a deep place: an abyss: a whirlpool: anything insatiable: a wide separation, e.g. between opponents' viewpoints.—*v.t* to engulf.—*v.i.* to flow like a gulf.—**gulf'weed** a large olive-brown seaweed (*Sargassum*) that floats unattached in great 'meadows' at the branching of the Gulf Stream and elsewhere in tropical oceans. [O.Fr *golfe*—Late Gr. *kolphos*—Gr. *kolpos*, the bosom.]

gull¹ *gul*, *n.* a sea-bird of the family Laridae, esp. of the genus Larus.—*n.* gull'ery a place where gulls breed. —*adj.* gull'-wing (of a motor-car door) opening upwards: (of an aircraft wing) having an upward-sloping short inner section and a long horizontal outer section. [Prob. W. *gwylan*.]

gull² *gul*, *n.* a dupe: an easily duped person.—*v.t.* to beguile, hoax.—*ns.* gull'er; gullibil'ity.—*adj.* gull'-ible easily deceived.

gullet *gul'it*, *n* the passage in the neck by which food is taken into the stomach: the throat. [O.Fr *goulet*, dim. of *goule* (Fr. *gueule*)—L. *gŭla*, the throat.]

gully, gulley *gul'i*, *n.* a channel worn by running water, as on a mountain-side: a ravine: a ditch: the position between point and slips (*cricket*).—*pl.* gull'ies, gull'-eys.—*v.t.* to wear a gully or channel in. [Prob. gullet.]

gulp *gulp*, *v t.* to swallow spasmodically or in large draughts.—*v.i.* to make a swallowing movement.—*n* a spasmodic or copious swallow: a movement as if of swallowing: a quantity swallowed at once: capacity for gulping. [Cf. Du. *gulpen*, gulp.]

gum¹ *gum*, *n.* the firm fleshy tissue that surrounds the bases of the teeth.—*adj.* gumm'y toothless.—**gum'-boil** a small abscess on the gum; gum'shield a soft pad worn by boxers to protect the teeth and gums [O.E. *gōma*, palate.]

gum² *gum*, *n.* a substance that collects in or exudes from certain plants, and hardens on the surface, dissolves or swells in water, but does not dissolve in alcohol or ether: a plant gum or similar substance used as an adhesive, a stiffener, or for other purpose: any gumlike or sticky substance: chewing-gum: a gumdrop (q.v.).—*v.t.* to smear, coat, treat, or unite with gum —*v.i.* to become gummy: to exude gum:—*pr.p.* gumm'ing; *pa.t.* and *pa.p.* gummed.—*adjs.* gumm'atous; gummif'erous producing gum.—*ns.* gumm'iness; gumm'ing act of fastening with gum: application of gum: becoming gummy.—*adjs.* gumm'-ous, gumm'y consisting of or resembling gum: producing or covered with gum.—**gum ammoniac, ammoniacum** a gum resin, inspissated juice of a Persian umbelliferous plant (*Dorema*), used in medicine and manufactures; gum arabic a gum obtained from various acacias; gum'boot a rubber boot; gum'drop a gelatinous type of sweet containing gum arabic; gum elastic rubber, gum resin a resin mixed with gum, gum'shoe (*U.S.*) a rubber overshoe: a shoe with rubber sole: a detective or policeman (*slang*).—Also *v.i.* (*slang*) to snoop, pry.—**gum tree** a tree that exudes gum, or gum resin, etc., esp. a Eucalyptus tree.—**gum up the works** (*coll.*) to make (e.g. a machine, a scheme) unworkable; up a gum tree in straits (from the opossum's refuge) [O.Fr *gomme* —L. *gummi*—Gr. *kommi*.]

gumbo *gum'bō*, *n.* the okra or its mucilaginous pods: a soup of which okra is an ingredient: a dish of okra pods seasoned: in central U.S. a fine soil which becomes sticky when wet.—*pl* gum'bos. [Angolan Negro (*ki*)*ngombo*.]

gumption *gum(p)'shən*, *n.* sense shrewdness commonsense —*adj.* gump'tious.

gun *gun*, *n.* a tubular weapon from which projectiles are discharged, usually by explosion: a cannon, rifle, revolver, etc.: a device for spraying, squirting, or otherwise propelling material: a signal by gun: one who carries a gun, a member of a shooting-party: a professional killer (*U.S. slang*): the throttle of an aircraft: the accelerator of a car.—*v.t.* to shoot: to shoot at: to provide with guns: to open the throttle of, to increase speed (also give the gun).—*v.i.* to shoot: to go shooting —*ns.* gunn'er one who works a gun: a private in the Artillery; gunn'ery the art of managing guns, or the science of artillery; gunn'ing.—gun barrel the tube of a gun; gun'boat a small vessel of light draught, fitted to carry one or more guns; gun-boat diplomacy show or threat of (orig. naval) force in international negotiation; gun carriage a carriage on which a cannon is mounted; gun'cotton an explosive prepared by saturating cotton with nitric and sulphuric acids; gun dog dog trained to work with a shooting-party; gun'fight fight involving two or more people with guns, esp in old American West.—Also *v.i.*—gun'fighter; gun'fire; gun'man a man who carries a gun, esp. an armed criminal; gun'metal an alloy of copper and tin in the proportion of about 9 to 1, once used in making cannon: an imitation thereof: the colour of the alloy; gun'play the use of guns, esp. in a fight or display of skill; gun'powder an explosive mixture of saltpetre, sulphur, and charcoal; gun'-room a room where guns are kept: on board ship, a mess-room for junior officers; gun'runner; gun'run-ning smuggling guns into a country; gun'ship an armed ship, helicopter, etc.; gun'shot the shot fired from a gun.—*adj.* caused by the shot of a gun.—*adj.* gun'-shy frightened by guns.—gun'slinger (*coll.*) a gunfighter; gun'smith a smith or workman who makes or repairs guns or small arms.—at gunpoint under, or using, the threat of injury from a gun; great gun a person of great importance (*coll.*; also big gun); gun for to seek, try to obtain: to seek to ruin; son of a gun a rogue, rascal (*slang*): used as an affectionate greeting: also *interj.* (*U.S.*); stand, stick, to one's guns to maintain one's position staunchly. [M.E. *gonne*, poss. from the woman's name *Gunhild*.]

gunge *gunj*, (*coll.*) *n.* any dirty, messy, or sticky substance.—*adj.* gun'gy. [Perh. a combination of goo and sponge.]

gung-ho *gung-hō'*, *adj.* (excessively or irrationally) enthusiastic, eager, zealous. [Chin. *kung*, work, *ho*, together.]

gunk *gungk*, (*coll.*) *n.* unpleasant, dirty, sticky material, or semi-solid usu valueless residue from a chemical process. [Orig. trademark of a grease-solvent.]

gunnel¹ *gun'l*, *n.* See gunwale.

gunnel² *gun'l*, a small long coast fish of the blenny family.

gunnery. See gun.

gunny *gun'i*, *n* a strong coarse jute fabric. [Hindi *ganī, gonī*, sacking—Sans *gonī*, a sack.]

gunter *gun'tər*, *n.* a Gunter's scale: a rig with topmast sliding on rings.—Gunter's chain a surveyor's chain of 100 links, 66 feet long (10 chains = 1 furlong; 10 sq. chains = 1 acre); Gunter's scale a scale graduated in several lines for numbers, log-arithmic sines, etc., so arranged that trigonomet-rical problems can be roughly solved by use of a pair of compasses, or in another form by sliding. [From the inventor, Edmund *Gunter* (1581–1626), astronomer]

gunwale, gunnel *gun'l*, *n.* the wale or upper edge of a ship's side next to the bulwarks, so called because the upper guns were pointed from it

gunyah *gun'ya*, (*Austr.*) *n* an Australian aboriginals' hut: a roughly-made shelter in the bush. [Aboriginal.]

guppy *gup'i*, *n.* a small West Indian fish (*Lebistes*) that multiplies very rapidly and feeds on mosquito larvae, also called *millions*. [From R J L *Guppy*, who sent it to the British Museum]

gurami. Same as **goramy.**

gurdwara *gûr'dwar-ə*, *n* a Sikh place of worship [Punjabi *gurduārā*—Sans *guru*, teacher, *dvāra*, door]

gurgle *gûr'gl*, *v i* to flow in an irregular noisy current· to make a bubbling sound —*n* the sound of gurgling. [Cf It. *gorgogliare*]

gurjun *gûr'jun*, *n* an East Indian tree yielding timber and a balsamic liquid used against leprosy [Hind *garjan*]

Gurkha *gōōr'kə*, *gûr'kə*, *n.* one of the dominant people of Nepal, a broad-chested fighting race claiming Hindu origin, but Mongolised, from whom regiments in the British and Indian armies were formed.

gurnard *gûr'nərd*, **gurnet** -*nit*, *ns* a fish with large angular head and three finger-like walking rays in front of the pectoral fin. [O Fr *gornard*, related to Fr. *grogner*, to grunt, from the sound they emit when taken.]

guru *gōō'rōō*, *gōō'*, *n.* a spiritual teacher (often *facet*) a revered instructor, mentor or pundit [Hind *gurū*—Sans *guru*, venerable]

gush *gush*, *v.i.* to flow out with violence or copiously: to be effusive, or highly sentimental —*v i.* to pour forth copiously —*n.* that which flows out. a violent issue of a fluid.—*n.* **gush'er** one who gushes an oil-well that does not have to be pumped —*adj* **gush'ing.**—*adv* **gush'ingly.**—*adj.* **gush'y** effusively sentimental [M.E. *gosshe, gusche*.]

gusset *gus'it*, *n.* the piece of chainmail covering a join in armour, as at the armpit· an angular piece inserted in a garment to strengthen or enlarge or give freedom of movement.—*v t.* to make with a gusset. to insert a gusset into [O.Fr. *gousset—gousse*, pod, husk.]

gust *gust*, *n* a sudden blast of wind· a violent burst of passion.—*v.t.* to blow in gusts.—*adjs.* **gust'ful, gust'y** stormy. irritable —*n.* **gust'iness.** [O.N *gustr*, blast]

gustation *gus-tā'sh(ə)n*, *n.* the act of tasting: the sense of taste.—*adjs* **gust'ative, gust'atory** of or pertaining to the sense of taste [L *gustus*, taste]

gusto *gus'tō*, *n.* exuberant enjoyment, zest [It — L. *gustus*, taste.]

gut *gut*, *n.* the alimentary canal. sheep's or other intestines or silkworm's glands prepared for violin-strings, etc . a narrow passage: the belly, paunch (*slang*): (in *pl*) the viscera: (in *pl*) the inner or essential parts: (in *pl.*) stamina, toughness of character, tenacity, staying power, endurance, forcefulness (*coll.*).—*adj.* (*coll*) of feelings or re-actions, strong, deeply personal: of issues, etc , having immediate impact, arousing strong feelings. —*v.t.* to take out the guts of: to remove the con-tents of: to reduce to a shell (by burning, dism-antling, plundering, etc.): to extract what is essential from:—*pr.p* **gutt'ing;** *pa.t.* and *pa.p* **gutt'ed.**—*adj./* **gutt'less** cowardly, lacking strength of character.—*n* **guts'iness** (*Scot*) greediness —*adj.* **guts'y** gluttonous (*Scot*): having pluck or nerve (*slang*): lusty, passionate (*slang*).—*n* **gutt'er.**— **hate someone's guts** (*slang*) to have a violent dislike for someone; **work, sweat, slog one's guts out** (*slang*) to work extremely hard [O E *guttas* (pl)]

gutta *gut'ə*, *n* a drop· a small drop-like ornament: a small round colour-spot (*zool*)·—*pl* **gutt'ae** (*-ē*) — *adjs* **gutt'ate, -d** containing drops. spotted [L *gutta*, drop]

gutta-percha *gut'ə-pûr'chə*, *n* a substance like rubber, but harder and not extensible, got chiefly from the latex of Malaysian trees (*Palaquium, Payena*, etc).— Also *adj*. [Malay *getah*, gum, *percha*, a tree pro-ducing it]

guttate, etc See **gutta.**

gutter *gut'ər*, *n.* a channel for conveying away water, esp at the roadside or at the eaves of a roof a furrow, groove loosely, the inner margins between two pages (*print*): slum-life, social degradation, or sordidness —*v.t* to cut or form into small hollows.—*v t.* to become hollowed: to trickle: to run down in drops, as a candle· (of flame) to be blown downwards, or threaten to go out —**gutter press journalism** sensational jour-nalism, **gutt'er-snipe** a street urchin: a neglected child from a slum area. [O Fr *goutiere—goute*—L *gutta*, a drop]

guttle. See **gut.**

guttural *gut'ər-əl*, *adj* pertaining to the throat. formed in the throat: throaty in sou.id —*n* a sound pro-nounced in the throat or (loosely) by the back part of the tongue (*phon*) a letter representing such a sound —*v.t* **gutt'uralise, -ize** to sound gutturally· to make guttural —*adv* **gutt'urally.** [L *guttur*, the throat]

guy[1] *gi*, *n* a rope, rod, etc . used to steady anything, or hold it in position —*v.t.* to keep in position by a guy — **guy'-rope.** [O.Fr. *guis, guie*; Sp *guia*, a guide]

guy[2] *gi*, *n* an effigy of *Guy* Fawkes, dressed up gro-tesquely on the anniversary of the Gunpowder Plot (5th Nov): an odd figure: a fellow (*coll.*): a joke, lark (*slang*).—*v t* to turn to ridicule, make fun of.

guzzle *guz'l*, *v.t* and *v i* to swallow greedily.—*n.* a bout of guzzling.—*n.* **guzz'ler.** [Perh. conn with Fr *gosier*, throat]

gwyniad, gwiniad *gwin'i-ad*, *n.* a whitefish (*Coregonus pennanti*), found in Bala Lake. [W *gwyniad—gwyn*, white]

gybe *jib*, *v i.* (of a sail) to swing over from one side to the other: to alter course in this way.—*v t* to cause to gybe —*n* a gybing.

gym *jim*, *n* and *adj.* a familiar shortening of **gymnasium, gymnastic, gymnastics.—gym shoe** a plimsoll; **gym slip, tunic** a belted pinafore dress worn by schoolgirls.

gymkhana *jim-ka'nə*, *n* a public place for athletic games, etc.· a meeting for such sports: now esp., a meeting for equestrian sports [Hindi *gend-khāna* (ball-house), racket-court, remodelled on *gymnastics*]

gymnasium *jim-nā'zi-əm*, *n* a place, hall, building, or school for gymnastics: orig. a public place or building where the Greek youths exercised themselves: (usu *gim-na'zi-ōōm*) a (German) secondary school:—*pl* **gymnā'siums, -ia,** for continental schools **gymnasien** (*gim-na'zi-ən*).—*adj.* **gymnā'sial.—*ns*** **gym'nast** (-*nast*) one skilled in gymnastics; **gymnas'tic** a system of training by exercise: (in *pl.* used as *sing.*) exercises devised to strengthen the body: (in *pl.*) feats or tricks of agility.—*adjs* **gymnas'tic, -al** pertaining to athletic exercises: athletic, vigorous.—*adv.* **gymnas'tically.** [Latinised from Gr. *gymnasion—gymnos*, naked.]

gymn(o)- *gim'n(ō)-, jim'n(ō)'-, -no'*, in composition, esp of bold terms, naked —*n.* **gym'nosperm** any of the lower or primitive group of seed-plants whose seeds are not enclosed in any ovary —*adj.* **gymnosper'-mous.** [Gr *gymnos*, naked]

(-)gyn-. See **gynaeco-.**

gynaeceum *gin-, jin-, jin-ē-sē'əm, n.* women's quarters in a house· the female organs of a flower (*bot.*) [Gr *gynaikeion*, women's quarters]

fāte; far, mē, hûr (her), mine, mōte, for, mûte, mōōn, fōōt, dhen (then), el'ə-mənt (element)

gynaeco-, in U.S **gyneco-**, *gin-*, *jin-*, *gin-*, *jin-ē'kō-*, or *-i-ko'-*, **gyno-**, *-ō-* or, *-o'*, (-)**gyn-** in composition, woman, female —*n* **gyn(aec)o'cracy** government by women or a woman.—*adjs.* **gyn(aec)ocrat'ic; gyn'aecoid** woman-like; **gynaecolog'ical.**—*ns.* **gynaecol'ogist; gynaecol'ogy** branch of medicine treating of women's diseases; **gynand'rism, gynandry** hermaphroditism.—*adj* **gynan'drous** hermaphrodtic with stamen concrescent with the carpels, as in orchids.—*n.* **gynan'dromorph** an animal combining male and female secondary characters —*adjs.* **gynandromorph'ic, gynandromorph'ous.**—*ns* **gynandromorph'ism, gynan'dromorphy; gyn(o)ecium** (*jin-*, *jin-ē'si-əm*) U.S. spellings of gynaeceum —*n.* **gyn'ophore** an elongation of the receptacle of a flower carrying carpels only. [Gr. *gynē*, *-aikos*, woman.]

gyno-. See gynaeco-.

gyp' *jip*, (*slang*) *n.* a swindle: a cheat.—*v.t* to swindle: —*pr.p.* **gypp'ing;** *pa.t.* and *pa.p.* **gypped.**

gyp' *jip*, (*slang*) *n.* pain, torture.—**give someone gyp** to cause someone pain [**gee up.**]

gyppie, gyppy. See **gippo.**

gypseous, gypsiferous. See **gypsum.**

Gypsophila *jip-sof'i-lə*, *n.* a genus of hardy perennials of chickweed-like aspect: (without *cap.*) a plant of this genus. [Gr. *gypsos*, chalk, *phileein*, to love.]

gypsum *jip'səm*, *gip'səm*, *n.* a soft mineral, hydrated calcium sulphate, source of plaster of Paris and other plasters.—*adjs.* **gyp'seous; gypsif'erous** producing or containing gypsum.—**gypsum block** a building block (usu. hollow) made of a gypsum plaster; (**gypsum**) **plasterboard** a building board consisting of a core of gypsum or anhydrous gypsum plaster between two sheets of paper [L.,—Gr *gypsos*, chalk.]

gypsy, gipsy *jip'si*, *n.* a Romany, a member of a wandering people of Indian origin: a cunning rogue: a dark-skinned person.—*adj* of the gypsies out-of-door: unconventional —**gypsy moth** a kind of tussock-moth [**Egyptian,** because once thought to have come from Egypt]

gyre *jir*, *n* a ring, circle: a circular or spiral turn or movement.—*adjs* **gyr'al, gyr'ant.**—*adv.* **gyr'ally.**—*v i* **gyrate'** to revolve, spin, whirl.—*adj.* **gyr'ate** curved round in a coil —*n* **gyrā'tion** a whirling motion: a whirl or twist (also *fig.*) a whorl.—*adjs.* **gyrā'tional; gyr'atory** revolving: spinning round: of traffic, revolving in one-way lines; **gyroid'al** spiral: rotatory; **gyr'ose** having a folded surface: marked with wavy lines or ridges; **gyr'ous.**—*n.* **gyr'us** a convoluted ridge between two grooves: a convolution of the brain.—*n.* **gyrocom'pass** a compass which indicates direction by the freely moving axis of a rapidly spinning wheel—owing to the earth's rotation, the axis assuming and maintaining a north and south direction.—*adj.* **gyromagnet'ic** pertaining to magnetic properties of rotating electric charges.—*ns.* **gyromag'netism; gyr'oscope** an apparatus in which a heavy flywheel or top rotates at high speed, the turning movement resisting change of direction of axis, used as a toy, an educational device, a compass, etc.—*adj.* **gyroscōp'ic.**—*ns.* **gyrostabilisā'tion, -z-; gyrostā'biliser, -z-** a gyroscopic device for countering the roll of a ship, etc.; **gyr'ostat** a gyroscope fixed in a rigid case.—*adj.* **gyrostat'ic.**—*n.sing.* **gyrostat'ics** the science of rotating bodies.—**gyromagnetic compass** a compass used in aircraft in which, in order to eliminate errors caused by changes of course and speed (greater in an aircraft than in a ship), a gyroscope is combined with a magnet system [L. *gyrus*—Gr. *gyros*, a circle, ring.]

gyrfalcon. See **gerfalcon.**

gyve *jiv*, earlier *giv*, *v.t.* to fetter.—*n.* a shackle: a fetter. [M.E. *gives*, *gyves*.]

H

H, h āch, sometimes spelt out **aitch,** n. the eighth letter in our alphabet, representing in Old English a guttural sound, gradually softened down to a spirant, and now often silent.—**H'-bomb** (H for *hydrogen*) hydrogen bomb.

ha *ha, interj.* denoting various emotions or responses, e.g. surprise, joy, exultation, dismay, enquiry, scepticism, encouragement, hesitation, and when repeated, laughter [Spontaneous utterance.]

haar *har,* (*East Coast*) n. a raw sea-mist. [O.N *härr,* hoary.]

habanera (*h*)a-ba-nā'rə, n. a Cuban Negro dance or dance-tune in 2-4 time. [*Habana* or Havana, in Cuba.]

habdabs hab'dabz, (*coll*) n.pl a state of extreme nervousness.—Also **ab'dabs.**

habeas-corpus hā'bi-əs-kor'pəs, n. a writ to a jailer to produce a prisoner in person, and to state the reasons of detention. [L., lit. have the body (*ad subjiciendum,* to be brought up before the judge).]

haberdasher hab'ər-dash-ər, n. a seller of small-wares, as ribbons, tape, etc., a men's outfitter (*U.S.*).—n. **hab'erdashery** (or *-dash'*) a haberdasher's goods, business, or shop [O Fr. *hapertas;* origin unknown.]

habergeon hab'ər-jən, n. a sleeveless mail-coat, orig. lighter than a hauberk [O.Fr. *haubergeon,* dim. of *hauberc*]

habile hab'il, adj. dexterous, adroit (*rare*). [M.E variant of **able,** later associated more closely with Fr. *habile*]

habiliment hə-bil'i-mənt, n attire (esp. in *pl.*) [Fr. *habiller,* to dress—L *habilis,* fit, ready—*habère.*]

habilitate hə-bil'i-tāt, v.t to equip or finance (as a mine) —v t to qualify, esp as a German university lecturer.—ns. **habilita'tion; habil'itātor.** [L L *habilitāre,* to enable—L. *habilis,* able.]

habit hab'it, n ordinary course of behaviour: tendency to perform certain actions: custom. familiarity bodily constitution· characteristic mode of development· the geometric form taken by a crystal (*crystal.*)· dress, esp official or customary· a garment, esp a riding-habit: an addiction to a drug, etc.—v t. to dress: to inhabit (*arch.*).—adj **hab'itable** that may be dwelt in.—ns. **habitabil'ity, hab'itableness.**—adv **hab'itably.**—ns **hab'itant** an inhabitant· (ab-ē-tã, Fr) a native of Canada or Louisiana of French descent (*pl* in this sense sometimes **habitans**); **habita'tion** act of inhabiting a dwelling or residence.—adj. **habit'ual** customary. usual: confirmed by habit —n one who has a habit a habitual drunkard, drug-taker, frequenter, etc — adv **habit'ually.**—v t. **habit'uāte** to accustom —ns. **habituā'tion** act of accustoming: process of becoming accustomed acquired tolerance for a drug, which thereby loses its effect. development of psychological, without physical, dependence on a drug; **hab'itūde** habit, **habitué** (*hab-it'ū-ā,* Fr *u-bē-tu-ā*) a habitual frequenter.—adj **hab'it-forming** of a drug, such as a taker will find it difficult or impossible to give up using [L *habitus,* state. dress— *habitāre,* to dwell]

habitat hab'i-tat, n the normal abode or locality of

an animal or plant (*biol.*): the physical environment of any community. the place where a person or thing can usually be found. [L., (it) dwells.]

habitation, habitual, etc. See **habit.**

hachure hash'ür, a-shur, n. a hill-shading line on a map. [Fr.]

hacienda as-i-en'də, (*Sp. Amer.*) n an estate or ranch: establishment· factory. [Sp.,—L. *facienda,* things to be done]

hack[1] hak, v.t. to cut with rough blows: to mangle: to notch: to kick the shins of.—v.i. to slash, chop: to cough.—n. act of hacking: gash: a notch: chap in the skin· a kick on the shin.—n. **hack'ing.**—adj. short and interrupted, as a broken, troublesome cough.—**hack'-saw** a saw for metals. [Assumed O E. *haccian,* found in composition *tō-haccian.*]

hack[2] hak, n. a horse (or formerly, still in U.S., a vehicle) kept for hire. esp. a poor one: an ordinary riding-horse: any person overworked on hire: a literary or journalistic drudge —adj. hired: hackneyed.—v.t. to make a hack of: to use as a hack: to hackney.—v.i to work as a hack: to journey on horseback.—**hack'ing-jacket, -coat** a waisted jacket with slits in the skirt and flapped pockets on a slant; **hack'-work** literary drudgery for publishers. [hackney.]

hack[3] hak, n. a grating or rack, as for feeding cattle: a bank for drying bricks. [O E *hæce, hæc,* grating, hatch; cf. **hatch**[1].]

hackamore hak'ə-mōr, -mor, n a halter used esp. in breaking in foals, consisting of a single length of rope with a loop to serve instead of a bridle. [Sp. *jáquima.*]

hackberry hak'ber-i, n. the hagberry: an American tree (*Celtis occidentalis*) allied to the elm [See **hagberry.**]

hackle hak'l, n a comb for flax or hemp. a cock's neck feather: this worn as a decoration in a cap, etc : (in *pl*) the hair of a dog's neck: an angler's fly made of a cock's hackle, or its frayed-out part.— v.t to dress with a hackle.—n. **hack'ler.**—adj. **hack'ly** rough and broken, as if hacked or chopped: jagged and rough (*min.*).—**make one's hackles rise** to make one angry. [Perh. partly from O E. *hacele, hæcele,* cloak, vestment.]

hackmatack hak'mə-tak, n an American larch [Indian word.]

hackney hak'ni, n a horse for general use, esp for hire. a horse with a high-stepping action, bred to draw light carriages —v.t. to use overmuch· to make commonplace.—adj. **hack'neyed** trite. dulled by overmuch use.—**hack'ney-carriage, -coach** a vehicle let out for hire. [O Fr *haquenée,* an ambling nag: further history unknown]

had had, pa t. and pa p of **have.**

haddock had'ək, n a sea-fish of the cod family. [M.E *haddok,* ety. unknown]

hade hād, (*min*) n. the angle between the plane of a fault. etc , and a vertical plane —v t to incline from the vertical

Hades hā'dēz, n the underworld the abode of the dead hell [Gr *Aidēs, Haidēs,* the god of the underworld the abode of the dead.]

hadith had'ith, ha-dēth', n the body of traditions

about Mohammed, supplementary to the Koran. [Ar *hadīth*.]

hadj, haj, hajj *haj, n* a Muslim pilgrimage to Mecca.— *n.* **hadj'i, haj'i, hajj'i** (*-ē, -i*) one who has performed a hadj: a Christian who has visited Jerusalem. [Ar. *hajj*, pilgrimage]

hadron *had'ron, n.* one of a class of subatomic particles, including baryons and mesons.—*adj.* **hadron'ic**. [Gr *hadros*, heavy, *-on* as in **proton**, etc.]

hadst. See **have.**

haeccelty *hek-sē'ɪ-ti, hēk-, n.* Duns Scotus's word for that element of existence on which individuality depends, hereness-and-nowness. [Lit. thisness, L. *haec.*]

haem- hēm-, hem-, haemat-, haemo- (in U.S. **hem-, hemat-, hemo-**) in composition, blood.—*n.* **haem** (also **hem, heme**) the pigment combined with the protein (globin) in haemoglobin.—*adj* **haemal, hemal** (*hē'məl*) of the blood or blood-vessels: ventral—opp. to *neural.—n.* **haematem'esis** (Gr. *emesis,* vomiting) vomiting of blood from the stomach.—*adj.* **haemat'ic** pertaining to blood.—*ns.* **hae'matin** a brown substance containing ferric iron obtainable from e.g. dried blood; **hae'matite** a valuable iron ore, often blood-red, with red streak; **hae'matocrit** a graduated capillary tube in which the blood is centrifuged, to determine the ratio, by volume, of blood cells to plasma (Gr. *krites,* judge); **haematol'ogist; haematol'ogy** the study of blood; **haematol'ysis** haemolysis; **haematō'ma** a swelling composed of blood effused into connective tissue; **haematū'ria** (Gr. *ouron,* urine) presence of blood in the urine; **haemocy'anin** (Gr *kuanos,* blue) a blue respiratory pigment with functions similar to haemoglobin, in the blood of Crustacea and Mollusca; **hae'mocyte** a blood cell, esp. a red one; **haemodial'ysis** the purifying of the blood (in e g. cases of kidney failure) by circulating it through an apparatus containing a semi-permeable membrane that blocks the passage of waste products (Gr. *dia,* through, *lysis,* dissolution); **haemoglō'bin** (L. *globus,* a ball) the red oxygen-carrying pigment in the red blood-corpuscles; **haemol'ysis** (Gr. *lysis,* dissolution) breaking up of red blood-corpuscles.—*adj.* **haemolyt'ic.—haemophil'ia** (Gr. *phileein,* to like) a constitutional tendency to excessive bleeding when any blood-vessel is even slightly injured; **haemophil'iac** one who suffers from haemophilia; **haemorrhage** (*hem'ər-ɪj;* Gr. *haimorrhagiā—rhēgnynai,* to burst) a discharge of blood from the blood-vessels.— Also *v i.—adj.* **haemorrhagic** (*-raj').—n* **haemorrhoid** (*hem'ər-oid;* Gr. *haimorrhois, -idos— rheein,* to flow) dilatation of a vein about the anus— usu. in *pl.,* piles.—*adj.* **haemorrhoid'al.—ns haemos'tasis** stoppage of bleeding or the flow of the blood; **hae'mostat** an instrument for stopping bleeding.—*n.* and *adj.* **haemostat'ic** (Gr. *statikos,* or hypothetical *states,* causing to stand) styptic. [Gr. *haima, -atos,* blood.]

hafnium *haf'ni-əm, n* an element (Hf; at numb 72) discovered in 1922 by Profs. Coster and Hevesy of Copenhagen. [L *Hafnia,* Copenhagen.]

haft *haft, n.* a handle.—*v t.* to set in a haft [O E. *hæft.*]

hag *hag, n.* an ugly old woman, originally a witch: one of the round-mouths, allied to the lamprey (also **hag'-fish**).—*adj.* **hagg'ish.—adv. hagg'ishly.—adj. hag'-ridden** ridden by witches, as a horse: troubled by nightmare· obsessed: troubled. [Perh. O E. *hægtesse,* a witch; cf. Ger. *Hexe.*]

hag² *hag,* (Scot.) *n.* any broken ground in a moss or bog: a relatively high and firm place in a bog [O.N *högg,* a gash, ravine, a cutting of trees.]

hagberry *hag'ber-ɪ,* **hackberry** *hak', ns* the bird-

cherry: the American hackberry. [Cf. O.N. *heggr,* bird-cherry.]

Haggada *hä-ga'də, n.* a free Rabbinical homiletical commentary on the whole Old Testament, forming, with the Halachah, the Midrash: the Passover ritual. —Also **Hagga'dah.**—*adj.* **Haggad'ic.** [Heb.]

haggard *hag'ərd, n.* an untamed hawk, or one caught when adult, esp. a female.—*adj.* untamed: intractable: lean: hollow-eyed, gaunt, from weariness, hunger, etc.—*adv.* **hagg'ardly.** [O.Fr. *hagard.*]

haggis *hag'is, n.* a Scottish dish made of the heart, lungs, and liver of a sheep, calf, etc., chopped up with suet, onions, oatmeal, etc., seasoned and boiled in a sheep's stomach-bag.

haggle *hag'l, v.i.* to bargain contentiously or wranglingly· to stick at trifles: to cavil.—*n.* **hagg'ler.** [Freq. of *hag,* to hack.]

hagi- *hag'ɪ-* (sometimes *haj'ɪ-*) in composition, holy: saint.—*n.* **hagioc'racy** government by holy ones.— *n.pl.* **Hagiog'rapha** those books which with the Law and the Prophets make up the Old Testament.—*ns.* **hagiog'rapher** a writer of the Hagiographa: a writer of saints' lives.—*adjs.* **hagiograph'ic, -al.—ns. hagiog'-raphist; hagiog'raphy** a biography of a saint: a biography which over-praises its subject; **hagiol'ater** a worshipper of saints; **hagiol'atry** (Gr. *latreiā,* worship).—*adjs.* **hagiolog'ic, -al.—ns. hagiol'ogist** a writer of, or one versed in, saints' legends; **hagiol'ogy; hag'ioscope** a squint in a church, giving a view of the high altar.—*adj.* **hagioscop'ic.** [Gr. *hagios,* holy.]

hah *hä, interj.* Same as **ha.**

ha-ha¹ *ha-ha, interj* in representation of a laugh.— *interj.* **ha-ha'** an expression of triumph, e.g. on discovering something. [Imit.]

ha-ha² *hä'hä,* **haw-haw** *ho'ho, ns.* a ditch or vertical drop e.g. between a garden and surrounding parkland, forming a barrier without interrupting the view. [Fr. *haha*]

haick. See **haik.**

haik, haick, *hīk, n* an oblong cloth worn by Arabs on head and body. [Ar. *hayk.*]

haiku *hī'koo, n.* a Japanese poem in three lines of 5, 7, 5 syllables, usu. comical. [From Jap.]

hail¹ *hāl, n* a call from a distance: a greeting: earshot. —*v.t.* to greet: to address: to call to: to summon.— *interj* of greeting or salutation.—*adj* **hail'-fellow** (**-well-met'**) readily friendly and familiar.—**hail Mary** (a recital of) the English version of the ave Maria.— **hail from** to belong to, come from (a particular place) [O N. *heill,* health, sound, cf. **hale¹, heal.**]

hail² *hāl, n.* frozen rain or grains of ice falling from the clouds· a shower, bombardment, of missiles, abuse, etc —*v i.* and *v.t* to shower hail: to shower vigorously or abundantly.—**hail'stone** a ball of hail; **hail'-storm.** [O E *hægl (hagol).*]

hair *hār, n* a filament growing from the skin of an animal: an outgrowth of the epidermis of a plant: a fibre: a mass or aggregate of hairs, esp. that covering the human head: anything very small and fine: a hair's-breadth: a locking spring or other safety contrivance in a firearm —*n* **hair'iness.—adjs. hair'less; hair'y** of or like hair: covered with hair: dangerous, risky (*coll.*).—**hair'-ball** a concretion of hair in the stomach, **hair'-band** a band, usu. of or incorporating elastic material, worn over the hair.—*adj.* **hair'-brained** same as **hare-brained.—hair'-brush** a brush for the hair; **hair'cloth** cloth made wholly or partly of hair; **hair'cut** a cutting of the hair or the style in which this is done; **hair'-do** (*coll.*) process or style of hairdressing:—*pl.* **hair'-dos; hair'dresser** one whose occupation is the cutting, colouring, arranging, etc. of hair: a barber; **hair'dressing; hair'-dryer, -drier** any of various types of hand-held or other apparatus producing a stream of warm air for drying the hair; **hair'-grass** a genus (*Aira*) of coarse grasses (perh. only a modification of the generic name); **hair'-grip** a short, narrow band of metal, bent double, worn in the hair to keep it in place; **hair'line** a line made of hair: a very fine line in writing, type, etc.: a finely striped cloth: the edge of the hair on the forehead.—*adj.* (of e.g. a crack) very thin: also *fig.*—**hair'-net** a net for confining a woman's hair; **hair'-oil** a scented oil for dressing the hair; **hair'-piece** a length of false hair, or a wig covering only part of the head; **hair'pin** a bent wire or the like used for fastening up the hair.—*adj.* narrowly U-shaped, as a bend on a road —*adj.* **hair'-rais'ing.**—**hair-restor'er** a preparation claiming to make hair grow on bald places, **hair'-shirt** a penitent's garment of haircloth; **hair's'-breadth,** the breadth of a hair, a minute distance.—*adj.* (of an escape, etc.) extremely narrow; **hair'-slide** a hinged clasp, often decorative, worn in the hair esp by young girls; **hair'-space** the thinnest metal space used by compositors; **hair'-splitt'er** a maker of over-fine distinctions; **hair'-splitt'ing;** **hair'-spray** lacquer sprayed on the hair to hold it in place, **hair'spring** a slender spring regulating a watch balance; **hair'streak** a butterfly (Thecla, etc.) with fine white band under the wing, **hair'-stroke** a hairline in penmanship, **hair'style** a particular way of cutting and arranging the hair; **hair'stylist; hair'-trigg'er** a trigger that releases the hair of a gun, **hair'-work** work done or something made with hair, esp. human.—**a hair of the dog that bit him** a smaller dose of that which caused the trouble: a morning glass after a night's debauch— a homoeopathic dose, **by the short hairs** in a powerless position, at one's mercy; **get in someone's hair** (*coll.*) to become a source of irritation to someone; **keep one's hair on** (*coll.*) to keep calm, **let one's hair down** to forget reserve and speak or behave freely; **make someone's hair curl** to shock someone; **make someone's hair stand on end** to frighten or astonish someone; **not turn a hair** not to be ruffled or disturbed; **split hairs** to make superfine distinctions, **tear one's hair** to display frenzied grief or (*coll.*) great irritation; **to a hair** exactly, with perfect nicety. [O.E. *hēr*, Ger. *Haar*, Du. and Dan *haar*, etc.; vowel perh. influenced by Fr. *haire*, a hair-shirt.]

haj, haji, hajj, hajji. See **hadj, hadji.**

hake *hāk, n.* a gadoid fish resembling the cod. [Prob Scand.; cf Norw. *hake-fisk*, lit. hook-fish]

Hakenkreuz *ha'kən-krouts, n.* the swastika. [Ger., hook-cross.]

hakim¹ *hä-kēm', n.* a physician. [Ar. *hakīm*]

hakim² *hä'kim, n.* a judge, governor, or official in Pakistan. [Ar. *hakim.*]

Halachah, Halakah, Halacha *ha-la'hha, -ka, n.* the legal element in the Midrash.—*adj.* **Halach'ic.** [Heb.,—*hālak,* to walk.]

halal *hāl-dl', v.t.* to slaughter according to Muslim law.—*n.* an animal that may lawfully be eaten as so slaughtered.—Also *adj.* [Ar. *halāl,* lawful.]

halation *hə-, ha-lā'shən, n.* blurring in a photograph by reflection and dispersion of light: a bright area around a bright spot on a fluorescent screen. [**halo.**]

halberd *hal'bərd, n.* an axe-like weapon with a hook or pick on its back, and a long shaft, used in the 15th and 16th centuries, in the 18th century denoting the rank of sergeant.—Also **hal'bert.**—*n.* **halberdier** (-dēr') one armed with a halberd. [O.Fr. *halebard*— M.H.G. *helmbarde*—*Halm,* stalk, or *Helm,* helmet, O.H.G. *barta,* axe.]

halcyon *hal'si-ən, n.* the kingfisher, once believed to make a floating nest on the sea, which remained calm during hatching.—*adj.* calm: peaceful. happy.— **halcyon days** a time of peace and happiness. [L

halcyōn—Gr. *alkyōn,* fancifully changed to *halkyōn* as if from *hals,* sea, *kyōn,* conceiving]

hale¹ *hāl, adj.* healthy: robust: sound of body — *n* **hale'ness.**—**hale and hearty** in good health [Northern, from O E. *hāl.*]

hale² *hāl, v t* to drag [O.Fr *haler*; Germanic in origin.]

half *haf, n* one of two equal parts. a half-year, term: a half-back· a halved hole in golf: half a pint, usu of beer (*coll*)·—*pl* **halves** (*havz*).—*adj* having or consisting of one of two equal parts: being in part· incomplete, as measures —*adv.* to the extent of onehalf: in part· imperfectly.—**half'-and-half** a mixture of two things in equal proportions —*adj.* and *adv* in the proportion of one to one, or approximately. in part one thing, in part another —**half'-back** in football, a player or position directly behind the forwards —in Rugby (*scrum half* and *stand-off half*), a link between forwards and three-quarters —*adj* **half's baked'** underdone: incomplete: crude immature half-witted.—**half'-beak** a fish with spear-like underjaw, **half'-bind'ing** a bookbinding with only·backs and corners of leather or the like; **half'-blood** relation between those who have only one parent in common. a half-breed.—*adj.* **half'-blood'ed.—half'-blue'** at university, a substitute for a full blue, or the colours awarded him or her; **half'-board** in hotels, etc., the providing of bed, breakfast and one main meal per day, demi-pension, **half'-boot** a boot reaching halfway to the knee, **half'-breed** one of mixed breed (esp a mixture of white and coloured races), **half's brother, half'-sister** a brother or sister by one parent only; **half'-caste** a half-breed, esp. a Eurasian, **half's cock'** the position of the cock of a gun drawn back halfway and retained by the first notch.—*adj* **half's cocked'.—half'-crown', half'-a-crown'** a coin worth two shillings and sixpence, from 1970 no longer legal tender, **half'-day'** a holiday of half a working day — *adj.* **half'-dead'** (*coll.*) very weary, exhausted —*n* and *adj.* **half'-doz'en** six.—*adjs.* **half'-hard'**y able to grow in the open air except in winter, **half'-heart'ed** lacking in zeal —*adv* **half'-heart'edly.—half's heart'edness; half'-hitch** a simple knot tied around an object; **half'-hol'iday** half of a working day for recreation; **half'-hour'** a period of 30 minutes —Also *adj* —*adj., adv.* **half-hour'ly** at intervals of 30 minutes.— **half-hunter** see **hunter; half'-landing** small landing at the bend of a staircase, **half'-leath'er** a half-binding for a book, with leather on back and corners, **half's length** portrait showing the upper part of the body.— *adj* of half the whole or ordinary length —**half'-life** the period of time in which activity of a radioactive substance falls to half its original value; **half'-light** dim light: twilight; **half'-mast'** the position of a flag partly lowered, in respect for the dead.—Also *adv.*— **half'-meas'ure** any means inadequate for the end proposed; **half'-mil'er** a runner specialising in races of half a mile; **half'-moon'** the moon at the quarters when half the disc is illuminated. anything semicircular; **half'-mourn'ing** mourning attire less than deep or full mourning; **half nelson** see **nelson; half's note** (*mus.*; *U.S.*) a minim, **half'-pay'** reduced pay, as of an officer not on active service —*adj.* **half'-pay** on half-pay —**halfpenny** (*hāp'ni*) a coin worth half a penny: its value:—*pl.* **halfpence** (*hā'pəns*), also **halfpennies** (*hāp'niz*).—*adj.* valued at a halfpenny —**halfpennyworth** (*hāp'ni-wûrth*—also **hap'orth** *hāp'ərth*) as much as is sold for or is worth a halfpenny, **half'-pint** (*slang*) a very small person; **half'-plate** see **plate; half'-price'** a charge reduced to half.—*adj.* and *adv* at half the usual price —*adj* and *adv* **half'-seas-o'ver** half-drunk.—**half'-sove'reign, half'-a-sove'reign** a gold coin worth ten shillings;

half'-step (*mus* ; *U S*) a semitone, **half'-term'** (a holiday taken at) the mid point of an academic term —*adj* **half'-tim'bered** built of a timber frame, with spaces filled in —**half'-time'** a short break halfway through a game (*sport*) in industry, half the time usually worked; **half'-tim'er** one who works half the full time, **half'-ti'tle** a short title preceding the title page or before a section of a book —*adj*. **half'-tone** representing light and shade photographically by dots of different sizes —*n*. (*mus*) a semitone — **half'-track** a motor vehicle with wheels in front and caterpillar tracks behind —Also *adj* —**half'-truth** a belief containing an element of truth· a statement conveying only part of the truth, **half'-voll'ey** see **volley.**—*adv* **halfway'** (sometimes *haf'wä*) midway· at half the distance imperfectly: slightly, barely (*coll*) —*adj* **half'way** equidistant from two points. —**halfway house** an inn, etc situated midway between two towns, points on a journey, etc : a midway point or state a centre offering accommodation and rehabilitation, **half'-wit** an idiot —*adj* **half'-witt'ed.**—**half'-year** six months —*adj* **half'-year'ly** occurring or appearing every half-year —*adv* twice a year —*n* a half-yearly publication —**at half-cock** only partially prepared, **by half** by a long way; **by halves** incompletely· half-heartedly, **go halves** to share equally, **half past one', two**, etc , **half after one, two**, etc (*U S*), **half one, two,** etc (*coll*) thirty minutes after one o'clock, two o'clock, etc., **how the other half lives** (*facet*) other (esp richer or poorer) people's way of life, **not half** (*slang*) very much, exceedingly, **one's other** or **better half** one's spouse [O E (Anglian) *half* (W S *healf*), side, half]

halibut *hal'i-bɔt*, *n*. a large flatfish, more elongated than flounder or turbot [App **holy**, and *butt*, a flatfish, as much eaten on holy days]

halide *hal'īd*, *n* a compound of a halogen with a metal or radical—a chloride, bromide, etc [Gr *hals*, salt]

halieutic *hal-i-ū'tik*, *adj* pertaining to fishing [Gr *halieutikos—halieus*, fisher—*hals*, sea]

Haliotis *hal-i-ō'tis*, *n* ear-shell or ormer, a genus of gasteropods with ear-shaped shell with perforations (without *cap*) a member of the genus:—*pl* **haliotis**. [Gr *hals*, sea, *ous, ōtos*, ear]

halite *hal'īt*, *n* rock-salt. [Gr *hals*, salt]

halitus *hal'i-tɔs*, *n* a vapour —*n* **halitō'sis** foul breath [L]

hall *hol*, *n* the main room in a great house: a building containing such a room. a manor-house: the main building of a college. in some cases the college itself an unendowed college· a licensed residence for students a college dining-room. a place for special professional education, or the conferring of diplomas, licences, etc : the headquarters of a guild, society, etc · a servants' dining-room and sitting-room (*servants' hall*)· a building or large chamber for meetings, concerts, exhibitions, etc : a large room entered immediately by the front door of a house: a passage or lobby at the entrance of a house —**hall'mark** the authorised stamp impressed on gold or silver articles at Goldsmiths' Hall or other place of assaying, indicating date, maker, fineness of metal, etc · any mark of authenticity or good quality.—*v t* to stamp with such a mark.—**hall'stand** a tall piece of furniture on which hats, coats and umbrellas can be left; **hall'way** an entrance hall.— **Liberty Hall** a place where everyone may do as he pleases; **the halls** music-halls [O E *hall* (*heall*), Du *hal*, O.N. *holl*, etc.]

hallal. Same as **halal.**

hallelujah, halleluiah *hal-ə-lōō'yə*, *n* and *interj*. the exclamation 'Praise Jehovah': a musical composition based on the word —Also **alleluia.** [Heb *hallelū*, praise ye. and *Jáh*, Jehovah.]

halliard. See halyard.

hallo, halloa *hɔ-lō', hu-lō', interj* expressing surprise, discovery, becoming aware· used also in greeting, accosting. calling attention.—*n*. a call of hallo:—*pl* **hallō(e)s', halloas.**—Also **hello, hullo.** [Imit]

halloo *hɔ-lōō'*, *n* a cry to urge on a chase or to call attention —*v t* to cry dogs on: to raise an outcry — *v t* to encourage with halloos: to hunt with halloos. —**don't halloo till you're out of the wood** keep quiet till you are sure you are safe [Imit.]

hallow *hal'ō*, *v t* to make holy· to reverence.—*n*. (*obs*) a saint —*ns* **Hallowe'en'** (esp *Scot*) the eve of, or the evening before, All Hallows, **Hall'owmas** the feast of All Hallows or All Saints, 1st November [O E *hālgian*, to hallow, *hālga*, a saint— *hālig*, holy]

Hallstatt *hal'shtat*, *adj* relating to a European culture transitional between Bronze Age and Iron Age [From finds at *Hallstatt* in upper Austria]

hallucinate *hɔl-ōō'sin-āt, hɔl-ū'*, *v t* to affect with hallucination —*v t* to experience hallucination —*n* **hallucinā'tion** a perception without objective reality. loosely, delusion —*adjs*. **hallu'cinative, hallu'cinatory.**—*n* **hallu'cinogen** a drug producing hallucinatory sensations —*adj*. **hallucinogen'ic** causing hallucinations [L *hallūcinārī* (better *ālūcinārī*), *-ātus*, to wander in the mind.]

hallux *hal'uks*, *n* the innermost digit of the hindlimb the great toe a bird's hind-toe —*pl* **halluces** (*-ū'sēz*). [Wrong form of L. (*h)allex, -icis*]

halm *ham* Same as **haulm.**

halma *hal'mə*, *n* in the Greek pentathlon, a long jump with weights in the hands (*hist*)· a game played on a board of 256 squares, in which the men move by jumps [Gr , a jump]

halo *hā'lō*, *n* a ring of light or colour, esp one round the sun or moon caused by refraction by ice-crystals: in paintings, etc such a ring round the head of a holy person an ideal or sentimental glory or glamour attaching to anything —*pl* **hā'loes, hā'los.**—*v t* to surround with a halo (*lit* and *fig*) —*pa.p* **hā'loed.** [Gr *halōs*, a threshing-floor, disc, halo]

haloid *hal'oid*, *n* a halide —*adj*· having the composition of a halide —*n* **halogen** (*hal'ə-jen*) any one of certain elements in the seventh group of the periodic table, fluorine, chlorine, bromine, iodine, and astatine (the first four defined in the 19th cent as forming salts by direct union with metals; astatine discovered in 1940) —*v t* **halogenate** (*-oj'*) to combine with a halogen —*adj*. **halog'enous.** [Gr *hals*, salt]

halt[1] *holt*, *v i* to come to a standstill to make a temporary stop —*v t* to cause to stop —*n* a standstill a stopping-place a railway station not fully equipped —**call a halt** (**to**) to stop, put an end (to) [Ger *Halt*, stoppage]

halt[2] *holt*, *v i* to limp (*arch*): to proceed lamely or imperfectly, as in logic, rhythm, etc.—*adj* (*arch*) lame —*n* and *adj* **halt'ing.**—*adv* **halt'ingly.** [O E *halt* (*healt*); Dan *halt*.]

halter *holt'ɔr*, *n* a rope for holding and leading an animal, or for hanging criminals: a woman's backless bodice held in place by straps round the neck and across the back —*v t* to put a halter on [O.E *hælftre*; Ger *Halfter*]

halteres *hal-tēr'ēz*, *n pl* the rudimentary hind-wings of flies [Gr *haltērēs*, dumb-bells held by jumpers —*hallesthai*, to jump]

halva(h) *hal'və*, *n* a sweetmeat, orig Turkish, containing sesame seeds, honey, etc [Yiddish *halva*, ult from Ar.]

halve *hav, v t* to divide in half. in golf, to draw. in carpentry, to join by cutting away half the thickness of each [**half**.]

halyard, hailiard *hal'yərd, n* a rope or purchase for hoisting or lowering a sail, yard, or flag. [For *halier* —**hale**, by association with **yard**[1].]

ham[1] *ham, n.* the back of the thigh or hock. the thigh of an animal, esp of a hog salted and dried —*adj* **hamm'y.**—*adjs* **ham'-fist'ed, ham'-hand'ed** clumsy [O E. *hamm*; cf dial. Ger. *hamme*.]

ham[2] *ham, (coll.) n.* an actor who rants and overacts. an amateur, esp. an amateur radio operator —*adj* given to overacting or ranting. amateur. clumsy, coarse. inexpert.—*v.i.* and *v.t.* to overact [Prob *hamfatter*, variety artist]

hamadryad *ham-ə-dri'ad, n* a wood-nymph who died with the tree in which she dwelt a large poisonous Indian snake, *Naja hamadryas.* a large baboon of Abyssinia:—*pl* **hamadry'ads, hamadry'ades** (*-ēz*). [Gr. *hamadryas—hama*, together, *drys*, (oak) tree]

Hamamelis *ham-ə-mē'lis, n* the American witch-hazel genus. [Gr. *hamamēlis*, medlar—*hama*, together with, *mēlon*, an apple.]

Hamburg *ham'bûrg, n.* a black variety of grape· a small blue-legged domestic fowl.—*n* **ham'burg(h)er** Hamburg steak, finely chopped meat. (a bread roll containing) this meat shaped into a round flat cake and fried: a large sausage. [*Hamburg* in Germany.]

hame *hām, n.* one of the two curved bars of a draughthorse's collar. [Cf. Du *haam*, L G. *ham*]

Hamite *ham'īt, n.* a descendant or supposed descendant of *Ham*, son of Noah. a member of a dark-brown long-headed race of N E. Africa (*Galla, Hadendoa*, etc.) a speaker of any language of a N. African family distantly related to Semitic (ancient Egyptian, Berber, etc.) —*adj.* **Hamitic** (*-it'ik*)

hamlet *ham'lit, n.* a cluster of houses in the country· a small village. [O.Fr. *hamelet*, dim of *hamel* (Fr *hameau*), from Gmc , cf. **home**.]

hammam *hum-am', hum'um, ham'am, n.* an Oriental bathing establishment, a Turkish bath [Ar *hammâm*.]

hammer *ham'ər, n* a tool for beating metal, breaking rock, driving nails, or the like: a striking-piece in the mechanism of a clock, piano, etc the apparatus that causes explosion of the charge in a firearm: the mallet with which an auctioneer announces that an article is sold: a small bone of the ear, the malleus: a metal ball weighing about 7 kg, attached to long handle of flexible wire, for throwing in competition (*athletics*) —*v t* to beat, drive, shape, or fashion with or as with a hammer: to contrive by intellectual labour, to excogitate (with *out*): to trounce or criticise severely: to teach by frequent and energetic reiteration (with *in* or *into*): to declare a defaulter on the Stock Exchange: to beat down the price of (a stock), to depress (a market) —*v i.* to use a hammer: to make a noise as of a hammer. to persevere pertinaciously (with *away*).—**hamm'er-beam** a horizontal piece of timber at or near the feet of a pair of rafters; **hamm'erhead** a shark with hammer-shaped head: a brown African bird akin to the storks; **hamm'erlock** a hold in wrestling in which opponent's arm is twisted upwards behind his back; **hamm'er-toe** a condition in which a toe is permanently bent upwards at the base and doubled down upon itself.—**(come) under the hammer** (come up for sale) by auction; **hammer and sickle** crossed hammer and sickle emblem of the Soviet Union, or of Communism; **hammer and tongs** with great noise and violence; **hammer home** to impress (a fact) strongly and effectively on someone [O E. *hamor*; Ger. *Hammer*, O N. *hamarr*.]

hammock *ham'ək, n* a cloth or netting hung by the ends. for use as a bed or couch [Sp. *hamaca*, from Carib.]

hamose *hā'mōs, adj.* hooked —*n* **hâm'ūlus** a small hook or hook-like process [L. *hāmus*, hook.]

hamper[1] *ham'pər, v t.* to impede: to distort. to curtail —*n.* essential but somewhat cumbrous equipment on a vessel (*naut*) [First in Northern writers, cf. Icel *hemja*, to restrain.]

hamper[2] *ham'pər, n* a large basket [O Fr *hanapier* —*hanap*, drinking-cup]

hamster, hampster *ham'stər, n.* a rodent (*Cricetus*) with cheek-pouches reaching almost to the shoulders [Ger.]

hamstring *ham'string, n* the great tendon at the back of the knee or hock of the hindleg —*v t* to lame by cutting the hamstring to make powerless.—*pa t* and *pa.p.* **ham'stringed, ham'strung.** [**ham**[1], **string**.]

hamza, hamzah *ham'za, ham'zə, n* in Arabic, the sign used to represent the glottal stop [Ar *hamzah*, a compression]

hand *hand, n.* in man the extremity of the arm below the wrist. any corresponding member in the higher vertebrates the forefoot of a quadruped the extremity of the hind-limb when it is prehensile. a pointer or index: a measure of four inches a division of a bunch of bananas: side, direction, quarter: a worker, esp in a factory or a ship: a performer: a doer, author, or producer· instrumentality. influence. share in performance. power or manner of performing· skill: touch· control: (often *pl*) keeping. custody: possession· assistance: style of handwriting. sign-nature pledge· consent to or promise of marriage, or tulfilment of such promise. the set of cards held by a player at one deal. the play of a single deal of cards: loosely, a game of cards: a round of applause (in *pl*) skill in handling a horse's reins.—*v t* to pass with the hand: to lead, escort, or help, esp in entering a carriage to transfer or deliver (often with *over*) —**hand**- in composition, by hand, or direct bodily operation (as **hand'-knitt'ed, hand'made**). for the hands (as **hand'-lotion, hand'towel**) operated by hand (as **hand'-punch**)· held in the hand (as **hand'-bask'et**) —**hand'ed** in composition, using one hand in preference to the other, as *left-handed* having a hand or hands as stated, as *one-handed* —n. **hand'ed-ness** the tendency to use one hand rather than the other· inherent asymmetry in particles, etc , e g causing twisting in one direction (*phys*.) —**-hander** in composition, a blow, etc with the hand or hands as stated, as *right-hander, back-hander.—n* **hand'ful** enough to fill the hand a small number or quantity: a charge that taxes one's powers:—*pl.* **hand'fuls.**—*adv* **hand'ily.**—*n* **hand'iness.**—*adjs.* **hand'iess** awkward, **hand'y** dexterous ready to the hand: convenient: near.—**hand'bag** a bag for small articles, carried by women, **hand'-ball** a game between goals in which the ball is struck with the palm of the hand· (**hand'ball**) a game similar to fives in which a ball is struck with the gloved hand against a wall or walls (usu. four), **hand'-barrow** wheelless barrow, carried by handles, **hand'bell** small bell with a handle, rung by hand; **hand'bill** a light pruning-hook: a bill or loose sheet bearing an announcement, **hand'book** a manual; **hand'-brake** a brake applied by hand-operated lever, **hand(s)'-breadth** the breadth of a hand; **hand'-cart** a light cart drawn by hand, **hand'-clap** a clap of the hands, **hand'craft** handicraft; **hand'-cuff** (esp. in *pl*) a shackle locked upon the wrist, **hand'-gall'op** an easy gallop, restrained by the bridlehand; **hand'-glass** a mirror or a lens with a handle; **hand'-grenade** a grenade to be thrown by hand; **hand'grip** something for the hand to grasp, **hand'-gun**

a gun which can be held and fired in one hand; **hand'-hold** a hold by the hand: a place or part that can be held by the hand, **hand'-line** a fishing-line without a rod, **hand'list** a list without detail, for handy reference —*adj* **hand'made.**—**hand'maid, hand'maiden** a female servant.—*adj* **hand'-me-down'** ready-made, usually cheap. second-hand.—*n* a cheap ready-made or second-hand garment.—**hand'-off** act or manner of pushing off an opponent in Rugby football, **hand's org'an** a barrel-organ, **hand'out** a portion handed out, esp. to the needy. an issue. a prepared statement issued to the press. a usu. free leaflet containing information, propaganda, etc ; **hand'over** a transfer, handing over —*v.t* **hand'-pick** to pick by hand: to select carefully for a particular purpose.—**hand'rail** a rail to hold for safety, support, etc., as on stairs: **hand'saw** a saw worked by hand, specif with a handle at one end; **hand'set** on a telephone, the part held by the hand, containing the mouthpiece and ear-piece; **hand'shake** a shaking of hands in greeting, etc (also **hand'shaking**), **hand'spike** a bar used as a lever; **hand'spring** a cartwheel or somersault with hands on the ground; **hand'stand** act of balancing one's body on the palms of one's hands with one's trunk and legs in the air, **hands'turn, hand's turn** (usu. with a negative) a single or least act of work, **hand'writing** writing, script. style of writing.—*adj.* **hand'written** written by hand, not typed or printed.—**hand'yman** a man for odd jobs.—**at first hand** directly from the source; **at hand** conveniently near: within easy reach: near in time; **at the hand of** by the act of, **by hand** by use of the hands, or tools worked by the hand, not by machinery or other indirect means: by personal delivery, not by post; **change hands** to pass to other ownership or keeping; **come to hand** to arrive: to be received; **for one's own hand** to one's own account; **get one's hand in** to get control of the play so as to turn one's cards to good use: to get into the way or knack; **good hands** good keeping: care of those who may be trusted to treat one well, **hand and foot** with assiduous attention, **hand and (or in) glove** on very intimate terms. in close co-operation; **hand down or on** to transmit in succession or by tradition, **hand in hand** with hands mutually clasped: with one person holding the hand of another: in close association. conjointly (*adj.* **hand'-in-hand'**), **hand it to someone** (*slang*) to admit his superiority, esp. as shown by his success in a difficult matter; **hand of God** unforeseen and unavoidable accident, as lightning, tempest; **hand out** to distribute, pass by hand to individuals (see also **handout**); **hand over** to transfer: to relinquish possession of; **hand over hand** by passing the hands alternately one before or above another, as in climbing a rope; **hand over fist** with steady and rapid gain, **hands down** with utter ease (as in winning a race); **hands off** keep off: do not touch or strike; **hands up** hold the hands above the head in surrender; **hand to hand** at close quarters (*adj* **hand'-to-hand'**); **hand to mouth** with provision for immediate needs only (*adj.* **hand'-to-mouth'**), **have one's hands full** to be preoccupied, very busy; **hold hands** see **hold**; **in hand** in preparation: under control; **keep one's hand in** see **keep**; **lay hands on** to seize: to obtain or find: to subject physically to rough treatment: to bless or to ordain by touching with the hand(s)—also to **lay on hands**; **laying on of hands** the touch of a bishop or presbyters in ordination, **lend a hand** to give assistance; **off one's hands** no longer under one's responsible charge; **old hand** see **old**; **on all hands**, every **hand** on all sides, by everybody, on **hand** ready, available: in one's possession, **on one's hands** under one's care or responsibility. remaining as a burden or encumbrance; **on the one hand ... on the other hand**

phrases used to introduce opposing points in an argument, etc , **out of hand** at once, without premeditation. out of control; **poor hand** an unskilful one; **set** or **put one's hand to** to engage in, undertake: to sign; **shake hands** see **shake**; **show of hands** a vote by holding up hands, **show one's hand** to expose one's purpose, **sit on one's hands** to take no action; **slow handclap** slow rhythmic clapping showing disapproval; **stand one's hand** (*slang*) to pay for a drink for another, **take in hand** to undertake, to take charge of in order to educate, etc , **take off someone's hands** to relieve someone of, **throw in one's hand** to give up a venture or plan; **tie someone's hands** to render someone powerless, **try one's hand at** to attempt: test one's prowess at; **under one's hand** with one's proper signature attached, **upper hand** mastery; **wash one's hands (of)** to disclaim responsibility (for) (Matt. xxvii, 24)   [O.E *hand*, in all Gmc. tongues, perh. rel. to Goth. *hinthan*, to seize.]

handicap *hand'i-kap*, *v t.* to impose special disadvantages or impediments upon, in order to offset advantages and make a better contest: to place at a disadvantage (*fig.*).—*n.* any contest so adjusted, or the condition imposed: amount added to or subtracted from one's score in stroke competitions (*golf*): a disadvantage (*fig*).—*adj.* **hand'icapped** suffering from some disability or disadvantage —*n.* **hand'icapper** one who handicaps.   [App. *hand i' cap*, from the drawing from a cap in an old lottery game.]

handicraft *hand'i-kräft*, *n* a manual craft or trade.—*n.* **hand'icraftsman** a man skilled in a manual art:—*fem.* **hand'icraftswoman.**   [O E. *handcræft*—*hand*, *cræft*, craft, assimilated to **handiwork.**]

handiwork, handywork *hand'i-wûrk*, *n.* work done by the hands, performance generally: work of skill or wisdom: creation. doing.   [O.E. *handgewerc*—*hand* and *gewerc* (*geweorc*), work.]

handkerchief *hang'kər-chif, -chêf, n.* a cloth or paper for wiping the nose, etc.: a neckerchief:—*pl.* **hand'kerchiefs.**   [**hand, kerchief.**]

handle *hand'l*, *v.t* to hold, move about, feel freely, with the hand, to make familiar by frequent touching: to manage: to deal with, treat: to trade or do business in —*n.* a part by which a thing is held: anything affording an advantage or pretext to an opponent.—*n.* **hand'ler** one who handles: a pugilist's trainer or second: one who trains, holds, controls, incites, or shows off an animal at a show, fight, etc.: one who trains and uses a dog or other animal which works for the police or an armed service.—**hand'lebar** the steering-bar of a cycle, or one half of it.—**a handle to one's name** a title, **fly off the handle** see **fly**; **handlebar moustache** a wide, thick moustache with curved ends thought to resemble handlebars. [O.E. *handle, handlian—hand.*]

hand of glory *hand əv glô'ri. glo'*, a charm made originally of mandrake root, afterwards of a murderer's hand from the gallows.   [A translation of Fr. *main de . gloire*—O.Fr *mandegloire*, mandrake—*mandragore*]

handsel, hansel *han(d)'səl, n.* an inaugural gift: an inauguration, as the first money taken, earnest-money, a first instalment, the first use of anything.—*v t.* to give a handsel to: to inaugurate: to make a beginning on.—*pr.p.* **han(d)'selling;** *pa.p.* and *pa.t.* **han(d)selled.**   [O.E. *handselen*, hand-gift, giving: or O.N. *handsal.*]

handsome *han'səm, adj* good-looking: well-proportioned: dignified. liberal or noble: generous: ample. —*adv* **hand'somely.**—*n.* **hand'someness.** [**hand** and suff. **-some;** cf Du *handzaam*]

handy. See **hand.**

handywork. See **handiwork.**

hanepoot han'ə-pōōt, (S Afr) n. a kind of grape.—Also **honeypot**. [Du. haane-poot—haan, cock, poot, foot.]

hang hang, v.t. to support from above against gravity: to suspend: to decorate with pictures, tapestry, etc , as a wall: to put to death by suspending by the neck: to suspend (meat and game) until mature: to fix, to fit (a door, etc.): to fasten, to stick (wallpaper, etc.): to exhibit (works of art): to prevent (a jury) from coming to a decision: (in the imper. and pass.) a euphemism for damn.—v.i. to be suspended, so as to allow of free lateral motion: to be put to death by hanging: to oppress (with over): to cling (with on followed by to): to drape well: to be undecided: to be in suspense: to hover: to impend: to linger: to hold back: to depend (on): to remain in close attention (with on):—pa.t. and pa.p. **hanged** (by the neck) or **hung** (in all senses).—n. action or mode of hanging: principle of connection, plan: knack of using: meaning: a declivity: euphemistically, a damn —n. **hangabil'ity**.—adj. **hang'able**.—n. **hang'er** one who hangs: that on which anything is hung: a wood on a hillside: a short sword.—adj. **hang'ing** suspending: suspended: drooping: downcast: deserving or involving death by hanging.—n. death by the halter: (esp in pl.) that which is hung, as drapery.—adj. **hung** (of an election, etc.) not decisive, producing no viable majority for any one party: (of a parliament) resulting from such an election.—**hang'dog** a low fellow.—adj. with a sneaking, cowed look.—**hang'er-on'** one who hangs on or sticks to a person or place: an important acquaintance: a dependant; **hang'-gliding** a sport in which one glides from a cliff-top, etc. hanging in a harness from a large kite; **hang'-glider** this apparatus, or the person using it; **hanging committee** a committee which chooses the works of art to be shown in an exhibition; **hanging garden** see garden; **hanging matter** a crime leading to capital punishment; **hanging valley** a tributary valley not graded to the main valley, a product of large-scale glaciation; **hang'man** a public executioner; **hang'out** a haunt; **hang'over** a survival: after-effects, esp of drinking (see also hung over below); **hang'-up** (slang) a problem about which one may be obsessed: an inhibition (see also hung up below); **hung'-beef** beef cured and dried; **hung jury** a jury that fails to agree.—**get the hang of** (coll.) to grasp the principle or meaning of; **hang about, around** to loiter: to stay, remain, persist; **hang back** to show reluctance; **hang by a thread** to depend upon very precarious conditions; **hang, draw, and quarter** to hang, cut down while still alive, disembowel and cut in pieces for exposure at different places; **draw, hang, and quarter** to drag on a hurdle or otherwise to the place of execution, then hang and quarter; **hang fire** to be long in exploding or discharging: to be slow in taking effect; **hang in the balance** to be in doubt or suspense; **hang in there** (coll.) to persist, persevere; **hang on** to wait; **hang on someone's lips** or **words** to give close, admiring attention to someone; **hang one's head** to look ashamed or sheepish; **hang out** to display, as a sign: to put outside on a clothes-line: to lodge or reside (slang); **hang out for** to insist on; **hang over** to project over or lean out from; **hang together** to keep united: to be consistent: to connect; **hang up** to suspend: to delay: to replace a telephone receiver, break off communication; **hung over** suffering from a hangover; **hung up** (coll.) in a state of anxiety, obsessed (with about or on); **let it all hang out** (coll.) to be completely uninhibited, relaxed. [O.E. hangian.]

hangar hang'ər, hang'gär, n a shed for aircraft, etc [Fr.]

hank hangk, n a coil or skein of a specified length,

varying with the type of yarn: a loop [O.N. hanki, a hasp.]

hanker hangk'ər, v i. to yearn (with after, for).—n. **hank'ering**. [Perh conn with hang; cf. Du. hunkeren.]

hankie, hanky hangk'i, n. a coll. dim. of **handkerchief**.

hanky-panky hangk'i-pangk'i, n. funny business, underhand trickery: faintly improper (esp. sexual) behaviour. [Arbitrary.]

Hanoverian han-ə-vē'ri-ən, adj. pertaining to Hanover: of the dynasty that came thence to the British throne in 1714.—n. a native of Hanover: a supporter of the house of Hanover, opp. to a Jacobite.

Hansard han'särd, n the printed reports of debates in parliament, from Luke Hansard (1752–1828), whose descendants continued to print them down to 1889.

Hanse hans, n. a league, esp. one of German commercial cities.—adjs. **Hanse, Hanseatic** (han-si-at'ik). [O.H.G. hansa, a band of men (M.H.G. hanse, merchants' guild)]

hansel. See handsel.

hansom han'səm, n. a light two-wheeled cab with driver's seat raised behind.—Also **han'som-cab**. [From the inventor, Joseph A. Hansom (1803–82).]

hanuman han-ōō-män', n. a long-tailed sacred monkey of India—the entellus monkey. [Hanumān, Hindu monkey god.]

hap hap, n. chance: fortune: accident.—v.i. to chance, happen—pr.p. **happ'ing**; pa.t. and pa.p. **happed**.—n. and adj. **hap'haz'ard** random: chance —adv. at random.—n. **haphaz'ardness**.—adj. **hap'less** unlucky: unhappy.—adv. **hap'lessly**.—n. **hap'lessness**.—adv **hap'ly** by hap: perhaps: it may be. [O.N. happ, good luck.]

hapax legomenon hap'aks leg-om'ən-on, (Gr.) lit. said once: a word or phrase that is found once only.

ha'pence hā'pəns, for **halfpence**.

ha'penny hāp'ni, for **halfpenny**.

haphazard, hapless. See hap.

haplo- in composition, single.—ns **haplography** (haplog'rə-fi) the inadvertent writing once of what should have been written twice; **haplol'ogy** omission in utterance of a sound resembling a neighbouring sound (as idolatry for idololatry)—adj. **hap'loid** (biol.) having the reduced number of chromosomes characteristic of the species, as in germ-cells (opp. to diploid).—n. **haploid'y**.—adj. **haploste'monous** (Gr. stēmōn, thread; bot.) with one whorl of stamens [Gr haploos, single, simple.]

haply. See hap.

hap'orth hā'pərth, for **halfpennyworth**.

happen hap'ən, v.i. to fall out: to come to pass: to take place: to chance.—ns. **happ'ening** event: a performance in which elements from everyday life are put together in a non-realistic way (theatre); **happ'enstance** chance: a chance circumstance.—**happen into, on, upon** to meet or come across by chance [hap.]

happy hap'i, adj. lucky: fortunate: expressing, or characterised by, content, wellbeing, pleasure, or good: apt· felicitous: mildly intoxicated (slang): in combination, delighted by the possession of or use of, as power-happy, bomb-happy—usu implying irresponsibility—or dazed as result of —adv **happ'ily** in a happy manner: in happiness: by chance· perhaps· I'm glad to say, luckily —n **happ'iness**.—adj. **happ'y-go-luck'y** easy-going: taking things as they come —adv. in any way one pleases.—**happy event** (now facet) a euphemism for a birth; **happy hour** in a club, bar, etc., a time, usu in the early evening, when drinks are sold at reduced prices; **happy hunting-ground** the Paradise of the Red Indian; **happy medium** a prudent or sensible middle course [hap.]

haptic *hap'tık, adj.* pertaining to the sense of touch.—*n. sing.* **hap'tics** science of studying data obtained by means of touch. [Gr. *haptein*, to fasten.]

hara-kiri *ha', há'ra-kē'rē, n.* ceremonious Japanese suicide by ripping the belly. [Jap. *hara*, belly, *kiri*, cut.]

harangue *hə-rang', n.* a loud speech addressed to a multitude: a pompous or wordy address.—*v.i.* to deliver a harangue.—*v.t.* to address by a harangue: —*pr.p.* **haranguing** (-*rang'ıng*); *pa.t.* and *pa.p.* **harangued** (-*rangd'*).—*n.* **harangu'er**. [O.Fr. *arenge, harangue*—O.H.G. *hring* (Ger *Ring*), ring (of auditors)]

harass *har'əs, v.t* to distress, wear out: to annoy, pester.—*adj.* **har'assed**.—*adv* **har'assedly**.—*n.* **har'asser**.—*n* and *adj.* **har'assing**.—*adv.* **har'assingly**.—*n.* **har'assment**. [O.Fr *harasser*; prob. from *harer*, to incite a dog.]

harbinger *har'bın-jər, n.* a forerunner, pioneer. [M.E. *herbergeour*.]

harbour (*in U.S.* **harbor**), *hàr'bər, n.* a refuge or shelter: a shelter, natural or artificial, for ships: a haven —*v.t.* to lodge, shelter, entertain, or give asylum to: to trace to its lair.—*v.ı.* to take shelter.—*ns.* **har'bourage** place of shelter: entertainment; **har'bourer**. —*n.pl.* **har'bour-dues** charges for the use of a harbour.—**har'bour-light** a guiding light into a harbour; **har'bour-master** an officer who has charge of a harbour. [O.E. *herebeorg*—*here*, army, *beorg*, protection.]

hard *hard, adj.* not easily penetrated or broken: unyielding to pressure: firm, solid: difficult to scratch (*min.*): difficult: strenuous: laborious: vigorous: difficult to bear: difficult to please: unfeeling: severe: rigorous: stiff: intractable: obdurate: troublesome: (of water) difficult to lather owing to calcium or magnesium salt in solution: harsh: brilliant and glaring: over-sharply defined: used as a classification of pencil-leads to indicate durability in quality and faintness in use: (of drink) (very) alcoholic: (of drug) habit-forming: (of news) definite, substantiated: (of letters) representing a guttural, not a sibilant, sound: (of radiation) penetrating.—*n.* a firm beach or foreshore: hard labour.—*adv.* with urgency, vigour, etc.: earnestly, forcibly: to the full extent (as **hard aport**): with difficulty: close, near, as in **hard by**.—*v.t.* **hard'en** to make hard or harder or hardy: to make firm: to strengthen: to confirm in wickedness: to make insensitive.—*v.ı.* to become hard or harder, *lit.* or *fig.*—*adj.* **hard'ened**.—*n.* **hard'ener**.—*adv.* **hard'ly** with difficulty: scarcely, not quite: severely, harshly.—*ns.* **hard'ness; hard'ship** a thing, or conditions, hard to bear: privation.—*adv.* **hard'-a-lee'** close to the lee-side, etc.—*adj.* **hard'-and-fast'** rigidly laid down and adhered to —**hard'-and-fast'ness; hard'back** a book with rigid covers —Also *adj.*—*adj.* **hard'backed**.—**hard'bake** almond toffee —*adj.* **hard'-bitt'en** given to hard biting, tough in fight: ruthless, callous.—**hard'board** a compressed fibreboard.—*adj.* **hard'-boiled** boiled until solid: callous or cynical.—**hard case** a person difficult to deal with or reform; **hard cash** specie: ready money, **hard cheese** (chiefly as *interj.*, *slang*) bad luck, **hard coal** anthracite; **hard copy** (*comput.*) output legible to the human reader, as distinct from coded material; **hard core** a durable, central part: something resistant to change, as, e.g. the most loyal members of a group.—*adj.* **hard'-core**.—**hard court** a tennis court laid with asphalt, concrete, etc., **hard currency** a currency not subject to depreciation; **hard drinker** one who drinks persistently and excessively.—*adj.* **hard'-earned** earned with toil.—**hard facts** undeniable facts.—*adjs.* **hard'-fav'oured, hard'-feat'ured** of coarse features; **hard'-fought** sorely contested.—**hard hat** a bowler-hat: a protective helmet worn by building workers: an obstinately conservative person; **hard'head** knapweed.—*adjs.* **hard'-head'ed** shrewd; **hard'-heart'ed** unfeeling: cruel.—*adv.* **hard'-heart'edly**.—**hard'-heart'edness**.—*adjs.* **hard'-hit'** seriously hurt as by a loss of money: deeply smitten with love, **hard'-hitt'ing** duly condemnatory, pulling no punches.—**hard labour** physical labour as an additional punishment to imprisonment, abolished in 1948, **hard landing** one made by a spacecraft, etc. in which the craft is destroyed on impact.—*adj* **hard'line** of an attitude or policy (**hard line**), definite and unyielding: having such an attitude or policy.—**hard'lin'er; hard lines** a hard lot: bad luck (usu. as *interj.*); **hard man** (*coll.*) a criminal specialising in acts of violence; **hard money** coin.—*adjs.* **hard'mouthed** with mouth insensible to the bit; **hard'nosed** (*coll.*) tough, unsentimental.—**hard pad** once considered a virus disease of dogs, now recognised as a symptom of distemper.—*adjs.* **hard'-pressed, hard'-pushed** in difficulties.—**hard sauce** sauce made with butter and sugar, and flavoured with rum or other liquor; **hard sell** aggressive and insistent method of promoting, advertising or selling; **hard shoulder** a surfaced strip forming the outer edge of a motorway, used when stopping in an emergency; **hard swearing** persistent and reckless swearing (by a witness): (often) perjury, **hard'tack** ship-biscuit.—*adj.* **hard'-up'** short of money, or of anything else.—**hard'ware** goods made of the baser metals, such as iron or copper. mechanical equipment including war equipment: mechanical, electrical or electronic components of a computer (compare *software*); **hard'-wareman**.—*adj* **hard'-wear'ing** lasting well in use, durable.—**hard wheat** wheat having a hard kernel with a high gluten content.—*adj.* **hard'-won** won with toil and difficulty.—**hard words** harsh words; **hard'wood** timber of deciduous trees, whose comparatively slow growth produces compact hard wood. —*adj.* **hard'work'ing** diligent, industrious.—**be hard going** see **going'; go hard with** turn out ill for, **hard as nails** very hard: callous: tough; **hard at it** working hard, very busy; **hard-luck** story a person's account of his own bad luck and suffering, usu. intended to gain sympathy; **hard of hearing** pretty deaf; **hard on the heels of** following immediately after; **hard put to it** in great straits or difficulty; **hold hard** to stop; **the hard way** through personal endeavour or salutary experience. [O.E. *hard* (*heard*); Du. *hard*, Ger. *hart*, Goth. *hardus*; allied to Gr. *kratys*, strong.]

hardy *hard'ı, adj.* brave: confident: able to bear cold, exposure, or fatigue.—*ns.* **hard'ihood** boldness: audacity.—*adv.* **hard'ily**.—*n.* **hard'iness.—hardy annual** an annual plant which can survive frosts: a story or topic of conversation which comes up regularly. [O.Fr. *hardi*—O.H.G. *hartjan*, to make hard]

hare *hàr, n.* a common very timid and very swift mammal of the order Rodentia or in some classifications the order Lagomorpha, in appearance like, but larger than, a rabbit.—*v.ı.* (*slang*) to run like a hare, hasten —**hare'-and-hounds'** a paper-chase; **hare'bell** the Scottish bluebell (*Campanula rotundifolia*).—*adjs.* **hare'-brained**, sometimes **hair'-brained**, giddy. heedless.—**hare'-lip** a fissured upper lip like that of a hare. —*adj.* **hare'-lipped**.—**hare's'-ear** an umbelliferous plant (*Bupleurum*, various species) with yellow flowers; **hare's'-foot** (tre'foil) a clover with long soft fluffy heads.—**first catch your hare** make sure you have a thing first before you think what to do with it; **hold (run) with the hare and run (hunt) with the hounds** to play a double game, to be with both sides at once; **raise, start a hare** to introduce an irrelevant topic, line of inquiry, etc. [O E. *hara*, Du *haas*, Dan *hare*, Ger. *Hase*]

harem *hä'rəm, ha-rēm'*, *n* women's quarters in a Muslim house: a set of wives and concubines: any Muslim sacred place [Ar. *harim*, *haram*, anything forbidden—*harama*, to forbid]

haricot *har'i-kō, -kot*, *n* a kind of ragout or stew of mutton and beans or other vegetables: (also **haricot bean**) the kidney-bean or French bean (plant or seed) [Fr. *haricot*]

hark *hark*, *v* i. to listen: to listen (to; also with *at*): to go in quest, or to follow (with *after*) —**hark'-back** a going back again (*lit.* and *fig.*).—**hark away, back, forward** cries to urge hounds and hunters; **hark back** to revert (to an earlier topic, etc) [See **hearken**.]

harken *här'kən*, *v.i* Same as **hearken**.

harl *härl*, **herl** *hûrl*, *ns*. a fibre of flax, etc : a barb of a feather, esp. one used in making an artificial fly for angling. [M.E. *herle*—L.G.]

harlequin *här'lə-kwin*, *n*. a pantomime character, in tight spangled dress, with visor and magic wand.—*n* **harlequinade'** part of a pantomime in which the harlequin plays a chief part.—**harlequin duck** a variegated northern sea-duck. [Fr *harlequin*, prob the same as O.Fr. *Hellequin*, a devil]

harlot *har'lət*, *n* a whore: a prostitute —*n.* **har'lotry** prostitution: unchastity. [O.Fr *herlot*, *arlot*, base fellow; ety. dub]

harm *harm*, *n.* injury: moral wrong.—*v t* to injure —*adj.* **harm'ful** hurtful —*adv.* **harm'fully**.—*n.* **harm'fulness**.—*adj.* **harm'less** not injurious, innocent —*adv.* **harm'lessly**.—*n.* **harm'lessness**.—**out of harm's way** in a safe place. [O E *herm (hearm)*; Ger *Harm*.]

harmattan *här-ma-tan'*, *har-mat'ən*, *n*. a dry, dusty N.E. wind from the desert in W Africa [Fanti *harmata*.]

harmonic *har-mon'ik*, *adj.* in harmonious proportion: pertaining to harmony. concordant: in accordance with the physical relations of sounds in harmony or bodies emitting such sounds (*math.*) —*n.* a component whose frequency is an integral multiple of the fundamental frequency: an overtone: a flutelike sound produced on a violin, etc., by lightly touching a string at a node and bowing: one of the components of what the ear hears as a single sound.—*n* **harmon'ica** the musical glasses, an instrument consisting of water-filled drinking-glasses (or revolving glass basins in Benjamin Franklin's mechanised version) touched on the rim with a wet finger: a mouth-organ. —*adv.* **harmon'ically**.—*n.sing* **harmon'ics** musical acoustics —*adj.* **harmonious** (*-mō'ni-əs*) in having, or producing harmony: in agreement: justly proportioned: concordant: congruous.—*adv.* **harmōn'iously**.—*ns.* **harmōn'iousness**; **harmonisation, -z-** (*här-mən-ī-zā'shən*).—*v.i.* **har'monise, -ize** to be in harmony: to sing in harmony to be compatible.—*v.t.* to bring into harmony: to reconcile: to provide parts to (*mus.*).—*ns.* **har'moniser, -z-**; **har'monist** one skilled in harmony (in theory or composition): a reconciler: one who seeks to reconcile apparent inconsistencies; **harmōn'ium** a reed-organ, esp. one in which the air is forced (not drawn) through the reeds; **harmōn'iumist**; **harmony** (*här'mən-i*) a fitting together of parts so as to form a connected whole: agreement in relation: in art, a normal and satisfying state of completeness and order in the relations of things to each other: a simultaneous and successive combination of accordant sounds (*mus.*): the whole chordal structure of a piece, as distinguished from its melody or its rhythm (*mus.*): concord: music in general: a collation of parallel passages to demon-

strate agreement—e g. of Gospels.—**harmonic mean** the middle term of three in harmonic progression, **harmonic minor** a minor scale with minor sixth and major seventh, ascending and descending; **harmonic motion** the motion along a diameter of a circle of the foot of a perpendicular from a point moving uniformly round the circumference; **harmonic progression** a series of numbers whose reciprocals are in arithmetical progression, such numbers being proportional to the lengths of strings that sound harmonics. [Gr. *harmonia—harmos*, a joint fitting]

harmony. See **harmonic**.

harness *har'nis*, *n*. tackle gear: equipment, esp now of a draught animal: an arrangement of straps, etc , for attaching a piece of equipment to the body, as a parachute harness, a baby's leading-strings, a seat belt, etc —*v t* to put harness on: to attach by harness: to control and make use of.—**har'ness-cask** (*naut.*) a cask for salt meat for daily use; **harness racing** trotting races between horses harnessed to a type of two-wheeled, one-person trap.—**in harness** occupied in the routine of one's daily work, not on holiday or retired. [O.Fr *harneis*, armour]

harp *harp*, *n* a musical instrument played by plucking strings stretched from a curved neck to an inclined sound-board —*v i* to play on the harp: to dwell tediously (on) —*ns* **harp'er**, **harp'ist** a player on the harp —**harp'-seal** the Greenland seal, a grey animal with dark bands curved like an old harp.—**harp on about** (*coll*) to dwell tediously or repeatedly on. [O E. *hearpe*; Ger *Harfe*]

harpoon *har-pōōn'*, *n*. a barbed dart, esp for killing whales —*v.t.* to strike with a harpoon —*n.* **harpoon'er**.—**harpoon'-gun**. [Fr *harpon*, a clamp—L *harpa*—Gr *harpē*, sickle]

harpsichord *harp'si-kord*, *n.* a keyboard instrument in which the strings are twitched by quills or leather points [O.Fr *harpechorde*; see **harp, chord**.]

harpy *har'pi*, *n.* a rapacious and filthy monster, part woman, part bird (*myth*): a large South American eagle (also **har'py-ea'gle**): a rapacious woman [Gr *harpyia*, lit snatcher—*harpazein*, to seize.]

harquebus *har'kwi-bus*, *n*. Same as **arquebus**.

harridan *har'i-dən*, *n* a vixenish old woman. [Prob O.Fr *haridelle*, a lean horse, a jade]

harrier[1] *har'i-ər*, *n* a medium-sized keen-scented dog for hunting hares: a cross-country runner. [**hare**, or **harry**.]

harrier[2]. See **harry**.

Harrovian *har-ō'vi-ən*, *adj.* pertaining to *Harrow* —*n* one educated at Harrow school.

harrow *har'ō*, *n.* a spiked frame or other contrivance for smoothing and pulverising land and covering seeds.—*v t* to draw a harrow over to tear or harass —*adj.* **harr'owing** acutely distressing —*adv* **harr'owingly**.—**harrowing** or **harrying of hell** Christ's delivery of the souls of patriarchs and prophets. [M.E. *harwe*.]

harrumph *hə-rumf'*, *v i.* to make a noise as of clearing the throat, usu. implying pomposity: to disapprove. [Imit.]

harry *har'i*, *v.t.* to plunder: to ravage: to destroy: to harass:—*pr.p.* **harr'ying**; *pa.t.* and *pa.p.* **harr'ied**.— *n.* **harr'ier** one who, or that which, harries: a kind of hawk (Circus) that preys on small animals.—**harrying of hell** see **harrow**. [O.E. *hergian*—*here*, army.]

harsh *härsh*, *adj.* rough: jarring on the senses or feelings: rigorous.—*adv* **harsh'ly**.—*n.* **harsh'ness**. [M.E *harsk*, a Northern word; cf Sw *härsk* and Dan *harsk*, rancid, Ger *harsch*, hard.]

harslet. See **haslet**.

hart *hart*, *n.* a male deer (esp red deer) esp over five years old, when the crown or surroyal antler begins to appear:—*fem.* **hind.**—**harts'horn** a solution of ammonia in water, orig. a decoction of the shavings of hart's horn (*spirit of hartshorn*); **hart's'-tongue** a fern with strap-shaped leaves [O.E *heort*]

hartal *här'tal, hŭr'tal*, (*India*) *n.* a stoppage of work in protest or boycott. [Hindi *hartāl*]

hartebeest *har'tǝ-bēst* (*Afrik* **hartbees** *hàrt'bēs*), *ns* a large South African antelope. [S.Afr.Du., hartbeast.]

harum-scarum *hā'rǝm-skā'rǝm, adj.* flighty: rash.—*n* a giddy, rash person [Prob from obs *hare*, to harass, and **scare.**]

haruspex *ha-rus'peks, n.* one (among the Etruscans) who foretold events from inspection of entrails of animals.—*pl* **harus'pices** (*-pi-sēz*) [L , perh from an Etruscan word and L *specēre*, to view.]

harvest *har'vist, n.* the time of gathering in crops: crops gathered in. fruits: the product of any labour or act —*v t* to reap and gather in —*v t.* to gather a crop.—*n* **har'vester** a reaper: a reaping-machine: any member of a class of Arachnida with very long legs (also **har'vestman, harvest spider**) —**har'vest-bug, -louse, -mite, -tick** a minute larval form of a mite abundant in late summer, a very troublesome biter, **har'vest-festival** a church service of thanksgiving for the harvest; **har'vest-home** a celebration of the bringing home of the harvest, **harvest moon** the full moon nearest the autumnal equinox, **harvest mouse** a very small mouse that nests in the stalks of corn. [O.E. *hærfest*, Ger. *Herbst*, Du *herfst*]

has *haz* See **have.**—**has'-been** a person or thing no longer as popular, influential, useful, etc. as before. —*pl.* **has'-beens.**

hash[1] *hash, v t* to mince to chop small —*n.* that which is hashed: a mixed dish of meat and vegetables in small pieces: a mixture and preparation of old matter: a mess.—**settle someone's hash** (*slang*) to silence or subdue someone [Fr. *hacher*—*hache*, hatchet.]

hash[2] *hash*, (*slang*) *n.* short for **hashish.**

hashish, hasheesh *hash'ish, -ēsh, n* leaves, shoots, or resin of hemp, smoked, or swallowed, as an intoxicant [Ar. *hashīsh.*]

Hasid *has'id, hhas'id, n.* a member of any of a number of extremely devout and often mystical Jewish sects existing at various times throughout history —*pl* **Hasidim** (*has'id-im, hha-sē'dim*).—Also **Hass'id, Chas(s)'id.**—*adjs.* **Has(s)id'ic, Chas(s)id'ic.** [Heb *hāsid*, (one who is) pious]

haslet *hāz'lit*, also *hās', has'*, **harslet** *hars', ns.* edible entrails, esp. of a hog. [O Fr *hastelet*, roast meat —*haste*, spit—L *hasta*, a spear.]

hasp *hasp, n* a clasp: a slotted part that receives a staple, as for a padlock —*v t* to fasten with a hasp [O E *hæpse*, Ger. *Haspe*, Dan *haspe*]

Hassid, Hassidic, etc. See **Hasid.**

hassle *has'l*, (*coll.*) *v.i* to be involved in a struggle or argument —*n.* bother. a difficulty: something requiring trouble: an argument.

hassock *has'ǝk, n.* a tussock of grass, etc . a stuffed stool —*adj.* **hass'ocky.** [O.E. *hassuc*]

hast *hast.* See **have.**

hastate, -d *hast'āt, -id, adjs* spear-shaped with basal lobes turned outward (*bot.*) [L *hastātus*—*hasta*, spear]

haste *hāst, n* urgency calling for speed: hurry inconsiderate speed —*vs t* **haste, hasten** (*hās'n*) to hurry on to drive forward.—*vs t* to move with speed. to hurry (**hasten**) to (wish to) do immediately (as in *I hasten to say that .*)—*adv* **hastily** (*hāst'i-li*).—*n* **hast'iness.**—*adj.* **hast'y** speedy quick rash: eager irritable —**hasty pudding** flour. milk, or oatmeal

and water porridge.—**make haste** to hasten. [O.Fr. *haste* (Fr *hâte*), from Gmc.]

hat *hat, n.* a covering for the head, often with crown and brim —*v.t* to provide with or cover with a hat: —*pa t.* and *pa.p.* **hatt'ed.**—*adj.* **hat'less.**—*n.* **hat'lessness.**—*adj* **hatt'ed** provided or covered with a hat —*ns* **hatt'er** a maker or seller of hats.— **hat'band** a ribbon round a hat; **hat'box; hat'brush; hat'pin** a long pin for fastening a hat to the hair; **hat'stand** a piece of furniture with hatpegs; **hat trick** the taking of three wickets by consecutive balls in cricket, or corresponding feat (as three goals) in other games: three successes in any activity —**a bad hat** (*slang*) a rascal, **hats off to** all honour to, **mad as a hatter** quite mad, **my hat!** an exclamation of surprise, **pass, send, round the hat** to take up a collection, solicit contributions, **take off one's hat to** to acknowledge in admiration (*fig*). to praise; **talk through one's hat** to talk wildly or at random, **throw one's hat into the ring see ring'; under one's hat** in confidence, **wear several hats** to act in several capacities. [O.E. *hæt*; Dan. *hat*]

hatch[1] *hach, n* a half-door. the covering of a hatchway a hatchway —**hatch'back** (a car with) a sloping rear door which opens upwards, **hatch'way** an opening in a deck, floor, wall, or roof.—**down the hatch** (*coll*) said when about to drink something, esp. an alcoholic beverage. [O.E. *hæcc, hæc*, grating, half-gate, hatch.]

hatch[2] *hach, v.t* to bring out from the egg: to breed. to originate, develop or concoct —*v.t.* to bring young from the egg. to come from the egg: to develop into young —*n.* act of hatching: brood hatched —*n* **hatch'ery** a place for artificial hatching, esp. of fish eggs.—**count one's chickens before they are hatched** to depend too securely on some uncertain future event [Early M.E. *hacchen.*]

hatch[3] *hach, v t.* to mark with fine lines, incisions, or inlaid or applied strips —*n* **hatch'ing** shading in fine lines [O Fr. *hacher*, to chop.]

hatchet *hach'it, n* a small axe for one hand.—*adj* **hatch'et-faced** having a narrow face with a profile like a hatchet.—**hatchet job** (*coll.*) the (attempted) destruction of a person's reputation or standing: a severely critical attack: a severe reduction; **hatchet man** (*coll.*) a militant journalist: one who does shady jobs for a politician or political party —**bury the hatchet** to end war (from a habit of North American Indians) [Fr *hachette*—*hacher*, to chop.]

hatchment *hach'mǝnt, n* the arms of a deceased person within a black lozenge-shaped frame, formerly placed on the front of his house [**achievement.**]

hate *hāt, v.t.* to dislike intensely.—*n.* extreme dislike: hatred object of hatred —*adjs.* **hat'able, hate'able;** **hate'ful** exciting hate: odious: detestable —*adv* **hate'fully.**—*ns.* **hate'fulness; hât'red** extreme dislike: enmity: malignity [O E *hete*, hate, *hatian*, to hate; Ger. *Hasz*]

hath. See **have.**

hatha yoga. See **yoga.**

hatter. See **hat.**

hauberk *ho'bǝrk, n.* a long coat of chain-mail sometimes ending in short trousers. [O Fr *hauberc*— O H G. *halsberg*—*hals*, neck, *bergan*, to protect.]

haughty *ho'ti, adj.* proud. arrogant. contemptuous — *adv* **haught'ily.**—*n.* **haught'iness.** [O.Fr. *halt, haut*, high—L *altus*, high]

haul *hol, v t.* to drag. to pull with violence or effort to transport (*U S*) —*v t* to tug. to try to draw something: to alter a ship's course: to change direction.—*n* act of pulling or of pulling in. contents of hauled-in net a take, gain, loot. a hauled load distance hauled —*ns* **haul'age** act of hauling transport, esp heavy road transport charge for hauling, **haul'er; haulier** (*hol'yər*) —**haul up** to call to account [A variant of **hale²**.]

haulm, halm *hom, ham, n.* a straw, stem stems of plants collectively. [O E *halm* (*healm*)]

haunch *honch, honsh, ns* the hip with buttock the leg and loin of venison, etc · the side or flank of an arch between the crown and the springing —**haunch bone** the innominate bone [O Fr *hanche*, prob of Gmc origin, cf O H.G *anchâ*, leg]

haunt *hont, v t.* to frequent· to intrude upon continually· to inhabit or visit (as a ghost) to cling, or keep recurring, to the memory of —*n* place much resorted to.—*adj* **haunt'ed** frequented, infested, esp by ghosts or apparitions obsessed· worried [O Fr *hanter*]

Hausa *how'sə, -zə, n* a Negroid peole living mainly in N Nigeria: a member of this people· their language

hausfrau *hows'frow, n* a housewife. esp a woman exclusively interested in domestic matters [Ger]

haut *ō,* (Fr) *adj.* high.—**haut monde** (*mɔ̃d*) high society —**de haut en bas** (*də ō tã ba*) with an air of superiority, contemptuously

hautboy (*h*)*ō'boi, n.* arch name for **oboe**: a large kind of strawberry (also **haut'bois**) [Fr. *hautbois*—*haut*, high, *bois*, wood]

haute *ōt,* (Fr) *adj* fem of **haut** —**haute couture** (*kōō'tur*) fashionable, expensive dress designing and dressmaking; **haute cuisine** (*kwē-zēn*) cookery of a very high standard; **haute école** (*ā-kol*) horsemanship of the most difficult kind; **haute vulgarisation** (*vulgar-ēz-as-yɔ̃*) popularisation of scholarly subjects

hauteur *ō'tər, ō-tœr, n* haughtiness· arrogance [Fr]

Havana *hə-van'ə, n.* a fine quality of cigar, made in *Havana* or *Cuba* generally

have *hav, v t.* to hold: to keep: to possess: to own: to hold in control to bear: to be in a special relation to (analogous to, if short of, ownership; e g *to have a son, an assistant, no government*): to be characterised by: to be in enjoyment of: to experience: to know· to entertain in the mind: to grasp the meaning or point of: to have received as information: to put, assert, or express. to suffer, endure, tolerate to hold or esteem· to cause or allow to be: to convey, take, cause to go: to accept, take: to remove (with *off, out*): to cause to be removed: to get: to obtain· to give birth to to be obliged. to get the better of, hold at a disadvantage or in one's power in a dilemma· to take in, deceive: to entertain in one's home (with *back, in, round, etc.*: *coll*): to ask to do a job in one's house, etc. (with *in, round, etc.*): as an auxiliary verb, used with the *pa.p.* in forming the perfect tenses:— *2nd pers* sing **hast; 3rd has,** *arch*. **hath;** *pl.* have; *pres subj.* **have;** *pa.t.* and *pa.p.* **had,** *2nd pers. pa.t* **hadst;** *pa.subj.* **had;** *pr.p.* **hav'ing.**—*n* one who has possessions:—*pl* **haves.**—*n.* **hav'ing** act of possessing: possession, estate; **have'-not** one who lacks possessions:—*pl.* **have'-nots; have-on'** a deception, a hoax —**had better, best** would do best to; **have at** (let me) attack: here goes, **had rather** would prefer; **have done** see **do'; have had it** (*coll.*) to be ruined: to have missed one's opportunities: to be doomed, beyond hope: to have been killed: (also **have had that**) not to be going to get or do (something); **have it** to prevail: to exceed in any way: to get punishment, unpleasant consequences; **have it coming (to one)** (*coll.*) to deserve the bad luck, punishment, etc. that one is getting or will get; **have it in for (someone)** to have a grudge against (someone); **have it in one** to have the courage or ability (to do something); **have it off, away** (**with**), **have off, away** (*slang*) to have sexual intercourse (**with**); **have it out** to discuss or express

explicitly and exhaustively, **have on** to wear. to take in, hoax, chaff· to have as an engagement or appointment, **have to do with** see **do'; have up** to call to account before a court of justice, etc , **have what it takes** to have the necessary qualities or capabilities to do something; **I have it!** I have found the answer (to a problem, etc.), **let (someone) have it** to attack (someone) with words, blows, etc. [O E *habban,* pa t *hæfde,* pa p *gehæfd;* Ger *haben,* Dan *have*]

havelock *hav'lək, n* a white cover for a military cap, with a flap over the neck [From Gen Henry *Havelock,* 1795–1857]

haven *hā'vn, n* an inlet affording shelter to ships a harbour· any place of retreat or asylum [O E *hæfen*]

haver¹ *hāv'ər, v t* to talk nonsense, or foolishly (*Scot.* and *Northern*) to waver, to be slow or hesitant in making a decision —*n* (usu in *pl Scot* and *Northern*) foolish talk: nonsense

haver² *hav'ər, n* (*Northern*) oats: the wild oat (grass) —*n* **hav'ersack** a bag worn over one shoulder for carrying provisions, etc , (orig horse's oats) on a journey [O N (pl) *hafrar;* cf Ger *Hafer, Haber,* oats.]

havildar *hav'il-dar, n* an Indian sergeant [Pers *hawāl-dâr*]

havoc *hav'ək, n* general destruction. devastation — **play havoc with** see **play.** [A.Fr *havok*—O Fr *havot,* plunder; prob Gmc]

haw¹ *ho, n* the fruit of the hawthorn —**haw'thorn** a small tree of the rose family, much used for hedges [O.E. *haga,* a yard or enclosure, a haw.]

haw² *ho, v i* to speak with hesitation or drawl.— *interj.* **haw'-haw'** a variant of **ha-ha¹.**—*v i* to guffaw [Imit.]

Hawaiian *ha-wī'(y)ən, adj* pertaining to Hawaii, to its citizens, or to its language —Also *n*

haw-haw. See **ha-ha², haw².**

hawk¹ *hok, n* a name given to many birds of prey of the family Accipitridae, esp to those of the sparrowhawk and goshawk genus· a predatory or a keensighted person· in politics, industrial relations, etc., a person who advocates aggressiveness rather than conciliation (opp to *dove*) —*v.t.* and *v i.* to hunt with trained hawks: to hunt on the wing.—*ns.* **hawk'er; hawk'ing** falconry —*adj* **hawk'ish.**—*adv* **hawk'ishly.**—**hawk'bit** a plant (Leontodon) close akin to the dandelion —*adj* **hawk'-eyed** sharpsighted —**hawk'-moth** any member of the Sphinx family, heavy moths with hovering flight —*adj.* **hawk'-nosed** hook-beaked —**hawk'weed** a genus (Hieracium) of yellow-headed composites.—**know a hawk from a handsaw** (prob for *heronshaw*) to be able to judge between things pretty well. [O.E. *hafoc;* Du *havik,* Ger *Habicht,* O N *haukr*]

hawk² *hok, v t* to force up from the throat.—*v.i* to clear the throat noisily.—*n* the act of doing so [Prob. imit]

hawk³. See **hawker.**

hawk⁴ *hok, n* a plasterer's slab with handle below

hawker *hok'ər, n.* one who goes about offering goods for sale —*v.t* **hawk** to convey about for sale. to cry for sale. [Cf L G. and Ger. *Hoker,* Du. *heuker.*]

hawse *hoz, n.* part of a vessel's bow in which the hawseholes are cut —**hawse'hole** a hole for a ship's cable, **hawse'pipe** a tubular casting, fitted to a ship's bows, through which the anchor chain or cable passes. [O.N. *hâls,* neck.]

hawser *ho'zər, n.* a small cable, a large rope used in warping [O Fr. *haucier, haulser,* to raise —L L. *altiâre*—L *altus,* high]

hawthorn. See **haw¹.**

hay *hā, n* grass, etc , cut down and dried for fodder or destined for that purpose —*v.t.* and *v.i* to make hay —**hay'box** an airtight box of hay used to continue the cooking of dishes already begun; **hay'cock** a conical pile of hay in the field; **hay fever** irritation by the pollen of the nose, throat, etc , with sneezing and headache; **hay'field; hay'fork** a long-handled fork used in turning and lifting hay, **hay'loft; hay'maker** one who makes hay: a wild swinging blow (*slang*); **hay'making; hay'mow** a rick of hay: a mass of hay stored in a barn; **hay'rick** a haystack; **hay'seed** grass seed dropped from hay: a rustic (*coll.*); **hay'stack; hay'wire** wire for binding hay.—*adj* (*slang*), crazy all amiss --Also *adv.*—**hit the hay** (*slang*) to go to bed; **make hay** to throw things into confusion (with *of*), **make hay while the sun shines** to seize an opportunity while it lasts [O.E *hieg, hig, heg;* Ger *Heu,* Du. *hooi;* O N *hey*]

hazard *haz' ard, n.* an old dicing game: chance· risk: the pocketing of the object ball (*winning* hazard), of the player's own ball after contact (*losing* hazard; *billiards*)· the side of the court into which the ball is served (*court tennis*)· any difficulty on golf links— bunker, water, etc: anything which might create danger, etc.—*v.t.* to risk: to venture: to venture to utter. —*adjs.* **haz'ardable; haz'ardous** dangerous: perilous: uncertain.—*adv.* **haz'ardously.**—*ns.* **haz'ardousness.** [O.Fr. *hasard;* prob. through the Sp from Ar. *al zār,* the die; according to William of Tyre from *Hasart,* a castle in Syria, where the game was invented during the Crusades.]

haze[1] *hāz, n* vapour or mist, often shining and obscuring vision: mistiness: lack of definition or precision.— *v t.* to make hazy.—*v.i.* to form a haze.—*adv.* **hā'zily.** —*n.* **hā'ziness.**—*adj.* **hā'zy.** [App. not O.E. *hasu, haswe,* grey.]

haze[2] *hāz, v.t.* to vex with needless or excessive tasks, rough treatment, practical jokes: to rag: to bully.— *ns.* **hā'zer; hā'zing.** [O.Fr. *haser,* to annoy.]

hazel *hā'zl, n.* a tree (Corylus) of the birch family· its wood.—*adj.* of hazel: light-brown, like a hazelnut.— **hazel grouse,** hen the ruffed grouse; **hā'zelnut** the edible nut of the hazel-tree. [O.E. *hæsel.*]

he *hē* (or when unemphatic *hi, ē, i*), nom. (irregularly, in *dial.,* or ungrammatically *accus.* or *dat*) *masc. pron.* of 3rd pers. the male (or thing spoken of as if male) named before, indicated, or understood:—*pl.* **they.**—*n.* a male:—*pl.* **hēs.**—*adj.* male (esp. in composition).—**he'-man** a man of exaggerated or extreme virility, or what some women take to be virility. [O.E. *hē, he.*]

head *hed, n.* the uppermost or foremost part of an animal's body: the brain: the understanding: self-possession: a chief or leader: a headmaster, principal: the place of honour or command: the front or top of anything: a rounded or enlarged end or top: a mass of leaves, flowers, hair, etc.: an individual animal or person as one of a group: a title, heading: energy of a fluid owing to height, velocity, and pressure: the highest point of anything: culmination: a froth on liquor poured out: point of suppuration: (in *pl.*) the obverse of a coin: one who takes hallucinogenic drugs (*slang*): (often in *pl.*) a ship's toilet (*naut. slang*): an electromagnetic device in tape recorders, etc. for converting electrical signals into the recorded form or vice versa, or erasing recorded material.—*adj* of, pertaining to, the head: for the head: chief, principal: at, or coming from, the front.—*v.t.* to remove the head or top from: to supply with a head, top, or heading: to be the head, or at the head of: to cause to face or front: to strike with the head.—*v.i* to shape one's course, make (for) —*n.* **head'er** one who or a machine which removes heads from or supplies heads for casks, etc.: a dive head foremost: a brick or stone at right angles to the wall surface: the act of heading a

ball —*adv* **head'ily.**—*ns* **head'iness; head'ing** a part forming a head: words placed at the head of a chapter, paragraph, etc —*adj.* **head'less.**—*adv* **head'long** with the head foremost or first: without thought, precipitately —*adj.* precipitate.—*adj.* **head'most** most advanced or forward.—*n.* **head'ship** the position or office of head or chief.—*adj.* **head'y** affecting the brain: intoxicating: rash: violent: exciting.—**head'ache** a pain in the head: a source of worry (*coll.*) —*adj.* **head'achy.**—**head'band** a band or fillet for the head; **head'board** an often ornamental board or panel at the head of a bed; **head'borough** (*hist.*) a petty constable; **head boy** the senior boy in a school; **head cold** a cold which affects parts of the head, as the eyes or nasal passages; **head count** (*coll.*) a count of people, bodies, etc.; **head'-dress** a covering for the head; **head'fast** a mooring rope at the bows of a ship; **head'gear** gear, covering, or ornament of the head; **head girl** the senior girl in a school.—*v.t.* **head'hunt** (*coll.*) to (attempt to) deprive a political opponent of power and influence (*U.S*): (also *v.t.*) to seek out and recruit (executives, etc.) for a business or organisation, esp. to do so professionally as e.g. a management consultant; **head'hunter; head'hunting** the practice of collecting human heads: the action of the verb *headhunt* (*coll.*); **head'land** a point of land running out into the sea: a cape: the border of a field where the plough passes, ploughed separately afterwards; **head'light, head'lamp** a light on the front of a vehicle; **head'line** line at the top of a page containing title, folio, etc.: title in a newspaper: a news item given very briefly (*radio, TV*); **head'liner** one whose name is made most prominent in a bill or programme; **head'man** a chief, a leader; **headmas'ter** the principal master of a school; **headmis'tress; head'note** a note placed at the head of a chapter or page.—*adj.* and *adv.* **head'-on** head to head, esp (of a collision) with the front of one vehicle, etc hitting the front of another: with head pointing directly forward: directly opposed.—**head'phone** (usu. in *pl.*) a telephone receiver worn in pairs on a headband, esp. for wireless listening; **head'piece** a top part: a decorative engraving at the beginning of a book, chapter, etc. (*print.*).—*n.pl.* and *n.sing.* **headquar'ters** the quarters or residence of a commander-in-chief or general: a central or chief office, etc.—**head'race** the race leading to a water-wheel; **head'rest** a support for the head: (also **head restraint**) a cushion fitted to the top of a car, etc. seat to prevent the head jerking back in a collision; **head-rhyme** alliteration; **head'room** uninterrupted space below a ceiling, bridge, etc.: space overhead; **head sea** a sea running directly against a ship's course, **head'set** a set of headphones, often with a microphone attached; **head'shake** a significant shake of the head; **head'shrinker** a headhunter who shrinks the heads of his victims: a psychiatrist (*coll.*); **heads'man** an executioner who cuts off heads; **head'square** a square cloth worn as a covering for the head; **head'stall** the part of a bridle round the head; **head'stock** (*mach.*) a device for supporting the end or head of a member or part; **head'stone** the principal stone of a building: cornerstone: gravestone; **head'-stream** a head-water: a high tributary· the stream forming the highest or remotest source —*adj.* **head'strong** obstinately self-willed.—**head waiter** a person placed over the waiters of a restaurant or hotel; **head-wat'er** the highest part of a stream, before receiving affluents; **head'way** motion ahead, esp. of a ship: progress: the time interval or distance between buses, trains, etc. travelling on the same route in the same direction; **head wind** a directly opposing wind; **head'word** a word serving as a heading: a word under which others are grouped, as in

a dictionary; **head'work** mental work; **head'work'er.**
—**above, over, one's head** beyond one's comprehension; **bring, come to a head** to cause to reach a climax or crisis; **get, take, it into one's head** to conceive the, esp. wrong or foolish, notion (that); **give a horse his head** to let him go as he chooses (now also *fig.* **give someone his head**); **go over someone's head** to take a complaint, etc. directly to a person more senior than someone; **go to one's head** to disturb one's sobriety or good sense; **have a head on one's shoulders** to have ability and balance; **have one's head screwed on the right way** to behave sensibly; **head and shoulders** very much, as if taller by a head and shoulders; **head first, foremost** with the head first; **head off** to get ahead of so as to turn back: to deflect from path or intention; **heads or tails** an invitation to guess how a coin will fall; **head over heels, headlong** as in a somersault: completely; **hit the headlines** to get prominent notice in the press; **hold up one's head** see hold¹; **keep, lose, one's head** to keep, lose, one's self-possession; **keep one's head above water** see water; **lay, put, heads together** to confer and co-operate; **off one's head** crazy; **on one's (own) head be it** one must, or will, accept responsibility for any unpleasant or undesirable consequences of one's actions; **out of one's head** of one's own invention; **over head and ears** deeply submerged or engrossed. [O.E. *hēafod*; cf. Du. *hoofd*, Ger. *Haupt*.]

-head. See **-hood.**

heal *hēl*, *v.t.* to make healthy: to cure: to restore to soundness: to remedy, amend —*v.i.* to grow sound. —*adj.* **heal'able.**—*n.* **heal'er.**—*n.* and *adj.* **heal'ing.** —*adv.* **heal'ingly.** [O.E. *hǣlan*—*hāl*, whole]

heald *hēld*, *n.* the same as **heddle.**

health *helth*, *n.* sound bodily or mental condition: soundness: well-being: state with respect to soundness: a toast.—*adj.* **health'ful** enjoying, indicating, or conducive to health —*adv.* **health'fully.**—*n.* **health'fulness.**—*adv.* **health'ily.**—*n.* **health'iness.**— *adjs.* **health'y** in good heath: morally or spiritually wholesome: conducive to or indicative of good health.—**health centre** centre for clinical and administrative health welfare work; **health farm** a place, usu in the country, where one goes to improve one's health by dieting, exercise, etc ; **health food** food thought to be particularly good for one's health, esp. that grown, prepared, etc. without artificial fertilisers, chemical additives, etc.; **health visitor** a nurse concerned mainly with health education and advice and preventive medicine rather than the treatment of disease, who visits esp. mothers with young children and the elderly in their own homes. [O.E. *hǣlth*— *hāl*, whole.]

heap *hēp*, *n.* a mass of things resting one above another: a mound: a great number, a great deal (often in *pl.*), a collection: an old dilapidated motor car.— *v.t.* to throw in a heap: to amass· to load with a heap or heaps: to pile high.—*adj.* **heap'ing** (*U.S* , of a spoonful, etc.) heaped.—*adv.* **heaps** (*coll.*) very much.—**knock, strike all of a heap** to confound utterly. [O.E. *hēap*; cf. O.N *hôpr*, Ger. *Haufe*, Du. *hoop.*]

hear *hēr*, *v.t.* to perceive by the ear. to accede to. to listen to: to try judicially: to be informed —*v.i* to have or exercise the sense of hearing: to listen: to have news (of or from).—*pa.t.* and *pa.p* **heard** (*hûrd*).—*adj.* **heard** (*hûrd*).—*ns.* **hear'er; hear'ing** power or act of perceiving sound: opportunity to be heard: audition: judicial investigation and listening to evidence and arguments, esp. without a jury: earshot. —**hear'ing-aid** any device, electrical or other, for enabling the deaf to hear or to hear better; **hear'say** common talk. report: rumour.—*adj.* of the nature of.

or based on, report given by others.—**hear, hear!** an exclamation of approval from the hearers of a speech; **hear out** to listen (to someone) until he has said all he wishes to say; **hear tell of** to hear some one speak of; **hear things** see thing; **will not hear of** will not allow. tolerate. [O.E. (Anglian) *hēran* (W. S. *hīeran*, *hȳran*).]

hearken *hark'n*, *v.i.* to hear attentively: to listen.—*n.* **heark'ener.** [O.E. *hercnian* (*heorcnian*).]

hearse *hûrs*, *n.* orig. a canopy or frame over a bier, designed to hold candles: a car for carrying the dead. [O.Fr. *herse*—L. *hirpex*, -*icis*, a harrow.]

heart *hârt*, *n.* the organ that circulates the blood: the innermost part: the core: the chief or vital part: the breast, bosom: the (imagined) seat of the affections, understanding, and thought, as opposed to the head, the seat of reason: courage. inmost feelings or convictions: vigour: a term of endearment or encouragement: a heart-shaped figure or object: a playing-card with heart-shaped pips: the centre of cabbage, lettuce, etc.· a diseased state of the heart —*v.i.* to form a compact head or inner mass, as a lettuce.—*adj.* **heart'ed** having a heart, esp. of a specified kind (*hardhearted*, etc.).—*v t.* **heart'en** to encourage, stimulate: to add strength to.—*v.i.* to take courage.—*adv.* **heart'ily.**—*n.* **heart'iness.**—*adj.* **heart'less** without heart, courage, or feeling: callous.—*adv.* **heart'lessly.**—*n.* **heart'lessness.**—*adj* **heart'y** heartfelt: cordial: robust: enthusiastic in, or indicating, good spirits, appetite, or condition· sound —*n.* a hearty fellow, esp. a sailor: a student who goes in for sports —**heart'ache** sorrow: anguish; **heart attack** a sudden failure of the heart to function correctly, often causing death; **heart'-beat** a pulsation of the heart: a throb; **heart'-block** a condition in which the ventricle does not keep time with the auricle; **heart('s)'-blood** blood of the heart: life, essence, **heart'break** a crushing sorrow or grief.—*adjs* **heart'-breaking; heart'broken.**—**heart'burn** a burning, acrid feeling in throat or breast, cardialgia, **heart disease** any morbid condition of the heart, **heart's failure** stoppage or inadequate functioning of the heart.—*adj* **heart'felt** felt deeply sincere — **heart'land** an area of a country that is centrally situated and/or vitally important; **heart murmur** an abnormal sound from the heart indicating a structural or functional abnormality.—*adj.* **heart'-rending** agonising.—**heart'-searching** examination of one's feelings; **heart's(-)ease** the pansy —*adjs.* **heart'-shaped** shaped like the conventional representation of the human heart; **heart'-sick** despondent.—**heart'-sick'ness.**—*adj.* **heart'-sore** sore at heart.—**heart'-string** orig. a nerve or tendon imagined to brace and sustain the heart: (in *pl.*) affections; **heart'-throb** (*slang*) one who is the object of sentimental adoration.—*adj* **heart'-to-heart'** candid, intimate, and unreserved.—*n.* a conversation of this sort.—*adjs.* **heart'warming** emotionally moving. gratifying, pleasing; **heart'-whole** sincere: with affections disengaged: undismayed —**heart'wood** the duramen or hard inner wood of a tree —**after one's own heart** exactly to one's own liking; **at heart** in real character, **break one's heart** to die of, or be broken down by, grief or disappointment: to cause deep grief to anyone, **by heart** by rote· in the memory; **cross one's heart** to emphasise the truth of a statement; **dear, near, to one's heart** which one feels a warm interest in or concern for, **find it in one's heart** to be able to bring oneself, **from the bottom of one's heart** most sincerely; **have a change of heart** to alter one's former opinion or viewpoint; **have a heart** (usu in *imper.*) to show pity or kindness; **have at heart** to cherish as a matter of deep interest, **have one's heart in it** (often in neg.) to have enthusiasm for what one is doing; **have one's heart in one's boots** to feel a sinking of the heart; **have one's heart in one's mouth** to be in trepidation, **have one's heart in the right place** to be basically decent, generous; **have one's heart set on** to desire earnestly; **have the heart** (usu. in neg.) to have the courage or resolution (to do something unpleasant); **heart and hand, heart and soul** with complete heartiness: with complete devotion to a cause; **heart-lung machine** a machine used in chest surgery to take over for a time the functions of the heart and lungs; **heart of heart(s)** the inmost feelings or convictions: deepest affections; **heart of oak** a brave, resolute heart; **in good heart** in sound or fertile condition: in good spirits or courage; **lay to heart** to store up in the mind for future guidance: to be deeply moved by something; **lose heart** to become discouraged; **lose one's heart to** to fall in love with; **set someone's heart at rest** to render easy in mind; **set one's heart on, upon** to come to desire earnestly; **take heart** to be encouraged; **take to heart** to lay to heart: to come to feel in earnest; **take to one's heart** to form an affection for; **to one's heart's content** as much as one wishes; **wear one's heart on one's sleeve** to show the feelings openly; **with all one's heart** most willingly.   [O.E. heorte.]

hearth harth, n. the part of the floor on which the fire is made: the fireside: the house itself: the home circle: the lowest part of a blast-furnace.—**hearth'-mon'ey, -penn'y, -tax** a tax on hearths; **hearth'-rug** a rug laid over the hearth-stone; **hearth'-stone** a stone forming a hearth: a soft stone used for whitening hearths, doorsteps, etc.   [O.E. heorth.]

heat hēt, n. that which excites the sensation of warmth: sensation of warmth, esp. in a high degree: degree of hotness: exposure to intense heat: a high temperature: the hottest time: redness of the skin: vehemence, passion: sexual excitement in animals, or its period. esp. in the female, corresponding to rut in the male: a single course in a race: a division of a contest from which the winner goes on to a final test: animation: pressure intended to coerce (coll.): period of intensive search, esp. by the police: trouble (coll.). —v.t. to make hot: to agitate —v.i. to become hot.— adj. **heat'ed.**—n. **heat'er** one who, or that which, heats: apparatus for heating a room or building.—n. and adj. **heat'ing.**—**heat barrier** difficulties caused by a thin envelope of hot air which develops round aircraft at high speeds and occasions structural and other problems; **heat engine** an engine that transforms heat into mechanical work; **heat exchanger** device for transferring heat from one fluid to another; **heat pump** a device (on the refrigerator principle) for drawing heat from water, air, or the earth, and giving it out to warm, e.g. a room.—adj. **heat'-resistant.**— **heat shield** an object or substance designed to protect against excessive heat, esp. that which protects a spacecraft re-entering the earth's atmosphere; **heat sink** something into which unwanted heat can be shot; **heat'spot** a spot or blotch on the skin caused by heat; **heat'stroke** exhaustion, illness, or prostration due to exposure to heat: sunstroke; **heat wave** heated state of atmosphere passing from one locality to another: a hot spell.—**in heat, on heat** of a female animal, ready to mate; **latent heat** the heat required to change solid to liquid, or liquid to gas, without change of temperature; **specific heat** see specify; **take the heat out of** to lessen the vehemence, or acrimony of (a situation, etc.); **turn on the heat** (slang) to use brutal treatment in order to coerce   [O.E. hǣtu, heat; hāt, hot; Ger. Hitze.]

heath hēth, n. barren open country, esp covered with low shrubs: any shrub of genus Erica, sometimes extended to heather.—adj. **heath'y.**   [O.E. hǣth.]

heathen hē'dhn, n. one who belongs to a people of some lower form of religion, esp. polytheistic, or of no religion: a pagan: one who is ignorant or unmindful of religion: an uncivilised person (coll.):— pl. **hea'then** (collectively), **hea'thens** (individually). —adj. pagan: irreligious.—ns. **hea'thendom.**—v.t. **hea'thenise, -ize** to make heathen or heathenish.— adj. **hea'thenish** relating to the heathen: uncivilised: cruel.—adv. **hea'thenishly.**—ns. **hea'thenishness; hea'thenism; hea'thenry.**   [O.E. hǣthen; Du. heiden.]

heather hedh'ər, n. ling, a common low shrub of the heath family: sometimes extended to the heaths (Erica).—adj of the purple colour of (red) heather: composed of or from heather.—adj **heath'ery.**— **heath'er-mix'ture** a woollen fabric speckled in colours like heather.—**set the heather on fire** to create a disturbance or a sensation, **take to the heather** to become an outlaw.   [Older Scots hadder.]

heather-bleat, heather-bleater hedh'ər-blēt', -ər, (Scot.) ns. a snipe.—Also **heather-bluiter, -blutter** (-blut', -blut'),   [O.E. haefer-blǣte—hæfer, goat. blǣtan, to bleat, from its cry; influenced by **heather;** cf. also Scots bluiter, bittern.]

Heath(-)Robinson hēth'rob'in-sən, used to describe an over-ingenious mechanical contrivance. [Heath Robinson (1872–1944), who drew such contraptions.]

heave hēv, v.t. to lift up, esp. with great effort: to throw: to haul: to force from the breast (as a sigh) — v.i. to rise like waves: to retch: to strive to lift or move something: to move, orig. of a ship:—pa.t. and pa.p. **heaved,** (naut.) **hōve.**—n an effort upward: a throw: an effort to vomit.—n. **heav'er.**—**give, get the heave-ho** (coll.) to dismiss, reject, be dismissed, rejected; **heave ho!** an orig. sailors' call to exertion, as in heaving the anchor; **heave in sight** to come into view; **heave to** to bring a vessel to a standstill.   [O E hebban, pa.t. hōf, pa.p. hafen.]

heaven hev'n, hevn, n. the vault of sky overhanging the earth (commonly in pl.): the upper regions of the air: a great and indefinite height: (often cap.) the dwelling-place of God or the gods, and the blessed: supreme happiness.—interj. (in pl.) expressing suprise, dismay, etc.—n. **heavenliness** (hev'n).—adj. **heavenly** (hev'n) of or inhabiting heaven: of or from God or the angels or saints: celestial: supremely blessed: excellent (coll.).—adj. **heav'enward.**—advs. **heav'enward, heav'enwards.**—adj. **heav'en-born** descended from heaven.—**heavenly bodies** the sun, moon, planets, comets, stars, etc.; **heavenly host** a multitude of angels.—adj. **heav'en-sent** sent by heaven: very timely.—**good heavens, heavens above** expressing surprise, dismay, etc.; **heaven forbid,** may it not happen (that); **heaven knows** God knows (q.v.), **in the seventh heaven** in a state of the most exalted happiness; **move heaven and earth** to do everything possible; **the heavens opened** there was a very heavy shower of rain.   [O.E. heofon.]

Heaviside layer. See Kennelly-Heaviside layer.

heavy hev'i, adj. weighty: laden: abounding: of high specific gravity: not easy to bear: oppressive: grave: dull, lacking interest: wanting in sprightliness: pompous: laborious: in low spirits: drowsy: with great momentum: deep-toned: massive: not easily digested: doughy: impeding the feet in walking: (of the ground) very wet and soft: heavy-armed (mil.): strong, as liquor: dark with clouds: pertaining to grave or serious roles (theat.): serious, important (slang): (of a market) with falling prices (commerce): —compar. **heav'ier;** superl. **heav'iest.**—adv. heavily. —n. the villain on stage or screen: a large, strong man employed for purposes of a violent nature (slang): in Scotland, a type of beer similar to, but not as strong

as, export.—*adv.* **heav'ily.**—*n.* **heav'iness.**—*adjs*
heav'ier-than-air' of greater specific gravity than air,
not sustained by a gasbag; **heav'y-armed** bearing
heavy armour or arms.—**heavy breather; heavy
breathing** loud and laboured breathing due to exertion, excitement, etc., sometimes associated with
anonymous obscene telephone calls.—*adjs* **heav'y-
du'ty** made to withstand very hard wear or use,
heav'y-hand'ed clumsy, awkward, oppressive,
heav'y-heart'ed weighted down with grief —**heavy
hydrogen** deuterium: also tritium, **heavy industry** see
industry.—*adj.* **heav'y-lad'en** with a heavy burden.—
heavy metal a metal of high specific gravity: guns or
shot of large size: a person to be reckoned with: a
particularly loud, simple and repetitive form of rock
(*mus.*); **heavy spar** barytes; **heavy water** water in
which deuterium takes the place of ordinary hydrogen, or a mixture of this and ordinary water,
heav'yweight a person or thing well above the average
weight: someone important or very influential
(*coll.*): one in the heaviest class (*sport*) in boxing
light-heavyweight over 11 st 6 lb. and not over 12 st 7
lb., amateur 11 st. 11 lb and 12 st. 10 lb. **heavyweight**
any weight above these —**be heavy going** see **going'**;
the heavies the more serious, newspapers, journals,
etc. (*coll.*). [O.E *hefig—hebban*, to heave,
O.H.G. *hebig.*]
hebdomad *heb'dō-mad, n.* a week.—*adj.* **hebdomadal**
(*dom'ə-dl*) weekly.—*adv* **hebdom'adally.** [Gr
hebdomas, -ados, a set of seven, a week—*hepta,*
seven.]
hebetate *heb'i-tāt, v.t.* to dull or blunt —*v.i* to
become dull.—*adj.* dull: blunt: soft-pointed [L
hebetāre, -ātum—hebes, -etis, blunt.]
Hebrew *hē'brōō, n* a Jew: the Semitic language of the
Hebrews.—*adj.* of the Hebrews or their language
—*adjs.* **Hebraic** (*hē-brā'ik*). **-al** relating to the Hebrews or to their language.—*adv.* **Hebrā'ically.**—
Hē'braism a Hebrew idiom; **Hē'braist** one skilled in
Hebrew. [O.Fr *Ebreu*—Aramaic *'ebrai,* lit. one
from the other side (of the Euphrates).]
Hebridean *heb-ri-dē'ən, adj.* of the Hebrides (*heb'ri-
dēz*).—*n.* a native of the Hebrides. [Due to a mis-
print of L. *Hebūdēs.*]
hecatomb *hek'ə-tom, -tōm* (sometimes *-tōōm*), *n.* a
great public sacrifice: any large number of victims.
[Gr. *hekatombē—hekaton,* a hundred, *bous,* an ox.]
heck *hek, n.* and *interj.* euphemistic for **hell.**
heckelphone *hek'l-fōn, n.* an instrument of the oboe
family, invented by W. *Heckel* (1856–1909), between
the cor anglais and the bassoon in pitch.
heckle *hek'l, v.i.* to comb out, of flax or hemp fibres
orig. *Scot.,* to ply with embarrassing questions (as
at an election).—*n.* a hackle.—*n.* **heck'ler.** [Cf.
hackle.]
hectare. See under **hecto-.**
hectic *hek'tik, adj.* affected with hectic fever: feverish,
agitated, rushed (*coll.*).—*n.* a hectic fever: a con-
sumptive: a flush.—*adv.* **hec'tically.**—**hectic fever**
fever occurring in connection with certain wasting
diseases of long duration. [Gr. *hektikos,* habitual—
hexis, habit.]
hecto- *hek'tō,* **hect-** in composition (esp. in the metric
system) 100 times.—*ns.* **hectare** (*hek'tar*) 100 ares or
10,000 sq. metres; **hec'togram(me)** 100 grammes; **hec'-
tograph** a gelatine pad for printing copies —*v.t* to
reproduce in this way —*adj.* **hectograph'ic.**—*ns* **hec'-
tolitre** 100 litres; **hec'tometre** 100 metres. [Fr contraction of Gr. *hekaton,* a hundred.]
hector *hek'tər, n.* a bully, a blusterer.—*v t.* to treat
insolently: to annoy —*v.i.* to play the bully' to bluster.—*n.* **hec'torer.** [Gr. *Hektōr,* the Trojan hero]
he'd *hēd,* a contraction of **he had** or **he would.**

heddle *hed'l, n* a series of vertical cords or wires, each
having in the middle a loop to receive a warp-thread,
and passing round and between parallel bars. [An
assumed O.E. *hefedl.*]
hedge *hej, n.* a close row of bushes or small trees serving as a fence: a barrier, protection (*fig.*): an act of
hedging.—*v t* to enclose with a hedge: to obstruct to
surround: to protect oneself from loss on, by compensatory transactions, e g bets on the other side —*v t.*
to make hedges: to shuffle, be evasive, as in argument.—*adj* living in or frequenting hedges, wayside,
low: debased —*n* **hedg'er** one who hedges or dresses
hedges —**hedge'hog** a small prickly-backed insectivorous animal that lives in hedges and bushes,
and has a snout like a hog: a small, strongly fortified,
defensive position.—*v.t* **hedge'-hop** (*airmen's slang*)
to fly low as if hopping over hedges —**hedge'-par'son,**
hedge'-priest a disreputable, vagrant, or illiterate
parson or priest, **hedge'pig** a hedgehog; **hedge'row** a
line of hedge, often with trees; **hedge'-school** an
open-air school, common in Ireland in 17th and 18th
centuries during the ban on Catholic education:
hedge'-schoolmaster; **hedge'-sparrow** formerly also
hedge'-warbler the dunnock (*Prunella modularis*),
superficially like a sparrow but with a more slender
bill. [O.E *hecg;* Du. *hegge,* Ger *Hecke.*]
hedonism *hē'dən-izm, n* in ethics, the doctrine that
pleasure is the highest good.—*adjs.* **hedonic** (*-don'*),
hēdonist'ic.—*n sing* **hēdon'ics** that part of ethics or
of psychology that treats of pleasure.—*n.* **hē'donist.**
[Gr. *hēdonē,* pleasure]
heebie (or **heeby**)-**jeebies** *hē'bi-jē'biz, n.pl.* (with *the*;
slang) a fit of nerves: the creeps [A coinage]
heed *hēd, v.t.* to observe, to look after: to attend to —
v.t. to mind, care.—*n* notice, caution, attention.—
adj. **heed'ful** attentive cautious.—*adv.* **heed'fully.**—
n **heed'fulness.**—*adj.* **heed'less.**—*adv.* **heed'lessly.**—
n. **heed'lessness.** [O.E. *hēdan*]
heehaw *hē'ho, v t.* to bray —*n.* a bray [Imit.]
heel¹ *hēl, n.* the hind part of the foot below the ankle·
the whole foot (esp. of beasts): the covering or
support of the heel· the hinder part of anything, as a
violin bow: a heel-like bend, as on a golf-club: the end
of a loaf. a cad (*slang*).—*v.t* to execute or perform
with the heel. to strike with the heel: to furnish with a
heel: to supply with a weapon, money, etc.—*v.t* to
move one's heels to a dance rhythm: to kick the ball
backwards out of the scrum with the heel (*Rugby
football*) —*adj* **heeled** provided with a heel: (often in
composition, as **well-heeled**) comfortably supplied
with money, etc.—**heel'-ball** a black waxy composition for blacking the heels and soles of shoes, and for
taking rubbings, **heel'-tap** a layer of material in a
shoe-heel. a small quantity of liquor left in the glass
after drinking.—**Achilles' heel** see under **Achillean;**
at, on, upon the heels of following close behind; **bring
to heel** to cause to come to heel; **come to heel** to obey
or follow like a dog: to submit to authority; **cool or
kick one's heels** to be kept waiting for some time; **dig
in one's heels** to behave stubbornly, **down at heel**
having the heels of one's shoes trodden down:
slovenly in poor circumstances; **heel and toe** with
strict walking pace, as opposed to running; **kick up
one's heels** to frisk, **show a clean pair of heels** to run
off, **take to one's heels** to flee; **turn on, upon, one's
heel** to turn sharply round, to turn back or away,
under the heel crushed, tyrannised over; **walk to heel**
(of a dog) to walk at one's heels, under control
[O E *hēla*]
heel² *hēl, i i* to incline, to lean on one side, as a ship
—*v t* to tilt [Earlier *heeld, hield,* O E *hieldan,* to
slope]
heft¹ *heft, n* weight (*U S.*) the greater part (*arch*) —

v.t. to lift: to try the weight of —*adj.* **heft'y** rather heavy: muscular· sizeable: vigorous.—*adv.* very [heave.]

Hegelian *hā-gēl'i-ən, adj.* of or pertaining to Wilhelm Friedrich *Hegel* (1770–1831) or his philosophy.—*n.* a follower of Hegel.—*n* **Hegel'ianism**.

hegemony *hi-gem'ən-i, n.* leadership: preponderant influence, esp. of one state over others. [Gr. *hēgemoniā—hēgemōn*, leader—*hēgeesthai*, to lead]

hegira, hejira *he', hij'i-rə, hi-jī'rə, ns* the flight of Mohammed from Mecca, A.D 622, from which is dated the Muslim era: any flight [Ar *hijrah*, flight, *hajara*, to leave]

he-he *hē-hē, interj* representing a high-pitched or gleeful laugh.—*n.* such a laugh.—*v.t* to laugh so [lmit.]

heifer *hef'ər, n* a young cow [O E *hēahfore, hēahfru, -fre*; lit. prob high-goer—*faran* to go]

heigh *hā* (or *hī*), *interj.* a cry of enquiry, encouragement, or exultation—also **hey, ha.**—*interj.* **heigh'-ho** an exclamation expressive of weariness. [Imit.]

height *hīt, n.* the condition of being high: degree of highness: distance upwards· angle of elevation: that which is elevated: a hill: a high place: elevation in rank or excellence: utmost degree —*v.t* and *v t.* **height'en** to make or become higher: to make or become brighter or more conspicuous, or (*fig.*) stronger or more intense.—**height of land** a watershed, esp. if not a range of hills; **height to paper** the standard height of type, blocks. etc , from foot to face (approx 0·918 in.). [From *highth*—O E *hiehtho, hēahthu—hēah*, high.]

heil! *hīl*, (Ger.) *interj* hail!

heinous *hā'nəs*, sometimes *hē'nəs, adj* wicked in a high degree, odious, atrocious —*adv* **hei'nously.**—*n* **hei'nousness**. [O.Fr *hainos* (Fr. *haineux*)—*hair*, to hate.]

heir *ār, n* in law, one who actually succeeds to property, title, etc., on the death of its previous holder: popularly, one entitled to succeed when the present possessor dies: a child, esp a first-born son: a successor to a position, e g. of leadership: inheritor of qualities, or of social conditions, or the past generally.—*ns.* **heir'dom, heir'ship; heir'ess** a female heir. a woman who has succeeded or is likely to succeed to a considerable fortune.—**heir'-appa'rent** the one by law acknowledged to be heir, no matter who may subsequently be born: a person expected to succeed the leader of a party, etc. (*fig.*); **heir'loom** any piece of furniture or personal property which descends to the heir by special custom: any object which is passed down through a family from generation to generation; **heir'-presump'tive** one who will be heir if no nearer relative should be born [O Fr *heir*—L. *hērēs* (vulgar accus. *hērem*), an heir.]

heist *hīst*, (*slang*) *v.t.* to steal or rob in a heist.—*n* a robbing or theft, esp. an armed hold-up. or a particularly clever or spectacular theft: one who robs or steals.—*n* **heist'er**. [Variant of **hoist**.]

hejira. See **hegira**.

held *pa.t* and *pa.p.* of **hold**[1].

Heldentenor *held' ən-ten'ər, held' ən-te-nōr', n.* (a man with) a powerful tenor voice, particularly suitable for roles in Wagnerian operas [Ger., hero tenor— *Held*, hero.]

heli- *hel-i-,* in composition, helicopter (as in *n* **hel'iport**, etc.).—*ns.* **hel'icopter** (Gr *pteron*, wing) a flying-machine sustained by a power-driven screw or screws revolving on a vertical axis.—*n.* **hel'ipad** a landing-place for a helicopter [Gr *helix*, screw.]

heliacal *hē-lī'ək-əl, adj* solar: coincident with that of the sun, or as nearly as could be observed —*adv* **heli'acally.—heliacal rising** the emergence of a star

from the light of the sun, **heliacal setting** its disappearance in it [Gr. *hēliakos—hēlios*, the sun]

Helianthus *hē-li-an'thəs, n.* the sunflower genus. [Gr. *hēlios*, sun, *anthos*, flower]

helical, etc. See **helix**.

Heliconian *hel-i-kō'ni-ən, adj* pertaining to *Helicon* (Gr. *Helikōn*). a mountain-range in Boeotia, favourite seat of the Muses.

helicopter. See **heli-**.

helio- *hē'li-ō-, hē-li-o'-*, in composition, sun —*adj* **heliocentric** (-*sen'trik*; Gr. *kentron*, centre; *astron.*) referred to the sun as centre —*adv* **heliocen'trically**. —*n* **he'liograph** (Gr *graphē*, a drawing) an apparatus for signalling by flashing the sun's rays· an engraving obtained photographically: an apparatus for photographing the sun: an instrument for measuring intensity of sunlight.—*v.t* and *v.t.* to communicate by heliograph —*adjs* **heliograph'ic, -al.**—*adv.* **heliograph'ically.**—*ns.* **heliog'raphy; heliogravure** (*-grəv-ūr', -grāv'yər*, Fr *héliogravure*) photoengraving; **heliom'eter** an instrument for measuring angular distances, as the sun's diameter; **he'liostat** (Gr. *statos*, fixed) an instrument by means of which a beam of sunlight is reflected in an invariable direction, for study of the sun or for signalling; **heliother'apy** (Gr. *therapeiā*, healing) medical treatment by exposure to the sun's rays, **heliotrope** (*hē'li-ō-trōp*; Gr *hēliotropion*) plant of the borage family, with small fragrant lilac-blue flowers: the colour of its flowers: a kind of perfume imitating that of the flower: a bloodstone (*min.*) —*adjs.* **heliotropic** (-*trop'ik*), **-al.**—*adv.* **heliotrop'ically.**—*ns.* **heliotropism** (-*ot'rə-pizm*), **heliot'ropy** the tendency of stem and leaves to bend towards (*positive heliotropism*), and roots from (*negative heliotropism*), the light; **he'liotype** (Gr. *typos*, impression) a photograph by heliotypy.—*adj.* **heliotypic** (-*tip'ik*).—*n.* **he'liotypy** (-*tī-pi*) a photo-mechanical process in which the gelatine relief is itself used to print from. [Gr. *hēlios*, the sun.]

heliography, etc. See **helio-**.

helium *hē'li-əm, n.* an element (He; at numb. 2). a very light inert gas, discovered (1868) by Lockyer in the sun's atmosphere, isolated (1895) by Ramsay from cleveite, and found in certain natural gases. [Gr *hēlios*, sun]

helix *hē'liks, n* a screw-shaped coil: a small volute or twist in the capital of a Corinthian column (*archit*)' (*cap.*; *zool.*) a genus of molluscs including the best-known land-snails—*pl.* **hē'lixes** or **helices** (*hel'i-sēz*). —*adj.* **helical** (*hel'ik-əl*).—*adv.* **hel'ically.**—*adj.* **hel'icoid** like a helix, screw-shaped. [Gr *hēlix*, a spiral—*helissein*, to turn round.]

Hell *hel, n.* the place of the dead in general: the place or state of punishment of the wicked after death: the abode of evil spirits: (the following meanings without *cap*) any place of vice or misery: (a state of) supreme misery or discomfort: anything causing misery, pain or destruction: ruin, havoc: commotion, uproar: severe censure or chastisement: used in various coll phrases expressing displeasure, emphasis, etc (as *what in hell?, get the hell out of here, I wish to hell he'd go away*): a gambling-house —*interj* expressing displeasure or emphasis —*n.* **hellion** (*hel'yən*) a troublesome, mischievous child —*adj* **hell'ish.**— *adv* **hell'ish(ly).**—*n* **hell'ishness.**—*adj* (*coll.*) **hell'-uva, hell'ova (hell of a)** great, terrific.—**hell'bender** a large American salamander· a reckless or debauched person.—*adj* **hell'-bent** (with *on*) recklessly determined.—*adv* with reckless determination — **hell'-cat** a malignant hag; **hell'-fire** the fire of hell: punishment in hell; **hell'-hole** the pit of hell, **hell'-hound** a hound of hell: an agent of hell, **hell's angel**

(often *cap.*) a member of any gang of young motor-cyclists who indulge in violent or antisocial behaviour.—*interjs.* **hell's bells, teeth,** etc. expressions of irritation, surprise, etc —**all hell breaks,** is **let loose** there is chaos or uproar; **as hell** absolutely very; **beat, kick, knock,** etc. **the hell out of** to beat, etc. severely; **come hell or high water** no matter what difficulties may be encountered; **for the hell of it** for fun or adventure, **give someone hell** to punish, castigate, rebuke someone severely: to cause someone pain or misery, **hell for leather** at a furious pace, **hell to pay** serious trouble, unpleasant consequences; **like hell** very much, very hard, very fast, etc.. (also **the hell, hell**) used to express strong disagreement or refusal, as in *like hell I will!, the hell I will!, will I hell!*); **not have a cat in hell's chance** see cat[1]; **not have a hope in hell** to have no hope at all; **play hell with** see **play; to hell with** an expression of angry disagreement with, intention to ignore, etc. (someone or something); **what the hell** it does not matter. [O.E. *hel, hell*; O.N. *hel*, Ger. *Hölle*.]

he'll *hēl*, contraction for **he will.**

Helladic *hel-ad'ik, adj.* Greek: of the Greek mainland Bronze Age. [Gr. *Helladikos,* Greek—*Hellas,* Greece.]

hellbender. See **Hell.**

hellebore *hel'i-bōr, -bor, n.* a plant of the buttercup family (as *black hellebore* or *Christmas rose, stinking hellebore, green hellebore*): a plant of the lily family (*American, false,* or *white hellebore,* known also as Indian poke or itchweed): the winter aconite (*winter hellebore*): the rhizome and roots of these prepared as a drug. [Gr *helleboros.*]

Hellene *hel'ēn, n.* a Greek.—*adj.* **Hellen'ic** (or *-en'*) Greek.—*v.i.* **hell'enise, -ize** (*-in-īz*; often with *cap.*) to conform, or tend to conform, to Greek usages.—*v.t.* to make Greek.—*ns.* **Hell'enism** a Greek idiom: the Greek spirit: Greek nationality: conformity to Greek ways, esp. in language; **Hell'enist** one skilled in the Greek language: one who adopted Greek ways and language, esp. a Jew.—*adj.* **Hellenist'ic** pertaining to the Hellenists: pertaining to Greek culture, affected by foreign influences after the time of Alexander —*adv.* **Hellenist'ically.** [Gr *Hellēn,* a Greek.]

hellion, etc. See **Hell.**

hello. Same as **hallo.**

helm[1] *helm, n.* steering apparatus.—**helms'man** a steersman. [O.E. *helma*; O.N. *hjālm,* a rudder, Ger. *Helm,* a handle.]

helm[2] *helm,* (*arch.*) *n.* a helmet.

helmet *hel'mit, n.* a covering of armour for the head any similar covering for the head, anything resembling a helmet, as a cloud on a mountain top, the top of a guinea-fowl's head, the hooded upper lip of certain flowers.—*adjs.* **hel'meted.** [O E. *helm,* Ger. *Helm,* cf. **helm.**]

helminth *hel'minth, n.* a worm.—*n.* **helminthi'asis** infestation with worms.—*adjs.* **helmin'thic; helmin'thoid** worm-shaped; **helmintholog'ic, -al.**—*ns* **helminthol'ogist; helminthol'ogy** the study of worms, esp. parasitic [Gr. *helmins, -inthos,* a worm]

helot *hel'ot, n.* one of a class of serfs among the ancient Spartans, deliberately humiliated and liable to massacre (*hist.*): a serf (*hist.*).—*ns.* **hel'otism; hel'otry** the whole body of the helots: any class of slaves [Gr. *Heilōtēs,* also *Heulōs, -ōtos.*]

help *help, v.t* to contribute towards the success of, aid, or assist: to give means for doing anything: to relieve the wants of: to provide or supply with a portion. to deal out: to remedy. to mitigate: to prevent, to keep from.—*v.t.* to give assistance: to contribute.—*n.* means or strength given to another for a

purpose: assistance relief: one who assists: a hired servant, esp domestic —*n.* **help'er** one who helps: an assistant —*adj.* **help'ful** giving help useful.—*n* **help'fulness.**—*adj.* **help'ing** giving help or support.— *n.* a portion served at a meal.—*adj* **help'less** without ability to do things for oneself. wanting assistance.— *adv.* **help'lessly.**—*n.* **help'lessness.—helping hand** assistance; **help'mate** a modification of **help'meet,** itself formed from the phrase in Gen ii. 18, 'an help meet for him', *specif.* a wife —**cannot help (be helped)** cannot avoid (be avoided), **help off with** to aid in taking off, disposing or getting rid of; **help on with** to help to put on, **help oneself (to)** to take for oneself without waiting for offer or authority; **help out** to supplement: to assist; **more than one can help** (illogically but idiomatically) more than is necessary; **so help me (God)** a form of solemn oath: on my word. [O.E *helpan,* pa.t. *healp* (pl. *hulpon*), pa.p. *holpen*; O.N *hjālpa*; Ger *helfen.*]

helter-skelter *hel'tər-skel'tər, adv.* in a confused hurry: tumultuously.—*n.* disorderly motion: a fair-ground spiral slide.—*adj.* confused. [Imit.]

helve *helv, n.* the handle of an axe or similar tool.—*v.t.* to furnish with a helve. [O.E. *helfe* (*hielfe*), a handle]

Helvetic *hel-vet'ik,* **Helvetian** *hel-vē'shən, adjs* Swiss. [L. *Helvētia,* Switzerland]

hem[1] *hem, n.* an edge or border: a border doubled down and sewed.—*v.t.* to form a hem on: to edge:— *pr.p.* **hemm'ing;** *pa t.* and *pa.p* **hemmed.—hem'-line** the height or level of the hem of a dress, skirt, etc.; **hem'-stitch** the ornamental finishing of the inner side of a hem, made by pulling out several threads adjoining it and drawing together in groups the cross-threads by successive stitches.—**hem in** to surround. [O.E. *hemm,* a border]

hem[2] *hem, hm, n* and *interj* a sort of half-cough to draw attention.—*v.i* to utter the sound *hem:*—*pr.p.* **hemm'ing;** *pa.t.* and *pa.p.* **hemmed.** [Sound of clearing the throat.]

hem-. See **haem-.**

he-man. See **he.**

hematite, etc. See **haematite,** etc. under **haem-.**

hemato-. See **haemato-** under **haem-.**

heme. See **haem** under **haem-.**

hemeralopia *hem-ər-ə-lō'pi-ə, n.* day-blindness. vision requiring dim light. [Gr. *hēmerā,* day, *alaos,* blind, *ōps,* eye.]

Hemerocallis *hem-ər-ō-kal'is, n.* a day-lily. [Gr *hēmerokalles—hēmerā,* day, *kallos,* beauty.]

hemi- *hem'i-,* in composition, half.—*n* **hemianops'ia** (Gr *an-,* priv *opsis,* sight) blindness in half of the field of vision.—*adj.* **hemianop'tic.**—*ns.* **hemi-demisem'iquaver** (*mus*) a note equal in time to half a demisemiquaver; **hemiplegia** (-*plē'ji-ə,* or -*gi-ə,* Gr. *plēgē,* a blow) paralysis of one side only —*adj.* **hemiplegic** (-*plej'* or -*plē'g'*) —Also *n.—n.pl.* **Hemip'tera** (Gr. *pteron,* a wing) an order of insects, variously defined, with wings (when present) often half leathery, half membranous—the bugs, cicadas, greenfly, etc —*adj* **hemip'terous.**—*n* **hem'isphere** (Gr. *hēmisphairion—sphaira,* a sphere) a half-sphere divided by a plane through the centre: half of the globe or a map of it one of the two divisions of the cerebrum —*adjs* **hemispher'ic, -al.**—*n* **hemistich** (*hem'i-stik;* Gr *hēmistichion—stichos,* a line) one of the two divisions of a line of verse.—*adj.* **hemi'stichal** (or *-is'*) —**Eastern and Western hemispheres** the eastern and western halves of the terrestrial globe, the former including Europe, Asia and Africa, the latter, the Americas [Gr *hēmi-,* half]

hemlock *hem'lok, n* a poisonous spotted umbelliferous plant (*Conium maculatum*). the poison got from it: extended to other umbelliferous plants, eg. water hemlock: a N. American tree (hemlock spruce) whose branches are fancied to resemble hemlock leaves. [O.E. *hymlīce* (Kentish *hemlīc*).]

hemo-. See **haemo-** under **haem-**.

hemp *hemp, n.* a plant (*Cannabis sativa*), classified by some as belonging to the mulberry family *Moraceae* but by many now placed in a separate family *Cannabinaceae*, yielding a coarse fibre, a narcotic drug, and an oil: the fibre itself: the drug: a similar fibre got from various other plants.—*adjs.* **hemp'en** made of hemp.—**hemp'-ag'rimony** a composite plant with hemp-like leaves; **hemp'-nett'le** a coarse bristly labiate weed. [O.E. *henep, hænep*; cf. Gr. *kannabis*.]

hen *hen, n.* a female bird: a female domestic fowl: applied loosely to any domestic fowl: the female of certain fishes and crustaceans.—**hen'bane** a poisonous plant (*Hyoscyamus niger*) of the nightshade family; **hen'-coop** a coop for a hen; **hen'-harr'ier** a bird, the common harrier.—*adj.* **hen'-heart'ed** faint-hearted: timid.—**hen'-house** a house for fowls; **hen'-party** a gathering of women only.—*v.t.* **hen'peck** to domineer over (said of a wife).—**hen'-roost** a roosting-place for fowls; **hen'-run** an enclosure for fowls.—*adj.* **hen'-toed'** with toes turned in.—**hen'-wife** a woman with charge of poultry. [O.E. *henn*, fem. of *hana*, a cock.]

hence *hens, adv.* from this place: from this time onward: in the future: from this cause or reason: from this origin.—*interj.* away! begone!—*advs.* **hence'forth**, **hencefor'ward** from this time forth or forward. [M.E. *hennes*, formed with genitive ending from *henne* —O.E. *heonan*, from the base of **he**.]

henchman *hench', hensh'man, n.* a servant: a page: a right-hand man: an active partisan, a thick-and-thin supporter:—*pl.* **hench'men**. [O.E. *hengest*, a horse, and *man*.]

hendecagon *hen-dek'ə-gon, n.* a plane figure of eleven angles and eleven sides.—*adj.* **hendecagonal** (-*ag'ən-l*). [Gr. *hendeka*, eleven, *gōniā*, an angle.]

hendecasyllable *hen'dek-ə-sil'ə-bl, n.* a metrical line of eleven syllables.—*adj.* **hendecasyllabic** (-*ab'ik*). [Gr. *hendeka*, eleven, *syllabē*, a syllable.]

hendiadys *hen-dī'ə-dis, n.* a rhetorical figure in which a notion, normally expressible by an adjective and a noun, is expressed by two nouns joined by *and* or another conjunction, as *clad in cloth and green* for *clad in green cloth*. [Mediaeval L.—Gr. *hen dia dyoin*, lit. one by two.]

henequen *hen'ə-kən, n.* a Mexican agave: its leaf-fibre, sisal-hemp used for cordage.—Also **hen'equin**, **hen'i-quin**. [Sp. *henequén, jeniquén*.]

henge *henj, n.* a circular or oval area enclosed by a bank and internal ditch, often containing burial chambers, or a circular, oval or horseshoe-shaped construction of large upright stones or wooden posts. [Back-formation from *Stonehenge*, a famous example.]

heniquin. See **henequen.**

henna *hen'ə, n.* a small Oriental shrub (*Lawsonia*) of the loosestrife family, with fragrant white flowers: a red or reddish-orange pigment made from its leaves for dyeing the hair and for skin decoration.—*adj.* **hennaed** (*hen'əd*) dyed with henna. [Ar. *hinnā'*.]

henotheism *hen'ō-thē-izm, n.* belief in one god, supreme or specially venerated but not the only god.— *n.* **henothe'ist**.—*adj.* **henotheist'ic**. [Gr. *heis, henos*, one, *theos*, god.]

henpeck. See **hen.**

henry *hen'ri, (elect.) n.* the unit of inductance, such that an electromotive force of one volt is induced in a circuit by current variation of one ampere per sec.:—*pl.* **hen'-ries** or **hen'rys**. [Joseph Henry, American physicist (1797–1878).]

hep *hep, (slang) adj.* knowing, informed, well abreast of fashionable knowledge and taste, esp. in the field of jazz.—**hep'-cat** (*slang*), a hipster (*q.v.*).—**be, get, hep to** to be, become informed about. [Perh. *hep*, left (command in drilling)—with ideas of being in step.]

hepar *hē'pär, n.* old name for liver-coloured compounds of sulphur.—*n.* **heparin** (*hep'ə-rin*) complex substance formed in tissues of liver, lung, etc , that delays clotting of blood, used in medicine and surgery. —*adj.* **hepatic** (*hi-pat'ik*) pertaining to, or acting on, the liver: liver-coloured.—*n.* a liverwort: a hepatic medicine.—*ns.* **Hepat'ica** a genus of plants with slightly liver-like leaf.—**hepati'tis** inflammation of the liver; **hepatol'ogist** a specialist in liver diseases; **hepatol'ogy**. [Gr. *hēpar, hēpatos*, liver.]

Hepplewhite *hep'l-(h)wīt, adj* belonging to a graceful school of furniture design typified by George *Hepplewhite* (d. 1786).

hepta- *hep'tə-, hep-ta', in composition, seven.—*ns.* **hep'tachord** (Gr. *chordē*, string) in Greek music, a diatonic series of seven tones, containing five whole steps and one half-step: an instrument with seven strings; **hep'tad** (Gr. *heptas, heptados*) a group of seven.—*adj.* **hep'taglot** (Gr. *heptaglōttos—glōtta*, tongue) in seven languages.—*n.* a book in seven languages.—*n.* **hep'tagon** (Gr. *heptagōnos—gōniā*, an angle) a plane figure with seven angles and seven sides. —*adj.* **heptag'onal**.—*ns.* **hepta'meter** (Gr. *metron*, measure) a verse of seven measures or feet; **hep'tane** a hydrocarbon, of the methane series; **hep'tarch** ruler in a heptarchy.—*adj.* **heptar'chic**.—*n.* **heptarchy** (*hep'tär-ki*; Gr. *archē*, sovereignty) a government by seven persons: a country governed by seven: a misleading term for a once supposed system of seven English kingdoms—Wessex, Sussex, Kent, Essex, East Anglia, Mercia, and Northumbria.—*adj.* **heptasyllab'ic** seven-syllabled.—*n.* **Hep'tateuch** (-*tūk*; Gr. *teuchos*, instrument, volume) the first seven books of the Old Testament. [Gr. *hepta*, seven.]

her *hûr, pron., gen.* (or *poss. adj.*), *dat.* and *acc.* of the pron. **she**: herself (*refl.; poet.* or *dial.*): she (*coll. nom.*). [O.E. *hire*, gen. and dat. sing. of *hēo*, she.]

herald *her'əld, n.* in ancient times, an officer who made public proclamations and arranged ceremonies: in mediaeval times, an officer who had charge of all the etiquette of chivalry, keeping a register of the genealogies and armorial bearings of the nobles: an officer whose duty is to read proclamations, to blazon the arms of the nobility, etc : a proclaimer: a forerunner: a name given to many newspapers.—*v.t.* to usher in: to proclaim —*adj.* **heraldic** (*her-, hər-al'dik*).—*adv.* **heral'dically**.—*ns.* **her'aldry** the art or office of a herald: the science of recording genealogies and blazoning coats of arms. [O.Fr. *herault*; of Gmc. origin.]

herb *hûrb n.* a plant with no woody stem above ground, distinguished from a tree or shrub: a plant used in medicine: an aromatic plant used in cookery.—*adj.* **herba'ceous** pertaining to, composed of, containing, or of the nature of, herbs: usu. understood as of tall herbs that die down in winter and survive in underground parts (*hort.*).—*ns.* **herb'age** herbs collectively: herbaceous vegetation covering the ground: right of pasture.—*adj.* **herb'al** composed of or relating to herbs.—*n.* a book containing descriptions of plants with medicinal properties.—*ns.* **herb'alist** one who studies, collects, sells, or administers herbs or plants: an early botanist; **herbärium** (a room, building, etc. for) a classified collection of preserved plants:—*pl.* **herbā'riums, herbä'ria.**—*adj.* **herbicid'al.**—*ns.* **herb'icide** (-*i-sīd*) a substance for killing weeds, etc., esp. a selective weedkiller; **herb'ist** a herbalist.—*n.pl.* **herbiv'ora** (ə-rə) grass-eating animals, esp ungulates.

For other sounds see detailed chart of pronunciation.

—*n.* **herb'ivore** (-*vōr*, -*vōr*).—*adj.* **herbiv'orous** eating or living on grass or herbage.—**herb'-benn'et** (L. *herba benedicta*, blessed herb) a plant, *Geum urbanum*, avens; **herb'-Chris'topher** baneberry; **herb'-garden; herb'-Par'is** a plant (*Paris quadrifolia*) of the lily family; **herb'-Pe'ter** cowslip; **herb'-Rob'ert** stinking cranesbill (*Geranium robertianum*), a plant with small reddish-purple flowers; **herb'-tea'** a drink made from aromatic herbs. [Fr. *herbe*—L. *herba*.]

Herculean *hûr-kū-lē'an, -kū'li-an, adj.* of or pertaining to *Hercules* (*hûr'kū-lēz*): (without *cap.*) extremely difficult or dangerous, as the twelve labours of Hercules.—**Hercules beetle** a gigantic S American beetle, *Dynastes hercules*.—**Pillars of Hercules** two rocks flanking the entrance to the Mediterranean at the Strait of Gibraltar.

herd¹ *hûrd, n.* a company of animals, esp large animals, that habitually keep together: a group of domestic animals, esp. cows or swine, with or without a guardian: a stock of cattle: the people regarded as a mass, as acting from contagious impulse, or merely in contempt.—*v.i.* to associate as in herds: to live like a beast in a herd.—*v.t.* to put in a herd: to drive together.—**herd'-book** a pedigree book of cattle or pigs, **herd instinct** the instinct that urges men or animals to act upon contagious impulses or to follow the herd; **herds'man** keeper of a herd. [O E. *heord*.]

herd² *hûrd, n.* a keeper of a herd or flock. [O.E *hirde, hierde*]

here *hēr, adv.* in this place: hither: in the present life or state.—*advs.* **here'about, -s** about this place; **here-af'ter** after this, in some future time, life, or state — *n* a future state —*advs.* **hereat'** at or by reason of this; **hereby'** not far off: by this; **herein'** in this; **hereinaf'ter** afterward in this (document, etc.)—opp to **hereinbefore'**.—*advs.* **hereof'** of this; **hereon'** on or upon this; **hereto'** to this: for this object, **here'tofore'** before this time: formerly; **hereund'er** under this, **here'unto** (also -*un'*) to this point or time, **here'upon'** on this: immediately after this; **herewith'** with this — **here and there** in this place, and then in that: thinly irregularly; **here goes!** an exclamation indicating that the speaker is about to do something; **here's to I** drink the health of, **here you are** (*coll.*) this is what you want: this is something for you: this way, **here we are** (*coll.*) this is what we are looking for: we have now arrived (at); **here we go again** (*coll.*) the same undesirable situation is recurring, **neither here nor there** of no special importance: not relevant. [O E *hēr*, from base of *hē*, he.]

heredity *hi-red'i-ti, n.* the transmission of characters to descendants: heritability.—*n* **hereditabil'ity**—*adj.* **hered'itable** that may be inherited —*n* **heredit'-ament** (*her-id-*) any property that may pass to an heir —*adv.* **hered'itarily.**—*n* **hered'itariness.**—*adj* **hered'itary** descending or coming by inheritance: transmitted to offspring: succeeding by inheritance according to inheritance. [L. *hēréditās, -ātis—hērēs, -ēdis*, an heir.]

Hereford *her'i-fard, adj.* of a breed of white-faced red cattle, originating in *Hereford*shire.—Also *n.*

heresy *her'i-si, n.* belief contrary to the authorised teaching of one's natural religious community: an opinion opposed to the usual or conventional belief: heterodoxy.—*ns.* **heresiarch** (*he-rē'zi-ark*) a leader in heresy; **heresiol'ogist** a student of, or writer on, heresies; **heresiol'ogy** the upholder of a heresy.—*adj.* **heretical** (*hi-ret'i-kl*)—*adv* **heret'ically.** [O.Fr *heresie*—L. *haeresis*—Gr *hairesis*, the act of taking, choice, set of principles, school of thought—*haireein*, to take.]

heriot *her'i-at, n* a fine due to the lord of a manor on the death of a tenant—originally his best beast or

chattel.—*adj.* **her'iotable.** [O.E. *heregeatu*, a military preparation—*here*, an army, *geatwe*, equipment.]

heritable *her'i-ta-bl, adj.* that may be inherited.—*n* **heritabil'ity.**—*adv* **her'itably.**—*ns.* **her'itor** one who inherits; **heritage** (*her'it-ij*) that which is inherited: inherited lot, condition of one's birth: anything transmitted from ancestors or past ages. [O.Fr. (*h*)*eritable*, (*h*)*eritage*—L.L. *hērēditāre*, to inherit—*hērēditas*; see **heredity**.]

herl. Same as **harl.**

herm *hûrm, -z, ns.* a head or bust (originally of *Hermes*) on a square base, often double-faced

hermaphrodite *hûr-maf'rad-īt, n.* an animal or plant with the organs of both sexes, whether normally or abnormally: a compound of opposite qualities.—*adj.* uniting the characters of both sexes: combining opposite qualities —*n* **hermaph'roditism** the union of the two sexes in one body —*adjs.* **hermaphrodit'ic, -al.**—**hermaphrodite brig** a brig square-rigged forward and schooner-rigged aft [Gr *Hermaphrodītos*, the son of *Hermēs* and *Aphrodītē*, who grew together with the nymph Salmacis into one person.]

hermeneutic, -al *hûr-ma-nū'tik, -l, adjs.* interpreting: concerned with interpretation.—*adv* **hermeneu'-tically.**—*n sing.* **hermeneu'tics** the science of interpretation —*n* **hermeneu'tist.** [Gr *hermēneutikos* —*hermēneus*, an interpreter, from *Hermēs*.]

hermetic, -al *hûr-met'ik, -l, adjs* belonging to magic or alchemy, magical: perfectly close, completely sealed: obscure, abstruse —*adv* **hermet'ically.**—*n. sing.* **hermet'ics** esoteric science: alchemy —**hermetically sealed** closed completely. made air-tight by melting the glass [Mediaeval L. *hermēticus*—*Hermēs Trismegistos*, Hermes the thrice-greatest, the Greek name for the Egyptian Thoth, god of science, esp. alchemy]

hermit *hûr'mit, n* a solitary religious ascetic: one who lives a solitary life.—*n* **her'mitage** a hermit's cell, a retired abode —**her'mit-crab** a soft-bodied crustacean that inhabits a mollusc shell [M.E *eremite*, through Fr. and L from Gr *erēmitēs*—*erēmos*, solitary]

hernia *hûr'ni-a, n* a protrusion through a weak place of part of the viscera, rupture —*adjs* **her'nial; her'ni-ated.** [L]

hero *hē'rō, n.* a man of distinguished bravery: any illustrious person: a person reverenced and idealised: the principal male figure, or the one whose career is the thread of the story, in a history or work of fiction: orig a man of superhuman powers, a demigod·—*pl* **hē'roes;** fem. **heroine** (*her'ō-in*).—*adj* **heroic** (*hi-rō'ik*) befitting a hero: of or pertaining to heroes: epic: supremely courageous: using extreme or elaborate means to obtain a desired result, as the preserving of life.—*n* a heroic verse: (in *pl.*) extravagant phrases, bombast —*adv.* **hero'ically.**—*v.t.* **hē'roïse, -ize** to treat as a hero, make a hero of.—*ns.* **heroism** (*her'ō-izm*) the qualities of a hero: courage: boldness.—**heroic age** any semi-mythical period when heroes or demigods were represented as living among men; **heroic couplet** a pair of rhyming lines of heroic verse —*adjs* **hero'i-com'ic, -al** consisting of a mixture of heroic and comic: high burlesque —**heroic poem** an epic, **heroic remedy** one that may kill or cure, **heroic verse** the form of verse in which the exploits of heroes are celebrated (in classical poetry, the hexameter, in English, the iambic pentameter, esp in couplets, in French, the alexandrine); **he'ro-worship** the worship of heroes: excessive admiration of great men, or of anybody —Also *v.t.* [Through O Fr and L from Gr. *hērōs*]

heroin *her'ō-in, hi-rō'in, n* a derivative of morphine

used in medicine and by drug-addicts. [Said to be from Gr. *hērōs*, a hero, from its effect.]

heron *her'ən*, *hûrn*, *hern*, *n.* a large long-legged, long-necked wading bird.—*n.* **her'onry** a place where herons breed. [O.Fr. *hairon*—O.H.G. *heigir*.]

heronshaw *her'ən*- or *hern'*-, *hûrn'-sho*, *-shoō*, *n.* a young heron: (esp. *dial.*) a heron [O.Fr. *herouncel*, confounded with **shaw** (wood).]

herpes *hûr'pēz*, *n.* a skin disease of various kinds, with spreading clusters of vesicles on an inflamed base—esp. *herpes zoster* or shingles.—*adj.* **herpetic** (*-pet'ik*) [Gr. *herpēs*—*herpein*, to creep]

herpetology *hûr-pi-tol'ə-ji*, *n.* the study of reptiles and amphibians.—*adjs.* **herpetolog'ic**, **-al.**—*adv.* **herpetolog'ically.**—*n.* **herpetol'ogist**. [Ger *herpeton*, a reptile—*herpein*, to creep.]

Herr *her*, *n.* lord, master, the German term of address equivalent to sir, or (prefixed) Mr.:—*pl* **Herr'en.**—*n.* **Herrenvolk** (*her'en-fölk*) lit. 'master race', fitted and entitled by their superior qualities to rule the world. [Ger.]

herring *her'ing*, *n.* a common small sea-fish (*Clupea harengus*) of great commercial value, found moving in great shoals or multitudes —*adj.* **herr'ing-bone** like the spine of a herring, applied to a kind of masonry in which the stones slope in different directions in alternate rows, to a zigzag stitch crossed at the corners, etc.: in skiing, of a method of climbing a slope, the skis being placed at an angle and leaving a herring-bone-like pattern in the snow.—*v.t.* to make or mark with herring-bone pattern: to climb a slope on skis by herring-bone steps.—**herr'ing-gull** a large white gull with black-tipped wings.—**red herring** see **red**. [O E. *hæring*, *hēring*; cf Ger. *Hering*.]

hers *hûrz*, *pron.* possessive of **she** (used without a noun)

herself *hûr-self'*, *pron.* an emphatic form for **she** or **her**: in real character: reflexive for **her**: predicatively (or *n.*) one having the command of her faculties, sane, in good form. [See **her**, **self**.]

hertz *hûrts*, *n.* the unit of frequency, that of a periodic phenomenon of which the periodic time is one second —sometimes called **cycle per second** in U.K.—**Hertzian waves** electromagnetic waves used in communicating information through space. [After Heinrich *Hertz* (1857–94), German physicist.]

he's *hēz* a contraction of **he is** or **he has**.

hesitate *hez'i-tāt*, *v.i.* to hold back or delay in making a decision: to be in doubt.—*ns.* **hes'itance**, **hes'itancy**, **hesita'tion** wavering: doubt: stammering: delay.—*adj.* **hes'itant** hesitating.—*adv.* **hes'itatingly.**—*adj* **hes'itative.**—*n.* **hes'itator.**—*adj.* **hes'itatory.** [L. *haesitāre*, *-ātum*, freq. of *haerēre*, *haesum*, to stick.]

Hesperus *-əs*, *n.* Venus as the evening star.—*adj.* **Hesperian** (*-pē'ri-ən*) western: of the Hesperides.—*n.pl.* **Hesperides** (*-per'i-dēz*) the sisters who guarded in their gardens in the west the golden apples which Hera had received from Gaea; **hesperid'ium** (*bot.*) a fruit of the orange type. [Gr. *hesperos*, evening, western.]

Hessian *hes'i-ən*, sometimes *hesh'(i)ən*, *adj.* of or pertaining to Hesse: mercenary (from the use of Hessian mercenaries by the British against the Revolutionaries) (*U.S.*).—*n.* a native or citizen of Hesse: (without *cap.*) a cloth made of jute.—**Hessian fly** a midge whose larva attacks wheat stems in America, once believed to have been introduced in straw for the Hessian troops. [*Hesse*, Ger. *Hessen*, in Germany.]

hest *hest*, (*arch.*) *n.* behest, command: vow. [O.E. *hæs*, a command—*hātan*, to command.]

hesternal *hes-tûr'nəl*, *adj.* of yesterday [L. *hesternus*.]

het *het*, (*U.S.* and *dial.*) *pa.p.* for **heated.**—**het up** agitated.

hetaira *he-tī'rə*, *n.* in Greece, a courtesan, esp. of a superior class:—*pl.* **hetai'rai** (*-rī*).—*n.* **hetai'rism** concubinage: the system of society that admitted hetairai: a supposed primitive communal marriage.—*adj.* **hetairis'mic.**—Also (Latinised) **hetaera** (*-tē'*; L. *-tī'*), etc. [Gr. *hetairā*, fem. of *hetairos*, companion.]

heter-, hetero- *het'ər-*, *-ō-*, or *-o'-*, in composition, other, different: one or other (often opposed to *homo-*, *auto-*).—*adjs.* **heterochromous** (*-krō'məs*; Gr. *chrōma*, colour) having different or varying colours, **het'eroclite** (*-klīt*; Gr. *heteroklitos—klitos*, inflected —*klīnein*, to inflect; *gram.*) irregularly inflected: irregular: having forms belonging to different declensions.—*n.* a word irregularly inflected: anything irregular.—*adjs.* **heterocyclic** (*-sī'klik*; Gr. *kyklos*, wheel) having a closed chain in which the atoms are not all alike (*chem.*); **het'erodox** (Gr *heterodoxos—doxa*, opinion—*dokeein*, to think) holding an opinion other than or different from the one generally received, esp. in theology: heretical —*n.* **het'erodoxy** heresy.—*adjs.* **het'erodyne** (*-ō-dīn*; Gr. *dynamis*, strength) in radio communication, applied to a method of imposing on a continuous wave another of slightly different length to produce beats; **heteroecious** (*-ē'shəs*).—*n* **heteroecism** (*-ē'sizm*; Gr *oikos*, a house) parasitism upon different hosts at different stages of the life-cycle.—*adj* **heterog'amous.**—*ns.* **heterog'amy** (Gr. *gamos*, marriage) alternation of generations (*biol.*)· reproduction by unlike gametes (*biol*): presence of different kinds of flower (male, female, hermaphrodite, neuter, in any combination) in the same inflorescence (*bot.*). indirect pollination (*bot.*); **heterogenē'ity.**—*adj.* **heterogeneous** (*-jē'ni-əs*; Gr *heterogenēs—genos*, a kind) different in kind: composed of parts of different kinds—opp. to *homogeneous.*—*adv.* **heteroge'neously.**—*ns.* **heteroge'neousness; heterogenesis** (*-jen'i-sis*; Gr. *genesis*, generation; *biol.*) spontaneous generation: alternate generation.—*adj* **heterogenetic** (*-ji-net'ik*).—*n.* **heterogeny** (*-oj'ən-i*) a heterogeneous assemblage: heterogenesis.—*adj.* **heterogonous** (*og'ə-nəs*; Gr *gonos*, offspring, begetting) having flowers differing in length of stamens (*bot.*): having alternation of generations (*biol*).—*ns* **heterog'ony**; **het'erograft** a graft of tissue from a member of one species to a member of another species.—*adj.* **heterologous** (*-ol'ə-gəs*) not homologous: different: of different origin abnormal.—*n.* **heterol'ogy** lack of correspondence between apparently similar structures due to different origin.—*adjs.* **heterom'erous** (Gr. *meros*, part) having different numbers of parts in different whorls (*bot.*): (of lichens) having the algal cells in a layer (*bot.*): having unlike segments (*zool.*); **heteromor'phic** (Gr. *morphē*, form) deviating in form from a given type: of different forms—also **heteromor'-phous.**—*ns.* **heteromor'phism**, **het'eromorphy.**—*adj* **heteron'omous** (Gr. *nomos*, law) subject to different laws: subject to outside rule or law—opp. to *autonomous.*—*ns.* **heteron'omy; het'eronym** a word of the same spelling as another but of different pronunciation and meaning.—*adj.* **heterophyllous** (*-fil'əs*; Gr. *phyllon*, a leaf) having different kinds of foliage leaf.—*ns* **het'erophylly; heteroplasia** (*plā'z(h)i-ə*, *-si-ə*; Gr. *plasis*, a forming) development of abnormal tissue or tissue in an abnormal place —*adj.* **heteroplastic** (*-plas'tik*).—*n.* **het'eroplasty** heteroplasia: grafting of tissue from another person. —*n.pl.* **Heterop'tera** (Gr. *pteron*, a wing) a suborder of insects, the bugs, Hemiptera with fore and hind wings (when present) markedly different.—*adj.* **heterop'terous.**—*adj.* **heterosex'ual** having, or pertaining to, sexual attraction towards the opposite sex. —*ns.* **heterosexual'ity; heterō'sis** cross-fertilisation: the increased size and vigour (relative to its parents) often found in a hybrid.—*adj.* **heterotact'ic.**—*ns.* **heterotax'is**, **het'erotaxy** (Gr. *taxis*, arrangement) anomalous arrangement of, e.g. parts of the body, etc.—*adj.* **heterotroph'ic.**—*n.* **heterot'rophy** (Gr. *trophē*, livelihood; *bot.*) dependence (immediate or ultimate) upon green plants for carbon (as in most animals, fungi, etc.) —*n.* **heterozygote** (-zī'gōt; Gr. *zygōtos*, yoked—*zygon*, yoke) a zygote or individual formed from gametes differing with respect to some pair of alternative characters (one dominant and one recessive).—*adj* **heterozy'gous.** [Gr. *heteros*, other, one or other.]

hetman *het'man*, (*hist.*) *n.* a Polish officer: the head or general of the Cossacks:—*pl.* **het'mans.** [Pol., —Ger *Hauptmann*, captain.]

heuristic *hū-ris'tik*, *adj.* serving or leading to find out: encouraging desire to find out: (of method, argument) depending on assumptions based on past experience: consisting of guided trial and error.—*n.* (in *pl.*) principles used in making decisions when all possibilities cannot be fully explored.—*adv.* **heur-is'tically.** [Irreg. formed from Gr *heuriskein*, to find.]

hevea rubber *hē'vē-ə rub'ər*, rubber from the S. American tree **hevea**, *Hevea brasiliensis*, used in electrical insulators for its good electrical and mechanical properties.

hew *hū*, *v.t.* to cut with blows: to shape, fell or sever with blows of a cutting instrument.—*v.t.* to deal blows with a cutting instrument:—*pa.t.* **hewed;** *pa.p.* **hewed** or **hewn.**—*n.* **hew'er.** [O.E. *hēawan*.]

hex *heks*, *n.* a witch: a wizard: a spell: something which brings bad luck.—*v t.* to bring misfortune, etc. to by a hex: to bewitch.—*n.* **hex'ing.** [Pennsylvania Dutch *hex*—Ger. *Hexe* (*fem.*), *Hexer* (*masc.*).]

hex-, hexa- *heks-, heks'ə, heks-a'-*, in composition, six.—*ns.* **hex'achord** (-*kòrd*) a diatonic series of six notes having a semitone between the third and fourth; **hexachlō'rophene**, **hexachlō'rophane** (or -*or'*) a bactericide, used in antiseptic soaps, deodorants, etc.—*n.* **hexad** (*heks'ad*; Gr. *hexas, -ados*) a series of six numbers: a set of six things: an atom, element, or radical with a combining power of six units (*chem.*).—*n.* **hex'agon** (Gr. *hexagōnon—gōnīā*, an angle) a figure with six sides and six angles.—*adj.* **hexagonal** (*ag'ən-l*).—*n.* **hex'agram** (Gr. *gramma*, figure) a figure of six lines, esp. a stellate hexagon.—*adj.* **hexahē'dral.**—*n.* **hexahē'dron** (Gr. *hēdrā*, a base) a solid with six sides or faces, esp. a cube.—*adj.* **hexam'erous** (Gr. *meros*, part) having six parts, or parts in sixes.—*ns.* **hexam'eter** (Gr. *metron*, measure) a verse of six measures or feet: in Greek and Latin verse such a line where the fifth is almost always a dactyl and the sixth a spondee or trochee, the others dactyls or spondees.—**hexane** (*heks'ān*) a hydrocarbon, sixth member of the methane series; **hex'apla** (Gr. *hexaplā*, contracted pl. neut. of *hexaploos*, sixfold) an edition (esp. of the Bible) in six versions.—*adj.* **hex'aplar.**—*n.* **hex'apod** (Gr. *pous, podos*, a foot) an animal with six feet.—*n.pl* **Hexap'oda** insects.—*ns.* **hexap'ody** a line or verse of six feet; **hexastyle** (*heks'ə-stīl*; Gr. *hexastylos—stylos*, a pillar) having six columns.—*n.* a building or portico having six columns in front.—*n.* **Hexateuch** (*heks'ə-tūk*; Gr. *teuchos*, tool, afterwards book) the first six books of the Old Testament.—*adj.* **hexateuch'al.**—*n.* **hex'ose** a sugar (of various kinds) with six carbon atoms to the molecule. [Gr. *hex*, six; cf L. *sex*, and six.]

hey *hā*, *interj.* expressive of joy or interrogation, or calling attention.—*interjs.* **hey'-pres'to** a conjuror's command in passing objects; **hey for** now for: off we go for [Imit.]

heyday *hā'dā*, *n.* culmination or climax of vigour, prosperity, gaiety, etc.: flush or full bloom.

hi *hī*, *interj.* calling attention: hey: hello. [Cf. **hey.**]

hiatus *hī-ā'təs*, *n.* a gap: an opening: a break in continuity, a defect: a concurrence of vowel sounds in two successive syllables (*gram.*):—*pl.* **hia'tuses.**—**hiatus hernia** one in which a part of the stomach protrudes through the opening in the diaphragm intended for the oesophagus. [L. *hiātus, -ūs—hiāre*, *hiātum*, to gape.]

hibernate *hī'bər-nāt*, *v.i* to winter: to pass the winter in a resting state.—*adj.* **hiber'nal** belonging to winter: wintry.—*n.* **hiberna'tion.** [L. *hibernāre*, -*ātum—hibernus*, wintry—*hiems*, winter.]

Hibernian *hī-bûr'ni-ən*, *adj.* relating to Hibernia or Ireland: Irish: characteristic of Ireland.—*n.* an Irishman.—*n.* **Hiber'nicism** (-*sizm*) an Irish idiom or peculiarity. [L. *Hibernia*, Ireland.]

Hibiscus *hib-is'kəs*, *n.* a genus of malvaceous plants, mostly tropical· (without *cap.*) a plant of this genus. [L.,—Gr. *ibiskos*, marsh-mallow.]

hic *hik, hēk*, (L.) this (*demons. pron.*).—**hic jacet** (*jā'set, ya'ket*) here lies; **hic sepultus** (*sə-pul'tus, se-pōōl'tōōs*) here be buried.

hiccup *hik'up*, *n.* the involuntary contraction of the diaphragm while the glottis is spasmodically closed: the sound caused by this: a temporary, and usu. minor, difficulty or setback (*fig.*).—*v.i.* to make a hiccup (*lit.* and *fig.*).—*v.t.* to say with a hiccup:—*pr.p.* **hicc'uping;** *pa.t.* and *pa.p.* **hicc'uped.**—Also **hiccough**, etc. [Imit.; an early form was *hicket*. The spelling *hiccough* is due to a confusion with *cough*.]

hick *hik*, *n.* a lout: a booby. [A familiar form of *Richard*.]

hickory *hik'ər-i*, *n.* a North American genus of the walnut family, yielding edible nuts and heavy strong tenacious wood. [Earlier· *pohickery*; of Indian origin.]

hidalgo *hi-dal'gō*, *n.* a Spanish nobleman of the lowest class: a gentleman:—*pl.* **hidal'gos.** [Sp. *hijo de algo*, son of something.]

hide *hīd*, *v.t.* to conceal: to keep in concealment: to keep secret or out of sight.—*v.i.* to go into, or to stay in, concealment:—*pa.t.* **hid** (*hid*); *pa.p.* **hidden** (*hid'n*), **hid.**—*n.* a hiding-place: a concealed place from which to observe wild animals, etc.—*adj.* **hidd'en** concealed: unknown.—*n.* **hidd'enness.**—*n.* **hid'ing** concealment: a place of concealment.—**hide'-and-(go-)seek'** a game in which one seeks the others, who have hidden themselves; **hide'-away** a place of concealment: a refuge; **hide'out** a retreat; **hid'ing-place; hid'y-hole, hid'ey-hole** a hiding-place. [O.E. *hȳdan*; cf. M.L.G. *hûden*, and (doubtfully) Gr. *keuthein*.]

hide *hīd*, *n.* the skin of an animal, esp. the larger animals, sometimes used derogatorily or facetiously for human skin.—*v.t.* to flog or whip: to skin.—*n.* **hid'ing** a thrashing.—*adj.* **hide'-bound** of animals, having the hide attached so closely to the back and ribs that it is taut, not easily moved: in trees, having the bark so close that it impedes the growth: stubborn, bigoted, obstinate.—**on a hiding to nothing** in a situation in which one is bound to lose, in spite of all one's efforts; **tan someone's hide** (*coll.*) to whip him. [O.E. *hȳd*; Ger. *Haut*, L. *cutis.*]

hide *hīd*, *n.* in old English law, a variable unit of area of land, enough for a household. [O.E. *hid*, contracted from *hīgid*; cf. *hīwan, hīgan*, household.]

hideous *hid'i-əs, adj.* frightful: horrible: ghastly· extremely ugly —*ns.* **hideos'ity, hid'eousness.**—*adv* **hid'eously.** [O.Fr. *hideus, hisdos—hide, hisde,* dread, poss.—L. *hispidus,* rough, rude.]

hidrosis *hid-rō'sis, n.* sweating, esp in excess.—*n.* and *adj.* **hidrotic** (-*rot'ik*) sudorific [Gr *hidrōs, -ōtos,* sweat.]

hie *hi, v.i.* to hasten (*arch.*).—*v t.* to urge (on): to pass quickly over (one's way).—*pr.p.* **hie'ing, hy'ing;** *pa.t.* and *pa.p.* **hied.** [O.E. *higian.*]

Hieracium *hi-ər-ā'shi-əm, n.* the hawkweed genus of Compositae· (without *cap.*) any plant of this genus [Latinised from Gr *hierākion,* hawkweed—*hierāx,* hawk.]

hierarch *hi'ər-ark, n* a ruler in holy things: a chief priest: a prelate.—*adjs.* **hi'erarch'ic, -al.**—*adv.* **hierarch'ically.**—*ns.* **hi'erarchism; hi'erarchy** the collective body of angels, grouped in three divisions and nine orders of different power and glory: each of the three main classes of angels. classification in graded subdivisions: a body or organisation classified in successively subordinate grades: (*loosely*) in an organisation so classified, the group of people who control that organisation· priestly government. [Gr. *hier-archēs—hieros,* sacred, *archein,* to rule.]

hieratic *hi-ər-at'ik, adj.* priestly: applying to a certain kind of ancient Egyptian writing which consisted of abridged forms of hieroglyphics; also to certain styles in art bound by religious convention. [L. *hieraticus* —Gr. *hierātikos—hieros,* sacred.]

hierocracy *hi-ər-ok'rə-si, n.* priestly government [Gr. *hieros,* sacred, *krateein,* to rule.]

hieroglyph *hi'ər-ō-glif, n.* a sacred character used in ancient Egyptian picture-writing or in picture-writing in general.—*adjs.* **hieroglyph'ic, -al.**—*n.* **hieroglyph'ic** a hieroglyph: (in *pl.*) hieroglyphic writing: (in *pl.*) writing that is difficult to read.—*adv.* **hieroglyph'ically.** [Gr. *hieroglyphikon—hieros,* sacred, *glyphein,* to carve.]

hierogram *hi'ər-ō-gram, n* a sacred or hieroglyphic symbol.—*n.* **hi'erograph** a sacred symbol. [Gr. *hieros,* sacred, *gramma,* a character, *graphein,* to write.]

hierolatry *hi-ər-ol'ə-tri, n.* the worship of saints or sacred things. [Gr. *hieros,* sacred, *latreiā,* worship]

hierology *hi-ər-ol'ə-ji, n.* the science of sacred matters, esp. ancient writing and Egyptian inscriptions —*adj.* **hierologic** (-ō-loj'ik).—*n* **hierol'ogist.** [Gr. *hieros,* sacred, *logos,* discourse.]

hierophant *hi'ər-ō-fant, n.* one who shows or reveals sacred things a priest: an expounder.—*adj.* **hierophant'ic.** [Gr. *hierophantēs—hieros,* sacred, *phainein,* to show.]

hi-fi, *hi'fi, n.* high-fidelity sound reproduction. equipment for this, e g. tape-recorder, record-player, etc.: the use of such equipment, esp. as a hobby.—Also *adj.*

higgledy-piggledy *hig'l-di-pig'l-di, adv* and *adj.* haphazard: in confusion

high *hi, adj.* elevated: lofty: tall: far up from a base, as the ground, sea-level, the zero of a scale, etc.: advanced in a scale: reaching far up· expressible by a large number of a height specified or to be specified of advanced degree of intensity: advanced, full (in time, e.g. *season, summer*): of a period, at its peak of development, as *High Renaissance*: of grave importance: advanced. exalted: eminent. chief· noble· haughty: extreme in opinion. powerful: loud violent acute in pitch. luxurious. elated: drunk over-excited under the influence of a drug. standing out· abstruse dear: for heavy stakes remote in time. of meat. etc , slightly tainted· florid.—*adv.* at or to an elevated degree aloft shrilly arrogantly· eminently

powerfully: luxuriously: dear: for heavy stakes.—*n.* that which is high: a high level: the maximum, highest level.—*adj.* **high'er,** *compar.* of **high.**—*v.t.* to raise higher: to lift.—*adj.* **high'est** *superl.* of **high.**—*adv.* **high'ly** in a high degree: in a high position.—*n.* **high'ness** the state of being high: dignity of rank· a title of honour given to princes, princesses, royal dukes, etc.—**high admiral** a high or chief admiral of a fleet; **high altar** see **altar; high bailiff** an officer who serves writs, etc.; **high'ball** (*U.S.*) whisky and soda or the like with ice in a tall glass.—*adj.* **high'-born** of noble birth.—**high'boy** (*U.S.*) a tallboy.—**high'-bred** of noble breed, training, or family.—**high'brow** an intellectual.—Also *adj.*—**high'browism; high camp** see **camp²; high'-chair** a baby or young child's tall chair, used esp. at mealtimes.—*adj.* **High Church** of a party within the Church of England that exalts the authority of the episcopate and the priesthood, the saving grace of sacraments, etc.: of similar views in other churches.—*n.* **High-Church'man.**—*adjs.* **high'-class** superior; **high-col'oured** having a strong or glaring colour: ruddy: over-vivid.—**high comedy** comedy set in refined sophisticated society, characterised more by witty dialogue, complex plot and good characterisation than by comical actions or situations; **high command** the commander-in-chief of the army together with his staff, or the equivalent senior officers of any similar force; **High Commission, Commissioner** see under **commission; high court** a supreme court; **high day** a holiday or festival; **higher criticism** see **criticism; higher education** education beyond the level of secondary education, e.g. at a university or college; **high'er-up** one occupying an upper position; **high'-explos'ive** a detonating explosive (e.g. dynamite, T.N.T.) of great power and exceedingly rapid action—also *adj.*; **high-falutin(g)** (-*lōōt'*) bombastic discourse.—*adj.* affected: pompous.—**high feather** high spirits; **high fidelity** good reproduction of sound.—*adj.* **high-fidel'ity.**—See also **hi-fi.**—**high'-fli'er, -fly'er** an ambitious person, or one naturally equipped to reach prominence.—*adjs.* **high'-flown** extravagant· elevated: turgid.—**high frequency** see **frequency.**—*adj.* **high'-gear** see **gear.**—**High German** that form of Germanic language affected by the second consonant shift, including the literary language of Germany.—*adjs.* **high'-grade** superior; **high'-hand'ed** overbearing: arbitrary.—**high'-hand'edness; high'-hat'** orig. a wearer of a top-hat: a snob or aristocrat: one who puts on airs: (**high'-hat**) a pair of cymbals on a stand, the upper one operated by a pedal so as to strike the lower one.—*adj.* affectedly superior.—*v.i.* to put on airs.—*v.t.* to adopt a superior attitude towards or to ignore socially.—*adj.* **high'-heeled'** having, wearing, high heels.—**high'jack, -er** see **hijack, -er; high jinks** boisterous play, jollity; **high kick** a dancer's kick high in the air, usu with a straight leg; **high'land** a mountainous district, esp. (in *pl.* **Highlands**) the north-west of Scotland, from Dumbarton to Stonehaven, or the narrower area in which Gaelic is or was recently spoken —*adj.* belonging to or characteristic of a highland, esp. (usu. with *cap.*) the Highlands, of Scotland —**High'lander, High'landman** an inhabitant or native of a mountainous region, esp. the Highlands of Scotland; **Highland cattle** a shaggy breed with very long horns; **Highland dress** kilt, plaid, and sporran; **Highland fling** a lively dance of the Scottish Highlands, danced by one person.—*adj* **high'-lev'el** at a high level, esp involving very important people —**high life** the life of fashionable society· the people of this society; **high'light** outstanding feature. (in *pl*) the most brightly lighted spots. (usu. in *pl.*) a portion or patch of the hair which reflects the light or which is artificially made lighter than the rest of the hair.—*v.t.* .to throw into relief by strong light. also *fig.*—**high living** luxurious living.—*adj* **high'ly-strung** nervously sensitive, excitable.—**high mass** a mass celebrated with music, ceremonies, and incense —*adj.* **high'-mind'ed** having lofty principles and thoughts.—**high'-mind'edness; high noon** exactly noon: the peak (*fig*)—*adjs.* **high'-oc'tane** (of petrol) of high octane number and so of high efficiency; **high'-pitched'** acute in sound, tending towards treble: steep (as a roof) —**high places** positions of importance; **high point** the most memorable, pleasurable, successful, etc. moment or occasion high spot; **high polymer** a polymer of high molecular weight.—*adjs.* **high'-pow'ered** very powerful: very forceful and efficient; **high'-press'ure** making or allowing use of steam or other gas at a pressure much above that of the atmosphere: involving intense activity.—**high priest** a chief priest; **high priestess; high'-priest'hood.**—**high'-ranker.**—*adj.* **high'-ranking** senior: eminent.—**high relief** bold relief, standing out well from the surface.—*adj.* **high'-rise** containing a large number of storeys.—**high'road** one of the public or chief roads: a road for general traffic, **high school** a secondary school, in U.K. formerly, often a grammar school; **high seas** the open ocean, **high society** fashionable, wealthy society—*adjs* **high'-sound'ing** pompous: imposing; **high'-speed** working, or suitable for working, at a great speed.— **high spot** an outstanding feature, place, etc ; **high's stepp'er** a horse that lifts its feet high from the ground: a person of imposing bearing or fashionable pretensions; **High Street** (sometimes without *cap.*) a common name for the main, or former main, street of a town.—*adj.* **high'-strung** (esp. *U.S.*) highly-strung —**high table** the don's table in a college dining-hall.— *v.i.* **high'tail** to hightail it (see below) —**high tea** a tea with meat, etc.; **high tech** a style or design of furnishing, etc. imitative of or using industrial equipment; **high technology** advanced, sophisticated technology in specialist fields, e.g. electronics, involving high investment in research and development.—*adj* **high'-ten'sion** high-voltage.—**high tide** high water' a tide higher than usual; **high time** quite time (that something were done).—*adj.* **high'-toned** high in pitch: morally elevated· superior, fashionable.—**high treason** treason against the sovereign or state; **high's up** one in high position (also *adj.*) —*adj* **high's vol'tage** of or concerning a voltage great enough to cause injury or damage.—**high water** the time at which the tide or other water is highest: the greatest elevation of the tide; **high'-wa'ter mark** the highest line so reached: a tide-mark; **high'way** a public road on which all have right to go: the main or usual way or course: a road, path or navigable river (*law*), **Highway Code** (the booklet containing) official rules and guidance on correct procedure for road-users, **high's-wayman** a robber who attacks people on the public way; **high wire** a tightrope high above the ground, **high words** angry altercation.—**for the high jump** (*coll.*): about to be reprimanded or chastised; **from on high** from a high place, heaven, or (*facet*) a position of authority; **high and dry** up out of the water, stranded; **high and low** rich and poor: up and down· everywhere; **high and mighty** (*ironically*) exalted· arrogant; **high as a kite** (*coll.*) over-excited, drunk, or very much under the influence of drugs, **high-level language** a computer-programming language, in which statements are written in a form similar to the user's normal language and which can be used in conjunction with a variety of computers (opp to *low-level language*), **high-speed steel** an alloy that remains hard when red-hot, suitable for metal-cutting tools,

high (old) time (*coll*) a time of special jollity or enthusiasm; **hightail it** (*coll.*) to hurry away, **hit the high spots** to go to excess to reach a high level; **on high** aloft: in heaven, **on one's high horse** in an attitude of fancied superiority very much on one's dignity [OE *hēah*]

hijacker, highjacker *hi'jak-ər, n* a robber or blackmailer of rum-runners and bootleggers: one who hijacks —*v t.* **hi'jack, high'jack** to stop and rob (a vehicle)· to steal in transit. to force a pilot to fly (an aeroplane) to an unscheduled destination· to force the driver to take (a vehicle or train) to a destination of the hijacker's choice —Also *v t*

hike *hīk, v.t.* (usually with *up, coll.*) to raise up with a jerk to increase (e g. prices), esp sharply and suddenly —*v i.* to hitch to tramp: to go walking and camp- ing with equipment on back· (of shirts, etc.) to move up out of place —*n* a walking tour, outing or march. an increase (in prices, etc)—*n* **hi'ker**. [Perh **hitch.**]

hilarious *hi-lā'ri-əs, adj.* extravagantly merry: very funny —*adv* **hilā'riously.**—*n.* **hilarity** (*hi-lar'*) gaiety· pleasurable excitement. [L *hilaris*—Gr *hilaros,* cheerful.]

Hilary *hil'ər-i, adj* the Spring term or session of the High Court of Justice in England: also the Spring term at Oxford and Dublin universities—from St *Hilary* of Poitiers (d *c* 367; festival, Jan 13).

hill *hil, n* a high mass of land, less than a mountain: a mound. an incline on a road.—*ns* **hill'iness; hill'ock** a small hill.—*adjs.* **hill'ocky; hill'y.**—**hill'-billy** (*U.S.*) a rustic of the hill country.—Also *adj* —**hill'-fort** a prehistoric stronghold on a hill; **hill'side** the slope of a hill; **hill station** a government station in the hills esp. of Northern India; **hill'top** the summit of a hill.—**old as the hills** (*coll.*) immeasurably old; **over the hill** past one's highest point of efficiency, success, etc . on the downgrade: past the greatest difficulty; **up hill and down dale** vigorously and persistently. [O E *hyll*; cf. L. *collis,* a hill, *celsus,* high]

hilt *hilt, n* the handle, esp. of a sword or dagger —*v t* to furnish with a hilt —**up to the hilt** completely, thoroughly, to the full [O E. *hilt*]

hilum *hi'ləm, n* the scar on a seed where it joined its stalk (*bot*)· the depression where ducts, vessels, etc.. enter an organ (*anat* , also **hi'lus**): —*pl* **hi'la.** [L *hīlum,* a trifle, 'that which adheres to a bean'.]

him *him, pron* the dative and accusative (objective) case of **he:** the proper character of a person. [O E. *him,* dat sing of *hē, he,* he, *hit,* it]

Himalaya(n) *him-ə-lā'ə(n), hi-mal'yə(n), adjs* pertaining to the Himalaya(s), the mountain range along the border of India and Tibet

himself *him-self'*, *pron* the emphatic form of **he, him:** in his real character: having command of his faculties. sane· in good form the reflexive form of **him** (*dat.* and *accus.*). [See **him, self.**]

hind¹ *hīnd, n.* the female of the stag or red deer [O.E *hind*]

hind² *hīnd,* (now *Scot.*) *n.* a farm-servant, with cottage on the farm: a rustic [O.E *hina, hīwna,* gen pl of *hīwan,* members of a household.]

hind³ *hīnd, adj.* placed in the rear pertaining to the part behind backward—opp to *fore.*—*adj* **hinder** (*hin'dər*) hind —*adjs* **hind'ermost, hind'most** farthest behind —*adv* **hindfore'most** with the back part in the front place.—**hind'leg.**—*n.pl* **hindquar'-ters** the rear parts of an animal —**hind'sight** wisdom after the event the rear sight on a gun, etc [O E *hinder,* backwards]

hinder *hin'dər, v t* to keep back· to stop, or prevent, progress of —*v i* to be an obstacle —*n* **hin'drance**

act of hindering: that which hinders: prevention obstacle. [O.E. *hindrian*; Ger *hindern*]

Hindi *hin'dē*, *n.* a group of Indo-European languages of Northern India, including Hindustani. a recent literary form of Hindustani, with terms from Sanskrit.—Also *adj* [Hindi *Hindī—Hind*, India]

hindmost. See **hind³**.

hindrance. See **hinder**.

Hindu, Hindoo *hin-dōō'*, or *hin'*, *n.* a member of any of the races of Hindustan or India (*arch.*). a believer in a form of Brahmanism.—Also *adj* —*n.* **Hindu'ism** (or *hin'*) the religion and customs of the Hindus [Pers *Hindū—Hind*, India]

Hindustani *hin-dōō-sta'nē*, *n* a form of Hindi containing elements from other languages —Also *adj*

hinge *hinj*, *n.* the hook or joint on which a door or lid turns. a joint as of a bivalve shell: a small piece of gummed paper used to attach a postage-stamp to the page of an album (also **stamp'-hinge**): a cardinal point: a principle or fact on which anything depends or turns.—*v.t.* to furnish with hinges: to bend —*v.t* to hang or turn as on a hinge: to depend (with *on*):—*pr.p.* **hinging** (*hinj'ing*); *pa t.* and *pa.p.* **hinged** (*hinjd*).—**hinge'-joint** (*anat.*) a joint that allows movement in one plane only. [Related to **hang**.]

hinny¹ *hin'i*, *n* the offspring of a stallion and she-ass [L. *hinnus*—Gr. *ginnos*, later *hinnos*, a mule.]

hinny² *hin'i*, *n.* a Scottish or N. Eng variant of **honey**.

hint *hint*, *n.* a distant or indirect indication or allusion: slight mention: insinuation. a helpful suggestion, tip —*v.t* to intimate or indicate indirectly.—*v t* to give hints.—**hint at** to give a hint, suggestion, or indication of. [O.E. *hentan*, to seize]

hinterland *hint'ər-land*, *-lant*, *n.* a region lying inland from a port or centre of influence. [Ger.]

hip¹ *hip*, *n.* the haunch or fleshy part of the thigh: the hip-joint: in archit., the external angle formed by the sides of a roof when the end slopes backwards instead of terminating in a gable.—*adjs.* **hipped** having a hip or hips: of a roof, sloping at the end as well as at the sides; **hipp'y** having large hips.—*n.* **hip'sters** trousers from the hips, not the waist.—**hip'-bath** a bath to sit in; **hip'-bone** the innominate bone; **hip'-flask** a flask carried in a hip-pocket, **hip'-joint** the articulation of the head of the thigh-bone with the ilium; **hip's pock'et** a trouser pocket behind the hip —**have, catch, on the hip** to get an advantage over someone (from wrestling). [O.E. *hype*; Goth *hups*, Ger. *Hufte*]

hip² *hip*, *ns.* the fruit of the dog-rose or other rose. [O.E *hēope*]

hip³ *hip*, *interj* an exclamation to invoke a united cheer—**hip'-hip'-hurrah'**.

hip⁴ *hip*, *adj.* a later form of **hep**.—*ns.* **hipp'y, hipp'ie** one of the hippies, successors of the beatniks as rebels against the values of middle-class society, who stress the importance of love, organise to some extent their own communities, and wear colourful clothes; **hip-ster** (*hip'stər*) one who knows and appreciates up-to-date jazz: a member of the beat generation (1950s and early 1960s).

hipp-, hippo- *hip(-ō)*, or (-*o*), in composition, a horse [Gr *hippos*, a horse]

hippeastrum *hip-i-as'trəm*, *n.* any plant of the S American genus **Hippeastrum**, bulbous, with white or red flowers. [Gr. *hippeus*, horseman, *astron*, star]

hippie. See **hip⁴**.

hippo *hip'ō*, *n.* a shortened form of **hippopotamus**:—*pl.* **hipp'os**.

hippocampus *hip-ō-kam'pəs*, *n.* a fish-tailed horse-like sea-monster (*myth.*). a genus of small fishes with horse-like head and neck, the sea-horse: a raised curved trace on the floor of the lateral ventricle of the brain (*anat.*):—*pl* **hippocamp'i**. [Gr. *hippokampos* —*hippos*, a horse, *kampos*, a sea-monster.]

hippocras *hip'ō-kras*, *n* spiced wine, formerly much used as a cordial [M E. *ypocras*, Hippocrates.]

Hippocratic *hip-ō-krat'ik*, *adj.* pertaining to the Greek physician *Hippocrates* (born about 460 B c) —**Hippocratic oath** an oath taken by a doctor binding him to observe the code of medical ethics contained in it—first drawn up (perhaps by Hippocrates) in the 4th or 5th century B.c

Hippocrene *hip-ō-krē'nē*, *hip'ō-krēn*, (*myth.*) *n.* a fountain on the northern slopes of Mount Helicon, sacred to the Muses and Apollo [Gr *hippokrēnē—hippos*, a horse, *krēnē*, a fountain]

hippodrome *hip'ə-drōm*, *n* a racecourse for horses and chariots (*ant.*) a circus: a variety theatre. [Gr *hippodromos—hippos*, a horse, *dromos*, a course.]

hippogriff, hippogryph *hip'ō-grif*, *n.* a fabulous mediaeval animal, a griffin-headed winged horse. [Fr. *hippogriffe*—Gr *hippos*, a horse, *gryps*, a griffin]

hippophagy *hip-of'ə-ji*, *-gi*, *n* feeding on horse-flesh. [**hippo-**, Gr *phagein* (aor.), to eat]

hippopotamus *hip-ō-pot'ə-məs*, *n.* a large African ungulate of aquatic habits, with very thick skin, short legs, and a large head and muzzle:—*pl.* **-muses** or **-mi**. [L.—Gr. *hippopotamos—hippos*, a horse, *potamos*, a river.]

hippy. See **hip¹,⁴**.

hipster, hipsters. See **hip¹,⁴**.

hircine *hûr'sin*, *adj.* goat-like [L. *hircus*, a he-goat.]

hire *hīr*, *n.* wages for service: the price paid for the use of anything. an arrangement by which use or service is granted for payment.—*v.t.* to procure the use or service of, at a price to engage for wages: to grant temporary use of for compensation (often with *out*) —*adjs.* **hir'able, hire'able**.—*n.* **hire'ling** a hired servant. one activated solely by material considerations.—*n.* **hir'er.**—**hire car** a rented car, usu. one rented for a short period; **hire'-pur'chase** a system by which a hired article becomes the hirer's property after a stipulated number of payments.—Also *adj.* —**on hire** for hiring [O.E. *hȳr*, wages, *hȳrian*, to hire.]

hirsute *hûr'sūt*, or *hər-sūt'*, *adj* hairy: rough: shaggy· having long, stiffish hairs (*bot.*).—*n.* **hirsute'ness**. [L. *hirsūtus—hirsus*, *hirtus*, shaggy.]

his *hiz*, *pron.*, *gen.* of **he** (or *possessive adj.*). [O.E. *his*, gen. of *hē*, *he*, *he*, and of *hit*, it]

Hispanic *his-pan'ik*, *adj* Spanish: of Spanish origin, e.g. Mexican.—Also *n* —*v.t.* **hispan'icise**, *-ize* (*-i-sīz*).—*n* **hispan'icism** a Spanish phrase. [L. *Hispānia*, Spain.]

Hispano- *his-pā'nō-*, in composition, Spanish, as *Hispano-American*, Spanish-American. [L. *Hispānus*.]

hispid *his'pid*, (*bot.* and *zool.*) *adj.* rough with, or having, strong hairs or bristles.—*n.* **hispid'ity**. [L *hispidus*.]

hiss *his*, *v.i* to make a sibilant sound like that represented by the letter *s*, as a goose, snake, gas escaping from a narrow hole, a disapproving audience, etc.—*v.t.* to condemn by hissing: to drive by hissing.—Also *n.* [Imit.]

hist *hist*, *st*, *interj.* demanding silence and attention· hush: silence. [Imit.]

hist-, histo- *hist-*, *-(i-)ō-*, *-o'-*, in composition, tissue: sail.—*n* **hist'amine** (*-ə-mēn*) a base present in all tissues of the body, being liberated into the blood, e g. when the skin is cut or burnt; **histogenesis** (*-jen'i-sis*) the formation or differentiation of tissues (*biol.*).—*adj.* **histogenetic** (*-ji-net'ik*).—*advs.* **histogenet'ically, histogen'ically.**—*adj.* **histogen'ic.**—*ns.*

histogeny (*his-toj'i-ni*) histogenesis —*adjs.* **histolog'ic, -al.**—*ns.* **histologist** (*-tol'*), **histol'ogy** the study of the minute structure of the tissues of organisms, **histol'ysis** (Gr *lysis*, loosing) the breakdown of organic tissues.—*adj.* **histolytic** (*-ô-lit'ik*).—*n.* **histopathol'ogist** a pathologist who studies effects of disease on tissues of the body.— *adj* **histopatholog'ical.**—*n.* **histopathol'ogy.** [Gr *histos*, a web]

history *hist'ar-i, n* an account of an event. a systematic account of the origin and progress of the world, a nation, an institution, etc.: the knowledge of past events: a course of events: a life-story: an eventful life, a past of more than common interest: a drama representing historical events.—*n.* **historian** (*histô'ri-an, -to'*) a writer of history (usu in the sense of an expert, an authority, on).—*adjs.* **historic** (*-tor'ik*) famous or important in history; **histor'ical** pertaining to history: containing history derived from history: associated with history: according to history: authentic (Formerly *historic* and *historical* were often used interchangeably.)—*adv* **histor'ically.**—*n* **histor'icism** a theory that all sociological phenomena are historically determined: a strong or excessive concern with, and respect for, the institutions of the past —*n* and *adj.* **histor'icist.**—*ns.* **historicity** (*hist-ar-is'i-ti*) historical truth or actuality, **historiog'rapher** a writer of history (esp an official historian).—*adjs.* **historiograph'ic, -al.**—*adv* **historiograph'ically,**—*n.* **historiog'raphy** the art or employment of writing history.— **historical novel** a novel having as its setting a period in history and involving historical characters and events; **historical present** the present tense used for the past, to add life and reality to the narrative.—**make history** to do that which will mould the future or have to be recognised by future historians: to do something never previously accomplished [L. *historia*—Gr *historiā*—*histōr*, knowing.]

histrionic, -al *his-tri-on'ik, -al, adjs.* relating to the stage or actors. stagy, theatrical: affected: melodramatic: hypocritical.—*adv.* **histrion'ically,**—*ns.* **histrion'icism,** **his'trionism** acting: theatricality.— *n.pl.* **histrion'ics** play-acting stagy action or speech: insincere exhibition of emotion. [L *histriōnicus*—*histriō*, an actor.]

hit *hit, v.t.* to strike. to reach with a blow or missile (also *fig*): to come into forceful contact with to knock (e.g. oneself, one's head) to inflict (a blow): to drive by a stroke to move on to (a road), reach (a place): (of news) to be published in (*coll*): to light upon, or attain, by chance: to imitate exactly: to suit, fit, conform to. to hurt, affect painfully (*fig.*).—*v i* to strike to make a movement of striking: to come in contact: to arrive suddenly and destructively: to come. by effort or chance, luckily (upon).—*pr.p* **hitt'ing;** *pa.t* and *pa p* **hit.**—*n* an act or occasion of striking: a successful stroke or shot: a lucky chance. a surprising success: an effective remark, e.g. a sarcasm. witticism something that pleases the public or an audience.—*adjs.* **hit'-and-miss'** hitting or missing, according to circumstances, **hit'-and-run'** (e.g. of an air raid) lasting only a very short time (of a driver) causing injury and running away without reporting the incident —**hit list** (*slang*) a list of people to be killed by gangsters or terrorists (also *fig*), **hit'-man** (*slang*) one employed to kill or attack others (also *fig.*).—*adj.* **hit'-or-miss'** random.—**hit'-parade** a list of currently popular songs: a list of the most popular things of any kind (*fig.*) —**hard hit** gravely affected by some trouble, or by love; **hit at** to aim a blow, sarcasm, jibe, etc , at; **hit below the belt** see **belt; hit it** to find, often by chance, the right answer, **hit it off** to agree, be compatible and friendly

(sometimes with *with*); **hit off** to imitate or describe aptly (someone, something); **hit on** or **upon** to come upon, discover. devise: to single out; **hit out** to strike out, esp. with the fist to attack strongly (absolute or with *at*); **hit the ceiling** or **roof** to be seized with, express, violent anger; **hit the hay** (*slang*) to go to bed; **hit the nail on the head** see **nail; hit the road** (*slang*) to leave, go away; **hit wicket** the act, or an instance, of striking the wicket with bat or part of the body (and thus being out) (*cricket*); **make a hit with** to become popular with: to make a good impression on [O E *hyttan*, app. O.N. *hitta*, to light on, to find.]

hitch *hich, v t* to move jerkily: to hobble or limp: to catch on an obstacle. to connect with a moving vehicle so as to be towed (*orig. U.S*): to travel by getting lifts.—*v t.* to jerk: to hook: to catch: to fasten: to tether: to harness to a vehicle: to make fast: to throw into place.—*n.* a jerk: a stoppage owing to a small or passing difficulty: a species of knot by which one rope is connected with another, or to some object (*naut.*). a lift in a vehicle —*n.* **hitch'er.**—*v t* **hitch'-hike** to hike with the help of lifts in vehicles —**hitch'-hike; hitch'-hiker; hitching post** a post, etc to which a horse's reins can be tied.—**get hitched** (*slang*) to get married; **hitch up** to harness a horse to a vehicle: to jerk up: to marry (*slang*).

hither *hidh'ar, adv* to this place —*adj* on this side or in this direction: nearer —*adj.* **hith'ermost** nearest on this side —*advs.* **hith'erto** up to this time —**hither and thither** to and fro: this way and that. [O.E. *hider.*]

Hitlerism *hit'lar-izm, n.* the principles, policy, and methods of Adolf *Hitler* (1889-1945), German Nazi dictator.—*ns.* and *adjs.* **Hit'lerist, Hit'lerite.**

Hittite *hit'īt, n* one of the Khatti or Heth, an ancient people of Syria and Asia Minor: an extinct language belonging to the Anatolian group of languages and discovered from documents in cuneiform writing.— Also *adj.* [Heb. *Hitti;* Gr. *Chettaios*]

hive *hiv, n* a box or basket in which bees live and store up honey: a colony of bees a scene of great industry: a teeming multitude or breeding-place —*v t.* to collect into a hive: to lay up in store (often with *away* or *up*) —*v i.* of bees, to enter or take possession of a hive: to take shelter together: to reside in a body — **hive off** to withdraw as if in a swarm: to assign (work) to a subsidiary company to divert (assets or sections of an industrial concern) to other concerns. [O E *hȳf.*]

hives *hivz, n* a popular term for nettlerash and similar diseases or for laryngitis

hiya *hi'ya, (slang) interj.* a greeting developed from **how are you.**

ho, hoa *hô, interj.* a call to excite attention, to announce destination or direction, to express exultation, surprise, or (repeated) derision or laughter. [Cf. O.N. *hô,* Fr *ho.*]

hoactzin. See hoatzin.

hoar *hôr, hor, adj.* white or greyish-white, esp. with age or frost.—*n.* hoariness: age.—*n.* **hoar'iness.**— *adj* **hoar'y** white or grey with age ancient: covered with short, dense, whitish hairs (*bot.*) —**hoar'-frost** rime or white frost, the white particles formed by the freezing of the dew. [O E. *hâr*, hoary, grey.]

hoard *hôrd, hord, n.* a store: a hidden stock: a treasure —*v.t* to store, esp. in excess to treasure up: to amass and deposit in secret.—*v i.* to store up: to collect and form a hoard.—*n.* **hoard'er.** [O E *hord.*]

hoarding *hôrd'ing, hord', n* a screen of boards, esp. for enclosing a place where builders are at work, or for display of bills. [O Fr *hurdis*—*hurt, hourt, hourd,* a palisade.]

hoarhound. See horehound.

hoarse *hōrs, hors, adj.* rough and husky: having a rough husky voice· discordant.—*adv* **hoarse'ly.**—*v.t* and *v.ı.* **hoars'en.**—*n.* **hoarse'ness.** [M.E *hors, hoors*—O.E. *hås,* inferred *hårs.*]

hoatzin *hō-at'sin,* **hoactzin** -*akt',* *ns.* the stink-bird, a S. American bird with occipital crest, great crop, and, in the tree-climbing and swimming young, clawed wings [Nahuatl *uatsin.*]

hoax *hōks, n.* a deceptive trick played as a practical joke.—Also *adj.*—*v.t* to trick, by a practical joke or fabricated tale —*n.* **hoax'er.** [App **hocus.**]

hob[1] *hob, n.* a surface beside a fireplace, on which anything may be laid to keep hot· the flat framework on top of a gas, etc. cooker on which pots are placed to be heated: a gear-cutting tool.—**hob'nail** a nail with a thick strong head, used in horseshoes, heavy workshoes, etc.—*adj* **hob'nailed.** [Cf. **hub.**]

hob[2] *hob, n.* a fairy or brownie (as Robin Goodfellow) a male ferret.—**hob'goblin** a mischievous fairy: a frightful apparition. [For *Robert.*]

Hobbesian *hobz'ı-ən, adj.* relating to Thomas *Hobbes* (1588–1679) or his political philosophy.—*n.* a follower of Hobbes

hobble *hob'l, v ı* to walk with short unsteady steps· to walk awkwardly: to move irregularly —*v.t.* to fasten the legs of (a horse) loosely together. to hamper —*n.* an awkward hobbling gait, anything used to hamper the feet of an animal.—**hobble skirt** a narrow skirt that hampers walking. [Cf. Du. *hobbelen, hobben,* to toss: and **hopple.**]

hobbledehoy *hob'l-di-hoı', n* an awkward youth, a stripling, neither man nor boy.—*ns.* **hobbledehoy'dom, hobbledehoy'hood, hobbledehoy'ism.**—*adj.* **hobbledehoy'ish.**

hobby[1] *hob'ı, n.* a small or smallish strong, active horse: a subject on which one is constantly setting off: a favourite pursuit followed as an amusement: a hobby-horse.—**hobb'y-horse** a stick or figure of a horse straddled by children: one of the chief parts played in the ancient morris-dance· the wooden horse of a merry-go-round: a rocking-horse: a hobby [M.E. *hobyn, hoby,* prob. *Hob,* a by-form of *Rob.*]

hobby[2] *hob'ı, n* a small species of falcon. [O Fr *hobe.*]

hobgoblin. See **hob**[2].

hobnail. See **hob**[1].

hobnob *hob'nob, v ı* to associate or drink together familiarly: to talk informally (with).—*pr p* **hob'-nobbing.** [Prob. *hab nab,* have or have not (we have); cf *Twelfth Night,* III, ıv 'Hob, nob, ıs his word, give 't or take 't'.]

hobo *hō'bō, n* an itinerant workman· a tramp.—*pl.* **ho'boes.**

Hobson's choice. See **choice.**

hock[1] *hok, n* joint on hindleg of a quadruped, between the knee and fetlock, corresponding to the ankle-joint in man. a piece of meat extending from the hock-joint upward —*v.t.* to hamstring. [O E *hōh,* the heel.]

hock[2] *hok,* (*slang*) *v.t.* to pawn.—**in hock** in debt: in prison. having been pawned, in pawn (*coll.*). [Du. *hok,* prison, hovel]

hock[3] *hok, n* properly, the wine made at *Hochheim,* on the Main, in Germany· now applied to all white Rhine wines [Obs *Hockamore*—Ger *Hochheimer.*]

hockey *hok'ı, n* a· ball game played with a club or stick curved at one end· ice hockey [Prob. O.Fr. *hoquet,* a crook.]

hocus-pocus *hō'kəs-pō'kəs, n.* a juggler's formula. jugglery. deception mumbo-jumbo.—*v ı* **hoc'us** to cheat: to stupefy with drink to drug (drink).—*pr.p*

hō'cus(s)ing; *pa.t* and *pa.p.* **hō'cus(s)ed.** [Sham Latin]

hod *hod, n* a V-shaped stemmed trough for carrying bricks or mortar on the shoulder a coal-scuttle. [Cf. dial. *hot, hott,* M.H G. *hotte,* obs Du. *hodde,* Fr. *hotte,* a basket.]

hodden *hod'n, n.* coarse, undyed homespun woollen cloth.

hodgepodge *hoj'poj, n.* see **hotchpotch.**

Hodgkin's disease *hoj'kınz dız-ēz', a disease in which the spleen, liver and lymph nodes become enlarged, and progressive anaemia occurs [After Thomas *Hodgkin,* 19th cent British physician.]

hodiernal *hō-dı-ûrn'əl, adj* of or pertaining to the present day. [L. *hodiernus*—*hodiē,* to-day = *hōc diē,* on this day.]

hodograph *hod'ə-graf, (math) n.* a curve whose radius vector represents the velocity of a moving point [Gr *hodos,* a way. *graphein,* to write.]

hodometer, now usu **odometer,** *hod-om'ı-tər, od-, ns* an instrument attached to a wheel for measuring distance travelled —*ns* **hodom'etry, odom'etry.** [Gr. *hodos,* a way. *metron,* a measure]

hoe *hō, n* an instrument for scraping or digging up weeds and loosening the earth —*v.t.* to scrape, remove, or clean with a hoe. to weed.—*v ı.* to use a hoe:—*pr.p.* **hoe'ing;** *pa t.* and *pa p.* **hoed.—hoe'-cake** (*U.S.*) a thin cake of Indian meal (originally baked on a hoe-blade), **hoe'down** a country-dance, esp. a square dance: a party at which such dances are performed. [O.Fr. *houe*—O.H.G. *houwâ* (Ger *Haue*), a hoe.]

hog *hog, n.* a general name for swine. a castrated boar: a pig reared for slaughter. a yearling sheep not yet shorn (also **hogg**): a greedy person: an inconsiderate boor: a person of coarse manners.—*v.t.* and *v i.* to eat hoggishly: to arch or hump like a hog's back, esp. of the hull of a ship.—*v.t.* to cut like a hog's mane: to take or use selfishly:—*pr.p.* **hogg'ing;** *pa.t.* and *pa.p.* **hogged.**—*adj.* **hogged** (*hogd*).—*n.* **hogg'et** a yearling sheep or colt.—*adj* **hogg'ish.**—*adv.* **hogg'ishly.**—*n* **hogg'ishness.—hog'back, hog's'-back** a hill-ridge, or other object, shaped like a hog's back, ı.e. curving down towards the ends; **hog'-chol'era** swine-fever; **hog'-fish** a fish having bristles on the head, **hog'-nose** an American snake (*Heterodon,* various species), **hog'-skin** leather made of the skin of swine —*v ı* **hog'tie** to tie (a person) up so as to be unable to move arms or legs (also *fig.*).—**hog'wash** the refuse of a kitchen, brewery, etc , given to pigs: thin worthless stuff: insincere nonsense, **hog'weed** the cow-parsnip: applied also to many other coarse plants.—**go the whole hog** see **whole; hog it** (*slang*) to eat greedily: to live in a slovenly fashion [O E *hogg*]

hogan *hō'gan, n.* a log hut, usu covered with earth, built by the Navaho tribe of North American Indians [Navaho.]

hogg, hogget, etc. See under **hog.**

Hogmanay *hog-mə-nā', (Scot) n.* the last day of the year: a refection or gift begged or bestowed then. [Prob from North Fr dial. *hoginane*—16th cent *aguillanneuf* (*-l'an neuf*) a gift at the New Year.]

hogshead *hogz'hed, n* a large cask: a measure of capacity = 52½ imperial gallons, or 63 old wine gallons, *of beer* = 54 gallons; *of claret* = 46 gallons; *of tobacco* (*U S.*) 750 to 1200 lb. [App. **hog's,** and **head.**]

hoick, hoik *hoık, n* a jerk —*v t* and *v ı.* to hitch up. (esp of aeroplanes) to jerk upwards. [Cf. **hike.**]

hoi polloi *hoı'-pə-loı', (Gr) the many: the rabble, the vulgar.

hoise *hoiz*, (*arch.*) *v.t.* to hoist—*pa.t* and *pa p*
hoised, hoist.—**hoist with his own petar(d)** caught in
his own trap. [Perh. Old Du *hijssen*, Du. *hijschen*,
to hoist.]

hoist *hoist*, *v t.* to lift: to heave upwards: to raise or
move with tackle.—*n* act of lifting: the height of a
sail: that part of a flag next to the mast a lift for heavy
goods. [Pa.t. and pa p. of **hoise** (q.v)]

hoity-toity *hoi'ti-toi'ti*, *interj.* an exclamation of surprise or disapprobation.—*adj.* superciliously
haughty. [From *hoit* (*obs.*), to romp]

hokum *hō'kəm*, (*U.S. slang*) *n.* something done for the
sake of applause: claptrap. [App **hocus-pocus**
combined with **bunkum.**]

hoky-poky, hokey-pokey *hō'ki-pō'ki*, *n.* hocus-pocus·
a kind of ice-cream sold on the streets.

Holarctic *hol-ärk'tik*, *adj* of the north temperate and
Arctic biological region [Gr. *holos*, whole,
arktikos, northern—*arktos*, a bear, the Great Bear
constellation.]

hold[1] *hōld*, *v.t.* to keep: to have: to grasp: to have in
one's possession, keeping, or power: to sustain· to
defend successfully: to maintain: to assert authoritatively: to think, believe: to occupy: to derive title to·
to bind: to contain· to have a capacity of: to enclose:
to confine: to restrain: to detain: to retain: to keep
the attention of: to catch: to stop: to continue: to
persist in: to celebrate, observe: to conduct: to carry
on: to convoke and carry on: to esteem or consider: to
aim, direct.—*v.i.* to grasp: to remain fixed: to be true
or unfailing: to continue unbroken or unsubdued: to
remain valid: to continue, to persist: to adhere: to
derive right: when making a telephone call, to wait,
without replacing the receiver, e.g. to be connected
to a person one wants to speak to (also **hold the line**):
—*pr.p.* **hōld'ing;** *pa.t.* **held;** *pa.p.* **held.**—*n.* act or
manner of holding: grip: power of gripping: tenacity:
a place of confinement: custody: stronghold: (a sign
for) a pause (*mus.*): a reservation (*U S.*): means of
influencing.—*ns.* **hold'er; hold'ing** anything held: a
farm held of a superior.—**hold'-all** an accommodating receptacle for clothes, etc., e.g a canvas bag;
hold'fast that which holds fast: a long nail: a catch: a
plant's fixing organ other than a root, **holding company** an industrial company that owns and controls
part or all of one or more other companies, usu. without having a direct hand in production; **holding pattern** a specific course which aircraft are instructed to
follow when waiting to land; **hold'-up** an attack with a
view to robbery: a highwayman: an act or state of
holding up: a stoppage.—**get hold of** to obtain: to get
in touch with; **hold against** (*coll.*) to remember as a
failing or as a misdemeanour on the part of; **hold back**
to restrain: to hesitate: to keep in reserve; **hold by** to
believe in: to act in accordance with; **hold down** to
restrain: to keep (a job) by carrying out its duties
efficiently, esp. in spite of difficulties; **hold forth** to
put forward: to show: to speak in public, to declaim;
hold good to remain the case; **hold hands** (of two
people) to be hand in hand or clasping both of each
other's hands: (of several people) each to clasp the
hand of the person on either side, thus forming a line,
circle, etc.; **hold hard!** stop; **hold in** to restrain, check:
to restrain oneself; **hold it!** keep the position exactly!;
hold off to keep at a distance: to refrain (from); **hold
on** to persist in something: to continue: to cling: to
keep (with *to*): stop (*imper.*): wait a bit; **hold one's
own** to maintain one's position; **hold one's peace,
tongue** to keep silence; **hold out** to endure, last: to
continue resistance: to offer; **hold out for** to wait
determinedly for something one wants or has asked
for; **hold out on** (*coll.*) to keep information from;
hold over to postpone, **hold the line** see **hold** above;

hold the road (of a vehicle) to remain stable and
under the driver's control e g in wet weather, at high
speeds or on bends; **hold to, hold someone to** to keep,
make someone keep, (a promise), adhere to (a
decision), etc ; **hold together** to remain united: to
cohere; **hold up** to raise: to keep back: to endure. to
bring to, or keep at, a standstill: to stop and rob: to
rob by threatening assault; **hold up one's head** to face
the world with self-respect; **hold water see water;**
hold with to take sides with, support: to approve of;
no holds barred not observing any rules of fair play
(*adj.* **no'-holds-barred'**). [O E. *haldan*.]

hold[2] *hōld*, *n.* the interior cavity of a ship used for the
cargo [**hole[1]**, with excrescent *d.*]

hole *hōl*, *n.* a hollow place: a cavity: an aperture. a gap:
a breach· a pit· a difficult situation: a scrape· an
animal's excavation or place of refuge: a miserable or
contemptible place· a cavity into which golf-balls are
played· the distance, or the part of the game, between
tee and hole· the score for playing a hole in fewest
strokes: a vacancy in an energy band, caused by
removal of an electron, which moves and is
equivalent to a positive charge (*electronics*).—*v.t.* to
form holes in: to put, send, play into a hole —*v.i.* to
go, play, into a hole —*adj* **holey** (*hōl'i*) full of holes.
—*adjs.* **hole'-and-cor'ner** secret: underhand: in
obscure places; **hole'-in-the-wall'** (*coll.*) small, insignificant, difficult to find.—**hole in one** in golf, a shot
from the tee that goes into the hole, and so completes
the hole with a single stroke, **hole out** (*golf*) to play
the ball into the hole, **hole in the heart** imperfect
separation of the left and right sides of the heart; **hole
up** (*coll.*) to go to earth, hide (also *fig.*); **in holes** full
of holes; **make a hole in** (e.g. one's pocket) to use up a
large amount of (e g. money); **toad in the hole** meat
baked in batter, etc [O.E *hol*, a hole, cavern]

holiday *hol'i-dā*, *n.* orig., a religious festival· a day or
season of idleness and recreation —*adj* befitting a
holiday: cheerful.—**holliday camp** an area, usu. at the
seaside, with chalets, hotels, entertainments, etc ,
for holidaymakers; **hol'idaymaker** one on holiday
away from home: a tourist. [**holy, day.**]

holism *hol'izm*, *hōl'izm*, *n.* the theory that the fundamental principle of the universe is the creation of
wholes, i.e. complete and self-contained systems
from the atom and the cell by evolution to the most
complex forms of life and mind.—*n.* **hol'ist.**—*adj.*
holist'ic. [Gr. *holos*, whole, coined by General
Smuts.]

holla *hol'a*, *interj* ho, there! attend! the usual
response to *ahoy!* (*naut*).—*n.* a loud shout. [Fr.
hola—*ho* and *là*—L. *illāc*, there.]

holland *hol'ənd*, *n.* a coarse linen fabric, unbleached or
dyed brown, which is used for covering furniture,
etc.: orig , a fine kind of linen first made in *Holland*
—*n.* **Holl'ander** a native or citizen of *Holland*: a
Dutch ship —*adj* **Holl'andish.**—*n* **holl'ands** gin
made in Holland.—**sauce hollandaise** (*sōs ol-ā-dez*,
Fr.) a sauce made of the yolk of an egg with melted
butter and lemon juice.

holler *hol'ər*, (*U S.* and *dial.*) *n* and *vb.* Same as **hollo.**
hollo *hol'ō*, *n.* and *interj.* a shout of encouragement or
to call attention· a loud shout:—*pl* **holl'o(e)s.**—*v t*
and *v.i.* to shout [Cf. **holla, hallo.**]

hollow *hol'ō*, *n.* a hole· a cavity: a depression: a vacuity: a groove: a channel.—*adj.* having an empty space
within or below. concave: sunken. unsound, unreal,
fleeting, deceptive: insincere: muffled, as if coming
from a hollow.—*v t.* (often with *out*) to make a hole
in. to make hollow. to excavate.—*adv.* completely:
clean.—*adv* **holl'owly.**—*n* **holl'owness.**—*adjs*
holl'ow-eyed having sunken eyes; **holl'ow-ground**
ground so as to have concave surface(s) —**holl'ow-**

ware, holl'oware hollow articles of iron, china, etc., as pots and kettles [O.E holh, a hollow place—hol; see hole.]

holly hol'ı, n an evergreen shrub having leathery, shining, and spinous leaves and scarlet or yellow berries, much used for Christmas decorations —holl'y-fern a spiny-leaved fern; holl'y-oak the holm-oak [O.E holegn.]

hollyhock hol'ı-hok, n. a plant of the mallow family brought into Europe from the Holy Land [M E holihoc—holı, holy, and O E. hoc, mallow.]

Hollywood hol'ı-wŏŏd, adj. of or belonging to Hollywood, a suburb of Los Angeles in California, a centre of the American cinema. typical of or resembling films made there, brash and romantic, presenting the image of an affluent or artificial society.

holm[1] hŏm, n. an islet, esp, in a river· rich flat land beside a river. [O.E. holm, Ger. Holm, etc]

holm[2] hŏm, n holly· the holm-oak.—holm'-oak' the evergreen oak (Quercus ılex), not unlike holly [M E. holin; see holly.]

holmium hŏl'mı-əm, n a metallic element (Ho, at numb 67). [Mod. L. Holmıa, Stockholm.]

holo- hol'ō-, hol- hol-, in composition, whole: wholly. —ns. hol'ocaust (-kost') a sacrifice, in which the whole of the victim was burnt: a huge slaughter or destruction of life (Gr. holokauston—kaustos, burnt); Holocene (hol'ə-sēn; geol.) the most recent period of geological time, approximating to the period since the last glaciation; hol'ogram a photograph made without use of a lens by means of interference between two parts of a split laser beam, the result appearing as a meaningless pattern until suitably illuminated, when it shows as a 3-D image (a number of pictures can be 'stored' on the same plate or film); hol'ograph (-graf) a document wholly written by the person from whom it proceeds.—Also adj —adj. holographic (-graf'ık)—n. holog'raphy (the technique or process of) making or using holograms —adj. holohē'dral (Gr. hedrâ, base).—ns holohē'drism (math.) the property of having the full number of symmetrically arranged planes crystallographically possible; holohē'dron a form possessing this property.—adj. holometabol'ic.—n holometab'olism complete metamorphosis.—adj. holophōt'al (Gr. phōs, phōtos, light).—ns. hol'ophote an apparatus by which all the light from a lighthouse is thrown in the required direction; hol'ophyte.—adj holophytic (-fît'ık; Gr. phyton, a plant) obtaining nutriment wholly in the manner of a green plant —n holophytism (-fît'izm). [Gr. holos, whole]

holothurian hol-ō-thōō'ri-ən, n. any member of the genus Holothu'ria or family Holothuroid'ea, a class of wormlike unarmoured echinoderms—the seacucumbers.—Also adj [Gr. holothourion, a kind of sea animal.]

hols holz, (school slang) n.pl. holidays.

holster hŏl'stər, n. a pistol-case, on saddle or belt.—adj. hol'stered. [Perh. Du. holster, pistol-case]

holt[1] hŏlt, n. a wood or woody hill: an orchard. [O E. holt, a wood.]

holt[2] hŏlt, n. a hold, grasp (U S. and dial)· a stronghold: an otter's den. [hold[1].]

holus-bolus hŏl'əs-bōl'əs, adv all at a gulp: altogether [Sham L.]

holy hŏ'lı, adj. perfect in a moral sense: pure in heart. religious: set apart to a sacred use: regarded with awe (often ironically): saintly: sanctimonious.—n. holy object, place.—adv. ho'lily.—n. ho'liness sanctity —adj. ho'lier-than-thou' offensively sanctimonious and patronising.—holy city Jerusalem: Rome. Mecca Benares: Allahabad, etc , holy day a religious festival

(see also holiday), Holy Family the infant Christ with Joseph, Mary, etc., Holy Ghost, Spirit the third person of the Christian Trinity; holy grail see grail; holy Joe (slang) a parson· a pious person, Holy Land Palestine, holy orders see order; ho'ly-rood Christ's cross: a cross, esp in R C churches over the entrance to the chancel, Holy Roller (derog) a preacher or follower of an extravagantly emotional religious sect, Holy See the Roman Catholic bishopric of Rome, ı e the Pope's see; ho'lystone a sandstone used by seamen for cleansing the decks, said to be named from cleaning the decks for Sunday, or from kneeling in using it, holy terror (coll) a formidable person, or one given to causing commotion or agitation; Holy Thursday Maundy Thursday Ascension Day (rare), holy war a war for the extirpation of heresy or a rival religion· a Crusade, holy water water blessed for religious uses, Holy Week the week before Easter, holy writ the Scriptures —holy of holies the inner chamber of the Jewish tabernacle; Holy Roman Empire the official denomination of the German Empire from 962 to 1806. [O.E. hālıg, lit whole—hāl, sound]

homage hom'ıj, n a vassal's acknowledgment that he is the man of his feudal superior anything done or rendered as such an acknowledgment: reverence, esp. shown by outward action. [O Fr homage—L L. homınātıcum—L homō, a man]

Homburg (-hat) hom'bûrg (-hat'), n a man's hat, of felt, with narrow brim and crown, dinted in at the top [First worn at Homburg.]

home hŏm, n habitual abode, or the place felt to be such: residence of one's family· the scene of domestic life, with its emotional associations a separate building occupied by a family. one's own country seat: habitat: natural or usual place of anything: the den or base in a game. the goal: an institution affording refuge, or residence· a private hospital in football pools, a match won by a team playing on their own ground.—adj pertaining or belonging to or being in one's own dwelling, country, or playingground: domestic near the dwelling or headquarters· coming or reaching home effective, searching —adv to home to the innermost or final position effectively—v ı to go home to find the way home to dwell: to be guided to a target or destination —v ı to send home. to set up in a home to guide to a target or destination.—adj. home'less.—n home'lessness.—n home'liness.—adj home'ly pertaining to home familiar plain. unpretentious ugly (U S.) —n hom'er a pigeon of a breed that can readily be trained to find its way home from a distance —advs home'ward, home'wards.—adjs home'ward in the direction of home, home'y, hom'y home-like, hom'ing trained to return home guiding home — Also n —adj home'-brewed brewed at home or for home use (n home'-brew') —home'-coming arrival at home· return home —home counties the counties over and into which London has extended— Middlesex, Essex, Kent, Surrey (Herts, Sussex), home'craft household arts arts practised at home or concerned with home life, Home Department that part of government which is concerned with the maintenance of the internal peace of England—its headquarters the Home Office, its official head the Home Secretary; home economics domestic science; home'-farm the farm attached to and near a great house —adj home'-grown produced in one's own country —home-guard' a member of a volunteer force for home-defence a force of the kind (first in war of 1939–45, Home Guard); home help a woman hired part-time to help with housework; home'land native land, fatherland mother-country: in Africa, an area reserved for Black African peoples (also

Bantustan).—*adj.* **home'-made** made at home: made in one's own country: plain.—**home'maker** a housewife, **home market** the market for goods in the country that produces them.—*adj.* **home'-produced** produced within the country, not imported.—**Home Rule** self-government, as that claimed by Irish (*hist*), Scottish, Welsh Nationalists, including a separate parliament to manage internal affairs.—*adj.* **home'sick** pining for home.—**home'sickness; home'-sig'nal** a signal at the beginning of a section of railway line showing whether or not the section is clear.—*adj.* **home'spun** spun or wrought at home not made in foreign countries: plain inelegant —*n.* cloth made at home —**home'stead** a dwelling-house with outhouses and enclosures immediately connected with it, **home'steading** (orig. *U.S*) a scheme by which people are permitted to live rent-free in or buy semi-derelict buildings and improve them with the help of Government grants, etc , **home'-stretch'** the last stretch of a racecourse (also *fig*); **home'-town** the town where one's home is or was, **home'-truth** a pointed, usually unanswerable, typically wounding, statement that strikes home —*adj.* **home'ward-bound** bound homeward or to one's native land —**home'work** work or preparation to be done at home, esp for school —**at home** in one's own house ready to receive a visitor feeling the ease of familiarity with a place or situation (**at-home'** a reception, **not at home** out of one's house or not receiving a visitor), **bring home to** to prove to, in such a way that there is no way of escaping the conclusion: to impress upon; **do one's homework** to prepare oneself, e.g for a discussion by acquainting oneself with the relevant facts; **eat out of house and home** to live at the expense of another so as to ruin him, **home and dry** having arrived, achieved one's aim, etc., **home from home** a place where one feels comfortable and at ease; **long home** the grave; **make oneself at home** to be as free and unrestrained as in one's own house; **nothing to write home about** (*coll.*) not very exciting. [O E *hām.*]

homeopathy, etc. Same as **homoeopathy,** etc., under **homo-.**

Homeric hō-mer'ik, *adj* pertaining to *Homer,* the great poet of Greece (*c* 850 B C) attributed to Homer. resembling Homer or his poetry. in the heroic or epic manner.—**Homeric question** the question of Homer's authorship of the *Iliad* and the *Odyssey* [Gr. *hōmērikos—Hōmēros,* Homer]

homicide hom'i-sīd, *n.* manslaughter: one who kills another —*adj.* **homici'dal** pertaining to homicide: murderous: bloody [L. *homicidium,* manslaughter, and *homicīda,* a man-slayer—*homō,* a man, *caedēre,* to kill.]

homily hom'i-li, *n* a plain expository sermon, practical rather than doctrinal. a hortatory discourse.—*adjs.* **homilet'ic, -al.**—*n sing.* **homilet'ics** the art of preaching. [Gr. *homīlia,* an assembly, a lecture or sermon—*homos,* the same, *īlē,* a company]

hominid hom'in-id, (*zool.*) *n* an animal of the family comprising man and his ancestors (also *adj*).—*n* and *adj* **hom'inoid.** [L. *homō, -inis,* man.]

hominy hom'i-ni, *n.* maize hulled, or hulled and crushed, boiled with water—a kind of Indian corn porridge [Amer Ind. origin]

homo hō'mō, *n.* man generically: (*cap.,* *zool*) the human genus —**Homo sapiens** the one existing species of man. [L. *homō, -inis,* man, human being.]

homo- hom'ō, hom-o', in many cases alternatively pronounced *hōm-,* in composition, same.—**homoeo-, homeo-, homoio-** hom'i-ō-, -oi'ō-, or -o'-, like, similar —*n* and *adj.* **homo** (*hō'mō, slang*) short for *homosexual:—pl.* **ho'mos** —*adjs* **homocentric** (-sen'-trik, Gr *homokentros—kentron,* centre, point) con-

centric. proceeding from or diverging to the same point: of rays, either parallel or passing through one focus (*phys.*), **homocyclic** (-sik'lik; Gr. *kyklos,* a ring; *chem.*) having a closed chain of like atoms —*n.* **hom(o)eopath** (*hom'* or *hōm'i-ə-path,* Gr. *pathos,* feeling), **hom(o)eopathist** (-*op'ə-thist*) one who believes in or practises homoeopathy.—*adj* **hom(o)eopathic** (-*path'*) —*adv.* **hom(o)eopath'ically.** —*ns.* **hom(o)eopathy** (-*op'ə-thi*) the system of treating diseases by small quantities of drugs that excite symptoms similar to those of the disease; **hom(o)eostasis** (*hom-i-os'ta-sis,* Gr *stasis,* a standing still) the tendency for the internal environment of the body to remain constant in spite of varying external conditions. a tendency towards health, stable conditions —*adjs.* **hom(o)eostat'ic; hom(o)eotherm'al, -ic, -ous** homothermous —Also **homoi'other'mal,** etc —*ns* **homoerot'icism, homoerot'ism** orientation of the libido towards one of the same sex —*adjs.* **homoerot'ic; homogamic** (-*gam'ik*), **homogamous** (*hom-og'ə-məs*).—*ns* **homogamy** (*hom-og'ə-mi,* Gr *gamos,* marriage) the condition of having all the flowers of an inflorescence sexually alike (*bot.*) simultaneous ripening of stamens and stigmas (*bot.*), **homogenate** (-*oj'ə-nāt*) a substance produced by homogenising, **homogeneity** (*hom-ō-ji-nē'i-ti*) the state or fact of being homogeneous —*adj* **homogeneous** (*hom-ō-jēn'i-əs,* also *hōm-, -jen'*; Gr *homogenēs—genos,* kind) of the same kind or nature. having the constituent elements similar throughout of the same degree or dimensions in every term (*math.*).—*n.* **homogē'neousness.**—*adj.* **homogenous** (*hom-oj'an-as*) similar owing to common descent.—*n* **homogenesis** (-*jen'i-sis,* Gr *genesis,* birth; *biol.*) a mode of reproduction in which the offspring is like the parent, and passes through the same cycle of existence —*adjs* **homogenet'ic, -al** homogenous.— *v.t.* **homog'enise, -ize** (or *hom'o-jən-īz*) to make homogeneous: to make (milk) more digestible by breaking up fat globules, etc to produce (milk) synthetically by mixing its constituents.—*ns.* **homogenisa'tion, -z-; homog'eniser, -z-; homog'eny** similarity owing to common descent, **homograft** (*hom'ō-graft*) a graft from one individual to an unrelated member of the same species; **homograph** (*hom'ō-graf,* Gr *graphein,* to write) a word of the same spelling and pronunciation as another, but of different meaning and origin —*adj.* **homoiousian** (*hom-oi-ōō'si-ən,* or -*ow',* Gr. *ousiā,* being) of similar (as distinguished from identical) essence: believing the Father and Son to be of similar essence —*n* a holder of such belief, a semi-Arian.—*v t.* **homol'ogate** (L L *homologāre, -ātum*—Gr *homologeein,* to agree—*logos,* speech) to confirm: to approve. to consent to: to ratify —*v.i* to agree —*n* **homologa'tion.**—*adj* **homological** (-*loj'*) —*adv.* **homolog'ically.**—*v.t* and *v i.* **homol'-ogise, -ize** (-*jīz*) —*adj* **homologous** (*hom-ol'ə-gəs*) agreeing of the same essential nature, corresponding in relative position, general structure, and descent.— *n.* **hom'ologue,** *U S.* **hom'olog,** (-*ə-log*) that which is homologous to something else, as a man's arm, a whale's flipper, a bird's wing —*ns* **homol'ogy** (-*ə-ji,* Gr. *homologos*) the quality of being homologous affinity of structure and origin, apart from form or use; **hom'omorph** (Gr *morphē,* form) a thing having the same form as another —*adjs.* **homomorph'ic, homomorph'ous** alike in form, esp if essentially different: uniform.—*ns.* **homomorph'ism; homomorphō'sis** regeneration of a lost part in the original form; **hom'onym** (Gr *homōnymos—onyma, onoma,* name) a word having the same sound and perhaps the same spelling as another, but a different meaning and origin a name rejected as preoccupied by another genus or species (*biol*): a namesake —*adjs.* **homonym'ic** pertaining to homonyms; **homon'ymous** having the same name having different significations and origins but the same sound: ambiguous. equivocal —*adv* **homon'ymously.**—*n.* **homon'ymy, homonym'ity.**—*adj* **homoousian, homousian** (*hom-*(ō-)ōō'si-ən, or -ow', Gr *ousiā*, being) of the same essence. believing the Son to be of the same essence as the Father —*n* a holder of such belief (according to the Nicene Creed) —*n* **homophone** (*hom'ə-fōn;* Gr. *phōnē,* sound) a character representing the same sound as another: a word pronounced alike with another but different in spelling and meaning —*adjs* **homophonic** (-*fon'*) sounding alike in unison: in the monodic style of music; **homophonous** (-*of'*) —*n* **homoph'ony.**—*adj* **homoplast'ic** (Gr *plastikos,* plastic, *plasma,* a mould; *biol.*) similar in structure and development owing to parallel or convergent evolution but not descended from a common source —*ns.* **hom'oplasmy** (-*plaz-mi*), **homop'lasy.**—*adj.* **homopō'lar** (*chem*) having an equal distribution of charge, as in a covalent bond.—*n* **homopolár'ity.**—*n.pl.* **Homoptera** (-*op'*; Gr *pteron,* a wing) an order of insects having wings of a uniform texture—cicadas, green-fly, etc —*adj.* **homop'terous.**—*adj.* **homosex'ual** having, or pertaining to, sexual propensity to one's own sex —Also *n.*—*ns.* **homosex'ualist; homosexual'ity.**—*adjs* **homotherm'al, homotherm'ic, homotherm'ous** (Gr *thermē,* heat) keeping the same temperature, warm-blooded —*ns* **homozygōs'is** the condition of having inherited a given genetical factor from both parents, so producing gametes of only one kind as regards that factor: genetical stability as regards a given factor; **homozy'gote** a zygote which is formed as a result of homozygosis.—*adj.* **homozy'gous.** [Gr *homos,* same, *homoios,* like, similar.] **homunculus** hō-*mung'kū-ləs,* *n* a tiny man capable of being produced artificially· a dwarf, manikin·—*pl.* **-li** —Also **homunc'ūle.** [L., dim of *homō.*] **hone** *hōn, n* a smooth stone used for sharpening instruments.—*v.t* to sharpen as on a hone [O E. *hān;* O.N. *hein;* allied to Gr. *kōnos,* a cone.] **honest** *on'ist, -əst, adj* full of honour· just: fair-dealing: upright: the opposite of thievish: free from fraud· candid: truthful: ingenuous: seemly. respectable (now only patronisingly): honourable.—*adv* **hon'estly** in an honest way: in truth.—*interj.* expressing annoyance, disbelief, etc.—*n.* **hon'esty** the state of being honest: integrity· candour: a garden-plant with shining silver or satiny white dissepiments —*adj.* **hon'est-to-God', hon'est-to-good'ness** genuine, out-and-out.—Also *adv.*—**honest Injun (Indian)** upon my honour; **make an honest woman of** to marry, where the woman has first been seduced [O.Fr *honeste*—L. *honestus*—*honor.*] **honey** *hun'i, n* a sweet, thick fluid elaborated by bees from the nectar of flowers: nectar of flowers: anything sweet like honey: a term of endearment: anything pleasant or delightful (*coll.*):—*v.t* to sweeten: to make agreeable:—*pr.p.* **hon'eying;** *pa.t* and *pa.p.* **hon'eyed** (-*id*).—*adjs* **hon'eyed, hon'ied** sweet: seductive; **hon'eyless.**—**hon'ey-badg'er** the ratel; **hon'ey-bee** the hive-bee; **hon'eybun, hon'eybunch** terms of endearment; **hon'ey-buzz'ard** a hawk (*Pernis apivora*) that feeds on the larvae and honey of bees, wasps, etc ; **hon'eycomb** (-*kōm*) a comb or mass of waxy cells formed by bees in which they store their honey: anything like a honeycomb: a bewildering maze of rooms, cavities, etc —*v.t.* to make like a honeycomb.—**hon'ey-dew** a sugar secretion from aphides or plants· ambrosia: a fine sort of tobacco moistened with molasses; **honeydew melon** a sweet-flavoured melon with smooth green or orange rind,

hon'ey-eat'er a honey-sucker; **honey fungus** a kind of honey-coloured edible mushroom; **hon'ey-guide** a bird of a mainly African family supposed to guide men to honey by hopping from tree to tree with a peculiar cry· a marking on a flower showing the way to the nectaries; **hon'eymoon** the first weeks after marriage. commonly spent on holiday, before settling down to the business of life: a period of (unusual) harmony at the start of a new business relationship, etc —Also *v i.*—**hon'eymooner; hon'eypot** a container for honey: anything that attracts people (*fig.*): (in *pl.*) a children's game: see also **hanepoot** (*S. Afr.*); **hon'ey-suck'er** any bird of a large Australian family, Meliphagidae, **hon'eysuckle** a climbing shrub with cream-coloured flowers, so named because honey is readily sucked from the flower (by long-tongued insects only) [O.E. *hunig.*] **honeypot** *hun'i-pot.* See **honey, hanepoot.** **honied.** See **honeyed.** **Honiton** *hon'i-tən,* local *hun',* adj. of a kind of pillow lace with sprigs, made at *Honiton,* Devon. **honk** *hongk, n* the cry of the wild goose: the noise of a motor horn.—Also *v i.* [Imit.] **honky, honkie** *hongk'i,* (*derog.,* orig. *U.S.*) *n.* a white man.—Also *adj.* **honky-tonk** *hongk'i-tongk,* (*slang*) *n.* a low drinking haunt: cheap entertainment: jangly piano music **honorarium** *on-ə-rā'ri-əm, hon-, n.* a voluntary fee paid, esp. to a professional man for his services.—*adj.* **honorary** (*on'*(ə-)*rə-ri*) conferring honour: holding a title or office without performing services or without reward —*n.* an honorary fee. [L. *honōrārius, honōrārium* (*dōnum*), honorary (gift)—*honor, -ōris,* honour] **honorific** (*h*)*on-ə-rif'ik, adj.* attributing or doing honour.—*n* an honorific form of title, address or mention —*adv.* **honorif'ically.** [L. *honōrificus*—*honor, -ōris,* honour, and *facěre,* to do, make.] **honoris causa** *hon-ōr'is* (-*ōr'*) *ko'zə, kow'zā,* (L.L.) as an honour, a token of respect.

honour, in U S **honor,** *on'ər, n* the esteem due or paid to worth: respect· high estimation: veneration: that which rightfully attracts esteem: that which confers distinction or does credit: self-respecting integrity: a scrupulous sense of what is due: chastity: virginity: distinction: exalted rank: any mark of esteem: privilege: a title or decoration: a title of respect in addressing or referring to judges, etc.: a prize or distinction: (in *pl.*) privileges of rank or birth: (in *pl.*) civilities paid: (in *pl.*) in universities, etc , a higher grade of distinction for meritorious, advanced, or specialised work· the right to play first from the tee (*golf*): any one of four (in whist) or five (in bridge) best trumps, or an ace in a no-trump hand: (in *pl.*) a score for holding these —*v.t.* to hold in high esteem: to respect: to exalt: to do honour to: to confer honour upon: to grace: to accept and pay when due.—*adj.* **hon'ourable** worthy of honour: illustrious: actuated by principles of honour: conferring honour: befitting men of exalted station: (*cap.*; written **Hon.**) prefixed to the names of various persons as a courtesy title.—*n.* **hon'ourableness.**—*adv* **hon'ourably.**—**honours list** a list of people who have or are to receive a knighthood, order, etc. from the monarch —**affair of honour** a duel; **birthday honours** honours granted to mark the monarch's birthday; **Companions of Honour** an order instituted in 1917 for those who have rendered conspicuous service of national importance; **debt of honour** see **debt; do the honours** to render civilities, esp. as host; **hon'our-bound', in honour bound** obliged by duty, conscience, etc. (to); **honour bright** a kind of interjectional minor oath or appeal to honour; **honours of war** the privileges granted to a capitulating force of marching out with their arms, flags, etc., **in honour of** out of respect for: celebrating, **last honours** funeral rites; **maid of honour** a lady in the service of a queen or princess. a bridesmaid (*U.S.*); **matron of honour** a married woman in the service of a queen or princess. a married woman performing the duties of a bridesmaid. **military honours** ceremonial tokens of respect paid by troops to royalty, or at the burial of an officer, etc., **point of honour** any scruple caused by a sense of duty: the obligation to demand and to receive satisfaction for an insult, esp. in the duel, **upon my honour** an appeal to one's honour in support of a statement, **word of honour** a promise which cannot be broken without disgrace. [A Fr. (*h*)*onour*—L. *honor, honôs, -ôris*]

hooch *hōōch* See **hootch.**

hood[1] *hood, n* a flexible covering for the head and back of the neck a covering for a hawk's head. a distinctive ornamental fold worn on the back over an academic gown. a folding roof for a carriage, etc . an overhanging or protective cover: the expansion of a cobra's neck. a motor-car bonnet (*U.S.*).—*v.t.* to cover with a hood: to blind.—**hood'ie-crow** the hooded crow (*Corvus cornix*) [O.E. *hôd.*]

hood[2] *hood,* (*slang*) a hoodlum

-hood *-hood, n. suff.* indicating state, nature, as *hardihood, manhood.* [O.E. *hâd,* Ger. *-heit,* state.]

hoodlum *hōod'lǝm, n.* a rowdy, street bully: a small-time criminal or gangster

hoodoo *hōo'dōo, n.* voodoo· a bringer of bad luck: bad luck.—*v.t.* to bewitch. to bring bad luck to [App. **voodoo.**]

hoodwink *hood'wingk, v.t.* to blindfold: to deceive, impose on [**hood**[1], **wink.**]

hooey *hōo'i,* (*slang*) *n.* nonsense

hoof *hōof, n.* the horny part of the feet of certain animals, as horses, etc : a hoofed animal: a foot (*coll*)—*pl.* **hoofs, hooves.**—*v t.* to strike with the hoof, to kick. to expel: (with *it*) to walk: (with *it*) to dance (*slang*)—**hoof'-mark, hoof'print.—on the hoof** alive (of cattle) [O.E. *hôf.*]

hoo-ha *hōo'ha', (slang) n.* noisy fuss [Imit.]

hook *hook, n* an object of bent form, such as would catch or hold anything: a sharply bent line: a snare· an advantageous hold. a curved instrument for cutting grain, branches, etc.: a boxer's blow with bent elbow the curve of a ball in flight (*sport*).—*v.t.* to catch, fasten, or hold with or as with a hook· to form into or with a hook. to ensnare: to pull the ball abruptly to one's left (*golf* and *cricket*): to obtain possession of (the ball) in the scrum (*rugby*).—*v.t.* to bend: to be curved: to pull abruptly.—*pa.p* or *adj.* **hooked** (*hookt*) physically dependent on drugs: (with *on, by*) addicted to a drug, activity, or indulgence: enthralled.—*n.* **hook'er** one who hooks: one whose part it is to hook the ball (*rugby*): a prostitute (*slang*). —*adj* **hook'y.**—*adj.* **hook'-nosed.—hook'-up** a connection: a temporary linking up of separate broadcasting stations for a special transmission; **hook'-worm** a parasitic nematode with hooks in the mouth· the disease it causes, ankylostomiasis or miner's anaemia.—**by hook or by crook** one way if not another, **hook and eye** a contrivance for fastening garments by means of a hook that catches in a loop or eye, **hook it** (*slang*) to decamp, make off, **hook, line and sinker** complete(ly), **off the hook** ready-made out of difficulty or trouble. [O.E. *hôc,* Du. *hoek.*]

hookah, hooka *hook'ǝ, n.* the water tobacco-pipe of Arabs, Turks, etc [Ar. *huqqah,* bowl, casket.]

hooker[1] *hook'ǝr, n.* a two-masted Dutch vessel. a small fishing-smack. [Du. *hoeker.*]

hooker[2]. See **hook.**

hookey, hooky *hook'i,* (*U.S*) *n* truant (in the phrase

play hookey) —**blind hookey** a gambling card-game.

hooligan *hool'i-gǝn, n.* a street rough: a (young) violent, rude person.—*n.* **hool'iganism.** [Said to be the name of a leader of a gang, poss *Houlihan* or *Hooley's gang.*]

hoop[1] *hoop, n.* a ring or circular band, esp. fo. holding together the staves of casks, etc.: a large ring of metal, etc., for a child to trundle, for leaping through, for holding wide a skirt, or other purpose: a ring: a croquet arch.—*v.t.* to bind with hoops to encircle —**hoop'-la** a fairground game in which small hoops are thrown over prizes —**go through the hoop** to suffer an ordeal, undergo punishment. [O.E *hôp.*]

hoop[2], **hooper, hooping-cough.** See under **whoop.**

hoopoe *hoop'ōo, n.* a crested bird (*Upupa epops*) an occasional visitor in Britain. [Earlier *hoop*—O.Fr. *huppe,* partly remodelled on L *ûpûpa*]

hoorah, hooray. Same as **hurrah.**

hoos(e)gow *hōos'gow, n.* (*U.S. slang*), a prison, jail [Sp *juzgado,* tribunal, courtroom.]

hoot *hoot, v.i.* (of an owl) to give a hollow cry to make a sound like an owl, usually expressing hostility or scorn: to laugh loudly: to sound a motor-horn, siren, or the like.—*v.t.* to greet or drive with such sounds.— *n.* the sound of hooting. the note of an owl, motor-horn, etc.: a whit (often *two hoots*): a hilarious performance, escapade, situation, etc. (*coll*) —*n.* **hoot'er** a factory or mine siren or steam whistle: a nose (*slang*). [Imit , prob. immediately Scand.]

hootch, hooch *hōoch, n.* a drink made by the Indians of N.W. America from fermented dough and sugar: whisky: liquor, esp. if illicitly got or made. [Said to be from *Hootchino,* an Alaskan tribe.]

hoot(e)nanny, hoota-, -le *hoot'(ǝ-)nan-ē, n* an informal concert with folk music.

Hoover® *hōo'vǝr, n* a vacuum-cleaner (also without *cap*).—*v.t.* and *v.i* to clean with a vacuum-cleaner. **hooves.** See **hoof.**

hop[1] *hop, v i.* to leap on one leg. to move in jumps like a bird to walk lame: to move smartly (in, out): to fly (in aircraft).—*v.t.* to jump or fly over: to board when in motion (*U.S.*):—*pr.p.* **hopp'ing;** *pa.t.* and *pa.p.* **hopped.**—*n.* a leap on one leg: a jump. a dance, dancing-party. a stage in a flying journey.—*n* **hopp'er** a hopping or leaping animal, esp. (*U.S.*) a grasshopper: a shaking or conveying receiver, funnel, or trough (originally a shaking one) in which something is placed to be passed or fed, as to a mill: a barge with an opening in its bottom for discharging refuse: a vessel in which seed-corn is carried for sowing: a device which holds and passes on punched cards to a feed mechanism (*comput.*).—**hop'-o'-my-thumb** (i.e. on my thumb) a pygmy —*adj.* **hopp'ing(-)mad'** (*coll.*) extremely angry.—**hop'-scotch** a game in which children hop over lines traced on the ground.—**hop it** (*slang*) to take oneself off; **hop, skip** (or **step**) **and jump** a leap on one leg, a skip, and a jump with both legs, **hop the twig** (*slang*) to escape one's creditors: to die; **on the hop** in a state of restless activity: unawares [O.E. *hoppian,* to dance.]

hop[2] *hop, n.* a plant of the mulberry family with a long twining stalk. (in *pl.*) its bitter catkin-like fruit-clusters used for flavouring beer and in medicine. opium (*slang*)· any narcotic (*slang*) —*v.t.* to mix or flavour with hops.—*v.i.* to gather hops.—*pr.p.* **hopp'ing;** *pa.t.* and *pa.p.* **hopped.**—*ns* **hopp'er** one who picks hops: a mechanical contrivance for stripping hops from the bines; **hopp'ing** the time of the hop harvest —*adj.* **hopp'y** tasting of hops.—**hop'bind, hop'bine** the stalk of the hop; **hop'-fly** a greenfly injurious to hops, **hop'-garden** a field of hops; **hop'-head** (*slang*) a drug addict —*adj.* **hopped'-up** (*slang*) drugged: artificially stimulated.—**hop'-pick'er** a hopper; **hop's pole** pole supporting hop-bine; **hop'(-)sack** sack for hops: (also **-sacking**) coarse fabric of hemp and jute, or woollen fabric with roughened surface. [Du. *hop.*]

hope[1] *hōp, v.i.* to cherish a desire of good with some expectation of fulfilment: to have confidence: to be hopeful.—*v.t.* to desire with belief in the possibility of fulfilment.—*n.* a desire of some good, with a certain expectation of obtaining it: confidence: anticipation: that on which hopes are grounded: that which is hoped for.—*adj.* **hope'ful** full of hope: having qualities which excite hope: promising good or success.—*n* a promising young person.—*adv.* **hope'-fully** in a hopeful manner: if all goes well (*coll.*).—*n.* **hope'fulness.**—*adj.* **hope'less** without hope: giving no ground to expect good or success: incurable.—*adv.* **hope'lessly.**—*n.* **hope'lessness.**—**hope'-chest** (*U.S.*) a repository of things stored by a woman for her marriage.—**hope against hope** to continue to hope when there is no (longer any) reason for this hope; **it is hoped** (*coll*) if all goes well; **no'-hop'er** (*slang*) a racehorse that is not good enough to have a chance of winning: any thing or person that has no chance of success; **some hope, what a hope** (*iron.*) that will never happen. [O.E. *hopian—hopa*, hope; Du. *hopen*, Ger. *hoffen*.]

hope[2]. See **forlorn hope**.

hoplite *hop'līt, n.* a heavy-armed Greek foot-soldier. [Gr. *hoplītēs.*]

hopple *hop'l, v.t.* to restrain by tying the feet together. —*n.* (chiefly in *pl.*) a fetter for horses, etc., when left to graze. [Cf. obs. Flem. *hoppelen.*]

hoppus (cubic) foot *hop'əs (kū'bik) fŏŏt,* a unit of volume for round timber. [E. *Hoppus.*]

horary *hō'rə-ri, ho', adj.* pertaining to an hour: noting the hours: hourly: continuing an hour. [L. *hōra,* an hour.]

Horatian *hor-ā'shən, adj.* pertaining to *Horace,* the Latin poet (65–8 B.C.), or to his manner or verse.

horde *hōrd, hôrd, n.* a migratory or wandering tribe or clan: a multitude.—*v.i.* to live together as a horde: to come together to form a horde. [Fr.,—Turk. *ordu,* camp.]

horehound, hoarhound *hōr', hôr'hownd, n.* a hoary labiate plant (*Marrubium vulgare*) once popular as a remedy for coughs. [O.E. *hār,* hoar, *hūne,* horehound.]

horizon *hər-ī'zən, n* the circle in which earth and sky seem to meet (*sensible, apparent,* or *visible horizon*): a plane through the earth's centre parallel to the sensible horizon (*rational horizon*), or the great circle in which it meets the heavens: a horizontal reflecting surface, as of mercury, used as a substitute for the horizon in taking an observation (*artificial horizon*) a stratigraphical level, characterised generally by some particular fossil or fossils (*geol.*): the limit of one's experience or apprehension.—*adj.* **horizontal** (*hor-i-zont'l*) pertaining to the horizon: parallel to the horizon: level: measured in the plane of the horizon: applying equally to all members of a group, aspects of an activity, etc —*n.* a horizontal line, position, or object.—*n.* **horizontal'ity.**—*adv* **horizon'-tally.** [Fr.,—L.,—Gr **horizōn** (*kyklos*), bounding (circle) —*horos,* a limit]

horme *hor'mē* (*psychol.*), *n* goal-directed or purposive behaviour. [Gr. *hormē,* animal impulse]

hormone *hōr'mōn, n* an internal secretion which on reaching some part of a plant or animal body exercises a specific physiological action.—*adj.* **hor'monal** (or *-mōn'*). [Gr **hormōn,** contracted pr p. of *hormaein,* to stir up.]

horn *hôrn, n.* a hard outgrowth on the head of an

animal, sometimes confined to the hollow structure on an ox, sheep, goat, etc., sometimes extended to a deer's antler, the growth on a rhinoceros's snout, etc.: a beetle's antenna: a snail's tentacle: any projection resembling a horn: a cusp: a crescent tip: an outgrowth visible to the eye of faith on a cuckold's forehead: the material of which horns are composed, keratin: an object made of or like a horn, as a drinking vessel: a wind instrument orig. made from a horn, now of brass, etc.: a sounding apparatus on motor vehicles.—*adj* made of horn.—*v.t.* to furnish with horns, real or visionary: to dishorn: to gore: to butt or push.—*ns.* **horn'iness.**—*adj.* **horn'y** like horn: of horn: hard: sexually aroused (*slang*): lecherous, lustful (*slang*).—**horn'beam** a tree (*Carpinus*) resembling a beech, with hard tough wood; **horn'bill** a bird with a horny excrescence on its bill; **horn'book** (*hist.*) a first book for children, which consisted of a single leaf set in a frame, with a thin plate of transparent horn in front to preserve it; **horned owl, horn owl** an owl with hornlike tufts of feathers on its head; **horned toad** a spiny American lizard (*Phrynosoma*): a S. American toad (*Ceratophrys*) with a bony shield on the back; **horn'fels** (*-fels;* Ger. *Fels,* rock) a compact rock composed of lime silicates.—*adj.* **horn'-rimmed** having rims of horn, or material resembling horn.— **horn'-rims** dark horn-rimmed spectacles; **horn'stone** a flinty chalcedony: hornfels.—*v.t.* **horn'swoggle** (*slang,* orig. *U.S.*) to trick, deceive: to cheat.— **horn'wort** a rootless water-plant with much-divided submerged leaves that turn translucent and horny.— **horn in** to interpose, butt in (on); **horn of plenty** see **cornucopia; horns of a dilemma** see **dilemma; pull or draw in one's horns** to abate one's ardour or pretensions: to curtail or restrict one's activities, spending, etc. [O.E. *horn.*]

hornblende *hôrn'blend, n.* a rock-forming mineral, essentially silicate of calcium, magnesium and iron, generally green to black. [Ger.; cf. **horn, blende.**]

hornet *hôrn'it, n.* a large kind of wasp.—**stir up a hornet's nest** to do something which causes a violent reaction. [O E. *hyrnet,* app.—*horn,* horn.]

hornfels. See **horn.**

hornpipe *hôrn'pīp, n.* an old Welsh musical instrument like a clarinet, prob. sometimes with a horn mouthpiece or bell: a lively English dance, usually by one person, popular amongst sailors: a tune for the dance. [**horn, pipe**.]

horologe *hor'ə-loj, n.* any instrument for telling the hours —*ns.* **horologer** (*-ol'ə-jər*), **horol'ogist** a maker of clocks, etc.—*adjs.* **horolog'ic, -al.**—*n.* **horol'ogy** the science of time measurement: the art of clockmaking. [L. *hōrologium*—Gr. *hōrologion—hōrā,* an hour, *legein,* to tell.]

horoscope *hor'ə-skōp, n.* a map of the heavens at the hour or on the day of a person's birth, by which the astrologer predicted the events of his life: a representation of the heavens for this purpose: any similar prediction about the future.—*adj.* **horoscopic** (*-skop'*).—*n.* **horos'copy** the art of predicting the events of a person's life from his horoscope: aspect of the stars at the time of birth. [Gr. *hōroskopos— hōrā,* an hour, *skopeein,* to observe.]

horrendous *hor-end'əs,* (*coll.*) *adj.* dreadful: frightful: horrible.—*adv.* **horrend'ously.** [L. *horrendus,* ger. of *horrēre,* to bristle.]

horrible *hor'i-bl, adj.* exciting horror. dreadful· detestable (*coll*)—*n.* **horr'ibleness.**—*adv.* **horr'ibly.** [L *horribilis—horrēre,* to shudder.]

horrid *hor'id, adj* bristling, rough (*poet.*): repellent, detestable (*coll*)—*adv.* **horr'idly.**—*n.* **horr'idness.** [L. *horridus—horrēre,* to bristle.]

horrify *hor'i-fī, v t* to strike with horror:—*pr.p.*

horr'ifying; *pa.t* and *pa.p.* **horr'ified.**—*adj.* **horrif'ic** exciting horror: frightful.—*advs.* **horrif'ically**; **horr'ifyingly.** [L *horrificus*—root of *horrēre*, to shudder, *facĕre*, to make.]

horripilation *hor-ɪ-pɪ-lā'shən, n.* a contraction of the cutaneous muscles causing erection of the hairs and goose-flesh.—*adj.* **horrip'ilant.** [L. *horripilātiō, -ōnis*—root of *horrēre*, to bristle, *pilus,* a hair.]

horrisonant *hor-ɪs'ən-ənt, adj.* sounding dreadfully. [From root of L *horrēre,* to bristle, *sonāns, -antis,* sounding.]

horror *hor'ər, n.* intense repugnance: power of exciting such feeling: a source of such feeling: anything mildly objectionable, ridiculous, grotesque, or distasteful (*coll.*).—*adj.* of a comic (i.e. strip cartoon), film, novel, etc., having gruesome, violent, horrifying, or bloodcurdling themes.—*adjs.* **horr'or-stricken, -struck.—the horrors** extreme depression [L *horror,* a shudder, bristling, etc.]

hors *or,* (Fr.) *prep.* out of, outside.—**hors concours** (*kȯ-kōōr'*) not in competition; **hors de combat** (*də kȯ-ba*) unfit to fight, disabled, **hors d'œuvre** (*pl.* **d'œuvre, d'œuvres;** *dœ-vr'*) savoury, e.g olives, sardines, etc., to whet the appetite before a meal.

horse *hors, n.* a solid-hoofed ungulate (*Equus caballus*) with flowing tail and mane: any member of the genus Equus (horse, ass, zebra, etc.) or the family Equidae: a male adult of the species. (*collec.*) cavalry: a gymnastic apparatus for vaulting, etc.: a horselike apparatus or support of various kinds (as *clothes-horse*): a mass of barren country interrupting a lode: heroin (*slang*):—*pl.* **horses** sometimes **horse.** —*v.t.* to mount or set as on a horse: to provide with a horse.—*v.i.* to get on horseback: to travel on horseback.—*adj.* **horse'less** mechanically driven.—*n.* **hors'iness.**—*adj.* **hors'y** of or pertaining to horses: horselike: devoted to horses, horse-racing, or breeding.—**horse'back** the back of a horse, **horse bean** a variety of broad bean: applied also to other beans; **horse block** a block or stage for mounting and dismounting by; **horse box** a trailer or railway car designed to carry horses: a stall on shipboard: a high-sided church pew (*facet*), **horse brass** a usu. brass ornament orig. for hanging on the harness of a horse; **horse'-break'er** one who breaks or tames horses, or teaches them to draw or carry; **horse chestnut** a smooth, brown, bitter seed or nut, perh. so called from its coarseness contrasted with the edible chestnut. the tree that produces it (*Aesculus hippocastanum*); **horse'-cloth** a cloth for covering a horse; **horse'-collar** a stuffed collar for a draught-horse, carrying the hames; **horse'-cop'er** one who deals in horses; **horse'-doc'tor** a veterinary surgeon, **horse'flesh** the flesh of a horse: horses collectively, **horse'fly** the forest-fly or other large fly that stings horses.—*n.pl.* **horse guards** horse soldiers employed as guards. (*cap.*) the cavalry brigade of the British household troops.—**horse'hair** a hair from a horse's mane or tail. a mass of such hairs: a fabric woven from horsehair.—*adj* made of or stuffed with horsehair.— **horse'hide; horse latitudes** two zones of the Atlantic Ocean (about 30°N and 30°S, esp. the former) noted for long calms; **horse'laugh** a harsh, boisterous laugh, **horse'-leech** a large species of leech, supposed to fasten on horses: a bloodsucker, **horse mackerel** the scad or allied fish: the tunny applied to various other fishes, **horse'man** a rider: one skilled in managing a horse. a mounted soldier. one who has charge of horses; **horse'manship; horse'meat** food for horses; **horse mushroom** a large coarse mushroom, **horse opera** a Wild West film; **horse pistol** a large pistol formerly carried in a holster by horsemen, **horse'play** rough, boisterous play, **horse'pond** a pond for watering horses at, **horse'power** the power a horse can exert, or its conventional equivalent (taken as 746 watt); **horse'-race** a race by horses; **horse'-racing; horse'radish** plant with a pungent root, used as a condiment, **horse'-rider; horse'-rid'ing; horse sense** (*coll.*) plain common sense; **horse'shoe** a shoe for horses, consisting of a curved piece of iron: anything of like shape.—*adj.* shaped like a horseshoe.— **horse'tail** a horse's tail: a Turkish standard, marking rank by number: a plant with hollow rush-like stems; **horse'-trading** hard bargaining, **horse'-train'er** one who trains horses for racing, etc.; **horse'whip** a whip for driving horses.—*v t.* to thrash with a horsewhip to lash.—**horse'-wom'an** a woman who rides on horseback, or who rides well.—**dark horse see dark; flog a dead horse** to try to work up excitement about a threadbare subject; **gift horse see gift; high horse see on one's high horse** (under **high**); **hold your horses** not so fast: wait a moment; **horse around** (*slang*) to fool about; **horses for courses** phrase expressing the view that each racehorse will do best on a certain course which peculiarly suits it; **horse of a different colour** another thing altogether; **put the cart before the horse see cart; (straight) from the horse's mouth** from a very trustworthy source (of information), **take horse** to mount on horseback; **white horse see white; willing horse** a willing, obliging, worker. [O.E. *hors*; O N. *hross*; O.H.G. *hros* (Ger. *Ross*.).]

horst *horst,* (geol.) *n.* a block of the earth's crust that has remained in position while the ground around it has either subsided or been folded into mountains by pressure against its solid sides. [Ger.]

horsy. See **horse.**

hortative *hȯrt'ə-tiv, adj.* inciting. encouraging: giving advice —Also **hort'atory.**—*n.* **horta'tion.** [L *hortārī, -ātus,* to incite.]

horticulture *hȯr'ti-kul-chər, n* the art of gardening.— *adj* **horticul'tural.**—*n.* **horticul'turist** one versed in the art of cultivating gardens. [L. *hortus,* a garden, *cultūra*—*colĕre,* to cultivate.]

hosanna *hō-zan'ə, n.* exclamation of praise to God. [Gr. *hōsanna*—Heb. *hōshī'āh nnā, hōshiā',* save, *nā,* I pray.]

hose *hōz, n* a covering for the legs or feet: stockings: socks: a flexible pipe for conveying water, etc., so called from its shape:—*pl.* **hose** in sense of pipe, *pl.* **hos'es.**—*v.t* to play a hose on (often with *down*).— *ns* **hosier** (*hōzh'(y)ər, hōz'yər*) a dealer in or a maker of hosiery; **hō'siery** hose collectively. knitted goods. —**hose'pipe; hose'-reel** a large revolving drum for carrying hoses [O.E *hosa,* pl. *hosan,* Du. *hoos,* Ger *Hose*.]

hospice *hos'pis, n.* a house of entertainment for strangers. a hostel: a home of refuge: a home for the care of the terminally ill [Fr.,—L. *hospitium*—*hospes, -itis,* a stranger, guest.]

hospitable *hos'pit-ə-bl,* or *hos-pit', adj.* kind to strangers: welcoming and generous towards guests.— *n.* **hos'pitableness** (or *-pit'*).—*adv.* **hos'pitably** (or *-pit'*).—*n.* **hospitality** see under **hospital.** [L.L *hospitāgium*—L. *hospes, -itis,* stranger, guest.]

hospital *hos'pit-l, n.* formerly, a charitable institution for the old or destitute, or for reception (and education) of the needy young: an institution for treatment of sick or injured: a building for any of these purposes.—*n.* **hospitalisa'tion, -z-.**—*v.t.* **hos'pitalise, -ize** to send to hospital —*ns.* **hospitality** (*-al'i-ti*) (friendly welcome and) entertainment of guests, **hos'pitaller** (*U S. -pitaler*) one of a charitable brotherhood for the care of the sick in hospitals: one of the Knights of St John (otherwise called Knights of Rhodes, and afterwards of Malta), an order which built a hospital for pilgrims at Jerusalem.—**hos'pital-**

ship a ship fitted out exclusively for the treatment and transport of the sick and wounded [O Fr. *hospital* —L.L. *hospitāle—hospes, -itis,* a guest.]

host[1] *hŏst, n.* one who entertains a stranger or guest at his house without (or with) reward: an innkeeper: an organism on which another lives as a parasite (also *fig*).—*v.t.* to receive and entertain as one's guest.— *ns.* **hŏst'ess** a female host: a paid female partner at a dance-hall, nightclub, etc.—**air'-hŏstess** one appointed to look after the comfort of the passengers in an aircraft; **reckon or count without one's host** to fail to take account of some important possibility, as the action of another. [O Fr. *hoste*—L. *hospes, hospitis*]

host[2] *hŏst, n* an army (*arch.*). a great multitude — **heavenly host** the angels and archangels, **Lord of hosts** a favourite Hebrew term for Jehovah, considered as head of the hosts of angels, etc [O.Fr *host*—L *hostis,* an enemy]

host[3] *hŏst, n.* (often *cap.*) in the R C Church, the consecrated wafer of the eucharist [L *hostia,* a victim]

Hosta *hŏst'ə, n* a genus of decorative perennial herbaceous plants (fam. *Liliaceae*) from Asia with ribbed basal leaves and blue, white, and lilac flowers: (without *cap*) any plant of the genus [After Austrian botanist N T. *Host*]

hostage *hos'tij, n.* one kept in the hands of an enemy as a pledge.—**hostages to fortune** the people and things one values most, of which the loss would be particularly painful. [O.Fr *hostage* (Fr *ôtage*)—L *obses, obsidis,* a hostage]

hostel *hos'tal, n* an inn: in some universities an extra-collegiate hall for students. a residence for students or for some class or society of persons, esp. one not run commercially. a youth hostel —*ns.* **hos'teler, hos'teller** keeper of a hostel: one who lives in, or uses, a hostel, **hos'telling** making sojourns in youth hostels; **hos'telry** an inn. [O.Fr. *hostel, hostellerie*—L *hospitâle.*]

hostess. See host[1].

hostile *hos'tīl,* in U S *-tal, adj.* pertaining to an enemy showing enmity or unfriendliness, or angry opposition resistant (to; esp. to new ideas, changes): (of place, conditions) inhospitable, harsh. engaged in hostilities. pertaining to hostilities.—*adv.* hos'tilely. —*n.* **hostility** (*-til'*) enmity:—*pl.* **hostil'ities** acts of warfare —**hostile witness** (*legal*) a witness who gives evidence against the party he/she was called by [L *hostilis—hostis.*]

hostler *hos'lar, n.* an ostler

hot *hot, adj* having a high temperature. very warm. fiery: pungent: giving a feeling suggestive of heat. animated: ardent violent: passionate: sexually excited: dangerously charged with electricity. dangerous: near the object sought. of news, fresh, exciting: of jazz, etc., music which is intensely played with complex rhythms and exciting improvisations: skilful (*coll.*): recently obtained dishonestly (*coll*): highly radioactive (*coll*) —*adv* hotly.—*v.t.* (*coll*) to heat —*adv* hot'ly.—*ns* hot'ness; hott'ie (*coll*) a hot-water bottle.—*adj* hott'ish.—**hot air** empty talk.— *adj* **hot'-air** making use of heated air.—**hot'bed** a glass-covered bed heated by a layer of fermenting manure for bringing forward plants rapidly: a place or conditions favourable to rapid growth or development, usu of a bad kind.—*adj* **hot'-blood'ed** having hot blood: homothermous: passionate: high-spirited. —**hot dog** a hot sausage sandwich, **hot favourite** in sports, races, etc., the most likely to win —*adv* **hot'foot** in haste (**hotfoot it** (*coll.*) to rush) —**hot gospeller** a loud, forceful proclaimer of a religious faith, **hot'head** an impetuous headstrong person.—

adj **hot'headed.—hot'house** a house kept hot for the rearing of tropical or tender plants: any heated chamber or drying-room, esp. that where pottery is placed before going into the kiln —*adj.* (*fig.*) (too) delicate, unable to exist in tough, or even normal, conditions. —**hot line** special telephone and teleprinter link with the Kremlin, orig one from Washington: any line of speedy communication ready for an emergency.—**hot metal** (*print*) used to describe machines or methods using type made from molten metal; **hot money** funds transferred suddenly from one country to another because conditions make transfer financially advantageous; **hot plate** the flat top surface of a stove for cooking: a similar plate, independently heated, for keeping things hot; **hot'pot** a dish of chopped mutton seasoned and stewed in a pot, with sliced potatoes, or similar mixture; **hot potato** see **potato; hot rod** a motor-car converted for speed by stripping off non-essentials and heightening in power, **hot seat** the electric chair (*U S slang*)· any uncomfortable situation (*fig*)—*adj.* hot'-short brittle when heated.— **hot'shot** a person who is (esp. showily) successful, skilful, etc., hot spot an area of (too) high temperature in an engine, etc.: a region of the earth where there is evidence of isolated volcanic activity; a nightclub (*coll*)· an area of potential trouble, esp. political (*fig.*): Hot'spur a violent, rash man like Henry Percy (1364–1403), so nicknamed; hot stuff (*slang*) any person, thing, or performance that is outstandingly remarkable, excellent, vigorous, or reprehensible —*adjs* hotted-up see hot up below; hot'· tem'pered having a quick temper.—hot water (*coll*) a state of trouble; hot well a spring of hot water· in a condensing engine, a reservoir for the warm water drawn off from the condenser —go, sell, like hot cakes to sell off or disappear promptly, hot-air balloon one containing air which is heated by a flame to maintain or increase altitude, hot cross-bun a bun bearing a cross, customarily eaten on Good Friday; hot on (*coll.*) fond of, interested in: good at, well-informed about, hot on the heels (of) (*coll.*) following, pursuing, closely; hot under the collar indignant, embarrassed, hot up (*coll*) to increase in excitement, energy, performance, etc (*adj* hott'ed-up'); hot-water bottle a container of hot water, used to warm a bed, make it hot for to make it unpleasant or impossible for [O E *hāt*]

hotchpotch *hoch'poch,* **hotchpot** *hoch'pot,* **hodge-podge** *hoj'poj, ns.* a confused mass of ingredients shaken or mixed together in the same pot· a kind of mutton-broth with vegetables of many kinds: a jumble —*n.* **hotchpot** a commixture of property in order to secure an equable division amongst children. [Fr. *hochepot—hocher,* to shake, and *pot,* a pot.]

hotel *hō-tel'* (old-fashioned *ō-tel'*), *n.* a house for the accommodation of strangers: an inn.—**hotelier** (*hō-tel'yər;* Fr *hôtelier; ōt-ə-lyā*) one who owns, runs a hotel; **hotel'-keeper.** [Fr *hôtel*—L. *hospitālia,* guest-chambers—*hospes*]

Hottentot *hot'n-tot, n.* one of a dwindling, nomad, pastoral, pale-brown-skinned race in S -W Africa. their language.—Also *adj.* [Du *imit* ; the language was unintelligible to them and sounded staccato.]

houdah. See **howdah.**

hound *hownd, n* a dog (*coll.*): a dog of a kind used in hunting: a contemptible scoundrel: a hunter, tracker, or assiduous seeker of anything· an addict, devotee— often in composition —*v t* to set on in chase: to drive by harassing.—**hound's'-tongue** a plant of the borage family (from its leaf); **hound's'-tooth** a textile pattern of broken checks.—*adj* —**master of hounds** the master of a pack of hounds; **ride to hounds** to hunt (on horseback). [O E. *hund.*]

For other sounds see detailed chart of pronunciation.

hour *owr, n.* 60 minutes, or the 24th part of the day the time as indicated by a clock, etc an hour's journey: a time or occasion· an angular unit (15°) of right ascension: (*in pl*) set times of prayer, the *canonical hours*, the offices or services prescribed for these, or a book containing them, often illustrated (also **book of hours**): (*pl*) the prescribed times for doing business —*adj* **hour'ly** happening or done every hour —*adv* every hour —**hour'-cir'cle** a great circle passing through the celestial poles· the circle of an equatorial which shows the right ascension; **hour'-glass** an instrument for measuring the hours by the running of sand through a narrow neck.—*adj* having the form of an hour-glass: constricted —**hour'-hand** the hand which shows the hour on a clock, etc —*adj.* and *adv.* **hour'long** lasting an hour —**at all hours** at irregular hours, esp late hours, **at the eleventh hour** at the last moment, **keep good hours** to go to bed and to rise early: to lead a quiet and regular life, **on the hour** at exactly one, two, etc o'clock [O.Fr *hore* (Fr *heure*) —L *hora*—Gr. *hōrā*]

houri *hōō'rı, how'rı, n.* a nymph of the Muslim paradise. a voluptuously alluring woman [Pers *hūri*— Ar *hūrıya*, a black-eyed girl]

house *hows, n.* a building for dwelling in: a building in general: a dwelling-place. an inn· a public-house a household: a family in line of descent. kindred a trading establishment. one of the twelve divisions of the heavens in astrology: a legislative or deliberative body or its meeting-place. a convent school boarding-house: pupils of such collectively· section of a school. an audience, auditorium, or performance: (**the House**) at Oxford, Christ Church, in London, the Stock Exchange, the Houses of Parliament.—*pl* **houses** (*howz'ız*).—*adj.* domestic —*v t.* **house** (*howz*) to protect by covering: to shelter: to store: to provide houses for.—*ns* **house'ful** (*pl* **house'fuls**), **housing** (*howz'ıng*) houses, accommodation, or shelter, or the provision thereof: a cavity into which a timber fits: anything designed to cover, protect, contain, etc. machinery or the like —Also *adj* —**house'- a'gent** one who arranges the buying, selling, and letting of houses; **house'-arrest'** confinement, under guard, to one's house, or to a hospital, etc , instead of imprisonment; **house'-boat** a barge with a deck-cabin that may serve as a dwelling-place; **house'-bote** a tenant's right to wood to repair his house.—*adj.* **house'- bound** confined to one's house because of illness, young children, etc.—**house'boy** a male domestic servant, usu African or Indian; **house'-breaker** one who breaks into and enters a house for the purpose of stealing: one whose work is demolishing old houses, **house'-breaking**; **house'-coat** a woman's long dress, formed like a coat, worn at home, **house'craft** skill in domestic activities, **house'-dog** a dog kept in a house: a watch-dog, **house'-fa'ther** the male head of a household or community a man in charge of children in an institution, **house'-flag** the distinguishing flag of a shipowner or shipping company; **house'-fly** the common fly universally distributed, **house guest** a guest in a private house; **house'hold** those who are held together in the same house, and compose a family.—*adj.* pertaining to the house and family. well-known to the general public, as in *household name, word.*—**house'holder** the holder or tenant of a house; **household gods** see **god**; **household troops** Guards regiments whose peculiar duty is to attend the sovereign and defend the metropolis; **household word** a familiar saying or name, **house'-husband** a married man who looks after the house and family and does not have a paid job; **house'keeper** a person employed to keep house: one who has the chief care of a house one who stays much at home, **house'keeping** the keep-

ing or management of a house or of domestic affairs: the money used for this —*adj* domestic —**house'- leek** a plant of the stonecrop family with succulent leaves, often growing on roofs, **house lights** (*theat.*) the lights illuminating the auditorium, **house'maid** a maid employed to keep a house clean, etc , **house-maid's knee** an inflammation of the sac between the knee-pan and the skin, to which those whose work involves frequent kneeling are specially liable; **house'-man** a recent graduate in medicine holding a junior resident post in a hospital; **house martin** a kind of black and white swallow with a slightly forked tail; **house'master** in schools, the head of a (boarding-)house, esp in connection with a public school (*fem* **house'mistress**), **house'-moth'er** a woman in charge of children in an institution, **house'-parent** a man or woman in charge of children in an institution; **house'-party** a company of guests spending some days in a country-house; **house plant** a plant that can be grown indoors as decoration.—*adj* **house'-proud** taking a pride in the condition of one's house.—**house'-room** room or place in a house (also *fig*); **house'-sur'geon** a resident surgeon in a hospital —so also **house'-physi'cian**.—*adj* **house'-to-house'** performed or conducted by calling at house after house —**house'top** the top or roof of a house —*adj* **house'-trained** of animals, taught to be cleanly indoors.—**house'-warming** an entertainment given after moving into a new house, **housewife** (*hows' wif*) the mistress and manager of a house a married woman who looks after the house and family and does not have a paid job (*huz'ıf*) a pocket sewing-outfit —*adj* **house'wifely**.—**housewifery** (*hows' wif-rı, -wif-rı*), **house'work** domestic work; **house'y-house'y** a game in which numbers are drawn at random and marked off on players' boards until one is clear—now usu called **bingo; housing estate** a planned residential area, esp. one built by a local authority, **hous'ing (joint)** a joint where the end of one board fits into a groove cut across another board; **housing scheme** a plan for the designing, building, and provision of houses, esp. by a local authority sometimes applied to an area coming under such a plan —**bring down the house** to evoke very loud applause in a place of entertainment; **full house** see **full'**; **house of cards** a situation, etc that is as unstable as a pile of playing cards, **house of correction** a jail, **house of God**, prayer or worship a place of worship; **house of ill-fame**, **ill repute** a brothel; **House of Commons, Lords, Peers, Representatives** see **common, lord, peer'**, **represent; House of Keys** see **Keys; keep a good house** to keep up a plentifully supplied table; **keep house** to maintain or manage an establishment, **keep open house** to give entertainment to all comers, **like a house on fire, afire** with astonishing rapidity; **on the house** of drinks, at the publican's expense: free, with no charge, **put, set, one's house in order** to settle one's affairs; **set up house** to start a domestic life of one's own; **the Household** the royal domestic establishment [O E *hūs*; Goth. *hūs*, Ger. *Haus.*]

housing' *howz'ıng, n* an ornamental covering for a horse· a saddle-cloth: (*in pl*) the trappings of a horse [O Fr *houce*, a mantle, of Gmc. origin]

housing². See **house.**

hove *pa.t.* and *pa p.* of **heave.**

hovel *hov'əl, huv'əl, n* a small or wretched dwelling: a shed.

hover *hov'ər, huv'ər, v ı.* to remain aloft flapping the wings. to remain suspended: to linger to move about near —*n.* act or state of hovering: in composition, describing vessels, vehicles, or stationary objects, resting on a cushion of air, e.g. **hov'ercraft** (a craft able to move at a short distance above the surface of sea or land supported by a down-driven blast of air); **hov'er-train, -bed** (which supports patient on film of warm air).—**hov'er-fly** a wasp-like fly that hovers and darts; **hov'erport** a port for hovercraft [Perh.—*hove*, to loiter]

how *how, adv* and *conj* in what manner: to what extent: by what means: in what condition: for what reason: to what an extent, in what a degree, that —*n* manner, method —**and how** (*U.S slang*) yes, certainly: very much indeed. I should think so indeed; **how about** what do you think of; **how are you** a conventional greeting to an acquaintance: sometimes specifically referring to his or her state of health, **how come** how does that come about; **how-do-you-do see do'**; **how now** what is this. why is this so; **how so** (*arch.*) how can this be so? why?, **how's that** (*how-zat'*, *cricket*) the appeal of the fielding side to the umpire to give the batsman out, **the how and the why** the manner and the cause. [O E *hū*, prob an adverbial form from *hwā*, who]

howbeit *how-bē'it, conj* be it how it may· notwithstanding· yet· however. [**how, be, it'.**]

howdah, houdah *how'da, n.* a pavilion or seat fixed on an elephant's back. [Ar *haudaj.*]

howdy *how'di, interj* a colloquial form of the common greeting. *How do you do?* —*n* **how'-d'ye-do', how'dy-do'** a troublesome state of matters.

however *how-ev'ar, adv* and *conj* in whatever manner or degree. nevertheless. at all events. [**how, ever.**]

howitzer *how'its-ar, n.* a short, squat gun, used for shelling at a steep angle, esp in siege and trench warfare. [Ger. *Haubitze*—Czech *houfnice*, a sling.]

howl *howl, v i.* to yell or cry, as a wolf or dog: to utter a long, loud, whining sound: to wail: to roar —*v.i* to utter with outcry:—*pr p*. **howl'ing;** *pa.t.* and *pa.p* **howled.**—*n.* a loud, prolonged cry of distress: a mournful cry: a loud sound like a yell, made by the wind. a wireless receiver, etc.—*n* **howl'er** one who howls: a S. American monkey, with prodigious power of voice: a glaring and amusing blunder (*coll.*) —*adj.* **howl'ing** tremendous (*coll.*). [O Fr *huller*—L. *ululāre*, to shriek or howl—*ulula*, an owl]

howsoever *how-sō-ev'ar, adv.* in what way soever· although: however [**how, so', ever;** and M E. *sum,* as.]

hoy' *hoi, n.* a large one-decked boat, commonly rigged as a sloop. [M.Du. *hoei*; Du. *heu*, Flem. *hui*]

hoy² *hoi, interj* ho! stop!

hoyden *hoi'dan, n.* a tomboy, a romp: formerly also *masc.*—*n.* **hoy'denism.**—*adj.* **hoy'denish.** [Perh Du. *heiden*, a heathen, a gypsy, *heide*, heath.]

huanaco. Same as **guanaco.**

hub *hub, n.* the nave of a wheel.—**hub'-cap** a metal covering over the end of an axle.—**hub of the universe.** [Prob a form of **hob',** place of most importance or interest]

hubble-bubble *hub'l-bub'l, n* a bubbling sound: tattle. confusion: a crude kind of hookah. [Redup from **bubble.**]

hubbub *hub'ub, n.* a confused sound of many voices· riot. uproar [App. of Irish origin.]

hubby *hub'i, (coll)* n a diminutive of **husband.**

hubris *hū'bris, n.* insolence: arrogance, such as invites disaster: overweening.—*adj* **hubris'tic.**—*adv* **hubris'tically.** [Gr. *hybris*.]

huckaback *huk'a-bak, n.* a coarse linen or cotton with raised surface, used for towels, etc

huckle *huk'l, n.* the haunch the hip.—*adjs.* **huck'le-backed** having the back round —**huckle'-bone** the hip-bone: the astragalus [Poss. conn. with **hook.**]

huckleberry *huk'l-bar-i, -ber-i, n.* a N. American shrub (*Gaylussacia*) akin to whortleberry: its fruit. [App for **hurtleberry.**]

huckster *huk'star, n.* a retailer of smallwares, a hawker or pedlar· a mean, haggling fellow.—*v.i.* to deal in small articles· to haggle meanly.

huddle *hud'l, v.t.* to jumble: to hustle, bundle: to drive, draw, throw or crowd together in disorder. to put hastily —*v i* to crowd in confusion.—*n* a confused mass: a jumble· confusion: a secret conference.—*adj* **hudd'led** jumbled crowded. crouching. [Poss. conn. with **hide'.**]

Hudibrastic *hū-di-bras'tik, adj.* similar in style to *Hudibras*, a metrical burlesque on the Puritans by Samuel Butler (1612–80).

hue' *hū, n.* appearance: colour tint: dye —*adjs.* **hued** having a hue. [O E. *hiow, hēow* (W S *hiw, hiew*).]

hue² *hū, n.* a shouting, clamour —**hue and cry** an outcry calling upon all to pursue one who is to be made prisoner (*hist.*): a proclamation or publication to the same effect (*hist*). the pursuit itself: a loud clamour about something. [Imit., perh. Fr *huer*]

huff *huf, n.* a fit of anger, sulks, or offended dignity· an act of huffing in draughts.—*v t* to give offence (in draughts) to remove from the board for omitting capture.—*v.t.* to take offence.—*adjs.* **huff'ish, huff'y** touchy: ready to take offence —*advs.* **huff'ishly, huff'ily.**—*ns.* **huff'ishness, huff'iness.**—**huffing and puffing** loud talk, noisy objections [Imit]

hug *hug, v.t.* to clasp close with the arms: to cherish: to keep close to, skirt.—*pr.p.* **hugg'ing;** *pa.t.* and *pa.p* **hugged.**—*n.* a close embrace: a particular grip in wrestling.—*adj.* **hugg'able.**—**hug'-me-tight** a close-fitting knitted garment.—**hug oneself** to congratulate oneself. [Ety obscure.]

huge *hūj, adj.* vast. enormous —*adv.* **huge'ly.**—**huge'ness.** [O.Fr *ahuge*]

hugger-mugger *hug'ar-mug'ar, n* secrecy. confusion.—*adj.* secret disorderly.—*adv* in secrecy or disorder.

Huguenot *hū'ga-not,* or *-nō, (hist.)* n a French Protestant.—Also *adj.* [Fr. —earlier *eiguenot*—Ger *Eidgenoss*, confederate]

huh *hu, interj* expressing disgust, disbelief, enquiry, etc [Imit.]

hula-hula *hōō'la-hōō'la, n.* a Hawaiian women's dance.—Also **hu'la.**—**hu'la-hoop** a light hoop used in the diversion of keeping the hoop in motion about the waist by a swinging movement of the hips [Hawaiian.]

hulk *hulk, n.* an unwieldy ship: a dismantled ship· a big lubberly fellow anything unwieldy:—*pl.* (with *the*) old ships formerly used as prisons.—*adjs.* **hulk'ing** big and clumsy. [O.E. *hulc*, perh Gr. *holkas*, a towed ship—*helkein*, to draw]

hull' *hull, n* a husk or outer covering.—*v.t.* to separate from the hull· to husk [O E. *hulu*, a husk, as of corn—*helan*, to cover]

hull² *hul, n* the frame or body of a ship: part of a flying-boat in contact with the water the heavily-armoured body of a tank.—*v.t.* to pierce the hull of.—*adv.* **hull'-down** so far away that the hull is below the horizon [Perh. same word as above]

hullabaloo *hul-a-ba-lōō', n.* an uproar. [Perh. **halloo**]

hullo *hu-lō', vb , n.* and *interj.* Same as **hallo.**

hum *hum, v i.* to make a sound like bees or that represented by *m.* to sing with closed lips without words or articulation: to pause in speaking and utter an inarticulate sound. to stammer through embarrassment. to be audibly astir: to have a strong, unpleasant smell (*slang*): to be busily active.—*v.t* to render by humming:—*pr p*. **humm'ing;** *pa.t* and *pa p* **hummed.**—*n* the noise of bees· a murmurous sound: an inarticulate murmur: the sound of humming.—**humm'ing-bird** any member of the tropical family Trochilidae, very small birds of brilliant plumage and rapid flight (from the humming sound of the wings); **humm'ing-top** a top that gives a humming sound as it spins —**hum and haw** (or **ha**) to make inarticulate sounds when at a loss to shilly-shally; **make things hum** to set things going briskly. [Imit ; cf. Ger *hummen*, *humsen*.]

hum² *hum*, *interj.* expressing doubt or reluctance to agree.

human-*hū'mən*, *adj.* belonging or pertaining to or of the nature of man or mankind· having the qualities of a man or the limitations of man: humane not invidiously superior· genial, kind.—*n* a human being —*adj* **humane** (*hū-mān'*) having the feelings proper to man: kind: tender· merciful. humanising, as *humane letters*, classical, elegant, polite —*adv* **humane'ly.**—*n.* **humane'ness.**—*v t* **humanise**, -**ize** (*hū'mən-īz*) to render human or humane: to soften to impart human qualities to, to make like that which is human or of mankind.—*ns* **humanisā'tion**, -**z**-; **hū'manist** at the Renaissance, a student of Greek and Roman literature: a student of human nature advocate of any system of humanism —Also *adj* —*n.* **hū'manism** literary culture: any system which puts human interests and the mind of man paramount, rejecting the supernatural, belief in a god, etc.—*adj* **humanist'ic.**—*n.* **hū'mankind** the human species — *adj* **hū'manlike.**—*adv.* **hū'manly** in a human manner· by human agency: having regard to human limitations· humanely.—*ns* **hū'manness; hū'manoid** one of the immediate kindred of man (closer than *anthropoid*): resembling, with the characteristics of, a human being —**human being** any member of the human race· a person, **humane society** a society promoting humane behaviour, usu to animals; **human interest** in newspaper articles, broadcasts, etc , reference to people's lives and emotions, **human nature** the nature of man· the qualities of character common to all men that differentiate them from other species· irrational, or, less than saintly, behaviour (often *facet*), **human rights** the right each human being has to personal freedom, justice, etc [Fr *humain*—L *hūmānus*—*homō*, a human being]

humanity *hū-man'it-i*, *n* the nature peculiar to a human being· humanness humaneness· the kind feelings of man: mankind collectively in Scottish universities, Latin language and literature (in *pl*) grammar, rhetoric, Latin, Greek and poetry, so called from their humanising effects —*n* **humanitarian** (*hū-man'i-tā'ri-ən*)· a philanthropist —*adj* of or belonging to humanity, benevolent —*n* **humanitā'rianism.** [Fr. *humanité*—L *hūmānitās*—*hūmānus* —*homō*, a man]

humble *hum'bl* (old-fashioned *um'bl*), *adj.* low: lowly. modest: unpretentious: having a low opinion of oneself or of one's claims abased —*v t* to bring down to the ground: to lower to abase to mortify· to degrade.—*n.* **hum'bleness** —*adv* **hum'bly.**—**your humble servant** an old formula used in subscribing a letter [Fr.,—L *humilis*, low—*humus*, the ground] **humble-bee** *hum'bl-bē*, *n* the bumble-bee (*Bombus*) [Perh from *humble*, freq. of **hum'.**] **humbles** see **umbles.**—**hum'ble-pie'** a pie made from the umbles of a deer.—**eat humble-pie** punningly. to humble, abase oneself, eat one's words, etc

humbug *hum'bug*, *n* an imposition under fair pretences: hollowness, pretence: one who so imposes a lump of toffee, peppermint drop, or the like —*v t* to deceive. to hoax to cajole —*pr p* **hum'bugging;** *pa.t.* and *pa.p* **hum'bugged.**—*n* **hum'buggery.** [Appears about 1750.]

humdinger *hum-ding'ər*, (*slang*) *n* an exceptionally excellent person or thing [Prob **hum¹** and *ding*, to beat.]

humdrum *hum'drum'*, *adj* dull· droning· monotonous commonplace.—*n* a stupid fellow· monotony tedious talk [**hum¹** and perh **drum¹**.]

Humean, Humian *hū'mi-ən*, *adj* pertaining to David *Hume*, or his philosophy —*n* a follower of Hume

humect *hū-mekt'*, *v t* and *v i* to make or become moist —*adj.* and *n* **humect'ant.** [L (*h*)*umectāre*—*ūmēre*, to be moist]

humerus *hū'mər-əs*, *n* the bone of the upper arm:—*pl.* **hū'meri.**—*adj* **hū'meral** belonging to the shoulder or the humerus [L. (*h*)*umerus*, shoulder]

humic. See under **humus.**

humid *hū'mid*, *adj.* moist· damp· rather wet —*ns* **humidificā'tion; humid'ifier** a device for increasing or maintaining humidity —*v t* **humid'ify** to make humid —*n.* **humid'ity** moisture: a moderate degree of wetness.—*adv* **hu'midly.**—*ns* **hu'midness; hum'idor** a chamber, etc , for keeping anything moist, as cigars [L (*h*)*ūmidus*—(*h*)*ūmēre*, to be moist]

humify *hū'mi-fī*, *v t.* and *v i* to make or turn into humus —*n* **humificā'tion.** [**humus.**]

humiliate *hū-mil'i-āt*, *v t* to humble· to mortify —*n* **humiliā'tion.** [L *humiliāre*, -*ātum*]

humility *hū-mil'i-ti*, *n* the state or quality of being humble· lowliness of mind modesty [O.Fr *humilite*—L *humilitās*—*humilis*, low]

hummock *hum'ək*, *n* a hillock a pile or ridge of ice — *adjs* **humm'ocked, humm'ocky.** [Origin unknown. at first nautical.]

hummus *hum'əs*, *hoo'məs*, *n* a Middle Eastern hors d'oeuvre of puréed chick-peas and sesame oil with garlic and lemon [Turk]

humour, in U S **humor**, *hū'mər*, *ū'mər*, *n* moisture (*arch*) a fluid. a fluid of the animal body, esp formerly any one of the four that in old physiology were held to determine temperament temperament or disposition of mind· state of mind (*good, ill humour*) disposition. caprice a mental quality which apprehends and delights in the ludicrous and mirthful that which causes mirth and amusement· playful fancy —*v t* to go along with the humour of· to gratify by compliance —*adj* **hū'moral** (*arch*) pertaining to a body fluid —*ns* **hūmoresque'** a musical caprice, **hū'morist** one who studies or portrays the humours of people one possessed of humour· a writer of comic stories —*adjs* **hūmoris'tic** humorous, **hū'morous** full of humour exciting laughter —*adv* **hū'morously.** —*n* **hū'morousness.**—*adj* **hū'mourless.**—**out of humour** out of temper, displeased [O Fr *humor* (Fr *humeur*)—L (*h*)*ūmor*—(*h*)*ūmēre*, to be moist]

humous. See under **humus.**

hump *hump*, *n* a hunch on the back· a protuberance: despondency (*slang*) —*v t* to bend in a hump· to exert oneself (*slang*) to vex or annoy (*slang*) to shoulder, to carry on the back —*v i* to put forth effort to have sexual intercourse (also *v i*) (*slang*) —*adj* **hump'y.**—**hump'back** a back with a hump or hunch a person with a humpback a whale with a humplike dorsal fin —*adjs* **hump'-back, hump's-backed** having a humpback —**over the hump** past the crisis or difficulty

humph *hmh, huh, hmf, interj* expressive of reserved doubt or dissatisfaction.

humpty *hum(p)'ti*, *n* a low padded seat

Humpty-dumpty *hum(p)'ti-dum(p)'ti*, *n* a short, squat, egg-like being of nursery folklore

humpy¹ *hum'pi*, (*Austr*) *n* an ·Aboriginal hut [Native *oompi*]

humpy². See **hump.**

humus *hūm'əs*, *n.* decomposed organic matter in the soil —*adjs* **hū'mic, hū'mous.** [L *humus*, cf Gr *chamai*, on the ground]

Hun *hun, n.* one of a powerful and savage nomad race of Asia who moved westwards, and under Attila (433–453) overran Europe: in U.S. formerly a Hungarian. a barbarian: a German (*slang*).—*adj.* **Hunn'-ish.** [O.E. (pl.) *Hūne, Hūnas.*]

hunch *hunch, hunsh, n.* a hump. a premonition: an intuitive feeling.—*v.t.* to hump, bend.—**hunch'back** one with a hunch on his back.—*adj.* **hunch'backed.**

hundred *hun'drəd, n.* the number of ten times ten. applied also to various other numbers used in telling: a set of a hundred things: a hundred pounds, dollars, etc.: (in *pl*) an unspecified large number: a division of a county in England orig. supposed to contain a hundred families (chiefly *hist.*):—*pl.* **hundreds** or, preceded by a numeral, **hundred.**—*adj.* to the number of a hundred: also used indefinitely, very many (*coll.*).—*adj., adv.,* and *n.* **hun'dredfold** a hundred times as much.—*adj.* **hun'dredth** last of a hundred: next after the ninety-ninth: equal to one of a hundred equal parts.—*n.* one of a hundred equal parts: a person or thing in hundredth position.—*adj.* **hun'dred-per-cent'** out-and-out: thorough-going (**not a hundred-per-cent** not in perfect health).—*n.pl.* **hun'dreds-and-thou'sands** little sweets used as an ornamental dressing.—**hun'dredweight** 1/20 of a ton, or 112 lb. avoirdupois (50·80 kg.; **long hundredweight**) orig. and still in U.S., 100 lb. (**short hundredweight**), 50 kg. (**metric hundredweight**), abbrev. *cwt.* (*c* standing for L. *centum, wt.* for weight).—**great** or **long hundred** usually six score: sometimes some other number greater than ten tens (as of herrings, 132 or 126): **not a hundred miles from** at, very near, **one, two,** etc. **hundred hours** one, two, etc., o'clock, from the method of writing hours and minutes 1.00, 2.00, etc. [O.E. *hundred*—old form *hund,* a hundred, with the suffix *-red,* a reckoning.]

hung *pa.t.* and *pa.p.* of **hang.**

Hungarian *hung-gā'ri-ən, adj.* pertaining to Hungary or its inhabitants —*n.* a person of Hungarian birth, descent, or citizenship: the Magyar or Hungarian language.

hunger *hung'gər, n* craving for food: need or lack of food: strong desire for anything.—*v i.* to crave food: to long.—*adv.* **hung'rily.**—*adj* **hung'ry** having eager desire for food (or anything else): greedy (with *for*): lean. poor.—in composition, eager for, in need of (as *land-hungry*).—**hunger march** a procession of unemployed or others in need, as a demonstration; **hunger'-marcher; hunger strike** prolonged refusal of all food by a prisoner, etc. as a form of protest, or a means to ensure release.—*v.i.* **hung'er-strike.**—**hung'er-striker.**—**go hungry** to remain without food. [O.E. *hungor* (n.), *hyngran* (vb.); cf. Ger *Hunger,* Du *honger,* etc]

hung over, hung up, etc. See under **hang.**

hunk¹ *hungk, n.* a lump· a strong or sexually attractive man (*coll*). [Same as **hunch.**]

hunk² *hungk,* (*U.S.*) *n.* goal or base in boys' games.—*adjs.* **hunk'y, hunk'y-do'ry** in good position or condition: all right. [Du. *honk*]

hunker *hungk'ər, v.i.* to squat down —*n.pl.* **hunk'ers** the hams. [Perh conn. with O.N *hūka,* to squat.]

hunky¹ *hungk'i,* (*U.S.*) *n.* a derogatory name for an unskilled workman, orig for one of East European descent [For **Hungarian.**]

hunky². See **hunk².**

hunt *hunt, v.t.* to chase or go in quest of for prey or sport: to seek or pursue game over. to ransack: to use in the hunt: to search for to pursue: to hound, drive —*v.i.* to go out in pursuit of game: to search: to oscillate or vary in speed (*mech.*).—*n.* a chase of wild animals: search: a pack of hunting hounds an association of huntsmen· the district hunted by a pack —*ns.*

hunt'er one who hunts:—*fem.* **hunt'ress;** a horse used in the chase: a watch whose face is protected with a metal case (a **half-hunter** if that case has a small circle of glass let in).—**hunt ball** a ball given by the members of a hunt, **hun'ter's-moon'** full moon following harvest-moon; **hunt'ing-box, -lodge** a temporary abode for hunting; **hunt'ing-cog** an extra cog in one of two geared wheels, by means of which the order of contact of cogs is changed at every revolution; **hunt'ing-horn** a horn used in hunting. a bugle; **hunt'ing-song** a song about hunting; **hunts'man** one who hunts: one who manages the hounds during the chase —**hunt'-the-slipp'er** a game in which one in the middle of a ring tries to catch a shoe passed around by the others.—*interj.* **good hunting!** good luck! (*coll.*). —**hunt after, for** to search for; **hunt down** to pursue to extremities: to persecute out of existence; **hunt out** or **up** to seek out. [O E. *huntian.*]

Huon-pine *hū'ən-pīn', n.* a Tasmanian conifer found first on the *Huon* river.

hurdle *hûr'dl, n.* a frame of twigs or sticks interlaced: a movable frame of timber or iron for gates, etc.: in certain races, a portable barrier over which runners jump: a rude sledge on which criminals were drawn to the gallows (*hist.*): an obstacle (*fig.*).—*v.t* to enclose with hurdles.—*n.* **hurd'ler** a maker of hurdles: a hurdle-racer. [O.E. *hyrdel;* Ger. *Hurde.*]

hurdy-gurdy *hûr'di-gûr'di, n.* a musical stringed instrument, whose strings are sounded by the turning of a wheel: a barrel-organ. [Imit.]

hurl *hûrl, v.t.* to fling with violence.—*v.i.* to play hurley.—*n.* act of hurling.—*ns.* **hurl'ey, hurl'ing** a game similar to hockey, of Irish origin, played by teams of 15, with broad-bladed sticks (**hurl'eys**) and a hide-covered cork ball. [Cf. L G *hurreln,* to hurl, precipitate; influenced by **hurtle** and **whirl.**]

hurly *hûr'li,* **hurly-burly** *hûr'li-bûr'li, ns.* tumult: confusion. [Perh. from **hurl.**]

hurrah, hurra *hŏŏr-a', hur-a',* **hurray** *-ā', interjs* an exclamation of approbation or joy.—Also *n.* and *v i.* [Cf. Norw , Sw., Dan. *hurra,* Ger *hurrah,* Du. *hoera.*]

hurricane *hur'i-kin, -kān, n.* a West Indian cyclonic storm of great violence: a wind of extreme violence: anything tempestuous (*fig.*): (*cap.*) a type of fighting aeroplane used in World War II.—**hurr'icane-lamp** an oil lamp encased so as to defy strong wind: also a protected electric lamp [Sp. *huracán,* from Carib.]

hurry *hur'i, v.t.* to urge forward: to hasten.—*v.i.* to move or act with haste, esp. perturbed or impatient haste:—*pr.p.* **hurr'ying;** *pa.t.* and *pa.p.* **hurr'ied.**—*n.* a driving forward: haste: flurried or undue haste. commotion: a rush: need for haste.—*adj.* **hurr'ied.**—*adv* **hurr'iedly.**—*n* **hurr'iedness.**—**hurr'y-scurr'y** confusion and bustle.—*adv* confusedly.—**in a hurry** in haste. speedily: soon: willingly; **hurry up** to make haste [Prob. imit ; cf. Old Sw. *hurra,* to whirl round.]

hurst *hûrst, n* a wood, a grove: a sand bank [O.E *hyrst*]

hurt *hûrt, v t.* to cause pain to: to damage: to injure: to wound, as the feelings.—*v.i.* to give pain. to be the seat of pain: to be injured:—*pa t.* and *pa.p.* **hurt.**—*n.* a wound: injury.—*adj.* injured: pained in body or mind.—*adj* **hurt'ful** causing hurt or loss: harmful —*adv.* **hurt'fully.**—*n.* **hurt'fulness.** [O.Fr *hurter* (Fr. *heurter*), to knock, to run against.]

hurtle *hûrt'l, v.t.* to dash: to hurl —*v.i.* to move rapidly with a clattering sound [Freq of **hurt** in its original sense.]

husband *huz'bənd, n* a man to whom a woman is married —*v t.* to manage with economy: to conserve.— *n.* **hus'bandage** allowance or commission of a ship's husband —*n* hus'bandry the business of a farmer tillage economical management thrift —hus'-bandman a working farmer one who labours in tillage —ship's husband an owner's agent who manages the affairs of a ship in port [O E *húsbonda*, O N *húsbōndi*—*hús*, a house, *búandi*, inhabiting, pr p of O N. *búa*, to dwell]

hush hush, *interj* or *imper* silence be still —*n* a silence, esp after noise.—*adj* for the purpose of concealing information (e.g *hush money*)—*v t* to become silent or quiet —*v t* to make quiet, to calm to procure silence or secrecy about (sometimes with *up*).—*n* hush'aby a lullaby used to soothe babies to sleep —Also *interj* —*adj* hush'-hush, hush'y (*coll*) secret —hush up to stifle, suppress: to be silent [imit]

husk husk, *n* the dry, thin covering of certain fruits and seeds, a case, shell, or covering, esp one that is worthless or coarse (in *pl*) refuse, waste —*v t* to remove the husk or outer integument from —*adv* husk'ily.—*ns.* husk'iness.—*adj* husk'y of the nature of husks: like a husk dry sturdy like a corn-husk with a dry, almost whispering voice [Perh conn with house.]

husky[1] hus'ki See husk.

husky[2] hus'ki, *n* an Eskimo sledge-dog: an Eskimo the Eskimo language [App —*Eskimo*]

hussar hə-, hōō-zar', *n* a soldier of a light cavalry regiment: orig a soldier of the national cavalry of Hungary in the 15th century [Hung *huszar*, through Old Serb.—It *corsaro*, a freebooter]

Hussite hus'it, hōōs'it, *n* a follower of the Bohemian reformer John *Hus*, martyred in 1415

hussy hus'i, huz'i, *n* a pert girl: a worthless wench [housewife.]

hustings hus'tingz, *n sing.* formerly the booths where the votes were taken at an election of an M P , or the platform from which the candidates gave their addresses. electioneering [O.E *hústing*, a council —O.N *hústhing*—*hús*, a house, *thing*, an assembly]

hustle hus'l, *v t.* to shake or push together to crowd with violence to jostle to thrust hastily to exert pressure on to obtain (money) illicitly (*slang*) —*v t* to act strenuously or aggressively to earn money illicitly (as a prostitute, *slang*) —*n* frenzied activity —*n.* hus'tler an energetic fellow a swindler (*slang*)· a prostitute (*slang*) [Du *hutselen*, to shake to and fro]

hut hut, *n.* a small or mean house a small temporary dwelling or similar structure —*v t* to quarter in or furnish with a hut or huts —*v t* to dwell in a hut or huts:—*pr p* hutt'ing; *pa t* and *pa p* hutt'ed.—*n* hut'ment an encampment of huts —hut'-cir'cle (*ant*) the remains of a prehistoric circular hut, a pit lined with stones, etc [Fr *hutte*—O H G *hutta*]

hutch huch, *n* a coop for rabbits a small, cramped house (*coll*): a trough used with some ore-dressing machines a low wagon in which coal is drawn up out of the pit [Fr *huche*, a chest—L L *hútica*, a box, prob Gmc]

Hutchinsonian huch-in-sōn'i-ən, *n* a follower of John *Hutchinson* (1674–1737), who held that the Hebrew Scriptures contain typically the elements of all rational philosophy, natural history, and true religion

huzza hōōz-a', huz-a', *interj* and *n* hurrah a shout of joy or approbation —*v t* to attend with shouts of joy —*v t* to utter shouts of joy or acclamation :—*pr p* huzza'ing; *pa t* and *pa p* huzzaed, huzza'd (-zad') [Perh Ger *hussa*]

hyacinth hi'ə-sinth, *n* a flower that sprang from the blood of Hyacinthus, a youth accidentally killed by Apollo (*myth*) a bulbous genus (*Hyacinthus*) of the lily family, much cultivated extended to others of the family, as wild hyacinth (the English bluebell), grape hyacinth (*Muscari*) a blue stone of the ancients (perh aquamarine) a red, brown, or yellow zircon: a purple colour, of various hues —*adj* hyacin'thine. [Gr *hyakinthos*, a species of larkspur, a blue stone]

Hyades hi'ə-dēz, Hyads hi'adz, *ns pl* a cluster of five stars in the constellation of the Bull, supposed by the ancients to bring rain when they rose with the sun [Gr *Hyâdēs, Hyádēs*, explained by the ancients as from *hyein*, to rain; more prob little pigs, *hys*, a pig]

hyaena. See hyena.

hyaline hi'ə-lin, -līn, *adj* of or like glass clear· transparent —*n* hyalinisa'tion, -z-.—*v t*, *v t* hy'alinise, -ize (*med*) of tissue, to change to a firm, glassy consistency —*n* hy'alite transparent colourless opal —*adj.* hy'aloid (*anat*) hyaline, transparent.—hyaline degeneration hyalinisation; hyaloid membrane the transparent membrane which encloses the vitreous humour of the eye [Gr *hyalos*, glass]

hybrid hi'brid, *n* an organism which is the offspring of a union between different races, species, genera or varieties a mongrel: a word formed of elements from different languages —*adj* produced from different species, etc. mongrel —*adj* hybridis'able, -z-.—*n* hybridisa'tion, -z-.—*v t* hy'bridise, -ize to cause to interbreed —*v t* to interbreed —*n* hy'bridism.—hybrid bill a public bill which affects certain private interests, hybrid computer one which combines features of digital and analog computers; hybrid vigour heterosis [L *hibrida*, offspring of a tame sow and wild boar; with associations of Gr *hybris*, insolence, overweening]

hydatid hi'də-tid, *n* a water cyst or vesicle in an animal body, esp one containing a tapeworm larva· the larva itself —*adj* hydatid'iform resembling a hydatid [Gr *hydatis*, -*idos*, a watery vesicle—*hydōr, hydatos*, water.]

hydr-. See hydro-.

Hydra hi'drə, *n* a water-monster with many heads, which when cut off were succeeded by others (*myth*.): a large southern constellation (without *cap*) any manifold evil (without *cap*) a freshwater hydrozoon remarkable for power of multiplication on being cut or divided [Gr *hydrā—hydōr*, water, akin to Sans *udra*, an otter.]

Hydrangea. See hydro-.

hydrate, hydraulic, etc See hydro-.

hydrazine hi'drə-zēn, *n* a fuming corrosive liquid used as a rocket fuel any of a class of organic bases derived from it [From hydr-, azo-.]

hydro hi'drō Short form of hydroelectric or hydropathic establishment (see under hydro-)·—*pl* hy'dros.

hydro- hi'drō'-, -dro'-, hydr- in composition, of, like, by means of, water (see also hydrogen).—*ns* Hydrangea (hi-drān'jə, -jyə, Gr *angeion*, vessel) a genus of shrubby plants with large globular clusters of showy flowers, natives of China and Japan (without *cap*) a plant of this genus, hydrant (hi'drənt) a connection for attaching a hose to a water-main or a fire-plug; hy'drate a compound containing water which is chemically combined and which can be expelled without affecting the composition of the other substance —*v t* to combine with water to cause to absorb water —*n* hydra'tion.—*adj* hydraulic (hi-drol'ik, -drol', Gr *aulos*, a pipe) relating to hydraulics· conveying water worked by water or other liquid in pipes setting in water —*adv* hydraul'ically.—*n sing* hydraul'ics the science of hydrodynamics in general, or its practical application to water-pipes, etc —*adj* hy'dric pertaining to an abundance of moisture see under hydrogen.—hy'drocele (-*sēl*, Gr *kělě*, a swelling, *med*) a swelling containing serous fluid, esp in the scrotum, **hydrocephalus** (-*sef'ə-ləs*, or -*kef'*; Gr *kephalě*, head) an accumulation of serous fluid within the cranial cavity —*adjs* **hydrocephal'ic, hydroceph'alous; hydrodynamic** (-*dīn-am'ik*, Gr *dynamis*, power), **-al.**—*n.* **hydrodynam'icist.**—*n sing* **hydrodynam'ics** the science of the motions and equilibrium of a material system partly or wholly fluid (called *hydrostatics* when the system is in equilibrium, *hydrokinetics* when it is not).—*adjs.* **hydroelast'ic see hydroelastic suspension** below, **hydroelec'tric.**—*ns* **hydroelectric'ity** electricity produced by means of water, esp by water-power, **hy'drofoil** a device on a boat for raising it from the water as its speed increases a boat fitted with this device; **hydrog'rapher** (Gr *graphein*, to write) —*adjs.* **hydrographic** (-*graf'ik*), **-al.** —*adv* **hydrograph'ically.**—*n* **hydrog'raphy** the investigation of seas and other bodies of water, including charting, sounding, study of tides, currents, etc —*adj* **hy'droid** like a Hydra: polypoid —*n* a hydrozoan: a hydrozoan in its asexual generation —*n sing.* **hydrokinet'ics** a branch of *hydrodynamics* (q v) —*adjs* **hydrolog'ic, -al.**—*ns.* **hydrol'ogist; hydrol'ogy** the study of water resources in land areas of the world— (*U.S.*) esp. underground water —*v t* **hydrolyse, -yze** (*hī'drō-līz*) to subject to hydrolysis.—Also *v.i* —*ns* **hydrolysis** (*hī-drol'i-sis*; Gr. *lysis*, loosing) chemical decomposition or ionic dissociation caused by water, **hy'drolyte** (-*līt*) a body subjected to hydrolysis —*adjs* **hydrolytic** (-*lit'ik*), **hydromagnet'ic.**—*n sing* **hydromagnet'ics** magneto-hydrodynamics —*n.* **hydromā'nia** a craving for water —*n sing.* **hydromechan'ics** hydrodynamics —*ns.* **hy'dromel** (Gr *hydromeli-meli*, honey) a beverage made of honey and water, **hydrom'eter** (Gr. *metron*, a measure) a float for measuring specific gravity.—*adjs* **hydrometric** (-*met'*), **-al.** —*ns.* **hydrom'etry; hy'dronaut** a person trained to work in an underwater vessel, e g. a submarine, **hydrop'athy** the treatment of disease by water, externally and internally —*adj* **hydropathic** (*hī-drō- path'ik*, Gr. *pathos*, suffering) of, for, relating to, practising, hydropathy —*n* (in full **hydropathic establishment;** *coll* **hy'dro**) a hotel (with special baths, etc.) where guests can have hydropathic treatment —*adv* **hydropath'ically.**—*ns.* **hydrop'athist** one who practises hydropathy, **hydrophane** (*hī'drō-fān*; Gr *phānos*, bright) a translucent opal transparent in water.—*adj* **hydrophil'ic** (*chem*) attracting water —*n* **hydrophō'bia** (Gr. *phobos*, fear) horror of water: inability to swallow water owing to a contraction in the throat, a symptom of rabies: rabies itself —*adjs* **hydrophō'bic** (or -*fob'*) pertaining to hydrophobia: repelling water (*chem.*).—*ns* **hy'drophone** (-*fōn*; Gr *phōnē*, voice) an apparatus for listening to sounds conveyed by water, **hy'drophyte** (-*fīt*, Gr *phyton*, plant) a plant growing in water or in very moist conditions —*adj* **hydrophytic** (-*fit'ik*) —*n* **hy'droplane** a light, flat-bottomed motor-boat which, at high speed, skims along the surface of the water. a seaplane.—*v.i* of a boat, to skim like a hydroplane of a vehicle, to skid on a wet road —*adj* **hydropneumat'ic** using water and air acting together —*n. sing* **hydroponics** (*hī-drō-pon'iks*, Gr. *ponos*, toil) the art or practice of growing plants in a chemical solution without soil —*ns* **hy'dropower** hydroelectric power, **hydroquinone** (-*kwin-ōn'*, or *kwin'*, or -*kwīn'*) quinol, **hydrosphere** (*hī'drō-sfēr*, Gr *sphaira*, sphere) the water on the surface of the earth—the seas and oceans —*adjs* **hydrostat'ic, hydrostat'ical.**—*adv* **hydrostat'ically.**—*n sing* **hydrostat'ics** a branch of *hydrodynamics* (q v) — **hydrother'apy, hydrotherapeu'tics** treatment of disease by the external use of water, e.g. treatment of disability by developing movement in water —*adjs*

hydrotherapeu'tic; hydrotrop'ic.—*n* **hydrot'ropism** (Gr. *tropos*, a turn) the turning of an organ towards (*positive*) or away from (*negative*) moisture —*adj* **hydrous** (-*hī'drəs, chem , min*) containing water — *n pl* **Hydrozō'a** (Gr *zōion*, an animal) a class of Coelenterata, chiefly marine organisms in which alternation of generations typically occurs, the hydroid phase colonial, giving rise to the medusoid phase by budding—the zoophytes, etc sometimes extended to include the true jellyfishes —*sing* **hydrozō'on.**—*n* and *adj* **hydrozō'an.**—**hydraulic brake** a brake in which the force is transmitted by means of a compressed fluid, **hydraulic press** a press operated by forcing water into a cylinder in which a ram or plunger works, **hydraulic ram** a device whereby the pressure head produced when a moving column of water is brought to rest is caused to deliver some of the water under pressure, **hydraulic suspension** a system of car suspension using hydraulic units, **hydroelastic suspension** a system of car suspension in which a fluid provides interconnection between the front and rear suspension units, **hydrostatic paradox** the principle that—disregarding molecular forces—any quantity of fluid, however small, may balance any weight, however great, **hydrostatic press** a hydraulic press [Gr *hydōr*, water]

hydrogen *hī'drō-jən, n.* a gas (symbol H, atomic number 1) which in combination with oxygen produces water, the lightest of all known substances, and very inflammable, of great importance in the moderation (slowing down) of neutrons.—*adj.* **hy'dric** of or containing hydrogen —*n.* **hy'dride** a compound of hydrogen with an element or radical.—*adjs* **hydriodic** (*hī-dri-od'ik*) of an acid composed of hydrogen and iodine, **hydrobrō'mic** applied to an acid composed of hydrogen and bromine, **hydrogen bromide** —*n* **hydrocar'bon** a compound of hydrogen and carbon with nothing else, occurring notably in oil, natural gas and coal —*adj* **hydrochloric** (-*klor'ik, -klôr', -klor'*) applied to an acid composed of hydrogen and chlorine, **hydrogen chloride**, still sometimes called *muriatic acid*.—*ns* **hydrochlor'ide** a compound of hydrochloric acid with an organic base, **hydrocor'tisone** one of the corticosteroids, a synthesised form of which is used to treat rheumatoid arthritis, etc —*adjs* **hydrocyanic** (-*sī-an'ik*) denoting an acid (*prussic acid*) composed of hydrogen and cyanogen; **hydrofluor'ic** applied to an acid composed of fluorine and hydrogen, **hydrogen fluoride** —*v t* **hydrogenate** (*hī'drō-jən-āt* or *hī-droj'ən-āt*) to cause to combine with hydrogen.—*n* **hydrogenā'tion.**—*adj* **hydrog'enous.**—*ns* **hydrosul'phide** a compound formed by action of hydrogen sulphide on a hydroxide, **hydrosul'phite** a hyposulphite (esp sodium hyposulphite) —*adj* **hydrosulphū'ric** formed by a combination of hydrogen and sulphur —*n* **hydrox'ide** a chemical compound which contains one or more hydroxyl groups —*adj* **hydrox'y** of a compound, contain- ing one or more hydroxyl groups (also *pfx* **hydrox'y-**) —*ns* **hydrox'yl** (Gr *hýlē*, matter) a compound radical consisting of one atom of oxygen and one of hydrogen —**hydrogen bomb**, or **H-bomb**, a bomb in which an enormous release of energy is achieved by converting hydrogen nuclei into helium nuclei—a fusion, not fission, process started by great heat, **hydrogen ion** an atom or molecule of hydrogen having a positive charge, esp an atom formed in a solution of acid in water—strong acids being highly ionised and weak acids only slightly, **hydrogen peroxide** see *peroxide*.—**heavy hydrogen** see *heavy* [Coined by Cavendish (1766) from Gr *hydōr*, water, and *gennaein*, to produce]

hyena, hyaena *hī-ē'nə, n* a carrion-feeding carnivore (genus *Hyae'na*, constituting a family **Hyae'nidae**)

with long thick neck, coarse mane and sloping body
—**hyena dog**, an African wild dog, blotched like a
hyena; **spotted hyena** an animal (*Crocuta*) resembling
a hyena, with a hysterical-sounding laugh [L
hyaena—Gr *hyaina*—*hȳs*, a pig]
hyetal *hī′t-ll, adj* pertaining to rain or rainfall [Gr
hȳetos, rain]
hygiene *hī′jēn, n* the science or art of preserving
health. sanitary principles —*adj* **hygienic** (*hī-jēn′ik*)
—*adv.* **hygien′ically.**—*n. sing* **hygien′ics** principles
of hygiene —*n* **hygienist** (*hī′jēn-ist*) one skilled in
hygiene [Fr *hygiène*—Gr *hygieinē* (*technē*).
hygienic (art)—*hygietā*, health. *hygiēs*, healthy]
hygro- *hī′grō-, -gro′*, in composition. wet. moist —*ns*
hygrol′ogy the study of the humidity of the air or
other gases, **hygrom′eter** an instrument for measuring the humidity of the air or of other gases —*adjs*
hygrometric (*-met′rik*), **-al** belonging to hygrometry
hygroscopic —*n.* **hygrom′etry** measurement of the
humidity of the air or of other gases.—*adjs*
hy′grophil, hygrophilous (*-grof′*, Gr *phileein*, to
love) moisture-loving: living where there is much
moisture.—*n* **hy′grophyte** (*-fīt*, Gr *phyton*, plant) a
plant adapted to plentiful water-supply —*adj.*
hygrophytic (*-fit′ik*)—*n* **hy′groscope** an instrument
that shows, without measuring, changes in the humidity of the air —*adjs* **hygroscopic** (*-skop′ik*), **-al** relating to the hygroscope. readily absorbing moisture
from the air· indicating or caused by absorption or
loss of moisture, as some movements of plants —*n*
hygroscopicity (*-skop-is′i-ti*) [Gr *hygros*, wet]
hylic *hī′lik, adj* material corporeal.—*adj* **hylomor′-
phic.**—*ns* **hylomor′phism** (*philos.*) the doctrine that
matter is the first cause of the universe, **hy′lotheism**
(Gr *theos*, god) the doctrine that there is no God but
matter and the universe, **hy′lotheist.**—*ns* **hylozo′ism**
(Gr *zōē*, life) the doctrine that all matter is endowed
with life, **hylozo′ist.** [Gr *hylikos*, material—*hȳlē*.
wood, matter]
Hymen *hī′men, n* the god of marriage (*myth*) marriage (*arch*) —*adj* **hymenē′al** —*n* wedding hymn
(in *pl.*) nuptials (*arch*) [Gr wedding-cry. perh
also a god]
hymen *hī′men, n* a thin membrane partially closing
the virginal vagina —*adj* **hy′menal.**—*n pl*
Hymenop′tera an order of insects with four transparent wings—ants, bees, wasps, etc —*n* and
adj **hymenop′teran.**—*adj.* **hymenop′terous.** [Gr
hymēn, membrane]
hymn *him, n* a song of praise —*v t* to celebrate in
song to worship by hymns —*v.i* to sing in adoration
—*pr.p* **hymning** (*him′ing*), *pa t* and *pa p* **hymned**
(*himd*) —*ns* **hym′nal** (*him′nəl*), **hym′nary** (*-nə-ri*) a
hymn-book —*adj* **hym′nic.**—*ns* **hym′nist;** **hym′-
nodist;** **hym′nody** hymns collectively **hymn-singing**
hymnology, **hymnog′rapher;** **hymnog′raphy** the art
of writing hymns the study of hymns, **hymnol′ogist;**
hymnol′ogy the study or composition of hymns
[Gr. *hymnos*]
hyoid *hī′oid, adj* having the form of the Greek letter
upsilon (υ), applied to a bone at the base of the
tongue [Gr *hyoeidēs—hȳ*, the letter upsilon; and
eidos, form.]
Hyoscyamus *hī-ō-sī′ə-məs, n* the henbane genus —*ns*
hy′oscine (*-sēn, -sən*, also called **scopolamine**; used as
a truth drug, for travel sickness, etc) and **hyo-
scy′amine** two poisonous alkaloids similar to
atropine, got from henbane [Gr *hyoskyamos*]
hypaethral *hip-ē′thrəl*, or *hip-, adj* roofless, open to
the sky —*n* **hypae′thron** an open court [Gr *hypo*,
beneath, *aithēr*, upper air, sky]
hypallage *hip-, hip-al′ə-jē*, (*rhet*) *n* a figure in which
the relations of words in a sentence are mutually in-

terchanged.—*adj* **hypallact′ic.** [Gr *hypo*, under,
allassein, to exchange]
hype *hīp*, (*slang*) *n* a hypodermic needle· a drug
addict something which stimulates artificially a
sales gimmick, etc a publicity stunt· the person or
thing promoted by such a stunt a deception —**hype
(up)** to inject oneself with a drug to stimulate artificially, **hyped up** artificially stimulated artificial,
fake [Abbrev of **hypodermic.**]
hyper- *hī′pər-, hī-pûr′*, in composition. over. excessive
more than normal —*n* **hyperacid′ity** excessive
acidity, esp in the stomach —*adj* **hyperac′tive**
(*med*) abnormally or pathologically active —*ns*
hyperactiv′ity; hyperaemia, in U S **hyperemia**,
(*-ē′mi-ə*, Gr *haima*, blood) congestion or excess of
blood in any part.—*adj* **hyperae′mic.**—*n* **hyper-
aesthesia**, in U S **hyperesthesia**, (*-ēs-* or *-es-thē′si-ə*,
-zi-ə; Gr *aisthēsis*, perception) excessive sensitivity to
stimuli. an abnormal extension of the bodily senses
assumed to explain telepathy and clairvoyance· exaggerated aestheticism —*adjs* **hyperaesthē′sic, hyper-
aesthetic** (*-thet′ik*) overaesthetic· abnormally or morbidly sensitive —*ns.* **hyper′baton** (Gr ,—root of
bainein, to go, *rhet*) a figure by which words are
transposed from their natural order, **hyper′bola** (Gr
hyperbolē, overshooting—*ballein*, to throw, *pl* usu
in *-s; geom*) one of the conic sections, the intersection of a plane with a cone when the plane cuts both
branches of the cone, **hyperbole** (*hī-pûr′bə-lē*) a
rhetorical figure which produces a vivid impression by
extravagant and obvious exaggeration —*adjs* **hyper-
bol′ic, -al** of a hyperbola or hyperbole —*adv* **hyper-
bol′ically.**—*v t* **hyper′bolise, -ize** to represent hyperbolically —*v i* to speak hyperbolically or with
exaggeration —*ns* **hyper′bolism; hyper′boloid** a
solid figure certain of whose plane sections are hyper-
bolas —*adj* **hyperborean** (*-bō′, -bo′*, Gr *Hyper-
boreoi*, a people supposed to live in sunshine beyond
the north wind—*Boreas*, the north wind) belonging
to the extreme north —*n* an inhabitant of the
extreme north —*n* **hypercrit′ic** one who is over-
critical: a carper —*adjs* **hypercrit′ic, -al.**—*adv*
hypercrit′ically.—*v t* **hypercrit′icise, -ize** (*-sīz*) —
ns **hypercrit′icism; hyperdulia** (*-dōō-lī′ə*) see **dulia;
hyperemia, hyperesthesia** see **hyperaemia, hyper-
aesthesia.**—*adjs* **hyperfo′cal** (*phot*) referring to the
minimum distance from a lens to the point from which
all objects can be focused clearly, **hyper′gamous**
pertaining to hypergamy.—*ns* **hypergamy** (*hī-
pûr′gə-mi*, Gr *gamos*, marriage) a custom that allows
a man but forbids a woman to marry a person of lower
social standing now sometimes more generally marriage of a man with a woman of higher social rank;
hyperglyc(a)emia (*-gli-sē′mi-ə*) abnormal rise in the
sugar content of the blood —*adjs* **hypergolic**
(*-gol′ik*) of two or more liquids, spontaneously
explosive on mixing —*ns* **hyperinflā′tion** rapid inflation uncontrollable by normal means; **hy′permarket**
a very large self-service store with a wide range of
goods —*adj* **hypermet′rical** beyond or exceeding the
ordinary metre of a line: having or being an additional
syllable —*n* **hypermetrō′pia** (Gr *metron*, measure,
ōps, eye) long-sightedness.—Also **hyperō′pia.**—*adj*
hypermetrōp′ic.—*n* **hy′peron** any particle with mass
greater than that of a proton or neutron —*adj* **hyper-
phys′ical** beyond physical laws supernatural —*n*
hyperpyrex′ia abnormally high body temperature —
v t **hypersens′itise, -ize** to increase the sensitivity of
—*adj* **hypersens′itive** excessively sensitive —*ns*
hypersens′itiveness; hypersensitivi′ity.—*adj* **hyper-
son′ic** (L *sonus*, sound) of speeds, greater than Mach
5 of sound-waves, having a frequency greater than
1000 million Hz —*n sing* **hyperson′ics.**—*ns* **hy′per-

space (*math.*) space having more than three dimensions; **hypersthene** (*hī'pər-sthēn*; Gr. *sthenos*, strength, rock-forming orthorhombic pyroxene, anhydrous silicate of magnesium and iron, generally dark green, brown, or black with metallic lustre; **hyperten'sion** blood pressure higher than normal: a state of great emotional tension.—*adjs.* **hyperten'sive**; **hyptherm'al**.—*ns.* **hypertherm'ia** (dangerous) overheating of the body; **hyperthyroidism** (*-thī'roid-izm*) overproduction of thyroid hormone by the thyroid gland, and the resulting condition.—*adjs* **hyperton'ic** of muscles, having excessive tone; of a solution, having a higher osmotic pressure than a specified solution, **hyper'trophied, hyper'trophous** (Gr *trophē*, nourishment). —*ns.* **hyper'trophy** overnourishment: abnormal enlargement; **hyperventila'tion** abnormally increased speed and depth of breathing.—**hyperbolic functions** in math., a set of six functions (sinh, cosh, tanh, etc.) analogous to the trigonometrical functions; **hyperbolic geometry** that involving the axiom that through any point in a given plane there can be drawn more than one line that does not intersect a given line; **hyperbolic logarithms** natural logarithms; **hyperfine structure** (*phys.*) the splitting of spectrum lines into two or more very closely spaced components. [Gr. *hyper*, over.]

Hypericum *hī-per'i-kəm, n.* the St John's wort genus of plants. [Gr. *hyperikon—hypo*, under, *ereikē*, heath.]

hypha *hī'fə, n.* a thread of fungus mycelium:—*pl* **hy'phae** (*-fē*).—*adj.* **hy'phal.** [Gr. *hyphē*, web.]

hyphen *hī'fən, n.* a short stroke (-) joining two syllables or words.—*v.t.* to join or separate by a hyphen.—*v.t.* **hy'phenate** to hyphen.—*adj.* **hy'phenated** hyphened: of mixed nationality, expressed by a hyphened word, as Irish-American.—*n.* **hyphena'tion.** [Gr. *hyphēn* —*hypo*, under, *hen*, one.]

hypn(o)- *hip'n(o, ō)-,* in composition, sleep or hypnosis —*n.* **hypnogen'esis** production of the hypnotic state.—*adjs.* **hypnogenet'ic, hypnogen'ic; hyp'noid, -al** like sleep: like hypnosis: esp. of a state between hypnosis and waking.—*ns.* **hypnol'ogy** the scientific study of sleep; **hypnopae'dia** learning or conditioning, by repetition of recorded sound during sleep (or semiwakefulness)—*adj.* **hypnopomp'ic** (Gr. *pompē*, a sending) dispelling sleep: pertaining to a state between sleep and wakefulness.—*ns.* **hypnō'sis** a sleeplike state in which the mind responds to external suggestion and can recover forgotten memories; **hypnother'apy** the treatment of illness by hypnotism. —*adj.* **hypnot'ic** of or relating to hypnosis: soporific —*n* a soporific: a person subject to hypnotism or in a state of hypnosis.—*adv.* **hypnot'ically.**—*adj.* **hypnotis'able, -z-.**—*ns.* **hypnotisabil'ity, -z-; hypnotisa'tion, -z-.**—*v.t.* **hyp'notise, -ize** to put in a state of hypnosis: to fascinate, dazzle, overpower the mind of (*fig.*).—*ns* **hyp'notism** the science of hypnosis: the art or practice of inducing hypnosis: hypnosis; **hyp'-notist** one who hypnotises. [Gr. *hypnos*, sleep.]

hypo- *hī'pō-, hıp'ō,* or *-o',* in composition, under: defective: inadequate —*n.* **hy'po** short for **hyposulph-**ite, in the sense of sodium thiosulphate, used as a fixing agent (*phot.*): short for **hypo**dermic syringe or injection (see also **hype**):—*pl* **hy'pos.**—*n.* **hypoblast** (*hıp', hıp'ō-blast*; Gr. *blastos*, bud, *zool*) the inner germ-layer of a gastrula —*adj* **hypoblast'ic.**—*ns* **hypocaust** (*hıp', hıp'ō-kost*; Gr. *hypokauston—hypo*, under, *kaiein*, to burn) a space under a floor for heating by hot air or furnace gases, esp in ancient Roman villas; **hypochlorite** (*hī-pō-klō'rīt, -klo'*) a salt of **hypochlo'rous acid**, an acid (HClO) with less oxygen than chlorous acid; **hypochondria** (*hıp-, hıp-*

ō-kon'dri-ə) originally the *pl.* of **hypochondrium** (see below): morbid anxiety about health: imaginary illness: a nervous malady, often arising from indigestion (*obs.*).—*adj* **hypochon'driac** relating to or affected with hypochondria: melancholy.—*n.* a sufferer from hypochondria.—*adj.* **hypochondri'acal.**—*n.* **hypochondri'asis** hypochondria; **hypochon'drium** (Gr *hypochondrion—chondros,* cartilage; *anat.*) the region of the abdomen on either side, under the costal cartilages and short ribs; **hypocorism** (*hip-, hīp-ok'ər-ızm* Gr. *hypokorisma—hypokorizesthai,* to use child-talk—*koros,* boy, *korē,* girl) a pet-name: a diminutive or abbreviated name.—*adj.* **hypocorist'ic.** —*adv.* **hypocorist'ically.**—*n.* **hypocotyl** (*hip-, hīp-ō-kot'ıl*) that part of the axis of a plant which is between the cotyledons and the primary root.—*adj* **hypocotylē'donary.**—*ns.* **hypocrisy** (*hi-pok'ri-si;* Gr. *hypokrisıā,* acting, playing a part) a feigning to be better than one is, or to be what one is not: concealment of true character or belief (not necessarily conscious): an instance or act of hypocrisy; **hypocrite** (*hıp'ə-krit;* Gr. *hypokritēs,* actor) one who practises hypocrisy.—*adj* **hypocrit'ical** practising hypocrisy: of the nature of hypocrisy.—*adv.* **hypocrit'ically.**—*n.* **hypocycloid** (*hī-pō-si'kloıd*) a curve generated by a point on the circumference of a circle which rolls on the inside of another circle.—*adj.* **hypocycloid'al.**— *ns.* **hypoderm** (*hıp' or hıp'ō-dûrm*), **hypoder'mis** (Gr. *derma,* skin; *bot.*) the tissue next under the epidermis.—*adjs.* **hypoderm'al; hypoderm'ic** pertaining to the hypodermis: under the epidermis: under the skin, subcutaneous, esp. of a method of injecting a drug in solution under the skin by means of a fine hollow needle to which a small syringe is attached —*n.* **hypoder'mic** a hypodermic injection: a drug so injected: a syringe for the purpose.—*adv.* **hypoder'mically.**— *adj.* **hypogastric** (*hip-* or *hip-ō-gas'trik;* Gr. *gastēr,* belly) belonging to the lower median part of the abdomen.—*n.* **hypogas'trium** the hypogastric region. —*adjs.* **hypogeal, -gaeal** (*-jē'əl*), **-ge'an, -gae'an, -ge'ous, -gae'ous** (Gr. *hypogeios, -gaios—gē* or *gaia,* the ground; *bot.*) underground: germinating with cotyledons underground; **hypogene** (*hip' or hıp'ō-jēn;* Gr *gennaein,* to engender; *geol.*) of or pertaining to rocks formed, or agencies at work, under the earth's surface, plutonic—opp. to *epigene.*—*n.* **hypogeum, hypogaeum** (*hıp-, hıp-ō-jē'əm*) an underground chamber: a subterranean tomb.—*pl.* **hypoge'a, -gae'a.**— *adj* **hy'poid** of a type of bevel gear in which the axes of the driving and driven shafts are at right angles but not in the same plane.—*ns.* **hypolim'nion** (Gr *lım-nion,* dim. of *limnē,* lake) a lower and colder layer of water in a lake; **hypomania** (*hip-, hīp-ō-mā'ni-ə; med.*) simple mania, a condition marked by overexcitability.—*adj.* **hypomā'nic** (or *-man'ik*).—*ns* **hyponasty** (*hip' or hip'ō-nas-tı;* Gr *nastos,* pressed close; *bot.*) increased growth on the lower side causing an upward bend—opp. to *epinasty;* **hypophosphite** (*hī-pō-fos'fīt*) a salt of **hypophos'phorous acid,** an acid with less oxygen than phosphorous acid; **hypophysis** (*hīp-, hıp-ōf'i-sıs,* Gr *hypophysis,* an attachment underneath—*phyein,* to grow); the pituitary body of the brain; **hypostasis** (*hıp-, hīp-os'tə-sıs;* Gr *hypostasis—stasis,* setting) orig. basis: foundation: substance, essence (*metaph.*): the essence or real personal subsistence or substance of each of the three divisions of the Trinity —*adjs.* **hypostatic** (*-stat'ık*), **-al.**—*adv* **hypostat'ically.**—*v.s.t* **hypos'tasise, -ize, hypos'tatise, -ize** to treat as hypostasis: to personify —**hypostyle** (*hıp', hıp'ō-stīl;* Gr *stȳlos,* a pillar; *archıt*) having the roof supported by pillars —Also *n* —*adj* **hypotac'tic.**—*ns* **hypotaxis** (*hıp-, hīp-ō-tak'-sıs,* Gr *taxıs,* arrangement, *gram*) dependent construction—opp to *parataxis*, **hypoten'sion** low blood-pressure —*adj.* **hypoten'sive.**—*n* a person with low blood-pressure —*ns* **hypotenuse** (*hīp-, hip-ot'ən-ūs,* or *-ūz*; Fr *hypoténuse*—L *hypoténūsa*—Gr. *hypoteinousa* —*teinein*, to stretch) the side of a right-angled triangle opposite to the right angle; **hypothalamus** (*hip-, hip-ō-thal'ə-məs*; L L , *med*) the part of the brain which makes up the floor and part of the lateral walls of the third ventricle.—*adj* **hypothalam'ic.**—*n.* **hypothec** (*hip-, hip-oth'ik*; Gr *hypothēkē,* a pledge) in Scots law, a lien or security over goods in respect of a debt due by the owner of the goods —*v.t* **hypoth'ecate** to place or assign as security under an arrangement: to mortgage.—*adj* **hypotherm'al.**—*ns.* **hypothermia** (*hip-, hip-ō-thúr'mi-ə*; Gr *thermē,* heat) subnormal body temperature, caused by exposure to cold or induced for purposes of heart and other surgery (see **freeze down**); **hypothesis** (*hī-poth'i-sis*; Gr *hypothesis*—*thesis,* placing) a supposition· a proposition assumed for the sake of argument: a theory to be proved or disproved by reference to facts: a provisional explanation of anything:—*pl.* **hypoth'esēs.**—*vs t.* and *vs i* **hypoth'esise, -ize, hypoth'etise, -ize.**—*adjs* **hypothet'ic, -al.**—*adv* **hypothet'ically.**—*adj* **hypothy'roid** pertaining to, or affected by, hypothyroidism —*n.* **hypothy'roidism** insufficient activity of the thyroid gland a condition resulting from this, cretinism, etc.—*adj* **hypoton'ic** of muscles, lacking normal tone of a solution, having lower osmotic pressure than a specified solution —*n* **hypox'ia** deficiency of oxygen reaching the body tissues —*adj.* **hypox'ic.** [Gr *hypo,* under]

hypo. See **hypo-**.

hypso- *hip'sō-,* in composition, height —*ns* **hypsography** (*-sog'rə-fi,* Gr *graphein,* to write) the branch of geography dealing with the measurement and mapping of heights above sea-level· a map showing topographic relief· a method of making such a map; **hypsometry** (*hip-som'ə-tri*; Gr *metron,* a measure) the art of measuring the heights of places on the earth's surface; **hypsom'eter** an instrument for doing this by taking the boiling point of water.—*adj* **hypsomet'ric.** [Gr *hypsos,* height]

Hyrax *hī'raks, n* a genus of mammals like marmots but really closer to the ungulates, living among rocks in Africa and Syria—the dassie or rock-rabbit: (without *cap*) any animal of this genus:—*pl.* **hy'raxes, hy'races** (*-sēz*) —*adj* **hy'racoid.** [Gr *hȳrax,* a shrew]

hyson *hī'son, n* a very fine sort of green tea [From Chin]

hyssop *his'əp, n* an aromatic labiate (*Hyssopus officinalis*): an unknown wall-plant used as a ceremonial sprinkler (*B*): a holy-water sprinkler [L *hyssōpus, -um*—Gr *hyssōpos, -on,* cf Heb *'ēzōb*]

hyster-, hystero- *his'tər-(o-),* in composition, womb —*ns* **hysterec'tomy** (Gr *ektomē,* a cutting out) surgical removal of the uterus [Gr *hysterā,* the womb]

hysteresis *his-tə-rē'sis, n* the retardation or lagging of an effect behind the cause of the effect· the influence of earlier treatment of a body on its subsequent reaction —*adj* **hysterēs'ic.** [Gr *hysterēsis,* a deficiency, coming late—*hysteros,* later]

hysteria *his-tē'ri-ə, n* a psychoneurosis in which repressed complexes become split off or dissociated from the personality, forming independent units, partially or completely unrecognised by consciousness, giving rise to hypnoidal states (amnesia, somnambulisms), and manifested by various physical symptoms, such as tics, paralysis, blindness, deafness, etc , general features being an extreme degree of emotional instability and an intense craving for affection· an outbreak of wild emotionalism —*adjs* **hysteric** (*his-ter'ik*), **-al** pertaining to, of the nature of, or affected with, hysterics or hysteria: like hysterics fitfully and violently emotional· (**hyster'ical**) extremely funny (*coll*).—*n* **hyster'ic** a hysterical person —*adv* **hyster'ically.**—*n pl* **hyster'ics** hysteric fits popularly, fits of uncontrollable laughter or crying, or of both alternately [Gr. *hysterā,* the womb, with which hysteria was formerly thought to be connected]

hysteron-proteron *his'tər-on-prot'ər-on, n* a figure of speech in which what would ordinarily follow comes first an inversion [Gr , lit latter-former]

I

I¹, i *ī, n.* the ninth letter of our alphabet. In Roman numerals I represents one; in mathematics *i* represents the imaginary square root of −1.—**I-beam** a metal girder I-shaped in section.

**I² ** *ī, pron.* the nominative singular of the first personal pronoun.—*n.* the object of self-consciousness, the ego. [M.E. *ich*—O.E. *ic.*]

i' *i, prep.* a form of **in.**

-ia *-ē'ə, -yə, suff.* used in naming (1) a pathological condition, (2) a genus of plants or animals, (3) (as L or Gr. *neut. pl.*) a taxonomic division, (4) (as *pl.*) things pertaining to (something specified).

iambus *ī-am'bəs, n.* a foot of two syllables, a short followed by a long, or an unstressed by a stressed:—*pl.* **iam'buses, iam'bi.**—Also **i'amb.**—*adj.* **iam'bic** consisting of iambuses: of the nature of an iambus: using iambic verse: satirical in verse.—*n.* an iambus: (in *pl*) iambic verse, esp satirical. [L. *iambus*—Gr. *iambos* —*iaptein,* to assail, this metre being first used by satirists.]

iatric, -al *ī-at'rik, -əl, adjs.* relating to medicine or physicians.—*adj.* **iatrogen'ic** (of disease) caused by treatment, esp for some other ailment.—*ns* **iatrogenic'ity; iatro'geny.** [Gr. *iātros, iātros,* a physician.]

Iberian *ī-bē'ri-ən, adj.* of Spain and Portugal: of the ancient inhabitants of these, or their later representatives: of a Mediterranean people of Neolithic culture in Britain, etc.—*n.* a member of any of these peoples. [L. *Ibēria*—Gr. *Ibēriā.*]

ibex *ī'beks, n.* a large-horned mountain wild-goat:—*pl.* **i'bexes,** also **ibices** (*ī'bi-sēz*). [L. *ibex, -icis.*]

ibidem *ib-ī'dəm, ib'i-dəm, i-bē'dem,* (L.) *adv.* in the same place.—Abbrev. **ib., ibid.**

ibis *ī'bis, n.* a wading bird with curved bill, akin to the spoonbills. [L. and Gr. *ibis,* prob. Egyptian.]

-ible *-ə-bl, adj. suff.* capable of being.—*n. suff.* **-ibility.** —*adv. suff.* **-ibly.**—See also **-able.**

Ibo *ē'bō, n.* a Negro people of S.E. Nigeria: a member of this people: their language, widely used in southern Nigeria:—*pl.* **I'bo, I'bos.**—Also *adj.*—Also **Igbo** (*ē'bō*).

ice *īs, n.* frozen water: any substance resembling this: concreted sugar on a cake, etc.: a frozen confection of fruit-juice, etc.: ice-cream: reserve, formality: coldness of manner: diamond(s) (*slang*).—*adj.* of ice. —*v.t.* to cover with ice: to freeze: to cool with ice: to cover with concreted sugar.—*v.i.* to freeze: to become covered with ice (with *up*):—*pr.p.* **ic'ing;** *pa.t.* and *pa.p.* **iced.**—*adj.* **iced** (*īst*) covered with or cooled with ice: encrusted with sugar.—*n.* **i'cer** one who makes icing.—*adv.* **ic'ily.**—*ns.* **ic'iness; ic'ing** covering with or of ice or concreted sugar.—*adj.* **ic'y** composed of, abounding in, or like ice: frosty: cold: chilling: without warmth of affection.—Also *adv.*—**ice age** (*geol.*) any time when a great part of the earth's surface has been covered with ice, esp. that in Pleistocene times; **ice'- axe** an axe used by mountain climbers to cut steps in ice; **ice'berg** (from Scand. or Du.) a huge mass of floating ice: a cold and unemotional person (*coll.*); **ice'blink** a gleam reflected from distant masses of ice; **ice'-blue** a very pale blue.—Also *adj.*—**ice'-boat** a boat for forcing a way through or sailing or being dragged over ice.—*adj.* **ice'-bound** bound, sur-

rounded, or fixed in with ice.—**ice'box** the freezing compartment of a refrigerator: a refrigerator (*U.S.*): a portable insulated box filled with ice, used for storing cold food and drink; **ice'-breaker** ship for breaking channels through ice: anything for breaking ice; **ice'- bucket** a receptacle with ice for cooling bottles of wine; **ice'-cap** a covering of ice over a convexity, as a mountain top, the polar regions of a planet.—*adj.* **ice'-cold** cold as, or like, ice.—**ice'-cream'** a sweet frozen food containing cream, or one of various substitutes, and flavouring (**ice'-cream soda** soda-water with ice-cream added); **ice'-cube** a small cube of ice used for cooling drinks, etc.; **ice dance, dancing** a form of ice-skating based on the movements of ballroom dancing; **ice'- field** a large area covered with ice, esp. floating ice; **ice'-floe** a large sheet of floating ice; **ice'-hock'ey** a form of hockey played on ice with a puck by skaters; **ice'-house** a house for keeping ice in; **ice'-loll'y** a lolli-pop consisting of water-ice on a stick; **ice'-machine** a machine for making ice in large quantity; **ice'man** a dealer in ice: a man who looks after an ice-rink; **ice'pack** drifting ice packed together: a pack prepared with ice; **ice'-pick** a tool with a pointed end used by climbers for splitting ice; **ice'plant** a plant (Mesembrianthemum) whose leaves glisten like ice in the sun; **ice'-rink** a skating rink of ice; **ice'-run** a tobogganing slide; **ice'-sheet** land-ice covering a whole region; **ice'- show** an entertainment or exhibition provided by skaters on ice; **ice'-skate** a skate for moving on ice (see **skate¹**); **ice'-water** water from melted ice: iced water; **icing sugar** sugar in the form of a very fine powder, for icing cakes, etc.—**break the ice** see **break¹; cut no ice** to count for nothing; **dry ice** solid carbon dioxide; **on ice** (*fig.*) kept or waiting in readiness: postponed: certain of achievement; (**skate) on thin ice** (to be) in a delicate, difficult or potentially embarrassing situation; **tip of the iceberg** the top of an iceberg, visible above the water, most of it being invisible below the surface: the small obvious part of a much larger problem, etc. (*fig.*). [O.E. *īs.*]

Iceland *īs'lənd, adj.* belonging to, originating in, *Iceland.*—*n.* **ice'lander** (or *īs-land'ər*) a native or citizen of Iceland: an Iceland falcon.—*adj.* **Icelandic** (*īs-land'ik*) of Iceland.—*n.* the modern language of the Icelanders: Old Norse.—**Iceland moss** a lichen of northern regions, used as a medicine and for food; **Iceland poppy** a dwarf poppy with flowers varying from white to orange-scarlet; **Iceland spar** a transparent calcite with strong double refraction.

I Ching *ī, ē ching,* an ancient Chinese system of divination, consisting of a set of symbols, 8 trigrams and 64 hexagrams, and the text, the *I Ching,* used to interpret them. [Chin., book of changes.]

ichneumon *ik-nū'mən, n.* any animal of the mongoose genus, esp. the Egyptian species that destroys crocodiles' eggs: (in full **ichneu'mon-fly**) any insect of a large family of Hymenoptera whose larvae are parasitic in or on other insects. [Gr. *ichneumōn,* lit. tracker.]

ichnite *ik'nīt,* **ichnolite** *ik'nə-līt, ns.* a fossil footprint.— *n.* **ichnography** (*ik-nog'rə-fi*) a ground plan: the art of drawing ground plans.—*adjs.* **ichnographic** (*-nō-graf'ik*), **-al.**—*adv.* **ichnograph'ically.** [Gr. *ichnos,* a track, footprint.]

For other sounds see detailed chart of pronunciation.

ichor i'kòr, n. the ethereal juice in the veins of the gods (*myth*)· a watery humour· colourless matter from an ulcer.—*adj.* i'chorous. [Gr *ìchōr*]

ichthy(o)- ik'thi-(ō-), in composition, fish —*adj* ich'thic.—*n* ichthyog'raphy a description of fishes —*adjs* ich'thyoid, -al fishlike; ichthyolog'ical.—*ns* ichthyol'ogist; ichthyol'ogy the branch of natural history that treats of fishes, ichthyophagist (-of'ə-jist, Gr *phagein*, to eat) a fish-eater, ichthyophagy (-of'ə-ji) the practice of eating fish; ichthyosaur (ik'thi-ō-sor; Gr. *sauros*, lizard) any member of the genus **Ichthyosaur'us** or of the order **Ichthyosaur'ia**, gigantic Mesozoic fossil fishlike marine reptiles — *adj.* ichthyosaur'ian.—*n.* ichthyō'sis a disease in which the skin becomes hardened, thickened, and rough.—*adj* ichthyōt'ic. [Gr. *ichthýs*, fish.]

icicle is'i-kl, n. a hanging, tapering piece of ice formed by the freezing of dropping water [O E *ísesgicel*— *íses*, gen ot *ís*, ice, *gicel*, icicle]

icing. See ice.

-icism. See -ism.

icky ik't, (*coll.*) *adj* sickly-sweet: repulsive [Perh —sickly.]

icon, ikon i'kon, n a portrait, carved, painted, etc · in the Eastern Churches a figure representing Christ, or a saint, in painting, mosaic, etc. (not sculpture): a symbol, representation: anybody or anything uncritically admired —*adj* icon'ic of images or icons. conventional in type.—*ns* icon'oclasm (Gr. *klaein*, to break) the act of breaking images· opposition to image-worship; icon'oclast a breaker of images· one opposed to image-worship, esp those in the Eastern Church, from the 8th century· one who assails old cherished errors and superstitions.—*adj* iconoclast'ic.—*ns.* iconog'raphy (Gr *graphiā*, a writing) the art of illustration· the study, description, cataloguing, or collective representation of portraits: the study of symbols used in a particular style of painting, etc., and their meaning; iconol'ogist; iconol'ogy the study of icons· symbolism —*adj.* iconomat'ic using pictures of objects to represent not the things themselves but the sounds of their names, as in a transition stage between picture-writing and a phonetic system —*ns* iconomat'icism (-i-sizm); iconom'eter an instrument for inferring distance from size or size from distance of an object, by measuring its image: a direct photographic view-finder, iconom'etry; icon'oscope a form of electron camera; iconos'tasis, icon'ostas (Gr *eikonostasis*—*stasis*, placing) in Eastern churches, a screen shutting off the sanctuary, on which the icons are placed.—**iconic memory** the persistence of a sense impression after the disappearance of the stimulus [L *icōn*—Gr. *eikōn*, an image]

icosahedron i-kos-ə-hē'dron, (*geom.*) n a solid with twenty plane faces.—*pl* icosahē'dra.—*adj* icosahē'dral.—*n.* icositetrahē'dron (*geom*) a solid figure with twenty-four plane faces —*pl* -dra. [Gr *eikosi*, twenty, *hedrā*, a seat]

icterus ik'tər-əs, n jaundice.—*adjs* icteric (-ter'ik), -al relating to or affected with jaundice —*ns* a medicine for jaundice [Gr. *ikteros*, jaundice]

ictus ik'təs, n a stroke (*med.*)· rhythmical or metrical stress (*pros.*)· a pulsation.—*pl* ic'tuses (or L *pl* ic'tūs -tōōs) —*adjs* ic'tal; ic'tic. [L , a blow]

I'd id, contracted from *I would*, or *I had*: also used for *I should*.

id¹ id, ide ïd, ns a fish of the same family as the carp, inhabiting fresh water in Northern Europe [Sw *id*.]

id² id, (*psych.*) n the sum total of the primitive instinctive forces in an individual subserving the pleasure-pain principle [L *id*, it]

ide. See id¹.

idea i-dē'ə, n an image of an external object formed by the mind a notion, thought, impression, any product of intellectual action, of memory and imagination· plan· an archetype of the manifold varieties of existence in the universe, belonging to the supersensible world (*Platonic*) one of the three products of the reason (the Soul, the Universe, and God) transcending the conceptions of the understanding (*Kantian*) the ideal realised, the absolute truth of which everything that exists is the expression (*Hegelian*).—*adjs.* ide'aed, ide'a'd provided with an idea or ideas, ide'al existing in idea· conceptual. existing in imagination only· highest and best conceivable: perfect, as opposed to the real, the imperfect: theoretical, conforming absolutely to theory.—*n* the highest conception of anything, or its embodiment: a standard of perfection· that which exists in the imagination only —*n* idealisā'tion, -z-.—*v t* ide'alise, -ize to regard or represent as ideal —*v t* to form ideals: to think or work idealistically —*ns.* ide'aliser, -z-; ide'alism the doctrine that in external perceptions the objects immediately known are ideas, that all reality is in its nature psychical· any system that considers thought or the idea as the ground either of knowledge or existence: a tendency towards the highest conceivable perfection, love for or search after the best and highest the habit or practice of idealising: impracticality: the imaginative treatment of subjects, ide'alist one who holds the doctrine of idealism one who strives after the ideal: an impractical person —*adj.* idealist'ic pertaining to idealists or to idealism —*adv.* idealist'ically.—*n* ideälity (-al'i-ti) an ideal state. ability and disposition to form ideals of beauty and perfection —*adv* ide'ally in an ideal manner. mentally.— *v.t.* ide'ate to form or have an idea of· to imagine: to preconceive —*v.i.* to form ideas.—*adj* produced by an idea.—*n.* the correlative or object of an idea.—*n.* ideā'tion the power of the mind for forming ideas: the exercise of such power —*adjs.* ideā'tional, ide'ative.—*adv* ideā'tionally.—**get, have, ideas** (*slang*) to become, be, overambitious: to have undesirable ideas; **have no idea** to be unaware of what is happening· to be ignorant or naïve, **not my**, etc **idea of** (*coll.*) the opposite of my, etc. conception of; **what's the big idea?** (*slang*) what's the intention, purpose? (usu. said in anger) [L *idéa*—Gr *idéā*; cf *idein* (aor), to see.]

ideal, idealise, etc See under idea.

idée ē-dā, (Fr.) n idea —idée fixe (*fēks*) a fixed idea, a monomania.

idem i'dem, i'dem, (L) *pron* the same —Abbrev. id.

identical. See under identity.

identify i-den'ti-fi, v t. to make, reckon, ascertain or prove to be the same. to ascertain or establish the identity of to assign to a species to bind up or associate closely to regard, or wish to regard, (oneself) as sharing (with a person or group) interests and experiences, or (because of an emotional tie, usu. abnormal) attitudes, characteristics and behaviour —*v i* to become the same. to see oneself as sharing experiences, outlook, etc (with):—*pr p.* iden'tifying; *pa t* and *pa p* iden'tified.—*adj* iden'tifiable.—*n* identificā'tion the act of identifying· the state of being identified: anything which proves one's identity: a process by which a person assumes the behaviour, ideas, etc., of someone else, particularly someone whom he admires (*psych*) —**identification card, disc,** etc a card, disc, etc , carried on one's person, with one's name, etc., on it, **identification parade** a group of people assembled by the police, from among whom a witness tries to identify a suspect [L L *identificāre* —*idem*, the same, *facēre*, to make]

identikit. See identity.

identity i-den'ti-ti, n. state of being the same sameness.

individuality: personality: who or what a person or thing is: an equation true for all values of the symbols involved (*math.*).—*adj.* **iden'tical** the very same: not different: expressing or resulting in identity.—*adv.* **iden'tically.**—*n.* **iden'ticalness.**—**identical twins** twins developing from one zygote; **iden'tikit** (orig. *U.S. Identi-Kit*) a device for building up a composite portrait from a large number of different features on transparent slips (also *fig*); **identity card, disc** a card, disc, etc., bearing the owner's or wearer's name, etc., used to establish his identity; **identity crisis** psychological confusion caused by inability to reconcile differing elements in one's personality. [L.L. *identitās, -ātis*—L. *idem,* resulting in same.]

ideogram *id'i-ō-gram,* or *īd',* **ideograph** *-graf, ns.* a written character or symbol that stands not for a word or sound but for the thing itself directly.—*adjs* **ideographic** (*-graf'ik*), **-al.**—*adv.* **ideograph'ically.**—*n.* **ideography** (*-og'rə-fi*). [Gr. *idéā,* idea, *gramma,* a drawing, *graphein,* to write.]

ideology *id-, i-di-ol'ə-ji, n.* the science of ideas, metaphysics: abstract speculation: visionary speculation: a body of ideas, usu. political and/or economic, forming the basis of a national or sectarian policy: way of thinking.—*adjs.* **ideologic** (*-loj'*), **-al** of or pertaining to an ideology: arising from, concerned with, rival ideologies.—*n.* **ideol'ogist** one occupied with ideas or an idea: a mere theorist or visionary: a supporter of a particular ideology—also **ideologue** (*i-dē'ō-log*). [Gr. *idéā,* idea, *logos,* discourse.]

Ides *īdz, n.pl.* in ancient Rome, the 15th day of March, May, July, October, and the 13th of the other months. [Fr. *ides*—L. *īdūs* (pl.).]

idiocy. See idiot.

id est *id est,* (L.) that is.—Abbrev. **i.e.**

idiolect *id'i-ō-lekt, n.* an individual's own distinctive form of speech.—*adjs.* **idiolec'tal, -tic.** [Gr *idios,* own, *legein,* to speak.]

idiom *id'i-əm, n.* a mode of expression peculiar to a language: an expression characteristic of a particular language not logically or grammatically explicable: a form or variety of language: a dialect: a characteristic mode of artistic expression of a person, school, etc.—*adjs.* **idiomat'ic, -al.**—*adv.* **idiomat'ically.** [Gr *idiōma, idiōtikon*—*idios,* own.]

idiomorphic *id-i-ō-mōr'fik, adj.* having the faces belonging to its crystalline form, as a mineral that has had free room to crystallise out. [Gr. *idios,* own, *morphē,* form.]

idiopathy *id-i-op'ə-thi, n.* a state or experience peculiar to the individual: a primary disease, one not occasioned by another (*med.*).—*adj.* **idiopathic** (*-path'ik*).—*adv.* **idiopath'ically.** [Gr. *idios,* own, *pathos,* suffering.]

idiosyncrasy *id-i-ō-sing'krə-si, n.* peculiarity of temperament or mental constitution: any characteristic of a person: hypersensitivity of an individual to a particular food, drug, etc. (*med.*).—*adjs.* **idiosyncratic** (*-krat'ik*), **-al.** [Gr. *idios,* own, *synkrāsis,* a mixing together—*syn,* together, *krāsis,* a mixing.]

idiot *id'i-ət, id'yət, n.* a person so defective in mind from birth as to be unable to protect himself against ordinary physical dangers: one afflicted with the severest grade of feeble-mindedness: a blockhead: a foolish or unwise person —*adj.* afflicted with idiocy. idiotic.—*n.* **id'iocy** (*-ə-si*), the state of being an idiot: imbecility: folly.—*adjs.* **idiotic** (*-ot'ik*), **-al** pertaining to or like an idiot: foolish.—*adv.* **idiot'ically.**—*adj* **id'iotish** idiotic.—*n.* **id'iotism** the state of being an idiot.—*adj* **id'iot-proof** of a tool, method of working, etc., so simple that even an idiot cannot make a mistake. [Fr.,—L. *idiōta*—Gr. *idiōtēs,* a private person, ordinary person, one who holds no public office

or has no professional knowledge—*idios,* own, private.]

idiot savant *ē-dyō'sa-vā, id'i-ət sav'ənt* a mentally retarded individual who demonstrates remarkable talent in some restricted area such as memorising or rapid calculation.

idle *i'dl, adj.* vain: baseless: trifling: unemployed: averse to labour: not occupied: useless: unimportant: unedifying.—*v.t.* to spend in idleness: to cause to be idle.—*v.i.* to be idle or unoccupied: of machinery, to run without doing work.—*ns.* **i'dleness; i'dler.**—*adv.* **i'dly.**—*adj.* **i'dle-head'ed** foolish.—*n.* **i'dle-pulley** a pulley which rotates freely and guides, or controls the tension of, a belt; **i'dle-wheel** a wheel placed between two others for transferring the motion from one to the other without changing the direction. [O.E. *īdel.*]

idol *i'dl, n.* an image, a semblance: a phantom: an image of a god: an object of worship: an object of love, admiration, or honour in an extreme degree.—*v.t.* **i'dolise, -ize** to make an idol of.—*ns.* **i'doliser, -z-; i'dolism** idol-worship: idolising. [L. *idōlum*—Gr. *eidōlon*—*eidos,* form—*idein* (aor.), to see.]

idolater *ī-dol'ə-tər, n.* a worshipper of idols: a great admirer:—*fem.* **idol'atress.**—*v.t.* and *v.i.* **idol'atrise, -ize** to worship as an idol: to adore.—*adj.* **idol'atrous.** —*adv.* **idol'atrously.**—*n.* **idol'atry** the worship of an image held to be the abode of a superhuman personality. excessive love. [Fr. *idolâtre*—Gr. *eidōlolatrēs*—*eidōlon,* idol, *latreuein,* to worship.]

idyll *id'il, īd'il, -əl, n.* a short pictorial poem, chiefly on pastoral subjects: a story, episode, or scene of happy innocence or rusticity: a work of art of like character in any medium.—Also **id'yl.**—*adjs.* **idyll'ian; idyll'ic.**—*n.* **i'dyllist.** [L. *īdyllium*—Gr. *eidyllion,* dim of *eidos,* image.]

if *if, conj.* on condition that: provided that: in case that: supposing that: whether.—*n.* a condition: a supposition.—**as if** as it would be if; **ifs and ans** things which might have happened, but which did not; **ifs and buts** objections. [O.E. *gif.*]

Igbo. See Ibo.

igloo *ig'lōō, n.* orig. a dome-shaped hut of snow: now usu. a dwelling of other materials: a dome-shaped place of storage or container for goods. [Eskimo.]

igneous *ig'ni-əs, adj.* of or like fire: produced by solidification of the earth's internal molten magma (*geol.*). [L. *ignis,* fire.]

ignis fatuus *ig'nis fat'ū-əs, fat'ōō-ōōs,* will-o'-thewisp—the light of combustion of marsh-gas, apt to lead travellers into danger: any delusive ideal that leads one astray:—*pl.* **ignes fatui** (*ig'nēz fat'ū-ī; ig'nās fat'ōō-ē*) [L. *ignis,* fire, *fatuus,* foolish.]

ignite *ig-nīt', v.t.* to set on fire: to heat to the point at which combustion occurs—*v.i.* to take fire.—*adj.* **ignit'able** (also **ignit'ible**).—*ns.* **ignitabil'ity** (**ignitibil'ity**); **ignit'er** one who ignites: apparatus for firing an explosive or explosive mixture; **ignition** (*-nish'ən*) an act of igniting: a means of igniting: the state of being ignited: the firing system of an internal-combustion engine.—**ignition key** in a motor vehicle, the key which is turned to operate the ignition system. [L. *ignīre, ignītum,* to set on fire, to make red-hot—*ignis,* fire.]

ignoble *ig-nō'bl, adj.* of low birth: mean or worthless: unworthy: dishonourable.—*ns.* **ignōbil'ity, ignō'bleness.**—*adv.* **ignō'bly.** [Fr.,—L. *ignōbilis*— *in-,* not, (*g*)*nōbilis,* noble.]

ignominy *ig'nə-min-i,* or *-nō-, n.* loss of good name: public disgrace: infamy.—*adj.* **ignomin'ious** deserving or marked with ignominy—*adv.* **ignomin'iously.** [L *ignōminia, in-,* not, (*g*)*nōmen, -inis,* name]

ignoramus *ig-nō-rā'məs, -nə-, n.* an ignorant person,

esp. one pretending to knowledge —*pl*
ignora'muses. [L *ignorāmus,* we are ignorant, in
legal use, we ignore, take no notice, 1st pers. pl. pres
indic. of *ignōrāre.*]

ignorant *ig'nər-ənt, adj* without knowledge, in general
or particular: uninstructed. uninformed. unaware:
showing, arising from, want of knowledge.—*n.* an
ignorant person.—*n.* **ig'norance** want of knowledge
—*adv.* **ig'norantly.** [Fr.,—L. *ignōrāns, -antis,* pr p
of *ignōrāre;* see **ignore.**]

ignoratio elenchi *ig-nə-rā'shō il-eng'kī, ig-nō-rat'i-ō el-
eng'kē,* (L.) ignoring the point in question. the fallacy
of arguing to the wrong point.

ignore *ig-nōr', -nor', v t.* wilfully to disregard: to set
aside —*adj.* **ignor'able.**—*ns.* **ignora'tion** ignoring;
ignor'er. [L. *ignōrāre,* not to know—*in-,* not, and
the root of (g)*nōscĕre,* to know.]

Iguana *i-gwa'nə, n.* a genus of large thick-tongued
arboreal lizards in tropical America loosely extended to others of the same family (**Iguan'idae**):
(without *cap.*) in South Africa a monitor lizard
[Sp., from Carib.]

Iguanodon *i-gwa'nə-don, n* a large, bipedal, bird-
hipped, Jurassic and Cretaceous herbivorous
dinosaur, with teeth like those of the iguana
[**iguana,** and Gr *odous, odontos,* tooth.]

ikebana *ē'ke-ba'nə, n.* the Japanese art of flower
arrangement [Jap., living flowers, arranged
flowers.]

ikon. Same as **icon.**

il- *il, pfx.* same as **in-,** the form used with words beginning with *l,* as in *illegible.*

ileac. See **ileum, ileus.**

ileum *il', il'i-əm, n.* the posterior part of the small
intestine—*pl* **il'ea.**—*adj.* **il'eac, il'iac.**—*n.* **ileitis**
(*il-, il-ə-i'tis*) inflammation of the ileum [L.L.
ileum, L. *ilia* (pl.), the groin, flank, intestines.]

ileus *il', il'i-əs, n.* obstruction of the intestine with
severe pain, vomiting, etc.:—*pl.* **il'euses.**—*adj.*
il'eac, il'iac. [L *īleos*—Gr. *ileos* or *eileos,* colic.]

ilex *i'leks, n* the holm-oak: (with *cap.*) the holly
genus:—*pl* **i'lexes, ilices** (*ī'li-sēz*) [L. *īlex,* holm-
oak.]

iliac. See **ileum, ileus, ilium.**

ilium *il', il'i-əm, n.* the bone that unites with the
ischium and pubis to form the innominate bone: (in
pl.) the flanks:—*pl.* **il'ia.**—*adj.* **il'iac.** [L. *ilium* (in
classical L only in pl *ilia*); see **ileum.**]

ilk *ilk, adj.* same.—*n.* type, kind.—**of that ilk** of that
same, i.e. of the estate of the same name as the
family. [O.E. *ilca,* same.]

I'll *il,* a contraction of **I will** or **I shall.**

ill *il, adj.* (*compar.* **worse;** *superl* **worst**) evil, bad:
wicked: producing evil. hurtful: unfortunate:
unfavourable. difficult: reprehensible: sick. diseased:
incorrect: cross, as temper.—*adv.* (*compar.* **worse;**
superl. **worst**) badly: not well: not rightly
wrongfully: unfavourably: amiss: with hardship with
difficulty.—*n* evil wickedness: misfortune: harm.
ailment.—*n.* **ill'ness** sickness' disease.—*adjs* **ill'-
advised'** imprudent. ill-judged, **ill'-affect'ed** not well
disposed; **ill'-assort'ed** incompatible: not matching,
ill'-behaved' behaving badly, ill-mannered.—**ill'-
blood', ill'-feel'ing** resentment, enmity —*adj* **ill'-
bred'** badly bred or educated uncivil —**ill'-
breed'ing.**—*adjs* **ill'-condit'ioned** in bad condition:
churlish; **ill'-consid'ered** badly thought out. miscon-
ceived, **ill'-defined'** having no clear outline (*lit* and
fig.), **ill'-disposed'** unfriendly inclined to evil —**ill'-
fame'** disrepute (see **house**).—*adjs* **ill'-fat'ed**
unlucky; **ill'-fa'voured** ill-looking deformed: ugly —
ill'-fa'vouredness; ill'-for'tune bad luck.—*adjs* **ill'-
found'ed** without foundation (*fig.*); **ill'-got', -gott'en**

procured by bad means.—**ill'-hu'mour.**—*adjs.* **ill'-
hu'moured** bad-tempered; **ill'-informed'** ignorant;
ill'-judged' not well judged.—**ill'-luck'** bad luck.—
adjs. **ill'-manned'** provided with too few men; **ill'-
mann'ered** rude: ill-bred —**ill'-na'ture.**—*adj.* **ill'-
na'tured** of a bad temper. cross: peevish —*adv.* **ill'-
na'turedly.**—**ill'-na'turedness.**—*adjs.* **ill'-ō'mened**
having bad omens: unfortunate; **ill'-spent** spent
amiss; **ill'-starred** born under the influence of an
unlucky star' unlucky.—**ill'-success'** lack of success,
ill-tem'per,—*adjs.* **ill'-tem'pered** having a bad temper: morose; **ill'-timed'** said or done at an unsuitable
time —*v t.* **ill-treat'** to treat ill' to abuse —**ill-treat'-
ment; ill'-turn'** an act of unkindness or enmity; **illus'age.**—*v t.* **ill'-use** to ill-treat.—*adjs* **ill-used'**
badly used or treated; **ill'-versed'** having scanty
knowledge or skill (with *in*).—**ill'-will'** unkind feeling: enmity.—*adj.* **ill'-wrest'ing** misinterpreting to
disadvantage.—**go ill with** to result in danger or misfortune to, **ill at ease** uneasy: embarrassed; **take it ill**
to be offended, **with an ill grace** ungraciously
[O.N. *illr.*]

illation *il-ā'shən, n.* the act of inferring from premises:
inference. conclusion.—*adj.* **illative** (*il'ə-tiv,* also *il-
ā'tiv*) pertaining to, of the nature of, expressing, or
introducing an inference: of a case in some Finno-
Ugric languages expressing direction into or towards
(*gram.*).—*n.* the illative case: a word in this case.—
adv. **ill'atively** (or *-ā'*). [L. *illātiō, -ōnis*—*illātus,*
used as pa.p. of *inferre,* to infer—*il-* (*in-*), in, *lātus,*
carried.]

illegal *il-ē'gl, adj.* contrary to law.—*v.t.* **ille'galise, -ize**
to render unlawful.—*n.* **illegality** (*-gal'i-ti*) the quality or condition of being illegal.—*adv.* **ille'gally.**
[Pfx. **il-** (**in-** (2)).]

illegible *il-ej'i-bl, adj.* that cannot be read: indistinct
—*ns.* **illeg'ibleness, illegibil'ity.**—*adv.* **illeg'ibly.**
[Pfx. **il-** (**in-** (2)).]

illegitimate *il-i-jit'i-mit, adj* not according to law: not
in the legal position of those born in wedlock or
legitimised. not properly inferred or reasoned: not
recognised by authority or good usage.—*n.* one born
out of wedlock —*v.t.* (*-māt*) to pronounce or render
illegitimate.—*n.* **illegit'imacy** (*-mə-si*).—*adv.* **illegit'imately.**—*n.* **illegitima'tion** the act of pronouncing or rendering, or state of being, illegitimate.
[Pfx. **il-** (**in-** (2)).]

illiberal *il-ib'ər-əl, adj.* niggardly: mean, narrow in
opinion or culture.—*v t.* **illib'eralise, -ize.**—*n.*
illiberality (*-al'i-ti*).—*adv.* **illib'erally.** [Pfx. **il-** (**in-**
(2)).]

illicit *il-is'it, adj* not allowable: unlawful: unlicensed.
—*adv.* **illic'itly.**—*n.* **illic'itness.** [L. *illicitus—il-
(in-),* not, *licitus,* pa.p of *licēre,* to be allowed.]

illimitable *il-im'it-ə-bl, adj.* that cannot be bounded:
infinite.—*n.* **illim'itableness.**—*adv.* **illim'itably.**—*n.*
illimita'tion.—*adj.* **illi'ited.** [Pfx. **il-** (**in-** (2)).]

illiquid *il-ik'wid, adj.* of assets, etc., not readily converted into cash: deficient in liquid assets.—*n* **illiquid'ity.** [Pfx. **il-** (**in-** (2))]

illiterate *il-it'ər-it, adj.* unacquainted with literature·
uneducated: ignorant: unable to read: of or characteristic of those who are without literary education:
ignorant in a particular field or subject —*n* an illiterate person.—*adv* **illit'erately.**—*ns* **illit'erateness, illit'eracy** (*-ə-si*) [Pfx **il-** (**in-** (2)).]

illocution *il-ə-kū'shən,* (*philos.*) *n* an act which is performed by a speaker in the actual utterance of words,
as an order, a promise (cf **perlocution**).—*adj* **illocū'-
tionary.** [Pfx **il-** (**in-** (1)).]

illogical *il-oj'i-kəl, adj.* contrary to the rules of logic
regardless of incapable of logic —*adv* **illog'ically.**—
n **illog'icalness.** [Pfx **il-** (**in-** (2)).]

illude il-ōōd', -ūd', v t. to trick [L illūdĕre—in, on, lūdĕre, lūsum, to play.]

illume il-ūm', -ōōm', v.t. a shortened poetic form of **illumine.**—v.t. **illum'inate** (-in-āt) to light up: to enlighten: to illustrate: to adorn with coloured lettering or illustrations: to confer power of vision upon.—adj. (-āt, -ıt) enlightened: pretending to enlightenment: admitted to a mystery.—n an initiate.—adj. **illu'minable** that may be illuminated.—adj. **illu'minant** enlightening —n. **illumină'tion** lighting up: enlightenment: intensity of lighting up: splendour: brightness: a decorative display of lights: adorning of books with coloured lettering or illustrations: divine inspiration or instance of it: the luminous flux per unit area expressed in lux (also **illu'minance**).—adj. **illu'minative** (-ə-tiv, -ā-tiv) giving light: illustrative or explanatory —n. **illu'minător.**—v t. **illu'mine** to make luminous or bright: to enlighten: to adorn.—n. **illu'miner** an illuminator. [L. illūmină̆re, -ātum, in, in, upon, lūmină̆re, to cast light]

illusion il-ōō'zhən, -ū', n. deceptive appearance· an apparition: false conception: delusion: a false sense-impression of something actually present (psych.).—ns. **illu'sionism** the doctrine that the external world is illusory· the production of illusion, esp the use of artistic techniques, as perspective, etc , to produce an illusion of reality; **illu'sionist** a believer in or practitioner of illusionism: one who produces illusions, a conjurer, prestidigitator.—adjs. **illu'sive** (-siv), **illu'sory** (-sər-i) deceiving by false appearances: false. —adv. **illu'sively.**—n. **illu'siveness.** [See illude.]

illustrate il'əs-trāt, v.t. to exemplify: to explain and adorn by pictures: to execute pictures for.—n. **illusträ'tion** the act of making lustrous or clear: the act of explaining: that which illustrates· exemplification, example: a picture or diagram elucidating, or at least accompanying, letterpress.—adj. **ill'ustrated** having pictorial illustrations.—n an illustrated periodical. —adjs. **illusträ'tional, illustrative** (il'əs-trā-tiv or -tra-, or il-us'trə-tiv), **illus'tratory** having the quality of making clear or explaining.—adv. **ill'ustratively** (or ill-us').—n **ill'ustrător.**—adj. **illus'trious** highly distinguished: noble: conspicuous.—adv. **illus'triously.**—n. **illus'triousness.** [L. illūstris; illūsträre, -ātum, lūsträre, to light up, prob.—lūx, light.]

illustrious, etc See illustrate.

Illyrian il-ır'ı-ən, adj. of, or pertaining to, Illyria, an ancient region to the East of the Adriatic Sea, its inhabitants, or their (prob Indo-European) language.—Also n.

im- im, pfx. same as **in-**, the form used with words beginning with b, m, or p, as in imbalance, immodest **I'm** im, a contraction of **I am.**

image im'ij, n. likeness: a statue: an idol: a representation in the mind, an idea: a picture or representation (not necessarily visual) in the imagination or memory· an appearance: that which very closely resembles anything: the figure of any object formed by rays of light reflected or refracted (opt.): an analogous figure formed by other rays (opt.): a metaphor or simile (rhet): (**public image**) the character, attributes, of a person, institution, etc., as perceived by the general public· a favourable self-representation of a public figure, etc —v t. to form an image of: to form a likeness of in the mind: to mirror· to imagine: to portray: to typify: to produce a pictorial representation of a part of the body for diagnostic medical purposes.—adjs **im'ageable; im'ageless** having no image.—ns. **imagery** (im'ij-ri, -ə-ri) the work of the imagination: mental pictures

figures of speech: images in general or collectively, **im'agism; im'agist** one of a twentieth-century school of poetry aiming at concentration, exact and simple language, and freedom of form and subject —Also adj —adj. **imagist'ic.**—**image orthicon** a kind of television camera tube [O Fr.,—L. imāgŏ, image; cf imitārī, to imitate]

imagine im-aj'ın, v.t. to form an image of in the mind: to conceive: to think: to think vainly or falsely. to conjecture: to contrive or devise.—v i to form mental images· to exercise imagination.—adj. **imag'inable.**—n **imag'inableness.**—adv. **imag'inably.**—adj **imag'inary** existing only in the imagination· not real: non-existent —n. **imagină'tion** the act of imagining: the faculty of forming images in the mind: the artist's creative power: that which is imagined: contrivance —adj. **imag'inative** (-ə-tiv, or -ā-tiv) full of imagination: suffused with imagination —ns. **imag'inativeness; imag'iner; imag'ining** that which is imagined.—**imaginary numbers, quantities,** non-existent quantities involving the square roots of negative quantities. [O.Fr. imaginer—L imāginārī —imāgŏ, an image.]

imagism, imagist. See image.

imago ı-mā'gŏ, -mā', n. the last or perfect state of insect life: an elaborated type, founded on a parent or other, persisting in the unconscious as an influence (psych.)·—pl. **imagines** (ı-mā'jın-ēz, -mā'gın-, -ma'), **ima'gos, -oes.** [L imāgŏ, -inis, image.]

imam ı-mam', **imaum** ı-möm', ns. the officer who leads the devotions in a mosque: (with cap.) a title for various Muslim potentates, founders, and leaders.—n. **imam'ate.** [Ar imăm, chief.]

imbalance im-bal'əns, n a lack of balance. [Pfx. **im-** (**in-** (2))]

imbecile im'bi-sēl, -sīl, -sıl, formerly im-bi-sēl', im-bes'il, adj. feeble (now generally in mind)· fatuous. —n. one who is imbecile: one whose defective mental state does not amount to idiocy, but who is incapable of managing his own affairs: loosely, a foolish, unwise or stupid person.—n. **imbecil'ity.** [Fr. imbécille (now imbécile)—L. imbēcillus]

imbed. Same as **embed.**

imbibe ım-bīb', v.t. to drink in: to absorb: to receive into the mind.—v.i. to drink, absorb —n **imbib'er.** [L. imbībĕre—in, in, into, bibĕre, to drink.]

imbricate im'bri-kāt, v.t to lay one overlapping another, as tiles on a roof.—v ı. to be so placed — adj. (-kit, -kāt) (of fish-scales, bird-scales, layers of tissue, teeth) overlapping like roof-tiles.—n. imbricā'tion. [L. imbrex, a tile, imbricāre, -ātum, to tile —imber, a shower of rain.]

imbroglio, embroglio ım-brŏl'yŏ, n a confused mass: a tangle: an embroilment: an ordered confusion (mus).—pl. **im-, embroglios.** [It , confusion—imbrogliare, to confuse, embroil]

imbrue ım-brōō', v t. to wet or moisten· to soak: to drench· to stain or dye —Also **embrue'.**—n. **imbrue'ment.** [O Fr. embreuver—bevre (Fr boire) —L bibĕre, to drink.]

imbue ım-bū', v.t to moisten: to tinge deeply: to fill, permeate (e.g. the mind) (with with). [O.Fr imbuer—L. imbuĕre—ın, and root of bibĕre, to drink]

imburse im-bûrs', v t to pay: to repay. [Pfx im- (**in-** (1)), and L bursa, a purse.]

imide im'īd, (chem) n any of a class of organic compounds formed from ammonia or a primary amine by replacing two hydrogen atoms by a metal or acid radical [Alteration of **amide.**]

imitate ım'i-tāt, v.t to strive to be like or produce

something like: to copy, not necessarily exactly: to mimic.—*n.* **imitability** (-*ə-bil'i-ti*).—*adj.* **im'itable** that may be imitated or copied.—*ns.* **im'itancy** the tendency to imitate; **im'itant** a counterfeit; **imitā'tion** the act of imitating: that which is produced as a copy, or counterfeit: a performance in mimicry: the repeating of the same passage, or the following of a passage with a similar one in one or more of the other parts of voices (*mus.*).—*adj.* sham, counterfeit: machine-made (as lace).—*adj.* **im'itative** inclined to imitate: formed after a model: mimicking.—*adv.* **im'itatively.**—*ns.* **im'itativeness; im'itator.** [L. *imitāri, -ātus.*]

immaculate *im-ak'ū-lit, adj.* spotless: unstained: pure. —*n.* **immac'ulacy** state of being immaculate.—*adv.* **immac'ulately.**—*n.* **immac'ulateness.**—**Immaculate Conception** the R.C. dogma that the Virgin Mary was conceived without original sin—first proclaimed as article of faith in 1854—not the same as the Virgin Birth. [L. *immaculātus*—*in-*, not, *maculāre*, to spot.]

immanent *im'ə-nənt, adj.* indwelling: pervading: inherent.—*ns.* **imm'anence, imm'anency** the pervasion of the universe by the intelligent and creative principle—a fundamental conception of pantheism. —*adj.* **immanental** (*-ent'l*).—*ns.* **imm'anentism** belief in an immanent God; **imm'anentist.** [L. *in*, in, *manēre*, to remain.]

Immanuel. See **Emmanuel.**

immaterial *im-ə-tē'ri-əl, adj.* not consisting of matter: incorporeal: unimportant.—*ns.* **immatē'rialism** the doctrine that there is no material substance; **immatē'rialist; immatērialITy** (*-al'*) the quality of being immaterial or of not consisting of matter.—*adv.* **immatē'rially.** [Pfx. **im-** (**in-** (2)).]

immature, immatured *im-ə-tyōōr(d)', -chōōr(d)', adjs.* not ripe: not perfect: come before the natural time: (**immature**) not fully developed (mentally, physically, etc.): (**immature**) (of behaviour, attitudes, etc.) childish.—*adv.* **immature'ly.**—*ns.* **immature'ness, immatur'ity.** [Pfx. **im-** (**in-** (2)).]

immeasurable *im-ezh'ər-ə-bl, adj.* that cannot be measured: very great.—*n.* **immeas'urableness.**—*adv.* **immeas'urably.** [Pfx. **im-** (**in-** (2)).]

immediate *im-ē'di-it, -dyət, -dyit, -jət, adj.* with nothing between: not acting by second causes: direct: present: without delay.—*n.* **immē'diacy** the state of being immediate: direct appeal to intuitive understanding.—*adv.* or *conj.* **immē'diately** (sometimes with *that*) as soon as.—*ns.* **immē'diateness; immē'diatism** immediateness: the policy of action at once, esp. (*U.S. hist.*) in abolition of slavery. [Pfx. **im-** (**in-** (2)).]

immedicable *im-(m)ed'i-kə-bl, adj.* incurable. [Pfx. **im-** (**in-** (2)).]

immemorial *im-i-mōr'i-əl, -mōr', adj.* ancient beyond the reach of memory.—*adv.* **immemō'rially.** [Pfx. **im-** (**in-** (2)).]

immense *i-mens', adj.* that cannot be measured: vast in extent: very large: fine, very good (*slang*).—*adv.* **immense'ly.**—*ns.* **immense'ness; immens'ity** an extent not to be measured: infinity: greatness. [Fr.,—L. *immēnsus*—*in-*, not, *mēnsus*, pa.p. of *metīrī*, to measure.]

immensurable *im-(m)en'shōōr-ə-bl, -syōōr-, -syər-, adj.* that cannot be measured.—*n.* **immensurabil'ity.** [Pfx. **im-** (**in-** (2)).]

immerse *im-(m)ûrs', v.t.* to dip under the surface of a liquid: to baptise by dipping the whole body: to engage or involve deeply.—*adj.* **immersed'** (*bot.*) embedded in the tissues.—*ns.* **immer'sion** the act of immersing: the state of being immersed: deep absorption or involvement: baptism by immersing: entry

into a position of invisibility as in eclipse or occultation (*astron.*): the application of liquid to a microscope object-glass: a method of teaching a foreign language by giving the learner intensive practice in a situation in which all communication is in the language concerned; **immer'sionism; immer'sionist** one who favours or practices baptism by immersion.—**immersion heater** an electrical apparatus directly immersed in the liquid, used for heating water. [From **in, merge.**]

immigrate *im'i-grāt, v.i.* to migrate or remove into a country with intention of settling in it.—*ns.* **imm'igrant** one who immigrates; **immigrā'tion.** [L. *immigrāre*—*in*, into, *migrāre, -ātum*, to remove.]

imminent *im'i-nənt, adj.* overhanging: intent: threatening: impending.—*ns.* **imm'inence; imm'inency.**—*adv.* **imm'inently.** [L. *imminēns, -entis*—*in*, upon, *minēre*, to project, jut.]

immiscible *im-(m)is'i-bl, adj.* not capable of being mixed.—*n.* **immiscibil'ity.** [Pfx. **im-** (**in-** (2)).]

immobile *im-(m)ō'bīl, -bēl, in U.S.-bil, adj.* immovable: not readily moved: motionless: stationary.—*n.* **immobilisā'tion, -z-.**—*v.t.* **immob'ilise, -ize** to render immobile: to put or keep out of action or circulation. —*n.* **immobil'ity.** [Pfx. **im-** (**in-** (2)).]

immoderate *im-od'ər-it, adj.* exceeding due bounds: extravagant: unrestrained.—*ns.* **immod'eracy, immod'erateness.**—*adv.* **immod'erately.**—*n.* **immoderā'tion** want of moderation: excess. [Pfx. **im-** (**in-** (2)).]

immodest *im-od'ist, adj.* wanting restraint: exceeding in self-assertion: impudent: wanting shame or delicacy: indecent.—*adv.* **immod'estly.**—*n.* **immod'esty.** [Pfx. **im-** (**in-** (2)).]

immolate *im'ō-lāt, im'əl-āt, v.t.* to offer in sacrifice.—*ns.* **immolā'tion** the act of sacrificing: the state of being sacrificed: that which is offered in sacrifice; **imm'olator.** [L. *immolāre, -ātum*, to sprinkle meal (on a victim), hence to sacrifice—*in*, upon, *mola*, meal.]

immoral *im-(m)or'əl, adj.* inconsistent with or disregardful of morality: sometimes esp. of sexual morality: wicked: licentious.—*ns.* **immor'alism** denial or rejection of morality; **immor'alist; immorality** (*im-or-, im-ər-al'i-ti*) the quality of being immoral: an immoral act or practice.—*adv.* **immor'ally.** [Pfx. **im-** (**in-** (2)).]

immortal *im-or'tl, adj.* exempt from death: imperishable: never to be forgotten.—*n.* one who will never cease to exist: (often with *cap.*) a god, esp. of the ancient Greeks and Romans: one whose works will always retain their supremacy.—*n.* **immortalisā'tion, -z-.**—*v.t.* **immor'talise, -ize** to make immortal.—*n.* **immortality** (*im-ör-, im-ər-tal'i-ti*).—*adv.* **immor'tally.**—**the Immortal Memory** a toast in memory of the Scottish poet, Robert Burns. [Pfx. **im-** (**in-** (2)).]

immortelle *im-or-tel', n.* an everlasting flower. [Fr. (*fleur*) *immortelle*, immortal (flower).]

immovable *im-ōōv'ə-bl, adj.* impossible to move: steadfast: unyielding: impassive: motionless: unalterable: not liable to be removed (*law*; commonly **immove'able**): real, not personal (*law*).—*n.* (*law*; usu. in *pl.* **immove'ables**) immoveable property.—*ns.* **immov'ableness, immovabil'ity.**—*adv.* **immov'ably.** [Pfx. **im-** (**in-** (2)).]

immune *im-ūn', adj.* exempt: not liable to danger, esp. infection: free from obligation.—*n.* one who is immune.—*n.* **immunisā'tion, -z-.**—*v.t.* **imm'unise, -ize** to render immune, esp. to make immune from a disease by injecting disease germs, or their poisons (either active or rendered harmless).—*n.* **imm'unity.** —**immuno-** in composition, immune, immunity, as in **immunochem'istry** (the chemistry of antibodies, antibody reactions, etc.).—*adj.* **immunolog'ical.**—*ns.* **immunol'ogist; immunol'ogy** the scientific study of immunity.—*adj.* **immunosuppress'ive** applied to drugs which lessen the body's rejection of e.g. transplanted organs.—*n.* **immunother'apy** the treatment of disease, now esp. cancer, by antigens which stimulate the patient's own natural immunity —**immune body** antibody. [L *immūnis*—*in*-, not, *mūnis*, serving.]

immure *im-ūr'*, *v.t.* to wall in: to shut up: to imprison (also *fig.*).—*n.* **immure'ment.** [L. *in*, in, *mūrus*, a wall.]

immutable *im-ūt'ə-bl*, *adj.* unchangeable.—*ns* **immūtabil'ity, immūt'ableness.**—*adv.* **immūt'ably.** [Pfx. **im-** (in- (2)).]

imp *imp*, *n.* a child: a mischievous child: a little devil or wicked spirit.—*v.t.* to graft, engraft (*arch*): to engraft feathers in (to mend a wing) (*falconry*).—*adj.* **imp'ish** like or characteristic of an imp, teasingly mischievous.—*adv.* **imp'ishly.**—*n.* **imp'ishness.** [O.E. *impa*—L.L. *impotus*, a graft—Gr. *emphytos*, engrafted.]

impact *im-pakt'*, *v.t.* to press firmly together: to drive close: to strike or collide.—*ns.* **im'pact** the blow of a body in motion impinging on another body: the impulse resulting from collision. the impulse resulting from a new idea or theory: strong effect, influence; **impac'tion** the act of pressing together, or of fixing a substance tightly in a body cavity: the condition so produced.—**impacted fracture** see **fract; impacted tooth** one wedged between the jawbone and another tooth and thus unable to come through the gum. [L. *impactus*, pa.p of *impingĕre*; see **impinge.**]

impair *im-pār'*, *v.t.* to diminish in quantity, value, or strength: to injure: to weaken.—*v.i.* to become worse: to decay.—*n.* impairing.—*n.* **impair'ment.** [O.Fr. *empeirer*, from L. *im-* (*in*-), intensive, *pējōrāre*, to make worse—*pējor*, worse.]

impala *im-pä'lə*, *n.* a large African antelope (*Aepyceros melampus*). [Zulu *i-mpālaj*.]

impale *im-pāl'*, *v.t.* to put to death by spitting on to a stake: to transfix: to combine palewise (*her.*).—Also **empale'.**—*n.* **impale'ment** the act or punishment of impaling: the marshalling side by side of two escutcheons combined in one (*her.*). [Fr. *empaler*—L. *in*, in, *pālus*, a stake.]

impalpable *im-pal'pə-bl*, *adj.* not perceivable by touch: extremely fine-grained: eluding apprehension. —*n.* **impalpabil'ity.**—*adv.* **impal'pably.** [Pfx. **im-** (in- (2)).]

impanel. See **empanel.**

impar(i)- *im-par-(i-)*, in composition, unequal.—*n.* **imparity** (*im-par'i-ti*) inequality.—*adj.* **imparisyllab'ic** having a syllable more in the other cases than in the nominative. [L. *impār*—*in*-, not, *pār*, equal.]

impart *im-pärt'*, *v.t.* to bestow a part of, or share out (*arch.*): to give (something abstract): to communicate, make known.—*v.i.* to give a part (of).—*ns.* **imparta'tion; impart'er.** [O.Fr. *empartir*—L. *impartīre*—*in*, on, *pars, partis*, a part.]

impartial *im-par'shl*, *adj.* not favouring one more than another: just.—*ns.* **impartiality** (*-shi-al'i-ti*), **impar'tialness.**—*adv.* **impar'tially.** [Pfx. **im-** (in- (2)).]

impartible *im-pärt'i-bl*, *adj.* not partible: indivisible. —*n.* **impartibil'ity.** [Pfx. **im-** (in- (2)).]

impassable *im-päs'ə-bl*, *adj.* not capable of being passed.—*ns.* **impassabil'ity, impass'ableness.**—*adv.* **impass'ably.**—*n.* **impasse** (*am-pas'*, *ē-pas*) a place from which there is no outlet: a deadlock. [Pfx. **im-** (in- (2)).]

impassible *im-pas'i-bl*, *adj.* incapable of suffering, injury, or emotion.—*ns* **impassibil'ity, impass'ibleness.**—*adv.* **impass'ibly.** [Church L. *impassibilis*—*in*-, not, *patī, passus*, to suffer.]

impassion *im-pash'ən*, *v.t.* to move with passion: to make passionate.—*adjs.* **impass'ionate** impassioned: dispassionate, **impass'ioned** moved by or charged with passion: animated [It. *impassionare*—L. *in*, in, *passiō, -ōnis*, passion.]

impassive *im-pas'iv*, *adj.* not susceptible of feeling: not showing feeling: imperturbable.—*adv.* **impass'ively.** —*ns.* **impass'iveness, impassiv'ity.** [Pfx. **im-** (in- (2)).]

impaste *im-pāst'*, *v.t.* to lay colours thick on.—*n.* **impasto** (*im-pas'tō*; It.) in painting and pottery, the thick laying on of pigments: the paint so laid on:—*pl.* **impast'os.**—*adjs.* **impast'oed, impast'o'd, impast'ed.** [L.L. *impastāre*—*in*, into, *pasta*, paste.]

impatient *im-pā'shənt*, *adj.* not able to endure or to wait: fretful: restless: intolerant (of).—*n.* **impā'tience.**—*adv.* **impā'tiently.** [L. *impatiēns, -entis*, impatient—*in*, not, *patiēns*, patient.]

impawn *im-pon'*, *v.t.* to put in pawn: to pledge: to risk. [Pfx **im-** (in- (1)).]

impeach *im-pēch'*, *v.t.* to disparage: to find fault with: to call in question: to arraign (esp. when a lower legislative house charges a high officer with grave offences before the upper house as judges): to turn king's evidence against, peach upon.—*adj.* **impeach'able.**—*ns.* **impeach'er; impeach'ment.** [O.Fr. *empech(i)er*, to hinder (Fr. *empêcher*)—L. *impedicāre*, to fetter—*in*, in, *pēdica*, fetter.]

impeccable *im-pek'ə-bl*, *adj.* not liable to sin: faultless. —*n.* one who is impeccable.—*adv.* **impecc'ably.**—*ns.* **impeccabil'ity, impecc'ancy.**—*adj.* **impecc'ant** without sin [Pfx. **im-** (in- (2)).]

impecunious *im-pi-kū'ni-əs, -nyəs, adj.* without money: short of money.—*n.* **impecunios'ity.** [Pfx. **im-** (in- (2)).]

impede *im-pēd'*, *v.t.* to hinder or obstruct.—*n.* **impe'dance** hindrance: an apparent increase of resistance to an alternating current owing to induction in a circuit (*elect.*).—*n.* **impediment** (*-ped'*) obstacle: a defect preventing fluent speech.—*n.pl.* **impediment'a** (L. *impedimenta*) military baggage: baggage generally: encumbrances.—*adjs.* **impediment'al, imped'itive** hindering. [L. *impedīre*—*in*, in, *pēs, pedis*, a foot.]

impel *im-pel'*, *v.t.* to urge forward: to excite to action: to instigate:—*pr.p.* **impell'ing**; *pa.t.* and *pa.p.* **impelled'.**—*adj.* **impell'ent** impelling or driving on —*n.* an impelling agent or power.—*n.* **impell'er** one who, or that which, impels: a rotor for transmitting motion. [L. *impellĕre, impulsum*—*in*, on, *pellĕre*, to drive.]

impend *im-pend'*, *v.i.* to threaten: to be about to happen.—*adjs.* **impend'ent, impend'ing.** [L. *impendēre* —*in*, on, *pendēre*, to hang.]

impenetrable *im-pen'i-trə-bl*, *adj.* not to be penetrated: impervious: inscrutable: occupying space exclusively (*phys.*).—*n.* **impenetrabil'ity.**—*adv.* **impen'etrably.** [Pfx. **im-** (in- (2)).]

impenitent *im-pen'i-tənt*, *adj.* not repenting.—*n.* one who does not repent: a hardened sinner.—*ns.* **impen'itence; impen'itency.**—*adv.* **impen'itently.** [Pfx. **im-** (in- (2)).]

imperative *im-per'ə-tiv*, *adj.* expressive of command, advice, or request: authoritative: peremptory: obligatory: urgently necessary: calling out for action.—*n.* that which is imperative: the imperative mood: a verb in the imperative mood.—*adv.* **imper'atively.**—

imp- for words beginning thus see also **emp.**

For other sounds see detailed chart of pronunciation.

categorical imperative see under **category**. [L. *imperātīvus—imperāre*, to command—*in*, in, *parāre*, to prepare.]

imperator *im-pər-ä'tər; L. im-per-ä'tor, n.* a commander: a ruler: an emperor.—*adj.* **imperatorial** (*im-per-ə-tō'ri-əl, -tö'*). [L. *imperător*, a general, later an emperor—*imperāre*, to command.]

imperceptible *im-pər-sep'ti-bl, adj.* not discernible by the senses: very small, slight or gradual.—*ns.* **impercep'tibleness, imperceptibil'ity.**—*adv.* **impercep'tibly.**—*adjs.* **impercep'tive, impercip'ient** not perceiving: having no power to perceive. [Pfx. **im-** (in- (2)).]

imperfect *im-pûr'fikt, adj* incomplete: defective: falling short of perfection: wanting any normal part, or the full normal number of parts: expressing continued or habitual action in past time (*gram.*): diminished, less by a semitone (*mus.*).—*n.* the imperfect tense: a verb in the imperfect tense.—*adj.* **imperfec'tible** that cannot be made perfect.—*ns.* **imperfectibil'ity; imperfection** (*-fek'shən*) the state of being imperfect: a defect.—*adj.* **imperfec'tive** denoting the aspect of the verb which indicates that the action described is in progress (*gram.*).—*advs.* **imperfec'tively** · (*gram.*); **imperfec'tly.**—*n.* **imper'fectness.—imperfect cadence** a cadence which is not resolved to the tonic key, esp. one passing from tonic to dominant chord. [Pfx. **im-** (in- (2)).]

imperforate *im-pûr'fə-rit, -d -rā-tid, adjs.* not pierced through or perforated: having no opening: abnormally closed (*med.*): without perforations for tearing apart, as a sheet of postage stamps. [Pfx. **im-** (in- (2)).]

imperial *im-pē'ri-əl, adj.* pertaining to, or of the nature of, an empire or emperor: sovereign, supreme: commanding, august: (of products, etc.) of superior quality or size.—*n.* a tuft of hair on lower lip: the top of a coach, carriage, or a trunk for carrying on it: a British size of paper, 22 × 30 in. (a U.S. size 23 × 33): a size of slates, 33 × 24 in.—*v.t.* **impē'rialise, -ize** to make imperial.—*ns.* **impē'rialism** the power or authority of an emperor: the policy of making or maintaining an empire: the spirit of empire; **impē'rialist.**—*adj.* **imperialist'ic.**—*n.* **imperiality** (*-al'i-ti*) imperial power, right, or privilege.—*adv.* **impē'rially.**—*adj.* **impē'rious** assuming command: haughty: tyrannical: domineering: peremptory: authoritative.—*adv.* **impē'riously.**—*n.* **impē'riousness.—imperial city** Rome; **imperial measure, weight** standard of measure, weight (**imperial gallon, yard, pound**) as fixed by parliament for the United Kingdom (final act 1963). [L. *impĕrium*, sovereignty.]

imperil *im-per'il, v.t.* to endanger:—*pa.p.* **imper'illed.** —*n.* **imper'ilment.** [Pfx. **im-** (in- (1)).]

imperious, etc. See **imperial.**

imperishable *im-per'ish-ə-bl, adj.* indestructible: everlasting.—*ns.* **imper'ishableness, imperishabil'ity.**—*adv.* **imper'ishably.** [Pfx. **im-** (in- (2)).]

imperium *im-pē'ri-əm, -per', n.* (the area, or extent, of) absolute sovereignty. [L. *impĕrium.*]

impermanence *im-pûr'mən-əns, n.* want of permanence.—*n.* **imper'manency.**—*adj.* **imper'manent.** [Pfx. **im-** (in- (2)).]

impermeable *im-pûr'mi-ə-bl, adj.* not permitting passage, esp. of fluids: impervious.—*ns.* **impermeabil'ity, imper'meableness.**—*adv.* **imper'meably.** [Pfx. **im-** (in- (2)).]

impermissible *im-pər-mis'i-bl, adj.* not permissible.— *n.* **impermissibil'ity.**—*adv.* **impermiss'ibly.** [Pfx. **im-** (in- (2)).]

impersonal *im-pûr'sən-əl, adj.* not having personality: used only in the third person singular (in English usu. with *it* as subject) (*gram.*): without reference to any particular person: objective, uncoloured by personal feeling.—*v.t.* **imper'sonalise, -ize.**—*n.* **impersonality** (*-al'i-ti*).—*adv.* **imper'sonally.** [Pfx. **im-** (in- (2)).]

impersonate *im-pûr'sən-āt, v.t.* to personify: to assume the person or character of, esp. on the stage.—*adj.* (*-it, -āt*) personified.—*ns.* **impersona'tion; imper'sonator.** [L. *in*, in, *persōna*, person; see **personate.**]

impertinent *im-pûr'ti-nənt, adj.* not pertaining to the matter in hand: trifling: intrusive: saucy: impudent. —*ns.* **imper'tinence, imper'tinency** that which is impertinent: intrusion: impudence, overforwardness: matter introduced into an affidavit, etc., not pertinent to the matter (*law*).—*adv.* **imper'tinently.** [Pfx. **im-** (in- (2)).]

imperturbable *im-pər-tûr'bə-bl, adj.* that cannot be disturbed or agitated: permanently quiet.—*n.* **imperturbabil'ity.**—*adv.* **impertur'bably.**— *n.* **imperturba'tion.** [L. *imperturbābilis—in-*, not, *perturbāre*, to disturb; see **perturb.**]

imperviable *im-pûr'vi-ə-bl, impervious im-pûr'vi-əs, adjs.* not to be penetrated: not easily influenced by ideas, arguments, etc., or moved or upset (with *to*).—*ns.* **imper'viableness, imperviabil'ity, imper'viousness.**—*adv.* **imper'viously.** [Pfx. **im-** (in- (2)).]

impetigo *im-pi-tī'gō, n.* a skin disease characterised by thickly-set clusters of pustules:—*pl.* **impetigines** (*-tij'i-nēz*), **impeti'gos.**—*adj.* **impetiginous** (*-tij'*). [L. *impetigō—impetĕre*, to rush upon, attack.]

impetus *im'pi-təs, n.* momentum: impulse: incentive: —*pl.* **im'petuses.**—*adj.* **impetuous** (*im-pet'ū-əs*) rushing on with impetus or violence: vehement: acting with headlong energy.—*n.* **impetuosity** (*-os'i-ti*). —*adv.* **impet'uously.**—*n.* **impet'uousness.** [L. *impetus* (pl. *impetūs*)—*in*, into, on, *petĕre*, seek.]

impi *im'pi, n.* a body of southern African native warriors. [Zulu.]

impiety *im-pi'ə-ti, n.* want of piety or veneration. [L. *impietās, -ātis—in*, not; cf. **piety.**]

impinge *im-pinj', v.i.* (with *on, upon, against*) to strike: to encroach.—*v.t.* to drive, strike:—*pr.p.* **imping'ing.**—*n.* **impinge'ment.**—*adj.* **imping'ent.** [L. *impingĕre—in*, against, *pangĕre*, to fix, drive in.]

impious *im'pi-əs* (also, esp. U.S., *im-pī'əs*), *adj.* irreverent: wanting in veneration, as for gods, parents, etc. [L. *impĭus—im-* (in-), not, *pĭus*; cf. **pious.**]

impish. See **imp.**

implacable *im-plak'ə-bl, -plāk', adj.* not to be appeased: inexorable: irreconcilable.—*ns.* **implac'ableness, implacabil'ity.**—*adv.* **implac'ably.** [Pfx. **im-** (in- (2)).]

implant *im-plänt', v.t.* to engraft: to plant firmly: to fix in: to insert: to instil or inculcate: to plant (ground, etc., with).—*n.* (*im'plänt*) something implanted in body tissue, as a graft, a pellet containing a hormone.—*n.* **implantā'tion.** [Pfx. **im-** (in- (1)).]

implausible *im-plöz'i-bl, adj.* not plausible.—*n.* **implausibil'ity.** [Pfx. **im-** (in- (2)).]

implement *im'pli-mənt, n.* a piece of equipment, a requisite: a tool or instrument of labour.—*v.t.* (often *-ment'*) to give effect to: to fulfil or perform.—*adj.* **implemen'tal** instrumental: effective.—*n.* **implementā'tion.** [L.L. *implēmentum—*L. *in*, in, *plēre*, to fill.]

implicate *im'pli-kāt, v.t.* to entwine together: to enfold: to involve: to entangle: to imply: to show to be, to have been, a participator.—*n.* a thing implied. —*adj.* (*-kit*) intertwined.—*n.* **implicā'tion.**—*adj.* **im'plicative** (or *im-plik'ə-tiv*) tending to implicate.— *adv.* **im'plicatively.**—*adj.* **implicit** (*im-plis'it*) implied: relying entirely, unquestioning: entangled, involved (*rare*).—*adv.* **implic'itly.**—*n.* **implic'itness.**

[L. *implicāre, -ātum*, also *-ītum—in*, in, *plicāre, -ātum* or *-itum*, to fold.]

implied, etc See **imply**.

implode *im-plōd'*, *v t* and *v i* to burst inwards: to sound by implosion —*ns*. **implod'ent** an implosive sound, **implosion** (*-plō'zhən*) bursting inward· in the formation of voiceless stops, compression of enclosed air by simultaneous stoppage of the mouth parts and the glottis (*phon.*): inrush of air in a suction stop (*phon.*) —*adj.* **implosive** (*-plōs'iv*, or *-plōz'*) —*n* an implosive consonant: a suction stop or (sometimes) a click [L *in*, in, *plōdĕre* (*plaudĕre*), to clap.]

implore *im-plōr'*, *-plor'*, *v.t* to ask earnestly· to entreat —Also *v i* —*n*. **implorā'tion.**—*adj* **imploratory** (*-plor'ə-tə-ri*) —*n* **implōr'er.**—*adv.* **implōr'ingly** in an imploring manner [L. *implōrāre*, to invoke with tears—*in*, in, *plōrāre*, to weep]

implosion. See **implode**.

imply *im-plī'*, *v t* to involve the truth or reality of to express indirectly: to insinuate: to signify:—*pr p* **ply'ing;** *pa t* and *pa p* **implied'.**—*adv* **impli'edly.** [O.Fr *emplier*—L *implicāre*]

impolder *im-pōl'dər*, *v t.* to make a polder of —Also **empol'der.** [Du *impolderen*, see **polder**.]

impolite *im-pə-līt'*, *adj* of unpolished manners· uncivil.—*adv* **impolite'ly.**—*n* **impolite'ness.** [Pfx. **im-** (**in-** (2)).]

impolitic *im-pol'i-tik*, *adj* not politic inexpedient — **impol'iticly.** [Pfx. **im-** (**in-** (2))]

imponderable *im-pon'dər-ə-bl*, *adj*. not able to be weighed or estimated without weight, immaterial without sensible weight —Also *n* —*ns* **impon'derableness, imponderabil'ity.**—*n pl* **impon'derables** factors in a situation whose influence cannot be gauged —*adj.* **impon'derous** weightless· very light [Pfx **im-** (**in-** (2))]

import *im-pōrt'*, *-port'*, *v t.* to bring in: to bring from abroad: to convey, as a word to signify: to betoken: to portend —Also *v i* —*n* **im'port** that which is brought from abroad meaning. importance. tendency.—*adj* **import'able.**—*ns* **import'ance** the fact of being important. extent of value or significance weight, consequence appearance of dignity —*adj* **import'ant** of great import or consequence: momentous. pompous —*adv.* **import'antly.**—*ns.* **importā'tion** the act of importing a commodity imported, **import'er.**—**invisible imports** such items in a national trade balance as money spent by tourists abroad, etc., opp to **visible imports** goods bought from foreign countries by traders [L *importāre, -ātum—in*, in, *portāre*, to carry]

importune *im-por-tūn'*, *-por'*, *v t* to urge or crave with troublesome application· to solicit for immoral purposes, make improper advances to —*v i* to be importunate.—*ns.* **impor'tunacy, import'unateness.**—*adj* **impor'tunate** (*-it, -āt*) troublesomely urgent· pressing. pertinacious —*v i.* to solicit pertinaciously — *advs.* **impor'tunately; importune'ly** (or *-por'*) —*ns.* **importun'er; importun'ing; importun'ity.** [L *importūnus*, inconvenient—*im-* (*in-*), not, *portus*, a harbour, cf. **opportune**.]

impose *im-pōz'*, *v t* to place upon something to lay on to enjoin· to set as a burden or task: to set up in or by authority. to pass off unfairly: to arrange or place in a chase, as pages of type (*print.*) —*v i* (with *on, upon*) to mislead, deceive. to lay a burden, as by encroaching, taking undue advantage of one's good nature· to act with constraining effect —*adj* **impos'able** capable of being imposed or laid on —*n* **impos'er.**—*adj* **impos'ing** commanding. impressive: adapted to impress forcibly: specious. deceptive — *adv.* **impos'ingly.**—*n* **impos'ingness.** [Fr *imposer*, see **compose**.]

imposition *im-pəz-ish'ən*, *n* a laying on· laying on of hands in ordination· a tax, a burden: a deception, a punishment task· the assembling of pages and locking them into a chase (*print*) [L. *impositiō, -ōnis—in*, on, *pōnĕre, pōsitum*, to place.]

impossible *im-pos'i-bl*, *adj* that cannot be: that cannot be done or dealt with: that cannot be true out of the question hopelessly unsuitable· beyond doing anything with —*n*. a person or thing that is impossible — *n* **impossibil'ity.** [Pfx **im-** (**in-** (2))]

impost[1] *im'pōst*, *n*. a tax, esp on imports· the weight carried by a horse in a handicap race (*coll*) [O Fr *impost* (Fr *impôt*)—L *impōnĕre, impōsitum*, to lay on]

impost[2] *im'pōst*, (*archit*) *n* the upper part of a pillar in vaults and arches, on which the weight of the building is laid a horizontal block resting on uprights [Fr *imposte*—It *imposta*—L *impōnĕre, impōsitum*]

impostor *im-pos'tər*, *n* one who assumes a false character or personates another.—Also **impost'er.**— *n* **impos'ture** (*-chər*) an imposition, fraud [L L.,— L *impōnĕre, impōsitum*, to impose.]

impotent *im'pə-tənt*, *adj* powerless helpless without sexual power —*ns* **im'potence, im'potency.**—*adv* **im'potently.** [Pfx **im-** (**in-** (2)).]

impound *im-pownd'*, *v t* to confine, as in a pound: to restrain within limits· to hold up in a reservoir to take legal possession of —*adj.* **impound'able.**—*ns* **impound'age; impound'er; impound'ment.** [Pfx **im-** (**in-** (1)), and **pound**[2]]

impoverish *im-pov'ər-ish*, *v t* to make poor (*lit* or *fig*) —*n* **impov'erishment.** [From O Fr. *empovrir, -iss,—L in*, in, *pauper*, poor.]

impracticable *im-prak'tik-ə-bl*, *adj* not able to be done: not able to be used or traversed —*ns* **impracticabil'ity, imprac'ticableness.**—*adv* **imprac'ticably.** [Pfx **im-** (**in-** (2))]

impractical *im-prak'ti-kl*, *adj* unpractical —*ns* **impracticality** (*-kal'*), **imprac'ticalness.** [Pfx **im-** (**in-** (2))]

imprecate *im'pri-kāt*, *v t* to call down by prayer (esp something evil) to invoke evil upon —*v i* to curse — *n* **imprecā'tion.**—*adj* **im'precatory** (*-kə-tə-ri*, or *-kā* or *kā'*) [L *imprecāri—in*, upon, *precāri, -ātus*, to pray]

imprecise *im-pri-sīs'*, *adj* not precise —*n*. **imprecis'ion.** [Pfx **im-** (**in-** (2))]

impregnable *im-preg'nə-bl*, *adj* that cannot be taken proof against attack —*n* **impregnabil'ity.**—*adv* **impreg'nably.** [Fr *imprenable*—L *in-*, not, *prendĕre, prehendĕre*, to take, *g*, a freak of spelling, has come to be pronounced]

impregnate *im'preg-nāt, -preg'*, *v t* to make pregnant to fecundate to fill or imbue (with the particles or qualities of another thing) to saturate (also *fig*) —*n* **impregnā'tion.** [L L *impraegnāre, -ātum—in*, in, *praegnāns*, pregnant]

impresario *im-pre-sa'ri-ō*, or *-za'*, *n* the manager of an opera company, etc a producer or organiser of entertainments a showman:—*pl* **impresa'rios, impresa'ri** (*-rē*) [It *—impresa*, enterprise]

imprescriptible *im-pri-skrip'ti-bl*, *adj* not liable to be lost by prescription, or lapse of time inalienable —*n* **imprescriptibil'ity.** [Pfx **im-** (**in-** (2))]

impress[1] *im-pres'*, *v t* to press. to apply with pressure, esp so as to leave a mark: to mark by pressure to produce by pressure: to stamp or print· to fix deeply in the mind: to affect the mind· to produce a profound effect upon, or upon the mind of —*v i.* to be impressive, make a good impression —*ns* **im'press** that which is made by pressure stamp distinctive mark, **impressibil'ity.**—*adj* **impress'ible** susceptible —*ns* **impression** (*im-presh'ən*) the act or result of impressing: pressure: a difference produced in a thing by action upon it: a single printing of a book: the effect of anything on the mind a profound effect on the emotions: a vague uncertain memory or inclination to believe: belief, generally ill-founded. an impersonation; **impressionabil'ity.**—*adj.* **impress'- ionable** able to receive an impression: very susceptible to impressions.—*n.* **impress'ionism** a nineteenth-century movement in painting, originating in France, aiming at the realistic representation of the play of light in nature, purporting to render faithfully what the artist actually saw, dispensing with the academic rules of composition and colouring (often with *cap.*) any similar tendency in other arts —*n* and *adj* **impress'ionist** an exponent of impressionism (often with *cap*): an entertainer who impersonates people —*adj* **impressionis'tic.**—*adv* **impressionist'ically.**—*adj.* **impressive** (-*pres'*) exerting or tending to exert pressure. capable of making a deep impression on the mind: solemn.—*adv.* **impress'ively.**—*n.* **impress'- iveness.**—**be under the impression** to think or believe without certainty. [*imprimère, -pressum—in, premère*]

impress² *im-pres'*, *v.t.* to force into service.—*n* **impress'ment** the act of impressing for service, esp in the navy. [Pfx im- (in- (1)), and cf **press²**.]

imprest *im'prest*, *n.* earnest-money: money advanced [Pfx. im- (in- (1)) and cf. **press²**.]

imprimatur *im-pri-mā'tər, n.* a licence or permission to print a book, etc [L *imprīmātur*, let it be printed, *subj.* pass of *imprimère—in*, on, *premère*, to press.]

imprint *im-print'*, *v t.* to print. to stamp. to impress: to fix in the mind —*n.* (*im'print*) that which is imprinted: the name of the publisher, time and place of publication of a book, etc , printed usu on the title-page: the printer's name on the back of the title-page or at the end of the book.—*n* **imprint'ing** a learning process in young animals in which their social preferences become restricted to their own species, or a substitute for this [Pfx. im- (in- (1)).]

imprison *im-priz'n*, *v.t.* to put in prison to shut up: to confine or restrain.—*n.* **impris'onment.** [Pfx. im- (in- (1)).]

improbable *im-prob'ə-bl*, *adj.* unlikely —*n.* **im- probabil'ity.**—*adv.* **improb'ably.** [Pfx im- (in- (2)).]

improbity *im-prōb'i-ti, -prob'*, *n.* want of probity [Pfx. im-. (in- (2)).]

impromptu *im-promp'tū, adj* improvised: off-hand —*adv* without preparation: on the spur of the moment —*n.* an extempore witticism or speech· an improvised composition: a musical composition with the character of an extemporisation [L. *impromptū* for *in promptū* (abl.), *in*, in, *promptus*, readiness.]

improper *im-prop'ər, adj.* not strictly belonging: not properly so called: not suitable: unfit: unbecoming unseemly: indecent.—*adv* **improp'erly.**—*n.* **im- prōpri'ety.**—**improper fraction** a fraction not less than unity. [L. *im-* (*in-*), not, *proprius*, own.]

improve *im-prōō'v'*, *v.t.* to make better.—*v.t* to grow better: to make progress: to make improvements: to follow up with something better (with *on*).—*ns* **improvabil'ity, improv'ableness.**—*adj.* **improv'- able.**—*adv.* **improv'ably.**—*ns.* **improve'ment** the act of improving: a change for the better: a thing changed, or introduced in changing, for the better: a better thing substituted for or following one not so good (often with *on*); **improv'er.**—*pr.p.* and *adj.* **improv'ing** tending to cause improvement: instructive: edifying: uplifting.—*adv.* **improv'- ingly.** [A.Fr. *emprower*—O.Fr. *en prou, preu*, into profit.]

improvident *im-prov'i-dənt, adj.* not provident or prudent· wanting foresight: thoughtless.—*n.* **improv'idence.**—*adv* **improv'idently.** [Pfx. im- (in- (2))]

improvise *im-prō-*, *-prə-vīz'*, or *im'*, *v t* to compose and recite, or perform, without preparation to bring about on a sudden: to make or contrive offhand or in emergency —*v t.* to perform extempore: to do anything offhand.—*n.* **improvisa'tion** (or *-prov'iz-*) the act of improvising. that which is improvised —*adjs* **improvisatō'rial** (-*iz-ə-*); **improvisatory** (-*iz'* or -*īz'*) —*n* **improvis'er.** [Fr. *improviser*—L. *in-*, not, *prōvīsus*, foreseen, see **provide.**]

imprudent *im-prōō'dənt, adj* wanting foresight or discretion· incautious: inconsiderate.—*n* **impru'- dence.**—*adv.* **impru'dently.** [Pfx. im- (in- (2))]

impudent *im'pū-dənt, adj* wanting shame or modesty brazen-faced· shamelessly bold. pert· insolent.—*n.* **im'pudence.**—*adv.* **im'pudently.** [L. *im-* (*in-*), not, *pudēns, -entis*, pr p of *pudēre*, to be ashamed.]

impugn *im-pūn'*, *v t* to oppose. to attack by words or arguments: to call in question.—*adj.* **impugnable** (-*pūn'*) —*ns.* **impugn'er; impugn'ment.** [L *impug- nāre*—in, against, *pugnāre*, to fight.]

impulse *im'puls*, *n* the act of impelling: the effect of an impelling force: force suddenly and momentarily communicated· a beat a single blow, thrust, or wave. a disturbance travelling along a nerve (**nerve impulse**) or a muscle an outside influence on the mind· a sudden inclination to act.—*n* **impul'sion** (-*shən*) impelling force: instigation —*adj.* **impuls'ive** having the power of impelling. acting or actuated by impulse: not continuous: given to acting upon impulse.—*adv* **impuls'ively.**—*n.* **impuls'iveness.**— **impulse buyer; impulse buying** the buying of goods on a whim rather than because of previous intent [L *impulsus*, pressure—*impellère*; see **impel.**]

impunity *im-pūn'i-ti, n* freedom or safety from punishment or ill consequences [L *impūnitās, -ātis—in*, not, *poena*, punishment]

impure *im-pūr'*, *adj* mixed with something else unclean materially, morally, or ceremonially —*adv.* **impure'ly.**—*ns* **impure'ness, impur'ity.** [Pfx. im- (in- (2))]

impute *im-pūt'*, *v t* to ascribe (usually evil). to charge to attribute vicariously (*theol*) —*adj* **imput'able** capable of being imputed or charged open to accusation· attributable.—*ns* **imput'ableness, imputabil'ity.**—*adv.* **imput'ably.**—*n* **imputā'tion** the act of imputing or charging· censure: reproach: the reckoning as belonging [Fr. *imputer*—L. *imputāre, -ātum—in*, in, *putāre*, to reckon]

in *in*, *prep.* expressing the relation of a thing to that which surrounds, encloses, includes, or conditions it, or to that which is assumed, held, maintained, or the relation of a right or possession to the person who holds or enjoys it: at: among: into: within: during: consisting of: by way of· because of: by or through· by the medium or method of. among the characteristics or possibilities of· wearing: belonging to —*adv.* within not out. at home· on the spot· in or to a position within or inward in or into office, parliament, etc.. in favour: in mutual favour: in intimacy. in fashion· in the market: in season. at the bat: as an addition· alight in pocket —*n* a member of the party in office or the side that is having its innings.—*adj* inward: proceeding inwards: that is fashionable, much in use, as **in-word, in-thing:** within a small group —**-in** in composition, indicating a (public) gathering of a group of people in one room, building, etc., orig as a form of protest (as in *sit-in, work-in*). now for any joint purpose (as in *love-in, teach-in*).— *adj* and *adv.* **in'-and-in'** (of breeding) from parents that are near akin —*adjs* **in'-built** built in, **in'-depth** of a survey, research, etc, detailed or penetrating thorough, comprehensive, not superficial —**in'-fighting** fighting or bitter rivalry, between individuals or within a group, that goes on more or less secretly (see also **infighting**—separate article) —*adj* **in'-flight** provided during an aeroplane flight —**in'group** a social group of people having the same interests and attitudes —*adj* and *adv* **in'-house'** within a particular company, establishment, etc —**in'-joke** a joke to be fully appreciated only by members of a particular limited group, **in'-off** (*billiards*) a losing hazard, **in'-patient** one lodged, fed and treated in a hospital.—*adjs* **in'-ser'vice** carried out while continuing with one's ordinary employment as *in-service training*. **in'shore** close to the shore. moving towards the shore —**in'-tray** a shallow container for letters, etc., still to be dealt with —**in as far as, in so far as,** insofar as to the extent that, **in as much as, inasmuch** as considering that; **in for** doomed to receive (esp unpleasant consequences): involved to the extent of entered for (see also **go**), **in for it** in for trouble committed to a certain course, **in it** in enjoyment of success in the running. **in itself** intrinsically. apart from relations, **in on** (*slang*) participating in, **ins and outs** (or **outs and ins**) turning this way and that. nooks and corners the whole details of any matter, those who repeatedly enter and leave, **in that** for the reason that, **in with** friendly with, associating much with enjoying the favour of, **nothing in it** no truth, no importance. no difficulty in the matter no important difference [O E. *in*]

in- *in-, pfx*, (1) in words derived from L and O E. used to form verbs with the sense in, into, sometimes used to form other parts of speech with this sense, sometimes used as an intensive or almost meaningless pfx, (2) in words derived from L, used to form negatives.

inability *in-ə-bil'i-ti, n* want of sufficient power incapacity [Pfx **in-** (2)]

in absentia *in ab-sensh'yə, ab-sent'i-a,* (L) in absence

inaccessible *in-ak-ses'i-bl,* or *-ək-, adj.* not to be reached, obtained, or approached —*ns.* **inaccessibil'ity, inaccess'ibleness.**—*adv* **inaccess'ibly.** [Pfx **in-** (2)]

inaccurate *in-ak'ūr-it, adj* not accurate incorrect —*n* **inacc'uracy** (*-ə-si*) —*adv* **inacc'urately.** [Pfx **in-** (2).]

inactive *in-akt'iv, adj* not active inert: having no power to move. sluggish idle lazy having no effect: not showing any action (*chem.*) —*n* **inac'tion.**—*adv* **inact'ively.**—*n.* **inactiv'ity** inaction inertness idleness [Pfx. **in-** (2)]

inadaptable *in-ə-dap'tə-bl, adj* that cannot be adapted.—*n* **inadaptā'tion** (*-ad-*) [Pfx **in-** (2)]

inadequate *in-ad'i-kwit, adj.* insufficient. short of what is required incompetent —Also *n* —*ns* **inad'equacy** (*-kwə-si*), **inad'equateness** insufficiency —*adv* **inad'equately.** [Pfx **in-** (2).]

inadmissible *in-əd-mis'i-bl, adj* not allowable —*n* **inadmissibil'ity.**—*adv.* **inadmiss'ibly.** [Pfx **in-** (2)]

inadvertent *in-əd-vûrt'ənt, adj* inattentive unintentional —*ns* **inadvert'ence, inadvert'ency** negligence oversight —*adv* **inadvert'ently.** [Pfx **in-** (2)]

inadvisable *in-əd-vi'zə-bl, adj* not advisable, unwise —*ns* **inadvisabil'ity, inadvis'ableness.** [Pfx **in-** (2)]

inalienable *in-āl'yən-ə-bl, -i-ən-ə-bl, adj* not capable of being transferred or removed —*n* **inalienabil'ity.**—*adv* **inal'ienably.** [Pfx **in-** (2)]

inalterable, -ability. Same as **unalterable,** etc

inane *in-ān', adj.* empty, void vacuous senseless characterless —*ns* **inanition** (*in-ə-nish'ən*) exhaus-

tion from want of food; **inanity** (*in-an'i-ti*) senselessness mental vacuity emptiness: an insipid empty-headed utterance [L *inānis*]

inanimate *in-an'i-mit,* **-d** *-māt-id, adjs* without animation without life: dead spiritless: dull —*ns* **inan'imateness, inanimā'tion.** [Pfx **in-** (2)]

inappellable *in-ə-pel'ə-bl, adj* incapable of being appealed against or challenged. [Pfx **in-** (2); see **appeal.**]

inapplicable *in-ap'lik-ə-bl, in-əp-lik', adj* not applicable —*n* **inapplicabil'ity.** [Pfx **in-** (2).]

inapposite *in-ap'ə-zit, adj* not apposite, suitable, or pertinent —*adv* **inapp'ositely.**—*n* **inapp'ositeness.** [Pfx **in-** (2)]

inappreciable *in-ə-prē'shə-bl, -shyə-bl, adj* too small or slight to be noticed, or to be important: priceless (*arch*) —*n* **inappreciation** (*-shi-ā'shən*) —*adj.* **inapprē'ciative** (*-shi-ə-tiv,* or *-shi-ā-tiv*) not valuing justly or at all [Pfx **in-** (2)]

inappropriate *in-ə-prō'pri-it, adj.* not appropriate, not suitable.—*adv* **inappro'priately.**—*n* **inappro'priateness.** [Pfx **in-** (2).]

inapt *in-apt', adj* not apt unfit, or unqualified —*ns.* **inapt'itude, inapt'ness** unfitness, awkwardness —*adv* **inapt'ly.** [Pfx. **in-** (2).]

inarticulate *in-ar-tik'ū-lit, adj.* not jointed or hinged indistinctly uttered or uttering. incapable of clear and fluent expression —*n* **inartic'ulacy.**—*adv* **inartic'ulately.**—*ns* **inartic'ulateness, inarticulā'tion** indistinctness of sounds in speaking [Pfx **in-** (2).]

in articulo mortis *in art-ik'ū-lō mor'tis, art-ik'ōō-lō,* (L) at the point of death.

inartistic, -al *in-ar-tis'tik, -əl, adjs.* not artistic: deficient in appreciation of art —*adv.* **inartis'tically.** [Pfx **in-** (2)]

inasmuch *in-az-much', -əz-.* See **in.**

inattentive *in-ə-ten'tiv, adj* careless: not fixing the mind to attention. neglectful —*ns* **inatten'tion, inatten'tiveness.**—*adv.* **inatten'tively.** [Pfx **in-** (2)]

inaudible *in-od'i-bl, adj* not able to be heard.—*ns* **inaudibil'ity, inaud'ibleness.**—*adv* **inaud'ibly.** [Pfx **in-** (2)]

inaugurate *in-o'gūr-āt, v t* to induct formally into an office: to cause to begin to make a public exhibition of for the first time —*adj* **inau'gural** pertaining to, or done at, an inauguration —*n* an inaugural address —*ns* **inaugurā'tion; inau'gurātor.**—*adj.* **inau'gura-tory** (*-ə-tər-i*) [L *inaugurāre, -ātum,* to inaugurate with taking of the auspices, see **augur.**]

inauspicious *in-o-spish'əs, adj* not auspicious. ill-omened: unlucky —*adv* **inauspic'iously.**—*n* **inauspic'iousness.** [Pfx **in-** (2)]

in-between *in-bi-twēn', adj* intervening. intermediate —*n* an interval an intermediary any thing or person that is intermediate

inboard *in'bōrd, -bord, adv* and *adj* within the hull or interior of a ship. [Pfx **in-** (1)]

inborn *in'born, adj* born in or with one: innate: implanted by nature [Pfx **in-** (1)]

inbreed *in'brēd, in-brēd', v.t* to breed or generate within to breed in-and-in—*pa p* and *adj* **in'bred** innate bred in-and-in —*n* **in'breeding.** [Pfx **in-** (1)]

Inca *ing'kə, n* an Indian of Peru a member of the old royal family of Peru a Peruvian king or emperor — Also *adj* [Quechua, prince]

incalculable *in-kal'kū-lə-bl, adj* not calculable or able to be reckoned too great to calculate unpredictable —*ns* **incalculabil'ity, incal'culableness.**—*adv* **incal'-culably.** [Pfx **in-** (2)]

in camera. See **camera.**

incandesce *in-kan-des', v t* to be luminous by heat — *n* **incandesc'ence** a white heat —*adj* **incandesc'ent**

white-hot.—*n*. **incandescent lamp** one whose light is produced by heating something to white heat [L *in*, in, *candēscēre—candēre*, to glow]

incantation *in-kan-tā'shən, n* a formula of words said or sung for purposes of enchantment the use of spells [L *incantāre*, to sing a magical formula over.]

incapable *in-kā'pə-bl, adj*. not capable unable (with *of*). incompetent helplessly drunk disqualified —*n* an incompetent person one who is helplessly drunk —*n* **incapabil'ity.**—*adv* **inca'pably.** [Pfx in- (2)]

incapacious *in-kə-pā'shəs, adj* not large, narrow: of small capacity —*n* **incapā'ciousness.**—*v t* **incapacitate** (*-pas'*) to disable to make unfit (for) to disqualify legally —*ns* **incapacità'tion** a disqualifying, **incapac'ity** want of capacity inability disability legal disqualification [L *incapāx, -ācis*]

incapsulate *in-kap'sūl-āt, v t* to enclose as in a capsule [Pfx in- (1)]

incarcerate *in-kar'sər-āt, v t* to imprison: to confine —*n* **incarcerā'tion** imprisonment obstinate constriction or strangulation (*surg*) [L *in*, in, *carcer*, a prison.]

incarnadine *in-kar'nə-dīn, -din, v t*. to dye red —*adj* carnation-coloured flesh-colour blood-red [Fr *incarnadin*—It. *incarnadino*, carnation, flesh-colour]

incarnate *in-kar'nāt*, or *in', v.t* to embody in flesh, give human form to: to personify (*fig*) —*v t* to form flesh, heal.—*adj* (*-kar'nit, -nat*) invested with flesh personified.—*n* **incarnā'tion** (often with *cap*) the act of embodying in flesh, esp of Christ an incarnate form manifestation, visible embodiment the process of healing, or forming new flesh (*surg.*) [L L *incarnāre, -ātum*—L *in*, in, *carō, carnis*, flesh.]

incautious *in-ko'shəs, adj* not cautious or careful — *ns* **incau'tion, incau'tiousness.**—*adv* **incau'tiously.** [Pfx. in- (2)]

incavo *in-ka'vō, n*. the incised part in an intaglio [It . —L *in*, in, *cavus*, hollow.]

incendiary *in-sen'di-ər-i, n* one who maliciously sets fire to property: one who inflames passions or promotes strife an incendiary bomb —*adj*. relating to incendiarism adapted or used for setting buildings, etc., on fire: tending to excite strife —*n* **incen'diarism**—**incendiary bomb** a bomb containing a highly inflammable substance and designed to burst into flames on striking its objective [L *incendiārius—incendium—incendēre*, to kindle]

incense[1] *in-sens', v t* to inflame with anger to incite, urge. [O Fr *incenser*—L *incendēre, incēnsum*, to kindle]

incense[2] *in'sens, n* material burned or volatilised to give fragrant fumes, esp in religious rites—usu a mixture of resins and gums, etc the fumes so obtained any pleasant smell.—*v t* to perfume or fumigate with incense to offer incense to [O Fr *encens*—L *incēnsum—incendēre*, to set on fire]

incentive *in-sent'iv, adj* inciting, encouraging —*n* that which incites to action [L *incentīvus*, striking up a tune—*incinēre—in*, in, *canēre*, to sing]

incentre *in'sen-tər, n* the centre of the inscribed circle or sphere [Pfx in- (1)]

inception *in-sep'shən, n* beginning —*adj* **incep'tive** beginning or marking the beginning. inchoative (*gram*) —*n* (*gram*) an inchoative verb [L *incipēre, inceptum*, to begin—*in*, in, on, *capēre*, to take]

incessant *in-ses'ənt, adj* uninterrupted continual — *adv*. **incess'antly** unceasingly [L *incessāns, -antis* —*in-*, not, *cessāre*, to cease]

incest *in'sest, n* sexual intercourse within the prohibited degrees of kindred —*adj* **incest'ous** per-taining to, or characterised by, incest, turned inward on itself, or of, or within. a small closely-knit group (*fig*) —*adv* **incest'uously.**—*n* **incest'uousness.** [L *incestum—in-*, not, *castus*, chaste]

inch[1] *inch, insh, n*. the twelfth part of a foot, equal to 2·54 cm the amount of e g rainfall that will cover a surface to the depth of one inch (now measured in millimetres) the amount of atmospheric pressure needed to balance the weight of a column of mercury one inch high (now measured in millibars), proverbially, a small distance or degree: (in *pl*) stature —*v t* and *v i* to move by slow degrees — **inch'-tape** a measuring tape divided into inches; **inch'-worm** a looper caterpillar —**by inches, inch by inch** by small degrees, **every inch** entirely, thoroughly [O E *ynce*, an inch—L *uncia*, a twelfth part, cf **ounce**[1].]

inch[2] *insh*, (*Scot*) *n* an island [Gael *innis*, island]

inchoate *in-kō'āt, in'kō-āt, adj* only begun. unfinished. rudimentary not established —*adj* **inchoative** (*in-kō'ə-tiv* or *in-kō-ā'tiv*) incipient denoting the beginning of an action (*gram*) —*n* (*gram*) an inchoative verb [L *inchoāre* (for *incohāre*), *-ātum*, to begin]

incident *in'si-dənt, adj* falling upon something liable to occur naturally belonging (to): consequent —*n* an event a subordinate action: that which naturally belongs to or is consequent on something else: a minor event showing hostility and threatening more serious trouble: a brief violent action, e g a bomb explosion —*n* **in'cidence** the frequency or range of occurrence the fact or manner of falling the falling of a ray on a surface the falling of a point on a line, or a line on a plane (*geom*) —*adj* **incidental** (*-dent'l*) incident: striking or impinging, liable to occur naturally attached accompanying: concomitant occasional, casual —*n* anything that occurs incidentally —*adv* **incident'ally** in an incidental way loosely, by the way, parenthetically, as a digression. —*n* **incident'alness.**—**incidental music** music accompanying the action of a play [L *incīdēns, -entis* —*in*, on, *cadēre*, to fall]

incinerate *in-sin'ər-āt, v t* to reduce to ashes.—*ns* **incinerā'tion; incin'erātor** a furnace for consuming anything [L *incinerāre, -ātum—in*, in, *cinis, cineris*, ashes]

incipient *in-sip'i-ənt, adj* beginning nascent —*ns* **incip'ience, incip'iency.**—*adv* **incip'iently.** [L *incipiēns, -entis*, pr p of *incipēre*, to begin]

incise *in-sīz', v t* to cut into to cut or gash: to engrave. —*adj* **incised'** cut engraved cut to about the middle (*bot*) —*n* **incision** (*in-sizh'ən*) the act of cutting in, esp (*surg*) into the body a cut: a notch trenchancy —*adj* **incisive** (*-sīs'*) having the quality of cutting in trenchant acute sarcastic —*adv* **inci'sively.**—*ns* **inci'siveness; incisor** (*-sīz'ər*) a cutting or fore-tooth [Fr *inciser*—L *incīdēre, incīsum—in*, into, *caedēre*, to cut]

incite *in-sīt', v t* to move to action to instigate —*ns* **incitā'tion** (*-sit-, -sīt-*) the act of inciting or rousing: an incentive, **incite'ment; incit'er,**—*adv* **incit'ingly.** [Fr .—L *incitāre—in*, in, *citāre*, to rouse—*ciēre*, to put in motion]

incivil *in-siv'il, adj* (*Shak*) uncivil —*n* **incivil'ity** want of civility or courtesy impoliteness: an act of discourtesy (in this sense *pl* **incivil'ities**) [Pfx in- (2)]

inclasp *in-klasp'* Same as **enclasp.**

inclement *in-klem'ənt, adj* severe stormy harsh —*n* **inclem'ency.**—*adv* **inclem'ently.** [Pfx in- (2)]

incline *in-klīn', v i* to lean forward or downward to bow or bend to deviate or slant: to slope to tend to be disposed —*v t* to cause to bend downwards to turn. to cause to deviate to slope to tilt to direct to dispose —*n* (*in'klin, in-klin'*) a slope a sloping tunnel or shaft (*min*) —*adj* **inclin'able** leaning. capable of being, tilted or sloped tending somewhat disposed favourably disposed —*ns* **inclin'ableness; inclinā'tion** (*in-klin-*) the act of inclining a bend or bow a slope or tilt a deviation angle with the horizon or with any plane or line tendency disposition of mind natural aptness favourable disposition, preference. affection —*adjs* **inclinā'tional; inclined'** bent sloping oblique having a tendency disposed —*n* **inclin'ing** inclination —*n* **inclinom'eter** (*-klin-*) an instrument for measuring slopes or inclination [L. *inclināre*, to bend towards—*in*, into, *clīnāre*, to lean]

inclose, inclosure. See **enclose.**

include *in-klōō d'*, *v t* to enclose to comprise as a part to classify, or reckon as part to take in —*adj* **includ'ed** enclosed. comprised not protruding (*bot*) —*prep* (or *pr p* merging in *prep*) **includ'ing** with the inclusion of —*adj* **includ'ible.**—*n* **inclusion** (*-klōō'zhən*) the act of including that which is included a foreign body enclosed in a crystal, or the like —*adj* **inclusive** (*-klōō'siv*) shutting in enclosing comprehensive including everything comprehending the stated limit or extremes, including (with *of*) included (*obs* or *loose*) —*adv* **inclu'sively.** [L. *inclūdere, inclūsum—in, in, claudēre,* to shut]

incognisable, incognizable *in-kog'niz-ə-bl,* or *in-kon'iz-ə-bl, adj* that cannot be known or distinguished —*adj* **incog'nisant, incog'nizant** not cognisant —*ns* **incog'nisance, incog'nizance** failure to recognise [See **cognition, recognise.**]

incognito *in-kog'ni-tō, in-kog-nē'tō, adj* unknown. unidentified disguised under an assumed title —*adv* under an assumed name with concealment, or feigned concealment. of identity —*n* concealment, real or feigned —*pl* **incognitos** [It .—L *incognitus—in-*, not. *cognitus,* known—*cognōscēre,* to recognise, come to know]

incognizable etc See **incognisable.**

incoherent *in-kō-hēr'ənt, adj* not coherent loose rambling —*ns* **incoher'ence, -ency.**—*adv* **incohēr'ently.**—*n* **incohē'sion.**—*adj* **incohē'sive** (*-siv*) [Pfx **in-** (2)]

incombustible *in-kəm-bust'i-bl, adj* incapable of combustion [Pfx **in-** (2)]

income *in'kum, in'kəm, ing'kəm, n* that which comes in profit, or interest from anything revenue —*n* **comer** (*in'kum-ər*) one who comes in one who comes to live in a place. not having been born there —*adj* **in'coming** coming in accruing ensuing, next to follow —*n* the act of coming in revenue —**incomes policy** a government policy of curbing inflation by controlling wages, **income tax** a tax directly levied on income or on income over a certain amount [Pfx **in-** (1)]

incommensurable *in-kəm-en'shə-ra-bl, -shōō-, adj* having no common measure incommensurate —*n* a quantity that has no common measure with another, esp with rational numbers —*ns* **incommensurabil'ity, incommen'surableness.**—*adj* **incommen'surably.**—*adj* **incommen'surate** disproportionate not adequate incommensurable —*adv* **incommen'surately.**—*n* **incommen'surateness.** [Pfx **in-** (2)]

incommode *in-kəm-ōd', v t* to cause trouble or inconvenience to —*adj* **incommō'dious** inconvenient (of e g a house) rather small —*adv* **incommō'diously.**—*n* **incommō'diousness.** [Fr *incommoder*—L *incommodāre—in-*, not, *commodus,* commodious]

incommunicable *in-kəm-ūn'i-kə-bl, adj* that cannot be communicated or imparted to others —*ns* **in-**

communicabil'ity, incommun'icableness.—*adv* **incommun'icably.** [Pfx **in-** (2)]

incommunicado *in-kəm-ūn-i-ka'dō, adj* and *adv* without means of communication in solitary confinement [Sp *incomunicado*]

incommutable *in-kəm-ūt'ə-bl, adj* that cannot be commuted or exchanged —*ns* **incommutabil'ity, incommut'ableness.**—*adv* **incommut'ably.** [Pfx **in-** (2)]

incomparable *in-kom'pər-ə-bl, adj* not admitting comparison matchless —*ns* **incomparabil'ity, incom'parableness.**—*adv* **incom'parably.** [Pfx **in-** (2)]

incompatible *in-kəm-pat'i-bl, adj* not consistent contradictory incapable of existing together in harmony or at all incapable of combination, co-operation, functioning together mutually intolerant or exclusive irreconcilable —*n* a thing incompatible with another (in *pl*) things which cannot co-exist —*ns* **incompatibil'ity** the state of being incompatible an incompatible feature. element. etc . **incompat'ibleness.**—*adv* **incompat'ibly.** [Pfx **in-** (2)]

incompetent *in-kom'pi-tənt, adj* wanting adequate powers· wanting the proper legal qualifications· grossly deficient in ability for one's work —*n* an incompetent person —*ns* **incom'petence, incom'petency.**—*adv* **incom'petently.** [Pfx **in-** (2)]

incomplete *in-kəm-plēt', adj* imperfect unfinished wanting calyx, corolla, or both (*bot*) —*adv* **incomplete'ly.**—*ns* **incomplete'ness; incompletion.** [Pfx **in-** (2)]

incomprehensible *in-kom-pri-hens'i-bl, adj* not capable of being understood not to be contained within limits (*theol*) —*ns* **incomprehensibil'ity, incomprehens'ibleness.**—*adv* **incomprehens'ibly.**—*n* **incomprehen'sion** lack of comprehension —*adj* **incomprehens'ive** not comprehensive —*n* **incomprehens'iveness.** [Pfx **in-** (2)]

incompressible *in-kəm-pres'i-bl, adj* not to be compressed into smaller bulk —*ns* **incompressibil'ity, incompress'ibleness.** [Pfx **in-** (2)]

inconceivable *in-kən-sēv'ə-bl, adj* that cannot be conceived by the mind· incomprehensible involving a contradiction in terms physically impossible: taxing belief or imagination (*coll*) —*ns* **inconceivabil'ity, inconceiv'ableness.**—*adv* **inconceiv'ably.** [Pfx **in-** (2)]

inconclusive *in-kən-klōōs'iv, adj* not settling a point in debate. indeterminate. indecisive —*adv* **inconclus'ively.**—*n* **inconclus'iveness.** [Pfx **in-** (2)]

incondite *in-kon'dit, -dīt, adj* not well put together. irregular, unfinished [L *inconditus—in-*, not, *condēre, conditum,* to build]

incongruous *in-kong'grōō-əs, adj,* inconsistent not fitting well together. disjointed unsuitable —Also **incong'ruent.**—*ns* **incongruity** (*-kong-* or *-kən-grōō'*), **incong'ruousness.**—*adv* **incong'ruously.** [Pfx **in-** (2)]

inconscionable *in-kon'shən-ə-bl, adj* unconscionable [Pfx **in-** (2)]

inconsequent *in-kon'si-kwənt, adj* not following from the premises illogical irrelevant· disconnected unrelated unimportant —*n* **incon'sequence.**—*adj* **inconsequential** (*-kwen'shl*) not following from the premises of no consequence or value —*adjs* **inconsequen'tially; incon'sequently.** [Pfx **in-** (2)]

inconsiderable *in-kən-sid'ər-ə-bl, adj* not worthy of notice unimportant of no great size —*n* **inconsid'erableness.**—*adv* **inconsid'erably.** [Pfx **in-** (2)]

inconsiderate *in-kən-sid'er-it, adj* not considerate thoughtless rash. imprudent —*adv* **inconsid'erately.** —*ns* **inconsid'erateness. inconsiderā'tion.** [Pfx **in-** (2)]

inconsistent *in-kən-sist'ənt, adj.* not consistent: not suitable or agreeing: intrinsically incompatible: self-contradictory: changeable, fickle.—*ns.* inconsist'ence, inconsist'ency.—*adv.* inconsist'ently. [Pfx. in- (2).]

inconsolable *in-kən-sōl'ə-bl, adj.* not to be comforted. —*n.* inconsol'ableness.—*adv.* inconsol'ably. [Pfx. in- (2).]

inconsonant *in-kon'sən-ənt, adj.* not consonant.—*n.* incon'sonance.—*adv.* incon'sonantly. [Pfx. in- (2).]

inconspicuous *in-kən-spik'ū-əs, adj.* not conspicuous. —*adv.* inconspic'uously.—*n.* inconspic'uousness. [Pfx. in- (2).]

inconstant *in-kon'stənt, adj.* subject to change: fickle. —*n.* incon'stancy.—*adv.* incon'stantly. [Pfx. in- (2).]

incontestable *in-kən-test'ə-bl, adj* too clear to be called in question: undeniable.—*n.* incontestabil'ity.—*adv* incontest'ably. [Pfx. in- (2).]

incontinent *in-kon'ti-nənt, adj.* not restraining the passions or appetites: unchaste: unable to restrain natural discharges or evacuations (*med.*).—*ns.* incon'-tinence, incon'tinency.—*adv.* incon'tinently. [L. *incontinēns, -entis—in,* not, *continēns;* see continent.]

incontrovertible *in-kon-trə-vûrt'i-bl, adj.* too clear to be called in question.—*n.* incontrovertibil'ity.—*adv.* incontrovert'ibly. [Pfx. in- (2)]

inconvenient *in-kən-vēn'yənt, adj.* unsuitable: causing trouble or uneasiness: increasing difficulty: incommodious.—*v.t.* inconvēn'ience to trouble or incommode.—*ns.* inconvēn'ience, inconvēn'iency.—*adv* inconvēn'iently. [Pfx. in- (2).]

inconvertible *in-kən-vûrt'i-bl, adj* that cannot be changed or exchanged.—*n.* inconvertibil'ity.—*adv* inconvert'ibly. [Pfx. in- (2).]

inco-ordinate (also incoor- in both words) *in-kō-ôrd'(i)-nit, adj.* not co-ordinate.—*n.* inco-ordination (*-i-nā'shən*) want or failure of co-ordination. [Pfx. in- (2).]

incorporate[1] *in-kor'pər-āt, v.t.* to form into a body: to combine into one mass, or embody: to merge: to absorb: to form into a corporation: to admit to a corporation.—*v.i.* to unite into one mass: to form a corporation.—*adj.* (*-it*) united in one body: constituted as an incorporation.—*adj.* incor'porating (*philol.*) combining the parts of a sentence in one word.—*n.* incorpora'tion the act of incorporating: the state of being incorporated: the formation of a legal or political body: an association: an incorporated society.—*adj.* incor'porative (*-ə-tiv, -ā-tiv*).—*n.* incor'porator. [L. *incorporāre, -ātum—in,* in, into, *corpus, -oris,* body.]

incorporate[2] *in-kōr'pər-it, -āt, adj.* without a body: unembodied.—*adj.* incorporeal (*-pō', -po'ri-əl*) not having a body: spiritual: intangible. [L. *incorporātus, incorporālis,* bodiless—*in-,* not, *corpus, -oris,* body.]

incorrect *in-kər-ekt', adj.* containing faults: not accurate: not correct in manner or character.—*adv.* incorrect'ly.—*n.* incorrect'ness. [Pfx. in- (2).]

incorrigible *in-kor'i-ji-bl, adj.* beyond correction or reform.—Also *n.*—*ns.* incorr'igibleness, incorrigibil'ity.—*adv.* incorr'igibly. [Pfx. in- (2).]

incorrupt *in-kər-upt', adj.* sound: pure: not depraved: not to be influenced by bribes—*adj.* incorrupt'ibly not capable of decay: that cannot be bribed: inflexibly just.—*ns.* incorrupt'ibleness, incorruptibil'ity.—*adv.* incorrupt'ibly.—*ns.* incorrup'tion, incorrupt'ness.—*adj.* incorrupt'ive.—*adv* incorrupt'ly. [Pfx. in- (2).]

increase *in-krēs', v.i.* to grow in size, number,—*v.t.* to make greater in size, number.—*n.* in'crease growth: increment: addition to the original stock profit produce: progeny (*arch.*).—*adj* increas'able.—*n.* in-

creas'er.—*n.* and *adj.* increas'ing.—*adv.* increas'-ingly. [M.E. *encressen*—A.Fr. *encresser*—L. *in-crēscēre—in, crēscēre,* to grow.]

incredible *in-kred'i-bl, adj.* surpassing belief: difficult to believe in: very great: unusually good (*coll.*).—*ns.* incredibil'ity; incred'ibleness.—*adv.* incred'ibly. [Pfx. in- (2).]

incredulous *in-kred'ū-ləs, adj.* hard of belief, sceptical: not believing.—*ns.* incredū'lity (*-krid-*) incred'ū-lousness.—*adv.* incred'ulously. [Pfx. in- (2)]

increment *ing'* or *in'kri-mənt, n.* increase: amount of increase: an amount or thing added: the finite increase of a variable quantity (*math.*): an adding of particulars towards a climax (*rhet.*).—*adj.* incremental (*-ment'l*). —unearned increment any exceptional increase in the value of land, houses, etc., not due to the owner's labour or outlay. [L. *incrēmentum—incrēscēre,* to increase.]

incriminate *in-krim'in-āt, v.t.* to charge with a crime or fault, to criminate: to implicate, involve in a charge.—*adj.* incrim'inatory. [Pfx. in- (1).]

incrust, incrustation. See encrust, encrustation.

incubate *in'* or *ing'kū-bāt, v.i.* to sit on eggs: to hatch: to undergo incubation.—*v.t* to hatch: to foster the development of (as bacteria, etc.) —*n.* incubā'tion the act of sitting on eggs to hatch them: hatching (natural or artificial): fostering (as of bacteria, etc.): the period between infection and appearance of symptoms (*med.*).—*adjs.* in'cubative, in'cubatory.—*n.* in'cubator a brooding hen: an apparatus for hatching eggs by artificial heat, for rearing prematurely born children, or for developing bacteria [L. *incubāre, -ātum* (usu. *-itum*)—*in,* on, *cubāre,* to lie, recline.]

incubus *in'* or *ing'kū-bəs, n.* the nightmare: a devil supposed to assume a male body and have sexual intercourse with women in their sleep: any oppressive person, thing, or influence:—*pl.* in'cubuses, in'cubi (*-bī*). [L. *incūbus,* nightmare—*in,* on, *cubāre,* to lie.]

incudes. See incus.

inculcate *in'kul-kāt* or *-kul', v.t.* to instil by frequent admonitions or repetitions.—*n.* inculcā'tion.—*adj.* inculc'ative (*-ə-tiv*).—*n.* in'culcātor.—*adj.* inculc'-atory. [L. *inculcāre, -ātum—in,* into, *calcāre,* to tread—*calx,* heel.]

inculpate *in'kul-pāt,* or *-kul', v.t.* to involve in a charge or blame: to charge.—*n.* inculpā'tion.—*adj.* incul'-patory (*-pə-tə-ri*) [L. L. *inculpāre, -ātum—*L. *in,* in, *culpa,* a fault.]

incumbent *in-kum'bənt, adj.* lying or resting: weighing on something: overlying (*geol.*): imposed or resting as a duty, lying along a surface, as a moth's wings at rest —*n.* one who holds an ecclesiastical benefice, or any office.—*n.* incum'bency the state or fact of being incumbent or an incumbent: a duty or obligation: the holding of an office: an ecclesiastical benefice.—*adv* incum'bently. [L. *incumbēns, -entis,* pr.p. of *incumbēre,* to lie upon]

incunabula *in-kū-nab'ū-lə, n.pl.* books printed in early period of the art, esp before the year 1501: the cradle, birthplace, origin of a thing:—*sing.,* incūnab'ūlum. [L. *incūnābūla,* swaddling-clothes, infancy, earliest stage—*in,* in, *cūnābula,* dim. of *cūnae,* a cradle.]

incur *in-kûr', v.t.* to become liable to: to bring upon oneself: to suffer:—*pr p.* incurr'ing; *pa.t.* and *pa.p* incurred'.—*adj.* incurr'able.—*n.* incurr'ence. [L *incurrēre, incursum—in,* into, *currēre,* to run.]

incurable *in-kûr'ə-bl, adj* not admitting of cure or correction.—*n.* one beyond cure.—*ns.* incur'-ableness, incurabil'ity.—*adv.* incur'ably. [Pfx. in- (2).]

incurious *in-kū'ri-əs, adj* not curious or inquisitive: inattentive: indifferent —*adv.* incū'riously.—*ns.* in-cū'riousness, incūrios'ity. [Pfx. in- (2).]

incursion *in-kûr'shən, n* a hostile inroad· the action of running in a sudden attack, invasion —*adj* **incur'sive** making inroads aggressive invading [L *incursiō,* *-ōnis—incurrère.*]

incurve *in-kûrv', v.t* and *v t* to curve· to curve inward —*n* **in'curve** a curve inwards [L *incurvāre,* to bend in, *incurvus,* bent.]

incus *ing'kəs, n* one of the bones in the middle ear, so called from its fancied resemblance to an anvil —*pl* **incudes** (*ing-kū'dēz,* or *ing'*) —*adj* anvil-shaped [L. *incūs, incūdis,* an anvil, see **incuse.**]

incuse *in-kūz', v t* to impress by stamping, as a coin — *adj* hammered.—*n.* an impression, a stamp [L *incūsus,* pa p. of *incūdère—in*[1], on, *cūdère,* to strike to work on the anvil]

indaba *in-da'bə, n* an important tribal conference an international Scout conference [Zulu]

indebted *in-det'id, adj* being in debt: obliged by something received —*n* **indebt'edness.** [Pfx in- (1)]

indecent *in-dē'sənt, adj* offensive to common modesty unbecoming: gross, obscene —*n* **indē'cency** the quality of being indecent anything violating modesty or seemliness —*adv* **indē'cently.—indecent assault** an assault accompanied by indecency, but not involving rape, **indecent exposure** the offence of indecently exposing part of one's body (esp the genitals) in public [Pfx. **in-** (2)]

indecipherable *in-di-sī'fər-ə-bl, adj* incapable of being deciphered. [Pfx **in-** (2)]

indecision *in-di-sizh'ən, n.* want of decision, or resolution· hesitation —*adj* **indecisive** (*-sī'siv*) settling nothing, inconclusive hesitant uncertain, indistinct —*adv* **indeci'sively.—**n* **indeci'siveness.** [Pfx **in-** (2)]

indeclinable *in-di-klīn'ə-bl,* (*gram*) *adj* not varied by inflection.—*adv* **indeclin'ably.** [Pfx **in-** (2)]

indecorous *in-dek'ə-rəs,* sometimes *-di-kō',* or *-ko', adj* unseemly: violating good manners.—*adv* **indec'orously.—ns* **indec'orousness, indecō'rum** want of propriety of conduct· a breach of decorum [L *indēcōrus*]

indeed *in-dēd', adv.* in fact: in truth in reality It emphasises an affirmation, marks a qualifying word, or clause, a concession or admission, or, used as an interj , it expresses surprise or interrogation. disbelief, or mere acknowledgment [**in, deed.**]

indefatigable *in-di-fat'i-gə-bl, adj* not to be wearied out unremitting in effort —*n* **indefat'igableness.—** *adv* **indefat'igably.** [Fr (obs),—L *indēfatigābilis —in-,* not, *dē,* from, *fatīgāre,* to tire]

indefeasible *in-di-fēz'i-bl, adj.* not to be made void — *n* **indefeasibil'ity.—**adv* **indefeas'ibly.** [Pfx **in-** (2)]

indefensible *in-di-fens'i-bl, adj* untenable, that cannot be defended (*lit.* or *fig*) that cannot be excused or justified —*n* **indefensibil'ity.—**adv* **indefens'ibly.** [Pfx **in-** (2)]

indefinable *in-di-fīn'ə-bl, adj* that cannot be defined —*adv* **indefin'ably.** [Pfx **in-** (2)]

indefinite *in-def'i-nit, adj* without clearly marked outlines or limits of a character not clearly distinguished not precise undetermined· not referring to a particular person or thing (*gram* , see also **article**) —*adv* **indef'initely.—**n.* **indef'initeness.** [Pfx **in-** (2)]

indehiscent *in-di-his'ənt,* (*bot*) *adj* not dehiscent (of fruits) not opening when mature.—*n* **indehisc'ence.** [Pfx **in-** (2)]

indelible *in-del'i-bl, adj* (making a mark) which cannot be erased —*ns* **indelibil'ity, indel'ibleness.—**adv* **indel'ibly.** [L *indēlēbilis—in-,* not, *dēlēre,* to destroy]

indelicate *in-del'i-kit, adj* immodest or verging on the immodest wanting in fineness of feeling or tact

coarse —*n* **indel'icacy.—**adv* **indel'icately.** [Pfx **in-** (2).]

indemnify *in-dem'ni-fī, v t.* to secure (with *against*)· to compensate to free, exempt (with *from*)—*pr p* **indem'nifying;** *pa.t.* and *pa.p.* **indem'nified.—**n* **indemnification** (*-fi-kā'shən*) [L. *indemnis,* unhurt (—*in-,* not, *damnum,* loss), and *facère,* to make]

indemnity *in-dem'ni-ti, n* security from damage or loss compensation for loss or injury: legal exemption from incurred liabilities or penalties [Fr *indemnité*—L *indemnis,* unharmed—*damnum,* loss]

indemonstrable *in-dem'ən-strə-bl,* or *in-di-mon', adj* that cannot be demonstrated or proved —*n* **indemonstrabil'ity.** [Pfx **in-** (2)]

indent *in-dent', v t* to cut into zigzags to divide along a zigzag line to notch to indenture. apprentice· (as a deed, contract, etc.) to draw up in exact duplicate· to begin farther in from the margin than the rest of a paragraph· to impress· to dent or dint —*v t* and *v t* to make out a written order with counterfoil or duplicate. to order (esp from abroad)· to requisition· (of a coastline, etc.) to penetrate, form recesses —*n* (*in'dent,* also *in-dent'*) a cut or notch a recess like a notch an indenture· an order for goods (esp from abroad) an official requisition for goods a dint —*n* **indent-ā'tion** a hollow or depression· the act of indenting or notching notch. recess —*adj* **indent'ed** having indentations serrated· zigzag.—*ns* **indent'er; indent'-tion** indentation blank space at the beginning of a line, **indent'ure** the act of indenting. indentation a deed under seal, with mutual covenants, where the edge is indented for future indentification (*law*). a written agreement between two or more parties a contract —*v t* to bind by indentures· to indent [Two different words fused together (1)—L L *indentāre*—L *in,* in, *dēns, dentis,* a tooth, (2)—English in and **dint, dent.**]

independent *in-di-pend'ənt, adj·* not dependent or relying on others (with *of*)· not subordinate completely self-governing (of a business, etc)· not affiliated or merged with a larger organisation· thinking or acting for oneself too self-respecting to accept help· not subject to bias. having or affording a comfortable livelihood without necessity of working or help from others· not depending on another for its value, said of a quantity or function (*math*)· (with *cap.*) belonging to the Independents —*n* (with *cap*) one who in ecclesiastical affairs holds that every congregation should be independent of every other and subject to no superior authority—a Congregationalist· a politician or other who commits himself to no party —*ns* **independ'ence** the state of being independent a competency, **independ'ency** independence· a sovereign state (with *cap*) Congregationalism — *adv* **independ'ently.—Independence Day** (see **Declaration of Independence**) a day when a country becomes self-governing or the anniversary of this event —**Declaration of Independence** the document (1776) proclaiming with reasons the secession of the thirteen colonies of America from the United Kingdom, reported to the Continental Congress, 4th July 1776—observed in the U S as a national holiday, **Independence Day.** [Pfx in- (2)]

indescribable *in-di-skrīb'ə-bl, adj* that cannot be described —*n* **indescribabil'ity.—**adv* **indes-crib'ably.** [Pfx in- (2)]

indestructible *in-di-struk'ti-bl, adj* that cannot be destroyed —*ns* **indestructibil'ity, indestruc'tibleness.—** *adv* **indestruc'tibly.** [Pfx in- (2)]

indeterminable *in-di-tûr'min-ə-bl, adj* not to be ascertained or fixed of argument, etc , that cannot be settled —*n* **indeter'minableness.—**adv* **indeter'-minably.—**n* **indeter'minacy.—**adj* **indeter'minate** not determinate or fixed uncertain having no defined or fixed value.—*adv.* **indeter'minately.**—*ns.* **indeter'-minateness, indetermina'tion** want of determination: want of fixed direction.—**indeterminacy principle** uncertainty principle [Pfx. **in-** (2).]

index *in'deks, n.* the forefinger (also **in'dex-fing'er**), or the digit corresponding. a pointer or hand on a dial or scale, etc. a moving arm, as on a surveying instrument: the gnomon of a sun-dial: the finger of a fingerpost: a figure of a pointing hand, used to draw attention (*print.*): an alphabetical register of subjects dealt with, usu. at the end of a book, with page or folio references: a similar list of other things: a list of prohibited books: a symbol denoting a power (*math*). a number, commonly a ratio, expressing some relation (as *cranial index*, the breadth of skull as a percentage of its length): a numerical scale showing the relative changes in the cost of living, wages, etc., with reference to some predetermined base level:—*pl.* of a book usu. **in'dexes;** other senses **indices** (*in'di-sēz*).—*v.t.* to provide with or place in an index: to link to an index, index-link.—*ns.* **indexa'tion, in'dexing** a system by which wages, rates of interest, etc. are directly linked (**in'dex-linked'**) to changes in the cost of living index, **in'dexer.**—*adjs.* **index'ical; in'dexless.**—*v.t.* **in'dex-link'.**—**in'dex-link'ing** indexation; **index number** a figure showing periodic movement up or down of a variable compared with another figure (usu 100) taken as a standard. [L. *index, indicis*—*indicāre,* to show.]

Indian *in'di-ən, adj.* of or belonging to India (with various boundaries), or its native population, or to the Indies, East or West, or to the aborigines of America, or to the Indians of South Africa: made of maize.—*n.* a member of one of the races of India: an aboriginal of America: in South Africa, a person belonging to the Asian racial group: one who carries out orders, a worker, etc. as opposed to a leader or organiser, as in *chiefs and Indians.*—*v.t.* **In'dianise, -ize** to make Indian: to assimilate to what is Indian.—*v.i.* to become Indian or like an Indian.—*adj.* **In'dic** originating or existing in India: of the Indian branch of the Indo-European languages.—**In'diaman** a large ship employed in trade with India; **Indian club** a bottle-shaped block of wood, swung in various motions by the arms to develop the muscles; **Indian corn** maize, so called because brought from the West Indies; **Indian fig** the banyan-tree: the prickly pear; **Indian file** see **file¹; Indian gift** a gift that is asked back or for which a return gift is expected; **Indian giver; Indian hemp** *Cannabis sativa* (*Cannabis indica* is a variety), source of drug variously known as hashish, marihuana, etc.; **Indian ink** see **ink; Indian meal** ground maize; **Indian millet** durra; **Indian pink** see under **pink²; Indian red** red ochre, or native ferric oxide, formerly imported from the East as a red pigment, also made artificially. **Indian rice** see **Zizania; Indian rope-trick** the supposed Indian trick of climbing an unsupported rope; **Indian runner** a breed of domestic duck; **Indian summer** (orig in America) a period of warm, dry, calm weather in late autumn, with hazy atmosphere; **Indian wrestling** a trial of strength in which two people in sitting position with elbows touching a table clasp hands, each trying to force the other's arm backwards; **India paper** a thin soft absorbent paper, of chinese or Japanese origin, used in taking the finest proofs (**India proofs**) from engraved plates: a thin tough opaque paper used for printing Bibles; **In'dia-rubb'er** an elastic gummy substance, the inspissated juice of various tropical plants: a piece of this material, esp. one used for rubbing out pencil marks.—**East Indian** an inhabitant or native of the East Indies, usually applied to a Eurasian, **Red Indian** one of the aborigines of America (from the coppery-brown colour of some tribes); **West Indian** a

native or an inhabitant of the West Indies [L. *India—Indus* (Gr *Indos*), the Indus]

Indic. See **Indian.**

indicate *in'di-kāt, v t.* to point out to show· to give some notion of· to be a mark or token of. to give ground for inferring to point to as suitable treatment (*med.*), also (usu in pass) as desirable course of action in any sphere.—*n.* **indica'tion** the act of indicating: mark: token: suggestion of treatment symptom.—*adj.* **indicative** (*in-dik'ə-tiv*) pointing out giving intimation: applied to the mood of the verb that expresses matter of fact (*gram*).—*n.* the indicative mood: a verb in the indicative mood.—*adv* **indic'atively.**—*n.* **in'dicator** one who or that which indicates: a pointer: a diagram showing names and directions of visible objects, as on a mountain top: a substance showing chemical condition by change of colour a measuring contrivance with a pointer or the like: any device for exhibiting condition for the time being.—*adj* **in'dicatory** (or *dik'*) [L. *indicāre, -ātum—in,* in, *dicāre,* to proclaim.]

indices. See **index.**

indict *in-dīt', v.t.* to charge with a crime formally or in writing.—*adj.* **indict'able.**—*ns.* **indictee'** one who is indicted, **indict'ment** a formal accusation the written accusation against one who is to be tried by jury: the form under which one is put to trial at the instance of the Lord Advocate (*Scots law*) [With Latinised spelling (but not pronunciation) from A.Fr. *enditer*—L. *in,* in, *dictāre,* to declare, freq of *dicēre,* to say]

indifferent *in-dif'ər-ənt, adj.* without importance: uninteresting: of a middle quality: not very good, inferior· neutral: unconcerned —*ns* **indiff'erence; indiff'erency; indiff'erentism** indifference: the doctrine that religious differences are of no moment (*theol.*); **indiff'erentist.**—*adv.* **indiff'erently** in an indifferent manner: tolerably: passably: without distinction, impartially. [Pfx. **in-** (2).]

indigenous *in-dij'in-əs, adj.* native born: originating or produced naturally in a country—opp. to *exotic.*—*adj.* and *n.* **in'digene** (*-jēn*) native, aboriginal —*n.* **indigenisa'tion, -z-.**—*v.t.* **indi'genise, -ize** to adapt or subject to native culture or influence: to increase the proportion of indigenous people in administration, employment, etc.—*adv.* **indig'enously.** [L. *indigena,* a native—*indu-,* in, and *gen-,* root of *gignēre,* to produce.]

indigent *in'di-jənt, adj.* in need, esp. of means of subsistence.—*ns.* **in'digence, in'digency.**—*adv.* **in'-digently.** [Fr.,—L. *indigēns, -entis,* pr.p. of *indigēre—indu-,* in, *egēre,* to need.]

indigestible *in-di-jest'-i-bl, adj* not digestible: not easily digested: not to be received or patiently endured.—*n.* **indigestibil'ity.**—*adv.* **indigest'ibly.**—*n.* **indigestion** (*in-di-jes'chən*) want of digestion: painful digestion.—*adj.* **indigest'ive** dyspeptic. [L. *indigestus,* unarranged—*in,* not, *dīgerēre,* to arrange, digest]

indignant *in-dig'nənt, adj.* feeling or showing justifiable anger (often mixed with scorn).— *adv.* **indig'nantly.**—*n.* **indigna'tion** righteous anger at injustice, etc.: feeling caused by an unjustified slight, etc., to oneself —*n.* **indig'nity** disgrace: dishonour: unmerited contemptuous treatment: incivility with contempt or insult. [L. *indignus,* unworthy—*in-,* not, *dignus,* worthy.]

indigo *in'di-gō, n.* a violet blue dye obtained from the leaves of the indigo plant, from woad, or synthetically: the indigo plant, any of various species of a tropical genus of Papilionaceae:—*pl.* **in'digos, in'digoes.**—*adj.* deep blue.—**indigo blue** the blue colouring matter of indigo; **indigo bird** an American finch, of which the male is blue. [Sp. *indico*, *indigo*—L. *indicum*—Gr *Indikon*, Indian (neut. adj.)]

indirect *in-di-rekt'*, or *-di-*, *adj* not direct or straight: not lineal or in direct succession: not related in the natural way, oblique: not straightforward or honest—*adv* **indirect'ly.**—*n.* **indirect'ness.**—**indirect object** (*gram.*) a substantival or pronominal word or phrase dependent on a verb less immediately than an accusative governed by it; **indirect speech** (L *ōrātiō obliqua*) speech reported with adjustment of the speaker's words to change of persons and time, **indirect tax** one collected not directly from the taxpayer but through an intermediate agent, as e.g. a customs duty (passed on in the form of higher price); **indirect taxation.** [Pfx. **in-** (2).]

indiscernible *in-di-sûrn'i-bl*, or *-zûrn'*, *adj.* not discernible.—*adv.* **indiscern'ibly.** [Pfx. **in-** (2).]

indiscipline *in-dis'i-plin*, *n.* want of discipline—*adj* **indisc'iplinable.** [Pfx **in-** (2).]

indiscreet *in-dis-krēt'*, *adj.* not discreet: imprudent: injudicious—*adv* **indiscreet'ly.**—*ns* **indiscreet'ness;** **indiscretion** (*-kresh'ən*) want of discretion: rashness: an indiscreet act, or one seemingly indiscreet: (esp formerly) an action breaking the moral code of society. [Pfx. **in-** (2).]

indiscrete *in-dis-krēt'*, or *-dis'*, *adj.* not separated or distinguishable in parts: homogeneous.—*adv.* **indiscrete'ly.**—*n.* **indiscrete'ness.** [Pfx. **in-** (2).]

indiscriminate *in-dis-krim'i-nit*, *adj.* not making distinctions: promiscuous.—*adv.* **indiscrim'inately.**—*adjs.* **indiscrim'inating** undiscriminating; **indiscrim'inative** (*-ə-tiv*) not discriminative.—*n* **indiscrimina'tion.** [Pfx. **in-** (2).]

indispensable *in-dis-pens'ə-bl*, *adj.* that cannot be dispensed with. absolutely necessary: of a law, etc., that cannot be set aside.—*ns.* **indispensabil'ity, indispens'ableness.**—*adv.* **indispens'ably.** [Pfx. **in-** (2).]

indispose *in-dis-pōz'*, *v.t.* to render indisposed, averse, or unfit.—*pa p.* and *adj.* **indisposed'** averse: slightly disordered in health.—*ns.* **indispos'edness; indisposition** (*-pə-zish'ən*) the state of being indisposed: disinclination: slight illness [Pfx. **in-** (2).]

indisputable *in-dis-pū'tə-bl*, also *-dis'*, *adj* beyond dispute.—*n.* **indisput'ableness.**—*adv.* **indisput'ably.** [Pfx. **in-** (2).]

indissociable *in-dis-ō'sh(y)ə-bl*, *adj.* incapable of being separated [Pfx. **in-** (2).]

indissoluble *in-dis-ol'ū-bl*, or *-dis'əl-*, *adj.* that cannot be broken or violated: inseparable: binding for ever.—*ns* **indissol'ubleness, indissolubility** (*-ol-ū-bil'*).—*adv.* **indissol'ubly.** [Pfx. **in-** (2).]

indistinct *in-dis-tingkt'*, *adj* not plainly marked: confused: not clear to the mind: dim.—*adj.* **indistinct'ive** not constituting a distinction.—*adv.* **indistinct'ively** indistinctly.—*n.* **indistinct'iveness.**—*adv.* **indistinct'ly.**—*ns.* **indistinct'ness; indistinc'tion** (*rare*) confusion: absence of distinction, sameness [Pfx **in-** (2).]

indistinguishable *in-dis-ting'gwish-ə-bl*, *adj.* that cannot be distinguished.—*n.* **indistin'guishableness.**—*adv.* **indistin'guishably.** [Pfx. **in-** (2).]

indite *in-dīt'*, *v.t.*, *v.i.* to compose or write.—*ns.* **indite'-ment; indit'er.** [O.Fr *enditer*; see **indict.**]

indium *in'di-əm*, *n.* a soft malleable silver-white metallic element (In; at. numb. 49). [From two *indigo*-coloured lines in the spectrum.]

individual *in-di-vid'ū-əl*, *adj.* not divisible without loss of identity: subsisting as one: pertaining to one only or to each one separately of a group: single, separate.—*n.* a single person, animal, plant, or thing considered as a separate member of its species or as having an independent existence: a person (*coll.*).—*n.* **indi-**

vidualisa'tion, -z-.—*v t* **individ'ualise, -ize** to stamp with individual character. to particularise.—*ns.* **individ'ualism** individual character. independent action as opposed to co-operation: that theory which opposes interference of the state in the affairs of individuals, opp to *socialism* or *collectivism·* the theory that looks to the rights of individuals, not to the advantage of an abstraction such as the state; **individ'ualist** one who thinks and acts with independence: one who advocates individualism.—Also *adj* —*adj* **individualist'ic.**—*n* **individuality** (*-al'i-ti*) separate and distinct existence: distinctive character.—*adv.* **individ'ually.**—*v.t* **individ'uate** to individualise. to give individuality to.—*adj.* undivided: inseparable. individuated —*n* **individua'tion.** [L. *indivīduus*—*in-*, not, *dīviduus*, divisible—*dīvidĕre*, to divide.]

indivisible *in-di-viz'i-bl*, *adj.* not divisible —*n.* (*math*) an indefinitely small quantity —*ns* **indivisibil'ity, indivis'ibleness.**—*adv.* **indivis'ibly.** [Pfx. **in-** (2).]

Indo- *in'dō-*, in composition, Indian.

Indo-Chinese *in'dō-chī-nēz'*, *adj* of or pertaining to Indo-China, the south-eastern peninsula of Asia

indoctrinate *in-dok'trin-āt*, *v t.* to instruct in any doctrine· to imbue with any opinion —*ns.* **indoctrina'tion; indoc'trinātor.** [Pfx **in-** (1).]

Indo-European *in'dō-ū-rō-pē'ən*, (*philol*) *adj.* of the family of languages, also called **Indo-Germanic** and sometimes **Aryan**, whose great branches are Aryan proper or Indian, Iranian, Armenian, Greek or Hellenic, Italic, Celtic, Tocharian, Balto-Slavonic, Albanian, Germanic, and probably Anatolian.

indolent *in'dəl-ənt*, *adj.* indisposed to activity: not painful (*med.*).—*ns.* **in'dolence, in'dolency.**—*adv* **in'dolently.** [L. *in-*, not, *dolēns, -entis*, pr.p of *dolēre*, to suffer pain]

indomitable *in-dom'it-ə-bl*, *adj.* not to be overcome.—*adv* **indom'itably.** [Pfx. **in-** (2).]

Indonesian *in-dō-nē'zi-ən*, *-zh(y)ən, -sh(y)ən, adj.* of the East Indian or Malay Archipelago, specif of the Republic of Indonesia, covering much of this territory· of a short, mesocephalic black-haired, light-brown race distinguishable in the population of the East Indian Islands· of a branch of the Austronesian family of languages chiefly found in the Malay Archipelago and Islands (Malay, etc.) —*n.* an Indonesian national, a member of the race or speaker of one of the languages: the official language of the Republic of Indonesia. [Gr. *Indos*, Indian, *nēsos*, island]

indoor *in'dōr, -dor, adj.* practised, used, or being within a building.—*adv.* **indoors'** inside a building [Pfx **in-** (1).]

indorse. See **endorse.**

indraught, indraft *in'dräft, n.* a drawing in: an inward flow of current. [in, draught.]

indrawn *in'drön, in-dron', adj.* drawn in [in, drawn.]

Indri(s) *in'drē(s), ns.* a genus of lemurs found in Madagascar: (without *cap.*) a member of a species of these.

indubitable *in-dū'bit-ə-bl, adj.* that cannot be doubted. certain.—*ns.* **indubitabil'ity; indū'bitableness.**—*adv* **indū'bitably** without doubt, certainly [Pfx. **in-** (2).]

induce *in-dūs', v.t.* to draw on: to prevail on: to bring into being: to initiate or speed up (labour) artificially, as by administering drugs (also *v.t.*) (*med.*): to cause, as an electric state, by mere proximity (*phys.*): to infer inductively (*log.*).—*v.i.* to reason or draw inferences inductively.—*ns.* **induce'ment** that which induces: incentive, motive: a statement of facts introducing other important facts (*law*); **induc'er.**—*adj.* **induc'ible.**—*n.* **induc'tion.**—**induced current** (*elect*) a current set in action by the influence of the surrounding magnetic field, or by the variation of an adjacent current. [L. *indūcĕre, inductum*—*in*, into, *dūcĕre*, to lead.]

induct *in-dukt'*, *v t.* to introduce to put in possession. as of a benefice, to install —*ns.* **induct'ance** the property of inducing an electromotive force by variation of current in a circuit a device having inductance.—*n* **induc'tion** a bringing or drawing in installation in office, benefice, etc a prelude· an introductory section or scene magnetising by proximity without contact the production by one body of an opposite electric state in another by proximity production of an electric current by magnetic changes in the neighbourhood reasoning from particular cases to general conclusions (*log*) —*adjs* **induc'tional**; **induct'ive.**—*adv* **induct'ively.**—*ns* **inductiv'ity**; **induct'or.**—**induction coil** an electrical machine consisting of two coils of wire, in which every variation of the current in one induces a current in the other, **induction motor** an electric motor in which currents in the primary winding set up an electromagnetic flux which induces currents in the secondary winding, interaction of these currents with the flux producing rotation [See **induce.**]

indue. See **endue.**

indulge *in-dulj'*, *v t.* to yield to the wishes of to favour or gratify to treat with favour or undue favour not to restrain to grant an indulgence to or on to grant some measure of religious liberty to (*hist*) —*v i* to gratify one's appetites freely, or permit oneself any action or expression (with *in*)· to partake, esp of alcohol (*coll*) —*n* **indulg'ence** gratification excessive gratification favourable or unduly favourable treatment in the R C Church, a remission, to a repentant sinner, of the temporal punishment which remains due after the sin and its eternal punishment have been remitted exemption of an individual from an ecclesiastical law —Also **indulg'ency.**—*adj* **indulg'ent** ready to gratify the wishes of others compliant not severe —*adv* **indulg'ently.**—*ns* **indulg'er; indult'** a licence granted by the Pope, authorising something to be done which the common law of the Church does not sanction [L *indulgēre*, to be kind to, indulge—*in*, in, and prob *dulcis*, sweet]

indult. See under **indulge.**

indurate *in'dū-rāt*, *v t* and *v i* to harden —Also *adj* — *n* **indura'tion.**—*adj* **in'durative.** [L *indūrāre*, *-ātum—in*, in, *dūrāre*, to harden]

indusium *in-dū'zi-əm*, *n* a protective membrane or scale, esp that covering a fern sorus an insect larvacase —*pl* **indu'sia.** [L *indūsium*, an undergarment]

industry *in'dəs-tri*, *n* the quality of being diligent assiduity steady application habitual diligence any branch of manufacture and trade, *heavy* industry relating to such basic industries as coalmining, steelmaking, shipbuilding, etc, involving heavy equipment, *light* industry to smaller factory-processed goods, e g knitwear, glass, electronics components, etc all branches of manufacture and trade collectively —*adj* **industrial** (*-dus'*) relating to or consisting in industry —*n* (in *pl*) stocks and shares in industrial concerns —*n* **industrialisā'tion, -z-.**—*v t* **indus'-trialise, -ize** to give an industrial character, or character of industrialism, to —*ns* **indus'trialism** devotion to labour or industrial pursuits that system or condition of society in which industrial labour is the chief and most characteristic feature, **indus'trialist** one who owns, or holds a powerful position in, industrial concern(s) —*adj* of or characterised by industry —*adv* **indus'trially.**—*adj* **indus'trious** diligent or active in one's labour laborious. diligent in a particular pursuit —*adv* **indus'triously.**—**industrial action** a strike or go-slow, **industrial archaeology** the study of industrial machines and buildings of the past, **industrial estate** a planned industrial area, with factories

organised to provide varied employment, **industrial relations** relations between management and workers, **industrial revolution** the economic and social changes arising out of the change from industries carried on in the home with simple machines to industries in factories with power-driven machinery—esp such changes (from about 1760) in Britain, the first country to be industrialised [L *industria*]

indwell *in-dwel'*, *v i* and *v t.* to dwell or abide in — *pa t* and *pa p* **indwelt'.**—*adj* **in'dwelling** dwelling within, abiding permanently in the mind or soul —*n* residence within, or in the heart or soul [Pfx **in-** (1)]

inebriate *in-ē'bri-āt*, *v t* to make drunk, to intoxicate to exhilarate greatly —*adj* (*-it, -ət*) drunk: intoxicated —*n* a drunk person a drunkard —*adj* **inē'briant** intoxicating —Also *n* —*ns* **inebria'tion, inebriety** (*in-ē-brī'i-ti*, or *in-i-*) drunkenness intoxication —*adj* **inē'brious** drunk [L *inēbriāre, -ātum—in*, intens, *ēbriāre*, to make drunk—*ēbrius*, drunk]

inedible *in-ed'i-bl*, *adj* unfit to be eaten —*n* **inedibil'ity.** [Pfx **in-** (2)]

ineducable *in-ed'ū-kə-bl*, *adj* incapable of education —*n* **ineducabil'ity.** [Pfx **in-** (2)]

ineffable *in-ef'ə-bl*, *adj* that cannot be described, inexpressible —*n* **ineff'ableness.**—*adv* **ineff'ably.** [L *ineffābilis—in-*, not, *effābilis*, effable]

ineffective *in-i-fek'tiv*, *adj* not effective useless —*adv* **ineffec'tively.**—*n* **ineffec'tiveness.**—*adj* **ineffec'tual** fruitless, ineffective, weak —*ns.* **ineffectual'ity, ineffec'tualness.**—*adv.* **ineffec'tually.** —*adj* **inefficacious** (*in-ef-i-kā'shəs*) not having power to produce an effect, or the desired effect —*adv* **inefficā'ciously.**—*n.* **inefficacy** (*-ef'i-kə-si*) want of efficacy —*n* **inefficiency** (*in-i-fish'ən-si*) —*adj* **inefficient** not efficient —*adv.* **ineffic'iently.** [Pfx **in-** (2)]

inelastic *in-i-las'tik*, *adj* not elastic incompressible — *n* **inelasticity** (*in-el-əs-tis'i-ti*) —**inelastic collision, scattering** see under **collide.** [Pfx **in-** (2)]

inelegance *in-el'i-gəns*, *n* want of gracefulness or refinement —Also **inel'egancy.**—*adj* **inel'egant.**—*adv* **inel'egantly.** [Pfx **in-** (2)]

ineligible *in-el'i-ji-bl*, *adj* not qualified for election not suitable for choice not rich enough or of the right social background to be chosen as a husband unsuitable —Also *n* —*n* **ineligibil'ity.**—*adv* **inel'-igibly.** [Pfx **in-** (2)]

ineloquent *in-el'ə-kwənt*, *adj* not eloquent —*n* **inel'o-quence.** [Pfx **in-** (2)]

ineluctable *in-i-luk'tə-bl*, *adj* not to be escaped from [L *inēluctābilis—in-*, not, *ē*, from, *luctāri*, to struggle]

inept *in-ept'*, *adj* unfit irrelevant and futile fatuous void (*law*) —*ns* **inept'itude, inept'ness.**—*adv* **inept'ly.** [L *ineptus—in-*, not, *aptus*, apt]

inequable *in-ek'wə-bl, -ēk'*, *adj* not equable, changeable [Pfx **in-** (2)]

inequality *in-ē-kwol'i-ti*, or *in-i-*, *n* want of equality difference inadequacy incompetency unevenness dissimilarity an uneven place [Pfx **in-** (2)]

inequitable *in-ek'wi-tə-bl*, *adj* unfair, unjust —*adv* **ineq'uitably.**—*n* **ineq'uity** lack of equity· an unjust action [Pfx **in-** (2)]

ineradicable *in-i-rad'i-kə-bl*, *adj* not able to be eradicated or rooted out —*adv* **inerad'icably.** [Pfx **in-** (2)]

inerrancy *in-er'ən-si*, *n* freedom from error —*adj* **inerr'ant** unerring [Pfx **in-** (2)]

inert *in-ûrt'*, *adj* without inherent power of moving, or of active resistance to motion passive chemically inactive sluggish disinclined to move or act —*n* **inertia** (*in-ûr'shi-ə, -shyə, -shə*) inertness the inherent property of matter by which it continues, unless constrained, in its state of rest or uniform motion in a straight line.—*adj.* **iner'tial** of, or pertaining to, inertia.—*adv.* **inert'ly.**—*n.* **inert'ness.**—**inert gas** one of several elements whose outer electron orbits are complete, rendering them inert to all the usual chemical reactions; **inertia-reel seat-belt** a type of self-retracting seat-belt in which the wearer is constrained only when violent deceleration of the vehicle causes the belt to lock; **inertia selling** sending unrequested goods to householders and attempting to charge for them if they are not returned. [L. *iners, inertis*, unskilled, idle—*in*-, not, *ars, artis*, art.]

inescapable *in-is-kā'pə-bl, adj.* unescapable: inevitable. [Pfx. **in**- (2).]

inessential *in-is-en'shl, adj.* not essential: not necessary: immaterial. [Pfx. **in**- (2).]

inestimable *in-es'tim-ə-bl, adj.* not able to be estimated or valued: priceless.—*adv.* **ines'timably.** [Pfx. **in**- (2).]

inevitable *in-ev'it-ə-bl, adj.* not to be evaded or avoided: certain to happen: exactly right, giving the feeling that the thing could not have been other than it is.—*ns.* **inevitabil'ity; inev'itableness.**—*adv.* **inev'itably.** [L. *inēvitābilis*—*in*-, not, *ē*, from, *vītāre*, to avoid.]

inexact *in-ig-zakt', adj.* not precisely correct or true: lax.—*ns.* **inexact'itude** lack of exactitude: an example of inexactitude; **inexact'ness.**—*adv.* **inexact'ly.** [Pfx. **in**- (2).]

in excelsis *in ek-sel'sis, ik-, eks-, iks-chel'sis,* or *-kel'sis, -sēs,* (L.L.) on high: in the highest degree.

inexcusable *in-ik-skūz'ə-bl, adj.* not justifiable: unpardonable.—*ns.* **inexcusabil'ity, inexcus'ableness.**—*adv.* **inexcus'ably.** [Pfx. **in**- (2).]

inexhaustible *in-ig-zós'tə-bl, adj.* not able to be exhausted or spent: unfailing.—*n.* **inexhaustibil'ity.**—*adv.* **inexhaust'ibly.**—*adj.* **inexhaust'ive** not exhaustive. [Pfx. **in**- (2).]

inexistence *in-ig-zist'əns, n.* non-existence.—*adj.* **inexist'ent.** [Pfx. **in**- (2).]

inexorable *in-eks'ər-ə-bl, adj.* not to be moved by entreaty: unrelenting: unyielding.—*ns.* **inex'orableness, inexorabil'ity.**—*adv.* **inex'orably.** [L.L. *inexōrābilis*—*in*-, not, *exōrāre*—*ex*, out of, *ōrāre*, to entreat.]

inexpedient *in-ik-spē'di-ənt, adj.* contrary to expediency: impolitic.—*ns.* **inexpe'dience, inexpe'diency.**—*adv.* **inexpe'diently.** [Pfx. **in**- (2).]

inexpensive *in-ik-spens'iv, adj.* not costly: not inclined to spend much.—*adv.* **inexpens'ively.**—*n.* **inexpens'iveness.** [Pfx. **in**- (2).]

inexperience *in-ik-spē'ri-əns, n.* want of experience.—*adj.* **inexpe'rienced** not having experience: unskilled or unpractised. [Pfx. **in**- (2).]

inexpert *in-eks'pûrt,* or *in-ik-spûrt', adj.* unskilled.—*n.* **inexpertness.** [Pfx. **in**- (2).]

inexplicable *in-eks'pli-kə-bl, -ik-splik', adj.* incapable of being explained or accounted for.—*ns.* **inexplicabil'ity, inexplicableness.**—*adv.* **inexplicably.** [Pfx. **in**- (2).]

inexplicit *in-ik-splis'it, adj.* not explicit: not clear. [Pfx. **in**- (2).]

inexpressible *in-ik-spres'i-bl, adj.* that cannot be expressed: unutterable: indescribable.—*adv.* **inexpress'ibly.**—*adj.* **inexpress'ive** inexpressible (*arch.*): unexpressive.—*n.* **inexpress'iveness.** [Pfx. **in**- (2).]

inexpungible *in-ik-spun'ji-bl, adj.* incapable of being expunged. [Pfx. **in**- (2).]

inextended *in-ik-stend'id, adj.* not extended: without extension.—*n.* **inextensibil'ity.**—*adj.* **inexten'sible** that cannot be extended or stretched.—*n.* **inexten'sion.** [Pfx. **in**- (2).]

inextinguishable *in-ik-sting'gwish-ə-bl, adj.* that cannot be extinguished, quenched, or destroyed.—*adv.* **inextin'guishably.** [Pfx. **in**- (2).]

in extremis *in ik-strē'mis,* or *ek-strā'mēs,* (L.L.) at the point of death: in desperate circumstances.

inextricable *in-eks'tri-kə-bl, -ik-strik', adj.* not able to be extricated or disentangled.—*adv.* **inex'tricably.** [L. *inextrīcābilis.*]

infall *in'föl, n.* falling in. [**in, fall**[1].]

infallible *in-fal'i-bl, adj.* incapable of error: certain to succeed: inevitable.—*ns.* **infall'ibilism** the doctrine of the Pope's infallibility; **infall'ibilist; infallibil'ity.**—*adv.* **infall'ibly.**—**the doctrine of infallibility** in the R.C. Church (defined in 1870) is that the Pope, when speaking *ex cathedra*, is kept from error in all that regards faith and morals. [Pfx. **in**- (2).]

infamous *in'fə-məs, adj.* having a reputation of the worst kind: publicly branded with guilt: notoriously vile: disgraceful.—*adv.* **in'famously.**—*n.* **in'famy** ill repute: public disgrace: an infamous act: extreme vileness. [L. *infāmāre*—*in*-, not, *fāma*, fame.]

infant *in'fant, n.* a babe: a person under the age of legal maturity (*Eng. law*).—*adj.* of or belonging to infants: of or in infancy.—*n.* **in'fancy** the state or time of being an infant: childhood: the beginning of anything.—*adj.* **infantile** (*in'fən-tīl,* in U.S. *-til,* also *-fant'*) pertaining to infancy or to an infant: having characteristics of infancy: no better than that of an infant: undeveloped.—*n.* **infant'ilism** persistence of infantile characters: an utterance or trait worthy of an infant.—**infantile paralysis** poliomyelitis; **infant mortality (rate)** the rate of) deaths in the first year of life; **infant school** a school for children up to about the age of seven. [L. *infāns, infantis*—*in*-, not, *fāns,* pr.p. of *fārī*, to speak; cf. Gr. *phanai.*]

infante *in-fan'tā, (hist.) n.* a prince of the blood royal of Spain or Portugal, esp. a son of the king other than the heir-apparent:—*fem.* **infant'a** a princess likewise defined: the wife of an infante. [Sp. and Port. from the root of **infant.**]

infanticide *in-fan'ti-sīd, n.* the murder of an infant: the murderer of an infant.—*adj.* **infanti'cidal** (or *-fant'*). [L. *infanticīdium*, child-killing, *infanticīda*, child-killer—*infāns*, an infant, *caedēre*, to kill.]

infantry *in'fant-ri, n.* foot-soldiers: a part of an army composed of such soldiers.—Also *adj.*—*n.* **in'fantryman.** [Fr. *infanterie*—It. *infanteria*—*infante*, youth, servant, foot-soldier—L. *infāns, -antis.*]

infarct *in-färkt', n.* a portion of tissue that is dying because blood supply to it has been cut off.—*n.* **infarc'tion.** [Mediaeval L. *infarctus*—*in*, in, *far(c)tus*—*farcīre*, to cram, stuff.]

infatuate *in-fat'ū-āt, v.t.* to turn to folly: to deprive of judgment: to inspire with foolish passion.—*adj.* **infatuated:**—*pa.p., adj.* **infat'uated.**—*n.* **infatua'tion.** [L. *infatuāre, -ātum*—*in*, in, *fatuus*, foolish.]

infeasible *in-fēz'i-bl, adj.* not feasible.—*n.* **infeasibil'ity.** [Pfx. **in**- (2).]

infect *in-fekt', v.t.* to taint, especially with disease: to corrupt: to spread to.—*n.* **infec'tion** (*-shən*) the act of infecting: that which infects or taints: an infectious disease.—*adjs.* **infec'tious** (*-shəs*), **infec'tive** (*-tiv*) having the quality of infecting: corrupting: apt to spread.—*adv.* **infec'tiously.**—*ns.* **infec'tiousness; infect'iveness; infect'or.** [L. *inficēre, infectum*—*in*, into, *facēre*, to make.]

infelicitous *in-fi-lis'i-təs, adj.* not felicitous or happy: inappropriate, inapt.—*n.* **infelic'ity.** [Pfx. **in**- (2).]

infer *in-fûr', v.t.* to derive as a consequence: to arrive at as a logical conclusion: to conclude: to entail or involve as a consequence: to imply:—*pr.p.* **inferr'ing;** *pa.t.* and *pa.p.* **inferred'.**—*adj.* **in'ferable** (or *-fûr'*; also **inferr'able, -ible**).—*n.* **in'ference** that which is inferred or deduced: the act of drawing a conclusion from premises: consequence. conclusion.—*adj* **inferential** (-*en'shl*) relating to inference: deducible or deduced by inference.—*adv.* **inferen'tially.** [L *inferre*—*in*, into, *ferre*, to bring.]

inferior *in-fē'ri-ər*, *adj.* lower in any respect: subordinate: poor or poorer in quality: somewhat below the line (*print*). of an ovary, having the other parts above it (*bot.*). of the other parts, below the ovary (*bot*): of a planet, revolving within the earth's orbit.—*n.* one lower in rank or station.—*n* **inferiority** (-*or'*) —*adv* **infe'riorly** in an inferior manner —**inferiority complex** a complex involving a suppressed sense of personal inferiority (*psych*): (*popularly*) a feeling of inferiority. [L. *inferior*, comp of *inferus*, low]

infernal *in-fûr'nəl*, *adj.* belonging to the lower regions resembling or suitable to hell: outrageous, very unpleasant (*coll*) —*n.* **infernality** (-*nal'*) —*adv* **infer'nally.**—*n.* **Infer'no** hell (*It.*) (also without *cap*) (without *cap.*) a conflagration.—*pl* **infer'nos.** [L *infernus*—*inferus.*]

infertile *in-fûr'tīl*, in U.S. -*til*, *adj* not productive· barren.—*n.* **infertility** (-*til'*). [Pfx. **in-** (2).]

infest *in-fest'*, *v t.* to disturb: to harass to haunt, beset, or swarm about, in a troublesome or injurious way — *n.* **infesta'tion** attack, or condition of being attacked, esp. by parasites [L *infestāre*, from *infestus*, hostile.]

infeudation *in-fū-dā'shən*, *n.* the putting of an estate in fee: the granting of tithes to laymen [Pfx **in-** (1), and **feud²**.]

infibulate *in-fib'ū-lāt*, *v.t* to fasten with a clasp.—*n* **infibula'tion** the act of confining or fastening, esp. the fastening or partial closing-up of the prepuce or the labia majora by a clasp, stitches, or the like. [Pfx. **in-** (1), and *fibula*, a clasp.]

infidel *in'fi-dl*, *adj.* unbelieving: sceptical. disbelieving Christianity or whatever be the religion of the user of the word.—*n.* one who rejects Christianity, etc . (*loosely*) one who disbelieves in any theory, etc.—*n* **infidel'ity** lack of faith or belief· disbelief in Christianity, etc.: unfaithfulness, esp. to the marriage contract: treachery. [O.Fr. *infidèle*—L *infidēlis*—*in*-, not, *fidēlis*, faithful—*fidēs*, faith]

infield *in'fēld*, *n.* in baseball, the space enclosed within the base-lines: the part of the field near the wicket (*cricket*): the players stationed in the infield.—*n* **in'fielder** a player on the infield. [**in, field.**]

infighting *in'fīt-ing*, *n.* boxing at close quarters.—See also under **in.** [**in, fighting.**]

infilling *in'fil-ing*, *n.* filling up or in: material used to fill up or level· building inside or alongside a house while staying within one's boundaries: infill development.— *v.t.* **in'fill** to fill in.—*n.* material for infilling —**infill housing, development** new houses built between or among older ones [**in, fill.**]

infiltrate *in'fil-trāt*, -*fil'*, *v t.* to cause to percolate· to cause to percolate into. to sift into: to permeate.—*v.i* to permeate by degrees: to sift or filter in.—*v t.* and *v.i.* of troops, agents, to enter (hostile area) secretly and for subversive purposes.—*ns.* **infiltra'tion; in'filtrator.** [Pfx. **in-** (1)]

infinite *in'fin-it*, *adj* without end or limit· greater than any quantity that can be assigned (*math.*) extending to infinity· vast: in vast numbers: inexhaustible.—*n* that which is not only without determinate bounds, but which cannot possibly admit of bound or limit. the Absolute, or God.—*adv.* **in'finitely.**—*n* **in'finiteness.**—*adj.* (orig. ordinal numeral) **infinitesimal** (-*es'*) infinitely small: (*loosely*) extremely small —*n* an infinitely small quantity.—*adv.* **infinites'imally.**— *ns* **infin'itude, infin'ity** boundlessness an infinite quantity: an infinite distance. vastness, immensity countless or indefinite number [Pfx **in-** (2)]

infinitive *in-fin'it-iv*, (*gram*) *adj* expressing, in the mood that expresses, ·the idea without person or number —*n.* the infinitive mood: a verb in the infinitive mood —*adj* **infiniti'val.**—*adv* **infin'itively.** [L. *infinītivus*—*in*-, not, *finīre*, to limit.]

infirm *in-fûrm'*, *adj* sickly weak: frail: unstable —*ns* **infirmary** a hospital or place for the treatment of the sick, **infirm'ity.**—*adv* **infirm'ly.**—*n.* **infirm'ness.** [L *infirmus*—*in*-, not, *firmus*, strong.]

infix *in-fiks'*, *v t.* to fix in: to set in by piercing: to insert an element within (a root) (*philol*).—*n* **in'fix** (*philol*) an element inserted within a root [L. *infixus*—*in*, in, *figēre*, *fixum*, to fix]

in flagrante delicto *in fla-gran'ti di-lik'tō*, *fla-gran'te dā-lik'tō*, (L) in the very act of committing the crime

inflame *in-flām'*, *v t* to cause to burn to make hot: to cause inflammation in to arouse passions in· to exacerbate.—*v t* to burst into flame to become hot, painful, red or excited· to undergo inflammation.—*adj* **inflamed'.**—*n.* **inflam'er.** [O.Fr *enflammer*—L *inflammāre*, see next.]

inflammable *in-flam'ə-bl*, *adj.* that may be set on fire (see **flammable**): easily kindled or excited.—*n.* an inflammable substance —*ns* **inflammabil'ity; inflamm'ableness.**—*adv* **inflamm'ably.**—*n* **inflammation** (-*fla-mä'shən*) the state of being in flame: heat of a part of the body, with pain, redness, and swelling· kindling of the passions —*adj.* **inflamm'atory** tending to·inflame· inflaming: exciting, tending to stir up trouble [L *inflammāre*—*in*, into, *flamma*, a flame]

inflate *in-flāt'*, *v.t* to well with air or gas: to puff up: to elate: to expand unduly: to increase excessively.—*v t.* to become full of air or gas: to distend —*adj* , *n.* **inflat'able** (any object) that can be inflated.—*adj* **inflat'ed** swollen or blown out: turgid· pompous· hollow, filled with air (*bot*) —*n.* **inflation** (*in-flā'shən*) the act of inflating: the condition of being inflated: undue increase in quantity of money in proportion to buying power, as on an excessive issue of fiduciary money : a progressive increase in the general level of prices —*adj.* **infla'tionary.**—*ns* **infla'tionism** the policy of inflating currency; **infla'tionist; inflat'or.** [L *inflāre*, -*ātum*—*in*, into, *flāre*, to blow]

inflect *in-flekt'*, *v t* to modulate, as the voice· to vary in the terminations (*gram*) —*n* **inflec'tion, inflex'ion** modulation of the voice· the varying in termination to express the relations of case, number, tense, etc (*gram*) —*adjs* **inflec'tional, inflex'ional; inflect'ive** subject to inflection. [L *inflectēre*—*in*, in, *flectēre*, *flexum*, to bend, *flexiō*, -*ōnis*, a bend]

inflexible *in-flek'si-bl*, *adj* that cannot be bent. unyielding: rigid· unbending —*ns* **inflexibil'ity, inflex'ibleness.**—*adv* **inflex'ibly.** [Pfx. **in-** (2).]

inflict *in-flikt'*, *v.t* to lay on to impose (as punishment, pain) —*n* **inflic'tion** the act of inflicting or imposing that which is inflicted [L. *infligēre*, *inflictum*—*in*, against, *fligēre*, to strike]

inflorescence *in-flor-es'əns*, -*flər*-, *n* mode of branching of a flower-bearing axis aggregate of flowers on an axis [L *inflōrēscēre*, to begin to blossom]

inflow *in'flō*, *n* the act of flowing in, influx that which flows in —*adj* **in'flowing** flowing in. [Pfx. **in-** (1)]

influence *in'floo-əns*, *n* the power· of producing an effect, esp unobtrusively the effect of power exerted that which has such power a person exercising such power ascendency, often of a secret or undue kind exertions of friends at court, wire-pulling, and the like —*v t* to have or exert influence upon· to affect —*adj* **in'fluent** inflowing exerting influence —*n* a tributary stream —*adj* **influential** (-*en'shl*) of the nature of influence having much influence effectively active (in bringing something about) —*adv*

influen'tially. [O.Fr.,—L.L *influentia*—L *in*, into, *fluĕre*, to flow.]

influenza *in-floō-en'zə*, *n.* an epidemic virus disease attacking esp. the upper respiratory tract.—*adj* **influen'zal.** [It., influence, influenza (as a supposed astral visitation)—L.L. *influentia*; see **influence.**]

influx *in'fluks*, *n* a flowing in: accession: that which flows in.—*n* **influxion** (*in-fluk'shən*). [L. *influxus* —*influĕre*.]

info *in'fō*, coll short form of **information.**

infold. See **enfold.**

inform *in-form'*, *v.t* to animate or give life to: to impart a quality to: to impart knowledge to: to tell.—*v.i.* to give information, make an accusation (with *against* or *on*).—*n.* **inform'ant** one who informs or gives intelligence.—*n. sing.* **informa'tics** information science: information technology.—*n* **information** (*in-far-mā'shən*) intelligence given: knowledge: an accusation given to a magistrate or court.—*adjs.* **informāt'ional; inform'ative** having power to form: instructive; **informed'** knowing, intelligent, educated. —*n.* **inform'er** one who gives information: one who informs against another: an animator—**information retrieval** the storage, classification, and subsequent tracing of (esp. computerised) information; **information science** (the study of) the processing and communication of data, esp by means of computerised systems; **information scientist; information technology** the (esp. computerised or electronic) technology related to the gathering, recording and communicating of information. [O.Fr. *enformer*— L *înformāre*—*in*, into, *fōrmāre*, to form, *fōrma*, form.]

informal *in-for'məl*, *adj.* not in proper form: irregular: unceremonious.—*n.* **informal'ity.**—*adv.* **inform'ally.** [L. *in*-, not, *fōrma*, form.]

infra *in'frə*, *ên'fra*, (L.) below: lower down on the page, or further on in the book —**infra dignitatem** (*dig-ni-tā'təm*, *-tā'tem*) below one's dignity (colloquially sometimes **infra dig.**).

infraction *in-frak'shən*, *n.* violation, esp of law: breach.—*v.t.* **infract'** to infringe.—*adjs.* **infract'ed** broken: interrupted: bent in.—*n.* **infrac'tor** one who infracts. [L. *înfringĕre*, *înfrāctum*—*in*, in, *frangĕre*, *frāctum*, to break.]

infrangible *in-fran'ji-bl*, *adj.* that cannot be broken: not to be violated.—*ns.* **infrangibil'ity**, **infran'gibleness.** [L. *in*-, not, *frangĕre*, to break.]

infra-red *in'fra-red'*, *adj.* beyond the red end of the visible spectrum: using infra-red radiation: sensitive to this radiation. [L. *infrā*, below.]

infrasonic *in-frə-son'ik*, (*acoustics*) *adj.* of frequencies, below the usual audible limit —*n.* **in'frasound.** [L *infrā*, below.]

infrastructure *in'frə-struk'chər*, *n.* inner structure, structure of component parts: a system of communications and services as backing for military, commercial, etc. operations. [L. *infrā*, below.]

infrequent *in-frē'kwənt*, *adj.* seldom occurring: rare: uncommon.—*ns.* **infrē'quence**, **infrē'quency.**—*adv.* **infrē'quently.** [Pfx. **in-** (2).]

infringe *in-frinj'*, *v.t.* to violate, esp. law: to neglect to obey —*n.* **infringe'ment.** [L *înfringĕre*—*in*, in, *frangĕre*, to break.]

infundibular *in-fun-dib'ū-lər*, *adj.* funnel-shaped [L. *infundibulum*, a funnel—*in*, in, *fundĕre*, to pour]

infuriate *in-fū'ri-āt*, *v t* to enrage: to madden [L. *in*, in, *furiāre*, *-ātum*, to madden—*furĕre*, to rave]

infuse *in-fūz'*, *v.t.* to pour in· to instil: to steep in liquor without boiling: to imbue.—*v.i.* to undergo infusion —*n* **infus'er** a device for making an infusion, esp of tea —*adj.* **infus'ible.**—*n* **infusion** (*in-fū'zhən*) pouring in· something poured in or introduced: the pouring

of water over any substance in order to extract its active qualities: a solution in water of an organic, esp. a vegetable, substance: inspiration: instilling —*adj.* **infusive** (*-fū'siv*) having the power of infusion, or of being infused. [L *infundĕre*, *înfūsum*—*in*, into, *fundĕre*, *fūsum*, to pour.]

infusible *in-fūz'i-bl*, *adj.* that cannot be fused: having a high melting-point.—*n* **infusibili'ity.** [Pfx. **in-** (2).]

ingathering *in'gadh-ar-ing*, *n.* collection: securing of the fruits of the earth: harvest. [Pfx **in-** (1).]

ingenious *in-jē'nyəs*, *-ni-əs*, *adj* skilful in invention or contriving· skilfully contrived —*adv.* **ingē'niously.**— *ns.* **ingē'niousness** power of ready invention: facility in combining ideas: curiousness in design; **ingē'nium** bent of mind [L. *ingenium*, mother-wit.]

ingénue *ē-zhã-nu*, (Fr.) *n.* a naive young woman, esp. on the stage:—*masc.* **ingénu.**

ingenuity *in-ji-nū'i-ti*, *n.* orig., ingenuousness: (by confusion with **ingenious**) ingeniousness. [L. *ingenuitās*, *-ātis*; see next word.]

ingenuous *in-jen'ū-əs*, *adj.* frank: honourable: free from deception.—*adv* **ingen'uously.**—*ns.* **ingen'uousness; ingenu'ity** (see previous word). [L. *ingenuus*, free-born, ingenuous]

ingest *in-jest'*, *v.t.* to take into the body.—*adj.* **ingest'ible.**—*n.* **ingestion** (*in-jes'chən*).—*adj.* **ingest'ive.** [L. *ingerĕre*, *ingestum*, to carry in—*in*, *gerĕre*, to carry.]

ingle *ing'gl*, (Scot. *ing'l*) *n.* a fire: fireplace.—**ing'le-nook** a chimney-corner; **ing'le-side** a fireside. [Possibly Gael. *aingeal*, or L. *igniculus*, dim. of *ignis*, fire.]

inglorious *in-glō'ri-əs*, *-glō'*, *adj.* not glorious: unhonoured: shameful.—*adv.* **inglō'riously.**—*n.* **inglō'riousness.** [Pfx. **in-** (2)]

ingoing *in'gō-ing*, *n.* a going in: entrance.—*adj.* going in: thorough, penetrating [**in**, **go**[1].]

ingot *ing'gət*, *-got*, *n.* a mass of unwrought metal, esp. gold or silver, cast in a mould. [Perh. O.E. *in*, in, and the root *got*, as in *goten*, pa.p. of *gēotan*, to pour.]

ingrain *in-grān'*, *v.t* the same as **engrain.**—*adj.* (pron. *in'grān* when attributive) dyed in the yarn or thread before manufacture: deeply fixed: through and through —*adj.* **ingrained'** (attrib. *in'grānd*). [Pfx. **in-** (1).]

ingrate *in-grāt'*, *in'grāt*, *adj.* ungrateful (*arch.*).—*n.* one who is ungrateful.—*adj.* **ingrate'ful** unthankful [L. *ingrātus*—*in*-, not, *grātus*, pleasing, grateful.]

ingratiate *in-grā'shi-āt*, *v.t.* to commend to someone's grace or favour (often reflexively; followed by *with*). —*adj* **ingra'tiating.** [L *in*, into, *grātia*, favour.]

ingratitude *in-grat'i-tūd*, *n.* unthankfulness. [L L. *ingrātitūdō*—L *ingrātus*, unthankful.]

ingredient *in-grē'di-ənt*, *n.* that which enters into a compound: a component. [L. *ingrediēns*, *-entis*, pr.p. of *ingredī*—*in*, into, *gradī*, to walk.]

ingress *in'gres*, *n* entrance: power, right, or means of entrance.—*n.* **ingression** (*in-gresh'ən*).—*adj.* **ingress'ive** (of speech sounds) pronounced with inhalation rather than exhalation of breath [L. *ingressus*—*ingredī*; see **ingredient.**]

ingrowing *in'grō-ing*, *adj.* growing inward: growing into the flesh: growing within —*adj* **in'grown.**—*n.* **in'growth** growth within or inward: a structure so formed [Pfx. **in-** (1).]

inguinal *ing'gwin-əl*, *adj* relating to the groin. [L. *inguinālis*—*inguen*, *inguinis*, the groin.]

inhabit *in-hab'it*, *v.t.* to dwell in: to occupy —*adj* **inhab'itable** that may be inhabited.—*ns.* **inhab'itance**, **inhab'itancy** the act of inhabiting: abode; **inhab'itant** one who inhabits: a resident.—*adj.* **resident.**—*ns.* **inhabitā'tion** the act of inhabiting: dwelling-place [L *inhabitāre*—*in*, in, *habitāre*, to dwell.]

inhale *in-hāl'*, *v t.* and *v i.* to breathe in· to draw in.— *adj.* **inhā'lant** inhaling. drawing in —*ns* **inhā'lant** an inhaling organ, structure or apparatus. a medicinal preparation to be inhaled; **inhalation** (*in-hǝ-lā'shǝn*) the act of drawing into the lungs. something to be inhaled; **inhalator** (*in'hǝ-lā-tǝr*, or -*lā'*) apparatus for enabling one to inhale a gas, etc ; **inhā'ler** one who inhales, one who habitually inhales tobacco smoke: an inhalator. a respirator or gas-mask [L *in*, upon, *hālāre*, to breathe (L *inhālāre* means to breathe upon).]

inharmonious *in-har-mō'ni-ǝs*, *adj* discordant, unmusical: disagreeing. marked by disagreement and dispeace.—*adjs.* **inharmonic** (*in-har-mon'ik*), **-al** wanting harmony inharmonious.—*adv.* **inharmō'niously.**—*ns.* **inharmō'niousness; inharmony** (*inhar'mǝn-i*). [Pfx. **in-** (2).]

inhere *in-hēr'*, *v.i.* (with *in*) to stick, remain firm in something: to be inherent —*adj.* **inhēr'ent** existing in and inseparable from something else: innate: natural. —*adv.* **inhēr'ently.** [L. *inhaerēre*, *inhaesum*—*in*, in, *haerēre*, to stick.]

inherit *in-her'it*, *v.t.* to get as heir. to possess by transmission from past generations. to have at second-hand from anyone (*coll.*): to have by genetic transmission from ancestors —*v i.* to succeed.—*adj.* **inher'itable** same as heritable.—*ns.* **inher'itance** that which is or may be inherited: hereditary descent, **inher'itor** one who inherits or may inherit an heir—*fem.* **inher'itress, inher'itrix.** [O.Fr *enhériter*—L.L. *inhērēditāre*, to inherit—L. *in*, in, *hērēs*, *hērēdis*, an heir]

inhibit *in-hib'it*, *v.t.* to hold in or back· to keep back: to check.—*ns.* **inhibi'tion** the act of inhibiting or restraining: the state of being inhibited· a restraining action of the unconscious will: the blocking of a mental or psychophysical process by another set up at the same time by the same stimulus: stoppage, complete or partial, of a physical process by some nervous influence; **inhib'itor** that which inhibits: a substance that interferes with a chemical or biological process.— *adjs.* **inhib'itive; inhib'itory** prohibitory. [L. *inhibēre*, -*hibitum*—*in*, in, *habēre*, to have.]

inhomogeneous *in-hom-ō-jēn'i-ǝs*, *adj.* not homogeneous —*n.* **inhomogeneity** (*-jǝn-ē'i-ti*) [Pfx. **in-** (2)]

inhospitable *in-hos'pit-ǝ-bl*, *adj* affording no kindness to strangers: (of a place) barren, not offering shelter, food, etc.—*ns.* **inhos'pitableness, inhospital'ity.**— *adv.* **inhosp'itably.** [Pfx. **in-** (2).]

inhuman *in-hū'mǝn*, *adj.* barbarous: cruel: unfeeling.— *n.* **inhumanity** (*in-hū-man'i-ti*).—*adv.* **inhū'manly.** [Pfx. **in-** (2).]

inhumane *in-hū-mān'*, *adj.* not humane, cruel. [Pfx **in-** (2).]

inimical *in-im'i-kl*, *adj.* unfriendly: hostile. unfavourable: opposed.—*adv* **inim'ically.**—*ns* **inim'icalness, inimical'ity.** [L *inimicālis*—*inimicus*, enemy—*in*-, not, *amicus*, friend.]

inimitable *in-im'it-ǝ-bl*, *adj.* that cannot be imitated· surpassingly excellent —*ns.* **inimitabil'ity, inim'itableness.**—*adv* **inim'itably.** [Pfx **in-** (2).]

iniquity *in-ik'wi-ti*, *n.* injustice. wickedness. a crime.— *adj* **iniq'uitous** unjust: scandalously unreasonable. wicked.—*adv* **iniq'uitously.** [Fr *iniquité*—L *iniquitās*, *-ātis*—*iniquus*, unequal—*in*-, not, *aequus*, equal]

initial *in-ish'l*, *adj.* beginning. of, at, or serving as the beginning· original.—*n* the letter beginning a word, esp. a name.—*v t.* to put the initials of one's name to —*pr.p.* **init'ialling;** *pa.t.* and *pa.p* **init'ialled.**—*adv* **init'ially.**—*v.t* **initiate** (-*ish'i-āt*), to begin, start to introduce (to) (e.g. someone) to admit (into), esp with rites, (as to a secret society, a mystery)—*v i.* to perform the first act or rite —*n* (-*it*) one who is initi-

ated —*adj.* initiated: belonging to one newly initiated —*n.* **initiā'tion.**—*adj* **init'iative** (-*i-ǝ-tiv*) serving to initiate. introductory.—*n.* the lead, first step, considered as determining the conditions for others: the right or power of beginning. energy and resourcefulness enabling one to act without prompting from others: the right to originate legislation.—*n.* **init'iátor** one who initiates —*adj.* **init'iatory** (-*i-ǝ-tǝ-ri*) tending or serving to initiate introductory —*n* introductory rite —**Initial Teaching Alphabet** a 44-character alphabet in which each character corresponds to a single sound of English, sometimes used for the teaching of reading [L *initiālis*—*initium*, a beginning, *inīre, initum*—*in*, into, *īre, itum*, to go]

inject *in-jekt'*, *v.t.* to force in: to inspire or instil. to fill by injection.—*ns.* **injec'tion** (-*shǝn*) the act of injecting or forcing in, esp. a liquid: a liquid injected into the body with a syringe or similar instrument: the spraying of oil-fuel into the cylinder of a compression-ignition engine by an injection pump: an amount of money added to an economy in order to stimulate production, expansion, etc.; **injec'tor.**—**injection moulding** moulding of thermoplastics by squirting from a heated cylinder into a water-chilled mould. [L. *injicēre*, *injectum*—*in*, into, *jacēre*, to throw.]

injudicious *in-jōō-dish'ǝs*, *adj.* not judicious: ill-judged. —*adv.* **injudic'ial** not according to law-forms.—*advs* **injudic'ially; injudic'iously.**—*n* **injudic'iousness.** [Pfx **in-** (2).]

Injun *in'jǝn*, (*coll.*) *n* an American Indian.—Also *adj.*

injunction *in-jungk'shǝn*, *n.* the act of enjoining or commanding: an order: a precept: an exhortation: an inhibitory writ by which a superior court stops or prevents some inequitable or illegal act being done [L L. *injunctiō*, *-ōnis*—*in*, in, *jungēre*, *junctum*, to join]

injure *in'jǝr*, *v.t.* to wrong: to harm: to damage: to hurt. —*n.* **in'jurer.**—*adj.* **injurious** (*in-jōō'ri-ǝs*) tending to injure. wrongful: hurtful: damaging to reputation — *adv* **inju'riously.**—*ns.* **inju'riousness; injury** (*in'jǝr-i*) that which injures. wrong: damage: hurt. impairment: annoyance.—**injury time** in ball games, extra time allowed for play to compensate for time lost as a result of injury during the game [L *injūria*, injury—*in*-, not, *jūs*, *jūris*, law.]

injustice *in-jus'tis*, *n.* violation or withholding of another's rights or dues: wrong: iniquity [Pfx. **in-** (2).]

ink *ingk*, *n* a black or coloured liquid used in writing, printing, etc. a dark liquid ejected by cuttle-fishes, etc —*v t* to daub, cover, blacken, or colour with ink —*ns.* **ink'er** one who inks: a pad or roller for inking type, etc , **ink'iness**—*adj.* **ink'y** consisting of or resembling ink: very black, blackened with ink.—**ink'-cap** any mushroom of the genus *Coprinus*; **ink'-erā'ser** india-rubber treated with fine sand, used for rubbing out ink-marks; **ink'stand** a stand or tray for ink-bottles and (usually) pens, **ink'stone** a kind of stone containing sulphate of iron, used in making ink, **ink'well** a reservoir for ink let into a desk.—**China ink, Chinese ink, Indian ink,** in U S. **India ink** (sometimes without *caps.*) a mixture of lamp-black and size or glue, usu kept in solid form and rubbed down in water for use· a liquid suspension of this, **ink-blot test** see **Rorschach test; ink in** to fill in in ink, **invisible** or **sympathetic ink** a kind of ink that remains invisible on the paper until it is heated [O Fr *enque* (Fr *encre*)—L L *encaustum*, the purple-red ink used by the later Roman emperors —Gr *enkauston*—*enkaiein*, to burn in, see **encaustic.**]

inkling *ingk'ling*, *n* a slight hint intimation a dim notion or suspicion [M E *inclen*, to hint at.]

inlaid. See **inlay.**

inland *in'land*, *in'lǝnd*, *n* the interior part of a country

—*adj.* remote from the sea: carried on, or produced, within a country: confined to a country.—*adv.* (also *in-land'*) landward: away from the sea: in an inland place.—*n.* **in'lander** one who lives inland —**inland navigation** passage of boats or vessels on rivers, lakes, or canals within a country; **inland revenue** internal revenue, derived from excise, stamps, income-tax, etc. [O.E *inland*, a domain—*in* and *land*]

in-law *in'lo*, (*coll*) *n.* a relative by marriage, e.g mother-in-law, brother-in-law:—*pl* **in'-laws.**

inlay *in'lā', in-lā', v.t.* to insert, embed: to ornament by laying in or inserting pieces of metal, ivory, etc : on television, to mix images electronically, using masks:—*pr.p.* **in'lay'ing;** *pa.t.* and *pa p.* **in'laid'.**—*n.* **in'lay** inlaying: inlaid work: material inlaid.—*adj.* **in'laid'** (or *in'lād,* or *in-lād'*) inserted by inlaying· decorated with inlay: consisting of inlay: having a pattern set into the surface —*ns.* **inlayer** (*in'lā-ər, in-lā'ər*), **inlaying.** [Pfx **in-** (1).]

inlet *in'let, -lət, n.* an entrance. a passage by which anything is let in: a place of ingress· a small bay or opening in the land: a piece let in or inserted **[in, let¹.]**

inlier *in'lī-ər,* (*geol.*) *n.* an outcrop of older rock surrounded by younger. [in, **lie².**]

in loco parentis *in lō'kō, lok'ō, pə-, pa-ren'tis,* (L) in the place of a parent.

inly *in'li, adj.* inward: secret.—*adv* inwardly: in the heart: thoroughly, entirely **[in.]**

inlying *in'lī-ing, adj.* situated inside or near a centre. **[in, lying.]**

inmate *in'māt, n.* one of those who live in a house, esp one confined to an institution. [in or inn, **mate¹.**]

in memoriam. See **memory.**

inmost. See **innermost** under **inner.**

inn *in, n.* a house open to the public for lodging and entertainment of travellers: a hostel: a hotel loosely, a public-house.—**inn'keeper** one who keeps an inn — **Inns of Court** the buildings of four voluntary societies that have the exclusive right of calling to the English bar (Inner Temple, Middle Temple, Lincoln's Inn and Gray's Inn): hence the societies themselves. [O.E. *inn,* an inn, house—*in, inn,* within (adv.), from the prep. *in,* in.]

innards *in'ərdz,* (*coll.*) *n.pl.* entrails: internal parts of a mechanism: interior **[inwards.]**

innate *in'āt, i-nāt', adj.* inborn: natural to the mind: inherent.—*adv.* **inn'ately** (or *-nāt'*).—*n.* **inn'ateness** (or *-nāt'*) [L *innātus*—*in-,* in, *nāscī, nātus,* to be born.]

inner *in'ər, adj.* (comp. of **in**) farther in: interior.—*n* (a hit on) that part of a target next the bull's-eye.—*adjs* **inn'ermost, in'most** (superl. of **in**) farthest in· most remote from the outside.—**inner city** the central part of a city, esp. with regard to its special social problems, e g. poor housing, poverty; **inner man** soul: mind: stomach (*facet.*); **inner space** the undersea region regarded as an environment; **inner tube** the rubber tube inside a tyre, which is inflated [O.E. *in,* comp *innera,* superl. *innemest.*]

innervate *in'ər-vāt, in-ûr'vāt, v.t* to supply with nerves or nervous stimulus.—Also **innerve'.**—*n* **innervā'tion.** [Pfx. **in-** (1).]

inning *in'ing, n.* (in *pl.*; in U S. sometimes in *sing.*) a team's turn of batting in cricket, etc.: hence, the time during which a person or a party is in possession of anything, a spell or turn.—**a good innings** a long life [in or **inn.**]

innocent *in'ə-sənt, adj.* not hurtful· inoffensive· blameless: harmless: guileless: simple: ignorant of evil: not legally guilty: devoid (with *of*): not malignant or cancerous (*med.*).—*n.* one free from fault: one with no knowledge of evil: a child: a simpleton: an idiot.—*n.* **inn'ocence** harmlessness: blamelessness: guileless-

ness: simplicity freedom from legal guilt.—*adv.* **inn'ocently.**—**Innocents' Day** see **Childermas.** [O Fr ,—L *innocēns, -entis*–*in-,* not, *nocēre,* to hurt.]

innocuous *in-ok'ū-əs, adj* harmless —*adv.* **innoc'uously.**—*ns.* **innoc'uousness, innocū'ity.** [L *innocuus* —*in-,* not, *nocuus,* hurtful—*nocēre,* to hurt]

innominate *i-nom'i-nāt, -nit, adj* having no name — **innominate bone** the hip-bone formed by fusion in the adult of the ilium, ischium, and pubis [L. *in-,* not, *nōmināre, -ātum,* to name]

innovate *in'ō-vāt, in'ə-vāt, v t* to introduce as something new —*v i.* to introduce novelties: to make changes —*ns* **innovā'tion** the act of innovating· a thing introduced as a novelty, **innovā'tionist.**—*adj* **inn'ovative.**—*n* **inn'ovātor.**—*adj* **inn'ovatory.** [L. *innovāre, -ātum*—*in,* in, *novus,* new.]

innoxious *in-ok'shəs, adj* not noxious.—*adv* **innox'iously.**—*n* **innox'iousness.** [Pfx **in-** (2).]

innuendo *in-ū-en'dō, n* insinuation: an indirect reference or intimation —*pl.* **innuen'do(e)s.** [L *innuendō,* by nodding at (i.e indicating).]

Innuit, Inuit *in'ū-it, in'ōō-it, n* the Eskimo people, esp those of Greenland, Canada and Northern Alaska· a member of this people: their language. [Eskimo, people, *pl.* of *inuk,* a person]

innumerable *in-(n)ū'mər-ə-bl, adj* that cannot be numbered countless —*ns* **innūmerabil'ity; innū'merableness.**—*adv.* **innū'merably.** [Pfx. **in-** (2)]

innumerate *in-(n)ūm'ər-it, adj* having no understanding of mathematics or science —Also *n.*—*n.* **innum'eracy.** [Coined 1959 by Sir Geoffrey Crowther (on analogy of *illiterate*)—L *numerus,* number.]

inobservant *in-əb-zûr'vənt, adj* unobservant: heedless —*adj.* **inobser'vable** incapable of being observed — *ns* **inobser'vance** lack of observance; **inobservā'tion** (*-ob-*). [Pfx **in-** (2).]

inoccupation *in-ok-ū-pā'shən,* n lack of occupation [Pfx **in-** (2)]

inoculate *in-ok'ū-lāt, v t.* to insert as a bud or graft: to graft to imbue: to introduce (e g. bacteria, a virus) into an organism: to give a mild form of (a disease) in this way: to make an inoculation in, esp for the purpose of safeguarding against subsequent infection.— *v.i* to practice inoculation —*n.* **inocula'tion** the act or practice of inoculating the insertion of the buds of one plant into another· the communication of disease by the introduction of a germ or virus, esp that of a mild form of the disease to produce immunity: the analogous introduction of anything. e g. nitrogen-fixing bacteria into soil, seed, a crystal into a supersaturated solution to start crystallisation —*adjs.* **inoc'ulative** (*-ə-tiv,* or *-ā-tiv*), **inoc'ulatory** (*-ə-tər-i*).—*ns.* **inoc'ulātor; inoc'ulum** material used for inoculating [L. *inoculāre, -ātum*—*in,* into, and *oculus,* an eye, a bud.]

inodorous *in-ō'dər-əs, adj* without smell.—*adv.* **ino'dorously.**—*n* **ino'dorousness.** [Pfx. **in-** (2).]

inoffensive *in-ə-fen'siv, adj* giving no offence: harmless —*adv.* **inoffen'sively.**—*n.* **inoffen'siveness.** [Pfx **in-** (2)]

inofficious *in-ə-fish'əs, adj* regardless of duty (*law*): inoperative [Pfx **in-** (2).]

inoperable *in-op'ər-ə-bl, adj* that cannot be operated on successfully, or without undue risk (*med.*): not workable —*ns.* **inoperabil'ity, inop'erableness.**—*adv.* **inop'erably.**—*adj.* **inop'erative** not in action: producing no effect —*n.* **inop'erativeness.** [Pfx **in-** (2).]

inopportune *in-op'ər-tūn, -tūn', adj.* unseasonable in time.—*adv* **inopp'ortunely** (or *-tūn'*).—*ns.* **inopportun'ity, inopp'ortuneness** (or *-tūn'*). [Pfx. **in-** (2).]

inordinate *in-ör'd'*(*i-*)*nit, adj.* unrestrained: excessive: immoderate.—*ns.* **inor'dinacy, inor'dinateness.**— *adv.* **inor'dinately.**—*n.* **inordina'tion** deviation from rule: irregularity. [L. *inordinātus—in-*, not, *ordināre, -ātum,* to arrange, regulate.]

inorganic *in-ör-gan'ik, adj.* not organic: not belonging to an organism: of accidental origin, not normally developed.—*adv.* **inorgan'ically.**—*adj.* **inor'ganised, -ized** unorganised.—**inorganic chemistry** the chemistry of all substances but carbon compounds, generally admitting a few of these also (as oxides of carbon, carbonates). [Pfx. **in-** (2).]

inornate *in-ör-nāt'*, or *-or'nit, adj.* not ornate: simple. [Pfx. **in-** (2).]

inosculate *in-os'kū-lāt, v t.* and *v.i.* to unite by mouths or ducts, as two vessels in a body: to anastomose.—*n.* **inoscula'tion.** [L. *in*, in, and *osculāri, -ātus,* to kiss.]

inositol *in-os'i-tol, n.* a member of the vitamin B complex, occurring in practically all plant and animal tissues. [Gr. *īs, īnos,* a sinew, muscle, and suffixes *-ite* and *-ol.*]

inotropic *in-ə-trop'ik, īn-, (med.) adj.* affecting, controlling muscular contraction, esp. in the heart. [Gr. *īs, īnos,* tendon, *tropos,* a turn.]

in pace *in pā'sē, pä'chä, pa-ke,* (L.) in peace.

in partibus infidelium *in par'ti-bas, in-fi-dē'li-əm, pär'ti-bŏŏs ēn-fi-dā'li-ōōm,* (L.) in unbelieving countries—a phrase formerly applied to titular bishops in countries where no Catholic hierachy had been set up

inpayment *in'-pā'mənt, n.* the payment of money into a bank account: the mount paid in. [**in, payment.**]

input *in'pŏŏt, n.* amount, material, or energy, that is put in: power, or energy, or coded information, stored or for storage: information available in a computer for dealing with a problem. process of feeding in data.— *adj.* relating to computer input —*v t.* to feed into, esp into a computer. [**in, put**[1].]

inquest *in'kwest, n.* inquiring: a judicial inquiry before a jury into any matter, esp any case of violent or sudden death: the body of men appointed to hold such an inquiry: the decision reached. [O Fr *enqueste*— L.L. *inquesta*—L *inquisīta (rēs)—inquīrēre,* to inquire.]

inquietude *in-kwī'i-tūd, n.* disturbance. uneasiness — *adj.* **inqui'et** unquiet.—*adv* **inqui'etly.** [Pfx. **in-** (2).]

inquire, enquire *in-kwīr', v.i.* to ask a question. to make an investigation.—*v.t.* to ask.—*n.* **inquir'er, enquir'er.**—*adj.* **inquir'ing** given to inquiry· eager to acquire information. (of e.g. a look) expressing inquiry.—*adv.* **inquir'ingly.**—*n.* **inquir'y, enquir'y** (or *ing'kwi-ri,* esp. *U S.*) the act of inquiring: a search for knowledge: investigation: a question. [O Fr *enquerre* (Fr. *enquérir*)—L *inquīrēre—in,* in, *quaerēre, quaesītum,* to seek.]

inquisition *in-kwi-zish'ən, n.* a searching examination: an investigation: a judicial inquiry: (with *cap.*) a tribunal in the R.C. church for discovery, repression, and punishment of heresy, unbelief, etc , 'the Holy Office', now the 'Congregation for Doctrine of the Faith'.—*adjs.* **inquisit'ional** searching or vexatious in making inquiry: relating to inquisition or the Inquisition; **inquisitive** (*-kwiz'i-tiv*) eager to know: apt to ask questions, esp. about other people's affairs. curious.—*adv.* **inquis'itively.**—*ns* **inquis'itiveness; inquis'itor** one who inquires, esp with undue pertinacity or searchingness: an official inquirer: a member of the Inquisition tribunal.—*adj.* **inquisito'rial** (or *-tor'*)—*adv.* **inquisito'rially.**—*ns.* **inquisito'rialness; inquis'itress** an inquisitorial woman.— **Grand Inquisitor** the chief in a court of Inquisition. [L. *inquīsītiō, -ōnis;* see **inquire.**]

in re *in rē, rä,* (L) in the matter (of).

inro *in'rō, n.* a small Japanese container for pills and medicines, once part of traditional Japanese dress:— *pl.* **in'rō.** [Jap., seal-box.]

inroad *in'rōd, n.* an incursion into an enemy's country: a raid: encroachment.—**make inroads into** to make progress with: to use up large quantities of. [**in and road** in sense of riding; cf. **raid.**]

inrush *in'rush, n.* an inward rush.—*n.* and *adj.* **in'rushing.** [**in, rush**[1].]

insalubrious *in-sə-lōō'bri-əs, -lū', adj.* unhealthy.— *adv.* **insalu'briously.**—*n.* **insalu'brity.** [Pfx. **in-** (2).]

insane *in-sān', adj.* not sane or of sound mind: crazy: mad: utterly unwise: senseless.—*adv.* **insane'ly.**—*ns.* **insane'ness** insanity: madness; **insanity** (*in-san'i-ti*) want of sanity: mental disorder causing one to act against the social or legal demands of society: madness. [L. *īnsānus.*]

insanitary *in-san'i-tər-i, adj.* not sanitary.—*ns* **insan'itariness, insanitā'tion.** [Pfx **in-** (2)]

insatiable *in-sā'sh(ə)-bl, adj.* that cannot be satiated or satisfied.—*ns* **insā'tiableness, insātiabil'ity.**—*adv.* **insā'tiably.**—*adj.* **insā'tiate** not sated: insatiable.— *adv.* **insā'tiately.**—*ns.* **insā'tiateness; insatiety** (*in-sə-tī'i-ti*) unsated or insatiable state. [Pfx. **in-** (2).]

inscribe *in-skrīb', v t* to engrave or otherwise mark: to engrave or mark on: to enter in a book or roll: to dedicate: in geom , to describe within another figure so as either to touch all sides or faces of the bounding figure or to have all angular points on it.— *adj.* **inscrib'able.**—*ns.* **inscrib'er; inscription** (*in-skrip'shən*) the act of inscribing: that which is inscribed: a dedication. a record inscribed on stone, metal, clay, etc —*adjs.* **inscrip'tional, inscrip'tive.**— *adv.* **inscrip'tively.** [L. *īnscrībēre, īnscrīptum—in,* upon, *scrībēre,* to write.]

inscrutable *in-skrōōt'ə-bl, adj.* that cannot be scrutinised or searched into and understood: inexplicable.— *ns.* **inscrutabil'ity, inscrut'ableness.**—*adv.* **inscrut'ably.** [L. *īnscrūtābilis—in-*, not, *scrūtāri,* to search into.]

insect *in'sekt, n.* a word loosely used for a small invertebrate creature, esp one with a body as if cut into, or divided into, sections: a member of the Insecta (*zool.*)· a small, wretched, insignificant person (*fig.*).—*n.pl.* **Insec'ta** a subphylum of arthropods sharply divided into head, thorax, and abdomen, with three pairs of legs attached to the thorax, usually winged in adult life, and commonly having a metamorphosis in the life-history.—*n* **insec'ticide** (*-i-sīd*): an insect-killing substance.—*n.* **insec'tifuge** a substance that drives away insects.—*n pl* **Insectiv'ora** an order of mammals, mostly terrestrial, insect-eating, nocturnal in habit, and small in size—shrews, moles, hedgehogs, etc.—*n.* **insect'ivore** a member of the Insectivora — *adj* **insectiv'orous** living on insects.—*ns.* **insectol'ogist; insectol'ogy** the study of insects.—**in'sectpow'der** powder for stupifying and killing insects: an insecticide or insectifuge [L. *īnsectum,* ·pa.p of *insecāre—in,* into, *secāre,* to cut.]

insecure *in-si-kūr', adj.* apprehensive of danger or loss: in anxious state because not well-adjusted to life: exposed to danger or loss unsafe: uncertain: not fixed or firm —*adv.* **insecure'ly.**—*n.* **insecur'ity.** [Pfx **in-** (2)]

inselberg *in'zəl-bûrg, in'səl-berg, (geol.) n.* a steep-sided eminence arising from a plain tract, often found in the semi-arid regions of tropical countries:—*pl.* **inselberge** (*-gə*). [Ger., island-hill.]

inseminate *in-sem'in-āt, v.t.* to sow: to implant: to introduce: to impregnate, esp. artificially—*ns.* **inseminā'tion; insem'inator.** [L. *īnsēmināre—in,* in, *sēmen, -inis,* seed.]

insensate *in-sen'sāt, -it, adj.* without sensation, inanimate: lacking sensibility or moral feeling: lacking in good sense.—*adv.* **insen'sately.**—*n.* **insen'sateness.** [L. *insēnsātus*—*in-*, not, *sēnsātus*, intelligent —*sēnsus*, feeling.]

insensible *in-sen'si-bl, adj.* not having feeling: not capable of emotion: callous: dull: unconscious: imperceptible by the senses.—*ns.* **insensibil'ity, insen'sibleness.**—*adv.* **insen'sibly.** [Pfx. **in-** (2).]

insensitive *in-sen'si-tiv, adj.* not sensitive.—*adv.* **insen'sitively.**—*ns.* **insen'sitiveness, insensitiv'ity.** [Pfx. **in-** (2).]

insentient *in-sen'sh(y)ənt, adj.* not having perception. —*ns.* **insen'tience, insen'tiency.** [Pfx. **in-** (2).]

inseparable *in-sep'ər-ə-bl, adj.* that cannot be separated.—*n.* (usu. used in *pl.*) an inseparable companion.—*ns.* **insep'arableness, inseparabil'ity.** —*adv.* **insep'arably.** [Pfx. **in-** (2).]

insert *in-sûrt', v.t.* to put in: to introduce (into) —*n.* **in'sert** something inserted in a proof, etc.: a paper placed within the folds of a periodical or leaves of a book.—*ns.* **insert'er; insertion** (*in-sûr'shən*) the act of inserting: that which is inserted.—*adj* **inser'tional.** [L. *īnserĕre, īnsertum*—*in*, serĕre, to join.]

insessorial *in-ses-ō'ri-əl, -ō', adj.* adapted for perching. [L *īnsessor*, adopted with the meaning percher—*īnsidĕre*—*in*, on, *sedĕre*, to sit.]

inset *in'set, n.* something set in, an insertion or insert, a leaf or leaves inserted between the folds of other leaves: a small map or figure inserted in a spare corner of another: a piece let in: the setting in of a current.—*v.t.* **inset'** to set in, to infix or implant. [**in, set.**]

inshore *in'shōr', -shör', adv.* near or toward the shore.—*adj.* (*in'shōr, -shör*) situated, carried on, or operating, near the shore, as fishing-grounds, fishing, or fishermen.

inside *in'sīd', in'sīd, n.* the side, space, or part within: (often in *pl.*) the entrails: inner nature: that which is not visible at first sight.—*adj.* being within: interior: indoor: working matters: from within: from a secret or confidential source: (of a criminal 'job') carried out by, or with the help of, someone trusted and/or employed by the victim (*coll.*).—*adv.* in or to the interior: indoors: on the inner side: in or into prison (*slang*).—*prep.* within: into: on inner side of.—*n.* **insi'der** one who is inside: one within a certain organisation, etc.: one possessing some particular advantage.—**inside left, right** in some games, a forward between the centre and outside; **insider dealing** using information not publicly available to deal on the Stock Exchange, generally considered a highly reprehensible practice.—**inside of** (esp. *U.S.*) in less than; **inside out** with the inner side turned outwards; **know (something) inside out** (*coll.*) to know thoroughly. [**in, side.**]

insidious *in-sid'i-əs, adj.* watching an opportunity to, intended to, entrap: deceptive: advancing imperceptibly: treacherous.—*adv.* **insid'iously.**—*n.* **insid'iousness.** [L. *īnsidiōsus*—*īnsidiae*, an ambush.]

insight *in'sīt, n.* power of seeing into and understanding things: imaginative penetration: practical knowledge: enlightenment: a view into anything: awareness, often of one's own mental condition (*psych.*): the apprehension of the principle of a task, puzzle, etc. (*psych.*).—*adj.* **insight'ful.** [**in, sight.**]

insignia *in-sig'ni-ə, n.pl.* in U.S. treated as *sing.*, signs or badges of office, honour, membership, occupation, etc.: marks by which anything is known. [L., neut. pl. of *īnsignis*—*in*, in, *signum*, a mark.]

insignificant *in-sig-nif'i-kənt, adj.* destitute of meaning: without effect: unimportant: petty.—*ns*

insignificance, insignificancy.—*adv.* **insignif'icantly.** [Pfx. **in-** (2).]

insincere *in-sin-sēr', adj.* not sincere.—*adv.* **insincere'ly.**—*n.* **insincerity** (*-ser'i-ti*). [Pfx. **in-** (2).]

insinuate *in-sin'ū-āt, v.t.* to introduce gently or artfully: to hint, esp. a fault: to work into favour.—*v.i.* to creep or flow in: to enter gently: to obtain access by flattery or stealth.—*adj.* **insin'uating.**—*adv.* **insin'uatingly.**—*n.* **insinua'tion.**—*adj.* **insin'uative** insinuating or stealing on the confidence: using insinuation.—*n.* **insin'uator.**—*adj.* **insin'uatory** (*-ə-tər-i*). [L. *īnsinuāre, -ātum*—*in*, in, *sinus*, a curve.]

insipid *in-sip'id, adj.* tasteless: without satisfying or definite flavour: wanting spirit or interest: dull.— *adv.* **insip'idly.**—*ns.* **insip'idness, insipid'ity.** [L.L. *insipidus*—L. *in-*, not, *sapidus*, well-tasted—*sapĕre*, to taste.]

insist *in-sist', v.i.* to speak emphatically and at length: to persist in pressing.—*v.t.* to maintain persistently. —*ns.* **insist'ence, insist'ency.**—*adj.* **insist'ent** urgent: prominent: insisting.—*adv.* **insist'ently.** [L. *īnsistĕre*—*in*, upon, *sistĕre*, to stand.]

in situ *in sī'tū, si'tōō,* (L.) in the original situation.

insobriety *in-sō-brī'ə-ti, n.* want of sobriety, drunkenness. [Pfx. **in-** (2).]

insofar. See **in**.

insole *in'sōl, n.* the inner sole of a boot or shoe—opp. to *outsole:* a sole of some material placed inside a shoe for warmth, dryness or comfort. [**in, sole**[1].]

insolent *in'səl-ənt, adj.* overbearing: insulting: rude: impudent.—*n* **in'solence.**—*adv.* **in'solently.** [L. *īnsolēns, -entis*—*in-*, not, *solēns*, pa.p. of *solēre*, to be wont.]

insoluble *in-sol'ū-bl, adj.* not capable of being dissolved: not to be solved or explained.—*ns.* **insolubil'ity, insol'ubleness.**—*adv.* **insol'ubly.** [Pfx. **in-** (2).]

insolvable *in-solv'ə-bl, adj.* not solvable.—*n.* **insolvabil'ity.**—*adv.* **insol'vably.** [Pfx. **in-** (2).]

insolvent *in-solv'ənt, adj.* not able to pay one's debts: bankrupt: pertaining to insolvent persons.—*n* one unable to pay his debts.—*n.* **insolv'ency** bankruptcy. [Pfx. **in-** (2).]

insomnia *in-som'ni-ə, n.* sleeplessness: prolonged inability to sleep.—*n.* **insom'niac** a person who suffers from insomnia.—*adj.* suffering from, causing, or caused by, insomnia. [L. *īnsomnis*, sleepless.]

insomuch *in-sō-much', adv.* to such a degree (with *as* or *that*): inasmuch (with *as*): so.

insouciant *in-sōō'si-ənt, ē-sōō-sē-ā, adj.* indifferent, unconcerned: heedless.—*n.* **insouciance** (*in-sōō'si-əns, ē-sōō-sē-äs*).—*adv.* **insouciantly** (*in-sōō'si-ənt-li, ē-sōō-sē-āt'li*). [Fr.]

inspect *in-spekt', v.t.* to look into: to examine: to look at narrowly, officially, or ceremonially.—*n.* **inspec'tion** the act of inspecting or looking into: careful or official examination.—*adjs.* **inspec'tional; inspec'tive.**—*ns.* **inspec'tor** one who inspects: an examining officer: a police officer ranking below a superintendent; **inspec'torate** a district under charge of an inspector: the office of inspector: a body of inspectors.—*adj.* **inspectō'rial.**—*ns.* **inspec'torship** the office of inspector; **inspec'tress** a female inspector. —**inspector general** the head of an inspectorate: a military officer who conducts investigations. [L. *īnspectāre*, freq. of *īnspicĕre, īnspectum*—*in*, into, *specĕre*, to look.]

inspire *in-spīr', v.t.* to breathe in or blow in (air, etc.): to draw or inhale into the lungs: to infuse into (the mind), esp. with an encouraging or exalting influence: (of divine influence, etc.) to instruct or guide: to instruct or affect with a particular emotion:

to bring about: to animate.—*v.i.* to draw in the breath.—*n.* **inspira'tion** (*in-spər-, -spir-, -spīr-*) the act of inspiring or breathing in: a breath: instruction, dictation, or stimulation by a divinity, a genius, an idea or a passion: an inspired condition: an object or person that inspires: an inspired thought or idea.—*adj.* **inspira'tional.**—*adv.* **inspira'tionally.**—*n.* **inspirator** (*in'spir-ā-tər*) an inspirer: an apparatus for injecting or drawing in vapour, liquid, etc.—*adj.* **inspiratory** (*in-spir'ə-tər-i,* or *in-spīr',* or *in'spir-*) belonging to or aiding inspiration or inhalation.—*adj.* **inspired'** actuated or directed by divine influence: influenced by elevated feeling: prompted by superior, but not openly declared, knowledge or authority: actually authoritative.—*n.* **inspir'er.**—*adv.* **inspir'ingly.** [L. *inspīrāre—in, in, into, spīrāre,* to breathe.]

inspirit *in-spir'it, v.t.* to infuse spirit into.—*adj.* **inspir'iting.**—*adv.* **inspir'itingly.** [Pfx. **in-** (1).]

inspissate *in-spis'āt, v.t.* to thicken, condense. [L *in,* in, *spissāre—spissus,* thick.]

instability *in-stə-bil'i-ti, n.* want of steadiness.—*adj.* **insta'ble** unstable. [Pfx. **in-** (2).]

install (also **instal**) *in-stol', v.t* to place in an office or order: to invest with any charge or office with the customary ceremonies: to set up and put in use:—*pr.p.* **install'ing;** *pa.t.* and *pa.p.* **installed'.**—*n.* **installa'tion** the act of installing: a placing in position for use: apparatus placed in position for use: the complete apparatus for electric lighting, or the like. [L.L. *installāre—in, in, stallum,* a stall—O.H.G. *stal*]

instalment, in U.S. **-stall-,** *in-stol'mənt, n.* one of a series of partial payments: a portion supplied or completed at one time, as of a serial story. [A.Fr. *estaler,* to fix, set; prob. influenced by **install.**]

instance *in'stəns, n.* solicitation, urging: occurrence: occasion: example: process, suit (*law*).—*v.t.* to mention as an example.—*n.* **in'stancy** insistency: urgency: imminence.—*adj.* **in'stant** immediate: without delay: present, current: (of food, drink) prepared so that little has to be done to it before use —*n.* the present moment of time: any moment or point of time: the present month.—*n.* **instantaneity** (*in-stant-ə-nē'i-ti*).—*adj.* **instantaneous** (*in-stənt-ā'ni-əs*) done in an instant: momentary: occurring or acting at once or very quickly: for the instant: at a particular instant.—*adv.* **instantan'eously.**—*n.* **instantan'eousness.**—*v.t.* **instan'tiate** to be or provide an example of.—*n.* **instantia'tion.**—*adv.* **in'stantly** at once.—**at the instance of** at the motion or solicitation of; **for instance** as an example; **in the first instance** firstly, originally; **on the instant** forthwith. [L. *instāns, instantis,* pr.p. of *instāre,* to be near, press upon, urge—*in,* upon, *stāre,* to stand.]

instar *in'stär, n.* the form of an insect between moult and moult. [L. *instar,* image.]

instate *in-stāt', v.t.* to put in possession: to install.—*n.* **instate'ment.** [Pfx. **in-** (1) and **state.**]

in statu quo *in stāt'ū, stat'ōō kwō,* (L L.) in the former state

instead *in-sted', adv.* in the stead, place, or room (of): as an alternative or substitute. [**in, stead.**]

instep *in'step, n.* the prominent arched part of the human foot near its junction with the leg: the corresponding part of a shoe, stocking, etc.: in horses, the hindleg from the ham to the pastern joint.

instigate *in'sti-gāt, v.t* to urge on, incite: to foment.—*n.* **instiga'tion** the act of inciting: impulse, esp. to evil.—*adj.* **in'stigative.**—*n.* **in'stigator** an inciter, generally in a bad sense. [L. *instīgāre, -ātum.*]

instil *in-stil', v.t.* to drop in: to infuse slowly into the mind:—*pr.p.* **instill'ing;** *pa.t.* and *pa.p.* **instilled'.**—

Also **instill.**—*ns.* **instilla'tion, instil'ment** the act of instilling or pouring in by drops: that which is instilled or infused. [L. *instillāre—in,* in, *stillāre,* to drop.]

instinct *in'stingkt, n* impulse: an involuntary prompting to action: intuition: the natural impulse by which animals are guided apparently independently of reason or experience.—*adj.* **instinct'ive** prompted by instinct: involuntary: acting according to or determined by natural impulse.—*adv.* **instinc'tively.**—*adj.* **instinc'tual** pertaining to instincts. [L. *instinctus—instinguere,* instigate]

institute *in'sti-tūt, v.t* to set up, establish: to set on foot —*n* anything instituted or formally established: established law: precept or principle: an institution: a literary and philosophical society or organisation for education, research, etc.: the building in which such an organisation is housed: a foundation for further education, esp. in technical subjects: (in *pl.*) a book of precepts, principles, or rules.—*n.* **institution** (*-tū'shən*) the act of instituting or establishing: that which is instituted or established: foundation: established order: enactment: a society or organisation established for some object, esp. cultural, charitable, or beneficent, or the building housing it: a custom or usage, esp. one familiar or characteristic: the act by which a bishop commits a cure of souls to a priest.—*adj.* **institu'tional** pertaining to institution, institutions, or institutes: being, or of the nature of, an institution: depending on or originating in institution: characterised by the possession of institutions.—*v.t.* **institu'tionalise, -ize** to make an institution of: to confine to an institution: (usu in *pass*) as a result of such confinement, to cause to become apathetic and dependent on routine.—*ns.* **institu'tionalism** the system or characteristics of institutions or institution life: belief in the nature of institutions; **institu'tionalist** a writer on institutes: one who sets a high value on institutionalism.—*adv.* **institu'tionally.**—*adj.* **institu'tionary** institutional.—*ns. in'stitutor, in'stitūter* one who institutes. [L. *instituere, -ūtum—in,* in, *statuere,* to cause to stand—*stāre,* to stand.]

instruct *in-strukt', v.t.* to inform: to teach: to direct: (of a judge) to give (a jury) guidance concerning the legal issues of a case: to order or command.—*adj.* **instruct'ible.**—*n.* **instruc'tion** the art of instructing or teaching: information: direction: command. (in *pl.*) special directions, commands.—*adjs.* **instruc'tional** relating to instruction: educational; **instruc'tive** affording instruction: conveying knowledge.—*adv.* **instruc'tively.**—*ns.* **instruc'tiveness; instruc'tor** a teacher: a college lecturer (*U.S.*):—*fem.* **instruc'tress.** [L. *instruere, instructum—in,* in, *struere,* to pile up]

instrument *in'strōō-mənt, n.* a tool or utensil: a contrivance for producing musical sounds: a writing containing a contract: a formal record: one who, or that which, is made a means or agency: a term generally employed to denote an indicating device but also other pieces of small electrical apparatus.—*v.t* (*-ment'*) to score for instruments: to equip with indicating, measuring, or control, etc., apparatus.—*adj.* for instruments: by means of instruments (as *instrument flight*).—*adj.* **instrumental** (*-ment'l*) acting as an instrument or means: serving to promote an object: helpful: of, for, belonging to, or produced by, musical instruments: serving to indicate the instrument or means (*gram.*).—*n.* the instrumental case (*gram.*): a piece of music for instruments only, i e without a vocal part.—*ns.* **instrument'alist** one who plays on a musical instrument; **instrumentality** (*-ment-al'i-ti*) agency.—*adv.* **instrument'ally.**—*n.*

instrumentā'tion the use or provision of instruments: the arrangement of a composition for performance by different instruments (*mus.*). [L. *instrūmentum—instruĕre*, to instruct; see **instruct**.]
insubordinate *in-sab-örd'*(*i-*)*nit, adj.* not subordinate or submissive.—*adv.* **insubord'inately.**—*n.* **insubordinā'tion.** [Pfx. **in-** (2).]
insubstantial *in-sab-stan'shal, adj.* not substantial: not real.—*n.* **insubstantiality** (*-shi-al'i-ti*).—*adv.* **insubstan'tially.** [Pfx. **in-** (2).]
insufferable *in-suf'ar-a-bl, adj.* that cannot be endured: detestable.—*adv.* **insuff'erably.** [Pfx. **in-** (2).]
insufficient *in-saf-ish'ant, adj.* inadequate.—*n.* **insuffic'iency.**—*adv.* **insuffic'iently.** [Pfx. **in-** (2).]
insular *in'sū-lar, adj.* belonging to an island: surrounded by water: standing or situated alone: narrow, prejudiced.—*ns.* **in'sūlarism, insūlarity** (*-lar'i-ti*) the state of being insular.—*adv.* **in'sūlarly.**—*v.t.* **in'sūlate** to cut off from connection or communication: to prevent the passing of heat, sound, electricity, etc. from (a body, area, etc.) to (another): to separate, esp. from the earth, by a non-conductor (*elect.*).—*ns.* **insūlā'tion; in'sūlator** one who, or that which, insulates: a non-conductor of electricity: a contrivance for insulating a conductor; **in'sūlin** an extract got from the islands or islets of Langerhans in the pancreas of animals, used for treating diabetes and also mental diseases.—**insulating tape** a usu. adhesive tape made from, or impregnated with, water-resistance insulating material, used for covering joins in electrical wires, etc.; **insulin shock, reaction** a state of collapse produced by an overdose of insulin. [L. *insula*, island.]
insult *in-sult', v.t.* to treat with indignity or contempt: to affront.—*n.* **in'sult** abuse: affront: contumely: injury, damage (*med.*, esp. *U.S.*).—*adjs.* **insult'able; insult'ing.**—*adv.* **insult'ingly.** [L. *insultāre—insilīre*, to spring at.]
insuperable *in-sū'par-a-bl, -sōō', adj.* that cannot be overcome or surmounted.—*ns.* **insuperabil'ity, insu'perableness.**—*adv.* **insu'perably.** [L *insuperābilis—in-*, not, *superāre*, to pass over—*super*, above.]
insupportable *in-sap-ört'a-bl, -ört', adj.* unbearable: not sustainable.—*adv.* **insupport'ably.** [Pfx. **in-** (2).]
insuppressible *in-sa-pres'i-bl, adj.* not to be suppressed or concealed.—*adv.* **insuppress'ibly.** [Pfx. **in-** (2).]
insure *in-shoor', v.t.* to make sure or secure: to guarantee: to make an arrangement for the payment of a sum of money in the event of loss or injury to.—*v.i.* to effect or undertake insurance.—*n.* **insurabil'ity.** —*adj.* **insur'able** that may be insured.—*ns.* **insur'ance** the act or system of insuring: a contract of insurance, a policy: the premium paid for insuring: the sum to be received; **insur'ant** an insurance policy holder; **insur'er** either party to a contract of insurance (now, strictly the insurance company). [O.Fr. *enseurer—en*, and *seur*, sure; see **ensure, sure**.]
insurgent *in-sûr'jant, adj.* rising: rushing in: rising in revolt.—*n.* one who rises in opposition to established authority: a rebel.—*ns.* **insur'gence, insur'gency.** [L. *insurgēns, -entis—in*, upon, *surgĕre*, to rise.]
insurmountable *in-sar-mownt'a-bl, adj.* not surmountable: that cannot be overcome.—*n.* **insurmountabil'ity.**—*adv.* **insurmount'ably.** [Pfx. **in-** (2).]
insurrection *in-sar-ek'shan, n.* a rising or revolt.—*adjs.* **insurrec'tional, insurrec'tionary.**—*ns.* **insurrec'tionary, insurrec'tionist; insurrec'tionism.** [L. *insurrēctiō, -ōnis—insurgĕre*; see **insurgent**.]

inswing *in'swing, n.* an inward swing or swerve.—*n.* **inswinger** (*in'swing-ar*) a ball bowled so as to swerve to leg (*cricket*): a ball kicked so as to swing in towards the goal or the centre of the pitch (*football*). [**in, swing.**]
intact *in-takt', adj.* untouched: unimpaired: whole: undiminished.—*n.* **intact'ness.** [L. *intactus—in-*, not, *tangĕre, tactum*, to touch.]
intaglio *in-täl'yō, n.* a figure cut into any substance: a stone or gem in which the design is hollowed out—opp. to *cameo*: a countersunk die:—*pl.* **intagl'ios.** —Also *v.t.*—*adj.* **intagl'iated** incised, engraved. [It., *—in*, into, *tagliare*, to cut.]
intake *in'tāk, n* that which is taken in: an airway in a mine: a place where water is taken in: a narrowing in a pipe: decrease by knitting two stitches together: the place where contraction occurs: a body of people taken into an organisation, as new recruits, or new pupils at a school: the point at which fuel mixture enters the cylinder of an internal-combustion engine. [**in, take.**]
intangible *in-tan'ji-bl, adj.* not tangible or perceptible to touch: insubstantial: eluding the grasp of the mind.—*n.* something intangible, e.g. a supplementary asset such as goodwill.—*ns.* **intan'gibleness, intangibil'ity.**—*adv.* **intan'gibly.** [See **intact**.]
integer *in'ti-jar, n.* a whole: a whole number, as opposed to a fraction (*arith.*).—*adjs.* **in'tegrable** (*-gra-bl*); **in'tegral** (*-gral*) entire or whole: not involving fractions: relating to integrals: unimpaired: intrinsic, belonging as a part to the whole.— *n.* a whole: the whole as made up of its parts: the value of the function of a variable whose differential coefficient is known (*math.*).—*adv.* **in'tegrally.**—*n.* **integral'ity.**—*adj.* **in'tegrant** making part of a whole: necessary to form an integer or an entire thing.—*v.t.* **in'tegrate** to make up as a whole: to make entire: to combine, amalgamate: to desegregate: to find the integral of (*math.*): to find the total value of.—*v. i.* to become integral: to perform integration.—*adj.* made up of parts: complete: whole.—*n.* **integrā'tion** the act or process of integrating (*math.*): unification into a whole, e.g. of diverse elements in a community, as white and coloured: the state of being integrated: the formation of a unified personality (*psych.*); **integrā'tionist** one who favours integration of a community.—Also *adj.*—*adj.* **in'tegrative** integrating: tending to integrate.—*ns.* **in'tegrator** one who integrates: an instrument for finding the results of integrations; **integrity** (*in-teg'ri-ti*) entireness, wholeness: the unimpaired state of anything: uprightness: honesty: purity.—**integral calculus** see **calculus; integrated circuit** a circuit consisting of an assembly of electronic elements in a single structure which cannot be subdivided without destroying its intended function [L. *integer—in-*, not, root of *tangĕre*, to touch.]
integument *in-teg'ū-mant, n.* an external covering, such as the skin, exoskeleton, etc.—*adj.* **integumentary** (*-ment'ar-i*). [L. *integumentum—in*, upon, *tegĕre*, to cover]
intellect *int'i-lekt, n.* the mind, in reference to its rational powers: the thinking principle.—*adj.* **intellectual** (*-lek'tū-al*) of or relating to the intellect: perceived or performed by the intellect: having the power of understanding: endowed with a superior intellect: appealing to, or (thought to be) intended for, intellectuals: intelligible only to a person with a superior intellect.—*n* a person of superior intellect or enlightenment.—*v.t.* **intellect'ualise, -ize** to reason intellectually: to endow with intellect: to give an intellectual character to.—*ns.* **intellect'ualism** the doctrine that derives all knowledge from pure

reason; **intellect'ualist; intellectuality** (-*al'i-ti*) intellectual power —*adv* **intellect'ually.** [L *intellēctus, -ūs—intelligēre, intellēctum,* to understand] **intelligent** *in-tel'i-jənt, adj* endowed with the faculty of reason: alert, bright, quick of mind: well-informed: cognisant· capable of performing some of the functions of a computer (*automation*) —*ns* **intell'igence** intellectual skill or knowledge. mental brightness· information communicated news intelligence department —*adj* **intelligential** (-*jen'-shl*) pertaining to the intelligence —*adv.* **intell'igently.** —*adj* **intell'igible** that may be understood: clear —*ns* **intell'igibleness, -igibil'ity.**—*adv* **intell'igibly.** —**intelligence department, service** a department of state or armed service for securing and interpreting information; **intelligence quotient** the ratio, commonly expressed as a percentage, of a person's mental age to his actual age (abbrev **I.Q.**), **intelligence test** a test by questions and tasks to determine a person's mental capacity, or the age at which his capacity would be normal. [L. *intelligēns, -entis,* pr.p of *intelligēre* (see preceding entry)]
intelligentsia, intelligentzia *in-tel-i-jent'si-ə,* or *-gent',* *n.* the intellectual or cultured classes, originally esp in Russia. [Russ.,—L *intelligentia*]
intelligible. See **intelligent.**
intemperance *in-tem'pər-əns, n* want of due restraint· excess of any kind· habitual overindulgence in intoxicating liquor —*adj* **intem'perate** indulging to excess in any appetite or passion: given to an immoderate use of intoxicating liquors passionate exceeding the usual degree· immoderate —*adv.* **intem'perately.**—*n* **intem'perateness.** [L. *intemperans,* intemperate]
intenable *in-ten'ə-bl, adj* untenable [Pfx. **in-** (2).]
intend *in-tend', v.t.* to purpose· to mean —*adj* **in-tend'ed** purposed.—*n.* (*coll.*) betrothed —*adv* **in-tend'edly** with intention or design. [O.Fr *entendre* —L. *intendēre, intentum* and *intēnsum—in,* towards, *tendēre,* to stretch]
intense *in-tens', adj* strained: concentrated, dense: extreme in degree: (of person, manner, etc.) earnestly or deeply emotional, or affecting to have deep feeling: of a photographic negative, opaque — *adv* **intense'ly.**—*ns.* **intense'ness, intens'ity; intensifica'tion; intens'ifier.**—*v t* **intens'ify** to make more intense —*v.i.* to become intense:—*pr.p* **intens'ifying;** *pa t.* and *pa.p.* **intens'ified.**—*n.* **intension** (*-ten'shən*) straining: intentness. intensity: the sum of the qualities implied by a general name (*logic*) —*adj* **intens'ive** concentrated, intense. strained· unremitting. relating to intensity or to intension: intensifying: intensified. giving force or emphasis (*gram.*).—*n* an intensive word —*adv.* **intens'ively.**—*n* **intens'iveness.**—**inten'sive** in composition, having, using, requiring, a great deal of something, as in *labour-intensive, capital-intensive.* —**intensive culture** getting the very most out of the soil of a limited area —**intensive care unit** an area in a hospital where a patient's condition is carefully monitored [See **intend.**]
intent *in-tent', adj* fixed with close attention· diligently applied —*n* the thing aimed at or intended· purpose, intention —*n* **intention** (*in-ten'shən*) design: purpose: application of thought to an object. a concept: (in *pl.*) purpose with respect to marriage (*coll.*).—*adj.* **inten'tional** with intention intended· designed: directed towards, or pertaining to the mind's capacity to direct itself towards, objects and states of affairs (*philos*) —*n* **inten-tional'ity.**—*adv* **inten'tionally** with intention· on purpose.—*adv* **intent'ly** earnestly diligently.—*n* **intent'ness.**—**to all intents (and purposes)** in every

important respect· virtually, **well-** (or **ill-**) **intentioned** having good (or ill) designs: meaning well (or ill), **with intent** (*law*) deliberately, with the intention of doing the harm, etc that is or was done. [See **intend.**]
inter *in-tûr', v t* to bury·—*pr.p* **interr'ing;** *pa.t.* and *pa.p* **interred'.**—*n.* **inter'ment** burial. [Fr. *enterrer* —L L *interrāre*—L *in,* into, *terra,* the earth.]
inter- *in'tər-, in-tûr', pfx* between, among, in the midst of. mutual, reciprocal· together. [L. *inter.*]
interact *in'tər-akt', v i* to act on one another —*ns* **interac'tant** a substance, etc which interacts; **inter-action** (*-ak'shən*) mutual action.—*adj.* **interac'tive** allowing, or capable of, mutual action: allowing continuous two-way communication between a computer and its user [Pfx **inter-.**]
interbreed *in-tər-brēd', v.t* and *v.i* to breed together, esp of different races —*pa.t.* and *pa p.* **interbred'.** —*n.* **interbreed'ing.** [Pfx **inter-.**]
intercalate *in-tûr'kə-lāt, v.t* to insert between others, as a day in a calendar: to interpolate.—*adj.* **inter'-calary** inserted between others.—*n* **intercala'tion.** —*adj* **inter'calative** (*-lā-tiv, -lə-tiv*). [L. *intercalāre, -ātum—inter,* between, *calāre,* to proclaim; see **calends.**]
intercede *in-tər-sēd', v.t.* to act as peacemaker between two: to plead (for one).—*adj.* **interced'ent.** —*n* **interced'er.** [L. *intercēdēre, -cēssum—inter,* between, *cēdēre,* to go]
intercept *in-tər-sept', v.t.* to stop and seize in passage: to cut off· to stop, alter, or interrupt, the progress of: to take or comprehend between (*math.*).—*ns.* **in'-tercept** (*math*) that part of a line that is intercepted; **intercep'ter, intercep'tor** one who or that which intercepts· a light, swift aeroplane for pursuit; **intercep'tion.**—*adj* **intercep'tive.** [L. *intercipēre, -cep-tum—inter,* between, *capēre,* to seize.]
intercession *in-tər-sesh'ən, n.* the act of interceding or pleading for another.—*adj.* **intercess'ional.**—*n.* **intercessor** (*-ses'ər*) one who intercedes: a bishop who acts during a vacancy in a see.—*adjs* **intercessōrial** (*-ōr', -ôr'*), **intercess'ory** interceding.—**intercession of saints** prayer offered on behalf of Christians on earth by saints [See **intercede.**]
interchange *in-tər-chānj', v t* to give and take mutually to exchange —*v i* to succeed alternately —*n* **in'terchange** mutual exchange. alternate succession. a road junction or series of junctions designed to prevent streams of traffic crossing one another.— *adj* **interchange'able** that may be interchanged.— *ns.* **interchange'ableness, interchangeabil'ity.**—*adv.* **interchange'ably.** [Pfx **inter-.**]
intercity *in-tər-sit'i, adj* between cities. [Pfx **inter-.**]
intercollegiate *in-tər-kə-lē'ji-āt, -ət, adj.* between colleges. [Pfx. **inter-.**]
intercom *in'tər-kom, n.* a telephone system within a building, aeroplane, tank, etc. [*Internal communication*]
intercommunicate *in-tər-ko-mūn-i-kāt, v.t.* and *v.i.* to communicate mutually or together· to have free passage from one to another —*ns* **intercommunica'tion; intercommun'ion** mutual communion or relation, esp between churches the permitting of members of one denomination to receive Holy Communion in the churches of another denomination. [Pfx **inter-.**]
interconnect *in-tər-kə-nekt', v t* to connect mutually and intimately, or by a multitude of ways.—*v i.* to be mutually connected —*n.* **interconnec'tedness, interconnec'tion, interconnex'ion.** [Pfx. **inter-.**]
intercontinental *in-tər-kon-ti-nen'tal, adj.* between or connecting different continents [Pfx **inter-.**]

intercostal *ın-tər-kost'əl, adj.* between the ribs or the leaf-veins [L. *inter,* between, *costa,* a rib]

intercourse *ın'tər-kōrs, -kors, n.* connection by dealings communication: commerce· communion. coition. [O Fr *entrecours*—L *intercursus,* a running between—*inter,* between, *currēre, cursum,* to run]

intercut *ın-tər-kut', (cinema) v.t.* to alternate (contrasting shots) within a sequence by cutting [Pfx **inter-.**]

interdenominational *ın-tər-dı-nom-ı-nāsh'(ə-)nl, adj* common to, with participation of, various religious denominations independent of denomination [Pfx **inter-.**]

interdental *ın-tər-dent'l, adj.* between the teeth. pronounced with the tip of the tongue between upper and lower teeth —*adv.* **interdent'ally.** [Pfx. **inter-.**]

interdepartmental *ın-tər-dē-part-ment'l, adj* between departments.—*adv* **interdepartment'ally.** [Pfx **inter-.**]

interdependence *ın-tər-dı-pend'əns, n* mutual dependence. dependence of parts one on another.—*adj* **interdepend'ent.** [Pfx. **inter-.**]

interdict *ın-tər-dıkt', v.t* to prohibit. to forbid: to forbid communion —*n* **in'terdict** prohibition a prohibitory decree.—*n* **interdic'tion** (*-shən*)—*adjs.* **interdic'tive, interdic'tory.** [L. *interdicēre, -dictum—inter,* between, *dicēre,* to say.]

interdigital *ın-tər-dıj'ı-tl, adj.* between digits —*v.t* and *v.t.* **interdig'itate** to interlock by finger-like processes, or in the manner of the fingers of clasped hands.—*n* **interdigitā'tion.** [Pfx. **inter-.**]

interdisciplinary *ın-tər-dı-sı-plın'ə-rı, adj.* involving two or more fields of study. [Pfx. **inter-.**]

interest *ınt'(ə-)rest, -rıst, n.* benefit. premium paid for the use of money: any increase: concern, importance. personal influence: a right to some advantage: claim to participate or be concerned in some way. stake. share behalf: partisanship or side: the body of persons whose advantage is bound up in anything: regard to advantage: a state of engaged attention and curiosity: disposition towards such a state. the power of arousing it: that in which one has interest or is interested.—*v.t.* to concern deeply. to cause to have an interest· to engage the attention of: to awaken concern in. to excite (on behalf of another) —*adj.* **in'terested** having an interest or concern. affected or biased by personal considerations, self-interest, etc.—*adv.* **in'terestedly.** —*adj* **in'teresting** engaging or apt to engage the attention or regard: exciting emotion or passion —*adv.* **in'terestingly.**—**interest group** a number of people grouped together to further or protect a common interest.—**in the interest(s) of** with a view to furthering or to helping. [From old word *interess,* influenced by O.Fr. *interest,* it concerns]

interface *ın'tər-fās, n* a surface forming a common boundary. a meeting-point or area of contact between objects, systems, subjects, etc. the connection or junction between two systems or two parts of the same system (*comput*) —*v t* to co-operate, communicate or interact (with) at an interface —*adj.* **interfacial** (*-fā'shl*) between plane faces of an interface [Pfx **inter-.**]

interfacing *ın'tər-fās-ıng, n.* firm material sewn between layers of fabric to shape and stiffen a garment [Pfx. **inter-.**]

interfere *ın-tər-fēr', v t* (of a horse) to strike a foot against the opposite leg in walking to intervene: to come in the way. to interpose to intermeddle. (of waves, rays of light, etc)to act reciprocally —*n* **interfer'ence** the act of interfering· the effect of combining similar rays of light, etc the spoiling of a wireless or television signal by others or by natural disturbances —*adj* **interferential** (*-fər-en'shl*) —*n* **interfer'er.**—

adv **interfer'ingly.**—*n.* **interferom'eter** an instrument which, by observing interference fringes, makes precision measurements, mainly of wavelengths; **interferom'etry; interfer'on** a protein produced naturally in the body, active against many viruses.—**interfere with** to meddle in: to get in the way of, hinder: to assault sexually [O Fr *entreferır*—L. *inter,* between, *ferīre,* to strike]

intergalactic *ın-tər-gal-ak'tık, adj.* between, or among, galaxies [Pfx **inter-.**]

interglacial *ın-tər-glā'sh(y)əl, (geol) adj* occurring between two periods of glacial action.

interim *ın'tər-ım, n.* the time between or intervening. the meantime: (with *cap.*) in the history of the Reformation, the name given to certain edicts of the German emperor for the regulation of religious and ecclesiastical matters, till they could be decided by a general council.—*adj.* temporary. [L.]

interior *ın-tē'rı-ər, adj.* inner: remote from the frontier or coast. inland. situated within or further in (sometimes with *to*): devoted to mental or spiritual life.—*n.* the inside of anything. the inland part of a country: a picture of a scene within a house: home affairs of a country. inner nature or character.—*n.* **interiority** (*-or'ı-tı*) —*adv.* **inter'iorly.**—**interior decoration,** design the construction and furnishing of the interior of a building.—*adj.* **inter'ior-sprung'** (of a mattress, etc)containing springs. [L., compar. of assumed *interus,* inward]

interject *ın-tər-jekt', v.t.* to throw between: to interpose: to exclaim in interruption or parenthesis: to insert.—*v.t* to throw oneself between.—*n.* **interjec'-tion** (*-shən*) a throwing between. a word thrown in to express emotion (*gram.*) —*adjs.* **interjec'tional, interjec'tionary, interjec'tural.**—*adv.* **interjec'-tionally.** [L. *ınter(j)ıcēre, interjectum—ınter,* between, *jacēre,* to throw.]

interlace *ın-tər-lās', v t.* to lace, weave, or entangle together.—*v ı.* to intermix.—*n.* **interlace'ment.—interlaced scanning** in television, the alternate scanning of an image in two sets of alternate lines. [Pfx. **inter-.**]

interlard *ın-tər-lard', v.t.* to mix in, as fat with lean: to diversify by mixture. [Pfx. **inter-.**]

interlay *ın-tər-lā', v t.* to lay between: to interpose [Pfx **inter-.**]

interleave *ın-tər-lēv', v t.* to put a leaf between: to insert blank leaves in —*n* **in'terleaf** a leaf so inserted:—*pl* **in'terleaves.** [Pfx. **inter-.**]

interline *ın-tər-lın', v.t.* to write in alternate lines: to insert between lines: to write between the lines of.—*adj* **interlinear** (*-lın'ı-ər*) written between lines [Pfx **inter-.**]

interlink *ın-tər-lingk', v t.* and *v.t* to link together [Pfx. **inter-.**]

interlock *ın-tər-lok', v.t.* to lock or clasp together: to connect so as to work together —*v.t.* to be locked together.—*n.* **in'terlock** an interlocked condition: synchronising mechanism. [Pfx **inter-.**]

interlocution *ın-tər-lo-kū'shən, n.* conference. an intermediate decree before final decision.—*n.* **interlocutor** (*-lok'ū-tər*) one who speaks in dialogue: a judge's decree (*Scots law*).—*adj.* **interloc'utory.**—*ns.* **interloc'utress, interloc'utrice, interloc'utrix** a female interlocutor. [L. *interlocūtiō, -ōnıs—ınter,* between, *loquı, locūtus,* to speak]

interloper *ın'tər-lō-pər, n.* one who trades without licence: an intruder.—*v ı.* and *v t.* **interlope'** (or *ın'*) to intrude into any matter in which one has no fair concern [Prob L. *ınter,* between, and **lope.**]

interlude *ın'tər-lōō d, -lūd, n.* a short piece introduced between the acts of the mysteries and moralities, etc , unconnected with the main theme and light in character: an early form of modern drama: a short piece of music played between the parts of a drama opera, hymn, etc.: an interval, any period of time or any happening different in character from what comes before or after. [L. *inter*, between, *lūdus*, play.]

interlunar *in-tər-lōō'nər, -lū'*, *adj.* belonging to the moon's monthly time of invisibility.—*n.* **interlunā'tion** (*-lōō-*) the dark time between old moon and new. [L *inter*, between, *lūna*, the moon.]

intermarry *in-tər-mar'ı*, *v.i.* to marry, esp. of different races or groups, or of near kin: to mingle by repeated marriage: (of a couple) to marry (*legal*): to marry (with *with*; *legal*).—*n.* **intermarr'iage**. [Pfx. **inter-**.]

intermediate *in-tər-mē'dyit, -di-it*, *adj.* placed, occurring, or classified between others, extremes, limits, or stages: of igneous rocks, between acid and basic in composition: intervening.—*n.* that which is intermediate: any compound manufactured from a primary that serves as a starting material for the synthesis of some other product (*chem.*).—*v.i.* (*-di-āt*) to interpose: to act between others.—*n.* **intermē'diacy** (*-ə-si*) the state of being intermediate.—*adj.* **intermē'diary** acting between others: intermediate.—*n.* an intermediate agent.—*adv.* **intermē'diately.**—*ns.* **intermēdia'tion** the act of intermediating; **intermē'diātor.**—*adj.* **intermē'diatory** (*-ə-tə-ri*).—**intermediate technology** technology which combines simple, basic materials with modern sophisticated tools and methods. [Pfx. **inter-**.]

interment. See **inter.**

intermezzo *in-tər-met'sō*, sometimes *-med'zō, n.* a short dramatic or musical entertainment as entr'acte: a short intermediate movement or the like (*mus.*):—*pl.* **intermez'zi** (*-zē*) or **-os.** [It.,—L. *intermedius*.]

interminable *in-tûr'min-ə-bl*, *adj.* without termination or limit: boundless: endless.—*n.* **inter'minableness.**—*adv.* **inter'minably.** [Pfx. **in-** (2).]

intermingle *in-tər-ming'gl*, *v.t.* and *v.i.* to mingle or mix together [Pfx. **inter-**.]

intermit *in-tər-mit'*, *v.t.* and *v.i.* to stop for a time.—*n.* **intermission** (*-mish'ən*) an act of intermitting: an interval: music played during a theatre or similar interval: pause: a respite.—*adj.* **intermissive** (*-mis'ıv*) coming and going: intermittent.—*ns.* **intermitt'ence**; **intermitt'ency.**—*adj.* **intermitt'ent** intermitting or ceasing at intervals.—*advs.* **intermitt'ently**; **intermitt'ingly.** [L. *intermittēre, -missum—inter*, between, *mittēre*, to cause to go.]

intermix *in-tər-miks'*, *v.t.* and *v.i.* to mix together.—*n.* **intermix'ture** a mass formed by mixture: something added and intermixed. [L. *intermiscēre, -mixtum—inter*, among, *miscēre*, to mix.]

intermolecular *in-tər-mol-ek'ū-lər*, *adj.* between molecules. [Pfx. **inter-**.]

intern *in-tûrn'*, *adj.* internal.—*n.* (also **interne**; Also *in'*; in U.S. *in'*) an inmate, as of a boarding-school: a resident assistant surgeon or physician in a hospital (*U.S.*).—*v.t.* to send into the interior of a country: to confine within fixed bounds without permission to leave the district, camp, port, or like limits.—*ns.* **internee'** one so restricted; **intern'ment** confinement of this kind. [Fr. *interne*—L. *internus*, inward.]

internal *in-tûr'nəl*, *adj.* in the interior: domestic as opposed to foreign: intrinsic: pertaining to the inner nature or feelings: inner.—Opp. to *external.*—*n.* (in *pl.*) inner parts.—*v.t.* **inter'nalise, -ize** to assimilate (an idea, etc.) into one's personality: to withdraw (an emotion, etc.) into oneself (rather than express it).—*p. adj.* **inter'nalised, -z-.**—*n.* **internality** (*-nal'i-ti*).—*adv.* **inter'nally.**—**internal evidence** evidence afforded by the thing itself.—**internal-combustion engine** an engine in which the fuel is burned within the working cylinder. [L. *internus—inter*, within.]

international *in-tər-nash'ən-l*, *adj.* between nations or

their representatives: transcending national limits: extending to several nations: pertaining to the relations between nations.—*n.* (with *cap.*) a short-lived association formed in London in 1864 to unite the working classes of all countries in efforts for their economic emancipation: (with *cap.*) a second organisation of socialists of all countries formed in 1889 as a successor to the first International—also (Fr.) **Internationale** (*ē-ter-na-syō-näl'*): (with *cap.*) a rival organisation (third International) operating from Moscow from 1919 to 1943: a game or contest between players chosen to represent different nations (*coll.*): a player who takes (or has taken) part in an international match.—*n.* **Internationale** (*ē-ter-na-syō-näl'*) an international communist song, composed in France in 1871: the second International.—*v.t.* **interna'tionalise, -ize** to make international: to put under international control.—*ns.* **interna'tionalism**; **interna'tionalist** one who favours the common interests, or action, of all nations: one who favours the principles of the International: one who represents his country in international contests: a specialist in international law.—*adj.* **internationalis'tic.**—*adv.* **interna'tionally.**—**international law** the law regulating the relations of states (**public international law**) or that determining what nation's law shall in any case govern the relations of private persons (**private international law**); **international master** (also with *caps.*) (a person holding) the second highest international chess title.—**International Date Line** the line east and west of which the date differs—the 180th meridian with deviations; **International Monetary Fund** an organisation, established in 1945 to promote international trade through increased stabilisation of currencies, which maintains a pool of money on which member countries can draw; **International Phonetic Alphabet** the alphabet of the International Phonetic Association, a series of symbols representing human speech sounds; **international system of units** see **S.I. units.** [Pfx. **inter-**.]

interne. See **intern.**

internecine *in-tər-nē'sīn*, *adj.* deadly: murderous: loosely, mutually destructive: involving conflict within a group. [L. *internecīnus, -īvus—internecāre—inter*, between (used intensively), *necāre*, to kill.]

internee. See **intern.**

interneural *in-tər-nū'rəl*, (*anat.*) *adj.* situated between the neural spines or spinous processes of successive vertebrae. [Pfx. **inter-**.]

internist *in-tûr'nist*, *n.* a specialist in internal diseases: a physician, in contrast to a surgeon. [*internal*, and **-ist**.]

internment. See **intern.**

internuncio *in-tər-nun'shi-ō*, *n.* a messenger between two parties: the Pope's representative at minor courts:—*pl.* **internun'cios.**—*adj.* **internun'cial** relating to an internuncio. [It. *internunzio*, Sp. *internuncio*, L. *ternuntius—inter*, between, *nuntius*, a messenger.]

interoceptor *in-tər-ō-sep'tər*, (*physiol.*) *n.* a sensory receptor of the viscera.—*adj.* **interocep'tive.** [*Interior* and re*ceptor.*]

interparietal *in-tər-pə-rī'ə-təl*, *adj.* situated between the right and left parietal bones of the skull. [Pfx. **inter-**.]

interpellation *in-tər-pel-ā'shən*, *n.* a question raised during the course of a debate.—*v.t.* **inter'pellate** (or *-pel'*) to question by interpellation. [Fr.,—L. *interpellāre, -ātum*, to disturb by speaking—*inter*, between, *pellēre*, to drive.]

interpersonal *in-tər-pûr'sən-əl*, *adj.* between persons—*adv.* **interper'sonally.** [Pfx. **inter-**.]

interphone *in'tər-fōn*, *n.* intercom. [Gr. *phōnē*, voice.]

interplanetary *in-tər-plan'ıt-ə-ri*, *adj.* between planets. [Pfx. **inter-**.]

interplay ın'tər-plā, n. mutual action: interchange of action and reaction. [Pfx. **inter-**.]

interplead ın-tər-plēd', (law) v.ı. to discuss adverse claims to property by bill of interpleader.—n. **interplead'er** one who interpleads: a form of process in the English courts intended to protect a defendant who claims no interest in the subject matter of a suit, while at the same time he has reason to know that the plaintiff's title is disputed by some other claimant. [Pfx. **inter-**.]

interpleural ın-tər-plōō'rəl, adj situated between the right and left pleural cavities. [Pfx **inter-**.]

Interpol ın'tər-pol, the *Inter*national Criminal Police Commission, directed to international co-operation in the suppression of crime.

interpolable. See **interpolate**.

interpolar in-tər-pō'lər, adj. between or connecting the poles [Pfx **inter-**.]

interpolate ın-tûr'pō-lāt, -pə-lāt, v.t. to insert unfairly, as a spurious word or passage in a book or manuscript: to tamper with, to corrupt by spurious insertions: to insert, intercalate, interject: to fill in as an intermediate term of a series (math)—adj **inter'polable**. —n. **interpolā'tion**.—adj. **inter'polative**.—n. **inter'polator**. [L. *interpolāre, -ātum—inter*, between, *polire*, to polish.]

interpose ın-tər-pōz', v t. to place between: to thrust in: to offer, as aid or services. to put in by way of interruption —v ı. to come between: to mediate: to interfere —ns. **interpos'al; interpos'er; interposition** (ın-tər-poz-ısh'ən) the act of interposing: intervention: mediation: in U.S., the right of a state to oppose the federal government for encroachment on the prerogatives of the state: anything interposed. [Fr. *interposer*—L *inter*, between, Fr *poser*, to place; see **pose¹**.]

interpret ın-tûr'prıt, v.t. to explain the meaning of, to elucidate, unfold, show the purport of· to translate into intelligible or familiar terms.—v ı. to practise interpretation.—adj. **inter'pretable** capable of being explained —n **interpretā'tion** the act of interpreting: the sense given by an interpreter: the representation of a dramatic part, performance of a piece of music, or the like, according to one's conception of it.—adjs. **inter'pretative** (-āt-ıv, -ət-ıv), **interpretive** inferred by or containing interpretation.—adv. **inter'pretatively**. —ns **inter'preter** one who translates orally for the benefit of two or more parties speaking different languages: an expounder: a machine which prints out on punched cards fed into it the data contained in the patterns of holes in the cards (*comput*.): a program which executes other programs (*comput*., cf compiler); **inter'pretership**. [L. *interpretārī, -ātus*]

interracial ın-tər-rā'sh(y)əl, -shı-əl, adj between races [Pfx. **inter-**.]

interregnum ın-tər-reg'nəm, n the time between two reigns: the time between the cessation of one and the establishment of another government: any breach of continuity in order, etc.:—pl. **interreg'na, interreg'-nums**. [L. *inter*, between, *regnum*, rule]

interrelation ın-tər-rı-lā'shən, n. reciprocal relation — n **interrelā'tionship**. [Pfx **inter-**.]

interrogate in-ter'ə-gāt, v t. to question to examine by asking questions: of a radar set, etc , to send out signals to (a radio-beacon) in order to ascertain position.— v.t. to ask questions —adj. **interr'ogable**.—ns **interr'ogant** a questioner, **interrogatee'** one who is interrogated, **interrogā'tion** the act of interrogating: a question put the mark placed after a question (?) (also **interrogation mark**).—adj **interrogative** (ın-tər-og'ə-tıv) denoting a question expressed as a question —n a word used in asking a question —adv **interrog'atively**.—ns **interr'ogator; interrog'atory** a

question or inquiry.—adj. expressing a question. [L. *interrogāre, -ātum—inter*, between, *rogāre*, to ask.]

interrupt in-tər-upt', v t. to break in between: to stop or hinder by breaking in upon: to break continuity in.— v ı. to make an interruption —adj **interrupt'ed** broken in continuity· irregular in spacing or size of parts (*biol*.).—adv. **interrupt'edly** with interruptions: irregularly.—ns. **interrup'ter** (also **interrup'tor**) one who interrupts: apparatus for interrupting, e.g. for breaking an electric circuit, for preventing the firing of a gun from an aircraft when the screw is in the line of fire; **interrup'tion** the act of interrupting: hindrance: temporary cessation.—adj. **interrup'tive** tending to interrupt.—adv. **interrup'tively**. [L. *interrumpêre, -ruptum—inter*, between, *rumpêre*, to break.]

interscapular ın-tər-ska'pū-lər, (anat.) adj. between the shoulder-blades. [Pfx. **inter-**.]

interscholastic ın-tər-skə-las'tık, adj between schools. [Pfx. **inter-**.]

intersect ın-tər-sekt', v t. to cut across· to cut or cross mutually: to divide into parts.—v.ı. to cross each other —ns **in'tersect** a point of intersection, **intersec'-tion** intersecting: the point or line in which lines or surfaces cut each other (*geom*). the set of elements which two or more sets have in common (*math*.): a crossroads —adj. **intersec'tional**. [L. *inter*, between, *secāre, sectum*, to cut]

intersex ın'tər-seks, (biol.) n. an individual developing some characters of the other sex.—adj. **intersex'ual** between the sexes: intermediate between the sexes.— n. **intersexûal'ity**. [Pfx. **inter-**.]

interspace ın'tər-spās, n. an interval —v.t. (-spās') to put intervals between. [Pfx. **inter-**.]

interspecific in-tər-spıs-ıf'ık, adj. between species [Pfx. **inter-**.]

intersperse ın-tər-spûrs', v.t to scatter or set here and there: to diversify —n. **interspersion** (-spûr'shən). [L. *interspergêre, -spersum—inter*, among, *spargêre*, to scatter]

interstate ın'tər-stāt, or -stāt', adj. pertaining to relations, esp·political and commercial, between states: between states —adv into or to another state. [Pfx. **inter-**.]

interstellar ın-tər-stel'ər, adj. beyond the solar system or among the stars: in the intervals between the stars. —Also **interstell'ary**. [L. *inter*, between, *stella*, a star.]

interstice in-tûr'stıs, n a small space between things closely set, or between the parts which compose a body. the time interval required by canon law before receiving higher orders (*R.C.*). a space between atoms in a lattice where other atoms can be located.—adj **interstitial** (-stish'l) occurring in interstices [L. *interstitium—inter*, between, *sistêre, stătum*, to stand, set.]

interstratification in-tər-strat-ı-fı-kā'shən, n. the state of lying between, or alternating with, other strata.— adj. **interstrat'ified**.—v t. and v ı. **interstrat'ify**. [Pfx **inter-**.]

intertarsal ın-tər-tar'sl, adj. between tarsal bones. [Pfx **inter-**.]

interterritorial ın-tər-ter-ı-tō'rı-əl, -to', adj between territories [Pfx **inter-**.]

intertidal ın-tər-tī'dl, adj between low-water and high-water mark [Pfx **inter-**.]

intertie ın'tər-tī, n in roofing, etc , a short timber binding together upright posts.

intertribal ın-tər-trī'bl, adj between tribes [Pfx **inter-**.]

intertrigo ın-tər-trī'gō, n an inflammation of the skin from chafing or rubbing:—pl **intertri'gos**. [L. *inter-trigō—inter*, between, *terêre, trītum*, to rub]

intertwine ın-tər-twīn', v t and v ı. to twine or twist

together.—*ns.* **in'tertwine** intertwining; **inter-twine'ment.**—*n.* and *adj.* **intertwin'ing.** [Pfx. inter-.]

interunion in-tər-ūn'yən, *n.* a blending together [Pfx. inter-.]

interurban in-tər-ûr'bən, *adj.* between cities [L *inter*, between, *urbs, urbis,* a city.]

interval in'tər-vəl, *n.* time or space between: a break between lessons, acts of a play, etc.: difference of pitch between any two musical tones (*mus.*). [L. *intervallum—inter*, between, *vallum*, a rampart]

intervene in-tər-vēn', *v.i.* to come or be between: to occur between points of time: to happen so as to interrupt: to interpose: to interpose in an action to which one was not at first a party (*law*)—*n.* **interven'er** one who intervenes.—Also (*law*) **interven'or.**—*adj.* **intervenient** (-vēn'yənt) being or passing between: intervening.—*ns.* **intervention** (-ven'shən) intervening: interference: mediation: interposition: a system of removing surplus produce from the market and storing it until prices rise; **interven'tionism; interven'tionist** one who advocates interference (also *adj.*).—**intervention price** the market price at which intervention occurs. [L. *inter*, between, *venīre*, to come.]

interview in'tər-vū, *n.* a formal meeting: a meeting between employer, board of directors, etc , and a candidate to ascertain by questioning and discussion the latter's suitability for a post, etc.: a meeting between a journalist, or radio or TV broadcaster, and a notable person to discuss the latter's views, etc., for publication or broadcasting: an article or programme based on such a meeting.—*v.t.* to have an interview with.—*ns.* **interviewee'** one who is interviewed, **in'terviewer.** [O.Fr. *entrevue—entre*, between, *voir*, to see.]

intervocalic in-tər-vō-kal'ik, *adj.* between vowels. [Pfx. inter-.]

interwar in-tər-wòr', *adj.* between wars. [Pfx. inter-.]

interweave in-tər-wēv', *v.t.* and *v.i* to weave together: to intermingle [Pfx. inter-.]

interzone in-tər-zōn', **interzonal** -zōn'əl, *adjs.* between zones (as of occupied country).—*n.* **in'terzone.** [Pfx. inter-.]

intestate in-tes'tāt, -tit, *adj.* dying without having made a valid will: not disposed of by will.—*n* a person who dies without making a valid will.—*n.* **intes'tacy** (-tə-si). [L. *intestātus—in-*, not, *testārī, -ātus*, to make a will.]

intestine in-tes'tin, *n.* (commonly in *pl.*) a part of the digestive system, divided into the smaller intestine (comprising duodenum, jejunum, and ileum) and the greater intestine.—*adj.* **intes'tinal** (also *-tīn'*) pertaining to the intestines of an animal body. [L. *intestīnus—intus*, within.]

intimate in'ti-mit, *-māt, adj.* innermost: internal: close: deep-seated: private: personal: closely acquainted: familiar: in illicit sexual connection: encouraging informality and closer personal relations through smallness, exclusiveness.—*n.* a familiar friend: an associate.—*v.t.* (*-māt*) to hint: to announce.—*n* **in'timacy** (*-mə-si*) the state of being intimate: close familiarity: illicit sexual intercourse.—*adv.* **in'timately.**—*n.* **intima'tion** indication: hint: announcement. [L. *intimāre, -ātum—intimus*, innermost—*intus*, within.]

intimidate in-tim'i-dāt, *v.t.* to strike fear into: to influence by threats or violence.—*n.* **intimida'tion** the act of intimidating: the use of violence or threats to influence the conduct or compel the consent of another: the state of being intimidated.—*adj.* **intim'idatory.** [L. *in*, into, *timidus*, fearful.]

into in'tōō, *prep.* to a position within: to a state of: used to indicate the dividend in dividing (*math.*): in contact or collision with: interested in or enthusiastic about (*slang*): to part of (*math.*).—*adj.* (*math.*) describing a

mapping of one set to a second set, involving only some of the elements of the latter. [in, to.]

intolerable in-tol'ər-ə-bl, *adj.* not to be endured.—*ns* **intolerabil'ity, intol'erableness.**—*adv.* **intol'erably.** —*ns.* **intol'erance, intolera'tion** state of being intolerant.—*adj.* **intol'erant** not able or willing to endure: not enduring difference of opinion: persecuting.—*adv.* **intol'erantly.** [Pfx. in- (2).]

intonate in'tōn-āt, *v.t.* and *v.i.* to intone.—*n.* **intona'tion** the opening phrase of any plainsong melody, sung usually either by the officiating priest alone, or by one or more selected choristers: pitching of musical notes: modulation or rise and fall in pitch of the voice: intoning.—*v.t* and *v.i.* **intone** (*in-tōn'*) to chant, read, or utter in musical tones, singsong, or monotone to begin by singing the opening phrase: to utter with a particular intonation. [L.L. *intonāre, -ātum*—L. *in*, in, *tonus*, tone.]

in toto in tō'tō, (L) entirely.

intoxicate in-toks'i-kāt, *v.t.* to make drunk: to excite to enthusiasm or madness: to elate excessively.—*adj.* **intox'icant** intoxicating.—*n.* an intoxicating agent.—*adj.* **intox'icating.**—*n.* **intoxica'tion** the state of being drunk: high excitement or elation. [L.L. *intoxicāre, -ātum—in*, in, *toxicum*—Gr. *toxikon*, arrow-poison—*toxon*, a bow.]

intra in'tra, in'trä, (L.) *within.*—**intra muros** (*mū'rōs, mōō'rōs*) within the wall; **intra vires** (*vī'rēz, wē*' or *vē'räs*) within the legal power of.

intra- in'trä-, in'trə-, in composition, within, as in **intra-abdom'inal** situated within the cavity of the abdomen; **intramū'ral** within walls: included within the college; **intra-ū'terine** within the uterus; **intravē'nous** within, or introduced into, a vein or veins. [L. *intrā*, within]

intractable in-trakt'ə-bl, *adj* unmanageable: obstinate.—*ns.* **intractabil'ity, intract'ableness.**—*adv.* **intract'ably.** [Pfx. in- (2).]

intrados in-trä'dos, (*archit.*) *n.* the soffit or under surface of an arch. [Fr.—L *intrā*, within, *dorsum*, the back.]

intramural. See intra-.

intransigent in-tran'si-jənt, -tran', -zi-, *adj.* refusing to come to any understanding, irreconcilable: obstinate.—*n.* one who is intransigent.—*ns.* **intran'sigence; intran'sigency.** [Fr. *intransigeant*—Sp. *intransigente*—L. *in-*, not, *transigēns, -entis,* pr.p. of *transigĕre*, to transact; see **transact.**]

intransitive in-tran'si-tiv, *-trän', -zi-, adj.* representing action confined to the agent, i.e. having no object (*gram.*).—*adv.* **intran'sitively.** [Pfx. in- (2).]

intransmissible in-trans-mis'i-bl, *-tranz-, -tränz-, adj.* that cannot be transmitted. [Pfx. in- (2).]

intransmutable in-trans-mūt'ə-bl, *-tranz-, -tränz-, adj.* that cannot be changed into another substance. —*n.* **intransmutabil'ity.** [Pfx. in- (2).]

intra-uterine, intravenous. See intra-.

intrench, intrenchment. See entrench.

intrepid in-trep'id, *adj.* without trepidation or fear: undaunted: brave.—*n.* **intrepid'ity** firm, unshaken courage.—*adv.* **intrep'idly.** [L. *intrepidus—in-*, not, *trepidus*, alarmed.]

intricate in'tri-kit, *-kāt* (also *-trik'it*), *adj.* involved: entangled: complex.—*ns.* **in'tricacy** (*-kə-si*; also *-trik'*), **intricateness.**—*adv.* **intricately.** [L. *intricātus—in-*, in, *tricāre*, to make difficulties—*trīcae*, hindrances.]

intrigue in-trēg', *n.* indirect or underhand scheming or plot: a private scheme: the plot of a play or romance: a secret illicit love affair.—*v.i.* to engage in intrigue.—*v.t.* to puzzle, to fascinate (orig. a Gallicism).—*n.* **intrigu'er.**—*ns.* and *adjs.* **intrig(u)ant** (*in'tri-gant, ē-trē-gä'*), (*fem.*) **intrig(u)ante** (*in-tri-*

gant', *ē-trē-gät*) —*adj* **intrigu'ing.**—*adv* **intrigu'-ingly.** [Fr , see **intricate.**]

intrinsic, -al *in-trin'sik, -əl, adjs* inward· genuine. inherent. essential, belonging to the point at issue.—*adv.* **intrin'sically.** [Fr. *intrinsèque*—L. *intrinsecus* —*intrā*, within, suff -*in, secus*, following]

intro *in'trō, n* contraction of **introduction**, used esp of the opening passage of a jazz or popular music piece —*pl* **in'tros.**

intro- *in'trō-, in-tro'-, pfx* within, into [L *intrō.*]

introduce *in-tra-dūs', v t.* to lead or bring in to conduct into a place. formally to make known or acquainted. to bring into notice or practice. to preface —*n* **introduc'er.**—*adj* **introduc'ible.**—*n* **introduction** (*-duk'shən*) the act of introducing preliminary matter to a book. a preliminary passage or section leading up to a movement (*mus*) a treatise introductory to a science or course of study —*adv* **introduc'torily.**— *adj.* **introduc'tory** serving to introduce preliminary prefatory [L *introdūcēre, -ductum*—*intrō*, inward, *dūcēre*, to lead]

introit *in-trō'it*, or *in'*, *-troit, n* the anthem sung at the beginning of Mass, immediately after the *Confiteor*, and when the priest has ascended to the altar (*R C.*). in other churches, an introductory hymn, psalm, or anthem [L *introïtus*—*introïre*—*intrō*, inwards, *ïre, ïtum*, to go]

introjection *in-trō-jek'shən, n* the taking into the self of persons or things from the outer world so as to experience a oneness with them and to feel personally touched by their fate —*v.t* and *v t.* **introject'.** [L *intrō*, within, *jacēre*, to throw]

intromit *in-trō-mit'*, or *-tra-, v t.* to send within: to admit: to permit to enter to insert —*v t* to have dealings (*Scots law*) to interfere, esp. with the effects of another (esp *Scots law*) —*pr.p* **intromitt'ing;** *pa.t* and *pa.p* **intromitt'ed.**—*ns.* **intromission** (*-mish'ən*) —*adjs* **intromiss'ive** pertaining to intromission. intromitting, **intromitt'ent** intromitting. adapted for insertion, esp (*zool*) in copulation —*n.* **intromitt'er.** [L *intrō*, inward, *mittēre, missum*, to send.]

introrse *in-trors', adj* turned or facing inward. (of an anther) opening towards the centre of the flower — *adv.* **introrse'ly.** [L. *introrsus*, toward the middle, inward—*intrō*, inward and *versus*—*vertēre*, to turn]

introspect *in-trō-spekt'*, or *-tra-, v.t.* to look into (esp the mind).—*v. t.* to practise introspection.—*ns.* **introspection** (*-spek'shən*) a viewing of the inside or interior. the act of observing directly the processes of one's own mind, **introspec'tionist.**—*adj* **introspec'tive.** [L. *intrō*, within, *specēre*, to look at]

introvert *in-trō-vûrt'*, or *-tra-, v.t* to turn inwards: to turn in upon itself. to turn inside out. to withdraw part within the rest of.—*n* **in'trovert** anything introverted a person interested mainly in his own inner states and processes—opp. to *extravert, extrovert* (*psych*).— *adj.* **introvers'ible.**—*n* **introver'sion** (*-shən*).—*adjs* **introver'sive; introver'tive.** [L. *intrō*, inwards, *vertēre, versus*, to turn.]

intrude *in-trōōd', v t.* to thrust oneself in to enter uninvited or unwelcome —*v t* to force in —*ns.* **intrud'er** one who or that which intrudes a military aircraft which raids enemy territory alone, **intrusion** (*-trōō'zhən*) the act of intruding. encroachment an injection of rock in a molten state among and through existing rocks: a mass so injected —*adj.* **intru'sive** (*-siv*) tending or apt to intrude. intruded. inserted without etymological justification· entering without welcome or right: of a rock, which has been forced while molten into cracks and fissures in other rocks — *n* an intrusive rock —*adv* **intru'sively.**—*n* **intru'siveness.** [L. *in*, in, *trūdere, trūsum*, to thrust]

intrust. A variant of **entrust.**

intubate *in'tū-bāt, v t* to insert a tube in to treat by insertion of a tube into, e g the larynx (*med.*).—*n* **intūbā'tion** insertion of a tube [L. *in*, in, *tubus*, a tube]

intuition *in-tū-ish'ən, n* the power of the mind by which it immediately perceives the truth of things without reasoning or analysis: a truth so perceived, immediate knowledge in contrast with mediate —*v t.* and *v t* **intuit** (*in'tū-it*) to know intuitively.—*adj.* **intu'ited.**— *adj.* **intuitional** (*-ish'ən-əl*).—*ns* **intuit'ion(al)ism** the doctrine that the perception of truth is by intuition: a philosophical system which stresses intuition and mysticism as opposed to the idea of a logical universe, **intuit'ion(al)ist.**—*adj* **intu'itive** perceived, perceiving, by intuition received or known by simple inspection and direct apprehension —*adv.* **intu'itively.** —*n* **intu'itivism.** [L *in*, into or upon, *tuēri, tuitus*, to look]

intumesce *in-tū-mes', v t* to swell up—*n.* **intumesc'ence.**—*adj* **intumesc'ent.** [L *in*, in, *tumēscēre*, to swell]

intussusception *in-təs-sə-sep'shən, n.* the passing of part of a tube (esp. the intestine) within the adjacent part. growth by intercalation of particles. [L. *intus*, within, *susceptiō, -ōnis*—*suscipēre*, to take up.]

Inuit. See **Innuit.**

inunction *in-ungk'shən, n* anointing· smearing or rubbing with an ointment or liniment [L. *inunctiō, -ōnis* —*inunguēre*, to anoint—*in*, in, on, *ung(u)ēre*, to smear]

inundate *in'un-dāt, v t* to flow upon or over in waves (said of water). to flood: to overwhelm (*fig.*): to fill with an overflowing abundance —*n* **inundā'tion.** [L. *inundāre, -ātum*—*in*, in, *undāre*, to rise in waves— *unda*, a wave.]

inurbane *in-ûr-bān', adj* not urbane.—*adv* **inurbane'ly.**—*n* **inurbanity** (*-ban'i-ti*) [Pfx **in-** (2).]

inure *in-ūr', v t* to accustom: to habituate. to harden to commit —*v t.* (*law*) to come into use or effect: to serve to one's use or benefit.—*n.* **inure'ment.** [Pfx **in-** (1), and obs. *ure*, use, practice.]

in utero *in ū'tar-ō, ōō'ter-ō*, (L.) in the womb

inutility *in-ū-til'i-ti, n* want of utility: uselessness: unprofitableness. something useless. [Pfx. **in-** (2).]

inutterable *in-ut'ər-ə-bl, adj* unutterable [Pfx. **in-** (2).]

in vacuo *in vak'ū-ō, vak'ōō-ō, wak'*, (L.) in a vacuum.

invade *in-vād', v.t* to enter as an enemy: to attack: to encroach upon: to violate. to seize or fall upon: to enter· to penetrate: to come upon. to rush into.—*ns* **invad'er; invasion** (*-vā'zhən*) the act of invading: an attack. an incursion: an attack on the rights of another: an encroachment: a violation.—*adj.* **invasive** (*-vā'siv*) making invasion aggressive: encroaching: infringing another's rights: entering, penetrating. [L *invādēre, invāsum*—*in*, in, *vādēre*, to go.]

invaginate *in-vaj'in-āt, v.t* to ensheath: to dint inwards, push or withdraw within, introvert.—*v.i.* to be introverted. to form a hollow ingrowth.—*n.* **invagina'tion.** [Pfx. **in-** (1), and L *vāgīna*, a sheath.]

invalid *in-val'id, adj* without validity, efficacy, weight, or cogency: having no effect void: null —*adj.* **invalid** (*in'və-lid, -lēd*) deficient in health, sick, weak: disabled: suitable for invalids.—*n* **in'valid** (*-id, -ēd, -ēd'*) one who is weak: a sickly person: one disabled for active service., esp a soldier or sailor.—*v.t.* **in'valid** (*-id, -ēd, -ēd'*) to make invalid or affect with disease: to enrol or discharge as an invalid.—*v.t.* **invalidate** (*-val'*) to render invalid· to make of no effect.—*ns.* **invalidā'tion; invalidhood** (*in'və-lid-hōōd*, or *-lēd-*, or *-lēd'*); **in'validing** the sending or return home, or to a more healthy climate, of those rendered incapable of active duty by wounds, sickness, etc —*ns.* **invalid'ity**

the state of being an invalid: lack of validity, **inval'id-ness** want of cogency or force.—adv **inval'idly.**—
invalidity pension a pension paid by the government to someone who has been unable to work through illness for over six months [Pfx **in-** (2)]
invaluable in-val'ū-ə-bl, adj. that cannot have a value set upon it· priceless: valueless (obs) —adv **inval'uably.** [Pfx. **in-** (2)]
Invar® in'var, in-vär', n. an alloy of iron, nickel and carbon, very slightly expanded by heat, used in the making of scientific instruments [From **invariable.**]
invariable in-vā'ri-ə-bl, adj. not variable: without alteration or change: unalterable: constantly in the same state.—ns. **invā'riableness, invāriabil'ity.**—adv. **invā'riably.**—n **invā'riant** that which does not change· an expression or quantity that is unaltered by a particular procedure (math) —Also adj.—n **invar'iance** invariableness: the theory of the constancy of physical laws. [Pfx **in-** (2).]
invasion, invasive. See **invade.**
invective in-vek'tiv, n. a severe or reproachful accusation brought against anyone: an attack with words: a violent utterance of censure: sarcasm or satire —adj railing abusive: satirical [See **inveigh.**]
inveigh in-vā', v i to make an attack with words: to rail: to revile [L invehēre, invectum—in, in, vehēre, to carry]
inveigle in-vē'gl, in-vā'gl, v t. to entice to ensnare by cajolery: to wheedle.—ns **invei'glement; invei'gler.** [Prob altered from A Fr enveogler (Fr. aveugler), to blind—L ab, from, oculus, the eye.]
invent in-vent', v.t. to devise or contrive· to design for the first time, originate· to frame by imagination· to fabricate (something false) —adj **inven'tible.**—n **inven'tion** that which is invented: contrivance· a deceit faculty or power of inventing· ability displayed by any invention or effort of the imagination: a short piece working out a single idea (mus.) —adj **inven'tive** able to invent: ready in contrivance —adv **inven'tively.**—ns. **inven'tiveness; inven'tor:**—fem. **inven'tress.**—**Invention of the Cross** a festival observed on 3rd May in commemoration of the alleged discovery of the true cross at Jerusalem in 326 by Helena, mother of Constantine the Great [L invenire, inventum—in, upon, venire, to come]
inventory in'vən-tər-i, n a list or schedule of articles comprised in an estate, etc.· a catalogue· stock, equipment: the total quantity of material in a nuclear reactor —v t. to make an inventory of: to amount to —v.t. to sum up.—adj. **invento'rial.** [L L inventōrium, a list of things found—invenire, to find]
inverse in'vûrs, in-vûrs', adj. inverted: upside down: in the reverse or contrary order· opposite related by inversion.—n. an inverted state: the result of inversion: a direct opposite.—adv **inverse'ly.**—n **inver'sion** (-shən) the act of inverting· the state of being inverted· a change or reversal of order or position: that which is got by inverting —adj. **inver'sive.**—**inverse proportion** (math.) a process by which one quantity decreases while another increases, their product remaining constant; **inverse ratio** the ratio of reciprocals. [L inversus, pa p of invertēre, inversum—in, in, and vertēre, to turn.]
invert in-vûrt', v t to turn in or about. to turn upside down· to reverse: to change the customary order or position of· to form the inverse of: to change by placing the lowest note an octave higher (mus)· to modify by reversing the direction of motion: to break up (cane-sugar) into dextrose and laevulose —n **in'vert** inverted sugar —n **in'vertase** (or -vär') an enzyme that inverts cane-sugar —adj **inver'ted** turned inwards· upside down· reversed· pronounced with tip of tongue turned up and back —adv **inver'tedly.**—ns **in-**

ver'ter, inver'tor. [L invertēre, inversum—in, in, vertēre, to turn]
invertebrate in-vûrt'i-brit, -brāt, adj without a vertebral column or backbone.—n. a member of the Invertebrata —n.pl **Invertebrā'ta** all animals other than vertebrates [Pfx. **in-** (2).]
invest in-vest', v t. to clothe: to envelop: to clothe with insignia of office: to settle or secure: to place in office or authority (with with or in): to adorn: to surround. to block up: to lay siege to: to lay out for profit, as by buying property, shares, etc.—v.i. (coll.) to lay out money, make a purchase (with in) —adj **inves'titive.**—ns **inves'titure** investing· the ceremony of investing; **invest'ment** the act of investing: putting on: covering: investiture: a blockade: the act of surrounding or besieging: any placing of money to secure income or profit: that in which money is invested; **inves'tor** one who invests, esp money. [L investire, -ītum—in, on, vestire, to clothe.]
investigate in-vest'i-gāt, v t. to search or inquire into with care and accuracy —v i to make investigation. —adj. **invest'igable** able to be investigated —n. **investigā'tion** the act of examining: research —adjs. **invest'igative, invest'igatory.**—n. **invest'igator.**—**investigative journalism** journalism involving the investigation and exposure of corruption, crime, inefficiency, etc [L investigāre, -ātum—in, in, vestigāre, to track]
inveterate in-vet'ər-it, adj firmly established by long continuance· deep-rooted, confirmed in any habit: stubborn. rootedly hostile.—adv. **invet'erately.**—ns **invet'erateness, invet'eracy** (-ə-si). [L. inveterātus, stored up, long continued—in, in, vetus, veteris, old]
invidious in-vid'i-əs, adj likely to incur or provoke ill-will· likely to excite envy, enviable: offensively discriminating.—adv. **invid'iously.**—n. **invid'iousness.** [L. invidiōsus—invidia, envy]
invigilate in-vij'i-lāt, v t and v i to supervise, esp. at examinations.—ns **invigilā'tion; invig'ilātor.** [L in, on, vigilāre, -ātum, to watch]
invigorate in-vig'ər-āt, v.t to give vigour to· to strengthen· to animate.—ns **invig'orant** an invigorating agent; **invigorā'tion; invig'orātor.** [Pfx **in-** (1)]
invincible in-vin'si-bl, adj that cannot be overcome: insuperable —ns **invin'cibleness, invincibil'ity.**—adv **invin'cibly.** [Pfx **in-** (2)]
inviolable in-vi'ə-lə-bl, adj that must not be profaned· that cannot be injured.—ns **inviolabil'ity, invi'olableness** the quality of being inviolable —adv. **invi'olably.**—adjs **invi'olate** (-lit, -lāt), -d (-lāt-id) not violated· unprofaned: uninjured —adv **invi'olately.**—n **invi'olateness.** [Pfx **in-** (2)]
invisible in-viz'i-bl, adj incapable of being seen: unseen· relating to services rather than goods (econ.). not shown in regular statements, as **invisible assets** (see **export, import;** finance)—n. an invisible export, etc —ns **invisibil'ity, invis'ibleness.**—adv **invis'ibly.** [Pfx **in-** (2)]
invite in-vit', v t to ask hospitably or politely to come to express affable willingness to receive or to have done: to be of such a kind as to encourage or tend to bring on· to offer inducement· to attract —n **in'vite** (coll) an invitation —n **invitation** (in-vi-tā'shən) the act of inviting an asking or solicitation the written or verbal form with which a person is invited: the brief exhortation introducing the confession in the Anglican communion office —adj. **invit'ing** alluring attractive —adv **invit'ingly.**—n **invit'ingness** attractiveness [L invitāre, -ātum]
in vitro in vit'rō, wit'rō, vit', (L) in glass in the test tube—opp. to **in vivo.**

in vivo *in vī'vō, wĕ'wō, vē'vō,* (L.) in the living organism.

invocate *in'vō-kāt, v.t* to invoke.—*n.* **invocā'tion** the act or the form of invoking or addressing in prayer or supplication: an appellation under which one is invoked: any formal invoking of the blessing or help of a god, a saint, etc.: an opening prayer in a public religious service or in the Litany: a call for inspiration from a Muse or other deity as at the beginning of a poem: an incantation or calling up of a spirit: a call or summons, esp. for evidence from another case (*law*) —*adj.* **invocatory** (*in-vok'ə-tə-ri*) making invocation [See **invoke.**]

invoice *in'vois, n.* a letter of advice of the despatch of goods, with particulars of their price and quantity.— *v.t.* to make an invoice of. [Prob pl. of Fr. *envoi.*]

invoke *in-vōk', v.t.* to call upon earnestly or solemnly: to implore assistance of: to address in prayer: to conjure up: to call to help, resort to. [Fr. *invoquer*—L. *invocāre, -ātum*—*in,* on, *vocāre,* to call.]

involucre *in'və-lōō-kər, -lū-, n.* an envelope (*anat.*): a ring or crowd of bracts around a capitulum, umbel, etc (*bot.*).—Also **involū'crum**—*adjs.* **involu'cral** of the nature of, pertaining to, an involucre; **involu'crate** having an involucre. [L. *involūcrum*—*involvēre,* to involve.]

involuntary *in-vol'ən-tər-i, adj.* not voluntary. not having the power of will or choice: not under control of the will: not done voluntarily.—*adv* **invol'untarily.**— **invol'untariness.** [Pfx. **in-** (2).]

involution *in-və-lū'shən, -lōō', n.* the state of being involved or entangled: complicated grammatical construction: raising to a power (*math.*): retrograde development, return to normal size (*zool.*).—*adj.* **involu'tional.** [See **involve.**]

involve *in-volv', v.t.* to coil: to wrap up: to envelop: to entangle: to complicate: to implicate: to comprehend: to entail or imply, bring as a consequence: to be bound up with: to concern: to raise to a power (*math.*): to make (oneself) emotionally concerned (in, with): to engage the emotional interest of.—*n.* **involve'ment.** [L. *involvēre*—*in,* in, *volvēre, volūtum,* to roll.]

invulnerable *in-vul'nər-ə-bl, adj.* that cannot be wounded: not vulnerable.—*ns.* **invulnerabil'ity, invul'nerableness.**—*adv* **invul'nerably.** [Pfx. **in-** (2).]

inward *in'wərd, adj.* placed or being within: internal: seated in the mind or soul, not perceptible to the senses: uttered as if within, or with closed mouth: secret, private (*arch.*).—*n.* (in *pl.;* often *in'ərdz*) entrails (also **innards**).—*adv.* toward the interior: into the mind or thoughts.—*adv.* **in'wardly** within: in the heart: privately: toward the centre.—*adv.* **in'wards** same as **inward.** [O.E. *inneweard* (adv.).]

iodine *ī'ə-dēn, or* ī'*ō-dēn,* also *-dīn, -din, n.* a halogen element (symbol I; at. numb. 53) giving a violet-coloured vapour.—*n.* **i'odate** a salt of iodic acid.—*adj.* **iodic** (ī-*od'ik*) pertaining to or caused by iodine.—*n.* **i'odide** a salt of hydriodic acid.—*v.t.* **i'odise, -ize** to treat with iodine.—*n.* **iodoform** (ī-*od', -ŏd'ə-fōrm*) a lemon-yellow crystalline compound of iodine (CHI₃) with a saffron-like odour, used as an antiseptic. [Gr. *ioeidēs,* violet-coloured—*ion,* a violet, *eidos,* form.]

ion *ī'ən, ī'on, n.* an electrically charged particle formed by loss or gain by an atom of electrons, effecting by its migration the transport of electricity.—*adj.* **ionic** (ī-*on'ik*).—*v.t.* **ionise, -ize** (ī'*ən-īz*) to produce ions in: to turn into ions.—*ns.* **ionisā'tion, -z-;** **ion'omer** the product of ionic bonding action between long-chain molecules, characterised by toughness and a high degree of transparency; **ion'opause** the region of the earth's atmosphere at the outer limit of the ionosphere; **ionophorē'sis** electrophoresis, esp. of small ions; **ion'osphere** the region of the upper atmosphere that includes the highly ionised Appleton and Kennelly-Heaviside layers.—*adj.* **ionosphēr'ic.**—**i'on-exchange** transfer of ions from a solution to a solid or another liquid, used in water-softening and many industrial processes; **ionic bond** a bond within a chemical compound achieved by transfer of electrons, the resulting ions being held together by electrostatic attraction; **ion implantation** the introduction of ions into a crystalline material by subjecting the material to bombardment with a stream of ions—an important element in the production of integrated circuits; **ionisation chamber** an instrument used to detect and measure ionising radiation, consisting of an enclosure containing electrodes between which ionised gas is formed. [Gr. *ion,* neut. pr.p. of *ienai,* to go.]

Ionian. See **Ionic.**

Ionic *ī-on'ik, adj.* relating to the Ionians, one of the main divisions of the ancient Greeks, to their dialect, to Ionia, the coastal district of Asia Minor settled by them, or to a style of Greek architecture characterised by the volute of its capital.—*n.* the Ionic dialect.—*adj.* and *n.* **Ionian** (ī-*ō'ni-ən*) Ionic: an Ionic Greek.—**Ionic dialect** the most important of the three main branches of the ancient Greek language (Ionic, Doric, Aeolic), the language of Homer and Herodotus, of which Attic is a development. [Gr. *Iōnikos, Iōnios.*]

ionomer, ionopause ... ionophoresis. See **ion.**

iota *ī-ō'tə, n.* the Greek letter I, ι, answering to I: a jot. [Gr. *iōta,* the smallest letter in the alphabet, I, ι.]

I O U *ī-ō-ū', n.* a memorandum of debt given by a borrower, requiring no stamp, but a holograph, usually dated, and addressed to the lender: any similar document. [Pronunciation of *I owe you.*]

ipecacuanha *ip-i-kak-ū-an'ə, n.* a valuable medicine or the Brazilian plant (*Cephaelis* or *Uragoga;* fam. Rubiaceae) whose root produces it—used as an emetic: applied to other roots used as substitutes.— Familiarly shortened to **ipecac'.** [Port. from Tupí.]

ipse dixit *ip'sē dik'sit, ip'se dēk'sit,* (L.) he himself said it: his mere word: a dogmatic pronouncement

ipsissima verba *ip-sis'ə-mə vûr'bə, ip-sis'i-ma ver', wer'ba,* (L.) the very words.

ipso facto *ip'sō fak'tō,* (L) by that very fact: thereby.

ir- *ir-, pfx.* same as **in-,** form used with words beginning with *r,* as in *irradiate.*

Iranian *i-, ī-rān'i-ən, or -rān', adj.* and *n.* Persian: (of) a branch of the Indo-European tongues including Persian.—Also **Iranic** (ī-*ran'ik*). [Pers. *Irān,* Persia.]

Iraqi *i-rä'kē, n* a native of Iraq: the form of Arabic spoken in Iraq.—*adj.* pertaining to the country of Iraq, its inhabitants or language. [Ar. *'Irāqī.*]

irascible *ir-as'i-bl, or* **ir-,** *adj.* susceptible of ire or anger: irritable.—*n.* **irascibil'ity.**—*adv.* **irasc'ibly.** [Fr.,— L. *irāscibilis*—*irāscī,* to be angry—*ira,* anger.]

ire *īr, n.* anger: rage: keen resentment.—*adj.* **irate** (ī-*rāt'* or **ir'āt**) enraged, angry.—*adv.* **irate'ly.** [L *īra,* anger.]

irenic *ī-rēn'ik, -ren', adj.* tending to create peace: pacific.—Also **iren'ical.**—*adv.* **iren'ically.**—*ns.* **iren'icism; iren'icon** same as **eirenicon.**—*n. sing.* **iren'ics** irenical theology (opp. to *polemics*). [Gr. *eirēnē,* peace.]

irid-. See **iris.**

iris *ī'ris, n.* the rainbow: an appearance resembling the rainbow: the contractile curtain perforated by the pupil, and forming the coloured part of the eye: the fleur-de-lis, or flag (Iris):—*pl.* **irides** (ī'*rid-ēz,* ir'), i'*rises.*—*ns.* **iridec'tomy** (*ir-* or ir-) surgical removal of part of the iris; **iridescence** (*ir-i-des'əns*) play of rainbow colours, caused by interference, as on bubbles, mother-of-pearl, some feathers —*adj* **iridesc'ent** coloured like the rainbow: glittering with

changing colours.—*adv.* **iridesc'ently**.—*adj.* **iridic**
(*i-rid'ik*, *ı*-) containing or consisting of iridium: of or
relating to the iris of the eye.—*ns.* **irid'ium** (*ır*- or *ır*-) a
very heavy steel-grey metallic element (symbol Ir; at.
numb. 77), with very high melting-point; **iridosmine**
(*ır-ıd-oz'mın*, or *ir*-, or *-os'*) **iridosmium** (*ır-ıd-oz'mı-*
əm, or *ir*-, or *-os'*) a native alloy of iridium and osmium
used for pen-points, also called *osmiridium*; **ir-**
idot'omy (*ır*- or *ir*-) surgical incision into the iris of the
eye.—*n.* **irit'is** inflammation of the iris of the eye.—
iris diaphragm an adjustable stop for a lens, giving a
continuously variable hole. [Gr. *Iris, -ıdos*, the
rainbow goddess.]

Irish *i'rısh, adj.* relating to, or produced in, or derived
from, Ireland: characteristic of Ireland, esp
blundering, self-contradictory, bull-making.—*n.* the
Celtic language of Ireland. an Irish commodity, esp.
whiskey: (as *pl.*) the natives or people of Ireland—*ns.*
I'rishism (also **I'ricism** *-sızm*, a faulty form) a Hiber-
nicism, an Irish phrase, idiom or characteristic, esp a
bull; **I'rishman**; **I'rish-woman**.—**Irish coffee** a
beverage made of sweetened coffee and Irish whiskey
and topped with cream; **Irish Guards** a regiment
formed in 1900 to represent Ireland in the Foot
Guards, **Irish moss** carrageen; **Irish stew** mutton.
onions, and potatoes stewed with flour, **Irish terrier** a
breed of dog with rough, wiry, reddish-brown coat

irk *ûrk, v t.* (now usu. used impersonally) to weary: to
disgust: to distress.—*adj.* **irk'some** tedious: burdensome —*adv.* **irk'somely**.—*n* **irk'someness.** [M E.
ırken.]

iron *i'ərn, n.* an element (symbol Fe; at. numb. 26), the
most widely used of all the metals. a weapon, instrument, or utensil made of iron: a pistol or revolver
(*slang*): a golf-club with an iron head: strength: a
medicinal preparation of iron: (in *pl.*) fetters, chains: a
theatre safety curtain (org. short for **iron curtain**, see
below): a stirrup —*adj.* formed of iron: resembling
iron: not to be broken: robust: insensitive: inflexible.
—*v.t.* to smooth with a flat-iron: to arm with iron: to
fetter: to smooth, clear up (with *out; fig.*).—*ns*
i'roner one who irons: an iron for pressing clothes;
i'roning the act or process of smoothing with hot irons:
clothes to be ironed.—*adj.* **i'rony** made, consisting of,
rich in iron: like iron: hard.—**Iron Age** the age in which
the ancient Greeks and Romans themselves lived,
regarded by them as a third step in degeneracy from the
Golden Age (*myth.*): the stage of culture of a people
using iron as the material for their tools and weapons
(*archaeol.*).—*adj.* **i'ron-clad** clad in iron: covered or
protected with iron.—*n.* a ship defended by iron
plates.—**i'ron-clay** clay ironstone; **Iron Cross** a Prussian war medal instituted in 1813, revived in 1870 and
1914 and reinstated by Hitler as a German war medal in
1939; **iron curtain** the safety curtain in a theatre, orig.
made of iron (*arch.*): an impenetrable barrier to observation or communication, esp. (with *caps.*) between
communist Russia with its satellites and the West,
i'ron-founder one who founds or makes castings in
iron; **i'ron-foundry**; **i'ron-glance** specular iron.—*adj.*
i'ron-gray', **-grey'** of a grey colour like that of iron
freshly cut or broken.—*n.* this colour.—**iron hand**
strict, despotic control (the iron hand is sometimes
hidden in the *velvet glove*, q.v).—*adj.* **i'ron-hand'ed.**
—**i'roning-board** a smooth board covered with cloth,
on which clothes are ironed; **iron lung** an apparatus
consisting of a chamber that encloses a patient's chest,
the air pressure within the chamber being varied rhythmically so that air is forced into and out of the lungs;
iron maiden an old instrument of torture, consisting of
a box lined with iron spikes in which a prisoner was
fastened, **i'ronmaster** a proprietor of ironworks; **i'ron-**
monger a dealer in ironmongery: loosely, in household

goods and equipment generally; **i'ronmongery** articles
made of iron hardware, **i'ron-ore**; **iron pyrites**
common pyrites, sulphide of iron; **iron ration** a ration
of concentrated food, esp. for an extreme emergency;
I'ronside, I'ronsides a nickname for a man of iron
resolution (as King Edmund, Oliver Cromwell): a
Puritan: (in *pl*) a name given to Cromwell's irresistible cavalry; **i'ronstone** any iron-ore, esp. carbonate;
i'ronware wares or goods of iron; **i'ronwood** timber of
great hardness, and many kinds of trees producing it,
i'ronwork the parts of a building, etc., made of iron:
anything of iron, esp. artistic work: (often in *pl.*) an
establishment where iron is smelted or made into
heavy goods.—**rule with a rod of iron** to rule with stern
severity; **strike while the iron is hot** to seize one's
opportunity while the circumstances are favourable to
one; **too many irons in the fire** too many things on hand
at once [O E *iren* (*isern, isen*)]

irony[1] *i'rən-ı, n.* the Socratic method of discussion by
professing ignorance: conveyance of meaning (generally satirical) by words whose literal meaning is the
opposite: a situation or utterance (as in a tragedy) that
has a significance unperceived at the time, or by the
person involved: a condition in which one seems to be
mocked by fate or the facts.—*adjs.* **ironic** (*i-ron'ik*),
iron'ical.—*adv.* **iron'ically.**—*v t.* and *v t.* **i'ronise,**
-ize.—*n* **i'ronist.** [L. *irōnia*—Gr. *eirōneiā,*
dissimulation.]

irony[2]. See **iron.**

Iroquoian *ır-ō-kwoı'ən, adj.* of, belonging to, the *Iro-*
quois, a confederation of American Indian tribes: of
the group of languages spoken by these tribes.—Also
n.

irradiate *ır-ā'di-āt, v.t.* to shed light or other rays upon
or into: to treat by exposure to rays: to light up: to
brighten: to radiate.—*v.i.* to radiate: to shine.—*adj.*
adorned with rays of light or with lustre.—*ns.* **irra'-**
diance, irra'diancy.—*adj.* **irra'diant**—*n.* **irradia'tion**
the act of irradiating: exposure to rays: that which is
irradiated: brightness: apparent enlargement of a
bright object by spreading of the excitation of the retina, or in a photograph by reflections within the emulsion: spread of a nervous impulse beyond the usual
area affected: intellectual light.—*adj.* **irra'diative.**
[Pfx. **ir-** (**in-** (1)).]

irrational *ır-ash'ən-əl, adj* not rational. not commensurable with natural numbers.—*n.* an irrational
being or number —*v t.* **irra'tionalise, -ize** to make
irrational.—*ns.* **irra'tionalism** an irrational system:
irrationality; **irra'tionalist.**—*adj.* **irrationalist'ic.**
—*n.* **irrational'ity.**—*adv* **irra'tionally.** [Pfx. **ir-** (**in-**
(2)).]

irreclaimable *ır-ı-klām'ə-bl, adj.* that cannot be
claimed back, brought into cultivation, or reformed:
incorrigible.—*ns.* **irreclaimabil'ity, irreclaim'-**
ableness.—*adv.* **irreclaim'ably.** [Pfx. **ir-** (**in-** (2)).]

irreconcilable *ır-ek-ən-sil'ə-bl, or ır-ek', adj.* incapable
of being brought back to a state of friendship or agreement: inconsistent.—*n.* an irreconcilable opponent:
an intransigent.—*ns.* **irreconcil'ableness, irrecon-**
cilabil'ity.—*adv* **irreconcil'ably.**—*adj.* **irrec'onciled**
not reconciled: not brought into harmony.—*n.* **ir-**
reconcile'ment. [Pfx. **ir-** (**in-** (2)).]

irrecoverable *ır-ı-kuv'ər-ə-bl, adj.* irretrievable: not re-
claimable: beyond recovery.—*n.* **irrecov'erableness.**
—*adv.* **irrecov'erably.** [Pfx. **ir-** (**in-** (2)).]

irrecusable *ır-ı-kū'zə-bl, adj.* that cannot be rejected —
adv. **irrecūs'ably.** [Fr.—L.L. *irrecūsābilis.*]

irredeemable *ır-ı-dēm'ə-bl, adj.* not redeemable: not
subject to be paid at the nominal value.—*ns.* **ir-**
redeem'ableness, irredeemabil'ity.—*n.pl.* **ir-**
redeem'ables undated government or debenture
stock.—*adv* **irredeem'ably.** [Pfx. **ir-** (**in-** (2)).]

Irredentist ır-ı-den′tıst, n one of an Italian party formed ın 1878, its aıms to gaın or regaın for Italy varıous regıons claımed on language and other grounds one who makes sımılar claıms for any natıon —Also *adj* —*n* **Irredent′ism**.—Often **irredentist, irredent-ism**. [It (*Italıa*) *ırredenta*, unredeemed (Italy)—L *ın-*, not, *redemptus*, pa p of *redımēre*, to redeem)

irreducible ır-ı-dūs′ı-bl, *adj* that cannot be reduced or brought from one degree, form, or state to another not to be lessened· not to be overcome —*n* **irreduc′ibleness**.—*adv* **irreduc′ibly**.—*ns* **ir-reducibil′ity, irreductibility** (-duk-tı-bıl′ı-tı) [Pfx **ir-** (**in-** (2))]

irrefragable ir-ef′rə-gə-bl, *adj*. that cannot be refuted unanswerable —*ns* **irrefragabil′ity, irref′ragable-ness**.—*adv* **irref′ragably**. [L *ırrefrăgăbılıs*—*ın-*, not, *re-*, backwards, *frangēre*, to break]

irrefutable ır-ef′ūt-ə-bl, also -ūt′, *adj* that cannot be refuted —*ns* **irrefutabil′ity, irref′utableness** (or -ūt′) —*adv* **irref′utably** (also -ūt′) [Pfx **ir-** (**in-** (2))]

irregular ır-eg′ū-lər, *adj* not regular· not conformıng to rule or to the ordinary rules: disorderly· uneven unsymmetrıcal· varıable· (of troops) not traıned under authorıty of a government (of a marrıage) not celebrated by a mınıster after proclamatıon of banns or of ıntentıon to marry —*n* an irregular soldıer.—*n* **irregularity** (-lar′ı-tı) a rough place or bump on an even surface· an ınstance of actıon, behavıour, etc not conforming to rules or regulatıons —*adv* **irreg′u-larly**. [Pfx **ir-** (**in-** (2))]

irrelevant ır-el′ə-vənt, *adj*. not relevant.—*ns* **irrel′-evance, irrel′evancy**.—*adv* **irrel′evantly**. [Pfx **ir-** (**in-** (2))]

irreligious ır-ı-lıj′əs, *adj* destitute of relıgıon: regardless of relıgıon: opposed to relıgıon: ungodly —*adv* **irrelig′iously**.—*ns* **irrelig′iousness, irrelig′ion** want of relıgıon· hostılıty to or dısregard of relıgıon [Pfx **ir-** (**in-** (2)).]

irremediable ır-ı-mē′dı-ə-bl, *adj*. beyond remedy or redress —*n*. **irremē′diableness**.—*adv* **irremē′diably**. [Pfx **ir-** (**in-** (2))]

irremissible ır-ı-mıs′ı-bl, *adj* not to be remitted or for-gıven —*ns* **irremissibil′ity, irremiss′ibleness, ir-remission** (-mısh′ən) —*adj* **irremiss′ive** unremitting [Pfx **ir-** (**in-** (2))]

irreparable ır-ep′ər-ə-bl, *adj* that cannot be made good or rectıfıed· beyond repaır —*ns* **irreparabil′ity, irrep′arableness**.—*adv* **irrep′arably**. [Pfx **ir-** (**in-** (2))]

irreplaceable ır-ı-plăs′ə-bl, *adj* whose loss cannot be made good: wıthout possıble substıtute —*adv* **ir-replace′ably**. [Pfx **ir-** (**in-** (2))]

irrepressible ır-ı-pres′ı-bl, *adj* not to be put down or kept under —*ns* **irrepressibil′ity, irrepress′ibleness**. —*adv* **irrepress′ibly**. [Pfx **ir-** (**in-** (2))]

irreproachable ır-ı-prōch′ə-bl, *adj* free from blame· faultless.—*ns* **irreproachabil′ity, irreproach′-ableness**.—*adv* **irreproach′ably**. [Pfx **ir-** (**in-** (2))]

irreprovable ır-ı-prōō′v′ə-bl, *adj* blameless —*adv*. **ir-reprov′ably**. [Pfx **ir-** (**in-** (2))]

irresistance ır-ı-zıst′əns, *n*. want of resıstance· passıve submıssıon —*adj* **irresist′ible** not to be opposed wıth success· resıstless overpowerıng: overmasterıng —*ns* **irresist′ibleness, irresistibil′ity**.—*adv* **irresist′-ibly**. [Pfx **ir-** (**in-** (2))]

irresoluble ır-ez′əl-ū-bl, -ōō-bl, *adj* that cannot be resolved ınto parts· that cannot be solved —*n* **irre-solubil′ity**.—*adv* **irres′olubly**. [Pfx **ir-** (**in-** (2))]

irresolute ır-ez′əl-ūt, -ōōt, *adj* not fırm ın purpose —*adv* **irres′olutely**.—*ns* **irres′oluteness, irresolution** (-û′shən, -ōō′shən) want of resolutıon [Pfx **ir-** (**in-** (2))]

irrespective ır-ı-spek′tıv, *adj* not havıng regard (wıth *of*) —Also *adv* —*adv* **irrespec′tively**. [Pfx. **ir-** (**in-** (2))]

irresponsible ır-ı-spons′ı-bl, *adj* not responsible· wıth-out sense of responsıbılıty. free from feelıng of respon-sıbılıty, lıght-hearted, carefree reprehensıbly careless· done wıthout feelıng of responsıbılıty —*ns* **irresponsibil′ity, irrespon′sibleness**.—*adv* **irre-spons′ibly**.—*adj* **irrespons′ive** not respondıng. not readıly respondıng —*adv* **irrespons′ively**.—*n* **irre-spons′iveness**. [Pfx. **ir-** (**in-** (2))]

irretrievable ır-ı-trēv′ə-bl, *adj* not to be recovered, ırreparable —*ns* **irretrievabil′ity, irretriev′-ableness**.—*adv* **irretriev′ably**. [Pfx. **ir-** (**in-** (2))]

irreverent ır-ev′ər-ənt, *adj*. not reverent. proceedıng from ırreverence —*n* **irrev′erence**.—*adj* **irrever-ential** (-en′shəl) —*adv* **irrev′erently**. [Pfx **ir-** (**in-** (2)).]

irreversible ır-ı-vûrs′ı-bl, *adj* not reversıble: that cannot proceed ın the opposıte dırectıon or ın both dırectıons: ıncapable of changıng back not alıke both ways. that cannot be recalled or annulled: (ınvolv-ıng damage whıch ıs) permanent (*med*) —*ns* **irre-versibil′ity, irrevers′ibleness**.—*adv* **irrevers′ibly**. [Pfx **ir-** (**in-** (2))]

irrevocable ır-ev′ək-ə-bl, *adj* that cannot be recalled or revoked —*ns*. **irrevocabil′ity, irrev′ocableness**.—*adv* **irrev′ocably**. [Pfx **ir-** (**in-** (2))]

irrigate ir′ı-gāt, *v.t* to wet or moısten: to water by means of canals or watercourses: to cause a stream of lıquıd to flow upon.—*n*. **irriga′tion**.—*adjs*. **irrig-ā′tional, irr′igative**.—*n*. **irr′igator** one who, or that whıch, ırrıgates: an applıance for washıng a wound, etc. [L *ırrıgāre, -ātum*, to water—*ın*, upon, *rıgāre*, to wet]

irritate ır′ı-tāt, *v t*. to excıte or stımulate: to rouse: to provoke: to make angry or fretful· to excıte a paınful, uncomfortable, or unhealthy condıtıon (as heat and redness) ın.—*n* **irritabil′ity** the qualıty of beıng easıly ırrıtated: the peculıar susceptıbılıty to stımulı pos-sessed by lıvıng matter —*adj*. **irr′itable** that may be ırrıtated· easıly annoyed· susceptıble of excıtement or ırrıtatıon —*n*. **irr′itableness**.—*adv* **irr′itably**.—*n* **irr′itancy**.—*adj*. **irr′itant** ırrıtatıng —*n* that whıch causes ırrıtatıon —*n* **irrita′tion** the act of irritating or excıtıng· anger, annoyance· stımulatıon· the term applıed to any morbıd excıtement of the vıtal actıons not amountıng to ınflammatıon, often, but not always, leadıng to that condıtıon (*med*) —*adj*. **irr′itative** tendıng to irritate or excite accompanıed wıth or caused by irritation —*n* **ir′ritātor**. [L. *irrītāre, -ātum*.]

irrupt ır-upt′, *v.i*. to break ın to make ırruptıon —*n* **irruption** (ır-up′shən) a breakıng or burstıng in: a sudden ınvasıon or ıncursıon —*adj*. **irrup′tive** rushing suddenly ın —*adv*. **irrup′tively**. [L *ırrumpēre, ır-ruptum*—ın, ın, *rumpēre*, to break]

Irvingite ûr′vıng-īt, *n* a popular name for a member of the Catholıc Apostolıc Church.—Also *adj* —*n*. **Ir′vingism**. [From Edward *Irvıng* (1792–1834)]

is ız, used as thırd pers sıng pres ındıc of **be**. [O E. *ıs*]

isagogic ī-sə-goj′ık, *-gog′ık*, *adj*. ıntroductory —*n*. **isagoge** (ī′sə-gō-jı, or -gō′) an academıc ıntroductıon to a subject —*n*. *sıng* **isagog′ics** that part of theologıcal study ıntroductory to exegesıs [Gr *eısagōgē*, an ıntroductıon—*eıs*, ınto, *ageın*, to lead]

isch(a)emia ıs-kē′mı-ə, *n* defıcıency of blood ın a part of the body —*adj* **isch(a)em′ic**. [Gr *ıscheın*, to re-straın, *haıma*, blood]

ischium ıs′kı-əm, *n* a posterıor bone of the pelvıc gırdle —*pl* **ıs′chia**.—*adjs* **ischiad′ic, is′chial, ischiat′ic**. [Latınısed from Gr *ıschıon*, the hıp-joınt]

For other sounds see detaıled chart of pronuncıatıon

-ise, -ize -īz, a suffix forming verbs from adjs., meaning to make, as equal*ise*, or from nouns, as botan*ise*, satir*ise*. [L. *-izāre*, from Gr *-izein*, Fr *-iser*]

isenergic is-en-ûr'jik, *adj.* in physics, denoting equal energy. [Gr. *isos*, equal, *energeia*, energy.]

isentropic ī-sen-trop'ik, *(phys.) adj.* of equal entropy [Gr. *isos*, equal, *entropē*, a turning about—*en*, in, *trepein*, to turn.]

-ish *-ish*, *adj.* suffix signifying somewhat, as brown*ish*, old*ish*, or signifying like or similar to, sometimes implying deprecation, as outland*ish*, child*ish*. [O.E *-isc.*]

isinglass ī'zing-glås, *n.* a material, mainly gelatine, got from sturgeons' air-bladders and other sources [App. from obs. Du *huizenblas*—*huizen*, a kind of sturgeon, *blas*, a bladder.]

Islam iz'läm, or is', or -lam', **Is'lamism**, *ns* the Muslim religion: the whole Muslim world—*adjs* **Islamic** (*-lam'ik*). **Islamitic** (*-lə-mit'ik*) —*v.t.* **Islam'icise, -ize** to Islamise.—*ns.* **Islam'icist** one who studies Islam, Islamic law, Islamic culture, etc.; **Islamisā'tion, -z-**.— *v.t* and *v.i* **Is'lamise, -ize** to convert, (cause to) conform to Islam. [Ar. *islām*, surrender (to God)]

island ī'lənd, *n.* a mass of land (not a continent) surrounded with water: anything isolated, detached, or surrounded by something of a different nature. a small raised traffic-free area in a street for pedestrians: tissue or cells detached and differing from their surroundings.—*adj.* of an island: forming an island.—*n.* **islander** (ī'lənd-ər) an inhabitant of an island.—**island universe** a spiral nebula regarded as forming a separate stellar system.—**islands of Langerhans** same as **islets of Langerhans**; **Islands of the Blest** in Greek mythology, the abode of the blessed dead, situated somewhere in the far west. [M E *iland*—O E *iegland*, *igland*, *ēgland*—*ieg*, *ig*, *ēg*, island and *land*; the s is due to confusion with *isle*.]

isle īl, *n.* an island.—*n.* **islet** (ī'lit) a little isle.—**isles'-man** an islander, esp. an inhabitant of the Hebrides— also **isle'man.**—**islets of Langerhans** (*lang'ar-håns*) groups of epithelial cells discovered by Paul *Langerhans*, a German anatomist (1847–88), in the pancreas, producing a secretion the lack of which causes diabetes. [M.E. *ile*, *yle*—O.Fr *isle* (Fr. *île*)—L *insula.*]

-ism -izm, **-asm** -azm, or (with **-ic**) **-icism** -i-sizm suffixes forming abstract nouns signifying condition, system, as ego*ism*, de*ism*, Calvin*ism*, pleon*asm*, Anglic*ism*, witticism [L. *-ismus*, *-asmus*—Gr. *-ismos*, *-asmos*.]

ism izm, *n.* any distinctive doctrine, theory, or practice —usually in disparagement [From the suffix *-ism.*]

Ismaili is-mà-ē'lē, or is-mā'i-li, *n.* one of a sect of Shiite Muslims whose imam or spiritual head is the Aga Khan.—Also *adj.*—*n.* and *adj.* **Ismailian** (is-mā-il'i-ən).—*n.* **Is'mailism.**—*adj.* **Ismailit'ic.**

isn't iz'ənt, for is not.

iso- ī'sō-, *pfx* equal: in chem. denoting an isomeric substance—e.g. **iso-oc'tane** one of the isomers of normal octane. [Gr. *isos*, equal.]

isobar ī'sō-bär, *n.* a curve running through places of equal pressure: esp. one connecting places, or their representations on a map, of equal barometric pressure (*meteor.*). (see **isobare**; *chem.*) —*adjs.* **isobaric** (*-bar'ik*), **isobaromet'ric.** [Pfx. iso-, and Gr *baros*, weight.]

isobare ī'sō-bär, *n.* either of two atoms of different chemical elements but of identical atomic mass (e.g an isotope of titanium and an isotope of chromium both of atomic mass 50).—Also **i'sobar.** [Same as **isobar** above.]

isobase ī'sō-bās, (*geol.*) *n.* a contour line of equal upheaval of the land. [Pfx. iso-, and Gr. *basis*, step.]

isobath ī'sō-bàth, *n.* a contour line of equal depth —

isobath'ic. [Pfx. iso-, and Gr *bathos*, depth.]

isocheim, isochime ī'sō-kīm, *n.* a contour line of mean winter temperature. [Pfx iso-, and Gr. *cheima*, winter weather.]

isochor, isochore ī'sō-kōr, -kor, *n.* a curve representing variation of some quantity under conditions of constant volume.—*adj.* **isochoric** (*-kor'ik*). [Pfx. iso-, and Gr. *chōrā*, space.]

isochromatic ī-sō-krō-mat'ik, *adj.* having the same colour (*optics*): orthochromatic (*phot.*) [Pfx iso-, and Gr. *chrōma*, *-atos*, colour]

isochronal ī-sok'rən-əl, **isoch'ronous** -əs, *adjs.* of equal time performed in equal times: in regular periodicity. —*advs.* **isoch'ronally, isoch'ronously.**—*n.* **is'ochrone** a line on a chart or map joining points associated with a constant time difference, e.g. in reception of radio signals —*v t.* **isoch'ronise, -ize**—*n* **isoch'ronism.** [Pfx. iso-, and Gr. *chronos*, time.]

isoclinal ī-sō-klī'nəl, *adj* folded with nearly the same dip in each limb (*geol.*): in terrestrial magnetism, having the same magnetic dip.—*n* an isoclinical line, or contour line of magnetic dip.—*n.* **i'socline** an area of rock strata with isoclinal folds. an isoclinal.—*adj* and *n.* **isoclinic** (*-klin'ik*) isoclinal. [Pfx. iso-, and Gr. *klīnein*, to bend.]

isocracy ī-sok'rə-si, *n.* (a system of government in which all people have) equal political power.—*adj.* **isocrat'ic.** [Pfx. iso-, Gr. *krateein*, to rule.]

isocyclic ī'sō-sī-klik, *adj.* homocyclic. [iso-, **cyclic.**]

isodiametric, -al ī-sō-dī-ə-met'rik, -əl, *adjs.* of equal diameters: about as broad as long. [Pfx. iso-.]

isodimorphism ī-sō-dī-morf'izm, (*crystal.*) *n.* isomorphism between each of the two forms of a dimorphous substance and the corresponding forms of another dimorphous substance.—*adjs* **isodimorph'ic, isodimorph'ous.** [Pfx iso-.]

isodont ī'sō-dont, (*zool.*) *adj.* having all the teeth similar in size and form.—Also **isodont'al.**—*n* an isodontal animal. [Gr *isos*, equal, *odous*, *odontos*, tooth.]

isodynamic ī-sō-dīn-am'ik, or *-din-*, *adj.* of equal strength, esp. of magnetic intensity.—*n* an isodynamic line on the earth or the map, a contour line of magnetic intensity. [Pfx. iso-, and Gr. *dynamis*, strenth.]

isoelectric ī-sō-i-lek'trik, *adj* having the same potential [iso-, **electric.**]

isoelectronic ī-sō-el-ik-tron'ik, *adj.* having an equal number of electrons, or similar electron patterns. [iso-, **electron.**]

isogeny ī-soj'ə-ni, *n.* likeness of origin.—*adjs.* **isogenetic** (ī-sō-ji-net'ik), **isog'enous.** [Pfx. iso-, and Gr *genos*, kind.]

isogeotherm ī-sō-jē'ō-thûrm, *n.* a subterranean contour of equal temperature.—*adjs.* **isogeotherm'al, isogeotherm'ic.**—*n.* an isogeotherm. [Pfx. iso-, and Gr *gē*, the earth, *thermē*, heat—*thermos*, hot.]

isogloss ī'sō-glos, *n.* a line separating one region from another region which differs from it in a particular feature of dialect —*adjs.* **isogloss'al, -glott'al, isoglott'ic.** [Pfx iso-, and Gr. *glōssa*, tongue.]

isogonic ī-sō-gon'ik, **isogonal** ī-sog'ən-əl, *adjs.* of equal angles, esp. of magnetic declination.—*ns.* an isogonic line or contour line of magnetic declination —*n.* **i'sogon** an equiangular polygon. [Pfx. iso-, and Gr *gōniā*, an angle.]

isogram ī'sō-gram, *n.* a line drawn on a map or diagram showing all points which have an equal numerical value with respect to a given climatic or other variable. —See also **isopleth.** [Pfx. iso-, and Gr. *gramma*, a letter.]

isohel ī'sō-hel, *n.* a contour line of equal amounts of sunshine. [Pfx iso-, and Gr. *hēlios*, sun.]

isohyet ī-sō-hī'ət, *n* a contour line of equal rainfall.—

adj. **isohy'etal.**—*n.* an isohyet. [Pfx iso-, and Gr. *hýetos*, rain—*hýein*, to rain.]

isolate *i'sō-lāt, v.t.* to place in a detached situation, like an island: to detach. to insulate to separate (esp those who might be infected) (*med.*). to seclude: to segregate. to obtain in an uncompounded state —*n.* **isolabil'ity.**—*adj.* **is'olable.**—*ns* **isola'tion; isola'tionism** the policy of avoiding political entanglements with other countries; **isola'tionist.**—*adj.* **i'solative** tending towards isolation· occurring without influence from outside —*n* **i'solātor.**—**isolating languages** those in which each word is a bare root, not inflected or compounded [It *isolare*—*isola*—L. *insula*, an island]

isoleucine *i-sō-lū'sīn, n.* an essential amino acid [iso-, leucine.]

isoline *i'sō-līn.* Same as **isopleth.**

isomagnetic *i-sō-mag-net'ik, adj.* having equal magnetic induction or force.—*n.* (*also* **isomagnetic line**) an imaginary line joining places at which the force of the earth's magnetic field is constant [iso-, magnetic.]

isomer *i'sō-mər,* (*chem*) *n.* a substance, radical, or ion isomeric with another. an atomic nucleus having the same atomic number and mass as another or others but a different energy state —*n.* **i'somère** (*zool.*) an organ or segment corresponding to or homologous with another.—*adj* **isomeric** (*-mer'ik; chem.*) identical in percentage composition and molecular weight but different in constitution or the mode in which the atoms are arranged· of nuclei, differing only in energy state and half-life —*v t.* and *v i* **isomerise, -ize** (*i-som'ər-īz*) to change into an isomer.—*ns.* **isomerīsā'tion, -z-; isom'erism** the property of being isomeric the existence of isomers. —*adj* **isom'erous** (*bot*) having the same number of parts (esp. in floral whorls) [Pfx iso-, and Gr *meros,* part]

isometric, -al *i-sō-met'rik, -əl, adjs* having equality of measure: pertaining to isometrics: having the plane of projection equally inclined to three perpendicular axes. of the cubic system, or referable to three equal axes at right angles to one another (*crystal*).—*n* **isomet'ric** (*also* **isometric line**) a line on a graph showing variations of pressure and temperature at a constant volume —*adv* **isomet'rically.**—*n sing* **isomet'rics** a system of strengthening the muscles and tuning up the body by opposing one muscle to another or to a resistant object.—*n.* **isom'etry** equality of measure [Pfx iso-, and Gr *metron,* measure.]

isomorph *i'sō-morf, n.* that which shows isomorphism.—*adj.* **isomorph'ic** showing isomorphism —*n* **isomorph'ism** similarity in unrelated forms (*biol.*) close similarity in crystalline form combined with similar chemical constitution (*crystal.*): a one-to-one correspondence between the elements of two or more sets and between the sums or products of the elements of one set and those of the equivalent elements of the other set or sets (*math.*).—*adjs* **isomorph'ic, isomorph'ous.** [Pfx iso-, and Gr. *morphē,* form.]

isonomy *i-son'ə-mi, n.* equal law, rights, or privileges —*adjs.* **isonom'ic, ison'omous.** [Gr. *isonomiā*—*isos,* equal, *nomos,* law.]

isopleth *i'sō-pleth, n.* an isogram, esp one on a graph showing variations of a climatic element as a function of two variables; cf. **nomogram.** [Pfx iso-, and Gr. *plēthos,* great number.]

isopolity *i-sō-pol'i-ti, n* reciprocity of rights of citizenship in different communities [Pfx iso-, and Gr. *polīteiā,* citizenship]

isoprene *i'sō-prēn, n* a hydrocarbon of the terpene group, which may be polymerised into synthetic rubber.

isosceles *i-sos'i-lēz,* (*geom*) *adj* having two equal sides, as a triangle [Gr *isoskelēs—isos,* equal, *skelos,* a leg]

isoseismal *i-sō-sīz'məl, n* a curve or line connecting points at which an earthquake shock is felt with equal intensity.—*adjs.* **isoseis'mal, isoseis'mic.** [Pfx iso-, and Gr. *seismos,* a shaking.]

isosporous *i-sos'pər-əs,* or *i-sō-spō'rəs, -spo', adj* having spores of one kind only (opp to *heterosporous*).—*n* **isos'pory.** [Pfx. iso-, and Gr. *sporos,* seed]

isostasy *i-sos'tə-si,* (*geol.*) *n* a condition of equilibrium held to exist in the earth's crust, equal masses of matter underlying equal areas, whether of sea or land down to an assumed level of compensation —*adj* **isostatic** (*i-sō-stat'ik*) in hydrostatic equilibrium from equality of pressure: in a state of isostasy: pertaining to isostasy —*adv* **isostat'ically.** [Gr *isos,* equal, *stasis,* setting, weighing, *statikos,* pertaining to weighing.]

isothere *i'sō-thēr, n* a contour line of equal mean summer temperature —*adj* **isotheral** (*i-soth'ər-əl, i-sō-thēr'əl*)—*n* an isothere [Gr *theros,* summer—*therein,* to make warm]

isotherm *i'sō-thûrm, n* a contour line of equal temperature.—*adj.* **isotherm'al** at constant temperature: pertaining to isotherms. —*n* an isothermal line, isotherm —*adv.* **isotherm'ally.** [Pfx. iso-, and Gr. *thermē,* heat—*thermos,* hot]

isotone *i'sō-tōn, n.* one of a number of nuclides having the same number of neutrons in the nucleus with differing numbers of protons. [Pfx iso-, and prob Gr *tonos,* tension.]

isotonic *i-sō-ton'ik, adj.·* having the same tone, tension, or osmotic pressure.—*n.* **isotonic'ity.** [Pfx iso-, and Gr *tonos,* tension, tone]

isotope *i'sō-tōp, n.* one of a set of chemically identical species of atom which have the same atomic number but different mass numbers; a natural element is made up of isotopes, always present in the same proportions —*adj.* **isotopic** (*-top'ik*) —*n* **isotopy** (*i-sot'ə-pi*) the fact or condition of being isotopic [Pfx iso-, and Gr *topos,* place (*scil* in the periodic table).]

isotype *i'sō-tīp, n* a presentation of statistical information by a row of diagrammatic pictures each representing a particular number of instances [Pfx iso-, and Gr *typos,* form]

I-spy *i'-spi', n.* a children's game of hide-and-seek, so called from the cry when one is spied: a word-game, in which one guesses objects in view, whose names begin with a certain letter of the alphabet [I, spy.]

Israeli *iz-rā'lē, n.* a citizen of the modern state of Israel —Also *adj* [See Israelite.]

Israelite *iz'ri-əl-īt, -rē-, n* a descendant of Israel or Jacob: a Jew: one of the elect (*fig*).—*adjs* **Israelit'ic, Israelit'ish.** [Gr *Isrāēlîtēs—Isrāēl,* Heb *Yisrāēl,* perh. contender with God—*sara,* to fight, *El,* God]

issue *ish'ū, -ōō, is'ū, n* a going or flowing out: an outlet: act of sending out· that which flows or passes out fruit of the body, children: produce, profits· a putting into circulation, giving out for use. a set of things put forth at one time: a single thing given out or supplied (chiefly *mil.*)· ultimate result, outcome: upshot critical determination: a point in dispute· a point on which a question depends· a question awaiting decision or ripe for decision a discharge or flux (*med*) —*v.i* to go, flow, or come out· to proceed, as from a source to spring· to be produced: to come to a point in fact or law (*law*)· to turn out, result, terminate.—*v.t.* to send out: to put forth: to put into circulation: to publish: to give out for use: to supply (*mil. jargon*).—*adj.* iss'uable capable of issuing, admitting of an issue —*n.* iss'uance the act of giving out, promulgation —*adj.* iss'ueless without issue: childless —*n.* iss'uer one who issues or emits —at issue in quarrel or controversy: in dispute; force the issue to hasten or compel a final decision on a matter; join, or take, issue to take an opposite position, or opposite positions, in dispute: to enter into dispute: to take up a point as basis of dispute; side issue a subordinate issue arising from the main business. [O.Fr. *issue—issir*, to go or flow out—L. *exire—ex*, out *ire*, to go.]

-ist -*ist*, *suff.* denoting the person who holds a doctrine or practises an art, as Calvin*ist*, chem*ist*, novel*ist*, art*ist*, royal*ist*. [L. -*ista*—Gr. -*istēs*.]

isthmus *is*(th)'*mas*, *n.* narrow neck of land connecting two larger portions (also *fig.*): a constriction —*adj.* isth'mian pertaining to an isthmus, esp. the Isthmus of Corinth. [L.,—Gr. *isthmos*.]

istle *ist'li*, ixtle *ikst'li*, *ns.* a valuable fibre obtained from Agave, Bromelia, and other plants. [Mexican Sp. *ixtle*—Nahuatl *ichtli*.]

it¹ *it*, *pron* the neut. of he, him (and formerly his) applied to a thing without life, a lower animal, a young child, rarely (except as an antecedent or in contempt) to a man or woman: used as an impersonal, indefinite, or anticipatory or provisional subject or object, as the object of a transitive verb that is normally an intransitive, or a noun: in children's games, the player chosen to oppose all others: that which answers exactly to what one is looking for (*coll.*): an indefinable crowning quality by which one carries it off—personal magnetism: sex-appeal (*slang*).—*gen.* its; *pl.* they, them. [O.E. *hit*, neut. (nom. and acc.) of *hē*.]

it² *it* Short for Italian vermouth.

itaconic acid *it-a-kon'ik*, or *īt-*, *a'sid* a white crystalline solid got by fermentation of sugar with Aspergillus mould, used in plastics manufacture. [Anagram of *aconitic*.]

Italian *i-tal'yan*, *adj.* of or relating to *Italy* or its people or language.—*n.* a native or citizen of Italy, or person of the same race: the language of Italy.—*adj.* Ital'ianate Italianised.—*v.t.* Ital'ianise, -ize to make Italian: to give an Italian character to.—*v.i.* to become Italian: to play the Italian: to speak Italian· to use Italian idioms: to adopt Italian ways.—*ns.* Italianisa'tion, -z-; Ital'ianism, Ital'icism (-*sizm*) an Italian idiom or habit: Italian sympathies; Ital'ianist one who has a scholarly knowledge of Italian: a person of Italian sympathies.—*adj.* Ital'ic pertaining to Italy, esp. ancient Italy: of or pertaining to Italic: (*without cap.*) of a sloping type introduced by the Italian printer Aldo Manuzio in 1501, used esp. for emphasis or other distinctive purpose.—*n.* a branch of Indo-European usu. considered to comprise Oscan, Umbrian, Latin, and related languages, but sometimes applied to either the Latin group or the Osco-Umbrian group alone: (without *cap.*, usu in *pl.*) an italic letter.—*n.* italicisa'tion, -z-.—*v.t* ital'icise, -ize to put in, or mark for, italics—Italian garden a formal garden with statues. [L. *Italiānus* and Gr. *Italikos*—L. *Italia*, Gr. *Italiā*, Italy.]

Italo- *i-tal'ō-*, *i'tal-ō-*, in composition, Italian.

itch *ich*, *n.* an irritating sensation in the skin: scabies, an eruptive disease in the skin, caused by a parasitic mite: a constant teasing desire.—*v.i.* to have an uneasy, irritating sensation in the skin: to have a constant, teasing desire.—*n.* itch'iness.—*adj.* itch'y pertaining to or affected with itch or itching [O E *giccan*, to itch.]

-ite -*īt*, *suff.* used to form (1) names of persons, indicating their origin, place of origin, affiliations, loyalties, etc. (e g. *Semite*, *Durhamite*, *Jacobite*, *Buchmanite*); (2) names of fossil organisms (e.g. *ammonite*), (3) names of minerals (e.g. *calcite*); (4) names of salts of acids with suff. -*ous* (e.g. *sulphite*, salt of sulphurous acid); (5) names of bodily parts (e g. *somite*). The nouns may be used also as adjs.

item *i'tam*, *adv.* likewise: also —*n* a separate article or particular in an enumeration a piece of news or other matter in a newspaper.—*v.t.* to set down in enumeration: to make a note of —*v.t.* i'temise -ize to give or list by items. [L. *item*, likewise.]

iterate *it'ar-āt*, *v.t.* to do again: to say again, repeat —*ns.* it'erance, itera'tion repetition.—*adjs.* it'erant, it'erative (-*a-tiv* or -*ā-tiv*) repeating.—*adv* it'eratively. [L. *iterāre*, -*ātum*—*iterum*, again.]

ithyphallus *ith-i-fal'as*, *n.* an erect phallus.—*adj.* ithyphall'ic of or with an ithyphallus: pertaining to the processions in honour of Dionysos in which an ithyphallus was carried, or to the hymns sung or the metres used: shameless. [Gr *ithyphallos—ithys*, straight, *phallos*, a phallus]

itinerant *i-tin'ar-ant*, also *ī-*, *adj.* making journeys from place to place: travelling.—*n.* one who travels from place to place, esp a judge, a Methodist preacher, a strolling musician, or a peddler: a wanderer.—*ns.* itin'eracy (-*a-si*), itin'erancy.—*adv* itin'erantly.—*adj* itin'erary travelling: relating to roads or journeys.—*n.* a plan or record of a journey: a road-book a route: an itinerant —*v.i* itin'erate to travel from place to place, esp. for the purpose of judging, preaching, or lecturing [L. *iter*, *itineris*, a journey.]

-itis -*i'tis*, *n. suff.* denoting a disease (now inflammation), as bronch*itis*: also jocularly, as jazz*itis* [Gr -*itis*.]

it'll *it'l*, a contraction of it will.

its *its*, possessive or genitive of it¹.—*pron* itself *it-self'*, the emphatic and reflexive form of it.—by itself alone, apart; in itself by its own nature.

it's *its*, a contraction of it is or it has.

itsy-bitsy *it'si-bit'si*, (*coll*) *adj.* tiny [Prob. a childish reduplicated form of little influenced by bit¹.]

I've *īv*, a contraction of I have.

ivory *i'va-ri*, *n.* dentine, esp. the hard white substance composing the tusks of the elephant, walrus, hippopotamus, and narwhal: an object of that material, as a billiard-ball, a piano-key, a dice: a tooth or the teeth (*slang*).—*adj.* made of, resembling, or of the colour of, ivory.—*adj.* i'voried made like ivory: furnished with teeth (*slang*).—*n* i'vorist a worker in ivory.— i'vory-nut the nut of Phytelephas or other palm, yielding vegetable ivory a substance like ivory; i'vory-palm; i'vory-por'celain a fine ware with an ivory-white glaze; ivory tower (*fig.*) a place of retreat from the world and one's fellows: a life-style remote from that of most ordinary people, leading to ignorance of practical concerns, problems, etc [O Fr *ivurie* (Fr. *ivoire*)—L. *ebur, eboris*, ivory.]

ivy *i'vi*, *n.* an evergreen plant that climbs by roots on trees and walls.—*adjs.* i'vied (also i'vy'd) overgrown or mantled with ivy.—i'vy-bush a bush or branch of ivy, esp. formerly one hung at a tavern-door, the ivy being sacred to Bacchus.—Ivy League a name given to eight eastern U.S universities of particular academic and social prestige.—*adj.* i'vy-leaved having five-lobed leaves like ivy. [O.E. *īfig*.]

ixia *ik'si-a*, *n.* any plant of the iridaceous genus *Ixia*, found in Southern Africa. [Mod. Latin, from Gr *ixos*, mistletoe, birdlime.]

ixtle. See istle.

-ize. See -ise.

J

J, j *jā,* (*Scot*) *jī, n.* the tenth letter in our alphabet, developed from I, specialised to denote a consonantal sound (*dzh* in English, *y* in German and other languages, *zh* in French, an open guttural in Spanish), I being retained for the vowel sound—a differentiation not general in English books till about 1630 —**J'-curve** (*econ*) a small initial deterioration, decrease, etc., followed by a larger sustained improvement, increase, etc , appearing on a graph as a J-shaped curve

jab *jab, v.t.* and *v.i.* to poke, stab.—*n.* a sudden thrust or stab: an injection (*coll.*). [Cf. **job.**]

jabber *jab'ər, v i* to gabble or talk rapidly.—*v t* to utter indistinctly.—*n.* rapid indistinct speaking.—*n* **jabb'erer**—*n* and *adj* **jabb'ering.**—*adv.* **jabb'eringly.** [Imit.]

jabberwock *jab'ər-wok, n.* a fabulous monster created by Lewis Carroll in his poem *Jabberwocky:* (also **jabb'erwocky**) nonsense, gibberish.

jabiru *jab'i-roo, -roo', n.* a large Brazilian stork: extended to other kinds. [Tupí *jabirú.*]

jabot *zha'bō, n.* a frill of lace, etc., worn in front of a woman's dress or on a man's shirt-front, esp (now) as part of full Highland dress. [Fr.]

jaçana *zhä-sə-na', jacana jak'ə-nə, ns.* a long-toed swamp bird of the tropics. [Port , from Tupí]

jacaranda *jak-ə-ran'də, n.* a tropical American, etc , tree of the Bignoniaceae, with lilac-coloured flowers, fern-like leaves and hard, heavy, brown wood [Port. and Tupí *jacarandá.*]

jacinth *jas'inth, jās', n.* originally, a blue gemstone, perhaps sapphire: a reddish-orange variety of transparent zircon—hyacinth (*min.*): a variety of garnet, topaz, quartz, or other stone (*jewellery*): a reddish-orange colour a slaty-blue fancy pigeon [**hyacinth.**]

jack *jak, n.* (with *cap.*) a familiar form or diminutive of John: (sometimes with *cap.*) an attendant, servant or labourer: (often with *cap*) a sailor: a machine or device which orig. took the place of a servant, as a boot-jack for taking off boots, an apparatus for raising heavy weights: a winch: a socket whose switching arrangements are such that the switch turns only when a jack plug is inserted (*telecomm.,* etc): the male of some animals: a jackass: a jack-rabbit: a jackdaw: a young pike: in keyboard instruments, part of the action that moves the hammer or carries the quill or tangent: a small flag indicating nationality, flown by a ship, usu at the bow or the bowsprit: a leather pitcher or bottle: a knave in cards: (in *pl.*) the game of dibs: a piece used in this game: the small white ball aimed at in bowls,—*v.t* to raise with, or as if with, a jack (with *up*): to act upon with a jack: to throw up or abandon promptly (also with *up or in*) (*slang*): to increase (as prices) (with *up*).—**Jack'-a-lan'tern, Jack'-o'-lan'tern** Will-o'-the-wisp; **jack'boot** a large boot reaching above the knee, to protect the leg, orig. covered with iron plates and worn by cavalry: military rule, esp when brutal (*fig*); **Jack Frost** frost personified, **Jack'-go-to-bed-at-noon'** the plant goat's-beard; **jack'hammer** a hand-held compressed-air hammer drill for rock-drilling.—*adj* and *adv.* **jack'-high** in bowls, as far as the jack.—**Jack'-in-the-box** a figure that springs up from a box when the lid is released; **Jack Ketch** a public hangman—from one so

named under James II; **jack'-knife** a large clasp-knife: a dive in which the performer doubles up in the air and straightens out again —*v.i.* and *v.t* to double up as a jack-knife does: (of connected vehicles or parts) through faulty control, to form, or cause to form, an angle of 90° or less —**Jack'-of-all'-trades** one who can turn his hand to anything; **jack'-o'-lantern** a will-o'-the-wisp a lantern made from a hollowed-out pumpkin, turnip, etc , with holes cut to resemble eyes, mouth, and nose; **jack'-plane** a large strong plane used by joiners, **jack plug** (*telecomm.*), etc) a one-pronged plug used to introduce an apparatus quickly into a circuit, **jack'pot** a poker game, played for the pot or pool (consisting of equal stakes from all the players), which must be opened by a player holding two jacks or better a money pool in card games, competitions, etc., that can be won only on certain conditions being fulfilled and accumulates till such time as they are (see also **hit the jackpot** below); a prize-money fund; **jack'-rabb'it** a long-eared American hare, **Jack Russell** (terrier) a breed of small terrier, introduced by *John Russell,* 19th-cent. parson; **Jack Sprat** a diminutive fellow, **jack'-staff** the staff on which the jack is hoisted.—*n.pl* **jack'-stays** ropes or strips of wood or iron stretched along the yards of a ship to bind the sails to.—**Jack'-straw, jack'-straw** a straw effigy: a man of straw, of no real significance a straw or slip used in the game of **jack'-straws'** or spillikins; **Jack tar** (also without *cap*) a sailor; **jack towel** a continuous towel passing over a roller.—**before you can say Jack Robinson** very quickly; **every man Jack** one and all, **hit the jackpot** to win a jackpot to have a big success. [App. Fr *Jacques,* the most common name in France, hence used as a substitute for *John,* the most common name in England; really = *James* or *Jacob*—L. *Jacōbus,* but possibly partly from *Jackin, Jankin,* dim. of *John*]

jackal *jak'öl, n.* a wild, gregarious animal closely allied to the dog—erroneously supposed to act as a lion's provider or hunting scout: hence, one who does another's dirty work: a drudge: one who would share the spoil without sharing the danger [Pers *shaghāl.*]

jackanapes *jak'ə-nāps, n.* an impudent fellow: a coxcomb: a forward child.

jackaroo, jackeroo *jak-ə-roo', (Austr.) n.* a newcomer, or other person, gaining experience on a sheep-station—*fem.* **jillaroo'.**—*v.i* to be a jackaroo. [App an imitation of **kangaroo** with **Jack.**]

jackass *jak'as, n* a he-ass: a blockhead, fool —**laughing jackass** an Australian kingfisher which has a laughter-like call, the kookaburra [**jack, ass.**]

jackdaw *jak'do, n* a daw, a small species of crow with greyish neck. [**jack, daw.**]

jackeroo. See **jackaroo.**

jacket *jak'it, n.* a short coat: an animal's coat: skin (of potatoes): a loose paper cover. outer casing of a boiler, pipe, etc. the aluminium or zirconium alloy covering of the fissile elements in a reactor.—*v.t* to furnish or cover with a jacket —*adj.* **jack'eted** wearing a jacket.—**dust someone's jacket** to beat someone [O Fr *jaquet,* dim. of *jaque*]

Jacob *jā'kəb, n.* (also **Jacob sheep**) a kind of sheep, piebald in colour, with 2 or 4 horns, originally imported to Britain from Spain. [From Gen. xxx. 40.]

Jacobean *jak-ō-bē'ən, adj.* of or characteristic of the period of James I of England (1603–25). [L *Jacōbus*, James.]

Jacobin *jak'ō-bin, n* a French Dominican monk, their original establishment being that of St *Jacques*, Paris: one of a society of revolutionists in France: an extremist or radical, esp. in politics.—*adjs.* **Jacobin'ic, -al.** [Fr.,—L *Jacōbus*, James]

Jacobite *jak'ō-bīt, n.* an adherent of James II and his descendants.—Also *adj.*—*adjs.* **Jacobit'ic, -al.**—*n.* **Jac'obitism.** [L. *Jacōbus*, James.]

Jacob's-ladder *jā'kəbz-lad'ər, n.* a ladder of ropes with wooden steps (*naut.*). a wild or garden plant (Polemonium) with ladder-like leaves: an endless chain of buckets used as an elevator [From the *ladder* seen by Jacob in his dream, Gen. xxviii, 12.]

Jacob's-staff *jā'kəbz-staf, n.* a pilgrim's staff: a staff with a cross-head used in surveying (*hist.*). [Prob. from the pilgrimage to St James (L *Jacōbus*) of Compostela.]

jaconet *jak'ə-net, n.* a cotton fabric, rather stouter than muslin—different from the fabric orig. so-named which was imported from *Jagannāth* (Puri) in India: a thin material with waterproof backing used for medical dressings.

jacquard *jak'ärd, jak-ärd', (often cap)n.* an apparatus with perforated cards for controlling the movement of the warp threads in weaving intricate designs. a fabric so woven.—**Jacq'uard-loom** a loom with jacquard [Joseph Marie *Jacquard* (1752–1834), the inventor.]

jactation *jak-tā'shən, n.* act of throwing: extreme restlessness in disease: bodily agitation. boasting [L *jactātiō, -ōnis,* tossing, boasting—*jactāre,* to throw.]

jactitation *jak-ti-tā'shən, n.* restless tossing in illness. bragging: public assertion, esp ostentatious and false —**jactitation of marriage** pretence of being married to another. [L L *jactitātiō, -ōnis*—L. *jactitāre, -ātum,* freq of *jactāre,* to throw]

Jacuzzi® *jə-kōō'zi, n.* a type of bath or small pool equipped with a mechanism that agitates the water to provide extra invigoration.

jade¹ *jād, n.* a sorry horse: a worthless nag. a woman, esp. perverse, ill-natured, or not to be trusted, often in irony.—*v.t.* to make a jade of: to weary, dull, cause to flag.—*v.t.* to become weary.—*adj* **jā'ded.**—*adv* **jā'dedly.**

jade² *jād, n.* a hard ornamental stone of varying shades of green and sometimes almost white—esp *nephrite* (silicate of calcium and magnesium) and **jade'ite** (silicate of aluminium and sodium)—once held to cure side pains —*adj.* **jade** of jade' of the colour of jade. [Fr.,—Sp *ijada,* the flank—L. *ilia*]

j'adoube *zha-dōō b,* (Fr.) I adjust (*chess;* a warning that only an adjustment is intended, not a move)

Jaeger® *yā'gər, n.* woollen material used in making clothes, originally containing no vegetable fibre [Dr Gustav *Jaeger,* the original manufacturer]

jaeger. See **jäger.**

Jaffa *jaf'ə, n.* (also **Jaffa orange**) an orange from *Jaffa* in Israel

jag¹ *jag, n.* a notch, slash, or dag in a garment, etc.: a ragged protrusion: a cleft or division (*bot.*): a prick (*Scot.*)· an inoculation, injection (chiefly *Scot.*).—*v.t.* to cut into notches: to prick or pierce:—*pr.p.* **jagg'ing;** *pa.p.* **jagged** (*jagd*) —*adj.* **jagg'ed** notched, rough-edged, uneven —*adv.* **jagg'edly.**—*n.* **jagg'edness.**—*adj.* **jagg'y** notched: slashed: prickly (*Scot.*).

jag² *jag, n.* a spree, bout of indulgence: one's fill of liquor or narcotics: a spell, fit.

jäger, jaeger *yā'gər, n.* a (German) huntsman: a German rifleman or sharpshooter: an attendant upon an

important or wealthy person, clad in huntsman's costume: (**jaeger**) a skua that chases and robs other gulls. [Ger., hunter—*jagen,* to hunt]

jaggery *jag'ə-ri, n.* a coarse, dark sugar made from palm-sap or otherwise. [Hindi *jāgrī,* Sans. *śarkarā;* cf **sugar, Saccharum.**]

jaguar *jag'war,* or *jag'ū-ar, -ər, n.* a powerful beast of prey, allied to the leopard, found in South America [Tupí *jaguāra.*]

jaguarundi, jaguarondi *ja-gwə-run'dē,* or *-ron', ns.* a South American wild cat. [Tupí—Guaraní.]

Jah *ya, ja, n.* Jehovah.—*n* **Jah'veh** same as **Yahweh.** [Heb. *Yah*]

jai alai *hī' (ə-)lī,* or *-lī', a* game resembling handball but played with a long curved basket strapped to the wrist [Sp.—Basque—*jai,* festival, *alai,* merry.]

jail, gaol *jāl, n.* a prison.—*v.t.* to imprison —*ns.* **jail'er, jail'or, gaol'er** one who has charge of a jail or of prisoners: a turnkey:—*fem.* **jail'eress,** etc.—**jail'-bird, gaol'-bird** a humorous name for one who is, has been, or should be much in jail; **jail'house** (*U.S.*) a prison.—**break jail, gaol** to force one's way out of prison (*ns.* **jail'-break, gaol'-break**) [O.Fr. *gaole* (Fr *geôle*)—L L. *gabiola,* a cage—L *cavea,* a cage—*cavus,* hollow.]

Jain *jīn, jān,* **Jaina** *jī'na, ns* an adherent of an Indian religion allied to Brahmanism and Buddhism.—Also *adjs —n.* **Jain'ism.** [Hind *jina,* a deified saint.]

jake *jāk, (coll.) adj.* honest· correct· first-rate

jalap *jal'ap, n.* the purgative root of an Ipomoea or *Exogonium,* first brought from *Jalapa* or Xalapa, in Mexico

jalop(p)y *jə-lop'i, n* an old motor-car or aeroplane.

jalousie *zhal-ōō-zē', or zhal', n* an outside shutter with slats —*adv.* **jal'ousied.** [Fr ,—*jalousie,* jealousy.]

jam¹ *jam, n.* a conserve of fruit boiled with sugar: good luck (*coll.*).—*v t* to spread with jam: to make into jam —*adj* **jamm'y** smeared or sticky with jam: like jam. lucky, excellent (*coll.*) —**jam'pot** a jar for jam (also **jam'jar**).—**jam tomorrow** better things promised for the future that remain in the future; **want jam on it** (*coll.*) to expect or want too much [Perh from next.]

jam² *jam, v t.* to press or squeeze tight: to crowd full. to block by crowding· to bring to a standstill by crowding or interlocking: to interfere with by emitting signals of similar wavelength (*radio*).—*v t* to become stuck, wedged, etc : to become unworkable: to press or push (as into a confined space): in jazz, to play enthusiastically, interpolating and improvising freely.—*pr p* **jamm'ing;** *pa.t.* and *pa.p* **jammed.**—*n.* a crush, squeeze a block or stoppage due to crowding or squeezing together: a jammed mass (as of logs in a river): a jamming of radio messages a difficult or embarrassing situation (*coll*)—**jam'-packed** completely full, crowded, etc , **jam session** a gathering of jazz musicians (orig an informal one) at which jazz as described at *v t* is played. [Cf. **champ**¹.]

jamahiriya(h) *ja-ma'hē-rē'ya, n.* people's state, state of the proletariat [Ar., connected with *jumhūriya,* republic—*jumhūr,* people.]

Jamaica *jə-mā'kə,* **Jamaican** *-kən, adjs* of the island of Jamaica.—*n* **Jamai'can** a native or inhabitant of Jamaica.—**Jamaica pepper** allspice, **Jamaica rum** slowly-fermented, full-bodied pungent rum.

jamb *jam, n.* the sidepiece or post of a door, fireplace, etc . leg-armour (in this sense also **jambe** *jam*) [Fr. *jambe,* leg.]

jambiya(h) *jam-bē'ya, n.* a type of Middle Eastern curved, double-edged dagger [Ar]

jamboree *jam-bə-rē', n.* a boisterous frolic, a spree: a great Scout rally

jammy. See **jam¹.**

jampan *jam'pan, n.* an Indian sedan-chair.—*n.* **jampanee', jampani** (*-ē'*) its bearer. [Beng *jhāmpān.*]

jangle *jang'gl, v.t.* and *v.i.* to sound with unpleasant tone, as bells.—*v.t.* to upset, irritate.—*v.i.* to wrangle or quarrel.—*n.* dissonant clanging: contention.—*ns.* **jang'ler; jang'ling.**—*adj* **jang'ly.** [O.Fr. *jangler.*]

janissary. See **janizary.**

janitor *jan'i-tər, n.* a doorkeeper: attendant or caretaker:—*fem.* **jan'itrix, jan'itress.**—*adj* **janitorial** (*-tō', -tō'*).—*n.* **jan'itorship.** [L. *jānitor—jānua,* a door.]

janizary *jan'i-zər-i, n.* a soldier of the old Turkish footguards (*c.* 1330–1826): a follower, supporter.—Also **jan'issary** (*-zər-i*), **jan'izar.**—*adj.* **janizā'rian.** [Fr. *Janissaire,* supposed to be—Turk, *yeni,* new, *tsheri,* soldiery]

jankers *jang'kərz,* (*mil. slang*) *n.pl.* defaulters: punishment: detention.

Jansenism *jan'sən-izm, n.* a system of evangelical doctrine deduced from Augustine by Cornelius *Jansen* (1585–1638), maintaining that human nature is corrupt, and that Christ died only for the elect, all others being irretrievably condemned to hell.—*n.* **Jan'senist** a believer in Jansenism

January *jan'ū-ər-i, n.* the first month of the year, dedicated by the Romans to Janus. [L. *Jānuārius.*]

Janus *jā'nəs, n.* the ancient Italian two-faced god of doors, whose temple in Rome was closed in time of peace. [L. *Jānus.*]

Jap *jap,* (*derog.*) *n.* and *adj.* Japanese.—**Jap'-silk** a thin kind of silk.

japan *jə-pan', adj* of Japan: japanned.—*n.* Japanese ware or work: a glossy black varnish of lacquer: japanned work —*v.t.* to varnish with japan, esp. in imitation of Japanese work: to make black.—*pr.p.* **japann'ing;** *pa.t.* and *pa.p* **japanned'.**—*adj.* **Japanese** (*jap-ə-nēz',* or *jap'*) of Japan, of its people, or of its language.—*n.* a native or citizen of Japan: the language of Japan:—*pl.* **Japanese.**—*adjs.* **Japanesque', Japanês'y** savouring of the Japanese.—*n.* **japann'er.**—**Japanese cedar** a very tall Japanese conifer (*Cryptomeria japonica*); **Japan laurel** a shrub (*Aucuba japonica*) of the dogwood family, with spotted yellow leaves; **Japan varnish** a varnish got from a species of sumach (*Rhus vernicifera*), extended to various other similar varnishes.

jape *jāp, v.i.* to jest, joke.—*v.t.* to mock.—*n.* a jest, joke, trick. [O.Fr. *japer,* to yelp.]

Japonic *jə-pon'ik, adj.* Japanese.—*n.* **japon'ica** the Japanese quince (*Chaenomeles japonica*), camellia, or other Japanese plant. [New L. *japonicus,* fem. *japonica,* Japanese.]

jar *jär, v.i.* to make a harsh discordant sound or unpleasant vibration: to give an unpleasant shock: to grate (on): to be discordant or distasteful: to be inconsistent.—*v.t.* to shake, as by a blow: to cause to vibrate unpleasantly: to grate on: to make dissonant: —*pr.p.* **jarr'ing;** *pa.t.* and *pa.p.* **jarred.**—*n.* a harsh sudden vibration: a dissonance: a grating sound or feeling: clash of interests or opinions, conflict.—*n.* **jarr'ing** the act of jarring: severe reproof.—Also *adj.* —*adv.* **jarr'ingly.** [Imit.]

jar *jär, n.* a wide-mouthed wide vessel: as much as a jar will hold: a drink (of an alcoholic beverage) (*coll.*).—*v.t.* to put in jars.—*n.* **jar'ful:**—*pl.* **jar'fuls.** [Fr. *jarre* or Sp. *jarra*—Ar. *jarrah.*]

jardinière *zhär'dē-nyer', n.* a vessel for the display of flowers, growing or cut: a dish including a mixture of vegetables. [Fr., gardener (fem.).]

jargon *jär'gən, n.* chatter, twittering: confused talk: slang· artificial or barbarous language: the terminology of a profession, art, group, etc.—*v.i.* to twitter, chatter: to speak jargon.—*ns.* **jargoneer', jar'gonist** one who uses jargon; **jargonisā'tion, -z-.**—*v.t.* **jargonise, -ize** to express in jargon.—*v.i.* to speak jargon. [Fr. *jargon.*]

jargon [2]. See **jargoon.**

jargonelle. See next word.

jargoon *jär'gōōn', jargon jär'gən, ns.* a brilliant colourless or pale zircon.—*n.* **jargonelle'** an early pear (orig. a gritty kind). [Fr. *jargon;* prob. conn. with **zircon.**]

jarl *yärl,* (*hist.*) *n.* a noble, chief, earl. [O.N.; conn with **earl.**]

jarrah *jar'ə, n.* a Western Australian timber tree, *Eucalyptus marginata.* [From a native name.]

jasmine *jas'min* or *jaz',* **jessamine** *jes'ə-min, ns.* a genus (*Jasminum*) of oleaceous shrubs, many with very fragrant flowers.—**red jasmine** a tropical American shrub akin to periwinkle—frangipani (*Plumeria*). [Fr. *jasmin, jasemin*—Ar. *yāsmin, yās-amin*—Pers. *yāsmin.*]

jasper *jas'pər, n.* a precious stone (*obs.*): an opaque quartz containing clay or iron compounds, used in jewellery or ornamentation and red, yellow, brown or green in colour: a fine hard porcelain (also **jas'perware**).—*adj.* of jasper.—*adjs.* **jaspe, jaspé** (*jasp, -ā*) mottled, variegated, or veined.—*n.* cotton or rayon cloth with a shaded effect used for bedspreads, curtains, etc.—*v.t.* **jasp'erise, -ize** to turn into jasper.—*adjs.* **jasp'erous, jasp'ery.** [O.Fr. *jaspe, jaspre*—L. *iaspis, -idis;* and directly from Gr *iaspis, -idos,* of Eastern origin.]

jataka *jä'tə-kə, n.* a nativity, the birth-story of Buddha. [Sans. *jātaka—jāta,* born.]

jato *jā'tō,* (*aero.*) *n.* a jet-assisted *t*ake-off, using a **jato** unit consisting of one or more rocket motors, usu. jettisoned after use:—*pl.* **jā'tos.**

jaundice *jön'dis n.* a disease in which there is yellowing of the eyes, skin, etc., by excess of bile pigment, the patient in rare cases seeing objects as yellow: a disease showing this condition: state of taking an unfavourable, prejudiced view.—*v.t.* to affect with jaundice, in any sense.—*adj.* **jaun'diced** affected with jaundice: feeling, or showing, prejudice, distaste, or jealousy. [Fr *jaunisse—jaune,* yellow—L. *galbīnus,* yellowish, *galbus,* yellow.]

jaunt *jönt v.i.* to go from place to place, now chiefly for pleasure: to make an excursion.—*n.* an excursion: a ramble.—*adj.* **jaunt'ing** strolling: making an excursion.—**jaunt'ing-car** a low-set, two-wheeled, open vehicle used in Ireland, with side-seats usu. back to back.

jaunty *jön'ti, adj.* having an airy or sprightly manner approaching swagger —*adv.* **jaunt'ily.**—*n.* **jaunt'iness.** [Fr. *gentil.*]

Java *jä'və, adj.* of the island of Java.—*adjs.* and *ns.* **Ja'van, Javanese'.**—**Java man** formerly Pithecanthropus erectus, now generally designated Homo erectus.

Javel(le) water *zha-* or *zhə-vel' wō'tər,* **eau de** (*ō də*) **Javel(le),** a solution of potassium chloride and hypochlorite used for bleaching, disinfecting, etc. [After *Javel,* former town, now part of the city of Paris.]

javelin *jav'(ə-)lin, n.* a throwing-spear. [Fr. *javeline;* prob. Celt.]

jaw *jö, n.* a mouth-structure for biting or chewing: one of the bones of a jaw: one of a pair of parts for gripping, crushing, cutting, grinding, etc.: (in *pl.*) a narrow entrance: talkativeness, scolding (*slang*).—*v.t.* (*slang*) to scold.—*v.i.* to talk, esp. in excess.—*adj.* **jawed** having jaws.—*n.* **jaw'ing** (*slang*) talk, esp. unrestrained, abusive, or reproving.—**jaw'bone** the bone of the jaw; **jaw'-break'er** a heavy-duty rock-breaking machine with hinged jaws (also **jaw'• crush'er**): a word hard to pronounce (*slang*; also **jaw'• twist'er**); **jaw lever** an instrument for opening the mouth of a horse or cow to admit medicine; **jaw'• tooth** a molar.—**hold one's jaw** to cease from talking or scolding.

ja wohl *ya vōl'*, (Ger) yes indeed.

jay[1] *jā, n.* a bird of the crow family with gay plumage: a stupid or awkward fellow (*U S slang*) —*adj.* (*U.S. slang*) stupid, inferior —*v.i.* **jay'walk.**—**jay'walker** a careless pedestrian whom motorists are expected to avoid running down; **jay'walking.** [O Fr. *jay.*]

jay[2] *jā, n.* tenth letter of the alphabet (J, j): object or mark of that shape.

jazz *jaz, n.* any of various styles of music with a strong rhythm, syncopation, improvisation, etc., originating in American Negro folk music: an art form and also various types of popular dance music derived from it: garish colouring, lively manner, vivid quality: insincere or lying talk (*slang*): talk, in general (*slang*) —Also *adj* —*v.t.* to impart a jazz character to (often with *up*).—*adv* **jazz'ily.**—*n.* **jazz'iness.**—*adj* **jazz'y.** —**jazz age** the decade following World War I, esp. in America; **jazz'man** a jazz musician

jealous *jel'əs, adj* suspicious of, or incensed at, rivalry envious: solicitous: anxiously heedful: mistrustfully vigilant: brooking no unfaithfulness —*adv* **jeal'ously.**—*ns.* **jeal'ousy, jeal'ousness.** [O Fr *jalous*—L *zēlus*—Gr. *zēlos,* emulation]

jean *jēn,* (esp. formerly) *jān, n.* a twilled-cotton cloth (also in *pl.*): (in *pl.*) trousers or overalls of jean: (in *pl.*) close-fitting, sometimes three-quarter length, casual trousers of jean or similar material. [O Fr. *Janne*—L. *Genua,* Genoa.]

jebel *jeb'əl, n.* in Arab countries, a hill or a mountain. [Ar., mountain.]

jeep *jēp, n.* a light military vehicle with great freedom of movement. [From G.P., for *general purpose*]

jeepers (creepers) *jē'pərz (krē'pərz), (U.S. slang)* *interj.* expressing suprise (for *Jesus Christ.*).

jeer *jēr, v.t* to make sport of· to treat with derision.— *v i.* (*usu* with *at*) to scoff: to deride: to make a mock —*n* a railing remark: biting jest: mockery.—*n* **jeer'er.**—*n.* and *adj.* **jeer'ing.**—*adv* **jeer'ingly.**

jehad. See **jihad.**

Jehovah *ji-hō'və, n* Yahweh, the Hebrew God, a name used by Christians—**Jehovah's Witnesses** a Christian fundamentalist sect which rejects all other religions and denominations, believes in the imminent end of the world, and refuses to accept civil authority where it clashes with its own principles—originally called the International Bible Students' Association [Heb.; for *Yĕhōwāh,* i.e *Yahweh* with the vowels of *Adōnāi.*]

Jehu *jē'hū, (coll) n* a driver, esp a furious whip [A reference to 2 Kings ix. 20.]

jejune *ji-jōōn', adj* empty: spiritless, meagre, arid: showing lack of information or experience: naive, immature, callow —*adv.* **jejune'ly.**—*ns* **jejune'ness, jejun'ity;** **jeju'num** the part of the small intestine between the duodenum and the ileum. [L *jejūnus,* hungry.]

Jekyll and Hyde *jek'il (or jek'il) and hīd,* the good side and the bad side of a human being—from R L. Stevenson, *The Strange Case of Dr Jekyll and Mr Hyde* (1886).

jell. See **jelly**[1].

jellaba. See **djellaba.**

jelly[1] *jel'i, n.* anything gelatinous: the juice of fruit boiled with sugar: a conserve of fruit, jam (*U.S.* and formerly *Scot.*)· a gelatinous preparation for the table.—*v i.* to set as a jelly: to congeal.—*v.t.* to make into a jelly —*v i.* and *v t* **jell** to jelly· to take distinct

shape (*coll.*).—*adjs.* **jell'ied** in a state of jelly· enclosed in jelly: **jell'iform.**—*v t.* **jell'ify** to make into a jelly.—*v.i.* to become gelatinous.—**jelly baby** a kind of gelatinous sweet in the shape of a baby; **jelly bag** a bag through which fruit juice is strained for jelly; **jell'ybean** a kind of sweet in the shape of a bean with a sugar coating and jelly filling; **jell'yfish** a marine coelenterate with jelly-like body: a person who lacks firmness of purpose [Fr *gelée,* from *geler*—L *gelāre,* to freeze; cf. **gel.**]

jelly[2] *jel'i, n.* a coll. shortening of **gelignite.**

jemmy *jem'i, n.* a burglar's short crowbar [A form of the name *James*]

je ne sais quoi *zhə nə se kwa,* an indefinable something. [Fr , I don't know what]

jennet *jen'it, n.* a small Spanish horse.—Also **genn'et, gen'et.** [O Fr. *genet*—Sp *jinete,* a light horseman, perh. of Arab origin.]

jenny *jen'i, n.* a wren or owl regarded as female: a she-ass: a travelling crane: a spinning-jenny.—**Jenny-long'-legs** (*Scot.*), **Jenn'y-spinner** (*dial.*) a crane-fly; **Jenny-wren'** a wren. [From the name *Jenny.*]

jeopardy *jep'ar-di, n.* hazard, danger: the danger of trial and punishment faced by the accused on a criminal charge (*U.S law*).—*v.t* **jeop'ardise, -ize** to put in jeopardy. [Fr. *jeu parti,* a divided or even game—L.L *jocus partītus*—L. *jocus,* a game, *partītus,* divided—*partīrī,* to divide]

jerbil. See **gerbil.**

jerboa *jûr-bō'ə, n* a desert rodent (family *Dipodidae*) that jumps like a kangaroo. [Ar. *yarbū'.*]

jeremiad *jer-i-mī'ad, n.* a lamentation: a tale of grief: a doleful story.—*n.* **Jeremi'ah** a person who continually prophesies doom [From *Jeremiah,* reputed author of the *Book of Lamentations.*]

jerfalcon. Same as **gerfalcon.**

jerk[1] *jûrk, n.* a short movement begun and ended suddenly: a twitch: an involuntary spasmodic contraction of a muscle: a movement in physical exercises: a useless person (*slang*).—*v.t.* to throw or move with a jerk —*v.i.* to move with a jerk: to utter abruptly —*ns.* **jerk'er; jerk'iness.**—*adj.* **jerk'y** moving or coming by jerks or starts, spasmodic.—**jerk off** (*vulg.*) to masturbate. [imit]

jerk[2] *jûrk, v.t.* to make into charqui.—*n.* charqui.— Also **jerk'ed-meat, jerk'y.** [charqui.]

jerkin *jûr'kin, n.* a jacket, a short coat or close waistcoat.

jerkinhead *jûr'kin-hed, (archit.) n.* the combination of a truncated gable with a lipped roof [Perh. from **jerk**[1].]

jeroboam *jer-ō-bō'əm, n* a very large bowl: a large bottle, esp. one for wine holding the equivalent of 6 normal bottles, or for champagne, the equivalent of 4 normal bottles. [Allusion to 1 Kings xi. 28.]

jerrican, jerrycan *jer'i-kan, n.* a kind of petrol-can, orig German.

Jerry, Gerry *jer'i, (war slang) n.* a German

jerry[1] *jer'i (slang) n* a chamber-pot [**jeroboam.**]

jerry[2] *jer'i, n (coll.)* a jerry-builder.—*adj* hastily made of bad materials —**jerr'y-builder** one who builds flimsy houses cheaply and hastily —**jerr'y-building.**—*adj.* **jerr'y-built.** [Prob the personal name]

jersey *jûr'zi, n* the finest part of wool: combed wool: a knitted woollen, etc upper garment: a fine knitted fabric in cotton, nylon, etc.· (with *cap.*) a cow of Jersey breed [From the island of *Jersey.*]

Jerusalem artichoke *jər-ōōs'ə-ləm är'ti-chōk,* see **artichoke.**

jess *jes, n* a short strap round the leg of a hawk.—*adj.* **jessed** having jesses on [O.Fr. *ges*—L *jactus,* a cast —*jacēre,* to throw]

---

fāte, far, mē, hûr (her), *mīne; mōte; for; mūte, mōōn; fōōt, dhen* (then), *el'ə-mənt* (element)

jessamine. See **jasmine.**

jest *jest, n.* something ludicrous: object of laughter: joke: fun: something uttered in sport.—*v.i* to make a jest: to joke —*v.t.* to jeer at, ridicule: to utter as a jest.—*n.* **jest'er** one who jests: a buffoon: a courtfool.—*adj.* **jest'ful** given to jesting —*n.* and *adj.* **jest'-ing.**—*adv.* **jest'ingly.** [Orig. a deed, a story, M.E. *geste*—O.Fr. *geste*—L. *gesta,* things done, doings— *gerēre,* to do.]

Jesuit *jez'ū-it, n.* a member of the famous religious order, the Society of *Jesus,* founded in 1534 by Ignatius Loyola: (*opprobriously*) a crafty person, an intriguer, a prevaricator.—*adjs.* **Jesuit'ic, -al.**—*adv* **Jesuit'ically.**—*ns.* **Jes'uitism, Jes'uitry** the principles and practices of or ascribed to the Jesuits.

Jesus *jē'zəs, n.* the founder of Christianity—also (in hymns, etc., esp. in the vocative) **Jesu** (*jē'zū*). [Gr. *Iēsous* (voc. and oblique cases *Iēsou*)—Heb. *Yēshūa',* contr. of *Yehōshūa',* Joshua.]

jet[1] *jet, n.* a rich black variety of lignite, very hard and compact, taking a high polish, used for ornaments: jet-black.—*adj.* of jet: jet-black.—*n.* **jett'iness.**— *adj.* **jett'y** of the nature of jet, or black as jet.—*adj.* **jet'-black'** black as jet.—Also *n.* [O.Fr. *jaiet*—L. and Gr. *gagātēs*—*Gagas* or *Gangai,* a town and river in Lycia, where it was obtained.]

jet[2] *jet, n.* a narrow spouting stream: a spout, nozzle or pipe emitting a stream or spray of fluid: a jet-plane.— *v.t.* and *v.i.* to spout —*v.i.* to travel by jet-plane:— *pr.p.* **jett'ing;** *pa.t.* and *pa.p.* **jett'ed.**—**jet'-drive.**— *adj.* **jet'-driven** driven by the backward emission of a jet of gas, etc.—**jet'foil** a hydrofoil powered by a jet of water; **jet lag** exhaustion, discomfort, etc., resulting from the body's inability to adjust to the rapid changes of time zone necessitated by high-speed longdistance air-travel; **jet'liner** an airliner powered by a jet engine; **jet'(-)plane** a jet-driven aeroplane.—*adj.* **jet'-propelled.**—**jet'-propulsion; jet'-setter** a member of the jet set.—*adj.* **jet'-setting** living in the style of the jet set.—**jet'(-)stream** very high winds more than 20000 feet above the earth: the exhaust of a rocket engine.—**the jet set** moneyed social set able to spend much of their time at fashionable resorts all over the world. [O.Fr. *jetter*—L. *jactāre,* to fling.]

jeté *zhə-tā,* (*ballet*) *n.* a leap from one foot to the other in which the free leg usu. finishes extended forward, backward, or sideways. [Fr., thrown.]

jetsam *jet'səm, n.* goods jettisoned from a ship and washed up on shore: according to some, goods from a wreck that remain under water (see **flotsam**).—*n.* **jett'ison** the act of throwing goods overboard.—*v.t.* to throw overboard, as goods in time of danger: to abandon, reject (*fig.*).—**flotsam and jetsam** often, unclaimed objects and ideas. [A.Fr. *jetteson*—L. *jactātiō, -ōnis,* a casting—*jactāre,* freq. of *jacĕre,* to cast.]

jetton, jeton *jet'ən, n.* a piece of stamped metal used as a counter in card-playing, casting accounts, etc. [Fr. *jeton—jeter,* to throw—L. *jactāre,* freq. of *jacĕre,* to throw.]

jetty *jet'i, n.* a projection: a pier. [O.Fr. *jettee,* thrown out; see **jet**[2].]

jeu *zhø,* (Fr.) *n.* a game.—**jeu de mots:**—*pl.* **jeux de mots** (*də mō*) a play on words, a pun; **jeu d'esprit:**— *pl.* **jeux d'esprit** (*des-prē*) a witticism.

jeunesse dorée *zhœ-nes do-rā,* (Fr.) gilded youth: luxurious, stylish, sophisticated young people.

Jew *jōō, n.* a person of Hebrew descent or religion: an Israelite: (*offensively*) a usurer, miser, etc :—*fem.* **Jew'ess.**—*v.t.* (*offensively*) to overreach, or to cheat. —*adj.* **Jew'ish** of the Jews or their religion.—*adv.* **Jew'ishly.**—*n.* **Jew'ishness.**—**Jew'-bait'ing** the persecuting of Jews; **jew'fish** a name for several very large American and Australian fishes; **Jew's'-ear** an ear-like fungus (Auricularia) parasitic on elder and other trees; **Jew's-harp', Jews'-harp'** (also without *cap.*) a small lyre-shaped instrument played against the teeth by twitching a metal tongue with the finger. [O.Fr. *Jueu*—L *Jūdaeus*—Gr. *Ioudaios*—Heb. *Yehūdāh,* Judah.]

jewel *jōō'əl, n.* a precious stone: a personal ornament of precious stones, gold, etc.: a hard stone (ruby, etc.) used for pivot bearings in a watch: an imitation of a gemstone: a glass boss: anything or anyone highly valued.—*v.t.* to adorn with jewels: to fit with a jewel: —*pr.p.* **jew'elling;** *pa.t.* and *pa.p.* **jew'elled.**—*ns.* **jew'eller** one who deals in, or makes, jewels; **jewellery** (*jōō'əl-ri*), **jew'elry** jewels in general.—**jew'el-case** a casket for holding jewels; **jew'elfish** an African cichlid, *Hemichromis bimaculatus,* popular in aquaria for its bright colours; **jew'el-house** a room in the Tower of London where the crown-jewels are kept. [O.Fr. *jouel* (Fr. *joyau*); either a dim. of Fr. *joie,* joy, from L. *gaudium,* joy—*gaudēre,* to rejoice—or derived through L.L. *jocāle,* from L. *jocārī,* to jest.]

Jewry *jōō'ri, n.* Judaea: a district inhabited by *Jews:* the Jewish world, community, or religion.

Jezebel *jez'ə-bəl, n.* a shameless painted woman. [From Ahab's wife, 2 Kings ix. 30.]

jib *jib, n.* a triangular sail borne in front of the foremast in a ship: the boom of a crane or derrick: an act of jibbing: a standstill.—*v.t.* to cause to gybe —*v.i.* (*usu.* with *at*) to gybe: (of a horse) to balk or shy: to refuse, show objective, boggle:—*pr.p.* **jibb'ing;** *pa.t.* and *pa.p.* **jibbed.**—**jib'-boom'** a boom or extension of the bowsprit, on which the jib is spread; **jib'-crane'** a crane with an inclined arm fixed to the foot of a rotating vertical post, the upper ends connected.— **the cut of one's jib** one's appearance.

jibe[1]. See **gibe.**

jibe[2] *jib* (chiefly *U.S.*) *v.i.* to agree, accord (with). [Poss. related to **chime**[1].]

jiffy *jif'i,* (*coll.*) *n.* an instant (sometimes shortened to **jiff**):

jig *jig, n.* a jerky movement: a lively dance usu. in 6-8 time: a dance-tune of like kind: a contrivance of various kinds, esp. one for catching fish by jerking hooks into its body, an appliance for guiding a tool, a miner's jigger.—*v.t.* and *v.i.* to jerk: to perform as a jig.—*v.t.* to work upon with a jig:—*pr.p.* **jigg'ing;** *pa.t.* and *pa.p.* **jigged.**—*ns.* **jigamaree', jigg'umbob** a what's-its-name: a gadget; **jigg'er** one who jigs in any sense: anything that jigs: one of many kinds of subsidiary appliances, esp. with reciprocating motion, as an oscillation transformer, an apparatus for separating ores by jolting in sieves in water, a warehouse crane: old-fashioned sloop-rigged boat: a jigger-mast (*naut.*): a sail on a jigger-mast (*naut.*): odd person: odd or despised contrivance: a small measure for drinks.—*v.t.* to jerk or shake: to form with a jigger: to ruin (sometimes with *up*).—*v.i.* to tug or move with jerks.—*adj.* **jigg'ered** (*coll.*) exhausted.— *n.* **jigg'ing.**—*adj.* **jigg'ish.**—*v.t.* and *v.i.* **jigg'le** to move with vibratory jerks.—*n.* a jiggling movement. —**jigg'er-mast** a four-masted ship's aftermost mast: a small mast astern; **jig'saw** a narrow reciprocating saw: a jigsaw puzzle.—*v.t.* and *v.i.* to cut with a jigsaw.—**jigsaw puzzle** a picture cut up into pieces, as by a jigsaw, to be fitted together.—**the jig is up** (*coll.*) the game is up, trick discovered, etc.

jigajig, etc. See **jig-jog.**

jigamaree. See **jig.**

jigger[1] *jig'ər, n.* a form of **chigoe.**

jigger[2]. See **jig.**

jiggered[1] *jig'ərd,* (*coll.*) *adj.* confounded.

jiggered[2]. See **jig.**

jiggery-pokery *jig'ə-ri-pō'kə-ri, n.* trickery: deception.

Jiggety-jog. See jig-jog.

Jiggle, jiggumbob. See jig.

jig-jog *jig'-jog'*, *adv.* with a jolting, jogging motion.— *n.* a jolting motion: a jog.—Also **jick'ajog'**, **jig'jig'**, **jig'ajig'**, **jig'ajog'**, **jigg'ety-jog'**. [jig, jog.]

jigot. Same as gigot.

jihad, jehad *jĕ-had'*, *n.* a holy war (for the Muslim faith): a stunt campaign. [Ar. *jihād*, struggle.]

jillaroo. See jackaroo.

jilt *jilt*, *n.* one, esp. a woman, who encourages and then rejects a lover.—*v.t.* to discard (a lover) after encouragement.

jimcrack. See gimcrack.

Jim Crow *jim krō*, (*derog.*) a generic name for the Negro: racial discrimination against Negroes.—**jim'- crow** a tool for bending or straightening iron rails or bars.—**Jim Crow car, school** etc., one for Negroes only. [From a Negro minstrel song with the refrain 'Wheel about and turn about and jump *Jim Crow*'.]

jiminy *jim'in-i interj.* expressing surprise.

jimjam *jim'jam*, *n.* a gimcrack: a gadget: an oddity: (in *pl.*) delirium tremens: (in *pl.*) the fidgets.

jimmy *jim'ı*, (chiefly *U.S.*) *n.* a burglar's jemmy. [James.]

jingbang *jing-bang'*, *jing'*, (*slang*) *n.* company: collection: lot.

jingle *jing'gl*, *n.* a succession of clinking sounds: that which makes a tinkling sound, esp. a metal disc on a tambourine: a short, simple verse, usu. with music, used to advertise a product, etc.—*v.t.* and *v.i.* to sound with a jingle.—*n.* **jing'ler**.—*adj.* **jing'ly**.— **jing'le-jang'le** a dissonant continued jingling: a jingling trinket. [Imit.]

jingo, Jingo *jing'gō*, *n.* used ın the mild oaths 'By jingo!', 'By the living jingo!' (*Scot.* 'By jings!'): from its occurrence in a music-hall song of 1878 that conveyed a threat against Russia, a (British) chauvinist. —*pl.* **jing'oes**.—*adjs.* **jing'o**, **jing'oish** chauvinist.— *ns.* **jing'oism**; **jing'oist**.—*adj.* **jingois'tic** characteristic of jingoism.—*adv.* **jingois'tically**.

jinjili. See gingili.

jink *jingk*, (orig. *Scot.*) *v.i.* to dodge nimbly.—*v.t.* to elude: to cheat.—*n.* a quick, illusory turn.—**high jinks** see high.

jinn *jin*, *n.pl.* (*sing.* **jinnee, jinni, djinni, genie** (*jin-ē'*, *jĕn'i*)) a class of spirits in Muslim mythology, assuming various shapes, sometimes as men of enormous size and portentous hideousness.—Also **djinn, ginn**. The *jinn* are often called *genii* by a confusion. A plural **jinns** is sometimes erroneously used. [Ar. *jinn*, sing., *jinnī*.]

jinricksha, jinrickshaw. See ricksha.

jinx *jingks*, *n.* a bringer of bad luck: an unlucky influence.—*adj.* **jinxed** beset with bad luck.

jism, gism *jiz'əm*, **jissom** *jis'əm*, *ns.* energy, force (*coll.*, chiefly *U.S.*): semen (*vulg.*).

jitter *jit'ər*, (orig. *U.S.*) *v.i.* to behave in a flustered way.—*n.pl.* **jitt'ers** a flustered state.—*adj.* **jitt'ery**. —**jitt'erbug** (*U.S.*) a violent spasmodic type of dancing to jazz music: one who dances so: (in Britain, by misunderstanding or extension) a scaremonger, alarmist.—*v.i.* to dance wildly and grotesquely.

jiu-jitsu. Same as ju-jitsu.

jive *jīv*, *n.* a style of jazz music: dancing thereto: jargon (*slang*).—*v.i.* to play or dance jive: to talk jargon (*slang*).

jizz *jiz*, *n.* the characteristic feature or features of behaviour, plumage or anatomy which serve to distinguish a bird from others which resemble ıt.

Job *jōb*, *n.* a person of great patience—from *Job* in the *Book of Job*.—*n.* **Jōba'tion** a tedıous scolding.—**Job's comforter** one who aggravates the distress of the unfortunate man he has come to comfort.

job *job*, *n.* any definite piece of work, esp. of a trifling or temporary nature: any undertaking or employment with a view to profit: an appointment or situation: state of affairs (*coll.*): an end accomplished by intrigue or wire-pulling: a criminal enterprise, esp. theft: a job-lot.—*adj.* employed, hired, or used by the job or for jobs: bought or sold lumped together. —*v.i.* to work at jobs: to buy and sell, as a broker: to practise jobbery.—*v.t.* to perform as a job: to put or carry through by jobbery: to deal in, as a broker.—*ns.* **jobb'er** one who jobs: one who buys and sells, as a broker; **jobb'ery** jobbing: unfair means employed to secure some private end.—*adj.* **jobb'ing** working by the job.—*n.* the doing of jobs: miscellaneous printing-work: buying and selling as a broker: stock-jobbing: jobbery.—*adj.* and *n.pl.* **job'less** (people) having no job.—**job centre, Jobcentre** (also without *cap.*) a government-run employment agency where information about available jobs is displayed; **job's lot** a collection of odds and ends, esp. for sale as one lot: any collection of inferior quality.—**a bad, good, job** a piece of work ill, or well, done: an unlucky, or lucky, fact; **have a job to** (*coll.*) to have difficulty in; **job of work** a task, bit of work; **jobs for the boys** jobs given to or created for associates or adherents; **just the job** (*coll.*) exactly what is wanted; **odd jobs** occasional pieces of work; **on the job** at work, in activity.

jobation. See Job.

Jock *jok*, *n.* a Scottish soldier (*slang*). [Jack.]

jockey *jok'i*, *n.* a man (orig. a boy) who rides in a horse-race.—*v.t.* to jostle by riding against: to manoeuvre: to trick by manoeuvring.—*v.i.* (often with *for*) to seek advantage by manoeuvring.—*ns.* **jock-ette'** (*facet.*) a female jockey; **jock'eyism**; **jock'ey-ship** the art or practice of a jockey.—**Jockey Club** an association for the promotion and ordering of horse-racing. [Dim. of Jock.]

jockstrap *jok'strap*, *n.* genital support worn by men participating in athletics. [Dial. *jock*, the male organ, strap.]

jocose *jō-kōs'*, *adj.* full of jokes: facetious: merry.— *adv.* **jocose'ly**.—*ns.* **jocose'ness, jocosity** (*-kos'i-ti*) the quality of being jocose. [L. *jocōsus—jocus*, a joke.]

jocular *jok'ū-lər*, *adj.* given to jokes: inclined to joke: of the nature of, intended as, a joke.—*n.* **jocularity** (*-lar'i-ti*).—*adj.* **joc'ularly**. [L. *joculāris—jocus*.]

jocund *jok'und*, *jok'und*, *-ənd*, *adj.* mirthful: merry: cheerful: pleasant.—*ns.* **jocundity** (*-kund'i-ti*), **joc'undness**.—*adv.* **joc'undly**. [O.Fr.—L.L. *jōcundus* for L. *jūcundus*, pleasant, modified by association with *jocus*.]

jodel *yō'dl*. Same as yodel.

jodhpurs *jod'pûrz*, *n.pl.* riding-breeches with a tight extension to the ankle (also **jodhpur breeches**): ankle-high boots worn with jodhpur breeches for riding (also **jodhpur boots, shoes**). [*Jodhpur* in India.]

joey *jō'i* (*Austr.*) *n.* a young animal, esp. kangaroo. [Australian *joe*.]

jog *jog*, *v.t.* to shake: to push with the elbow or hand: to stimulate, stir up, as the memory.—*v.i.* to move by jogs: to trudge: to run at a slow, steady pace, as a form of exercise:—*pr.p.* **jogg'ing**; *pa.t.* and *pa.p.* **jogged**.—*n.* a slight shake: a push or nudge: a spell of jogging.—*ns.* **jogg'er** a person who jogs for exercise; **jogg'ing** running at a slow, steady pace, esp. for exercise.—**jog'-trot** a slow jogging trot: humdrum routine.—**jog along** to proceed at a slow but steady pace, esp. of life, events, etc.

joggle *jog'l*, *n.* a tooth, notch, or pin to prevent sliding of surfaces ın contact: a joint so made.—*v.t.* to join with a joggle. [Perh. conn. with **jag**.]

joggle² *jog'l*, *v t.* to jog or shake slightly: to jostle.— *v.i.* to shake:—*pr.p.* **jogg'ling;** *pa.t.* and *pa.p.* **jogg'led.** [App. dim. or freq of **jog.**]

John *jon*, *n* a proper name, a diminutive of which, **Johnny** (also **John'ie**), is sometimes used in slang for a simpleton, an empty-headed man-about-town or fellow generally: (without *cap.*) a lavatory (*slang*). —*n.* **johnn'ie, johnny** (*slang*) a condom.—**John Barleycorn** malt liquor personified; **John Bull** a generic name for an Englishman, from Arbuthnot(t)'s *History of John Bull*, 1712; **John Bullism** the typical English character, or any act or word expressive of it, **John Citizen** a typical citizen; **John Collins** an alcoholic drink based on gin; **Johnn'y-come-late'ly** a newcomer; **Johnn'y-raw** a beginner: a greenhorn; **John Thomas** (*slang*) the penis. [L. *Jōhannēs*]

joie de vivre *zhwa də vē-vr'*, (Fr.) joy of living exuberance.

join *join*, *v.t* to connect: to unite: to associate: to add or annex· to become a member of: to come into association with or the company of: to go to and remain with, in, or on: to draw a straight line between (*geom.*) —*v.i.* to be connected: to combine, unite: to run into one· to grow together: to be in, or come into, close contact.—*n.* a joining: a place where things have been joined: a mode of joining.—*ns* **joind'er** (esp. *law*) joining, uniting; **join'er** one who joins or unites: a worker in wood, esp. one who makes smaller structures than a carpenter: one who joins many societies; **join'ery** the art of the joiner: joiner's work; **join'ing** the act of joining: a seam: a joint; **joint** a joining: the place where, or mode in which, two or more things join: a place where two things (esp bones) meet with power of movement as of a hinge: a node, or place where a stem bears leaves, esp. if swollen: a segment: a piece of an animal's body as cut up for the table: a crack intersecting a mass of rock (*geol.*): the place where adjacent surfaces meet: condition of adjustment at a joint (in the phrase *out of joint*): a low resort: a place, esp. a public house or hotel: a cigarette containing marijuana (*coll.*).—*adj.* joined, united, or combined: shared among more than one: sharing with another or others.—*v t.* to unite by joints: to fit closely: to provide with joints or an appearance of joints: to fill the joints of. to divide into joints.—*v.i.* to fit like or by joints.—*adj.* **joint'ed** having joints: composed of segments: constricted at intervals.—*n.* **joint'er** the largest kind of plane used by a joiner: a bricklayer's tool for putting mortar in joints.—*adj* **joint'less.**—*adv.* **joint'ly** in a joint manner: unitedly or in combination: together —*ns* **joint'ness; joint'ure** property settled on a woman at marriage to be enjoyed after her husband's death —*v t* to settle a jointure upon.—*ns.* **joint'uress, joint'ress** a woman on whom a jointure is settled —**joint account** a bank account held in the name of more than one person, any of whom can deposit or withdraw money, **joint'-heir** one who inherits jointly with another or others; **joint'ing-rule** a long straight-edged rule used by bricklayers; **joint'-stock** stock held jointly or in company (**joint'-stock company** one in which each shareholder can transfer shares without consent of the rest), **joint'-ten'ancy; joint'-ten'ant** one who is owner of land or goods along with others —**join issue** to begin to dispute: to take up the contrary view or side; **join up** to enlist, esp. in participation in a general movement; **out of joint** dislocated disordered (*fig*), **put someone's nose out of joint** to supplant someone in another's love or confidence· to disconcert· to rebuff; **universal joint** a contrivance by which one part is able to move freely in all directions, as in the ball-and-socket joint [O Fr *joindre*—L *jungēre, junctum*, to join]

joist *joist*, *n.* a beam supporting the boards of a floor or the laths of a ceiling.—*v.t.* to fit with joists. [O.Fr. *giste—gesir*—L. *jacēre*, to lie.]

jojoba *hō-hō'bə*, *n.* a desert shrub of the box family, native to Mexico, Arizona and California, whose edible seeds yield a waxy oil chemically similar to spermaceti [Mex. Sp]

joke *jōk*, *n.* a jest: a witticism anything said or done to excite a laugh: anything provocative of laughter: an absurdity.—*v.t.* to cast jokes at: to banter· to make merry with —*v.i.* to jest: to be merry: to make sport —*n* **jok'er** one who jokes or jests: a fifty-third card in the pack, used at poker, etc.: an unforeseen factor affecting a situation: a fellow (*slang*).—*adjs* **joke'some; jō'key, jō'ky.**—*adv* **jok'ingly** in a joking manner.—**joke'smith** a maker of jokes —**joking apart** if I may be serious, seriously; **no joke** a serious or difficult matter. [L. *jocus.*]

jolly *jol'i*, *adj.* merry: expressing or exciting mirth, jovial: comely, robust: used as an indefinite expression of approbation (*coll.*).—*v.t.* to make fun of: to put or keep in good humour, beguile.—*adv* (*coll.*) very —*n.* a marine (*slang*): a jollification (*coll.*).—*n* **jollifica'tion** a making jolly: noisy festivity and merriment.—*v.i.* **joll'ify.**—*adv.* **joll'ily.**—*ns.* **joll'iness, joll'ity.**—**Jolly Roger** the pirates' black flag with white skull and crossbones. [O Fr *jolif, joli*]

jollyboat *jol'i-bōt*, *n.* a ship's boat.

jolt *jōlt*, *v.i* to shake or proceed with sudden jerks.— *v.t* to shake with a sudden shock.—*n.* a sudden jerk: a shock, a stimulating shock.—*n.* **jolt'er.**—*adv.* **jolt'-ingly** in a jolting manner.—*adj* **jolt'y.**

Jonah *jō'nə*, *n.* a bringer of ill-luck on shipboard or elsewhere. [From the prophet *Jonah.*]

jongleur *zh5-glər'*, *n.* a wandering minstrel a mountebank. [Fr.,—O.Fr *jogleor*—L *joculātor*; cf **juggler.**]

jonquil *jong'kwil*, *n.* a name given to certain species of narcissus with rush-like leaves. [Fr *jonquille*—L *juncus*, a rush.]

jorum *jōr'əm, jor'*, *n.* a large drinking-bowl a great drink. [Poss from *Joram* in 2 Sam. viii 10]

josh *josh*, *v.t* to ridicule: to tease —*n* a hoax: a derisive jest: a fool.—*n* **josh'er.**

joss *jos*, *n.* a Chinese idol: luck: fate.—*n* **joss'er** a clergyman (*Austr*): a fellow (*slang*): a blunderer (*slang*) —**joss'-house** a temple; **joss'-stick** a stick of gum which gives off a perfume when burned, used as incense in India, China, etc [Port *deos*, god—L *deus.*]

jostle *jos'l*, **justle** *jus'l*, *vs.t.* and *vs i.* to shake or jar by collision. to hustle: to elbow —*ns* an act of jostling. —*ns.* **jos'tlement, jos'tling.** [Freq. of **joust, just.**]

jot *jot*, *n.* an iota, a whit, a tittle —*v.t.* to set down briefly· to make a memorandum of—*pr.p.* **jott'ing;** *pa.t* and *pa.p.* **jott'ed.**—*ns* **jott'er** one who jots a book or pad for rough notes, **jott'ing** a memorandum· a rough note [L. *iōta* (read as *jōta*)—Gr *iōta*, the smallest letter in the alphabet, equivalent to *i*; *Heb yōd.*]

jota *hhō'ta*, *n.* a Spanish dance in triple time [Sp]

joule *jōōl*, *n* orig. unit of energy, now of energy, work and heat in the MKS and SI systems, equal to work done when a force of 1 newton advances its point of application 1 metre (1 joule = 10⁷ ergs) [After the physicist J P *Joule* 1818–89).]

jounce *jowns*, *v.t* and *v i* to jolt, shake

jour *zhōōr* (Fr.) *n* a day —**jour de fête** (*də fet*) a feast day, esp a saint's day

journal¹ *jûr'nəl*, *n* a daily register or diary a book containing a record of each day's transactions: a newspaper published daily (or otherwise) a magazine. the transactions of any society —*n* **journalese'**

the jargon of bad journalism —v.t **jour'nalise, -ize** to write for or in a journal —v t to enter in a journal —ns **journ'alism** the profession of conducting or writing for public journals writing of fleeting interest or hasty character, **jour'nalist** one who writes for or conducts a newspaper or magazine: one who keeps a journal —adj **journalist'ic.** [Fr ,—L diurnális, see **diurnal.**]

journal² jûr'nal, (mech) n that part of a shaft or axle which rests in the bearings —v t to provide with or fix as a journal —**jour'nal-box** a box or bearing for a journal

journey jûr'ni, n any travel· tour excursion movement from end to end of a fixed course —pl **jour'neys.**—v t **jour'ney** to travel —pr p **jour'neying;** pa.t and pa p **jour'neyed** (-nid) —n. **jour'neyer.**—**jour'neyman** one who works by the day: any hired workman one whose apprenticeship is completed [Fr .journée—jour, a day—L diurnus]

joust, just just (joost and jowst are recent pronunciations due to the spelling), n the encounter of two knights on horseback at a tournament —v t to tilt [O Fr. juste, jouste, joste—L juxtā, nigh to]

Jove jōv, n another name for the god Jupiter.—adj **jovial** (jō'vi-əl) joyous full of jollity and geniality (cap) of Jupiter· (cap) influenced by Jupiter —ns **joviality** (-al'i-ti), **jō'vialness.**—adv **jō'vially.**—adj **Jō'vian** of the god, or the planet, Jupiter —**by Jove** an exlamation of surprise, admiration, etc [L Jovis (in the nom. usu Juppiter, Jupiter), the god Jove or Jupiter, or the planet Jupiter, an auspicious star]

jovial, Jovian. See Jove.

jowl jowl, n. the jaw the cheek a pendulous double chin a dewlap: a head —adj **jowled.**

joy joi, n intense gladness· rapture mirth. a cause of joy a beloved one —v t to rejoice to be glad to exult —v t to give joy to —pr p **joy'ing;** pa t. and pa p. **joyed.**—adj **joy'ful** full of joy feeling, expressing, or giving joy —adv **joy'fully.**—n **joy'-fulness.**—adj **joy'less** without joy not giving joy —adv **joy'lessly.**—n **joy'lessness.** adj **joy'ous** joyful —adv **joy'ously.**—n **joy'ousness.**—**joy'-ride** (slang) a pleasure-drive, esp reckless or surreptitious, often in a stolen car; **joy'-rider; joy'-riding; joy'-stick** (slang) the control-lever of an aeroplane — **no joy** (slang) no news, reply, information, luck [Fr. joie (cf. It gioja)—L gaudium.]

jubate joo'bāt, (zool , etc) adj maned. [L. jubātus —juba, mane]

jubbah joob'ə, jub'ə, n a long loose outer garment worn by Muslims. [Ar jubbah]

jube joob A coll. shortening of **jujube.**

jubilant joo'bi-lənt, adj shouting for joy: uttering songs of triumph: rejoicing —ns **ju'bilance, ju'bilancy** exultation.—adv **ju'bilantly.**—v t **ju'bilate** to exult, rejoice —ns **jubilate** (joo-bi-lā'tē, yoo-bi-la'te) the third Sunday after Easter: also the 100th Psalm, **jubila'tion** a shouting for joy the declaration of triumph: rejoicing [L jūbilāre, to shout for joy]

jubilee joo'bi-lē, n among the Jews, every fiftieth year, a year of release of slaves, cancelling of debts, return of property to its former owners, proclaimed by the sound of a trumpet the celebration of a fiftieth anniversary—e.g of a king's accession, a bishop's conse cration, etc · in the R C. Church, a year (every twenty-fifth—ordinary jubilee) of indulgence for pilgrims and others, an extraordinary jubilee being specially appointed by the Pope any season or condition of great joy and festivity. joyful shouting exultant joy.—**silver, golden, diamond jubilee** respectively a twenty-fifth, fiftieth, sixtieth anniversary [Fr jubilé—L. jūbilaeus—Heb yōbēl, a ram, ram's horn]

Judaean, Judean joo-de'ən, adj of Judaea or the Jews —n a native of Judaea a Jew [L Judaea]

Judaic, -al joo-dā'ik, -əl, adjs pertaining to the Jews — adv. **Juda'ically.**—n **Judáisa'tion, -z-.**—v t **Ju'daise, -ize** to conform to, adopt, or practise Jewish customs or Judaism —ns **Ju'daiser, -z-; Ju'daism** the doctrines and rites of the Jews conformity to the Jewish rites, **Ju'daist** one who holds the doctrines of Judaism —adj. **Judaist'ic.**—adv. **Judaist'ically.** [L Jūdaicus—Jūda, Judah, a son of Israel]

Judas joo'dəs, n a traitor. (also without cap) a Judashole used attributively, as in Judas goat, denoting an animal or bird used to lure' others.—**Ju'das-hole, Ju'das-window** (also without caps.) a spy-hole in a door, etc , the **Ju'das-kiss** any act of treachery under the guise of kindness (Matt xxvi 48, 49) [Judas Iscariot]

judder jud'ər, n a vibratory effect in singing produced by alternations of greater or less intensity of sound. aircraft or other vibration —Also v t [Prob **jar'** and **shudder.**]

judge juj, v t to exercise the office of judge: to point out or declare what is just or law to try and decide questions of law or guiltiness, etc to pass sentence to compare facts to determine the truth to form or pass an opinion to distinguish —v t to hear and determine authoritatively to sit in judgment on to pronounce on the guilt or innocence of: to sentence to decide the merits of. to be censorious towards to condemn (B) to decide to award to estimate. to form an opinion on to conclude to consider (to be) —n one who judges. one appointed to hear and settle causes, and to try accused persons one chosen to award prizes, to decide doubtful or disputed points in a competition, etc. an arbitrator· one who can decide upon the merit of anything one capable of discriminating well (cap , pl) title of 7th book of the O T — ns **judge'ship** the office of a judge, **judg'ment** (also **judge'ment**) act of judging. the comparing of ideas to elicit truth faculty by which this is done, the reason. opinion formed discrimination good taste sentence· condemnation doom a misfortune regarded as sent by Providence in punishment —**judge'-ad'vocate** the crown-prosecutor at a court-martial, **Judges' Rules** in English law, a system of rules governing the behaviour of the police towards suspects, e g the cautioning of a person about to be charged, **judg'ment-day** the day of final judgment on mankind, **judg'ment-seat** the seat or bench in a court from which judgment is pronounced —**judgment of Solomon** a judgment intended to call the bluff of the false claimant—like that of Solomon in 1 Kings iii 16–28, **judgment reserved** decision delayed after the close of a trial [A Fr juger—L jūdicāre—jūs, law, and dicēre, to say, to declare]

judicature joo'di-kə-chər, n power of dispensing justice by legal trial. jurisdiction the office of judge· the body of judges a court. a system of courts —adj **ju'dicable** that may be judged or tried.—n. **judica'tion** judgment —adj **ju'dicative** having power to judge —ns **ju'dicator** one who judges, **ju'dicatory** (-kə-tər-i) judicature: a court —adj pertaining to a judge distributing justice [L jūdicāre, -ātum, to judge]

judicial joo-dish'əl, adj pertaining to a judge or court of justice established by statute arising from process of law of the nature of judgment judge-like, impartial critical —adj **judic'ially.**—**judicial separation** the separation of two married persons by order of the Divorce Court [L jūdiciālis—jūdicium]

judiciary joo-dish'ər-i, -i-ər-i, adj pertaining to judgment, judges, or courts of law —n a body of judges a system of courts [L jūdiciārius]

judicious jōō-dish'əs, adj. according to sound judgment: possessing sound judgment: discreet.—adv. **judic'iously**.—n. **judic'iousness**. [Fr. judicieux—L. jūdicium.]

judo jōō'dō, n. a modern variety of ju-jitsu.—n. **judogi** (jōō'dō-gi or -dō'gi) the costume (jacket and trousers) worn by a **ju'dōist** or **judoka** (jōō'dō-kə or -dō'kə), a person who practises, or is expert in, judo. [Jap. ju, gentleness, do, way.]

Judy jōō'di, n. Punch's wife in the puppet-show: (without cap.) a girl (dial. or slang). [From the name Judith.]

jug[1] jug, n. a vessel with a handle and a spout or lip for pouring liquids: a jugful.—v.t. to boil or stew as in a closed jar:—pr.p. **jugg'ing**; pa.t. and pa.p. **jugged**.—n. **jug'ful** as much as a jug will hold:—pl. **jug'fuls**.—**jugged hare** hare cut in pieces and stewed with wine and other seasoning.

jug[2] jug, (slang) n. prison.

jugate jōō'gāt, adj. paired (bot.): having the leaflets in pairs (bot.): joined side by side or overlapping. [L. jugāre, -ātum, to join—jugum, a yoke.]

Jugendstil yōō'gənd-shtēl, n. the German term for art nouveau. [Ger. Jugend, youth (the name of a magazine first appearing in 1896), Stil, style.]

Juggernaut jug'ər-not, ns. an incarnation of Vishnu, beneath the car of whose idol at Puri devotees were supposed by Europeans to immolate themselves: hence, any relentless destroying force or object of devotion and sacrifice: (without cap.) a very large lorry. [Sans. Jagannātha, lord of the world.]

juggins jug'inz, (slang) n. a simpleton.

juggle jug'l, v.i. to amuse by sleight-of-hand, conjure —now usu. to manipulate balls or other objects with great dexterity (also fig.): to practise artifice or imposture: to tamper or manipulate.—v.t. to transform, render, put by jugglery.—n. a trick by sleight-of-hand: an imposture.—ns. **jugg'ler**; **jugg'lery** (-lə-ri) art or act of a juggler: legerdemain: trickery. —n. and adj. **jugg'ling**.—adv. **jugg'lingly** in a deceptive manner. [O.Fr. jogler—L. joculārī, to jest—jocus, a jest.]

Jugoslav. Same as Yugoslav.

jugular jug', jōōg'ū-lər, adj. pertaining to the neck.—n one of the large veins on each side of the neck.—v.t. **jug'ulate** to cut the throat of: to strangle, check by drastic means (fig.). [L. jugulum, the collar-bone —jungēre, to join.]

juice jōōs, n. the sap of vegetables: the fluid part of animal bodies: interesting quality: piquancy: electric current, petrol vapour, or other source of power (slang).—adj. **juice'less**.—ns. **juic'er** (esp. U.S.) a juice extractor; **juic'iness**.—adj. **juic'y**.—**juice extractor** a kitchen device for extracting the juice from fruit, etc.—**step on the juice** (slang) to accelerate a motor-car. [Fr. jus, broth, lit. mixture.]

ju-jitsu, **jiu-jitsu** jōō-jit'sōō, n. a system of fighting barehanded developed by the samurai in Japan: a sport founded on it. [Jap. jū-jutsu.]

ju-ju, juju jōō'jōō, n. an object of superstitious worship in West Africa: a fetish or charm. [App. Fr. joujou, a toy.]

jujube jōō'jōōb, n. a spiny shrub or small tree (Zizyphus) of the buckthorn family: its fruit, which is dried as a sweetmeat: a lozenge made of sugar and gum in imitation of the fruit. [Fr. jujube or L.L. jujuba— Gr. zizyphon.]

juke jōōk (slang) v.i. to dance.—**juke'-box** a slot machine that plays gramophone records; **juke'-joint** a resort for dancing and drinking. [Gullah juke, disorderly—W. African dzug, to lead a careless life.]

julep jōō'ləp, n. a sweet drink, often medicated: an American drink of spirits, sugar, ice, and mint (also mint'-julep). [Fr.,—Sp julepe—Ar. julāb—Pers. gulāb—gul, rose, āb, water.]

Julian jōōl'yən, adj. pertaining to Julius Caesar (100–44 B.C.).

julienne jōō-li-en', zhu-lyen, n. a clear soup, with shredded herbs: any foodstuff which has been shredded. [Fr. name.]

July jōō-lī', jōō'li, n. the seventh month of the year [L. Jūlius, from Julius Caesar, who was born in it.]

jumble jum'bl, v.t. to mix confusedly: to throw together without order: to shake up, jolt —v i. to be mixed together confusedly: to be agitated: to flounder.—n. a confused mixture: confusion: things sold at a jumble-sale: jolting.—n. **jum'bler**.—adv **jum'blingly** in a confused or jumbled manner —adj **jum'bly**.—**jum'ble-sale** a sale of miscellaneous articles, rubbish, etc., often for charity.

jumbo jum'bō, n. anything very big of its kind: an elephant (after a famous large one so named): a jumbo jet:—pl. **jum'bos**.—adj. huge: colossal.—**jumbo jet** a large jet airliner. [Prob. mumbo-jumbo.]

jumbuck jum'buk, (Austr.) n. a sheep. [Aboriginal.]

jump jump, v.i. to spring or bound: to move suddenly to bounce: to rise suddenly: to pass discontinuously: to throb: to agree, coincide (with).—v.t to cause or help to leap: to toss: to leap over, from, or on to: to skip over: to spring or start, as game: to appropriate, as when the owner has failed to satisfy conditions or has abandoned his claim: to attack (slang).—n act of jumping: a bound: an obstacle to be jumped over: height or distance jumped: a sudden rise or movement: a start: (in pl.) convulsive movements, chorea, delirium tremens, or the like: a bounce: a discontinuity —n. **jump'er**.—adv. **jump'ily**.—n. **jump'iness**.—adj **jump'y** nervy, inclined to start.—adj **jumped'-up** (coll.) upstart.—**jump'ing-bean** the seed of a Mexican plant (Sebastiania), which an enclosed larva causes to move or jump; **jump'ing-deer** the black-tailed American deer; **jump'ing-jack** a toy figure whose limbs can be moved by pulling a string; **jump'-jet** a fighter plane able to land and take off vertically, **jump leads** two electrical cables for supplying power to start a car from another battery; **jump'-off** (U.S.) the start: starting-place: see **jump off** below; **jump'-seat** a movable carriage-seat: a folding seat; **jump suit** a one-piece, trouser and jacket or blouse, garment for either sex.—**jump at** to accept with eagerness; **jump down someone's throat** to assail someone with violent rating, **jumping-off place** the terminus of a route: the point where one sets forth into the wilds, the unknown, etc , **jump off** in showjumping, to compete in another, more difficult round, when two or more competitors have an equal score after the first (n. **jump'-off**); **jump on** to jump so as to come down heavily upon: to censure promptly and vigorously; **jump (one's) bail** to abscond, forfeiting one's bail; **jump ship** (coll.) (of a sailor) to leave one's ship while still officially employed, in service, etc.; **jump start** to start a car by pushing it and engaging the gears while it is moving (n. **jump'-start**; also **bump start**); **jump the gun** (i.e. the starting-gun in a race) to get off one's mark too soon, act prematurely, take an unfair advantage; **jump the queue** to get ahead of one's turn (lit. and fig.); **jump to conclusions** to form inferences prematurely; **jump to it!** hurry! [Prob onomatopoeic.]

jump[2] jump, n. a short coat: (in pl.) stays: clothes.—n jump'er a knitted upper garment, originally one loose at the waist: a pinafore dress (U.S.). [Perh. from Fr. juppe, now jupe, a petticoat.]

junco jung'kō, n. a North American snow-bird:—pl junc'oes, junc'os. [Sp. junco—L. juncus, rush.]

junction jung'shən, jungk', n. a joining, a union or combination: place or point of union, esp. of railway lines.—**junction box** a casing for a junction of electrical wires. [L. *junctiō, -ōnis*; see **join**.]

juncture *jungk'chər, n.* a joining: a union: a critical or important point of time. [L. *junctūra*; see **join**.]

June *jōon, n.* the sixth month.—**June'berry** the fruit of the shad-bush. [L. *Jūnius.*]

Jungian *joong'i-ən, adj* of, according to, the theories of the Swiss psychologist, Carl Gustav *Jung* (1875–1961).

jungle *jung'gl, n.* originally waste ground: a dense tropical growth of thickets, brushwood, etc : dense tropical forest: a jumbled assemblage of large objects: a confusing mass of, e.g. regulations: a place or situation where there is ruthless competition, or cruel struggle for survival.—*adj.* **jung'ly.**—**jungle fever** a severe malarial fever; **jungle fowl** the wild parent of the barndoor fowl; **jungle juice** (*slang*) alcoholic liquor, esp. of poor quality, or home-made.—*adj.* **jun'gle-green** very dark green [Sans. *jāngala*, desert.]

junior *joon'yər, adj* younger: less advanced: of lower standing.—*n.* one younger, less advanced, or of lower standing: a young person.—*adj.* **juniority** (*-ı-or'ı-tı*)—**junior common room** (*abbrev.* **J.C.R.**) in some universities, a common room for the use of students, as opposed to a senior common room, for the use of staff; **junior service** the Army. [L. *jūnior*, compar of *juvenis*, young.]

juniper *joo'nı-pər, n* an evergreen coniferous shrub whose berries are used in making gin. [L *jūniperus.*]

junk¹ *jungk, n.* a Chinese vessel, with high fore-castle and poop, sometimes large and three-masted. [Port. *junco*, app.—Javanese *djong.*]

junk² *jungk, n.* rubbish generally: nonsense (*fig.*): a narcotic.—*v.t.* to treat as junk: to discard, abandon as useless.—*n.* **junk'er, junk'ie, junk'y** a narcotics addict.—**junk'-dealer, junk'man** a dealer in junk; **junk food** food of little nutritional value, usu. easily available and quick to prepare; **junk mail** unsolicited advertising material and the like, delivered by the Post Office along with the regular mail; **junk'-shop** a place where junk is sold; **junk'-yard** a yard in which junk is stored or collected for sale.

junker *yoongk'ər, n.* a young German noble or squire. an overbearing, narrow-minded, reactionary aristocrat.—*ns.* **junk'erdom; junk'erism.** [Ger.,—*jung,* young. *Herr*, lord.]

junket *junk'ıt, n.* a rush-basket (*dial.*): a cream cheese: curds mixed with cream, sweetened and flavoured: a feast or merrymaking, a picnic, an outing, a spree—*v t* to feast, banquet, take part in a convivial entertainment or spree—*v.t.* to feast, regale, entertain—*pr.p* **junk'eting;** *pa.p.* **junk'eted.**—*n* (often in *pl*) **junk'eting** a merry feast or entertainment, picnicking [A.Fr *jonquette*, rush-basket—L *juncus*, a rush.]

junkie, junky. See **junk².**

Juno *joo'nō, n* in Roman mythology, the wife of Jupiter, identified with the Greek Hera, protectress of marriage and guardian of woman [L *Jūnō, -ōnis*]

junta *jun'tə, hoon'ta, n* a meeting, council: a Spanish grand council of state: a body of men joined or united for some secret intrigue a government formed by a usu small group following a coup d'état [Sp., L. *jungēre, junctum*, to join]

Jupiter *joo'pı-tər, n* the chief god among the Romans, the parallel of the Greek Zeus (also *Jove*): the largest and, next to Venus, the brightest of the planets [L *Jūpiter, Juppiter*, Father (*pater*) Jove]

Jurassic *joo-ras'ık,* (*geol*) *adj.* of the middle division of the Mesozoic rocks, well-developed in the *Jura*

Mountains.—*n.* the Jurassic period or system.—Also **Ju'ra.**

jurat¹ *joo'rat, n.* the official memorandum at the end of an affidavit, showing the time when and the person before whom it was sworn. [L. *jūrātum*, sworn—*jūrāre*, to swear.]

jurat² *joo'rat, n.* a sworn officer, as a magistrate. [Fr.,—L. *jūrāre, -ātum,* to swear.]

juridical *joo-rid'ık-əl,* **jurid'ic** *adjs.* relating to the distribution of justice: pertaining to a judge: used in courts of law.—*adv.* **jurid'ically.** [L *jūridicus—jūs, jūris*, law, *dīcere*, to declare.]

jurisconsult *joo'rıs-kon-sult', n* one who is consulted on the law: a lawyer who gives opinions on cases put to him: one learned in law [L *jūris cōnsultus—jūs, jūris*, law, *cōnsulēre, cōnsultus*, to consult]

jurisdiction *joo-ris-dık'shən, n.* the distribution of justice: legal authority: extent of power: district over which any authority extends.—*adjs* **jurisdic'tional, jurisdic'tive.** [L. *jūrisdictiō, -ōnis.*]

jurisprudence *joo-ris-proo'dəns, n.* the science or knowledge of law —*adj.* **jurispru'dent** learned in law —*n.* one who is learned in law. [L. *jūrisprūdentia—jūs, jūris*, law, *prūdentia,* knowledge.]

jurist *joo'rıst, n.* one who is versed in the science of law, esp. Roman or civil law: a student of law: a graduate in law: a lawyer (*U.S.*).—*adjs.* **jurist'ic, -al.**—*adv.* **jurist'ically.** [Fr. *juriste.*]

jury *joo'ri, n.* a body of persons sworn to declare the truth on evidence before them: a committee of adjudicators or examiners —*n.* **ju'ror** one who serves on a jury (also **ju'ryman, ju'rywoman;**—*pl.* **ju'rymen, ju'rywomen**).—**ju'ry-box** the place in which the jury sits during a trial [A.Fr *juree—jurer*—L. *jūrāre*, to swear.]

just¹ *just.* Same as **joust.**

just² *just, adj.* righteous (*B.*): fair. impartial: according to justice: due: in accordance with facts: well-grounded: accurately true: exact.—*adv* precisely: exactly: so much and no more: barely: only: merely: quite (*coll.*)—*adv.* **just'ly** in a just manner: equitably accurately: by right.—*n.* **just'ness** equity: fittingness: exactness —**just about** nearly: more or less; **just now** precisely at this moment: hence, a little while ago, or very soon; **just so** exactly, I agree: in a precise, neat manner. [Fr *juste,* or L. *jūstus—jūs,* law.]

justice *jus'tıs, n.* the quality of being just: integrity: impartiality: rightness: the awarding of what is due: a judge. a magistrate.—*ns.* **jus'ticer** a vindicator or administrator of justice; **jus'ticeship** the office or dignity of a justice or judge; **justiciar** (*-tish'ı-ər; hist*) an administrator of justice: a chief-justice, **justiciary** (*-tish'ı-ə-ri*) a judge· a chief-justice: jurisdiction of a justiciar or justiciary.—*adj.* pertaining to the administration of justice.—**chief'-jus'tice** in the Commonwealth, a judge presiding over a supreme court: in the U S., a judge who is chairman of a group of judges in a court, **do justice to** to give full advantage to: to treat fairly· to appreciate (a meal, etc.) fully (*coll.*), **European Court of Justice** an EEC institution whose function is to ensure that the laws embodied in the EEC treaties are observed, and to rule on alleged infringements, **Justice of the Peace** (abbrev **J.P.**) a local minor magistrate commissioned to keep the peace [Fr ,—L. *jūstitia*]

justify *jus'tı-fī, v t* to make just· to prove or show to be just or right. to vindicate to absolve: to adjust by spacing (*print.*)·—*pr.p* **jus'tifying;** *pa.t* and *pa p* **jus'tified.**—*adj* **jus'tifiable** (or *-fī'*) that may be justified or defended —*n.* **jus'tifiableness** (or *-fī'*) —*adv* **jus'tifiably** (or *-fī'*) —*n* **justification** (*jus-tı-fi-kā'shən*) act of justifying that which justifies· vindication: absolution: a plea of sufficient reason.—*adjs.* **jus'tificātive, justificatory** (*jus-tif'i-kə-tə-ri* or *jus'ti-fi-kā-tə-ri*, or *-kā'*) having power to justify.—*ns.* **jus'tificātor, jus'tifier** one who defends or vindicates: he who pardons and absolves from guilt and punishment.—**justifiable homicide** the killing of a person in self-defence, or to prevent an atrocious crime.— **justification by faith** the doctrine that men are justified by faith in Christ. [Fr. *justifier* and L. *jūstificāre*—*jūstus*, just, *facĕre*, to make.]

Justle. See Jostle.

jut *jut*, *n.* a projection.—*v.i.* to project:—*pr.p.* **jutt'ing;** *pa.t.* and *pa.p.* **jutt'ed.**—*adj.* **jutt'ing.**— *adv.* **jutt'ingly.** [A form of **jet²**.]

Jute *jōōt*, *n.* the fibre of *Corchorus capsularis* and *C. olitorius* (fam. Tiliaceae), plants of Bangladesh, etc., used for making sacks, mats, etc.: the plant itself.— Also *adj.* [Bengali *jhuṭo*—Sans. *jūṭa*, matted hair.]

juvenescent *jōō-vən-es'ənt*, *adj.* becoming youthful.— *n.* **juvenesc'ence.** [L. *juvenēscĕre*, to grow young.]

juvenile *jōō'və-nīl*, *adj.* young: pertaining or suited to youth or young people: having or retaining characteristics of youth: childish.—*n.* a young person: a book written for the young: an actor who plays youthful parts.—*n.* **ju'venileness.**—*n.pl.* **juvenilia** (*-il'yə*) writings or works of one's childhood or youth. —*n.* **juvenility** (*-il'i-ti*) juvenile character.—**juvenile court** a special court for the trial of children and young persons aged under seventeen; **juvenile delinquent, juvenile offender** a young law-breaker, in Britain under the age of seventeen. [L. *juventlis— juvenis*, young.]

juxtaposition *juks-tə-pə-zish'ən*, *n.* a placing or being placed close together.—*v.t.* **jux'tapose** (or *-pōz'*) to place side by side.—*adj.* **juxtaposi'tional.** [L. *juxtā*, near, and **position, pose¹**.]

For other sounds see detailed chart of pronunciation.

K

K, k *kā, n.* the eleventh letter in our alphabet, derived from Greek kappa, representing a back voiceless stop, formed by raising the back of the tongue to the soft palate: in thermometry K stands for the Kelvin scale. often used as a symbol for a thousand (from **kilo-**): a unit of 1024 words, bytes or bits (*comput.*).

Kaaba *ka'ba, n.* the holy building at Mecca into which the Black Stone is built. [Ar. *ka'bah—ka'b*, cube.]

kabala. Same as **cabbala.**

Kabbala(h). Same as **cabbala.**

kabuki *ka-bōō-kē', n.* a popular Japanese dramatic form, historical, classical, eclectic, with music

Kabyle *ka-bīl', n.* one of a branch of the great Berber people of North Africa: a dialect of Berber [Fr ,— Ar. *qabā'il*, pl. of *qabīlah*, a tribe]

kachahri, kacheri *kuch'ə-rı, kuch-er'ı, n* an Indian magistrate's office or courthouse. [Hındı *kacahrī*]

kack-handed. See **cack-handed.**

Kaddish *kad'ısh, n.* a Jewish form of thanksgiving and prayer, used at funerals, etc. [Aramaic *qaddīsh.*]

kade. See **ked.**

kadi *ka'di, n.* Same as **cadi.**

Kaffir, Kaffer *kaf'ər, kuf'ər, n.* name applied to certain indigenous peoples of S. Africa including the Xhosa (*hist*). now often used derogatorily· any of the languages spoken by them (*hist.*)·' (*pl*) S. African mining shares.—Also *adj.*—**kaffir bread** the pith of S. African cycads (*Encephalartos*); **kaffir corn** sorghum. [**Kafir** (q.v.).]

kaffiyeh *kaf-ē'ye, n* a Bedouin shawl for the head.— Also **kuffi'yeh, kufi'ah, kufi'ya(h).** [Ar. *kaffiyah.*]

Kafir *kaf'ər, n* an infidel (*offensive*) a native of Kafiristan (in Afghanistan): a Kaffir [Ar *kāfir*, unbeliever]

Kafkaesque *kaf'kə-esk', adj.* in the style of, reminiscent of, the ideas, work, etc of the Czech novelist Franz Kafka (1883–1924), esp in his vision of man's isolated existence in a dehumanised world

kaftan. Same as **caftan.**

kagool, kagoul(e). See **cagoul(e).**

kai *kā'ē, kī, (N Zealand,* etc) *n* food.—*n* **kai'kai** food: feast.—*v.t* to eat [Maori]

kail. See **kale.**

kainite *kī'nīt, kā'nīt, kā'ın-īt, n.* hydrous magnesium sulphate with potassium chloride, found in salt deposits, used as a fertiliser. [Ger *Kaınıt*—Gr *kainos,* new, recent]

Kainozoic. Same as **Cainozoic.**

kaiser *kī'zər, n* an emperor, esp. a German Emperor.— *ns* **kai'serdom; kai'serism; kai'sership.—the Kaiser's war** the war of 1914–18 (Kaiser Wilhelm II). [Ger , —L *Caesar.*]

kaka *ka'kə, n.* a New Zealand parrot (*Nestor meridionalis*) —*n* **ka'kapo** the New Zealand owl-parrot, large-winged but almost flightless.—*pl* **ka'kapōs.** [Maori *kaka*, parrot, *po*, night.]

kakemono *kak-i-mō'nō, n* a Japanese wall-picture or calligraphic inscription on a roller:—*pl* **kakemō'nos.** [Jap *kake,* to hang, *mono*, thing]

kala-azar *ka'lä-a-zar', n* a tropical fever, characterised by bloodlessness, and ascribed to a protozoan parasite [Assamese *kālā*, black, *āzār*, disease]

kale, kail *kāl, n* a cabbage with open curled leaves cabbage generally broth of which kale is a chief

ingredient, and also dinner (*Scot.*).—*ns.* **kail'-pot'; kail'yard'** a cabbage-patch.—**Kailyard school** a set of Scottish sentimental story-writers. [Northern form of **cole.**]

kaleidoscope *kə-lī'də-skōp, n.* an optical toy in which one sees an ever-changing variety of beautiful colours and forms.—*adj.* **kaleidoscopic** (*-skop'ık*) pertaining to a kaleidoscope: showing constant change. [Gr. *kalos,* beautiful, *eıdos,* form, *skopeein,* to look.]

kalendar, kalends. Same as **calendar, calends.**

Kalevala *ka'le-và-la, n.* the great Finnish epic, pieced together from oral tradition by Dr. Elias Lonnrot in 1835–49. [Finnish *kaleva*, a hero, *-la,* denoting place.]

kali *kal'ı,* or *kā'lī, n.* the prickly saltwort or glasswort (*Salsola kalı*) —*ns* **kalinite** (*kal'ın-īt*) native potash alum; **kā'lium** potassium [Ar. *qili* as in root of **alkali.**]

Kalmia *kal'mı-ə, n* a genus of North American evergreen shrubs of the heath family, including the mountain laurel or calico-bush· (without *cap*) a shrub of the genus. [From Peter *Kalm*, pupil of Linnaeus]

Kalmuck *kal'muk, n* a member of a Mongolian race in China and Russia: their language —Also *adj.* [Turki and Russ]

kalong *ka'long, n.* a large fruit-bat. [Malay *kālong*]

kalpa *kal'pə, n.* a day of Brahma, a period of 4320 million years. [Sans , formation.]

kame *kām, n* a low irregular ridge like a cock's comb: an esker, a bank or ridge of gravel, sand, etc., associated with the glacial deposits of Scotland (*geol.*) [Northern form of **comb¹.**]

kamerad *kam-ər-ad', interj* comrade (said to have been a German form of surrender or appeal for quarter) — *v.i.* to surrender [Ger·,—Fr. *camarade,* comrade.]

kamikaze *ka-mı-ka'zē, n* (a Japanese airman, or plane, making) a suicidal attack [Jap , divine wind.]

kampong *kam'pong, kam-pong', n.* an enclosed space: a village. [Malay.]

kamseen, kamsin. Same as **khamsin.**

kanaka *kən-ak'a, kan'ə-ka, n* a South Sea Islander, esp an indentured or forced labourer [Hawaiian, a man.]

Kanarese *kan-ər-ēz', adj.* of Kanara in western India.— *n* one of the people thereof: their Dravidian language, now called *Kannada,* akin to Telugu

kandy *kan'di, n.* Same as **candy².**

kanga, khanga *kang'gə, n* in East Africa, a piece of cotton cloth, usually brightly decorated, wound around the body as a woman's dress. [Swahili.]

kangaroo *kang-gə-rōō', n* a large marsupial of Australia, with very long hind-legs and great power of leaping.—**kangaroo closure** the method of allowing the chairman to decide which clauses shall be discussed and which passed or leaped over; **kangaroo court** a court operated by a mob, by prisoners in jail, by any improperly constituted body· a tribunal before which a fair trial is impossible. a comic burlesque court, **kangaroo'-rat'** a North American rodent (*Dipodomys*) akin to the jerboa. [Supposed to be a native name]

Kannada *kun'ə-də, n* an important Dravidian language. [Kanarese, *Kannada*]

Kantian *kant'ı-ən, adj* pertaining to the German philosopher Immanuel *Kant* (1724–1804) or his philosophy

—*ns* **Kan'tianism, Kant'ism** the doctrines or philosophy of Kant, **Kant'ist** one who is a disciple or follower of Kant.

kaolin, kaoline *kā'ō-lın, n* China clay, esp. that composed of kaolinite.—*v t.* and *v ı.* **ka'olinise, -ize** to turn into kaolin.—*n* **ka'olinite** a hydrated aluminium silicate occurring in minute monoclinic flakes, a decomposition product of feldspar, etc. [From the mountain *Kao-ling* (high ridge) in China]

kaon *kā'on* A type of meson (q v.)

kapellmeister *kə-pel'mīs'tər, n* the director of an orchestra or choir. [Ger. *Kapelle*, chapel, orchestra, *Meister*, master]

kapok *kāp', kap'ok, n* very light, waterproof, oily fibre covering the seeds of a species of silk-cotton tree, used for stuffing pillows, life-belts, etc. [Malay *kāpoq*.]

kappa *kap'ə, n* the tenth (earlier eleventh) letter of the Greek alphabet (K, κ).

kaput, kaputt *kə-pŏŏt', adj (slang)* ruined: broken: smashed [Ger]

karabiner *ka-rə-bēn'ər, (mountaineering)n.* a steel link with a spring clip in one side. [Ger.]

karakul, caracul *kar'ə-kōōl, -kōōl', n* (often with cap.) an Asiatic breed of sheep: a fur prepared from the skin of very young lambs of the Karakul or Bukhara breed, or of kids: a cloth imitating it. [Russ *Kara Kul*, a lake near Bukhara]

karat. U.S. spelling of **carat.**

karate *ka-ra'tı, n* a Japanese combative sport using blows and kicks.—**karate chop** a sharp downward blow with the side of the hand.

karma *kur'mə, kar'mə, n* the conception (Buddhist, etc.) of the quality of actions, including both merit and demerit, determining the future condition of all sentient beings the theory of inevitable consequence generally· the result of the actions of a life —*adj.* **kar'mic.** [Sans *karma*, act.]

Karoo, Karroo *ka-rōō', n.* a high inland pastoral tableland (*S. Afr.*): a series of strata in South Africa of Permian and Trias age (*geol.*). [Believed to be of Hottentot origin.]

kaross *ka-ros', n.* a S African skin blanket. [Perh. a Hottentot modification of Du. *kuras*, cuirass.]

karri *kar'ē, n* a Western Australian gum-tree (*Eucalyptus diversicolor*): its red timber. [Native name.]

Karroo. See **Karoo.**

karst *kàrst, n.* rough limestone country with underground drainage. [From the *Karst* district, east of the Adriatic.]

kart *kart, n* go-kart (q.v.).—*n.* **kart'ing** go-kart racing.

karyokinesis *ka-rı-ō-kin-ē'sis, (biol) n.* mitosis. [Gr *karyon*, kernel, and *kinēsis*, movement]

karyoplasm *ka'rı-ō-plazm, n.* the protoplasm of a cell-nucleus [Gr *karyon*, kernel, and *plasma*, that which is formed]

kasba(h), casbah, *kaz'ba, n* a castle or fortress in a N. African town or the area round it, esp. in Algiers.

Kashmir. Same as **Cashmere** (which, without *cap* , is the usual English spelling when reference is to the fabric) [Region in north-west of Indian subcontinent.]

katabasis *kat-ab'ə-sıs, n.* a going down —*adj* **katabatic** (-*ə-bat'ik*) [Gr.]

katabolism, *kat-ab'ə-lızm, (biol.) n.* the disruptive processes of chemical change in organisms—destructive metabolism, opposed to *anabolism* —*adj* **katabolic** (*kat-ə-bol'ık*). [Gr *katabolē*—*kataballein*, to throw down—*kata*, down, *ballein*, to throw.]

katakana *kat-a-ka'nà, n* a Japanese syllabary [Jap.]

katathermometer *ka-tə-thər-mom'ı-tər, n* an alcohol thermometer for measuring the cooling power of the air. [Gr. *kata*, down, and **thermometer**.]

kation. See **cation.**

katydid *kā'tı-did, n* an American insect akin to the grasshopper. [Imit. of its note.]

katzenjammer *kat'sən-jam-ər, or -jam', n.* a hangover: a similar state of emotional distress (*fig.*): an uproar, clamour. [Ger., meaning 'cats' misery'.]

kauri *kow'ri*, or **kauri-pine,** *n* a splendid coniferous forest-tree of New Zealand, source of **kau'ri-gum,** a resin used in making varnish. [Maori.]

kava *ka'və, n.* a species of pepper (*Piper methysticum*): a narcotic drink prepared from its root and stem [Polynesian.]

kay. See **quay.**

kayak *kī'ak, n.* an Eskimo seal-skin canoe: a canvas, fibreglass, etc. canoe built in this style. [Eskimo]

kayo(e) *kā-ō' (slang).* Stands for **K.O.** (knockout (q.v.)) *n.* and *v t.:—pl.* **kayos', -oes'.**

kazoo *ka-zōō', n.* a would-be musical instrument, a tube with a strip of catgut, plastic, etc., that resonates to the voice. [Prob imit.]

kea *kā'a, kē'd, n* a New Zealand parrot that sometimes kills sheep. [Maori.]

kebab *kə-bab, ns.* (also used in *pl.*) small pieces of meat cooked with vegetables, etc , esp (from Turkish **shish kebab**) when on a skewer. [Ar. *kabab*.]

keblah. See **kiblah.**

keck *kek, v.ı.* to retch, feel loathing.—*n.* a retching. [Imit]

ked *ked,* **kade, kād, ns.** a sheep-tick.

kedge *kej, n.* a small anchor for keeping a ship steady, and for warping the ship.—*v.t.* to move by means of a kedge, to warp —*n* **kedg'er** a kedge.

kedgeree *kej'ə-rē, n* an Indian dish of rice, cooked with butter and dal, flavoured with spice, shredded onion, etc.· a similar European dish made with fish, rice, etc. [Hind. *khichrī*]

keek *kek, (Scot.) v.i.* to peep.—*n.* a peep.—*n.* **keek'er** one who peeps or spies: an eye: a black eye [M.E. *kyke*.]

keel[1] *kēl, n* the part of a ship extending along the bottom from stem to stern, and supporting the whole frame: a longitudinal member running along the under side of an airship's hull or gas-bag: any narrow prominent ridge.—*v.t.* or *v.ı.* to navigate: to turn keel upwards —*adj.* **keeled** having a ridge on the back.—*v.t* **keel'haul** to punish by hauling under the keel of a ship by ropes from the one side to the other: to rebuke severely.—**keel'hauling.—on an even keel** calm(ly); **keel over** to stagger, fall over. [O.N. *kjolr.*]

keel[2] *kel, n* a low flat-bottomed boat: a ship.—Also **keel'boat.**—*ns.* **keel'er, keel'man** one who works on a barge. [Du *kiel*, ship, prob.—O.E. *cēol*, ship.]

keelson *kel'sən, kēl', kelson kel'sən, ns.* a ship's inner keel, which binds the floor-timbers to the outer keel. [keel[1].]

keen[1] *kēn, adj.* eager. sharp, having a fine edge: piercing: acute of mind: penetrating: intense —*adv* **keen'ly.**—*n.* **keen'ness.—keen prices** very low prices. —**keen on** (*coll.*) devoted to: fond of: much interested in. very desirous of. [O E *cēne*, bold, fierce, keen.]

keen[2] *kēn, n.* a lamentation over the dead.—*v.ı.* to wail over the dead.—*n.* **keen'er** a professional mourner [Ir. *caoine*]

keep *kēp, v t* to tend to have the care of: to guard: to maintain. to manage, conduct, run: to attend to the making of records in: to retain: to retain as one's own: to have in one's custody: to have habitually in stock for sale· to support, supply with necessaries: to have in one's service. to remain in or on· to adhere to: to continue to follow or hold to: to continue to make. to maintain hold upon: to restrain from departure, to hold back· to prevent: to reserve: to preserve in a certain state: to observe. to celebrate: to conform to the requirements of: to fulfil —*v i* to remain to continue to be or go: to be or remain in a specified condition: to remain fresh or good: to last or endure: to continue: to refrain: to confine or restrict oneself:— *pr.p.* **keep'ing;** *pa.t.* and *pa.p.* **kept** (*kept*).—*n.* care (*arch.*): a charge: condition: that which keeps or protects: subsistence: food: the innermost and strongest part of a castle, the donjon: a stronghold.—*ns.* **keep'er** one who or that which keeps, in any sense: an attendant, esp. upon the insane, or upon animals in captivity: a custodian: a gamekeeper: the title of certain officials: a wicket-keeper: the socket that receives the bolt of a lock: the armature of a magnet: a guard-ring; **keep'ership** office of a keeper; **keep'ing** care: preservation: retention: observance: custody: charge: just proportion: harmonious consistency.—**keep'net** a cone-shaped net suspended in a river, etc , in which fish caught by anglers can be kept alive; **keep'sake** something given to be kept for the sake of the giver: an annual gift-book; **kept woman** a woman maintained financially by a man as his mistress.—**for keeps** as a permanent possession: for good: permanently; **how are you keeping?** how are you?; **keep at it** to persist in anything; **keep back** to withhold: to keep down, repress; **keep body and soul together** to maintain life; **keep down** to restrain: to repress: to remain low; **keep from** to abstain from: to remain away from; **keep in** to prevent from escaping: to confine in school after school hours: to conceal: to restrain; **keep in with** to maintain the confidence or friendship of someone, often with the suggestion of unworthy means; **keep off** to hinder or prevent from approaching or making an attack, etc.: to stay away or refrain from; **keep on** to continue; **keep on about** to continue talking about; **keep on at** to nag, badger (*coll.*); **keep one's countenance** to avoid showing one's emotions; **keep one's hand in** to retain one's skill by practice; **keep someone going in something** to keep someone supplied with something; **keep tab(s) on** to keep a check on, to keep account of; **keep time** to observe rhythm accurately, or along with others: to go accurately (as a clock); **keep to** to stick closely to: to confine oneself to; **keep under** to hold down in restraint; **keep up** to retain one's strength or spirit: to support, prevent from falling: to continue, to prevent from ceasing: to maintain in good condition: to continue to be in touch (with): to keep pace (with; also *fig.*, **as keep up with the Joneses** to keep on social equality with one's neighbours, e.g. by having possessions of like quality in like quantity); **keep wicket** to act as a wicket-keeper. [O.E. *cēpan*.]

kef *kāf, n.* a state of dreamy repose: something, as Indian hemp, smoked to produce this.—Also **kif** (*kif, kēf*). [Ar. *kaif*, pleasure.]

kefuffle. See **carfuffle.**

keg *keg, n.* a small cask: a metal cask in which beer is kept under gas pressure.—**keg beer** any of various types of beer kept in and served from pressurised kegs. [Earlier *cag*—O.N. *kaggi*.]

keir. See **kier.**

keloid, cheloid *kē'loid, n.* a hard growth of scar tissue in skin that has been injured.—*adj.* **keloid'al, cheloid'al.** [Gr. *chēlē,* claw.]

kelp *kelp, n.* any large brown seaweed, wrack: the calcined ashes of seaweed, a source of soda, iodine, etc. [M.E *culp.*]

kelpie, kelpy *kel'pi, n* a malignant water-sprite haunting fords (*Scot.*): a kind of collie (*Austr.*).

kelson. Same as **keelson.**

kelt *kelt, n.* a salmon, etc , that has just spawned

Kelt, Keltic. Same as **Celt, Celtic.**

Kelvin *kel'vin, adj.* applied to a thermometer scale with absolute zero for zero and centigrade degrees.— *n.* **kel'vin** (SI units) the unit of temperature (formerly

'degree Kelvin'). [Sir William Thomson, Lord *Kelvin* (1824–1907), physicist.]

kemp *kemp, n.* the coarse, rough hairs of wool: (in *pl.*) knotty hair that will not felt. [O.N. *kampr,* beard.]

ken *ken, v.t.* to know (mainly *Scot.*):—*pa.t.* and *pa.p.* **kenned, kent.**—*n.* range of sight or knowledge.—*ns.* **kenn'er; kenn'ing** range of vision: a periphrastic formula in Old Norse or other old Germanic poetry. —*adj.* **kent** known.—**beyond one's ken** outside the limits of one's knowledge. [O.E. *cennan,* causative of *cunnan.*]

kendo *ken'dō,* or *-dō', n.* Japanese art of swordsmanship practised with bamboo staves, in 18th-cent.-style armour, and observing strict ritual. [Jap. *kendō.*]

kennel *ken'l, n.* a house for dogs: a pack of hounds: (in *pl.*) an establishment where dogs are boarded. —*v.t.* to put or keep in a kennel.—*v.i.* to live in a kennel:—*pr.p.* **kenn'elling;** *pa.t.* and *pa.p.* **kenn'elled.** —**kenn'el-maid, kenn'el-man** an attendant upon dogs. [From an O.N. Fr. form answering to Fr. *chenil*—L. *canīle—canis,* a dog.]

kenning. See **ken.**

kenspeckle *ken'spek-l,* (*Scot.* and *dial.*) *adj.* easily recognised: conspicuous.—Also **ken'speck.** [Appar. O.N. *kennispeki,* power of recognition.]

kent. See **ken.**

Kentish *kent'ish, adj.* of *Kent.*—*n.* the dialect of Kent, Essex, etc.

kentledge *kent'lij, n.* pig-iron in a ship's hold for ballast.

kephalic *ki-fal'ik.* Same as **cephalic.**

kepi *kāp'ē, n.* a flat-topped forage-cap with a straight peak. [Fr. *képi.*]

kept. *pa.t.* and *pa.p.* of **keep.**

keramic *ki-ram'ik.* Same as **ceramic.**

keratin *ker'ə-tin, n.* a nitrogenous compound, the essential ingredient of horny tissue, as of horns, nails, etc.—*v.t., v.i.* **ker'atinise, -ize** to make or become horny.—*n.* **keratinisa'tion, -z-** formation of keratin: becoming horny.—*adj.* **keratinous** (*kə-rat'i-nəs*) horny.—*n.* **kerati'tis** inflammation of the cornea.— *adjs.* **keratogenous** (*-oj'i-nəs*) producing horn or keratin; **ker'atoid** resembling horn or keratin.—*n.* **ker'-atoplasty** grafting of part of a healthy cornea to replace a piece made opaque by disease, etc.—*adj.* **ker'atose** (esp. of certain sponges) having a horny skeleton.—*n.* **keratō'sis** a horny growth on or over the skin, e.g. a wart: a skin condition producing this. [Gr. *keras, -atos,* a horn.]

kerb, also (chiefly *U.S.*) **curb** (q.v.), *kûrb, n.* a hearth fender: a kerbstone, pavement edge: a kerb market: an edging or margin of various kinds.—**kerb'-crawling** driving along slowly with the intention of enticing people into one's car; **kerb drill** the safe procedure for crossing a road adopted by some pedestrians; **kerb'-merchant, -trader, -vendor** one who sells on or beside the pavement; **kerb'side** (also *adj.*); **kerb'stone** a stone placed edgeways as an edging to a path or pavement [Fr. *courbe*—L. *curvus,* bent.]

kerchief *kûr'chif, n.* a square piece of cloth worn to cover the head, neck, etc.: a handkerchief. [O.Fr. *cuevrechief* (Fr *couvrechef*)—*covrir,* to cover, *chef,* the head.]

kerf *kûrf, n.* a cut: a notch: the groove made by a saw: the place where a cut is made. [O.E. *cyrf,* a cut.]

kermes *kûr'mēz, n.* the female bodies of a coccus insect used as a red dyestuff: the oak (**kermes oak;** *Quercus coccifera*) on which they breed. [Pers. and Ar. *qirmiz.*]

kermis *kûr'mis, n.* a fair in the Low Countries: in America, an indoor fair.—Also **ker'mess, kir'mess.** [Du *kermis*—*kerk,* church, *mis,* mass]

kern *kûrn*, (*print.*) *n.* part of a type that projects beyond the body and rests on an adjoining letter. [Fr. *carne*, a projecting angle—L. *cardō*, *-ınıs*.]

kern(e) *kûrn*, *n.* an Irish foot-soldier: a boor.—*adj.* **ker'nish.** [From Ir.—Old Gael.]

kernel *kûr'nl*, *n.* a seed within a hard shell: the edible part of a nut: a nucleus: the important part of anything. [O.E. *cyrnel—corn*, grain, and dim. suffix *-el*.]

kerosine *ker'ō-sēn*, *n* paraffin-oil obtained from shale or by distillation of petroleum This spelling is now used commercially; **kerosene** is the older spelling. [Gr *kēros*, wax]

kersey *kûr'zı*, *n.* a coarse woollen cloth. [Perh. from *Kersey* in Suffolk.]

kerseymere *kûr'zı-mēr*, or *-mēr'*, *n.* twilled cloth of the finest wools [For **cashmere**.]

kerygma *ka-rig'ma*, *n.* (preaching of) the Christian gospel, esp. in the way of the early Church.—*adj.* **kerygmat'ic.** [Gr. *kērygma*, proclamation, preaching.]

kestrel *kes'trəl*, *n.* a small species of falcon. [O.Fr. *cresserelle*.]

keta *kē'ta*, *n.* a Pacific salmon, the dog-salmon. [Russ *keta*.]

ketch *kech*, *n.* a small two-masted vessel. [Earlier *catch*, perh. from the vb. **catch.**]

ketchup *kech'əp*, *n.* a sauce made from tomatoes, mushrooms, etc —Also **catch'up, cat'sup.** [Malay *kēchap*, perh. from Chinese.]

ketone *kē'tōn*, *n.* an organic compound consisting of a carbonyl group united to two like or unlike alkyl radicals.—*n.* **ketō'sis** the excessive formation in the body of ketone or acetone bodies, due to incomplete oxidation of fats—occurs in e.g. diabetes. [Ger. *Keton*, from *Aketon*, acetone]

kettle *ket'l*, *n.* a vessel for heating or boiling liquids, esp. one with a spout and a lid for domestic use: a cauldron.—*n.* **kett'leful.**—**kett'ledrum** a musical instrument, consisting of a hollow metal hemisphere with a parchment head, tuned by screws; **kett'le-drumm'er; kett'le-holder** a little cloth, etc , for lifting a hot kettle.—**a kettle of fish** (ironically—often **a pretty kettle of fish**) an awkward mess. [O.E *cetel*.]

kewpie doll *kū'pı dol*, a plump baby doll with a top-knot of hair. [**Cupid.**]

key¹ *kē*, *n.* an instrument for locking or unlocking, winding up, turning, tuning, tightening or loosening: a wedge: a piece inserted to prevent relative motion. a tapered piece of metal for fixing the boss of a wheel, etc : to a shaft a spanner: the middle stone of an arch: a piece of wood let into another piece crosswise to prevent warping: in musical instruments, a lever or piston-end pressed to produce the sound required: a similar part in other instruments for other purposes, as in a typewriter or calculating machine: a lever to close or break an electrical circuit: a dry winged fruit, as of ash or maple, often hanging with others in bunches: a fret pattern: preparation of a surface to take plaster, glue, or the like: a system of tones definitely related to one another in a scale: that which gives command of anything or upon which success turns: a scheme or diagram of explanation or identification: a set of answers to problems: a crib translation: that which leads to the solution of a problem: a leading principle: general tone of voice, emotion, morals, etc.—*v.t* to lock or fasten with a key: to furnish with a key: to give an advertisement a feature that will enable replies to it to be identified: to mark the position on the layout of something to be printed, using symbols (*print.*): to attune (with *to*): to stimulate (to a state of nervous tension and excitement), raise (in pitch or standard), increase (with *up*).—*adj.* vital essential: crucial.—*adjs.* **keyed** furnished with a key or keys: set to a particular key: in a state of tension or readiness; **key'less** without a key: not requiring a key.—**key'board** a range of keys or levers in a musical or other instrument: (in *pl.*) usu. in pop groups, musical instruments, esp. electronic, incorporating keyboards; **key'-fruit** a winged fruit; **key'-hole** the hole in which a key of a lock is inserted; **key industry** an industry indispensable to others and essential to national economic welfare and independence; **key man** an indispensable worker, essential to the continued conduct of a business, etc.; **key money** a premium, fine, or sum additional to rent, demanded for the grant, renewal, or continuance of a tenancy; **key'note** the fundamental note or tonic: any central principle or controlling thought —*adj.* of fundamental importance.—**key pad** a device incorporating push-button controls by which a television, etc., can be operated; **key'-ring** a ring for holding a bunch of keys; **key signature** the indication of key by marking sharps, flats or naturals where the key changes or at the beginning of a line; **key'stone** the stone at the apex of an arch: the chief element or consummation: that on which all else depends; **key'-stroke** the operation of a key on a typewriter or other machine using keys.—**have the key of the street** (*coll.*) to be locked out: to be homeless; **key in, into** (*comput*) to transfer, store, etc. data by operating a keyboard. [O.E. *cæg*.]

key² *kē*, *n.* a low island or reef.—Also **cay.** [Sp. *cayo*.]

Keys *kēz*, *n.pl.* in full **House of Keys**, the lower house of the Manx Court of Tynwald. [App. **key¹**, not Manx *kiare-as-feed*, four-and-twenty.]

khaddar *kud'ər*, *n.* in India, hand-spun, hand-woven cloth.—Also **khadi.** [Hind. *khâdar*, *khâdî*.]

khaki *ka'kı*, *adj.* dust-coloured, dull brownish or greenish yellow.—*n.* a light drab cloth used for military uniforms. [Urdu and Pers. *khâkî*, dusty.]

khalif. See **caliph.**—*ns.* **khalifa, khalifah** (*ka-lē'fa*) a caliph, **khalifat, khalifate** (*kâl'ı-fat*, *-fât*) the caliphate. [Ar. *khalīfah.*]

khamsin *kam'sın*, *-sēn'*, *n.* a hot S. or S.E. wind in Egypt, blowing for about fifty days from mid-March. —Also **kamseen', kam'sin.** [Ar. *khamsīn—khamsūn*, fifty.]

khan¹ *kan*, *n.* an Eastern inn, a caravanserai. [Ar. *khan.*]

khan² *kan*, *n.* in N. Asia, a prince or chief: in Persia, a governor. [Turkı (and thence Pers.) *khân*, lord or prince.]

khanga. See **kanga.**

khedive *ke-dēv'*, *n.* the title (1867–1914) of the viceroy of Egypt.—*ns.* **khedi'va** his wife; **khedi'v(i)ate** the khedive's office or territory.—*adjs.* **khedi'v(i)al.** [Fr. *khédive*—Turk. *khidīv*, *hudīv*—Pers. *khidīw*, prince]

Khmer *kmûr*, *n.* a member of a people inhabiting Cambodia: their language, the official language of Cambodia.—Also *adj.*

khotbah, khotbeh. See **khutbah.**

khutbah *kōōt'ba*, *n.* a Muslim prayer and sermon delivered in the mosques on Fridays.—Also **khot'bah, khot'beh.** [Ar.]

kiang, kyang, *kyang, ki-ang'*, *n.* a Tibetan wild ass. [Tibetan *rkyang.*]

kibble¹ *kıb'l*, *n.* the bucket of a draw-well.—**kibb'le-chain** the chain for drawing up a bucket. [Cf. Ger. *Kubel.*]

kibble² *kıb'l*, *v.t.* to grind cereal, etc., fairly coarsely.

kibbutz *kē-bōōts'*, *n.* a Jewish communal agricultural settlement in Israel:—*pl.* **kibbutzim** (*ke̅-bōo̅ts-ēm'*). —*n.* **kibbutz'nik** a person who lives and works on a kibbutz. [Heb.]

kibe *kīb, n.* chilblain, esp. on heel. [Cf. W. *cibwst.*]

kibitzer *kib'it-sər, n.* onlooker (at cards, etc.) who gives unwanted advice.—*v.i.* **kib'itz.** [Yiddish.]

kiblah *kib'lä, n.* the point toward which Muslims turn in prayer.—Also **keb'lah.** [Ar. *qiblah.*]

kibosh, kybosh *kī'bosh, ki-bosh', (coll.) n.* nonsense, rot.—*v.t.* to dispose of finally.—**put the kibosh on** to kibosh.

kick *kik, v.t.* to hit with the foot: to put or drive by blows with the foot: to start or work by foot on a pedal: to achieve by a kick or kicking: to free oneself from (e.g. a habit) (*slang*).—*v.i.* to thrust out the foot with violence: to show opposition or resistance: to recoil violently: to jerk violently: to move as if kicked: to be exposed to kicking, lie around (often with *about*).—*n.* a blow or fling with the foot: the recoil of a gun: a jerk: kicking power: resistance: resilience: stimulus, pungency (*coll.*): thrill (*coll.*): dismissal (esp. with *the*; *slang*): an enthusiastic but short-lived interest: a phase of such interest.—*adj.* **kick'able.**—*n.* **kick'er** one who kicks, esp. a horse.— **kick'back** part of a sum received paid to another by confidential agreement for favours past or to come: money paid in return for protection: a strong reaction (*fig.*); **kick'down** a method of changing gear in a car with automatic gear transmission, by pressing the accelerator pedal right down; **kick'-off** the first kick in a game of football; **kick pleat** a pleat at the back of a narrow skirt from knee-level to hem, for greater ease in walking; **kick'-start** the starting of an engine by a treadle.—**for kicks** for thrills; **kick around** to move around from place to place; **kick out** (*coll.*) to eject with force: to dismiss; **kick over the traces** to throw off control; **kick the bucket** see **bucket**; **kick up a dust** or **row** to create a disturbance; **kick upstairs** to promote (usu. to a less active or less powerful position). [M.E. *kiken.*]

kickshaws *kik'shōz,* **kickshaw** *-shō, ns.* a trinket, a cheap, worthless article: a delicacy (*arch.*). [Fr. *quelque chose,* something.]

kid¹ *kid, n.* a young goat: extended to young antelope, etc.: a child or young person (*coll.*): leather of kidskin, or a substitute.—*adj.* made of kid leather or imitation kid leather.—*v.t.* and *v.i.* to bring forth (of a goat):—*pr.p.* **kidd'ing;** *pa.t.* and *pa.p.* **kidd'ed.**— *ns.* **kidd'y** dim. of kid:—*pl.* **kidd'ies; kiddy'wink, kidd'iewink, -ie** (*facet.*) extended forms of **kiddy,** a child; **kid'ling** a young kid.—**kid'-glove'** a glove of kid.—*adj.* as if done by one wearing kid-gloves: overnice, delicate.—**kid'-skin; kids' stuff** (*coll.*) something only suitable for children: something very easy. [O.N. *kith.*]

kid² *kid, (coll.) v.t.* and *v.i.* to hoax: to pretend, esp. banteringly: to tease.—*n.* a deception.—*ns.* **kidd'er;** **kidology** (*kid-ol'ə-ji; coll.*) the art of kidding, sometimes to gain a psychological advantage. [Perh. conn. with **kid¹**, a child.]

Kidderminster *kid'ər-min-stər, n.* a two-ply or ingrain carpet formerly made at *Kidderminster.*—Also *adj.*

kiddle *kid'l, n.* a stake-fence set in a stream for catching fish. [O.Fr. *quidel.*]

kiddy, etc. See **kid¹.**

kidnap *kid'nap, v.t.* to steal (a human being), often for ransom:—*pr.p.* **kid'napping;** *pa.t.* and *pa.p.* **kid'napped.**—*n.* an instance of this.—*n.* **kid'napper.** [**kid¹**, a child.]

kidney *kid'ni, n.* one of two flattened glands that secrete urine: temperament, humour, disposition— hence, sort or kind.—**kid'ney-bean** the French bean: a red variety of runner bean; **kidney machine** an apparatus used, in cases where the kidney functions badly, to remove by dialysis harmful substances from the blood; **kid'ney-stone** a hard deposit in the kidney. [M.E. *kidenei* (pl. *kideneiren*), perh. a compound of *ei* (pl. *eiren*), egg, confused sometimes with *nere*, kidney.]

kidology. See **kid².**

kie-kie *ke̅'ä-ke̅-ä, ke̅'ke̅, n.* a New Zealand high-climbing shrub (*Freycinetia banksii*). [Maori.]

kier, keir, *ke̅r, n.* a bleaching vat. [Cf. O.N. *ker,* tub.]

kieselguhr *ke̅'zl-gōo̅r, n.* diatomite. [Ger.,—*Kiesel,* flint, *Guhr,* fermentation.]

kif. See **kef.**

kike *kīk, (offensive slang) n.* and *adj.* Jew. [Possibly from the *-ki* ending of many E. European Jewish immigrants' names in U.S. at the end of the 19th cent.]

kilderkin *kil'dər-kin, n.* a small barrel: a liquid measure of 18 gallons. [Old Du. *kindeken, kinneken,* dim. of *kintal*—L.L. *quintāle,* quintal.]

kilerg *kil'ûrg, n.* a thousand ergs. [Gr. *chilioi,* thousand, **erg.**]

kill *kil, v.t.* to put to death, to slay: to deprive of life: to destroy: to nullify or neutralise, to render inactive, to weaken or dilute: to reject, discard, defeat: to fascinate, overcome: to spoil: to muffle or still: to exhaust: to cause severe pain: to consume completely (*coll.*).—*v.i.* to murder, slaughter.—*n.* an act or instance of killing, destroying, etc.: prey or game killed.—*n.* **kill'er** one who kills: one who murders readily or habitually: a slaughterer or butcher: an instrument for killing: a neutralising agent: the grampus or other ferocious delphinid (also **killer whale**).— *adj.* **kill'ing** depriving of life: destructive: deadly, irresistible: exhausting: fascinating: irresistibly funny (*coll.*).—*n.* slaughter: a severe handling.—**kill'joy** a spoil-sport.—*adj.* austere.—**in at the kill** (*fig.*) present at the culminating moment; **kill by inches** to kill gradually, as by torture; **kill off** to exterminate; **kill the fatted calf** to prepare an elaborate feast, etc., for a homecoming or welcome; **kill time** to occupy oneself with amusements, etc., in order to pass spare time or to relieve boredom; **kill two birds with one stone** to effect one thing by the way, or by the same means with which another thing is done; **make a killing** (*coll.*) to make a lot of money, a large profit; **to kill** (*coll.*) in an irresistible manner. [M.E. *killen* or *cullen.*]

killdeer *kil'dēr, n.* the largest North American ringplover.—Also **kill'dee.** [Imit.]

killick, killock *kil'ik, -ək, ns.* a small anchor: its fluke.

kiln *kiln, kil, n.* a large oven for drying, baking, or calcining corn, hops, bricks, pottery, limestone, etc. —*v.t.* to dry, fire, etc. in a kiln.—*v.t.* **kiln'-dry** to dry in a kiln:—*pa.p.* and *adj.* **kiln'-dried.**—**kiln'-hole** the mouth of a kiln. [O.E. *cyln, cylen*—L. *culīna,* a kitchen.]

kilo *ke̅l'ō, n.* a shortened form of **kilogram(me)** or sometimes of other word with the prefix **kilo-**:—*pl.* **kil'os.**

kilo- *kil'ə-, kil'ō-, pfx.* denoting 1000 times the unit to which it is attached, e.g. **kil'obar** = 1000 bars; **kil'obit** (*comput.*) 1024 bits; **kil'ocalorie** 1000 calories, used to measure energy content of food; **kil'ogram(me)** SI base unit of mass, the mass of a platinum-iridium cylinder at Paris, 2·205 lb; **kil'ogram-calorie** same as **kilocalorie; kil'ohertz** 1000 cycles of oscillation per second, used to measure frequency of sound and radio waves; **kil'ometre** (also *-om'-*) 1000 metres, 0·6214 or about ⅝ mile; **kil'oton** a measure of explosive force equivalent to that of 1000 tons of TNT; **kil'ovolt** 1000 volts; **kil'owatt** 1000 watts, the power dissipated by one bar of the average electric fire;

kil'owatt hour the energy consumed by a load of one kilowatt in one hour of use (3·6 megajoules), the unit by which electricity is charged to the consumer. [Gr. *chīlioi*, a thousand.]

kilt *kilt, n.* a man's short pleated skirt, usu. of tartan, forming part of Highland dress.—*v.t.* to tuck up (skirts): to pleat vertically.—*adj.* **kilt'ed** dressed in a kilt: tucked up: vertically pleated.—*n.* **kilt'y, kilt'ie** a wearer of a kilt. [Scand.]

kilter *kil'tər, n.* good condition.—**out of kilter** out of order, not functioning properly.

kimberlite *kim'bər-līt, n.* a mica-peridotite, an eruptive rock, the matrix of the diamonds found at *Kimberley* and elsewhere in South Africa.

kimono *ki-mō'nō, n.* a loose robe with wide sleeves, fastening with a sash, an outer garment in Japan: a dressing-gown of similar form:—*pl.* **kimō'nos.** [Jap.]

kin *kin, n.* persons of the same family: relatives: relationship: affinity.—*adj.* related.—*adj.* **kin'less** without relations.—*ns.* **kinsfolk** (*kinz'fōk*) folk or people kindred or related to one another (also **kinfolk, kins'folks**); **kin'ship** relationship.—**kins'man** a man of the same kin or race as another:—*fem.* **kins'woman.—next of kin** the relatives of a deceased person, among whom his personal property is distributed if he dies intestate: the person(s) most closely related to an individual by blood or marriage, or a legal ruling. [O.E. *cynn;* cog. with L. *genus,* Gr. *genos.*]

-kin a noun suffix denoting a diminutive, as lamb*kin,* mani*kin;* also in proper names, as Jen*kin* (*John*), Wil*kin* (*William*) [Prob. Du. or L.G.; cf. Ger *-chen.*]

kinaesthesis, in U.S **kinesthesis,** *kin-ēs-thē'sis, kin-, -es-, n.* sense of movement or of muscular effort.— Also **kinaesthē'sia** (*-zi-ə, -zya*)—*adj.* **kinaesthetic** (*-thet'ik*) pertaining to kinaesthesis. [Gr *kineein,* to move, *aisthēsis,* sensation.]

kinase *kī'nāz, kin'āz, n.* a biochemical agent, e.g. a metal ion or a protein, which converts a zymogen to an enzyme, and so acts as an activator. [*kinetic,* -*ase.*]

kincob *king'kob, n.* a rich silk fabric embroidered with gold or silver thread, made in India. [Hind. and Pers *kimkhāb.*]

kind *kind, n.* those of kin, a race· sort or species, a particular variety: fundamental qualities (of a thing). produce, as distinguished from money.—*adj.* having or springing from the feelings natural for those of the same family: disposed to do good to others: benevolent.—*adv.* **kind'ly** in a kind manner: a (rather peremptory) substitute for please (for the *adj.,* see sep. art.).—*n.* **kind'ness** the quality or fact of being kind: a kind act.—*adj.* **kind'-heart'ed.—kind'-heart'edness.—after (its) kind** according to (its) nature; **in kind** in goods instead of money: tit for tat; **kind of** (*coll.*) of a kind, somewhat, to some extent, as it were—used adjectivally and adverbially. [O.E. (*ge*)*cynde—cynn,* kin]

kindergarten *kin'dər-gär-tn, n.* an infant school on Froebel's principle (1826), in which object-lessons and games figure largely. [Ger.,—*Kinder,* children, *Garten,* garden.]

kindle *kin'dl, v t.* to set fire to: to light: to inflame, as the passions: to provoke: to incite.—*v.i.* to take fire: to begin to be excited: to be roused.—*ns.* **kin'dler; kin'dling** the act of causing to burn: materials for starting a fire. [Cf. O.N. *kyndill,* a torch—L *candēla,* candle.]

kindly *kind'li, adj.* inclined to kindness: benign: genial· comfortable.—*adv.* in a kind or kindly manner (see also under **kind**).—*n* **kind'liness.—take it**

kindly to feel it as a kindness; **take kindly to** (often with *neg.*) to take a favourable view of, or to adopt (a practice) with enthusiasm. [O.E. *gecyndelic;* cf. **kind.**]

kindred *kin'drid, n.* relationship by blood, less properly, by marriage: relatives: a group of relatives, family, clan.—*adj.* akin: cognate: congenial.—*ns.* **kin'dredness; kin'dredship.** [M.E. *kinrede*—O.E. *cynn,* kin, and the suffix *-rœden,* expressing mode or state.]

kine *kin, (B.) n.pl.* cows. [M.E. *kyen,* a doubled plural of O.E. *cū,* a cow, the plural of which is *cy̆.*]

kinematics *kin-i-mat'iks,* or *kin-, n.* sing the science of motion without reference to force.—*adjs.* **kinemat'ic, -al.** [Gr. *kinēma,* motion—*kineein,* to move.]

kinesis *ki-nē'sis,* or *ki-, n.* movement, change of position, *specif.* under stimulus and with direction not precisely determined —*n.* sing. **kine'sics** (study of) body movements which convey information in the absence of speech.—*ns.* **kinesiol'ogist; kinesiol'ogy** scientific study of human movement, relating mechanics and anatomy. [Gr. *kinēsis,* movement.]

kinesthesis, etc. U.S. spelling of **kinaesthesis,** etc.

kinetics *kī-net'iks* or *ki-, n* sing. the science of the action of force in producing or changing motion.— *adjs.* **kinet'ic, -al** pertaining to motion or to kinetics: due to motion.—**kinetic art, sculpture** art, sculpture, in which movement (produced by air currents, or electricity, or sound, etc.) plays an essential part; **kinetic energy** energy possessed by a body by virtue of its motion. [Gr. *kinetikos—kineein,* to move.]

kinfolk. Same as **kinsfolk,** under **kin.**

king *king, n.* a hereditary chief ruler or titular head of a nation: a monarch: a playing-card having the picture of a king: the most important piece in chess: a crowned man in draughts: one who is pre-eminent among his fellows: (*cap.; pl.*) the title of two historical books of the Old Testament:—*fem.* **queen.**— *v.t* to make king: to furnish with a king: to play king (with object *it*).—**king-** in composition, most important.—*n.* **king'dom** the state or attributes of a king: a monarchical state: a region that was once a monarchical state: one of the three grand divisions of natural history (animal, vegetable, mineral).—*n.* **king'hood** kingship: kingliness.—*adj.* **king'less.—***ns* **king'liness; king'ling** a petty king.—*adj.* **king'ly** belonging or suitable to a king: royal: king-like.—Also *adv.*—*n.* **king'ship** the state, office, or dignity of a king.—**king'-bird** an American flycatcher; **king's bolt, -rod** a metal rod in a roof connecting the tiebeam and the ridge; **king'-co'bra** a large Asiatic species of cobra; **king'-crab** Limulus, a curious large marine arachnoid, with convex horseshoe-shaped buckler; **king'cup** the buttercup: the marsh-marigold; **king'fish** the opah; **king'fisher** a fish-eating bird with very brilliant plumage, the halcyon; **king'maker** one who has the creating of kings or other high officials in his power; **king'-of-arms** (sometimes **-at-arms**) a principal herald; **king'-penguin** a large penguin, smaller than the emperor; **king'-pin** a tall pin, or one prominently placed: a pin on which swivels an axle of the type of that of an automobile front-wheel: the most important person of a group engaged in an undertaking: the key issue; **king'post** a perpendicular beam in the frame of a roof rising from the tie-beam to the ridge; **king prawn** a large prawn; **King's Bench** (Queen's Bench in a queen's reign) a division of the High Court of Justice; **king's counsel** (or **queen's counsel**) an honorary rank of barristers and advocates; **king's English** (or **queen's English**) correct standard speech; **king's-e'vil** a scrofulous disease formerly supposed to be healed by the touch of the king.—*adj.* **king'-size(d)** of large size.—**King's Regulations** (or **Queen's Regulations**) the regulations governing the British Armed Forces; **king's speech** (or **queen's speech**) the sovereign's address to parliament at its opening and closing.—**kingdom come** (*slang*) the state after death; **king of beasts** the lion; **king of birds** the eagle; **king of kings** a powerful monarch with other monarchs subject to him: (*cap.*) God, Christ; **king of metals** gold; **king of terrors** death; **king of the castle** (orig. from a children's game) the most important, powerful person in a group; **king of the forest** the oak. [O.E. *cyning—cynn*, a tribe, with suffix *-ing*; cog. with **kin**.]

kinin *ki'nin*, (*biol.*) *n.* a plant hormone which promotes cell-division and is used commercially as a preservative for cut flowers: any of a group of polypeptides in the blood, causing dilation of the blood vessels and contraction of smooth muscles. [Gr. *kin(ēsis)*, movement.]

kink *kingk*, *n.* a twisted loop in a string, rope, etc.: a mental twist: a crick: a whim: an imperfection.—*v.i.* to form a kink.—*v.t.* to cause a kink in.—*n.* **kink'le** a slight kink.—*adj.* **kink'y** twisted: curly: eccentric (*coll.*): mad (*coll.*): out of the ordinary in an attractive and sophisticated way (*coll.*): homosexual, or sexually perverted (*coll.*). [Prob. Du. *kink.*]

kinkajou *king'ka-jōō*, *n.* a South American animal allied to the raccoon. [App. from a North Amer. Indian word misapplied.]

kinkle, kinky. See **kink**.

kino *kē'nō*, *n.* an astringent exudation from various tropical trees:—*pl.* **kin'os.** [App. of W. African origin.]

kinsfolk, kinship, etc. See **kin**.

kiosk *kē'osk*, *ki-osk'*, *n.* an Eastern garden pavilion: a small roofed stall for sale of papers, sweets, etc., either out-of-doors or inside a public building: a bandstand: a public telephone box. [Turk. *kioshk, keushk*—Pers. *kūshk.*]

kip¹ *kip*, *n.* the skin of a young animal.—**kip'-skin** leather made from the skin of young cattle, intermediate between calfskin and cowhide.

kip² *kip*, *n.* a level or slight incline at the end of an underground way, on which the tubs of coal stand till hoisted up the shaft.

kip³ *kip*, (*slang*) *n.* a lodging-house: a bed: a nap.—*v.i.* to go to bed: to lie.—**kip down** to go to bed. [Cf. Dan. *kippe*, a low alehouse.]

kip⁴ *kip*, (*Austr.*) *n.* a short flat stick used to throw up pennies in the game of two-up.

kipper *kip'ər*, *n.* a male salmon during the spawning season after spawning: a salmon or (esp.) herring split open, seasoned, and dried.—*v.t.* to cure or preserve, as a salmon or herring.—*n.* **kipp'erer**.

Kirbigrip®, *kirby-grip*, **kirbigrip** *kûr'bi-grip*, *n.* a kind of hair-grip. [From **Kirby**, the name of one of the original manufacturers.]

kirk *kirk*, *kûrk*, (*Scot.*) *n.* church, in any sense: by English Episcopalians sometimes specially applied to the Church of Scotland. [A Northern Eng. form of **church**.—O.N. *kirkja*—O.E. *cirice*.]

kirmess. See **kermis**.

kirn *kirn*, (*Scot.*) *n.* the cutting of the last sheaf or handful of the harvest: a harvest-home.—**kirn'-ba'by, corn'-ba'by, kirn'-doll'ie, corn'-doll'ie, corn'-maiden** a dressed-up figure made of the last handful of corn cut: (esp. **corn-dollie**) any of a number of straw decorations usu. of traditional design.

kirschwasser *kêrsh'väs-ər*, *n.* a liqueur made from the wild cherry.—Also **kirsch.** [Ger., cherry water.]

kirtle *kûr'tl*, (*hist.*) *n.* a sort of gown or outer petticoat: a mantle.—*adj.* **kir'tled.** [O.E. *cyrtel*; app.—L. *curtus*, short.]

kismet *kiz'met*, or *kis'*, *n.* fate, destiny. [Turk. *qismet*—Ar. *qisma.*]

kiss *kis*, *v.t.* to caress or salute with the lips: to touch gently—*v.i.* to salute with the lips: to collide.—*n.* a caress or salute with the lips.—*n.* **kiss'er** one who kisses: the mouth (*slang*).—**kiss'-curl** a small curl at the side of the forehead; **kissing cousin** a more or less distant relation with whom one is on terms familiar enough to kiss on meeting.—**kiss hands** to kiss the sovereign's hands on acceptance of office, **kiss of death** (*coll.*) something that causes failure, destruction, etc.; **kiss of life** a mouth-to-mouth method of restoring breathing: a means of restoring vitality or vigour (*fig.*), **kiss of peace** a kiss of greeting between the members of the early, and some branches of the modern, Church. [O.E. *cyssan*, to kiss—*coss*, a kiss.]

kit¹ *kit*, *n.* a small wooden tub: an outfit: equipment: material, tools, instructions, assembled in a container for some specific purpose: the container itself.—*v.t.* (sometimes with *out*) to provide with kit.—**kit'-bag** a strong canvas bag for holding one's kit or outfit (*mil.*): a knapsack: a strong canvas grip; **kit'-boat, -car** a boat, car, put together, from standard components, by an amateur builder [Prob. Middle Du. *kitte*, a hooped beer-can.]

kit² *kit*, *n.* a small pocket violin.

kitchen *kich'ən*, *n.* a place where food is cooked: cooking department or equipment:—*ns* **kitch'endom** the domain of the kitchen, **kitch'ener** a person employed in the kitchen: a cooking-stove; **kitchenette'** a tiny kitchen: a compact combined kitchen and pantry.—**kitch'en-gar'den** a garden where vegetables are cultivated for the kitchen, **kitch'en-gar'dener;** **kitch'en-maid** a maid or servant whose work is in the kitchen; **kitch'en-midd'en** a prehistoric rubbish-heap, **kitch'en-range** a kitchen grate with oven, boiler, etc., attached, for cooking.—*adj.* **kitch'en-sink'** (of plays, etc.) dealing with sordid real-life situations.—**kitchen tea** in Australia, a bride's shower, the gifts being kitchen utensils, etc.; **kitchen unit** a set of up-to-date kitchen fitments. [O E. *cycene*—L. *coquina—coquĕre*, to cook]

kite *kit*, *n.* a rapacious bird of the hawk kind: a rapacious person: a light frame covered with paper or cloth for flying in the air: a more complicated structure built of boxes (*box-kite*), often for carrying recording instruments or a man in the air: a rumour or suggestion given out to see how the wind blows, test public opinion, or the like: an aircraft (*airmen's slang*).—**kite'-balloon'** an observation-balloon designed on the principle of the kite to prevent revolving, etc.; **kite'-flying** sending up and controlling a kite: the dealing in fictitious accommodation paper to raise money: testing public opinion by circulating rumours, etc. (**fly a kite** to take part in kite-flying), **kite'-mark** a kite-shaped mark on goods indicating conformity in quality, size, etc., with the specifications of the British Standards Institution. [O. E. *cyta.*]

kith *kith*, *n.* knowledge: native land: acquaintance—obs. except in **kith and kin,** friends (originally home-country) and relatives. [O.E. *cȳth—cunnan,* to know.]

kitsch *kich*, *n.* trash: work in any of the arts that is pretentious and inferior or in bad taste.—*adj.* **kitsch'y.**—*adv.* **kitsch'ly.** [Ger.]

kitten *kit'n*, *n.* a young cat (*dim.* **kitt'y**): sometimes the young of another animal.—*v.t.* and *v.i.* (of a cat) to bring forth—*adjs.* **kitt'enish, kitt'eny** frolicsome: skittish: affectedly playful.—**have kittens** to be in a state of excitement or anger. [M.E. *kitoun,* dim. of **cat.**]

kittiwake *kit'i-wāk*, *n.* a species of gull with long wings

fāte; fär; mē; hûr (her); *mine; mōte; för; mūte; mōōn; fōōt; dhen* (then); *el'ə-mənt* (element)

pad with loop for the forehead; **tie someone (up) in knots** to confuse, bewilder somone completely. [O.E. *cnotta*.]

knout *knōōt*, also *nowt*, *n.* whip formerly used as an instrument of punishment in Russia: punishment inflicted by the knout.—*v.t.* to flog. [French spelling of Russ. *knut*.]

know *nō*, *v.t.* to be informed of: to be assured of: to be acquainted with: to recognise.—*v.i.* to possess knowledge:—*pr.p.* **know'ing;** *pa.t.* **knew** (*nū*, *U.S.* *nōō*); *pa.p.* **known** (*nōn*.)—*n.* possession of the relevant facts.—*adj.* **know'able** capable of being known, discovered, or understood.—*ns.* **know'ableness; know'er.**—*adj.* **know'ing** intelligent: skilful: cunning. —*adv.* **know'ingly** in a knowing manner: consciously: intentionally.—*n.* **know'ingness** the quality of being knowing or intelligent: shrewdness.—**know'-all** one who thinks he knows everything; **know'-how** the faculty of knowing the right thing to do in any contingency: specialised skill; **know'-noth'ing** one who is quite ignorant.—*adj.* completely ignorant.—**in the know** in possession of private information: initiated; **I wouldn't know** I am not in a position to know; **know all the answers** to be completely informed on everything, or to think one is; **know better** to be too wise, well-instructed (to do this or that); **know how many beans make five** to be sensible, aware, have one's wits about one; **known as** going by name of; **know the ropes** to understand the detail or procedure, as a sailor does his rigging; **know what's o'clock, know what's what** to be wide awake; **know which side one's bread is buttered on** to be fully alive to one's own interest; **what do you know?** what is the news?: a greeting or expression of incredulity; **you never know** (*coll.*) perhaps. [O.E. *cnāwan*.]

knowledge *nol'ij*,*n.* assured belief: that which is known: information, instruction: enlightenment: learning: practical skill: acquaintance.—*adj.* **knowl'edgeable** possessing knowledge: intelligent.—*adv.* **knowl'-edgeably.**—**to one's knowledge** so far as one knows. [M.E. *knowleche*, where *-leche* is unexplained; see **know.**]

knubble, nubble *nub'l*, **knobble** *nob'l*, *vs.t.* to beat with the fists: to knock. [**knob.**]

knuckle *nuk'l*, *n.* projecting joint of a finger: the kneejoint of a calf or pig (*cook.*).—*v.i.* to yield (usu. with *down* or *under*): to bend the knuckles or knee.—*v.t.* to touch with the knuckle.—**knuck'le-bone** any with a rounded end: (in *pl.*) the game of dibs; **knuck'leduster** a metal covering for the knuckles, for attack or defence; **knuck'le-head** (*coll.*) idiot; **knuck'le-joint** a joint where the forked end of a connecting-rod is joined by a bolt to another piece of the machinery; **knuckle sandwich** (*slang*) a blow with the fist.— **knuckle down (to)** to set oneself to hard work: see also above; **knuckle under** to yield to authority, pressure, etc.; **near the knuckle** on the verge of the indecent. [M.E. *knokel*, not recorded in O.E.]

knur, knurr, nur, nurr *nûr*,*n.* an excrescence on a tree: a hard ball or knot of wood. [M.E. *knurre*.]

knurl, nurl *nûrl*, *n.* a small excrescence, or protuberance: a ridge or bead, esp. in series.—*v.t.* to make knurls on, to mill.—*adj.* **knurled** covered with knurls.—*n.* **knurl'ing** mouldings or other woodwork elaborated into a series of knobs.—*adj.* **knurl'y** gnarled. [Prob. a dim. of **knur.**]

koa *kō'a*, *n.* a Hawaiian acacia. [Hawaiian.]

koala *kō-ä'la*, *kōō'la*, *n.* an Australian marsupial, like a small bear, called also **koala bear, native bear.** [Australian *kūlā*.]

koan *kō'än*, *n.* in Zen Buddhism, a nonsensical question given to students as a subject for meditation. [Jap , a public proposal or plan.]

kobold *kō'bold*, *n.* in German folklore, a spirit of the mines: a domestic brownie. [Ger.]

Kodiak bear *kō'di-ak bār*, the largest variety of brown bear, *Ursus arctos*, found in Alaska and the Aleutian Islands. [From *Kodiak* Island, Alaska.]

kohl *kōl*, *n.* a fine powder of native stibnite (formerly known as antimony) which is black in colour, used in the East for staining the eyelids. [Ar. *koh'l*.]

kohlrabi *kōl'rä'bi*, *n.* a cabbage with a turnip-shaped stem. [Ger.,—It. *cavolo rapa*—L. *caulis*, cabbage, *rapa*, turnip.]

Koine *koi'nē*, *n.* a Greek dialect developed from Attic, in use in the Eastern Mediterranean in Hellenistic and Byzantine times: (often without *cap.*) any dialect which has spread and become the common language of a larger area. [Gr. *koinē* (*dialektos*) common (dialect).]

kola. See **cola.**

kolinsky *ko-lin'ski*, *n.* (the fur of) the polecat or mink. [Russ. *kolinski*, of the Kola Peninsula.]

kolkhoz *kol-hhoz'*, *n.* a collective or co-operative farm. [Russ. abbrev. of *kollektivnoe khozyaistvo*.]

Komodo dragon or **lizard** *kə-mō'dō drag'ən, liz'ərd*, a very large monitor lizard of some Indonesian islands. [From *Komodo* Island, Indonesia.]

Komsomol *kom'sō-mol*, *n.* the Communist youth organisation of Russia. [Russ. abbrev. of *Kommunisticheskii Soyuz Molodezhi*.]

konimeter *kon-im'i-tər*, *n.* an instrument for measuring dust in air.—*ns.* **koniol'ogy** the study of dust in the air and its effects; **kon'iscope** an instrument for estimating the dustiness of air. [Gr. *konis*, dust, *metron*, measure, *skopeein*, to look at.]

koodoo. See **kudu.**

kook *kōōk*, (*slang*) *n.* a person who is mad, foolish, or eccentric and amoral.—*adj.* **kook'ie, kook'y** with the qualities of a kook: (of clothes) smart and eccentric. [Prob. from **cuckoo.**]

kookaburra *kōōk'ə-bur'ə*, *n.* the laughing jackass. [Native Australian name.]

kopeck, copeck *kō-pek', kō'pek*, *n.* a Russian coin, the hundredth part of a rouble. [Russ. *kopeika*.]

kopje. Older form of **koppie.**

koppie *kop'i*, *n.* a low hill. [Cape Du. *kopje*—*kop*, head.]

Koran *kō-rän', kō-*, sometimes *kō'rən, kō', n.* the Muslim Scriptures.—*adj.* **Koranic** (*-rän'ik*). [Ar. *qurān*, reading.]

korfball *kōrf'böl, körf', n.* a game of Dutch origin resembling basket-ball played by teams of six men and six women a side. [Du. *korfbal*—*korf*, basket, *bal*, ball.]

kosher *kō'shər*, *adj.* pure, clean, according to the Jewish ordinances—as of meat killed and prepared by Jews: legitimate, proper, genuine (*coll.*). [Heb. *kāshēr*, right.]

kosmos. Same as **cosmos.**

koto *kō'tō*, *n.* a Japanese musical instrument consisting of a long box with thirteen silk strings:—*pl.* **kō'tos.** [Jap.]

koulan, koumiss, kourbash, kouskous. See **kulan, kumiss, kurbash, couscous.**

kowhai *kō'hī*, *-(h)wī*, *n.* a papilionaceous shrub (*Sophora tetraptera*) of New Zealand, etc.: the New Zealand glory-pea (*Clianthus*). [Maori.]

kowtow *kow-tow', n.* the Chinese ceremony of prostration.—*v.i.* to perform that ceremony: to abase oneself before (with *to*). [Chin. *k'o*, knock, *t'ou*, head.]

kraal *kral*, *n.* a S. African native village: loosely, a single hut: a corral.—*v.t.* to pen. [Du. *kraal*—Port. *curral*—L. *currēre*, to run.]

kraft *kräft*, *n.* a type of strong brown wrapping paper

made from pulp treated with a sulphate solution. [Ger. *Kraft*, strength.]
krait *krīt*, *n.* a deadly Indian rock snake. [Hind. *karait*.]
kraken *krä'kən*, *n.* a fabled sea-monster. [Norw.]
krantz *kränts*, (*S.Afr.*) *n.* a crown of rock on a mountain-top: a precipice.—Also **krans, kranz**. [Du. *krans*, a wreath.]
kraut *krowt*, (often *cap.*; *slang*) *n.* a German. [From *sauerkraut*.]
kremlin *krem'lin*, *n.* a citadel, specially (with *cap.*) that of Moscow: (with *cap.*) the Russian government.—*ns.* **Kremlinol'ogist; Kremlinol'ogy** the study of the Russian government and its policies. [Russ. *kreml'*.]
kriegspiel, kriegsspiel *krēg'spēl*, *n.* a war-game played on a map to train officers. [Ger. *Kriegsspiel—Krieg*, war, *Spiel*, game.]
Krilium® *kril'i-əm*, *n.* an improver of soil structure, consisting of synthetic polymers.
krill *kril*, *n.* whaler's name for species of *Euphausia* (fam. *Euphausiaceae*), phosphorescent shrimps.
krimmer *krim'ər*, *n.* tightly curled grey or black fur from a Crimean type of lamb. [Russ. *Krim*, Crimea.]
kris *krēs*, *n.* a Malay dagger with wavy blade:—*pl.* **kris'es.**—*v.t.* to stab with a kris. [Malay.]
Krishna *krish'nə*, *n.* a deity in later Hinduism, a form of Vishnu.—*n.* **Krish'naism** (also called **Krishna Consciousness**) belief in, worship of, Krishna. [Sans.]
krone *krō'nə*, *n.* (*pl.* **kro'ner**) in Denmark and Norway, and **krona** *krōō'na* (*pl.* **kro'nor**) in Sweden, a silver coin and monetary unit equal to 100 öre. [Cf. **crown**.]
Kronos *kron'os*, *n.* a supreme god of the Greeks, son of Ouranos and Gaia, dethroned by his son Zeus.
Krugerrand *krōō'gər-rand*, *n.* a South African coin containing one troy ounce of fine gold and bearing a portrait of President *Kruger*.—Also **Kruger Rand, rand**. [*rand*.]
krummhorn, krumhorn, crumhorn *krōōm'hörn*, *n.* an old double-reed wind instrument with curved end: an organ reed-stop. [Ger., curved horn.]
krypton *krip'ton*, *n.* an inert gas discovered in the air (where it is present in extremely small quantity) by Sir W. Ramsay in 1898 (Kr; atomic number 36). [Gr. *krypteïn*, to hide.]
kudos *kū'dos*, Gr. *kü'dos*, *n.* credit, fame, renown, prestige. [Gr. *kÿdos*, glory.]
kudu, koodoo *kōō'dōo*, *n.* an African antelope with long spiral horns. [From Hottentot.]
kudzu *kōōd'zōō*, *n.* an ornamental papilionaceous plant of China and Japan (*Pueraria thunbergiana*) with edible root tubers and a stem yielding a fibre. [Jap.]
kufiyeh, kufiah, kuffya(h). See **kaffiyeh.**
Ku-Klux Klan *kōō'*, *kū'kluks klan*, or **Ku-Klux** or the **Klan** a secret organisation in several Southern U.S. states after Civil War of 1861–65, to oppose Northern influence, and prevent Negroes from enjoying their rights as freemen—revived in 1916 to deal drastically with Jews, Catholics, Negroes, etc., and to preserve white Protestant supremacy.—*n.* **Klan'sman** a member of this organisation. [Gr. *kyklos*, a circle, and **clan**.]
kukri *kōōk'rē*, *n.* a sharp, curved Gurkha knife or short sword. [Hindi *kukrī*.]
kulak *kōō-lak'*, *n.* in Tsarist times, a rich peasant: later, an exploiter. [Russ., fist.]
kulan, koulan *kōō'län*, *n.* the onager, or a nearly related wild ass of the Kirghiz Steppe. [Kirghiz.]
kumara *kōō-mä'rə*, *n.* sweet potato. [Maori.]
kumiss, koumiss *kōō'mis*, *n.* fermented mares' milk.

[Russ. *kumis*—Tatar *kumiz*.]
kümmel *küm'l*, *kim'l*, *kōōm'l*, *n.* a liqueur flavoured with cumin and caraway seeds. [Ger.,—L. *cumīnum* —Gr. *kymīnon*, cumin.]
kumquat *kum'kwot*, *n.* a small kind of orange. [Cantonese, gold orange.]
kung fu *kung fōō*, the art of unarmed combat and self-defence developed in ancient China. [Chin., combat skill.]
Kuo-yü *kwō'*, *gwō'yü*, *n.* lit. 'national language', a form of Mandarin taught all over China.
kurbash, kourbash *kōōr'bash*, *n.* a hide whip used in the East.—*v.t.* to whip with a kurbash. [Ar. *qurbāsh*.]
kurchatovium *kûr-chə-tō'vi-əm*, *n.* element 104 named by Russians (who claimed its discovery in 1966) after a Russian physicist.
Kurd *kōōrd*, *kûrd*, *n.* one of the people of Kurdistan, Iranian in speech.—*adj.* and *n.* **Kurd'ish.**
kurrajong *kur'ə-jong*, *n.* an Australian name for various trees with fibrous bark.—Also **curr'ajong.** [Native name.]
kursaal *kōōr'zäl*, *n.* the reception-room of a spa. [Ger., lit. cure-saloon.]
kurta *kōōr'tä*, *n.* a loose-fitting collarless shirt or tunic worn in India. [Hindi.]
kurtosis *kər-tō'sis*, (*statistics*) *n.* the relative degree of sharpness of the peak on a frequency-distribution curve. [Gr. *kurtōsis*, bulging, swelling—*kurtos*, curved.]
Kushitic. Same as **Cushitic.**
kvass *kväs*, *n.* rye-beer. [Russ. *kvas*.]
kvetch *kvech*, *v.i.* to complain, whine, esp. incessantly. —*ns.* **kvetch, kvetch'er** a complainer, fault-finder. [Yiddish.]
kwacha *kwach'ə*, *n.* the basic unit of currency in Zambia and Malawi. [Native name, meaning 'dawn'.]
kwashiorkor *kwä-shi-ör'kör*, or *kwosh'*, *n.* a widespread nutritional disease of children in tropical and subtropical regions due to deficiency of protein. [Ghanaian name.]
kwela *kwä'la*, *n.* Zulu folk-music of jazz type. [Bantu, lift, from leaping upward in dancing to the music.]
kyang. See **kiang.**
kyanise, -ize *kī'ə-nīz*, *v.t.* to preserve from dry-rot by injecting corrosive sublimate into the pores of (wood). [From John H. *Kyan* (1774–1830).]
kyanite *kī'ə-nīt*, *n.* a mineral, an aluminium silicate, generally sky-blue. [Gr. *kyanos*, blue.]
kybosh. See **kibosh.**
kydst (*Spens.*). See **kythe.**
kyle *kīl*, *n.* a narrow strait. [Gael. *caol*.]
kylie, kyley *kī'li*, *n.* a boomerang. [Western Australian word.]
kyllosis *kil-ō'sis*, *n.* club-foot. [Gr. *kyllōsis*.]
kyloe *kī'lō*, *n.* one of the cattle of the Hebrides.
kymograph *kī'mō-gräf*, *n.* an instrument for recording the pressure of fluids, esp. of blood in a blood-vessel. —*adj.* **kymographic** (*-graf'ik*). [Gr. *kÿma*, a wave, *graphein*, to write.]
kyphosis *kī-fō'sis*, *n.* a hunchbacked condition.—*adj.* **kyphotic** (*-fot'ik*). [Gr. *kÿphōsis—kÿphos*, a hump.]
Kyrie eleison *kēr'i-e el-ā'i-son*, *kir'*, *kīr'i-e el-e-ē'son*, *el-e-ā'son*, etc., (abbrev. **Kyrie**) a form of prayer in all the ancient Greek liturgies, retained in the R.C. mass, following immediately after the introit (including both words and music): one of the responses to the commandments in the Anglican ante-communion service. [Gr. *Kÿrie, eleēson*, Lord, have pity.]

L

L, l *el*, *n.* the twelfth letter in our alphabet, representing a lateral liquid sound, the breath passing the side or sides of the tongue: anything shaped like the letter: used as a sign for pound (L. *libra*).—**L-dopa** see **dopa.**

la[1] *lä, interj.* lo! see! behold! ah! indeed! [Cf. **lo, law**[3].]

la[2] *lä, n.* the sixth note of the scale in sol-fa notation—also spelt **lah.** [See **Aretinian.**]

laager *lä'gər, n.* in South Africa, a defensive ring of ox-wagons: any extemporised fortication: an encampment: a defensive group of people drawn together by similarity of opinion, etc.—*v.t.* and *v.i.* to arrange or camp in a laager. [Cape Du. *lager*—Ger. *Lager*, a camp.]

lab *lab, n.* a familiar contraction of **laboratory.**

labarum *lab'ə-rəm, n.* the imperial standard after Constantine's conversion—with a monogram of the Greek letters XP (ChR), for Christ: a similar ecclesiastical banner borne in processions: any moral standard or guide. [L.,—Late Gr. *labaron.*]

label *lä'bl, n.* a small slip placed on or near anything to denote its nature, contents, ownership, destination, etc.: a paper annexed to a will, as a codicil (*law*): a dripstone (*archit.*): a characterising or classificatory designation (*fig.*).—*v.t.* to affix a label to: to describe by or on a label:—*pr.p.* **la'belling;** *pa.t.* and *pa.p.* **la'belled.** [O.Fr. *label*, perh.—O.H.G. *lappa*, flap.]

labellum *lə-bel'əm, n.* the lower petal of an orchid: applied also to other lip-like structures in flowers:—*pl.* **labell'a.** [L., dim of *labrum*, lip]

labial *lä'bi-əl, adj.* of or formed by the lips: sounded by impact of air on a lip-like projection, as an organ flue-pipe (*mus.*).—*n.* a sound formed by the lips.—*v.t.* **la'bialise, -ize** to make labial: to pronounce with rounded lips.—*adv.* **la'bially.**—*adj.* **la'biate** lipped: having a lipped corolla.—*n.* **la'bium** a lip or lip-like part:—*pl.* **la'bia.**—*adj.* and *n.* **labiodent'al** (a sound) produced by the lips and teeth together, as *f* and *v.*—**labia majora (minora)** the two outer (inner) folds of skin surrounding the vaginal orifice in human females. [L. *labium*, lip.]

labile *lä'bil,* in U.S. *-əl, adj.* unstable: apt to slip or change. [L. *labilis*—*labi*, to slip.]

laboratory *lə-bor'ə-tə-ri, lab'ə-rə-tə-ri, n.* orig a chemist's workroom: a place for experimental work or research. [L. *labōrāre*—*labor*, work.]

laborious, etc. See **labour.**

labour, in U.S. **labor,** *lä'bər, n.* toil: work: pains: duties: a task requiring hard work: effort toward the satisfaction of needs: workers collectively: supply or services of workers, esp. bodily workers: the Labour Party or its cause, principles, or interest: the pangs and efforts of childbirth: heavy pitching or rolling of a ship.—*adj.* of labour or the Labour Party —*v.t.* to undergo labour: to work: to take pains· to be oppressed: to move slowly: to be in travail: to pitch and roll heavily (*naut.*).—*v.t.* to strain, over-elaborate.—*adj.* **laborious** (*lə-bō', -bo'ri-əs*) involving or devoted to labour: strenuous: arduous.—*adv.* **labo'riously.**—*n.* **labo'riousness.**—*adj.* **la'boured** bearing marks of effort in execution: strained: over-elaborated.—*ns*

la'bourer one who labours: one who does work requiring little skill.—**labour camp** a penal institution where the inmates are forced to work: temporary accommodation for workers; **Labour Day** in many countries the 1st of May, a day of labour demonstrations: in U.S., the first Monday in September; **Labour Exchange** see **employment exchange; labour force** the number of workers employed in an industry, factory, etc.; **Labour Party** a party aiming at securing for workers by hand or brain the fruits of their industry and equitable distribution thereof.—*adj.* **la'boursav'ing** intended to supersede or lessen labour.—**hard labour** compulsory work imposed in addition to imprisonment, abolished in U.K. in 1948; **labour of love** work undertaken without hope of emolument; **labour** with to take pains to convince. [O.Fr. *labour, labeur*—L. *labor.*]

Labrador *lab'rə-dòr,* or *lab-rə-dòr', n.* a mainland region of Newfoundland and Quebec.—Also *adj.*—*n.* **lab'radorite** (or *-dor'*) a feldspar with fine play of colours found on the Labrador coast.—**Labrador (dog, retriever)** a sporting dog about twenty-two inches in height, either black or (**yellow** or **golden Labrador**) from red to fawn in colour.

labrum *lä'brəm, n.* a lip: a lip-like part:—*pl.* **la'bra.**—*n.* **la'bret** a lip ornament. [L. *labrum*, a lip.]

laburnum *lə-bûr'nəm, n.* a small poisonous papilionaceous tree, a native of the Alps. [L.]

labyrinth *lab'i-rinth, n.* orig a building with intricate passages: a maze: a tangle of intricate ways and connections: a perplexity: the cavities of the internal ear (*anat.*).—*adjs.* **labyrinth'al, labyrinth'ian, labyrinth'ic, -al, labyrinth'ine** (-*in*, -*in*).—*ns.* **labyrinth'itis** inflammation of the inner ear. [Gr. *labyrinthos.*]

lac *lak, n.* a dark-red transparent resin produced on the twigs of trees in the East by coccid insects (**lac insects**). [Hind. *lākh*—Sans. *lākṣā*, 100 000, hence the (teeming) lac insect.]

laccolite *lak'ō-līt, n.* a mass of igneous rock that has risen in a molten condition and bulged up the overlying strata to form a dome.—Also **lacc'olith** (*-lith*) —*adjs.* **laccolitic** (*-lit'ik*), **laccolith'ic.** [Gr. *lakkos*, a reservoir, *lithos*, a stone.]

lace *läs, n.* a string for passing through holes: an ornamental fabric made by looping, knotting, plaiting, or twisting threads into definite patterns.—*v.t.* to fasten with a lace (often with *up*): to compress or pinch by lacing: to adorn with lace: to streak: to thrash: to reprimand severely (often with *into*): to intermix, as coffee with brandy, etc.: to intertwine.—*v.i.* to have lacing as mode of fastening —*adj.* **laced.**—*n.* **lacet** (*läs-et'*) a kind of braidwork.—*n.* and *adj.* **lac'ing.**—*adj.* **lac'y** (also **lac'ey**) like lace —**lace'-frame** a machine used in lace-making; **lace'-leaf** same as **lattice-leaf** under **lattice; lace'-pill'ow** a cushion held on the knees by lacemakers; **lace'-ups** boots or shoes having laces; **lace'-wing** a neuropterous insect with gauzy wings and brilliant golden eyes. [O.Fr. *las*, a noose—L. *laqueus.*]

lacerate *las'ə-rāt, v.t.* to tear: to rend: to wound: to afflict.—*n.* **lacerā'tion.**—*adj.* **lac'erative** tearing: having power to tear [L. *lacerāre*, *-ātum*, to tear—*lacer*, torn.]

lacet, lacey. See **lace.**

laches *lach'ız*, (*law*) *n.* negligence or undue delay, esp. such as to disentitle to remedy. [A.Fr. *lachesse*.]

lachrymal *lak'rı-məl*, *adj.* of or for tears.—*n* a bone near the tear-gland: (in *pl.*) lachrymal organs: (in *pl.*) weeping fits.—*adjs.* **lach'rymary, lach'rymatory** lachrymal: causing tears to flow.—*ns.* a tear-bottle.—*ns.* **lachryma'tion** the secretion of tears; **lach'rymátor** a substance that causes tears to flow, as tear-gas: a contrivance for letting it loose.—*adj.* **lach'rymose** shedding tears: given to weeping: lugubrious.—*adv.* **lach'rymosely.**—Also **lacrymal, lacrimal**, etc.—**lachryma Christi** (*lak'rimə kris'tē*; L., Christ's tear) a sweet but piquant wine from grapes grown on Vesuvius; **lachrymal duct** a duct that conveys tear-water from the inner corner of the eye to the nose; **lachrymal gland** a gland at the outer angle of the eye that secretes tears. [From *lachryma*, a mediaeval spelling of L. *lacrima*, tear.]

lacinia *la-sın'ı-ə, n.* a long narrow lobe in a leaf, etc.: —*pl.* **lacin'iae** (*-ē*).—*adjs.* **lacin'iate, -d** cut into narrow lobes, slashed.—*n.* **lacinia'tion.** [L., a lappet, tag.]

lack *lak, n.* want, deficiency: a thing absent or in short supply.—*v.t.* to be without: to be short of or deficient in: to need.—*v.i.* (now usu. in *pr.p.*) to be wanting, absent: to be deficient.—*adj.* **lack'ing.**—*adj.* **lack'-lus'tre** dull, without brightness, sheen or vitality.—Also *n.* [Cf M.L.G. and Du. *lak*, blemish.]

lackadaisical *lak-ə-dā'zi-kl, adj.* affectedly pensive: vapidly sentimental: listless: languishing. [Old word *alack-a-day*, alas.]

lackey, lacquey *lak'ı, n.* a footman or valet: a servile follower:—*pl.* **lack'eys, lacqu'eys.**—*v.t.* and *v.i.* to serve or attend as or like a footman. [O.Fr. *laquay* (Fr. *laquais*)—Sp. *lacayo*, a lackey.]

Laconian *la-kō'nyən, -ni-ən,* **Laconic** *la-kon'ik, adjs.* of Laconia or Lacedaemonia, Spartan.—*n.* **Laco'nian.**—*adjs.* **laconic, -al** expressing or expressed in few words after the manner of the Laconians: sententiously brief.—*adv.* **lacon'ically.** [Gr *lakōnikos*.]

lacquer *lak'ər, n.* a solution of film-forming substances in a volatile solvent, esp. a varnish of lac and alcohol: a similar substance sprayed on the hair to hold it in place: a covering of one of these: an article, or ware, so coated.—*v.t.* to cover with lacquer: to varnish.—*ns.* **lacq'uerer; lacq'uering** varnishing with lacquer: a coat of lacquer varnish. [Fr. *lacre*—Port. *lacre, laca*; *lacrymal*, see **lac**.]

lacquey. See **lackey**.

lacrimal, etc. Variants of **lachrymal**, etc.

lacrosse *la-, lä-kros', n.* a team game (orig. N. American) in which the ball is driven through the opponents' goal by means of a crosse. [Fr.]

lacteal *lak'tı-əl, adj.* of milk: conveying chyle.—*n.* a lymphatic conveying chyle from the intestines to the thoracic ducts.—*ns.* **lactase** (*lak'tās*) an enzyme that acts on lactose (*lak'tāte* a salt of lactic acid.—*v.i.* (also *lak-tāt'*) to secrete milk.—*n.* **lacta'tion** secretion or yielding of milk: the period of suckling. —*adj.* **lac'teous** milky.—*n.* **lactesc'ence.**—*adjs.* **lactesc'ent** turning to milk: producing milky juice; **lac'tic** pertaining to milk; **lactif'ic** producing milk or milky juice; **lactogen'ic** inducing lactation.—*n.* **lac'tose** milk-sugar $C_{12}H_{22}O_{11} + H_2O$, obtained by evaporating whey.—**lactic acid** an acid obtained from milk, $CH_3CH(OH)COOH$. [L. *lac, lactis*, milk.]

lacuna *la-, la-kū'nə, n.* a gap or hiatus: an intercellular space (*biol.*): a cavity: a depression in a pitted surface:—*pl.* **lacu'nae** (*-nē*)—*adjs.* **lacun'al, lacun'-** **ary, lacun'ate** pertaining to, or including, lacunae; **lacu'nose** having lacunae: pitted. [L. *lacūna*, hollow, gap.]

lacustrine *la-kus'trīn, adj.* pertaining to lakes: dwelling in or on lakes: formed in lakes. [L. *lacus*, a lake.]

lacy. See **lace**.

lad *lad, n* a boy· a youth: a stable-man: a dashing fellow.—*n.* **ladd'ie** a little lad· a boy. [M.E *ladde*, youth, servant.]

ladanum *lad'ə-nəm, n.* a resin exuded from Cistus leaves in Mediterranean countries. [L. *lādanum, lēdanum*—Gr. *lādanon, lēdanon*—*lēdon*, the Cistus plant, prob.—Pers. *lādan.*]

ladder *lad'ər, n.* a contrivance, generally portable, with rungs between two supports, for going up and down: anything of similar form, as a run in knitwear where the breaking of a thread gives an appearance of rungs: a contrivance for enabling fish to ascend a waterfall (*fish-ladder, salmon-ladder*): means of attaining a higher status (*fig.*).—*v.t.* to develop a ladder.—*adjs.* **ladd'ered, ladd'ery.** [O.E. *hlǣder.*]

laddie. See **lad**.

lade *lād, v.t.* to load: to burden: to put on board: to ladle or scoop: to empty, drain, as with a ladle.—*v.i.* to take cargo aboard:—*pa.t.* **lad'ed;** *pa.p.* **lad'en, lad'ed.**—*adj.* **lad'en** loaded: burdened.—*n.* **lad'ing** the act of loading: that which is loaded: cargo: freight. [O.E. *hladan*, load, draw water.]

laden. See **lade**.

la-di-da, lah-di-dah *lä-dı-dä', (slang), adj.* affectedly fine, esp. in speech or bearing.

Ladin *lä-dēn', n.* a Romance tongue spoken in the upper Inn valley: a general name for the Rhaeto-Romanic languages or dialects. [L. *Latīnus*, Latin.]

Ladino *lä-dē'nō, n.* a Spanish-American of mixed white and Indian blood:—*pl.* **Ladin'os.** [Sp.,—L. *Latīnus*, Latin.]

ladle *lād'l, n.* a large spoon for lifting liquid: the float-board of a mill-wheel: a long-handled pan or bucket for holding and conveying molten metal.— *v.t.* to transfer or distribute with a ladle.—*n.* **lad'leful** as much as a ladle will hold:—*pl.* **lad'lefuls.—ladle out** to distribute generously. [O.E. *hlǣdel*—*hladan*, to lade.]

lady (*cap.* when prefixed), *lā'di, n.* the mistress of a house: used as the feminine of **lord** and of **gentleman**, and ordinarily as a less formal substitute for **dame**: any woman of refinement of manners and instincts: a lady-love or object of chivalric devotion: a girl-friend, mistress, etc.: used also as a feminine prefix.—in composition, denoting a woman who performs a certain job, etc., as *tea-lady*:—*pl.* **ladies** (*lā'diz*); old genitive **la'dy.**—*n.* **ladies'** ladies' public lavatory.—*n.* **la'dyhood** condition, character of a lady.—*adj.* **la'dylike** like a lady in manners: refined: soft, delicate: often implying want of touch with reality and sincerity—genteel.—*n.* **la'dyship** the title of a lady.—**ladies' companion** a small bag used for a woman's needlework; **ladies' fingers** see **lady's fingers**(s) below; **ladies' gallery** a gallery in the House of Commons; **ladies' man** one fond of women's society; **la'dybird** any member of the family Coccinellidae, little round beetles, often brightly spotted, preying on greenfly, etc.—also **la'dybug, la'dycow, la'dyfly; lady chapel** a chapel dedicated to the Virgin Mary, usually behind the high altar, at the end of the apse; **Lady Day** 25th March, the day of the annunciation of the Virgin; **la'dy-in-wait'ing** an attendant to a lady of royal status; **la'dy-killer** a man who is, or fancies himself, irresistible to women; **la'dy-love** a lady or woman loved: a sweetheart; **la'dy's-cu'shion** the mossy saxifrage; **la'dy's finger, fingers** a name for many plants, esp. the kidney-vetch: gumbo, okra. a finger-shaped cake; **la'dy's-maid** a female attendant on a lady, esp. for the toilet; **la'dy's-mantle** a genus of rosaceous plants with small, yellowish-green flowers and leaves like folded drapery; **la'dy's-slipp'er** a genus of orchids with large slipper-like lip; **la'dy's-smock, la'dy-smock** the cuckoo-flower, a cruciferous meadow-plant, with pale lilac-coloured flowers; **lady's (or ladies') tresses** (*sing.* or *pl*) an orchid with small white flowers —**find the lady** see **three-card trick** under **three; our Lady** the Virgin Mary. [O.E. *hlǽfdige*, lit app. the bread-kneader—*hlāf*, loaf, and a lost word from the root of **dough.**]

laevo-, levo- *lē-vō-*, in composition, on, or to, the left. [L. *laevus*, left.]

laevorotatory, levorotatory *lē-vō-rō'tə-tə-ri, -rō-tā'*, *adj.* counterclockwise: rotating the plane of polarisation of light to the left.—*n.* **laevorota'tion.** [L. *laevus*, left, *rotāre*, to rotate.]

laevulose *lēv'ū-lōs*, or *lev'*, *n* fructose, a laevorotatory sugar ($C_6H_{12}O_6$).—Also **levulose.** [L. *laevus*, left.]

lag *lag*, n. he who, or that which, comes behind: the fag-end: (esp in *pl.*) dregs: a retardation or falling behind: the amount by which one phenomenon is delayed behind another: delay.—*v.i.* to move or walk slowly: to loiter: to fall behind:—*pr.p.* **lagg'ing;** *pa.t.* and *pa.p.* **lagged.**—*adj.* **lagg'ard** lagging.—*ns.* **lagg'ard,** **lagg'er** one who lags behind.—*n.* and *adj.* **lag'ging.**—*adv* **lagg'ingly.**—**lag of the tides** the progressive lengthening of the interval between tides as neap-tide is approached—opp. to *priming.*

lag *lag*, *n.* a stave: a lath: boarding: a wooden lining: a non-conducting covering: a perforated wooden strip used instead of a card in weaving.—*v.t.* to furnish with a lag or lagging.—*ns.* **lagg'er** one who insulates pipes, machinery, etc. against heat loss; **lagg'ing** boarding, as across the framework of a centre for an arch, or in a mine to prevent ore falling into a passage: a non-conducting covering for pipes, etc. to minimise loss of heat. [Prob O.N. *lögg*, barrel-rim.]

lag *lag*, (*slang*) *v.t.* to steal: to carry off: to arrest: to send to penal servitude.—*n* a convict: an old convict: a term of penal servitude or transportation.

lagan *lag'ən*, *n.* wreckage or goods at the bottom of the sea: later taken to mean such goods attached to a buoy with a view to recovery.—Also **ligan** (*lī'gən*). [O.Fr. *lagan*, perh. Scand. from the root of **lay²**, **lie²**; falsely associated with L. *ligāmen*, a tying.]

lager *lä'gər*, *n.* (in full **lager beer**) a light beer kept for up to six months before use. [Ger. *Lager-bier—Lager*, a storehouse.]

lagomorph *lag'o-mórf*, *n.* an animal of the order *Lagomorpha* of gnawing mammals having two pairs of upper incisors, e.g. hares, rabbits.—*adjs.* **lagomor'phic, lagomor'phous.** [Gr. *lagōs*, hare, *morphē*, form.]

lagoon *lə-gōōn'*, *n.* a shallow lake, esp. one near or communicating with the sea or a river. [It. *laguna—* L. *lacūna.*]

lagrimoso *läg-ri-mō'sō,· (mus.) adj.* and *adv.* plaintive(ly). [It.,—L. *lacrimōsus*, tearful—*lacrima*, a tear.]

lah. Same as la².

lahar *lä'här*, *n.* a mud-lava or other mud-flow.

lah-di-dah. See **la-di-da.**

laic, laical, laicise. See **lay⁴.**

laid *lād*, *pa.t.* and *pa.p.* of **lay.**—*adj.* put down, prostrate· pressed down.—*adj.* **laid'-back', laid back** (*slang*) relaxed: easy-going: unhurried.—**laid paper** such as shows the marks of the close parallel wires on which the pulp was laid—opp. to *wove*; **laid work** in embroidery, couching of the simplest kind

laika *lī'kə*, *n* any of several similar breeds of working dog, originating in Finland, small and reddish-brown.

lain *pa p* of **lie².**

lair *lār*, *n.* a lying-place, esp. the den or retreat of a wild beast: an enclosure for beasts: the ground for one grave in a burying-place (*Scot.*) —*v t.* to put in a lair.—*v.i* to lie: to go to a lair —*n.* **lair'age** a place where cattle are housed or laired, esp. at markets and docks. [O.E. *leger*, a couch—*licgan*, to lie down.]

laird *lārd*, (*Scot.*) *n.* a landed proprietor.—*n.* **laird'ship.** [Northern form of **lord.**]

laisse *les*, *n.* a tirade or string of verses on one rhyme. [Fr.]

laissez-aller *les'ā-al'ā*, *n.* unconstraint.—Also **laiss'er-all'er.** [Fr , let go.]

laissez-faire *les'ā-fer'*, *n.* a general principle of non-interference —Also **laiss'er-faire'.** [Fr., let do.]

laissez-passer *les'ā-pās'ā*, *n.* pass, special passport. [Fr., let pass.]

laity. See **lay⁴.**

lake¹ *lāk*, *n.* a reddish pigment originally got from lac: a coloured substance got by combination of a dye with a metallic hydroxide: its colour: carmine.—*adj.* **lak'y. [lac.]**

lake² *lāk*, *n.* a large or considerable body of water within land: a large quantity, an excess, as of wine, etc. (*econ.*)—*n.* **lake'let** a little lake.—**lake'-basin** a hollow now or once containing a lake: the area drained by a lake; **Lake District** a picturesque and mountainous region in (formerly) Cumberland, Westmorland, and Lancashire (now in Cumbria), with many lakes; **lake'-dweller; lake'-dwelling** a settlement, esp. prehistoric, built on piles in a lake. [M.E. *lac*, either—O E. *lacu*, stream, confused in sense with L. *lacus*, lake, or from *lacus* itself, directly or through Fr *lac.*]

Lalique glass *lal-ēk'glās*, ornamental glassware, esp. with bas-relief decoration of figures, flowers, etc. [Named after René *Lalique* (d. 1945), Fr. designer of jewellery and glassware.]

lallan *lal'*, *lâl'ən*, *adj.* and *n.* a form of **lowland.**—*n.* **Lallans** Broad Scots: a form of Scots developed by modern Scottish writers.

lallygag, lolly- *lal'*, *lol'i-gag*, (*coll.*), *vs.i.* to idle, loiter: to caress, esp. publicly.

lam *lam*, *v.t.* to beat.—*n.* **lamm'ing.** [Cf. O.E. *lemian*, to subdue, lame, O.N. *lemja*, to beat, lit. lame.]

lama *lä'mə*, *n.* a Buddhist priest in Tibet.—*ns.* **Lamaism** (*lä'mə-izm*) the religion prevailing in Tibet and Mongolia, being Buddhism corrupted by Sivaism, and by Shamanism or spirit-worship; **La'maist.**—*adj.* **lamaist'ic.**—*ns.* **la'masery** (or *lä-mä'sə-ri*), **lamaserai** (*-rī*) a Tibetan monastery. [Tibetan, *blama*, the b silent]

Lamarckism *lä-märk'izm*, *n.* the theory of the French naturalist J. B. P. A. de Monet de *Lamarck* (1744–1829) that species have developed by the efforts of organisms to adapt themselves to new conditions—also **Lamarck'ianism.**—*adj.* and *n.* **Lamarck'ian.**

lamasery, lamaserai. See **lama.**

lamb *lam*, *n.* the young of a sheep: its flesh as a food: lambskin: one simple, innocent or gentle as a lamb.—*v.t.* and *v.i.* to bring forth as sheep· to tend at lambing.—*adj.* **lamb'-like** like a lamb: gentle.—**lamb'skin** the skin of a lamb dressed with the wool on: the skin of a lamb dressed as leather: a woollen cloth resembling this: a cotton cloth with raised surface and deep nap; **lamb's'-lett'uce** corn-salad; **lamb's'-tails'** hazel catkins; **lamb's'-wool** fine wool, specif. wool obtained from the first shearing of a (yearling) lamb.—**like a lamb to the slaughter** meekly, innocently, without resistance; **the Lamb, Lamb of God** applied to Christ, in allusion to the paschal lamb and John i. 29. [O.E. *lamb*.]

lambast *lam-bast'*, *v.t.* to thrash: to reprimand severely.—Also **lambaste** (*lam-bāst'*). [Perh. **lam** and **baste**.]

lambda *lam'də*, *n.* the Greek letter (Λ, λ) corresponding to Roman *l*: used as a symbol for wavelength: the meeting of the sagittal and lambdoid sutures of the skull.—**lambda particle** a subatomic particle, the lightest of the hyperons. [Gr. *lambda*, properly *labda*—Heb. *lāmedh*.]

lambent *lam'bənt*, *adj.* licking: moving about as if touching lightly: gliding over: flickering: softly radiant, glowing: (esp. of wit) light and brilliant.—*n.* **lam'bency** the quality of being lambent: a flicker.—*adv.* **lam'bently**. [L. *lambēre*, to lick.]

lambert *lam'bərt*, *n.* a unit of brightness, one lumen per square centimetre. [After J. H. *Lambert* (1728–77), German scientist.]

lamboys *lam'boiz*, (*ant.*) *n.pl.* kilted flexible steelplates worn skirt-like from the waist. [Perh. Fr. *jambeaux*, flaps; or a blunder for *jambeaux*.]

lambrequin *lam'bər-kin*, or *-brı-kın*, *n.* a veil over a helmet: mantling: a strip of drapery over a window, doorway, from a mantelpiece, etc. [Fr.]

lame[1] *lām*, *adj.* disabled, esp. in the use of a leg: hobbling: unsatisfactory: imperfect.—*v t.* to make lame: to cripple.—*adv.* **lame'ly**.—*n.* **lame'ness**.—*adj.* **lam'ish** a little lame: hobbling. [O.E. *lama*, lame.]

lame[2] *lām*, *n.* a thin plate, esp. of metal, as in armour. —*n.* **lamé** (*lä'mä*) a fabric in which metal threads are interwoven. [Fr.,—L. *lāmina*, a thin plate.]

lamella *lə-mel'ə*, *n.* a thin plate or layer:—*pl.* **lamell'ae** (*-ē*).—*adjs.* **lamell'ar** (or *lam'ı-lər*); **lam'ellate** (or *-el'*), **-d**; **lamell'iform**; **lamell'old**; **lamell'ose**.—*n.* **lamell'ibranch** (*-brangk*; L. *branchiae*, gills) any member of the **Lamellibranchiā'ta**, bivalve molluscs, from their plate-like (nutritive) gills.—*adj.* **lamellibranch'iate**.—*n.* **lamell'icorn** (L. *cornū*, horn) a member of a very numerous group of beetles—the cockchafer, etc., with the ends of the antennae expanded in flattened plates. [L. *lāmella*, dim. of *lāmina*.]

lament *lə-ment'*, *v t* to utter grief in outcries: to wail: to mourn.—*v.t.* to mourn for: to deplore.—*n.* sorrow expressed in cries: an elegy or dirge: a musical composition of like character —*adj.* **lamentable** (*lam'ənt-ə-bl*) deserving or expressing sorrow: sad: pitiful: worthless (*coll.*).—*adv.* **lam'entably**.—*n.* **lamenta'tion** act of lamenting: audible expression of grief: wailing: (*cap.*; *pl.*) a book of the Old Testament traditionally attributed to Jeremiah.—*adj* **lament'ed**.—*n.* and *adj.* **lament'ing**.—*adv.* **lament'ingly**. [L. *lāmentārī*.]

lamina *lam'i-nə*, *n.* a thin plate or layer: a leaf blade: a thin plate of bone: a plate of sensitive tissue within a hoof:—*pl.* **lam'inae** (*-nē*).—*adjs.* **lam'inable** suitable for making into thin plates; **lam'inar**, **lam'inary** consisting of or like thin plates or layers. of or relating to a fluid, streamlined flow.—*v.t.* **lam'inarise**, **-ize** to make (a surface, etc) such that a flow over it will be laminar.—*adj.* **lam'inate**, **-d** in laminae or thin plates: consisting of scales or layers, over one another: made by laminating.—*v t* **lam'inate** to make into a thin plate: to separate into layers: to make by putting layers together.—*n* a laminated plastic, or other material similarly made.—*ns* **lamina'tion** arrangement in thin layers. a thin layer; **lam'inator** one who manufactures laminates; **lamini'tis** inflammation of a horse's lamina —**laminar flow** viscous flow: a fluid flow in which the particles move smoothly without turbulence, esp., as in aircraft,

such a non-impeding flow over a streamlined surface (*phys.*); **laminated plastic** sheets of paper, canvas, linen, or silk, impregnated with a resin, dried and pressed together. [L. *lāmina*, a thin plate.]

Lammas *lam'əs*, *n.* the feast of first fruits on 1st August.—**Lamm'as-tide** season of Lammas. [O.E. *hlāf-mæsse*, *hlāmmæsse*—*hlāf*, loaf, *mæsse*, feast.]

lammergeier, **lammergeyer** *lam'ər-gī-ər*, *n.* the great bearded vulture of southern Europe, etc. [Ger. *Lämmergeier*—*Lämmer*, lambs, *Geier*, vulture.]

lamp *lamp*, *n.* a vessel for burning oil with a wick, and so giving light: any structure containing a source of artificial light: any source of light: an eye (*arch.* and *slang*).—*v.t.* to illumine.—**lamp'-black** soot from a lamp, or from the burning of bodies rich in carbon (mineral oil, turpentine, tar, etc.) in a limited supply of air: a pigment made from it.—*v.t.* to blacken with lamp-black.—**lamp'-burner** that part of a lamp from which the flame proceeds; **lamp'-chimney**, **lamp's glass** a glass funnel placed round the flame of a lamp; **lamp'holder** a socket for an electric bulb; **lamp'light** the light shed by a lamp or lamps; **lamp'lighter** a person employed to light street-lamps; **lamp'post**, **lamp'-standard** the pillar supporting a street-lamp; **lamp'shade** a structure for moderating or directing the light of a lamp; **lamp'-shell** a brachiopod, esp. Terebratula or kindred genus, from its shell like an antique lamp.—**smell of the lamp** to show signs of great elaboration or study. [Fr. *lampe*, and Gr. *lampas*, *-ados*—*lampein*, to shine.]

lampas *lam'pas*, *n.* a material of silk and wool used in upholstery. [Fr.]

lampern *lam'pərn*, *n.* a river lamprey. [O.Fr. *lamprion*.]

lampoon *lam-pōōn'*, *n.* a personal satire.—*v.t.* to assail with personal satire.—*ns* **lampoon'er**; **lampoon'ery**; **lampoon'ist**. [O.Fr. *lampon*, perh. from a drinking-song with the refrain *lampons*, let us drink.]

lamprey *lam'pri*, *n.* a genus of cyclostomes that fix themselves to stones by their mouths:—*pl.* **lam'preys**. [O.Fr. *lamproie*—L.L. *lamprēda*, *lampetra*.]

lanate *lā'nāt*, **lanose** *lā'nōs*, *-nōz*, *adjs.* woolly. [L. *lānātus*—*lāna*, wool.]

Lancastrian *lang-kas'tri-ən*, *adj.* pertaining to *Lancaster*, or Lancashire, or the dukes or house of Lancaster —*n.* a native of Lancaster or Lancashire: an adherent of the house of Lancaster.

lance[1] *lans*, *n.* a cavalry weapon with a long shaft, a spearhead, and a small flag: a similar weapon for other purposes: a surgeon's lancet: a blade in a cutting tool to sever the grain in advance of the main blade· the bearer of a lance.—*v.t.* to pierce, as with a lance: to open with a lancet.—Also **launce**.—*ns.* **lance'let** any of the narrow, translucent, backboned marine animals of the genera Amphioxus and Asymmetron; **lanc'er** a light cavalry soldier armed with a lance, or of a regiment formerly so armed. (*pl*) a popular set of quadrilles, first in England about 1820, or its music.—*adj.* **lanc'iform** shaped like a lance.—**lance'-corporal** acting corporal· the military rank between private and corporal (*army slang*, **lance's jack**); **lance'-sergeant** a corporal acting as a sergeant; **lance'-wood** a wood of various kinds, strong and elastic, brought from Jamaica, Guyana, etc [Fr ,—L *lancea*.]

lance[2]. See **launce**.

lanceolate, **-d** *lan'sı-ə-lāt*, *-ıd*, *adjs* shaped like a lance-head lancet-shaped: tapering toward both ends and two or three times as long as broad (*bot.*) [L *lanceolātus*—*lanceola*, dim. of *lancea*, lance]

lancet *lan'sıt*, *n.* a surgical instrument used for opening veins, abscesses, etc a lancet window a lancet arch —*adj* shaped like a lancet, narrow and pointed.—

adj. **lan'ceted.**—**lancet arch** high and narrow pointed arch; **lancet window** a tall, narrow, acutely arched window. [O.Fr. *lancette*, dim. of lance¹; see lance².]
lancinate *lān'sin-āt, v.t.* to lacerate: to pierce.—*adj.* **lan'cinating** (of pain) shooting, darting.—*n.* **lancinā'tion** sharp, shooting pain. [L. *lancināre, -ātum,* to tear.]
land *land, n.* the solid portion of the surface of the globe: a country: a district: a nation or people: real estate: ground: soil: a group of dwellings or tenements under one roof and having a common entry (*Scot.*).—*v.t.* to set on land or on shore: to set down: to deposit, drop, or plant: to cause to arrive: to bring ashore: to capture: to secure: to attach to one's interest.—*v.i.* to come on land or on shore: to alight: to arrive, find oneself, end by being.—*adj.* of or on the land: land-dwelling: terrestrial.—*adj.* **land'ed** possessing land or estates: consisting in or derived from land or real estate.—*n.* **land'ing** disembarkation: a coming to ground: alighting: putting ashore: setting down: a place for getting on shore or upon the ground: the level part of staircase between flights of steps or at the top.—*adj.* relating to the unloading of a vessel's cargo, or to disembarking, or to alighting from the air.—*adjs.* **land'less; land'ward** lying towards the land: inland.—*advs.* **land'ward, -s** towards the land.—**land'-agent** a person employed to let farms, collect rents, etc.: an agent or broker for buying and selling of land; **land'-army** a body of women organised for farm-work in wartime; **land'-bridge** (*geol.*) a connection by land allowing terrestrial plants and animals to pass from one region to another; **landed interest** the combined interest of the land-owning class in a community; **land'fall** an approach to land after a journey by sea or air: the land so approached; **land'fill** the disposal of refuse by burying it under the soil: refuse disposed of in this way: a place where landfill is practised; **land'filling, land'-girl** a girl who does farm-work; **land'-grabbing; land grant** a grant of public land (to a college, etc.); **land'holder** a tenant or proprietor of land.—*adj.* **land'holding.**—**land'ing-beam** a radio beam by which an aircraft is guided in to land; **land'ing-carriage** the wheeled structure on which an aeroplane runs when starting or landing; **land'ing-craft** a small, low, open vessel, or vessels, for landing troops and equipment on beaches; **land'ing-field** a field that allows aircraft to land and take-off safely; **land'ing-gear** wheels, floats, etc., of an aircraft used in alighting; **land'ing-ground** a piece of ground prepared for landing aircraft as required; **land'ing-net** a kind of scoop-net for landing a fish that has been hooked; **land'ing-place** a place for landing; **land'ing-ship** a ship whose forward part can be let down in order to put vehicles ashore; **land'ing-speed** the minimum speed at which an aircraft normally lands; **land'ing-stage** a platform, fixed or floating, for landing passengers or goods; **land'ing-strip** a narrow hard-surfaced runway; **land'lady** a woman who has tenants or lodgers: the mistress of an inn; **land'-line** overland line of communication or transport.—*adj.* **land'-locked** almost or quite shut in by land: cut off from the sea.—**land'lord** a man who has tenants or lodgers: the master of an inn; **land'-lordism** the authority, policy, behaviour, or united action of the landowning class: the system of land-ownership; **land'-lubber** (*naut.*; in contempt) a landsman.—*adj.* **land'-lubberly.**—**land'man** a countryman: a landsman; **land'mark** any land-boundary mark: any conspicuous object on land marking a locality or serving as a guide: an event of outstanding moment in history, thought, etc.; **land'mass** a large area of land unbroken by seas; **land'-mine** a type of bomb laid on or near the surface of the ground, to

explode when an enemy is over it: a large bomb dropped by parachute.—*v.t.* to lay land-mines.—**land'-mining; land'owner** one who owns land; **land'-ownership.**—*adj.* **land'-owning.**—**land'race** a large white Danish breed of pig; **land'rail** the corncrake; **Land'-rover®** a sturdy motor-vehicle used for driving over rough ground; **land'slide** a landslip (orig. *U.S.*): a great transference of votes; **land'slip** a fall of land or rock from a hillside or cliff: a portion so fallen; **land's'man** one who lives or serves on land: one inexperienced in seafaring; **land'-spring** a shallow intermittent spring; **land'-steward** a person who manages a landed estate; **land'-survey'ing** measurement and mapping of land; **land'-survey'or; land'-tax** a tax upon land; **land'-val'ue** (usu. in *pl.*) the economic value of land, a basis of taxation; **land-yacht(ing)** see yacht.—**land of milk and honey** a land of great fertility promised to the Israelites by God: any region of great fertility; **land of Nod** the state of slumber (*coll.*); **land with** to encumber with (a burden, difficult situation, etc.); **see how the land lies** to find out in advance how matters stand. [O.E. *land.*]
land² *land,* (*U.S.*) *n.* and *interj.* euphemism for lord.
Land *länt, n.* a state or province in Germany and Austria functioning as a unit of local government:—*pl.* **Länder** (*len'dər*). [Ger. *Land,* land.]
landau *lan'dö, n.* a carriage with folding top.—*n.* **land-aulet'**, **-ette** a motor-car whose enclosed part can be uncovered: a small landau. [*Landau* in Germany, where it is said to have been first made.]
lande *lād, n.* a heathy plain or sandy tract (now forested) along the coast in S.W. France. [Fr.]
ländler *lent'lər, n.* a South German dance, or its tune, like a slow waltz. [Ger.,—*Landl,* a nickname for Upper Austria.]
land-louper *land'lowp-ər,* **landloper, land-loper** *-lōp-ər, ns.* a vagabond or vagrant. [Du. *landlooper* —*land,* land, *loopen,* to ramble.]
landscape *land'skāp, n.* the appearance of that portion of land which the eye can view at once: the aspect of a country, or a picture representing it: the painting of such pictures.—*v.t.* to improve by landscape-gardening.—Also *v.i.*—**land'scape-gar'dening** the art of laying out grounds so as to produce the effect of a picturesque landscape; **land'scape-paint'er, land'-scapist** a painter of landscapes; **land'scape-paint'ing.** [Du. *landschap,* from *land* and *-schap,* suffix = *-ship.*]
landsknecht *länts'knehht,* (*hist.*) *n.* a mercenary foot-soldier of the 16th century. [Ger.,—*lands,* gen. of *Land,* country, *Knecht,* servant, soldier.]
Landsmaal, -mål *läns'möl, n.* a literary language based on Norwegian dialects by Ivar Aasen (1850), now called Nynorsk, new Norse. [Norw.,—*land,* land, *maal,* speech.]
Landtag *länt'tähh, n.* the legislative assembly of a German state or land: the Diet of the Holy Roman Empire, or of the German Federation. [Ger.,—*Land,* country, *Tag,* diet, day.]
Landwehr *länt'vār, n.* an army reserve. [Ger.,—*Land,* land, *Wehr,* defence.]
lane *lān, n.* a narrow passage or road: a passage through a crowd or among obstructions: a division of a road for a single stream of traffic: a channel: a prescribed course. [O.E. *lane, lone.*]
lang *lang, adj.* a Scottish form of long.—*adv.* **lang syne** (*sīn*) long since, long ago.—*n.* time long past.
langlauf *läng'lowf, n.* cross-country skiing. [Ger. *lang,* long and *Lauf,* race, run, leap.]
Langobard *lang'gō-bärd.* See Lombard.
langouste *lä-gōost', n.* the spiny lobster.—*n.* **langoustine** (*-ēn'*) the Norway lobster (see lobster), larger than a prawn but smaller than a lobster. [Fr.]
langrage, langridge *lang'grij, n.* shot consisting of a

canister containing irregular pieces of iron, formerly used to damage sails and rigging.

language *lang'gwij, n.* human speech: a variety of speech or body of words and idioms, esp. that of a nation: mode of expression: diction: any manner of expressing thought or feeling: an artificial system of signs and symbols, with rules for forming intelligible communications, for use in e.g. a computer.—**language laboratory** a room in which pupils in separate cubicles are taught a language by means of material recorded on tapes.—**bad language** swearing; **dead language** one no longer spoken, as opp. to **living language; speak the same language** to come within one's range of understanding: to have the same tastes or habit of mind. [Fr. *langage*—*langue*—L. *lingua*, the tongue.]

langue *läg,* (*linguistics*) *n.* language viewed as a general or abstract system, as opposed to **parole**. [Fr.,—L. *lingua*, tongue.]

langue de chat *läg-də-sha',* a very thin finger-shaped biscuit or piece of chocolate. [Fr., cat's tongue.]

Langue d'oc *läg dok,* a collective name for the Romance dialects of southern France, often used as synonymous with Provençal, one of its chief branches. The name itself survives in the province *Languedoc.—adj.* **Languedocian** (*lang-gə-dö'shi-ən*). —**Langue d'oïl** (*läg do-ël, doil*), the Romance dialect of northern France, the main element in modern French. [O.Fr. *langue*—L. *lingua*, tongue; *de,* of; Prov. *oc,* yes—L. *hōc,* this; O.Fr. *oil, oui,* yes—L. *hōc illud,* this (is) that, yes.]

languet, languette *lang'gwet, -get, -get', n.* a tongue-like object or part. [Fr. *languette,* dim. of *langue,* tongue.]

languid *lang'gwid, adj.* slack: flagging: inert: listless: faint: relaxed: spiritless.—*adv.* **lang'uidly.**—*n.* **lang'uidness.** [L. *languidus*—*languēre,* to be weak.]

languish *lang'gwish, v.i.* to become or be languid, inert, depressed: to lose strength and animation: to pine: to flag, droop: to look languishingly.—*adj.* **lang'uished** sunken in languor.—*ns.* **lang'uisher; lang'uishing.—adj.** expressive of languor, or merely sentimental emotion: lingering.—*adv.* **lang'uishingly.**—*n.* **lang'uishment** the act or state of languishing: tenderness of look. [Fr. *languiss-* (serving as part. stem of *languir*)—L. *languēscēre*—*languēre,* to be faint.]

languor *lang'gər, n.* pining: languidness: listlessness: lassitude: dreamy inertia: tender softness.—*adj.* **lang'uorous** full of or expressing languor: languishing. [L. *languor, -ōris.*]

langur *lung-gōōr', n.* the entellus monkey or other of its genus. [Hindi *lāgūr.*]

laniard. See **lanyard.**

laniferous *lan-if'ər-əs, adj.* wool-bearing.—Also **lanigerous** (*-ij'*). [L. *lānifer, lāniger*—*lāna,* wool, *ferre, gerĕre,* to bear.]

lank *langk, adj.* flabby: drooping: flaccid: limp: thin: (of hair) straight and flat.—*n.* **lank'iness.**—*adv.* **lank'ly.**—*n.* **lank'ness.**—*adj.* **lank'y** lean, tall, and ungainly: long and limp. [O.E. *hlanc.*]

lanner *lan'ər, n.* a kind of falcon, esp. the female.—*n.* **lann'eret** the male lanner. [Fr. *lanier,* possibly—L. *laniārius,* tearing, or from *lānārius,* a weaver (a mediaeval term of reproach).]

lanolin(e) *lan'ō-lin, -lēn, n.* fat from wool, a mixture of palmitate, oleate, and stearate of cholesterol. [L. *lāna,* wool, *oleum,* oil.]

lanose. See **lanate.**

lant *lant.* Same as **launce.**

lantern *lant'ərn, n.* a case for holding or carrying a light: the light-chamber of a lighthouse: a magic lantern: an open structure like a lantern, esp. one

surmounting a building, giving light and air.—*adj.* **lan'tern-jawed** hollow-faced.—**lantern jaws** thin long jaws. [Fr. *lanterne*—L. *lanterna*—Gr. *lamptēr* —*lampein,* to give light.]

lanthanum *lan'thə-nəm, n.* a metallic element (at. numb. 57; symbol La).—*n.pl.* **lan'thanides** the rare-earth elements. [Gr. *lanthanein,* to escape notice, because it lay hid in rare minerals till 1839.]

lanugo *lan-ū'gō, n.* down: an embryonic woolly coat of hair:—*pl.* **lanū'gos.**—*adjs.* **lanū'ginose** (*-jin-*), **lanūginous** downy: covered with fine soft hair. [L. *lānūgō, -inis,* down—*lāna,* wool.]

lanyard, laniard *lan'yərd, n.* a short rope used as a fastening or handle (*naut.*): a cord for hanging a knife, whistle, or the like about the neck. [Fr. *lanière,* origin doubtful; confused with **yard.**]

Laodicean *lā-od-i-sē'ən, adj.* lukewarm in religion, like the Christians of *Laodicea* (Rev. iii. 14–16).—*n.* **Laodicē'anism.** [Gr. *Lāodikeia,* Laodicea.]

Laotian *la-ō'shən, adj.* of Laos or its people.—*n.* a native of Laos.

lap¹ *lap, v.t.* to scoop up with the tongue (often with *up*): to take in greedily or readily (*fig.*) (usu. with *up*): to wash or flow against.—*v.i* to drink by licking up: to make a sound or movement as of lapping:—*pr.p.* **lapp'ing;** *pa.t.* and *pa.p.* **lapped.**—*n.* a motion or sound of lapping: that which may be lapped: thin liquor.—*n.* and *adj.* **lapp'ing.** [O.E. *lapian.*]

lap² *lap, n.* a flap: a lobe (of the ear): a fold: a hollow: part of a garment disposed to hold or catch: the fold of the clothes and body from waist to knees of a person sitting: place where one is nurtured (*fig.*; in phrases): a round, as of a race-course, or of anything coiled: an overlap: amount of overlap: a polishing disc, cylinder, or the like: the length of material needed to go round a drum, etc.: a layer or sheet of (cotton, etc.) fibres.—*v.t.* to wrap, enfold, surround: to lay overlappingly: to polish with a lap: to unite accurately: to get or be a lap ahead of: to traverse as a lap or in laps: to hold in the lap.—*v.i.* to lie with an overlap: to overlap: to extend beyond some limit.—*n.* and *adj.* **lapp'ing.—lap'-board** a flat wide board resting on the lap, used by tailors and seamstresses; **lap'dog** a small dog fondled in the lap: a pet dog.—*adj.* **lap'-joint'ed** having joints formed by overlapping edges.—**lap of honour** a ceremonial circuit of field, track, show ring, made by the victor(s) in a contest; **the lap of luxury** luxurious conditions; **in the lap of the gods** of a situation, such that the result cannot be predicted. [O.E. *læppa,* a loosely hanging part.]

laparoscopy *lap-ər-os'kəp-i, n.* surgical examination by means of a **laparoscope** (*lap'ər-əs-kōp*), a tube-shaped optical instrument which permits examination of the internal organs from outside. [Gr. *laparā,* flank, *skopeein,* to see.]

lapel *la-, lə-pel', n.* part of a coat folded back continuing the collar.—*adj.* **lapelled'.** [Dim. of **lap².**]

lapis *lap'is, n.* a stone (the Latin word, used in certain phrases only).—*adj.* **lapidar'ian** pertaining to stones: inscribed on stones: learned in stones.—*ns.* **lap'idarist** (*-ə-rist*) an expert in gems; **lap'idary** (*-ə-ri*) a cutter of stones, esp. gem-stones.—*adj.* pertaining to stones: dwelling in stone-heaps (as a kind of bee): inscribed on stone: suitable for inscription.—*adj.* **lapid'eous** stony; **lapidic'olous** (L. *colĕre,* to inhabit) living under or among stones.—*n.pl.* **lapilli** (*lä-pil'lē*) small fragments (in size from a pea to a walnut) of lava ejected from a volcano (*pl.* of It. *lapil'lo;* also of L. *lapil'lus*).—*adj.* **lapill'iform.—lapis laz'uli** a beautiful stone consisting of calcite and other minerals coloured ultramarine by lazurite, etc., commonly spangled with iron pyrites (see **azure,**

lazulite, lazurite).—lapis lazuli blue a deep blue, sometimes veined with gold, used in decoration and in porcelain; **lapis lazuli ware** a pebble ware veined with gold upon blue. [L. *lapis, -idis,* a stone.]

Lapp *lap,* **Lap'lander** *-ləndər, ns.* a native or inhabitant of Lapland: one of the race or people inhabiting Lapland.—*adjs.* **Lapp, Lap'landish; Lapp'ish.**—*ns.* the language of the Lapps.

lappet *lap'it, n.* a little lap or flap.—*adj.* **lapp'eted.**— **lappet moth** a moth of the Lasiocampidae whose caterpillar has lappets on its sides. [Dim. of **lap²**.]

lapse *laps, v.i.* to slip or glide: to pass by degrees: to fall away by cessation or relaxation of effort or cause: to fall from the faith: to fail in virtue or duty: to pass into disuse: to pass or fail owing to some omission or non-fulfilment: to become void.—*n.* a slip: passage (of time): a falling away: a failure (in virtue, attention, memory, etc.): a vertical gradient as of atmospheric temperature.—*adjs.* **laps'able** liable to lapse; **lapsed** having slipped or passed or been let slip: fallen away (esp. in the Christian Church, from the faith).— **lapse rate** (*meteor.*) rate of change in temperature in relation to height in the atmosphere. [L. *lāpsāre,* to slip, *lāpsus,* a slip—*lābi, lāpsus,* to slip.]

lapsus *lap'səs, lap'sŏŏs,* (L.) *n.* a slip.—**lapsus calami** (*kal'ə-mī, ka'la-mē*) a slip of the pen; **lapsus linguae** (*ling'gwē, 'gwī*) a slip of the tongue; **lapsus memoriae** (*me-mōr'i-ē* or *mōr'* or *'ri-ī*) a slip of the memory.

lapwing *lap'wing, n.* a bird of the plover family, the peewit. [M.E. *lappewinke*—O.E. *lǣpewince, hlēapewince, hlēapewince:* modified by folk ety.]

larceny *lär'sə-ni, n.* the legal term in England and Ireland for stealing: theft.—*ns.* **lar'cener, lar'cenist** a thief.—*adj.* **lar'cenous.**—*adv.* **lar'cenously.** [O.Fr. *larrecin* (Fr. *larcin*)—L. *latrōcinium—latrō,* a robber.]

larch *lärch, n.* any tree of the coniferous genus Larix, distinguished from cedar by the deciduous leaves. [Ger. *Lärche*—L. *larix, -ícis.*]

lard *lärd, n.* the rendered fat of the hog.—*v.t.* to smear or enrich with lard: to stuff with bacon or pork: to fatten: to mix with anything: to stuff or load: to interlard, interpenetrate: to garnish, strew.—*n.* **lar'don, lardoon'** a strip of bacon used for larding.—*adj.* **lar'dy.**—**lar'dy-cake** esp. in S. England, a rich sweet cake made of bread dough, with lard, dried fruit, etc. [O.Fr.,—L. *lāridum, lārdum.*]

larder *lärd'ər, n.* a place where food is kept: stock of provisions.—*n.* **lard'erer** one in charge of a larder. [O.Fr. *lardier,* bacon-tub; see **lard.**]

lardo(o)n, lardy(-cake). See **lard**.

large *lärj, adj.* great in size: extensive: bulky: broad: copious: abundant: generous: magnanimous: loftily affected or pretentious: in a great way: (of the wind) having a favouring component (*naut.*).—*adv.* before the wind (*naut.*): ostentatiously.—*adv.* **large'ly** in a large manner: in great measure.—*n.* **large'ness.**— *adj.* **larg'ish** fairly large, rather big.—*adjs.* **large's heart'ed** having a large heart: of liberal disposition or comprehensive sympathies: generous; **large'-mind'ed** magnanimous: characterised by breadth of view.—**as large as life** actually, really; **at large** at liberty: at random: in general: in full. [Fr.,—L. *largus,* abounding.]

largess, largesse *lärj'es, n.* a bestowal or distribution of gifts: generosity. [Fr. *largesse.*]

largo *lär'gō, (mus.) adj.* broad and slow.—Also *adv.*— *n.* a movement to be so performed:—*pl.* **lar'gos.**— *adj.* **larghet'to** somewhat slow: not so slow as largo.— *n.* a somewhat slow movement:—*pl.* **larghet'tos.** [It.,—L. *largus.*]

lariat *lar'i-ət, n.* a picketing rope, a lasso. [Sp. *la,* the, *reata,* picketing rope.]

lark¹ *lärk, n.* a well-known bird (*Alauda*) that flies high as it sings: extended to various similar birds.— *v.i.* to catch larks.—*adj.* **lark'-heeled** having a long hind-claw.—**lark's'-heel** the Indian cress: the larkspur; **lark'spur** any plant of the genus Delphinium, from the spurred flowers.—**get up with the lark** to rise very early in the morning. [M.E. *laverock*— O.E. *lǣwerce, lāwerce.*]

lark² *lärk, n.* a frolic: a piece of mischief.—*v.i.* to frolic.—*ns* **lark'er; lark'iness.**—*adjs.* **lark'ish; lark'y** (*coll.*). [Perh. from the preceding (cf. **skylarking**).]

larmier *lär'mi-ər, n.* a corona or other course serving as a dripstone (*archit.*): a tear-pit (*zool.*). [Fr.,— *larme*—L. *lacrima,* a tear.]

larn *lärn,* (*dial.* or *facet.*) *v.t.* and *v.i.* to learn: to teach. [**learn.**]

larrigan *lar'i-gən, n.* a long boot made of oiled leather worn by lumbermen, etc.

larrup *lar'əp,* (*coll.*) *v.t.* to flog, thrash. [Cf. Du. *larpen,* thresh with flails.]

larva *lär'və, n.* an animal in an immature but active state markedly different from the adult, e.g. a caterpillar:—*pl.* **larvae** (*lär'vē;* L. *-vī*).—*adjs.* **lar'val; larvici'dal** destroying larvae.—*n.* **lar'vicide.** —*adj.* **lar'viform.** [L. *lārva, lārua,* a spectre, a mask.]

larynx *lar'ingks, n.* the upper part of the windpipe:— *pl.* **larynges** (*lar'in-jēz,* or *lar-in'jēz*) or **lar'ynxes.**— *adjs.* **laryngal** (*lar-ing'gl*), **laryngeal** (*lar-in'ji-əl*).— *n.* **laryngectomy** (*-jek*) surgical removal of the larynx.—*adj.* **laryngitic** (*-jit'ik*).—*n.* **laryngitis** (*-jī'tis*) inflammation of the larynx.—*adjs.* **laryngological** (*-ing-ga-loj'*).—*ns.* **laryngol'ogist; laryngology** (*-gol'ə-ji*) the science of the larynx; **laryng'oscope** a mirror for examining the larynx and trachea.—*adj.* **laryngoscop'ic.**—*ns.* **laryngos'copist; laryngos'copy; laryngot'omy** the operation of cutting into the larynx. [Gr. *larynx, -yngos.*]

lasagne *lä-zän'yə, -sän', la-, lə-, n.pl.* flat pieces of pasta: (*sing.*) a baked dish of this with tomatoes, cheese, meat.—Also **lasagna.** [It.; *sing. lasagna.*]

lascar *las'kər, -kär,* or *las-kär', n.* an Oriental (originally Indian) sailor or camp-follower. [Hind. and Pers. *lashkar,* army, or *lashkarī,* a soldier.]

lascivious *lə-siv'i-əs, adj.* wanton: inclining or tending to libidinousness.—*adv.* **lasciv'iously.**—*n.* **lasciv'iousness.** [L.L. *lascīviōsus*—L. *lascīvus,* playful.]

laser *lāz'ər, n.* a device which amplifies an input of light, producing an extremely narrow and intense monochromatic beam.—Also *adj.*—*v.i.* **lase** (of a crystal, etc.) to be, or become, suitable for use as a laser. [*Light amplification by stimulated emission* of *radiation.*]

lash¹ *lash, n.* the flexible part of a whip: a scourge: an eyelash: a stroke with a whip or anything pliant: a sweep or flick: a stroke of satire.—*v.t.* to strike with, or as if with, a lash: to dash against: to drive, urge, or work by blows of anything flexible, or figuratively: to whisk or flick with a sweeping movement: to secure with a rope or cord: to scourge with sarcasm or satire. —*v.i.* to dash: to make a rapid sweeping movement or onset: to use the whip.—*ns.* **lash'er** one who lashes or whips: a rope for binding one thing to another; **lash'- ing** act of whipping: a rope for making things fast: (colloquial, esp. in *pl.*) an abundance of anything.— **lash'-up** (*slang*) a mess, fiasco: an improvisation.— **lash out** to kick out, fling out, hit out without restraint: to spend extravagantly. [Perh. several different words, with possible connections with **latch, lash²** and **lace.**]

lash² *lash, adj.* soft: insipid.—*n.* **lash'er** a weir: a waterfall from a weir: a pool below a weir. [M.E. *lasche*, slack—O.Fr. *lasche*—L. *laxus*, lax.]

lashkar *lash'kār*, *n.* a body of armed Indian tribesmen, a force. [Hind., army, camp; cf. **lascar**.]

lasket *las'kit*, *n.* a loop at the foot of a sail, to fasten an extra sail. [Perh. **latchet**.]

lass *las*, *n.* a girl: a sweetheart.—*n.* (dim.) **lassie** (*las'i*) the ordinary Scots word for a girl.

Lassa fever *la'sə fē'vər*, an infectious tropical virus disease, often fatal, transmitted by rodents. [From *Lassa*, in Nigeria, where it was first recognised.]

lassitude *las'i-tūd*, *n.* faintness: weakness: weariness: languor. [L. *lassitūdō—lassus*, faint.]

lasso *la-sōō'*, *las'ō*, *n.* a long rope with a running noose for catching wild horses, etc.:—*pl.* **lasso(e)s'** (or *las'*). —*v.t.* to catch with the lasso:—*pr.p.* **lasso'ing** (or *las'*); *pa.p.* **lassoed** (*las-ōōd'* or *las'*). [S. Amer. pron. of Sp. *lazo*—L. *laqueus*, a noose.]

last[1] *läst*, *n.* a shoemaker's model of the foot on which boots and shoes are made or repaired. [O.E. *lǣste*, last, *lǣst*, footprint]

last[2] *läst*, *v.i.* to continue, endure: to escape failure: to remain fresh, unimpaired: to hold out: to survive.— *n.* **last'er** one who has staying power: a thing that keeps well.—*adj.* **last'ing** enduring: durable.—*n.* endurance.—*adv.* **last'ingly**.—*n.* **last'ingness.—last out** to last as long as or longer than: to last to the end or as long as is required. [O.E. *lǣstan*, to follow a track, keep on, suffice, last, see foregoing word.]

last[3] *läst*, *n.* a load, cargo: a varying weight, generally about 4000 lb.—*n.* **last'age** the lading of a ship: room for stowing goods in a ship. [O.E. *hlæst*.]

last[4] *läst*, *adj.* latest: coming or remaining after all the others: final: immediately before the present: utmost: ending a series: most unlikely, least to be preferred.—Also *adv.*—*adv.* **last'ly** finally.—*adj.* **last'-ditch** (of an attempt, etc) made at the last moment or in the last resort.—*adj.* **last'-minute** made, done, or given at the latest possible time.—**last post** (*mil.*) second of two bugle-calls denoting the hour of retiring for the night: farewell bugle-call at military funerals; **last rites** religious rites performed for those near death; **last straw** (the straw that breaks the camel's back) that beyond which there can be no endurance; **last word** final remark in an argument: final decision: the most up-to-date of its kind (*coll.*). —**at last** in the end; **at long last** after long delay; **breathe one's last** to die; **first and last** altogether; **last thing** after doing everything else, **on one's last legs** on the verge of utter failure or exhaustion; **see (hear) the last** of see (hear) for the last time; **the Last Day** the Day of Judgment; **the Last Supper** the supper partaken of by Christ and his disciples on the eve of the crucifixion; **to the last** to the end: till death. [O.E. *latost*, superl. of *læt*, slow, late.]

latch *lach*, *n.* a door catch lifted from without by a lever or string: a light door-lock, opened from without by a key.—*v.t.* and *v.i.* to fasten with a latch.—*ns.* **latch'key**, **latch'-string** a key, string, for opening a latched door.—**latchkey child** one who regularly returns home to an empty house; **latch on to** (*coll.*) to attach oneself to: to gain comprehension of; **on the latch** not locked, but to be opened by a latch [O.E. *læccan*, to catch.]

late *lāt*, *adj.* (*compar.* **lāt'er**; *superl.* **lāt'est**) tardy: behindhand: coming, remaining, flowering, ripening, producing, etc., after the due, expected, or usual time: long delayed: far advanced towards the close: deceased: departed: out of office: former: not long past: most recent —Also *adv.*—*adv.* **late'ly** recently. —*v.t.* and *v.i* **lāt'en** to make or grow late.—*n.* **late'ness.—*n.* **lāt'est** (*coll.*; with *the*) the latest news.— *adj.* and *adv.* **lāt'ish.—late'-comer** a person who

arrives late.—**at (the) latest** not later than (a stated time); **late in the day** (*fig.*) at an unreasonably late stage of development, etc.; **of late** recently. [O.E. *læt*, slow.]

lateen *la-tēn'*, *adj.* applied to a triangular sail, common in the Mediterranean, the Lake of Geneva, etc. [Fr. (*voile*) *latine*—L. *Latīnus*, Latin.]

La Tène *la ten*, of a division of the Iron Age exemplified at *La Tène* near Neuchâtel in Switzerland, later than Hallstatt.

latent *lā'tənt*, *adj.* hid: concealed: not visible or apparent: dormant: undeveloped, but capable of development.—*ns.* **lā'tence**, **lā'tency**.—*adv.* **lā'tently.—latent period** the time between stimulus and reaction: that between contracting a disease and appearance of symptoms. [L. *latēns*, *-entis*, pr.p. of *latēre*, to lie hid.]

lateral *lat'ə-rəl*, *adj.* belonging to the side.—*n.* **laterality** (*-ral'i-ti*) the state of belonging to the side: physical one-sidedness, either right or left.—*adv.* **lat'erally.—lateral thinking** thinking which seeks new ways of looking at a problem and does not merely proceed by logical steps from the starting-point of what is known or believed. [L. *laterālis—latus*, *lateris*, a side.]

Lateran *lat'ə-rən*, *adj.* pertaining to the Church of St John *Lateran* at Rome, the Pope's cathedral church, on the site of the splendid palace or basilica of Plautius Lateranus (executed A D 66).—**Lateran Councils** five general councils of the Western Church, held in the Lateran basilica (1123, 1139, 1179, 1215, and 1512–17), regarded by Roman Catholics as ecumenical; **Lateran Treaty** restored the papal state (1929).

laterigrade *lat'ə-ri-grād*, *adj.* running sideways, like a crab. [L. *latus*, *-ēris*, side, *gradus*, step]

laterite *lat'ə-rīt*, *n.* a clay formed by weathering of rocks in a tropical climate, composed chiefly of iron and aluminium hydroxides. [L. *later*, *latēris*, a brick.]

latex *lā'teks*, (*bot.*) *n.* the milky juice of some plants, e.g. rubber trees:—*pl.* **lā'texes**, **lā'tices**. [L. *lătex*, *lăticis*.]

lath *lath*, *n.* a thin slip of wood: a substitute for such a slip, used in slating, plastering, etc.: anything long and thin:—*pl.* **laths** (*lädhz*, *läths*).—*v.t.* to cover with laths —*adj* **lathen** (*läth'ən*).—*n.* **lath'ing** the act or process of covering with laths: a covering of laths.— *adj.* **lath'y** like a lath. [O.E. *lætt*.]

lathe *lādh*, *n* a machine for turning and shaping articles of wood, metal, etc.: the swing-frame of a loom carrying the reed for separating the warp threads and beating up the weft.

lather *ladh'ər*, *ladh'ər*, *n.* a foam made with water and soap: froth from sweat. a state of agitation (*coll.*).— *v.t.* to spread over with lather: to thrash (*coll.*).—*v.i.* to form a lather.—*adj.* **lath'ery**. [O.E. *lēathor*.]

lathi, lathee *la-tē'*, *n.* a heavy stick. [Hind. *lāṭhī*.]

Latin *lat'in*, *adj.* pertaining to ancient Latium (esp. Rome) or its inhabitants, or its language, or to those languages that are descended from Latin, or to the peoples speaking them, esp. (*popularly*) of Central, Portuguese and Italians or the inhabitants of Central and South America of Spanish, etc extraction: of or denoting the temperament considered characteristic of the Latin peoples, passionate, excitable, volatile: written or spoken in Latin: Roman Catholic.—*n.* an inhabitant of ancient Latium: the language of ancient Latium, and esp. of Rome: a person belonging to a Latin people: a Roman Catholic.—*adj.* **Lat'inate** imitating Latin style· (of vocabulary) borrowed from Latin.—*ns.* **Lat'inism** a Latin idiom· the use or inclination towards use of Latin idioms, words, or ways;

communities; **law of nature** the invariable order of nature: natural law; **law of the jungle** the rules for surviving, succeeding, etc. in a competitive or hostile situation by the use of force, etc.; **law of the land** the established law of a country; **law of the Medes and Persians** see **Median**; **lay down the law** to state authoritatively or dictatorially; **take the law into one's own hands** to obtain justice, or what one considers to be justice, by one's own actions, without recourse to the law, the police, etc.; **the law** (coll.) the police: a policeman. [M.E. *lawe*—late O.E. *lagu*, of O.N. origin, from the same root as **lie²**, **lay²**.]
law² *lö*, (Scot.) n. a hill, esp rounded or conical. [Northern form of **low**, O.E. *hlāw*.]
law³ *lo*, interj. expressing surprise (dial.). [Partly for **la** or **lo**, partly **lord** (q.v.).]
lawn¹ *lön*, n. a sort of fine linen or cambric: extended to some cottons.—adj. made of lawn [Prob. from *Laon*, near Rheims]
lawn² *lön*, n. an open space between woods (arch.): a smooth space of ground covered with grass, generally beside a house.—adj. **lawn'y**.—**lawn'-mower** a machine for cutting grass on a lawn; **lawn'-sprink'ler** a machine for watering a lawn by sprinkling; **lawn tennis** a game derived from tennis, played by one or two a side on an unwalled court (hard or of turf), the aim being to hit the ball over the net and within the court, if possible so as to prevent like return. [Old word *laund*—O.Fr. *launde*.]
lawrencium *lö-ren'si-əm*, n. the name given to element 103 (symbol Lr) first produced at Berkeley, California. [Ernest O. *Lawrence* (1901–58), scientist.]
lax *laks*, adj. slack: loose: soft, flabby: not strict in discipline or morals: loose in the bowels.—adj. **lax'a-tive** having the power of loosening the bowels.—n. a purgative or aperient medicine.—ns. **lax'ativeness**; **laxa'tor** a muscle that relaxes an organ or part; **lax'ity**, **lax'ness**.—adv. **lax'ly**. [L. *laxus*, loose.]
lay¹ *lā*, pa.t. of **lie²**.
lay² *lā*, v.t. to cause to lie: to place or set down: to beat down: to spread on a surface: to spread something on: to cover: to apply: to cause to subside: to exorcise: to deposit: to set on the table: to wager: to put forward: to cause to be: to set: to produce and deposit: to station: to locate: to set in position: to waylay: to impose: to attribute, impute: to set material in position for making: to form by setting in position and twisting (as a rope): to design, plan: to layer (hort.): to have sexual intercourse with (slang.).—v.i. to produce eggs: to wager, bet: to deal blows: to lie (arch., naut., and illit.):—pr.p. **lay'ing**; pa.t. and pa.p. **laid**. —n. a situation, a lying-place: an oyster-bed: a mode of lying: a disposition, arrangement or plan: a layer: a mode of twisting: laying activity: an act of sexual intercourse (slang): a partner, usually female, in sexual intercourse (slang).—n. **layer** (lā'ər, lār) one who or that which lays—e.g. a hen, a bricklayer: (lār) a course, bed, or stratum: a distinctively coloured space between contour-lines on a map: a shoot bent down to earth in order to take root.—v.t. and v.i. to propagate by layers.—v.t. to put in layers.—v.i. to be laid flat, lodge.—adj. **lay'ered** in or with layers.—ns. **lay'ering**; **lay'ing** the first coat of plaster: the act or time of laying eggs: the eggs laid.—**lay'about** a lounger, loafer; **lay'away** goods on which a deposit has been paid, kept for a customer until he completes payment (as vb. **lay away**).—**lay'-by** an expansion of a roadway to allow vehicles to draw up out of the stream of traffic:—pl. **lay'-bys**; **lay'er-cake** a cake built up in layers; **lay'-off** the act of laying off or period of time during which someone lays off or is laid off; **lay'-out** that which is laid out: a display: an outfit: the disposition, arrangement, plan, esp. of buildings

or ground: the general appearance of a printed page: a set, unit, organisation; **lay'-shaft** an auxiliary geared shaft in a machine, esp. the secondary shaft in an automobile gear-box; **lay'-up** the time or condition of being laid up.—**lay about one** to deal blows vigorously or on all sides; **lay a course** to succeed in sailing to the place required without tacking; **lay aside, away** to discard: to put apart for future use (see also **lay-away** above); **lay bare** to make bare, disclose; **lay before** to submit to, as of plans; **lay by** to keep for future use: to dismiss: to put off; **lay down** to give up: to deposit, as a pledge: to formulate: to assert (law, rule): to store: to plant: to lay on (print.); **lay hold of**, or **on**, to seize; **lay in** to get in a supply of; **lay into** to beat thoroughly; **lay it on** to charge exorbitantly: to do anything, as to exaggerate, or to flatter, with profuseness; **lay off** to dismiss temporarily: to cease (coll.); **lay on** to install a supply of: to provide: to deal blows with vigour; **lay oneself open to** to make oneself vulnerable to, or open to, (criticism, etc.); **lay open to** make bare, to show, expose: to cut open: **lay out** to display: to expend: to plan: to dispose according to a plan: to prepare for burial: to fell; **lay siege to** to besiege: to importune; **lay the table** to put dishes, etc on the table in preparation for a meal; **lay to** to apply with vigour: to bring a ship to rest; **lay under** to subject to, **lay up** to store up, preserve: (usu. in *pass*) to confine to bed or one's room: to put in dock for cleaning, repairs, etc. or because no longer wanted for or fit for service; **lay wait** to lie in wait, or in ambush; **lay waste** to devastate. [O.E *lecgan*, to lay, causative of *licgan*, to lie.]
lay³ *lā*, n. a short narrative poem: a lyric: a song [O.Fr. *lai*.]
lay⁴ *lā*, adj pertaining to the people: not clerical: non-professional· not trumps (cards).—n the laity.—adj. **laic** (lā'ik) lay.—n. a layman.—adj **la'ical**.—n. **laicisa'tion**, -z-.—v.t. **laicise**, **-ize** (lā'i-sīz) to make laical: to open to the laity.—n. **la'ity** the people as distinguished from some particular profession, usu. the clerical.—**lay brother**, **sister** one under vows of celibacy and obedience, who serves a religious house, but is exempt from the studies and choir duties of monks or nuns; **lay'man** one of the laity: a non-professional man: one not an expert; **lay reader** in the Anglican Church, a layman authorised to read part of the service. [O.Fr. *lai*—L. *lāicus*—Gr. *lāikos*—*lāos*, the people.]
lay-day *lā'dā*, n. one of a number of days allowed for loading and unloading of cargo.—**lay'time** the total time allowed. [Perh. **delay** and **day**, **time**.]
layer. See **lay²**.
layette *lā-et'*, n. a baby's complete outfit. [Fr.]
lay-figure *lā'-fig'ər*, n. a jointed model used by painters: a living person or a fictitious character wanting in individuality.—Also (earlier) **lay'man**. [Du. *leeman*—*led* (now *lid*), joint, *man*, man.]
lazar *laz'ər*, n. one afflicted with a loathsome and pestilential disease like *Lazarus*, the beggar (Luke xvi. 20).—**lazar house** a lazaretto.
lazaretto *laz-ə-ret'ō*, n. a hospital for infectious diseases, esp. leprosy: a place of quarantine: a place for keeping stores on a ship:—pl. **lazarett'os**.—Also **laz'aret**. [It. *lazzaretto*.]
lazulite *laz'ū-līt*, n. a blue mineral. [L.L. *lazulum*—Pers. *lājward*; cf. **azure**, **lapis lazuli**, **lazurite**.]
lazurite *laz'ū-rīt*, n. a blue cubic mineral, a constituent of lapis lazuli. [L.L. *lazur*—Pers. *lājward*; cf. **azure**, **lapis lazuli**, **lazulite**.]
lazy *lā'zi*, adj. disinclined to exertion: averse to labour: sluggish.—v.i. **laze** to be idle (back-formation).—adv. **la'zily**.—n. **la'ziness**.—**la'zy-bones** (coll.) a lazy person, an idler; **lazy Susan** a revolving

tray with a number of separate dishes or sections for foods, intended to be placed on a dining-table, etc.—*n.pl.* **la'zy-tongs** a series of diagonal levers pivoted together at the middle and ends, capable of being extended by a movement of the scissors-like handles so as to pick up objects at a distance.—*adj.* constructed on the model of lazy-tongs.

lea[1] *lē, n.* open country—meadow, pasture, or arable. [O.E. *lēah.*]

lea[2] *lē, adj.* and *n.* fallow: arable land under grass or pasture.—**lea'-rig** an unploughed rig or grass field. [O.E. *læge*, found in *læghrycg*, lea-rig.]

leach *lēch, v.t.* to allow (a liquid) to percolate through something: to subject (something) to percolation so as to separate soluble constituent(s): to drain away by percolation.—*v.i.* to percolate through or out of: to pass out of by the action of a percolating liquid: to lose soluble elements by the action of a percolating liquid.—*ns.* **leach'ate** a liquid that has percolated through or out of some substance: a solution got by leaching; **leach'ing.**—*adj.* **leach'y** liable to be leached.—**bacterial leaching** the use of selected strains of bacteria to accelerate the acid leach of sulphide minerals. [O.E. *leccan*, to water, irrigate, moisten.]

lead[1] *lēd, v.t.* to show the way by going first: to precede: to guide by the hand: to direct: to guide: to conduct: to convey: to induce: to live: to cause to live or experience: to adduce (*Scots law*): to have a principal or guiding part or place in: to play as the first card of a round (*cards*).—*v.i.* to be first or among the first: to be guide or chief: to act first: to cart crops to the farmyard (often with *in*): to afford a passage (to), or (*fig.*) tend towards: of a newspaper, etc., to have as its main story, feature, etc. (with *with*):—*pa.t.* and *pa.p.* **led.**—*n.* first place: precedence: the amount by which one is ahead: direction: guidance: an indication: a precedent or example: a chief rôle: the player of a chief rôle: leadership: initiative: the act or right of playing first, or the play of him who plays first: the first player of a side (*curling*, etc.): a leash: a watercourse leading to a mill: a channel among ice: a main conductor in electrical distribution.—*adj.* chief: main: leading.—*ns.* **lead'er** one who leads or goes first: a chief: the principal first violin: the head of a party, expedition, etc.: the leading editorial article in a newspaper (also **leading article**): a horse in a front place in a team: a tendon: a translucent connection between a fishing-line and bait: a line of dots to guide the eye (*print.*): the principal wheel in any machinery: an alternative name for conductor (of orchestra, etc.) (*U.S.*); **lead'ership** the office of leader or conductor: ability to lead; **lead'ing** guidance: spiritual guidance: leadership: carting (crops, etc.).—*adj.* acting as leader: directing, controlling: principal: preceding.—**lead'-in** the cable connecting the transmitter or receiver to the elevated part of an aerial: the introduction to, or introductory passage of, a commercial, discussion, newspaper article, piece of music, etc.—Also *adj.*—**leading business** the acting of the principal parts or rôles in plays (by the **leading lady** and the **leading man**); **leading case** (*law*) a case serving as a precedent; **leading edge** the edge first met: the foremost edge of an aerofoil or propeller blade: rising amplitude portion of a pulse signal (*telecomm.*); **leading lady, man** see **leading business; leading light** a very influential member; **leading question** a question so put as to suggest the desired answer; **lead'-ing-strings** strings used to lead children beginning to walk: vexatious care or custody; **lead time** (orig. *U.S.*) the time between the conception or design of a product, factory, alteration, etc. and its production, completion, implementation, etc.—**lead astray** to

draw into a wrong course: to seduce from right conduct, **lead by the nose** to make one follow submissively; **lead off** to begin or take the start in anything; **lead on** to persuade to go on, to draw on: to persuade to a foolish course: to hoax in jest; **lead out** to conduct to execution or a dance: to proceed to play out (*cards*); **lead the way** to go first and guide others; **lead up to** to bring about by degrees, to prepare for by steps or stages: to play in challenge to, or with a view to weakness in (*cards*). [O.E. *lǣdan*, to lead, lǣd, a way.]

lead[2] *led, n.* a heavy soft bluish-grey metal (symbol Pb; at. numb. 82): a plummet for sounding: a thin plate of lead separating lines of type: a leaden frame for a window-pane: extended loosely to blacklead: a stick of blacklead for a pencil: (*pl.*) sheets of lead for covering roofs, or a flat roof so covered.—*adj.* made of lead.—*v.t.* to cover, weight, or fit with lead: to separate the lines of with leads (*print.*).—*adjs.* **lead'ed** fitted or weighted with or set in lead: separated by leads (*print.*); **lead'en** made of lead: leadcoloured: inert: depressing: heavy: dull.—*v.t.* and *v.i.* to make or become leaden.—*adv.* **lead'enly.**—*n.* **lead'enness.**—*adjs.* **lead'less; lead'y** like lead.—**lead'-glance** galena; **lead'-line** a sounding-line; **lead'-paint** paint with red lead or white lead as base; **lead'-pencil** a blacklead pencil for writing or drawing; **lead poisoning** poisoning by the absorption of lead into the system: death by shooting (*slang*); **leads'man** a seaman who heaves the lead.—**swing the lead** (*naut.* and *mil. slang*) to invent specious excuses to evade duties. [O.E. *lēad.*]

leaf *lēf, n.* one of the lateral organs developed from the stem or axis of the plant below its growing-point, esp. one of those flat green structures that perform the work of transpiration and carbon-assimilation, but also more generally any homologous structure, as a scale, a petal: the condition of having leaves: leaves collectively: anything beaten thin like a leaf: two pages of a book on opposite sides of the same paper: a broad thin part or structure, hinged, sliding, or inserted at will, as of folding doors, window-shutters, table-tops, drawbridges, etc.:—*pl.* **leaves** (*lēvz*).—*v.t., v.i.* (with *through*), to turn the pages of (a book etc.).—*v.i.* (also **leave**) to produce leaves:—*pr.p.* **leaf'ing;** *pa.p.* **leafed.**—*adj.* in the form of leaves.—*n.* **leaf'age** foliage.—*adj.* **leafed** (*lēft*) having leaves (also **leaved** *lēvd*).—*n.* **leaf'iness.**—*adj.* **leaf'less** destitute of leaves.—*n.* **leaf'let** a little leaf: a division of a compound leaf: a single sheet of printed political, religious, advertising, etc. matter, flat or folded, or several sheets folded together.—*v.t.* to distribute leaflets to.—*v.i.* to distribute leaflets:—*pr.p.* **leaf'-leting,** less correctly **leaf'letting;** *pa.t.* and *pa.p.* **leaf'leted,** less correctly **leaf'letted.**—*adj.* **leaf'-like.** —*adjs.* **leaf'y, leav'y** covered with or abounding in leaves: leaf-like.—**leaf'-base** the base of a leaf-stalk, where it joins the stem; **leaf'-curl** a plant disease of various kinds characterised by curling of the leaves; **leaf'-cutter** an insect (ant or bee) that cuts pieces out of leaves; **leaf'-cutt'ing** a leaf used as a cutting for propagation; **leaf'-hopper** a name for various hopping orthopterous insects that suck plant juices; **leaf'-in'sect** an insect with wing-covers like leaves; **leaf'-met'al** metal, especially alloys imitating gold and silver, in very thin leaves, for decoration; **leaf'-mosa'ic** a name for various virus diseases of potato, tobacco, etc., in which the leaf is mottled; **leaf'-mould** earth formed from decayed leaves, used as a soil for plants.—*adj.* **leaf'-nosed** having a leaf-like structure on the nose, as certain bats.—**leaf'-roll** a potato disease; **leaf'-stalk** the petiole of a leaf.—**take a leaf out of someone's book** see **book; turn over a new**

leaf to begin a new and better course of conduct. [O.E. *léaf*.]

league[1] *lēg, n.* a nautical measure, 1/20th of a degree, 3 international nautical miles, 3·456 statute miles (5·556 km.): an old measure of length, varying in extent, in general, e.g. in poetry, taken to be about 3 miles (4·828 km.). [L.L. *leuga, leuca*, Gallic mile of 1500 Roman paces; poss. Gaulish.]

league[2] *lēg, n.* a bond or alliance: a union for mutual advantage: an association or confederacy: an association of clubs for games: a class or group.—*v.t.* and *v.i.* to join in league.—*n.* **lea'guer** a member of a league.—**league match** a match between two clubs in the same league; **league table** a table in which clubs in a league are placed according to their performances, or (*fig.*) any grouping made to reflect relative success, importance, etc.—**in league with** having made an alliance with, usu. for a bad purpose; **League of Nations** an international body, under a covenant drawn up in 1919, to secure peace, justice, scrupulous observance of treaties, and international co-operation generally—superseded in 1945 by the United Nations; **not in the same league** as not of the same calibre, ability, importance, etc. as; **top, bottom, of the league** (*fig.*) highest, lowest, in a particular field of achievement, or in quality. [Fr. *ligue*—L.L. *liga*—L. *ligāre*, to bind.]

leak *lēk, n.* a crack or hole in a vessel through which liquid may pass: passage through such an opening: urination (*slang*): a place, means, instance, of unintended or undesirable admission or escape (*lit.* and *fig.*): the usu. unauthorised, but sometimes only apparently unauthorised, divulgation of secret information: a high resistance, esp. serving as a discharging path for a condenser (*elect.*).—*v.i.* to have a leak: to pass through a leak.—*v.t.* to cause to leak: to let out or in by, or (*fig.*) as if by, a leak: to divulge (secret information) without, or apparently without, authorisation, or to cause this to be done.—*ns.* **leak'-age** a leaking: that which enters or escapes by leaking: an allowance for leaking; **leak'er; leak'iness.**—*adj.* **leak'y.**—**leak out** to find vent: (of secret information) to be divulged to the public without, or apparently without, authorisation; **spring a leak** to become leaky. [O.E. *hlec*, leaky; or perh. reintroduced from Du. or L.G. *lek*, leak; or O.N. *leka*, to leak.]

lean[1] *lēn, v.i.* to incline: to be or become inclined to the vertical: to rest sideways against something: to bend over: to swerve: to abut: to have an inclination: to rely.—*v.t.* to cause to lean:—*pa.t.* and *pa.p.* **leaned** (*lēnd*) or **leant** (*lent*).—*n.* an act or condition of leaning: a slope.—*n.* and *adj.* **lean'ing.**—**lean'-to** a shed or penthouse propped against another building or wall:—*pl.* **lean'-tos.**—**lean on** (*slang*) to put pressure on, to use force on (a person). [O.E. *hléonian, hlinian,* and causative *hlǽnan.*]

lean[2] *lēn, adj.* thin, wanting flesh: not fat: without fat: unproductive.—*n.* flesh without fat.—*adv.* **lean'ly.**—*n.* **lean'ness.** [O.E. *hlǽne.*]

leap *lēp, v.i.* to move with bounds: to spring upward or forward: to rush with vehemence: to pass abruptly or over a wide interval.—*v.t.* to bound over: to cause to take a leap:—*pr.p.* **leap'ing;** *pa.t.* and *pa.p.* **leaped** *lēpt,* or **leapt** *lept.*—*n.* an act of leaping: a bound: the space passed by leaping: a place of leaping: an abrupt transition: a wide gap or interval.—*n.* **leap'er** a steeplechaser: one who leaps.—**leap day** an intercalary day in the calendar (29th February); **leap'-frog** a sport in which one person in turn places his hands on the back of another stooping in front of him, and vaults over him —*v.t.* and *v.i.* to jump (over) as in leap-frog (also *fig.*). to go in advance of each other alternately:—*pr.p.* **leap'-frogging;** *pa.t.* and *pa.p.* **leap'-frogged.**—

adj. and *n.* **leap'-frogging.**—**leap year** a year with an intercalary day (perh. because any anniversary after that day misses or leaps over a day of the week).—**by leaps and bounds** by a large amount or extent: very quickly; **leap in the dark** an act of which we cannot foresee the consequences. [O.E. *hléapan.*]

learn *lûrn, v.t.* to be informed: to get to know: to gain knowledge, skill, or ability in: to teach (now *illit.*).—*v.i.* to gain knowledge or skill:—*pa.t.* and *pa.p.* **learned** (*lûrnd*) or **learnt** (*lûrnt*).—*adjs.* **learn'able** that may be learned; **learned** (*lûrn'id*) having learning: versed in literature, etc.: skilful.—*adv.* **learn'edly.**—*ns.* **learn'edness; learn'er** one who learns: one who is yet in the rudiments; **learn'ing** what is learned: knowledge: scholarship: skill in languages or science. [O.E. *leornian.*]

leary. Same as **leery** under **leer.**

lease *lēs, n.* a contract letting or renting a house, farm, etc., for a term: tenure or rights under such a contract: duration of such tenure: a hold upon, or prospect of continuance of, life, enjoyment, health, etc.—*v.t.* to grant or take under lease.—*adj.* **leas'able.**—*ns.* **leas'er** a lessee.—**lease'back** the selling of a building, etc. to a person or organisation from whom the seller then leases it.—Also **sale and leaseback;** **lease'hold** a tenure by lease: land, etc., so held.—*adj.* held by lease.—**lease'holder.**—*n.* and *adj.* **lease'-lend** see **lend-lease** under **lend.** [Fr. *laisser,* to leave —L. *laxāre,* to loose, *laxus,* loose.]

leash *lēsh, n.* a line for holding a hawk or hound: control by a leash, or as if by a leash: a set of three, especially animals.—*v.t.* to hold by a leash: to bind. [O.Fr. *lesse,* a thong to hold a dog by—L. *laxus,* loose.]

least *lēst, adj.* (serving as superl. of **little**) little beyond all others: smallest.—*adv.* in the smallest or lowest degree.—*n.* the smallest amount: the lowest degree.—*advs.* **least'aways, least'ways** (*dial.*), **-wise** (*rare* or *U.S.*) at least: however—used to tone down a preceding statement.—**at least,** or **at the least at** the lowest estimate: at any rate. [O.E. *lǽst* (adj. and adv.); compar. *lǽssa* (adj.), *lǽs* (adv.); no positive.]

leather *ledh'ər, n.* a tanned, tawed, or otherwise dressed skin: a strap or other piece of leather: the ball in certain games: (in *pl.*) riding breeches made from leather.—*adj.* of leather.—*v.t.* to apply leather to: to thrash (*coll.*).—*ns.* **leatherette'** cloth or paper made to look like leather; **leath'ering** (*coll.*) a thrashing.—*adjs.* **leath'ern** of or like leather; **leath'ery** resembling leather: tough.—**leath'er-back** a large variety of seaturtle; **leath'er-cloth** a fabric coloured on one face so as to resemble leather—called also *American cloth;* **leath'er-jacket** one of various fishes: a grub of the crane-fly.—*adjs.* **leath'er-lunged** strong-lunged, able to shout vigorously; **leath'er-mouthed** (*-mowdhd*) of certain fish, having a mouth like leather, smooth, and toothless.—**leath'er-neck** a sailors' name for a soldier or marine (from the leather stock he once wore), esp. now a U.S. marine.—**artificial leather** any of certain plastic materials treated so as to simulate leather. [O.E. *lether,* leather.]

leave[1] *lēv, n.* permission: a formal parting: a farewell: permission to depart or be absent: permitted absence from duty: the time of this: holidays.—**leave'-taking** bidding farewell.—**leave of absence** permission to be absent, or the (time of) permitted absence; **take leave** to assume permission; **take (one's) leave (of)** to depart (from), say farewell (to); **take leave of one's senses** to become irrational. [O.E. *léaf,* permission.]

leave[2] *lēv, v.t.* to allow, or cause, to remain: to abandon, resign: to quit or depart from: to have remaining at death: to bequeath: to refer for decision, action, etc.—*v.i.* to desist: to cease: to depart:—*pr.p.*

leav'ing; *pa.t.* and *pa.p.* left.—*n.pl.* leav'ings things left: relics: refuse.—be left with to have remaining; leave a little (much) to be desired to be slightly (very) inadequate or unsatisfactory; leave alone to let remain undisturbed; leave be to leave undisturbed; leave behind to forget to bring, or leave intentionally or accidentally: to go away from (also *fig.*); leave go (*coll.*) to let go; leave it at that to take no further action, make no further comment, etc.; leave off to desist, to terminate: to give up using; leave out to omit; leave unsaid to refrain from saying. [O E *læfan*]

leave³, leaved, leaves, leavy. See leaf.

leaven lev'n, *n.* the ferment, e.g. yeast, that makes dough rise: anything that makes a general change.— *v.t.* to raise with leaven: to permeate with an influence —*n.* leav'ening. [Fr. *levain*—L. *levāmen* —*levāre*, to raise—*levis*, light.]

Lebensraum *lāb'ənz-rowm*, (Ger)*n.* room to live (and, if necessary, expand).

lecher lech'ər, *n.* a man addicted to lewdness.—*v.i.* to practise lewdness.—*adj.* lech'erous lustful: provoking lust.—*adv.* lech'erously.—*ns.* lech'erousness; lech'ery. [O.Fr. *lecheor—lechier*, to lick.]

lecithin les'i-thin, *n.* a very complex substance containing phosphorus, found in yolk of egg, brain, blood, etc. [Gr. *lekithos*, egg-yolk.]

lectern lek'tərn, *n.* a church reading-desk from which the lessons are read [L.L. *lectrīnum—lectrum*, a pulpit—Gr. *lektron*, a couch.]

lection lek'shən, *n.* a reading: a lesson read in Church.— *n.* lec'tionary a book of church lessons for each day. [L. *lectiō, -ōnis—legĕre, lectum*, to read.]

lector lek'tor, -tər, *n.* a reader, esp. in a college. an ecclesiastic in one of the minor orders, lowest in the Orthodox, next above doorkeeper, in the Roman Catholic.—*ns.* lec'torate; lec'torship. [L. *lector, -ōris—legĕre, lectum*, to read.]

lecture lek'chər, *n.* a lesson or period of instruction: a discourse on any subject, esp. a professorial or tutorial discourse: an expository and discursive religious discourse: an endowed lectureship: a formal reproof. —*v.t.* to instruct by discourses: to instruct authoritatively: to reprove.—*v.i.* to give a lecture or lectures.— *ns.* lec'turer one who lectures: a college or university instructor of lower rank than a professor; lec'tureship the office of a lecturer: the foundation of a course of lectures. [L. *lectūra—legĕre, lectum*, to read.]

lecythus les'i-thəs, *n* the Latinised form of lekythos. [See lekythos.]

led *led, pa.t.* and *pa.p.* of lead¹.—*adj.* under leading or control, esp. of a farm or place held along with another by a non-resident.

lederhosen *lā'dər-hōz-ən, n.pl.* short leather trousers with braces. [Ger., leather trousers.]

ledge *lej, n.* an attached strip: a shelf-like projection: a ridge or shelf of rocks: a lode.—*adj.* ledg'y abounding in ledges. [M.E. *legge*, prob. from the root of lay².]

ledger lej'ər, *n.* the principal book of accounts among merchants, in which the entries in all the other books are entered: a horizontal timber in scaffolding· a flat grave-slab.—*adj.* resident, stationary —*v.i.* to fish with a ledg'er-line.—ledg'er-bait fishing bait that lies on the bottom, the ledg'er-tackle being weighted; ledg'er-line a line fixed in one place (*angling*): a short line added above or below the stave where required (often leger-line; *mus*). [App from O.E. *licgan*, to lie, *lecgan*, to lay.]

lee *lee, n.* shelter: the sheltered side: the quarter toward which the wind blows —*adj.* (opp. to *windward* or *weather*) sheltered: on or towards the sheltered side —*adj.* lee'ward (also *naut. lū'ərd, loo'ərd*) pertaining to, or in, the direction towards which the wind blows —*adv.* towards the lee.—lee'-board a board lowered

on the lee-side of a vessel, to lessen drift to leeward; lee'-ga(u)ge position to leeward—opp. to *weather-gage*, lee side the sheltered side; lee tide a tide in the same direction as the wind; lee'way leeward drift.— make up leeway to make up for lost time, ground, etc. [O.E. *hlēo(w)*, gen. *hlēowes*, shelter.]

leech¹ *lēch, n.* the side edge of a sail. [Cf. O.N. *līk*; Dan. *līg*; Sw *lik*, a bolt-rope.]

leech² *lēch, n* a blood-sucking worm: a physician (*arch.*): one who attaches himself to another for personal gain —*v t.* to apply leeches to: to cling to like a leech: to drain.—*v.i.* (usually with *on*) to cling to. [O.E. *læce*, perh. orig two different words.]

leechee. Same as lychee.

leek *lēk, n.* a vegetable of the onion genus—national emblem of Wales. [O E. *lēac*, leek, plant.]

leer *lēr, n.* a sly, sidelong, or lecherous look —*v.i.* to glance sideways: to look lecherously.—*n.* and *adj* leer'ing.—*adv.* leer'ingly.—*adj.* leer'y cunning: wary (with *of*). [O.E. *hlēor*, face, cheek.]

lees *lēz, n pl.* sediment or dregs of liquor.—*sing.* (*rare*) lee. [Fr. *lie*—L.L *lia*]

leet *lēt*, (*Scot.*) *n.* a selected list of candidates for an office.—short leet a select list for the final choice.

left¹ *left, pa.t.* and *pa.p.* of leave².—*adjs.* left'-off laid aside, discarded; left'-o'ver remaining over from a previous occasion.—*n.* a thing left over: a survival: food uneaten at a meal (usu in *pl.*).

left² *left, adj.* on, for, or belonging to that side, or part of the body, etc. on that side, which in man has normally the weaker and less skilful hand: on that side from the point of view of a person looking downstream, a soldier looking at the enemy, a president looking at an assembly, an actor looking at the audience: relatively liberal, democratic, progressive, innovating in politics: inclined towards socialism or communism.—*n.* the left side: the region to the left side: the left hand: a blow with the left hand: a glove, shoe, etc., for the left hand or foot, etc.: the more progressive, democratic, socialist, radical or actively innovating party or wing (from its sitting in some legislatures to the president's left).—*adv.* on or towards the left.—*adj.* and *n.* left'ie, left'y (often *derog.*) (a) leftist —*adj.* and *n* left'ist.—*adj.* and *adv.* left'ward towards the left: on the left side: more left-wing.— *advs.* left'wardly, left'wards.—Left Bank the artistic quarter of Paris on the south bank of the Seine.—*adjs.* left'-bank; left'-footed performed with the left foot: having more skill or strength in the left foot; left'-hand on the left side: towards the left: with thread or strands turning to the left: performed with the left hand; left'- hand'ed having the left hand stronger and readier than the right: for the left hand: counter-clockwise: forming a mirror-image of the right-handed form: awkward: unlucky: dubious (as *a left-handed compliment*): morganatic.—*adv.* left'-hand'edly.— left'-hand'edness; left'-hand'er a blow with the left hand: a left-handed person; left'-hand'iness awkwardness; left wing the political left: the wing on the left side of an army, football pitch, etc.—*adj.* left'-wing playing on the left wing: belonging to the more leftwardly inclined section· (having opinions which are) progressive, radical, socialist, etc.—left'- wing'er a person with left-wing views or who supports the left wing of a party, etc.: a player on the left wing. —have two left feet to be clumsy or awkward, e g. in dancing; left-hand drive a driving mechanism on the left side of a vehicle which is intended to be driven on the right-hand side of the road; left, right, and centre in, from, etc all directions everywhere. [M E. *lift, left*—O E. (Kentish) *left*, weak, worthless.]

leg *leg, n* a walking limb the human hind-limb, or sometimes the part between knee and ankle: a long, slender support of anything, as of a table: in cricket, that part of the field, or that fielder, on or behind a line straight out from the batsman on the on side (also *adj.*): a branch or limb of anything forked or jointed, as a pair of compasses: the part of a garment that covers the leg: a distinct part or stage of any course, e.g. of a flight: in sports, one event or part in a contest consisting of two or more parts or events.—*v.t.* and *v.i.* to walk vigorously (*v.t.* with *it*): to propel through a canal tunnel by pushing with the feet on wall or roof.—*adj.* **legged** (*legd, leg'id*; usu. in composition) having (a certain type, number, etc. of) legs.—*ns.* **legg'iness; legg'ing** an outer and extra gaiter-like covering for the lower leg.—*adjs.* **legg'y** having noticeably long and lank legs; **leg'less** having no legs: very drunk (*coll.*).—*n.* **leg'lessness.—leg'-break** (*cricket*) a ball that breaks from the leg side towards the off side on pitching: a ball bowled to have this deviation: spin imparted to a ball to cause such a deviation; **leg'-bye** in cricket, a run made when the ball touches any part of the batsman's person except his hand; **leg'-guard** a cricketer's pad; **leg'-iron** a fetter for the leg.—*adj.* **leg-of-mutt'on** shaped like a leg of mutton, as a triangular sail, a sleeve tight at the wrist and full above.—**leg'-pull** a bantering attempt to impose on someone's credulity; **leg'-puller; leg's pulling; leg'-rest** a support for the legs; **leg'room** space for one's legs, as in a car; **leg'-show** an entertainment depending mainly on the exhibition of women's legs; **leg side** (or **the leg;** *cricket*) that half of the field nearest the batsman's legs (opp. to *off side*); **leg'-slip** (*cricket*) a fielder or position on the leg side somewhat behind the batsman; **leg'-spin** (*cricket*) (a) leg-break; **leg'-spinner** (*cricket*) one who bowls leg-breaks; **leg theory** (*cricket*) the policy of bowling on the striker's legs with a trap of leg-side fielders: body-line; **leg'-warmers** long footless socks; **leg'work** (*coll.*) work involving much travelling, searching, etc.—**a leg up** a help or hoist in mounting, climbing, or generally; **feel one's legs** to begin to support oneself on the legs; **find one's legs** to become habituated, to attain ease; **fine, long, short, square leg** (*cricket*) fielding positions respectively fine from, far from, near to, square to, the batsman on the leg side; **leg before (wicket)** in cricket, a way of being given out as penalty for stopping with the leg (or any part of the body except the hand) a straight or off-break ball that would have hit the wicket (**l.b.w.**); **not have a leg to stand on** to have no case at all; **pull someone's leg** to make a playful attempt to impose upon someone's credulity; **shake a leg** (*coll.*) to hurry up; **show a leg** to make an appearance: to get up. [O.N. *leggr*, a leg.]

legacy *leg'ə-si, n.* that which is left to one by will: a bequest of personal property.—*ns.* **leg'atary** a legatee; **legatee'** one to whom a legacy is left; **legator** (*li-gā'tər*) a testator. [L. *lēgāre*, -*ātum*, to leave by will.]

legal *lē'gl, adj.* pertaining to, or according to, law: lawful: created by law.—*n.* **lēgalisā'tion**, -*z*-.—*v.t.* **lē'galise, -ize** to make lawful.—*ns.* **lē'galism** strict adherence to law: in theol., the doctrine that salvation depends on strict adherence to the law, as distinguished from the doctrine of salvation by grace: the tendency to observe letter or form rather than spirit, or to regard things from the point of view of law; **lē'galist** one inclined to legalism: one versed in law.—*adj.* **lēgalis'tic.—*adv.* **lēgalist'ically.—*n.* **lēgality** (*-gal'i-ti*).—*adv.* **lē'gally.—legal aid** financial assistance given to those unable to pay the full costs of legal proceedings; **legal tender** that which a creditor cannot refuse in payment of a debt; **legal year** see **year**. [L. *lēgālis—lēx, lēgis*, law.]

legate *leg'it, n.* an ambassador, esp. from the Pope: a delegate, deputy, esp. orig. a Roman general's lieutenant: the governor of a Papal province (*hist.*).—*n.* **leg'ateship.—*n.* **legation** (*li-gā'shən*) a diplomatic mission, body of delegates, or its official abode: the office or status of legate: a Papal province (*hist.*). [L. *lēgātus—lēgāre*, to send with a commission.]

legatee. See **legacy.**

legato *le-gä'tō*, (*mus.*) *adj.* and *adv.* smooth, smoothly, the notes running into each other without a break (*superl.* **legatis'simo**).—*n.* a legato passage or manner:—*pl.* **legat'os**. [It., bound, tied—L. *ligāre*, -*ātum*, to tie.]

legend *lej'ənd, n.* a story of a saint's life: a collection of such stories: a traditional story: a body of tradition: an untrue or unhistorical story: a person having a special place in public esteem because of striking qualities or deeds, real or fictitious: the body of fact and fiction gathered round such a person: a motto, inscription, or explanatory words (with e.g. a picture).—*adj.* **leg'endary** pertaining to, of the nature of, consisting of, or described in, legend: romantic: fabulous. [Fr. *légende*—L.L. *legenda*, to be read.]

legerdemain *lej-ər-də-mān', n.* sleight-of-hand: jugglery.—*adj.* juggling: tricky. [Lit. light of hand—Fr. *léger*, light, *de*, of, *main*, hand.]

leger-line—better ledger-line. See **ledger.**

leghorn *leg'horn, li-gorn', n.* fine straw plait made in Tuscany: a hat made of it: (*li-gorn'*) a small breed of domestic fowl. [*Leghorn* (It. *Legorno*, now *Livorno*, L. *Liburnus*) in Italy.]

legible *lej'i-bl, adj.* clear enough to be deciphered: easy to read.—*ns.* **leg'ibleness; legibil'ity.—*adv.* **leg'ibly.** [L. *legibilis—legēre*, to read.]

legion *lē'jən, n.* in ancient Rome, a body of three to six thousand soldiers: a military force: applied especially to several in French history: a great number.—*adj.* (*rare*) multitudinous.—*adj.* **le'gionary** of, or consisting of, a legion or legions: containing a great number.—*n.* a member of a legion.—*n.* **lēgionnaire** (*-när*'; Fr. *légionnaire*) a member of the British, Foreign, etc. Legion.—**American Legion** an association of U.S. war veterans; (**Royal**) **British Legion** an ex-servicemen's and -women's association; **Foreign Legion** a body of foreigners, esp. that in the French army organised in 1831; **Legionnaire's** or **Legionnaires' Disease** a severe, sometimes fatal, pneumonia-like disease (so named after an outbreak of the disease at an American Legion convention in Philadelphia in 1976); **Legion of Honour** a French order instituted in 1802 by Napoleon I; **their name is Legion** they are beyond numbering (from Mark v. 9). [L. *legiō*, -*ōnis*—*legēre* to levy.]

legislate *lej'is-lāt, v.t.* to make laws.—*n.* **legislā'tion.** —*adj.* **leg'islative** (or *-lə-tiv*) law-making: having power to make laws: pertaining to legislation.—*n.* law-making power: the law-making body.—*adv.* **leg'islatively.—*n.* **leg'islator** a lawgiver: a member of a legislative body.—*adj.* **legislatorial** (*-lə-tō'ri-əl, -tō'*) of or pertaining to, or of the nature of, a legislator, legislature, or legislation.—*n.* **leg'islatorship;** **leg'islature** a law-making body. [L. *lēx, lēgis*, law, *latum*, serving as supine to *ferre*, to bear.]

legist *lē'jist, n.* one skilled in the laws. [Fr. *légiste.*]

legit *lij-it'*, coll. shortening of **legitimate.**

legitimate *li-jit'i-mit, -māt, adj.* lawful: lawfully begotten, born in wedlock, or having the legal status of those born in wedlock: related, derived, or transmitted by birth in wedlock or subsequently legitimated: as used by believers in the theory of divine right, according to strict rule of heredity and primogeniture: logically inferred: following by natural sequence: genuine: conforming to an accepted standard.—*v.t.* (*-māt*) to make lawful: to give the rights of a legitimate child to.—*n.* legit'imacy (*-mə-si*) the fact or state of being legitimate.—*adv.* legit'imately.—*ns.* legit'imateness; legitimā'tion the act of rendering legitimate, esp. of conferring the privileges of lawful birth.—*v.t.* legit'imise, -ize to legitimate.—*n.* legit'imist one who believes in the right of royal succession according to the principle of heredity and primogeniture. [L.L. *lĕgitimāre, -ātum*—L. *lĕgitimus*, lawful—*lēx*, law.]

legume leg'ūm, li-gūm', *n.* a pod (as in pea, bean, etc.) of one carpel: a vegetable used as food.—*n.pl.* Legūminō'sae (*-sē*) an order of angiosperms characterised by the legume.—*adj.* legū'minous pertaining to pulse: of or pertaining to the Leguminosae: bearing legumes. [L. *legūmen*, pulse.]

lei¹. See leu.

lei² lā'ē, *n.* a garland, wreath. [Hawaiian.]

Leibni(t)zian lĩb-nit'si-ən, *adj.* pertaining to the great German philosopher and mathematician Gottfried Wilhelm *Leibniz* (1646–1716).—*n.* Leibni(t)z'ianism the philosophy of Leibniz—the doctrine of primordial monads, pre-established harmony, fundamental optimism on the principle of sufficient reason.

Leicester les'tər, *adj.* of a long-woolled breed of sheep that originated in *Leicestershire*.—*n.* a sheep of that breed.

Leishmania lēsh-mān'i-ə, -man'i-ə, *n.* a genus of Protozoa (fam. Trypanosomidae): (without *cap.*) any protozoon of the genus Leishmania, or any protozoon of the Trypanosomidae in a non-flagellated form:—*pl.* leishmān'ia, -iae (*-i-ē*), -ias.—*ns.* leishmaniasis (*lēsh-mən-i'ə-sis*), leishmaniō'sis any of various diseases, such as kala-azar, due to infection with Leishmania:—*pl.* -ses. [Named after Sir William *Leishman* (1865–1926), who discovered the cause of kala-azar.]

leisure lezh'ər, (*U.S.* and old-fashioned) lēzh'ər, *n.* time free from employment: freedom from occupation: convenient opportunity.—*adj.* free from necessary business: for casual wear.—*adj.* leis'urable leisured: leisurely.—*adv.* leis'urably.—*adv.* leis'ured having much leisure.—*adj.* and *adv.* leis'urely not hasty or hastily.—at (one's) leisure free from occupation: at one's ease or convenience. [O.Fr. *leisir*—L. *licēre*, to be permitted.]

leitmotiv līt'mō-tēf', *n.* a theme associated with a person or a thought, recurring when the person appears on the stage or the thought becomes prominent in the action: a recurring theme (*fig.*).—Also leitmotif. [Ger.,—*leiten*, to lead, and *Motiv*, a motif.]

lek lek, *n.* a unit of Albanian currency = 100 qintars: a coin or note of this value.

lekythos lē'ki-thos, (*ant.*) *n.* a narrow-necked Greek flask. [Gr. *lēkythos*.]

lem, or **LEM** lem, *n.* abbrev. for lunar excursion module.

lemma lem'ə, *n.* a preliminary proposition (*math.*): a premise taken for granted (*math.*): a theme, argument, heading, or head-word:—*pls.* lemm'as, lemm'ata. [Gr. *lēmma, -atos*, from the root of *lambanein*, to take.]

lemming lem'ing, *n.* a northern rodent (*Lemmus* and other genera) near allied to voles. [Norw.]

lemon¹ lem'ən, *n.* a pale yellow oval citrus fruit with acid pulp: the tree that bears it: a pale yellow colour: something disappointing, worthless, unattractive, unpleasant (*slang*).—*adj.* flavoured with lemon: (coloured) pale yellow.—*v.t.* to flavour with lemon. —*n.* lemonade' a drink (still or aerated) made with lemon juice or more or less flavoured with lemons.— *adj.* lem'ony.—lemon cheese, curd a soft paste of lemons, eggs, and butter.—*adj.* lem'on-coloured.— lemon drop a hard lemon-flavoured sweet; lemon peel the skin of lemons, candied or not; lemon squash a highly concentrated lemon drink; lemon squeezer a small hand-press for extracting the juice of lemons.— *n.* and *adj.* lem'on-yell'ow.—hand someone a lemon (*slang*) to swindle someone. [Fr. *limon* (now the lime); cf. Pers. *līmūn*; cf. lime².]

lemon² lem'ən, *n.* a species of sole (lem'on-sole', or sand sole): a kind of dab resembling a sole (lem'on-dab', lem'on-sole', also called smear-dab or smooth dab). [Fr. *limande*.]

lemur lē'mər, *n.* any member of a group of mammals akin to the monkeys, forest dwellers, mainly nocturnal in habits, common in Madagascar.—*ns.* and *adjs.* lemurian (*lem'ū-ri-ən*), lemurine (*lem'ū-rīn*), lem'uroid. [L. *lēmŭrēs*, ghosts.]

lend lend, *v.t.* to give the use of for a time: to afford, grant, or furnish, in general: to let for hire.—*v.i.* to make a loan:—*pr.p.* lend'ing; *pa.t.* and *pa.p.* lent.— *ns.* lend'er; lend'ing the act of giving in loan.—lend's lease an arrangement authorised by Congress in 1941 by which the President could supply war materials to other countries whose defence he deemed vital to the United States.—Also *adj.*—lend an ear (*coll.*) to listen; lend itself to to be able to be used for. [O.E. *lǣnan*—*lǣn*, lān, a loan.]

lenes. See lenis.

length length, *n.* quality of being long: extent from end to end: the longest measure of anything: long continuance: prolixity: time occupied in uttering a vowel or syllable: the quantity of a vowel: any definite portion of a known extent: a stretch or extent: distance (chiefly *Scot.*): a suitable distance for pitching a cricket ball: the lengthwise measurement of a horse, boat, etc. (*racing*).—*v.t.* and *v.i.* length'en to increase, in length.—*adv.* length'ily.—*n.* length'iness. —*advs.* length'ways, length'wise in the direction of the length.—*adj.* length'y of great or tedious length: rather long.—at length in full: fully extended: at last; go (to) great lengths, go to all lengths, any length(s) to do everything possible (sometimes more than is ethical) to achieve a purpose; length of days prolonged life. [O.E. *lengthu—lang*, long.]

lenient lēn'yənt, -ni-ənt, *adj.* mild: merciful.—*ns.* lē'nience, lē'niency.—*adv.* lē'niently.—to mitigate, to assuage.—*adj.* lenitive (*len'*) mitigating: laxative.— *n.* any palliative: an application for easing pain (*med.*).—*n.* lenity (*len'*) mildness: clemency. [L. *lēniēns, -entis*, pr.p. of *lēntre*, to soften—*lēnis*, soft.]

Leninism len'in-izm, *n.* the political, economic and social principles and practices of the Russian revolutionary leader, *Lenin* (Vladimir Ilyich Ulyanov; 1870–1924), esp. his theory of government by the proletariat.—*ns.* Len'inist, Len'inite.

lenis lē'nis, (*phon.*) *adj.* of a consonant, articulated with relatively little muscular effort and pressure of breath (opp. to *fortis*).—Also *n.*:—*pl.* lē'nes (*-ēz*).— *n.* lenition (*li-nish'ən*) a softening of articulation, common in Celtic languages. [L., soft.]

lenitive, lenity. See lenient.

leno lē'nō, *n.* a thin muslin-like fabric:—*pl.* lē'nos. [Perh. Fr. *linon*.]

lens lenz, *n.* a piece of transparent matter causing regular convergence or divergence of rays passing through it (*opt.*): the refracting structure (*crystalline lens*) between the crystalline and vitreous humours of the eye:—*pl.* lens'es.—*n.* lent'icle (*geol.*) a lenticular mass.—*adj.* lenti'cular shaped like a lens or lentil seed: double-convex.—*adv.* lentic'ularly.—*adjs.* lent'iform, lent'oid. [L. *lēns, lentis*, lentil.]

Lent lent, *n.* the time from Ash Wednesday to Easter observed as a time of fasting in commemoration of Christ's fast in the wilderness (Matt. iv. 2).—*adj.* Lent'en (also without *cap.*) of Lent: sparing: fleshless.—**lent'-lil'y** the daffodil. [O.E. *lencten*, the spring.]

lent *pa.t.* and *pa.p.* of **lend**.

lentamente, lentando, lenti. See **lento**.

lentic *len'tik, (ecology) adj.* associated with standing water: inhabiting ponds, swamps, etc [L. *lentus*, slow.]

lentiform, etc. See **lens**.

lentigo *len-tī'gō, n.* a freckle: (usu) freckles:—*pl.* **lentigines** (*len-tij'i-nēz*).—*adjs.* **lentig'inose, lentig'inous** (*bot.*) minutely dotted. [L *lentīgō, -inis*, a freckle.]

lentil *len'til, n* an annual papilionaceous plant common near the Mediterranean: its seed used for food [O.Fr. *lentille*—L. *lēns, lentis*, the lentil.]

lentisk *len'tisk, n.* the mastic tree. [L. *lentiscus*]

lento *len'tō, (mus) adj* slow —*adv.* slowly.—*n* a slow passage or movement:—*pl.* **len'tos, len'ti** (*-tē*). —*adv.* **lentamen'te** (*-tā*).—*adj.* and *adv.* **lentan'do** slowing.—*adj.* and *adv* **lentiss'imo** very slow(ly) [It.,—L. *lentus*, slow.]

lentoid. See **lens**.

Leo *lē'ō, n.* the Lion, a constellation between Cancer and Virgo: the 5th sign of the zodiac, in which it used to be (the constellation is now in the sign Virgo) — *adj.* **lē'onine** lionlike. [L. *leō, -ōnis*, lion]

leopard, *fem.* **leop'ardess,** *lep'ərd, -es, n* a large spotted animal of the cat kind found in Africa and Asia: in America, the jaguar.—**leop'ard-cat** a spotted wild cat of India; **snow leopard** the ounce [O Fr ,— L. *leopardus*—Gr. *leopardos* (for *leontopardos*)— *leōn*, lion, *pardos*, pard.]

leotard *lē'ə-tard, n* a skin-tight garment worn by dancers and acrobats, sleeveless or long-sleeved, legs varying from none at all to ankle-length [Jules *Léotard*, 19th-century French trapeze artist.]

leper *lep'ər, n.* one affected with leprosy: a tainted person (*fig.*): an outcast.—*n.* **lep'ra** leprosy· a scurfy, mealy substance on some plants (*bot.*) —*adj.* **lep'rose** (*-rōs*) scaly: scurfy —*ns* **leprosity** (*-ros'i-ti*) scaliness; **lep'rosy** (*-rə-si*) a name formerly widely applied to chronic skin diseases: now to one caused by a bacillus and occurring in two forms, tubercular, beginning with spots and thickenings of the skin, and anaesthetic, attacking the nerves, with loss of sensation in areas of skin.—*adj* **lep'rous** or of affected with leprosy· scaly: scurfy. [O.Fr. *lepre* and Gr. *leprā*— *lepros*, scaly—*lepos*, or *lepis*, a scale, *lepein*, to peel.]

lepid-, lepido- *lep'id-, -ō-, -o', in* composition, scale — *n.pl.* **Lepidop'tera** (Gr *pteron*, wing) an order of insects, with four wings covered with fine scales— butterflies and moths.—*ns.* **lepidop'terist** a student of butterflies and moths; **lepidopterol'ogy.**—*adj.* **lepidop'terous.** [Gr *lepis, -idos*, a scale]

leporine *lep'ə-rīn, adj* pertaining to or resembling the hare [L. *leporīnus—lepus, lepōris*, the hare.]

lepra. See **leper.**

leprechaun, leprechawn *lep'rə-hhòn, n* a little brownie, who helps Irish housewives, mends shoes, grinds meal, etc [Prob Old Ir *luchorpán, lu,* small, *corpan, corp,* a body.]

leprosy, leprous, etc. See **leper.**

-lepsy *-lep-si, (med)* in composition, a seizing, seizure, as in *catalepsy* —**-leptic** adjectival combining form [Gr *lēpsis—lambanein*, to seize, take]

lepton *lep'ton, n* the smallest ancient Greek coin, translated mite in the N T · a modern Greek coin, 1/100th of a drachma —*pl.* **lep'ta:** any of a group of subatomic particles with weak interactions, electrons, negative muons and neutrinos (opp to **baryon**) (*pl* **lep'tons**).—*adj.* **leptocephal'ic** (Gr *kephālē,* head) narrow-skulled —*n* **lep'tosome** (Gr *sōma*, body) a person with a slight, slender physical build: an asthenic.—*adjs.* **leptosō'mic, leptosomatic** (*-sə-mat'ik*).—*n.* **leptospirō'sis** (Gr *speira*, a coil) a disease of animals or man caused by bacteria of the genus **Leptospi'ra.** [Gr. *leptos,* neut. *lepton,* slender.]

les. See **lez(z).**

Lesbian *lez'bi-ən, adj.* of the island of *Lesbos:* amatory, erotic: (also without *cap.*) homosexual (of women).—*n.* (also without *cap.*) a woman homosexual.—*n.* **Les'bianism.**

lese-majesty, leze-majesty *lēz'-maj'is-ti, n.* an offence against the sovereign power, treason. [Fr. *lèse majesté*, transl. of L *laesa mājestās,* injured majesty —*laedēre,* to hurt.]

lesion *lē'zhən, n.* a hurt: a physical change in the body caused by disease or injury, esp an injury or wound (*med.*). [Fr. *lésion*—L. *laesiō, -ōnis—laedēre, laesum,* to hurt.]

less *les, adj.* (used as *comp* of **little**) smaller (not now used of material things): in smaller quantity: minor: fewer (*arch.* and *coll.*): inferior, lower in estimation: younger —*adv.* not so much: in a lower degree.—*n.* a smaller portion or quantity.—*prep.* without: with diminution of, minus —**much less** often used by confusion for much more; **no less** (usu. *iron.*) a phrase used to express admiration; **nothing less than** (formerly) anything rather than: (now) quite as much as. [O.E. *lǣssa,* less, *lǣs* (adv);apparentlynotconn. with **little.**]

-less *-les, -lis, adj.* suffix, free from, wanting, as guilt-*less,* godless. [O E *-lēas.*]

lessee *les-ē', les'ē, n.* one to whom a lease is granted. [**lease.**]

lessen *les'n, v.t.* to make less, in any sense: to lower in estimation: to disparage: to belittle —*v.i.* to become less, shrink [**less.**]

lesser *les'ər, adj* less: smaller: inferior: minor. [Double comp. from **less.**]

lesson *les'n, n.* a portion of Scripture read in divine service: a spell, instalment, or prescribed portion of instruction: an exercise· an instructive or warning experience or example: a severe reproof [Fr. *leçon*— L *lectiō, -ōnis—legēre,* to read.]

lessor *les'or, n.* one who grants a lease [**lease.**]

lest *lest, conj.* that not· for fear that. [M E *leste*— O.E *thý lǣs the,* the less that—*thý* instrum. case; see **the**[2].]

let[1] *let, v.t.* to allow to go or come· to allow, permit, suffer (usu with infin. without *to*): to grant to a tenant or hirer: in the imper. with accus and infin. without *to,* often used virtually as an auxiliary with imperative or optative effect:—*pr p.* **lett'ing;** *pa.t* and *pa.p.* **let.**—*n.* a letting for hire.—*ns* **lett'er** one who lets, esp on hire; **lett'ing.**—**let'-down** an act or occasion of letting down. a disappointment; **let'-out** a chance to escape, avoid keeping (an agreement, contract, etc.); **let'-up** cessation: abatement: alleviation —**let alone** not to mention, much less: to refrain from interference with· (*imper*) trust (*arch.*); **let be** to leave undisturbed; **let down** to allow to fall: to lower· to leave in the lurch, fail to back up at need, betray trust; **let fall** to drop; **let fly** to fling, discharge, shoot; **let go** to cease holding· to slacken (*naut.*); **let in** to allow to enter· to betray into or involve in (*for*) anything vexatious to insert· to leak inwards; **let in on** (*coll*) to allow to take part in; **let into** to admit to the knowledge of· to throw into one with; **let loose** to set free; **let off** to allow to go free or without exacting all to fire off, discharge, **let on** (*coll*) to allow to be believed, to pretend to betray awareness: to reveal, divulge, **let someone know** to inform someone; **let oneself go** (*coll*) to allow one's appearance, life-style, etc , to deteriorate to act without restraint; **let**

loose to let go restraint, to indulge in extravagant talk or conduct; **let out** to allow to get free, or to become known: to widen, slacken, enlarge: to put out to hire· to leak outwards; **let up** (*coll.*) to become less: to abate, **let up on** (*coll*) to cease to have to do with; **let well alone** to let things remain as they are from fear of making them worse; **to let** available for hire. [O.E. *lētan*, to permit, pa.t. *lēt*; pa.p. *lǣten*.]

let[2] *let, n.* obstruction by the net, or other ground for cancelling a service (*lawn-tennis*, etc.): a service so affected. [O.E. *lettan*, to hinder—*lǣt*, slow.]

-let *-lit, -lət, n.* suffix used to form diminutives, as brace*let*, leaf*let*, stream*let*.

lethal *lē'thəl, adj.* death-dealing: deadly: mortal. [L. *lēt*(*h*)*ālis*—*lēt*(*h*)*um*, death]

lethargy *leth'ər-ji, n* heavy unnatural slumber. torpor —*adjs.* **lethargic** (*-är'*), *-al* pertaining to lethargy· unnaturally sleepy: torpid.—*adv* **lethar'gically.**—*adj.* **leth'argied.**—*v.t.* **leth'argise, -ize.** [Gr. *lēthārgiā*, drowsy forgetfulness—*lēthē*, forgetfulness, *ārgos*, idle.]

Lethe *lē'thē, n.* a river of the underworld causing forgetfulness of the past to all who drank of it: oblivion.—*adj.* **lethē'an.** [Gr. *lēthē*, forgetfulness.]

Lett *let, n.* a member of a people inhabiting **Lett'land** (Latvia): a native or citizen of Latvia.—*adjs.* **Lett'ic** of the group (also called *Baltic*) of languages to which Lettish belongs, incl. Lithuanian and Old Prussian; **Lett'ish.**—*n* language of Letts [Ger *Lette*—Lettish *latvis* (now *latvietis*).]

letter[1] *let'ər, n* a conventional mark primarily used to express a sound of speech: a written or printed message: literal meaning: printing-type: (in *pl.*) learning, literary culture.—*v.t.* to stamp letters upon: to mark with a letter or letters.—*adj.* **lett'ered** marked with letters: educated: versed in literature: literary.—*ns.* **lett'erer; lett'ering** the act of impressing or marking with letters: the letters impressed: their style or mode of formation.—**lett'er-bomb** a device inside an envelope which explodes when the envelope is opened; **lett'er-box** a box for receiving letters for or from the post; **lett'er-card** a card folded and gummed like a letter, with perforated margin for opening; **lett'er-clip** an appliance for gripping letters or papers to keep them together; **lett'er-file** arrangement for holding letters for reference; **lett'erhead** a printed heading on notepaper, etc.: a piece of notepaper with such heading.—**lett'erpress** printed reading matter: a copying-press: a method of printing in which ink on raised surfaces is pressed on to paper.—*n.pl.* **lett'ers-patent** a writing conferring a patent or privilege, so called because written on open sheets of parchment —**lett'er-stamp** an instrument for cancelling postage-stamps: a stamp for imprinting dates, etc.—**letter of credit** a letter authorising credit or cash to a certain sum to be given to the bearer; **letter of the law** literal interpretation of the law; **letters of credence, letters credential** a diplomat's formal document accrediting him to a foreign government; **to the letter** exactly, in every detail. [Fr. *lettre*—L. *littera, litera*.]

letter[2], **letting.** See **let**[1].

lettre *le-tr', (*Fr.*) n.* a letter.—**lettre de cachet** (*də ka-she*) a letter under the royal signet: a royal warrant for arrest and imprisonment.

lettuce *let'is, n.* a composite plant (*Lactuca sativa*) with milky juice: its leaves used as a salad: extended to other (inedible) plants of the genus. [Appar. from some form (perh. the pl.) of A.Fr. *letue* (Fr *laitue*)—L. *lactūca—lac*, milk.]

leu *le'oo, n.* the monetary unit of Rumania:—*pl.* **lei** (*lā*). [Rum., lion.]

leuc-, leuco-, leuk-, leuko- *lūk-, lōōk-, lūs-, lōōs-, lū'kō, lōōk'ō-, -ko'-* (*-c-* and *-k-* are in most inter-

changeable, and, except in the first case, *-k-* forms have not been given below), in composition, white.—*ns.* **leucaemia, leukaemia,** (*lū-kē'mi-ə;* Gr *haima*, blood) a sometimes fatal cancerous disease in which too many leucocytes are accumulated in the body, associated with changes in the lymphatic system and enlargement of the spleen; **leucocyte** (*-kō-sīt;* Gr *kytos*, container, used as if cell) a white corpuscle of the blood or lymph; **leucotomy** (*lū-, lōō-kot'ə-mi;* Gr. *tomē*, a cutting) a surgical scission of the white association fibres between the frontal lobes of the brain and the thalamus to relieve cases of severe schizophrenia and manic-depressive psychosis. [Gr *leukos*, white.]

leucin(e) *lū', lōō'sin, -sēn, n.* a decomposition product of proteins. [Gr. *leukos*, white.]

leuco-. See **leuc-.**

leucoma *lū-, lōō-kō'mə, n.* a white opacity of the cornea. [Gr. *leukōma—leukos.*]

leuk(o)-. Alternative form of **leuc(o)-.** See **leuc-.**

lev, lew *lef, n* the monetary unit or franc of Bulgaria. —*pl.* **leva** (*lev'ä*) [Bulg., lion.]

Levant *li-vant', n.* the eastern Mediterranean and its shores: (without *cap.*) the levanter wind: (without *cap.*) a kind of morocco leather.—*adj.* (without *cap.*) (*lev'ənt*) eastern.—*n* **Levant'er** an inhabitant of the Levant: (without *cap.*) a boisterous easterly wind in the Levant.—*adj.* **Levant'ine** (or *lev'ən-tīn*) of the Levant. [Fr. *levant* or It. *levante*, east, lit. rising— L. *levāre*, to raise.]

levant *li-vant', v.t.* to decamp.—*n.* **levan'ter** one who absconds, esp. with bets unpaid. [Sp. *levantar*, to move.—L *levāre*, to raise.]

levator *le-vā'tər, -tor, n.* a muscle that raises—opp. to *depressor.* [L. *levātor*, a lifter—*levāre.*]

levee[1] *lev'i, li-vē', n.* a morning (or comparatively early) reception of visitors, esp. by a person of distinction. [Fr. *levée, lever*—L. *levāre*, to raise.]

levee[2] *lev'i, li-vē', n.* a natural or artificial riverside embankment, esp. on the Lower Mississippi: a quay. [Fr. *levée*, raised; see the foregoing]

level *lev'l, n.* an instrument for testing horizontality: a horizontal position: a condition of horizontality: a horizontal plane or line: a nearly horizontal surface or region with no considerable inequalities: the horizontal plane, literal or figurative, that anything occupies or reaches up to: height: a horizontal mine-gallery: an ascertainment of relative elevation: a levelling survey: natural or appropriate position or rank: a condition of equality: a ditch or channel for drainage, esp. in flat country.—*adj.* horizontal: even, smooth: even with anything else: uniform: well-balanced, sound of judgment: in the same line or plane: filled to a level with the brim: equal in position or dignity.—*adv.* in a level manner: point-blank.—*v.t.* to make horizontal: to make flat or smooth: to lay low: to raze: to aim: to make equal: to direct: to survey by taking levels.—*v.i.* to make things level: to aim.—*v.t.* and *v.i.* to change in spelling or pronunciation, making one word, form, the same as another: —*pr.p.* **lev'elling;** *pa.t.* and *pa.p.* **lev'elled.**—*ns.* **lev'eller** one who levels in any sense: one who would remove all social or political inequalities, esp. (*cap.*) one of an ultra-republican party in the parliamentary army, crushed by Cromwell in 1649; **lev'elling.**—**level best** (*coll.*) one's utmost; **lev'el-cross'ing** a place at which a road crosses a railway at the same level.—*adj.* **lev'el-head'ed** having sound common sense.—**lev'el-pegg'ing(s)** equal state of two rivals, contestants, etc. (often in the form **be level-pegging with**).—*adj.* at the same level, equal.—**find one's level** to come to equilibrium in one's natural position or rank; **level down** or **up** to lower or raise to the same level or status; **level off** to make flat or even· to reach and maintain equilibrium. **level with** (*slang*) to tell the truth; **on the level** fair: honestly speaking [O Fr. *livel*, *liveau* (Fr. *niveau*)—L. *libella*, a plummet, dim of *libra*, a balance.]

lever *lē'vər, n.* a bar turning on a support or fulcrum for imparting pressure or motion from a source of power to a resistance —*v t.* to move with a lever —*n.* **le'verage** the mechanical power gained by the use of the lever: advantage gained for any purpose —**le'ver·watch** a watch having a vibrating lever in the mechanism of the escapement. [O Fr *leveor—lever*—L *levāre*, to raise]

leveret *lev'ə-rit, n.* a hare in its first year. [O Fr *leverette* (Fr. *lièvre*)—L *lepus, lepŏris*, a hare]

leviable. See **levy.**

leviathan *le-vī'ə-thən, n.* anything of huge size, esp. a ship or a man: (after Hobbes's book, 1651) the state —*adj* gigantic, formidable. [Heb *livyāthān.*]

levigate *lev'i-gāt, v.t* to smooth. to grind to fine powder, esp. with a liquid —*n.* **leviga'tion.** [L *lēvigāre*, *-ātum—lēvis*, smooth.]

levirate *lev'* or *lev'i-rāt, n.* the (ancient Hebrew and other) custom of compulsory marriage with a childless brother's widow.—*adjs.* **lev'irate, leviratical** (*-rat'-i-kl*) [L *lēvir*, a brother-in-law.]

Levis® *lē'vīz, n.pl.* (also without *cap.*) heavy, close-fitting denim, etc , trousers, with low waist, reinforced at points of strain with copper rivets

levitation *lev-i-tā'shən, n* the act of rising by virtue of lightness: act of rendering light. the floating of heavy bodies in the air, according to spiritualists. raising and floating on a cushion of air.—*v.t , v.i* **lev'itate** to (cause to) float [On the model of *gravitate*—L *levis*, light.]

Levite *lē'vīt, n* a descendant of *Levi*: an inferior priest of the ancient Jewish Church.—*adjs.* **levitic** (*li-vit'ik*), **-al.**—*adv.* **levit'ically.**—*n.* **Levit'icus** the third book of the Old Testament.

levity *lev'it-i, n.* lightness of temper or conduct: thoughtlessness. disposition to trifle: vain quality [L. *levitās, -ātis—levis*, light.]

levo-. Same as **laevo-.**

levulose. Same as **laevulose.**

levy *lev'i, v t* to raise, collect, as an army or tax: to call for to impose. to begin to wage:—*pr.p.* **lev'ying;** *pa t* and *pa p.* **lev'ied.**—*n.* the act of levying: a contribution called for from members of an association: a tax: the amount collected: troops levied.—*adj.* **leviable** (*lev'i ə-bl*) able to be levied or assessed —**to levy war** to make war. [Fr *levée—lever*—L. *levāre*, to raise.]

lew. See **lev.**

lewd *lōōd, lūd, adj.* lustful: unchaste.—*adv* **lewd'ly.**—*n* **lewd'ness.** [O E *lǣwede*, ignorant]

lewis *lōō'is, n* a dovetail iron tenon for lifting blocks of stone (also **lew'isson**)

Lewis gun *lōō'is gun,* a light machine-gun invented by Col Isaac Newton *Lewis.*

lewisite *lōō'is-īt, n* a vesicant liquid, an arsine derivative, used in chemical warfare [Named after W L *Lewis*, American chemist.]

lewisson. See **lewis.**

lexeme *lek'sēm,* (*gram*) *n.* a word or other essential unit of vocabulary in its most abstract sense [*lexicon*, and -*eme*]

lexicon *leks'i-kən, n* a word-book or dictionary: a vocabulary of terms used in connection with a particular subject —*adj* **lex'ical** belonging to a lexicon: pertaining to the words of a language as distinct from its grammar and constructions —*adv* **lex'ically.**—*n.* **lexicographer** (*-kog'rə-fər*).—*adjs* **lexicographic** (*-kə-graf'ik*), **-al.**—*ns.* **lexicog'raphist; lexicog'raphy**

the writing and compiling of dictionaries; **lexicol'ogist; lexicol'ogy** the study of the history and meaning of words [Gr *lexikon*, a dictionary—*lexis*, a word, *legein*, to speak]

lexigraphy *leks-ig'rə-fi, n* a system of writing in which each sign represents a word —*n.* **lex'igram** a sign which represents a word —*adjs.* **lexigraphic** (*-graf'ik*), **-al.** [Gr *lexis*, word, *graphein*, to write]

ley *lā, n.* (also **ley line**) one of the straight lines between features of the landscape, possibly pathways, or perhaps having scientific or magical significance in prehistoric times. [Var. of **lea¹.**]

Leyden jar *lā'dən jar,* a condenser for electricity, a glass jar coated inside and outside with tinfoil or other conducting material [*Leyden* in Holland, where it was invented.]

leze-majesty. See **lese-majesty.**

lez(z), **les, lezzy** *lez, lez'i,* (*coll.*) *n* short forms of **lesbian.**

lhasa apso *la'sə ap'sō,* a Tibetan (breed of) small, longhaired terrier.—*pl.* **lhasa apsos.** [*Lhasa*, the capital of Tibet.]

liable *lī'ə-bl, adj* subject to an obligation: exposed to a possibility or risk: responsible (*for*) tending (usually with *to*): apt: likely (*to*).—*n.* **liabil'ity** state of being liable: that for which one is liable, a debt, etc — **limited liability** a principle of modern statute law which limits the responsibilities of shareholders in a partnership, joint-stock company, etc , by the extent of their personal interest therein. [App.—Fr *lier*—L *ligāre*, to bind]

liaison *lē-ā'zn, -zō, lyez-ō, n.* union, or bond of union· connection illicit union between the sexes: in French, the linking in pronunciation of a final (and otherwise silent) consonant to a vowel beginning the next word: effective conjunction with another unit or force (*mil.*) —*v i.* **liaise** (*lē-āz'*, back-formation) to form a link (*with*): to be or get in touch (*with*).— **liaison officer** an officer forming a link with another unit or force. [Fr ,—L *ligātiō, -ōnis—ligāre*, to bind.]

liana *lē-a'nə,* **liane** *lē-an', ns.* any climbing plant, especially any contorted woody kind festooning tropical forests [Fr *liane*, Latinised or Hispanicised as *liana*, app —*lier*—L *ligāre*, to bind.]

liar. See **lie¹.**

Lias *lī'as,* (*geol.*) *n.* and *adj.* Lower Jurassic —*adj* **Liassic** (*lī-as'ik*). [A Somerset quarryman's word, app.—O Fr *liois* (Fr *liais*), a kind of limestone]

lib. See **liberate.**

libation *lī-bā'shən, li-, n* the pouring forth of wine or other liquid in honour of a god, or (*facet*) for other purpose: the liquid poured. [L *lībāre, -ātum,* to pour, sip, touch.]

libber. See **liberate.**

libel *lī'bl, n.* a written accusation: any malicious defamatory publication or statement: written defamation (*English law,* distinguished from *slander* or spoken defamation, in Scots law both are slander) the statement of a plaintiff's grounds of complaint — *v.t* to defame by libel to satirise unfairly: to proceed against by producing a written complaint (*law*) — *pr.p* **li'belling;** *pa.t.* and *pa.p* **li'belled.**—*ns* **li'bellant** one who brings a libel; **li'beller** a defamer; **li'belling.**—*adj* **li'bellous** containing a libel defamatory —*adv* **li'bellously.** [L. *lībellus,* dim of *liber*, a book]

liberal *lib'ə-rəl, adj* directed towards the cultivation of the mind for its own sake, disinterested (opposed to *technical* and *professional*): generous noble-minded broad-minded. not bound by authority or traditional orthodoxy. looking to the general or broad sense rather than the literal candid free free from re-

straint: ample: (*cap.*) of the Liberal Party (see below).
—*n.* one who advocates greater freedom in political
institutions: one whose views in theology are liberal.—
n. **liberalisa'tion**, -z-.—*v.t.* and *v.i.* **lib'eralise, -ize** to
make or become liberal, or enlightened.—*ns.*
lib'eralism the principles of a liberal in politics or
religion; **lib'eralist**.—*adj.* **liberalist'ic**.—*n.* **liberality**
(-*al'i-ti*) the quality of being liberal: generosity: largeness or nobleness of mind: candour: freedom from
prejudice.—*adv.* **lib'erally**.—**liberal arts** the studies
that make up a liberal education; **Liberal Party**
successors of the Whigs, including the Radicals, advocates of democratic reform and liberty. [L. *liberālis*,
befitting a freeman—*liber*, free.]
liberate *lib'ə-rāt, v.t.* to set free: to release from restraint, confinement, or bondage: to give off.—*ns*
libera'tion setting free, releasing: freeing from social
disadvantages and prejudices (*coll.* shortening **lib**);
libera'tionism; libera'tionist one who supports the
cause of social freedom and equality for sections of
society believed to be underprivileged or discriminated against (*coll.* shortening **libb'er**); **lib'erātor**.
[L. *liberāre, -ātum—liber*, free.]
liberty *lib'ər-ti, n.* freedom from constraint, captivity,
slavery, or tyranny: freedom to do as one pleases: the
unrestrained enjoyment of natural rights: privilege:
permission: free range: leisure: disposal: presumptuous or undue freedom: speech or action violating ordinary civility.—*n* **liberta'rian** a believer in free-will:
one who believes in the maximum amount of freedom
of thought, behaviour, etc.—Also *adj.*—*ns*
liberta'rianism; lib'ertinage (also -*ûrt'*) debauchery;
lib'ertine (-*tēn, -tin, -tīn*) formerly one who professed
free opinions, esp. in religion: one who leads a licentious life, a rake or debauchee.—*adj.* unrestrained:
licentious.—*n.* **lib'ertinism**.—**liberty bodice** an
undergarment like a vest formerly often worn by
children; **liberty cap** see **cap**; **Liberty Hall** (*coll.*; also
without *cap.*) a place where one may do as one likes;
liberty horse a circus horse that, as one of a group and
without a rider, carries out movements on command.
—**at liberty** free: unoccupied: available; **civil liberty**
freedom of an individual within the law: individual
freedom as guaranteed by a country's laws; **liberty of
the press** freedom to print and publish without government permission, **take liberties with** to treat with
undue freedom or familiarity, or indecently: to falsify;
take the liberty to venture, presume. [Fr. *liberté*—
L. *libertās, -ātis*, liberty: L. *libertīnus*, a freedman—
liber, free]
libido *li-bē'dō, li-bi'dō, n.* vital urge, either in general
or as of sexual origin (*psych.*): sexual impulse:—*pl.*
libid'os.—*adjs.* **libidinal** (-*bid'*) pertaining to the
libido, **libid'inous** lustful, lascivious, lewd.—*ns*
libidinos'ity, libid'inousness.—*adv.* **libid'inously**.
[L *libīdō, -inis*, desire—*libet, lubet*, it pleases.]
libra *lī'bra*, L. *lē', n.* a Roman pound (*ant.*; used in
contraction lb. for the British pound, and £ for a pound
in money): (*cap.*) the Balance, a constellation
between the Virgin and the Scorpion: the seventh sign
of the zodiac in which it used to be (it is now in Scorpio)
[L *libra*.]
library *lī'brə-ri, n.* a collection of books: a building or
room containing it: a publisher's series: also a collection of gramophone records, etc.; a collection of
computer programmes.—*ns.* **libra'rian** the keeper of a
library, **libra'rianship**.—**library edition** an edition of a
book with high-quality binding, etc.—**lending library**
one from which people may take books away on loan
[L. *librārium*, a bookcase—*liber*, a book.]
librate *lī'brāt, v.i.* to oscillate: to be poised.—*n* **libra'tion**.—**libration of the moon** a slight turning of the
moon to each side alternately so that more than half of

its surface is visible one time or other. [L. *librāre,
-ātum—libra*, balance.]
libretto *li-bret'ō, n.* the text or book of words of an
opera, oratorio, or ballet:—*pl* **librett'i** (-*ē*),
librett'os.—*n.* **librett'ist** a writer of libretti. [It.,
dim. of *libro*—L. *liber*, a book.]
Libyan *lib'i-ən, adj.* of Libya in North Africa.—*n.* a
native thereof. [Gr. *Libyē*, Libya.]
lice *lis*, plural of **louse**.
licence, in U.S. **license**, *lī'səns, n.* a being allowed:
leave: grant of permission: the document by which
authority is conferred: excess or abuse of freedom:
licentiousness, libertinage, debauchery: a departure
for effect from a rule or standard in art or literature:
tolerated freedom.—*v.t.* **li'cense** to grant licence to: to
permit to depart, dismiss: to authorise or permit.—
Also **licence**.—*adjs.* **li'censable; li'censed** holding a
licence: permitted, tolerated.—*ns.* **licensee'** one to
whom a licence is granted, esp. to sell alcoholic drink;
li'censer, (chiefly *U.S.*) **li'censor** one who grants
licence or permission: one authorised to license;
li'censure act of licensing, **licentiate** (*lī-sen'shi-āt*)
among Presbyterians, a person authorised by a Presbytery to preach: a holder of an academic diploma of
various kinds: in some European universities, a graduate ranking between bachelor and doctor.—*adj.*
licentious (-*sen'shəs*) indulging in excessive freedom:
given to the indulgence of the animal passions.
dissolute.—*adv.* **licen'tiously**.—*n.* **licen'tiousness**.—
license plate (*U.S.*) a number plate. [Fr. *licence*—L.
licentia—licēre, to be allowed.]
lich *lich, n* a body, living or dead (*obs*).—**lich'gate,
lych'gate** a roofed churchyard gate to rest the bier
under; **lich'wake** see **lykewake**. [M.E. *lich, liche*
(Southern), *like* (Northern)—O E. *līc*.]
lichee. Same as **lychee**.
lichen *lī'kən, lich'ən, n.* a compound plant consisting of
a fungus and an alga living symbiotically, forming
crusts and tufts on stones, trees, and soil: an eruption
on the skin.—*ns.* **li'chenist, lichenol'ogist** one versed
in lichenol'ogy, the study of lichens.—*adjs.* **li'chenoid;
li'chenose, li'chenous** abounding in, or pertaining to,
of the nature of, lichens, or lichen. [L. *lichēn*—Gr.
leichēn, -enos.]
lichgate, etc. See **lich**.
lichi. See **lychee**.
licit *lis'it, adj.* lawful, allowable.—*adv.* **lic'itly**. [L
licitus.]
lick *lis'it, v.t.* to pass the tongue over: to take in by the
tongue: to lap: to put or render by passing the tongue
over: to pass over or play upon in the manner of a
tongue: to smear to beat (*slang*).—*v i* (*slang*) to go at
full speed —*n.* an act of licking a quantity licked up,
or such as might be imagined to be licked up: a slight
smearing or wash: a place where animals lick salt:
vigorous speed (*coll.*).—*ns* **lick'er; lick'ing** a
thrashing —**a lick and a promise** a perfunctory
wash; **lick into shape** to mould into due form; **lick
one's lips** to recall or look forward with pleasure; **lick
one's wounds** to retire from a defeat, failure, etc., esp
in order to try to recover one's strength, pride, etc ,
lick someone's boots to toady; **lick the dust** to be slain.
to be abjectly servile. [O E *liccian*.]
licorice. Another spelling (chiefly *U.S*) for **liquorice**.
lictor *lik'tor, -tər, n* an officer who attended a Roman
magistrate, bearing the fasces [L *lictor*.]
lid *lid, n.* a cover, hinged or separate, for the opening of
a receptacle: the movable cover of the eye: an effective
restraint (*fig.*): a hat (*slang*) —*adjs* **lidd'ed** having a
lid or lids; **lid'less**.—**put the lid on it** to end the matter
to be a culminating injustice, misfortune, etc., **take,
lift, blow the lid off** to uncover, reveal (a scandal,
etc) [O.E *hlid*.—*hlīdan*, to cover]

lido *lē'dō*, *n.* a bathing beach: an open-air swimming-pool:—*pl.* **lid'os**. [From the *Lido* at Venice—L. *lĭtus*, shore.]

lie¹ *lī*, *n.* a false statement made with the intention of deceiving: anything misleading or of the nature of imposture: (with *the*) an accusation of lying.—*v.i.* to utter falsehood with an intention to deceive: to give a false impression:—*pr.p.* **ly'ing**; *pa.t.* and *pa.p.* **lied**.—*n.* **li'ar** one who lies, esp. habitually.—*adj.* **ly'ing** addicted to telling lies.—*n.* the habit of telling lies.—*adv.* **ly'ingly**.—**lie detector** an instrument claimed to detect lying by recording abnormal involuntary bodily reactions in a person not telling the truth.—**give someone the lie (in his throat)** to charge someone to his face of lying; **give the lie to** to charge with lying: to prove false; **lie in one's throat** to lie shamelessly; **white lie** a minor falsehood; esp. one uttered for reasons of tact, etc. [O.E. *lyge* (noun), *lēogan* (strong vb.).]

lie² *lī*, *v.i.* to be in a horizontal or nearly horizontal posture: to assume such a posture: to lean: to press: to be situated: to have a position or extent: to remain: to be or remain passively: to abide: to be still: to be incumbent: to depend: to consist: to be sustainable (*law*):—*pr.p.* **ly'ing**; *pa.t.* **lay**; *pa.p.* **lain**.—*n* mode or direction of lying: slope and disposition: relative position: general situation: a spell of lying: an animal's lurking-place or favourite station: position from which a golf-ball is to be played.—*n.* **li'er**.—**lie'-abed'** one who lies late.—Also *adj.*—**lie-down'** see **lie down** below; **lie'-in'** a longer than usual stay in bed in the morning; **ly'ing-in'** confinement during child-birth:—*pl.* **ly'ings-in'**.—Also *adj.*—**lie at someone's door** to be directly imputable to someone; **lie back** to lean back on a support: to rest after a period of hard work; **lie by** to be inactive: to keep out of the way: to lie to (*naut.*); **lie down** to place oneself in a horizontal position, esp. in order to sleep or rest (*n.* **lie'-down'**); **lie hard** or **heavy on, upon, to** to oppress, burden; **lie in** to be in childbed: to stay in bed later than usual; **lie in wait** to lie in ambush; **lie low** to keep quiet or hidden: to conceal one's actions or intentions; **lie of the land** (*fig.*) the current situation; **lie on, upon** to be incumbent on; **lie on one's hands** to remain unwanted, unclaimed, or unused; **lie out of** to remain without the good of, without payment of; **lie over** to be deferred to a future occasion; **lie to** to be or become nearly stationary with head to wind; **lie under** to be subject to or oppressed by; **lie up** to abstain from work: to take to or remain in bed: of a ship, to go into or be in dock; **lie with** to have sexual intercourse with: to rest with as a choice, duty, etc.; **take it lying down** to endure without resistance or protest. [O.E. *licgan*.]

lied *lēt*, *n.* a German lyric or song, esp. an art-song:—*pl.* **lieder** (*lē'dər*). [Ger.; cf. O.E. *lēoth*, a song.]

lief *lēf*, (*arch.*) *adv.* willingly [O.E. *lēof*.]

liege *lēj*, *adj.* free except as within the relations of vassal and feudal lord: under a feudal tenure.—*n.* one under a feudal tenure: a vassal: a loyal vassal, subject: a lord or superior (also in this sense, **liege'-lord**).—*n.* **liege'man** a vassal: a subject. [O.Fr *līge.*]

lien *lē'ən, lēn*, (*law*) *n.* a right to retain possession of another's property until the owner pays a debt. [Fr.,—L. *ligāmen*, tie, band.]

lier. See **lie²**.

lierne *li-ûrn'*, *n.* a cross-rib or branch-rib in vaulting [Fr.]

lieu *lū, loo*, *n.* place, stead, chiefly in the phrase 'in lieu of'. [Fr.,—L. *locus*, place.]

lieutenant *lef-*, *lif-*, *laf-ten'ant*, also (esp. *navy*) *le-, lə-, loo-ten'-*, *arch.* *loot'nənt*, in U.S., *loo-*, *n* one representing, or performing the work of a superior (form. also *fig.*): an officer holding the place of another in his absence: a commissioned officer in the army next below a captain, or in the navy next below a lieutenant-commander and ranking with captain in the army: one holding a place next in rank to a superior, as in the compounds **lieuten'ant-col'onel, lieuten'ant-command'er, lieuten'ant-gen'eral**.—*ns.* **lieuten'ancy, lieuten'antship** office or commission of a lieutenant: the body of lieutenants; **lieuten'ant-gov'ernor** a State governor's deputy (*U.S., Austr.*): a governor subordinate to a governor-general: a governor (Isle of Man, Jersey, Guernsey); **lieuten'ant-gov'ernorship**.—**Lord Lieutenant** a permanent governor of a county, head of the magistracy and the chief executive authority:—*pl.* **Lords Lieutenant, Lord Lieutenants, Lords Lieutenants**. [Fr.; see **lieu** and **tenant**.]

life *līf*, *n.* state of being alive: conscious existence: existence: the sum of the activities of plants and animals· continued existence, activity, or validity of anything: the period of usefulness of machinery, etc.: the period between birth and death: a continued opportunity of remaining in the game: career: present state of existence: manner of living: moral conduct: animation: liveliness: appearance of being alive: a living being: living things: social state: human affairs: narrative of a life: that on which continued existence depends: one who imparts animation: the living form and expression, living semblance: a life sentence (*coll.*): an insured person:—*pl.* **lives** (*līvz*).—*adj.* (and in composition) for the duration of life: of life.—*adj.* **life'less** dead: insensible: without vigour: insipid: sluggish.—*adv.* **life'lessly**.—*n.* **life'lessness**.—*adj.* **life'like** like a living person or the original.—*n.* **lif'er** a person sentenced for life: a life sentence.—*adj.* **life'-and-death'** critical: determining between life and death.—**life'-annu'ity** a sum paid to a person yearly during life; **life'-assur'ance, life'-insur'ance** insurance providing a sum of money for a specified beneficiary in the event of the policy-holder's death, and for the policy-holder if he reaches a specified age; **life'belt** a buoyant belt for sustaining a person in the water: any aid to survival (*fig.*); **life'-blood** the blood necessary to life: that which gives strength or life; **life'boat** a boat for saving shipwrecked persons; **life'-buoy** a float for supporting a person in the water till he can be rescued; **life'-cycle** (*biol.*) the round of changes in the life and generations of an organism, from zygote to zygote, **life'-force'** a directing principle supposed to be immanent in living things.—*adj.* **life'-giving** imparting life: invigorating.—**life'guard** a bodyguard: one employed to rescue bathers in difficulties: (*cap., pl.*) two horse regiments formed in 1660; **life'-his'tory** the history of a life: the succession of changes from zygote to maturity and death: the life-cycle; **life'-jack'et** a buoyant jacket, a lifebelt; **life'-line** a rope for saving or safeguarding life: a vital line of communication.—*adj.* **life'long** lasting throughout life.—**life'-peer** a peer whose title is not hereditary; **life'-peer'age; life'-peeress; life raft** a raft kept on board a ship for use in an emergency; **life'-rock'et** a rocket for carrying a line to a ship in distress; **life'-saver** one who saves from death, esp. from drowning: one employed to rescue bathers in difficulty: something, or someone, that comes to one's aid at a critical moment (*fig.*); **life'-sav'ing**.—*adj.* designed to save life, esp. from drowning.—**life'-school** a school where artists work from living models; **life sciences** the sciences (biology, medicine, etc.) concerned with living organisms; **life sentence** a prison sentence to last for the rest of the prisoner's natural life (usu now lasting approx. 15 years).—*adjs.* **life'-size(d)** of the size of the object represented.—**life'-**

span the length of time during which a person or animal normally lives, or a machine, etc., functions, **life style** way of living, i.e. one's material surroundings, attitudes, behaviour, etc.: the (characteristic) way of life of a group or individual; **life-support machine, system** a device or system of devices designed to maintain human life in adverse conditions, e.g. in space, during illness, etc.; **life'time** time during which one is alive; **life'-work** the work to which one's life is or is to be devoted.—**bring to life** to confer life upon: to reanimate; **come to life** to become alive: to be reanimated, **for life** for the whole period of one's existence; **for the life of him** though it were to save his life: do what he might; **high life** fashionable society or its manner of living; **not on your life** (*coll.*) on no account; **see life** to see how other people live, esp. the disreputable; **the life and soul** the one who is the chief source of merriment, etc., esp. at a party; **the life of Riley** (*rī'li*) an easy, troublefree life; **to the life** very closely like the original. [O.E. *līf*.]

lift *lift, v.t.* to bring to a higher position: to take up: to elate: to take and carry away: to hold up, support: to arrest (*slang*): to steal: to plagiarise: to remove or revoke.—*v.i.* to rise.—*n.* act of lifting: lifting power: vertical distance of lifting: the component of the aerodynamic force on an aircraft acting upwards at right angles to the drag: that which assists to lift: an enclosed platform moving in a well to carry persons or goods up and down: one of the layers of material in a shoe heel, esp. an extra one to increase the wearer's height: a contrivance for raising or lowering a vessel to another level of a canal: a step in advancement: help on one's way by taking upon a vehicle.—*adj.* **lift'able**.—*n.* **lift'er**.—**lift'-off** the take-off of an aircraft or rocket: the moment when this occurs; **lift'-pump** any pump that is not a force-pump.—**lift a, one's hand (to)** to raise it in hostility; **have one's face lifted** to undergo an operation for smoothing and firming it. [O.N. *lypta—lopt*, the air.]

ligament *lig'ə-mənt, n.* anything that binds: the bundle of fibrous tissue joining bones or cartilages (*anat.*): a bond of union.—*adjs.* **ligamental** (*-ment'l*), **ligament'ary**, **ligament'ous**.—*ns.* **ligand** (*lig'ənd, lī'*) an atom, molecule, radical, or ion which forms a complex with a central atom; **ligature** (*lig'ə-chər*) anything that binds: a bandage: a tie or slur (*mus.*): a type of two or more letters (e.g. æ, ﬀ) (*print.*): a cord for tying the blood-vessels, etc. (*med.*).—*v.t.* to bind with a ligature. [L. *ligāre*, to bind.]

ligan; ligate, etc. See **lagan; ligament**.

light¹ *līt, n.* the agency by which objects are rendered visible: electromagnetic radiation capable of producing visual sensation: that from which it proceeds, as the sun, a lamp: a high degree of illumination: day: a gleam or shining from a bright source: a gleam or glow in the eye or on the face: means of igniting or illuminating: a lighthouse: mental or spiritual illumination (*fig.*): enlightenment: a hint, clue, help towards understanding: knowledge: open view: aspect: a conspicuous person: an aperture for admitting light: a vertical division of a window.—*adj.* not dark: bright: whitish: well lighted.—*v.t.* to give light to: to set fire to: to attend with a light.—*v.i.* to become light or bright:—*pr.p.* **light'ing**; *pa.t.* and *pa.p.* **light'ed** or **lit**.—*n.* **light'er** one who sets alight: a means of igniting.—*n.* **light'ing** illumination: ignition, kindling: disposal or quality of lights.—Also *adj.*—*adjs.* **light'ish**; **light'less**.—*n.* **light'ness**.—*adj.* **light'some** full of light.—**light bulb** a glass bulb containing a metal filament which glows when an electric current is passed through it, the usual method of electric lighting; **light'house** a building with a light to guide or warn ships or aircraft; **light'houseman, light-**

(house)keep'er the keeper of a lighthouse.—*n.* and *adj.* **light'ing-up** (**lighting-up time** the time of day from which vehicles must show lights).—**light meter** (*phot.*) an exposure meter; **light pen** (*comput.*) a pen-like photoelectric device that can enter or alter data on a visual display unit; **light'ship** ship serving the purpose of a lighthouse; **light'-year** distance light travels in a year (about 6 000 000 000 000 miles).—**according to one's lights** as far as one's knowledge, spiritual illumination, etc., enable one to judge; **bring to light** to reveal; **come to light** to be revealed; **inner light** spiritual illumination, light divinely imparted; **in one's, the, light** between one and the source of illumination; **in the light of** considering, taking into account; **light of nature** intellectual perception or intuition: man's capacity of discovering truth unaided by revelation (*theol.*); **lights out** (*mil.*) bugle or trumpet call for extinction of lights: the time at which lights are turned out for the night, in a boarding-school, barracks, etc.; **light up** to light one's lamp, pipe, cigarette, etc.: to turn on the light: to make or become light or bright; **northern (southern) lights** aurora borealis (australis); **see the light** to come into view or being: to be converted; **shed, throw, light on** to clarify. [M.E. *liht*—O.E. *leht, lēht*.]

light² *līt, adj.* not heavy: of short weight: easily suffered or performed: easily digested: well risen, as bread: containing little alcohol: not heavily armed: active: not heavily burdened: unimportant: not dense or copious or intense: slight: scanty: gentle: delicate: nimble: facile: frivolous: unheeding: gay, lively: amusing: unchaste: loose, sandy: giddy, delirious: idle: worthless: falling short in the number of tricks one has contracted to make (*bridge*).—*adv.* lightly.—*v.t.* **light'en** to make lighter.—*v.i.* to become lighter.—*ns.* **light'er** a large open boat used in unloading and loading ships; **light'erage** unloading by lighters: the payment for such unloading; **light'erman**.—*adj.* **light'ish**.—*adv.* **light'ly** in a light manner: slightly: promptly.—*n.* **light'ness**.—*n.pl.* **lights** the lungs of an animal (as lighter than adjoining parts).—*adj.* **light'some** light, gay, lively, cheering.—*n.* **light'someness**.—*adjs.* **light'-armed** armed in a manner suitable for activity; **light'er-than-air** of aircraft, sustained by a gas-bag; **light'-fing'ered** light or active with one's fingers: thievish; **light'-foot, -ed** nimble, active; **light'-hand'ed** with light, delicate, or dexterous touch: insufficiently manned; **light'-head'ed** giddy in the head: delirious: thoughtless: unsteady.—**light'-head'edness**.—*adj.* **light'-heart'ed** free from anxiety: cheerful.—*adv.* **light'-heart'edly**.—**light'-heart'edness**.—**light'-horse** light-armed cavalry; **light industry** see **industry**; **light'-in'fantry** light-armed-infantry; **light-middleweight** see under **middle**.—*adj.* **light'-mind'ed** frivolous or unstable: inconsiderate.—**light'-mind'edness; light'weight** a man or animal between the middleweight and the featherweight, as a boxer over 9 st. and not over 9 st. 9 lb. (amateur 7 lb.): a person of little importance or influence: a light article of any kind, esp. a motorcycle.—*adj.* light in weight: lacking substance, solemnity, etc. (*fig.*).—**make light of** to treat as of little consequence. [O.E. *līht*.]

light³ *līt, v.i.* to dismount: to come down as from a horse or vehicle or from fall or flight: to alight: to settle: to rest: to come by chance:—*pr.p.* **light'ing**; *pa.t.* and *pa.p.* **light'ed** or **lit**.—**light into** (*coll.*) to attack, with blows or words; **light out** to decamp. [O.E *lihtan*, to dismount, lit. make light; see preceding.]

lighten¹ *līt'n, v.t.* to make light or lighter, or brighter: to illuminate.—*v.i.* to become light, lighter, or brighter: to flash as lightning.—*ns.* **light'ening** a linen and wool mixed, or inferior wool with cotton.—*adj*. of linen and wool: neither one thing nor another [Perh. **line**[1], **wool**, and possibly *say*, a woollen material.]

lint *lint*, *n*. scraped linen or a cotton substitute for dressing wounds: cotton fibre: raw cotton.—*adj*. **lint'y.** [M.E. *lynt*, *lynet*, perh.—L. *linteus*, of linen—*līnum*, flax.]

lintel *lint'l*, *n*. a timber or stone over a doorway or window —*adj*. **lint'elled.** [O.Fr. *lintel* (Fr. *linteau*) —a dim of L. *līmes*, *-itis*, border.]

lion *lī'ən*, *n*. a large, fierce, tawny, loud-roaring animal of the cat family, the male with shaggy mane: a man of unusual courage (*fig.*)· (*cap.*) the constellation or the sign Leo (*astron.*):—*fem*. **li'oness.**—*v.t* **li'onise, -ize** to treat as a lion or object of interest: to go around the sights of: to show the sights to.—*n*. **li'onism** lionising· lion-like appearance in leprosy.—*adjs*. **li'on-like, li'only.**—**li'on-cub** a young lion; **li'on-heart** one with great courage.—*adj*. **li'on-heart'ed.**—**li'on-hunt'er; lion's mouth** (*fig.*) a dangerous position; **lion's share** the whole or greater part; **li'on-tā'mer.** [A.Fr. *liun* —L. *leō*, *-ōnis*—Gr. *leōn*, *-ontos*.]

lip *lip*, *n*. either of the muscular flaps in front of the teeth and surrounding the mouth: any similar structure, as each of the two divisions of a labiate corolla: the edge or rim of an orifice, cavity, or vessel: part of such a rim bent outwards like a spout: impudent talk, insolence (*slang*).—*v.t.* to touch with the lips. to kiss. to wash, overflow, or overrun the edge of: to lap or lave: to form a lip on: to edge: to utter with the lips.—*v.i.* to manage the lips in playing a wind-instrument· to lap at the brim: to have water lapping over:—*pr.p* **lipp'ing;** *pa.t* and *pa.p.* **lipped.**—*adj* of the lip. formed or sounded by the lips: (in composition) from the lips only, not sincere.—*adjs*. **lip'less; lipped** (*lipt*) having a lip or lips: labiate; **lipp'y** with hanging lip· saucy (*slang*) —**lip'gloss** a substance applied to the lips to give them a glossy appearance.—*v.i.* **lip'-read.** —**lip'-reader; lip'-read'ing** gathering what a person says by watching the movement of the lips; **lip'-rounding** rounding of the lips, as in pronouncing *o*; **lip'salve** ointment for the lips: blandishment; **lip'-service** insincere praise or worship; **lip'stick** colouring for the lips in the form of a stick.—*v.t.* and *v.i.* to paint with lipstick.—**bite one's lip** to show annoyance or disappointment: to repress an emotion or utterance; **hang on someone's lips** to listen eagerly to all that he has to say; **(keep) a stiff upper lip** (to show) a face of resolution, with no yielding to emotion. [O.E. *lippa*.]

lip-, lipo- *lip-*, *līp-*(*ō-*), in composition, fat —*ns*. **lip'ase** (*-ās*, *-āz*) an enzyme that breaks up fats; **lip'id(e)** a fat or wax, etc., found in living cells.—*adj*. **lip'oid** fat-like.—*n*. a fat-like substance: a lipid.—*ns* **lipō'ma** a fatty tumour:—*pl*. **lipō'mata; lipomatō'sis** the excessive growth of fat.—*adj*. **lipō'matous.**—*n* **lipoprō'tein** a water-soluble protein found in the blood, which carries cholesterol.—*adj*. **liposō'mal.**—*n*. **lip'ōsome** (Gr. *sōma*, body) a substance consisting of lipids and water in droplets, used in the treatment of various diseases. [Gr. *lipos*, fat.]

liparite *lip'ə-rīt*, *n*. rhyolite. [From the *Lipari* Islands, where it occurs.]

Lipizzaner *lip-it-sä'nər*, *n*. a breed of horses (usu. grey or white in colour) particularly suited for displays of haute école.—Also **Lippizaner, Lippizzaner, Lippizana** (*-nə*), **Lippizzana.** [*Lipizza* (*Lippiza*, *Lippizza*), near Trieste, where orig. bred.]

liquate *lik'wāt*, *v.t.* to melt: to subject to liquation.—*adj*. **liq'uable.**—*n*. **liquā'tion** melting: separation of metals with different melting-points. [L. *liquāre*, *-ātum*, to liquefy.]

liquefy *lik'wi-fī*, *v.t.* to make liquid.—*v.i.* to become liquid:—*pr.p.* **liq'uefying;** *pa.t.* and *pa.p.* **liq**
—*n*. and *adj*. **liquefacient** (*-fā'shənt*) —*n* **liquefa**
(*-fak'shən*).—*adj*. **liq'uefiable.**—*n*. **liq'uefier.**—
liquefied petroleum gas propane or butane under moderate pressure, used in vehicles in place of petrol or diesel oil. [L *liquefacĕre*—*liquēre*, to be liquid, *facĕre*, to make.]

liquesce *lik-wes'*, *v.i.* to become liquid: to merge.—*ns*. **liquesc'ence, liquesc'ency.**—*adj*. **liquesc'ent.** [L. *liquēscĕre*—*liquēre*, to be liquid]

liqueur *lik-ūr'*, or *lē-kœr'*, *n*. an alcoholic preparation flavoured or perfumed and sweetened—as chartreuse, cherry brandy.—*v t* to flavour with a liqueur.—*adj*. (of brandy or whisky) that may be drunk as a liqueur.—**liqueur'-glass** a very small drinking-glass. [Fr.,—L *liquor*, see **liquor.**]

liquid *lik'wid*, *adj*. flowing: fluid. watery: in phys., in a state between solid and gas, in which the molecules move freely about one another but do not fly apart: clear· moist: of sound, etc., free from harshness: indisputable: unfixed: readily converted into cash.—*n* a liquid substance: a flowing consonant sound, as *l*, *r*.—*v.t.* **liq'uidate** to clear up or off: to wind up (a commercial firm, etc)· to dispose of: to wipe out, do away with (*slang*): to kill off (*slang*) —*v.i.* to go into liquidation —*ns* **liquidā'tion; liq'uidator.**—*v.t.* **liq'uidise, -ize** to render liquid: to purée (food).—*ns*. **liq'uidiser, -z-** a machine which purées foodstuffs; **liquid'ity** the state of being liquid: the condition of having liquid assets.—*adv*. **liq'uidly.**—*n* **liq'uidness.**—**liquid crystal** a liquid which is anisotropic, like a crystal, over a definite range of temperature above its freezing point.—**go into liquidation** (of a commercial firm, etc.) to be wound up, become bankrupt; **liquid crystal display** a display, esp. in electronic calculators, based on the changes in reflectivity of a liquid crystal cell when an electric field is applied [L *liquidus*, liquid, clear—*liquēre*, to be clear.]

liquor *lik'ər*, *n*. anything liquid, esp. the product of cooking or other operation: a liquid secretion: a beverage, esp. alcoholic· strong drink: a strong solution. any prepared solution —*v.t* to apply liquor or a solution to [O Fr *licur*, *licour* (Fr *liqueur*)—L *liquor*, *-ōris*]

liquorice, licorice *lik'ə-ris*, (in U S. also *-rish*), *n* a papilionaceous plant (*Glycyrrhiza glabra*, or other species) of Europe and Asia: its long sweet root used in medicine: an extract from the root. confectionery made from it. [A.Fr. *lycorys*—L.L. *liquirītia*, a corr of Gr *glykyrrīza*—*glykys*, sweet, *rhīza*, root.]

lira *lē'rə*, *n*. Italian monetary unit: the monetary unit of Turkey, equivalent to 100 piastres —*pl*. **lire** (*lē'rā*), **lir'as.** [It ,—L. *lībra*, a pound]

lisle *līl*, *n* a long-stapled, hard-twisted cotton yarn.—Also *adj*. [Old spelling of *Lille*, France.]

lisp *lisp*, *v.i.* to speak with the tongue against the upper teeth or gums, as in pronouncing *th* for *s* or *z*: to articulate as a child: to utter imperfectly —*v.t.* to utter with a lisp.—*n*. the act or habit of lisping: a defect of speech by which one lisps.—*n*. **lisp'er.**—*adj*. and *n*. **lisp'ing.**—*adv* **lisp'ingly.** [O E *wlisp* (adj.), stammering.]

lissome, lissom *lis'əm*, *adj*. lithesome, nimble, flexible. —*n* **liss'om(e)ness.** [**lithesome.**]

list[1] *list*, *n*. the selvage on woven textile fabrics: a border: a stripe: a strip. a strip cut from an edge: material composed of cut-off selvages: (in *pl.*) the boundary of a tilting-ground or the like, hence the ground itself, combat.—*adj*. made of strips of woollen selvage —*v t.* to border. to put list on: to remove the edge from.—*adj*. **list'ed** enclosed for tilting or the like: fought in lists —**enter the lists** to come forward for contest [O.E. *līste*.]

making or becoming lighter or brighter; **light'ning** the electric flash usually followed by thunder.—*adj*. characterised by speed and suddenness.—**light'ning-conduc'tor, -rod** a metallic rod for protecting buildings from lightning; **lightning strike** an industrial strike without warning. [**light**[1].]

lighten[2]. See **light**[2].

lightsome. See **light**[1,2].

ligne *līn*, (Fr *lēn-y'*), *n*. a measure of watch movement (Swiss ligne = 2·256 mm.). [Fr.]

lignum *lig'nəm*, *n*. wood.—*adj*. **lig'neous** woody: wooden.—*n*. **lignificā'tion.**—*v t.* and *v.i* **lig'nify** to turn into wood or woody:—*pr p.* **lig'nifying;** *pa.t.* and *pa.p.* **lig'nified.**—*ns*. **lig'nin** a complicated mixture of substances deposited in thickened cell-walls of plants; **lig'nite** (*-nīt*) brown coal, a stage in the conversion of vegetable matter into coal.—*adjs*. **lignitic** (*-nit'ik*) —**lig'num-vitae** (*vī'tē*; L. *lig'nŏŏm wē'tī*, *vē'*; wood of life) the wood of Guaiacum. [L. *lignum*, wood.]

ligule *lig'ūl*, *n*. (*bot.*) a scale at the top of the leaf-sheath in grasses: a similar scale on a petal: a strap-shaped corolla in composite plants.—*n* **lig'ula** a tongue-like part or organ: the anterior part of an insect's labium, or lower lip.—*adjs*. **lig'ular; lig'ulate** (*bot.*) like a strap: having ligules. [L. *ligula*, dim. of *lingua*, a tongue]

like[1] *līk*, *adj*. identical, equal, or nearly equal in any respect: similar, resembling: suiting, befitting (often in compound *adjs*. as *ladylike*): characteristic of (sometimes in compound *adjs*.): inclined, likely, probable (*dial.*).—*n*. one of the same kind: the same thing: a stroke bringing the total to the same as the other side's (*golf*): an exact resemblance.—*adv*. in the same manner: nearly (*coll.*): sometimes used meaninglessly (*dial.*).—*conj*. (now *illit.*) as: as if.—*prep*. in the same manner as: to the same extent as.—*ns*. **like'lihood** probability: promise of success or of future excellence; **like'liness** likelihood.—*adj*. **like'ly** like the thing required: promising: probable: credible.—*adv*. probably.—*v.t.* **lik'en** to represent as like or similar: to compare.—*n*. **like'ness** resemblance: semblance: guise: one or that which has a resemblance: a portrait.—*adv*. **like'wise** in the same or similar manner: moreover: too.—*adj* **like'-mind'ed** having similar opinions, values, etc.—**feel like** to be disposed or inclined towards; **had like** was likely, came near to; **look like** to show a likelihood of: to appear similar to; **something like a** a fine specimen, a model of what the thing should be; **such like** of that kind; **the like** (*coll*) similar things; **the likes of (them)** people like (them). [O E. *līc*, seen in *gelīc*.]

like[2] *līk*, *v.t.* to be pleased with: to approve: to enjoy. —*n* a liking, chiefly in phrase 'likes and dislikes'.—*adj*. **lik(e)'able** lovable· amiable —*ns*. **lik'er; lik'ing** affection, inclination: taste: satisfaction. [Orig. impersonal—O E. *līcian*, to please, to be suitable—*līc*, like, suitable, likely.]

lilac *lī'lək*, *n*. a European tree (*Syringa vulgaris*) of the olive family, with light-purple or white flowers, or other species of the genus: a light purple colour —*adj*. of that colour. [Fr. (*obs.*; now *lilas*) and Sp.,—Ar *līlāk*, *līlāk*—Pers. *līlak*, *nīlak*, bluish]

liliaceous, lilied etc. See **lily.**

Lilliputian *lil-i-pū'sh(y)ən*, *n*. an inhabitant of **Lill'iput** (*-put*), an imaginary country described by Swift in his *Gulliver's Travels*, inhabited by pygmies: a midget, pygmy.—*adj* (also without *cap*) diminutive

Lilo® *lī'lō*, *n* (also without *cap*) an inflatable mattress, often used in camping, etc

lilt *lilt*, *v.i* to sing or play, esp merrily, or vaguely and absent-mindedly, giving the swing or cadence rather than the structure of the melody: to hum —*v t.* to sing or play in such a manner.—*n*. a cheerful song or air: cadence, movement of a tune or the like. [M.E. *lulte*; origin unknown.]

lily *lil'i*, *n*. any plant or flower of the genus **Lil'ium,** typical genus of **Liliā'ceae:** extended to other plants: the fleur-de-lis: a person or thing of great purity or whiteness (*fig.*).—*adj*. white: pale.—*adjs*. **liliā'ceous; lil'ied** adorned with lilies: resembling lilies; **lil'y-liv'ered** cowardly —**lily pad** a leaf of a waterlily. —*adj* **lil'y-white.**—**lily of the valley** Convallaria, with two long oval leaves and spikes of white bell-shaped flowers. [O.E. *lilie*—L. *līlium*—Gr. *leirion*, lily.]

lima *lē'mə*, *n*. (in full **Lima bean**) a bean akin to the French bean. [*Lima* in Peru.]

limb[1] *lim*, *n*. an arm, leg, or wing: a prudish euphemism for leg: a projecting part: a main branch of a tree or of anything else: a member of a body of people, as 'a limb of the law': an imp, scapegrace, as 'a limb of Satan'.—*adjs*. **limbed** furnished with limbs; **limb'less.**—**out on a limb** in a hazardous position on one's own (*fig*). [O.E. *lim*.]

limb[2] *lim*, *n*. an edge or border, as of the sun, etc.: the edge of a sextant, etc.: the free or expanded part of a floral or other leaf (*bot*).—*adjs*. **lim'bate** bordered; **lim'bous** overlapping. [L. *limbus*, a border.]

limber[1] *lim'bər*, *n*. the shaft of a vehicle (*dial.*): the detachable fore-part of a gun-carriage (*mil.*).—*v.t.* to attach to the limber. [Poss. Fr. *limonière*.]

limber[2] *lim'bər*, *adj*. pliant, flexible.—*v.t.* to make limber.—**limber up** to tone up the muscles in preparation for physical effort of some sort.

limber[3] *lim'bər*, (*naut.*) *n*. (usu. *pl.*) channel or hole on either side of the keelson for drainage. [Fr. *lumière* —L. *lumināria*, windows.]

Limbo, limbo *lim'bō*, *n*. the borderland of Hell, assigned to the unbaptised (*Limbus patrum* for the righteous who died before Christ, *Limbus infantum* for children): any unsatisfactory place of consignment or oblivion: an uncertain or intermediate state: prison:—*pl* **Lim'bos, lim'bos.**—Also **Lim'bus** (*-bəs*). [From the Latin phrase *in limbo*, *in*, in, *limbus*, border]

limbo *lim'bō*, *n*. a West Indian dance in which the dancer bends backwards and passes under a bar which is progressively lowered:—*pl*. **lim'bos.** [Perh. **limber**[1].]

Limburger (cheese) *lim'bûrg-ər* (*chēz*), *n*. a white cheese from *Limburg* in Belgium, of strong taste and smell.

Limbus patrum, infantum. See **Limbo.**

lime[1] *līm*, *n*. any slimy or gluey material (*dial.*): bird-lime. the white caustic earth (calcium oxide, quicklime, caustic lime) got by calcining calcium carbonate (as limestone): calcium hydroxide (slaked lime) got by adding water to quicklime: loosely, limestone or calcium carbonate —*adj*. of lime.—*v t.* to cover with lime: to treat with lime: to manure with lime· to ensnare (also *fig.*) —*ns*. **līm'iness; līm'ing** the soaking of skins in limewater to remove hair· application of lime.—*adj*. **līm'y** smeared with, containing, like, of the nature of, lime.—**lime'kiln** a kiln or furnace in which calcium carbonate is calcined to lime, **lime'light** light produced by a blowpipe-flame directed against a block of quicklime: the glare of publicity (*fig.*); **lime'stone** a sedimentary rock of calcium carbonate; **lime'wash** a milky mixture of slaked lime and water, used for coating walls, etc.; **lime'water** a suspension of calcium hydroxide in water [O E *līm*.]

lime[2] *līm*, *n*. a tropical citrus tree, *C aurantifolia*· its small nearly globular fruit, with acid pulp: the colour of the fruit, a yellowish green —*n*. **lime'y** (*slang*) a

British sailor or ship (from the use of lime-juice on British ships to prevent scurvy): any British person.—**lime'-juice.** [Fr.,—Sp. *lima*; cf. **lemon**[1].]

lime[3] *līm*, *n.* the linden tree (*Tilia europaea*), or other of the genus.—**lime'-tree; lime'-wood.** [**lind.**]

limen *lī'men*, (*psych.*) *n.* the threshold of consciousness: the limit below which a stimulus is not perceived.—*adj.* **liminal** (*līm'*, *lim'in-əl*). [L. *līmen*, *-inis*, threshold.]

limerick *lim'ə-rik*, *n.* a form of humorous verse in a five-line jingle. [Said to be from a refrain formerly used, referring to *Limerick* in Ireland.]

limit *lim'it*, *n.* boundary: that which may not be passed: restriction: a value, position, or figure, that can be approached indefinitely (*math.*): that which is bounded, a region or division: (with *the*) the unspeakable extreme of endurability (*coll.*)—*v.t.* to confine within bounds: to restrict.—*adj.* **lim'itable.**—*adj.* **lim'itary** (*-ə-ri*) of a boundary: placed at the boundary: confined within limits.—*n.* **limitā'tion** a limiting: a disability, lack of talent: in law a specified period within which an action must be brought, etc.—*adjs.* **lim'itātive** tending to limit; **lim'ited** within limits: narrow: restricted.—*n.* a limited company.—*adv.* **lim'itedly.**—*ns.* **lim'itedness; lim'iter** the person or thing that limits or confines.—*n.* and *adj.* **lim'iting.**—*adj.* **lim'itless** having no limits: boundless: immense: infinite.—*adv.* **lim'itlessly.**—*n.* **lim'itlessness.**—**limited edition** an edition, esp. of a book, of which only a certain number of copies is printed or made; **limited (liability) company** one whose owners enjoy limited liability.—**off limits** out of bounds; **statute of limitations** an act specifying the period within which certain action must be taken; **within limits** to a limited extent. [L. *līmes*, *-itis*, boundary.]

limitrophe *lim'i-trōf*, *adj.* near the frontier: border. [L. *limitrophus*—*līmes*, *-itis*, border, Gr. *trophos*, feeder.]

limnetic *lim-net'ik*, *adj* living in fresh water.—*adj.* **limnolog'ical.**—*ns.* **limnol'ogist; limnol'ogy** the scientific study (embracing physical, geographical, biological, etc., characteristics) of lakes and other freshwater bodies.—*adj.* **limnoph'ilous** living in ponds or marches. [Gr. *limnē*, a pool or marsh.]

limonite *lī'mən-īt*, *n* brown iron ore, hydrated ferric oxide, a deposit in bogs and lakes (*bog-iron*) or a decomposition product in rocks.—*adj.* **limonitic** (*-it'ik*). [Gr. *leimōn*, a meadow.]

Limousin *lē-mōō-zē*, *n.* a breed of cattle.—*n.* **limousine** (*lim'ōō-zēn*) large closed motor-car (orig with the driver's seat outside but covered by the roof) which has a partition separating driver and passengers: loosely, any large motor-car (sometimes used ironically). [*Limousin*, a district in France.]

limp[1] *limp*, *adj.* wanting stiffness: flaccid: drooping: of a cloth binding for books, not stiffened by boards

limp[2] *limp*, *v.i.* to halt: to drag a leg: (of damaged ship, aircraft) to proceed with difficulty.—*n.* a limping gait: a halt.—*n* and *adj.* **limp'ing.**—*adv.* **limp'ingly.** [There is an O.E. adj. *lemp-healt*, halting.]

limpet *lim'pit*, *n.* a gasteropod (Patella, etc.) with conical shell, that clings to rocks: one not easily ousted.—**limpet mine** an explosive device attached to a ship's hull by a magnet, etc. [O E. *lempedu*, lamprey.]

limpid *lim'pid*, *adj.* clear· transparent.—*n.* **limpid'ity.**—*adv.* **lim'pidly.** [L. *limpidus*]

limy. See **lime**[1].

lin. See **linn.**

linchpin *linch'*, *linsh'pin*, *n.* a pin used to keep a wheel on its axle: a person or thing essential to a plan, organisation, etc. (*fig.*). [O.E. *lynis*, axle, and **pin.**]

Lincoln-green *lingk'ən-grēn*, *n.* a bright green cloth once made at *Lincoln*: its colour.

linctus *lingk'təs*, *n.* a syrup-like medicine:—*pl.* **linc'tuses.**—*n.* **linc'ture.** [L. *linctus*, *-ūs*, a licking.]

lind *lind*, **linden** *lin'dən*. Same as **lime**[3]. [O.E. *lind*.]

line[1] *līn*, *v.t.* to cover on the inside: to fill, stuff: to reinforce, strengthen (esp. books): to be placed along the side of: to serve as a lining.—*adj.* **lined** having a lining.—*ns.* **lin'er** that which serves as a lining: one who lines; **lin'ing** the action of one who lines: material applied to a surface, esp. material on the inner surface of a garment, etc.: contents.—**line one's pocket(s)** to make a profit, esp. dishonestly. [O.E. *līn*, flax, cognate with or derived from L. *līnum*; cf. next word.]

line[2] *līn*, *n.* a thread, string, cord, rope, esp. one for fishing, sounding, hanging clothes, or guidance: that which has length without breadth or thickness (*math.*): a long narrow mark: a streak, stroke, or narrow stripe: draughtsmanship: a row: a row of printed or written characters, ships, soldiers, etc.: a verse, such as is usu. written in one row: a series or succession, as of progeny: a service of ships, buses, etc. or a company running them: a course, route, system: a railway or tramway track or route: a stretch or route of telegraph, telephone, or power wires or cables: an order given to an agent for goods: such goods received: trade in, or the stock on hand of, any particular goods: a lineament: a rank: a short letter or note: a wrinkle: a trench: limit: method: policy: a rule or canon: (with *the*; often cap.) the equator: lineage: direction: occupation: course: province or sphere of life, interest, or taste: regular army: line of battle (see below): relevant information (*coll.*): glib talk (*slang*): in TV, the path traversed by the electron beam or scanning spot in moving once from side to side (horizontal scanning) or from top to bottom (vertical scanning) of the picture: (in *pl.*) **lines** marriage or church membership certificate: words of an actor's part: a school imposition.—*v.t.* to mark out with lines: to cover with lines: to put in line: to form a line along: to delineate, sketch (sometimes verbally).—*v.i.* to take a place in line.—*ns.* **linage, lineage** (*līn'ij*) measurement or payment by the line; **lineage** (*lin'i-ij*), ancestry.—*adj.* **lineal** (*lin'i-əl*) of or belonging to a line or lines or one dimension: composed of lines: in the direction of a line: in, of, or transmitted by, direct line of descent, or legitimate descent.—*n.* **lineality** (*-al'i-ti*).—*adv.* **lin'eally.**—*n.* **lineament** (*lin'i-ə-mənt*) feature: distinguishing mark in the form, esp. of the face.—*adj.* **linear** (*lin'i-ər*) of or belonging to a line: of one dimension: consisting of, or having the form of, lines: long and very narrow, with parallel sides: capable of being represented on a graph by a straight line: of a system, in which doubling the cause doubles the effect.—*n.* **linearity** (*lin-i-ar'i-ti*).—*adv.* **lin'early.**—*adjs.* **lin'eate, -d** marked with lines.—*n.* **lineā'tion** marking with lines: arrangement of or in lines.—*adj.* **lined** (*līnd*) marked with lines: having a line.—*adj.* **lineolate** (*lin'i-ə-lāt*) marked with fine lines.—*ns.* **lin'er** one who makes, marks, draws, paints, or writes lines: a paint-brush for making lines: a line-fisher: a line-fishing boat: a vessel or aircraft of a line: colouring matter used to outline the eyes; **lin'ing** alignment: the making of a line: use of a line. marking with lines.—**linear accelerator** apparatus in

...erated while travelling down ...by means of electromagnetic ... a multinomial equation in the ...**otor** an electric motor which ...ust, without the use of gears; ... that which enables a computer to ...esult when fed with a number of un...es, used in determining the most efficient a...ent of e g. an industrial process; **line block** a printing block consisting of black and white only, without gradations of tone; **line'-engrav'er; line'-engrav'ing** the process of engraving in lines, steel or copperplate engraving: an engraving so done, **line'-fish** one taken with the line rather than the net; **line'-fish'er, -fish'erman; line'-fish'ing; line'man** one who attends to lines of railway, telegraph, telephone, or electric-light wires, etc.; **line'-out** (*Rugby football*) method of restarting play when the ball has gone into touch, the forwards of each team lining up behind each other facing the touch line and trying to catch the ball when it is thrown in; **linesman** (*līnz'*) lineman: in Association football, one who marks the spot at which the ball goes into touch: in lawn-tennis, one who decides on which side of a line the ball falls, **line'-up'** an arrangement in line: putting or coming into line: a queue.—**all along the line** at every point (*lit.* or *fig.*); **bring into line** to cause to conform, **end of the line** (*fig*) a point beyond which it is useless or impossible to proceed; **get a line on** (*slang*) to get information about; **in line** in a straight line: in agreement or harmony (*with*): in the running (with *for*): in a line of succession (with *to*); **lay it on the line** to speak out firmly and frankly; **lay on the line** to risk, stake (a reputation, etc.); **line up** to bring into alignment: to make a stand (in support of, or against): to gather together in readiness: to secure, arrange (for a person); **one's line of country** one's field of study or interest; **on the lines of** in a (specified) manner or direction; **read between the lines** to infer what is not explicitly stated. [Partly from O E *line*, cord (from or cognate with L. *līnum*, flax), partly through Fr *ligne*, and partly directly from L *līnea*, cf preceding word]

lineage, lineal, linear, etc See **line**[2].

lined. See **line**[1,2].

linen *lin'ən*, *n* cloth made of lint or flax· underclothing, orig. of linen: articles of linen, or of other materials as cotton, rayon, etc.—table-linen, bed-linen, body-linen —*adj.* of or like linen.—**wash one's dirty linen at home, in public** to keep secret, to expose, sordid family affairs. [O.E. *linen* (adj)—*līn*, flax; see **line**[1].]

lineolate. See **line**[2].

-ling *-ling*, noun suffix denoting a diminutive as duck*ling*, hence expressing affection as dar*ling* (O E *dēorling*), sometimes implying deprecation, as under*ling*.

ling[1] *ling*, *n.* a fish (*Molva*) of the cod family. [Prob conn. with **long.**]

ling[2] *ling*, *n.* heather.—*adj.* **ling'y.** [O N *lyng*.]

lingam *ling'gam*, *n* the Hindu phallus, a symbol of Siva —Also **ling'a.** [Sans.]

linger *ling'gər*, *v.i.* to remain long: to delay in reluctance to tarry: to loiter: to be protracted: to remain alive, although gradually dying.—*v.t.* to pass in tedium or dawdling.—*n.* **ling'erer.**—*n* and *adj* **ling'ering.**—*adv.* **ling'eringly.** [Freq. from O E *lengan*, to protract—*lang*, long.]

lingerie *lēzh-ə-rē*, *n.* women's underclothing. [Fr.,—*linge*, linen—L. *līnum*, flax, thread, linen.]

lingo *ling'gō*, *n.* language, esp one despised or not understood:—*pl.* **ling'oes.** [Prov *lengo*, *lingo*, or some other form of L. *lingua*, language]

lingua *ling'gwə*, *n.* the tongue: a tongue-like struc... —*adj.* **ling'ual.**—*adv.* **ling'ually.**—*adj.* **ling'uiform** tongue-shaped.—*ns.* **ling'uist** one who has a good knowledge of languages. one who studies linguistics.—*adjs.* **linguist'ic, -al** pertaining to languages or knowledge or study of languages.—*adv.* **linguist'ically.**—*n.* **linguistic'ian** a student of linguistics.—*n.sing.* **linguist'ics** the scientific study of language in its widest sense, in every aspect and in all its varieties.—*ns.* **ling'uistry; lingula** (*ling'gū-lə*) a little tongue-like part.—*adjs* **ling'ular** pertaining to a lingula; **ling'ulate** tongue-shaped.—**lingua franca** (*ling'gwə frangk'ə*; It., Frankish language) a mixed Italian trade jargon used in the Levant: a language chosen as a medium of communication among speakers of different languages: any hybrid language used for the same purpose [L *lingua* (for *dingua*), the tongue]

liniment *lin'i-mənt*, *n.* a thin ointment: an embrocation. [L. *linimentum*—*linīre*, *linĕre*, to smear.]

lining. See **line**[1,2].

link[1] *lingk*, *n.* a ring of a chain, chain-mail, etc.: anything connecting (also *fig.*): a unit in a communications system: the 1/100th part of the surveyor's chain, 7·92 inches (approx. 20 cm): a segment or unit in a connected series: a cufflink —*v t.* to connect.—*v i* to be or become connected: to go arm-in-arm.—*n* **link'age** an act or mode of linking: the fact of being linked: a system of links: a chemical bond.—**link man** one who provides a connection as by passing on information, or by holding together separate items of a broadcast programme, **link'-mo'tion** reversing gear of a steam-engine: a system of pieces moving as a linkage, **link'-up** a connection, union; **link'work.**—**missing link** any point or fact needed to complete a series or a chain of argument: an intermediate form in the evolution of man from simian ancestors. [Prob. from an O N. form cog. with O E *hlencan* (pl.), armour.]

link[2] *lingk*, *n* a torch of pitch and tow.—**link'boy, link'man** an attendant carrying a link in dark streets.

link[3] *lingk*, *n* (in *pl* often treated as *sing*) a stretch of flat or gently undulating ground along a seashore, hence a golf-course [O.E *hlinc*, a ridge of land, a bank]

linn, lin *lin*, *n* a waterfall a cascade pool· a dee... ravine. [O.E. *hlynn*, a torrent, combined wi... Gael *linne*, Ir. *linn*, W *llyn*, pool]

Linnaean, Linnean *lin-ē'ən*, *adj.* pertaining to *Li... naeus* or *Linné*, the Swedish botanist (1707–1778), to his artificial system of classification

linnet *lin'it*, *n.* *Linota cannabina*, a common fin... feeding on flax-seed —**green linnet** the greenfi... [O Fr. *linette*, *linot*—*lin*, flax—L *līnum*]

linoleic *lin-ō-lē'ik*, **linolenic** *lin-ō-lēn'ik* (or *-len'*), ...*as'id*, highly unsaturated fatty acids obtained ... the glycerides of certain fats and oils, as linsee... and constituting Vitamin F.

linoleum *lin-ō'li-əm*, *-lyəm*, *n.* floor-covering m... impregnating a fabric with a mixture of oxidis... seed-oil, resins, and fillers (esp. cork).—Also ... Also **lino** (*lī'nō*) (*coll.*):—*pl* **lī'nos.**—**linocut** ...*kut*) a design cut in relief in linoleum: a pri... such a block. [L *līnum*, flax, *oleum*, oil.]

Linotype® *līn'ō-tīp*, *n* a machine for pr... stereotyped lines a slug or line of printing-... in one piece

linseed *lin'sēd*, *n.* flax seed—also **lint'seed.**—... **cake** the cake remaining when the oil is pres... lint or flax seed, used as a food for sheep ... **lin'seed-oil** oil from flax seed. [O E *līn*, ... seed.]

linsey *lin'zi*, *n* cloth made of linen and w... *adj.*—**lin'sey-woolsey** (*-wŏŏl'zi*) a thin co...

list[2] *list, n.* a catalogue, roll, or enumeration.—*v.t.* to place in a list or catalogue. to enrol (as soldiers).—*v.i.* to enlist (also *'list*, as if for **enlist**) —*n* **list'ing** a list: position in a list: a print-out of all the data stored in a file (*comput*): an official quotation for stock so that it can be traded on the Stock Exchange.—**listed building** one officially listed as being of special architectural or historic interest, which cannot be demolished or altered without (local) government consent; **list price** the price of an article as shown in a catalogue or advertisement —**active list** the roll of those liable for active service; **List D schools** since 1969 the name given in Scotland to community homes (formerly approved schools) [O.F *liste*, of Gmc origin, ultimately same word as above, from the sense of a strip of paper.]

list[3] *list, n.* a fillet (*archit*): a division of parted hair [It. *lisia, lustello*; ult the same as **list**[1,2].]

list[4] *list, v.t.* to desire: to like or please: to choose: to cause to heel over (*naut*).—*v i* to heel over:—*pa.t* **list'ed, list**; *pa.p.* **list'ed**; *3rd pers sing pr t*. **list, lists, listeth**.—*n.* desire: inclination: choice: heeling over —*adj.* **list'less** having no desire or wish: uninterested. languid.—*adv* **list'lessly**.—*n* **list'lessness**. [O.E *lystan*, impers., to please—*lust*, pleasure]

list[5] *list, (arch. or poet.) v.t.* to listen. [O.E. *hlystan*]

listen *lis'n, v.i.* to give ear or hearken to follow advice. —*n.* act of listening —*adj* **list'enable** pleasant to listen to —*n* **listener** (*lis'nər*) one who listens or hearkens.—**list'ening-in.**—**listen in** to listen to a wireless broadcast: to overhear intentionally a message intended for another [O E *hlysnan*, recorded in the Northumbrian form *lysna*.]

lit. *Pa.t* and *pa.p.* of **light**[1-3].

litany *lit'əni, n.* a prayer of supplication, esp in processions: an appointed form of responsive prayer in public worship in which the same thing is repeated several times: a long list or catalogue, evocative or merely boring. [L L. *litania*—Gr *litaneia*—*litesthai*, to pray.]

litchi. See **lychee**.

lite pendente *li'te pen-den'te, le'te pen-den'te,* (L.) pending the suit.

liter. American spelling of **litre**.

literacy. See **literate**.

literal *lit'ə-rəl, adj.* pertaining to letters of the alphabet: of the nature of a letter: according to the letter: not figurative or metaphorical: following word for word inclined to use or understand words in a matter-of-fact sense.—*n* a misprint of a letter —*v.t.* **lit'eralise, -ize**. —*ns.* **lit'eraliser, -z-;** **lit'eralism** strict adherence to the letter: interpretation that is merely verbal: exact and unimaginative rendering (*art*), **li'teralist;** **literality** (*-al'i-ti*).—*adv.* **lit'erally** (often used by no means literally) —*n* **lit'eralness**. [L. *litterālis—littera* (*litera*), a letter.]

literary *lit'ər-ə-ri, adj* pertaining to, of the nature of, versed in, or practising literature or the writing of books: bookish: of language, formal.—*adv* **lit'erarily.**—*ns.* **lit'erariness; lit'eraryism** a bookish expression.—**literary agent** one who deals with the business affairs of an author; **literary criticism** the art of making judgments on literary works; **literary executor** one appointed to deal with unpublished material after an author's death. [L. *litterārius— litera* (*littera*), a letter.]

literate *lit'ər-it, -āt, adj* learned: able to read and write —*n.* one who is literate. an educated person without a university degree, esp. a candidate for orders —*n* **lit'eracy** condition of being literate.—*n pl* **literati** (*-a'te*) men of letters, the learned.—*sing.* **litera'tus** (L), **literato** (*-a'tō.* It) [L *litera, literātus* (L), *literātum, literōsus—litera* (*littera*), letter.]

literature *lit'(ə-)rə-chər, n.* the art of composition in prose and verse: the whole body of literary composition universally, or in any language, or on a given subject, etc.: literary matter: printed matter: humane learning: literary culture or knowledge [L. *literāt-ūra—litera* (*littera*), a letter.]

lith-, litho- *lith-, -ō-, -a-, o-,* in composition, stone: calculus —*ns* **lithi'asis** (Gr *lithiāsis*) formation of calculi in the body —*adj.* **lith'ic** pertaining to or got from stone or calculi —*ns.* **lith'ite** a calcareous body secreted in an animal cell, esp. with a sensory function; **lith'ocyst** (*-ō-sist;* Gr. *kystis,* a bladder) a sac containing a lithite.—*adj.* **lithogenous** (*-oj'i-nəs*) rock-building —*ns.* **lith'oglyph** (*-ə glif;* Gr *glyphein,* to carve) an engraving on stone, esp. a precious stone, **lith'ograph** (*-graf;* Gr. *graphein,* to write) a print from stone (**lithographic stone** or **slate** a fine-grained slaty limestone), or a substitute (as zinc or aluminium), with greasy ink —*v.t.* and *v.i* to print so.—*n.* **lithographer** (*-og'rə-fər*).—*adjs.* **lithographic** (*-ə-graf'ik*), **-al.**—*adv* **lithograph'ically.**—*n.* **lithog'raphy.**—*adjs* **litholog'ic, -al.**—*ns* **lithol'ogist; lithol'ogy** the science of rocks as mineral masses: the department of medicine concerned with calculi.—*adj.* **lithophilous** (*-of'i-ləs;* Gr. *philos,* friend) growing, living, or sheltering among stones.—*n.* **lith'ophyte** (*-fit;* Gr. *phyton,* plant) a plant that grows on rocks or stones: a stony organism, as coral.—*adj.* **lithophytic** (*-fit'ik*).— *ns.* **lithoprint** (*li'thō-*) a print made by lithography; **lith'osphere** (*-ō sfēr;* Gr. *sphaira,* sphere) the rocky crust of the earth.—*adj.* **lithospheric** (*-sfer'ik*).—*n* **lith'otome** (*-ō-tōm;* Gr. *tomos,* cutting) an instrument for lithotomy; **lithot'omy** cutting for stone in the bladder [Gr. *lithos,* stone.]

litharge *lith'arj, n.* lead monoxide, such as is got in refining silver. [Fr.—Gr. *lithargyros—lithos,* a stone, *orgyros,* silver.]

lithe *lidh, adj.* supple, limber.— *adv.* **lithe'ly.**—*n* **lithe'ness.** [O.E *lithe,* soft, mild.]

lithia *lith'i-ə, n* oxide of lithium (from its mineral origin, unlike soda and potash).— Also *adj.*—*adj.* **lith'ic** pertaining to or got from lithium —*n.* **lithium** (*-i-əm*) the lightest metallic element (symbol Li; at. numb 3). [Gr. *lithos,* stone.]

litho *lith'ō, n. (pl. li'thos), adj.* short for **lithograph, -graphic. -graphy** (see under **lith-**)

lithotrity *lith-ot'ri-ti,* **lithotripsy** *lith'ō-trip-si. ns.* the operation of crushing a stone in the bladder, so that its fragments may be removed through the urethra. [Gr *lithōn thryptika,* breakers of stones; reconstructed as from Gr *tripsis,* rubbing, or L. *tritus,* rubbing.]

Lithuanian *li-thū-ā'ni-ən, adj* pertaining to the U.S.S.R. republic of *Lithuania* on the Baltic Sea, or its people. or their language.—*n.* the Lithuanian language. a native or inhabitant of Lithuania.

litigate *lit'i-gāt, v.t.* and *v.i* to dispute, esp. by a lawsuit.—*adjs.* **lit'igable; lit'igant** contending at law: engaged in a lawsuit.—*n.* a person engaged in a lawsuit.—*n.* **litiga'tion.**—*adj.* **litigious** (*-ij'əs*) pertaining to litigation: inclined to engage in lawsuits: disputable: open to contention.—*adv.* **litig'iously.**— *n.* **litig'iousness.** [L. *litigāre, -ātum—lis, litis,* strife, *agère,* to do.]

litmus *lit'məs, n.* a substance obtained from certain lichens, turned red by acids, blue by alkalis.—**litmus paper** a test-paper dipped in litmus solution: **litmus test** (*fig*) an event seen as an indicator of underlying attitudes, factors, etc [O.N. *litmosi* herbs used in dyeing—*litr,* colour. *mosi,* moss.]

litotes *li'tō- or lit'ō-tēz, (rhet.) n.* meiosis or understatement: esp. affirmation by negation of the contrary. [Gr. *litotēs,* simplicity—*litos,* plain.]

litre *lē'tər, n* the metric unit of capacity, orig. intended to be 1 cubic decimetre: (1901) volume of a kilogram of water at 4°C, under standard atmospheric pressure (1·00028 cu. dm.): (1964) 1 cubic decimetre.—-**litre** in composition, denoting the capacity of the cylinders of a motor-vehicle engine (as *three-litre*). [Fr ,—L.L. *lītra*—Gr. *lītrā*, a pound.]

litter *lit'ər*, *n*. a heap of straw, bracken, etc , esp. for animals to lie upon: materials for a bed: any scattered or confused collection of objects, esp. of little value: a state of confusion and untidiness with things strewn about: wastage, rubbish: a couch carried by men or beasts: a stretcher: a brood of animals: an occasion of birth of animals —*v t*. to cover or supply with litter: to scatter carelessly about: to give birth to (said of animals) —*v.i.* to produce a litter or brood: to strew rubbish, etc. untidily.—*adj*. **litt'ered.**—*adj*. **litt'ery** in condition of litter: addicted to litter.—**litt'er-basket, -bin** a receptacle for rubbish, **litt'er-bug, -lout** one who wilfully drops litter. [O.Fr *litiere*—L.L *lectāria*—L. *lectus*, a bed.]

little *lit'l*, *adj*. small in size, extent, quantity, or significance: petty: small-minded: young: resembling or reminiscent of something else, but on a small(er) scale.—*n*. (or *adj*. with a noun understood) that which is small in quantity or extent. a small quantity a small thing.—*adv*. in a small quantity or degree: not much.—**less, least** serve as compar. and superl to the adv. and to some extent, along with **lesser**, to the adj —*n*. **litt'leness.**—**Little Bear** Ursa Minor; **litt'le-ease** a confined space in which a prisoner can neither sit, stand nor lie; **little man** a man of no importance, an underdog; **little people** the fairies, or a traditional race of pygmies, **little woman** (*facet*.) one's wife.—**by little and little, little by little** by degrees, **make little of** to treat as of little consequence, belittle: to comprehend only slightly; **twist, wind, wrap someone round one's little finger** to control someone completely, or influence someone to a great extent [O E *lȳtel*]

littoral *lit'ər-əl*, *adj* belonging to the seashore, to lands near the coast, the beach. the space between high and low tidemarks, or water a little below low-water mark: inhabiting the shore or shallow water in a lake or sea.—*n*. the strip of land along it. [L. *littorālis* for *lītorālis*—*lītus*, *lītoris*, shore]

liturgy *lit'ər-ji*, *n*. the form of service or regular ritual of a church—strictly, that used in the celebration of the eucharist.—*adjs*. **liturgic** (*-ûrj'ik*), **-al.**—*adv*. **liturgically.**—*n*. *sing* **litur'gics** the doctrine of liturgies. [Gr. *leitourgiā*.]

live[1] *liv*, *v.i* to have, or continue in, life, temporal, spiritual, or figurative: to last. to enjoy life: to direct one's course of life: to be supported, subsist, get a living: to escape destruction or oblivion: to dwell.—*v.t.* to spend or pass. to act in conformity to: to express by one's life, make one's life the same thing as:—*pr.p.* **liv'ing;** *pa.t.* and *pa.p.* **lived** (*livd*).—*adjs* **liv'able, live'able** worth living, capable of being lived: habitable.—*n*. **liv'er.**—*adjs*. **liv'able(-with)** such as one could endure to live with, **live'-in'** of an employee, living at the place of work: of a sexual partner, sharing the same dwelling.—**live and let live** to give and expect toleration or forbearance, **live down** to live so as to allow to be forgotten; **live for** to attach great importance to: to long for; **live in, out** to dwell in, away from, one's place of employment; **live it up** to go on the spree: to live rather too intensely; **live on** to live by feeding upon, or with expenditure limited to: **live on air** to have no apparent means of sustenance; **live out** to survive; **live to** to live long enough to, come at last to, **live together** to cohabit. **live up to** to rule one's life in a manner worthy of to spend up to the scale of; **live well** to live luxuriously,

live with to cohabit with: to accept and adapt to as an inescapable part of one's life. [O.E. *lifian*.]

live[2] *liv*, *adj*. having life: alive, not dead: active: stirring: unquarried or unwrought: charged with energy (as by electricity, chemicals, etc.) and still capable of discharge: burning: vivid: of the theatre, etc., concerned with living performance as distinct from filming, broadcasting, or televising: of a broadcast, made directly from the actual event, not from a recording. fully operational (*comput.*).—**-lived** (*-livd*, sometimes *-livd*) in composition, having life (as *long-lived*).—*v.t.* **liv'en** to enliven.—*v i* to become lively.—**live'-birth'** birth in a living condition (opposed to *still-birth*)—*adj*. **live'-born.**—**live'-box** a glass box for examining living objects under the microscope: a box for live fish.—**live'-rail, live'-wire** one carrying electric current; **live'-wire** (*fig*) a person of intense energy or alertness; **live'stock** domestic animals, esp. horses, cattle, sheep, and pigs; **live'ware** all the people working with a computer system, **live'-weight** weight of living animals **[alive.]**

livelihood *liv'li-hood*, *n*. means of living: support. [O.E *liflād*—*lif*. life, *lād*, course.]

livelong[1] *liv'long*, also *liv'long*, *adj* very long: protracted: enduring. [*lief*, used intensively, **long**.]

livelong[2] *liv'long*, *n*. the orpine, a plant difficult to kill. [**live**[1], **long**[3].]

lively *liv'li*, *adj*. brisk: active. sprightly. spirited: vivid —*adv* vivaciously: vigorously—*adv*. **live'lily.**—*n* **live'liness.**—**look lively!** make haste. [O E. *liflic*—*lif*, life.]

liven. See **live**[2].

liver[1] *liv'ər*, *n* a large gland that secretes bile, formerly regarded as seat of courage, love, etc · its substance as food. a disordered state of the liver (*coll*) —*adj* **liver-colour**—*adjs* **liv'ered** having a liver, as *lily-livered*, cowardly; **liv'erish, liv'ery** suffering from disordered liver: irritable.—*n* and *adj*. **liv'er-col'our** dark reddish brown —*adj* **liv'er-coloured.**—**liv'er-fluke** a trematode worm that infects the bile-ducts of sheep and other animals; **liv'er-rot** a disease caused by liver-flukes; **liver salts** mineral salts taken to cure indigestion, **liver sausage** a rich sausage made of liver, **liver spot** a liver-coloured mark on the skin appearing in old age; **liv'erwort** (*-wûrt*) any plant of the Hepaticae, forming with the mosses the Bryophyta, some kinds having once been used medicinally in diseases of the liver; **liv'erwurst** (*-wûrst*) liver sausage. [O.E *lifer*]

liver[2]. See **live**[1].

Liverpudlian *liv-ər-pud'li-ən*, *adj* belonging to Liverpool.—*n*. a native of Liverpool. [*Liverpool*, influenced by *puddle*.]

livery[1] *liv'ər-i*, *n* the feeding, care, and stabling of a horse at a certain rate. the distinctive dress or badge of a great man's household (*hist*.): the distinctive garb of a person's servants, esp. men-servants, or of a body, e g. a trade-guild: any characteristic garb: the distinctive decoration used for all its aircraft, etc by an airline, etc.: a body of liverymen or of livery-servants —*adj*. **liv'eried** clothed in livery.—**liv'ery-com'pany** a guild of the city of London; **liv'eryman** a man who wears a livery: a freeman of the city of London entitled to wear the livery and enjoy other privileges of his company: one who keeps or works at a livery-stable; **liv'ery-servant** a servant who wears a livery; **liv'ery-stable** a stable where horses are kept at livery and for hire.—**at livery** of a horse, kept at the owner's expense at a livery stable. [A Fr *liveré*, lit handed over—*livrer*—L *liberāre*, to free.]

livery[2]. See **liver**[1].

lives *livz*, *n* plural of **life**.

livid *liv'id*, *adj* black and blue of a lead colour·

discoloured: pale, ashen: extremely angry (*coll.*).— *ns.* **livid'ity, liv'idness, livor** (*lī'vər*, -*vör*). [L. *lividus*—*livēre*, to be of a lead colour.]

living *liv'ing, adj.* live: alive: having vitality: lively: in present life, existence, activity, or use.—*n.* means of subsistence: manner of life: a property: a benefice. —**living death** a life of unrelieved misery; **living memory** the memory of anybody or somebody still alive; **liv'ing-room** a sitting-room for all-round use: **living wage** a wage on which it is possible for a workman and his family to live fairly. [Pr.p. of **live**[1].]

livor. See **livid.**

lixiviation *liks-iv-i-ā'shən, n.* leaching.—*v.t.* **lixiv'iate.** —*n.* **lixiv'ium** lye. [L. *lixivium*, lye.]

lizard *liz'ərd, n.* any member of the Lacertilia, an order of scaly reptiles, usually differing from snakes in having four legs, movable eyelids, and non-expansible mouths.—*adj.* **liz'ard-hipped** (of dinosaurs) having a pelvis slightly similar to a lizard's, the pubis extending forwards and downwards from the limb socket, saurischian. [O.Fr. *lesard* (Fr. *lézard*)—L. *lacerta*.]

'll *l.* Shortened form of **will, shall.**

llama *lä'ma, n.* a S. American transport animal of the camel family, a domesticated guanaco: its wool: cloth made thereof. [Sp., from Quechua.]

llano *lyä'nō,* or *lä'nō, n.* one of the vast steppes or plains in the northern part of South America:—*pl.* **lla'nos.** [Sp.,—L. *plānus*, plain.]

lo *lō, interj.* look: behold:—*pl.* **los.** [O.E. *lā.*]

loach *lōch, n.* a small river-fish of a family (*Cobitidae*) akin to the carps. [Fr. *loche*.]

load *lōd, n.* that which is carried: that which may or can be carried at one time or journey: a burden: a freight or cargo: a definite quantity, varying according to the goods: weight carried: power output of an engine, etc.: work imposed or expected: power carried by an electric circuit: a large quantity borne: that which burdens or grieves: a weight or encumbrance: abundance (*coll.*, esp. in *pl.*).—*v.t.* to burden: to charge: to put a load on or in: to put on or in anything as a load: to put film in (a camera): to put on overmuch: to weigh down: to overburden: to supply, present, or assail overwhelmingly or lavishly: to weight: to give weight or body to, by adding something: to mix with white: to lay on in masses (*painting*): to add charges to (*insurance*): (of wine) to doctor, drug, adulterate, or fortify.—*v.i.* to put or take on a load: to charge a gun: to become loaded or burdened.—*adj.* **load'ed** rich, wealthy: under the influence of drink or drugs (*slang*): weighted in discussion in a certain direction: charged with contentious material.—*ns.* **load'er; load'ing** the act of lading: that with which anything is loaded.—*adj.* **load'-bearing** of a wall, etc., supporting a structure, carrying weight.—**loaded question** a question designed to make an unwilling answerer commit himself to some opinion, action, or course; **loading gauge** a suspended bar that marks how high a railway truck may be loaded; **load'-line** a line on a ship's side to mark the depth to which her cargo may be allowed to sink her; **load shedding** temporarily reducing the amount of electricity sent out by a power station.—**a load off one's mind** relief from anxiety; **get a load of** (*slang*) to listen to, look at, pay attention to; **load dice** to make one side heavier than the other so as to influence their fall for purposes of cheating; **load the dice against someone** (*fig.*) to deprive someone of a fair chance of success. [O.E. *lād*, course, journey, conveyance.]

loadstar, loadstone. Same as **lodestar, lodestone.**

loaf[1] *lōf, n.* a portion of bread baked in one mass: a moulded portion of food, esp. bread or meat. a

conical mass of sugar: a cabbage-head: the head, or brains (*slang*):—*pl.* **loaves** (*lōvz*); **loaf'-sug'ar** refined sugar moulded in the form of a great cigar.— **half loaf** a loaf of half the standard weight. [O.E. *hlāf*, bread.]

loaf[2] *lōf, v.i.* to loiter or stand idly about, pass time idly.—*n.* **loaf'er** one who loafs: a casual shoe, often resembling a moccasin.—*n.* and *adj.* **loaf'ing.** [Poss.—Ger. *Landläufer*, tramp, vagabond.]

loam *lōm, n.* a soil consisting of a natural mixture of clay and sand, with animal and vegetable matter: a composition basically of moist clay and sand used in making bricks.—*v.t.* to cover with loam.—*n.* **loam'-iness.**—*adj.* **loam'y.** [O.E. *lām.*]

loan *lōn, n.* anything lent, esp. money at interest: the act of lending: the condition of being lent: an arrangement for lending: permission to use.—*v.t.* to lend.—*adj.* **loan'able.**—**loan'-office** a public office at which loans are negotiated, received, or recorded: a pawnshop; **loan'-shark** a usurer; **loan'-society** a society organised to subscribe money to be lent; **loan translation** a compound, phrase, etc. that is a literal translation of a foreign expression—also called a calque; **loan'-word** one borrowed from another language. [O.N. *lán*.]

loath. Same as **loth.**

loathe *lōdh, v.t.* to dislike intensely: to feel disgust at. —*adj.* **loathed.**—*ns.* **loath'edness; loath'er.**—*adj.* **loath'ful** loathsome: reluctant.—*ns.* **loath'fulness; loath'ing** extreme hate or disgust: abhorrence.—*adj.* hating.—*adv.* **loath'ingly.**—*n.* **loath'liness.**—*adj.* **loathsome** (*lōth'. lōdh'səm*) exciting loathing or abhorrence: detestable.—*adv.* **loath'somely.**—*n.* **loath'someness.** [O.E. *lāthian*; cf. **loth.**]

loave, loaves. See **loaf**[1].

lob *lob, n.* in cricket, a slow, high underhand ball: in lawn-tennis, a ball high overhead, dropping near the back of the court.—*v.t.* to bowl or strike as a lob.— *pa.t.* and *pa.p.* **lobbed..** [Cf. Fris. and Du. *lob.*]

lobar, lobate, etc. See **lobe.**

lobby *lob'i, n.* a small hall or waiting-room: a passage serving as a common entrance to several apartments: the ante-chamber of a legislative hall: a corridor into which members pass as they vote (also **divis'lon-** lobb'y): a group of persons who campaign to persuade legislators to make regulations favouring their particular interests.—*v.t.* to seek to influence in the lobby.—*v.i.* to frequent the lobby in order to influence members or to collect political intelligence.—*ns.* **lobb'ying; lobb'yist.—lobby correspondent** reporter on parliamentary affairs; **lobby system** the giving of political information to lobby correspondents on condition that the source is not revealed. [L.L. *lobia*—M.H.G. *loube* (Ger. *Laube*), a portico, arbour—*Laub*, a leaf; cf. **lodge.**]

lobe *lōb, n.* a broad, esp. rounded, segmental division, branch, or projection: the soft lower part of the ear: a division of the lungs, brain, etc.: a division of a leaf—*adjs.* **lob'ar, lob'ate, lobed, lob'ose.**— **lobec'tomy** surgical excision of a lobe of any organ or gland of the body; **lobe'let, lobule** (*lob'ūl*) small lobe; **lob'ing** formation of, possession of, or provision with, lobes.—*v.t.* **lobot'omise, -ize** to perform a lobotomy on: to render dull, bland or inoffensive (*fig.*).—*n.* **lobot'omy** surgical incision into a lobe of an organ or gland: (loosely) leucotomy.—*adjs.* **lob'ular, -ulate(d).** [Gr. *lobos*, lobe.]

Lobelia *lō-bē'lyə, n.* a genus of garden plants: (without *cap.*) a plant of this genus. [Named after the botanist Matthias de *Lobel* (1538-1616).]

lobster *lob'stər, n.* a large strong-clawed edible crustacean (*Homarus*). red when boiled: extended to kindred kinds.—**lob'ster-pot** a basket for trapping lobsters. [O.E. *loppestre*—L. *locusta*, a lobster; cf. locust.]

lobular, etc. See lobe.

lobworm *lob'wûrm*, *n*. a lugworm: sometimes an earthworm. [lob, worm.]

local *lō'kl*, *adj*. pertaining to position in space: of or belonging to a place: confined to a place or places.—*n*. someone or something local, as an inhabitant, a public-house: a place: (*lō-käl'*; erroneously locale, for Fr. *local*) the scene of some event.—*n*. **localis- a'tion**, -z-.—*v.t*. **lo'calise**, **-ize** to assign, limit, to a place.—*n*. **lo'caliser**, -z- something that localises, esp. a radio transmitter used in effecting a blind landing.—Also *adj*. **lo'calism** the state of being local: affection for place: provincialism; **locality** (*lō-kal'i-ti*) place: position: district.—*adv*. **lo'cally**.—*v.t*. **locate'** to place: to set in a particular position: to designate or find the place of.—*n*. **loca'tion** act of locating: a farm: a claim or place marked off (for native occupation, etc.): position, site: site for filming outside the studio (*cinema*): a leasing on rent (*law*): (a position in a memory which can hold) a unit of information, e.g. a word (*comput*.).—*adj*. **locative** (*lok'ə-tiv*) pertaining to the location: denoting place where (*gram*.).—*n*. the locative case: a word in the locative case.—**local anaesthesia** anaesthesia affecting a restricted area only of the body; **local anaesthetic**; **local authorities** elected bodies for local government, e.g. town councils, county councils; **local call** a telephone call made to another number on the same exchange or group of exchanges; **local colour** faithful, characteristic details of particular scenery, manners, etc., giving verisimilitude in works of art and fiction; **local government** self-administration (in local affairs) by towns, counties, and the like, as opp. to *national* or *central government*; **local radio** radio (programmes) broadcast from a local station to a relatively small area, often on local themes; **local time** the time of a place as measured by the passage of the sun over the meridian passing through that place.—**on location** outside the studio (of filming or sound-recording). [L. *localis*—*locus*, a place.]

locate, location, etc. See under local.

loch *lohh*, *n*. a lake: an arm of the sea.—*n*. **loch'an** (*Gael*.) a lakelet. [Gael. *loch*.]

Lochaber-axe *lohh-ä'bar-aks*, *n*. a long-handled Highland variety of halberd. [*Lochaber* district in Inverness-shire.]

lochan. See loch.

lochia *lok'i-ə*, or *lōk'*, *n.pl*. a discharge from the uterus after childbirth.—*adj*. **lo'chial**. [Gr. *lochia* (pl.).]

loci. Plural of locus (q.v.).

lock[1] *lok*, *n*. a fastening device, esp. one in which a bolt is moved by mechanism, with or without a key: an enclosure for raising or lowering boats: the part of a firearm by which it is discharged: a grapple in wrestling: in Rugby football, one of the two inside men in the second row of a scrum (also **lock'-for'ward**): a state of being jammed, or immovable: an assemblage of things mutually engaged: any narrow, confined place: locking up: the full extent of the turning arc of the front wheels of a motor vehicle.—*v.t*. to fasten (door, chest, etc.) with a lock: to fasten so as to impede motion: to engage: to jam: to shut up: to close fast: to embrace closely: to furnish with locks.—*v.i*. to become fast: to unite closely: to become locked.—*ns*. **lock'age** the locks of a canal: the difference in the levels of locks: materials used for locks: water lost by use of a lock: tolls paid for passing through locks; **lock'er** box, small cupboard, properly one that may be locked; **locket** (*lok'it*) a little ornamental case usually containing a miniature or memento, and hung from the neck.—**lock'er-room** a room for changing clothes and for storing belongings in lockers; **lock's gate** a gate for opening or closing a lock in a canal, river, or dock-entrance; **lock'house** a lock-keeper's house; **lock'(ing)-nut** a nut screwed on top of another one to prevent it loosening; **lock'-jaw** tetanus: loosely, trismus; **lock'-keeper** the attendant at a lock; **lock'out'** the act of locking out, esp. used of the locking out of employees by the employer during an industrial dispute; **lock'smith** one who makes and mends locks; **lock'stitch** a sewing-machine stitch formed by the locking of two threads together; **lock'-up** a place for locking up prisoners, motor-cars, etc.: a locking up.—*adj*. capable of being locked up.—**lock away** to hide, usu. by locking up out of sight; **lock horns** to engage in combat, physical or otherwise; **lock in, out** to confine, keep out, by locking doors; **lock on (to)** of a radar beam, to track (an object) automatically; **lock, stock, and barrel** the whole: altogether; **lock up** to confine: to lock securely: to lock whatever is to be locked: to make inaccessible or unavailable (*fig*.); **under lock and key** locked up: imprisoned. [O.E. *loc*.]

lock[2] *lok*, *n*. a tuft or ringlet of hair, wool, etc.: (in *pl*.) dreadlocks (q.v.). [O.E. *locc*.]

loco[1] *lō'kō*, (*U.S.*) *adj*. mad.—*n*. (also **lo'co-plant**, **-weed**) Astragalus or other leguminous plant:—*pl*. **lō'co(e)s**. [Sp. *loco*, mad.]

loco[2] *lō'kō*. Short for locomotive:—*pl*. **lo'cos.—lō'co-man** a railway engine driver.

loco citato *lō'kō si-tä'tō*, *ki-tä'tō*, (L.) in the passage cited—abbrev. **loc. cit.**

locomotive *lō-kə-mō'tiv*, *adj*. moving from place to place: capable of, or assisting in, locomotion.—*n*. a locomotive machine: a railway engine.—*adj*. **loco-mo'bile** (*-bil*) having power of changing place: self-propelling.—*n*. a locomobile vehicle.—*ns*. **locomo-tion** (*-mō'shən*); **locomotiv'ity**; **locomo'tor**.—*adjs*. **locomo'tor, locomo'tory**. [L. *lŏcus*, a place, *movēre*, *mōtum*, to move.]

loculus *lok'ū-ləs*, *n*. a small compartment (*bot*., *anat*., *zool*.):—*pl*. **loc'uli** (*-lī*).—Also **loc'ule** (*-ūl*):—*pl*. **loc'ules**.—*adjs*. **loc'ular**, **loc'ulate** having loculi. [L. *loculus*, dim. of *locus*, a place.]

locum (tenens) *lō'kəm* (*tēn'*, *ten'enz*) *n*. a deputy or substitute, esp. for a clergyman or doctor:—*pl*. **lō'cum-tenentes** (*ten-en'tēz*, *-tās*), **locums.**—*n*. **lō'cum-ten'ency** the holding by a temporary substitute of a post. [L. *lŏcum*, accus. of *lŏcus*, a place, *tenēns*, pr.p. of *tenēre*, to hold.]

locus *lō'kəs*, *lok'ŏŏs*, *n*. a place, locality, location: a passage in a writing: the line or surface constituted by all positions of a point or line satisfying a given condition (*math*.):—*pl*. **loci** (*lō'sī*, *lok'ē*).—**locus classicus** (*klas'i-kəs*, *-kŏŏs*) the classical passage, the stock quotation; **locus standi** (*stan'dī*, *-dē*) a place for standing: a right to interfere. [L. *lŏcus*, place.]

locust *lō'kəst*, *n*. a name for several kinds of migratory winged insects akin to grasshoppers, highly destructive to vegetation: extended to various similar insects: a devourer or devastator (*fig*.): a locust-bean: a locust-tree.—*n*. **locust'a** a grass spikelet:—*pl*. **locust'ae** (*-ē*).—**lo'cust-bean'** the carob-bean; **lo'cust-tree'** the carob: the false acacia: a large West Indian tree. [L. *locusta*, lobster, locust; cf. **lobster**.]

locution *lok-ū'shən*, *n*. act or mode of speaking: expression, word, or phrase.—*adj*. **locu'tionary** of or pertaining to an utterance.—*n*. **loc'utory** a room for conversation, esp. in a monastery [L. *loquī*, *locūtus*, to speak.]

lode *lōd*, *n*. a vein containing metallic ore: a reach of water: an open ditch.—**lode'star**, **load'star** the star that guides, the Pole Star—often used figuratively; **lode'stone**, **load'stone** a form of magnetite which exhibits polarity, behaving, when freely suspended, as a magnet: a magnet—often figuratively. [O.E *lād*, a course; cf. **load**.]

loden *lō'dən*, *n*. a thick waterproof woollen cloth with a short pile· (also **loden coat**) a coat made of this cloth. [Ger.]

lodge *loj*, *n*. an abode, esp. if secluded, humble, small, or temporary: a house in the wilds for sportsmen: a gate-keeper's cottage: a college head's residence: a porter's room: the meeting-place of a branch of some societies, as freemasons: the branch itself: an American Indian's abode: the dwelling-place of a beaver, otter, etc.: a retreat: often, a villa (as part of its name): a loggia: a box in a theatre.—*v.t* to furnish with a temporary dwelling: to place: to deposit: to infix to vest: to settle. —*v.i.* to dwell, esp for a time, or as a lodger: to pass the night: to come to rest in a fixed position.—*ns.* **lodg'er** one who lodges: one who lives in a hired room or rooms; **lodg'ing** temporary habitation: (often in *pl.*) a room or rooms hired in the house of another: harbour; **lodg'ment** (also **lodge'ment**) act of lodging, or state of being lodged: accumulation of something that remains at rest.—**lodge'-gate'** a gate with a lodge; **lodge'-keeper**; **lodge'pole** a pole used in making an Amer. Indian lodge, **lodg'ing-house** a house where lodgings are let: a house other than a hotel where travellers lodge: a house where vagrants may lodge. [O Fr. *loge*—O.H.G. *lauba*, shelter, cf. **lobby**, **loggia**.]

loess, **löss** *læs*. *n*. a loamy deposit. [Ger. *Löss*.]

loft *loft*, *n*. a room or space immediately under a roof: a gallery in a hall or church: an upper room: a room for pigeons: a stroke that causes a golf-ball to rise: a backward slope on a golf-club head for the purpose of lofting: a lifting action.—*v.t.* to strike up (*golf*): to toss: to propel high into the air or into space.—*n.* **loft'er** a golf iron for lofting.—*adv* **loft'ily**.—*n.* **loft'iness**.—*adj.* **loft'y** very high in position, character, sentiment, manner, or diction: stately: haughty. [Late O.E. *loft*—O.N. *lopt*, sky, an upper room.]

log[1] *log*, *n*. short for **logarithm**.—**log tables** a book of tables setting out logarithmic values.

log[2] *log*, *n*. a bulky piece of wood: a clog or impediment: an inert or insensitive person (*fig.*): an apparatus (originally a block of wood) for ascertaining a ship's speed: a record of a ship's, or other, performance and experiences, a log-book.—*adj.* consisting of logs.—*v.t.* to cut or haul in the form of logs: to enter in a log-book, or record otherwise: to cover a distance of, according to the log: to record the name and punishment of: to punish.—*adj* **logged** (*logd*) reduced to the inactivity of helplessness of a log: waterlogged: cleared of logs.—*ns.* **logg'er** a lumberman: (also **data logger**) a device which automatically records data; **logg'ing**.—**log'-book** a book containing an official record of a ship's progress and proceedings on board, or of a journey made by an aircraft or car, or of any progress: a headmaster's record of attendances, etc.: the registration documents of a motor vehicle; **log'-cab'in** a hut built of hewn or unhewn logs; **log'-canoe'** a boat made by hollowing out the trunk of a tree; **logg'er-head** a blockhead: a large sea-turtle.—**log'-house** a log-cabin: a prison (*U.S.*); **log'-hut'**; **log'-jam** jamming that brings floating logs to a standstill: congestion of events, etc., leading to a complete cessation of action (*fig.*): such cessation of action; **log'-line** the line fastened to the log, and marked for finding the speed of a vessel; **log'-man** one who cuts and removes logs; **log'-reel** a reel on which the log-line is wound.—*v.t.* and *v.i.* **log'-roll**.—**log'-roller**;

log'-rolling a gathering of people to facilitate the collection of logs after the clearing of a piece of land, or for rolling logs into a stream: the sport of trying to dislodge another person standing on the same floating log: mutual aid among politicians, esp. trading in votes to secure passage of legislation, **log's saw** a bow-saw; **log'wood** a tropical American tree of the Caesalpinia family, exported in logs: its dark-red heartwood: an extract from it used in dyeing.—**at loggerheads** at issue, quarrelling; **sleep like a log** to be very deeply asleep.

logan *log'ən*, *n*. a rocking-stone —Also **log'an-stone**, **logg'an-stone**, **logg'ing-stone**. [Dialect word *log*, to rock; poss. conn. with Dan *logre*, to wag the tail.]

loganberry *lō'gən-ber-i*, *-bər-i*, *n*. a supposed hybrid between raspberry and a Pacific coast blackberry, obtained by Judge J. H. *Logan* (d. 1928).

logarithm *log'ə-ridhm*, *-rithm*, *n*. the power of a fixed number (called the base of the system, usu. 10 or *e*) that equals the number in question.—*adjs.* **logarith'-mic**, **-al**.—*adv.* **logarith'mically**. [Gr *logos*, ratio, reckoning, *arithmos*, number.]

loggan-stone. See **logan**.

loggat, **logger**, **loggerhead**, etc. See **log**[2].

loggia *loj'(y)ə*, *n*. a covered open arcade:—*pl.* **loggie** (*loj'ā*), **loggias**. [It.; cf. **lodge**.]

logging-stone. See **logan**.

logic *loj'ik*, *n*. the science and art of reasoning correctly: the science of the necessary laws of thought: the principles of any branch of knowledge: sound reasoning: individual method of reasoning: convincing and compelling force (as of facts, events): basis of operation as designed and effected in a computer, comprising **logical elements** which perform specified elementary arithmetical functions. —*adj.* **log'ical** of or according to logic: rightly reasoning. following necessarily from facts or events: of, used in, logic circuits (*comput.*).—*ns* **logical'ity**, **log'icalness**.—*adv.* **log'ically**.—*n.* **logician** (*loj-ish'ən*) one skilled in logic.—*v.i.* **logic circuit** (*comput.*) an electronic circuit with usu. two or more inputs and one output, which performs a logical operation, e.g. *and*, *not*; **logic diagram** (*comput.*) a diagram showing logical elements and interconnections without engineering details. [Gr. *logikē* (*technē*), logical (art)—*logos*, speech, reason.]

logistic, **-al** *loj-is'tik*, *-əl*, *adjs.* pertaining to reasoning, to calculation, or to logistic(s): proportional.—*n.* **logis'tic** the art of calculation.—*n.* **logistician** (*-tish'ən*) one skilled in logistics.—*n.sing.* or *pl.* **logis'tics** the art of movement and supply of troops: the handling of the practical detail of any large-scale enterprise or operation.—**logistics vessel** a ship designed for the transport of troops and vehicles, and for their landing directly on to beaches. [Gr. *logistikos—logizesthai*, to compute; influenced by Fr. *loger*, to lodge.]

loglog *log'log*, *n*. the logarithm of a *logarithm*.—Also **lō'log**.

logo. See **logotype**.

logogram *log'ō-gram*, **logograph** *-gräf*, *ns.* a single sign for a word: a logogriph. [Gr. *logos*, word, *gramma*, letter, *graphein*, to write.]

logogriph *log'ō-grif*, *n*. a riddle in which a word is to be found from other words made up of its letters, or from synonyms of these. [Gr. *logos*, word, *griphos*, a net, riddle.]

Logos *log'os*, *n*. in the Stoic philosophy, the active principle living in and determining the world: the Word of God incarnate (*Christian theol.*). [Gr. *logos*, word.]

logotype *log'ō-tīp*, *n*. a type of a word or several

letters cast in one piece: a single piece of type comprising a name and/or address, trademark, or design: an identifying symbol consisting of a simple picture or design and/or letters.—Also **log'o:**—*pl* **log'os.** [Gr. *logos*, word, *typos*, an impression.]

-logy *-lo-ji*, *suffix* indicating science, theory: discourse, treatise. [Gr. *logos*, word, reason]

loin *loin, n.* the back of a beast cut for food: (usu. in *pl.*) the reins, or the lower part of the back: (in *pl.*) generating source.—**loin'-cloth** a piece of cloth for wearing round the loins.—**gird up one's loins** to prepare for energetic action, as if by tucking up one's clothes. [O.Fr. *loigne*—L. *lumbus*, loin.]

loiter *loi'tər*, *v.i* to proceed lingeringly: to dawdle: to linger.—*n.* **loi'terer.**—*n.* and *adj.* **loi'tering.**—*adv.* **loi'teringly.** [Du. *leuteren*, to dawdle.]

loll *lol*, *v.i.* to lie lazily about, to lounge, sprawl. to dangle, hang (now mainly of the tongue).—*v.t.* to let hang out.—*n.* **loll'er.**—*adv.* **loll'ingly.**—*v i.* **loll'op** to lounge, idle: to bound clumsily along. [Perh imit.; cf. Du *lollen*, to sit over the fire]

Lollard *lol'ərd, n.* a follower of Wycliffe: an idler.—*ns* **Loll'ardy, Loll'ardry, Loll'ardism.** [M.Du. *lollaerd*, mutterer, droner—*lollen*, to mew, bawl, mutter; combined with **lolier** (see **loll**).]

lollipop *lol'i-pop, n.* a sweetmeat made with sugar and treacle. a large hard sweetmeat impaled on a stick: (usu. in *pl.*) a sweetmeat in general (also *fig.*).—Also **loll'y**—as *slang*, money.—**lollipop man, woman, lady** one appointed to conduct children across a busy street, distinguished by carrying a pole with a disc on the end. [Perh. Northern dial. *lolly*, tongue]

lollop. See **loll.**

lolly. See **lollipop.**

lollygag. See **lallygag.**

lolog. Same as **loglog.**

Lombard *lom'bərd, n.* an inhabitant of *Lombardy* in N Italy: (also **Langobard** *lang'gō-bard,* **Longobard** *long'*) one of the Langobardi, or Longobardi, a Germanic tribe, which founded a kingdom in Lombardy (568), overthrown by Charlemagne (774).—*adjs.* **Lom'bard, Lombardic** (*-bard'ik*).—**Lombard Street** the chief centre of the banking interest in London; **Lombardy poplar** a variety of black poplar with erect branches. [O.Fr.,—L. *Langobardus, Longobardus.*]

lomentum *lō-ment'əm, n.* a pod that breaks in pieces at constrictions between the seeds:—*pl.* **loment'a.**—Also **lō'ment** (*-mənt*).—*adj.* **lomentā'ceous.** [L *lōmentum*, bean-meal (used as a cosmetic)—*lavāre, lōtum*, to wash.]

Londoner *lun'dən-ər, n.* a native or citizen of *London.*—**London Clay** a Lower Eocene formation in southeastern England; **London Pride** a hardy perennial saxifrage—also *none-so-pretty* and *St Patrick's cabbage:* formerly applied to other plants.

lone *lōn, adj.* isolated: solitary: unfrequented, uninhabited: unmarried, or widowed.—*ns.* **lone'ness; lon'er** a lone wolf.—*adj.* **lone'some** solitary: feeling lonely.—Also *n.—adv* **lone'somely.**—*n.* **lone'someness.**—**lone wolf** (*fig.*) one who prefers to act on his own and not to have close friends or confidential relationships. [**alone.**]

lonely *lōn'li, adj.* unaccompanied: isolated: uninhabited, unfrequented: uncomfortably conscious of being alone.—*n.* **lone'liness.**—**lonely heart** a usu. unmarried person without close friends and consequently lonely and unhappy —*adj* **lone'ly-heart.** [**alone.**]

long *long, adj.* not short: of a specified (or to be specified) length: extended in space in the direction of greatest extension: far-extending. extended in time: of extended continuance: of distant date: requiring much time in utterance or performance: *loosely*, accented: *loosely*, in a long syllable: numerically extensive. of more than average number (as a suit of cards) exceeding the standard value (see **dozen, hundred**): having a large holding in a commodity, etc (*finance*): tedious —*compar.* **longer** (*long'gər*), *superl.* **longest** (*long'gist*).—*n* a long time: a long syllable (*pros.*): the long summer university vacation (*coll*): an obsolete note equal to two (in 'perfect' time three) breves (*mus* ; L *longa*): (in *pl*) long trousers: (in *pl.*) long-dated securities.—*adv.* for, during, or by, a great extent of time: throughout the whole time:—*compar.* and *superl* as for *adj.*—*v i.* to yearn.—**long** in composition, of a specified length (as *year-long, mile-long*).—*n.* **long'ing** an eager desire, craving.—*adj.* yearning.—*adv.* **long'-ingly.**—*adj.* **longish** (*long'ish, -gish*).—*advs.* **long'-ways, -wise** lengthwise —*adj.* **long'-ago'** of the far past.—*n.* the far past —**long arm** far-reaching power; **long'boat** the largest and strongest boat of a ship, **long'bow** a bow drawn by hand—opp. to **crossbow; longcase clock** grandfather clock.—*n.pl.* **long'-clothes** long garments for a baby.—*adj.* **long'-da'ted** of securities, due for redemption in more than fifteen years.—**long'-divi'sion** division in which the working is shown in full; **long dozen,** thirteen.—*adj.* **long'-drawn (-out')** prolonged: unduly protracted.—**long drink** a large thirst-quenching drink (sometimes alcoholic) in a tall glass.—*adjs.* **long'-eared** with long ears or earlike feather-tufts, **long'-faced** dismal-looking —**long face** a dismal expression, **long'-field** (*cricket*) a fielder or station near the boundary on the bowler's side.—*adj.* **long'-haired** highbrow: unconventional, hippy.—**long'hand** ordinary writing—opp. to *shorthand;* **long haul** a journey over a great distance —*adjs.* **long'-haul; long'-headed** dolichocephalous. shrewd: sagacious.—**long'-head'edness; long home** the grave; **long'horn** an animal with long horns or antennae, as a longicorn beetle; **long'-house** a long communal house, esp. of American Indians, **long johns** long underpants; **long jump** a jump for distance along the ground; **long'-leg** (*cricket*) a fieldsman, or his station, far out behind the batsman and a little to his left —*adj* **long'-legged** having long legs.—**long'-legs** a crane-fly.—*adjs.* **long'-life** of foodstuffs, treated so as to prolong freshness; **long'-lived** (*-livd'*, also *-līvd'*) having a long life.—**long odds** in betting, a remote chance, unfavourable odds in terms of risk, favourable in terms of potential gain; **long'-off, long'-on** (*cricket*) the fielders in the long-field to the off and on of the batsman respectively: their position; **long'-pig'** (from cannibal term) human flesh as food.—*adjs.* **long'-playing** of a gramophone record, giving length in reproduction because of the extremely fine groove, **long'-range** long in range: covering a long future time or long distance.—**long'ship** (*hist.*) a long vessel of the old Norsemen; **long shot** (a bet, entry, venture, etc., with) a remote chance of success: a shot taken at a distance from the object filmed.—*adj.* **long'-sight'ed** able to see far but not close at hand: hypermetropic: presbyopic: having foresight: sagacious.—**long'-sight'edness; long'-slip** (*cricket*) a fielder some distance behind the batsman on the off side.—*adjs.* **long'-spun** long-drawn, tedious; **long'-stand'ing** of long existence or continuance; **long'-stay** staying permanently or semi-permanently, as patients in a hospital.—**long'-stop** one who stands behind the wicket-keeper to stop balls missed by him (*cricket*): a person or thing that acts as a final safeguard or check (*fig.*).—*adj.* **long'-suff'ering** enduring long and patiently.—*n.* long endurance or patience.—**long suit** the suit with most cards in a hand: an advantageous quality or talent (*fig.*).—*adj.* **long'-term** extending over a long time: of a policy, concerned with time ahead as distinct from the immediate present.—**long vacation** a long holiday during the summer, when schools, etc., are closed; **long view** the taking into consideration of events, etc , in the distant future.— adj. **long'-waist'ed** having a long waist: long from the armpits to the hips; **long'-wave** (radio) of, or using, wavelengths over 1000 metres; **long'-wind'ed** long-breathed: tediously wordy and lengthy.—**long's wind'edness.**—**as long as** provided only that; **before long, ere long** soon, **long on** well supplied with; **make a long nose** to cock a snook or put a thumb to the nose, **no longer** not now as formerly; **not long for this world** near death, **so long!** (coll.) good-bye; **so long as** provided only that; **the long and the short (of it)** the sum of the matter in a few words. [O.E. lang, long (adj), lange, longe (adv)]

longaeval, -aevous. See longevity.

longan long'gan, n. a tree (Nephelium longana) akin to the lychee: its fruit. [Chin. lung-yen, dragon's eye.]

longanimity long-ga-nim'i-ti, n. forbearance.—adj. **longanimous** (-gan'). [L. longanimitās, -ātis— longus, long. animus, spirit.]

longe. Same as lunge².

longevity long-jev'i-ti, n. great length of life —adjs **longaeval, -geval, longaevous. -gevous** (-jēv') [L longaevitās, -ātis—longus, long, aevum, age.]

longicorn lon'ji-korn, n. any beetle of the family Cerambycidae, with very long antennae.—Also adj. [L. longus, long, cornū, horn.]

longitude lon'ji-tūd, long'gi-, n length: arc of the equator between the meridian of a place and a standard meridian (usually that of Greenwich) expressed in degrees E. or W · the arc of the ecliptic between a star's circle of latitude and the first point of Aries or vernal equinox, measured eastwards (astron.) —adj. **longitud'inal** of or in length or longitude. lengthwise —adv. **longitud'inally.** [L. longitūdō, -inis, length —longus, long]

Longobard. See Lombard (second meaning).

longshore long'shōr, -shor, adj. existing or employed along the shore.— **long'shoreman** a stevedore: one who makes a living along the shore [alongshore.]

Lonsdale belt lonz'dāl belt, award (see belt) for gaining the same boxing title three times in succession. [Lord Lonsdale.]

loo¹ lōō, (coll.) n. a lavatory

loo² lōō, n. a card game. [From lanterloo, name of another game]

loofah lōō'fä, n. a tropical genus (Luffa) of the gourd family: the fibrous network of its fruit, used as a flesh-brush.—Also **loofa, luffa** (luf') [Ar. lūfah.]

look lōōk, v.i. to direct the sight with attention. to give attention: to face to seem. to seem: to be: to have an appearance: to tend.—v.t. to make sure: to see to it. to ascertain by a look: to look at: to expect: to seem likely: to render by a look. to express by a look. to refer to, turn (up) —n. the act of looking: view: air. appearance: (in pl.) beauty, comeliness (also good looks).—imper. or interj. see: behold.—ns. **look'er** one who looks: an observer: one who has good looks (coll); **look'ing.**—adj. (in composition) having the appearance of.—**look'-alike** a person who closely resembles another in personal appearance, a double; **look'-in'** a chance of doing anything effectively or of sharing. a short casual call; **look'ing-glass** a mirror, **look'out** a careful watch a place to observe from: one set to watch: prospect: concern, **look'-see** (slang) a look around.—**look after** to take care of; **look alive** (coll.) to bestir oneself; **look down on** to despise; **look down one's nose** to regard with contempt; **look for** to search for: to expect; **look forward to** to anticipate with pleasure; **look here!** I say! attend to this!, **look in**

to make a short call: to watch television; **look into** to inspect closely: to investigate; **look on** to regard, view, think: to be a spectator; **look out** to be watchful: to be on one's guard. to look for and select; **look over** to examine cursorily: to overlook or pass over; **look sharp** (coll.) be quick about it; **look small** to appear or feel foolish and ashamed; **look to** to look at, towards: to watch: to take care of· to depend on (for). to expect (to do); **look up** to search for, refer to: to take courage: to improve, to have taken a turn for the better· to seek out and call upon, visit (coll); **look up to** to feel respect or veneration for; **not much to look at** (coll) plain, unattractive [O E. lōcian, to look.]

loom¹ lōōm, n. a machine for weaving: the shaft of an oar [O.E gelōma, a tool.]

loom² lōōm, v.i to appear indistinctly or as in a mirage, esp. in an exaggerated or magnified form to take shape, as an impending event.—n an indistinct or mirage-like appearance

loon¹ lōōn. n. in north-east of Scotland, a boy (also **loon'ie**): a simple-minded or eccentric person (coll.)

loon² lōōn, any of an order of northern diving birds — n **loon'ing** their cry. [O N. lōmr.]

loony lōōn'i, n. and adj. for lunatic.—**loon'y-bin** (slang) a lunatic asylum

loop¹ lōōp, n. a doubling of a cord, chain, etc., leaving a space. an ornamental doubling in fringes: anything of like form, as an element in fingerprints: a branch of anything that returns to the main part a set of instructions used more than once in a program (comput.) an intra-uterine contraceptive device shaped like a loop (also **Lippes loop**) —v.t. to fasten in or with a loop. to ornament with loops: to make a loop of.—v i. to travel in loops —adj. **looped.**—n. **loop'er** a geometrid caterpillar, from its mode of walking.—n. and adj. **loop'ing.**—adj. **loop'y** having loops· slightly crazed (slang).—**loop the loop** to move in a complete vertical loop or circle, head downwards at the top of the curve

loop² lōōp, loophole lōōp'hōl, ns. a slit in a wall: a means of escape or evasion.—v.t. **loop'hole** to make loopholes in [Perh. M.Du. lūpen, to peer]

loose lōōs, adj. slack· free: unbound: not confined· not compact. unattached: untied: not close-fitting: not tight: relaxed. inexact: indefinite: vague: not strict: unrestrained: lax: licentious: inattentive: dispersedly or openly disposed: not serried: in Rugby football, referring to all play except for the set scrums and line-outs —adv. loosely.—n. an act or mode of loosing, esp. an arrow. the loose state. unrestraint. freedom: abandonment: an outbreak of self indulgence: loose play (Rugby football).—v.t. to make loose. to set free. to unfasten: to untie' to dis connect: to relax: to slacken· to discharge.—v i. to shoot.—adv. **loose'ly.**—v.t. **loos'en** to make loose: to relax: to make less dense: to open, as the bowels.— v i. to become loose: to become less tight.—n **loose'- ness** the state of being loose: diarrhoea.—adj. **loose'- bod'ied** flowing. **loose-fitting:** loose in behaviour.— **loose -box** a part of a stable where horses are kept untied: **loose change** coins kept about one's person for small expenditures; **loose'-cover** a detachable cover, as for a chair, **loose fish** one of irregular, esp. lax habits.—adjs **loose'-leaf** having a cover such that leaves may be inserted or removed; **loose'-limbed'** having supple limbs —**break loose** to escape from confinement, **let loose** to set at liberty: **loosen up** to become less shy or taciturn; **on the loose** indulging in a bout of unrestraint: freed from confinement [O N laus, O E léas, see less.]

loosestrife lōōs'strīf, n a plant (Lysimachia vulgaris) of the primrose family, or other member of the genus (as yellow pimpernel, creeping Jenny): a tall waterside plant (*Lythrum salicaria*, purple loosestrife). [Intended as a translation of Gr. *lȳsimacheion*, common loosestrife (as if from *lyein*, to loose, *machē*, strife), which may be from the personal name *Lȳsimachos*.]

loot *lōōt*, *n.* plunder: money (*slang*).—*v.t.* or *v.i.* to plunder.—*n.* **loot'er.** [Hindi *lūt*.]

lop[1] *lop*, *v.i.* to hang down loosely.—*adj.* **lop'-eared** having drooping ears.—*adj.* **lop'-sid'ed** ill-balanced: heavier, bigger, on one side than the other. [Perh. conn. with **lob.**]

lop[2] *lop*, *v.t.* to cut off the top or ends of, esp. of a tree: to cut away, as superfluous parts:—*pr.p.* **lopp'ing;** *pa.t.* and *pa.p.* **lopped.**—*n.* twigs of trees cut off: an act of looping.—*ns.* **lopp'er;** **lopp'ing** a cutting off: that which is cut off. [O.E. *loppian*.]

lope *lōp*, *v.i.* to leap: to run with a long stride. [O.N. *hlaupa*; cf. **leap**[1].]

lopper, lopping. See **lop**[2].

loquacious *lō-kwā'shas*, *adj.* talkative.—*adv.* **loquā'ciously.**—*ns.* **loquā'ciousness, loquacity** (*-kwas'*). [L. *loquāx*, *-ācis*—*loqui*, to speak.]

loquat *lō'kwot*, *-kwat*, *n.* a Chinese and Japanese tree (*Eriobotrya japonica*) of the rose family: its small, yellow fruit. [Chinese *luh kwat*.]

lor, lor'. See **lord.**

loran *lō'*, *lō'rän*, *n.* a long-range radio-navigation system. [*Long-range navigation*.]

lord (**Lord,** when prefixed), *lōrd*, *n.* a master: a feudal superior (also **lord'-supe'rior;** *hist.*): a ruler: the proprietor of a manor (*hist.*): a titled nobleman: a bishop, esp. if a member of the House of Lords: a judge of the Court of Session: used as part of various official titles: (with *cap.*) God: (with *cap.*) Christ.— *v.t.* (with *it*) to play the lord, tyrannise.—*interj.* expressing surprise (*coll.* **lor, lor', law, lordy**).—*adj.* **lord'ly** like, becoming, or of a lord: magnificent: lavish: lofty: haughty: tyrannical.—Also *adv.*—*n.* **lord'ship** state or condition of being a lord: dominion: authority: used in referring to, addressing, a lord (with *his, your*), or a woman sheriff or judge (with *her, your*).—**Lord's Day** Sunday; **Lord's Prayer** prayer Christ taught his disciples (Matt. vi. 9–13); **lords spiritual** the archbishops and bishops in the House of Lords; **Lord's Supper** holy communion; **Lord's table** the communion table; **lords temporal** the lay peers.—**drunk as a lord** extremely drunk; **House of Lords** upper house of British parliament; **live like a lord** to live in luxury; **Lord knows (who, what, etc.)** I don't know, and I question if anybody does; **lords and ladies** common arum; **Lord of Session** a judge of the Court of Session. [M.E. *lovered, laverd*—O.E. *hlāford—hlāf*, bread, *ward*, keeper, guardian.]

lordosis *lōr-dō'sis*, *n.* abnormal curvature of the spinal column, the convexity towards the front.—*adj.* **lordot'ic** affected with, relating to lordosis. [Gr. *lordōsis—lordos*, bent back.]

lore[1] *lōr, lōr*, *n.* learning: now esp. learning of a special, traditional, or out-of-the-way miscellaneous kind. [O.E. *lār*.]

lore[2] *lōr, lōr*, *n.* the side of the head between eye and bill (*ornithology*). [L. *lōrum*, thong.]

lorgnette *lōrn-yet'*, *n.* eyeglasses with a handle: an opera-glass.—*n.* **lorgnon** (*lōrn'yõ*) an eyeglass: eyeglasses. [Fr. *lorgner*, to look sidelong at, to ogle.]

lorica *lō-*, *lō-*, *la-rī'ka*, *n.* leather corslet: the case of a protozoan, rotifer, etc.:—*pl.* **lori'cae** (*-sē*). [L. *lōrica*, a leather corslet—*lōrum*, a thong.]

lorikeet *lor-i-kēt'*, *n.* a small lory. [From **lory,** on analogy of **parakeet.**]

lorimer *lor'i-mar*, **loriner** *-nar*, *ns.* a maker of the metal

parts of horse-harness. [O.Fr. *loremier, lorenier*— L. *lōrum*, a thong.]

loris *lō'*, *lō'ris*, *n.* the slender lemur of Sri Lanka: an East Indian lemur (*Nycticebus* or *Bradycebus tardigradus*, the *slow loris*). [Fr. *loris*; said to be from Du.]

lorry *lor'i*, *n.* a long wagon without sides, or with low sides.

lory *lō'*, *lō'ri*, *n.* any parrot of a family with brushlike tongues, natives of New Guinea, Australia, etc.: in South Africa a touraco. [Malay *lūrī*.]

lose *lōōz*, *v.t.* to fail to keep or get possession of: to be deprived or bereaved of: to cease to have: to cease to hear, see or understand: to mislay: to waste, as time: to miss: to be defeated in: to cause the loss of: to cause to perish: to bring to ruin.—*v.i.* to fail, to be unsuccessful: to suffer waste or loss: of a clock or watch, to go too slowly:—*pr.p.* **los'ing;** *pa.t.* and *pa.p* **lost** (*lost*).—*adj.* **los'able.**—*n.* **los'er.**—*n.* and *adj.* **los'ing.**—*adj.* **los'ingly.**—*adj.* **lost** (*lost*) parted with: no longer possessed: missing: thrown away: squandered: ruined: confused, unable to find the way (*lit.* and *fig.*).—**losing game** a game that is going against one: a game played with reversal of the usual aim; **lost cause** a hopeless endeavour; **lost soul** a damned soul, an irredeemably evil person; **lost tribes** the tribes of Israel that never returned after deportation by Sargon of Assyria in 721 B.C —**get lost!** (*slang*) go away and stay away!: stop annoying or interfering!; **lose oneself** to lose one's way: to become rapt or bewildered; **lose out** (*coll.*) to suffer loss or disadvantage: (also with *on*) to fail to acquire something desired; **lost to** insensible to. [O.E. *losian*, to be a loss.]

loss *los*, *n.* losing: diminution: bereavement: destruction: defeat: deprivation: detriment: that which is lost.—**loss adjuster** an assessor employed by an insurance company, usu. in fire damage claims; **loss'-leader** a thing sold at a loss to attract other custom.— **at a loss** running in deficit: off the scent: at fault: nonplussed: perplexed. [O.E. *los*, influenced by **lost.**]

löss. See **loess.**

lost. See **lose.**

lot *lot*, *n.* an object, as a slip of wood, a straw, drawn or thrown out from among a number in order to reach a decision by chance: decision by this method: a prize so to be won: destiny: that which falls to any one as his fortune: a separate portion: a parcel of ground: a set: a set of things offered together for sale: the whole: a plot of ground allotted or assigned to any person or purpose, esp. for building: a large quantity or number.—*v.t.* to allot: to separate into lots:—*pr.p.* **lott'ing;** *pa.t.* and *pa.p.* **lott'ed.—across lots** (*U.S.*) by short cuts; **bad lot** a person of bad moral character; **cast or throw in one's lot with** to share the fortunes of; **cast or draw lots** to draw from a set alike in appearance in order to reach a decision; **lots of** (*coll.*) many; **the lot** the entire number or amount. [O.E. *hlot*, lot —*hlēotan*, to cast lots.]

loth, loath *lōth*, *adj.* reluctant, unwilling.—**nothing loth** not at all unwilling. [O.E. *lāth*, hateful; cf. **loathe.**]

lotion *lō'shan*, *n.* a liquid preparation for external application, medicinal or cosmetic. [L. *lōtiō, -ōnis*, a washing—*lavāre, lōtum*, to wash.]

lottery *lot'ar-i*, *n.* an arrangement for distribution of prizes by lot: a matter of chance: a card game of chance.—*n.* **lott'o, lō'to** a game played by covering on a card each number drawn till a line of numbers is completed:—*pl.* **lott'os, lō'tos.** [It. *lotteria, lotto*, of Gmc origin; cf. **lot.**]

lotus *lō'tas*, *n.* an Egyptian or Indian water-lily of various species: a tree (possibly the jujube) in North Africa, whose fruit induced in the eater a state of blissful indolence and forgetfulness: an architectural ornament like a water-lily.—**lotus position** a seated position used in yoga, cross-legged, with each foot resting on the opposite thigh. [Latinised Gr. *lōtos*.]

louche *loosh, adj.* squinting: ambiguous: shady, sinister.—*adv.* **louche'ly.** [Fr.]

loud *lowd, adj.* making a great sound: noisy: obtrusive: vulgarly showy.—*advs.* **loud, loud'ly.**—*v.t.* and *v.i.* **loud'en** to make or grow louder.—*adj.* **loud'ish.**—*n.* **loud'ness.**—**loudhail'er** a portable megaphone with microphone and amplifier.—*adjs.* **loud'-lunged; loud'mouthed.**—**loud'mouth** (*coll.*) one who talks too much or too offensively: a boaster; **loud'speak'er** an electro-acoustic device which amplifies sound.—*adj.* **loud'-voiced.** [O.E. *hlūd.*]

lough *lohh, n.* the Irish form of **loch.**

lounge *lownj, v.i.* to loll: to idle.—*v.t.* to idle (away).—*n.* an act, spell, or state of lounging: an idle stroll: a sitting-room in a private house: a room in a public building for sitting or waiting, often providing refreshment facilities: (also **lounge'-bar**) a more expensive and luxurious bar in a public house: a kind of sofa, esp. with back and one raised end: (also **lounge chair**) an easy chair suitable for lolling in.—*n.* **loung'er** one who lounges: a woman's long loose dress for wearing indoors: an extending chair or light bed for relaxing on.—*n.* and *adj.* **loung'ing.**—*adv.* **loung'ingly.**—**lounge'-liz'ard** one who loafs with women in hotel lounges, etc.; **lounge'-suit** a man's matching jacket and trousers for (formal) everyday wear.

loupe *loop, n.* a small jeweller's and watchmaker's magnifying glass, worn in the eye-socket. [Fr.]

lour, lower *lowr, low'ər, v.i.* to look sullen or threatening: to scowl, glare: a gloomy threatening appearance.—*n.* and *adj.* **lour'ing, lower'ing.**—*adv.* **lour'ingly, lower'ingly.**—*adj.* **lour'y, lower'y.** [M.E. *louren*; cf. Du. *loeren*.]

louse *lows, n.* a wingless parasitic insect (Pediculus), with a flat body, and short legs: extended to similar animals related and unrelated: a person worthy of contempt (*slang; pl.* **louses**):—*pl.* **lice** (*līs*).—*v.t.* (*lowz*) to remove lice from: to spoil, make a mess of (with *up*; *slang*).—*adv.* **lou'sily** (*-zi-*).—*n.* **lous'iness.**—*adj.* **lousy** (*low'zi*) infested with lice: swarming or full (with *with*; *slang*): inferior, bad, unsatisfactory (*slang*). [O.E. *lūs*, pl. *lýs.*]

lout[1] *lowt, n.* a bumpkin: an awkward boor.—*adj.* **lout'ish** clownish: awkward and boorish.—*adv.* **lout'ishly.**—*n.* **lout'ishness.**

louvre, louver *loo'vər, n.* a turret-like structure on a roof for escape of smoke or for ventilation: an opening or shutter with louvre-boards: a louvre-board.—*adj.* **lou'vred, lou'vered.**—**lou'vre-, lou'ver-board** a sloping slat placed across an opening; **lou'vre-, lou'ver-door, -win'dow** a door, open window crossed by a series of sloping boards. [O.Fr. *lover, lovier.*]

lovage *luv'ij, n.* an umbelliferous salad plant (*Levisticum officinale*) of Southern Europe akin to Angelica: any plant of the kindred genus *Ligusticum,* including *Scottish lovage.* [O.Fr. *luvesche*—L.L. *levisticum,* L. *ligusticum,* lit. Ligurian.]

lovat *luv'ət, n.* a greyish- or bluish-green colour, usu. in tweed or woollen cloth: cloth of this colour (also **lov'at-green'**).—Also *adj.* [From *Lovat,* in Inverness-shire.]

love *luv, n.* fondness: charity: an affection of the mind caused by that which delights: strong liking: devoted attachment to one of the opposite sex: sexual attachment: a love-affair: the object of affection: used as a term of endearment or affection: in some games, no score.—*v.t.* to be fond of: to regard with affection: to

delight in with exclusive affection: to regard with benevolence.—*v.i.* to have the feeling of love.—*adjs.* **lov'able, love'able** (*luv'ə-bl*) worthy of love: amiable; **love'less.**—*n.* **love'liness.**—*adj.* **love'ly** exciting admiration: attractive: extremely beautiful: delightful (*coll.*).—*adv.* delightfully, very well (*coll.*).—*n.* (*coll.*) a beautiful woman, esp. showgirl, model.—*ns.* **lov'er** one who loves, esp. one in love with a person of the opposite sex (in the singular usually of the man): a paramour: one who is fond of anything; **lov'ey** (*coll.*) a term of endearment.—*n.* and *adj.* **lov'ing.**—*adv.* **lov'ingly.**—*n.* **lov'ingness.**—**love'-affair'** an amour honourable or dishonourable; **love'-apple** the tomato; **love'bird** a small African parrot (*Agapornis*), strongly attached to its mate: extended to other kinds; **love'-charm** a philtre; **love'-child** an illegitimate child; **love'-feast** the agape, or a religious feast in imitation of it; **love'-game** (*lawn-tennis*) a game in which the loser has not scored (poss. from Fr. *l'œuf,* egg—cf. **duck**[3] in cricket); **love'-in-a-mist'** a fennel-flower (*Nigella damascena*): a West Indian passion-flower; **love'-knot, lov'er's-knot** an intricate knot, used as a token of love; **love'-letter** a letter of courtship; **love'-lies-bleed'ing** a kind of amaranth with drooping red spike; **love'light** a lustre in the eye expressive of love.—*adj.* **love'lorn** forsaken by one's love: pining for love.—**love'-maker; love'-making** amorous courtship: sexual intercourse; **love'-match** a marriage for love, not money; **love'-nest** a place where lovers, often illicit, meet or live; **love'-potion** a philtre.—*adj.* **love'sick** languishing with amorous desire.—**love'-song** a song expressive of or relating to love; **love'-story** a story whose subject-matter is romantic love; **lov'ing-cup** a cup passed round at the end of a feast for all to drink from; **lov'ing-kind'ness** (*B.*) kindness full of love: mercy.—*adj.* **lovey-dovey** (*luv'i-duv'i; coll.*) loving, sentimental.—**fall in love** to become in love (with); **for love or money** in any way whatever; **for the love of it** for the sake of it: for the pleasure of it; **for the love of Mike** (*slang*) for any sake; **in love (with)** romantically and sexually attracted, devoted (to); **make love to** to try to gain the affections of: to have sexual intercourse with; **play for love** to play without stakes; **there's no love lost between them** they have no liking for each other. [O.E. *lufu,* love.]

low[1] *lō, v.i.* to make the noise of oxen.—*n.* sound made by oxen.—*n.* **low'ing.** [O.E. *hlōwan.*]

low[2] *lō, adj.* occupying a position far downward or not much elevated: not reaching a high level: not tall: reaching far down: of clothes, cut so as to expose the neck (and bosom): quiet, soft, not loud: grave in pitch, as sounds produced by slow vibrations: produced with part of the tongue low in the mouth (*phon.*): in shallow relief: expressed in measurement by a small number: of numbers, small: of small value, intensity, quantity, or rank: weak in vitality or nutrition: scanty, deficient: attributing lowness: dejected: debased: base: mean: vulgar: humble: socially depressed: little advanced in organisation or culture: of latitude, near the equator:—*compar.* **lower** (*lō'ər*); *superl.* **lowest** (*lō'ist*), **low'ermost.**—*n.* that which is low or lowest: an area of low barometrical pressure: a low or minimum level: low gear.—*adv.* in or to a low position, state, or manner: humbly: with a low voice or sound: at low pitch: at a low price: in small quantity or to small degree.—*v.t.* **low'er** to make lower: to let down: to lessen.—*v.i.* to become lower or less.—*n.* **low'ering** the act of bringing low or reducing.—*adj.* letting down: sinking: degrading.—*adj.* **low'ermost** lowest.—*adv.* **low'lily** (*-li-li*).—*n.* **low'liness.**—*adj.* **low'ly** humble: modest: low in stature or in organisation.—*n.* **low'ness.**—*adj.* **low'-born** of humble birth.

—adj. **low'-bred** ill-bred: unmannerly.—**low'-brow** one who is not intellectual or makes no pretensions to intellect.—Also adj.—adj. **Low Church** of a party within the Church of England setting little value on sacerdotal claims, ecclesiastical constitutions, ordinances, and forms, holding evangelical views of theology—opp. to *High Church*.—**Low-Church'ism**; **Low-Church'man**; **low comedy** comedy of farcical situation, slapstick, low life.—adjs. **low'-cost** cheap; **low'-country** lowland (**the Low Countries** Holland and Belgium); **low'-down** (coll.) base: dishonourable.—n. (slang) information, esp. of a confidential or damaging nature —**low'er-case** (print.) lit. kept in a lower case, small as distinguished from capital, **low'er-class** pertaining to persons of the humbler ranks.—**low'er-deck** deck immediately above the hold. ship's crew (as opposed to officers).—Also adj —**lower house, chamber** the larger more representative of two legislative chambers, **lower regions** Hades, hell —adj. **low'-key'** in painting or photography, in mostly dark tones or colours, with few, if any, highlights: undramatic, under-stated, restrained: of a person, not easily excited, showing no visible reaction.—**low'land** land low with respect to higher land (also adj.), **low'lander** (also cap) a native of lowlands, esp. the **Lowlands** of Scotland; **low life** sordid social circumstances: persons of low social class: **low'-loader** a low sideless wagon for very heavy loads, **low mass** mass without music and incense.—adjs **low'-mind'ed** moved by base or gross motives· vulgar, **low'-necked** of a dress, cut low in the neck and away from the shoulders, décolleté, **low'-paid'** (of worker) receiving, (of job) rewarded by, low wages, **low'-pitched** of sound, low in pitch: of a roof, gentle in slope: having a low ceiling; **low'-press'ure** employing or exerting a low degree of pressure (viz. less than 50 lb. to the sq. inch), said of steam and steam-engines: having low barometric pressure.—**low profile** a manner or attitude revealing very little of one's feelings, intentions, activities, etc —adj. **low-pro'file**.—**low relief** same as **bas-relief**.—adjs. **low'-rise** of buildings, having only a few storeys, in contrast to *high-rise* (q.v.); **low'-spir'ited** having the spirits low or cast down: not lively: sad. —**low'-spir'itedness**; **Low Sunday** the first Sunday after Easter. —adj. **low technology** simple, unsophisticated technology used in the production of basic commodities.—adjs **low'-ten'sion** using, generating or operating at a low voltage; **low tide, water** the lowest point of the tide at ebb; **low'-wat'ermark** the lowest line reached by the tide: anything marking the point of greatest degradation, decline, etc. (fig.) —**an all-time low** the lowest recorded level; **lay low** to overthrow, fell, kill; **low-level language** any computer-programming language that is designed as a machine code rather than as a language comprehensible to the user (opp to *high-level language*). [O.N. lâgr, Du. laag, low.]

lower lowr. See **lour**.

lower lō'er. See **low²**.

lox¹ loks, n. liquid oxygen, used as a rocket propellant.

lox² loks, n. a kind of smoked salmon [Yiddish laks, from M.H.G. lahs, salmon.]

loxodrome loks ə-drōm, n. a line on the surface of a sphere which makes equal oblique angles with all meridians, a rhumb-line—also **loxodromic curve, line** or **spiral**. [Gr loxos, oblique, dromos, a course.]

loyal loi'əl, adj faithful: true as a lover: firm in allegiance: personally devoted to a sovereign or monarch: being sovereign: manifesting loyalty.—n. **loy'alist** a loyal adherent, esp. of a king or of an established government. (also with cap.) in Northern Ireland, a supporter of the British government: (also with cap.) in English history, a partisan of the Stuarts: (also with cap) in the American war of Independence, one that sided with the British.—adv. **loy'ally**.—n. **loy'alty**. [Fr ,—L. legālis—lēx, lēgis, law.]

lozenge loz'inj. n. a diamond-shaped parallelogram or rhombus: a small sweetmeat, medicated or not, originally diamond-shaped.—adj. **loz'enge-shaped**. [Fr. losange (of unknown origin).]

LP el-pē', (coll.) n. a long-playing record

LSD. See under **lysis**.

lubber lub'ər, **lubbard** lub'ərd, ns. an awkward, clumsy fellow: a lazy, sturdy fellow.—adj. **lubberly** —adj and adv. **lubb'erly**.

lubfish lub'fish, n. a kind of stockfish [**lob.**]

lubricate lōō', lū'bri-kāt, v.t to make smooth or slippery: to supply with oil or other matter to overcome friction: to supply with liquor: to bribe —adj. **lu'bricant** lubricating.—n a substance used to reduce friction —n **lubrica'tion**.—adj. **lu'bricative**.—ns **lu'bricator**; **lubricity** (-bris'i-ti) slipperiness. smoothness: instability: lewdness [L. lūbricus, slippery.]

lucarne lōō-, lū-karn', n. a dormer-window, esp in a church spire. [Fr. (of unknown origin).]

luce lōōs, lūs, n. a freshwater fish, the pike. [O.Fr. lus —L.L lūcius.]

lucent lōō', lū'sənt, adj shining: bright.—n. lu'cency. [L. lūcēns, -entis, pr.p. of lūcēre, to shine—lūx, lūcis, light]

lucerne lōō-. lū-sûrn', n. purple medick, a plant resembling clover, also called alfalfa (esp U S), valuable as fodder for cattle, etc. [Fr. luzerne.]

luces. See **lux**.

lucid lōō', lū'sid, adj. shining: transparent: easily understood· intellectually bright: not darkened with madness —ns. **lucid'ity**, **lu'cidness**.—adv. **lu'cidly**. —**lucid intervals** times of sanity in madness, of quietness in fever, turmoil, etc [L. lūcidus—lūx, lūcis, light.]

Lucifer lōō', lū'si-fər, n the planet Venus as morning-star· Satan (without cap.) a match of wood tipped with a combustible substance to be ignited by friction —also **lu'cifer-match'**. [L. lūcifer, light-bringer—lūx, lūcis, light, ferre, to bring]

luck luk, n. fortune: good fortune: an object with which a family's fortune is supposed to be bound up —adv **luck'ily** in a lucky way· I'm glad to say, fortunately.—n. **luck'iness**.—adj. **luck'less** without good luck. unhappy.—adv **luck'lessly**.—n. **luck'lessness**.—adj. **luck'y** having, attended by, por tending, or bringing good luck.—**luck'-penny** a trifle returned for luck by a seller: a coin carried for luck, **luck'y-bag** a bag sold without disclosing its contents a bag in which one may dip and draw a prize (also **luck'y-dip**): a receptacle for lost property on board a man-of-war; **lucky charm** an object which is supposed to promote good fortune; **lucky strike** a stroke of luck.—**push one's luck** (coll.) to try to make too much of an advantage, risking total failure; **tough luck** an expression of real or affected sympathy for someone s predicament: **try one's luck (at)** to attempt something; **worse luck** unfortunately. [Prob L G or Du luk.]

lucre lōō', lū'kər, n. sordid gain: riches —adj. lu'crative (-krə-tiv) profitable.—adv. **lu'cratively**. [L lucrum, gain.]

lucubrate lōō', lū'kū-brāt, v.i. to study by lamplight: to discourse learnedly or pedantically.—ns. **lucubrā'tion** study or composition protracted late into the night: a product of such study: a composition that smells of the lamp; **lu'cubrator**. [L lūcubrāre, -ātum—lūx, light.]

luculent lōō', lū'kū-lənt, adj. bright: clear: convincing —adv lu'culently. [L. lūculentus—lūx, light.]

Luddite lud'īt, n one of a band of destroyers of

machinery in northern England about 1812–18·
hence, any opponent of technological innovation,
etc.—Also *adj.*—*n.* **Ludd'ism.** [Said to be from
one Ned *Ludd*, who had smashed stocking-frames at
a slightly earlier date.]

ludicrous *lōō', lū'di-krəs, adj.* adapted to excite laughter: ridiculous, absurd: laughable.—*adv.* **lu'di-
crously.**—*n.* **lu'dicrousness.** [L. *lūdicrus—lūdĕre*,
to play.]

ludo *lōō', lū'dō, n.* a game in which counters are
moved on a board according to the fall of dice:—*pl*
lud'os. [L. *lūdō*, I play.]

lues *lōō', lū'ēz, n.* a pestilence: now confined to
syphilis.—*adj.* **luetic** (-*et'ik*). [L. *lūēs.*]

luff *luf, n.* the windward side of a ship: the act of
sailing a ship close to the wind: the loof, or the after-
part of a ship's bow where the planks begin to curve
in towards the cut-water.—*v.i.* to turn a ship towards
the wind.—*v.i.* to turn nearer to the wind: to move
(the jib of a crane) in and out. [M.E. *luff, lof(f)*—
O.Fr. *lof*; possibly from a conjectured M.Du. form
loef (modern Du. *loef*).]

luffa. See **loofah.**

luftwaffe *lōōft'vá-fə,* (Ger.) *n.* air force.

lug¹ *lug, v.t.* to pull: to drag heavily: of sailing-ships,
to carry too much sail.—*v.i.* to pull:—*pr.p.* **lugg'ing;**
pa.t. and *pa.p.* **lugged.**—*n.* **lugg'age** the trunks and
other baggage of a traveller.—**lugg'age-van** a railway wagon for luggage.—**lug in** to introduce without
any apparent connection or relevance. [Cf. Sw
lugga, to pull by the hair; perh. conn. with **lug³**.]

lug² *lug,* **lugsail** *lug'sāl, lug'sl, ns.* a square sail bent
upon a yard that hangs obliquely to the mast.—*n.*
lugg'er a small vessel with lugsails.

lug³ *lug, n.* the flap or lappet of a cap: the ear (*coll.*;
chiefly *Scot.*): an earlike projection or appendage: a
handle: a loop.—*adj.* **lugged** (*lugd*) having lugs or a
lug. [Perh. conn. with **lug¹**.]

lug⁴ *lug,* **lugworm** *lug'wûrm, ns.* a sluggish worm
found in the sand on the seashore, much used for
bait.

luge *lōōzh, lüzh, n.* a light toboggan.—*v.i* to glide on
such a sledge.—*pa.p.* and *n.* **lug'ing, luge'ing.**
[Swiss Fr.]

Luger® *lōō'gər,* (Ger.) *n.* a type of pistol.

luggage. See **lug¹.**

lugger. See **lug².**

lugubrious *lōō-gōō'bri-əs,* or *-gü', adj.* mournful:
dismal.—*adv.* **lugu'briously.** [L. *lūgubris—lūgēre*,
to mourn.]

lugworm. See **lug⁴.**

luke *lōōk,* (*dial.*) *adj.* moderately warm: tepid.—*adjs.*
luke'warm luke: half-hearted; **luke'warmish.**—*adv.*
luke'warmly.—*ns.* **luke'warmness, luke'warmth.**
[M.E. *luek, luke.*]

lull *lul, v.t.* to soothe: to compose: to quiet.—*v.i.* to
become calm: to subside.—*n.* an interval of calm: a
calming influence.—*n.* **lull'aby** (*-ə-bī*) a song to lull
children to sleep, a cradle-song.—*v t* to lull to
sleep. [Cf. Sw. *lulla.*]

lulu *lōō'lōō,* (*slang*) *n.* thing, person, that is outstandingly bad or good.

lumbago *lum-bā'gō, n.* a rheumatic affection of the
muscles or fibrous tissues in the lumbar region:—*pl*
lumbā'gos.—*adj.* **lumbaginous** (-*baj'i-nəs*). [L
lumbāgō, lumbago—*lumbus,* loin.]

lumbar *lum'bər, adj.* of or relating to the section of
the spine between the lowest rib and the pelvis.—
lumbar puncture the process of inserting a needle
into the lower part of the spinal cord to take a
specimen of cerebrospinal fluid, inject drugs, etc.
[L. *lumbus,* loin.]

lumber¹ *lum'bər, n.* furniture stored away out of use:

anything cumbersome or useless: timber, esp. sawn
or split for use (*U.S.* and *Canada*).—*v.t.* to fill with
lumber: to heap together in confusion: to cumber: to
cut the timber from.—*v.t.* to work as a lumberman.
—*ns.* **lum'berer** a lumberjack; **lum'bering** felling,
sawing and removal of timber.—**lum'ber-camp** a
lumberman's camp; **lum'berjack, lum'berman** one
employed in the felling, sawing, etc., of timber;
lum'ber-jacket a man's longish, loose-fitting, sometimes belted jacket fastened right up to the neck and
usu. in bold-patterned heavy material: a woman's
cardigan of like fastening; **lum'ber-mill** a sawmill;
lum'ber-yard a timber-yard. [Perhaps from **lumber²**.]

lumber² *lum'bər, v.i.* to move heavily and clumsily: to
rumble.—*n.* **lum'berer.** [M.E. *lomeren,* perh. a
freq. formed from *lome,* a variant of **lame¹**; but cf.
dial. Sw. *lomra,* to resound.]

lumen *lōō', lū'men, n.* a unit of luminous flux—the
light emitted in one second in a solid angle of one
steradian from a point-source of uniform intensity of
one candela· the cavity of a tubular organ (*anat.*):
the space within the cell-wall (*bot.*):—*pl.* **lu'mina,
lu'mens.**—*adjs.* **lu'menal, lu'minal** of a lumen.—*n*
lu'minance luminousness: the measure of brightness
of a surface, measured in candela/cm² of the surface
radiating normally.—*adj.* **lu'minant** giving light.—*n.*
an illuminant.—*ns.* **lu'minarism; lu'minarist** one
who paints luminously, or with skill in lights: an impressionist or plein-airist; **lu'minary** a source of
light, esp. one of the heavenly bodies: one who illus-
trates any subject or instructs mankind.—Also *adj.*
—*n.* **luminā'tion** a lighting up.—*v.i.* **luminesce'** to
show luminescence.—*n.* **luminescence** (-*es'əns*) emission of light otherwise than by incandescence and so
at a relatively cool temperature: the light so
emitted.—*adj.* **luminesc'ent.**—*ns* **lu'minist** a lu-
minarist, **luminosity** (-*os'i-ti*) luminousness: the
measure of the quantity of light actually emitted by
a star, irrespective of its distance.—*adj.* **lu'minous**
giving light: shining: lighted: clear: lucid.—*adv.*
lu'minously.—*n.* **lu'minousness.** [L. *lūmen, -inis,*
light—*lūcēre,* to shine.]

luminaire *lū-min-er', n.* the British Standards Institution term for a light fitting. [Fr.]

lumme, lummy *lum'i, interj.* (Lord) love me

lummox *lum'əks,* (*coll.*) *n.* a stupid, clumsy person.

lump *lump, n.* a shapeless mass: a protuberance: a
swelling, a feeling as if of a swelling in the throat: a
considerable quantity: the whole together: the gross:
an inert, dull, good-natured, or fair-sized person: a
lumpfish.—*v.t.* to throw into a confused mass: to
take in the gross: to include under one head: to
endure willy-nilly: to put up with: to dislike.—*v.i* to
be lumpish: to gather in a lump: to stump along.—*n.*
lumpec'tomy the surgical removal of a lump, caused
by cancer, in the breast, esp. as opposed to removal
of the entire breast.—*adv.* **lump'ily.**—*n.* **lump'iness.**
—*adjs.* **lump'ing** in a lump: heavy: bulky; **lump'ish**
like a lump: heavy: gross: dull: sullen.—*adv.* **lump'-
ishly.**—*n.* **lump'ishness.**—*adj.* **lump'y** full of lumps:
like a lump.—**lump'fish, lump'sucker** a clumsy sea-
fish (*Cyclopterus*) with pectoral fins transformed
into a sucker; **lump'-su'gar** loaf-sugar broken in
small pieces or cut in cubes; **lump sum** a single sum
of money in lieu of several.—**If you don't like it** you
may **lump it** take it as you like: but there is no
remedy; **the lump** system of using for a particular
job self-employed workmen, esp. in order to evade
tax and national insurance payments.

lumpen *lum'pən, adj.* pertaining to a dispossessed
and/or degraded section of a social class, as in
lumpen proletariat (also as one word), the very poor

lowest-class down-and-outs. stupid, boorish. [From Ger *Lumpen*, a rag.]

lunacy, lunar, lunate, lunatic, etc. See **lune**.

lunch *lunch*, *lunsh*, *n*. a slight repast between breakfast and midday meal: midday meal: snack at any time of day (*U.S.*).—*v t*. to take lunch —*v.t*. to provide lunch for.—*n*. **lunch'eon** lunch —**lunch'eon-bar** a counter where luncheons are served; **lunch'eon-basket** basket for carrying lunch, with or without cutlery, etc , **lunch'eon-meat** a type of pre-cooked meat containing preservatives, usually served cold; **lunch(-eon) voucher** a ticket or voucher given by employer to employee to be used to pay for the latter's lunch; **lunch'-hour, lunch'-time** the time of, or time set apart for, lunch. an interval allowed for lunch. [Perh altered from **lump**; or from Sp. *lonja*, slice of ham, etc.]

lune *lōōn*, *lūn*, *n*. anything in the shape of a half-moon. —*n* **lunacy** (usu *lōō'nə-si*) a form of insanity once believed to come with changes of the moon: insanity generally: extreme folly —*adj* **lunar** (usu *lōō'nər*) belonging to the moon: measured by the moon's revolutions: caused by the moon: like the moon.—*adjs* **lu'nate**, -**d** crescent-shaped; **lunatic** (*lōō'nə-tik*) affected with lunacy.—*n*. a person so affected: a madman.—*ns*. **luna'tion** a synodic month; **lunette'** a crescent-shaped ornament: a semi-circular or crescent-shaped space where a vault intersects a wall or another vault, often occupied by a window or by decoration. an arched opening in a vault: a detached bastion (*fort.*): a small horseshoe: in the R C Church, a moon-shaped case for the consecrated host; **lu'nula** a lunule: a crescent-like appearance, esp. the whitish area at the base of a nail: a Bronze Age crescent-shaped gold ornament forming part of a necklace —*adjs*. **lu'nular**; **lu'nulate**, -**d** shaped like a small crescent (*bot.*): having crescent-shaped markings.—*n* **lu'nule** anything in form like a small crescent: a geometrical figure bounded by two arcs of circles.—**lunar cycle** see **metonic cycle**; **Lunar Excursion Module (LEM, lem)** module for use in the last stage of the journey to land on the moon; **lunatic asylum** a former, now offensive, name for a mental hospital, **lunatic fringe** the more nonsensical, extreme-minded, or eccentric members of a community or of a movement. [L *lūna*, the moon—*lūcēre*, to shine.]

lung *lung*, *n*. a respiratory organ in animals that breathe atmospheric air: an open space in a town (*fig.*).—*adj*. **lunged.**—**lung'-fish** one of the Dipnoi, having lungs as well as gills. [O.E. *lungen*.]

lunge[1] *lunj*, *n*. a sudden thrust as in fencing: a forward plunge.—*v.t*. to make a lunge: to plunge forward.—*v.t*. to thrust with a lunge:—*pr.p*. **lunge'ing, lung'ing.** [Fr. *allonger*, to lengthen—L. *ad*, to, *longus*, long]

lunge[2], **longe** *lunj*, *n*. a long rope used in horse-training: training with a lunge: a training-ground for horses.—*v.t*. to train or cause to go with a lunge. [Fr. *longe*—L. *longus*, long.]

lungi *loon'gē*, *n*. a long cloth used as loincloth, sash, turban, etc. [Hind and Pers *lungī*.]

lupin, lupine *lōō'*, *lū'pin*, *n*. (a plant of) a genus (*Lupinus*) of Papilionaceae, with flowers on long spikes: its seed [L. *lupīnus*.]

lupine *lōō'*, *lū'pin*, *adj*. of a wolf: like a wolf: wolfish. [L. *lupīnus—lupus*, a wolf.]

lupus *lōō'*, *lū'pəs*. *n*. a chronic tuberculosis of the skin, often affecting the nose [L. *lupus*, a wolf]

lur. See **lure**[2].

lurch[1] *lûrch*, *n*. in various games, a situation in which one side fails to score at all. or is left far behind: a discomfiture.—**leave someone in the lurch** to leave someone in a difficult situation without help. [O Fr *lourche*]

lurch[2] *lûrch*, *n*. *v.t*. to lurk, prowl about.—*n*. **lurch'er** one who lurches: a dog with a distinct cross of greyhound, esp a cross of greyhound and collie. [Connection with **lurk** difficult; influenced apparently by foregoing.]

lurch[3] *lûrch*, *v.i* to roll or pitch suddenly forward or to one side.—*n*. a sudden roll or pitch

lurdan, lurdane, lurden *lûr'dən*, *n*. a dull, heavy, stupid or sluggish person —Also *adj* [O Fr *lourdin*, dull —*lourd*, heavy]

lure[1] *lōōr*, *lūr*, *n*. any enticement: bait decoy: a bunch of feathers used to recall a hawk.—*v.t*. to entice: decoy [O.Fr. *loerre* (Fr. *leurre*)—M H G *luoder* (Ger *Luder*), bait]

lure[2], **lur** *lōōr*, *n*. a long curved Bronze Age trumpet still used in Scandinavian countries for calling cattle, etc. [O N. *luthr*, Dan and Norw. *lur*.]

Lurex® *lū'reks*, *n* (fabric made from) a plastic-coated aluminium thread.

lurid *lōō'*, *lū'rid*, *adj* glaringly, wanly, or dingily reddish-yellow or yellowish-brown gloomily threatening: ghastly pale: ghastly: melodramatically sensational.—*adv* lu'ridly.—*n* lu'ridness. [L *lūridus*]

lurk *lûrk*, *v i* to lie in wait: to be concealed: to skulk: to go or loaf about furtively.—*n*. a prowl: a lurking-place: a swindling dodge.—*n* **lurk'er**.—*n*. and *adj*. **lurk'ing.—lurk'ing-place**. [Perh. freq from **lour**.]

luscious *lush'əs*, *adj*. sweet in a great degree: delightful: fulsome voluptuous.—*adv*. **lusc'iously**.—*n*. **lusc'iousness**. [Origin unknown; **delicious**, influenced by **lush**[1], has been suggested.]

lush[1] *lush*, *adj*. rich and juicy: luxuriant —*adv*. **lush'ly**. —*n*. **lush'ness**. [Perh. a form of **lash**[2].]

lush[2] *lush*, a drinker or drunkard [Perh from foregoing.]

lust *lust*, *n*. appetite: relish: longing eagerness to possess: sensual desire: sexual desire, now always of a degraded kind —*v.i* to desire eagerly (with *after, for*): to have carnal desire: to have depraved desires.—*n*. **lust'er**.—*adj* **lust'ful** having lust: inciting to lust. sensual —*adv* **lust'fully**.—*n*. **lust'fulness**.—*ns*. **lust'iness**.—*adv*. **lust'ily**.—*adj* **lust'y** vigorous: healthful: stout: bulky. [O.E. *lust*, pleasure]

lustrate *lus'trāt*, *v.t* to purify by sacrifice.—*n* **lustra'tion**. [L. *lūstrum*, prob —*luēre*, to wash, to purify]

lustre, *U.S.* **luster** *lus'tər*, *n*. characteristic surface appearance in reflected light: sheen: gloss: brightness: splendour: renown (*fig.*): a candlestick, vase, etc , ornamented with pendants of cut glass: a dress material with cotton warp and woollen weft, and highly finished surface: a metallic pottery glaze.—*v.t*. to impart a lustre to.—*v i* to become lustrous.—*adj* **lus'treless**.—*n*. **lus'tring**.—*adj*. **lus'trous** bright: shining: luminous.—*adv* **lus'trously**.—**lus'treware** pottery, etc with a metallic glaze. [Fr ,—L *lūstrāre*, to shine on.]

lustring *lus'tring*, *n* a glossy silk cloth.—Also **lus'trine**. **lutestring** (*lōōt'*, *lūt'string*). [Fr. *lustrine*—It *lustrino*.]

lusty. See **lust**.

lute[1] *lōōt*, or *lūt*, *n*. an old stringed instrument shaped like half a pear.—*ns*. **lut'anist, lut'enist, lut'er, lut'ist** player on lute, **luthier** (*lūt'i-ər*) maker of lutes, etc.—**lute'string** string of lute (see also **lustring**). [O.Fr *lut* (Fr. *luth*)—from Ar. *al*, the, *'ûd*, wood, the lute.]

lute[2] *lōōt*, *lūt*, *n*. clay, cement or other material used as a protective covering, an airtight stopping, or the like a rubber packing-ring for a jar —*v.t*. to close or coat with lute —*n* **lut'ing**. [L *lutum*, mud—*luēre*, to wash.]

luteal. See **lutein**.

lutecium. Same as **lutetium**.

lutein _lōōt'ē-in_, _lūt'_, _n._ a yellow colouring-matter in yolk of egg.—_adj._ **luteal** (_lōō'ti-əl_) pertaining to (the formation of) the corpus luteum.—_n._ **luteinisā'tion**, **-z-** the process of stimulation to the ovary, whereby ovulation occurs and a corpus luteum is formed.—_v.t._ and _v.i._ **lu'teinise**, **-ize**.—**luteinising hormone** a hormone that, in females, stimulates ovulation and the formation of the corpus luteum (q.v.), and in males, the production of androgen. [L. _lūteus_, yellow, _lūteum_, egg-yolk.]

lutenist. See lute[1].

lutestring. See lustring, lute.

lutetium _lōō-tē'shi-əm_, _lū-_, _n._ metallic element (Lu; at. numb. 71) first separated from ytterbium by Georges Urbain, a Parisian. [L. _Lutetia_, Paris.]

Lutheran _lōō'thər-ən_, _adj._ pertaining to Martin _Luther_, the great German Protestant reformer (1483-1546), or to his doctrines.—_n._ a follower of Luther.—_ns._ **Lu'ther(an)ism**; **Lu'therist**.

luthier. See lute[1].

Lutine bell _lōō-tēn'_, _lōō'_, _bel_, a bell recovered from the frigate _Lutine_, and rung at Lloyd's of London before certain important announcements.

lutz _lōōts_, _n._ in figure-skating, a jump (with rotation) from the back outer edge of one skate to the back outer edge of the other. [Poss. Gustave _Lutzsi_ of Switzerland, born 1898, the first exponent.]

lux _luks_, _n._ a unit of illumination, one lumen per square metre:—_pl._ **lux**, **luxes**, **luces** (_lōō'sēs_).—**lux'meter** instrument for measuring illumination. [L. _lūx_, light.]

luxate _luks'āt_, _v.t._ to put out of joint: to displace.—_n._ **luxā'tion** a dislocation. [L. _luxāre_, _-ātum_—_luxus_—Gr. _loxos_, slanting.]

luxe. See deluxe.

luxmeter. See lux.

luxury _luk'shə-ri_, also _lug'zhə-ri_, _n._ abundant provision of means of ease and pleasure: indulgence, esp. in costly pleasures: anything delightful, often expensive, but not necessary: a dainty.—_adj._ relating to or providing luxury.—_ns._ **luxuriance** (_lug-zhōō'ri-əns_, _-zū'_, _-zhū'_, or _luk-_, etc.), **luxu'riancy** growth in rich abundance or excess: exuberance: overgrowth: rankness.—_adj._ **luxu'riant** exuberant in growth: overabundant: profuse: erroneously, for luxurious.—_adv._ **luxu'riantly**.—_v.i._ **luxu'riate** to be luxuriant (_obs._): to live luxuriously: to enjoy luxury: to enjoy, or revel in, free indulgence.—_n._ **luxuriā'tion**.—_adj._ **luxu'rious** of luxury: given to luxury: ministering to luxury: furnished with luxuries: softening by pleasure —_adv._ **luxu'riously**.—_ns._ **luxu'riousness**. [O.Fr. _luxurie_—L. _luxuria_, luxury—_luxus_, excess.]

lycanthropy _lī-_, _li-kan'thrə-pi_, _n._ power of changing oneself into a wolf: a kind of madness, in which the patient fancies himself to be a wolf.—_ns._ **lycanthrope** (_lī'kan-thrōp_, or _-kan'_), **lycan'thropist** a wolf-man or werewolf: one affected with lycanthropy.—_adj._ **lycanthropic** (_-throp'_). [Gr. _lykos_, a wolf, _anthrōpos_, a man.]

lycée _lē'sā_, _n._ a state secondary school in France. [Fr , lyceum.]

Lyceum _lī-sē'əm_, _n._ a gymnasium and grove beside the temple of Apollo at Athens, in whose walks Aristotle taught: (without _cap._) a college: (without _cap._) a place or building devoted to literary studies, lectures, etc.: —_pl._ **lyce'ums**. [L. _Lȳcēum_—Gr. _Lykeion_—_Lykeios_, an epithet of Apollo (perh. wolf-slayer, perhaps the Lycian).]

lychee, litchi, lichee, lichi _lī'chē_, _lē'chē_, **leechee** _lē'chē_, _ns._ a Chinese fruit, a nut or berry with a fleshy aril: the tree (_Litchi chineasis_; fam. Sapindaceae) that bears it. [Chin. _li-chi_.]

lychgate. Same as lichgate.

Lydian _lid'i-ən_, _adj._ pertaining to _Lydia_ in Asia Minor: of music, soft and slow, luxurious and effeminate.—_n._ native of Lydia: the language of ancient Lydia, apparently akin to Hittite. [Gr. _Lȳdiā_, Lydia.]

lye _lī_, _n._ a strong alkaline solution: a liquid used for washing: a solution got by leaching. [O.E. _lēah_, _lēag_]

lying. See lie[1,2].

lykewake _līk'wāk_, **lyke'walk**, **like-** _-wok_, (_Scot._; _Eng._ **lichwake** _lich'_) _ns._ a watch over the dead, often with merrymaking. [O.E. _līc_, and **wake**.]

Lymeswold® _līmz'wōld_, _n._ a kind of mild, blue, full-fat soft cheese.

lymph _limf_, _n._ pure water: a colourless or faintly yellowish fluid collected into the lymphatic vessels from the tissues in animal bodies, of a rather saltish taste, and with an alkaline reaction: a vaccine.—_adj._ **lymphangial** (_-anj'əl_; Gr. _angeion_, vessel) pertaining to the lymphatic vessels.—_n._ **lymphangitis** (_-an-jī'tis_) inflammation of a lymphatic vessel.—_adj._ **lymphat'ic** pertaining to lymph: of a temperament or bodily habit once supposed to result from excess of lymph: disposed to sluggishness and flabbiness.—_n._ a vessel that conveys lymph.—_adv._ **lymphat'ically**.—_ns._ **lymph'ocyte** (_-ō-sīt_) a kind of leucocyte formed in the lymph nodes and spleen; **lymphog'raphy** radiography of the lymph glands, recorded on a **lymph'ogram**; **lymphō'ma** a tumour consisting of lymphoid tissue.— **lymphatic system** the network of vessels that conveys lymph to the venous system; **lymph gland, node** any of the small masses of tissue sited along the lymphatic vessels, in which lymph is purified, and lymphocytes are formed. [L. _lympha_, water; _lymphāticus_, mad.]

lynch _linch_, _linsh_, _v.t._ to judge and put to death without the usual forms of law.—**lynch'-law**. [Captain William _Lynch_ of Virginia.]

lynchpin. A variant of **linchpin**.

lynx _lingks_, _n._ an animal of the cat family, high at the haunches, with short tail and tufted ears:—_pl._ **lynx'es**: (with _cap._) the genus to which this cat belongs.—_adj._ **lynx'-eyed**. [L., —Gr. _lynx_, _lynkos_.]

Lyon _lī'ən_, _n._ the chief herald of Scotland.—Also **Lord Lyon, Lyon King-of-arms** (or **-at-arms**).—**Lyon Court** the court over which he presides, having jurisdiction in questions of coat-armour and precedency. [From the heraldic _lion_ of Scotland.]

lyophil, lyophile _lī'ō-fil_, _-fil_, **lyophilic** _-fil'ik_, _adjs._ of a colloid, readily dispersed in a suitable medium.— _n._ **lyophilisā'tion**, **-z-** freeze-drying.—_v.t._ **lyoph'ilise**, **-ize** to dry by freezing.—_adjs._ **ly'ophobe** (_-fōb_), **lyophobic** (_-fob'_) of a colloid, not readily dispersed. [Gr. _lȳe_, separation, _phileein_, to love, _phobeein_, to fear.]

lyre _līr_, _n._ a musical instrument like the harp, anciently used as an accompaniment to poetry—a convex sound-chest with a pair of curved arms connected by a cross-bar, from which the strings were stretched over a bridge to a tailpiece.—_adjs._ **ly'rate**, **-d** lyre-shaped: having the terminal lobe much larger than the lateral ones (_bot._).—_adj._ **lyric** (_lir'_) pertaining to the lyre: fitted to be sung to the lyre: of poems or their authors, expressing individual or private emotions.—_n._ a lyric poem: a song: (in _pl._) the words of a popular song.— _adj._ **lyrical** (_lir'_) lyric: song-like: expressive, imaginative: effusive.—_adv._ **lyr'ically**.—_ns._ **lyricism** (_lir'i-sizm_) a lyrical expression: lyrical quality.—_adj._ **lyriform** (_lī'_) shaped like a lyre.—_n._ **lyr'ism** (_lir'_, _lir'_) lyricism: singing; **lyrist** (_lir'_ or _lir'_) a player on the lyre or harp: (_lir'_) a lyric poet.—**lyre'-bird** an Australian passerine bird about the size of a pheasant, having the 16 tail-feathers of the male arranged in the form of a lyre —**wax lyrical** to grow expressive or effusive in praise of something. [L. _lyra_—Gr. _lyrā_.]

lysis *lī'sis, n.* the gradual abatement of a disease, as distinguished from *crisis*: breaking down as of a cell (*biol.*): the action of a lysin.—*v.t.* **lyse** (*līz*) to cause to undergo lysis.—**-lysis** (*-lis'is*) in composition, the action of breaking down, or dividing into parts.— **-lyse, -lyze** (*-līz*) verb combining form.—**-lyst** (*-list*), **-lyte** (*-līt*) noun combining forms.—**-lytic, -lytical** (*-lit'*) adjectival combining forms.—**lysergic acid** (*lī-sûr'jik*) a substance, $C_{16}H_{16}O_2N_2$, got from ergot, causing (in the form of lysergic acid diethylamide— **LSD** or **ly'sergide**) a schizophrenic condition, with hallucinations and thought processes outside the normal range. [Gr. *lysis*, dissolution—*lyein*, to loose.]

maestro *mi'strō, mä-es'trō, n.* a master, esp. an eminent musical composer or conductor:—*pl.* **maestros** (*mi'strōz*), **maestri** (*mä-es'trē*). [It.]

Mae West *mā west,* an airman's pneumatic life-jacket. [From its supposed resemblance, when inflated, to the figure of an American actress of that name.]

Mafia *mä'fē-ə, n.* a spirit of opposition to the law in Sicily, hence a preference for private and unofficial rather than legal justice: a secret criminal society originating in Sicily, controlling many illegal activities, e g., gambling, narcotics, etc., in many parts of the world, and particularly active in the U.S. —Also called **Cosa Nostra**.—*n.* **Mafioso** (*-fē-ō'sō, -zō*) a member of the Mafia (also without *cap.*):—*pl.* **Mafiosi** (*-sē, -zē*) [Sicilian Italian *mafia.*]

ma foi *ma fwa,* (Fr.) my goodness (*lit.* upon my faith).

mag. Short for **magazine** (periodical publication) (*coll.*).

magazine *mag-ə-zēn', also mag', n.* a storehouse: a place for military stores: a ship's powder-room: a compartment in a rifle for holding extra cartridges: a periodical publication or broadcast containing articles, stories, etc., by various people.—**magazine'-gun, -rifle** one from which a succession of shots can be fired without reloading. [Fr. *magasin*—It. *magazzino*—A1. *makhāzin,* pl. of *makhzan,* a store-house.]

Magdalen, Magdalene *mag'də-lən, -lēn* (in the names of Oxford and Cambridge colleges, *môd'lın*) *ns* (without *cap.*) a repentant prostitute: an institution for receiving such persons (abbrev. for *Magdalene hospital, asylum*). [From Mary *Magdalene,* i.e (Gr.) *Magdalēnē,* of Magdala (Luke viii. 2), on the assumption that she was the woman of Luke vii. 37–50.]

Magdeburg hemispheres *mag'de-bûrg hem'i-sfērz,* two hemispherical cups held together by atmospheric pressure when the air is pumped out from between them. [Invented at *Magdeburg* in Germany]

mage *māj.* See **Magus.**

Magellanic clouds *mag-el-an'ık, or maj-, klowdz,* two galaxies in the southern hemisphere, appearing to the naked eye like detached portions of the Milky Way, the nearest galaxies to the earth.

magenta *mə-jen'tə, n.* the dyestuff fuchsine: its colour, a reddish purple.—*adj.* reddish purple. [From its discovery about the time of the battle of *Magenta* in North Italy, 1859.]

maggot *mag'ət, n.* a legless grub, esp. of a fly.—*adj.* **[maggo]ty** full of maggots.—*n.* **maggotorium** (*-tō', [-ri-əm] w]here** maggots are bred for sale to fisher-**[men].** [oss. a modification of M E. *maddok, mathek,* dim., see **mawk.**]

Magi, Magian. See **Magus.**

magic *maj'ik, n.* the art of producing marvellous results by compelling the aid of spirits, or by using the secret forces of nature, such as the power supposed to reside in certain objects as 'givers of life': enchantment: sorcery: art of producing illusions by legerdemain: a secret or mysterious power over the imagination or will.—*v.t.* to affect by, or as if by, magic:—*pr.p.* **mag'icking**; *pa.t.* and *pa.p.* **mag'icked**.—*adjs.* **mag'ic** pertaining to, used in, or done by, magic: causing wonderful or startling results: marvellous. exciting (*coll.*); **mag'ical** pertaining to magic: wonderful, enchanting.—*adv.* **mag'ically**.—*n.* **magician** (*mə-jish'ən*) one skilled in magic: a wizard: an enchanter: a wonder-worker.—**magic bullet** a drug. etc. which is capable of destroying bacteria, cancer cells, etc. without adversely affecting the host; **magic carpet** one that, in fairy stories, can transport people magically through the air; **magic eye** a miniature cathode ray tube in a radio receiver which helps in tuning the receiver by indicating, by means of varying areas

of luminescence and shadow, the accuracy of the tuning; **magic lantern** an apparatus for projecting pictures on slides upon a screen; **magic square** a square filled with rows of figures so arranged that the sums of all the rows will be the same, perpendicularly, horizontally or diagonally—as the square formed from the three rows 2, 7, 6; 9, 5, 1; 4, 3, 8; **magic circles, cubes, cylinders, spheres,** are similarly arranged.— **black magic** the black art, magic by means of evil spirits; **natural magic** the art of working wonders by a superior knowledge of the powers of nature power of investing a work of art with an atmosphere of imagination: legerdemain; **sympathetic magic** magic aiming at the production of effects by mimicry, as bringing rain by libations, injuring a person by melting his image or sticking pins in it; **white magic** magic without the aid of the devil. [Gr *magikē* (*technē*), magic (art). See **Magus.**]

magilp, megilp *mə-gilp', n.* a vehicle used by oil-painters, consisting of linseed-oil and mastic varnish.

magister *mə-jis'tər, n.* one licensed to teach in a mediaeval university: still used in the degree titles of *Magister Artium,* etc.—*adj.* **magisterial** (*maj-is-tē'ri-al*) pertaining or suitable to, or in the manner of, a teacher, master artist, or magistrate: of the rank of a magistrate; authoritative: dictatorial: of a magistery. —*adv.* **magiste'rially**.—*ns* **magiste'rialness; mag'istracy** (*-trə-si*) the office or dignity of a magistrate: a body of magistrates.—*adj.* **magistral** (*mə-jis'tral,* or *maj'is-*) of or pertaining to a master masterly: authoritative: specially prescribed for a particular case as a medicine: effectual.—*n* **mag'istrate** one who has power of putting the law in force, esp a justice of the peace, a provost, or a bailie.—*adjs.* **magistratic** (*-trat'ik*), **-al**.—*n.* **mag'istrature**.— **Magister Artium** (*mə-jis'tər ä1'shi-əm*) Master of Arts. [L. *magister,* master.]

Maglemosian *mag-li-mō'zi-ən,* (*archaeol*) *adj.* of a culture represented by finds at *Muglemose* in Denmark, transitional between Palaeolithic and Neolithic.

magma *mag'mə, n.* a pasty or doughy mass: molten or pasty rock material: a glassy base of a rock:—*pl* **mag'mata** (*-mə-tə*), **mag'mas.**—*adj* **magmatic** (*-mat'ik*). [Gr. *magma, -atos,* a thick unguent]

Magna Carta (**Charta**) *mag'nə kar'tə,* the Great Charter obtained from King John, 1215, the basis of English political and personal liberty: any document establishing rights. [L.]

magna cum laude *mag'nə kum lō'dē, mag'nä kōōm low'de,* (L.) with great distinction (*laus, laudis,* praise).

magnanimity *mag-nə-nim'i-ti, n.* greatness of soul that quality of mind which raises a person above all that is mean or unjust: generosity.—*adj.* **magnanimous** (*-nan'*)—*adv* **magnan'imously.** [L. *magnanimitās*—*magnus,* great, *animus,* mind.]

magnate *mag'nāt, -nit, n.* a noble: a man of rank or wealth, or of power. [L. *magnās, -ātis*—*magnus,* great.]

magnesium *mag-nē'z(h)i-əm, -z(h)yəm, -shi-əm. -shyəm, n* a metallic element (symbol Mg, at. numb. 12) of a bright, silver-white colour, burning with a dazzling white light.—*n.* **magne'sia** a light white powder, oxide of magnesium: basic magnesium carbonate, used as a medicine.—*adj.* **magne'sian** belonging to, containing, or resembling magnesia.—*n.* **magnesite** (*mag'nəs-īt*) native magnesium carbonate. [From *Magnesia,* in Thessaly.]

magnet *mag'nit, n.* the lodestone (**natural magnet**): a bar or piece of steel, etc., to which the properties of the lodestone have been imparted: anything or anyone that attracts (*fig*).—*adjs.* **magnetic** (*mag-*

net'ik), **-al** pertaining to the magnet: having, or capable of acquiring, the properties of the magnet: attractive: strongly affecting others by personality: hypnotic.—*adv.* **magnet'ically.**—*n.* **magnetician** (*-ish'ən*) one versed in magnetism.—*n.pl.* or *sing.* **magnet'ics** the science of magnetism.—*adj.* **magnetis'able, -z-.**—*n.* **magnetisā'tion, -z-.**—*v.t.* **mag'-netise, -ize** to render magnetic: to attract as if by a magnet: to hypnotise.—*ns.* **mag'netiser, -z-; mag'-netism** the cause of the attractive power of the magnet: the phenomena connected with magnets: the science which treats of the properties of the magnet: attraction: influence of personality; **mag'netite** magnetic iron ore (Fe_3O_4), called lodestone when polar, **magneto** (*mag-nē'tō*; for *magneto-electric machine*) a small generator with permanent magnet, used for ignition in an internal-combustion engine, etc.:—*pl.* **magnē'tos.**—**magneto-** in composition, magnetic pertaining to magnetism: magneto-electric —*adjs.* **magnē'to-elec'tric, -al** pertaining to magneto-electricity.—*ns.* **magnē'to-electric'ity** electricity produced by the action of magnets: the science thereof; **magnē'tograph** an instrument for recording the variations of the magnetic elements; **magnetometer** (*mag-ni-tom'i-tər*) an instrument for measuring the strength or direction of a magnetic field, esp the earth's.—*adj.* **magnētomō'tive** producing a magnetic flux —*ns.* **magnet'osphere** the region surrounding the earth or other body corresponding to its magnetic field; **mag'netron** a vacuum tube combined with a magnetic field to deflect electrons.—**animal magnetism** Mesmer's name for hypnotism: power to hypnotise: sexual power of attraction due entirely to physical attributes, **artificial magnet** a magnet made by rubbing with other magnets; **bar magnet** a magnet in the form of a bar, **horse-shoe magnet** a magnet bent like a horse-shoe, **magnetic battery** several magnets placed with their like poles together, so as to act with great force; **magnetic disc** (*comput.*) a disc, disc file; **magnetic drum** (*comput.*) a storage device consisting of a rotating cylinder with a magnetic coating; **magnetic equator** the line round the earth where the magnetic needle remains horizontal; **magnetic field** the space over which magnetic force is felt; **magnetic flux** the surface integral of the product of the permeability of the medium and the magnetic field intensity perpendicular to the surface; **magnetic flux density** the product of the field intensity and the permeability of the medium; **magnetic ink** ink with magnetic quality used, e.g. in printing cheques that are to be sorted by machine; **magnetic mine** a mine sunk to the sea-bottom, detonated by a pivoted magnetic needle when a ship approaches; **magnetic needle** the light bar in the mariner's compass which, because it is magnetised, points always to the north; **magnetic north** the direction indicated by the magnetic needle; **magnetic poles** two nearly opposite points on the earth's surface, where the dip of the needle is 90°; **magnetic storm** a disturbance in the magnetism of the earth; **magnetic tape** flexible plastic tape, coated on one side with magnetic material, used to register for later reproduction television images, or sound, or computer data, **permanent magnet** a magnet that keeps its magnetism after the force which magnetised it has been removed; **personal magnetism** power of a personality to make itself felt and to exercise influence, **terrestrial magnetism** the magnetic properties possessed by the earth as a whole [Through O Fr. or L., from Gr *magnētis* (*lithos*), Magnesian (stone), from *Mag-nēsiā*, in Lydia or Thessaly.]

magnifiable. See **magnify.**

Magnificat *mag-nif'i-kat*, *n.* the song of the Virgin Mary, Luke i 46–55, beginning in the Vulgate with this word. [L. '(my soul) doth magnify', 3rd pers. sing. pres. ind. of *magnificāre.*]

magnification. See **magnify.**

magnificence *mag-nif'i-səns*, *n.* the quality of being magnificent.—*adj.* **magnif'icent** great in deeds or in show. noble: pompous: displaying greatness of size or extent: very fine (*coll.*)—*adv.* **magnif'icently.** [L. *magnificēns, -entis*, lit. doing great things.]

magnify *mag'ni-fī*, *v.t.* to make great or greater: to enlarge: to cause to appear greater: to exaggerate: to praise highly:—*pr p.* **mag'nifying;** *pa.t* and *pa.p.* **mag'nified.**—*adj.* **mag'nifiable** that may be magnified.—*ns.* **magnification** (*-fi-kā'shən*) act or power of magnifying: state of being magnified: enlarged appearance or state or copy: extolling; **mag'nifier** (*-fī-ər*) one who, or that which, magnifies or enlarges, esp. a pocket-lens (**magnifying glass**) one who extols [L. *magnificāre—magnus*, great, *facēre*, to make.]

magniloquent *mag-nil'ə-kwənt*, *adj.* speaking in a grand or pompous style: bombastic —*n.* **magnil'o-quence.**—*adv.* **magnil'oquently.** [L. *magnus*, great, *loquēns, -entis*, pr.p. of *loquī*, to speak.]

magnitude *mag'ni-tūd*, *n* greatness: size: extent importance: a measure of the intensity of a star's brightness.—**of the first magnitude** (*astron.*) (of a star) of the first degree of brightness: of a very important, significant or catastrophic kind (*fig.*). [L. *magnitūdō—magnus.*]

Magnolia *mag-nōl'i-ə*, or *yə*, *n* an American and Asiatic genus of trees with beautiful foliage, and large solitary flowers: (without *cap.*) any tree of this genus.—*adj.* **magnolia'ceous.** [From Pierre *Magnol* (1638–1715), a Montpellier botanist]

magnum *mag'nəm*, *n.* a two-quart bottle or vessel: as a bottle-size of champagne or other wine, the equivalent of two ordinary bottles, containing usu. 1½ litres:—*pl.* **mag'nums.** [L. *magnum* (neut), big.]

magnum opus *mag'nəm ōp'əs, mag'nŏŏm op'ŏŏs*, (L.) a great work, esp. of literature or learning, esp a writer's greatest achievement or the culmination of his efforts

magpie *mag'pī*, *n.* the pie (*Pica rustica*), a black-and-white chattering bird allied to the crow: extended to other black-and-white or pied birds (in Australia, a piping crow): a chattering person: one who hoards or steals trifles (*fig*) [*Mag*, shortened form of *Margaret*, and **pie'.**]

maguey *mag'wā, ma-gā'i*, *n.* agave [Sp.]

Magus *mā'gəs*, *n.* ancient Persian priest, a magician· (without *cap*) a magician: one of the wise men from the East who brought gifts to the infant Christ'—*pl.* **Mā'gi** (*-jī*) —*n.* **mage** (*māj*) a magus or sorcerer.—*adj* **Mā'gian** pertaining to the Magi or to a sorcerer —*n.* a magus. a sorcerer. [L ,—Gr *magos*—O.Pers *magus*]

Magyar *mag'yar*, *n.* one of the prevailing people of Hungary, the speech of Hungary.—*adj.* (without *cap.*) of a garment, cut with the sleeves in a piece with the rest. [Magyar]

maharaja, maharajah *ma-ha-ra'ja, mə-ha-ra'jə, n* formerly, a great Indian prince, esp. a ruler of a state —*fem.* **maharani, maharanee** (*-ra'nē*). [Hind., from Sans *mahat*, great, *rājan*, king, *rānī*, queen.]

maharishi *ma-ha-rē'shi*, *n* a leading instructor in the Hindu faith [Sans. *mahat*, great, *rishi*, sage]

mahatma *mə-hat'ma, -hat'mə*, *n.* one skilled in mysteries or religious secrets. an adept. ə wise and holy leader [Sans *mahātman*, high-souled]

Mahdi *ma'dē*, *n.* the great leader of the faithful Muslims, who is to appear in the last days: a title of various insurrectionary leaders, esp. in the Sudan. [Ar *mahdīy*]

mah-jongg *mä-jong'*, *n.* an old Chinese table game for four, played with small painted bricks or 'tiles'. Also **mah-jong**. [Chin.]

mahlstick. See **maulstick**.

mahogany *ma-hog'a-ni*, *n.* a tropical American tree (*Swietenia mahogoni*): its timber, valued for furniture-making: the colour of the timber, a dark reddish brown: a dining-table (*coll.*).

Mahommedan, Mahometan. See **Mohammedan**.

mahout *mä-howt'*, *n.* the keeper and driver of an elephant. [Hind. *mahâut, mahâwat*.]

mahseer, mahsir *mä'sēr*, *n.* a large fish found in the rivers of Northern India. [Hind. *mahâsir*.]

maid *mäd*, *n.* an unmarried woman, esp. one who is young: a virgin: a female servant: a young skate.—**maid'-servant** a female servant.—**maid-of-all-work** a maid who does general housework; **maid of honour** see **honour**; **old maid** a woman left unmarried: a card game. [Shortened from **maiden**.]

maiden *mäd'n*, *n.* a maid: a horse that has never won a race.—*adj.* unmarried: virgin: female: fresh: new: unused: in the original or initial state: that has never been captured, climbed, trodden, penetrated, pruned, etc.: that has never won a race (of a horse): first.—*ns.* **maid'enhead** virginity: the hymen; **maid'enhood** the state or time of being a maiden: **maidenhead**.—*adjs.* **maid'enish** (*deprecatorily*) like a maiden; **maid'enlike**.—Also *adv.*—*n.* **maid'enliness**.—*adj.* **maid'enly** maidenlike: becoming a maiden: gentle: modest.—Also *adv.*—**maid'enhair** a fern (*Adiantum*), with fine footstalks; **maiden name** the family name of a married woman before her marriage; **maiden over** in cricket, an over in which no runs are made; **maiden speech** one's first speech, esp. in Parliament; **maiden stakes** in horse-racing, the prize in a race between horses that have not won before the date of entry; **maiden voyage** a first voyage. [O.E *mægden*.]

maieutic *mī-* or *mä-ūt'ik*, *adj.* helping birth, esp. of thoughts.—*n.sing.* **maieut'ics** the Socratic art. [Gr *maieutikos—maia*, good woman, a midwife.]

maigre *mä'gər*, *meg'r'*, *adj.* made without flesh: belonging to a fast-day or to a fast.—*n.* (also **meagre** *mē'gər*) a large Mediterranean fish (*Sciaena aquila*) noted for the sound it emits. [Fr. *maigre*, lean—L. *macer*.]

mail[1] *mäl*, *n.* defensive armour for the body, formed of steel rings or network: armour generally: protective covering of an animal.—*v.t.* to clothe in mail.—*adj.* **mailed** protected by mail.—*adj.* **mail'-clad** clad with a coat of mail.—**mailed fist** physical force. [Fr. *maille*—L. *macula*, a spot or a mesh.]

mail[2] *mäl*, *n.* a bag for the conveyance of letters, etc.: the contents of such a bag: post (esp. for long distances): correspondence: a batch of letters, etc.: the person or the carriage by which the mail is conveyed. —*v.t.* to post: to send by post.—*adj.* **mail'able** capable of being sent by mail.—**mail'-bag** a bag in which letters are carried; **mail'-boat** a boat that carries the public mails; **mail'-box** (*U.S.*) a letter-box; **mail'-coach, -car, -carriage, -drag, -gig, -van** a conveyance that carries the public mails; **mailing list** a list of the names and addresses of those to whom advertising material, information, etc. is to be posted; **mail'man** also **mail'-carrier** a postman; **mail order** an order for goods to be sent by post (also *adj.* as in *mail-order firm, house*); **mail'-plane**, **mail'-train** one that carries the public mails. [O.Fr. *male*, a trunk, a mail—O.H.G. *malha, malaha*, a sack.]

maillot *mä-yō*, *n.* tights for ballet-dancer, etc.: one-piece close-fitting swimsuit. [Fr., *lit.* swaddling-clothes.]

maim *mäm*, *v.t.* to disable: to mutilate: to lame or cripple: to render defective.—*n.* serious bodily injury: a lameness.—*adj.* **maimed**.—*ns.* **maimedness** (*mämd', mä'mid-nis*); **maiming**. [O.Fr. *mahaing*.]

main *män*, *n.* might: strength: the principal part: the mainland: the high sea: a principal pipe or conductor in a branching system distributing water, gas, electricity, etc.: (*pl.*) the water, gas or electricity supply available through such a system: that which is essential: the most part.—*adj.* strong (*Milt.*): sheer (as in *main force*): great: extensive: important: chief, principal: first in importance or extent: leading: general.—*adv.* **main'ly** chiefly, principally.—**main'-brace** the brace attached to the mainyard (see **splice**); **main clause** (*gram.*) a principal clause; **main'-course** mainsail; **main'-deck** the principal deck of a ship; **main'door** a door giving independent access to a house, distinguished from one opening upon a common passage; **main'frame** the central processing unit and storage unit of a computer.—*adj.* (of a computer) of the large, powerful type rather than the small-scale kind.—**main'land** (*-land, -land*) the principal or larger land, as opposed to neighbouring islands, **main'lander**; **main line** a railway line between important centres: an important vein (*slang*).—*adj.* **main'line**.—*v.i.* (*slang*) to take narcotics intravenously.—**main'liner**; **main'lining**; **main'mast** (*-mast, -mäst*) the principal mast, usually second from the prow; **main'sail** (*-sl, -sâl*) the principal sail, generally attached to the mainmast; **main'spring** the spring that gives motion to any piece of machinery, esp. that of a watch or a clock: principal motive, motivating influence (*fig.*); **main'stay** a rope stretching forward and down from the top of the mainmast: chief support; **main store** the memory or store (q.v.) of a computer; **main stream** a river with tributaries: the chief direction or trend in any historical development, including that of an art.—*adj.* **main'stream** pertaining to the main stream (*lit.* and *fig.*): of swing, coming in the line of development between early and modern (*jazz*): in accordance with what is normal or standard.—*v.t.* (*education*) to integrate (handicapped children) into classes of normal children.—**main'yard** the lower yard on the mainmast.—**in the main** for the most part: on the whole; **might and main** utmost strength. [Partly O.E. *mægen*, strength, partly O.N. *meginn*, strong.]

maintain *män-tän'*, *mən-*, *men-*, *v t.* to observe or practise: to keep in existence or in any state: to preserve from capture, loss, or deterioration: to uphold: to carry on: to keep up: to support: to make good: to support by argument: to affirm: to defend: to support in an action in which one is not oneself concerned (*law*).—*adjs.* **maintain'able**; **maintained'** financially supported, e.g. (of a school, etc.) from public funds. —*ns.* **maintain'er**; **maintenance** (*män'tən-əns*) the act of maintaining, supporting, or defending: continuance: the means of support: defence, protection. —**main'tenance-man** one keeping machines, etc., in working order. [Fr. *maintenir*—L. *manû* (abl.) *tenêre*, to hold in the hand.]

maiolica. See **majolica**.

maisonnette, maisonette *mez-on-et'*, *n.* a small house or flat. [Fr. *maisonnette*.]

maître d'hôtel *metr' dō-tel*, a house-steward, major domo: manager or head-waiter of a hotel.

maize *mäz*, *n.* a staple cereal (*Zea mays*) in America, etc., with large ears (corncobs)—called also *Indian corn*, or *mealies*: the yellow colour of maize.—Also *adj.* [Sp. *maiz*—from Haitian.]

majesty *maj'is-ti*, *n.* greatness and glory of God grandeur: dignity: elevation of manner or style: royal state: a title of monarchs (*His, Her, Your, Majesty*;

Their, Your, Majesties): a representation of God (sometimes Christ) enthroned.—*adjs.* **majestic** (*mə-jes'tik*), **-al** having or exhibiting majesty: stately: sublime.—*adv.* **majes'tically** in a majestic manner. [Fr. *majesté*—L. *mājestās, -ātis—mājor, mājus,* compar. of *magnus,* great.]

Majlis *māj-lis', n.* the Iranian parliament: in various Middle-Eastern countries, (appeal to) an assembly. —Also **Mejlis'**. [Pers. *majlis.*]

majolica *mə-jol'i-kə,* or -*yol', * **maiolica** *yol', ns.* glazed or enamelled earthenware. [Perh. from *Majorca.*]

major *mā'jər, adj.* greater in number, quantity, size, value, importance, dignity: in boys' schools, senior: greater (than minor) by a semitone (*mus.*): involving a major third (see below; *mus.*).—*n.* a person of full legal age (in U.K., before 1970, 21 years; from 1970, 18 years): an officer in rank between a captain and lieutenant-colonel: anything that is major opposed to minor: a student's special subject (*U.S.*).—*v.i.* to specialise in a particular subject at college (with *in*; *U.S.*): to specialise in a particular product, etc. (with *in, on*).—*v.i.* to channel or concentrate (one's activities, efforts, etc.) in a particular direction.—*ns.* **majorette'** a member of a group of girls who march in parades, etc., wearing a decorative approximation to military uniform, sometimes twirling batons, playing instruments, etc.; **majority** (*mə-jor'i-ti*) pre-eminence: the greater number: the difference between the greater and the less number: full age (see **major** above).—Also *adj.*—*n.* **mā'jorship.**—**ma'jor-dō'mō** an official who has the general management in a large household: a general steward; **ma'jor-gen'eral** an officer in the army next in rank below a lieutenant-general; **majority verdict** the verdict reached by the majority in a jury, as distinct from a unanimous verdict; **major key, major, scale** one with its third a major third above the tonic; **major orders** in the R.C. Church, the higher degrees of holy orders, i.e. bishop, priest and deacon; **major premise** (*log.*) that in which the major term occurs; **major suit** (*bridge*) spades or hearts, valued more highly than diamonds or clubs; **major term** the term which is the predicate of the conclusion; **major third** (*mus.*) an interval of four semitones.—**go over to,** or **join, the majority** to die. [L. *mājor,* comp. of *magnus.*]

majuscule *mə-jus'kūl,* or *maj'əs-kūl,* (*palaeog.*) *n.* a large letter whether capital or uncial.—Also *adj.*— *adj.* **majus'cular.** [L. (*littera*) *mājuscula,* somewhat larger (letter).]

make *māk, v.t.* to fashion, frame, construct, compose, or form: to create: to bring into being: to produce: to conclude, contract: to bring about: to perform: to force: to cause: to result in: to cause to be: to convert or turn: to appoint: to render: to represent as doing or being: to reckon: to get as result or solution: to occasion: to bring into any state or condition: to establish: to prepare: to obtain, gain earn: to score: to constitute: to amount to: to count for: to turn out: to be capable of turning or developing into or serving as: to reach, succeed in reaching: to accomplish, achieve: to attempt, offer, or start: to be occupied with: to do: to cause, assure, success of: to persuade (a woman) to have sexual intercourse with one (*slang*): to have sexual intercourse with (*slang*).—*v.i.* to behave (as if), esp. in order to deceive: to proceed: to tend:— *pr.p.* **māk'ing;** *pa.t.* and *pa.p.* **māde.**—*n.* form or shape: structure, texture: build: formation: manufacture: brand: type: making: quantity made.—*adj.* **mak(e)'able.**—*ns.* **māk'er** one who makes: (*cap.*) the Creator; **māk'ing** the act of forming (often in composition, as in *bread-making, cabinetmaking*): structure: form: (in *pl.*) gains: (in *pl.*) that from which something can be made.—*v.i.* **make'-believe** to pre-

tend, feign: to play at believing.—*n.* feigning (also **make'-belief**).—*adj.* feigned.—*adj.* **make'-do** make-shift; **make'-ready** preparation of a letterpress sheet for printing, so as to obtain evenness of impression; **make'shift** a temporary expedient or substitute.— *adj.* of the nature of or characterised by temporary expedient.—**make'-up** the way anything is arranged, composed, or constituted, or the ingredients in its constitution: one's character, temperament, mental qualities: an actor's materials for personating a part or a woman's, esp. cosmetics, for self-beautification: the effect produced thereby; **make'-weight** that which is thrown into a scale to make up the weight: a person or thing of little value added to supply a deficiency.— **make a face** to grimace, contort the features; **make after** to follow or pursue; **make amends** to render compensation or satisfaction; **make an ass of oneself** to behave like a fool; **make a night (day) of it** to extend an, esp. enjoyable, activity through the whole night (day); **make as if,** or **though** to act as if, to pretend that; **make certain (of)** to find out: to put beyond doubt: to secure; **make do (with)** to manage (with the means available—usually inferior or inadequate); **make for** to set out for, seek to reach; **make free with see free; make friends** to become friendly: to acquire friends; **make head or tail of** to find any sense in; **make it** to reach an objective: to succeed in a purpose: to become a success (*coll.*): to have one's way sexually (with) (*vulg.*); **make much of** to treat with fondness, to cherish, to foster: to turn to great account: to find much sense in, succeed in understanding; **make nothing of** to think it no great matter, have no hesitation or difficulty: to be totally unable to understand; **make of** to construct from (as material): to understand by; **make off** to decamp; **make off with** to run away with; **make one's way** to proceed: to succeed; **make or break, make or mar** to be the crucial test that brings success or failure to (*adj.* **make'-or-break'**); **make out** to descry: to discern: to decipher: to comprehend, understand: to prove: to seek to make it appear: to draw up: to succeed: to engage in love-making (with) (*slang*); **make over** to remake, reconstruct: to transfer; **make sail** to increase the quantity of sail: to set sail; **make sure (of)** to ascertain: to put beyond doubt or risk: to secure: to feel certain; **make the best of** to turn to the best advantage: to take in the best spirit; **make the most of** to use to the best advantage; **make up** to fabricate: to feign: to collect: to put together: to parcel: to put into shape: to arrange: to become friends again (after a quarrel, etc.): to constitute: to repair: to complete, supplement: to adjust one's appearance (as an actor for a part): to apply paint and powder, etc., to the face: to make good: to compensate; **make up one's mind** to come to a decision; **make up to** to make friendly, adulatory, or amorous approaches to: to compensate; **on the make** (*coll.*) bent on self-advancement or promotion. [O.E. *macian.*]

mako [1] *mā'kō, n.* any of several sharks of the genus *Isurus:—pl.* **ma'kos.**—Also **mako shark.** [Maori.]

mako [2] *mā'kō, n.* a small tree of New Zealand with red berries that turn purple as they ripen:—*pl.* **ma'kos.** [Maori.]

mal *mal,* (Fr.) *n.* pain, sickness.—**mal de mer** (*də mer*) sea-sickness; **mal du pays** (*dü pā-ē*) homesickness.

mal- *mal-, pfx.* bad, badly. [Fr.—L. *male,* badly.]

Malacca-cane *məl-ak'ə-kān, n.* a brown walking-cane made from a rattan. [*Malacca,* a centre of the trade.]

malachite *mal'ə-kīt, n.* a green mineral, basic copper carbonate. [Gr. *malachē,* mallow, as of the colour of a mallow leaf.]

maladaptation *mal-ad-ap-tā'shən, n.* faulty adaptation.—*adjs.* **maladap'ted; maladap'tive.** [Pfx. **mal-.**]

maladjusted *mal-ə-just'id, adj.* poorly or inadequately adjusted, esp. to one's environment or circumstances —*n.* **maladjust'ment.** [Pfx. **mal-.**]

maladministration *mal-ad-min-is-trā'shən, n.* bad management, esp. of public affairs.—*v.t.* **maladmin'ister.** [Pfx. **mal-.**]

maladroit *mal'ə-droit* (or *-droit'*), *adj.* not dexterous. unskilful: clumsy —*adv* **maladroit'ly.**—*n.* **maladroit'ness.** [Fr]

malady *mal'ə-di, n.* illness: disease, either of the body or of the mind: a faulty condition. [Fr. *maladie—malade,* sick—L. *male habitus,* in ill condition—*male,* badly, *habitus,* pa.p. of *habēre,* to have, hold.]

Malagasy *mal-ə-gas'i, adj.* of or pertaining to Madagascar or its inhabitants.—*n.* a native of Madagascar: the language of Madagascar

malaise *mal-āz', n.* uneasiness: a feeling of discomfort or of sickness. [Fr. *malaise*]

malamute. See **malemute.**

malapropism *mal'ə-prop-izm, n.* misapplication of words without mispronunciation, from Mrs *Malaprop* in Sheridan's play, *The Rivals,* who uses words *malapropos*

malapropos *mal'a-pro-pō mal-ə-prō-po', adj.* out of place: unsuitable: inapt.— *adv* inappropriately: unseasonably. [Pfx. **mal-.**]

malar *mā'lər, adj.* pertaining to the cheek.—*n* the cheek-bone. [L. *māla,* the cheek—*mandēre,* to chew.]

malaria *mə-lā'ri-ə, n.* poisonous air arising from marshes, once believed to produce fever: miasma: the fever once attributed thereto, actually due to a protozoan parasite transmitted by mosquitoes —*adjs* **malā'rial, malā'rian, malā'rious.**—*ns.* **malārio'logist; malārio'logy** the study of malaria. [It. *mal' aria—*L *malus,* bad, *āēr, āēris,* air.]

malark(e)y *mə-lar'ki, (U.S) n.* unfounded story: nonsense

Malathion® *mal-ə-thī'on, n.* a phosphorus-containing insecticide used chiefly in the house and garden.]

Malay, -an *mə-lā', -ən, ns* a member of a race inhabiting Malaysia, Singapore and Indonesia (formerly known as the Malay Archipelago): the language of the Malays.—*adjs* of the Malays, their language, or their countries.—*adj.* **Malay'sian** (*-si-ən, -zhən, -shən*) relating to the Malay Archipelago or esp. to Malaysia.—Also *n* [Malay *malāyu.*]

Malayala(a)m *ma-lə-ya'ləm, n.* the Dravidian language of Kerala.—Also *adj.*

malcontent *mal'kən-tent, adj.* discontented, dissatisfied, esp. in political matters.—*n.* one discontented —*adj.* **malcontent'ed.**—*adv.* **malcontent'edly.**—*n.* **malcontent'edness.** [O Fr *malcontent.*]

mal de mer. See under **mal.**

male *māl, adj.* masculine: of or pertaining to the sex that begets (not bears) young, or produces relatively small gametes: staminate (*bot*): adapted to fit into a corresponding hollow part (*mach.*).—*n* one of the male sex.—**male chauvinist** (pig) (*coll. derog.*) a man who believes in the superiority of men over women and acts accordingly (*abbrev.* MCP); **male rhymes** those in which only the final syllables correspond. [O.Fr. *male—*L. *masculus,* male—*mās,* a male]

Malebolge *ma-lā-bol'jā, n.* the eighth circle of Dante's Hell. [It , bad holes or pits, lit pockets]

malediction *mal-i-dik'shən, n.* cursing: a calling down of evil.—*adjs.* **maledic'tive, maledic'tory.** [L *maledicēre, -dictum—male,* ill, *dicēre,* to speak.]

malefactor *mal'i-fak-tər, n.* an evil-doer: a criminal —*adjs.* **malefac'tory, malefic** (*mə-l-ef'ik*) doing mischief: producing evil —*adv.* **malef'ically.**—*n.* **mal-**

eficence (*-ef'i-səns*).—*adj.* **malef'icent** hurtful: wrong-doing [L *malefacēre,* to do evil.]

maleic. See under **malic.**

malemute *māl'ə-mūt, n.* an Eskimo dog —Also **mal'-amute.** [From a tribe on the Alaskan coast]

malevolent *mal-ev'ə-lənt, adj* wishing evil: ill-disposed towards others, rejoicing in another's misfortune.—*n.* **malev'olence.**—*adv.* **malev'olently.** [L *malevolēns, -entis,* ill disposed, wishing evil]

malfeasance *mal-fē'zəns, n.* an illegal deed, esp. of an official (*law*).—*adj.* **malfea'sant.** [Fr *malfaisance* —L. *mal,* ill, *facēre,* to do.]

malformation *mal-for-mā'shən, n.* faulty structure: deformity —*adj* **malformed'.** [Pfx. **mal-.**]

malfunction *mal-fungk'shən, n* the act or fact of working imperfectly.—*v i* to work or function imperfectly.—*n* **malfunc'tioning.** [Pfx **mal-.**]

malic *mā'lik, mal'ik, adj* obtained from apple juice — applied to an acid ($H_6C_4O_5$) found in unripe fruits —*adj.* **maleic** (*mə-lē'ik*) —**maleic acid** an acid got from malic acid. [L. *mālum,* an apple.]

malice *mal'is, n.* ill-will: spite, disposition or intention to harm another or others a playfully mischievous attitude of mind.—*adj.* **malicious** (*mə-lish'əs*) bearing ill-will or spite: moved by hatred or ill-will: mischievous.—*adv* **mali'ciously.**—*n.* **mali'ciousness.**—**malice aforethought** (*law*) the predetermination to commit a crime esp. against the person, i.e. serious injury or murder. [Fr ,—L *malitia—malus,* bad]

malign *mə-līn', adj.* baleful: injurious: malignant.— *v t.* to speak evil of, especially falsely and rancorously, to defame —*ns.* **malign'er; malignity** (*mə-lig'ni-ti*) state or quality of being malign: great hatred, virulence: deadly quality —*adv.* **malign'ly.** [Fr. *malin,* fem *maligne—*L. *malignus* for *maligenus,* of evil disposition—*malus,* bad, and *gen-,* root of *genus.*]

malignant *mə-lig'nənt, adj* disposed to do harm baleful: actuated by great hatred, tending to cause death, or to go from bad to worse, esp cancerous (*med*).—*ns.* **malig'nance, malig'nancy.**—*adv.* **malig'nantly.** [L *malignāns, -antis,* pr p. of *malignāre,* to act maliciously.]

malinger *mə-ling'gər, v.i.* to feign sickness in order to avoid duty —*ns.* **maling'erer; maling'ery** feigned sickness. [Fr. *malingre,* sickly.]

mall *mōl,* or *mal. n.* a large wooden hammer: a mallet for the old game of pall-mall' the game itself: a pall-mall alley' (from a former alley of the kind in London) a level shaded walk: a public walk' a street, area, etc. of shops, along which vehicles are not permitted [See **maul** and **pall-mall.**]

mallard *mal'ərd, n.* a kind of wild duck common in the northern hemisphere—the male has a shiny green head. [O.Fr *mallart, malart;* origin obscure.]

malleate *mal'i-āt, v t* to hammer: beat thin —*adj.* **mall'eable** able to be beaten, rolled, etc , into a new shape (also *fig.*) —*ns.* **mall'eableness, malleabil'ity; mallea'tion** hammering: a hammer-mark.—*adj.* **malleiform** (*mal'ē-i-form*) hammer-shaped.—*n.* **malleus** (*mal'i-əs*) one of the small bones of the middle ear in mammals. [L. *malleus,* a hammer.]

mallee *mal'ē, n.* dwarf Eucalyptus, esp. *E. dumosa.* —**mall'ee-bird, -fowl, -hen** an Australian moundbird; **mall'ee-scrub'** a thicket formation of mallee. [Australian word.]

malleiform. See **malleate.**

malleolus *mə-lē'ə-ləs, n* a bony protuberance on either side of the ankle —*adj* **mallē'olar** (or *mal'i-*) [L. *malleolus,* dim. of *malleus,* hammer.]

mallet *mal'it, n.* a hammer with a large head, e g. of

wood: a soft-headed stick used to beat a gong, etc. (*mus.*): a long-handled hammer for playing croquet or polo. [Fr. *maillet*, dim. of *mail*, a mall.]

malleus. See **malleate.**

mallow *mal'ō*, *n.* any plant of the genus Malva, from its emollient properties or its soft downy leaves: extended to other genera of Malvaceae: a mauve colour [O.E. *m(e)alwe*—L. *malva*; Gr. *malachē—malassein*, to soften.]

malm *mäm*, *n.* calcareous loam, earth specially good for brick: an artificial mixture of clay and chalk [O.E. *m(e)alm* (*-stān*), a soft (stone).]

malmsey *mam'zı*, *n.* a sort of grape: a strong and sweet wine, first made in Greece and exported from *Monembasia*. [L.L. *malmasia*.]

malnutrition *mal-nū-trish'ən*, *n.* imperfect or faulty nutrition. [Pfx. **mal-**.]

malodour *mal-ō'dər*, *n.* an ill smell.—*adj.* **malo'dorous.**—*n.* **malo'dourousness.** [Pfx. **mal-**.]

malpractice *mal-prak'tis*, *n.* an evil or improper practice' professional misconduct: treatment falling short of reasonable skill or care: illegal attempt of a person in position of trust to benefit himself at others' cost —*n.* **malpractitioner** (*-tish'ən-ər*). [Pfx. **mal-**.]

malstick. See **maulstick.**

malt *mòlt*, *n.* barley or other grain steeped in water, allowed to sprout, and dried in a kiln, used in brewing ale, etc.: malt liquor —*v.t.* to make into malt: to treat or combine with malt.—*adj.* containing or made with malt.—*n* **malt'ase** an enzyme that produces grape-sugar from maltose.—*adj.* **malt'ed** containing or made with malt.—*ns.* **malt'ing** a building where malt is made; **malt'ose** a hard, white crystalline sugar, formed by the action of malt or diastase on starch; **malt'ster** a maltman.—*adj.* **malt'y.—malt'-ex'tract** a fluid medicinal food made from malt; **malt'-floor** a perforated floor in the chamber of a malt-kiln, through which heat rises, **malt'-house**, **malt'-kiln**; **malt liquor** a liquor, as ale or porter, formed from malt; **malt'man** one whose occupation it is to make malt [O.E. *m(e)alt*.]

Malta *mol'*, *mol'tə*, *adj.* of the island of Malta.—*adj* **Maltese** (*-tēz'*) of Malta, its people, or language.—*n.* one of the people of Malta (*pl.* **Maltese**): an official language of Malta—Arabic with a strong Italian infusion —**Maltese cross** the badge of the knights of Malta, a cross with two-pointed expanding limbs. [L. *Melita*, Gr. *Melitē*.]

Malthusian *mal-thūz'i-ən*, *adj.* relating to Thomas Robert *Malthus* (1766–1834), or to his teaching that the increase-of population tends to outstrip that of the means of living.—*n.* a disciple of Malthus.—*n.* **Malthus'ianism.**

maltreat *mal-trēt'*, *v.t.* to use roughly or unkindly.—*n.* **maltreat'ment.** [Fr. *maltraiter*—L. *male*, ill, *tractāre*, to treat.]

Malva *mal'və*, *n.* the mallow genus, giving name to the family **Malvä'ceae**, including hollyhock, cotton, etc. —*adj.* **malvä'ceous.** [L.; cf. **mallow.**]

malversation *mal-vər-sä'shən*, *n.* misbehaviour in office as by bribery, extortion, embezzlement: corrupt administration (of funds). [Fr.—L. *male*, badly, *versārī*, *-ātus*, to occupy oneself.]

mam *mam*, (*dial.*) *n.* mother.

mama. See **mamma**[1].

mamba *mam'bə*, *n.* a large, deadly African snake, black or green. [Kaffir *im mamba*, large snake.]

mambo *mam'bō*, *n* a voodoo priestess: a West Indian dance, or dance-tune, like the rumba'—*pl.* **mam'bos.** —*v ı.* to dance the mambo. [Amer. Sp., prob. from Haitian.]

mamelon *mam'ə-lən*, *n.* a rounded hill or protuberance. [Fr , nipple.]

Mameluke *mam'ə-lōōk*, *n.* one of a military force originally of Circassian slaves—afterwards the ruling class and sultans of Egypt: a slave, esp. white. [Ar. *mamlūk*, a purchased slave—*malaka*, to possess.]

mamilla, *U.S.* **mammilla**, *mam-il'ə*, *n.* the nipple of the mammary gland: a nipple-shaped protuberance: —*pl.* **mamill'ae** (*-ē*).—*adjs.* **mam'illar**, **mam'illary** pertaining to the breast: nipple-shaped: studded with rounded projections. [L. *mam(m)illa*, dim. of *mamma*.]

mamma[1], **mama** *ma-ma'* (in U S. *ma'mə*), *n.* mother— used chiefly by young children.—*n.* **mammy** (*mam'ı*) a child's word for mother: a coloured nurse (*U.S.*). [Repetition of *ma*, a child's natural utterance.]

mamma[2] *mam'ə*, *n.* the milk gland: the breast:—*pl.* **mamm'ae** (*-ē*).—*adjs.* **mamm'ary** of the nature of, relating to, the mammae or breasts; **mamm'ate** having breasts, **mammif'erous** having mammae; **mamm'iform** having the form of a breast.—*n.* **mammog'raphy** radiological examination of the breast [L. *mamma*]

mammal *mam'əl*, *n.* a member of the **Mammalia** (*mə-mā'li-ə*), the class of animals that suckle their young.—*adj.* **mammä'lian.** [L. *mammālis*, of the breast—*mamma*, the breast.]

mammary, **mammate.** See **mamma**[2].

mammiform. See **mamma**[2].

mammilla. Same as **mamilla.**

mammography. See **mamma**[2].

mammon *mam'ən*, *n.* riches: (with *cap.*) the god of riches.—*adj.* **mamm'onish** devoted to money-getting —*ns.* **mamm'onism** devotion to gain; **mamm'onist**, **mamm'onite** a person devoted to riches.—*adj.* **mammonist'ic.** [L.L. *mam(m)ōna*—Gr *mam(m)ōnās*—Aramaic *māmōn*, riches.]

mammoth *mam'əth*, *n.* an extinct species of elephant —*adj.* resembling the mammoth in size: gigantic [Former Russ. *mammot* (now *mamant* or *mamont*).]

mammy. See **mamma**[1].

mamselle. See **mademoiselle.**

man *man*, *n.* a human being: mankind. a grown-up human male: a male attendant or servant: a workman, employee: a vassal. a follower: an uncommissioned soldier: one possessing a distinctively manly character: a husband, or man living as a husband with a woman: a piece used in playing chess or draughts or similar game: a cairn or rock pillar: a ship, as in *man-of-war*: a word of familiar address:—*pl.* **men.**—*adj.*, also in composition, male —*v.t.* to furnish with a man or men: to provide with a (human) worker, operator, etc.-—*pr.p* **mann'ing**; *pa.t.* and *pa.p* **manned** (*mand*).—*adj.* **man'ful** having the good qualities of a man: manly: bold: courageous vigorous: stout: noble-minded.—*adv.* **man'fully.**—*ns.* **man'fulness**; **man'hood** state of being a man: manly quality: human nature; **man'kind'** the human race, the mass of human beings: (*man'kīnd*) human males collectively —*adj.* **man'-like** having the appearance or qualities of a human being or of an adult human male.—*adv.* in the manner of a man: in a way that might be expected of a male person: manfully.—*n.* **man'liness**—*adjs.* **man'ly** befitting a man: brave: dignified: noble: pertaining to manhood: not childish or womanish. **manned** (*mand*); **mann'ish** like or savouring of a male or grown-up man (usu. depreciatory): masculine.—*n* **mann'ishness.—man'-about-town'** a fashionable, sophisticated man; **man'-at-arms'** a soldier, esp. mounted and heavy-armed; **man'-child** a male child: a boy'—*pl.* **men'-children; man'-day** a day's work of one man:—*pl.* **man'-days; man'-eater** a cannibal a tiger or other animal that has acquired the habit of eating men: a woman given to chasing, catching and devouring men (*coll.*), **Man Friday** a factotum or

servile attendant—from Robinson Crusoe's man.—
v.t. **man'handle** to move by manpower. to handle,
treat, roughly (*orig. slang*) —**man'hole** a hole large
enough to admit a man, esp. to a sewer, cable-duct, or
the like; **man'-hour** an hour's work of one man:—*pl.*
man'-hours; man'hunt an organised search for a person, esp. one mounted by police, etc. for a criminal;
man'-jack', man jack individual man (as *every man-
jack*).—*adj.* **man'-made** made by man: humanly made
or originated: (of fibre, fabric, etc.) artificial.
synthetic.—**man'-of-war', man'-o'-war'** a warship:—
pl **men'-of-war', men'-o'-war'; man'power** the
agency or energy of man in doing work: the rate at
which a man can work: available resources in population or in able-bodied men; **man'-servant** a male servant:—*pl.* **men'-servants; man'shift** the work done by
one man in one shift or work period.—*adj.* **man'-
size(d)** suitable for, or requiring, a man: very big
(*coll*).—**man'slaughter** the slaying of a man: unlawful homicide without malice aforethought (*law*); **man'-
trap** a trap for catching trespassers: any source of
potential danger; **man'folk(s)** male people, esp. a
woman's male relatives.—**as one man** all together
unanimously; **be one's own man** to be independent, not
answerable to anyone else; **be someone's man** to be
exactly the person someone is seeking for a particular
purpose; **man alive!** an exclamation of surprise; **man in
the moon** a fancied semblance of a man seen in the
moon; **man in the street** the ordinary, everyday man—
Tom, Dick, or Harry; **man of God** a holy man: *a* clergyman; **man of letters** a scholar: a writer; **man of straw**
a person of no substance (esp. financially): one nom-
inally, but not really, responsible: a sham opponent or
argument set up for the sake of disputation; **man of the
match** the most outstanding player in a cricket, football. etc. match (also *fig.*); **man of the moment** the man
(most capable of) dealing with the present situation;
man of the world one accustomed to the ways and
dealings of men; **man to man** one man to another as
individuals in fight or talk: frank and confidential; **to a
man** without exception. [O.E. *mann*.]

mana *ma'nä,* (*anthrop.*) *n.* a mysterious power associated with persons and things. [Maori.]

manacle *man'ə-kl, n.* a handcuff.—*v.t.* to handcuff: to
shackle [O Fr. *manicle*—L. *manicula,* dim. of
manica, sleeve, glove, handcuff—*manus,* hand.]

manage *man'ij, v.t.* to train by exercise, as a horse: to
handle: to wield: to conduct: to control: to administer,
be at the head of: to deal tactfully with: to contrive
successfully: to have time for: to be able to cope with:
to manipulate: to contrive: to bring about —*v.i.* to
conduct affairs: to get on, contrive to succeed.—*n*
manageabil'ity the quality of being manageable.—
adj. **man'ageable** that can be managed: governable.—
n. **man'ageableness.**—*adv.* **man'ageably.**—*ns.* **man'-
agement** the art or act of managing: manner of directing or of using anything: administration: skilful treatment: a body of managers; **man'ager** one who
manages: in an industrial firm or business, a person
who deals with administration and with the design and
marketing, etc. of the product, as opposed to its actual
construction. one who organises other people's doings: a domestic contriver: a person legally appointed
to manage a business, property, etc. as receiver:—
fem. **man'ageress; man'agership.**—*adjs.* **manage'rial**
of or pertaining to a manager, or to management:
man'aging handling. controlling: administering: contriving. domineering.—**management consultant** one
who advises firms on the most efficient procedures
applicable to particular businesses or industries [It
maneggio—L. *manus,* the hand.]

mañana *man-yä'nə. man-ya'nä,* (Sp.) *n.* and *adv* tomorrow: an unspecified time in the future.

manatee, manati *man-ə-tē', n.* a sirenian (*Manatus* or
Trichechus) of the warm parts of the Atlantic and the
rivers of Brazil. [Sp. *manati*—Carib *manatoui.*]

Manchester *man'chis-tər, adj.* belonging to or made in
Manchester, or similar to goods made in Manchester,
applied esp. to cotton cloths.

manchineel *manch-i-nēl', n.* a tropical American tree
(*Hippomane*) of the spurge family, with poisonous
latex. [Sp. *manzanilla,* dim. of *manzana,* apple.]

Manchu *man-chōō', or man', n.* one of the race from
which Manchuria took its name, and which governed
China from the 17th to the 20th century: their language —*adj.* of or pertaining to Manchuria or to its
inhabitants.—*n.* **Manchu'ria.**—*adj.* **Manchur'ian.**
[Manchu, pure.]

maniciple *man'si-pl, n.* a steward: a purveyor, particularly of a college or an inn of court. [O.Fr.,—L
manceps, -cipis, a purchaser: see foregoing.]

Mancunian *man(g)-kūn'i-ən, adj.* belonging to Manchester —*n.* a Manchester person. [Doubtful L
Mancunium, a Roman station in Manchester. *Mam-
ucium* is probably right.]

-mancy *-man-si, -man-si.* in composition, divination.—
-mantic adjective combining form. [Gr. *manteiā.*]

mandala *mun'da-lə, n.* in Buddhism, etc., a symbol of
the universe, varying a little but having an enclosing
circle, usu. images of deities, used as an aid to religious
meditation: in the psychology of Jung, symbol of the
wholeness of the self (in imperfect form shows lack of
harmony in the self) [Sans. *maṇḍala.*]

mandamus *man-dā'məs, n.* a writ or command issued by
a higher court to a lower:—*pl.* **manda'muses.** [L.
mandāmus, we command.]

mandarin *man'də-rin, -rēn, n.* a member of any of nine
ranks of officials under the Chinese Empire (*hist.*): a
statuette of a seated Chinese figure, often with a
movable head (a *nodding mandarin*): (*cap.*) the most
important form of the Chinese language: a man in
office, bureaucrat: a person of standing in the literary
world, often one who tends to be reactionary or pedantic (also **man'darine**) a small kind of orange (of
Chinese origin): its colour.—*adj.* pertaining to a mandarin: of style or language, formal and ornate.—*n*
man'darinate office of mandarin: mandarins as a
group.—**mandarin collar** a high, narrow, stand-up
collar the front ends of which do not quite meet;
mandarin duck a crested Asiatic duck (*Aix gal-
ericulata*). [Port. *mandarim*—Malay (from Hind)
mantrī, counsellor—Sans *mantra,* counsel.]

mandate *man'dāt, n.* a charge: a command from a
superior official or judge to an inferior, ordering him
how to act: a right given to a person to act in name of
another: the sanction held to be given by the electors to
an elected body, to act according to its declared
policies, election manifesto, etc : the power conferred
upon a state by the League of Nations in 1919 to govern
a region elsewhere: (also with *cap.*) any of the regions
governed in this way (also **mandated territory**).—*v.t*
mandate' to assign by mandate: to invest with
authority.—*ns.* **man'datary, man'datory** (*-də-tə-ri*)
the holder of a mandate: a mandate; **manda'tor** the
giver of a mandate.—*adj.* **man'datory** containing a
mandate or command: of the nature of a mandate
bestowed by mandate: compulsory. allowing no
option. [L. *mandātum*—*mandāre*—*manus,* hand,
dāre, give.]

mandible *man'di-bl, n* a jaw or jaw-bone, esp the
lower: either part of a bird's bill: an organ performing
the functions of a jaw in the lower animals.—*adjs*
mandib'ular relating to the jaw; **mandib'ulate, -d.**
[L. *mandibula*—*mandere,* to chew.]

mandilion. See mandylion.

mandoline, mandolin *man'də-lin, -lēn, n* a round-backed instrument like a lute, sustained notes being played by repeated plucking.—*ns.* **mandō'la,** mandō'ra a large mandoline. [It. *mandola, mandora,* dim. *mandolino.*]

mandrake *man'drāk, n.* a poisonous plant (*Mandragora*) of the potato family, subject of many strange fancies. [L. *mandragora*—Gr. *mandragorās.*]

mandrel, mandril *man'drəl, n.* a bar of iron fitted to a turning-lathe on which articles to be turned are fixed: the axle of a circular saw. [Fr. *mandrin.*]

mandrill *man'dril, n.* a large West African baboon. [Prob. **man**[1] **and drill**[2].]

mandylion *man-dil'i-ən, n.* a loose outer garment worn e.g. by soldiers over their armour (also **mandil'ion**) (*hist.*): (with *cap.*) the name of a cloth supposed to bear the imprint of the face of Jesus. [M.Fr. *mandillon,* cloak, and Late Gr. *mandylion,* cloth; cf. ultimately L. *mantel(l)um,* napkin or cloak, and L. *mantele, mantelium,* napkin.]

mane *mān, n.* long hair on the back of the neck and neighbouring parts, as in the horse and the lion: a long bushy head of hair.—*adjs.* **maned; mane'less.** [O.E. *manu.*]

manège *man-ezh', n.* the managing of horses: the art of horsemanship or of training horses: a horse's actions and paces as taught him: a riding-school.—*v.t.* to train, as a horse. [Fr.; cf. manage.]

manes *mā'nēz,* (*Roman myth.*) *n.pl.* the spirits of the dead. [L. *mānēs.*]

maneuver. U.S. spelling of manoeuvre.

mangabey *mang'gə-bā, n.* the white-eyelid monkey, any species of the mainly West African genus *Cercocebus,* esp. the sooty mangabey. [From a district in Madagascar, where, however, they are not found.]

manganese *mang-gə-nēz', mang', n.* a hard brittle greyish-white metallic element (Mn; at. numb. 25): (originally and commercially) its dioxide (*black manganese*) or other ore.—*n.* **mang'anate** a salt of manganic acid.—**manganese steel** a very hard, shock-resistant steel containing a higher than usual percentage of manganese. [Fr. *manganèse*—It. *manganese*—L. *magnēsia.*]

mange. See mangy.

mangel-wurzel, mangold-wurzel *mang'gl-wûr'zl, n.* a variety of beet cultivated as cattle food.—Also **mang'el, mang'old.** [Ger. *Mangold,* beet, *Wurzel,* root.]

manger *mānj'ər, n.* a trough in which food is laid for horses and cattle. [O.Fr. *mangeoire*—L. *mandūcāre,* to chew, eat.]

mangetout *māzh-tōō, n.* a type of pea, the pod of which is also eaten.—Also **mangetout pea, sugar pea.** [Fr., *lit.,* eat-all.]

mangey. See mangy.

mangle[1] *mang'gl, v.t.* to hack to raggedness: to tear in cutting: to mutilate: to bungle (*fig.*): to distort.—*n.* **mang'ler.** [A.Fr. *mangler, mahangler,* prob. a freq. of O.Fr. *mahaigner,* to maim—*mahaing,* a hurt.]

mangle[2] *mang'gl, n.* a rolling-press for smoothing linen: a wringer.—*v.t.* to smooth with a mangle: to wring (clothes).—*n.* **mang'ler.** [Du. *mangel*—Gr. *manganon.*]

mango *mang'gō, n.* a tropical, orig. East Indian, tree (*Mangifera indica*) of the cashew-nut family: its fleshy fruit:—*pl.* **mang'oes.** [Port. *manga*—Malay *manggā*—Tamil *mān-kāy,* mango-fruit.]

mangold, mangold-wurzel. See mangel-wurzel.

mangonel *mang'gə-nel, n.* a mediaeval engine for throwing stones, etc. [O.Fr.,—L.L. *mangonum*—Gr. *manganon.*]

mangrove *mang'grōv, n.* a tree that grows in muddy swamps covered at high tide or on tropical coasts and estuary shores.

mangy, mangey *mānj'i, adj.* scabby: affected with mange: shabby, seedy: mean.—*ns.* **mange** (*mānj*; a back-formation) inflammation of the skin of animals caused by mites; **mang'iness.** [Fr. *mangé,* eaten, pa.p. of *manger*—L. *mandūcāre,* to chew.]

manhandle. See man.

Manhattan *man-hat'ən, n.* a cocktail containing vermouth, whisky, bitters, etc. [*Manhattan,* New York.]

manhole, manhood, manhunt. See man.

mania *mā'ni-ə, n.* a mental illness characterised by euphoria, excessively rapid speech and violent, destructive actions (*psychiatry*): the elated phase of manic-depressive psychosis (*psychiatry*): excessive or unreasonable desire: a craze.—*-mania* in composition, an abnormal and obsessive desire or inclination, or, more loosely, an extreme enthusiasm, for a specified thing.—**mániac** noun and adjective combining form.—*n.* **mā'niac** a person affected with mania: a madman.—*adj.* affected by, relating to, mania: raving mad.—*adj.* **maniacal** (*mə-nī'ə-kl*).—*adv.* **mani'acally.**—*adj.* **manic** (*mān'ik* or *man'ik*) of or affected by mania.—*adv.* **man'ically.**—**man'ic-depress'ive** one suffering from manic-depressive psychosis.—Also *adj.*—**manic-depressive psychosis** a form of mental illness characterised by phases of depression and elation, either alone or alternately, with lucid intervals. [L.,—Gr. *maniā.*]

manicure *man'i-kūr, n.* the care of hands and nails: professional treatment for the hands and nails: one who practises this.—*v.t.* to apply manicure to.—*n.* **man'icurist.** [L. *manus,* hand, *cūra,* care.]

manifest *man'i-fest, adj.* that may be easily seen by the eye or perceived by the mind.—*v.t.* to make clear or easily seen: to put beyond doubt: to reveal or declare.—*n.* an open or public statement: a list or invoice of the cargo of a ship or aeroplane to be exhibited at the custom-house: a list of passengers carried by an aeroplane.—*adj.* **manifest'able, manifest'ible** that can be manifested or clearly shown.—*n.* **manifesta'tion** act of disclosing what is dark or secret: that by which something is manifested.—*adv.* **man'ifestly.** [L. *manifestus.*]

manifesto *man-i-fest'ō, n.* a public written declaration of the intentions, opinions, or motives of a sovereign or of a leader, party, or body:—*pl.* **manifest'o(e)s.** [It.; see **manifest.**]

manifold *man'i-fōld, adj.* various in kind or quality: many in number: having many features: performing several functions.—*n.* a pipe with several lateral outlets to others: a carbon-copy.—*v.t.* to multiply: to make simultaneous copies of. [many, and suff. -fold.]

manihoc. See manioc.

manikin, mannikin *man'i-kin, n.* a dwarf: an anatomical model: a mannequin. [Du. *manneken,* a double dim. of *man.*]

manil(l)a *mə-nil'ə, n.* cheroot made in *Manila:* abaca: strong paper orig. made from abaca.—**Manil(l)a hemp** abaca.

manioc *man'i-ok, n.* cassava: meal therefrom.—Also **man'ihoc.** [Tupi *mandioca.*]

maniple *man'i-pl, n.* in the Western Church, a eucharistic vestment, a narrow strip worn on the left arm. [L. *manipulus*—*manus,* the hand, *plēre,* to fill.]

manipulate *mə-nip'ū-lāt, v.t.* to work with the hands: to handle or manage: to give a false appearance to: to turn to one's own purpose or advantage.—*n.* **manipula'tion.**—*adjs.* **manip'ul(āt)able** capable of being manipulated; **manip'ular, manip'ulative, manip'ula-**

tory.—*n.* **manip'ulâtor** one who manipulates: a mechanical device for handling small, remote, or radioactive objects. [L.L. *manipulâre, -âtum*; see **maniple**.]

manito *man'i-tō, n.* a spirit or object of reverence among American Indians:—*pl.* **man'itos.**—Also **manitou** (*-tōō*). [Algonkin.]

man-jack, mankind. See man.

manky *mang'ki,* (*dial.*) *adj.* dirty, rotten.

manly. See man.

manna *man'ə, n.* the food miraculously provided for the Israelites in the wilderness (*B.*): delicious food for body or mind: anything advantageous falling one's way as by divine bounty: a sugary exudation from the **mann'a-ash** (*Fraxinus ornus*), and other trees. [Heb. *mân hû,* what is it? or from *man,* a gift.]

mannequin *man'i-kin, n.* a dummy figure: a person, usu. a woman, employed to wear and display clothes. [Fr.,—Du.; see **manikin**.]

manner *man'ər, n.* the way in which anything is done: method: fashion: personal style of acting or bearing: custom: style of writing or of thought: sort (of): style (*pl.*) social conduct: (*pl.*) good behaviour.—*adj.* **mann'ered** having manners (esp. in compounds, as *well-* or *ill-mannered*): affected with mannerism: artificial: stilted.—*ns.* **mann'erism** a constant sameness of manner: stiltedness: a marked peculiarity or trick of style or manner, esp. in literary composition: manner or style becoming wearisome by its sameness; **mann'erist** one addicted to mannerism.—*adj.* **manneris'tic**.—*adv.* **manneris'tically**.—*n.* **mann'erliness**. —*adj.* **mann'erly** showing good manners: well-behaved: not rude.—*adv.* with good manners: civilly: respectfully: without rudeness.—**by no manner of means** under no circumstances whatever; **in a manner** in ɛ certain way; **shark's manners** rapacity; **to the manner born** accustomed from birth. [Fr. *manière* —*main*—L. *manus,* the hand.]

mannikin. See manikin.

manning, mannish. See man.

manoeuvre, in U.S. **maneuver,** *ma-nōō'vər,* or *-nū',n.* a piece of dexterous management: a stratagem: a skilful and clever movement in military or naval tactics: (usu. *pl.*) a large-scale battle-training exercise of armed forces.—*v.i.* and *v.t.* to perform a manoeuvre: to manage with art: to change the position of troops or of ships: to effect or to gain by manoeuvres.—*ns.* **manoeu'vrer; manoeuvrabil'ity**.—*adj.* **manoeu'vrable**.—In U.S. **maneuverer,** etc. [Fr. *manœuvre*— L. *manû,* by hand, *opera,* work.]

manometer *man-om'i-tər, n.* an instrument for measuring and comparing the pressure of fluids.—*adjs.* **manometric** (*man-ō-met'rik*), **-al**. [Gr. *manos,* rare, thin, *metron,* measure.]

manor *man'ər, n.* the land belonging to a nobleman, or so much as he formerly kept for his own use.—*adj.* **manorial** (*ma-nō'ri-əl, -nō'*) pertaining to a manor.— **man'or-house, -seat** the house or seat belonging to a manor. [O.Fr. *manoir*—L. *manêre, mânsum,* to stay.]

manqué *mä-kā,* (Fr.) *adj.* unsuccessful, not having realised promise or expectation—placed after the noun.

mansard *man'särd, n.* a roof having the lower part steeper than the upper.—Usually **man'sard-roof'**. [Employed by François *Mansard* or *Mansart* (1598–1666).]

manse *mans, n.* an ecclesiastical residence, esp. that of a parish minister or that of the Church of Scotland.—**son of the manse** a minister's son. [L.L. *mansus, mansa,* a dwelling—*manêre, mânsum,* to remain.]

mansion *man'shən, n.* a large house: a manor-house: a house (*astrol.*): (in *pl.*) a large building let in flats.— **man'sion-house** a mansion (**the Mansion House** the official residence of the Lord Mayor of London). [O.Fr.,—L. *mânsiō, -ōnis*—*manêre, mânsum,* to remain, to stay.]

manslaughter. See man.

manta *man'tə, n.* a blanket: a cloak: a horse-cloth: (with *cap.*) a genus of gigantic rays. [Sp.]

manteau *man'tō, n.* (17th–18th cent.) a woman's loose gown:—*pls.* **man'teaus** (*-tōz*), **man'teaux** (*-tō, -tōz*). [Fr. *manteau*—L. *mantellum.*]

mantel *man'tl, n.* a manteltree: a mantelpiece: a mantelshelf.—*n.* **man'telet** a mantlet.—**man'telpiece** the ornamental structure over and in front of a fireplace: a mantelshelf; **man'telshelf** the ornamental shelf over a fireplace. [mantle.]

mantelet. See under mantel, mantle.

mantic *man'tik, adj.* relating to divination: prophetic. —See also **-mancy**. [Gr. *mantikos*—*mantis,* a prophet.]

mantilla *man-til'ə, n.* a small mantle: a kind of veil covering the head and falling down upon the shoulders. [Sp.; dim. of *manta*.]

Mantis *man'tis, n.* a genus of orthopterous insects carrying their large spinous forelegs in the attitude of prayer: (without *cap.*) an insect of this or a related genus. [Gr. *mantis, -eōs,* prophet.]

mantissa *man-tis'ə, n.* the fractional part of a logarithm. [L., make-weight.]

mantle *man'tl, n.* a cloak or loose outer garment (*arch.*): a covering: symbol of the spirit or authority: a fold of the integument of a mollusc or a brachiopod secreting the shell: a hood or network of refractory material that becomes incandescent when exposed to a flame: the part of the earth immediately beneath the crust, constituting the greater part of the earth's bulk, and presumed to consist of solid heavy rock.— *v.t.* to cover: to obscure: to disguise.—*v.i.* to spread like a mantle.—*ns.* **man'tlet, man'telet** a small cloak for women; **man'tling** cloth suitable for mantles: the drapery of a coat-of-arms (*her.*).—**mantle rock** loose rock at the earth's surface. [Partly through O.E. *mentel,* partly through O.Fr. *mantel* (Fr *manteau*)— L. *mantel(l)um.*]

mantra *man'trə, n.* a Vedic hymn: a sacred text used as an incantation: a word, phrase, etc. chanted or repeated inwardly in meditation. [Sans., instrument of thought.]

mantrap. See man.

mantua *man'tū-ə, n.* (17th–18th cent.) a woman's loose outer gown. [**manteau**, confused with *Mantua,* in Italy.]

manual *man'ū-əl, adj.* of the hand: done, worked, or used by the hand, as opposed to automatic, computer-operated, etc.: working with the hands.— *n.* drill in the use of weapons, etc : a handbook or handy compendium of a large subject or treatise: a key or keyboard played by hand.—*adv.* **man'ually**.— **manual alphabet** the signs for letters made by the deaf and dumb; **manual exercise** drill in handling arms. [L. *manuâlis*—*manus,* the hand.]

manufacture *man-ū-fak'chər, v.t.* to make, originally by hand, now usu. by machinery and on a large scale: to fabricate, concoct: to produce unintelligently in quantity.—*v.i.* to be occupied in manufactures.—*n.* the practice, act, or process of manufacturing: anything manufactured.—*n.* **manufac'turer** one who owns a factory: one who makes, concocts, or invents. —*adj.* **manufac'turing** pertaining to manufactures [Fr.,—L. *manû* (abl.) by hand, *factûra,* a making, from *facêre, factum,* to make.]

manuka *mà'nōō-ka, n.* an Australian and New Zealand tree (*Leptospermum*) of the myrtle family, with hard wood, its leaves a substitute for tea. [Maori.]

manumit *man-ū-mit', v.t.* to release from slavery: to

set free:—*pr.p.* **manumitt'ing**; *pa.t.* and *pa.p* **manumitt'ed**.—*n.* **manumission** (*-mish'∂n*). [L. *manūmittĕre* or *manŭ mittĕre* or *ēmittĕre*, to send from one's hand or control—*manus*, the hand, *mittĕre*, *missum*, to send.]

manure *man-ūr'*, *v.t.* to enrich with any fertilising substance.—*n.* any substance applied to land to make it more fruitful.—*n* **manūr'er**.—*adj.* **manūr'ial**.—*n.* **manūr'ing**. [A Fr *maynoverer* see **manoeuvre**.]

manus *mā'nəs*, *ma'nōōs*, *n* the hand or corresponding part of an animal. [L. *mānus*, pl. *-ūs*]

manuscript *man'ū-skript*, *adj.* written by hand or typed, not printed.—*n.* a book or document written by hand before invention of printing: copy for a printer, in handwriting or typed: handwritten form. —Abbrev. MS. [L *manū* (abl), by hand, *scrībĕre*, *scriptum*, to write.]

Manx *mangks*, *n* the language of the Isle of *Man*, belonging to the Gadhelic branch of Celtic.—*adj.* pertaining to the Isle of Man or to its inhabitants.— **Manx cat** a breed of cat with only a rudimentary tail: **Manx'man**—*fem.* **Manx'woman**.

many *men'i*, *adj* (*compar.* **more** *mōr*, *mor*; *superl* **most** *mōst*) consisting of a great number: numerous —*n* many persons: a great number (usu. with omission of *of*).—*adjs* **man'y-coloured**, **man'y-eyed** having many colours, eyes; **man'y-sid'ed** having many qualities or aspects: having wide interests or varied abilities.—**man'y-sid'edness.—many a** many (with singular noun and verb), **the many** the crowd [O E *manig.*]

manyplies *men'i-pliz*, *n.* *sing.* and *pl.* the third stomach of a ruminant. [**many, ply**[1].]

manzanilla *man-zə-nil'ə*, *-nē'yə.* *n.* a very dry, light sherry [Sp.]

Maoist *mow'ist*, *n.* one who adheres to the Chinese type of communism as set forth by Mao Tse-tung.—*n.* **Mao'ism**.

Maori *mow'ri*, *ma'ō-ri*, *n.* a member of the brown race of New Zealand: the language of this race:—*pl* **Mao'ris**.—Also *adj.* [Maori.]

map *map*, *n.* a representation in outline of the surface features of the earth. the moon, etc , or of part of it, usu. on a plane surface: a similar plan of the stars in the sky. a representation, scheme, or epitome of the disposition or state of anything —*v.t* to make a map of to place (the elements of a set) in one-to-one correspondence with the elements of another set (*math.*):—*pr.p.* **mapp'ing**; *pa.t.* and *pa.p* **mapped**.— *ns* **mapp'er**; **map'-reading** the interpretation of what one sees in a map.—**map out** to plan, divide up, and apportion; **off the map** out of existence: negligible: of a location, remote from main thoroughfares, etc.; **on the map** to be taken into account. [L. *mappa*, a napkin. a painted cloth]

maple *mā'pl*, *n.* any tree of the genus *Acer*, from the sap of some species of which sugar and syrup can be made, its timber.—*adj.* of maple.—**maple sugar; maple syrup; maple leaf** the emblem of Canada [O.E. *mapul*, maple.]

maquette *ma-ket'*, *n.* a small model of something to be made, esp. a model in clay or wax of a piece of sculpture. [Fr.]

maquillage *ma-kē-yazh*, *n.* (art of using) cosmetics, make-up. [Fr.]

maquis *ma'kē'*, *n.sing.* and *pl.* a thicket formation of shrubs, as in Corsica and on Mediterranean shores (*bot.*): (often *cap.*) French guerrilla bands (1940–45). or a member of one [Fr.,—It. *macchia*—L. *macula*, mesh.]

mar *mar*, *v.t.* to spoil: to impair: to injure: to damage to disfigure:—*pr.p.* **marr'ing**; *pa.t.* and *pa p.* **marred**. [O.E. *merran*.]

marabou(t) *mar'ə-bōō*(*t*), *n.* an adjutant bird, esp. an African species: its feathers: a plume or trimming of its feathers. [Same as next word.]

marabout *mar'ə-bōōt.* *n* a Muslim hermit, esp. in N. Africa: a Muslim shrine. [Fr.,—Ar. *murābit*, hermit.]

maraca *mə-rak'ə*, *n.* a dance-band instrument, a gourd or substitute, containing beans, beads, shot, or the like [Carib.]

maraschino *mar-ə-skē'nō*, *-shē'nō*, *n.* a liqueur distilled from a cherry grown in Dalmatia.—*pl.* **maraschi'nos**. —**maraschino cherry** a cherry preserved in real or imitation maraschino and used for decorating cocktails, etc. [It.,—*marasca*, *amarasca*, a sour cherry—L. *amārus*, bitter.]

marasmus *mə-raz'məs*, *n* a wasting away of the body. —*adj.* **maras'mic**. [Latinised—Gr *marasmos*— *marainein*, to decay.]

Marathon *mar'ə-thon*, *-thən*, *n.* scene of the Greek victory over the Persians, 490 B C , 22 miles from Athens: (without *cap.*) a marathon race: (without *cap.*) a test of endurance —*adj* (without *cap.*) of great length in time, or distance, etc.: displaying powers of endurance and stamina.—*n* **mar'athoner**. —**marathon race** a long-distance foot-race (usually 26 miles 385 yards—42·7 kilometres), commemorating the tradition that a Greek ran from Marathon to Athens with news of the victory. a long-distance race in other sports, e.g swimming. [Gr. *Marathōn*.]

maraud *mə-rod'*, *v.i.* to rove in quest of plunder.—*v.t.* to harry.—*n.* raiding: plundering.—*n.* **maraud'er**. [Fr. *maraud*, rogue.]

marble *mär'bl*, *n* a granular crystalline limestone: loosely, any rock of similar appearance taking a high polish: a slab, work of art, tombstone, tomb, or other object made of marble: a little hard ball (originally of marble) used by boys in play: marbling: anything hard, cold, polished, white, or otherwise like marble (*fig*): (in *pl.*) a game played with little balls. (in *pl.*) one's wits (*coll*)—*adj.* composed of marble: shining. unyielding: hard: insensible: marbled.—*v.t.* to stain or vein like marble.—*adj.* **mar'bled** irregularly mottled and streaked like some kinds of marble: wrought in marble. furnished with marble.—*ns.* **mar'bler; mar'bling** a marbled appearance or colouring: the act of veining or painting in imitation of marble.—*adv.* **mar'bly** like marble.—*adjs.* **mar'ble-edged** having the edges marbled, as a book; **mar'ble-heart'ed** hard-hearted, insensible.—**Elgin marbles** a collection of marbles obtained chiefly from the Parthenon by Lord *Elgin* in 1811, now in the British Museum. [O.Fr. *marbre*—L. *marmor*; cf Gr. *marmaros*—*marmairein*, to sparkle.]

marc *mark*, Fr *mar*, *n* fruit-refuse in wine- or oil-making.—**marc brandy** brandy made from marc. [Fr]

marcasite *mur'kə-sit*, *n.* sulphide of iron in orthorhombic crystals (in the gem trade can be pyrite. polished steel, etc.) [L L *marcasita*—Ar *marqashit*(*h*)ə; origin unknown.]

marcato *mar-ka'tō*, *adj.* marked: emphatic strongly accented—*superl.* **marcatis'simo**.—Also *adv.* [It . —*marcare*, to mark.]

March *märch*, *n.* the third month of the year (in England until 1752 the year began on 25th March).— **March hare** a hare gambolling in the breeding season, proverbially mad [L. *Martius* (*mēnsis*), (the month) of Mars.]

march[1] *march*, *n.* a boundary: border: a border district —used chiefly in *pl.* **march'es**.—*v.i.* to have a common boundary.—*n.* **march'er** an inhabitant or lord of a border district.—**march'man** a borderer, **march'-stone** a boundary stone —**riding the marches**

a ceremony of riding round the bounds of a municipality. [Fr *marche*; of Gmc. origin.]
march² *märch*, *v.i* to walk in a markedly rhythmical
military manner, or in a grave, stately, or resolute
manner: to advance steadily or irresistibly.—*v.t* to
cause to march. to force to go.—*n.* a marching
movement: an act of marching: distance traversed at
a stretch by marching: regular advance: a piece of
music fitted for marching to, or similar in character
and rhythm —**marching orders** orders to march: (as
from employment, etc.) dismissal (*coll.*); **march past**
the march of a body in front of one who reviews it —
forced march a march vigorously pressed forward for
combative purposes; **on the march** afoot and journeying; **rogue's march** music played in derision of a
person expelled; **steal a march on** to gain an advantage over, esp. in a sly or secret manner [Fr
marcher, to walk, prob —L *marcus*, a hammer]
marchioness *mar'shan-es, -is, n* the wife of a marquis,
marquess: a woman who holds a marquisate in her
own right. [L.L. *marchiōnissa*, fem of *marchiō*,
-ōnis, a lord of the marches.]
marchpane *march'pän, n* until 19th cent., name of
marzipan (q.v) [It *marzapane*]
Mardi Gras *mär-dē gra*, (Fr.) Shrove Tuesday.
mare¹ *mär, n.* the female of the horse.—**mare's'-nest** a
supposed discovery that turns out to have no reality,
mare's'-tail a tall marsh plant of the genus Hippuris:
(in *pl.*) long straight fibres of grey cirrus cloud
[O.E *mere*, fem. of *mearh*, a horse.]
mare² *mä'rē, ma're, n.* any of various darkish level
areas in (*a*) the moon, (*b*) Mars.—*pl.* **maria** (*mä'ri-ə,
ma'ri-a*) [L , sea.]
maremma *mar-em'ə, n.* seaside marshland [It ,—L
maritima, seaside]
marg. See **margarine**.
margarine *mär'jər-ēn, -gər-* (cont. **marg** *marg*, **marge**
marj), *n.* a butterlike substance made from vegetable
oils and fats, etc —*n* **mar'garite** a pearly-lustred
mineral sometimes reckoned a lime-alumina mica.—
adjs. **margaric** (*-gar'*), **margarit'ic**. [Gr *margarītēs*,
a pearl]
margay *mar'gā, n.* a spotted S American tiger-cat.
[Fr (or Sp).—Tupi *mbaracaia*]
marge¹ *marj, n* margin, brink [Fr ,—L *margō*,
-inis.]
marge². See **margarine**.
margin *mar'jin, n* an edge, border: the blank edge on
the page of a book: something allowed more than is
needed: a deposit to protect a broker against loss
difference between selling and buying price.—*v.t.* to
furnish with margins: to enter on the margin.—*adj*
mar'ginal pertaining to a margin: in or on the margin:
barely sufficient.—*n.* marginal constituency.—*n.pl*
margina'lia notes written on the margin.—*v.t.* **mar'-
ginalise, -ize** to furnish with notes —*adv.* **mar'-
ginally**.—*adjs.* **mar'ginate, -d** having a well-marked
border; **mar'gined**.—**marginal constituency, seat,
ward** a constituency, ward that does not provide a
safe seat for any of the political parties; **marginal land**
less fertile land which will be brought under cultivation only if economic conditions justify it [L.
margō, marginis]
margrave *mar'grāv, n.* a German nobleman of rank
equivalent to an English marquis.—*fem.* **margravine**
(*mar'grə-vēn*). [M Du *markgrave* (Du *markgraaf*,
Ger. *Markgraf*)—*mark*, a border, *grave* (mod
graaf), a count.]
marguerite *mar-gə-rēt', n.* the ox-eye daisy or other
single chrysanthemum. [Fr , daisy—Gr. *margarītēs,* pearl]
maria. See **mare²**.
Marian *mä'ri-ən, adj* relating to the Virgin *Mary* or to

Queen *Mary* (Tudor or Stewart).—*n.* a devotee,
follower, or defender of Mary: an English Roman
Catholic of Mary Tudor's time.—*n* **Mariol'atry**
(excessive) worship of the Virgin Mary. [L. *Marīa*.]
mariculture *mar'i-kul-chər, n.* the cultivation of plants
and animals of the sea in their own environment
[L. *mare*, sea.]
marigold *mar'i-gōld, n.* a composite plant (*Calendula*)
or its orange-yellow flower: extended to other yellow
flowers. [From the Virgin *Mary* and O.E. *golde*,
marigold.]
marijuana, marihuana *ma-ri-(hh)wa'nə, n* hemp: its
dried flowers and leaves smoked as an intoxicant
[Amer Sp]
marimba *ə-rim'bə, n.* an African xylophone, adopted
by Central Americans and jazz musicians. [African
origin.]
marine *mə-rēn', adj.* of, in, near, concerned with, or
belonging to, the sea: done or used at sea: inhabiting,
found in or got from the sea.—*n.* a soldier serving on
shipboard: shipping, naval or mercantile, fleet: nautical service —*ns.* **marina** (*mə-rē'nə*) a yacht, etc
station, prepared with every kind of facility for a
sailing holiday; **marinade** (*mar-i-nād'*) a liquor or
pickle in which fish or meat is steeped before cooking,
to improve the flavour, tenderise, etc —*vs.t.*
mar'inade, mar'inate to steep in wine, oil, herbs, etc.
—*n* **mar'iner** a sailor.—**marine engine** a ship's
engine; **marine insurance** insurance of ships or cargoes —**tell that to the marines** a phrase expressive of
disbelief and ridicule [Fr ,—L *marinus—mare*,
sea]
Mariolatry, etc. See **Marian**.
marionette *mar-i-ə-net', n.* a puppet moved by strings.
[Fr , dim. of the name *Marion*, itself a dim of *Marie*,
Mary.]
Marist *mar'ist, n.* a member of a modern R C congregation for teaching, preaching, and foreign missions
—*adj.* devoted to the service of the Virgin [Fr.
Mariste]
marital *mar'i-təl, mə-ri'təl, adj.* pertaining to a husband, or to a marriage of the nature of a marriage.—
adv. **mar'itally** (or *mə-ri'*). [L. *maritālis—maritus*,
a husband.]
maritime *mar'i-tīm, adj.* pertaining to the sea. relating
to sea-going or sea-trade: having a sea-coast: situated
near the sea: living on the shore: having a navy and
sea-trade. [L. *maritimus—mare*, sea.]
marjoram *mar'jə-rəm, n.* an aromatic labiate plant
(*Origanum*) used as a seasoning. [O.Fr. *majorane*]
mark¹ *mark, n.* a boundary (*arch*): a limit (*arch*): a
boundary stone, post, or the like: an object indicating
position or serving as a guide· an object to be aimed
at, striven for, or attained, as a butt, a goal: a suitable
victim (*slang*)· that which exactly suits one (*slang*): a
visible indication or sign· a symbol: a distinctive
device· a brand: a set, group, or class, marked with
the same brand: a type, model, issue, etc (usu.
numbered, as in *mark 1*)· a stamp: a token: a
substitute for a signature: a distinguishing characteristic: an impression or trace· a discoloured spot,
streak, smear, or other local modification of appearance: note: distinction: noteworthiness: a point
awarded for merit: a footprint: the impression of a
Rugby football player's heel on the ground on making
a fair catch.—*v.t.* to make a mark on: to indicate: to
record· to put marks on (a child's, student's, etc. written work) to show where it is correct or incorrect: to
make emphatic, distinct, or prominent: to characterise in a specified way· to impress with a sign: to
note· to regard· in football, hockey, etc , to remain
close to (one's opponent) in order to try and prevent
his obtaining or passing the ball (also *v i*)—*v.t.* to

take particular notice —*adj.* **marked** having marks: indicated: noticeable: prominent: emphatic: watched and suspected: doomed.—*adv.* **mark'edly** (*mar'kid-li*) noticeably.—*ns.* **mark'er** a person or tool that marks: something that marks a position, as a stationary light, a flare: one who marks the score at games, as at billiards: a counter or other device for scoring: a bookmark: the soldier who forms the pivot round which a body of soldiers wheels; **mark'ing** the act of making a mark or marks: (esp. in *pl.*) disposition of marks —Also *adj.*—**mark'er-bea'con**, **-bomb**, **-flag**; **mark'ing-ink** indelible ink, used for marking clothes; **marks'man**, **marks'woman** one good at hitting a mark: one who shoots well.—**(God) bless or save the mark** a phrase expressing ironical astonishment or scorn, from the usage of archery; **make one's mark to** make a notable impression: to gain great influence, **mark down** to set down in writing: to label at a lower price or to lower the price of (*n.* **mark'-down**): to note the position of: to destine for one's own; **mark off** to lay down the lines of: to graduate: to mark as attended to, disposed of, **mark of the Beast** see under **beast**; **mark out** to lay out the plan or outlines of: to destine; **mark time** to move the feet alternately in the same manner as in marching, but without changing ground: to keep things going without progressing; **mark up** to raise the price of (*n.* **mark'-up**); **off the mark** well away from the start in a race; **on your mark(s)** said before a race begins to prepare the runners for the starting command or signal; **soft mark** an easy dupe: one easy to cope with; **up to the mark** satisfactory, up to standard: fit and well. [O.E. (Mercian) *merc* (W.S. *mearc*), a boundary, a limit.]

mark² *märk, n* a coin of Germany (in 1924 officially named the Reichsmark; in 1948 the Deutsche mark), of Finland (the *markka, pl markkaa*, originally equivalent to a franc), and formerly of various countries. [O.E. *marc.*]

market *mär'kit, n.* a periodic concourse of people for the purposes of buying and selling: a building, square, or other public place used for such meetings: a shop (orig. *U.S.*): a region in which there is a demand for goods: buying and selling: opportunity for buying and selling: demand: state of being on sale: bargain: sale: rate of sale: value.—*adj.* relating to buying and selling.—*v.t.* to deal at a market: to buy and sell.—*v.t.* to put on the market:—*pr.p.* **mar'keting**; *pa.t.* and *pa.p.* **mar'keted.**—*adj.* **mar'ketable** fit for the market: saleable.—*ns.* **marketabil'ity**, **mar'ketableness; marketeer'** one who buys or sells at a market: a supporter of Britain's entry into the Common Market; **mar'keter** one who goes to market, buys or sells at a market; **mar'keting** the act or practice of buying and selling in market.—**mar'ket-cross'** a cross or similar structure anciently set up where a market was held; **mar'ket-day** the fixed day on which a market is held; **mar'ket-gar'den** a garden in which fruit and vegetables are grown for market; **mar'ket-gar'dener; mar'ket-gar'dening; mar'ket-hall, mar'ket-house** a building in which a market is held; **mar'ket-place** the market-square: broadly, the world of commercial transactions; **mar'ket-square'** the open space in a town where markets are held; **mar'ket-price', mar'ket-val'ue** the current price, **market research** research to determine consumers' preferences and what they can afford to buy; **mar'ket-town** a town having the privilege of holding a public market.—**in the market for** desirous of buying; **on the market** available for buying: on sale [Late O.E. *market*—O.N.Fr. *market* (Fr. *marché*, It. *mercato*), from L. *mercātus*, trade, a market—*merx*, merchandise.]

marl *marl, n.* a limy clay often used as manure. the

ground (*poet.*).—*v.t.* to cover with marl.—*adj* **mar'ly** like marl: abounding in marl. [O.Fr. *marle* (Fr. *marne*)—L.L. *margila*, a dim. of L. *marga*, marl.]

marlin *mär'lin, n.* a large oceanic fish of the genus *Makaira* akin to the swordfishes. [**marline-spike**.]

marline *mär'lin, n.* a small rope for winding round a larger one to keep it from wearing.—**mar'line-spike** a spike for separating the strands of a rope in splicing. —Also spelt **marlin. marlinspike.** [Du. *marling*, vbl. n. from *marlen*, or *marlijn—marren*, and *lijn*, rope]

marls. See meril.

marly. See marl.

marm. See ma'am.

marmalade *mär'mə-lād, n* a jam or preserve generally made of the pulp (and rind) of oranges, originally of quinces. [Fr *marmelade*—Port. *marmelada—marmelo*, a quince—L. *melimēlum*—Gr. *melimēlon*, a sweet apple—*meli*, honey. *mēlon*, an apple.]

marmite *mär'mīt, mär-mēt', n.* a metal or earthenware cooking vessel, esp for soup. [Fr.. pot or kettle]

marmoreal *mär-mōr'i-al, -mōr', adj.* of, or like, marble [L. *marmor*, marble; Gr. *marmaros*.]

marmoset *mär'mə-zet, n.* a very small American monkey. [Fr. *marmouset*, grotesque figure.]

marmot *mär'mət, n.* a genus of stout burrowing rodents (*Marmota* or *Arctomys*), in America called woodchuck. [It. *marmotto*—Romansch *murmont* —L *mūs, muris*, mouse, *mons, montis*, mountain.]

marocain *mar'ə-kān, n.* a dress material finished with a grain surface like morocco-leather. [Fr. *maroquin*, morocco-leather.]

maroon¹ *mə-rōōn', n.* a brownish crimson: a detonating firework.—*adj.* of the colour maroon. [Fr. *marron*, a chestnut—It *marrone*, a chestnut.]

maroon² *mə-rōōn', n.* a fugitive slave: a marooned person.—*v.t.* to put and leave ashore on a desolate island: to isolate uncomfortably.—*ns.* **maroon'er; maroon'ing.** [Fr. *marron*—Sp. *cimarrón*, wild.]

marque¹ *märk, n* a privateer.—**letter(s)-of-marque** a privateer's licence to commit acts of hostility. [Fr.]

marque² *märk, n.* a brand, mark. [Fr.]

marquee *mär-kē', n.* a large tent. [From **marquise**, as if *pl.*]

marquess, etc. See **marquis**.

marquetry, marqueterie *mark'i-tri, n.* work inlaid with pieces of various-coloured wood, ivory, metal, etc. [Fr. *marqueterie—marqueter*, to inlay—*marque*, a mark.]

marquis or (spelling used by some holders of the title) **marquess** *mär'kwis, n.* a title of nobility next below that of a duke:—*fem.* **marchioness** (*mär'shən-es, -is*). —*ns.* **mar'quisate, -quessate** the lordship of a marquis; **marquise** (*mär-kēz'*) in France, a marchioness. a marquee: a ring set with gems arranged to form a pointed oval: a gem cut into the shape of a pointed oval; **mar'quisette** a woven clothing fabric, used also for curtains and mosquito nets. [O.Fr. *marchis*, assimilated later to Fr. *marquis*—L.L. *marchēnsis*, a prefect of the marches.]

marram *mar'əm, n.* a seaside grass (*Ammophila*, or *Psamma, arenaria*), a binder of sand-dunes. [O.N. *marr*, sea, *halmr*, haulm.]

marrels. See meril.

marriage *mar'ij, n.* the ceremony, act, or contract by which a man and woman become husband and wife. the union of a man and woman as husband and wife. a close union (*fig.*).—*adj.* **marr'iageable** suitable for marriage.—*n.* **marr'iageableness.—marr'iage-bed** the bed of a married couple: marital intercourse: the rights and obligations of marriage; **marr'iage-broker** one who, for a fee, arranges a marriage contract;

... certain parts of the ...val or feast-day, as in ... *Martinmas*, etc. [O E ... L. *mittĕre*, to send away, perh ... the close of service, *ite, missa est* ... (the congregation) is dismissed]

...*as'ə-kər*, n. indiscriminate slaughter, esp ...ruelty: carnage —*v.t.* to kill with violence and ...elty: to slaughter · [Fr.}

massage *ma'sazh, mə-sazh'*, n. a system of treatment for painful muscles, etc by pressing, tapping, kneading, friction, etc.—*v t* to subject to massage —*ns* **massa'gist**, **masseur** (*-sœr'*, or *-sûr'*).—*fem* **masseuse** (*-sœz'*) [Fr., from Gr *massein*, to knead]

massé *mas'ā*, n in billiards, a sharp stroke made with the cue vertical or nearly so   [Fr]

masseur, masseuse. See **massage.**

massif *ma-sēf', mas'if*, n a central mountain mass [Fr]

massive, massy, etc See **mass¹.**

mast¹ *mast*, n a long upright pole, esp one for carrying the sails of a ship —*v.t* to supply with a mast or masts —*adjs* **mast'ed**; **mast'less.**—**mast'head** the top of a mast the name of a newspaper or periodical in the typographical form in which it normally appears, or a similar block of information regularly used as a heading —**before the mast** as a common sailor (whose quarters are in the forecastle)   [O E *mæst*.]

mast² *mast*, n the fruit of the oak, beech, chestnut, and other trees, on which swine feed· nuts, acorns —*adjs* **mast'ful**; **mast'less**; **mast'y** of the nature of mast· as if well fed on mast —*adj* **mast'-fed.** [O E *mæst*]

mastaba *mas'tə-bə*, n an ancient Egyptian tomb in which offerings were made in an outer chamber communicating with an inner one where was the figure of the dead man, with a shaft descending to the actual grave   [Ar *mastabah*, a bench]

mastectomy. See **mastoid.**

master *mas'tər*, n one who commands or controls a lord or owner a leader or ruler a teacher an employer the commander of a ship: one eminently skilled in anything, esp art· one who has complete knowledge (with *cap*) formerly prefixed to a name or designation as Mr is now, now only of a boy in this use (usu with *cap*) a title of dignity or office—a degree conferred by universities, as *Master of Arts*, etc , the head of some corporations, etc , of a lodge of freemasons, etc an original (film, record, etc) from which copies are made —*adj* chief: controlling: predominant. of a master. of the rank of a master· original.—*v t* to become master of. to overcome· to gain control over: to acquire a thorough knowledge of to become skilful in to rule as master —*adj* **mas'terful** exercising the authority or power of a master: imperious: masterly (*rare*) —*adv* **mas'terfully.**—*ns* **mas'terfulness; mas'terhood; mas'tering** action of verb *master*.—*adj.* **mas'terless** without a master or owner: ungoverned. unsubdued. beyond control —*n* **mas'terliness.**—*adj* **mas'terly** like a master: with the skill of a master —*ns.* **mas'tership** the condition, authority, status, office, or term of office of master rule or dominion: superiority; **mas'tery** the power or authority of a master: upper hand control· masterly skill or knowledge.—**mas'ter-build'er** a chief builder one who directs or employs others, **mas'ter-card** the card that commands a suit; **mas'ter-class** the dominant class in a society: a lesson, esp. in music, given to talented students by a renowned expert, **mas'ter-key** a key that opens many (different) locks, esp all the locks in a certain building a clue able to guide one out

of many difficulties (*fig.*); **mas'ter-mar'iner** the captain of a merchant-vessel or fishing-vessel; **mas'ter-ma'son** a freemason who has attained the third degree; **mas'termind** a mind, or a person having a mind, of very great ability· the person conceiving or directing a project —*v t.* to originate, think out, and direct —**mas'terpiece** piece of work worthy of a master· one's greatest achievement; **mas'terstroke** a stroke or performance worthy of a master: an effective, well-timed act; **mas'terswitch** a switch for controlling the effect of a number of other switches or contactors; **master-slave manipulator** a manipulator, esp. one used to handle, from behind a protective screen, radioactive material; **old masters** a term applied collectively to the great painters about the time of the Renaissance, esp the Italians, **passed master** one who has passed as a master: a qualified or accomplished master, a thorough proficient (also **pastmaster**)   [Partly O.E *mægester*, partly O Fr *maistre* (Fr *maître*), both from L. *magister*, from root of *magnus*, great.]

mastic, mastich *mas'tik, n.* a pale yellow gum resin from the lentisk and other trees, used for varnish, cement, liquor a tree exuding mastic: a bituminous or oily cement of various kinds   [Fr *mastic*—L L *mastichum*—Gr *mastichē*]

masticate *mas'ti-kāt, v t* to chew to knead mechanically, as in rubber manufacture —*adj.* **mas'ticable** that may be chewed —*ns* **mastica'tion; mas'ticātor** one who masticates a machine for grinding· a machine for kneading india-rubber —*adj* **mas'ticatory** (*-kə-tə-ri*) chewing adapted for chewing.—*n* a substance chewed to increase the saliva   [L *masticāre, -ātum*, cf Gr *mastax*, jaw, *mastichaein*, to grind the teeth]

mastiff *mas'tif, n* a thick-set and powerful variety of dog used as a watch-dog   [O Fr *mastin*, app —L *mansuētus*, tame]

mastitis. See **mastoid.**

Mastodon *mas'tə-don*, n a genus of extinct elephants, so named from the teat-like prominences of the molar teeth (without *cap*) an animal of this genus   [Gr *mastos*, breast. *odous, odontos*, a tooth]

mastoid *mas'toid, adj* like a nipple or a teat —*n* a process of the temporal bone behind the ear (also **mastoid bone, process**).—*ns* **mastect'omy** surgical removal of a breast, **masti'tis** inflammation of the mammary gland —*adj* **mastoid'al.**—*n.* **mastoidi'tis** inflammation of the air cells of the mastoid processes —**radical mastectomy** the surgical removal of a breast together with some pectoral muscles and lymph nodes of the armpit   [Gr *mastos*, a nipple]

masturbation *mas-tər-bā'shən*, n stimulation, usually by oneself, of the sexual organs by manipulation, etc., so as to produce orgasm —*v t* **mas'turbate.**—*n* **mas'turbātor.** [L *masturbārī*]

masty. See **mast².**

mat¹ *mat*, n a piece of fabric of sedge, rushes, straw, coarse fibre, etc . or of rubber, wire, or other material, for cleaning shoes, for covering a floor, hearth, threshold, for protection, packing, for standing, sleeping, etc , on, or for other purpose· a rug: a small piece of cloth, wood, etc , for placing under a vase, dish, or other object· a closely interwoven or tangled mass, as of hair, of vegetation —*v t* to cover with mats. to interweave to tangle closely —*v t* to become tangled in a mass—*pr p* **matt'ing;** *pa t* and *pa p* **matt'ed.**—*n* **matt'ing** mat-making becoming matted· covering with mats' material used as mats —**mat'grass, mat'weed** a small, tufted, rushlike moorland grass (*Nardus stricta*) marram —**on the mat** on the carpet (*fig.*).   [O E *matt(e), meatte*—L *matta*, a mat]

mat² *mat, adj.* dull or lustreless.—Also **matt, matte.** —*n* **mat** a dull uniform finish or surface—*v.t* to produce a dull surface on: to frost (glass). [Fr *mat.*]

matador, matadore *mat'ə-dör, -dör, n.* the man who kills the bull in bullfights. [Sp *matador—matar,* to kill—L. *mactāre,* to kill, to honour by sacrifice—*mactus,* honoured.]

match¹ *mach, n.* a piece of inflammable material which easily takes or carries fire: a short stick of wood or other material tipped with an easily ignited material —**match'box** a box for holding matches, **match'-maker; match'stick** the wooden shaft of a match.— *adj.* very thin, like a matchstick: (of figures in a drawing, etc.) having limbs suggested by single lines —**match'wood** touchwood. wood suitable for matches: splinters. [O.Fr *mesche.*]

match² *mach, n.* that which tallies or exactly agrees with another thing: an equal: one able to cope with another: a condition of exact agreement. compatibility or close resemblance, esp. in colours equality in contest. a formal contest or game: a pairing: a marriage: one to be gained in marriage.— *v.t.* to be exactly or nearly alike: to correspond. to form a union· to compete or encounter (esp. on equal terms).—*v.t.* to be equal to. to be a counterpart to: to be compatible with, or exactly like, in colour. etc.. to be able to compete with: to find an equal or counter-part to. to pit or set against another in contest or as equal: to treat as equal: to fit in with: to suit. to join in marriage.—*adjs.* **match'able; matched.**—*n* **match'er.**—*adjs.* **match'ing; match'less** having no match or equal: superior to all.—*adv.* **match'lessly.** —*n.* **match'lessness.—match'board** a board with a tongue cut along one edge and a groove in the oppo-site edge; **match'maker** one who plans to bring about marriages: one who arranges boxing matches, **match'-making; match'-play** scoring in golf according to holes won and lost rather than the number of strokes taken; **match point** the stage at which another point wins the match: the point that wins the match: a unit of scoring in bridge tournaments.—**to match** in accordance, as in colour. [O.E. *gemæcca.*]

match-maker. See **match¹.**
matchmaker. See **match².**

mate¹ *māt, n.* a companion: an equal· a fellow work-man: a friendly or ironic form of address: a husband or wife: an animal with which another is paired: one of a pair: a ship's officer under the captain or master: an assistant, deputy (as *plumber's mate*).—*v.t.* to marry: to pair (esp. animals): to couple: to fit.—*v.i* to marry: to pair:—*adjs.* **mate'less** without a mate or companion; **mat(e)'y** (*coll.*) friendly and familiar, esp. in a studied or overdone manner. [Prob M.L.G. *mate* or earlier Du. *maet* (now *maat*).]

mate² *māt, v.t.* to checkmate.—*n.* and *interj* **checkmate** [O.Fr. *mat,* checkmated; see **check-mate.**]

mate³, maté *ma tā, n.* a South American species of holly (*Ilex paraguayensis*): an infusion of its leaves and green shoots, Paraguay tea [Sp *mate*—Que-chua *mati,* a gourd (in which it is made)]

matelot. See **matlo.**

mater *mā'tər, ma'ter, n.* mother (*slang*). [L *māter.*]
material *mə-tē'ri-əl, adj.* relating to matter: consisting of matter. corporeal, not spiritual: bodily· physical· gross, lacking spirituality: relating to subject-matter relevant: of serious importance, esp. of legal impor-tance.—*n.* that out of which anything is or may be made: that which may be made use of for any pur-pose· one who is suitable for a specified occupation, training, etc . a fabric —*n.* **materialisa'tion, -z·.—** *v.t.* **mate'rialise, -ize** to render material to cause to assume bodily form: to reduce to or regard as matter.

to render materialistic —*v.i.* to take [illegible] become actual (*coll.*).—*ns.* **mate'rialism** the [illegible] that denies the independent existence of spirit, an maintains that there is but one substance—matter. the explanation of history as the working out of economic conditions: blindness to the spiritual. excessive devotion to bodily wants or financial success, **mate'rialist.**—Also *adj —adjs.* **materi-alist'ic, -al.—***advs* **materialist'ically; mate'rially** in material manner: in respect of matter or material conditions, or material cause. in a considerable or important degree. —*ns.* **mate'rialness, materiality** (*-al'i-ti*).—**dialectical materialism** Karl Marx's view of history as a conflict between two opposing forces, thesis and antithesis, which is resolved by the forming of a new force, synthesis, present conditions are due to a class struggle between the capitalists, whose aim is private profit, and the workers, who resist exploita-tion. [L *māteriālis—māteria,* matter]

maternal *mə-tür'nəl, adj* of a mother motherly on the mother's side: of the nature, or in the person, of a mother —*adv.* **mater'nally.**—*n* **mater'nity** the fact of being in the relation of mother motherhood — *adj.* of or for women at or near the time of childbirth. [Fr. *maternel* (It *maternale*) and *maternité*—L. *māternus—māter,* mother.]

matey. See **mate¹.**

mathematic, -al *math-i-mat'ik, -əl, adjs.* pertaining to, or done by, mathematics very accurate —*adv* **mathemat'ically.**— *ns.* **mathematician** (*-mə-tish'ən*) one versed in mathematics, **mathemat'icism** the be-lief that everything can be described or explained ult-imately in mathematical terms —*n* sing. or pl. **mathe-mat'ics** (*coll.* **maths,** in U S **math**) the science of magnitude and number, and of all their relations [Gr *mathēmatikē* (*epistēmē,* skill. knowledge*) re-lating to learning—*mathēma—root* of *manthanein,* to learn.]

Matilda *mə-til'də, (Austr) n.* a bushman's swag — **walk, waltz Matilda** to travel around carrying one's swag

matin *mat'in, n.* (in *pl.*; often *cap.*) one of the seven canonical hours of the R.C. Church, usually sung between midnight and daybreak, or now by anticip-ation the afternoon or evening before. (in *pl*) the daily morning service of the Church of England.— *adj.* **mat'inal.**—*n* **matinée, matinee** (*mat'i-nā, mat(-ə)-nā'*) a public entertainment or reception usually held in the afternoon.—**matinée coat, jacket** a baby's coat or jacket made of wool or similar mater-ial; **matinée idol** a handsome actor, popular esp. among women [Fr *matines* (fcm. pl.)—L *mātū-tinus,* belonging to the morning—*Mātūta,* goddess of morning. prob. akin to *mātūrus,* early]

matlo, matlow *mat'lō,* (*slang*) *n* a seaman, sailor.— *pl.* **mat'los, mat'lows.**—Also **matelot** (*mat'lō*) [Fr. *matelot*]

matrass *mat'ras, n* a long-necked chemical flask: a hard-glass tube closed at one end [Fr. *matras.*]

matriarchy *mā'tri-ar-ki, n.* government by a mother or by mothers: an order of society in which descent is reckoned in the female line.—*n* **ma'triarch** a patri-arch's wife: a woman of like status to a patriarch: an elderly woman who dominates her family or associ-ates. an old woman of great dignity —*adj.* **matriar'-chal.** [Formed on the analogy of **patriarchy**—L. *māter,* mother.]

matricide *mā'* or *mat'ri-sīd, n.* a murderer of his (or her) own mother. the murder of one's own mother,— *adj.* **matrici'dal.** [L. *mātricida, mātricidium— māter,* mother, *caedēre,* to kill]

matricula *mə-trik'ū-lə, n.* a register of members, students, etc.—*v.t* **matric'ulate** to admit to membership by entering one's name in a register, esp. in a college.—*v.i.* to become a member of a college, university, etc., by being enrolled.—*ns.* **matricula'-tion** the act of matriculating: the state of being matriculated: an entrance examination (familiarly **matric'**), **matric'ulator**.—*adj.* **matricula'tory**. [L L. *mātricula*, a register, dim. of L *mātrix*.]

matrilineal *mat-ri-lin'i-əl*, **matrilinear** *-ər*, *adjs.* reckoned through the mother or through females alone.—*adv.* **matrilin'eally**.—*n.* **mat'riliny** (or *-lī'ni*). [L. *māter*, a mother, *linea*, a line.]

matrimony *mat'ri-mən-i, n.* wedlock: a card game of chance in which one of the winning combinations is that of king and queen: the combination of king and queen in that and in various other games.—*adj.* **matrimonial** (*-mō'ni-əl*) relating to marriage. [L. *mātrimōnium—māter*, *mātris*, mother.]

matrix *mā'triks*, or *mat'riks, n.* the womb (*anat.*): the cavity in which anything is formed: that in which anything is embedded, as cementing material: the bed on which a thing rests: a mould: a rectangular array of quantities or symbols (*math.*):—*pl.* **ma'trices** (*-tris-ēz*, or *-iz*) or **ma'trixes**. [L. *mātrix, -īcis*, a breeding animal, later, the womb—*māter*, mother.]

matron *mā'trən, n.* a married woman: an elderly lady of staid and sober habits: one in charge of nursing and domestic arrangements in a hospital, school, or other institution —*ns.* **mā'tronage**, **mā'tronhood** state of being a matron: a body of matrons.—*adjs.* **mā'tronal** pertaining or suitable to a matron· motherly: grave, **mā'tronly** like, becoming, or belonging to a matron: elderly: sedate· plump.—*n.* **mā'tronship**. [Fr. *matrone*—L *mātrōna—māter*, mother.]

matronymic. See metronymic.

matt. Same as mat[2].

mattamore *mat-ə-mōr'*, *-mor'* or *mat'*, *n.* a subterranean chamber. [Fr. *matamore*—Ar. *matmūrah*.]

matte *mat*, *adj.* Same as **mat[2].**

matted. See mat[1].

matter *mat'ər, n* that which occupies space, and with which we become acquainted by our bodily senses: that out of which anything is made, material: subject or material of thought, speech, writing, dispute, etc.: substance (opp. to *form*): anything engaging the attention: affair: thing: that with which one has to do: cause or ground: thing of consequence: something that is amiss: importance: an approximate amount: pus.—*v.i* to be of importance: to signify: to form or discharge pus.—*adjs.* **matt'erful** full of matter, pithy; **matt'erless; matt'ery** purulent: containing, discharging, or covered ·with pus.—*adj.* **matter'-of-fact'** adhering to literal, actual or pedestrian fact: not fanciful: prosaic.—**as a matter of fact** really; **for that matter** as for that: indeed; **matter of course** a thing occurring in natural time and order, as to be expected; **matter of form** a (mere) official procedure or conventional etiquette; **no matter** it does not matter: it makes no difference. [O.Fr. *matiere*—L. *māteria*, matter.]

matting. See mat[1].

mattock *mat'ək, n.* a kind of pickaxe with cutting end instead of a point. [O.E. *mattuc*.]

mattress *mat'ris, n.* a bed made of a stuffed bag, or a substitute or supplementary structure of wire, hair, etc.: a mass of brushwood, etc., used to form a foundation for roads, etc., or for the walls of embankments, etc. [O.Fr. *materas* (Fr. *matelas*)—Ar. *mat-rah*, a place where anything is thrown.]

mature *mə-tūr'*, *adj.* fully developed: having the mental, emotional and social development appropriate to an adult: perfected: ripe: well thought out: due.—*v.t.* to bring to ripeness, full development or perfection.—*v.i.* to come to or approach ripeness,

full development, or perfection: to become due.—*adj.* **matur'able** capable of being matured.—*v.t.* **maturate** (*mat'*) to make mature: to promote the suppuration of (*med.*).—*v.i.* (*med.*) to suppurate perfectly.—*n.* **matura'tion** a bringing or a coming to maturity: the process of suppurating fully: the final stage in the production of a germ-cell.—*adjs.* **matu-rā'tional; matur'ative** (or *mat'*) promoting ripening: promoting suppuration.—*adv.* **mature'ly**.—*ns.* **mature'ness; matur'ity** ripeness: full development: the time of becoming due, as of a bill. [L. *mātūrus*, ripe.]

matutinal *mat-ū-tī'nl* (or *mə-tū'ti-nl*), *adj.* pertaining to the morning: happening early in the day.—Also **matutine** (*mat'ū-tīn*) [L. *mātūtīnālis, mātūtīnus*; see **matin.**]

maty. See mate[1].

matzo *mat'sə, -sō, n.* unleavened bread: a wafer of it:—*pl.* (with verb *sing.* or *pl.*) **mat'zoth, -zos.**—Also **mat'-zoh**, **mat'za(h):**—*pls.* **mat'zot(h), mat'za(h)s.** [Yiddish *matse*; from Heb.]

maudlin *mod'lin, adj.* silly: sickly-sentimental: fuddled, half-drunk. [M.E. *Maudelein*, through O.Fr. and L. from Gr. *Magdalēnē*, from the assumption that Mary Magdalene was the penitent woman of Luke vii. 38.]

maul *möl, n.* a heavy wooden hammer: a loose scrimmage (*Rugby football*).—*v t.* to beat with a maul or heavy stick: to handle roughly, batter, maltreat.—*v.i.* to thrust forward in a close mass. [**mall.**]

maulstick *mol'stik, n.* a stick used by painters as a rest for the hand.—Also **mahl'stick, mal'stick.** [Du *maalstok—malen*, to paint, *stok*, stick, assimilated to **stick.**]

maunder *mön'dər, v.i.* to grumble: to drivel: to wander idly.—*ns.* **maun'derer; maun'dering** drivelling talk.

maundy *mon'di, n.* the religious ceremony of washing the feet of the poor, in commemoration of Christ's washing the disciples' feet (John xiii)—long practised by some monarchs.—**maundy money** the dole given away on **Maundy Thursday,** the day before Good Friday, by the royal almoner, usu. a silver penny for each year of sovereign's age—the small silver coins specially minted since 1662. [Fr *mandé*—L. *man-dātum*, command (John xiii. 34).]

mausoleum *mö-so-lē'əm, n.* a magnificent tomb or monument.—*adj.* **mausolē'an.** [L. *mausōlēum*—Gr. *Mausōleion*, the magnificent tomb of *Mausōlos* (d. 353 B C) at Halicarnassus.]

mauve *möv, möv, n.* a purple aniline dye: its colour, that of mallow flowers.—*adj.* of the colour of mauve.—*n.* **mauv(e)'in(e)** mauve dye. [Fr.,—L. *malva*, mallow.]

maverick *mav'ər-ik, n* a stray animal without an owner's brand, esp. a calf: one who does not conform [From Samuel *Maverick*, a Texas cattle-raiser.]

mavis *mā'vis, n.* the song-thrush. [Fr. *mauvis.*]

maw *mo, n.* the stomach, esp. in the lower animals: inward parts: any insatiate gulf or receptacle (*fig.*). [O.E. *maga*]

mawk *mök,* (now *dial.*) *n.* a maggot.—*adj.* **mawk'ish** (orig.) maggoty· disgusting: squeamish: insipid: sickly: sickly-sentimental, maudlin.—*adv.* **mawk'-ishly.**—*n.* **mawk'ishness.** [O.N. *mathkr.* maggot.]

maxi- *mak'si-,* in composition, (very) large, long (abbrev. of **maximum**) as in e.g. the following:—**max'i-coat, -skirt, -dress** a coat, skirt, dress reaching the ankle; **max'i-single** a gramophone record longer than an ordinary single.

maxi *mak'si, n.* short for **maxi-coat,** etc —*adj. (coll.)* (extra) large or long.

maxilla *maks-il'ə, n* a jawbone, esp. the upper: in arthropods, an appendage close behind the mouth, modified in connection with feeding:—*pl* **maxill'ae** (-*ē*).—*adj.* **maxill'ary** (or **maks'**) pertaining to a jaw or maxilla.—*n.* a bone forming the posterior part of the upper jaw. [L. *maxilla*, jawbone]

maxim *maks'im*, *n.* a general principle, serving as a rule or guide: a pithy saying: a proverb. [Fr. *maxime* —L. *maxima* (*sententia*, or some other word), greatest (opinion, etc.), fem., superl. of *magnus*, great.]

maximum *maks'i-məm*, *adj.* greatest.—*n.* the greatest number, quantity, or degree: the highest point reached: the value of a variable when it ceases to increase and begins to decrease (*math.*):—*pl.* **max'ima**.—opp. to *minimum*.—*adj.* **maxi'mal** of the highest or maximum value.—*adv.* **max'imally**.—*v.t* **max'imise, -ize** to raise to the highest degree.— **maximum and minimum thermometer** a thermometer that shows the highest and lowest temperatures that have occurred since last adjustment [L., superl neut. of *magnus*, great.]

maxixe *ma-shē'shā*, *n.* a Brazilian dance: a tune for it. [Port.]

maxwell *maks'wəl*, *n.* the cgs unit of magnetic flux, equal to 10^{-8} weber. [James Clerk-*Maxwell* (1831–79), Scottish physicist.]

may *mā*, *vb.* expressing ability, permission, freedom, possibility, contingency, chance, competence, or wish, or softening a blunt question—used with infin. without *to*:—infin. and participles obsolete: *3rd pers.* **may**; *pa.t.* **might**.—*adv.* **may'be** perhaps, possibly.— *n.* a possibility.—*adv.* **may'hap** (or **-hap'**) perhaps. [O.E. *mæg*, pr.t. (old pa.t.) of *magan*, to be able, pa.t. *mihte*.]

May *mā*, *n.* now the fifth month of the year (see **March**): the early or gay part of life: (*without cap.*) may-blossom.—*v.i.* (also without *cap.*) to gather may on Mayday: to participate in May sports.—*n.* **may'ing** the observance of Mayday customs.—*adj.* **may-bee'tle, may'-bug** the cockchafer; **may'-bloom', -bloss'om** the hawthorn flower; **May'day** the first day of May, given to sports and to socialist and labour demonstrations. —Also *adj.*—**May'-dew'** the dew of May, esp. that of the morning of the first day of May, said to whiten linen, and beautify faces; **May'fair** the aristocratic West End of London, at one time scene of a fair in May; **may'flower** the hawthorn or other flower that blooms in May; **may'fly** a short-lived insect (Ephemera) that appears in May: the caddis-fly; **may'pole** a pole erected for dancing round on Mayday; **May'-queen'** a young woman crowned with flowers as queen on Mayday; **May'-time** the season of May; **may tree** the hawthorn. [O.Fr. *Mai*—L. *Māius* (*mēnsis*), prob. (month) sacred to *Māia*, mother of Mercury.]

Maya *mä'ya*, *n.* one of an Indian people of Central America and Southern Mexico who developed a remarkable civilisation.—*adjs.* **Ma'ya, Ma'yan**.

maybe. See **may**.

mayday *mā'dā*, the international radiotelephonic distress signal for ships and aircraft. [Fr. (*infin.*) *m'aider*, pron *mā-dā*, help me.]

Mayday. See **May**.

mayhap. See **may**.

mayhem *mā'hem*, *mā'əm*, *n.* maiming: malicious damage (*legal* and *U.S.*). [**maim**.]

mayonnaise *mā-ə-nāz'*, or *mā'*, *n.* a sauce composed of the yolk of eggs, salad-oil, and vinegar or lemon-juice, seasoned: any cold dish of which it is an ingredient. [Fr.]

mayor *mā'ər*, *mār*, *n.* the chief magistrate of a city or borough in England, Ireland, etc., whether man or woman: the head of a municipal corporation.—*adj* **may'oral**.—*ns.* **may'oralty, may'orship** the office of a mayor; **may'oress** a mayor's wife, or other lady who

performs her social and ceremonial functions. [Fr. *maire*—L. *major*, compar. of *magnus*, great.]

mayweed *mā'wēd*, *n.* stinking camomile (*Anthemis cotula*): corn feverfew (*Matricaria inodora*; a scentless mayweed): applied to various similar plants [O E. *mægtha*, mayweed, and **weed**[1].]

mazarine *maz-ə-rēn'*, *n.* a rich blue colour. a blue gown or stuff.

maze *māz*, *n.* bewilderment: a labyrinth: a set of intricate windings.—*v.t.* to bewilder: to confuse.—*adv* **mā'zily**.—*n* **mā'ziness**.—*adj.* **mā'zy**.

mazurka *mə-zōōr'kə*, or *-zûr'*, *n.* a lively Polish dance: music for it, in triple time [Pol., Masurian woman.]

Mc. See **Mac**.

McCarthyism *mə-kar'thi-izm*, *n.* the hunting down and removal from public employment of all suspected of Communism.—*adj* **McCar'thyite** of, relating to, this kind of purge [From Joseph *McCarthy* (1909–1957), U.S. politician.]

MCP. Abbrev. for **male chauvinist pig** (see **male**).

me[1] *mē*, *mi*, *pers. pron.* the accusative and dative of I. [O.E. *mē*.]

me[2]. An anglicised spelling of **mi**.

mea culpa *mē'ə kul'pə*, *mā'a kōōl'pa*, (L.) by my own fault—an acknowledgement of one's guilt or mistake.

mead[1] *mēd*, *n.* honey and water fermented and flavoured. [O.E. *meodu*.]

mead[2] *mēd*, (*poet.*), and **meadow** *med'ō*, *ns.* a level tract producing grass to be mown down: a rich pasture-ground, esp. beside a stream.—*adj.* **mead'owy**. —**mead'ow-grass** any grass of the genus Poa; **mead'ow-lark'** (*U.S.*) a name for various species of birds of the genus *Sturnella*; **meadow pipit** *Anthus pratensis*, a common brown and white European songbird; **mead'ow-saff'ron** *Colchicum autumnale*—also autumn-crocus, or naked lady. [O.E. *mæd*, in oblique cases *mædwe*—*māwan*, to mow.]

meadow-sweet *med'ō-swēt*, *n.* the rosaceous plant *Spiraea ulmaria*, a tall fragrant plant of watery meadows. [Earlier *mead-sweet* which may be from **mead**[1] or from **mead**[2].]

meagre *mē'gər*, *adj.* having little flesh: lean: poor: without richness or fertility: barren: scanty: without strength: jejune.—*adv.* **mea'grely**.—*n.* **mea'greness**. [Fr. *maigre*—L. *macer, macra, -rum*, lean.]

meal[1] *mēl*, *n.* the food taken at one time: the act or occasion of taking food, as a breakfast, dinner, or supper.—**meals'-on-wheels'** a welfare service taking cooked, usu. hot, meals to old people in need of such help; **meal ticket, meal'-ticket** a ticket that can be exchanged for a meal (esp. at reduced price): someone or something that is the source of one's expenses or income: someone who can be depended upon; **meal'-time** the time for a meal.—**make a meal of** to consume as a meal: to enjoy to the full: to treat or perform in an unnecessarily laborious or meticulous way. [O.E. *mæl*, time, portion of time.]

meal[2] *mēl*, *n.* grain ground to powder: other material in powder: a powdery surface-covering —*v.t.* to cover with meal: to grind into meal.—*v i.* to yield or be plentiful in meal.—*n.* **meal'iness**.—*adj.* **meal'y** like meal, powdery: covered with meal or with something like meal: whitish.—**meal'-worm** the larva of a beetle (Tenebrio) abounding in granaries and flour-stores; **meal'y-bug** a hothouse pest, a coccus insect with a white powdery appearance.—*adj.* **meal'y-mouthed** (-*mowdhd*) smooth-tongued: over-squeamish, esp. in choice of words.—**meal'y-mouth'-edness**. [O.E. *melu, melo*.]

mealie *mēl'i*, *n.* (esp. in South Africa) an ear of maize: (esp. in *pl.*) maize.—Also **meal'y**.—**mealie meal** finely ground maize. [S.Afr. Du. *milie*, millet.]

mean[1] *mēn*, *adj.* low in rank or birth: low in worth or estimation: of little value or importance: poor, humble: inconsiderable: despicable: ungenerous: malicious, bad-tempered: skilful, excellent (*slang*). —*n.* **mean'ie, -y** (*coll*) an ungenerous, ungracious, small-minded, or malicious person.—*adv.* **mean'ly**. —*n.* **mean'ness**.—*adjs.* **mean'-born; mean'-spir'ited**. —**mean'-spir'itedness**. [O.E. *gemǣne*; L. *commūnis*, common.]

mean² *mēn, adj.* intermediate: average.—*n.* that which is between or intermediate: an average amount, or value: a middle state or position: an intermediate term in a progression: an instrument or medium:—*pl.* in form **means** that by whose instrumentality anything is caused or brought to pass: (treated as *sing.* or *pl.*) way to an end: (treated as *pl.*) pecuniary resources: what is required for comfortable living.—*ns.* **mean'time, mean'while** the intervening time.—*advs.* in the intervening time.—**means** test the test of private resources, determining or limiting claim to concession or allowance.—*v.t.* **means'-test**.—**arithmetic(al) mean** the sum of a number of quantities divided by their number; **by all means** certainly; **by any means** in any way; **by means of** with the help or use of; **by no means** certainly not; **geometric(al) mean** the *n*th root of the product of *n* quantities; **golden mean** the middle course between two extremes: a wise moderation. [O.Fr. *meien* (Fr. *moyen*)—L. *mediānus—medius*, middle.]

mean³ *mēn, v.t.* to have in mind as signification: to intend, to purpose: to destine, design: to signify.— *v.t.* (with *well, ill*) to have good, bad, intentions or disposition: (with *much, little*, etc.) to be of much, little, importance (to):—*pr.p.* **mean'ing**; *pa.t* and *pa.p* **meant** (*ment*).—*n.* **mean'ing** that which is in the mind or thoughts: signification: the sense intended: purpose.—*adj.* significant.—*adjs.* **mean'ingful; mean'ingless** senseless: expressionless: without significance—*adv.* **mean'ingly** significantly: intentionally. [O.E. *mǣnan*.]

meander *mi-an'dər, n.* a winding course: a maze: an intricate fret pattern: perplexity.—*v.i.* to wind about: to be intricate: to wander listlessly (with some reminiscence of *maunder*).—*adjs.* **mean'dered** formed into or covered with mazy passages or patterns; **mean'dering** winding. [L. *Maeander*—Gr. *Maiandros*, a winding river in Asia Minor.]

means. See **mean²**.

meant *ment, pa.t.* and *pa.p.* of **mean³**.

measles *mē'zlz, n. sing.* an infectious fever accompanied by eruptions of small red spots upon the skin: a disease of swine and cattle, caused by larval tapeworms —*adj.* **mea'sled** measly.—*n.* **mea'sliness**. —*adj.* **mea'sly** infected with measles, or with tapeworm larvae: spotty: paltry, miserable.—**German measles** rubella. [M.E. *maseles*.]

measure *mezh'ər, n.* the ascertainment of extent by comparison with a standard: a system of expressing the result of such ascertainment: the amount ascertained by comparison with a standard: that by which extent is ascertained or expressed: size: a standard or unit: a quantity by which another can be divided without remainder: an instrument for finding the extent of anything, esp. a graduated rod or tape for length, or a vessel of known content for capacity: the quantity contained in a vessel of known capacity—often a bushel: adequacy or due amount: some amount or degree, a portion: proportion: moderation: extent: that which is meted out to one, treatment: a means to an end· an enactment or bill: rhythm: a unit of verse —one foot or two feet: metre: strict time: a bar of music: the width of a page or column, usually in *ems* (*print*.): (in *pl.*) a series of beds or strata (*geol.*).— *v.t* to ascertain or show the dimensions or amount of

(sometimes with *out* or *up*): to mark out or lay off (often with *off* or *out*): to mete (out): to proportion: to pit: to traverse —*v.i.* to be of the stated size: to take measurements.—*adj.* **meas'urable** that may be measured or computed: moderate: in small quantity or extent.—*n.* **meas'urableness**.—*adv.* **meas'urably**. —*adj.* **meas'ured** determined by measure: mensurable: rhythmical: with slow, heavy, steady rhythm: considered: restrained.—*adv.* **meas'uredly**.—*adj.* **meas'ureless** boundless.—*ns.* **meas'urement** the act of measuring: the quantity found by measuring; **meas'urer**.—*n.* and *adj.* **meas'uring**.—**meas'uring-rod, -tape** one for measuring with.—**above**, or **beyond, measure** to an exceedingly great degree; **be the measure of (something)** to be standard by which the quality, etc. of something may be judged; **for good measure** as something extra or above the minimum necessary; **get, have, someone's measure** to take someone's measure, esp by seeing through a façade; **hard measures** harsh treatment; **in a measure, in some measure** to some degree; **made to measure** see **made**; **measure one's length** to fall or be thrown down at full length; **measure up** (sometimes with *to*) to reach a certain, or a required, standard, to be adequate; **short measure** less than the due and professed amount; **take measures** to adopt means to gain an end; **take someone's measure** to estimate someone's character and abilities; **tread a measure** to go through a dance; **within measure** moderately; **without measure** immoderately. [O.Fr. *mesure*—L. *mēnsūra*, a measure—*mētīrī, mēnsum*, to measure.]

meat *mēt, n.* anything eaten as food: the edible part of anything: the flesh of animals used as food—sometimes beef, mutton, pork, veal, etc., as opposed to poultry, fish, etc.: food for thought, substance, pith (*fig.*).—*n.* **meat'iness**.—*adjs.* **meat'less** foodless: without butcher's meat; **meat'y** full of meat (*lit.* and *fig.*); fleshy: flesh-like in taste or smell: pithy.— **meat'-ball** a ball of minced meat; **meat'-eater** one who eats butcher's meat: a carnivore; **meat loaf** a loaf-shaped mass of chopped or minced meat, cooked and usually eaten cold; **meat'-paste; meat'-pie; meat'-plate** a large, esp. oval, plate on which meat is served: **meat'-safe** a receptacle for storing meat. [O.E. *mete*.]

meatus *mi-ā'tos*, (*anat.*) *n.* a passage or canal:—*pl.* **mea'tuses**.—*adj.* **mea'tal**. [L. *meātus* (pl. *-ūs*)— *meāre*, to go.]

Mecca *mek'ə, n.* the birthplace of Mohammed, a place of pilgrimage for Muslims: any outstanding place reverenced or resorted to—e.g. St. Andrews, Mecca of golf.

Meccano® *mi-kä'nō, n.* small metal plates, rods, nuts and bolts, etc., with which models can be constructed.

mechanic *mi-kan'ik, adj* mechanical.—*n.* a handicraftsman: a skilled worker, esp. one who makes or maintains machinery.—*adj.* **mechan'ical** pertaining to machines or mechanics: dynamical: worked or done by machinery or by mechanism: acting or done by physical, not chemical, means: machine-like: of the nature of a machine or mechanism: without intelligence or conscious will: performed simply by force of habit: reflex: skilled in mechanism: manually employed: mechanistic.—*adv.* **mechan'ically**.—*n.* **mechanician** (*mek-ən-ish'ən*) a machine-maker: one skilled in the structure of machines.—*n.sing.* **mechan'ics** dynamics, the science of the action of forces on bodies, including kinetics and statics: the art or science of machine construction: the details of making or creating by manual or other process (also *n.pl.*): the system on which something works (also *n.pl.*).—*n.pl.* routine procedure(s).—*n.* **mechanis-**

á'tion, -z-.—*v.t.* **mech'anise, -ize** to make mechanical: to adapt to mechanical working: to provide with armoured armed vehicles.—*ns.* **mech'anism** the construction of a machine: the arrangement and action by which a result is produced: a philosophy that regards the phenomena of life as explainable by mechanical forces: the means adopted unconsciously towards a subconscious end (*psych.*); **mech'anist** a mechanician: a believer in philosophical mechanism. —*adj.* **mechanist'ic.**—*adv* **mechanist'ically.**—**mechanical powers** the elementary forms or parts of machines—three *primary,* the lever, inclined plane, and pulley; and three *secondary,* the wheel-and-axle, the wedge, and the screw; **mechanical tissue** any tissue that gives a plant power of resisting stresses. [Gr. *mēchanikos—mēchanē,* a contrivance.]

Mechlin mek', or *mehh'lin, adj.* produced at Mechlin or Malines, in Belgium.—*n* lace made at Mechlin.

meconic *mi-kon'ik, adj.* denoting an acid obtained from poppies.—*ns.* **mecō'nium** the first faeces of a newborn child; **Meconops'is** a genus of largely Asiatic poppies: (without *cap.*) a plant of this genus:—*pl.* **meconops'ēs.** [Gr. *mēkōn,* the poppy.]

medal med'l, *n.* a piece of metal usu. in the form of a coin bearing some device or inscription, struck or cast usually in commemoration of an event or as a reward of merit.—*v.t.* to decorate with a medal:—*pr.p.* **med'-alling;** *pa.t* and *pa.p.* **med'alled.**—*adj.* **medallic** (*mi-dal'ik*) —*ns.* **medallion** (*mi-dal'yən*) a large medal: a bas-relief of a round (sometimes a square) form: a round ornament, panel, tablet, or design of similar form.—*n.* **med'allist** one with expert knowledge of medals, or a collector of medals: a designer or maker of medals: one who has gained a medal.—**medal play** golf scored by strokes for the round, not by holes [Fr. *médaille—*It. *medaglia;* through L.L. from L. *metallum,* metal.]

meddle med'l, *v.i.* to interfere unnecessarily, temerariously, (with, in): to tamper (with).—*n.* **medd'ler.**—*adj.* **medd'lesome** given to meddling.—*n.* **medd'lesomeness.**—*n.* and *adj.* **medd'ling.** [O.Fr *medler,* a variant of *mesler* (Fr. *mêler*)—L.L. *musculāre—*L. *miscēre,* to mix.]

media mē'di-ə, *n.* a voiced stop consonant, or a letter representing it: the middle coat of a blood-vessel:— *pl.* **mē'diae** (-ē).—See also **medium.** [L. *media,* middle, fem. of *medius,* middle.]

mediacy. See **mediate.**

mediaeval, medieval med-i-ē'vl, *adj.* of the Middle Ages.—*ns.* **medi(a)e'valism** the spirit of the Middle Ages: devotion to mediaeval ideals; **medi(a)e'valist** one versed in the history, art, etc., of the Middle Ages: one who follows mediaeval practices.—*adv.* **medi(a)e'vally.** [L. *medius,* middle, *aevum,* age.]

medial mē'di-əl, *adj.* intermediate: occurring within a word: median: pertaining to a mean or average.— *adv.* **me'dially.** [L.L. *mediālis—*L. *medius,* middle.]

median mē'di-ən, *adj.* in the middle, running through the middle: situated in the straight line or plane (*median line, plane*) that divides anything longitudinally into symmetrical halves.—*n.* a straight line joining an angular point of a triangle with the middle point of the opposite side: in a series of values, the value middle in position (not usu. in magnitude) [L. *mediānus—medius,* middle.]

mediant mē'di-ənt, *n.* the third tone of a scale, about midway between tonic and dominant. [L.L. *mediāns, -antis,* pr.p. of *mediāre,* to be in the middle.]

mediastinum mē-di-ə-stī'nəm, *n.* a membranous septum, or a cavity, between two principal portions of an organ, esp. the folds of the pleura and the space between the right and left lungs.—*adj* **mediasti'nal.**

[Neut of L.L. *mediastīnus,* median (in classical L. *mediastinus* is a drudge)—*medius.*]

mediate mē'di-ıt, *adj.* middle: intervening: indirect: related or acting through something intervening.— *v.t.* (-āt) to interpose between parties as a friend of each. to act as intermediary: to intercede: to be or act as a medium: to hold a mediate position.—*v.t.* to bring about, end, promote, obtain, or communicate by friendly intervention, or by intercession, or through an intermediary: to be the medium or intermediary of: to transmit, convey, pass on.—*n.* **mē'diacy** mediateness.—*adv.* **mē'diately.**—*n.* **mē'diateness** the state of being mediate; **media'tion** the act of mediating or coming between: an entreaty for another; **mē'diātor** one who mediates between parties at strife.—*adj.* **mē'diatory.** [L.L. *mēdiāre, -ātum,* to be in the middle—L. *mēdius.*]

medic¹ med'ik, *n.* medical student (*slang*).—**medico-** combining form, relating to medicine or medical matters, as in *adjs.* **med'ico-chirur'gical** relating to both medicine and surgery; **med'ico-le'gal** relating to the application of medicine to questions of law. [L. *medicus.*]

medic². See **medick.**

Medicaid med'i-kād, (also without *cap.*) *n.* in the U.S., a scheme providing assistance with medical expenses for people with low incomes. [*Medical aid.*]

medical med'i-kl, *adj.* relating to the art of healing: relating to the art of the physician, distinguished from surgery.—*n.* a medical examination to ascertain the state of one's physical health.—*adv.* **med'ically.**— **medical certificate** a certificate from a doctor stating that a person is, or has been, unfit for work, etc., or that a person has, or has not, passed a medical examination; **medical officer** a doctor in charge of medical treatment, etc. in an armed service or other organisation. [L.L. *medicālis—*L. *medicus,* a physician—*medērī,* to heal.]

medicament med-ik'ə-mənt, or med', *n.* a substance used in curative treatment, esp. externally.—*v.t.* to treat with medicaments.—*adjs.* **medicamental** (-ment'l), **medicament'ary.**—*adv.* **medicament'ally.** [L. *medicāmentum—medicāre.*]

Medicare med'i-kār, (also without *cap.*) *n.* in the U.S, a scheme providing medical insurance for people aged 65 and over. [*Medical care.*]

medicate med'i-kāt, *v t.* to treat with medicine: to impregnate with anything medicinal: to drug, doctor, tamper with —*adj.* **med'icable** that may be healed.— *adj.* **med'icated.**—*n.* **medicā'tion.**—*adj.* **med'icative.** [L. *medicāre, -ātum,* to heal—*medicus.*]

medicine med'sin, -sn, also (esp. *U.S.*) med'i-sin, -sn, *n.* any substance used (esp. internally) for the treatment or prevention of disease: a drug: the art or science of prevention and cure of disease, esp. nonsurgically: remedial punishment: a charm, magic: anything of magical power.—*adjs.* **medicinable** (med'-sin-ə-bl) having a healing power; **medicinal** (med-is'i-nl, sometimes med-i-sī'nl) used in medicine: curative: relating to medicine: like medicine.—*adv.* **medic'inally.**— **med'icine-ball** a heavy ball tossed and caught for exercise, **med'icine-bott'le; med'icine-chest** a chest for keeping a selected set of medicines; **med'icine-dropp'er; med'icine-man** among savages, a witch-doctor or magician.—**a dose, taste, of one's own medicine** harsh or unpleasant treatment given, often in revenge, to one used to giving such treatment to others. [L. *medicina—medicus.*]

medick, in U.S. **medic,** med'ik, *n.* any species of *Medicago,* a genus distinguished from clover by its spiral or sickle-shaped pods and short racemes— including lucerne. [L. *mēdica—*Gr. *Mēdikē (poā),* Median (herb), i.e. lucerne.]

medico *med'ik-ō,* (*slang*) *n.* a medical practitioner or student:—*pl.* **med'icos.** [It. *medico,* or Sp *médico* —L. *medicus,* a physician.]

medico-. See **medic¹.**

medieval. Same as **mediaeval.**

medio- *mē' di-ō-,* (in compounds) middle [L. *medius,* middle.]

mediocre *mē' di-ō-kər,* or *-ō',* adj. of middling goodness (usu. disparagingly).—*n.* **medioc'rity** (*-ok'*) a middling degree: a mediocre person. [Fr. *médiocre*—L *mediocris—medius,* middle.]

meditate *med'i-tāt, v.t.* to consider thoughtfully (with *on, upon*): to engage in contemplation, esp. religious. —*v t* to consider deeply, reflect upon. to revolve in the mind: to intend.—*adj.* **med'itated.**—*n.* **meditā'tion** the act of meditating: deep thought: serious continuous contemplation esp. on a religious or spiritual theme· a meditative discourse: a meditative treatment of a literary or musical theme.—*adj.* **med'itative.**—*adv.* **med'itatively.**—*n.* **med'itativeness.** [L *meditārī,* prob. cog. with L. *medērī,* to heal]

mediterranean *med-i-tə-rā'ni-ən, adj.* situated in the middle of earth or land: land-locked: of the **Mediterranean Sea** (so called from being in the middle of the land of the Old World) or its shores [L. *mediterrāneus—medius,* middle, *terra,* earth.]

medium *mē' di-əm, n.* the middle the middle place or degree: a middle course: any intervening means, instrument, or agency. instrumentality: a substance through which any effect is transmitted: that through which communication is maintained· (*pl.* **media**) a channel (as newspapers, radio, television) through which information, etc is transmitted to the public (also **mass medium**): (*pl.* usu. **media**) any material, e.g punched cards, paper tape, on which data is recorded (*comput.*): an enveloping substance or element in which a thing exists or lives: environment. a vehicle for paint, etc.: a nutritive substance on which a culture (as of bacteria, tissue, etc) may be fed: (*pl.* **mediums**) in spiritualism, the person through whom spirits are said to communicate with the material world: (*pl.* **mediums**) a person of supernormal sensibility:—*pl.* **me'dia,** or **me'diums.**—*adj.* intermediate: between fast and slow, long and short, etc.—*adj.* **mediumis'tic** of or pertaining to spiritualistic mediums.—*adjs* **me'dium-da'ted** of securities, redeemable in five to fifteen year's time; **me'dium-term** intermediate between short-term and long-term —**medium waves** (*radio*) electromagnetic waves of between 200 and 1000 metres. [L *medium,* neut. of *medius,* middle.]

medlar *med'lər, n.* a small tree (*Mespilus,* or *Pyrus, germanica*) akin to the apple: its fruit. [O.Fr *medler. mesler*—L. *mespilum*—Gr *mespilon.*]

medley *med'li, n.* a mingled and confused mass: a miscellany: a song or piece of music made up of bits from various sources: a cloth woven from yarn of different colours. [O Fr *medler, mesler,* to mix.]

medulla *me-dul'a, n.* the inner portion of an organ, hair, or tissue: bone-marrow: pith: a loose or spongy mass of hyphae:—*pl.* **medull'ae** (*-ē*), **medull'as.**—*adjs* **medull'ar, -y** consisting of, or resembling, marrow or pith: **medull'ate** having medulla, **med'ullated** provided with a medullary sheath.—**medulla oblongā'ta** (or *-a'tə*) that part of the brain that tapers off into the spinal cord; **medullary sheath** a thin layer surrounding the pith (*bot.*): a whitish fatty membrane covering an axis-cylinder (*anat.*) [L. *medulla,* marrow.]

Medusa *me-dū'zə, n.* one of the three Gorgons, whose head, with snakes for hair, turned beholders into stone, but was cut off by Perseus: (without *cap*) a jellyfish:—*pl* **medū'sae** (*-zē*), **medū'sas.**—*adj.*

medū'san.—*n.* a medusa —*adjs.* **medū'siform** like a jellyfish; **medū'soid** like a medusa. [L. *Medūsa* —Gr *Medousa,* the Gorgon *Medusa* (lit ruler).]

meed *mēd, n.* wages (*arch*): reward. [O E. *mēd.*]

meek *mēk, adj.* mild and gentle of temper· submissive —*v.t* **meek'en** to render meek.—*v.t* to become meek —*adv.* **meek'ly.**—*n.* **meek'ness** the state or quality of being meek. [O N *mjūkr*]

meerkat *mēr'kat, n* a South African carnivore (*Cynictis penicillata*), akin to the ichneumon· a lemur.— Also **meer'cat.** [Du *meerkat,* monkey, as if 'overseas cat', from *meer,* sea, *kat,* cat.]

meerschaum *mēr'shəm, n* a fine light whitish clay: a tobacco-pipe made of it [Ger.,—*Meer,* sea, *Schaum,* foam]

meet¹ *mēt, adj.* fitting: qualified —*adv* **meet'ly.**—*n* **meet'ness.**

meet² *mēt, v.t* to come face to face with: to come into the company of: to become acquainted with, be introduced to: to encounter in conflict: to find or experience: to be suitable to: to satisfy, as by payment: to receive, as a welcome· to cause to meet, bring into contact: to await the arrival of, keep an appointment with.—*v i.* to come together from different points: to assemble· to come into contact· to have an encounter. to balance, come out correct:—*pa t.* and *pa.p* **met.**— *n.* a meeting, as of huntsmen: an assembly for racing ·-*n.* **meet'ing** a coming face to face for friendly or hostile ends: an interview· an assembly. an organised assembly for transaction of business: an assembly for religious worship· a place of meeting: a junction.— **meet'ing-house** a house or building where people, esp. Quakers, meet for public worship.—**meet half-way** to make concessions in compromise, **meet the ear,** or **eye** to be readily apparent; **meet up (with)** to meet, by chance or arrangement; **meet with** to come to or upon, esp. unexpectedly· to meet (U.S.). to undergo, chance to experience, **race-'meet'ing** a stated occasion for horse-racing; **well met** an old complimentary greeting [O E *mētan,* to meet— *mōt, gemōt,* a meeting]

meg(a)-, megalo- *meg(ə-)(lō-),* in composition, big in names of units, a million. as *megabar, meganewton, megohm, megawatt,* etc —*ns.* **meg'abar; meg'abit; meg'abyte.**—*adj* **megacephalous** (*-sef'ə-ləs*). largeheaded.—*ns* **meg'acurie; meg'acycle** a million cycles· a million cycles per second; **meg'adeath** death of a million people, a unit in estimating casualties in nuclear war; **meg'adyne; megafar'ad; meg'agauss; meg'ahertz; meg'ajoule; meg'alith** a huge stone, as in prehistoric monuments —*adj.* **megalith'ic.**—*n* **megaloma'nia** the delusion that one is great or powerful: a mania, or passion, for big things —*n* and *adj* **megaloma'niac.**—*ns* **megalop'olis** a widespreading, thickly-populated urban area; **meg'alosaur, megalosau'rus** a gigantic Jurassic and Cretaceous dinosaur, carnivorous in mode of life —*adj.* **megalosau'rian.**—*ns.* **meg'anewton; meg'aparsec; meg'aphone** a funnel-shaped device for directing, or increasing volume of. sound —*v t.* and *v t* to communicate by megaphone.—*ns.* **meg'apode** (Gr. *pous, podos,* foot) a mound-bird; **meg'arad; meg'aton** (*-tun*) one million tons: a unit of explosive power equalling a million tons of TNT (**megaton bomb** a bomb of this force); **meg'avolt; meg'awatt** (**megawatt day** the unit of energy used in speaking of nuclear power reactors (day = 24 hours)); **meg'ohm.** [Gr. *megas,* fem. *megalē,* neut *mega,* big.]

megilp *mə-gilp'.* See **magilp.**

megohm. See under **meg(a)-.**

megrim *mē'grim.* See **migraine.**

meiosis *mī-ō'sis, n* understatement as a figure of speech (*rhet*) litotes: cell-division with reduction of the number of chromosomes towards the development of a reproductive cell (*biol.*):—*pl.* **melō'ses.**—*adj.* **meiotic** (*-ot'ik*). [Gr. *meiōsis*, diminution]

Meissen (**china, porcelain, ware**). Same as **Dresden.**

Meistersinger *mīs'tər-zing-ər*, *-sing-ər, n.* one of the burgher poets and musicians of Germany in the 14th–16th centuries:—*pl.* **Meistersinger, -s.** [Ger., master-singer.]

Majlis. Same as **Majlis.**

melamine *mel'ə-mēn, n.* a white crystalline organic substance used in forming **melamine resins**, thermosetting plastics used as adhesives, coatings, etc. [Ger. *Melamin*.]

melancholy *mel'ən-kol-i, -kəl-i, n.* black bile, an excess thereof, or the mental condition of temperament supposed to result therefrom (*obs.*): continued depression of spirits: indulgence in thoughts of pleasing sadness: pensiveness.—*adj.* prone to, affected by, expressive of, or causing, melancholy: depressed: pensive: deplorable.—*ns.* **melanchō'lia** a mental state characterised by dejection and misery; **melanchō'liac** a sufferer from melancholia.—Also *adj.*—*adj.* **melancholic** (*-kol'ik*) affected with, or caused by, melancholy or melancholia; dejected: mournful. [Gr. *melancholiā—melās, -ānos, black, cholē, bile.]

Melanesian *mel-ən-ēz'i-ən, -ēz'yən, -ēzh'(y)ən, adj.* pertaining to *Melanesia*, a group of islands lying N.E. of Australia, in which the dominant race is dark-skinned.—*n.* a native, or a language, of these islands. [Gr. *melās, -ānos,* black, *nēsos,* an island.]

mélange *mā-lāzh', n.* a mixture: a medley. [Fr.]

melanic *mi-lan'ik, adj.* black or dark in pigmentation.—*ns.* **melanin** (*mel'ə-nin*) the dark pigment in skin, hair, etc.; **mel'anism** more than normal development of dark colouring matter.—*adj.* **melanist'ic.**—*ns.* **melano** (*mi-lä'nō, mel'ə-nō;* on the analogy of *albino*) a person or animal abnormally dark:—*pl.* **melanos; melanō'ma** any skin tumour consisting of melanin-pigmented cells: a malignant tumour consisting of melanin-pigmented cells, which usually develops from a mole:—*pl.* **melanō'mata, melanō'mas; melanō'sis** an abnormal deposit of melanin: the associated condition of body. [Gr. *melās, -ānos,* black.]

melba toast *mel'bə tōst* very thin crisp toast.—**melba sauce** a sauce for puddings, made from raspberries. [Named after Dame Nellie *Melba* (1861–1931), Australian operatic singer.]

meld[1] *meld,* (*obs.* except in cards) *v.t.* and *v.i.* to declare: to announce.—Also *n.* [O.E. *meldan*.]

meld[2] *meld, v.t.* and *v.i.* to merge, blend, combine.—Also *n.* [Poss. **melt** and **weld**.]

mêlée *mel'ā, n.* a fight in which the combatants are mingled together: a confused conflict: an affray. [Fr.,—*mêler,* to mix.]

meliorate *mē'li-ə-rāt, v.t.* to make better.—*v.i.* to grow better.—*n.* **meliorā'tion.**—*adj.* **mē'liorative** tending towards improvement.—*ns.* **mē'liorator; mē'liorism** the doctrine that the world is capable of improvement, as opposed to *optimism* and *pessimism;* **mē'liorist; meliority** (*-or'i-ti*) betterness. [L.L. *meliōrāre, -ātum—L. melior,* better.]

meliphagous *mel-if'ə-gəs, adj.* feeding upon honey. [Gr. *meli,* honey, *phagein* (aor.), to eat.]

melisma *mel-iz'mə, n.* a song: a tune: a melodic embellishment:—*pl.* **melis'mata, melis'mas.** [Gr. *melisma, -matos,* a song, tune.]

melliferous *mel-if'ə-rəs, adj.* honey-producing.—*ns.* **mellificā'tion** honey-making; **mellif'luence** a flow of sweetness: a smooth sweet flow.—*adjs.* **mellif'luent, mellif'luous** flowing with honey or sweetness: smooth.—*advs.* **mellif'luently, mellif'luously.**—*adj.* **melliv'orous** eating honey. [L. *mel, mellis,* honey.]

mellow *mel'ō, adj.* soft and ripe: well matured: soft to

the touch, palate, ear, etc.: genial: half-tipsy.—*v.t.* to soften by ripeness or age: to mature.—*v.i.* to become soft: to be matured, ripened: to become gentler and more tolerant—*adv.* **mell'owly.**—*n.* **mell'owness.**—*adj.* **mell'owy** mellow. [Prob. O.E. *melu,* meal, influenced by *mearu,* soft, tender.]

melodrama *mel'ō-drä-mə,* or *-drä', n.* a kind of romantic and sensational drama, crude, sentimental, and conventional, with strict attention to poetic justice and happy endings.—*adj.* **melodramat'ic** (*-drə-mat'ik*) of the nature of melodrama: overstrained: sensational.—*n.* **melodramatist** (*-dram'ə-tist*) a writer of melodramas. [Gr. *melos,* a song, *drāma,* action.]

melody *mel'ə-di, n.* an air or tune: music: an agreeable succession of single musical sounds, as distinguished from *harmony.*—*n.* **melodeon, melodion** (*mi-lō'di-ən*) a small reed-organ: an improved accordion.—*adj.* **melodic** (*mi-lod'ik*).—*n.sing.* **melod'ics** the branch of music concerned with melody.—*adj.* **melō'dious** full of melody: agreeable to the ear.—*adv.* **melō'diously.**—*n.* **melō'diousness.**—*v.i.* **mel'odise, -ize** to make melody: to perform a melody.—Also *v.t.*—*n.* **mel'odist.** [Fr., through L.L.,—Gr. *melōidiā.*]

melon *mel'ən, n.* any of several juicy gourds: the plant bearing it. [Fr.,—L. *mēlō, -ōnis—Gr. mēlon,* an apple.]

melt *melt, v.i.* to become liquid from the solid state, esp. by heat: to fuse: to dissolve: to stream with liquid: to lose distinct form: to blend: to shade off: to become imperceptible: to disperse, be dissipated, disappear (sometimes with *away*): to be softened emotionally.—*v.t.* to cause to melt in any sense.—*n.* the act of melting: the state of being melted: molten material: the quantity melted.—*n.* and *adj.* **melt'ing.**—*adv.* **melt'ingly.**—*n.* **melt'ingness.**—*adj.* **mōlt'en** melted: made of melted metal.—*adv.* **mōlt'enly.**—**melt'down** the process in which, due to a failure of the cooling system, the radioactive fuel in a nuclear reactor overheats, melts through its insulation, and is released into the environment; **melt'ing-point** the temperature at which a given solid begins to become liquid; **melt'ing-pot** a vessel for melting things in: a state of dissolution preparatory to shaping anew (*fig.*); **melt'-water** water running off melting ice or snow. [O.E. *meltan* (intrans. strong vb.), and *mæltan, meltan* (causative weak vb.).]

melton *mel'tən, n.* a strong cloth for overcoats. [*Melton* Mowbray, in Leicestershire.]

member *mem'bər, n.* a distinct part of a whole, esp. a limb of an animal: one of a society: a representative in a legislative body.—*adj.* **mem'bered** having limbs.—*n.* **mem'bership** the state of being a member or one of a society: the members of a body regarded as a whole.—*adj.* **mem'bral** pertaining to the limbs rather than the trunk.—**member of parliament** a member of the House of Commons, M.P. [Fr. *membre—L. membrum.*]

membrane *mem'brān, -brin, n.* a thin flexible solid sheet or film: a thin sheet-like structure, usually fibrous, connecting other structures or covering or lining a part or organ (*biol.*): a skin of parchment.—*adjs.* **membranaceous** (*-brə-nā'shəs*), **mem'branous** (*-brə-nəs*) like or of the nature of a membrane: thin, translucent, and papery (*bot.*). [L. *membrāna—membrum.*]

memento *mi-men'tō, n.* something kept or given as a reminder:—*pl.* **memen'tos** or *-toes.*—**memento mori** (*mō'rī, mo'rē*) remember that you must die: anything to remind one of mortality. [L., imper. of *meminisse,* to remember.]

memo *mem'ō, n.* a contraction for **memorandum:**—*pl.* **mem'os.**

memoir *mem'wär, -wôr, n.* (usu. in *pl.*) a written record set down as material for history or biography: a biographical sketch: a record of a study of some subject investigated by the writer: (in *pl.*) the transactions of a society.—*ns.* **mem'oirism** the act or art of writing memoirs: **mem'oirist** a writer of memoirs. [Fr. *mémoire*—L. *memoria*, memory—*memor*, mindful.]

memorabilia, memorable, etc. See memory.

memorandum *mem-ə-ran'dəm, n.* something to be remembered: a note to assist the memory: a brief note of some transaction (*law*): a summary of the state of a question (*diplomacy*):—*pl.* **memoran'dums, memoran'da.** [L., a thing to be remembered, neut. gerundive of *memorāre*, to remember.]

memory *mem'ə-ri, n.* the power of retaining and reproducing mental or sensory impressions: an impression so reproduced: a having or keeping in the mind: time within which past things can be remembered: commemoration: a religious service in commemoration: remembrance: of computers, a store (q.v.).—*n.pl.* **memorabil'ia** (from L.) things worth remembering: noteworthy points.—*n.* **memorabil'ity.**—*adj.* **mem'orable** deserving to be remembered: remarkable: easily remembered.—*n.* **mem'orableness.**—*adv.* **mem'orably.**—*adj.* **memorial** (*ōr', ·ór'*) serving or intended to preserve the memory of anything: done in remembrance of a person, event, etc.: pertaining to memory.—*n.* that which serves to keep in remembrance: a monument: a note to help the memory: a written statement of facts: a record: (in *pl.*) historical or biographical notices.—*v.t.* **memor'ialise, -ize** to present a memorial to: to commemorate: to petition by a memorial.—*n.* **memor'ialist** one who writes, signs, or presents a memorial.—*n.* **memorisā'tion, -z-.**—*v.t.* **mem'orise, -ize** to commit to memory—**memory bank** (*comput.*) a memory or store (q.v.); **memory trace** (*psych.*) a hypothetical change in the cells of the brain caused by the taking-in of information, etc.—**in living memory** within the memory of people still alive; **in memor'iam** to the memory of: in memory. [L. *memoria*, memory.]

mem-sahib *mem'-sä-ib, n.* in India, a married European lady. [ma'am and sahib.]

men plural of man.—**menfolk(s)** see under **man.**

menace *men'əs, -is, n.* a threat or threatening: a show of an intention to do harm: a threatening danger.—*v.t.* to threaten.—*v.i.* to act in a threatening manner.—*adj.* **men'acing.**—*adv.* **men'acingly.** [Fr.,—L. *mināciae* (pl.), threats—*minae*, overhanging parts, threats.]

ménage *mā-näzh', n.* a household: the management of a house.—**ménage à trois** (*a trwä*) a household composed of a husband and wife and the lover of one of them. [Fr.,—L. *mānsiō*, dwelling.]

menagerie *mi-naj'ə-ri, n.* a collection of wild animals in cages for exhibition: the place where these are kept. [Fr. *ménagerie*—*ménage.*]

mend *mend, v.t.* to remove a fault from: to repair: to make better: to correct: to improve: to improve upon.—*v.i.* to grow better: to reform.—*n.* a repair: a repaired place: an act of mending.—*ns.* **mend'er; mend'ing** the act of repairing: a repair: things requiring to be mended.—**mend one's ways** to reform one's behaviour; **on the mend** improving, recovering. [amend.]

mendacious *men-dā'shəs, adj.* lying.—*adv.* **mendā'ciously.**—*n.* **mendacity** (*-das'i-ti*) lying: a falsehood. [L. *mendāx, -ācis,* conn. with *mentīrī,* to lie.]

mendelevium *men-de-lē', -lā'vi-əm, n.* the element (symbol Md) of atomic number 101, artificially produced in 1955 and named after the Russian D. I. *Mendeleev* (1834–1907), who developed the periodic table of elements.

Mendelian *men-dēl'i-ən, adj.* pertaining to the Austrian-German Gregor *Mendel* (1822–84), or his teaching on heredity.—*n.* a believer in Mendel's theory.—*n.* **Men'delism** (*-də-lizm*).

mendicant *men'di-kənt, adj.* begging.—*n.* a beggar.—*ns.* **men'dicancy, mendicity** (*-dis'i-ti*) the condition of a beggar: begging. [L. *mendicāns, -antis,* pr.p. of *mendicāre,* to beg—*mendīcus,* a beggar.]

menhaden *men-hā'dn, n.* an oily fish (*Brevoortia tyrannus*) of the herring family, found off the east coast of the United States. [From an Indian name.]

menhir *men'hēr, n.* an ancient monumental standing stone. [Breton *men,* stone, *hir,* long.]

menial *mē'ni-əl, adj.* of or pertaining to servants or work of a humiliating or servile nature: servile.—*n.* a servant: one performing servile work: a person of servile disposition. [A.Fr. *menial.*]

meninx *mē'ningks, n.* any of three membranes that envelop the brain and spinal cord:—*pl.* **meninges** (*men-in'jēz*).—*adj.* **mening'eal.**—*ns.* **meningitis** (*-ji'*) inflammation of the meninges; **meningocele** (*mening'gō-sēl*) protrusion of the meninges through the skull. [Gr. *mēninx, -ingos,* a membrane.]

meniscus *men-is'kəs, n.* a crescent-shaped figure: a convexo-concave lens: a liquid surface curved by capillarity:—*pl.* **menis'ci** (*-kī* or *-sī*) or **menis'cuses.** [Gr. *mēniskos,* dim. of *mēnē,* the moon.]

Mennonite *men'ən-īt, n.* one of a Protestant sect combining some of the distinctive characteristics of the Baptists and Friends. [From *Menno* Simons (d. 1559), their chief founder.]

menopause *men'ō-pöz, n.* the ending of menstruation, change of life.—*adj.* **menopaus'al** of, relating to, or experiencing, the menopause. [Gr. *mēn,* month, *pausis,* cessation.]

menorah *mə-nō'rə, -nō'rə, n.* (also with *cap.*) a candelabrum with a varying number of branches, usu. seven, used in Jewish religious ceremony. [Heb. *menōrāh.*]

menses *men'sēz, n.pl.* the monthly discharge from the uterus. [L. *mēnsēs,* pl. of *mēnsis,* month.]

Menshevik *men'shə-vik,* (*hist.*) *n.* a moderate or minority socialist in Russia—as opp. to *Bolshevik* [Russ. *menshye,* smaller, *-(v)ik,* agent suffix.]

menstruum *men'strōō-əm, n.* a solvent (from a fancy of the alchemists):—*pl.* **men'strua,** or **men'struums** (menstrua also the menses).—*adj.* **men'strual** monthly: pertaining to the menses.—*v.i.* **men'struate** to discharge the menses.—*n.* **menstruā'tion.**—*adj.* **men'struous.** [L. neut. of *mēnstruus,* monthly—*mēnsis.*]

mensurable *men'sh(y)ər-ə-bl,* or *-sūr-, adj.* measurable: having a fixed relative time-value for each note (*mus.*).—*n.* **mensurabil'ity.**—*adj.* **men'sural** pertaining to measure, measurable (*mus.*).—*n.* **mensurā'tion** the act or art of finding by measurement and calculation the length, area, volume, etc., of bodies.—*adj.* **men'surative.** [L. *mēnsūrāre,* to measure.]

mental *men'tl, adj.* pertaining to the mind: done in the mind, esp. in the mind alone, without outward expression: suffering from, or provided for, or involved in the care of, disease or disturbance of the mind: mentally unbalanced (*slang*).—*ns.* **men'talism** the process of mental action: idealism; **men'talist; mentality** (*-tal'i-ti*) mind: mental endowment: a cast of mind: a way of thinking; **menta'tion** mental activity.—*adv.* **men'tally.**—**mental age** the age in years, etc., at which an average child would have reached the same stage of mental development as the individual under consideration; **mental cruelty** conduct in marriage, not involving physical cruelty or violence, that wounds feelings or personal dignity; **mental deficiency** mental retardation; **mental home, hospital**; **mental patient**; **mental retardation** retarded development of learning ability, whether arising from innate defect or from some other cause. [Fr.,—L. *mēns, mentis*, the mind.]

menthol *men'thol, n.* a camphor got from oil of peppermint, used as a local analgesic.—*adj.* **men'tholated** containing menthol. [L. *mentha*, mint.]

mention *men'shən, n.* a brief notice: the occurrence or introduction of name or reference.—*v.t.* to notice briefly: to remark: to name.—*adj.* **men'tionable** fit to be mentioned: worth mentioning.—**honourable mention** an award of distinction not entitling to a prize; **not to mention** to say nothing of—a parenthetical rhetorical pretence of refraining from saying all one might say. [L. *mentiō, -ōnis*.]

mentor *ment'ər, -tŏr, n.* a wise counsellor. [Gr. *Mentōr*, the tutor by whom Telemachus was guided.]

menu *men'ū, n.* a bill of fare: a list of subjects, options, etc. (*fig.* or *comput.*). [Fr.,—L. *minūtus*, small.]

meow *mi-ow', myow.* A form of miaow.

mepacrine *mep'ə-krēn, n.* a bitter yellow powder derived from acridine dye compounds, formerly used against malaria—also **atabrin, atebrin.**

Mephistopheles *mef-is-tof'i-lēz, n.* the devil in the *Faust* story.—Also **Mephistoph'ilis, Mephostoph'ilus**, etc.: abbrev. **Mephis'tō.**—*adjs.* **Mephistophelē'an, Mephistophē'lian, Mephistophelic (-fel')** cynical, scoffing, fiendish.

mephitis *me-fī'tis, n.* a poisonous exhalation: a foul stink.—*adjs.* **mephitic (-fit')**, **-al.** [L. *mephītis.*]

meprobamate *mep-rō-bam'āt, n.* a drug used as a muscle relaxant and as a sedative.

mercantile *mûr'kən-tīl, adj.* pertaining to merchants: having to do with trade: commercial: mercenary.—*ns.* **mer'cantilism**; **mer'cantilist.**—**mercantile law** the law relating to the dealings of merchants with each other; **mercantile marine** the ships and crews of any country employed in commerce. [Fr.,—It. *mercantile*—L. *mercārī*; cf. **merchant.**]

mercaptan *mər-kap'tan, n.* a substance analogous to an alcohol, with sulphur instead of oxygen. [L. *mercūrium captāns*, laying hold of mercury.]

Mercator *mər-kā'tər, mer-kä'tŏr, n.* a Latin translation of the name of the Flemish-born German cartographer Gerhard Kremer (lit. shopkeeper; 1512–94).—**Mercator's projection** a representation of the surface of the globe in which the meridians are parallel straight lines, the parallels straight lines at right angles to these, their distances such that everywhere degrees of latitude and longitude have the same ratio to each other as on the globe itself.

mercenary *mûr'sin-ər-i, adj.* hired for money: actuated by the hope of reward: too strongly influenced by desire of gain: sold or done for money.—*n.* one who is hired: a soldier hired into foreign service.—*adv.* **mer'cenarily.**—*n.* **mer'cenarism** the state of being a mercenary. [L. *mercēnārius*—*mercēs*, hire.]

mercer *mûr'sər, n.* a dealer in textiles, esp. the more costly: a dealer in small wares.—*n.* **mer'cery** the trade of a mercer: the goods of a mercer. [Fr. *mercier.*]

mercerise, -ize *mûr'sər-īz, v.t.* to treat (cotton) so as to make it appear like silk.—*ns.* **mercerisā'tion, -z-**; **mer'ceriser, -z-.** [From John Mercer (1791–1866), the inventor of the process.]

merchant *mûr'chant, n.* a trader, esp. wholesale: a shopkeeper: a fellow, esp. one who specialises or behaves in some specified way (*slang*).—*adj.* commercial.—*v.i.* to trade.—*v.t.* to trade in.—*n.* **mer'chandise (-dīz)** goods bought and sold for gain:

dealing.—*v.t.* (also **-ize**) to buy and sell: to plan the advertising of, selling campaign for.—Also *v.i.* (also **-ize**).—*n.* **mer'chandising, -z-.**—*adj.* **mer'chantable** fit or ready for sale: marketable.—*n.* **mer'chantry** the business of a merchant: merchants collectively.—**mer'chantman** a trading ship:—*pl.* **mer'chantmen; merchant navy**, service the mercantile marine; **merchant ship** a ship that carries merchandise. [Fr. *marchand.*]

mercury *mûr'kū-ri, n.* a silvery metallic element (Hg; atomic number 80) liquid at ordinary temperatures, also called *quicksilver*: the column of mercury in a thermometer or barometer: a plant of the spurge family: a messenger: a common title for newspapers: (*cap.*) the Roman god of merchandise, theft, and eloquence, messenger of the gods, identified with the Greek Hermes: (*cap.*) the planet nearest the sun.—*adj.* **mercū'rial** containing mercury: of or like mercury: caused by mercury: (*cap.*) of or pertaining to Mercury the god or the planet: (sometimes *cap.*) having the qualities attributed to persons born under the planet—eloquent, etc.: active, sprightly, often changing.—*n.* a drug containing mercury.—*adv.* **mercū'rially.**—*adjs.* **mercū'ric** containing bivalent mercury; **mer'curous** containing univalent mercury. [L. *Mercūrius*, prob. *merx, mercis*, merchandise.]

mercy *mûr'si, n.* forbearance towards one who is in one's power: a good thing regarded as derived from God: a happy chance (*dial.*): a forgiving disposition: clemency: compassion for the unfortunate.—*interj.* an expression of surprise (for *God have mercy*).—Also **mercy on us.**—*adj.* **mer'ciful** full of, or exercising, mercy.—*adv.* **mer'cifully.**—*n.* **mer'cifulness.**—*adj.* **mer'ciless** without mercy: unfeeling: cruel.—*adv.* **mer'cilessly.**—*ns.* **mer'cilessness.**—**mercy killing** killing, esp. painlessly, to prevent incurable suffering; **mer'cy-seat** the covering of the Jewish Ark of the Covenant: the throne of God.—**at the mercy of** wholly in the power of; **for mercy's sake!** an earnest conjuration in the form of an appeal to pity; **leave (a person) to someone's tender mercies or mercy** (*ironic*) to leave (a person) exposed to unpleasant treatment at someone's hands; **sisters of mercy** members of female religious communities who tend the sick, etc. [Fr. *merci*, grace—L. *mercēs, -ēdis*, the price paid, wages, later favour.]

mere[1] *mēr, n.* a pool or lake. [O.E. *mere*, sea, lake, pool.]

mere[2] *mēr, adj.* only what is said and nothing else, nothing more, nothing better.—*adv.* **mere'ly** simply: only: without being more or better. [L. *merus*, unmixed.]

mere[3], **meri** *mer'i, n.* a war-club: a greenstone trinket in the form of a war-club. [Maori.]

merel, merell. Same as **meril.**

meretricious *mer-i-trish'əs, adj.* of the nature of harlotry: characteristic or worthy of a harlot: flashy: gaudy.—*adv.* **meretric'iously.**—*n.* **meretric'iousness.** [L. *meretrīx, -īcis*, a harlot—*merēre*, to earn.]

merfolk. See **mermaid.**

merganser *mûr-gan'sər, n.* any bird of the genus *Mergus* (goosander, smew, etc.). [L. *mergus*, a diving bird, *ānser*, a goose.]

merge *mûrj, v.t.* to cause to be swallowed up or absorbed in something greater or superior: to cause to coalesce, combine, or amalgamate.—*v.i.* to be swallowed up, or lost: to coalesce: to lose identity in something else: to combine or amalgamate.—*ns.* **mer'gence; mer'ger** (*law*) a sinking of an estate, title, etc., in one of larger extent or of higher value: a combine, an absorption. [L. *mergēre, mersum.*]

meri. See **mere**[3].

meridian *mə-rid'i-ən, adj.* of or at midday: on the

meridian: pertaining to a meridian or the sun or other body on the meridian: at culmination or highest point.—*n.* midday: an imaginary great circle through the poles of the earth, the heavens, or any spherical body or figure, or its representation on a map: in particular, that cutting the observer's horizon at the north and south points, which the sun crosses at local noon: culmination or highest point, as of success, splendour, power, etc.—*adj.* **merid'ional** pertaining to the meridian: in the direction of a meridian: midday: culminating: southern: characteristic of the south.—*adv.* **merid'ionally.**—**prime** (or **first**) **meridian** the meridian from which longitudes are measured east or west, specif. that through Greenwich. [L. *meridiānus, meridiōnālis*—*merīdiēs* (for *medīdiēs*), midday—*medius*, middle, *diēs*, day.]

meril, merel, merell *mer'əl, n.* a counter used in the game of merils: (in *pl.*) a rustic game played by two persons with counters on a figure marked on the ground, a board, etc., consisting of three squares, one within another, the object to get three counters in a row at the intersection of the lines joining the corners and the mid-points of the sides.—Also **marls, marr'-els, morr'is.—fivepenny morris** the game as played with five pieces each; **ninepenny morris, nine men's morris** with nine. [O.Fr. *merel*, counter.]

meringue *mə-rang', n.* a crisp cake or covering made of a mixture of sugar and a white of eggs. [Fr.]

merino *mə-rē'nō, n.* a sheep of a fine-woolled Spanish breed (also **merino sheep**): a fine dress fabric, originally of merino wool: a fine woollen yarn, now mixed with cotton: knitted goods of this:—*pl.* **meri'nos.**—*adj.* belonging to the merino sheep or its wool: made of merino. [Sp., a merino sheep, also a governor—L. *mājōrīnus*, greater, also (L.L.) a head-man—L. *mājor*, greater.]

meristem *mer'is-tem, n.* the formative tissue of plants, distinguished from the permanent tissues by the power its cells have of dividing and forming new cells. —*adj.* **meristematic** (*-sti-mat'ik*). [Gr. *meristos*, divisible, *merizein*, to divide—*meros*, a part.]

merit *mer'it, n.* excellence that deserves honour or reward: worth: value: desert: (in *pl.*, esp. in *law*) the intrinsic right or wrong.—*v.t.* to earn: to have a right to claim as a reward: to deserve.—*ns.* **meritoc'racy** (government by) the class of persons who are in prominent positions because of their ability, real or apparent; **mer'itōcrat.**—*adjs.* **meritōcrat'ic; meritorious** (*-tōr', -tōr*) possessing merit or desert: deserving of reward, honour, or praise.—*adv.* **meritor'iously.**—*n.* **meritor'iousness.—order of merit** arrangement in which the best is placed first, the next best second, and so on: (*caps.*) a strictly limited British order (O.M.), instituted in 1902, for eminence in any field. [L. *meritum—merēre, -itum*, to obtain as a lot, to deserve.]

merle, merl *mûrl, (arch.* or *literary Scot.*) *n.* the blackbird. [Fr.,—L. *merula.*]

merlin *mûr'lin, n.* a species of small falcon, *Falco columbarius.* [A.Fr. *merilun*—O.Fr. *esmerillon.*]

merlon *mûr'lən, (fort.) n.* the part of a parapet between embrasures. [Fr. *merlon*—It. *merlone—merlo*, battlement.]

mermaid *mûr'mād, n.* a sea-woman, a woman to the waist, with fish's tail.—**mer'child; mer'folk; mer'maid'en; mer'maid's-purse'** the egg-case of skate, etc; **mer'man; mer'people.** [O.E. *mere*, lake, sea, *mægden*, maid.]

merome *mer'ōm, n.* a merosome. [Gr. *meros*, part.]

merosome *mer'ō-sōm, n.* one of the serial segments of which a body is composed, as the ring of a worm. [Gr. *meros*, part, *sōma*, body.]

Merovingian *mer-ō-vin'ji-ən, adj.* pertaining to the first dynasty of Frankish kings in Gaul, founded by Clovis.—*n.* a member of this family. [L. *Merovingi*—*Merovaeus* or *Merovech*, king of the Salian Franks (448–457), grandfather of Clovis.]

merpeople. See mermaid.

merry *mer'i, adj.* sportive: cheerful: noisily gay: causing laughter: enlivened by drink: lively: used as an intensifier of *hell*, as in *play merry hell with.*—*adv.* **merr'ily.—*ns.* merr'iment** gaiety with laughter and noise: mirth: hilarity; **merr'iness.—merr'y-an'drew** a quack's zany: a buffoon: one who makes sport for others; **merry England** an idealistically jovial picture of life in England in the past, esp. in Elizabethan times; **merr'y-go-round** a revolving ring of wooden horses, etc. for riding at a funfair: a roundabout: a whirl of activity, etc. (*fig.*): any activity inclined to circularity (*fig.*); **merr'y-make** a merrymaking.—*v.i.* to make merry.—**merr'ymaker; merr'ymaking** a merry entertainment: a festival; **merr'yman** a zany: a jester: (in *pl.*; **merry men**) followers, in arms or in outlawry; **merr'ythought** a fowl's wishbone.—**make merry** to hold festival: to indulge in enjoyment: to turn to ridicule (with *with* or *over*); **the merry monarch** Charles II. [O.E. *myr(i)ge.*]

mesa *mā'sə, n.* a table-shaped hill. [Sp.,—L. *mēnsa*, table.]

mesal. See mesial.

mésalliance *mā-zal-yās*, (Fr.) *n.* an unsuitable marriage: marriage with one of lower station.

mescal *mes-kal', n.* the peyote cactus, chewed or drunk in infusion as an intoxicant in Mexico: an intoxicant distilled from Agave.—*ns.* **mescalin** (*mes'kəl-in*) the principal alkaloid ($C_{11}H_{17}NO_3$) in mescal, producing hallucinations and schizophrenia; **mescal'ism** addiction to mescal. [Sp. *mescal, mezcal*—Nahuatl *mexcalli.*]

mesdames *mi-däm', Mesdemoiselles.* See **madam, mademoiselle.**

meseems *mi-sēmz', (poet.) v.impers.* it seems to me:—*pa.t.* **meseemed'.** [me¹ (dat.) and **seem.**]

Mesembrianthemum, conventionally **Mesembryanthemum,** *mi-zem-bri-an'thi-məm, n.* a genus of succulent plants (family Aizoaceae), mostly South African (Hottentot fig, ice-plant, Livingstone daisy): (without *cap.*) a plant of this genus. [Gr. *mesēmbriā*, midday—*mesos*, middle, *hēmerā*, day, and *anthemon*, a flower: some are open only about midday.]

mesencephalon *mes-en-sef'ə-lon, n.* the mid-brain.—*adj.* **mesencephalic** (*-si-fal'ik*). [Gr. *mesos*, middle, and **encephalon.**]

mesentery *mes'ən-tər-i,* or *mez', n.* a fold of the peritoneum, keeping the intestines in place: in coelenterates, a vertical inward fold of the body wall.—*adjs.* **mesenterial** (*-tē'ri əl*), **mesenteric** (*-ter'ik*).—*n.* **mesenteron** (*-en'tər-on*) the mid-gut. [Gr. *mesos*, middle, *enteron*, intestines.]

mesh *mesh, n.* the opening between the threads of a net: the threads and knots bounding the opening: a network: a trap: the engagement of geared wheels or the like.—*v.t.* to catch in a net: to provide or make with meshes.—*v.i.* to become engaged, as gear-teeth: to become entangled.—*n.* **mesh'ing.—adj.** **mesh'y** formed like network. [Perh. M.Du. *maesche.*]

mesial *mē'zi-əl, adj.* middle: in or towards the median plane or line—also **mē'sal, mē'sian.—advs.** **mē'sally, mē'sially.** [Gr. *mesos*, middle.]

mesic. See meson.

mesmerise, -ize *mez'mər-īz, v.t.* to hypnotise: loosely, to fascinate, dominate the will or fix the attention of. —*adjs.* **mesmeric** (*-mer'ik*), **-al.—ns.** **mesmerisā'tion, -z-; mes'meriser, -z-, mes'merist; mes'merism** hypnotism as expounded, with some fanciful notions, from 1775 by Friedrich Anton or Franz *Mesmer*, a German physician (1734-1815): hypnotic influence.

mesne *měn*, (*law*) *adj.* intermediate. [Law Fr. *mesne*, middle; cf. **mean**².]

mes(o)- *mes*(*-ō* or *-o*), *mez-*, *mē-*, in composition, middle.—*n.* **mes'oblast** the middle germinal layer.— *adj.* **mesoblas'tic**.—*n.* **mes'ocarp** the middle layer of a pericarp.—*adjs.* **mesocephalic** (*-si-fal'ik*), **-cephalous** (*-sef'ə-ləs*) mesencephalic.—*ns.* **mesoceph'aly**; **mes'oderm** the mesoblast or tissues derived from it.—*adj.* Mesolith'ic intermediate between Palaeolithic and Neolithic.—*n.* **mes'omorph** (*-mórf*) a person of muscular bodily type.—*adjs.* **mesomor'phic**, **mesomor'phous** relating to a mesomorph: relating to an intermediate state of matter between solid and liquid (*chem.*).—*ns.* **mes'omorphy**; **mes'ophyll** the spongy tissue within a leaf; **mes'o-phyte** (*-fīt*; Gr. *phyton*, plant) a plant intermediate between a xerophyte and a hydrophyte.—*adj.* **meso-phytic** (*-fit'ik*).—*ns.* **mes'osphere** the region of the earth's atmosphere above the stratosphere; **meso-thēliō'ma** a rare malignant tumour of the lining of the chest or abdomen, sometimes caused by blue asbestos dust.—*adj.* Mesozō'ic of the Secondary geological period, including the Triassic, Jurassic, and Cretaceous systems. [Gr. *mesos*, middle.]

meson *měz'on*, *mes'on*, *n.* a short-lived subatomic particle of smaller mass than a proton.—*adjs.* **mes'ic**, **meson'ic**. [Gr. *meson*, neut. of *mesos*, middle.]

mesophyll ... **Mesozoic.** See under **mes(o)-**.

mesquite, **mesquit** *mes-kēt'*, *mes'kēt*, *n.* a leguminous tree or shrub (*Prosopis*) of America, with nutritious pods. [Mex. Sp. *mezquite*.]

mess *mes*, *n.* a dish of food, course, or meal (*arch.*): a number of persons who take their meals together, esp. in the fighting services: a place where a group of persons in a fighting service take their meals together: a quantity (*U.S.*): a dish of soft, pulpy or liquid stuff: liquid, pulpy or smeary dirt: a mixture disagreeable to the sight or taste: a medley: disorder: confusion: embarrassment: a bungle.—*v.t.* to supply with a mess: to make a mess of (usu. with *up*): to muddle: to befoul.—*v.i.* to eat of a mess: to eat at a common table: to belong to a mess: to make a mess: to meddle, involve oneself (with, in) (*coll.*; esp. *U.S.*): to tangle (with) (*coll.*; esp. *U.S.*).—*adv.* **mess'ily**.—*n.* **mess'iness**.—*adj.* **mess'y** confused, untidy (also *fig.*): involving, or causing, dirt or mess: bungling.—**mess's room**; **mess'-tin** a soldier's utensil serving as plate, cup, and cooking-vessel; **mess'-up** a mess, muddle, bungle, or confusion.—**mess about or around** (*coll.*) to potter about: to behave in a foolish or annoying way: to meddle or interfere (with): to upset, put into a state of disorder or confusion; **mess of pottage** a material advantage accepted in exchange for something of higher worth, as by Esau (Gen. xxv. 29 ff.). [O.Fr. *mes* (Fr. *mets*), a dish—L. *mittĕre, missum*, to send, in L.L. to place.]

message *mes'ij*, *n.* any communication sent from one person to another: an errand: an official communication of a president, governor, etc., to a legislature or council: the teaching that a poet, sage, prophet, has to communicate to the world.—*v.t.* to send as a message: to transmit as by signalling.—*n* **mess'enger** (*-ən-jər*) one who brings a message: one employed to carry messages and perform errands: a forerunner.— **mess'age-boy**, **-girl** an errand boy or girl; **mess'age-stick** (*Austr.*) a carved stick carried as identification by an aborigine messenger; **messenger RNA** (*bio-chemistry*) a short-lived, transient form of RNA which serves to carry genetic information from the DNA of the genes to the ribosomes where the requisite proteins are made—also **m-RNA; mess'enger**

wire a wire supporting an overhead cable.—**get the message** (*slang*) to understand. [Fr.,—L.L. *mis-sāticum*—L. *muttĕre, missum*, to send.]

Messiah *mə-sī'ə*, *n.* the expected deliverer of the Jews: by Christians, applied to Jesus: a hoped-for deliverer, saviour, or champion generally.—*adj.* **Messianic** (*mes-1-an'ik*).—*ns.* **Messi'anism** belief in a Messiah; **Messi'anist.** [Gr. *Messīās*—Aram. *m'shīhā*, Heb. *māshīah*, anointed—*māshah*, to anoint.]

Messieurs *mes-yø*, *pl.* of **Monsieur**; contracted and anglicised as **Messrs** (*mes'ərz*) and used as *pl.* of **Mister.**

mestee *mes-tē'*, *ns.* the offspring of a white person and a quadroon.—*n.* **mestizo** (*mes-tē'zō*) a half-caste, esp of Spanish and American Indian parentage.—*pl.* **mesti'zos**; *fem.* **mesti'za**, *pl.* **mesti'zas**. [Sp. *mestizo* —a L.L. derivative of L. *mixtus*, mixed.]

met *pa.t.* and *pa.p.* of **meet**².

met. *met.* Abbrev. for *meteorology*.—**met'cast** a weather forecast; **met man** a weather forecaster; **Met Office** the Meteorological Office.

met(a)- *met(-ə)-*, in composition, among, with: after, later: often implies change, as *metamorphose*: beyond, above, as *metamathematics*. In *chem.* meta-indicates (1) a derivative of, or an isomer or polymer of, the substance named, or (2) an acid or hydroxide derived from the ortho- form of the substance by loss of water molecules, or (3) a benzene substitution product in which the substituted atoms or groups are attached to two carbon atoms which are themselves separated by one carbon atom.—*adj.* and *n.* **meta-carp'al**.—*ns.* **metacarp'us** the part of the hand (or its bones) between the wrist and the fingers, or its corresponding part, e.g. the foreleg of a horse between 'knee' and fetlock; **met'acentre** the point of intersection of a vertical line through the centre of gravity of a body floating in equilibrium and that through the centre of gravity of the displaced liquid when the body is slightly displaced.—*adj.* **metacen'tric**.—*ns.* **met'a-language** a language or a system of symbols used to discuss another language or symbolic system; **met'amer** (*chem.*) a compound metameric with another; **met'amere** (*-mēr*; *zool.*) a segment, merosome, or somite.—*adj.* **metamer'ic**.—*ns.* **metam'erism** a particular form of isomerism in which different groups are attached to the same central atom (*chem.*): segmentation of the body along the primary axis, producing a series of homologous parts (*zool.*).—*adj.* **metapsycholog'ical**.—*ns.* **metapsy-chol'ogy** theories and theorising on psychological matters, such as the nature of the mind, which cannot be verified or falsified by experiment or reasoning; **metastabil'ity** a state which appears to be chemically stable, often because of the slowness with which equilibrium is attained—said of, e.g., a supersaturated solution: a metastable state.—*adjs.* **metastable** (*met'ə-stā-bl*) having metastability (**metastable state** an excited state, esp. of an atom which has, however, insufficient energy to emit radiation); **metatarsal** (*-tär'sl*)—Also *n.* **metatar'sus** that part of the foot, or its bones, between the tarsus and the toes.—*n.pl.* **Metazoa** (*met-ə-zō'ə*; also without *cap.*; Gr. *zōion*, animal) many-celled animals (opp. to single-celled *Protozoa*):—*sing.* **metazō'on**.—*adj.* and *n.* **metazō'an**.—*adj.* **metazō'ic.** [Gr. *meta*, among, with, beside, after.]

metabolism *met-ab'əl-izm*, *n.* the sum total of chemical changes of living matter: metamorphosis.— *adj.* **metabolic** (*-bol'ik*) exhibiting or relating to metabolism.—*v.t.* and *v.i.* **metab'olise, -ize.**—*n.* **metab'olite** a product of metabolism. [Gr. *metabolē*, change.]

metacarpus, etc., **metacentre**, etc. See **met(a)-**.

metage *mēt'ij, n.* official weighing of coal, grain, etc.: the charge for such weighing. [**mete**[1].]

metal *met'l, n.* an opaque elementary substance, possessing a peculiar lustre, fusibility, conductivity for heat and electricity, readiness to form positive ions, etc., such as gold, etc.: an alloy: that which behaves chemically like a true metal: courage or spirit (now spelt *mettle*): intrinsic quality: or or argent as a tincture (*her.*): molten material for glass-making: broken stones used for macadamised roads or as ballast for railways: (*pl.*) the rails of a railroad. —*adj.* made of metal.—*v.t.* to furnish or cover with metal:—*pr.p.* **met'alling;** *pa.t.* and *pa.p.* **met'alled.** —*adjs.* **met'alled** covered with metal, as a road; **metallic** (*mi-tal'ik*) pertaining to, or like, a metal: consisting of metal: of a colour, etc., having the lustre characteristic of metals: of a sound, like the sound produced by metal when struck.—*adv.* **metall'ically.**—*adjs.* **metallif'erous** bearing or yielding metal; **met'alline** of, like, consisting of, or mixed with, metal.—*ns.* **met'alling** road-metal, broken stones; **metallisā'tion, -z-.**—*v.t.* **met'allise, -ize** to make metallic: to deposit thin metal films on glass or plastic.—*ns.* **met'allist** a worker in metals; **metallog'eny** (*geol.*) (the study of) the origin and distribution of mineral deposits, esp. with regard to petrological, etc. features; **metallog'rapher.**—*adj.* **metallograph'ic.**—*ns.* **metallog'raphy** the study of the structure and constitution of metals; **met'alloid** a non-metal: an element resembling a metal in some respects, as selenium, tellurium.—*adjs.* **met'alloid, metalloid'al** pertaining to, or of the nature of, the metalloids.—**met'al-work, -er, -ing.** [O.Fr.,—L. *metallum*—Gr. *metallon*, a mine.]

metalanguage. See **met(a)-**.

metallic. See **metal.**

metallurgy *met'əl-ūr-ji, met-al'ər-ji, n.* art and science applied to metals, including extraction from ores, refining, alloying, shaping, treating, and the study of structure, constitution, and properties.—*adjs.* **metallur'gic, -al** pertaining to metallurgy.—*n.* **met'allurgist** (or, now more usu., *-al'*). [Gr. *metallourgeein*, to mine—*metallon*, a mine, *ergon*, work.]

metamere, metamerism. See **met(a)-**.

metamorphosis *met-ə-mōr'fəs-is,* sometimes *-fōs'is, n.* change of shape, transformation: transformation of a human being to a beast, stone, tree, etc. (*folklore*): the marked change which some living beings undergo in the course of growth, as caterpillar to butterfly, tadpole to frog:—*pl.* **metamor'phoses** (*-sēz,* or *-fō'sēz*).—*adj.* **metamor'phic** showing or relating to change of form: formed by alteration of existing rocks by heat, pressure, or other processes in the earth's crust (*geol.*).—*n.* **metamor'phism** transformation of rocks in the earth's crust.—*v.t.* **metamor'phose** (*-fōz, -fōs*) to transform: to subject to metamorphism or metamorphosis: to develop in another form.—*v.i.* to undergo metamorphosis. [Gr. *metamorphōsis*—*meta* (see **met(a)-**) and *morphē*, form.]

metaphor *met'ə-fər, n.* a figure of speech by which a thing is spoken of as being that which it only resembles, as when a ferocious man is called a tiger.—*adjs.* **metaphoric** (*-for'ik*), **-al.**—*adv.* **metaphor'ically.** —*n.* **met'aphorist.**—**mixed metaphor** an expression in which two or more metaphors are confused, as *to take arms against a sea of troubles.* [Gr. *metaphorā* —*meia* (see **met(a)-**) and *pherein*, to carry.]

metaphrase *met'ə-frāz, n.* a turning of prose into verse or verse into prose: a rendering in a different style or form: an altered wording: a word for word translation—also **metaphrasis** (*-af'rə-sis*). [Gr. *metaphrasis*—*meta* (see **met(a)-**) and *phrasis*, a speaking.]

metaphysics *met-ə-fiz'iks, n. sing.* the branch of philosophy which investigates the first principles of nature and thought: ontology or the science of being: loosely and vaguely applied to anything abstruse, abstract, philosophical, subtle, transcendental, occult, supernatural, magical.—*adj.* **metaphysical.**—*adj.* **metaphys'ical** pertaining to metaphysics: abstract: beyond nature or the physical: supernatural: fanciful: addicted to far-fetched conceits.—*adv.* **metaphys'ically.**—*n.* **metaphysician** (*-ish'ən*) one versed in metaphysics. [Originally applied to those writings of Aristotle which in the accepted order came after (Gr. *meta*) those dealing with natural science (*ta physika—physis*, nature).]

metastasis *met-as'ta-sis, n.* removal from one place to another: transition: transformation:—*pl.* **metas'tases.**—*v.i.* **metas'tasise, -ize** to pass to another part of the body, as a tumour.—*adj.* **metastatic** (*-stat'ik*). [Gr. *metastasis*, change of place—*meta* (see **met(a)-**) and *stasis*, a standing.]

metatarsus, -al. See **met(a)-**.

metathesis *met-ath'ə-sis, n.* transposition or exchange of places, esp. between the sounds or letters of a word:—*pl.* **metath'eses.**—*adjs.* **metathetic** (*met-ə-thet'ik*), **-al.** [Gr.,—*metatithenai*, to transpose—*meta* (see **met(a)-**) and *tithenai*, to place.]

Metazoa, etc. See **met(a)-**.

metcast. See **met.**

mete[1] *mēt, v.t.* to measure: to apportion. [O.E. *metan.*]

mete[2] *mēt, n.* a boundary or limit. [L. *mēta*, a goal or boundary.]

metempsychosis *met-emp-si-kō'sis, n.* the passing of the soul after death into some other body:—*pl.* **metempsychō'ses.** [Gr. *metempsychōsis*—*meta* (see **met(a)-**), *en,* in, *psychē,* soul.]

meteor *mē'tyər, mē'ti-ər, n.* one of numberless small bodies travelling through space, revealed to observation when they enter the earth's atmosphere as aerolites, fireballs, or shooting-stars: anything brilliant or dazzling but short-lived.—*adj.* **meteoric** (*mē-ti-or'ik*) influenced by weather: of or pertaining to meteors in any sense: of the nature of a meteor: transiently flashing like a meteor: rapid (*fig.*).—*adv.* **meteor'ically** in manner of a meteor.—*n.* **me'teorite** a meteor that has fallen to earth as a lump of stone or metal.—*adj.* **meteorit'ic.**—*n.* **me'teoroid** a meteor that has not reached the earth's atmosphere.—*adjs.* **meteorolog'ic, -al.**—*ns.* **meteorol'ogist;** **meteorol'ogy** the study of weather and climate.— **meteoric showers** or **meteor showers, storms** showers of meteors; **Meteorological Office** a government department issuing weather forecasts, etc. [Gr. *ta meteōra,* things on high—*meta* and the root of *aeirein,* to lift.]

meter[1] *mē'tər, n.* a measurer: an apparatus for measuring, esp. quantity of a fluid, or of electricity, used: a gauge or indicator: a parking meter.—*v.t.* to measure by a meter. [**mete**[1].]

meter[2]. American spelling of **metre**[1,2].

-meter *-mi-tər* or *-mē-*, in composition, an instrument for measuring.—**-metric, -al** (*-met'rik, -l*) adjective combining forms.—**-met'rically** adverb combining form.—**-metry** (*-mi-tri*) noun combining form. [Gr. *metron,* measure.]

methadone *meth'ə-dōn, n.* a synthetic addictive drug similar to morphine. [di*methyl*amino-, *d*iphenyl, heptan*one.*]

methane *mē'thān, meth'ān, n.* marsh-gas (CH$_4$), the simplest hydrocarbon, found wherever the decomposition of vegetable matter is taking place under water, also in coal-mines, forming when mixed with air the deadly fire-damp. [**methyl**.]

methanol *meth'ə-nol*, *n*. methyl alcohol, wood spirit. [methane, -ol, suffix—L. *oleum*, oil.]

Methedrine® *meth'ə-drēn*, *n*. a former proprietary name for an amphetamine, used by drug addicts.

methinks *mi-thingks'*, *v.impers.* it seems to me: I think. [O.E. *mē thyncth*, it seems to me; *thyncan*, to seem, has been confused with *thencan*, to think.]

method *meth'əd*, *n*. the mode or rule of accomplishing an end: orderly procedure: manner: orderly arrangement: methodicalness: classification: a system, rule: manner of performance.—*adjs.* **methodic** (*mithod'ik*), **-al** arranged with method: disposed in a just and natural manner: observing method: formal.—*adv.* **method'ically**.—*n.* **method'icalness**.—*v.t.* **meth'odise, -ize** to reduce to method: to dispose in due order.—*ns.* **Meth'odism** the principles and practice of the Methodists; **meth'odist** one who observes method: (*cap.*) a follower of the Wesleys—a name given first to a group of students at Oxford 'for the regularity of their lives as well as studies'.—*adjs.* **Methodist'ic, -al** resembling the Methodists, esp. as viewed by opponents: strict in religious matters.—*n.* **methodol'ogy** a system of methods and rules applicable to research or work in a given science or art: evaluation of subjects taught and principles and techniques of teaching them.—**method acting** acting as a personal living of a part, contrasted with mere technical performance (also called the **method**). [Gr. *methodos*—*meta*, after, *hodos*, a way.]

meths *meths*, *n. sing.* short for **methylated spirits**.

Methuselah *mi-thū'zə-lə, -thoō'*, *n.* a patriarch said to have lived 969 years (Gen. v. 27): any very aged person.

methyl *meth'il, mē'thil*, (*chem.*) *n.* the radical (CH_3) of wood (or methyl) alcohol (CH_3·OH).—*n.* **methylamine** (*-a-mēn'*) an inflammable gas (CH_3·NH_2).—*v.t.* **meth'ylate** to mix or impregnate with methyl alcohol: to introduce the radical CH_3 into.—*n.* a methyl alcohol derivative: a compound with a methyl group.—*ns.* **methyla'tion**; **meth'ylene** the hypothetical compound CH_2.—*adj.* **methyl'ic.**—**methylated spirit(s)** alcohol made unpalatable with methyl alcohol, and usually other things; **methyl chloride** a refrigerant and local anaesthetic. [Gr. *methu*, wine, *hȳlē*, wood.]

meticulous *me-tik'ū-ləs*, *adj.* scrupulously careful: (*popularly*) overcareful.—*adv.* **metic'ulously**.—*n.* **metic'ulousness.** [L. *meticulōsus*, frightened—*metus*, fear.]

métier *mā'tyā*, *n.* one's calling or business: that in which one is specially skilled. [Fr.,—L. *ministerium*.]

metif *mā'tēf*, *n.* (sometimes with *cap.*) the offspring of a white and a quadroon.—*n.* **métis** (*mā-tēs'*; sometimes with *cap.*) a person of mixed descent, esp., in Canada, a half-breed of French and Indian parentage:—*pl.* **métis** (*-tēs'* or *-tēz'*); *fem.* **métisse** (sometimes with *cap.*). [Fr.; cf. **mestizo.**]

metol *mē'tol*, *n* *p*-methylaminophenol sulphate, the basis of a rapid developer for photographic negatives. [From *Metol*, a trademark]

Metonic *mi-ton'ik*, *adj.* pertaining to the Athenian astronomer *Mēton* or his cycle (**Metonic cycle** beginning on 27th June, 432 B.C.) of 19 years after which the moon's phases recur on the same days of the year.

metonym *met'ə-nim*, *n.* a word used in a transferred sense.—*adjs.* **metonym'ic, -al**.—*adv.* **metonym'ically**.—*n.* **metonymy** (*mi-ton'i-mi*) a trope in which the name of one thing is put for that of another related to it, the effect for the cause, etc., as 'the bottle' for 'drink'. [Gr. *metōnymiā*—*meta*, indicating change, and *onyma* = *onoma*, a name.]

metope *met'o-pē*, also *met'ōp*, (*archit.*) *n.* the slab, plain or sculptured, between the triglyphs of a Doric frieze. [Gr. *metōpē*—*meta* and *ōpē*, an opening for a beam-end.]

metre[1] (*U.S.* **meter**) *mē'tər*, *n.* that regulated succession of certain groups of syllables (long and short, stressed and unstressed) in which poetry is usually written: a scheme of versification, the character of a stanza as consisting of a given number of lines composed of feet of a given number, arrangement, and kind: musical time.—*v.t.* and *v.i.* to versify.—*adjs.* **metred** (*mē'tərd*) rhythmical; **metric** (*met'rik*), **-al** pertaining to metre: in metre: consisting of verses.—*adv.* **met'rically**.—*n.* **metrician** (*me-trish'ən*) a metricist.—*v.t.* **met'ricise, -ize** (*-sīz*) to analyse the metre of.—*n.* **met'ricist** (*-sist*) one skilled in metres: one who writes in metre.—*n. sing.* **met'rics** the art or science of versification (also *n.* **met'ric**).—**metrification** metrical structure: the act of making verses; **met'rifier** a versifier; **met'rist** one skilled in the use of metres: a student of metre. [O.E. *mēter* and O.Fr. *metre*, both—L. *metrum*—Gr. *metron*, measurement, metre; and partly directly.]

metre[2] (*U.S.* **meter**) *mē'tər*, *n.* the fundamental unit of length in the metric system—orig. intended to be one ten-millionth of distance from pole to equator: later the distance between two marks on a platinum-iridium bar in Paris: defined more recently in terms of the wavelength of the orange radiation of the krypton-86 atom: 1 yard equals 0·9144 metre.—*adj.* **metric** (*met'rik*) pertaining to the metre, or to the metric system.—*v.t., v.i.* **met'ricate** to convert, change to the metric system.—*n.* **metrica'tion**; **metre-kilogram(me)-second** (contr. M.K.S. or MKS) system a system of scientific measurement having the metre, etc., as units of length, mass, time; **metric system** a decimal system of weights and measures. [Fr. *mètre*—Gr. *metron*, measure.]

metric[1] *met'rik*, *adj.* quantitative.—*adj.* **met'rical** pertaining to measurement.—*n. sing.* **met'rics** the theory of measurement.—*ns.* **metrol'ogist**; **metrol'ogy** the science of weights and measures, or of weighing and measuring. [Gr. *metron*, measure.]

metric[2]. See **metre**[1].

metric[3]. See **metre**[2].

metricate. See **metre**[2].

metrician, etc., **metrifier, metrist**. See **metre**[1].

métro *mā'trō*, *n.* (often *cap.*) an underground railway, esp. the Paris subway:—*pl.* **mét'ros**.—Also **metro, Metro.** [Fr. *métro*. Abbrev. for *chemin de fer métropolitain*, metropolitan railway.]

metrology. See **metric**[1].

metronome *met'rə-nōm*, *n.* an instrument with an inverted pendulum that can be set to beat so many times a minute, the loud ticking giving the right speed of performance for a piece of music.—*adj.* **metronomic** (*-nom'ik*). [Gr. *metron*, measure, *nomos*, law.]

metronymic *met-rə-nim'ik, adj.* derived from the name of one's mother or other female ancestor: indicating the mother: using such a system of naming.—*n.* an appellation so derived (cf. *patronymic*).—Also **matronymic.** [Gr. *mētēr, -tros*, mother, *onyma* = *onoma*, name.]

metropolis *mi-trop'ə-lis*, *n.* the capital of a country, county, etc.: the chief cathedral city, as Canterbury of England, or chief see of a province: a chief centre, seat or focus:—*pl.* **metrop'olises**.—*adj.* **metropolitan** (*met-rə-pol'i-tən*) of a metropolis: of the mother-church.—*n.* the bishop of a metropolis, presiding over the other bishops of a province.—*n.* **metropol'itanate**.—*adj.* **metropolit'ical.**—**metropolitan county, district** a county or district in a heavily-populated industrial area of England, the district running more, and the county fewer, public services than other districts or counties. [Gr. *metropolis—metēr*, mother, *polis*, city.]

mettle *met'l*, *n.* temperament: ardent temperament: spirit: sprightliness: courage.—*adj.* **mett'led**, **mett'lesome** high-spirited: ardent.—*n.* **mett'lesomeness.—put (someone) on his mettle** to rouse (a person) to put forth his best efforts. [metal.]

mew[1] *mū*, *n.* a gull. [O.E. *mǣw*; Du. *meeuw*, O.N. *mār*, Ger. *Mòwe*.]

mew[2] *mū*, *v.i.* to cry as a cat.—*n.* the cry of a cat. [Imit.]

mew[3] *mū*, *v.t.* to shed, moult, or cast: to confine, as in a cage.—*v.i.* to cast the antlers or feathers: to moult.— *n.* a cage for hawks, esp. while mewing: a coop: a place of confinement: a retreat: a hiding-place.—*n.* **mews** (*mūz*; orig. *pl.* of mew, now commonly as *sing.* with new *pl.* **mews'es**) a street or yard of stabling (often converted into dwelling-houses or garages)— from the king's mews at Charing Cross when hawks were succeeded by horses. [O.Fr. *muer*—L. *mūtāre*, to change.]

mewl *mūl*, *v.i.* to mew: to cry feebly, as a child. [Imit.]

mews. See mew[3].

Mexican *meks'i-kən*, *adj.* of Mexico and its people.— *n.* a native or citizen of Mexico: an Aztec: the Nahuatl language. [Sp. *Mexicano*, now *Mejicano*.]

mezuza(h) *mə-zōōz'ə*, *n.* a parchment scroll containing scriptural texts placed in a case and fixed to the doorpost by some Jewish families as a sign of their faith:—*pl.* **-zu'zahs, -zuzoth** (*-zōō-zŏt'*). [Heb., doorpost.]

mezzanine *mez'ə-nēn*, *n.* an entresol (*archit.*): a room below the stage.—Also *adj.* [Fr.,—It. *mezzanino— mezzano*—L. *mediānus—medius*, middle.]

mezzo-forte *met'sō-, med'zō-fòr'tä*, *adj.* and *adv.* rather loud. [It.]

mezzo-soprano *met'sō-, med'zō-sō-prä'nō*, *n.* a voice between soprano and contralto: low soprano: a part for such a voice: a person possessing it:—*pl.* **mez'zo-sopra'nos.** [It. *mezzo*, middle, and *soprano*.]

mezzotint *met'sō-, med'zō-tint*, *n.* a method of copper-plate engraving giving an even gradation of tones by roughening a plate and removing the bur for lights: an impression from a plate so produced.—Also **mezzotinto** (*-tin'tō*):—*pl.* **mezzotin'tos.** [It. *mezzo-tinto—mezzo*, middle, half, *tinto*, tint—L. *tingěre*, *tinctum*, to dye.]

mho *mō*, *n.* formerly a unit of electric conductance, that of a body with a resistance of one ohm (now **siemens**):—*pl.* **mhos.** [**ohm** spelt backwards.]

mi *mē*, *n.* the third note of the scale in sol-fa notation— also anglicised in spelling as **me**. [See Aretinian.]

miaow *mi-ow'*, *myow'*. Same as **mew**[2].

miasma *mi-* or *mī-az'mə*, *n.* an unwholesome exhalation—also **mī'asm**:—*pls.* **mias'mata, mias'mas, mī'asms.—adjs. mias'mal, miasmat'ic, mias'matous, mias'mic, mias'mous.** [Gr. *miasma, -atos*, pollution —*miainein*, to stain, pollute.]

miaul *mi-öl'*, *mi-owl'*, *v.i.* to cry as a cat.—*n.* a mew. [Fr. *miauler*; imit.]

mica *mī'kə*, *n.* a rock-forming mineral with perfect basal cleavage, the laminae flexible and elastic, and usu. transparent, of various colours, used as an electric insulator and as a substitute for glass:—*pl.* **mī'cas.—adj. micaceous** (*-kā'shəs*).—**mī'ca-schist', -slate'** a metamorphic rock consisting of alternate folia of mica and quartz. [L. *mīca*, a crumb; use probably influenced by association with *mīcāre*, to glitter.]

mice *mīs*, plural of **mouse.**

micelle *mi-sel'*, **micella** *mī-sel'ə*, *ns.* a group of molecular chains, a structural unit found in colloids. —*adj.* **micell'ar.** [Dim. of L. *mīca*, crumb, grain.]

Michaelmas *mik'əl-mas*, *n.* the festival of St *Michael*, Sept. 29.—**Mich'aelmas-dai'sy** a wild aster: any of several garden plants of genus Aster with clusters of small purple, pink, blue, etc. flowers; **Michaelmas term** the autumn term at Oxford and Cambridge and some other universities. [mass[2].]

mick, mickey, micky *mik'(i)*, *ns.* an Irishman (*rather offensive*).—**Mickey (Finn)** (*slang*) a doped drink: that which is added to the drink, usu. a stupefying drug or a strong laxative; **Mickey Mouse** an animated cartoon character created by Walt Disney, 1928.— *adj.* (*slang*) simple, easy, often derisively so: unimportant, insignificant: (of music, a band, etc.) trite, corny.—**mick'ey-taking** (*slang*).—**take the mick, mickey (micky) out of** (*slang*; perhaps with different origin) to annoy: to make game of. [*Michael*.]

mickle *mik'l*, (*arch.*) *adj.* much: great.—*n.* a great quantity.—*adv.* much.—*Scot.* **muck'le.—many a little (or pickle) makes a mickle** (*often absurdly* **many a mickle makes a muckle**) every little helps. [O.E. *micel, mycel*.]

micky. See **mick.**

micro *mi'krō*, (*coll.*) *n.* short for **microprocessor:—*pl.* mi'cros.**

micr(o)- *mī-kr(ō)-, mī-kr(ə)-*, in composition, (1) (a) abnormally or extremely small: (b) using, or used in, or prepared for, microscopy: (c) dealing with minute quantities, objects or values: (d) dealing with a small area: (e) magnifying, amplifying: (f) reducing, or reduced, to minute size: (2) a millionth part, as in **mi'croampere** a millionth part of an ampere, **mi'crobar** one-millionth of a bar of pressure, **mi'crofarad, mi'crogram, and many others.** [Gr. *mikros*, little.]

microanalysis *mī-krō-ə-nal'i-sis*, *n.* chemical analysis of minute quantities.—*adj.* **microanalyt'ical.** [micro- (1c).]

microbalance *mī'krō-bal-əns*, *n.* a balance for measuring very small weights. [micro- (1c).]

microbe *mī'krōb*, *n.* a microscopic organism, esp. a disease-causing bacterium.—*adjs.* **micrō'bial, micrō'bian, micrō'bic.—ns. microbiol'ogist; microbiol'ogy** the biology of microscopic or ultramicroscopic organisms, as bacteria, viruses, fungi. [Fr.,—Gr. *mikros*, little, *bios*, life.]

microcephalous *mī-krō-sef'ə-ləs*, *adj.* abnormally-small-headed.—Also **microcephalic** (*-si-fal'ik*).—*n.* **microceph'aly** abnormal smallness of head. [Gr. *mikros*, little, *kephalē*, head.]

microchemistry *mī-krō-kem'is-tri*, *n.* chemistry dealing with very small quantities. [micro- (1c).]

microchip *mī'krō-chip*, *n.* a chip (q.v.) of silicon, etc. [micro- (1f).]

microcircuit *mī'krō-sûr-kit*, *n.* an electronic circuit with components formed in one unit of semiconductor crystal. [micro- (1f).]

microclimate *mī'krō-klī-māt, -klī-mət*, *n.* the climate of a small or very small area, esp. if different from that of the surrounding area. [micro- (1d).]

microcomponent *mī'krō-kəm-pō'nənt*, *n.* a minute component of e.g. a microcircuit. [micro- (1a).]

microcomputer *mī-krō-kəm-pū'ter*, *n.* a tiny computer containing a microprocessor, often used as the control unit for some instrument, tool, etc.: the microprocessor itself. [micro- (1f).]

microcopying *mī-krō-kop'i-ing*, *n.* copying on microfilm.—*n.* **mi'crocopy.** [micro- (1f).]

microcosm *mī'krō-kozm*, *n.* a little universe or world: man, who was regarded by ancient philosophers as a model or epitome of the universe.—*adjs.* **microcos'-mic, -al** pertaining to the microcosm.—**in microcosm**

on a small scale, as an exact copy or representative model of a larger group, etc. [Gr. *mikros*, small, *kosmos*, world.]

microdot mī′krə-dot, *n.* photograph of usu. secret material reduced to size of large dot: a small pill containing concentrated LSD (*slang*). [micro- (1f).]

microeconomics mī-krō-ēk-ə-nom′iks, -ek-, *n. sing.* that branch of economics dealing with individual households, firms, industries, commodities, etc.— *adj.* **microeconom′ic.** [micro- (1d).]

microelectronics mī-krō-el-ik-tron′iks, -ē-lik-, *n. sing.* the technology of electronic systems involving micro-miniaturisation, microcircuits or other microelectronic devices.—*adj.* **microelectron′ic.** [micro- (1f).]

microfiche mī′krə-fēsh, *n.* a sheet of microfilm suitable for filing:—*pl.* **mī′crofiche, mī′crofiches** (-fēsh). [micro- (1f), and Fr. *fiche*, slip of paper, etc.]

microfilm mī′krə-film, *n.* a photographic film for preserving a microscopic record of a document, which can be enlarged in projection.—*v.t.* to record on microfilm. [micro- (1f).]

microform mī′krə-förm, *n.* any of the media of reproduction by microphotography, as microfiche, microfilm, videotape, etc. [micro- (1f).]

microgram mī′krə-gram, *n.* a micrograph—a photograph or drawing of an object under the microscope: a message typed and photographically reduced for sending by air, enlarged on receipt and printed on a card: the card concerned. [micro- (1f).]

micrograph mī′krə-gräf, *n.* a pantograph instrument for minute writing or drawing: a minute picture: a drawing or photograph of a minute object as seen through a microscope.—*n.* **micrographer** (mī-krog′rə-fər) one who draws or describes microscopic objects.—*adj.* **micrographic** (mī-krə-graf′ik) pertaining to micrography: minutely written or delineated—*n.* **microg′raphy** study with the microscope: the description of microscopic objects. [micro- (1f) and Gr. *graphein*, to write.]

microgroove mī′krə-grōōv, *n.* the fine groove of long-playing gramophone records. [micro- (1a).]

microlight mī′krə-līt, *n.* a very light miniature aircraft. [micro- (1a).]

microlite mī′krə-līt, *n.* a mineral composed of calcium, tantalum, and oxygen, occurring in very small crystals: an incipient crystal, detected under the microscope by polarised light.—*n.* **mī′crolith** a microlite: a very small stone implement of the Stone Age, usu. used with a haft.—*adjs.* **microlith′ic; microlitic** (-lit′ik). [micro- (1a) and Gr. *lithos*, a stone.]

micrology mī-krol′ə-ji, *n.* the study of microscopic objects.—*adjs.* **micrologic** (-loj′), -al.—*adv.* **microlog′ically.**—*n.* **microl′ogist.** [Gr. *mikros*, little, *logos*, discourse.]

micro-manipulation mī-krō-mə-nip-ū-lā′shən, *n.* the technique of using delicate instruments, as **microneedles** and **micropipettes,** to work on cells, bacteria, etc. under high magnifications, or of working with extremely small quantities in microchemistry. [micro- (1b, c).]

micrometer mī-krom′i-tər, *n.* an instrument, often attached to a microscope or telescope, for measuring very small distances or angles: (also **micrometer gauge, micrometer calliper(s))** an instrument which measures small widths, lengths, etc. to a high degree of accuracy.—*adjs.* **micrometric** (mī-krə-met′rik), -al.—*n.* **microm′etry** measuring with a micrometer. [micro- (1c).]

micrometre. See micron.

microminiature mī-krō-min′i-(-ə)-chər, *adj.* made on an extremely small scale.—*n.* **microminiaturisa′tion,** -z- reduction to extremely small size of scientific or

technical equipment or any part of it.—*v.t.* **microminia′turise, -ize.** [micro- (1f).]

micron mī′kron, *n.* (better **mī′crometre**) one millionth of a metre (denoted by μ). [Gr. *mikron*, neut. of *mikros*, little.]

microneedle. See micro-manipulation.

Micronesian mī-krə-nē′zh(y)ən, -zyən, -zi-ən, *adj.* pertaining to *Micronesia,* a group of small islands in the Pacific, north of New Guinea.—*n.* a native of the group. [Gr. *mikros*, little, *nēsos,* an island.]

micro-organism mī-krō-ör′gən-izm, *n.* a microscopic (or ultramicroscopic) organism. [micro- (1a).]

microphone mī′krə-fōn, *n.* an instrument for intensifying sounds: a sensitive instrument (pop. contracted **mike** mīk), similar to a telephone transmitter, for picking up sound-waves to be broadcast or amplified and translating them into a fluctuating electric current.—*adj.* **microphonic** (-fon′ik). [Gr. *mikros*, small, *phōnē,* voice.]

microphotograph mī-krə-fōt′ə-gräf, *n.* strictly, a photograph reduced to microscopic size: loosely, a photomicrograph, or photograph of an object as magnified by the microscope.—*n.* **microphotographer** (-og′rə-fər).—*adj.* **microphotographic** (-ə-graf′ik).— *n.* **microphotog′raphy.** [micro- (1f).]

micropipette. See micro-manipulation.

microprint mī′krō-print, *n.* a microphotograph of e.g. printed text, reproduced on paper, card, etc.—*adj.* **mī′croprinted.**—*n.* **mī′croprinting.** [micro- (1f).]

microprocessor mī-krō-prō′ses-ər, *n.* an integrated circuit on a silicon chip, or a number of these, acting as the central processing unit of a computer. [micro- (1f).]

micropyle mī-krə-pīl, *n.* the orifice in the ovule through which the pollen-tube commonly enters (*bot.*): an opening by which a spermatozoon may enter an ovum (*zool.*).—*adj.* **micropy′lar.** [Gr. *mikros*, little, *pylē,* gate.]

microscope mī′krə-skōp, *n.* an instrument for magnifying minute objects.—*adjs.* **microscopic** (-skop′ik), -al pertaining to a microscope or to microscopy: magnifying: able to see minute objects: invisible or hardly visible without the aid of a microscope: minute.—*adv.* **microscop′ically.**—*ns.* **microscopist** (mī-kros′kop-ist, mī-krəs-kō′pist); **micros′copy.**—**acoustic microscope** one in which ultrasonic waves passed through the specimen are scanned by a laser beam; **come under the microscope** to be subjected to minute examination; **compound microscope,** **simple microscope** microscopes with respectively two lenses and a single lens; **electron, proton, ultraviolet microscope** one using a beam of electrons, protons, or ultraviolet rays. [Gr. *mikros*, little, *skopeein,* to look at.]

microstructure mī-krō-struk′chər, or mī′, *n.* structure, especially of metals and alloys, as revealed by the microscope. [micro- (1a, b).]

microsurgery mī-krō-sûr′jə-ri, *n.* surgery performed on cells or other very small plant or body structures, requiring the use of a microscope.—*n.* **microsur′geon.** [micro- (1b).]

microtechnology mī-krō-tek-nol′əj-i, *n.* microelectronic technology. [micro- (1f).]

microtome mī′krə-tōm, *n.* an instrument for cutting thin sections of objects for microscopic examination. —*adjs.* **microtomic, -al** (-tom′ik, -l).—*ns.* **microtomist** (-krot′ə-mist); **microt′omy.** [Gr. *mikros*, little, *tomē,* a cut.]

microtone mī′krə-tōn, (*mus.*) *n.* an interval less than a semitone.—*n.* **microtonal′ity.** [micro- (1a).]

microwave mī′krə-wāv, *n.* in radio communication, one of very short wavelength: now usu. a wave in the radiation spectrum between normal radio waves and infrared.—Also *adj.*—**microwave oven** an oven in which food is cooked by the heat produced by microwaves passing through it. [**micro-** (1a).]

micturition *mik-tū-rish'ən, n.* the frequent desire to pass urine: (*loosely*) the act of urinating.—*v.i.* **mic'-turate** to urinate [L. *micturīre, -ītum,* desiderative of *mingĕre, mi(n)ctum,* to pass urine, *mi(n)ctiō, -ōnis,* urination.]

mid- *mid-,* in composition, the middle part of: of or in the middle of. [From **mid,** adj.; not always hyphened.]

mid *mid, adj.* middle: situated between extremes: uttered with the tongue in a position between high and low (*phon.*).—*n.* the middle.—*n.* **midst** middle —*adv.* in the middle.—*prep* (also **'midst** as if for **amidst**) amidst.—*adj.* **mid'most** middlemost.—*n.* the very middle —*adv.* in the very middle.—*prep.* in the very middle of.—**mid-air'** a region somewhat above the ground: the midst of a course through the air.— Also *adj.*—**mid'brain** the part of the brain derived from the second brain vesicle of the embryo: **mid'day** noon.—*adj.* of, at, or pertaining to, noon.—**mid'field** the middle area of a football, etc. pitch, not close to either team's goal: the players who operate in this area, acting as links between a team's defending and attacking players; **mid'-gut** that part of the alimentary canal formed from the original gastrula cavity and lined with endoderm: also, the small intestine.—*adj.* **mid'land** in the middle of, or surrounded by, land: distant from the coast: inland.—*n.* the interior of a country: (*pl.*) esp. (*cap.*) the central parts of England.—**mid-life crisis** the feeling of panic, pointlessness, etc. experienced at middle age by those who are concerned that they are no longer young; **mid'-mor'ning, mid'night** the middle of the night: twelve o'clock at night: pitch darkness.—*adj.* of or at midnight: dark as midnight.—**midnight sun** the sun visible at midnight in the polar regions; **mid'-o'cean; mid-off', mid-on'** (*cricket*) a fieldsman on the *off,* or *on,* side nearly in line with the bowler: his position; **mid'rib** the rib along the middle of a leaf; **mid'-seas'on** (also *adj.*).—*adj.* **mid'ship** in the middle of a ship.—**mid'shipman** once the title of a young officer (orig. quartered *amidships*) entering the navy, since 1957 only a shore ranking during training.— **midstream'** the middle of the stream.—*adv.* in the middle of the stream.—**mid'summer** (also -*sum'*) the middle of the summer: the summer solstice, about the 21st of June; **Midsummer day** the 24th of June, a quarter-day; **midsummer madness** madness attributed to the hot sun of midsummer; **mid'-term'** the middle of an academic term, term of office, etc.— Also *adj.*—**mid'way** the middle of the way or distance: a middle course.—*adj.* in the middle of the way or distance.—*adv.* half-way.—*prep.* half-way along or across.—*adj.* **mid'-week** in the middle of the week. —**Mid'west** Middle West; **mid'-wick'et** a fieldsman on the on side, about midway between mid-on and square leg: his position; **mid-win'ter** the middle of winter: the winter solstice (21st or 22nd December), or the time near it. [O.E. *midd.*]

'mid, mid, for **amid.**

Midas *mī'das, n.* a king of Phrygia whose touch turned all to gold, and on whom Apollo bestowed ass's ears. —**Midas touch** the ability to make money easily.

midden *mid'ən, n.* a dunghill: a refuse-heap. [Scand., as Dan. *mödding—mög,* dung; cf. **muck.**]

middle *mid'l, adj.* equally distant (in measurement or in number of steps) from the extremes: avoiding extremes, done as a compromise: intermediate: intervening: (*cap.*; of languages) between Old and Modern (as *Middle English, Middle High German*). —*n.* the middle point, part, or position: midst: the central portion, waist: the middle term (*log.*): a middle article.—**midd'le-age'.**—*adj.* **midd'le-aged'** (-*ājd'*) between youth and old age, variously reckoned to suit the reckoner.—**middle-age(d) spread** a thickening of the body attributable to the onset of middle-age; **Middle Ages** the time between the fall of the Western Roman empire and the Renaissance (5th–15th cent.); **Middle America** the countries lying between the United States of America and Colombia, sometimes including the West Indies: the American middle-class, esp. the conservative elements of it.— *n.* and *adj* **Middle-Amer'ican.**—*adjs.* **midd'le-brack'et** in a midway grouping in a list; **midd'lebrow** midway between highbrow and lowbrow.—Also *n.*— **middle C** the C in the middle of the piano keyboard: the first line below the treble or above the bass stave; **middle class** that part of the people which comes between the aristocracy and the working-class.— Also *adj.*—**middle distance** in a picture, the middle ground.—*adj.* **midd'le-dis'tance** in athletics, of or denoting a race of 400, 800, or 1500 metres, or an athlete who takes part in such a race.—**middle ear** the part of the ear containing the malleus, incus and stapes; **midd'le-earth'** the earth, considered as placed between the upper and lower regions; **Middle East** formerly the countries from Iran to Burma: now generally used of an area including the Arabic-speaking countries around the eastern end of the Mediterranean Sea and in the Arabian Peninsula, along with Greece, Turkey, Cyprus, Iran and the greater part of N. Africa.—*adj.* **Midd'le-East'ern.**—**Midd'le-East'-erner; Middle English** see **English; middle ground** the part of a picture between the foreground and background: a compromise position.—*adj.* **midd'le-in'come** having, or relating to those who have, an average income which makes them neither rich nor poor.—**midd'leman** one occupying a middle position: an intermediary, esp. between producer and consumer; **middle management** the junior managerial executives and senior supervisory personnel in a firm. —*adj.* **midd'lemost** nearest the middle.—**middle name** any name between a person's first name and surname: the notable quality or characteristic of a specified thing or person (*facet.*).—*adj.* **midd'le-of-the-road'** midway between extremes.—**middle school** a school for children between the ages of about 9 to 13: in some secondary schools, an administrative unit usu. comprising the third and fourth forms.—*adj.* **midd'le-sized** of average size.—**middle term** (*log.*) that term of a syllogism which appears in both premises but not in the conclusion; **middle watch** that from midnight to 4 a.m.; **midd'leweight** a boxer (over 10 st 7 lb. and not over 11 st. 6 lb.—professional only) of intermediate weight; **Middle West** the region between the Appalachians and the Rockies, the Mississippi basin as far south as Kansas, Missouri, and the Ohio River.—**in the middle of** occupied with, engaged in (doing something): during: while. [O.E. *middel* (adj.); see **mid.**]

middling *mid'ling, adj.* moderate (*coll.*): indifferent: mediocre: fairly good.—*adv.* (*coll.*) fairly: fairly well. [Orig. Scots—mid and suff. **-ling.**]

middy *mid'i,* (*Austr. slang*) *n.* a measure of beer, varying in amount from one place to another: the glass containing it.

Midgard *mid'gärd,* (*Scand. myth.*) *n.* the abode of men, middle-earth. [O.N. *mithgarthr,* mid-yard.]

midge *mij, n.* a small gnat-like fly: a very small person. —*n.* **midg'et** something very small of its kind: a very small person. [O.E. *mycg, mycge.*]

Midi *mē-dē', n.* the south (of France).—*n.* **midinette** (-*net'*) a Paris work-girl or a shop-girl in the millinery or fashion trade (noticeable at lunch-hour). [Fr.

midi, midday; *midinette* is said to be from *midi* and *dînette*, snack.]

midi- *mid'i-*, in composition, of middle size, length, etc., as **mid'i-skirt**, one reaching to about mid-calf. [**mid**; cf. **mini-**.]

midi *mid'i*, *n.* short for **midi-skirt**.

midland, midmost, midnight, etc. See **mid**.

midriff *mid'rif*, *n.* the diaphragm: the part of a woman's garment that fits over the diaphragm. [O.E. *mid*, middle, *hrif*, belly.]

midshipman, midst. See **mid**.

midwife *mid'wif*, *n.* a woman, or (*rarely*) a man, who assists women in childbirth:—*pl.* **midwives** (*mid'wivz*).—*v.t.* (also *mid'wive*; *-wiv*) to help in bringing forth (a child) (also *fig.*):—*pr.p.* **-wifing**, **-wiving**; *pa.t.*, *pa.p.* **-wifed**, **-wived**.—*n.* **mid'wifery** (*-wif-ə-ri*, *-wif-ri*, *-if-ri*, *-wif'ri*) the art or practice of a midwife: assistance at childbirth: obstetrics. [O.E. *mid*, with *wif*, woman.]

mien *mēn*, *n.* an air or look, manner, bearing (*literary*). [Perh. **demean**, influenced by Fr. *mine*.]

miff *mif*, (*coll.*) *n.* a slight feeling or fit of resentment. —*v.t.* to put out of humour.—*v.i.* to take offence.— *n.* **miff'iness**.—*adj.* **miff'y** ready to take offence: touchy. [Cf. Ger. *muffen*, to sulk.]

might [1] *mit*, *pa.t.* of **may**.—**might'-have-been** one who, or that which, might have been, or might have come to something.

might [2] *mit*, *n.* power: ability: strength: energy or intensity of purpose or feeling.—*adv.* **might'ily**.—*n.* **might'iness** the state of being mighty: power: greatness: great amount: a title of dignity: excellency.—*adj.* **might'y** having greater power: strong: valiant: very great: important: exhibiting might: wonderful.—*adv.* (now *coll.*, usu. with a tinge of irony except in *U.S.*) very.—**might and main** utmost strength. [O.E. *miht*, *meaht*; cf. **may**.]

mignon *mē-nyõ*, (Fr.) *adj.* small and dainty:—*fem.* **mignonne** (*mē-nyon*).

mignonette *min-yə-net'*, *n.* a sweet-scented Reseda: a fine kind of lace. [Fr. *mignonette*, fem. dim. of *mignon*, daintily small, a darling.]

migraine *mē'grān*, *mī'*, **megrim** *mē'grim*, *ns.* a pain affecting only one half of the head or face and usu. accompanied by nausea: a condition marked by recurring migraines. [Fr. *migraine*—Gr. *hēmikrāniā*—*hēmi*, half, *krānion*, skull.]

migrate *mī-grāt'*, *v.i.* to pass from one place to another: to change one's abode to another country, college, etc.: to change habitat periodically: to move (as parasites, etc.) to another part of the body: to pass in a stream (as ions, particles).—*n.* **mi'grant** a person or animal that migrates or is migrating.—Also *adj.*— *adj.* **mi'gratory** (*-grə-tə-ri*) migrating or accustomed to migrate: wandering.—*ns.* **migra'tion** a change of abode: a removal from one country or climate to another, esp. in a body: a number removing together; **migra'tionist** one who emigrates: one who explains facts by a theory of migration; **mi'grātor**. [L. *migrāre*, *-ātum*; cf. **meāre**, to go.]

mihrab *mē-räb'*, or *mēhh'*, *n.* a niche or slab in a mosque marking the direction of Mecca. [Ar. *mihrāb*.]

mikado *mi-kä'dō*, *n.* a title given by foreigners to the Emperor of Japan:—*pl.* **mika'dos**. [Jap., exalted gate.]

mike *mik*, *n.* a contraction of **microphone**.

mil *mil*, *n.* a unit (1/1000 in.) in measuring the diameter of wire: in pharmacy, a millilitre: a unit of angular measurement, used esp. with artillery, equal to 1/6400 of a circle or 0.05625°. [L. *mille*, a thousand.]

milady, miladi *mi-lād'i*, *n.* a French-English term for

an English lady of quality. [Fr. modification of *my lady*.]

milage. See **mile**.

milch *milch*, *milsh*, *adj.* giving milk.—**milch'-cow** a cow yielding milk or kept for milking: a ready source of gain or money (*fig.*). [O.E. *milce*; cf. **milk**.]

mild *mild*, *adj.* gentle in temper and disposition: not sharp or bitter: acting gently: gently and pleasantly affecting the senses: soft: calm.—*n.* mild ale.—*v.t.* **mild'en** to render mild.—*v.i.* to become mild.—*adv.* **mild'ly**.—*n.* **mild'ness**.—**mild ale** ale with less hop flavouring than pale ale.—*adj.* **mild'-spok'en** having a mild manner of speech.—**mild steel** steel with little carbon.—**put it mildly** to understate the case. [O.E. *milde*, mild.]

mildew *mil'dū*, *n.* a disease on plants, caused by the growth of minute fungi: a similar appearance on other things or of another kind: a fungus causing the disease.—*v.t.* to taint with mildew.—*adj.* **mil'dewy**. [O.E. *meledēaw*, *mildēaw*.]

mile *mil*, *n.* a Roman unit of length, 1000 (double) paces (*mille passūs* or *passuum*; about 1611 English yards): applied to various later units, now in Britain and U.S. to one of 1760 yards or 5280 feet (1.61 km.) —*statute mile*.—*ns.* **mil'age**, **mile'age** distance in miles: (also **mil(e)age allowance**) travelling allowance at so much a mile: miles travelled per gallon of fuel: use, benefit (*fig. coll.*); **mil'er** a runner of a mile race. —**mile'-castle** one of a series of small forts placed at mile intervals along a Roman wall; **mileom'eter**, **milom'eter** an instrument that records the number of miles that a vehicle, etc. has travelled; **mile'stone** a stone or mark showing distance in miles: a stage or reckoning-point: an important event, stage, etc. (*fig.*).—**geographical** or **nautical mile** one minute of longitude measured along the equator—6082.66 feet: in British practice, *Admiralty measured mile*, 6080 feet (1.8532 km.); *international nautical mile*—official unit in U.S. since 1954—6076.1033 feet, or 1.852 km. [O.E. *mil*—L. *milia*, pl. of *mille* (*passuum*) a thousand (paces).]

milfoil *mil'foil*, *n.* yarrow or other species of Achillea: extended to other plants with finely divided leaves, as **wat'er-mil'foil**. [O.Fr.,—L. *millefolium*—*mille*, a thousand, *folium*, a leaf.]

miliary *mil'i-ər-i*, *adj.* like a millet-seed: characterised by an eruption like millet-seeds. [L. *miliārius*—*milium*, millet.]

milieu *mēl-yø'*, *n.* environment, setting, medium, element:—*pl.* **milieus'**, or **milieux'** (*-yø*). [Fr., middle.]

militant *mil'it-ənt*, *adj.* fighting: engaged in warfare: actively contending: combative: using violence: militaristic.—*n.* one who takes active part in a struggle: one who seeks to advance a cause by violence.—*n.* **mil'itancy**.—*advs.* **mil'itantly**; **mil'-itarily**.—*n.* **militarisa'tion**, *-z-*.—*v.t.* **mil'itarise**, *-ize* to reduce or convert to a military model or method: to make militaristic: to subject to military domination. —*ns.* **mil'itarism** an excess of the military spirit: domination by an army, or military class or ideals: belief in such domination: a tendency to overvalue military power or to view things from the soldier's point of view; **mil'itarist** a student of military science: one imbued with militarism.—*adjs.* **militaris'tic**; **mil'itary** pertaining to soldiers, armies, or warfare: warlike.—*n.* soldiery: the army.—*v.i.* **mil'itate** to contend: to have weight, tell (esp. with *against*): to fight for a cause.—**military academy** a training-college for army officer cadets; **military band** a band of brasses, woodwinds, and percussion; **military cross** a decoration (M.C.) awarded since 1914 to army officers (below major) and warrant officers; **military**

honours see **honour; military medal** a medal awarded since 1916 to non-commissioned and warrant officers and serving men; **military police** a body of men and women functioning as a police force within the army; **military policeman, -woman.** [L. *miles, -itis*, a soldier, *militāris*, military, *militāre, -ātum*, to serve as a soldier.]

militaria mil-i-tā'ri-ə, *n.pl.* weapons, uniforms, and other things connected with wars past and present. [*military*, and noun suffix -*ia*; or L., things military, neut. pl. of *militāris*, military.]

militarise, etc. See **militant**.

militia mi-lish'ə, *n.* a body of men enrolled and drilled as soldiers: the National Guard and its reserve (*U.S.*): a territorial force: troops of the second line.— **milit'iaman.** [L. *mīlitia*, military service or force— *mīles*, a soldier.]

milk milk, *n.* a white liquid secreted by female mammals for the nourishment of their young: a milklike juice or preparation: lactation.—*v.t.* to squeeze or draw milk from: to supply with milk: to extract money, venom, etc., from: to extract: to manipulate as if milking a cow.—*v.i.* to yield milk.—*n.* **milk'er** one who milks cows, etc.: a machine for milking cows: a cow that gives milk.—*adv.* **milk'ily.**—*ns.* **milk'iness** cloudiness: mildness; **milk'ing** the act or art of milking (*lit.* or *fig.*): the amount of milk drawn at one time.—Also *adj.*—*adjs.* **milk'less; milk'like; milk'y** made of, full of, like, or yielding, milk: clouded: soft: gentle.—*adj.* **milk'-and-wa'ter** insipid: wishy-washy. —**milk'-bar** a shop where milk, milk-shakes, and the like are sold for drinking on the spot; **milk chocolate** eating chocolate made from cocoa, cocoa-butter, sugar, and condensed or dried milk; **milk'-cow** a milch-cow; **milk-denti'tion** the first set of teeth; **milk'-float** a vehicle in which milk-bottles are carried; **milk'-gland** a mammary gland; **milk'ing-stool** a stool on which the milker sits; **milk'ing-time; milk'maid** a woman who milks; **milk'man** a man who sells or delivers milk; **milk'-pudd'ing** rice, tapioca, etc., cooked with milk; **milk'-run** a milkman's morning round (also **milk round**): a routine flight (*airmen's slang*); **milk'-shake'** milk shaken up with a flavouring; **milk'sop** a piece of bread sopped or soaked in milk: a soft, unadventurous, effeminate fellow; **milk'-su'gar** lactose; **milk'-tooth** one of the first set of teeth.—*adj.* **milk'-white.**—**milk'wood** any of various trees with latex; **milk'wort** a plant (*Polygala*) supposed by some to promote production of milk; **Milky Way** the Galaxy.—**milk and honey** abundance, plenty: luxury; **milk of magnesia** a suspension of magnesium hydroxide in water. [O.E. (Mercian) *milc* (W.S. *meolc*), milk.]

mill mil, *n.* a machine for grinding by crushing between hard, rough surfaces, or for more or less similar operations: a building or factory where corn is ground, or manufacture of some kind is carried on.— *v.t.* to grind: to press, stamp, roll, cut into bars, full, furrow the edges of, or otherwise treat in a mill.—*v.i.* to move round in a curve: to practise the business of a miller: (often with *about, around*; of crowd) to move in an aimless and confused manner.—*adj.* **milled** prepared by a grinding-mill or a coining-press: transversely grooved on the edge (as a coin or screw-head): treated by machinery, esp. smoothed by calendering rollers in a paper-mill.—*ns.* **mill'er** one who owns or works a mill; **mill'ing** the business of a miller: the act of passing anything through a mill: the act of fulling cloth: the process of turning and ridging the edge of a screw-head or coin: a gruelling: aimless and confused movement of a crowd.—**mill'-board** stout pasteboard, used esp. in binding books; **mill'er's-thumb** the bull-head; **mill'-girl; mill'-hand** a factory worker;

milling machine a machine-tool for shaping metal, with rotating cutters; **mill'-owner; mill'pond** a pond to hold water for driving a mill (proverbially smooth); **mill'race** the current of water that turns a mill-wheel, or the channel in which it runs; **mill'stone** one of the two stones used in a mill for grinding corn: a very heavy burden (*fig.*); **mill'stone-grit** a hard, gritty sandstone suitable for millstones: (*cap.*) a series of grits, sandstones, shales, underlying the British Coal Measures; **mill'-stream** the stream of water that turns a mill-wheel; **mill'-wheel** a waterwheel · used for driving a mill; **mill'-work** the machinery of a mill: the planning and putting up of machinery in mills; **mill'-wright** a wright or mechanic who builds and repairs mills.—**go, put, through the mill** to undergo, subject to, probationary hardships, suffering or experience, or severe handling. [O.E. *myln*—L.L. *molīna*—L. *mola*, a mill—*molĕre*, to grind.]

mille mēl, (Fr.) *n.* thousand.—*ns.* **millefeuille(s)** (*mēl-fœy'*; Fr. *feuille*, leaf) a layered cake made with puff-pastry.

millenary mil'in-ər-i (also -ēn', or -en'), *n.* a thousand: a thousand years: a thousandth anniversary: a believer in the millennium.—*adj.* consisting of a thousand, or a thousand years: pertaining to the millennium or to belief in it.—*adj.* **millenā'rian** pertaining to the millennium.—*n.* a believer in the millennium.—*ns.* **millenā'rianism, mill'enārism.** [L. *millēnārius*, of a thousand—*mille*.]

millennium mil-en'i-əm, *n.* a thousand years: a thousandth anniversary, millenary: the thousand years after the second coming of Christ: (usu. *ironical*) a coming golden age:—*pl.* **millenn'ia, millenn'iums.**—*adj.* **millenn'ial.**—*ns.* **millenn'ialist** a believer in the millennium; **millenn'ianism, millenn'iarism.** [L. *mille*, a thousand, *annus*, a year.]

millepede. See **millipede.**

millesimal mil-es'im-əl, *adj.* thousandth: consisting of thousandth parts.—*adv.* **milles'imally.** [L. *millēsimus*—*mille*, a thousand.]

millet mil'it, *n.* a food-grain (*Panicum miliaceum*): extended to other species and genera.—**mill'et-seed'.**— *adj.* of the size or appearance of seeds of millet: miliary. [Fr. *millet*—L. *milium*.]

milli- mil'i-, in composition, in names of units, a thousandth part. [L. *mille*, a thousand.]

milliard mil'yärd, *n.* a thousand million. [Fr.,—L. *mille*, a thousand.]

milliner mil'in-ər, *n.* orig. a dealer in goods made in *Milan*—'fancy goods': one who makes or sells women's headgear, trimmings, etc.—*n.* **mill'inery** the articles made or sold by milliners: the industry of making them. [*Milaner*, a trader in Milan wares.]

million mil'yən, *n.* a thousand thousands (1 000 000): a very great number: a million pounds, dollars, etc.— Also *adj.*—*n.* **millionaire** (-*ār'*) a man worth a million pounds, dollars, etc. (more or less):—*fem.* **millionair'ess.**—*adj.* and *n.* **mill'ionth** the ten hundred thousandth. [Fr.,—L.L. *milliō, -ōnis*—L. *mille*, a thousand.]

millipede, millepede mil'i-pēd, *n.* any myriapod of the class Chilognatha, vegetarian cylindrical animals with many joints, most of which bear two pairs of legs. [L. *millepeda*, a woodlouse—*mille*, a thousand, *pēs, pĕdis*, a foot.]

millometer. See **mileometer.**

milor, milord mi-lōr(d)', *n.* a rich Englishman. [Fr. modification of *my lord*.]

milt milt, *n.* the spleen (also, in Jewish cookery, **miltz** *milts*): the semen, or soft roe, of male fishes.—*v.t.* (of fishes) to impregnate.—*n.* **milt'er** a male fish, esp. in the breeding season. [O.E. *milte*, spleen.]

Miltonic mil-ton'ik, *adj.* relating to *Milton*

(1608–1674), or relating to his poetry, or in his manner.

miltz. See **milt**.

mimbar mim′bàr, **minbar** mɪn′, ns. a mosque pulpit. [Ar. minbar.]

mime mīm, n. an ancient farcical play of real life, with mimicry (esp. in its Latin form): an actor in such a farce: a play without dialogue, relying solely on movement, expression, etc.: an actor in such a play: mimicry without words: a mimic: a buffoon.—v.t. and v.i. to act as a mime: to act with mimicry: to mimic.—ns. **mim′er; mimesis** (mɪm- or mīm-ē′sis) imitation or representation in art: the rhetorical use of a person's supposed or imaginable words: simulation of one disease by another (med.): mimicry (biol.); **mime′ster.**—adjs. **mimet′ic, -al** (mim- or mīm-) imitative: mimic: pertaining to, showing mimicry, mimesis or miming.—adv. **mimet′ically.**—n. **mimic** (mim′ik) one who imitates, esp. one who performs in ludicrous imitation of others' speech and gestures: an unsuccessful imitator or imitation: a plant or animal exemplifying mimicry.—adj. imitative: mock or sham.—v.t. to imitate, esp. in ridicule or so as to incur ridicule: to ape: to produce an imitation of: to resemble deceptively:—pr.p. **mim′icking;** pa.t. and pa.p. **mim′icked.**—ns. **mim′icker; mimicry** (mim′) an act of mimicking: an advantageous superficial resemblance to some other species or object (biol.). [Gr. mīmos, a mime, mīmēsis, imitation, mīmētēs, an imitator.]

mimeograph mim′i-ō-gräf, n. an apparatus on which handwritten or typescript sheets can be reproduced from a stencil: a copy so produced.—v.t. to produce a copy or copies of (something) in this way. [Mimeograph, formerly a trademark.]

mimer, mimetic, mimic, mimicker, mimicry, etc. See **mime.**

Mimosa mim-ō′zə, n. the sensitive plant genus: (without cap.) a plant of this genus: (without cap.) popularly extended to Acacia and other genera of the **Mimosā′ceae** (mim- or mīm-) a regular-flowered family of Leguminosae.—adj. **mimosā′ceous** (mim- or mīm-). [Gr. mīmos, a mimic.]

Mimulus mim′ū-ləs, n. the musk and monkey-flower genus of the figwort family: (without cap.) a plant of the genus. [Gr. mīmos, a mime, with L. dim. suffix -ulus.]

mina. Same as **myna.**

minar min-àr′, n. a tower.—n. **min′aret** a mosque tower, from which the call to prayer is given. [Ar. manār, manārat, lighthouse—nār, fire.]

minatory min′ə-tə-ri (or mīn′), adj. threatening. [L. minārī, -ātus, to threaten.]

minbar. See **mimbar.**

mince mins, v.t. to cut into small pieces: to chop fine: to diminish or suppress a part of in speaking: to pronounce affectedly.—v.i. to walk with affected nicety: to speak affectedly:—pr.p. **minc′ing;** pa.t. and pa.p. **minced** (minst).—n. minced meat: mincemeat.—n. **minc′er.**—adj. **minc′ing** not speaking fully out: speaking or walking with affected nicety.—Also n.—adv. **minc′ingly.**—**mince′meat** meat chopped small—hence anything thoroughly broken or cut to pieces: a chopped mixture of raisins, peel, and other ingredients; **mince-pie′** a pie made with mincemeat, esp. in latter sense.—**make mincemeat of** to destroy utterly (esp. fig.); **mince matters, words** to speak of things with affected delicacy, or to soften an account unduly. [O.Fr. mincier, minchier—L. minūtus; cf. **minute**¹.]

mind mīnd, n. memory: thought: judgment: opinion: inclination: attention: direction of the will: the state of thought and feeling: wits, right senses, sanity: consciousness: intellect: that which thinks, knows, feels, and wills: soul: personality: a thinking or directing person.—v.t. to attend to: to tend, have care or oversight of: to be careful about: to beware of: to be troubled by, object to, dislike.—v.i. to attend: to care: to look out, take heed: to be troubled, object.—interj. be careful, watch out!—adj. **mind′ed** inclined: disposed.—**-mind′ed** in composition, having a mind of such-and-such a kind or inclined towards this or that.—**-mind′edness** in composition, inclination.—**mind′er** one who minds a machine, child, etc.: a criminal's bodyguard (slang).—adj. **mind′ful** bearing in mind: taking thought or care: attentive: observant.—adv. **mind′fully.**—n. **mind′fulness.**—adj. **mind′less** without mind: stupid: unmindful.—adv. **mind′lessly.**—n. **mind′lessness.**—**mind′-bender** a brain-teaser, a puzzle.—adjs **mind′-bending** permanently inclining the mind towards certain beliefs, etc.: forcing the mind to unwonted effort, teasing the brain; **mind′-blowing** (of a drug) producing a state of ecstasy: (of an exhilarating experience, etc.) producing a similar state; **mind′-boggling** astonishing: incomprehensible.—**mind′-reading** thought-reading; **mind's eye** visual imagination, mental view, contemplation.—**absence of mind** inattention to what is going on owing to absorption of the mind in other things; **cast one's mind back** to think about, try to recall past events, etc.; **change one's mind** to come to a new resolution or opinion; **cross one's mind** see **cross; do you mind?** an interjection expressing annoyance or disagreement; **do, or would, you mind?** please do: do you object?; **have a (good, great) mind** to wish or to be inclined strongly; **have a mind of one's own** to be strong-willed and independent, unwilling to be persuaded or dissuaded by others; **have half a mind** to be somewhat inclined; **if you don't mind** if you have no objection; **in two minds** wavering; **know one's own mind** to be sure of one's intentions and opinions: to be self-assured; **make up one's mind** to come to a decision; **mind one's p's and q's** to be watchfully accurate and punctilious; **mind out** (often with for) to beware (of), look out (for); **mind you** an expression used to introduce a qualification added to something already said; **mind your own business** this is none of your affair; **never mind** do not concern yourself: it does not matter: you are not to be told; **of one** (or **a,** or **the same**) **mind** agreed; **of two minds** uncertain what to think or do; **on one's mind** weighing upon one's spirit; **out of mind** forgotten: out of one's thoughts; **out of one's mind** mad; **presence of mind** a state of calmness in which all the powers of the mind are on the alert and ready for action; **put in mind** to remind (of); **put out of one's mind** to think no more about, forget about; **set one's mind on** to fix a settled desire upon; **set, put one's mind to** to focus one's attention on; **speak one's mind** to say plainly what one thinks; **take someone's mind off** to distract someone from; **time out of mind** from time immemorial; **to my,** etc. **mind** to my, etc. thinking, in my, etc. opinion: to my, etc. liking. [O.E. gemynd—munan, to think.]

mine¹ mīn, pron., genitive of **I,** used predicatively or absolutely, belonging to me: my people: that which belongs to me. [O.E. mīn.]

mine² mīn, n. a place from which minerals are dug: a burrowing animal's gallery, as an insect's in a leaf: an excavation dug under a position to give secret ingress, to subvert it, or to blow it up (mil.): an explosive charge therefor: a submerged or floating charge of explosives in a metal case to destroy ships: a landmine: a rich source.—v.t. to excavate, tunnel, make passages in or under: to obtain by excavation: to work as a mine: to bring down or blow up by a mine: to beset with mines: to lay mines in or under.—*v.i.* to dig or work a mine or mines: to tunnel: to burrow: to lay mines: to proceed secretly, insidiously (*fig.*).—*n.* **mi'ner** one who works in a mine: a soldier who lays mines.—*n.* and *adj.* **min'ing.—mine'-detector** an apparatus for detecting explosive mines; **mine'-field** an area beset with mines (also *fig.*); **mine'-hunter** a ship for locating mines; **mine'-layer** a ship for laying mines; **mine'-owner; miner's lamp** a lamp carried by a miner, commonly on his cap; **mine'-sweeper** a vessel for removing mines; **mine'-worker** a miner. [Fr. *mine* (noun), *miner* (verb).]

mineola. See **min(n)eola.**

mineral *mun'ər-l, n.* a substance produced by processes of inorganic nature: a substance got by mining: ore: a substance neither animal nor vegetable: a mineral water (in a wide sense).—*adj.* relating to minerals: having the nature of minerals: impregnated with minerals, as water: of inorganic substance or nature.—*n.* **mineralisā'tion, -z-.**—*v.t* **min'eralise, -ize** to make into a mineral: to give the properties of a mineral to: to go looking for and examining minerals.—*ns.* **min'eralis'er, -z-** one who, that which, mineralises: an element that combines with a metal to form an ore, as sulphur; **min'eralist** one versed in or employed about minerals.—*adj.* **mineralog'ical** pertaining to mineralogy.—*adv.* **mineralog'ically.**—*v.i.* **mineralogise, -ize (-al')** to collect or study minerals.—*ns.* **mineral'ogist** one versed in mineralogy; **mineral'ogy** the science of minerals.—**mineral kingdom** that department of nature which comprises substances that are neither animal nor vegetable; **mineral oil** any oil of mineral origin; **mineral spring, well** a spring of mineral water; **mineral water** spring water impregnated with minerals: an artificial imitation thereof: loosely, an effervescent non-alcoholic beverage; **mineral wool** a mass of fibres got by blowing steam through molten slag. [Fr. *minéral*—*miner*, to mine; cf. **mine**[2].]

Minerva *min-ûr'və, n.* the Roman goddess of wisdom, identified with the Greek Athena. ' [L., prob. from root of *mēns*, the mind.]

minestrone *min-i-strōn'i, n.* a thick vegetable soup with pieces of pasta, etc. [It.]

minever. See **miniver.**

Ming *ming, n.* a Chinese dynasty (1368–1643).—*adj.* of the dynasty, its time, or esp. its pottery and other art.

mingle *ming'gl, v.t.* and *v.i.* to mix.—*n.* a mixture: a medley.—*ns.* **ming'lement; ming'ler; ming'ling.**—*adv.* **ming'lingly.** [O.E. *mengan*.]

mingy *min'ji, (coll.) adj.* niggardly.—*n.* **min'giness.** [Perh. a portmanteau-word from **mangy** or **mean**[1] and **stingy**.]

mini- *min'i-,* in composition, small (abbrev. of **miniature**) as in e.g. the following (also often without hyphen):—**min'i-bus** a small motor bus; **min'i-cab** a small motor vehicle plying for hire; **min'ipill** a low-dose oral contraceptive containing no oestrogen; **min'i-skirt** a skirt whose hem-line is well above the knees; **min'i-sub('marine).**

mini *min'i, n.* short for **mini-car, mini-skirt.**—*adj.* (*coll.*) small, miniature.

miniature *min'i(-ə)-chər, min'yə-tūr, -tyər, n.* manuscript illumination: a painting on a very small scale, on ivory, vellum, etc.: the art of painting in this manner: a small or reduced copy, type or breed of anything.—*adj.* on a small scale: minute.—*n.* **miniaturisā'tion, -z-.**—*v.t.* **min'iaturise, -ize** to make very small: to make something on a small scale.—*n.* **min'iaturist** one who paints miniatures.—**in miniature** on a small scale. [It. *miniatura*—L. *minium*, red lead; meaning affected by association with L. *minor, minimus*, etc., and their derivatives.]

minim *min'im, n.* a least part: a note, formerly the shortest, equal to two crotchets (*mus.*): apothecaries' measure, one-sixtieth of a fluid drachm: apothecaries' weight, a grain: a short down-stroke in handwriting.—*adj.* **min'imal** of least, or least possible, size, amount, or degree: of the nature of a minimum.—*ns.* **min'imalism; min'imalist** a person advocating a policy of the least possible action, intervention, etc.: a practitioner of minimal art; **minimisā'tion, -z-.**—*v.t.* **min'imise, -ize** to reduce to the smallest possible amount: to make as light as possible: to estimate at the lowest possible: loosely, to lessen, diminish: loosely, to belittle.—*n.* **min'imum** the least quantity or degree, or the smallest possible: the lowest point or value reached: in math., a value of a variable at which it ceases to diminish and begins to increase—opp. of *maximum*:—*pl.* **min'ima.**—*adj.* smallest or smallest possible.—**minimal art** art whose practitioners reject such traditional elements as composition and interrelationship between parts of the whole; **minim rest** a rest of the duration of a minim; **minimum wage** the lowest wage permitted by law or regulation for certain work: a fixed bottom limit to workers' wages in various industries. [L. *minimus, -a, -um,* smallest.]

minion *min'yən, n.* a darling, a favourite, esp. of a prince: a flatterer: a servile dependant. [Fr. *mignon, mignonne*.]

minipill. See **mini-.**

miniscule. A wrong spelling of **minuscule.**

minister *min'is-tər, n.* one who administers or proffers, in service or kindness: one who serves at the altar: a clergyman: the head, or assistant to the head, of several religious orders: one transacting business for another: the responsible head of a department of state affairs: the representative of a government at a foreign court.—*v.i.* to give attentive service (to): to perform duties: to supply or do things needful.—*adj.* **ministē'rial** pertaining to a minister or ministry (in any sense): on the government side: administrative: executive: instrumental.—*adv.* **ministē'rially.**—*adjs.* **min'istering** attending and serving; **min'istrant** administering: attendant.—Also *n.*—*n.* **ministrā'tion** the act of ministering or performing service: office or service of a minister.—*adj.* **min'istrative (-trə-tiv,** or **-trā-tiv)** serving to aid or assist: ministering.—*ns.* **min'istress** a female who ministers; **min'istry** act of ministering: service: office or duties of a minister: the clergy: the clerical profession: the body of ministers who manage the business of the country: a department of government, or the building it occupies: term of office as minister.—**Minister of State** an additional, non-Cabinet, minister in an exceptionally busy government department; **Minister of the Crown** a government minister in the Cabinet; **Minister without Portfolio** a government minister, a member of the cabinet having no specific department. [L. *minister*—*minor*, less.]

miniver, minever *min'i-vər, n.* white fur, orig. a mixed or variegated fur: the ermine in winter coat. [O.Fr. *menu*, small—L. *minūtus*, and *vair*, fur—L. *varius*, particoloured.]

mink *mingk, n.* a small animal (of several species) of the weasel kind: its fur: a coat or jacket made from its fur. [Perh. from Sw. *mänk*.]

min(n)eola *min-i-ō'lə, n.* a variety of citrus fruit developed from a tangerine and a grapefruit and resembling an orange, grown in the U.S. and elsewhere. [Poss. *Mineola* in Texas.]

minnesinger *min'i-sing-ər,* Ger. *-zing-ər, n.* one of a 12th–13th cent. school of German amatory lyric poets, mostly of noble birth. [Ger. *Minne*, love, *Singer*, singer.]

minnow *min'ō, n.* a very small freshwater fish (*Phoxinus phoxinus*) close akin to chub and dace: loosely extended to other small fish: a small, unimportant person or thing (*fig.*).

Minoan *min-ō'ən, min-, adj.* pertaining to prehistoric Crete and its culture.—*n.* a prehistoric Cretan. [Gr. *Mīnōs*, a legendary king of Crete.]

minor *mī'nər, adj.* lesser: inferior in importance, degree, bulk, etc.: inconsiderable: lower: smaller (than major) by a semitone (*mus.*): in boys' schools, junior: Franciscan.—*n.* a person under age: the minor term, or minor premise (*log.*): anything that is minor opposed to major.—*n.* **minority** (*min-* or *mīn-or'ı-ti*) the condition of fact of being little or less: the state or time of being under age (also **mī'norship**): the smaller number: less than half: the party, social group, section of the population, etc., of smaller numbers: the number by which it falls short of the other party— opp to *majority*.—*adj.* of the minority.—**minority carrier** (*electronics*) in a semiconductor, the electrons or holes which carry the lesser degree of measured current; **minority group** a section of the population with a common interest, characteristic, etc., which is not common to most people; **minor key, mode, scale** one with its third a minor third above the tonic; **minor orders** the lower degrees of holy orders, i.e. porter, exorcist, lector, acolyte; **minor planet** a small planet, any one of many hundreds with orbits between those of Mars and Jupiter; **minor poet** a genuine but not great poet; **minor premise** (*log.*) that in which the minor term occurs; **minor prophets** the twelve from Hosea to Malachi in the Old Testament; **minor suit** in bridge, clubs or diamonds; **minor term** (*log.*) the term which is the subject of the conclusion; **minor third** (*mus.*) an interval of three semitones. [L. *minor*, less; cf. **minus**.]

Minotaur *min'* or *mīn'ə-tör, n.* the bull-headed monster in the Cretan Labyrinth, offspring of Pasiphae, wife of Minos. [Gr. *Mīnōtauros—Mīnōs*, Minos, *tauros*, bull.]

minster *min'stər, n.* an abbey church or priory church: often applied to a cathedral or other great church without any monastic connection. [O.E. *mynster—* L. *monastērium*, a monastery.]

minstrel *min'strəl, n.* a musician: a mediaeval harper who sang or recited his own or others' poems: one of a troupe of entertainers with blackened faces.—*n.* **min'strelsy** (*-si*) the art or occupation of a minstrel: music: a company or body of minstrels: a collection of songs. [O.Fr. *menestrel—*L.L. *ministeriālis—*L. *minister*, attendant.]

mint¹ *mint, n.* a place where money is coined, esp. legally: a vast sum of money.—*v.t.* to coin: to invent: to stamp.—*adj.* in mint condition.—*ns.* **mint'age** coining: coinage: stamp: duty for coining; **mint'er.—mint condition, state** the condition of a new-minted coin: perfect condition, as if unused; **mint'-mark** a mark showing where a coin was minted. [O.E. *mynet*, money—L. *monēta*; see **money**.]

mint² *mint, n.* any plant of the aromatic labiate genus Mentha, as spearmint, peppermint: any sweet flavoured with mint.—*adj.* **mint'y.—mint'-ju'lep** see **julep; mint'-sauce'** chopped spearmint or other mint mixed with vinegar and sugar, used as a sauce for roast lamb. [O.E. *minte—*L. *mentha—*Gr. *minthē*, *mintha*.]

minuend *min'ū-end, n.* the number from which another is to be subtracted. [L. *minuendus* (*numerus*)—*minuĕre*, to lessen.]

minuet *min-ū-et', n.* a slow, graceful dance in triple measure, invented in the 17th century: the music for such a dance. [Fr. *menuet—menu*, small—L. *minūtus*, small.]

minus *mī'nəs, prep.* diminished by (*math.*): deficient in respect of, deprived of, without (*coll.*).—*adj.* negative.—*n.* a deficiency or subtraction: a negative quantity or term: the sign (also **minus sign**) of subtraction or negativity (–) opposed to *plus*. [L. *minus*, neut. of *minor*, less.]

minuscule *min'əs-kūl*, or *-us', n.* a small cursive script, originated by the monks in the 7th–9th centuries: a lower-case letter (*print.*): opposed to *majuscule.—adj.* very small, very unimportant.—*adj.* **minus'cular**. [L. (*littera*) *minuscula*, smallish (letter).]

minute¹ *min-ūt'*, or *min-ūt', adj.* extremely small: having regard to the very small: exact.—*adv.* **minute'ly.—*n.* **minute'ness.** [L. *minūtus*, pa.p. of *minuĕre*, to lessen.]

minute² *min'ıt, n.* the sixtieth part of an hour: the sixtieth part of a degree: an indefinitely small space of time: a particular moment: a brief jotting or note: (in *pl.*) a brief summary of the proceedings of a meeting: a minute's walk, or distance traversed in a minute.—*v.t.* to make a brief jotting or note of: to record in the minutes.—**min'ute-bell** a bell sounded every minute, in mourning; **min'ute-book** a book of minutes or short notes; **min'ute-gun** a gun discharged every minute, as a signal of distress or mourning; **min'ute-hand** the hand that indicates the minutes on a clock or watch; **min'uteman** (often *cap.*) a man ready to turn out at a minute's warning, as in the American war of independence (*hist.*): a member of an armed right-wing organisation in the U.S., formed to take prompt action against Communist activities: a three-stage intercontinental ballistic missile; **minute steak** a small thin piece of steak which can be cooked quickly. —**up to the minute** right up to date. [Same word as foregoing.]

minutia *mi-nū'shi-ə, n.* a minute particular or detail:— *pl.* **minū'tiae** (*-ē*).—*adj.* **minū'tiose** (*-shi-ōs*). [L. *minūtia*, smallness.]

minx *mingks, n.* a pert young girl.

Miocene *mī'ō-sēn, (geol.) adj.* of the Tertiary period preceding the Pliocene and having a smaller proportion of molluscan fossils of species now living.—*n.* the Miocene system, period, or strata. [Gr. *meiōn*, smaller, *kainos*, recent.]

miosis *mī-ō'sıs, n.* a variant spelling of **meiosis** and of **myosis**.

miracle *mir'ə-kl, n.* a supernatural event: hyperbolically, a marvel, a wonder: a miracle play.—*adj.* **miraculous** (*-ak'ū-ləs*) of the nature of a miracle: done by supernatural power: very wonderful: able to perform miracles.—*adv.* **mirac'ulously.—*n.* **mirac'ulousness.—miracle play** a mediaeval form of drama founded on Old or New Testament history, or the legends of the saints. [Fr.,—L. *mīrāculum— mīrāri, -ātus*, to wonder at.]

mirage *mi-räzh', n.* an appearance of objects raised or depressed, erect or inverted, single or double, owing to the varying refractive index of layers of hot and cold air, the sky often simulating the appearance of water: something illusory (*fig.*). [Fr. *mirer*, to look at—L. *mīrāri*, to wonder at.]

mire *mīr, n.* deep mud.—*v.t.* to plunge and fix in mire: to soil with mud—*v.i.* to sink in mud.—*n.* **mir'iness.** —*adj.* **mir'y** consisting of mire: covered with mire. [O.N. *mýrr*, bog.]

mirepoix *mēr-pwa', n.* sautéed vegetables used for making sauces, etc. [Prob. after the Duc de Mirepoix, 18th-cent. French general.]

mirk, etc. Same as **murk**.

mirror *mir'ər, n.* a looking-glass: a reflecting surface: a faithful representation (*fig.*): an example, good or bad.—*v.t.* to reflect an image of, as in a mirror: to furnish with a mirror.—*pr.p.* **mirr'oring;** *pa.p.*

mirr'ored.—*adj.* and *adv.* **mirr'orwise** with interchange of left and right.—**mirr'or-im'age** an image with right and left reversed as in a mirror; **mirror symmetry** the symmetry of an object and its reflected image; **mirr'or-writing** writing which is like ordinary writing as seen in a mirror. [O.Fr. *mireor, mirour*—L. *mīrārī, -ātus*, to wonder at.]

mirth *mûrth, n.* merriness: pleasure: delight: noisy gaiety: jollity: laughter.—*adj.* **mirth'ful** full of mirth: causing mirth: merry: jovial.—*adv.* **mirth'fully.**—*n.* **mirth'fulness.**—*adj.* **mirth'less.**—*adv.* **mirth'lessly.**—*n.* **mirth'lessness.** [O.E. *myrgth*—*myrige*, merry.]

miry. See **mire.**

mis- *mis, pfx.* wrong, ill, e.g. **misbehave, misdeed,** **mis-lead.** [O.E. *mis-*; cf. **miss**[1].]

misadventure *mis-əd-ven'chər, n.* ill-luck: mishap: accidental killing. [M.E.—O.Fr., *mesaventure.*]

misadvise *mis-əd-vīz', v.t.* to advise ill.—*adj.* **misadvised'.**—*adv.* **misadvi'sedly.**—*n.* **misadvis'edness.** [Pfx. **mis-**.]

misalliance *mis-ə-lī'əns, n.* an unsuitable alliance, esp. marriage with one of a lower rank.—*adj.* **misallied'.** [Fr. *mésalliance.*]

misandry *mis'ən-dri, n.* hatred of men.—*n.* **mis'andrist.** [Gr. *misandria*—*misandros*, hating men.]

misanthrope *mis'ən-thrōp, n.* a hater of mankind, one who distrusts everyone else—also **misanthropist** (*mis-an'throp-ist*).—*adjs.* **misanthropic, -al** (*mis-ən-throp'ik, -əl*) hating or distrusting mankind.—*adv.* **misanthrop'ically.**—*n.* **misan'thropy** hatred or distrust of mankind. [Gr. *mīsanthrōpos* —*mīseein*, to hate, *anthrōpos*, a man.]

misapply *mis-ə-plī', v.t.* to apply wrongly: to use for a wrong purpose.—*n.* **misapplica'tion** (*-ap-*). [Pfx. **mis-**.]

misapprehend *mis-ap-ri-hend', v.t.* to apprehend wrongly: to take or understand in a wrong sense.— *n.* **misapprehen'sion.**—*adj.* **misapprehen'sive.**—*adv.* **misapprehen'sively** by or with misapprehension or mistake.—*n.* **misapprehen'siveness.** [Pfx. **mis-**.]

misappropriate *mis-ə-prō'pri-āt, v.t.* to put to a wrong use: to take dishonestly for oneself.—*n.* **misappropria'tion.** [Pfx. **mis-**.]

misarrange *mis-ə-rānj', v.t.* to arrange wrongly: to put in wrong order.—*n.* **misarrange'ment.** [Pfx. **mis-**.]

misbegot, misbegotten *mis-bi-got', -got'n, adj* unlawfully begotten: monstrous. [Pfx. **mis-**, and *pa.p.* of *beget.*]

misbehave *mis-bi-hāv', v.t.* (*refl.*) and *v.i.* to behave ill or improperly.—*n.* **misbehav'iour.** [Pfx. **mis-**.]

misbelieve *mis-bi-lēv', v.t.* to believe wrongly or falsely.—*ns.* **misbelief'** (or *mis'*) belief in false doctrine; **misbeliev'er.**—*adj.* **misbeliev'ing.** [Pfx. **mis-**.]

miscalculate *mis-kal'kū-lāt, v.t.* and *v.i.* to calculate wrongly.—*n.* **miscalcula'tion.** [Pfx. **mis-**.]

miscall *mis-köl', v.t.* to call by a wrong name: to call by an ill name: to abuse or revile. [Pfx. **mis-**.]

miscarriage *mis-kar'ij, n.* an act or instance of miscarrying: failure: failure to reach the intended result or destination: act of bringing forth prematurely, esp. of expelling a foetus between the third and seventh months.—*v.i.* **miscarr'y** to be unsuccessful: to fail of the intended effect: to bring forth before the proper time: to be born prematurely.— **miscarriage of justice** failure of the courts to do justice. [Pfx. **mis-**.]

miscast *mis-käst', v.t.* and *v.i.* to cast (in any sense) amiss or blameworthily. [Pfx. **mis-**.]

miscegenation *mis-i-jin-ā'shən, n.* mixing of race: interbreeding, intermarriage, or sexual intercourse between different races. [L. *miscēre*, to mix, *genus*, race.]

miscellaneous *mis-əl-ān'i-əs, adj.* mixed or mingled: consisting of several kinds.—*adj.* **miscellanarian** (*-ən-ā'ri-ən*).—*n.* a writer of miscellanies.—*adv.* **miscellan'eously.**—*ns.* **miscellan'eousness; miscellanist** (*mis-el'ən-ist*, or *mis'əl*) a writer of miscellanies; **miscellany** (*mis-el'*, or *mis'əl-*) a mixture of various kinds: a collection of writings on different subjects or by different authors.—*n.pl.* **miscella'nea** (L. *neut. pl.*) a miscellany. [L. *miscellāneus*—*miscellus*—*miscēre*, to mix.]

mischance *mis-chäns', n.* ill-luck: mishap. [M.E.—O.Fr. *meschance.*]

mischief *mis'chif, n.* an ill consequence: evil: injury: damage, hurt: the troublesome fact: a source of harm: petty misdeeds or annoyance: pestering playfulness: a mischievous person.—*adj.* **mischievous** (*mis'chiv-əs*) causing mischief: injurious: prone to mischief.—*adv.* **mis'chievously.**—*n.* **mis'chievousness.**—**mis'chief-maker** one who stirs up strife.— *n.* and *adj.* **mis'chief-making.** [O.Fr. *meschef,* from *mes-* (From L. *minus,* less) and *chef*—L. *caput,* the head.]

miscible *mis'i-bl, adj.* that may be mixed.—*n.* **miscibil'ity.** [L. *miscēre*, to mix.]

misconceive *mis-kən-sēv', v.t.* and *v.i.* to conceive wrongly: to mistake.—*n.* **misconcep'tion** [Pfx **mis-**.]

misconduct *mis-kon'dukt, n.* bad conduct: wrong management: adultery: behaviour, not necessarily morally reprehensible, such as would lead any reasonable employer to dismiss an employee (*legal*).—*v.t.* **misconduct** (*-kən-dukt'*). [Pfx. **mis-**.]

misconstrue *mis-kən-strōō', or -kon'strōō, v.t.* to construe or to interpret wrongly. [Pfx. **mis-**.]

miscount *mis-kownt', v.t.* to count wrongly: to misjudge.—*n.* a wrong counting. [Pfx. **mis-**.]

miscreant *mis'kri-ənt, n.* orig. a misbeliever, a heretic or infidel: a vile wretch, a detestable scoundrel.—*adj.* depraved, ill-doing. [O.Fr. *mescreant* —*mes-* (from L. *minus,* less) and L. *crēdēns, -entis,* pr.p. of *crēdēre,* to believe]

miscue *mis-kū', n.* at billiards, a stroke spoiled by the slipping off of the cue.—Also *v.t.* (*lit.* and *fig.*) [Pfx. **mis-**, or **miss**[1].]

misdate *mis-dāt', v.t.* to date wrongly.—*n.* a wrong date [Pfx. **mis-**.]

misdeal *mis-dēl', n.* a wrong deal, as at cards.—*v.t.* and *v.i.* to deal wrongly: to divide improperly:— *pa.t.* and *pa.p.* **misdealt** (*-delt'*). [Pfx. **mis-**.]

misdeed *mis-dēd', n.* wrong-doing, an evil deed. [O.E. *misdǣd.*]

misdemean *mis-di-mēn', v.t.* (*refl.*) and *v.t.* to misbehave.—*ns.* **misdemean'ant** one guilty of petty crime, or misconduct; **misdemean'our,** in U.S. **misdemean'or,** bad conduct: a misdeed: formerly a legal offence of less gravity than a felony. [Pfx. **mis-**, **demean**[1].]

misdevotion *mis-di-vō'shən, n.* ill-directed devotion. [Pfx. **mis-**.]

misdid. See **misdo.**

misdirect *mis-di-rekt', v.t.* to direct wrongly.—*n.* **misdirec'tion.** [Pfx. **mis-**.]

misdo *mis-dōō', v.t.* to do wrongly or badly.—*v.i.* to act amiss:—*pa.t.* **misdid'**; *pa.p.* **misdone'**.—*ns.* **misdo'er; misdo'ing.** [Pfx. **mis-**.]

misdoubt *mis-dowt', v.t.* to have a doubt, suspicion, misgiving, or foreboding of or about.—*n.* suspicion: misgiving.—*adj.* **misdoubt'ful.** [Pfx. **mis-**.]

misdraw *mis-drö', v.t.* to draw or draft badly.—*n.* **misdraw'ing.** [Pfx. **mis-**.]

mise *mēz, mīz, n* a stake in gambling: the lay-out of

cards.—**mise(-)en(-)scène** (*mē-zä-sen*) the act, result, or art, of setting a stage scene or arranging a pictorial representation (also *fig.*). [O.Fr. *mise*, placing or setting—L. *mittēre*, *missum*.]

miseducation *mis-ed-ū-kā'shən*, *n.* improper or hurtful education. [Pfx. **mis-**.]

misemploy *mis-im-ploi'*, *v.t.* to employ wrongly or amiss: to misuse.—*n.* **misemploy'ment**. [Pfx. **mis-**.]

miser *mī'zar*, *n.* one who lives miserably in order to hoard wealth: a niggard.—*n.* **mi'serliness**.—*adj.* **mi'serly**. [L. *miser*, wretched.]

miserable *miz'ə-rə-bl*, *adj.* wretched: exceedingly unhappy: causing misery: extremely poor or mean: contemptible.—*n.* a wretch.—*n.* **mis'erableness**.—*adv.* **mis'erably**. [Fr. *misérable*—L. *miserābilis*—*miser*.]

mistère *mē-zer'*, *miz-ār'*, *n.* in card games, an undertaking to take no tricks. [Fr. *misère*, misery.]

Miserere *miz-e-rē'ri*, *mis-e-rā're*, *n.* the 50th Psalm of the Vulgate (51st in A.V.)—from its first word: a musical setting of it. [L., 2nd pers. sing. imper. of *miserēri*, to have mercy, to pity—*miser*, wretched.]

misericord, misericorde *miz-er'i-körd*, or *miz'ər-*, or *-körd'*, *n.* a relaxation of monastic rule: a room in a monastery where some relaxation of rule was allowed: a bracket on a turn-up seat in a choir-stall, allowing the infirm some support when standing, often intricately carved: a narrow-bladed dagger for killing a wounded foe. [O.Fr. *misericorde*—L. *misericordia*—*misericors*, *-cordis*, tender-hearted.]

miserly. See **miser**.

misery *miz'ər-i*, *n.* wretchedness: extreme pain: miserable conditions: very unhappy experience: a doleful person (*coll.*). [O.Fr.,—L. *miseria*.]

misfeasance *mis-fēz'əns*, (*law*) *n.* the doing of a lawful act in a wrongful manner, as distinguished from *malfeasance*.—*n.* **misfeas'or**. [O.Fr. *mesfaisance*—pfx. *mes-* (from L. *minus*, less) *faisance*—*faire*—L. *facēre*, to do.]

misfile *mis-fīl'*, *v.t.* to file (information) under the wrong headings, etc. [Pfx. **mis-**.]

misfire *mis-fīr'*, *v.i.* to fail to go off, explode, or ignite, at all or at the right time: to fail to have the effect intended (*fig.*).—*n.* a failure to fire, or to achieve effect. [**miss'**, **fire**.]

misfit *mis'fit*, *n.* a bad fit: a thing that fits badly: a person who cannot adjust himself to his social environment, or his job, etc.—*v.t.* and *v.i.* (*mis-fit'*) to fit badly. [Pfx. **mis-**.]

misfortune *mis-för'tūn*, *n.* ill-fortune: an evil accident: calamity. [Pfx. **mis-**.]

misgive *mis-giv'*, *v.t.* to suggest apprehensions to, fill with forebodings: to give amiss.—*v.i.* to have apprehensive forebodings:—*pa.t.* **misgave'**; *pa.p.* **misgiv'en**.—*n.* **misgiv'ing** mistrust: a feeling that all is not well. [Pfx. **mis-**.]

misgovern *mis-guv'ərn*, *v.t.* to govern badly or unjustly.—*ns.* **misgov'ernment**; **misgov'ernor**. [Pfx. **mis-**.]

misguide *mis-gīd'*, *v.t.* to guide wrongly: to lead into error.—*n.* **misguid'ance**.—*adj.* **misguid'ed** erring: misdirected: ill-judged.—*adv.* **misguid'edly**.—*n.* **misguid'er**. [Pfx. **mis-**.]

mishandle *mis-han'dl*, *v.t.* to handle amiss or unskilfully: to maltreat. [Pfx. **mis-**.]

mishap *mis-hap'*, *mis'*, *n.* ill chance: unlucky accident: misfortune. [Pfx. **mis-**.]

mishear *mis-hēr'*, *v.t.* and *v.i.* to hear wrongly. [Pfx. **mis-**.]

mishit *mis-hit'*, *v.t.* to hit faultily.—*n.* (*mis'hit*) a faulty hit. [Pfx. **mis-**.]

mishmash *mish'mash*, *n.* a hotch-potch, medley. [Redup. of **mash**.]

Mishnah, Mishna *mish'nä*, *n.* the Jewish oral law, finally redacted A.D. 220:—*pl.* **Mishnayôth'**.—*adjs.* **Mishnā'ic, Mish'nic**. [Heb. *mishnāh—shānāh*, to repeat, teach, learn.]

misinform *mis-in-förm'*, *v.t.* to inform or tell incorrectly.—*ns.* **misinform'ant; misinforma'tion; misinform'er**. [Pfx. **mis-**.]

misinterpret *mis-in-tûr'prit*, *v.t.* to interpret wrongly: to explain wrongly.—*ns.* **misinterpretā'tion; misinter'preter**. [Pfx. **mis-**.]

misjudge *mis-juj'*, *v.t.* and *v.i.* to judge wrongly.—*n.* **misjudg'ment**—also **misjudge'ment**. [Pfx. **mis-**.]

mislay *mis-lā'*, *v.t.* to place amiss: to lay in a place not remembered: to lose:—*pa.t.* and *pa.p.* **mislaid'**. [Pfx. **mis-** and **lay²**.]

mislead *mis-lēd'*, *v.t.* to draw into error: to cause to mistake:—*pa.t.* and *pa.p.* **misled'**.—*n.* **mislead'er**.—*adj.* **mislead'ing** deceptive.—*adv.* **mislead'ingly**. [Pfx. **mis-**.]

mismake *mis-māk'*, *v.t.* to make amiss, shape ill.—*pa.p.* and *adj.* **mismade'**. [Pfx. **mis-**.]

mismanage *mis-man'ij*, *v.t.* to conduct badly: to conduct carelessly.—*n.* **misman'agement**. [Pfx. **mis-**.]

mismatch *mis-mach'*, *v.t.* to match unsuitably.—*n.* a bad match.—*n.* **mismatch'ment**. [Pfx. **mis-**.]

misname *mis-nām'*, *v.t.* to call by an unsuitable or wrong name. [Pfx. **mis-**.]

misnomer *mis-nō'mər*, *n.* a misnaming: a wrong or unsuitable name. [O.Fr. from *mes-* (from L. *minus*, less) and *nommer*—L. *nōmināre*, to name.]

miso *mē'sō*, *n.* a paste, used for flavouring, prepared from soy beans and fermented in brine:—*pl.* **mi'sos**. [Jap.]

miso- *mis-ō-*, *mīs-ō-*, in composition, hater of, hating. —*ns.* **misogamist** (*-og'ə-mist*) a hater of marriage; **misog'amy; misogynist** (*-oj'i-nist*, *-og'*) a womanhater.—*adjs.* **misogynist'ical, misog'ynous**.—*ns.* **misog'yny; misology** (*-ol'ə-ji*) hatred of reason, reasoning, or knowledge; **misol'ogist**. [Gr. *mīseein*, to hate.]

mispickel *mis'pik-əl*, *n.* arsenical pyrites, a mineral composed of iron, arsenic, and sulphur. [Ger.]

misplace *mis-plās'*, *v.t.* to put in a wrong place: to mislay: to set on an improper object (*fig.*), or indulge in in unsuitable circumstances (*fig.*).—*n.* **misplace'ment**. [Pfx. **mis-**.]

misplay *mis-plā'*, *n.* a wrong play.—Also *v.t.* and *v.i.* [Pfx. **mis-**.]

misprint *mis-print'*, *v.t.* to print wrong.—*n.* (*mis'print, mis'print'*) a mistake in printing. [Pfx. **mis-**.]

misprise, misprize *mis-prīz'*, *v.t.* to scorn: to slight: to undervalue.—*n.* scorn: failure to value. [O.Fr. *mespriser*—pfx. *mes-* (from L. *minus*, less), L.L. *pretiāre*—L. *pretium*, price, value.]

misprision¹ *mis-prizh'ən*, *n.* mistake: criminal oversight or neglect in respect to the crime of another (*law*): any serious offence, failure of duty—*positive* or *negative*, according as it is maladministration or mere neglect.—**misprision of heresy, treason**, etc., knowledge of and failure to give information about heresy, treason, etc. [O.Fr. *mes-* (from L. *minus*, less), L.L. *prēnsiō, -ōnis*—L. *praehendere*, to take.]

misprision² *mis-prizh'ən*, *n.* failure to appreciate. [misprise, after the model of **misprision¹**.]

mispronounce *mis-prə-nowns'*, *v.t.* to pronounce incorrectly.—*n.* **mispronunciation** (*-nun-si-ā'shən*) wrong or improper pronunciation. [Pfx. **mis-**.]

misquote *mis-kwōt'*, *v.t.* to quote wrongly.—*n.* **misquotā'tion**. [Pfx. **mis-**.]

misread *mis-rēd'*, *v.t.* to read wrongly.—*n.* **mis'-read'ing**. [Pfx. **mis-**.]

misrelate *mis-ri-lāt'*, *v.t.* to relate incorrectly.—*n.* **misrelā'tion**.—**misrelated participle** a participle which the grammatical structure of the sentence insists on attaching to a word it is not intended to qualify (e.g. *Lost in thought, the bus passed me without stopping*). [Pfx. **mis-**.]

misremember *mis-ri-mem'bər*, *v.t.* and *v.i.* to remember wrongly or imperfectly. [Pfx. **mis-**.]

misreport *mis-ri-pört'*, *-pört'*, *v.t.* to report falsely, misleadingly, or wrongly.—*n.* false reporting or report. [Pfx. **mis-**.]

misrepresent *mis-rep-ri-zent'*, *v.t.* to represent falsely: to give a misleading interpretation to the words or deeds of: to be an unrepresentative representative of. —*n.* **misrepresentā'tion.** [Pfx. **mis-**.]

misrule *mis-rōōl'*, *n.* disorder: bad or disorderly government.—*v.t.* and *v.i.* to govern badly. [Pfx. **mis-**.]

Miss *mis*, *n.* a title prefixed to the name of an unmarried woman or girl: also prefixed to a representational title, esp. in beauty contests, e.g. *Miss World*: vocatively used alone in displeasure, real or assumed, or (*coll.*) to address a waitress, female teacher, etc.: (without *cap.*) a schoolgirl, or girl or woman with the faults attributed to schoolgirls: a person between a child and a woman: a kept mistress (*obs.*):—*pl.* **miss'es**—either 'the Miss Hepburns' or 'the Misses Hepburn' may be said, but the latter is more formal.—*n.* **miss'y** (usu. subervient) the little girl. [Shortened form of **mistress**.]

miss[1] *mis*, *v.t.* to fail to hit, reach, find, meet, touch, catch, get, have, take advantage of, observe, see: to avoid (a specified danger): to omit: to discover the absence of: to feel the want of: to leave out.—*v.i.* to fail to hit or obtain: to fail.—*n.* the fact or condition or an act or occasion of missing: failure to hit the mark: loss: (the source of or reason for) a feeling of loss or absence.—*adj.* **miss'ing** not to be found: not in the expected place: wanting: of unascertained fate (*mil.*). —**missing link** a hypothetical extinct creature thought to be intermediate between man and the anthropoid apes: any one thing required to complete a series.—**go missing** to disappear, esp. unexpectedly and inexplicably: to be mislaid; **miss out** to omit: (with *on*) to fail to experience or benefit from; **miss the bus** (or **boat**) (*coll.*) to lose one's opportunity. [O.E. *missan*.]

miss[2]. See **Miss**.

missa (also *cap.*) *mis'ə*, *-a*, (L.) *n.* the Mass (*R.C.*). —**missa, Missa solemnis** (*sol-em'nis*) high mass.

missal *mis'l*, *n.* a book containing the complete service for mass throughout the year. [L.L. *missāle*, from *missa*, mass.]

missel *mis'l*, *miz'l*, *n.* the missel-thrush.—**miss'el-thrush** a large thrush fond of mistletoe berries. [O.E. *mistel*, *mistil*, mistletoe.]

misshape *mis-shāp'*, *v.t.* to shape ill: to deform.—*n.* deformity.—*adjs.* **misshap'en, misshaped'** ill-shaped. —*n.* **misshap'enness.** [Pfx. **mis-**.]

missile *mis'il*, *mis'l*, *adj.* capable of being thrown or projected: pertaining to a missile.—*n.* a weapon or object for throwing by hand or shooting from a bow, gun, or other instrument, esp. a rocket-launched weapon, often nuclear-powered.—*n.* **miss'ile(e)ry** (*-il-ri*, *-l-ri*) missiles collectively: their design, manufacture and use. [L. *missilis*—*mittĕre*, *missum*, to throw.]

missing. See **miss**[1].

mission *mish'ən*, *n.* an act of sending, esp. to perform some function: a flight with a specific purpose, as a bombing raid or a task assigned to an astronaut or astronauts: the errand or purpose for which one is sent: that for which one has been or seems to have been sent into the world, vocation: a sending out of persons on a political or diplomatic errand, for the spread of a religion, or for kindred purpose: an organisation that sends out missionaries: its activities: a station or establishment of missionaries: any particular field of missionary enterprise: the body of persons sent on a mission: an embassy: a settlement for religious, charitable, medical, or philanthropic work in a district.— *adj.* of a mission or missions, esp. characteristic of the old Spanish missions in California.—*n.* **miss'ionary** one sent upon a mission, esp. religious.—*adj.* pertaining to missions.—**mission architecture** the style of the old Spanish missions in California, etc.; **missionary position** in sexual intercourse, the face-to-face position with the male on top. [L. *missiō*, *-ōnis*—*mittĕre*, to send.]

missis, missus *mis'is*, *-iz*, *n.* (*illit.*, *coll.*) mistress of the house: wife. [**mistress**.]

missive *mis'iv*, *n.* that which is sent, as a letter. [L.L. *missīvus*—L. *mittĕre*, *missum*, to send.]

misspell *mis-spel'*, *v.t.* and *v.i.* to spell wrongly:—*pa.t.* and *pa.p.* **misspelt'**, **misspelled'**.—*n.* **misspell'ing** a wrong spelling. [Pfx. **mis-**.]

misspend *mis-spend'*, *v.t.* to spend ill: to waste or squander:—*pa.t.* and *pa.p.* **misspent'**. [Pfx. **mis-**.]

misstate *mis-stāt'*, *v.t.* to state wrongly or falsely.—*n.* **misstate'ment.** [Pfx. **mis-**.]

misstep *mis-step'*, *v.i.* to make a false step: to make a mistake.—*n.* a mistake in conduct, etc. [Pfx. **mis-**.]

missus. See **missis**.

mist *mist*, *n.* watery vapour seen in the atmosphere: cloud in contact with the ground: thin fog: rain in very fine drops: a suspension of liquid in a gas: a dimness or dim appearance: anything that dims or darkens the sight or the judgment.—*v.t.* to obscure or veil with mist or as with mist.—*v.i.* to become misty or veiled.— *adj.* **mist'ful** misty.—*adv.* **mist'ily.**—*ns.* **mist'iness;** **mist'ing** mist.—*adj.* **misty:** hazy: dimming.—*adj.* **mist'y** full of, covered with, obscured by, mist: like mist: dim: obscure: clouded: vague: not perspicuous. [O.E. *mist*, darkness, dimness.]

mistake *mis-tāk'*, *v.t.* to understand wrongly: to take for another thing or person: to be wrong about: to think wrongly.—*v.i.* to err in opinion or judgment: to do amiss:—*pa.t.* **mistook'**; *pa.p.* **mistak'en**—*n.* a taking or understanding wrongly: an error: (*mis'*) a faulty shot in cinematography.—*adjs.* **mistak'able;** **mistak'en** understood wrongly: guilty of or under a mistake: erroneous: incorrect: ill-judged.—*adv.* **mistak'enly.**—*n.* **mistak'enness.**—**mistaken identity** an error in identifying someone.—**and no mistake** (*coll.*) assuredly; **be mistaken** to make or have made a mistake: to be misunderstood. [M.E. *mistaken*—O.N. *mistaka*, to take wrongly—*mis-*, wrongly, *taka*, to take.]

Mister *mis'tər*, *n.* a title prefixed to a man's name, and to certain designations (as Mr Justice, Mr Speaker), written **Mr:** (without *cap.*) sir (*coll.*, *illit.*). [**master.**]

mistery. Same as **mystery**[2].

mistime *mis-tīm'*, *v.t.* to time wrongly. [Pfx. **mis-**.]

mistle. Same as **missel**.

mistletoe *mis'l-tō*, or *miz'*, *n.* a partly parasitic evergreen shrubby plant (*Viscum album*) with white viscous fruits, growing on the apple, apricot, etc. (very rarely on the oak): extended to other species of its genus or family (Loranthaceae). [O.E. *misteltān*— *mistel*, *mistil*, mistletoe, *tān*, twig; see **missel**.]

mistook *mis-tōōk'*, *pa.t.* of **mistake**.

mistral *mis'tral*, *n.* a violent cold dry north-east wind in southern France. [Fr.,—Prov. *mistral*—L. *magistrālis*, masterful, *magister*, master.]

mistranslate *mis-trans-lāt'*, *v.t.* and *v.i.* to translate incorrectly.—*n.* **mistransla'tion.** [Pfx. **mis-**.]

mistreat *mis-trēt'*, *v.t.* to treat ill.—*n.* **mistreat'ment.** [Pfx. **mis-**.]

mistress *mis'tris*, *n.* (*fem.* of **master**) a woman employer of servants or head of a house or family: a woman (or anything personified as a woman) having power of ownership: a woman teacher, esp. in a school: a woman well skilled in anything: a woman loved and courted: a concubine: (with *cap.*; *mis'ız*; now usu. written **Mrs**; *fem.* of **Mister**, **Mr**) a title prefixed to the name, once of any woman or girl, now ordinarily of a married woman, sometimes also prefixed to a designation. [O.Fr. *maistresse* (Fr. *maîtresse*)—L.L. *magistrissa*, fem. from L. *magister*, master.]

mistrial *mis-trī'əl*, *n.* a trial void because of error: an inconclusive trial (*U.S.*). [Pfx. **mis-**.]

mistrust *mis-trust'*, *n.* distrust.—*v.t.* to distrust: to suspect.—*v.i.* to have suspicion.—*adj.* **mistrust'ful**.—*adv.* **mistrust'fully**.—*n.* **mistrust'fulness**.—*adv.* **mistrust'ingly**.—*adj.* **mistrust'less**. [Pfx. **mis-**.]

misty. See **mist**.

misunderstand *mis-und-ər-stand'*, *v.t.* to take in a wrong sense: to fail to appreciate the true nature, motives, etc. of:—*pa.t.* and *pa.p.* **misunderstood'**.—*n.* **misunderstand'ing** a mistake as to meaning: a slight disagreement.—*adj.* **misunderstood'**. [Pfx. **mis-**.]

misuse *mis-ūs'*, *n.* improper use: application to a bad purpose.—*v.t.* **misuse** (*mis-ūz'*) to use for a wrong purpose or in a wrong way: to treat ill.—*ns.* **misus'age** ill-usage: wrong use; **misus'er**. [Pfx. **mis-**.]

mite[1] *mīt*, *n.* a very small acaridan arachnid.—*adj.* **mīt'y** infested with mites. [O.E. *mīte*.]

mite[2] *mīt*, *n.* orig. an old Flemish coin of very small value: vaguely, a very small amount: a jot: a diminutive person: a small child. [M.Du. *mīte* (Du. *mijt*); perh. ult. the same as the preceding.]

miter. American spelling of **mitre**[1,2].

Mithras *mith'ras*, **Mithra** *-rä*, *ns.* the ancient Persian light-god, whose worship became popular in the Roman Empire.—*adj.* **Mithrā'ic**.—*ns.* **Mithrā'icism**, **Mith'raism** (*-rä-izm*); **Mith'raist**. [L. and Gr. *Mithrās*—O.Pers. *Mithra*.]

mithridate *mith'ri-dāt*, *n.* an antidote to poison, *Mithridates*, king of Pontus (reigned *c.* 120–63 B.C.), having traditionally made himself proof against poisons.—*n.* **mith'ridatism** (*-dāt-izm*) acquired immunity to a poison.

mitigate *mit'i-gāt*, *v.t.* to mollify, appease: to make more easily borne: to lessen the severity, violence, or evil, of: to temper.—*adjs.* **mit'igable**; **mit'igant** mitigating.—*n.* **mitigā'tion**.—*n.* and *adj.* **mit'igative**.—*n.* **mit'igator**.—*adj.* **mit'igatory**. [L. *mītigāre*, *-ātum—mītis*, mild.]

mitochondrion *mīt-*, *mit-ō-kon'dri-ən*, *n.* an energy-producing body, thread-like to spherical in shape, present in cytoplasm:—*pl.* **mitochon'dria**.—*adj.* **mitochon'drial**. [Gr. *mitos*, thread, *chondros*, granule.]

mitosis *mī-*, *mi-tō'sis*, *n.* an elaborate process of cell-division involving the arrangement of protoplasmic fibres in definite figures.—*adj.* **mitotic** (*-tot'ik*). [Gr. *mitos*, fibre.]

mitre[1] *mī'tər*, *n.* a woman's head-fillet: an eastern hat or turban: a high head-dress, cleft on top, worn by archbishops and bishops, and by some abbots.—*adjs.* **mī'tral** of or like a mitre: of the mitral valve; **mit'riform** (*mīt'*, or *mit'*) mitre-shaped.—**mitral valve** a mitre-shaped valve of the heart; **mi'tre-wort** bishop's cap. [Fr.,—Gr. *mitrā*, fillet.]

mitre[2] *mī'tər*, *n.* a joint (also **mi'tre-joint**) in which each piece is cut at an angle of 45° to its side, giving a right angle between the pieces: sometimes applied to any joint where the plane of junction bisects the angle: an angle of 45°: a gusset, a tapered insertion.—*v.t.* to join with a mitre: to turn a corner in, by cutting out a triangular piece and joining (*needlework*).

[Prob. same as above.]

mitt *mit*, *n.* a mitten: a hand (*slang*): a padded leather glove worn in baseball. [Abbrev. of **mitten**.]

mitten *mit'n*, *n.* a kind of glove, without a separate cover for each finger: a glove for the hand and wrist, but not the fingers.—*adj.* **mitt'ened** covered with a mitten or mittens. [O.Fr. *mitaine*.]

mittimus *mit'i-məs*, *n.* a warrant granted for sending to prison a person charged with a crime (*law*). [L., we send—*mittĕre*, to send.]

mix *miks*, *v.t.* to combine so that the parts of one thing or things of one set are diffused among those of another: to prepare or compound in like manner: to blend: to mingle: to join: to combine in one film (*cinematography*): to confound: to associate: to interbreed, cross: to involve.—*v.i.* to become, or to be capable of becoming, mixed: to be joined: to associate: to have intercourse.—*n.* a mixing, mingling: a mixture, esp. a standard mixture: a formula giving constituents and proportions: a jumble, a mess.—*adj.* **mixed** (*mikst*) mingled: of or for both sexes: miscellaneous: confused: not select: combining characters of two or more kinds.—*adv.* **mix'edly** (or *mikst'li*).—*ns.* **mix'edness** (or *mikst'*); **mix'er** one who mixes: that by which or in which things are mixed: one who is easily sociable in all sorts of company: one who mixes drinks: a soft drink for adding to an alcoholic one; **mix'ture** (*-chər*) act of mixing: state of being mixed: the product of mixing: a product of mixing in which the ingredients retain their properties—distinguished from *compound* (*chem.*): a mixture of petrol vapour and air (*motoring*).—*adj.* **mix'y** mixed.—*adj.* **mixed'-ability** of classes, etc. accommodating members who differ in (esp. academic) ability.—**mixed bag** any assortment of diverse people, things, characteristics, etc.; **mixed blessing** something which has both advantages and disadvantages; **mixed crystal** a crystal formed from two or more distinct compounds; **mixed doubles** tennis matches with a male and a female player as partners on each side; **mixed farming** farming of both crops and livestock; **mixed foursome** a golf match with a male and female player as partners on each side; **mixed grill** see **grill**; **mixed marriage** one between persons of different religions or races.—*adj.* **mixed'-me'dia** of a work in the arts, combining traditional forms, e.g. acting, dance, painting, and electronic media, e.g. tape recording.—**mixed metaphor** see **metaphor**.—*adj.* **mixed'-up** socially confused, bewildered, and ill-adjusted.—**mix'-up** confusion: a confused jumble.—**mix it** (*slang*) to fight forcefully. [L. *miscēre*, *mixtus*, to mix.]

mizzen, **mizen** *miz'n*, *n.* in a three-masted vessel, the hindmost of the fore-and-aft sails.—*adj.* belonging to the mizzen: nearest the stern.—**mizz'en-course**; **mizz'en-mast**; **mizz'en-sail**. [Fr. *misaine*, foresail, foremast—It. *mezzana*, mizzen-sail—L.L. *medi-ānus*, middle—L. *medius*, middle; the development of meaning is puzzling.]

mizzle[1] *miz'l*, *v.i.* to rain in small drops.—*n.* fine rain.—*n.* **mizz'ling**.—*adj.* **mizz'ly**. [Cf. L.Ger. *miseln*, mist.]

mizzle[2] *miz'l*, (*slang*) *v.i.* to decamp.

mneme *nē'mē*, *n.* a memory-like capacity of living matter for after-effect of stimulation of the individual or an ancestor.—*adj.* **mnē'mic** pertaining to the mneme.—*ns.* **mne'mon** a hypothetical unit of memory; **mnemonic** (*ni-mon'ik*) a device, e.g. verse, to help memory: (in *pl.*, treated as *sing.*) art of assisting memory.—*adj.* pertaining to the mneme.—*adj.* **mnemon'ical**.—*ns.* **mnē'monist** a teacher or practitioner of mnemonics: one from whose memory nothing is erased. [Gr. *mnēmē*, memory, *mnēmōn*, mindful, *Mnēmosynē*, Mnemosyne.]

mo. See **moment.**

-mo -*mō*, the final syllable of certain Latin ordinal numbers, used in composition with English cardinal numbers to denote the number of leaves in a gathering of a book; see **twelvemo, sixteenmo** under **twelve, sixteen.**

moa *mō'ə*, n. a gigantic extinct bird of New Zealand. [Maori.]

moan *mōn*, n. lamentation: a lament: a complaint: a grumble (*coll.*): a low murmur of pain: a sound like a murmur of pain.—*v.t.* to lament: to bemoan: to utter with moans.—*v.t.* to make or utter a moan: to grumble (*coll.*).—*n.* **moan'er.**—*adj.* **moan'ful** expressing sorrow: lamentable.—*adv.* **moan'fully.** [Unrecorded O.E *mān* (noun) answering to the verb *mǣnan.*]

moat *mōt*, n. a deep trench round a castle or fortified place, sometimes filled with water.—*v.t.* to surround with a moat —*adj.* **moat'ed.** [O.Fr. *mote,* mound.]

mob *mob*, n. the mobile or fickle common people: the vulgar: the rabble: a disorderly crowd: a riotous assembly: a gang: a crowd, mixed collection, large herd or flock (*Austr.*).—*adj.* of or relating to the Mob.—*v.t.* to attack in a disorderly crowd: to crowd around, esp. with vexatious curiosity or attentions: to drive by mob action.—*v.t.* and *v.t.* to form into a mob:—*pr.p.* **mobb'ing;** *pa.t.* and *pa.p.* **mobbed.**—*adjs.* **mobbed** crowded (*coll.*); **mobb'ish.**—*ns.* **mob-oc'racy** (*slang*) rule or ascendency exercised by the mob; **mob'ocrat.**—*adj.* **mobocrat'ic.**—*n.* **mob'ster** gangster.—*adj.* **mob-hand'ed** in large numbers: constituting a large group.—**the mob, the Mob** (*U.S. slang*) the Mafia: organised crime in general. [L. *mōbile* (*vulgus*), fickle (multitude); *movere,* to move.]

mob-cap *mob'kap,* n. a woman's indoor morning cap with puffy crown, a broad band, and frills (*hist.*). [Perh. *Mab,* for *Mabel;* but cf. O.Du. *mop;* mod.Du. *mopmuts,* a woman's nightcap.]

mobile *mō'bīl, -bēl, -bil, adj.* movable: able to move about: easily, speedily moved: not fixed: changing rapidly: of a liquid, characterised by great fluidity.— *n.* a moving or movable body or part: an artistic structure, orig. consisting of dangling forms, now sometimes having a base, in which movement is caused by air currents: short for mobile police, library, etc.—*n.* **mobilisation,** -*z*- (*mō-* or *mo-bil-i-zā'shən,* or *-ī-*).— *v.t.* **mō'bilise, -ize** to make movable, mobile, or readily available: to put in readiness for service in war: to call into active service, as troops.—*v.i.* to make armed forces ready for war: to undergo mobilisation.—*n.* **mobility** (*mō-bil'i-ti*), quality of being mobile.—**mobile home** a caravan or other vehicle with sleeping, cooking, etc. facilities; **mobile shop, library,** etc. one set up in a motor vehicle, driven to customers' homes; **mobility allowance** money paid by the government to disabled people to compensate for their travel costs. [Fr.,—L. *mōbilis* —*movēre,* to move.]

Möbius strip *mœ'bē-əs strip,* (*math.*) the one-sided surface formed by joining together the two ends of a long rectangular strip, one end being twisted through 180 degrees before the join is made. [August F. Mobius (1790–1868), mathematician.]

mobocracy, mobster, etc. See **mob**[1].

moccasin, mocassin *mok'ə-sin,* n. a North American Indian's shoe of deerskin or other soft leather: a shoe or slipper more or less resembling it: a venomous North American pit-viper.—**mocc'asin-flow'er** a lady's-slipper orchid. [American Indian.]

Mocha *mok'ə, mō'kə, n.* a fine coffee. [*Mocha,* on the Red Sea.]

mock *mok,* v.t. to deride: to scoff at derisively: to make sport of: to mimic in ridicule: to simulate: to defy, set at naught, tantalise, disappoint, deceive, befool, as if in mockery (*fig.*).—*v.i.* to jeer: to scoff: to speak or behave as one not in earnest.—*n.* ridicule: a bringing into ridicule: a scoff: a mockery: a thing mocked.—*adj.* sham: false: resembling, or accepted as a substitute for, the true or real.—*adj.* **mock'able** worthy of derision.—*ns.* **mock'er; mock'ery** derision: ridicule: subject of ridicule: mimicry: imitation, esp. a contemptible or insulting imitation: false show: insulting or ludicrous futility.—*n.* and *adj.* **mock'ing.** —*adv.* **mock'ingly.**—*adj.* **mock'-hero'ic** burlesquing the heroic style.—*n.* a mock-heroic composition: (in *pl.*) mock-heroic verses: (in *pl.*) sham heroic utterances or pose.—*adj.* **mock-hero'ical.**—*adv.* **mock'-hero'ically.**—**mock'ing-bird, mock'ingbird** an American bird (*Mimus*) of the thrush family, that mimics other birds' songs and other sounds; **mock moon** a paraselene, or bright spot in the moon's halo, 22° to right or left of the moon, due to refraction from ice crystals floating vertically; **mock'-or'ange** a tall shrub (*Philadelphus,* commonly called syringa) of the saxifrage family with strong-scented flowers; **mock sun** a spot in the sun's halo; **mock'-up** a full-size dummy model: a fabrication.—Also *adj.*—**mock turtle soup** an imitation of turtle soup, made of calf's head or veal; **put the mockers on** (*slang*) to put an end to, put paid to. [O.Fr. *mocquer.*]

mod *mod, mōd, mŏd,* n. a Highland literary and musical festival. [Gael. *mòd*—O.N. *mót;* cf. **moot.**]

Mod *mod,* n. a member of teenage faction in (originally) the 1960s distinguished by special dress (typically neat), etc., from their rivals, the Rockers.

mod. con. mod *kon,* modern convenience, any item of up-to-date plumbing, heating, etc.

mode *mōd,* n. way or manner of acting, doing, happening, or existing: kind: form: manifestation: state of being: that which exists only as a quality of substance: a mood (*gram.*): character as necessary, contingent, possible or impossible (*log.*): a mood (*log.*): the value of greatest frequency (*statistics*): modality: fashion: that which is fashionable: fashionableness: the method of dividing the octave according to the position of its steps and half-steps (*mus.*): in old music, the method of time-division of notes.— *adj.* **modal** (*mōd'l*) relating to mode.—*n.* **modality** (*mōd-al'i-ti*) fact or condition of being modal: mode: method, terms, style: any of the primary methods of sensation: classification of propositions as to whether true, false, necessary, possible or impossible (*log.*)— *adv.* **mod'ally.**—*adj.* **modish** (*mōd'ish*) fashionable: affectedly, foolishly, or absurdly fashionable.—*adv.* **mod'ishly.**—*ns.* **mod'ishness; mod'ist** a follower of the fashion; **modiste** (*mō-dēst;* Fr.) a professedly fashionable dressmaker or milliner. [L. *modus;* partly through Fr. *mode.*]

model *mod'l,* n. a preliminary solid representation, generally small, or in plastic material, to be followed in construction: something to be copied: a pattern: an imitation of something on a smaller scale: a person or thing closely resembling another: one who poses for an artist, photographer, etc.: one who exhibits clothes for a shop by wearing them: a pattern of excellence: an article of standard design or a copy of one: structural type.—*adj.* of the nature of a model: set up for imitation: completely suitable for imitation, exemplary.—*v.t.* to form after a model: to shape: to make a model or copy of: to form in some plastic material: of a mannequin, to display (a garment) by wearing it.—*v.i.* to practise modelling:— *pr.p.* **mod'elling;** *pa.t.* and *pa.p.* **mod'elled.**—*ns.* **mod'eller; mod'elling** the act or art of making a model of something, a branch of sculpture: rendering of solid form: working as a model. [O.Fr. *modelle*— It. *modello*, dim. of *modo*—L. *modus*, a measure.]

modem mō'dəm, (*comput.*) n. an electronic device used to transmit and receive data as a frequency-modulated tone over a communications system. [*modulator, demodulator.*]

moderate mod'ə-rāt, v.t. to keep within measure or bounds: to regulate: to reduce in intensity: to make temperate or reasonable: to pacify: to preside as moderator over or at.—v.i. to become less violent or intense: to preside or act as a moderator.—adj. (-rit) kept within measure or bounds: not excessive or extreme: temperate: of middle rate, average.—n. one whose views are far from extreme.—adv. mod'erately. —ns. mod'erateness; modera'tion act of moderating: state of being moderated or moderate: freedom from excess: self-restraint: the process of slowing down neutrons in an atomic pile: (in *pl.*) the first public examination for B.A. at Oxford (*coll.* mods); mod'eratism moderate opinions in religion or politics; mod'erator one who, or that which, moderates: a president, esp. in Presbyterian church courts: an officer at Oxford and Cambridge who superintended degree examinations: a moderations examiner at Oxford: the material in which neutrons are slowed down in an atomic pile:—*fem.* mod'eratrix; mod'erator-ship. [L. *moderāri*, *-ātus*—*modus*, a measure.]

moderato mod-ə-rä'tō, (*mus.*) adj. and adv. at a moderate speed. [It.]

modern mod'ərn, adj. of or characteristic of present or recent time: not ancient or mediaeval: in education, mainly or wholly concerned with subjects other than Greek and Latin: (*cap.*), of a language, of or near the form now spoken and written, distinguished from *Old* and *Middle*.—n. one living in modern times, esp. distinguished from the ancient Greeks and Romans: a modernist.—n. modernisa'tion, -z-.—v.t. mod'ernise, -ize to adapt to the present time, conditions, needs, language, or spelling.—v.i. to adopt modern ways.— ns. mod'erniser, -z-; mod'ernism modern usage, expression, or trait: modern spirit or character: a tendency to adjust Christian dogma to the results of science and criticism; mod'ernist an admirer of modern ideas, ways, literature, studies, etc.: one who favours modernism; modernis'tic; modern'ity.—adv. mod'ernly.—n. mod'ernness.—modern jazz a style of jazz which evolved in the early 1940s, characterised by greater rhythmic and harmonic complexity than previously. [L.L. *modernus*—*modo*, just now, orig. abl. of *modus*.]

modest mod'ist, adj. restrained by a sense of seemliness: unobtrusive: unpretentious: unassuming: diffident: decent: chaste: pure and delicate, as thoughts or language: not excessive or extreme: moderate.—adv. mod'estly.—n. mod'esty the quality or fact of being modest: a slight covering for a low neck. [L. *modestus*—*modus*, a measure.]

modicum mod'i-kəm, n. a small quantity:—*pl.* mod'-icums. [L. neut. of *modicus*, moderate—*modus*.]

modify mod'i-fī, v.t. to moderate: to change the form or quality of: to alter slightly: to vary: to differentiate: of a word or phrase, to limit or qualify the sense of (*gram.*):—*pr.p.* mod'ifying; *pa.t.* and *pa.p.* mod'ified.—adj. mod'ifiable.—n. modification (-fi-kā'shən) act of modifying or state of being modified: result of alteration or change: changed shape or condition.—*adjs.* mod'ificative, mod'ificatory tending to modify: causing change of form or condition.—adj. mod'ified (-fīd) altered by modification.—n. mod'ifier (-fī-ər). [Fr. *modifier*—L. *modificāre*, *-ātum*—*modus*, a measure, *facēre*, to make.]

modish, modist, modiste. See mode.

mods. See under moderate.

modulate mod'ū-lāt, v.t. to regulate, adjust: to inflect: to soften: to vary the pitch or frequency of: to impress characteristics of signal wave on (carrier wave) (*radio*): to vary velocity of electrons in electron beam. —v.i. (*mus.*) to pass from one key into another using a logical progression of chords that links the two keys.— adj. mod'ular of or pertaining to mode or modulation, or to a module.—ns. modula'tion; mod'ulator one who, or that which, modulates: any device for effecting modulation (*radio*): a chart used in the tonic sol-fa notation on which modulations are shown; mod'ule a small measure or quantity: a unit of size, used in standardised planning of buildings and design of components: a self-contained unit forming part of a spacecraft or other structure: a standard unit or part of machinery, etc. in a system: a set course forming a unit in an educational scheme: an assembly within a geometrical framework of electronic units functioning as a system: a measure, often the semidiameter of a column, for regulating proportions of other parts (*archit.*).—n. mod'ulus a constant multiplier or co-efficient (*math.*): a quantity used as a divisor to produce classes of quantities, each class distinguished by its members yielding the same remainders (*math.*): the positive square root of the sum of the squares of the real and imaginary parts of a complex number (*math.*): a quantity expressing the relation between a force and the effect produced:—*pl.* moduli (mod'ū-lī). [L. *modulārī*, *-ātus*, to regulate, *modulus*, dim. of *modus*, a measure.]

modus mō'dəs, mo'dōos, n. manner, mode: the way in which anything works:—*pl.* mō'dī.—modus operandi (op-ər-an'dī, -an'dē) mode of operation, way of working; modus vivendi (vi-ven'dī, -dē, wē-wen'dē) way of life or living: an arrangement or compromise by means of which those who differ may get on together for a time. [L. *mōdus*, manner.]

meggy, moggie, mog mog'i, mog. ns. a cat (*slang*). [Perh. *Maggie*.]

Mogul mō'gul, mō-gul', n. a Mongol or Mongolian, esp. one of the followers of Baber, the conqueror of India (1483–1530): (without *cap.*) an influential person, magnate.—adj. pertaining to the Mogul Empire, architecture, etc. [Pers. *Mughul*, properly a Mongol.]

mohair mō'hār, n. the long, white, fine silken hair of the Angora goat: other hair as a substitute for it: cloth made of it. [Ar. *mukhayyar*; influenced by hair.]

Mohammedan mō-ham'i-dən, **Mahommedan** mə-hom', **Mahometan** mə-hom'it-ən, **Muhammadan, Muhammedan** mōō-ham'a-dən, -i-dən, adjs. pertaining to Mohammed (formerly popularly rendered as Mahomet) or to his religion, Islam.—n. a follower of Mohammed, a Muslim: one who professes Mohammedanism, Islam.—v.t. and v.i. Mohamm'edanise, -ize, etc., to convert to, or conform to, Mohammedanism, Islam.—ns. Mohamm'edanism, Mohamm'edism, etc., Islam, the religion of Mohammed, contained in the Koran. These terms are felt to be offensive by many Muslims, who prefer Muslim, Islam, Islamic, etc. [Ar. *Muhammad*, the great prophet of Arabia (c. 570–632); lit. praised.]

mohel mō'(h)el, n. an official Jewish circumciser. [Heb.]

Mohs scale mōz skāl, a scale of numbers from 1 to 10 (1 representing talc, 10 representing diamond) in terms of which the relative hardness of solids can be expressed. [F. *Mohs* (1773–1839), German mineralogist.]

moiety moi'ə-ti, n. half: one of two parts or divisions. [O.Fr. *moite*—L. *medietās*, *-tātis*, middle point, later half—*medius*, middle.]

moil moil, (*arch.*) v.t. to wet: to bedaub: to defile.—v.i.

(*dial.*) to toil: to drudge.—*n.* (*dial.* and *arch.*) a spot: a defilement: labour: trouble: turmoil.—*n.* **moll'er.** [O.Fr. *moillier* (Fr. *mouiller*) to wet—L. *mollis*, soft.]

moire *mwàr*, also *mwor, môr, moir, n.* orig. watered mohair: now watered silk or other fabric with watered appearance (also **moire antique**).—*adj.* **moiré** (*mwar'ā, moi'ri*) watered.—*n.* a watered appearance on cloth or metal surface: sometimes for moire, the material. [Fr., from English **mohair**.]

moist *moist, adj.* damp: humid: rainy: watery.—*v.t.* **moisten** (*mois'n*) to make moist: to wet slightly.—*adv.* **moist'ly.**—*ns.* **moist'ness; moist'ure** moistness: that which makes slightly wet: liquid, esp. in small quantity.—*adj.* **moist'ureless.**—*v.t.* **moist'urise, -ize** to add or restore moisture to.—Also *v.i.*—*n.* **moist'-uriser, -z-.** [O.Fr. *moiste* (Fr. *moite*), perh.—L. *mustum*, juice of grapes, new wine, perh. L. *mūcidus*, mouldy.]

moke *mōk*, (*slang*) *n.* a donkey.

mol, molal, etc., **molar,** etc. See **mole**[1].

molar *mō'lar, adj.* used for grinding: pertaining to a grinding tooth.—*n.* a grinding tooth, or back tooth. [L. *molāris—mola*, a millstone—*molĕre*, to grind.]

molasses *mo-las'iz, n.sing.* a thick treacle that drains from sugar. [Port. *melaço* (Fr. *mélasse*)—L.L. *mellāceum—mel, mellis*, honey.]

mold. See **mould**[1,2,3].

mole[1] *mōl, n.* the amount of substance that contains as many (specified) entities (e.g. atoms, molecules, ions, photons) as there are atoms in 12 grams of carbon-12 (abbrev. **mol** *mōl*): formerly defined as equal to gram-molecule.—*adj.* **mol'al** of, relating to, or containing, a mole.—*n.* **molal'ity** the concentration of a solution expressed as the number of moles of dissolved substance per thousand grams of solvent.—*adj.* **mol'ar** of, or relating to, a mole: per mole: per unit amount of substance: of, or relating to molecules: of or pertaining to mass or masses or to large masses.—*n.* **molar'ity** the concentration of a solution expressed as the number of moles of dissolved substance per litre of solution. [Ger., —*Molekül*, molecule; both words (Ger. and Eng.) ult. from L. *mōlēs*, mass.]

mole[2] *mōl, n.* a spot: a small spot or elevation on the skin, often coloured and hairy. [O.E. *māl*.]

mole[3] *mōl, n.* a small insectivorous animal (Talpa) with very small eyes and soft fur, which burrows in the ground and casts up little heaps of mould: extended to kindred or similar animals: one who works in darkness or underground: a spy who successfully infiltrates a rival organisation, esp. one not engaging in espionage until firmly established and trusted: one who sees badly (*fig.*).—**mole'cast** a molehill; **mole'catcher** one whose business it is to catch moles; **mole'-crick'et** a burrowing insect of the cricket family; **mole'hill** a little hill or heap of earth cast up by a mole; **mole'rat** a name for several burrowing rodents (*Spalax, Bathyergus*, etc.); **mole'skin** the skin of a mole: mole's fur: a superior kind of fustian, double-twilled, cropped before dyeing: (in *pl.*) clothes, esp. trousers, made of this fustian.—**make a mountain out of a molehill** to magnify a trifling matter. [M.E. *molle, mulle*.]

mole[4] *mōl, n.* a massive breakwater. [Fr. *môle*—L. *mōlēs*, mass.]

molecule *mol'i-kūl*, or *mōl', n.* the smallest particle of any substance that retains the properties of that substance: a gram-molecule.—*adj.* **molecular** (*mol-ek'ū-lar*).—*n.* **molecularity** (*mol-ek-ū-lar'i-ti*).—*adv.* **molec'ularly.**—**molecular biology** study of the molecules of the substances involved in the processes of life; **molecular weight** weight of a molecule rela-

tively to that of an atom of carbon-12 taken as 12. [Fr. *molécule,*—L. *mōlēs*, mass.]

molest *mə-, mō-lest', v.t.* to vex: to interfere with in a troublesome or hostile way: to annoy.—*n.* annoyance.—*ns.* **molestă'tion** (*mo-, mō-*); **molest'er.**—*adj.* **molest'ful.** [Fr. *molester*—L. *molestāre—molestus,* troublesome.]

moline *mō'līn, -lin', (her.) adj.* like a millstone rind—applied to a cross with each arm ending in two outward curving branches.—*n.* a moline cross. [L. *mola*, a mill.]

moll *mol, n.* (with *cap.*) a familiar form of *Mary*: a gangster's girl-friend: a prostitute.

mollify *mol'i-fī, v.t.* to soften: to assuage: to cause to abate: to appease.—*v.t.* to become soft: to relax in severity or opposition:—*pr.p.* **moll'ifying;** *pa.t.* and *pa p.* **moll'ified.**—*ns.* **mollification** (*-fi-kā'shən*); **moll'ifier.** [Fr. *mollifier*—L. *mollificāre—mollis,* soft, *facĕre,* to make.]

mollusc, mollusk *mol'əsk, n.* one of the **Mollusca** (*-us'kə*), a large phylum of invertebrates, without segments or limbs, usually having a mantle or fold of skin that secretes a shell—lamellibranchs, gasteropods, cephalopods, and some smaller groups: a person of inert habit.—*adjs.* **mollus'can, mollus'cous** of or belonging to the Mollusca; like a mollusc. [L. *molluscus,* softish—*mollis,* soft.]

molly *mol'i, n.* (with *cap.*) dim. of *Mary*: a milksop.—*n.* **moll'ycoddle** an effeminate fellow.—*v.t.* to coddle.

Moloch *mō'lok, n.* a Semitic god to whom children were sacrificed (also **Mo'lech**): any cause to which dreadful sacrifice is made or destruction due. [Gr. and L. *Moloch*—Heb. *Mōlek.*]

Molotov cocktail *mol'ə-tof kok'tāl*, a crude form of hand-grenade consisting of a bottle with inflammable liquid, and a wick to be ignited just before the missile is thrown. [V. M. *Molotov,* Russian statesman.]

molt. See **moult.**

molten. See **melt.**

molto *mol'tō, (mus.) adv.* very: much. [It.]

moly *mō'li, n.* a magic herb given by Hermes to Odysseus as a counter-charm against the spells of Circe: a species of wild onion, *Allium moly*. [Gr. *mōly*.]

molybdenum *mol-ib'din-əm* (also *mol-ib-dē'nəm*), *n.* silvery-white metallic element (symbol Mo; atomic number 42).—*ns.* **molyb'date** a salt of molybdic acid; **molybdēn'ite** or *-ib'dən-īt*) a mineral, molybdenum disulphide.—*adj.* **molyb'dic.**—*n.* **molybdō'sis** lead-poisoning.—*adj.* **molyb'dous.**—**molybdic acid** H_2MoO_4. [Latinised neuter—Gr. *molybdaina,* a lump of lead, a leadlike substance—*molybdos,* lead.]

mom *mom, (U.S. coll.) n.* mother.—Also **momm'a, momm'y.** [See **mamma**[1].]

moment *mō'mənt, n.* a point of time: a time so short that it may be considered as a point: a very short time (abbrev. in slang, **mo**): a second: a precise instant: the present, or the right, instant: importance, consequence: a stage or turning-point: an element or factor: a measure of turning effect—the *moment of a force* about a point is the product of the force and the perpendicular on its line of action from the point.—*adv.* **mo'mentarily** for a moment: every moment: at any moment.—*n.* **mo'mentariness.**—*adj.* **mo'mentary** lasting for a moment: short-lived.—*adv.* **mo'mently** every moment: for a moment.—*adj.* occurring every moment: of a moment.—*adj.* **momentous** (*-ment'*) of great consequence.—*adv.* **moment'ously.**—*ns.* **moment'ousness; moment'um** the quantity of motion in a body measured by the product of mass and velocity: force of motion gained in movement, impetus (*coll.*):—*pl.* **moment'a.**—**moment of truth** the climax of the bullfight: a moment when, suddenly and dramatically, one is face to face with stark reality—often a testing moment (*fig.*) [L. *mōmentum*, for *movimentum—movēre*, *mōtum*, to move.]

momma, mommy. See **mom.**

mon-. See **mon(o)-.**

monacid *mon-as'id*, **monoacid** *mon-ō-as'id*, *adjs*. having one replaceable hydrogen atom: capable of replacing one hydrogen atom of an acid. [**mon(o)-.**]

monad *mon'ad*, *n*. the number one: a unit: an ultimate unit of being, material and psychical: a spirit: God: a hypothetical primitive living organism or unit of organic life: a flagellate of the genus Monas or akin to it: a univalent element, atom, or radical.—Also *adj.* —*adjs.* **monad'ic, -al; monad'iform** like a monad.— *n* **mon'as** a monad: (with *cap.*) a genus of flagellates. [Gr. *monas, -ados*, a unit—*monos*, single, alone.]

monadelphous *mon-a-del'fas*, *adj.* of stamens, united by the filaments in one bundle: of a flower or plant, having all the stamens so united. [Gr *monos*, single. alone, *adelphos*, brother.]

monandrous *mon-an'dras*, *adj.* having or allowing one husband or male mate (at a time): having one stamen or one antheridium (*bot.*).—*n.* **monan'dry** the condition or practice of being monandrous. [Gr. *monos*, single, alone, *anēr, andros*, a man, male]

monarch *mon'ark*, *n*. a sole hereditary head of a state, whether titular or ruling.—*adjs.* **monarchal** (*-ark'al*), **monarch'ial, monarch'ic, -al.**—*v.t.* **mon'archise, -ize** to rule over as a monarch: to convert into a monarchy. —*ns.* **mon'archism** the principles of monarchy: love of monarchy; **mon'archist** an advocate of monarchy: a believer in monarchy.—Also *adj.*—*adj.* **monarchist'ic.**—*n* **mon'archy** a kind of government of which there is a monarch: a state with monarchical government: the territory of a monarch. [Gr. *monarchēs—monos*, single, alone, *archein*, to rule.]

Monarda *mon-ar'da*, *n*. a genus of North American aromatic herbs of the mint (Labiatae) family: (without *cap.*) a plant of this genus [N. *Monardes* (d. 1589), Spanish botanist.]

monas. See **monad.**

monastery *mon'as-tar-i, -tri*, *n*. a house for monks, or (*rarely*) nuns.—*adjs.* **monastē'rial, monastic** (*-as'tik*), **-al** pertaining to monasteries, monks, and nuns: recluse: solitary.—*n.* **monas'tic** a monk.—*adv.* **monas'tically.**—*n.* **monas'ticism** (*-sizm*) the corporate monastic life or system of living. [Late Gr. *monastērion—monastēs*, a monk—*monos*, single, alone.]

monatomic *mon-a-tom'ik*, *adj.* consisting of one atom: having one replaceable atom or group: univalent [**mon(o)-.**]

monaural *mon-o'ral*, *adj.* having or using only one ear: pertaining to one ear: of a gramophone record, etc., giving the effect of sound from a single direction—not stereophonic. [**mon(o)-.**]

monazite *mon'az-it*, (*min.*) *n*. a phosphate of cerium, lanthanum, neodymium, praseodymium, and usually thorium, a source of thorium. [Gr. *monazein*, to be solitary—on account of its rarity.]

Monday *mun'di, n.* the second day of the week.—*adj.* **Mon'dayish** having the feelings normal after Sunday's activities or inactivities with the prospect of the week's work.—**Monday Club** a right-wing group of Conservatives. [O.E. *mōnandæg, mōnan*, gen. of *mōna*, moon, *dæg*, day.]

mondial *mon'di-al, adj.* of the whole world, world-wide. [Fr —L. *mundus*, world.]

moneious. Same as **monoecious.**

Monel metal® *mō-nel' met'l*, a nickel-base alloy with high strength and resistance to corrosion.

monetary *mon'* or *mun'i-tar-i, adj.* of or relating to

money: consisting of money.—*ns.* **mon'etarism; mon'etarist** one who advocates an economic policy based chiefly on the control of a country's money supply; **monetisa'tion, -z-.**—*v.t.* **mon'etise, -ize** to give the character of money to, to coin as money. [L. *monēta* (see **money**).]

money *mun'i, n.* coin: pieces of stamped metal used in commerce: any currency used in the same way: wealth:—*pl.* **moneys** (*arch.* and *legal*) sums of money: money.—*adjs.* **mon'eyed, mon'ked** having money: rich in money: consisting in money; **mon'eyless** having no money.—**money'-bag** a bag for or of money: (*pl.*) a rich man; **money'-box** a box for collecting or saving money, usu. with a slit for insertion; **mon'ey-broker** one who carries out transactions in money for others; **mon'ey-changer** one who exchanges one currency for another; **mon'ey-grubber** a sordid accumulator of wealth; **mon'ey-lender** a professional lender of money at interest; **mon'ey-lending** money-maker one who acquires riches: anything that brings profit; **mon'ey-making** act of gaining wealth.—*adj.* lucrative, profitable —**mon'ey-market** (the dealers in) the market for short-term loans for business, etc.; **mon'ey-or'der** an order for money deposited at one post-office, and payable at another; **mon'ey-spi'der** a small spider supposed to bring luck; **mon'ey-spinner** a money-spider: a successful speculator anything that brings much money: **mon'ey's-worth** something as good as money: full value.—**for my, our, money** if I, we, were to choose, express an opinion, etc., **hard money** coin; **in the money** among the prize-winners (*racing*, etc.): well-off; **make money** to acquire wealth: to make a profit; **money down** money paid on the spot; **money for jam, old rope**, etc., money obtained without effort; **money of account** a monetary unit (not represented by current coins) used in keeping accounts; **money talks** the wealthy have much influence; **pot(s) of money** a large amount of money; **put money into** to invest in; **put money on** to place a bet on; **put one's money where one's mouth is** to support one's judgment by betting money; **ready money** money paid for a thing at the time at which it is bought: money ready for immediate payment [O.Fr. *moneie* (Fr. *monnaie*)—L. *monēta*, money, a mint, *Monēta* (the reminder) being a surname of Juno, in whose temple at Rome money was coined.]

'mong, 'mongst aphetic for **among, amongst.**

monger *mung'gar, n.* (chiefly in composition) a dealer —except in a few instances, as *ironmonger*, one who traffiks in a petty, or discreditable way, or in unpleasant subjects.—*ns.* **mong'ering, mong'ery.** [O.E. *mangere*—L. *mangō, -ōnis*, a furbisher, slave-dealer—Gr. *manganeuein*, to use trickery.]

Mongol *mong'gol, n.* a member of Genghis Khan's clan, or of the various populations under him: one of the people of Mongolia: their language: a member of a broad-headed, yellow-skinned, straight-haired, small-nosed human race: (often without *cap.*) a person affected by Mongolism.—*adj.* of the Mongols, Mongolia, or Mongolian.—*adj.* **Mongolian** (*mong-gō'li-an*) of Mongolia, the Mongols, or their language.—*n.* the language of Mongolia.—*adj.* **Mongolic** (*-gol'ik*) Mongolian: of Mongolian type.—*n.* **Mong'olism** (often without *cap.*) a congenital disease caused by chromosomal abnormality, in which there is mental deficiency and a broadening and flattening of the features, now more usu. called **Down's syndrome.**—*adj.* **Mong'oloid** of Mongolian race or type: (often without *cap.*) affected with Mongolism. —*n.* a person of Mongolian type: (often without *cap.*) a person affected by Mongolism. [Said to be from Mongol *mong*, brave.]

mongoose *mong'*, *mung'gōōs*, *n.* an Indian animal of the civet family, a great slayer of snakes and rats: any other species of the genus, including the ichneumon: a Madagascan lemur:—*pl.* **mong'ooses**. [Marathi *mangūs*.]

mongrel *mung'grəl*, *n.* an animal, esp. a dog, of a mixed breed (usu. in contempt): a person, thing, or word of mixed or indefinite origin or nature: that which is neither one thing nor another.—*adj.* mixed in breed: ill-defined.—*v.t.* **mong'relise**, **-ize**.—*n.* **mong'relism**. —*adj.* **mong'relly**. [Prob. from root of O.E. *mengan*, to mix.]

moni(c)ker *mon'i-kər*, (*slang*; orig. tramps' slang) *n.* an alias, nickname, or real name.

monied, monies. See **money**.

monism *mon'izm*, *n.* a philosophical theory that all being may ultimately be referred to one category; thus *idealism*, *pantheism*, *materialism* are monisms— as opposed to the dualism of matter and spirit.—*n.* **mon'ist**.—*adjs.* **monist'ic**, **-al**. [Gr. *monos*, single, alone.]

monition *mon-ish'ən*, *n.* a reminding or admonishing: warning: notice.—*adj.* **mon'itive** conveying admonition.—*n.* **mon'itor** one who admonishes: an adviser: a senior pupil who assists in school discipline: apparatus for testing transmission in electrical communication: a person employed to monitor: a genus (Varanus) of very large lizards of Africa, Asia, and Australia (from a fancy that they give warning of the presence of a crocodile): a detector for radioactivity: an instrument used in a production process to keep a variable quantity within prescribed limits by transmitting a controlling signal: a screen in a television studio showing the picture being transmitted: —*fem.* **mon'itress**.—*v.t.* to act as monitor to: to check (as the body and clothing of persons working with radioactive materials) for radioactivity: to track, or to control (an aeroplane, guided missile, etc.): to watch, check, supervise.—*v.i.* (*radio*) to tap on to a communication circuit, usu. in order to ascertain that the transmission is that desired: to listen to foreign broadcasts in order to obtain news, code messages, etc.—*adj.* **monitorial** (*-ōr'*, *-ór'*) relating to a monitor.—*adv.* **monito'rially**.—*n.* **mon'itorship**.—*adj.* **mon'itory** giving admonition or warning. [L. *monēre*, *-itum*, to remind.]

monk *mungk*, *n.* formerly, a hermit: a man (other than a friar, but loosely often applied to a friar also) of a religious community living together under vows.— *adj.* **monk'ish** (*depreciatory*) pertaining to a monk: like a monk: monastic.—**monk'fish** the angel fish (shark): any of several types of angler-fish; **monk's cloth** a type of heavy cotton cloth; **monks'hood** a poisonous plant (*Aconitum*) with a large hoodlike posterior sepal. [O.E. *munuc*—L. *monachus*—Gr. *monachos*—*monos*, alone.]

monkey *mungk'i*, *n.* any mammal of the Primates except man and (usually) the anthropoid apes: an ape: a name of contempt, esp. for a mischievous person, also of playful endearment: the falling weight of a pile-driver: a large hammer: 500 pounds, or dollars (*slang*): anger (*slang*): a liquor-vessel of various kinds:—*pl.* **monk'eys**.—*v.i.* to meddle with anything, to fool.—*v.t.* to imitate as a monkey does.—*adj.* **monk'eyish**.—**monk'ey-bread** the baobab tree or its fruit; **monkey business** underhand dealings: mischievous behaviour; **monk'ey-en'gine** a pile-driving engine; **monk'ey-flow'er** a species of Mimulus; **monk'ey-gland** ape's testicle, grafted experimentally on man (1920–30s) to effect rejuvenescence; **monk'ey-jacket** a close-fitting jacket; **monk'ey-nut** the pea-nut or ground-nut (Arachis); **monk'ey-puzz'le** the so-called Chile pine, *Araucaria imbricata*, with close-set prickly leaves; **monk'ey-shine** (*U.S. slang*) a monkeyish trick; **monk'ey-suit** a man's evening suit; **monk'ey-trick**; **monk'ey-wrench** a wrench with a movable jaw.—**have a monkey on one's back** to be addicted to drugs; **have, get, one's monkey up** to be angry; **make a monkey (out) of** to make a fool of; **not to give a monkey's** (*vulg. slang*) not to care, be interested, at all. [Perh. from M.L.G. *moneke*, conn. Sp., Port. *mono*, monkey.]

mon(o)- *mon'(-ó)-*, in composition, single. [Gr. *monos*, single, alone.]

mono *mon'ō*, (*coll.*) *n.* a monaural gramophone record: monaural reproduction:—*pl.* **mon'os**.—Also *adj.*

monoacid. Same as **monacid**.

monoamine *mon-ō-am'in*, *-ēn*, *n.* an amine containing only one amino-group. [**mon(o)-**.]

monobasic *mon-ō-bā'sik*, *adj.* capable of reacting with one equivalent of an acid: (of an acid) having one replaceable hydrogen atom. [**mon(o)-**.]

monocarpellary *mon-ō-kär'pəl-ə-ri*, or *-pel'*, *adj.* of or with only one carpel. [**mon(o)-**.]

monocarpic *mon-ō-kärp'ik*, *adj.* fruiting once only.— *n.* **mon'ocarp** a monocarpic plant.—*adj.* **monocarp'-ous** monocarpic: having only one ovary: producing one fruit. [Gr. *monos*, single, alone, *karpos*, fruit.]

monochlamydeous *mon-ō-klə-mid'i-əs*, (*bot.*) *adj.* having a one-whorled perianth.—*n.pl.* **Monochlamyd'eae** a division of the Archichlamydeae, usually with perianth in one whorl. [**mon(o)-**.]

monochord *mon'ō-körd*, *n.* an acoustical instrument with one string, sound-board and bridge. [**mon(o)-**.]

monochroic *mon-ō-krō'ik*, *adj.* of one colour. [Gr. *monochroos*—*monos*, *chrōs*, colour.]

monochromatic *mon-ō-krō-mat'ik*, *adj.* of one colour or wavelength only: completely colour-blind: done in monochrome.—*ns.* **monochro'masy** complete colour-blindness; **monochro'mat**, **-mate** one who sees all colours as differing in brilliance only; **monochro'-matism** monochromatic vision; **monochro'mator** a device capable of isolating and transmitting monochromatic or nearly monochromatic light; **mon'o-chrome** representation in one colour: a picture in one colour: black and white: monochromy: **mono-chro'mist** one who practises monochrome; **mon'o-chromy** the art of monochrome. [Gr. *monochrōmatos*—*monos*, single, alone, *chrōma*, *-atos*, colour.]

monocle *mon'ə-kl*, *n.* a single eyeglass. [Fr. *monocle* —Gr. *monos*, L. *oculus*, eye.]

monocline *mon'ō-klīn*, (*geol.*) *n.* a fold in strata followed by resumption of the original direction.— *adj.* **monoclin'al**. [Gr. *monos*, single, alone, *klinein*, to cause to slope.]

monoclinic *mon'ō-klin-ik*, (*crystal.*) *adj.*, referable to three unequal axes, two intersecting each other obliquely and at right angles to the third. [Gr. *monos*, single, alone, *klinein*, to incline.]

monoclinous *mon'ō-klī-nəs* or *-klī'*, (*bot.*) *adj.* hermaphrodite. [Gr. *monos*, single, alone, *klinē*, bed.]

mono-compound *mon-ō-kom'pownd*, (*chem.*) *n.* a compound containing one atom or group of that which is indicated. [**mon(o)-**.]

monocoque *mon-ō-kok'*, *-kók'*, (*aero.*) *n.* a fuselage or nacelle in which all, or nearly all, structural loads are carried by the skin: a motor vehicle structure in which body and chassis are in one and share stresses: the hull of a boat made in one piece. [Fr., lit. single shell.]

monocotyledon *mon-ō-kot-i-lē'dən* *n.* a plant of the Monocotyle'dones (*-ēz*), or Monocot'ylae, one of the two great divisions of the Angiosperms, the embryos with one cotyledon, leaves commonly parallel-veined, the parts of the flower usually in threes, the vascular bundles scattered.—*adj.* **monocotyle'donous.** [mon(o)-.]

monocracy *mon-ok'rə-si, n.* government by one person.—*n.* **mon'ecrat** (-ō-krat).—*adj.* **monocrat'ic.** [Gr. *monos*, single, alone, *kratos*, power.]

monocrystal *mon'ō-kris-təl, n.* a single crystal —*adj.* **monocrys'talline.** [mon(o)-.]

monocular *mon-ok'ū-lər, adj.* one-eyed: of, for, or with, one eye.—Also **monoc'ulous.** [Gr. *monos*, single, alone, L. *oculus*, an eye.]

monoculture *mon'ō-kul-chər, n.* the growing of one kind of crop only, or a large area, over which it is grown. [mon(o)-.]

monodrama *mon'ō-drä-mə, n.* a dramatic piece for a single performer.—*adj.* **monodramatic** (-drə-mat'ik). [mon(o)-.]

monody *mon'ə-di, n.* a mournful ode or poem in which a single mourner bewails: a song for one voice: a manner of composition in which one part or voice carries the melody, the others accompanying.—*adjs.* **monodic** (-od'), **-al.**—*n* **mon'odist** one who writes monodies. [Gr. *monōidiā—monos*, single, alone, *ōidē*, song.]

monoecious *mon-ē'shəs, adj.* hermaphrodite: having separate male and female flowers on the same plant. —*n.* **monoecism** (-ē'sizm). [Gr. *monos*, single, alone, *oikos*, a house.]

monofil *mon'ō-fil, n.* a single strand of synthetic fibre. —Also **monofil'ament.** [Gr. *monos*, single, alone, L. *filum*, a thread.]

monogamy *mon-og'ə-mi, n.* the rule, custom, or condition of marriage to one wife or husband at a time, or (now rarely) in life.—*adjs.* **monogamic** (*mon-ō-gam'ik*), **monogamous** (-og'əm-).—*n.* **monog'amist.** [Gr. *monos*, single, alone, *gamos*, marriage.]

monogenesis *mon-ō-jen'i-sis, n.* development of offspring from a parent like itself: asexual reproduction: community of origin.—*adj.* **monogenet'ic.**—*ns.* **monogenism** (-oj'ən-izm) the doctrine of the common descent of all living things, or of any particular group (esp. mankind) from one ancestor or pair; **monog'enist.**—*adjs.* **monogenist'ic; monog'enous.**—*n.* **monog'eny** descent from one common ancestor or pair: asexual reproduction. [mon(o)-.]

monoglot *mon'ō-glot, n.* one who knows only one language.—Also *adj.* [Gr. *monos*, single, alone, *glōtta*, tongue.]

monogony *mon-og'ən-i, n.* asexual reproduction. [Gr. *monos*, single, alone, *gonos*, begetting.]

monogram *mon'ə-gram, n.* a figure consisting of several letters interwoven or written into one.—*adj.* **monogrammatic** (-grə-mat'ik). [Gr. *monos*, single, alone, *gramma*, *grammatos*, a letter.]

monograph *mon'ə-gräf, n.* a treatise written on one particular subject or any branch of it: a systematic account.—*v.t.* to write a monograph upon.—*ns.* **monographer** (*mon-og'rə-fər*), **monog'raphist** a writer of monographs.—*adjs.* **monographic** (-graf'), **-al** pertaining to a monograph or a monogram. [Gr. *monos*, single, alone, *graphein*, to write.]

monogyny *mon-oj'i-ni, or -og', n.* the custom, practice, or condition of having only one wife: marriage with one wife: the habit of mating with one female.—*adj.* **monog'ynous** having one wife: practising monogyny. [Gr. *monos*, single, alone, *gynē*, woman.]

monohull *mon'ō-hul, n.* a vessel with one hull, as opp. to catamaran, trimaran. [mon(o)-.]

monolingual *mon-ō-ling'gwəl, adj.* expressed in one language: speaking only one language.—*ns.* **monoling'ualism; monoling'uist.** [Gr. *monos*, single, L. *lingua*, tongue.]

monolith *mon'ō-lith, n.* a pillar, or column, of a single stone: anything resembling a monolith in uniformity, massiveness or intractability.—*adj.* **monolith'ic** pertaining to or resembling a monolith: of a state, an organisation, etc., massive, and undifferentiated throughout: intractable for this reason. [Gr. *monos*, single, alone, *lithos*, a stone.]

monologue *mon'ə-log, n.* a composition put into the mouth of one person, or intended to be spoken by one person: a harangue that engrosses conversation.—*adjs.* **monologic** (-loj'), **-al.**—*v.i.* **monologise, -ize** (*mon-ol'ə-jīz*) to indulge in this.—Also **monol'oguise, -ize** (-gīz).—*ns.* **monol'ogist** one who talks in monologue (also **mon'ologuist); monol'ogy** the habit of doing so. [Gr. *monos*, single, alone, *logos*, speech.]

monomania *mon-ō-mā'ni-ə, n.* madness confined to one subject: an unreasonable interest in any particular thing.—*n.* **monoma'niac** one affected with monomania.—*adjs.* **monomā'niac, monomaniacal** (-mə-nī'ə-kl). [Gr. *monos*, single, alone, *maniā*, madness.]

monomark *mon'ō-märk, n.* a particular combination of letters, figures, etc. as a mark of identification. [mon(o)-.]

monomer *mon', mōn'ə-mər, n* the simplest of any series of compounds having the same empirical formula—opp. to *polymer*.—*adj.* **monomer'ic.** [Gr. *monos*, single, alone, *meros*, part.]

monometallic *mon-ō-mi-tal'ik, adj.* involving or using but one metal as a standard of currency.—*ns.* **monometallism** (-met'əl-izm); **monomet'allist.** [mon(o)-.]

monomial *mon-ō'mi-əl, n.* an algebraic expression of one term only.—Also *adj.* [Ill-formed from Gr. *monos*, single, alone, L. *nōmen*, name.]

monomorphic *mon-ō-mör'fik, adj.* existing in one form only.—*adj.* **monomor'phous.** [Gr. *monos*, single, alone, *morphē*, form.]

mononuclear *mon-ō-nū'kli-ər, adj.* having a single nucleus.—*n.* (med.) **mononucleosis** (*mon-ō-nūk-li-ō'sis*) the presence in the blood of an abnormally large number of a type of leucocytes.—See also **infectious mononucleosis** under *infect*. [mon(o)-.]

monophasic *mon-ō-fāz'ik, adj* (of electric current) single-phase (also **mon'ophase**): having one period of rest and one of activity during the 24 hours (*biol.*). [mon(o)-.]

monophobia *mon-ō-fō'bi-ə, n.* morbid dread of being alone.—*adj.* **monophō'bic.** [mon(o)-.]

monophonic *mon-ō-fon'ik, adj.* homophonic: monaural (opp. to *stereophonic*).—*n.* **monoph'ony.** [Gr. *monos*, single, alone, *phōnē*, voice, sound.]

monophthong *mon'of-thong, n.* a simple vowel sound. —*adj.* **monophthongal** (-thong'gəl). [Gr. *monophthongos—monos*, single, alone, *phthongos*, sound, vowel.]

Monophysite *mō-nof'i-zīt, -sīt, n.* one who holds that Christ had but one composite nature.—*adj.* **Monophysitic** (-sit'ik, -zit'ik).—*n.* **Monoph'ysitism.**—All words also without *cap.* [Gr. *monos*, single, alone, *physis*, nature.]

monoplane *mon'ə-plān, n.* an aeroplane or glider with one set of planes or wings. [mon(o)-.]

monoplegia *mon-ō-plē'ji-ə, n.* paralysis limited to a single part. [Gr. *monos*, single, alone, *plēgē*, stroke.]

monopoly *mon-op'ə-li, n.* sole power, or privilege, of dealing in anything: exclusive command or possession: that of which one has such a sole power, privilege, command, or possession: (with *cap.*; ®) a board-game for two or more players, their object being the acquisition of property.—*v.t.* **monop'olise, -ize** to have a monopoly of: to keep to oneself: to engross.—*ns.* **monop'oliser, -z-, monop'olist.**—*adj.* **monopolis'tic.—Monopolies and Mergers Commis-**

sion a body set up by the government to investigate monopolies, etc., where a monopoly is defined as 25 per cent of the market. [L. *monopōlium*—Gr. *monopōlion*—*monos*, single, alone, *pōleein*, to sell.]

monopsony *mon-op'sə-ni*, *n.* a situation where only one buyer exists for the product of several sellers, or where one of several buyers is large enough to exert undue influence over the price of a product.—*n.* **monop'sonist**.—*adj.* **monopsonis'tic**. [Gr. *monos*, single, alone, *opsonia*, a purchase—*opsonein*, to buy.]

monorail *mon'ō-rāl*, *n.* a railway with carriages running astride of, or suspended from, one rail.—Also *adj.* [mon(o)-.]

monosaccharide *mon-ō-sak'ə-rīd*, *n.* a simple sugar that cannot be hydrolysed. [mon(o)-.]

monosepalous *mon-ō-sep'ə-ləs*, (*bot.*) *adj.* having the sepals all united. [mon(o)-.]

mono-ski *mon'ō-skē*, *n.* a ski on which both feet are placed.—*v.i.* to use a mono-ski.—*n.* **mon'o-skier** [mon(o)-.]

monosodium glutamate *mon-ō-sō'di-əm glōō'tə-māt*, a white crystalline salt which brings out the flavour of meat (*glutamate*, a salt of glutamic acid).

monosyllable *mon-ə-sil'ə-bl*, *n.* a word of one syllable. —*adj.* **monosyllabic** (-*ab'ik*).—*n.* **monosyll'abism**. [mon(o)-.]

monotheism *mon'ō-thē-izm*, *n.* the belief in only one God.—*n.* **mon'otheist**.—*adjs.* **monotheist'ic**, **-al**. [Gr. *monos*, single, alone, *theos*, God.]

monotint *mon'ə-tint*, *n.* drawing or painting in a single tint. [mon(o)-.]

monotone *mon'ə-tōn*, *n.* a single, unvaried tone or utterance: a succession of sounds having the same pitch: continued or extended sameness: sameness in colour.—*adj.* in monotone.—*v.t.* and *v.i.* to sing, declaim, speak, utter, in monotone.—*adjs.* **monotonic** (-*ton'ik*) in monotone: of a function or sequence, having the property of either never increasing or never decreasing; **monotonous** (*mon-ot'ə-nəs*) uttered in one unvaried tone: marked by dull uniformity.— *adv.* **monot'onously**.—*ns.* **monot'onousness**; **monot'ony** dull uniformity of tone or sound: want of modulation in speaking or reading: irksome sameness or want of variety (*fig.*). [Gr. *monos*, single, alone, *tonos*, a tone.]

Monotremata *mon-ō-trē'mə-tə*, *n.pl.* the lowest order of Mammalia, having a single opening for the genital and digestive organs.—*adj.* **monotre'matous**—also **mon'otreme**.—*n.* **mon'otreme** a member of the Monotremata. [Gr. *monos*, single, alone, *trēma*, -*atos*, a hole.]

monotype *mon'ə-tīp*, *n.* a sole type, a species forming a genus by itself: a single print made from a picture painted on a metal or glass plate: (with *cap.*; ℞) the name of a machine that casts and sets type, letter by letter. —Also *adj.*—*adj.* **monotypic** (-*tip'ik*). [mon(o)-.]

monovalent *mon-ō-vā'lənt*, *mon-ov'əl-ənt*, *adj.* univalent.—*ns.* **monova'lence**, **monova'lency**. [mon(o)-.]

monoxide *mon-ok'sīd*, *n.* an oxide with one oxygen atom in the molecule. [mon(o)-.]

monozygotic *mon-ō-zī-got'ik*, *adj.* developed from one zygote. [mon(o)-.]

Monseigneur *m̄ɔ̃-sen-yœr*, *n.* my lord: a title in France given to a person of high birth or rank, esp. to bishops, etc. (written *Mgr*):—*pl.* **Messeigneurs** (*me-sen-yœr*).—*n.* **Monsieur** (*mə-syø*) sir: a title of courtesy in France = *Mr* in English (printed *M.* or in full): a Frenchman generally: a French gentleman:—*pl.* **Messieurs** (Fr. *mes-yø*, written *MM.*; Eng. *mes'ərz*, written **Messrs**) and (of **monsieur**) **messieurs**. [Fr.

mon seigneur, *sieur*, my lord—L. *meum seniōrem* (accus.), my elder.]

Monsignor *mon-sēn'yər* (It. *mon-sēn-yōr'*), **Monsignore** (-*yō'rā*) *ns.* a title conferred on prelates and on dignitaries of the papal household.—*pls.* **Monsignors** (-*sēn'*), **Monsigno'ri** (-*rē*). [It.—Fr.]

monsoon *mon-sōōn'*, *n.* a periodical wind of the Indian Ocean, S.W. from April to October, and N.E. the rest of the year: a similar wind elsewhere: in N. and W. India, the rains accompanying the S.W. monsoon. —*adj.* **monsoon'al**.—**break of the monsoon** the first onset of the monsoon rain. [Port. *monção*—Malay *mūsim*—Ar. *mausim*, a time, a season.]

mons pubis *monz pū'bis*. Same as **mons veneris**:—*pl.* **montes pubis** (*mon'tēz*). [L., hill of the pubis.]

monster *mon'stər*, *n.* anything out of the usual course of nature: a prodigy: a fabulous animal: an abnormally formed animal or plant: a grotesque animal: a gigantic animal: anything gigantic: anything horrible from ugliness or wickedness.—*adj.* gigantic, huge.—*n.* **monstrosity** (-*stros'i-ti*) the state or fact of being monstrous: marked abnormality: an abnormally formed animal, plant, part, or object: anything outrageously constructed.—*adj.* **mon'strous** out of the common course of nature: enormous: wonderful: horrible: outrageous: preposterous.—*adv.* **mon'strously**.—*n.* **mon'strousness**. [Fr. *monstre*—L. *mōnstrum*, an evil omen, a monster— *monēre*, *monitum*, to warn.]

monstrance *mon'strəns*, *n.* the ornamental receptacle in which the consecrated host is exposed in R.C. churches for the adoration of the people. [O.Fr.,— L. *mōnstrāre*, to show.]

mons veneris *monz ven'ə-ris*, the mound of flesh over the pubis on the female human body:—*pl.* **montes veneris** (*mon'tēz*). [L., hill of Venus.]

montage *mɔ̃-täzh'*, *n.* selection and piecing together of material for a cinematograph film with a view to effect: (act or process of making) a composite photograph: setting-up, assemblage, superimposition: a picture made partly by sticking objects on the canvas. [Fr.,—*monter*, to mount.]

montane *mon'tān*, *adj.* mountainous: mountain-dwelling. [L. *montānus*—*mōns*, *montis*, a mountain.]

Montbretia *mon(t)-brēsh'yə*, *n.* a genus of S. African iridaceous plants: (without *cap.*) a plant of this genus: (without *cap.*) a plant (*Crocosmia*) of the iris family bearing bright orange-coloured flowers: (without *cap.*) a plant of the genus Tritonia. [After a French botanist, Coquebert de *Montbret* (1780–1801).]

monte *mon'tā*, -*ti*, *n.* a shrubby tract, a forest: a Spanish-American gambling card-game.—**three-card monte** a Mexican three-card trick. [Sp., mountain, scrub, cards remaining after a deal—L. *mōns*, *montis*, a mountain.]

Montessorian *mon-tes-ōr'i-ən*, -*ōr'*, *adj.* pertaining to Dr Maria *Montessori* or her method (*c.* 1900) of education, insisting on spontaneity and freedom from restraint.

Montezuma's revenge *mon-tə-zōōm'əz ri-venj'*, diarrhoea caused by travelling in Mexico and/or eating Mexican food. [*Montezuma II*, a 15th-cent. Mexican ruler.]

month *munth*, *n.* the moon's period: one of the twelve conventional divisions of the year, or its length—a *calendar* month.—*adj.* **month'ly** performed in a month: done, recurring, or appearing once a month. —*n.* a monthly publication: (*pl.*) the menses (*coll.*). —*adv.* once a month: in every month.—**lunar month** a month reckoned by the moon; **a month of Sundays** see Sunday; **solar month** one-twelfth of a solar year. [O.E. *mōnath*—*mōna*, moon.]

monticulus *mon-tik'ū-ləs*, *n.* a little elevation—also

mon'ticle and mon'ticule.—*adjs.* montic'ulate, montic'ulous having small projections. [L. *monticulus*,
dim. of *mons*, mountain.]
monture *mon'tūr, mō-tūr, n.* a mounting, setting,
frame. [Fr.]
monument *mon'ū-mənt, n.* anything that preserves the
memory of a person or an event, a building, pillar,
tomb, tablet, statue, etc.: any structure, natural or
artificial, considered as an object of beauty or of interest as a relic of the past: a historic document or
record: a stone, post, river, etc. marking a boundary
(*U.S.*): a relic, indication, or trace: a notable or
enduring example.—*adj.* monumental (-*ment'əl*) of
or relating to or of the nature of a monument, tomb,
memento, or token: memorial: massive and lasting:
vast: impressive: amazing: loosely, very large —*adv.*
monument'ally. [L. *monumentum, monimentum*—
monēre, to remind.]
mony *mun'i*, a Scots form of many.
moo *mōō, v.i.* to low.—*n.* a cow's low. [Imit.]
mooch *mōōch, v.i.* to slouch about: to skulk: to loiter,
wander (about): to sponge.—*v.t.* to pilfer: to beg,
cadge.—*n.* the act of mooching.—*n.* mooch'er.
[Perh. O.Fr. *muchier*, to hide.]
mood[1] *mōōd. n.* a form of the verb to express the mode
or manner of an action or of a state of being (*gram.*):
the form of the syllogism as determined by the quantity and quality of its three constituent propositions
(*log.*). [mode.]
mood[2] *mōōd, n.* temporary state of the emotions or of
attitude: state of gloom or sullenness.—*adv.* mood'-
ily.—*n.* mood'iness sullenness.—*adj.* mood'y indulging in moods: sullen. [O E. *mōd*, mind.]
Moog synthesizer® *mōōg sin'thi-sīz-ər*, an electronic
musical instrument with a keyboard, that can produce
a wide range of sounds. [Developed by Robert
Moog, an American engineer.]
mooi *mō'i*, (*Afrik.*) *adj.* fine—a general word of
commendation. [From Du.]
moola(h) *mōō'lə*, (*slang*) *n.* money.
moon *mōōn, n.* (often with *cap.*) the earth's satellite: a
satellite: a month: anything in the shape of a moon or
crescent.—*v.i.* to wander about or gaze vacantly at
anything (usu. with *around, about*)—*adj.* mooned
marked with the figure of a moon.—*n.* moon'er one
who moons about.—*adjs.* moon'ish like the moon:
variable: inconstant: moon'less destitute of moonlight; moon'y of or relating to the moon: moon-like:
crescent-shaped: bearing a crescent: round and
shining: moonlit: inclined to moon: fatuous.—moon'-
beam a beam of light from the moon; moon'calf a
false conception or fleshy mass formed in the womb: a
dolt; moon'face a full, round face—a point of beauty
in the East.—*adj.* moon'-faced.—moon'-fish the
opah or other silvery disc-shaped fish; moon'-flower
the oxeye daisy; moon'-god, -goddess a god or goddess
representing or associated with the moon; moon'light
the light of the moon—sunlight reflected from the
moon's surface: smuggled spirit.—*adj.* lighted by the
moon: occurring in moonlight.—moon'lighter a
moonshiner: one who takes work in the evening in
addition to his normal day's work, esp. when the income from this is not declared for tax assessment;
moonlight flit(ting) a removal by night, with rent
unpaid; moon'lighting.—*adj.* moon'lit lit or illu-
mined by the moon.—moon'-mad'ness lunacy, once
thought to be connected with the moon's changes;
moon'quake a tremor of the moon's surface; moon'-
raking the following of crazy fancies; moon'rise the
rising of the moon; moon'scape the physical appearance of the surface of the moon, or a representation
of it; moon'set the setting of the moon; moon'shine
moonlight: show without reality (*fig.*): nonsense

(*coll.*): spirits illicitly distilled or smuggled.—*adj.*
lighted by the moon: made of moonlight, bodiless
(*fig.*).—moon'shiner a smuggler or illicit distiller of
spirits.—*adj.* moon'shiny lighted by the moon:
visionary, unreal.—moon'shot act or process of
launching an object or vehicle into orbit, or land on, the
moon; moon'stone an opalescent orthoclase feldspar,
perh. sometimes selenite; moon'strike the act or process of landing a spacecraft on the surface of the
moon.—*adj.* moon'struck (also moon'-stricken)
affected by the moon, lunatic, crazed.—over the
moon (*coll.*) delighted. [O.E. *mōna*.]
moor[1] *mōōr, n.* a wide tract of untilled ground, often
covered with heath, and having a poor, peaty soil: a
heath.—*adjs.* moor'ish, moor'y resembling a moor:
sterile: marshy: boggy.—moor'buzz'ard the marsh-
harrier; moor'cock, moor'fowl red, or black, grouse;
moor'hen water-hen: female moorfowl; moor'land a
tract of moor: moorish country.—*adj.* of moorland.
—moor'log a deposit of decayed woody material
under a marsh, etc.; moor'man a dweller in moors.
[O.E. *mōr*.]
moor[2] *mōōr, v.t.* to fasten by cable or anchor.—*v.i.* to
make fast a ship, boat, etc.: to be made fast.—*ns.*
moor'age condition of being moored: act of mooring:
a due paid for mooring: a place for mooring; moor'ing
act of mooring that which serves to moor or confine a
ship: (in *pl.*) the place or condition of a ship thus
moored. [Prob. from an unrecorded O.E. word
answering to M.Du. *māren.*]
Moor *mōōr, n.* a member of the mixed Arab and Berber
people of Morocco and the Barbary coast: one of the
Arab and Berber conquerors and occupants of Spain
from 711 to 1492: in some countries, a Muslim: a
dark-coloured person generally, a Negro:—*fem.*
Moor'ess.—*adj.* Moor'ish. [Fr. *More, Maure*—L.
Maurus, doubtfully connected with Byzantine Gr
mauros, black.]
moose *mōōs, n.* the American elk:—*pl.* moose. [Al-
gonquian *mus, moos.*]
moot *mōōt, n.* orig. a meeting: a deliberative or
administrative assembly or court (*hist.*). its meeting-
place: discussion: a law student's discussion of a
hypothetical case.—*v.t.* to argue, dispute: to propose
for discussion.—*v.i.* to dispute, plead.—*adj.* debat-
able —*adj.* moot'able.—*ns.* moot'er; moot'ing.—
moot case a case for discussion: a case about which
there may be difference of opinion; moot'-court a
meeting for discussion of hypothetical cases; moot's
hall, -house a town-hall or council chamber: a hall for
moot-courts; moot point an undecided or disputed
point. [O.E. (*ge*)*mot* (n.), *mōtian* (vb.), akin to
mētan, to meet.]
mop *mop, n.* a bunch of rags, yarn, or the like, on the
end of a stick, for washing, removing dust, soaking up
liquid, etc.: any similar instrument, as for cleansing a
wound, polishing, etc.: a thick or bushy head of hair:
an act of mopping.—*v.t.* to wipe, dab, soak up, or
remove with a mop or as if with a mop: to clear away
or dispose of as residue:—*pr.p.* mopp'ing; *pa.t.* and
pa.p. mopped.—*ns.* mopp'er; mopp'et a rag-doll: a
doll-like woman: (a term of endearment or contempt
for) a little girl or child.—*adj.* mop'-head'ed having a
shaggy, unkempt head of hair.—mop'stick the handle
of a mop: a hand-rail nearly circular in section: a rod
for raising a piano damper; mop'-up' an action of
mopping up.—mop up to clear away or clean up with
a mop: to clear away, dispose of: to absorb (e.g.
surplus credit): to capture or kill (enemy stragglers)
after a victory, etc.; Mrs Mop(p) a cleaner,
charwoman. [Possibly from O.Fr. *mappe*—L.
mappa, a napkin.]
mope *mōp, v.i.* to go aimlessly and listlessly: to yield to

low spirits.—*n.* a listless person: (esp. in *pl.*) moping —*adv.* **mop'ingly.**—*adj.* **mop'ish** dull: spiritless.— *adv.* **mop'ishly.**—*ns.* **mop'ishness; mop'us** one who mopes.—*adj.* **mop'y.**

moped *mō'ped, n.* a motor-assisted *pedal* cycle.

mopoke *mō'pōk, n.* an Australian and S. Asian bird akin to the goatsuckers: a New Zealand owl: a silly person. —Also **mope'hawk, more'-pork.** [From the cry of the owl and of a kindred Australian species, mistakenly attributed to the frogmouth]

Mopp, Mrs. See under **mop.**

mopper, etc. See **mop.**

mopus. See **mope.**

moquette *mō-ket', n.* a carpet and soft furnishing material with a loose velvety pile, the back made of thick canvas, etc. [Fr.]

mora¹ *mō'rə, mó', n.* delay, esp. unjustifiable (*law*). [L., delay.]

mora², morra *mor'ə, n.* the game of guessing how many fingers are held up. [It. *mora.*]

moraine *mo-rān', n.* a continuous marginal line of débris borne on or left by a glacier: a garden imitation of this.—*adjs.* **morain'al, morain'ic.** [Fr.]

moral *mor'əl, adj.* of or relating to character or conduct considered as good or evil: ethical: conformed to or directed towards right, virtuous: esp. virtuous in matters of sex: capable of knowing right and wrong: subject to the moral law: supported by evidence of reason or probability.—*n.* in *pl.* writings on ethics: the doctrine or practice of the duties of life: moral philosophy or ethics: principles and conduct, esp. sexual: in *sing.* the practical lesson that can be drawn from anything: an exposition of such lesson by way of conclusion: a symbol: a certainty (*slang*): (spelt **morale** to look French and to suggest the Fr. pron. *mor-äl'*) condition with respect to discipline and confidence, pride, fixity of purpose, faith in the cause fought for, etc. (usu. *mil.*).—*ns.* **morale** *mor-äl'* see above, **moralisa'tion, -z-** act of moralising, explanation in a moral sense.—*v.t.* **mor'alise, -ize** to apply to a moral purpose: to explain in a moral sense: to make moral: to furnish with matter of morality.—*v.i.* to speak or write on moral subjects: to make moral reflections.—*ns.* **mor'aliser; mor'alism** a moral maxim: moral counsel: morality as distinct from religion; **mor'alist** one who teaches morals, or who practises moral duties: a moral as distinguished from a religious man: one who prides himself on his morality.—*adj.* **moralist'ic.**—*n.* **morality** (*mor-al'i-ti*) quality of being moral: that which renders an action right or wrong: the practice of moral duties apart from religion: virtue: the doctrine of actions as right or wrong: ethics: a mediaeval allegorical drama in which virtues and vices appear as characters (also **moral'ity-play**).—*adv.* **mor'ally** in a moral manner: in respect of morals: to all intents and purposes, practically.—**moral agent** one who acts under a knowledge of right and wrong; **moral certainty** a likelihood great enough to be acted on, although not capable of being certainly proved; **moral courage** power of facing disapprobation and ridicule; **moral defeat** a success so qualified as to count as a defeat, or to point towards defeat; **moral faculty** moral sense; **moral law** a law or rules for life and conduct, founded on what is right and wrong: the law of conscience: that part of the Old Testament which relates to moral principles, esp. the ten commandments; **moral philosophy** ethics; **Moral Rearmament** a movement succeeding the Oxford Group in 1938, advocating absolute private and public morality (abbrev. M.R.A.); **moral sense** that power of the mind which knows or judges actions to be right or wrong, and determines conduct accordingly; **moral support** the help afforded by approbation; **moral theology** ethics

treated with reference to a divine source; **moral victory** a defeat in appearance, but in some important sense a real victory. [L. *mōrālis—mōs, mōris,* manner, custom, (esp. in *pl.*) morals.]

morass *mə-ras', n.* a tract of soft, wet ground: a marsh. —*adj.* **morass'y.** [Du. *moeras*—O.Fr. *maresc,* influenced by Du. *moer,* moor.]

moratorium *mor-ə-tō'ri-əm, -tō', n.* an emergency measure authorising the suspension of payments of debts for a given time: the period thus declared: a temporary ban on, or decreed cessation of, an activity: —*pl.* **morator'ia, morator'iums.**—*adj.* **moratory** (*mor'ə-tə-ri*) delaying: deferring. [Neut. of L.L. *morātōrius,* adj. from *mora,* delay.]

Moravian *mo-rā'vi-ən, adj.* pertaining to *Moravia* or the Moravians.—*n.* one of the people of Moravia: one of a small body of Protestants of extraordinary missionary energy, founded in the 15th century.—*n.* **Mora'vianism.** [L. *Moravia,* Moravia—*Morava,* the river March.]

moray *mō'rā, mō-rā', mur'i, mur-ā', n.* an eel of the family Muraenidae. [Port. *moreia*—L. *mūraena*— Gr. *(s)mȳraina,* fem. of *(s)mȳros,* eel.]

morbid *mōr'bid, adj.* sickly: unwholesome: inclined to dwell on unwholesome or horrible thoughts: relating to, or of the 'nature of, disease.—*n.* **morbid'ity** sickliness: unwholesomeness: ratio of sickness.—*adv.* **mor'bidly.**—*n.* **mor'bidness.**—**morbid anatomy** the science or study of diseased organs and tissues. [L. *morbidus—morbus,* disease.]

morbiferous, etc. See **morbus.**

morbilli *mōr-bil'ī, n.pl.* measles.—*adjs.* **morbill'iform, morbill'ous.** [L.L. dim. of L. *morbus,* disease.]

morbus *mor'bəs, n.* disease (L.; used in phrases).—*adjs.* **morbif'erous** disease-bringing; **morbif'ic** disease-causing. [L.]

morceau *mōr'sō, n.* a morsel: a fragment: a piece of music: a short literary composition:—*pl.* **mor'ceaux** (*-sō*). [Fr.; see **morsel.**]

mordacious *mōr-dā'shəs, adj.* given to biting: biting in quality (*lit.* or *fig.*).—*adv.* **morda'ciously.**—*ns.* **mordacity** (*-das'i-ti*), **mordancy** (*mōr'dən-si*).—*adj.* **mor'dant** biting: incisive: serving to fix dyes, paints, gold-leaf.—*n.* a corroding substance: any substance that combines with and fixes a dyestuff in material that cannot be dyed direct: a substance used to cause paint or gold-leaf to adhere.—*v.t.* to treat with a mordant. —*adv.* **mor'dantly.** [L. *mordēre,* to bite.]

mordent *mōr'dənt,* (*mus.*) *n.* a grace note in which the principal note is preceded in performance by itself and the note below or itself and the note above. [Ger.,— It. *mordente.*]

more *mōr, mór, adj.* (serving as *compar.* of **many** and **much**) in greater number or quantity: additional: other besides.—*adv.* to a greater degree: rather: again: longer: further: moreover.—*n.* a greater thing: something further or in addition:—*superl., adj.* and *adv.* **most** (*mōst*).—*adj.* **mo'rish, more'ish** such that one wants more.—**any more** anything additional: further; **more and more** continually increasing; **more or less** about: in round numbers; **no more** nothing in addition: never again: no longer in existence: dead. [O.E. *māra,* greater.]

morel¹ *mor-el', n.* any edible fungus of the genus Morchella. [Fr *morille.*]

morel² *mor-el', mor'əl,* **morell'o** (*-ō; pl.* **morell'os**) *ns.* a dark-red cherry, much used in cooking and for cherry brandy. [Possibly—It. *morello,* dark-coloured.]

moreover *mōr-ō'vər, mor-, adv.* more over or beyond what has been said: further: besides: also. [**more, over.**]

more-pork. See **mopoke.**

mores *mō', mo'rēz, mō'räs, n pl.* customs, manners [L. *mōs, mōris*, custom.]

morganatic *mor-gən-at'ik, adj.* of, by, or of the nature of, a left-handed marriage, that is, a marriage (in some countries) between persons of unequal rank (latterly only where one is of a reigning house), the marriage being valid, the children legitimate, but unable to inherit the higher rank, the wife (if the lower-born) not being granted the husband's title —*adv* **morganat'ically.** [L.L. *morganātica*, a gift from a bridegroom to his bride.]

morgen *mor'gən, n* a unit of land-measurement—in Holland, S Africa, and parts of the U.S.A , a little over two acres; in Norway, Denmark, and Prussia, about two-thirds of an acre. [Du and Ger , perh *morgen*, morning, hence a morning's ploughing.]

morgue *morg, n.* a place where dead bodies are laid out for identification a place, as in a newspaper office, where miscellaneous material for reference is kept [Fr]

moribund *mor'i-bund, adj.* about to die in a dying state.—*n.* **moribund'ity.** [L *moribundus—morī*, to die]

Morisco *mo-ris'kō, n* a Moor, esp a Christianised Moor in Spain after the fall of Granada in 1492. (without *cap.*) a morris-dance or dancer an arabesque:—*pl.* **Moris'co(e)s.**

morish. See **more.**

Mormon *mor'mən, n.* one of a religious sect with headquarters since 1847 in Salt Lake City, polygamous till 1890, calling itself *The Church of Jesus Christ of Latter-day Saints*, founded in 1830 by Joseph Smith, whose *Book of Mormon* was given out as translated from the golden plates of *Mormon*, a prophet.—*ns.* **Mor'monism; Mor'monite.**

morn *mòrn, (poet., dial.) n.* the first part of the day: morning.—**the morn** (*Scot*) tomorrow; **the morn's morn** or **morning** (*Scot.*) tomorrow morning; **the morn's nicht** (*Scot.*) tomorrow night. [M.E. *morwen*—O.E. *morgen.*]

mornay (sauce) *mor'nā (sos), n.* a cream sauce with cheese flavouring. [Perh. Philippe de *Mornay*, Fr Huguenot leader.]

morning *mòrn'ing, n.* the first part of the day, until noon, or the time of the midday meal: the early part of anything —*adj.* of the morning: taking place or being in the morning.—*adv.* **morn'ings** (*coll.* or *dial.*) in the morning.—**morn'ing-dress** dress, esp. formal dress, worn in early part of day, as opp. to *evening-dress*; **morn'ing-glo'ry** a plant of the genus *Ipomoea* (esp. *Ipomoea purpurea*) or *Convolvulus*, with showy flowers of various colours; **morn'ing-gown** a gown for wearing in the morning, **morn'ing-prayer** prayer in the morning: matins; **morn'ing-room** a sitting-room for use in the morning; **morn'ing-sick'ness** nausea and vomiting in the morning, common in the early stages of pregnancy; **morn'ing-star** a planet, esp. Venus, when it rises before the sun: a precursor· a mediaeval weapon, a spiky ball attached directly or by a chain to a handle; **morn'ing-tide** the morning time: early part; **morn'ing-watch** the watch between 4 and 8 a m — **morning-after pill** a contraceptive pill taken within a specified time after intercourse, **the morning after** (*coll.*) the unpleasant after-effects of a night of excessive drinking, etc. [Contr of M E *morwening*; cf *morn.*]

Moro *mōr'ō, mor'ō, n.* one of any of the tribes of Muslim Malays in the Philippine Islands.—*pl* **Moro(s).** [Sp., lit. moor, L *Maurus.*]

morocco *mə-rok'ō, n* a fine goat-skin leather tanned with sumac, first brought from *Morocco* (also **morocco leather**). a sheep-skin leather imitation of it —*pl* **morocc'os.**—*adj* consisting of morocco —

French morocco an inferior kind of Levant morocco, with small grain, **Levant morocco** a fine quality of morocco, with large grain, **Persian morocco** a morocco finished on the grain side

moron *mōr'on, mor', n* a somewhat feeble-minded person: a former category of mental retardation, describing a person with an 1 Q. of 50–69, i.e. one who remains throughout life at the mental age of eight to twelve.—Also *adj* —*adj* **moron'ic.** [Gr *mōros*, foolish.]

morose *mə-rōs', adj* sour-tempered gloomy: severe —*adv* **morose'ly.**—*n* **morose'ness.** [L *mōrōsus*, peevish—*mōs, mōris*, manner]

morph¹ *morf, (zool , etc.) n* a variant form of an animal, etc. [Gr. *morphē*, form]

morph² See **morphic.**

-morph *-morf,* **morph(o)-** *mor'fō-,* in composition, of a specified form, shape or structure —**morph'ic** adjective combining form.—**-morph'ism** noun combining form. [Gr *morphē,* form.]

morphia *mor'fi-ə, n* morphine —*ns* **mor'phine** (*-fēn*) the principal alkaloid in opium, used as a hypnotic, **mor'phinism** the effect of morphine on the system· the habit of taking morphine; **morphinomā'nia; morphinomā'niac.** [Gr. *Morpheus*, god of dreams.]

morphic *mor'fik, adj.* relating to form, morphological —*ns* **morph** (*linguistics*, a back-formation from **morpheme**) a part of a spoken or written word corresponding to or representing a morpheme; **morpheme** (*mor'fēm*) a linguistic unit (word or part of word) that has meaning.—*adj.* **morphēm'ic.**—*n.sing* **morphēm'ics** the study of morphemes.—*n.* **morphogenesis** (*-fə-jen'i-sis*) the origin and development of a part, organ, or organism.—*adj* **morphogenet'ic.** —*ns.* **morphogeny** (*-foj'i-ni*) morphogenesis; **morphographer** (*-fog'rə-fər*); **morphog'raphy** descriptive morphology.—*adjs.* **morpholog'ic, -al.**—*ns.* **morphol'ogist; morphol'ogy** the science of form, esp. that of the outer form, inner structure, and development of living organisms and their parts: also of the external forms of rocks and land-features: also of the forms of words. [Gr. *morphē,* form]

morphine, etc. See **morphia.**

morra. See **mora².**

morris¹ *mor'is,* **morr'is-dance** *ns* a dance, according to some of Moorish origin, which came to be associated with May games, with (latterly) Maid Marian, Robin Hood, the hobby-horse, and other characters, who had bells attached to their dress: a tune for the dance —*v.i.* **morr'is** to perform by dancing.—*n.* **morr'is-dancer.** [**Moorish.**]

morris². See **meril** (for **nine men's morris,** etc.).

Morris chair *mor'is chār,* a kind of armchair with an adjustable back [From William *Morris*, 19th cent. English designer and architect.]

Morrison shelter *mor'i-sən shel'tər,* a kind of portable steel air-raid shelter for use inside a house or other building, developed during World War II and named after the then Secretary of State for Home Affairs and Home Security, Herbert S. *Morrison.*

morro *mor'ō, n.* a rounded hill or headland:—*pl.* **morr'os.** [Sp]

morrow *mor'ō, n.* the day following the present: tomorrow. the next following day· the time immediately after any event [M E *morwe* for *morwen*; cf. *morn.*]

Morse *mors, n* signalling by a code in which each letter is represented by a combination of dashes and dots or long and short light-flashes, sound signals, etc , invented by Sam F B *Morse* (1791–1872).—Also *adj*

morsel *mor'səl, n* a bite or mouthful: a small piece of food· a choice piece of food, a dainty. a small piece of anything. [O.Fr. morsel (Fr. morceau, It. morsello), dim. from L. morsus—mordēre, morsum, to bite.]

mortal mör'tl, adj. liable to death: causing death: deadly: fatal: punishable with death: involving the penalty of spiritual death, as opposed to venial: to the death: implacable: human: very great (coll.): tediously long (coll.): without exception (coll.): very drunk (slang).—n. a human being.—adv. (dial. or coll.) extremely: confoundedly.—v.t. mor'talise, -ize to make mortal.—n. mortality (-tal'i-ti) condition of being mortal: death: frequency or number of deaths, esp. in proportion to population: the human race, nature, or estate.—adv. mor'tally. [L. mortālis—mori, to die.]

mortar mör'tər, n. a vessel in which substances are pounded with a pestle: a short piece of artillery for throwing a heavy shell, a bomb, a life-line, etc.: a mixture of cement, sand, and water.—v.t. to join or plaster with mortar: to bombard with a mortar.—mor'tar-board a square board, with a handle beneath, for holding mortar: a square-topped college cap. [O.E. mortere—L. mortārium, a mortar, matter pounded.]

mortgage mör'gij, n. a conditional conveyance of, or lien upon, land or other property as security for the performance of some condition (as the payment of money), becoming void on the performance of the condition: the act of conveying, or the deed effecting it: the amount of money advanced by a building society, bank, etc., on the security of one's property.—v.t. to pledge as security for a debt.—ns. mortgagee' one to whom a mortgage is made or given: one who gives or grants a mortgage; mort'gagor (-jər) one who mortgages his property.—Also (sometimes) mort'gager. [O.Fr.,—mort, dead, gage, a pledge.]

mortice. See mortise.

mortician mör-tish'ən, (U.S.) n. an undertaker. [L. mors, mortis, death.]

mortify mör'ti-fī, v.t. to destroy the vital functions of: to deaden: to subdue by severities and penance: to vex in a humiliating way.—v.i. to lose vitality: to become gangrenous: to be subdued: to practise asceticism:—pr p. mor'tifying; pa.t. and pa.p. mor'tified.—adj. mortif'ic death-bringing: deadly.—n. mortification (mör-ti-fi-kā'shən) act of mortifying or state of being mortified: the death of part of the body: a bringing under of the passions and appetites by a severe or strict manner of living: humiliation: chagrin: that which mortifies or vexes.—adj. mor'tified.—n. mor'tifier.—adj. and n. mor'tifying. [Fr. mortifier—L.L. mortificāre, to cause death to—mors, mortis, death, facēre, to make.]

mortise mör'tis, n. a hole made to receive a tenon—also mor'tice.—v.t. to cut a mortise in: to join by a mortise and tenon.—mor'tise-lock, mor'tice-lock a lock whose mechanism is covered by being sunk into the edge of a door, etc. [Fr. mortaise.]

mortmain mört'mān, (law) n. the transfer of property to a corporation, which is said to be a dead hand, i.e. one that can never part with it again. [Fr. morte (fem.), dead, main—L. manus, hand.]

mortuary mört'ū-ər-i, adj. connected with death or burial.—n. a place for the temporary reception of the dead. [L. mortuārius—mortuus, dead, mori, to die.]

norula mör'ū-lə, n. a solid spherical mass of cells resulting from the cleavage of an ovum.—adj. mor'ular. [L. mōrum, a mulberry.]

norwong mör'wong, n. an Australian and N.Z. food fish. [Native name.]

Mosaic mō-zā'ik, adj. pertaining to Moses, the great Jewish lawgiver.—n. Mō'saism.—Mosaic Law the law of the Jews given by Moses at Mount Sinai.

mosaic mō-zā'ik, n. the fitting together in a design of small pieces of coloured marble, glass, etc.: a piece of work of this kind: anything of similar appearance, or composed by the piecing together of different things: a leaf-mosaic: leaf-mosaic disease (or mosaic disease): a hybrid with the parental characters side by side and not blended.—adj. relating to, or composed of, mosaic.—adv. mosā'ically.—ns. mosā'icism (-i-sizm) presence side by side of patches of tissue of unlike constitution; mosā'icist (-i-sist) a worker in mosaic. [Fr. mosaïque —L.L. mosaicum, mūsaicum—mūsa—Gr. mousa, a muse; cf. L.L. mūsaeum or mūsivum (opus), mosaic (work).]

moschatel mos-kə-tel', n. a small plant (Adoxa moschatellina), with pale-green flowers and a supposed musky smell [Fr. moscatelle—It. moschatella—moscato, musk.]

Moselle mō-zel', n. white wine from the district of the river Moselle, with an aromatic flavour

Moses basket mō'zəz bäs'kit, a portable cot for babies. [Story of Moses in the bulrushes, Exod. ii. 3.]

mosey mō'zi, (slang) v.i. to move along gently: to jog: to make off: to hurry. [Perh for vamoose.]

moshav mō-shäv', n. an agricultural settlement in Israel: (also moshav ovdim ŏv-dēm') a joint association of privately-owned farms, on which machinery and marketing are usually operated communally:—pl. moshavim (-shə-vēm'), moshvei ovdim (mosh-vā'). [Heb., dwelling.]

Moslem moz'lem, -ləm, n. and adj. Same as Muslim.

mosque mosk, n. a Muslim place of worship. [Fr. mosquée—It. moschea—Ar. masjid (in N. Africa pron. masgid)—sajada (sagada), to pray.]

mosquito mos-kē'tō, n. loosely, any small biting or stinging insect: any of several long-legged insects of the family Culicidae, the females of which have their mouth-parts adapted for bloodsucking and can therefore transmit disease incl. malaria:—pl. mosqui'to(e)s.—mosquito canopy, curtain, net an arrangement of netting to keep out mosquitoes. [Sp. dim. of mosca, a fly—L musca.]

moss mos, n. boggy ground or soil: any of the Musci, a class of Bryophyta, small plants with simply constructed leaves, and no woody material, attached by rhizoids, the zygote growing into a small spore-bearing capsule that grows parasitically on the parent plant: a mass of such plants: a moss-like growth, covering, or excrescence: loosely extended to plants of similar appearance to true mosses.—v.t. to cover with moss: to clear of moss.—v.i. to gather moss.—n. moss'iness. —adj. moss'y overgrown or abounding with moss: like moss: boggy.—moss'-ag'ate chalcedony with moss-like inclusions of chlorite, manganese oxide, etc; moss'-back a person of antiquated views.—adj. moss'-grown covered with moss.—moss'land wet, peaty land; moss'plant a plant of moss: the sexual generation in the life-history of a moss, on which the asexual generation is parasitic; moss'-rose a variety of rose having a moss-like growth on and below the calyx; moss stitch a knitting stitch—alternate plain and purl stitches along each row and in succeeding rows; moss'-troop'er one of the freebooters that used to infest the mosses of the Border. [O.E. mōs, bog.]

mossbunker mos'bung-kər, n. the menhaden. [Du. mars-banker, the scad or horse-mackerel.]

mossie mos'i, mozzie moz'i, (coll.) ns. short for mosquito.

most mōst, adj. (superl. of more) greatest: in greatest quantity or number.—adv. in the highest degree: almost (U.S. and dial.; perhaps aphetic).—n. the greatest number or quantity.—adv. most'ly for the most part.—at (the) most at the utmost computation; for the most part chiefly: in the main. [The Northumbrian form mǎst may have occurred in O.E. beside the ordinary form *mæst*; or the vowel may come from analogy with the comparative; cf. Ger. *meist*.]

-most -*mōst* in composition, indicating superlative, e.g. *hindmost*, *farthermost*. [O.E. superl. suffix. -*mæst*, -*mest*.]

mot *mō*, (Fr.) *n*. a word: a pithy or witty saying.—le mot juste (*lə mō zhüst*) the word which fits the context exactly.

MOT em-ō-tē', *n*. a compulsory annual check made by order of the Ministry of Transport on vehicles of more than a certain age.—Also **MOT test**.

mote *mōt, n*. a particle of dust: a speck: a seed or other foreign particle in wool or cotton: a stain or blemish: anything very small.—*adjs.* **mōt'ed**, **mote'y** containing a mote or motes.—mote spoon a perforated spoon formerly used to remove tea-leaves from a tea-cup. [O.E. *mot*.]

motel *mō-tel', n*. hotel made up of units, each accommodating a car and occupants: a hotel with accommodation and servicing facilities for cars.—*n.* **motel'ler** owner or manager of a motel. [mo(tor), (ho)tel.]

motet, motett *mō-tet', n*. a polyphonic choral composition, usually unaccompanied, with biblical or similar prose text: loosely, an anthem or church cantata.—*n.* **motett'ist**. [Fr. *motet*, dim. of *mot*.]

motey. See mote.

moth *moth, n*. the cloth-eating larva of the clothes-moth: the imago of the same kind: any member of the Heterocera, a popular and unscientific division of the Lepidoptera, broadly distinguished from butterflies by duller colouring, thicker body, antennae not clubbed, wings not tilted over the back in rest, and by the habit of flying by night: that which eats away gradually and silently: a fragile, frivolous creature, readily dazzled into destruction (*fig.*): a light aero-plane:—*pl.* **moths** (*moths*).—*adjs.* **mothed** (*motht*) moth-eaten; **moth'y** full of moths: moth-eaten.—**moth'ball** a ball of naphthalene or other substance for keeping away clothes-moths.—*v.t.* to lay up in mothballs: to spray with a plastic and lay up (a ship, etc.): to lay aside temporarily, postpone work on, keep in readiness for eventual use.—*adjs.* **moth'-eaten** eaten or cut by moths (also *fig.*); **moth'-proof** (of clothes, etc.) chemically rendered resistant to moths.—Also *v.t.*—(put) in mothballs (to put) temporarily in abeyance. [O.E. *moththe, mohthe.*]

mother[1] *mudh'ər, n*. a female parent: a matron: that which has produced anything: the female head of a religious house or other establishment: a familiar term of address to, or prefix to the name of, an old woman: extended to an ancestress, a stepmother, mother-in-law, foster-mother.—*adj.* received by birth, as it were from one's mother: being a mother: acting the part of a mother: originating: used to produce others from.—*v.t.* to give birth to: to acknowledge, to adopt, to treat as a son or daughter: to foster: to attribute the maternity or authorship of (with *on* or *upon*): to find a mother for.—*ns.* **moth'erhood** state of being a mother; **moth'ering** a rural English custom of visiting the mother church or one's parents on Mid-Lent Sunday (Mothering Sunday).—*adj.* **moth'erless** without a mother.—*n.* **moth'erliness**.—*adj.* **moth'erly** pertaining to, or becoming, a mother: like a mother.—**moth'er-cell'** (*Biol.*) a cell that gives rise to others by division; **moth'er-church** the church from which others have sprung: a principal church; **moth'er-cit'y** one from which another was founded as a colony; **moth'er-coun'try, -land** the country of one's birth: the country from which a colony has gone out; **moth'ercraft** knowledge and skill required for care of child; **moth'er-fig'ure** an older woman who symbolises for

one the qualities and authority of one's mother; **moth'er-in-law** the mother of one's husband or wife:—*pl.* **moth'ers-in-law.**—**mother lode** (*mining*) the main lode of any system.—*adj.* **moth'er-na'ked** naked as at birth.—**moth'er-of-pearl** the nacreous internal layer of the shells in some molluscs (also *adj.*); **Mother's Day** a day for honouring of mothers, as, in U.S., second Sunday in May; also used for Mothering Sunday; **mother's help** one employed to help a mother with domestic duties, esp. the supervision of children; **moth'er-ship** a ship having charge of torpedo-boats or small craft: a ship which provides a number of other, usu. smaller, ships with services, supplies, etc.; **mother's (or mothers') ruin** (*slang*) gin; **mother superior** the head of a convent or any community of nuns; **moth'er-to-be'** a woman who is pregnant, esp. with her first child; **moth'er-tongue** native language: a language from which another has its origin; **moth'er-wa'ter** residual liquid, still containing certain chemical substances, left after others have been crystallised or precipitated from it; **moth'er-wit** native wit: common sense.—**be mother** (*facet.*) to pour the tea; **every mother's son** every man without exception; **Mother Carey's chicken, goose** the storm petrel, or similar bird; **the mother and father** (or **father and mother**) (**of**) (*coll.*) the biggest, greatest (usu. *fig.*), as in *the mother and father of an argument* (or *all arguments*). [O.E. *mōdor.*]

mother[2] *mudh'ər, n*. dregs: scum: a slimy mass of bacteria that oxidises alcohol into acetic acid (in full, **mother of vinegar**).—*v.i.* to become mothery.—*adj.* **moth'ery** like or containing mother. [Poss. the same as the foregoing; or poss.—Du. *modder*, mud; cf. **mud**.]

mothering, motherly. See mother[1].

motif *mō-tēf', n*. a theme or subject: an element in a composition, esp. a dominant element: a figure, subject, or leitmotif (*mus.*): an ornament added to a woman's garment, often symbolic. [Fr. *motif*; see **motive.**]

motile *mō'til*, in U.S. *-til, adj.* capable of moving spontaneously as a whole: characterised by motion.—*n.* **motility** (*-til'i-ti*). [L. *mōtus*, movement.]

motion *mō'shən, n*. the act, state, manner, of changing place: a single movement: change of posture: power of moving or of being moved: agitation: a working in the mind: a feeling: an emotion: a formal proposal put before a meeting: an application to a court, during a case before it, for an order or rule that something be done, esp. something incidental to the progress of the cause rather than its issue: evacuation of the intestine: a piece of mechanism: (in *pl.*) faeces.—*v.t.* to direct or indicate by a gesture: to move, propose: to give motion to.—*v.i.* to offer a proposal.—*adj.* **mō'tional**.—*n.* **mō'tionist** one who is skilled in motions.—*adj.* **mō'tionless** without motion.—**mō'tion-pic'ture** a cinematograph film; **motion sickness** same as travel sickness.—**go through the motions** to make a half-hearted attempt: to pretend; **laws of motion** Newton's three laws: (1) Every body continues in its state of rest, or of uniform motion in a straight line, except so far as it may be compelled by force to change that state; (2) Change of motion is proportional to force applied, and takes place in the direction of the straight line in which the force acts; (3) To every action there is always an equal and contrary reaction. [Fr. *motion*—L. *mōtiō, -ōnis*—*movēre, mōtum*, to move.]

motive *mō'tiv, adj.* causing motion: having power to cause motion: concerned with the initiation of action. —*n.* an incitement of the will: a consideration or emotion that excites to action.—*v.t.* **mo'tivate** to provide with a motive: to induce.—*n.* **motiva'tion** motivating force, incentive.—*adjs.* **motiva′tional** pertaining to motivation; **mo′tiveless**.—*n.* **mo′tivelessness**.—*adj.* **motiv′ic** of, having or concerning a musical motif.—*n.* **motiv′ity** power of moving or of producing motion.—**motivation(al) research** research into motivation, esp. into consumer reaction, carried out scientifically; **motive-power** the energy or source of the energy by which anything is operated. [L.L. *mōtīvus*—L. *movēre*, *mōtum*, to move.]

motley *mot′li*, *adj.* particoloured: variegated: made of, or dressed in, motley: heterogeneous.—*n.* a particoloured garb, such as a jester wore.

motocross *mō′tō-kros*, *n.* a form of scrambling, motorcycle racing round a very rough circuit. [**motor**.]

motor *mō′tar*, *n.* a mover: that which gives motion: a machine whereby some source of energy is used to give motion or perform work, esp. an internal-combustion engine or a machine for converting electrical into mechanical energy: a motor-car: a muscle, or a nerve, concerned in bodily movement.—*adj.* giving or transmitting motion: driven by a motor: of, for, with, relating to, motor vehicles: concerned with the transmission of impulses: initiating bodily movement: pertaining to muscular movement or the sense of muscular movement.—*v.t.* and *v.i.* to convey, traverse, or travel by a motor vehicle.—*adjs.* **mo′torable** of roads, able to be used by motor vehicles; **moto′rial** motory.—*n.* **motorisa′tion**, *-z-*.—*v.t.* **mo′torise**, *-ize* to furnish with, or adapt to the use of, a motor or motors: to interpret or imagine in terms of motor sensation.—*ns.* **mo′torist** one who drives a motor-car, esp. for pleasure; **moto′rium** that part of the nervous system concerned in movement.—*adj.* **mo′tory** causing, conveying, imparting motion: motor.—**mo′tor-bi′cycle**, **-bike**, **-boat**, **-bus**, **-car**, **-coach**, **-cy′cle**, **-launch**, **-lorr′y**, **-ship** one driven by a motor; **motorcade** (*mō′tar-kād*; after **cavalcade**) a procession of motorcars; **motor caravan** a motor vehicle with living, sleeping, etc. facilities, like a caravan; **mo′tor-cy′cling**; **mo′tor-cyclist**.—*adj.* **mo′tor-driven** driven by a motor.—**motor generator** an electrical generator driven by an electric motor, whereby one voltage, frequency or number of phases, i.e. those of the motor, can be used to produce a different voltage, frequency or number of phases, i.e. those of the generator; **mo′torman** a man who controls a motor, esp. that of a tram-car or electric train; **mo′tor-scoo′ter** a small motor-cycle, usu. with an engine of 150 h.p. or less; **mo′tor-trac′tion** the conveyance of loads, including passengers, by motor vehicles; **mo′tor-trac′tor** an internal-combustion engine for hauling loads, esp. for drawing agricultural implements; **mo′torway** a road for motor traffic, esp. one for fast traffic with no crossings on the same level.—**motorway madness** (*coll.*) reckless driving in bad conditions on motorways, esp. in fog. [L. *mōtor*—*movēre*, to move.]

motorail *mō′tō-rāl*, *n.* a system of carrying cars and passengers by train on certain routes. [**motor**.]

mottle *mot′l*, *v.t.* to variegate blotchily.—*n.* a blotched appearance, condition, or surface.—*adj.* **mott′led**.—*n.* **mott′ling**. [Prob. from **motley**.]

motto *mot′ō*, *n.* a short sentence or phrase adopted as representative of a person, family, etc., or accompanying a coat of arms: a passage prefixed to a book or chapter shadowing forth its matter: a scrap of verse or prose enclosed in a cracker or accompanying a sweetmeat:—*pl.* **mott′oes** (*-ōz*).—*adj.* **mott′o′d**, **mott′oed**. [It.,—L. *muttum*, a murmur.]

moue *mōō*,. (Fr.) *n.* a grimace of discontent, pout.

moufflon, **mouflon**, **muflon** *mōōf′lon*, *n.* a wild sheep of the mountains of Corsica, etc.: extended to large big-horned wild sheep of other kinds:—*pl.* **moufflon**, etc. or **-s**. [Fr. *mouflon*—L.L. *mufrō*, *-ōnis*.]

mouillé *mōō′yā*, *adj.* (of *l* and *n*) sounded in a liquid manner, palatalised—as *gl* in 'seraglio', *ñ* in 'señor'. [Fr. moistened.]

moujik *mōō-zhik′*, *mōō′zhik*, *n.* Same as **muzhik**.

mould¹ (*U.S.* **mold**) *mōld*, *n.* loose soft earth: earth, considered as the material of which the body is formed or to which it turns: the earth of the grave: soil rich in decayed matter.—*v.t.* to cover with soil.—*v.i.* **mould′er** to crumble to mould: to turn to dust: to waste away gradually.—*v.t.* to turn to dust.—*adj.* **mould′y** like, or of the nature of, mould.—**mould′-board** the curved plate in a plough which turns over the soil. [O.E. *molde*.]

mould² (*U.S.* **mold**) *mōld*, *n.* a woolly growth on bread, cheese, or other vegetable or animal matter: any one of various small fungi of different classes, forming such growths.—*v.i.* to become mouldy.—*v.t.* to cause or allow to become mouldy.—*n.* **mould′iness**.—*adj.* **mould′y** overgrown with mould: like mould: stale: musty. [M.E. *mowle*.]

mould³ (*U.S.* **mold**) *mōld*, *n.* a templet: matrix in which a cast is made: a formed surface from which an impression is taken: the foundation upon which certain manufactured articles are built up: a thing formed in a mould, esp. a jelly or blancmange: nature: form: model: a pattern: that which is or may be moulded.—*v.t.* to knead: to shape: to model: to form in a mould.—*adj.* **mould′able**.—*ns.* **mould′er**; **mould′ing** the process of shaping, esp. any soft substance: anything formed by or in a mould: an ornamental edging or band projecting from a wall or other surface, as a fillet, astragal, bead, etc.: a strip of wood that can be applied for the purpose.—**mould′ing-board** a baker's board for kneading dough. [O.Fr. *modle*, *molle* (Fr. *moule*)—L. *modulus*, a measure.]

moult (*U.S.* **molt**) *mōlt*, *v.i.* to cast feathers or other covering: to be shed.—*v.t.* to shed.—*n.* the act, process, condition, or time of moulting.—*n.* **moult′ing**. [O.E. (*bi*)*mūtian*, to exchange—L. *mūtāre*; the *l*, first a freak of spelling, afterwards sounded.]

mound¹ *mownd*, *n.* a bank of earth or stone raised as a protection: a hillock: a heap.—*v.t.* to fortify with an embankment: to heap in a mound.—**mound′-bird** a megapode, or bird of the Australian family Megapodidae, gallinaceous birds that build large mounds as incubators; **mound′-builder** one of the Indians who in early times built great mounds in the eastern United States: a mound-bird.

mound² *mownd*, *n.* a king's orb. [Fr. *monde*—L. *mundus*, the world.]

mount¹ *mownt*, *n.* a mountain (*arch.* except **Mount**, as prefix to a name): a small hill or mound, natural or artificial: a fleshy protuberance on the hand. [O.E. *munt*—L. *mōns*, *montis*, mountain.]

mount² *mownt*, *v.i.* to go up: to climb: to get upon horseback, bicycle, or the like: to extend upward: to extend backward in time: to rise in level or amount.—*v.t.* to climb, ascend: to get up on: to cover or copulate with: to cause to rise, to lift, raise, erect: to place upon anything high: to put on horseback, or the like: to furnish with an animal, bicycle, etc., to ride on: to fix in a setting, on a support, stand, or mount: to furnish with accessories: to put in position and state of readiness for use or exhibition: to stage: to carry, wear, or put on: to put into operation, carry out.—*n.* a rise: an act of mounting: manner of mounting: a step to mount by: a signal for mounting: a riding animal or cycle: that upon which a thing is placed or in which it is set for fixing, strengthening, embellishing, esp. the card surrounding a picture: the slide, cover-glass, etc., used in mounting an object for the microscope.—*adj.* **mount′ed** on horseback: furnished with horses: set on high: set up: set (also in composition).—*ns.* **mount′er**;

mount'ing; mount'y, mount'ie (*coll.*) a Canadian mounted policeman.—**mount'ing-block** a block or stone to enable one to mount a horse.—**mount guard** see **guard**. [Fr. *monter*, to go up—L. *mōns, montis*, mountain.]

mountain *mownt'in, n.* a high hill: a large quantity, excess, esp. of agricultural, dairy, etc. products bought up by an economic community to prevent a fall in prices.—*adj.* of a mountain: growing, dwelling, etc. on or among mountains.—*adj.* **mount'ained.**—*n.* **mountaineer'** an inhabitant of mountain country: a climber of mountains.—*v.i.* to climb mountains.—*n.* **mountaineer'ing** mountain climbing.—*adj.* **mount'-ainous** full of, characterised by, mountains: large as a mountain: huge.—**mount'ain-ash'** the rowan-tree; **mount'ain-cat'** a catamount, a wild-cat; **mount'ain-chain'** a range of mountains forming a long line; **mount'ain-dew'** whisky; **mount'ain-hare'** a smaller species of hare, grey in summer, usually white in winter.—*adv.* and *adj.* **mount'ain-high', mount'ains-high'** high as a mountain (hyperbolically).—**mount'-ain-lau'rel** kalmia; **mount'ain-li'on** the puma; **mount'ain-rail'way** a light narrow-gauge railway for mountainous regions, usually a rack-railway; **mount'-ain-sheep'** the bighorn of the Rocky Mountains; **mount'ain-sick'ness** sickness brought on by breathing rarefied air; **mount'ain-side** the slope of a mountain; **mount'ain-top.** [O.Fr. *montaigne*—L. *mōns, montis*, mountain.]

mountant *mownt'ənt, n.* an adhesive paste for mounting photographs, etc.: any substance in which specimens are suspended on a microscope slide. [Fr. *montant*, pr.p. of *monter*, to mount.]

mountebank *mown'ti-bangk, n.* a quack who harangues and plays the fool: a buffoon: a charlatan.—*v.i.* (or *it*) with *it*) to play the mountebank.—*ns.* **moun'tebankery, moun'tebanking, moun'tebankism.** [It. *montimbanco, montambanco*—*montare*, to mount, *in*, on, *banco*, bench.]

mourn *mōrn, mōrn, v.i.* to grieve: to be sorrowful: to wear mourning: to murmur as in grief.—*v.t.* to grieve for: to utter in a sorrowful manner.—*n.* **mourn'er** one who mourns: one who attends a funeral, especially a relative of the deceased: a person hired to lament or weep for the dead.—*adj.* **mourn'ful** causing, suggesting, or expressing sorrow: feeling grief.—*adv.* **mourn'fully.**—*n.* **mourn'fulness.**—*adj.* **mourn'ing** grieving: lamenting.—*n.* the act of expressing grief: the dress of mourners, or other tokens of mourning. —*adv.* **mourn'ingly.**—**mourn'ing-band** a band of black material worn round the sleeve to signify that one is in mourning; **mourn'ing-dove'** an American pigeon with plaintive note; **mourn'ing-stuff** a lustreless black dress fabric, as crape, cashmere, etc., for making mourning clothes.—**in mourning** wearing black (in China, white) in token of mourning: with eyes blackened (*slang*). [O.E. *murnan.*]

mousaka. Same as **moussaka.**

mouse *mows, n.* a little rodent animal (*Mus*) found in houses and in the fields: extended to various voles and other animals more or less like the mouse: a black eye, or discoloured swelling (*slang*): a timid, shy, colourless person:—*pl.* **mice** (*mīs*).—*v.i.* (*mowz*) to hunt for mice or as if for mice: to prowl.—*v.t.* to treat or to tear as a cat does a mouse.—*ns.* **mous'kin, mous'ie** a young or little mouse; **mouser** (*mowz'er*) a cat good at catching mice; **mousery** (*mows'ər-i*) a resort of mice.—*n.* and *adj.* **mousing** (*mowz'ing*).—*v.t.* **mousle** (*mowz'l*) to pull about roughly or disrespectfully.—*adj.* **mous(e)y** (*mows'i*) like a mouse in colour or smell: abounding with mice: noiseless, stealthy: of hair, limp and dull greyish-brown: of person, uninteresting, too unassertive.—**mouse'-colour**

the grey colour of a mouse.—*adjs.* **mouse'-colour, -ed.—mouse'-deer** a chevrotain.—**mouse-eared bat** a kind of bat, *Myotis myotis*, found chiefly in continental Europe and Western Asia; **mouse'-hole** a hole made or used by mice: a small hole or opening; **mouse'-trap** a trap for mice: any cheese of indifferent quality. [O.E. *mūs*, pl. *mȳs.*]

moussaka, mousaka *mōō-sä'ka, n.* a Greek dish consisting of minced meat, aubergines, tomatoes and cheese.

mousse *mōōs, n.* a dish made with whipped cream, eggs, etc., flavoured and usu. eaten cold. [Fr., moss.]

mousseline *mōōs-lēn', n.* fine French muslin: a very thin glassware: a claret-glass made of it.—**mousseline-de-laine** (-*də-len'*) an all-wool muslin; **mousseline-de-sole** (-*də-swä'*) a silk muslin.—**mousseline sauce** a kind of sauce hollandaise made light by added whipped cream or egg-white. [Fr.]

moustache, mustache *məs-, mus-, mōōs-täsh', n.* the hair upon the upper lip—also **mustachio** (-*tä'shō*; *pl.* **musta'chios**).—Also in *pl.*—*adj.* **moustached', mustach'ioed; moustach'ial.—moustache'-cup** a cup with the top partly covered, formerly used to keep the moustache from getting wet. [Fr. *moustache*—It. *mostaccio*—Doric Gr. *mystax, -ākos*, the upper lip, moustache.]

mouth *mowth, n.* the opening in the head of an animal by which it eats and utters sound: opening or entrance, as of a bottle, river, etc.: a consumer of food: a speaker: a spokesman: cry, voice, utterance: a wry face, a grimace: backchat, insolence:—*pl.* **mouths** (*mowdhz*).—*v.t.* (*mowdh*) to utter: to utter with exaggerated, affectedly pompous, or self-conscious action of the mouth: to form (words) silently by moving the lips: to declaim or spout: to take in the mouth.—*v.i.* to declaim, rant: to grimace.—*adjs.* **mouthable** (*mowdh'ə-bl*) lending itself to elocutionary utterance; **mouthed** (*mowdhd*) having a mouth.—*ns.* **mouther** (*mowdh'ər*) one who mouths; **mouth'ful** (*mowth'fəl*) as much as fills the mouth: a small quantity: a big word: a momentous utterance (*slang*):—*pl.* **mouth'fuls.—*adjs.* **mouth'less; mouthy** (*mowdh'i*) ranting: affectedly over-emphatic.— **mouth-breather** (*mowth'-brē'dhər*) one who habitually breathes through the mouth; **mouth'-breeder** a cichlid fish that carries its young in its mouth for protection.—*adj.* **mouth-filling** (*mowth'*) full-sounding. —**mouth'-harp** a mouth-organ; **mouth music** music (usually accompanying dance) sung, not played on instrument(s); **mouth'-organ** a small musical instrument encasing metallic reeds, played by the mouth— a harmonica; **mouth'piece** the piece of a musical instrument, tobacco-pipe, mask, etc., held to or in the mouth: a spokesman —*adj.* **mouth'-to-mouth'** of a method of artificial respiration in which a person breathes air directly into the patient's mouth to inflate the lungs.—**mouth'wash** an antiseptic solution for cleansing the mouth and for gargling with.—*adj.* **mouth'watering** causing the release of saliva in the mouth, highly appetising.—**be all mouth** (*slang*) to be unable to support one's boastful talk with action; **have a big mouth** (*coll.*) to (habitually) talk indiscreetly, loudly, or too much; **make a poor mouth** to profess poverty; **shoot one's mouth off** (*slang*) to talk freely, inaccurately, tactlessly, etc.; **shut, stop the mouth of** to silence. [O.E. *mūth.*]

move *mōōv, v.t.* to cause to change place or posture: to set in motion: to impel: to excite to action: to cause (the bowels) to be evacuated: to persuade: to instigate: to arouse: to provoke: to touch the feelings of: to propose formally before a meeting: to recommend. —*v.i.* to go from one place to another: to change place or posture: to walk, to carry oneself: to change residence: to make a motion as in an assembly: to begin to act: to take action: to become active or exciting (*coll.*): to go about one's activities, live one's life, pass one's time: in chess, draughts, etc., to transfer a piece in one's turn to another square:—*pr.p.* **mov'ing**; *pa.t.* and *pa.p.* **moved**.—*n.* an act of moving: a beginning of movement: a proceeding or step: play in turn, as at chess: turn to play, in chess, draughts, etc.: the manner in which a chessman, or the like, can be moved.—*adj.* **movable** (*mōōv'ə-bl*) **mobile**: changeable: not fixed.—Also (esp. *law*) **move'able**.—*n.* (esp. in *pl.*) a portable piece of furniture: a piece of movable or moveable property.—*ns.* **mov'ableness** (**move'ableness**); **mov(e)abil'ity**.—*adv.* **mov'ably** (**move'ably**).—*adj.* **move'less** motionless: immovable.—*adv.* **move'lessly**.—*ns.* **move'lessness** **move'ment** act or manner of moving: change of position: activity: impulse: the moving parts in a mechanism, esp. the wheelwork of a clock or watch: tempo or pace: a main division of an extended musical composition, with its own more or less independent structure: the suggestion of motion conveyed by a work of art: a general tendency or current of thought, opinion, taste or action, whether organised and consciously propagated or a mere drift; **mov'er**; **mov'ie**, **mov'y** (*slang*) a moving picture, a cinematograph film: a showing of such: (in *pl.*, **movies**, usu. with **the**) motion pictures in general, or the industry that provides them.—Also *adj.*—*adj.* **mov'ing** causing motion: changing position: affecting the feelings: pathetic.—*adv.* **mov'ingly**.—**movable feast** a church feast whose date depends on that of Easter, as Shrove-Tuesday, Good Friday, etc.; **moving pictures** the cinematograph: cinematograph films; **moving staircase** an escalator.—**get a move on** to hurry up: to make progress; **move heaven and earth** *see* **heaven**; **on the move** changing or about to change one's place: travelling: progressing. [A.Fr. *mover*, O.Fr. *movoir* (Fr. *mouvoir*)—L. *movēre*, to move.]

mow *mō*, *v.t.* to cut down, or cut the grass upon, with a scythe or a grass-cutting machine: to cut down in great numbers:—*pr.p.* **mow'ing**; *pa.t.* **mowed** (*mōd*); *pa.p.* **mowed** or **mown** (*mōn*).—*adjs.* **mowed**, **mown**. —*ns.* **mow'er** one who mows grass, etc.: a machine with revolving blades for mowing grass; **mow'ing** the act of cutting: land from which grass is cut.— **mow'ing-machine'**. [O.E. *māwan*.]

Moygashel® *moi'gə-shel*, *n.* (also found without *cap.*) a type of linen manufactured in Northern Ireland. [Placename.]

Mozartian, -ean *mō-tsär'ti-ən*, *adj.* of or like (the style, etc. of) Wolfgang Amadeus *Mozart* (1756–1791), Austrian composer.

mozzarella *mot-sə-rel'ə*, *n.* a softish Italian cheese. [It.]

mozzie. *See* **mossie.**

Mr, Mrs. *See* **Mister, Mistress.**

Ms. *miz*, *n.* a title substituted for **Mrs** or **Miss** before the name of a woman, to avoid distinguishing between the married and the unmarried.

MS. *See* **manuscript.**

mu *mū*, *mōō*, *mü*, *n.* the Greek letter M, μ, equivalent to M: used as a symbol for **micron** and **micro-** (2).— **mu-** (or **μ-**) **meson** a subatomic particle, classed formerly as the lightest type of meson, now as the heaviest type of lepton, having unit negative charge, now largely superseded by **mu'on** (*mū'* or *mōō'*) (*q.v.*). [Gr. *mȳ*.]

much *much* (*compar.* **more**; *superl.* **most**), *adj.* in great quantity.—*adv.* in a great degree: to a great extent: in nearly the same way: by far.—*n.* a great deal: anything of importance or worth.—*adv.* (*arch.* and *jocular*) **much'ly**.—(**as**) **much as** although, even

though; **make much of** *see* **make**; **much about it** something like what it usually is; **much of a muchness** just about the same value or amount; **not up to much** (*coll.*) not very good; **too much for** more than a match for; **too much of a good thing** more than can be tolerated. [M.E. *muche*, *muchel*—O.E. *micel*, *mycel*.]

mucid, mucilage. *See under* **mucus.**

muck *muk*, *n.* dung: manure: wet or clinging filth: anything contemptible or worthless: dirt, debris, rubble: rubbishy reading matter: a mess.—*v.t.* to clear of muck: to manure with muck: to befoul: to make a mess of, to bungle (with *up*).—*v.i.* (usu. with *about*; *coll.*) to potter: to act the fool.—*ns.* **muck'er** one who mucks: a coarse, unrefined person; **muck'iness**.—*adj.* **muck'y** nasty, filthy: of the nature of muck: like muck.—**muck'-heap** a dunghill; **muck'-midd'en**; **muck'-rake** a rake for scraping filth.—*v.i.* to seek out and expose scandals or supposed scandals, whether for worthy or unworthy motives.—**muck'-raker**; **muck'-raking**; **muck'-sweat** profuse sweat.—**make a muck of** (*coll.*) to make dirty: to mismanage, **muck in** (with) (*coll.*) to share with: to help, participate (in) [Prob. Scand.]

muckle *muk'l*, a Scottish form of **mickle.**

muckluck, mukluk, mucluc *muk'luk*, *n.* an Eskimo sealskin boot. [Eskimo.]

Mucor *mū'kər*, *n.* a genus of fungi including some of the commonest moulds (without *cap.*) any mould of this genus. [L., mould.]

mucus *mū'kəs*, *n.* the slimy fluid secreted by the mucous membrane of the nose or other parts.—*adjs.* **mu'cid** mouldy, musty; **muciferous** (*-sif'*) secreting or conveying mucus.—*n.* **mu'cigen** (*-si-jen*) a substance secreted by the cells of mucous membrane, converted into mucin.—*n.* **mu'cilage** (*-si-lij*) a gluey mixture of carbohydrates in plants: any sticky substance: gum used as an adhesive.—*adj.* **mucilaginous** (*-laj'*).—*ns.* **mucilag'inousness;** **mu'cin** any one of a class of albuminous substances in mucus.—*adjs.* **mucoid** (*mū'koid*) like mucus; **mucopū'rulent** of mucus and pus.—*ns.* **mucosa** (*mū-cō'za*) the mucous membrane: —*pl.* **mucō'sae** (*-sē*); **mucos'ity.**—*adjs.* **mu'cous** like mucus: slimy: viscous: producing mucus; **mu'culent** like mucus.—**mucous membrane** a lining of various tubular cavities of the body, with glands secreting mucus. [L. *mūcus*, nose mucus; cf. *mungĕre*, to wipe away.]

mud *mud*, *n.* wet soft earth: a mixture of earthy or clayey particles with water: a similar mixture with certain added chemicals used as a lubricant in drilling oil-wells: something worthless or contemptible.—*v.t* to bury in mud: to clog with mud: to plaster with mud: to befoul: to make turbid: to supply with mud.—*v.i.* to hide in the mud.—*adv.* **mudd'ily**.—*n.* **mudd'iness.** —*adj.* **mudd'y** foul with mud: containing mud: covered with mud: of the nature of mud: like mud: mud-coloured: confused: stupid.—*v.t.* and *v.i.* to make or become muddy:—*pr.p.* **mudd'ying**; *pa.t.* and *pa.p.* **mudd'ied.**—**mud'-bath** a bath in mud, esp. as a remedy: an outdoor event taking place in muddy conditions (*coll.*); **mud'-fish** a fish that burrows in mud, esp. a lung-fish; **mud'-flap** a flap fixed behind the wheels of a vehicle to prevent mud, etc., being thrown up behind; **mud'-flat** a muddy stretch submerged at high water; **mud'-guard** a screen to catch mud-splashes from a wheel; **mud'-hole** a hole with mud in it: an opening for removing sediment from a boiler, etc.; **mud'lark** a name for various birds that frequent mud: one who picks up a living along the banks of tidal rivers: a street-arab.—*v.i.* to work or play in mud.—**mud'pack** a cosmetic paste one ingredient of which is fuller's earth; **mud'-pie** a moulded mass of mud made by children in play, **mud'-pupp'y** (*U S*) the axolotl a hellbender, **mud'-skipper** a goby that can skip about on bare mud, **mud'-slinger; mud'-slinging** vilification; **mud'-volca'no** a vent that emits mud —**clear as mud** not at all clear, **his, her,** etc , **name is mud** he, she, etc , is out of favour, **mud in your eye** good health' (used as a toast), **throw, fling mud at** to insult, to slander [Cf Old Low Ger *mudde*, Du *modder*]

muddle *mud'l*, *v t* to render muddy· to confuse to bungle to mix —*v.i* to potter about· to blunder —*n* confusion, mess mental confusion, bewilderment — *n* **mudd'lehead** a blockhead.—*adj* **muddlehead'ed.** —*adv* **muddlehead'edly.**—*ns* **muddlehead'edness; mudd'ler.**—**muddle away** to squander or fritter away confusedly; **muddle through** to get through difficulties blunderingly [Freq of **mud.**]

mueddin. See **muezzin.**

muesli *mōō'zli*, *mu'zli*, *n.* a dish of rolled oats, nuts, fruit, etc. eaten esp. as a breakfast cereal [Swiss Ger]

muezzin *mōō-ez'in*, *n.* the Muslim official who calls to prayer —Also **muedd'in.** [Ar *mu'adhdhin*]

muff[1] *muf*, *n.* a cylinder of fur or the like for keeping the hands warm· a similar contrivance for the feet, ear, etc [Prob. from Du *mof*]

muff[2] *muf*, *n.* one who is awkward or unskilful, esp in sport. a duffer: a bungler· an unpractical person· a failure, esp to hold a ball —*v t.* to perform awkwardly to bungle· to miss.—*v.i* to act clumsily, esp in letting a ball slip out of the hands [Poss. **muff**[1].]

muffin *muf'in*, *n.* a soft, porous cake, eaten hot, with butter.—**muff'in-man** one who goes round selling muffins

muffle[1] *muf'l*, *n.* the thick naked upper lip and nose, as of a ruminant. [Fr. *mufle.*]

muffle[2] *muf'l*, *v t.* to envelop, for warmth, concealment, stifling of sound, etc : to deaden or dull the sound of.—*n.* a means of muffling: a receptacle, oven, or compartment in which things can be heated in a furnace without contact with the fuel and its products· a muffled state· a muffled sound —*adj.* **muff'-led.**—*n.* **muff'ler** a scarf for the throat: any means of muffling· one who muffles: a silencer (*U.S*) [App. Fr *mouffle*, mitten.]

muflon. See **moufflon.**

mufti *muf'ti*, *n* an expounder of Muslim law: the civilian dress of one who wears a uniform when on duty· plain clothes: a civilian [Ar. *muftī.*]

mug[1] *mug*, *n.* a cup with more or less vertical sides· its contents—*n* **mug'ful** (*-fəl*):—*pl.* **mug'fuls.**

mug[2] *mug*, *n* the face: the mouth —**mug'shot, mug shot** (*coll.*) a photograph of a person's face, esp one taken for police records [Poss. from the grotesque face on a drinking-mug.]

mug[3] *mug*, (*coll.*) *n.* a simpleton: an easy dupe.—a mug's game something only fools would do

mug[4] *mug*, (*coll.*) *v t.* and *v i.* (often with *up*) to study hard: to swot up

mug[5] *mug*, (*slang*) *v t.*, *v.i* to attack from behind, seizing by the throat: to attack suddenly with the intention of robbing —*ns* **mugg'er; mugg'ing.** [Perh **mug**[2].]

muggins *mug'inz*, *n* a children's card-game· a form of dominoes· a simpleton

muggy *mug'i*, *adj* foggy close and damp, as weather [Perh. O N *mugga*, mist]

mugwort *mug'wûrt*, *n* a common British wormwood [O E. *mucgwyrt*, lit midge-wort]

mugwump *mug'wump*, *n* an Indian chief· a person of great importance, or one who thinks himself so. [Algonquian *mugquomp*, a great man.]

Muhammedan. See Mohammedan.

mujik. See muzhik.

mukluk. See muckluck.

mulatto *mū-lat'ō*, *n* the offspring of a Negro and a person of European stock (also *adj*)·—*pl* **mulatt'os:** —*fem* **mulatt'a, mulatt'ress.** [Sp *mulato*, dim of *mulo*, mule, Fr *mulâtre*]

mulberry *mul'bar-i*, *n* the edible multiple fruit of any tree of the genus Morus (family Moraceae)· the tree bearing it, with leaves on which silkworms feed extended to various fruits or plants more or less similar superficially or really the colour of the fruit, dark purple —*adj* mulberry-coloured [Prob O H G *mulberi* (Mod Ger *Maulbeere*)—L *mōrum*]

mulch, mulsh *mulch, mulsh, ns* loose material, strawy dung, etc , laid down to protect the roots of plants — *v t* to cover with mulch —*adj* soft [Cf Ger dial *molsch*, soft, beginning to decay; O E *melsc*]

mulct *mulkt*, *n* a fine· a penalty —*v t* to fine to swindle to deprive (with *of*)·—*pa p* **mulct'ed, mulct.** [L *mulcta*, a fine]

mule[1] *mūl*, *n* the offspring of the ass and horse (esp he-ass and mare): a hybrid· a cross between a canary and another finch: a cotton-spinning machine· an obstinate person —*adj* hybrid —*n.* **muleteer** (*mūl-i-tēr'*) a mule-driver.—*adj.* **mul'ish** like a mule obstinate —*adv* **mul'ishly.**—*n* **mul'ishness.** [O.E. *mūl*—L *mūlus* was superseded by O.Fr *mul* (masc ; in Mod Fr the dim *mulet* is used), *mule* (fem)—L *mūlus, mūla*]

mule[2] *mūl*, *n* a loose slipper. [Fr *mule*]

mulga *mul'gə*, *n* an Australian acacia, typically found in arid, uninhabited regions.—**mulga wire** (*Austr.*) bush telegraph [Native word.]

muliebrity *mū-li-eb'ri-ti*, *n.* womanhood. [L *muliebritās, -tātis—mulier*, a woman.]

mull[1] *mul*, (*Scot.*) *n.* a promontory [Prob Gael. *maol* or O N. *mūli*, snout.]

mull[2] *mul*, *n.* a soft muslin.—Also **mul'mul(l).** [Hind. *malmal*.]

mull[3] *mul*, *v i.* (often with *over*) to cogitate, ponder, turn over in the mind

mull[4] *mul*, *v t.* to warm, spice, and sweeten (wine, ale, etc.).—*adj* **mulled.**—*n.* **mull'er.**

mullah *mul'ə, mōō'l'ə*, *n.* a Muslim learned in theology and law: a Muslim schoolmaster or teacher· a fanatical preacher of war on the infidel. [Pers., Turk , Hind *mullā*—Ar. *maulā*.]

mullein *mul'in*, *n* a tall, stiff, yellow-flowered woolly plant (Verbascum)—popularly known as *hag-taper, Adam's flannel, Aaron's rod, shepherd's club* [A Fr. *moleine*.]

muller *mul'ər*, *n.* a pulverising tool. [Perh. O.Fr *moloir—moldre* (Fr *moudre*), to grind.]

mullet *mul'it*, *n* a fish of the genus Mugil, palatable, nearly cylindrical: another fish (*Mullus*), slightly compressed—**red mullet.** [O.Fr. *mulet*, dim.—L. *mullus*, red mullet]

mulligatawny *mul-i-gə-to'ni*, *n.* an East Indian curry-soup. [Tamil *milagu-tannīr*, pepper-water]

mullion *mul'yən*, *n* an upright division between the lights of windows, etc.—*adj* **mull'ioned.**

mullock *mul'ək*, *n.* rubbish, esp. mining refuse [From obs. or dial. *mull*, dust, cf. O.E *myl*]

mulmul(l). See mull[2].

mulsh. Same as **mulch.**

mult(i)-, *-mult-*, *-mul-ti-*, in composition, much, many. —*adjs* **multang'ular** having many angles; **multicell'-ular** having or made up of many cells.—*n* **multicolour** (*mul'ti-kul-ər*) diversity or plurality of colour —*adj* many-coloured —*adj.* **mul'ticoloured; multiden'tate** many-toothed, **multidigitate** (*-dij'i-tāt*) many-fingered, **multidimen'sional** (*math.*) of more than three dimensions; **multidisciplin'ary** involving a combination of several (academic) disciplines, methods, etc.; **multifac'eted** (of a gem) having many facets: having many aspects, characteristics, etc.—*n.* **mul'tifil** a multiple strand of synthetic fibre (also **multifil'ament**).—*adjs.* **multiflo'rous** many-flowered, **multifo'liate** with many leaves; **mul'tiform** having many forms, polymorphic.—*n.* that which is multiform.—*ns* **multiform'ity; mul'tihull** a sailing vessel with more than one hull.—*adjs* **multilat'eral** many-sided: with several parties or participants.—*ns.* **multilat'eralism; multilat'eralist** one who favours multilateral action, esp. in abandoning or reducing production of nuclear weapons.—*adjs* **multilineal** (-*lin'*), **multilin'ear** having many lines; **multilingual** (-*ling'gwal*) in many languages: speaking several languages: (of a country, state, or society) in which several languages are spoken —*n.* **multimé'dia** the use of a combination of different media of communication (in e.g. entertainment, education): simultaneous presentation of several visual and/or sound entertainments.—Also *adj.*—*ns* **multimillionaire'** one who is a millionaire several times over; **multinat'ional** a large business company which operates in several countries.—*adj.* of this type of company.— **multi-own'ership** ownership of property on the principle of time-sharing (q.v.) —*adj.* **multipar'tite**, divided) divided into many parts: much cut up into segments.—*n.* **mul'tiplex** (*telecomm.*) a system enabling two or more signals to be sent simultaneously on one communications channel —Also *adj.*—*ns.* **mul'tiplexer; multipro'gramming** (*comput.*) a technique of handling several programs simultaneously by interleaving their execution through time-sharing.— *adjs.* **mul'tipur'pose; multira'cial** embracing, consisting of, many races.—*n.* **multira'cialism** the policy of recognising the rights of all in a multiracial society. —*adjs.* **mul'ti-stage** in a series of distinct parts: of a rocket, consisting of a number of parts that fall off in series at predetermined places on its course; **mul'titor(e)y; mul'ti-track** of a recording, made up of several different tracks blended together.—*ns.* **multivā'lence** (or -*tiv'ə-*), **multivā'lency** (or -*tiv'ə-*). —*adj.* **multivā'lent** (or -*tiv'ə-; chem.*) having a valency greater than one. [L. *multus*, much.]

multifarious *mul-ti-fā'ri-əs, adj.* having great diversity: made up of many parts: manifold: in many rows or ranks (*bot.*).—*adv.* **multifa'riously.**—*n.* **multifa'riousness** the state of being multifarious: multiplied variety. [L. *multifārius*; poss. from *fāri*, to speak.]

multipara *mul-tip'ər-ə, n.* a woman who has given birth for the second or later time, or is about to do so—opp. to *primipara.*—*n.* **multiparity** (-*par'i-ti*) condition of being a multipara: condition of being multiparous.— *adj.* **multip'arous** pertaining to a multipara: producing more than one at a birth (*zool.*). [multi-, -*para*—L. *parĕre*, to bring forth.]

multiple *mul'ti-pl, adj.* consisting of many elements or components, esp. of the same kind: manifold: compound: multiplied or repeated: allowing many messages to be sent over the same wire (*teleg.*).—*n* a quantity which contains another an exact number of times.—*adv.* **multiply** (*mul'ti-pli*).—*adj.* **mul'tiple-choice'** of an examination question, accompanied by several possible answers from which the correct answer is to be chosen.—**multiple cinema** a cinema which has been converted into two or more separate cinemas; **multiple fruit** a single fruit formed from several flowers in combination, as a pineapple, fig, mulberry; **multiple sclerosis** disseminated sclerosis; **multiple shop, store** one of many shops belonging to the same firm, often dispersed about the country;

multiple star group of stars so close as to seem one.— **common multiple** number or quantity, that can be divided by each of several others without a remainder; **least common multiple** the smallest number that forms a common multiple. [Fr.;—L.L *multiplus*—root of L *plēre*, to fill.]

multiplex[1] *mul'ti-pleks, adj.* multiple [L. *multiplex* —*plicāre*, to fold.]

multiplex[2]. See under **mult(i)-**.

multiply *mul'ti-pli, v.t.* to increase the number of: to accumulate: to reproduce: to obtain the product of (*math*).—*v.i.* to become more numerous: to be augmented: to reproduce: to perform the mathematical process of multiplication:—*pr.p.* **mul'tiplying;** *pa t* and *pa.p.* **mul'tiplied.**—*adjs* **mul'tipliable, mul'tiplicable** (or -*plik'*).—*n.* **mul'tiplicand** (or -*kand'*) a quantity to be multiplied by another.—*adj.* **mul'tiplicate** (or *tip'*) consisting of more than one: in many folds.—*n.* the condition of being in many copies: one of these copies.—*n.* **multiplica'tion** the act of multiplying or increasing in number: increase of number of parts by branching (*bot.*): the rule or operation by which quantities are multiplied.—*adj.* **mul'tiplicative** (or -*plik'ə-tiv*) tending or having power to multiply.—*ns.* **mul'tiplicator** (*math.*) a multiplier; **multiplicity** (-*plis'i-ti*) the state of being manifold: a great number; **mul'tiplier** one who multiplies: a quantity by which another is multiplied: a device or instrument for intensifying some effect.— **multiplication table** a tabular arrangement giving the products of pairs of numbers usually up to 12. [Fr. *multiplier*—L. *multiplicāre*—*plicāre*, to fold.]

multiply[2] *mul'ti-pli.* See under **multiple.**

multitude *mul'ti-tūd, n.* the state of being many: a great number: a crowd: the mob.—*adj.* **multitud'inous.**—*adv.* **multitud'inously.**—*n.* **multitud'inousness.** [L. *multitūdō, -inis—multus.*]

mum[1] *mum, adj.* silent.—*n* silence.—*interj.* not a word.—*v.i.* (also **mumm**) to act in dumb show: to act in a mummers' play: to masquerade:—*pr.p.* **mumm'ing;** *pa.t.* and *pa.p.* **mummed.**—*ns.* **mumm'er** an actor in a folk-play, usu at Christmas: a masquerader: an actor; **mumm'ery** mumming: great show without reality: foolish ceremonial; **mumm'ing.**— **mum's the word** not a word. [An inarticulate sound with closing of the lips; partly O.Fr. *momer*, to mum, *momeur*, mummer.]

mum[2] *mum, mummy mum'i, ns.* childish words for mother. [Cf. **mamma**[1].]

mum[3] *mum.* See **ma'am.**

mumble *mum'bl, v.t.* and *v.i* to say, utter, or speak indistinctly, softly, or perfunctorily: to mouth with the lips, or as with toothless gums.—*n.* **mum'bler.**— *n.* and *adj.* **mum'bling.**—*adv.* **mum'blingly.** [Frequentative from **mum**[1].]

Mumbo-jumbo *mum'bō-jum'bō, n.* a god or bugbear of West Africa: (without *cap.*) any object of foolish worship or fear: mummery or hocus-pocus:—*pl.* **mum'bo-jum'bos.** [Said to be Mandingo.]

mummy[1] *mum'i, n.* an embalmed or otherwise preserved dead body: the substance of such a body, formerly used medicinally: dead flesh: anything pounded to a formless mass: a bituminous drug or pigment.—*v.t.* to mummify:—*pr.p.* **mumm'ying;** *pa.t.* and *pa.p.* **mumm'ied.**—*ns.* **mumm'ia** mummy as a drug; **mummifica'tion.**—*adj.* **mumm'iform.**—*v.t* **mumm'ify** to make into a mummy:—*pr.p.* **mumm'-ifying;** *pa t.* and *pa.p.* **mumm'ified.** [O.Fr *mumie* —L.L. *mumia*—Ar. and Pers *mūmiyā*—Pers. *mūm*, wax]

mummy[2]. See **mum**[2].

mump *mump, v.i.* (*dial.*) to mumble. to sponge: to sulk: to mope: to grimace —*n.* **mump'er.**—*adj.*

mump'ish having mumps: dull: sullen.—*adv.* **mump'-ishly.**—*n.* **mump'ishness.**—*n. sing.* mumps an acute infectious disease characterised by a painful swelling of the parotid gland: gloomy silence. [Cf. **mum**[1] and Du. *mompen*, to cheat.]

munch *munch, munsh, v.t.* and *v.i.* to chew with marked action of the jaws, esp. with a crunching noise.—*n.* **munch'er.** [Prob. imit.]

mundane *mun-dān', adj.* worldly: earthly: cosmic: ordinary, banal.—*adv.* **mundane'ly.**—*n.* **mundanity** (*-dan'i-ti*). [L. *mundānus—mundus*, the world.]

mung bean *mŏong, mung, bēn,* a leguminous Asian plant, *Phaseolus aureus,* or its seeds, grown for forage and as a source of bean sprouts. [Hindi *mūng.*]

mungo *mung'gō, n.* the waste produced in a woollen-mill from hard spun or felted cloth, or from tearing up old clothes, used in making cheap cloth:—*pl.* **mun'gos.**

municipal *mū-nis'i-pl, adj.* pertaining to home affairs: pertaining to (the government of) a borough, town or city.—*n.* **municipalisa'tion, -z-.**—*v.t.* **munic'ipalise, -ize** to erect into a municipality: to bring under municipal control or ownership.—*ns.* **munic'ipalism** concern for the interests of one's municipality: belief in municipal control; **municipality** (*-pal'i-ti*) a self-governing town: a district governed like a city.—*adv.* **munic'ipally.** [L. *mūnicipālis—mūniceps, -ipis,* an inhabitant of a *mūnicipium,* a free town—*mūnia,* official duties, *capēre,* to take.]

munificence *mū-nif'i-səns, n.* magnificent liberality in giving: bountifulness.—*adj.* **munif'icent.**—*adv* **munif'icently.** [L. *mūnificentia—mūnus,* a present, *facēre,* to make.]

munify *mū'ni-fī, v.t.* to fortify. [L. *mūnīre,* to fortify, *facēre,* to make.]

muniment *mū'ni-mənt, n.* a means of defence: a record fortifying or making good a claim: (in *pl.*) furnishings, equipment, things provided.—*v.t.* **munit'ion** to supply with munitions.—*ns.* **munition** (*-nish'ən*; commonly in *pl.*) fortification: defence: material used in war: weapons: military stores; **munitioneer', munit'ion-work'er** a worker engaged in making munitions. [L. *mūnīre, -ītum,* to fortify; *mūnīmentum,* fortification, later, title-deeds—*moenia,* walls.]

Munro *mun-rō', n.* a designation orig. of Scottish (now also English, Irish and Welsh) mountains over 3000 feet:—*pl.* **Munros'.** [Orig. list made by H.T *Munro.*]

muntjak, muntjac *munt'jak, n.* a name for a group of small deer of the Oriental region. [From the Malay name.]

muon. See **mu.**—*adj.* **mūon'ic.**—*n.* **muonium** (*mū-ōn'i-əm*), an isotope of hydrogen.—**muonic atom** (*mū-on'ik*) a hydrogen-like atom, formed by the slowing-down of an energetic muon by ionisation as it traverses matter.

muraena, murena *mū-rē'nə, n.* a favourite food-fish of the Romans, a moray: **Muraena** the moray genus, giving name to a family of eels, **Murae'nidae.** [L. *mūraena;* see **moray.**]

mural *mū'rəl, adj.* of, on, attached to, or of the nature of, a wall.—*n.* mural decoration, esp. painting.— **mural painting** a painting executed, especially in distemper colours, upon the wall of a building. [L *mūrālis—mūrus,* a wall.]

murder *mûr'dər, n.* the act of putting a person to death intentionally and unlawfully: excessive or reprehensible slaughter not legally murder: hyperbolically, torture, excessive toil or hardship.—*v.t.* to kill (ordinarily a person) unlawfully with malice aforethought: to slaughter: hyperbolically, to torture: to beat, defeat utterly (*coll.*): to destroy (*coll.*): to mangle in performance (*coll.*).—*n.* **mur'derer:—**

fem. **mur'deress.**—*adj.* **mur'derous.**—*adv.* **mur'der-ously.**—**cry, scream blue murder** (*coll.*) to make an exaggerated outcry; **get away with murder** to do as one pleases yet escape punishment or censure; **murder will out** murder cannot remain hidden: the truth will come to light. [O.E. *morthor—morth,* death.]

murena. See **muraena.**

Murex *mū'reks, n.* a genus of gasteropod molluscs, some of which yielded purple dye: (without *cap.*) a mollusc of this genus.—*pl.* **mu'rexes, mu'rices** (*-ri-sēz*). [L. *mūrex, -icis.*]

Muridae *mū'ri-dē, n.pl.* the mouse family. [L. *mūs, mūris,* a mouse.]

murine *mūr'īn, -in, adj.* mouselike: of the mouse family or subfamily.—*n.* a murine animal. [L *mūrīnus—mūs, mūris,* mouse.]

murk, mirk *mûrk, n.* darkness (*lit., fig.*).—*adj.* dark gloomy: obscure.—*adv.* **murk'ily.**—*n.* **murk'iness.**—*adj.* **murk'ish.**—*adjs.* **murk'some; murk'y** dark obscure: gloomy. [O.E. *mirce* (n. and adj.).]

murmur *mûr'mər, n.* a low, indistinct sound, like tha of running water: an abnormal rustling sound from the heart, lungs, etc.: a muttered or subdued grumble or complaint.—*v.i.* to utter a murmur: to grumble.— *v.t.* to say or utter in a murmur.—*ns.* **murmura'tion** murmuring; **mur'murer.**—*n.* and *adj.* **mur'muring.**— *adv.* **mur'muringly.**—*adj.* **mur'murous.**—*adv.* **mur'murously.** [Fr. *murmure*—L. *murmur;* cf. Gr. *mor mÿrein,* to surge.]

murphy *mûr'fi, (coll.) n.* a potato:—*pl.* **mur'phies** [From the common Irish name *Murphy.*]

murrain *mur'in, -ən, n* a cattle-plague, esp foot-anc mouth disease.—*adj.* affected with murrain.—*adj.* **murr'ained.** [O.Fr. *morine,* pestilence, carcass.]

murram *mur'əm.* Same as **marram.**

Musak. See **Muzak.**

Musca *mus'kə, n.* the house-fly genus.—*adj.* **musci** (*mus'id*) of the house-fly family **Muscidae** (*mus'i-dē* —n. a member of the family.—*muscae volitante* (*mus'ē vol-i-tan'tēz, mŏŏs'kī wo-li-tan'tās;* L., flu tering flies) ocular spectra like floating black spo before the eyes. [L. *musca,* a fly.]

muscadel *mus-kə-del', mus'.* Same as **muscatel.**

muscat *mus'kat, n.* muscatel wine. a musky grape or i vine [Prov. *muscat.*]

muscatel *mus-kə-tel', or mus', n.* a rich spicy wine, various kinds: a grape of musky smell or taste: th vine producing it: a raisin from the muscatel grape.- Also **muscadel.** [O.Fr. *muscatel, muscadel*—Pro *muscat,* musky.]

Musci *mus'ī, n.pl.* mosses, one of the two gre divisions of the Bryophyta, the other being th Hepaticae or liverworts.—*n.* **muscology** (*-kol'ə-* bryology.—*adjs.* **mus'coid** (*-koid*), **mus'cose** mos like. [L. *muscus,* moss.]

muscid. See **Musca.**

muscle *mus'l, n.* a contractile structure by which bodi movement is effected: the tissue forming it: bodi strength: power, strength of other kinds (financi political, etc.) (*coll.*).—*v.i.* to force one's wa thrust.—*adj.* **muscled** (*mus'ld*) having muscles. *n.* **musc'ling,** delineation of muscles, as in a pictu —*adj.* **muscular** (*mus'kū-lər*) pertaining to a musc consisting of muscles: having strong muscles. brawi strong: vigorous.—*n.* **muscularity** (*-lar'i-ti*).—*ac* **mus'cularly.**—*ns.* **muscula'tion** muscular actic musculature; **mus'culature** provision, disposition a system of muscles.—*adj.* **musc'le-bound** having t muscles stiff and enlarged by over-exercise.— **musc'le-man,** a man of extravagant physical devel ment, esp. one employed as an intimidator.—A *fig.*—**muscular dystrophy** (*dis'trə-fī*) any of the for of a hereditary disease in which muscles progr sively deteriorate.—**muscle in** (*coll.*) to push in: to grab a share. [Fr. *muscle*, or directly—L. *mūsculus*, dim. of *mūs*, a mouse, muscle.]

muscology, muscoid, muscose. See **Musci.**

muscovado *mus-kō-vä'dō*, *n.* unrefined sugar, after evaporating the cane-juice and draining off the molasses:—*pl.* **muscova'dos.** [Sp. *mascabado.*]

Muscovy *mus'kə-vi*, (*hist.*) *n.* the old principality of Moscow: extended to Russia in general.—*ns.* and *adjs.* **Muscovian** (*-kō'vi-ən*) Muscovite; **Mus'covite** of Muscovy: Russian: a Russian.—**mus'covy-duck** see **musk.** [*Moscovia*, Latinised from Russ. *Moskva*, Moscow.]

muscular. See **muscle.**

muse *mūz*, *v.i.* to study in silence: to be absent-minded: to meditate.—*v.t.* to meditate on: to say musingly.—*n.* deep thought: contemplation: a state or fit of absence of mind.—*adje.* **mused** bemused, muzzy, fuddled; **muse'ful** meditative.—*adv.* **muse'-fully.**—*n.* **mus'er.**—*n.* and *adj.* **mus'ing.**—*adv.* **mus'ingly.** [Fr. *muser*, to loiter, in O.Fr. to muse.]

Muse *mūz*, *n.* one of the nine goddesses of the liberal arts—daughters of Zeus and Mnemosyne (**Calliope** of epic poetry; **Clio** of history; **Erato** of love poetry; **Euterpe** of music and lyric poetry; **Melpomene** of tragedy; **Polyhymnia** of sacred lyrics; **Terpsichore** of dancing; **Thalia** of comedy; **Urania** of astronomy): an inspiring goddess more vaguely imagined: poetic character: poetry or art. [Fr.,—L. *Mūsa*—Gr. *Mousa.*]

museology, museology. See **museum.**

musette *mū-zet'*, *n.* an old French bagpipe: a small (esp. army) knapsack. [Fr., dim. of *muse*, a bagpipe.]

museum *mū-zē'əm*, *n.* orig. a temple, home or resort of the Muses: a place of study: a resort of the learned: an institution or repository for the collection, exhibition, and study of objects of artistic, scientific, historic, or educational interest: a collection of curiosities: —*pl.* **muse'ums.**—*ns.* **museol'ogist; museol'ogy** the study of museums and their organisation.—**muse'um-piece** a specimen so fine as to be suitable for exhibition in a museum, or so old-fashioned as to be unsuitable for anything else. [L. *mūsēum*—Gr. *mouseion*; see **Muse.**]

mush[1] *mush*, *n.* meal boiled in water: anything pulpy: sloppy sentimentality (*coll.*): rubbish.—*v.t.* to reduce to mush: to crush the spirit of, wear out (*dial.*).—*adv.* **mush'ily.**—*n.* **mush'iness.**—*adj.* **mush'y.** [Prob. **mash.**]

mush[2] *mush*, (*Can.* and *U.S.*) *v.i.* to travel on foot with dogs over snow.—*n.* a journey of this kind.—*interj.* and *imper.* a command to dogs to start moving or move faster.—*n.* **mush'er.** [Prob. Fr. *marcher*, to walk.]

mushroom *mush'rōōm*, *n.* an edible fungus (*Agaricus*, or *Psalliota*, *campestris*, or kindred species) of toadstool form: any edible fungus: any fungus of umbrella shape whether edible or not: any fungus: an object shaped like a mushroom: anything of rapid growth and decay (*fig.*).—*adj.* of or like a mushroom.—*v.i.* to expand like a mushroom cap: to gather mushrooms: to increase, spread with disconcerting rapidity.—*n.* **mush'roomer.**—**mushroom cloud** a mushroom-shaped cloud, esp. one resulting from a nuclear explosion. [O.Fr. *mousseron*, perh. *mousse*, moss, which may be of Germanic origin.]

music *mū'zik*, *n.* the art of expression in sound, in melody, and harmony, including both composition and execution: sometimes specially of instrumental performance to the exclusion of singing: the science underlying it: the performance of musical compositions: compositions collectively: a connected series of (sweet) sounds: melody or harmony: pleasing sound: sound of definite pitch, not mere noise: written or printed representation of tones, expression, etc., or of what is to be played or sung: sheets or books of parts or scores collectively: harmonious character.— *adj.* of or for music.—*v.i.* to perform music:—*pr.p.* **mu'sicking.**—*adj.* **mu'sical** pertaining to, of, with, or producing, music: pleasing to the ear: of definite pitch (unlike mere noise): melodious: having skill in, or aptitude or taste for, music.—*n.* a musical person, party, or performance, esp. a theatrical performance or film in which singing and usu. dancing play an important part—a successor to musical comedy with less frivolous plot.—*ns.* **musicale** (*mū-zi-käl'*,) a social gathering with music, or the programme of music for it; **musicality** (*-al'i-ti*).—*adv.* **mu'sically.**— *ns.* **mu'sicalness; musician** (*mū-zish'ən*) one skilled in music: a performer or composer of music, esp. professional.—*adj.* **musi'cianly** characteristic of, or becoming, a musician.—*n.* **musi'cianship.**—*adj.* **musicolog'ical.**—*ns.* **musicol'ogist; musicol'ogy** academic study of music in its historical, scientific, and other aspects; **musicother'apy** the treatment of (esp. mental) illness by means of music.—**musical box** a toy that plays tunes automatically, by projections from a revolving barrel twitching a comb; **musical chairs** the game of prancing round a diminishing row of chairs and securing one when the music stops; **musical comedy** a light dramatic entertainment with sentimental songs and situations held together by a minimum of plot; **musical director** the conductor of an orchestra (in a theatre, etc.); **mu'sic-box** a musical box: jocularly, a piano; **mu'sic-case**, **-fo'lio** a roll, portfolio, etc., for carrying sheet music; **music centre** a unit consisting of a record player, tape-recorder, and radio, with loudspeakers; **mus'ic-dra'ma** that form of opera introduced by Wagner in which the relations of music and drama are reformed; **mu'sic-hall** orig. and still sometimes a concert-hall, usu. now a hall for variety entertainments; **mu'sic-holder** a music-case: a clip, rack, or desk for holding music during performance; **mu'sic-house** concert-hall: firm dealing in music or musical instruments; **mu'sic-master**, **-mistress**, **-teacher** a teacher of music; **mu'sic-paper** paper ruled for writing music; **mu'sic-pen** a five-channelled pen for drawing the stave; **mu'sic-rack** a rack attached to a musical instrument for holding the player's music; **mu'sic-roll** a case for carrying music rolled up: a roll of perforated paper for mechanical piano-playing; **mu'sic-room** a room in which music is performed; **mu'sic-seller** a dealer in printed music; **mu'sic-stand** a light adjustable desk for holding music during performance; **mu'sic-stool** a piano-stool.—**music of the spheres** see **spheres; music to one's ears** anything that one is very glad to hear. [Fr. *musique*—L. *mūsica*—Gr. *mousikē* (*technē*) musical (art)—*Mousa*, a Muse.]

musique concrète *mū-zēk kɔ̃-kret*, (Fr.) a kind of mid-20th cent. music, made up of odds and ends of recorded sound variously handled.

musk *musk*, *n.* a strong-smelling substance, used in perfumery, got chiefly from the male musk-deer: the odour thereof: the musk-deer: a species of Mimulus, said once to have smelt of musk.—*adj.* (or prefix to the names of many animals and plants) supposed to smell of musk.—*v.t.* to perfume with musk.—*adj.* **musked** (*muskt*) smelling, or tasting, like musk.— *adv.* **musk'ily.**—*n.* **musk'iness.**—*adj.* **musk'y** having the odour of musk.—**musk'-bag**, **-cod**, **-pod**, **-pouch**, **-sac** a musk-gland; **musk'-deer** a hornless deer (*Moschus moschiferus*) of Asia, chief source of musk; **musk'-duck** (also by confusion **muscovy-duck**) a large musky-smelling South American duck (*Cairina* *moschata*); **musk'-gland** a skin pit in some animals producing musk, **musk'-mel'on** the common melon (apparently transferred from a musky-scented kind); **musk'-ox** a long-haired ruminant (*Ovibos moschatus*) of northern Canada and Greenland, exhaling a strong musky smell; **musk'-rat** the musquash: a musk-shrew: its skin; **musk'-rose** a fragrant species of rose; **musk'-shrew** the desman: a musky-smelling Indian shrew. [Fr. *musc*—L. *muscus*, Gr. *muschos*, prob.—Pers *mushk*, perh.—Sans. *muṣka*, a testicle (for which the gland has been mistaken).]

muskeg *mus-keg'*, (*Can.*) *n.* swamp, bog, marsh. [Cree Indian word.]

muskellunge *mus'kə-lunj*, *n.* a large North American freshwater fish of the pike family. [Algonquian.]

musket *mus'kit*, *n.* a male sparrow-hawk: a military hand firearm, esp. of an old-fashioned smooth-bore kind.—*ns.* **musketeer'** a soldier armed with a musket, **musketoon'** a short musket: a soldier armed with one, **mus'ketry** muskets collectively: practice with, or the art of using, small arms: a body of troops armed with muskets.—**mus'ket-rest** a forked support for the heavy 16th-century musket. [O.Fr. *mousquet*, musket, formerly a hawk—It. *moschetto*, perh.—L *musca*, a fly.]

Muslim *muz'*, *mŏŏz'*, *mus'lim*, *n.* a follower of the Islamic religion, a Mohammedan.—*adj.* of, belonging to, the followers of Islam, Mohammedans.—*n.* **Mus'limism.**—Also **Mos'lem, Mos'lemism.** [Ar. *muslim*, pl. *muslimīn*—*salma*, to submit (to God); cf. **Islam.**]

muslin *muz'lin*, *n.* a fine soft cotton fabric, gauzy in appearance, but woven plain.—*adj.* made of muslin.—*adj.* **mus'lined** clothed with muslin.—*n.* **muslinet'** a coarse kind of muslin. [Fr. *mousseline*—It. *mussolino*, from It. *Mussolo*, the town of Mosul in Mesopotamia.]

musquash *mus'kwosh*, *n.* a large aquatic American animal akin to the voles, very destructive to dams and waterways (also *musk-rat*): its fur. [From an Amer Ind. word.]

muss, musse *mus*, *n.* disturbance: confusion, disorder· a mess.—*v.t.* and *v.t.* to disarrange: to mess.—*n* **muss'iness.**—*adj.* **muss'y** disordered.

mussel *mus'l n.* a marine lamellibranch shellfish of the family Mytilidae: a freshwater lamellibranch of the Unionidae: the shell of any of these.—**muss'el-shell'.** [O.E. *mūs(c)le*; from L. *mūsculus*, dim of *mūs*, mouse.]

Mussulman, Musulman *mus'l-mən*, *-man'*, *n.* a Muslim:—*pl.* **Muss'ulmans.** [Pers. *musulmān*—Ar. *musulmān*, *moslim*, Muslim.]

mussy. See **muss.**

must¹ *must*, *v.t.* am, is, are obliged physically or morally: cannot but: insist upon (with *inf* without *to*):—used only in the present (orig. past) indic.:—*3rd pers. sing.* **must.**—*n.* an essential, a necessity: a thing that should not be missed or neglected. [O.E. *mōste*, pa.t. of *mōt*.]

must² *must*, *n.* new wine: unfermented, or only partially fermented, grape-juice or other juice or pulp for fermentation: process of fermentation.—*adj.* **must'y.** [O.E. *must*—L. *mustum* (*vīnum*) new (wine).]

must³ *must*, *n.* mustiness. mould. [App. back formation—**musty².**]

must⁴, musth *muṣt*, *n.* dangerous frenzy in some male animals, as elephants.—*adj.* in such a state.—*adj.* **must'y** in a frenzy. [Pers. and Hind. *mast*, intoxicated.]

mustache, mustachio. Same as **moustache.**

mustang *mus'tang*, *n.* the feralised horse of the American prairies. [Sp. *mestengo*, now *mesteño*,

belonging to the *mesta* or graziers' union, combined with *mostrenco*, homeless, stray.]

mustard *mus'tard*, *n.* any of various species of the *Sinapis* section of the genus Brassica: their (powdered) seeds. a pungent condiment prepared from the seeds: the brownish-yellow colour of the condiment. —**mus'tard-gas** the vapour from a poisonous blistering liquid, $(CH_2Cl \cdot CH_2)_2S$, got from ethylene and sulphur chloride; **mus'tard-plas'ter** a plaster made from black and white mustard flour —**black mustard** *Brassica nigra*; **French mustard** mustard prepared for table by adding salt, sugar, vinegar, etc ; **mustard and cress** a salad of seedlings of white mustard and garden cress; **white mustard** *Brassica alba*; **wild mustard** charlock —**keen as mustard** (*slang*) intensely enthusiastic. [O.Fr. *mo(u)starde* (Fr. *moutarde*)—L. *mustum*, **must²** (because the condiment was prepared with must)]

muster *mus'tər*, *n.* an assembling or calling together, esp. of troops, as for inspection, verification, etc.: inspection: an assembly: a register: a round-up (*Austr.*).—*v.t.* and *v.t* to assemble: to enroll: to number.—*v.t.* to summon up (often with *up*).—*v.t.* to pass muster.—**muster in** (*U.S*) to enroll, receive as recruits; **muster out** (*U.S.*) to discharge from service; **pass muster** to bear examination, be well enough. [O.Fr. *mostre*, *moustre*, *monstre*—L. *mōnstrum*— *monēre*, to warn.]

musth. See **must⁴.**

musty¹. See **must²,⁴.**

musty² *must'i*, *adj.* mouldy: spoiled by damp: stale in smell or taste: deteriorated from disuse.

Musulman. Same as **Mussulman.**

mutable *mū'tə-bl*, *adj.* that may be changed: subject to change: variable: inconstant, fickle.—*ns.* **mutabil'ity**, **mū'tableness.**—*adv.* **mū'tably.**—*n.* **mū'tagen** (*biol.*) a substance that produces mutations.—*adj.* **mutagen'ic.**—*v.t.* **mū'tagenise, -ize** to treat with mutagens.—*ns.* **mutan'dum** something to be altered:—*pl.* **mutan'da; mū'tant** a form arising by mutation —*v.t.* and *v.i.* **mutate'** to cause or undergo mutation.—*ns.* **muta'tion** change: umlaut: discontinuous variation or sudden inheritable divergence from ancestral type (*biol.*); **muta'tionist** a believer in evolution by mutation.—*adjs.* **mu'tative, mu'tatory** changing: mutable.—*n.* **mū'ton** the smallest element of a gene capable of giving rise to a new form by mutation. [L. *mūtāre*, *-ātum*, to change—*movēre*, *mōtum*, to move.]

mutatis mutandis *mū-tā'tis mū-tan'dis*, *mŏŏ-ta'tēs mŏŏ-tan'dēs*, (L.) with necessary changes.

mutch *much*, (*Scot.*) *n.* a woman's close cap [M.Du. *mutse*; Du *muts*, Ger. *Mutze*.]

mute *mūt*, *adj.* dumb: silent: refusing to plead (*law*): without vocal utterance: unpronounced or faintly pronounced: pronounced by stoppage of the breath-passage.—*n.* a dumb person: a silent person· one who refuses to plead (*law*): a funeral attendant: a dumb servant in an Eastern house: an actor with no words to speak: a stop-consonant· a clip, pad, or other device for subduing the sound of a musical instrument.—*v t.* to deaden the sound of with a mute: to silence.—*adj.* **mut'ed** (of e.g. sound, colour) softened, not loud, harsh, or bright.—*adv* **mute'ly.**—*ns.* **mute'ness; mut'ism** dumbness.—**mute swan** the common swan [L. *mūtus*.]

mutilate *mū'ti-lāt*, *v.t.* to maim: to remove a material part of: to deform by slitting, boring, or removing a part.—*ns.* **mutila'tion; mu'tilător.** [L. *mutilāre*, *-ātum—mutilus.*]

mutiny *mū'tin-i*, *n.* insurrection against constituted authority, esp. naval or military· revolt, tumult, strife.—*v.i.* to rise against authority, esp. in military or naval service:—*pr.p.* **mu'tinying**; *pa.t* and *pa.p* **mu'tinied.**—*n.* **mutineer'** one who mutinies.—*v.i.* to mutiny.—*adj.* **mu'tinous** disposed to mutiny: of the nature of, or expressing, mutiny.—*adv.* **mu'tinously.** —*n.* **mu'tinousness.** [Fr *mutin*, riotous—L. *movēre*, *mōtum*, to move.]

muton. See **mutable.**

mutt *mut*, (slang, orig *U.S*) *n* a blockhead: a dog, esp a mongrel [Perh. for **mutton-head.**]

mutter *mut'ər*, *v.i.* to utter words in a low, indistinct voice: to murmur, esp in hostility, grumbling, mutiny, or menace: to sound with a low rumbling.— *v.i.* to utter indistinctly —*n.* indistinct utterance. low rumbling: subdued grumbling.—*n* **mutt'erer.**—*n* and *adj.* **mutt'ering.**—*adv.* **mutt'eringly.** [Prob imit.]

mutton *mut'n*, *n.* sheep's flesh as food.—*adj* **mutt'ony.**—**mutt'on-bird** an Australasian shear-water, esp. the short-tailed; **mutt'on-chop.**—*adj.* shaped like a mutton-chop (of whiskers).—**mutt'on-cut'let; mutt'on-head** a heavy, stupid person —*adj.* **mutt'on-head'ed** stupid.—**mutton dressed as lamb** (*coll.*) elderly woman dressing or behaving in style suitable to a young one. [O.Fr. *moton* (Fr. *mouton*), a sheep—L.L. *multō*, *-ōnis*; perh. of Celt origin.]

mutual *mū'tū-əl*, *adj.* interchanged: reciprocal: given and received: common, joint, shared by two —*n.* **mutualisa'tion, -z-.**—*v.i.* **mu'tualise, -ize** to put upon a mutual footing.—*ns.* **mu'tualism** symbiosis: theory that mutual dependence is necessary for the welfare of the individual and society: practice based on this; **mutuality** (*-al'i-ti*).—*adv.* **mu'tually.**—**mutual funds** (*U.S.*) unit trusts; **mutual insurance** the system of a company in which the policy-holders are the share-holders. [Fr. *mutuel*—L. *mūtuus*—*mūtāre*, to change.]

muu-muu *mōō'mōō*, *n.* a simple loose dress worn chiefly in Hawaii. [Hawaiian *mu'u mu'u*.]

Muzak® *mū'zak*, *n.* one of the kinds of piped music (q.v.).—Also (erroneously) **Musak.**

muzhik, moujik, mujik *mōō-zhik'*, *mōō'zhik*, *n.* a Russian peasant. [Russ. *muzhik*.]

muzzle *muz'l*, *n.* the projecting jaws and nose of an animal: a strap or a cage for the mouth to prevent biting: the extreme end of a gun, etc.—*v.t* to put a muzzle on: to keep from hurting: to gag or silence.— *v.t.* and *v.i.* to touch, thrust, or investigate with the muzzle.—*n.* **muzz'ler** one who muzzles: a blow on the mouth: a muzzle-loader; **muzz'le-load'er** a firearm loaded through the muzzle—opp. to *breech-loader* —*adj.* **muzz'le-load'ing.**—**muzz'le-veloc'ity** the velocity of a projectile the moment it leaves the muzzle of a gun. [O.Fr. *musel* (Fr. *museau*)—L.L. *mūsellum*, dim. of *mūsum* or *mūsus*, beak.]

muzzy *muz'i*, *adj.* dazed, bewildered. tipsy: blurred: hazy.—*adv.* **muzz'ily.**—*n.* **muzz'iness.**

M-way. See **M.**

my *mī* (sometimes *mi*), *poss adj* or gen of *pron* I, of or belonging to me.—*interj.* expressing surprise (perh. for **my word**, or **my God**). [**mine¹**—O E *mīn* (gen.), of me.]

myal. See **myalism.**

myalgia *mī-al'ji-ə*, *n.* pain in muscle.—*adj* **myal'gic.** [Gr. *mȳs*, muscle, *algos*, pain.]

myalism *mī'əl-izm*, *n.* West Indian Negro witchcraft. —*adj.* **my'al.** [Prob. of West African origin.]

myall¹ *mī'ol*, *n.* a wild Australian aboriginal —*adj* wild [Australian *mail*, the black people]

myall² *mī'ol*, *n.* an Australian acacia of various species with hard, scented wood: their wood [Australian *maiāl*.]

myasthenia *mī-əs-thē'ni-ə*, *n* muscular weakness

or debility.—*adj.* **myasthenic** (*-then'*). [Gr *mys*, muscle, **asthenia.**]

mycelium *mī-sē'li-əm*, *n.* the white thread-like mass of hyphae forming the thallus of a fungus.—*pl* **mycē'lia.**—*adj.* **mycē'lial.** [Gr *mȳkēs*, a mush-room]

Mycenaean *mī-sē-nē'ən*, *adj.* of the ancient city state of *Mȳcēnae* (Gr *Mȳkēnai*) in Argolis, Agamemnon's kingdom, or its culture culminating in the Bronze Age

mycetes *mī-sē'tēz*, *n.pl.* (*rare* except in composition) fungi —*ns.* **mycetol'ogy** mycology. [Gr *mȳkēs*, *-ētos*, pl. *mȳkētēs*, a mushroom.]

myc(o)- *mik-*, *mī-kō-*, in composition, fungus. mush-room. See also terms under **mycetes.**—*adjs* **mycologic** (*mī-kə-loj'ik*), **-al.**—*ns.* **mycologist** (*-kol'*); **mycol'ogy** the study of fungi; **mycophagist** (*mī-kof'ə-jist*) a toadstool-eater; **mycoph'agy; mycosis** (*-kō'sis*) a disease due to growth of a fungus —*adj.* **mycotic** (*-kot'ik*).—*ns* **mycotoxicosis** (*-tok-si-kō'sis*) poisoning caused by a mycotoxin; **mycotoxin** (*-tok'sin*) any poisonous substance produced by a fungus.—*adj.* **mycotroph'ic** (*-trof'ik*) (of a plant) liv-ing in symbiosis with a fungus. [Gr *mȳkēs*, *-ētos*, pl *mȳkētēs*, a mushroom.]

myelitis *mī-ə-lī'tis n.* inflammation of the spinal cord, or sometimes of the bone-marrow —*n* **my'elin** the substance forming the medullary sheath of nerve-fibres.—*adj* **my'eloid** like, pertaining to, of the nature of, marrow.—*ns.* **myeloma** (*-lō'mə*) a tumour of the bone marrow, or composed of cells normally present in bone marrow; **my'elon** the spinal cord [Gr *myelos*, marrow]

myna, mynah, mina *mī'nə*, *n.* a common black, brown and white Indian bird of the starling family. applied also to several allied kinds, including some that can be taught to talk. [Hind. *mainā*.]

mynheer *min-hār'*, Du *mən-ār'*, *n.* my lord: Dutch for *Mr* or *sir*: a Dutchman [Du. *mijn*, my, *heer*, lord]

myo- *mi'ō-*, *mī-o'-*, in composition, muscle.—*n.* **my'oblast** a cell producing muscle-tissue.—*adjs.* **myoblast'ic; myocar'dial** (myocardial infarction de-struction of the myocardium due to interruption of blood supply to the area).—*ns.* **myocardi'tis** inflam-mation of the myocardium, **myocar'dium** the mus-cular substance of the heart, **my'ogram** a myographic record; **my'ograph** an instrument for recording mus-cular contractions —*adjs.* **myograph'ic, -al.**—*ns* **myog'raphist; myog'raphy.**—*adjs.* **my'oid** like muscle; **myolog'ical.**—*ns.* **myol'ogist; myol'ogy** the study of muscles; **myō'ma** a tumour composed of muscular tissue; **my'osin** a protein that contributes to the process of contraction in muscles; **myosi'tis** inflammation of a muscle. [Gr. *mȳs*, *mȳos*, muscle.]

myopia *mī-ō'pi-ə*, *n.* shortness of sight.—*adj.* **myopic** (*-op'*) short-sighted (also *fig.*) —*n.* a short-sighted person.—*ns.* **my'ops** (*-ops*), **my'ope** (*-ōp*) a short-sighted person [Gr *myōps*, short-sighted—*myein*, to shut, *ōps*, the eye.]

myosin, myositis. See **myo-.**

myosis *mī-ō'sis*, *n.* abnormal contraction of the pupil of the eye.—*adjs* **myosit'ic; myotic** (*-ot'*).—Also *n.* [Gr *myein*, to close, blink]

Myosotis *mī-os-ō'tis*, *n* the forget-me-not genus of the borage family —*ns* **myosō'tis, my'osote** a plant of this genus [Gr *myosōtis*—*mȳs*, *mȳos*, a mouse, *ous*, *ōtos*, an ear]

myria- *mir'i-ə-*, in composition, ten thousand: a very large number. See **myriad, myriapod.**

myriad *mir'i-əd*, *n* any immense number.—*adj.* numberless. [Gr. *mȳrias*, *-ados*, ten thousand.]

myriapod *mir'i-ə-pod*, *n.* a member of the Myriapoda. —*n pl* **Myriapoda** (*-ap'ə-də*) a class of Arthropoda with many legs, centipedes and millipedes. [Gr. *myriopous*, *-podos*, many-footed—*myrios*, numberless, *pous*, *podos*, a foot.]

myrmecoid *mûr'mik-oid*, *adj*. ant-like.—*adjs*. **myrmecolog'ic**, **-al**.—*ns*. **myrmecol'ogist**; **myrmecol'ogy** the study of ants. [Gr. *myrmēx*, *-ēkos*, ant.]

Myrmidon *mûr'mi-dən*, *n*. one of a tribe of warriors who accompanied Achilles to Troy: (without *cap*.) one of a ruffianly band under a daring leader: one who carries out another's orders without fear or pity. —*adj*. **myrmidō'nian**. [Gr. *Myrmidōnēs* (pl.).]

myrobalan *mī-rob'ə-lən*, or *mi-*, *n*. the astringent fruit of certain Indian mountain species of Terminalia (Combretaceae): a variety of plum. [Gr. *myrobalanos*—*myron*, an unguent, *balanos*, an acorn.]

myrrh *mûr*, *n*. a bitter, aromatic, transparent gum, exuded from the bark of Commiphora: sweet cicely. —*adj*. **myrrh'ic**.—*n*. **myrrh'ol** the volatile oil of myrrh. [O.E. *myrra*—L. *myrrha*—Gr. *myrrā*.]

myrtle *mûr'tl*, *n*. an evergreen shrub with beautiful and fragrant leaves: extended to various other plants. [O.Fr. *myrtil*, dim. of *myrte*—L. *myrtus*—Gr. *myrtos*.]

myself *mī-self'*, or *mi-self'*, *pron*. I or me, in person (used for emphasis, almost always in apposition): me (reflexively): [me[1], self.]

mystery[1] *mis'tər-i*, *n*. a secret doctrine: (usu. in *pl*.) in ancient religions, rites known only to the initiated: (in *pl*.) the secrets of freemasonry, etc.: anything very obscure: that which is beyond human knowledge to explain: anything artfully made difficult: a miracle play (also **mys'tery-play'**):—*pl*. **mys'teries**.—*adj*. **mystē'rious** containing mystery: having an air of mystery: obscure: secret: incomprehensible.—*adv*. **mystē'riously**.—*n*. **mystē'riousness**.—**mys'tery-tour'** an excursion to a destination which remains secret until the journey's end. [L. *mystērium*—Gr. *mystērion*—*mystēs*, one initiated—*myeein*, to initiate—*myein*, to close the eyes.]

mystery[2], **mistery** *mis'tər-i*, *n*. craft, art, trade (*arch*.): a trade guild (*hist*.). [L.L. *misterium*—L. *ministērium*—*minister*, servant; confused with *mystērium* and prob. with **mastery**.]

mystic, **-al** *mis'tik*, *-əl*, *adj*. relating to mystery, the mysteries, or mysticism: mysterious: sacredly obscure or secret: involving a sacred or a secret meaning hidden from the eyes of the ordinary person, only revealed to a spiritually enlightened mind: allegorical.—*n*. **mys'tic** one who seeks or attains direct intercourse with God in elevated religious feeling or ecstasy.—*adv*. **mys'tically**.—*ns*. **mys'ticalness**; **mys'ticism** (*-sizm*) the habit or tendency of religious thought and feeling of those who seek direct communion with God or the divine: fogginess and unreality of thought (with suggestion of **mist**); **mystifica'tion**; **mys'tifier** one who or that which mystifies: a hoaxer.—*v.t.* **mys'tify** to make mysterious,

obscure, or secret: to involve in mystery: to bewilder: to puzzle: to hoax:—*pr.p.* **mys'tifying**; *pa.t.* and *pa.p.* **mys'tified**. [L. *mysticus*—Gr. *mystikos*—*mystēs*, an initiate; cf. **mystery**[1].]

mystique *mis-tēk'*, *mēs-tēk*, *n*. incommunicable spirit, gift, or quality: secret (of an art) as known to its inspired practitioners: sense of mystery, remoteness from the ordinary, and power or skill surrounding a person, activity, etc. [Fr.]

myth *mith*, *n*. an ancient traditional story of gods or heroes, esp. one offering an explanation of some fact or phenomenon: a story with a veiled meaning: mythical matter: a figment: a commonly-held belief that is untrue, or without foundation.—*adjs*. **myth'ic**, **-al** relating to myths: fabulous: untrue.—*adv*. **myth'ically**.—*v.t.* **myth'icise**, **-ize** (*-i-siz*) to make the subject of myth: to explain as myth.—*ns*. **myth'icism** (*-sizm*) theory that explains miraculous stories as myth; **myth'iciser**, **-z-**, **myth'icist**.—*ns*. **mythol'oger**, **mythol'gian** a mythologist.—*adjs*. **mytholog'ic**, **-al** relating to mythology, fabulous.—*adv*. **mytholog'ically**.—*v.t.* **mythol'ogise**, **-ize** to interpret or explain the mythological character of: to render mythical.—*ns*. **mythol'ogiser**, **-z-**; **mythol'ogist**; **mythol'ogy** a body of myths: the scientific study of myths; **mythomā'nia** (*psychiatry*) lying or exaggerating to an abnormal extent; **mythomā'niac**.—*adjs*. **mythopoeic** (*mith-ō-pē'ik*; Gr. *poieein*, to make), **mythopoetic** (*-pō-et'ik*) myth-making.—*ns*. **mythopoe'ist** a myth-maker; **mythopō'et** a myth-maker: a writer of poems on mythical subjects; **mythus** (*mith'əs*; L.), **mythos** (*mith'os*; Gr.) myth: mythology: theme, scheme of events: the characteristic or current attitudes of a culture or group, expressed symbolically (through poetry, art, drama, etc.). [Gr. *mythos*, talk, story, myth.]

Mytilus *mit'i-ləs*, *n*. the common mussel genus, giving name to the family **Mytilidae** (*mī-til'i-dē*).—*adjs*. **mytil'iform**, **myt'iloid**. [L. *mytilus*, *mitulus*, *mūtulus*.]

myxoedema *mik-sē-dē'mə*, *n*. a diseased condition due to deficiency of thyroid secretion, characterised by loss of hair, increased thickness and dryness of the skin, increase in weight, slowing of mental processes, and diminution of metabolism.—Also **myxedema**. [Gr. *myxa*, mucus, *oidēma*, swelling.]

myxoma *mik-sō'mə*, *n*. a tumour of jelly-like substance:—*pl*. **myxō'mata**.—*adj*. **myxō'matous**.—*n*. **myxomatō'sis** a contagious virus disease of rabbits. [Gr. *myxa*, mucus.]

Myxomycetes *mik-sō-mī-sē'tēz*, *n.pl*. slime-fungi, a class of very simple plants creeping on wet soil, on rotten wood, etc.—*n.sing.* **myxomycete** (*-sēt'*). [Gr. *myxa*, mucus, *mykētēs*, pl. of *mykēs*, a mushroom.]

myxovirus *mik'sō-vī-rəs*, *n*. any of a group of related viruses causing influenza, mumps, etc. [Gr. *myxa*, mucus, **virus**.]

N

N, n *en, n* the fourteenth letter of our alphabet, thirteenth of the Greek, representing a point nasal consonant sound, or before *g* or *k* a back nasal (as in *sing, sink*): an indefinite number, esp in a series (*math*): a unit of measurement (**en**) = half an em (*print*): an indefinite number, (*coll.*) a large number —*adj.* **n**[th], **nth.—to the n**[th] (**nth**) to any power hence (*coll*) to an unlimited degree

'n' a coll. shortening of **and.**

Naafi *na'fi, n.* an organisation for providing canteens for servicemen and -women: one of the canteens — Also **NAAFI.** [From the initials of Navy, Army, and Air-Force Institute(s).]

naartje. Same as **nartjie.**

nab *nab, v t.* to seize, snatch· to arrest (*coll*)·—*pr p* **nabb'ing;** *pa t.* and *pa.p* **nabbed.**—*n* **nabb'er.**

nabob *na'bob, n* a European who has enriched himself in the East (*ar.h.*, used in Europe only): in Europe, any man of great wealth, an important person [Hind *nawwāb;* see **nawab.**]

nacarat *nak'ə-rat, n.* a bright orange-red: a fabric so coloured. [Fr.]

nacelle *na-sel', n.* the car of a balloon· a body on an aircraft housing engine(s), etc. [Fr.—L L *nāvicella,*—L. *nāvis,* ship]

nacre *nā'kər, n.* mother-of-pearl or a shellfish yielding it —*adj.* **nā'creous** (also **nā'crous**) [Fr ; prob of Eastern origin.]

nadir *nā'dēr, -dər, n* the point of the heavens diametrically opposite to the zenith the lowest point of anything [Fr.—Ar. *nadīr* (*nazīr*), opposite to.]

naevus *nē'vəs,* L. *nī'vōŏs, n.* a birthmark: a pigmented spot or an overgrowth of small blood-vessels in the skin.—*pl* **naevi** (*nē'vī,* L. *nī'vē*).—*adj* **nae'void.** [L.]

nag[1] *nag, n.* a horse, esp. a small one: a riding-horse, or an inferior horse. [M.E *nagge.*)]

nag[2] *nag, v.t.* or *v t.* to find fault with urge (to do something), cause pain to, or worry, constantly: (with *at*) to worry or annoy continually·—*pr.p.* **nagg'ing;** *pa t* and *pa p.* **nagged.**—*ns* **nag, nagg'er** a scold [Cf. Norw *nage,* to grow, rankle, Sw *nagga,* to gnaw]

naga *na'gə, n* a snake, esp the cobra (*Ind*) a divine snake (*Hind. myth.*). [Sans *nāga*]

nagana *na-ga'nə, n.* a disease of horses and cattle caused by a trypanosome transmitted by tsetse flies [Zulu *nakane.*]

nagari *nä'gə-rē, n.* devanagari: the group of alphabets to which devanagari belongs [Sans. *nāgarī,* townscript—*nāgaran,* town; addition of *deva-* to form *devanagari* was a later development.]

nagor *nā'gor, n.* a West African antelope (*Redunca redunca*). [Fr., arbitrarily formed by Buffon from earlier *nanguer.*]

Nahuatl *na'wat-l, n.* the language of the Aztecs — Also *adj.*

naiad *nī'ad, nā'əd, n.* a river or spring nymph:—*pl.* **nai'ades, nai'ads.**—*n.* **Nai'as** a genus of water-plants, giving name to a family **Naiadā'ceae** akin to or including the pondweeds [Gr. *nāias, -ados,* pl. *-adēs,* from *naein,* to flow.]

naif *na-ēf', now usu. **naive** *na-ēv', adjs.* with natural or unaffected simplicity, esp in thought, manners, or speech· artless: ingenuous.—*adv* **naive'ly.**—*ns* **naiveté** (*na-ēv'tā*), **naivety** (*na-ēv'ti*) natural simplicity and unreservedness of thought, manner, or speech: ingenuosity —Also **naif, naive,** etc [Fr *naif,* fem. *naive*—L *nātīvus,* native—*nāscī, nātus,* to be born]

nail *nāl, n.* a horny plate at the end of a finger or toe, usu distinguished from a claw as being flattened· a claw: a small spike, usu of metal, and with a head, used for fastening wood, etc : a nail-shaped excrescence, esp one at the tip of a bird's bill: a measure of length (2¼ inches) —*v t.* to fix to pin down, hold fast: to catch or secure (*slang*).—*ns* **nail'er** a maker of nails; **nail'ery** a place where nails are made —**nail'-bed** that portion of the true skin on which a finger-, toe-nail rests; **nail'-biting** chewing off the ends of one's fingernails —*adj* of an event or experience, which induces nail-biting (as a sign of anxiety, excitement or tension).—**nail'-bomb** an explosive device containing gelignite and packed with long nails; **nail'-brush** a brush for cleaning the nails, **nail'-file** a file for trimming finger- or toe-nails; **nail gun** an implement used to put in nails, **nail'-head** the head of a nail: an ornament shaped like it, **nail polish** nail-varnish, **nail'-scissors** small scissors designed for trimming the finger- and toe-nails, **nail'-varnish** varnish for finger- or toe-nails —**a nail in one's, the, coffin** any event, experience, etc which has the effect of shortening one's life: a contributory factor in the downfall of anything; **hard as nails** callous, unsympathetic, unsentimental, **hit the nail on the head** to touch the exact point; **nail a lie to the counter** to expose it and put it out of currency, from the old custom of shopkeepers with counterfeit coins, **nail one's colours to the mast see colour; on the nail** on the spot [O.E *nægel;* Ger. *Nagel.*]

nainsook *nān'sŏŏk, n.* a kind of muslin like jaconet [Hind. *nainsukh—nain,* eye, *sukh,* pleasure]

naira *nī'rə, n.* the standard unit of currency in Nigeria

naive. See **naif.**

naked *nā'kid, adj.* without clothes· uncovered: bare exposed· unconcealed: evident defenceless. unprovided: simple: without the usual covering —*adv.* **na'kedly.**—*n* **na'kedness.**—**naked eye** the eye unassisted by glasses of any kind; **naked lady** the meadow-saffron. [O.E. *nacod;* Ger *nackt*]

naker *nā'kər, n* a kettledrum. [O Fr *nacre*—Ar *naqāra.*]

namby-pamby *nam'bi-pam'bi, adj* feebly wishy-washy· prettily or sentimentally childish.—*n.* namby-pamby writing or talk: a namby-pamby person [Nickname given by Carey or by Swift to *Ambrose* Philips (1674-1749), whose simple odes to children were despised by 18th-century Tories]

name *nām, n.* that by which a person or a thing is known or called: a designation· reputation· fame: a celebrity: family or clan: seeming or pretension without reality. authority: behalf: assumed character (of) —*v t* to give a name to: to mention the name of: to designate: to speak of or to call by name: to state or specify: to utter (with cognate object): to mention for a post or office. to nominate: to mention formally by name in the House of Commons as guilty of disorderly conduct to make known the name of (someone implicated in a crime, an accomplice, etc) to the police, etc.—*adjs* **nam'able, name'able** capable, or worthy, of being named, **named; name'less** without a name. anonymous; undistinguished: indescribable: unspeakable —*adv* **name'lessly.**—*n* **name'lessness.** —*adv* **name'ly** by name. that is to say —**name brand** a make of an article bearing a manufacturer's distinguishing name; **name'-calling** abuse, **name'-child** a person called after one; **name'-day** the day of the saint of one's name: the day when a ticket bearing the buyer's name, etc , is given to the seller (*Stock Exchange*). the day on which a name is bestowed, **name'-dropping** trying to impress by casual mention of important or well-known persons as if they were one's friends; **name'-dropper.**—*v.i* **name'-drop.—name's part** the part that gives title to a play, title-rôle; **name'-plate** an attached plate bearing the name of occupant, owner, manufacturer, etc , **name'sake** one bearing the same name as another, **name'-tape** a short piece of cloth tape attached to a garment, etc , marked with the owner's name.—**call names** to abuse, **in name** fictitiously, as an empty title; **in name of** on behalf of: by the authority of; **name after** a person (*U.S.* **name for**) to give the same name to in honour of a person, **name the day** to fix a day, esp. for a marriage, **no names, no pack-drill** (*coll.*) mention no names, then no-one gets into trouble, **proper name** a name given to a particular person, place, or thing; **take a name in vain** to use a name lightly or profanely, **the name of the game** (*coll.*) the thing that is important or essential; the central :rend or theme, what it's all about (usu. *derog.*), **you name it** this applies to whatever you mention, want, etc , **to one's name** belonging to one. [O.E. *nama*]

nan *nan, n* a type of slightly leavened bread, as baked in India and Pakistan, similar to pitta bread. [Hindi]

nana. See **nanny.**

Nancy *nan'sı,* (also without *cap*) *n.* an effeminate young man a homosexual—also **Nan'cy-boy** (also without *cap*).—Also *adj* [From the girl's name.]

nankeen *nan'kĕn,* or *-kēn', n.* a buff-coloured cotton cloth first made at *Nanking* in China· (in *pl.*) clothes, esp breeches, made of nankeen.—Also **nan'kin** (or *-kın'*).

nanny *nan'ı, n* a she-goat (also **nanny'-goat**): a children's nurse, esp. one trained to take care of children. a pet name for a grandmother.—Also **nana, nanna.**—*v ı* to nurse. [From the woman's name]

nano- *nān-ō-, nan-ō-,* in composition, one thousand millionth, 10^{-9}, as in **nan'ogram, nan'osecond:** of microscopic size, as in **nanoplankton.** [Gr. *nānos,* a dwarf.]

nap¹ *nap, v.t.* to take a short or casual sleep.—*pr.p* **napp'ing;** *pa.p.* **napped.**—*n.* a short or casual sleep.— **catch someone napping** to detect someone in error that might have been avoided. to catch someone off his guard or unprepared. [O.E *hnappian.*]

nap² *nap, n* a woolly surface on cloth. now (distinguished from *pile*) such a surface raised by a finishing process, not made in the weaving· a downy covering or surface on anything.—*v.t.* to raise a nap on: to remove nap from.—*adj.* **nap'less.**—*n.* **napp'i-ness.**—*adj.* **napp'y** downy. shaggy. [M.E. *noppe,* app —M Du or M L G *noppe.*]

nap³ *nap, n* the card-game *Napoleon*: in that game a call of five: the winning of five tricks: a racing tip that professes to be a certainty—one that one may 'go nap' on —*v t.* to name (a particular horse) as certain to win. **—go nap** to undertake to win all five tricks: to risk all

napalm *nā'pam, na', n* a petroleum jelly, highly inflammable, used in bombs and flame-throwers. [*naphthenate palmitate.*]

nape *nāp, n* the back of the neck.

Naperian. See **Napierian.**

napery *nāp'ə-ri,* (*arch* and *Scot.*) *n.* linen, esp. for the table. [O.Fr. *naperie*—L. *mappa,* a napkin.]

naphtha *naf'thə* (sometimes *nap'thə*), *n.* rock-oil: a vague name for the liquid inflammable distillates from coal-tar, wood, etc ,esp the lighter and more volatile —*n.* **naph'thalene** a hydrocarbon got by distillation of coal-tar, crystallising in plates, used for killing moths, etc —*adj.* **naphthal'ic** (*naf-thal'ik*) pertaining to, or derived from, naphthalene [Gr. *naphtha.*]

Napierian, Naperian *nā-pē'rı-ən, adj.* pertaining to John *Napier* of Merchiston (1550–1617), or to his system of logarithms. now applied to natural logarithms.— **Napier's bones,** or **rods** an invention of Napier's for multiplying and dividing mechanically by means of rods.

napkin *nap'kin, n.* a small square of linen, paper, etc., used at table for wiping the mouth and hands, or otherwise: a pad of disposable material or a folded square of towelling, muslin, etc. placed between a baby's legs and kept in place by a fastening at the waist, for absorbing urine and faeces (usu. shortened to **nappy** (*nap'i*)).—**nap'kin-ring** a ring in which a table-napkin is rolled. [Dim. of Fr. *nappe*—L. *mappa.*]

napoleon *nə-pōl'yən,* or *-ı-ən, n.* a twenty-franc gold coin issued by *Napoleon*. a French modification of the game of euchre, each player receiving five cards and playing for himself (commonly **nap**).—*adj.* **Napoleonic** (*-ı-on'ik*) relating to *Napoleon* I 1769–1821, Emperor of the French.—*ns.* **Napol'eonism; Napol'eonist.**

nappe *nap, n.* a sheet of rock brought far forward by recumbent folding or thrusting (*geol.*). a sheet (*math.*): one of the two sheets on either side of the vertex forming a cone (*math.*). [Fr *nappe,* table-cloth—L. *mappa.*]

nappy¹. See **napkin.**

nappy² *nap'i, adj* of liquor, having a head; heady, strong.—*n.* strong ale. [Perh. from **nappy,** shaggy: see **nap².**]

Narcissus *nar-sıs'əs, n.* the daffodil genus of the Amaryllis family. (without *cap.*) a plant of this genus, esp. *N poeticus* (the poet's narcissus):—*pl.* **narciss'uses** or **narciss'i.**—*ns* **narciss'ism** sensual gratification found in one's own body· excessive self-admiration; **narciss'ist.**—*adj* **narcissis'tic.** [L .—Gr *Narkissos,* a youth who pined away for love of his own image, and was transformed into the flower.]

narco-analysis, etc. See **narcotic.**

narcolepsy *när'kō-lep-si, n.* a condition marked by short attacks of irresistible drowsiness. [Gr. *narkē,* numbness, and *lēpsis,* seizure.]

narcotic *nar-kot'ık, adj.* producing torpor, sleep, or deadness: affecting the central nervous system so as to produce dizziness, euphoria, loss of memory and of neuromuscular co-ordination, and eventually unconsciousness.—*n.* anything having a narcotic effect, e.g a drug, alcohol, an inert gas.—*n.* **narcosis** (*-kō'sis*) drowsiness, unconsciousness or other effects to the central nervous system produced by a narcotic:—*pl* **narco'ses** (*-sēz*).—*adv.* **narcot'ically.**—*v.t.* **nar'-cotise, -ize** to subject to the influence of a narcotic.— *ns.* **nar'cotism** the influence of narcotics, **nar'cotist.**— **nar'co-analysis** hypnoanalysis when narcotics are used in producing the hypnotic state; **nar'cosyn'thesis** the bringing out of repressed emotions by narcotics so that they become freely accepted into the self. [Gr. *nar-kōtikos*—*narkē,* numbness, torpor.]

nard *närd, n.* spikenard: a name for matweed.—*v.t.* to anoint with nard. [L. *nardus*—Gr. *nardos.*]

nare *när, n.* (*arch.*) a nostril, esp. a hawk's.—*n.pl.* **när'ĕs** (L.) nostrils.—*adjs.* **när'ial, när'ine** (*-īn*) [L *nāris,* pl. *-ēs,* nostril.]

narghile *nar'gıl-i, n.* a hookah.—Also **nargile(h),**

narg(h)il(l)y. [Pers *nārgīleh—nārgīl*, a coconut (from which it used to be made)]

narial, etc See **nare.**

nark *nark*, (*slang*) *n* an informer a police spy, as *copper's nark* a persistent fault-finder an annoying or baffling circumstance —*v i* to grumble —*v i* to annoy to tease —*adjs.* **nark'y** irritable, **narked** annoyed —**nark at** to fret with persistent criticism [Romany *nāk*, nose]

narrate *nə-* or *na-rāt'*, *v t* to tell of (a series of events) to give a running commentary on (a film, etc) —*v i* to recount or relate events —*adj* **narrāt'able.**—*n* **narrā'tion** the act of telling, that which is told an orderly account of a series of events —*adj* **narrative** (*nar'ə-tiv*) narrating, giving an account of any occurrence· inclined to narration story-telling —*n* that which is narrated a continued account of any series of occurrences story —*adv* **narr'atively.**—*n* **narrā'tor.**—*adj* **narr'atory.** [L *narrāre, -ātum,* prob — *gnārus,* knowing]

narrow *nar'ō, adj* of little breadth of small extent from side to side closely confining, limited contracted in mind or outlook bigoted not liberal parsimonious, with little to spare close strict, precise keen· tense (*phon*) —*n* a narrow part or place (usu in *pl*) narrow passage, channel, or strait —*adv* narrowly —*v t* to make narrow to contract or confine — *v.i* to become narrow to reduce the number of stitches in knitting —*adv* **narr'owly.**—*n* **narr'owness.**—**narr'ow-boat** a canal-boat —*v t* **narr'owcast.** —**narr'owcasting** cable television the production and distribution of material on video tapes, cassettes, etc . **narrow escape** an escape only just managed —*adjs* **narr'ow-gauge** of a railway, less than 4 ft 8½ in (about 1 4 metres) in gauge, **narr'ow-mind'ed** of a narrow or illiberal mind —**narr'ow-mind'edness; narrow seas** the seas between Great Britain and the Continent, **narrow squeak** a narrow escape [O E *nearu*]

narthex *nar'theks, n* a western portico or vestibule in an early Christian or Oriental church or basilica, to which women and catechumens were admitted a vestibule between the church porch and the nave [Gr *narthēx,* giant fennel, a cane or stalk, a casket, a narthex]

nartjie (orig. **naartje**) *nar'chı,* (*Afrık*) *n.* a small sweet orange like the mandarin. [Prob conn with **orange.**]

narwhal *nar'wəl, n* a kind of whale (Monodon) with one large projecting tusk (occasionally two tusks) in the male [Dan. *narhval*, O N *nāhvalr,* may be from *nār,* corpse, *hvalr,* whale, from its pallid colour.]

nary *nār'ı,* (*U S* and *dial*) for **ne'er a** never a, not one

nasal *nā'zl, adj* belonging to the nose. affected by, or sounded through, the nose —*n.* a sound uttered through the nose a letter representing such a sound — *n* **nasalisation, -z-** (*nā-zə-lī-zā'shən*) —*v t* and *v i* **na'salise, -ize** to render nasal, as a sound —*n* **nasality** (*nā-zal'ı-tı*) —*adv* **na'sally.** [L *nāsus,* the nose]

nascent *nas'ənt, nās'ənt, adj* coming into being —*ns* **nasc'ence** (*rare*), **nasc'ency.** [L *nāscēns, -entıs,* pr p of *nāscī, nātus,* to be born]

naso- *nā'zō-,* in composition, nose of the nose (and something else), as *adjs* **nasofront'al** pertaining to the nose and the frontal bone, **nasolac'rymal** pertaining to the nose and tears, as the duct that carries tears from the eye and the nose [L *nāsus,* nose]

nastic *nas'tık, nas', adj* (of plant movements) not related to the direction of the stimulus [Gr *nastos,* close-pressed]

Nasturtium *nas-tûr'shəm, n* the water-cress genus of Cruciferae (without *cap* , in popular use) the Indian cress (*Tropaeolum majus*), a garden climber [L *nāsus,* nose, *torquēre,* to twist (from its pungency)]

nasty *nas'tı, adj* disgustingly foul obscene threatening ill-natured difficult to deal with unpleasant —*n* (*coll*) something or someone unpleasant or intractable —*adv* **nas'tily.**—*n* **nas'tiness** —**a nasty piece, bit, of work** a person very objectionable in character and conduct [Perh for earlier *nasky* (cf Sw dial *naskug, naskeı*), or perh connected with Du *nestıg,* dirty]

natal *nā'tl, adj* of or connected with birth native —*n* **natality** (*nə-, nā-tal'ı-tı*) birth birth-rate [L *nātālıs* —*nāscī, nātus,* to be born]

natant *nāt'ənt, adj* floating swimming —*n* **natation** (*nat-* or *nāt-ā'shən*) swimming —*adjs* **nātato'rial, nā'tatory** pertaining to swimming having the habit of swimming, adapted or used for swimming —*n* **nātato'rium** (*U S.*) a swimming-pool [L *natāns, -antıs,* pr p of *natāre,* freq of *nāre,* to swim]

natch *nach,* (*slang*) *adv* of course, short for **naturally.**

nates *nā'tēz, n pl* the buttocks [L *natıs,* pl *-ēs*]

nathless, natheless *nāth', (arch*) *adv* and *prep* notwithstanding [O E *nā,* never, *thȳ,* by that (instrum case), *lǣs,* less]

nation *nā'shən, n* a body of people marked off by common descent, language, culture, or historical tradition the people of a state an American Indian tribe or federation of tribes a set of people, animals, etc (in *pl*) the heathen or Gentiles —*adj* **national** (*nash'nəl, -ə-nəl*) pertaining to a nation or nations belonging or peculiar to, characteristic of, or controlled by, a nation public general attached to one's own country —*n* a member or fellow-member of a nation —*n* **nationalisā'tion, -z-.**—*v t* **nat'ionalise, -ize** to make national to make the property of the nation to bring under national management to naturalise to make a nation of —*ns* **nat'ionalism; nat'ionalist** one who favours or strives after the unity, independence, interests, or domination of a nation. a member of a political party specially so called, e g the Irish Nationalist party who aimed at Home Rule.—Also *adj —adj* **nationalist'ic.**—*adv* **nationalist'ically.**—*n* **nationality** (*-al'-ıt-ı*) membership of, the fact or state of belonging to, a particular nation nationhood a group or set having the character of a nation· national character —*adv* **nat'ionally.**—*n* **nationhood** (*nā'*) the state or fact of being a nation —**national anthem** an official song or hymn of a nation, sung or played on ceremonial occasions; **national debt** money borrowed by the government of a country and not yet paid back, **national grid** the grid (q v) of power-lines in, or of lines on maps of, Great Britain, **National Guard** a force which took part in the French Revolution, first formed in 1789· organised militia of individual States (*U S*), **national insurance** a system of compulsory insurance paid for by weekly contributions by employee and employer, and yielding benefits to the sick, retired, unemployed, etc , **national park** area owned by or for the nation, set apart for preservation and enjoyment of the beautiful or interesting, **national service** compulsory service in the armed forces, **National Socialism** the policies of the National Socialist Party. **National Trust** an organisation for preserving historic or beautiful sites —*adj* **na'tionwide** covering the whole nation —**National Health Service** in Britain, the system under which medical, dental, etc treatment is available free, or at a nominal charge, to all, paid for out of public taxation, **National Savings Bank** a department of the Post Office with which money may be deposited to accumulate interest, **National Socialist (German Workers') Party** an extreme nationalistic fascist party in Germany, led by Adolf Hitler [L *nātıō, -ōnıs—nāscī, nātus,* to be born]

native *nā'tıv, adj* belonging naturally innate natural in a natural state occurring naturally as a mineral (not manufactured), or naturally uncombined (as an element): belonging by birth. having a right by birth· born or originating in the place: being the place of birth or origin· belonging to the people originally or at the time of discovery inhabiting the country. esp. when they are not yet fully civilised.—*n* one born in any place one born and long dwelling in a place: a member of a native race: a coloured person (*coll derog* ; *no longer common*): an indigenous species, variety, or breed, or an individual of it.—*adv* **na'tively.**—*ns* **na'tiveness; na'tivism** the belief that the mind possesses some ideas or forms of thought that are inborn and not derived from sensation; **na'tivist.**—*adj.* **nativis'tic.**—*n.* **nativity** (*nǝ-tiv'i-ti*) the state or fact of being born· the time, place, and manner of birth: the birth of Christ, hence the festival commemorating it—Christmas, or a picture representing it: a horoscope.—**native bear** the koala —*adj* **na'tive-born** born in the country.—**native rock** unquarried rock.—**go native** see go. [L *nātīvus*—*nāscī, nātus*, to be born.]

Nato *nä'tō, n* the North Atlantic Treaty Organisation (see **north**).

natron *nä'trǝn, n.* a hydrated carbonate of sodium found on some lake borders. [Ar. *natrūn*—Gr *nitron*]

natter *nat'ǝr, v.i* to rattle on in talk, esp. grumblingly: to chatter, talk much about little (*coll.*) —Also *n*

natterjack *nat'ǝr-jak, n.* a toad with a yellow stripe down the back.

natty *nat'i, (coll)* adj. dapper: spruce: clever, ingenious.—*adv.* **natt'ily.**—*n.* **natt'iness.** [Possibly connected with **neat**².]

natural *nach'(ǝ)rǝl, adj.* pertaining to, produced by, or according to nature: furnished by or based on nature: not miraculous: not the work of man: not interfered with by man: inborn. having the feelings that may be expected to come by nature, kindly: normal: happening in the usual course: spontaneous: not acquired: without affectation: physical: life-like, like nature: related by actual birth (not adoption, etc): illegitimate: in a state of nature, ·inregenerate: according to the usual diatonic scale, not sharp or flat (*mus.*).—*n.* an idiot: one having a natural aptitude (for), or being an obvious choice (for): a thing assured by its very nature of success, a certainty: a tone that is neither sharp nor flat (*mus.*)· a character (♮) cancelling a preceding sharp or flat (*mus.*): a white key in a keyboard musical instruments —*n* **naturalisā'tion, -z-.**—*v.t.* **nat'uralise, -ize** to make natural or easy· to cause an introduced species of plant, animal, etc. to adapt to a different climate or to different conditions of life: to grant the privileges of natural-born citizens to: to adopt into the language: to admit among accepted institutions, usages, etc.—*v.i.* to acquire citizenship in another country: to study natural history in the field: of a plant, animal, etc., to adapt to a new environment.—*ns.* **nat'uralism** following of nature: a close following of nature without idealisation: the theory that this should be the aim of art and literature, esp. the form of realism advocated or practised by Emile Zola: a world-view that rejects the supernatural; **nat'uralist** one who studies nature. more particularly zoology and botany, esp zoology, and esp. in the field: a believer in naturalism.—*adj* **naturalist'ic** pertaining to, or in accordance with, nature, natural history, or naturalism.—*advs.* **naturalist'ically; nat'urally** in a natural manner: by nature. according to nature or one's own nature: in a life-like manner: normally: in the ordinary course of course. —*n.* **nat'uralness.**—*adj.* **nat'ural-born** native — **natural death** death owing to disease or old age, not violence or accident; **natural gas** gases issuing from the earth, whether from natural fissures or bored wells, applied particularly to the hydrocarbon gases associated with the production of petroleum and used as domestic or industrial fuel; **natural history** originally the description of all that is in nature, now used of the sciences that deal with the earth and its productions—botany, zoology, and mineralogy, esp. field zoology; **natural law** a law of nature: the sense of right and wrong which arises from the constitution of the mind of man, as distinguished from the results of revelation or legislation; **natural logarithm** one to the base *e*; **natural magic** see **magic; natural numbers** the whole numbers 1, 2, 3, and upwards; **natural order** in botany, a category now usually called a family, **natural philosophy** the science of the physical properties of bodies· physics, or physics and dynamics; **natural resources** features, properties, etc of the land such as minerals, an abundance of water, timber, etc. that occur naturally and can be exploited by man; **natural science** the science of nature, as distinguished from mental and moral science and from mathematics; **natural selection** evolution by the survival of the fittest with inheritance of their fitness by next generation, **natural wastage** (reduction of staff by) non-replacement of those who leave, e.g through retirement; **natural year** see **year.** [L. *nātūrālis*—*nātūra*, nature.]

nature *nä'chǝr, n.* the power that creates and regulates the world: the power of growth: the established order of things: the external nature, esp. as untouched by man: the qualities of anything which make it what it is: essence: being: constitution: kind or order· naturalness: normal feeling: conformity to truth, or reality: inborn mind, character, instinct, or disposition: course of life: nakedness: a primitive undomesticated condition: the strength or substance of anything.—*adj.* **na'tured** having a certain temper or disposition (esp in compounds, as *good-natured*).— *ns.* **na'turism** communal nudity practised in the belief that it encourages self-respect, respect for others and a feeling of being in harmony with nature: natureworship; **na'turist.**—*adj.* **naturist'ic.**—*n.* **nat'uropath** one who practises naturopathy.—*adj* **naturopath'ic.**—*n.* **nāturop'athy** (also *na-*) the promotion of health and natural healing by a system of diet, exercise, manipulation, care, and hydrotherapy: the philosophy of the system.—**na'ture-cure** the practice of, or treatment by, naturopathy; **na'ture-study** a branch of school work intended to cultivate the powers of seeing and enjoying nature by the observation of natural objects, e.g. plants, animals, etc.; **na'ture-worship, na'turism** worship of the powers of nature.—**in the nature of** the same sort as, that amounts to [Fr.,—L. *nātūra*—*nāscī, nātus*, to be born.]

naturopath, -pathy. See **nature.**

naught *nöt, n* nothing: a nought (q v.).—*adj (arch.)* good for nothing· worthless· ruined.—**bring to naught** to frustrate, baffle; **come to naught** to come to nothing, to fail, **set at naught** to treat as of no account, to despise —Also **nought.** [O E *nāht, nāwiht*—*nā*, never, *wiht*, whit.]

naughty *nöt't, adj.* bad· ill-behaved: verging on the indecorous· now chiefly applied to children in censure.—*adv.* **naught'ily.**—*n* **naught'iness.** [**naught.**]

nauplius *no'pli-ǝs, n.* a larval form in many Crustacea, with one eye and three pairs of appendages:—*pl* **nau'plii (-ī).** [L , a kind of shellfish—Gr *Nauplios*, a son of Poseidon—*naus*, a ship, *pleein*, to sail]

nausea *nö'si-ǝ, -shi-ǝ, -zhǝ, n.* a feeling of inclination to vomit: sickening disgust or loathing —*v i.* **nau'seate** to feel nausea or disgust.—*v t* to loathe: to strike

with disgust —*adj*. **nau'seàting** causing nausea or
(*fig*.) disgust —*adj* **nau'seous** (*-shэs, -shı-эs, -sı-эs*)
producing nausea: disgusting·loathsome —*adv* **nau'-**
seously.—*n*. **nau'seousness.** [L.,—Gr *nausiā*, sea-
sickness—*naus*, a ship]

nautch *noch, ns*. ın India, a performance of dancing
women known as **nautch'-girls.** [Hınd *nâch*,
dance.]

nautical *not'ik-эl, adj* of or pertaınıng to ships, to
sailors, or to navigation.—*adv* **nau'tically.—Nau-**
tical Almanac a perıodıcal book of astronomıcal
tables specıally useful to saılors; **nautical mile** see
mile. [L *nautıcus*—Gr *nautıkos—nautēs*, saılor,
naus, a ship]

nautilus *no-tı-lэs, n* a cephalopod (**pearly nautilus**) of
southern seas, with a chambered external shell: a
Mediterranean cephalopod (**paper nautilus** or
argonaut) wrongly believed by Arıstotle to use its
arms as saıls·—*pl*. **nau'tiluses**, or **nau'tili.** [L ,—
Gr. *nautilos*, a sailor, a paper nautilus—*naus*, ship.]

naval *nâ'vl, adj* pertaınıng to warships or a navy.—
naval officer an officer ın the navy: a custom-house
officer of high rank (*U S.*). [L *nâvâlıs—nâvis*, a
ship]

navarin *nav'э-rın, nav-a-rē, n*. a stew of mutton or
lamb, with turnıp and other root vegetables   [Fr.]

nave[1] *nâv, n*. the middle or maın body of a basılıca,
rısing above the aisles: the main part of a church,
generally west of the crossing, including or excluding
its aisles. [L. *nâvıs*, a ship.]

nave[2] *nâv, n*. the hub or central part of a wheel,
through which the axle passes. [O.E. *nafu*.]

navel *nâ'vl, n*. the umbilicus or depression ın the centre
of the abdomen: a central point.—**na'vel-or'ange** a
variety of orange with a navel-lıke depression, and a
smaller orange enclosed; **na'vel-string** the umbılıcal
cord; **na'velwort** pennywort. [O.E *nafela*, dim. of
nafu, nave of a wheel.]

navicular *nav-ık'ū-lэr, adj*. boat-shaped: pertaining to
the navicular bone.—*n*. the navicular bone —
navicular bone a boat-shaped bone on the thumb sıde
of the wrist joınt, the seaphoid bone a corresponding
bone ın the ankle joınt; **navicular disease** ınflammatıon of the navicular bone in horses [L *nâvıcula*,
dim of *nâvıs*, a ship.]

navigate *nav'ı-gât, v.ı*. to conduct or manage a ship,
aircraft, motor vehıcle, etc , ın saılıng, flyıng or
moving along: to fınd one's way and keep one's
course, esp. by water or aır. to saıl.—*v.t*. to direct the
course of: to saıl, fly, etc., over, on, or through —*n*
navigability (*-gэ-bil'ı-tı*).—*adj* **nav'igable** that may
be passed by ships, etc.: dırıgıble —*ns* **nav'ig-**
ableness; naviga'tion the act, science, or art of con-
ductıng ships or aircraft, etc , esp. the fındıng of posı-
tion and determination of course by astronomıcal
observations and mathematical computatıons· travel
or traffic by water or air —*adj*. **naviga'tional** pertaınıng to navıgatıon.—*n*. **nav'igator** one who
navigates or saıls· one who dırects the course of a
ship, etc · one who describes the route to, and dırects,
the driver ın car rally or race: an explorer by sea   [L
nâvigâre, -âtum—nâvıs, a ship, *agère*, to drıve]

navvy *nav'ı, n* a labourer: a machine for dıggıng out
earth, etc —*v.ı* to work as a navvy, or lıke a navvy·—
pr.p. **navv'ying;** *pa.t* and *pa.p.* **navv'ied.**
[navigator.]

navy *nâ'vi, n* a fleet of shıps: the whole of a nation's
shıps-of-war· the officers and men belongıng to a
nation's warshıps —*adj*. of, used by, such as is
supplied to, the navy —*n* and *adj*. **na'vy-blue'** dark
blue as ın naval dress —**na'vy-list'** a lıst of officers
and ships of a navy; **na'vy-yard** (*U.S.*) a government
dockyard. [O.Fr. *navıe*—L. *nâvıs*, a ship.]

nawab *nэ-wab', -wob', n*. a deputy or viceroy in the
Mogul empıre· a Muslım prınce or noble: an honorary
tıtle bestowed by the Indian government   [Hınd
nawwâb—Ar. *nawwâb*, respectful pl. of *nä'ib*,
deputy.]

nay *nâ, adv* no: not only so, but· yet more· ın point of
fact —*n* a denial: a vote against   [M.E *nay, naı*.]

Nazarene *naz'э-rēn, n* an ınhabıtant of *Nazareth*, ın
Galilee: a follower of Jesus of Nazareth, orıgınally
used of Chrıstıans ın contempt: an early Jewısh
Christian.—Also **Naz'arite.**

Nazarite *naz'э-rīt, n* a Jewish ascetic under a vow (see
Num. vi) (also **Naz'irite**)· a Nazarene [Heb
nâzar, to consecrate.]

naze *nâz, n*. a headland or cape. [O.E *næs*; cf **ness.**]

Nazi *nä'tsē, n* and *adj*. for Ger *Natıonal-sozıalıst*,
National Socialist. Hıtlerıte —*ns* **Naz'ism, Naz'iism.**
—*v ı , v ı* **Naz'ify.** [Ger]

nazir *na'zir, n* formerly, an Indian court official who
served summonses, etc an official of varıous kınds
[Ar. *nâzir*, overseer.]

Nazirite. See **Nazarite.**

Neanderthal *nı-an'dэr-tal, adj* of a Palaeolıthıc
species of man whose remains were first found in 1857
ın a cave in the *Neanderthal*, a valley between Düssel-
dorf and Elberfeld

neanic *nē-an'ik*, (*zool*) *adj*. pertaınıng to the adolescent perıod in the lıfe-history of an individual. [Gr.
neanikos, youthful.]

neap *nēp, adj* of tides, of smallest range —*n* a neap
tıde —*v ı* to tend towards the neap.—*adj*. **neaped**
left aground between sprıng tides —**neap'tide, neap**
tide a tide of mınımum amplitude, occurrıng when the
sun and moon are working against each other.
[O E. *nēp*, app. meanıng helpless; *nēpflōd*, neap
tıde.]

Neapolitan *nē-э-pol'ı-tэn, adj*. of the cıty or the former
kıngdom of Naples.—*n*. a natıve, cıtızen, or ınhabıtant of Naples.—**Neapolitan ice** ice-cream made in layers of dıfferent colours and flavours, **Neapolitan**
violet a scented double varıety of sweet vıolet. [L
Neâpolıtânus—Gr *Neâpolıs*, new town—*neos, -â,
-on*, new, *polıs*, cıty]

near *nēr, adv* to or at no great dıstance close: closely·
nearly: almost: narrowly.—*prep* close to.—*adj* not
far away ın place or tıme: close ın kın, friendship,
imıtatıon, approxımatıon, or ın any relation: close,
narrow, so as barely to escape· short, as a road:
stingy· of horses, vehıcles. etc., left, left-hand·—
compar **near'er;** *superl* **near'est.** (also *advs*. and
preps) —*v ı* and *v ı* to approach: to come nearer.—
adv **near'ly** at or within a short distance: closely:
scrutınısıngly, parsımonıously: almost: approxı-
mately but rather less —*n* **near'ness.**—*adj* **near'-by**
neıghbourıng —*adv* (usu **near-by'**) close at hand —
prep. (also **near by**) close to.—**Near East** formerly, an
area ıncludıng the Balkans and Turkey, and sometimes also the countrıes to the west of Iran· now
synonymous with **Middle East** (q v).—**near miss** (*lıt.*
and *fig*) a mıss that ıs almost a hit; **near'side** the sıde
of a vehıcle nearer to the kerb e g when it is beıng
driven, ın Brıtaın the left sıde· the left side of a horse
or other animal, or of a team of horses —Also *adj.*—
adj **near'-sight'ed** short-sighted.—*n* **near'-sight'ed-**
ness.—**a near thing** a narrow escape; **near as dammit**
(*coll*) very nearly [O.E. *nēar*, compar of *nēah*,
nıgh (*adv*), and O.N. *nær*, compar. (but also used as
positive) of *nä*, nigh.]

Nearctic *nē-ark'tık, adj* of the New World part of the
Holarctıc regıon [Gr. *neos*, new, *arktıkos*,
northern]

neat[1] *nēt*, (*dıal*) *n*. an ox, cow, bull, etc :—*pl* **neat.—**
neat'-cattle; neat'-herd; neat'-house; neat'-stall;

neat's leather leather made of the hides of neat.—
neat's-foot oil an oil obtained from the feet of oxen
[O.E *nēat*, cattle, a beast—*nēotan*, *nīotan*, to use]
neat² *nēt*, *adj* unmixed: undiluted. elegant: trim: tidy
adroit well and concisely put· ingenious. effective.
economical in effort or method.—*adv.* neatly.—*v.t.*
neat'en to make neat. tidy.—*adv* **neat'ly.**—*n* **neat'-
ness.**—*adj* **neat'-hand'ed** dexterous [Fr *net*,
clean. tidy—L *nitidus*. shining. bright—*nitēre*, to
shine]
neath, 'neath *nēth*, (*dial* and *poet.*) *prep* beneath
[Aphetic for **beneath**, or dial. *aneath*]
neb *neb*, *n*. a beak or bill. the nose the sharp point of
anything [O E *nebb*, beak, face, cog with Du
neb, beak.]
nebbich *neb'thh*, **nebbish** -*ish*, *ns.* a colourless, incompetent person. a perpetual victim.—Also *adj*
[Yiddish]
nebula *neb'ū-lə*, *n* a slight opacity of the cornea. a
liquid for spraying: a faint. misty appearance in the
heavens produced either by a group of stars too distant to be seen singly, or by diffused gaseous matter.
—*pl.* **neb'ulae** (-*lē*) —*adj.* **neb'ular** pertaining to
nebulae. like or of the nature of a nebula.—*n*
nebulos'ity.—*adj.* **neb'ulous** hazy, vague, formless
(*lit* , *fig*) cloudlike: like. of the nature of, or surrounded by, a nebula—*adv.* **neb'ulously.**—*n*
neb'ulousness.—**nebular hypothesis** the theory of
Laplace that the solar system was formed by the contraction and breaking up of a rotating nebula [L.
nebula, mist]
necessary *nes'is-ə-ri*, *adj* that must be: that cannot be
otherwise: unavoidable: indispensable. (of agent) not
free.—*n*. that which cannot be left out or done without (food, etc)—used chiefly in *pl.*: money (*coll*).—
n. and *adj* **necessă'rian.**—*n* **necessă'rianism** the doctrine that the will is not free, but subject to causes
without. which determine its action.—*adv.* **nec'es-
sarily** (or *nes-is-e'rə-li*) as a necessary consequence:
inevitably: (*loosely*) for certain —*n*. **nec'essariness.**
—**necessary truths** such as cannot but be true. [L
necessārius.]
necessity *ni-ses'i-ti*, *n* a state or quality of being necessary: that which is necessary or unavoidable
unavoidable compulsion. great need: poverty.—*n*.
and *adj.* **necessită'rian.**—*n* **necessită'rianism** neces-
sarianism.—*v t.* **necess'itate** to make necessary. to
render unavoidable: to compel.—*n.* **necessită'tion.**—
adj. **necess'itous** in necessity: very poor: destitute.—
adv **necess'itously.**—*n*. **necess'itousness.—of** necessity necessarily. [L. *necessitās*, *-ātis*.]
neck *nek*, *n*. the part connecting head and trunk: the
flesh of that part regarded as food: anything resembling that part: the part connecting head and body of
anything, e.g. a violin. the plain lower part of the
capital of a column: any narrow connecting part, e.g
an isthmus. anything narrow and throatlike, as the
upper part of a bottle: the part of a garment on or
nearest the neck: a neck's length: impudence,
audacity (*slang*)—*v t*. to make a neck on.—*v t*
(*slang*) to embrace.—*adj.* **necked** having a neck.—*ns*
neck'ing the neck of a column (*archit.*): a moulding
between the capital and shaft of a column, gorgerin
(*archit.*): embracing, petting (*slang*), **neck'let** a
simple form of necklace.—**neck'-band** the part of a
shirt, etc , encircling the neck: a band worn on the
neck; **neck'-bone** a cervical vertebra; **neck'-cloth** a
piece of folded cloth worn round the neck by men as a
band or cravat; **neck'erchief** a kerchief for the neck,
neck'lace (-*lis*, -*ləs*) a lace, chain, or string of beads or
precious stones worn on the neck; **neck'line** the
boundary-line of a garment at the neck; **neck'-mould-
ing** a moulding where the capital of a column joins the

shaft. **neck'tie** a scarf or band tied round the neck.
neck'wear apparel for the neck—**get it in the neck** to
be severely dealt with. hard hit, **neck and crop**
completely bodily: in a heap: summarily and unceremoniously, **neck and neck** exactly equal. side by
side, **neck of the woods** (*coll.*) a particular area, part
of the country, **neck or nothing** risking everything:
stick one's neck out to put oneself at risk, expose
oneself to trouble. danger. or contradiction; **talk
through (the back of) one's neck** to talk wildly or
absurdly wide of the truth. **up to one's neck** deeply
involved. esp. in a troublesome situation [O E
hnecca, Ger. *Nacken*]
necro- *nek'rō-*, *-ro'*, in composition. dead. dead body
—*ns.* **necrōbiō'sis** degeneration of living tissue,
necrol'ater; necrol'atry worship of, or morbid or
sentimental reverence for, the dead—*adjs*
necrōlog'ic, -al.—*ns* **necrol'ogist;** necrol'ogy an
obituary list; **nec'rōmancer** a sorcerer, **nec'rōmancy**
the art of revealing future events by calling up and
questioning the spirits of the dead enchantment —
adj **necrōman'tic.**—*adv* **necrōman'tically.**—*adj*
necroph'agous feeding on carrion.—*ns* **nec'rophile**
(-*fil*) one who is morbidly attracted to corpses,
necrophilia (-*fil'*) necrophilism.—*adjs*. **necrophil'iac,
-phil'ic.**—*ns*. **necroph'ilism,** necroph'ily a morbid
liking for dead bodies—*adj*. **necroph'ilous.**—*ns*
necrōphō'bia a morbid horror of corpses, **nec-
rop'olis** a cemetery, **nec'ropsy** (or *-rop'*) a post-
mortem examination —*adj* **necrōscop'ic.**—*n*. **nec-
ros'copy** a post-mortem examination. autopsy [Gr
nekros, dead body. dead.]
necrosis *nek-rō'sis*, *n*. death of part of the living body
—*v.t.* and *v.t.* **necrose** (*nek-rōs'*) to affect with or
undergo necrosis —*adj* **necrōt'ic.**—*v t*. and *v t*
nec'rōtise, -ize to necrose [Gr *nekros*, dead body]
nectar *nek'tər*, *n* the name given by Homer, etc.. to
the beverage of the gods, giving life and beauty a
delicious beverage. the honey of the glands of plants
—*adjs* **nectă'rean,** nectă'reous, nec'tarous of or like
nectar.—*n*. **nec'tarine** (-*ēn*, -*in*) a variety of peach
with a smooth skin.—*n*. **nec'tary** a glandular organ
that secretes nectar.—[Gr *nektar*.]
neddy *ned'i*, *n* a donkey [From *Edward*.]
née *nā*, *adj* (of a woman) born—used in stating a
woman's maiden name [Fr , fem pa p. of *naître*, to
be born]
need *nēd*, *n*. want of something which one cannot well
do without. necessity. a state that requires relief
want of the means of living.—*v.t* to have occasion
for. to want: to require (used before the infinitive
with *to*, or in negative, interrogative. conditional,
etc. sentences without *to*) to require or be obliged (to
do something): (used before a verbal noun) to require
(to be dealt with in a particular way) —*v.t* (*arch*) to
be necessary —*n*. **need'er.**—*adj* **need'ful** necessary
requisite —*adv*. **need'fully.**—*n*. **need'fulness.**—*adv*
need'ily.—*n*. **need'iness.**—*adj*. **need'less** not needed:
unnecessary.—*adv*. **need'lessly.**—*n* **need'lessness.**—
adv. **needs** of necessity. indispensably —*adj*. **need'y**
very poor—**must needs, needs must** (often *iron*)
must inevitably, **the needful** (*slang*) ready money.
[O.E. *nēd, nied, nȳd*]
needle *nēd'l*, *n*. a small, sharp instrument for sewing
any similar slender, pointed instrument, as for knitting, etching, playing gramophone records, dissection, (hooked) for crochet: the suspended magnet of
a compass or galvanometer: a pointer on a dial: the
pointed end of a hypodermic syringe: anything sharp
and pointed: a pinnacle of rock an obelisk. a long
slender crystal: a strong beam passed through a wall
as a temporary support: a long, narrow, stiff leaf
irritation —*adj* (of a contest) intensely keen and

acutely critical —*v t* to sew. to pass through to underpin with needles· to irritate. goad. heckle —*v t* to pass out and in. to sew —**need'le-book** a needle-case in book form; **need'le-case** a case for holding needles; **need'lecord** a cotton material with closer ribs and flatter pile than corduroy, **need'le-craft** the art of needlework, **need'le-point** a very sharp point lace made with a needle embroidery on canvas, done with woollen yarns, used on chair-covers. etc —**needle time** the amount of time allowed to a radio channel for the broadcasting of recorded music, **need'lewoman** a woman who does needlework, **need'lework** work done with a needle· the business of a seamstress —**get the needle** (*coll*) to be irritated, **look for a needle in a haystack** to engage in a hopeless search [O E *nædl*; Ger *Nadel*. cog with Ger *nahen*, to sew, L *nēre*, to spin]

neep *nēp*, (*Scot*)*n* a turnip [O E *nǣp*—L *nāpus*]

ne'er *nār*, *adv* contr of *never.*—*adj* and *n* **ne'er'-do-well** good-for-nothing

nefarious *ni-fā'ri-əs*, *adj* extremely wicked villainous —*adv* **nefa'riously.**—*n* **nefa'riousness.** [L *nefārius*—*nefās*, wrong, crime—*ne*-, not, *fās*, divine law]

neg. *neg* Abbrev. of **negative.**

negate *ni-gāt'*, *v t.* to deny· to nullify to imply the non-existence of to make ineffective —*ns* **negation** (-*gā'shən*) the act of saying no denial a negative proposition (*log*) something that is the opposite (of a positive quality, state, etc) a thing characterised by the absence of qualities, **nega'tionist** one who merely denies, without offering any positive assertion —*adj* **negative** (*neg'ə-tiv*) denying· expressing denial, refusal, or prohibition (opp to *affirmative*) denying the connection between a subject and a predicate (*log.*). lacking positive quality opposite, contrary to, neutralising, that which is regarded as positive defeatist less than nothing (*math*): reckoned or measured in the opposite direction to that chosen as positive (*math*): of, having. or producing negative electricity (*elect* , see below) having dark for light and light for dark (*opt* , *phot*) in complementary colours (*opt* , *phot*) in a direction away from the source of stimulus (*biol*) —*n* a word or statement by which something is denied a word or grammatical form that expresses denial the side of a question or the decision which denies what is affirmed an image in which the lights and shades are reversed a photographic plate bearing such an image —*v t* to prove the contrary of to veto to reject by veto to deny· to neutralise —*adv* **neg'atively.**—*ns* **neg'ativeness; neg'ativism** the doctrine or attitude of a negationist, **negativ'ity.**—*adj* **neg'atory** expressing denial —**negative electricity** electricity arising from the excess of electrons, **negative pole** that pole of a magnet which turns to the south when the magnet swings freely, **negative sign** the sign (–, read *minus*) of subtraction. [L *negāre*, -*ātum*, to deny]

neglect *ni-glekt'*, *v t* to treat carelessly to pass by without notice to omit by carelessness to fail to bestow due care upon —*n* disregard slight omission· uncared-for state —*adj* **neglect'able** (*rare*) negligible —*ns* **neglect'edness; neglect'er.**—*adj* **neglect'ful** careless accustomed to omit or neglect things. slighting —*adv* **neglect'fully.**—*n* **neglect'fulness.** [L *neglegĕre*, *neglectum*—*neg*- or *nec*-, not, *legĕre*, to gather]

négligé *nā'glē-zhā*, *n* easy undress —*adj* carelessly or unceremoniously dressed· careless —*n* **negligee** (*neg'li-zhā*) a woman's loose decorative dressing-gown of flimsy material [Fr , neglected]

negligence *neg'li-jəns*, *n* the fact or quality of being negligent want of proper care habitual neglect a

slight carelessness about dress, manner, etc : omission of duty, esp such care for the interests of others as the law may require —*adj* **neg'ligent** neglecting· careless inattentive· disregarding ceremony or fashion —*adv* **neg'ligently.**—*n* **negligibil'ity.**—*adj* **neg'ligible** (sometimes **neg'ligeable**) such as may be ignored because very little or very unimportant —*adv* **neg'ligibly.** [L *negligentia* for *neglegentia*—*neglegĕre*, to neglect]

negotiate *ni-gō'shi-āt*, *v t* to traffic to bargain· to confer for the purpose of mutual arrangement —*v t* to arrange for by agreement· to manage to transfer or exchange for value to cope with successfully (*coll*) —*n* **negotiabil'ity.**—*adj* **nego'tiable.**—*ns* **negotiā'tion; nego'tiator.** [L *negōtiārī*, -*ātus*—*negōtium*, business—*neg*-, not, *ōtium*, leisure]

Negrillo *ni-gril'ō*, *n* an African Negrito —*pl* **Negrill'os.** [Sp , dim of *negro*, black]

Negrito *ni-grē'tō*, *n* a member of any of a number of pygmy negroid peoples of S -E Asia and Africa —*pl.* **Negri'tos.** [Sp , dim of *negro*, black]

Negro *nē'grō*, *n* a member of any of the dark-skinned peoples of Africa or a person racially descended from one of these —*pl* **Ne'groes.**—*adj* of or pertaining to Negroes —*n* **Ne'gress** (sometimes *derog*) a Negro woman or girl —*adj* **ne'groid** of Negro type having physical characteristics associated with Negro races, e g full lips, tightly curling hair, etc —*n* one who is of Negro type· one who is a Negro in a broad sense only —*adj* **negroid'al.**—*n* **ne'grōism** any peculiarity of speech among Negroes, esp in the southern U S devotion to the cause of the Negroes [Sp *negro*—L *niger*, *nigra*, *nigrum*, black]

negus[1] *nē'gəs*, *n* port or sherry with hot water, sweetened and spiced [From Colonel *Negus*, its first maker]

negus[2] *nē'gəs*, *n* the king of Abyssinia [Amharic]

neigh *nā*, *v i* to utter the cry of a horse —*n* the cry of a horse [O E *hnǣgan*]

neighbour *nā'bər*, *n* a person who dwells near another a person or thing that is near another —*v t* and *v t* to live or be near —*n* **neigh'bourhood** a set of neighbours a district, locality, esp with reference to its inhabitants as a community a district a region lying near a near position all the points that surround a given point in a specified degree of closeness (*math*) —*adj* **neigh'bouring** being near· adjoining —*n* **neigh'bourliness.**—*adj* **neigh'bourly** like or becoming a neighbour friendly social —**in the neighbourhood of** approximately, somewhere about, **neighbourhood law centre** see under **law**[1]. [O E *nēahgebūr*—*nēah.* near. *gebūr* or *būr*, a farmer]

neither *nī'dhər*, or *nē'dhər*, *adj* and *pron* not either —*conj* not either and not· nor yet —*adv* not at all: in no case [O E *nāther*, *nāwther*, abbrev of *nā-hwæther*—*nā*, never, *hwæther*, whether]

nekton *nek'ton*, *n* the assemblage of actively swimming organisms in a sea, lake, etc [Gr *nēkton* (neut), swimming]

nellie, nelly, not on your (*nel'i*, *slang*) not on any account—said to be from *not on your Nellie Duff*, rhyming with *puff*, meaning 'life'

nelly *nel'i*, *n* a large petrel [Perh the woman's name]

nelson *nel'sən*, *n* a wrestling hold in which the arms are passed under both the opponent's arms from behind, and the hands joined so that pressure can be exerted with the palms on the back of his neck —Also **full nelson.—half nelson** this hold applied on one side only, i e with one arm under one of the opponent's arms a disabling restraint (*fig*) [From the proper name]

nematocyst *nem'ət-ō-sist*, or -*at'*, *n* a stinging organ in jellyfishes, etc , a sac from which a stinging thread can be everted. [Gr *nēma, -atos,* a thread, *kystis,* a bladder.]

nematode *nem'ə-tōd, n* a round-worm or thread-worm.—Also *adj.—adj.* **nem'atoid.**—*n*. **nema-tol'ogist; nematol'ogy** the study of nematodes. [Gr *nēma, -atos,* thread, *eidos,* form]

Nembutal® *nem'bū-təl, n.* proprietary name for sodium dimethylmethylbutyl barbiturate, used as a seda-tive, hypnotic, and antispasmodic.

Nemean *nem-ē'ən, nem'i-ən, nēm'i-ən, adj.* of Nemea (Gr. *Nēmeā*), valley of Argolis, famous for its games held in the second and fourth years of each Olympiad, and for the lion slain by Herakles

Nemertinea *nem-ər-tin'i-ə, n pl.* a phylum of worm-like animals mostly marine, often brightly coloured.—Also **Nemer'tea.** [Gr. *Nēmertēs,* one of the nereids]

Nemesia *nem-ē'zh(y)ə, -sh(y)ə, -si-ə, n.* a S. African genus of the figwort family, including some brightly coloured garden flowers: (without *cap.*) a plant of this genus. [Gr. *nemesion,* a kind of catchfly.]

Nemesis *nem'i-sis, (myth.) n.* the Greek goddess of retribution: (without *cap.*) retributive justice. [Gr *nemesis,* retribution—*nemein,* to deal out, dispense.]

nemine contradicente *nem'ə-nē kon-trə-di-sen'tē, nā'mi-ne kon-trạ-dē-ken'te,* (L.; often abbrev. **nem. con.**) without opposition: no-one speaking in opposi-tion; **nemine dissentiente** *(di-sen-shi-en'tē, -ti-en'te)* no-one dissenting.

Nemophila *nem-of'i-lə, n.* a N. American genus of *Hydrophyllaceae,* favourite garden annuals, esp. one with blue, white-centred flowers: (without *cap.*) a plant of this genus. [Gr. *nemos,* a glade, wooded pasture. *phileein,* to love.]

neo- *nē'ō-,* in composition, new, young, revived in a new form —*adj* **neoclass'ical** belonging to a revival of classicism, or classicism as understood by those who would revive it, e.g. in the 18th century.—*ns* **neoclass'icism** *(-i-sizm),* **neoclass'icist; neocolón'-ialism** the policy of a strong nation of obtaining con-trol over a weaker through economic pressure, etc., **Neo-Dar'winism** a later development of Darwinism. laying greater stress upon natural selection and denying the inheritance of acquired characters —*ns* and *adjs.* **Neo-Darwin'ian, Neo-Dar'winist.**—*ns* **neodymium** *(-dim'i-əm)* a metal (Nd; at numb 60), the chief component of the once-supposed element *didymium* (q v). **Neofascism** *(-fash'izm)* a move-ment attempting to reinstate the policies of fascism, **Neofasc'ist; Neohell'enism** the modern Hellenism inspired by the ancient. the devotion to ancient Greek ideals in literature and art, esp in the Italian Renaissance —*adj* **Neolithic** *(-lith'ik,* Gr *lithos,* a stone) of the later or more advanced Stone Age —*ns* **ne'olith** a Neolithic artefact, **neol'ogy** (Gr *logos,* a word) the introduction of new words, or new senses of old words a neologism —*v.t* **neol'ogise,-ize** to intro-duce new words or doctrines —*ns.* **neol'ogism** a new word or phrase: the use of old words in a new sense, **neol'ogist.**—*adjs* **neologis'tic, -al; neonăt'al** per-taining to the newly born —*adj.* and *n* **ne'onate** (one) newly born.—*n* **neophyte** *(nē'ō-fīt,* Gr *neophytos,* newly planted—*phyein,* to produce) a new convert one newly baptised: a newly ordained priest. a novice in a religious order: a tiro or beginner.—*adj.* **neo-phytic** *(-fit'ik).*—*n.* **neo'plasm** (Gr. *plasma,* form, mould) a morbid new growth or formation of tissue —*adj.* **neoplas'tic.**—*n.* **Neoplă'tonism** a combination of Platonism with Oriental elements.—*adj* **Neo-platonic** *(-plə-ton'ik).*—*ns.* **neoplă'tonist; neoprene** *(nē'ō-prēn)* an oil-resisting and heat-resisting synthetic rubber made by polymerising chloroprene;

neoteny *(nē-ot'ən-i,* Gr. *teinein,* to stretch) prolonged retention of larval or immature character or charac-ters in the adult form.—*adjs* **neotenic** *(nē-ō-ten'ik),* **neot'enous; Neotrop'ical** *(biol.)* of tropical America, **Neozoic** *(nē-ō-zō'ik,* Gr. *zōikos,* of animals) later than Palaeozoic· later than Mesozoic [Gr *neos,* new.]

neon *nē'on, n.* a gaseous element (Ne, at. numb. 10) found in the atmosphere by Sir Wm Ramsay (1852–1916) —**neon lamp, light** an electric discharge lamp containing neon, giving a red glow. used e g for advertising signs: *(loosely)* one of a variety of tubular fluorescent lamps giving light of various colours; **neon lighting.** [Neuter of Gr. *neos,* new.]

neonatal to **neoteny.** See **neo-.**

neoteric *nē-ō-ter'ik, adj.* of recent origin, modern — *adv* **neoter'ically.** [Gr. *neōterikos—neōteros,* compar of *neos,* new.]

Neozoic. See **neo-.**

nepenthe *ni-pen'thē, n* a sorrow-lulling drink or drug *(poet.):* the plant yielding it.—*adj* **nepen'thean.**—*n.* **Nepen'thes** *(-thēz)* nepenthe. the pitcher-plant genus. [Gr. *nepenthēs, -es—pfx. nē-,* not, *penthos,* grief.]

nephelometer *nef-ə-lom'i-tər, n* an instrument for measuring cloudiness. esp. in liquids.—*adj* **ne-phelomet'ric.**—*n.* **nephelom'etry.** [Gr. *nephelē,* cloud, *metron,* measure.]

nephew *nev'ū,* or *nef'ū, n* the son of a brother or sister: extended to a like relation by marriage:—*fem* **niece.** [(O.)Fr. *neveu*—L *nepōs, nepōtis,* grandson, cf. O.E *nefa,* Ger. *Neffe,* nephew]

nephology *nef-ol'ə-ji, n.* the study of clouds in meteorology.—*adjs.* **nephologic** *(-ə-loj'),* **-al.**—*n* **nephol'ogist.** [Gr. *nephos,* cloud.]

nephr(o)- *nef-r(o)-, -r(ō)-,* in composition, kidney.—*n.* **neph'rite** the mineral jade, in the narrower sense—an old charm against kidney disease.—*adj.* **nephrit'ic** pertaining to the kidneys, or nephritis.—*n.* **nephri'tis** inflammation of the kidneys.—*adj.* **nephrolog'ical.**—*ns.* **nephrol'ogist; nephrology** the science concerned with structure, functions, diseases, of the kidneys.—*n.* **nephrot'omy** incision into the kidney. [Gr *nephros,* a kidney]

nepit. See **nit⁴.**

neplusultra *nē plus ul'trə, nā plŏŏs ŏŏl'tra,* (L) nothing further. the uttermost point or extreme perfection of anything

nepotism *nep'o-tizm, n* undue patronage to one's rela-tions. orig by a pope —*adjs* **nepotic** *(ni-pot'ik).* **nepotis'tic.**—*n.* **nep'otist.** [L *nepōs, nepōtis,* a grandson.]

Neptune *nep'tūn, n* the Roman sea-god, identified with the Greek Poseidon. a remote planet of the solar system, discovered in 1846 —*adj.* **Neptū'nian.**—*n* **neptū'nium** an element (Np, at numb 93) named as next after uranium, as Neptune is next after Uranus [L. *Neptūnus.*]

nereid *nē'rē-id, n.* a sea-nymph. daughter of the sea-god *Nereus* (Gr. *myth*): a marine worm. [Gr *nērēis* or *nērēis—Nēreus*]

Nerine *ni-rī'nē, n* a South African amaryllid genus. with scarlet or rose-coloured flowers, including the Guernsey lily: (without *cap.*) a plant of this genus [L. *nērinē,* a nereid.]

nerka *nûr'kə, n.* the sockeye salmon.

nero-antico *nā-rō-an-tē'kō, n.* a deep-black marble found in Roman ruins [It , ancient black]

neroli *ner'ə-lē, n.* an oil distilled from orange flowers—also **neroli oil.** [Said to be named from its discoverer, an Italian princess.]

Neronian *nē-rō'ni-ən, adj.* pertaining to *Nero,* Roman emperor from A D. 54 to 68: excessively cruel and tyrannical. [L. *Nērō, -ōnis.*]

nerve nûrv, *n.* a sinew (now chiefly *fig*). a cord that conveys impulses between the brain or other centre and some part of the body (*anat.*)· a leaf-vein or rib (*bot*). a nervure in an insect's wing (*entom*). a vault rib cool courage impudent assurance, audacity (*coll*)· (in *pl*) nervousness —*v t* to give strength, resolution, or courage to —*adjs* **ner've** (of leaf) having veins nerved, **nerved** furnished with nerves, **nerve'less** without nerves or nervures without strength inert slack, flabby —*ns* **nerve'lessness; nerv'iness.**—*adj.* **nerv'ous** pertaining to the nerves having the nerves easily excited or weak, agitated and apprehensive (often with *of*)· shy timid in a jumpy state —*adv* **nerv'ously.**—*ns.* **nerv'ousness; nerv'ure** a leaf-vein a chitinous strut or rib supporting and strengthening an insect's wing (*entom*) a rib of a groined vault —*adj* **nerv'y** nervous jumpily excited or excitable —**nerve'-cell** any cell forming part of the nervous system. a neuron, **nerve'-cen'tre** an aggregation of nerve-cells from which nerves branch out in an organisation, the centre from which control is exercised (*fig*), **nerve'-fi'bre** an axon, **nerve gas** any of a number of gases, prepared for use in war, having a deadly effect on the nervous system, esp on nerves controlling respiration —*adj* **nerve'-rack'ing, -wrack'ing** distressfully straining the nerves —**nerve, nervous, impulse** the electrical impulse passing along a nerve fibre when it has been stimulated, **nervous breakdown** a loose term indicating nervous debility following prolonged mental or physical fatigue a euphemism for any mental illness, **nervous system** the brain, spinal cord, and nerves collectively —**bundle of nerves** (*coll.*) a very timid, anxious person, **get on one's nerves** to become oppressively irritating, **live on one's nerves** to be in a tense or nervous state. to be of an excitable temperament, **lose one's nerve** to lose confidence in one's ability to become suddenly afraid, **war of nerves** see **war.** [L *nervus*, sinew, cf Gr *neuron*]

nescience nesh'i-əns, nesh'əns, nes'i-əns, -yəns, *n* want of knowledge.—*adj* **nesc'ient.** [L *nescientia* —*nescire*, to be ignorant—*ne-*, not, *scîre*, to know]

ness nes, *n* a headland [O.E. næs, næss.]

nest nest, *n* a structure prepared for egg-laying, brooding, and nursing, or as a shelter a place of retreat or residence a den a comfortable residence a place where anything teems, or is fostered the occupants of a nest, as a brood, a swarm, a gang· a set of things (as boxes, tables) fitting one within another a set of buildings divided into blocks and units —*v t* to build or occupy a nest to go bird's-nesting —*v t* and *v t* to lodge, settle —**nest'-egg** an egg. real or sham, left or put in a nest to encourage laying something laid up as the beginning of an accumulation money saved; **nest'ing-box** a box set up for birds to nest in — **feather one's nest** see **feather.** [O.E. *nest*]

nestle nes'l, *v t* to lie or press close or snug as in a nest to settle comfortably or half hidden —*v t* to thrust close to provide a nesting-place for —*n* **nestling** (nes'ling) a young bird in the nest —Also *adj* [O E *nestlian—nest*]

Nestor nes'tor, -tər, *n* an old king of Pylos, a Greek hero at Troy remarkable for eloquence, wisdom, and long life [Gr *Nestor*]

net¹ net, *n* an open fabric, knotted into meshes a piece or bag, or a screen or structure, of such fabric used for catching fish, butterflies, etc , carrying parcels, stopping balls, retaining hair, excluding pests machine-made race of various kinds a snare —*adj* of or like net or network —*v t* to form into network to mark or cover with network. to set with nets: to form by making network to take with a net to capture — *v t* to form network —*pr p* **nett'ing;** *pa t* and *pa p*

nett'ed.—*n* **net'ful** enough to fill a net —*adj* **nett'ed** made into a net reticulated. caught in a net: covered with a net —*n* **nett'ing** the act or process of forming network a piece of network —*adj* **nett'y** like a net —**net'ball** a game in which the ball is thrown into a net hung from a pole, **net'-play** (in tennis, etc) play near the net, **net'-player; nett'ing-need'le** a kind of shuttle used in netting.—**net'work** any structure in the form of a net a system of lines, e g railway lines, resembling a net a system of units, as, e g buildings, agencies, groups of persons, constituting a widely spread organisation and having a common purpose an arrangement of electrical components a system of stations connected for broadcasting the same programme (*radio* and *TV*) —*v t* to broadcast on radio or T V stations throughout the country, as opposed to a single station covering only one region [O E *net, nett*, Du *net*, Ger *Netz*.]

net², **nett** net, *adj* clear of all charges or deductions (opp to *gross*) of weight, not including that of packaging lowest, subject to no further deductions.—*v t* to gain or produce as clear profit —*pr p* **nett'ing;** *pa t* and *pa p* **nett'ed.** [neat².]

nether nedh'ər, *adj* lower —*adj* **neth'ermost** lowest [O E *neothera*, adj —*nither*, adv , from the root *ni-*, down]

Netherlander nedh'ər-land-ər, *n* an inhabitant of the *Netherlands*, formerly also Belgium —*adjs* **Netherland'ic; Neth'erlandish** Dutch

netsuke net'skē, -skā, ne'tsoō-ke', *n* a small Japanese carved ornament, once used to fasten small objects, e g a purse or pouch for tobacco, medicines, etc , to a sash [Jap *ne*, root, bottom, *tsuke—tsukeru*, to attach]

nett. See **net².**

nettle net'l, *n* a common weed (Urtica) with stinging hairs —*v t* to sting to annoy —**nett'lerash** a rash of red or white weals with irritation like nettle-stings urticaria —**grasp the nettle** to set about an unpleasant task, duty, etc with firmness and resolution [O E *netele*, Ger *Nessel*.]

netty, network, etc See **net¹.**

neume nūm, *n* in mediaeval music, a succession of notes sung to one syllable a sign giving a rough indication of rise or fall of pitch —Also **neum.** [O Fr , —Gr *pneuma*, breath]

neur- nûr-, **neuro-** nū'rō-, in composition, pertaining to a nerve-cell, to a nerve-fibre, to nerve-tissue, or to the nervous system (esp the brain and spinal cord) pertaining to the nerves and some other system (e g *adjs* **neuromus'cular, neurovas'cular**). concerned with, dealing with, the nervous system (e.g. **neurophysiol'ogy; neurosur'gery**) —*adj* **neu'ral** of, or relating to, nerves dorsal (opp to *haemal*).—*n* **neuralgia** (nū-ral'jə, -jyə, Gr *algos*, pain) paroxysmal intermittent pain along the course of a nerve.—*adj* **neural'gic.**—*ns* **neurasthenia** (nū-rəs-thē'ni-ə, Gr *astheneia*, weakness) nervous debility, **neurasthè'niac** one suffering from neurasthenia.—*adj.* **neurasthenic** (-*then'ik*, or -*thēn'ik*) —Also *n* a neurastheniac —*ns* **neurâ'tion** nervation; **neurec'tomy** the surgical excision of part of a nerve, **neurilemm'a, neurolemm'a** (Gr *eilēma*, covering) the external sheath of a nerve-fibre —*adj.* **neuritic** (-*it'ik*) —*ns* **neuri'tis** inflammation of a nerve, **neurog'lia** (Gr. *glia*, glue) the supporting tissue of the brain and spinal cord, etc —*adj* **neurolog'ical.**—*ns* **neurol'ogist; neurol'ogy** orig the study of the nervous system that branch of medicine concerned with the diagnosis and treatment of diseases of the nervous system, **neu'ron, neu'rone** a nerve-cell with its processes —*adj* **neurôn'al.**—*n* **neur'opath** (-*path*, Gr *pathos*, suffering) one whose nervous system is

diseased or abnormal —*adjs* **neuropath'ic, -al.**—*ns*
neuropathist (*nūr-op'ə-thıst*) a specialist in nervous
diseases, **neuropathol'ogy** the pathology of the nervous system; **neurop'athy** nervous disease generally,
neuró'sis functional derangement through disordered
nervous system, esp without lesion of parts' mental
disturbance characterised by a state of unconscious
conflict, usually accompanied by anxiety and obses-
sional fears (also called *psychoneurosis*)· (*loosely*) an
obsession:—*pl* **neuróses** (*-sēz*) —*adj* **neurotic**
(*-ot'ık*) of the nature of, characterised by, or affected
by, neurosis· (*loosely*) obsessive hypersensitive —*n*
a person with neurosis a medicine for nerve diseases
(*arch.*) —*ns* **neurot'icism** (*-sızm*), **neurotomy**
(*-ot'ə-mi*) the surgical cutting of a nerve [Gr
neuron, a nerve]

Neuroptera *nū-rop'tə-rə, n.* a former order of insects,
pl. now placed in a superorder, **Neuropteroidea** (*nū-
rop-tə-roi'dı-ə*), the insects generally having four net-
veined wings.—*adj* **neurop'terous.** [Gr *neuron*, a
nerve, *pteron*, a wing, *eidos*, form]

neuter *nū'tər, adj* neither masculine nor feminine
(*gram*). sexless sexually undeveloped· castrated
without, or without a functional, androecium or
gynaeceum —*n* a neuter word, plant, or animal esp
a worker bee, ant, etc · a castrated cat —*v t* to
castrate. [L *neuter*, neither—*ne*, not, *uter*, either]

neutral *nū'trəl, adj.* indifferent· taking no part on
either side: not siding with either party pertaining to
neither party: not involved in a war or dispute: belonging to neither, esp. of two adjoining countries of
no decided character: having no decided colour with
no noticeable smell: belonging to neither of two
opposites, as acid and alkaline, electrically positive
and negative: neuter without transmission of motion.—*n.* a person or nation that takes no part in a
contest: a position of gear in which no power is transmitted: a neuter.—*n* **neutralisa'tion, -z-.**—*v t*
neu'tralise, -ize to declare neutral: to make inert· to
render of no effect: to counteract.—*ns* **neu'traliser,**
-z-; **neu'tralism** the policy of not entering into alliance with other nations or taking sides ideologically;
neu'tralist; neutrality (*-tral'ı-tı*) the fact or state of
being neutral —*adv.* **neu'trally.** [L *neutrālis—*
neuter, neither]

neutron *nū'tron,* (*phys.*) *n.* an uncharged particle of
about the same mass as the proton —*n* **neutrino**
(*-trē'nō*) an uncharged particle with zero mass when
at rest:—*pl* **neutri'nos** —**neutron bomb** a type of
nuclear bomb which destroys life by immediate intense radiation, without blast and heat effects to destroy buildings, etc.; **neutron number** the number of
neutrons in the nucleus of an atom; **neutron star** a
supposed heavenly body of very small size and very
great density, an almost burnt out and collapsed star
[L. *neuter*, neither.]

névé *nā'vā, n.* firn: the snow lying on the surface of a
glacier [Fr.,—L. *nix, nivis*, snow]

never *nev'ər, adv.* not ever: at no time: in no degree
not —*adjs.* **nev'er-end'ing; nev'er-fad'ing; nev'er-**
fail'ing.—*adv* **nev'ermore** at no future time —*n*
nev'er-nev'er the hire-purchase system (*coll*)
(**-land**) an imaginary place, imaginary conditions, too
fortunate ever to exist in reality —*advs* **nevertheless'**
notwithstanding· in spite of that —**never so** (*arch*)
ever so [O E *næfre—ne*, not, *æfre*, ever]

new *nū, adj* lately made or produced young fresh
not much used: having lately happened or begun to
be: recent, modern· not before seen or known· only
lately discovered or experienced. other than the
former or preceding, different: additional strange,
unaccustomed: lately begun beginning afresh· renewed: reformed or regenerated· restored or re-

sumed —*n* that which is new newness —*adv* (often
joined by hyphen to an adj) newly anew —*adj*
new'ish.—*adv* **new'ly** very lately —*n* **new'ness.**—
new birth renewal, esp spiritual, **new blood** (a person
with) fresh talent a revitalising force —*adjs* **new'-**
blown just come into bloom, **new'born** newly born —
new broom (*fig*) see **new brooms sweep clean** under
broom.—*adj* **new'come** recently arrived —**new'-**
comer one who has lately come, **New Englander** a
native or citizen of any of the New England states —
adjs **newfangled** see separate article, **new's**
fash'ioned made in a new way or fashion lately come
into fashion, **new'-found** newly discovered or
devised —**New Jerusalem** the heavenly city —*adj*
new'-laid —**New Learning** the new studies
of the Renaissance, **New Left** an extreme left-wing
movement among students, etc , in the 1960s, **New**
Light a member of a relatively more advanced religious school; **new look** a change in women's fashions
(1947), notably to longer and fuller skirts· a radical
modification in the appearance of something —*n*
and *adj* **new'ly-wed** (a person who is) recently married, **new maths** a method of teaching mathematics
which is more concerned with basic structures and
concepts than numerical drills, **new moon** the
moment when the moon is directly in line between the
earth and sun, and therefore invisible· the time when
the waxing moon becomes visible: the narrow waxing
crescent itself, **new rich** the recently enriched: par-
venus; **New'speak** a type of English described by
George Orwell in his book, *Nineteen Eighty-four*
(1949), developed by reducing vocabulary to such a
point, and forming new words of such ugliness and so
little emotive value, that literature and even thought
will be impossible: (also without *cap*) any type of
language considered similar in style, etc (esp *pejorative*); **New Style** see **style; new town** a town planned
and built by the government to aid housing conditions
in near-by large cities, stimulate development, etc ,
New Wave see **Nouvelle Vague:** a slightly later
movement in jazz aiming at freedom from set patterns and styles: (also without *caps*) any similar
artistic, musical, cultural, etc movement or grouping, **New World** North and South America, **New Year**
the first few days of the year —**New Model Army** the
Parliamentary army as remodelled by Cromwell
(1645), **New Year's Day** the first day of the year
[O E. *nīwe, nēowe*, Ger *neu*, Ir *nuadh*, L *novus*,
Gr. *neos*]

Newcastle disease *nū'ka-səl dız-ēz', an acute, highly
contagious viral disease of chickens and other domestic and wild birds, first recorded at *Newcastle*-upon-
Tyne in 1926—also called **fowl-pest.**

newel *nū'əl, n* the upright column about which the
steps of a circular staircase wind. an upright post at
the end or corner of a stair handrail (also **newel post**)
—*adj* **new'elled.** [O Fr *nual* (Fr *noyau*),
fruitstone—L L *nucālis*, nutlike—L *nux, nucis*, a
nut]

newfangled *nū-fang'gld, adj* unduly fond of new
things newly but superfluously devised —*adv* **new-**
fang'ledly.—*n* **newfang'ledness, newfang'leness.**
[M E *newefangel—newe* (O E *nīwe*), new, *fangel*,
ready to catch]

Newfoundland *nū-fownd'lənd, n* a very large, intelligent breed of dog from *Newfoundland*, originally
black, a strong swimmer

newmarket *nū-mar'kıt, or nū', n* a card game in which
the stakes go to those who succeed in playing out
cards whose duplicates lie on the table a close-fitting
coat, originally a riding-coat, for men or women
[*Newmarket*, the racing town]

news *nūz, n* (*orig pl*) tidings a report of a recent

event something one had not heard before matter suitable for newspaper readers —*n* **news'iness.**—*adj* **news'y** gossipy —**news agency** an organisation which collects material for newspapers, magazines, etc , **news'agent** one who deals in newspapers, **news'boy, news'girl** a boy or girl who delivers or sells newspapers, **news'cast** a news broadcast or telecast, **news'casting; news'caster** one who gives newscasts; an apparatus which gives a changing display of news headlines, etc ; **news'hound** a reporter in search of news, **news'letter** orig a written or printed letter containing news sent by an agent to his subscribers—the predecessor of the newspaper a sheet of news supplied to members of a particular group, **news'man, -woman** a bringer, collector, or writer of news; **news'monger** one who deals in news: one who spends much time in hearing periodically for circulating news. etc , **news'paper-man, -woman** a journalist. **news'print** paper for printing newspapers, **news'* reader** one who reads news on radio or television, **news'reel** film showing, or a programme commenting on, news items, **news'room** a reading-room with newspapers room. etc , where news is made ready for newspaper, newscast, etc , **news'-sheet** a printed sheet of news, esp an early form of newspaper, **news'-stand** a stall for the sale of newspapers, **news'* theatre** a cinema showing chiefly newsreels, **news'* value** interest to the general public as news, **news'* vendor** a seller of newspapers; **newswoman** see **newsman.**—*adj* **news'worthy** sufficiently interesting to be told as news —**news'worthiness; news'-writer** a reporter or writer of news —**New Blood scheme, appointment,** etc (an appointment under) a University Grants Committee scheme to finance a number of extra university posts in certain fields [Late M E *newes*; Fr. *nouvelles*]

newt *nūt, n* a tailed amphibian of the salamander family—formed with initial *n*, borrowed from the article **an,** from *ewt,* a form of **eft¹.** [O E *efeta, efete*]

newton *nū'tən, n* the SI unit of force—it is equal to the force which, acting on a mass of one kilogramme, produces an acceleration of one metre per second per second —*adj* **Newtonian** *(nū-tō'ni-ən)* relating to, according to, formed or discovered by, Sir Isaac *Newton* (1642–1727).—**Newtonian telescope** a form of reflecting telescope

next *nekst, adj* nearest in place, in kinship or other relation· nearest following (or preceding if explicitly stated) in time or order.—*adv* nearest immediately after. on the first occasion that follows· in the next place.—*adv* **next'ly.**—*adj* **next best, biggest,** etc , next in order after the best, biggest, etc.—*adj* **next'-door** dwelling in or occupying the next house, shop, etc · at or in the next house neighbouring —*adv* **next-door'.** —**next friend** a person appointed, or permitted, by a court of law to act on behalf of a minor or other person under legal disability —**next door to** in the next house to: near, bordering upon. very nearly, **next of kin** see **kin; next to** adjacent to almost, **next to nothing** almost nothing at all [O E *nēhst (niehst),* superl of *nēh (nēah),* near]

nexus *nek'səs, n.* a bond a linked group [L *nexus,* pl -*ūs*—*nectĕre,* to bind]

ngaio *ni'ō, n* a New Zealand tree with white wood — *pl* **ngai'os.** [Maori]

niacin *ni'ə-sin, n* nicotinic acid

nib *nib, n* something small and pointed a pen-point a bird's bill a peak· a projecting point or spike· a timber carriage pole. a handle on a scythe's shaft *(dial)·* (in *pl*) crushed cocoa-beans· (in *pl*) included particles in varnish, wool, etc —*v t* to furnish with a

nib to point to mend the nib of to reduce to nibs — *adj* **nibbed** having a nib [**neb.**]

nibble *nib'l, v t* to bite gently or by small bites to eat a little at a time —*v i* to bite gently to show signs of accepting, as an offer, or of yielding (with *at*): to find fault —*n* the act of nibbling a little bit —*ns* **nibb'ler; nibb'ling.**—*adv* **nibb'lingly.** [Origin obscure, cf L G *nibbelen,* Du *knibbelen*]

niblick *nib'lik, n* a golf-club with a heavy head with wide face, used for lofting—a number eight or nine iron

nibs *nibz* **his nibs** *(iron)* himself, his mightiness

niccolite *nik'əl-īt, n* a hexagonal mineral, nickel arsenide, also called kupfernickel, copper-nickel [See **nickel.**]

nice *nis, adj* hard to please fastidious. forming or observing very small differences calling for very fine discrimination done with great care and exactness, accurate delicate dainty agreeable, delightful. respectable —*adj* **nice'ish.**—*adv* **nice'ly.**—*ns* **nice'ness; nicety** *(nis'i-ti)* the quality of being nice precision fineness of perception or feeling critical subtlety a matter of delicate discrimination or refinement fastidiousness —**nice and** used adverbially— pleasantly, **to a nicety** with great exactness [O Fr *nice,* foolish, simple—L *nescius,* ignorant]

Nicene *ni'sēn, adj* pertaining to the town of *Nicaea,* in Bithynia, where a council in 325 dealt with the Arian controversy —**Nicene Creed** the creed based on the results of the first Nicene Council

niche *nich, nēsh, n* a recess in a wall· a suitable or actual place or condition in life —*v t* to place in a niche —*adj* **niched** placed in a niche [Fr ,—It *nicchia,* niche, of doubtful origin]

Nichrome® *ni'krōm, n* trademark for a nickel-chromium alloy with high electrical resistance and ability to withstand high temperatures

nick *nik, n* a notch: a cut the precise moment of time: a prison, a police-office *(slang)* —*v t* to notch: to mark by cutting, carve out to cut· to snip. to catch *(slang)* to arrest *(slang)* to steal *(slang)* to make a cut in a horse's tail muscle, so that the tail is carried higher.—*v i* of breeding animals, to mate well —**in good nick** *(coll)* in good health or condition; **in the nick** (now usu **nick of time**) just in time: at the critical moment [Possibly connected with **nock, notch.**]

Nick *nik, n.* the devil, esp **Old Nick.**—Also *(Scot)* **Nickie-ben'.** [Apparently for *Nicholas*]

nickel *nik'l, n* an element (symbol Ni, at. numb 28), a white, magnetic, very malleable and ductile metal largely used in alloys a 5-cent piece (of copper and nickel, *U S*) —*adj* of nickel —*v t* to plate with nickel —*pr p* **nick'elling;** *pa t* and *pa p* **nick'elled.** —**nick'el-plat'ing** the plating of metals with nickel; **nick'el-sil'ver** an alloy of copper, nickel and zinc, white like silver, **nick'el-steel'** a steel containing some nickel [Ger *Kupfer-nickel,* niccolite—*Kupfer,* copper, *Nickel,* a mischievous sprite, goblin, because the ore looked like copper-ore but yielded no copper]

nickelodeon *nik-ə-lō'di-on, n* a five-cent entertainment· a juke-box [See **nickel, odeon.**]

nicker *nik'ər, (slang) n* £1

nick-nack, etc Same as **knick-knack,** etc

nickname *nik'nām, n* a name given in contempt or sportive familiarity —*v t* to give a nickname to [M E *neke-name,* for *eke-name,* with *n* from the indefinite article, see **eke¹, name.**]

nicol *nik'l, n* a crystal of calcium carbonate so cut and cemented as to transmit only the extraordinary ray, used for polarising light —Also **Nicol('s) prism.** [From William *Nicol* *(c 1768–1851)* of Edinburgh, its inventor]

Nicotiana ni-kō-shi-a'nə, n the tobacco genus (without cap) a plant of the genus —ns **nicotinamide** (-tin') a member of the vitamin B complex, **nicotine** (nik'ə-tēn) a poisonous alkaloid got from tobacco leaves —adj **nicotinic** (-tin'ik) —n **nic'otinism** a morbid state induced by excessive use of tobacco —**nicotinic acid** a white crystalline substance, a member of the vitamin B complex, deficiency of which is connected with the development of pellagra [Jean Nicot, who sent tobacco to Catherine de Medici]

nictate nik'tāt, v i to wink—also **nic'titate.—**ns **nicta'tion, nictita'tion.—nictitating membrane** the third eyelid, developed in birds, etc , a thin movable membrane that passes over the eye [L nictāre, -ātum and its L L freq nictitāre, -ātum, to wink]

nidal, etc See **nidus.**

nidicolous nid-ik'ə-ləs, adj (of young birds) staying long in the nest [L nīdus, a nest, colēre, to inhabit]

nidificate. See **nidify.**

nidifugous nid-if'ū-gəs, adj (of young birds) leaving the nest soon after hatching [L nīdus, nest, fugēre, to flee]

nidify nid'i-fī, v i to build a nest —Also **nidificate** (nid'i-fi-kāt) —n **nidifica'tion.** [L nīdus, nest, facēre, to make]

nidus ni'dəs, n a nest or breeding-place a place where anything is originated, harboured, developed, or fostered a place of lodgment or deposit a point of infection a nerve-centre —pl **ni'di.—**adj **ni'dal** pertaining to a nest or nidus [L nīdus, a nest]

niece nēs, n a brother's or sister's daughter extended to a like relation by marriage —masc **nephew.** [O Fr , —L nepus, granddaughter]

niello ni-el'ō, n a method of ornamenting metal by engraving, and filling up the lines with a black composition, a work so produced the compound used in niello-work —pl **niell'i** (-ē), **niell'os.—**v i to decorate with niello —pr p **niell'oing;** pa t and pa p **niell'oed.** [It niello—L L nigellum, a black enamel —L niger, black]

Niersteiner nēr's(h)tīn-ər, n a Rhine wine, named from Nierstein, near Mainz

Nietzschean nēch'i-ən, adj of Friedrich Nietzsche (1844-1900) or his philosophy —n a follower of Nietzsche —n **Nietzsch'eanism.**

niff nif, (dial or slang) n a stink —adj **niff'y.**

nifty nif'ti, (slang) adj. fine. spruce sharp, neat smart quick agile —n **nift'iness.**

Nigella ni-jel'ə, n a genus of plants, with finely dissected leaves, and whitish, blue, or yellow flowers—Nigella damascena is called love-in-a-mist (without cap) a plant of the genus [Fem of L nigellus, blackish—niger, black, from the black seeds]

niggard nig'ərd, n one who grudges to spend or give away —adj niggardly —n **nigg'ardliness.—**adj **nigg'ardly** stingy

nigger nig'ər, n derogatorily, a Negro, or a member of any very dark-skinned race —adj Negro blackish brown —**nigger in the wood-pile** a hidden evil influence, **work like a nigger** to toil hard [Fr nègre —Sp negro, see **Negro.**]

niggle nig'l, v i to busy oneself with petty scrupulosity to move in a fidgety or ineffective way to gnaw to criticise in a petty way —ns a minor criticism —ns **nigg'ler; nigg'ling** fussiness petty elaboration —adj petty fussy —adj **nigg'ly.** [Cf Norw nigle]

nigh nī, (poet , dial , or arch) adj , adv , prep , near [O E nēah, nēh]

night nīt, n the end of the day the time from sunset to sunrise the dark part of the twenty-four-hour day darkness obscurity, ignorance, evil, affliction, or sorrow death the experience of a night a night set apart for some purpose, esp receiving visitors —adj belonging to night occurring or done in the night working or on duty by night.—adj **night'less.—**adj and adv **night'long** lasting all night.—adj **night'ly** done or happening by night or every nigh —adv by night every night —adv. **nights** (coll) at, by night —n **night'y, night'ie** a nightgown —**night'-bell** a door-bell for use at night, **night'-bird** a bird that flies or that sings at night a person who is active or about at night, **night'-blind'ness** inability to see in a dim light, nyctalopia, **night'cap** a cap worn at night in bed a drink taken before going to bed, **night'-cart** (hist) a cart used to remove the contents of privies before daylight, **night'-club** a club open between nightfall and morning for amusement or dissipation, **night'dress** attire for the night, esp a nightgown, **night'fall** the fall or beginning of the night the close of the day evening, **night's glass** a spy-glass with concentrating lenses for use at night, **night'(-)gown** a loose robe for sleeping in, for men or women, **night'jar** a goatsucker, **night'-latch** a door-lock worked by a key without and a knob within, **night life** activity in the form of entertainments at night, **night'-light** lamp, candle that gives a subdued light all night the faint light of the night, the light of phosphorescent sea-animals, **night'mare** (O E mære, M E mare, the nightmare incubus, cf O H G mara, O N mara) an unpleasant dream a horrifying experience —adj **night'marish.—night'-owl** an exclusively nocturnal owl one who sits up very late, **night'-school** a school held at night, esp for those at work during the day, **night'-shift** a gang or group of workers that takes its turn by night the time it is on duty a nightdress (arch), **night'shirt** a man's shirt for sleeping in, **night'-soil** (hist) the contents of privies, cesspools, etc , generally carried away at night and sometimes used for fertiliser, **night'spot** (coll) a night-club, **night'-time** the time when it is night, **night'-watch** a watch or guard at night one who is on watch by night time of watch in the night, **night'-watch'man** one who is on watch by night, esp on industrial premises and building sites a batsman, not a high scorer, put in to defend a wicket until the close of play (cricket) —**make a night of it** to spend the night, or a large part of it, in amusement or celebration, **of a night, of nights** in the course of a night some time at night [O E niht, Ger Nacht, L nox, Gr nyx]

nightingale nīt'ing-gāl, n a small bird of the thrush family celebrated for the rich love-song of the male heard chiefly at night a person with a beautiful singing voice [O E nihtegale—niht, night, galan, to sing, Ger Nachtigall]

nightjar, nightmare. See **night.**

nightshade nīt'shād, n a name given to various plants, chiefly of the Solanaceae and chiefly poisonous or narcotic —**deadly nightshade** belladonna, **woody nightshade** bittersweet [O E nihtscada, app —niht, night, scada, shade]

nightshirt, nightspot. See **night.**

nigrescence nī- or ni-gres'əns, n blackness dark colouring or pigmentation blackening —adj **nigresc'ent** growing black or dark blackish [L niger, black]

nihilism nī'hil-izm, -il-, n belief in nothing denial of all reality, or of all objective growth of truth extreme scepticism nothingness in tsarist Russia, a terrorist movement aiming at the overturn of all the existing institutions of society, **ni'hilist.—**adj **nihilist'ic.—**n **nihility** (-hil') nothingness a mere nothing [L nihil, nothing]

nihil ad rem nī', ni'hil ad rem, (L) nothing to the point, **ni'hil obstat** (ob'stat) nothing hinders—a book censor s form of permission to print

-nik -nik, in composition, a person who does, practises, etc something, as in beatnik, kibbutznik [Russ suffix, influenced in meaning by Yiddish suffix denoting an agent]

nil *nil, n* nothing zero [L *nil, nihil,* nothing.]

Nile green *nil grēn,* a very pale green colour, thought of as the colour of the River *Nile*

nilgai *n* a large Indian antelope, the male slaty-grey, the female tawny [Pers and Hind *nil,* blue, Hind *gāi,* Pers *gāw,* cow]

Nilot *nil'ot,* **Nilote** *-ōt, ns* an inhabitant of the banks of the Upper Nile: a Hamitised Negro of the Upper Nile —*adj.* **Nilotic** (*-ot'ik*) of the Nile [Gr *Neilōtēs*]

nim *nim, n.* an old and widespread game, perh orig. Chinese, in which two players take alternately from heaps or rows of objects (now usu matches) [Perh. O E. *niman,* to take]

nimbi. See **nimbus.**

nimble *nim'bl, adj.* light and quick in motion: active: swift.—*n.* **nim'bleness.**—*adv* **nim'bly.**—*adjs* **nim'ble-fing'ered; nimbl'e-foot'ed; nim'ble-witt'ed.** [App O E *næmel, numol—niman,* to take]

nimbus *nim'bəs, n* a cloud or luminous mist investing a god or goddess: a halo. a rain-cloud —*pl.* **nim'bi, nim'buses.**—*n* **nimbostratus** (*-strā', -stra'*) a low, dark-coloured layer of cloud, bringing rain [L.]

niminy-piminy *nim'i-ni-pim'i-ni, adj* affectedly fine or delicate —*n* affected delicacy [Imit]

Nimrod *nim'rod, n.* any great hunter [From the son of Cush, Gen x 8–10]

nincompoop *nin(g)'kəm-pōōp, n* a simpleton: a booby

nine *nīn, n.* the cardinal number next above eight. a symbol representing it (9, ix, etc.) a set of that number of things or persons (as a baseball team): a shoe or other article of a size denoted by 9 a card with nine pips a score of nine points, tricks, etc. the ninth hour after midday or midnight: the age of nine years —*adj.* of the number nine nine years old —*adj* **ninth** (*ninth*) last of nine. next after the eighth: equal to one of nine equal parts —*n.* a ninth part: a person or thing in ninth position an octave and a second (*mus*) a tone at that interval (*mus.*) —*adv* **ninth'ly** in the ninth place —*adjs* **nine'-foot, -inch, -mile,** etc, measuring 9 feet, etc, **nine'-hole** having nine holes, **nine'-pin** a bottle-shaped pin set up with eight others for the game of **nine'pins** in which players bowl a ball at these pins (see **skittles**) —*n* and *adj* **nine'score** nine times twenty —**nine days' wonder** see **wonder; nine men's morris** see **meril; nine points of the law** worth nine-tenths of all the points that could be raised (proverbially of possession); **to the nines** fully, elaborately [O E *nigon*]

nineteen *nin-tēn', or nīn'tēn, n.* and *adj* nine and ten. —*n.* and *adj* **nine'teenth** (or *-tēnth'*) —*adv* **nine'teenth'ly.—nineteenth hole** a golf club-house, esp the bar or restaurant —**nineteen to the dozen** with great volubility [O.E *nigontēne* (*-tiene*), see **nine, ten.**]

ninety *nīn'ti, n* and *adj* nine times ten —*n pl* **nine'ties** the numbers ninety to ninety-nine: the years so numbered in a life or a century. a range of temperature from ninety to just less than one hundred degrees —*adj.* **nine'tieth** last of ninety next after the eighty-ninth equal to one of ninety equal parts —*n* a ninetieth part a person or thing in ninetieth position [O E *nigontig (hundnigontig)*]

ninny *nin'i, n* a simpleton [Possibly from **innocent;** poss —It *ninno,* child]

ninon *nē-nɔ̃', n.* a silk voile or other thin fabric [Fr *Ninon,* a woman's name.]

ninth. See **nine.**

Niobe *ni'ō-bē, n* a daughter of Tantalus, turned into stone as she wept for her children, slain by Artemis and Apollo —*adj* **Niobe'an.** [Gr. *Niobē.*]

niobium *ni-ō'bi-əm, n* a metallic element (symbol Nb, at numb. 41) discovered in the mineral tantalite —*adj.* **nio'bic.** [See **Niobe.**]

nip[1] *nip, n* a small quantity of spirits —*v t* to take a dram

nip[2] *nip, v t* to pinch: to press between two surfaces: to remove or sever by pinching or biting (often with *off*): to check the growth or vigour of to give a smarting or tingling feeling to. to snatch —*v.i* to pinch: to smart to go nimbly —*pr p* **nipp'ing;** *pa t.* and *pa p.* **nipped** (*nipt*).—*n* an act or experience of nipping: the pinch of cold: a nipping quality —*n* **nipp'er** one who, or that which, nips. a great claw, as of a crab: a horse's incisor, esp of the middle four: a little boy or (sometimes) girl. (in *pl*) any of various pincer-tools. —*adj* **nipp'y** pungent, biting. nimble (*coll.*). (esp of weather) very cold, frosty. —**nip in the bud** see **bud**[1]. [Prob related to Du. *nijpen,* to pinch]

Nip. See **Nippon.**

Nipa *nē', ni'pə, n.* a low-growing East Indian palm of brackish water: an alcoholic drink made from it. [Malay *nīpah*]

nipple *nip'l, n* the pap of the breast: a teat: a small projection with an orifice, esp for regulating flow or lubricating machinery —**nipp'lewort** a tall composite weed with small yellow heads [A dim. of **neb** or **nib.**]

Nippon *nip-on', n.* the Japanese name of Japan.—*n* and *adj* **Nipp'onese.**—*n.* **Nip** (*slang*) a Japanese [Jap. *ni,* sun, *pon—hon,* origin]

nippy. See **nip**[2].

nirvana *nir-va'nə, n* the cessation of individual existence—the state to which a Buddhist aspires as the best attainable (*loosely*) a blissful state [Sans *nirvāna,* a blowing out]

nisei *nē-sā', n.* a resident in the Americas born of Japanese immigrant parents [Jap., second generation]

nisi *ni'si, adj* to take effect unless, after a time, some condition referred to, be fulfilled [The L *conj nisi,* unless.]

nisi prius *ni'si pri'əs, ni'si pri'ōōs,* (L) unless previously—a name (from the first words of the writ) given to the jury sittings in civil cases

Nissen *nis'ən, adj* designed by Col P N *Nissen* (1871–1930), applied to a semi-cylindrical corrugated-iron hut

nit[1] *nit, n* the egg of a louse or other vermin a young louse —*adj* **nitt'y** full of nits —**nit'-picking** (*coll*) petty criticism of minor details —*v t* **nit'-pick.** [O E *hnitu*]

nit[2] *nit,* (*coll*) *n* a fool [Poss. foregoing, or an abbrev of **nitwit.**]

nit[3] *nit, n* the unit of luminance, one candela per square metre [L. *nitor,* brightness.]

nit[4] *nit,* (*comput.*) *n* a unit of information (1·44 bits)—also **nep'it.** [Napierian *digit*]

niterie, nitery *nit'ə-ri,* (*coll*) *n* a nightclub [**night,** -**ery.**]

nitid *nit'id, adj* shining gay [L *nitidus—nitēre,* to shine]

nitraniline. See **nitro-.**

nitre *ni'tər, n* potassium nitrate or saltpetre (**cubic nitre** is sodium nitrate, or **Chile saltpetre**) —*n.* **ni'trate** a salt of nitric acid a fertiliser—natural (potassium or sodium) or synthetic (calcium) nitrate —*v t* to treat with nitric acid or a nitrate to convert into a nitrate or nitro-compound.—*ns.* **nitratine** (*ni'trə-tin*) sodium nitrate as a mineral; **nitra'tion.**—*adj* **ni'tric.**—*n* **ni'tride** a compound of nitrogen with another element.—*v t.* to turn into a nitride to case-harden by heating in ammonia gas.—*ns.* **ni'triding; ni'trile** (*-tril, -trēl, -trīl*) any of a group of organic cyanides; **nitrifica'tion** treatment with nitric acid: conversion into nitrates, esp. by bacteria through the intermediate condition of nitrites.—*v t.* and *v.i* **ni'trify** to subject to or suffer nitrification:—*pr.p.* **ni'trifying**; *pa.t* and *pa.p* **ni'trified**.—*n* **ni'trite** a salt of nitrous acid.—*adj.* **ni'trous**.—**nitric acid** HNO₃; **nitric anhydride** N₂O₅; **nitric oxide** NO, **nitrous acid** HNO₂; **nitrous oxide** laughing gas, N₂O [Fr.,—L. *nitrum*—Gr. *nitron*, sodium carbonate, prob. of Eastern origin.]

nitride, nitrile, nitrify, etc. See **nitre**.

nitro- *ni-trō-*, in composition, indicating nitration.— *n.pl.* **ni'trobacte'ria** bacteria that convert ammonium compounds into nitrites, and (esp.) those that convert nitrites into nitrates.—*ns.* **nitroben'zene** a yellow oily liquid (C₆H₅NO₂) got from benzene and nitric acid concentrated sulphuric acid; **nitrocell'ulose** cellulose nitrate, used as an explosive, in lacquers, glues, etc.; **ni'tro-com'pound** a compound in which one or more hydrogens of an aromatic or aliphatic compound are replaced by nitro-groups; **ni'trocott'on** guncotton, **nitroglyc'erine** a powerfully explosive compound produced by the action of nitric and sulphuric acids on glycerine, **ni'tro-group** the radical NO₂; **nitrome'thane** a liquid (CH₃NO₂) obtained from methane and used as a solvent and as rocket-fuel

nitrogen *ni'trō-jən, n* a gaseous element (symbol N, at. numb. 7) forming nearly four-fifths of common air, a necessary constituent of every organised body, so called from its being an essential constituent of nitre —*v t* **nitrogenise, -ize** (*-troy'*) to combine or supply with nitrogen.—*adj.* **nitrog'enous** of or containing nitrogen.—**nitrogen cycle** the sum total of the transformations undergone by nitrogen and nitrogenous compounds in nature—from free nitrogen back to free nitrogen, **nitrogen fixation** the bringing of free nitrogen into combination [Gr *nitron*, sodium carbonate (but taken as if meaning nitre), and the root of *gennaein*, to generate]

nitrous. See **nitre**.

nitty. See **nit¹**.

nitty-gritty *nit'i-grit'i, (coll.) n* the basic details, the fundamentals, esp in phrase *get down to the nitty-gritty* [Origin uncertain; perhaps from **grit**.]

nitwit *nit'wit, (slang) n.* a blockhead —*adj* **nit'witted**. [Poss. Ger dial *nit*, not, and **wit**.]

nix¹ *niks, (Gmc myth.) n.* a water-spirit, mostly malignant:—*fem.* **nix'ie, nix'y**. [Ger. *Nix*]

nix² *niks, (slang) n* nothing: short fo · 'nothing doing, you'll get no support from me' [Coll Ger and Du for Ger *nichts*, nothing]

nix³ *niks, interj.* a cry to give warning of an approaching policeman, master, etc

no¹ *nō, adv.* not so. not: (with *compar*) in no degree, not at all —*n* a denial: a refusal: a vote or voter for the negative:—*pl* **noes**.—*n* **no'-no** (*coll*) a failure, non-event: something which must not be done, said, etc.:—*pl* **no'-nos, -no's, -noes**.—**no more** destroyed: dead: never again [O E *nā—ne*, not, *ā*, ever, cf **nay**.]

no² *nō, adj.* not any not one by no means properly called.—*adj* **no-account'** (*U S*) worthless. insignificant —**no'-ball'** (*cricket*) a ball bowled in such a way that it is disallowed by rules, **no'-man's-land** a waste region to which no one has a recognised claim neutral or disputed land, esp between entrenched hostile forces (also *fig*) —*adj.* **no-non'sense** sensible, tolerating no nonsense —**no-side'** the end of a game at Rugby football; **no'-trump'**, **no'-trumps'** (*bridge*) a call for the playing of a hand without any trump suit —*adj.* **no'-trump'**.—**no-trump'er** a no-trump call. a hand suitable for this. one addicted to calling no-trumps —*advs.* **no'way, no'ways, no'wise** in no way,

manner, or degree (see also below) —**no-claim bonus, discount** a reduction in the price of an insurance policy because no claims have been made on it; **no doubt** surely, no **end, no go, no-hoper** see **end, go¹, hope; no joke** not a trifling matter; **no one** no single, **no time** a very short time, **no way** (*coll.*) under no circumstances, absolutely not. [O E. *nān*, none See **none**.]

no³ *nō*, (*mod. Scot.*) *adv.* not [Perh. from *nocht*; see **not, nought**.]

no⁴, **nō, noh** *nō, n.* (often with *cap.*) the Japanese drama developed out of a religious dance [Jap. *nō.*]

nob¹ *nob, n* head (*coll*). the knave of turn-up suit in cribbage —**one for his nob** a point scored for holding the nob a blow on the head [Perh. **knob**.]

nob² *nob, n* a superior person —*adv* **nobb'ily**.—*n.* **nobb'iness**.—*adj* **nobb'y** smart

nobble *nob'l, (slang) v t.* to get hold of, esp. dishonestly: to win over, as by bribery: to swindle. to injure or drug (a racehorse) to prevent it from winning. to prevent from doing something. to seize [Perh **nab**.]

nobbut *nob'ət, (dial.) adv* only —*prep.* except — *conj* except that. [no¹·², but¹.]

Nobel prize *nō-bel' priz'*, one of the annual prizes for work in physics, chemistry, medicine, literature, and the promotion of peace instituted by Alfred B. *Nobel* (1833–96), Swedish discoverer of dynamite

nobelium *nō-bel'i-əm, -bēl', n* the name given to a transuranic element (symbol No, at. numb. 102) in 1957 when its production at the *Nobel* Institute, Stockholm, was claimed

nobiliary. See under **nobility**.

nobility *nō-bil'i-ti, n.* the quality of being noble· high rank. dignity. excellence· greatness of mind or character: noble descent· nobles as a body —*adj* **nobil'iary** of nobility.—**nobiliary particle** a preposition forming part of a title or some names, e g Ger. *von*, Fr *de*, It. *di* [See next word]

noble *nō'bl, adj* illustrious. high in rank or character of high birth· stately. generous: excellent.—*n.* a person of exalted rank a peer. an obsolete gold coin — *n* **no'bleness**.—*adv.* **no'bly**.—**noble gas** an inert gas, **no'bleman** a man who is noble or of rank· a peer—*pl* **no'blemen**; *fem* **no'blewoman**; **noble metal** one that does not readily tarnish on exposure to air, as gold, silver, platinum (opposed to *base metal*) —*adj* **no'ble-mind'ed**.—**no'ble-mind'edness; noble savage** a romantic and idealised view of primitive man —**most noble** the style of a duke [Fr *noble*—L. (*g*)*nōbilis* —(*g*)*nōscēre*, to know]

noblesse *nō-bles', n.* nobility: nobleness: a body of nobility —**noblesse oblige** (*ō-blēzh*) rank imposes obligations [Fr]

nobody *nō'bə-di, n* no person no-one· a person of no account —**like nobody's business** very energetically or intensively [no², **body**.]

nock *nok, n* a notch. or a part carrying a notch. esp on an arrow or a bow the forward upper end of a sail that sets with a boom —*v t* to notch: to fit (an arrow) on the string [Origin obscure—poss. connected with Sw *nock*, tip.]

nocti- *nokt-*, **nocti-** *nok-ti-*, in composition, night [L *nox, noct-*]

noctambulation *nok-tam-bū-lā'shən, n* sleep-walking —*ns* **noctam'bulism; noctam'bulist.** [L *nox, noctis*, night, *ambulāre, -ātum*, to walk]

noctilucent *nok-ti-lōō'sənt, adj* phosphorescent. shining in the dark [L *nox, noctis*, night, *lūcēre*, to shine]

noctivagant *nok-tiv'ə-gənt, adj* wandering in the night —*n* **noctivagā'tion**.—*adj* **noctiv'agous.** [L *nox, noctis*, night, *vagāri*, to wander.]

Noctua *nok'tū-ə, n.* a generic name sometimes used (without *cap.*) as a general name for any member of the **Noctū'idae**, a large family (or group of families) of mostly nocturnal, strong-bodied moths, the owlet-moths.—*n.* **noc'tūid.** [L. *noctūa*, an owl—*nox*, night.]

noctule *nok'tūl, n.* the great bat, the largest British species. [Fr.,—It *nottola*, L. *nox, noctis*, night.]

nocturn *nok'tərn, n.* any one of the three sections of the office of Matins.—*adj* **nocturn'al** belonging to night: happening, done, or active by night.—*adv.* **nocturn'ally.**—*n.* **nocturne** (*nok'tûrn* or *-tûrn'*) a dreamy or pensive piece, generally for the piano: a moonlight or night scene (*paint*). [L. *nocturnus—nox*, night.]

nod *nod, v.i.* to give a quick forward motion of the head, esp. in assent, salutation, or command: to let the head drop in weariness: to bend or curve downward: to dance or bob up and down: to make a careless slip.—*v.t.* to incline: to signify or direct by a nod:—*pr.p.* **nodd'ing;** *pa.t.* and *pa.p.* **nodd'ed.**—*n.* a quick bending forward of the head: a slight bow: a movement of the head as a gesture of assent or command.—*n.* **nodd'er.**—*n.* and *adj.* **nodd'ing.**—*v.t* and *v.i.* **nodd'le** to nod slightly: to keep nodding.—**nodding acquaintance** slight acquaintance: someone with whom one is only slightly acquainted.—**Land of Nod** sleep (in punning allusion to the biblical land, Gen. iv. 16); **nod off** (*coll.*) to fall asleep; **nod through** in parliament, to allow to vote by proxy; **on the nod** (*slang*) on tick: by general assent, i.e. without the formality of voting, etc [M.E. *nodde*, not known in O.E.]

nodal, etc. See node.

noddle *nod'l, n.* jocular, the head.

noddy *nod'i, n.* a simpleton, noodle: an oceanic bird (*Anous*) akin to the terns, unaccustomed to man and therefore easily taken and deemed stupid.

node *nōd, n.* a knob or lump: a swelling, a place, often swollen, where a leaf is attached to a stem: a point of intersection of two great circles of the celestial sphere, esp. the orbit of a planet or the moon and the ecliptic: a point at which a curve cuts itself, and through which more than one tangent to the curve can be drawn (*geom.*): a similar point on a surface, where there is more than one tangent-plane (*geom.*): a point of minimum displacement in a system of stationary waves.—*adjs.* **nō'dal** of or like a node or nodes; **nodical** (*nōd'* or *nod'*) pertaining to the nodes of a celestial body: from a node round to the same node again; **nodose** (*nōd-ōs', nōd'ōs*) having nodes, knots or swellings: knotty.—*n* **nodosity** (*nō-dos'i-ti*) knottiness: a knotty swelling.—*adj.* **nodular** (*nod'ū-lər*) of or like a nodule: in the form of nodules: having nodules or little knots; **nod'ulated** having nodules.—*ns.* **nodulā'tion; nod'ūle** a little rounded lump: a swelling on a root inhabited by symbiotic bacteria.—*adjs.* **nod'ūled; nod'ūlose, nod'ūlous.**—*n.* **nod'us** (L.) a knotty point, difficulty, complication:—*pl* **nod'i** (*-ī*). [L. *nōdus*; dim. *nōdulus*.]

Noel. See Nowel.

noesis *nō-ē'sis, n.* the activity of the intellect —*adj.* **noetic** (*nō-et'ik*) purely intellectual [Gr *noēsis—noeein*, to perceive, think.]

nog[1] *nog, n.* egg-nog or similar drink

nog[2] *nog, n.* a stump or snag, a wooden peg: a brick-sized piece of wood inserted in a wall to receive nails —*n.* **nogg'ing** a brick filling between timbers in a partition.

noggin *nog'in, n.* a small mug or wooden cup: its contents, a dram of about a gill: a drink (of beer, spirits, etc.) (*coll.*): the head (*coll.*).

noh. Same as no[4].

nohow *nō'how, adv.* not in any way, not at all. in no definable way —*adj.* (*coll.*, also **no'howish**) out of sorts.

noils *noilz, n pl.* short pieces of fibre separated from the longer fibres by combing

noise *noiz, n.* sound of any kind: an unmusical sound: an over-loud or disturbing sound: din: frequent or public talk: interference in an electrical current, etc. or communication channel.—*v.t.* (usu. with *about, abroad*) to spread by rumour.—*adj.* **noise'less.**—*adv* **noise'lessly.**—*n.* **noise'lessness.**—*adv.* **nois'ily.**—*n.* **nois'iness.**—*adj.* **nois'y** making a loud noise or sound: attended with noise: clamorous: turbulent.—**a big noise** a person of great importance, **make a noise in the world** to achieve great notoriety [Fr. *noise*, quarrel; perh. from L. *nausea*, disgust, but possibly from L. *noxia*, hurt—*nocēre*, to hurt]

noisette[1] *nwa-zet', n.* a hybrid between China rose and musk-rose [From Philippe *Noisette*, its first grower.]

noisette[2] *nwa-zet', n* a small choice piece of meat specially cooked: a nutlike or nut-flavoured sweet. [Fr., hazelnut.]

noisome *noi'səm, adj.* injurious to health: disgusting to sight or smell.—*adv.* **noi'somely.**—*n.* **noi'someness.** [*noy*, aphetic for **annoy.**]

nolens volens *nō'lenz vō'lenz, nō'läns vō', wō'läns,* (L.) willynilly.

noli-me-tangere *nō-li-mē-tan'jə-ri* (**noli me tangere** *nō-lē mā tang'ge-rā*; Vulgate, John xx. 17) *n.* a warning against touching: a species of balsam, that ejects its ripe seeds at a light touch. [L. *nōlī* do not, *mē*, me, *tangere* to touch.]

nolle prosequi *no'le pros'ə-kwī,* (L.; *law*) (an entry on a record to the effect that) the plaintiff or prosecutor will proceed no further with (part of) the suit.

nolo contendere *nō'lō kon-ten'də-ri,* (L.) I do not wish to contend (*lit.*)—a legal plea by which the accused does not admit guilt, but accepts conviction.

nom *nɔ̃,* (Fr.) *n* name.—**nom de guerre** (*də ger*) an assumed name: pseudonym.

noma *nō'mə, n* a destructive ulceration of the cheek, esp. that affecting debilitated children. [L. *nomē,* ulcer—Gr *nemein,* to consume.]

nomad *nōm'ad, n.* one of a wandering pastoral community. a rover.—Also *adj.*—**nomadic** (*nōm-* or *nom-ad'ik*).—*adv* **nomad'ically.**—*n.* **nomadisā'tion, -z-.**—*v.t.* **nom'adise, -ize** to lead a nomadic or vagabond life.—*v.t.* to make nomadic.—*n.* **nom'adism.** [Gr. *nomas, nomados—nemein,* to drive to pasture.]

nombril *nom'bril,* (*her.*) *n.* a point a little below the centre of a shield. [Fr., navel.]

nom de plume *nɔ̃ də plum', plōōm',* or *nom,* a pen-name, pseudonym. [Would-be Fr —Fr. *nom,* name, *de,* of, *plume,* pen.]

nomen *nō'men,* (L) *n.* a name, esp. of the gens or clan, a Roman's second name as Gaius *Julius* Caesar:—*pl.* **nō'mina.**

nomenclator *nō'mən-klā-tər, n.* one who bestows names, or draws up a classified scheme of names: one who announces or tells the names of persons, esp. (*hist.*) in canvassing for a Roman election.—*n.* **nō'menclāture** (or *nō-men'klə-chər*) a system of names: terminology: a list of names: mode of naming. [L. *nōmenclātor—nōmen,* a name, *calāre* to call.]

-nomic. See **-nomy.**

nominal *nom'in-əl, adj.* pertaining to, or of the nature of, a name or noun: of names: by name: only in name. so-called, but not in reality: inconsiderable, hardly more than a matter of form.—*n.* a noun or phrase, etc. standing as a noun (*gram.*).—*ns* **nom'inalism** the doctrine that general terms have no corresponding reality either in or out of the mind, being mere words;

nom'inalist.—*adj* nominalist'ic.—*adv* nom'inally by name: as a noun: in name only —nominal par, nominal value see par¹. [L *nōmnālis*–*nōmen*, *-inus*, a name]

nominate *nom'in-āt, v t.* to name to mention by name to appoint to propose formally for election —*adj* nom'inable namable: fit to be named —*n.* nomina'tion the act or power of nominating: state of being nominated. naming —*adj.* nominatival (*nom-in-ə-tī'vl,* or *nom-nə-*)—*adv* nominati'vally.—*adj.* nominative (*nom'in-ə-tiv, nom'nə-tiv, gram.*) naming the subject· in the case in which the subject is expressed (also *nom'in-ā-tiv*) nominated, appointed by nomination —*n* the nominative case: a word in the nominative case —*adv* nom'inatively.—*n.* nom'inātor one who nominates.—nominative absolute a nominative combined with a participle, but not connected with a finite verb or governed by any other word. [L. *nōmnāre, -ātum,* to name—*nōmen*]

nominee *nom-in-ē', n.* one who is nominated by another one on whose life an annuity or lease depends: one to whom the holder of a copyhold estate surrenders his interest. [L. *nōmnāre, -ātum,* to nominate, with *-ee* as if from Fr]

nomography *nom-* or *nōm-og'rə-fi, n* the art of making nomograms —*n* nom'ogram a chart or diagram of scaled lines or curves used to help in calculations, comprising three scales in which a line joining values on two determines a third —Also called nom'ograph, isopleth.—*adjs.* nomograph'ic, nomograph'ical. [Gr *nomos,* law, *graphein,* to write.]

nomothete *nom'ō-thēt, n.* a lawgiver —*adjs.* nomothetic (*-thet'ik*). nomothet'ical. [Gr. *nomothetēs—nomos,* law, and the root *the-,* as in *tithenai,* to set.]

-nomy *-nə-mi,* in composition, a science or field of knowledge, or the discipline of the study of these —-nōm'ic adjective combining form. [Gr. *-nomia,* administration, regulation.]

non¹ *non,* a Latin word used as a prefix, not: sometimes used of someone or something with pretensions who, which, is ludicrously unworthy of the name mentioned, e.g non-hero, non-event; the words given below include the most common words with *non-* but the prefix is living and many other words using it may be formed —*ns.* non-accept'ance; non-ac'cess (*law*) want of opportunity for sexual intercourse; non-aggress'ion abstention from aggression (also *adj*)—*adjs* non-alcohol'ic not alcoholic· not containing alcohol; non-aligned' not aligned: not ta'cing sides in international politics, esp not supporting either of the main international blocs, i.e the Warsaw Pact countries or the USA and the western European democracies.—*ns* non-align'ment; non-appear'ance failure or neglect to appear, esp in a court of law, non-arri'val; non-attend'ance a failure to attend· absence, non-Chris'tian (also *adj*); non'-claim a failure to make claim within the time limited by law.—*adj* non-cog'nisable of an offence, that cannot be judicially investigated.—*n* non-com'batant any one connected with an army who is there for some purpose other than that of fighting, as a surgeon, a chaplain: a civilian in time of war.—*adjs.* non-commiss'ioned not having a commission, as an officer in the army below the rank of commissioned officer or warrant officer; non-committ'al not committing one, or refraining from committing oneself, to any particular opinion or course of conduct: free from any declared preference or pledge: implying nothing, one way or the other.—*n.* non-commun'icant one who does not take communion on any particular occasion or in general, esp formerly according to the rites of the Church of England: one who has not yet communicated; non-complī'ance.—*adj* non-

conduct'ing not readily conducting, esp heat or electricity —*n* non-conduct'or a substance or object that does not readily conduct heat or electricity —*adj* nonconform'ing.—*ns.* nonconform'ist one who does not conform esp one who refused to conform or subscribe to the Act of Uniformity in 1662· usu applied in England (*cap*) to a Protestant separated from the Church of England (also *adj*), nonconform'ity; non'-content one not content in House of Lords, one giving a negative vote —*adj* non-contrib'utory not based on contributions.—*ns* non-co-operā'tion failure or refusal to co-operate, esp (in India before 1947) with the government, non-deliv'ery.—*adjs* non-denominā'tional not exclusively belonging to or according to the beliefs of any single denomination of the Christian church, non-drip' (of paint) thixotropic, of such a consistency that it does not drip when being applied; non-effect'ive unfitted or unavailable for service —*n* a member of a force who is unfitted or unavailable for active service —*n* non-e'go in metaphysics, the not-I, the object as opposed to the subject, whatever is not the conscious self.—*adjs* non-elec'tive not chosen by election, non-essen'tial not essential· not absolutely required —*n* something that is not essential, or is not of extreme importance —*adj.* non-Euclid'ean not according to Euclid's axioms and postulates.—*ns* non-event' see above at non; non-exist'ence.—*adj* non-exist'ent.—*n* non-feasance see separate article —*adjs.* non-ferr'ous containing no iron: other than iron: relating to metals other than iron: non-fic'tion of a literary work, without any deliberately fictitious element; non-fic'tional; non-flamm'able not capable of supporting flame, though combustible.—*ns.* non-fulfil'ment not fulfilling or not being fulfilled; non-interven'tion a policy of systematic abstention from interference in the affairs of other nations, non-involve'ment.—*adj.* nonjur'ing not swearing allegiance.—*n.* nonjur'or one who refuses to swear allegiance, esp (with *cap*) one of the clergy in England and Scotland who would not swear allegiance to William and Mary in 1689.—*adjs.* non-lin'ear; non-marr'ying not readily disposed to marry —*ns* non'-mem'ber one who is not a member; non'-met'al an element that is not a metal. —*adjs* non-metall'ic; non-mor'al; non-nat'ural; non-objec'tive (*paint.*) non-representational —*n* non-observ'ance.—*adjs* non-operā'tional; non-partic'ipating not taking part: (of shares, etc.) not giving the right to a share in profits; non-partisan' (or *-part'*); non-par'ty independent of party politics —*ns* non-pay'ment; non-perform'ance; non'-per'son one previously of political, etc., eminence, now out of favour· a complete nonentity —*adjs.* non-play'ing (of e g· the captain of a team), non-prof'it-making not organised or engaged in with the purpose of making a profit —*n.* non-proliferā'tion lack of proliferation, esp a limit imposed on the proliferation of (usu nuclear) weapons —*adj* non-representā'tional not aiming at the depicting of objects.—*n.* non-res'idence the fact of not residing at a place, esp where one's official or social duties require one to reside or where one is entitled to reside.—*adj.* and *n.* non-res'ident.—*n.* non-resist'ance the principle of not resisting violence by force, or of not resisting authority: passive submission.—*adjs.* non-resist'ant, non-resist'ing; non-restric'tive (*gram.*) used of a relative clause that does not restrict its antecedent; non-return'able of a bottle, jar or other container, on which a returnable deposit has not been paid; non-sched'uled of an airline, operating between specified points but not to a specific schedule of flights; non-skid', non-slip' designed to reduce chance of slipping to a minimum —*n* non-smo'ker one who does not smoke: a railway compartment in which smoking is forbidden —*adjs.* **non-smok'ing; non-spec'ialist.**— Also *n* —*adj* **non-specif'ic** not specific. of a disease, not caused by any specific agent.—*n.* **non-start'er** a horse which, though entered for a race, does not run. a person, idea, etc., with no chance at all of success — *adj* **non-stick'** of e.g a pan, treated so that food or other substance will not stick to it —*adj* and *adv.* **non'-stop'** uninterrupted(ly): without any stop or halt —*adjs* **non-U** see **U; non-u'nion** not attached to a trade union: employing, or produced by, non-union workers —*n* **non-vi'olence** (the ideal or practice of) refraining from violence on grounds of principle.— *adjs* **non-vi'olent; non-vo'ting** not voting: of shares, etc., not giving the right to vote on company decisions —*n.* **non-white'** (a member of) a race other than the white race (also *adj*) [L *nôn*, not]

non² *non, nôn,* (L) not.—**non obstante** (*ob-stan'tē, ob-stan'te*) not hindering. notwithstanding

nonage *non'ij, nôn'ij, n* legal infancy, minority. time of immaturity generally —*adj* **non'aged.** [O Fr *nonage*—pfx *non-* (L. *nôn*) and *age*, age]

nonagenarian *nôn-* or *non-ə-ji-nā'ri-ən, n* one who is ninety years old or between ninety and a hundred.— *adj.* of that age [L. *nônāgēnārius*, relating to ninety —*nônāgintā*, ninety]

nonagon *non'ə-gon, n.* an enneagon. [L *nônus*, ninth, Gr *gōnia*, angle.]

nonary *non'ə-ri, adj.* based on nine. [L *nônārius*]

nonce *nons, n.* (almost confined to the phrase *for the nonce*) the occasion: the moment, time being.— **nonce'-word** a word coined for use at the moment [From *for the nones*, i.e *for then ones*, for the once, *then* being the dative of *the* and *ones* the genitive of *one* substituted for the dative.]

nonchalance *non'shə-ləns, n* unconcern. coolness: indifference —*adj.* **non'chalant.**—*adv.* **non'chalantly.** [Fr.,—*non*, not, *chalour*, to matter, interest]

nonconformist, -ity. See **non¹.**

nondescript *non'di-skript, adj.* not easily classified: not distinctive enough to be described: neither one thing nor another.—*n.* a person or thing not easily, described or classed [L. *nôn*, not, *dēscrĭbĕre, -scrīptum,* to describe.]

none *nun, pron* (*pl.* or *sing.*) not one: no person or persons: not any: no portion or amount.—*adj.* (separated from the noun) no.—*adv.* in no degree: by no means: not at all.—*adv.* **none'-the-less'** (or **none the less**) nevertheless —**none other** (often with *than*) no other person; **none the** (followed by *compar* adjective) in no way, to no degree, **none too** (*coll*) not very [O.E. *nân—ne*, not, *ân*, one.]

nonentity *non-en'ti-ti, n* the state of not being: a thing not existing: a person or thing of no importance [L *nôn*, not, *entitās* (see **entity**).]

Nones *nônz, n pl.* in the Roman calendar, the ninth day before the Ides (both days included)—the 7th of March, May, July, and October, and the 5th of the other months: a church office originally for the ninth hour, or three o'clock, afterwards earlier [L *nônae —nônus,* ninth]

non(e)such *non', nun'such, n* a unique, unparalleled, or extraordinary thing: black medick [none, such.]

nonet *nô-net', (mus.) n* a composition for nine performers. [It. *nonetto.*]

non-feasance *non-fē'zəns, n.* omission of something which ought to be done. [Pfx. *non-,* not, O Fr *faisance,* doing—*faire*—L *facĕre,* to do]

nonillion *nô-nil'yən, n* a million raised to the ninth power: one thousand raised to the tenth power (*U.S.*) —*adj.* **nonill'ionth.** [L *nônus,* ninth, in imitation of **million, billion**.]

nonjuring, etc See **non¹.**

nonpareil *non-pə-rel', -rāl', non', n.* a person or thing without equal: a fine variety of apple: a kind of comfit. —*adj.* unequalled· matchless. [Fr. *non*, not, *pareil,* from a L.L. dim. of L. *pār*, equal.]

nonplus *nonplus', n* a state in which no more can be done or said: great difficulty: perplexity —*v.t.* to perplex completely. make uncertain what to say or do:— *pr p* **nonpluss'ing;** *pa.t* and *pa.p.* **nonplussed'.** [L *nôn*, not, *plūs*, more.]

nonsense *non'sans, n* that which has no sense: language without meaning: absurdity· trifling: foolery· humbug· trivial things: that which is manifestly false: absurd, illogical, or unintelligible statement or action.— Also *interj.*—*adj.* **nonsensical** (*-sens'*) without sense: absurd.—*ns* **nonsensicality** (*non-sens-i-kal'i-ti*). **nonsens'icalness.**—*adv* **nonsens'ically.**—**nonsense verse** verse deliberately written to convey an absurd meaning, or without obvious meaning at all.—**no-nonsense** see **no².** [Pfx *non-*, not, and **sense**.]

non-sequitur *non-sek'wi-tər, n.* (the drawing of) a conclusion that does not follow logically from the premises (*loosely*) a remark, action, that has no relation to what has gone before —Also **non sequitur.** [L *nôn*, not, and *sequitur,* follows, 3rd sing pres ind. of *sequi,* to follow.]

nonsuch. See **non(e)such.**

nonsuit *non'sūt, -sōōt, n.* in England, the stopping of a suit by voluntary withdrawal of the plaintiff, or by the judge when the plaintiff has failed to make out cause of action or to bring evidence —*v t.* to subject to a nonsuit [A.Fr. *no(u)nsute,* does not pursue]

noodle¹ *nōōd'l, n.* a simpleton: a blockhead.

noodle² *nōōd'l, n.* a flat, usu. ribbon-shaped, pasta, usu made with eggs. [Ger. *Nudel.*]

nook *nŏŏk, n.* a corner: a narrow place formed by an angle: a recess· a secluded retreat. [M.E. *nok, noke,* prob. Scand]

noon *nōōn, n.* the ninth hour of the day in Roman and ecclesiastical reckoning, three o'clock p.m.: afterwards (when the church service called *Nones* was shifted to midday) midday: middle: greatest height.— *adj* belonging to midday· meridional.—**noon'day** midday: the time of greatest prosperity —*adj.* pertaining to midday· meridional.—**noon'tide** the time of noon, midday —*adj.* pertaining to noon: meridional. [O.E. *nôn*—L. *nôna (hôra),* the ninth (hour).]

no-one *nô'-wun, n.* and *pron.* nobody.—Also **no one.**

noose *nōōs,* also *nōō z, n.* a loop with running knot which ties the firmer the closer it is drawn: a snare or bond generally —*v.t.* to tie or catch in a noose.—**put one's head in a noose** to put oneself into a dangerous or vulnerable situation [Perh O.Fr *nous*, pl of *nou* (Fr. *nœud*)—L *nōdus*, knot.]

nopal *nô'pəl, -pal, n.* a Central American cactus used for rearing cochineal insects. [Sp. *nopal*—Mex. *nopalli.*]

nope *nôp, adv.* an emphatic, originally American, form of **no¹**, pronounced with a snap of the mouth

nor *nôr, conj* and not· neither—used esp in introducing the second part of a negative proposition— correlative to *neither*. [App from *nother*, a form of **neither.**]

nor' *nor,* a shortened form of **north.**

noradrenalin *nor-ə-dren'ə-lin,* **noradrenaline** *-lin, -lēn, ns* an amine related to adrenalin, used as a heart resuscitant —Also (esp *U.S.*) **norepinephrine** (*nôr-ep-i-nef'rin, -rēn*)

Nordic *nor'dik, adj.* of a tall, blond, dolichocephalic type of (generally Germanic) peoples in N.W. Europe: loosely used by Nazis.—Also *n.*—**Nordic skiing** competitive skiing involving cross-country and jumping events. [Fr *nord,* north.]

norepinephrine. See **noradrenalin.**

Norfolk *nor'fɔk, adj* belonging to the English county of *Norfolk*.—**Norfolk jacket** a loose pleated coat with a waistband [O E *northfolc,* north folk]

noria *nō'ri-ə, no',* n an endless chain of buckets on a wheel for water-raising [Sp *noria*—Ar *nā'ūrah*]

norm *norm, n* a rule a pattern an authoritative standard the ordinary or most frequent value or state an accepted standard of behaviour —*adj* **nor'mal** according to the not deviating from the standard ordinary well-adjusted functioning regularly. (of a solution) having one gramme-equivalent of dissolved substance to a litre. perpendicular (*geom*) —*n* a perpendicular.—*ns.* **nor'malcy** normality. often of political, economic, etc , conditions, **normalisā'tion, -z-.**—*v t* **nor'malise, -ize** to make normal to heat (steel) in order to refine the crystal structure and to relieve internal stress —*v i* to become normal. regular —*n* **normal'ity.**—*adv* **nor'mally** in a normal manner usually —*adj* **nor'mative** of. or pertaining to, a norm establishing a standard. prescriptive — **normal distribution** (*statistics*) a frequency distribution represented by a symmetrical, bell-shaped curve. **normal school** a training-college for teachers, **normal solution** see above and also **standard solution.** [L *norma,* a rule]

normal, etc See **norm.**

Norman *nor'mən, n* a native or inhabitant of Normandy one of that Scandinavian people which settled in northern France about the beginning of the 10th century, founded the Duchy of Normandy, and conquered England in 1066 the Norman-French dialect —*pl* **Nor'mans.**—*adj* pertaining to the Normans or to Normandy.—**Norman architecture** a massive Romanesque style, prevalent in Normandy (10th–11th cent) and England (11th–12th), the churches with semicircular apse and a great tower, **Norman Conquest** the conquest of England by Duke William of Normandy (1066) —*n* and *adj* **Nor'man-French'** French as spoken by the Normans [O Fr *Normanz, Normans,* nom and accus pl of *Normant,* Northman, from Scand.]

normative. See **norm.**

Norn *norn,* (*Scand myth*) *n* one of the three Fates [O N *norn.*]

Norse *nors, adj* Norwegian ancient Scandinavian — *n* the Norwegian language the language of the ancient Scandinavians—also **Old Norse.**—*n* **Norse'-man.** [Perh Du *noor(d)sch*]

north *north, adv* in the direction of that point of the horizon or that pole of the earth or heavens which at equinox is opposite the sun at noon in Europe or elsewhere on the same side of the equator, or towards the sun in the other hemisphere in the slightly different direction (*magnetic north*) in which a magnetic needle points —*n* the point of the horizon in that direction the region lying in that direction the part placed relatively in that direction the north wind —*adj.* lying towards the north forming the part that is towards the north blowing from the north (of a pole of a magnet, usually) north-seeking —*ns* **norther** (*north'ər*) a wind or gale from the north, **north'erliness** (-*dh*-) —*adj* **north'erly** (-*dh*-) being toward the north blowing from the north —*adv* toward or from the north —*n* a north wind —*adj* **north'ern** (-*dh*-) pertaining to the north being in the north or in the direction toward it proceeding from the north —*n* a native of the north —*n* **north'erner** (-*dh*-) a native of, or resident in, the north, esp of the northern United States —*adj* **north'ernmost** (-*dh*-) most northerly —*ns* **north'ing** (-*th*-) motion, distance, or tendency northward distance of a heavenly body from the equator northward difference of latitude made by a ship in sailing deviation towards the

north —*adjs , advs ,* and *ns* **north'ward, nor'ward, norward** (*north'wərd, nor'wərd, nor'əd*) —*adj* and *adv* **north'wardly.**—*adv* **north'wards.**—*adjs* **north'-bound** bound for the north travelling northwards, **north'-country** belonging to the northern part of the country. esp of England —**north-coun'try-man.**—*adjs* and *advs* **north-east', nor'-east** (also *north', nor'*) midway between north and east —*ns* the direction midway between north and east. the region lying in that direction the wind blowing from that direction —**north-east'er, nor'-east'er** a strong wind from the north-east —*adj* and *adv* **north-east'erly** towards or from the north-east —*adj* **north'-east'ern** belonging to the north-east being in the north-east, or in that direction —*adj* and *adv* **north-east'ward** toward the north-east —*n* the region to the north-east —*adj* and *adv* **north-east'wardly.**—*adv* **north-east'wards.**—**northern lights** the aurora borealis, **north'land** (also *adj*) land, or lands, of the north, **North'man** an ancient Scandinavian —*ns , adjs ,* and *advs* **north-north-east'; north-north-west'** (in) a direction midway between north and north-east or north-west —**north pole** the end of the earth's axis in the Arctic regions. its projection on the celestial sphere· (usually) that pole of a magnet which when free points to the earth's north magnetic pole, **North Star** a star very near the north pole of the heavens, the Pole Star —*adjs* and *advs* **north-west', nor'-west'** (also *north', nor'*) midway between north and west —*ns* the direction midway between north and west the region lying in that direction the wind blowing from that direction —**north-, nor'-west'er** a strong north-west wind —*adjs* and *advs* **north'-west'erly** toward or from the north-west, **north'-west'ern** belonging to the north-west being in the north-west or in that direction —*adj , adv ,* and *n* **north-west'ward.**—*adj* and *adv.* **north-west'wardly.**—*adv* **north-west'wards.**—**North Atlantic Treaty Organisation** a political alliance linking the United States and Canada to a group of European States, established by the **North Atlantic Treaty,** 4th April 1949 (abbrev **Nato**), **North-east Passage** a passage for ships along the north coasts of Europe and Asia to the Pacific, **North-west Passage** a sea-way from the Atlantic into the Pacific north of North America [O E *north,* cf Ger *Nord*]

Northumbrian *nor-thum'bri-ən, n* a native of the modern *Northumberland,* or of the old kingdom of *Northumbria* (O E *Northhymbre, Northhymbra-land*) stretching from the Humber to the Forth the dialect of Old English spoken in Northumbria, later Northern English (including Scots) —*adj* of Northumberland or Northumbria

norward, etc Same as **northward,** etc

Norway *nor'wâ, adj* Norwegian —**Norway rat** the brown rat, **Norway spruce** *Picea excelsa* its wood

Norwegian *nor-wē'j(y)ən, adj* of Norway, its people. or its language —*n* a native or citizen of Norway the language of Norway [L L *Norvegia,* Norway— O N *Norvegr* (O E *Northweg*)—O N *northr,* north, *vegr,* way]

nose *nōz, n* the projecting part of the face used in breathing, smelling, and to some extent in speaking the power of smelling flair, a faculty for tracking out. detecting, or recognising scent, aroma, esp the bouquet of wine a projecting fore-part of anything a projection a beak a nozzle an informer (*slang*) — *v t* to smell to examine by smelling or as if by smelling. to track out, detect, or recognise (often with **out**). to touch, press, or rub with the nose to thrust the nose into to make (way) by feeling or pushing with the nose —*v i* to pry to nuzzle to move nosefirst —*adj* **nosed** having a nose—esp in composition.

as *bottle-nosed, long-nosed,* etc.—*adjs.* **nose′less;
nos′ey, nos′y** long-nosed: large-nosed. prying: ill-smelling: fragrant.—*n.* a nickname for a nosey person.—*adv.* **nos′ily.**—*n.* **nos′iness** a tendency to pry.—*n.* **nos′ing.**—**nose′bag** a bag for food, hung on a horse's head; **nose′-band** the part of the bridle coming over the nose, attached to the cheek-straps; **nose′-bleed** a bleeding at the nose; **nose′-cone** the front, usu. conical, part of a spacecraft, etc., **nose′-dive** a headlong plunge.—*v.i* to plunge nose-first.—**nose′-flute** a flute blown by the nose, **nose′-piece** a nozzle: the end of a microscope tube carrying the objective. a nose-band: the nasal in armour; **nose′-rag** (*slang*) a handkerchief; **nose′-ring** an ornament worn in the septum of the nose or in either of its wings: a ring in the septum of the nose for controlling a bull, swine, etc.; **nose′-wheel** the single wheel at the front of a vehicle, etc., esp. an aircraft; **Nos′ey Parker** (*coll.*, also without *caps.*) a prying person.—**cut off one's nose to spite one's face** to injure oneself rather than fail to injure another; **follow one's nose** to go straight forward; **get up someone's nose** (*coll.*) to annoy, irritate someone; **keep one's nose clean** (*coll.*) to keep out of trouble, i.e. not to behave badly or dishonestly; **lead by the nose** see **lead**[1]; **look down one's nose at** to look at in a supercilious way; **make a long nose, thumb one's nose** see **long, thumb; nose to tail** closely following one another; **nose to the grindstone** see **grind; not see beyond, further than, (the end of) one's nose** to see only what is immediately in front of one, i.e. not to see the long-term consequences of one's actions, etc.; **on the nose** (in horse-race betting) to win only (not to come second or third); **put someone's nose out of joint** see **join; rub someone's nose in it** (*coll.*) to remind someone continually of something he has done wrong; **through the nose** exorbitantly; **thrust, poke, stick one's nose into** to meddle officiously with; **turn up one's nose at** to refuse or receive contemptuously; **under one's very nose** in full view: close at hand; **with one's nose in the air** in a haughty, superior manner. [O.E. *nosu.*]

nosegay *nōz′gā, n.* a bunch of fragrant flowers: a posy or bouquet. [**nose, gay.**]

nosh *nosh,* (*slang*) *v.i.* to nibble, eat between meals: to eat.—*n.* food.—**nosh′-up** (*slang*) a (large) meal. [Yiddish.]

nosography *nos-og′rə-fi, n.* the description of diseases.—*n.* **nosog′rapher.**—*adj.* **nosographic** (*nos-ə-graf′ik*). [Gr. *nosos,* disease, *graphein,* to write.]

nosology *nos-ol′ə-ji, n.* the science of diseases: the branch of medicine which treats of the classification of diseases.—*adj.* **nosological** (*-ə-loj′*).—*n.* **nosol′ogist.** [Gr. *nosos,* disease, *logos,* discourse.]

nostalgia *nos-tal′ji-ə, n.* home-sickness: sentimental longing for past times.—*adj.* **nostal′gic.**—*adv.* **nostal′gically.** [Gr. *nostos,* a return, *algos,* pain.]

Nostoc *nos′tok, n.* a genus of blue-green Algae, beaded filaments forming gelatinous colonies on damp earth, etc., once thought derived from stars: (without *cap.*) an alga of this genus [Appar. coined by Paracelsus.]

Nostradamus *nos-trə-dā′məs, n.* one who professes to foretell the future.—*adj.* **nostradamic** (*-dam′ik*). [From the French astrologer (1503–1566).]

nostril *nos′tril, n.* one of the openings of the nose [M.E. *nosethirl*—O.E. *nosthyr(e)l*—*nosu,* nose, *thyrel,* opening.]

nostrum *nos′trəm, n* any secret, quack, or patent medicine: any favourite remedy or scheme. [L. *nostrum* (neut.), our own—*nōs,* we.]

nosy. See **nose.**

not *not, adv.* a word expressing denial, negation, or refusal:—enclitic form **-n't.**—**not′-being** the state or fact of not existing; **not′-I** that which is not the conscious ego.—*adj.* and *adv.* **not-out′** (*cricket*) still in: at the end of the innings without having been put out.—**not on** (*coll.*) not possible: not morally, socially, etc. acceptable. [Same as **naught, nought.**]

nota bene *nō′tə ben′i, bēn′, no′tä ben′e,* (L.) mark well, take notice—often abbrev. **N.B.**

notable *nō′tə-bl, adj.* worthy of being known or noted: remarkable: memorable: distinguished: noticeable: considerable.—*n.* a person or thing worthy of note, esp. in *pl.* for persons of distinction and political importance in France in pre-Revolution times.—*ns.* **notabil′ity** the fact of being notable: a notable person or thing; **no′tableness.**—*adv.* **no′tably.** [L. *notābilis*—*notāre,* to mark.]

notaphily *nō-taf′i-li, n.* the collecting of bank-notes, cheques, etc. as a hobby.—*adj.* **notaph′ilic.**—*ns.* **notaph′ilism; notaph′ilist.** [Cf. **note, phil-.**]

notary *nō′tə-ri, n.* an officer authorised to certify deeds, contracts, copies of documents, affidavits, etc. (generally **notary public**): anciently, one who took notes or memoranda of others' acts.—*adj.* **notā′rial.**—*adv.* **notā′rially.**—*v.t.* **no′tarise, -ize** to attest to, authenticate (a document, etc.) as a notary. [L. *notārius.*]

notation *nō-tā′shən, n.* a system of signs or symbols: the act of notating or writing down.—*v.t.* **notate′** to write (music, etc.) in notation.—*adj.* **notā′tional.** [L. *notātiō, -ōnis*—*notāre, -ātum,* to mark.]

notch *noch, n.* a nick: an indentation: a narrow pass.—*v.t.* to make a nick in: to record by a notch: (often with *up*) to score, achieve.—*adj.* **notched** nicked.—*n.* **notch′ing** a method of joining timbers, by fitting into a groove or grooves. [Supposed to be from Fr. *oche* (now *hoche*) with *n* from the indefinite article.]

note *nōt, n.* a distinguishing mark: a sign or symbol: a mark of censure: an observation or remark: a comment attached to a text: a jotting set down provisionally for use afterwards: an impression: a short statement or record: a memorandum: a short informal letter: a diplomatic paper: a small size of paper used for writing: a mark representing a sound (**whole note,** a semibreve) (*mus.*): a key of a piano or other instrument: the sound or tone represented by the printed or written note: the song, cry, or utterance of a bird or other animal: a paper acknowledging a debt and promising payment, as a bank-note: notice: attention: cognisance: distinction: importance: consequence.—*v.t.* to make a note of: to notice: to attend to: to indicate: to mark: to mention: to record in writing or in musical notation: to annotate.—*adjs.* **nōt′ed** marked: well known: celebrated: eminent: notorious.—*adv.* **not′edly.**—*n.* **nōt′edness.**—*adj.* **note′less.**—*ns.* **note′let** a short annotation or letter: a folded sheet of notepaper, usu. with printed decoration, for short letters; **nōt′er.**—**note′book** a book for keeping notes or memoranda; **note′-case** a pocket-book for bank-notes; **note′-pad** a pad of paper for writing notes on; **note′paper** writing-paper intended for letters; **note row** a tone row; **note′worthiness.**—*adj.* **note′worthy** worthy of note or of notice.—**note of hand** promissory note; **of note** well-known, distinguished: significant, worthy of attention; **strike the right (a false) note** to act or speak appropriately (inappropriately); **take note** to observe carefully, closely (often with *of*). [Fr.,—L. *nota,* a mark.]

nothing *nuth′ing, n.* no thing: the non-existent: zero number or quantity: the figure representing it, a nought: a thing or person of no significance or value: an empty or trivial utterance: a low condition: a trifle: no difficulty or trouble.—*adv.* in no degree: not at all.—*n* **noth′ingness** non-existence: the state of being

nothing: worthlessness: insignificance vacuity· a thing of no value.—**be nothing to** not to be important to or concern (someone); **come to nothing** to have little or no result: to turn out a failure; **for nothing** in vain: free of charge; **make nothing of** see **make**; next **to nothing** almost nothing; **nothing but** only; **nothing doing** an emphatic refusal: an expression of failure; **nothing for it but** no alternative but; **nothing if not** primarily, above all: at the very least; **nothing on** (*slang*) no claim to superiority over: no information about (used esp. by police of criminals)· no engagement; **nothing to it** having nothing in it worth while: easy; **nothing less than, short of** at least: downright, **stop, stick at nothing** to be ruthless, unscrupulous, **sweet nothings** (esp. whispered) words of affection and endearment; **to say nothing of** not to mention (see **mention**); **think nothing of** to regard as easy or unremarkable: to have a low opinion of [no², thing.]

notice *nō'tis*, *n*. intimation: announcement: information: warning: a writing, placard, board, etc., conveying an intimation or warning: time allowed for preparation: cognisance: observation: heed: a dramatic or artistic review: civility or respectful treatment —*v.t.* to mark or observe: to regard or attend to: to make observations upon: to show sign of recognition of: to treat with civility.—*adj*. **no'ticeable** that can be noticed: likely to be noticed.—*adv*. **no'ticeably.**—**no'tice-board** a board for fixing a notice on.—**at short notice** with notification only a little in advance; **give notice** to warn beforehand: to inform: to intimate, esp. the termination of an agreement [Fr *notice*—L. *nōtitia*—*nōscĕre*, *nōtum*, to get to know.]

notify *nō'ti-fī*, *v.t.* to make known: to declare: to give notice or information of:—*pr.p*. **no'tifying;** *pa t.* and *pa.p*. **no'tified.**—*adj*. **no'tifiable** (of diseases) that must be reported to public health authorities.—*ns* **notification** (*-fi-kā'shən*); **not'ifier.** [Fr. *notifier*— L. *nōtificāre*, *-ātum*—*nōtus*, known, *facĕre*, to make.]

notion *nō'shən*, *n*. a concept in the mind of the various marks or qualities of an object: an idea: an opinion, esp. one not very well founded: a caprice or whim: a liking or fancy: a small article ingeniously devised, usually in *pl.*—*adj*. **no'tional** of the nature of a notion: having a full meaning of its own, not merely contributing to the meaning of a phrase: theoretical: ideal: fanciful: imaginary, unreal —*n*. **no'tionalist** a theorist.—*adv*. **no'tionally.** [Fr ,—L. *nōtiō*, *-ōnis*— *nōscĕre*, *nōtum*, to get to know.]

notochord *nō'tō-körd*, *n*. a simple cellular rod, foreshadowing the spinal column, persisting throughout life in many lower vertebrates.—*adj*. **notochord'al.** [Gr. *nōtos*, back, *chordē*, a string.]

notorious *nō-tō'ri-əs*, *-tō'*, *adj*. publicly known (now only in a bad sense): infamous.—*n* **notori'ety** the state of being notorious: publicity· public exposure. —*adv*. **noto'riously.**—*n*. **noto'riousness.** [L.L *nōtōrius*—*nōtus*, known.]

Notornis *no-tör'nis*, *n*. a genus of flightless rails, long thought extinct, but found surviving in New Zealand in 1948: (without *cap.*) a bird of this genus [Gr. *notos*, south, *ornis*, a bird.]

no-trump(s). See **no²**.

notwithstanding *not-with-stand'ing*, or *-widh-*, *prep* in spite of.—*conj*. in spite of the fact that, although —*adv*. nevertheless, however, yet. [Orig. a participial phrase in nominative absolute = L *non obstante*.]

nougat *nōō'gà*, *nug'ət*, *n*. a confection made of a sweet paste filled with chopped almonds or pistachio nuts [Fr.,—L. *nux*, *nucis*, a nut.]

nought *nöt*, *n*. not anything: nothing: the figure 0.—

adv. in no degree.—**noughts and crosses** a game in which one seeks to make three noughts. the other three crosses, in a row in the spaces of crossed parallel lines; **set at nought** to despise, disregard, flout [Same as **naught**.]

noumenon *nōō'* or *now'mi-non*, *n*. an unknown and unknowable substance or thing as it is in itself:—*pl* **nou'mena.**—*adj* **nou'menal.** [Gr *nooumenon*, neuter of pr.p pass. of *noeein*, to think.]

noun *nown*, (*gram*) *n*. a word used as a name: formerly including the adjective —*adj* **noun'al.**—**noun clause** a clause equivalent to a noun. [A Fr *noun* (O Fr *non*; Fr *nom*)—L *nōmen*, *nōminis*, a name.]

nourish *nur'ish*, *v.t* to feed to furnish with food: to support: to help forward the growth of in any way· to allow to grow: to bring up· to cherish —*adj* **nour'ishable.**—*n* **nour'isher.**—*adj*. **nour'ishing.**—*n*. **nour'ishment** the act of nourishing. the state of being nourished: that which nourishes: nutriment [O Fr *norir*, *nourir*, *-iss-* (Fr. *nourrir*)—L *nūtrīre*, to feed]

nous *nows*, *n*. intellect· common sense (*slang*, *nows*) [Gr. *nous*, contracted from *noos*.]

nouveau *nōō-vō*, fem **nouvelle** *-vel*, (Fr) *adj* new — **nouveau riche** (*rēsh*) one who has only lately acquired wealth, but who has not acquired good taste or manners: an upstart·—*pl*. **nouveaux riches; nouvelle cuisine** a style of simple French cooking that does not involve rich creamy sauces, etc.; **Nouvelle Vague** (*vàg*) a movement in the French cinema (beginning just before 1960) aiming at imaginative quality in films —**art nouveau** see **art**.

nova *nō'və*, *n*. a star that suddenly flares up with explosive violence:—*pl* **no'vae** (*-vē*), **no'vas.** [L. *nōva* (*stella*), new (star); fem. of *novus*, new.]

novation *nō-vā'shən*, *n* the substitution of a new obligation for the one existing: innovation [L *novātiō*, *-ōnis*—*novus*, new.]

novel *nov'l*, *adj*. new and strange: of a new kind: felt to be new.—*n* a fictitious prose narrative or tale presenting a picture of real life, esp of the emotional crises in the life-history of the men and women portrayed.—*n* **novelette'** a short novel, esp. one that is feeble, trite, and sentimental: Schumann's name for a short piano piece in free form.—*adj*. **novelett'ish.**—*n*. **novelett'ist.**—*adj* **nov'elish** savouring of a novel.—*n*. **nov'elist** a novel-writer —*adj* **novelist'ic.** —*ns*. **novella** (*-el'la*, It), a tale, short story: (*-e'lə*) in recent times, a short novel (*pl* **novelle, novellas** *-lä. -əs*); **nov'elty** newness: unusual appearance: anything new, strange, or different from what was known or usual before: a small, usually cheap, manufactured article of unusual or gimmicky design:—*pl*. **nov'elties.** [Partly through O Fr *novelle* (Fr *nouvelle*), partly through It. *novella*, partly direct, from L *novellus*, fem. *novella*—*novus*, new]

November *nō-vem'bər*, *n* the eleventh month, ninth of the most ancient Roman year [L. *November— novem*, nine]

novena *nō-vē'nə*, *n* a devotion lasting nine days, to obtain a particular request, through the intercession of the Virgin or some saint [L. *novēnus*, nine each, *novem*, nine.]

novice *nov'is*, *n*. one new in anything: a beginner: a new convert or church member. an inmate of a religious house who has not yet taken the vows: a competitor that has not yet won a recognised prize — *ns*. **nov'icehood; nov'iceship; noviciate, novitiate** (*-ish'i-āt*) the state of being a novice: the period of being a novice the novices' quarters in a religious house: a novice [Fr.,—L *novīcius—novus*, new]

Novocain(e)® *nō'və-kān*, *n* a proprietary name for procaine (q.v.).

now *now*, *adv* at the present time, or the time in question, or a very little before or after: as things are: used meaninglessly, or with the feeling of time lost or nearly lost, in remonstrance, admonition, or taking up a new point.—*adj.* present.—*n.* the present time or the time in question —*conj.* at this time when and because it is the fact: since at this time.—*interj.* expressing admonition, warning or (when repeated) reassurance —**now and then, or again,** sometimes' from time to time; **now ... now** at one time . at another time; **now then!** interjection expressing admonition or rebuke. [O.E *nū*; Ger *nun,* L *nunc,* Gr. *nȳn.*]

nowadays *now'ə-dāz, adv.* in these times —Also *adj.* [now and days, O.E *dæges,* gen of *dæg,* day, to which the prep. **a** (O.E. *on* was later added]

noway, noways, nowise. See no².

Nowel(l), Noël *nō-el'*, (*obs.* except in Christmas carols) *n.* Christmas. [O.Fr.—L. *nātālis,* belonging to a birthday.]

nowhere *nō'(h)wâr, adv* in or to no place: out of the running.—*n.* a non-existent place.—**nowhere near** not nearly. [no², where.]

nowt *nowt,* (*dial.*) *n.* nothing. [naught.]

noxious *nok'shəs, adj.* hurtful.—*adv.* **nox'iously.**—*n.* **nox'iousness.** [L. *noxius—noxa,* hurt—*nocēre,* to hurt.]

noyade *nwà-yàd', n.* wholesale drowning, as by Carrier at Nantes, 1793–94. [Fr.,—*noyer,* to drown.]

noyau *nwa-yō', n.* a liqueur flavoured with bitter almonds or peach-kernels. [Fr.,— fruit-stone—L. *nucālis,* nutlike—*nux, nucis,* a nut.]

nozzle *noz'l, n.* an outlet tube, or spout: an open end of a tube. [Dim. of nose.]

-n't. Shortened (enclitic) form of **not.**

nth. See N.

nu *nū, nü, n.* the thirteenth letter (N, *v*) of the Greek alphabet, answering to N. [Gr. *nȳ.*]

nuance *nü-ās, nwās, nū-āns', n.* a delicate degree or shade of difference. [Fr.,—L. *nūbēs, nūbis,* a cloud.]

nub *nub, n.* the point or gist [Prob. from knub, a lump.]

nubble. See **knubble.**

nubile *nū'bīl, -bil, adj.* (esp. of a woman) marriageable: sexually mature: sexually attractive —*n.* **nubility** (-bil'i-ti). [L. *nūbilis—nūbēre,* to veil oneself, hence to marry.]

nucha *nū'kə, n.* the nape of the neck.—*adj.* **nū'chal.** [L.L. *nucha—*Ar. *nukhā',* spinal marrow.]

nuciferous *nū-sif'ər-əs, adj.* nut-bearing. [L. *nux, nucis,* nut, *ferre,* to bear.]

nucivorous *nū-siv'ə-rəs, adj.* nut-eating. [L. *nux, nucis,* nut, *vorāre,* to devour.]

nuclear, etc. See **nucleus.**

nucleus *nū'kli-əs, n.* a central mass or kernel: that around which something may grow: the densest part of a comet's head or a nebula: a rounded body in the protoplasm of a cell, the centre of its life (*biol.*): the massive part of an atom, distinguished from the outlying electrons (*phys.*): a stable group of atoms to which other atoms may be attached so as to form series of compounds (*phys.*):—*pl.* **nuclei** (*nū'kli-ī*). —*adj.* **nu'clear** (-*kli-ər*) of, or of the nature of, a nucleus: pertaining to the nucleus of an atom, nuclei of atoms: pertaining to, or derived from, fission or fusion of atomic nuclei.—*n.* **nu'clease** any of a number of enzymes inducing hydrolysis in nucleic acids.—*v.t.* and *v.i.* **nu'cleate** (-*kli-āt*) to form into, or group around, a nucleus.—*v.t.* to act, in a process of formation, as a nucleus for (e.g. *to nucleate crystals*) —*adjs.* **nu'cleate, -d** having a nucleus.—*n.* **nuclea'tion** the action or process of nucleating: seeding clouds to control rainfall and fog formation.—*adjs.*

nucle'olar of, or of the nature of, a nucleolus. **nu'cleolate, -d** having a nucleus or a nucleolus (of a spore) containing one or more conspicuous oil-drops.—*ns.* **nucle'olus** a body (sometimes two bodies) observed within a cell nucleus, indispensable to growth:—*pl* **nucle'oli** (-*lī*); **nu'cleon** a general name for a neutron or a proton.—*n.sing.* **nucleon'ics** nuclear physics, esp. its practical applications —*ns.* **nu'cleo-pro'tein** any of a group of compounds containing a protein molecule combined with a nuclein—important constituents of the nuclei of living cells; **nuc'leotide** any of a number of compounds of sugar, phosphoric acid, and a purine or pyrimidine base, the principal constituents of nucleic acids; **nuclide** (*nū'klīd, -klid*) a species of atom of any element distinguished by the number of neutrons and protons in its nucleus, and its energy state.—**nuclear energy** a more exact term for *atomic energy,* energy released or absorbed during reactions taking place in atomic nuclei; **nuclear family** the basic family unit consisting of the mother and father with their children; **nuclear fission** spontaneous or induced splitting of atomic nucleus; **nuclear fuel** material, as uranium or plutonium, consumed to produce atomic energy, **nuclear fusion** the creation of a new nucleus by merging two lighter ones, with release of energy; **nuclear physics** the science of forces and transformations within the nucleus of the atom; **nuclear power** power obtained from a controlled nuclear reaction (*adj.* **nu'clear-pow'ered**); **nuclear reaction** a process in which an atomic nucleus interacts with another nucleus or particle, producing changes in energy and nuclear structure; **nuclear reactor** an assembly of uranium, with moderator, in which a nuclear chain reaction can develop; **nuclear warfare; nuclear warhead; nuclear weapon; nucleic acid** any of the complex acid components of nucleo-proteins.—**nuclear magnetic resonance** resonance which can be produced in nuclei of most isotopes of the elements and from which a clue can be obtained to the particular atoms involved [L. *nucleus—nux, nucis,* a nut.]

nude *nūd, adj.* naked: bare: undraped: without consideration (*law*).—*n.* a nude figure or figures: undraped condition.—*adv.* **nude'ly.**—*ns.* **nude'ness; nu'dibranch** shell-less marine gasteropod with gills exposed on the back and sides of the body; **nu'dism** the practice of going naked: (esp. *U.S.*) naturism; **nu'dist** one who goes naked, or approves of going naked: (esp. *U.S.*) a naturist.—Also *adj* —*n.* **nu'dity** the state of being nude: a nude figure. [L. *nūdus,* naked.]

nudge *nuj, n.* a gentle poke or push, as with the elbow. —*v.t.* to poke or push gently, esp. to draw someone's attention to something. [Origin obscure; perh connected with Norw. *nugge,* to rub.]

nugatory *nū'gə-tə-ri, adj.* trifling: worthless: inoperative: unavailing: futile.—*n.* **nu'gatoriness.** [L. *nūgātōrius—nūgae,* trifles, trumpery.]

nuggar *nug'ər, n.* a large boat used to carry cargo on the Nile. [Ar. *nuqqār.*]

nugget *nug'it, n.* a lump. esp. of gold: anything small but valuable.—*adj.* **nugg'ety** (*Austr.*) stocky, thickset.

nuisance *nū'səns, n.* that which annoys or hurts, esp. if there be some legal remedy: that which is offensive to the senses: a person or thing that is troublesome or obtrusive in some way.—*n.* **nui'sancer.** [Fr.,—L. *nocēre,* to hurt.]

nuke *nūk,* (*slang*) *n.* a nuclear weapon.—*v.t.* to attack using nuclear weapons. [Contr. of **nuclear.**]

null *nul, adj.* of no legal force: void: invalid: empty of significance: amounting to nothing.—*ns.* **null'ity** the state of being null or void: nothingness: want of existence, force, or efficacy. **null'ness.** [L *nullus*, not any, from *ne*, not, *ullus*, any]

nulla(h) *nul'ə*, *n* a ravine· a water-course, not necessarily a dry one [Hind *nālā*]

nulla-nulla *nul'ə-nul'ə*, *n* an Australian aborigine's hard-wood club —Also **null'a.** [Native word]

nullifidian *nul-ı-fıd'ıən*, *adj* having no faith, esp religious —*n*. one who has no faith [L *nullus*, none, *fıdēs*, faith]

nullify *nul'ı-fī*, *v t* to make null, to annul· to render void or of no force —*pr.p* **null'ifying;** *pa t* and *pa p* **null'ified.**—*ns* **nullification** (*-fı-kā'shən*), **null'ifier** (*-fī-ər*) [Late L. *nullıfıcāre—nūllus*, none, *facēre*, to make]

nullipara *nul-ıp'ə-rə*, *n* a woman who has never given birth to a child, esp if not a virgin —*adj* **nullip'arous.**—*n*. **nulliparity** (*-ı-par'ı-tı*) [L *nūllus*, none, *parēre*, to bring forth]

nullipore *nul'ı-pōr, -por, n* a coralline seaweed [L *nūllus*, none, *porus*, a passage, pore]·

nullity, nullness. See null.

numb *num, adj*. having diminished power of sensation or motion: powerless to feel or act stupefied —*v t* to make numb: to deaden —*pr p* **numbing** (*num'ıng*), *pa t*. and *pa p* **numbed** (*numd*)— **numbskull** see numskull. [O E *numen*, pa p of *nıman*, to take]

numbat *num'bat, n* a small Australian marsupial (*Myrmecobıus fascıatus*) which feeds on termites [Native name]

number *num'bər, n.* that by which single things are counted or reckoned: quantity reckoned in units a particular value or sum of single things or units a representation in arithmetical symbols of such a value or sum· a full complement a specified or recognised set, class, or group· some or many of the persons or things in question (often in *pl*). more than one numerousness: (in *pl*) numerical superiority numerability· a numerical indication of a thing's place in a series, or one assigned to it for reference, as in a catalogue a label or other object bearing such an indication: a person or thing marked or designated in such a way an item· an issue of a periodical or serial publication: an integral portion of an opera or other composition: arithmetical faculty, (in *pl*) rhythm, verses, music: the property in words of expressing singular and plural (*gram*.) a single item in a programme, esp of popular music and/or variety turns an item of merchandise on show, usu of clothing (*coll*): a girl (*slang*). (with *cap* , in *pl*.) the fourth book of the Old Testament, in which an account of a census is given.—*v.t.* to count. to apportion to have lived through. to reckon as one. to mark with a number or assign a number to to amount to.—*v t* to be reckoned in the number to be of like number —*n* **num'berer.**—*adj*. **num'berless** without number. more than can be counted —**number one** chief. most important. he or that whose number is one, the first in the numbered series. self, oneself (*slang*) lieutenant, first officer (under the rank of commander, *naut slang*), **number plate** the plaque on a motor vehicle showing its registration number. **number system** (*math*) any set of elements which has two binary operations called addition and multiplication, each of which is commutative and associative, and which is such that multiplication is distributive with respect to addition; **number ten** (*coll*) 10 Downing St , official residence of the Prime Minister; **number two** second-in-command.—**any number of** many, beyond, without number too many to be counted, **by numbers** (of a procedure, etc.) performed in simple stages, each stage being identified by a number; **have,** or **get someone's number** to size someone up, **his number is up** he

is doomed, has not long to live, **one's (its) days are numbered** one's (its) end is imminent [Fr. *nombre* —L. *numerus*]

numdah *num'da, n* an embroidered felt rug made in India. [Cf **numnah.**]

numen. See **numinous.**

numerable *nū'mər-ə-bl, adj* that may be numbered or counted.—*n* **numerabil'ity.**—*adv* **nu'merably.**—*n* **nu'meracy** the state of being numerate —*adj* **nu'meral** pertaining to, consisting of, or expressing number —*n* a figure or mark used to express a number, as 1, 2, I, V, etc a word used to denote a number (*gram*)—*v t* **nu'merate** to read off as numbers (from figures) —*adj* (*-ıt*) having some understanding of mathematics and science. able to solve arithmetical problems (see also **innumerate**) —Also *n* —*n*. **numera'tion; nu'merātor** one who numbers, the upper number of a vulgar fraction, which expresses the number of fractional parts taken —*adj* **numerical** (*-mer'ı-kl*) belonging to, expressed in, or consisting in, number in number independently of sign —*adv* **numer'ically.**—*n* **numerol'ogy** the study of numbers as supposed to show future events —*adj* **nu'merous** great in number or quantity many consisting of or pertaining to a large number.— *adv* **nu'merously.**—*n* **nu'merousness.**—**numerical analysis** the study of methods of approximation and their accuracy, etc , **numerical control** automatic control of operation of machine tools by means of numerical data stored on magnetic or punched tape or on punched cards [L *numerus*, number]

numinous *nū'mın-əs, adj* pertaining to a divinity suffused with feeling of a divinity —*ns* **numen** (*nū'men*) a presiding deity·—*pl*. **nu'mina** (*-ın-ə*); **nu'minousness.** [L *nūmen, -ınıs*, divinity]

numismatic *nū-mız-mat'ık, adj* pertaining to money, coins, or medals.—*n sing* **numismat'ics** the study or collection of coins and medals —*ns* **numis'matist; numismatol'ogist; numismatol'ogy.** [L *numısma*— Gr *nomısma*, current coin—*nomızein*, to use commonly—*nomos*, custom]

nummary *num'ə-rı, adj* relating to coins or money — *adj* **numm'ūlar** coin-shaped —*n*. **numm'ūlite** a large coin-shaped fossil protozoon, forming limestones — *adj* **nummūlitic** (*lıt'ık*) [L *nummus*, a coin]

numnah *num'nə, n.* a felt or, now usu , sheepskin, cloth or pad placed under a saddle to prevent chafing [Hind *namdā*]

numskull *num'skul, n* a blockhead —Also **numb'skull. [numb, skull.]**

nun *nun, n* a woman who, under a vow, has secluded herself in a religious house, to give her time to devotion. a kind of pigeon with feathers on its head like a nun's hood a blue tit a male smew —*n* **nunn'ery** a house for nuns —*adj* **nunn'ish.**—*ns* **nunn'ishness.**— **nun's'-veil'ing** a woollen cloth, soft and thin, used by women for veils and dresses [O E *nunne*—L.L *nunna, nonna*, a nun]

nunatak *nōō'na-tak, n* a point of rock appearing above the surface of land-ice [Eskimo]

nunc dimittis *nungk dı-mıt'ıs*, the song of Simeon (Luke II 29–32) in the R C Breviary and the Anglican evening service [From the opening words, *nunc dīmıttıs*, now lettest thou depart]

nuncio *nun'shı-ō, n* an ambassador from the pope — *pl*. **nun'cios.**—*n* **nun'ciature** a nuncio's office or term of office [It (now *nunzıo*)—L *nūntıus*, a messenger]

nuncupate *nung'kū-pāt, v t* to declare orally —*n* **nuncūpa'tion.**—*adj* **nunc'ūpātive.** [L *nuncupāre*, to call by name—prob from *nōmen*, name, *capere*, to take.]

nunnery. See **nun.**

nuptial *nup'shəl, adj* pertaining to marriage· pertaining to mating (*zool*) —*n* (usu in *pl*) marriage wedding ceremony —*n* **nuptiality** (-shi-al'i-ti) nuptial character or quality: marriage-rate (in *pl*) wedding ceremonies and festivities. [L *nuptiālis—nuptiae*, marriage—*nubēre, nuptum*, to marry]

nur, nurr. See **knur.**

nurl. See **knurl.**

nurse[1] *nûrs, n* one who suckles a child one who tends a child· one who has the care of the sick, feeble, or injured, or who is trained for the purpose a worker bee, ant, etc , that feeds the young one who or that which feeds, rears, tends, saves, fosters, or develops anything, or preserves it in any desired condition the state of being nursed (in the phrases *at nurse, out to nurse*) —*v t* to suckle, to tend, as an infant or a sick person· to bring up to cherish to manage with care and economy to play skilfully, manipulate carefully, keep watchfully in touch with, in order to obtain or preserve the desired condition to hold or carry as a nurse does a child —*adj* **nurse'like**.—*n* **nurs(e)'ling** that which is nursed or fostered· an infant, **nurs'er; nurs'ery** a place for nursing an apartment for children, a place where young animals are reared, or where the growth of anything is promoted a piece of ground where plants are reared for sale or transplanting a race for two-year-old horses (also **nursery stakes**) —*adj* pertaining to a nursery, or to early training —**nurse'maid** a maid servant who takes care of children, **nurs'erymaid** a maid employed in keeping a nursery· a nursemaid, **nurs'eryman** a man who owns or works a nursery one who is employed in cultivating plants, etc , for sale, **nursery rhyme** a traditional rhyme known to children, **nursery school** a school for very young children (aged two to five), **nursery slopes** slopes set apart for skiing novices, **nurs'sing-chair** a low chair without arms, used when feeding a baby, **nursing home** a private hospital; **nursing officer** any of several grades of nurses having administrative duties —**put (out) to nurse** to commit to a nurse, usu away from home to put (an estate) under trustees [O Fr *norrice* (Fr *nourrice*)—L *nūtrix, -icis—nūtrīre*, to nourish]

nurse[2] *nûrs, n* a shark· a dogfish [Earlier *nuss*, perh for (*an*) *huss, husk*, a dogfish]

nurture *nûr'chər, n* upbringing· rearing training whatever is derived from the individual's experience, training, environment, distinguished from *nature*, or what is inherited (*v t* to nourish· to bring up to educate —*adjs* **nur'tural; nur'turant**.—*n* **nur'turer**. [O.Fr *noriture* (Fr *nourriture*)—L L *nūtritūra*—L *nūtrīre*, to nourish]

nut *nut, n* popularly, any fruit with seed in a hard shell a hard dry indehiscent fruit formed from a syncarpous gynaeceum (*bot*), often the hazel-nut, sometimes the walnut the head (*slang*) a hardheaded person, one difficult to deal with, a tough: a crazy person (also a **nut'-case**, **nut'case**; *slang*) a small block, usu of metal, for screwing on the end of a bolt· the ridge at the top of the fingerboard on a fiddle, etc (*mus*) the mechanism for tightening or slackening a bow (*mus*) a small lump of coal a small biscuit or round cake the testicles (in *pl* , *slang*) — *v t* to look for and gather nuts'—*pr p* **nutt'ing;** *pa t* and *pa p* **nutt'ed**.—*adj* **nuts** crazy (*slang*)—Also *interj*. expressing defiance, contempt, disappointment, etc —*ns* **nutt'er** one who gathers nuts· a crazy person (*slang*), **nutt'iness; nutt'ing** the gathering of nuts —*adj* **nutt'y** abounding in nuts having the flavour of nuts mentally unhinged (*slang*) —*adj* **nut'•brown** brown, like a ripe hazel-nut —**nut'-butt'er** a butter-substitute made from nuts, **nut'cracker** a bird (*Nucifraga*) of the crow family: (usu in *pl*)

an instrument for cracking nuts —*adj* like a pair of nutcrackers, as toothless jaws —**nutcracker man** a type of early man found in Tanzania in 1959, by some distinguished as a separate species *Zinjanthropus*, **nut'-gall** a nut-like gall, produced by a gall-wasp, chiefly on the oak, **nut'hatch** a bird (Sitta) that hacks nuts and seeks insects on trees like a creeper, **nuthouse** (*slang*) a mental asylum a place where people's behaviour is crazy, **nut'-oil** an oil got from walnuts or other nuts, **nut'-pine** the stone-pine or other species with large edible seeds, **nut'shell** the hard covering of a nut, **nut'-tree** any tree bearing nuts, esp the hazel, **nut'-wee'vil** a weevil whose larvae live on hazelnuts —**a (hard) nut to crack** a difficult problem, **be nuts on, about** (*slang*) to be very fond of, **do one's nut** (*slang*) to become extremely angry, to rage, **in a nutshell** in very small space briefly, concisely, **not for nuts** not even incompetently, **nuts and bolts** the basic facts, the essential, practical details, **off one's nut** (*slang*) mentally unhinged, crazy [O E *hnutu*]

nutant *nū'tənt, adj* nodding drooping —*v i* **nu'tate** to nod, to droop to perform a nutation —*n* **nutā'tion** a nodding a fluctuation in the precessional movement of the earth's pole about the pole of the ecliptic (*astron*) the sweeping out of a curve by the tip of a growing axis (*bot*) —*adj* **nutā'tional.** [L *nūtāre*, to nod]

nutmeg *nut'meg, n* the aromatic kernel of an East Indian tree, much used as a seasoning in cookery — *adjs* **nut'megged; nut'meggy.** [M E *notemuge*—nut and interred O Fr *mugue*, musk—L *muscus*, musk]

nutria *nū'tri-ə, n* the coypu its fur [Sp *nutria*, otter —L *lutra*]

nutrient *nū'tri-ənt, adj* feeding nourishing —*n* any nourishing substance —*n* **nu'triment** that which nourishes food —*adj* **nutrimental** (-ment'l) —*n* **nutri'tion** the act or process of nourishing food — *adj* **nutri'tional.**—*n*. **nutri'tionist** an expert in foods and their nutritional values —*adj* **nutri'tious** nourishing —*adv* **nutri'tiously.**—*n* **nutri'tiousness.**—*adj* **nu'tritive** nourishing concerned in nutrition — *adv* **nu'tritively.** [L *nūtrīre*, to nourish]

nux vomica *nuks vom'ik-ə.* a seed that yields strychnine, the East Indian tree (*Strychnos nux-vomica*) that produces it [L *nux*, a nut, *vomēre*, to vomit]

nuzzle *nuz'l, v t* and *v i* to poke, press, burrow, root, rub, sniff, caress, or investigate with the nose —*v i* to thrust in (the nose or head) —*v i* to snuggle [Freq vb from **nose.**]

nyctalopia *nik-tə-lō'pi-ə, n* properly, night-blindness, abnormal difficulty in seeing in a faint light by confusion sometimes, day-blindness —*adj* **nyctalōp'ic.** [Gr *nyktalōps*, night-blind, day-blind—*nyx, nyktos*, night, *alaos*, blind, *ōps*, eye, face]

nyctitropism *nik-tit'ro-pizm, n* the assumption by plants of certain positions at night —*adj* **nyctitropic** (-*trop'*) [Gr *nyx, nyktos*, night, *tropos*, turning]

nyctophobia *nik-tō-fō'bi-ə, n* morbid fear of the night or of darkness [Gr *nyx, nyktos*, night, and **phobia.**]

nylon *nī'lən, -lon, n* any of numerous polymeric amides that can be formed into fibres, bristles, or sheets any material made from nylon filaments or fibres a stocking made of nylon [Formerly a trademark]

nymph *nimf, n* one of the divinities who lived in mountains, rivers, trees, etc (*myth*) a young and beautiful maiden (often ironical), an immature insect, similar to the adult but with wings and sex-organs undeveloped —*n pl* **nymphae** (-ē) the labia minora —*adjs* **nymph'al; nymphe'an.**—*n* **nymph'et** a young nymph, a young girl with strong sex-attraction.—*adj.* **nymph'-like.**—*ns.* **nymph'o** a nymphomaniac:—*pl.* **nym'phos**; **nymph'olepsy** a species of ecstasy or frenzy said to have seized those who had seen a nymph: a yearning for the unattainable; **nymph'olept** a person so affected.—*adj.* **nympholept'-ic.**—*n.* **nymphomā'nia** morbid and uncontrollable sexual desire in women.—*n.* and *adj.* **nymphomā'niac.** [L. *nympha*—Gr. *nymphē*, a bride, a nymph.]

nystagmus *nis-tag'məs, n.* a spasmodic, lateral oscillatory movement of the eyes, found in miners, etc.—*adjs.* **nystag'mic; nystag'moid.** [Latinised from Gr. *nystagmos*—*nystazein*, to nap.]

O

O¹, o ō, *n.* the fifteenth letter of our alphabet: in telephone, etc., jargon, nought or nothing:—*pl.* **Oes, O's, oes, o's** (*ōz*): prefixed *o-* stands for *ortho-* (chem.).—**O'-level** *n.* (examination at end of school course) requiring ordinary, i.e. less than A-level, knowledge of a school subject: a pass in an O-level.— Also *adj.*

O², oh ō, *interj* used in addressing or apostrophising, marking the occurrence of a thought, reception of information, or expressing wonder, admiration, disapprobation, surprise, protest, pain, or other emotion. The form O is chiefly used in verse (*O for, O that*).

o', o ō, ə, a worn-down form of **of** and of **on.**

oaf *ōf, n.* a changeling: a dolt: an idiot: a lout:—*pl.* **oafs,** (*rarely*) **oaves.**—*adj.* **oaf'ish** idiotic, doltish: lubberly: loutish. [O.N. *ālfr,* elf; cf. **elf.**]

oak *ōk, n.* a genus (*Quercus*) of trees of the beech family: its timber, valued in shipbuilding, etc.. extended to various other trees, as **poison-oak, she-oak** (qq.v.).—*adj.* of oak.—*adj.* **oak'en** of oak.—*adj.* **oak'y** like oak, firm: abounding in oaks.—**oak'-apple** a gall caused by an insect on an oak, **oak'-gall** a gall produced on the oak, **oak'-mast** acorns collectively, **oak'-nut** a gall on the oak; **oak'-tree; oak'-wood.** [O.E. *āc.*]

oakum *ōk'əm, n.* old (usu. tarred) ropes untwisted and teased out for caulking the seams of ships. [O.E. *ācumba* (*æcumbe*) from *ā-,* away from, and the root of *cemban,* to comb.]

oar *ōr, or, n.* a light bladed pole for propelling a boat: a stirring-pole: a swimming organ: an oarsman —*v.t* to impel as by rowing.—*v.i.* to row.—*adjs.* **oared** furnished with oars; **oar'less; oar'y** having the form or use of oars —**oar'-fish** a ribbon-fish (*Regalecus*).— *adj.* **oar'-footed** having swimming feet.—**oars'man, oars'woman** a rower: one skilled in rowing. **oars'manship** skill in rowing —**lie or rest on one's oars** to abstain from rowing without removing the oars from the rowlocks: to rest, take things easily· to cease from work; **put in one's oar** to interpose when not asked. [O.E. *ār.*]

oasis *ō-ā'sis,* sometimes *ō'ə-sis, n.* a fertile spot or tract in a sandy desert: any place of rest or pleasure in the midst of toil and gloom: (with *cap.;* ®) a block of soft permeable material used to hold cut flowers, etc in place in a flower arrangement:—*pl.* **oases** (*-sēz*) [Gr. *oasis,* an Egyptian word; cf. Coptic *ouahe.*]

oast *ōst, n.* a kiln to dry hops or malt.—*n.* **oast'-house.** [O.E. *āst.*]

oat *ōt* (oftener in *pl.* **oats** *ōts*), *n.* a well-known genus (*Avena*) of grasses, esp. *A. sativa,* whose seeds are much used as food: its seeds.—*adj.* **oat'en** consisting of an oat stem or straw: made of oatmeal.—**oat'cake** a thin hard dry cake made with oatmeal.—**oat'-grass** a grass of *Avena* or kindred genus used more as fodder than for the seed; **oat'meal** meal made of oats —*adj* of the colour of oatmeal.—**feel one's oats** to be frisky or assertive; **get one's oats** (*slang*) to have sexual intercourse; **off one's oats** without appetite, off one's food (*coll.*); **sow one's wild oats** to indulge in youthful dissipation or excesses. [O.E. *āte,* pl. *ātan.*]

oath *ōth, n.* a solemn appeal to a god or something holy or reverenced as witness or sanction of the truth of a statement: the form of words used: a more or less similar expression used lightly, exclamatorily, decoratively, or in imprecation: a swear-word: a curse:—*pl.* **oaths** (*ōdhz*).—**on, under, upon oath** sworn to speak the truth: attested by oath; **take an oath** to have an oath administered to one. [O E. *āth.*]

obbligato *ob-*(b)*li-ga'tō, n* a musical accompaniment of independent importance, esp that of a single instrument to a vocal piece:—*pl.* **obbliga'tos, -ti** (*-tē*) [It.]

obcompressed *ob'kəm-prest,* (*bot*) *adj.* flattened from front to back. [L pfx *ob-,* towards; in mod. L , in the opposite direction, reversed.]

obconic, -al *ob-kon'ik, -əl,* (*bot*) *adjs.* conical and attached by the point. [L pfx *ob-,* as in **obcompressed.**]

obcordate *ob-kor'dāt,* (*bot.*) *adj.* inversely heartshaped, as a leaf [L pfx. *ob-,* as in **obcompressed.**]

obdurate *ob'dū-rāt, adj.* hardened in heart or in feelings· difficult to influence, esp. in a moral sense: stubborn: hard.—*n* **ob'dūracy** (or *ob-dū'rə-si*) state of being obdurate: invincible hardness of heart.— *adv.* **ob'dūrately** (or *-dū'*)—*ns.* **ob'dūrateness** (or *-dū'*), **obdūrā'tion.** [L. *obdūrāre, -ātum—ob-,* intens., against, *dūrāre,* to harden—*dūrus,* hard]

obeah. See **obi¹.**

obedience *ō-bē'dyəns, -di-əns, n* the act of doing what one is told: the state of being obedient. willingness to obey commands: dutifulness —*adjs* **obē'dient** obeying: ready to obey, **obediential** (*ō-bē-di-en'shi*) pertaining to, of the nature of, obedience —*adv* **obē'diently.** [L. *obēdientia,* see **obey.**]

obeisance *ō-bā'səns, n* a bow or act of reverence· an expression of respect.—*adj.* **obei'sant.** [Fr. *obéissance—obéir—*L. root as **obey.**]

obelus *ob't-ləs, n* a sign (– or –) used in ancient manuscripts to mark suspected, corrupt, or spurious words and passages: a dagger-sign (†) used esp. in referring to footnotes (**double obelus ‡,** *print.*):—*pl.* **ob'eli** (*-lī*).—*n.* **ob'elisk** a tall, four-sided, tapering pillar, usually of one stone, topped with a pyramid: an obelus [L. *obelus—*Gr *obelos* (dim. *obeliskos*), a spit.]

obese *ō-bēs', adj* abnormally fat —*ns.* **obese'ness, obesity** (*-bēs'-, -bes'-*). [L. *obēsus—ob-,* completely, *edēre, ēsum,* to eat.]

obey *ō-bā', v.t* to render obedience: to do what one is told: to be governed or controlled —*v.t* to do as told by: to comply with to be controlled by [Fr *obéir—* L. *obēdīre—ob-,* towards, *audīre,* to hear]

obfuscate *ob-fus'kāt, v.t.* to darken: to obscure —*adj* **obfuscat'ed** (*coll.*) drunk.—*n* **obfusca'tion.** [L. *obfuscāre, -ātum—ob-,* intens., *fuscus,* dark.]

obi¹ *ō'bi,* **obeah** *ō'bi-ə, ns.* witchcraft and poisoning practised by Negroes of the West Indies, Guyana, etc a fetish or charm.—**o'bi-man; o'bi-woman.** [Of W. African origin]

obi² *ō'bi, n.* a broad sash worn with a kimono by the Japanese [Jap. *obi—obiru,* to wear.]

obit *ob'it,* or *ō'bit, n.* an anniversary or other commemoration of a death.—*adj.* **obit'uary** relating to or recording the death of a person or persons.—*n* an account of a deceased person, or a notice of his death a collection of death-notices in a newspaper often extended to include notices of births and marriages, etc [L L *obitus—obire. -itum*, to die—*ob*, in the way of, *ire*, to go]

obiter *ob'*, *ōb'it-ar, ob'it-er*, (L.) *adv* by the way, cursorily —**obiter dictum** (*dik'tam, -tōōm*) something said by the way, a cursory remark —*pl* **obiter dicta** (*dik'ta*)

object *ob'jikt, n* a material thing that which is thought of, regarded as being outside, different from, or independent of, the mind (opposed to *subject*): that upon which attention, interest, or some emotion is fixed, an oddity or deplorable spectacle: that towards which action or desire is directed, an end: part of a sentence denoting that upon which the action of a transitive verb is directed, or standing in an analogous relation to a preposition (*gram*)—*v.t.* **object** (*ab-jekt', ob-*) to offer in opposition· to bring as an accusation.—*v.i.* to be opposed, feel or express disapproval (with *to, that, against*) to refuse assent —*n.* **objectifica'tion** (*-jekt-*).—*v t* **object'ify** to make objective —*n.* **objec'tion** act of objecting: anything said or done in opposition argument or reason against (with *to, against*) inclination to object, dislike, unwillingness.—*adj* **objec'tionable** that may be objected to· requiring to be disapproved of: distasteful.—*adv* **objec'tionably.**—*adj.* **object'ive** (also *ob'*) relating to or constituting an object· of the nature of, or belonging to, that which is presented to consciousness (opposed to *subjective*), exterior to the mind, self-existent, regarding or setting forth what is external, actual, practical, uncoloured by one's own sensations or emotions denoting the object (*gram.*): in the relation of object to a verb or preposition: objecting: (of lenses) nearest the object.—*n.* (*-jekt'*) the case of the grammatical object: a word in that case: an object-glass the point to which the operations (esp. of an army) are directed. a goal, aim.—*adv.* **object'ively.**—*n.* **object'iveness.**—*v t.* **object'ivise, -ize** to objectify —*ns.* **object'ivism** a tendency to lay stress on what is objective: a theory that gives priority to the objective, **object'ivist.**—*adj.* **objectivist'ic.**—*n.* **objectiv'ity.**—*adj* **ob'jectless** having no object: purposeless.—*n.* **object'or.**— **ob'ject-finder** a device in microscopes for locating an object in the field before examination by a higher power; **ob'ject-glass** in an optical instrument, the lens or combination of lenses at the end next to the object; **ob'ject-less'on** a lesson in which a material object is before the class: a warning or instructive experience. —**money**, etc , **no object** money, etc , not being a thing aimed at; distance, etc , **no object** distance, etc., not being reckoned worth consideration (perh. by confusion with the foregoing), **object of virtu** an article valued for its antiquity or as an example of craftsmanship, etc [L. *objectus*, pa.p. of *ob(j)icĕre*, or partly the noun *objectus, -ūs* (found in the abl), or the freq. vb *objectāre—ob*, in the way of, *jacĕre*, to throw.]

objet *ob-zhã*, (Fr.) *n.* an object.—**objet d'art** (*dar*) an article with artistic value, **objet de vertu** (*da ver-tū*) a Gallicised (by the English) version of object of virtu (q.v.); **objet trouvé** (*trōō-vā*) a natural or man-made object displayed as a work of art, either exactly as found or touched up ('composed').—*pls* **objets** (*-zhā*) **d'art, de vertu, trouvés** (*-vā*).

objure *ob-jōō'r, v.t* to swear —*v.t.* to bind by oath· to charge or entreat solemnly.—*n.* **objura'tion** act of binding by oath: a solemn charge. [L. *objurāre*, to bind by oath—*ob-*, down, *jūrāre*, to swear.]

objurgate *ob'jar-gāt, or -jûr'*, *v t.* and *v.i.* to chide.—*n.* **objurga'tion.** [L. *objurgāre, -ātum*, to rebuke—*ob-*, intens., *jurgāre*, to chide.]

oblanceolate *ob-lan'si-ō-lāt, (bot.) adj.* like a lance-head reversed, as a leaf—about three times as long as broad, tapering more gently towards base than apex. [Pfx. *ob-*, as in **obcompressed.**]

oblate[1] *ob'lāt, ob-lāt', adj.* dedicated: offered up.—*n.* a dedicated person, esp. one dedicated to monastic life but not professed, or to a religious life.—*n.* **ob-lā'tion** act of offering: a sacrifice: anything offered in worship, esp a eucharistic offering: an offering generally.—*adjs.* **oblā'tional; oblatory** (*ob'la-ta-ri*). [L. *oblātus*, offered up, used as pa.p. of *offerre*, to offer; see **offer.**]

oblate[2] *ob'lāt, ob-lāt', ō-blāt', adj.* flattened at opposite sides or poles, as a spheroid—shaped like an orange (opp. to *prolate*).—*n.* **oblateness.** [On analogy of **prolate;** L. pfx *ob-*, against, or (mod. L.) in the opposite direction.]

oblige *ō-blīj', a-blīj', v.t.* to bind morally or legally: to constrain: to bind by some favour rendered, hence to do a favour to.—*v.i.* (*coll.*) to do something as a favour —*v.t.* **ob'ligate** (*-li-gāt*) to bind by contract or duty: to bind by gratitude (*arch* or *coll*)—*n.* **obligation** (*ob-li-gā'shan*) act of obliging: a moral or legal bond, tie, or binding power: that to which one is bound: a debt of gratitude: a favour: a bond containing a penalty in case of failure (*law*).—*adv.* **obligatorily** (*ob'lig-a-tar-i-li* or *o-blig'*, *a-*).—*n.* **ob'ligatoriness** (or *o-blig'*, *a-*).—*adj.* **ob'ligatory** (or *o-blig'*, *a-*) binding: imposing duty: imposed as an obligation: obligate.—*n.* **oblige'ment** a favour conferred.—*adj.* **oblig'ing** disposed to confer favours ready to do a good turn: courteous.—*adv.* **oblig'ingly.**—*n.* **oblig'ingness.** [Fr. *obliger*—L. *obligāre, -ātum—ob-*, down, *ligāre*, to bind.]

oblique *ō-blēk', a-blēk', adj.* slanting: neither perpendicular nor parallel: not at right angles: not parallel to an axis: not straightforward: indirect. underhand: not a right angle (*geom.*): having the axis not perpendicular to the plane of the base: skew: unsymmetrical about the midrib (*bot.*): monoclinic (*crystal.*).—*n.* an oblique line, figure, muscle, etc.: an oblique movement or advance. esp. one about 45° from the original direction —*v.i.* to advance obliquely by facing half right or left and then advancing.—*ns.* **obliqueness** (*-blēk'*), **obliquity** (*ob-lik'wi-ti*) state of being oblique: a slanting direction: crookedness of outlook, thinking, or conduct, or an instance of it.—*adv.* **oblique'ly.**—**oblique case** any case other than nominative and vocative. [L. *oblīquus—ob-*, intens., and the root of *līquis*, slanting.]

obliterate *ō-blit'a-rāt, v.t.* to blot out, so as not to be readily or clearly readable: to efface.—*n.* **obliterā'tion.**—*adj.* **oblit'erative.** [L. *oblitterāre, -ātum—ob-*, over, *littera* (*lītera*), a letter.]

oblivion *ab-liv'i-an, ob-, n.* forgetfulness: a state of having forgotten: amnesty: a state of being forgotten.—*adj.* **obliv'ious** forgetful: prone to forget: raptly or absent-mindedly unaware (with *of, to*).—*adv.* **obliv'iously.**—*n.* **obliv'iousness.** [L. *oblīviō, -ōnis*, from the root of *oblīviscī*, to forget.]

oblong *ob'long, adj.* long in one way: longer than broad: nearly elliptical, with sides nearly parallel, ends blunted, two to four times as long as broad (*bot.*).—*n.* a rectangle longer than broad: any oblong figure, whether angular or rounded. [L. *oblongus—ob-* (force obscure), and *longus*, long.]

obloquy *ob'la-kwi, n.* reproachful language: censure: calumny: disgrace. [L. *obloquium—ob*, against, *loquī*, to speak.]

obnoxious *ob-nok'shas, ab-, adj.* objectionable: offensive: noxious, hurtful (*erron.*).—*adv.* **obnox'iously.**—*n.* **obnox'iousness.** [L. *obnoxius—ob*, exposed to, *noxa*, hurt.]

ture, either fixed or mobile, used in offshore drilling to support the rig and to keep stores, **oil'-rig** the complete plant (machinery, structures, etc) required for oil-well drilling loosely, a mobile oil platform, **oil sand** sand or sandstone occurring naturally impregnated with petroleum tar sand, **oil'-seed** and seed that yields oil, **oil'-shale** a shale containing diffused hydrocarbons in a state suitable for distillation into mineral oils, **oil'skin** cloth made waterproof by means of oil a garment made of oilskin, **oil slick** a patch of oil forming a film on the surface of water or (*rarely*) a road, etc , **oil'stone** a whetstone used with oil, **oil'-tanker** a vessel constructed for carrying oil in bulk, **oil'-well** a boring made for petroleum —**oil someone's palm** to bribe a person, **oil the wheels** (*fig*) to do something in order to make things go more smoothly, successfully, etc   [O Fr *oile* (Fr *huile*) —L *oleum*—Gr *elaion*—*elaiā*, olive-tree, olive]

oino- *oi-nō-*, in composition, an occasional variant in words beginning **oeno-**.

ointment *oint'mənt, n* anything used in anointing any greasy substance applied to diseased or wounded parts (*med*)· an unguent   [Fr *oint*, pa p of *oindre* —L *unguère*, to anoint]

Oireachtas *er'əhh-thəs, n* the legislature of the Republic of Ireland (President, Seanad, and Dáil) [Ir., assembly.]

OK, okay *ō-kā', (coll) adj* all correct: all right satisfactory.—*adv* yes, all right, certainly.—*n.* approval sanction· endorsement:—*pl* OK's, okays.—*v t* to mark or pass as right· to sanction:—*pr p* **OK'ing,** **OKing, okaying;** *pa t* and *pa p* **OK'd, OKed,** **okayed.**   [Various explanations of the letters have been given]

okapi *ō-ka'pē, n* an animal of Central Africa related to the giraffe.—*pl* **oka'pis.**   [Native name]

oke *ōk, (slang) adv* same as **OK.**—*adj* and *adv* **okey-** **dokey** (*ō'ki-dō'ki, slang*) OK

okra *ok'rə, ōk'rə, n* gumbo.   [From a W African name]

old *ōld, adj* advanced in years· having been long or relatively long in existence, use, or possession· of a specified (or to be specified) age, of long standing, worn or worn out· out of date: superseded or abandoned former: old-fashioned, antique, ancient early· belonging to later life· belonging to former times, denoting anyone or anything with whom or with which one was formerly associated, as *old school*, etc.: (of a language) of the earliest, or earliest known, stage long practised or experienced, having the characteristics of age: familiar, accustomed: in plenty, in excess, or wonderful (esp in *high old*; *coll*)· a general word of familiar or affectionate approbation or contempt (often *good old* or *little old*, *coll*). reckoned according to Old Style (see **style**):— *compar.* **old'er, eld'er** (q.v), *superl* **old'est, eld'est.** —*n.* an old person· olden times —*adj* **old'en** old, ancient.—*n* **old'ie** (*coll.*) an old person· a film, song, etc produced, popularised, etc a considerable time ago —*ns* **old'ness;** **old'ster** a man getting old (*coll*) —**old age** the later part of life, **Old Bailey** the Central Criminal Court in London; **old bird** (*fig*) an experienced person, **old boy** one's father, husband, etc (*coll.*): an old or oldish man, esp. one in authority, or one who has some air of youthfulness· a former pupil an affectionately familiar term of address to a male of any age (*coll* , also **old bean, old chap, old fellow, old man, old thing**):—*fem* **old girl; Old Catholic** a member of a body that broke away from the Roman Catholic Church on the question of papal infallibility, **old'-clothes'man** one who buys cast-off garments; **old country** the mother-country; **old dear** (*slang*) an old lady —*adjs* **old'-estab'lished** long established; **olde-**

worlde (*ō'ldi-wûrld'i*) self-consciously imitative of the past or supposed past —*adj* **old'-fash'ioned** in a fashion like one of long ago out of date clinging to old things and old styles with manners like those of a grown-up person (said of a child) knowing —**old'-** **fash'ionedness.—old gang, guard** old and conservative element in party, etc , **Old Glory** the Stars and Stripes, **old gold** a dull gold colour like tarnished gold, used in textile fabrics; **old hand** an experienced performer an old convict, **Old Harry, Nick, One,** **Poker, Scratch** the devil —*adj* **old hat** out-of-date — **old lady** (*coll*) a person's mother or wife, **old maid** a spinster, esp one who is likely to remain a spinster a woman, or more often a man, of the character supposed to be common among spinsters—fussy, prim, conventional, over-cautious, methodical a simple game played by passing and matching cards also the player left with the odd card —*adj* **old'-** **maid'ish** like the conventional old maid, prim —**old man** a person's husband, father, or employer (*coll*) the captain of a merchant ship a familiar friendly or encouraging term of address, **old master** (often *caps*) any great painter or painting of a period previous to the 19th cent (esp of the Renaissance), **old salt** an experienced sailor, **old school** those whose ways or thoughts are such as prevailed in the past —Also *adj* —**old story** something one has heard before, something that happened long ago, or has happened often —*adj* **old'-time** of or pertaining to times long gone by of long standing· old-fashioned —**old'-tim'er** one who has long been where he is an experienced person, veteran· an old-fashioned person: (esp as a form of address; *U S*) an old man, **old wife** an old woman one who has the character ascribed to old women, a fish of various kinds—sea-bream, file-fish, etc , **old woman** a person's wife or mother (*coll.*)· an oldwomanish person —*adjs.* **old'-wom'anish** like an old woman, esp fussy; **old'-world** belonging to earlier times, old-fashioned and quaint: (*cap*) of the Old World —*n* **Old World** the Eastern hemisphere —**an** **old-fashioned look** a knowing or quizzically critical look; **of old** long ago: in or of ancient times formerly, **old age pension** a pension for one who has reached old age, esp under a national system (first instituted in Britain in 1908); **old age pensioner; Old Boy network** (also without *caps*) the members of a society (usu upper-class), closely interconnected, who share information, and secure advantages for each other this form of association, **old man's beard** a name for several plants including traveller's joy, **old school tie** a distinctive tie worn by old boys of a school the emblem of (esp upper-class) loyalties shown by such people to each other   [O E *ald*]

olden, etc. **oldster.** See **old.**

oleaginous *ō-li-aj'in-əs, adj.* oily —*n.* **oleag'inousness.**   [L *oleāginus*—*oleum,* oil]

oleander *ō-li-an'dər, n.* an evergreen shrub with lance-shaped leathery leaves and beautiful red or white flowers, the rose-bay or rose-laurel   [L L *oleander*]

oleaster *ō-li-as'tər, n* properly the true wild olive extended to the so-called wild olive, Elaeagnus   [L *oleáster—olea,* an olive-tree—Gr. *elaiā*]

oleate *ō'li-āt, n* a salt of oleic acid —*ns* **o'lefin, -fine** (*-fin, -fēn*) any hydrocarbon of the ethylene series — *adjs* **ole'ic** (or *ō'li-ik*) pertaining to or got from oil (as in **oleic acid** $C_{18}H_{34}O_2$), **oleif'erous** producing oil, as seeds —*ns* **olein** (*ō'li-in*) a glycerine ester of oleic acid; **oleo** (*ō'li-ō*) a contraction for oleograph or for oleomargarine —*pl* **o'leos; o'leograph** a print in oil-colours to imitate an oil-painting; **oleog'raphy; oleomar'garine** margarine (*U S.*): a yellow fatty substance got from beef tallow and used in the manufacture of margarine. soap. etc.—*adj.* **oleo-phil'ic** having affinity for oils: wetted by oil in preference to water. [L *oleum*, oil.]

olefin(e), oleic, olein, etc See **oleate.**

oleo. See **oleate.**

oleraceous *ol-ər-ā'shəs, adj* of the nature of a pot-herb, for kitchen use. [L. (*h*)*oleráceus*—(*h*)*olus*, (*h*)*oleris*, a pot-herb, vegetable.]

olfactory *ol-fak'tə-ri, adj* pertaining to, or used in, smelling.—*n.* **olfac'tion.**—*adj.* **olfac'tive.** [L. *olfacère*, to smell—*olère*, to smell, *facère*, to make.]

olibanum *ol-ib'ə-nəm, n.* a gum-resin flowing from incisions in species of *Boswellia*, esp. species in Somaliland and Arabia, frankincense. [L L., prob. —Gr *libanos*, frankincense.]

olig(o)- *ol-ig-, -i-gō, -i-gə-,* in composition, little, few. —*n.* ol'igarch (-*ark*; Gr. *archē*, rule) a member of an oligarchy —*adjs.* **oligarch'al, oligarch'ic, -ical.**—*n.* **ol'igarchy** (*-ar-ki*) government by a small exclusive class: a state so governed: a small body of men who have the supreme power of a state in their hands.— *adj* **Oligocene** (*ol'i-gō-sēn, geol.*; Gr. *kainos*, new, as having few fossil molluscs of living species) between Eocene and Miocene.—*n.* the Oligocene system, period, or strata.—*adj.* **oligopolist'ic.**—*ns.* **oligopoly** (*ol-i-gop'o-li*, Gr. *pôleein*, to sell) a situation in which there are few sellers, and a small number of competitive firms control the market—opp. to **oligopsony** (*ol-i-gop'sə-ni*; Gr. *opsônia*, purchase of food) a situation in which there are few buyers, each competitive buyer influencing the market.—*adjs.* **oligopsonist'ic; oligotrophic** (*-trof'*; Gr. *trophē*, nourishment) (of a lake) having steep, rocky shores and scanty littoral vegetation, lacking in nutrients but rich in oxygen at all levels. [Gr. *oligos*, little, few]

olio *ō'li-ō, n.* a savoury dish of different sorts of meat and vegetables. a mixture· a medley: a miscellany: a variety entertainment:—*pl.* **o'lios.** [Sp. *olla*—L. *ōlla*, a pot; cf. **olla.**]

olive *ol'iv, n.* a tree (*Olea europaea*) cultivated round the Mediterranean for its oily fruit: extended to many more or less similar trees: the fruit of the olive-tree: a colour like the unripe olive: a person of olive-coloured complexion an olive-shaped or oval object of various kinds: a rolled lump of seasoned meat (usu. in *pl.*).—*adj.* of a brownish-green colour like the olive.—*adjs.* **oliva'ceous** olive-coloured. olive-green, **ol'ivary** olive-shaped.—**olive branch** a symbol of peace: something which shows a desire for peace or reconciliation; **olive drab** the olive green of American uniforms, **olive green** a dull dark yellowish green, **ol'ive-oil** oil pressed from the fruit of the olive [Fr.. —L *olīva*]

Oliver. See **Bath.**

olla (L.) *ol'a, ōl'a,* (Sp.) *ol'ya, n.* jar or urn: an olio.— **olla-podrida** (*ol'ya-po-drē'da*; Sp., rotten pot) a Spanish mixed stew or hash of meat and vegetables: any incongrous mixture or miscellaneous collection. [L. *ōlla* and Sp. *olla*, pot, Sp. *podrida*—L *putrida* (fem)—*puter, putris*, rotten.]

olm *olm, ōlm, n.* a European blind, cave-dwelling, eel-like salamander (*Proteus anguinus*). [Ger.]

-ology. The combining element is properly **-logy** (q.v.) —*n.* **ology** (*ol'ə-ji*) a science whose name ends in -ology: any science.

oloroso *ol-ə-rō'sō, -zō, ōl-, n.* a golden-coloured medium-sweet sherry:—*pl* **oloro'sos.** [Sp , fragrant.]

Olympus *ol-im'pəs, n.* the name of several mountains, esp. of one in Thessaly, abode of the greater Greek gods heaven.—*ns.* **Olym'piad** in ancient Greece, a period of four years, being the interval from one celebration of the Olympic games to another, used in

reckoning time (the traditional date of the first Olympiad is 776 B C): a celebration of the Olympic games: a celebration of the modern Olympic games: (sometimes without *cap.*) an international contest in bridge or other mental exercise; **Olym'pian** a dweller on Olympus, any of the greater gods, esp. Zeus: a godlike person: a competitor in the Olympic games —*adj.* of Olympus. godlike.—*adj.* **Olym'pic** of Olympia: of the Olympic games.—*n.pl.* **Olym'pics** the Olympic games, esp. those of modern times: (sometimes without *cap*) an international contest in some mental exercise such as chess.—**Olympic games** the ancient games celebrated every four years at Olympia, in Greece: quadrennial international athletic contests held at various centres since 1896, **Winter Olympics** international contests in skiing, skating, and other winter sports, held in the same years as the Olympics. [Gr. *Olympos.*]

-oma *-ō-mə, n. suff.* a tumour, as *sarcoma, glaucoma:* —*pl* **-ō'mas, -ō'mata.** [Gr. *-ōma.*]

omasum *ō-mā'səm, n.* a ruminant's third stomach, the psalterium or manyplies:—*pl.* **omā'sa.**—*adj* **omā'sal.** [L *omāsum*, ox tripe; a Gallic word.]

ombrometer *om-brom'i-tər, n.* a rain-gauge. [Gr *ombros*, a rain-storm, *metron*, measure.]

Ombudsman *om'boõdz-man, -man, n.* (also without *cap*) (orig in Sweden and Denmark) a 'grievance man , an official who is appointed to investigate complaints against the Administration: in Britain officially 'Parliamentary Commissioner for Administration': (often without *cap.*) any official with a similar function:—*pl* **-men.** [Sw.]

-ome *-ōm, n. suff.* a mass, as in *rhizome, biome.* [Gr *-ōma*]

omega *ō'mig-ə, U.S. -mēg', n.* the last letter of the Greek alphabet—long ō (Ω, ω): the conclusion [Late Gr. *ō mega*, great O; opposed to omicron; the earlier Gr. name of the letter was *ō.*]

omelet, omelette *om'lit, -let, n.* a pancake made of eggs, beaten up, and fried in a pan (with or without cheese, herbs, ham, jam, or other addition). [Fr. *omelette*, earlier *amelette*, apparently by change of suffix and metathesis from *alemelle* (*l'alemelle* for *la lemelle*), a thin plate—L. *lāmella, lāmina,* a thin plate.]

omen *ō'mən, n.* a sign of some future event, either good or evil: threatening or prognosticating character.— *v t.* to portend.—*adj.* **o'mened** affording or attended by omens, esp. in composition, as *ill-omened.* [L. *ōmen, -inis.*]

omentum *ō-men'təm, n* a fold of peritoneum proceeding from one of the abdominal viscera to another:—*pl.* **omen'ta.** [L. *ōmentum.*]

omicron *ō-mi'krən, U.S. ōm'i-, om', n.* the fifteenth letter of the Greek alphabet—short o (O, o) [Late Gr. *o mícron*, little O; opposed to omega, the earlier Greek name of the letter was *ou.*]

ominous *om'in-əs, adj.* pertaining to, or containing, an omen: portending evil: inauspicious.—*adv.* **om'inously.**—*n.* **om'inousness.** [See **omen.**]

omit *ō-mit', v.t.* to leave out: to fail (to). to fail to use, perform:—*pr.p.* **omitt'ing;** *pa.t.* and *pa.p.* **omitt'ed.** —*adj.* **omiss'ible** that may be omitted.—*n.* **omission** (*-mish'n*) the act of omitting: a thing omitted. [L *omittère, omissum—ob-,* in front, *mittère*, to send.]

ommateum *om-ə-tē'əm, n.* a compound eye:—*pl.* **om-mate'a.**—*ns.* **ommatid'ium** a simple element of a compound eye:—*pl.* **ommatid'ia.** [Gr. *omma, -atos,* an eye.]

omni- *om-ni-,* in composition, all.—*n.* **omnicom'petence** competence in all matters.—*adjs.* **omnicom'petent; omnidirec'tional** acting in all directions.—*ns* **omnip'otence, omnip'otency** unlimited power —*adj.*

omnip'otent all-powerful.—*adv.* **omnip'otently.**—*n.* **omnipres'ence** the quality of being present everywhere at the same time.—*adj.* **omnipres'ent.**—*n.* **omniscience**(*om-nis'i-əns,-nish'əns,-yəns*)knowledge of all things.—*adj.* **omnisc'ient** all-knowing.—*adv.* **omnisc'iently.**—*n.* **om'nivore.**—*adj.* **omniv'orous** all-devouring: feeding on both animal and vegetable food (*zool.*). [L. *omnis,* all.]

omnibus *om'ni-bəs, n.* a large road-vehicle carrying a considerable number of passengers of the general public, or hotel guests (shortened form **bus**): an omnibus book. a waiter's or waitress's assistant:—*pl.* **om'nibuses.**—*adj.* widely comprehensive: of miscellaneous contents.—**omnibus book** a book containing reprints of several works or items, usually by a single author, or on a single subject, or of the same type; **omnibus clause** one that covers many different cases; **omnibus train** one that stops at every station. [Lit. for all, dative pl. of L. *omnis.*]

omnicompetence ... omnipotence ... omniscience. See **omni-.**

omnium *om'ni-əm, n.* a Stock Exchange term for the aggregate value of the different stocks in which a loan is funded.—**om'nium-gath'erum** (*coll.; sham Latin*) a miscellaneous collection. [L., of all; gen. pl. of *omnis,* all.]

omnivore, omnivorous. See **omni-.**

on *on, prep.* in contact with the upper, supporting, outer, or presented surface of: to a position in contact with such a surface of: in or to a position or state of being supported by: having for basis, principle, or condition: subject to: in a condition or process of: towards or to: against: applied to: with action applied to: with inclination towards: close to, beside: exactly or very nearly at: at the time, date, or occasion of: very little short of: just after: concerning, about: with respect to: by (in oaths and adjurations): at the risk of: assigned to: in addition to: at the expense of, to the disadvantage of (*coll.*).—*adv.* in or into a position on something: towards something: in advance: forward: in continuance: in, or into, or allowing connection, supply, activity, operation, or validity: in progress: on the stage, the table, the fire, the programme, the menu, or anything else: not off.—*interj.* forward!, proceed!—*adj.* on the side on which the batsman stands (normally the bowler's right) (*cricket*): in a condition expressed by the adverb on: agreed upon: willing to participate.—*n.* the on side.—*v.i.* to go on (*coll.*): (with *with*) to put on (*coll.*).—**on'coming** an approach.—*adj.* advancing: approaching.—**on'-drive** (*cricket*) a drive to the on side.—Also *v.i.* and *v.t.*—**on'fall** an attack, onslaught; **on'flow** a flowing on: an onward flow; **on'going** a going on: a course of conduct: an event: (*pl.*) proceedings, behaviour, esp. misbehaviour.—*adj.* (*on'-going*) currently in progress: continuing: which will not stop.—**on'-licence** a licence to sell alcoholic liquors for consumption on the premises.—*adj.* **on'-line** (*comput.*) attached to, and under the direct control of, the central processing unit: got from or by means of on-line equipment.—**on'looker** a looker on, observer.—*adjs* **on'looking; on'-off'** (of a switch, etc.) which can be set to one of only two positions, either *on* or *off.*—**on'rush** a rushing onward; **on'set** a violent attack: an assault: the beginning, outset.—*adj.* **onshore** (*on'-shōr, -shōr'*) towards the land.—*adv.* **on'-shore.**—*adj.* and *adv.* **on'side** not offside.—*n.* (*cricket*) see **on** *adj.*—*adj.* and *adv.* **on'-stream** of an industrial plant, etc., in, or going into, operation or production.—*prep.* **onto** see **on to:** to the whole of (*math.*).—*adj.* (*math.*) describing a mapping of one set to a second set, involving every element of the latter.—*adj.* **on'ward** (*on'wərd*) going on: advancing: advanced.—*adv.* (also **on'wards**) towards a place or time in advance or in front: forward: in continuation of forward movement.—**on to** to a place or position on (also **on'to**): forward to: aware of, cognisant of (*coll.*); **on and off** same as **off and on; on and on** (and **on**) used in phrases containing the particle *on* to emphasise duration, distance, etc.; **on stream** same as **on-stream.** [O.E. *on.*]

onager *on'ə-jər, n.* the wild ass of Central Asia: an ancient military engine for throwing great stones. [L.,—Gr. *onagros—onos,* an ass, *agrios,* wild—*agros,* a field.]

onanism *ō'nən-izm, n.* coitus interruptus: masturbation.—*n.* **o'nanist.**—*adj.* **onanist'ic.** [See Gen. xxxviii. 9.]

once *wuns, adv.* a single time: on one occasion: at a former time: at any time.—*n.* one time.—*adj.* former.—*conj.* when once: as soon as.—*n.* **onc'er:** a £1 note (*slang*).—*adj.* **once'-for-all'** done, etc. once and for all.—*n.* **once-o'ver** a single comprehensive survey.—**at once** without delay: alike: at the same time; **for once** on one occasion only; **once and again** more than once: now and then; **once (and) for all** once only and not again; **once in a way, while** occasionally: rarely; **once or twice** a few times, **once upon a time** at a certain time in the past—the usual formula for beginning a fairy-tale. [O.E. *ānes,* orig. gen. of *ān,* one, used as adv.]

onchocerciasis *ong-kō-sər-kī'-ə-sis, n.* a disease of man, also known as river blindness, common in tropical regions of America and Africa, caused by infestation by a filarial worm (*Onchocerca volvulus*) which is transmitted by various species of black fly, and characterised by subcutaneous nodules and very often blindness. [Gr. *onkos,* a hook, *kerkos,* a tail.]

oncology *ong-kol'ə-ji, n.* the study of tumours.—*adj.* **oncogenic** (*-kō-jen'*) causing tumours.—*n.* **oncol'ogist.** [Gr. *onkos,* bulk, mass, tumour.]

on-dit *ō-dē, n.* rumour: hearsay:—*pl.* **on-dits** (*-dē, -dēz*) [Fr.]

one *wun, adj.* single: of unit number: undivided: the same: a certain: a single but not specified: first.—*n.* the number unity: a symbol representing it: an individual thing or person: a thing bearing or distinguished by the number one.—*pron.* somebody: anybody.—*ns.* **one'ness** singleness: uniqueness: identity: unity: homogeneity, sameness; **oner** (*wun'ər;* all meanings *coll.* or *slang*) a person or thing unique or outstanding in any way: an expert: a heavy blow: a big lie.—Also **one'-er, wunn'er.**—*pron.* **oneself', one's self** the emphatic and reflexive form of **one.**—*adjs.* **one'-eyed; one'-hand'ed** with, by, or for, one hand; **one'-horse** drawn by a single horse: petty, mean, inferior; **one'-legged.—one'-lin'er** (*coll.*) a short pithy remark: a wisecrack, quip.—*adjs.* **one'-man** of, for, or done by, one man; **one'-off'** made, intended, etc. for one occasion only.—Also *n.*—*adjs* **one'-one** one-to-one, **one'-piece** made in one piece; **one'-shot** (intended to be) done, used, etc. on only one occasion or for one particular purpose or project. **one-off:** not part of a serial.—Also *n.*—*adj.* **one's-sid'ed** limited to one side: partial: developed on one side only: turned to one side.—*adv.* **one'-sid'edly.**—**one'-sid'edness; one'step** a dance of U.S. origin danced to quick march time.—*v.i.* to dance a one-step.—*adjs.* **one'-time** former, erstwhile; **one'-to-one'** corresponding each one uniquely to one; **one'-track'** incapable of dealing with more than one idea or activity at a time: obsessed with one idea to the exclusion of others.—**one'-two** (*coll*) in boxing, etc., a blow with one fist followed by a blow with the other (also *fig.*): in football, a movement in which a player passes the ball to another player then runs forward to receive the ball which is immediately passed back to him —**one-up'manship** (*facet* , *Stephen Potter*) the art of being one up, i e scoring or maintaining an advantage over someone —*adj.* **one'-way** proceeding, or permitting, or set apart for traffic, in one direction only —**a, the, one** a person special or remarkable in some way (*coll.*), **a one for** an enthusiast for, **all one** just the same of no consequence, at **one** of one mind. reconciled (with), **be one up on** to score an advantage over (another). **(all) in one** combined as one unit, object, etc , **just one of those things** an unfortunate happening that must be accepted, **one and all** everyone without exception, **one-armed bandit** a fruit machine (q v.), **one by one** singly in order, **one day** on a certain day at an indefinite time; **one-horse race** (*fig.*) a race, competition, etc in which one particular competitor or participant is certain to win, **one-man band** a musician who carries and plays many instruments simultaneously (also **one-man show**) an organisation, activity, etc run very much by one person who refuses the help of others (*fig*), **one-night stand** a performance or performances, or anything similar, given on one single evening in one place by one or more people who then travel on to another place an amorous relationship lasting only one night (*coll*); **one or two** a few, **one-parent family** a family in which, due to death, divorce, etc , the children are looked after by only one parent, **one-way glass** glass which can be looked through from one side but which appears from the other side to be a mirror. [O.E *ān.*]

oneiric ō-nī'rik, *adj.* belonging to dreams.—Also **oni'ric.** [Gr *oneiros*, a dream.]

onerous on'ə-rəs, ō'nər-əs, *adj* burdensome. oppressive —*adv.* **on'erously.**—*n* **on'erousness.** [L. *onerōsus*—*onus*, a burden]

onfall, ongoing. See on.

onion un'yən, *n* a pungent edible bulb of the lily family: the plant yielding it applied also to some kindred species —*adj* **on'iony** —**onion dome** a bulb-shaped dome having a sharp point, characteristic of Eastern Orthodox, esp Russian, church architecture —**know one's onions** to know one's subject or one's job well (*coll.*) [Fr *oignon*—L. *ūniō, -ōnis,* union, a large pearl, an onion.]

oniric. See **oneiric.**

on-licence to **onlooking.** See under **on.**

only ōn'li, *adj.* single in number: without others of the kind without others worthy to be counted.—*adv* not more, other, or otherwise than alone: merely barely just.—*conj.* but: except that —**if only** (I, he, etc.) wish (wished, etc.) ardently that; **only too** very, extremely. [O.E *ānlic* (adj.)—*ān,* one, *-līc,* like]

onomastic on-ə-mas'tik, *adj.* pertaining to a name, esp pertaining to the signature to a paper written in another hand.—*n.sing* **onomas'tics** the study of the history of proper names [Gr *onomastikos, -on—onoma,* a name.]

onomatopoeia on-ō-mat-ō-pē'ə, *n* the formation of a word in imitation of the sound of the thing meant. a word so formed. the use of words whose sounds help to suggest the meaning (*rhet*) —Also **onomatopoesis** (*-pō-ē'sis*) or **onomatopoiesis** (*-poi-ē'sis*).—*adjs* **onomatopoeic** (*-pē'ik*), **onomatopoetic** (*-pō-et'ik*) [Gr. *onomatopoiiā, -poiēsis—onoma, -atos,* a name, *poieein,* to make.]

onrush to **onshore.** See under **on.**

onslaught on'slot, *n* an attack or onset assault [Prob. Du *aanslag* or Ger. *Anschlag,* refashioned as Eng.]

on-stream to **onto.** See under **on.**

ontogenesis on-tō-jen'i-sis, *n.* the history of the individual development of an organised being, as distinguished from *phylogenesis* —Also **ontogeny** (*ontoj'i-ni*) —*adjs* **ontogenet'ic, ontogen'ic.**—*advs* **ontogenet'ically, -gen'ically.** [Gr *ōn, ontos,* pr p of *einai,* to be. *genesis,* generation]

ontology on-tol'ə-ji, *n* the science that treats of the principles of pure being that part of metaphysics which treats of the nature and essence of things —*adjs* **ontologic** (*-tə-loj'ik*), **-al.**—*adv* **ontolog'ically.** [Gr *ōn, ontos,* pr p of *einai,* to be, *logos,* discourse]

onus ō'nəs, *n* burden responsibility [L. *ōnus, -eris*]

onward, etc See under **on.**

onyx on'iks, *n* an agate formed of alternate flat layers of chalcedony, white or yellow and black, brown or red, used for making cameos (*min*) onychite, onyx-marble a fingernail-like opacity in the cornea of the eye —**on'yx-mar'ble** a banded travertine or stalagmite, also called oriental alabaster [Gr *onyx, onychos,* nail, claw, onyx]

oo- ō'ə-, ō-o-, in composition, egg —*n* **oolite** (ō'ə-līt, Gr *lithos,* a stone, *geol*) a kind of limestone composed of grains like the eggs or roe of a fish: (with *cap.*) stratigraphically the upper part of the Jurassic in Britain, consisting largely of oolites —*adj* **oolitic** (ō-ə-lit'ik) —*ns* **oology** (ō-ol'ə-ji, Gr *logos,* discourse) the science or study of birds eggs; **ool'ogist.** [Gr *oion,* egg.]

oodles ōō'dlz, *n sing.* or *pl* abundance —Also **ood'-lins.** [Perh **huddle.**]

ooh ōō, *interj* expressing pleasure, surprise, etc.—Also *n.* and *v t* [Imit.]

oolong, oulong ōō'long, *n* a variety of black tea with the flavour of green. [Chin *wu-lung,* black dragon.]

oomia(c)k, oomiac. Same as **umiak.**

oompah ōōm'pa, *n* a conventional representation of the deep sound made by a large brass musical instrument such as a tuba.—Also *v i.* and *v t.*

oomph ōōmf, ōōmf, (*slang*) *n* vitality: enthusiasm: sex-appeal: personal magnetism

oops ōōps, *interj.* an exclamation drawing attention to, apologising for, etc. a mistake.

ooze ōōz, *n* gentle flow, as of water through sand or earth slimy mud a fine-grained, soft, deep-sea deposit, composed of shells and fragments of foraminifera, diatoms, and other organisms.—*v.i.* to flow gently: to percolate, as a liquid through pores or small openings: to leak —*v.t* to exude.—*adv* **ooz'ily.**—*n* **ooz'iness.**—*adj* **ooz'y** resembling ooze slimy: oozing [Partly O.E *wōs,* juice, partly O.E *wāse,* mud.]

op *op.* Short for **operation** and (in **op art,** see below) **optical:** abbrev for **opus.**

opacity. See under **opaque.**

opah ō'pə, *n* the kingfish (*Lampris*), a large sea-fish with laterally flattened body, constituting a family of uncertain affinities [West African origin.]

opal ō'pl, *n.* amorphous silica with some water, usually milky white with fine play of colour, in some varieties precious, opal-glass. the colouring of opal —*adj.* of opal: like opal —*adj* **o'paled.**—*n.* **opalesc'ence** a milky iridescence —*adj* **opalesc'ent.**—*adj* **o'paline** (*-ēn, -īn*) relating to, like, or of, opal.—*n* opal-glass. a photographic print fixed on plate-glass —*adj* **o'palised, -z-** converted into opal opalescent — **o'pal-glass'** white or opalescent glass [L *opalus,* Gr *opallios,* perh —Sans *upala,* gem.]

opaque ō-pāk', *adj.* shady: dark dull. that cannot be seen through impervious to light or to radiation of some particular kind obscure, hard to understand (*fig.*). impervious to sense doltish —*v t* to make opaque —*n.* **opacity** (ō-pas'i-ti) opaqueness.—*adv* **opaque'ly.**—*n.* **opaque'ness.** [L. *opācus*]

op art *op art*, art using geometrical forms precisely executed and so arranged that movement of the observer's eye, or inability to focus, produces an illusion of movement in the painting. [optical]

ope *ōp, adj , (poet.) v t.* and *v.t* a short form of **open**.

open *ō'pn, adj* not shut: allowing passage out or in. exposing the interior: unobstructed free· unenclosed exposed: uncovered. liable: generally accessible· available: ready to receive or transact business with members of the public· willing to receive or accept (with *to*)· public: free to be discussed obvious: unconcealed: undisguised: unfolded, spread out, expanded: unrestricted: not restricted to any class of persons, as *open championship* (of a town) without military defences: not finally decided, concluded, settled, or assigned: not dense in distribution or texture: widely spaced: loose: much interrupted by spaces or holes: showing a visible space between (*naut.*): clear· unfrozen: not frosty· not hazy· free from trees: frank: unreserved unstopped (*mus*) without use of valve, crook, or key: (of an organ pipe) not closed at the top: (of a vowel sound) low, with wide aperture for the breath: (of a consonant) without stopping of the breath stream. (of a syllable) ending with a vowel.—*v.t.* to make open: to make as an opening· to make an opening in: to clear· to expose to view: to expound: to declare open: to begin.—*v t.* to become open: to have an opening, aperture, or passage: to serve as passage· to begin to appear: to begin: to give tongue· to speak out —*n.* a clear space: public view: open market. an opening —*ns* **o'pener; o'pening** the act of causing to be, or of becoming. open: an open place: an aperture: a gap: a street or road breaking the line of another: a beginning: a first stage· a preliminary statement of a case in court· the initial moves, or mode of beginning, in a game, etc : the two pages exposed together when a book is opened: an opportunity for action: a vacancy —Also *adj.—adv.* **o'penly.—n. o'penness —open access** public access to the shelves of a library —*adjs.* **o'pen-air** outdoor; **o'pen-and-shut'** simple, obvious, easily decided, **o'pen-armed'** cordially welcoming —**open book** anything that can be read or interpreted without difficulty; **o'pen-cast'** in mining, an excavation open overhead.—Also *adj.* and *adv.—***open court** a court proceeding in public —*adjs* **o'pen-door'; o'pen-end'(ed)** not closely defined, general and adaptable to suit various contingencies: (of question, debate, etc) allowing free unguided answers or expressions of opinion: (of investment trust) offering shares in unlimited numbers, redeemable on demand: (**o'pen-end'ed**) without fixed limits, **o'pen-eyed** astonished fully aware of what is involved —**open fire** an exposed fire on a domestic hearth —*adj* **o'pen-hand'ed** with an open hand: generous: liberal.—**o'pen-hand'edness.**—*adj* **o'pen-heart'ed** with an open heart: frank: generous —**o'pen-heart'edness.**—*adj.* **o'pen-hearth** making use of, or having, a shallow hearth of reverberating type.—**open house** hospitality to all comers; **opening time** the time when bars, public houses, etc. can begin selling alcoholic drinks; **open letter** a letter addressed to one person but intended for public reading; **open market** a market in which buyers and sellers compete without restriction; **open mind** freedom from prejudice: readiness to receive and consider new ideas.—*adj.* **o'pen-mind'ed.**—**o'pen-mind'edness.**—*adj.* **o'pen-mouthed'** gaping. expectant: greedy: clamorous —**open note** a note produced by an unstopped string, open pipe, or without a crook, etc —*adj.* **o'pen-plan'** having few, or no, internal walls, partitions, etc.—**open prison** a prison without the usual close security, allowing prisoners considerably more freedom of movement than in con-ventional prisons; **open question** a matter undecided; **open sandwich** one which has no bread, etc , on top; **open sea** unenclosed sea, clear of headlands, **open season** a time of the year when one may kill certain game or fish (also *fig.*), **open secret** a matter known to many but not explicitly divulged; **open sesame** a spell or other means of making barriers fly open—from the story of Ali Baba and the Forty Thieves in the *Arabian Nights*, **open side** the part· of the field between the scrum. etc. and the farther touch-line (*rugby*), **open skies** the open air. reciprocal freedom for aerial inspection of military establishments; **open university** (also with *caps.*) a British university (1971) having no fixed entry qualifications, whose teaching is carried out by correspondence and by radio and television; **open verdict** a verdict that a crime has been committed without specifying the criminal; **o'pen-work** any work showing openings through it.—*adj* open-cast —**open fire** to begin to shoot; **open-heart** surgery surgery performed on a heart which has been stopped and opened up while blood circulation is maintained by a heart-lung machine, **open out** to make or become more widely open: to expand: to disclose: to unpack: to develop: to bring into view: to open the throttle, accelerate: **open up** to open thoroughly or more thoroughly· to lay open: to disclose· to make available for traffic, colonisation, or the like: to accelerate: to begin firing, **with open arms** cordially [O E *open*; prob related to **up.**]

opera[1] *op'ə-rə, n* musical drama: a company performing opera —*adj* used in or for an opera.—*adj.* **operatic** (*-at'ik*) pertaining to or resembling opera —*adv* **operat'ically.—opéra comique** (*kom-ēk*) (Fr.) opera with some spoken dialogue: **comic opera** opéra comique: opera of an amusing nature: an absurd emotional situation; **grand opera** opera without dialogue, esp if the subject is very dramatic or emotional: **light opera** a lively and tuneful opera: an operetta (q.v), **soap opera** see **soap.—op'era-glass(es)** a small binocular telescope for use in the theatre; **op'era-house** a theatre for opera; **op'era-sing'er.** [It.—L. *opera*; cf **operate.**]

opera[2] *op'ə-rə, pl.* of **opus.**

operate *op'ə-rāt, v.i* to exert strength. to produce any effect: to exert moral power: to be in activity, act, carry on business: to take effect upon the human system (*med*)· to perform some surgical act upon the body with the hand or an instrument.—*v t.* to effect, bring about, cause to occur: to work: to conduct, run, carry on.—*adj.* **op'erable** admitting of a surgical operation. able to be operated: practicable.—*n* **op'erand** something on which an operation is performed, e g a quantity in mathematics.—*adj* **op'erant** operative: ۠active: effective.—*n.* an operator.—*adj* **op'erating.**—*n.* **opera'tion** the act or process of operating: that which is done or carried out: agency: influence: a method of working: action or movements a surgical performance —shortened to **op** esp. in military or surgical sense —*adjs.* **opera'tional** relating to operations: ready for action, **opera'tions** relating to problems affecting operations, esp. military (as in *operations research*), **op'erative** having the power of operating or acting· exerting force: producing effects: efficacious.—*n* a workman in a factory: a labourer.—*adv.* **op'eratively.—ns. op'erativeness; op'erator** one who, or that which, operates: one charged with the operation of a machine, instrument, or apparatus: one who deals in stocks: a symbol, signifying an operation to be performed (*math.*). —**operating table, theatre** one set apart for use in surgical operations, **operational, operations, research** research to discover how a weapon, tactic, or strategy can be altered to give better results: similar research to promote maximum efficiency in industrial spheres. **operative words** the words in a deed legally effecting the transaction (e g *devise and bequeath* in a will) (*loosely*, often in *sing*) the most significant word or words [L *operāri, -ātus—opera,* work, closely connected with *opus, operis,* work.]

operculum ō-pûr′kū-ləm, *n* a cover or lid (*bot*). the plate over the entrance of a shell (*zool*). the gillcover of fishes —*pl.* **oper′cula.** **oper′culate, -d** having an operculum [L *operculum—operīre,* to cover]

opere citato op′ə-rē sit-ā′tō, op′er-e kit-a′tō, (L) in the work cited.—abbrev **op. cit.**

operetta op-ə-ret′ə, *n.* a short, light, rather trivial, musical drama often esp formerly, light opera (see **opera¹**) —*n.* **operett′ist** a composer of operettas [It , dim of *opera*]

ophi(o)- of-i(-ō)-, -o′-, in composition, snake —*n* **oph′icleide** (-klīd, Fr *ophicléide*—Gr *kleis, kleidos,* key) a keyed wind-instrument developed from the serpent, a bass or alto keybugle —*n pl* **Ophid′ia** (Gr *ophidion,* dim) the snakes as an order or suborder of reptiles —*n* and *adj* **ophid′ian.**—*ns* **ophiol′ogist; ophiol′ogy** the study of snakes —*ns* **ophioph′ilist** a snake-lover. **oph′ite** a name given to various rocks mottled with green —*adj* **ophitic** (of-it′ik) [Gr *ophis,* snake]

ophthalm(o)- of-thal-m(ō)-, -o′-, in composition, eye —*n* **ophthal′mia** inflammation of the eye, esp of the conjunctiva —*adj* **ophthal′mic** pertaining to the eye —*ns* **ophthal′mist** an ophthalmologist, **ophthalmi′tis** ophthalmia —*adj* **ophthalmolog′ical.**—*ns* **ophthalmol′ogist; ophthalmol′ogy** the science of the eye, its structure, functions, and diseases, **ophthal′moscope** an instrument for examining the interior of the eye —*adjs* **ophthalmoscop′ic, -al.**—*n* **ophthalmos′copy** examination of the interior of the eye with the ophthalmoscope —**ophthalmic optician** an optician qualified both to prescribe and to dispense spectacles, etc [Gr *ophthalmos,* eye.]

opiate ō′pi-āt, -ət, *n* a drug containing opium to induce sleep that which dulls sensation, physical or mental —*adj* inducing sleep —*v t* (ō′pi-āt) to treat with opium to dull —*adj* **o′piated.** [opium.]

opine ō-pīn′, *v t* to suppose to form or express as an opinion [Fr *opiner*—L *opināri,* to think]

opinion ō-pin′yən, *n* what seems to one to be probably true judgment estimation favourable estimation —*adjs* **opin′ionâted, opin′ionâtive, opin′ioned** unduly attached to one′s own opinions stubborn —**a matter of opinion** a matter about which opinions differ [L *opīniō, -ōnis*]

opisometer op-i-som′i-tər, *n* a map-measuring instrument with a wheel that traces a line on the map and then runs backward along a straight scale until the wheel reaches its original position on the screw that holds it [Gr *opisō,* backward, *metron,* measure]

opium ō′pi-əm, *n* the dried narcotic juice of the white poppy anything considered to have a stupefying or tranquillising effect on people′s minds, emotions, etc —**opium den** a resort of opium-smokers, **o′pium-eat′er, -smoker** one who makes a habitual use of opium [L *ōpium*—Gr *opion,* dim from *opos,* sap]

opossum ō-pos′əm, *n* any member of the American genus *Didelphys,* or family Didelphyidae, small marsupials, often pouchless, mainly arboreal, with prehensile tail in Australia, a phalanger. opossum-fur —Also (*U S*) **possum, ′possum.**—**play possum** to feign death [American Indian]

oppidan op′i-dən, *n* a townsman in university towns, one who is not a member of the university, or a student not resident in a college at Eton (formerly elsewhere) a schoolboy who is not a foundationer or colleger —*adj* urban [L *oppidānus—oppidum,* town.]

opponent o-pō′nənt, *adj* opposing. placed opposite or in front —*n* one who opposes a course of action, belief, person, etc —*n* **oppo′nency.** [L *oppōnēns, -entis,* pr p of *oppōnēre—ob,* in the way of, *pōnēre,* to place]

opportune op′ər-tūn, or -tūn′ *adj* occurring at a fitting time conveniently presented: timely. convenient suitable opportunist —*adv* **opportune′ly** (or *op′*) —*ns* **opportune′ness** (or *op′*), **opportun′ism** (or *op′*) the practice of regulating actions by favourable opportunities rather than consistent principles, **opportun′ist** (or *op′*) one (e.g a politician) who waits for events before declaring his opinions, or shapes his conduct or policy to circumstances of the moment a person without settled principles —Also *adj* —*n* **opportun′ity** an occasion offering a possibility advantageous conditions [Fr *opportun*—L *opportūnus—ob,* before. *portus, -ūs,* a harbour]

oppose o-pōz′, *v t* to place in front or in the way (with *to*) to place or apply face to face or front to front· to set in contrast or balance to set in conflict to place as an obstacle to face. to resist to contend with —*v t* to make objection.—*n* **opposabil′ity.**—*adjs* **oppos′able** that may be opposed· capable of being placed with the front surface opposite (to—as a thumb to other fingers), **oppo′sing.**—*n* **oppos′er.** [Fr *opposer*—L *ob,* against, Fr *poser,* to place—L *pausāre,* to rest, stop, see **pose¹.**]

opposite op′ə-zit, *adj* placed, or being, face to face, or at two extremities of a line facing on the other side of leaves, in pairs at each node, with the stem between (*bot*) of floral parts, on the same radius directly contrary. diametrically opposed opposed corresponding.—*adv* in or to an opposite position or positions —*prep* in a position facing, opposing, contrary to, etc. as a lead in the same film or play as (another lead) (*theat* , etc)—*n* that which is opposed or contrary an opponent —*adv* **opp′ositely.**—*n* **opp′ositeness**—*adj* **oppositive** (-poz′) characterised by opposing adversative inclined to oppose —**opposite number** one who has a corresponding place in another set one who is allotted to another as partner, opponent, etc [Fr ,—L *oppositus—ob,* against, *pōnere, positum,* to place]

opposition op-ə-zish′ən, *n* the act of opposing or of setting opposite the state of being opposed or placed opposite opposed or opposite position an opposite contrast contradistinction resistance a difference of quantity or quality between two propositions having the same subject and predicate (*logic*) a body of opposers the party that opposes the ministry or existing administration the situation of a heavenly body, as seen from the earth. when it is directly opposite to another. esp the sun (*astron*) —*adj* of the parliamentary opposition —*adj* **opposi′tional.** [L *oppositiō, -ōnis,* cf **opposite.**]

oppress o-pres′, *v t.* to press against or upon. to overwhelm to distress· to lie heavy upon to treat with tyrannical cruelty or injustice to load with heavy burdens —*n* **oppression** (o-presh′ən) an act of oppressing tyranny a feeling of distress or of being weighed down dullness of spirits —*adj* **oppress′ive** tending to oppress. overburdensome. tyrannical heavy overpowering —*adv* **oppress′ively.**—*ns* **oppress′iveness; oppress′or.** [Fr *oppresser*—L L *oppressāre,* freq of L *oprimēre, oppressum—ob,* against, *premēre,* to press]

opprobrium o-prō′bri-əm, *n* disgrace, reproach, or imputation of shameful conduct infamy anything that brings such reproach —*adj* **oppro′brious**

reproachful, insulting, abusive.—*adv.* **oppro'briously.**—*n.* **oppro'briousness.** [L. *opprobrium—ob*, against, *probrum*, reproach.]

oppugn *o-pūn'*, *v.t.* to assail, esp. by argument: to oppose: to call in question.—*adj.* **oppug'nant** (-*pug'*) opposing: hostile.—*n.* an opponent.—*n.* **oppugner** (*o-pūn'ər*). [L. *oppugnāre*, to attack—*ob*, against, *pugna*, a fight.]

ops. A contraction of **operations.**

opt *opt*, *v.i.* where there is more than one possibility, to decide (to do), to choose (with *for*).—*n.* **opt'ant** one who opts: one who has exercised a power of choosing, esp. his nationality.—*adj* **optative** (*opt'ə-tiv*, or *op-tā'tiv*) expressing a desire or wish.—*n.* (*gram.*) a mood of the verb expressing a wish.—*adv.* **op'tatively.**—**opt out (of)** to choose not to take part (in). [L. *optāre, -ātum,* to choose, wish.]

optic, -al *op'tik, -əl, adjs.* relating to sight, or to the eye, or to optics: (**optical**) constructed to help the sight: acting by means of light: amplifying radiation: visual.—*n.* **op'tic** an eye (now mainly *facet.*): a lens, telescope, or microscope (*obs.*): a device in, or attached to, a bottle, for measuring liquid poured out.—*adv.* **op'tically.**—*n.* **optician** (*op-tish'ən*) formerly one skilled in optics: one who makes or sells optical instruments.—*n.sing.* **op'tics** the science of light.—*ns.* **optom'eter** an instrument for testing vision; **optom'etrist; optom'etry** the science of vision and eye-care: the practice of examining the eyes and vision: the prescription and provision of optical appliances, etc. for the improvement of vision.—**optical fibre** a thin strand of glass through which light waves may be bounced, used e.g. in some communications systems, fibre optics, etc.; **optical microscope, telescope** one which operates by the direct perception of light from the object viewed, as opposed to an electron microscope or radio telescope; **optic lobe** part of the mid-brain concerned with sight. [Gr. *optikos,* optic, *optos,* seen.]

optimal, etc. See **optimism.**

optimism *op'ti-mizm, n.* a belief that everything is ordered for the best: a disposition to take a bright, hopeful view of things: hopefulness.—Opp. to *pessimism.*—*adj.* **op'timal** optimum.—*v.t.* **op'timalise, -ize** to bring to the most desirable or most efficient state.—*n.* **optimalisā'tion, -z-.**—*v.t.* **op'timise, -ize** to make the most or best of: to make as efficient as possible, esp. by analysing and planning processes: to prepare or revise (a computer system or programme) so as to achieve greatest possible efficiency.—*n.* **optimisā'tion, -z-.**—*n.* **op'timist** one who believes in optimism: commonly, a sanguine person.—*adj.* **optimist'ic.**—*adv.* **optimist'ically.** [L. *optimus,* best.]

optimum *op'ti-məm, n.* that point at which any condition is most favourable:—*pl.* **op'tima.**—*adj.* (of conditions) best for the achievement of an aim or result: very best. [L., neut. of *optimus,* best]

option *op'shən, n.* an act of choosing: the power or right of choosing: a thing that may be chosen: an alternative for choice: a power (as of buying or selling at a fixed price) that may be exercised at will within a time-limit.—*adj.* **op'tional** left to choice: not compulsory: leaving to choice.—*adv.* **op'tionally.**—**keep, leave one's options open** to refrain from committing oneself (to a course of action, etc.). [L. *optiō, -ōnis* —*optāre,* to choose.]

optometry, etc. See **optic.**

opulent *op'ū-lənt, adj.* wealthy: loaded with wealth luxuriant: over-enriched.—*n.* **op'ulence** riches abounding riches.—*adv.* **op'ulently.** [L. *opulentus.*]

Opuntia *ō-pun'shi-ə, n.* the prickly-pear genus of the cactus family: (without *cap.*) a plant of this genus. [L. *Opūntia* (*hera,* plant), of *Opūs* (Gr. *Opous*), a town of Locris where Pliny said it grew.]

opus *ō'pəs, op'əs, op'ōōs, n.* a work, esp. a musical composition—esp. one numbered in order of publication, as opus 6 (abbrev. op. 6): used in naming various styles of Roman masonry:—*pl.* **o'puses, opera** (*op'ə-rə*) [L *ŏpus, -eris,* work]

opuscule *o-pus'kūl, n.* a little work. [L. dim. of *opus.*]

or[1] *ŏr, conj.* marking an alternative. [M.E. *other.*]

or[2] *ŏr,* (*her.*) *n.* the tincture gold or yellow. [Fr.,—L. *aurum,* gold.]

orach, orache *or'ich, n.* a genus of the goosefoot family, sometimes used as spinach is. [O.Fr. *arace* (Fr. *arroche*)—L. *atriplex*—Gr. *atraphaxys.*]

oracle *or'ə-kl, n.* a medium or agency of divine revelation: a response by or on behalf of a god: the place where such responses are given: the Jewish sanctuary: the word of God: a person with the repute or air of infallibility or great wisdom: an infallible indication: a wise or seeming-wise or mysterious utterance: (with *cap.:* ®) the teletext (q.v.) service of the Independent Broadcasting Authority.—*adj* **oracular** (*or-ak'ū-lər*) of the nature of an oracle: like an oracle: seeming to claim the authority of an oracle: delivering oracles: equivocal. ambiguous: obscure. [L. *ōrāculum*—*ōrāre,* to speak.]

oracy. See **oral.**

oral *ō'rəl, o'rəl, adj.* relating to the mouth: near the mouth: uttered by the mouth: spoken, not written: taken through the mouth: pertaining to the infant stage of development when satisfaction is obtained by sucking.—*n.* an oral examination.—*n.* **o'racy** skill in self-expression and ability to communicate freely with others by word of mouth.—*adv.* **o'rally.**—**oral contraception** inhibition of the normal process of ovulation and conception by taking orally, and according to a specified regimen, any of a number of hormone-containing pills; **oral contraceptive** a pill of this type; **oral history** (the study of) information on events, etc. of the past, obtained by interviewing people who participated in them. [L. *ōs, ōris,* the mouth.]

orang. See **orang-utan.**

orange *or'inj, n.* a gold-coloured fruit with tough skin, within which are juicy segments: the tree (*Citrus* genus of family Rutaceae) on which it grows: extended to various unrelated but superficially similar fruits and plants: a colour between red and yellow.—*adj.* pertaining to an orange: orange-coloured.—*ns.* **orangeade** (*or-in-jād'*) a drink made with orange juice; **or'angery** (-*ri,* -*ər-i*) a building for growing orange-trees in a cool climate.—**or'ange-bloss'om** the white blossom of the orange-tree, worn by brides: that of the mock-orange, similarly used.—*adj* **or'ange-col'oured.**—**or'ange-flower** orange-blossom (**orange-flower water** a solution of oil of neroli); **or'ange-peel** the rind of an orange, often candied; **orange squash** a highly concentrated orange drink; **or'ange-squeezer** an instrument for squeezing out the juice of oranges—**or'ange-tip'** a butterfly (*Euchloe* or kindred) with an orange patch near the tip of the forewing.—**or'ange-tree.**—**bitter, Seville,** or **sour, orange** *Citrus aurantium,* **sweet orange** *Citrus sinensis,* native of China and south-east Asia, or any cultivated fruit derived from it. [Fr ult. from Ar *nāranj;* the loss of the *n* may be due to confusion with the indef. art. (*una, une*), the vowel changes to confusion with L. *aurum,* Fr. *or,* gold.]

Orange *or'inj, adj.* relating to the family of the princes of *Orange,* a former principality in southern France from the 11th century, passing by an heiress to the house of Nassau in 1531, the territory ceded to France in 1713: favouring the cause of the Prince of Orange in Holland or in Great Britain and Ireland: of or favouring the Orangemen: extreme Protestant Irish Conservative.—*n.* **Or'angism** (**Or'angism**).— **Or'angeman** a member of a society revived and organised in Ireland in 1795 to uphold Orange principles.

orang-utan *ō-, o-rang'-ōō-tan', ō', ō'rang-ōō'tan,* **orang-outang** *ō-, o-rang'-ōō-tang' ns.* an anthropoid ape, found only in the forests of Sumatra and Borneo, reddish-brown.—Also **orang'**. [Malay *ōranghūtan,* man of the woods (said not to be applied by the Malays to the ape)—*ōrang,* man, *hūtan,* wood, wild.]

oration *ō-, ō-rā'shan, n.* a formal speech: a harangue.— *v.i.* **orate'** (*facet.*) to harangue, hold forth. [L. *ōrātiō, -ōnis—ōrāre,* to pray.]

orator *or'ə-tər, n.* a public speaker: a man of eloquence:—*fem.* **or'atress, oratrix** (*or-ā'triks,* or *or'ə-triks*).—*adjs.* **oratorical** (*or-ə-tō'ri-əl, -to'*) of an orator, oratory, or an oratory, **orato'rian** of an oratory.—*n.* a priest of an oratory.—*adj.* **oratorical** (*-tor'*) characteristic of an orator: addicted to oratory: rhetorical: relating to or savouring of oratory.— *adv.* **orator'ically**.—*n.* **or'atory** the art of the orator: rhetoric: rhetorical utterances or expression: a place for private prayer: a lectern for praying at. [L. *ōrātor, -ōris—ōrāre,* to pray.]

oratorio *or-ə-tō'ri-ō, -tō', n.* a story, usually Biblical, set to music, with soloists, chorus, and full orchestra (scenery, costumes, and acting, however, being dispensed with): the form of such composition:—*pl.* **orato'rios**.—*adj.* **orato'rial**. [It. *oratorio*—L. *ōrātōrium,* an oratory, because they developed out of the singing at devotional meetings in church oratories.]

orb *ōrb, n.* a circle: a sphere: anything round: a celestial body: an eyeball: the mound or globe of a king's regalia.—*adjs.* **orbed** in the form of an orb: circular: **orbic'ular** approximately circular or spherical: round: having the component minerals crystallised in spheroidal aggregates (*petr.*). [L. *orbis,* circle.]

orbis terrarum *ōr'bis ter-ā'ram, ter-a'rōōm,* the circle of lands, the whole world. [L.]

orbit *or'bit, n.* the path in which a heavenly body moves round another, or an electron round the nucleus of an atom (also **or'bital**), or the like: a path in space round a heavenly body: a regular course or beat, sphere of action: the hollow in which the eyeball rests (also **or'bita**): the skin round a bird's eye.—*v.t.* of an aircraft, to circle (a given point): to circle (the earth, etc.) in space: to put into orbit.—*adj.* **or'bital**. —*n.* **or'biter** a spacecraft which orbits the earth, etc. [L. *orbita,* a wheel-track—*orbis,* a ring, wheel.]

orc *ōrk, n.* a fierce sea-monster: a killer-whale: an ogre. [L. *orca.*]

Orcadian *ōr-kā'di-ən, adj.* of Orkney.—*n.* an inhabitant or a native of Orkney. [L. *Orcadēs*—Gr. *Orkadēs,* Orkney (Islands).]

orchard *or'chərd, n.* an enclosed garden of fruit-trees. —*n.* **or'chardman** one who grows and sells orchard fruits. [O.E. *ort-geard,* prob. L. *hortus,* garden, and O.E. *geard;* see **yard²**. Some connect the first part with O.E. *wyrt;* see **wort¹**.]

orchel, orchella. See **archil**.

orchestra *ōr'kis-trə,* form. *-kes', n.* in the Greek theatre, the place in front of the stage where the chorus danced: now the part of a theatre or concert-room in which the instrumental musicians are placed. a large company of musicians (strings, woodwinds, brasses, and percussion) playing together under a conductor: loosely applied to a small group, as in a restaurant.—*adj.* **orchestral** (*-kes'*) of or for an orchestra.—*n.* **orches'tralist** an orchestral composer.

—*v.t.* **or'chestrate** to compose or arrange (music) for performance by an orchestra: to organise so as to achieve the best effect (*fig.*).—Also *v.i* —*ns* **orchestra'tion;** or'chestrator.—*adj.* orches'tric orchestral.—**orchestra stalls** theatre seats just behind the orchestra [Gr *orchēstrā—orcheesthai,* to dance.]

orchid *or'kid, n.* any plant, or flower, of a family of monocotyledons, including many tropical epiphytes, often with showy flowers.—*adjs.* **orchida'ceous, orchid'eous**.—*ns.* **or'chidist** a fancier or grower of orchids; **orchidol'ogist; orchidol'ogy** the knowledge of orchids.—**or'chid-house** a place for growing orchids. [Gr. *orchis, -ios* or *-eōs,* a testicle (from the appearance of the root-tubers; the *d* is a blunder, as if the genitive were *orchidos.*]

orchil, orchilla. See **archil**.

orchitis *ōr-kī'tis, n.* inflammation of a testicle.—*adj.* **orchitic** (*-kit'ik*).—*ns.* **orchidec'tomy, orchiec'tomy** (*-ki-ek'*) excision of one or both testicles. [Gr. *orchis, -ios* or *-eōs,* testicle.]

ordain *ōr-dān', v.t.* to arrange: to establish: to decree: to destine: to order: to assign, set apart: to appoint: to set apart for an office: to invest with ministerial functions: to admit to holy orders.—*adj.* **ordain'able**.— *ns* **ordain'er; ordain'ment; ordinee'** one who is being, or has just been, ordained. [O.Fr. *ordener* (Fr. *ordonner*)—L. *ordināre, -ātum—ordō, -inis,* order.]

ordeal *ōr'děl,* less justifiably *or-děl'* or *ōr-dē'əl, n.* an ancient form of referring a disputed question to the judgment of God, by lot, fire, water, etc.: any severe trial or examination. [O.E. *orděl, ordāl*—pfx. *or-,* out, *dǣl,* deal, share.]

order *ōr'dər, n.* arrangement: sequence: due condition: the condition of normal or due functioning: a regular or suitable arrangement: a method: a system: tidiness: a restrained or undisturbed condition: a form of procedure or ceremony: the accepted mode of proceeding at a meeting: a practice: grade, degree, rank, or position, esp. in a hierarchy: a command: a written instruction to pay money: a customer's instruction to supply goods or perform work: a pass for admission or other privilege: a class of society: a body of persons of the same rank, profession, etc.: a fraternity, esp. religious or knightly: a body modelled on a knightly order, to which members are admitted as an honour: the insignia thereof: a group above a family but below a class (*biol.*): one of the different ways in which the column and its entablature with their various parts are moulded and related to each other (*archit.*): one of the successively recessed arches of an archway: the position of a weapon with butt on ground, muzzle close to the right side: (*pl.*) the several degrees or grades of the Christian ministry.—*v.t.* to arrange: to set in order: to put in the position of order (*mil.*): to regulate: to command: to give an order for.—*v.i.* give command: to request the supply of something, esp. food.—*interj.* used in calling for order or to order.—*ns.* **or'derer; or'dering** arrangement: management: the act or ceremony of ordaining, as priests or deacons; **or'derliness**.—*adj.* **or'derly** in good order: regular: well regulated: of good behaviour: quiet: being on duty.—*adv.* regularly: methodically. —*n.* a non-commissioned officer who carries official messages for his superior officer: a hospital attendant: a street cleaner.—**or'der-book** a book for entering the orders of customers, the special orders of a commanding officer, or the motions to be put to the House of Commons, **order form** a printed form on which the details of a customer's order are written; **orderly officer** the officer on duty for the day; **orderly room** a room for regimental, company, etc., business; **order paper** paper showing order of deliberative business.—**full orders** the priesthood; **holy orders** an institution, in the Roman and Greek Churches a sacrament, by which one is specially set apart for the service of religion: the rank of an ordained minister of religion; **in order with** the purpose (with *to, that*): in accordance with rules of procedure at meetings, appropriate, suitable, likely: (also in **good, working,** etc. **order**) operating, or able to operate, well or correctly: in the correct, desired, etc. order; **in, of, the order of** more or less of the size, quantity or proportion stated; **on order** having been ordered but not yet supplied; **order about, around** to give orders to in a domineering fashion; **order of battle** arrangement of troops or ships in preparation for a fight; **order of the day** business set down for the day something necessary, normal, prevalent, especially popular, etc. at a given time (*fig.*); **out of order** not in order; **sealed orders** instructions not to be opened until a specified time; **take orders** to be ordained; **tall, large, order a** very great task or demand; **to order** according to, and in fulfilment of, an order [Fr. *ordre*—L. *ordō, -inis.*]

ordinal *or'din-əl, adj.* indicating order of sequence relating to an order.—*n.* an ordinal numeral (first, second, third, etc.—distinguished from *cardinal*): a service-book: a book of forms of consecration and ordination. [L L. *ordinālis*—L. *ordō, -inis,* order.]

ordinance *or'din-əns, n.* that which is ordained by authority, fate, etc.: regulation: artistic arrangement, planning: a decree a religious practice enjoined by authority, esp. a sacrament —*ns.* **or'dinand** a candidate for ordination; **or'dinate** a straight line parallel to an axis cutting off an abscissa. the *y*-co-ordinate in analytical geometry.—*v.t.* to ordain: to co-ordinate or order.—*adv.* **ord'inately** in an ordered manner restrainedly. with moderation.—*n.* **ordinā'tion** the act of ordaining: admission to the Christian ministry by the laying on of hands of a bishop or a presbytery: established order [L. *ordināre, -ātum*—*ordō,* order.]

ordinary *ord'(i-)nə-ri, adjs.* according to the common order: usual: of the usual kind: customary: of common rank: plain: undistinguished: commonplace: plain-looking (*coll.*): (of a judge or jurisdiction) by virtue of office, not by deputation: (of a judge in Scotland) of the Outer House of the Court of Session (**Lord Ordinary**).—*n.* a judge of ecclesiastical or other causes who acts in his own right, as a bishop or his deputy: something settled or customary: the common run, mass, or course: one of a class of armorial charges, figures of simple or geometrical form, conventional in character (*her.*): a reference-book of heraldic charges.—*adv.* **or'dinarily.**—**ordinary level** see **O**[1]; **ordinary seaman** a seaman ranking below an able seaman; **ordinary shares** shares which rank last for receiving dividend, but which may receive as large a dividend as the profits make possible (**preferred ordinary shares** have limited priority).—**in ordinary** in regular and customary attendance; **out of the ordinary** unusual. [L. *ordinārius*—*ordō, -inis,* order.]

ordinee. See **ordain.**

ordnance *ōrd'nəns, n.* munitions: great guns, artillery: a department concerned with supply and maintenance of artillery.—**Ordnance datum** the standard sea-level of the Ordnance Survey, now mean sea-level at Newlyn, Cornwall; **Ordnance Survey** the preparation of maps of Great Britain and N. Ireland by the *Ordnance Survey (Department).* [**ordinance.**]

ordonnance *or'də-nəns, n.* co-ordination, esp. the proper disposition of figures in a picture, parts of a building, etc. [Fr.; cf. **ordinance.**]

ordure *ōrd'yər, n.* dirt: dung: anything unclean (*fig.*).—*adj.* **or'durous.** [Fr., —O.Fr. *ord,* foul—L. *horridus,* rough.]

ore *ōr, ór, n* a solid, naturally-occurring mineral aggregate, of economic interest, from which one or more valuable constituents may be recovered by treatment. [O E *ār,* brass, influenced by *ōra,* unwrought metal]

ore *œ'rə, n.* a coin and money of account in Sweden and (**øre**) Norway and Denmark.—*pl.* **öre, øre.** See **krone.**

oregano *o-ri-ga'nō, o-reg'ə-nō, n.* origanum:—*pl* **oreganos.** [Amer. Sp. *orégano,* wild marjoram—L. *origanum*; see **Origanum.**]

oreide. See **oroide.**

oreography, oreology, etc. See **orography.**

orfe *orf, n.* a golden-yellow semi-domesticated variety of id. [Ger. *Orfe*—Gr *orphōs,* the great sea-perch.]

organ *or'gən, n* an instrument or means by which anything is done: a part of a body fitted for carrying on a natural or vital operation: a means of communicating information or opinions. a keyboard wind instrument consisting of a collection of pipes made to sound by means of compressed air: a system of pipes in such an organ, having an individual keyboard, a partial organ: a musical instrument in some way similar to a pipe-organ, incl. pipeless organ a barrel-organ —*n.* **organelle** a specialised part of a cell serving as an organ —*adjs* **organic** (*or-gan'ik*), **-al** pertaining to, derived from, like, of the nature of, an organ (in any sense). of an organism or organisation: organised: inherent in organisation. structural: formed as if by organic process (*art*): instrumental. mechanical: containing or combined with carbon (*chem*): concerned with carbon compounds: of crops, crop production, etc., produced without, or not involving, the use of fertilisers and pesticides not wholly of plant or animal origin.—*adv* **organ'ically.**—*n.* **organisabil'ity, -z-.**—*adj.* **organis'able, -z-.**—*n.* **organisā'tion, -z-** the act of organising: the state of being organised: the manner in which anything is organised: an organised system, body, or society.—*adj.* **organisā'tional, -z-.**—*v.t.* **or'ganise, -ize** to supply with organs: to form into an organic whole: to co-ordinate and prepare for activity: to arrange: to obtain (*slang*) —*v.i.* to become organic: to be active in organisation —*adj.* **or'ganised, -z-** having or consisting of parts acting in co-ordination: having the nature of a unified whole: organic.—*ns.* **or'ganiser, -z-**; **or'ganism** organic structure, or that which has it: that which acts as a unified whole: a living animal or vegetable.—*adj.* **organis'mal.**—*ns* **or'ganist** one who plays on an organ; **organity** (*-gan'*) an organised whole.—**or'gan-gallery** a gallery where an organ is placed; **or'gan-grinder** one who plays a hand-organ by a crank; **or'gan-pipe** one of the sounding pipes of a pipe-organ; **or'gan-screen** an ornamented stone or wood screen on which an organ is placed.—**organic chemistry** the chemistry of carbon compounds; **organic disease** a disease accompanied by changes in the structures involved; **organic sensation** sensation from internal organs, as hunger.—**organ of Corti** (*kor'ti*) the organ in the cochlea which contains the auditory receptors [L. *organum*—Gr. *organon* —*ergon,* work.]

organdie *or'gən-di, n.* fine muslin: book muslin.—*n* **organ'za** material transparently thin but made of silk, rayon or nylon, not cotton. [Fr. *organdi*]

organ(o)- *ōr-gən(-ō)-, -ə', -ō',* in composition, organ: (also *or-gan'ō-*) organic, as in organometallic compounds. —*ns.* **organogeny** (*or-gən-oj'i-ni*), **organogen'esis** the development of living organs; **organog'raphy** a description of the organs of plants or animals.—*adjs.* **organolep'tic** affecting a bodily organ or sense: concerned with testing the effects of a substance on the senses, esp. of taste and smell (Gr. root of *lambanein,* to seize); **organometall'ic** (or *-gan'*) consisting of a metal and an organic radical: relating to compounds of this type.—*n.* **organother'apy** treatment of disease by administration of animal organs or extracts of them. esp of ductless gland extracts [L *organum*, see **organ**.]

organza. See **organdie.**

organzine *or'gən-zēn*, *n* a silk yarn of two or more threads thrown together with a slight twist [Fr *organsin*—It *organzino*, poss —*Urgenj*, Turkestan]

orgasm *or'gazm*, *n* immoderate excitement culmination of sexual excitement —*adjs* **orgas'mic**, or**gas'tic.** [Gr *orgasmos*, swelling]

orgy *or'ji*, *n* a secret rite, as in the worship of Bacchus (usu in *pl*): esp a frantic unrestrained celebration. a celebration in general a riotous, licentious, or drunken revel —Also (properly *pl.*) **or'gia.**—*n* **or'giast** one who takes part in orgies —*adjs* **orgias'tic, or'gic.** [Fr *orgies*—L —Gr *orgia* (pl)]

oribi *or'i-bi*, *n* a small South African antelope, the palebuck [Afrik., app from some native language]

oriel *ō'*, *o'ri-əl*, *n* a small room or recess with a polygonal window, built out from a wall, resting on the ground or (esp.) supported on brackets or corbels the window of an oriel (in full **o'riel-win'dow**).—*adj* **o'rielled.** [O Fr *oriol*, porch. recess. gallery]

orient *ō'*, *o'ri-ənt*, *adj* rising, as the sun eastern bright or pure in colour —*n* the part where the sun rises: sunrise: purity of lustre in a pearl an orient pearl. (with *cap*) the East (with *cap*) the countries of the East —*v.t* **o'rient** (or *-ent'*) to set so as to face the east to build (lengthwise) east and west: to place in a definite relation to the points of the compass or other fixed or known directions: to determine the position of, relatively to fixed or known directions to acquaint (someone, oneself) with the present position relative to known point(s), or (*fig.*) with the details of the situation —*adj* **oriental, Oriental** (*-ent'əl*) eastern: pertaining to, in, or from the east orient.—*n.* a native of the east' an Asiatic.—*v.t* **orient'alise, -ize.**—*ns* **Orient'alism** an eastern expression, custom, etc scholarship in eastern languages, **Orient'alist** one versed in eastern languages, **orientality** (*-al'i-ti*).—*adv.* **orient'ally.**—*v.t* **o'rientate** to orient.—*v t.* to face the east: to be oriented —*ns* **orientā'tion** the act of orienting or orientating the state of being oriented. determination or consciousness of relative direction the assumption of definite direction in response to stimulus: **o'rientător** an instrument for orientating —*adjs* **o'riented** (or *-ent'*), **o'rientated** directed (towards), often used in composition as second element of *adj* normally aware of the elements of one's situation—time, place, persons (*psychiatry*, also *fig*) —*n* **orienteer'ing** the sport of making one's way quickly across difficult country with the help of map and compass.—**orientation table** an indicator of tabular form for showing the direction of various objects—mountains and the like [L *oriēns, -entis*, pr p of *oriri*, to rise.]

orifice *or'i-fis*, *n* a mouth-like opening, esp small — *adj* **orificial** (*-fish'əl*). [Fr.—L *ōrificium—ōs, ōris*, mouth, *facĕre*, to make]

oriflamme *or'i-flam*, *n* a little banner of red silk split into many points, borne on a gilt staff—the ancient royal standard of France [Fr ,—L L *auriflamma* —L *aurum*, gold, and *flamma*, a flame]

origami *or-i-gam'ē*, *n* the orig Japanese art of folding paper so as to make bird forms, etc [Jap , paperfolding,—*ori*, folding, *kami*, paper]

Origanum *or-ig'ə-nəm*, *n* the marjoram genus of labiates. (without *cap*) any of various aromatic herbs, of this or other genus, used in cookery —*n* **or'igan(e)** (*-gan*) marjoram, esp wild marjoram —See also **oregano.** [L *origanum*—Gr *origanon*]

origin *or'i-jin*, *n* the rising or first existence of anything that from which anything first proceeds the fixed starting-point or point from which measurement is made (*math*). the point or place from which a muscle, etc arises (*anat*) source derivation —*adj* **orig'inal** pertaining to the origin or beginning existing from or at the beginning being such from the beginning. innate standing in relation of source not derived, copied, imitated, or translated from anything else originative novel creative independent in invention odd in character —*n* that which is not itself, or of which something else is, a copy, imitation, or translation a real person, place, etc , serving as model for one in fiction an inhabitant, member, etc , from the beginning a person of marked individuality or oddity —*n* **original'ity.**—*adv* **orig'inally.**—*v t* **orig'inate** to give origin to to bring into existence — *v t* to have origin to begin —*n* **originā'tion.**—*adj* **orig'inātive** having power to originate or bring into existence originating —*n* **orig'inātor** —**original sin** innate depravity and corruption held to be transmitted to Adam's descendants in consequence of his sin [L *origō, -inis—oriri*, to rise]

oriole *ōr'i-ōl*, *or'*, *n* a golden yellow bird (*Oriolus galbula*, the **golden oriole**) with black wings, or other member of the genus or of the Old World family **Oriol'idae**, related to the crows in America applied to birds of the Icteridae (see **Baltimore**) [O Fr *oriol*—L *aureolus*, dim of *aureus*, golden—*aurum*, gold]

orison *or'i-zən*, *n* a prayer [O Fr *orison* (Fr *oraison*)—L *ōrātiō, -ōnis—ōrāre*, to pray]

Oriya *ō-rē'ya*, *o-*, *n* the language of Orissa in India a member of the people speaking it —Also *adj*

orle *orl*, (*her*) *n* a border within a shield at a short distance from the edge a number of small charges set as a border [O Fr , border, from a dim formed from L *ōra*, border]

orlop (deck) *or'lop (dek)*, *n* the lowest deck in a ship, a covering to the hold [Du *overloop*, covering]

ormer *or'mər*, *n* an ear-shell or sea-ear, esp the edible *Haliotis tuberculata*, common in the Channel Islands [Channel Island Fr *ormer* (Fr *ormier*)—L *auris maris*, sea-ear]

ormolu *or'mo-loo*, *n* an alloy of copper, zinc, and sometimes tin gilt or bronzed metallic ware goldleaf prepared for gilding bronze, etc [Fr *or*—L *aurum*, gold, and Fr *moulu*, pa p of *moudre*, to grind—L *molĕre*, to grind]

ornament *or'nə-mənt*, *n* anything meant to add grace or beauty or to bring credit additional beauty a mark of honour (usu in *pl*.) articles used in the services of the church (*Pr Bk*) —*v t* (*or-nə-ment'*, *or'nə-ment*) to adorn to furnish with ornaments.—*adj* **orna-ment'al** serving to adorn decorative, pleasantly striking in dress and general appearance —*n* a plant grown for ornament or beauty —*adv* **ornament'ally.** —*ns* **ornamentā'tion** the act or art of ornamenting ornamental work, **ornament'er; ornament'ist.** [Fr *ornement*—L *ornāmentum—ornāre*, to adorn]

ornate *or-nāt'*, *or'nāt*, *adj* decorated much or elaborately ornamented —*adv* **ornate'ly** (or *or'*) —*n* **ornate'ness** (or *or'*) [L *ornāre, -ātum*, to adorn]

ornery *or'nə-ri*, (*U S*) *adj* touchy, cantankerous (*coll*) stubborn (*coll*) mean, contemptible (*coll*) [A variant of **ordinary**.]

ornis *or'nis*, *n* the birds collectively of a region, its avifauna —*adj* **ornithic** (*or-nith'ik*) relating to birds —*n pl* **Ornithischia** (*-this'ki-ə*, Gr *ischion*, hip joint) the order of bird-hipped dinosaurs. herbivorous and often heavily armoured —*n* and *adj* **ornithis'chian.**—*adj* **ornitholog'ical.**—*adv* **ornitholog'ically.**—*ns* **ornithol'ogist; ornithol'ogy** the study of birds.—*ns.* **or'nithopod** a member of the **Ornithop'oda**, a suborder of bipedal ornithischian dinosaurs; **Ornithorhynchus** (*-ō-ring'kəs*; Gr. *rhynchos*, snout) the duckbill genus' (without *cap*) the duckbill; **ornithosaur** (*ör-nī'thō-sor*; Gr *sauros*, lizard) a pterodactyl; **ornitho'sis** psittacosis [Gr *ornis, ornithos*, a bird.]

orogenesis *or-ō-jen'i-sis, ör-, or-,* **orogeny** *or-oj'ə-ni, ör-, ör-, ns.* mountain-building —*adjs* **orogenet'ic, orogen'ic** [Gr *oros*, mountain. *genesis*, production.]

orography *or-og'rə-fi, n.* the description of mountains —also **oreography** (*or-i-og'*).—*adjs.* **or(e)ographic** (*-graf'ik*), **-al.**—*ns.* **orol'ogy, oreology** (*or-i-ol'*) the scientific study of mountains —*adjs* **or(e)olog'ical.**—*ns.* **or(e)ol'ogist.** [Gr. *oros, -eos*, mountain, *graphein*, to write, *logos*, discourse.]

oroide *ō'rō-īd, ō', n.* an alloy of copper and zinc or tin, etc., imitating gold.—*n* **o'reide** a similar or identical alloy. [Fr. *or*—L *aurum*, gold, Gr. *eidos*, form]

orology, etc. See **orography.**

orotund *o', ō', ō'rō-tund, adj* full and round in utterance: pompously mouthed or mouthing.—Also **o'rorotund.**—*ns.* **o(ro)rotund'ity.** [L *ōs, ōris,* mouth, *rotundus,* round.]

orphan *ör'fən, n* one bereft of father or mother, or (usually) of both.—Also *adj.*—*v.t.* to make an orphan.—*ns.* **or'phanage** the state of being an orphan a house for orphans; **or'phanhood, or'phanism.** [Gr. *orphanos,* akin to L. *orbus,* bereaved.]

Orpheus *ör'füs, -fi-əs, n.* a mythical Thracian musician and poet who could move inanimate objects by the music of his lyre, founder or interpreter of the ancient mysteries.—*adjs.* **Orphē'an** pertaining to Orpheus; **Or'phic** pertaining to the mysteries associated with Orpheus: esoteric —*n.* **Or'phism** the system taught in the Orphic mysteries: an early 20th-cent. style of abstract art using brilliant colour—also **Orphic Cubism.**

orphrey *ör'fri, n.* gold or other rich embroidery, esp bordering a vestment. [O.Fr. *orfreis*—L *auriphrygium,* Phrygian gold.]

orpiment *ör'pi-mənt, n.* a yellow mineral, arsenic trisulphide, used as a pigment. [O.Fr.—L. *auripigmentum—aurum,* gold, *pīgmentum,* paint.]

orpine, orpin *ör'pin, n.* a purple-flowered, broadleaved stonecrop. [Fr. *orpin*]

Orpington *ör'ping-tən, n.* a breed of poultry (white, black, or buff). [*Orpington* in W. Kent.]

orrery *or'ər-i, n.* a clockwork model of the solar system [From Charles Boyle, fourth Earl of *Orrery* (1676–1731) for whom one was made.]

orris *or'is, n.* the Florentine or other iris: its dried rootstock (**orr'is-root'**) smelling of violets, used in perfumery. [Perh. **iris.**]

ort *ört, n.* a fragment, esp. one left from a meal—usually *pl.* [Cf. Low Ger. *ort,* refuse of fodder.]

ortanique *ör'tan-ēk, n.* a cross between the orange and the tangerine, or its fruit. [Portmanteau word and suff. *-ique.*]

orthicon *örth'i-kon, n.* a television camera tube more sensitive than the earlier iconoscope; a further development is the **image orthicon.** [ortho-, iconoscope.]

ortho- *ör-thō-,* in composition, straight: upright: perpendicular: right: genuine: derived from an acid anhydride by combination with the largest number of water molecules (distinguished from *meta-*; *chem*): having substituted atoms or groups attached to two adjacent carbon atoms of the benzene ring (distinguished from *meta-* and *para-* —in this sense commonly represented by *o-*; *chem*).—*ns.* **orthocaine** (*-kā'in, -kān*) a white crystalline substance used as a

local anaesthetic; **or'thocentre** the point of intersection of the altitudes of a triangle —*adj.* **orthochromat'ic** (Gr *chrōma,* colour) correct in rendering the relation of colours, without the usual photographic modifications —*ns* **or'thoclase** (*-klās, -klāz;* Gr *klasis,* fracture) common or potash feldspar, monoclinic, with cleavages at right angles, **or'thocompound; orthodontia** (*-don'shi-ə;* Gr. *odous, odontos,* tooth) rectification of abnormalities in the teeth Also **orthodont'ics.**—*adj* **orthodont'ic.**—*n* **orthodont'ist.**—*adj.* **or'thodox** (Gr. *doxa,* opinion) sound in doctrine: believing, or according to, the received or established doctrines or opinions, esp in religion (*cap*) of the Eastern Church —*n* **or'thodoxy.**—*adjs* **orthoepic** (*-ep'ik,* Gr *epos,* a word), **orthoep'ical.**—*ns* **ortho'epist; orth'o'epy** (the study of) correct pronunciation; **orthogen'esis** (Gr *genesis,* generation) the evolution of organisms systematically in definite directions and not accidentally in many directions: determinate variation —*adjs* **orthogenet'ic; orthogonal** (Gr *gōniā,* angle) right-angled (**orthogonal projection** projection by lines perpendicular to the plane of projection) —*adv.* **orthog'onally.**—*ns* **or'thograph** a drawing in orthographic projection, esp of the elevation of a building; **orthog'rapher** one skilled in orthography: a speller —*adjs* **orthograph'ic, -al** pertaining or according to spelling: spelt correctly: in perspective projection, having the point of sight at infinity.—*adv* **orthograph'ically.**—*ns* **orthog'raphist** an orthographer; **orthog'raphy** (Gr. *orthographia,* spelling, elevation—*graphein,* to write) the art or practice of spelling words correctly· spelling, orthographic projection —*adjs.* **orthopae'dic, -al, orthopē'dic, -al.**—*n. sing* **orthopaedics, orthopēdics** (*-pē'diks;* Gr *pais, paidos,* a child) the art or process of curing deformities arising from disease or injury of bones, esp in childhood.—*n.* **orthopae'dist, -pē'dist.**—*n.pl.* **Orthop'tera** (Gr *pteron,* wing) the cockroach order of insects with firm fore-wings serving as covers to the fan-wise folded hind-wings —*n.* and *adj.* **orthop'teran.**—*adjs.* **orthop'terous** pertaining to the Orthoptera; **orthop'tic** (Gr. *optikos,* optic) relating to normal vision.—*ns.* **orthop'tics** the treatment of defective eyesight by exercises and visual training; **orthop'tist.**—*adjs.* **orthorhom'bic** (Gr. *rhombos,* rhomb, *crystal*) referable to three unequal axes at right angles to each other, **orthoscop'ic** (Gr. *skopeein,* to look at) having or giving correct vision, true proportion, or a flat field of view; **orthot'ic** or of relating to orthotics —*n sing* **orthot'ics** the branch of medical science dealing with the rehabilitation of injured or weakened joints or muscles through artificial or mechanical support.—*n* **or'thotist** one skilled in orthotics.—*adjs.* **orthoton'ic** taking an accent in certain positions but not in others—also **or'thotone; orthotrop'ic** (Gr *tropos,* a turn) manifesting orthotropism: (of a material, as wood) having elastic properties varying in different planes.—*ns.* **orthot'ropism** growth in the direct line of stimulus, esp of gravity; **orthot'ropy** (of a material, as wood) the state of being orthotropic. [Gr *orthos,* straight, upright, right]

ortolan *or'tə-lan, n.* a kind of bunting, common in Europe, and considered a great table delicacy. [Fr., —It. *ortolano*—L. *hortulānus,* belonging to gardens —*hortulus,* dim. of *hortus,* a garden]

Orwellian *ór-wel'i-ən, adj.* relating to or in the style of the English writer George *Orwell* (1903–50): characteristic of the dehumanised authoritarian society described in his novel *1984*

Oryx *or'iks, n.* an African genus of antelopes: (without *cap.*) an antelope of this genus. [Gr *oryx, -ygos,* a pick-axe, an oryx antelope.]

Osage *ō-sāj', ō'sāj, n.* an Indian of a tribe living in

Oklahoma, etc.—*adj.* O**sage.—Osage orange** a hedge-tree (*Maclura*) of the mulberry family, first found in the Osage country: its orange-like inedible fruit.

Oscan *os'kən*, *n.* one of an ancient Italic people in southern Italy: their language akin to Latin.—also *adj.*

Oscar *os'kər*, *n.* a gold-plated statuette awarded by the American Academy of Motion Picture Arts and Sciences to a film writer, actor, director, etc., for the year's best performance in his or her particular line: any similar award. [Name fortuitously given, possibly after an Academy employee's uncle.]

oscillate *os'il-āt*, *v.i.* to swing to and fro like a pendulum: to vibrate: to radiate electromagnetic waves: to vary between certain limits: to fluctuate.—*v.t.* to cause to swing or vibrate.—*adj.* **osc'illating.**—*n* **oscilla'tion.**—*adj.* **osc'illative** having a tendency to vibrate: vibratory.—*n.* **osc'illator** one who oscillates: apparatus for producing oscillations.—*adj.* **oscillatory** (*os'il-ə-tə-ri*) swinging: moving as a pendulum does: vibratory.—*ns.* **oscill'ogram** a record made by an oscillograph; **oscill'ograph** an apparatus for producing a curve representing a number of electrical and mechanical phenomena which vary cyclically, **oscill'oscope** an instrument which shows on a fluorescent screen the variation with time of the instantaneous values and waveforms of electrical quantities, including voltages translated from sounds or movements. [L. *ōscillāre*, *-ātum*, to swing]

Oscines *os'i-nēz*, *n.pl.* the song-birds, forming the main body of the Passeriformes.—*adj.* **osc'inine** or (faultily formed) **osc'ine.** [L. *oscen*, *oscinis*, a singing-bird.]

osculant *os'kū-lənt*, *adj.* kissing: adhering closely: intermediate between two genera, species, etc., linking (*biol.*).—*adj.* **os'cular** pertaining to the mouth or osculum, or to kissing: osculating.—*v.t.* **os'culate** to kiss: to have three or more coincident points in common with (*math.*).—*v.i* to be in close contact: to form a connecting link —*n.* **oscula'tion.**—*adj.* **os'culatory** of or pertaining to kissing or osculation —*n.* a carved tablet kissed by the priest and (now rarely) by the people at mass. [L. *ōsculārī*, *-ātus*—*ōsculum*, a little mouth, a kiss, dim. of *ōs*, mouth]

osier *ōzh'(y)ər*, *ōz'i-ər*, *ōz'yər*, *n.* any willow whose twigs are used in making baskets, esp. *Salix viminalis* —*adj.* made of or like osiers.—**o'sier-bed** a place where osiers grow. [Fr. *osier* of unknown origin; there is a L.L. *ausāria* or *osāria*, willow bed.]

Osmanli *os-man'li*, *adj.* of the dynasty of *Osmān*, who founded the Turkish empire in Asia, and reigned 1288–1326: of the Turkish empire: of the western branch of the Turks or their language.—*n.* a member of the dynasty: a Turk of Turkey. [Cf. **Ottoman.**]

osmium *oz'*, *os'mi-əm*, *n.* a grey-coloured metal (Os; atomic number 76) the heaviest substance known.—*n.* **osmirid'ium** iridosmium. [Gr. *osmē*, smell.]

osmosis *os-mō'sis*, or *oz-*, *n.* diffusion of liquids through a porous septum.—Also **os'mose.**—*v.t.* and *v.i.* **osmose'** to (cause to) undergo osmosis.—*n.* **osmom'eter** an apparatus for measuring osmotic pressure.—*adj.* **osmotic** (*-mot'ik*).—*adv.* **osmot'ically.—osmotic pressure** the pressure exerted by a dissolved substance in virtue of the motion of its molecules, or a measure of this in terms of the pressure which must be applied to a solution in order just to prevent osmosis into the solution. [Gr. *ōsmos* = *ōthismos*, impulse—*ōtheein*, to push.]

osprey *os'pri*, *-prā*, *n.* a bird of prey (*Pandion haliaetus*) that feeds on fish: an egret or other plume used in millinery, not from the osprey. [Supposed to be from L. *ossifraga*, misapplied; see **ossifrage.**]

osseous *os'i-əs*, *adj.* bony: composed of, or like, bone: of the nature or structure of bone.—*ns.* **ossā'rium** an ossuary; **ossein** (*os'i-in*) the organic basis of bone; **osselet** (*os'ə-let*, *os'let*) a hard substance growing on the inside of a horse's knee; **oss'icle** a little bone or bone-like plate.—*n.* **ossifica'tion** the process or state of being changed into a bony substance.—*v.t.* **oss'ify** to make into bone or into a bone-like substance.—*v.i.* to become bone: to become hardened, inflexible, set in a conventional pattern (*fig.*):—*pr.p.* **oss'ifying**; *pa.t.* and *pa.p.* **oss'ified.** [L. *os*, *ossis*, bone.]

ossia *ō-sē'a*, (It.) *conj.* or (giving an alternative in music).

ossifrage *os'i-frāj*, *n.* the lammergeier: the osprey: the bald eagle (*U.S.*). [L. *ossifraga*, prob. the lammergeier—*os*, *ossis*, bone, and the root of *frangēre*, to break.]

ossuary *os'ū-ə-ri*, *n.* a place where bones are laid, e.g. a vault or charnel-house: an urn for bones. [L. *ossuārium*—*os*, bone.]

ostensible *os-tens'i-bl*, *adj.* outwardly showing or professed.—*n.* **ostensibil'ity.**—*adv* **ostens'ibly.**—*adj.* **ostens'ive** showing: deictic: ostensible.—*adv.* **ostens'ively.**—*n.* **ostentā'tion** (*-tən-*) act of showing: display to draw attention or admiration: boasting.—*adj.* **ostentā'tious** given to show: fond of self-display: showy.—*adv.* **ostentā'tiously.**—*n.* **ostentā'tiousness.** [L. *ostendēre*, *ostēnsum* (*ostentum*), to show, and its freq *ostentāre*—pfx. *obs-*, in front, *tendēre*, to stretch.]

oste(o)- *os-ti(-ō)-*, in composition, bone.—*adj.* **osteal** (*os'ti-əl*) relating to bone: sounding like bone on percussion.—*ns.* **osteitis** (*os-ti-ī'tis*) inflammation of a bone, **osteo-arthri'tis** a form of arthritis in which the cartilages of the joint and the bone adjacent are worn away; **osteoarthrō'sis** chronic non-inflammatory disease of bones: osteo-arthritis, **os'teoblast** (Gr. *blastos*, a shoot) a bone-forming cell; **osteoclasis** (*os-ti-ok'lə-sis*, Gr *klasis*, fracture) fracture of a bone for correction of a deformity: absorption and destruction of bone tissue by osteoclasts; **os'teoclast** a surgical instrument for fracturing bone: a bone-destroying cell; **osteogen'esis**, **osteogeny** (*-oj'*) formation of bone.—*adjs.* **osteogenet'ic**, **osteogen'ic**, **osteog'enous.** —*n.* **osteog'raphy** description of bones.—*adjs.* **ost'eoid** bone-like; **osteolog'ical.**—*ns.* **osteol'ogist**; **osteol'ogy** the study of bones, part of anatomy; **osteō'ma** a tumour composed of bone or bone-like tissue; **osteomyelitis** (*-mī-ə-lī'tis*; Gr. *myelos*, marrow) inflammation of bone and bone-marrow; **os'teopath** (*-path*), **osteop'athist** (*-ə-thist*) a practitioner of osteopathy.—*adj.* **osteopathic** (*ost-i-ō-path'ik*).—*n.* **osteop'athy** a system of healing or treatment consisting largely of massage and manipulation.—*adj* **osteoplast'ic.**—*ns.* **os'teoplasty** a plastic operation by which a loss of bone is remedied; **osteoporō'sis** (root as **pore**¹) development of a porous structure in bone; **osteot'omy** the surgical cutting of a bone. [Gr. *osteon*, bone.]

ostinato *os-tin-ä'tō*, (*mus.*) *n.* a ground-bass:—*pl.* **ostina'tos.** [It.; root as **obstinate.**]

ostium *os'ti-əm*, *n.* the mouth of a river: a mouth-like opening:—*pl.* **os'tia.**—*adj.* **os'tial.** [L. *ostium.*]

ostler, **hostler** *os'lər*, *n* one who attends to horses at an inn:—*fem.* **ost'leress.** [**hosteler.**]

Ostpolitik *ōst'po-li-tēk*, *n.* the West German policy of establishing normal trade and diplomatic relations with the East European communist countries: any similar policy. [Ger., Eastern policy.]

ostrakon, **ostracon** (*os'trə-kon*, *n.* a potsherd or tile, esp. one used in ostracism in Greece or for writing on in ancient Egypt:—*pl.* **os'traka**, **-ca.**—*adjs.* **ostracean** (*os-trā'shən*), **ostrā'ceous** of the nature of an oyster.

fāte; *fär*; *mē*, *hûr* (her); *mīne*; *mōte*; *for*; *mūte*, *mōōn*; *fōōt*, *dhen* (then); *el'ə-mənt* (element)

—*v.t.* **os'tracise, -ize** (-*sīz*) in ancient Greece, to banish by the vote of the people written on potsherds: to exclude from society, or from one's social group.—*ns.* **os'tracism** (-*sizm*) banishment by ostracising: expulsion from society. [Gr. *ostrakon*, a shell, tile, potsherd.]

Ostrea *os'tri-ə*, *n.* the oyster genus.—*adj.* **ostrea'ceous.** —*ns.* **ostreicul'ture** (*os-trē-i-*) oyster culture; **ostreicul'turist.** [L. *ostrea*—Gr. *ostreon*, oyster.]

ostrich *os'trich*, *-trij*, *n.* the largest living bird (*Struthio*), found in Africa, remarkable for its speed in running, and prized for its feathers.—*n.* **os'trichism** (*fig.*) the habit or policy of ignoring and refusing to face unpleasant facts.—*adj.* and *adv.* **os'trich-like** (usu. in reference to the supposed habit of hiding its head when in danger). [O.Fr. *ostruche* (Fr. *autruche*)—L. *avis*, bird, L.L. *struthiō*—Gr. *strouthiōn*, an ostrich, *strouthos*, a bird.]

Ostrogoth *os'trō-goth*, *n.* one of the tribe of east Goths who established their power in Italy in 493, and were overthrown in 555.—*adj.* **Os'trogothic.**

Ostyak, Ostiak *os'ti-ak*, *n.* a member of a Ugrian people of Siberia: their language.—Also *adj.*

otalgia *ō-tal'ji-ə*, *n.* earache—also **otal'gy.** [Gr. *ous*, *ōtos*, ear, *algē*, pain.]

otary *ō'-tə-ri*, *n.* a sea-lion or sea-bear, a seal with external ears:—*pl.* **o'taries.**—*adj.* **ot'arine.** [Gr. *ōtaros*, large-eared—*ous*, *ōtos*, ear.]

other *udh'ər*, *adj.* orig., one of two: second: alternate: different: different from or not 'the same as the one in question (often with *than*): not the same: remaining: additional.—*pron.* (or *n.*) other one: another.—*adv.* otherwise.—*n.* **oth'erness.**—*adv.* **oth'erwise** in another way or manner: by other causes: in other respects: under other conditions.—*conj.* else: under other conditions.—*n.* **oth'erworld** a world other than, better than, or beyond this.—Also *adj.*—*adj.* **oth'erworld'ish.**—*n.* **otherworld'liness.**—*adj.* **otherworld'ly** concerned with the world to come, or with the world of the imagination, to the exclusion of practical interests.—**other ranks** members of the armed services not holding commissions.—**every other** each alternate: **rather . . . than otherwise** rather than not; **someone (something) or other** an undefined person or thing; **the other day, etc.,** on an unspecified day, etc., not long past. [O.E. *ōther*.]

otic *ō'tik*, *adj.* of or pertaining to the ear.—*ns.* **oti'tis** inflammation of the ear; **otol'ogist; otol'ogy** knowledge of the ear; **otorhinolaryngology** (-*ri-nō-lar-ing-gol'ə-ji*; Gr. *rhīs, rhīnos*, nose, *larynx, -yngos*, larynx) knowledge of ear, nose, and larynx and their diseases, often shortened to **otolaryngol'ogy; otorrhoea** (*ō-tō-rē'ə*; Gr. *rhoiā*, flow) a discharge from the ear; **o'toscope** an instrument for examining the ear. [Gr. *ous, ōtos*, ear.]

otiose *ō'shi-ōs*, *adj.* unoccupied: indolent: functionless: futile: superfluous.—*n.* **otiosity** (*-os'i-ti*) ease, idleness. [L. *ōtiōsus*—*ōtium*, leisure.]

otitis ... otolaryngology ... otology. See **otic.**

-otomy. The combining element is properly **-tomy** (q.v.).

otorhinolaryngology ... otoscope. See **otic.**

ottar *ot'ər.* See **attar.**

ottava *ōt-tä'vä*, *ō-tä'və*, *n.* an octave.—**ottava rima** (*rē'mä*) an Italian stanza consisting of eight hendecasyllabic lines, rhyming *a b a b a b c c*. [It.; cf. **octave.**]

otter *ot'ər*, *n.* an aquatic fish-eating carnivore (*Lutra vulgaris*) of the weasel family: its brown short fur: a board travelling edge-up, manipulated on the principle of the kite, to carry the end of a fishing-line (or several hooked and baited lines) in a lake, or to keep open the mouth of a trawl (also **ott'er-board**): a par-

avane.—*v.i.* or *v.t.* to fish with an otter-board.— **ott'er-hound** a dog of a breed used in otter-hunting; **ott'er-trawl'** a trawl with otter-boards; **ott'er-trawl'ing.** [O.E. *otor*, akin to **water.**]

otto *ot'ō.* See **attar.**

Ottoman *ot'ō-mən*, *adj.* pertaining to the Turkish Empire, founded by *Othmān* or *Osmān*: Osmanli.— *n.* a Turk of Turkey: (the following defs. without *cap.*) a cushioned seat for several persons sitting with their backs to one another: a low, stuffed seat without a back: a variety of corded silk.

oubliette *ōō-bli-et'*, *n.* a dungeon with no opening but at the top: a secret pit in the floor of a dungeon into which a victim could be precipitated. [Fr.,—*oublier*, to forget—L. *oblīvīscī.*]

ouch[1] *owch*, *n.* a brooch: a clasped ornament: the socket of a precious stone. [O.Fr. *nouche.*]

ouch[2] *owch*, *interj.* expressing pain. [Ger. *autsch.*]

Oudenarde *ōō'də-närd*, *n.* a tapestry representing foliage, etc., once made at *Oudenarde* in Belgium.

ought[1] *ōt*, *n.* a variant of **aught.**

ought[2] *ōt*, *v.* an auxiliary verb (with time expressed by tense of the principal verb) should: is or was proper or necessary.

Ouija® *wē'jə*, *n.* a board with an alphabet, used with a planchette.—Also without *cap.* [Fr. *oui*, Ger. *ja*, yes.]

oolong. Same as **oolong.**

ounce[1] *owns*, *n.* the twelfth part of the (legally obsolete) pound troy = 480 grains: $\frac{1}{16}$ of a pound avoirdupois: a minute quantity (*fig.*).—**fluid ounce** $\frac{1}{20}$ pint: $\frac{1}{16}$ U.S. pint. [O.Fr. *unce*—L. *uncia*, the twelfth part; cf. **inch**[1].]

ounce[2] *owns*, *n.* originally, and still sometimes, a lynx: now generally the snow leopard: the jaguar: the cheetah: sometimes vaguely any moderate-sized wild beast of the cat tribe. [Fr. *once*, perh. for *lonce* (as if *l'once*)—Gr. *lynx.*]

our *owr*, *pron.* (*gen.*) or *poss. adj.* pertaining or belonging to us—when used absolutely, **ours** (*owrz*), *dial.* **ourn** (*owrn*).—*reflex.* and *emphatic* **ourself** myself (regally or editorially):—*pl.* **ourselves** (*-selvz'*). [O.E. *ūre*, gen. of *wē*, we.]

ourali *ōō-rä'lē*, **ourari** *ōō-ra'rē.* See **wourali.**

ousel. See **ouzel.**

oust *owst*, *v.t.* to eject or expel.—*n.* **oust'er** (*law*) ejection, dispossession. [A.Fr. *ouster*, to remove.]

out (see also **out-**) *owt*, *adv.* (shading into *adj.* predicatively), not within: forth: abroad: to, towards, or at the exterior or a position away from the inside or inner part or from anything thought of as enclosing, hiding, or obscuring: from among others: from the mass: beyond bounds: away from the original or normal position or state: at or towards the far end, or a remote position: seawards: away from home or a building: in or into the open air: in or into a state of exclusion: not in office: not in use or fashion: ruled out, not to be considered: no longer in the game: no longer in as a batsman, dismissed: not batting: out of the contest and unable to resume in time: in the condition of having won: away from the mark: at fault: in error: not in form or good condition: at a loss: in or into a disconcerted, perplexed, or disturbed state: not in harmony or amity: in distribution: in or into the hands of others or the public: on loan: to or at an end: in an exhausted or extinguished state: completely: thoroughly: subjected to loss: in or to the field: in quest of or expressly aiming at something: in rebellion: on strike: in an exposed state: no longer in concealment or obscurity: in or into the open: before the public: in or into society: on domestic service: in existence: at full length: in an expanded state: in bloom: in extension: loudly and clearly: forcibly:

unreservedly —*adj* external: outlying. remote: played away from home· outwards· not batting: exceeding the usual: in any condition expressed by the adverb *out*.—*n* one who is out that which is outside: a projection or outward bend (as in *outs and ins*) a way out.—*prep.* forth from (now usu. *from out*): outside of (now *rare*) —*v t* to put out: to knock out: (with *with*) to bring out: (with *with*) to say suddenly or unexpectedly.—*v.i* to go out —*interj* away, begone you are, he is, out: alas: shame (usu *out upon*; *arch*).—*n* **out′age** amount of a commodity lost in transport or storage· amount of fuel used on a flight. stoppage of a mechanism due to failure of power· period during which electricity fails or is cut off —*adj.* **out′er** (O E *úterra*, comp) more out or without: external—opp. to *inner* (**outer bar** the junior barristers who plead outside the bar in court, as opposed to King's (Queen's) Counsel and others who plead within the bar) —*n.* the outermost ring of a target, a shot striking it.—*adjs* **out′ermost**, **out′most** (*-most*, *-mōst*, O.E *ūtemest*, superl) most or farthest out most distant.—*n.* **out′ing** an outdoor excursion or airing.—*adj.*, *adv.*, *prep.*, *n* **outside** see separate article.—*adv.* **out′ward** toward the outside. on the outside **outer**: external: exterior appearing externally: apparent: formal —*adv* toward the exterior away from port: to a foreign port superficially —*adv.* **out′wardly** in an outward manner: externally· in appearance.—*n.* **out′wardness** externality objectivity — *adv* **out′wards** in an outward direction.—*adj.* **out′and-out** thorough-going: thorough-paced: utter: absolute: unqualified —*adv* **out-and-out′** finally and completely: definitely unreservedly.—*n.* **out-and-out′er** any person or thing that is a complete or extreme type: a thorough-going partisan· a great lie —*adj* and *adv.* **out′back** (*Austr.*) in, to, or of, the back-country —*n.* the back-country.—**out′building** a building separate from, but used in connection with, a dwelling-house or a main building: an outhouse, **outer space** the immeasurable expanse beyond the solar system, or, loosely, at a distance from the earth reached only by rocket, **out′erwear** clothes, as suits, dresses, worn over other clothes; **out′field** at cricket and baseball, the outer part of the field· the players who occupy it; **out′fielder** one of such players; **out′-guard** a guard at a distance, or at the farthest distance, from the main body, **out′house** a separate building subsidiary to a main building —*adj.* **outland′ish** queer, bizarre: out-of-the-way —*adv* **out-land′ishly**.—**outland′ishness**; **out′line** the outer line· the line by which any figure or object as seen is bounded: a sketch showing only the main lines· representation by such lines: a general statement without details: a statement of the main principles: a set-line in fishing —*v.t.* to draw the exterior line of: to delineate or sketch.—*adjs* **out-of-date′** not abreast of the times: obsolete: no longer valid, **out-of-door(s)′** out-door (see **out-**): outside of parliament —*n.* **out-of-doors′** the open air.—*adv.* (without hyphens; see below) — *adj.* **out-of-the-way′** uncommon: singular· secluded. remote —*n.pl.* and *adj* **out-of-work′** unemployed (persons).—**out′-patient** a hospital patient who is not an inmate; **out′post** a post or station beyond the main body or in the wilds: its occupants. a remote settlement; **out′rigger** a projecting spar for extending sails or any part of the rigging: a projecting contrivance ending in a float fixed to the side of a canoe against capsizing: an iron bracket fixed to the outside of a

boat carrying a rowlock at its extremity to increase the leverage of the oar: a light racing-boat with projecting rowlocks· a projecting beam for carrying a suspended scaffold in building· a projecting frame to support the controlling planes of an aeroplane —*adj* **out′right** out-and-out unqualified· unmitigated downright: direct —*adv* **outright′** directly· straight ahead· unreservedly· undisguisedly at once and completely.—*adj.* and *n* **out′size** (a size, or a garment, etc , that is) exceptionally large —**out′skirt** (usu in *pl*) the border area, **out′sole** the outer sole of a boot or shoe which rests on the ground, **out′-tray′** a shallow container for letters, etc , ready to be dispatched —*prep.* **outwith** (*owt′with*, *ōō′t′with*, *-with*, *Scot.*) outside of.—**out′work** a work outside the principal wall or line of fortification· outdoor work, field work: work done away from the shop or factory, **out′worker.—from out** to come from; **murder will out** see **murder; out and about** able to go out, convalescent. active out of doors; **out and away by far**· beyond competition, **out for** abroad in quest of: aiming at obtaining, achieving, dismissed from batting with a score of; **out of** from within· from among: not in· not within. excluded from from (as source, material, motive, condition, possession, language, etc.): born of: beyond the bounds, range, or scope of: deviating from, in disagreement with· away or distant from: without, destitute or denuded of; **out of doors** in or into the open air; **out of it** excluded from participation: without a chance, **out on one's feet** as good as knocked out: done for, but with a semblance of carrying on; **out to** aiming, working resolutely, to; **out with** away with: not friendly with: to utter, ejaculate, divulge: to bring out, whip out, **out′ward-bound** bound outwards or to a foreign port [O.E *úte*, *út*.]

out- (see also **out**) in composition, (1) meaning 'away from the inside or inner part', *lit* and *fig* ; (2) with prepositional force, meaning 'outside of', e.g *outboard*, *outdoor*; (3) meaning 'through, throughout', or 'beyond', or 'completely', e.g. *outwatch*, *outflank*, *outweary*; (4) indicating the fact of going beyond a norm, standard of comparison, or limit, 'more than', 'more successfully than', 'farther than', 'longer than', etc., e.g *outweigh*, *outmanoeuvre*, *outstep*, *outlast* (Words in which **out** has the adjectival senses of 'outside, not within', 'outlying', are given at **out**).—*vs t* **outbal′ance** to outweigh, **outbar′gain** to get the better of in a bargain; **outbid′** to make a higher bid than. —*adj.* **out′board** outside of a ship or boat: towards, or nearer, the ship's side: having engines outside the boat.—*adv.* outside of, or towards the outside of.— *adj* **out′bound** bound for a distant port —*n* **out′break** a breaking out: a disturbance —*adj* **out′bred** resulting from outbreeding —*v.i* **outbreed′**.—*ns* **outbreed′ing** breeding from parents not close akin, **out′burst** a bursting out· an eruption or explosion: a sudden violent expression of feeling; **out′cast** one who is cast out of society or home: anything rejected, eliminated, or cast out; **out′caste** one who is of no caste or has lost caste —*v.t.* **outclass′** to surpass so far as to seem in a different class —*adj* **outclassed′**.—*n* **out′come** the issue· consequence: result; **out′crop** the cropping out of a rock· a sudden emergence or occurrence; **out′cry** a loud cry of protest, distress, etc : a confused noise· a public auction —*vs t* **outdare′** to surpass in daring: to defy; **outdate′** to put out of date. —*adj.* **outdat′ed**.—*vs t* **outdis′tance** to leave far behind· to outstrip; **outdo′** to surpass· to excel to

For many words beginning out-, see **out** *or* **out-**.

fāte; fär; mē; hûr (her); mīne, mōte; for, mûte; mōōn, fōōt; dhen (then), el′ə-mənt (element) overcome —*adj.* **out'door** outside the door or the house: in or for the open air —*adv* **outdoors'** out of the house· abroad —*n* the world outside dwellings, the open air —*adj* **outdoor'sy** of, characteristic of, suitable for or having a liking for the outdoors.—*v.t* **outface'** to stare down: to confront boldly —*ns* **outfall** (*owt'fol*) the outlet of a river, drain, etc. a sortie, **out'fit** the act of fitting out for an enterprise complete equipment: a set of (esp selected and matching) clothes: expenses for fitting out: a company travelling, or working, together for any purpose, esp in charge of cattle (*U S*) any set of persons, a gang.—*v.t* to fit out, equip —*v t* to get an outfit.—*ns* **out'fitter** one who furnishes outfits one who deals in clothing, haberdashery, sporting equipment, etc, **out'fitting.**—*v.t.* **outflank'** to extend beyond or pass round the flank of· to circumvent —*n* **out'flow** a flowing out. an outward current outfall· amount that flows out.—*vs t* **outfox'** to get the better of by cunning to outwit; **outgen'eral** to get the better of by generalship· to prove a better general than —*n.* **out'giving** a disbursement. an utterance. a declaration of policy.—*v t.* **outgo'** to outstrip: to surpass: to pass or live through.—*v.i.* to go out: to come to an end·—*pa.t* **outwent'**; *pa.p.* **outgone'.**—*ns.* **out'go** (*pl.* **out'goes**) that which goes out· expenditure—opp to *income*; **out'going** act or state of going out: extreme limit: expenditure —*adj.* departing—opp to *incoming*, as a tenant —*v t.* **outgrow'** to surpass in growth: to grow out of, grow too big for. to eliminate or become free from in course of growth.— *n.* **out'growth** that which grows out from anything: an excrescence· a product.—*vs t.* **outgun'** to defeat by means of superior weapons, forces (*lit* and *fig.*), **out-Her'od** to overact the part of (*Herod*) in violence (*Hamlet* III, ii)· to outdo, esp in what is bad, **outlast'** to last longer than.—*n* **out'lay** that which is laid out: expenditure.—*v.t* **outlay'** to lay out in view: to expend: to surpass in laying.—*n* **out'let** the place where or means by which anything is let out, provided or sold: the passage outward, vent —*v t* **outlie'** to surpass in telling lies to lie beyond —*n* **out'lier** one who lodges or lies apart from others or from a place with which he is connected. a detached portion of anything lying some way off or out: an isolated remnant of rock surrounded by older rocks (*geol*).—*v t.* **outlive** (*-liv'*) to live longer than· to survive to live through: to live down —*n.* **out'look** a place for looking out from: a view, prospect: a prospect for the future: mental point of view —*adj.* **out'lying** lying out or beyond: lodging apart· remote. on the exterior or frontier· detached.—*vs t* **outman'** to outnumber in men; **outmanoeu'vre** to surpass in or by manoeuvring; **outmode'** to put out of fashion —*adj* **outmod'ed.**—*vs.t* **outmove'** to move faster than to get the better of by moving, **outnum'ber** to exceed in number; **outpace'** to walk faster than: to outstrip, **outplay'** to play better than, and so defeat; **outpoint'** to score more points than.—*ns* **out'pouring** a pouring out. a passionate or fluent utterance, **out'put** quantity produced or turned out. data in either printed or coded form after processing by a computer: punched tape or printed page by which processed data leave a computer signal delivered by a telecommunications instrument or system —*v.t* (of a computer, etc.) to send out, supply (data, etc).—*vs.t.* **outrank'** to rank above, **outreach'** to reach or extend beyond: to overreach. to stretch forth, **outride'** to ride beyond: to ride faster than. to ride safely through (a storm).—*n* **out'rider** a man who rides beside a carriage as a guard one sent ahead as a scout, or to ensure a clear passage. —*v t* **outrun'** to go beyond in running to exceed. to get the better of or to escape by running —*n.* **out'runner.**—*vs.t* **outsail'** to leave behind in sailing: to sail beyond, **outsell'** to fetch a higher price than: to exceed in value to surpass in the number or amount of sales —*ns.* **out'set** a setting out· beginning: an outward current, **out'setting.**—Also *adj.*—*v.t.* **outsit'** to sit beyond the time of: to sit longer than.—*adj.* **out'size** over normal size —*n.* an exceptionally large size· anything, esp a garment, of exceptionally large size —*adj.* **out'sized.**—*vs.t.* **outsleep'** to sleep longer than. to sleep through. to sleep to or beyond the time of, **outsmart'** (*coll, orig. U.S*) to show more cleverness or cunning than, to outwit —*adjs.* **outspent'** thoroughly tired out, **outspo'ken** frank or bold of speech uttered with boldness.—*n.* **outspo'kenness.**—*v.t* and *v.i* **outspread'** to spread out or over. —*adj.* **out'spread** (or *owt-spred'*) spread out.—*n* an expanse —*adj* **outspread'ing.**—*v t.* **outstand'** to withstand to stand or endure through or beyond.— *v.i.* to stand out or project: to stand out (to sea). to stand over, remain —*adj.* **outstand'ing** prominent. excellent, superior. unsettled: unpaid: still to be attended to or done —*adv.* **outstand'ingly.**—*vs.t.* **outstare'** to face the stare of unabashed: to gaze at without being blinded, **outstay'** to stay beyond or throughout to stay longer than: to endure longer than, **outstep'** to step beyond, overstep, **outstretch'** to stretch out. to reach forth: to spread out: to stretch to the end of: to stretch beyond; **outstrip'** to outrun: to leave behind to surpass.—*ns.* **out'swing** an outward swing or swerve; **out'swinger** a ball bowled to swerve from leg to off (*cricket*). a ball kicked to swerve away from the goal or from the centre of the pitch; **out'turn** the amount of anything turned out, produced or achieved —*vs t* **outvote'** to defeat by a greater number of votes; **outweigh'** to exceed in weight or importance.—**outwent'** see **outgo.**—*v.t.* **outwit'** to surpass in wit or ingenuity: to defeat by superior ingenuity:—*pr p* **outwitt'ing;** *pa.t* and *pa.p.* **outwitt'ed.**—*adj.* **outworn'** (or *owt'*) worn out. obsolete.

outlaw *owt'lo, n* one deprived of the protection of the law (loosely) a bandit —*v.t* to place beyond the law: to deprive of the benefit of the law to ban —*n.* **out'lawry** the act of putting a man out of the protection of the law. state of being an outlaw. [O.E. *ūtlaga*—O N. *ūtlāgi—ūt*, out, *log*, law.]

outrage *owt'rij, n.* gross or violent injury: an act of wanton mischief. an atrocious act: gross offence to moral feelings: great anger or indignation. violation: rape —*v t* to treat with excessive abuse: to shock grossly to injure by violence, esp. to violate, to ravish.—*adj* **outrageous** (*owt-rā'jas*) violent. furious.

---

turbulent: atrocious: monstrous: immoderate.—*adv*
outrā'geously.—*ns.* **outrā'geousness.** [O.Fr. *ultrage*
—*outre*, beyond—L. *ultrā*; the word is not connected
with **out** and **rage** but influenced by them.]
outrance *ōō-träs*, *n.* the utmost extremity: the bitter
end (**à outrance** to the bitter end of a combat—
erroneously in Eng. use, **à l'outrance**). [Fr ,—*outre*,
beyond.]
outré *ōō'trā*, *adj.* beyond what is customary or proper:
extravagant, fantastic. [Fr.]
outside *owt'sīd'*, *owt'sīd*, *owt-sīd'*, *n.* the outer side.
the farthest limit: the outer surface: the exterior: an
outside passenger: the outer part.—*adj.* on or from
the outside: carried on the outside: exterior: superficial: external: extreme: 'beyond the limit: not
enjoying membership: (of a criminal activity) carried
out by person(s) not having contacts with someone
near the victim: of a position near(er) the edge of the
field (*Rugby*, etc.).—*adv.* **outside'** (sometimes *owt'*)
on or to the outside: not within: out of prison —*prep.*
out'side' outside of: (*Rugby*, etc.) in a position nearer
the edge of the field than.—*n.* **outsid'er** one who (or
that which) is not a member of a particular company,
profession, etc., a stranger, a layman: one not considered fit to associate with: one who is not an inmate:
one who is not participating: a racehorse, competitor,
team, etc. not included among the favourites in the
betting: one whose place in a game, at work, etc., is
on the outside: (in *pl.*) a pair of nippers for turning a
key in a keyhole from the outside.—**outside
broadcast** a broadcast not made from within a studio;
outside chance a remote chance; **outside half** (*Rugby*)
a stand-off half; **outside left, right** in some games, a
forward player on the extreme left, right.—**get outside of** (*coll.*) to eat or drink; **outside in** turned so that
outside and inside change places: intimately,
thoroughly (of knowing anything); **outside of** in or to
a position external to: apart from, except (*coll.*, esp.
U.S.). [**out, side.**]
ouvrage *ōō-vräzh*, (Fr.) *n.* work.
ouzel, ousel *ōō'zl n.* a blackbird (*arch.*).—**ring'-ou'zel** a
blackish thrush with a broad white band on the
throat; **wa'ter-ou'zel** the dipper. [O.E. *ōsle*.]
ouzo *ōō'zō*, *n.* an aniseed liqueur:—*pl.* **ou'zos.** [Mod.
Gr. *ouzon*.]
ova. See **ovum**, under **ov(i)-.**
oval *ō'vəl*, *adj.* strictly, egg-shaped, like an egg in the
round or in projection, rounded, longer than broad,
broadest near one end: loosely, elliptical or ellipsoidal,
or nearly: rounded at both ends, about twice as long as
broad, broadest in the middle (*bot.*).—*n.* an oval
figure or thing, e.g. an oval field.—*adv.* **o'vally** [L.
ōvum, egg; *ōvālis* is modern Latin.]
ovalbumin, ovarian, ovary, etc. See **ov(i)-.**
ovate *ov'āt*, *n.* an Eisteddfodic graduate neither a bard
nor a druid. [W. *ofydd*, a philosopher, or lord.]
ovation *ō-vā'shən*, *n.* in ancient Rome, a lesser triumph:
an outburst of popular applause, an enthusiastic
reception. [L. *ōvātiō*, *-ōnis—ōvāre*, to exult.]
oven *uv'n*, *n.* an arched cavity or closed chamber for
baking, heating, or drying: a small furnace.—**o'ven-
bird** a name for various birds that build oven-shaped
nests, esp. the South American genus *Furnarius*; **oven
glove** a type of thick reinforced glove worn when
handling hot dishes.—*adj.* **ov'en-ready** of food, prepared beforehand so as to be ready for cooking in the
oven immediately after purchase.—**ov'enware**
dishes, as casseroles, that will stand the heat of an
oven. [O.E. *ofen*.]

over *ō'vər*, **o'er**, *ōr*, *ōr*, *preps.* above in place, rank,
power, authority, contention, preference, value,
quantity, number, etc.: in excess of: above and from
one side of to the other: down from or beyond the
edge of: from side to side or end to end of: along:
throughout the extent of: during: until after: across:
on or to the other side of: on, on to, about, or across
the surface of, or all or much of: in discussion,
contemplation, study of, or occupation with: concerning: on account of: recovered from the effects of:
in a sunk, submerged, or buried state beyond the level
of.—*adv.* on the top: above: across: to or on the other
side: from one person, party, condition, etc., to
another: into a sleep: outwards so as to overhang, or
to fall from: away from an upright position: through,
from beginning to end, esp. in a cursory or exploratory way: throughout: into a reversed position: across
the margin: again, in repetition: too much: in excess:
left remaining: at an end.—*interj.* (over) in telecommunications, indicates that the speaker now expects a
reply.—*adj.* (usu. treated as a prefix) upper or
superior: surplus: excessive.—*n.* (**over**) the series of
balls (as *six-ball*, *eight-ball*, *over*) or the play,
between changes in bowling from one end to the
other (*cricket*): anything that is over: a surplus copy,
etc.: an excess, overplus.—**all over** at an end: everywhere: at his, her, its, most characteristic: covered
with, besmeared or bespattered with; **be all over** (one)
to make a fuss of, fawn on (one); **over again** anew;
over against opposite; **over and above** in addition to:
besides; **over and over** (**again**) many times: repeatedly; **over head and ears** completely submerged;
over seas to foreign lands. [O.E. *ofer*; cf. **up.**]
over- in composition, used with certain meanings of
over *prep.*, *adv.*, or *adj.*, as (1) above, across, across
the surface; (2) beyond an understood limit; (3)
down, away from the upright position; (4) upper; (5)
beyond what is usual or desirable; (6) completely.—
v.i. **overachieve'** to do better than predicted or expected —*v.t.* **overact'** to act with exaggeration, to
overdo the performance of.—Also *v.i.*—*adv.*
overall', **over-all'** above all: altogether: over the
whole.—*adj.* **o'verall** including everything: everything being reckoned: all-round.—*n.* **o'verall** a protective garment worn over ordinary clothes for dirty
work or weather: (*pl.*) trousers or leggings or
combined shirt and trousers of this kind.—*adj.*
o'veralled.—*v.t.* **overarch'** to arch over: to form
above into an arch.—*v.i.* to hang over like an arch.—
adj. and *adv.* **o'verarm** with the arm raised above the
shoulder.—*vs.t.* **overawe'** to daunt by arousing fear
or reverence; **overbal'ance** to exceed in weight, value,
or importance: to cause to lose balance.—*v.i.* to lose
balance, fall over.—*n.* excess of weight or value.—
v.t. **overbear'** to bear down, overpower: to overwhelm: to overrule (objections, an objector).—*adj.*
overbear'ing inclined to domineer: haughty and dog-
matical: imperious.—*adv.* **overbear'ingly.**—*n.* **overbear'ingness.**—*v.t.* **overbid'** to outbid: to make a bid
that is greater than or counts above: to bid more than
the value of.—Also *v.i.*—*n.* (**o'**) a higher bid: an unduly high bid.—*ns.* **overbidd'er; overbidd'ing.**—*v.i.*
overblow' to blow with too much violence: to produce
a harmonic instead of the fundamental tone, by excess of wind-pressure (*mus.*).—*v.t.* to blow (an
instrument) too strongly (*mus.*).—*adv.* **overboard'**
over the board or side: from on board: out of a ship
(**go overboard about** or **for** (*slang*) to go to extremes
of enthusiasm about or for).—*vs.t.* **overbook'** to

---

overabound' *v.i.* over- (5).   o'ver-anxi'ety *n.* over- (5).   **overboil'** *v.t.*, *v.i.* over- (2), (5).
overabound'ing *adj.* over- (5).   o'ver-anx'ious *adj.* over- (5).   **overbold'** *adj.* over- (5).
overabun'dance *n.* over- (5).   o'verblanket *n.* over- (1).

---

make more reservations than the number of places (in a plane, ship, hotel, etc.) actually available (also *v.i.*); **overbuild'** to build in excess: to build too much upon or in; **overburd'en** to burden overmuch.—*n.* (*ŏ'vər-*) an excessive burden.—*adj.* **overbus'y** too busy: officious.—*v.t.* **overbuy'** to buy too much:—*pa.t.* and *pa.p.* **overbought'**.—*v.t.* **overcall'** (*bridge*) to outbid: to bid above: to bid too high on: to rank as a higher bid than.—*n.* (*ŏ'*) a higher bid than the opponent's preceding one.—*n.* **overcapitalisā'tion, -z-.**—*v.t.* **overcap'italise, -ize** to fix the capital to be invested in, or the capital value of, too high; **overcast'** to overthrow: to cast as a covering: to cast a covering over: to sew stitches over (a raw edge): to compute too high, overestimate.—*v.t.* to grow dull or cloudy —*adj.* clouded over.—*n.* (*ŏ*) a cloudy covering.—*n.* **overcast'ing.**—*v.t.* **overcloud'** to cover over with clouds: to cause gloom or sorrow to.—Also *v.i.*—*v.t.* **over-club'** (*golf*) to hit (a shot) too far through using a club with insufficient loft.—Also *v.i.*—*ns.* **o'vercoat** an outdoor coat worn over all else, a topcoat; **o'vercoating** cloth for overcoats.—*v.t.* **overcome'** to get the better of: to conquer or subdue: to surmount. —*v.i.* to be victorious.—*v.t.* **overcom'pensate** to allow too much in compensation of.—Also *v.i.* (with *for*).—*n.* **overcompensā'tion.**—*v.t.* **overcorrect'** to apply so great a correction to as to deviate in the opposite way.—*n.* **overcorrec'tion.**—*v.t.* **o'vercrop** to take too much out of by cultivation.—*adjs.* **overdat'ed** out of date; **over-deter'mined** too firmly resolved (to): too resolute, stubborn: having more than the necessary determining data or factors.—*v.t.* **overdo'** to do overmuch: to overact: to exaggerate: to carry too far: to harass, to fatigue: to cook too much: to excel.—*n.* **overdo'er.**—*adj.* **overdone'.**—*ns.* **overdos'age; o'verdose** an excessive dose of drugs, medicine, etc.—*v.t.* and *v.i.* **overdose'.**—*ns.* **o'verdraft** the act of overdrawing: the excess of the amount drawn over the sum against which it is drawn.—*v.t.* **overdraw'** to exaggerate in drawing: to exaggerate: to draw beyond one's credit.—*v.t.* and *v.i.* **overdress'** to dress too ostentatiously or elaborately.—*n.* **o'verdrive** a gearing device which transmits to the driving shaft a speed greater than engine crankshaft speed.— *adjs.* **overdue'** (or *ŏ'vər-*) behind time for arrival: still unpaid after the time it is due; **overear'nest** too earnest.—*v.i.* **overeat'** to eat too much.—*v.t.* **overexpose'** to expose too much, esp. to light.—*n.* **o'verfall** a rippling or race of water: a sudden increase of depth: a place or structure for overflow of surplus waters.—*v.t.* **overfall'** to fall on or over: to assail.— *adv.* **overfar'** too far.—*n.* **o'verflight** a flight above and over.—*v.t.* **o'verflour'ish** to cover with blossom, or with flourishes or ornament; **overflow'** to flow over the edge of: to flow over the surface of: to flood: to flow over and beyond: to cause to run over: (of e.g. people) to fill and then spread beyond (e.g. a room): —*pa.t.* **overflowed'**; *pa.p.* **overflowed'**, formerly and

still sometimes **overflown'**.—Also *v.i.*—*n.* **o'verflow** a flowing over: that which flows over, *lit.* and *fig.* (**overflow meeting** a supplementary meeting of those unable to find room in the main meeting): a pipe or channel for spare water, etc.: an inundation: a superabundance.—*adj.* **overflow'ing** flowing over: running over: overfull: overabounding: exuberant.—Also *n.* —*v.t.* **overfly'** to fly over.—*adj.* **overfond'** too fond: too fond (of).—*n.* **o'vergarment** a garment worn on top of others.—*v.t.* **overglaze'** to glaze over: to cover speciously.—*n.* **o'verglaze** an additional glaze given to porcelain, etc.—*v.t.* **overgo'** to exceed: to surpass: to overpower: to go over: to pass over, traverse: to spread over: to pass over, forbear to speak of.—*v.i.* to go over: to pass on:—*pa.t.* **overwent'**.—*n.* **overgo'ing** passing over: crossing, traversing: transgression.— *adj.* **overgrown** (*ŏ'vər-grōn*, or *-grōn'*) grown beyond the natural size: covered over with a growth.—*ns.* **o'vergrowth** excessive or abnormally great growth: excess or superfluity resulting from growth: that which grows over and covers anything; **o'verhair** the long hair overlying the fur of many animals.—*adv.* **overhand'** (or *ŏ'*) with hand above the object: palm downwards: with hand or arm raised above the shoulders or (in swimming) coming out of the water over the head: with stitches passing through in one direction and back round the edges (*needlework*).— *adj.* **o'verhand** done or performed overhand (**overhand knot** the simplest of all knots, tied by passing the end over the standing part and through the bight).— *adj.* and *adv.* **overhand'ed** with hand above: with too many hands.—*v.t.* **overhang'** to hang over: to project over: to impend over: to cover with hangings.—*v.i.* to hang over, lean out beyond the vertical.—*n.* **o'verhang** a projecting part: degree of projection.—*v.t.* **overhaul'** to haul or draw over: to turn over for examination: to examine: to overtake or gain upon (*naut.*).—*n.* **o'verhaul** examination, esp. with a view to repair.—*adv.* **overhead'** above one's head: aloft: in the zenith: in complete submergence.—*adj.* **o'verhead** above one's head: well above ground level: all-round, general, average.—*n.* (often in *pl.*; also **overhead costs, charges**) the general expenses of a business—as distinct from the direct cost of producing an article: that which is overhead (**overhead projector** one which, set up on a speaker's desk, projects transparencies on a screen behind him).—*vs.t.* **overhear'** to hear without being meant to hear: to hear by accident; **overheat'** to heat to excess.—*v.i.* to become too hot.—*v.t.* and *v.i.* to make or become agitated.—*adj.* **overhung'** overhanging: suspended from above: covered over, adorned with hangings.— *n.* **overinsur'ance.**—*vs.t.* **overinsure'** to insure for more than the real value; **overissue'** to issue in excess, as bank-notes or bills of exchange.—*n.* **o'verissue** excessive issue.—*v.t.* **overjoy'** to fill with great joy: to transport with delight or gladness.—*ns.* **o'verjoy** joy to excess, transport; **o'verkill** something, esp. power

For other sounds see detailed chart of pronunciation.

for destruction, in excess of what is necessary or desirable.—*vs.t.* **overla'bour** to labour excessively over: to be too nice with: to overwork; **overlaid** *pa.p.* of **overlay**; **overlain** *pa.p.* of **overlie**.—*adj.* **overland** passing entirely or principally by land.—*adv.* **overland'** (or *ō'*) by or over land.—*v.t.* **overlap'** to extend over and beyond the edge of: to reach from beyond, across the edge, and partly rest on: to coincide in part with: to ripple over.—*v.i.* (*Soccer, Rugby,* etc.) to advance down the flank as an attacking manoeuvre. —*n.* **o'verlap** an overlapping part or situation: a disposition of strata where the upper beds extend beyond the boundary of the lower beds of the same series (*geol.*).—*vs.t.* **overlard'** to smear over as with lard: to overload with fulsomeness; **overlay'** to cover by laying or spreading something over: to cover to excess, encumber: by confusion, to overlie:—*pa.t.* and *pa.p.* **overlaid'**.—*ns.* **o'verlay** a covering: anything laid on or over for the purpose of visual alteration; **overlay'ing** a superficial covering: that which overlays: plating.—*adv.* **overleaf'** on the other side of the leaf of a book.—*v.t.* **overlie'** to lie above or upon: to smother by lying on:—*pr.p.* **overly'ing**; *pa.t.* **overlay'**; *pa.p.* **overlain'**.—*n.* **o'verlier** (or *-lī'*).—*v.t.* **overlive** (*-liv'*) to survive: to outlive: to outlive the appropriate date of, or usefulness of (*refl.*).—*v.i.* to survive: to live too long.—*v.t.* **overload'** to load or fill overmuch.—*n.* (*ō'*) an excessive load.—*v.t.* **overlook'** to look over: to see from a higher position: to view carefully: to oversee, superintend: to fail to notice or take into account: to pass by without cognisance or punishment.—*ns.* **overlook'er**; **o'verlord** a lord over other lords: a feudal superior; **o'verlordship**.—*adv.* **o'verly** (*-li*; *coll.*) excessively, too.—*adj.* **overly'ing** lying on the top.—*n.* **o'verman** an overseer in mining, the man in charge of work below ground: superman. —*v.t.* **overman'** to furnish with too many men.—*n.* **o'vermantel** an ornamental structure, often with a mirror, set on a mantel-shelf.—*vs.t.* **overmas'ter** to gain or have the mastery of: to overpower: to dominate; **overmatch'** to be more than a match for: to defeat, overcome.—*ns.* **o'vermatch** one who is more than a match; **overmeas'ure** (or *ō'*) something given over the due measure.—*v.t.* (*-mezh'*) to measure above the true value.—*adj.* and *adv.* **o'vermuch** (or *-much'*) too much.—*v.t.* **overmul'tiply** to become too numerous.—*n.* **overmultiplica'tion**.—*adj.* **overnice'** too fastidious.—*adv.* **overnight'** all night: during the night: in the course of the night: on the evening of the day just past.—*adj.* done or occurring or existing overnight: for the time from afternoon till next morning: (**overnight bag, case** a small case for carrying the clothes, toilet articles, etc., needed for an overnight stay).—*adv.* **overpage'** overleaf.—*vs.t.* **overpaint'** to put too much paint on: to depict with exaggeration; **overpass'** to pass over: to pass by without notice: to exceed.—*v.i.* to pass over: to elapse.—*n.* (*ō'*) a road bridging another road or railway, canal, etc.—*adj.* **overpast'** over: at an end.—*v.t.* **overpay'** to pay too much: to be more than an ample reward for.—*n.* **overpay'ment**.—*v.t.* **overpitch'** to pitch too far, or beyond the best distance.—*adj.* **overpitched'** steeply pitched, as a roof: (of a cricket ball) bowled so that it pitches too near the stumps.—*v.t.* **overplay'** to overemphasise the importance, value, of: to try to gain more than one's assets (*lit.* and *fig.*) can be ex-

pected to yield (**overplay one's hand;** *fig.*).—*v.t.* and *v.i.* to exaggerate (an emotion, acting rôle, etc.): to hit the ball beyond (the putting green) (*golf*).—*n.* **o'verplay**.—*v.t.* **overpower'** to overcome, reduce to helplessness, by force: to subdue: to overwhelm: to furnish with too much power.—*adj.* **overpower'ing** excessive in degree or amount: irresistible.—*adv.* **overpower'ingly.**—*v.t.* **overpress'** to burden too heavily: to put too much pressure on.—*n.* **overpress'ure** excessive pressure, esp. of work.—*v.t.* **overprint'** to print too strongly or dark: to print too many copies of: to print over already printed matter (esp. a postage stamp).—*n.* **o'verprint** an offprint: that which is printed over an already printed surface, as on a postage stamp.—*v.t.* **overprize'** to value too highly.— *v.t.* and *v.i.* **overproduce'**.—*n.* **overproduc'tion** excessive production: production in excess of the demand.—*adj.* **overproof'** (or *ō'*) containing more alcohol than does proof-spirit.—*v.t.* **overreach'** to reach or extend beyond: to overtake: (*refl.*) to defeat by one's own oversubtlety or by attempting too much.— *v.i.* to strike the hindfoot against the forefoot, as a horse.—*adj.* **overread** (*-red'*) having read too much. —*v.t.* and *v.i.* **overreck'on** to compute too highly.— *v.t.* **override'** to injure or exhaust by too much riding: to ride over: to trample down on horseback: to slide or mount on the top or back of: to pass over: to overlap: to set aside: to be valid against: to be more important than, prevail over.—*n.* **o'verride** an auxiliary (esp. manual) control capable of temporarily prevailing over the operation of another (esp. automatic) control.—*n.* **o'verrider** an attachment on the bumper of a motor vehicle to prevent another bumper becoming interlocked with it.—*adj.* **overrid'ing** dominant, stronger than anything else.—*v.t.* and *v.i.* **overruff'** to trump with a higher trump.—*n.* **o'verruff.**—*vs.t.* **overrule'** to modify or to set aside by greater power: to prevail over the will of, against a previous decision of: to impose an overriding decision upon: to prevail over and set aside: to annul, declare invalid (*law*): to rule against: to disallow; **overrun'** to run over, crush underfoot or under wheel: to spread over: to infest, swarm over: to infect widely: to spread over and take possession of: to run beyond: to exceed the limit of: to carry beyond a limit: to carry over into another line or page: to adjust the type of by overrunning: to outdo in running: to escape from by running faster: (*refl.*) to injure or exhaust by too much running.—*v.i.* to run over, overflow: to run beyond a limit:—*pr.p.* **overrun'ning**; *pa.t.* **overran'**; *pa.p.* **overrun'**.—*ns.* **o'verrun** an act or occasion of overrunning; **overrun'er**.—*v.t.* **overscore'** to score or draw lines across: to obliterate in this way.—*adjs.* **o'versea, o'verseas** across, beyond, or from beyond the sea.—*adv.* **oversea(s)'** in or to lands beyond the sea: abroad.—*n.* **oversea'** foreign lands.—*v.t.* **oversee'** to see or look over: to superintend: to overlook, disregard: to see without being meant to see.—*n.* **o'verseer** (*-sēr, -sē-ar*) one who oversees: a superintendent: the manager of a plantation of slaves.—*v.t.* and *v.i.* **oversell'** to sell too dear: to sell more of than is available: to exaggerate the merits of:—*p.adj.* **oversold'**.—*vs.t.* **o'versew** (or *-sō'*) to sew together overhand; **overshade'** to throw a shade or shadow over: to darken; **overshad'ow** to throw a shadow over: to cast into the shade by surpassing, to outshine: to darken. to shelter or protect.—*n.* o'vershoe a shoe, esp of waterproof, worn over another.—*v.t* overshoot' to shoot over or beyond, as a mark: to pass beyond, exceed, fail to stop at: to shoot, dart, or fly across overhead: to surpass in shooting: to injure or exhaust by too much shooting (**overshoot oneself,** to venture too far, to overreach oneself):—*pa.t.* and *pa.p.* overshot'.—Also *v.i.*—*n.* o'vershoot a going beyond the mark —*adj* overshot' shot over: too much shot over: surpassed: overdone: in error by overshooting the mark —*ns.* o'versight superintendence a failure to notice mistake: omission; o'versize a large or larger size.—*adj.* o'versized (or -sīzd').—*v.t* oversleep' to indulge in sleeping too long: to sleep beyond.—*v.i* to sleep too long.—*n* o'verslip a close-fitting under-bodice —*vs.t* oversow' to sow after something has been already sown: to sow over; overspend' to spend beyond: to exhaust or cripple by spending.—*v.i.* to spend too much.—*adj.* overspent' excessively fatigued.—*ns.* o'verspill that which is spilt over: population leaving a district, or displaced by changes in housing, etc.; o'verspin the spinning of a flying ball in the same direction as if it were rolling on the ground.—*vs.t.* overstaff' to provide too many people as staff for; overstate' to state too strongly: to exaggerate.—*n.* overstate'ment; o'versteer tendency of a motor-car to exaggerate the degree of turning applied by the steering-wheel.—*v.t.* overstep' to step beyond: to exceed: to transgress.—*v.t.* and *v.i* overstrain' to strain too much: to strain beyond the elastic limit.—*n.* o'verstrain too great strain —*adj.* overstrained' strained to excess' exaggerated.—*v.t.* overstretch' to stretch to excess: to exaggerate —*adjs.* overstrung' too highly strung: (of a piano) having two sets of strings crossing obliquely to save space, o'verstuffed covered completely with well-stuffed upholstery.—*v.t.* oversubscribe' to subscribe for beyond what is offered.—*n.* oversubscrip'-tion.—*vs.t.* overtake' to come up with: to move past (something or someone travelling in the same direction) to catch up with: to catch: to come upon: to take by surprise; overtax' to tax overmuch: to require too much of.—*adj.* o'ver-the-count'er (of securities, etc) not listed on or traded through a stock exchange, but traded directly between buyers and sellers: (of drugs, etc.) able to be bought or sold without a prescription or licence.—*v.t.* overthrow' to throw over, overturn, upset: to ruin, subvert: to defeat utterly: to throw too far or too strongly.—*ns.* o'verthrow act of overthrowing or state of being overthrown: a ball missed at the wicket and returned from the field (*cricket*): a run scored in consequence; o'vertime time employed in working beyond the regular hours: work done in such time: pay for such work.—*adj.* and *adv* , during, for, or concerning, such time.—*v t.* (ō-vər-tīm') to time too long (esp. of a photographic exposure) —*ns.* o'vertimer one who works overtime, o'vertone a harmonic or upper partial. a subtle meaning, additional to the main meaning, conveyed by a word or statement: implicit quality, or constant association.—*v.t.* overtop' to rise over the top of: to be higher than: to surpass: to exceed.—*v.i.* over-trade' to trade overmuch or beyond capital to buy in more than can be sold or paid for.—*n.* over-trad'ing (one's capital, etc).—*v.t* overtrain' to train so far as to do harm to train too high.—*n.* o'vertrick (*bridge*) a trick in excess of those contracted for —*vs t* overtrump' to trump with a higher card than one

already played, overturn' to throw down or over: to upset' to subvert.—*ns.* o'verturn an overturning. a turnover; overvalua'tion; o'vervalue.—*v t.* overval'ue to set too high a value on.—*ns.* o'verview a general survey; o'verwash a washing over: material carried by glacier-streams over a frontal moraine (*geol.*).—Also *adj.*—*v.t.* overwear'y to overcome with weariness, weary out —*adj.* excessively weary.—*v.i.* overween' to expect too much: to be presumptuous or arrogant: to think too highly, esp. of oneself.—*adj.* and *n.* overween'ing.—*n* o'verweight weight beyond what is required or what is allowed: preponderance.—*adjs.* overweight' above the weight required: above the ideal or desired weight; over-weight'ed not fairly balanced in presentation —*vs.t.* overweight' to weigh down: to put too heavy a burden on; overwent' see overgo; overwhelm' to overspread and crush by something heavy or strong: to flow over the bear down: to reduce to helplessness to overpower: to ply overpoweringly.—*n.* and *adj* overwhel'ming.—*adv* overwhel'mingly.—*v t.* overwind (-wīnd') to wind too far:—*pa.t.* and *pa.p.* overwound.—*v i.* overwin'ter to pass the winter.—*adj* overwise' wise overmuch: affectedly wise: wise in one's own estimation.—*v.t.* and *v.i.* overwork' to work overmuch.—*n* o'verwork additional work: (o'verwork') excess of work.—*adj.* overworn' (-wō', -wo') worn out. subdued by toil: spoiled by use: threadbare: trite: exhausted of meaning or freshness by excessive use: out of date: spent or past; overwound' *pa.t.* and *pa.p.* of overwind.—*v.t.* overwrite' to write too much about: to write in a laboured manner —*v t* to write too much or too artificially.—*adj.* overwrought' worked too hard: too highly excited: with highly strained nerves: worked or embellished all over: overdone.

overachieve . . . to . **oversubscription.** See **over-**.

overt *ō'vûrt, ō-vûrt', adj.* open to view, not concealed. public evident —*adv.* **overtly** —**overt act** something obviously done in execution of a criminal intent [Fr. *ouvert,* pa p of *ouvrir,* to open.]

overtake . to . **overtrump.** See **over-**.

overture *o'vər-tūr, n.* an opening of negotiations: an offer or proposal: an opening or opportunity: an opening or beginning: an instrumental prelude to an opera, oratorio, etc., or an independent composition in similar form (sonata form). [O.Fr *overture* (Fr. *ouverture*), opening.]

overturn . to . **overwrought.** See **over-**

ovibos *ōv'i-bos, ov'i-bōs, n.* the musk-ox. —*adj.* **ovibo'vine.** [L. *ōvis,* sheep, *bōs, bovis,* ox.]

ov(i)- *ōv-, ō-vi-,* in composition, egg: ovum.—*ns.* **ovalbumin** (*-al'bū-min, -bū'*) the albumin in egg whites; **ovary** (*ō'və-ri*) the female genital gland: the part of the gynaeceum that contains the ovules (*bot.*).—*adj.* **ova'rian** of or pertaining to the ovary.—*ns.* **ovariot'omy** (Gr. *tomē,* a cut; *surg*) the cutting of an ovary: usu the removal of ovaries because of a tumour, **ovari'tis** inflammation of the ovary.—*adj.* **ō'vate** egg-shaped: shaped in outline like an egg, broadest below the middle (*bot*) —*n.* **oviduct** (*ō'vi-dukt*) the tube by which the egg escapes from the ovary (*zool.*; L *ducĕre, ductum,* to convey) —*adjs* **oviform** (*ō'vi-form*) egg-shaped (L *fōrma,* form); **oviparous** (*ō-vip'ə-rəs*) egg-laying (L *parĕre,* to bring forth). —*n.* **ovipar'ity** (*-par'i-ti*) —*adv.* **ovip'arously.**—*n* **ovipositor** (*ō-vi-poz'i-tər*) an egg-laying organ (L *positor—pōnĕre,* to place) —*adj* **ovoid** (*ō'void*)

---

oversimplifica'tion *n* over- (5)	overspecialisa'tion, -z- *n* over- (5)	overstress' *v t.* over- (5)
oversim'plify *v.t* over- (5)	overspread' *v.t* over- (1)	overuse' *v t* over- (5)
o'verskirt *n* over- (4).	overstay' *v t* over- (2)	o'veruse *n.* over- (5)
overspec'ialise, -ize *v.i.* over- (5)	o'verstock *v t* over- (5)	

For other sounds see detailed chart of pronunciation

egg-shaped and solid in form (sometimes also of a plane figure): egg-shaped and attached by the broad end (*bot.*) —*n* an egg-shaped figure or body (Gr. *eidos*, form).—*adj.* **ovoid'al** ovoid.—*n.* **ovotest'is** (*pl.* **-tes** *tēz*) an organ which produces both ova and spermatozoa.—*adjs.* **ovoviviparous** (ō-vō-vī-vip'ə-rəs, or -vī-) producing eggs which are hatched in the body of the parent (L. *vīvus*, living, *parēre*, to bring forth); **ov'ular** of or pertaining to an ovule.—*v.i* **ovulate** (ov'ūl-āt, ōv'-) to release ova from the ovary: to form ova.—*n* **ovulā'tion.**—*n.* **ovule** (ōv'ūl) in flowering plants, the body which on fertilisation becomes the seed, answering to the megasporangium and consisting of the nucellus and its integuments with the embryo-sac (megaspore): an undeveloped seed (from mod. L dim. of *ovum*) —*adj.* **ov̆ulif'erous** carrying ovules.—*n.* **ovum** (ō'vəm) an egg: the egg-cell, or female gamete (*biol.*).—*pl.* **o'va.** [L. *ōvum*, egg]

oviform² ov'ı-form, ō'vı-, *adj.* like a sheep: ovine.— *adj.* **ovine** (ō'vīn) of sheep: sheep-like. [L. *ōvis*, sheep, *fōrma*, form.]

oviform² . . . to . . . **ovoidal.** See ov(i)-.

ovolo ō'vō-lō, *n.* a moulding with the rounded part composed of a quarter of a circle, or of an arc of an ellipse with the curve greatest at the top (*archit.*):—*pl* **ō'voli** (-lē). [It.,—L. *ōvum*, an egg.]

ovotestis . . . to . . . **ovum.** See ov(i)-.

owe ō, *v.t.* to be indebted for: to be under an obligation to repay or render: to feel as a debt or as due: to have to thank: to concede or be bound to concede as a handicap.—*v.i.* to be in debt:—*pa.t.* and *pa.p.* **owed.** [O.E. *āgan*, to own, possess]

owing ō'ıng, *adj.* due: to be paid: imputable.—**owing to** because of: in consequence of

owl owl, *n.* any member of the Strigiformes, nocturnal predaceous birds with large broad heads, flat faces, large eyes surrounded by disks of feathers, short hooked beaks, silent flight, and howling or hooting cry: one who sits up at night: one who sees badly, or who shuns light: a solemn person: a wiseacre: a dullard: an owl-like breed of pigeon.—*n.* **owl'et** an owl: a young owl: a moth of the Noctuidae.—*adj.* **owl'ish** like an owl: solemn: blinking: stupid: dull-looking.—*n.* **owl'ishness.**—*adj.* **owl'y** owlish.—*adj.* **owl'-eyed** having blinking eyes like an owl.—**owl'-moth** a gigantic South American moth of the Noctuidae; **owl'-parr'ot** the kakapo; **owl'-train** (U.S.) a night train. [O.E. *ūle.*]

own¹ ōn, *v.t.* to possess, have belonging to one: to acknowledge as one's own: to confess: to allow to be true: to admit, concede: to acknowledge, recognise —*v.i.* to confess (with *to*).—*n.* **own'er** possessor, proprietor.—*adj.* **own'erless.**—*n.* **own'ership.**— **own'er-occupa'tion**—*adj.* **own'er-occ'upied.**— **own'er-occ'upier** one who owns the house he lives in. —**own up** to confess freely [O.E. *āgnıan*—*āgen*, one's own; cf. own².]

own² ōn, *adj.* belonging to oneself: sometimes used as an endearment.—**come into one's own** to take possession of one's rights: to have one's talents, merits, realised; **get one's own back** to retaliate, get even; **on one's own** on one's own account: on one's own initiative: by one's own efforts or resources: independently: set up in independence: alone, by oneself. [O.E. *āgen*, pa.p. of *āgan*, to possess; cf. **owe.**]

ox *oks*, *n.* a general name for male or female of common domestic cattle (bull and cow), esp. a castrated male of the species: extended to kindred animals:—*pl.* **ox'en** used for both male and female.—**ox'-bird** the dunlin: the ox-pecker: an African weaver-bird: applied also to various other birds; **ox'blood** a dark reddish-brown colour.—Also *adj.*—**ox'-bot** a warble-fly larva infesting cattle; **ox'-bow** (-bō) a collar for a yoked ox: a

river-bend returning almost upon itself (forming an *ox-bow lake* when the neck is pierced and the bend cut off); **ox'-eye** a name for various birds, esp. the great titmouse: a wild chrysanthemum with yellow disc and white ray (*ox-eye daisy*): sometimes (*yellow ox-eye*) the corn marigold: an elliptical dormer window.—*adj.* **ox'-eyed** having large, ox-like eyes.—**ox'-pecker** an African genus (*Buphaga*) of birds akin to starlings, that eat the parasites on cattle—also **beefeater**; **ox'tail** the tail of an ox, esp. as used for soup, stew, etc.; **ox'-tongue** the tongue of an ox, used as food [O E *oxa*, pl. *oxan.*]

Oxalis *oks'ə-lıs*, *n.* the wood-sorrel genus: (without *cap.*) a plant of this genus.—*adj.* **oxalic** (-al'ık) applied to an acid ($C_2H_2O_4$) obtained from woodsorrel.—*n.* **ox'alate** a salt of oxalic acid [Gr. *oxalıs* —*oxys*, sharp, acid.]

Oxbridge *oks'brıj*, *n* and *adj.* (pertaining to) *Ox*ford and *Camb*ridge regarded as typifying an upper-class-oriented kind of education, or as a road to unfair advantages, e.g. in obtaining jobs, or as the home of particular academic attitudes.

Oxford *oks'fərd*, *adj.* belonging to the city, county, or university of Oxford.—**Oxford bags** very wide trousers; **Oxford blue** a dark blue (see also **blue¹**); **Oxford English** a form of standard English in which certain tendencies are (sometimes affectedly) exaggerated, widely believed to be spoken at Oxford; **Oxford movement** the Tractarian movement; **Oxford (shoe)** a low shoe, usu. laced. [O.E. *Oxnaford*, lit oxen's ford.]

oxide *oks'ıd*, *n.* a compound of oxygen and some other element or radical.—*ns.* **ox'idant** a substance acting as an oxidiser; **oxidā'tion** oxidising.—*adj.* **oxidis'able**, **-z-.**—*v.t.* and *v.i.* **ox'idise**, **-ize** to combine with oxygen: to make, or become, rusty: to put a protective oxide coating on (a metal surface). —*n.* **oxidis'er**, **-z-** an oxidising agent. [Fr. *oxide* (now *oxyde*), formed from *oxygène*, oxygen.]

oxlip *oks'lip*, *n.* originally a hybrid between primrose and cowslip: now, a species of Primula (*P. elatior*) like a large pale cowslip. [O.E. *oxanslyppe*—*oxan*, gen. of *oxa*, ox, and *slyppe*, slime, a slimy dropping; cf. **cowslip.**]

Oxonian *oks-ō'ni-ən*, *adj.* of or pertaining to *Ox*ford or to its university.—*n.* an inhabitant, native, student, or graduate of Oxford: a kind of shoe. [L. *Oxonia*, Oxford—O.E. *Oxnaford.*]

oxonium *oks-ō'nı-əm*, *n.* a univalent basic radical, H_3O, in which oxygen is tetravalent, forming organic derivatives, **oxonium salts.** [*oxygen* and *ammonium.*]

oxy- *oks-i-*, in composition, sharp: pointed: acid: oxygen —*adj.* **ox'y-acet'ylene** involving, using, or by means of, a mixture of oxygen and acetylene, esp in cutting or welding metals at high temperatures.—*ns* **ox'y-a'cid**, **ox'y-com'pound**, **ox'y-salt**, etc., an acid, compound, salt, etc., containing oxygen: one in which an atom of hydrogen is replaced by a hydroxyl-group. [Gr. *oxys*, sharp.]

oxygen *oks'ı-jən*, *n.* a gas (atomic number 8; symbol O) without taste, colour, or smell, forming part of the air, water, etc., and supporting life and combustion.—*v.t* **ox'ygenate** (or *oks-ij'*) to oxidise: to impregnate or treat with oxygen.—*ns.* **oxygenā'tion**; **ox'ygenator** an apparatus performing functions of heart and lungs during an operation: that which supplies oxygen.—*v.t.* **ox'ygenise**, **-ize** to oxygenate —*adj.* **oxyg'enous.**—**oxygen debt** a depletion of the body's store of oxygen occurring during bursts of strenuous exercise, replaced after bodily activity returns to normal levels; **oxygen mask** a masklike breathing apparatus through which oxygen is supplied in rarefied atmospheres to aviators and mountaineers, **oxygen tent** tent-like enclosure in which there is a controllable flow of oxygen, erected round a patient to aid breathing [Gr *oxys*, sharp, acid, and the root of *gennaein*, to generate, from the old belief that all acids contained oxygen.]

oxymoron *oks-i-mō'ron, -mo'*, *n* a figure of speech by means of which contradictory terms are combined, so as to form an expressive phrase or epithet, as *cruel kindness, falsely true*, etc. [Gr. neut. of *oxymōros*, lit. pointedly foolish—*oxys*, sharp, *mōros*, foolish.]

oxytocin *oks-i-tō'sin, n.* a pituitary hormone that stimulates uterine muscle contraction. [Gr. *oxys*, sharp, *tokos*, birth.]

oxytone *oks'i-tōn, adj* having the acute accent on the last syllable —*n.* a word so accented. [Gr. *oxys*, sharp, *tonos*, tone.]

oyez, oyes *ō-yes', ō'yes, interj.* the call of a public crier, or officer of a law-court, for attention before making a proclamation. [O.Fr. *oyez*, imper of *oir* (Fr *ouir*), to hear.]

oyster *ois'tər, n.* bivalve shellfish (*Ostrea*) used as food: secretive person: source of advantage.— **oys'ter-bank, -bed, -farm, -field, -park** place where oysters breed or are bred; **oys'ter-catcher** a black and white wading bird, with red bill and feet, feeding on limpets and mussels (not oysters), **oys'ter-fish'ery** the business of catching oysters, **oys'ter-knife** a knife for opening oysters, **oys'ter-patt'y** a small pie or pasty made from oysters, **oys'ter-plant** salsify, or a seaside plant, *Mertensia maritima*—both supposed to taste like oysters, **oys'ter-shell**.—*n.pl.* **oys'ter-tongs** a tool for gathering oysters —**the world is my** (Shak , *Merry Wives* II, ii. 2, **world's mine), his,** etc., **oyster** the world lies before me, etc , ready to yield profit or success [O Fr. *oistre* (Fr *huitre*)—L *ostrea*—Gr. *ostreon*, an oyster—*osteon*, a bone]

Ozalid® *oz'əl-id, n.* a method of duplicating printed matter onto chemically treated paper: a reproduction made by this process

ozokerite *ō-zō'kər-īt, -kēr'īt,* **ozocerite** *ō-zos'ər-īt, ō-zō-sēr'īt, ns.* a waxy natural paraffin. [Gr. *ozein*, to smell, *kēros*, wax.]

ozone *ō'zōn, n.* a form (O_3) of oxygen present in the atmosphere, once regarded as health-giving, but harmful in concentration such as may occur in industrial areas: (see also **ozonosphere**) —*ns.* **ozon'o-sphere, ozone layer** a layer of the upper atmosphere where ozone is formed in quantity, protecting earth from the sun's ultraviolet rays [Gr. *ozōn*, pr.p. of *ozein*, to smell.]

For other sounds see detailed chart of pronunciation.

P

P, p pē, n. the sixteenth letter of our alphabet, representing a voiceless labial stop: in chem. p- is an abbreviation for para-.—**P-Celt, P-Kelt** see Celt.

pa pä, n. a childish or vulgar word for father. [**papa.**]

pabulum pab'ū-, -yə-, -ləm, n. food of any kind, esp. that of lower animals and of plants: provender: fuel: nourishment for the mind.—adjs. **pab'ūlar, pab'ūlous.** [L. pābulum—pāscĕre, to feed.]

paca pä'kə, n. the so-called spotted cavy of South America. [Sp. and Port.,—Tupí paca.]

pace¹ pās, n. a stride: a step: the space between the feet in walking, about 30 inches, or (among the Romans), the space between two successive positions of the same foot, over 58 inches: gait: rate of walking, running, etc. (of a man or beast): rate of speed in movement or work, often applied to fast living: a mode of stepping in horses in which the legs on the same side are lifted together: amble: a step of a stair, or the like. —v.t. to traverse with measured steps: to measure by steps (often with out): to train to perform paces: to set the pace for: to perform as a pace or paces.—v.i. to walk: to walk slowly and with measured tread: to amble.—adj. **paced** having a certain pace or gait.—n. **pac'er** one who paces: a horse whose usual gait is a pace: a horse trained to pace in harness racing.—adj. **pac'(e)y** (coll.) fast: lively, smart.—**pace'maker** one who sets the pace as in a race (also fig.): a small mass of muscle cells in the heart which control the heartbeat electrically: an electronic device (in later models, with radioactive core) used to correct weak or irregular heart rhythms; **pace'-setter** a pacemaker, except in anatomical and electronic senses.—**go the pace** to go at a great speed: to live a fast life; **keep, hold pace with** to go as fast as: to keep up with; **make, set the pace** to regulate the speed for others by example; **put someone through his paces** to set someone to show what he can do; **show one's paces** to show what one can do; **stand, stay the pace** to keep up with the pace or speed that has been set. [Fr. pas—L. passus, a step—pandĕre, passum, to stretch.]

pace² pā'sē, prep. with or by the leave of (expressing disagreement courteously). [L., abl. of pāx, peace]

pachisi pä-chē'sē, -zē, n. an Indian game like backgammon or ludo. [Hindi pacīsī, of twenty-five—the highest throw.]

pachy- pak'i-, in combination, thick.—n. **pach'yderm** (Gr. derma, skin) strictly, any animal of the Pachydermata, but usually an elephant, rhinoceros, or hippopotamus: an insensitive person.—n.pl. **Pachyderm'ata** in old classification, those ungulates that do not ruminate—elephant, horse, pig, etc. [Gr. pachys, thick.]

pacify pas'i-fī, v.t. to appease: to calm: to bring peace to.—adjs. **pac'ifiable; pacif'ic** peacemaking: appeasing: inclining towards peace: peaceful: mild: tranquil (with cap.) of, or pertaining to the ocean between Asia and America, so called by Magellan, because he happened to cross it in peaceful weather conditions.—n. (with cap.) the Pacific Ocean.—adj. **pacif'ical** pacific.—adv. **pacif'ically.**—v.t. **pacif'icate** to give peace to.—ns. **pacifica'tion** peacemaking: conciliation: appeasement: a peace treaty.—adj. **pacif'icatory** (-ə-tə-ri) tending to make peace.—ns. **pac'ifism** (-izm); **pac'ifist** (-ist) one who

is opposed to war, or believes all war to be wrong; **pac'ifier** a person or thing that pacifies. [Partly through Fr. pacifier—L. pācificus, pacific—pācificāre—pāx, pācis, peace, facĕre, to make.]

pack¹ pak, n. a bundle, esp orig. one made to be carried on the back by a pedlar or pack-animal: a collection, stock, or store: a bundle of some particular kind or quantity: a complete set of playing cards: a number of animals herding together or kept together for hunting: the forwards in a Rugby football team: a group of Cub Scouts or Brownies: a worthless, disreputable or otherwise objectionable set of persons: a mass of pack-ice: a sheet for folding round the body to allay inflammation, fever, etc.: the use or application of such a sheet: a cosmetic paste: act of packing or condition of being packed: mode of packing: a compact package, esp. of something for sale: a group of e.g. submarines acting together.—v.t. to make into a bundled pack: to place compactly in a box, bag, or the like: to press together closely: to compress: to fill tightly or compactly: to fill with anything: to cram: to crowd: to envelop: to surround closely: to fill the spaces surrounding: to prepare (food) for preservation, transport and marketing: to send away, dismiss (usu. with off): to form into a pack: to load with a pack: to carry in packs: to carry, wear (a gun).—v.t. to form into a pack: to settle or be driven into a firm mass: to form a scrum: to admit of being put into compact shape: to put one's belongings together in boxes, bags, etc., as for a journey (often with up): to travel with a pack: to take oneself off, to depart in haste (usu. with off).—n. **pack'age** the act, manner, or privilege of packing: a bundle, packet, or parcel: a case or other receptacle for packing goods in: a composite proposition, scheme, offer, etc. in which various separate elements are all dealt with as essential parts of the whole (see also **package deal**): a computer programme in general form, to which the user adds such data as is applicable in a particular case.—v.t. to put into a container or wrappings, or into a package.—adj. **pack'aged** (lit. and fig.).—ns. **pack'aging** anything used to package goods: the total presentation of a product for sale, i.e its design, wrapping, etc.; **pack'er** one who packs: one who packs goods for sending out: an employer or employee in the business of preparing and preserving food: a machine or device for packing; **pack'et** a small package: a carton: a ship or vessel employed in carrying packets of letters, passengers, etc.: a vessel plying regularly between one port and another (also **pack'et-boat, pack'et-ship,** etc.): a large amount of money (coll.): a small group: a block of coded data (comput.; see **packet-switching** below) —v.t. to parcel up.—n. **pack'ing** the act of putting into packs or of tying up for carriage or storing: material for packing: anything used to fill an empty space or to make a joint close.—**package deal** a deal which embraces a number of matters and has to be accepted as a whole, the less favourable items along with the favourable, **package holiday, tour** one whose details are arranged by the organiser before he advertises it and for which he is paid a fixed price which covers all costs (food, travel, etc.); **pack'-animal** a beast used to carry goods on its back; **pack'-drill** a military punishment of marching about laden with full equipment, **pack'et-switching** (*comput.*) a system of communication in which packets of data are transmitted between computers of varying types and compatability, **pack'-horse** a horse used to carry goods on its back· a drudge; **pack'-ice** a mass of large pieces of floating ice driven together by winds and currents; **pack'ing-box, -case** a box or framework for packing goods in, **pack'-load** the load an animal can carry; **pack'man** a pedlar or a man who carries a pack; **pack'-rat** a kind of long-tailed rat, native to the western part of North America, **pack's saddle** a saddle for pack-horses, pack-mules, etc , **pack'staff** a staff for supporting a pedlar's pack when he rests (see also **pike¹**); **pack'-train** a train of loaded pack-animals; **pack'way** a narrow path fit for packhorses —**pack a punch** to be capable of giving a powerful blow, **pack it in, up** (*slang*) to stop, give up, doing something; **pack up** (*slang*) to stop. to break down; **send someone packing** to dismiss summarily [M E *packe, pakke,* app —M Flem *pac* or Du or L Ger *pak.*]

pack² *pak, v.t.* to fill up (a jury, meeting, etc) with persons of a particular kind for one's own purposes [Prob. **pact.**]

package, packet. See pack¹.

paco *pa'kō, n* an alpaca:—*pl.* **pa'cos.** [Sp ,—Quechua *paco*]

pact *pakt, n* that which is agreed on· an agreement, esp. informal or not legally enforceable —**Warsaw Pact** a treaty of friendship, assistance and co-operation signed in Warsaw in May 1955 by the USSR and seven other European communist states. [L *pactum—paciscère, pactum,* to contract.]

pad¹ *pad, v.i.* to walk on foot: to trudge along: to walk with quiet or dull-sounding tread:—*pr p* **padd'ing;** *pa t.* and *pa.p.* **padd'ed.** [Du. *pad,* a path]

pad² *pad, n* anything stuffed with a soft material, to prevent friction, pressure, or injury, for inking, for filling out, etc.: a soft saddle: a cushion: a number of sheets of paper or other soft material fastened together in a block: a leg-guard for cricketers, etc · the fleshy, thick-skinned undersurface of the foot of many animals, as the fox the foot of a beast, esp of chase: its footprint· a water-lily leaf (*U.S.*). a rocketlaunching platform. a bed, room, or home, esp one's own (*slang*): a device built into a road surface, operated by vehicles passing over it, controlling changes of traffic lights (**vehicle-actuated signals**) so as to give passage for longer time to the greater stream of traffic —*v.t.* to stuff, cover, or fill out with anything soft: to furnish with padding: to track by footprints: to impregnate, as with a mordant.—*pr p* **padd'ing;** *pa t.* and *pa.p.* **padd'ed.**—*ns* **padd'er** one who pads, or cushions; **padd'ing** stuffing matter of less value introduced into a book or article in order to make it of the length desired· the process of mordanting a fabric.—**pad'-cloth** a cloth covering a horse's loins; **padded cell** a room with padded walls in a mental hospital, **pad'-saw** a small saw-blade with detachable handle, often used for cutting curves and awkward angles. [Origin obscure; possibly connected with **pod¹.**]

paddle¹ *pad'l, v.i.* to wade about or dabble in liquid or semi-liquid: to walk unsteadily or with short steps — *n.* **padd'ler** one who paddles: (in *pl.*) a protective garment worn by children when paddling. [Cf **pad¹,** and L Ger *paddeln,* to tramp about]

paddle² *pad'l, n* a small, long-handled spade: a short, broad, spoon-shaped oar, used for moving canoes· the blade of an oar: one of the boards of a paddlewheel or water-wheel: a paddle-shaped instrument for stirring, beating, etc —*v i* to use a paddle, progress by use of paddles: to row gently: to swim about

like a duck —*v t* to propel by paddle· to strike or spank with a paddle or the like (esp *U S*).—*ns* **padd'ler; padd'ling.**—**padd'le-boat** a paddlesteamer, **padd'le-board** one of the boards of a paddlewheel, **padd'le-steam'er** a steamer propelled by paddle-wheels, **padd'le-wheel** the wheel of a steamvessel, which by turning in the water causes the boat to move —**paddle one's own canoe** to progress independently

paddock¹. See puddock.

paddock² *pad'ək, n* an enclosed field under pasture, orig near a house or stable a small field in which horses are kept before a race. [Apparently from earlier *parrock*—O E *pearroc,* park.]

paddy *pad'i, n* growing rice· rice in the husk —**padd'y-bird** the Java sparrow or rice-bird, **padd'y-field.** [Malay *pādi,* rice in the straw]

Paddy *pad'i, n* a familiar name for an Irishman· (without *cap*) a rage (*coll.*) —**paddy wagon** a black Maria

padishah *pa'di-sha, n* chief ruler: great king, a title of the Shah of Persia, and formerly of the Sultan of Turkey, the Great Mogul, or the (British) Emperor of India [Pers *pad,* master, *shāh,* king]

padlock *pad'lok, n* a movable lock with a link turning on a hinge or pivot at one end, catching the bolt at the other.—Also *v.t* [Origin uncertain, possibly dial. Eng *pad,* a basket, and **lock¹.**]

padre *pa'drä, n* father, a title given to priests: an army chaplain. a person. [Port (also Sp. and It) *padre*—L *pater,* a father]

paean *pē'ən, n.* a song of thanksgiving or triumph. exultation.—Also **pē'an.** [L *paeân*—Gr. *paiân,* a hymn —*Paiān, -ānos,* Apollo.]

paed(o)-, ped(o)- *pēd-, pē-dō-,* also sometimes **paid(o)-** *pīd-, pī-dō-,* in composition, child, boy.—*adj* **paedagog'ic** see **pedagogic.**—*ns* **paed'agogue** see **pedagogue; paed'erast** (Gr *erastēs,* lover) one who practises paederasty.—*adj* **paederast'ic.**—*ns.* **paed'erasty** sexual relations of a male with a male, esp a boy; **paedeut'ic, paideut'ic** (also *n sing.* **paed-, paideutics**) educational method or theory —*adj* **paediat'ric** (Gr *iātrikos,* medical) relating to the medical treatment of children —*n.sing* **paediat'rics** the treatment of children's diseases.—*ns.* **paediatrician** (*-ə-trish'ən*), **paedi'atrist; paedi'atry; paedobap'tism** infant baptism, **paedobap'tist.**—*adj.* **paedolog'ical.**—*ns.* **paedol'ogist; paedol'ogy** the study of the growth and development of children.— *adj* **paedomor'phic** of paedomorphism or paedomorphosis.—*ns.* **paedomorph'ism** (Gr *morphē,* form) retention of juvenile characters in the mature stage; **paed'ophile** (*-fīl*) one affected with paedophilia; **paedophilia** (*-fil'*) sexual desire whose object is children —*adjs* and *ns* **paedophil'iac, -phil'ic.** [Gr *pais, paidos,* boy, child; *paideutēs,* teacher]

paella *pī-el'ə, pa-el'ya, n* a stew containing saffron, chicken, rice, vegetables, etc [Sp.,—L. *patella,* pan.]

paeony. Same as peony.

pagan *pā'gən, n* a heathen: one who is not a Christian, Jew, or Muslim more recently, one who has no religion: one who sets a high value on sensual pleasures —Also *adj* —*v t.* **pā'ganise, -ize** to render pagan or heathen: to convert to paganism.—*adj.* **pa'ganish** heathenish —*n* **pā'ganism** heathenism: the beliefs and practices of the heathen. [L *pāgānus,* rustic, peasant, also civilian (because the Christians reckoned themselves soldiers of Christ)—*pāgus,* a district.]

page¹ *pāj, n* a boy attendant a boy in buttons employed as a messenger in hotels, clubs, etc : a messenger, boy or girl, in the U S Congress, etc.· a youth training for knighthood, receiving education and performing services at court or in a nobleman's household (*hist.*).—*v.t.* to attend as a page: to seek or summon by sending a page around, by repeatedly calling aloud for, or by means of a pager.—*n.* **pa'ger** an electronic device which pages a person (cf. **bleeper**).—**page'-boy** a page: (also **page-boy hairstyle, haircut**) a hairstyle in which the hair hangs smoothly to approx. shoulder-level and curls under at the ends. [Fr. *page.*]

page² *pāj, n.* one side of a leaf of a book, etc.: the type, illustrations, etc., arranged for printing one side of a leaf: a leaf of a book thought of as a single item: rhetorically, writings, literature: an incident, episode, or whatever may be imagined as matter to fill a page.—*v.t.* to number the pages of: to make up into pages (*print.*).—*adj.* **paginal** (*paj'*).—*v.t.* **paginate** (*paj'*) to mark with consecutive numbers, to page.— *ns.* **paginā'tion** the act of paging a book: the figures and marks that indicate the numbers of pages; **pā'ging** the marking or numbering of the pages of a book.— **page-proof** a proof of matter made up into pages; **page three** (*coll.*) a photograph of a scantily-clad, attractive, young woman in an alluring pose, found esp. on page three of certain daily newspapers. [Fr.,—L. *pāgina*, a page.]

pageant *paj'ənt, n.* a spectacle, esp. one carried around in procession: a series of tableaux or dramatic scenes connected with local history or other topical matter, performed either on a fixed spot or in procession: a piece of empty show: display.—*n.* **page'antry** splendid display: pompous spectacle: a fleeting show. [Origin obscure; Anglo-L. *pāgina* may be the classical word transferred from page to scene in a MS; or *pāgina*, in the sense of slab, may have come to mean boarding, framework.]

paginal, paginate, etc. See **page².**

pagoda *pə-gō'də, n.* an Eastern temple, esp. in the form of a many-storied tapering tower, each story with a projecting roof: an ornamental building in imitation of this. [Port. *pagode*—Pers. *but-kadah*, idol-house, or some other Eastern word.]

pah *pä, interj.* an exclamation of disgust.

paid *pād, pa.t.* and *pa.p.* of **pay¹**.—*adj.* **paid-up'** paid in full: having fulfilled financial obligations.—**put paid to** to finish: to destroy chances of success in.

paid-. See **paed-**.

pail *pāl, n.* an open cylindrical or conical vessel with a hooped handle, for holding or carrying liquids (also ice, coal, etc.), a bucket: a pailful.—*n.* **pail'ful** as much as fills a pail. [O.E. *pægel,* a gill measure, apparently combined with or influenced by O.Fr. *paele,* a pan—L. *patella,* a pan, dim. of *patera—patēre,* to be open.]

paillasse. Same as **palliasse.**

pain *pān, n.* penalty: suffering: bodily suffering: (now only in *pl.*) great care or trouble taken in doing anything: (in *pl.*) the throes of childbirth: a tiresome or annoying person (*coll.*).—*v.t.* to cause suffering to. —*adjs.* **pained** showing or expressing pain: suffering pain: distressed; **pain'ful** full of pain: causing pain: requiring labour, pain, or care: distressing, irksome. —*adv.* **pain'fully.**—*n.* **pain'fulness.**—*adj.* **pain'less** without pain.—*adv.* **pain'lessly.**—*n.* **pain'lessness.**— **pain'-killer** anything that does away with pain; **pains'taker.**—*adj.* **pains'taking** taking pains or care. —*n.* careful diligence.—**be at pains, take pains, (to)** to put oneself to trouble, be assiduously careful (to); **for one's pains** as reward or result of trouble taken (usu. ironical); **pain in the neck** (*fig.*) a feeling of acute discomfort: an exasperating circumstance: a thoroughly tiresome person; **under or on pain of** under liability to the penalty of. [Fr. *peine*—L. *poena,* satisfaction—Gr. *poinē,* penalty.]

paint *pānt, v.t.* to cover over with colouring matter: to represent in a coloured picture: to produce as a coloured picture: to apply with a brush: to apply anything to, with a brush: to describe or present as if in paint (*fig.*): to colour: to apply coloured cosmetics to: to adorn, diversify: to represent speciously or deceptively.—*v.i.* to practise painting.—*n.* a colouring substance spread or for spreading on the surface: a cake of such matter: coloured cosmetics.—*adj.* **paint'-able** suitable for painting.—*adj.* **painted** covered with paint: ornamented with coloured figures: marked with bright colours: feigned.—*n.* **paint'er** one who paints: an artist in painting: one whose occupation is painting: a house-decorator: a vivid describer.—*ns* **paint'iness; paint'ing** the act or employment of laying on colours: the act of representing objects by colours: a painted picture: vivid description in words.—*adj.* **paint'y** overloaded with paint, with the colours too glaringly used: smeared with paint.—**paint'-box** a box in which different paints are kept in compartments; **paint'-brush** a brush for putting on paint; **painted lady** the thistle-butterfly, orange-red spotted with white and black: the painted cup; **paint roller** roller used in house-painting instead of a brush.—*n.sing.* **paint'works** a paint-making factory.—**paint the town red** to break out in a boisterous spree. [O.Fr. *peint,* pa.p. of *peindre,* to paint—L. *pingĕre,* to paint.]

painter *pānt'ər, n.* a rope for fastening a boat.—**cut the painter** to sever ties; **lazy painter** a small painter for use in fine weather only.

pair *pār, n.* two things equal, or suited to each other, or growing, grouped or used together: a set of two equal or like things forming one instrument, garment, etc, as a pair of scissors, tongs, trousers: the other of two matching things: a set of like things generally: a couple: husband and wife: two persons betrothed to or in love with each other: a male and a female animal mated together: two persons or things associated together: two horses harnessed together: two cards of like designation: two voters on opposite sides who have an agreement to abstain from voting;—*pl.* **pairs, pair** (*coll.*)—*v.t.* to couple: to sort out in pairs.—*v.i.* to be joined in couples: to be a counterpart or counterparts: to mate: of two opposing voters, to arrange to abstain, on a motion or for a period (also *v.t.,* usu. *pass.*).—*adj.* **paired** arranged in pairs: set by twos of a like kind: mated.—*n.* **pair'ing.**—*adv.* **pair'-wise** in pairs.—**pair'-bond** a continuing and exclusive relationship between a male and female; **pair'-bonding; pair'-roy'al** three cards of the same denomination, esp. in cribbage: a throw of three dice all falling alike: a set of three (also **pairt'al, pri'al)**— **pair of colours** two flags carried by a regiment, one the national ensign, the other the flag of the regiment: hence an ensigncy; **pair off** to arrange, set against each other, or set aside in pairs: to become associated in pairs. [Fr. *paire,* a couple—L. *paria,* neut. pl. of *pār,* afterwards regarded as a fem. sing., equal.]

paisa *pī'sā, n.* in India and Pakistan, (a coin worth) one one-hundredth of a rupee:—*pl.* **paise** (*-sā*): in Bangladesh, (a coin worth) one one-hundredth of a taka.

paisano *pī-zä'no, n.* among people of Spanish or American descent in America, a person from the same area or town: hence, a friend:—*pl.* **paisan'os.** [Sp.,—Fr. *paysan,* peasant.]

paisley *pāz'li, n.* a woollen or other fabric with a pattern resembling Paisley pattern.—**paisley pattern, design** a type of pattern whose most characteristic feature is an ornamental device known as a 'cone' (rather like a tree cone), used in the **Paisley shawl,** a shawl made in *Paisley,* Scotland in the 19th cent.

pajamas. See **pyjamas.**

pak-choi cabbage *pak'-choi kab'ij*, same as **Chinese cabbage.**

Pakhtu, Pakhto. See **Pushtu.**

Pakistani *pa-kis-tan'i, n.* a citizen of Pakistan: an immigrant from, or a person whose parents, etc. are immigrants from, Pakistan.—Also *adj*—*n* **Paki** (*pak'i; derog. British slang*) a Pakistani.—Also *adj*

pal *pal,* (*coll.*) *n.* a partner, mate: chum.—*v i.* to associate as a pal:—*pr.p.* **pal'ling;** *pa.t.* and *pa p.* **palled** (*pald*).—*adj.* **pally** (*pal'i*) —*adj* **pal'sy(-wal'sy)** (*coll.*) over-friendly: ingratiatingly intimate. [Gypsy.]

palace *pal'is, n.* the house of a king or a queen: a very large and splendid house: a bishop's official residence: a large and usually showy place of entertainment or refreshment.—**palace revolution** a revolution within the seat of authority —**palais de danse** (*pa-le də däs;* Fr.) a dance-hall [Fr *palais*—L *Palátium,* the Roman emperor's residence on the *Palatine* Hill at Rome.]

paladin *pal'ə-din,* (*hist*) *n.* one of the twelve peers of Charlemagne's household. a knight-errant, or paragon of knighthood. [Fr ,—It *paladino*—L *palátinus,* belonging to the palace, cf **palatine.**]

palae-, palaeo-, in U S. also **pale-, paleo-,** *pal-i-, -ŏ-,* also *pál-,* in composition, old: of, concerned with, the very distant past as **palaeoclimatology, -geography,** etc.—*adj.* **palaeanthrop'ic** (Gr. *anthrōpos,* man) of the earliest types of man —*n* **palaeanthropol'ogy** the study of the earliest types of man.—*adj.* **Palaearc'tic** of the Old World part of the Holarctic region —*ns* **palaeobot'anist; palaeobot'any** the study of fossil plants.—*adj* **Pal'aeocene** (*geol.*) of or from the oldest epoch of the Tertiary period (also *n.*).—*n.* **palaeog'rapher** (Gr. *graphein,* to write) one skilled in palaeography —*adjs.* **palaeograph'ic, -al.**—*ns* **palaeog'raphist; palaeog'raphy** ancient modes of writing. the study of ancient modes of handwriting —*adj.* **Palaeolith'ic** of the earlier Stone Age —*ns* **palaeontol'ogist; palaeontol'ogy** (Gr. *onta,* neut. pl of *pr* p of *einai,* to be, *logos,* discourse) the study of fossils —*adjs* **Palaeozo'ic** (Gr. *zōē,* life) of the division of the fossiliferous rocks, from Cambrian to Permian, **palaeozoolog'ical.**—*ns* **palaeozool'ogist; palaeozool'ogy** the study of fossil animals [Gr *palaios,* old.]

palafitte *pal'ə-fit, n* a prehistoric lake dwelling. [It *palafitta*—*palo* (—L *pālus*), a stake, *fitto,* pa p of *figgere* (—L *figère*), to fix.]

palais de danse. See **palace.**

palamino. Same as **palomino.**

palanquin, palankeen *pal-ən-kēn', n* a light litter for one, a box borne on poles on men's shoulders [Port. *palanquim,* cf Hind *palang,* a bed—Sans *palyanka,* a bed]

palate *pal'it, -ət, n* the roof of the mouth, consisting of the *hard palate* in front and the *soft palate* behind sense of taste relish mental liking. ability to appreciate the finer qualities of wine, etc. (also *fig*) —*adj.* **pal'atable** pleasant to the taste acceptable to mind or feelings —*ns* **palatabil'ity, pal'atableness.**—*adv* **pal'atably.**—*adj* **pal'atal** pertaining to the palate uttered by bringing the tongue to or near the hard palate —*n* a sound so produced —*v t* **pal'atalise, -ize** to make palatal —*adj* **pal'atō-alvē'olar** (*phon*) produced by bringing the tongue to a position at or close to the hard palate and the roots of the upper teeth —**cleft palate** a congenital defect of the palate, leaving a longitudinal fissure in the roof of the mouth [L. *palātum*]

palatial *pə-lā'shl, adj* of or like a palace [See **palace.**]

palatine *pal'ə-tīn, adj.* of the Palatine Hill or the palace of emperors there: of a palace: having royal privileges or jurisdiction· of a count or earl palatine (see below) —*n* an officer of the palace a noble invested with royal privileges and jurisdiction: a subject of a palatinate —*n.* **palat'inate** (or *pa'lat-*) the office or rank of a palatine. the province of a palatine, esp an electorate of the ancient German Empire.—**count, earl,** etc , **palatine** a feudal lord with supreme judicial authority over a province; **county palatine** the province of such a lord [L *palātīnus;* cf **palace.**]

palaver *pə-la'vər, n* a conference, esp. orig with African or other native tribespeople a talk or discussion· idle copious talk. talk intended to deceive —*v i* to hold a palaver to prate —*v t* to flatter —*n.* **palav'erer.** [Port *palavra,* word—L *parabola,* a parable, later a word, speech—Gr *parabolē,* cf **parable, parabola.**]

pale[1] *pāl, n.* a stake of wood driven into the ground for fencing: any thing that encloses or fences in: a limit. the limit of what can be accepted as decent or tolerable (*fig*). an enclosure a marked-off district a broad stripe from top to bottom of a shield (*her.*) —*v.t* to enclose with stakes· to fence —*adv* **pale'wise** (*her*) vertically, like a pale —*n.* **pāl'ing** the act of fencing· wood or stakes for fencing a fence of stakes connected by horizontal pieces an upright stake or board in a fence —*adj* **pāl'y** (*her*) divided by vertical lines —**beyond the pale** intolerable unacceptable [Fr *pal*—L *pālus,* a stake]

pale[2] *pāl, adj* whitish not ruddy or fresh wan of a faint lustre, dim wanting in colour —*v t* to make pale.—*v.t.* to turn pale —*n* paleness —*adv* **pale'ly.** —*n.* **pale'ness.**—*adj* **pāl'ish** somewhat pale —**pale ale** a light-coloured pleasant bitter ale, **pale'buck** the oribi; **pale'face** (attributed to American Indians) a white person [O.Fr *palle,* pale (*Fr pâle*)—L *pallidus,* pale.]

pale-. See **palae-.**

paleobotany, etc Same as **palaeobotany,** etc

Palestinian *pal-is-tin'i-ən, adj* pertaining to *Palestine* (Gr *Palaistīnē*) —*n* a native or inhabitant of Palestine a member of a guerrilla movement or political body one of whose aims is to reclaim former Arab lands from Israelis. [Cf **Philistine.**]

palette *pal'it, n.* a little board, usu with a thumb-hole, on which a painter mixes his colours· the assortment or range of colours used by a particular artist or for any particular picture a range or selection (*fig*)· a plate against which one leans in working a drill —**pal'ette-knife** a thin round-ended knife for mixing colours, cooking ingredients, etc [Fr ,—It. *paletta* —*pala,* spade—L *pāla,* a spade]

palfrey *pol'fri,* (*arch* or *poet*) *n* a saddle-horse, esp for a lady [O Fr *palefrei*—L L *paraverēdus*]

Pali *pa'lē, n* the sacred language of the Buddhists of India, etc , close akin to Sanskrit [Sans *pāli,* canon]

palimony *pal'i-mən-i,* (*coll*) *n* alimony or its equivalent demanded by one partner when the couple have been cohabiting without being married [**pal, alimony.**]

palimpsest *pal'imp-sest, n* a manuscript in which old writing his been rubbed out to make room for new a monumental brass turned over for a new inscription [Gr *palimpsēston*—*palin,* again, *psāein,* to rub]

palindrome *pal'in-drōm, n.* a word, verse, or sentence that reads alike backward and forward —*adjs* **palindromic** (*-drom', -drōm'*), **-al.**—*n* **pal'indromist** (or *pə-lin'*) an inventor of palindromes [Gr *palindromos,* running back]

paling. See under **pale**[1].

palingenesis *pal-in-jen'i-sis, n* a new birth reincarnation: a second creation: regeneration: unmodified inheritance of ancestral characters: the new-formation of a rock by refusion. [Gr. *palin*, again, *genesis*, birth.]

palisade *pal-i-sād'*, *n.* a fence of stakes: a stake so used (*mil.*).—*v.t.* to surround or defend with a palisade. [Fr. *palissade* and Sp. *palizada*—L. *pālus*, a stake.]

palish. See **pale**[2].

palki, palkee *pāl'kē*, *n.* a palanquin. [Hind. *pālkī*.]

pall[1] *pöl*, *n.* a covering of rich cloth: a cloth spread over a coffin or tomb: a cloak, mantle, outer garment: a curtain, covering, or cloak, as of smoke, darkness (*fig.*).—*v.t.* to cover with, or as with, a pall. —**pall'-bearer** one of the mourners at a funeral who used to hold up the corners of the pall. [O.E. *pæll*, a rich robe—L. *pallium*; see **pallium**.]

pall[2] *pöl*, *v.i.* to become vapid, insipid, or wearisome to lose relish.—*v.t.* to make vapid: to cloy. [Prob. from **appal**.]

palladium *pə-lā'di-əm*, *n.* a metallic element (symbol Pd; at. numb. 46) resembling platinum, remarkable for power of occluding hydrogen.—*adjs.* **palladic** (*-lad'*), **pallā'd(i)ous** containing palladium in smaller or greater proportion respectively. [Named by its discoverer Wollaston (in 1803 or 1804) after the newly discovered minor planet *Pallas*.]

pallescent *pə-les'ənt*, *adj.* turning pale.—*n.* **pallesc'ence.** [L. *pallēscēns*, *-entis*, pr.p. of *pallēscēre*, to turn pale.]

pallet[1] *pal'it*, *n.* a palette: a flat wooden tool with a handle, as that used for shaping pottery: in a timepiece, the surface or part on which the teeth of the escape wheel act to give impulse to the pendulum or balance: a valve of an organ wind-chest, regulated from the keyboard: a board for carrying newly moulded bricks: a piece of wood built into a wall for the nailing on of joiner-work: a platform or tray for lifting and stacking goods, used with the fork-lift truck, and having a double base into which the fork can be thrust.—*adj.* **pall'eted** carried on pallet(s).—*n.* **palletisa'tion,** -**z**- the adoption of pallets for moving goods: the packing of goods on pallets.—*v.i.* and *v.t.* **pall'etise, -ize.** [**palette**.]

pallet[2] *pal'it*, *n.* a mattress, or couch, properly a mattress of straw: a small or mean bed. [Dial. Fr. *paillet*, dim. of Fr. *paille*, straw—L. *palea*, chaff.]

palliasse *pal-i-as'*, *pal-yas'*, *pal'*, *n.* a straw mattress: an under-mattress.—Also **paillasse.** [Fr. *paillasse* —*paille*, straw—L. *palea*.]

palliate *pal'i-āt*, *v.t.* to excuse, extenuate: to soften by pleading something in favour: to mitigate: to alleviate.—*n.* **pallia'tion** the act of palliating.—*adj.* **pall'iative** (*-ə-tiv*) serving to extenuate: mitigating: alleviating.—*n.* that which lessens pain, etc., or gives temporary relief.—*adj.* **pall'iatory.** [L. *palliāre*, *-ātum*, to cloak—*pallium*, a cloak.]

pallid *pal'id*, *adj.* pale, wan.—*ns.* **pallid'ity, pall'idness.**—*adv.* **pall'idly.** [L. *pallidus*, pale.]

pallium *pal'i-əm*, *n.* a white woollen vestment like a double Y, embroidered with crosses, worn by the Pope, and conferred by him upon archbishops:—*pl.* **pall'ia.** [L. *pallium*.]

pallor *pal'ər*, *n.* paleness. [L. *pallēre*, to be pale.]

pally. See **pal**.

palm[1] *päm*, *n.* the inner surface of the hand between wrist and fingers: the corresponding part of a forefoot, or of a glove: a sailmaker's instrument used instead of a thimble: a flat expansion, as of an antler, or the inner surface of an anchor fluke: an act of palming.—*v.t.* to touch, or stroke with the palm: to hold or conceal in the palm: to impose, pass off (esp. with *off*, and *on* or *upon*): to bribe.—*adjs.* **palmar** (*pal'mər*) relating to the palm; **palmate** (*pal'*), -**d**

hand-shaped: having lobes radiating from one centre (*bot.*): web-footed (*zool.*).—*adv.* **pal'mately.**—*n.* **palmā'tion** palmate formation. a palmate structure or one of its parts or divisions.—*adj.* **palmed** (*pämd*) having a palm: held or concealed in the palm.—*ns.* **palmiped** (*pal'mi-ped*), **palmipede** (*-pēd*) a web-footed bird.—*adj.* web-footed.—*ns.* **palmist** (*päm'ist*) one who tells fortune from the lines on the palm; **palm'istry.**—**grease someone's palm** to bribe someone; **in the palm of one's hand** in one's power: at one's command. [L. *palma*.]

palm[2] *päm*, *n.* any tree or shrub of the **Palmae** (*pal'mē*), a large tropical and sub-tropical family of usually branchless trees with a crown of pinnate or fan-shaped leaves: a leaf of this tree borne in token of rejoicing or of victory: emblematically, pre-eminence, the prize: a branch of willow or other substitute in symbolic or ceremonial use.—*adj.* **palmaceous** (*pal-mā'shəs*) of the palm family.—*ns.* **palmifica'tion** (*pal-*) artificial fertilisation of dates by hanging a wild male flower-cluster on a cultivated female tree; **palmitate** (*pal'*) a salt of **palmit'ic acid**, a fatty acid ($C_{15}H_{31}$·COOH) got from palm-oil, etc.; —*adj.* **palm'y** bearing palms: flourishing: palmlike. —**pal'ma Christi** castor-oil; plant **palm'-branch** a palm-leaf; **palm'-butt'er** palm-oil in a solid state; **palm'-cat'**, **palm'-civ'et** the paradoxure; **palm'-hon'ey** evaporated coquito-palm sap; **palm'house** a glass house for palms and other tropical plants; **palmitic acid** see **palmitate** above; **palm'-oil** an oil or fat obtained from the pulp of the fruit of palms, esp. of the oil-palm; **palm'-su'gar** jaggery; **Palm Sunday** the Sunday before Easter, in commemoration of the strewing of palm-branches when Christ entered Jerusalem; **palm'-tree**; **palm'-wine** fermented palm sap. [O.E *palm*, *palma*, *palme*, also directly L. *palma*, palm-tree, from the shape of its leaves; see preceding.]

palmar, palmate, etc. See **palm**[1].

palmer *päm'ər*, *n.* a pilgrim carrying a palm-leaf in token of having been in the Holy Land: a bristly artificial fly. [**palm**[2].]

palmitin, etc. See **palm**[2].

palmipede, palmist, etc. See **palm**[1].

palmy. See **palm**[2].

palmyra *pal-mī'ra*, *n.* an African and Asiatic palm (*Borassus flabellifer*) yielding toddy, jaggery, and **palmy'ra-nuts.**—**palmy'ra-wood** properly the wood of the palmyra palm: any palm timber. [Port. *palmeira*, palm-tree, confused with *Palmyra* in Syria.]

palolo *pa-lō'lō*, *n.* an edible sea-worm that burrows in coral-reefs:—*pl.* **palo'los.**—Also **palolo worm.** [Samoan.]

palomino *pal-ə-mē'nō*, *n.* a horse of largely Arab blood, pale tan, yellow, or gold, with white or silver mane and tail:—*pl.* **palomin'os.** [Amer. Sp.,—Sp., of a dove.]

palooka *pa-lōō'kə*, (*U.S. slang*) *n.* a stupid or clumsy person, esp. in sports.

palp[1] *palp*, *n.* a jointed sense-organ attached in pairs to the mouth-parts of insects and crustaceans (also **pal'pus**:—*pl.* **pal'pi**). **pal'pal.** [L.L. *palpus*, a feeler (L. a stroking)—L. *palpāre*, to stroke.]

palp[2] *palp*, *v.t.* to feel, examine, or explore by touch —*n.* **palpabil'ity.**—*adj.* **palp'able** that can be touched or felt: perceptible: easily found out, as lies, etc.: obvious, gross.—*n.* **palp'ableness.**—*adv* **palp'ably.**—*v.t.* **palp'ate** to examine by touch.—*n* **palpā'tion.** [L. *palpāre*, *-ātum*, to touch softly, stroke, caress, flatter.]

palpi. See **palp**[1].

palpitate *pal'pi-tāt*, *v i.* to throb: to beat rapidly: to pulsate: to quiver.—*v.t.* to cause to throb.—*adj*

pal'pitant palpitating.—n. **palpitā'tion** the act of palpitating: abnormal awareness of heart-beat. [L. *palpitāre, -ātum*, freq. of *palpāre*; cf. **palp**[1,2].]

palpus. See palp[1].

palsy *pöl'zi*, n. loss of control or of feeling, more or less complete, in the muscles of the body: paralysis.— v.t. to affect with palsy: to deprive of action or energy: to paralyse.—adj. **pal'sied**. [From **paralysis**.]

palsy(-walsy). See pal.

paltry *pöl'tri*, adj. mean: trashy: trumpery: not worth considering.—adv. **pal'trily**.—n. **pal'triness**. [Cf. Dan. *pialter*, rags, L.G. *paltrig* ragged.]

paludal *pal-ū'dl, -ōō'*, also *pal*[1], *(rare) adj.* pertaining to marshes: marshy: malarial.—adjs. **palu'dic** of marshes; **palustral** (*-us'trǝl*), **palus'trian**, **palus'trine** (*-trīn*) of marshes: inhabiting marshes. [L. *palūs, palūdis*, a marsh; *palūster, -tris*, marshy.]

paly. See under pale[2].

pampa *pam'pǝ* (usu. in *pl.* **pampas**), n. a vast treeless plain in southern S. America.—**pampas grass** a tall, ornamental, reed-like grass (*Gynerium*, or *Cortaderia*) with large thick silvery panicles. [Sp., —Quechua *pampa, bamba*, plain.]

pamper *pam'pǝr*, v.t. to gratify to the full; to over-indulge.—ns. **pam'peredness**; **pam'perer**. [A freq. from (*obs.*) *pamp, pomp*; cf. Ger. dial. *pampen*, to cram.]

pamphlet *pam'flit*, n. a small book stitched but not bound: a separately published tractate, usu. controversial, on some subject of the day.—n. **pamphleteer'** a writer of pamphlets.—v.i. to write pamphlets.—n. and adj. **pamphleteer'ing**. [Anglo-L. *panfletus*, possibly from a Latin erotic poem *Pamphilus* (—Gr. *Pamphilos*, beloved of all) very popular in the Middle Ages.]

pan[1] *pan*, n. a broad, shallow vessel for use in the home or in arts or manufactures: anything of like shape, as the upper part of the skull (*brain-pan*), the patella (*knee-pan*): a lavatory bowl: a hollow in the ground, a basin, in which water collects in the rainy season, leaving a salt deposit on evaporation: a salt-pan: a salt-work: the part of a firelock that holds the priming: a hard layer (*hard-pan*) in or under the soil: a small ice-floe: a hollow metal drum as played in a steel band: a panful.—v.t. to wash in a gold-miner's pan: to obtain by evaporating in a pan: to yield: to obtain: to cook and serve in a pan: to review, criticise, harshly.—v.i. to wash earth for gold: to yield gold (usu. with *out*): to result, turn out (with *out*): to come to an end, be exhausted (with *out*): to cake:—pr.p. **pann'ing**; *pa.t.* and *pa.p.* **panned**.—ns. **pan'ful**; **pann'-ikin** a small metal cup: a little pan or saucer; **pann'ing** washing for gold: the gold so got: harsh criticism.— **pan'cake** a thin cake of eggs, flour, sugar, and milk, fried in a pan: see **pancake (make-up)** below: an aeroplane descent or landing with wings nearly horizontal (also *adj.*).—v.i. to descend or alight so.—**pan'-handle** a strip of territory stretching out from the main body like the handle of a pan.—**flash in the pan** a mere flash in the pan of a flint-lock without discharge: a fitful show of brilliance without accomplishing anything; **pancake ice** polar sea ice in thin flat slabs, found as winter draws near; **pancake (make-up)** cosmetic in cake form, moist, or moistened before application; **Pancake Tuesday** Shrove Tuesday. [O.E. *panne.*]

pan[2] *pān*, *pawn pon, ns.* betel leaf: betel. [Hind. *pān.*]

pan[3] *pan*, v.t to move (a cinema or television camera) about, or as if pivoting about, an axis while taking a picture so as to follow a particular object or to produce a panoramic effect.—Also *v.i.:—pr.p.* **pann'-** ing; *pa.t.* and *pa.p.* **panned.** [pan(orama).]

Pan *pan*, n. the Greek god of pastures, flocks, and woods, with goat's legs and feet, and sometimes horns and ears: later (from association with *pān*, the whole) connected with pantheistic thought.—**Pan'-pipes, Pan's pipes** the syrinx, a musical instrument attributed to Pan, made of reeds of different lengths, fastened in a row. [Gr. *Pān.*]

pan-, pant-, panto- in composition, all. [Gr. *pās, pāsa, pān*, gen. *pantos, pāsēs, pantos.*]

panacea *pan-ǝ-sē'ǝ*, n. a universal medicine. [Gr. *panakeia—akos*, cure.]

panache *pa-nāsh', -nash'*, n. a plume: knightly splendour: swagger: grand manner, theatricality, sense of style. [Fr.,—It. *pennacchio—penna*, feather.]

panada *pǝ-nä'dǝ*, n. a dish made by boiling bread to a pulp in water, and flavouring: a thick binding sauce of breadcrumbs or flour and seasoning. [Sp. *pan* (L. *pānis*), bread.]

Pan-African *pan-af'ri-kǝn*, adj. including or relating to all Africa, esp. concerning policies of political unity among African states.—n. **Pan-Af'ricanism**. [**pan-** and **African**.]

Panama *pan-ǝ-mä'*, n. a republic, town, and isthmus of Central America.—Also *adj.*—n. and *adj.* **Panam-anian** (*-mä'ni-ǝn*).—**panama (hat)** a hand-plaited hat made, not in Panama but in Ecuador, of plaited strips of the leaves of a South American plant: an imitation thereof. [Sp. *Panamá.*]

Pan-American *pan-ǝ-mer'i-kǝn*, adj. including all America or Americans, North and South.—n. **Pan-Amer'icanism**. [**pan-** and **American**.]

Pan-Arab *pan-ar'ǝb*, **Pan-Arabic** *-ik*, adjs. of or relating to the policy of political unity between all Arab states.—n. **Pan-Ar'abism**. [**pan-** and **Arab**.]

panatella *pan-ǝ-tel'ǝ*, n. a long, thin cigar. [American Sp. *panetela*, a long, thin biscuit,—It., small loaf—L. *pānis.*]

panchax *pan'chaks*, n. any of several kinds of brightly coloured fish, genus *Aplocheilus*, native to Africa and S.E. Asia—often stocked in aquariums. [L., former generic name.]

panchayat *pun-chä'yǝt*, n. a village or town council. [Hindi *pañcāyat*—Sans. *pañca*, five.]

panchromatic *pan-krō-mat'ik*, adj. equally or suitably sensitive to all colours: rendering all colours in due intensity.—n. **panchro'matism**. [Gr. *chrōma, -atos*, colour.]

pancratium *pan-krā'shi-ǝm*, n. a combination of boxing and wrestling.—adj. **pancrā'tian**.—n. **pancrā'tiast** (*-shi-ast*) a competitor or victor in the pancratium.—adj. **pancratic** (*-krat'ik*) of the pancratium: excelling all round in athletics or accomplishments: of a lens, adjustable to different degrees of magnification.—n. **pan'cratist**. [Gr. *pankration—kratos*, strength.]

pancreas *pan(g)'kri-ǝs*, n. the sweetbread, a large gland discharging into the duodenum and containing islands of endocrine gland tissue.—adj. **pancreat'ic**. —ns. **pan'creatin** the pancreatic juice: a medicinal substance to aid the digestion, prepared from extracts of the pancreas of certain animals; **pancreati'tis** inflammation of the pancreas.—**pancreatic juice** the alkaline secretion from the pancreas into the duodenum to aid the digestive process. [Gr. *kreas, -atos*, flesh.]

panda *pan'dǝ*, n. a raccoon-like animal (*Ailurus fulgens*) of the Himalayas (also **common** or **lesser panda**): (also, more correctly, **giant panda**) a larger beast (*Ailuropoda melanoleuca*) of Tibet and China, apparently linking the lesser panda with the bears.— **panda car** a car used by policemen on the beat. [Said to be its name in Nepal.]

Pandaemonium. See **Pandemonium.**

Pandean *pan-dē'ən, adj.* of the god Pan· or Pan-pipes [Irregularly formed from *Pân.*]

pandect *pan'dekt, n* a treatise covering the whole of any subject.—*n.* **pandect'ist.** [L. *pandecta*—Gr *pandektēs—pās, pān,* all, *dechesthai,* to receive]

pandemic *pan-dem'ik, adj* incident to a whole people, epidemic over a wide area —*n.* a pandemic disease.— *n.* **pandemia** (*-dē'mi-ə*) a widespread epidemic [Gr. *pandēmios—dēmos,* people.]

Pandemonium, Pandaemonium *pan-di-mō'ni-əm, n.* the capital of Hell in Milton's *Paradise Lost.* (without *cap.*) any very disorderly or noisy place or assembly. (without *cap.*) tumultuous uproar —*adj* **Pandemonic** (*-mon'ik:* also no *cap.*). [Gr. *pās, pān,* all, *daimōn,* a spirit]

pander *pan'dər, n.* one who procures for another the means of gratifying his base passions a pimp.—*v t* to play the pander for —*v i* to act as a pander to minister to the passions. to indulge, gratify (with *to*). [*Pandarus,* in the story of Troilus and Cressida as told by Boccaccio (*Filostrato*), Chaucer, and Shakespeare]

pandit. Same as **pundit.**

Pandora *pan-dō', -do'rə, n.* the first woman, made for Zeus so that he might through her punish man for the theft by Prometheus of heavenly fire, given a box from which escaped and spread all the ills of human life —**Pandora's box** any source of great and unexpected troubles. [Gr *pās, pān,* all, *dōron,* a gift.]

pane[1] *pān, n.* a rectangular compartment: a panel. a slab of window glass: a flat side or face: a length of wall: the side of a quadrangle: a rectangular piece of ground: a large sheet of stamps issued by the Post Office· half such a sheet separated from the other half by a gutter. a page of a book of stamps.—*v.t* to insert panes or panels in —*adj.* **paned** (*pānd*) made of panes or small squares· variegated [Fr *pan*—L *pannus,* a cloth, a rag.]

pane[2]. Same as **peen.**

panegyric *pan-i-jir'ik (U.S.* sometimes) *-jīr' n.* a eulogy, esp. public and elaborate (on, upon)· laudation —*adjs.* **panegyr'ic, -al.**—*adv.* **panegyr'ically.** —*v t.* **pan'egyrise, -ize** (or *-ej'ər-*) to write or pronounce a panegyric on. to praise highly.—*n* **pan'egyrist** (or *-jir',* or *-ej'ər-*) [Gr *panēgyrikos,* fit for a national festival—*pās, pān,* all, *agyris* (*agorā*), an assembly]

panel *pan'l, n* a rectangular piece of any material: rectangular divisions on a page, esp for the illustrations in children's comics: a compartment. a bordered rectangular area: a thin flat piece sunk below the general surface of a door, shutter, wainscot, or the like, often with a raised border: a compartment or hurdle of a fence: a strip of material inserted in a dress· a slip of parchment such a slip containing a list of names, esp. of jurors: a jury prior to the introduction of the national health service, a list of doctors available to treat those who paid into a national health insurance scheme: such a doctor's list of patients. a thin board on which a picture is painted: a large long photograph a group of persons chosen for some purpose, as to judge a competition, serve on a brains trust, or be the guessers in radio and television guessing games (**panel games**).—*v.t* to furnish with a panel or panels —*pr p* **pan'elling;** *pa t* and *pa.p* **pan'elled.**—*ns.* **pan'elling** panel-work, **pan'ellist** a member of a panel, esp. in panel games —**panel beating** the shaping of metal plates for vehicle bodywork, etc ; **panel beater; panel doctor** a doctor who was on the panel or had a panel, **panel heating** indoor heating diffused from floors, walls, or ceilings, **panel pin** a light, narrow-headed nail of small dia

meter used chiefly for fixing plywood or hardboard to supports, **panel saw** a fine saw for cutting very thin wood [O Fr.,—L.L *pannellus*—L *pannus,* a cloth]

pang *pang, n.* a violent but not long-continued pain. a painful emotion [Poss. **prong; pronge, prange,** have been found]

panga *pang'gə, n.* a broad, heavy African knife used as a tool and as a weapon

Pan-German *pan-jûr'mən, adj* pertaining to or including all Germans —*n.* **Pan-Ger'manism** a movement for a Greater Germany or union of all German peoples [**pan-** and **German.**]

Panglossian *pan-glos'i-ən,* **Panglossic** *-ik, adjs* taking an over-cheerful and optimistic view of the world as did Dr **Pan'gloss** in Voltaire's *Candide.*

pangolin *pang-gō'lin, n.* the scaly ant-eater, an edentate mammal (Manis, order *Pholidota*) of Asia and Africa. [Malay *peng-gōling,* roller, from its habit of rolling up.]

pangrammatist *pan-gram'ə-tist, n* one who contrives verses or sentences containing all the letters of the alphabet —*n.* **pan'gram** a sentence containing all the letters of the alphabet, e g. *the quick fox jumps over the lazy brown dog* [Gr. *gramma, -atos,* letter]

panhandle. See **pan[1].**

panhellenic *pan-hel-ēn'ik,* or *-en', adj,* pertaining to all Greece including all Greeks. (with *cap*) of or relating to Panhellenism.—*ns.* **Panhell'enism** (*-ən-izm*) a movement or aspiration for Greek union; **Panhell'enist.**—*adj* **Panhellenis'tic.** [Gr *Hellēnikos,* Greek—*Hellas,* Greece]

panic[1] *pan'ik, n* frantic or sudden fright· contagious fear· great terror without any visible ground or foundation.—*adj* relating or due to the god Pan· of the nature of a panic inspired by panic.—*v.t* to throw into a panic —*v.i* to be struck by panic:—*pr.p* **pan'icking;** *pa.t* and *pa.p* **pan'icked.**—*adj* **pan'icky** inclined to, affected by, resulting from, or of the nature of, panic —**pan'ic-bolt'** an easily moved bolt for emergency exits —*v.i.* and *v.t* **pan'ic-buy'** to buy up stocks of a commodity which threatens to be in short supply (often precipitating a greater shortage than might otherwise have occurred).—*adjs.* **pan'ic-strick'en, -struck** struck with a panic or sudden fear [Gr *pānikos,* belonging to Pan, *pānikon* (*deima*), panic (fear), fear associated with the god Pan.]

panic[2] *pan'ik, n* any grass of the genus Panicum (see below), or of various closely related genera (also **pan'ic-grass'**): the edible grain of some species.— Also **pan'ick, pann'ick.**—*n* **pan'icle** a raceme whose branches are themselves racemes: loosely, a lax irregular inflorescence —*adjs* **pan'icled, pan- ic'ūlate, -d** furnished with, arranged in, or like, panicles —*adv* **panic'ūlately.**—*n* **Pan'icum** a large genus of grasses having the one- or two-flowered spikelets in spikes, racemes or panicles—including several of the millets [L. *pānicum,* Italian millet]

panislam *pan-iz'lam, n* the whole Muslim world: pan-islamism.—*adj* **panislam'ic.**—*ns* **panis'lamism** an aspiration or movement for the union of all Muslims, **panis'lamist.** [**pan-** and **Islam.**]

Panjabi. Same as **Punjabi.**

panjandrum *pan-jan'drəm, n* an imaginary figure of great power and importance, a burlesque potentate, from the Grand Panjandrum in a string of nonsense made up by Samuel Foote, 18th cent English wit, actor and dramatist —Also **panjan'darum.**

panne *pan, n* a fabric resembling velvet, with a long nap [Fr]

pannick. See **panic[2].**

pannier *pan'yər,* or *pan'i-ər, n* a provision-basket a basket carried on the back one of a pair of baskets slung over a pack-animal's back or over the back of a motor-cycle, etc.: a sculptured basket (*archit.*): a contrivance formerly used for puffing out a woman's dress at the hips: the part so puffed out: a piece of basket-work for protecting archers, or, when filled with gravel or sand, for forming and protecting dikes, embankments, etc.: a covered basket of medicines and surgical instruments (*mil.*): hence (blunderingly) an ambulance (*mil.*).—*adj.* **pann'iered.** [Fr. *panier* —L. *pānārium*, a bread-basket—*pānis*, bread.]

pannikin. See **pan¹.**

pannose *pan'ōs*, (*bot.*) *adj.* like felt. [L. *pannōsus*—*pannus*, cloth.]

panocha *pā-nō'chə*, *n.* a Mexican coarse sugar. [Sp.]

panophobia *pan-ō-fō'bi-ə*, *n.* a form of melancholia marked by groundless fears: erroneously used for **pantophobia.** [Gr. *Pān*, the god who inspired fears, *phobos*, fear.]

panoply *pan'ə-pli*, *n.* complete armour: a full suit of armour: full or brilliant covering or array.—Also *fig.* —*adj.* **pan'oplied** in panoply. [Gr. *panopliā*, full armour of a hoplite—*pās*, *pān*, all, *hopla* (pl.), arms.]

panoptic *pan-op'tik*, *adj.* all-embracing: viewing all aspects.—Also **panop'tical.** [Gr. *panoptēs*, all-seeing.]

panorama *pan-ə-rä'mə*, *n.* a wide or complete view: a picture disposed around the interior of a room, viewed from within in all directions: a picture unrolled and made to pass before the spectator.—*adj.* **panoramic** (-*ram'ik*).—**panorama head** a swivel device fitted to the head of a camera tripod to permit the sideways swinging motion of the camera when taking panning shots; **panoramic camera** one which takes very wide angle views, generally by rotation about an axis and by exposing a roll of film through a vertical slit; **panoramic sight** a gun sight that can be rotated, so enabling the user to fire in any direction [Gr. *horāma*, a view, from *horaein*, to see.]

Pan-Slav *pan-släv'*, *adj.* of, including, or representing, all Slavs.—*adj.* **Pan-Slav'ic.**—*ns.* **Pan-Slav'ism** a movement for the union of all Slav peoples; **Pan-Slav'ist.**—*adj.* **Pan-Slavon'ic.** [**pan-** and Slav.]

pansophy *pan'sə-fi*, *n.* universal knowledge.—*adjs.* **pansophic** (-*sof'ik*), **-al.**—*ns.* **pan'sophism; pan'-sophist.** [Gr. *sophiā*, wisdom.]

panspermatism *pan-spûr'mə-tizm*, **panspermism** *-mizm*, **panspermy** *-mi*, **panspermia** *-mi-ə*, *ns.* the theory that life could be diffused through the universe by means of germs carried by meteorites.—*adjs.* **panspermat'ic, -sper'mic.**—*ns.* **pansper'matist, -mist.** [Gr. *sperma*, *-atos*, seed.]

pansy *pan'zi*, *n.* a name for various species of violet, esp. the heart's-ease (*Viola tricolor*) and garden kinds derived from it, as well as other species with up-turned side petals and large leafy stipules: a soft bluish-purple: an effeminate or namby-pamby man: a male homosexual.—*adj.* bluish-purple: effeminate. [Fr. *pensée*—*penser*, to think—L. *pēnsāre*, to weigh.]

pant *pant*, *v.i.* to gasp for breath: to run gasping: to throb: to wish ardently, to long, to yearn (with *for*): to bulge and shrink successively, as ships' hulls, etc.—*v.t.* to gasp out.—*n.* **pant** a gasping breath: a throb.—*n.* and *adj.* **pant'ing.**—*adv.* **pant'ingly.** [Apparently related to O.Fr. *pantoisier*, to pant.]

pant-. See **pan-.**

pantagraph. See **pantograph.**

Pantagruelism *pan-tə-grōō'əl-izm*, *-tag'rōō-*, *n.* the theories and practice of *Pantagruel* as described by Rabelais (*d.* 1553): burlesque ironical buffoonery as a cover for serious satire.—*adj.* and *n.* **Pantagruelian** (*-el'i-ən*).

pantalets, pantalettes *pan-tə-lets'*, *n.pl.* long frilled drawers, worn by women and children in the first half of the 19th century: a detachable ruffle for these, or one simulating these: extended to various trouser-like. garments worn by women.—Also **pantalettes.**—*adj.* **pantalett'ed.** [Dim. of **pantaloons.**]

Pantaloon *pan-tə-lōōn'*, or *pan'*, *n.* a character in Italian comedy, and afterwards in pantomime, a lean old man (originally a Venetian) more or less a dotard: (without *cap.*; in *pl.*) various kinds of trousers worn by or suggesting the stage pantaloon, as wide breeches of the Restoration, later combined breeches and stockings, later 18th-century trousers fastened below the calf or under the shoe, children's trousers resembling these, (usu. **pants**) trousers generally or long woollen underpants.—*adj.* **pantalooned'.**—*n.* **pantaloon'ery** buffoonery. [Fr. *pantalon*—It. *pantalone*, from St *Pantaleone*, a favourite saint of the Venetians.]

pantechnicon *pan-tek'ni-kon*, *n.* orig., a building in London intended for the sale of all kinds of artistic work, turned into a furniture-store: a furniture-van (in full **pantech'nicon-van'**): (*loosely*) a receptacle holding a large number of miscellaneous objects. [Gr. *technē*, art.]

pantheism *pan'thē-izm*, *n.* the doctrine that identifies God with the universe.—*n.* **pan'theist.**—*adjs.* **pan-thēist'ic, -al.**—*n.* **Pantheon** (*pan'thi-on, pan-thē'on*) a temple of all the gods, esp. the rotunda erected by Hadrian at Rome (on the site of Agrippa's of 27 B.C.), now the church of Santa Maria Rotonda, a burial-place of great Italians: a building serving as a general burial-place or memorial of the great dead, as Sainte Geneviève at Paris: all the gods collectively: a complete mythology. [Gr. *theos*, a god, *pantheion*, a Pantheon.]

panthenol *pan'thin-ol*, *n.* a vitamin of the B-complex, affecting the growth of hair.

Pantheon. See **pantheism.**

panther *pan'thər*, *n.* a leopard, esp. a large one or one in its black phase, formerly believed to be a different species: a puma (*U.S.*):—*fem.* **pan'theress.**—*adjs.* **pan'therine** (*-īn*), **pan'therish.** [Gr. *panthēr.*]

panties. See **pants.**

pantihose *pan'ti-hōz*, *n.pl.* tights worn by women or children with ordinary dress, i.e. not theatrical, etc. [**panty, hose.**]

pantile *pan'tīl*, *n.* a roofing tile whose cross-section forms an ogee curve: a tile concave or convex in cross-section.—*adj.* **pan'tiled.**—*n.* **pan'tiling.** [**pan¹, tile.**]

panto. See **pantomime.**

panto-. See **pan-.**

Pantocrator *pan-tok'rə-tər*, *n.* the ruler of the universe, esp. Christ enthroned, as in icons, etc. [Gr. *kratos*, power.]

pantograph *pan'tə-gräf*, *n.* a jointed framework of rods, based on the geometry of a parallelogram, for copying drawings, plans, etc., on the same, or a different, scale: a similar framework for other purposes, as for collecting a current from an overhead wire.—*n.* **pantographer** (*-tog'rə-fər*).—*adjs.* **pantographic** (*-tō-graf'ik*), **-al.**—*n.* **pantog'raphy.**—Also (*faulty*) **pan'tagraph,** etc. [Gr. *graphein*, to write.]

pantomime *pan'tə-mīm*, *n.* a play or an entertainment in dumb show: a theatrical entertainment, usu. about Christmas-time, developed out of this, no longer in dumb show, with showy scenery, topical allusions, songs of the day, buffoonery and dancing strung loosely upon a nursery story, formerly ending with a transformation scene and a harlequinade: dumb show.—*adj.* of pantomime: pantomimic.—**pan'to** coll. for pantomime:—*pl.* **pan'tos.**—*adjs.* **pantomimic** (*-mim'ik*), **-al.**—*adv.* **pantomim'ically.**—*n.* **pan'tomimist** an actor in or writer of pantomime.

[L. *pantomimus*—Gr. *pantomimos*, imitator of all—*pās*, *pantos*, all, *mimos*, an imitator.]

pantophagy *pan-tof'ə-jı*, *n.* omnivorousness.—*n.* **pantoph'agist.**—*adj.* **pantoph'agous** (-*gəs*). [Gr *phagein*, to eat.]

pantophobia *pan-tə-fō'bı-ə*, *n.* morbid fear of everything: (by confusion with **panophobia**) causeless fear. [Gr. *pās*, *pantos*, all, *phobos*, fear.]

pantoscope *pan'tə-skōp*, *n.* a panoramic camera: a very wide-angled photographic lens.—*adj.* **pantoscopic** (-*skop'ik*) giving a wide range of vision: bifocal [Gr. *skopeein*, to look at.]

pantothenic *pan-to-then'ik*, *adj* lit. from all quarters. applied to an acid, a member of the vitamin B complex, so ubiquitous that the effects of its deficiency in man are not known. [Gr. *pantothen*, from everywhere.]

pantry *pan'trı*, *n.* a room or closet for provisions and table furnishings, or where plate, knives, etc., are cleaned.—*ns.* **pan'trymaid; pan'tryman.** [Fr *paneterie*—L.L. *pānιtāria*—L. *pānıs*, bread.]

pants *pants*, *n.pl.* trousers (esp. *U.S.*): drawers.—*n.pl.* **pant'ies** very short drawers for children and women. —**pant(s) suit** (esp. *U.S.*) a woman's suit of trousers and jacket.—**(be caught) with one's pants down** (*coll.*) (to be caught) at an embarrassing and unsuitable moment, in a state of unpreparedness [**pantaloons**.]

panty girdle *pan'tı gûr'dl*, a woman's foundation garment consisting of panties made of elasticated material. [**panties**.]

panzer *pant'sər*, (Ger.) *n.* armour: a tank.—**panzer division** an armoured division.

pap[1] *pap*, *n.* soft food for infants, as of bread boiled with milk: trivial ideas, entertainment, etc. (*fig.*): mash: pulp.—*v.t.* to feed with pap.—*adj.* **papp'y.** [Imit]

pap[2] *pap*, (*dial.*) a nipple: in place-names, a round conical hill. [App. Scand.]

papa *pə-pa'* (*U.S.* *pa'pə*), *n.* father (*old-fashioned hypocoristic* or *genteel*): a priest of the Greek Church [Partly through Fr. *papa*, partly directly from L.L. *pāpa*, Gr. hypocoristic *papās*, *pappās*, father.]

papacy *pā'pə-sı*, *n.* the office of pope: a pope's tenure of office: papal government. [L L *pāpātia*—*pāpa*, pope]

papain *pə-pā'ın*, *n.* a digestive enzyme in the juice of papaw (Carıca) fruits and leaves [Sp *papaya*, papaw]

papal *pā'pl*, *adj.* of the pope or the papacy —*ns* **pa'palism** the papal system; **pa'palist** a supporter of the pope and of the papal system.—*adv.* **pa'pally.**—**papal cross** a cross with three cross-bars; **Papal knighthood** a title of nobility conferred by the Pope; **Papal States** States of the Church (see **state**) [L.L. *pāpālıs*—*pāpa*, pope.]

Papanicolaou smear, test *pap-ə-nık'o-low, -nēk'*, *smēr*, *test*, a smear test for detecting cancer, esp. of the womb, devised by George *Papanıcolaou*, 20th cent U.S. anatomist.—Abbrev **Pap smear, test.**

paparazzo *pa-pa-rat'sō*, *n.* a photographer who specialises in harassing famous people in order to obtain photographs of them in unguarded moments, etc.:—*pl.* **paparazz'i.** [It.]

Papaver *pə-pā'vər*, *n.* the poppy genus, giving name to the family **Papaverā'ceae.**—*adj.* **papaveraceous** (*pə-pav-*, or *-pāv-ə-rā'shəs*) of the poppy family.—*n.* **papaverine** (*pə-pav'ə-rēn*, *-rīn*, or *-pāv'*) an alkaloid got from poppy juice and used medicinally. [L. *papāver*, the poppy.]

papaw *pə-po'*, *po'po*, *n* the tree *Asımına trıloba* (of the custard-apple family) or its fruit, native to the U.S.: the papaya.—Also **paw'paw'.** [Prob. variant

of **papaya.**]

papaya *pə-pa'yə*, *n.* the tree *Carıca papaya*, or its fruit, native to South America but common in the tropics, the trunk, leaves, and fruit yielding papain, the leaves forming a powerful anthelmintic.—Also called **papaw.** [Sp. *papayo* (tree), *papaya* (fruit) app. from Carib.]

paper *pā'pər*, *n.* a material made in thin sheets as an aqueous deposit from linen rags, esparto, wood-pulp, or other form of cellulose, used for writing, printing, wrapping, and other purposes: extended to other materials of similar purpose or appearance, as to papyrus, rice-paper, to the substance of which some wasps build their nests, to cardboard, and even to tinfoil ('silver paper'): a piece of paper a written or printed document or instrument, note, receipt, bill, bond, deed, etc · a newspaper: an essay or literary contribution, esp. one read before a society: a set of examination questions. paper-money: paper-hangings for walls: a wrapping of paper: a quantity of anything wrapped in or attached to a paper.—*adj.* consisting of made of paper: papery: on paper —*v.t.* to cover with paper. to fold in paper: to treat in any way by means of paper, as to sandpaper, etc.—*n* **pa'pering** the operation of covering with paper: the paper so used —*adj* **pa'pery** like paper.— **pa'perback** a book with paper cover, **pa'perboard** a type of strong, thick cardboard· pasteboard; **pa'perboy, -girl** one who delivers newspapers; **pa'per-chase** the game of hare and hounds, in which some runners (*hares*) set off across country strewing paper by which others (*hounds*) track them; **pa'per-clip** a clip of bent wire or the like, for holding papers together: a letter-clip; **pa'per-cutter** a paper-knife: a machine for cutting paper in sheets, for trimming the edges of books, etc., **pa'per-day** (*law*) one of certain days in each term for hearing cases down in the paper or roll of business; **pa'per-fastener** a button with two blades that can be forced through papers and bent back; **pa'per-file** an appliance for filing papers; **pa'per-hanger** one who papers walls, **pa'per-hangings** paper for covering walls, **pa'per-knife** a thin, flat blade for cutting open the leaves of books and other folded papers; **pa'per-maker** a manufacturer of paper; **pa'per-making; pa'per-mill** a mill where paper is made; **paper money** pieces of paper stamped or marked by government or by a bank, as representing a certain value of money, which pass from hand to hand instead of the coin itself; **paper nautilus** the argonaut (see **nautilus**); **pa'per-pulp** pulpy material for making paper; **pa'per-reed** the papyrus, **pa'per-rul'er** one who, or an instrument which, makes straight lines on paper, **pa'per-sail'or** an argonaut, **paper tape** (*comput*) a paper data-recording tape, which records information by means of punched holes, **paper tiger** a person, organisation, that appears to be powerful but is in fact the reverse; **pa'per-weight** a small weight for keeping loose papers from being displaced; **paper work** clerical work keeping of records as part of a job.—**on paper** planned, decreed, existing theoretically only: apparently, judging by statistics, but perhaps not in fact, **paper over (the cracks)** to create the impression that there is or has been no dissent, error, or fault. [A.Fr. *papır*, O.Fr (Fr) *papıer*—L. *papyrus*—Gr. *papyros*, papyrus.]

papier collé *pa-pyā kol-ā*, scraps of paper and odds and ends pasted out as a help to cubist composition. [Fr , glued paper.]

papier-mâché *pap'yā-ma'shā*, *n.* a material consisting of paper-pulp or of sheets of paper pasted together, often treated so as to resemble varnished or lacquered wood or plaster —*adj* of papier-mâché. [Would-be French,—Fr. *papıer* (see **paper**) *mâché*, chewed—L. *mastıcātus*.]

Papilio *pə-pil'i-ō, n.* the swallow-tailed butterfly genus: (without *cap.*) a butterfly of this genus:—*pl.* **papil'ios.**—*adj.* **papilionā'ceous** of butterflies: butterfly-like: of a form of corolla somewhat butterfly-like: of a family of flowers characterised by such a corolla, including pea, bean, clover, gorse, laburnum, etc. [L. *pāpiliō, -ōnis,* butterfly.]

papilla *pə-pil'ə, n.* a small nipple-like protuberance: a minute elevation on the skin, esp. of the finger-tips and upper surface of the tongue, in which a nerve ends: a protuberance at the base of a hair, feather, tooth, etc.. a minute conical protuberance as on the surface of a petal:—*pl.* **papill'ae** (*-ē*).—*adjs.* **papill'ar, papill'ary** like, of the nature of, or having, papillae; **papill'ate, -d, papillif'erous** (*pap-*) having papillae; **papill'iform** in the form of a papilla.—*n.* **papillō'ma** a tumour formed by hypertrophy of a papilla or papillae, as a wart, etc. [L., dim. of *papula.*]

papillon *pap-ē-yō, n.* a breed of toy spaniel with erect ears. [Fr., butterfly.]

papillote *pap'il-ōt, n.* a curl-paper: frilled paper used to decorate the bones of chops, etc. (*cook.*): oiled or greased paper in which meat is cooked and served (*cook.*). [Fr., app.—*papillon,* butterfly—L. *pāpiliō, -ōnis.*]

papist *pā'pist, n.* an adherent of the pope: a name slightingly given to a Roman Catholic.—*n.* **pā'pism** popery.—*adjs.* **pāpist'ic, -al** pertaining to popery, or to the Church of Rome, its doctrines, etc.—*adv.* **pāpist'ically.**—*n.* **pā'pistry** popery. [L.L. *pāpa,* pope.]

papoose *pə-pōōs', n.* a North American Indian baby or young child.—Also **pappoose'.** [Narraganset *papoos.*]

pappadom. See pop(p)adum.

pappus *pap'əs, n.* a ring or parachute of fine hair or down, respresenting the calyx limb, which grows above the seed and helps in wind-dissemination in composites and some other plants (*bot.*). [L. *pappus*—Gr. *pappos,* a grandfather, down, a pappus.]

pappy[1]. See **pap**[1].

pappy[2] *pap'i, (U.S. coll.) n.* father. [**papa**.]

paprika *pap'ri-kə, pa-prēk'ə, n.* Hungarian red pepper, a species of Capsicum. [Hung.]

papula *pap'ū-lə,* **papule** *pap'ūl, ns.* a pimple: a papilla:—*pl.* **pap'ūlae** (*-lē*), **pap'ules.**—*adj.* **pap'ūlar.** [L. *papula,* a pimple.]

papyrus *pə-pī'rəs, n.* the paper-reed (*Cyperus papyrus,* or kindred species), a tall plant of the sedge family, once common in Egypt: its pith cut in thin strips and pressed together as a writing material of the ancients: a manuscript on papyrus:—*pl.* **papy'ri** (*-rī*).—*ns.* **papyrologist** (*pap-i-rol'ə-jist*); **papyrol'ogy** the study of ancient papyri. [L. *papyrus*—Gr. *papyros;* probably Egyptian.]

par[1] *pär, n.* state of equality: equal value: norm or standard: state or value of bills, shares, etc., when they sell at exactly the price marked on them—i.e. without *premium* or *discount*: equality of condition: the number of strokes that should be taken for a hole or a round by good play, two putts being allowed on each green (*golf*).—**par value** value at par.—**above par** at a premium, or at more than the nominal value; **at par** at exactly the nominal value; **below par** at a discount, or at less than the nominal value: out of sorts (*fig.*); **on a par with** equal to; **par for the course** a normal, average result or (*coll. fig.*) occurrence, state of affairs, etc.; **par of exchange** the value of currency of one country expressed in that of another [L. *pār,* equal.]

par[2] *par, n.* Same as **parr.**

para[1] *par'ə, n.* a small Turkish coin: the 40th part of a piastre: in Yugoslavia the 100th part of a dinar. [Turk. *pārah.*]

para[2] *par'ə, n.* a colloquial short form of **paratrooper, paragraph.**

Pará *pa-ra', n.* a city, state, and estuary of Brazil.—**pará grass** piassava; **pará nut** Brazil nut; **pará rubber** that got from *Hevea brasiliensis.*

para-[1] *par'ə,* in composition, beside: faulty: disordered: abnormal: false: a polymer of: a compound related to: closely resembling, or parallel to (as in *adj.* and *n.* **paramed'ic,** *adj.* **paramed'ical** (a person) helping doctors or supplementing medical work; *adj.* and *n.* **paramilitary** (see separate entry)): in organic chem., having substituted atoms or groups attached to two opposite carbon atoms of the benzene ring—commonly represented by *p-.*—**pa'ra-compound.** [Gr. *para,* beside.]

para-[2] *par'ə, pfx.,* parachute, as in *ns* **par'abrake** a parachute used to help brake an aircraft when it has landed; **par'adoctor** a doctor who parachutes to patients; **par'afoil** a form of steerable parachute, consisting of air-filled nylon cells; **par'aglider** a glider with inflatable wings; **par'agliding** the sport of being towed through the air by plane while fitted with a modified type of parachute, then allowed to drift to the ground; **par'amedic(o)** a paradoctor.

parable *par'ə-bl, n.* a similitude: a fable or story of something which might have happened, told to illustrate some doctrine, or to make some duty clear.—*v.t.* to represent by a parable.—*ns.* **parabola** (*pə-rab'ə-lə*) a curve, one of the conic sections, the intersection of a cone and a plane parallel to its side, or the locus of a point equidistant from a fixed point (the *focus*) and a fixed straight line (the *directrix*): its equation with vertex as origin $y^2 = 4ax$: generalised to include any curve whose equation is $y^n = px^m$:—*pl.* **parab'olas; parab'ole** (*-lē*) in rhetoric, a similitude, simile, or metaphor.—*adjs.* **parabol'ic** (*par-ə-bol'ik*), **-al,** of or like a parable or a parabola or a parabole: expressed by a parable: belonging to, or of the form of, a parabola.—*adv.* **parabol'ically.** [Gr. *parabolē,* a placing alongside, comparison, parabola, etc.—*para,* beside, beyond, *ballein,* to throw.]

parablepsis *par-ə-blep'sis, n.* false vision: oversight.—Also **par'ablepsy.**—*adj.* **parablep'tic.** [Gr., looking askant—*para,* beside, beyond, *blepein,* to see.]

parabola, etc. See **parable.**

paracentesis *par-ə-sen-tē'sis, (surg.) n.* tapping. [Gr. *parakentēsis*—*para,* beside, beyond, *kenteein,* to pierce.]

paracetamol *par-ə-sēt'ə-mol, n.* a mild analgesic and antipyretic drug, often used instead of aspirin. [Gr. *para,* beside, beyond, *acetami*de.]

parachronism *par-ak'rən-izm, n.* an error in dating, esp. when anything is represented as later than it really was. [Gr. *para,* beside, beyond, *chronos,* time.]

parachute *par'ə-shōōt, n.* an apparatus like an umbrella for descending safely from a height (*coll.* short form **chute**): any structure serving a like purpose.—*v.i.* to descend by parachute.—*n.* **par'achutist.** [Fr. *parachute*—It *para,* imper. of *parare,* to ward—L. *parāre,* to prepare, and Fr. *chute,* fall.]

paraclete *par'ə-klēt, n.* an advocate or legal helper, or intercessor—applied (with *cap.*) to the Holy Ghost (John xiv. 26). [Gr. *paraklētos—parakaleein,* to call in, also to comfort.]

paracme *par-ak'mē, n.* the stage of decline or senescence after the culmination of development. [Gr. *para,* beside, beyond, *akmē,* a point.]

paracrostic *par-ə-kros'tik, n.* a poem whose initial letters reproduce its first verse. [**para-**[1] and **acrostic.**]

parade *pǝ-rād'*, *n.* show: display: ostentation: an assembling in order for exercise, inspection, etc.: a procession: ground for parade of troops: a public promenade: a parry (*fencing*).—*v.t.* to show off: to thrust upon notice: to lead about and expose to public attention: to traverse in parade: to marshal in military order.—*v.i.* to march up and down as if for show: to pass in military order: to march in procession: to show off.—**parade'-ground**. [Fr.,—Sp. *parada—parar*, to halt—L. *parāre*, *-ātum*, to prepare]

paradigm *par'ǝ-dim*, *n.* an example, exemplar: an example of the inflection of a word (*gram.*): a basic theory, a conceptual framework within which scientific theories are constructed.—*adjs.* **paradigmatic** (*-dig-mat'ik*), **-al**—*adv.* **paradigmat'ically**. [Fr. *paradigme*—Gr. *paradeigma—paradeiknynai*, to exhibit side by side—*para*, beside, beyond, *deiknynai*, to show.]

paradise *par'ǝ-dīs*, *n.* the garden of Eden: heaven: the abode (intermediate or final) of the blessed dead: any place of bliss.—*adjs.* **paradisaic** (*par-ǝ-dis-ā'ik*), **-al**, **paradisal** (*-dī'sǝl*), **paradisean** (*-dis'i-ǝn*), **paradisiac** (*-dis'i-ak*, *-diz'i-ak*), **paradisiacal** (*-dis-i'ǝ-kl*), **paradisial** (*-dis'*, *-diz'*), **paradisian** (*-dis'*, *-diz'*), **paradisic** (*-dis'*, *-diz'*).—**par'adise-fish** a Chinese freshwater fish (*Macropodus*), often kept in aquaria for its beauty of form and colouring.—**bird of paradise** any bird of the family **Paradise'idae**, inhabitants chiefly of New Guinea, close akin to the crows but extremely gorgeous in plumage. [Gr. *paradeisos*, a park—O.Pers. *pairidaēza*, park.]

paradox *par'ǝ-doks*, *n.* that which is contrary to received opinion: that which is apparently absurd but is or may be really true: a self-contradictory statement: paradoxical character.—*adj.* **paradox'al**.—*n.* **par'adoxer**.—*adj.* **paradox'ical**.—*adv.* **paradox'ically**.—*ns.* **par'adoxist; paradoxol'ogy** the utterance or maintaining of paradoxes; **par'adoxy** the quality of being paradoxical. [Gr. *paradoxos*, *-on*, contrary to opinion—*para*, beside, beyond, *doxa*, opinion.]

paradoxure *par-ǝ-dok'sūr*, *n.* a civet-like carnivore of Southern Asia and Malaysia, the palm-cat of India. [Gr. *paradoxos*, paradoxical, and *ourā*, tail.]

paraesthesia, in U.S. **paresthesia**, *par-ēs-thē'si-ǝ*, or *-es-*, *n.* abnormal sensation. [Gr. *para*, beyond, *aisthēsis*, sensation.]

paraffin *par'ǝ-fin*, *n.* originally, paraffin-wax—so named by its discoverer, Reichenbach, from its having little chemical affinity for other bodies: generalised to mean any saturated hydrocarbon of the methane series, gaseous, liquid, or solid, the general formula being C_nH_{2n+2}: paraffin-oil.—Also **par'affine**.—*v.t.* to treat with paraffin.—*adjs.* **paraffin'ic**, **par'affinoid**, **par'affiny**.—**par'affin-oil** any of the mineral burning oils associated with the manufacture of paraffin, mixtures of liquid paraffin and other hydrocarbons; **par'affin-wax'** a white transparent crystalline substance got by distillation of shale, coal, tar, wood, etc., a mixture of solid paraffins.—**liquid paraffin** a liquid form of petrolatum, used as a mild laxative. [L. *parum*, little, *affinis*, having affinity.]

parafoil. See para-².

parage *par'ij*, *n.* high birth or rank: equality among persons of whom one does homage for all, the others holding of him (*feudal law*). [Fr.]

paragenesis *par-ǝ-jen'i-sis*, **paragenesia** *par-ǝ-jin-ē'zi-ǝ*, (*geol.*) *ns.* the development of minerals in such close contact that their formation is affected and they become a joined mass.—*adj.* **paragenet'ic**. [para-¹, genesis.]

paraglider, **paragliding**. See para-².

paragon *par'ǝ-gon*, *-gǝn*, *n.* a model of perfection or supreme excellence. [O.Fr *paragon*—It. *paragone*,

touchstone.]

paragram *par'ǝ-gram*, *n.* a play upon words by change of initial (or other) letter. [Gr. (*skōmmata*) *para gramma*, (jokes) by letter.]

paragraph *par'ǝ-graf*, *n.* a sign (in ancient MSS. a short horizontal line, in the Middle Ages ℂ, now ¶, ℙ) marking off a section of a book, etc a distinct part of a discourse or writing marked by such a sign or now usually by indenting: a short passage, or a collection of sentences, with unity of purpose: a musical passage forming a unit: a short separate item of news or comment in a newspaper.—*v.t.* to form into paragraphs: to write or publish paragraphs about.—*ns.* **par'agrapher**, **par'agraphist** one who writes paragraphs, esp. for newspapers.—*adjs.* **paragraphic** (*-graf'*), **-al**.—*adv.* **paragraph'ically**. [Gr. *paragraphos*, written alongside—*para*, beside, beyond, *graphein*, to write.]

paragraphia *par-ǝ-graf'i-ǝ*, *n.* writing of wrong words and letters, owing to disease or injury of the brain.—*adj.* **paragraphic** (*-graf'ik*). [Gr. *para*, beside, beyond, *graphein*, to write]

Paraguay *par-ǝ-gwī'*, *-gwä'*, *n.* a country and river of South America.—**Paraguay tea** maté.

parakeet, **parrakeet** *par'ǝ-kēt*, *n.* a small long-tailed parrot of various kinds. [Sp. *periquito*, It. *parrocchetto*, or O.Fr *paroquet* (Fr. *perroquet*); the origin and relations of these are not determined.]

paralalia *par-ǝ-lā'*, *-lā'li-ǝ*, *n.* a form of speech disturbance, particularly that in which a different sound or syllable is produced from the one intended. [Gr. *para*, beside, beyond, *lalia*, speech.]

paralanguage *par-ǝ-lang'gwij*, *n* elements of communication other than words, i.e. tone of voice, gesture, facial expression, etc.—*adj.* **paralinguist'ic**.—*n.sing.* **paralinguist'ics** the study of paralanguage. [para-¹, and language, linguistic(s).]

paraldehyde *par-al'di-hīd*, *n.* a polymer, $(C_2H_4O)_3$, of acetaldehyde, used to induce sleep. [para-¹ and aldehyde.]

paraleipsis, **paralipsis** *par-ǝ-līp'sis*, *-lip'*, *n.* a rhet. figure by which one fixes attention on a subject by pretending to neglect it, as 'I will not speak of his generosity', etc —*n.* **paral(e)ipom'enon** a thing left out, added in supplement:—*pl.* **paral(e)ipom'ena**, esp. (in the Septuagint, etc.) the Books of Chronicles. [Gr. *paraleipsis*, *paraleipomenon* (neut. pr. part. pass.)—*paraleipein*, to leave aside.]

paralexia *par-ǝ-lek'si-ǝ*, *n.* a defect in the power of seeing and interpreting written language, with meaningless transposition of words and syllables. [Gr. *para*, beside, beyond, *lexis*, a word.]

paralinguistic(s). See **paralanguage**.

paralipsis, etc. See **paraleipsis**.

parallax *par'ǝ-laks*, *n.* an apparent change in the position of an object caused by change of position in the observer: in astron., the apparent change (measured angularly) in the position of a heavenly body when viewed from different points—when viewed from opposite points on the earth's surface this change is called the *daily* or *diurnal* or *geocentric parallax*; when viewed from opposite points of the earth's orbit, the *annual* or *heliocentric parallax*.—*adjs.* **parallac'tic**, **-al**. [Gr. *parallaxis—para*, beside, beyond, *allassein*, to change—*allos*, another.]

parallel *par'ǝ-lel*, *adj.* extended in the same direction and equidistant in all parts: analogous, corresponding: alongside in time: having a constant interval (major and minor being reckoned alike; *mus.*).—*n.* a parallel line: a line of latitude: an analogue, or like, or equal: an analogy: a tracing or statement of resemblances: parallel arrangement.—*v.t.* to place so as to be parallel: to conform: to represent as parallel: to liken in detail: to find a parallel to: to match: to be or run parallel to.—*v.i.* to be or run parallel:—*pr.p.* **par'alleling;** *pa.t.* and *pa.p.* **par'alleled.**—*v.t.* **par'allelise, -ize** to furnish a parallel to.—*ns.* **par'allelism** the state or fact of being parallel: resemblance in corresponding details: a balanced construction of a verse or sentence, where one part repeats the form or meaning of the other: comparison: development along parallel lines; **par'allelist** one who draws a parallel or comparison.—*adj.* **parallelis'tic.**—*advs.* **par'allelly; par'allelwise.**—**parallel bars** a pair of fixed bars used in gymnastics; **parallel motion** a name given to any linkage by which circular motion may be changed into straight-line motion; **parallel ruler** or **rulers** rulers joined by two pivoted strips, for ruling parallel lines.—**in parallel** of electrical apparatus, so arranged that terminals of like polarity are connected together. [Gr. *parallēlos,* as if *par' allēloin,* beside each other.]

parallelepiped *par-ə-lel-ep'i-ped* (or *-lel'ə-,* or *-ə-pī'*), *n.* a solid figure bounded by six parallelograms, opposite pairs being identical and parallel.—Also improperly **parallelopi'ped.** [Gr *parallēlepipedon—parallēlos, epipedon,* a plane surface—*epi,* on, *pedon,* ground.]

parallelogram *par-ə-lel'ō-gram, n.* a plane four-sided figure whose opposite sides are parallel.—*adjs.* **parallelogrammat'ic, -al, parallelogramm'ic, -al.** —**parallelogram of forces** a figure in which the direction and amount of two component forces are represented by two sides of a parallelogram, those of their resultant by the diagonal. [Gr. *parallēlogrammon —grammē,* a line.]

paralysis *pə-ral'i-sis, n.* palsy, a loss of power of motion, or sensation, in any part of the body: deprivation of power of action.—*v.t.* **paralyse,** in U.S. **paralyze** (*par'ə-līz*) to afflict with paralysis: to deprive of power of action.—*n.* **par'alyser,** in U.S. **-z-.**—*adj.* **paralytic** (*par-ə-lit'ik*) of or pertaining to paralysis: afflicted with or inclined to paralysis. helplessly drunk (*slang*).—*n.* one who is affected with paralysis. [Gr. *paralysis,* secret undoing, paralysis—*lyein,* to loosen.]

paramatta, parramatta *par-ə-mat'ə, n.* a fabric like merino made of worsted and cotton. [App. from *Parramatta* in New South Wales.]

paramedic(al). See **para-**[1], **para-**[2].

parameter *pə-ram'i-tər, n.* a line or quantity which serves to determine a point, line, figure, or quantity in a class of such things (*math.*): a constant quantity in the equation of a curve: in conic sections, a third proportional to any diameter and its conjugate diameter: the latus rectum of a parabola: the intercept upon an axis of a crystal face chosen for purpose of reference (the *parametral plane*): a quantity to which an arbitrary value may be given as a convenience in expressing performance or for use in calculations (*elect.*): variable: a variable which is given a series of arbitrary values in order that a family of curves of two other related variables may be drawn: any constant in learning or growth curves that differs with differing conditions (*psych.*): a boundary or limit (*lit.* and *fig.*). —*adjs.* **param'etral, parametric** (*par-ə-met'rik*), **-al.** [Gr. *para,* beside, beyond, *metron,* measure.]

paramilitary *par-ə-mil'i-tər-i, adj.* on military lines and intended to supplement the strictly military: organised as a military force.—Also *n.* [**para-**[1] and **military** (see **militant**).]

paramnesia *par-am-nē'zh(y)ə, n.* a memory disorder in which words are remembered but not their proper meaning: the condition of believing that one remembers events and circumstances which have not previously occurred. [Gr. *para,* beside, beyond, and the root of *mimnēskein,* to remind.]

paramo *pà'rä-mō, n.* a bare wind-swept elevated plain in South America:—*pl.* **par'amos.** [Sp. *páramo.*]

paramount *par'ə-mownt, adj.* superior to all others: supreme.—*n.* a paramount chief: a superior.—*n.* **par'amount(t)cy.**—*adv.* **par'amountly.**—**paramount chief** a supreme chief. [O.Fr. *paramont, par* (L. *per*) *à mont* (L. *ad montem*); see **amount.**]

paramour *par'ə-mōōr, n.* a lover of either sex, formerly in an innocent, now usually in the illicit, sense. [Fr. *par amour,* by or with love.]

paranephros *par-ə-nef'ros, n.* the suprarenal gland, near the kidney.—*adj.* **paraneph'ric.** [Gr *para,* beside, beyond, *nephros,* kidney.]

parang *par'ang, n.* a heavy Malay knife. [Malay.]

paranoia *par-ə-noi'ə, n.* a form of mental disorder characterised by fixed delusions, esp. of grandeur, pride, persecution: intense (esp. irrational) fear or suspicion.—*adj.* **paranoi'ac** of paranoia.—*n.* a victim of paranoia.—Also **paranoe'ic, paranoic** (*-no'ik*).— *adjs.* **par'anoid, paranoid'al** resembling paranoia. [Gr. *paranoiā—para,* beside, beyond, *noos,* mind.]

paranormal *par-ə-nör'məl, adj.* abnormal, esp. psychologically: not susceptible to normal explanations. [**para-**[1] and **normal.**]

paranthelion *par-an-thē'li-on, n.* a diffuse whitish image of the sun, having the same altitude, at an angular distance of 90° to 140°:—*pl.* **paranthe'lia.** [Gr. *para,* beside, beyond, *anti,* against, *hēlios,* the sun.]

parapet *par'ə-pit, n.* a bank or wall to protect soldiers from the fire of an enemy in front: a low wall along the side of a bridge, edge of a roof, etc.—*adj.* **par'apeted** having a parapet. [It. *parapetto,* from pfx. *para-* (see **parachute**) and It. *petto*—L. *pectus,* the breast.]

paraph *par'af, n.* a mark or flourish under one's signature.—*v.t.* to append a paraph to, to sign with initials. [Fr. *paraphe;* cf. **paragraph.**]

paraphasia *par-ə-fā'zh(y)ə, n.* a form of aphasia in which one word is substituted for another.—*adj.* **paraphasic** (*-fā'zik, -sik*). [**para-**[1] and **aphasia.**]

paraphernalia *par-ə-fər-nāl'yə, -i-ə, n.pl.* formerly, property other than dower that remained under a married woman's own control, esp. articles of jewellery, dress, personal belongings: (the following all now usu. *n.sing.*) ornaments of dress of any kind: trappings: equipment: miscellaneous accessories. [Late L. *paraphernālia—parapherna*—Gr., from *para,* beside, beyond, *phernē,* a dowry—*pherein,* to bring.]

paraphonia *par-ə-fō'ni-ə, n.* a morbid change of voice: an alteration of the voice, as at puberty.—*adj.* **paraphonic** (*-fon'ik*). [Gr. *para,* beside, beyond, *phōnē,* voice.]

paraphrase *par'ə-frāz, n.* expression of the same thing in other words: an exercise in such expression: a verse rendering of a biblical passage for church singing, esp. in the Church of Scotland.—*v.t.* to express in other words.—*v.i.* to make a paraphrase.—*ns.* **par'aphraser, par'aphrast** (*-frast*) one who paraphrases. —*adjs.* **paraphrast'ic, -al.**—*adv.* **paraphrast'ically.** [Gr *paraphrasis—para,* beside, beyond, *phrasis,* a speaking—*phrazein,* to speak.]

paraplegia *par-ə-plē'j(y)ə, n.* paralysis of the lower part of the body.—*adjs.* **paraplectic** (*-plekt'ik*), **paraplegic** (*-plēj'* or *-plej'*; also *n.*). [Ionic Gr. *paraplēgiē,* a stroke on the side—*para,* beside, beyond, *plēgē,* a blow.]

parapsychology *par-ə-sī-kol'ə-ji, n.* psychical research: the study of phenomena such as telepathy and clairvoyance which seem to suggest that the mind can gain knowledge by means other than the normal perceptual processes.—*n.* **parapsychologist.** [**para-**[1] and **psychism.**]

paraquat *par'ə-kwat*, *n.* a weed-killer very poisonous to human beings [**para-**[1] and *quat*ernary, part of its formula.]

parasailing *par'ə-sā-lıng*, *n.* a sport similar to para-gliding, the participant wearing water-skis and a modified type of parachute, and being towed into the air by motor-boat. [**para-**[2], **sailing**.]

parascending *par'ə-sen-dıng*, *n.* a sport similar to para-gliding, the participant being towed into the wind behind a motor vehicle. [**para-**[2], **ascending**.]

paraselene *par-ə-se-lē'nē*, *n.* a mock moon:—*pl.* **para-selē'nae** (*-nē*). [Gr. *para*, beside, beyond, *selēnē*, moon.]

parasite *par'ə-sīt*, *n.* a hanger-on or sycophant who frequents another's table: one who lives at the expense of society or of others and contributes nothing. an organism that lives in or on another organism and derives subsistence from it without rendering it any service in return: in literary but not scientific use extended to an epiphyte.—*adjs* **para-sitic** (*-sıt'ık*), **-al** of, of the nature of, caused by, or like, a parasite.—*adv.* **parasit'ically.**—*ns* **para-sit'icalness; parasiticide** (*-sıt'i-sīd*), that which destroys parasites —*v t.* **par'asitise, -ize** to be a parasite on (another organism): to infect or infest with para-sites.—*ns* **par'asitism** (*-sīt-ızm*) the act or practice of being a parasite, **parasitol'ogist; parasitol'ogy.** [Gr *parasītos—para*, beside, and *sītos*, corn, bread, food]

parasol *par'ə-sol*, or *-sol'*, *n.* a sunshade [Fr.,—It. *parasole—para*, imper. of *parare*, to ward—L *parāre*, to prepare, and *sole*—L. *sōl*, *sōlis*, the sun.]

parasuicide *par-ə-sū'ı-sīd*, *-sōō'*, *n.* a deliberate harmful act against one's own person (such as taking an overdose of drugs) which appears to be an attempt at suicide but which was probably not intended to be successful. a person who performs such an act [**para-**[1], **suicide**.]

parasympathetic *par-ə-sım-pə-thet'ık.* See **sympathy.**

parasynthesis *par-ə-sın'thı-sıs*, *n.* derivation of words from compounds, as *come-at-able*, where *come* and *at* are first compounded and then the derivative suffix *-able* added.—*adj* **parasynthetic** (*-thet'ık*).—*n* **parasyn'theton** a word so formed:—*pl.* **parasyn'-theta.** [Gr]

parataxis *par-ə-tak'sıs*, (*gram.*) *n.* the arrangement of clauses or propositions without connectives —*adjs.* **paratac'tic, -al.**—*adv.* **paratac'tically.** [Gr ,— *para*, beside, beyond, *taxis*, arrangement]

paratha *pə-ra'tə*, *-ta*, *n.* a thin cake of flour, water and ghee, originating in India [Hindi.]

parathyroid *par-ə-thī'roıd*, *adj.* beside the thyroid.— *n* any of a number of small ductless glands apparently concerned with calcium metabolism. [**para-**[1] and **thyroid.**]

paratroops *par'ə-trōōps*, *n pl.* troops carried by air, to be dropped by parachute.—*n.* **par'atrooper.** [**para-**[2] and **troop.**]

paratyphoid *par-ə-tī'foıd*, *n.* a disease (of various types) resembling typhoid. —Also *adj* [**para-**[1].]

paravane *par'ə-vān*, *n.* a fish-shaped device, with fins or vanes, towed from the bow, for deflecting mines along a wire and severing their moorings—sometimes called an 'otter' an explosive device of similar design for attacking submerged submarines [**para-**[1] and **vane.**]

Parazoa *par-ə-zō'ə*, *n pl* a division of the animal kingdom, the sponges, co-ordinate with *Protozoa* and *Metazoa* (also without *cap*).—*n.* and *adj* **parazō'an.** —*n* **parazō'on** any member of the group Parazoa — *pl* **-zō'a.** [Gr *zōa*, beside, beyond, *zōıon*, animal]

parboil *par'boıl*, *v t.* orig., to boil thoroughly: (now, by confusion) to boil slightly [O Fr *parboıllır—*

L.L. *perbullīre*, to boil thoroughly, influenced by confusion with **part.**]

parbuckle *par'buk-l*, *n* a purchase made by making fast a rope in the middle and passing the ends under and then over a heavy object to be rolled up or down: a sling made by passing both ends of a rope through its bight —*v.t* to hoist or lower by a parbuckle [Earlier *parbunkel*, *parbuncle*; origin unknown.]

parcel *par'sl*, *n* a little part: a portion: a quantity: a group: a set: a pack (depreciatively): a lot: a sum of money lost or won (*coll.*): a package, esp. one wrapped in paper and tied with string a continuous stretch of land —*v.t* to divide into portions (esp. with *out*). to make up into parcels or a parcel (esp. with *up*): to cover with tarred canvas (*naut.*):—*pr.p.* **par'celling;** *pa.t.* and *pa.p.* **par'celled.**—*adv.* **par'cel-wise** by parcels, piecemeal.—**parcel post** (also, formerly, **parcels post**) a Post Office service forwarding and delivering parcels. [Fr. *parcelle* (It. *particella*)—L. *particula*, dim. of *pars*, *partis*, a part.]

parcener *par'sən-ər*, *n.* a co-heir.—*n.* **par'cenary** (*-ə-ri*), co-heirship. [A.Fr. *parcener*—L.L. *partōnārıus—pars*, part.]

parch *parch*, *v.t* to make hot and very dry: to roast slightly: to scorch.—*v ı.* to be scorched: to become very dry.—*adj.* **parched.**—*adv* **parch'edly.**—*n.* **parch'edness** (or *parchı'*).

parchment *parch'mənt*, *n* the skin of a sheep, goat, or other animal prepared for writing on, etc.: a piece of this material: a manuscript written on it: a parch-ment-like membrane or skin.—*adj* of parchment.— *v.t.* **parch'mentise, -ize** to make like parchment, esp by treating with sulphuric acid —*adj* **parch'menty** like parchment.—**parchment paper** or **vegetable parchment** unsized paper made tough and transpar-ent by dipping in sulphuric acid [Fr *parchemin*— L. *pergamēna* (*charta*), Pergamene (paper)—from Gr. *Pergamos*, Bergama, in Asia Minor]

pard[1] *pard*, *n.* the leopard. [L. *pardus*—Gr *pardos*; prob. of Eastern origin.]

pard[2] *pard*, **pard'ner** *-nər*, (*U S.*) *ns* slang forms of **partner.**

pardon *par'dn*, *v.t.* to forgive: to allow to go unpun-ished: to excuse: to tolerate: to grant in remission, refrain from exacting or taking: to grant remission of sentence to (even if the condemned has been found innocent).—*v ı.* to forgive: to grant pardon.—*n.* forgiveness, either of an offender or of his offence: remission of a penalty or punishment: forbearance' a warrant declaring a pardon· a papal indulgence.— *adj.* **par'donable** that may be pardoned: excusable.— *n.* **par'donableness.**—*adv.* **par'donably.**—*n* **par'-doner** one who pardons: a licensed seller of papal indulgences (*hıst.*).—*n.* and *adj.* **par'doning.**—**I beg your pardon, pardon?** what did you say?; **pardon me** excuse me—used in apology and to soften a con-tradiction. [Fr. *pardonner*—L.L *perdōnāre*—L *per*, through, away, *dōnāre*, to give.]

pare *pār*, *v t.* to cut or shave off the outer surface or edge of: to trim: to remove by slicing or shaving: to diminish by littles.—*ns.* **pār'er; pār'ing.** [Fr *parer* —L *parāre*, to prepare.]

paregoric *paı-ı-gor'ık*, *adj.* soothing, lessening pain.— *n.* a medicine that soothes pain an alcoholic solution of opium, benzoic acid, camphor, and oil of anise [Gr *parēgorıkos—parēgoreein*, to exhort, comfort]

pareira *pə-rā'rə*, *n* orig , a tropical climbing plant (*Cis-sampelos pareıra*) or its root (now called **false pareira**). a South American plant of the same family (*Chondro-dendron tomentosum*, **pareira brava** *bra'və*, i.e wild): a tonic diuretic drug derived from its root.—**white par-eira** (*Abuta rufescens*) another South American plant of the same family [Port *parreıra*, wallclimber]

parella pə-rel'ə, n. a crustaceous lichen (*Lecanora parella*) yielding archil: extended to others of like use.— Also **parelle'**. [Fr. *parelle*.]

parencephalon par-en-sef'ə-lon, n. a cerebral hemisphere. [Gr. *para*, beside, beyond, *enkephalon*, brain.]

parent pā'rənt, n. one who begets or brings forth: a father or a mother: one who, or that which, produces: that from which anything springs or branches: an author: a cause.—*v.t.* and *v.t.* to be, act as, a parent (to).—n. **pā'rentage** descent from parents: extraction: rank or character derived from one's parents or ancestors: the relation of parents to their children: the state or fact of being a parent.—*adj.* **parental** (pə-rent'əl).—*adv.* **parent'ally.**—*ns.* **pā'renthood** the state of being a parent: the duty or feelings of a parent; **pā'renting.**—*adj.* **pā'rentless** without a parent. [Fr. *parent*, kinsman—L. *parēns, -entis*, old pr.p. of *parēre*, to bring forth.]

parenteral par-en'tər,əl, adj. not intestinal: not by way of the alimentary tract (said of the administration of a drug).—*adv.* **paren'terally.** [Gr. *para*, beside, and **enteral.**]

parenthesis pə-ren'thi-sis, n. a word or passage of comment or explanation inserted in a sentence which is grammatically complete without it: a figure of speech consisting of the use of such insertion: a digression: an interval, space, interlude: (usu. in *pl.*) a round bracket () used to mark off a parenthesis:—*pl.* **paren'theses** (-sēz).—*v.i.* **parenth'esise, -ize.**—*adjs.* **parenthetic** (par-ən-thet'ik), **-al,** of the nature of a parenthesis: using or over-using parenthesis.—*adv.* **parenthet'ically.** [Gr.,—*para*, beside, beyond, *en*, in, *thesis*, a placing.]

paresis par'i-sis, n. a diminished activity of function—a partial form of paralysis.—*adj* **paretic** (-et'ik). [Gr.,—*parienai*, to relax.]

paresthesia. See **paraesthesia.**

par excellence pàr ek'se-lās, ek'sə-ləns, as an example of excellence: superior to all others of the same sort. [Fr., lit. by excellence.]

parfait pär-fe', n. a kind of frozen dessert containing whipped cream and eggs. [Fr., lit. perfect.]

parget pär'jit, v.t. to plaster over: to cover with ornamental plaster-work: to decorate the surface of: to bedaub:—*pr.p.* **par'geting;** *pa.t.* and *pa.p.* **par'geted.** —n. plaster spread over a surface: cow-dung plaster for chimney flues: ornamental work in plaster: surface decoration.—*ns.* **par'geter; par'geting.** [App. O.Fr. *parjeter*, to throw all over.]

parhelion par-hēl'i-ən, n. a mock sun:—*pl.* **parhē'lia.** —*adjs.* **parhelic** (-hē'lik, -he'lik), **parheliacal** (-hē-lī'ə-kl). [Irregularly—Gr. *parēlion—para*, beside, beyond, *hēlios*, sun.]

pariah pə-rī'ə, par'i-ə, pär', n. a member of a caste in Southern India lower than the four Brahminical castes: one of low or no caste: a social outcast: an ownerless cur of Eastern towns (in full **pariah dog**), a pye-dog. [Tamil *paraiyar*.]

parial. Same as **pairial;** see under **pair.**

parietal pə-rī'i-tl, adj. of a wall or walls: of, attached to, or having connection with, the side, or the inside of the wall, of a cavity, esp. a plant ovary: pertaining to or near the parietal bone.—n. a bone (**parietal bone**), forming with its fellow part of the sides and top of the skull, between the frontal and the occipital. [L. *parietālis—pariēs, parietis*, a wall.]

pari-mutuel par-ē-mū-tū-el, n. a betting-machine which automatically pools stakes and distributes winnings—a totalisator. [Fr., lit. mutual bet.]

pari passu pä'rī pas'ū, pa'rē pas'ōō, (L.) with equal pace: together.

paripinnate par-i-pin'it, -āt, (bot.) adj. pinnate without a terminal leaflet. [L. *pār*, equal.]

Paris par'is, n. the capital of France.—*adj.* of, originating in, Paris.—*adj.* **Parisian** (pə-rī'zyən, -zhyən, -zhən) of or pertaining to Paris.—n. a native or resident of Paris:—*Fr. fem.* **Parisienne** (pa-rē-zē-en, -zyen').—**Paris green** copper arsenite and acetate, a pigment and insecticide. [L. *Parisiī*, the Gallic tribe of the Paris district.]

parish par'ish, n. a district having its own church and minister or priest of the Established Church: a district assigned by a church to a minister or priest: a division of county for administrative and local government purposes (not now in Scotland).—*adj.* belonging or relating to a parish: employed or supported by the parish: for the use of the parish.—n. **parishioner** (pə-rish'ə-nər) one who belongs to or is connected with a parish: a member of a parish church.—**parish church** the church of the establishment for a parish; **parish clerk** the clerk or recording officer of a parish: the one who leads the responses in the service of the Church of England; **parish council** a body elected to manage the affairs of a parish; **parish councillor; parish minister, priest** a minister or priest who has charge of a parish; **parish pump** the symbol of petty local interests; **parish register** a book in which the baptisms, marriages, and burials in a parish are recorded.—**on the parish** in receipt of poor-relief. [A.Fr. *paroche* (Fr. *paroisse*)—L. *parochia*—Gr. *paroikiā*, an ecclesiastical district—*para*, beside, *oikos*, a dwelling; altered by confusion with Gr. *parochos*, a purveyor.]

parison par'i-sən, n. a lump of glass before it is moulded into its final shape. [Fr. *paraison—parer*, to prepare,—L. *parāre*.]

parisyllabic par-i-si-lab'ik, adj. having the same number of syllables. [L. *pār*, equal.]

parity par'i-ti, n. equality in status: parallelism: equivalence: a standard equivalence in currency: of numbers, the property of being odd or even (*math.*). [Fr. *paritē*—L. *paritās—pār*, equal.]

park pärk, n. an enclosed piece of land for beasts of the chase: a tract of land surrounding a mansion, kept as a pleasure-ground: hence often part of the name of a house, street, or district: a piece of ground for public recreation: a football, etc. pitch (*coll.*): a piece of country kept in its natural condition as a nature-reserve or the like: a place occupied by artillery, wagons, etc. (*mil.*): a piece of ground where motor-cars or other vehicles may be left untended: an enclosed basin for oyster-culture.—*v.t.* to enclose in a park: to make a park of: to bring together in a body, as artillery: to place and leave in a parking-place: to deposit and leave (*coll.*).—*v.i.* to use a car park or parking-place.—*ns.* **park'er** one who parks a vehicle; **park'ing** the action of the verb park.—**park'ing lot** (*U.S.*) a car park; **parking meter** a coin-operated meter that charges for motor-car parking-time; **park'ing-place** a place where one may temporarily stop and leave a vehicle; **park'ing-ticket** a notice of a fine, or summons to appear in court, for a parking offence; **park'-keeper** a park-officer; **park'land, -s** parklike grassland dotted with trees; **park'-off'icer** the keeper of a park; **park'way** a broad road adorned with turf and trees, often connecting the parks of a town. [O.Fr. *parc*, of Gmc. origin; cf. O.E. *pearruc, pearroc*.]

parka pärk'ə, n. a fur shirt or coat with a hood, or a similar garment made of a wind-proof material.—Also **parkee, parki** (pärk'ē). [Aleutian Eskimo word.]

parkin pär'kin, **perkin** pûr'kin, (*Northern*) ns. a biscuit or gingerbread of oatmeal and treacle.

Parkinson's disease pär'kin-sənz diz-ēz', shaking palsy, a disease characterised by rigidity of muscles, tremor of hands, etc.; studied by James *Parkinson* (1755-1824).—Also **Par'kinsonism.**

Parkinson's Law *par'kin-sənz lo,* (*facet.*) any one of the laws propounded by C. Northcote *Parkinson,* esp. the law that in officialdom work expands so as to fill the time available for its completion.

parkleaves *pàrk'lèvz, n.* tutsan [App. **park, leaf.**]

parky *pàr'ki,* (*coll.*) *adj.* chilly.

parlance. See under **parle.**

parlando *pàr-làn'dō,* (*mus.*) *adj.* and *adv.* in declamatory style: recitative. [It., speaking; cf **parle.**]

parle *pärl,* (*arch.*) *v.i.* to parley —*n.* **par'lance** diction, phraseology, jargon, mode of speech.—*v.t.* **par'ley** to speak with another: to confer: to treat with an enemy. —*n.* talk: a conference with an enemy: a conference. [Fr. *parler,* to speak—L.L. *parlāre—parabolāre—* Gr. *parabolē,* a parable, word.]

parliament *par'lə-mənt, n.* a legislative body.—*n.* **parliamenta'rian** an adherent of Parliament in opposition to Charles I: one skilled in the ways of parliament.—*adj.* on the side of parliament.—*adv.* **parliamentarily** (*-ment'ər-i-li*).—**parliament'arism** the principles of parliamentary government: the parliamentary system.—*adj.* **parliament'ary** pertaining to parliament: enacted, enjoined, or done by parliament: according to the rules and practices of legislative bodies: (of language) civil, decorous: for Parliament against the Royalists.—**parliamentary agent** a person employed by private persons or societies for drafting bills or managing business to be brought before parliament; **par'liament-house** a building where parliament sits or has sat.—**act of parliament** a statute that has passed through both the House of Commons and the House of Lords, and received the formal royal assent; **Parliamentary Commissioner for Administration** see **Ombudsman.** [Fr. *parlement— parler,* to speak.]

parlour *par'lər, n.* a room where conversation is allowed in a monastery or nunnery: a private room for conversation or conference in a public building, office, etc.: a more or less private room in an inn or tavern: a family sitting-room or living-room.—*adj.* used in or suitable for a parlour.—**parlour game** an (esp. informal) indoor game; **par'lour-maid** a maidservant who waits at table; **parlour tricks** minor social accomplishments: performances intended to impress. —**milking parlour** a special room or building in which cows are milked. [A.Fr. *parlur* (Fr. *parloir)—parler,* to speak.]

parlous *par'ləs, adj.* perilous.—*adv.* (*arch* and *facet.*) extremely. [A form of **perilous.**]

Parmesan *par-mi-zan',* or *par', adj.* pertaining to *Parma* in N. Italy.—*n.* Parmesan cheese, a hard dry cheese made from skimmed milk mixed with rennet and saffron.—**Parma violet** Neapolitan violet.

Parnassus *pàr-nas'əs, n.* a mountain in Greece, sacred to Apollo and the Muses: a collection of poems.— *adj.* **Parnass'ian** of Parnassus: of the Muses: of a school of French poetry supposed to believe in art for art's sake (from the collections published as *Le Parnasse contemporain,* 1866-76).—*n.* a member of the Parnassian school.

paroccipital *par-ok-sip'i-tl, adj.* near the occiput [**para-¹** and **occiput.**]

parochial *pə-rō'ki-əl, adj.* of or relating to a parish: restricted or confined within narrow limits—of sentiments, tastes, etc.—*v.t.* **parō'chialise, -ize** to make parochial: to form into parishes.—*v.t.* to do parish work.—*ns.* **parō'chialism** a system of local government which makes the parish the unit: provincialism, narrowness of view; **parōchiality** (*-al'*).—*adv* **parō'chially.** [L. *parochiālis—parochia;* see **parish.**]

parody *par'ə-di, n.* a burlesque or satirical imitation.— *v.t.* to make a parody of:—*pr.p.* **par'odying;** *pa.t.* and *pa.p.* **par'odied.**—*adjs.* **parod'ic(al).**—*n.* **par'odist.**— *adj.* **parodist'ic.** [Gr. *parōidià—para,* beside, *ōidē,* an ode.]

parol. See **parole.**

parole *pə-rōl', n.* word of mouth: word of honour (esp. by a prisoner of war, to fulfil certain conditions; *mil.*): the condition of having given one's word of honour, or privilege of having it accepted: conditional release of a prisoner: officers' daily password in a camp or garrison: language as manifested in the speech of individuals, as opposed to *langue* (*linguistics*).—*adj.* pertaining to parole: (usu. **parol,** usu. *par'*) given by word of mouth—opp. to *documentary,* as *parol* evidence.—*v.t.* **parole'** to put on parole: to release on parole.—*v.i.* to give parole. [Fr. *parole,* word—L. *parabola,* a parable, saying—Gr.; see **parable.**]

paronomasia *par-on-o-mā'sya, -zya, -zh(y)ə, n.* a play upon words—also **paronom'asy** (*-ə-si, -ə-zi*).—*adjs.* **paronomastic** (*-mas'tik*), **-al.**—*n.* **paronym** (*par'o-nim*) a word from the same root, or having the same sound, as another.—*adj.* **paron'ymous.**—*n.* **paron'ymy.** [Gr. *para,* beside, *onoma, onyma,* name.]

paronychia *par-o-nik'i-ə, n.* a whitlow.—*adj.* **paronych'ial.** [Gr. *para,* beside *onyx, onychos,* nail.]

parotid *pə-rot'id, -rōt', adj* near the ear.—*n.* the parotid gland, a salivary gland in front of the ear. [Gr. *parōtis, -idos—para,* beside, *ous, ōtus,* ear.]

parousia *pə-rōō'zi-ə,* or *-row',* (*theol.*) *n.* the second coming of Christ [Gr. *parousià,* presence, arrival.]

paroxysm *par'oks-izm, n.* a fit of acute pain: a fit of passion, laughter, coughing, etc.: any sudden violent action.—*adj.* **paroxys'mal.** [Gr. *paroxysmos— para,* beyond, *oxys,* sharp.]

paroxytone *par-ok'si-tōn, adj.* having the acute accent on the last syllable but one.—*n.* a word so accented. [Gr. *paroxytonos—para,* beside, *oxys,* acute, *tonos,* tone.]

parpen *pär'pən, n.* a stone passing through a wall from face to face: a wall of such stones: a partition: a bridge parapet. [O.Fr. *parpain.*]

parquet *pär'kā, -kit, pär-kā', -ket', n.* a floor-covering of wooden blocks fitted in a pattern.—*adj.* of parquetry.—*v.t.* to cover or floor with parquetry:—*pa.p.* **par'queted, parquett'ed.**—*n.* **par'quetry** (*-ki-tri*) flooring in parquet. [Fr. *parquet,* dim. of *parc,* an enclosure.]

parr *pär, n* a young salmon before it becomes a smolt: the young of several other kinds of fish.

parrakeet. See **parakeet.**

parramatta. See **paramatta.**

parricide *par'i-sīd, n.* the murder of a parent or near relative, or the murder of anyone to whom reverence is considered to be due: one who commits such a crime.—*adj.* **parricid'al.** [Fr.,—L. *parricidium, pāricidium* (the offence), *parricida, pāricida* (the offender)—*caedēre,* to slay; the connection with *pater,* father, is apparently fanciful.]

parrot *par'ət, n.* one of a family of tropical and subtropical birds with brilliant plumage, hooked bill, and zygodactyl feet, good imitators of human speech: an uncritical repeater of the words of others.—*v.t.* to repeat by rote: to teach to repeat by rote —*v.i.* to talk like a parrot (also *v.t.* with *it*):—*pa.p.* **parr'oted.**— *ns.* **parr'oter; parr'otry** unintelligent imitation.— *adj.* **parr'oty** like a parrot or parrot-coal.—**parr'ot-cry'** a catch-phrase senselessly repeated from mouth to mouth.—*adv.* **parr'ot-fashion** by rote.—**parr'ot-fish** a name applied to various fishes, esp. of the wrasse family and the kindred Scaridae, from their colours or their powerful jaws [Possibly Fr. *Perrot,* dim. of *Pierre,* Peter.]

fàte, fàr, mè; hûr (her); *mine; mōte; for, mûte; mōōn; fōōt; dhen* (then); *el'ə-mənt* (element)

parry *par'i*, *v.t.* to ward or keep off: to turn aside, block or evade: to avert:—*pr.p.* **parr'ying;** *pa.t.* and *pa.p.* **parr'ied.**—*n.* a turning aside of a blow or a thrust or of an attack of any kind, e.g. an argument or a jibe. [Perh. from Fr. *parez*, imper. of *parer*—L. *parāre*, to prepare, in L.L. to keep off.]

parse *pärz*, also *pärs*, (*gram.*) *v.t.* to describe (a word) fully from point of view of classification, inflexion, and syntax: to analyse (a sentence).—*ns.* **pars'er; pars'ing.** [L. *pars* (*ōrātiōnis*), a part (of speech).]

parsec *pär'sek* or *pär-sek'*, *n.* the distance (about 19 billion miles) at which half the major axis of the earth's orbit subtends an angle of one second, a unit for measurement of distances of stars. [**par**allax, **sec**ond.]

Parsee, Parsi *pär'sē*, or *-sē'*, *n.* a descendant of the Zoroastrians who emigrated from Persia to India in the 8th century.—*n.* **Par'seeism, Par'sism** (or *-sē'*), **Par'sism** their religion. [Pers. *Pārsī*—*Pārs*, Persia.]

parsimony *pär'si-mən-i*, *n.* sparingness in the spending of money: praiseworthy economy in use of means to an end: avoidance of excess: frugality: niggardliness.—*adj.* **parsimonious** (*-mō'ni-əs*).—*adv.* **parsimō'niously.**—*n.* **parsimō'niousness.** [L. *parsimōnia*—*parcĕre*, *parsus*, to spare.]

parsley *pärs'li*, *n.* a bright green umbelliferous herb (*Carum petroselinum*) with finely divided, strongly scented leaves, used in cookery.—**parsley fern** a fern (*Cryptogramma crispa*) with bright green crisped leaves not unlike parsley. [O.E. *petersilie*, modified by Fr. *persil*, both—L. *petroselīnum*—Gr. *petroselīnon*—*petros*, a rock, *selinon*, parsley.]

parsnip *pärs'nip*, *n.* an umbelliferous plant or its edible carrot-like root. [L. *pastināca*—*pastinum*, a dibble; prob. affected by neep.]

parson *pär'sn*, *n.* the priest or incumbent of a parish: a rector: any minister of religion: one who is licensed to preach.—*ns.* **par'sonage** the residence appropriated to a parson.—*adjs.* **parsonic** (*-son'ik*), **-al.**—**par'son-bird** a New Zealand honey-bird of glossy blue-black plumage with tufts of white at the neck, the tui; **parson's nose** the pope's nose (q.v.). [O.Fr. *persone*—L. *persōna*, a person, prob. in legal sense, or a mouthpiece.]

part *pärt*, *n.* a portion: that which along with others makes up, has made up, or may at some time make up, a whole: a constituent: a component: a member or organ: an equal quantity: share: region: direction, hand, or side: participation: concern: interest: a rôle or duty: a side or party: a character taken by an actor in a play: the words and actions of a character in a play or in real life: a voice or instrument in concerted music: that which is performed by such a voice or instrument: a copy of the music for it: a constituent melody or succession of notes or harmony: a section of a work in literature (see also **partwork** below), or in music: a separately published portion or number (see also **partwork** below): an inflected form of a verb: (in *pl.*) intellectual qualities, talents, or conduct.—*adj.* in part: partial.—*adv.* in part: partly.—*v.t.* to divide: to separate: to break: to set in different directions: to distribute: to share.—*v.i.* to become divided or separated: to separate: to go different ways: to depart: to come or burst apart: to relinquish (with *with*).—*adjs.* **part'ed** divided: separated: sundered: departed: assigned a part: deeply cleft, as a leaf (*bot.*); **part'ible** that may be parted: separable.—*ns.* **partibil'ity; part'ing** the action of the verb to part: a place of separation or division: a dividing line: a line of skin showing between sections of hair brushed in opposite directions on the head: leave-taking.—*adj.* separating: dividing: departing: leave-taking: of or at leave-taking.—*adv.* **part'ly** in part: in some degree.

—**part-exchange'** a transaction in which an article is handed over as part of the payment for another article.—Also *adj.* and *adv.*—**part'-own'er** a joint owner; **part'-pay'ment** payment in part; **part'-singing; part'-song** a melody with parts in harmony, usu. unaccompanied.—*adj.* **part'-time** for part of working time only.—Also *adv.*—**part'-tim'er; part'-work** one of a series of publications (esp. magazines) issued at regular intervals, eventually forming a complete course or book.—**for my part** as far as concerns me; **for the most part** commonly; **in bad,** or **ill, part** unfavourably; **in good part** favourably: without taking offence; **in great part** to a great extent; **in part** partly: so far as part is concerned: not wholly but to some extent; **on the part of** so far as concerns: as done or performed by: in the actions of: on the side of; **part and parcel** essentially a part; **part company** to separate; **parting of the ways** a point at which a fateful decision must be made; **part of speech** one of the various classes of words; **take part in** to share or to assist in; **take part with** to take the side of; **take someone's part** to support, side with, someone (in an argument, etc.). [O.E. and Fr. *part*—L. *pars*, *partis*.]

partake *pär-*, *pər-tāk'*, *v.i.* to take or have a part or share (usu. with *of* or *in*): to take some, esp. of food or drink: to have something of the nature or properties (of).—*v.t.* to have a part in: to share: to have a share in the knowledge (of).—*pr.p.* **parta'king;** *pa.t.* **partook'**; *pa.p.* **parta'ken.**—*ns.* **parta'ker; parta'king.** [Back-formation from **partaker**—**part**, **taker**.]

parterre *pär-ter'*, *n.* an arrangement of flower-beds: the pit of a theatre, esp. the part under the galleries. [Fr.,—L. *per*, along, *terra*, the ground.]

parthenogenesis *pär-thi-nō-jen'i-sis*, *n.* reproduction by means of an unfertilised ovum.—*adj.* **parthenogenetic** (*-ji-net'ik*). [Gr. *parthenos*, a virgin, *genesis*, production.]

Parthian *pär'thi-ən*, *adj.* of Parthia.—*n.* a native of Parthia.—**a Parthian shot** a parting shot, from the Parthian habit of turning round in the saddle to discharge an arrow at a pursuer.

parti *par-tē*, (Fr.) *n.* a group of people: a decision: a marriageable person considered as a match or catch. —**parti pris** (*prē*) bias, preconceived opinion.

partial *pär'shl*, *adj.* relating to a part only: not total or entire: inclined to favour one person or party: having a preference or fondness (with *to*): component: subordinate (*bot.*).—*n.* a partial tone, one of the single-frequency tones which go together to form a sound actually heard.—*ns.* **par'tialism; par'tialist** one who is biased: one who sees or knows only part; **partiality** (*-shi-al'i-ti*).—*adv.* **par'tially.** [Fr.,—L.L. *partiālis*—L. *pars*, a part.]

participate *pär-tis'i-pāt*, *v.i.* to have a share, or take part (in): to have some of the qualities (of).—*adj.* **partic'ipant** participating: sharing.—*n.* a partaker.—*adj.* **partic'ipating** of insurance, entitling policyholders to a share of the company's additional profits.—*n.* **participa'tion** the act of participating: (as in the phrase **worker participation**) the involvement of employees at all levels in the policy-making decisions of a company, etc.—*adj.* **partic'ipative** capable of participating.—*n.* **partic'ipator** one who participates: a person who has a share in the capital or income of a company. [L. *participāre*, *-ātum*—*pars*, *partis*, part, *capĕre*, to take.]

participle *pär'ti-sip-l*, *n.* a word combining the functions of adjective and verb.—**present participle, past** or **perfect participle** referring respectively to an action roughly contemporaneous or past; the present participle is active, the past usually passive.—*adj.* **particip'ial.**—*adv.* **particip'ially.** [O.Fr. (Fr.

particle),—L. *participium—pars, partis,* a part, *capère,* to take.]

particle *par'ti-kl, n.* a little part a very small portion a clause of a document' a minute piece of matter: a little hard piece: a material point (*mech*) a smallest amount: a short, usu. indeclinable word, as a preposition, a conjunction, an interjection a prefix or suffix a crumb of consecrated bread or a portion used in the communion of the laity (*R C Church*) —*adj.* **particular** (*par-tik'ū-lər*) relating to a part predicating of part of the class denoted by the subject (*log*) pertaining to a single person or thing: individual. special. worthy of special attention detailed. noteworthy definite: concerned with or marking things single or distinct: minutely attentive and careful fastidious in taste· particularist —*n.* a distinct or minute part. a single point. a single instance: a detail: an item.—*n* **particularisā'tion, -z-.—***v t* **partic'ularise, -ize** to render particular. to mention the particulars of· to enumerate in detail: to mention as a particular or particulars.—*v.t.* to mention or attend to minute details.—*ns.* **partic'ularism** attention to one's own interest or party: a minute description the doctrine that salvation is offered only to particular individuals, the elect, and not to the race. attention to the interest of a federal state before that of the confederation. the policy of allowing much freedom in this way.—*n.* and *adj* **partic'ularist**—*adj* **particularist'ic.**—*n* **par-ticularity** (*-lar'i-ti*) the quality of being particular: minuteness of detail: a single instance or case: a detail: peculiarity.—*adv.* **partic'ularly** in a particular manner: individually: severally. in detail· in the manner of a particular proposition. intimately notably: in a very high degree.—*n.* **partic'ularness.**—*adj.* **partic'ulate** having the form of or relating to particles — *n.* a particulate substance.—**in particular** especially: in detail. [L. *particula,* dim. of *pars, partis,* a part]

parti-coated, parti-coloured. See under **party.**

particular, etc See **particle.**

partisan, partizan *par-ti-zan', par'ti-zan, n* an adherent, esp. a blind or unreasoning adherent, of a party or a faction. a light irregular soldier who scours the country and forays: in World War II, an irregular resister within the enemy occupation lines —Also *adj.*—*n.* **par'-tisanship** (or *-zan'*). [Fr *partisan,* from a dialect form of It. *partigiano—parte* (L *pars, partis*), part.]

partita *par-tē'tə,* (*mus.*) *n.* (esp. 18th cent.) a suite: a set of variations [It.]

partite *par'tīt, adj* divided· cut nearly to the base.—*n* **partition** (*-tish'ən*), the act of dividing: the state of being divided: a separate part. that which divides: a wall between rooms. a barrier, septum or dissepiment: a score (*mus*).—*v.t.* to divide into shares: to divide into parts by walls, septa, or the like —*ns* **parti'tioner** one who partitions property; **parti'-tionist** one who favours partition; **parti'tionment.**—*adj.* **par'titive** parting dividing: distributive: indicating that a part is meant (*gram.*).—*n.* a partitive word.—*adv.* **par'titively.—parti'tion-wall'** an internal wall. [L. *partītus,* pa.p. of *partīrī* or *partīre,* to divide—*pars,* part.]

partly. See **part.**

partner *part'nər, n* a sharer: an associate: one engaged with another in business: one who plays on the same side with another in a game one who dances or goes in to dinner with another: a husband or wife: an associate in commensalism or symbiosis: (in *pl* ; *naut.*) a wooden framework round a hole in the deck, supporting a mast, etc.—*v t* to be the partner of.—*n* **part'nership** the state of being a partner. a contract between persons engaged in any business [Prob. a form of **parcener.**]

partook *par-tŏŏk', pa.t.* of **partake.**

partridge *par'trij, n* any member of a genus (*Perdix*) of game-birds of the pheasant family extended to many other birds —*pl* **partridge(s)** [Fr *perdrix—* L *perdix*—Gr *perdix*]

parturient *par-tū'ri-ənt, adj* bringing, or about to bring, forth of parturition —*n* **partüri'tion** the act of bringing forth [L *parturire,* desiderative from *parère,* to bring forth]

party *par'ti, n* a side in a battle, game, lawsuit, or other contest: a body of persons united in favour of a political or other cause a small body of persons associated together in any occupation or amusement. a detachment· a company: a meeting or entertainment of guests one concerned in any affair a person who enters into a contract, e g of marriage: a possible match in marriage· a person (*coll*) —*adj* pertaining to party. parted or divided (*her*).—*v t* to attend, hold or take part in parties or similar entertainments —*adjs* **par'ti-coat'ed, par'ty-coat'ed** having on a coat of various colours, **par'ti-col'oured, par'ty-col'oured** variegated.—**par'ty-line'** a telephone exchange line shared by two or more subscribers. boundary between properties the policy rigidly laid down by the party leaders; **par'ty-man'** a partisan; **par'ty-pol'itics** politics viewed from a party standpoint, or arranged to suit the views or interests of a party, **par'ty-spir'it** the unreasonable spirit of a party-man.—*adj* **par'ty-spir'ited.—par'ty-ver'dict** a joint verdict, **par'ty-wall** a wall between two adjoining properties or houses.—**the party's over** a favourable, enjoyable, carefree, etc situation has ended [Fr *partie,* fem. (and also *parti,* masc.), pa.p. of *par-tir*—L. *partire, partīrī,* to divide—*pars,* a part.]

parulis *pə-rōō'lis,* (*med*) *n.* a gumboil [Gr *para,* beside, *oulon,* the gum]

parure *pa-rur', n.* a set of ornaments, etc [Fr.]

parvanimity *par-və-nim'i-ti, n.* littleness of mind [L *parvus,* little, *animus,* mind.]

parvenu *par'və-nu, -nū, n.* an upstart: one newly risen into wealth, notice, or power, esp. if vulgar or exhibiting an inferiority complex.—Also *adj.* [Fr pa.p of *parvenir*—L. *pervenire,* to arrive]

parvis, parvise *par'vis, par'vēs, ns.* an enclosed space, or sometimes a portico, before a church: a room over a church porch (*erron*) [O Fr. *parevis;* same root as **paradise.**]

parvovirus, Parvo virus *par'vō-vī-rəs, n.* any of a group of viruses which contain DNA and which are the causes of various animal, including canine, diseases. [L. *parvus,* little, and **virus.**]

pas *pa, n.* a step: a dance: action: precedence:—*pl.* **pas** (*pa*).—**pas de chat** (*də sha*) a ballet leap in which each foot is raised in turn to the opposite knee, **pas de deux** (*də dø*), a dance of two persons; **pas redoublé** (*rə-dōōblä*), a quickstep; **pas seul** (*sœl*) a dance for one person, a solo dance [Fr.,—L *passus,* cf. **pace.**]

pascal *pas'kal, n.* a unit of pressure, the newton per square metre, a supplementary SI unit [Blaise *Pascal,* French philospher and scientist]

Pasch *pask, n* the Passover: Easter (*arch*).—*adj* **pasch'al.** [L. *pascha*—Gr *pascha*—Heb *pesach,* the Passover—*pāsach,* to pass over.]

pash *pash, n* a slang contraction of **passion.**

pasha *pa'shə, pa-sha', n* a Turkish title (abolished 1934) given to governors and high military and naval officers [Turk *pāshā;* cf. **bashaw.**]

pashm *push'əm, n* the fine underfleece of the goats of Northern India, used for making rugs, shawls, etc.— Also **pashim** (*push'ēm*), **pashmina** (*push-mē'nə*) [Pers , wool.]

Pashto, Pashtu. See **Pushtu.**

paso doble *pa'sō dō'blä,* (Sp) a march usu. played at bullfights. a two-step: the music for this dance.

pasque-flower *pask'flowr, n* a species of anemone (*Anemone pulsatilla*) extended to some other species [Fr *passefleur*, apparently—*passer*, to surpass, modified after **pasch,** as flowering about Easter]

pass *pas, v ı* to proceed to go or be transferred from one place to another: to transfer the ball to another player (*football*, etc) to make one's way to reach, extend, or have a course to undergo change from one state to another: to be transmitted· to change ownership to change to be astır to circulate to be accepted or reputed or known to go by to go unheeded or neglected to elapse, to go away. to disappear, come to an end, fade out. to die· to move over, through or onwards· to go or get through an obstacle, difficulty, test, ordeal, examination, etc to get through an examination without honours to be approved: to meet with acceptance· to be sanctioned to be made law: to be talented to come through to be voided. to happen: to be communicated or transacted to sit or serve (upon a jury): to adjudicate· to be pronounced: to exceed bounds· to perform a pass (see noun below): to abstain from making a call or declaration (*cards*)—*v.t.* to go or get by, over, beyond, through, etc to undergo, experience· to undergo successfully. to spend (as time) to omit: to disregard: to exceed. to surpass. to cause or allow to pass· to transfer, transmit: to transfer (the ball) to another player (*football*, etc.): to hand: to utter to circulate. to pledge (as one's word): to emit, discharge to perform a pass with or upon. ▸o perform as a pass to esteem (*obs.*).—*pa.t* and *pa.p* **passed** (*past*), rarely **past.**—*n* a way by which one may pass or cross: a narrow passage, esp through or over a range of mountains or other difficult region: a narrow defile. an act of passing: the passing of an examination, esp. without honours. event, issue, fulfilment, consummation: a state or condition (as in *pretty, sad pass*)· a predicament, critical position: a passport: a written permission to go somewhere or do something: permission to be in a certain area (*S Afr*): a free ticket: a thrust (*fencing*) transference of the ball to another team-member (*football*, etc.): transference in a juggling trick· an amorous advance (*coll.*): a movement of the hand over anything, as by a mesmerist —*adj* **pass'able** that may be passed, travelled over, or navigated: that may bear inspection: that may be accepted or allowed to pass: tolerable —*n* **pass'ableness.**—*adv.* **pass'ably.**—*adj* **passing** (*pas'ıng*) going by, through, or away. transient, fleeting· happening now. incidental: casual —*n* the action of the verb to pass a place of passing: a coming to an end. death —**pass'-book** a book that passes between a trader and his customer, in which credit purchases are entered: a bank-book: a booklet containing permission to be in a certain area, and other documents (*S.Afr.*), **passed pawn** (*chess*) a pawn having no opposing pawn before it on its own or an adjacent file, **pass'er-by** one who passes by or near:— *pl.* **pass'ers-by; pass'ing-note** (*mus.*) one forming an unprepared discord in an unaccented place in the measure; **pass'key** a key enabling one to enter a house a key for opening several locks; **pass laws** (*S Afr*) laws restricting the movements of blacks, **pass'man** one who gains a degree without honours — *adj* **pass'out** entitling one who goes out to return.— **pass'word** (*mil.*) a secret word by which a friend may pass or enter a camp, etc —**bring to pass** to bring about, cause to happen; **come to pass** to happen (apparently originally a noun in these expressions), **in passing** while doing, talking about, etc. something else; **make a pass at** to aim a short blow at, especially ineffectually (*coll*): to make an amorous advance to

(*coll.*), **pass as, for** to be mistaken for or accepted as, **pass away** to come to an end, go off to die: to elapse, **pass by** to move, go beyond or past to ignore or overlook, **pass off** to impose fraudulently, to palm off. to take its course satisfactorily to disappear gradually, **pass on** to go forward to proceed· to die to transmit, hand on; **pass on,** or **upon,** to give judgment or sentence upon to practise artfully, or impose, upon to palm off, **pass out** to distribute to die. to faint, become unconscious or dead drunk (*slang*): to go off: to complete military, etc training, **pass over** to overlook, to ignore· to die, **pass the time of day** to exchange any ordinary greeting of civility, **pass through** to undergo, experience, **pass up** to renounce, to have nothing to do with. to neglect (an opportunity) [Fr *pas*, step, and *passer*, to pass—L *passus*, a step]

passacaglia *pas-a-kal'ya*, (*mus*) *n* a slow solemn old Spanish dance-form, slower than the chaconne, in triple time. usually on a ground-bass [Italianised from Sp *pasacalle—pasar*, to pass, *calle*, street, appar. because often played in the streets]

passade *pa-sād', n* the motion of a horse to and fro over the same ground. [Fr *passade*, Sp *pasada*—L *passus*, step]

passage[1] *pas'ıj, n.* an act of passing transit· a crossing. migration: transition. a journey (now only by water or air, or *fig*): right of conveyance: possibility of passing: lapse, course: transmission: evacuation of the bowels. the passing of a bill: a means or way of passing: an alley. a corridor or lobby· a navigable channel or route· a crossing-place, ford, ferry, bridge, or mountain-pass. that which passes: an occurrence, incident, episode: transaction, interchange of communication or intercourse, dealings together: a continuous but indefinite portion of a book, piece of music, etc , of moderate length a run, figure, or phrase in music —**pass'age-boat** a boat plying regularly for passengers; **pass'age-money** fare; **pass'-ageway** a way of access a corridor: an alley.—**bird of passage** a migratory bird· a transient visitor (*fig*); **passage of arms** any feat of arms: an encounter, esp. in words. [Fr. *passage*—L. *passus*, step.]

passage[2] *pas-azh', pas'ıj, v.ı* to go sideways.—*v.t* to cause (a horse) to go sideways [Fr *passager—pass-éger*—It *passeggiare*, to walk—L *passus*, step]

passant *pas'ənt,* (*her*) *adj* walking towards the dexter side, with dexter fore-paw raised [Fr]

passé, *fem.* **passée,** *pa-sā,* (Fr) *adj.* past one's best, faded: nearly out of date.

passement, passment *pas'mənt,* **passament** *-ə-mənt, ns.* decorative trimming —*n* **passementerie** (*pas-mâ-t-*(*ə*)*-rē,* Fr.) [Fr]

passenger *pas'ın-jər, n* one who passes: one who travels in a private or public conveyance (as opposed to one who drives or operates the vehicle, etc): one carried along by others' efforts (*fig*)—*adj.* of or for passengers [Ô Fr *passagier* (Fr *passager*), with inserted *n*, as in *messenger, nightingale*]

passe-partout *pas-par-tōō', n* a means of passing anywhere a master-key: a card or the like cut as a mount for a picture. a kind of simple picture-frame, usually of pasteboard, the picture being fixed by strips pasted over the edges: adhesive tape or paper [Fr , a master-key, from *passer*, to pass, *par*, over, *tout,* all.]

Passeres *pas'ə-rēz, n.pl* an old order of birds —*n.pl* **Passerifor'mes** the huge order of perching birds (sparrow-like in form) including amongst others all British songsters.—*adj* and *n* **pass'erine** (*-īn*) [L *passer,* a sparrow]

passible *pas'ı-bl, adj* susceptible of suffering, or of impressions from external agents.—ns. **passibil'ity, pass'ibleness.** [L. *passibilis—patī, passus,* to suffer.]

passim *pas'im,* (L.) *adv.* everywhere: throughout.

passion *pash'n, n.* the sufferings (esp. on the Cross) and death of Christ: martyrdom: suffering: a painful bodily ailment (as *iliac passion*): the fact, condition, or manner of being acted upon: passivity: a passive quality: strong feeling or agitation of mind, esp. rage, often sorrow: a fit of such feeling, esp. rage: an expression or outburst of such feeling: ardent love: sexual desire: an enthusiastic interest or direction of the mind: the object of such a feeling.—*adj* **pass'ional.**—*ns.* **pass'ional, pass'ionary** a book of the sufferings of saints and martyrs.—*adj.* **pass'ionate** moved by passion: showing strong and warm feeling: easily moved to passion: intense, fervid.—*v.t.* to express with passion: to imbue with passion: to impassion.—*adv.* **pass'ionately.**—*n.* **pass'ionateness.**—*adjs.* **pass'ioned** moved by passion: expressing passion: expressed with passion; **pass'ionless** free from passion: not easily excited to anger.—**pass'ionflower** any flower or plant of genus Passiflora, consisting mostly of climbers of tropical and warm temperate America, from a fancied resemblance of parts of the flower to the crown of thorns, nails, and other emblems of Christ's Passion: the plant itself; **pass'ion-fruit** the granadilla: any edible passionflower fruit; **Pass'ion-play** a religious drama representing the sufferings and death of Christ; **Pass'ion-Sunday** the fifth Sunday in Lent; **Pass'ion-tide** the two weeks preceding Easter; **Pass'ion-week** Holy week: the week before Holy week. [O.Fr. *passiun* and L. *passiō, -ōnis—patī, passus,* to suffer.]

passive *pas'iv, adj.* acted upon, not acting: inert: lethargic: not actively resisting: not actively resisting: bearing no interest: (of that voice) which expresses the suffering of an action by the person or thing represented by the subject of the verb (*gram.*).—*n.* the passive voice: a passive verb: a passive person.—*adv.* **pass'ively.**—*ns* **pass'iveness; pass'ivism** passive resistance; **pass'ivist** a passive resister; **passiv'ity.**—**passive resistance** deliberate refusal (from scruples of conscience) to do what law or regulation orders, and submission to the consequent penalties; **passive resister.** [L. *passīvus—patī, passus,* to suffer.]

passman. See pass.

Passover *päs'ō-vər, n.* annual feast of the Jews, to commemorate the exodus of the Israelites from captivity in Egypt, so named from the destroying angel passing over the houses of the Israelites when he slew the first-born of the Egyptians.—*adj.* pertaining to the Passover.

passport *päs'pōrt, pōrt, n* a permit for entering a country: that which gives privilege of entry to anything (*fig.*). [Fr. *passeport*; cf. **pass, port³.**]

past *päst, adj.* bygone: elapsed: ended: in time already passed: expressing action or being in time that has passed, preterite (*gram.*): just before the present: past one's best: having served a term of office.—*n.* time that has passed: things that have already happened: (one's) early life or bygone career, esp. if marked by tragedy or scandal: the past tense: a verb or verbal form in the past tense.—*prep.* after: after the time of: beyond, in place, etc.: beyond the possibility of.—*adv.* by.—*v.t.* and *v.i.* an unusual pa.p. of **pass.**—**past'master** one who has held the office of master (as among freemasons): hence, a thorough proficient (see also **passed master** under **master**).—**past it** (*coll.*), **past one's best** having decreased strength, ability, etc. due to advancing age; **I,** etc. **would not put it past him** (*coll.*) I, etc. regard him as (esp. morally) capable of (some act). [An old pa.p. of **pass.**]

pasta *päs', pas'tə, n.* flour dough in fresh, processed (e.g spaghetti), and/or cooked form. [It., paste.]

paste *päst, n.* a soft plastic mass: dough for piecrust, etc.: a doughy sweetmeat: a smooth preparation of food suitable for spreading on bread: a cement made of flour, water, etc.: material for making pottery: the basis of a man's character (*fig.*): a fine kind of glass for making artificial gems.—*adj.* of paste.—*v.t.* to fasten or cover with paste: to thrash (*slang*).—*n.* **past'iness.**—*adj.* **past'y** like paste.—**paste'board** a stiff board made of sheets of paper pasted together: a visiting-card, playing-card, or ticket (*slang*).—*adj.* of pasteboard: sham: trumpery.—*adj.* **past'y-faced** pale and dull of complexion. [O.Fr. *paste* (Fr. *pâte*)—L.L. *pasta*—Gr. *pasta,* barley porridge.]

pastel *pas'tal, -tel, n.* chalk mixed with other materials and coloured for crayons: a drawing made with pastels: the process or art of drawing with pastels.—*adj.* in pastel: (of colour) soft, quiet.—*n.* **pastellist** (*pas', or -tel'*). [Fr. *pastel*—It. *pastello*—L. *pasta,* paste.]

pastern *pas'tərn, n.* the part of a horse's foot from the fetlock to the hoof, where the shackle is fastened. [O.Fr. *pasturon* (Fr. *paturon*)—O.Fr. *pasture,* pasture, a tether for a horse; cf. **pester.**]

Pasteurian *pas-tûr'i-ən, adj.* relating to Louis *Pasteur* (1822–95) or his methods.—*n.* **pasteurisa'tion, -z-** sterilisation of milk, etc., by heating.—*v.i.* **pas'teurise, -ize.**—*ns.* **pasteuris'er, -z-** an apparatus for sterilising milk, etc.

pastiche *pas-tēsh', n.* a jumble: a pot-pourri: a composition (in literature, music, or painting) made up of bits of other works or imitations of another's style. [Fr. (from It.) and It.—It. *pasta,* paste; see **paste.**]

pastille *pas'til, pas-tēl', n.* a small cone of charcoal and aromatic substances, burned as incense, or for fumigation, fragrance: a small (often medicated) sweetmeat. [Fr.,—L. *pāstillus,* a little loaf.]

pastime *päs'tim, n.* that which serves to pass away the time: recreation. [**pass, time.**]

pastis *pas-tēs', n.* an alcoholic drink similar in flavour to absinthe. [Fr.]

pastor *päs'tər, n.* one who has care of a flock or of a congregation: a clergyman: the rose-coloured starling.—*adj.* **pas'toral** relating to shepherds or to shepherd life: of the nature of pastureland: of or pertaining to the pastor of a church and his obligations to his congregation: addressed to the clergy of a diocese by their bishop.—*n.* a poem, play, romance, opera, piece of music, or picture depicting the life of (usually idealised or conventionalised) shepherds, or rural life in general: such writing as a genre: a pastoral letter: a book on the care of souls: a pastoral staff.—*ns.* **pastorale** (*päs-to-rä'lä;* It.) a pastoral composition in music: a pastoral, rustic, or idyllic opera or cantata; **pas'toralism** pastoral character, fashion, cult, mode of writing; **pas'toralist.**—*adv.* **pas'torally.**—*n.* **pas'torate** the office of a pastor: a pastor's tenure of office: a body of pastors.—*adj.* **pas'torly** becoming a pastor.—*n.* **pas'torship.**—**pastoral address or letter** an address or a letter by a pastor to his people, or by a bishop to his clergy; **pastoral staff** a crosier: a tall staff forming part of a bishop's insignia, headed like a shepherd's crook. [L. *pāstor—pāscĕre, pāstum,* to feed.]

pastrami *pas-trä'mi, n.* a smoked, highly seasoned (esp. shoulder) cut of beef. [Yiddish—Rumanian *pastramă—a pāstra,* to serve.]

pastry *päs'tri, n.* articles made of paste or dough collectively: crust of pies, tarts, etc.: a small cake.—**pas'trycook** a maker or seller of pastry. [paste.]

pasture *päs'chər, n.* grazing: growing grass for grazing: grazing land: a grazing ground, piece of grazing land.

—*v.i.* to graze.—*v.t.* to put to graze: to graze on.— *adj.* **past'urable** fit for pasture.—*n.* **past'urage** the business of feeding or grazing cattle: pasture-land: grass for feeding: right of pasture.—*adjs.* **past'ural** of pasture; **past'ureless.**—**past'ure-land** land suitable for pasture. [O.Fr. *pasture* (Fr. *pâture*)—L. *pāstūra* —*pāscēre*, *pāstum*, to feed.]

pasty[1] *păs'ti*, *adj.* See under **paste.**

pasty[2] *pas'ti*, *n.* a meat-pie baked without a dish. [O.Fr. *pastée*—L. *pasta*; see **paste.**]

pat[1] *pat*, *n.* a gentle stroke with a flat surface, as the palm of the hand: such a stroke as a caress or mark of approbation: a sound as of such a stroke: a small lump, esp. of butter, such as might be moulded by patting.—*v.t.* to strike (now only to strike gently) with the palm of the hand or other flat surface: to shape by patting.—*v.i.* to tap: to make the sound of pats, as with the feet:—*pr.p.* **patt'ing;** *pa.t* and *pa.p.* **patt'ed.**—*adv.* and *adj.* hitting the mark to a nicety: at the right time or place: exactly to the purpose: with or ready for fluent or glib repetition.—*adv.* **pat'ly** (*rare*) fitly, conveniently: glibly, fluently.—*n.* **pat'- ness.**—**pat'ball** rounders: gentle hitting in other games.—**pat on the back** a mark of encouragement or approbation, **stand pat** in poker, to decide to play one's hand as it is: to refuse to change [Prob. imit.]

patch *pach*, *n.* a piece put on or to be put on to mend a defect: a piece of plaster for a cut or sore: a pad for a hurt eye: a piece of ground, period of time, etc.: a small piece of black silk, etc., stuck by ladies on the face, to bring out the complexion by contrast: a small- ish area differing in colour or otherwise from its sur- roundings: a plot of ground: a scrap or fragment: a scrap pieced together with others: a group of instruc- tions added to a computer program to correct a mis- take (*comput.*).—*v.t.* to mend with a patch: to put a patch on: to apply as a patch: to join in patchwork: to mend or construct hastily, clumsily, or temporarily (commonly with *up*): to construct as a patchwork: to mark with patches.—*adj.* **patch'able.**—*adj.* **patched.** —*n* **patch'er.**—*adv* **patch'ily.**—*n* and *adj.* **patch'- ing.**—*adj.* **patch'y** covered with patches: diversified in patches: inharmonious, incongruous —**patch'- board** (*telecomm.*, etc) a panel with multiple electric terminals into which wires may be plugged to form a variety of electric circuits; **patch'-pocket** a flat, usu. square piece of material attached to the outside of a garment, **patch test** a test for allergy in which allergenic substances are applied to areas of skin which are later examined for signs of irritation; **patch- up'** a provisional repairing; **patch'work** work formed of patches or pieces sewed together: an incongruous combination: work patched up or clumsily executed: a surface diversified in patches.—**hit, strike a bad patch** to experience a difficult time, encounter unfavourable conditions, etc ; **not a patch on** not fit to be compared with [M.E. *pacche*; origin unknown; poss conn with **piece.**]

patchouli, patchouly *pach'ōō-le*, also *pə-chōō'le*, *n.* a labiate shrub (*Pogostemon patchouly*) of S.E. Asia: a perfume got from its dried branches. [Tamil *paccilı*]

pate *pāt*, *n.* the crown of the head. the head —*adj* **pāt'ed** having a pate. [Origin unknown]

pâté *păt'-*, *pat'ā*, *n* orig a pie, pastry: now usu. a paste made of blended meat, herbs, etc.—**pâté de foie gras** (*da fwa grä*) orig. a pasty of fat goose liver: now usu the goose liver paste filling. [Fr]

patella *pə-tel'ə*, *n* a little pan (*ant.*): the knee-cap (*anat.*):—*pl.* **patell'ae** (*-ē*).—*adjs.* **patell'ar** of the kneecap; **patell'ate** (or *pat'*) saucer-shaped: limpet- shaped; **patell'iform.** [L., dim. of *patina*, a pan.]

paten *pat'ən*, *n.* a plate: a communion plate: a chalice- cover: a metal disc. [O.Fr. *patene*—L. *patena*, *patina*, a plate—Gr. *patanē.*]

patent *pā'tənt*, or (esp. in *letters-patent* and *Patent Office*, and in U.S.) *pat'ənt*, *adj.* lying open: con- spicuous, obvious, evident: generally accessible: pro- tected by a patent: spreading (*bot.*): expanding: in- genious (*slang*).—*n.* an official document, open, and having the Great Seal of the government attached to it, conferring an exclusive right or privilege, as a title of nobility, or the sole right for a term of years to the proceeds of an invention: something invented and protected by a patent: a privilege: a certificate.—*v t* to secure a patent for.—*n.* **pā'tency** openness: obviousness.—*adj.* **pā'tentable.**—*n.* **pātentee'** one who holds a patent, or to whom a patent is granted.— *adv.* **pā'tently** openly, obviously.—*n.* **pā'tentor** one who grants a patent.—**patent leather** finely varnished leather; **patent medicine** (*strictly*) a medicine protec- ted by a patent: (*loosely*) any proprietary medicine, esp. one liable to stamp duty, as made by secret pro- cess or for other reason; **Patent Office** an office for the granting of patents for inventions, **pā'tent-right** the exclusive right reserved by letters-patent.—*n.pl.* **pā'tent-rolls** the register of letters-patent issued in England [L. *patēns*, *-entis*, pr.p. of *patēre*, to lie open.]

pater *pā'tər*, (*slang*) *n.* father [L *păter.*]

paterfamilias *pā-tər-fə-mil'i-as*, or *pat'ər-*, *n* the father or head of a family or household:—*pl.* strictly **patres- famil'ias** (*-tras-*), sometimes **paterfamil'iases.** [L *păter*, a father, *familiās*, old gen of *familia*, a household]

paternal *pə-tûr'n(ə)l*, *adj.* of a father: on the father's side: derived or inherited from the father: fatherly: showing the disposition or manner of a father —*n* **pater'nalism** a system or tendency in which provident fostering care is apt to pass into unwelcome inter- ference.—*adv.* **pater'nally.**—*n.* **pater'nity** the state or fact of being a father: fatherhood: the relation of a father to his children: origin on the father's side: ori- gination or authorship —**paternity leave** leave of absence from work granted to a husband so that he can be with his wife and assist her during and after childbirth. [L. *pater* (Gr. *patēr*) a father.]

paternoster *pat-ər-nos'tər*, or *păt'*, *n* the Lord's Prayer a muttered formula or spell: a large bead in a rosary, at which, in telling, the Lord's Prayer is re- peated: a rosary: anything strung like a rosary: a lift for goods or passengers, consisting of a series of cars moving on a continuous belt, the floors remaining horizontal at the top and bottom of travel [L *Pater noster*, 'Our Father', the first words of the Lord's Prayer.]

path *path*, *n.* a way trodden out by the feet. a foot- path: a course, route, line along which anything moves: a course of action, conduct:—*pl.* **paths** (*padhz*).—**path'finder** one who explores the route, a pioneer. a radar device used as an aircraft navig- ational aid: a radar device for guiding missiles into a target area, **path'way** a path in neurology, the route of a sensory impression to the brain, or of a motor impulse from the brain to the musculature [O E. *pæth.*]

Pathan *pə-tan'*, *put-(h)an'*, *n.* an Afghan proper: one of Afghan race settled in India —Also *adj*

pathos *pā'thos*, *n.* the quality that raises pity.—*adj* **pathetic** (*pə-thet'ik*) affecting the emotions of pity, grief, sorrow: touching. sadly inadequate: con- temptible, derisory (*coll.*) —See also **-pathetic** below.—*n.* that which is pathetic: the style or manner fitted to excite emotion: (*in pl.*) attempts at pathetic expression —*adj.* **pathet'ical.**—*adv.* **pathet'ically.**— **-path** in composition, a sufferer from a particular disorder: a therapist for a particular disorder; **path'o-** in composition, disease, disorder; **-pathy** in composition, mental or emotional sensitivity or receptiveness: disease, disorder: therapy for a particular disorder; **-pathet'ic**, **-path'ic** adjective combining forms; **-pathist** noun combining form, a therapist for a particular disorder.—*ns.* **pathogen** (*path'ō-jen*) an organism or substance that causes disease; **pathogen'esis**, **pathogeny** (*pə-thoj'ə-ni*) (mode of) production or development of disease.—*adjs.* **pathogenetic** (*path-ō-ji-net'ik*), **pathogenic** (*-jen'ik*), **pathog'enous** producing disease.—*n.* **pathogenicity** (*-is'i-ti*) the quality of producing, or the ability to produce, disease.—*adjs.* **patholog'ic**, **-al** relating to pathology —*adv.* **patholog'ically**.—*ns.* **pathol'ogist** one skilled in pathology, usu. having as one of his duties the performing of post-mortems; **pathol'ogy** the study of diseases or abnormalities or, more particularly, of the changes in tissues or organs that are associated with disease: a deviation from the normal, healthy state; **-pathy** in composition, see above.—**pathetic fallacy** the reading of one's own emotion into external nature. [Gr. *pathos*, experience, feeling, pathos.]

patible *pat'i-bl*, *adj.* capable of suffering or being acted on: passible. [L. *patibilis—patī*, to suffer.]

patience *pā'shəns*, *n* the quality of being able calmly to endure suffering, toil, delay, vexation, or the like: sufferance: a card-game of various kinds, generally for one person, the object being to fit the cards, as they turn up, into some scheme.—*adj.* **pa'tient** sustaining pain, delay, etc., without repining: not easily provoked: persevering in long-continued or minute work: expecting with calmness: long-suffering: enduring: susceptible (of an interpretation). —*n.* one who bears or suffers: a person under medical or surgical treatment: a physician's client.—*adv.* **pa'tiently**. [Fr.,—L. *patientia—patī*, to bear.]

patina *pat'i-nə*, *n.* a eucharistic paten: a film of basic copper carbonate that forms on exposed surfaces of copper or bronze: a similar film of oxide, etc., on other metals: a film or surface appearance that develops on other substances (wood, flint, etc.) on long exposure or burial: a sheen acquired from constant handling or contact (also *fig.*).—*adj.* **pat'inated**.—*n.* **patinā'tion**.—*adj.* **pat'ined**. [L. *patina*, a dish.]

patio *pa'ti-ō*, *-tyō*, *n.* a courtyard: a paved area usu. adjoining a house, where outdoor meals can be served, etc.:—*pl.* **pat'ios**. [Sp., a courtyard.]

pâtisserie *pa-tēs'rē*, (Fr.) *n.* a pastry shop: pastry.

patois *pat'wä*, *n.* illiterate or provincial dialect:—*pl.* **patois** (*-wäz*). [Fr.: origin disputed, some suggesting corr. of *patrois*—L.L. *patriensis*, a local inhabitant.]

patresfamilias. See **paterfamilias**.

patrial *pā'*, *pa'tri-əl*, *adj.* pertaining to one's native land: (of a word) denoting a native or inhabitant of the place from whose name the word was formed: pertaining to the legal right to enter and stay in the U.K., or to one who has this right.—*n.* a patrial word: a citizen of the U.K., a British colony or the British Commonwealth, who for certain reasons, e.g. because a parent was born in the U.K., has a legal right to enter and stay in the U.K.—*v.t.* **pa'trialise, -ize**.—*ns.* **patrialisā'tion, -z-**; **pa'trialism**; **patrial'ity** the condition of being a patrial. [Obs. Fr.—L. *patria*, fatherland.]

patriarch *pā'tri-ärk*, *n.* one who governs his family by paternal right: one of the early heads of families from Adam downwards to Abraham, Jacob, and his sons (*B.*): a bishop ranking above primates and metropolitans: the head of certain Eastern Churches: a father or founder: a venerable old man: an oldest

inhabitant: an old leader of a flock: the most imposing and greatest of its kind.—*adj.* **patriarch'al** belonging, or subject, to a patriarch: like a patriarch: of the nature of a patriarch.—*ns.* **patriarch'alism** the condition of tribal government by a patriarch; **pa'triarchate** the province, dignity, office, term, or residence of a church patriarch: patriarchy; **pa'triarchism** government by a patriarch; **pa'triarchy** a community of related families under the authority of a patriarch: the patriarchal system.—**patriarchal cross** a cross with two horizontal bars. [Gr. *patriarchēs—patriā*, family—*patēr*, father, *archē*, rule.]

patriation *pā-tri-ā'shən*, *n.* the transferring of responsibility for the Canadian constitution (as enshrined in the British North America Act of 1867) from the British parliament to the Canadian parliament.—*v.t.* **pāt'riate**. [L. *patria*, fatherland.]

patrician *pə-trish'ən*, *n.* a member or descendant by blood or adoption of one of the original families of citizens forming the Roman people (opp. to *plebeian*): a nobleman of a new order nominated by the emperor in the later Roman Empire: an imperial Roman provincial administrator in Italy or Africa: a hereditary noble: an aristocrat.—Also *adj.*—*adj.* **patri'cianly**.—*n.* **patriciate** (*pə-trish'i-āt*) the position of a patrician: the patrician order. [L. *patricius —pater, patris*, a father.]

patricide *pat'ri-sīd*, *n.* the murder of one's own father: one who murders his father.—*adj.* **patrici'dal**. [Doubtful L. *patricīda*, as if from *pater, patris*, father, *caedēre*, to kill; prob. an error for *parricīda*; see **parricide**.]

patriclinic, patriclinous, etc. See **patroclinic.**

patrifocal *pat'ri-fō-kəl*, (*anthrop.*, etc.) *adj.* centred on the father: (of societies, families, etc.) in which authority and responsibility rest with the father.—*n.* **patrifocal'ity**. [L. *pater, patris*, father, *focus*, a hearth.]

patrilineal *pat-ri-lin'i-əl*, **patrilinear** *-ər*, *adjs.* reckoned through the father or through males alone. [L. *pater, patris*, father, *līnea*, line.]

patrilocal *pat-ri-lō'kl*, *adj.* (of a form of marriage) in which the wife goes to live with the husband's group. [L. *pater, patris*, father, *locālis—locus*, place.]

patrimony *pat'ri-mən-i*, *n.* an inheritance from a father or from ancestors: a church estate or revenue.—*adj.* **patrimonial** (*-mō'ni-əl*).—*adv.* **patrimō'nially**. [L. *patrimōnium*, a paternal estate—*pater, patris*, a father.]

patriot *pā'tri-ət*, sometimes *pat'*, *n.* one who truly, though sometimes injudiciously, loves and serves his fatherland.—*adj.* devoted to one's country.—*adj.* **patriotic** (*pat-ri-ot'ik*, or *pāt-*) like a patriot: actuated by a love of one's country: directed to the public welfare.—*adv.* **patriot'ically**.—*n.* **pā'triotism** (or *pat'*). [Gr. *patriōtēs*, fellow-countrymen—*patrios—patēr*, a father.]

patristic, -al *pə-tris'tik*, *-əl*, *adjs.* pertaining to the fathers of the Christian Church. [Gr. *patēr, pat(e)ros*, a father.]

patrol *pə-trōl'*, *v.i.* to move systematically round, an area, for purpose of watching, repressing, protecting, inspecting, etc.: to be on duty on a beat.—*v.t.* to keep (an area) under surveillance by patrolling: to perambulate:—*pr.p.* **patroll'ing**; *pa.t.* and *pa.p.* **patrolled'**. —*n.* the act or service of patrolling: perambulation: a person or group of people patrolling an area: a body of aircraft, ships, etc. having patrolling duties: a small detachment of soldiers, etc. sent on reconnaissance or to make an attack, etc.: one of the units of eight or so Scouts or Guides forming a troop.—*n.* **patroll'er**. —**patrol car** that used by police to patrol an area; **patrol'man** a policeman on duty on a beat (*U.S.*): a policeman without rank (*U S.*). (or **patrol**) a man on patrol to help motorists in difficulties —*fem* **patrol'woman.** [O.Fr *patrouiller*, to patrol, orig to paddle in the mud.]

patron pā'trən, *n* a protector: one who countenances or encourages. a customer. a habitual attender. an upholder a proprietor of a restaurant, etc . one who has the right to appoint to any office, esp to a living in the church a guardian saint.—*fem* **pā'troness.**—*n* **patronage** (*pat'*) support given by a patron guardianship of saints the right of bestowing offices, privileges, or church benefices habitual commercial dealings —*adj* **patronal** (*pa-, pa-trō'nl, pāt', pat'rən-l*) —*v t* **patronise, -ize** (*pat', U S pāt'*) to act as a patron toward· to give encouragement to to assume the condescending air of a patron toward· to give one's custom to, or to frequent, habitually —*n.* **pat'roniser, -z-.**—*adj* **pat'ronising, -z-.**—*adv* **pat'ronisingly, -z-.**—*adj* **pā'tronless.**—**patron saint** a saint regarded as the protector of a particular group, nation, etc. [L *patrōnus*—*pater, patris*, a father]

patronymic pat-rə-nim'ik, *adj* derived from the name of a father or an ancestor —*n* a name so derived [Gr *patrōnymikos*—*patēr*, a father, *onyma (onoma)*, a name]

patsy pat'si, (slang) *n* an easy victim, a sucker a scapegoat, fall guy

patten pat'n, *n* a wooden shoe: a wooden sole mounted on an iron ring to raise the shoe above the mud the base of a pillar (*archit.*) —*adj* **patt'ened** with pattens [O Fr *patin*, clog (now skate), perh —*patte*, paw]

patter[1] pat'ər, *v.i* to pat or strike often, as hailstones to make the sound of a succession of light pats· to run with short quick steps.—*n* the sound of pattering [Freq of **pat.**]

patter[2] pat'ər, *v i.* to talk or sing rapidly and glibly. to talk thus, esp on the stage, as accompaniment to action or for comic effect —*v.t* to repeat hurriedly, to gabble.—*n* glib talk, chatter: the cant of a class —**patt'er-song** a comic song in which a great many words are sung or spoken very rapidly [**paternoster.**]

pattern pat'ərn, *n* a person or thing to be copied: a model. a design or guide with help of which something is to be made (e.g a dressmaker's paper pattern). a model of an object to be cast, from which a mould is prepared: a sample: a typical example. a decorative design· a particular disposition of forms and colours: a design or figure repeated indefinitely the distribution of shot on a target —*v t* to take as a pattern: to fashion after a pattern: to make a pattern upon.—**patt'ern-maker** one who makes the patterns for moulders in foundry-work, **pattern race** a race open only to horses in a particular category, e g. of a certain age or weight; **patt'ern-shop** the place in which patterns for a factory are prepared, **patt'ern-wheel** the count-wheel in a clock [Fr *patron*, patron, pattern; cf **patron.**]

patty pat'i, *n.* a little pie. a small flat cake of minced beef or other food —**patt'y-pan** a pan for baking patties. [Fr *pâté*; cf **pasty.**]

paucity po'sit-i, *n* fewness. smallness of quantity [L *paucitās, -ātis*—*paucus*, few]

Pauline pol'in, *adj* of the apostle *Paul* —*n* a member of any religious order named after him a scholar of St Paul's School, London.—*adj* **Paulinian** (*-in'i-ən*) Pauline —*ns* **Paul'inism** the teaching or theology of Paul, **Paul'inist.**—*adj* **Paulinist'ic.**—**Paul Jones** (*jōnz*) a dance in the course of which each man takes a number of partners in succession—perh from the Scottish-American seaman Paul Jones (1747–92), who exc lled in the capture of prizes [L *Paulus, Paullus*, a Roman cognomen, meaning 'little']

paunch ponch, ponsh, *n* the belly: a protuberant belly the first and largest stomach of a ruminant· a rope mat to prevent chafing (*naut*) —*adj* **paunch'y** big-bellied [O Fr *panche*]

pauper po'pər, *n.* a destitute person· one not required to pay costs in a law suit· one supported by charity or by some public provision —*fem* **pau'peress.**—*n* **pauperisā'tion, -z.**—*v t* **pau'perise, -ize** to reduce to pauperism to accustom to expect or depend on support from without —*n.* **pau'perism** the state of being a pauper [L , poor]

pause poz, *n* intermission. a temporary stop cessation caused by doubt hesitation. a mark for suspending the voice. a continuance of a note or rest beyond its time, or a mark indicating this (*mus*).—*v.i* to make a pause —*v i* to cause to stop —*adjs* **paus'al; pause'ful.**—*adv* **pause'fully.**—*adj* **pause'less.**—*adv* **pause'lessly.**—*n* **paus'er.**—*n* and *adj.* **paus'ing.**—*adv* **paus'ingly.**—**give pause** to cause to hesitate [Fr ,—L *pausa*—Gr *pausis*, from *pauein*, to cause to cease]

pavan pav'ən, (hist) *n* a slow dance, much practised in Spain music for it, in 4-4 time.—Also **pav'ane** (or *pav-an'*). [Fr *pavane*, or Sp or It. *pavana*, prob — L *pāvō, -ōnis*, peacock.]

pave pāv, *v t* to cover with slabs or other close-set pieces, so as to form a level surface for walking on. to cover with anything close-set. to be such a covering for —*adj* **paved.**—*n* **pave'ment** a paved surface, or that with which it is paved: a footway by the side of a street (sometimes even when unpaved) paved road (*U S.*).—*v.t.* to pave: to be a pavement for.—*adj.* **pā'ven** paved —*n.* and *adj* **pā'ving.**—*n* **pā'viour** one who lays pavement or rams sets. a paving-stone — Also **pā'ver, pā'vior.**—**pavement artist** one who seeks a living by drawing coloured pictures on the pavement; **pavement light** a window of glass blocks in the pavement to light a cellar, **pa'ving-stone** a slab of stone or concrete used in a pavement, etc.—**pave the way for** to prepare the way for· to make easier: to help to bring on [Fr *paver*, prob. a back-formation from *pavement*—L *pavimentum*—*pavīre*, to beat hard.]

pavé pa-vā, (Fr) *n.* pavement: a setting of jewellery with the stones close together, covering the metal

pavement, paven. See **pave.**

pavilion pə-vil'yən, *n.* a tent, esp a large or luxurious one: a tent-like covering. a light building for players and spectators of a game an ornamental or showy building for pleasure purposes: a projecting section of a building, usually with a tent-like roof and much decorated· a hospital block: an exhibition building an ornamental building often turreted or domed· in gem-cutting, the under-surface of a brilliant, opposite to the crown: the bell of a horn· the outer ear.— *v.t.* to furnish with pavilions to cover, as with a tent [Fr *pavillon*—L. *pāpiliō, ōnis*, a butterfly, a tent]

pavior, paviour. See **pave.**

pavlova pav-lō'və, (also with *cap*) *n* a type of sweet dish consisting of a meringue base topped with whipped cream and fruit [Named in honour of the Russian ballerina Anna *Pavlova.*]

Pavlovian pav-lō'vi-ən, (*psych., physiol*) *adj* relating to the work of the Russian physiologist, Ivan *Pavlov*, on conditioned reflexes (of reactions, responses, etc) automatic, unthinking

paw po, *n.* a clawed foot: a hand (*facet* or *derog*) — *v i.* to draw the forefoot along the ground to strike the ground with the forefoot to strike out with the paw to feel about or over anything, esp offensively —*v t* to scrape, feel, handle, or strike with the forefoot or hand to handle grossly, coarsely, or clumsily [O Fr *poe, powe*, prob Gmc]

For other sounds see detailed chart of pronunciation.

pawl *pöl, n.* a catch engaging with the teeth of a ratchet wheel to prevent backward movement. [Origin obscure; poss. conn. with Du. or Fr. *pal,* L *pālus,* stake.]

pawn[1] *pön, n.* something deposited as security for re-payment or performance: the state of being pledged (as *in* or *at pawn*).—*v.t.* to give in pledge: to pledge —*ns.* **pawnee**' one who takes anything in pawn; **pawn'er** one who gives a pawn or pledge as security for money borrowed.—**pawn'broker** a broker who lends money on pawns; **pawn'broking; pawn'shop** a shop of a pawnbroker. [O.Fr. *pan.*]

pawn[2] *pon, n.* a small piece in chess of lowest rank and range: a humble tool or lightly valued agent (*fig.*) [O.Fr. *paon,* a foot-soldier—L.L. *pedō, -ōnis*—L *pēs, pedis,* the foot.]

pawn[3]. See **pan**[2].

pawnee. See under **pawn**[1].

pawpaw. See **papaw.**

pax[1] *paks, n.* the kiss of peace: an osculatory.—*interj.* truce. [L. *pāx,* peace.]

pax[2] *paks,* (L.) *n.* peace.—**pax vobiscum** (*vo-bis'kəm, vō-, wō-bēs'kōōm*) peace be with you.

pay[1] *pā, v.t.* to give what is due (in satisfaction of a debt, in exchange, in compensation, in remuneration, etc.) to (the person, etc. to whom it is owed): to give (money, etc.) in satisfaction of a debt, in exchange, compensation, remuneration, etc.: to settle, dis-charge (a claim, bill, debt, etc.): to hand over money, etc., for: (of a sum of money, etc.) to be or yield satisfactory remuneration or compensation for, or enough to discharge: to yield (a certain sum, profit, etc.): to be profitable to, to benefit: to render, confer (attention, heed, court, a visit, etc.): of a rope, to allow or cause to run out (*naut.*).—*v.t.* to hand over money or other equivalent, compensation, etc. (with *for*): to afford, constitute, an equivalent or means of making payment (with *for*): to be worth one's trouble: to be profitable: to suffer or be punished (with *for*): to be the subject of payment:—*pr.p.* **pay'ing;** *pa.t.* and *pa.p.* **paid,** (*obs.* except in the nau-tical sense) **payed** (*pād*).—*n.* money given for service: salary, wages: receipt of wages, etc., service for wages, etc., hire (esp. for an evil purpose).—*adj.* **paid** see separate article.—*adj.* **pay'able** that may or should be paid: due: profitable.—*ns.* **payee'** one to whom money is paid; **pay'er.**—*n.* and *adj.* **pay'ing.**—*n.* **pay'ment** the act of paying: the discharge of a debt by money or its equivalent in value: that which is paid: recompense: reward: punishment.—**pay'-as-you-earn'** a method of income-tax collection in which the tax is paid by deduction from earnings before they are received:—abbrev. **P.A.Y.E.**—**pay bed** a bed, specif. in a National Health Service hospital, avail-able to a patient who pays for its use and for his own treatment; **pay'-day** a regular day for payment, as of wages; **pay'-dirt, -grav'el** gravel or sand containing enough gold to be worth working (**pay-dirt** also *fig.*); **pay'-list, -roll** a list of persons entitled to receive pay, with the amounts due to each: (**pay'-roll**) the money for paying wages; **pay'-load** that part of the cargo of an aeroplane or other conveyance for which revenue is obtained: the part of a rocket's equipment that is to fulfil the purpose of the rocket, as a warhead, or apparatus for obtaining information; **pay'master** the master who pays: one who pays workmen, soldiers, etc.; **pay'-off** (time of) payment—reward or punish-ment: outcome: an esp. useful or desirable result: dénouement; **pay-out** see **pay out** below; **pay'-phone** a coin-operated public telephone; **pay'-roll** see **pay'-list; pay'-slip** a note to a worker (giving an analysis) of the sum he has been paid.—**in the pay of** receiving payment in return for services, used esp. in a sinister

sense; **pay back** to pay in return (a debt): to give tit for tat; **pay down** to pay (e.g. a first instalment) in cash on the spot; **pay for** to make amends for: to suffer for: to bear the expense of; **pay in** to contribute to a fund: to deposit money in a bank-account; **pay off** to pay in full and discharge: to take revenge upon: to requite: to fall away to leeward (*naut.*): to yield good results, justify itself (see also **pay-off** above); **pay one's** or **its, way** to have, or bring, enough to pay expenses: to compensate adequately for initial outlay; **pay out** to cause to run out, as rope: to disburse (*n.* **pay'-out**): to punish deservedly; **pay the piper** see **pipe**; **pay through the nose** to pay dearly; **pay up** to pay in full: to pay arrears: to accept the necessity and pay. [Fr. *payer*—L. *pācāre,* to appease; cf. *pāx,* peace.]

pay[2] *pā, v.t.* to smear with tar, etc.:—*pa.t.* and *pa.p.* **payed.** [O.Fr. *peier*—L. *picāre,* to pitch.]

payola *pā-ō'lə, n.* secret payment, a bribe, to se-cure a favour, esp. the promotion of a commercial product by a disc-jockey. [Facetiously coined from **pay**[1] and Victrola, a make of gramophone, or pian-ola.]

paysage *pā-ē-zazh', n.* a landscape, a landscape paint-ing.—*n.* **paysagist** (*pā'zə-jist*) a landscape-painter [Fr.]

paz(z)azz. See **piz(z)azz.**

pea[1] *pē, n.* a new singular formed from **pease** (q.v.) which was mistaken for a plural, with a new plural **peas**—the nutritious seed of the papilionaceous climbing plants *Pisum sativum* (garden pea) and *P. arvense* (field pea): the plant itself (also **pea'-plant**): extended to various similar seeds and plants and to various rounded objects, e.g. roe of salmon.—*n.* and *adj.* **pea'-green** (or *-grēn'*) yellowish-green, the colour of soup made from split peas: bright green like fresh peas.—**pea'nut** monkey-nut or ground-nut (Arachis): (*in pl.*) something very trifling or insignificant, esp. a meagre sum of money (*coll.*); **peanut butter** a paste made from ground roasted peanuts; **pea'pod'; pea'-shooter** a small tube for blowing peas through, used as a toy weapon, **pea'-soup** see **pease-soup; pea-soup'er** a fog like pea-soup; **pea'-trainer** an erection for pea-plants to climb on; **split peas** peas stripped of their membranous covering, dried and halved. [See **pease.**]

pea[2] *pē, n.* an obs. term for a **pea'-fowl**—a male or female peacock.—**pea'-chick** a young pea-fowl; **pea'-hen** the female of the peacock. [O.E. *pēa* (*pāwa*)—L. *pāvō.*]

peace *pēs, n.* a state of quiet: freedom from disturb-ance: freedom from war: cessation of war: a treaty that ends a war: freedom from contention: ease of mind or conscience: tranquillity: quiet: stillness: silence.—*adj.* **peace'able** disposed to peace: peace-ful.—*n.* **peace'ableness.**—*adv.* **peace'ably.**—*adj.* **peace'ful** enjoying peace: tending towards or favouring peace: inclined to peace: belonging to time of peace: consistent with peace: tranquil: calm: serene.—*adv.* **peace'fully.**—*n.* **peace'fulness.**—*adv.* **peace'less.**—*n.* **peace'lessness.**—**Peace Corps** in the U.S., a government agency that sends volunteers to developing countries to help with agricultural, technological and educational schemes; **peace'-keeper.**—*adj.* **peace'-keeping** (peace-keeping force a military force sent into an area with the task of pre-venting fighting between opposing factions).—**peace'maker** one who makes or produces peace: one who reconciles enemies; **peace'making; peace'-off'ering** a gift offered towards reconciliation, pro-pitiation, or deprecation; **peace'-off'icer** an officer whose duty it is to preserve the peace: a police-officer; **peace'-pipe** the calumet; **peace'time** time when there is no war —*adj* of peacetime —**at peace** in a state of peace not at war, **hold one's peace** to remain silent, **in peace** in enjoyment of peace, **keep the peace** to refrain from disturbing the public peace to refrain from, or to prevent, contention, **make one's peace with** to reconcile or to be reconciled with, **make peace** to end a war. [O.Fr. *pais* (Fr. *paix*)—L. *pāx*, *pācis*, peace]

peach[1] *pēch, v.i.* (with *on*) to betray one's accomplice: to become informer [Conn. with **impeach**.]

peach[2] *pēch, n.* a sweet, juicy, velvety-skinned stone-fruit: the tree bearing it, close akin to the almond extended to other fruits and fruit-trees: anything regarded as a very choice example of its kind, esp. a girl (*slang*): a yellow slightly tinged with red —*adj* of the peach: of the colour of a peach.—*adj* **peach'y.**— **peach'-blow** a pinkish glaze on porcelain, esp. Chinese porcelain.—Also *adj.*—**peach'-brand'y** a spirit distilled from the fermented juice of the peach —*adj.* **peach'-coloured** of the colour of a ripe peach (yellowish, tinged with red) or of peach-blossom (pink).—**peach Melba** a dish named in honour of the Australian soprano Dame Nellie *Melba*, consisting of peach halves served with ice-cream and usu a raspberry sauce, **peach'-stone; peach'-tree.** [O.Fr *pesche* (Fr. *pêche*, It *persica, pesca*)—L *Persicum* (*mālum*), the Persian (apple); its native country is unknown.]

pea-chick. See **pea**[2].

pea-coat. Same as **pea-jacket.**

peacock *pē'kok, n.* a genus (Pavo) of large birds of the pheasant kind, consisting of the common peacock (*P cristatus*) and the Javan (*P. muticus*), noted for gay plumage, esp., in the former, the deep iridescent greenish blue in the neck and tail-coverts: the male of either species: a vainglorious person: peacock-blue (also *adj*).—*v.t.* to make like a peacock.—*v.i.* to strut about or behave like a peacock —*n.* **peacock'ery** vainglorious ostentation.—*adjs.* **pea'cockish; pea'- cock-like; pea'cocky.**—**pea'cock-blue'** the deep greenish blue of the peacock's neck —Also *adj.*— **pea'cock-butt'erfly** a butterfly (*Vanessa io*) with spots like those of the peacock's train. [**pea**[2] and **cock,** etc]

pea-fowl; pea-hen. See **pea**[2].

pea-jacket *pē'-jak'it, n.* a sailor's coarse thick over-coat.—Also **pea'-coat.** [Du *pie* (now *pij*), coat of coarse stuff, and **jacket, coat.**]

peak[1] *pēk, n.* a point: the pointed end or highest point of anything the top of a mountain, esp. when sharp a summit. a maximum point in a curve or the corresponding value in anything capable of being represented by a curve, e g a point or time of maximum use by the public of a service, etc : a sharp projection. the projecting front of a cap a projecting point of hair on the forehead: a pointed beard. the upper outer corner of a sail extended by a gaff or yard (*naut.*): the upper end of a gaff (*naut*).—*adj.* maximum. of a maximum.—*v.i.* to rise in a peak: to reach the height of one's powers, popularity, etc : of prices, etc , to reach a highest point or level (sometimes with *out*) —*adj* **peaked** having a peak or peaks —*adj.* **peak'y** having a peak or peaks: like a peak.— **peak'-load** the maximum demand of electricity, or load on a power-station —**pea**[2]: **(viewing, listening) hours, time** the period in the day when the maximum number of people are watching television (approximately 5.00 p.m.–10.00 p.m.) or listening to the radio. [Found from the 16th cent (*peked* in the 15th); app. connected with **pike**[1].]

peak[2] *pēk, v.i.* to droop, to look thin or sickly.—*adjs.* **peaked, peak'ing, peak'y** having a pinched or sickly look, sharp-featured.

peal *pēl, n.* a loud sound: a number of loud sounds one after another a set of bells tuned to each other. a chime or carillon. the changes rung upon a set of bells.—*v.t.* to resound in peals —*v t.* to give forth in peals [Apparently aphetic for **appeal.**]

pean[1]. Same as **paean.**

pean[2]. Same as **peen.**

peanut. See **pea**[2].

pear *pār, n* an esteemed fruit, a pome tapering to-wards the stalk and bulged at the end: the tree (*Pyrus communis*) bearing it, of the apple genus. extended to various fruits (**alligator-, anchovy-pear, prickly-pear,** etc): in gem-cutting, a pear-shaped brilliant —**pear'-drop** a pear-shaped pendant a pear-shaped, pear-flavoured sweetmeat, **pear'-tree.** [O.E. *pere, peru* —L.L. *pira*—L. *pirum* (wrongly *pyrum*), pear]

pearl[1] *pûrl, n* a concretion of nacre formed in a pearl-oyster, pearl mussel, or other shellfish, around a for-eign body or otherwise, prized as a gem nacre: a paragon or finest example: a lustrous globule: a gran-ule —*adj.* of or like pearl granulated: of an electric light bulb, made from a frosted, rather than clear, glass as a precaution against glare.—*v.t* to set or adorn with pearls or pearly drops. to make pearly: to make into small round grains.—*v.i.* to take a rounded form: to become like pearls to fish for pearls —*adj.* **pearl'ed.**—*ns.* **pearl'er** a pearl-fisher or his boat; **pearl'iness**—*n* and *adj* **pearl'ing.**—*adj.* **pearl'y** like pearl, nacreous rich in pearls.—*n.* (in *pl.*) pearl-but-tons: (in *pl.*) costermongers' clothes covered with pearl-buttons. a costermonger, or a member of his family, wearing such clothes:—*pl.* **pearl'ies.**—**pearl'-bar'ley** see **barley**[1]; **pearl'-butt'on** a mother-of-pearl button, **pearl'-div'er** one who dives for pearls.— **pearl'-fisher** one who fishes for pearls; **pearl'-fishery; pearl'-fishing; pearl'-gray', -grey'** a pale grey.—Also *adj* —**pearl'-mill'et** the bulrush millet or spiked mil-let, a grain much grown in India; **pearl'-muss'el** a freshwater mussel that yields pearls; **pearl'-oys'ter** any oyster that produces pearls, **pearl'-shell** mother-of-pearl: pearly or pearl-bearing shell; **pearl'- tapio'ca** tapioca granulated and graded acc. to its size: a potato-starch imitation; **pearl'-wort** a member of a genus (Sagina) of small plants akin to chickweed, **pearly gates** (Rev. xxi) entrance to heaven; **pearly king** a costermonger whose costume is considered the most splendidly decorated with pearl-buttons:—*fem.* **pearly queen.**—**cultured pearl** a true pearl formed by artificial means, as by planting a piece of mother-of-pearl wrapped in oyster epidermis in the body of an oyster; **false, imitation, simulated pearl** an imitation. as, for instance, a glass bulb coated with pearl essence [Fr. *perle*, prob from dim. of L. *perna*, leg, leg-of-mutton-shaped, cf It dial. *perna*, pearl, It. *pernocchia*, pearl-oyster.]

pearl[2] *pûrl, n* a small loop on the edge of lace, ribbon, etc. [Cf. **purl**[3].]

pearlite *pûr'līt, n* a constituent of steel composed of alternate plates of ferrite and cementite.—*adj.* **pear-lit'ic.** [**pearl**[1].]

pearmain *pār'mān, n* a variety of apple. [App. O.Fr *parmain, permain.*]

peasant *pez'ənt, n* a small farmer: a tiller of the soil: a countryman: a rustic: an ignorant or low fellow (*derog.*) —*adj.* of or relating to peasants, rustic, rural: rude —*n* **peas'antry** the body of peasants: the condition of quality of a peasant. [O.Fr *paisant* (Fr. *paysan*)—*pays*—assumed L. *pāgēnsis*—*pāgus*, a district]

pease *pēz, n.* orig., a pea or pea-plant (old *pl.* **peason** *pēz'ən*). now almost wholly superseded by the new singular **pea** (q.v.) and plural **peas** except in a collec-tive sense.—**pease'-cod, peas'cod** the pod of the pea;

pease'-meal, pease'-porr'idge, pease'-pudd'ing meal, porridge, or pudding made from pease; **pease'-soup, pea'-soup** soup made from pease: a thick yellow heavy-smelling fog (also **pea'-soup'er**). [M.E. *pēse*, pl. *pēsen*—O.E. *pise*, pl. *pisan*—L L. *pisa*, L *pīsum*—Gr. *pison* or *pisos*.]

peat *pēt*, *n* a shaped block dug from a bog and dried or to be dried for fuel: the generally brown or nearly black altered vegetable matter (chiefly bog-moss) found in bogs, from which such blocks are cut.—*ns*. **peat'ary, peat'ery, pēt'ary, peat'-bank, -bed, -bog, -moor, -moss** a region, bog, moor, etc , covered with peat: a place from which peat is dug—*adj*. **peat'y** like, of the nature of, abounding in, or composed of, peat. [From the 13th cent. in S E Scotland in Anglo-Latin as *peta*, a peat; possibly of British origin; cf. **piece**.]

peau de soie *pō-də-swa'*, a type of smooth silk or rayon fabric. [Fr., lit. skin of silk.]

peavey, peavy *pē'vi*, (*U.S.*) *n.* a lumberman's spiked and hooked lever. [Joseph *Peavey*, its inventor.]

pebble *peb'l*, *n.* a small roundish stone, esp. water-worn: transparent and colourless rock-crystal: a lens made of it: a semi-precious agate: a grained appearance on leather, as if pressed by pebbles.—*adj.* of pebble.—*v.t.* to stone or pelt: to impart pebble to (leather) —*adjs.* **pebb'led; pebb'ly** full of pebbles.—*n.* **pebb'ling.**—**pebble dash** a method of coating exterior walls with small pebbles set into the mortar. [O.E. *papol* (*-stān*), a pebble (*-stone*).]

pec *pek*, *n.* a photoelectric cell. [From the initials]

pecan *pi-kan'*, *n.* a North American hickory (also **pecan'-tree**): its nut (**pecan'-nut'**). [Indian name; cf Cree *pakan*.]

peccable *pek'ə-bl*, *adj.* liable to sin.—*ns* **peccabil'ity; pecc'ancy** sinfulness: transgression.—*adj.* **pecc'ant** sinning: offending: morbid.—*adv.* **pecc'antly.** [L *peccāre, -ātum*, to sin.]

peccadillo *pek-ə-dil'ō*, *n.* a trifling fault, a small misdemeanour:—*pl.* **peccadill'os** (or **peccadill'oes**). [Sp. *pecadillo*, dim. of *pecado*—L. *peccātum*, a sin.]

peccant, etc. See **peccable.**

peccary *pek'ə-ri*, *n.* either of two species of hog-like South American animals. [Carib *pakira*.]

peck[1] *pek*, *n.* formerly a measure of capacity for dry goods, 2 gallons, or one-fourth of a bushel: a measuring vessel holding this quantity: an indefinitely great amount (as *a peck of troubles*). [M.E *pekke, pek*—O.Fr. *pek*, generally a horse's feed of oats.]

peck[2] *pek*, *v.t.* to strike or pick up with the point of the beak or other sharp instrument: to make (a hole, etc.), render or cause to be (damaged, etc.) by quick movement of the beak, etc.: to eat sparingly or with affectation of daintiness or (*slang*) eat in general: to kiss with dabbing movement.—*v.i.* to strike or feed with the beak or in similar manner: to eat daintily or sparingly (with *at*): to cavil (with *at*): to nag, criticise (with *at*).—*n.* an act of pecking: a hole made by pecking: a kiss: food (*slang*).—*ns.* **peck'er** that which pecks: a woodpecker: a kind of hoe: a part with an up-and-down movement in a telegraph instrument: spirit (as in *keep your pecker up*; *slang*); **peck'ing.**—*adj.* **peck'ish** somewhat hungry —*n.* **peck'ishness.**—**pecking order, peck order** a social order among poultry (or other birds) according to which any bird may peck a less important bird but must submit to being pecked by a more important one: order of prestige or power in a human social group. [App a form of **pick**[1].]

pecten *pek'tan*, *n.* a comb-like structure of various kinds, e.g. in a bird's or reptile's eye:—*pl.* **pec'tines** (*-tin-ēz*).—*adjs.* **pec'tinate, -d** toothed like a comb. having narrow parallel segments or lobes: like the teeth of a comb —*n* **pectinā'tion.** [L. *pecten, -inis*, a comb]

pectic *pek'tik*, *adj* of, relating to, or derived from, pectin —*n* **pec'tin** a mixture of carbohydrates found in the cell-walls of fruits, important for the setting of jellies.—*n.* **pec'tose** a substance yielding pectin contained in the fleshy pulp of unripe fruit [Gr. *pēktikos*, congealing—*pēgnynai*, to fix.]

pectinaceous, pectineal, pectines, etc. See **pecten.**

pectoral *pek'tə-rəl*, *adj.* of, for, on, or near, the breast or chest: coming from the heart or inward feeling (*fig.*).—*n.* armour for the breast of man or horse: an ornament worn on the breast, esp. the breastplate worn by the ancient Jewish high-priest, and the square of gold, embroidery, etc., formerly worn on the breast over the chasuble by bishops during mass: a pectoral cross: a pectoral fin: either of the two muscles (*pectoralis major, pectoralis minor*) situated on either side of the top half of the chest and responsible for certain arm and shoulder movements.—*adv* **pec'torally.**—**pectoral cross** a gold cross worn on the breast by bishops, etc.; **pectoral fins** the anterior paired fins of fishes. [L. *pectorālis—pectus, pectoris*, the breast.]

pectose. See **pectic.**

peculate *pek'ū-lāt*, *v.t* and *v.i.* to appropriate dishonestly to one's own use, pilfer, embezzle.—*ns* **pecula'tion; pec'ulātor.** [L. *pecūlārī, -ātus—pecūlium*, private property, akin to *pecūnia*, money.]

peculiar *pi-kū'lyər*, *adj.* own: of one's own: belonging exclusively: privately owned: appropriated: preserved: characteristic: special: very particular: odd, strange.—*n.* a parish or church exempt from the jurisdiction of the ordinary or bishop in whose diocese it is placed: anything exempt from ordinary jurisdiction.—*v.t.* **peculiarise, -ize** to set apart.—*n.* **peculiarity** (*-li-ar'i-ti*) quality of being peculiar or singular: that which is found in one and in no other: that which marks anything off from others: individuality: oddity.—*adv.* **pecu'liarly.**—*n.* **pecu'lium** private property, esp. that given by a father to a son, etc.—**peculiar motion** see **proper motion** under **proper.** [L *pecūlium*, private property.]

pecuniary *pi-kū'nyə-ri, -ni-ə-ri, adj* relating to money: consisting of money [L *pecūnia*, money, from the root that appears in L. *pecudēs* (pl.), cattle, and **fee.**]

ped-[1]. See **paed**(o)-.

ped-[2]. See **ped**(i)-.

-ped *-ped*, **-pede** *-pēd*, in composition, foot.—**-pedal** (*-ped'l*) adjective combining form. [L. *pēs, pedis* foot.]

pedagogue *ped'ə-gog*, *n.* a teacher. a pedant.—*adjs.* **pedagogic** (*-gog', -goj'*), **-al.**—*adv.* **pedagog'ically.**—*n.sing.* **pedagog'ics** (*-gog', -goj'*) the science and principles of teaching.—*n.* **ped'agoguery** (*-gog-ə-ri*) schoolmastering: pedagoguishness.—*adj.* **ped'agoguish** like a pedagogue.—*ns* **ped'agog(u)ism** (*-gizm, -jizm*) the spirit or system of pedagogy: teaching; **ped'agogy** (*-gog-i, -goj-i*) the science of teaching: instruction: training [Partly through Fr. and L from Gr. *paidagōgos*, a slave who led a boy to school.]

pedal *ped'l* (*zool.* also *pē'dəl*), *adj.* of the foot: of the feet of perpendiculars: of, with, or pertaining to, a pedal or pedals.—*n.* (*ped'l*) a lever pressed by the foot.—*v.i.* to use a pedal or pedals: to advance by use of the pedals.—*v.t.* to drive by the pedals:—*pr.p.* **ped'alling;**—*pa t.* and *pa.p.* **ped'alled.**—*ns* **ped'aller** one who uses pedals, **ped'alling.**—**ped'al-organ** the division of an organ played by means of pedals, **ped'al-point** organ point, a tone or tones (usu. tonic and dominant) sustained normally in the bass, while other parts move independently; **ped'al-pushers**

women's knee-length breeches, gathered below the knee. [L. *pedālis—pēs, pedis,* foot]

pedaller, etc See **pedal.**

pedant *ped'nt, n.* an over-learned person who parades his knowledge: one who attaches too much importance to merely formal matters in scholarship.—*adjs.* **pedantic** (*pid-ant'ik*), **-al** schoolmasterly: of the character or in the manner of a pedant.—*adv.* **pedant'ically.**—*ns* **ped'antism** pedantry. pedanticism; **ped'antry** the character or manner of a pedant: a pedantic expression: unduly rigorous formality [It *pedante* (perh. through Fr. *pédant*); connection with **pedagogue** not clear.]

pedate *ped'āt, adj* footed: foot-like: palmately lobed with the outer lobes deeply cut, or ternately branching with the outer branches forked (*bot.*) — *adv.* **ped'ately.** [L. *pedātus,* footed—*pēs, pedis,* foot.]

peddle *ped'l, v.i* to go about as a pedlar: to trifle.— *v.t.* to sell or offer as a pedlar —*n* (esp. *U.S*) **pedd'ler.** [App partly a back-formation from **pedlar,** partly from **piddle.**] **-pede.** See **-ped.**

pederasty, etc See **paed(o)-.**

pedestal *ped'is-tl, n.* the support of a column, statue, vase, etc.: the fixed casting which holds the brasses in which a shaft turns, called also *axle-guard* or *pillow-block —v.t* to place on a pedestal.—*adj.* **ped'-estalled.** [Fr. *piédestal*—It. *piedistallo,* for *piè di stallo,* foot of a stall—*piè,* foot (L. *pēs, pedis*), *di,* of (L. *dē*), *stallo,* stall (see **stall**).]

pedestrian *pi-des'tri-ən, adj* on foot. of walking. prosaic, uninspired: flat or commonplace.—*n* a walker. one who practises feats of walking or running.—*v.t* **pedes'trianise, -ize** to convert (street) to use by pedestrians only.—*n.* **pedestrianisā'tion, -z-.**—*n.* **pedes'trianism** walking, esp. as an exercise or athletic performance· pedestrian quality (*fig.*).—**pedestrian crossing** a part of a roadway (often controlled by traffic lights) marked for the use of pedestrians who wish to cross, and on which they have right of way; **pedestrian precinct** see **precinct.** [L. *pedester, -tris—pēs, pedis.*]

ped(i)- *ped('i)-,* in combination, foot [L. *pēs, pedis,* foot]

pediatrics. See **paed(o)-.**

pedicab *ped'i-kab, n* a light vehicle consisting of a tricycle with the addition of a seat, usu behind, covered by a half hood, for passenger(s) [L *pēs, pedis,* the foot, and **cab.**]

pedicel *ped'i-sel, n* the stalk of a single flower in an inflorescence: the stalk of a sedentary animal: the stalk of an animal organ, e g a crab's eye [Botanists' dim. of L *pēs, pedis,* the foot.]

pedicle *ped'i-kl, n.* a little stalk —*adjs.* **ped'icled; pedic'ūlate; pedic'ulated.** [L. *pediculus,* a little foot —*pēs, pedis,* foot.]

pedicure *ped'i-kūr, n* the treatment of corns, bunions, or the like: one who treats the feet.—*n* **ped'icurist.** [L *pēs, pedis,* foot, *cūra,* care]

pedigree *ped'i-grē, n.* a line of ancestors: a scheme or record of ancestry. lineage. genealogy. distinguished and ancient lineage derivation, descent succession, series, set.—*adj.* of known descent, pure-bred, and of good stock.—*adj* **ped'igreed** having a pedigree [App. Fr. *pied de grue,* crane's-foot, from the arrowhead figure in a stemma]

pediment *ped'i-mənt, (archit.) n.* a triangular structure crowning the front of a Greek building, less steeply sloped than a gable. in later architecture a similar structure, triangular, rounded, etc , over a portico, door, window, or niche.—*adjs.* **pedimental** (*-ment'l*), **ped'imented** furnished with a pediment: like a pedi-

ment. [Earlier *periment,* prob for **pyramid.**]

pedlar *ped'lər, n.* one who goes about with a pack of goods for sale one who peddles.—*n.* **ped'lary** the wares or occupation of a pedlar. [Prob. from *pedder,* a pedlar with inserted *l,* as in *tinkler* from *tinker*]

pedo-. See **paed(o)-.**

pedology *ped-ol'ə-ji, n.* the study of soils.—*adj* **pedological** (*-ə-loj'*).—*n.* **pedol'ogist.** [Gr. *pedon,* ground, *logos,* discourse.]

pedometer *pid-om'i-tər, n.* an instrument for counting paces and so approximately measuring distance walked [L *pēs, pedis,* foot—Gr *metron,* measure.]

peduncle *pi-dung'kl, n* the stalk of an inflorescence or of a solitary flower. the stalk by which a sedentary animal is attached. a narrow stalk-like connecting part. a tract of white fibres in the brain.—*adjs.* **pedun'-cular, pedun'culate, -d.** [Botanists' L *pedunculus* —L. *pēs, pedis,* the foot]

pee *pē, (coll.) v i.* to urinate —Also *n* [For **piss.**]

peek *pēk, n.* a sly look, a peep.—*v i.* to peep.—*n.* **peek'abo(o)'** a child's peeping game

peel¹ *pēl, v.t.* to strip off the skin, bark, or other covering from to strip off: to cause (someone else's ball) to go through a hoop (*croquet*).—*v.i.* to come off as the skin: to lose the skin: to undress (*coll*).—*n.* rind, esp that of oranges, lemons, etc., in the natural state or candied.—*adj.* **peeled** pillaged: bald: tonsured: stripped of skin, rind, or bark.—*ns.* **peel'er** one who peels: a plunderer: an instrument or machine for peeling or decorticating; **peel'ing** the act of stripping: a piece, strip, or shred stripped off.—**peel off** (*aero.*) to leave a flying formation by a particular manoeuvre. (of ship) to veer away from a convoy. [O.E. *pilian*—L. *pilāre,* to deprive of hair—*pilus,* a hair; perh. influenced by Fr *peler,* to skin; cf **pill².**]

peel² *pēl, n.* a shovel, esp. a baker's wooden shovel: an instrument for hanging up paper to dry [O.Fr. *pele* —L. *pāla,* a spade.]

peeler *pēl'ər, n.* a policeman, from Sir Robert *Peel* who established the Irish police (1812–18) and improved those in Britain (1828–30).

peen, pean, pein, pene *pēn,* **pane** *pān, ns.* the end of a hammerhead opposite the hammering face —*v.t.* to strike or work with a peen. [Origin uncertain, cf. Norw *pen,* Ger. *Pinne,* Fr. *panne.*]

peep¹ *pēp, v.t.* to cheep like a chicken.—*n.* a high feeble sound.—*n.* **peep'er** a young bird —**not a peep** (*coll.*) no noise, not a sound. [Imit.]

peep² *pēp, v i* to look through a narrow opening: to look out from concealment to look slyly, surreptitiously, or cautiously to be just showing: to begin to appear —*v i.* to put forth from concealment as if to take a view· to direct as if to view.—*n* a sly look. a beginning to appear· a speck of light or flame: a glimpse —*n* **peep'er** one that peeps: a prying person· the eye (*slang*). a glass, for various purposes (*slang*). —**peep'-hole** a hole through which one may look without being seen, **peeping Tom** a prying fellow, esp one who peeps in at windows, **peep'-show** a small show viewed through a small hole, usually fitted with a magnifying glass.—**peep of day** the first appearance of light in the morning.

peepul. See **pipal.**

peer¹ *pēr, n* an equal: a fellow. a nobleman of the rank of baron upward generally, a nobleman· a member of the House of Lords: one of Charlemagne's paladins: a member of any similar body.—*fem.* **peer'ess.** —*adj* **peer** pertaining to a peer group —*n* **peer'age** the rank or dignity of a peer: the body of peers: a book of the genealogy, etc., of the different peers.—*adj* **peer'less** unequalled. matchless.—*adv* **peer'lessly.**— *n* **peer'lessness.**—**peer group** a group of people equal in age, rank, merit, etc.—**spiritual peer** a bishop or archbishop qualified to sit in the House of Lords; **temporal peer** any other member. [O.Fr. (Fr. *pair*) —L. *pār, paris*, equal.]

peer[3] *pēr, v.i.* to look narrowly or closely: to look with strain, or with half-closed eyes: to peep: to appear.—*adj.* peer'y inclined to peer: prying: sly.

peevish *pēv'ish, adj.* wayward: fretful.—*v.t.* **peeve** (back-formation) to irritate.—*v.i.* to be fretful: to show fretfulness.—*n.* a fretful mood: a grievance, grouse.—*adj.* **peeved** (*coll.*) annoyed.—*adv.* **peev'ishly.**—*n.* **peev'ishness.**

peewit, pewit *pē'wit,* also *pū'it, n.* the lapwing [Imit.]

peg *peg, n.* a pin (esp. of wood): a fixture for hanging a hat or coat on: a pin for tuning a string (*music*): a small stake for securing tent-ropes, marking a position, boundary, claim, etc.: a pin for scoring as in cribbage: a pin in a cup to show how far down one may drink: hence a drink, esp. of brandy and soda: a degree or step: a wooden or other pin used in shoemaking: a turtle harpoon: a clothes-peg: a pegtop: a wooden leg (*coll.*): a leg (*coll.*): a theme (*fig.*). —*v.t.* to fasten, mark, score, furnish, pierce, or strike with a peg or pegs: to insert or fix like a peg: to score (as at cribbage): to keep from falling or rising by buying or selling at a fixed price (*stock-exchange*): to hold (prices, pensions, etc.) at a fixed level, or directly related to the cost of living: to stabilise: to throw.—*v.i.* to keep on working assiduously: to make one's way vigorously:—*pr.p.* **pegg'ing;** *pa.t.* and *pa.p.* **pegged.**—*adj.* **pegged.**—*n.* **pegg'ing.**—**peg'board** a board having holes into which pegs are placed, used for playing and scoring in games or for display or storage purposes; **peg'-box** part of the head of a musical instrument in which the pegs are inserted; **peg'-leg** a simple wooden leg: a man with a wooden leg.—**off the peg** of a garment, (bought) ready to wear from an already-existing stock: not adjusted to suit the circumstances, etc. (*fig.*) (*adj.* **off'-the-peg'**); **peg away** to work on assiduously; **peg down** to restrict (someone) to an admission, following a certain course of action; **peg out** in croquet, to finish by driving the ball against the peg: in cribbage, to win by pegging the last hole before show of hands: to mark off with pegs: to become exhausted, be ruined, or die (*slang*); **round peg in a square hole** or **square peg in a round hole** one who is unsuited to the particular position he occupies; **take down a peg** (or **two**) to take down, to humble, to snub. [Cf. L.G. *pigge,* Du. dial. *peg,* Dan. *pig.*]

pegmatite *peg'mə-tīt, n.* graphic granite: a very coarsely crystallised granite, as in dykes and veins: any very coarse-grained igneous rock occurring in like manner.—*adj.* **pegmatitic** (-*tit'ik*). [Gr. *pēgma,* a bond, framework, from the root of *pēgnynai,* to fasten.]

peignoir *pen'wär, n.* a woman's dressing-gown. [Fr., —*peigner*—L. *pectināre,* to comb.]

pein. See **peen.**

peirastic *pī-ras'tik, adj.* experimental: tentative.— *adv.* **peiras'tically.** [Gr. *peirastikos*—*peira,* a trial.]

pejorate *pē'jər-āt, pi', v.t.* to make worse.—*n.* **pejora'tion** a making or becoming worse: deterioration.— *adj.* **pejor'ative** (or *pē'*) depreciating, disparaging.— *n.* a depreciating word or suffix.—*adv.* **pejor'atively** (or *pē'*). [L. *pējor,* worse.]

pekan *pek'ən, n.* the wood-shock, a large North American marten. [Canadian Fr. *pékan*—Algonquin *pékané.*]

Pekingese, Pekinese *pē-kin(g)-ēz', adjs.* of Peking, China.—*n.* a native or inhabitant of Peking: the chief dialect of Mandarin: a dwarf pug-dog of a breed brought from Peking (also *coll.* short form **peke**).—

Pekin (**duck**) a large white breed of duck, bred esp. for food; **Peking man** a type of fossil man first found (1929) S.W. of Peking, related to Java man.

pekoe *pēk'ō, pek'ō, n.* a scented black tea. [Chin. *pek-ho,* white down]

pelage *pel'ij, n.* a beast's coat of hair or wool [Fr.]

Pelagian *pi-lā'ji-ən, n.* a follower of Pelagius, a 5th-cent British monk, who denied original sin.—Also *adj.*—*n.* **Pelā'gianism.**

pelagic *pi-laj'ik, adj.* oceanic: of, inhabiting, or carried out in, the deep or open sea: living in the surface waters or middle depths of the sea: deposited under deep-water conditions.—*adj.* **pelagian** (*pi-lā'ji-ən*) pelagic.—*n.* a pelagic animal. [Gr. *pelagos,* sea.]

Pelargonium *pel-ər-gō'ni-əm, n.* a vast genus of the Geraniaceae, having clusters of red, pink or white flowers, often cultivated under the name of geranium: (without *cap.*) any plant of this genus. [Gr. *pelargos,* stork, the beaked capsules resembling a stork's head.]

pelerine *pel'ə-rin, -rēn, n.* a woman's tippet or cape, esp. one with long ends coming down in front. [Fr. *pèlerine,* tippet, pilgrim (fem.); see **pilgrim.**]

pelf *pelf, n.* riches (in a bad sense): money. [O.Fr. *pelfre,* booty; cf. **pilfer.**]

pelham *pel'əm,* (often with *cap.*) *n.* on a horse's bridle, a type of bit, a combination of the curb and snaffle designs. [Perh name *Pelham.*]

pelican *pel'i-kən, n.* a large water-fowl, with enormous pouched bill.—**pelican crossing** a type of pedestrian-operated street crossing which includes an orange flashing light, during the showing of which motorists may proceed only if the crossing is clear; **pel'ican-fish** a deep-sea fish (Eurypharynx) with enormous mouth and very little body; **pel'ican's-foot'** a marine gasteropod mollusc (Aporrhaïs pes-pelicani): its shell, with a lip like a webbed foot. [L.L. *pelicānus* —Gr. *pelekan, -ānos,* pelican.]

pelisse *pe-lēs', n.* orig. a fur-lined or fur garment, esp. a military cloak: a lady's long mantle. [Fr.,—L.L. *pellicea* (*vestis*)—L. *pellis,* a skin.]

pelite *pē'līt, n.* any rock derived from clay or mud.— *adj.* **pelitic** (*-lit'ik*).—*n.* **pelother'apy** treatment by mud baths and the like. [Gr. *pēlos,* clay, mud.]

pellagra *pel-ag'rə, -āg'rə, n.* a deadly deficiency disease marked by shrivelled skin, wasted body, and insanity. —*n.* **pellag'rin** one afflicted with pellagra.—*adj.* **pellag'rous** connected with, like, or afflicted with, pellagra. [Gr. *pella,* skin, *agrā,* seizure; or It. *pelle agra,* rough skin.]

pellet *pel'it, n.* a little ball: a small rounded boss: a small rounded mass of compressed iron ore, waste material, etc.: a small pill: a ball of shot: a mass of undigested refuse thrown up by a hawk or owl.—*v.t.* to form (seeds) into a pellet by surrounding with an inert substance which breaks down with moisture, to make planting easier.—*vs.t.* **pell'etify, pell'etise, -ize** to form (esp. solid waste material, iron ore, etc.) into pellets.—*n.* **pelletisā'tion, -z-.** [O.Fr. *pelote*—L. *pila,* a ball.]

pellicle *pel'i-kl, n.* a thin skin or film: a film or scum on liquors.—*adj.* **pellic'ular.** [L. *pellicula,* dim. of *pellis,* skin.]

pellitory[1] *pel'i-tə-ri, n.* a plant of the nettle family, growing on old walls (called *pellitory of the wall*), or other member of the genus. [L. (*herba*) *parietāria*— *parietārius*—*pariēs, parietis,* a wall.]

pellitory[2] *pel'i-tə-ri, n.* a North African and South European plant, known as *pellitory of Spain,* akin to camomile: extended to various similar plants, as yarrow, feverfew. [M.E. *peletre*—L. *pyrethrum*—Gr. *pyrethron,* pellitory of Spain; see **pyrethrum.**]

pell-mell *pel'-mel', adv.* confusedly, promiscuously:

headlong helter-skelter vehemently.—*adj* confusedly mingled. promiscuous, indiscriminate headlong —*n* disorder confused mingling a hand-to-hand fight [O Fr *pesle-mesle* (Fr. *pêle-mêle*), *-mesle* being from O Fr *mesler* (Fr *mêler*), to mix, meddle—L L. *misculāre*—L *miscēre*, and *pesle*, a rhyming addition, perh influenced by Fr *pelle*, shovel]

pellucid *pe-lū'sid, -lōō'sid, adj* perfectly clear. transparent —*ns* **pellucid'ity, pellu'cidness.**—*adv* **pellu'cidly.** [L *pellūcidus—per*, through, *lūcidus*, clear—*lūcēre*, to shine]

Pelmanism *pel'mən-izm, n* a system of mind training to improve the memory (usu without *cap*) a card game in which the cards are spread out face down and must be turned up in matching pairs [The *Pelman* Institute, founded 1898, which devised the system.]

pelmet *pel'mit, n* a fringe, valance, or other device hiding a curtain rod [Perh Fr *palmette*]

Peloponnesian *pel-ō-pə-nē'sh(y)ən, -zh(y)ən, -zyən, adj* of the *Peloponnesus* or Peloponnese, the southern peninsula of Greece —*n* a native thereof —**Peloponnesian War** a war between Athens and Sparta, 431–404 B C [Gr *Peloponnēsos*, Peloponnese—*Pelops* (see foregoing), *nēsos*, an island.]

pelorus *pel-ōr'əs, -or', n* a kind of compass from which bearings can be taken [Perh *Pelorus*, Hannibal's pilot.]

pelota *pel-ō'tə, n.* a ball-game, of Basque origin, resembling fives, using a basket catching and throwing device. [Sp. *pelota*, ball]

pelotherapy. See **pelite.**

pelt[1] *pelt, n* a raw hide. a hawk's prey when killed, especially when torn —*n* **pelt'ry** the skins of animals with the fur on them: furs.—**pelt'monger** a dealer in skins. [App a back-formation from *peltry*—O.Fr *pelleterie*—L. *pellis*, a skin.]

pelt[2] *pelt, v.t* to assail (formerly with repeated blows, now usu) with showers of missiles, or of words, reproaches, pamphlets, etc . to drive by showers of missiles. to shower —*v t*. to shower blows or missiles. to beat vigorously, as rain, hail: to speak angrily to speed.—*n.* a blow. a pelting: a downpour, as of rain: a storm of rage a rapid pace —*n* **pelt'er** one who or that which pelts: a shower of missiles· a sharp storm of rain, of anger, etc.—*v.t* to go full pelt: to pelt (*dial.*).—*n* and *adj* **pelt'ing** —**(at) full pelt** at full speed

peltry. See **pelt**[1].

pelvis *pel'vis, n* the bony cavity at the lower end of the trunk the bony frame enclosing it. the cavity of the kidney: the basal part of a crinoid cup —*pl.* **pel'ves** (*-vēz*).—*adj.* **pel'vic.**—**pelvic fin** a fish's paired fin homologous with a mammal's hindleg, **pelvic girdle** or **arch** the posterior limb-girdle of vertebrates, with which the hind-limbs articulate, consisting of the haunch-bones (ilium, pubis and ischium united), which articulate with the sacrum [L *pelvis*, a basin]

pemmican, pemican *pem'i-kən, n* a North American Indian preparation of lean flesh-meat, dried, pounded, and mixed with fat and other ingredients highly condensed information or reading-matter (*fig*) [Cree *pimekan*.]

pemphigus *pem'fi-gəs, n* an affection of the skin with watery vesicles.—*adjs* **pem'phigoid, pem'phigous.** [False Latin—Gr *pemphix, -igos,* blister]

pen[1] *pen, n* a small enclosure, esp for animals a dam or weir animals kept in, and enough to fill, a pen —*v t* to put or keep in a pen to confine to dam —*pr p* **penn'ing;** *pa t* and *pa p* **penned** or **pent.**—**pen'fold** a fold for penning cattle or sheep. a pound —

submarine pen a dock for a submarine, esp if protected from attack from above by a deep covering of concrete [O E. *penn*, pen]

pen[2] *pen, n* a large feather a flight-feather: a quill: a cuttle-bone: an instrument used for writing (with ink or otherwise), formerly made of a quill, but now of other materials: a nib· a nib with a holder. writing literary style. an author.—*v t* to write, to commit to paper—*pr.p* **penn'ing;** *pa t* and *pa.p* **penned.**—*n* **pen'ful** as much ink as a pen can take at a dip: as much as the reservoir of a fountain-pen can hold: what one can write with one dip of ink.—*adj.* **penned** written quilled.—**pen'-and-ink'** writing materials. a pen drawing.—*adj* writing written· executed with pen and ink, as a drawing —**pen'-case** a receptacle for a pen or pens; **pen'craft** penmanship. the art of composition, **pen'-friend, -pal** an otherwise unknown person (usu abroad) with whom one corresponds; **pen'-holder** a rod on which a nib may be fixed; **pen'knife** orig. a knife for making or mending pens. a small pocket-knife, **pen'light** a small pen-shaped electric torch (**penlight battery** a long, thin battery, as used in a penlight), **pen'man** one skilled in handwriting· a writer or author:—*fem* **pen'woman; pen'manship; pen name** a writer's assumed name, **pen'-nib** a nib for a pen [O.Fr *penne*—L *penna*, a feather]

pen[3]. Slang short form of **penitentiary.**

pen[4] *pen, n* a female swan

penal *pē'nl, adj* pertaining to, liable to, imposing, constituting, or used for, punishment: constituting a penalty: very severe —*n.* **pēnalisā'tion, -z-.**—*v.t* **pē'nalise, -ize** to make punishable: to put under a disadvantage —*adv.* **pē'nally.**—**penal code** a codified system of law relating to crime and punishment; **penal laws** laws imposing penalties, esp. (*hist*) in matters of religion; **penal servitude** hard labour in a prison under different conditions from ordinary imprisonment, substituted in 1853 for transportation, abolished 1948; **penal settlement** a settlement peopled by convicts. [L. *poenālis—poena*—Gr *poinē*, punishment]

penalty *pen'l-ti, n.* punishment. suffering or loss imposed for breach of a law: a fine or loss agreed upon in case of non-fulfilment of some undertaking: a fine: a disadvantage imposed upon a competitor for breach of a rule of the game, for want of success in attaining what is aimed at, as a handicap, or for any other reason arising out of the rules: a penalty kick: a loss or suffering brought upon one by one's own actions or condition: a score for an opponent's failure to make his contract or for the bidder's success when the call is doubled (*bridge*).—**penalty area, box** in association football, the area in front of the goal in which a foul by the defending team may result in a penalty kick being awarded against them; **penalty goal** one scored by a penalty kick, **penalty kick** a free kick, or the privilege granted to a player to kick the ball as he pleases, because of some breach of the rules by the opposing side —**death penalty** punishment by putting to death —**under** or **on penalty of** with liability in case of infraction to the penalty of [L.L *poenālitās*, see foregoing]

penance *pen'əns, n.* an act of mortification undertaken voluntarily or imposed by a priest to manifest sorrow for sin the sacrament by which absolution is conveyed (involving contrition, confession, and satisfaction, *R C* and *Orthodox*)· expiation hardship [O.Fr , cf **penitence.**]

penannular *pen-an'ū-lər,* or *pēn-, adj* in the form of an almost complete ring [L *paene*, almost, *annulāris*, annular.]

pence *pens, n* a plural of **penny:** a new penny (*coll.*)

penchant *pä'shä, n* inclination decided taste: bias

[Fr., pr p. of *pencher*, to incline—assumed L.L. *pen-dicāre*—L. *pendēre*, to hang.]

pencil *pen'sl*, *n*. a fine paint-brush: a small tuft of hairs: a writing or drawing instrument that leaves a streak of blacklead, chalk, slate, or other solid matter, esp. one of blacklead enclosed in wood and sharpened as required: a small stick of various materials shaped like a lead-pencil, for medical, cosmetic, or other purpose: the art of painting or drawing: a system of straight lines meeting in a point (*geom.*): a set of rays of light diverging from or converging to a point: a narrow beam of light.—*v.t.* to paint, draw, write, or mark with a pencil: to apply a pencil to:—*pr.p.* **pen'cilling**; *pa.t.* and *pa.p.* **pen'cilled.**—*adj.* **pen'cilled** painted, drawn, written or marked with a pencil: marked as if with a pencil: showing fine concentric streaking: having pencils of rays: radiated: tufted.—*ns.* **pen'ciller**; **pen'cilling** the art or act of painting, writing, sketching, or marking with a pencil: marks made with a pencil: fine lines on flowers or feathers: a sketch: the marking of joints in brickwork with white paint.—**pen'cil-case** a case for pencils: metal case receiving a movable piece of blacklead or the like, used as a pencil; **pen'cil-lead** graphite for pencils: a stick of it for a metal pencil-case; **pen'cil-sharpener** an instrument for sharpening lead-pencils by rotation against a blade or blades; **pencil skirt** a straight, close-fitting skirt; **pen'cil-stone** a clay mineral used for making slate-pencils. [O Fr. *pincel* (Fr. *pinceau*)—L. *pēnicillum*, a painter's brush, dim. of *pēnis*, a tail.]

pencraft. See pen².

pend *pend*, *v.i.* to hang, as in a balance, to impend.—*adj.* **pend'ing** hanging: impending: remaining undecided: not terminated.—*prep.* during: until, awaiting. [Fr. *pendre* or L. *pendēre*, to hang; sometimes aphetic for **append** or for **depend.**]

pendant, sometimes **pendent**, *pen'dənt*, *n* anything hanging, especially for ornament: a hanging ornament worn on the neck: the hanging (esp. decorated) end of a waist-belt: an earring: a lamp hanging from the roof: an ornament of wood or of stone hanging downwards from a roof: a pennant: a pendant-post: anything attached to another thing of the same kind, an appendix: a companion picture, poem, etc.—*n.* **pen'dency** undecided state: droop.—*adj.* **pen'dent**, sometimes **pen'dant**, hanging: dangling: drooping: overhanging: not yet decided: grammatically incomplete, left in suspense —*n.* **pendentive** (*-dent'*) a spherical triangle formed by a dome springing from a square base (*archit.*).—*adv.* **pen'dently.** [Fr. *pendant*, pr.p. of *pendre*, to hang—L. *pendēns*, *-entis*—pr.p. of *pendēre*, to hang.]

pendente lite *pen-den'tē lī'tē*, *pen-den'te li'te*, (L) during the process of litigation.

pendulum *pen'dū-ləm*, *n.* any weight so hung from a fixed point as to swing freely: the swinging weight which regulates the movement of a clock: anything that swings or is free to swing to and fro:—*pl.* **pen'dulums.**—*adj.* **pen'dular** relating to a pendulum.—*n.* **pendulos'ity.**—*adj.* **pen'dulous** hanging loosely: swinging freely: drooping: dangling: overhanging: suspended from the top: floating in air or space.—*adv.* **pen'dulously.**—*n.* **pen'dulousness.** [Neut. of L. *pendulus*, hanging—*pendēre*, to hang.]

pene. See peen.

peneplain *pē'ni-plān*, or *-plān'*, *n.* a land surface so worn down by denudation as to be almost a plain.— Also *pe'neplane.* [L. *paene*, almost, and **plain².**]

penes. See penis.

penetrate *pen'i-trāt*, *v.i.* to thrust or force a way into the inside of: to pierce into or through: to permeate: to reach the mind or feelings of: to pierce with the eye

or understanding, see into or through (*fig.*): to understand.—*v.i.* to make way or pass inwards.—*ns.* **penetrability** (*-tra-bil'i-ti*), **pen'etrableness.**—*adj.* **pen'etrable.**—*adv.* **pen'etrably** so as to be penetrated.—*ns.* **pen'etrance** (*genetics*) the frequency, expressed as a percentage, with which a gene exhibits an effect; **pen'etrancy.**—*adj.* **pen'etrant** penetrating.—*n.* (*chem*) a substance which increases the penetration of a liquid into porous material or between contiguous surfaces, by lowering its surface tension — *adj.* **pen'etrating** piercing: having keen and deep insight: sharp: keen: discerning —*adv.* **pen'etratingly.** —*n* **penetra'tion** the act or power of penetrating or entering: acuteness: discernment: the space-penetrating power of a telescope.—*adj.* **pen'etrative** tending or able to penetrate: piercing: having keen and deep insight: reaching and affecting the mind.— *adv.* **pen'etratively.**—*ns.* **pen'etrativeness**; **pen'etrator.** [L. *penetrāre*, *-ātum*—*penes*, in the house, possession, or power of.]

penfold. See pen¹, and cf. **pinfold.**

penguin *peng'gwin*, *pen'*, *n.* any bird of the *Sphenisciformes*, flightless sea birds of the Southern Hemisphere, of peculiar structure.—*n.* **pen'guinery**, **pen'guinry** a penguin breeding-place. [According to some, W. *pen*, head, *gwyn*, white, or the corresponding Breton words: conjectures are *pin-wing*, and L. *pinguis*, fat.]

penholder. See pen².

penial. See penis.

penicillate *pen-i-sil'it*, *-āt*, *pen'*, *adj.* tufted: forming a tuft: brush-shaped.—*adj.* **penicill'iform** paint-brush-shaped.—*ns.* **penicill'in** a group of substances that stop the growth of bacteria, extracted from moulds, esp. *Penicillium notatum*, of the genus of fungi, **Penicill'ium** (Ascomycetes; see ascus), which includes also the mould of jam, cheese, etc. (*P glaucum*). [L. *pēnicillus*, paintbrush, dim. of *pēnis*, tail.]

penile. See penis.

penillion. Same as **pennillion.**

peninsula *pen-in'sū-lə*, *n.* a piece of land that is almost an island.—*adj.* **penin'sular.**—*n.* **peninsular'ity.**— **Peninsular War** the war in Spain and Portugal carried on by Great Britain against Napoleon's marshals (1808–14). [L. *paeninsula*—*paene*, almost, *insula*, an island.]

penis *pē'nis*, *n.* the external male organ:—*pl.* **pē'nises**, **pē'nes** (*-nēz*)—*adjs.* **pē'nial**, **pē'nile.**—**penis envy** (*psych*) the Freudian concept of a woman's subconscious wish for male characteristics. [L. *pēnis*, orig. a tail.]

penitent *pen'i-tənt*, *adj.* suffering pain or sorrow for sin with will to amend: contrite: repentant: expressing sorrow for sin: undergoing penance: appropriate to penance.—*n.* one who sorrows for sin: one who has confessed sin, and is undergoing penance: a member of one of various orders devoted to penitential exercises and work among criminals, etc.—*ns.* **pen'itence**; **pen'itency** (*rare*) —*adj.* **penitential** (*-ten'shl*) of the nature of, pertaining to, or expressive of, penitence. —*n.* a book of rules relating to penance: a penitent: (in *pl.*) the behaviour or garb of a penitent: black clothes (*coll.*).—*adv.* **peniten'tially.**—*adj.* **penitentiary** (*-ten'sha-ri*) relating to penance: penitential. penal and reformatory.—*n.* an office (under the *Grand Penitentiary*) at Rome dealing with cases of penance, dispensations, etc : a book for guidance in imposing penances a reformatory prison or house of correction: a prison (*U.S.*).—*adv.* **pen'itently.** [L. *paenitēns*, *-entis*, pr p of *paenitēre*, to cause to repent, to repent.]

penknife, penman. See under pen².

penna *pen'ə*, *n.* a feather, esp. one of the large feathers of the wings or tail:—*pl.* **penn'ae** (-*ē*).—*adj.* **penn'ate** pinnate: winged, feathered, or like a wing in shape. [L. *penna*, feather, wings.]

pennant *pen'ant*, (*naut.*) *pen'ən, n.* a dangling line with a block (*naut.*): a long narrow flag: a signalling flag: a pennon.—**broad pennant** a long swallow-tailed flag flown by a commodore. [A combination of **pendant** and **pennon**.]

pennate. See **penna**.

penniless. See **penny**.

pennill *pen'il*, W. *pen'ıhl, n.* a form of Welsh improvised verse:—*pl.* **pennill'ion**. [Welsh.]

pennon *pen'ən, n.* a flag or streamer attached to a lance: a flag: a long narrow flag or streamer. [O.Fr *penon*, streamer, arrow-feather, prob.—L. *penna*, feather.]

penn'orth. See **penny**.

penny *pen'i, n.* a coin, originally silver, later copper, bronze from 1860, formerly worth 1/12 of a shilling, or 1/240 of a pound, now (**new penny**) equal to a hundredth part of £1: its value: applied to various more or less similar coins: a cent (*U.S.*): a small sum: money in general: (*pl.* **pennies** *pen'iz*, as material objects; **pence** *pens*, as units of value).—*adj.* sold for a penny: costing a penny.—*adj.* **penn'iless** without a penny: without money: poor.—*n.* **penn'ilessness**.—**penny-a-lin'er** a hack writer of the worst, or worst-paid, kind; **penny-a-lin'erism** a hack writer's expression; **penny arcade** an amusement arcade with slot machines orig. operated by a penny; **penny black** the first adhesive postage stamp, issued by Britain, 1840; **penn'ycress** a cruciferous plant of the genus *Thlaspi*, with round flat pods; **penny dreadful** see **dread**; **penn'y-far'thing** an old-fashioned bicycle with a big wheel and a little one.—*adj.* **penny'-in-the-slot** worked by putting a penny in a slot.—**penn'y-piece** a penny.—*adjs.* **penn'y-pinch'ing** miserly, too concerned with saving money; **penn'y-plain** plain, straightforward, unpretentious (from 19th cent. children's paper cut-out figures for toy theatres, costing one penny if plain, twopence if coloured; hence, **penny-plain, twopence-coloured** used of any two basically similar articles, one having a more attractive appearance).—**penn'yweight** twenty-four grains of troy weight (the weight of a silver penny); **penn'y-whist'le** a tin whistle or flageolet.—*adj.* **penn'y-wise** saving small sums at the risk of larger: niggardly on improper occasions.—**penn'y-wort** a name given to various plants with round leaves; **penn'yworth** a penny's worth of anything: the amount that can be got for a penny: a good bargain—also **penn'orth** (*pen'ərth*; *coll.*).—**a penny for your thoughts** (*coll.*) what are you thinking so deeply about?; **a pretty penny** a considerable sum of money; **in penny numbers** a very few, or a very little, at a time; **pennies from heaven** money obtained without effort and unexpectedly; **Peter's pence** Rome-scot, a tax or tribute of a silver penny paid to the Pope —in England perhaps from the time of Offa of Mercia, in Ireland from Henry II, abolished under Henry VIII: a similar tax elsewhere: a voluntary contribution to the Pope in modern times; **spend a penny** (*euph.*) to urinate; **the penny drops** now I (etc.) understand; **turn an honest penny** to earn some money honestly; **two a penny** in abundant supply and of little value. [O.E. *penig*.]

pennyroyal *pen-i-roi'əl, n.* a species of mint once esteemed in medicine. [M.E. *puliol real*—A.Fr. *puliol real*—L. *pūleıum, pūlegium*, pennyroyal, and *regālis, -e*, royal.]

pennywinkle. Same as **periwinkle**[2].

penology, poenology *pē-nol'ə-ji, n.* the study of punishment in its relation to crime: the management of prisons.—*adj.* **penological** (-*nə-loj'*).—*n.* **penologist**

(-*nol'ə-jist*). [Gr. *poinē*, punishment, *logos*, discourse.]

pensile *pen'sıl, -sil, adj.* hanging: suspended: overhanging: of birds, building a hanging nest.—*ns.* **pen'sileness, pensility** (-*sil'i-ti*). [L. *pēnsilis*—*pendēre*, to hang.]

pension *pen'shən, n.* an allowance of money as a bribe for future services, as a mark of favour, or in reward of one's own or another's merit: an allowance to one who has retired or has been disabled or reached old age or has been widowed or orphaned, etc.: (now pronounced as Fr., *pä-syɔ̃*) a Continental boarding-house: board.—*v.t.* to grant a pension to.—*adjs.* **pen'sionable** entitled, or entitling, to a pension; **pen'sionary** receiving a pension: of the nature of a pension.—*n.* one who receives a pension: one whose interest is bought by a pension.—*n.* **pen'sioner** one who receives a pension: a dependent: one who pays out of his own income for his commons, chambers, etc., at Cambridge University = an Oxford *commoner*.—**pension off** to dismiss, or allow to retire, with a pension. [Fr.,—L. *pēnsiō, -ōnis*—*pendēre, pēnsum*, to weigh, pay.]

pensive *pen'siv, adj.* meditative: expressing thoughtfulness with sadness.—*adv.* **pen'sively**.—*n.* **pen'siveness**. [Fr. *pensif, -ive*—*penser*, to think—L *pēnsāre*, to weigh—*pendēre*, to weigh.]

Penstemon. See **Pentstemon**.

penstock *pen'stok, n.* a sluice. [**pen**[1], **stock**.]

pensum *pen'sam, n.* a task. [L. *pēnsum*.]

pent[1] *pa.t.* and *pa.p.* of **pen**[1], to shut up.—*adj.* **pent'-up** held in: repressed.

pent[2] *pent, n.* a penthouse: a sloping or overhanging covering.—**pent'roof** a roof that slopes one way only [From **penthouse**, app influenced by Fr. *pente*, slope.]

pent-, penta- in composition, five.—*ns.* **pentachord** (*pen'tə-kòrd*; Gr. *chordē*, string) a musical instrument with five strings: a diatonic series of five notes; **pentacle** (*pent'ə-kl*; L.L. *pentaculum*, app.—Gr. *pente*; according to some, O.Fr. *pentacol—pendre*, to hang, *à*, on, *col*, the neck) a pentagram or similar figure (sometimes a hexagram) or amulet used as a defence against demons.—*adj.* **pentacy'clic** (Gr. *kyklos*, wheel) having five whorls.—*n.* **pent'ad** (Gr. *pentas, -ados*) a set of five things: a period of five years or five days.—Also *adj.*—*adjs* **pentad'ic**; **pentadac'tyl, pentadac'tyle** (-*til*; Gr. *daktylos*, finger, toe) having five digits.—*n.* a person with five fingers and five toes.—*adjs.* **pentadactyl'ic, pentadac'tylous**.—*ns.* **pentadac'tylism; pentagon** (*pen'tə-gon*; Gr. *pentagōnon—gōniā*, angle) a rectilineal plane figure having five angles and five sides (*geom.*): a fort with five bastions: (with *cap.*) the headquarters of the U.S. armed forces at Washington —from the shape of the building.—*adj.* **pentagonal** (*pen-tag'ən-əl*).—*adv.* **pentag'onally**.—*ns.* **pen'tagram** (Gr. *pentagrammon—gramma*, a letter) a stellate pentagon or five-pointed star: a magic figure of that form; **pentahe'dron** (Gr. *hedrā*, seat) a five-faced solid figure.—*pl.* **pentahe'drons, -dra**.—*adj.* **pentahe'dral**.—*n.* **pentam'erism** (Gr. *meros*, part) the condition of being pentamerous.—*adj.* **pentam'erous** having five parts or members: having parts in fives.—*ns.* **pentam'ery; pentam'eter** (Gr. *pentametros—metron*, a measure) a verse of five measures or feet; **pentane** (*pent'ān*) a hydrocarbon (C_5H_{12}), fifth member of the methane series; **pent'angle** a pentacle: a pentagon.—*adjs.* **pentang'ular; pentapodic** (*pent-ə-pod'ik*).—*ns.* **pentapody** (*pen-tap'ə-di*; Gr. *pous, podos*, foot) a measure of five feet; **pent'aprism** a five-sided prism that corrects lateral inversion by turning light through an angle of 90°, used on reflex cameras to allow eye-level viewing; **pentarchy** (*pent'-ärk-ı*) government by five persons: a group of five kings, rulers, states, or governments; **pentastich** (*pent'ə-stık*; Gr. stichos, row, line) a group of five lines of verse:—*pl.* **pentastichs** (*-stiks*).—*adjs.* **pentastichous** (*pen-tas'ti-kəs*) five-ranked; **pentasyllabic** five-syllabled.—*n.* **Pentateuch** (*pen-tə-tūk*; Gr. *pentateuchos*, five-volumed—*teuchos*, a tool; later, a book) the first five books of the Old Testament.—*adj.* **pentateuch'al**.—*ns.* **pentath'lete** a competitor in the **pentath'lon** (Gr. *penthalon—athlon*, contest) a contest in five exercises—wrestling, disc-throwing, spear-throwing, leaping, running: a five-event contest at the modern Olympic games from 1906–1924: a five-event Olympic games contest for women: (**modern pentathlon**) an Olympic games contest consisting of swimming, cross-country riding and running, fencing and revolver-shooting—also (Latin) **pentath'lum**.—*adjs.* **pentatomic** (*pent-ə-tom'ik*; Gr *atomos*, atom) having five atoms, esp. five atoms of replaceable hydrogen; **pentavalent**; **pentatonic** (*pent-ə-ton'ik*; Gr. *tonos*, tone) consisting of five tones or notes—applied esp. to a scale, a major scale with the fourth and seventh omitted; **pentavalent** (*pen-tə-vā'lənt, pen-tav'ə-lent*) having a valency of five. [Gr. *pente*, five.]

Pentecost *pent'i-kost*, *n.* a Jewish festival held on the fiftieth day after the second day of the Passover: the festival of Whitsuntide, seven weeks after Easter.—*adj.* **Pentecost'al** of or relating to Pentecost: of or relating to any of several fundamentalist Christian groups placing great emphasis on the spiritual powers of the Holy Spirit.—*n.* a Pentecostalist: (in *pl.*) offerings formerly made to the parish priest at Whitsuntide.—*n.* **Pentecost'alist** a member of a Pentecostal church. [Gr. *pentēkostē* (*hēmerā*), fiftieth (day).]

penteteric *pen-tı-ter'ik*, *adj.* occurring every fourth (by the old mode of reckoning, fifth) year [Gr. *pentetērikos—etos*, a year.]

penthouse *pent'hows*, *n.* a shed or lean-to projecting from or adjoining a main building: a separate room or dwelling on a roof: a roofed corridor surrounding the court in real tennis: a (small) sextet top flat: a protection from the weather over a door or a window: anything of similar form, as an eyebrow:—*pl.* **pent'-houses** (*-how-ziz*).—*v.t.* to provide or cover with, or as with, a penthouse. [For *pentice*—Fr. *appentis*—L.L. *appendicium*, an appendage.]

pentimento *pen-ti-men'tō*, *n.* something painted out of a picture which later becomes visible again:—*pl.* **-ti** (*tē*) [It.—*pentirsi*, to repent.]

pentode *pent'ōd*, *n.* a thermionic tube with five electrodes. [Gr. *pente*, five, *hodos*, way]

pentose *pent'ōs*, *n.* a sugar (of various kinds) with five oxygen atoms. [Gr. *pente*, five.]

Pentothal® *pen'tō-thal*, *n.* registered trademark for thiopentone, an intravenous anaesthetic, a sodium thiobarbiturate compound.—Also **Pentothal sodium.**

pentoxide *pent-ok'sīd*, (chem.) *n.* a compound having 5 atoms of oxygen combined with another element or radical. [Gr. *pente*, five, and **oxide**.]

pentroof. See **pent²**.

Pentstemon *pen(t)-stē'mən*, *n.* a mainly North American showy-flowered genus of Scrophulariaceae, with a sterile fifth stamen: (without *cap.*) a plant of this genus.—Also, and now more usu., **Penstē'mon**. [Gr. *pente*, five, *stēmōn*, warp, as if stamen.]

penuche, penuchi. Same as **panocha.**

penuchle. See **pinochle.**

penult *pi-nult'*, also *pē'nult*, **penult'ima** *-im-ə*, *ns.* the syllable last but one.—*adj.* **penult'imate** last but one —*n.* the penult: the last but one. [L *paenultima*

(*syllaba*, etc.)—*paene*, almost, *ultimus*, last.]

penumbra *pen-um'brə*, *n.* a partial or lighter shadow round the perfect or darker shadow of an eclipse: the less dark border of a sun-spot or any similar spot: the part of a picture where the light and shade blend into each other.—*adjs.* **penum'bral, penum'brous.** [L *paene*, almost, *umbra*, shade.]

penury *pen'ū-ri*, *n.* want: great poverty —*adj.* **penū'-rious** niggardly: miserly.—*adv.* **penū'riously.**—*n* **penū'riousness.** [L. *paenūra*]

peon *pē'on*, *n.* a day-labourer, esp formerly in Spanish-speaking America, ˈone working off a debt by bondage: in India (*pūn*), a foot-soldier (*hist*), a policeman (*hist.*), a messenger.—*ns.* **pē'onage, pē'onism** agricultural servitude of the above kind [Sp. *peón* and Port. *peão*—L L *pedō, -ōnis*, a foot-soldier —L. *pēs, pedis*, a foot]

peony, paeony *pē'ə-ni*, *n.* any plant of the genus *Paeonia*, of the buttercup family, with large showy crimson or white globular flowers: its flower [O.E. *peonie* and O.Fr (Northern) *pione* (Fr. *pivoine*)—L. *paeōnia*—Gr *paiōniā—Paiōn, Paiān*, physician of the gods from its use in medicine.]

people *pē'pl*, *n.* a nation· a community: a body of persons held together by belief in common origin, speech, culture, political union, or other bond: a set of persons: transferred to a set of animals as if forming a nation—in these senses used as *sing.* with a *pl.* **peo'ples** (*B.* **peo'ple**): a body of persons linked by common leadership, headship, etc.: subjects: retainers: followers: employees: servants: congregation: attendants: near kindred: members of one's household: parents: ancestors and descendants. inhabitants of a place: transferred to animal inhabitants: the persons associated with any business: laity: the mass of the nation: general population: populace: the citizens: voters: (approaching a *pron.*) they, one, folks—in these senses used as *pl.*—*v.t.* to stock with people or inhabitants: to inhabit: to occupy as if inhabiting.—**people's front** same as **popular front.** [O.Fr. *poeple*—L. *pōpulus*.]

pep *pep*, (*coll*) *n.* vigour, go, spirit.—*v.t* to put pep into (usu. with *up*).—*adjs.* **pep'ful, pepp'y.**—**pep pill** a pill containing a stimulant drug; **pep talk** a strongly-worded talk designed to arouse enthusiasm for a cause or course of action. [**pepper**.]

peplos *pep'los*, **peplus** *pep'ləs*, *ns.* a draped outer robe worn usu. by women in ancient Greece —*n.* **pep'lum** a peplos. an overskirt supposed to be like the peplos a short skirt-like section attached to the waist-line of a dress, blouse or jacket. [Gr. *peplos*.]

pepo *pē'pō*, *n.* the type of fruit found in the melon and cucumber family, a large many-seeded berry usually with hard epicarp:—*pl* **pē'pos.** [L. *pēpō, -ōnis*.]

pepper *pep'ər*, *n.* a pungent aromatic condiment consisting of the dried berries of the pepper plant, entire or powdered (*black pepper*), or with the outer parts removed (*white pepper*): any plant of the genus Piper, esp *P nigrum*, or of the family Piperaceae: a plant of the genus Capsicum or one of its pods (*red or green pepper*; also called **sweet pepper**)· cayenne (also **cay'enne-pepper**): extended to various similar condiments and the plants producing them —*v t* to sprinkle or flavour with pepper: to sprinkle: to pelt with shot, etc. to pelt thoroughly: to do for —*v.t* to pelt: to shower: to discharge shot, etc , in showers —*ns.* **pepp'eriness; pepp'ering.**—*adj* **pepp'ery** having the qualities of pepper: pungent: hot, choleric, irritable —*adj.* **pepper-and-salt** mingled black and white. of hair, flecked with grey —**pepp'ercorn** the dried berry of the pepper plant· something of little value.—*adj* like a peppercorn, as the small tight knots in which certain African peoples wear their hair: trivial, nominal, as *peppercorn rent*; **pepp'ermill** a small handmill in which peppercorns are ground; **pepp'ermint** an aromatic and pungent species of mint (*Mentha piperita*): a liquor distilled from it: a lozenge flavoured with it; **peppermint cream** a sweet creamy peppermint-flavoured substance: a sweet made of this; **pepp'ermint-drop** a peppermint-flavoured, usu hard, sweet; **pepp'er-pot** a pot or bottle with a perforated top for sprinkling pepper: a West Indian dish of cassareep, flesh or dried fish, and vegetables, esp green okra and chillies. [O.E *pipor*—L. *piper*—Gr. *peperi*—Sans. *pippali*.]

peppy. See **pep.**

pepsin, pepsine *pep'sin*, *n.* any of a group of closely allied proteins, digestive enzymes of the gastric juice of vertebrates.—*adj* **pep'tic** relating to or promoting digestion: having a good digestion: of or relating to pepsin or the digestive juices.—*ns* **pep'tide** any of a number of substances formed from amino-acids in which the amino-group of one is joined to the carboxyl group of another; **pep'tone** a product of the action of enzymes on albuminous matter —**peptic ulcer** an ulcer of the stomach or duodenum, etc [Gr. *pepsis*, digestion—*peptein*, to digest.]

per¹ *pûr*, *par*, *prep.* for each, a· (chiefly commercial) by.—**as per usual** (*coll* or *illit.*) as usual. [L. and O.Fr. *per*]

per² *pûr*, *per*, (L) through, by means of, according to —**per annum (diem, mensem)** (*an'əm*, *-ōōm*, *di'əm*, *dē'em*, *men'sam*, *men'sem*) yearly (daily, monthly), **per ardua ad astra** (*ar'dū-ə ad as'trə*, *ar'dōō-ä ad as'trä*) by steep and toilsome ways to the stars—Air Force motto; **per capita** (*kap'i-tə*, *kap'i-ta*), **per caput** (*kap'ōōt*) (counting) by heads: all sharing alike; **per contra** (*kon'tra*, *kon'tra*) on the contrary: as a set-off; **per impossibile** (*im-po-si'bi-lē*, *im-po-si'bi-le*) by an impossibility: if it were so, which it is not; **per procurationem** (*prok-ū-rā-shi-ō'nem*, *prō-kōō-rä-ti-ō'nem*) by the agency of another, by proxy; **per se** (*sē*, *sä*) by himself, etc.: essentially: in itself).

per- *pûr-*, *par-*, in composition (1) in chemistry, indicating the highest degree of combination with oxygen or other element or radical; (2) in words from Latin, through, beyond, or thoroughly, or indicating destruction.

peradventure *pûr-əd-ven'chər*, *adv.* by chance: perhaps. [O.Fr. *per* (or *par*) *aventure*, by chance.]

perai *pē-rī'*. See **piranha.**

perambulate *par-am'bū-lāt*, *v.t* to walk through, about, around, up and down, or over: to pass through for the purpose of surveying: to beat the bounds of: to patrol: to wheel in a perambulator.—*v.i* to walk about.—*ns.* **perambulā'tion**; **peram'bulātor** one who perambulates: a wheel for measuring distances on roads: a light carriage for a child (now usu. **pram**).— *adj.* **peram'bulatory.** [L. *perambulāre*, *-ātum*—*per*, through, *ambulāre*, to walk.]

Perca. See **perch¹.**

percale *per-käl'*, *par-käl'*, *n.* a closely woven French cambric.—*n.* **percaline** (*pûr-kə-lēn'*, or *pûr'-*) a glossy cotton cloth. [Fr.; cf. Pers. *purgâlah*, rag.]

perceive *par-sēv'*, *v.t.* to become or be aware of through the senses: to get knowledge of by the mind: to see: to understand: to discern.—**perceived noise decibel** a unit used to measure the amount of annoyance caused to people by noise. [O.Fr *percever*—L. *percipĕre*, *perceptum*—pfx. *per-*, thoroughly, *capĕre*, to take]

per cent (usu. written or printed with a point after it as if an abbreviation for *per centum*, but pronounced as a complete word, *pər-sent'*) in the hundred: for each hundred or hundred pounds.—*n.* a percentage· (in *pl.*, in composition) securities yielding a specified percentage (as *three-percents*).—*n.* **percent'age** rate

per hundred: an allowance of so much for every hundred· a proportional part· commission (*coll*): profit, advantage (*coll*).—*adjs* **percent'al, percen'tile.**—*n* **percen'tile** the value below which falls a specified percentage (as 25, 50, 75) of a large number of statistical units (e.g. scores in an examination): percentile rank —**percentile rank** grading according to percentile group. [L *per centum*]

percept *pûr'sept*, *n.* an object perceived by the senses: the mental result of perceiving —*n* **perceptibil'ity.** —*adj* **percep'tible** that can be perceived: that may be known by the senses: discernible.—*adv* **percep'tibly.** —*n.* **percep'tion** the act or power of perceiving. discernment: apprehension of any modification of consciousness: the combining of sensations into a recognition of an object direct recognition. a percept· reception of a stimulus (*bot*) —*adjs.* **percep'-tional; percep'tive** able or quick to perceive: discerning: active or instrumental in perceiving —*ns* **percep'tiveness; perceptiv'ity.**—*adj* **percep'tual** of the nature of, or relating to, perception [L *percipĕre*, *perceptum*; see **perceive.**]

perch¹ *pûrch*, *n.* a spiny-finned fresh-water fish of the genus Perca (*pûr'kə*): extended to various fishes of the same or kindred family, or other.—*adj* **per'coid** (*-koid*). [L *perca* (partly through Fr. *perche*)—Gr. *perkē*, a perch]

perch² *pûrch*, *n* a rod for a bird to alight, sit, or roost on· anything serving the purpose for a bird, a person, or anything else: a high seat: a rod or pole, a measure of 5½ yards (5·03 metres).—*v i.* to alight, sit or roost on a perch: to be set on high to be balanced on a high or narrow footing· to settle —*v.t* to place, as on a perch: to stretch, examine, or treat on a perch —*adj* **perch'ing** with feet adapted for perching —**perching birds** the Passeriformes. [Fr *perche*—L. *pertica*, a rod.]

perchance *pər-châns'*, *adv* by chance· as it may happen: perhaps [A.Fr. *par chance*.]

percheron *per'shə-rō*, *pûr'shə-ron*, *n.* a draught-horse of a breed originating in La *Perche* in Southern Normandy.—Also *adj.* [Fr.]

perchloric *pər-klō-rik*, *-klo'rik*, *adj* containing more oxygen than chloric acid—applied to an oily explosive acid, $HClO_4$ —*n.* **perchlo'rate** a salt of perchloric acid [per- (1)]

percipient *pər-sip'i-ənt*, *adj* perceiving having the faculty of perception —*n.* one who perceives or can perceive. one who receives impressions telepathically or otherwise supersensibly —*ns* **percip'ience**, (*rare*) **percip'iency.** [L. *percipiēns*, *-entis*, pr p of *percipĕre*; cf. **perceive, percept.**]

percoid *pûr'koid.* See **perch¹.**

percolate *pûr'kə-lāt*, *v.t* and *v i* to pass through pores, small openings. etc : to filter —*n* a filtered liquid — *ns* **percolation** (*pûr-kō-lā'shən*), **per'colător** an apparatus for percolating, esp for making coffee [L. *percōlāre*, *-ātum*—*per*, through, *cōlāre*, to strain.]

percuss *pər-kus'*, *v.t.* to strike so as to shake: to tap for purposes of diagnosis.—*n.* **percussion** (*-kush'ən*) striking: impact: tapping directly or indirectly upon the body to find the condition of an organ by the sound (*med.*): massage by tapping· the striking or sounding of a discord, etc , as distinguished from preparation and resolution (*mus*): collectively, instruments played by striking—drum, cymbals, triangle, etc. (*mus*): a device for making an organ-pipe speak promptly by striking the reed (*mus.*) —*adj.* **percuss'ional.**—*n.* **percuss'ionist** a musician who plays percussion instruments.—*adj.* **percussive** (*-kus'*).—*adv.* **percuss'ively.**—*n.* **percuss'or** a percussion hammer —*adj.* **percutient** (*-kū'shyent*) striking or having power to strike —*n* that which strikes or has power to strike.—**percuss'ion-bull'et** a bullet that explodes on striking; **percuss'ion-cap** a metal case containing a fulminating substance which explodes when struck, formerly used for firing rifles, etc.: a small paper case of the same type, used to make children's toy guns sound realistic (usu. **cap**); **percuss'ion-fuse** a fuse in a projectile that acts on striking; **percuss'ion-hamm'er** a small hammer for percussion in diagnosis; **percuss'ion-lock** a gun lock in which a hammer strikes a percussion-cap.—**bulb of percussion** see **bulb**. [L. *percussiō*, *-ōnis*—*percutēre*, *percussum*—pfx. *per-*, thoroughly, *quatēre*, to shake.]

percutaneous *pər-kū-tā'ni-əs, adj.* done or applied through the skin.—*adv.* **percutā'neously**. [per- (2), L. *cutis*, the skin.]

percutient. See **percuss**.

perdendo *per-den'dō, (mus.) adj.* and *adv.* dying away in volume of tone and in speed.—Also **perden'dosi** (*-sē*). [It.]

perdition *pər-dish'ən, n.* the utter loss of happiness in a future state: hell. [L. *perditiō, -ōnis*—*perdēre*, *per-ditum*—pfx. *per-*, entirely, *dāre*, to give, give up.]

père *per*, (Fr) *n.* father.—**Père David's** (*dā'vidz, dā'vēdz, -vēdz'*) **deer** a breed of large grey deer discovered in China by Father A *David*, 19th cent. French missionary, and now surviving only in captivity.

peregrine *per'i-grin, adj.* applied to a species of falcon (*Falco peregrinus*), so named because taken not from the (inaccessible) nest (as an eyas is) but while in flight from it.—*n.* a peregrine falcon.—*v.i.* per'-egrinate to travel about: to live in a foreign country. to go on pilgrimage.—*v.t.* to traverse.—*ns.* peregrinā'tion travelling about: wandering: pilgrimage: a complete and systematic course or round: a sojourn abroad; per'egrinator one who travels about. [L. *peregrinus*, foreign—*peregre*, abroad—*per*, through, *ager*, field.]

pereira *pə-re'rə, n.* a Brazilian tree, the bark of which is used medicinally: the bark itself.—Both also **pereira bark**. [From Jonathan *Pereira*, 19th. cent. English pharmacologist.]

peremptory *pər-em(p)'tə-ri,* or *per'əm(p)-, adj.* imperious: arrogantly commanding.—*adv.* **peremp'torily** (or *per'*).—*n.* **peremp'toriness** (or *per'*). [L. *peremptōrius—perimēre, peremptum,* to destroy, prevent—pfx. *per-,* entirely, and *emēre,* to take, to buy.]

perennial *pər-en'yəl, adj.* lasting through the year: perpetual: never failing: growing constantly: lasting more than two years (*bot.*): of insects, living more than one year.—*n.* a plant that lives more than two years.—*adv.* **perenn'ially**.—*n.* **perennial'ity**. [L. *perennis—per,* through, *annus,* a year.]

perfect *pūr'fekt, -fikt, adj.* done thoroughly or completely: completed: mature: complete: having all organs in a functional condition: having androecium and gynaeceum in the same flower: completely skilled or versed: thoroughly known or acquired: exact: exactly conforming to definition or theory: flawless: having every moral excellence: sheer, utter: of the simpler kind of consonance (*mus.*).—*n.* the perfect tense: a verb in the perfect tense.—*v.t.* per'-fect (*pər-fekt'*, or *pūr'*) to make perfect: to finish: to teach fully, to make fully skilled in anything.—*ns.* perfect'er (or *pūr'*); perfectibil'ity capability of becoming perfect.—*adj.* perfect'ible capable of becoming perfect.—*ns.* perfec'tion state of being perfect: a quality in perfect degree: the highest state or degree: an embodiment of the perfect: loosely, a degree of excellence approaching the perfect.—*v.t.* perfec'tionate to bring to perfection.—*ns.* perfec'tion-

ism; perfec'tionist one who claims to be perfect: one who aims at or calls for nothing short of perfection: one who thinks that moral perfection can be attained in this life.—*adj.* perfect'ive tending to make perfect. of a verb aspect, denoting completed action (*gram.*). —*advs.* perfect'ively; per'fectly.—*ns.* per'fectness the state or quality of being perfect: completeness, perfect'o (Sp., perfect; *pl.* perfect'os) a large tapering cigar.—**perfect binding** an unsewn book-binding in which the backs of the gathered sections are sheared off and the leaves held in place by glue; **perfect cadence** one passing from the chord of the dominant to that of the tonic; **perfect fifth** the interval between two sounds whose vibration frequencies are as 2 to 3; **perfect fourth** the interval between sounds whose vibration frequencies are as 3 to 4; **perfect insect** the imago or completely developed form of an insect; **perfect interval** the fourth, fifth, or octave, **perfect number** a number equal to the sum of its aliquot parts, as $6 = 1 + 2 + 3, 28 = 1 + 2 + 4 + 7 + 14$; **perfect pitch** (*mus.*) a term often used for *absolute pitch*; **perfect tense** a tense signifying action completed in the past (e.g. *I have said*) or at the time spoken of (**past perfect, pluperfect** e.g. *I had said*; **future perfect** e.g. *I shall have left by then*).—**to perfection** perfectly. [M.E. *parfit*—O.Fr. *parfit*; assimilated to L. *perfectus,* pa.p. of *perficēre*—pfx. *per-,* thoroughly, *facēre,* to do.]

perfervid *pər-fūr'vid, (poet.) adj.* very fervid. ardent: eager.—*ns.* **perfervidity** (*pûr-fər-vid'i-ti*), **perfer'-vidness;** perfer'vour, -or. [L. *perfervidus—prae,* before, *fervidus,* fervid.]

perfidious *pər-fid'i-əs, adj.* faithless: unfaithful. basely violating faith.—*adv.* perfid'iously.—*ns.* perfid'-iousness, perfidy (*pûr'fid-i*). [L. *perfidiōsus—per-fidia,* faithlessness—pfx. *per-,* implying destruction, *fidēs,* faith.]

perfoliate *pər-fō'li-āt, adj.* (of a leaf) having the base joined around the stem, so as to appear pierced by the stem—orig. said of the stem passing through the leaf, or of the plant.—*n.* perfolia'tion. [per- (2), L. *folium,* a leaf.]

perforate *pûr'fə-rāt, v.t.* to bore through or into. to pierce or to make a hole through: to penetrate: to pass through by a hole.—*adj.* pierced by a hole or holes: having an aperture. pierced by rows of small holes for easy separation (as postage-stamps) (more usually per'forated).—*adj* per'forable.—*ns.* per'-forans the long flexor muscle of the toes, or the deep flexor muscle of the fingers, whose tendons pass through those of the perforatus; perforation (*pûr-fə-rā'shən*) the act of making a hole: the forma-tion of a hole or aperture: the condition of being perforated: a hole through or into anything: a series, or one of a series, of small holes, as for ease in tearing paper.—*adj.* per'forative having the power to pierce. —*ns.* per'forator one who bores: a boring instrument or organ; perforatus (*pûr-fə-rā'təs*) the short flexor of the toes or the superficial flexor of the fingers. [L. *perforāre, -ātum—per,* through, *forāre,* to bore.]

perforce *pər-fōrs', -fors', adv.* by force: of necessity. [O.Fr. *par force.*]

perform *pər-form', v.t.* to do. to carry out duly: to act in fulfilment of: to fulfil: to bring about: to render. to execute: to go through duly: to act: to play in due form.—*v.i.* to do what is to be done: to execute a function: to act, behave: to act a part: to play or sing: to do feats, tricks, or other acts for exhibition.—*adj.* perform'able capable of being performed: practic-able.—*n.* perform'ance the act of performing: a carrying out of something: something done: a piece of work: manner or success in working: execution, esp as an exhibition or entertainment: an act or action: an instance of awkward, aggressive, embarrassing, etc., behaviour (*coll.*).—*adj.* **perform'ative** of a statement or verb, that itself constitutes the action described, e.g. *I confess my ignorance.*—*n.* such a statement (opp. of **constative**).—*n.* **perform'er** one who performs: one who does or fulfils what is required of him: an executant: one who takes part in a performance or performances: one who does feats or tricks, esp. in exhibition.—*adj.* **perfor'ming** that performs: trained to perform tricks.—*n.* performance.—**performance art** a theatrical presentation in which several art forms, such as acting, music, photography, etc., are combined; **performing arts** those in which an audience is present, as drama, ballet, etc.; **performing right** the right to give a public performance of a piece of music or play. [A.Fr. *parfourner*, app. an altered form of *parfourner*—O.Fr. *parfournir*, *par*—L. *per*, through, *fournir*, to furnish.]

perfume *pûr'fūm*, formerly and still sometimes *pər-fūm'*, *n.* sweet-smelling smoke or fumes from burning: any substance made or used for the sake of its pleasant smell: fragrance—*v.t.* **perfume** (*pər-fūm'*, sometimes *pûr'fūm*) to scent.—*adjs.* **per'-fumed** (or *pər-fūmd'*); **per'fumeless** (or *-fūm'*).—*ns.* **perfū'mer** one who fumigates: a maker or seller of perfumes; **perfū'mery** perfumes in general: the art of preparing perfumes: the shop or place in a shop where perfumes are sold.—*adj.* **per'fumy.** [Fr. *parfum*—L. *per*, through, *fūmus*, smoke.]

perfunctory *pər-fungk'tə-ri*, *adj.* done merely as a duty to be got through: done for form's sake, or in mere routine: acting without zeal or interest: merely formal: hasty and superficial.—*adv.* **perfunc'torily.** —*n.* **perfunc'toriness.** [L. *perfunctōrius*—*perfunctus*, pa.p. of *perfungī*, to execute—pfx. *per-*, thoroughly, *fungī*, to do.]

perfuse *pər-fūz'*, *v.t.* to pour or diffuse through or over: to force, as a liquid, through an organ or tissue. —*n.* **perfusion** (*-fū'zhən*).—*adj.* **perfusive** (*-fū'siv*). [L. *perfūsus*, poured over—*per*, through, *fundēre*, *fūsus*, to pour.]

pergola *pûr'gə-lə*, *n.* a structure with climbing plants along a walk. [It.—L. *pergula*, a shed.]

perhaps *pər-haps'*, *adv.* it may be: possibly: as it may happen. [From the pl. of **hap**, after the model of **peradventure, perchance.**]

peri- *per'i-*, *pə-ri'-*, in composition, (1) around; (2) esp. in astron., near. [Gr. *peri*, around.]

perianth *per'i-anth*, (*bot.*) *n.* calyx and corolla together, esp. when not clearly distinguishable.—Also *adj.* [**peri-** (1), Gr. *anthos*, flower.]

periblem *per'i-blem*, (*bot.*) *n.* the layer of primary meristem from which the cortex is formed, covering the plerome. [Gr. *periblēma*, garment, mantle—*peri, ballein*, to throw.]

pericardium *per-i-kàr'di-əm*, (*anat.*) *n.* the sac round the heart.—*adjs.* **pericar'diac, pericar'dial, pericar'-dian.**—*n.* **pericardi'tis** inflammation of the pericardium. [Latinised from Gr. *perikardion*—*peri, kardiā*, heart.]

pericarp *per'i-kàrp*, (*bot.*) *n.* the wall of a fruit, derived from that of the ovary. [Gr. *perikarpion*—*peri, karpos*, fruit.]

perichondrium *per-i-kon'dri-əm*, *n.* the fibrous investment of cartilage. [**peri-** (1), Gr. *chondros*, cartilage.]

periclase *per'i-klāz, -klàs*, *n* native magnesia. [Gr. pfx. *peri-*, very, *klasis*, fracture (from its perfect cleavage).]

periclinal *per-i-klī'nəl*, *adj.* quaquaversal (*geol.*): parallel to the outer surface (*bot.*). [Gr. *periklīnēs*, sloping on all sides—*peri, klīnein*, to slope.]

pericranium *per-i-krā'ni-əm*, *n.* the membrane that surrounds the cranium: (*loosely*) skull or brain.—*adj.* **pericrā'nial.** [Latinised from Gr. *perikrānion*—*peri, krānion*, skull.]

pericycle *per'i-sī-kl*, (*bot.*) *n.* the outermost layer or layers of the central cylinder.—*adj.* **pericy'clic.** [Gr. *perikyklos*, all round—*peri, kyklos*, a circle.]

pericynthion *per-i-sin'thi-ən*, *n.* Same as **perilune.** [**peri-** (2), *Cynthia*, a name of the goddess of the moon.]

periderm *per'i-dûrm*, *n* the horny cuticular covering of a hydroid colony: the cork-cambium with the cork and other tissues derived from it, forming a protective outer covering in plants—*adj.* **periderm'al.** [**peri-** (1), Gr. *derma*, skin.]

peridesmium *per-i-des'mi-əm*, (*anat.*) *n.* the areolar tissue round a ligament. [**peri-** (1), Gr. *desmos*, a band.]

peridot *per'i-dot*, **peridote** *-dōt*, *ns.* olivine: a green olivine used in jewellery.—*adj.* **peridot'ic.**—*n.* **peridotite** (*-dō'tīt*) a coarse-grained igneous rock mainly composed of olivine, usually with other ferro-magnesian minerals but little or no feldspar [Fr. *péridot.*]

periegesis *per-i-ē-jē'sis*, *n.* a description in manner of a tour: a progress or journey through. [Gr. *periēgēsis* —*peri, hēgeesthai*, to lead.]

perigastric *per-i-gas'trik*, *adj.* surrounding the alimentary canal.—*n.* **perigastri'tis** inflammation of the outer surface of the stomach. [**peri-** (1), Gr. *gastēr*, belly.]

perigee *per'i-jē*, (*astron.*) *n.* the point of the moon's, or any artificial satellite's, orbit at which it is nearest the earth—opp. to *apogee.*—*adjs.* **perigē'al, perigē'an.** [Gr. *perigeion*, neut. of *perigeios*, round or near the earth—*peri, gē*, earth.]

Perigordian *per-i-gòr'di-ən*, *adj.* pertaining to the Palaeolithic epoch to which the Lascaux Cave paintings and other examples of primitive art belong. [*Périgord*, region in S.W. France.]

perihelion *per-i-hē'li-ən*, *n.* the point of the orbit of a planet or a comet at which it is nearest to the sun— opp. to *aphelion:* culmination (*fig.*).—Also *adj.* [**peri-** (2), Gr. *hēlios*, the sun.]

perihepatic *per-i-hi-pat'ik*, *adj.* surrounding the liver. —*n.* **perihepatitis** (*-hep-ə-tī'tis*) inflammation of the peritoneum covering the liver. [**peri-** (1), Gr. *hēpar, hēpatos*, liver.]

peril *per'il*, *n.* danger.—*v.t.* to expose to danger: —*pr.p.* **per'illing;** *pa.t* and *pa.p.* **per'illed.**— *adj.* **per'ilous** dangerous.—*adv.* **per'ilously.**—*n.* **per'ilousness.** [Fr. *péril*—L. *periculum.*]

perilune *per'i-lūn*, *-lōōn*, *n.* the point in a spacecraft's orbit round the moon where it is closest to it—also **pericynthion.** [**peri-** (2), Fr. *lune*—L. *luna*, moon]

perimeter *pər-im'i-tər*, *n.* the circuit or boundary of any plane figure, or the sum of all its sides (*geom.*): an instrument for measuring the field of vision (*med.*): the boundary of a camp or fortified position: the outer edge of any area—*adj.* **perimetric** (*per-i-met'-rik*).—*n.* **perim'etry.** [Gr. *perimetros—peri, metron*, measure.]

perimysium *per-i-miz'i-əm*, *n.* the connective tissue which surrounds and binds together muscle fibres [**peri-** (1), *-mysium*—Gr. *mus*, muscle.]

perinaeum, perineum *per-i-nē'əm*, *n.* the lower part of the body between the genital organs and the anus.— *adj.* **perinae'al, perinē'al.** [Latinised from Gr. *perinaion.*]

perinatal *per-i-nā'tl*, *adj.* pertaining to the period between the seventh month of pregnancy and the first week of life. [**peri-** (1), and **natal'**.]

perinephrium *per-i-nef'ri-əm*, *n* the fatty tissue surrounding the kidney.—*adj.* **perineph'ric.**—*n.*

perinephri'tis inflammation of the perinephrium. [**peri-** (1), Gr. *nephros*, kidney.]

perineum. See **perinaeum.**

perineurium *per-i-nū'ri-əm, n.* the sheath of connective tissue about a bundle of nerve fibres.—*adj.* **perineu'ral.**—*n.* **perineuri'tis** inflammation of the perineurium. [**peri-** (1), Gr. *neuron*, nerve.]

period *pē'ri-əd, n.* the time in which anything runs its course: an interval of time at the end of which events recur in the same order: the time required for a complete oscillation—reciprocal of the frequency: the time of a complete revolution of a heavenly body about its primary: the difference between two successive values of a variable for which a function has the same value: the recurring part of a circulating decimal: a set of figures (usu. three) in a large number marked off e.g. by commas: a series of chemical elements represented in a horizontal row of the periodic table: a stretch of time: a long stretch, an age: one of the main divisions of geological time: a stage or phase in history, in a man's life and development, in a disease, or in any course of events: a time: a division of the school day, the time of one lesson: the end of a course: a recurring time: (the time of) menstrual discharge: a complete sentence, esp. one of elaborate construction: in music, a division analogous to a sentence: (in *pl.*) rounded rolling rhetoric: a mark (.) at the end of a sentence—a full stop: a rhythmical division in Greek verse.—*adj.* (of e.g. architecture, furniture, a play) characteristic, representative, imitative of, belonging to, or dealing with, a past period.—*adjs.* **periodic** (*pēr-i-od'ik*) relating to a period or periods: of revolution in an orbit: having a period: recurring regularly in the same order: (*loosely*) occurring from time to time: characterised by or constructed in periods: pertaining to periodicals (*rare*); **period'ical** periodic: published in numbers at more or less regular intervals: of, for, or in such publications.—*n.* a magazine or other publication that appears at stated intervals (not usually including newspapers).—*adv.* **period'ically** at regular intervals: in a periodic manner: in a periodical publication: (*loosely*) from time to time.—*ns.* **periodicity** (*-dis'-*) the fact or character of being periodic: frequency; **periodisa'tion, -iza'tion** division into periods.— **periodic function** (*math.*) one whose values recur in a cycle as the variable increases; **periodic system** the classification of chemical elements according to this law; **periodic table** a table of chemical elements in order of atomic number arranged in horizontal series and vertical groups, showing how similar properties recur at regular intervals; **period piece** an object belonging to a past age esp. with charm or value: a person ludicrously behind the times: a play, novel, etc., set in a past time. [Fr. *période*—L. *periodus*—Gr *periodos*—*peri, hodos,* a way.]

periodontal *per-i-ō-dont'əl, adj.* (pertaining to tissues or regions) round about a tooth.—*ns.* **periodon'tics** (*n. sing.*), **periodontol'ogy** the branch of dentistry concerned with periodontal diseases; **periodon'tist.** [**peri-** (1), *odous, odontos,* tooth.]

perionychium *per-i-o-nik'i-əm, n.* the skin surrounding a fingernail or toenail. [**peri-** (1), Gr. *onux*, a nail]

periosteum *per-i-os'ti-əm, n.* a tough fibrous membrane covering the surface of bones.—*adjs.* **perios'teal; periostit'ic.**—*n.* **periostit'tis** inflammation of the periosteum. [Gr. *periosteon* (neut. adj.)—*peri, osteon,* a bone.]

peripatetic *per-i-pə-tet'ik, adj.* walking about: of e.g. a teacher, itinerant.—*n.* a pedestrian: an itinerant.— *adj.* **peripatet'ical.** [Gr. *peripatētikos*—*peripatos,* a walk—*peri, pateein,* to walk.]

peripet(e)ia *per-i-pe-tī'ə, n.* a sudden change of

fortune, esp. in drama. [Gr. *peripeteia*—*peri,* and *pet-* the root of *piptein,* to fall.]

periphery *pər-if'ə-ri, n.* bounding line or surface: the outside of anything· a surrounding region.—*adj.* **periph'eral** of or relating to a periphery: not of the most important: incidental: minor.—*n.* a peripheral unit.—**peripheral units, devices** in a computer system, the input (e.g. card reader), output (e.g magnetic tape), and storage devices, which are computer-controlled. [Gr. *periphereia*—*peri, pherein,* to carry.]

periphrasis *pər-if'rə-sis, n.* round-about expression:— *pl.* **periph'rases** (*-sēz*).—*n.* **periphrase** (*per'i-frāz*) periphrasis:—*pl* **periphrás'es.**—*v.t.* to say with circumlocution.—*v.t.* to use circumlocution.—*adjs* **periphrastic** (*per-i-fras'tik*), **-al** using periphrasis: using at least two words instead of a single inflected form, esp. of a verb tense involving an auxiliary.— *adv* **periphras'tically.** [Gr. *periphrasis*—*peri, phrasis,* speech.]

periplast *per'i-plast,* (*zool.*) *n.* intercellular substance: the ectoplasm of flagellates: cuticle covering the ectoplasm. [**peri-** (1), Gr. *plastos,* moulded.]

perique *pə-rēk', n.* a strongly-flavoured tobacco from Louisiana. [Perh. *Périque,* nickname of a grower.]

periscope *per'i-skōp, n.* a tube with mirrors by which an observer in a trench, a submarine, etc., can see what is going on above.—*adj.* **periscopic** (*-skop'ik*). [Gr. *periskopeein,* to look around.]

perish *per'ish, v.i.* to pass away completely: to waste away: to decay: to lose life: to be destroyed: to be ruined or lost.—*v.t* to destroy: to ruin: to cause to decay: to distress with cold, hunger, etc.—*n.* **perishabil'ity.**—*adj.* **per'ishable** that may perish: subject to speedy decay.—*n.* that which is perishable: (in *pl.*) food or other stuff liable to rapid deterioration.—*n.* **per'ishableness.**—*adv.* **per'ishably.**—*adj.* **per'ished** distressed by cold, hunger, etc. (*coll.* or *dial.*): of materials such as rubber, weakened or injured by age or exposure.—*n.* **per'isher** (*slang*) a reprehensible and annoying person.—*adj.* **per'ishing** (*coll.* or *dial.*) freezing cold· vaguely used as a pejorative.—Also *adv.*—*adv.* **per'ishingly.** [O.Fr. *perir,* pr p. *perissant*—L. *perire, peritum,* to perish— pfx. *per-, ire,* to go.]

perisperm *per'i-spûrm,* (*bot.*) *n.* nutritive tissue in a seed derived from the nucellus.—*adjs.* **perispermal, perisper'mic.** [**peri-** (1), Gr. *sperma,* seed.]

perissodactyl *pər-is-ō-dak'til, adj* having an odd number of toes.—*n.* an animal of the **Perissodac'tyla,** a division of ungulates with an odd number of toes— horse, tapir, rhinoceros, and extinct kinds (distinguished from the *Artiodactyla*).—*adjs.* **perissodac'tylate, perissodactyl'ic, perissodac'tylous.** [Gr *perissos,* odd, *daktylos,* a finger, toe.]

peristalith *pər-is'tə-lith, n* a stone circle. [Irregularly formed from Gr. *peri, histanai,* to set up, *lithos,* a stone.]

peristaltic *per-i-stalt'ik, adj.* forcing onward by waves of contraction, as the alimentary canal and other organs do their contents.—*n.* **peristal'sis.**—*adj.* **peristalt'ically.** [Gr. *peristaltikos*—*peristellein,* to wrap round—*peri, stellein,* to place.]

peristyle *per'i-stīl, n.* a range of columns round a building or round a square: a court, square, etc., with columns all round.—*adj.* **peristy'lar.** [L. *peristyl(i)um*—Gr. *peristylon*—*peri, stylos,* a column.]

peritoneum, peritonaeum *per-i-tan-ē'əm, n.* a serous membrane enclosing the viscera in the abdominal and pelvic cavities.—*adjs.* **peritone'al, peritonae'al; peritonitic** (*-it'ik*) of peritonitis, suffering from peritonitis.—*n.* **peritoni'tis** inflammation of the peritoneum. [Gr. *peritonaion*—*peri, teinein,* to stretch.]

perityphlitis *per-i-tif-lī'tis, n.* inflammation of some part near the blind-gut. [peri- (1), Gr. *typhlos*, blind.]

periwig *per'i-wig, (hist.) n.* a wig. [Earlier *perwyke, perwig, perywig,* etc.—Fr. *perruque*; see **peruke, wig**¹.]

periwinkle¹ *per'i-wingk-l, n.* a creeping evergreen plant, growing in woods: the light blue colour of some of its flowers.—*adj.* of this colour. [M.E. *peruenke* —O.E. *peruince,* from L. *pervinca.*]

periwinkle² *per'i-wingk-l, n.* an edible gasteropod (*Littorina littorea*) abundant between tide-marks, or other member of the genus: extended to other kinds. —Also **pennywinkle.** [O.E. (pl.) *pinewinclan* (or perh. *winewinclan*)—*wincle,* a whelk.]

perjure *pûr'jər, v.t.* to forswear oneself (*refl.*): to cause to swear falsely.—*v i.* to swear falsely.—*adj.* **per'-jured** having sworn falsely: being sworn falsely, as an oath.—*n.* **per'jurer.**—*adjs* **perjurious** (*-jōō'ri-əs*), **per'jurous** (*arch.*) guilty of or involving perjury.—*n.* **per'jury** false swearing: the breaking of an oath: the crime committed by one who, when giving evidence on oath or affirmation as a witness in a court of justice, gives evidence which he knows to be false (*law.*). [O.Fr. *parjurer*—L. *perjūrāre*—*per-, jūrāre,* to swear.]

perk¹ *pûrk, (arch.) v.i.* to bear oneself with self-confidence or self-assertion.—*adv.* **perk'ily.**—*n* **perk'-iness.**—*adj.* **perk'y** self-assertive: cocky: pert: in good spirits.—**perk up** to recover spirits or energy, esp. in sickness: to jerk up, cock up: to decorate so as to look newer, more interesting, etc., to smarten up.

perk² *pûrk, (coll.) n.* Short for **perquisite.**

perk³ *pûrk, v.t.* and *n.* Short for **percolate, percolator** (of coffee).

perkin. See parkin.

perky. See perk¹.

perlite *pûr'līt, n.* any acid volcanic glass with perlitic structure: pearlite.—*adj.* **perlitic** (*-it'ik*) showing little concentric spheroidal or spiral cracks between rectilineal ones. [Fr. *perle,* Ger. *Perle,* pearl.]

perlocution *pûr-lə-kū'shən, (philos.) n.* an act that is the effect of an utterance, as frightening, persuading, comforting, etc. (cf. **illocution**).—*adj.* **perlocū'tionary.** [per- (2) and **locution.**]

perm¹ *pûrm, (coll.) n.* short for of **permutation.**—*v.t.* to permute: to arrange a forecast according to some defined system of combination or permutation.

perm² *pûrm, (coll.) n.* short for of **permanent wave.**— *v.t.* (*coll.*) to impart a permanent wave to.

permafrost *pûr'mə-frost, n.* permanently frozen subsoil. [**permanent, frost.**]

permalloy *pûrm'a-loi, n.* any of various alloys of iron and nickel, often containing other elements, e.g copper, molybdenum, chromium, which has high magnetic permeability. [**permeable alloy.**]

permanent *pûr'mə-nənt, adj.* remaining, or intended to remain, indefinitely.—*ns.* **per'manence** the fact or state of being permanent; **per'manency** permanence: a thing that is permanent.—*adv.* **per'manently.**— **permanent teeth** the adult teeth, which come after the milk-teeth lost in childhood; **permanent wave** a long-lasting artificial wave in hair. [L. *permanēns, -entis,* pr.p. of *permanēre*—*per,* through, *manēre,* to continue.]

permanganate *pər-mang'gə-nāt, n.* a salt of permanganic acid (HMnO₄), esp. **potassium permanganate** (KMnO₄) which is used as an oxidising and bleaching agent and as a disinfectant. [per- (1), and **manganese.**]

permeate *pûr'mi-āt, v.t.* to pass through the pores of: to penetrate and fill the pores of: to pervade: to saturate.—*v.i.* to diffuse.—*n.* **permeabil'ity**—*adj* **per'meable.**—*adv.* **per'meably.**—*n.* **per'meance** the

act of permeating: the reciprocal of the reluctance of a magnetic circuit; **permea'tion.**—*adj.* **per'meative** having power to permeate.—**magnetic permeability** the ratio of flux-density to magnetising force. [L. *permeāre*—*per,* through, *meāre,* to pass]

Permian *pûr'mi-ən, (geol.) n.* the uppermost Palaeozoic system.—*adj.* of that system. [*Perm,* in Russia, where it is widely developed.]

permissible, etc. See **permit.**

permit *pər-mit', v.t.* to allow.—*v.t.* to allow—*pr.p* **permitt'ing;** *pa.t.* and *pa.p.* **permitt'ed.**—*n.* (*pûr'*) permission, esp. in writing.—*n.* **permissibil'ity.**—*adj* **permiss'ible** that may be permitted: allowable.—*adv* **permiss'ibly.**—*n.* **permission** (*-mish'ən*) an act of permitting: leave.—*adj.* **permiss'ive** granting permission or liberty: permitted, optional: lenient, indulgent: allowing much freedom in social conduct (as in the **permissive society**—from c. 1960)—*adv* **permiss'ively.** —*n* **permiss'iveness.** [L. *permittĕre, -missum,* to let pass through—*per, mittĕre,* to send.]

permute *pər-mūt', v.t.* to interchange: to transmute: to subject to permutation.—*n* **permūtabil'ity.**—*adj.* **permūt'able** interchangeable.—*v.t.* **per'mūtate** to subject to permutation.—*n.* **permūta'tion** transmutation. the arrangement of a set of things in every possible order (*math.*). any one possible order of arrangement of a given number of things taken from a given number: immediate inference by obversion (*logic*): esp. in football pools, a forecast of a specified number of results from a larger number of matches based on some defined system of combination or permutation (often shortened to **perm**). any such system. [L. *permūtāre,* to change thoroughly —pfx. *per-, mūtāre,* to change.]

pernancy *pûr'nən-si, (law) n.* receiving [A Fr *pernance* (O.Fr. *prenance*)]

pernicious *pər-nish'əs, adj* destructive. highly injurious: malevolent —*adv.* **perni'ciously.**—*n* **perni'ciousness.**—**pernicious anaemia** see **anaemia.** [L *perniciōsus*—pfx. *per-, nex, necis,* death by violence.]

pernickety *pər-nik'i-ti, adj.* finical: exacting minute care.—*n.* **pernick'etiness.** [Scots; origin unknown.]

pernoctation *pûr-nok-tā'shən, n.* passing the night· a watch, vigil [per- (2), L *nox, noctis,* night]

Pernod 109 *per'nō, n.* an alcoholic drink made in France, flavoured with aniseed.

perone *per'o-nē, n.* the fibula.—*adj* **perone'al.**—*n* **perone'us** one of several fibular muscles [Gr. *peronē*]

peroration *per-ə-rā'shən, -ō-, -o-, n.* the conclusion of a speech: a rhetorical performance.—*v.i.* **per'orate** to make a peroration. to harangue (*coll*). [L *perōrātiō, -ōnis*—*per,* through, *ōrāre,* to speak.]

peroxide *pər-oks'īd, n.* an oxide with the highest proportion of oxygen: one that yields hydrogen peroxide on treatment with an acid: colloquially, the bleach hydrogen peroxide, H₂O₂.—*v.t* to treat or bleach with hydrogen peroxide. [per- (1), and **oxide.**]

perpendicular *pûr-pən-dik'ū-lər, adj.* erect: vertical· upright: in the direction of gravity or at right angles to the plane of the horizon: at right angles (to a given line or surface; *geom*).—*n.* an instrument for determining the vertical line: a straight line or plane perpendicular to another line or surface: verticality or erectness: in a ship, a vertical line from each end of the water-line.—*n.* **perpendicularity** (*-lar'i-ti*) the state of being perpendicular.—*adv.* **perpendic'ularly.** [L. *perpendicūlāris*—*perpendiculum,* a plumb-line—pfx. *per-, pendēre,* to hang.]

perpetrate *pûr'pi-trāt, v.t.* to execute or commit (esp. an offence, a poem, or a pun).—*ns.* **perpetra'tion,** **per'petrātor.** [L. *perpetrāre, -ātum*—pfx. *per-, patrāre,* to achieve.]

perpetual *pər-pet′ū-əl, adj.* never ceasing: everlasting not temporary: incessant: unintermitting: continuously blooming. **perennial** —*adv* **perpetually** —*n.* a perennial: a continuously blooming hybrid rose —*ns* **perpet′ualism; perpet′ualist** one who advocates the perpetual continuation of anything; **perpetuality** (*-al′i-ti*) —*adv* **perpet′ually.**—**perpetual motion** a machine, or motion of a machine, that should do work indefinitely without receiving new energy from without, **perpetual screw** an endless screw [L. *perpetuālis*—*perpetuus*, continuous]

perpetuate *pər-pet′ū-āt, v t* to cause to last for ever or for a very long time: to preserve from extinction or oblivion, to pass on, cause to continue to be believed, known, etc.—*ns.* **perpet′uance** perpetuation, **perpetua′tion** continuation or preservation for ever, or for a very long time. preservation from extinction or oblivion, **perpet′uātor.** [L *perpetuāre, -ātum—perpetuus,* perpetual]

perpetuity *pûr-pi-tū′i-ti, n* the state of being perpetual: endless time duration for an indefinite period: something lasting for ever: the sum paid for a perpetual annuity. the annuity itself: an arrangement whereby property is tied up, or rendered inalienable, for all time or for a very long time [L. *perpetuitās, -ātis—perpetuus,* perpetual]

perplex *pər-pleks′, v.t.* to embarrass or puzzle with difficulties or intricacies. to bewilder: to tease with suspense or doubt: to complicate. to interweave: to tangle —*adv.* **perplex′edly.**—*n* **perplex′edness.**—*adj.* **perplex′ing.**—*adv.* **perplex′ingly.**—*n.* **perplex′ity** the state of being perplexed: confusion of mind arising from doubt, etc.: embarrassment doubt: intricacy: tangle. [L *perplexus,* entangled—*pfx. per-, plexus,* involved, pa.p. of *plectĕre*]

perquisite *pûr′kwi-zit, n.* a casual profit: anything left over that a servant or other has by custom a right to keep: a tip expected upon some occasions: emoluments. something regarded as falling to one by right:—often shortened (*coll.*) to **perk.**—*n* **perquisition** (*-zish′ən*) a strict search: diligent inquiry [L. *perquīsitum,* from *perquīrĕre,* to seek diligently—pfx *per-, quaerĕre,* to ask]

perron *per′ən, per-õ′, n.* a raised platform or terrace at an entrance door: an external flight of steps leading up to it. [Fr ,—L *petra,* stone]

perruque, perruquier. See **peruke.**

perry *per′i, n.* a drink made from fermented pear juice [O.Fr. *peré*—L.L *pēra* (L. *pirum*), pear.]

perse *pûrs, adj* dark blue, bluish-grey.—*n.* a dark-blue colour: a cloth of such colour. [O.Fr. *pers*]

persecute *pûr′si-kūt, v.t.* to harass, afflict, hunt down, or put to death, esp. for religious or political opinions.—*n* **persecū′tion.**—*adj* **per′secūtive.**—*n* **per′secūtor.**—*adj.* **per′secūtory.**—**persecution complex** (*psych*) a morbid fear that one is being plotted against by other people [L. *persequī, persecūtus*—pfx. *per-, sequī,* to follow]

persevere *pûr-si-vēr′, v.i.* to continue steadfastly: to keep on striving —*n.* **persevē′rance** the act or state of persevering: continued application to anything which one has begun: a going on till success is met with.—*adj* **persev′erant** steadfast —*v.i* **persev′erate** to recur or tend to recur (*psych.*) to repeat the same actions or thoughts.—*ns.* **perseveration** (*pûr-sev-ər-ā′shən*) meaningless repetition of an action, utterance, thought, etc. the tendency to experience difficulty in leaving one activity for another; **persev′erātor.**—*adj* **persevē′ring.**—*adv.* **persevē′ringly.** [Fr *persévérer*—L *perseverāre*—*persevērus,* very strict—pfx *per-, sevērus,* strict]

Persian *pûr′shən, -shyən, -zhən, -zhyən, adj* of, from,

or relating to *Persia* (now Iran), its inhabitants, or language.—*n.* a native or citizen of Persia: the language of Persia· a Persian cat.—*v.t* and *v i* **Per′sian-ise, -ize.**—**Persian blinds** persiennes, **Persian carpet** a rich, soft carpet of the kind woven in Persia, **Persian cat** a kind of cat with long, silky hair and bushy tail, **Persian lamb** a lamb of the Karakul or Bukhara breed its black, curly fur used to make coats, hats, etc

persienne *per-si-en′, n* an Eastern cambric or muslin with coloured printed pattern (in *pl.*) Persian blinds, outside shutters of thin movable slats in a frame [Fr , Persian (fem.)]

persiflage *pûr-si-flazh′, pûr′, n* banter: flippancy [Fr ,—*persifler,* to banter—L *per,* through, Fr *siffler*—L *sībilāre,* to whistle, to hiss.]

persimmon *pər-sim′ən, n* a date-plum or date-plum tree [From an Amer -Indian word]

persist *pər-sist′, v i* to continue steadfastly or obstinately, esp. against opposition (often with *in*). to persevere· to insist to continue to exist· to remain in the mind after the external cause is removed —*v t* to assert or repeat insistently —*ns* **persis′tence, persis′-tency** the quality of being persistent: perseverance· obstinacy duration, esp of an effect after the exciting cause has been removed.—*adj* **persis′tent** persisting pushing on, esp. against opposition tenacious: fixed· constant or constantly repeated remaining after the usual time of falling off, withering, or disappearing (*zool , bot.*): continuing to grow beyond the usual time.—Also *n.*—*advs.* **persis′-tently; persis′tingly.** [L *persistĕre*—*per, sistĕre,* to cause to stand, to stand—*stāre,* to stand]

person *pûr′sn, n* a character represented, as on the stage: a capacity in which one is acting: a living soul or self-conscious being: a personality· a human being, sometimes used slightingly or patronisingly: the outward appearance, etc.: bodily form: human figure (often including clothes): bodily presence or action: a hypostasis of the Godhead (*theol.*): a form of inflexion or use of a word according as it, or its subject, represents the person, persons, thing, or things speaking (*first person*), spoken to (*second person*), or spoken about (*third person*) (*gram.*):—*pl* in the sense of an individual human being, *usu.* **people** (*pē′pl*): in formal, technical, etc. use, **per′sons.**—**-person** (*-pûr-sn*), in composition, used instead of **-man** to avoid illegal or unnecessary discrimination on grounds of sex, e.g *chairperson.*—*n* **persona** (*pər-sōn′ə*) Jung's term for a person's manner assumed when dealing with the world, masking one's inner thoughts, feelings, etc.: a character in fiction, esp in drama·—*pls* **-æ** (*-ē, -ī*) **-s.**—*adj.* **per′sonable** having a well-formed body or person: of good appearance —*ns.* **per′sonableness; per′sonage** bodily frame or appearance: a person: an exalted or august person: a character in a play or story.—*adj* **per′sonal** of the nature of a person: of or relating to a person or personality: relating, referring, or pointing to a particular person or persons· aiming offensively at a particular person or persons: belonging or peculiar to a person. own: one's own of private concern: relating to private concerns: bodily: in bodily presence: (of telephone call) made to a particular person· by one's own action: indicating person (*gram*) tailored to the needs of a particular person. done in person: opposed to *real,* passing at death not to the heir (as real property) but to the executor —*n.pl* **personalia** (*-ā′li-ə*) notes, anecdotes, or particulars relating to persons —*n* **personalisā′tion, -z-.**—*v t* **per′sonalise, -ize** to personify. to apply to, or take as referring to, a definite person: to mark with a person's name, initials, monogram, etc · to tailor to, or cater for, the desires of a particular person. to give a mark or character to (something) so that it is identifiable as belonging to a certain person (*coll.*) —*ns.* **per'sonalism** the character of being personal; **per'sonalist** one who writes personal notes; **personal'ity** the fact or state of being a person or of being personal: existence as a person· individuality: distinctive or well-marked character: a person: direct reference to, or an utterance aimed at, a particular person or persons, esp. of a derogatory nature: the integrated organisation of all the psychological, intellectual, emotional, and physical characteristics of an individual, especially as they are presented to other people (*psych.*).—*adv.* **per'sonally** in a personal or direct manner: in person. individually: for my part (*coll.*).—*n.* **per'sonalty** (*law*) all the property which, when a man dies, goes to his executor or administrator, as distinguished from the realty, which goes to his heir.—*v.t.* **per'sonate** to assume the likeness or character of. to play the part of: to mimic· to pass oneself off as: to represent in the form of a person: to symbolise.—*ns.* **per'sonating; persona'tion; per'sonator.**—*v.t.* **per'sonise, -ize** to personify.—*n.* **personnel'** the persons employed in any service: (*loosely*) people in general: an office or department that deals with employees' appointments, records, welfare. etc. —**personal chair** a university chair created for the period of tenure of a particular person; **personal column** a newpaper column containing personal messages, advertisements, etc., **personal estate,** property the things legally belonging to one, excluding land; **personal identity** the continued sameness of the individual person, through all changes, as testified by consciousness, **personality cult** excessive adulation of the individual, orig. in Communist usage; **personality disorder** (*psych.*) any of various types of mental illness in which one tends to behave in ways which are harmful to oneself or others; **personal pronoun** (*gram.*) a pronoun which stands for a definite person or thing; **personal rights** rights which belong to a person as a living, reasonable being; **personal service** attention or service of the proprietor of a concern, rather than one of his employees or assistants—*adj.* **per'son-to-per'son** (of telephone call) personal: involving meeting or contact.—Also *adv* —**in person** in actual bodily presence: by one's own act, not by an agent or representative. [L. *persōna*, a player's mask.]

persona¹. See **person.**

persona² *pər-sōn'ə*, -*a*, (L.) person.—**persona grata** *grā'*, *grä'tə*, -*a*, person who is acceptable, esp. diplomatically acceptable to a foreign government, **persona non grata** opp. of **persona grata.**

personage, personal, etc. See **person.**

personify *pər-son'i-fī*, *v.t.* to represent as a person: to ascribe personality to. to be the embodiment of:—*pr.p.* **person'ifying;** *pa.t.* and *pa.p.* **person'ified.**—*ns.* **personificā'tion; person'ifier.** [L. *persōna*, a person, *facĕre*, to make: see foregoing.]

personnel. See **person.**

perspective *pər-spek'tiv*, *n.* the art or science of drawing objects on a surface, so as to give the picture the same appearance to the eye as the objects themselves: appearance, or representation of appearance, of objects in space, with effect of distance, solidity, etc.: just proportion in all the parts: a picture in perspective: a vista: a prospect of the future.—*adj.* pertaining or according to perspective.—*n.* **perspec'tivism** the theory that things can only be known from an individual point of view at a particular time (*philos.*): the use of subjective points of view in literature and art.—**perspective plane** the surface on which the picture of the objects to be represented in perspective is

drawn.—**in, out of, perspective** according to, against, the laws of perspective: in just, unjust, proportion. in, out of, prospect (*obs.*) [L (*ars*) *perspectīva,* perspective (art)—*perspicĕre, perspectum—per, specĕre,* to look]

Perspex® *pûr'speks*, *n.* a proprietary thermoplastic resin of exceptional transparency and freedom from colour, used for windscreens, etc.

perspicacious *pûr-spi-kā'shəs, adj.* clear-minded.— *adv.* **perspicā'ciously.**—*n.* **perspicacity** (-*kas'i-ti*). [L *perspicāx, -ācis;* see **perspective.**]

perspicuous *pər-spik'ū-əs, adj.* lucid —*n.* **perspicū'ity.** —*adv.* **perspic'ūously.**—*n.* **perspic'ūousness.** [L *perspicuus;* see preceding.]

perspire *pər-spīr', v.t.* to exude· to sweat.—*n.* **perspiration** (-*spir-ā'shən*) the act of perspiring: sweat. [L. *perspīrāre, -ātum—per, spīrāre,* to breathe.]

persuade *pər-swād', v.t.* to induce by argument, advice, etc . to bring to any particular opinion: to convince. —*v.i.* to use persuasive methods —*adj.* **persuad'able.** —*ns.* **persuad'er; persuasibility** (-*swās-i-bil'i-ti*).— *adj.* **persuas'ible** capable of being persuaded.—*n.* **persuasion** (-*swā'zhən*) the act, process, method, art, or power of persuading: an inducement: the state of being persuaded: settled opinion: a creed: a party adhering to a creed: a kind (*facet.*).—*adj.* **persuasive** (-*swās'*) having the power to persuade: influencing the mind or passions —*n.* that which persuades or wins over.—*adv.* **persuā'sively.**—*n.* **persuā'siveness.** —*adj.* **persuas'ory** persuasive [L. *persuādēre, -suāsum*—pfx. *per-, suādēre,* to advise.]

pert *pûrt, adj.* forward. saucy: impertinent: presumingly free in speech.—*adv.* **pert'ly.**—*n.* **pert'ness.** [Aphetic for **apert.**]

pertain *pər-, pûr-tān', v.i.* to belong: to relate (with *to*) —*ns* **per'tinence, per'tinency** (*pûr'*) the state of being pertinent.—*adj.* **per'tinent** pertaining or related· to the point· fitted for the matter on hand: fitting or appropriate.—*n.* (chiefly *Scot.*) anything that goes along with an estate.—*adv.* **per'tinently.** [O Fr *partenir*—L. *pertinēre*—pfx. *per-, tenēre,* to hold.]

pertinacious *pûr-ti-nā'shəs, adj.* thoroughly tenacious: holding obstinately to an opinion or a purpose: obstinate: unyielding.—*adv.* **pertinā'ciously.**—*ns.* **pertinā'ciousness; pertinacity** (-*nas'i-ti*) the quality of being pertinacious or unyielding: obstinacy. resoluteness. [L. *pertināx, -ācis,* holding fast—pfx. *per-, tenāx,* tenacious—*tenēre,* to hold.]

pertinence, pertinent, etc. See **pertain.**

perturb *pər-tûrb', v.t.* to disturb greatly: to agitate.— *adj.* **pertur'bable.**—*ns.* **pertur'bance** perturbation; **perturb'ant** anything that perturbs.—*adj.* **perturbing.**—*n.* **perturbā'tion** the act of perturbing or state of being perturbed: disquiet of mind: irregularity: the disturbance produced in the simple elliptic motion of one heavenly body about another by the action of a third body, or by the non-sphericity of the principal body (*astron.*): a perturbing agent.—*adjs.* **perturbā'tional; pertur'bative.**—*n.* **per'turbător.**—*adj.* and *n.* **pertur'batory.**—*adj.* **perturbed'.**—*adv.* **perturb'edly.**—*n.* **pertur'ber.** [L. *perturbāre, -ātum*—pfx. *per-, turbāre,* to disturb—*turba,* a crowd.]

pertussis *pər-tus'is, n.* whooping-cough.—*adj.* **pertuss'al.** [per- (2), L. *tussis,* cough.]

Peru *pə-rōō', n.* a country of S. America.—*adj.* **Peru'vian** of Peru.—*n.* a native, or inhabitant, of Peru.— **Peruvian bark** cinchona bark. [Sp. *Perú.*]

peruke *pər-ōōk',* formerly *per', n.* a wig.—Also **perruque.** (Fr. *per-uk*)—*n.* **perru'quier** (-*ōō k'yər,* Fr. *-uk-yä*) a wigmaker. [Fr. *perruque*—It. *parrucca* (Sp. *peluca*); connection with L. *pīlus,* hair, very doubtful.]

peruse *pǝr-ōōz'*, *v.t.* to examine in detail: to revise: to read attentively or critically: (*loosely*) to read.—*ns.* **perus'al; perus'er.** [L. pfx. *per-*, thoroughly, *ūtī, ūsus*, to use.]

Peruvian. See Peru.

perv *pûrv.* A coll. short form of a (sexual) pervert.

pervade *pǝr-vād', v.t.* to diffuse or extend through the whole of.—*n.* **pervasion** (*-vā'zhǝn*).—*adj.* **pervasive** (*-vā'siv*) tending or having power to pervade.—*adv.* **perva'sively.**—*n.* **perva'siveness.** [L. *pervādēre—per*, through, *vādēre*, to go]

perverse *pǝr-vûrs', adj.* turned aside from right or truth: obstinate in the wrong: capricious and unreasonable in opposition: froward: wrong-headed wayward: against the evidence or judge's direction or point of law.—*adv.* **perverse'ly.**—*ns.* **perverse'ness; perversion** (*-vûr'shǝn*) the act of perverting: the condition of being perverted: the product of the process of perverting: a diverting from the true object: a turning from right or true: a distortion: a misapplication: a pathological deviation of sexual instinct: the formation of a mirror-image (*math.*). the mirror-image itself; **pervers'ity** the state or quality of being perverse.—*adj.* **pervers'ive** tending to pervert.—*v t.* **pervert'** to turn wrong or from the right course: to wrest from the true meaning: to corrupt: to turn from truth or virtue: to form a mirror-image of (*math*) — *v.i.* to go wrong or out of the right course —*ns.* **pervert** (*pûr'vûrt*) one who has abandoned the doctrine assumed to be true: one whose sexual instinct is perverted; **pervert'er.**—*adj.* **pervert'ible.** [Partly through Fr.—L. *pervertēre, perversum*—pfx. *per-*, wrongly, *vertēre*, to turn.]

pervious *pûr'vi-ǝs, adj* perr ble: passable: penetrable: open.—*adv.* **per'vic .ly.**—*n.* **per'viousness.** [L. *pervius—per*, through, *i ia*, a way.]

Pesach, Pesah *pā'sahh, n.* the festival of Passover [Heb.]

pesade *pǝ-zad, -säd', -zäd', n.* dressage manoeuvre in which a horse rears up on its hindlegs without forward movement. [Fr.; from It.]

peseta *pe-sā'ta, -ǝ, n.* the standard monetary unit of Spain. [Sp., dim. of *pesa*, weight.]

pesewa *pǝ-sōō'a, -ǝ, n.* a Ghanaian unit of currency:—*pls.* **-a, -as,** etc.—See **cedi.**

pesky *pes'ki,* (*coll.*) *adj.* annoying.—*adv.* **pes'kily.** [Perh. **pest.**]

peso *pā'sō, n.* a Spanish five-peseta piece: a Mexican dollar: in S. and Central America and the Philippines a coin of various values:—*pl.* **pe'sos.** [Sp.,—L. *pēnsum*, weight.]

pessary *pes'ǝ-ri, n.* a surgical plug, or medicated device, esp. one worn in the vagina. [Fr. *pessaire*—L.L. *pessārium*—Gr. *pessos*, a pebble, pessary.]

pessimism *pes'i-mizm, n.* the doctrine that the world is bad rather than good (*philos.*): a temper of mind that looks on the dark side of things: a depressing view of life: (*loosely*) despondency, hopelessness.—*n.* **pess'imist** one who believes that everything is tending to the worst: one who looks too much on the dark side of things—opp. to *optimist.*—*adjs.* **pessimis'tic, -al.**—*adv.* **pessimis'tically.** [L. *pessimus*, worst.]

pest *pest, n.* any deadly epidemic disease: plague: any insect, fungus, etc., destructive of cultivated plants: troublesome person or thing.—*ns.* **pesticide** (*pes'ti-sīd*), a substance for killing pests, **pest'ilence,** any deadly epidemic disease: bubonic plague: anything that is hurtful to the morals.—*adjs.* **pest'ilent,** deadly: producing pestilence: hurtful to health and life: pernicious: mischievous: vexatious; **pestilential** (*-len'shl*), of the nature of pestilence: producing or infested with pestilence: destructive: baneful: detestable: pestering.—*advs.* **pestilen'tially, pest'ilently.**

—*adj.* **pestolog'ical.**—*ns.* **pestol'ogist; pestol'ogy** the study of agricultural pests and methods of combating them.—**pest'house** (*hist.*) a hospital for plague or other infectious or contagious disease [Fr. *peste* and *pestilence*—L. *pestis, pestilentia.*]

pester *pes'tǝr, v.t.* to annoy persistently.—*n.* an annoyance —*n.* **pes'terer.**—*adv.* **pes'teringly.** [App from O.Fr. *empestrer* to entangle; influenced by **pest.**]

pesticide, pestiferous, pestilence, etc. See **pest.**

pestle *pes'l,* also *pest'l, n.* an instrument for pounding: a leg, esp as food (now *dial.*).—*v.t* to pound.—*v.i* to use a pestle. [O.Fr *pestel*—L. *pistillum,* a pounder—*pinsēre, pistum,* to pound.]

pestology. See pest.

pet¹ *pet, n.* a cherished tame animal· an indulged favourite: used as an endearment.—*adj.* kept as a pet: indulged: cherished: favourite.—*v.t* to treat as a pet: to fondle· to pamper· to indulge.—*v i. (coll.*) to indulge in amorous caressing:—*pr.p.* **pett'ing;** *pa.t.* and *pa.p.* **pett'ed.**—*adj* **pett'ed.**—*ns* **pett'er; pett'ing.**—**pet aversion,** hate a chief object of dislike, **pet name** a name used in familiar affection

pet² *pet, n* a slighted and offended feeling: a slight, or childish, fit of aggrieved or resentful sulkiness the sulks, huff.—*v i.* to be peevish, to sulk —*adj* **pett'ed in a pet·** apt to be in a pet.—*adv.* **pett'edly.** —*n.* **pett'edness.**—*adj.* **pett'ish** peevish: sulky· inclined to sulk: of the nature of or expressive of sulkiness.—*adv.* **pett'ishly.**—*n.* **pett'ishness.**

petal *pet'l, n.* a corolla leaf. [Gr *petalon,* a leaf]

pétanque *pā-tāk', n.* a French (Provençal) game in which steel bowls are rolled or hurled towards a wooden marker ball.

petard *pe-tar(d)', n.* a case containing an explosive, used for blowing in doors, etc : a moving firework.— **hoist with his own petard** see **hoise.** [O.Fr —*péter,* to crack or explode—L *pēdĕre,* to break wind]

petcock *pet'kok, n.* a small tap or valve for draining condensed steam from steam-engine cylinders, or for testing the water-level in a boiler [Poss. obs *pet,* to fart, or *petty,* and *cock,* a tap.]

petechia *pe-tē'ki-ǝ, n.* a small red or purple spot on the skin:—*pl.* **pete'chiae** (*-ē*).—*adj* **petech'ial.** [Latinised from It. *petecchia.*]

peter¹ *pē'tǝr, v.i* to dwindle away to nothing, be dissipated or exhausted (with *out*) [Orig U.S mining slang.]

peter² *pē'tǝr, n* the Blue Peter (flag): call for trumps. —*v.i.* to signal that one has a short suit (by throwing a higher card than necessary).—**Peter's pence** see **penny.**

peter³ *pē'tǝr, (slang) n* a safe: a prison cell —**pe'terman** a safe-blower.

Peter Pan a character in J. M. Barrie's play of that name (1904), the type of the person who never grows up.—**Peter Pan collar** a flat collar with rounded ends.

petersham *pē'tǝr-shǝm, n.* a heavy greatcoat designed by Lord *Petersham:* rough-napped cloth generally dark blue of which it was made. a heavy corded ribbon used for belts, hat-bands, etc

pethidine *peth'ǝ-dēn, n.* a synthetic analgesic and hypnotic, having action similar to that of morphine [Perh. mixture of *piperidine, ethyl.*]

pétillant *pā-tē-yä,* (Fr) *adj.* of wine, slightly sparkling

petiole *pet'i-ōl, n.* a leaf-stalk (*bot.*): a stalk-like structure, esp that of the abdomen in wasps, etc. (*zool.*). —*adjs.* **pet'iolar** of, or of the nature of, a petiole; **pet'iolate, -d,** **pet'ioled** stalked. [L. *petiolus,* a little foot, a petiole]

petit formerly *pet'it,* now *pet'i, pǝ-tē',* or as Fr. *pǝ-tē,* *adj.* a form of **petty** (q.v.), *obs.* except in legal and other French phrases:—*fem.* **petite** (*pǝ-tēt'*) applied to a woman, small-made (with a suggestion of neatness).—**petit bourgeois** (*bŏŏr-zhwä*) a member of the lower middle class; **petite bourgeoisie** (*bŏŏr-zhwä-zē*) the lower middle class; **petit four** (*fŏr, fŏr, fŏŏr*) a small very fancy biscuit; **petit jury** (*legal*) a 12-man jury, in Britain now the only form of jury (also **petty jury**; see **grand jury**); **petit mal** (*mal*) a mild form of epilepsy without convulsions; **petit point** (*point, pwē*) work in tent stitch; **petits pois** (*pǝ-tē pwä*) small green peas. [Fr. *petit, -e.*]

petition *pǝ-tish'ǝn, n.* a supplication: a prayer: a formal request to an authority: a written supplication signed by a number of persons: a written application to a court of law: the thing asked for.—*v.t.* to address a petition to: to ask for.—*adj.* **peti'tionary.**—*ns.* **peti'-tioner; petit'ioning; peti'tionist.**—*adj.* **petitory** (*pet'i-tǝ-ri*) petitioning. [L. *petitiō, -ōnis–petēre,* to ask.]

petitio principii *pe-tish'i-ō prin-sip'i-ī, pe-tē'ti-ō prēn-kip'i-ē,* (*log.*) a begging of the question. [L. *petitiō principiī.*]

petitory. See **petition.**

Petrarchan *pe-trär'kǝn,* **Petrarchian** *-ki-ǝn, adjs.* pertaining to, imitating, the Italian poet Francesco *Petrarca* or *Petrarch* (1304–74).

petre *pē'tǝr,* (*coll.*) *n.* short for **saltpetre.**

petrel *pet'rǝl, n.* any bird of the genus Procellaria akin to the albatrosses and fulmars, esp. the **storm** (popularly **stormy**) **petrel** or Mother Carey's chicken, a dusky sea-bird, rarely landing except to lay its eggs, the smallest web-footed bird known. [L. *Petrus,* Peter, from its seeming to walk on the water; see Matt. xiv. 29.]

Petri, or **petri, dish** *pē'tri, pā'tri, pet'ri dish,* a shallow glass dish with an overlapping cover used for cultures of bacteria.—Also **Petri plate.** [R. J. *Petri,* German bacteriologist.]

petrify *pet'ri-fī, v.t.* to turn into stone: to fossilise (*geol.*): loosely, to encrust with stony matter: to make hard like a stone: to fix in amazement, horror, etc.—*v.i.* to become stone, or hard like stone:—*pr.p.* **pet'rifying;** *pa.t.* and *pa.p.* **pet'rified.**—*n.* **petrifac'-tion** turning or being turned into stone: a petrified object: a fossil.—*adjs.* **petrifac'tive, petrif'ic** petrifying.—*n.* **petrifica'tion** petrifaction. [L. *petra* —Gr. *petrā,* rock, L. *facēre, factum,* to make.]

Petrine *pē'trīn, adj.* pertaining to, or written by, the Apostle *Peter.* [L. *Petrinus–Petrus,* Gr. *Petros,* Peter.]

petro-[1] *pet'rō-,* in composition, petroleum.—*n.* and *adj.* **petrochem'ical** (of or relating to) any chemical obtained from petroleum.—*ns.* **pet'rocurr'ency, pet'romoney, pet'rodollars, pet'ropounds** currency, etc., acquired by the oil-producing countries as profit from the sale of their oil to the consumer countries. [petroleum.]

petro-[2] *pet-rō-, pi-tro'-,* in composition, rock.—*n.* **petrogen'esis** (the study of) the origin, formation, etc., of rocks.—*adj.* **petrogenet'ic.**—*n.* **pet'róglyph** (Gr. *glyphein,* to carve) a rock-carving, esp. prehistoric.—*adj.* **petróglyph'ic.**—*ns.* **petróg'raphy** (Gr. *graphein,* to write) the systematic description and classification of rocks; **petróg'rapher.**—*adjs.* **petrograph'ic(al).**—*n.* **petról'ogy** (Gr. *logos,* discourse) the science of the origin, chemical and mineral composition and structure, and alteration of rocks.—*adj.* **petrolog'ical.**—*n.* **petról'ogist.** [Gr. *petrā,* rock.]

petrol *pet'rol, -rǝl, n.* formerly, petroleum: now a mixture of light volatile hydrocarbons got by fractional distillation or cracking of petroleum, used for driving motor-cars, aeroplanes, etc. (U.S. **gasoline**).—*v.t.* to supply with petrol:—*pr.p.* **pet'rolling;** *pa.t.* and *pa.p.*

pet'rolled.—*ns.* **pet'rolage** treatment with petrol to stamp out mosquitoes; **petrolatum** (*-ā'tam*) petroleum jelly.—*adj.* **petroleous** (*pi-trō'li-ǝs*) containing, or rich in, petroleum.—*ns.* **petroleum** (*pi-trō'li-ǝm*) a (usu. liquid) mineral oil containing a mixture of hydrocarbons got from oil-wells, and used to make petrol, paraffin, lubricating oil, fuel oil, etc.—*adjs.* **petrolic** (*pi-trol'ik*) of petrol or petroleum; **petrolif'erous** (*pet-*) yielding petroleum.—**petrol blue** a vibrant blue colour; **petrol bomb** a petrol-filled Molotov cocktail or the like, **petroleum jelly** soft paraffin, a mixture of petroleum hydrocarbons used in emollients, as a lubricant, etc. (see also **liquid paraffin** at **liquid**); **petrol pump** a machine for transferring measured amounts of petrol to motor vehicles; **petrol station** a garage which sells petrol. [L. *petra,* rock, *oleum,* oil.]

petrous *pet'rǝs, adj.* stony. [L. *petrōsus–petra*–Gr. *petrā,* rock.]

pe-tsai cabbage *pä-tsī' kab'ij.* Same as **Chinese cabbage.**

petticoat *pet'i-kōt, n.* a short or small coat (*orig.*): a skirt, esp. an under-skirt, or a garment of which it forms part: any garment or drapery of similar form: a bell-shaped structure, as in telegraph insulators, etc. —*adj.* feminine: female: of women.—*adj.* **pett'-icoated.**—**pett'icoat-tails'** small cakes of shortbread; **pett'icoat** government domination by women. [petty, coat.]

pettifogger *pet'i-fog-ǝr, n.* a paltry cavilling lawyer.— *v.i.* **pett'ifog** to play the pettifogger.—*n.* **pett'ifoggery.**—*n.* and *adj.* **pett'ifogging** paltry, trivial, cavilling (behaviour). [petty; origin of second part obscure.]

pettish. See **pet**[2].

petty *pet'i, adj.* small: of less importance: minor: trifling: lower in rank, power, etc.: inconsiderable, insignificant: contemptible: small-minded.—*adv.* **pett'ily.**—*n.* **pett'iness.**—**petty bourgeois, bourgeoisie** variants of **petit bourgeois, petite bourgeoisie**; **petty cash** miscellaneous small sums of money received or paid: a sum of money kept for minor expenses which usu. do not need to be referred to a higher authority; **petty jury** see **petit jury; petty larceny** see **larceny; petty officer** a naval officer ranking with a non-commissioned officer in the army. [Fr. *petit.*]

petulant *pet'ū-lǝnt, adj.* orig. wanton, lascivious: showing peevish impatience, irritation, or caprice: forward, impudent in manner.—*ns.* **pet'ulance, pet'ulancy.**—*adv.* **pet'ulantly.** [L. *petulāns, -antis* —assumed *petulāre,* dim. of *petēre,* to seek]

Petunia *pē-tū'nyǝ, -ni-ǝ, n.* South American genus of ornamental plants near akin to tobacco: (without *cap.*) a plant of this genus [Tupí *petun,* tobacco.]

pew *pū, n.* an enclosed compartment or fixed bench in a church: formerly, a place for a preacher or reader: a box or stall in another building: a seat (*slang*). [O.Fr. *puie,* raised place, balcony—L. *podia,* pl. of *podium*—Gr. *podion,* dim. of *pous, podos,* foot]

pewit *pē'wit, pū'it.* Same as **peewit.**

pewter *pū'tǝr, n.* formerly, an alloy of three to nine parts of tin and one of lead: now tin with a little copper, antimony, and/or bismuth: a vessel made of pewter, esp. a beer-tankard: the bluish-grey colour of pewter: prize-money (*slang*).—*adj.* made of pewter. —*n.* **pew'terer** one who works in pewter —**pew'termill** a lapidary's pewter polishing-wheel for amethyst, agate, etc. [O.Fr. *peutre.*]

peyote *pā-yō'tā, n.* a Mexican intoxicant made from cactus tops—also called **mescal.** [Nahuatl *peyotl.*]

pfennig *pfen'ig, -ihh, n.* a German coin, the hundredth part of a mark.

pH (value) *pē-āch'* (*val'ū*), *n.* a number used to express degrees of acidity or alkalinity in solutions, related by formula to a standard solution of potassium hydrogen phthalate, which has value 4 at 15°C.

phacoid *fak'* or *fāk'oid*, **phacoidal** *fə-koi'dl*, *adjs.* lentil-shaped, lens-shaped. [Gr. *phakos*, a lentil, *eidos*, form.]

Phaedra complex *fēd'rə kom'pleks*, (*psych.*) the difficult relationship which can arise between a new step-parent and the (usu. teenage) son or daughter of the original marriage. [Greek story of *Phaedra* who fell in love with her stepson and committed suicide after being repulsed by him.]

phaeic *fē'ik*, *adj.* dusky.—*n.* **phae'ism** duskiness, incomplete melanism (in butterflies). [Gr. *phaios*, dusky.]

phaen(o)- *fē-n(ō)-*. Now usu. **phen(o)-**.

phaeton *fā'(ı-)tn*, *n.* an open four-wheeled carriage for one or two horses. [From the foregoing.]

phag-, -phaga. See **phag(o)-**.

phage. Short for **bacteriophage.**

-phage. See **phag(o)-**.

phag(o)- *fag(-ō)-*, in composition, used to denote 'feeding', 'eating', as in *phagocyte*.—**-phaga** in zoological names, 'eaters'; **-phage** (*-fāj, -fazh*) eater, or destroyer; **-phagous** (*-fəg-əs*) feeding on; **-phagus** (*-fəg-əs*) one feeding in a particular way, or on a particular thing; **-phagy** (*-fə-ji*) eating of a specified nature. [Gr. *phagein*, to eat.]

phagedaena, phagedena *faj-* or *fag-i-dē'nə*, *n.* rapidly spreading destructive ulceration, once common in hospitals—hospital gangrene.—*adj.* **phagedae'nic, phagedē'nic.** [Gr. *phagedaina—phagein*, to eat.]

phagocyte *fag'ō-sīt*, *n.* a white blood-corpuscle that engulfs bacteria and other harmful particles.—*adjs.* **phagocytic** (*-sit'*), **-al.**—*n.* **phag'ocytism** (*-sīt-*) the nature or function of a phagocyte.—*n.* **phagocytō'sis** destruction by phagocytes. [Gr. *phagein*, to eat, *kytos*, a vessel.]

-phagous, -phagus, -phagy. See **phag(o)-**.

phalange, etc. See **phalanx.**

phalanger *fal-an'jər*, *n.* any one of a group of small arboreal Australasian marsupials. [Gr. *phalangion*, spider's web, from their webbed toes.]

phalanx *fal'angks* (or *fāl'*), *n.* a solid formation of ancient Greek heavy-armed infantry: a solid body of men, etc.: a solid body of supporters or partisans: a bone of a digit: the part of a finger or toe answering to it: a joint of an insect's leg: a bundle of stamens:—*pl.* **phal'anxes** or (*biol.*) **phalanges** (*fal-an'jēz*).—*adj.* **phalangal** (*fal-ang'gl*) phalangeal.—*n.* **phalange** (*fal'anj*) a phalanx (in biological senses): the Falange, Primo de Rivera's Spanish fascist party: the Christian right-wing group in Lebanon, modelled on the Spanish Falange:—*pl.* **phal'anges.**—*adj.* **phalan'geal.**—*ns.* **phalangid** (*fal-an'jid*) a harvestman; **phalan'gist** a Spanish falangist: a member of the Lebanese phalange. [Gr. *phalanx, -angos*, a roller, phalanx, phalange, spider.]

phalarope *fal'ə-rōp*, *n.* a wading bird (*Phalaropus*) with coot-like feet. [Gr. *phalaris*, a coot, *pous*, a foot.]

phallus *fal'əs*, *n.* the penis: the symbol of generation in primitive religion:—*pl.* **phall'i**, **phall'uses.**—*adj.* **phall'ic.** [L.,—Gr. *phallos.*]

Phanariot *fa-nar'i-ot*, *n.* one of the Greeks inhabiting the *Fanar* quarter of Constantinople, or of a Greek official class—in Turkish history mostly diplomatists, administrators, and bankers.—*adj.* **Phanar'iot.**—Also **Fan-.** [Gr. *phānarion*, lighthouse, from that on the Golden Horn.]

phanerogam *fan'ər-ō-gam*, *n.* a spermatophyte.—*adjs.* **phanerogam'ic**, **phanerog'amous.** [Gr. *phaneros,*

visible, *gamos*, marriage.]

phantasm *fan'tazm*, *n.* a vain, airy appearance: a fancied vision: an apparition: a spectre —Also **phantas'ma:**—*pl.* **phan'tasms**, **phantas'mata.**—*adjs.* **phantas'mal; phantasmā'lian** (*rare*).—*n.* **phantasmal'ity.**—*adv.* **phantas'mally.**—*adjs.* **phantas'mic, -al.** [Gr. *phantasma—phantazein*, to make visible.]

phantasmagoria *fan-taz-mə-gō'ri-ə, -gō'*, *n* a fantastic series of illusive images or of real forms.—*adjs* **phantasmago'rial** pertaining to or resembling a phantasmagoria; **phantasmagōr'ic, -al.** [A name given to a show of optical illusions in 1802, from Fr *phantasmagorie*—Gr. *phantasma*, an appearance, and perh *agorā*, an assembly.]

phantasy, phantastic, phantastry. Same as **fantasy,** etc.

phantom *fan'təm*, *n.* a deceitful appearance: an immaterial form: a visionary experience: a show without reality.—*adj.* illusive: unreal: spectral: imaginary: ghostly-looking: transparent and hardly visible. [O.Fr. *fantosme*—Gr. *phantasma*.]

Pharaoh *fā'rō*, *n.* a title of the kings of ancient Egypt. —*adj.* **pharaonic** (*fā-rā-on'ik*).—**Pharaoh('s) ant** a tiny yellow-brown tropical ant which has spread through many countries and infests heated buildings, e.g. hospitals, restaurants, blocks of flats; **Pharaoh's serpent** the coiled ash of burning mercuric thiocyanate; **Pharaonic circumcision** the ancient practice of female circumcision by the removal of the clitoris and labia majora and minora. [L. and Gr. *pharaō*— Heb. *par'ōh*—Egypt. *pr-'o*, great house.]

Pharisee *far'i-sē*, *n.* one of a party among the Jews, marked by its legalistic interpretation of the Mosaic law, which by the time of Jesus had degenerated into an obsessive concern with the mass of rules covering the details of everyday life: any one more careful of the outward forms than of the spirit of religion: a very self-righteous or hypocritical person.—*adjs* **pharisā'ic, -al** pertaining to, or like, the Pharisees: hypocritical.—*adv.* **pharisā'ically.**—*ns.* **pharisā'icalness;** **phar'isaism** (also **phar'iseeism**). [O.E. *phariseus*— L.L. *pharisaeus*—Gr. *pharisaios*—Heb. *pārūsh*, separated.]

pharmaceutic, -al *fär-mə-sū'tik* (or *-kū'tik*), *-əl*, *adjs.* pertaining to the knowledge or art of preparing medicines.—*n.* **pharmaceu'tical** a chemical used in medicine.—*adv.* **pharmaceu'tically.**—*n.sing.* **pharmaceu'tics** the science of preparing medicines.—*n.* **pharmaceu'tist.** [Gr. *pharmakeutikos.*]

pharmacology, etc. See **pharmacy.**

pharmacopoeia *far-mə-kə-pē'-(y)ə*, *n.* a book or list of drugs with directions for their preparation: a collection of drugs. [Gr. *pharmakopoiiā—pharmakon*, a drug, *poieein*, to make]

pharmacy *fär'mə-si*, *n.* a department of the medical art which consists in the collecting, preparing, preserving, and dispensing of medicines: the art of preparing and mixing medicines: a druggist's shop: a dispensary. —*ns.* **phar'macist** (*-sist*) a druggist, one skilled in pharmacy: one legally qualified to sell drugs and poisons.—*ns.* **pharmacol'ogist; pharmacol'ogy** the science of drugs. [Gr. *pharmakeiā*, use of drugs, *pharmakon*, a drug.]

pharynx *far'ingks*, *n.* the cleft or cavity forming the upper part of the gullet, lying behind the nose, mouth, and larynx:—*pl.* **phar'ynges** (*-in-jēz*), **phar'ynxes.**—*adjs.* **pharyngal** (*fa-ring'gl*), **pharyngeal** (*fa-rin'ji-əl* or *-jē'əl*).—*n.* **pharyngitis** (*far-in-ji'tis*) inflammation of the mucous membrane of the pharynx.—*ns.* **pharyngol'ogy** the study of the pharynx and its diseases; **pharyngoscope** (*fa-ring'gə-skōp*) an instrument for inspecting the pharynx; **pharyngoscopy** (*far-ing-gos'kə-pi*); **pharyngot'omy** the operation of making an incision into the pharynx. [Gr. *pharynx, -ygos,* later *-yngos.*]

phase¹ *fāz, n.* the appearance at a given time of the illuminated surface exhibited by the moon or a planet —also **phasis** (*fā'sis*): the aspect or appearance of anything at any time: the stage of advancement in a periodic change, measured from some standard point: a stage in growth or development (*lit.* and *fig.*): —*pl.* **phases** (*fā'zız, -sēz*).—*v.t.* to do by phases or stages.—*adjs.* **phased** adjusted to be in the same phase at the same time: by stages, **phā'sic** (or *-sık*).— **phase-contrast, phase-difference, microscope** one in which the clear detail is obtained by means of a device that alters the speed of some of the rays of light, so that staining is unnecessary.—**in, out of, phase** in the same phase together, or in different phases; **phase in, out** to begin, cease, gradually to use, make, etc. [Gr. *phasis—phaein,* to shine]

phase². See **feeze.**

phasic, phasis. See **phase¹.**

phasis. See **phatic.**

phatic *fat'ık, adj* using speech for social reasons, to communicate feelings rather than ideas.—*n.* **phasis** (*fā'sis*). [Gr. *phasis,* utterance.]

pheasant *fez'nt, n.* a richly-coloured gallinaceous bird, a half-wild game-bird in Britain: extended to others of the same or kindred genus (as *golden, silver, Argus, Amherst's* pheasant) and to other birds: the flesh of the bird as food:—*pl.* **pheasant(s).**—*n.* **pheas'-antry** an enclosure for rearing pheasants.—**pheas'-ant's-eye** a plant with deep-red dark-centred flowers. [A.Fr. *fesant*—L. *phāsiānus*—Gr. *phāsiānos* (*ornis,* bird), from the river Phasis, in Colchis.]

pheeze, pheese. Same as **feeze.**

phellem *fel'əm,* (*bot.*) *n.* cork.—*ns.* **phell'oderm** (Gr. *derma,* skin) a layer of secondary cortex formed by the phellogen on its inner side; **phellogen** (*fel'ō-jen*) a layer of meristem that forms cork without, otherwise cork-cambium. [Gr. *phellos,* cork.]

phen-, pheno- *fēn-, fēn-ō-,* in composition, showing: visible: related to benzene. [Gr. *phainein,* to show.]

phenacetin *fın-as'i-tin, n.* an antipyretic drug, $C_{10}H_{13}NO_2$. [**acetic** and **phene.**]

phene *fēn, n.* an old name for benzene. [Gr *phainein,* to show, because obtained in the manufacture of illuminating gas.]

phenobarbitone *fē-nō-bar'bi-tōn, n.* a sedative and hypnotic drug.

phenocryst *fē'nō-krist, n.* a larger crystal in a porphyritic rock. [Gr. *phainein,* to show, and **crystal.**]

phenol *fē'nol, n.* carbolic acid, got from coal-tar, a powerful disinfectant: extended to the class of aromatic compounds with one or more hydroxyl groups directly attached to the benzene nucleus, weak acids with reactions of alcohols.—*n.* **phenol-phthalein** (*fē-nol-fthal'i-in,* or *-thal'*) a substance got from phenol and phthalic anhydride, brilliant red in alkalis, colourless in acids, used as an indicator. [See **phene;** **-ol** from **alcohol.**]

phenology *fē-nol'ə-ji, n.* the study of organisms as affected by climate, esp. dates of seasonal phenomena, as opening of flowers, arrival of migrants.—*adj.* **phenological** (*-ə-loj'*).—*n* **phenol'ogist.** [Gr. *phainein,* to show, *logos,* discourse.]

phenomenon *fi-nom'i-nən* or *-non, n.* anything directly apprehended by the senses or one of them: an event that may be observed: the appearance which anything makes to our consciousness, as distinguished from what it is in itself: loosely, a remarkable or unusual person, thing, or appearance, a prodigy:—*pl.* **phenom'ena** (sometimes used *erron* for *n. sing.*).— *adj.* **phenom'enal** pertaining to a phenomenon: of the

nature of a phenomenon.—*v.t.* **phenom'enalise, -ize** to represent as a phenomenon.—*ns.* **phenom'enalism** the philosophical doctrine that phenomena are the only realities, or that knowledge can only comprehend phenomena—also *externalism;* **phenom'enalist.**—*adj* **phenomenalist'ic.**—*n.* **phenomenality** (*-al'ı-tı*) the character of being phenomenal.—*adv* **phenom'enally.**—*adj.* **phenom-enolog'ical.**—*ns.* **phenomenol'ogist; phenomenol'ogy** the science, or a description, of phenomena· the philosophy of Edmund Husserl (1859–1938), concerned with the experiences of the self. [Gr. *phainomenon,* pl *-a,* neut. pr p pass. of *phainein,* to show]

phenotype *fēn'ō-tip, n* the observable characteristics of an organism produced by the interaction of genes and environment: a group of individuals having the same characteristics of this kind.—*adjs.* **phenotypic(al)** (*-tıp'*) [Gr. *phainein,* to show, and **type.**]

phenyl *fē'nıl, n.* an organic radical, C_6H_5, found in benzene, phenol, etc.—*adj.* **phenyl'ic.**—*ns.* **phenylal'anin(e)** an amino-acid present in most food proteins; **phenylbut'azone** (*-būt'ə-zōn*) an analgesic and antipyretic used in the treatment of rheumatic disorders and also, illegally, in horse-doping; **phenyl-ketonuria** (*-kē-tō-nū'ri-ə*) an inherited metabolic disorder in infants in which there is an inability to break down phenylalanine, commonly later resulting in mental defect, unless a· phenylalanine-free diet is given; **phenylketonū'ric** one who suffers from phenyl-ketonuria.—Also *adj.* [**phene,** and Gr. *hȳlē,* material.]

pheromone *fer'ə-mōn, n.* a chemical substance secreted by an animal which influences the behaviour of others of its species, e.g. queen bee substance [Gr. *pherein,* to bear, and **hormone**]

phese. See **feeze.**

phew *fū, interj.* an exclamation of petty vexation, unexpected difficulty, impatience, relief, contempt, etc. [A half-formed whistle.]

phi *fi, fē, n.* the twenty-first letter (*Φ, φ*) of the Greek alphabet. [Gr. *phei.*]

phial *fi'əl, n.* a vessel for liquids, esp. now a small medicine-bottle. [L *phiala*—Gr. *phialē,* a broad shallow bowl.]

Phi Beta Kappa *fi'* or *fē', bē'* or *bā'tə kap'ə,* the oldest of the American college societies. [Gr. Φ.Β.Κ., the initial letters of its motto—*Philosophiā biou kyber-nētēs,* Philosophy is the guide of life.]

phil- *fil-,* **philo-** *fil-ō-,* in composition, used to denote loving: lover.—**-phil** *-fil,* **-phile** *-fil,* lover of: loving; **-philia, -phily** love of; **-philic** (also, as *n.* suffix, lover of), **-philous** loving; **-philus** in zoological names, lover of (usu. a specified food). [Gr. *philos,* friend— *phileein,* to love.]

philabeg. See **fillibeg.**

Philadelphian *fil-ə-del'fi-ən, adj.* of the Pergamene city of Philadelphia: of Philadelphia, Pennsylvania. —*n.* a native or inhabitant of Philadelphia. [**phil-,** Gr. *adelphos,* a brother, *adelphē,* a sister.]

philander *fil-an'dər, n.* a lover: a dangler after women: a male flirt: a philandering.—*v.i.* to make love: to flirt or coquet.—*n.* **philan'derer.** [Gr. *philandros,* fond of men or of a husband, misapplied as if meaning a loving man.]

philanthropy *fil-an'thrə-pı, n.* love of mankind esp. as shown in services to general welfare.—*ns.* **phil-anthrope** (*fil'ən-thrōp*), **philan'thropist** one who tries to benefit mankind.—*adjs.* **philanthropic** (*-throp'ık*), **-al** doing good to others, benevolent.— *adv.* **philanthrop'ically.** [Gr. *philanthrōpiā— anthrōpos,* a man]

philately *fil-at'i-li, n.* the study and collection of postage and revenue stamps and labels —*adj* **philatelic** (*fil-ə-tel'ik*).—*n.* **philat'elist.** [Fr. *philatélie,* invented in 1864—Gr. *atelēs,* tax-free—*a-,* priv , *telos,* tax.]

-phile. See **phil-.**

philharmonic *fil-àr-mon'ik,* also *-har-, -ər-, adj.* loving music. [**phil-,** Gr. *harmoniā,* harmony.]

philhellenic *fil-hel-ēn'ik,* or *-en'ik, adj.* loving Greece, esp. Greek culture: favouring the Greeks.—*ns.* **philhellene** (*-hel'ēn*), **philhellenist** (*-hel'in-ist*) a supporter of Greece. esp. in 1821–32; **philhell'enism.** [**phil-,** Gr. *Hellēn,* a Greek.]

-philia. See **phil-.**

philibeg. Same as **fillibeg.**

Philippian *fil-ip'i-ən, n.* a native of *Philippi* . in Macedonia.—Also *adj.*

Philippic *fil-ip'ik, n* one of the three orations of Demosthenes against Philip of Macedon: (without *cap.*) any discourse full of invective. [Gr. *philippikos, philippizein—Philippos,* Philip.]

Philistine *fil'is-tīn* (*U.S. fil-is'tīn*), *n.* one of the ancient inhabitants of south-west Palestine, enemies of the Israelites: (also without *cap.*) a person of material outlook, indifferent or hostile to culture.— Also *adj.* **Phil'istine** (sometimes without *cap.*).—*v.t.* **Phil'istinise, -ize** (*-tin-*).—*n.* **Phil'istinism** (sometimes without *cap.*). [Gr *Philistīnos, Palaistīnos*— Heb. *P'lishtīm.*]

phillabeg, phillibeg. Same as **fillibeg.**

phillumeny *fil-ōō'mən-i, n.* a fantastic word for collecting matchbox labels.—*n.* **phillu'menist.** [L *lūmen, -inis,* light.]

philo-. See **phil-.**

philogyny *fil-oj'i-ni, n.* love of women —*adj.* **philog'ynous.**—*n.* **philog'ynist.** [Gr. *philogyniā—gynē,* a woman.]

philology *fil-ol'ə-ji, n.* the science of language: the study of etymology, grammar, rhetoric, and literary criticism: orig., the knowledge which enabled men to study and explain the languages of Greece and Rome. —*ns.* **philol'oger, philologian** (*-ə-lō'*), **philol'ogist, phil'ologue** (*-log*) one versed in philology.—*adjs.* **philologic** (*-ə-loj'ik*), **-al.**—*adv.* **philolog'ically.— comparative philology** the study of languages by comparing their history, forms, and relationships with each other. [Gr. *philologiā—phil-* (q.v.). *logos,* word.]

philosopher *fi-los'ə-fər, n.* a lover of wisdom· one versed in or devoted to philosophy: a metaphysician: one who acts calmly and rationally in the affairs and changes of life.—*adjs.* **philosophic** (*-sof'* or *-zof'*), **-al** pertaining or according to philosophy: skilled in or given to philosophy: befitting a philosopher: rational· calm.—*adv.* **philosoph'ically.**—*v.t.* **philos'ophise, -ize** to reason like a philosopher: to form philosophical theories.—*n.* **philos'ophiser, -z-** a would-be philosopher.—*adjs.* **philosophist'ic, -al.**—*n.* **philos'ophy** orig., pursuit of wisdom and knowledge: investigation of the nature of being: knowledge of the causes and laws of all things: the principles underlying any department of knowledge: reasoning: a particular philosophical system: calmness of temper.— **philosopher's stone** an imaginary stone or mineral compound, long sought after by alchemists as a means of transforming other metals into gold.— **moral, natural, philosophy** see **moral, natural.** [Gr. *philosophos—sophiā,* wisdom.]

-philous. See **phil-.**

philtre, philter *fil'tər, n.* a drink, or (rarely) a spell, to excite love. [Fr. *philtre—*L. *philtrum—*Gr. *philtron—phileein,* to love, *-tron,* agent-suffix.]

-phily. See **phil-.**

phimosis *fi-mō'sis, n* narrowing of the preputial orifice [Gr. *phimōsis,* muzzling—*phimos,* a muzzle]

phiz *fiz,* **phizog** *fiz-og',* (*slang*) *ns* the face [**physiognomy.**]

phlebitis *fli-bī'tis, n* inflammation of a vein.—*n* **phlebolite** (*fleb'ə-līt;* Gr. *lithos,* stone) a calcareous concretion found in a vein —*v t* **phlebot'omise, -ize** (Gr. *tomē,* a cut) to bleed.—*ns.* **phlebot'omist** a blood-letter, **phlebot'omy** blood-letting. [Gr *phleps, phlebos,* a vein.]

phlegm *flem, n* the thick, slimy matter secreted in the throat, and discharged by coughing, regarded in old physiology as one (cold and moist) of the four humours or bodily fluids: the temperament supposed to be due to its predominance, sluggish indifference: calmness.—Following words pron *fleg-* unless indicated otherwise—*adjs.* **phlegmat'ic, -al** abounding in or generating phlegm. cold and sluggish: not easily excited.—*adv.* **phlegmat'ically.**—*adj.* **phlegmy** (*flem'i*). [By later return to Greek spelling, from M.E *fleem, fleme, flemme—*O.Fr. *flemme, fleume* —L. *phlegma—*Gr. *phlegma, -atos,* flame, inflammation. phlegm (regarded as produced by heat), inflammation—*phlegein,* to burn]

phloem *flō'əm, n.* the bast or sieve-tube portion of a vascular bundle, by which elaborated food materials are transported in a plant. [Gr. *phloos,* bark]

Phlox *floks, n* a Siberian and American genus of Polemoniaceae, well-known garden plants: (without *cap.*) a plant of this genus:—*pl* **phlox** or **phlox'es.** [Gr *phlox,* flame, wallflower—*phlegein,* to burn.]

phobia *fō'bi-ə,* **phobism** *fō'bizm, ns.* a fear, aversion, or hatred, esp. morbid and irrational.—**-phobe** in composition, one who has a (specified) phobia.— **-phobia** in composition, fear or hatred of (a specified object, condition, etc.).—*adj.* **phō'bic** like or pertaining to a phobia.—*n.* **phō'bist.** [Gr *phobos,* fear]

phoebe *fē'bi, n* a N. American flycatcher of the genus *Sayornis.* [Imit.]

Phoenician *fi-nish'ən, -yən, adj* of Phoenicia, on the coast of Syria, its people, colonies (including Carthage), language, and arts.—*n.* one of the people of Phoenicia: their Semitic language. [Gr. *Phoinix, -īkos.*]

phoenix *fē'niks, n.* a fabulous Arabian bird, worshipped in ancient Egypt, the only individual of its kind, that burned itself every 500 years or so and rose rejuvenated from its ashes: hence anything that rises from its own or its predecessor's ashes. [O.E. *fenix,* later assimilated to L *phoenix—*Gr. *phoinix.*]

phon *fon, n.* a unit of loudness level.—In composition **phon-, phono-** (*fōn-, fō'nō-, fō-nō-*) sound, voice — *v.i* **phōnate'** to produce vocal sound, to utter voice —*n.* **phōnā'tion.**—*adj.* **phōn'atory** (or *fō-nā'tər-i*)— *n.* **phone** (*fōn*) an elementary speech sound: a telephone receiver: (also **'phone;** *coll.*) a telephone.— *v.t., v.i.* (also **'phone;** *coll.*) to telephone.—**-phone** adj and noun combining form, speaking, or one who speaks (a given language), as in *Francophone.*—*n.* **phoneme** (*fōn'ēm;* Gr. *phōnēma,* a sound) a group or family of speech sounds felt in any one language to be merely variants of one sound.—*adj* **phonemic** (*-nēm'* or *-nem'*).—*adv.* **phonem'ically.**—*n.sing.* **phonēm'ics** the science of phonemic groups and contrasts.—*adj* **phonetic** (*fō-net'ik, fə-*) of, concerning, according to, or representing the sounds of spoken language.— Also **phonet'ical.**—*adv* **phonet'ically** according to pronunciation.—*n.* **phonetician** (*fō-ni-tish'ən*) one versed in phonetics.—*v.t* **phonet'icise, -ize** to make phonetic: to represent phonetically —*n sing.* **phonet'ics** that branch of linguistic science that deals with pronunciation, speech production, etc —*n.pl.* phonetic representations.—*adj* **phòn'ic** (or *fon'ık*) of sound, esp. vocal sound: voiced.—*n. sing.* **phòn'ics** (or *fon'iks*) the science of sound, or of spoken sounds. —*ns.* **phonogram** (*fō'nə-gram*) a character representing a sound: a phonographic record; **phonograph** (*fō'nə-graf*; Gr. *graphein*, to write) a character used to represent a sound: Edison's instrument for recording sounds on a cylinder and reproducing them: the ordinary word for any gramophone (*U.S*); **phonographer** (*fō-nog'rəəfər*), **phonog'raphist** a writer of phonographic shorthand.—*adj.* **phonographic** (*fō-nə-graf'ik*) phonetic: of phonography: of or by means of the phonograph.—*adv.* **phonograph'ically.** —*ns.* **phonog'raphy** (*fō-nog'rə-fi*) the art of representing each spoken sound by a distinct character: Pitman's phonetic shorthand: the use of the phonograph; **phonology** (*fō-nol'ə-ji*; Gr. *logos*, discourse) (the study of) the system of sounds in a language, and sometimes the history of their changes.—*adj.* **phonolog'ical.**—*ns.* **phonol'ogist; phonom'eter** (Gr. *metron*, measure) apparatus for estimating the loudness level of a sound in phons by subjective comparison.—*n.sing.* **phonotac'tics** (Gr.,—*tassein*, to arrange) (the study of) the ways in which the sounds of a language can appear in the words of that language.—**phone'-in** a radio programme which consists mainly of telephone calls from listeners on selected topics; **pho'ner-in'; phonetic alphabet** a system (used in voice communications) in which letters of the alphabet are identified by means of code words: a list of symbols used in phonetic transcriptions; **phonetic spelling** the writing of a language by means of a separate symbol for every sound: often applied to a compromise, or a departure from conventional spelling more or less adapted as a guide to pronunciation; **phonic method** a method of teaching reading through the phonetic value of letters and groups of letters. [Gr. *phōnē*, voice, sound.]

phonate, phone, phonemic, etc., phonetic, etc. See **phon.**

phoney, phony *fō'ni*, (*slang*), *n.* and *adj.* counterfeit: unreal.—*v.t.* to fake, counterfeit, achieve by faking. —*n.* **phon'eyness, phon'iness.**

phono-. For words beginning thus, see **phon.**

phony. See **phoney.**

phooey *foo'i*, *interj.* an exclamation of contempt, scorn, disbelief, etc. [Perh. conn. with **phew.**]

-phore *-fōr, -for, -phor -fòr,* in composition used to denote 'carrier', as *semaphore, chromatophore.—* **-phoresis** noun combining form denoting a transmission, migration, as *electrophoresis.* [Gr. *phoros,* bearing—*pherein.*]

phosgene *fos'jēn, n.* a poisonous gas, carbonyl chloride (COCl₂). [Gr. *phōs,* light, and the root of *gignesthai,* to be produced.]

Phosphorus *fos'far-əs, n.* a non-metallic element (symbol P; at. numb. 15) a waxy, poisonous, and inflammable substance giving out light in the dark.—*n.* **phosphate** (*fos'fāt*) a salt of phosphoric acid.—*adj.* **phosphatic** (*fos-fat'ik*) of the nature of, or containing, a phosphate.—*ns.* **phos'phide** (*-fīd*) a compound of phosphorus and another element; **phos'-phine** (*-fēn, -fīn*) phosphuretted hydrogen gas (PH₃): extended to substances analogous to amines with phosphorus instead of nitrogen; **phos'phite** a salt of phosphorous acid; **phosphopro'tein** any of a number of compounds formed by a protein with a substance containing phosphorus, other than a nucleic acid or lecithin.—*v.t.* **phos'phorate** to combine or impregnate with phosphorus: to make phosphorescent.—*v.i.* **phosphoresce'** to shine in the dark like phosphorus.—*n.* **phosphoresc'ence.**—*adj.* **phos-**

phoresc'ent.—*n.*—*adjs.* **phos'phoretted** (or *-et'*) see **phosphuretted; phosphoric** (*fos-for'ik*) of or like phosphorus: phosphorescent: containing phosphorus in higher valency (*chem.*).—*v.t.* **phos'phorise, -ize** to combine or impregnate with phosphorus, to make phosphorescent.—*adjs.* **phos'phorous** phosphorescent· containing phosphorus in lower valency (*chem.*); **phos'phuretted** (or *-et'*) combined with phosphorus (**phosphuretted or phosphoretted hydrogen** phosphine). [L *phosphorus*—Gr. *phōsphorus,* light-bearer—*phōs,* light, *phoros,* bearing, from *pherein,* to bear]

phot *fot, fōt, n.* the CGS unit of illumination, 1 lumen per cm².—*adj.* **photic** (*fōt'ik*) of light: light-giving sensitive to light: accessible to light (as e.g the uppermost layer of sea) —*n* **phot'ism** sensation of light accompanying another sensation or thought. [Gr *phōs, phōtos,* light.]

phot- *fōt-,* **photo-** *fō'tō-,* in composition, light.—*adj* **photoac'tive** affected physically or chemically by light or other radiation.—*ns.* **pho'tocall** a session in which prominent people are photographed for publicity purposes; **pho'tocell** a photoelectric cell—*adj.* **photochem'ical.**—*ns.* **photochem'ist; photochem'-istry** the part of chemistry dealing with changes brought about by light, or other radiation, and with the production of radiation by chemical change — *adjs* **photoconduct'ing, -ive** pertaining to, or showing, photoconductivity.—*ns.* **photoconductivity** (*-kon-duk-tiv'i-ti*) the property of varying conductivity under influence of light; **photodi'ode** a two-electrode semiconductor device, used as an optical sensor; **photoelectric'ity** electricity or a change of electric condition, produced by light or other electromagnetic radiation —*adj.* **photoelectric** (*-i-lek'*) pertaining to photoelectricity, to photoelectrons, or to electric light (**photoelectric cell** any device in which incidence of light of suitable frequency causes an alteration in electrical state, esp. by photo-emission). —*ns.* **photoelec'trode** an electrode which is activated by light; **photoelec'tron** an electron ejected from a body by the incidence of ultra-violet rays or X-rays upon it —*n.sing.* **photoelectron'ics** the science dealing with the interactions of electricity and electromagnetic radiations, esp. those that involve free electrons.—*n.* **photo-emiss'ion** emission of electrons from the surface of a body on which light falls.—*adj.* **photogenic** (*-jen'* or *-jēn'*) producing light: produced by light: having the quality of photographing well: (*loosely*) attractive, striking.—*ns.* **photokinesis** (*-ki-, -kī-nē'sis;* Gr *kinēsis,* movement) movement occurring in response to variations in light intensity; **photolysis** (*fō-tol'i-sis;* Gr. *lysis,* loosing— *lyein,* to loose) decomposition or dissociation under the influence of radiation (*chem.*): the grouping of chloroplasts in relation to illumination (*bot.*) —*adj.* **photolytic** (*fō-tō-lit'ik*).—*n.* **photom'eter** an instrument for measuring luminous intensity, usu. by comparing two sources of light.—*adj.* **photomet'ric.** —*ns.* **photom'etry** (the branch of physics dealing with) the measurement of luminous intensity; **photopsia, photopsy** (*fō-top'si-ə, -top'si*; Gr. *opsis,* appearance) the appearance of flashes of light, owing to irritation of the retina; **photo-recep'tor** a nerve-ending receiving light stimuli.—*adjs.* **photo-resist'** of an organic material) that polymerises on exposure to ultraviolet light and in that form resists attack by acids and solvents.—*v.t.* **photosens'itise, -ize** to make photosensitive by chemical or other means —*n.* **photosens'itiser, -ize**—*adj.* **photosens'itive** affected by light, visible or invisible.—*ns.* **photosensitiv'ity; photosphere** (*fō'tō-sfēr*) the luminous envelope of the sun's globe, the source of light; **photosynthesis**

photo- 738 phyco-

(*fō-tō-sin'thi-sis*; *bot.*) the building up of complex compounds by the chlorophyll apparatus of plants by means of the energy of light.—*adj.* **photosynthet'ic**.—*n.* **phototaxis** (*fō-tō-taks'is*; Gr. *taxis*, arrangement; *biol.*) a change of place under stimulus of light.—*adj.* **phototac'tic**.—*ns.* **phototelegraph** (*fō-tō-tel'i-gräf*) an instrument for transmitting drawings, photographs, etc., by telegraphy; **phototeleg'raphy**.—*ns.* **phototropism** (*fōt-ot'rap-izm*; Gr. *tropos*, turning) orientation in response to the stimulus of light (*bot.*): reversible colour change on exposure to light (*chem.*); **phototrope** (*fō'tō-trōp*) a substance that changes thus.—*adj.* **phototropic** (*fō-tō-trop'ik*).—*n.* **phototropy** change of colour due to wavelength of incident light.—*adj.* **photovoltaic** (*fō-tō-vol-tā'ik*) producing an electromotive force across the junction between dissimilar materials when it is exposed to light or ultraviolet radiation.—*n.sing.* **photovolta'ics** the science and technology of photovoltaic devices and substances. [Gr. *phōs*, *phōtos*, light.] **photo-** *fō'tō-*, in composition, photographic: made by, or by the aid of, photographic means.—*n.*, *v.t.*, *adj.* **photo** a coll. shortening of **photograph**(ic, -al):—*pl.* **pho'tos**.—*ns.* **pho'tocomposition** (*print.*) setting of copy by projecting images of letters successively on a sensitive material from which printing plates are made; **pho'tocopier** a machine which makes photocopies; **photocopy** (*fō'tō-ko-pi*) a photographic reproduction of written matter.—*v.t.* to make a photocopy.—*ns.* **pho'tocopying**; **pho'to-engraving, -etching** any process of engraving by aid of photography, esp. from relief plates; **pho'to-finish** a race finish in which a special type of photography is used to show the winner, etc.: a neck and neck finish of any contest; **Pho'to-fit®** a method of making identification pictures, an alternative to identikit (q.v.); **pho'togram** a type of picture produced by placing an object on or near photographic paper which is then exposed to light; **photogravure** (*fō-tō-grə-vūr'*; Fr. *gravure*, engraving) a method of photo-engraving in which the design etched on the metal surface is intaglio not relief: a picture produced by this method; **photolithography** (*fō-tō-li-thog'rə-fi*) a process of lithographic printing from a photographically produced plate.—*n.* and *v.t.* **photolith'ograph** (*-o-gräf*).—*n.* **photolithog'rapher**.—*adj.* **photolithographic** (*-graf'ik*).—*ns.* **photomicrograph** (*fō-tō-mī'krō-gräf*; Gr. *mikros*, little, *graphein*, to write) an enlarged photograph of a microscopic object taken through a microscope; **photomicrographer** (*-krog'rə-fər*).—*adj.* **photomicrographic** (*-krō-graf'ik*).—*ns.* **photomicrog'raphy**; **photomon'tage** (*-tazh*) (the art of making) a picture by cutting up photographs, etc., and arranging the parts so as to convey, without explicitly showing, a definite meaning; **pho'tosetting** photocomposition; **Photostat®** (*fō'tō-stat*; Gr. *statos*, set, placed) a photographic apparatus for making facsimiles of MSS., drawings, etc., directly: a facsimile so made.—*v.t.* and *v.i.* to photograph by Photostat.—**phototype** (*fō'tō-tīp*; Gr. *typos*, impression) a printing block on which the material is produced photographically: a print made from such a block: the process of making such a block.—*v.t.* to reproduce by phototype.—*adj.* **phototypic** (*-tip'ik*).—*n.* **phototypy** (*fō'tō-tī-pi* or *fō-tot'i-pi*. [**photograph**.] **photography** *fō-tog'rə-fi*, *n.* the art or process of producing permanent and visible images by the action of light, or other radiant energy, on chemically prepared surfaces.—*n.* **photograph** (*fō'tə-gräf*) an image so produced.—*v.t.* to make a picture of by means of photography.—*v.i.* to take photographs: to be capable of being photographed.—*n.* **photog'rapher**.—*adjs.* **photographic** (*-graf'ik*), **-al.**—*adv.* **photo-**

graph'ically.—*n.* **photog'raphist**. [Gr. *phōs*, *phōtos*, light, *graphein*, to draw.] **phrase** *frāz*, *n.* manner of expression in language: an expression: a group of words generally not forming a clause but felt as expressing a single idea or constituting a single element in the sentence: a pithy expression: a catchword: an empty or high-sounding expression: a short group of notes felt to form a unit (*mus.*).—*v.t.* to express in words: to style: to mark, bring out, or give effect to the phrases of (*mus.*).—*adjs.* **phras'al** consisting of, of the nature of, a phrase; **phrase'less** incapable of being described.—*ns.* **phraseogram** (*frā'zi-ō-gram*) a single sign, written without lifting the pen, for a whole phrase (esp. in shorthand); **phra'seograph** a phrase that is so written; **phraseol'ogy** style or manner of expression or arrangement of phrases: peculiarities of diction: a collection of phrases in a language; **phra'sing** the wording of a speech or passage: the grouping and accentuation of the sounds in performing a melody (*mus.*).—*adj.* **phra'sy** inclining to emptiness and verbosity of phrase.—**phrasal verb** a phrase, consisting of a verb and one or more additional words, having the function of a verb; **phrase'-book** a book containing or explaining phrases of a language.—**turn of phrase** an expression: one's manner of expression. [Gr. *phrāsis*—*phrazein*, to speak.] **phratry** *frā'tri*, *n.* a social division of a people, often exogamous. [Gr. *phrātriā*.] **phreatic** *frē-at'ik*, *adj.* pertaining to underground water supplying, or probably able to supply, wells or springs, or to the soil or rocks containing it, or to wells: (of underground gases, etc.) present in, or causing, volcanic eruptions.—*n.* **phreat'ophyte** a deep-rooted plant drawing its water from the water table or just above it. [Gr. *phrear*, well, *phreātia*, cistern.] **phrenesis** *fri-nē'sis*, *n.* phrenitis: delirium: frenzy.—For *adj.*, *n.* **phrenetic**, *adj.* **phrenetical**, *adv.* **phrenetically**, see **frenetic**.—*adjs.* **phrenic** (*fren'ik*) of or near the midriff; **phrenit'ic** of or affected with phrenitis.—*n.* **phreni'tis** inflammation of the brain: brain-fever.—*adjs.* **phrenolog'ic** (*fren-*), **-al.**—*adv.* **phrenolog'ically**.—*v.t.* **phrenol'ogise, -ize** to examine phrenologically.—*ns.* **phrenol'ogist**; **phrenol'ogy** a would-be science of mental faculties supposed to be located in various parts of the skull and investigable by feeling the bumps on the outside of the head. [Gr. *phrēn*, *phrenos*, midriff, supposed seat of passions, mind, will.] **Phrygian** *frij'i-ən*, *adj.* pertaining to *Phrygia* in Asia Minor, or to its people.—*n.* a native of Phrygia: a Montanist: the language of the ancient Phrygians.—**Phrygian cap** a conical cap with the top turned forward. **phthalic** (*f*)*thal'ik*, *adj.* applied to three acids, $C_6H_4(COOH)_2$, and an anhydride, derived from naphthalene.—*ns.* **phthal'ate** a salt or ester of phthalic acid; **phthal'ein** (*-i-in*) any one of a very important class of dye-yielding materials formed by the union of phenols with phthalic anhydride. [**naphthalene**.] **phthisis** *thī'sis*, also *fthī'*, *tī'*, *n.* wasting disease: tuberculosis, esp. of the lungs.—*n.* **phthisic** (*tiz'ik*, sometimes *thī'sik*, *fthī'sik*, *tī'sik*) phthisis: vaguely, a lung or throat disease.—*adjs.* **phthisical** (*tiz'*), **phthis'icky**. [Gr. *phthisis*—*phthi*(*n*)*ein*, to waste away.] **phut** *fut*, *n.* a dull sound esp. of collapse, deflation, etc.—Also *adv.*, as in **go phut** to break, become unserviceable: to come to nothing. [Hind. *phatnā*, to split.] **pH value.** See **pH**. **phyco-** *fī-kō-*, in composition, seaweed.—*ns.*

phycologist (-kol'ə-jist); **phycol'ogy** the study of algae. [Gr. *phykos*, seaweed.]

phyla. See **phylum.**

phylactery fi-lak'tə-rı, n. a charm or amulet: among the Jews, a slip of parchment inscribed with certain passages of Scripture, worn in a box on the left arm or forehead: a reminder: ostentatious display of religious forms: a case for relics: in mediaeval art, a scroll at the mouth of a figure in a picture bearing the words he is supposed to speak.—*adjs.* **phylacteric** (-ter'ık), **-al.** [Gr. *phylaktērion—phylax*, a guard.]

phyletic fi-let'ik, adj. pertaining to a phylum: according to descent. [Gr. *phyletikos—phylē*, a tribe.]

phyllary fil'ə-rı, (bot.) n. an involucral bract. [Gr. *phyllarion*, dim. of *phyllon*, leaf.]

phylloclade fil'ō-klād, n. a branch with the form and functions of a leaf. [Gr. *phyllon*, leaf, *klados*, shoot.]

phyllode fil'ōd, n. a petiole with the appearance and function of a leaf-blade. [Gr. *phyllon*, leaf.]

phyllomania fil-ō-mā'ni-ə, n. excessive production of leaves, at the expense of flower or fruit production [Gr. *phyllon*, leaf, *maniā*, madness.]

phylloquinone fil-ō-kwin'ōn, or -ōn', n. vitamin K₁ [Gr. *phyllon*, leaf, and **quinone.**]

phyllotaxis fil-ō-tak'sis, n. the disposition of leaves on the stem.—Also **phyll'otaxy.**—*adjs.* **phyllotact'ic, -al.** [Gr. *phyllon*, a leaf, *taxis*, arrangement.]

Phylloxera fil-ok-sē'rə, n. a genus of insects of a family akin to green-fly, very destructive to vines: (without *cap.*) an insect of this genus. [Gr. *phyllon*, a leaf, *xēros*, dry.]

phylogeny fi-loj'ı-nı, n. evolutionary pedigree or genealogical history—also **phylogenesis** (fi-lō-jen'ı-sis).—*adj.* **phylogenet'ic.**—*adv.* **phylogenet'ically.** [Gr. *phylon*, race, *genesis*, origin.]

phylum fi'lam, n. a main division of the animal or the vegetable kingdom:—*pl.* **phy'la.** [Mod. L.—Gr. *phylon*, race.]

Physalia fi-sā'li-ə, n. a genus of large oceanic colonial hydrozoans with a floating bladder—including the Portuguese man-of-war: (without *cap.*) a member of the genus. [Gr. *physallis*, a bladder, *physētēr*, a blower, a whale, bellows—*physaein*, to blow.]

physic fiz'ik, n. orig. natural philosophy, physics: the science, art, or practice of medicine: a medicine: anything healing or wholesome.—*adj.* **phys'ical** pertaining to the world of matter and energy, or its study, natural philosophy: material: bodily: requiring bodily effort: involving bodily contact.—*ns.* **phys'icalism** the theory that all phenomena are explicable in spatiotemporal terms and that all statements are either analytic or reducible to empirically verifiable assertions; **phys'icalist; physical'ity** preoccupation with the bodily.—*adv.* **phys'ically.**—*ns.* **physician** (fi-zish'n) one skilled in the use of physic or the art of healing: one legally qualified to practice medicine. one who makes use of medicines and treatment, distinguished from a surgeon who practices manual operations: a doctor: a healer or healing influence (fig.); **physic'ianship; phys'icism** (-sizm) belief in the material or physical as opposed to the spiritual, **phys'icist** (-sist) one versed in physics: one who believes the phenomena of life are purely physical.—*adjs.* **phys'icky** like medicine; **physicochem'ical** relating to or involving both physics and chemistry: pertaining to physical chemistry (see below).—*n. sing* **phys'ics** orig. natural science in general: now, the science of the properties (other than chemical) of matter and energy.—**physical astronomy** the study of the physical condition and chemical composition of the heavenly bodies; **physical chemistry** the study of the dependence of physical properties on chemical composition, and of the physical changes accompanying chemical reactions; **physical force** force applied outwardly to the body, as distinguished from persuasion, etc.; **physical geography** the study of the earth's natural features—its mountain-chains, ocean-currents, etc.; **physical jerks** (coll.) bodily excercises. [Gr. *physikos*, natural—*physis*, nature.]

physi(o)- fiz-i-(ō-) in composition, nature.—*ns.* **phys'io** short for physiotherapist:—*pl.* **phys'ios; physiocracy** (-ok'rə-si; Gr. *krateein*, to rule) government, according to François Quesnay (1694–1774) and his followers, by a. natural order inherent in society, land and its products being the only true source of wealth, direct taxation of land being the only proper source of revenue, **phys'iocrat** (-ō-krat) one who maintains these opinions.—*adj.* **physiocrat'ic.**—*ns.* **physiography** (-og'rə-fi; Gr. *graphein*, to describe) description of nature, descriptive science: physical geography; **physiog'rapher.**—*adjs.* **physiographic** (-ō-graf'ik), **-al.**—*n.* **physiology** (-ol'ə-ji; Gr. *logos*, discourse) the science of the processes of life in animals and plants.—*adjs.* **physiologic** (-ə-loj'ik), **-al.** —*adv* **physiolog'ically.**—*ns.* **physiol'ogist; physiol'ogus** a bestiary; **physiotherapy** (-ō-ther'ə-pi; Gr *therapeiā*, treatment) treatment of disease by remedies such as massage, fresh air, electricity, rather than by drugs.—Also *n.sing.* **physiotherapeutics** (-pūt'iks).—*adj.* **physiotherapeut'ic.**—*ns* **physiother'apist.** [Gr *physis*, nature]

physiognomy fiz-i-on'ə-mı or -og'nə-mi, n. the art of judging character from appearance, esp. from the face: the face as an index of the mind: the face (coll.): the general appearance of anything: character, aspect.—*adj.* **physiognomic** (-nom'), **-al.**—*adv* **physiognom'ically.**—*n.* **physiogn'omist.** [Gr. *physiognōmiā*, a shortened form of *physiognōmoniā* —*physis*, nature, *gnōmōn, -onos*, an interpreter.]

physique fiz-ēk', n. bodily type, build, or constitution. [Fr]

phyto- fi-tō-, -to-, in composition, plant.—**-phyte** in composition, used to indicate a plant belonging to a particular habitat, or of a particular type.—**-phytic** (-fit-ik) adjective combining form.—*ns.* **phytogen'esis, phytogeny** (-toj'ı-nı) evolution of plants —*adjs.* **phytogenet'ic, -al** relating to phytogenesis; **phytogenic** (-jen'ik) of vegetable origin.—*n.* **phytog'rapher.**—*adj.* **phytograph'ic.**—*n.* **phytog'-raphy** descriptive botany —*adj.* **phytolog'ical.**—*ns* **phytol'ogist** a botanist; **phytol'ogy** botany, **phytonadione** (fi-tō-nə-dī'ōn) phylloquinone, vitamin K₁, **phytopathol'ogist; phytopathology** (Gr. *pathos*, suffering) the study of plant diseases; **phyto'sis** the presence of vegetable parasites or disease caused by them; **phytot'omist; phytotomy** (-tot'ə-mı, Gr. *tomē*, a cut) plant anatomy.—*adj.* **phytotox'ic** poisonous to plants: pertaining to a phytotoxin.—*ns.* **phytotoxic'ity** harmfulness to plants; **phytotox'in** a toxin produced by a plant. [Gr. *phyton*, plant.]

pi¹ pi, pē, n. the sixteenth letter (Π, π) of the Greek alphabet, answering to the Roman P: a symbol for the ratio of the circumference of a circle to the diameter, approx 3·14159 (math.) —**pi-** (or π-) **meson** the source of the nuclear force holding protons and neutrons together (phys.).—Also **pion.** [Gr. *pei, pi.*]

pi² (print). Same as **pie².**

pi³ pī, (slang) adj an abbreviation of **pious**: religious sanctimonious.—*n.* a pious, religious, or sanctimonious person or talk.—**pi'-jaw** sermonising an admonition.

pia pi'ə, pē'a, (L) adj. pious—**pia fraus** (froz, frows) pious fraud

piacevole pyə-chā'vo-lā, (mus) adj pleasant, playful [It.]

piaffe *pi-af'*, *pyaf*, *v.i.* in horsemanship, to advance at a piaffer.—*n.* **piaff'er** a gait in which the feet are lifted in the same succession as a trot, but more slowly.—Also *Spanish-walk*. [Fr. *piaffer*]

pia mater *pī'ə mā'tər*, the vascular membrane investing the brain. [L. *pia māter*, tender mother, a mediaeval translation of Ar. *umm raqīqah*, thin mother.]

pianoforte *pya'nō-for-ti*, *pē-a'*, *pyä'*, *pē-a'*, shortened to **piano** (*pya'*, *pē-a'*, or *-a'*), *n.* a musical instrument with wires struck by hammers moved by keys:—*pl.* **pia'nofortes**, **pian'os**.—*ns* **pianette** (*pē-ə-net'*), **pianino** (*pya-nē'nō*, *pē-ə-nē'nō*, *pl.* **piani'nos**) a small upright piano.—*adj.* and *adv.* **pianissimo** (*pya-nēs'si-mō*, *pē-ə-nis'i-mō*) very soft —*n.* **pianist** (*pē'ə-nist*, *pyan'*; also *pē-an'ist*) one who plays the pianoforte, esp. expertly.—*adj.* **pianist'ic**.—*adv.* **pianist'ically**.—*adj.* and *adv.* **piano** (*pya'nō*, *pē-ä'nō*) soft, softly.—*n.* a soft passage.—*n.* **Pianola**® (*pyan-ō'lə*, *pē-ə-*) a pneumatic contrivance for playing the piano by means of a perforated roll (a **piano roll**).—**pia'no-accord'ion** an elaborate accordion with a keyboard like a piano; **pia'no-or'gan** a piano like a barrel-organ, played by mechanical means, **pian'o-play'er** a mechanical contrivance for playing the piano: a pianist; **pian'o-stool** a stool usually adjustable in height for a pianist; **pian'o-wire** wire used for piano strings, and for deep-sea soundings, etc.—**player piano** a piano with a piano-player [It.—*piano*, soft —L. *plānus*, level, and *forte*, loud—L. *fortis*, strong.]

piassava *pē-əs-d'və*, **plassaba** *-bə*, *ns.* a coarse stiff fibre used for making brooms, etc., got from Brazilian palms, *Attalea* (coquilla) and *Leopoldinia* (chiqui-chiqui): the tree yielding it. [Port. from Tupi.]

piastre *pi-as'tər*, *n.* a unit of currency in current or former use in several N. African and Middle Eastern countries, equal to 1/100 of a (Sudanese, Egyptian, etc.) pound: a coin of this value: piece of eight. [Fr.,—It. *piastra*, a leaf of metal; see **plaster**.]

piazza *pē-āt'sə*, also *pē-ad'zə*, *pē-az'ə*, *n.* a place or square surrounded by buildings: (*erroneously*) a walk under a roof supported by pillars: a veranda (*U.S.*).—*adj.* **piazz'ian**. [It.,—L. *platea*—Gr. *plateia*, a street (fem. of *platys*, broad).]

pibroch *pē'brohh*, *n.* the classical music of the bagpipe, free in rhythm and consisting of theme and variations. [Gael. *piobaireachd*, pipe-music—*piobair*, a piper—*piob*, from Eng. **pipe**.]

pic *pik*, *n.* a coll. short form of **picture**; cf. **pix²**.

pica *pī'kə*, (*print.*) *n.* an old type size, approximately, and still used synonymously for, 12-point, giving about 6 lines to the inch, much used in typewriters. [Possibly used for printing *pies*; see **pie²**.]

Pica *pī'kə*, *n.* the magpie genus: (without *cap.*) a craving for unsuitable food. [L. *pīca*, magpie.]

picador *pik-ə-dòr'*, *-dor'*, now usu. *pik'ə-dör*, *n.* a mounted bull-fighter with a lance. [Sp.,—*pica*, a pike.]

picamar *pik'ə-mär*, *n.* a bitter oily liquid got from tar. [L. *pix*, *picis*, pitch, *amārus*, bitter.]

picaresque. See **picaroon**.

picaroon *pik-ə-rōōn'*, *n.* one who lives by his wits: a cheat: a pirate.—*adj.* **picaresque** (*-resk'*).—**picaresque novels** the tales of Spanish rogue and vagabond life, much in vogue in the 17th century: novels of this type. [Sp. *picarón*, augmentative of *pícaro*, rogue.]

picayune *pik-ə-ūn'*, *n.* a small coin worth 6½ cents, current in United States before 1857: a five-cent piece, or other small coin: anything of little or no value.—*adj.* petty.—*adj.* **picayun'ish**. [Prov. *picaioun*, an old Piedmontese copper coin.]

piccalilli *pik-ə-lil'i*, *n.* a pickle of various vegetable substances with mustard and spices.

piccaninny, pickaninny *pik-ə-nin'i*, *n.* a little child: a Negro child.—*adj.* very little. [Port. *pequenino*, dim. of *pequeno*, little, or possibly Sp. *pequeño niño*, little child.]

piccolo *pik'ə-lō*, *n.* a small flute, an octave higher than the ordinary flute: an organ stop of similar tone:—*pl.* **picc'olos**. [It., little.]

pice *pīs*, *n.sing.* and *pl.* a money of account and coin, ¼ anna.—**new pice** 1/100 rupee. [Hind. *paisā*.]

piceous *pis'i-əs*, *pish'(i-)əs*, *adj.* like pitch: inflammable: black: reddish black. [L *piceus—pix*, pitch.]

pichurim *pich'ōō-rim*, *n.* a S. American tree of the laurel family: its aromatic kernel (also **pichurim bean**). [Port. *pichurim*—Tupi *puchury*.]

pick *pik*, *n.* a tool for breaking ground, rock, etc., with head pointed at one end or both, and handle fitted to the middle: a pointed hammer: an instrument of various kinds for picking: an act, opportunity, or right of choice· a portion picked: the best or choicest.—*v.t.* to break up, dress, or remove with a pick: to make with a pick or by plucking: to poke or pluck at, as with a sharp instrument or the nails: to clear, to remove, or to gather, by single small acts: to detach, extract, or take separately and lift or remove: to pluck: to pull apart: to cull: to choose: to select, esp. one by one or bit by bit: to peck, bite, or nibble: to eat in small quantities or delicately: to open (as a lock) by a sharp instrument or other unapproved means: to rifle by stealth: to seek and find a pretext for (as a quarrel).—*v.i.* to use a pick: to eat by morsels: to pilfer.—*adj.* **picked** (*pikt*) selected, hence the choicest or best: plucked, as flowers or fruit.—*ns.* **pick'edness**; **pick'er** one who picks or gathers up: a tool or machine for picking: one who removes defects from and finishes electrotype plates: a pilferer; **pick'ing** the action of the verb to pick: the quantity picked: that which is left to be picked: dabbing in stoneworking: the final finishing of woven fabrics by removing burs, etc.: removing defects from electrotype plates: (in *pl.*) odd gains or perquisites.—*adj.* **pick'y** (*coll.*) excessively fussy or choosy.—**pick'lock** an instrument for picking or opening locks: one who picks locks; **pick'-me-up** a stimulating drink: a medicinal tonic; **pick'-pocket** one who picks or steals from other people's pockets; **pick'-up** an act of picking up: reception: a stop to collect something or someone: a recovery: a thing picked up: accelerating power: a device for picking up an electric current: (also **pick-up head**) a transducer, activated by a sapphire or diamond stylus following the groove on a gramophone record, which transforms the mechanical into electrical impulses: a light motor vehicle with front part like private car and rear in form of truck: a man's chance, informal acquaintance with a woman, usu implying a sexual relationship: the woman in such a relationship.—*adj.* for picking up: picked up.—**pick a hole in someone's coat, pick holes in someone** to find fault with someone; **pick at** to find fault with; **pick oakum** to make oakum by untwisting old ropes; **pick off** to select from a number and shoot: to detach and remove; **pick on** to single out, esp. for anything unpleasant: to nag at: to carp at; **pick one's way** to choose carefully where to put one's feet, as on dirty ground; **pick out** to make out, distinguish: to pluck out: to select from a number: to mark with spots of colour, etc.; **pick over** to go over and select; **pick someone's brains** to make use of another's brains or ideas for one's own ends; **pick to pieces** to pull asunder: to criticise adversely in detail; **pick up** to lift from the ground, floor etc.: to improve gradually: to gain strength bit by bit: to take into a vehicle, or into one's company: to scrape acquaintance informally with, esp. of a man with a woman to acquire as occasion offers· to gain: to come upon, make out, distinguish (as a signal, a track, a comet, etc.); **pick up the pieces** to restore (esp emotional) matters to their former equilibrium after they have been brought to disarray or collapse

pickaback pık'ə-bak, adv and adj. on the back like a pack. of a vehicle or plane, conveyed on top of another.—n. a ride on one's back —Also **pick'back, pick'apack, pigg'yback**. [Connection with **pick** (pitch), **pack** and **back** obscure]

pickaninny. See **piccaninny.**

pickaxe pık'aks, n. a picking tool, with a point at one end of the head and a cutting blade at the other, used in digging [M E pıkoıs—O Fr pıcoıs, a mattock, pıquer, to pierce, pıc a **pick**]

pickerel pık'ər-əl, n. a young pike [**pike.**]

picket pık'ıt, n. a pointed stake or peg driven into the ground: a surveyor's mark· a small outpost, patrol, or body of men set apart for some special duty· picket-duty a person or group set to watch and dissuade those who go to work during a strike —v t to tether to a stake· to strengthen or surround with pickets· to peg down: to post as a picket· to deal with as a picket or by means of pickets: to place pickets at or near — v.t. to act as picket—pr p **pick'eting**; pa.t and pa.p **pick'eted.**—n. **pick'eter** one who pickets in a labour dispute —**pick'et-duty; pick'et-fence** (U S) a fence of pales; **pick'et-guard** a guard kept in readiness in case of alarm; **pick'et-line** a line of people acting as pickets in a labour dispute. [Fr pıquet, dim of pıc, a pickaxe.]

pickle pık'l, n. a liquid, esp brine or vinegar, in which food is preserved: an article of food preserved in such liquid: (in pl.) preserved onions, cucumber, etc , as a condiment: acid or other liquid used for cleansing or treatment in manufacture: a plight (coll)· a troublesome child (coll.) —v t to preserve with salt, vinegar, etc.: to rub with salt or salt and vinegar, as an old naval punishment: to clean or treat with acid or other chemical —adj. **pick'led** treated with a pickle: drunk (slang).—n **pick'ler** one who pickles· a vessel for pickling: an article suitable, or grown, for pickling — **pick'le-herring** a pickled herring. a merry-andrew (obs.) —**have a rod in pickle** to have a punishment ready [M E pekılle, pykyl, pekkyll, pykulle, cf Du pekel; Ger. Pokel.]

picnic pık'nık, n. orig. a fashionable social entertainment, towards which each person contributed a share of the food. an open-air repast of a number of persons on a country excursion: an undertaking that is mere child's play, often ironically —adj. of or for a picnic picnicking —v.t to have a picnic—pr p. **pic'nicking**; pa.t. and pa p. **pic'nicked.**—n **pic'nicker.**—adj **pic'nicky.** [Fr. pıque-nıque]

pico- pē-kō-, pī-kō-, in composition, a millionth of a millionth part, a million millionth, as in **pıcocurie, pıcosecond**, etc [Sp pıco, a small quantity]

picot pē'kō, n. a loop in an ornamental edging a raised knot in embroidery.—v t. to ornament with picots.—adj. **picoté** (pē-kō-tā) [Fr pıcot, point, prick.]

picotee pık-ə-tē', n. a florists' variety of carnation. orig speckled, now edged with a different colour [Fr pıcoté, prickled]

picra pık'rə, n. short for hıera-pıcra.—n **pıc'rate** a salt (highly explosive) of pıcrıc acıd.—adj **pıc'rıc** (pıcrıc acıd C₆H₂(NO₂)₃.OH, trinitrophenol. used as a yellow dye-stuff and as the basis of high explosives) [Gr. pıkros, bitter.]

Pict pıkt, n. one of an ancient people of obscure affinities, in Britain, esp north-eastern Scotland —adj. **Pict'ish.**—n. the language of the Picts —**Picts' house** an earth-house. [L Pıctī, Pıcts: possibly the same as

pictī, pa p. of pıngēre, to paint.]

pictograph pık'tə-graf, n a picture used as a symbol in picture-writing —n **pic'togram** a pictograph: a graphic representation —adj **pictographic** (-graf'ik) —adv **pictograph'ically.**—n. **pictography** (pık-tog'rə-fi) picture-writing [L. pıctus, painted, Gr. graphein, to write, gramma, a letter, figure.]

pictorial pık-tō'rı-əl, -tō', adj of a painter: of or relating to painting or drawing of, by means of, like, or of the nature of, a picture, or pictures.—n a periodical in which pictures are prominent.—adv **picto'rially.** [L pıctor, -ōrıs, painter—pıngēre, pıctum, to paint.]

picture pık'chər, n. the art or act of painting: an imitative representation of an object on a surface: (loosely) a photograph· a portrait: a tableau: a visible or visual image: a mental image: (an image on) a television screen· a person as like another as his own portrait: an impressive or attractive sight, like a painting or worthy of being painted: a visible embodiment: a vivid verbal description: a cinema film: (in pl) a cinema show, or the building in which it is given —v t to depict, represent in a picture: to form a likeness of in the mind: to describe vividly in words.—adj. **pic'tural** relating to, illustrated by, or consisting of pictures.—**pic'ture-book** a book of pictures; **pic'ture-card** a court card; **pic'ture-frame** a frame for surrounding a picture; **pic'ture-gallery** a gallery, hall, or building where pictures are exhibited; **pic'ture-house, -palace** a building for cinema shows; **picture postcard** a postcard bearing a picture, commonly a local view, **pic'ture-restorer** one who cleans and restores and sometimes ruins old pictures, **pic'ture-rod, -rail, -mould'ing** a rod, moulding, from which pictures may be hung; **pic'ture-win'dow** a usu. large window designed to act as a frame to an attractive view; **pic'ture-writ'ing** the use of pictures to express ideas or relate events —**get the picture** (coll.) to understand the situation; **in the picture** having a share of attention: adequately briefed; **put me** (etc.) **in the picture** give me (etc.) all the relevant information [L pıctūra—pıngēre, pıctum, to paint]

picturesque pık-chə-resk', adj. like a picture· such as would make a striking picture, implying some measure of beauty with much quaintness or immediate effectiveness: of language, vivid and colourful, or (facet) vulgar: having taste or feeling for the picturesque —adv **picturesque'ly,**.—n. **picturesque'ness.** [It pıttoresco—pıttura, a picture— L pıctūra]

piddle pıd'l, v t. to deal in trifles· to trifle· to eat with little relish: to urinate (coll) —n **pidd'ler** a trifler. —adj **pidd'ling** trifling, paltry

pidgin pıj'ın, n a Chinese corruption of **business** (also **pidg'eon, pig'eon**)· affair, concern (coll , also **pidg'eon, pig'eon**)· any combination and distortion of two languages as a means of communication —**pidgin English** a jargon, mainly English in vocabulary with Chinese arrangement, used in communication between Chinese and foreigners: any jargon consisting of English and another language

pi-dog, pie-dog. See **pye-dog.**

pie¹ pī, n. a magpie: a chatterer [Fr.,—L pīca]

pie², pi pī, n type confusedly mixed· a mixed state. confusion

pie³ pī, n a quantity of meat, fruit, or other food baked within or under a crust of prepared flour· an easy thing (slang). a welcome luxury, prize, or spoil (coll) —**pie chart, diagram, graph** a circle divided into sections by radii so as to show relative numbers or quantities; **pie'crust** the paste covering or enclosing a pie; **piecrust table** a Chippendale table with carved raised edge; **pie′dish** a deep dish in which pies are made.—*adj.* **pie′-eyed** (*coll.*) drunk.—**pie′man** one who sells pies, esp. in the street; **pie′-shop.**—**pie in the sky** some improbable future good promised without guarantee (from early 20th-cent. song).

piebald pī′böld, *adj.* black and white in patches: (*loosely*) of other colours in patches: motley: heterogeneous.—*n.* a piebald horse or other animal. [**pie¹, bald.**]

piece *pēs, n.* a part or portion of anything, esp. detached: a separate lump, mass, body, of any material, considered as an object: a distance: a span of time: a single article: a definite quantity, as of cloth or paper: a literary, dramatic, musical, or artistic composition: a production, specimen of work: an example: an exemplification or embodiment: a coin: a gun: a man in chess, draughts, or other game (in chess sometimes excluding pawns): a person—now usually (often disrespectfully) a woman.—*v.t.* to enlarge by adding a piece: to patch: to combine.—**piece** in composition, consisting of a given number of separate parts, pieces, members, etc., as in *three-piece suite.*—*adv.* **piece′meal** in pieces: to pieces: bit by bit.—*adj.* done bit by bit: fragmentary.—*n.* a small piece: bit by bit proceeding.—**piece′-goods** textile fabrics made in standard lengths; **piece′-rate** a fixed rate paid according to the amount of work done; **piece′-work** work paid for by the piece or quantity, not by time.—**all to pieces** into a state of disintegration or collapse; **a piece** each; **a piece** of an instance of: a bit of, something of; **a piece of one′s mind** a frank outspoken rating; **go to pieces** to break up entirely (*lit.* and *fig.*): to lose completely ability to cope with the situation; **in pieces** in, or to, a broken-up state; **of a piece** as if of the same piece, the same in nature: homogeneous, uniform: in keeping, consistent (with *with*); **piece of work** a task: a fuss, ado: person (usually with **nasty**, etc.); **piece together** to put together bit by bit. [O.Fr. *piece*—L.L. *pecia, petium,* a fragment, a piece of land—thought to be of Celtic (Brythonic) origin.]

pièce *pyes,* (Fr.) *n.* a piece, item.—**pièce de résistance** (*də rā-zē-stäs*) the substantial course at dinner, the joint: the best item; **pièce d′occasion** (*do-ka-zyɔ̄*) something, usu. a literary or musical work, composed, prepared, or used for a special occasion.

pied *pīd, adj.* variegated like a magpie: of various colours.—*n.* **pied′ness.** [**pie¹.**]

pied-à-terre pyä-da-ter, (Fr.) *n.* a dwelling kept for temporary, secondary, or occasional lodging:—*pl.* **pieds-à-terre.**

pier *pēr, n.* the mass of stone-work between the openings in the wall of a building: the support of an arch, bridge, etc.: a masonry support for a telescope or the like: a buttress: a gate pillar: a mass of stone, iron-work, or woodwork projecting into the sea or other water, as a breakwater, landing-stage, or promenade: a jetty or a wharf.—*n.* **pier′age** toll paid for using a pier.—**pier′-glass** orig., a mirror hung between windows: a tall mirror; **pier′-head** the seaward end of a pier. [M.E. *pēr,* L.L. *pēra.*]

pierce *pērs, v.t.* to thrust or make a hole through: to enter, or force a way into: to touch or move deeply: to penetrate: to perforate: to make by perforating or penetrating.—*v.i.* to penetrate.—*n.* a perforation: a stab: a prick.—*adj.* **pierce′able** capable of being pierced.—*adj.* **pier′ced** perforated: penetrated.—*n.* **pierc′er.**—*adj.* **pierc′ing** penetrating: very acute: keen.—*adv.* **pierc′ingly.**—*n.* **pierc′ingness.** [O.Fr. *percer.*]

Pierrot pē′ə-rō, pyer-ō, *n.* a white-faced buffoon with loose long-sleeved garb: (without *cap*; formerly) a member of a group of entertainers in similar dress at seaside resorts, etc.:—*fem.* **Pierrette′.** [Fr., dim of *Pierre,* Peter.]

pietà pyā-tä′, *n.* a representation of the Virgin with the dead Christ across her knees. [It.,—L. *pietās, -ātis,* pity.]

pietra-dura pyā′trə-dōō′rə, *n.* inlaid work with hard stones—jasper, agate, etc. [It , hard stone.]

piety pī′i-ti, *n.* the quality of being pious: dutifulness: devoutness: sense of duty towards parents, benefactors, etc.: dutiful conduct—*ns.* **pi′etism; pi′etist** one marked by strong devotional feeling: a name first applied to a sect of German religious reformers of deep devotional feeling (end of 17th century).—*adjs.* **pietist′ic, -al.** [O.Fr. *piete*—L. *pietās, -ātis.*]

piezo- pī′i-zō-, pī-ē′zō-, in composition, pressure.—*adj.* **piezo** short for **piezoelectric.**—*n.* **piezochem′istry** the chemistry of substances under high pressure.—*adj.* **piezoelec′tric.**—*n.* **piezoelectri′city** electricity developed in certain crystals by mechanical strain, and the effect of an electric field in producing expansion and contraction along different axes. [Gr. *piezein,* to press.]

piffle pif′l, *n.* nonsense: worthless talk.—*v.t.* to trifle: to act ineffectually.—*adj.* **piff′ling** trivial, petty.—*n.* **piff′ler.**

pig pig, *n.* any mammal of the family Suidae, omnivorous ungulates with thick, bristly skin, esp. the domesticated *Sus scrofa,* a farm animal bred as food for humans: a swine: a young swine: swine′s flesh as food, esp. that of the young animal: one who is like a pig, dirty, greedy, gluttonous, or cantankerous (also used mildly in reproach): an oblong mass of unforged metal, as first extracted from the ore: the mould into which it is run, esp. one of the branches, the main channel being the *sow:* a cleaning brush, scraper, etc., for pipes or ducts: a policeman (*slang*): a segment of an orange (*slang*): something very difficult (*slang*).—*v.i.* to bring forth pigs: to live, herd, huddle, sleep, or feed like pigs: to eat (*slang*):—*pr.p.* **pigg′ing;** *pa.t.* and *pa.p.* **pigged.**—*n.* **pigg′ery** a place where pigs are kept: piggishness.—*adj.* **pigg′ish** like a pig: greedy: dirty: cantankerous.—*adv.* **pigg′ishly.**—*ns.* **pigg′ishness; pigg′le, pigg′y, pigg′let, pigg′ling** a little pig.—*adj.* **pigg′y** like a pig.—**pig′-deer** the babiroussa.—*adjs.* **pig′-eyed** having small dull eyes with heavy lids; **pig′-faced.**—**pig′feed** food for pigs; **piggyback** see separate entry; **pigg′y-bank** a child′s money-box, shaped like a pig: sometimes a child′s money-box of any design.—*adj.* **pig′head′ed** having a pig-like head: stupidly obstinate.—*adv.* **pig′head′edly.**—*adj.* **pig′head′edness.**—*adj.* **pig′-ig′norant** (*coll., derog.*) very ignorant.—**pig′(gy)-in-the-midd′le** a children′s game in which a person standing between two others tries to intercept a ball, etc. passing back and forth between them: one caught between opposing viewpoints, strategies, etc. (*fig.*); **pig′-iron** iron in pigs or rough bars; **pig′meat** bacon, ham or pork; **pig′-nut** the earth-nut (*Conopodium*); **pig′pen** a pigsty; **pig′-rat** the bandicoot rat; **pig′skin** the skin of a pig prepared as a strong leather: a saddle (*slang*); **pig′-sticker; pig′-sticking** boar-hunting with spears; **pig′sty** a pen for keeping pigs; **pig′s whisper** a low whisper (*dial.*): a very short space of time; **pig swill, pig′swill** kitchen, etc. waste fed to pigs; **pig′tail** the tail of a pig: the hair of the head plaited behind in a queue or queues: a roll of twisted tobacco.—**a pig in a poke** see **poke¹**; **make a pig of oneself** (*coll.*) to overindulge in food or drink; **make a pig′s ear of (something)** (*coll.*) to make a mess of something, to do something badly or clumsily; **pig it** (*coll.*) to live in dirty surroundings; **when pigs fly** (*coll.*) never. [M.E. *pigge.*]

pigeon¹ pij′ən, *-in, n.* orig., a young dove: a dove: any bird of the dove family: extended to various other birds (e.g. the *Cape pigeon*): one who is fleeced (slang).—v.t. to gull.—n. **pig'eonry** a place for keeping pigeons.—adj. **pig'eon-breast'ed, -chested** having a narrow chest with breast-bone thrown forward.—**pig'eon-fancier** one who keeps and breeds pigeons for racing or exhibiting.—adj. **pig'eon-heart'ed** timid.—**pig'eon-hole, pig'eonhole** a niche for a pigeon's nest: a hole of similar appearance: a compartment for storing and classifying papers, etc.: a compartment of the mind or memory.—v.t. to furnish with or make into pigeon-holes: to put into a pigeon-hole: to classify methodically, or too rigidly: to lay aside and treat with neglect.—**pig'eon-house** a dovecot; **pig'eon-pea** dal; **pig'eon-post** transmission of letters by pigeons; **pig'eon's-blood** a dark red colour, ruby; **pigeon's milk** partly digested food regurgitated by pigeons to feed their young.—adj. **pig'eon-toed** intoed. [O.Fr. pijon—L. pīpiō, -ōnis—pīpīre, to cheep.]

pigeon². Same as **pidgin**.

piggin pig'in, n. a small pail or bowl of staves and hoops, one stave usually prolonged as a handle: a vessel of various other kinds. [Poss. from Scot. pig, an earthenware crock or other vessel.]

piggy. See **pig**.

piggyback pig'i-bak, adv., adj., and n. a variant of **pickaback**.—adj. of a method of heart transplant surgery in which the patient's own heart is not removed and continues to function in tandem with that of the donor.

pigmean. See **pygmy**.

pigment pig'mənt, n. paint: any substance used for colouring: that which gives colour to animal and vegetable tissues.—adjs. **pigmental** (-men'tl) **pig'mentary, pig'mented**.—n. **pigmentā'tion** coloration or discoloration by pigments in the tissues. [L. pigmentum—pingĕre, to paint.]

pigmy. Same as **pygmy**.

pi-jaw. See **pi⁵**.

pika pī'kə, n. the tailless hare (Ochotona), a small mammal of the order Rodentia or, in some classifications, Lagomorpha, found in mountain regions. [Tungus piika.]

pike¹ pīk, n. a sharp point: a weapon with a long shaft and a sharp head like a spear, formerly used by footsoldiers: a spiked staff: a sharp-pointed hill or summit: a voracious freshwater fish (Esox lucius) with pointed snout; extended to various other fishes. —v.t. to kill or pierce with a pike.—adj. **piked** (pīkt, pīk'id) spiked: ending in a point.—n. **pik'er** one who bets, gambles, speculates, or does anything else in a very small way.—**pike'man** a man armed with a pike: one who wields a pick; **pike'staff** the staff or shaft of a pike: a staff with a pike at the end.—**plain as a pikestaff** (orig. **packstaff**), perfectly plain or clear. [O.E. pīc, pick, spike; but also partly from Fr. pic with the same meaning, and pique the weapon, and prob. partly from Scand.]

pike² pīk, n. a turnpike: a toll: a main road (U.S.). [Short for **turnpike**.]

pilaff. See **pilau**.

pilaster pi-las'tər, n. a square column, partly built into, partly projecting from, a wall.—adj. **pilas'tered**. [Fr. pilastre—It. pilastro—L. pīla, a pillar.]

pilau pi-low', n. a highly spiced Eastern dish of rice with a fowl, meat, or the like, boiled together or separately.—Also **pilau', pilaw', pilaff'** (or pil'), **pilow'**. [Pers. pilāw, Turk. pilāw, pilāf.]

pilchard pil'chərd, n. a sea-fish like the herring, but smaller, thicker, and rounder, common off Cornwall.

pilcorn pil'körn, n. the naked oat, a variety in which the glume does not adhere to the grain. [For **pilled** (= peeled, husked) **corn**.]

pile⁵ pīl, n. a set of things fitted or resting one over

another, or in a more or less regular figure: a set of weights fitting one within another: a stack of arms: a set of wrought-iron bars placed together for welding and rolling into one: a series of alternate plates of two metals for generating an electric current: a great amount of money, a fortune (slang): a large supply (coll.): a tall building: an atomic pile.—v.t. to lay in a pile or heap: to collect in a mass: to heap up: to load with heaps: to accumulate.—v.i. to come into piles: to accumulate: to go in crowds: to get in or out (with in or out).—n. **pil'er**.—**pile'-up** a collision involving several motor vehicles, players in Rugby, etc.—**pile it on** (coll.) to overdo, exaggerate (something); **pile on, up, the agony** (coll.) to overdo painful effects by accumulation, etc.; **pile up** to run ashore: to form a disorderly mass or heap: to become involved in a pile-up (q.v.): to accumulate. [Fr.,—L. pīla, a pillar.]

pile² pil, n. a large stake or cylinder driven into the earth to support foundations.—v.t. to drive piles into: to support with or build on piles.—**pile'-driver** an engine for driving in piles: in games, a very heavy stroke, kick, etc.; **pile'-dwelling** a dwelling built on piles, esp. a lake-dwelling; **pile shoe** the iron or steel point fitted to the foot of a pile to give it strength to pierce the earth and so assist driving. [O.E. pīl—L. pīlum, a javelin.]

pile³ pil, n. a covering of hair, esp. soft, fine, or short hair: down: human body-hair: a single hair: a raised surface on cloth—now distinguished from nap as made not in finishing but in weaving, either by leaving loops (which may be cut) or by weaving two cloths face to face and cutting them apart.—adjs. **pilif'erous**, bearing hairs: ending in a hair-like point; **pil'iform**, hair-like. [L. pīlus, a hair.]

pile⁴ pil, n. (usu. in pl.) a haemorrhoid. [L. pīla, a ball.]

pileate. See **pileum**.

pileum pī'li-əm, n. the top of a bird's head:—pl. **pil'ea**. —n. **pil'eus** the expanded cap of a mushroom or toadstool, or other fungus:—pl. **pilei** (pī'li-ī).—adjs. **pi'leate, -d** cap-shaped: capped: crested. [L. pileum, pileus, for pilleum, pilleus, a felt cap; cf. Gr. pilos, felt, a felt cap.]

pilfer pil'fər, v.i. and v.t. to steal in small quantities.— ns. **pil'ferage, pil'fering, pil'fery** petty theft; **pil'ferer**.—adv. **pil'feringly**. [Prob. connected with **pelf**.]

pilgrim pil'grim, n. one who travels to a distance to visit a holy place: allegorically or spiritually, one journeying through life as a stranger in this world: a Pilgrim Father.—adj. of or pertaining to a pilgrim: like a pilgrim: consisting of pilgrims.—n. **pil'grimage** the journeying of a pilgrim: a journey to a shrine or other holy place or place venerated for its associations: the journey of life: a lifetime.—adj. visited by pilgrims.—v.i. to go on pilgrimage: to wander.—**Pilgrim Fathers** the Puritans who sailed for America in the Mayflower, and founded Plymouth, Massachusetts, in 1620. [Assumed O.Fr. pelegrin (Fr. pèlerin)—L. peregrīnus, foreigner, stranger; see **peregrine**.]

pili pē-lē', n. the nut (also **pili'-nut**) of trees of the genus Canarium. [Tagálog.]

piliferous, piliform. See **pile³**.

pill¹ pil, n. a little ball of medicine: a ball, e.g. a cannon-ball, tennis-ball, or (in pl.) billiards (facet.): anything disagreeable that must be accepted: a tiresome person: a doctor (slang; also in pl.).—**pill'-box** a box for holding pills: a small blockhouse (mil. slang): a small round brimless hat.—**the pill** any of various contraceptive pills (see **oral contraception**); **on the pill** taking contraceptive pills regularly. [L. pīla, perh. through O.Fr. pile, or from a syncopated form of the dim. pilūla.]

pill² *pil, v.t.* and *v.i.* to plunder (*arch.*).—*n.* **pill'age** the act of plundering: plunder.—*v.t.* and *v.i.* to plunder.—*n.* **pill'ager.** [O.E. *pylian* and O.Fr. *peler*, both—L. *pilāre*, to deprive of hair; cf. peel.]

pillar *pil'ər, n.* a detached support, not necessarily cylindrical or of classical proportions (*archit.*): a structure of like form erected as a monument, ornament, object of worship, etc.: a tall upright rock: a mass of coal or rock left in a mine to support the roof: anything in the form of a column: a supporting post: the post supporting a bicycle saddle: a cylinder holding the plates of a watch or clock in position: a pillar-box: one who, or anything that, sustains.— **pill'ar-box** a short hollow pillar for posting letters in (**pillar-box** red the bright red colour of most British pillar-boxes).—**from pillar to post** from one state of difficulty to another: hither and thither. [O.Fr. *piler* (Fr. *pilier*)—L.L. *pilāre*—L. *pila*, a pillar.]

pillau. See **pilau.**

pillion *pil'yən, n.* a pad or light saddle for a woman: a cushion behind a horseman for a second rider (usu. a woman) or for a bag: the passenger-seat of a motorcycle, or a baggage-carrier, usable as an extra seat.— *adv.* on a pillion.—*v.t.* to seat on or furnish with a pillion.—*ns.* **pill'ionist, pill'ion-rider** one who rides pillion; **pill'ion-seat.** [Prob. Ir. *pillin,* Gael. *pillin, pillean,* a pad, a pack-saddle—*peall,* a skin or mat, L. *pellis,* skin.]

pillory *pil'ə-ri, n.* a wooden frame, supported by an upright pillar or post, with holes through which the head and hands were put as a punishment, abolished in England in 1837.—*v.t.* to set in the pillory: to hold up to ridicule:—*pr.p.* **pill'orying;** *pa.t.* and *pa.p.* **pill'-oried.**—Also **pill'orise, -ize.** [O.Fr. *pilori.*]

pillow *pil'ō, n.* a cushion for a sleeper's head: any object used for the purpose: a cushion for lace-making: a support for part of a structure.—*v.t.* to lay or rest for support: to serve as pillow for: to furnish or prop with pillows.—*v.i.* (*arch.*) to rest the head.— *adjs.* **pill'owed** supported by, or provided with, a pillow; **pill'owy** like a pillow: round and swelling: soft. —**pill'ow-case, -slip** a cover for a pillow; **pillow-block** see **pedestal; pill'ow-cup** a last cup before going to bed; **pill'ow-fight, pill'ow-fighting** the sport of thumping one another with pillows; **pill'ow-lace** lace worked with bobbins on a pillow. [O.E. *pyle,* also *pylu*—L. *pulvīnus.*]

pilose *pi'lōs, adj.* hairy: having scattered soft or moderately stiff hairs.—*adj.* **pi'lous** hairy.—*n.* **pilosity** (*-los'i-ti*). [L. *pilōsus—pilus,* hair.]

pilot *pi'lət, n.* one who conducts ships in and out of a harbour, along a dangerous coast, etc.: one who actually operates the flying controls of an aircraft, etc.: one who is qualified to act as pilot: a guide: a pilot film or broadcast.—*adj.* pertaining to pilot(s): acting as guide or control: trial (of e.g. a model on a smaller scale) serving to test the qualities or future possibilities of a machine, plant, etc. or (of a film or broadcast) to test the popularity of a projected radio or television series.—*v.t.* to act as pilot to.—*n.* **pi'lotage** piloting: a pilot's fee.—*adj.* **pi'lotless** without a pilot: not requiring a pilot, as an automatic aeroplane.—**pi'lot-balloon** a small balloon sent up to find how the wind blows; **pi'lot-boat** a boat used by pilots on duty; **pilot burner, jet, light** (see also below) a small gas-burner kept alight to light another; **pi'lot-fish** a fish that accompanies ships and sharks; **pi'lot-flag, -jack** the flag hoisted at the fore by a vessel needing a pilot; **pi'lot-house** a shelter for steering-gear and pilot—also *wheel-house;* **pi'lot-jacket** a pea-jacket; **pilot lamp, light** a small electric light to show when current is on, or for other purpose; **pilot officer**

in the Air Force, an officer ranking with an army second-lieutenant; **pi'lot-plant** prototype machinery set up to begin a new process; **pilot scheme** a scheme serving as a guide on a small scale to a full-scale scheme. [Fr. *pilote*—It. *pilota,* app. for earlier *pedota,* which may be—Gr. *pēdon,* oar, in pl. rudder.]

pilous. See **pilose.**

pilow. See **pilau.**

pils(e)ner *pulz', pils'nər,* (also with *cap.*) *n.* a light beer. [Ger., from *Pilsen,* a city in Czechoslovakia.]

pilule *pil'ūl, n.* a little pill.—Also **pil'ula.**—*adj.* **pil'-ular.** [L. *pilŭla,* dim. of *pila,* ball.]

pimento *pi-ment'ō, n.* formerly Cayenne pepper: now allspice or Jamaica pepper, the dried unripe fruits of a W. Indian tree (*Pimenta officinalis*) of the myrtle family: the tree itself: its wood:—*pl.* **pimen'tos.**—*n.* **pimiento** (*pi-mē-en'tō*) the sweet, red, or green, pepper, capsicum:—*pl.* **pimien'tos.** [O.Fr. *piment,* Sp. *pimiento*—L. *pigmentum,* paint.]

pimp *pimp, n.* one who procures gratifications for the lust of others, a pander: a man who lives with and sometimes solicits for, a prostitute and lives off her earnings, or one who solicits for a prostitute or brothel and is paid for his services.—*v.i.* to pander.

pimpernel *pim'pər-nel, n.* a plant of the primrose family, with scarlet (or blue, etc.) flowers; **water pimpernel** brookweed; **yellow pimpernel** the wood loosestrife (*Lysimachia nemorum*). [O.Fr. *pimpernelle,* mod. Fr. *pimprenelle,* and It. *pimpinella,* burnet.]

pimple *pim'pl, n.* a pustule: a small swelling, protuberance, or hill.—*adjs.* **pim'pled, pim'ply** having pimples.

pin *pin, n.* a piece of wood or of metal used for fastening things together: a peg or nail: a sharp-pointed piece of wire with a rounded head for fastening clothes, etc.: an ornamental elaboration of this: a cylindrical part inserted into something, as the stem of a key, or part of a lock that a hollow-stemmed key fits: the projecting part of a dovetail joint: a peg aimed at in quoits: a peg in the centre of an archery target: the rod of a golf flag: a skittle or ninepin: a tuning peg in a stringed instrument: a leg (*coll.*): short for clothes-pin, rolling-pin, etc.: an act of pinning or state of being pinned: anything of little value —*v.t.* to fasten with a pin: to fix, to fasten, to enclose, to hold down (*fig.*): to make a small hole in:—*pr.p.* **pinn'ing;** *pa.t.* and *pa.p.* **pinned.**—**pin'ball** a form of bagatelle: a scoring game, played on a slot-machine, in which a ball runs down a sloping board set with pins or other targets; **pin curl** a lock of hair made to curl by winding it around one's finger, etc., and securing it with a hairpin; **pin'-cushion** a cushion for holding pins; **pin'-feather** a young, unexpanded feather; **pin'-head,** the head of a pin: a stupid person (*slang*); **pin'-hole** a hole for or made by a pin, or such as a pin might make; **pinhole camera; pinhole photography** the taking of photographs by the use of a pinhole instead of a lens; **pin'-man** a seller of pins: a match-stick drawing, in which the limbs and body are represented by single lines; **pin'-money** money allotted to a wife for private expenses, ostensibly to buy pins; **pin'-point** the point of a pin: anything very sharp or minute.—*v.t.* to place, define, very exactly.—**pin'-prick** the prick of a pin: (an act of) petty irritation; **pin'-stripe** a very narrow stripe in cloth: cloth with such stripes.—*adj.* **pin'-striped.**—**pin'table** a pinball machine; **pin'tail** a duck, with a pointed tail: a sand-grouse.—*adj.* **pin'tailed** having a long, narrow tail.— **pin'-tuck** a very narrow ornamental tuck.—*adj.* **pin'-up** such as might have her portrait pinned up on a wall for admiration.—*n.* a girl of such a kind: a portrait so pinned up.—**pin'-wheel** a wheel with pins at right angles to its plane, to lift the hammer of a striking clock: a paper toy windmill: a revolving firework.—**on pins and needles** in agitated expectancy; **pin it on (to) (someone)** to prove, or seem to prove, that he did it; **pin one's faith on** to put entire trust in; **pin one's hopes on** to place one's entire hopes on; **pins and needles** a tingling feeling in arm, hand, leg, foot, due to impeded circulation (see also above); **pin someone down** to get someone to commit himself (to), to make someone express a definite opinion. [O.E. *pinn*, prob —L *pinna*, a feather, a pinnacle.]

pinafore pin'ə-fōr, -for, n. a loose covering over a dress, esp. a child's.—*adj.* **pin'afored.**—**pinafore dress, skirt** a skirt hung from the shoulders, combined with a sleeveless bodice [**pin, afore.**]

pinaster pī- or pī-nas'tər, n. the cluster-pine [L *pināster—pīnus*, pine.]

pinball. See **pin.**

pince-nez pēs'-nā, n a pair of eye-glasses with a spring for catching the nose:—*pl.* **pince'-nez** (-*nāz*, -*nā*) — *adj* **pince'-nezed** (-*nād*). [Fr., pinch nose.]

pincer pin'sər, n. a grasping claw or forceps-like organ: (in *pl.*) a gripping tool with jaws and handles on a pivot, used for drawing out nails, squeezing, etc.: (in *pl.*) a twofold advance that threatens to isolate part of an enemy's force (*fig.*) —*v.t.* to pinch with pincers.—**pin'cer-movement.** [(O.)Fr. *pincer*, to pinch.]

pinch pinch, pinsh, v t. to compress a small part of between fingers and thumb or between any two surfaces, to nip: to squeeze: to crush: to nip off: to bring or render by squeezing or nipping. to affect painfully or injuriously, as cold or hunger: to cause to show the effects of such pain or injury: to harass: to hamper: to restrict: to stint: to purloin (*slang*): to arrest (*slang*)· to over-urge (*horse-racing*): to pluck, play pizzicato (*U.S.*).—*v.i.* to nip or squeeze: to be painfully tight: to encroach: to carp: to live sparingly: to narrow, taper off (*mining*) —*n.* an act or experience of pinching: a critical time of difficulty or hardship: an emergency: a place of narrowing, folding, difficulty, or steepness: a quantity taken up between the finger and thumb.—*adj.* **pinched** having the appearance of being tightly squeezed: hard pressed by want or cold: (of the face, or general appearance) haggard with cold, tiredness, hunger, etc.: narrowed: straightened.—*n.*—*n.* and *adj.* **pinch'ing.**—*adv* **pinch'ingly.**—**pinch'cock** a clamp that stops the flow of liquid by pinching a tube —*v.i.* **pinch'-hit** (*baseball*) to bat in place of another in an emergency: also *fig.*—**pinch'-hitter.**—**at a pinch** in a case of necessity; **feel the pinch** (*coll.*) to be in financial difficulties, to find life, work, etc difficult because of lack of money; **know where the shoe pinches** to know by direct experience what the trouble or difficulty is. [O.Fr. *pincier*; prob. Gmc.]

pinchbeck pinch', pinsh'bek, n. a yellow alloy of copper with much less zinc than ordinary brass, simulating gold, invented by Christopher *Pinchbeck* (*c* 1670-1732), watchmaker.—*adj.* sham: in bad taste

pin-cushion. See **pin.**

Pindaric pin-dar'ik, adj. after the manner or supposed manner of the Greek lyric poet *Pindar.*—*n.* a Pindaric ode. [Gr. *pindarikos—Pindaros.*]

pine[1] pīn, n. any tree of the north temperate coniferous genus Pinus, with pairs or bundles of needle-leaves on short shoots and scale-leaves only on long shoots extended to various more or less nearly allied trees and to some plants only superficially like: the timber of the pine: a pineapple plant or its fruit.—*adj.* of pines or pine-wood.—*ns.*—*adj.* **pi'ny** (wrongly **pī'ney**) of, like, or abounding in pine-trees.—**pine'-**

apple a large South American multiple fruit shaped like a pine-cone: the plant (Ananas) bearing it: a finial shaped like a pine-cone or a pineapple. a bomb (*slang*)· a hand-grenade (*slang*); **pine'-beau'ty, -car'pet** kinds of moths whose larvae feed on pine-trees; **pine'-beet'le** any beetle that attacks pine-trees, esp. the **pine'-chā'fer; pine'-cone** the cone or strobilus of a pine-tree; **pine'-finch** an American finch like the goldfinch. a large grosbeak of pine-forests; **pine'-ker'nel** the edible seed of a pine-tree of various species; **pine'-mar'ten** a British species of marten, *Mustela martes*, now rare, dark brown, with yellowish throat, and partly arboreal in habit; **pine'-need'le** the acicular leaf of the pine-tree; **pine tar** a dark, oily substance obtained from pine-wood, used in paints, etc., and medicines; **pine'-tree; pine'-wood** a wood of pine-trees· pine timber. [O E. *pin*—L *pīnus*]

pine[2] pīn, v.i. to waste away, esp. under pain or mental distress· to languish with longing: to long: to repine. [O.E *pīnian*, to torment—L *poena*, punishment.]

pineal pin'i-əl or pīn', adj. shaped like a pine-cone: connected with the pineal body.—**pineal body** or **gland** a small body at the end of an upgrowth from the optic thalami of the brain; **pineal eye** a vestigial third eye in front of the pineal body, best developed in the tuatara [L. *pinea*, a pine-cone—*pīnus*, pine.]

pineapple, piney. See **pine**[1].

ping ping, n. a sharp ringing or whistling sound as of a bullet —*v.i.* to make such a sound —*v.t.* to cause to make such a sound —*n.* **ping'er** an acoustic transmitter for the study of ocean currents: (®; with *cap*) a domestic clockwork device set to give a warning signal at a chosen time: any of various devices sending out an acoustic signal for directional, timing, etc. purposes.—**Ping'-Pong'®** a trademark for table tennis.—*adj.* (without *cap*) moving backwards and forwards, to and fro (*fig.*). [Imit.]

pinguid ping'gwid, adj fat [L. *pinguis*, fat]

pinguin ping'gwin, n. a West Indian plant, *Bromelia pinguin*· its fruit [Perh. L. *pinguis*, fat; confused with **penguin.**]

pinhead, pinhole. See **pin.**

pinion[1] pin'yən, n. a wing: the last joint of a wing: a flight feather, esp. the outermost.—*v.t.* to cut a pinion of. to confine the wings of: to confine by holding or binding the arms [O Fr *pignon*—L *pinna* (*penna*), wing.]

pinion[2] pin'yən, n. a small wheel with teeth or 'leaves'. [Fr. *pignon*, pinion, in O.Fr. battlement—L. *pinna*, pinnacle]

pink[1] pingk, v.t. to decorate by cutting small holes or scallops· to make a serrated edge on —*n.* a stab: an eyelet.—*adj.* **pinked** pierced or worked with small holes.—**pink'ing-shears** scissors with serrated cutting edges. [Cf L.G. *pinken*, to peck]

pink[2] pingk, n. any plant or flower of the genus Dianthus, including carnation and sweet-william: extended to some other plants: the colour of a wild pink, a light red· a scarlet hunting-coat or its colour: the person wearing it: one who is something of a socialist but hardly a red (also **pink'o**, pl **pink'o(e)s**). the fine flower of excellence· the most perfect condition. the highest point, the extreme —*adj.* of the colour pink: slightly socialistic —*v.t* and *v.i* to make or become pink.—*ns.* **pink'iness; pink'ing** the reddening of gem-stones by heat.—*adj.* **pink'ish** somewhat pink.—*ns.* **pink'ishness; pink ness.**—*adj.* **pink'y** inclining to pink.—**pink'-eye** acute contagious conjunctivitis: an acute contagious infection in horses due to a filterable virus, the eye sometimes becoming somewhat red: a red discoloration in salt fish, etc.—**pink elephants** see **elephant; pink gin** gin with angostura bitters; **pink'root** Indian pink, Carolina pink, or other species of Spigelia. its root, a vermifuge.—**in the pink** in perfect health or condition, **pink of perfection** the acme of perfection.

pink² *pingk*, *n*. a tinkling sound. a chaffinch's note· a chaffinch —*v.ı.* (of an engine) to detonate or knock [Imit]

Pinkerton *ping'kər-tən*, *n*. a private detective.—Also without *cap*. [Allan *Pinkerton*, 1819–84, American detective.]

pinko, pinky. See **pink²**.

pinna *pin'ə*, *n*. a leaflet of a pinnate leaf, or similar expansion: a wing, fin, feather, or similar expansion the outer ear, esp. the upper part.—*pl* **pinn'ae** (-*ē*) —*adjs*. **pinn'ate, -d** shaped like a feather: having a row of leaflets on each side of the rachis, or other expansions arranged in like manner: (usu **pennate**) having wings, fins, or wing-like tufts.—*adv*. **pinn'-ately.**—*adjs*. **pinnatifid** (*pin-at'ı-fid*) pinnately cut nearly or about half-way down; **pinnat'iped** of birds, with lobate feet.—*adjs*. **pinn'ūlate, -d.**—*n*. **pinn'ūle** a lobe of a leaflet of a pinnate leaf· a branchlet of a crinoid arm.—Also **pinn'ūla**. [L. *pinna*, a feather, dim. *pinnula*.]

pinnace *pin'is*, -*əs*, *n*. a small vessel with oars and sails a boat with eight oars: a man-of-war's tender boat. (*vaguely*) a small boat. [Fr. *pinasse*]

pinnacle *pin'ə-kl*, *n* a slender turret or spiry structure in architecture. a high pointed rock or mountain like a spire: the highest point.—*v.t.* to be the pinnacle of: to set on a pinnacle: to raise as a pinnacle: to furnish with pinnacles.—*adj* **pinn'acled.** [Fr. *pinacle*— L.L. *pinnāculum*, dim. from L *pinna*, a feather]

pinnate, etc. See **pinna**.

pinnie *pin'i*, *n*. short for **pinafore**.

pinnatiped, pinnule etc See **pinna**.

pinny *pin'ı*, *n*. short for **pinafore**.

pinochle, pinocle, penuchle *pin'*, *pēn'ək-l*, *n*. a game like bezique: a declaration of queen of spades and knave of diamonds.

pinole *pē-nō'lā*, *n*. parched Indian corn or other seeds ground and eaten with milk: a mixture of vanilla and aromatic substances in chocolate. [Sp.,—Aztec *pinolli*.]

piñon *pin'yon*, *pēn'yōn*, (*U S.*) *n* an edible pine seed· the tree bearing it [Sp.]

pinpoint. See **pin**.

pinscher. See **Doberman pinscher**.

pint *pīnt*, *n*. a measure of capacity = half a quart or 4 gills—in imperial measure (liquid or dry), about 568 cubic centimetres, 0 568 litre, 20 fluid ounces—in U.S. measure (liquid) 473 cc, 16 U.S fluid ounces, (dry) 551 cc: a pint of beer (*coll.*).—*n*. **pint'a** (*coll* ; **pint of**) a drink, esp. a pint, of milk.—**pint'-pot** a pot for holding a pint, esp. a pewter pot for beer, a seller or drinker of beer.—*adj*. **pint'-size(d)** (*coll.*) very small. [Fr. *pinte*.]

pinta¹. See **pint**.

pinta² *pin'tə*, *n*. a contagious skin disease occurring in the tropics, characterised by loss of skin pigmentation —also called **mal del pinto** (*mal del pin'to*; Sp., disease of the spotted person). [Sp.,—L.L. *pinctus* —L. *pictus*, painted.]

pintable. See **pin**.

pintado *pin-ta'dō*, *n*. a kind of petrel, the Cape pigeon the guinea-fowl:—*pl*. **pinta'dos**. [Port , painted]

pintail. See **pin**.

pintle *pin'tl*, *n*. a bolt or pin, esp. one on which something turns: the plunger or needle of the injection valve of an oil engine, opened by oil pressure on an annular face, and closed by a spring. [O.E. *pintel*.]

pinto *pin'tō*, (*U.S.*) *adj*. mottled: piebald.—*n*. a piebald horse:—*pl*. **pin'tos**.—**pinto bean** a kind of bean resembling a kidney bean, mottled in colour

[Sp , painted]

pinxit *pingk'sit*, (L.) painted (this)

piny. See **pine¹**.

Pinyin *pin'yin'*, *n* an alphabetic system (using Roman letters) for the transcription of Chinese, esp Mandarin. [Chin ,phonetic, alphabetic (transcription)]

piolet *pyo-lā'*, *pyô-lā'*, *n*. an ice-axe, spiked staff for climbing or (*obs*) skiing [Fr ,—Piedmontese dialect *piola*.]

pion. See **pi¹**.

pioneer *pī-ə-nēr'*, *n*. a military artisan, employed in peace-time in painting and repairing barracks, and such work, in war in preparing the way for an army, and minor engineering works, as trenching. an excavator: a labourer one who is among the first in new fields of enterprise, exploration, colonisation, research, etc.—*v t*. to act as pioneer to: to prepare as a pioneer [O Fr *peonier* (Fr *pionnier*)—*pion*, a foot-soldier—L L *pedō*, *pedōnis*—L. *pēs*, *pedis*, a foot.]

pious *pī'əs*, *adj* dutiful showing, having, or proceeding from piety professing to be religious.—*adv* **pi'ously.**—**pious fraud** a deception practised with a good end in view a religious humbug (*coll.*) [L *pius*.]

pip¹ *pip*, *n*. roup in poultry, etc . spleen, hump, disgust, offence (*coll.*) —*v.t* to affect with the pip.— **give someone the pip** (*coll*) to annoy or offend someone [App —M Du *pippe*—L L *pipita*—L *pituita*, rheum]

pip² *pip*, *n* a small hard body (seed or fruitlet) in a fleshy fruit —*adjs*. **pip'less; pipp'y**. [App from **pippin**.]

pip³ *pip*, *pēp*, *n* a spot on dice, cards, dominoes: a star as a mark of rank (*coll.*): a speck. on radar screen, indication, e.g spot of light, of presence of object: a single blossom or corolla in a cluster

pip⁴ *pip*, *n*. a signal sounding like the word 'pip'

pip⁵ *pip*, (slang) *v t*. to blackball: to pluck, plough, reject, or fail in an examination: to foil, thwart, get the better of to win with a bullet or the like: to wound to kill.—*pr p*. **pipp'ing;** *pa.t*. and *pa p* **pipped.—pipped at the post** defeated at the point when success seemed certain [Perh. from **pip²**.]

pip⁶ *pip*, *v.ı.* to chirp, as a young bird [Cf. **peep¹**.]

Pipa *pē'pə*, *n*. a genus of S American toads which carry their young on their back: (without *cap*) a toad of this genus, the Surinam toad. [Surinam dialect]

pipage. See **pipe¹**.

pipal, pipul, peepul *pē'pul*, -*pəl*, *n* the bo tree [Hind. *pīpul*]

pipe¹ *pip*, *n*. a musical wind instrument, or part of an instrument, consisting of or including a tube: any tube, or tubular part or thing, natural or artificial· a pipe-like volcanic vent, mass of ore, etc : an entrance to a decoy: a tube with a bowl at one end for smoking. a fill of tobacco: the smoking of a fill of tobacco: the note of a bird: a voice, esp a high voice: (usu. in *pl.*) the windpipe: a boatswain's whistle: (often in *pl.*) a bagpipe.—*v.ı* to play upon a pipe: to whistle, as the wind, or a boatswain: to speak or sing, esp. in a high voice· to peep or sing, as a bird. to weep: to become pipy.—*v.t* to play on a pipe. to lead, call, by means of a pipe (with *in*) to accompany in with pipe music· to render, or cause to be, by playing a pipe: to propagate by piping (*hort.*): to ornament with piping· to supply with pipes: to convey by pipe to transmit (television, radio signals) by electricity along a wire.—*n*. **pip'age** conveyance or distribution by pipe.—*adj*. **piped** (*pipt*) tubular or fistulous: transported by means of a pipe —*n* **pipe'ful** enough to fill a pipe.—*adjs* **pipe'less; pipe'like**.—*n* **pip'er** a player on a pipe, esp a bagpipe.—*adj*. **pip'ing** playing a pipe: sounding like a pipe· whistling· thin and high-pitched: hissing hot· very hot.—*n.* the action of the verb pipe in any sense. pipe-playing· a system of pipes: tubing small cord used as trimming for clothes: strings and twists of sugar ornamenting a cake: a slip or cutting from a joint of a stem: hydraulicking.—*adj* **pip′y,** pipe-like: having pipes: piping.—**pipe′clay** a fine white, nearly pure, kaolin, free from iron, used for making tobacco-pipes and fine earthenware, and for whitening belts, etc.—*v t.* to whiten with pipeclay —**pipe cleaner** a length of wire with tufts of fabric twisted into it, used to clean pipe-stems, **piped music** continuous background music played in a restaurant, or piped from a central studio to other buildings, **pipe′-dream** a futile and unreal hope or fancy such as one has when relaxing while smoking a pipe (orig. an opium-smoker's fantasy); **pipe′-dreamer; pipe′fish** a fish (of several species) of the sea-horse family, a long thin fish covered with hard plates, the jaws forming a long tube, **pipeless organ** a musical instrument, played like an organ, in which sounds, built up from whatever harmonics may be chosen, are produced by a loud-speaker, **pipe′-line, pipe′line** a long continuous line of piping to carry water from a reservoir, oil from an oil-field, etc a line of piping to carry solid materials: a line of communication, or supply, or of progress and development (*fig.*): see also **in the pipeline** below; **pipe major** the chief of a band of bagpipers, **pipe′-organ** a musical organ with pipes; **pipe′-rack** a rack for tobacco-pipes; **pipe′-stem** the tube of a tobacco-pipe; **pipe′stone** a red argillaceous stone used by North American Indians for making tobacco-pipes; **pipe′work** a vein of ore in the form of a pipe· piping or pipes collectively, as in an organ; **pipe′s wrench** a wrench that grips a pipe when turned one way; **piping crow** an Australian bird (*Gymnorhina*) called a magpie, really akin to the shrikes.—**boatswain's pipe see whistle; in the pipeline** waiting to be considered or dealt with: in preparation; **pay the piper** to bear the expense (and so call the tune, have control): to have to pay heavily; **pipe down** to dismiss from muster, as a ship's company (the final order of the day): to subside into silence; **pipe of peace** see **calumet; pipe up** (*coll.*) to interject: to begin to speak; **piping hot** hissing hot, usu. hyperbolically; **put that in your pipe and smoke it!** (*coll.*) there! how do you like that? (of something unpleasant) [O.E *pípe*—L. *pipare,* to cheep]

pipe² *pīp, n.* a cask or butt (of wine), of two hogsheads, varying according to the wine, ordinarily about 105 gallons in Britain, 126 U.S. gallons: this measure. [O.Fr. *pipe,* cask, tube; cf. preceding.]

Piper *pip′ər, n.* the pepper genus.—*ns.* **piper′azine** a crystalline nitrogen compound used in medicine, insecticides and anti-corrosion substances; **piper′idine** a liquid base ($C_5H_{11}N$) got from piperine; **pip′erine** an alkaloid ($C_{17}H_{19}O_3N$) found in pepper; **pī′peronal** a phenolic aldehyde of very pleasant odour, used as a perfume and in flavourings, etc.—also called **heliotropin.** [L. *piper,* pepper.]

pipette *pip-et′, n.* a tube for transferring and measuring fluids.—*v.t.* to transfer or measure, using a pipette. [Fr., dim. of *pipe,* pipe.]

piping. See under **pipe¹.**

pipistrelle *pip-is-trel′, n.* a small reddish-brown bat, the commonest British bat [Fr.,—It. *pipistrello,* a form of *vespertilio*—L. *vespertiliō,* bat—*vesper,* evening.]

pipit *pip′it, n.* any member of a lark-like genus (*Anthus*) of birds akin to wagtails [Prob. imit]

pipkin *pip′kin, n* a small pot, now only of earthenware: a piggin (*U.S.*). [Poss. a dim. of **pipe.**]

pippin *pip′in, n.* an apple of various varieties. [O Fr *pepin.*]

pippy. See **pip².**

pipsqueak *pip′skwēk,* (*slang*) *n* something or someone insignificant, contemptible

pipul. Same as **pipal.**

pipy. See under **pipe¹.**

piquant *pē′kənt, adj* stinging· pleasantly pungent· appetising kindling keen interest —*n* **piq′uancy.**—*adv* **piq′uantly.** [Fr , pr.p. of *piquer,* to prick.]

pique¹ *pēk, n.* animosity or ill-feeling: offence taken a feeling of anger or vexation caused by wounded pride resentment of a slight dudgeon —*v t* to wound the pride of· to nettle: to arouse, stir, provoke: (*refl*) to pride oneself (on, upon) [Fr *pique,* a pike, pique, *piquer,* to prick]

pique² *pēk, n.* in piquet, the scoring of 30 points in one hand before the other side scores at all.—*v t* to score a pique against —*v.t.* to score a pique. [Fr *pic,* see **piquet.**]

piqué *pē′kā, n* a stiff corded cotton fabric: inlaid work of gold or silver in point or strip (sometimes with mother-of-pearl) on tortoise-shell or ivory.—*v t* to stitch.—Also *adj* —**piqué work** inlaying in piqué· needlework with raised design made by stitching [Fr., pa p. of *piquer,* to prick]

piquet *pi-ket′, n* a game for two with 32 cards, with scoring for declarations and tricks [Fr.]

piracy. See **pirate.**

piranha, piraña *pē-ran′ya,* **piraya** *pē-ra′ya,* **perai** *pe-rī′,* **pirai** *pē, ns.* a ferocious South American river-fish (*Serrasalmo* or *Pygocentrus*) of the Characinidae. [Port. from Tupi *piranya, piraya*]

pirate *pī′rət, -rit, n* one who, without authority, attempts to capture ships at sea: a sea-robber: a pirates' ship: one who publishes without authority of the owner of the copyright: a private bus, or its driver, plying on the recognised route of others: one who, in ordinary life, shows the predatory spirit of the sea rovers: a person who runs an unlicensed radio station. —*adj* operating illegally.—*v t* to rob as a pirate to publish without permission. to copy recordings without copyright consent.—*n.* **piracy** (*pī′rə-si, pī′*) the crime of a pirate: robbery on the high seas: unauthorised publication: infringement of copyright.—*adjs* **piratic** (*pī-rat′ik*), **-al** pertaining to a pirate: practising piracy.—*adv.* **pirat′ically.** [L *pīrāta*—Gr *peiratēs*—*peiraein,* to attempt.]

piraya. See **piranha.**

pirl. See **purl¹.**

pirouette *pir-ōō-et′, n.* a spinning about on tiptoe.—*v.i.* to spin round on tiptoe.—*n.* **pirouett′er.** [Fr]

Pisces *pis′ēz, pis′ēz, pis′kēz, pisk′ās, n.pl.* the class of fishes (*zool.*): the Fishes, the twelfth sign of the zodiac, or the constellation that formerly coincided with it (*astron.*) —*n.* **piscary** (*pisk′ə-ri*) the right of fishing. a fishing pond.—*adjs.* **piscatorial** (*pis-kə-tō′ri-əl, -ʼo′*), **piscatory** (*pis′kə-tə-ri*) relating to fishing: fishing.—*ns* **pis′ciculture** the rearing of fish by artificial methods; **pis′ciculturist; piscifau′na** the assemblage of fishes in a region, formation, etc.— *adjs.* **pis′ciform** having the form of a fish; **piscine** (*pis′īn*) of fishes: of the nature of a fish. [L. *piscis,* a fish; pl *piscēs; piscātor,* fisher.]

piscina *pis-ē′nə, pis-ī′nə, n.* a fish-pond: a swimming-pool (as in Roman baths): a basin and drain in old churches, usu in a niche south of an altar, into which was emptied water used in washing the sacred vessels. —*pl.* **pisci′nas,** or **-ae.**—Also **piscine** (*pis′ēn,* or *-ēn′*) [L. *piscina—piscis,* fish.]

piscine¹, piscivorous. See **Pisces.**

piscine². See **piscina.**

pisé *pē′zā, n.* rammed earth or clay for walls or floors —Also *adj.* [Fr.]

pish *pish, interj.*, of impatience or contempt.—*n.* an utterance of the exclamation.—*v.t.* to pooh-pooh. [Imit.]

pisiform *pi'si-förm, piz'i-förm, adj.* pea-shaped.—*n.* a pea-shaped bone of the carpus. [L. *pisum*, pea, *förma*, shape.]

pisky. See **pixie.**

piss *pis, (coll.) v.i.* to discharge urine.—*v.t.* to discharge as urine: to urinate on.—*n.* urine.—*adj.* **pissed** *(slang)* extremely drunk.—*n.* **pissoir** *(pē-swär; Fr.)* a public urinal.—**piss off** *(interj.; vulg.)* go away. [Fr *pisser.*]

pissasphalt *pis'as-falt, n.* a semi-liquid bitumen [Gr. *pissa*, pitch, *asphaltos*, asphalt.]

pissoir. See **piss.**

pistachio *pis-ta'chi-ō, -shi-ō, -chyō*, or *pis-tà'*, or *pis-tä'*, *n.* the almond-flavoured fruit-kernel of a small western Asiatic tree *(Pistacia vera)* of the same genus of the cashew family as the mastic tree:—*pl.* **pista'chios.** [Sp. *pistacho* and It. *pistacchio*—L.L. *pistāquium*—Gr. *pistākion*—Pers. *pistah.*]

piste *pēst, n.* a beaten track, esp. a ski trail in the snow [Fr.]

pistil *pis'til, (bot.) n.* the ovary of a flower, with its style and stigma.—*adjs.* **pis'tillary; pis'tillate** having a pistil but no (functional) stamens, female. [L *pistillum*, a pestle.]

pistol *pis'tl, n.* a small hand-gun, held in one hand when fired.—*v.t.* to shoot with a pistol:—*pr.p.* **pis'tolling;** *pa.t.* and *pa.p.* **pis'tolled.**—**pistol grip** a handle (usu. with a trigger mechanism) for a camera, etc., shaped like the butt of a pistol; **pis'tol-shot.**—*v.t.* **pis'tol-whip** to hit (someone) with a pistol.—**hold a pistol to someone's head** *(fig.)* to force someone to act according to one's wishes. [Through Fr. and Ger. from Czech.]

pistole *pis-tōl', n.* an old Spanish gold coin. [O.Fr *pistole*, earlier *pistolet.*]

piston *pis'tən, n.* a cylindrical piece moving to and fro in a hollow cylinder, as in engines and pumps: a valve mechanism for altering the effective length of tube in brass and musical instruments: a push-key for combining a number of organ stops.—**piston ring** a split ring fitted in a circumferential groove around a piston rim forming a spring-loaded seal against the cylinder wall; **pis'ton-rod** the rod to which the piston is fixed, and which moves up and down with it. [Fr.,—It. *pistone*—*pestare*, to pound—L. *pinsēre*, *pistum.*]

pit[1] *pit, n.* a hole in the earth: a mine shaft: a mine, esp. a coal-mine: a place whence minerals are dug: a prison, esp. a castle prison entered from above *(arch.)*: a cavity in the ground or in a floor for any purpose, as reception of ashes, inspection of motor-cars, a bottom-sawyer: a place beside the course where cars in a race can be refuelled and repaired: a hole for storing root-crops: a covered heap of potatoes, etc.: a grave, esp. one for many bodies: hell, or its lowest depths: a hole used as a trap for wild beasts: an enclosure in which animals are kept (esp. bears): an enclosure for cockfights or the like: the ground floor of a theatre, or its occupants, or the part of the ground floor behind the stalls: the area in front of the stage reserved for the orchestra in a theatre (also **orchestra pit**): a bed *(slang)*: any hollow or depression, as the *pit of the stomach* below the breastbone: an indentation left by smallpox: a minute depression in a surface: a hollow made by a raindrop:—*v t* to mark with little hollows: to lay in a pit: to set to fight, as cocks in a cockpit: to match *(with against)*.—*v.i.* to become marked with pits: to retain an impression for a time after pressing *(med.)*:—*pr.p.* **pitt'ing;** *pa t* and *pa.p.* **pitt'ed.**—*adj.* **pitt'ed** marked with small

pits.—**pit'-brow** the top of a shaft; **pit'fall** a lightly covered hole as a trap: a hidden danger *(fig.)*; **pit'-head** the ground at the mouth of a pit, and the machinery, etc., on it; **pit'man** a man who works in a coal-pit or a saw-pit, esp. at sinking, repair, and inspection of shafts and at pumping in a mine; **pit'-pony** a pony employed for haulage in a coal-mine; **pit'-prop** a, usu. timber, support in the workings of a coalmine; **pit'-stop** a stop a racing-car makes during a motor race when it goes into the pits for repairs; **pit'-vi'per** any member of an American group of snakes, including the rattlesnake, with a pit between eye and nose.—**the pits** *(slang)* the absolute worst place, thing, etc possible. [O.E. *pytt*—L. *puteus*, a well.]

pit[2] *pit, n.* a fruit-stone.—*v.t.* to remove the stone from [App. Du. *pit.*]

pita[1] *pē'tə, n.* the fibre of various species of Bromelia, Agave, etc.—Also **pi'ta-flax', -hemp'.** [Sp.,—Quechua *pita*, fine thread.]

pita[2]. See **pitta.**

pitapat *pit'ə-pat,* **pitty-pat,** *pit'i-pat,* **pit-pat** *pit'pat', advs.* with palpitation or pattering.—*adjs.* fluttering: pattering.—*ns.* a light, quick step: a succession of light taps: a patter.—*vs.i.* to step or tread quickly: to patter: to palpitate. [Imit.]

pitch[1] *pich, n.* the black shining residue of distillation of tar, etc.: extended to various bituminous and resinous substances, as Burgundy pitch.—*v.t.* to smear, cover, or caulk with pitch.—*n.* **pitch'iness.**—*adj.* **pitch'y** like or characteristic of pitch: smeared with pitch: abounding in pitch: black —*adj.* **pitch'-black** black as pitch.—**pitch'blende** a black mineral of resinous lustre, fundamentally composed of uranium oxides, a source of uranium and radium.—*adj.* **pitch's dark'** utterly dark.—**pitch'pine** a name for several American pines that yield pitch and timber *(Pinus palustris, P. rigida*, etc.). [O.E. *pic*—L. *pix, picis.*]

pitch[2] *pich, v.t.* to thrust or fix in the ground: to set up: to establish: to set or plant firmly: to set in position to lay out for sale: to set, cover, stud, or face: to pave with stones set on end or on edge: to make a foundation of stones for: to pit in opposition: to set in a key, to give this or that musical pitch, emotional tone, or degree of moral exaltation, etc., to: to fling, throw, or toss, esp in such a manner as to fall flat or in a definite position: to loft so as not to roll much on falling *(golf)*: to deliver to the batsman by an overhand or underhand throw *(baseball)*.—*v.i.* to settle: to alight: to fix the choice (on): to encamp: to plunge forward: to oscillate about a transverse axis: to slope down: to descend or fall away abruptly: to interlock —*n* the act or manner of pitching: a throw or cast. degree, esp. of elevation or depression: highest point *(fig.; lit., arch)*: height: a descent. slope: ground between the wickets *(cricket)*: a place set apart for playing or practising a game: the point where a ball alights: a station taken by a street trader, etc · a salesman's particular line of persuasive talk: the degree of acuteness of sound: a standard of acuteness for sounds: degree of intensity: distance between successive points or things, as the centres of teeth in a wheel or a saw, the threads of a screw. (of a propeller) the angle between the chord of the blade and the plane of rotation· the distance a propeller would advance in one revolution —*ns* **pitch'er** one who pitches: a paving-stone or sett a baseball player who delivers the ball to the batsman: one who pitches a stall: a cutting or stake intended to take root; **pitch'-ing** the action of the verb to pitch· a facing of stone: a foundation of stone for a road surface: a cobble-stone surface of a road —**pitch-and-toss'** a game in which coins are thrown at a mark, the player who throws nearest having the right of tossing all, and keeping those that come down heads up; **pitch circle** in a toothed wheel, an imaginary circle along which the tooth pitch is measured and which would put the wheel in contact with another that meshed with it; **pitched battle** a deliberate battle on chosen ground between duly arranged sides (also *fig.*); **pitch'fork** a fork for pitching hay, etc.: a tuning-fork.—*v.t.* to lift with a pitchfork: to throw suddenly into any position. —**pitch'pipe** a small pipe to pitch the voice or tune with; **pitch'-wheel** a toothed wheel which operates with another of the same design.—**pitch in** to set to work briskly: to join in, cooperate; **pitch into** to assail vigorously: to throw oneself into (work, a task, etc.); **pitch (up)on** to let one's choice fall (up)on.

pitcher[1] *pich'ər, n.* a vessel, usu. of earthenware, for holding or pouring liquids: a modified leaf or part of a leaf in the form of a pitcher, serving to catch insects. —*n.* **pitch'erful.**—**pitch'er-plant** an insectivorous plant with pitchers, esp. Nepenthes, also Sarracenia, Darlingtonia, etc. [O.Fr. *picher*—L.L. *picārium,* a goblet—Gr. *bīkos,* a wine-vessel.]

pitcher[2]. See **pitch**[2].

pitchy. See **pitch**[1].

piteous *pit'i-əs, adj.* fitted to excite pity.—*adv.* **pit'eously.**—*n.* **pit'eousness.** [O.Fr *pitos, piteus,* cf. **pity**.]

pitfall. See **pit**[1].

pith *pith, n.* the soft tissue within the ring of vascular bundles in the stems of dicotyledonous plants: similar material elswhere, as the white inner skin of an orange: spinal marrow: innermost part: condensed substance, essence: mettle: vigour: significant meaning: importance.—*v.t.* to remove the pith of: to sever, pierce, or destroy the marrow or central nervous system of: to kill (animals) in this way.—*adv.* **pith'ily.**—*n.* **pith'iness.**—*adjs.* **pith'ful; pith'less; pith'like; pith'y** full of pith: forcible: strong: energetic: sententious and masterful.—**pith hat, helmet** a sun-helmet of sola pith; **pith'-tree** a tropical African tree whose very pithlike wood is used for floats, canoes, etc. [O.E. *pitha.*]

pithead. See **pit**[1].

Pithecanthropus *pith-ə-kan'thro-pəs, pith-ē-kan-thrō'pəs, n.* a fossil hominid discovered in Java in 1891–92, a former genus of primitive man, now included in the genus Homo [Gr. *pithēkos,* ape, *anthrōpos,* man.]

pithecoid *pith-ē'koid, adj.* ape-like. [Gr. *pithēkos,* ape, *eidos,* form.]

pitiable, pitiless, etc. See **pity**.

pitman. See **pit**[1].

piton *pē'ton,* Fr. *pē-tɔ̃, n.* an iron peg or stanchion to which a rope may be attached, used in mountaineering. [Fr.]

Pitta *pit'ə, n.* a genus of birds, the so-called antthrushes of the Old World: (without *cap.*) a bird of this genus. [Telugu *pitta.*]

pitta (bread), pita (bread) *pit'ə (bred)* a type of slightly leavened bread, originating in the Middle East, in the form of a hollow flat cake. [Mod. Gr., a cake.]

pittance *pit'əns, n.* a very small portion or quantity: a miserable pay. [O.Fr. *pitance*—L. *pietās,* pity]

pitter *pit'ər, v.i.* to make a sound like a grasshopper.— *adv.* **pitt'er-patt'er** with light pattering sound.—*v.t.* to make, or move with, such a sound.—Also *n* [Imit.]

pitty-pat. See **pitapat.**

pituita *pit-ū-ī'tə,* **pituite** *pit'ū-īt, (arch.) n* phlegm, mucus.—*adj.* **pitū'itary** of or relating to phlegm, mucus (*arch.*): of or relating to the pituitary gland.— *n.* **pitū'itrin** a hormone produced by the pituitary body.—**pituitary gland, body** a ductless endocrine gland at the base of the brain affecting growth, once

thought to produce mucus. [L. *pītuīta.*]

pity *pit'i, n.* a feeling for the sufferings and misfortunes of others. a cause or source of pity or grief: an unfortunate chance: a matter for regret.—*v.t* to feel pity for: to feel grief at:—*pr.p.* **pit'ying;** *pa.t.* and *pa.p.* **pit'ied.**—*adj.* **pit'iable** to be pitied: miserable, contemptible.—*n.* **pit'iableness.**—*adv.* **pit'iably.**—*n.* **pit'ier.**—*adj.* **pit'iful** feeling pity: compassionate: exciting pity. sad: despicable.—*adv.* **pit'ifully.**—*n.* **pit'ifulness.**—*adj.* **pit'iless,** without pity: cruel.— *adv.* **pit'ilessly.**—*n.* **pit'ilessness.**—*adv.* **pit'yingly.** [O.Fr. *pite* (Fr. *pitié,* It. *pietà*)—L. *pietās, pietātis* —*pius,* pious.]

pityriasis *pit-i-rī'i-sis, n.* a branny scaliness of the skin [Gr. *pityron,* bran.]

più *pyoo, pē'oo,* (It.) *adv.* more.—**più mosso** (*mō'sō, mo'so*) quicker.

pivot *piv'ət, n.* a pin on which anything turns: a soldier upon whom, or position on which, a body wheels: a centre-half in football: that on which anything depends or turns: a man of cardinal importance in an industry: a movement of the body as if on a pivot.— *adj.* of the nature of a pivot: cardinal: serving as a pivot.—*v.t.* to mount on a pivot.—*v.i.* to turn on or as if on a pivot.—*adj.* **piv'otal.**—*adv.* **piv'otally.**—*adj.* **piv'oted.**—*ns.* **piv'oter; piv'oting** the pivot-work in machines —**piv'ot-bridge** a swing-bridge moving on a vertical pivot in the middle; **piv'ot-man** a man on whom a body of soldiers turns: a man of cardinal importance in industry, etc. [Fr. *pivot,* perh. related to It. *piva,* pipe, peg, pin.]

pix[1] *piks, n.* Same as pyx.

pix[2] *piks, (coll.) n pl.* short for **pictures,** usu. in sense of photographs:—*sing.* **pic.**

pixel *pik'səl, n.* one of the minute units which make up the picture on a cathode-ray tube, video display, etc [**pix**[2], element.]

pixie, pixy *pik'si, (dual.;* S W. England) **pisky** *pis'ki, ns.* a small fairy.—*adj.* **pix'ilated, pix'illated** bemused, bewildered: slightly crazy: intoxicated.— **pix'ie-hood** a hood with a point. [Origin obscure, cf. Sw. *pysk, pyske,* a small fairy.]

pizazz. See **piz(z)azz.**

pizza *pēt'sə, n.* an open pie of bread dough with tomatoes, cheese, etc —*n* **pizzeria** (*pēt-sə-rē'ə*) a bakery or restaurant where pizzas are sold and/or made. [It.]

piz(z)azz, paz(z)azz *pə-zaz', (coll.) n.* a combination of flamboyance, panache and vigour, in behaviour, display or performance.

pizzicato *pit-si-ka'tō, (mus.) adj* played by plucking the string, not with the bow—contradicted by *arco* or *col arco.*—*adv.* by plucking.—*n.* a tone so produced. a passage so played: the manner of playing by plucking:—*pl.* **pizzica'tos.** [It., twitched—*pizzicare,* to twitch.]

placable *plak'* or *plāk'ə-bl, adj.* that may be appeased: relenting: willing to forgive.—*ns.* **placabil'ity, plac'-ableness.**—*adv.* **plac'ably.**—*v t.* **placate** (*plə-kāt', plā-kāt', plak', plāk'āt*) to conciliate.—*n.* **placa'tion** propitiation.—*adj* **placatory** (*plak'* or *plāk'ə-tə-ri, plə-kā'*) conciliatory. [L *plācāre,* to appease, akin to *placēre.*]

placard *plak'ard, n.* a written or printed paper stuck upon a wall or otherwise displayed as an intimation: a notice written or printed on wood, cardboard or other stiff material, and carried, hung, etc., in a public place.—*v.t.* (sometimes *plə-kard'*) to publish or notify by placard: to post or set up as a placard: to put placards on or in. [O.Fr *plackart, placard,* etc.— *plaquier,* to lay flat, plaster—M. Flem. *placken,* to plaster]

placate, etc. See **placable.**

place *plās*, *n.* an open space in a town, a market-place or square: in street names, vaguely a row or group of houses, often short, secluded, or mean· a portion of space: a portion of the earth's surface, or any surface: a position in space, or on the earth's surface, or in any system, order, or arrangement: a building, room, piece of ground, etc , assigned to some purpose (as *place of business, entertainment, worship*): a particular locality: a town, village, etc : a dwelling or home: a mansion with its grounds: a seat or accommodation in a theatre, train, at table, etc.: space occupied: room: the position held by anybody, employment, office, a situation, esp. under government or in domestic service: due or proper position or dignity: that which is incumbent on one: precedence: position in a series: high rank: position attained in a competition or assigned by criticism: position among the first three in a race: stead.—*v.t.* to put in any place: to assign to a place: to find a place, home, job, publisher, etc., for: to lay (before) (*fig.*): to induct: to identify: to invest: to arrange (loan, bet, etc.): to put (trust, etc., in).—*adjs.* **placed** set in place or in a place: having a place: among the first three in a race: inducted to a charge; **place'less** without place or office.—*ns.* **place'ment** placing or setting: assigning to places: assigning to a job; **plac'er**.—**place card** a card placed before each setting on the table at a banquet, formal dinner, etc., with the name of the person who is to sit there; **place'-kick** in football, a kick made when the ball has been placed on the ground for that purpose; **place name** a geographical proper name, **place setting** each person's set of crockery, cutlery and glassware at a dining table.—**give place (to)** to make room (for): to be superseded (by); **in place** in position: opportune; **in place of** instead of; **in the first place** firstly, originally; **out of place** out of due position: inappropriate, unseasonable; **put someone in his, her place** to humble someone who is arrogant, presumptuous, etc.; **take place** to come to pass: to take precedence; **take someone's place** to act as substitute for, or successor to, someone; **take the place of** to be a substitute for. [Partly O.E. (Northumb.) *plæce*, market-place, but mainly Fr *place*, both from L *platea*—Gr. *plateia* (*hodos*), broad (street).]

placebo *pla-sē'bō*, *n.* vespers for the dead: a medicine given to humour or gratify a patient rather than to exercise any physically curative effect: a pharmacologically inactive substance administered as a drug either in the treatment of psychological illness or in the course of drug trials:—*pl.* **placê'bos.** [From the first words of the first antiphon of the office, *Placēbō Dominō*, I shall please the Lord.]

placenta *pla-sen'ta*, *n.* the structure that unites the unborn mammal to the womb of its mother and establishes a nutritive connection between them: the part of the carpel that bears the ovules (*bot.*): a structure bearing sporangia:—*pl.* **placen'tae** (-*tē*).—*adj.* **placen'tal.**—*n.pl.* **Placent-alia** (*plas-ən-tā'li-a*) the Eutheria or placental mammals. [L. *placenta*, a flat cake.]

placer *plas'ər, pläs'ər, n.* a superficial deposit from which gold or other mineral can be washed.—**plac'er-gold.** [Sp. *placer*, sandbank—*plaza*, place.]

placet *plā'set, pla'ket, n.* a vote of assent in a governing body: permission given, esp. by a sovereign, to publish and carry out an ecclesiastical order, as a papal bull or edict. [L. *plācet*, it pleases, 3rd sing. pres. indic. of *placēre*, to please.]

placid *plas'id, adj.* calm.—*ns.* **placid'ity, plac'idness.**—*adv.* **plac'idly.** [L. *placidus—placēre*, to please.]

placket *plak'it, n.* in armour, a breastplate or backplate, or a leather doublet with strips of steel: an opening in a skirt, for a pocket, or at the fastening: a piece of material sewn behind this: a pocket, esp. in a skirt.

placoderm *plak'ō-dûrm, adj* covered with bony plates, as some fossil fishes —*n* a fish so covered. [Gr *plax, plakos,* anything flat, *derma,* skin.]

placoid *plak'oid, adj.* plate-like: having placoid scales, irregular plates of hard bone, not imbricated, as sharks [Gr. *plax, plakos,* anything flat and broad, *eidos,* form.]

plafond *pla-fɔ̄, n.* a ceiling, esp decorated: a soffit: a game like contract bridge. [Fr., ceiling, score above the line in bridge—*plat,* flat, *fond,* bottom.]

plage *pläzh, n.* a fashionable beach: a bright or dark area seen on certain types of photograph of the sun, showing respectively an area of heated or cool gas on the sun's surface. [Fr]

plagiary *plā'ji-a-ri, n.* (*arch.*) one who steals the thoughts or writings of others and gives them out as his own: the crime of plagiarism.—*v.t.* **pla'giarise, -ize** to steal from the writings or ideas of another.—*ns.* **pla'giarism** the act or practice of plagiarising; **pla'giarist.** [L *plagiārius,* a kidnapper, plagiary—*plāga,* a net.]

plagioclase *plā'ji-ō-klās, -klāz,* or *plaj', n* a feldspar whose cleavages are not at right angles. [Gr. *plagios,* oblique, *klasis,* a fracture.]

plagiostome *plā'ji-ō-stōm, n.* a plagiostomous fish, one of the cross-mouthed fishes, sharks and rays, having the mouth as a transverse slit on the under side of the head.—*adjs* **plagiostom'atous, plagios'tomous.** [Gr. *plagios,* crosswise, *stoma, -atos,* mouth.]

plague *plāg, n* an affliction regarded as a sign of divine displeasure: a deadly epidemic or pestilence, esp. a fever caused by a bacillus (*B pestis*) transmitted by rat-fleas from rats to man, characterised by buboes, or swellings of the lymphatic glands, by carbuncles and petechiae: murrain: any troublesome thing or person· trouble (*coll*).—*v.t.* to pester or annoy — *adj.* **plague'some** (*coll.*) troublesome, annoying — *adv.* **pla'guily** confoundedly.—*adj* **plagu(e)y** (*plā'gi*) of, or of the nature of, plague: vexatious: troublesome: confounded.—**plague on** may a curse rest on. [O.Fr. *plague*—L. *plāga,* a blow.]

plaice *plās, n.* a yellow-spotted flatfish.—**plaice's mouth** a mouth placed awry —*adj.* wry-mouthed. [O.Fr. *plais* (Fr *plie*)—L.L. *platessa,* a flatfish.]

plaid *plād* (by the English also *plad*), *n.* a long piece of woollen cloth, worn over the shoulder, usually in tartan as part of Highland dress, or checked as formerly worn by Lowland shepherds: cloth for it.—*adj.* like a plaid in pattern or colours.—*adj.* **plaid'ed** wearing a plaid: made of plaid cloth.—*n.* **plaid'ing** a strong woollen twilled fabric. [Perh. Gael. *plaide,* a blanket; but that may be from the Scots word.]

plain¹ *plān,* (*arch.*), *v.t., v.i* to complain —*n* **plain'-ant** a plaintiff. [O.Fr *plaigner* (Fr *plaindre*)—L *plangēre,* to beat the breast, lament.]

plain² *plān, adj.* flat: level: even: unobstructed: clear: obvious: simple: downright, utter: not ornate: unembellished: unvariegated: uncoloured: unruled: without pattern, striation, markings, etc.: without gloss: uncurled: not twilled: in knitting, denoting a straightforward stitch with the wool passed round the front of the needle (opp. to *purl*): not elaborate· without addition: not highly seasoned deficient in beauty· without subtlety: candid: outspoken: straightforward: undistinguished: ordinary· other than a court card: other than trumps.—*n.* an extent of level land: the open country, esp. as a field of battle or as a setting for pastoral or romantic literature (*poetic*) .—*adv* clearly: distinctly —*adv.* **plain'ly** —*n* **plain'-ness.**—**plain'-chant** plainsong; **plain chocolate** dark chocolate, made with some sugar added but without milk.—*adj.* **plain'-clothes** wearing ordinary clothes, not uniform, as a policeman on detective work.— **plain'-deal'er** one who is candid and outspoken.—*n.* and *adj.* **plain'-deal'ing.—plain Jane** (*coll.*) a plain, dowdy girl; **plain language** straightforward, understandable language; **plain sailing** sailing in open, unrestricted waters (*naut.*): an easy, straightforward task, affair, etc. (*fig.*): see also **plane²**; **plains'man** a dweller in a plain, esp. in N. America; **plain'song** unmeasured music sung in unison in ecclesiastical modes from early times, and still in use in R.C. and some Anglican churches: a simple melody: that to which a descant can be added; **plain'-speaking** straightforwardness or bluntness of speech.—*adj.* **plain'-spoken** plain, rough, and sincere.—**plain'work** plain needlework, as distinguished from embroidery —**plain as a pikestaff** see **pike¹**. [Fr.,—L. *plānus*, plain.]

plainant. See **plain¹**.

plaint *plānt, n.* lamentation: a statement of grievance, esp. the exhibiting of an action in writing by a complainant in a court of law.—*n.* **plaint'iff** (*Eng. law*) one who commences a suit against another— opp. to *defendant.*—*adj.* **plaint'ive** mournful.—*adv.* **plaint'ively.**—*n.* **plaint'iveness.** [O.Fr. *pleinte* (Fr. *plainte*)—L. *plangĕre, planctum,* to beat the breast, lament.]

plait *plat, plăt, plēt, n.* a pleat or zigzag fold (usu. **pleat,** and pron *plēt* even when spelt plait): a braid in which strands are passed over one another in turn: material so braided: a braided tress or queue (in these senses usu. *plat,* and sometimes spelt *plat*).—*v.t.* to pleat (usu. *plēt*): to braid or intertwine (usu. *plat*).— *adj.* **plait'ed.**—*ns.* **plait'er; plait'ing.** [O.Fr. *pleit, ploit* (Fr. *pli*)—L. *plicāre, -itum, -ātum,* to fold.]

plan *plan, n.* a figure or representation of anything projected on a plane or flat surface, esp. that of a building, floor, etc., as disposed on the ground: a large-scale detailed map of a small area: a scheme for accomplishing a purpose: a purposed method: a scheme drawn up beforehand: a scheme of arrangement: in the Methodist churches, a quarterly programme of services with preachers for each church in the circuit.—*v.t.* to make a plan of: to design: to lay plans for: to devise: to purpose.—*v.i.* to make plans: —*pr.p.* **plann'ing;** *pa.t.* and *pa.p.* **planned.**—*adjs.* **planned** intended: in accordance with, or achieved by, a careful plan made beforehand; **plan'less.**—*n.* **plann'er.—planning permission** permission from a local authority to erect or convert a building or to change the use to which a building or piece of land is put. [Fr.,—L. *plānus,* flat.]

planchet *plan'shit, n.* a blank to be stamped as a coin. —*n.* **planchette** (*plä-shet, plan-shet'*) a board mounted on two castors and a pencil-point, used as a medium for automatic writing and supposed spirit-messages. [Fr. *planche*—L. *planca.*]

plane¹ *plān, n.* any tree of the genus Platanus: in Scotland, the great maple.—**plane'-tree.** [Fr. *plane*—L. *platanus;* see **platane.**]

plane² *plān, n.* a surface on which, if any two points be taken, the straight line joining them will lie entirely (*geom.*): any flat or level material surface: one of the thin horizontal structures used as wings and tail to sustain or control aeroplanes in flight: short for aeroplane or airplane (also **'plane**): an act of planing or soaring: in mines, a main road for transport of coal or other mineral: any grade of life or of development or level of thought or existence.—*adj.* having the character of a plane: pertaining to, lying in, or confined to a plane: level: smooth.—*v.t.* to make plane or smooth (see also **plane³**).—*v.i.* to travel by aero-

plane: to soar: to volplane: of a boat, to skim across the surface of the water.—*adj.* **planar** (*plān'ər*).—*ns.* **planation** (*plə-nā'shən*) making level; **planer** (*plān'ər*) one who levels or makes plane: a smoothing instrument (see also **plane³**); **planigraph** (*plan'i-graf*) an instrument for reducing or enlarging drawings; **planimeter** (*plan-im'itər*) an instrument for measuring the area of a plane figure.—*adjs.* **planimetric** (*plān-, plan-i-met'rik*), **-al.**—*ns.* **planimetry** (*plan-im'i-tri*) the mensuration of plane surfaces; **planisphere** (*plan'*) a sphere projected on a plane: a map of the celestial sphere, which can be adjusted so as to show the area visible at any time.— *adjs.* **planispher'ic; plā'no-con'cave** plane on one side and concave on the other; **plā'no-con'vex** plane on one side and convex on the other.—*ns.* **planom'eter** (*plan-*) a plane surface used in machine-making as a gauge for plane surfaces.—**planar diode** one with plane parallel electrodes; **plane chart** a chart used in plane sailing, the lines of longitude and latitude being projected onto a plane surface, so being represented parallel; **plane sailing** the calculation of a ship's place in its course as if the earth were flat instead of spherical: see also **plain sailing** under **plain²**. [L. *plānum,* a flat surface, neut. of *plānus,* flat; cf. **plain²** and next word.]

plane³ *plān, n.* a carpenter's tool for producing a smooth surface by paring off shavings: a tool or machine for smoothing other things.—*v.t.* to smooth or remove with a plane (see also **plane²**).—*n.* **plā'ner** one who uses a plane: a tool or machine for planing. —**plān'ing-machine'** a machine for planing wood or metals. [Fr. *plane*—L.L. *plāna—plānāre,* to smooth.]

planet *plan'it, n.* a body (other than a comet or meteor) that revolves about the sun (including the earth) reflecting the sun's light and generating no heat or light of its own: a satellite of a planet (*secondary planet*): an astrological influence vaguely conceived.—*n.* **planetā'rium** a machine showing the motions and orbits of the planets, often by projecting of their images on to a (domed) ceiling: a hall or building containing such a machine:—*pl.* **planetā'ria.**—*adj.* **plan'etary** pertaining to the planets or a planet, or this planet: consisting of, or produced by, planets: under the influence of a planet: erratic: revolving in an orbit.—*adjs.* **planetic** (*plan-et'ik*), **-al.**—*n.* **plan'etoid** a minor planet: an artificial body put into orbit.—*ns.* **planetol'ogy** the science of the planets; **planetol'ogist.—minor planets** the numerous group of very small planets between the orbits of Mars and Jupiter. [Fr. *planète*—Gr. *planētēs,* wanderer— *planaein,* to make to wander.]

plangent *plan'jənt, adj.* resounding: noisy, clangorous: resounding mournfully.—*adv.* **plan'gently.**—*n.* **plan'gency.** [L. *plangēns, -entis,* pr.p. of *plangĕre,* to beat.]

planigraph, planimeter, etc. See **plane².**

planish *plan'ish, v.t.* to polish (metal, etc.): to flatten. —*n.* **plan'isher** a tool for planishing. [Obs. Fr. *planir, -issant—plan,* flat.]

planisphere. See **plane².**

plank *plangk, n.* a long piece of timber, thicker than a board: one of the principles or aims that form the platform or programme of a party.—*v.t.* to cover with planks: to pay down or table (with *down*).—*n.* **plank'-ing** the act of laying planks: a series of planks: work made up of planks.—**walk the plank** to walk (compulsorily) along a plank projecting over the ship's side into the sea. [L. *planca,* a board.]

plankton *plangk'tən, n.* the drifting organisms in oceans, lakes or rivers.—*adj.* **planktonic** (*-ton'ik*). [Neut. of Gr. *planktos, -ē, -on,* wandering.]

plano-concave, etc., **planometer**. See **plane**[2].

plant *plànt*, *n.* a vegetable organism, or part of one, ready for planting or lately planted: a slip, cutting, or scion: any member of the vegetable kingdom, esp. (*popularly*) one of the smaller kinds: something deposited beforehand for a purpose: equipment, machinery, apparatus, for an industrial activity: factory: a deceptive trick, put-up job (*slang*).—*v.t.* to put into the ground for growth: to introduce: to insert: to place firmly: to set in position: to station, post: to found: to settle: to locate: to place or deliver (as a blow, a dart): to leave in the lurch: to bury (*slang*): to hide (*slang*): to place stolen goods, etc., in another's possession so as to incriminate him: to place as a spy, etc. (*slang*): to instil or implant: to furnish with plants: to colonise: to stock: to furnish or provide (with things disposed around).—*v.i* to plant trees, colonists, or anything else.—*adj.* **plant'able.**—*ns.* **planta'tion** a place planted, esp. with trees: a colony: an estate used for growing cotton, rubber, tea, sugar, or other product of warm countries: a large estate (*Southern U.S.*): the act or process of introduction: **plant'er** one who plants or introduces: the owner or manager of a plantation: a pioneer colonist: a settler: an instrument for planting: an ornamental pot or other container for plants.—*adj* **plant'igrade** walking on the soles of the feet.—*n.* an animal that walks so.—*n.* **plant'ing** the act of setting in the ground for growth: the art of forming plantations of trees.—**plant'-louse** an aphis or greenfly:—*pl.* **plant'-lice.**—**plant'-pot** a pot for growing a plant in.—**plant out** to transplant to open ground, from pot or frame: to dispose at intervals in planting. [O.E *plante* (n.)—L. *planta*, shoot, slip, cutting, and O.E. *plantian* (vb.), and partly from or affected by Fr. *plante* and L. *planta*, plant, also (perh. a different word) sole.]

plantain[1] *plan'tin*, *n.* a roadside plant that presses its leaves flat on the ground.—**plantain lily** a plant of the Hosta genus [L. *plantägö*, *-inis—planta*, the sole of the foot.]

plantain[2] *plan'tin*, *n.* a plant akin to the banana. its fruit, a coarse banana: in India, a banana.—**plan'tain-eater** an African bird, a touraco.

plap *plap*, *n.* a flatter sound than a plop.—*v.i.* to make, or move with, such a sound. [Imit.]

plaque *plak*, *plák*, *n.* a plate, tablet, or slab hung on, applied to, or inserted in, a surface as an ornament, memorial, etc.: a tablet worn as a badge of honour: a patch, such as a diseased area (*med.*): a film of saliva and bacteria formed on teeth (*dentistry*): an area in a bacterial or tissue culture where the cells have been destroyed by infection with a virus. [Fr.]

plash[1] *plash*, *v.t.* to interweave by partly cutting through, bending and twining the branches: to bend down: to break down: to make, mend, or treat, by cutting, bending, and interweaving stems and branches.—*n.* a plashed branch: a plashed place.—*n.* **plash'ing.** [O.Fr *plassier*—L. *plectêre*, to twist; cf. **pleach.**]

plash[2] *plash*, *n.* a shallow pool: a puddle. [O E *plæsc.*]

plash[3] *plash*, *n.* a dash of water: a splashing sound.—*v.i.* to dabble in water: to splash.—*v.t.* to splash.—*adj.* **plash'y.** [Cf. M.L.G. *plaschen*, early Mod. Du. *plasschen*; perh. conn. with preceding.]

plasm *plazm*, *n.* a mould or matrix: protoplasm: plasma.—*n.* **plas'ma** plasm: a bright green chalcedony: protoplasm: the liquid part of blood, lymph, or milk: a very hot ionised gas, having approximately equal numbers of positive ions and of electrons, highly conducting.—*adjs.* **plasmat'ic, -al,** **plas'mic** of, or occurring in, plasma: protoplasmic.—

n. **plas'mid** a circular piece of DNA which can exist and reproduce autonomously in the cytoplasm of cells. [Gr. *plasma*, *-atos*, a thing moulded—*plassein*, to mould.]

plaster *plås'tər*, *n.* a fabric coated with an adhesive substance for local application as a remedy, for protection of a cut, etc.: a pasty composition that sets hard, esp. a mixture of slaked lime, sand, and sometimes hair, used for coating walls, etc.: plaster of Paris: calcium sulphate.—*adj* made of plaster —*v t* to apply plaster, or a plaster, to: to treat with plaster. to bedaub: to smear: to cover excessively, injudiciously, or meretriciously: to stick (on or over) to reduce to plaster or a sticky mass: to damage by a heavy attack: to smooth down: to smooth (over): to treat with gypsum: to attach with plaster —*adj* **plas'tered** daubed, treated, etc., with plaster: shattered intoxicated (*slang*).—*ns.* **plas'terer** one who plasters, or one who works in plaster; **plas'tering.**—*adj.* **plas'tery** like plaster.—*n.* **plas'teriness** a building slab of plaster faced with paper or fibre: gypsum plasterboard; **plaster cast** a copy got by pouring a mixture of plaster of Paris and water into a mould formed from the object: an immobilising and protective covering of plaster of Paris for a broken limb, etc.; **plas'ter-work** —**plaster of Paris** gypsum (originally found near *Paris*) partially dehydrated by heat, which dries into a hard substance when mixed with water. [O.E. *plaster* (in medical sense) and O.Fr. *plastre* (builder's plaster) both—L.L. *plastrum*—L. *emplastrum*—Gr. *emplastron* for *emplaston*—*en*, on, *plassein*, to mould, apply as a plaster.]

plastic *plas'*, *plás'tik*, *adj.* having power to give form: shaping, formative: mouldable: of or pertaining to moulding or modelling: modifiable: capable of permanent deformation without giving way: capable of, or pertaining to, metabolism and growth. made of plastic.—*n.* a mouldable substance, esp. now any of a large number of polymeric substances, most of them synthetic, mouldable at some stage under heat or pressure, used to make domestic articles and many engineering products: the art of modelling or of sculpture (usu. **plastics**).—*n* **Plas'ticine®** (*-ti-sēn*) a substitute for modelling clay.—*n.sing* **plas'tics** plastic surgery: the art of modelling or sculpture —*adj.* dealing with plastic materials (as *the plastics industry*).—*v.t.* and *v.t* **plas'ticise, -ize** (*-ti-sīz*) to make or become plastic.—*ns.* **plasticis'er, -z-** substance that induces plasticity; **plasticity** (*-tis'i-ti*) the state or quality of being plastic: the quality in a picture of appearing to be three-dimensional.—**plastic art** the art of shaping (in three dimensions), as sculpture, modelling: art which is, or appears to be, three-dimensional; **plastic bomb** a bomb made with a certain explosive chemical that can be moulded; **plastic clay** clay from which earthenware and bricks are made; **plastic money** (*coll.*) credit cards; **plastic operation** a surgical operation which restores a lost part, or repairs a deformed or disfigured part, of the body; **plastic surgery** the branch of surgery concerned with plastic operations [Gr. *plastikos—plassein*, to mould]

plastron *plas'tron*, *n.* a breastplate worn under the hauberk: a fencer's wadded breast-shield: the front of a dress-shirt: a separate ornamental front part of a woman's bodice. [Fr. *plastron*—It. *piastrone—piastra*, breastplate]

plat *plat*. Same as **plait.**

platane, platan *plat'ən*, *n.* a plane-tree. [L. *platanus* —Gr. *platanos—platys*, broad.]

plat du jour *pla du zhōōr*, a dish on a restaurant menu specially recommended that day [Fr]

plate *plāt*, *n.* a sheet, slab, or lamina of metal or other hard material, usually flat or flattish: metal in the form of sheets: a broad piece of armour: a separate portion of an animal's shell: a broad thin piece of a structure or mechanism: a plate-like section of the earth's crust; a piece of metal, wood, etc , bearing or to bear an inscription to be affixed to anything: an engraved piece of metal for printing from: an impression printed from it, an engraving: a whole-page separately printed and inserted illustration in a book: a mould from type, etc., for printing from, as an electrotype or stereotype: part of a denture fitting the mouth and carrying the teeth: a device worn in the mouth by some children in order to straighten the teeth: a film-coated sheet of glass or other material to photograph on: a plate-rail: a horizontal supporting timber in building: a five-sided white slab at the home base (*baseball*): wrought gold or silver: household utensils in gold or silver: table utensils generally: plated ware: a cup or other prize for a race or other contest: a race or contest for such a prize: a shallow dish: a plateful: a portion served on a plate: a church collection: (in *pl.*) the feet (*slang*; orig. rhyming slang for *plates of meat*).—*v.t.* to overlay with metal: to armour with metal: to cover with a thin film of another metal: to make a printing plate of.—*adj.* **plä'ted** covered with plates of metal: covered with a coating of another metal, esp. gold or silver: armoured with hard scales or bone (*zool.*).—*ns.* **plate'ful** as much as a plate will hold; **plate'let** a minute body in blood, concerned in clotting; **plä'ter** one who, or that which, plates: a moderate horse entered for a minor, race; **plä'ting**.—*adj.* **plä'ty**, plate-like: separating into plates.—**plate'-arm'our** protective armour of metal plates; **plate'-glass** a fine kind of glass used for mirrors and shop-windows, orig. poured in a molten state on an iron plate.—*adj.* made with, consisting of, plate-glass: of a building, having large plate-glass windows, appearing to be built entirely of plate-glass: hence, of any very modern building or institution, esp. recently-founded British universities.—**plate'-layer** one who lays, fixes, and attends to the rails of a railway; **plate'-rail** a flat rail with a flange; **plate'-room** a room where silver-plated goods or printing plates are kept; **plate tectonics** (*geol.*) the theory that the earth's crust consists of continually moving plates forming the continental land-masses.—**half'-plate** in photography, a size of plate measuring 4¾ by 6½ in. (4½ by 5½ in U.S.); **quar'ter-plate** 3¼ by 4¼ in., **whole'-plate** 6½ by 8½ in.; **handed to one on a plate** (*fig.*) obtained by one without the least effort; **on one's plate** (*fig.*) in front of one, waiting to be dealt with. [O.Fr. *plate*, fem. (and for the dish *plat*, masc.), flat—Gr. *platys*, broad.]

plateau *pla'tō, pla-tō'*, *n.* a tableland: an ornamented tray, plate, or plaque: a temporary stable state reached in the course of upward progress: the part of a curve representing this:—*pl.* **plateaux** (*-tōz*), also **plateaus**.—*v.t.* to reach a level, even out (sometimes with *out*). [Fr.,—O.Fr. *platel*, dim. of *plat*.]

platen *plat'n*, *n.* the work-table of a machine-tool: a flat part that in some printing-presses pushes the paper against the forme: the roller of a typewriter. [Fr. *platine*—*plat*, flat.]

platform *plat'förm*, *n.* a scheme of church government or of administrative policy: a party programme: a site: a basis: a raised level surface: a terrace: a raised floor for speakers, musicians, etc.: those who have seats on the platform at a meeting: public speaking or discussion (*fig.*): a medium for discussion: a deck for temporary or special purpose: a position prepared for mounting a gun: a raised walk in a railway station giving access to trains: a floating installation, usu.

moored to the sea-bed, for drilling for oil, marine research, etc.: flooring outside an inner entrance to a bus, tram-car, or sometimes a railway carriage.—*adj.* **on**, relating to, admitting to, etc., a platform: of shoes, boots, etc., having a very thick sole (**platform sole**), giving extra height.—*v.t.* to furnish with a platform: to sketch, plan: to place on, or as on, a platform [Fr. *plateforme*, lit. flat form.]

platinum *plat'in-əm*, *n.* a noble metal (at. numb. 78; symbol Pt), a steel-grey element, very valuable, malleable and ductile, very heavy and hard to fuse.—*adj.* made of platinum.—*adj.* **platinic** (*pla-tin'ik*) of platinum, esp. tetravalent.—*v.t.* **plat'inise, -ize** to coat with platinum.—*ns.*—*adj.* **plat'inous** of bivalent platinum.—**platinum blonde** a woman with metallic silvery hair; **platinum lamp** an electric lamp with a platinum filament. [Sp. *platina—plata*, silver.]

platitude *plat'ı-tūd*, *n.* flatness: a dull commonplace or truism: an empty remark made as if it were important.—*v.i.* **plat'itudinise, -ize.**—*adj.* **platitud'inous.** [Fr.,—*plat*, flat.]

Platonic *pla-ton'ik*, *adj.* pertaining to Plato, the Greek philosopher, or to his philosophy: (often without *cap.*) of love, without sensual desire: relating to or experiencing Platonic love.—*ns.* **Pla'tonism** the philosophy of Plato: **Pla'tonist** a follower of Plato.— **Platonic solid** any of the five regular polyhedrons (tetrahedron, hexahedron, octahedron, dodecahedron, and icosahedron); **Platonic year** see **year.** [Gr. *platōnikos—Platōn, -ōnos*, Plato.]

platoon *pla-tōōn'*, *n.* a subdivision of a company of soldiers: a squad. [Fr. *peloton*, ball, knot of men— L. *pila*, ball.]

platter *plat'ər*, *n.* a large flat plate or dish: a gramophone record (*slang*, esp. *U.S.*). [A.Fr. *plater— plat*, a plate.]

platy. See **plate.**

platy- *plat'i-*, in composition, flat, broad. [Gr. *platys*, broad.]

platypus *plat'i-pəs, -poōs*, *n.* the duck-bill:—*pl.* **plat'ypuses.** [Gr. *pous, podos*, a foot.]

platyrrhine *plat'i-rīn*, **platyrrhinian** *plat-i-rin'i-ən*, *adjs.* broad-nosed: belonging to the division of the monkeys found in South America.—*ns.* a New World monkey. [Gr. *platyrrīs, -inos—rhīs, rhīnos*, nose.]

plaudit *plö'dit*, *n.* (now usu. in *pl.*) an act of applause: also praise bestowed, enthusiastic approval.—*adj.* **plaud'itory.** [Shortened from L. *plaudite*, applaud, an actor's call for applause at the end of a play, pl. imper. of *plaudēre, plausum*, to clap the hands.]

plausible *plö'zi-bl*, *adj.* likely, reasonable, seemingly true: seemingly worthy of approval or praise: fair-showing: specious: ingratiating and fair-spoken.—*ns.* **plausibil'ity, plaus'ibleness.**—*adv.* **plaus'ibly** in a plausible manner. [L. *plaudēre*, to clap the hands.]

play *plā*, *v.i.* to move about irregularly, lightly, or freely: to have some freedom of movement: to flicker, flutter, shimmer, pass through rapid alternations: to move in, discharge, or direct a succession, stream, or shower (as of water, light, waves, missiles): to engage in pleasurable activity: to perform acts not part of the immediate business of life but in mimicry or rehearsal or in display: to amuse oneself: to sport: to make sport: to trifle: to behave without seriousness: to behave amorously or sexually: to take part in a game: to proceed with the game, perform one's part in turn: to send a ball or the like in the course of a game: to gamble: to perform on a musical instrument: to give forth music: to come forth as music: to act a part.—*v.t.* to perform: to ply, wield: to cause or allow to play: to set in opposition, pit: to send, let off, or discharge in succession or in a stream or shower: to give a limited freedom of movement to: hence, to manage: to allow (a fish) to tire itself by its struggles to get away: to engage in (a game or recreative mimicry): to oppose (in a game, sport, etc.): to proceed through (a game, part of a game—as a stroke, trick—or an aggregate of games—as a rubber, set): to stake or risk in play: to gamble on (*coll.*): to bring into operation in a game, as by striking (a ball), throwing on the table (a card), moving (a man): to compete against in a game: to compete on the side of (with *for*): to act (e.g. comedy, a named play): to act the part of, in a play or in real life: to act, perform, in (e.g. a circuit of theatres, halls): to make-believe in sport: to perform music on· to perform on a musical instrument: to lead, bring, send, render, or cause to be by playing.—*n.* activity. operation: action of wielding: light fluctuating movement or change: limited freedom of movement: scope: recreative activity: display of animals in courtship: amusement: dalliance: the playing of a game: manner of playing: procedure or policy in a game: gambling: a drama or dramatic performance· manner of dealing, as *fair play* (fig.).—*adj.* **play'able** capable (by nature or by the rules of the game) of being played, or of being played on.—*n.* **play'er** one who plays: an actor: a trifler: an instrumental performer: a professional cricketer: a mechanism for playing a musical instrument.—*adj* **play'ful** sportive: high-spirited, humorous.—*adv.* **play'fully**.—*ns* **play'fulness; play'let** a short play.—**play'-acting** performance of plays: pretence; **play'-actor, -actress** (usu. in contempt) professional actor, actress; **play'back** the act of reproducing a recording of sound or visual material, esp. immediately after it is made: a device for doing this (see also **play back** below), **play'bill** a bill announcing a play; **play'boy** a lighthearted irresponsible person, esp. rich and leisured —*adj.* **played'-out** exhausted. used up: no longer good for anything.—**play'er-pian'o** see **pianoforte**; **play'fellow** a playmate; **play'ground** a place for playing in, esp. one connected with a school: a holiday region; **play'group** an informal, usu. voluntarily-run group having morning or afternoon sessions attended by preschool children and mothers, for creative and co-operative play; **play'house** a theatre. a child's toy house, usu. big enough to enter; **play'ing-card** one of a pack (e.g. of fifty-two cards, divided into four suits) used in playing games; **play'ing-field** a grass-covered space set apart, marked out, and kept in order for games; **play'leader** a person trained to supervise and organise children's play in a playground, etc.; **play'mate** a companion in play, esp child's play; **play'-off** a game to decide a tie: a game between the winners of other competitions: see also **play off** below; **play'-pen** an enclosure within which a young child may safely play; **play'room** a room for children to play in; **play'school** a nursery school or playgroup; **play'thing** a toy: a person or thing treated as a toy; **play'time** a time for play; **play'wright, play's writer** a dramatist.—**bring, come, into play** to bring, come, into exercise, operation, use; **hold in play** to keep occupied, esp. to gain time or detain; **in, out of, play** in, out of, such a position that it may be played, **make a play for** (*coll.*) to try to get; **make great play with, of** to make a lot of: to treat, talk of, as very important; **play about, around** to behave irresponsibly, not seriously, **play along (with)** to cooperate, agree with, usu. temporarily; **play a part (in)** to be instrumental, help in doing: to act a theatrical rôle (in) (also fig.); **play at** to engage in the game of to make a pretence of: to practise without seriousness; **play back** to play a sound, video, etc. recording that has just been made; **play ball** to co-operate, **play it, one's cards, close to the chest** to be secretive about

one's actions or intentions in a particular matter; **play down** to treat (something) as less important than it is, **play fair** (sometimes with *with*) to act honestly; **play fast and loose** to act in a shifty, inconsistent, and reckless fashion; **play for safety** to play safe, **play for time** to delay action or decision in the hope or belief that conditions will become more favourable later; **play hard to get** to make a show of unwillingness to co-operate with a view to strengthening one's position; **play havoc, hell with** to upset, disorganise: to damage; **play into the hands of** to act so as to give, usu. unintentionally, an advantage to; **play it** (*coll* ; usu. followed by an *adj.*) to behave in, manage, a particular situation in a stated way, as in *play it cool*, **play it by ear** to improvise plan of action to meet the situation as it develops; **play off** to manipulate so·as to counteract: to play from the tee (*golf*); **play on** to direct one's efforts to the exciting of, work upon; **play out** to play to the end: to wear out, to exhaust; **play safe** to take no risks; **play the field** (*coll.*) to spread one's interests, affections or efforts over a wide range of subjects, people, activities, etc., rather than concentrating on any single one, **play the game** to act strictly honourably; **play up** to strike up, begin the music: to redouble one's efforts, play more vigorously: to show up well in a crisis or emergency: to give (esp undue) prominence to, or to boost: to fool; **play (up)on** to practise upon, work upon, **play (up)on words** a pun or other manipulation of words depending on their sound; **play up to** to act so as to afford opportunities to (another actor)· to flatter; **play with** to play in company of, or as partner or opponent to. to dally with.   [O.E. *pleg(i)an*, vb., *plega*, n.]

playa *plä'ya*, *n.* a basin which becomes a shallow lake after heavy rainfall and dries out again in hot weather. [Sp.]

plaza *plä'za*, *n.* a public square or open, usu. paved, area in a city or town   [Sp.]

plea *plē*, *n.* a prisoner's or defendant's answer to a charge or claim: an excuse: a pretext. urgent entreaty.—**plea('-)bargaining** the esp. U.S. legal practice of arranging more lenient treatment by the court in exchange for the accused's admitting to the crime, turning State's evidence, etc., **plea('-)bargain**.   [O.Fr. *plai*, *plaid*, *plait*—L L. *placitum*, a decision— L. *placēre*, *-itum*, to please.]

pleach *plēch*, *v.t.* to intertwine the branches of, as a hedge: to plash.   [From form of O.Fr *pless(i)er*—L *plectĕre*; see **plash¹**.]

plead *plēd*, *v.i.* to carry on a plea or lawsuit: to argue in support of a cause against another: to put forward an allegation or answer in court: to implore.—*v.t* to maintain by argument: to allege in pleading: to put forward as a plea to offer in excuse·—*pa t.*, *pa.p* **plead'ed** also (*Scot.*, *U.S.*, and *dial*) **pled**.—*n* **plead'er**.—*adj.* **plead'ing** imploring.—*n.* the act of putting forward or conducting a plea: (in *pl.*) the statements of the two parties in a lawsuit: entreaty.— *adv.* **plead'ingly**.—**plead guilty or not guilty** to state that one is guilty, or innocent, of a crime with which one is charged; **special pleading** unfair or one-sided argument aiming rather at victory than at truth   [O.Fr. *plaidier*; cf. **plea.**]

please *plēz*, *v.t* to give pleasure to. to delight· to satisfy: to choose, to will (to do) —*v.i.* to give pleasure: to like, think fit, choose (originally impersonal with dative, e.g *it pleases* (to) *me*; later *me pleases*; then *I please*).—*adj* **pleas'ant** pleasing agreeable inoffensive: affable   good-humoured cheerful.—*adv*   **pleas'antly**.—*ns.*   **pleas'antness; pleas'antry** jocularity. a facetious utterance or trick —*pl* **pleas'antries**.—*adj* **pleased** (*plēzd*) grateful. delighted.—*adj* and *n.* **pleas'ing**.—*adv* **pleas'ingly**.

—*adj.* **pleasurable** (*plezh'ər-ə-bl*) able to give pleasure: delightful: gratifying.—*n.* **pleas'urableness.**—*adv.* **pleas'urably.**—*n.* **pleasure** (*plezh'ər*) agreeable emotions: gratification of the senses or of the mind: sensuality: dissipation: a source of gratification: what the will prefers: purpose: command.—*v.t.* (*arch.*) to give pleasure to.—**pleas'ure-boat** a boat used for pleasure or amusement; **pleas'ure-ground** ground laid out in an ornamental manner for pleasure; **pleas'ure-seeker** one who seeks pleasure: a holiday-maker; **pleas'ure-seeking; pleas'ure-trip** an excursion for pleasure.—**at pleasure** when, if, or as, one pleases; **if you please** if you like: a polite formula of request or acceptance: forsooth (*ironically*); **may it please you, so please you** deferential or polite formulas of address or request; **please,** also (now *rare*) **please to,** a polite formula equivalent to **if you please,** now felt as imperative; **pleased as Punch** delighted; **please yourself** do as you like. [O.Fr. *plaisir* (Fr. *plaire*)—L. *placēre,* to please.]

pleat *plēt, n.* a fold sewn or pressed into cloth.—*v.t.* to make pleats in. [From **plait.**]

pleb. See **plebeian.**

plebeian *pli-bē'ən adj.* of the Roman plebs: of the common people: low-born: undistinguished: vulgar-looking: vulgar.—*n.* a member of the plebs of ancient Rome: a commoner: a member of a despised social class.—*n.* **pleb** (*coll.*) a person of unpolished manners which are attributed to his low rank in society.—*adj.* **plebb'y** (*coll.*). [L. *plēbēius—plēbs, plēbis.*]

plebiscite *pleb'i-sit, -sīt, n.* a direct vote of the whole nation or of the people of a district on a special point: an ascertainment of general opinion on any matter.—*adj.* **plebisc'itary.** [Partly through Fr. *plébiscite*—L. *plēbiscītum—plēbs,* plebs, *scītum,* decree—*scīscēre,* to vote for.]

plebs *plebz, n.* one of the two divisions of the Roman people, originally the less privileged politically.—See also **plebeian.** [L. *plēbs, plēbis.*]

plectrum *plek'trəm, n.* a pointed device held in the fingers or on the thumb, with which the strings of e.g. a guitar are struck. [L. *plēctrum*—Gr. *plēktron—plēssein,* to strike.]

pled *pled.* See **plead.**

pledge *plej, n.* something given as a security: a gage: a token or assuring sign: a child, as a token of love or binding obligation: a solemn promise: a friendly sentiment expressed by drinking: a state of being given, or held, as a security.—*v.t.* to give as security: to bind by solemn promise: to vow: to give assurance of: to drink a toast in response to: to drink at the invitation of another: to drink to the health of.—*adj.* **pledge'able.**—*ns.* **pledgee'** the person to whom a thing is pledged; **pledger, pledg(e)or** (*plej'ər*).—**take or sign the pledge** to give a written promise to abstain from intoxicating liquor. [O.Fr. *plege* (Fr. *pleige*)—L.L. *plevium, plivium,* prob. Gmc.]

pledget *plej'it, n.* a wad of lint, cotton, etc., as for a wound or sore: an oakum string used in caulking.

pledgor. See **pledge.**

-plegia *-plē-ji-ə,* in composition, paralysis, as in *paraplegia.*—adjective and noun combining form **-plēgic.** [Gr. *plēgē,* stroke—*plēssein,* to strike.]

Pleiad *plī'ad, n.* any one of the seven daughters of Atlas and Pleione, changed into stars (one 'lost' or invisible): a brilliant group of seven, esp. seven Alexandrian tragic poets or (usu. as Fr., **Pléiade** *plā-ē-äd*) the poets Ronsard, Du Bellay, Baïf, Daurat, and others variously selected.—*pl.* **Plei'ads, Pleiades** (*plī'ə-dēz*) a group of six naked-eye and a multitude of telescopic stars in the shoulder of the constellation Taurus. [Gr. *pleias, plēias, -ados,* pl. *-adēs.*]

plein-air *plen'-er', adj.* open-air: attaching importance to painting in the open air.—*n.* **plein-air'ist** a plein-air painter. [Fr. *en plein air,* in the open air.]

pleio-, plio-, *plī'ō, plī-o', *pleo-* plē'ō, plē-o',* in composition, more. [Gr. *pleiōn* or *pleōn,* compar. of *polys,* many, much.]

Pleiocene. Same as **Pliocene.**

Pleistocene *plīs'tō-sēn, adj.* of the geological period following the Pliocene, having the greatest proportion of fossil molluscs of living species.—*n.* the Pleistocene system, period, or strata. [Gr. *pleistos,* most (numerous), *kainos,* recent—from the proportion of living species of molluscs.]

plenary *plē'nə-ri, adj.* full: entire: complete: passing through all its stages—opp. to *summary* (*law*): having full powers.—*adv.* **plē'narily.**—*n.* **plē'narty** the state of a benefice when occupied.—**plenary indulgence** in the Roman Catholic Church, full or complete remission of temporal penalties to a repentant sinner; **plenary powers** full powers to carry out some business or negotiations. [L.L. *plēnārius*—L. *plēnus,* full—*plēre,* to fill.]

plenipotentiary *plen-i-pō-ten'sh(y)ə-ri, adj.* having full powers.—*n.* a person invested with full powers, esp. a special ambassador or envoy to some foreign court. [L. *plēnus,* full, *potentia,* power.]

plenitude *plen'i-tūd, n.* fullness: completeness: plentifulness: repletion.—*adj.* **plenitud'inous.** [L. *plēnitūdō, -inis—plēnus,* full.]

plenty *plen'ti, n.* a full supply: all that can be needed: abundance.—*adj.* in abundance.—*adv.* (*coll.*) abundantly.—*adj.* **plenteous** (*plen'tyəs*) fully sufficient: abundant: fruitful: well provided: rich: giving plentifully.—*adv.* **plen'teously.**—*n.* **plen'teousness.**—*adj.* **plen'tiful** copious: abundant: yielding abundance.—*adv.* **plen'tifully.**—*n.* **plen'tifulness.**—**horn of plenty** see **cornucopia; in plenty** abundant, as *food in plenty.* [O.Fr. *plente*—L. *plēnitās, -ātis—plēnus,* full.]

plenum *plē'nəm, n.* a space completely filled with matter—opposed to *vacuum:* a full assembly.—**plenum system, ventilation** (*archit.*) an air-conditioning system in which the air propelled into a building is maintained at a higher pressure than the atmosphere. [L. *plēnum* (*spatium*) full (space).]

pleo-. See **pleio-.**

pleomorphic *plē-ō-mör'fik, adj.* polymorphic.—Also **pleomor'phous.**—*ns.* **pleomorph'ism, plē'omorphy.**

pleonasm *plē'o-nazm, n.* redundancy, esp. of words: a redundant expression.—*adjs.* **pleonas'tic, -al.**—*adv.* **pleonas'tically.** [Gr. *pleonasmos—pleōn,* more.]

pleroma *pli-rō'mə, n.* fullness: abundance: in Gnosticism, divine being.—*adj.* **pleromatic** (*-mat'ik*). [Gr. *plērōma—plērēs,* full.]

plerome *plē'rōm,* (*bot.*) *n.* the central part of the apical meristem. [Gr. *plērōma,* filling.]

plesiosaur *plē'si-ō-sör, n.* a great Mesozoic fossil reptile with long neck, short tail, and four flippers. [Gr. *plēsios,* near, *sauros,* lizard.]

plessor, plessimeter, etc. See **plexor.**

plethora *pleth'ər-ə,* sometimes *pli-thō'rə, -thō', n.* excessive fullness of blood: over-fullness in any way.—*adjs.* **plethoric** (*pli-thor'ik;* sometimes *pleth'ər-ik*), **plethor'ical.**—*adv.* **plethor'ically.** [Gr. *plēthōrā,* fullness—*pleos,* full.]

pleura *plōō'rə, n.* a delicate serous membrane that covers the lung and lines the cavity of the chest: a side-piece, esp. pleuron:—*pl.* **pleu'rae** (*-rē*).—*adj.* **pleu'ral.**—*n.* **pleurisy** (*plōō'ri-si*) inflammation of the pleura.—*adjs.* **pleurit'ic, -al** of, affected with, or causing pleurisy.—*n.* a sufferer from pleurisy.—*ns.* **pleurī'tis** pleurisy; **pleurodynia** (*plōō-rō-dīn'i-ə;* Gr. *odynē,* pain) neuralgia of the muscles between the ribs; **pleurōt'omy** (*med.*) incision into the pleura. [Gr. *pleurā* and *pleuron,* rib, side.]

plexiform. See **plexus.**

plexor *pleks'ər,* **plessor** *ples'ər, ns.* a percussion hammer.—*ns.* **plexim'eter, plessim'eter,** a small plate to receive the tap in examination by percussion.—*adjs.* **pleximet'ric, plessimet'ric.**—*ns.* **plexim'etry, plessim'etry.** [Gr. *plēxis,* a stroke, *plēssein,* to strike.]

plexus *pleks'əs, n.* a network:—*pl.* **plex'uses** or **plex'us** (L. *plexūs*).—*adj.* **plex'iform** in the form of a network: complex. [L. *plexus, -ūs,* a weaving.]

pliable *plī'ə-bl, adj.* easily bent or folded: flexible: adaptable: easily persuaded: yielding to influence —*ns.* **pliabil'ity, pli'ableness.**—*adv.* **pli'ably.**—*ns.* **pli'ancy, pli'antness.**—*adj.* **pli'ant** bending easily: flexible: tractable: easily influenced.—*adv.* **pli'antly.** [See **ply**[1].]

plié *plē'ā, n.* a movement in ballet, in which the knees are bent while the body remains upright. [Fr , bent.]

plied, plier, pliers, plies. See **ply**[1,2].

plight[1] *plīt, v.t.* to pledge:—*pa.p* **plight'ed,** also **plight.** [O.E. *pliht,* risk.]

plight[2] *plīt, n.* evil state. [Assimilated in spelling to the foregoing, but derived from O.Fr. *plite*—L. *plicāre, plicitum*; see **plait.**]

plimsoll, plimsole *plim'səl, -sol, n.* a rubber-soled canvas shoe.—**Plimsoll line** or **mark** a ship's load-line, or set of load-lines for different waters and conditions, required by the Merchant Shipping Act (1876) passed at the instance of Samuel *Plimsoll* (1824–98).

plink *plingk, n.* a short, relatively high-pitched, sound, as of the string of a musical instrument being plucked. [Imit.]

plinth *plinth, n.* the square block under the base of a column: a block serving as a pedestal: a flat-faced projecting band at the bottom of a wall: a similar projecting base in furniture. [L. *plinthus,* Gr. *plinthos,* a brick, squared stone, plinth.]

plio-. See **pleio-.**

Pliocene *plī'ō-sēn, (geol.) adj.* of the Tertiary period following the Miocene, and having a greater proportion of molluscan species now living.—*n.* the Pliocene system, period, or strata. [Gr. *pleiōn,* greater, more numerous, *kainos,* recent.]

plissé *plē-sā, (Fr.) adj.* (of a fabric) chemically treated to produce a shirred effect.

plod *plod, v.i.* to walk heavily and laboriously: to study or work on steadily and laboriously.—*v.t.* to traverse or make by slow and heavy walking:—*pr.p.* **plodd'-ing;** *pa.t.* and *pa.p.* **plodd'ed.**—*n.* a heavy walk: a thud.—*n.* **plodd'er** one who plods on: a dull, heavy, laborious man: one who gets on more by sheer toil than by inspiration.—*adj.* and *n.* **plodd'ing.**—*adv.* **plodd'ingly.** [Prob. imit.]

plonk[1] *plongk, v.t.* to put down, etc., so as to make a hollow or metallic sound.—*v.i.* to plump.—Also *n.,* *adv., interj.*—*n.* **plonk'er** anything large, esp. a smacking kiss *(coll.).*—*adj.* **plonk'ing** *(coll.)* used to denote great size, often with *great.* [Imit.]

plonk[2] *plongk, n.* (orig. *Austr. slang)* wine, esp. cheap.

plop *plop, n.* the sound of a small object falling vertically into water: the sound of the movement of small bodies of water: the sound of a cork coming out of a bottle, or of a bursting bubble.—*adv.* with a plop: plump.—*v.i.* to make the sound of a plop: to plump into water.—*v.t.* to set with a plop:—*pr.p.* **plopp'ing;** *pa.t.* and *pa.p.* **plopped.** [Imit.]

plosive *plō'siv, -ziv, (phon.) adj., n.* explosive.—*n.* **plo'sion** *(phon.)* explosion.

plot *plot, n.* a small piece of ground: a ground-plan of a building, plan of a field, etc.: the story or scheme of

connected events running through a play, novel, etc.: a secret scheme, usually in combination, to bring about something, often illegal or evil, a conspiracy: a stratagem or secret contrivance.—*v.t.* to lay out in plots, dispose: to make a plan of: to represent on or by a graph: to conspire or lay plans for.—*v.i.* to conspire:—*pr.p.* **plott'ing;** *pa.t.* and *pa.p.* **plott'ed.**—*n.* **plott'er.**—*n.* and *adj.* **plott'ing.** [O.E. *plot,* a patch of ground; influenced by (or partly from) Fr. *complot,* a conspiracy.]

plough, plow, *n.* an instrument for turning up the soil in ridges and furrows: a joiner's plane for making grooves: agriculture *(fig.)*: a plough-team: ploughed land: (with *cap.)* seven stars of the Great Bear.—*v.t.* to turn up with the plough: to make furrows or ridges in: to make with a plough: to put into or render with a plough (also *fig.*): to tear, force, or cut a way through: to furrow: to wrinkle: to reject in an examination *(university slang)*: to fail in (a subject) *(university slang)*.—*v.i.* to work with a plough: to fail *(slang).*—**plough'boy** a boy who drives or guides horses in ploughing; **plough'land** land suitable for tillage: as much land as could be tilled with one plough (with a proportionate amount of pasture) *(hist.)*; **plough'-man** a man who ploughs:—*pl.* **plough'men**; **plough-man's lunch** a cold meal of bread, cheese, cold meat, pickle, etc.; **plough'share** (O.E. *scear,* ploughshare—*scieran,* to shear, cut) the detachable part of a plough that cuts the under surface of the sod from the ground; **plough'-team** the team of horses, oxen, etc. (usu. two), that pulls a simple plough; **plough'wright** one who makes and mends ploughs.—**plough a lonely furrow** to be separated from one's former friends and associates and go one's own way; **plough back** *(fig.)* to reinvest (profits of a business) in that business; **plough in** to cover with earth by ploughing, **put one's hand to the plough** to begin an undertaking. [Late O.E. *plōh, plōg,* a ploughland.]

plover *pluv'ər, n.* a general name for birds of the family (Charadriidae) to which the lapwing and dotterel belong: extended to some related birds. [Fr. *pluvier*—L. *pluvia,* rain; possibly from their restlessness before rain.]

plow *plow* (chiefly American). Same as **plough.**

plowter. See **plouter.**

ploy *ploi, n.* an employment, doings, affair, frolic, escapade, engagement for amusement: a method or procedure used to achieve a particular result: a manoeuvre in a game, conversation, etc. [Prob. **employ.**]

pluck *pluk, v.t.* to pull off, out, or away: to pull forcibly: to snatch away: to rescue: to pull: to tug: to twitch: to strip, as of feathers: to despoil, fleece: to swindle *(slang)*.—*v.i.* to make a pulling or snatching movement (at).—*n.* a single act of plucking: the heart, liver, and lungs of an animal—hence heart, courage, spirit.—*adj.* **plucked** subjected to plucking: having pluck.—*adv.* **pluck'ily.**—*n.* **pluck'iness.**—*adj.* **pluck'y** having courageous spirit and pertinacity. —**pluck up** to pull out by the roots: to summon up, as courage: to gather strength or spirit. [O.E. *pluccian.*]

plug *plug, n.* a peg stopping, or for stopping, a hole: a bung: a stopper: a mechanism releasing the flow of water in a water-closet: filling for a tooth: volcanic rock stopping a vent: a fitting for a socket for giving electrical connection: a piece of wood inserted in a wall to take nails: a fire-plug; a sparking-plug: a blow or punch: a compressed cake of tobacco: a piece of it cut for chewing: a piece of favourable publicity, esp. one incorporated in other material *(coll.)*: anything worn-out or useless: a dogged plodding.—*v.t.* to stop with a plug or as a plug: to insert a plug in: to insert as a plug: to shoot (*slang*): to punch with the fist (*slang*)· to force into familiarity by persistent repetition, esp for advertising purposes (*slang*): to din into the ears of the public.—*v.i.* (*slang*) to go on doggedly:—*pr.p.* **plugg'ing**; *pa.t.* and *pa.p.* **plugged**.—*ns.* **plugg'er** one who plugs in any sense: that which plugs, esp. a dentist's instrument; **plugg'ing** the act of stopping with a plug, or punching (*slang*), or promoting (*slang*): material of which a plug is made—**plug'-ug'ly** (*U.S.*) a street ruffian.—**plug in** to complete an electric circuit by inserting a plug.—*adj.* **plug'-in.** [App. Du. *plug*, a bung, a peg.]

plum *plum*, *n.* a drupe or stone-fruit, or the tree producing it (*Prunus domestica* or kindred species) of the rose family: extended to various fruits and trees more or less similar (as *sapodilla plum, coco-plum, date-plum*): a raisin as a substitute for the true plum: plum-colour: a sugar-plum: something choice that may be extracted or attained to.—*adj.* plum-colour: choice, cushy.—*adj.* **plumm'y** full of plums: plum-like: desirable, profitable: (of voice) too rich and resonant.—**plum'-cake** a cake containing raisins, currants, etc.—*n.* and *adj.* **plum'-colour** dark purple.—**plum'-duff** a flour-pudding boiled with raisins; **plum'-pudd'ing** a national English dish made of flour and suet, with raisins, currants, and various spices; **plum'-stone**; **plum'-tree.** [O.E. *plûme*—L *prûnum.*]

plumage *plōōm'ij*, *n.* a natural covering of feathers: feathers collectively.—*adj.* **plum'aged.** [Fr., *plume*—L. *plûma*, a feather, down.]

plumassier, plumate. See plume.

plumb *plum*, *n.* a heavy mass, as of lead, hung on a string to show the vertical line, or for other purpose: verticality: a sounding lead, plummet.—*adj.* vertical: level, true (*cricket*): sheer, thorough-going, out-and-out.—*adv.* vertically: precisely: utterly (esp. *U.S.*). —*v t.* to test by a plumb-line: to make vertical: to sound as by a plumb-line: to pierce the depth of, fathom, by eye or understanding: to weight with lead: to seal with lead: to do or furnish the plumber-work of.—*v.i.* to hang vertically: to work as a plumber —*n.* **plumbate** (*plum'bāt*) a salt of plumbic acid.—*adj.* **plumbeous** (*plum'bi-əs*) leaden: lead-coloured: lead-glazed.—*ns.* **plumber** (*plum'ər*) orig. a worker in lead: now one who instals and mends pipes, cisterns, and other fittings for supply of water and gas and for household drainage; **plumb'ery** plumber-work: a plumber's workshop.—*adjs.* **plumbic** (*plum'bik*) due to lead: of quadrivalent lead; **plumbiferous** (-*bif'*) yielding or containing lead.—*ns* **plumbing** (*plum'ing*) the operation of making plumb: the craft of working in lead: the system of pipes in a building for gas, water and drainage: (the design, style, working, etc. of) lavatories (*euph.*): the work of a plumber; **plum'bism** (-*bizm*) lead poisoning; **plum'-bite** (-*bīt*) a salt of the weak acid lead hydroxide.—*adjs.* **plumb'less** incapable of being sounded; **plum-bous** (*plum'bəs*) of bivalent lead.—**plumb bob** a weight at the end of a plumb-line; **plumb'er-work**; **plumbic acid** an acid of which lead dioxide is the anhydride; **plumb'-line** a line to which a bob is attached to show the vertical line: a vertical line: a plummet.—*adj.* **plumb'-rule** a board with plumbline and bob, for testing the verticality of walls, etc. [Fr. *plomb* and its source L. *plumbum*, lead.]

plumbago *plum-bā'gō*, *n.* graphite:—*pl.* **plumbā'gos**. —*adj.* **plumbaginous** (-*baj'i-nəs*). [L. *plumbāgō*, -*inis*—*plumbum*, lead.]

plumbate, etc., **plumber**, etc. See under **plumb**.

plume *plōōm*, *n.* a feather: a large showy feather: the vane of a feather: a bunch or tuft of feathers: a feather, or anything similar, used as an ornament,

symbol, crest, etc : a feather as a token of honour· the plumule of a seed: anything resembling a feather, as smoke, etc.—*v.t.* to preen: (*refl.*) to pride, take credit to (with *on, upon; fig.*): to adorn with plumes. —*n.* **plumassier** (*plōō-mă-sēr'*) a worker in feathers: a feather-seller —*adjs.* **plum'ate, plu'mose, plu'mous** feathered: feathery: plume-like; **plumed** feathered. adorned with a plume.—*adj.* **plume'less.**—*ns* **plume'let** a plumule: a little tuft; **plum'ery** plumes collectively.—*adj.* **plu'my** covered or adorned with down or plume: like a plume.—**plume'-bird** a long-tailed bird of paradise; **plume'-grass** a tall grass (*Erianthus*) akin to sugar-cane, with great silky panicles, grown for ornament. [O.Fr.,—L *plûma*, a small soft feather.]

plummet *plum'it*, *n.* leaden or other weight. esp. on a plumb-line, sounding-line, or fishing-line: plumb-rule.—*v t.* to fathom, sound.—*v.i.* to plunge head-long. [O.Fr. *plomet*, dim. of *plomb*, lead; see **plumb.**]

plump[1] *plump*, *v.i.* to fall or drop into liquid, esp vertically, passively, resoundingly, without much disturbance: to flop down: to come suddenly or with a burst: to give all one's votes without distribution: to choose, opt, decisively or abruptly (with *for*).—*v.t.* to plunge, souse· to fling down or let fall flat or heavily: to blurt.—*n.* the sound or act of plumping: a sudden heavy fall of rain (esp. *Scot.*).—*adj.* and *adv.* with a plump: in a direct line: downright: in plain language: without hesitation, reserve, or qualification. [L.G. *plumpen* or Du. *plompen*, to plump into water; prob. influenced by **plumb** and **plump**[2].]

plump[2] *plump*, *adj.* pleasantly fat and rounded: well filled out.—*v.t.* and *v.i.* to make or grow plump: to swell or round.—*adj.* **plump'ish**.—*n.* **plump'ness.** [App. the same word as Du. *plomp*, blunt, L.G *plump.*]

plumula *plōōm'ū-lə*, *n.* a plumule:—*pl.* **plum'ulae** (-*lē*).—*adjs.* **plumulā'ceous, plum'ular; plum'ulate** downy.—*n.* **plum'ule** a little feather or plume: a down feather: the embryo shoot in a seed —*adj.* **plum'ulose.** [L. *plûmula*, dim. of *plûma*, a feather.]

plumy. See **plume.**

plunder *plun'dər*, *v.t.* to carry off the goods of by force: to pillage: to carry off as booty: to carry off booty from.—*v.i* to pillage, carry off plunder.—*n.* pillage: booty.—*ns* **plun'derage** the stealing of goods on board ship; **plun'derer**.—*adj.* **plun'derous.** [Ger. *plündern*, to pillage—*Plunder*, household stuff, now trash.]

plunge *plunj*, *v.t.* to put or thrust with suddenness under the surface of a liquid, or into the midst of, the thick of, or the substance of, anything: to immerse.— *v.i.* to fling oneself or rush impetuously, esp into water, downhill, or into danger or discourse: to turn suddenly and steeply downward: to fire down upon an enemy from a height: to gamble or squander recklessly: to pitch as a ship: to pitch suddenly forward and throw up the hindlegs.—*n* act of plunging.—*n.* **plung'er** one who plunges: part of a mechanism with a plunging movement, as the solid piston of a force-pump: a suction instrument for cleaning blockages in pipes.—*adj.* and *n.* **plung'ing.—plunge bath** a bath large enough to immerse the whole body; **plunging neckline** (in woman's dress) a neckline which is cut low.—**take the plunge** to commit oneself definitely after hesitation. [O.Fr. *plonger*—L. *plumbum*, lead.]

plunk *plungk*, *v.t.* to twang: to pluck the strings of (a banjo, etc.): to plonk.—*v.i* to plump —Also *n.*, *adv.*, *interj.* [Imit.]

pluperfect *plōō-pûr'fekt*, -*fikt*, or *plōō'*, (*gram.*) *adj.* denoting that an action happened before some other past action referred to.—*n.* the pluperfect tense: a pluperfect verb or form. [L. *plūs quam perfectum* (*tempus*) more than perfect (tense).]

plural *plōōr'l, adj.* numbering more than one: more than onefold: expressing more than one, or, where dual is recognised, more than two (*gram.*).—*n.* (*gram.*) the plural number: a plural word form.—*n.* **pluralisā'tion, -z-.**—*v.t.* **plur'alise, -ize** to make plural.—*ns.* **plur'alism** plurality: the holding by one person of more than one office at once, esp. ecclesiastical livings: a system allowing this: a philosophy that recognises more than one principle of being (opp. to *monism*) or more than two (opp. to *monism* and *dualism*): a (condition of) society in which different ethnic, etc., groups preserve their own customs, or hold equal power; **plur'alist** one who holds more than one office at one time: a believer in pluralism.—*adj.* **pluralist'ic.**—*n.* **plurality** (-*al'i-ti*) the state or fact of being plural: numerousness: a plural number: the greater number, more than half: the holding of more than one benefice at one time: a living held by a pluralist.—*adv.* **plu'rally.**—**plural society** one in which pluralism is found. [L. *plūrālis* —*plūs, plūris,* more.]

pluri- *plōōr'i-,* in composition, several: usu. more than two. [L. *plūs, plūris,* more.]

plus *plus,* (*math.* and *coll.*) *prep.* with the addition of. —*adj.* positive: additional: having an adverse handicap.—*n.* an addition: a surplus: a positive quality or term: the sign (also **plus sign**) of addition or positivity (+); opposed to *minus* (−). [L. *plūs,* more.]

plus-fours *plus'-förz', -förz, n.pl.* baggy knickerbockers or knickerbocker suit. [**plus, four**; from the four additional inches of cloth required.]

plush *plush, n.* a fabric with a longer and more open pile than velvet: (in *pl.*) footman's breeches.—*adj.* of plush: pretentiously luxurious (also **plush'y**). [Fr. *pluche* for *peluche*—L. *pila,* hair; cf. **pile**[3].]

Pluto *plōō'tō, n.* the Greek god of the underworld: a planet beyond Neptune, discovered 1930.—*n.* **plutō'nium** the element (Pu) of atomic number 94, named as next after neptunium (93), as the planet Pluto is beyond Neptune. [L. *Plūtō, -ōnis*—Gr. *Ploutōn, -ōnos,* Pluto.]

Plutus *plōō'tas, n.* the Greek god of wealth.—*ns.* **plutocracy** (*plōō-tok'ra-si*) government by the wealthy: a ruling body or class of rich men; **plutocrat** (*plōō'tō-krat*) one who is powerful because of his wealth.—*adj.* **plutocrat'ic.** [L. *Plūtus,* Gr. *Ploutos* (Gr. *ploutos,* wealth).]

pluvial *plōō'vi-al, adj.* of or by rain: rainy.—*n.* a period of prolonged rainfall (*geol.*).—*n.* **pluviom'eter** a rain-gauge.—*adjs.* **plu'vious, plu'viose** rainy.—**pluvius insurance** insurance cover taken out, e.g. by the organiser of a fête, against loss of takings due to rain. [L. *pluvia,* rain.]

ply[1] *plī, n.* a fold: a layer or thickness: a layer of hard rock or of hard or soft in alternation (*min.*): a bend: a bend or set: a strand:—*pl.* **plies.**—*v.t.* and *v.i.* to bend or fold:—*pr.p.* **ply'ing;** *pa.t.* and *pa.p.* **plied;** *3rd pers. sing.* **plies.**—*n.* **pli'er** one who plies: (in *pl.*) small pincers for bending or cutting wire, etc.—**ply'wood** boarding made of thin layers of wood glued together, the grain of each at right-angles to that of the next. [(O.)Fr. *pli,* a fold, *plier,* to fold—L. *plicāre.*]

ply[2] *plī, v.t.* to work at steadily: to use or wield diligently or vigorously: to keep supplying or assailing (with): to importune: to row, sail, over habitually.— *v.i.* to work steadily: to make regular journeys over a route: to be in attendance for hire: to beat against the wind: to make one's way, direct one's course:—*pr.p.* **ply'ing;** *pa.t.* and *pa.p.* **plied;** *3rd pers. sing.* **plies.**— *n.* **pli'er** one who plies. [Aphetic, from **apply.**]

Plymouth *plim'ath, n.* a port in Devon: a port named after it in Massachusetts, with the supposed landing-place of the Pilgrims (**Plymouth Rock**).—**Plymouth Brethren** a religious sect, founded in Dublin *c.* 1825, out of a reaction against High Church principles and against a dead formalism associated with unevangelical doctrine—its first congregation was established at Plymouth in 1831.

plywood. See **ply**[1].

pneuma *nū'ma, n.* breath: spirit, soul.—*adjs.* **pneumatic** (-*mat'ik*) relating to air or gases: containing or inflated with air: worked or driven by compressed air: containing compressed air: with air-cavities (*zool.*): spiritual.—*adv.* **pneumatically.**—*n.* **pneumaticity** (*nū-ma-tis'i-ti*) the condition of having air-spaces.—*n. sing.* **pneumat'ics** the science of the properties of gases.—*n.* **pneumatom'eter** an instrument for measuring the quantity of air breathed or the force of breathing. [Gr. *pneuma, -atos,* breath —*pneein.*]

pneum(o)-, pneumon(o)- *nū'm(o)-, -mon-(o)-,* in composition, lung.—**pneumococc'us** a bacterium in the respiratory tract which is a causative agent of pneumonia; **pneumoconiosis** (*nū-mō-kō-ni-ō'sis;* Gr. *konia,* dust) any of various diseases caused by habitually inhaling mineral or metallic dust, as in coal-mining.—*n.* **pneumō'nia** inflammation of the lung.— *adj.* **pneumonic** (-*mon'-*) pertaining to the lungs.—*n.* a medicine for lung diseases.—*ns.* **pneumoni'tis** pneumonia; **pneumotho'rax** (*med.*) the existence, or introduction of, air between the lung and chest-wall: lung collapse resulting from the escape of air from the lung into the chest cavity—a potential hazard of working in compressed air, e.g. deep-sea diving. [Gr. *pneumōn, -ōnos,* lung—*pneein,* to breathe.]

po *pō,* (*coll.*) *n.* A shortening of **chamber pot:**—*pl.* **pos.** [**pot**—prob. from a euph. French pronunciation.]

poach[1] *pōch, v.t.* to cook slowly in boiling liquid.—*n.* **poach'er** one who poaches eggs: a vessel with hollows for poaching eggs in. [App. Fr. *pocher,* to pocket— *poche,* pouch, the white forming a pocket about the yolk.]

poach[2] *pōch, v.i.* to intrude on another's preserves in order to pursue or kill game, or upon another's fishing to catch fish (also *fig.*): to encroach upon another's rights, profits, areas of influence, etc., or on a partner's place or part in a game: to seek an unfair advantage.—*v.t.* to take illegally on another's ground or in another's fishing: to seek or take game or fish illegally on: to take in unfair encroachment.—*ns.* **poach'er; poach'iness; poach'ing.** [A form of **poke**[2] or from O.Fr. *pocher,* to poke.]

pochaise. See **pochay.**

pochard *pōch', poch'ard, n.* a red-headed diving-duck esp. the male, the female being the dun-bird.

pochay *pō'shā, po'chaise -shāz.* See **post-chaise** (under **post**[3]).

pochette *posh-et', n.* a small bag, esp. one carried by women: a pocket note-case or wallet. [Fr., dim. of *poche,* pocket.]

pock *pok, n.* a small elevation of the skin containing pus, as in smallpox.—*adjs.* **pocked; pock'y** marked with pustules: infected with pox.—**pock'mark, pock'-pit** the mark, pit, or scar left by a pock.—*adjs.* **pock'-marked, pock'pitted.** [O.E. *poc,* a pustule; see **pox.**]

pocket *pok'it, n.* a little pouch or bag, esp. one attached to a garment or a billiard-table or the cover of a book: a cavity: a rock cavity filled with ore, etc.: a portion of the atmosphere differing in pressure or other condition from its surroundings: a small isolated area or patch, as of military resistance, unemployment, etc.: the innermost compartment of a pound-net.—*adj.* for the pocket: of a small size.—*v.t.* to put in one's pocket or a pocket: to appropriate: to take stealthily: to conceal: to enclose: to hem in: to play into a pocket (*billiards*).—*v.i.* to form a pocket·—*pr.p.* **pock'eting;** *pa.t.* and *pa.p.* **pock'eted.**—*n* **pock'etful** as much as a pocket will hold:—*pl.* **pock'etfuls.—pocket battleship** a small battleship, built to specifications limited by treaty, etc.; **pock'et-book** a notebook: a wallet for papers or money carried in the pocket: a small book for the pocket: a handbag (*U.S.*); **pocket gopher** any American burrowing rodent with outward-opening cheek-pouches; **pock'et-handk'erchief; pock'et-knife** a knife with one or more blades folding into the handle for the pocket; **pock'et-money** money carried for occasional expenses: an allowance, esp. to a boy or girl; **pocket mouse** a small rodent of genus *Perognathus,* native to the N. American desert.—*adj.* **pock'et-sized** small enough for the pocket.—**in one's pocket** (*fig.*) under one's control or influence; **in,** or **out of, pocket** with, or without, money: the richer, or the poorer, by a transaction (*adj.* **out'-of-pock'et** of expenses, etc., paid in cash); **line one's pockets** to make a dishonest profit from business entrusted to one; **pick a person's pocket** to steal from his pocket; **pocket an insult, affront,** etc., to submit to or put up with it without protest; **pocket one's pride** to humble oneself to accept a situation. [A.Fr. *pokete* (Fr. *pochette,* dim. of *poche,* pocket).]

pocky, etc. See **pock.**

poco *pō'kō,* (It.) *adj.* little.—*adj.* **pococuran'te** (-*kōō-ran'tā,* -*kū-ran'ti;* It. *curante, pr.p.* of *curare,* to care) uninterested: indifferent: nonchalant.—*n.* a habitually uninterested person.—*ns.* **pococurant'ism** (-*kū-rant'izm*), **pococuranteism** (-*kū-rant'i-ism*); **pococurant'ist.—poco a poco** little by little.

poculiform *pok'ū-li-förm, adj.* cup-shaped. [L. *pōculum,* cup.]

pod¹ *pod, n.* the fruit, or its shell, in peas, beans, and other leguminous plants—the legume: sometimes extended to the siliqua: a silk cocoon: a musk-bag: a paunch: a groove along an auger or bit: the socket into which a bit, etc., fits: a protective housing for (external) engineering equipment, e.g. aircraft engines, nuclear reactor, space or submarine instruments, or for weapons carried externally e.g. on an aircraft: a decompression compartment.—*v.t.* to shell or hull.—*v.i.* to form pods: to fill as pods:—*pr.p.* **podd'ing;** *pa.t.* and *pa.p.* **podd'ed.**

pod² *pod, n.* a school, esp. of whales or seals.

podagra *pod-ag'rə,* also *pod', n.* gout, properly in the feet.—*adjs.* **podag'ral, podag'ric, -al, podag'rous** gouty. [Gr. *podagrā—pous, podos,* foot, *agrā,* a catching.]

pod(o)- *pod(ŏ)-, pŏd(ŏ)-,* in composition, foot.—*adjs.* **pō'dal, podal'ic** of the feet.—*ns.* **podiatry** (*pod-ī'ə-tri;* Gr. *iātros, iātros,* physician) treatment of disorders of the foot; **podi'atrist; podol'ogist; podol'ogy** scientific study of the feet. [Gr. *pous, podos,* foot.]

podge *poj,* **pudge** *puj, ns.* a squat, fat, and flabby person or thing.—*ns.* **podg'iness, pudg'iness.—adjs. podg'y, pudg'y.**

podiatrist, podiatry. See **pod(o)-.**

podium *pō'di-əm, n.* a continuous pedestal, a stylobate: a platform, dais: a foot or hand (*anat.*):—*pl.* **pō'dia.—adj. pō'dial.** [Latinised from Gr. *pŏdion,* dim. of *pous, podos,* foot.]

podo-. See **pod(o)-.**

podsol, podzol *pod-zol', n.* a bleached sand soil, poor in humus. [Russ.,—*pod,* under, *zola,* ash.]

poe-bird, poy-bird *pō'i-bûrd, n.* the New Zealand

parson-bird or tui [Captain Cook's name from Tahitian *poe,* pearl beads, taken by him to mean earrings, on account of the side-tufts of the bird's neck.]

poem *pō'im, -em, n.* a composition in verse: a composition of high beauty of thought or language and artistic form, typically, but not necessarily, in verse: anything supremely harmonious and satisfying (*fig.*). [Fr. *poème*—L. *poēma*—Gr. *poiēma—poieein,* to make.]

poenology. Same as **penology.**

poesy *pō'i-zi, n.* poetry collectively or in the abstract. [Fr. *poésie*—L. *poēsis.*—Gr. *poiēsis—poieein,* to make.]

poet *pō'it, -et, n.* the author of a poem or (formerly) of any work of literary art: a verse-writer: one skilled in making poetry: one with a poetical imagination:—*fem.* **pō'etess.—adjs. poetic** (*pō-et'ik*), **-al** of the nature or having the character of poetry: pertaining or suitable to a poet or to poetry: expressed in poetry: in the language of poetry: imaginative.—*ns.sing.* **poet'ic(s)** the branch of criticism that relates to poetry.—*adv* **pōet'ically.**—*v t.* and *v.i.* **poet'icise, -ize** to make poetic: to write poetry about: to write, speak, or treat, poetically.—*ns.* **pō'etry** the art of the poet: the essential quality of a poem: poetical composition or writings collectively (rarely in *pl.*): poetical quality; **pō'etship.—poetic justice** ideal administration of reward and punishment; **poetic licence** a departing from strict fact or rule by a poet for the sake of effect; **Poet Laureate** see **laureate.—poetry in motion** exceedingly beautiful, harmonious, rhythmical, etc. movement. [Fr. *poète*—L. *poēta*—Gr. *poiētēs—poieein,* to make.]

po-faced *pō'fāst,* (*coll.*) *adj.* stupidly solemn and narrow-minded: stolid, humourless. [Perh. *pot-faced* or *poor-faced.*]

pogo stick *pō'gō stik,* a child's toy consisting of a stick with a crossbar on a strong spring on which one stands in order to bounce along the ground. [*Pogo,* a trademark.]

pogrom *pog'rom, pog-rom', n.* an organised massacre, orig. (late 19th cent.) esp. of Russian Jews. [Russ., destruction, devastation.]

poignant *poin'(y)ənt, adj.* stinging, pricking: sharp: acutely painful: penetrating: pungent: piquant: touching, pathetic.—*n.* **poign'ancy.—adv. poign'antly.** [O.Fr. *poignant, pr.p.* of *poindre*—L. *pungēre,* to sting.]

poikilitic *poi-kil-it'ik, adj.* mottled.—*adjs.* **poikilotherm'al, poikilotherm'ic** having variable blood-temperature—'cold-blooded'.—*n.* **poikilotherm'y** cold-bloodedness. [Gr. *poikilos,* variegated.]

Poinciana *poin-si-a'nə, n.* a tropical genus of the Caesalpinia family—flamboyant tree, etc.: (without cap.) a tree of this genus. [After De *Poinci,* a French West Indian governor]

poinsettia *poin-set'i-ə, n.* a spurge, *Euphorbia pulcherrima,* with petal-like bracts, usu. scarlet, and small yellow flowers, orig. from Mexico and Central America. [From Joel Roberts *Poinsett* (1779–1851), American Minister to Mexico.]

point *point, n.* a dot: a small mark used in Semitic alphabets to indicate a vowel, to differentiate a consonant, or for other purpose: a dot separating the integral and fractional parts of a decimal: a mark of punctuation: that which has position but no magnitude (*geom.*): a place or station, considered in relation to position only: a place or division in a scale, course, or cycle (as *boiling point, dead-point*): a moment of time, without duration: a precise moment: a state: a juncture: a critical moment: the verge: a culmination: a conclusion: a unit in scoring, judging, or measurement: a character taken into account in judging: a distinctive mark or characteristic: a unit of measurement of type, approximately 1/72 inch: one of thirty-two divisions of the compass (**points of the compass**) or the angle between two successive divisions (⅛ of a right angle): a unit in rationing by coupon: a particular: a head, clause, or item: a position forming a main element in the structure of an argument or discourse: a matter in debate, under attention, or to be taken into account: that which is relevant: that upon which one insists or takes a stand: the precise matter: the essential matter: that without which a story, joke, etc., is meaningless or ineffective: a clearly defined aim, object, or reason: a particular imparted as a hint: lace made with a needle (also **point'-lace**): a sharp end: a tip, or free end: a thing, part, or mark with a sharp end: a piercing weapon or tool: an etching-needle: the sharp end of a sword: a tine: a spike: a cape or headland: the tip of the chin (*boxing*): a horse's or other animal's extremity: a nib: a movable rail for passing vehicles from one track to another: a tapering division of a backgammon board: a fielder or his position, on the off-side straight out from and near the batsman (as if at the point of the bat) (*cricket*): a socket for making connection with electric wiring: pointedness: pungency: sting: the act or position of pointing: the vertical rising of a hawk, indicating the position of the prey: pointe: 1/100 part of a carat.—*adj.* (*phon.*) articulated with the tip of the tongue.—*v.t.* to insert points in: to mark with points: to mark off in groups of syllables for singing: to sharpen: to give point to: to prick in or turn over with the point of a spade: to show the position or direction of or draw attention to (now usu. with *out*): to place in a certain direction, direct (with *at*): to indicate: to insert white hairs in (a fur): to rake out old mortar from, and insert new mortar in, the joints of: to ration by points.—*v.i.* to have or take a position in a direction (with *at, to, toward*, etc.: to indicate a direction or position by extending a finger, a stick, etc.: of dogs, to indicate the position of game by an attitude: to hint: to aim.—*adj.* **point'ed** having a sharp point: sharp: keen: telling: epigrammatic: precise: explicit: aimed at particular persons: having marked personal application.—*adv.* **point'edly.**—*ns.* **point'edness; point'er** one who points, in any sense: a rod for pointing to a blackboard, map, screen, etc : an index-hand: a hint, tip, suggestion, indication: a tool for clearing out old mortar from joints: a breed of dogs that point on discovering game: (in *pl*) two stars of the Great Bear nearly in a straight line with the Pole Star; **point'ing.**—*adj.* **point'less.**—*adv.* **point'lessly.**—*n.* **point'lessness.**—**point'-duty** the duty of a policeman stationed at a particular point to regulate traffic; **point'-lace** (see above).—*adj.* **point'-of-sale'** of, relating to, or occurring at the place where a sale is made.—**points'man** one on point-duty: one in charge of rail points.—*adj.* **point'-to-point'** from one fixed point to another: across country.—*n.* a cross-country race, a steeplechase.—**at the point of** on the verge of; **carry one's point** to gain what one contends for; **in point** apposite; **in point of** in the matter of; **point of fact** as a matter of fact; **make a point of** to treat as essential, make a special object of; **not to put too fine a point on it** to speak bluntly; **on the point of** close upon: very near; **point for point** exactly in all particulars; **point of no return** that point on a flight from which one can only go on, for want of fuel to return.—Also *fig.*; **point of order** a question raised in a deliberative society, whether proceedings are according to the rules; **point of view** the position from which one looks at anything, literally or figuratively; **point out** to point to, show, bring someone's attention to; **point up** to emphasise; **score points off someone** to

advance at the expense of another: to outwit, get the better of someone in an argument or repartee; **stand upon points** to be punctilious; **stretch** (or **strain**) **a point** to go further (esp. in concession) than strict rule allows; **to the point** apposite; **up to a point** partly, not wholly. [Partly Fr. *point*, point, dot, stitch, lace, partly Fr. *pointe*, sharp point, pungency—L. *punctum* and L L. *puncta*, respectively—L *pungĕre*, *punctum*, to prick.]

point-blank *point'-blangk'*, *adj.* aimed directly at the mark without allowing for the downward curve of the trajectory: permitting such an aim, i.e. at very close range: direct: straightforward: blunt.—*adv.* with point-blank aim: directly: bluntly: flat.—*n.* a point-blank shot or range. [App. from **point** (vb.) and **blank** (of the target).]

pointe *pwēt*, (Fr.) *n.* in ballet, the extreme tip of the toe, or the position of standing on it.

pointillism *pwan'til-izm*, Fr. **pointillisme** *pwē-tē-yēzm*, *ns.* in painting, the use of separate dots of pure colour instead of mixed pigments.—*adj.* **pointillé** (*pwē-tē-yā*) ornamented with a pattern of dots made by a pointed tool.—*n.* and *adj.* **poin'tillist,** Fr. **pointilliste** (-*tē-yēst*). [Fr. *pointillisme—pointille*, dim. of *point*, point.]

poise *poiz*, *v.t.* to hold so as to get some notion of the weight: to ponder, weigh in the mind (*rare*) to balance: to carry or hold in equilibrium.—*v.i.* to hang in suspense: to hover.—*n.* balance: equilibrium: bias: carriage or balance of body: dignity and assurance of manner: suspense.—*adj.* **poised** having or showing poise, composure: balanced —*n.* **pois'er.** [O.Fr. *poiser* (Fr. *peser*)—L. *pēnsāre*, freq of *pendēre*, to weigh, and O.Fr. *pois*—L *pēnsum*, weight.]

poison *poi'zn*, *n.* any substance which, taken into or formed in the body, destroys life or impairs health: any malignant influence: a substance that inhibits the activity of a catalyst (*chem.*): a material that absorbs neutrons and so interferes with the working of a nuclear reactor.—*v t.* to administer poison to: to injure or kill with poison: to put poison on or in: to taint: to mar: to embitter: to corrupt.—*adj.* poisonous —*adj* **poi'sonable.**—*n.* **poi'soner.**—*adj* **poi'sonous** having the quality or effect of poison: noxious: offensive (*coll.*) —*adv.* **poi'sonously.**—*n.* **poi'sonousness.**—**poi'son-fang** one of two large tubular teeth in the upper jaw of venomous snakes, through which poison passes from glands at their roots when the animal bites; **poi'son-gas** any injurious gas used in warfare, **poi'son-gland** a gland that secretes poison; **poi'son-ivy, poi'son-oak, poi'son-sumac(h)** names for various North American sumacs with ulcerating juice; **poi'son-nut** nux vomica; **poison pen** a writer of malicious anonymous letters.—**what's your poison?** (*coll*) what would you like to drink? [O Fr. *puison*, poison —L. *pōtiō, -ōnis*, a draught—*pōtāre*, to drink; cf. **potion.**]

poke[1] *pōk*, *n.* (now chiefly *dial.*) a bag: a pouch: a pokeful: a pocket.—**a pig in a poke** a blind bargain, as of a pig bought without being seen. [M E. *poke.*]

poke[2] *pōk*, *n.* a projecting brim or front of a bonnet: a poke-bonnet.—**poke'-bonnet** a bonnet with a projecting front. [Perh. from foregoing, or from following word]

poke[3] *pōk*, *v.t* to thrust or push the end of anything against or into: to prod or jab: to cause to protrude: to thrust forward or endwise: to make, put, render, or achieve by thrusting or groping: to stir up, incite.—*v.i.* to thrust, make thrusts: to protrude: to feel about, grope: to bat gently and cautiously (*cricket*): to potter: to stoop: to pry about: to live a dull or secluded life.—*n.* an act of poking.—*n.* **pō'ker** one who pokes: a rod for poking or stirring a fire: an

instrument for doing poker-work: a stiff person.—
adj. **pō'kerish** like a poker: stiff.—*adj.* **pō'king** pottering: petty: confined: stuffy: shabby.—*adj.* **pō'ky** poking.—**pō'ker-work** work done by burning a design into wood with a heated point.—**poke fun at** to banter; **poke one's nose** to pry; **red-hot poker** Kniphofia or Tritoma. [M.E. *pōken*; app. of L.G. origin.]

poke⁴ *pōk, n.* a name for various American species of Phytolacca (also **poke'weed, poke'berry**): American or white hellebore (**Indian poke**) [Of American Indian origin]

poker *pō'kər, n.* a round game at cards —**po'ker-face** an inscrutable face, useful to a poker-player: its possessor.—*adj.* **po'ker-faced.**

Polack *pōl'ak, (slang;* usu. *derog.) n.* a Pole.—*adj* Polish. [Pol. *Polak;* Ger. *Polack.*]

polar *pō'lər, adj* of, or pertaining to, a pole (see **pole¹**) or poles: belonging to the neighbourhood of a pole: referred to a pole: of the nature of, or analogous to, a pole: axial: having polarity: directly opposed.—*ns.* **polarim'eter** an instrument for measuring the rotation of the plane of polarisation of light, or the amount of polarisation of light.—*adj.* **polarimetric** (*pō-lar-ı-met'rık*).—*ns.* **polarimetry** (*pō-lar-ım'ı-trı*); **Polaris** (*pō-lā'ris*) the Pole Star; **polarisation, -z-** (*pō-lar-ı-zā'shən*) act of polarising: the state of being polarised: development of poles: loosely, polarity. the effect of deposition of products of electrolysis upon electrodes, resulting in an opposing electromotive force: the restriction (according to the wave theory) of the vibrations of light to one plane, **polariscope** (*pō-lar'ı-skōp*) an instrument for showing phenomena of polarised light.—*v.t* **polarise, -ize** (*pō'lər-ız*) to subject to polarisation: to give polarity to: to develop new qualities or meanings in (*fig.*).—*v.ı.* to acquire polarity.—*adj* **po'larised, -z-.**—*ns* **po'lariser, -z-** a device for polarising light; **polarity** (*pō-lar'ı-tı*) state of having two opposite poles: the condition of having properties different or opposite in opposite directions or at opposite ends: particular relation to this or that pole or opposed property rather than the other directedness (*fig.*): opposedness or doubleness of aspect or tendency.—*adj* **Po'laroid®** a trademark applied to photographic equipment, light-polarising materials, etc.—**polar bear** a large white bear found in the Arctic regions; **polar circle** the Arctic or the Antarctic Circle; **polar co-ordinates** co-ordinates defining a point by means of a radius vector and the angle which it makes with a fixed line through the origin; **polar equation** an equation in terms of polar co-ordinates. [L. *polāris—polus;* see **pole¹**.]

polder *pōl'dər, n.* a piece of low-lying reclaimed land the first stage in its reclamation.—Also *v t.* [Du.]

pole¹ *pōl, n.* the end of an axis, esp. of the earth, the celestial sphere, or any rotating sphere: either of the two points of a body in which the attractive or repulsive energy is concentrated, as in a magnet: an electric terminal or electrode: a fixed point (*geom.*): a point from which a pencil of rays radiates: an opposite extreme (*fig.*).—**Pole Star** Polaris, a star near the N. pole of the heavens: a guide or director.—**poles apart, asunder** widely separated, very different. [L. *polus*—Gr. *polos,* pivot, axis, firmament.]

pole² *pōl, n.* a long rounded shaft, rod, or post, usu. of wood: a single shaft to which a pair of horses may be yoked: a measure of length, 5½ yards, of area, 30¼ square yards: the position next to the inner boundary-fence in a racecourse (now usu. **pole position**).—*v.t.* to propel, push, strike, or stir with a pole: to furnish or support with poles.—*v.ı.* to use a pole.—*n.* **pō'ling** supplying, propelling, or stirring with a pole or poles: poles collectively.—**pole'-vault** an athletic event in

which the competitor uses a pole to achieve great height in jumping over a cross-bar.—Also *v.i.*—**pole'-vaulter; pole position** the most advantageous position in any competition, race, etc. (see also above).—**up the pole** (*slang*) in a predicament: drunk: crazed [O.E. *pāl*—L. *pālus,* a stake.]

Pole *pōl, n.* a native or citizen of Poland: a Polish-speaking inhabitant of Poland

pole-axe, -ax *pōl'aks, n.* a battle-axe, originally short-handled: a long-handled axe or halbert: a sailor's short-handled axe for cutting away rigging a butcher's axe with a hammer-faced back.—*v.t* to strike or fell with (or as if with) a pole-axe. [Orig *pollax,* from *poll,* head, and **axe,** confused with **pole²**.]

polecat *pōl'kat, n.* a large relative of the weasel, which emits a stink. [M.E *polcat;* poss Fr *poule,* hen, and **cat.**]

polemic *po-lem'ik, adj.* given to disputing: controversial.—*n.* a controversialist. a controversy: a controversial writing or argument.—*adj.* **polem'ical.**—*adv.* **polem'ically.**—*ns.* **polem'icist, pol'emist** one who writes polemics or engages in controversy.—*n sing.* **polem'ics** the practice or art of controversy. [Gr. *polemikos—polemos,* war.]

polenta *po-len'tə, n.* an Italian porridge of maize, barley, chestnut, or other meal [It.,—L *polenta,* peeled barley.]

police *pal-ēs', n.* a body of men and women employed to maintain order, etc.: its members collectively.—*adj.* of the police —*v.t* to control as police: to furnish with police: to guard or to put or keep in order —**police'-con'stable** a policeman of ordinary rank, **police'-dog'** a dog trained to help the police; **police'-force** a separately organised body of police; **police'-inspect'or** a superior officer of police who has charge of a department, next in rank to a superintendent, **police'man** a member of a police-force; **police'-off'ice, -stā'tion** the headquarters of the police of a district, used also as a temporary place of confinement, **police'-off'icer** an ordinary policeman; **police'-state'** a country in which secret police are employed to detect and stamp out any opposition to the government in power, **police'woman** a woman member of a police-force [Fr ,—L *politīa*—Gr *politeiā*—*politēs,* a citizen—*polis,* a city.]

policy¹ *pol'ı-sı, n.* a course of action: a system of administration guided more by interest than by principle. dexterity of management: prudence: cunning. in Scotland (sometimes in *pl.*), the pleasure-grounds around a mansion. [O.Fr. *policie* (Fr. *police*)—L *politīa*—Gr. *politeiā* (see **police**); in Scots perh influenced by L. *politus,* embellished.]

policy² *pol'ı-sı, n* a writing containing a contract of insurance.—**pol'icy-holder** one who holds a contract of insurance. [Fr *police,* policy, app —L.L *apodissa,* a receipt—Gr *apodeixis,* proof.]

poliomyelitis *pōl-ı-ō-mī-ə-lī'tıs* (or *pol-*), *n.* inflammation of the grey matter of the spinal cord: infantile paralysis.—*n.* **polio** (*pōl'ı-ō, pol'*) short for poliomyelitis: a sufferer therefrom:—*pl.* **pol'ios.**—Also *adj.* [Gr. *polios,* grey, *myelos,* marrow.]

Polish *pō'lısh, adj* of Poland, or its people or its language.—*n.* the Slavonic language of the Poles.

polish *pol'ısh, v.t.* to make smooth and glossy by rubbing: to bring to a finished state: to impart culture and refinement to.—*v.i.* to take a polish.—*n.* an act of polishing: gloss: refinement of manners: a substance applied to produce a polish —*adjs.* **pol'ishable; pol'ished** cultured, refined: accomplished.—*n.* **pol'isher.—pol'ishing-paste; pol'ishing-powder; polishing'-slate** a slaty stone used for polishing glass, marble, and metals.—**polish off** (*coll.*) to finish off:

to dispose of finally, **polish up (on)** to work at, study in order to improve. [O.Fr. *polir, polissant*—L *polire*, to polish.]

Politburo, -bureau *po-lit'bū-rō*, or *pol'*, *n* in Communist countries, the policy-making committee, effectively the most powerful organ of the Communist Party's executive [Russ. *politicheskoe*, political, *byuro*, bureau.]

polite *po-lit'*, *adj*. refined: of courteous manners.—*adv*. **polite'ly**.—*ns*. **polite'ness**; **politesse** (*pol-ė-tes'*, Fr) superficial politeness. [L *politus*, pa.p. of *polire*, to polish.]

politic *pol'i-tik*, *adj*. in accordance with good policy acting or proceeding from motives of policy: prudent: discreet: astutely contriving or intriguing.—*adj*. **polit'ical** pertaining to policy or government: pertaining to parties differing in their views of government interested or involved in politics.—*adv*. **polit'ically**.—*ns*. **politician** (*-tish'ən*) one versed in the science of government· one engaged in political life or statesmanship: one interested in party politics: a politic person: one who makes a profession or a game of politics; **politicisā'tion, -z-**.—*v.t*. **polit'icise, -ize** (*-i-siz*) to make political.—*v.t*. to play the politician: to discuss politics.—*n*. **pol'iticking** engaging in political activity, as seeking votes.—*v.t*. **pol'itick**. —*adv*. **pol'iticly**.—**politico-** noun and adjective combining form denoting politics or political, as in *politico-economic, politico-industrial*.—*adj*. **polit'ico-econom'ic** of political economy: of politics and economics.—*n*. **pol'itics** (*sing*.) the art or science of government: (*sing*.) the management of a political party: (*sung*. or *pl*.) political affairs or opinions: (*pl*.) manoeuvring and intriguing: (*pl*.) policy-making, as opposed to administration.—**political economy** the science of the production, distribution, and consumption of wealth; **political geography** that part of geography which deals with the division of the earth for purposes of government, as states, colonies, countries, and the work of man, as towns, canals, etc ; **political prisoner** one imprisoned for his or her political beliefs, activities etc. **political science** the science or study of government, as to its principles, aims, methods, etc.; **political status** the status of a political prisoner. [Gr. *politikos—politēs*, a citizen.]

politico *pō-lit'i-kō*, (*coll*.) *n*. a politician, or a person who is interested in politics (usu. *derog*.):—*pl*. **polit'ico(e)s**. [It. or Sp.]

polity *pol'i-ti*, *n*. political organisation: form of political organisation, constitution: a body of people organised under a system of government. [Gr *politeiā*.]

polka *pōl'kə, pol'*, *n*. a Bohemian dance or its tune, in 2-4 time with accent on the third quaver, invented about 1830 —**pol'ka-dot** a pattern of dots. [Perh. Czech *pùlka*, half-step; or from Pol. *polka*, a Polish woman.]

poll *pōl*, *n*. the head: the hair of the head: the blunt end of the head of a hammer, miner's pick, etc.: a head as a unit in numbering, an individual: a register, esp. of voters: a voting: an aggregate of votes: the taking of a vote: a taking of public opinion by means of questioning (also **opinion poll**): a polled animal.—*adj*. polled: cut evenly (as in **deed poll**, opp. to *indenture*).—*v.t*. to cut the hair, horns, top (of a tree), edge (of a deed) from: to receive or take the votes of: to receive, take, or cast (a vote): to receive (a stated number of votes): to question (someone) in a poll.—*v.t*. to vote.—*adj*. **polled** shorn: pollarded: deprived of horns: hornless.—*ns*. **poll'er**; **poll'ing** (*comput*.) a technique by which each of several terminals connected to the same central computer is periodically

interrogated in turn by the computer to determine whether it has a message to transmit; **poll'ster** one who carries out, or puts his faith in, a public opinion poll.—**poll'ing-booth** the place, esp. the partially-enclosed cubicle, where a voter records his vote; **poll'-money, poll'-tax** a tax of so much a head—i.e on each person alike.—**at the head of the poll** having the greatest number of votes at an election [Cf obs. Du and L.G. *polle*, top of the head.]

pollack *pol'ak*, *n*. a common fish of the cod family —Also **poll'ock**.

pollan *pol'ən*, *n* an Irish whitefish, esp that found in Lough Neagh [Perh Ir. *poll*, lake; cf **powan**.]

pollard *pol'ərd*, *n*. a tree having the whole crown cut off, leaving it to send out new branches from the top of the stem. a hornless animal of horned kind.—*adj*. pollarded: awnless: bald.—*v.t*. to make a pollard of [poll.]

pollen *pol'ən*, *n*. the fertilising powder formed in the anthers of flowers.—*v.t* **poll'inate** to convey pollen to.—*ns*. **pollinā'tion**; **poll'inator**.—*adjs*. **pollin'ic** of or pertaining to pollen, **pollinif'erous** bearing, producing, pollen.—**poll'en-basket** a hollow in a bee's hindleg in which pollen is carried; **pollen count** the amount of pollen in the atmosphere, estimated from deposits on slides exposed to the air; **poll'en-sac** a cavity in an anther in which pollen is formed. [L. *pollen, -inis*, fine flour.]

pollex *pol'eks*, *n*. the thumb or its analogue:—*pl*. **pollices** (*pol'i-sēz*).—*adj*. **poll'ical**. [L. *pollex, -icis*.]

polliwig, -wog. See **pollywog**.

pollock. Same as **pollack**.

pollster. See **poll**.

pollute *po-lōōt', -lūt'*, *v.t*. to befoul physically: to contaminate, make (any feature of the environment) offensive or harmful to human, animal, or plant life· to make unclean morally: to defile ceremonially, profane.—*adj*. defiled.—*n*. **pollu'tant** something that pollutes.—*adj*. **pollut'ed**.—*adv*. **pollut'edly**.—*ns* **pollut'edness; pollut'er; pollution** (*po-lōō'shən, -lū'*). —*adj*. **pollu'tive** causing pollution. [L. *polluēre, pollūtus—pol-*, a form of *prō* or *per, luēre*, to wash.]

Polly *pol'i*, *n*. a form of **Molly**: a parrot.

pollywog, polliwog *pol'i-wog*, **pollywig, polliwig** *-wig*, *ns*. a tadpole.—Also **porwigg'le**. [M.E. *pollwyggle* —poll, wiggle.]

polo *pō'lō*, *n*. a game like hockey on horseback—of Oriental origin: a similar aquatic (*water-polo*), bicycle (*bicycle polo*), or skating (*rink polo*) game: a jersey with a polo neck:—*pl*. **pō'los**.—*n*. **po'loist**.—**polo neck** a pullover collar fitting the neck closely and doubling over, as orig. in a polo jersey. [Balti (Tibetan dial. in Kashmir) *polo*, polo ball; Tibetan *pulu*.]

polonaise *pol-ə-nāz'*, *n*. a woman's bodice and skirt in one piece, showing an underskirt: a Polish national dance or promenade of slow movement in 3-4 time: a musical form in the same rhythm. [Fr., Polish (fem.).]

Polonia *pol-ō'ni-ə*, *n*. the mediaeval Latin name for Poland.—*n*. **polonium** (*pol-ō'ni-əm*) a radioactive element (at. numb. 84; symbol Po) discovered by Mme Curie (a Pole).

polony *po-lō'ni*, *n*. a dry sausage of partly cooked meat. [Prob. *Bologna*, in Italy; perh. *Polonia*.]

poltergeist *pōl', pol'tər-gīst*, *n*. a mysterious invisible agency asserted to throw things about: a noisy ghost [Ger. *polter*, to make a racket, *Geist*, ghost.]

poltroon *pol-trōōn'* *n*. a dastard. [Fr. *poltron*—It *poltrone—poltro*, lazy.]

poly *pol'i*, *n*. and *adj*. a coll. shortening of **polytechnic(al)** (see below):—*pl*. **pol'ys**.

poly- *pol'i-, pol-i'-*, in composition, many: several:

much: denoting a polymer, as *polyethylene* (see below): affecting more than one part (*med.*).—*adjs.* pol'yact (Gr *aktīs, -īnos,* ray), polyactī'nal (or *-akt'in-al*), polyact'ine many rayed —*n.* polyam'ide a polymeric amide, as nylon —*adj.* polyan'drous having or allowing several husbands or male mates (at a time): having a large and indefinite number of stamens or of antheridia (*bot*) —*ns.* pol'yandry (or *-an'*) the condition or practice of being polyandrous: the social usage of some peoples in certain stages of civilisation in which a woman normally has several husbands; polyan'thus (Gr *anthos,* flower) a many-flowered supposed hybrid between cowslip and primrose: also applied to certain hybrid roses:—*pl.* polyan'thuses.—*adjs.* polyatom'ic (*chem*) having many atoms, or replaceable atoms or groups: multivalent; polyax'ial (L. *axis*) having many axes or several axis cylinders, polybas'ic capable of reacting with several equivalents of an acid: of acids, having several replaceable hydrogen atoms.—polycarp'ic (Gr *karpos,* fruit) fruiting many times, or year after year; polycarp'ous polycarpic, pol'ychrome (*-krōm*; Gr. *chrōma,* colour) many-coloured.—*n.* a work of art (esp a statue) in several colours: varied colouring.—*adjs.* polychromat'ic, polychrom'ic.—*ns.* pol'ychromy the art of decorating in many colours; pol'yclinic a general clinic or hospital.—*adj.* and *n.* pol'ycotton (of) a material made from polyester and cotton.—*adjs.* polycotyle'donous with more than two cotyledons; polycyclic (*-sī'klik*; Gr *kyklos,* wheel) having many circles, rings, whorls, turns, or circuits: containing more than one ring of atoms in the molecule; polydac'tyl having more than the normal number of fingers or toes.—Also *n.*—*ns.* polydac'tylism, -dac'tyly.—*adj.* polydac'tylous.—*ns.* polyes'ter any of a range of polymerised esters, some thermoplastic, some thermosetting; polyeth'ylene, pol'ythene a generic name for certain thermoplastics, polymers of ethylene.—polygamist (*pol-ig'*).—*adj.* polyg'amous.—*adv.* polyg'amously.—*ns* polygamy (*pol-ig'a-mi*) the rule, custom, or condition of marriage to more than one person at a time: mating with more than one in the same breeding season (*zool.*): occurrence of male, female, and hermaphrodite flowers on the same or on different plants (*bot.*); pol'ygene (*-jēn*) any of a group of genes that control a single continuous character (e.g. height).—*adj.* pol'yglot (Gr. *polyglōttos—glōtta,* tongue) in, of, speaking, or writing, many languages.—*n.* one who speaks or writes many languages: a collection of versions in different languages of the same work, esp a Bible.—Also pol'yglott.—*adjs.* polyglott'al.—*n* pol'ygon (*-gon, -gan*; Gr. *gōniā,* angle) a plane figure bounded by straight lines, esp more than four: an object in the form of a polygon, esp. in the building of earthworks and fortifications.—*adj.* polyg'onal.—*n.* pol'ygraph a copying, multiplying, or tracing apparatus: a copy: an instrument which measures very small changes in body temperature, pulse rate, respiration, etc and which is often used as a lie detector —*adjs* polygraph'ic; polygynous (*-lij'* or *-lig'i-nas*) having several wives: mating with several females having several styles —*n* polygyny (*-lij'* or *-lig'*) the custom, practice, or condition of having a plurality of wives or styles: the habit of mating with more than one female —*adjs* polyhěd'ral; polyhedric (*-hěd', -hed'*).—*ns.* polyhěd'ron (or *-hed',* Gr *hedrā,* seat) a solid figure or body bounded by plane faces (esp more than six); polyhy'brid a cross between parents differing in several heritable characters.—*adj* polyhy'dric having several hydroxyl groups.—*n* pol'ymath (Gr *polymathēs*—the root of *manthanein,* to learn) one who knows many arts and

sciences.—*adj* polymath'ic.—*ns.* polym'athy much and varied learning; pol'ymer (Gr. *meros,* part; *chem.*) one of a series of substances alike in percentage composition, but differing in molecular weight, especially one of those of higher molecular weight as produced by polymerisation —*adj.* polymeric (*-mer'ik*) of, in a relation of, or manifesting, polymerism —*ns.* polym'eride a polymer; polymerisā'-tion, -z-.—*v.t.* polym'erise, -ize to combine to form a more complex molecule having the same empirical formula as the simpler ones combined· to render polymerous —*v.i.* to change into a polymer.—polym'erism.—*adj* polym'erous having many parts: having many parts in a whorl (*bot.*) —*ns.* polym'ery condition of being polymerous, pol'ymorph (Gr *polymorphos,* many-formed—*morphē,* form) any one of several forms in which the same thing may occur. an organism occurring in several forms: a substance crystallising in several systems.—*adj.* polymorph'ic.—*n.* polymorph'ism.—*adjs.* polymorph'-ous; Polynē'sian (Gr *nēsos,* an island) of *Polynesia,* its prevailing race of brown people, or their languages (a division of the Austronesian).—*n* a native of Polynesia· a member of the brown race of Polynesia.—*n.* polyneuritis (*-nûr-ī'tis*; Gr. *neuron,* a nerve) simultaneous inflammation of several nerves.—*adj.* and *n* polynō'mial multinomial —*ns.* polynō'mialism; polyp, polype (*pol'ip*; L. *polypus, -ī,* adopted, and transformed to 2nd declension, from Gr. *polypous, -podos—pous,* foot; see polypus) an individual of a colonial animal: a pedunculated tumour growing from mucus membrane:—*pl.* pol'yps, polypes (*pol'ips*), polypi (*pol'i-pī*; L); pol'ypary the common investing structure of a colony of polyps; polypep'tide a peptide in which many amino-acids are linked to form a chain; polyphagia (*-fā'ji-a*; Gr. *phagein* (aorist), to eat) bulimia: the habit of eating many different kinds of food.—*adj* polyphagous (*po-lif'a-gas*) eating many different kinds of food: eating much.—*n* polyph'agy (*-ji*) the character of being polyphagous.—*adjs.* pol'yphase having several alternating electric currents of equal frequency with uniformly spaced phase differences; polyphasic (*-fāz'ik*) going through several phases of activity followed by rest in any twenty-four hours.—*adj.* polyphonic (*-fon'ik*) many-voiced of polyphony.—*ns.* pol'yphonist a contrapuntist; polyph'ony composition of music in parts each with an independent melody of its own.—*adj* polyploid (*pol'i-ploid*; on the analogy of *haploid, diploid*) having more than twice the normal haploid number of chromosomes.—*ns.* pol'yploidy the polyploid condition, polypod (*pol'i-pod*) an animal with many feet. polypody; polypody (*pol'i-pod-i*) any fern of the genus Polypodium, esp. *P. vulgare.*—*adj.* pol'ypoid like polypus.—*ns.* polypō'sis the presence or development of polyps —*adj.* pol'ypous of the nature of a polyp.—*ns* polyprop'ylene a polymer of propylene, similar in properties to polyethylene; polyprō'todont (Gr. *prōtos,* first, *odous, odontos,* tooth) any member of the suborder of marsupials, including opossums, dasyures, etc , with many small incisors; polyptych (*pol'ip-tik*; Gr. *ptychos,* a fold) a picture, altarpiece, etc. consisting of four or more panels hinged or folding together —polypus (*pol'i-pas,* Gr. *polypous*) a pedunculated tumour growing from mucous membrane —*pl.* (L) pol'ypi; pol'yrhythm the simultaneous combination of different rhythms in a piece of music.—*adj* polyrhyth'mic.—*ns* polysaccharide (*-sak'a-rīd*) a carbohydrate of a class including starch, insulin, etc that hydrolyses into more than one molecule of simple sugars; pol'yseme (*-sēm*) a word with more than one meaning; pol'ysemy.—*adj.*

polysep'alous having the sepals separate from each other.—*ns.* **pol'ysome** a group of ribosomes linked by a molecule of ribonucleic acid and functioning as a unit in the synthesis of proteins; **pol'ysomy** a condition in which one or more extra chromosomes, are present in the cells of the body; **polysty'rene** a polymer of styrene having good mechanical properties, resistant to moisture and to chemicals.—*adjs.* **polysyllabic** (-*ab'ik*), **-al.**—*ns.* **polysyll'able** a word of many or of more than three syllables; **polysyndeton** (*pol-ι-sin'di-tən*; Gr. *syndeton*, a conjunction—*syn*, together, *deein*, to bind; *rhet.*) figurative repetition of connectives or conjunctions; **polysynthesis** (-*sin'thι-sis*).—*adjs.* **polysynthet'ic**, **-al** made up of many separate elements: combining many simple words of a sentence in one, as in the native languages of America—also called *incorporating* (*phιlol.*).—*adv.* **polysynthet'ically.**—*ns.* **polysynthet'icism** (-*i-sιzm*), **polysyn'thetism** the character of being polysynthetic.—*adj.* **polytechnic** (-*tek'nιk*; Gr. *technikos—technē*, art) of many arts or technical subjects.—*n.* a school where such subjects are taught to an advanced level.—*adj.* **polytech'nical.**—*n.* **polytetrafluor(o)eth'ylene** a plastic with non-adhesive surface properties; **polytheism** (*pol'i-thē-izm*; Gr. *theos*, a god) the doctrine of a plurality of gods; **pol'ytheist.**—*adjs.* **polytheist'ic**, **-al.**—*adv.* **polytheist'ically.**—*n.* **pol'ythene** see **polyethylene.**—*adjs.* **polytocous** (*pol-it'ə-kəs*; Gr. *tokos*, birth) producing many or several at a birth or in a clutch; **polyton'al.**—*n.* **polytonal'ity** use at the same time of two or more musical keys.—*adj.* **polyunsat'urated** (*chem.*) containing more than one carbon-carbon double bond in the molecule (**polyunsaturated fats, oils** glycerides of polyunsaturated fatty acids).—*n.* **polyur'ethane** any of a range of resins, both thermoplastic and thermosetting, used in production of foamed materials, coatings, etc —*adj.* **polyvalent** (*pol-i-vā'lənt, pol-ιv'ə-lənt*) multivalent.—*n.* **polyvi'nyl** a vinyl polymer.—Also *adj.* (**polyvinyl chloride** a vinyl plastic used as a rubber substitute for coating electric wires, cables, etc., and as a dress and furnishing fabric; abbrev. **PVC**).—*n.* **pol'ywater** a supposed form of water, said to be a polymer, with properties different from those of ordinary water. [Gr. *polys, poleia, poly*, much.]

polyact . . . to . . . Polynesian. See **poly-**.

polynia, polynya *pol-in'i-ə, -in'yə, n.* open water among sea ice, esp. Arctic. [Russ. *polyn'ya*.]

polynomial . . . to . . . polywater. See **poly-**.

pom¹ *pom*, (*coll.*) *n.* short for Pomeranian dog.

pom², **Pom** *pom*, (*Austr.*) *n.* and *adj.* short for **pommy** (q.v.).

pomace *pum'is, n.* crushed apples for cider-making, or the residue after pressing: anything crushed to pulp, esp. after oil has been expressed. [App. L.L. *pōmācium*, cider—L. *pōmum*, apple, etc.]

pomaceous. See **pome.**

pomade *pom-ād', n.* ointment for the hair—Latinised as **pomā'tum.** [Fr. *pommade*—It. *pomada, pomata*, lip-salve—L. *pōmum*, an apple.]

pomander *pom-* or *pom-an'dər, n.* a ball of perfumes, or a perforated globe or box in which it is kept or carried. [O.Fr. *pomme d'ambre*, apple of amber.]

pomatum. Same as **pomade.**

pombe *pom'be, n.* any of various Central and East African alcoholic drinks. [Swahili.]

pome *pōm, n.* a fruit constructed like an apple, the enlarged fleshy receptacle enclosing a core formed from the carpels.—*adj.* **pomaceous** (-*ā'shəs*) relating to, consisting of, or resembling, apples: of the apple family or the apple section of the rose family.—*n.* **pom'iculture.**—*adjs.* **pomif'erous** bearing apples,

pomes, or fruit generally; **pomolog'ical.**—*ns.* **pomol'ogist; pomol'ogy** the study of fruit-growing. [L. *pōmum*, a fruit, an apple.]

pomegranate *pom'i-gran-it, pom'ə-, pom', formerly* pom-, pum-gran'it, *n.* an Oriental fruit much cultivated in warm countries, with a thick leathery rind and numerous seeds with pulpy edible seed-coats: the tree bearing it. [O.Fr. *pome grenate*—L *pōmum*, an apple, *grānātum*, having many grains.]

pomelo *pum', or pom'il-ō, n.* the shaddock: the grapefruit:—*pl.* **pom'elos.**

Pomeranian *pom-i-rā'ni-ən, 'adj.* of Pomerania.—*n.* a native of Pomerania: a spitz or Pomeranian dog, a cross from the Eskimo dog, with a sharp-pointed face and an abundant white, creamy, or black coat

pomeroy. See **pome.**

Pomfret a spelling representing the older pronunciation (*pum'frιt*) of **Pontefract** *pon'tι-frakt*, a town in Yorkshire —**Pomfret-** (*pum', pom'*), **Pon'tefract-cake** a round flat liquorice sweetmeat made there. [A.Fr. *Pontfret*, L *pōns, pontis*, bridge, *fractus*, broken.]

pomiculture, etc. See **pome.**

pommel *pum'l, n.* a ball-shaped finial: a knob on a sword-hilt: the high part of a saddle-bow. a heavy-headed ramming tool: either of two handles on top of a gymnastics horse —*v t* (usu spelt **pummel**, q v) [O.Fr *pomel* (Fr *pommeau*)—L *pōmum*, an apple.]

pommy *pom'ι, (Austr)* n. an immigrant from the British Isles: a British (esp. English) person in general.—Also *adj.* [Origin obscure; perh. from **pomegranate**, alluding to the colour of the immigrants' cheeks.]

pomologist, etc See **pome.**

pomp *pomp, n.* great show or display: ceremony: ostentation: worldly vanity. consequential bearing. —*n.* **pomposity** (-*os'ι-tι*) solemn affectation of dignity: a ridiculously pompous action, expression, or person.—*adj.* **pomp'ous** solemnly consequential.— *adv.* **pomp'ously.**—*n.* **pomp'ousness.** [Fr. *pompe*—L. *pompa*—Gr *pompē*, a sending, escort, procession.]

pompadour *pom'pə-dōōr, n* a fashion of dressing women's hair by rolling it back from the forehead over a cushion —*adj* in, pertaining to, the style of hairdressing or dress described above, associated with Mme de Pompadour's time. [Marquise de *Pompadour*, 1721–64.]

pompano *pomp'ə-nō, n.* a general name for carangoid fishes, esp. American food-fishes of the genus *Trachynotus*:—*pl.* **pomp'ano(s).** [Sp *pámpano*, a fish of another family.]

pompier *pom'pι-ər,* or (Fr.) *pō-pyā, adj.* of art, conventional, traditional, uninspired. [Fr *pompier*, fireman—*pompe*, pump.]

pompom¹ *pom'pom, (coll.)* n. a machine-gun: a usu multi-barrelled anti-aircraft gun. [Imit]

pompom² *pom'pom, pom'pon, ns.* a jewelled hair ornament on a pin: a fluffy or woolly ball, tuft, or tassel worn on a shoe, hat, etc. [Fr *pompon*]

pomposity, pompous. See **pomp.**

ponce *pons, n.* a man who lives on the immoral earnings of a woman.

ponceau *pɔ̃-sō', n.* and *adj* poppy colour.—*n* a red dye:—*pl.* **ponceaux** (-*sōz'*). [Fr.]

poncho *pon'chō, n.* a South American cloak, a blanket with a hole for the head: a cyclist's waterproof cape of like form: any similar garment:—*pl* **pon'chos.** [Sp. from Araucanian.]

pond *pond, n.* a small, usually artificial lake: the stretch of water between locks in a canal: (with *cap.*) the Atlantic (*facet.*).—*n.*—**pond'-life'** animal life in ponds; **pond'-lily** a water-lily; **pond'-snail** a pond-dwelling snail, esp. Limnaea; **pond'weed** any plant of the genus Potamogeton. [M.E. *ponde*; cf **pound²**.]

ponder *pon'dər*, *v.t.* to weigh, now only in the mind: to think over: to consider.—*v.i.* to think (often with *on* and *over*).—*n.* **ponderabil'ity.**—*adjs* **pon'derable** that may be weighed: having sensible weight; **pon'deral** pertaining to weight: ascertained by weight.—*ns.* **pon'derance, pon'derancy** weight.—*v.t.* and *v i* **pon'derate** to weigh: to ponder.—*ns.* **ponderā'tion** weighing; **pon'derer.**—*adv.* **pon'deringly.**—*ns.* **pon'derment; ponderosity** (-*os'i-ti*).—*adj.* **pon'derous** heavy: weighty: massive: unwieldy: lumbering: solemnly laboured—*adv.* **pon'derously.**—*n.* **pon'derousness.** [L *ponderāre*, and *pondus, ponderis*, a weight.]

pone¹ *pōn*, (*U.S.*) *n.* maize bread: a maize loaf or cake [Algonquian *pone*.]

pone² *pō'ni, pōn*, (*cards*) *n.* the player to the right of the dealer who cuts the cards: sometimes the player to the left. [L. *pōnĕ*, imper. of *pōnĕre*, to place]

pong *pong*, *v.i.* to smell bad.—*n.* a bad smell. [Prob. Romany *pan*, to stink.]

pongee *pun-, pon-jē'*, *n.* a soft silk, made from cocoons of a wild silkworm: a fine cotton. [Perh. Chin. *punchī*, own loom.]

pongo *pong'gō*, *n* an anthropoid ape, orig. prob. the gorilla, but transferred to the orang-utan: a monkey:—*pl.* **pong'os**, (*Austr.*) **pong'oes.**—*adj.* and *n.* **pon'gid** (-*jid*). [Congo *mpongi*.]

poniard *pon'yərd*, *n.* a small dagger.—*v.t.* to stab with a poniard. [Fr. *poignard*—*poing*—L. *pugnus*, fist.]

pons *ponz*, (*anat.*) *n.* a connecting part, esp. the *pons Varolii*, a mass of fibres joining the hemispheres of the brain:—*pl.* **pon'tes.**—*adjs.* **pon'tal, pon'tic, pon'tile** relating to the pons of the brain. [L. *pōns, pontis*, a bridge.]

pons asinorum *ponz as-i-nōr'əm, -nōr', pōns as-i-nōr'ōom*, (L.) the asses' bridge (see **ass**): any severe test of a beginner.

pontal. See **pons.**

Pontefract. See **Pomfret** (former spelling).

pontes; pontic. See **pons.**

pontifex *pon'ti-feks*, *n.* in ancient Rome a member of a college of priests that had control of matters of religion, their chief being *Pontifex Maximus*: a pontiff·—*pl.* **pontifices** (-*tif'i-sēz, -kās*).—*n.* **pon'tiff** a pontifex: a high-priest: a bishop, esp. the pope or *sovereign pontiff (R.C.)*.—*adjs.* **pontif'ic, -al** of or belonging to a pontiff: splendid: pompously dogmatic.—*ns.* **pontif'ical** an office-book for bishops, **pontifical'ity.**—*adv.* **pontif'ically.**—*n.* *pl.* **pontif'icals** the dress of a priest, bishop, or pope.—*n.* **pontif'icate** the dignity of a pontiff or high-priest: the office and dignity or reign of a pope.—*v.i.* to perform the duties of a pontiff: to play the pontiff.—*v.i.* **pon'tify** to play the pontiff.—**pontifical mass** mass celebrated by a bishop while wearing his full vestments. [L. *pontifex, pontificis* (partly through Fr *pontife*), which was supposed to be from *pōns, pontis*, a bridge, *facĕre*, to make, but is possibly from an Oscan and Umbrian word *puntis*, propitiatory offering.]

pontile. See **pons.**

pontlevis *pont-lev'is, p5-lə-vē, n.* a drawbridge. [Fr.]

pontoon¹ *pon-tōōn', n.* a flat-bottomed boat, a ferryboat, barge, or lighter: such a boat, or a float, used to support a bridge: a bridge of boats: a low vessel carrying plant, materials, and men for work at sea or on rivers: the floating gate of a dock: a boat-like float of a seaplane: a float.—**pontoon'-bridge** a platform or roadway supported upon pontoons. [Fr. *ponton*—L. *pontō, -ōnis*, a punt, pontoon—*pōns*, a bridge.]

pontoon² *pon-tōōn', n.* a card game of chance. [vingt-

et-un (q.v)]

pony *pō'ni, n.* a small horse—usu one less than 14 2 hands high. £25 (*slang*). a small glass, esp. of beer.—*v.t.* and *v.i.* to pay or settle (with *up*).—**pony express** in the U S., a former method of long-distance postal delivery employing relays of horses and riders; **po'ny-tail** a woman's hair style in which the hair is gathered together at the back and hangs down like a pony's tail, **po'ny-trekking** cross-country pony-riding in groups as a pastime. [Scots *pown(e)y, pownie*, prob.—O.Fr *poulenet*, dim. of *poulain*—L L *pullānus*, a foal—L *pullus*, a young animal.]

pooch *pōōch*, (*slang*) *n.* a dog, esp a mongrel

poodle *pōōd'l, n.* a breed of pet dog which has curly hair (often clipped to a standard pattern).—**pood'le-dog** a poodle: an assiduous follower [Ger *Pudel*; L G *pudeln*, to paddle, splash.]

poof, pouf(fe), puff *pōōf, pōōf, puf*, (*slang*) *ns.* a male homosexual —Also **poof'tah, poof'ter, poufter** (-*tə(r)*). [Fr. *pouffe*, puff.]

pooh *pōō, pōō, interj.* of disdain.—*v t.* **pooh-pooh'** to make light of: to ridicule, dismiss contemptuously. [Imit.]

pool¹ *pōōl, n.* a small body of still water: a temporary or casual collection of water or other liquid: a puddle: a deep part of a stream: an underground accumulation (in the pores of sedimentary rock) of petroleum or gas. [O.E. *pōl*.]

pool² *pōōl, n.* the stakes in certain games: the collective stakes of a number of persons who combine in a betting arrangement: an organised arrangement for betting in this way: a group of persons so combining: a game, or a set of players, at quadrille, etc.: a game or contest of various kinds in which the winner receives the pool: any of various games played on a billiard-table, each player trying to pocket a number of (esp. coloured and numbered) balls· a common stock or fund: a combination of interest: a combine: an arrangement for eliminating competition: a group of people who may be called upon as required, e g., a pool of typists: (in *pl.*) football pools, betting by post on the results of a number of football games.—*v.t* to put into a common fund or stock—*v.t* to form a pool. [Fr *poule*, a hen, also stakes (possibly through an intermediate sense of plunder), but associated in English with **pool¹**.]

poop¹ *pōōp, n.* the after part of a ship: a high deck at the stern.—*v.t.* to break over the stern of: to ship over the stern —*adj.* **pooped** having a poop. [Fr *poupe*—L *puppis*, the poop.]

poop². Abbrev. for **nincompoop.**

poop³ *pōōp, v.t.* (*slang*) to make out of breath: to exhaust.—*v.i.* (*slang*) to become winded or exhausted: (often with *out*) to cease.

poor *pōōr, adj.* possessing little or nothing: without means: needy: deficient· lacking: unproductive: scanty: mere: inferior: sorry: spiritless: in sorry condition: (in modest or ironical self-depreciation) humble: unfortunate, to be pitied (esp. of the dead) —*adj.* **poor'ish.**—*adv.* **poor'ly** in a poor manner badly: inadequately. in a small way: meanly —*adj.* in ill-health.—*n.* **poor'ness.**—**poor'-box** a money-box for gifts for the poor; **Poor Clare** see **Clare**; **poor'-house** a house established at the public expense for sheltering the poor—a workhouse; **poor'-law** (often in *pl.*) the law or laws relating to the support of the poor.—Also *adj.*—**poor'-rate** a rate or tax for the support of the poor; **poor relation** any person or thing similar but inferior or subordinate to another; **poor's relief** money, food, etc. for the poor.—*adj.* **poor's spir'ited** lacking in spirit —**poor white** a member of a class of poor, improvident, and incompetent white people in the Southern States of America, South

Africa and elsewhere, called by the Negroes *poor white trash*. [O.Fr. *poure, povre* (Fr. *pauvre*)—L. *pauper*, poor.]

poorwill *pōōr'wil, n.* a Western North American night-jar (*Phalaenoptilus*), smaller than the whippoorwill [From its note.]

poove *pōōv,* (*slang*) *n.* same as **poof** (q.v.).—*n.* **poo'very.**—*adj.* **poo'vy.**

pop¹ *pop, n.* a mild explosive sound, as of drawing a cork: a shot: a pistol (*slang*): ginger-beer, champagne or other effervescing drink (*slang*): pawn, or an act of pawning (*slang*).—*v.i.* to make a pop: to shoot: to burst with a pop: to protrude: to come, go, slip, or pass, suddenly, unexpectedly, or unobtrusively: to pitch or alight.—*v.t.* to cause to make a pop or to burst with a pop: to shoot: to thrust or put suddenly or quickly: to pawn (*slang*):—*pr.p.* **popp'ing;** *pa.t.* and *pa.p.* **popped.**—*adv.* with a pop: suddenly.—*n.* **popp'er** one who pops: anything that makes a pop: a press-stud: a utensil for popping corn.—**pop'corn** maize burst open and swelled by heating: a kind of maize suitable for this.—*adj.* **pop'-eyed** having prominent or protruding eyes: open-eyed, agog (as from interest, excitement, etc.).—**pop-fastener** (*-fäs'nər*) a press-stud; **pop'-gun** a tube for shooting pellets by compressed air: a contemptible gun; **pop'over** a thin hollow cake or pudding made from batter; **popp'ing-crease** see **crease.**—*adj.* **pop'-up** (of appliances, books, etc.) having mechanisms, pages, etc. that rise or move quickly upwards.—**pop off** to make off: to die: to fall asleep; **pop the question** to make an offer of marriage. [Imit.]

pop² *pop,* (*coll.*) *adj.* popular.—*n.* currently popular music (also **pop'-music**), esp. the type characterised by a strong rhythmic element and the use of electrical amplification.—**pop art** art drawing deliberately on commonplace material of modern urbanised life; **pop'-concert** a concert at which pop-music is played; **pop'-festival; pop'-group** a (usu. small) group of musicians who play pop-music; **pop'-record; pop's singer; pop'-song.**—**top of the pops** (of a record) currently (among) the most popular in terms of sales: currently very much in favour (*fig.*).

pop³. See **poppa, poppet, popular.**

pop(p)adum *pop'ə-dəm, n.* a thin strip or circle of dough fried in oil, etc.—Many variant spellings. [Tamil, Malayalam, *poppatam.*]

pope¹ *pōp,* (often *cap.*) *n.* the bishop of Rome, head of the R.C. Church: a person wielding, assuming, or thought to assume authority like that of the pope: the ruff (fish).—*ns.* **pope'dom** the office, dignity, or jurisdiction of the pope: a pope's tenure of office; **pope'hood, pope'ship** the condition of being pope; **pope'ery** a hostile term for Roman Catholicism or whatever seems to savour of it.—*adj.* **pop'ish** (*hostile*) relating to the pope or to popery.—**pope's eye** the gland surrounded with fat in the middle of the thigh of an ox or a sheep; **pope's nose, parson's nose** the fleshy part of a (esp. cooked) bird's tail. [O.E. *pāpa* —L.L. *pāpa*—Gr. *pappas* (late Gr. *papās*), hypocoristic for father.]

pope² *pōp, n.* a parish priest in the Greek Orthodox Church. [Russ. *pop*—Late Gr. *papās;* cf preceding.]

popinjay *pop'in-jā, n.* a parrot: a figure of a parrot set up to be shot at: a fop or coxcomb. [O.Fr. *papegai;* cf. L.L. *papagallus;* Late Gr. *papagallos* (also *papagas*), a parrot; prob. Eastern; influenced by jay.]

poplar *pop'lər, n.* a genus (*Populus*) of trees of the willow family. [O.Fr. *poplier*—L. *pōpulus,* poplar-tree.]

poplin *pop'lin, n.* a corded fabric with silk warp and

worsted weft: an imitation in cotton or other material. [Perh. Fr. *popeline*—It. *papalina,* papal, from the papal town of Avignon, where it was made.]

popliteal *pop-lit'i-əl,* often *pop-lit-ē'əl, adj.* of the back of the knee.—Also **poplit'ic.** [L. *poples, -itis.*]

poppa, popper *pop'ə(r),* (*coll. U.S.*) *n.* papa.—Abbrev **pop, pops.**

poppadum. See **popadum.**

poppet *pop'it, n.* a puppet: a darling (abbrev. **pop**): a timber support used in launching a ship: a lathe-head: a valve that lifts bodily (also **popp'et-valve**): a type of bead. [An earlier form of **puppet.**]

popple *pop'l, v.i.* to flow tumblingly: to make the sound of rippling or bubbling, or of repeated shots.—*n.* a poppling movement or sound [Imit., or a freq. of **pop.**]

poppy *pop'i, n.* a cornfield plant (of several species) or its large scarlet flowers: any other species of the genus Papaver, as the opium poppy, or of kindred genera: extended to various unrelated plants.—**popp'y-head** a capsule of the poppy: a finial in wood, esp. at a pew end; **Flanders poppy** an emblem, from 1st World War, of British fallen; **Poppy Day** orig. Armistice Day (q.v.), later the Saturday nearest Armistice Day, or (later) Remembrance Sunday (q.v.), when artificial poppies are sold for war charity. [O.E. *popig*—L. *papāver,* poppy.]

poppycock *pop'i-kok,* (*slang*) *n.* balderdash. [Du. *pappekak,* lit. soft dung.]

popsy *pop'si, n.* term of endearment for a girl.—Also **pop'sy-wop'sy.** [Prob. dim. abbrev. of **poppet.**]

populace *pop'ū-ləs, n.* the common people: those not distinguished by rank, education, office, etc. [Fr.,—It. *popolazzo*—L. *pōpulus,* people.]

popular *pop'ū-lər, adj.* of the people: pleasing to, enjoying the favour of, or prevailing among, the people: liked by one's associates: suited to the understanding or the means of ordinary people: democratic.—*n.* a popular or moderate-priced concert, newspaper, etc. (abbrev. **pop;** cf. **pop²**).—*n.* **popularisa'tion, -z-.**—*v.t.* **pop'ularise, -ize** to make popular: to democratise: to present in a manner suited to ordinary people: to spread among the people.—*ns.* **pop'ulariser, -z-;** **popularity** (*-lar'i-ti*) the fact or state of being popular.—*adv.* **pop'ularly.** —*v.t.* **pop'ulate** to people: to furnish with inhabitants.—*ns.* **popula'tion** the act of populating: the number of the inhabitants: the number of inhabitants of a particular class: the plants or animals in a given area: a group of persons, objects, items, considered statistically.—**pop'ulism; pop'ulist** one who believes in the right and ability of the common people to play a major part in governing themselves: a supporter, wooer or student of the common people.—*adj.* **pop'ulous** full of people: numerously inhabited.—*adv.* **pop'ulously.**—*n.* **pop'ulousness.—popular front** an alliance of the more progressive or leftward political parties in the state. [L. *pōpulus,* the people.]

poral *pō'rəl, pö'.* See **pore¹.**

porbeagle *pör'bē-gl, n.* a North Atlantic and Mediterranean shark. [From Cornish dialect.]

porcelain *pörs'lin, pors', -lən, n.* a fine earthenware, white, thin, transparent or semi-transparent, first made in China.—*adj.* of porcelain.—*adj.* **porcell'anous** (or *pör', por'*) like porcelain—also **porcella'neous, porc'elainous, porcelaineous** (*pör-, pör-sə-lā'ni-əs*).—**porcelain cement** cement for mending china; **porcelain clay** kaolin. [O.Fr. *porcelaine* —It. *porcellana,* cowrie.]

porch *pörch, porch, n.* a building forming an enclosure or protection for a doorway: a portico or colonnade. [O.Fr. *porche*—L. *porticus*—*porta,* a gate.]

fāte; fär; mē; hûr (her); *mīne; mōte; for; mūte; mōōn; fōōt, dhen* (then); *el'ə-mənt* (element)

positron *poz'i-tron, n.* a particle differing from the electron in having a positive charge: a *positive electron.*—Also **pos'iton.**

posology *pos-ol'ə-ji, n.* the science of quantity: the science of dosage.—*adj.* **posological** (-ə-loj'i-kl). [Gr. *posos,* how much, and *logos,* a word, discourse.]

poss *adj.* A slang shortening of **possible.**

posse *pos'i, n.* power: possibility: a force or body (of constables).—**In posse** in potentiality. [L. *posse,* to be able.]

possess *poz-es', v.t.* to have or hold as owner, or as if owner: to have: to seize: to obtain: to maintain: to control: to be master of: to occupy and dominate the mind of: to put in possession (with *of,* formerly *in*): to inform, acquaint: to imbue: to impress with the notion or feeling.—*adj.* **possessed'** in possession: self-possessed: dominated by a spirit that has entered one, or other irresistible influence.—*n.* **possession** (*poz-esh'ən*) the act, state, or fact of possessing or being possessed: a thing possessed: a subject foreign territory.—*adjs.* **possess'ionary; possess'ionate** holding or allowed to hold possessions (opp. to *mendicant*).—*n.* a possessionate monk.—*adjs.* **possess'ioned; possess'ive** pertaining to or denoting possession: unwilling to share what one has with others: reluctant to allow another person to be independent of oneself, too inclined to dominate: genitive (*gram.*).—*n.* (*gram.*) a possessive adjective or pronoun: the possessive case or a word in it.—*adv.* **possess'ively.**—*ns.* **possess'iveness** extreme attachment to one's possessions: desire to dominate another emotionally; **possess'or.** —*adj.* **possess'ory.**—**what possesses him,** etc.? what malign influence causes him, etc., to act so foolishly? [O.Fr. *possesser*—L. *possidēre, possessum.*]

posset *pos'it, n.* a dietetic drink, milk curdled with e.g. wine, ale, or vinegar. [M.E. *poschot, possot.*]

possible *pos'i-bl, adj.* that may be or happen: that may be done: not contrary to the nature of things: contingent: potential: practicable: such as one may tolerate, accept, or get on with.—*n.* a possibility: that which or one who is possible: the highest possible score: (in *pl.*) necessaries (*slang*).—*ns.* **poss'ibilism** the policy of confining efforts to what is immediately possible or practicable; **poss'ibilist; possibil'ity** the state of being possible: that which is possible: a contingency: (in *pl.*) potential, promise for the future.— *adv.* **poss'ibly** perhaps: by any possible means [L. *possibilis*—*posse,* to be able.]

possum, 'possum *pos'əm, n.* a colloquial aphetic form of **opossum.**—**play possum** to feign death: to dissemble.

post¹ *pōst, n.* a stout, stiff stake or pillar of timber or other material, usually fixed in an upright position: an upright member of a frame: a winning-post, starting-post, etc.: the pin of a lock: a solid thickish stratum: a pillar of coal left in a mine as a support.— *v.t.* to stick up on a post, hence on a board, door, wall, hoarding, etc.: to announce, advertise, or denounce by placard: to placard as having failed in an examination, or failed to be classed: to announce as overdue: to affix a bill or bills to.—*n.* **post'er** a bill-sticker: a large printed bill or placard for posting.—*v.t.* to stick bills on: to advertise or publish by posters.—**poster colours** matt water-colours for designing posters and other reproduction work.—**between you and me and the (bed-, lamp-, gate-,** etc.) **post** in confidence; **first past the post** having reached the winning-post first, having won the race (see also **first-past-the-post** under **first**). [O.E. *post*—L. *postis,* a doorpost— *pōnĕre,* to place.]

post² *pōst, n.* a fixed place or station, esp. a place where a soldier or body of soldiers is stationed: a fixed place or stage on a road, for forwarding letters and change of horses: a body of men stationed at a post: a trading station: an office, employment, or appointment: a messenger carrying letters by stages or otherwise: an established system of conveying letters: a mail-coach: a despatch, delivery, or batch of letters: a post-office, or post-office letter-box: full rank as naval captain (see **post-captain** below): a bugle-call (*first* or *last*) summoning soldiers to their quarters or (*last post*) performed at a military funeral: a stake in a game.—*v.t.* to station: to entrust to the post-office for transmission: to transfer to another book, or enter in a book, or carry to an account (*book-k.*): to supply with necessary information: to appoint to a post: to send or appoint (to a ship) as full captain: to move (personnel, a military unit, etc.) to a new location: to stake.—*v.i.* to travel with posthorses or with speed: to move up and down in the saddle, in time with the horse's movements.—*adv.* with posthorses: with speed.—*n.* **post'age** money paid for conveyance by post.—*adj.* **post'al** of or pertaining to the mail-service.—*n.* and *adj.* **post'ing.**—**post'age-stamp** an embossed or printed stamp or an adhesive label to show that the postal charge has been paid: something very tiny in area (*facet.*); **postal ballot** the submission of votes by post; **postal order** an order issued by the postmaster authorising the holder to receive at a post-office payment of the sum printed on it; **postal union** an association of the chief countries of the world for international postal purposes; **postal vote** a vote submitted by post rather than placed directly into a ballot-box; **post'-bag** a mail-bag: a term used collectively for letters received; **post'-box** a letter-box; **post'-bus** a small bus used for delivering mail and for conveying passengers, esp. in rural areas; **post'-cap'tain** formerly, a naval officer posted to the rank of captain, a full captain distinguished from a commander (called captain by courtesy); **post'card** a card on which a message may be sent by post.—**post'-chaise** (popularly **po''chay, po'chay, po''chaise**) a carriage, usually four-wheeled, for two or four passengers with a postilion, used in travelling with posthorses; **Postcode, postal code** a short series of letters and numbers denoting a very small area used for sorting mail by machine.—*adj.* and *adv* **post'-free'** without charge for postage: with postage prepaid.— **post'haste** (from the old direction on letters, *haste, post, haste*) haste in travelling like that of a post.— *adj.* speedy: immediate.—*adv.* with utmost haste or speed.—**post'-horn** a postman's horn: a long straight brass horn blown by a coach guard; **post'horse** a horse kept for posting; **post'house** an inn, orig. where horses were kept for posting; **post'man** a letter-carrier; **post'mark** the mark stamped upon a letter at a post-office defacing the postage-stamp or showing the date and place of expedition or of arrival; **post'master** the manager or superintendent of a post-office: one who supplies posthorses; **Post'master-Gen'eral** formerly, the minister at the head of the post-office department; **post'mistress; post'-office** an office for receiving and transmitting letters by post, and other business: **Post Office** formerly, a department of the government which had charge of the conveyance of letters, converted in 1969 into a public corporation, the **Post Office Corporation.**—*adj* **post'-paid'** having the postage prepaid.—**post'-road** a road with stations for posthorses; **post'woman** a female letter-carrier —**general post** a game in which the players change places simultaneously; **postman's knock** a parlour kissing-game; **post-office box** a box in the post-office into which are put the letters addressed to a particular person or firm. [Fr *poste* —It *posta* and *posto*—L *pōnĕre, positum,* to place.]

post- *pōst-, pfx.* after—as *post-classical, post-*

Reformation, post-war, etc.: behind—as *post-nasal.* —*v.t* **post'date'** to date after the real time: to mark with a date (as for payment) later than the time of signing.—*adjs.* **post'-doc'toral** pertaining to academic work carried out after obtaining a doctorate, **post'-exil'ian, post-exil'ic** after the time of the Babylonian captivity of the Jews.—*ns.* **post'face** something added by way of a concluding note at the end of a written work (opp. to *preface; rare*); **post'fix** a suffix.—*adjs.* **post-gla'cial** after the glacial epoch; **post-grad'uate** belonging to study pursued after graduation.—Also *n.* —*adj.* **post-hypnot'ic** (**post-hypnotic suggestion** a suggestion made to a hypnotised subject but not acted upon till some time after he emerges from his trance). —*n.* **Post-Impress'ionism** a movement in painting that came after Impressionism, aiming at the expression of the spiritual significance of things rather than mere representation.—*n. and adj.* **Post-Impress'ionist.**—*n.* **post'lude** a concluding movement or voluntary.—*adj.* **post-merid'ian** coming after the sun has crossed the meridian: in the afternoon—*n.* **post-millenä'rian** a believer in post-millennialism.—*adj.* **post-millenn'ial.**—*n.* **post-millenn'ialism** the doctrine that the Second Advent will follow the millennium.—*adj* **post'-mor'tem** (L. *mortem*, acc. of *mors, mortis*, death) after death.—*n.* a post-mortem examination, autopsy: an after the event discussion, as at the end of a hand of cards.—*adjs.* **post-na'tal** after birth.—*adjs* **post-op'erative** relating to the period just after a surgical operation; **post'-pran'dial** (L. *prandium*, a repast) after-dinner.—*ns.* **postsce'nium** the part of the stage behind the scenery; **post'script** (L. *scriptum*, written, *pa.p.* of *scribere*, to write) a part added to a letter after the signature: an addition to a book after it is finished: a talk following, e.g. a news broadcast: additional comment or information provided.—*adj.* **post'-war'** (**post-war credit** a portion of income-tax credited to an individual for repayment after World War II). [L. *post*, after, behind.]

postage, postal. See **post²**.

poster. See **post¹·².**

poste restante *pōst res-tät*, a department of a postoffice where letters are kept till called for. [Fr., remaining post.]

posterior *pos-tē'ri-ər, adj.* coming after: later: hinder: on the side next the anus (*bot.*).—*n.* hinder parts, buttocks.—*n.* **posteriority** (*pos-tē-ri-or'i-ti*).—*adv.* **postē'riorly.**—*n.* **posterity** (*-ter'i-ti*) those coming after: succeeding generations: a race of descendants. [L. *postĕrior*, compar. of *posterus*, coming after— *post*, after.]

postern *pōst'ərn, n.* a back door or gate: a small private door: a sally-port.—*adj.* back: private. [O.Fr. *posterne, posterie*—L. *posterula*, a dim. from *posterus*, coming after.]

posthorse, posthouse. See **post²**.

posthumous *post'ū-məs, adj.* after death: born after the father's death: published after the author's or composer's death.—*adv.* **post'humously.** [L. *posthumus, postumus,* superl. of *posterus,* coming after— *post*, after; the *h* inserted from false association with *humāre*, to bury.]

postiche *pos-tēsh', adj.* superfluously and inappropriately superadded to a finished work: counterfeit or false.—*n.* a superfluous and inappropriate addition: a false hairpiece, wig. [Fr.,—It. *posticio*—L. *posticus*, hinder.]

postilion *pos-* or *pōs-til'yən, n.* one who guides posthorses, or horses in any carriage, riding on one of them.—Also **postill'ion.** [Fr. *postillon*—It *postiglione*—*posta*, post.]

postliminy *pōst-lim'i-ni, n.* the right of a returned exile, prisoner, etc., to resume his former status: the right by which persons or things taken in war are restored to their former status.—*adj.* **postlimin'iary.** [L. *postliminum*, lit. return behind the threshold— *limen, -inis,* threshold.]

postlude. See **post-.**

postmaster. See **post²**.

post meridiem *pōst mer-id'i-em, -ĕd',* (L.) after noon.

postpone *pōs(t)-pōn', v.t.* to put off to a future time: to defer: to delay: to subordinate.—*ns.* **postpone'ment; postpōn'er; postposition** (*pōst-poz-ish'ən*) placing, or position, after: a word or particle placed after a word, usu. with the force of a preposition.—*adjs.* **postposi'tional; postpositive** (*-poz'*).—*advs* **postposi'tionally, postpos'itively.** [L. *postpōnĕre, -positum—post,* after, *pōnĕre,* to put.]

postscenium, postscript. See **post-.**

postulate *pos'tū-lāt, v.t.* to claim: to take for granted, assume: to assume as a possible or legitimate operation without preliminary construction (*geom.*).—*v.i.* to make demands.—*n.* a stipulation: an assumption: a fundamental principle: a position assumed as self-evident: an operation whose possibility is assumed (*geom.*): an axiom (*geom.*): a necessary condition.— *ns.* **pos'tulancy** the state, or period, of being a postulant; **pos'tulant** a petitioner: a candidate, esp. for holy orders, or admission to a religious community; **postulā'tion.**—*adj.* **postula'tional.**—*adv.* **postulā'tionally.**—*adj.* **pos'tulatory** supplicatory: assuming or assumed as a postulate. [L. *postulāre, -ātum,* to demand—*poscĕre,* to ask urgently.]

posture *pos'chər, n.* relative disposition of parts, esp. of the body: carriage, attitude, pose.—*v.t.* to place in a particular manner.—*v.i.* to assume a posture: to pose: to attitudinise.—*adj.* **pos'tural.**—*n.* **pos'turer** one who attitudinises. [Fr.,—L. *positūra—pōnĕre, positum,* to place.]

posy *pō'zi, n.* a motto, as on a ring: a bunch of flowers [poesy.]

pot *pot, n.* a deep or deepish vessel for manufacturing, cooking or preserving purposes, or for growing plants, or holding jam, etc., or holding or pouring liquids: the contents, or capacity, of such a vessel: a chamber-pot: a pocket, or a stroke in which the object ball enters a pocket (*billiards*): a prize (*coll.*): a large sum of money: an important person (usu. *big pot*): a pot-shot: a wicker trap for lobsters, etc.: cannabis, marijuana (*slang*).—*v.t.* to put up in pots for preserving: to put in pots: to cook in a pot: to plant in a pot: to drain, as sugar: to shoot for the pot, by a pot-shot, or generally, to bag, win, secure: to pocket (as a billiard-ball).—*v.i.* to have a pot-shot:—*pr.p.* **pott'ing;** *pa.t.* and *pa.p.* **pott'ed.**—**pot'ful** as much as a pot will hold:—*pl.* **pot'fuls.**—*adj.* **pott'ed** condensed, concentrated: abridged: (of music, etc.) recorded for reproduction.—*n.* **pott'y** a chamber-pot (esp. as a child's expression or *facet.*): a similar article especially intended for children too young to use a full-size toilet.—**pot'-bar'ley** barley whose outer husk has been removed by mill-stones.—*adj.* **pot'-bellied.**—**pot'-bell'y** a protuberant belly; **pot'-boiler** a work in art or literature produced merely to secure the necessaries of life: a producer of such works; **pot'-boiling.**—*adj.* **pot'-bound** having roots compressed in a mass without room for growth.—**pot'-herb** a vegetable (esp.) for flavouring—e.g. parsley; **pot'-hole** a hole worn in rock in a stream bed by eddying detritus: a deep hole eroded in limestone: a hole worn in a road surface; **pot'-holing** the exploration of limestone potholes; **pot'hook** a hook for hanging a pot over a fire: a hooked stroke in writing; **pot'-lid** the cover of a pot; **pot'-liquor** a thin broth in which meat has been boiled; **pot'-luck** what may happen to be in the pot, or available, for a meal, without special preparation for guests (also *fig.*); **pot'-metal** an alloy of copper and lead: scraps of old iron pots, etc.; **pot'-plant** a plant grown in a pot; **pot'-roast** braised meat.—*v.t.* to braise.—**pot'-shot** a shot within easy range: a casual or random shot; **pot'-still** a still in which heat is applied directly to the pot containing the wash (opp. to *patent still*); **pott'ing-shed** a garden shed in which plants are grown in pots before being planted out in beds.—**go to pot** to go to ruin: to go to pieces (orig. in allusion to the cooking-pot, not the melting-pot); **keep the pot (a-)boiling** to procure the necessaries of life: to keep going briskly without stop. [Late O.E. *pott*.]

potable *pō'tə-bl,* adj. fit to drink. [L. *pōtābilis—pōtāre,* to drink.]

potage *po'tāzh, n.* thick soup. [Fr.]

potamic *pot-am'ik, adj.* of rivers.—*ns.* **potamologist** (*-mol'ə-jist*); **potamol'ogy** the scientific study of rivers. [Gr. *potamos,* a river.]

potash *pot'ash, n.* a powerful alkali, potassium carbonate, originally got in a crude state by lixiviating wood *ash* and evaporating in *pots*—hence **pot-ashes, pot-ash:** potassium hydroxide (*caustic potash*): sometimes the monoxide or (vaguely) other compound of potassium.—*adj.* containing, or rich in, potassium.—*adj.* **potass'ic** of potassium.—*n.* **potass'ium** an element (symbol K, for *kalium;* at. numb. 19), an alkali metal discovered by Davy in 1807 in potash.—**potassium-argon dating** estimating the date of prehistoric mineral formation from the proportion of potassium-40 to argon-40, the latter having developed from the former by radioactive decay and being trapped in the rock. [Eng. *pot, ash,* or the corresponding Du. *pot-asschen* (mod. *potasch*).]

potassium. See under **potash.**

potation *pō-tā'shən, n.* drinking: a draught: liquor.—*adj.* **pota'tory.** [L. *pōtātiō, -ōnis—pōtāre, -ātum,* to drink.]

potato *pə-* or *pō-tā'tō, n.* originally the sweet-potato, plant or tuber (see under **sweet**): now usu. a S. American plant, *Solanum tuberosum,* widely grown in temperate regions, or its tuber:—*pl.* **pota'toes.**—**pota'to-app'le** the fruit of the potato; **pota'to-blight** a destructive disease of the potato caused by the parasitic fungus *Phytophthora infestans;* **pota'to-chips'** long pieces of potato fried in fat: potato crisps (*U.S.* and elsewhere); **potato crisps** very thin, crisp, fried slices of potato, widely produced commercially.—**hot potato** (*slang*) a contentious issue: a tricky problem or assignment that one would prefer not to touch; **small potatoes** (*U.S.*) anything of no great worth. [Sp. *patata*—Haitian *batata,* sweet-potato.]

potatory. See **potation.**

poteen, potheen *po-tyēn', -chēn', -tēn', n.* Irish whiskey illicitly distilled. [Ir. *poitín,* dim. of *pota,* pot, from Eng. *pot* or Fr. *pot.*]

potent *pō'tant, adj.* powerful: mighty: strongly influential: cogent: formed of or terminating in crutch-heads (*her.*): (of a male) capable of sexual intercourse.—*n.* **po'tence** a structure shaped like a gibbet: in watchmaking, a bracket for supporting the lower pivot.—*adj.* **po'tencé** (*-sā*) in heraldry, potent.—*n.* (*her.*) a marking of the shape of T.—*ns.* **po'tency** power: potentiality: a wielder of power: in a male, the ability to have sexual intercourse; **po'tentate** one who possesses power: a prince.—*adj.* **potential** (*-ten'shl*) powerful, efficacious: latent: existing in possibility, not in reality.—*n.* anything that may be possible: a possibility: of a point in a field of force, the work done in bringing a unit (of mass, electricity, etc.) from infinity to that point: potentiality: power or resources not yet developed.—*n.* **potentiality** (*pō-ten-shi-al'i-ti*).—*adv.* **poten'tially.**—*n.* **potentiom'eter** an instrument

for measuring difference of electric potential: a rheostat.—*adj.* **potentiomet'ric.**—*adv.* **po'tently.**—**potential difference** a difference in the electrical states existing at two points, which causes a current to tend to flow between them; **potential energy** the power of doing work possessed by a body in virtue of its position. [L. *potēns, -entis,* pr.p. of *posse,* to be able—*potis,* able, *esse,* to be.]

Potentilla *pō-tən-til'ə, n.* a genus of the rose family, including silverweed and barren strawberry: (without *cap.*) any plant of this genus. [L.L., dim. of L. *potēns,* powerful, from its once esteemed medicinal virtues.]

potentiometer. See **potent.**

potheen. See **poteen.**

pother *podh'ər, n.* a choking smoke or dust: fuss: commotion: turmoil.—*v.i.* to fluster, to perplex.—*v.i.* to make a pother.

pothole, pothook. See **pot.**

potion *pō'shən, n.* a draught: a dose of liquid medicine or poison. [Fr.,—L. *pōtiō, -ōnis—pōtāre,* to drink.]

potlach *pot'lach, n.* in north-west U.S., an Indian winter festival, the occasion for emulation in extravagant gift-giving and, in one tribe, even property-destruction: any feast or gift (*coll.*). [Chinook.]

pot-pourri *pō-pōō'ri, pō', or -rē', n.* orig. mixed stew: a mixture of sweet-scented materials, chiefly dried petals: a selection of tunes strung together: a literary production composed of unconnected parts: a hotchpotch. [Fr. *pot,* pot, *pourri,* rotten.—*pa.p.* of *pourrir*—L. *putrēre,* to rot.]

potsherd *pot'shûrd, n.* a piece of broken pottery. [**pot, shard.**]

pottage *pot'ij, n.* vegetables boiled with or without meat (*arch.*): a thick soup: soup. [Fr. *potage,* food cooked in a pot, later, soup—*pot,* jug, pot.]

potter *pot'ər, n.* one who makes articles of baked clay, esp. earthenware vessels.—*n.* **pott'ery** articles of baked clay collectively, esp. earthenware vessels: a place where such goods are manufactured: the art of the potter. [**pot.**]

potter *pot'ər, v.i.* to busy oneself in a desultory way: to dawdle.—*n.* pottering: diffuse talk.—*n.* **pott'erer.**—*n.* and *adj.* **pott'ering.**—*adv.* **pott'eringly.** [Old word **pote,** to poke.]

pottle *pot'l, n.* a chip basket for strawberries. [O.Fr. *potel,* dim. of *pot,* pot.]

potto *pot'ō, n.* a member of a West African genus (*Perodicticus*) of lemurs: also applied to the kinkajou:—*pl.* **pott'os.** [Said to be a West African name.]

potty *pot'i,* (*coll.*) *adj.* trifling: petty: crazy: dotty.

potty[2]. See **pot.**

pouch *powch, n.* a poke, pocket, or bag: any pocketlike structure, as a kangaroo's marsupium, a monkey's cheek-pouch, etc.—*v.t.* to pocket: to form into a pouch: to tip.—*v.i.* to form a pouch: to be like a pouch.—*adj.* **pouched** having a pouch.—*n.* **pouch'ful:** —*pl.* **pouch'fuls.**—*adj.* **pouch'y** baggy. [O.N.Fr. *pouche* (O.Fr. *poche*); cf. **poke**[1].]

pouf, pouffe, *pōōf, n.* in dressmaking, material gathered up into a bunch: a soft ottoman or large hassock. [Fr. *pouf.*]

pouf(fe). Less common spelling of **poof.**

pouftah, poufter. Other spellings of **pooftah, poofter.**

poulard *pōō-lärd', n.* a fattened or spayed hen. [Fr. *poularde—poule,* hen.]

poulp, poulpe *pōōlp, n.* the octopus. [Fr. *poulpe*—L. *pōlypus*—Doric Gr. *pōlypos = polypous;* see **polyp.**]

poult *pōlt, n.* a chicken: the young of the common domestic fowl or of other farmyard or game bird.—*ns.* **poult'erer** one who deals in dead fowls and game; **poult'ry** domestic or farmyard fowls collectively.—

poult'ry-farm, -yard a farm, yard, where poultry are confined and bred. [Fr. *poulet*, dim. of *poule*—L.L. *pulla*, hen, fem. of L. *pullus*, young animal.]

poultice *pōl'tis*, *n.* a usu. hot, soft composition applied on a cloth to the skin, to reduce inflammation.—*v.t.* to put a poultice on. [L. *pultēs*, pl. of *puls, pultis* (Gr. *poltos*), porridge.]

pounce[1] *powns*, *n.* a hawk's claw: a sudden spring or swoop with attempt to seize.—*v.t.* to emboss by blows on the other side: to puncture (*obs.*): to ornament with small holes: to seize with the claws.—*v.i.* to make a pounce: to dart: to fix suddenly upon anything. [Derived in some way from L. *punctiō, -ōnis —pungĕre, punctum*, to prick; cf. **puncheon**[1].]

pounce[2] *powns*, *n.* fine powder for preparing a writing surface or absorbing ink: coloured powder shaken through perforations to mark a pattern on a surface beneath.—*v.t.* to prepare with pounce: to trace, transfer, or mark with pounce.—**pounce'-bag, pounce'-box** a perforated bag, box, for sprinkling pounce. [Fr. *ponce*, pumice—L. *pūmex, pūmicis*.]

pouncet-box *pown'sit-boks*, *n.* a pomander (also shortened to **poun'cet;** *Shak.*): sometimes used for **pounce-box** (see above). [Prob. for *pounced-box*, i.e. perforated box; see **pounce**[1].]

pound[1] *pownd*, *n.* a unit of weight of varying value, long used in western and central Europe, more or less answering to the Roman *libra*, whose symbol *lb.* is used for pound: in avoirdupois weight, 16 ounces avoirdupois, 7000 grains, or 0·45359237 kilogram: formerly, in troy weight, 12 ounces troy, 5760 grains, or about 373·242 grams: a unit of money, originally the value of a pound-weight of silver: formerly 20 shillings, now 100 (new) pence (the pound sterling, written £, for *libra*): the Australian (formerly), New Zealand (formerly), and Jamaican pound (written £A, £NZ, £J): the *pound scots* (at Union, 1s. 8d.): the unit of currency in certain other countries, including Israel, Egypt, Syria, Lebanon and Turkey:—*pl.* formerly **pound,** now **pounds** (except *coll.* and in compounds and certain phrases).—*ns.* **pound'age** a charge or tax made on each pound: a commission, or a share in profits, of so much a pound; **pound'al** the foot-pound-second unit of force; **pound'er** a specimen weighing a pound: in composition, anything weighing, or worth, or carrying, or one who has, receives, or pays, so many pounds.—**pound'-cake** a sweet cake containing proportionally about a pound of each chief ingredient.—*adj.* **pound'-fool'ish** neglecting the care of large sums in attending to little ones.—**pound'-weight** as much as weighs a pound: a weight of one pound used in weighing.—**pound of flesh** strict exaction of one's due in fulfilment of a bargain, etc., to the point of making the other party suffer beyond what is reasonable (see Shak., *Merch. of Ven.* I, iii. 150, IV, i. 99 ff., etc.). [O.E. *pund*— L. (*libra*) *pondō*, (pound) by weight, *pondō*, by weight—*pendĕre*, to weigh.]

pound[2] *pownd*, *n.* an enclosure in which strayed animals are confined, or distrained goods kept: any confined place: a level part of a canal between two locks: the last compartment of a pound-net.—*v.t.* to put in a pound: to enclose, confine.—**pound'-net** an arrangement of nets for trapping fish. [O.E. *pund* (in compounds), enclosure.]

pound[3] *pownd*, *v.t.* to beat into fine pieces: to bruise: to bray with a pestle: to thump.—*v.i.* to beat: to thump: to beat the ground: to make one's way heavily: to struggle on.—*n.* the act or sound of pounding.—*n.* **pound'er.** [O.E. *pūnian*, to beat; *-d* excrescent, as in **sound**[3], **bound**[4].]

pour *pōr, pôr*, *v.t.* to cause or allow to flow in a stream: to send forth or emit in a stream or like a stream.—

v.i. to stream: to rain heavily: to pour out tea, coffee, etc.: (of a vessel) to allow liquid contents to run out duly.—*n.* a pouring: an amount poured at a time.—*n.* **pour'er.**—*n.* and *adj.* **pour'ing.**—**it never rains but it pours** things never happen singly; **pouring wet** raining hard; **pour oil on troubled waters** to soothe or calm a person or situation. [M.E. *pouren.*]

pourboire *pŏŏr-bwàr'*, *n.* a tip. [Fr.,—*pour*, for, *boire*, to drink.]

pourpoint *pŏŏr'point*, *n.* a mediaeval quilted doublet. [Fr.]

pousse-café *pŏŏs-ka-fâ*, *n.* a cordial, liqueur, or combination of several in layers, served after coffee. [Fr., push-coffee.]

poussette *pŏŏs-et'*, *n.* a figure in country-dancing in which couples hold both hands and move up or down the set, changing places with the next couple.—*v.i.* to perform a poussette. [Fr., dim. of *pousse*, push.]

pousowdie. See **powsowdy.**

poussin *pŏŏ-sē'*, *n.* a chicken reared for eating. [Fr.]

pout[1] *powt*, *v.i.* to push out the lips, in sullen displeasure or otherwise: to protrude.—*v.t.* to protrude. —*n.* a protrusion, esp. of the lips.—*ns.* **pout'er** one who pouts: a variety of pigeon having its breast inflated; **pout'ing.**—*adv.* **pout'ingly.** [M.E. *powte.*]

pout[2] *powt*, *n.* a fish, the bib—also **whit'ing-pout.**—*n.* **pout'ing** the whiting-pout. [O.E. *(æle-) pūte*, (eel-) pout—perh conn. with foregoing with reference to the bib's inflatable membrane on the head.]

poverty *pov'ar-ti*, *n.* the state of being poor: necessity: want: lack: deficiency.—*adj.* **pov'erty-stricken** suffering from poverty.—**poverty trap** a poor financial state from which there is no escape as any increase in income would result in a diminution or withdrawal of low-income government benefits. [O.Fr. *poverte* (Fr. *pauvreté*)—L. *paupertàs, -àtis—pauper*, poor.]

powan *pow'an, pô'an*, *n.* a species of whitefish (Coregonus) found in Loch Lomond and Loch Eck. [Scots form of **pollan.**]

powder *pow'dar*, *n.* dust: any solid in fine particles: gunpowder: hair-powder: face-powder: a medicine in the form of powder.—*v.t.* to reduce to powder: to sprinkle, daub, or cover with powder: to salt by sprinkling: to sprinkle.—*v.i.* to crumble into powder: to use powder for the hair or face.—*adjs.* **pow'dered** reduced to powder e.g., of food, through dehydration and crushing: sprinkled, or daubed, or dusted with powder: salted; **pow'dery** of the nature of powder: covered with powder: dusty: friable.—**pow'der-box** box for face-, hair-powder, etc.; **pow'der-flask, pow'der-horn** a flask (originally a horn) for carrying gunpowder; **pow'der-mag'azine** a place where gunpowder is stored; **pow'der-monk'ey** a boy carrying powder to the gunners on a ship-of-war; **pow'der-puff** a soft, downy ball, etc. for dusting powder on the skin; **pow'der-room** a ship's powder-magazine: a room for powdering the hair (also **pow'dering-room**): a ladies cloakroom.—**keep one's powder dry** to keep one's energies ready for action, play a waiting game: to observe all practical precautions. [O.Fr. *poudre* —L *pulvis, pulveris*, dust.]

power *pow'ar, powr*, *n.* ability to do anything—physical, mental, spiritual, legal, etc.: capacity for producing an effect: strength: energy: faculty of the mind: moving force of anything: authority: rule: influence: control: governing office: permission to act: potentiality: a wielder of authority, strong influence, or rule: that in which such authority or influence resides: a spiritual agent: a being of the sixth order of the celestial hierarchy: a state influential in international affairs: a great deal or great many (now *dial.* or *coll.*): the rate at which a system absorbs energy from, or passes energy into, another system, esp. the rate of doing mechanical work, measured in watts or other unit of work done per unit of time (*mech., physics*, etc.): an instrument serving as means of applying energy (see **mechanical**): the product of a number of equal factors, generalised to include negative and fractional numbers (*math.*): the potency of a point with respect to a circle (*geom.*): magnifying strength, or a lens possessing it (*opt.*).—*adj.* concerned with power: worked, or assisted in working, by mechanical power: involving a high degree of physical strength and skill.—*v.t.* to equip with mechanical energy.—*v.i.* and *v.t.* (*slang*) to move, or propel, with great force, energy or speed.—*adjs.* **pow'ered; pow'erful** having great power: mighty: forcible: efficacious: intense: impressive, esp. in a disagreeable way: very great (*coll.*).—*adv.* (*coll.*) exceedingly.—*adv.* **pow'erfully.**—*n.* **pow'erfulness.**—*adj.* **pow'erless** without power: weak: impotent: helpless.—*adv.* **pow'erlessly.**—*n.* **pow'erlessness.**—*adj.* **pow'er-assist'ed** helped by, using, mechanical power —**power block** a politically important and powerful group or body; **pow'erboat** a boat propelled by a motor, a motorboat; **power cut** an interruption of, or diminution in, the electrical supply in a particular area; **pow'er-dive** a usu. steep dive of an aeroplane, made faster by use of engine(s).—Also *v.i., v.t.*— **pow'er-diving.**—*adj.* **pow'er-driven** worked by mechanical power.—**power'-house** (also *fig.*), **-station** a place where mechanical power (esp. electric) is generated; **pow'er-drill, -lathe, -loom, -press** a drill, lathe, loom, press, worked by mechanical power, as water, steam, electricity; **power pack** a device for adjusting an electric current to the voltages required by a particular piece of electronic equipment; **pow'er-plant** an industrial plant for generating power: the assemblage of parts generating motive power in a motor-car, aeroplane, etc.; **pow'er-point** a point at which an appliance may be connected to the electrical system; **pow'er-politics** international politics in which the course taken by states depends upon their knowledge that they can back their decisions with force or other compulsive action; **power steering** a type of steering system in a vehicle, in which the rotating force exerted on the steering wheel is supplemented by engine power.—**in one's power** at one's mercy: within the limits of what one can do; **in power** in office; **the powers that be** the existing ruling authorities (from Rom. xiii. 1). [O.Fr. *poer* (Fr. *pouvoir*)—L.L. *potēre* (for L. *posse*), to be able.]

powwow *pow'wow, n.* a conference.—*v.i.* **powwow'** to hold a powwow: to confer. [Algonquian *powwaw, powah.*]

pox *poks, n. (pl.* of **pock**) pustules: an eruptive disease, esp. smallpox or syphilis (as *sing.*): sheep-pox.—*v.t.* to infect with pox.—*interj.* plague.

poy-bird. See poe-bird.

pozzolana *pot-sō-lä'nə,* **pozzuolana** *-swō-, ns.* a volcanic dust first found at *Pozzuoli,* near Naples, which forms with mortar a cement that will set in air or water.

praam. Same as pram¹.

practic *prak'tik, n.* (esp. in *pl.*) practices, doings: legal usage or case-law (esp. *Scots law*).—*n.* **practicabil'ity.**—*adj.* **prac'ticable** that may be practised, carried out, accomplished, used, or followed: passable, as a road: (of a stage window, light-switch, etc.) functioning.—*n.* **prac'ticableness.**—*adv.* **prac'-ticably.**—*adj.* **prac'tical,** in relating to, concerned with, well adapted to, or inclining to look to, actual practice, actual conditions, results, or utility: practised: practising, actually engaged in doing something: efficient in action: workable: virtual: (of a piece of stage equipment, esp. electric lights, etc.)

that can be operated on stage (*theat.*).—*n.* a practical examination.—*ns.* **prac'ticalism** devotion to what is practical; **prac'ticalist; practical'ity** practicalness: a practical matter or feature, aspect, of an affair.—*adv.* **prac'tically** in a practical way: by a practical method: to all intents and purposes: very nearly, as good as.—*ns.* **prac'ticalness; prac'tice** (*-tis*) action, performance: actual doing: proceeding: habitual action: custom: legal procedure: repeated performance as a means of acquiring skill, esp. in playing a musical instrument: form so acquired: the exercise of a profession: a professional man's business, as a field of activity or a property: scheming: plotting: trickery: working upon the feelings; **practician** (*-tish'ən*) a practiser or practitioner: a practical man.—*v.t.* **practise** (*prak'tis,* formerly *-tiz'; U.S.* **practice**) to put into practice: to perform: to carry out: to do habitually: to exercise, as a profession: to exercise oneself in, or on, or in the performance of, in order to acquire or maintain skill: to train by practice: to put to use.—*v.i.* to act habitually: to be in practice (esp. medical or legal): to exercise oneself in any art, esp. instrumental music: to proceed, esp. to seek to injure, by underhand means: to tamper, work (with *upon, on*): to scheme: to have dealings: to use artifices: to work by artifice (on the feelings).—*adj.* **prac'tised** skilled through practice.—*n.* **prac'tiser.**—*adj.* **prac'tising** actually engaged, e.g. in professional employment: holding the beliefs, following the practices, demanded by a particular religion, etc.—*n.* **practitioner** (*-tish'ən-ər*; irreg. from *practician*) one who is in practice, esp. in medicine: one who practises.—**practical joke** a joke that consists in action, not words, usually an annoying trick.—**general practitioner** one who practises medicine and surgery without specialising. [Obs. Fr. *practique*—L. *practicus*—Gr. *prāktikos,* fit for action—*prāssein,* to do.]

prae-; praecoces, praecocial. See pre-; precocious.

praenomen *prē-nō'mən, prī-nō'men, n.* the name prefixed to the family name in ancient Rome, as *Gaius* in Gaius Julius Caesar: the generic name of a plant or animal. [L. *praenōmen—nōmen,* name.]

praesidium. See presidial.

praeter-. See preter-.

praetor *prē'tər, -tōr, prī'tor, n.* a magistrate of ancient Rome next in rank to the consuls.—*adj.* **praetorian** (*-tō', tō').*—*n.* a former praetor or man of like rank: a member of the emperor's bodyguard.—**praetorian gate** the gate of a Roman camp in front of the general's tent, and nearest to the enemy; **praetorian guard** the bodyguard of the Roman Emperor. [L. *praetor,* for *praeitor—prae,* in front of, and *īre, itum,* to go.]

pragmatic *prag-mat'ik, adj.* relating to affairs of state: relating to, or of the nature of, pragmatism: having concern more for matters of fact than for theories: pragmatical.—*adj.* **pragmat'ical** active: practical: matter of fact: interfering with the affairs of others: officious: meddlesome: self-important: opinionative: pragmatic.—*n.* **pragmatical'ity.**—*adv.* **pragmat'ically.**—*n.* **pragmat'icalness.**—*v.t.* **prag'matise, -ize** to interpret or represent as real: to rationalise.—*ns.* **prag'matiser, -z-; prag'matism** pragmatical quality: matter-of-factness: concern for the practicable rather than for theories and ideals: a treatment of history with an eye to cause and effect and practical lessons: humanism or practicalism, a philosophy, or philosophic method, that makes practical consequences the test of truth (*philos.*); **prag'matist** a pragmatic person: one who advocates the practicable rather than the ideal course: a believer in pragmatism. [Gr. *prāgma, -atos,* deed—*prāssein,* to do.]

prahu *prä'(h)ōō.* Same as **prau.**

prairie *prā'ri*, *n.* a treeless plain, flat or rolling, naturally grass-covered.—**prai'rie-chick'en**, **-hen** an American genus of grouse: the sharp-tailed grouse of the western United States; **prai'rie-dog** a gregarious burrowing and barking North American marmot (*Cynomys*); **prai'rie-schoon'er** an emigrants' long covered wagon; **prai'rie-wolf** the coyote. [Fr.,—L.L. *prātaria*—L. *prātum*, a meadow.]

praise *prāz*, *v.t.* to speak highly of: to commend: to extol: to glorify, as in worship.—*n.* commendation: glorifying: the musical part of worship: that for which praise is due.—*n.* and *adj.* **prais'ing.**—*advs.* **prais'-ingly; praise'worthily.**—*n.* **praise'worthiness.**—*adj.* **praise'worthy** worthy of praise: commendable. [O.Fr. *preiser*—L.L. *preciāre* for L. *pretiāre*, to prize—*pretium*, price.]

Prakrit *prā'krit*, *n.* a collective name for languages or dialects in an immediate relation to Sanskrit.—*adj.* **Prakrit'ic.** [Sans. *prākṛta*, the natural—*prakṛti*, nature.]

praline *prā'lēn*, *n.* an almond or nut kernel with a brown coating of sugar, or a similar confection made with crushed nuts. [Fr. *praline*, from Marshal Duplessis-*Praslin*, whose cook invented it.]

pram¹, praam *prām*, *n.* a flat-bottomed Dutch or Baltic lighter: a flat-bottomed dinghy with squared-off bow: a barge fitted as a floating battery. [Du. *praam.*]

pram² *pram*, *n.* a shortening (formerly *coll.*) of **perambulator**: a milkman's hand-cart.

prance *prāns*, *v.i.* to bound from the hind legs: to go with a capering or dancing movement: to move with exaggerated action and ostentation: to swagger: to ride a prancing horse.—*v.t.* to cause to prance.—*n.* an act of prancing: swagger.—*n.* **pranc'er.**—*adj.* and *n.* **pranc'ing.**—*adv.* **pranc'ingly.** [M.E. *praunce*.]

prandial *pran'di-əl*, (esp. *facet.*) *adj.* relating to dinner. [L. *prandium*, a morning or midday meal.]

prang *prang*, (*slang*) *n.* a crash: a bombing-attack.—*v.t.* to crash or smash: to bomb heavily: to crash into (e.g. another car).

prank¹ *prangk*, *n.* a trick: a practical joke: a frolic.—*n.* **prank'ster.**

prank² *prangk*, (*arch.*) *v.t.* to dress or adorn showily. [Akin to Du. *pronken*, Ger. *prunken*, to show off; cf. **prink**.]

praseodymium *prāz-i-ō-dim'i-əm*, *n.* aɴ element (symbol Pr; at. numb. 59), a metal with green salts, separated from the once-supposed element didymium. [Gr. *prasios*, leek-green—*prason*, leek, and *didymium*.]

prat¹ *prat*, (*slang*) *n.* the buttocks.—*n.* **prat'fall** a fall landing on the prat: a humiliating blunder or experience.

prat² *prat*, (*slang*) *n.* used abusively, a fool, an ineffectual person. [Poss. conn. with **prat¹**.]

prate *prāt*, *v.i.* to talk foolishly: to talk boastfully or insolently: to tattle: to be loquacious.—*v.t.* to utter pratingly: to blab.—*n.* **pra'ter.**—*n.* and *adj.* **pra'ting.**—*adv.* **pra'tingly.** [Cf. L.G. *praten*, Dan. *prate*, Du. *praaten*.]

pratie, praty *prā'ti*, *n.* an Anglo-Irish form of **potato.**

pratincole *prat'ing-kōl*, *n.* a bird akin to the plovers, with swallow-like wings and tail. [L. *prātum*, meadow, *incola*, an inhabitant.]

pratique *prat'ik*, *-ēk'*, *n.* permission to hold intercourse or to trade after quarantine or on showing a clean bill of health. [Fr.]

prattle *prat'l*, *v.i.* to talk much and idly: to utter child's talk.—*v.t.* to utter in a prattling way.—*n.* empty talk.

—*n.* **pratt'ler.** [Dim. and freq. of **prate**.]

prau *prä'ōō*, **prow, prahu** *prä'(h)ōō*, **proa** *prō'ə*, *ns.* a Malay sailing- or rowing-boat, esp. a fast sailing-vessel with both ends alike, and a flat side with an outrigger kept to leeward. [Malay *prāū.*]

prawn *prön*, *n.* a small edible shrimp-like crustacean.—*v.i.* to fish for prawns. [M.E. *prayne*, *prane.*]

praxis *praks'is*, *n.* practice: an example or a collection of examples for exercise: a model or example. [Gr. *prāxis*—*prāssein*, to do.]

pray *prā*, *v.i.* to ask earnestly (often with *for*): to entreat: to express one's desires to, or commune with, a god or some spiritual power.—*v.t.* to ask earnestly and reverently, as in worship: to supplicate: to present as a prayer: to render, get, put, or cause to be, by praying:—*pa.t.* and *pa.p.* **prayed.**—*interj.* (often *iron.*) I ask you, may I ask.—*ns.* **pray'er** one who prays: (*prār*, *prā'ər*) the act of praying: entreaty: a petition to, or communing with, a god or spiritual power: the wish put forward or the words used: a form used or intended for use in praying: public worship: (in *pl.*) (a time set aside for) worship in a family, school, etc.: a petition to a public body, e.g. a legislature: in Parliament, a motion addressed to the Crown asking for the annulment of an order or regulation: the thing prayed for.—*adj.* **prayerful** (*prār'fŏōl*) given to prayer: in a spirit or mental attitude of prayer.—*adv.* **prayer'fully.**—*n.* **prayer'fulness.**—*adj.* **prayer'less** without or not using prayer.—*n.* and *adj.* **pray'ing.**—(Position of accent on following compounds depends on whether one says **prār'** or **prā'ər**) **prayer'-bead** one of the beads on a rosary: a jequirity bean; **prayer'-book** a book containing prayers or forms of devotion, esp. the Book of Common Prayer of the Church of England; **prayer'-meeting** a shorter and simpler form of public religious service, in which laymen often take part; **prayer'-rug** a small carpet on which a Muslim kneels at prayer; **prayer'-wheel** a drum wrapped with strips of paper inscribed with prayers deemed by Buddhists of Tibet to be proffered when the drum is turned; **praying insect** the mantis. [O.Fr. *preier* (Fr. *prier*), to pray, and O.Fr. *preiere*, prayer (—L.L. *precāria*)—L. *precārī*—*prex*, *precis*, a prayer.]

pre- (as living prefix), **prae-** (L. spelling more common formerly) *prē*, *prī-*, *pfx.* (1) in front, in front of, the anterior part of, as *predentate*, *presternum*; (2) before in time, beforehand, in advance, as *prehistoric*, *pre-war*, *prewarn*; (3) surpassingly, to the highest degree, as *pre-eminent*.—used without hyphen as *prep.* (*coll.*) before, prior to. [L. *prae*, in front of.]

preach *prēch*, *v.i.* to deliver a sermon: to discourse earnestly: to give advice in an offensive, tedious, or obtrusive manner.—*v.t.* to set forth in religious discourses: to deliver, as a sermon: to proclaim or teach publicly: to render or put by preaching.—*n.* (*coll.*) a sermon.—*ns.* **preach'er** one who discourses publicly on religious matter: a minister or clergyman: an assiduous inculcator or advocate.—*v.i.* **preach'ify** to preach tediously: to sermonise: to weary with lengthy advice.—*adj.* **preach'y** given to tedious moralising: savouring of preaching. [Fr. *prêcher*—L. *praedicāre*, *-ātum*, to proclaim.]

preadmonish *prē-ad-mon'ish*, *v.t.* to forewarn.—*n.* **preadmoni'tion.** [Pfx. **pre-** (2).]

preamble *prē-am'bl*, *n.* preface: introduction, esp. that of an Act of Parliament, giving its reasons and purpose: a prelude.—Also *v.t.* and *v.i.* [Fr. *préambule*—L. *prae*, *ambulāre*, to go.]

preaudience *prē-ö'di-əns*, *n.* right to be heard before

preadapta'tion *n.* pre- (2).　　**preappoint'** *v.t.* pre- (2).　　**prearrange'ment** *n.* pre- (2).
preannounce' *v.t.* pre- (2)　　**prearrange'** *v.t.* pre- (2).

fāte; fär; mē; hûr (her); *mīne; mōte; fòr; mūte; mōōn; fŏōt; dhen* (then), *el'ə-mənt* (element) another: precedence at the bar among lawyers. [Pfx. **pre-** (2).]

prebend *preb'ənd, n.* the share of the revenues of a cathedral or collegiate church allowed to a clergyman who officiates in it at stated times.—*adj.* **prebendal** (*pri-bend'l*).—*n.* **preb'endary** a resident clergyman who enjoys a prebend, a canon: the honorary holder of a disendowed prebendal stall. [L.L. *praebenda*, an allowance—L. *praebēre*, to allow, grant.]

Pre-Cambrian *prē-kam'bri-ən*, (*geol.*) *adj.* and *n.* (of or relating to) the earliest geological era: Archaean. [Pfx. **pre-** (2).]

pre-cancel *prē-kan'səl, v.t.* to cancel a postage stamp (e.g. by applying a postmark) before use.—Also *n.* [Pfx. **pre-** (2).]

pre-cancerous *prē-kan'sər-əs, adj.* that may become cancerous. [Pfx. **pre-** (2).]

precarious *pri-kā'ri-əs, adj.* depending upon the will of another: depending on chance: insecure: uncertain: dangerous, risky.—*adv.* **preca'riously.**—*n.* **preca'riousness.** [L. *precārius*—*precārī*, to pray.]

precast *prē'käst', adj.* of concrete blocks, etc., cast before putting in position. [Pfx. **pre-** (2).]

precatory *prek'ə-tə-ri, adj.* of the nature of, or expressing, a wish, request, or recommendation.—*adj.* **prec'ative** supplicatory: expressing entreaty (*gram.*). [L. *precārī*, pray.]

precaution *pri-kö'shən, n.* a caution or care beforehand: a measure taken beforehand.—*adjs.* **precau'tional, precau'tionary, precau'tious.** [Pfx. **pre-** (2).]

precede *prē-sēd', v.t.* to go before in position, time, rank, or importance: to cause to be preceded.—*v.i.* to be before in time or place.—*ns.* **precedence** (*pres'i-dəns; prēs'*, also *pri-sē'dəns*) the act of going before in time: the right of going before: priority: the state of being before in rank: the place of honour: the foremost place in ceremony—also **precedency** (*pres'i-, prēs'i-, pri-sē'dən-si*); **precedent** (*pres'i-dənt*; also *prēs'*) that which precedes: a past instance that may serve as an example: a previous judicial decision or proceeding.—*adj.* (*pri-sē'dənt*) preceding.—*adjs.* **precedented** (*pres'*; also *prēs'*) having a precedent: warranted by an example; **precedential** (*pres-i-den'shl*) of the nature of a precedent; **prec'eding** going before in time, rank, etc.: antecedent: previous: foregoing: immediately before.—**take precedence of,** over to precede in ceremonial order. [Fr. *précéder*—L. *praecēdēre, -cēssum,—prae, cēdēre,* go.]

precentor *pri-* or *prē-sen'tər, n.* the leader of the singing of a church choir or congregation: in some English cathedrals, a member of the chapter who deputes this duty to a succentor:—*fem.* **precen'tress, precen'trix.**—*n.* **precen'torship.** [L.L. *praecentor, -ōris*—L. *prae, canēre,* to sing.]

precept *prē'sept, n.* a rule of action: a commandment: a principle, or maxim: the written warrant of a magistrate (*law*): a mandate: an order to levy money under a rate.—*adj.* **precep'tive** containing or giving precepts: directing in moral conduct: didactic.—*n.* **precep'tor** one who delivers precepts: a teacher: an instructor: the head of a school:—*fem.* **precep'tress.**—*adjs.* **precepto'rial** (*prē-*); **precep'tory** (*pri-*) giving precepts. [L. *praeceptum,* pa.p. neut. of *praecipĕre,* to take beforehand—*prae, capĕre,* to take.]

precession *pri-sesh'ən, n.* the act of going before: a moving forward: the precession of the equinoxes (see below): the analogous phenomenon in spinning-tops and the like, whereby the wobble of the spinning object causes its axis of rotation to become cone-shaped.—*adj.* **precess'ional.—precession of the equinoxes** a slow westward motion of the equinoctial points along the ecliptic, caused by the greater attraction of the sun and moon on the excess of matter at the equator, such that the times at which the sun crosses the equator come at shorter intervals than they would otherwise do. [L.L. *praecessiō, -ōnis—praecēdēre;* see **precede.**]

precinct *prē'singkt, n.* a space, esp. an enclosed space, around a building or other object (also in *pl.*): a district or division within certain boundaries: a district of jurisdiction or authority: a division for police or electoral purposes (*U.S.*): (in *pl.*) environs.—**pedestrian precinct** a traffic-free area of a town, esp. a shopping centre; **shopping precinct** a shopping centre, esp. if traffic-free. [L.L. *praecinctum,* pa.p. neut. of *praecingĕre—prae, cingĕre* to gird.]

precious *presh'əs, adj.* of great price or worth: cherished: very highly esteemed: often used in irony for arrant, worthless, 'fine': affecting an over-refined choiceness.—*adv.* extremely, confoundedly (*coll.*).—*n.* **preciosity** (*presh-i-os'i-ti,* or *pres-*) fastidious over-refinement.—*adv.* **prec'iously.**—*n.* **prec'iousness.—precious metals** gold, silver (sometimes mercury, platinum, and others of high price); **precious stone** a stone of value and beauty for ornamentation: a gem or jewel. [O.Fr. *precios* (Fr. *précieux*)—L. *pretiōsus—pretium,* price.]

precipice *pres'i-pis, n.* a high vertical or nearly vertical cliff.—*adj.* **precip'itable** (*chem.*) that may be precipitated.—*ns.* **precip'itance, precip'itancy** the quality of being precipitate: a headlong fall: headlong haste or rashness: an impulsively hasty action.—*adj.* **precip'itant** falling headlong: rushing down with too great velocity: impulsively hasty.—*n.* anything that brings down a precipitate.—*adv.* **precip'itantly.**—*v.t.* **precip'itate** to hurl headlong: to force into hasty action: to bring on suddenly or prematurely: to bring down from a state of solution or suspension.—*v.i.* to rush in haste: to come out of solution or suspension: to condense and fall, as rain, hail, etc.—*adj.* (*-āt* or *-it*) falling, hurled, or rushing headlong: sudden and hasty: without deliberation: rash.—*n.* (*-āt, -it*) a substance separated from solution or suspension, usually falling to the bottom: moisture deposited as rain, snow, etc.—*adv.* **precip'itately.**—*n.* **precipita'tion** the act of precipitating: a headlong fall or rush: an impulsive action: great hurry: rash haste: impulsiveness: rain, hail, and snow (sometimes also dew): the amount of rainfall, etc.: the formation or coming down of a precipitate: separation of suspended matter: a precipitate.—*adj.* **precip'itative.**—*ns.* **precip'itator** one who precipitates: a precipitating agent: an apparatus or tank for precipitation.—*adj.* **precip'itous** like a precipice: sheer.—*adv.* **precip'itously.**—*n.* **precip'itousness.** [L. *praeceps, praecipitis,* headlong, *praecipitium,* precipice, *praecipitāre, -ātum,* to precipitate—*prae, caput, -itis,* head.]

précis *prā'sē, n.* an abstract:—*pl.* **précis** (*-sēz*).—*v.t.* to make a précis of:—*pr.p.* **précising** (*prā'sē-ing*); *pa.t.* and *pa.p.* **précised** (*prā'sēd*). [Fr.]

precise *pri-sīs', adj.* definite: exact: accurate: free from vagueness: very, identical: scrupulously exact: scrupulous in religion: puritanical: over-exact: prim: formal.—*adv.* **precise'ly.**—*ns.* **precise'ness; precisian** (*pri-sizh'ən*) an over-precise person: a formalist; **prec'isianism; precis'ianist** a precisian; **prec'ision** the quality of being precise: exactness: minute accuracy.—*adj.* for work of, carried out with, accuracy.—*n.* **precis'ionist** one who insists on precision: a purist.

prechris'tian *adj.* pre- (2). **preclass'ical** *adj.* pre- (2).

[Fr. *précis*, *-e*—L. *praecīsus*, pa.p. of *praecīdĕre*— *prae, caedĕre*, to cut.]

preclude *pri-klōōd'*, *v.t.* to close beforehand: to shut out beforehand: to hinder by anticipation: to prevent. —*n.* **preclusion** (*pri-klōō'zhən*).—*adj.* **preclusive** (*-klōō'siv*) tending to preclude: hindering beforehand. [L. *praeclūdĕre*, *-clūsum*—*claudĕre*, to shut.]

precocious *pri-kō'shəs*, *adj.* early in reaching some stage of development, as flowering, fruiting, ripening, mental maturity: precocial: flowering before leaves appear: showing early development.— *n.pl.* **praecoces** (*prē'kō-sēz*, *prī'ko-kās*) praecocial birds (opp. to *altrices*).—*adj.* **precocial, praecocial** (*-kō'shl*, *-shyəl*) hatched with complete covering of down, able to leave the nest at once and seek food: premature: forward.—*adv.* **precō'ciously**.—*ns.* **precō'ciousness, precocity** (*pri-kos'i-ti*) the state or quality of being precocious: early development or too early ripeness of the mind. [L. *praecox*, *-ōcis*—*prae, coquĕre*, to cook, ripen.]

precognition *prē-kog-nish'ən*, *n.* foreknowledge: a preliminary examination of witnesses as to whether there is ground for prosecution (*Scots law*): evidence so obtained.—*adj.* **precog'nitive** (*pri-*). [Pfx. pre- (2).]

preconceive *prē-kən-sēv'*, *v.t.* to conceive or form a notion of, before having actual knowledge.—*ns.* **preconceit'** a preconceived notion; **preconcep'tion** the act of preconceiving: a previous opinion formed without actual knowledge. [Pfx. pre- (2).]

precondition *prē-kən-dish'ən*, *n.* a condition that must be satisfied beforehand.—*v.t.* to prepare beforehand. [Pfx. pre- (2).]

preconise, -ize *prē'kən-īz*, *v.t.* to proclaim: to summon publicly: (of the pope) to proclaim and ratify the election of as bishop.—*n.* **preconisation, -z-** (*prē-kən-ī-zā'shən*, or *-kon-i-*). [L. *praecō, -ōnis*, a crier, a herald.]

precook *prē-kook'*, *v.t.* to cook partially or completely beforehand. [Pfx. pre- (2).]

precursor *prē-kur'sər*, a forerunner: a predecessor: an indication of the approach of an event.—*adjs.* **precur'sive**; **precur'sory**. [L. *praecurrĕre, -cursum*—*currĕre*, to run.]

predacious, (*irreg.*) **predaceous** *pri-dā'shəs*, *adj.* living by prey: predatory.—*ns.* **preda'ciousness, predac'ity**; **pred'ator**.—**pred'atorily**.—*n.* **pred'atoriness**.—*adj.* **pred'atory** of, relating to, or characterised by, plundering: living by plunder. [L. *praeda*, booty.]

predate *prē-dāt'*, *v.t.* to date before the true date: to antedate: to be earlier than. [Pfx. pre- (2).]

predator, etc. See **predacious**.

predecease *prē-di-sēs'*, *n.* death before another's death, or before some other time.—*v.t.* to die before. —*adj.* **predeceased'** deceased at an earlier time. [Pfx. pre- (2).]

predecessor *prē-di-ses'ər*, *n.* one who has been before another: a thing that has been supplanted or succeeded: an ancestor. [L., *praedēcessor*—*dē-cessor*, a retiring officer—*dē*, away, *cēdĕre*, to go, depart.]

predella *pri-del'ə*, *n.* the platform or uppermost step on which an altar stands: a retable: a painting or sculpture, on the face of either of these: a painting in a compartment along the bottom of an altarpiece or other picture. [It., prob.—O.H.G. *pret*, board.]

predentate *prē-den'tāt*, *adj.* having teeth in the forepart of the jaw only. [Pfx. pre- (1).]

predestine *prē-* or *prē-des'tin*, *v.t.* to destine or decree beforehand: to foreordain.—*adj.* **predestin'arian** believing in, or pertaining to, the doctrine of pre-

destination.—*n.* one who holds the doctrine of predestination.—*ns.* **predestina'tion** the act of predestinating: God's decree fixing unalterably from all eternity whatever is to happen, esp. the eternal happiness or misery of men (*theol*): fixed fate; **predes'tiny** irrevocably fixed fate. [Pfx. pre- (2).]

predetermine *prē-di-tûr'min*, *v.t.* to determine or settle beforehand.—*adjs.* **predeter'minable**; **predeter'minate** determined beforehand.—*n.* **predetermina'tion**. [Pfx. pre- (2).]

predicable *pred'i-kə-bl*, *adj.* that may be predicated or affirmed of something: attributable.—*n.* anything that can be predicated of another, or esp. of many others: one of the five attributes—genus, species, difference, property, and accident (*log.*).—*n.* **predicabil'ity**. [L. *praedicabilis*—*praedicāre*, to proclaim, *-abilis*, able.]

predicament *pri-dik'ə-mənt*, *n.* a condition: an unfortunate or trying position. [L.L. *praedicāmentum*, something predicated or asserted.]

predicant *pred'i-kənt*, *adj.* preaching.—*n.* a preaching-friar or Dominican. [L. *praedīcāns, -antis*, pr.p. of *praedicāre*; see next.]

predicate *pred'i-kāt*, *v.t.* to affirm: to assert: to state as a property or attribute of the subject (*log.*).—*n.* (*-it*) that which is predicated of the subject (*log.*): the word or words by which something is said about something (*gram.*).—*n.* **predica'tion**.—*adj.* **predicative** (*pri-dik'ə-tiv*, or *pred'i-kā-tiv*) expressing predication or affirmation: affirming: asserting.—*adv.* **predicatively**.—*adj.* **pred'icatory** affirmative. [L. *praedicāre, -ātum*, to proclaim—*prae*, forth, *dīcāre*, (orig.) to proclaim.]

predict *pri-dikt'*, *v.t.* to foretell.—*adj.* **predic'table** that can be predicted: happening, or prone to act, in a way that can be predicted.—*ns.* **predictabil'ity, predic'tableness; prediction** (*-shən*).—*adj.* **predic'tive** foretelling: prophetic.—*n.* **predic'tor** that which predicts: an anti-aircraft rangefinding and radar device. [L. *praedictus*, pa.p. of *praedīcĕre*—*dīcĕre*, to say.]

predigest *prē-di-jest'* or *-dī-*, *v.t.* to digest artificially before introducing into the body.—*n.* **predigestion** (*-jest'yən*) digestion beforehand. [Pfx. pre- (2).]

predikant *prä-di-kant'*, *n.* a Dutch Reformed preacher, esp. in South Africa. [Du.,—L *praedī-cāns, -antis*; see **predicant, preach**.]

predilection *prē-di-lek'shən*, *pred-i-*, *n.* favourable prepossession of mind: preference. [L. *prae, dīligĕre, dīlectum*, to love—*dī-*, *dis-*, apart, *legĕre*, to choose.]

predispose *prē-dis-pōz'*, *v.t.* to dispose or incline beforehand: to render favourable: to render liable.— *n.* **predisposition** (*-pəz-ish'ən*). [Pfx. pre- (2).]

predominate *pri-dom'in-āt*, *v.t.*—*v.i.* to surpass in strength or authority: to be most numerous or abounding: to have a commanding position.—*ns.* **predom'inance, predom'inancy**.—*adj.* **predom'inant** ruling: having superior power: ascendant: preponderating: prevailing: commanding in position or effect.—*adv.* **predom'inantly**.—*n.* **predomina'tion**. [Pfx. pre- (3).]

pre-eclampsia *prē-i-klamp'si-ə*, *n.* a toxic condition occurring in late pregnancy, characterised by high blood pressure, excessive weight gain, proteins in the urine, oedema, and sometimes severe headaches and visual disturbances. [Pfx. pre- (2), and **eclampsia**.]

pre-elect *prē-i-lekt'*, *v.t.* to choose beforehand.—*n.* **pre-elec'tion**.—*adj.* before election. [Pfx. pre- (2).]

pre-eminent *prē-em'in-ənt*, *adj.* more important or influential than others: surpassing others in good or

preconstruct'*v.t.*pre-(2) predevel'op *v.t.*, *v.i.* pre- (2) predevel'opment *n.* pre- (2).
preconstruc'tion *n.* pre-(2)

fāte; fär; mē; hûr (her); *mīne; mōte; fōr; mūte; mōōn; fŏŏt; dhen* (then); *el'ə-mənt* (element) bad qualities: outstanding: extreme.—*n.* **pre-em'inence.**—*adv.* **pre-em'inently.** [Pfx. pre- (3).]

pre-emption *prē-em(p)'shən, n.* the act or right of purchasing in preference to others: a belligerent's right to seize neutral contraband at a fixed price: seizure: the act of attacking first to forestall hostile action.—*v.t.* **pre-empt** (*prē-empt', -emt'*) to secure as first-comer: to secure by pre-emption: to take possession of.—*v.i.* (*bridge*) to make a pre-emptive bid.—*adjs.* **pre-empt'ible; pre-empt'ive.**—*n.* **pre-empt'or.**—**pre-emptive bid** (*bridge*) an unusually high bid intended to deter others from bidding. [L *prae, emptiō, -ōnis,* a buying—*emēre,* to buy.]

preen *prēn, v.t.* (of a bird) to clean and arrange (the feathers), or to clean and arrange the feathers of (a part of the body): to adorn, dress or slick (oneself) (*fig.*): to plume, pride or congratulate (oneself) (with *on*)—**preen gland** the uropygial gland that secretes oil used in preening the feathers. [App. **prune**[2] assimilated to the following word.]

pre-establish *prē-is-tab'lish, v.t.* to establish beforehand. [Pfx. pre- (2)]

pre-exilic *prē-eg-zil'ik, adj* before the exile—of O.T writings prior to the Jewish exile (*c.* 586–538 B.C.).—Also **pre-exil'ian.** [Pfx. pre- (2).]

pre-exist *prē-ig-zist', v.i.* to exist beforehand, esp. in a former life.—*n.* **pre-exist'ence.**—*adj.* **pre-exist'ent.** [Pfx. pre- (2).]

prefabricate *prē-fab'ri-kāt, v.t.* to make standardised parts of beforehand, for assembling later.—*adj.* **prefab'ricated** composed of such parts.—*ns.* **prefabrica'tion; prefab'ricator; pre'fab** (*coll.*) a prefabricated house. [Pfx. pre- (2).]

preface *pref'is, n.* something said by way of introduction or preliminary explanation: a statement, usually explanatory, placed at the beginning of a book, not regarded as forming (like the introduction) part of the composition: the ascription of glory, etc., in the liturgy of consecration of the eucharist: anything preliminary or immediately antecedent.—*v.t.* to say by way of preface: to introduce by a preface.—*v.i.* to make preliminary remarks.—*adjs.* **prefatorial** (*pref-ə-tō'ri-əl, -tō'*) serving as a preface or introduction; **pref'atory** pertaining to a preface: serving as an introduction: introductory. [Fr. *préface*—L.L. *prēfātia* for L. *praefātiō*—*prae, fārī, fātus,* to speak.]

prefect *prē'fekt, n.* one placed in authority over others (also **praefect**): a commander or magistrate (*Rom hist.*; also **praefect**): a school pupil with some measure of authority over others: the administrative head of a department in France, of a province in Italy, or of any similar administrative district elsewhere.—*adj.* **prefectorial** (*prē-fek-tō'ri-əl, -tō'*).—*n.* **pre'fectship.**—*adj.* **prefect'ural** (*pri-*).—*n.* **pre'fecture** the office, term of office, or district of a prefect: in Japan, any of 46 administrative districts headed by a governor: the house or office occupied by a prefect. [O.Fr. *prefect* (Fr. *préfet*) and L. *praefectus,* pa.p. of *praeficĕre*—*prae, facĕre,* to make.]

prefer *pri-fûr', v.t.* to put forward, offer, submit, present, for acceptance or consideration: to promote: to advance: to hold in higher estimation: to choose or select before others: to like better (with *to,* or *rather than;* not with *than* alone):—*pr.p.* **preferring** (*pri-fûr'ing*); *pa.t.* and *pa.p.* **preferred** (*pri-fûrd'*).—*n.* **preferabil'ity** (*pref-*).—*adj.* **pref'erable** to be preferred: having priority.—*adv.* **pref'erably** by choice: in preference.—*n.* **pref'erence** the act of choosing, favouring, or liking one above another: estimation above another: the state of being preferred: that which is preferred: priority: an advantage given to

one over another.—*adj.* **preferential** (*pref-ər-en'shl*) having, giving, or allowing, a preference.—*adv.* **preferen'tially.**—*n.* **prefer'ment** advancement: promotion: superior place, esp. in the Church.—**preference shares** or **stock** shares or stock on which the dividends must be paid before those on other kinds. [Fr. *préférer*—L. *praeferre*—*ferre,* to bear.]

prefigure *prē-fig'ər, v.t.* to imagine beforehand: to foreshadow by a type.—*n.* **prefigura'tion.** [Pfx. pre- (2).]

prefix *prē-fiks', prē'fiks, v t.* to put before, or at the beginning: to fix beforehand—*n* **pre'fix** a particle to add as a prefix put before, and usually joined to, a word to affect its meaning: a title placed before a name, as *Mr, Sir* [L. *praefigĕre, -fixum—figĕre,* to fix.]

preform *prē-form', v.t.* to determine the shape of beforehand.—*n.* **preforma'tion.** [Pfx. pre- (2).]

prefrontal *prē-front'l, -frunt'l, adj.* in front of, or in the forepart of, the frontal bone, lobe, scale, etc . pertaining to such a part —*n.* a bone or scale so situated [Pfx. pre- (1)]

preggers *preg'ərz,* (*coll.,* esp. upper-class) *adj.* pregnant

pre-glacial *prē-glā'shl, adj* earlier than the glacial period. [Pfx pre- (2).]

pregnable *preg'nə-bl, adj* that may be taken by assault or force: vulnerable. [Fr *prenable—prendre,* to take; see **impregnable.**]

pregnant *preg'nənt, adj* with child or young· fruitful: fruitful in results: momentous: significant: threatening: freighted: swelling: full of thoughts, ready-witted, inventive: full of promise: full of meaning: pithy and to the purpose: weighty· cogent· obvious: clear.—*n.* **preg'nancy.**—*adv* **preg'nantly.** [L. *praegnāns, -antis,* from earlier *praegnās, -ātis,* app — *prae* and the root of *gnāscī,* to be born, but in some meanings from or confused with O Fr. *preignant,* pr.p. of *preindre—*L. *premĕre,* to press]

preheat *prē-hēt', v.t.* to heat before using, before heating further, or before subjecting to some other process or treatment. [Pfx. pre- (2).]

prehensile *pri-hen'sīl, adj.* capable of grasping—also **prehen'sive, prehensō'rial** (*prē-*), **prehen'sory** (*pri-*).—*ns.* **prehensility** (*prē-hen-sil'i-ti*); **prehension** (*pri-hen'shən*). [L. *praehendĕre, -hensum,* to seize.]

prehistoric, -al *prē-his-tor'ik, -əl, adjs.* of a time before extant historical records.—*n.* **prehistō'rian.**—*adv.* **prehistor'ically.**—*n.* **prehis'tory.** [Pfx. pre- (2).]

pre-ignition *prē-ig-nish'ən, n.* too-early ignition of the charge in an internal combustion engine. [Pfx. pre- (2).]

prejudge *prē-juj', v.t.* to judge or decide upon before hearing the whole case: to condemn unheard.—*n* **prejudg'ment** (also **prejudge'ment**) —*adj* **prejudicant** (*prē-jōō'd'i-kənt*).—*v.t.* **prejud'icate** to judge beforehand.—*v.t* to form an opinion beforehand — *n.* **prejudica'tion.** [L. *praejūdicāre.*]

prejudice *prej'ōō-dis, n.* a judgment or opinion formed beforehand or without due examination: pre-possession in favour of or (usu.) against anything: bias: injury or hurt: disadvantage.—*v.t.* to fill with prejudice: to prepossess: to bias the mind of: to injure or hurt.—*adjs.* **prej'udiced** having prejudice: biased; **prejudicial** (*-dish'l*) injurious: detrimental: (*prē-jōō-*) relating to matters to be decided before a case comes into court.—*adv.* **prejudic'ially.**—**without prejudice** a phrase used to require an understanding that nothing said at this stage is to detract from one's rights, to damage claims arising from future developments, or to constitute an admission of liability.

pre'flight' *adj.* pre- (2).

[Fr. *préjudice*, wrong, and L. *praejúdicium—júdicium*, judgment.]

prelate *prel'it*, *n.* an ecclesiastic of high rank: a chief priest: a clergyman.—*ns* **prelacy** (*prel'ə-si*) the office of a prelate: the order of bishops or the bishops collectively: church government by prelates: episcopacy; **prel'ateship**.—*adjs.* **prelatial** (*pri-lā'shəl*) of a prelate; **prelatic** (*pri-lat'ik*), **-al** pertaining to prelates or prelacy: (*in hostility*) episcopal or episcopalian —*ns.* **prel'atism** (*usu. hostile*) episcopacy or episcopalianism: domination by prelates; **prel'atist** an upholder of prelacy. [Fr. *prélat* —L. *praelātus—prae*, before and *lātus*, borne.]

preliminary *pri-lim'in-ə-ri*, *adj.* introductory: preparatory: preceding or preparing for the main matter.— *n.* that which precedes: an introduction (often in *pl.*, **prelim'inaries**): a preliminary or entrance examination (in student slang shortened to **prelim'** or **prē'-lim**; often in *pl.*): (in *pl.*) preliminary pages—titles, preface, contents, introduction, etc. (in printers' slang **prelims'** or **prē'lims**). [L *prae*, *līmen*, *-inis*, threshold.]

prelude *prel'ūd*, *n* a preliminary performance or action: an event preceding and leading up to another of greater importance: a preliminary strain, passage, or flourish, often improvised (*mus.*): an introduction or first movement of a suite: a movement preceding a fugue: an overture: an introductory voluntary: a short independent composition such as might be the introduction to another, or developed out of the prelude in the literal sense.—*v.t.* (*prel'ūd*, formerly and still by some *pri-lūd'*, *-lōōd'*) to precede as a prelude, serve as prelude to: to introduce with a prelude: to perform as a prelude.—*v.i.* to furnish a prelude: to perform a prelude: to serve as a prelude.—*adjs.* **prelusive** (*-lōō'* or *-lū'siv*) of the nature of a prelude: introductory; **prelu'sory** (*-sə-ri*) introductory. [Fr. *prélude*—L.L *praelūdium*—L. *lūdēre*, to play.]

premarital *prē-mar'i-təl*, *adj.* before marriage. [Pfx. **pre-** (2).]

premature *prem'ə-tūr*, *prēm'*, or *-tūr'*, *adj.* ripe before the time: unduly early: of a human baby, born less than 37 weeks after conception, or (sometimes) having a birth weight of between 2½ and 5½ pounds irrespective of length of gestation.—*adv.* **prematurely**.—*ns.* **prematureness**; **prematur'ity**. [L. *praemātūrus—prae*, *mātūrus*, ripe.]

premedical *prē-med'i-kl*, *adj.* of or pertaining to a course of study undertaken before medical studies.— *adj.* **prē'med** (*coll.*) short for **premedical**.—*n.* (also **premed'ic**) a premedical student: premedical studies: premedication.—*v.t.* **premed'icate**.—*n* **premedicā'tion** drugs given to sedate and prepare a patient, esp. for the administration of a general anaesthetic. [Pfx. **pre-** (2).]

premeditate *prē-med'i-tāt*, *v.t.* to meditate upon beforehand: to design previously.—*v.i.* to deliberate beforehand —*adv.* **premed'itatedly**.—*n.* **premeditā'-tion**.—*adj.* **premed'itative**. [L. *praemeditārī*, *-ātus—prae*, *meditārī*, to meditate]

premenstrual *prē-men'strōō-əl*, *adj.* preceding menstruation.—**premenstrual tension** a state of emotional anxiety, etc. caused by hormonal changes preceding menstruation (abbrev. **PMT**). [Pfx. **pre-** (2).]

premia. See **premium**.

premier *prem'i-ər*, *-yər*, by some *prēm'i-ər*, formerly also *pri-mēr'*, *adj.* prime or first: chief.—*n* the first or chief: the prime minister.—*n.* **première** (*prəm-yer'*, *prem'yər*; from the Fr. *fem.*) a leading actress, dancer, etc.: the first performance of a play or film—also *adj.*—*v.t.* to give a first performance of

—Also *v i.*—*n.* **prem'iership**. [Fr ,—L. *prīmārius*, of the first rank—*prīmus*, first.]

premillenarian *prē-mil-ən-ā'ri-ən*, *n.* a believer in the premillennial coming of Christ.—Also *adj* —*n.* **premillena'rianism**. [Pfx **pre-** (2).]

premillennial *prē-mil-en'yəl*, *adj.* before the millennium.—*ns.* **premillenn'ialism** premillenarianism; **premillenn'ialist**. [Pfx. **pre-** (2).]

premise *prem'is*, *n.* a proposition stated or assumed for after-reasoning, esp. one of the two propositions in a syllogism from which the conclusion is drawn (*log.*, also **prem'iss**): (usu. in *pl.*) the matter set forth at the beginning of a deed: (in *pl.*) the beginning of a deed setting forth its subject-matter· (in *pl.*) the aforesaid, hence, a building and its adjuncts, esp. a public-house: a presupposition (also **prem'iss**) —*v.t.* **premise** (*pri-mīz'*, also *prem'is*) to mention or state first, or by way of introduction: to prefix: to state or assume as a premise: to perform or administer beforehand (*med.*). [Fr *prémisse* and L. (*sententia*, etc.) *praemissa*, (a sentence, etc.) put before—*mittēre*, *missum*, to send]

premium *prē'mi-əm*, *n.* a reward: a prize: a bounty: payment made for insurance: a fee for admission as a pupil for a profession: excess over original price or par (opp. to *discount*): anything offered as an incentive:—*pl.* **pre'miums**, (*rare*) **pre'mia.—Premium (Savings) Bond** a Government bond, the holder of which gains no interest, but is eligible for a money prize allotted by draw held at stated intervals.—**at a premium** above par. [L. *praemium—prae*, above, *emēre*, to buy.]

premolar *prē-mō'lər*, *adj.* in front of the true molar teeth.—*n.* tooth between the canine and molars (called molar or milk-molar in the milk dentition). [Pfx. **pre-** (1).]

premonition *prē-mən-ish'ən*, or *prem-*, *n.* a forewarning: a feeling that something is going to happen.— *adjs.* **premonitive** (*pri-mon'*), **premon'itory** giving warning or notice beforehand. [On the model of **admonish**—L. *praemonēre—monēre*, to warn.]

Premonstratensian *pri-mon-strə-ten'sh*(*y*)*ən*, *-si-ən*, *adj.* of an order of canons regular founded by St Norbert, in 1119, at *Prémontré*, near Laon, or of a corresponding order of nuns.—*n.* a member of the order.— Also (*n.* and *adj.*) **Premon'strant**. [L *prātum mōn-strātum*, the meadow pointed out, or (*locus*) *praemōnstrātus*, (the place) foreshown (in a vision), i.e. *Prémontré*.]

premorse *pri-mōrs'*, *adj.* ending abruptly, as if bitten off. [L. *praemorsus*, bitten in front—*prae*, *mordēre*, *morsum*, to bite.]

premosaic *prē-mō-zā'ik*, *adj.* before the time of *Moses* [Pfx. **pre-** (2), **Mosaic**.]

prenatal *prē-nā'tl*, *adj.* before birth. [Pfx. **pre-** (2)]

prentice, 'prentice *pren'tis*, aphetic for **apprentice**.

preoccupy *prē-ok'ū-pī*, *v.t* to occupy, fill, beforehand or before others: to take or have possession of to the exclusion of others or other things: to fill the mind of. —*n.* **preoccupā'tion**.—*adj.* **preoc'upied** already occupied: lost in thought, abstracted: having one's attention wholly taken up by (with *with*): of a genus or species name, not available for adoption because it has already been applied to another group [Pfx. pre- (2).]

preordain *prē-or-dān'*, *v.t.* to ordain, appoint, or determine beforehand.—*n* **preordain'ment**.—*v.t* **preor'der** to arrange or ordain beforehand —*ns.* **preor'dinance** a rule previously established: that which is ordained beforehand; **preordinā'tion** preordaining [Pfx pre- (2).]

---

premix' *v t* pre- (2).

---

prep *prep*, *adj.* coll. short form of *preparatory*.—*n.* school slang for *preparation* of lessons: a preparatory school (also **prep school**): a pupil in a preparatory school.—Also *v.t.*—*adj.* **prepp'y** (*U.S.*) vaguely denoting the values, mores, dress, etc of a class of people who (might wish to seem to) have attended a (U.S.) preparatory school (q.v.).

prepack *prē'pak'*, *v.t.* to pack (e.g. food) before offering for sale.—*p.adj.* **prē'packed'**. [Pfx. pre- (2).]

prepaid. See prepay.

prepare *pri-pār'*, *v.t.* to make ready or fit: to bring into a suitable state: to dispose: to adapt: to train, as for an examination: to get up, learn: to make a preliminary study of (work prescribed for a class): to subject to a process for bringing into a required state: to make, produce: to cook and dress: to lead up to.—*v.i.* to make oneself ready: to make preparation.—*n.* **preparation** (*prep-ə-rā'shən*) the act of preparing: a preliminary arrangement: the process or course of being prepared: the preliminary study of prescribed classwork: readiness: that which is prepared or made up, as a medicine: an anatomical or other specimen prepared for study or preservation.—*adj.* **preparative** (*pri-par'ə-tiv*) serving to prepare: preliminary.—*n.* that which prepares the way: preparation.—*adj.* **preparatory** preparing: previous: introductory.—*adv.* **preparatorily** (with *to*).—*adj.* **prepared** (*pri-pārd'*) made ready, fit, or suitable: ready.—*adv.* **prepa'redly.**—*ns.* **prepa'redness**; **prepa'rer.**—**preparatory school** one which prepares pupils for a public or other higher school: a private school that prepares young people for college (*U.S.*).—**be prepared** to be ready, or be willing, to (do something). [Fr. *préparer*—L. *praeparāre*—*prae*, *parāre*, to make ready.]

prepay *prē'pā'*, *v.t.* to pay before or in advance:—*pa.t.* and *pa.p.* **prē'paid'.**—*adj.* **pre'paid'.**—*adj.* **pre'payable.**—*n.* **pre'pay'ment.** [Pfx. pre- (2).]

prepense *pri-pens'*, *adj.* premeditated: intentional, chiefly in the phrase 'malice prepense' = malice aforethought or intentional. [Ō.Fr. *purpense*.]

preponderate *pri-pon'dər-āt*, *v.i.* to weigh more: to turn the balance: to prevail or exceed in number, quantity, importance, influence, or force (with *over*)—*v.t.* (*lit.* or *fig.*) to outweigh.—*ns.* **prepon'derance**, **prepon'derancy.**—*adj.* **prepon'derant.**—*adv.* **prepon'derantly.** [L. *praeponderāre*, *-ātum—prae*, *ponderāre*, *-ātum*, to weigh—*pondus*, a weight.]

preposition *prep-ə-zish'ən*, *n.* a word placed usually before a noun or its equivalent to mark some relation: (*prē-*) position in front.—*adj.* **preposi'tional** (*prep-*).—*adv.* **preposi'tionally.**—*adj.* **prepositive** (*pri-poz'i-tiv*) put before: prefixed. [L. *praepositiō*, *-ōnis—praepōnēre*, *-positum—prae*, *pōnēre*, to place.]

prepossess *prē-poz-es'*, *v.t.* to fill beforehand, as the mind with some opinion or feeling: to preoccupy: to bias or prejudice, esp. favourably.—*adjs.* **prepossessed'** biased, prejudiced; **prepossess'ing** tending to prepossess: making a favourable impression.—*adv.* **prepossess'ingly.**—*n.* **prepossession** (*-esh'ən*) previous possession: preoccupation: bias, usually favourable. [Pfx. pre- (2).]

preposterous *pri-pos'tə-rəs*, *adj.* contrary to the order of nature or reason: utterly absurd.—*adv.* **prepos'terously.**—*n.* **prepos'terousness.** [L. *praeposterus*—*prae*, before, *posterus*, after—*post*, after.]

prepotent *prē-pō'tənt*, *adj.* powerful in a very high degree.—*ns.* **prepo'tence**, **prepo'tency.** [Pfx. pre- (3).]

preppy. See prep.

prepuce *prē'pūs*, *n.* the loose skin of the penis, the foreskin: a similar fold of skin over the clitoris.—*adj.*

preputial (*pri-pū'shyəl*, *-shəl*). [L. *praepūtium*.]

prequel *prē'kwəl*, (*coll*) *n* a film produced after some other film has proved a box-office success, based on the same leading characters but depicting events happening before those of the first film [Pfx. pre- (2), and **sequel.**]

Pre-Raphaelite *prē-raf'ā-ə-līt*, *n.* one who seeks to return to the spirit and manner of painters before the time of *Raphael* (1483–1520): a member of a group (the Pre-Raphaelite Brotherhood, or 'P.R.B.', 1848) of painters and others (D. G. Rossetti, W. Holman Hunt, J. E. Millais, etc.) who practised or advocated a truthful, almost rigid, adherence to natural forms and effects.—Also *adj.* [Pfx. pre- (2), *Raphael*, and suff. **-ite.**]

pre-Reformation *prē-ref-ər-mā'shən*, *adj.* before the Reformation: dating from before the Reformation. [Pfx. pre- (2).]

prerelease *prē-ri-lēs'*, *n.* the release of a cinematograph film before the normal date: the exhibition of a film so released.—Also *adj* [Pfx. pre- (2).]

prerequisite *prē-rek'wi-zit*, *n.* a condition or requirement that must previously be satisfied.—*adj.* required as a condition of something else. [Pfx. pre- (2).]

prerogative *pri-rog'ə-tiv*, *n.* a peculiar privilege shared by no other: a right arising out of one's rank, position, or nature.—*adj.* arising out of, or held by, prerogative.—**royal prerogative** the rights which a sovereign has by right of office, which are different in different countries. [L. *praerogātīvus*, asked first for his vote—*prae*, *rogāre*, *-ātum*, to ask.]

presa *prā'sa*, *-sə*, *-za*, *n* a symbol ($\cdot \dot{X} \cdot$, $\cdot S$ or Σ) used to indicate the points at which successive voice or instrumental parts enter a round, canon, etc.:—*pl.* **pre'se** (*-sā*, *-zā*). [It., an act of taking up.]

presage *pres'ij*, formerly also *pri-sāj'*, *n.* a prognostic: an omen: an indication of the future: a foreboding: a presentiment.—*v.t.* **presage** (*pri-sāj'*) to portend: to forebode: to warn of as something to come: to forecast: to have a presentiment of [L. *praesāgium*, a foreboding—*prae*, *sāgus*, prophetic.]

presbyopia *prez-bi-ō'pi-ə*, *n.* difficulty in accommodating the eye to near vision, a defect increasing with age—also **pres'byopy.**—*n.* **pres'byope** one so affected.—*adj.* **presbyopic** (*-op'ik*). [Gr. *presbys*, old, *ōps*, *ōpos*, the eye.]

presbyter *prez'bi-tər*, *n.* an elder: a minister or priest in rank between a bishop and a deacon: a member of a presbytery.—*adj.* **presbyterial** (*-tē'ri-əl*) of a presbytery: of church government by elders.—*adv.* **presbytē'rially.**—*adj.* **Presbytē'rian** pertaining to, or maintaining the system of, church government by presbyters: of a church so governed.—*n.* a member of such a church: an upholder of the Presbyterian system.—*ns.* **Presbytē'rianism** the form of church government by presbyters; **pres'bytership**; **pres'bytery** a church court ranking next above the kirk-session, consisting of the ministers and one ruling elder from each church within a certain district: the district so represented: the Presbyterian system: part of a church reserved for the officiating priests, the eastern extremity: a priest's house (*R.C.*). [Gr. *presbyteros*, compar. of *presbys*, old.]

preschool *prē'skōōl'*, *adj.* before school: not yet at school.—*n.* **prē'schooler** a preschool child.

prescience *prē'sh(y)əns*, *-shi-əns*, *prē'*, *-si-əns*, *n.* foreknowledge: foresight.—*adj.* **pre'scient.**—*adv.* **pre'sciently.** [L. *praesciēns*, *-entis*, pr.p of *praescīre—prae*, *scīre*, to know.]

prescind *pri-sind'*, *v t.* to cut off, cut short, separate: to abstract.—*v.i.* to withdraw the attention (usu. with

prepro'grammed *adj.* pre- (2). **pre'record'** *v.t.* pre- (2).

For other sounds see detailed chart of pronunciation.

from).—*n*. **prescission** (*pri-sish'ən*). [L. *praescindĕre*, to cut off in front.]

prescribe *pri-skrīb'*, *v.t.* to lay down as a rule or direction: to give as an order: to appoint: to give directions for, as a remedy (*med.*): to limit, set bounds to.—*v.i.* to lay down rules: to give or make out a prescription (*med.*).—*n*. **prescrip'tion** the act of prescribing or directing: a written direction for the preparation of a medicine (*med.*): a recipe: any claim based on long use, or an established custom taken as authoritative. —*adj*. **prescrip'tive** prescribing, laying down rules: consisting in, or acquired by, custom or long-continued use: customary.—*adv*. **prescrip'tively.**—*n*. **prescrip'tiveness.** [L. *praescrībĕre*, *-scrīptum*, to write before, lay down in advance, demur to—*prae*, *scrībĕre*, to write.]

preselect *prē-si-lekt'*, *v.t.* to select beforehand.—*ns*. **preselec'tion; preselec'tor** a component of a radio receiver, improving reception. [Pfx. pre- (2).]

presence *prez'əns*, *n*. the fact or state of being present (opp. to *absence*): immediate neighbourhood: the impression made by one's bearing, esp. imposing bearing: military or political representation or influence: something felt or imagined to be present. —**presence of mind** the power of keeping one's wits about one: coolness and readiness in emergency, danger, or surprise; **real presence** the true and substantial presence, according to the belief of Roman Catholics, Eastern Orthodox, etc., of the body and blood of Christ in the eucharist. [O Fr.,—L. *praesentia*; see present[1,2,3].]

presension. See **presentient.**

present[1] *prez'ənt*, *adj*. in the place in question or implied (opp. to *absent*): at hand: ready: found or existing in the thing in question: before the mind: now under view or consideration: now existing: not past or future: denoting time just now, or making a general statement (*gram.*): in or of the present tense: immediate.—*n*. that which is present: the present time: the present tense: a verb in the present tense: the present business or occasion: the present document or (in *pl.*) writings.—*adv*. **pres'ently** at present, now (*obs*. or *Scot*. and *U.S.*): before long: directly, immediately, necessarily.—*n*. **pres'entness.**—*adj*. **pres'ent-day'** belonging to or found in the present time, contemporary.—**at present** at the present time, now; **for the present** for the moment: now for the time being. [O.Fr.,—L. *praesēns*, *-sentis*, present.]

present[2] *prez'ənt*, *n*. a gift. [O.Fr. *present*, orig. presence, hence gift (from the phrase *mettre en present à*, to put into the presence of, hence to offer as a gift to).]

present[3] *pri-zent'*, *v.t.* to set before (someone), introduce into presence or to notice, cognisance, or acquaintance: to introduce at court: to introduce to the public, as on the stage: to put on the stage: to exhibit to view: to have as a characteristic: to put forward: to proffer: to make a gift of: to appoint to a benefice: to nominate to a foundation: to put forward or bring up for examination, trial, dedication, a degree, consideration, etc.: to deliver: to bestow something upon, endow (with *with*): to represent, depict, or symbolise: to point, direct, aim, turn in some direction: to apply: to hold vertically in front of the body in salute to a superior (*mil.*): (*refl.*) to come into presence, attend, appear: (*refl.*) to offer (oneself): (*refl.*) to offer (itself), occur.—*v.i.* to make presentation to a living: to offer: to be directed, to be in position for coming first (*obstetrics*).—*n*. the position of a weapon in presenting arms or in aiming.—*n*. **presentabil'ity.** —*adj*. **present'able** capable of being presented: fit to be presented: fit to be seen: passable.—*adv*. **present'ably.**—*ns*. **present'ableness; presentation**

(*prez-ən-tā'shən*) the act of presenting: the mode of presenting: the right of presenting: that which is presented: immediate cognition: a setting forth, as of a truth: representation.—*adj*. that has been presented: of or for presentation.—**presenter** (*pri-zent'ər*); **present'ment** the act of presenting: a statement: a jury's statement to a court of matters within its knowledge: a representation: an image, delineation, picture: a presentation to consciousness.—**present arms** to bring the weapon to a vertical position in front of the body. [O.Fr. *presenter*—L. *praesentāre*—*praesēns*, present (in place or time).]

presentient *prē-ser.'sh(y)ənt*, *adj*. having a presentiment.—*n*. **presen'sion.** [Pfx. pre- (2).]

presentiment *pri-zent'i-mənt*, sometimes *-sent'*, *n*. a foreboding, esp. of evil. [Pfx. pre- (2).]

presentment. See **present[3]**.

preserve *pri-zûrv'*, *v.t.* to keep safe from harm or loss: to keep alive: to keep in existence: to retain: to maintain, keep up: to guard against shooting or fishing by unauthorised persons: to keep sound: to keep from or guard against decay: to pickle, season, or otherwise treat for keeping.—*v.i.* to preserve game, fish, ground, or water, etc.—*n*. preserved fruit or jam (often in *pl.*): a place or water where shooting or fishing is preserved: anything regarded as closed or forbidden to outsiders: (in *pl.*) spectacles to protect the eyes from dust or strong light.—*n*. **preservabil'ity.**—*adj*. **preserv'able.**—*ns*. **preservā'tion** (*prez-*); **preservā'tionist** one who is interested in preserving traditional and historic things.—*adj*. **preserv'ative** serving to preserve.—*n*. a preserving agent: a safeguard: a prophylactic.—*adj*. and *n*. **preserv'atory.**—*n*. **preserv'er.**—**preserv'ing-pan** a large pan usu. with a hooped handle and a lip, in which jams, etc. are made —**well preserved** (*coll.*; of a person) not showing the signs of ageing one would expect in a person of such an age. [Fr. *préserver*—L. *prae*, *servāre*, to keep.]

pre-shrink *prē'-shringk'*, *v.t.* to shrink (cloth) before it is made up into garments, etc. [Pfx. pre- (2).]

preside *pri-zīd'*, *v.i.* to be in the chair: to be at the head: to superintend: to be at the organ or piano (orig. as a kind of conductor).—*ns*. **presidency** (*prez'i-dən-si*) the office of a president, or his dignity, term of office, jurisdiction, or residence; **pres'ident** one who is chosen to preside over the meetings of a society, conference, etc.: the elected head of a republic: the head of a board, council, or department of government: the title of the head of certain colleges, universities, and other institutions: the head of an organisation generally (*U.S.*).—*adj*. **presidential** (*-den'shl*) presiding: of a president or presidency.— **presiding officer** a person in charge of a polling-place. —**Lord President** the presiding judge of the Court of Session; **Lord President of the Council** a member of the House of Lords who presides over the privy council [Fr. *présider*—L. *praesidēre*—*prae*, *sedēre*, to sit.]

presidial *pri-sid'i-əl*, *adj*. pertaining to a garrison, a presidio, or a president.—*n*. **presid'ium** a standing committee in the Soviet system (also **praesidium**):— *pl*. **-diums** or **-dia.** [L. *praesidium*, a garrison— *praesidēre*, to preside.]

press[1] *pres*, *v.t.* to exert a pushing force upon: to squeeze: to compress: to clasp: to thrust onwards or downwards: to squeeze out: to imprint, stamp, print: to flatten, condense, dry, shape, or smooth by weight or other squeezing force: to put to death by application of heavy weights: to bear heavily on: to harass: to beset: to urge strongly: to invite with persistent warmth: to offer urgently or abundantly (with *upon*): to throng, crowd: to present to the mind with earnestness: to lay stress upon: to hurry on with great speed.—*v.i.* to exert pressure: to push with force: to crowd: to go forward with violence: to be urgent in application, entreaty, or effort: to strive: to strain: to strive to do too much, to the loss of ease and effectiveness (*golf*).—*n.* an act of pressing: pressure: a crowd: crowding: the thick of a fight: stress: urgency: a cupboard or shelved closet or recess: a bookcase: an apparatus for pressing: a printing-machine: printing: a printing organisation: often extended to a publishing house: printing activities: newspapers and periodicals collectively: the journalistic profession: (with *cap.*) a common name for a newspaper: (favourable or unfavourable) reception by newspapers and periodicals generally (also *fig.*).—*ns.* **press'er**; **press'ing** the action of verb to press: an article, articles, esp. gramophone records, made from the same mould or press.—*adj.* urgent: importunate: crowding.—*adv.* **press'ingly.**—**press'-agent** one who arranges for newspaper advertising and publicity, esp. for an actor or theatre; **press'-box** an erection provided for the use of reporters at sports, shows, etc.; **press'-button** a push-button.—Also *adj.*—**press conference** a meeting of a public personage with the press for making an announcement or to answer questions; **press'-cutt'ing** a paragraph or article cut out of a newspaper or magazine; **press'-fastener**, **press'-stud** a form of button fastening in two parts, one of which can be pushed partly into the other; **press'-gall'ery** a reporters' gallery; **press'man** one who works a printing-press: a journalist or reporter; **press release** an official statement or report supplied to the press; **press'-room** a room where printing-presses are worked: a room for the use of journalists; **press'-up** a gymnastic exercise in which the prone body is kept rigid while being raised and lowered by straightening and bending the arms.—**at press, in the press** in course of printing: about to be published; **go to press** to begin to print or to be printed; **liberty, freedom, of the press** right of publishing material without submitting it to a government authority for permission; **press ahead, forward, on** to continue, esp. energetically, often in spite of difficulties or opposition; **the press** printed matter generally, esp. newspapers: journalists as a class. [Fr. *presser*—L. *pressāre*—*premĕre*, *pressum*, to press.]

press² *pres*, *v.t.* to carry off and force into service, esp. in the navy: to requisition: to turn to use in an unsuitable or provisional way.—*n.* impressment: authority for impressing.—**press'-gang** a gang or body of sailors under an officer, empowered to impress men into the navy.—Also *v.t.* (also *fig.*). [Old word *prest*, to enlist for service.]

pressure *presh'ər*, *n.* the act of pressing or squeezing: the state of being pressed: constraining force or influence: that which presses or afflicts: urgency: a strong demand: a force directed towards the thing it acts upon, measured as so much weight upon a unit of area.—*v.t.* to apply pressure to: to compel by pressure (with *into*).—*v.t.* **pressurise, -ize** (of an aeroplane, etc.) to fit with a device that maintains nearly normal atmospheric pressure: to subject to pressure: to force by pressure (into doing something).—**press'ure-cab'in** a pressurised cabin in an aircraft.—*v.t.* **press'ure-cook'** to cook in a pressure cooker.—**pressure cooker** an autoclave, esp. one for domestic use; **pressure group** a set putting pressure on a government for a particular purpose; **press'ure-hel'met** an airman's helmet for use with a pressure-suit; **pressure point** any of various points on the body on which pressure may be exerted to relieve pain, control bleeding, etc.; **press'ure-suit** an automatically inflating suit worn by airmen against pressure-cabin

failure at very high altitudes. [L *pressura*—*premĕre*, to press.]

Prestel® *pres'tel*, *n.* the viewdata (q.v.) system of the Post Office.

prestidigitation *pres-ti-dij-i-tā'shən*, *n.* sleight-of-hand. —*n.* **prestidig'itator.** [Fr. *prestidigitateur*—*preste*, nimble, L. *digitus*, finger.]

prestige *pres-tēzh'*, *n.* standing or ascendancy in people's minds owing to associations, station, success, etc.—*adj.* consisting in, or for the sake of, prestige: considered to have or give prestige: superior in quality, style, etc.—*adj.* **prestigious** (*-tij'əs*) having prestige, esteemed. [Fr ,—L. *praestigium*, delusion.]

presto *pres'tō*, (*mus.*) *adj.* very quick.—*n.* a presto movement or passage:—*pl.* **pres'tos.**—*adv.* quickly, quicker than *allegro*.—*adv.* or *interj.* (usu. **hey presto** as in conjuring tricks) at once. [It.,—L. *praestō*, at hand.]

pre-stressed *prē-strest'*, *adj.* (of concrete) strengthened with stretched wires or rods instead of large steel bars as in reinforced concrete. [Pfx. pre- (2).]

presume *pri-zūm'*, *-zōōm'*, *v.t.* to take as true without examination or proof: to take for granted: to assume provisionally: to take upon oneself, esp. with overboldness.—*v.i.* to venture beyond what one has ground for: to act forwardly or without proper right: to rely, count (with *on*, *upon*), esp. unduly.—*adj.* **presum'able** that may be presumed or supposed to be true.—*adv.* **presum'ably.**—*adj.* **presūm'ing** venturing without permission: unreasonably bold.—*conj.* (often with *that*) making the presumption that.—*n.* **presumption** (*-zum'shən*, *-zump'shən*) the act of presuming: supposition: strong probability: that which is taken for granted: an assumption or belief based on facts or probable evidence: confidence grounded on something not proved: a ground or reason for presuming: conduct going beyond proper bounds.—*adj.* **presumptive** (*-zump'*, *-zum'tiv*) grounded on probable evidence: giving grounds for presuming.—*adj.* **presumptuous** (*-zump'tū-əs*, or *-zum'*) presuming.—*adv.* **presump'tuously.**—*n.* **presump'tuousness.** [L. *praesūmĕre*, *-sūmptum*—*prae*, *sūmĕre*, to take—*sub*, under, *emĕre*, to buy.]

presuppose *prē-sə-pōz'*, *v.t.* to assume or take for granted: to involve as a necessary antecedent.—*n.* **presupposition** (*prē-sup-ə-zish'ən*). [Pfx. pre- (2).]

pretend *pri-tend'*, *v.t.* to profess, now only falsely: to feign: to allege falsely: to make believe: to venture, attempt, undertake.—*v.i* to aspire: to be a suitor: to make a claim: to feign: to make believe.—*n.* **pretence'** (*U.S.* **pretense'**) an act of pretending: something pretended: an allegation: an aim, purpose: the thing aimed at: appearance or show to hide reality: false show: a false allegation: a sham: pretentiousness: a pretext: claim.—*n.* **preten'dant** (or **-ent**) a claimant: a suitor: a pretender.—*adj.* **preten'ded.**—*ns.* **preten'der** a claimant, esp. to a throne: a candidate: one who pretends; **preten'dership.** —*adv.* **preten'dingly.**—*n.* **preten'sion** pretence: show: pretext: claim: aspiration, esp. to marriage: pretentiousness.—*adj.* **preten'tious** (*-shəs*) overassuming: seeming to claim much, or too much.—*adv.* **preten'tiously.**—*n.* **preten'tiousness.**—**Old Pretender, Young Pretender** the son, grandson, of James II and VII as claimants to the British throne. [L. *praetendĕre*—*prae*, *tendĕre*, *tentum*, *tēnsum*, to stretch.]

preter-, (L. spelling occurring chiefly in obs. words) **praeter-**, *prē'tar-*, in composition, beyond.—*adj.* **preternat'ural** out of the ordinary course of nature: abnormal: supernatural. [L. *praeter*.]

preterite, preterit *pret'ə-rit*, *adj.* past —*n.* (a word in) the past tense.—*adj.* **pret'erite-pres'ent** pertaining to a verb which has an original preterite still preterite in form but present in meaning.—Also *n.* [L. *praeteritus—ire, itum*, to go.]

preterm *prē'tûrm'*, *adj.* born prematurely. [Pfx. **pre-** (2).]

pretermit *prē-tar-mit'*, *v.t.* to pass by to omit: to leave undone: to desist from for a time:—*pr.p.* **prētermitt'ing**; *pa.t.* and *pa.p.* **prētermitt'ed.**—*n.* **pretermission** (*-mish'ən*). [L. *praetermittĕre, -missum—mittĕre*, to send.]

pretext *prē'tekst*, *n.* an ostensible motive or reason, put forward as excuse or to conceal the true one. [L. *praetextus, -ūs*, pretext, outward show, *praetextum*, pretext.]

pretty *prit'i*, *adj.* (esp. ironically) fine: commendable: pleasing in a moderate way but not deeply: having some superficial attractiveness but not striking beauty: beautiful without dignity: insipidly graceful: considerable.—*n.* a pretty thing or person: a knick-knack: the fluted part of a glass.—*adv.* fairly: prettily (*coll.* or *illit.*).—*n.* **prettifica'tion.**—*v t.* **prett'ify** to trick out in an excessively ornamental or namby-pamby way.—*adv.* **prett'ily** in a pretty manner: pleasingly: elegantly: neatly.—*ns.* **prett'iness**; **prett'y-prett'y** (*coll.*) a knick-knack.—*adj.* namby-pamby: insipidly pretty, overpretty.—**a pretty penny** a good large sum; **pretty much** very nearly; **pretty well** almost entirely; **sitting pretty** in an advantageous position. [O.E. *prættig*, tricky—*prætt*, trickery.]

pretzel *pret'səl*, *n.* a crisp salted biscuit made in rope shape and twisted into a kind of loose knot. [Ger.]

prevail *pri-vāl'*, *v.i.* to gain the victory: to succeed: to have the upper hand: to urge successfully (with *on, upon*): to be usual or most usual: to hold good, be in use, be customary.—*adj.* **prevail'ing** having great power: controlling: bringing about results: very general or common: most common.—*adv.* **prevail'-ingly.**—*ns.* **prevalence** (*prev'ə-ləns*), **prev'alency** the state of being prevalent or widespread: superior strength or influence: preponderance: effective influence.—*adj.* **prev'alent** prevailing: having great power: victorious: widespread: most common.—*adv* **prev'alently.** [L. *praevalēre—prae, valēre*, to be powerful.]

prevaricate *pri-var'i-kāt*, *v.i.* to evade the truth: to quibble.—*ns.* **prevarica'tion**; **prevar'icātor.** [L. *praevāricāri, -ātus*, to walk straddlingly or crookedly, to act collusively—*prae, vāricus*, straddling—*vārus*, bent.]

prevent *pri-vent'*, *v.t.* to balk: to preclude: to stop, keep, or hinder effectually: to keep from coming to pass.—*n.* **prevē'nience.**—*adj.* **prevē'nient** antecedent: predisposing: preventive.—*n.* **prevent-abil'ity.**—*adj.* **preven'table** (also **-ible**).—*ns.* **preven'ter**; **preven'tion** the act of preventing: anticipation or forethought: obstruction.—*adjs.* **preven'tive** (also, irregularly, **preven'tative**) tending to prevent or hinder: prophylactic.—*ns.* that which prevents: a prophylactic.—**preventive detention** specially prolonged imprisonment for persistent offenders of 30 or over for periods of from 5 to 14 years. [L. *praevenire, -ventum—venire*, to come.]

preverbal *prē-vûr'bl*, *adj.* occurring or standing before a verb: pertaining to a time before the development of speech. [Pfx. **pre-** (2).]

preview *prē'vū*, *n.* a view of a performance, exhibition, etc., before it is open to the public: an advance showing to the public of excerpts from a film, play, etc.—*v.t.* (*prē-vū'*) to look at beforehand: to foresee:

(*prē'vū*) to give a preview of. [Pfx. **pre-** (2)]

previous *prē'vi-əs*, *adj.* going before in time: already arranged: former: premature (*facet.*)—*adv.* previously (usu. with *to*)—*adv.* **prē'viously.**—*n.* **prē'-viousness.**—**previous question** in parliament, a motion 'that the question be not now put' If the decision be 'ay', the debate is ended without a vote on the main issue In public meetings the carrying of the 'previous question' means that the meeting passes on to the next business. [L. *praevius—prae, via*, a way.]

previse *prē-vīz'*, *v.t* to foresee: to forewarn.—*n.* **prevision** (*-vizh'ən*) foresight: foreknowledge. [L. *praevidēre, -vīsum—prae, vidēre*, to see.]

prey *prā*, *n.* booty, plunder: an animal that is, or may be, killed and eaten by another: a victim (with *to*): depredation.—*v.i.* (commonly with *on* or *upon*) to make depredations: to take plunder: to seek, kill, and feed: to live (*on*) as a victim: to waste, eat away, distress —**beast, bird, of prey** one that devours other animals, esp higher animals. [O.Fr. *preie* (Fr *proie*)—L. *praeda*, booty.]

prezzie *prez'i*, (*coll.*) *n.* a present or gift

prial *prī'əl.* Same as **pair-royal.**

Priapus *prī-ā'pəs*, *n.* an ancient deity personifying male generative power, guardian of gardens, later regarded as the chief god of lasciviousness and sensuality.—*adjs.* **Priapean** (*prī-ə-pē'ən*); **Priapic** (*-ap'ik*) of or relating to Priapus: (without *cap.*) of, relating to, exhibiting, etc. a phallus: (without *cap.*) overly concerned or preoccupied with virility and male sexuality.—*n.* **pri'apism** persistent erection of the penis: licentiousness, lewdness. [Latinised from Gr. *Priāpos.*]

price *prīs n.* the amount, usually in money, for which a thing is sold or offered: that which one forgoes or suffers for the sake of or in gaining something: money offered for capture or killing of anybody: (the size of) the sum, etc., by which one can be bribed: betting odds.—*v.t.* to fix, state, or mark the price of: to ask the price of (*coll.*).—*adjs.* **priced** having a price assigned: valued at such-and-such a price; **price'less** beyond price: invaluable: supremely and delectably absurd.—*adv.* **price'lessly.**—*n.* **price'lessness.**—*adj.* **pric'ey** sometimes **pric'y**, (*coll.*) expensive:—*compar.* **pri'cier**; *superl.* **pri'ciest.**—*n* **priciness.**—**price control** the fixing by a government of maximum, or sometimes minimum, prices chargeable for goods or services; **price'-cutting** lowering of prices to secure custom; **price'-fixing** the establishing of the price of a commodity, etc. by agreement between suppliers or by government price control, rather than by the operation of a free market; **price index** an index number which relates current prices to those of a base period or base date, the latter usu. being assigned the value of 100; **price'-list** a list of prices of goods offered for sale; **price ring** a group of manufacturers who co-operate for the purpose of raising or maintaining the price of a commodity above the level that would be established by a free market; **price'-tag** a tag or the like showing price (also *fig.*).—**above, beyond price** so valuable that no price can or would be enough; **at a price** at a somewhat high price; **price-earnings ratio** the ratio of the market price of a common stock share to its earnings; **price of money** the rate of discount in lending or borrowing capital; **price oneself out of the market** to charge more than customers or clients are willing to pay; **price on one's head** a reward for one's capture or slaughter; **what price—?** what about (this or that) now?: what do you think of?; **without price** priceless [O.Fr. *pris* (Fr.

pre'-war' *adj.*, *adv.* **pre-** (2).

prix)—L. *pretium*, price; cf. **praise, prize**[3].]

prick *prik*, *n.* anything sharp and piercing, as a thorn, spine, goad: the act, experience, or stimulus of piercing or puncturing: a puncture: a mark or wound made by puncturing: the centre of an archery target: a mark or target: a hare's footprint: a penis (*vulg.*).—*v.t.* to pierce slightly with a fine point: to give a feeling as of pricking: to make by puncturing: to urge with, or as with, a spur or goad: to trace with pricks: to pin: to pick with a point: to insert (e.g. seedlings) in small holes (usu. with *in, out*, etc.): to stick, stick over: to erect, cock, stick up (sometimes with *up*): to incite (*fig.*): to deck out: to pain.—*v.i.* to pierce, make punctures: to have a sensation of puncture or prickling: to begin to turn sour: to stand erect: to ride with spurs, or quickly.—*ns.* **prick'er; prick'ing; prickle** (*prik'l*) a little prick: a sharp point growing from the epidermis of a plant or from the skin of an animal.—*v.t.* and *v.i.* to prick slightly.—*v.i.* to have a prickly feeling.—*n.* **prick'liness.**—*n.* and *adj.* **prick'ling.**—*adj.* **prick'ly** full of prickles: tingling as if prickled: easily annoyed.—*adj.* **prick'-eared** having erect or noticeable ears.—**prick'ly-heat** a skin disease, inflammation of the sweat-glands with intense irritation; **prick'ly-pear** a cactaceous genus (Opuntia) with clusters of prickles: its pear-shaped fruit.—**kick against the pricks** to hurt oneself by resisting someone or something, to no avail (Acts ix. 5); **prick up one's ears** to begin to listen intently. [O.E. *prica*, point.]

pride *prid*, *n.* the state or feeling of being proud: too great self-esteem: haughtiness: a proper sense of what is becoming to oneself and scorn of what is unworthy: a feeling of pleasure on account of something worthily done or anything connected with oneself: that of which one is proud: splendour: a peacock's attitude of display: a company of lions.—*v.t.* (*refl.*) to take pride in (with *on*).—**pride of place** the culmination of an eagle's or hawk's flight: the distinction of holding the highest position; **take (a) pride in** to make (a thing) an object in which one's pride is concerned. [O.E *prȳde, prȳte*—*prūd, prūt*, proud.]

prie-dieu *prē'dyø'*, *n.* a praying-desk or chair for praying on. [Fr., pray-God.]

priest *prēst*, *n.* an official conductor of religious rites: a mediator between a god and worshippers (*fem.* **priest'ess**): a minister above a deacon and below a bishop: a clergyman.—*ns.* **priest'craft** priestly policy directed to worldly ends; **priest'hood** the office or character of a priest: the priestly order.—*adj.* **priest'ly** pertaining to or like a priest.—**priest's hole, priest hole** a secret room for a priest in time of persecution or repression. [O.E. *prēost*—L. *presbyter*—Gr. *presbyteros*, an elder.]

prig *prig*, *n.* a precisian: a person of precise morals without a sense of proportion.—*n.* **prigg'ery.**—*adj.* **prigg'ish.**—*adv.* **prigg'ishly.**—*n.* **prigg'ishness.**

prim[1] *prim*, *adj.* exact and precise: stiffly formal.—*v.t.* to deck with great nicety: to form, set or purse into primness.—*v.i.* to look prim: to prim the mouth:—*pr.p.* **primm'ing;** *pa.t.* and *pa.p.* **primmed.**—*adv.* **prim'ly.**—*n.* **prim'ness.** [Late 17th-cent. cant.]

prim[2] *prim*, *n.* med. coll. contraction of **primigravida** as in **elderly prim** one of 25 and over.

prima. See **primo.**

primacy *prī'mə-si*, *n.* the position of first: the chief place: the office or dignity of a primate.

primaeval. Same as **primeval.**

prima facie *prī'ma fāsh'ē(-ē), prē'ma fak'i-ā*, (L.) on the first view: at first sight: (of evidence) sufficient to support the bringing of a charge (*law*): (of a case) supported by prima facie evidence (*law*).

primal. See **prime**[1].

primary *prī'mə-ri*, *adj.* first: original: of the first order (e.g. in a system of successive branchings): firstformed: primitive: chief: elementary: fundamental: belonging to the first stages of education: of a feather, growing on the manus: relating to primaries (*U.S.*): (with *cap.*) Palaeozoic (*geol.*).—*n.* that which is highest in rank or importance: a primary feather: a primary school: a substance obtained directly, by extraction and purification, from natural, or crude technical, raw material—cf. *intermediate:* a meeting of the voters of a political party in an electoral division to nominate candidates, or to elect delegates to a nominating convention representing a larger area (*U.S politics*).—*adv.* **pri'marily.**—*n.* **pri'mariness.** —**primary battery, cell** one producing an electric current by irreversible chemical action; **primary colours** those from which all others can be derived—physiologically red, green, violet, or blue, for pigments red, yellow, blue: also red, orange, yellow, green, blue, indigo, and violet; **primary planet** a planet distinguished from a satellite. [L. *primārius*—*primus*, first.]

primate *prī'māt, -mit*, *n.* one who is first: a bishop or archbishop to whose see was formerly annexed the dignity of vicar of the holy see (*R.C. Church*): an archbishop over a province (*Ch. of Eng.*): a member of the order Primates (*zool.*).—*n.pl.* **Primates** (*prī-mā'tēz*) the highest order of mammals, including lemurs, monkeys, anthropoid apes, and man.—*n.* **pri'mateship.**—*ns.* **primatol'ogist; primatol'ogy** the study of the Primates. [L.L. *primās, -ātis*—L. *primus*, first.]

prime[1] *prim*, *adj.* first in order of time, rank, or importance: primary: chief: main: of the highest quality: of the time of broadcasting of a radio or television programme, occurring during peak viewing or listening time and (therefore) having the highest advertising rates: original: (of a number other than one) divisible by no whole number except unity and itself (*arith.*): (of two or more numbers) relatively prime (with *to*; *arith.*).—*n.* the first of the lesser hours of the Roman breviary: the time of this office, about six in the morning, or sometimes sunrise: the time from the beginning of the artificial day to terce (about nine): the beginning: the best part: the height of perfection: full health and strength: a prime number: a first subdivision or symbol marking it (') (*math.* etc.): the first guard against sword-thrusts, also the first and simplest thrust (*fencing*).—*adj.* **pri'mal** first: primitive: original: chief, fundamental.—**prime (lending) rate** the lowest rate of interest charged by a bank at any given time, usu. available only to large concerns with high credit ratings, and forming the base figure on which other rates are calculated; **prime meridian** that chosen as zero for reference; **prime minister** the chief minister of state; **prime mover** the main cause or instigator of an action, project, etc. (*fig.*); **prime number** a number, other than one, divisible only by itself or unity.—**relatively prime** (*arith.*) having no common integral factor but unity. [L. *primus*, first; partly through O.E. *prim*—L. *prima* (*hōra*), first (hour).]

prime[2] *prim*, *v.t.* to charge, fill: to supply with powder or other means of igniting the charge (of a firearm, bomb, etc.): to lay a train to: to bring into activity or working order by a preliminary charge (as a man by giving him liquor, a pump by pouring in water, an internal-combustion engine by injecting gas or oil): to post up, coach, cram beforehand with information or instructions: to put on a primer in painting.—*v.i.* to prime a gun: (of a boiler) to send water with the steam into the cylinder: (of the tides) to recur at progressively shorter intervals.—*ns.* **pri'mer** one who primes: a priming-wire: a detonator: a preparatory first coat of paint, etc.: the particular type of paint used for this; **pri'ming** the action of the verb in any sense: the progressive shortening of the interval between tides as spring tide approaches: a detonating charge that fires a propellant charge: a tube for priming an internal-combustion engine: a priming-wire: a first coat of paint.—**pri'ming-iron, -wire** a wire passed through the touch-hole of a cannon to clear it and pierce the cartridge; **pri'ming-pow'der** detonating powder: a train of powder.

primer *prī'mər*, or *prim'ər*, *n.* a small book of hours or prayer book for laymen, used also for teaching reading: a first reading-book: an elementary introduction to any subject. [L. *prīmārius*, primary.]

primeval, primaeval *prī-mē'vl*, *adj.* belonging to the first ages. [L. *primaevus—prīmus*, first, *aevum*, an age.]

primigravida *prī-mi-grav'i-də*, *n.* a woman pregnant for the first time:—*pl.* **primigrav'idae** (*-dē*) or **-as.** [L. fem. adjs. *prīma*, first, *gravida*, pregnant.]

primipara *prī-mip'ə-rə*, *n.* a woman who has given birth for the first time only, or is about to do so:—*pl.* **primip'arae** (*-rē*) or **-as.** [L. *prīma* (fem.), first, *parēre*, to bring forth.]

primitiae *prī-mish'i-ē*, *n.pl.* first-fruits: the first year's revenue of a benefice.—*adj.* **primitial** (*-mish'l*) of first-fruits: (*loosely*) primeval, original. [L. *prīmitiae—prīmus*, first.]

primitive *prim'i-tiv*, *adj.* belonging to the beginning, or to the first times: original: ancient: antiquated, old-fashioned: crude: not derivative: fundamental: first-formed, of early origin (*biol.*): (of a culture or society) not advanced, lacking a written language and having only fairly simple technical skills.—*n.* that from which other things are derived: a root-word: a painter or picture of pre-Renaissance date or manner: a 19th- and 20th-century school of painting, characterised by a complete simplicity of approach to subject and technique.—*adv.* **prim'itively.**—*ns.* **prim'itiveness; prim'itivism** approbation of primitive ways, primitive Christianity, primitive art, etc.; **prim'itivist.** [L. *prīmitīvus*, an extension of *prīmus*.]

primo *prē'mō*, *adj.* first:—*fem.* **pri'ma.**—*n.* (*mus.*) the first or principal part in a duet or trio:—*pl.* **pri'mos.**—**prima ballerina** (*bal-ə-rēn'ə*, It. *ba-le-rē'na*) the leading ballerina:—*pls.* **prima ballerinas, prime** (*-ā*) **ballerine; prima donna** (*don'ə* It. *don'na*) the leading female singer in an opera company: a person, esp. a woman, who is temperamental, over-sensitive and hard to please:—*pls.* **prima donnas, prime** (*-ā*) **donne.** [It.,—L. *prīmus.*]

primogeniture *prī-mō-jen'i-chər*, *n.* the state or fact of being first-born: inheritance by or of the first-born child or (*male primogeniture*) son. [L. *prīmōgenitus —prīmō*, first (adv.), *genitus*, born.]

primordial *prī-mör'di-əl*, *adj.* existing from the beginning: original: rudimentary: first-formed.—*n.* the first principle or element.—*ns.* **primor'dialism; primordiality** (*-al'i-ti*).—*adv.* **primor'dially.** [L. *prīmordium—prīmus*, first, *ordīrī*, to begin.]

primp *primp*, *v.i.* to dress in a fussy or affected manner: to preen, titivate.—Also *v.t.* [Conn. **prim.**]

primrose *prim'rōz*, *n.* a plant (*Primula vulgaris*), or its flower, common in spring in woods and meadows: extended to others of the genus Primula: formerly some other (and brighter) flower.—*adj.* pale yellow, like a primrose. [O.Fr. *primerose*, as if—L., *prīma rosa*; perh. really through M.E. and O.Fr. *primerole* —L.L. *prīmula—prīmus*, first.]

Primula *prim'ū-la*, *n.* the genus of flowers including

the primrose, cowslip, oxlip, etc.: (without *cap.*) a plant of this genus. [L.L.,—L. *prīmus*, first.]

primus¹ *prī'məs*, *prē'mŏŏs*, *n.* a presiding bishop in the Scottish Episcopal Church. [L., first.]

primus² *prī'məs*, *prē'mŏŏs*, (L.) first.—**primus inter pares** (*in'tər pā'rēz*, *pār'ĕs*) first among equals.

Primus® *prī'məs*, *n.* a portable cooking stove burning vaporised oil.—Also **Primus stove.**

prince *prins*, *n.* one of the highest rank: a sovereign (of some small countries): a male member of a royal or imperial family: a title of nobility, as formerly in Germany (*Fürst*): a chief: anybody or anything that is first in merit or demerit, or most outstanding.—*ns.* **prince'dom** a principality: the estate, jurisdiction, sovereignty, or rank of a prince; **prince'ling** a petty prince.—*adj.* **prince'like** like a prince: becoming a prince.—*n.* **prince'liness.**—*adj.* **prince'ly** of a prince or princess: of the rank of prince: princelike: becoming a prince: magnificent: sumptuous: lavish. —Also *adv.*—*n.* **prin'cess** (or *-ses'*) *fem.* of prince: a prince's wife (of recognised rank): a woman's garment with skirt and bodice in one piece—in this sense also (Fr.) **princesse** (*prin'*, or *-ses'*), **princess(e)-dress, -skirt**, etc., the style being known as **princess line.**— **prince'-con'sort** a prince who is husband of a reigning queen; **prin'cess-roy'al** a title which may be conferred on the eldest daughter of a sovereign.—**prince of darkness, prince of this world** Satan; **Prince of Peace** Christ: the Messiah; **Prince of Wales** since 1301, a title usu. conferred on the eldest son of the English, and later British, sovereign. [Fr.,—L. *princeps— prīmus*, first, *capĕre*, to take.]

principal *prin'si-pl*, *adj.* taking the first place: highest in rank, character, or importance: chief: of the nature of principal or a principal.—*n.* a principal person: the head of a college or university, or sometimes of a school: one who takes a leading part: money on which interest is paid: a main beam, rafter, girder, or timber: the person who commits a crime, or one who aids and abets him in doing it (*law*): a person for whom another becomes surety (*law*): a person who employs another to do an act which he is competent himself to do (*law*): one who fights a duel: an organstop like the open diapason but an octave higher (*mus.*).—*n.* **principality** (*-pal'i-ti*) the status, dignity, or power of a prince: the condition of being a prince: the territory of a prince or the country that gives him title: a member of one order of angels.—*adv.* **prin'- cipally.**—*n.* **prin'cipalship.**—**principal boy** (*theat.*) an actress (now sometimes an actor) who plays the role of the hero in pantomime; **principal clause** a clause which could function as an independent sentence; **principal parts** those forms (of a verb) from which all other forms may be deduced. [L. *prīncipālis—prīnceps, -ipis*, chief.]

principate *prin'si-pāt*, *n.* princehood: principality: the Roman empire in its earlier form in which something of republican theory survived. [L. *prīncipātus—*the emperor's title *prīnceps* (*cīvitātis*), chief (of the city or state).]

principle *prin'si-pl*, *n.* a source, root, origin: that which is fundamental: essential nature: a theoretical basis: a faculty of the mind: a source of action: a fundamental truth on which others are founded or from which they spring: a law or doctrine from which others are derived: a settled rule of action: consistent regulation of behaviour according to moral law: a component: a constituent part from which some quality is derived (*chem.*).—*v.t.* to establish in principles: to impress with a doctrine.—*adj.* **prin'cipled** holding certain principles: having, or behaving in accordance with, good principles: invoking or founded on a principle.—**first principles** fundamental principles, not deduced from others; **in principle** so far as general character or theory is concerned without respect to details or particular application; **on principle** on grounds of principle: for the sake of obeying or asserting a principle. [L. *prīncipium*, beginning— *prīnceps*.]

prink *pringk*, *v.t.* and *v.i.* to deck up, smarten. [App. conn. with **prank**[2].]

print *print*, *n*. an impression: a mould or stamp: printed state: printed characters or lettering: an edition: a printed copy: a printed picture: an engraving: a newspaper: a positive photograph made from a negative (or negative from positive): a printed cloth, esp. calico stamped with figures: a plaster-cast in low relief (*archit.*): a fingerprint.—*adj.* of printed cotton.— *v.t.* to mark by pressure: to impress on paper, etc., by means of types, plates, or blocks: to produce or reproduce by such means: to cause to be so printed: to stamp a pattern on or transfer it to: to produce as a positive picture from a negative, or as a negative from a positive (*phot.*): to write in imitation of type.—*v.i.* to practise the art of printing: to publish a book: to yield an impression, or give a positive, etc.—*adj.* **print'able** capable of being printed: fit to print.— *ns.* **print'er** one who, or that which, prints: one who is employed in printing books, etc.: a device for printing, as telegraph messages, photographs, etc.; **print'ing** the act, art, or business of the printer: the whole number of copies printed at one time, an impression.—**printed circuit** a wiring circuit, free of loose wiring, formed by printing the design of the wiring on copper foil bonded to a flat base and etching away the unprinted foil; **printer's mark** an engraved device used by printers as a trademark; **print'ing-house** a building where printing is carried on: a printing-office; **print'ing-ink** ink used in printing—a usually thickish mixture of pigment (as carbon black) with oil and sometimes varnish; **print'ing-machine** a printing-press worked by power; **print'ing-office** an establishment where books, etc., are printed; **print'ing-press** a machine by which impressions are taken in ink upon paper from types, plates, etc.; **print'-out** the printed information given out by a computer, etc.; **print'-run** a single printing of a book, etc.—**in print** existing in printed form: printed and still to be had; **out of print** no longer in print; no longer available from a publisher; **print out** to print: to produce a print-out of. [M.E. *print, prente*, etc. —O.Fr. *preinte, priente—preindre, priembre*—L. *premēre*, to press.]

prior *prī'ər*, *adj.* previous.—*adv.* previously (with *to*). —*n*. the officer next under the abbot in an abbey (*claustral prior*): the head of a priory of monks (*conventual prior*) or of a house of canons regular or of friars:—*fem.* **pri'oress**.—*n*. **priority** (*prī-or'i-ti*) the state of being first in time, place, or rank: preference: the privilege of preferential treatment: something that ought to be considered, dealt with, in the earliest stage of proceedings.—*adj.* having, entitling to, or allowed to those who have, priority.—*ns.* **pri'orship**; **pri'ory** a convent of either sex subject to an abbey. [L. *prior, -ōris*, former.]

prise. See **prize**[1].

prism *prizm*, *n*. a solid whose ends are similar, equal, and parallel polygons, and whose sides are parallelograms (*geom.*): an object of that shape, esp. a triangular prism of glass or the like for resolving light into separate colours: (*loosely*) prismatic colours or spectrum.—*adjs.* **prismat'ic, -al** resembling or pertaining to a prism: built up of prisms: separated or formed by a prism.—*n*. **pris'moid** a figure like a prism, but with similar unequal ends.—**prismatic colours** the seven colours into which a ray of white light is refracted by a

prism—red, orange, yellow, green, blue, indigo, and violet; **prismatic compass** a surveying instrument which by means of a prism enables the compass-reading to be taken as the object is sighted. [Gr. *prisma, -atos*, a piece sawn off.]

prison *priz'n*, *n*. a building for the confinement of criminals or others: a jail: any place of confinement: confinement.—*v.t.* to shut in prison: to enclose: to restrain.—*n*. **pris'oner** one under arrest or confined in prison: a captive, esp. in war: anyone involuntarily kept under restraint.—**prison officer** the official title of a warder (still so-called unofficially) in prison.— **prisoner of conscience** see **conscience**; **prisoner of war** a person captured during a war, esp. a member of the armed forces, but also including militia, irregular troops and, under certain conditions, civilians; **take prisoner** to capture. [O.Fr. *prisun*—L. *prēnsiō, -ōnis*, for *praehēnsiō*, seizure—*praehendēre, -hēnsum*, to seize.]

prissy *pris'i*, *adj.* prim, prudish, fussy: effeminate. [Prob. **prim** and **sissy**.]

pristine *pris'tīn, -tēn*, *adj.* original: former: belonging to the earliest time. [L. *prīstinus*; cf. *prīscus*, antique, *prior*, former.]

prithee *pridh'ē, -i, interj.* for (I) **pray thee**.

privacy *priv'ə-si*, or *prīv'*, *n*. seclusion: a place of seclusion: retreat: retirement: avoidance of notice or display: secrecy: a private matter. [**private**.]

private *prī'vit*, *adj.* apart from the state: not in public office: (of member of parliament) not holding government office: (of soldier) not an officer or non-commissioned officer: peculiar to oneself: belonging to, or concerning, an individual person or company: not part of, not receiving treatment under, etc. the National Health Service or any similar state scheme: independent: own: relating to personal affairs: in an unofficial capacity: not public: not open to the public: not made known generally: confidential: retired from observation: alone.—*n*. privacy: (in *pl.*) private parts: a private soldier.—*adv.* **pri'vately.**—*n*. **privatisa'tion, -z-.**—*v.t.* **pri'vatise, -ize** to make private: to denationalise.—**private company** a company, with restrictions on the number of shareholders, whose shares may not be offered to the general public; **private detective** see **detective** under **detect**; **private enterprise** an economic system in which individual private firms operate and compete freely; **private eye** (*coll.*) a private detective; **private income** private means; **private investigator** (esp. *U.S.*) a private detective; **private means** income from investments, etc. as opposed to salary or fees for work done; **private parts** the external sexual organs; **private school** a school run independently by an individual or a group, especially for profit; **private sector** the part of a country's economy owned, operated, etc., by private individuals and firms (opp. to *public sector*).—**in private** not in public: away from public view: secretly; **private member's bill** one introduced and sponsored by a private member in parliament. [L. *prīvātus*, pa.p. of *prīvāre*, to deprive, to separate.]

privateer *prī-və-tēr'*, *n*. a private vessel commissioned to seize and plunder an enemy's ships: the commander or one of the crew of a privateer.—*v.i.* to cruise in a privateer.—*ns.* **privateer'ing**; **privateers'man**. [**private**.]

privation *prī-vā'shən*, *n*. the state of being deprived of something, esp. of what is necessary for comfort: the absence of any quality (*log.*).—*adj.* **privative** (*priv'ə-tiv*) causing privation: consisting in the absence or removal of something: expressing absence or negation (*gram.*).—*n*. that which is privative or depends on the absence of something else: a term denoting the absence of a quality (*log.*): a privative affix or word (*gram.*).—*adv.* **priv'atively.** [L. *privātio, -ōnis, privātivus—privāre,* to deprive.]

privet *priv'it, n.* European shrub of the olive family, used for hedges: also applied to other members of the genus.

privilege *priv'i-lij, n.* an advantage, right or favour granted to or enjoyed by an individual, or a few: freedom from burdens borne by others: a happy advantage: a prerogative: a sacred and vital civil right.—*v.t.* to grant a privilege to: to exempt: to authorise, license.—*adj.* **priv'ileged** enjoying a privilege or privileges.—**breach of privilege** any interference with or slight done to the rights or privileges of a legislative body; **privilege of parliament, parliamentary privilege** special rights or privileges enjoyed by members of parliament, as freedom of speech (not subject to slander laws), and freedom from arrest except on a criminal charge. [Fr. *privilège—*L. *privilēgium—privus,* private, *lēx, lēgis,* a law.]

privy *priv'i, adj.* private: pertaining to one person: for private uses: secret: appropriate to retirement: sharing the knowledge of something secret (with *to*).—*n.* a person having an interest in an action, contract, conveyance, etc. (*law*): a room set apart with container in which to evacuate body waste products (esp. one in an outhouse).—*adv.* **priv'ily** privately: secretly.—**privy council** (also with *caps.*) originally the private council of a sovereign to advise in the administration of government—its membership now consisting of all present and past members of the Cabinet and other eminent people, but with its functions mainly formal or performed by committees, etc.; **privy councillor,** or **counsellor** (also with *caps.*); **privy purse** (also with *caps.*) an allowance for the private or personal use of the sovereign; **privy seal** see **seal**[1].—**Lord Privy Seal** see under **seal**[1]. [Fr. *privé—*L. *privātus,* private.]

prize[1], **prise** *prīz, v.t.* to force (esp. up or open) with a lever. [Fr. *prise,* hold, grip.]

prize[2], *prīz, n.* that which is taken by force, or in war, esp. a ship.—*v.t.* to make a prize of.—**prize'-crew** a crew put aboard a prize to bring her to port; **prize'-money** share of the money or proceeds from any prizes taken from an enemy. [Fr. *prise,* capture, thing captured—L. *praehēnsa—praehendēre,* to seize.]

prize[3] *prīz, n.* a reward or symbol of success offered or won in competition by contest or chance, or granted in recognition of excellence: anything well worth striving for: a highly valued acquisition.—*adj.* awarded, or worthy of, a prize.—*v.t.* to value: to value highly.—*adjs.* **prīz'able** valuable; **prized.**—**prize'-list** a list of winners; **prize'-man** a winner of a prize, esp. an academic prize; **prize'-winner.** [A differentiated form of **price** and **praise**—O.Fr. *pris* (n.), *prisier* (vb.)—L. *pretium,* price.]

prize[4] *prīz, n.* a match.—*n.* **prīz'er** a contestant in a prize or match.—**prize'-fight** a public boxing-match for money; **prize'-fighter** orig. one who fights for a prize: now, a professional pugilist; **prize'-fighting; prize'-ring** a ring for prize-fighting: the practice itself. [Possibly from the foregoing.]

pro[1] *prō,* (L.) *prep.* for.—**pro bono publico** (*bo'nō pub'li-kō, bō'nō pōō'bli-kō*) for the public good; **pro forma** (*för'mə, för'mä*) as a matter of form: (also with *hyphen*) of an account, etc., made out to show the market price of specified goods: with goods being paid for before dispatch; **pro patria** (*pā'tri-ə, pä'tri-ä*) for one's country; **pro rata** (*rā'tə, rä'tä*) in proportion; **pro tempore** (*tem'pə-rē, tem'po-re*) for the time being.

pro[2] *prō, n.* a coll. contraction of **professional** (golfer, cricketer, actor, etc.), of **probationary** (nurse), and of **prostitute:**—*pl.* **pros** (*prōz*).—*adj.* of or pertaining

to a pro or pros.—*adj.* **pro'-am'** involving both professionals and amateurs.

pro[3] *prō, n.* one who favours or votes for some proposal: a reason or argument in favour:—*pl.* **pros** (*prōz*).—**pros and cons** reasons or arguments for and against. [L. *prō,* for.]

pro-[1] *prō, Gr. pfx.* before (in time or place): earlier than: in front of: the front part of: primitive: rudimentary. [Gr. prep. *prŏ,* before; cf. L. *prō,* Eng. **for, fore.**]

pro-[2] *prō, L. pfx.* used (*a*) as an etymological element with the senses before (in place or time), forward, forth, publicly; (*b*) as a living pfx. with the sense instead of; (*c*) as a living pfx. (in new formations) with the sense in favour of—as *pro-Boer; pro-German; pro-Negro; pro-slavery.* [L. prep. *prō,* earlier *prōd,* in comp. sometimes *prō-;* cf. preceding.]

proa *prō'ə.* See **prau.**

pro-am. See **pro**[2].

probable *prob'ə-bl, adj.* having more evidence for than against: giving ground for belief: likely: colourable, plausible.—*n.* probable opinion: one that has a good chance, or is likely to turn out or become the thing in question.—*n.* **probabil'ity** the quality of being probable: the appearance of truth: that which is probable: the chance or likelihood of something happening:—*pl.* **probabil'ities.**—*adv.* **prob'ably.**—**in all probability** quite probably. [Fr.,—L. *probābilis—probāre, -ātum,* to prove.]

probang *prō'bang, n.* an instrument for pushing obstructions down the oesophagus. [Called *provang* by its inventor; prob. influenced by **probe.**]

probate *prō'bāt, -bit, n.* the proof before a competent court that a written paper purporting to be the will of a person who has died is indeed his lawful act: the official copy of a will, with the certificate of its having been proved.—*adj.* relating to the establishment of wills and testaments.—*n.* **probation** (*prə-, prō-bā'shən*) testing: proof: a preliminary time or condition appointed to allow fitness or unfitness to appear: noviciate: suspension of sentence, allowing liberty under supervision on condition of good behaviour, (esp. to young, or first, offenders): time of trial: moral trial.—*adjs.* **proba'tional** relating to, serving purpose of, probation or trial; **proba'tionary** probational: on probation.—*n.* a probationer.—*ns.* **proba'tioner** one who is on probation or trial: an offender under probation: a novice: one licensed to preach, but not ordained to a pastorate (esp. *Scot.*); **proba'tionership.**—*adj.* **probative** (*prō'bə-tiv*) testing: affording proof.—**probation officer** one appointed to advise and supervise offenders under probation. [L. *probāre, -ātum,* to test, prove.]

probe *prōb, n.* an instrument for exploring a wound, locating a bullet, and the like: an act of probing: an exploratory bore: a prod: an investigation: any of various instruments of investigation in space research (as a multi-stage rocket), electronics, etc.: a pipelike device attached to an aircraft for making connection with a tanker aeroplane so as to refuel in flight: a device used in docking two space modules.—*v.t.* to examine with or as with a probe: to examine searchingly.—*v.t.* and *v.i.* to pierce. [L. *proba,* proof, later examination—*probāre,* to prove.]

probity *prob'i-ti,* or *prōb', n.* uprightness: moral integrity: honesty. [L. *probitas, -ātis—probus,* good, honest.]

problem *prob'ləm, n.* a matter difficult of settlement or solution: a question or puzzle propounded for solution: a source of perplexity.—*adjs.* **problemat'ic, -al** of the nature of a problem: questionable: doubtful.—*adv.* **problemat'ically.**—*n.pl.* **problemat'ics** matters that are problematic.—**problem child** one whose character presents an exceptionally difficult problem to parents, teachers, etc. [Gr. *problēma*, *-atos*—*pro*, before, *ballein*, to throw.]

proboscis *prə-*, *prō-bos'is*, *n.* a trunk or long snout: a trunk-like process, as the suctorial mouth-parts of some insects: a nose (*facet.*):—*pls.* **probos'ises**, **probos'ides** (*-ı-dēz*).—*n.pl.* **Proboscid'ea** the elephant order of mammals.—*adjs.* and *ns.* **proboscid'ean**, **proboscid'ian.—proboscis monkey** a very long-nosed monkey (*Nasalis larvatus*). [L.,—Gr. *proboskis*, a trunk—*pro*, expressing motive, *boskein*, to feed.]

procaine *prō'kān*, *n.* a crystalline substance used as a local anaesthetic. [pro-[2] (*b*), **cocaine**.]

procathedral *prō-kə-thē'drəl*, *n.* a church used temporarily as a cathedral. [Pfx. pro-[2] (*b*).]

proceed *prə-*, *prō-sēd'*, *v.i.* to go on: to continue: to advance: to begin and go on: to act according to a method: to go from point to point: to prosper: to come forth: to result: to be descended: to take measures or action: to take legal action.—*v.t.* to say in continuation.—*n.* **prō'ceed** (usu. in *pl.*) outcome: money got from anything.—*adj.* **procedural** (*-sēd'yə-rəl*).—*ns.* **procé'dure** a mode of proceeding: a method of conducting business, esp. in a law case or a meeting: a course of action: a step taken or an act performed; **proceed'ing** a going forward. progress: advancement: a course of conduct: a step: an operation: a transaction: (in *pl.*) a record of the transactions of a society. [Fr. *procéder*—L. *prōcēdère*—*prō*, before, and *cēdère*, *cēssum*, to go.]

process *prō'ses*, sometimes (esp. in U.S.) *pros'*, *n.* a state of being in progress or being carried on: course: a series of actions or events: a sequence of operations or changes undergone: a writ by which a person or matter is brought into court (*law*): an action, suit, or the proceedings in it as a whole: progression: proceeding: a projecting part, esp. on a bone (*biol.*).—*v.t.* to serve a summons on: to sue or prosecute: to subject to a special process: to prepare (e.g. agricultural produce) for marketing, by some special process e.g. canning or bottling: to arrange (documents, etc.) systematically: to examine and analyse: (of a computer) to perform operations on (data supplied): to subject (data) to such operations.—*n.* **prō'cessor** a person or thing that processes something: a device which processes data (*comput.*): a central processing unit (*comput.*).—*adj.* **prō'cessed** produced by a special process, as synthetically, photo-mechanically, etc.—**data processing** the handling and processing of information by computers.—**in (the) process of** carrying out or on (an activity), or being carried out or on. [Fr. *procès*—L. *prōcessus*, *-ūs*, advance; cf. **proceed**.]

procession *prə-*, *prō-sesh'ən*, *n.* the act of proceeding: a train of persons, boats, etc. moving forward together as in ceremony, display, demonstration, etc.: the movement of such a train.—*v.i.* to go in procession.—*v.t.* to go through or around in procession: to celebrate by a procession.—*v.i.* **process** (*prō-ses'*) to go in procession.—*adj.* **process'ional**.—*n.* a book of litanies, hymns, etc., for processions: a hymn sung in procession.—*n.* **process'ionalist**.—*adj.* **process'ionary**.—**processionary moth** a European moth whose caterpillars go out seeking food in great processions [L. *prōcessiō*, *-ōnis*; cf. **proceed**.]

prochronism *prō'kron-izm*, *n.* a dating of an event before the right time. [Gr. *pro*, before, *chronos*, time.]

proclaim *prə-*, *prō-klām'*, *v.t.* to cry aloud. to publish abroad: to announce officially: to denounce: to announce the accession of—*n* **proclaim'** a proclamation: a proclaiming.—*ns.* **proclaim'ant**; **proclaim'er**; **proclamation** (*prok-lə-mā'shən*) the act

of proclaiming: that which is proclaimed: official notice given to the public.—*adj.* **proclamatory** (*-klam'ət-ər-i*). [Fr. *proclamer*—L. *prōclāmāre*, *prōclāmāre*—*prō*, out, *clāmāre*, to cry.]

proclitic *prō-klit'ik*, *adj.* so closely attached to the following word as to have no accent.—*n.* a proclitic word. [A modern coinage on the analogy of **enclitic** —Gr. *pro*, forward, *klīnein*, to lean.]

proclivity *prə-*, *prō-kliv'i-ti*, *n.* inclination: propensity. [L. *prōclīvis*—*prō*, forward, *clīvus*, a slope.]

proconsul *prō-kon'sl*, *n.* a Roman magistrate with almost consular authority outside the city, orig. one whose consulate had expired, often governor of a province: sometimes applied to a colonial or dominion governor.—*adj.* **procon'sular** (*-sū-lər*).—*ns.* **procon'sulate** (*-sū-lit*, *-lāt*), **procon'sulship** (*-sl-ship*) the office, or term of office, of a proconsul. [L. *prōcōnsul*.]

procrastinate *prō-kras'ti-nāt*, *v.i.* to defer action.—*n.* **procrastina'tion**—*adjs.* **procras'tinative**, **procras'-tinating**, **procras'tinatory**.—*ns.* **procras'tinativeness**; **procras'tinator**. [L. *procrāstināre*, *-ātum*—*prō*, onward, *crāstinus*, of tomorrow—*crās*, tomorrow.]

procreate *prō'kri-āt*, *v.t.* to engender: to beget: to generate.—*v.i.* to produce offspring.—*n.* **prō'creant** (*-kri-ənt*) a generator.—*adj.* generating: connected with or useful in reproduction.—*n.* **prōcrea'tion.**—*adj.* **prō'creative** having the power to procreate: generative: productive.—*ns.* **prō'creativeness**; **prō'-creator** a parent. [L. *prōcreāre*, *-ātum*—*prō*, forth, *creāre*, to produce.]

Procrustean *prō-krus'ti-ən*, *adj.* violently making conformable to a standard—from *Procrustes* (Gr. *Prōkroustēs*) a legendary Greek robber, who stretched or cut his captives' legs to make them fit a bed.—Hence, **Procrustean bed** (*fig*). [Gr. *prokrouein*, to lengthen out.]

proctal *prok'tl*, *adj.* anal.—*ns.* **proctalgia** (*-al'ji-ə*; Gr. *algos*, pain) neuralgic pain in the rectum; **procti'tis** inflammation of the rectum; **proc'toscope** an instrument for examining the rectum. [Gr. *prōktos*, anus]

proctor *prok'tər*, *n.* a procurator or manager for another: an attorney in the spiritual courts: a representative of the clergy in Convocation: an official in the English universities whose functions include enforcement of university regulations.—*adj.* **proctо'rial** (*-tōr'*, *-tōr'ı-əl*).—*adv.* **procto'rially.**—*n* **proc'torship.—king's**, **queen's**, **proctor** an official who intervenes in divorce cases in England if collusion or fraud is suspected. [**procurator**.]

procumbent *prō-kum'bənt*, *adj* lying or leaning forward: prone: prostrate: lying on the ground (*bot.*) [L. *prōcumbēns*, *-entis*, pr.p. of *prōcumbēre*—*prō*, forward, *cumbēre*, to lie down.]

procurator *prok'ū-rā-tər*, *n.* a financial agent in a Roman imperial province, sometimes administrator of part of it: one who manages affairs for another: one authorised to act for another: an agent in a law court. —*adj* **procuratorial** (*-rə-tō'ri-əl*, *-tor'*).—*ns.* **proc'u-ratorship; proc'uratory** (*-rə-tər-ı*) authorisation to act for another.—**proc'urator-fis'cal** see **fisc**. [L *prōcūrātor*, *-ōris*; see next word.]

procure *prə-*, *prō-kūr'*, *v.t.* to contrive to obtain or bring about: to bring upon someone: to induce: to obtain for another's immoral purposes.—*v.i.* to pander, pimp.—*adj* **procur'able** to be had—*ns* **procuracy** (*prok'ū-rə-si*) the office of a procurator; **procura'tion** the management of another's affairs: the instrument giving power to do so: a sum paid by incumbents to the bishop or archdeacon on visitations: a procuring; **procure'ment** the act of procuring in any sense, **procur'er** one who procures: a pander:—*fem.* **procur'ess** a bawd [Fr. *procurer*—L *prŏcûrâre*, to manage—*prŏ*, for, *cûrâre*, -*âtum*, to care for.]

prod *prod*, *v.t.* to prick: to poke, as with the end of a stick:—*pr.p.* **prodd'ing;** *pa.t.* and *pa.p.* **prodd'ed.**—*n.* an act of prodding: a sharp instrument, as a goad, an awl, a skewer. [Origin unknown; O.E. *prodbor* seems to mean auger.]

prodigal *prod'i-gl*, *adj.* wasteful of one's means: squandering: lavish.—*n.* a waster: a spendthrift.—*n.* **prodigality** (-*gal'i-ti*) the state or quality of being prodigal: extravagance: profusion: great liberality.—*adv.* **prod'igally.** [Obs. Fr.,—L *prŏdigus*—*prŏ-digĕre*, to squander.]

prodigy *prod'i-ji*, *n.* any person or thing that causes great wonder: a wonder: a child of precocious genius or virtuosity.—*n.* **prodigios'ity.**—*adj.* **prodig'ious** astonishing: more than usually large in size or degree.—*adv.* **prodig'iously.**—*n.* **prodig'iousness.** [L. *prŏdigium*, a prophetic sign.]

produce *pra-*, *prŏ-dūs'*, *v.t.* to bring forward or out: to extend: to bring into being: to bring forth: to yield: to bring about: to make: to put on the stage: to prepare for exhibition to the public.—*v.i.* to yield: to create value.—*ns.* **produce** (*prod'ūs*) that which is produced: product: proceeds: crops: yield, esp. of fields and gardens; **produc'er** one who produces, esp commodities, or a play or similar exhibition: one who exercises general control over, but does not actually make, a motion picture (cf. **director**).—*adj.* **pro-duc'ible** that may be produced.—*ns.* **product** (*prod'əkt*, -*ukt*) a thing produced: a result: a work: offspring: a quantity got by multiplying (*math.*): a substance obtained from another by chemical change (*chem.*); **productibil'ity** (*pra-dukt-*) the capability of being produced.—*n.* **produc'tion** the act of producing: that which is produced: fruit: product: a work, esp. of art: a putting upon the stage: a bringing out: the creation of values (*pol. econ.*): extension.—*adjs.* **produc'tional; produc'tive** having the power to produce: generative: that produces: producing richly: fertile: efficient.—*adv.* **produc'tively.**—*ns.* **produc'tiveness; productiv'ity** (*prod-*, *prŏd-*) the rate or efficiency of work, esp. in industrial production.—**pro-ducer gas** a combustible gas, chiefly a mixture of hydrogen and carbon monoxide diluted with nitrogen.—**producer(s') goods** goods, such as raw materials and tools, used in the production of consumer(s') goods; **production line** an assembly line (q.v.); **production platform** an oil platform (q.v.); **productivity deal** an agreement whereby employees receive increased wages or salaries if they agree to improve their efficiency and increase their output.—**make a production (out) of** (*coll.*) to make an unnecessary fuss or commotion about (something). [L. *prŏdūcĕre*, -*ductum*—*prŏ*, forward, *dûcĕre*, to lead.]

proem *prŏ'em*, *n.* an introduction: a prelude: a preface. [Fr. *proème*—L. *prooemium*—Gr. *prooimion*—*pro*, before, *oimē*, a song, *oimos*, a way.]

prof *prof*, *n.* a familiar contraction of **professor.**

profane *pra-*, *prŏ-fān'*, *adj.* not sacred: secular: showing contempt of sacred things: uninitiated: unhallowed: ritually unclean or forbidden.—*v.t.* to treat with contempt or insult in spite of the holiness attributed: to desecrate: to violate: to put to an unworthy use.—*n.* **profanation** (*prof-ə-nā'shən*).—*adj.* **profanatory** (*prŏ-fan'ə-tər-i*).—*adv.* **profane'ly.**—*ns.* **profane'ness; profan'er; profanity** (-*fan'*) irreverence: that which is profane: profane language or conduct. [L. *profânus*, outside the temple, not sacred, unholy—*prŏ*, before, *fânum*, a temple.]

profess *pra-*, *prŏ-fes'*, *v.t.* to make open declaration of: to declare in strong terms: to claim (often insincerely) to have a feeling of: to pretend to: to claim to be expert in: to receive into a religious order by profession (*R C.*).—*v.i.* to enter publicly into a religious state.—*adj.* **professed'** openly declared: avowed: acknowledged: having made profession.—*adv.* **profess'edly.**—*adj.* **profess'ing** avowed: pretending, soidisant.—*n.* **profession** (-*fesh'ən*) the act of professing: an open declaration: an avowal: religious belief: a pretence: an employment not mechanical and requiring some degree of learning: a calling, habitual employment: the collective body of persons engaged in any profession: entrance into a religious order: the vow then taken.—*adj.* **profess'ional** pertaining to a profession: engaged in a profession or in the profession in question: competing for money prizes or against those who sometimes do so: undertaken as a means of subsistence, as opp. to *amateur*: showing the skill, artistry, demeanour, or standard of conduct appropriate in a member of a profession or of a particular profession.—*n.* one who makes his living by an art, or makes it his career: one who engages in sport for livelihood or gain.—*n.* **professionalisâ'tion, -z-.**—*v.t.* **profess'ionalise, -ize** to give a professional character to: to give over to professionals.—*n.* **profess'-ionalism** the status of professional: the competence, or the correct demeanour, of those who are highly trained and disciplined: the outlook, aim, or restriction of the mere professional: the predominance of professionals in sport.—*adv.* **profess'ionally.**—*ns.* **professor** (*pra-fes'ər*) one who professes: one who openly declares belief in certain doctrines: a teacher of the highest grade or, in the U.S., of any grade (as *associate professor, assistant professor*), in a university or sometimes a college (prefixed to the name); **profess'orate** professoriate.—*adj.* **professorial** (*prof-es-ō'ri-al*, -*ō'ri-əl*).—*adv.* **professo'rially.**—*ns.* **professo'riate** the office or chair of a professor: his period of office: body of professors; **profess'orship.** [L. *professus*, perf.p. of *profitēri*—*prŏ*, publicly, *fatēri*, to confess.]

proffer *prof'ər*, *v.t.* to offer for acceptance, to tender, present: to offer to undertake:—*pr.p.* **proff'ering;** *pa.t.* and *pa.p.* **proff'ered.**—*n.* an offer, tender: an incipient act.—*n.* **proff'erer.** [A.Fr. *proffrir*—L. *prŏ*, forward, *offerre*; see **offer.**]

proficient *pra-*, *prŏ-fish'ənt*, *adj.* competent: well-skilled: thoroughly qualified.—*n.* an adept: an expert.—*n.* **profi'ciency.**—*adv.* **profi'ciently.** [L. *prŏficiēns*, -*entis*, pr.p. of *prŏficĕre*, to make progress.]

profile *prŏ'fīl*, -*fēl*, -*fil*, *n.* an outline: a head or portrait in a side-view: the side-face: the outline of any object without foreshortening: a drawing of a vertical section of country, an engineering work, etc.: a graph: a short biographical sketch, e.g. in a newspaper or magazine: an outline of the characteristic features (of e.g. a particular type of person): an outline of the course of an operation: one's manner, attitude or behaviour considered with regard to the extent to which it attracts attention to oneself and one's activities or reveals one's feelings, intentions, etc., or the extent of one's involvement, etc. (as in *low, high*, etc. *profile*).—*v.t.* to draw in profile: to make an outline of: to show in profile: to give a profile to: to shape the outline of: to write or give a profile of. [It. *profilo*—L. *prŏ*, before, *filum*, a thread.]

profit *prof'it*, *n.* gain: the gain resulting from the employment of capital: the excess of selling price over first cost: advantage. addition to good or value: benefit: improvement.—*v.t.* to benefit or to be of advantage to.—*v.i.* to gain advantage: to receive profit: to be of advantage.—*n.* **profitabil'ity.**—*adj.* **prof'-itable** yielding or bringing profit or gain: lucrative: productive.—*n.* **prof'itableness.**—*adv.* **prof'itably.**

—*n.* **profiteer'** one who takes advantage of an emergency to make exorbitant profits.—*v.i.* to act as a profiteer.—*ns.* **profiteer'ing; prof'iter; prof'iting.** —*adj.* **prof'itless** without profit.—**prof'it-sharing** a voluntary agreement under which the employee receives a share, fixed beforehand, in the profits of a business. [Fr.,—L. *prŏfectus,* progress—*prŏficĕre, prŏfectum,* to make progress.]

profiterole *prə-fit'ə-rōl, n.* a small puff of choux pastry with filling. [Fr.; perh.—*profiter,* to profit.]

profligate *prof'li-git, -gāt, adj.* abandoned to vice: dissolute: prodigal, rashly extravagant.—*n.* one leading a profligate life: one who is recklessly extravagant or wasteful.—*adv.* **prof'ligacy** (*-gə-si*).—*adv.* **prof'-ligately.** [L. *prŏflīgātus,* pa.p. of *prŏflīgāre—prō,* forward, *flīgĕre,* to dash.]

pro-forma. See **pro forma** under **pro¹.**

profound *prə-, prō-fownd', adj.* deep: deep-seated: far below the surface: intense: abstruse: intellectually deep: penetrating deeply into knowledge.—*adv.* **pro-found'ly.**—*ns.* **profound'ness, profundity** (*-fund'*) the state and quality of being profound: depth of place, of knowledge, etc.: that which is profound. [Fr. *profond*—L. *profundus—pro,* forward, *fundus,* bottom.]

profuse *prə-, prō-fūs', adj.* liberal to excess: lavish: extravagant: over-abounding.—*adv.* **profuse'ly.** —*ns.* **profuse'ness; profusion** (*-fū'zhən*) the state of being profuse: extravagance: prodigality. [L. *prŏfūsus,* pa.p. of *prŏfundĕre—prō,* forth, *fundĕre,* to pour.]

progenitor *prō-jen'i-tər, n.* an ancestor.—*n.* **progeny** (*proj'ə-ni*) offspring: descendants: race.—Also fig. [L. *prŏgenitor, prŏgeniēs—prōgignĕre—prō,* before, *gignĕre, genitum,* beget.]

progesterone *prō-jes'tər-ōn, n.* a female sex hormone that prepares the uterus for the fertilised ovum and maintains pregnancy.—*ns.* **proges'tin** (**pro-¹,** gestation, *-in*) any hormone concerned with changes before pregnancy, esp. **proges'togen,** any of a range of hormones of the progesterone type; several synthetic progestogens are used in oral contraceptives. [*progestin, sterol, -one.*]

prognathous *prog'nə-thəs,* also *prog-* or *prŏg-nā'thəs, adj.* with projecting jaw. [Gr. *pro,* forward, *gnathos,* a jaw.]

prognosis *prog-nō'sis, n.* a forecasting, or forecast, esp. of the course of a disease:—*pl.* **prognōs'es** (*-ēz*) —*n.* **prognostic** (*prog-, prag-nost'ik*) a foretelling: an indication of something to come: a presage: a symptom on which prognosis can be based.—*adj.* indicating what is to happen by signs or symptoms: of prognosis.—*v.t.* **prognos'ticate** to foretell: to indicate as to come.—*n.* **prognostica'tion.**—*adj.* **prog-nos'ticative.**—*n.* **prognost'icator** a predictor, esp. a weather prophet. [Gr. *prognōsis—pro,* before, *gig-nōskein,* to know.]

programme, (esp. *U.S.,* and usu. also in speaking of computers) **program,** *prō'gram, n.* a paper, booklet, or the like, giving a scheme of proceedings arranged for an entertainment, conference, course of study, etc., with relevant details: the items of such a scheme collectively: a broadcast performance, entertainment, etc.: a plan of things to be done: the sequence of actions to be performed by an electronic computer in dealing with data of a certain kind: a course of instruction (by book or teaching machine) in which subject-matter is broken down into logical sequence of short items of information, and a student can check immediately the suitability of his responses.—*v.t.* to provide with, enter in, etc., a programme: to prepare a program(me) for (an electronic computer, etc.): to create a certain pattern of thought, reaction, etc. in

the mind of (*fig.*).—*n.* **programmabil'ity** (*comput.*). —*adj.* **programm'able** (*comput.*).—*n.* (*comput.*) a programmable calculator.—*adj.* **programmatic** (*-grə-mat'ik*) of a programme: of, or of the nature of, programme music.—*adj.* **pro'grammed.**—*ns.* **pro'-grammer** (*comput.*); **pro'gramming.**—**programme music** music that seeks to depict a scene or tell a story [Gr. *programma,* proclamation—*pro,* forth, *gramma,* a letter.]

progress *prō'gres,* sometimes (esp in U.S.) *pro', n.* a forward movement: an advance to something better or higher in development: a gain in proficiency: a course: a passage from place to place.—*v i.* **progress'** to go forward: to make progress: to go on, continue: to travel in state: to go.—*n* **progression** (*prə-, prō-gresh'ən*) motion onward: the act or state of moving onward: progress. movement by successive stages: a regular succession of chords (*mus.*): movements of the parts in harmony: a change from term to term according to some law (*math.*): a series of terms so related (see **arithmetic, geometry, harmony**).—*adjs.* **progress'ional; progress'ive** moving forward: making progress: of the nature of progress: advancing by successive stages: (in games, e.g. **progressive whist**) played by several sets of players, some of whom move round from table to table after each hand according to rule: advancing towards better and better or higher and higher: in favour of progress—applied (usu. with *cap.*) to various parties in municipal and national politics more or less favouring reform: of such a party.—*n.* one who favours progress or reform: (usu. with *cap*) a member of a party called progressive.— *adv.* **progress'ively.**—*n.* **progress'iveness.—in progress** going on: in course of publication. [Fr. *progresse* (now *progrès*)—L. *prōgressus, -ūs—prō,* forward, *gradi, gressus,* to step.]

prohibit *prə-, prō-hib'it, v.t.* to forbid: to prevent.— *ns.* **prohib'iter, -or; prohibition** (*prō-hi-bi'shən* or *prō-i-*) the act of prohibiting, forbidding, or interdicting: an interdict: the forbidding by law of the manufacture and sale of alcoholic drinks.—*adj.* **prohibi'-tionary.**—*ns.* **prohibi'tionism; prohibi'tionist** one who favours prohibition, esp. of the manufacture and sale of alcoholic drinks.—*adj.* **prohibitive** (*-hib'*) tending to make impossible or preclude.—*adv.* **pro-hib'itively.**—*n.* **prohib'itiveness.**—*adj.* **prohib'itory** that prohibits or forbids: forbidding. [L. *prohibēre, prohibitum—prō,* before, *habēre,* to have.]

project *proj'ekt, n.* a scheme of something to be done: a proposal for an undertaking: an undertaking.—*v.t.* **project** (*prə-jekt', prō-jekt'*) to throw out or forward: to speak or sing in such a way as to aim the voice at the rear of the auditorium (*theat.*): to throw, propel: to cause to jut out, stretch out: to scheme, plan, devise: to cast (as a light, a shadow, an image) upon a surface or into space: to throw an image of: to show outlined against a background: in geom., to derive a new figure from, so that each point corresponds to a point of the original figure according to some rule: to externalise: to make objective.—*v.i.* to jut out.—*adj.* **projec'tile** caused by projection: impelling: capable of being thrown or thrust forth.—*n.* a body projected by force: a missile, esp. one discharged by a gun.—*n.* and *adj.* **projec'ting.**—*n.* **projec'tion** (*-shən*) an act or method of projecting: the fact or state of being projected: planning: that which is projected: a jutting out: that which juts out: the standing out of a figure: a figure got by projecting another (*geom.*): a method of representing geographical detail upon a plane, or the representation so obtained (also **map projection**): a projected image: the reading of one's own emotions and experiences into a particular situation (*psych.*): a person's unconscious attributing to other people of certain attitudes towards himself, usu. as a defence against his own guilt, inferiority, etc. (*psych.*).—*adj.* **projec'tional.**—*n.* **projec'tionist** one who projects, makes projections, esp. in map-making: an operator of a film-projector: an operator of certain television equipment.—*adj.* **projec'tive** projecting: of projection: derivable by projection: unchanged by projection.—*ns.* **projectivity** (*proj-ǝk-tiv'i-ti*); **projec'tor** one who projects enterprises: a promoter of speculative schèmes for money-making: an apparatus for projecting, esp. an image or a beam of light: a straight line joining a point with its projection (*geom.*); **projec'ture** a jutting out. [L. *prōjicĕre, prōjectum—prō*, forth, *jacĕre*, to throw.]

prokaryon *prō-kar'i-ǝn*, (*biol.*) *n.* the nucleus of a blue-green alga, bacterium, etc., with no membrane separating the DNA-containing area from the rest of the cell (cf. *eukaryon*).—*n.* **prokar'yot(e)** (*-ōt, -ǝt*) a cell or organism with such a nucleus or nuclei.—Also *adj.*—*adj.* **prokaryōt'ic.** [**pro-**[1], and Gr. *karyon*, a kernel.]

prolapse *prō-laps'*, or *prō'laps*, (*med.*) *n.* a falling down, or out of place.—Also **prolap'sus.**—*v.i.* **prolapse'** to slip out of place. [L. *prōlābī, prōlāpsus*, to slip forward—*prō*, forward, *lābī*, to slip.]

prolate *prō'lāt*, rarely *prō-lāt'*, *adj.* drawn out along the polar diameter, as a spheroid (opp. to *oblate*): widespread.—*adj.* **prolative** (*prō-lā'tiv, prō'lǝ-tiv; gram.*) completing the predicate. [L. *prōlātus*, produced—*prō*, forward, *lātus*, used as perf.p. of *ferre*, to carry.]

prole *prōl*, (*coll.*) *n.* and *adj.* proletarian.

proleg *prō'leg*, *n.* an insect larva's abdominal leg, distinguished from a thoracic or 'true' leg. [Pfx. **pro-**[2] (*b*), **leg.**]

prolegomena *prō-leg-om'in-ǝ*, *n.pl.* an introduction, esp. to a treatise:—*sing.* **prolegom'enon.**—*adjs.* **prolegom'enary, prolegom'enous.** [Gr. *prōlegomenon*, pl. *-a*, pass. part. neut. of *prolegein—pro*, before, *legein*, to say.]

prolepsis *prō-lep'sis*, or *-lēp'*, *n.* anticipation: the rhetorical figure of anticipation, use of a word not literally applicable till a later time: a figure by which objections are anticipated and answered:—*pl.* **prolep'sēs.**—*adjs.* **prolep'tic, -al.**—*adv.* **prolep'tically.** [Gr. *prōlēpsis—pro*, before, *lambanein*, to take.]

proletarian *prō-li-tā'ri-ǝn*, *adj.* of the poorest labouring class: of the proletariat: having little or no property.—*n.* a member of the poorest class: a member of the proletariat.—*n.* **proletarianisā'tion, -z-.**—*v.t.* **proleta'rianise, -ize.**—*n.* **proleta'riat** (*-ǝt*), **-ate** the proletarian class: the wage-earning class, esp. those without capital. [L. *prōlētārius*, (in ancient Rome) a citizen of the sixth and lowest class, who served the state not with his property but with his *prōlēs*, offspring.]

proliferate *prō-lif'ǝ-rāt*, *v.i.* to grow by multiplication of parts (cells, buds, shoots, etc.): to reproduce by proliferation: to reproduce abundantly: to increase in numbers greatly and rapidly.—*v.t.* to produce by proliferation.—*n.* **prolifera'tion.**—*adjs.* **prolif'erative, prolif'erous.**—*adv.* **prolif'erously.** [L. *prōlēs*, progeny, *ferre*, to bear.]

prolific *prǝ-*, *prō-lif'ik*, *adj.* reproductive: fertilising: fertile: producing much offspring (also *fig.* as of an author): fruitful: abounding.—*n.* **prolif'icacy** (*-ǝ-si*).—*adv.* **prolif'ically.**—*ns.* **prolifica'tion** the generation of young: development of a shoot by continued growth of a flower (*bot.*); **prolificity** (*-is'i-ti*), **prolif'icness.** [L. *prōlēs*, offspring, *facĕre*, to make.]

prolix *prō'liks*, or *-liks'*, *adj.* long and wordy: long-winded: dwelling too long on particulars.—*n.* **prolix'ity.**—*adv.* **prolix'ly** (or *prō'*).—*n.* **prolix'ness** (or

prō'). [L. *prōlixus—pro*, forward, *līquī*, to flow.]

prolocutor *prō-lok'ū-tǝr*, *n.* a spokesman: a chairman, esp. of the lower house of Convocation:—*fem.* **prōloc'utrix.**—*ns.* **prolocu'tion** (*prō-* or *pro-*) an introductory speech or saying; **prōloc'utorship.** [L. *prōlocūtor—prōloquī, -locūtus*, to speak out—*loquī*, to speak.]

prologue *prō'log*, *n.* in a Greek play, the part before the entry of the chorus: an introduction to a poem, etc.: a speech before a play: the speaker of a prologue: an introductory event or action.—*v.t.* to introduce: to preface.—*v.i.* **pro'logise, -ize** (*-gīz, -jīz*) to speak a prologue—also **pro'loguise, -ize.** [Fr.,—L. *prologus—*Gr. *prologos—logos*, speech.]

prolong *prǝ-, prō-long'*, *v.t.* to lengthen out.—*v.i.* to lengthen out.—*adj.* **prolongable** (*prō-long'ǝ-bl*).—*v.t.* **prolongate** (*prō'long-gāt*) to lengthen.—*ns.* **prolongation** (*-long-gā'shǝn*) lengthening out: a piece added in continuation: continuation. [L. *prōlongāre—prō*, before, *longus*, long.]

prolusion *prō-lōō'zhǝn, -lū'*, *n.* a preliminary performance, activity, or display: an essay preparatory to a more solid treatise.—*adj.* **prolu'sory** (*-sǝ-ri*). [L. *prōlūsiō, -ōnis—prō*, before, *lūdĕre, lūsum*, to play.]

prom *prom*, *n.* a contraction of **promenade**: a promenade concert.

pro-marketeer *prō-mär-ki-tēr'*, *n.* a person in favour of Britain's entry into, or continued membership of, the European Common Market. [Pfx. **pro-**[2] (*c*).]

promenade *prom-i-näd'* or *-näd'*, *n.* a walk, ride, or drive for pleasure, show, or gentle exercise: a processional dance: a place where people walk to and fro: a paved terrace on a sea-front: an esplanade.—*v.i.* to walk, ride, or drive about: to make a promenade.—*v.t.* to lead about and exhibit: to walk, ride or drive about or through.—*n.* **promenader** (*-äd'ǝr*) one who promenades: a member of the standing portion of the audience at a promenade concert.—**promenade concert** one in which part of the audience stands throughout and can move about; **promenade deck** a deck on which passengers walk about. [Fr.,—*promener*, to lead about (*se promener*, to take a walk)—L. *prōmināre*, to drive forwards.]

Promethean *prō-mē'thi-ǝn, -thyǝn*, *adj.* pertaining to *Prometheus* (*-thūs*), who stole fire from heaven, for which Zeus chained him to a rock, to be tortured by a vulture.—*n.* **prome'thium** (formerly **prome'theum**) element 61 (symbol Pm). [Gr. *Promētheus*.]

prominent *prom'i-nǝnt*, *adj.* standing out: projecting: most easily seen: catching the eye or attention: in the public eye.—*ns.* **prom'inence** state or quality of being prominent: a prominent point or thing: a projection; **prom'inency** a prominence.—*adv.* **prom'inently.** [L. *prōminēns, -entis*, pr.p. of *prōminēre*, to jut forth—*prō*, forth, *minae*, projections, threats.]

promiscuous *prō-mis'kū-ǝs*, *adj.* confusedly or indiscriminately mixed: indiscriminate (now usu. referring to one indulging in indiscriminate sexual intercourse): haphazard: belonging to a mixed set: casual, accidental (*coll.*).—*n.* **promiscū'ity** (*prom-*) mixture without order or distinction: promiscuous sexual intercourse.—*adv.* **promis'cuously.** [L. *prōmiscuus—prō*, intens., *miscēre*, to mix.]

promise *prom'is*, *n.* an engagement to do or keep from doing something: expectation, or that which raises expectation: a ground for hope of future excellence.—*v.t.* to engage by promise to do, give, etc.: to betroth: to encourage to expect: to afford reason to expect: to assure: to engage to bestow.—*v.i.* to make a promise or promises: to afford hopes or expectations.—*n.* **promisee'** the person to whom a promise is made.—*n.* **prom'iser.**—*adj.* **prom'ising** affording ground for hope or expectation: likely to turn out well.—*adv.* **prom'isingly.**—*n* **prom'isor** (*law*) the person making a promise.—*adj.* **prom'issory** containing a promise of some engagement to be fulfilled.—**promised land** the land promised by God to Abraham and his seed: Canaan: heaven; **promissory note** a written promise to pay a sum of money on some future day or on demand. [L. *prōmissum*, neut. pa.p. of *promittĕre*, to send forward.]

prommer *prom'ər*, (*coll.*) *n.* a (regular) attender of promenade concerts, esp. a promenader.

promontory *prom'ən-tər-i*, *-tri*, *n.* a headland or high cape: a projection, ridge, or eminence (*anat*) [L.L. *prōmontōrium.*]

promote *prə-*, *prō-mōt'*, *v.t.* to further. to further the progress of: to raise to a higher grade: to take steps for the passage or formation of: to set in motion (as the office of a judge in a criminal suit): to encourage the sales of by advertising.—*t.s.* **promo'ter** one who promotes: one who takes part in the setting up of companies: the organiser of a sporting event, esp. a boxing match: a substance that increases the efficiency of a catalyst; **promotion** (*-mō'shən*) the act of promoting: advancement in rank or in honour. encouragement: preferment: a venture, esp. in show business: advertising in general, or an effort to publicise and increase the sales of a particular product. [L. *prōmovēre*, *-mōtum*—*prō*, forward, *movēre*, to move.]

prompt *prom(p)t*, *adj.* ready in action: performed at once: paid or due at once: ready for delivery.—*adv.* promptly, punctually, to the minute.—*v.t.* to incite: to instigate: to move to action: to supply forgotten words to, esp. in a theatrical performance: to help with words or facts when one is at a loss: to suggest to the mind.—*n.* a time limit for payment: an act of prompting: words furnished by the prompter.—*ns.* **prompt'er** one who prompts, esp. actors; **prompt'ing**; **prompt'itude** promptness: readiness: quickness of decision and action—*adv.* **prompt'ly.**—*n* **prompt'ness.** [L. *prōmptus—prōmĕre*, to bring forward.]

promulgate *prom'əl-gāt* (U.S. *prə-mul'*) *v.t.* to proclaim, publish abroad: to make widely known: to put in execution by proclamation (as a law).—*ns.* **promulgā'tion; prom'ulgātor.** [L. *prōmulgāre*, *-ātum*]

prone *prōn*, *adj.* with the face, ventral surface, or palm of the hand downward: prostrate: directed downward: loosely, lying or laid flat: descending steeply: disposed, inclined, naturally tending: willing.—*-prone* in composition, liable to suffer a specified thing, as in *accident-prone*. [L. *prōnus*, bent forward.]

prong *prong*, *n.* a tine, tooth, or spike of a fork or forked object: a tine, spur, or projection, as on an antler.—*adj.* **pronged** having prongs.—**prong'buck** the pronghorn (properly the male); **prong'horn** an American antelope-like ruminant with deciduous horns pronged in front. [M E. *prange*.]

pronoun *prō'nown*, *n.* a word used instead of a noun, i.e. to indicate without naming.—*adj.* **pronominal** (*prə-*, *prō-nom'in-əl*) belonging to, or of the nature of, a pronoun.—*adv.* **pronom'inally.**

pronounce *prə-*, *prō-nowns'*, *v.t.* to proclaim: to utter formally: to utter rhetorically: to declare: to utter: to articulate.—*v.i.* to pass judgment: to articulate one's words.—*adjs.* **pronounce'able** capable of being pronounced; **pronounced'** marked with emphasis: marked.—*adv.* **pronoun'cedly.**—*ns.* **pronounce'ment** a confident or authoritative assertion or declaration: the act of pronouncing; **pronoun'cer.**—*n.* and *adj.* **pronoun'cing.**—*n.* **pronunciation** (*prō-nun-si-ā'shən*) mode of pronouncing: articulation. [Fr *prononcer* —L. *prōnūntiāre—prō*, forth, *nūntiāre*, to announce—*nūntius*, a messenger.]

pronto *pron'tō*, (*slang*) *adv.* promptly, quickly. [Sp. *pronto*—L. *prōmptus*, at hand.]

pronunciamento *prō-nun-si-ə-men'tō*, *n.* a manifesto: a proclamation:—*pl.* **-os.** [Sp. *pronunciamiento.*]

pronunciation. See **pronounce.**

proof *prōōf*, *n.* that which proves or establishes the truth of anything: the fact, act, or process of proving or showing to be true: demonstration: evidence that convinces the mind and goes toward determining the decision of a court: an instrument of evidence in documentary form: a checking operation (*arith*): a test testing, esp. of guns: ability to stand a test invulnerability: impenetrability: a standard strength of spirit (alcohol and water of relative density 12/13 at 51°F —i.e. 49·28 per cent of alcohol): an impression taken for correction (*print*): an early impression of an engraving: a coin, intended for display, etc., rather than circulation, struck from polished dies on polished blanks (also **proof coin**): the first print from a negative (*phot*):—*pl* **proofs.**—*adj.* impervious: invulnerable: of standard strength (of alcohol).—*v.t.* to make impervious, esp. to water: to take a proof of: to test —**-proof** in composition, (to make) able to withstand or resist, as in *waterproof*, *childproof*, *weatherproof*, etc.—*n.* **proof'ing** the process of making waterproof, gasproof, etc : material used for the purpose.—**proof'-mark** a mark stamped on a gun to show that it has stood the test —*v.t.* and *v.i.* **proof'-read** to read and correct in proof.—**proof'-reader** one who reads printed proofs to discover and correct errors; **proof'-reading; proof'-sheet** an impression taken on a slip of paper for correction before printing finally; **proof'-spirit** a standard mixture of alcohol and water; **proof'-text** a passage of the Bible adduced in proof of a doctrine —**artist's proof** a first impression from an engraved plate or block; **over, under proof** containing in 100 volumes enough alcohol for so many volumes more, or less, than 100. [O Fr *prove* (Fr. *preuve*); see prove.]

prop[1] *prop*, *n.* a rigid support: a supplementary support: a stay: a strut: a timber supporting a mineroof a supporter, upholder in Rugby football, either of the two forwards at the ends of the front row of the scrum (also **prop'(-)for'ward**)—*v.t* to hold up by means of something placed under or against: to support or to sustain: to keep (a failing enterprise, etc.) going: to hit straight or knock down (*slang*).—**prop'-root** a root growing down from a trunk or branch, serving to prop up a tree. [M.E. *proppe*]

prop[2] *prop*, *n.* a coll. or slang abbrev of (aircraft) propeller, (theatrical) property.—*n.pl.* **props** stage properties.—*n.sing.* a property-man.

propaedeutic *prō-pē-dū'tik*, *n.* (often in *pl.*) a preliminary study.—*adjs.* **propaedeut'ic, -al.** [Gr. *propaideuein*, to teach beforehand]

propagate *prop'ə-gāt*, *v t.* to increase by natural process: to multiply: to pass on: to transmit: to spread from one to another —*v.t.* to multiply: to breed — *adj* **prop'agable.**—*n.* **propagan'da** a congregation of the Roman Catholic Church, founded 1622, charged with the spreading of Catholicism (*dē propāgandā fidē*, 'concerning the faith to be propagated'): any association, activity, plan, etc., for the spread of opinions and principles, esp. to effect change or reform: the information, etc., spread by such an association —*v.t.* and *v i.* **propagand'ise, -ize.**—*ns.* **propagand'ism** practice of propagating tenets or principles: zeal in spreading one's opinions: proselytism; **propagand'ist**—also *adj.*—*n.* **propagā'tion.**—*adj.* **prop'agative.**—*n* **prop'agator** one who, or that which, propagates: a heated, covered box in which plants may be grown from seed or cuttings —**propaganda machine** all the means employed in the process of spreading opinions: the process itself. [L. *prōpāgāre*, *-ātum*.]

propane *prō'pān*, *n*. a hydrocarbon gas (C_3H_8), third member of the methane series. [**propionic**.]

proparoxytone *prō-par-ok'si-tōn*, *adj*. having the acute accent on the third last syllable.—*n*. a word thus accented. [Gr. *proparoxytonos*; see **paroxytone**.]

propel *pra-*, *prō-pel'*, *v.t.* to drive forward:—*pr.p.* **propell'ing**; *pa.t.* and *pa.p.* **propelled'**.—*n.* **propell'ant** that which propels: an explosive for propelling projectiles: the fuel used to propel a rocket, etc.: the gas in an aerosol spray.—*adj*. **propell'ent** driving.—*n.* a driving agent: a motive.—*ns.* **propell'er** one who, or that which, propels: driving mechanism: a shaft with spiral blades (*screw-propeller*) for driving a ship, aeroplane, etc.: a helical blower (*air-propeller*, *propeller fan*); **propel'ment** propulsion: propelling mechanism.—**propell'er-blade'**; **propell'er-shaft'** the shaft of a propeller: the driving shaft between gear-box and rear axle in a motor vehicle; **propelling pencil** one having a replaceable lead held within a casing that can be turned to push the lead forward as it is worn down. [L. *prōpellēre—prō*, forward, *pellēre*, to drive.]

propene. Same as **propylene**.

propensity *prō-pen'si-ti*, *pra-*, *n*. inclination of mind: tendency to good or evil. [From *propense*, inclined —L. *prōpendēre*, *-pēnsum*, to hang forward.]

proper *prop'ar*, *adj*. own: appropriate: peculiar: confined to one: in natural colouring (*her.*): strict: strictly applicable: strictly so-called (usu. after *n.*): thorough, out-and-out (now *coll.* or *slang*): actual, real: befitting: decorous, seemly: conforming strictly to convention: goodly: belonging to only one: comely.—*adv.* (*coll.*) very, exceedingly.—*adj*. **prop'erly** in a proper manner: strictly: entirely, extremely (*coll.*).—*n.* **prop'erness**.—**proper fraction** a fraction that has a numerator of a lower value than the denominator; **proper motion** a star's apparent motion relative to the celestial sphere, due partly to its own movement (peculiar motion), partly to that of the solar system (parallactic motion); **proper noun**, **name** the name of a particular person, animal, thing, place, etc.—opp. to *common* noun. [Fr. *propre—*L. *prōprius*, own.]

property *prop'ar-ti*, *n*. that which is proper to any person or thing: a quality that is always present: a characteristic: that which is one's own: the condition of being one's own: a piece of land owned by somebody: right of possessing, employing, etc.: ownership: an article required on the stage (abbrev. *prop*).—*adj*. of the nature of a stage property.—*adj*. **prop'ertied** possessed of property.—**prop'erty-man**, **-mas'ter** one who has charge of stage properties; **prop'erty-room** the room in which stage properties are kept; **property tax** a tax levied on property, at the rate of so much per cent. on its value. [O.Fr. *properte*; see **propriety**.]

prophecy *prof'i-si*, *n*. inspired or prophetic utterance: prediction. [O.Fr. *prophecie—*L. *prophētīa—*Gr. *prophēteia—prophētēs*, prophet.]

prophesy *prof'i-sī*, *v.i.* to utter prophecies: to speak prophetically: to foretell the future.—*v.t.* to foretell: —*pa.t.* and *pa.p.* **proph'esied**.—*ns.* **proph'esier**; **proph'esying**. [A variant of **prophecy**.]

prophet *prof'it*, *n*. a spokesman of deity: one who proclaims a divine message: an inspired teacher, preacher, or poet: the spokesman of a group, movement, or doctrine: a minister of the second order of the Catholic Apostolic Church: a foreteller, whether claiming to be inspired or not:—*fem.* **proph'etess**.—*ns.* **proph'ethood**, **proph'etship**.—*adjs.* **prophetic** (*pra-fet'ik*), **-al**.—*adv.* **prophet'ically**.—**prophet of doom** a person who continually predicts unfortunate events, disasters, etc.; **the Prophet** Mohammed.

[Fr. *prophète—*L. *prophēta—*Gr. *prophētēs—pro*, for, *phanai*, to speak.]

prophylactic *pro-fi-lak'tik*, *adj*. guarding against disease.—*n*. a preventive of disease: a condom (usu. *U.S.*).—*n*. **prophylaxis** preventive treatment against diseases, etc. [Gr. *prophylaktikos—pro*, before, *phylax*, a guard.]

propinquity *pra-ping'kwi-ti*, *n*. nearness. [L. *propinquitās*, *-ātis—propinquus*, near—*prope*, near.]

propionic acid *prō-pi-on'ik as'id* one of the fatty acids, $C_2H_5 \cdot COOH$. [Pfx. *pro-*[1], *piŏn*, *-on*, fat.]

propitiate *pra-pish'i-āt*, *v.t.* to render favourable: to appease.—*adj*. **propi'tiable**.—*n*. **propitia'tion** act of propitiating: atonement: atoning sacrifice.—*adj*. **propi'tiātor**.—*adv*. **propi'tiato-rily** (*-shi-a-tar-t-li*).—*adjs.* **propi'tiatory** propitiating: expiatory; **propitious** (*-pish'as*) favourable: disposed to be gracious: of good omen.—*adv*. **propi'tiously**.—*n*. **propi'tiousness**. [L. *propitiāre*, *-ātum*, to make favourable—*propitius*, well-disposed.]

prop-jet *prop'-jet*, (*aero.*) *adj*. and *n*. (a jet aeroplane) having a turbine-driven propeller. [**prop**(eller) and **jet**.]

propolis *prop'a-lis*, *n*. bee-glue, a brown sticky resinous substance gathered by bees from trees and used by them as cement and varnish. [Gr. *propolis*.]

propone *pra-pōn'*, (now *Scot.*) *v.t.* to propose.—*n*. **pro-pōn'ent** a propounder or proposer: a favourer, advocate. [L. *prōpōnēre—prō*, forward, *pōnēre*, to place.]

proportion *pra-pōr'shan*, *-pōr'*, *n*. the relation of one thing to another in magnitude: fitness of parts to each other: due relation: relation of rhythm or of harmony: ratio: the identity or equality of ratios (*math.*): equal or just share: relative share, portion, inheritance: contribution, quota, fortune: 'a part or portion (*coll.*): (in *pl.*) dimensions.—*v.t.* to adjust or fashion in due proportion: to regulate the proportions of: to divide proportionally.—*adjs.* **propor'tionable** that may be proportioned: having a due or definite relation; **propor'tional** relating to proportion: in proportion: having the same or a constant ratio (*math.*): proportionate, in suitable proportion.—*n*. (*math.*) a number or quantity in a proportion.—*n*. **propor-tional'ity**.—*adv*. **propor'tionally**.—*adj*. **propor'-tionate** in fit proportion: proportional.—*v.t.* to adjust in proportion.—*adv*. **propor'tionately**.—*n*. **propor'tioning** adjustment of proportions.—*adj*. **propor'tionless** ill-proportioned.—**proportional representation** a system intended to give parties in an elected body a representation as nearly as possible proportional to their voting strength: often loosely applied to the system of transferred vote.—**in proportion** (often with *to*) in a (given) ratio: having a correct or harmonious relation (with something): to a degree or extent which seems appropriate to the importance, etc. of the matter in hand; **out of (all) proportion** not in proportion. [L. *prōportiō*, *-ōnis—prō*, in comparison with, *portiō*, part, share.]

propose *pra-pōz'*, *v.t.* to offer for consideration or acceptance: to suggest or lay before one as something to be done: to purpose or intend: to move formally: to nominate: to invite the company to drink (a health): to enunciate.—*v.i.* to form or put forward an intention or design: to offer, especially marriage.—*ns.* **propōs'al** an act of proposing: an offer, esp. of marriage: anything proposed: a plan; **propōs'er**. [Fr. *proposer—*pfx. *pro-*, *poser*, to place; see **pose**[1].]

proposition *prop-a-zish'an*, *n*. an act of propounding or (more rarely) proposing: the thing propounded or proposed: a statement of a judgment: a form of statement in which a predicate is affirmed or denied of a subject (*log.*): a premise, esp. a major premise: a statement of a problem or theorem for (or with) solution or demonstration (*math.*): any situation, thing, or person considered as something to cope with, as an enterprise, job, opponent, etc. (*slang*, orig. *U.S.*): an invitation to sexual intercourse (*coll.*).—*v.t.* to make a proposition to someone, esp. to solicit a woman for sexual relations.—*adj.* **proposi'tional.** [L. *prōpositiō, -ōnis*—*prō*, before; see **position.**]

propound *prə-pownd'*, *v.t.* to offer for consideration: to set forth as aim or reward: to produce for probate (*law*).—*n.* **propound'er.** [**propone.**]

propraetor *prō-prē'tər, -tör, prō-prī'tor, n.* a magistrate of ancient Rome, who, after acting as praetor in Rome, was appointed to the government of a province. [L. *prōpraetor—prō praetōre*, for the praetor.]

proprietor *prō-prī'ə-tər, n.* an owner:—*fem.* **propri'etress, propri'etrix.**—*adj.* **propri'etary** of the nature of property: legally made only by a person or body of persons having special rights: owning property.—*adj.* **proprietorial** (*-tō', -tō'ri-əl*).—*n.* **propri'etorship.** [L.L. *proprietārius—proprius,* own; **proprietor** has been formed irregularly; it is not a Latin word.]

propriety *prō-prī'ə-ti, n.* rightness, as in the use of words: appropriateness: seemliness: decency: conformity with good manners: conformity with convention in language and conduct. [Fr. *propriété*—L *proprietās, -ātis—proprius,* own.]

proprioceptive *prō-pri-ō-sep'tiv, adj.* of, pertaining to, or made active by, stimuli arising from movement in the tissues.—*n.* **propriocep'tor** a sensory nerve-ending receptive of such stimuli.—**proprioceptive sense** the sense of muscular position. [L. *proprius,* own, after **receptive.**]

propulsion *prə-pul'shən, n.* driving forward.—*adjs.* **propul'sive, propul'sory.** [L. *prōpellēre, prōpulsum,* to push forward; see **propel.**]

propyl *prō'pil, n.* the alcohol radical C₃H₇.—*ns.* **pro'pylamine** an amine of propyl; **pro'pylene, pro'pene** a gaseous hydrocarbon (C₃H₆).—*adj.* **propyl'ic.** [**propionic** and Gr. *hylē,* matter.]

prorate *prō-rāt', prō'rāt,* (mainly *U S.*) *v.t.* to distribute proportionately.—*n.* **prora'tion.** [**pro rata.**]

prorogue *prə-, prō-rōg', v.t.* to discontinue the meetings of for a time without dissolving.—*n.* **proroga'tion.** [L. *prōrogāre, -ātum—prō,* forward, *rogāre,* to ask.]

prosaic, -al *prō-zā'ik, -əl, adjs.* like prose: unpoetical: matter-of-fact: commonplace: dull.—*adv.* **prosa'ically.**—*ns.* **prosā'icalness; prosā'icness** quality of being prosaic. [L. *prosa,* prose.]

proscenium *prō-sē'ni-əm, n.* the front part of the stage: the curtain and its framework, esp. the arch that frames the more traditional type of stage (**proscenium arch**). [Latinised from Gr. *proskēnion—pro,* before, *skēnē,* stage.]

prosciutto *pro-shōō'tō, n.* finely cured uncooked ham, often smoked:—*pl.* **prosciut'ti, prosciutt'os.** [It , lit. pre-dried.]

proscribe *prō-skrīb', v.t.* to put on the list of those who may be put to death: to outlaw: to prohibit.—*ns.* **prōscrib'er; prō'script** one who is proscribed; **prōscrip'tion.**—*adj.* **prōscrip'tive.** [L. *prōscribēre—prō-,* before, publicly, *scribēre, scriptum,* to write.]

prose *prōz, n.* ordinary spoken and written language with words in direct straightforward arrangement without metrical structure: all writings not in verse: a passage of prose for translation from or, usu., into a foreign language, as an exercise —*adj.* or in prose: not poetical: plain: dull.—*v.t.* to write prose: to speak or write tediously.—*v.t.* to compose in prose: to turn into prose.—*n.* **prō'ser.**—*adv.* **prō'sily.**—*ns.* **prō'siness; prō'sing** speaking or writing in a dull or prosy

way.—*adj.* **prō'sy** dull, tedious, humdrum: addicted to prosing.—**prose poem** a prose work or passage having some of the characteristics of poetry; **prose writer.** [Fr., —L. *prōsa—prorsus,* straightforward —*prō,* forward, *vertēre, versum,* to turn.]

prosecute *pros'i-kūt, v.t.* to follow onwards or pursue, in order to reach or accomplish: to pursue by law: to bring before a court —*v.i.* to carry on a legal prosecution.—*adj.* **pros'ecūtable.**—*ns.* **prosecū'tion** the act of prosecuting in any sense: the prosecuting party in legal proceedings; **pros'ecūtor** one who prosecutes or pursues any plan or business: one who carries on a civil or criminal suit:—*fem.* **pros'ecūtrix** (modern L.):—*pl.* **pros'ecūtrixes, prosecutrices** (*-kū-trī'sēz, -kū'tri-sēz*).—**director of public prosecutions, public prosecutor** one appointed to conduct criminal prosecutions (in U.S., **prosecuting attorney, district attorney**). [L. *prōsequī, -secūtus —prō,* onwards, *sequī,* to follow]

proselyte *pros'i-līt, n.* one who has come over from one religion or opinion to another: a convert, esp. from paganism to Judaism.—*v.t.* **pros'elytise, -ize** to convert.—*v.i.* to make proselytes.—*ns* **pros'elytiser, -izer; pros'elytism** being, becoming, or making a convert: conversion. [Gr. *prosēlytos,* a newcomer, resident foreigner—*pros,* to, and the stem *elyth-,* used to form aorists for *erchesthai,* to go.]

prosencephalon *pros-en-sef'ə-lon, n.* the fore-brain, comprising the cerebral hemispheres and olfactory processes. [Gr *pros,* to, used as if for *pro,* before, *enkephalon,* brain—*en,* in, *kephalē,* head.]

prosimian *prō-sim'i-ən, n.* a primate of the suborder **Prosimii,** e.g. the lemur, loris, tarsier.—Also *adj* [pro-¹, L. *simia,* ape.]

prosit *prō'sit, interj.* good luck to you, a salutation in drinking healths customary among German students [L. *prōsit,* used as 3rd pers sing. pres subj. of L *prōdesse,* to be of use—*prōd(-), esse,* to be.]

prosody *pros'ə-di, n.* the study of versification —*adjs* **prosodial** (*pros-, prəs-ō'di-əl*), **prosodic** (*-od'ik*), **-al.** —*ns.* **prosō'dian, pros'odist** one skilled in prosody. [L *prosōdia,* Gr *prosōdiā—pros,* to, *ōidē,* a song]

prosopography *pros-ō-pog'rə-fi, n.* a biographical sketch, description of a person's appearance, character, life, etc.: the compiling or study of such material. —*adj.* **prosopograph'ical.** [Gr *prosōpon,* face, person, *graphein,* to write.]

prospect *pros'pekt, n* outlook: direction of facing: a wide view: view, sight, field of view: a scene: a pictorial representation, view: a survey or mental view: outlook upon the probable future: expectation: chance of success: a wide street (*Russ prəs-pyekt'*): a place thought likely to yield a valuable mineral (*mining*): a sample, or a test, or the yield of a test of a sample from such a place a probable source of profit —*v i.* **prospect'** to look around (*prəs-pekt'*; *U.S. pros'*) to make a search, esp for chances of mining to promise or yield results to the prospector.—*v.t.* (*-pekt', pros'pekt*) to explore, search, survey, or test for profitable minerals.—*ns.* **prospect'ing** (*U.S pros'*) searching a district for minerals with a view to further operations; **prospec'tion** looking to the future: foresight.—*adj.* **prospec'tive** probable or expected future looking forward: yielding distant views: looking to the future.—*n* prospect.—*adv.* **prospec'tively.**—*ns.* **prospec'tiveness; prospec'tor** (*U.S. pros'*) one who prospects for minerals; **pros'pec'tus** the outline of any plan submitted for public approval, particularly of a literary work or of a joint-stock concern: an account of the organisation of a school:—*pl* **prospec'tuses.** [L. *prōspectus, -ūs— prōspicēre, prōspectum—prō-,* forward, *specēre,* to look]

prosper *pros'par, v.t* to thrive· to experience favourable circumstances: to flourish. to turn out well.—*v.t* to cause to prosper.—*n.* prosperity (*-per'i-ti*) the state of being prosperous: success. good fortune. —*adj.* **pros'perous** thriving: successful.—*adv.* **pros'perously.**—*n.* **pros'perousness.** [L. *prosper, prosperus.*]

prostaglandins *pros-ta-gland'inz, n.pl.* a group of chemical substances secreted by various parts of the body into the bloodstream and found to have a wide range of effects on the body processes, e.g on muscle contraction [*prostate gland,* a major source of these.]

prostate *pros'tāt, n.* a gland in males at the neck of the bladder.—Also **prostate gland.**—*rj.* prostatec'tomy surgical removal of (part of) the prostate gland.— *adj.* prostatic (*pros-tat'ik*). [Gr. *prostatēs,* one who stands in front, the prostate—*pro,* before, *sta,* root of *histanai,* to set up]

prosthesis *pros'tha-sis, pros-thē'sis, n.* addition of a prefix to a word, e.g. for ease of pronunciation (*linguistics;* also **prothesis,** q.v): the fitting of artificial parts to the body: such an artificial part:—*pl.* **prostheses** (*-sēz*).—*adj.* **prosthetic** (*-thet'ik*) relating to prosthesis —*n.* an artificial part of the body.—*n. sing.* **prosthet'ics** the surgery or dentistry involved in supplying artificial parts to the body.—*n.* **pros-thet'ist.** [Gr. *prosthesis,* adj *prosthetikos*—*pros,* to, *thesis,* putting.]

prosthodontia *pros-thō-don'shi-a, n.* provision of false teeth —Also *n. sing.* **prosthodon'tics.**—*n.* **pros-thodon'tist.** [Gr. *prosthesis,* addition—*pros,* to, *thesis,* putting, and *odous, odontos,* tooth.]

prostitute *pros'ti-tūt, v.t.* to devote to, or offer or sell for, evil or base use: to hire out for sexual intercourse: to devote to such intercourse as a religious act: to degrade by publicity or commonness.—*adj.* openly devoted to lewdness: given over (to evil): basely venal.—*n.* a person (usu. a woman or a homosexual man) who accepts money in return for sexual intercourse: a base hireling.—*ns.* **prostitū'tion** the act or practice of prostituting: devotion to base purposes, **pros'titūtor.** [L. *prostituĕre, -ūtum,* to set up for sale—*prō,* before, *statuĕre,* to place.]

prostrate *pros'trāt, adj.* prone: lying or bent with face on the ground: loosely, lying at length: procumbent, trailing (*bot.*). lying at mercy: reduced to helplessness: completely exhausted.—*v t.* **prostrate'** (or *pros'*) to throw forwards on the ground: to lay flat: to overthrow. to reduce to impotence or exhaustion: to bend in humble reverence (*refl.*).—*n.* **prostrā'tion.** [L. *prōstrātus,* pa.p. of *prōsternĕre*—*prō,* forwards, *sternĕre,* to spread.]

prosy. See **prose.**

prot-. See **proto-.**

protactinium *prōt-ak-tin'i-am, n* radioactive element (at. numb. 91; symbol Pa) that yields actinium on disintegration. [Gr. *prōtos,* first, and **actinium.**]

protagonist *prō-tag'an-ist, n.* the chief actor, character, or combatant: loosely, a champion, advocate [Gr. *prōtos,* first, *agōnistēs,* a combatant, actor]

protamine *prō'ta-mēn, n.* any of the simplest proteins, found esp. in the sperm of certain fish. [**proto-, amine.**]

protasis *prot'a-sis, n.* the conditional clause of a conditional sentence—opp to *apodosis·* the first part of a dramatic composition:—*pl.* prot'asēs. [Gr *protasis,* proposition, premise, *protasis*—*pro,* before, *tasis,* a stretching, *teinein,* to stretch.]

Protea *prō'ti-a, n.* a large South African genus of shrubs or small trees, with big cone-shaped heads of flowers: (without *cap.*) a plant of the genus. [**Proteus;** from the varied character of the family]

Protean, protean. See **Proteus.**

protease. See **protein.**

protect *pra-, prō-tekt', v.t.* to shield from danger, injury, change, capture, loss: to defend: to strengthen: to seek to foster by import duties: to screen off for safety (e.g. machinery).—*adjs.* **protect'ed; protect'ing.**—*ns.* **protec'tion** act of protecting: state of being protected: defence: that which protects: a fostering of home produce and manufactures by import duties: patronage: concubinage; **protec'tionism;** **protec'tionist** one who favours the protection of trade by duties on imports—also *adj.*—*adj.* **protec'tive** affording protection: intended to protect: defensive: sheltering.—*n.* that which protects: a condom.—*adv.* **protec'tively.**—*ns.* **protec'tiveness;** **protec'tor** one who protects from injury or oppression: a protective device: a means of protection: a guard: a guardian: a regent: the head of the state during the Commonwealth (*Lord Protector*):—*fem.* **protec'tress, protec'trix**—*adj.* **protec'toral** of a protector or a regent.—*n.* **protec'torate** the position, office, term of office, or government of a protector: (*cap.*) the Commonwealth period (*hist.*): guardianship: authority over a vassal state: relation assumed by a state over a territory which it administers without annexation and without admitting the inhabitants to citizenship.—*adjs.* **protectorial** (*prō-tek-tōr'i-al, -tor'i-al*); **protec'torless.**—*ns.* **protec'torship; protec'-tory** an institution for destitute or delinquent children.—**protection money** money extorted from shopkeepers, businessmen, etc., as a bribe for leaving their property, business, etc., unharmed; **protective coloration** likeness in the colour of animals to their natural surroundings tending to prevent them from being seen by their enemies; **protective custody** detention of a person for his personal safety or from doubt as to his possible actions. [L. *prōtegĕre, -tēctum*—*prō-,* in front, *tegĕre,* to cover.]

protégé *prō', or pro'ta-zhā, n.* one under the protection or patronage of another: a pupil: a ward:—*fem.* **pro'tégée** (*-zhā*). [Fr.,—pa.p. of *protéger,* to protect— L. *prōtegĕre.*]

protein *prō'tē-in, -tēn, n.* any member of a group of complex nitrogenous substances that play an important part in the bodies of plants and animals, compounds of carbon, hydrogen, oxygen, nitrogen, usually sulphur, often phosphorus, etc., easily hydrolysed into mixtures of amino-acids.—*n.* **pro'tease** (*-tē-ās, -āz*) any enzyme that splits up proteins.—*adjs.* **proteinaceous** (*prō-tēn-ā'shas*), **proteinic** (*prō-tēn'ik*), **protein'ous.** [Gr. *prōteios,* primary—*prōtos,* first.]

Proterozoic *prot-ar-ō-zō'ik,* or *prōt-, n.* and *adj.* orig., Lower Palaeozoic (Cambrian to Silurian): Pre-Cambrian: Upper Pre-Cambrian. [Gr. *proteros,* earlier, *zōē,* life.]

protest *pra-, prō-test', v.i.* to express or record dissent or objection: to make solemn affirmation, professions, or avowal.—*v.t.* to make a solemn declaration of: to declare: to note, as a bill of exchange, on account of non-acceptance or non-payment: to make a protest against.—*n.* **prō'test** an affirmation or avowal: a declaration of objection or dissent: the noting by a notary-public of an unpaid or unaccepted bill.—*adj.* expressing, in order to express, dissent or objection.—*n* **Protestant** *prot'is-tant,* one of those who, in 1529, protested against an edict of Charles V and the Diet of Spires denouncing the Reformation: a member, adherent, or sharer of the beliefs of one of those churches founded by the Reformers.—*adj.* of, or pertaining to, Protestants, or more usually, Protestantism —*v.t.* **Prot'estantise, -ize**—*ns.* **Prot'estantism** the Protestant religion: the state of being a Protestant, **protestation** (*prō-tes-tā'shən*) an avowal: an asseveration: a declaration in pleading: **protest'er, -or** one who protests —*adv* **protest'ingly.** [Fr. *protester*—L. *prōtestārī, -ātus*, to bear witness in public—*prō*, before, *testārī—testis*, a witness.]

Proteus *prō'tūs, n.* an ancient Greek sea-god who assumed many shapes to evade having to foretell the future.—*adj.* **Protean, protean** (*prō-tē'ən* or *prō'ti-ən*) readily assuming different shapes: variable: inconstant [Gr *Prōteus*]

prothesis *proth'i-sis, n.* in the Greek Church the preliminary oblation of the eucharistic elements before the liturgy: the table used: the chapel or northern apse where it stands development of an inorganic initial sound (*linguistics*).—*adj.* **prothetic** (*prə-, prō-thet'ik*) [Gr. *prothesis—pro*, before, and the root of *tithenai*, to place.]

Protista *prō-tis'tə, n.pl* a large group of unicellular organisms on the border-line between plants and animals: a proposed term for a biological kingdom including Protozoa and Protophyta.—*n.* **prō'tist.** [Gr. *prōtistos*, very first—*prōtos*, first]

protium *prō'ti-əm, -shi-əm, n.* ordinary hydrogen of atomic weight 1, distinguished from deuterium and tritium. [Gr. *prōtos*, first.]

proto- *prō'tō-, prot- prōt-* in composition, first: first of a series: first-formed: primitive: ancestral: denoting a protolanguage. [Gr. *prōtos*, first.]

protocol *prō'tō-kol, n.* an original note, minute, or draft of an instrument or transaction: a draft treaty: an official or formal account or record: an official formula: a body of diplomatic etiquette.—*v.t.* to issue, form, protocols.—*v t* to make a protocol of:—*pr.p.* **pro'tocolling;** *pa.t.* and *pa p.* **pro'tocolled.**—Also **prō'tocolise, -ize.** [Fr. *protocole*—L L. *prōtocollum*—Late Gr. *prōtokollon*, a glued-on descriptive first leaf of a MS.—Gr. *prōtos*, first, *kolla*, glue.]

proto-historic *prō-tō-his-tor'ik, adj.* belonging to the earliest age of history, just after the prehistoric and before the development of written records, etc —*n* **proto-his'tory.** [proto-.]

protolanguage *prō'tō-lang-gwij, n.* a hypothetical language (as *Proto-Indo-European*) regarded as the ancestor of other recorded or existing languages, and reconstructed by comparing these. [proto-.]

protomartyr *prō'tō-mār-tər, n.* the first martyr in any cause, esp St Stephen. [Late Gr. *prōtomartyr.*]

proton *prō'ton, n.* an elementary particle of positive charge and unit atomic mass—the atom of the lightest isotope of hydrogen without its electron.—*adj.* **protonic** (*-ton'ik*). [Gr., neut. of *prōtos*, first.]

protopathic *prō-tə-path'ik, adj.* of or relating to a certain type of nerve which is only affected by the coarser stimuli, e.g pain: of or relating to this kind of reaction.—**protop'athy.** [proto-, pathic.]

Protophyta *prōt-of'i-tə, n.pl.* a group of unicellular plants.—*n.* **protophyte** (*prō'tə-fīt*) one of the Protophyta.—*adj.* **protophytic** (*-fit'ik*) [proto-, and Gr *phyton*, a plant.]

protoplasm *prō'tə-plazm, n.* living matter, the physical basis of life.—*adjs.* **protoplasm'ic, protoplas'mal, protoplasmat'ic.** [proto-, and Gr. *plasma*, form—*plassein*, to form.]

Prototheria *prō-tə-thē'ri-ə, n.pl.* the monotremes — *adj.* **protothē'rian.** [proto-, Gr *thēr*, wild beast.]

prototype *prō'tə-tīp, n.* first or original type or model from which anything is copied: exemplar: pattern: ancestral form.—*adjs.* **pro'totypal, prototypical** (*-tip'*). [Fr.,—Gr. *prōtos*, first, *typos*, a type.]

Protozoa *prō-tō-zō'ə, n.pl.* the lowest and simplest of animals, unicellular forms or colonies multiplying by fission.—*ns.* **protozō'an, protozō'on** one of the Protozoa:—*pls.* **-zō'ans, -zō'a.**—*adjs.* **protozōan; proto-**

zō'ic pertaining to the Protozoa [**proto-**, and Gr *zōion*, an animal]

protract *prō-trakt', v t.* to draw out or lengthen in time to prolong: to lengthen out: to protrude: to draw to scale —*adj* **protrac'ted** drawn out in time. prolonged: lengthened out: drawn to scale.—*adv* **protrac'tedly.**—*adjs* **protrac'tile** (*-tīl*, in U S. *-til*), **protrac'tible** susceptible of being thrust out —*n* **protrac'tion** (*-shən*) act of protracting or prolonging: the delaying of the termination of a thing: the plotting or laying down of the dimensions of anything on paper: a plan drawn to scale —*adj.* **protrac'tive** drawing out in time prolonging. delaying.—*n.* **protrac'tor** one who, or that which, protracts: an instrument for laying down angles on paper: a muscle whose contraction draws a part forward or away from the body [L *prōtrahēre, -tractum—prō*, forth, *trahēre*, to draw.]

protrude *prō-trōōd', v.t* to thrust or push out or forward: to obtrude.—*v t* to stick out, project —*n* **protru'sion** (*-zhən*) the act of protruding: the state of being protruded: that which protrudes.—*adj* **protru'sive** thrusting or impelling forward: protruding. —*adv.* **protru'sively.**—*n.* **protru'siveness.** [L. *prōtrūdēre, -trūsum—prō*, forward, *trūdēre*, to thrust.]

protuberance *prō-tūb'ər-əns, n.* a bulging out: a swelling.—*adj.* **protū'berant.**—*adv.* **protū'berantly.**—*v.i* **protū'berate** to bulge out.—*n* **protūberā'tion.** [L. *prōtūberāre, -ātum—prō*, forward, *tūber*, a swelling.]

proud *prowd, adj* having excessive self-esteem: arrogant: haughty: having a proper sense of self-respect. having an exulting sense of credit due to or reflected upon oneself: having a glowing feeling of gratification (because of; with *of*): giving reason for pride or boasting. manifesting pride: having an appearance of pride, vigour, boldness, and freedom: stately. mettlesome: swelling: projecting, standing out, as from a plane surface, e.g. a nail-head —*adj* **proud'ish** somewhat proud —*adv* **proud'ly.**—**proud flesh** a growth or excrescence of flesh in a wound — **do someone proud** (*coll*) to treat someone sumptuously: to give honour to someone. [O.E. *prūd, prūt*, proud; perh. from a L L. word connected with L. *prōdesse*, to be of advantage.]

prove *prōōv, v.t* to test, experience, suffer: to test the genuineness of: to ascertain: to establish or ascertain as truth by argument or otherwise: to demonstrate: to check by the opposite operation (*arith.*): to obtain probate of: to cause or allow (dough) to rise.—*v.i* to make trial: to turn out: to be shown afterwards: (of dough) to rise:—*pa.p.* **proved.**—Also *pa.p.* **prov'en** surviving as the usu. form in U.S. (*prōōv'n*) and becoming commoner in Britain: already retained specif. for *Scots law* (*prōv'n*) —*adj.* **prov(e)'able.**—*adv* **prov(e)'ably.**—*n* **prov'er.**—*adj.* **prov'ing** testing, as in **proving ground** a place for testing scientifically (also *fig.*), **proving flight** test flight.— **the exception proves the rule** the making of an exception proves that the rule holds good otherwise. [O.Fr. *prover*—L. *probāre—probus*, excellent; partly perh.—O.E. *prōfian*, to assume to be—L. *probāre.*]

proven *prōv'n, prōōv'n.* See prove.—**not proven** a Scottish legal verdict declaring that guilt has been neither proved nor disproved.

provenance *prov'i-nəns, n.* source, esp. of a work of art [Fr.,—L. *prō-*, forth, *venīre*, to come.]

Provençal *prov-ä-säl, adj* of or pertaining to *Provence*, in France, or to its inhabitants or language.— *n.* a native or the language of Provence, *langue d'oc.* —*adj* **Provençale** (*prov-ä-säl*) in cooking, prepared with oil and garlic and usu tomatoes [L. *prōvinciālis—prōvincia*, province]

provender *prov'in-dər, -ən-dər, n* food: dry food for

beasts, as hay or corn: esp. a mixture of meal and cut straw or hay.—*v.t.* and *v.i.* to feed. [O.Fr. *proven-dre* for *provende*—L.L. *provenda*.]

provenience *prō-vē'ni-əns, n.* provenance. [L. *prō-venīre*; see **provenance**.]

proverb *prov'ərb, n.* a short familiar sentence expressing a supposed truth or moral lesson: a byword: (in *pl.* with *cap.*) a book of maxims in the Old Testament.—*adj.* **prover'bial** (*prə-vûr'bi-əl*) like or of the nature of a proverb: expressed or mentioned in a proverb: notorious.—*adv.* **prover'bially.** [Fr. *proverbe*—L. *prōverbium*—*prō-*, publicly, *verbum*, a word.]

provide *prə-, prō-vīd', v.t.* to supply: to appoint or give a right to a benefice, esp. before it is actually vacant: to stipulate.—*v.i.* to procure supplies, means, or whatever may be desirable, make provision: to take measures (for or against).—*adj.* **provi'dable.**—*pa.p.* or *conj.* **provi'ded,** *pres.p.* or *conj.* **provi'ding** (often with *that*) on condition: upon these terms: with the understanding.—*n.* **provi'der.** [L. *prōvidēre*—*prō,* before, *vidēre,* to see.]

providence *prov'i-dəns, n.* foresight: prudent manage-ment and thrift: timely preparation: the foresight and benevolent care of God (*theol.*). God, considered in this relation (usu. with *cap.*) (*theol.*).—*adjs.* **prov'i-dent** seeing beforehand, and providing for the future: prudent: thrifty: frugal: **providential** (*-den'shl*) affected by, or proceeding from, divine providence.—*advs.* **providen'tially; prov'idently.**—**provident society** same as **friendly society.** [L. *prōvidēns, -entis,* pr.p. of *prōvidēre*—*prō,* before, *vidēre,* to see.]

province *prov'ins, n.* a portion of an empire or a state marked off for purposes of government or in some way historically distinct: the district over which an archbishop has jurisdiction: a territorial division of the Jesuits, Templars, and other orders: a faunal or floral area: a region: vaguely, a field of duty, activity, or knowledge: a department: (in *pl.*) all parts of the country but the capital (esp. *theat.* and *journalism*)—*adj.* **provincial** (*prə-vin'shl*) relating to a province belonging to a province or the provinces: local showing the habits and manners of a province: unpolished: narrow.—*n.* an inhabitant of a province or country district: an unpolished person: the super-intendent of the heads of the religious houses in a province (*R.C.*).—*v.t.* **provin'cialise, -ize** to render provincial.—*ns.* **provin'cialism** a manner, a mode of speech, or a turn of thought peculiar to a province or a country district: a local expression: state or quality of being provincial: ignorance and narrowness of inter-ests shown by one who gives his attention entirely to local affairs; **provinciality** (*-shi-al'i-ti*).—*adv.* **pro-vin'cially.** [Fr.,—L. *prōvincia,* an official charge, hence a province.]

provision *prə-vizh'ən, n.* act of providing: that which is provided or prepared: measures taken beforehand: a clause in a law or a deed: a stipulation: a rule for guidance: an appointment by the pope to a benefice not yet vacant: preparation: previous agreement: a store or stock: (commonly in *pl.*) store of food: (in *pl.*) food.—*v.t.* to supply with provisions or food.—*adj.* **provi'sional** provided for the occasion: to meet necessity: (of e.g. arrangement) adopted on the understanding that it will probably be changed later containing a provision.—*n.* **Provi'sional** a member of the Provisional Irish Republican Army, the militant breakaway wing of the Official IRA (coll. shortening **Prō'vō:**—*pl.* **Pro'vos**).—*adv.* **provi'sionally.**—**pro-visional order** an order granted by a secretary of state, which, when confirmed by the legislature, has the force of an act of parliament. [Fr.,—L. *prōvisiō,*

-ōnis—prōvidēre; see **provide.**]

proviso *prə-, prō-vī'zō, n.* a provision or condition in a deed or other writing: the clause containing it: any condition:—*pl.* **provi'sos, provi'soes** (*-zōz*).—*adv.* **provi'sorily** (*-zə-ri-li*).—*adj.* **provi'sory** containing a proviso or condition: conditional: making provision for the time: temporary. [From the L. law phrase *prōvisō quod,* it being provided that.]

Provo. See **Provisional** under **provision.**

provocable, etc. See **provoke.**

provoke *prə-vōk', v.t.* to call forth, evoke (feelings, desires, etc.): to excite, stimulate: to incite, bring about: to excite with anger or sexual desire: to annoy, exasperate.—*adj.* **provocable** (*prov'ək-ə-bl*), **pro-vōk'able.**—*ns.* **provocateur** (*pro-vo-ka-tœr*; Fr.) one who provokes unrest and dissatisfaction for political ends, **provoca'tion** act of provoking: that which pro-vokes: any cause of danger.—*adj.* **provocative** (*-vok'*) tending, or designed, to provoke or excite.—*n.* any-thing that provokes.—*adv* **provoc'atively.**—*ns.* **pro-voc'ativeness; prov'ocător.**—*adjs.* **provoc'atory; pro-vōk'able** (older spelling **-vōc'-**).—*adj.* **provōk'ing** irritating.—*adv.* **provōk'ingly.** [L *prōvocāre, -ātum—prō-,* forth, *vocāre,* to call.]

provost *prov'əst, n* the dignitary set over a cathedral or collegiate church: in certain colleges, the head: in Scotland, the chief magistrate of a burgh, answering to mayor in England —*n.* **prov'ostship.**—**provost-mar'shal** (*prə-vō'*; U.S. *prō'*) head of military police, an officer with special powers for enforcing discipline and securing prisoners until trial (*army*): officer (master-at-arms) having charge of prisoners (*navy*); **provost-ser'geant** (*prə-vō'*) sergeant of military police.—**Lord Provost** chief magistrate of Edinburgh, Glasgow, Perth, Aberdeen, or Dundee, **Lady Provost** the wife (or other female relative) of a Lord Provost as supporting him in certain of his official duties. [O.E. *profast* (*prafost*), O.Fr *provost* (Fr. *prévôt*)—L.L. *prōpositus—prō-* for *prae,* at the head, *positus,* set.]

prow[1] *prow,* formerly sometimes *prō, n.* the forepart of a ship: the nose of an aeroplane: a projecting front part. [Fr *proue,* or Port., Sp , or Genoese *proa*—L *prōra*—Gr *prōrā.*]

prow[2] *prow, adj.* (*arch.*) valiant.—*n* **prow'ess** bravery: valour: daring: accomplishment. [O.Fr. *prou* (Fr. *preux*).]

prowl *prowl,* earlier *prōl, v.t.* to keep moving about as if in search of something: to rove in search of prey or plunder —*n.* the act of prowling.—*n.* **prowl'er.**—*n.* and *adj.* **prowl'ing.**—*adv.* **prowl'ingly.**—**on the prowl** occupied in prowling. [M.E. *prollen.*]

proximate *proks'i-mit, -māt, adj.* nearest or next. without anything between, as a cause and its effect. near and immediate.—*adj.* **prox'imal** (*biol*) at the near, inner, or attached end (opp. to *distal*).—*advs.* **prox'imally; prox'imately.**—*ns.* **proximā'tion, prox-im'ity** immediate nearness in time, place, rela-tionship, etc.—*adv* **prox'imo** next month—often written **prox.** (for L. *proximō mēnse*). [L. *prox-imus,* next, superl. from *propior* (compar.)—*prope,* near.]

proxy *prok'si, n.* the agency of one who acts for another: one who acts or votes for another: the writing by which he is authorised to do so: a substitute. [procuracy.]

prude *prōōd, n.* a person of priggish or affected modesty: one who pretends extreme propriety —*n* **pru'dery** manners of a prude.—*adj* **pru'dish.**—*adv* **pru'dishly.**—*n.* **pru'dishness.** [O.Fr. *prode,* fem of *prou, prod,* excellent; cf **prow**[2], **proud.**]

prudent *prōō'dənt, adj.* cautious and wise in conduct. discreet· characterised by, behaving with, showing, having, or dictated by forethought.—*n.* **pru'dence** quality of being prudent: wisdom applied to practice: attention to self-interest: caution.—*adj.* **prudential** (-*den'shl*) having regard to considerations of prudence: relating to prudence: prudent.—*n.* (generally *pl.*) a matter or consideration of prudence: a prudent maxim.—*n.* **prudentiality** (-*den-shi-al'i-ti*). —*advs.* **pruden'tially; pru'dently.** [L. *prūdens,* *prūdentis,* contr. of *prōvĭdens,* pr.p. of *prōvĭdēre,* to foresee.]

prudery, prudish, etc. See **prude.**

pruina *prŏō-i'nə,* (*bot.*) *n.* a powdery bloom or waxy secretion.—*adj.* **pruinose** (*prŏō'i-nŏs*). [L. *pruīna,* hoar-frost.]

prune[1] *prŏōn, v.t.* to trim by lopping off superfluous parts: to divest of anything superfluous (*fig.*): to remove by pruning.—*ns.* **pru'ner; pru'ning** the act of pruning or trimming.—**pru'ning-bill, -hook** a hooked bill for pruning with; **pru'ning-knife** a large knife with a slightly hooked point for pruning.—*n.pl.* **pru'ning-shears** shears for pruning shrubs, etc. [O.Fr. *proignier.*]

prune[2] *prŏōn, n.* a dried plum: the dark purple colour of prune-juice: a dud pilot (*airmen's slang*).—*adj.* of colour of prune-juice. [Fr.,—L. *prūna,* pl. of *prūnum* (taken for a *sing.*); cf. Gr. *prou*(m)*non,* plum.]

prunella *prŏō-nel'ə,* *n.* a strong or woollen stuff, formerly used for academic and clerical gowns and women's shoes.—*adj.* of prunella. [App. Fr. *prunelle,* sloe, dim. of *prune,* plum.]

prunt *prunt, n.* a moulded glass ornament on glass: a tool for making it.—*adj.* **prunt'ed.**

prurient *prŏō'ri-ənt, adj.* itching: uneasily or morbidly interested, curious, or craving: dallying with lascivious thoughts.—*ns.* **pru'rience, pru'riency.**—*adv.* **pru'riently.** [L. *prūriēns, -entis,* pr.p. of *prūrīre,* to itch.]

prurigo *prŏō-rī'gō, n.* an eruption on the skin, causing great itching:—*pl.* **pruri'gos.**—*adjs.* **pruriginous** (-*rij'i-nəs*); **prurit'ic** pertaining to pruritus.—*n.* **pruri'tus** itching. [L. *prūrĭgō, -inis, prūrītus, -ūs—prūrīre,* to itch.]

Prussian *prush'ən, adj.* of or pertaining to Prussia, a former state of N. Central Europe.—*n.* an inhabitant, native, or citizen of Prussia.—*v.t.* and *v.i.* **Pruss'-ianise, -ize** to make or become Prussian.—*ns.* **Pruss'-ianiser, -z-; Pruss'ianism** spirit of Prussian nationality: often used for arrogant militarism; **prussiate** (*prus'* or *prush'i-āt*) a cyanide: a ferricyanide: a ferrocyanide.—*adj.* **pruss'ic** (also sometimes *prŏŏs'*), pertaining to Prussian blue.—**Prussian** (also without *cap.*) **blue** ferric ferrocyanide, a colour pigment, discovered in Berlin: the very dark blue colour of this; **prussic acid** hydrocyanic acid, a deadly poison, first obtained from Prussian blue.

pry *prī, v.i.* to peer or peep into that which is private (also *fig.*): to examine things with impertinent curiosity:—*pr.p.* **prying;** *pa.t.* and *pa.p.* **pried;** *3rd pers. sing. pr.t.* **pries.**—*n.* **pri'er** one who pries—also **pry'er.**—*n.* and *adj.* **pry'ing.**—*adv.* **pry'ingly.**—**pry out** to investigate or find out by prying. [M.E. *prien.*]

Przewalski's horse *pr-zhe-val'skiz hörs,* a wild horse discovered in Central Asia by Nikolai Przewalski (1839–88).—Various other spellings exist.

psalm *säm, n.* a devotional song or hymn, esp. one of those included in the Old Testament **Book of Psalms.** —*n.* **psalmist** (*säm'ist*) a composer of psalms, esp. (with *cap.*) David.—*adjs.* **psalmodic** (*sal-mod'ik*), **-al** pertaining to psalmody.—*ns.* **psalmodist** (*sal',* *sä'mə-dist*) a singer of psalms; **psalmody** (*sal',* or *säm';* Gr. *psalmōidiā,* singing to the harp) the singing

of psalms, esp. in public worship: psalms collectively. —**psalm'-book.** [O.E. (*p*)*salm,* (*p*)*sealm*—L.L *psalmus*—Gr. *psalmos,* music of or to a stringed instrument.]

Psalter *söl'tər, n.* the **Book of Psalms,** esp when separately printed.—*n.* **psal'tery** an ancient and mediaeval stringed instrument like the zither, played by plucking. [O.E. *saltere*—L. *psaltērium*—Gr. *psaltērion,* a psaltery.]

psalterium *söl-tē'ri-əm, n.* the third division of a ruminant's stomach, the omasum or manyplies:—*pl.* **psaltē'ria.** [From the appearance of its lamellae, like a stringed instrument; see the foregoing.]

psephism (*p*)*sē'fizm, n.* (*ant.*) a decree of the Athenian assembly (from the voting with pebbles).— *ns.* **pse'phite** a rock composed of pebbles, a conglomerate; **psephol'ogy** sociological and statistical study of election results and trends—also **psephoanal'ysis.**—*adj.* **psepholog'ical.**—*n.* **psephol'ogist.** [Gr. *psēphos,* a pebble.]

pseud- (*p*)*sūd-,* **pseudo-** *sū'dō-,* in U S. *sŏō'dō-,* in composition, sham, false, spurious: deceptively resembling: isomerous with: temporary, provisional.—As a separate word, *adj.* **pseu'do,** *pseud* (*coll.*) false, sham, pretentious.—*n.* **pseud** (*coll.*) a pretender, pretentious fraud.—*n.* **pseu'dery** (*coll.*) falseness.— *ns.* **pseudaesthe'sia** imaginary feeling, as in an amputated limb; **pseudepig'rapha** (*pl.*) books ascribed to Old Testament characters, but not judged genuine by scholars.—*adjs.* **pseudepigraph'ic, -al, pseudepig'-raphous.**—**pseu'docarp** a fruit formed from other parts in addition to the gynaeceum; **pseu'dograph** a writing falsely ascribed; **pseu'domorph** a portion of a mineral showing the outward form of another which it has replaced by molecular substitution or otherwise.—*adjs.* **pseudomor'phic, pseudomor'phous.**— *ns.* **pseudomor'phism; pseu'donym** a fictitious name assumed, as by an author; **pseudonym'ity.**—*adj.* **pseudon'ymous.**—*adv.* **pseudon'ymously.** [Gr. *pseudēs,* false.]

pshaw *pshō, shō, pshə, interj.* expressing contempt or impatience.—*v.i.* to say 'pshaw'.—*v.t.* to say 'pshaw' at. [Spontaneous expression.]

psi (*p*)*sī,* (*p*)*sē, n.* the twenty-third letter (185,161) of the Greek alphabet, equivalent to *ps.*—*adj.* **psion'ic.**— **psi particle** an elementary particle with a very long life, formed by an electron-positron collision; **psi phenomena** the phenomena of parapsychology. [Gr. *psei.*]

psilocybin *sī-lō-sī'bin, n.* a hallucinogenic drug, obtained from Mexican mushrooms. [Gr. *psīlos,* bare, *kybē,* head.]

psilosis (*p*)*sī-lō'sis, n.* loss of hair: sprue (from loss of epithelium).—*adj.* **psilot'ic** pertaining to psilosis. [Gr. *psīlōsis—psīlos,* bare.]

psionic. See **psi.**

Psittacus (*p*)*sit'ə-kəs, n.* the grey parrot genus.—*adj.* **psitt'acine** (-*sīn*) of or like parrots.—*n.* **psittacosis** (-*kō'sis*) a contagious disease of birds, strictly of parrots, also used of other birds, communicable to man. [Gr. *psittakos,* parrot.]

psoas (*p*)*sō'əs, n.* a muscle of the loins and pelvis: the tenderloin.—*n.* (*pl.*) *psoai,* the accus. *psoäs,* being mistaken for a nom. sing.]

psora (*p*)*sō', sō'rə, n.* scabies, itch.—*n.* **psori'asis** a skin disease in which red scaly papules and patches appear.—*adjs.* **psoriat'ic; pso'ric.** [Gr. *psōrā,* *psōriāsis,* itch.]

psyche *sī'kē, n.* the soul, spirit, mind: the principle of mental and emotional life, conscious and unconscious.—*v.t.* **psych, psyche** (*sīk; slang*) to subject to psychoanalysis: to work out a problem, the intentions of another person, etc., psychologically (often with *out*): to defeat or intimidate by psychological means (sometimes with *out*): to get (oneself) psychologically prepared for (usu. with *up*): to stimulate (usu. with *up*).—*n.* **psychedelia** (*-děl'i-ə*) (production of) psychedelic experiences.—*adjs.* **psychedelic** see **psychodelic; psychiat'ric(al).**—*ns.* **psych'atrist** one who is medically qualified to treat diseases of the mind; **psych'iatry.**—*adjs.* **psych'ic, -al** pertaining to the psyche, soul, or mind; spiritual: spiritualistic: beyond, or apparently beyond, the physical: sensitive to or in touch with that which has not yet been explained physically.—*n.* **psych'ic** that which is of the mind or psyche: a spiritualistic medium.—*adv.* **psych'ically.**—*n.sing.* **psy'chics** the science of psychology: psychical research.—**psychical research** investigation of phenomena apparently implying a connection with another world; **psychic force** a power not physical or mechanical, supposed to cause certain so-called spiritualistic phenomena. [Gr. *psychē*, soul, butterfly.]

psych(o)- *sīk-(ō-)*, in composition, soul, spirit: mind, mental: psychological.—*n.* **psych'o** coll. shortening of **psychopath** (*pl.* **psych'os**).—*adj.* **psychoac'tive** of a drug, affecting the brain and influencing behaviour (also **psychotrop'ic**).—*v.t.* **psychoan'alyse, -yze** to subject to psychoanalysis.—*ns.* **psychoanal'ysis** a method of investigation and psychotherapy whereby nervous diseases or mental ailments are traced to forgotten hidden concepts in the patient's mind and treated by bringing these to light; **psychoan'alyst** one who practises psychoanalysis.—*adjs.* **psychoanalyt'ic, -al; psychodel'ic** (the irregularly formed **psychedelic** (*sī-kə-del'ik, -děl'ik*) is commoner) pertaining to a state of relaxation and pleasure, with heightened perception and increased mental powers generally: pertaining to drugs which cause, or are believed to cause, the taker to enter such a state: pertaining to visual effects and/or sound effects whose action on the mind is a little like that of psychedelic drugs: dazzling in pattern.—*n.* **psychodram'a** a method of mental treatment in which the patient is led to objectify and understand his difficulty by spontaneously acting it out.—*adjs.* **psychodramat'ic; psychodynam'ic** pertaining to mental and emotional forces, their source in past experience, and their effects.—*ns.* **psychodynam'ics; psychogen'esis** (the study of) the origin or development of the mind: origination in the mind.—*adjs.* **psychogenet'ic, -al; psychogen'ic** having origin in the mind or in a mental condition; **psychogeriat'ric.**—*n.* **psychogeriat'ric'ian.**—*n.sing.* **psychogeriat'rics** the study of the psychological problems of old age.—*adj.* **psychohistor'ical.**—*ns.* **psychohis'tory** history studied from a psychological point of view; **psychokinē'sis** movement by psychic agency.—*adj.* **psychokinet'ic.**—*n.* **psycholing'uist.**—*adj.* **psycholinguis'tic.**—*n.sing.* **psycholinguis'tics** the study of language development, language in relation to the mind, thought, etc.—*adjs.* **psycholog'ic, -al.**—*adv.* **psycholog'ically.**—*ns.* **psychol'ogist** one who has studied and qualified in psychology; **psychol'ogy** science of mind: study of mind and behaviour: attitudes, etc., characteristic of individual, type, etc., or animating specific conduct; **psychom'eter** one who has occult power of psychometry: instrument for measuring reaction-times, etc.—*adjs.* **psychomet'ric, -al.**—*ns.* **psychometrician** (*-trish'ən*), **psychom'etrist.**—*n.sing.* **psychomet'rics** branch of psychology dealing with measurable factors.—*n.* **psychom'etry** psychometrics: occult power of divining properties of things by mere contact.—*adj.* **psy'chomotor** pertaining to such mental action as induces muscular contraction.—*n.* **psychoneurō'sis** mental disease without any apparent

anatomical lesion: a functional disorder of the mind in one who is legally sane and shows insight into his condition:—*pl.* **psychoneurō'ses.**—*n.* and *adj.* **psychoneurot'ic.**—*n.* **psy'chopath** (*-path*) one who shows a pathological degree of specific emotional instability without specific mental disorder: one suffering from a behavioural disorder resulting in inability to form personal relationships and in indifference to or ignorance of his obligations to society, often manifested by anti-social behaviour, as acts of violence, sexual perversion, etc.—*adj.* **psychopath'ic** pertaining to psychopathy (also *n.*).—*ns.* **psychopathol'ogist; psychopathol'ogy** the branch of psychology that deals with the abnormal workings of the mind; **psychop'athy** derangement of mental functions; **psychoprophylax'is** a method of training for childbirth aimed at making labour painless.—*adj.* **psychosex'ual** of or relating to the psychological aspects of sex, e.g. sexual fantasies.—*n.* **psychō'sis** mental condition: a serious mental disorder characterised by e.g. illusions, delusions, hallucinations, mental confusion and a lack of insight into his condition on the part of the patient:—*pl.* **psychō'ses.**—*adjs.* **psychosō'cial** of or relating to matters both psychological and social; **psychosomat'ic** (Gr. *sōma*, body) of mind and body as a unit: concerned with physical diseases having a psychological origin.—*ns.* **psychosur'gery** brain-surgery in the treatment of mental cases; **psychotherapeut'ics, -ther'apy** treatment of mental illness by hypnosis, psychoanalysis and similar psychological means; **psychother'apist.**—*adj.* **psychot'ic** pertaining to psychosis.—*n.* one suffering from a psychosis.—*n.* **psychot'icism.**—*adj.* **psychotrop'ic** same as **psychoactive** (also *n.*).—**psychological block** an inability to think about, remember, etc., a particular subject, event, etc., for psychological reasons; **psychological moment** properly the psychological element or factor, misunderstood by a French translator from German and applied to the moment of time when the mind could best be worked upon: hence now often the very moment, the nick of time; **psychological warfare**, the use of propaganda to influence enemy opinion or morale. [Gr. *psychē*, soul, butterfly.]

psychrometer *sī-krom'i-tər*, *n.* originally a thermometer: now a wet-and-dry-bulb hygrometer.—*adjs.* **psychrometric** (*sī-krō-met'rik*), **-al.**—*n.* **psychrom'etry.** [Gr. *psýchros*, cold, *metron*, a measure.]

ptarmigan *tär'mi-gən*, *n.* a mountain-dwelling grouse, white in winter: extended to other species of *Lagopus*, as willow-grouse. [Gael. *tàrmachan.*]

pter-(o)- *p)ter'(-o)-*, in composition, feather, wing.—**-ptera** in zoological names, organism(s) having specified type or number of wings or wing-like parts.—adjective combining form **-pteran, -pterous.** [Gr. *pteron*, wing.]

pteranodon (*p)ter-an'ə-don*, *n.* a toothless flying reptile of the Cretaceous period with a horn-like crest [Gr. *pteron*, wing, *an-*, without, *odous, odontos*, tooth.]

pteridology. See **Pteris.**

pteridophyte (*p)ter'id-ō-fīt*, *n.* a vascular cryptogam or a member of the **Pteridophyta** (*-of'i-ta*), one of the main divisions of the vegetable kingdom—ferns, horsetails, etc. [Gr. *pteris, -idos*, a fern, *phyton*, a plant.]

pterin (*p)ter'in*, *n.* any of a group of substances occurring as pigments in butterfly wings, important in biochemistry.—**pteroic** ((*p)ter-ō'ik*) **acid** the original folic acid found in spinach; **pteroylglutamic** ((*p)ter'ō-il-gloō-tam'ik*) **acid** the folic acid that is therapeutically active in pernicious anaemia. [Gr. *pteron*, a wing.]

pterion (*p*)*ter'*, or (*p*)*tēr'i-on*, *n*. in craniometry, the suture where the frontal, squamosal, and parietal bones meet the wing of the sphenoid:—*pl.* **pter'ia**. [Gr. dim. of *pteron*, wing.]

Pteris (*p*)*ter'is*, (*p*)*tē'ris*, *n*. a genus of ferns with spore-clusters continuous along the pinnule margin, usually taken to include bracken, which some separate as **Pterid'ium**.—*ns.* **pteridol'ogist**; **pteridol'ogy** the science of ferns; **pteridoph'ilist** a fern-lover. [Gr. *pteris, -idos,* or *-eōs,* male-fern—*pteron*, a feather.]

pterodactyl, pterodactyle (*p*)*ter-ə-dak'til, n.* a fossil (Jurassic and Cretaceous) flying reptile with large and bird-like skull, long jaws, and a flying-membrane attached to the long fourth digit of the forelimb. [Gr. *pteron*, wing, *daktylos*, finger.]

pterosaur (*p*)*ter'ə-sör, n.* a member of the **Pterosaur'ia**, an extinct order of flying reptiles, including the pterodactyls. [Gr. *pteron*, wing, *sauros*, lizard.]

pterygium (*p*)*tar-ij'i-əm, n.* a vertebrate limb: a wing-like growth: a wing-shaped area of thickened conjunctiva which spreads over part of the cornea and sometimes over the eyeball:—*pl.* **pteryg'ia**.—*adj.* **pteryg'ial**.—*n.* a bone in a fin. [Latinised from Gr. *pterygion*, dim. of *pteryx, -ygos*, wing.]

pterygoid (*p*)*ter'i-goid, adj.* wing-like: of or near the pterygoid.—*n.* (in full, **pterygoid bone, plate, process**) in various vertebrates, a paired bone of the upper jaw. [Gr. *pteryx, -ygos*, wing.]

ptisan *tiz'n, tiz-an', n.* a medicinal drink made from barley: a decoction.—Also **tisane**. [Gr. *ptisanē*, peeled barley, barley-gruel—*ptissein*, to winnow.]

Ptolemaic *tol-i-mā'ik, adj.* pertaining to the *Ptolemies*, Greek kings of Egypt (from Alexander's general to Caesar's son), or to *Ptolemy* the astronomer (fl. A.D. 150)—also **Ptolemaean** (*-mē'ən*).

ptomaine *tō'mān, tō-mān', n.* a loosely used name for amino-compounds, some poisonous, formed from putrefying animal tissues.—**ptomaine poisoning** (*arch.*) food poisoning—formerly thought to be caused by ptomaines, few of which are now known to be poisonous if eaten. [It. *ptomaina*—Gr. *ptōma*, a corpse.]

ptosis (*p*)*tō'sis, n.* downward displacement: drooping of the upper eyelid. [Gr. *ptōsis*—*piptein*, to fall.]

pub *pub,* (*slang*) *n.* short for **public house**.—**pub'-crawl** a progression from pub to pub.—Also *v.i.*

puberty *pū'bər-ti, n.* the beginning of sexual maturity. —*adjs.* **pū'beral, pū'bertal**.—*ns.* **pū'bes** (*-bēz*) the lower part of the hypogastric region: the hair growing thereon at puberty; **pūbescence** (*-es'əns*) puberty: a soft downy covering, esp. in plants, of adpressed hairs.—*adjs.* **pūbes'cent**; **pū'bic** of the pubes or the pubis.—*n.* **pūbis** (for L. *os pūbis*, bone of the pubes) a bone of the pelvis which in man forms the anterior portion of the innominate bone:—*pl.* **pū'bises**.—As a prefix **pū'bio-** (wrongly **pū'bo-**). [L. *pūber* and *pūbēs, -eris,* grown-up, downy, and *pūbēs, -is,* grown-up youth, the pubes.]

public *pub'lik, adj.* of or belonging to the people: pertaining to a community or a nation: general: common to, shared in by, or open to, all: generally known: in open view, unconcealed, not private: engaged in, or concerning, the affairs of the community: devoted or directed to the general good (now *rare* except in *public spirit*): international: open to members of a university as a whole, not confined to a college: of a public house.—*n.* the people: the general body of mankind: the people, indefinitely: a part of the community regarded from a particular viewpoint, e.g. as an audience or a target for advertising: public view of a public place, society, or the open.—*ns.* **pub'lican**

the keeper of an inn or public house: a tax-farmer (*Roman hist.*): a tax-collector (*Roman hist.*); **publicā'tion** the act of publishing or making public: a proclamation: the act of sending out for sale, as a book: that which is published as a book, etc.—*v.t.* **pub'licise, -ize** (*-sīz*) to give publicity to: to make known to the general public, to advertise.—*ns.* **pub'licist** (*-sist*) one who publicises: an advertising agent; **publicity** (*-lis'i-ti*) state of being open to the knowledge of all: notoriety: acclaim: the process of making something known to the general public: advertising.—*adv.* **pub'-licly**.—*n.* **pub'licness** (*rare*).—**public bar** one usu. less well appointed than a lounge bar; **public company** one whose shares can be purchased on the stock exchange by members of the public; **public convenience** see **convenience**; **public corporation** one owned by the government and run on business principles, being for the most part self-ruling; **public enemy** someone whose behaviour is considered to be a menace to a community in general; **public funds** government funded debt; **public holiday** a general holiday; **public house** one chiefly used for selling alcoholic liquors to be consumed on the premises: an inn or tavern; **public image** see **image**; **public law** law governing relations between public authorities, as the state, and the individual; **public nuisance** an illegal act harming the general community rather than an individual: an annoying, irritating person (*coll.*); **public ownership** ownership by the state as of nationalised industry; **public prosecutor** an official whose function is to prosecute persons charged with offences; **public relations** the relations between a person, organisation, etc., and the public: the business of setting up and maintaining favourable relations: a department of government, an industrial firm, etc., dealing with this.—Also *adj.*—**public school** school under the control of a publicly elected body: an endowed classical school for providing a liberal education for such as can afford it—Eton, Harrow, Rugby, etc.—*adj.* **pub'lic-school'**.—**public sector** government-financed industry, social service, etc.; **public servant** a person employed by the government; **public spending** spending by the government.—*adj.* **pub'lic-spir'ited** having a spirit actuated by regard to the public interest: with a regard to the public interest.—**public transport**; **public utility** a service or supply provided in a town etc., for the public, as gas, electricity, water, transport: (in *pl.*) public utility shares.—**go public** to become a public company; **in public** openly, publicly; **public address system** a system that enables (large) groups of people to be addressed clearly, consisting of some or all of the following—microphones, amplifiers, loud speakers, sound projectors; **public health inspector** designation in England of an official whose duty is to enforce regulations regarding e.g. food-handling in shops, maintenance of a clean water-supply, waste-disposal, and to ascertain the fitness of dwellings for human habitation, formerly known as sanitary inspector; **public lending right** an author's right to payment when his/her books are borrowed from public libraries; **public opinion poll** a taking of public opinion based on the answers of scientifically selected elements in the community to questioning. [L. *pūblicus*—*pop*(u)*lus*, the people.]

publican, publication. See under **public**.

publish *pub'lish, v.t.* to proclaim: to send forth to the public: to put forth and offer for sale books, newspapers, etc.: to put into circulation: of an author, to get published.—*v.i* to publish a work, newspaper, etc.—*adj.* **pub'lishable**.—*ns.* **pub'lisher** one who publishes books: one who attends to the issuing and distributing of a newspaper. [Fr. *publier*—L.

pūblicāre, with *-ish* on the model of other verbs]
puce *pūs, n.* and *adj.* brownish-purple. [Fr *puce*—L.
pūlex, -icis, a flea.]
puck[1] *puk, ns.* a goblin or mischievous sprite.—*adj.*
puck'ish impish: full of mischief. [O.E. *pūca*.]
puck[2] *puk, n.* a rubber disc used instead of a ball in
ice-hockey.
pucka, pukka *puk'ə,* (*Anglo-Ind.*) *adj.* out-and-out
good: thorough: complete: solidly built: settled: durable: permanent: full-weight: straightforward:
genuine: sure.—**pucka sahib** a gentleman. [Hind
pakkā, cooked, ripe.]
pucker *puk'ər, v.t.* to wrinkle: to make gathers in.—
Also *v.i.—n.* a corrugation or wrinkle: a group of
wrinkles, esp. irregular ones: agitation, confusion
(*coll.*).—*adj.* **puck'ery** astringent: tending to
wrinkle. [Cf. **poke**[1].]
puckish. See **puck**[1].
pud *pŏŏd,* (*coll.*) *n.* Short for **pudding**.
pudden, puddening, etc. See **pudding.**
pudding *pŏŏd'ing, n.* a skin or gut filled with seasoned
minced meat and other materials (as blood, oatmeal),
a kind of sausage: meat, fruit, etc., cooked in a casing
of flour: a soft kind of cooked dish, usually farinaceous, commonly with sugar, milk, eggs, etc.: a pad of
rope, etc., used as a fender on the bow of a boat or
elsewhere (also **pudd'ening**): material gain (*fig.*): a
fat, dull, or heavy-witted person (*coll.*).—Also (now
coll. or *dial.*) **pudden** (*pŏŏd'n, pud'n*).—*adj.* **pudd'-
ingy** (*-ing-i*).—*adj.* **pudd'ing-faced** having a fat,
round, smooth face.—**pudd'ing-plate** a shallow bowl-
like plate, usu. smaller than a soup-plate; **pudd'ing-
sleeve** a large loose sleeve gathered in near the wrist.
—**in the pudding club** (*slang*) pregnant [M.E.
poding.]
puddle *pud'l, n.* a small muddy pool: a non-porous
mixture of clay and sand: a muddle (*coll.*): a muddler
(*coll.*).—*v.t.* to make muddy: to work into puddle, to
stir and knead: to cover with puddle: to make
watertight by means of clay: to convert from pig-iron
into wrought-iron by stirring in a molten state.—*v.i.*
to make a dirty stir.—*ns.* **pudd'ler, pudd'ling.**—*adj.*
pudd'ly full of puddles. [App. dim. of O.E. *pudd*,
ditch.]
puddock *pud'ək,* **paddock** *pad'ək,* (*arch.* and *Scot.*) *ns.*
a toad or frog. [Dim. from late O.E. *pade, padde*,
toad.]
pudendum *pū-den'dəm, n.* (and *pl.* **puden'da**) the external genital organs, esp. female. [L. *pudēre*, to
make (or be) ashamed, *pudendum*, something to be
ashamed of.]
pudge *puj,* **pudgy** *puj'i.* Same as **podge, podgy.**
pueblo *pweb'lŏ, n.* a town or settlement (in Spanish-
speaking countries): a communal habitation of the
Indians of New Mexico, etc.: an Indian of the pueb-
los:—*pl.* **pueb'los.** [Sp., town—L. *populus*, a
people.]
puer *pūr, n.* and *v.t.* Same as **pure** (in tanning).
puerile *pū'ər-īl,* in U.S. *-il, adj.* childish: trifling: silly.
—*n.* **puerility** (*-il'i-ti*). [L. *puerīlis—puer*, a boy.]
puerperal *pū-ûr'pər-əl, adj.* relating to childbirth.—
puerperal fever fever occurring in connection with
childbirth: now confined to morbid conditions owing
to introduction of organisms into the genital tract.
[L. *puerpera*, a woman in labour—*puer*, a child, *parēre*, to bear.]
puff *puf, v.i.* to blow in whiffs: to breathe out vehemently or pantingly: to emit puffs: to issue in puffs: to
make the sound of a puff: to go with puffs: to swell
up.—*v.t.* to drive with a puff: to blow: to emit in
puffs: to play (as a wind instrument) or smoke (as a
pipe) with puffs: to inflate or swell: to elate unduly:
to extol, esp. in disingenuous advertisement: to put

out of breath.—*n.* a sudden, forcible breath, blast, or
emission: a gust or whiff: a cloud or portion of
vapour, dust, air, etc., emitted at once: a sound of
puffing: a downy pad for powdering: anything light
and porous, or swollen and light: a biscuit or cake of
puff-paste or the like: laudation intended as, or serving as, advertisement.—*adj.* **puffed** distended:
inflated: gathered up into rounded ridges, as a sleeve
out of breath.—*ns.* **puff'er** one who puffs: a steam-
engine: a steamboat.—*adv* **puff'ingly.**—*adj.* **puff'y**
puffed out with air or any soft matter. tumid: bombastic. coming in puffs: puffing: short-winded —
puff'-adder a thick, venomous African snake (*Bitis
arietans* or kindred species) that distends its body
when irritated; **puff'ball** a fungus with ball-shaped
fructification filled when ripe with a snuff-like mass
of spores; **puff'-box** a box for toilet powder and puff;
puff'er(fish) a globe-fish; **puff'-paste** a flour paste in
thin layers: pastry made thereof (**puff'-pastry**).—
puffed quite out of breath: inflated, distended,
expanded; **puffed up** swollen with pride, presumption, or the like. [O.E. *pyffan*, or kindred form.]
puffin *puf'in, n.* a sea-bird (Fratercula) of the auk
family, with brightly coloured parrot-like beak.
[Origin obscure: connection with **puff** is conjectured.]
pug[1] *pug, n.* a monkey: a fox: a pug-dog.—*adjs.*
pugg'ish, pugg'y like a monkey or a pug-dog:
snub-nosed.—*ns.* **pug'-dog** a small short-haired dog
with wrinkled face, upturned nose, and short curled
tail; **pug'-engine** a shunting engine.—*adj.* **pug'-faced**
monkey-faced.—**pug'-nose** a short, thick nose with
the tip turned up.—*adj.* **pug'-nosed.** [Connection
with **puck**[1] is conjectured.]
pug[2] *pug, n.* clay ground and worked with water.—*v.t.*
to beat: to grind with water and make plastic: to pack
with pugging.—*n.* **pugg'ing** clay, sawdust, plaster,
etc., put between floors to deaden sound.
puggy. See **pug**[1].
pugilism *pū'jil-izm, n.* the art or practice of boxing:
prize-fighting.—*adjs.* **pu'gilist.**—*adjs.* **pugilist'ic, -al.**—
adv. **pugilist'ically.** [L. *pugil*, a boxer.]
pugnacious *pug-nā'shəs, adj.* given to fighting: combative: quarrelsome.—*adv.* **pugna'ciously.**—*ns.* **pugna'-
ciousness, pugnacity** (*-nas'i-ti*) inclination to fight:
fondness for fighting: quarrelsomeness. [L. *pug-
nāx, -ācis—pugnāre*, to fight.]
puisne *pū'ni. adj.* an obsolete form of **puny**, surviving
as applied to certain judges—junior.—*n.* a puisne
judge. [O.Fr. (Fr. *puîné*), from *puis*—L. *posteā*,
after, *né*—L. *nātus*, born.]
puissant, puissaunt *pū'is-ənt, pwis', (poet.) pū-is', adj.*
powerful.—*n.* **puissance, -aunce** (*-əns, -ŏns', -ăns'*)
power (*arch.*): (usu. *pwēs'ăs, -ăns*) (a showjumping
competition with very high jumps showing) the power
of a horse.—*adv.* **puissantly** (*-ənt-li*). [Fr. *puissant,*
app. formed as a pr.p. from a vulgar L. substitute for
L. *potēns, -entis*; see **potent.**]
puja *pōō'jə, n.* worship: reverential observance: a festival. [Sans. *pūjā*, worship.]
puke[1] *pūk, v.t.* and *v.i.* to vomit.—*n.* vomit: a despicable person (*slang*). [Poss. connected with Flem.
spukken, Ger. *spucken*.]
pukka. Same as **pucka.**
pulchritude *pul'kri-tūd, n.* beauty.—*adj.* **pul-
chritud'inous.** [L. *pulchritūdō, -inis—pulcher*,
beautiful.]
pule *pūl, v.t.* and *v.i.* to pipe: to whimper or whine.—
n. **pū'ler.**—*n.* and *adj.* **pū'ling.**—*adv.* **pū'lingly.**—
adj. **pū'ly** whining: sickly. [Imit.; cf. Fr. *piauler*.]
pulka *pul'kə, n.* a Laplander's boat-shaped sledge.—
Also **pulk, pulk'ha.** [Finnish *pulkka*, Lappish
pulkke, bulkke.]

pull *pōōl*, *v.t.* to pluck: to remove by plucking: to extract: to pick by hand: to strip, deprive of feathers, hair, etc.: to draw: to move, or try or tend to move, towards oneself or in the direction so thought of: to render, or bring to be, by pulling: to row: to transport by rowing: to move in a particular direction when driving (usu. with *out*, *over*, etc.): to stretch: to hold back (as a boxing blow, a racehorse to prevent its winning): to take as an impression or proof, orig. by pulling the bar of a hand-press: to strike to the left (right for left-handed person; *cricket*, *golf*): to bring down: to take a draught of: to draw or fire (a weapon): to snatch, steal (*slang*): to arrest (*slang*): to raid (*slang*): to attract (e.g. a crowd) (*slang*).—*v.i.* to give a pull: to perform the action of pulling anything: to tear, pluck: to drag, draw: to strain at the bit: to exert oneself: to go with a pulling movement: to move in a particular direction, esp. when in a motor vehicle (usu. with *away*, *out*, *over*, etc.): to row: to suck: to strike the ball to the left, etc.—*n.* an act, bout, or spell of pulling: a pulling force: a row: a stiff ascent: a draught of liquor: a proof, single impression (*print*): advantage: influence: an apparatus for pulling: the quantity pulled at one time: resistance.—*n.* **pull'er**. —**pull'-back** a retreat, withdrawal; **pull'-in** a stopping-place (also *adj.*): a transport café (see also **pull in** below).—*adj.* **pull'-on** requiring only to be pulled on, without fastening.—*n.* a pull-on garment of any kind.—*adj.* **pull'-out** a section of a magazine, etc., that can be removed and kept separately (see also **pull out** below).—**pull'over** a jersey, a jumper, a body garment put on over the head.—**pull a bird** (*slang*) to succeed in forming a (sexual) relationship with a girl; **pull about** to distort: to treat roughly; **pull a face** to grimace; **pull a fast one on** (*slang*) to take advantage of by a sudden trick; **pull apart**, **to pieces** to bring asunder by pulling: to criticise harshly; **pull back** to retreat, withdraw (see also *n.* **pull'-back** above); **pull down** to take down or apart: to demolish: to bring down: to reduce in health or vigour; **pull for** to row for: to support; **pull in** to draw in: to make tighter: to draw a motor vehicle into the side of the road and halt (see also *n.* and *adj.* **pull'-in** above): to arrest: to earn: of a train, to arrive at a station; **pull off** to carry through successfully; **pull oneself together** to regain one's self-control: to collect oneself, preparing to think or to act; **pull one's weight** to give full effect to one's weight in rowing: to do one's full share of work, cooperate wholeheartedly; **pull out** to draw out: to drive a motor vehicle away from the side of the road or out of a line of traffic: of a train, to leave a station: to abandon a place or situation which has become too difficult to cope with (*coll.*; *n.* **pull'-out**; see also above); **pull round** to bring, or come, back to good health or condition or to consciousness; **pull through** to bring or get to the end of something difficult or dangerous with some success; **pull together** (*fig.*) to cooperate; **pull up** to pull out of the ground: to tighten the reins: to bring to a stop: to halt: to take to task: to gain ground: to arrest. [O.E *pullian*, to pluck, draw.]

pullet *pōōl'it*, *n.* a young hen, esp. from first laying to first moult. [Fr. *poulette*, dim. of *poule*, a hen—L.L. *pulla*, a hen, fem. of L. *pullus*, a young animal.]

pulley *pōōl'i*, *n.* a wheel turning about an axis, and receiving a rope, chain, or band on its rim, used for raising weights, changing direction of pull, transmission of power, etc.: a block: a combination of pulleys or blocks:—*pl.* **pull'eys**. [M.E. *poley*, *puly*—O.Fr. *polie* (Fr. *poulie*)—L.L. *polegia*.]

Pullman *pōōl'mən*, *n.* a railway saloon or sleeping-car, first made by George M. *Pullman* (1831–97) in America.—In full, **Pullman car**.

pullulate *pul'ū-lāt*, *v.i.* to sprout: to sprout or breed abundantly: to teem: to increase vegetatively.—*n.* **pullula'tion**. [L. *pullulāre*, *-ātum*—*pullulus*, a young animal, sprout—*pullus*.]

pulmonary *pul'-mən-ər-i*, *adj.* of the lungs or respiratory cavity: leading to or from the lungs: of the nature of lungs: having lungs: diseased or weak in the lungs. —*adj.* **pulmonic** (*-mon'ik*) of the lungs. [L. *pulmō*, *-ōnis*, lung.]

pulp *pulp*, *n.* any soft fleshy part of an animal, e.g. the tissue in the cavity of a tooth: the soft part of plants, esp. of fruits: any soft structureless mass: the soft mass obtained from the breaking and grinding of rags, wood, etc., before it is hardened into paper: crushed ore: nonsense (*fig.*): sentimentality (*fig.*): a cheap magazine printed on wood-pulp paper, or of a paltry and sentimental or sensational character (also **pulp('-)magazine**).—*v.t.* to reduce to pulp: to make pulpy: to deprive of pulp.—*v.i.* to become pulp or like pulp.—*n.* **pulp'er** a machine for reducing various materials to pulp.—*adj.* **pulp'y**.—**pulp'board** cardboard made directly from a layer of pulp; **pulp's cav'ity** the hollow of a tooth containing pulp; **pulp'mill** a machine or factory for pulping wood, roots, or other material; **pulp'wood** wood suitable for paper-making: a board of compressed wood-pulp and adhesive. [L. *pulpa*, flesh, pulp.]

pulpit *pōōl'pit*, *n.* a raised structure for preaching from (also *fig.*): an auctioneer's desk or the like. [L. *pulpitum*, a stage.]

pulpy. See **pulp**.

pulque *pōōl'kā*, *-kě*, *n.* a fermented drink made in Mexico from agave sap. [Sp. Amer.]

pulsate *pul'sāt*, or *-sāt'*, *v.i.* to beat, throb: to vibrate: to change repeatedly in force or intensity: to thrill with life or emotion.—*n.* **pul'sar** (for 'pulsating star') any of a number of interstellar sources of regularly pulsed radiation which may be rotating neutron stars. —*adj.* **pul'satile** (*-sə-til*, in U.S. *-til*) capable of pulsating: pulsatory: rhythmical: played by percussion (*mus.*).—*n.* **pulsa'tion** a beating or throbbing: a motion of the heart or pulse: any measured beat: vibration.—*adj.* **pulsative** (*pul'sə-tiv* or *-sāt'*).—*n.* **pulsa'tor** (or *pul'sə-tər*) a machine, or part of a machine, that pulsates or imparts pulsation, as for separating diamonds from earth, for regulating the rhythmical suction of a milking machine, for pumping.—*adj.* **pulsatory** (*pul'sə-tər-i*, or *-sā'*) beating or throbbing. [L. *pulsāre*, *-ātum*, to beat.]

pulse¹ *puls*, *n.* a beating or throbbing: a measured beat or throb: a vibration: a single variation, beat or impulse: a signal of very short duration (*radio*): the beating of the heart and the arteries: a thrill (*fig.*).— *v.i.* to beat, as the heart: to throb: to pulsate.—*v.t.* to drive by pulsation: to produce, or cause to be emitted, in the form of pulses.—*adjs.* **pulsed**; **pul'sific** producing a single pulse.—*ns.* **pulsim'eter**, **pulsom'eter** an instrument for measuring the strength or quickness of the pulse.—**pulse'-rate** the number of beats of a pulse per minute; **pulse'-wave** the expansion of the artery, moving from point to point, like a wave, as each beat of the heart sends the blood to the extremities.—**feel someone's pulse** to test or measure someone's heart-beat, usu. by holding his wrist: to explore a person's feelings or inclinations in a tentative way; **keep one's finger on the pulse** (*fig.*) to keep in touch with current events, ideas, etc. [L. *pulsus* —*pellěre*, *pulsum*; partly O.Fr. *pouls*, *pous*, remodelled on Latin.]

pulse² *puls*, *n.* seeds of leguminous plants as food collectively—beans, pease, lentils, etc.: the plants yielding them. [L. *puls*, *pultis*, porridge; cf. Gr. *poltos*, and **poultice**.]

pulverise, -ize *pul'və-rīz, v.t.* to reduce to dust or fine powder: to defeat thoroughly, destroy (*fig.*).—*v.i.* to fall into dust or powder.—*adj.* **pul'verisable, -z-,** (or **-iz'**).—*n.* **pulverisā'tion, -z-.**—*n.* **pul'veriser, -z-** one who pulverises: a machine for pulverising or for spraying.—*adj.* **pul'verous** dusty or powdery.—*n.* **pulverulence** (-*vûr'ū-lans*).—*adj.* **pulver'ūlent** consisting of fine powder: powdery: dusty-looking: readily crumbling. [L. *pulvis, pulveris,* powder.]

puma *pū'mə,* n. the cougar (*Felis concolor*), a large reddish-brown American cat—also called **mount'ain-li'on**—*pl.* **pu'mas.** [Peruv. *puma.*]

pumelo. Same as **pomelo.**

pumice *pum'is, pū'mis,* n. an acid glassy lava so full of gas-cavities as to float in water: a frothy portion of any lava: a piece of such lava used for smoothing or cleaning.—*v.t.* to smooth or clean with pumice-stone—also **pumicate** (*pū'mi-kāt; rare*).—*adj.* **pumiceous** (-*mish'əs*).—**pum'ice-stone.** [O.E. *pumic* (-*stān*), pumice (-stone): reintroduced—O.Fr. *pomis*; both—L. *pūmex, -icis.*]

pummel *pum'l,* n. a less usual spelling of **pommel.**—*v.t.* (the usual spelling) to beat, pound, bethump, esp. with the fists:—*pr.p.* **pumm'elling;** *pa.t* and *pa.p.* **pumm'elled.** [pommel.]

pump *pump,* n. a machine for raising and moving fluids, orig. esp. bilge-water in ships, or for compressing, rarefying, or transferring gases: a stroke of a pump: an act of pumping.—*v.t* to raise, force, compress, exhaust, empty, remove, or inflate with a pump: to discharge by persistent effort: to move in the manner of a pump: to subject to, or elicit by, persistent questioning: to put out of breath (esp. in *pass.*; often with *out; coll.*).—*v.i.* to work a pump: to work like a pump: to move up and down like a pump-handle: to spurt: to propel, increase the speed of, a sailing-boat by rapidly pulling the sails in and out (*naut.*).—*n.* **pump'er.**—**pump gun** a gun whose chamber is fed by a pump-like movement; **pump priming** starting a pump working efficiently by introducing fluid to drive out the air: investing money in order to stimulate commerce, local support, etc.; **pump'-room** the apartment at a mineral spring in which the waters are drunk; **pump'-water** water from a pump; **pump'-well** a well from which water is got by pumping: the compartment in which a pump works.

pump² *pump,* n. a light shoe without fastening, worn esp. for dancing.

pumpernickel *pōōmp'ər-nik-l,* n. rye bread, much used in Westphalia. [Ger.; the Ger. word means a rackety goblin, a coarse lout, rye bread (poss. from its giving forth a sound like *pump* when struck).]

pumpkin *pum(p)'kin,* n. a plant of the gourd family, or its fruit.—Also **pump'ion.** [O.Fr. *pompon*—L *pepō*—Gr. *pepōn,* ripe.]

pun¹ *pun, v.t.* to ram: to consolidate by ramming:—*pr.p.* **punn'ing;** *pa.t.* and *pa.p.* **punned.**—*n.* **punn'er** a tool for punning, a ram. [See **pound³.**]

pun² *pun, v.i.* to play upon words alike or nearly alike in sound but different in meaning:—*pr p.* **punn'ing;** *pa.t.* and *pa.p.* **punned.**—*n.* a play upon words.—*ns.* **punn'ing; pun'ster** a maker of puns. [A late-17th-century word; origin unknown; It. *puntiglio,* fine point, has been conjectured.]

punch¹ *punch, punsh,* (*dial.*) *adj.* short and thick.—*n.* a short-legged, round-bodied horse, long bred in Suffolk [Poss. shortened from **puncheon¹,** or from **Punchinello,** or a variant of **bunch.**]

punch² *punch, punsh,* n a drink ordinarily of spirit, water, sugar, lemon-juice, and spice (with variations).—**punch'-bowl** a large bowl for making punch in; **punch'-ladle** a ladle for filling glasses from a punch-bowl [Traditionally from the five original

ingredients, from Hindi *pāc,* five—Sans. *pañca.*]

punch³ *punch, punsh, v.t.* to prod: to poke: to strike with a forward thrust, as of the fist: to thump: to stamp, pierce, perforate, indent, by a forward thrust of a tool or part of a machine: to make, obtain, or remove by such a thrust: to press in vigorously the keys or button of: to record by pressing a key.—*v.t.* to perform an act of punching: to clock (*in* or *out*).—*n.* a vigorous thrust or forward blow: striking power: effective forcefulness: a tool or machine for punching: a die: a prop for a mine-roof.—*n.* **punch'er** one who punches: an instrument for punching.—*adj.* **punch'y** vigorous, powerful: punch-drunk (*coll.*).—**punch'-ball** a suspended ball used for boxing practice; **punch'-card, punched card** a card with perforations representing data, used in the operation of automatic computers.—*adj.* **punch'-drunk** having a form of cerebral concussion from past blows in boxing, with results resembling drunkenness: dazed (*coll. abbrev.* **punch'y**).—**punched tape** (*comput.*) same as **paper tape; punch line** the last line or conclusion of a joke, in which the point lies: the last part of a story, giving it meaning or an unexpected twist; **punch'-up** a fight with fists.—**pull one's punches** to hold back one's blows (also *fig.*). [**pounce¹**; or from **puncheon¹**; possibly in some senses for **punish.**]

puncheon¹ *pun'chn, -shn,* n. a tool for piercing, or for stamping: a short supporting post: a split trunk with one face smoothed for flooring, etc. [O.Fr. *poinson*—L. *pungĕre, punctum,* to prick.]

puncheon² *pun'chn, -shn, n.* a cask: a liquid measure of from 70 to 120 gallons. [O.Fr. *poinson,* a cask.]

Punchinello *punch-, punsh-i-nel'ō,* n. a hook-nosed character in an Italian puppet-show: a buffoon, any grotesque personage:—*pl.* **Punchinell'o(e)s.** [It. *Pulcinella,* a Neapolitan buffoon, of doubtful origin.]

punchy. See **punch³.**

punctate, -d *pungk'tāt, -id, adjs.* dotted: pitted.—*n.* **puncta'tion.** [L. *punctum,* a point, puncture—*pungĕre, punctum,* to prick.]

punctilio *pungk-til'i-ō, -yō,* n. a nice point in behaviour or ceremony: a point about which one is scrupulous: nicety in forms: exact observance of forms:—*pl.* **punctilios.**—*adj.* **punctil'ious** attentive to punctilio: scrupulous and exact.—*adv.* **punctil'iously.**—*n.* **punctil'iousness.** [It. *puntiglio* and Sp. *puntillo,* dims. of *punto*—L. *punctum,* a point.]

punctual *pungk'tū-al, adj.* of the nature of a point: pertaining to a point, or points (*math.*): of punctuation: punctilious: exact in keeping time and appointments: done at the exact time: up to time.—*n.* **punctuality** (-*al'i-ti*).—*adv.* **punc'tually.** [L.L. *punctuális*—*punctum,* a point.]

punctuate *pungk'tū-āt, v.t.* to mark with points: to mark off with the usual stops, points of interrogation, and the like: to intersperse: to emphasise.—*n.* **punctua'tion** the act or art of dividing sentences by points or marks.—*adj.* **punc'tuative.**—*n.* **punc'tuator.** [L.L. *punctuāre, -ātum,* to prick—L. *punc-tum.*]

punctum *pungk'təm,* (*anat.*) n. a point, dot: a minute aperture:—*pl.* **punc'ta.** [L. *punctum*—*pungĕre, punctum,* to prick.]

puncture *pungk'chər,* n. a pricking: a small hole made with a sharp point: perforation of a pneumatic tyre.—*v.t.* to make a puncture: to deflate someone's pride, self-confidence, etc. (*fig.*).—*v.i.* to get a puncture.—*adj.* **punc'tured** perforated: pierced: marked with little holes: consisting of little holes.—*n.* **punctura'tion.** [L. *punctūra*—*pungĕre,* to prick]

pundit, pandit *pun'dit,* n. one who is learned in the

language, science, laws, and religion of India: any learned man: an authority, now, commonly, one who considers himself or herself an authority.—*n.* pun'dltry. [Hindi *pan d it*—Sans. *pan d ita*.]

pungent pun'jənt, *adj.* sharp: ending in a hard sharp point (*bot.*): pricking or acrid to taste or smell: keenly touching the mind: painful: sarcastic.—*n.* pun'gency.—*adv.* pun'gently. [L. *pungēns, -entis,* pr.p. of *pungĕre,* to prick.]

Punic pū'nik, *adj.* of ancient Carthage: Carthaginian: faithless, treacherous, deceitful (as the Romans alleged the Carthaginians to be).—Punic faith treachery. [L. *Pūnicus—Poenī,* the Carthaginians.] punily. See puny.

punish pun'ish, *v.t.* to cause (someone) to suffer for an offence: to cause someone to suffer for (an offence): to handle, beat, severely (*coll.*): to consume a large quantity of (*coll.*).—*v.i.* to inflict punishment.—*n.* punishabil'ity.—*adj.* pun'ishable.—*adj.* pun'ishing causing suffering or retribution: severe, testing (*coll.*).—*n.* pun'ishment act or method of punishing: penalty imposed for an offence: severe handling (*coll.*). [Fr. *punir, punissant*—L. *pūnīre,* to punish—*poena,* penalty.]

punition pū-nish'ən, *n.* punishment.—*adjs.* pu'nitive (*-ni-tiv*) concerned with, inflicting, or intended to inflict, punishment; pu'nitory. [L. *pūnīre,* to punish.]

Punjabi, Panjabi pun-jä'bē, *n.* a native or inhabitant of the Punjab in India and Pakistan: the language of the Punjab.—*adj.* of the Punjab. [Hindi *Pañjābī.*]

punk¹ pungk, *n.* anything or anyone worthless: balderdash: a foolish person: a follower of punk rock, often recognisable by the use of cheap, utility articles, e.g. razor blades, plastic rubbish bags, safety-pins, as clothes or decoration.—punk rock a style of popular music of the late 1970s, rhythmical and aggressive, with violent, often obscene lyrics, inspired by a feeling of despair at the cheapness and ugliness of life—also called new wave.

punk² pungk, *n.* touchwood: tinder: a preparation of amadou used as tinder. [Poss. spunk; or poss. of American Indian origin.]

punka, punkah pung'kə, *n.* a fan: palm-leaf fan: a large mechanical fan for cooling a room. [Hindi *pākhā,* a fan.]

punner, punning, punster. See pun¹,².

punnet pun'it, *n.* a small shallow basket for fruit, as strawberries.

punt¹ punt, *n.* a flat-bottomed boat with square ends.—*v.t.* to propel by pushing a pole against the bottom: to transport by punt.—*v.i.* to go in a punt: to go shooting in a punt: to pole a punt or boat.—*n.* punt'er.—punt'-pole a pole for propelling a punt; punt's man a sportsman who uses a punt. [O.E. *punt*—L. *pontō, -ōnis,* punt, pontoon; cf. pontoon¹.]

punt² punt, *v.i.* to stake against the bank: to back a horse.—*n.* punt'er one who punts: a professional gambler: customer (*coll.*): an ordinary person (*coll.*). [Fr. *ponter.*]

punt³ punt, *n.* the act of kicking a dropped football before it touches the ground.—*v.t.* to kick in this manner.

punt⁴ pōōnt, *n.* the Irish pound.

puny pū'ni, *adj.* stunted: feeble:—*compar.* pu'nier; *superl.* pu'niest.—*adv.* pu'nily.—*n.* pu'niness. [puisne.]

pup pup, *n.* a shortened form of puppy.—*v.t.* and *v.i.* to whelp:—*pr.p.* pupp'ing; *pa.t.* and *pa.p.* pupped.—buy a pup to be swindled; in pup of a bitch, pregnant; sell a pup to inveigle someone into a specious bad bargain: to swindle.

pupa pū'pə, *n.* an insect in the usually passive stage

between larva and imago: an intermediate stage of development in some other invertebrates:—*pl.* pupae (pū'pē), pū'pas.—*adj.* pū'pal of a pupa.—*v.i.* pū'pate to become a pupa.—*n.* pūpā'tion. [L. *pūpa,* a girl, a doll.]

pupil¹ pū'pl, -pil, *n.* a ward (*law*); one who is being taught: one who is being or has been taught by a particular teacher.—*adj.* under age.—*ns.* pu'pillage the state of being a pupil or student: the time during which one is a pupil or student; pupillar'ity the state or time of being legally a pupil.—*adjs.* pu'pillary pertaining to a pupil or ward, or one under academic discipline. (The above words are sometimes spelt with one *l.*)—pupil teacher a pupil who does some teaching as part of his training for later entry into the profession. [Fr. *pupille*—L. *pūpillus, pūpilla,* dims. of *pūpus,* boy, *pūpa,* girl.]

pupil² pū'pl, -pil, *n.* the apple of the eye: the round opening in the eye through which the light passes: a central spot, esp. within a spot.—*adjs.* pu'pillary; pu'pillate (*zool.*) having a central spot of another colour. (The above words sometimes with one *l.*) [L. *pūpilla,* pupil of the eye, orig. the same as in the preceding, from the small image to be seen in the eye.]

puppet pup'it, *n.* a doll or image moved by wires or hands in a show: a marionette: one who acts just as another tells him.—*adj.* behaving like a puppet: actuated by others.—*ns.* puppeteer' one who manipulates puppets; pupp'etry play of, or with, puppets: puppets collectively: puppet-like action: puppet-shows: anything like or associated with puppets.—pupp'et-show; pupp'et-valve see poppet. [Earlier poppet; cf. O.Fr. *poupette,* dim. from L. *pūpa.*]

puppodum pup'ə-dəm. Same as popadum.

puppy pup'i, *n.* a young dog: a whelp: a young seal: a conceited young man.—*v.t.* and *v.i.* to pup.—*ns.*—pupp'y-dog; pupp'y-fat temporary fatness in childhood or adolescence.—*adj.*—puppy love same as calf-love. [App. Fr. *poupée,* a doll or puppet—L. *pūpa.*]

pur pūr, (Fr.) *adj.* pure.—pur sang (*sā*) pure blood: thoroughbred: total.

Purana pōō-rä'nə, *n.* any one of a class of sacred books in Sanskrit literature, legendary, religious, etc.—*adj.* Puranic (*-rän'ik*). [Sans. *purāna—purā,* of old.]

purblind pûr'blīnd, *adj.* orig. apparently wholly blind: nearly blind: dim-sighted, esp. spiritually.—*adv.* pur'blindly.—*n.* pur'blindness. [pure (or perh. O.Fr. intens. pfx. *pur-*), and blind.]

purchase pûr'chəs, *v.t.* to acquire: to get in any way other than by inheritance (*law*): to buy: to obtain by labour, danger, etc.: to raise or move by a mechanical power.—*v.i.* to make purchases.—*n.* act of purchasing: that which is purchased: acquisition: annual rent: any mechanical advantage in raising or moving bodies or apparatus: advantageous hold, or means of exerting force advantageously.—*adj.* pur'chasable.—*n.* pur'chaser.—purchase tax formerly, a British form of sales-tax levied on specified goods and at differential rates.—so many years' purchase value, price, of a house, an estate, etc., equal to the amount of so many years' rent or income. [O.Fr. *porchacier,* to seek eagerly, pursue.]

purdah pûr'də, *n.* a curtain, esp. for screening women's apartments: seclusion of women.—Also *fig.* [Urdu and Pers. *pardah.*]

pure pūr, *adj.* clean: unsoiled: unmixed: free from guilt or defilement: chaste: free from bad taste, meretriciousness, solecism, barbarism: modest: mere: that and that only: utter, sheer: of a study, confined to that which belongs directly to it: non-empirical, involving an exercise of mind alone, without admixture of the results of experience: homozygous, breeding true (*biol.*): unconditional (*law*).— *n.* purity: dog's dung or similar substance used by tanners (also **puer**).—*adv.* purely: without admixture.—*v.t.* to cleanse, refine: to treat with pure (also **puer**).—*adv.* **pure'ly** chastely: unmixedly: unconditionally: wholly, entirely.—*ns.* **pure'ness**; **purism** (q.v.).—*adjs.* **pure'-blood**, **-ed**, **pure'-bred** of unmixed race.—**pure mathematics** mathematics treated without application to observed facts of nature or to practical life; **pure science** science considered apart from practical applications. [Fr. *pur* —L. *pūrus*, pure.]

purée pū'rā, *n.* food material reduced to pulp and passed through a sieve: a soup without solid pieces.— *v.t.* to make a purée of. [Fr.]

purfle pûr'fl, *v.t.* to ornament the edge of, as with embroidery or inlay.—*n.* a decorated border.—*n.* **pur'fling** a purfle, esp. around the edges of a fiddle. [O.Fr. *pourfiler*—L. *prō*, before, *fīlum*, a thread.]

purge pûrj, *v.t.* to purify: to remove impurities from: to clear of undesirable elements or persons: to remove as an impurity: to clarify: fo clear from accusation: to expiate: to evacuate, as the bowels: to make (someone) evacuate the bowels.—*v.i.* to become pure by clarifying: to evacuate the bowels: to have frequent evacuations: to take a purgative.—*n.* act of purging: an expulsion or massacre of those who are not trusted: a purgative.—*n.* **purgation** (-gā') purging: a clearing away of impurities: the act of clearing from suspicion or imputation of guilt (*law*): a cleansing.—*adj.* **purgative** (pûrg'ə-tiv) cleansing: having the power of evacuating the intestines.—*n.* a medicine that evacuates.—*adv.* **pur'gatively.**—*adjs.* **purgato'rial, purgato'rian** pertaining to purgatory: purgatory purging or cleansing: expiatory.—*n.* a place or state in which souls are after death purified from venial sins (*R.C.*): any kind or state of suffering for a time: intense discomfort (*coll.*).—*n.* and *adj.* **purging** (pûrj'). [Fr. *purger*—L. *pūrgāre*, *-ātum*— earlier *pūrigāre*—*pūrus*, pure.]

purify pū'ri-fī, *v.t.* to make pure: to cleanse from foreign or hurtful matter: to free from guilt, from ritual uncleanness or from improprieties or barbarisms in language.—*v.i.* to become pure:—*pr.p.* **pu'rifying**; *pa.t.* and *pa.p.* **pu'rified.**—*n.* **purifica'tion.**—*adj.* **pu'rificative.**—*adj.* **pu'rificatory** tending to purify or cleanse.—*n.* **pu'rifier.** [Fr. *purifier*—L. *pūrificāre*—*pūrus*, pure, *facēre*, to make.]

purim pū'rim, *pōōr-ēm'*, *n.* the Feast of Lots held about 1st of March, in which the Jews commemorated their deliverance from the plot of Haman, as related in Esther (see esp. iii. 7). [Heb. *pūrīm* (sing. *pūr*), lots.]

purin, purine pū'rin, *-ēn*, *ns.* a white crystalline substance C$_5$H$_4$N$_4$, which with oxygen forms uric acid (C$_5$H$_4$N$_4$O$_3$) and is the nucleus of many other derivatives. [Contracted from L. *pūrum ūricum* (*acidum*), pure uric (acid).]

purism pū'rizm, *n.* fastidious, esp. over-fastidious, insistence upon purity (esp. of language in vocabulary or idiom).—*n.* and *adj.* **pūr'ist.**—*adjs.* **pūris'tic, -al.** [L. *pūrus*, pure.]

Puritan pū'ri-tan, *n.* one who in the time of Elizabeth and the Stuarts wished to carry the reformation of the Church of England further by purifying it of ceremony: an opponent of the Church of England on account of its retention of much of the ritual and belief of the Roman Catholics: an opponent of the Royalists in the 17th century: (the following meanings also without *cap.*) a person of like views with, or in sympathy with, the historical Puritans: a person

strictly moral in conduct: slightingly, one professing a too-strict morality: an advocate of purity in any sense.—*adj.* (also without *cap.*) pertaining to the Puritans.—*adjs.* **pūritanic** (*-tan'ik*), **-al** (usu. *derog.*).—*adv.* **pūritan'ically.**—*n.* **pūr'itanism.** [L. *pūrus*, pure.]

purity pūr'i-ti, *n.* condition of being pure: freedom from mixture of any kind, sin, defilement, or ritual uncleanness: chastity: sincerity: freedom from foreign or improper idioms or words. [L. *pūritās, -ātis*—*pūrus*.]

purl[1] pûrl, *v.i.* to flow with a murmuring sound: to flow in eddies: to curl or swirl.—*n.* a trickling rill: a movement or murmuring as of a stream among stones: an eddy or ripple (also **pirl**).—*n.* and *adj.* **purl'ing.** [Cf. Norw. *purla*, to babble, Sw. dial. *porla*, to purl, ripple.]

purl[2] pûrl, *v.i.* to spin round: to capsize: to go head over heels: to fall headlong or heavily.—*v.t.* to throw headlong.—*n.* a heavy or headlong fall: an upset.—*n.* **purl'er** a headlong or heavy fall or throw, esp. in phrases *go, come, a purler.* [Perh. conn. with **purl**[2].]

purl[3] pûrl, *v.t.* to embroider or edge with gold or silver thread: to fringe with a waved edging, as lace.—*v.t.* and *v.i.* to knit with a purl stitch.—*n.* twisted gold or silver wire: a loop or twist, esp. on an edge (also **pearl**): a succession of such loops, or a lace or braid having them: a fold, pleat, or frilling: knitting with a purl stitch.—*adj.* (also **pearl**) in knitting, denoting an inverted stitch made with the wool passed behind the needle (opp. to *plain*).

purlieu pûr'lū, *n.* (in *pl.*) borders or outskirts. [A.Fr. *puralee*, land severed by perambulation—O.Fr. *pur* (= L. *prō*), *allee*, going; infl. by Fr. *lieu*, place.]

purlin, purline pûr'lin, *n.* a piece of timber stretching across the principal rafters to support the common or subsidiary rafters.

purloin pur-loin', pûr', *v.t.* to filch, steal.—*v.i.* to practise theft. [A.Fr. *purloigner*, to remove to a distance.]

purple pûr'pl, *n.* crimson (*hist.*): the Tyrian crimson dye, got in ancient times from various shellfish (*hist.*): the animal yielding it: a crimson cloth or garment anciently worn by kings and emperors (*hist.*): the dignity of king or emperor: cardinalate (from the red hat (former) and robes): bishops (with **the**): now, any mixture of blue and red: a purple pigment: (in *pl.*) purpura.—*adj.* of the colour purple, mixed red and blue: blood-red, bloody (*hist.*).—*v.t.* to make purple. —*v.i.* to become purple.—*adjs.* **pur'plish, pur'ply** somewhat purple.—**purple heart** the purple-coloured wood of species of Copaifera (fam. Caesalpiniaceae) (also **purple wood**): a mauve heart-shaped tablet of a stimulant drug of amphetamine type: (with *caps.*) a U.S. decoration for wounds received on active service; **purple patch** a passage of fine, or (often) over-ornate, writing; **purple prose** writing of this sort. —**born in the purple** born in the purple chamber (see **Porphyrogenite**): hence, of exalted birth. [O.E. (Northumb.) *purpl(e)*, purple (adj.)—*purpur* (n.)— L. *purpura*—Gr. *porphȳra*, purple-fish.]

purport pûr'part, *-pôrt, -pôrt, n.* meaning conveyed: substance, gist, tenor.—*v.t.* **purport'** (also *pûr'*) to give out as its meaning: to convey to the mind: to seem, claim, profess (to mean, be, etc.).—*adv.* **purport'edly.** [O.Fr., from *pur* (Fr. *pour*)—L. *prō*, for *porter*—L. *portāre*, to carry.]

purpose pûr'pas, *n.* idea or aim kept before the mind as the end of effort: power of seeking the end desired: act or fact of purposing: an end desired: a useful function: a definite intention.—*v.t.* to intend.—*adjs.* **pur'posed** intentional: intended: purposeful; **pur'poseful** directed towards a purpose: actuated by pur pose.—*adv.* **pur'posefully.**—*n.* **pur'posefulness.**—*adv.* **pur'posely** intentionally.—*adj.* **pur'posive** directed towards an end: showing intention or resolution, purposeful.—*adj.* **pur'pose-built** specially made or designed to meet particular requirements.—**on purpose, of set purpose** with design, intentionally; **to good** (or **some**) **purpose** with good effect; **to the purpose** to the point, or material to the question. [O.Fr. *pourpos, propos*—L. *prōpositum*, a thing intended—*prō*, forward, *pōnĕre, positum*, to place; cf. **propose.**]

purpura *pûr'pū-rə*, *n.* purples, an eruption of small purple spots, caused by extravasation of blood. [L. *purpura*—Gr. *porphўrā.*]

purr *pûr*, *v.i.* to utter a low, murmuring sound, as a cat when pleased.—*v.t.* to say or utter with or by purring.—*ns.* **purr; purr'ing.**—*adv.* **purr'ingly.** [Imit.]

purse *pûrs*, *n.* a small bag for carrying money: a sum of money in a purse: a sum given as a present or offered as a prize: funds: a woman's handbag (*U.S.*): a purse-like receptacle or cavity.—*v.t.* to contract as the mouth of a purse: to draw into folds or wrinkles.—*v.i.* to pucker.—*ns.* **purs'er** formerly a naval paymaster: an officer in charge of cabins, stewards, etc.; **purs'ership.**—**purse'-bearer** one who carries in a bag the Great Seal for the Lord Chancellor, or the royal commission for the Lord High Commissioner; **purse'-net** a bag-shaped net that closes by a drawstring at the neck; **purse'-seine** a seine-net that can be drawn into the shape of a bag; **purse'-seiner** a fishing-vessel equipped with such nets; **purse'-strings** the strings fastening a purse (usu. *fig.*).—**privy purse** an allowance for a sovereign's private expenses; **public purse** the nation's finances. [O.E. *purs*, app.—L.L. *bursa* —Gr. *byrsa*, a hide.]

purslane *pûrs'lin*, *n.* a pot and salad herb: any member of its genus or family.—Also **purslain.** [O.Fr. *porcelaine*—L. *porcilāca, portulāca.*]

pursue *pər-sū'*, *-sōō'*, *v.t.* to harass, persecute, persist in opposing or seeking to injure: to follow in order to overtake and capture or kill: to chase: to hunt: to follow up: to follow the course of: to be engaged in: to carry on: to seek to obtain or attain: to proceed with.—*v.i.* to follow: to go on or continue: to act as a prosecutor at law.—*adj.* **pursu'able.**—*ns.* **pursu'al,** (more often) **pursu'ance** pursuit: act of carrying out or (e.g. *in pursuance of this policy*) following out.—*adj.* **pursu'ant** pursuing: in pursuance (with *to*; approaching an *adv.*).—*n.* and *adj.* **pursu'er** one who pursues.—*n.* and *adj.* **pursu'ing.** [A.Fr. *pursuer, pursiwer*—popular L. forms *pro-, persequĕre, -ire,* for L. *prōsequi, persequi—prō-, per-* (the prefixes being confused), and *sequi,* to follow.]

pursuit *pər-sūt'*, *-sōōt'*, *n.* the act of pursuing: endeavour to attain: occupation: employment: that which is pursued.—**pursuit plane** a type of military aeroplane used in pursuing enemy aeroplanes. [A.Fr. *purseute,* fem. pa.p.; see **pursue.**]

pursuivant *pûr's(w)i-vənt*, *n.* an attendant or follower: a state messenger with power to execute warrants: an officer ranking below a herald. [Fr. *poursuivant,* pr.p. of *poursuivre,* to pursue.]

pursy *pûrs'i*, *adj.* puffy: fat and short: short-winded.—*n.* **purs'iness.** [O.Fr. *poulsif,* broken-winded—*poulser* (Fr. *pousser*)—L. *pulsāre,* to drive.]

purtenance *pûr'tən-əns*, *n.* that which pertains or belongs. [Earlier form of **pertinence.**]

purulent *pū'rū-lənt, -rōō-*, *adj.* consisting of, of the nature of, forming, full of, characterised by, or like pus.—*ns.* **pū'rulence,** *adj.* **pū'rulency.**—*adv.* **pū'rulently.** [L. *pūrulentus*—*pūs, pūris,* pus.]

purvey *pûr-vā'*, *v.t.* to provide, furnish: to supply.—*v.i.* to furnish provisions or meals as one's business.—*ns.* **purvey'ance** the act of purveying: a procuring of victuals: that which is supplied; **purvey'or** one whose business is to provide victuals or meals: an officer who formerly exacted provisions for the use of the king's household. [A.Fr. *purveier* (Fr. *pourvoir*)—L. *prōvidēre;* see **provide.**]

purview *pûr'vū*, *n.* the body or enacting part of a statute distinguished from the preamble: enactment: scope: range: field of activity or view: competence. [A.Fr. *purveu,* provided, pa.p. of *purveier;* see **purvey.**]

pus *pus*, *n.* a thick yellowish fluid formed by suppuration, consisting of serum, white blood cells, bacteria, and debris of tissue. [L. *pūs, pūris;* cf. Gr. *pyon.*]

push *pŏŏsh*, *v.t.* to thrust or press against: to drive by pressure: to press or drive forward: to urge: to press hard: to advance, carry to a further point: to promote, or seek to promote, vigorously and persistently: to make efforts to promote the sale of: to effect by thrusting forward: to peddle (drugs): to come near (an age or number).—*v.i.* to make a thrust: to exert pressure: to make an effort: to press forward: to make one's way by exertion: to be urgent and persistent.—*n.* a thrust: an impulse: pressure: a help to advancement: enterprising or aggressive pertinacity: an effort: an onset: an offensive: dismissal (*coll.*).—*adj.* **pushed** in a hurry (*coll.*): short of money (*coll.*).—*n.* **push'er** one who pushes: a machine or part that pushes: a child's table implement, or a finger of bread, used for pushing food on to a fork: a self-assertive person: one who assiduously seeks social advancement: a dope pedlar.—*adjs.* **push'ful** energetically or aggressively enterprising; **push'ing** pressing forward in business: enterprising: self-assertive; **push'y** aggressive: self-assertive.—**push'-bicycle** (*coll.* **-bike**), **-cycle** one propelled by foot; **push'-button** a knob which when pressed puts on or cuts off an electric current, as for bells, etc. (*adj.* operated by, or using, push-button, -buttons); **push'-chair** a folding-chair with wheels, for a child; **push'-over** an easy thing: a person or side easily overcome.—*adj.* **push'-pull** of any piece of apparatus in which two electrical or electronic devices act in opposition to each other, as, e.g., of an amplifier in which two thermionic valves so acting serve to reduce distortion.—*v.t.* **push'-start** to start (a motor-car) by pushing it while it is in gear.—*n.* the act of starting the car thus.—**at a push** when circumstances urgently require: if really necessary; **give, get the push** to dismiss, be dismissed, from a job; **push along** (*coll.*) to depart, to go on one's way; **push around** to bully; **push for** to make strenuous efforts to achieve; **push off** of a rower or a boat, to leave the bank, shore, etc.: to depart (*coll.*); **push one's luck see luck; push out** (of person, boat) to row or be rowed out towards open water; **push through** to compel acceptance of; **push up the daisies** to be dead and buried. [Fr. *pousser*—L. *pulsāre,* freq. of *pellĕre, pulsum,* to beat.]

Pushtu, Pashtu, Pushtoo *push'tōō,* **Pushto, Pashto** *-tō,* **Pakhtu** *puhh'tōō,* **Pakhto** *-tō, ns.* the language of the Afghans proper. [Afghan *Pashtō, Pakhtō.*]

pusillanimous *pū-si-lan'i-mas, adj.* wanting firmness of mind: mean-spirited: cowardly.—*adv.* **pusillan'imously.**—*n.* **pusillanim'ity.** [L. *pusillanimis*—*pusillus,* very little, *animus,* mind.]

puss *pŏŏs,* *n.* a familiar name for a cat: a hare, in sportsmen's language: a playfully pejorative name for a child or a girl.—*n.* **puss'y** a dim. of **puss** (also **puss'y-cat**): anything soft and furry: a willow-catkin: the female genitalia (*slang*).—**puss'-moth** a thick-bodied hairy moth whose caterpillar feeds on willow or poplar leaves; **Puss'yfoot** U.S. nickname of William E. Johnson (1862–1945) from his stealthy ways as a revenue officer: (without *cap.*) hence, from his prohibitionist campaigns, a prohibitionist—*v.i.* (without *cap.*) to go stealthily: to act timidly or cautiously.—**puss'yfooter; puss'y-will'ow** a common American willow, *Salix discolor* or other species with silky spring catkins. [Cf. Du. *poes*, puss; Ir. and Gael. *pus*, a cat.]

pustule *pus'tūl, n.* a pimple containing pus: a pimple-like or warty spot or elevation.—*adjs.* **pus'tular, pus'-tulous.** [L. *pustula.*]

put[1] *pŏŏt, v.t.* to push or thrust: to cast, throw, hurl (esp. by a thrusting movement of the hand from the shoulder): to place, or cause to be, in such and such a position, state, predicament, relation, etc.: to apply: to append, affix: to connect: to add: to commit: to assign: to assign or suggest a course of action to (with *on*, as a diet, a study, a track; or *to*, as a task): to subject: to reduce: to convert: to render: to express: to assert, have: to propound: to submit to a vote: to impose: to impute: to call upon, oblige, stake, venture, invest: to repose (as trust, confidence).—*v.i.* to proceed, make one's way (*naut.*): to set out, esp. hurriedly:—*pr.p.* **putting** (*pŏŏt'*); *pa.t* and *pa p* **put.**—*n.* a push or thrust: a cast, throw, esp. of a heavy stone from the shoulder: on the stock exchange, an option of selling within a certain time certain securities or commodities, at a stipulated price (also **put option**).—*ns.* **putter** (*pŏŏt'ər*) one who puts; **putt'ing** the act or sport of hurling a heavy stone or weight from the hand by a sudden thrust from the shoulder (also **putting the shot**).—**put'-down** a snub: an action intended to assert one's superiority; **put'-in** (*Rugby football*) the act of throwing the ball into a set scrum; **put'-off** an excuse, a makeshift, evasion: a postponement; **put'-on** a hoax.—*adj.* **put-up'** speciously preconcerted.—**put about** to change the course, as of a ship: to publish, circulate; **put across** to carry out successfully, bring off: to perform so as to carry the audience with one, **put an end** or **a stop to** to cause to discontinue; **put away** to renounce: to divorce: to stow away, pack up, set aside: to put into the proper or desirable place: to imprison: to eat; **put back** to push backward: to delay: to repulse: to turn and sail back for port (*naut.*): to reduce one's finances (*coll.*); **put by** to store up; **put down** to crush, quell: to kill, esp. an old or ill animal: to snub, humiliate: to enter, write down on paper: to reckon: to attribute: to surpass, outshine: of an aeroplane, to land (often with *at*): to pay (a deposit): to put (a baby) to bed (*coll.*); **put forth** to extend: to propose: to publish: to exert: to display: to lend at interest: to set out from port: to produce, extrude; **put forward** to propose: to advance; **put in** to introduce: to insert: to lodge, deposit, hand in: to make a claim or application (*for*): to enter: to enter a harbour: to interpose: to perform towards completing a total: to spend, pass, fill up with some occupation: to appoint; **put in an appearance** see **appearance; put in mind** to remind; **put it across someone** to defeat someone by ingenuity; **put it on** to pretend (to be ill, etc.); **put it past someone** to judge it inconsistent with someone's character; **put off** to lay aside: to lay aside the character of: to palm off: to turn aside with evasions, excuses, or unsatisfying substitutes: to divert, turn aside from a purpose: to postpone: to disconcert: to cause aversion or disinclination: to push from shore; **put on** to don, clothe with: to assume, esp. deceptively: to mislead, deceive: to superpose: to impose: to affix, attach, apply: to add (as weight, charges, etc.): to stake: to move forward: to set to work: to set in operation: to incite: to turn on the supply of: to score: to stage; **put on to** to make aware of: to connect with by telephone; **put out** to expel: to dismiss from a

game and innings: to send forth: to stretch forth: to extinguish: to place at interest: to expand: to publish: to disconcert: to put to inconvenience: to offend: to dislocate: to exert: to produce: to place with others or at a distance: to go out to sea, leave port: to remove bodily or blind (an eye). to render unconscious (*slang*); **put over** to carry through successfully: to impress an audience, spectators, the public, favourably with: to impose, pass off; **put through** to bring to an end: to accomplish: to put in telephonic communication: to process (*comput*), **putting the shot, stone, weight** putting (q v.), **put to** to apply: to add to: to connect with: to harness: to shut: to set to; **put to death** see **death; put to it** to press hard: to distress; **put to rights** see **rights; put to sea** to begin a voyage; **put two and two together** to draw a conclusion from various facts, **put up** to sheathe: to compound: to accommodate with lodging: to take lodgings: to nominate or stand for election: to expose for sale: to present (as a good game, fight, or defence, a prayer): to preconcert; **put-up job** a dishonest scheme prearranged usu. by several people; **put upon** to take undue advantage of: to impose upon; **put up to** to incite to: to make conversant with, supply with useful information or tips about; **put up with** to endure; **stay put** to remain passively in the position assigned. [Late O.E. *putian* (found in the verbal-noun *putung*, instigation).]

put[2] *put.* See **putt.**

putative *pū'tə-tiv, adj.* supposed: reputed: commonly supposed to be. [L. *putātīvus—putāre, -ātum,* to suppose.]

putlog *put'log* **putlock** *-lok, ns.* a cross-piece in a scaffolding, the inner end resting in a hole left in the wall.

putois *pu-twa', n.* a brush of polecat's hair, or substitute, for painting pottery. [Fr.]

putrefy *pū'tri-fī, v.t.* to cause to rot: to corrupt.—*v.i.* to rot:—*pr.p.* **pu'trefying;** *pa.t.* and *pa.p.* **pu'trefied.** —*adj.* **putrefacient** (*-fā'shənt*) causing putrefaction. —*n.* **putrefaction** (*-fak'shən*) rotting.—*adjs.* **putrefac'tive; putrefi'able.**—*n.* **putrescence** (*-tres'əns*) incipient rottenness.—*adjs.* **putresc'ent; pu'trid** rotten: wretchedly bad (*slang*).—*adv.* **pu'tridly.**—*ns.* **putrid'ity, pu'tridness.** [L. *putrefacēre, putrēscēre, putridus—puter, putris,* rotten.]

putsch *pŏŏch, n.* a sudden revolutionary outbreak. [Swiss Ger. dialect.]

putt *also* **put** *put, v.t.* to hurl in putting (as a weight, stone; *Scot.*; see **put**): to strike in making a putt (*golf*).—*v.i.* to make a putt or putts:—*pr.p.* **putting** (*put'*); *pa.p.* and *pa.t.* **putted** (*put'*).—*n.* a throw or cast (*Scot.*; see **put**): a delicate stroke such as is made with a putter on, or sometimes near, a putting-green, with the object of rolling the ball, if possible, into the hole (*golf*).—*ns.* **putter** (*put'ər*) one who putts or can putt: a short stiff golf-club with upright striking-face, used in putting; **putt'ing** the exercise of hurling a heavy weight (*Scot.*; see **put**; *also* **putting the shot**): the act or art of making a putt.—**putt'ing-green** the turf, made firm and smooth for putting, round each of the holes of a golf-course: by the rules all within 20 yards of the hole, hazards excluded: an area of smooth grass with holes, like a small golf-course, on which only putting is allowed; **putt'ing-stone** see **put.** [A Scottish form of **put.**]

puttee, puttie *put'ē, -i, n.* a cloth strip wound round the leg from ankle to knee, as a legging. [Hindi. *patti.*]

putto *pŏŏt'ō, n.* very young boy, often winged, in Renaissance or Baroque art:—*pl.* **putti** (*pŏŏt'ē*). [It.]

putty *put'i, n.* orig. putty-powder (*polishers'* or *jewellers' putty*): a cement of whiting and linseed oil (*glaziers'* or *painters' putty*): a fine cement of slaked lime and water only (*plasterers' putty*): a yellowish grey colour: a weak-willed, easily manipulated person (*fig.*).—*v.t.* to fix, coat, or fill with putty:—*pr.p.* **putt'ying**; *pa.t.* and *pa.p.* **putt'ied.**—*n* **putt'ier** a glazier.—*adjs.* **putt'y-coloured; putt'y-faced** having a putty-coloured face.—**putt'y-knife** a blunt, flexible tool for laying on putty; **putt'y-pow'der** stannic oxide (often with lead oxide) used for polishing glass. [Fr. *potée*, potful, putty-powder—*pot.*]

puzzle *puz'l*, *v.t.* to perplex: to bewilder: to afford difficulty of solution to: to set a problem that gives difficulty to: to entangle, complicate: to solve by systematic or assiduous thinking (with *out*).—*v i.* to be bewildered: to labour at solution: to search about. —*n.* bewilderment: perplexity: anything that puzzles: a problem: a riddle or a toy designed to try ingenuity.—*ns.* **puzz'lement** the state of being puzzled; **puzz'ler.**—*adj.* **puzz'ling** posing: perplexing.—*adv.* **puzz'lingly.**

puzzolana *pŏŏt-sō-lä'na.* Same as **pozzolana.**

pyaemia *pī-ē'mi-a*, *n.* infection of the blood with bacteria from a septic focus, with abscesses in different parts of the body.—Also **pye'mia.**—*adj.* **pyae'mic.** [Gr. *pyon*, pus, *haima*, blood]

pycnic. Same as **pyknic.**

pycno-, pykno- *pik'nō-, pik-no'-* in composition, dense, close. [Gr. *pyknos*, dense.]

pyebald. See **piebald.**

pye-dog *pī'-dog*, *n.* an ownerless or pariah dog.—Also **pi'-dog, pie'-dog.** [Hind. *pāhī*, outsider.]

pyelitis *pī-a-lī'tis*, *n.* inflammation of the pelvis of the kidney.—*adj.* **pyelitic** (*-lit'ik*).—*n.* **pyelonephritis** (*-nef-rī'tis*) inflammation of the kidney and the renal pelvis.—*adj* **pyelonephritic** (*-rit'ik*). [Gr. *pyelos*, a trough.]

pyemia. See **pyaemia.**

pygal *pī'gal*, *adj.* belonging to the rump or posteriors of an animal.—*n.* the posterior median plate of a chelonian carapace. [Gr. *pȳgē*, rump.]

pygmy, pigmy *pig'mi*, *n.* a member of any of the actual dwarf human races, negritos, negrillos, and others: a dwarf: any person, animal or thing relatively diminutive or in some way insignificant.—*adj.* dwarfish: diminutive: of the pygmies.—*adjs.* **pygmaean; pyg-, pigmean** (*-mē'an*); **pyg'mold.** [Gr. *pygmaios*, measuring a *pygmē* (13½ inches, distance from elbow to knuckles).]

pygostyle *pī'gō-stil*, *n.* the bone of a bird's tail. [Gr. *pȳgē*, rump, *stȳlos*, a column.]

pyjamas *pa-*, *pi-*, or *pī-ja'maz*, *n.pl.* loose trousers tied round the waist, worn by Indians: (in European use) a sleeping-suit.—Also (*U.S.*) **paja'mas.**—*adj.* **pyja'ma'd, pyja'maed** wearing pyjamas.—**pyja'ma-jacket, -trousers.** [Pers and Hind. *pāējāmah—pāe*, leg, *jāmah*, clothing.]

pyknic *pik'nik*, *adj.* characterised by short squat stature, small hands and feet, relatively short limbs, domed abdomen, short neck, round face. [Gr *pyknos*, thick.]

pylon *pī'lon*, *n.* a gateway, gate-tower, gatehouse, or mass of building through which an entrance passes, esp. the gateway of an Egyptian temple (*archit.*): a guiding mark at an aerodrome: a structure for support of power-cables: an artificial leg: an external structure on an aeroplane for attaching an engine, etc.:— *pl.* **py'lons.** [Gr. *pylōn, -ōnos—pylē*, a gate.]

pylorus *pī-, pi-lō'ras, -lö'*, *n.* the opening from the stomach to the intestines —*adj.* **pylor'ic** (*-lor'*). [L ,—Gr. *pylōros*, gate-keeper, pylorus—*pylē*, an entrance, *ōrā*, care; cf. *ouros*, a guardian]

pyogenic *pī-a-jen'ik*, *adj.* pus-forming.—*n.* **pyogen'esis.**—*adj.* **py'oid** purulent.—*n.* **pyorrhoea** (*-rē'a*; Gr. *rhoiā*, flow) discharge of pus: now, suppur-

ation in the sockets of teeth.—*adjs.* **pyorrhoe'al, pyorrhoe'ic.** [Gr. *pyon*, pus.]

pyracanth *pī'ra-kanth*, **pyracantha** *-kan'tha*, *ns* a thorny evergreen shrub of the genus *Pyracantha*, near akin to hawthorn. [Gr. *pȳrakantha—pȳr*, fire, *akanthos*, thorn]

pyramid *pir'a-mid*, *n.* a solid figure on a triangular, square, or polygonal base, with triangular sides meeting in a point' any object or structure of that or similar form, esp. a great Egyptian monument: a crystal form of three or more faces each cutting three axes (*crystal.*): (in *pl*) a game played on a billiard-table in which the balls are arranged in pyramid shape.—*adjs.* **pyram'idal, pyramid'ic, -al** having the form of a pyramid.—*advs.* **pyram'idally, pyramid'ically.**—*n.* **pyram'idist** one who studies the Egyptian Pyramids. —**pyramid selling** a method of distributing goods by selling batches to agents who then sell batches at increased prices to sub-agents, and so on. [Gr. *pyramis, -idos*]

pyrargyrite *pīr-*, or *pir-ar'jir-īt*, *n.* ruby-silver ore, sulphide of silver and antimony. [Gr *pȳr*, fire, *argyros*, silver.]

pyre *pīr*, *n.* a pile of combustibles for burning a dead body. [L *pyra—*Gr *pȳrā—pȳr*, fire.]

Pyrenean, Pyrenaean *pir-a-nē'an*, *adj.* of the *Pyrenees*, the mountains between France and Spain.—*n.* a native of the Pyrenees.—**Pyrenean mountain dog** a large dog with a dense white coat, bred in the Pyrenees to guard flocks. [L. *Pȳrēnaeus—*Gr. *Pȳrēnaios.*]

Pyrethrum *pī-rēth'ram, pī-reth'ram, pir-eth'ram*, *n.* a former genus of composite plants now merged in Chrysanthemum, including feverfew: (without *cap.*) still applied to various garden flowers, esp. varieties of *Chrysanthemum coccineum*: (without *cap.*) insect-powder of flower-heads of various species of pyrethrum: (without *cap.*) in pharmacy, the root of pellitory of Spain.—*n.* **pyreth'rin** (or *-rē'*) either of two insecticidal oily esters prepared from pyrethrum flowers. [L.,—Gr. *pȳrēthron*, pellitory of Spain.]

pyretic *pī-ret'ik, pir-et'ik*, *adj.* of, of the nature of, for the cure of, fever.—*ns.* **pyretol'ogy** study of fevers; **pyretother'apy** treatment by inducing high body temperature; **pyrex'ia** fever.—*adjs.* **pyrex'ial, pyrex'ic.** [Gr. *pȳretikos*, feverish—*pȳretos*, fever; and *pȳress-ein*, to be feverish—*pȳr*, fire.]

Pyrex® *pī'reks*, *n.* a type of glassware containing oxide of boron and so resistant to heat. [Gr. *pȳr*, fire, and L. *rēx*, king.]

pyrexia. See **pyretic.**

pyridine *pir'*, or *pir'i-dēn, -dīn*, *n.* a strong-smelling, colourless, strongly basic liquid, C_5H_5N, got in distillation of bone-oil, coal-tar, etc —*ns.* **pyridox'in(e)** a pyridine derivative, a member of the vitamin B complex; **pyrim'idine** one of a group of heterocyclic compounds forming an essential part of nucleic acids. [Gr. *pȳr*, fire.]

pyrimethamine *pi-ri-meth'a-mēn*, or *pī-*, *n.* a powerful anti-malaria drug [Gr. *pȳr*, fire, *methyl*, and *amine.*]

pyrimidine. See **pyridine.**

pyrites *pīr-, pir-ī'tēz*, *n.* a brassy yellow mineral, iron disulphide. (also called **pyrite** *pī'rīt*, **iron pyri'tes**): extended to a large class of mineral sulphides and arsenides —*adjs.* **pyritic** (*pir-, pīr-it'ik*), **-al; pyritif'erous; pyr'itous.** [Gr. *pȳrītēs*, striking fire— *pȳr*, fire, and]

pyro- *pī'rō-*, in composition, fire, heat, fever: obtained by heating or as if by heating, or by removing (theoretically) a molecule of water (*chem.*).—*adj.* **pyrochem'ical** relating to, producing, or produced by chemical changes at high temperatures.—*v.t.*

py'rolyse (*U.S.* **-lyze**) to decompose by pyrolysis.
—*n.* **pyrolysis** (*pi-rol'is-is*; Gr. *lysis*, loosing) decomposition of a substance by heat.—*adj.* **pyrolytic** (*-lit'ik.*). [Gr. *pŷr*, in compounds *pŷr-*, fire.]

pyro *pi'rō*, (*photog.*) *n.* a familiar short form of **pyrogallol**.

pyro-electric *pi-rō-i-lek'trik*, *adj.* becoming positively and negatively electrified at opposite poles on heating or cooling: of pyro-electricity.—*n.* **pyro-electricity** (*-el-ik-tris'i-ti*) the property of being pyroelectric: the study of the phenomena shown by pyroelectric crystals. [Gr. *pŷr*, fire, and **electric**.]

pyrogallol *pi-rō-gal'ol*, *n.* a phenol got by heating gallic acid, used in photographic developing—also called **pyrogall'ic acid**.

pyrogenic *pi-rō-jen'ik*, **pyrogenetic** *-jin-et'ik*, **pyrogenous** *-roj'ə-nəs*, *adjs.* produced by, or producing, heat or fever.—*n.* **py'rogen** a substance causing heat or fever. [Gr. *pŷr*, fire, root of *gignesthai*, to become.]

pyrognostic *pi-rog-nos'tik*, *adj.* pertaining to testing of minerals by flame. [Gr. *pŷr*, fire, *gnōstikos*, discriminating.]

pyrography *pi-rog'rə-fi*, *n.* poker-work.—*n.* **pyrogravure**'. [Gr. *pŷr*, fire, *graphein*, to write.]

pyrolysis, pyrolytic. See **pyro-**.

pyromania *pi-rō-mā'ni-ə*, *n.* an incendiary mania.—*n.* and *adj.* **pyromā'niac.**—*adj.* **pyromaniacal** (*-mə-nī'ə-kl*). [Gr. *pŷr*, fire, and **mania**.]

pyrometer *pi-rom'i-tər*, *n.* an instrument for measuring high temperatures.—*adjs.* **pyrometric** (*pi-rō-met'rik*), **-al.**—*n.* **pyrom'etry.** [Gr. *pŷr*, fire, *metron*, measure.]

pyrope *pi'rōp*, *n.* a fiery red gemstone: a red magnesia-alumina garnet, used in jewellery (*min.*). [Gr. *pŷrōpos*, fiery-eyed—*ōps*, *ōpos*, eye, face.]

pyroscope *pi'rō-skōp*, *n.* an instrument for measuring the intensity of radiant heat. [Gr. *pŷr*, fire, *skopeein*, to view.]

pyrosis *pi-rō'sis*, *n.* water-brash. [Gr. *pŷrōsis—pŷr*, fire.]

pyrostat *pi'rō-stat*, *n.* a type of thermostat for use at high temperatures.—*adj.* **pyrostat'ic**. [Gr. *pŷr*, fire, and thermo*stat*.]

pyrotechnics *pi-rō-tek'niks*, *n.* (*sing.*) the art of making fireworks: (*sing.* or *pl.*) display of fireworks: (*sing.* or *pl.*) showy display in talk, music, etc.—*adjs.* **pyrotech'nic**, **-al.**—*adv.* **pyrotech'nically.**—*ns.* **pyrotech'nist** a maker of fireworks: one skilled in, or given to, pyrotechnics; **py'rotechny**

pyrotechnics. [Gr. *pŷr*, fire, *technikos*, skilled —*technē*, art.]

pyroxene *pi'rok-sēn*, a general name for a group of minerals, metasilicates of calcium, magnesium, aluminium, and other metals, usually green or black, very common in igneous rocks.—*adj.* **pyroxenic** (*-sen'ik*).—*n.* **pyrox'enite** (*-ən-it*, or *-ēn'it*) a rock compound essentially of pyroxene. [Gr. *pŷr*, fire, *xenos*, stranger (because Haüy thought that pyroxene crystals in lava had only been accidentally caught up).]

Pyrrhic *pir'ik*, *adj.* of or pertaining to *Pyrrhus*, king of Epirus (318–272 B.C.).—**Pyrrhic victory** a victory gained at too great a cost, in allusion to Pyrrhus's exclamation after his defeat of the Romans at Heraclea on the Siris (280), 'Another such victory and we are lost'.

Pyrrhonism *pir'ən-izm*, *n.* the complete scepticism of *Pyrrhō* (Gr. *Pyrrōn*) of Elis (3rd cent. B.C.).—*adj.* and *n.* **Pyrrhonian** (*pir-ō'ni-ən*).—*adj.* **Pyrrhonic** (*-on'ik*).—*n.* **Pyrrh'onist**.

pyrrhous *pir'əs*, *adj.* reddish. [Gr. *pyrros*, flame-coloured—*pŷr*, fire.]

Pythagorean *pi-* or *pī-thag-ər-ē'ən*, *adj.* pertaining to *Pythagoras* (of Samos; 6th cent. B.C.), the Greek philosopher, or to his philosophy: transformed, as if by transmigration of the soul (taught by Pythagoras): vegetarian.—*n.* a follower of Pythagoras.—*ns.* **Pythagorē'anism**, **Pythag'orism** his doctrines.—**Pythagorean theorem** that the square on the hypotenuse of a right-angled triangle is equal to the sum of the squares on other two sides.

python *pi'thən*, *n.* a large snake that crushes its victims, esp. and properly one of the Old World genus *Python*, akin to the boas. [Gr. *Pythōn*, the great snake killed by Apollo at Delphi.]

pyx *piks*, *n.* a box: a vessel in which the host is kept after consecration, now usu. that in which it is carried to the sick (*R.C.*): a box at the Mint in which sample coins are kept for testing.—*v.t.* to test the weight and fineness of, as the coin deposited in the pyx.—*ns.* **pyxid'ium** (*bot.*) a capsule that opens by a transverse circular split:—*pl.* **pyxid'ia**; **pyx'is** a little box or casket as for jewels, drugs, toilet materials, etc.:—*pl.* **pyx'ides** (*-id-ēz*).—**trial of the pyx** trial by weight and assay of gold and silver coins by a jury of goldsmiths: periodic official testing of sterling coinage. [L. *pyxis*, a box—Gr. *pyxis*, *-idos*, dim. *pyxidion—pyxos*, box-tree.]

pzazz. Same as **pizazz**.

Q

Q, q *kū, n.* the seventeenth letter of our alphabet, in English followed by *u* (*qu* being sounded as *kw*.).— Q'-**boat** a naval vessel disguised as a merchant ship or fishing-boat, to deceive and destroy submarines; Q'**-fever** an acute disease characterised by fever and muscular pains, transmitted by the rickettsia *Coxiella burnetii*. [L. *cū*.]

qa-, qe-, qi-, qo-, qu-. Arabic and Hebrew words spelt thus are in most cases given at **k-** or **c-**.

Qaddish, qadi. Same as **Kaddish, cadi.**

qanat *kä-nät', n.* an underground tunnel for carrying irrigation water. [Ar. *qanāt*, pipe.]

qibla. Same as **kiblah.**

Qoran. Same as **Koran.**

qua *kwä, kwä, adv.* in the capacity of. [L. *quā*, adverbial abl. fem. of *quī*, who.]

quack¹ *kwak, n.* the cry of a duck.—*v.i.* to make the sound of a quack. [Imit.]

quack² *kwak, n.* a shortened form of **quacksalver**: a charlatan.—Also *adj.*—*n.* **quack'ery** the pretensions or practice of a quack, esp. in medicine.—**quack'salver** a boastful pretender to knowledge and skill (esp. in medicine) that he does not possess.—*adj.* **quack'salving.** [Du. *quacksalver* (now *kwakzalver*), perh. one who quacks about his salves.]

quad *kwod, n.* a shortening of **quadrangle, quadraphonics, quadrat, quadruplet.**—*adj.* short for **quadruple.**

quadragenarian *kwod-rə-ji-nā'ri-ən, n.* one who is forty years old, or between forty and fifty.—Also *adj.* [L. *quadrāgēnārius—quadrāgintā*, forty each.]

Quadragesima *kwod-rə-jes'i-mə, n.* the first Sunday in Lent.—*adj.* **quadrages'imal.** [L. *quadrāgēsimus, -a, -um,* fortieth—*quadrāgintā,* forty—*quattuor,* four.]

quadrangle *kwod-rang'gl,* also *kwod', n.* a plane figure with four angles (and therefore four sides): an object or space of that form: a court or open space, usually rectangular, enclosed by a building (as a college).—*adj.* **quadrang'ular** (*-gū-lər*).—*adv.* **quadrang'ularly.** [Fr.,—L. *quadrangulum—quattuor,* four, *angulus,* an angle.]

quadrant *kwod'rənt, n.* the fourth part of a circle or its circumference, a sector or an arc of 90°: an area, object, street, of that form: an instrument with an arc of 90° for taking altitudes.—*adj.* **quadrantal** (*-rant'l*). [L. *quadrāns, -antis* a fourth part—*quattuor,* four.]

quadraphonics, quadrophonics *kwod-rə-fon'iks, -ro-, n. sing.* a system of sound transmission using a minimum of four speakers fed by four, or sometimes three, separate channels.—Also **quadrophony** (*-rof'*), **quadraph'ony.**—*adj.* **quadraphon'ic, quadrophon'ic.**

quadrat *kwod'rat, n.* a piece of type-metal lower than the letters, used in spacing between words and filling out blank lines (commonly **quad**)—distinguished as *en* and *em.*—*adj.* **quad'rate** (*-rāt, -rit*) square: rectangular: squarish: square, as a power or root.—*n.* a square or quadrate figure or object: the quadrate bone, suspending the lower jaw in vertebrates other than mammals.—*v.t.* and *v.i.* to square: to conform. —*adj.* **quadratic** (*-rat'ik*) of or like a quadrate: involving the square but no higher power.—*n.* a

quadratic equation.—*ns.* **quad'rature** (*-rə-chər*) the finding of a square equal to a given figure: an angular distance of 90°: the position of a heavenly body at such an angular distance, or the time of its being there; **quadra'tus** the name of several quadrangular muscles.—**quadrature of the circle** see **square.** [L. *quadrātus,* pa.p. of *quadrāre,* to square—*quattuor,* four.]

quadrennium, etc. See **quadr(i)-.**

quadr(i)- *kwod-r(i)* in composition, four: square.— *adj.* **quad'ric** of the second degree.—*n.* **quadriceps** (*kwod'ri-seps;* L. *caput, -itis,* head) the great thigh muscle that extends the leg (from its four heads).— *adj.* **quadricipital** (*-sip'i-tl*).—*n.* **quadriennium** (*kwod-ri-en'i-əm;* L. *annus,* year) four years:—*pl.* **quadrienn'ia.**—*adj.* **quadrienn'ial** lasting four years: once in four years.—*n.* a quadriennial event.—*adv.* **quadrienn'ially.**—The forms **quadrenn'ium,** etc., are etymologically incorrect but now usual.—*adjs.* **quadrifid** (*kwod'ri-fid;* L. from the root of *findĕre,* to cleave) cleft in four; **quadrilateral** (*kwod-ri-lat'ər-l;* L. *latus, lateris,* a side) four-sided.—*n.* a plane figure bounded by four straight lines (*geom.*): a group of four fortresses, esp. Mantua, Verona, Peschiera, and Legnaga.—*adj.* **quadrilingual** (*-ling'gwəl;* L. *lingua,* tongue) using four languages.—*n.* **quadrillion** (*kwod-, kwəd-ril'yən;* modelled on **million**) a million raised to the fourth power, represented by a unit and 24 ciphers: in U.S., a thousand to the fifth power, a unit with 15 ciphers.—*n.* and *adj.* **quadrill'ionth.**— *adj.* **quadrinomial** (*kwod-ri-nō'mi-əl;* irregularly from L. *nōmen, -inis,* a name; *alg.*) of four terms.—*n.* an expression of four terms.—*adj.* **quadripartite** (*kwod-ri-pàr'tīt;* L. *partīrī, -ītum,* to divide) in four parts: having four parties: deeply cleft into four parts, as a leaf (*bot.*): divided, as a vault, into four compartments (*archit.*).—*n.* **quadriparti'tion.**—*n.* **quadriplegia** (*kwod-ri-plēj'(i)ə, -plēj'yə;* Gr. *plēgē,* a blow) paralysis of both arms and both legs.—*n.* and *adj.* **quadripleg'ic.**—*n.* **quadrireme** (*kwod'ri-rēm;* L. *rēmus,* an oar) an ancient ship with four sets of oars. —*adj.* **quadrivalent** (*kwod-riv'ə-lənt,* or *-vä'lənt*) having a valency of four.—*ns.* **quadriv'alence** (or *-vä'*); **quadrivium** (*kwod-riv'i-əm;* L., the place where four roads meet—*via,* a way) in mediaeval education, the four branches of mathematics (arithmetic, geometry, astronomy, music).—*adj.* **quadriv'ial.** [L. *quadri—quattuor,* four.]

quadrille¹ *kwə-dril'* or *kə-, n.* a square dance for four couples or more, in five movements: music for such a dance. [Fr.,—Sp. *cuadrilla,* a troop, app.—L. *quadra,* a square.]

quadrille² *kwə-dril'* or *kə-, n.* a four-handed game with 40 cards. [Fr., perh.—Sp. *cuatrillo,* the game of quadrille, or *cuartillo,* fourth part.]

quadrillion . . . quadrivium. See **quadr(i)-.**

quadroon *kwod-rōōn', n.* a person of one-quarter Negro descent: extended to refer to any person or animal of similarly mixed ancestry. [Sp. *cuarterón —cuarto,* a fourth.]

quadrophonics, -phony. See **quadraphonics.**

quadru- *kwod-rōō-,* a variant of **quadr(i)-.**—*adj.* **quadrumanous** (*kwod-rōō'mən-əs;* L. *manus,* a hand) four-handed: of the Primates other than man.—*n.*

quadruped (*kwod'rōō-ped*; L. *pēs*, *pedis*, a foot) a four-footed animal, usu. a mammal, esp. a horse.—*adj.* four-footed.—*adj.* **quadrupedal** (*-rōō'pi-dǝl*).

quadruple *kwod'rōō-pl*, also (esp. in Scotland) *-rōō'*, *adj.* fourfold: having four parts, members, or divisions.—*n.* four times as much.—*v.t.* to increase fourfold: to equal four times.—*v.i.* to become four times as much.—*n.* **quad'ruplet** (or *-rōō'*) a combination of four things: a group of four notes performed in the time of three: a cycle for four riders: one of four born at a birth.—*adv.* **quad'ruply** (*-pli*, or *-rōō'pli*) in a fourfold manner.—**quadruple time** (*mus.*) a time with four beats to the bar. [Fr.,—L. *quadruplus*, from the root of *plēre*, to fill.]

quadru'plicate *kwod-rōō'pli-kit*, *adj.* fourfold.—*n.* one of four corresponding things: fourfoldness.—*v.t.* (*-kāt*) to make fourfold.—*ns.* **quadruplica'tion**; **quadruplicity** (*-plis'i-ti*). [L. *quadruplex*, *-icis*, fourfold—*plicāre*, *-ātum* to fold.]

quaere *kwē'rē*, *kwī're*, (L. imper. of *quaerēre*, *quaesītum*, to inquire) *v.imper.* inquire (suggesting doubt, or desirability of investigation).—*n.* a query, question.—See also **query**.

quaestor *kwēs'tōr*, *-tǝr*, *kwīs'tor*, *n.* an ancient Roman magistrate, in early times an investigator, prosecutor, or judge in murder cases, later a treasurer with various other functions.—*adj.* **quaestorial** (*-tō'ri-ǝl*, *-tō'*). —*n.* **quaes'torship**. [L. *quaestor*, *-ōris*—*quaerēre*, *quaesītum*, to seek.]

quae vide. See **quod¹**.

quaff *kwäf*, *kwof*, *v.t.* to drink or drain in large draughts.—*v.i.* to drink largely.—*n.* a draught.—*n.* **quaff'er**.

quag *kwag*, *kwog*, *n.* a boggy place, esp. one that quakes underfoot.—*n.* **quagg'iness**.—*adj.* **quagg'y**. [Cf. **quake**.]

quagga *kwag'ǝ*, *n.* an extinct S. African wild ass (*Equus quagga*), less fully striped than the zebras, to which it was related. [Perh. Hottentot *quacha*.]

quagmire *kwag'mīr*, or *kwog'*, *n.* wet, boggy ground that yields or quakes under the feet. [App. **quag**, **mire**.]

quahog, **quahaug** *kwö'hog*, *-hōg*, *n.* an edible Venus mollusc (*Venus mercenaria*) of the N. American Atlantic coast—also known as round clam. [Narraganset Ind. *poquauhock*.]

quaich, **quaigh** *kwähh*, (*Scot.*) *n.* a drinking-cup, orig. of staves and hoops, now usu. of silver or pewter. [Gael. *cuach*, a cup.]

quail¹ *kwāl*, *v.i.* to flinch: to fail in spirit. [M.E. *quayle*; origin obscure.]

quail² *kwāl*, *n.* a genus (*Coturnix*) of small birds of the partridge family: in America extended to various similar small game-birds. [O.Fr. *quaille*; prob. Gmc.]

quaint *kwānt*, *adj.* pleasantly odd: whimsical.—*adv.* **quaint'ly**.—*n.* **quaint'ness**. [O.Fr. *cointe*—L. *cognitus*, known; perh. confused with *comptus*, neat.]

quake *kwāk*, *v.i.* to quiver or vibrate, as the earth or a quagmire: to tremble, esp. with cold or fear.—*n.* a tremor: an earthquake: a shudder.—*ns.* **qua'kiness**; **qua'king**.—*adv.* **qua'kingly**.—*adj.* **qua'ky** shaky.—**quaking ash** the aspen; **qua'king-grass** a moorland grass of the genus *Briza*, with pendulous, panicled tremulous spikelets. [O.E. *cwacian*; perh. allied to **quick**.]

Quaker *kwā'kǝr*, *n.* one of the Religious Society of Friends, founded by George Fox (1624–91): a dummy cannon (also **Quaker gun**).—*adj.* of Quakers.—*ns.* **Qua'kerdom**; **Qua'keress**; **Qua'kerism**.—*adjs.* **Qua'kerish**, **Qua'kerly** like a Quaker.—**Qua'ker-bird** the sooty albatross. [Nickname given them because Fox bade others *quake* at the word of the Lord.]

qualify *kwol'i-fī*, *v.t.* to ascribe a quality to: to characterise: to render capable or suitable: to furnish with legal power: to limit by modifications: to moderate. —*v.t.* to take the necessary steps to fit oneself for a certain position, activity, or practice: to fulfil a requirement: to have the necessary qualities or qualifications:—*pr p* **qual'ifying**; *pa.p.* and *pa t.* **qual'ified**.—*adj.* **qual'ifiable** (*-fī-ǝ-bl*).—*n.* **qualification** (*-fi-kā'shǝn*) qualifying: modification: restriction: that which qualifies: a quality that fits a person for a place, etc.: a necessary condition.—*adj.* **qual'ificatory**.—*adj.* **qual'ified** (*-fīd*) fitted: competent: having the necessary qualification: modified: limited.—*adv.* **qual'ifiedly** (*-fīd-li*).—*n.* **qual'ifier** (*-fī-ǝr*).—*n.* and *adj.* **qual'ifying**.—**qualifying round** a preliminary round in a competition, to limit the number of competitors. [Fr *qualifier* or L.L. *quālificāre*—L. *quālis*, of what sort, *facēre*, to make.]

quality *kwol'i-ti*, *n.* nature: character: kind: property: attribute: social status: high social status: persons of the upper class collectively: grade of goodness: excellence: skill, accomplishment: timbre, that character of a sound that depends on the overtones present, distinguished from loudness and pitch: the character of a proposition as affirmative or negative (*log.*).—*adj.* of high grade of excellence.—*adj.* **qual'itative** relating to, or concerned with, quality, esp. opp. to *quantitative*.—*adv.* **qual'itatively**.—**quality control** inspection, testing, etc., of samples of a product to ensure maintenance of high standards. [O.Fr. *qualité*—L. *quālitās*, *-tātis*—*quālis*, of what kind.]

qualm *kwäm*, also *kwöm*, *n.* an access of faintness or sickness: an uneasiness, as of conscience: a misgiving. —*adj.* **qualm'ish**.—*adv.* **qualm'ishly**.—*n.* **qualm'ishness**.—*adjs.* **qualm'less**; **qualm'y**. [Perh. O.E. *cwealm*, death, murder, torment, pain.]

quandang. See **quandong**.

quandary *kwon'dǝ-ri*, *n.* a state of perplexity: dilemma.

quand même *kā mem*, (Fr.) nevertheless, whatever the consequences may be.

quandong *kwan'* or *kwon'dong*, *n.* a small Australian tree of the sandalwood family: its edible drupe (*native peach*) or edible kernel (**quan'dong-nut**).— Also **quan'dang**, **quan'tong**.

quango *kwang'gō*, *n.* a board funded by, and with members appointed by, central government, to supervise or develop activity in areas of public interest:—*pl.* **quan'gos**. [*quasi-autonomous non-governmental* (sometimes *national government*) *organisation*.]

quant *kwant*, *kwont*, (*Kent, E.Anglia*) *n.* a punting or jumping pole, with a flat cap.—*v.t.* to punt. [Poss. conn. with L. *contus*, Gr. *kontos*.]

quanta, **quantal**. See **quantum**.

quantic *kwon'tik*, (*math.*) *n.* a rational integral homogeneous function of two or more variables.—*adj.* **quan'tical**. [L. *quantus*, how great.]

quantify *kwon'ti-fī*, *v.t.* to qualify (a term in a proposition) by stating the quantity (*log.*): to fix or express the quantity of: to express as a quantity.—*adj.* **quan'tifiable**.—*ns.* **quantification** (*-fi-kā'shǝn*); **quan'tifier**. [L. *quantus*, how great, *facēre*, to make.]

quantise, **-ize**. See **quantum**.

quantity *kwon'ti-ti*, *n.* the amount of anything: size: a sum: a determinate amount: an amount, portion: a considerable amount, portion: length or shortness of duration of a sound or syllable: extension (*log.*): the character of a proposition as universal or particular: anything which can be increased, divided, or measured.—*adj.* **quan'titative** (less justifiably **quan'titive**) relating to, or concerned with, quantity, esp.

opp. to *qualitative* —*adv.* **quan'titătively.** —**quantity surveyor** one who estimates quantities required, obtains materials, evaluates work done, etc , for construction work.—**unknown quantity** a quantity whose mathematical value is not known: a factor, person or thing whose importance or influence cannot be foreseen. [O Fr *quantité*—L *quantitās*, *-tātis*—*quantus*, how much]

quantong. See **quandong.**

quantum *kwon'təm*, *n.* quantity· amount· a naturally fixed minimum amount of some entity which is such that all other amounts of that entity occurring in physical processes in nature are integral multiples thereof (*phys.*):—*pl.* **quan'ta.**—*adj.* **quan'tal** of, or pertaining to, a quantum (*phys.*): having one of only two possible states or values.—*n.* **quantisā'tion, -z-.** —*v t* **quan'tise, -ize** to express in terms of quanta or in accordance with the quantum theory —**quantum jump** the sudden transition of an electron, atom, etc , from one energy state to another a sudden spectacular advance, **quantum mechanics** a branch of mechanics based on the quantum theory, used in predicting the behaviour of elementary particles; **quantum number** any of a set of integers or half-integers which together describe the state of a particle or system of particles; **quantum theory** Planck's theory of the emission and absorption of energy not continuously but in finite steps. [L. *quantum*, neut of *quantus*, how much.]

quaquaversal *kwā-kwə-vûr'sl*, *kwa-kwa-*, *adj.* dipping outward in all directions from a centre (*geol.*): facing or bending all ways.—*adv.* **quaquaver'sally.** [L *quāquā*, whithersoever, *vertēre*, *versum*, to turn.]

quarantine *kwor'ən-tēn*, *n.* a time (orig. for a ship forty days) of compulsory isolation or detention to prevent spread of contagion or infection: isolation or detention for such a purpose· the place where the time is spent: any period of enforced isolation.—*v.t* to subject to quarantine.—**quarantine flag** a yellow flag displayed by a ship in quarantine, with a black spot if there be contagious disease on board. [It. *quarantina*—*quaranta*, forty—L. *quadrāginiā*.]

quark *kwork*, *kwark*, *n* any of a triplet of particles, not yet found, suggested as the units out of which all other subatomic particles are formed [From word coined by James Joyce in *Finnegans Wake*.]

quarrel¹ *kwor'l*, *n.* a square-headed arrow as for a cross-bow: a diamond pane of glass: a square tile — **quarr'el-pane.** [O Fr *quarrel* (Fr *carreau*)—L.L *quadrellus*—*quadrus*, a square.]

quarrel² *kwor'l*, *n.* ground of complaint or action: a cause contended for: an unfriendly contention or dispute: a breach of friendship.—*v.i.* to cavil, find fault (with): to dispute violently· to fall out to disagree violently:—*pr.p.* **quarr'elling;** *pa.t.* and *pa.p.* **quarr'elled.**—*n.* **quarr'eller.**—*n.* and *adj* **quarr'elling.**—*adj.* **quarr'elsome** disposed to quarrel.—*adv* **quarr'elsomely.**—*n* **quarr'elsomeness.** [O.Fr. *querele*—L *querēla*—*querī*, *questus*, to complain.]

quarry¹ *kwor'i*, *n.* an open excavation for building-stone, slate, etc . any source of building-stone, etc.. a source from which information can be extracted — *v.t.* to dig from, or as from, a quarry: to cut into or cut away:—*pr.p* **quarr'ying;** *pa.t* and *pa p* **quarr'ied.**— *adj.* **quarr'iable.**—*n.* **quarr'ier** a quarryman— **quarr'yman** one who works in a quarry; **quarr'y-master** the owner of a quarry. [L L. *quareia*, for *quadrāria*—L. *quadrāre*, to square.]

quarry² *kwor'i*, *n* orig. a deer's entrails given on a hide, to the dogs (*obs.*): a hunted animal prey: a victim: a hunter's heap of dead game [O Fr *cuiree*, *curee*, said to be from *cuir*—L. *corium*. hide.]

quarry³ *kwor'i*, *n.* a quarrel of glass: a square paving-tile or slab.—**quarry tile** a square unglazed floor tile [A form of **quarrel¹**; or perh from O.Fr. *quarré*—L *quadrātus*, squared.]

quart¹, **quarte** *kart*, *n* a sequence of four cards in piquet, etc . the fourth of eight parrying or attacking positions in fencing [Fr *quarte*]

quart² *kwort*, *n* the fourth part of a gallon, or two pints (1·14 litres)· a vessel containing two pints: as much as will fill it —*n.* **quartā'tion** the mixing of gold with three parts of silver as a stage towards purification [Fr *quart*, *-e*—L *quārtus*, *-a*, *-um*, fourth— *quattuor*, four]

quartan *kwor'tən*, *adj* occurring every third (by inclusive reckoning fourth) day, as a fever.—*n* quartan malaria [L *quārtānus*, of the fourth.]

quarte. See **quart¹.**

quarter *kwor'tər*, *n.* a fourth part: the fourth part of a cwt = 28 (*U.S.* 25) lb. avoirdupois:·8 bushels (perh. orig a fourth of a ton of corn): the fourth part of an hour—of the year—(or the moon's period (or the moon's position at the end of it)—of the world, etc . 25-cent piece: a limb with adjacent parts of the trunk, esp of the dismembered body of one who has been executed, or of a beast's carcass: a haunch: one of the four parts of a quartered shield (*her.*)· an ordinary occupying one-fourth of the field (*her.*)· a cardinal point, or any point, of the compass· the region about any point of the compass: hence a region generally, and also figuratively· a town district inhabited by a particular class: lodging, as for soldiers, esp. in *pl.*: an assigned station: mercy granted to an antagonist (perh. from sending to quarters): the part of a ship's side abaft the beam —*v t.* to divide into four equal parts: to divide into parts or compartments: to station, lodge· or impose in quarters: to bear, place, or divide quarterly (*her.*): to beat or range as for game: to search thoroughly.—*v.i.* to be stationed: to lodge· to range for game: of the wind, to blow on to a ship's quarter.—In composition, **quar'ter-**, *adjectivally*, one-fourth part (of), *adverbially*, to the extent of one-fourth.—*n.* **quar'terage** a quarterly payment quarters, lodging.—*adjs.* **quar'tered;** **quar'tering** sailing nearly before the wind: striking on the quarter of a ship, as a wind.—*n.* assignment of quarters: series of small upright posts for forming partitions, lathed and plastered only, or boarded also (*archit.*): the division of a coat by horizontal and vertical lines (*her.*): one of the divisions so formed: the marshalling of coats in these divisions, indicating family alliances· any one of the coats so marshalled —*adj* **quar'terly** relating to a quarter, esp. of a year: recurring, or published, once a quarter· divided into or marshalled in quarters (*her.*) —*adv* once a quarter: in quarters or quarterings (*her.*).—*n.* a quarterly periodical.— **quart'er-back** in American football, a player between the forwards and the half-backs, who directs the attacking play of his team.—*adj* **quar'ter-bound** having leather or cloth on the back only, not the corners.—**quar'ter-boy, quar'ter-jack** an automaton that strikes the quarter-hours, **quar'ter-day** the first or last day of a quarter, on which rent or interest is paid, **quar'ter-deck** the part of the deck of a ship abaft the mainmast—used by cabin passengers and by superior officers (and saluted on warships), **quar'ter-fi'nal** the round before the semi-final in a knockout competition; **quar'ter-horse** (*U S*) a horse that can run a quarter of a mile or so at great speed; **quarter (of an) hour** a period of fifteen minutes —*adv* **quar'ter-hour'ly.**—**quar'ter-jack** a quarter-boy a quartermaster (*slang*); **quarter light** a small window in a car, beside the front seat, for ventilation; **quar'termaster** an officer who finds quarters for soldiers, and attends to supplies: a petty officer who attends to the helm, signals, etc. (*naut.*):—*fem.* **quar'termistress** (or **quartermaster**); **quar'termaster-gen'eral** a staff-officer who deals with questions of transport, marches, quarters, fuel, clothing, etc.; **quar'termaster-ser'geant** a non-commissioned officer who assists the quartermaster; **quar'ter-mil'er** an athlete whose speciality is the quarter-mile race; **quar'ter-note** a crotchet (*U.S.*): a quarter-tone; **quar'ter-plate** see **plate**; **quar'ter-sessions** a court held quarterly by justices of the peace (superseded in 1972 by crown courts); **quar'ter-staff** a long wooden pole, an old weapon of defence: play with this weapon; **quar'ter-tone** half a semitone.—(**a**) **quarter after**, **past** (an hour) fifteen minutes after that hour; (**a**) **quarter to** fifteen minutes before the hour; **at close quarters** in very near proximity: hand-to-hand. [O.Fr. *quarter*—L. *quārtārius*, a fourth part—*quārtus*, fourth.]

quartern *kwör'tə(r)n*, *n.* a quarter, esp. of a peck, a stone, a pound (weight), a pint, or a hundred.—**quar'tern-loaf** a four-pound loaf, as is made from a quarter of a stone of flour. [A.Fr. *quartrun*, O.Fr. *quarteron*—*quart*(*e*), fourth part.]

quartet, quartette, quartett *kwör-tet'*, *n.* a set of four: a composition for four voices or instruments: a set of performers or instruments for such compositions. [It. *quartetto*, dim. of *quarto*—L. *quārtus*, fourth.]

quartic *kwor'tik*, (*math.*) *adj.* of the fourth degree — *n.* a function, curve, or surface of the fourth degree. [L. *quārtus*, fourth.]

quartile *kwör'til*, *n.* an aspect of planets when their longitudes differ by 90° (*astrol.*): in frequency-distribution, a value such that a fourth, a half, or three-quarters of the numbers under consideration fall below it.—Also *adj.* [L. *quārtus*, fourth.]

quarto *kwör'tō*, *adj.* having the sheet folded into four leaves or eight pages (often written 4to).—*n.* a book of sheets so folded, or of such a size:—*pl.* **quar'tos.** [L. (*in*) *quārtō*, (in) one-fourth.]

quartz *kwörts*, *n.* the commonest rock-forming mineral, composed of silica, occurring in hexagonal crystals (clear and colourless when pure) or crypto-crystalline.—*adj.* of quartz.—*adj.* **quartzif'erous** quartz-bearing.—*n.* **quartz'ite** a metamorphosed sandstone with the grains welded together.—*adjs.* **quartzitic** (*-it'ik*); **quartz'y.**—**quartz crystal** a disc or rod cut in certain directions from a piece of piezoelectric quartz and ground so that it vibrates naturally at a particular frequency; **quartz glass** fused quartz resistant to high temperatures and transparent to ultraviolet radiation.—**quartz-crystal clock, watch** one in which a quartz crystal, energised by a microcircuit, does the work of the pendulum or hairspring of the traditional clock or watch; **quartz-iodine lamp,** using iodine, a compact source of light used for high-intensity flooding of large areas, car (fog-)lamps, cine-projectors, etc. [Ger. *Quarz.*]

quasar *kwä'sər*, *n.* a point (star-like) source of radiation (radio waves, etc.) outside our galaxy, usu. with a very large red-shift; quasars are the most distant and most luminous bodies so far known. [*quasi*-stellar object.]

quash *kwosh*, *v.t.* to crush: to subdue or extinguish suddenly and completely: to annul. [O.Fr. *quasser* (Fr. *casser*)—L. *quassāre*, intens. of *quatēre*, to shake.]

quasi *kwä'sī, kwä'zē*, *adv.* as if, as it were.—In composition, **quasi-**, in a certain manner, sense, or degree: in appearance only, as **quasi-historical, quasi-stellar**. [L.]

quassia *kwosh'(y)ə*, *n.* a South American tree (*Quassia amara*), whose bitter wood and bark are used as a tonic: now generally a West Indian tree of the same family (*Picraena excelsa*). [Named by Linnaeus from a Negro *Quassi*, who discovered its value against fever.]

quatercentenary *kwot-, kwat-ər-sen-tēn'ər-i, -sin-, -ten'ər-i, -sen'tin-, n.* a 400th anniversary, or its celebration. [L. *quater*, four times.]

quaternary *kwo-tûr'nər-i, adj.* consisting of four: by fours: in fours· of the fourth order. based on four: with four variables: (*cap , geol.*) Post-Tertiary.—*n.* the number four: a set of four: (*cap. , geol.*) the Post-Tertiary era or group of strata (Pleistocene and Recent).—*ns.* **quater'nion** a set or group of four· in mathematics, the operation of changing one vector into another, or the quotient of two vectors, depending on four geometrical elements and expressible by an algebraical quadrinomial, **quatern'ity** fourfoldness. a set of four: a fourfold godhead. [L. *quaternī*, four by four]

quatorze *kə-torz', n.* the four aces, kings, queens, knaves, or tens in piquet, counting 14 [Fr. *quatorze, quatorzaine.*]

quatrain *kwot'rān, n.* a stanza of four lines usually rhyming alternately. [Fr.]

quatrefoil *kat'ər-foil*, or *kat'rə-foil, n* a four-petalled flower or leaf of four leaflets: an openwork design or ornament divided by cusps into four lobes (*archit*) [O Fr *quatre*, four, *foil* (Fr. *feuille*), leaf]

quattrocento *kwat-rō-chen'tō, n* the 15th century in Italian art and literature.—*ns* **quattrocent'ism**; **quattrocen'tist.** [It., four (for fourteen) hundred.]

quaver *kwā'vər, v.i.* to tremble, quiver: to speak or sing with tremulous uncertainty to trill.—*v.t* to utter or sing tremulously.—*n.* a trembling, esp. of the voice: half a crotchet (*mus.*) —*n* **quā'verer.**—*n.* and *adj.* **quā'vering.**—*adv.* **quā'veringly.**—*adj.* **quā'very.** [Freq. from obs. or dial. *quave*, M.E. *cwavien*, to shake.]

quay *kē, n.* a landing-place: a wharf for the loading or unloading of vessels —*n.* **quay'age** provision of quays: space for, or system of, quays: payment for use of a quay.—*n.* and *adj.* **quay'side.**—Earlier forms **kay** (*kā*), **key.** [O.Fr. *kay, cay, perh Celtic, partly assimilated to mod. Fr. spelling *quai*]

quean *kwēn, n.* a saucy girl: a woman of worthless character: a girl (*Scot*). [O E. *cwene*, woman, cf **queen** (O.E. *cwēn*).]

queasy, queazy *kwē'zi, adj* uneasy causing nausea. squeamish: inclined to vomit: fastidious.—*adv* **quea'sily.**—*n.* **quea'siness.** [Poss. O Fr *coisier*, to hurt; poss. O.N. *kveisa*, a boil.]

Quebec(k)er *kwi-bek'ər, n* an inhabitant of *Quebec*, in Canada —*n.* **Québecois** (*kā-bek-wa*; Fi) an inhabitant of Quebec, esp. a French-speaking one —Also *adj.*

quebracho *kā-bra'chō, n.* name of several S. American trees yielding very hard wood: their wood or bark:—*pl.* **quebra'chos.** [Sp.,—*quebrar*, to break, *hacha*, axe.]

Quechua *kech'wə, n.* a Peruvian Indian of the race that was dominant in the Inca empire: the language of the Quechua.—Also *adj.*—*adj.* **Quech'uan.**—Also *n.* [Sp. *Quechua, Quichua.*]

queen *kwēn, n.* the consort or wife of a king: female monarch: a presiding goddess: a woman or (*fig*) anything that is pre-eminent in excellence, beauty, etc : a sexually functional female social insect: female cat: male homosexual adopting female role (*slang*): a playing-card bearing the figure of a queen, in value next below a king: in chess, a piece that can be moved any distance in any straight line.—*v.t.* to make a queen of: to substitute a queen for: to play the queen (with *it* (*up*)).—*ns.* **queen'craft; queen'dom; queen'hood; queen'ing** an apple, of various varieties.—*adj.*

queen'-like.—*n.* queen'liness.—*adj.* queen'ly becoming or suitable to a queen: like a queen.—*n* queen'ship.—queen'-bee a fertile female bee: a woman who dominates her associates: a woman in an important business position, queen'-cake a small, soft, sweet cake with currants; queen'-con'sort the wife of a reigning king; queen'-dow'ager a king's widow; queen'-moth'er a queen-dowager that is mother of the reigning king or queen: a queen or queen-bee that is a mother; queen'-post one of two upright posts in a trussed roof, resting upon the tie-beam, and supporting the principal rafter; queen'-rè'gent a queen who reigns as regent; queen'-reg'nant a queen reigning as monarch.—*adj.* queen'-size larger than standard size, but smaller than the largest sizes, used of furnishings, etc.—queen's ware cream-coloured Wedgwood ware.—Queen Anne's Bounty a fund for augmenting poor livings of the Church of England; Queen Anne's dead that is old news; Queen Anne style (*archit.*) the simplified Renaissance manner of the early 18th century, or an imitation of it, plain and simple, with classic cornices and details; Queen of Heaven Ashtoreth: Juno: the Virgin Mary (*R.C.*); queen of puddings a pudding made with egg, breadcrumbs, fruit or jam, etc., topped with meringue; Queen of the May May Queen.—For Queen's Bench, Counsel, etc., see under king. [O.E. *cwēn*; Goth. *qēns*; O.N. *kvæn*, *kvän*; Gr. *gynē*; cf. quean.]

Queensberry Rules *kwēnz'bar-i rōōlz*, rules applied to boxing, originally drawn up in 1867 and named after the Marquess of *Queensberry*, who took a keen interest in sport: (*loosely*) standards of proper behaviour in any fight, physical or verbal.

Queensland-nut *kwēnz'land-nut*, *n.* a proteaceous tree of *Queensland* and New South Wales: its edible nut.

queer *kwēr*, *adj.* odd, singular, quaint: open to suspicion: counterfeit: slightly mad: having a sensation of coming sickness: homosexual (*slang*).—*v.t.* (*slang*) to spoil.—*n.* (*slang*) a male homosexual.—*adj.* queer'ish.—*adv.* queer'ly.—*n.* queer'ness.—Queer Street the feigned abode of persons in debt or other difficulties.—queer someone's pitch to spoil someone's chances. [Perh. Ger. *quer*, across, cf. thwart.]

quell *kwel*, *v.t.* to extinguish: to crush: to subdue.—*n.* quell'er. [O.E. *cwellan*, to kill, causal of *cwelan*, to die; cf. quail (vb.).]

quench *kwen(t)sh*, *v.t.* to put out: to put out the flame, light, or sight of: to stop (a discharge of electrically charged particles): to cool with liquid: to slake: to damp down: to put an end to: to put to silence: to destroy.—*n.* quenching.—*adj.* quench'able.—*n.* quench'er one who, or that which, quenches: a draught or drink.—*n.* and *adj.* quench'ing.—*adj.* quench'less not to be extinguished.—*adv.* quench'lessly. [O.E. *cwencan*, found only in the compound *ācwencan*, to quench.]

quenelle *kə-nel'*, *n.* a forcemeat ball of chicken, veal, or fish. [Fr.]

querist. See query.

quern *kwûrn*, *n.* a stone handmill.—quern'stone. [O.E. *cweorn*.]

querulous *kwer'ū-ləs*, also *-ōō-*, *-ə-*, *adj.* complaining: peevish.—*adv.* quer'ulously.—*n.* quer'ulousness. [L.L. *querulōsus*—*querī*, to complain.]

query, formerly often quaere, *kwē'ri*, *n.* an inquiry: doubt: interrogation mark (?).—*v.t.* to inquire into: to question: to doubt: to mark with a query.—*v.i.* to question:—*pa.t.* and *pa.p.* que'ried.—*n.* que'rist an inquirer.—*n.* and *adj.* que'rying.—*adv.* que'ryingly. [L. *quaere*, imper. of *quaerĕre*, *quaesītum*, to inquire.]

quest *kwest*, *n.* the act of seeking: search: an undertaking with the purpose of achieving or finding some definite object: the object sought for.—*v.i.* to go in search: of dogs, to search for game.—*v.t.* to go in quest of or after.—*n.* and *adj.* quest'ing.—*adv.* quest'ingly. [O.Fr. *queste*—L. (*rēs*) *quaesīta*, (a thing) sought.]

question *kwes'chən*, *n.* an inquiry: an interrogation: the putting of a problem: a demand for an answer: an interrogative sentence or other form of words in which it is put: a unit task in an examination: a problem: a subject of doubt or controversy: a subject of discussion, esp. the particular point actually before the house, meeting, or company. subjection to examination: examination by torture (*hist.*): objection: doubt: the measure to be voted upon: vaguely, a relevant matter.—*v.t.* to put questions to: to call to account: to examine by questions: to inquire: to inquire concerning: to throw doubt upon: to challenge, take exception to.—*v.i.* to ask questions: to inquire.—*adj.* quest'ionable that may be questioned: doubtful: open to suspicion.—*ns.* quest'ionableness; questionabil'ity.—*adv.* quest'ionably.—*n.* quest'ioner.—*n.* and *adj.* quest'ioning.—*adv.* quest'ioningly.—*adj.* quest'ionless.—*n.* questionnaire (*kwes-chən-ār'*, *kes-tē-on-er'*) a series of questions: a prepared set of written questions, for purposes of compilation or comparison.—ques'tion-begg'ing begging the question (see beg²).—Also *adj.*—ques'tion-mark a point of interrogation (?); ques'tion-mas'ter one who presides at a gathering whose purpose is the putting and answering of questions; question time in parliament, a period during each day when members can put questions to ministers.—in question under consideration: in dispute, open to question; out of question doubtless; out of the question not to be thought of; question of fact (*Eng. law*) that part of the issue which is decided by the jury; question of law that part decided by the judge. [O.Fr.,—L. *quaestiō*, *-ōnis*—*quaerĕre*, *quaesītum*, to ask.]

quetzal *ket-säl'*, *k(w)et'səl*, *n.* a golden green Central American bird with long tail-feathers: the Guatemalan currency unit, or dollar. [Aztec *quetzalli*.]

queue *kū*, *n.* a pendent braid of hair at the back of the head, a pigtail: a file of persons, etc., awaiting their turn.—*v.i.* to form, or take one's place in, a queue.—*n.* queu'ing, queue'ing.—*v.i.* queue'-jump'.—queue'-jump'ing going straight to the head of a queue instead of taking one's proper place in it (*lit.* and *fig.*). [Fr.,—L. *cauda*, a tail.]

quibble *kwib'l*, *n.* an evasive turning away from the point in question into matters irrelevant, merely verbal, or insignificant: a pun: a petty conceit.—*v.i.* to evade a question by a play upon words: to cavil: to trifle in argument: to pun.—*n.* quibb'ler.—*n.* and *adj.* quibb'ling.—*adv.* quibb'lingly. [Perh. dim. of obs. *quib*, quibble, which may be—L. *quibus*, dat. or abl. pl. of *quī*, who, a word frequent in legal use; or a variant of quip.]

quiche *kēsh*, *n.* a shell of unsweetened pastry filled with egg custard and cheese, etc. [Fr.,—Ger. dial. *küche*, dim. of *Kuche*, cake.]

quick *kwik*, *adj.* living (*arch.*): lively: swift: nimble: ready: sensitive: readily responsive: ready-witted: prompt in perception: hasty: pregnant (*arch.*).—*adv.* without delay: rapidly: soon.—*n.* the living (*arch.*): a living plant, esp. hawthorn in a hedge (also collectively): the sensitive parts, esp. under the nails: the tenderest feelings.—*v.t.* quick'en to give life to: to stimulate: to impart energy or liveliness to: to revive: to accelerate.—*v.i.* to become alive or lively: to revive: to be stimulated: to reach the stage in pregnancy when the mother becomes conscious of the movement of the child: to move faster.—*n.* **quick'ener.**—*n.* and *adj.* **quick'ening.**—*n.* **quick'ie** (*coll.*) something that takes, or is to be done in, a short time: an alcoholic drink to be rapidly consumed.—Also *adj.*—*adv.* **quick'ly.**—*n.* **quick'ness.**—**quick assets** readily realisable assets.—*adjs.* **quick'-change** quick in making a change, esp. (of a performer) in appearance (**quick-change artist** such a performer: a person who changes rapidly or frequently in mood or opinion); **quick'-fire, -firing** designed to allow a quick succession of shots.—**quick'-fire** rapid and continuous gunfire; **quick'-firer; quick'-freeze** very rapid freezing of food so that its natural qualities are unimpaired.—Also *vb.*—*adj.* **quick'-frozen.**—**quick'lime** unslaked lime; **quick march** (*mil.*) a march at a fast pace.—*interj.* the command to start such a march.—**quick'sand** a loose watery sand ready to swallow those who walk on it, boats, etc.: anything similarly treacherous.—*adjs.* **quick'-sandy; quick'-selling; quick'set** formed of living plants.—*n.* a living plant, slip, or cutting, esp. of hawthorn, or a series of them, set to grow for a hedge: a quickset hedge.—*adj.* **quick'-sighted** having quick sight or discernment.—**quick'-sight'edness; quick'silver** mercury.—*adj.* of mercury.—*v.t.* to overlay or to treat with quicksilver or amalgam.—*adj.* **quick'silvered.**—**quick'silvering** the mercury on the back of a mirror.—*adjs.* **quick'-silverish, quick'silvery.**—**quick'step** a march step or tune in fast time: a fast foxtrot.—*adj.* **quick'-tem'pered** irascible.—**quick'thorn** hawthorn; **quick time** (*mil.*) a rate of about 120 steps per minute in marching; **quick'-trick** a card that should win a trick in the first or second round of the suit.—*adj.* **quick'-witt'ed** having a ready wit.—**quick'-witt'edness.**—**a quick one** a quick drink; **quick on the draw** swift to draw a gun from its holster: prompt in response or action. [O.E. *cwic*; O.N. *kvikr*, living.]

quid[1] *kwid, n.* something chewed or kept in the mouth, esp. a piece of tobacco. [**cud.**]

quid[2] *kwid,* (*slang*) *n.* a pound (£1): formerly, a guinea:—*pl.* **quid—quids in** (*slang*) in a very favourable or profitable situation.

quiddity *kwid'i-ti, n.* the essence of anything: any trifling nicety: quibble. [Schoolman's L. *quidditās, -tātis.*]

quidnunc *kwid'nungk, n.* a newsmonger: a gossip. [L. *quid nunc?,* what now?]

quid pro quo *kwid prō kwō,* (L.) something for something: something given or taken as equivalent to another, often as retaliation: action or fact of giving or receiving thus.

quiesce *kwi-es', kwi-, v.i.* to become quiet or silent.—*ns.* **quiesc'ence, quiesc'ency** rest: inactivity: silence of a consonant.—*adj.* **quiesc'ent** resting: not sounded: inactive: still.—*adv.* **quiesc'ently.** [L. *quiēscĕre,* to rest.]

quiet *kwi'ət, adj.* at rest: calm: undisturbed: unaccompanied by disturbance: without loudness, gaudiness, ostentation, formality, or obtrusiveness of any kind: still: without bustle or restlessness: without much activity: peaceable: gentle: inoffensive.—*n.* rest: repose: calm: stillness: peace: freedom from noise or disturbance.—*v.t.* and *v.i.* to make or become quiet.—*v.t.* and *v.i.* **qui'eten** to quiet.—*n.* and *adj.* **qui'etening.**—*n.* **qui'eter.**—*n.* and *adj.* **qui'eting.**—*ns.* **qui'etism** mental tranquillity: the doctrine that religious perfection on earth consists in passive and uninterrupted contemplation of the Deity; **qui'etist.**—*adj.* **quietist'ic.**—*adv.* **qui'etly.**—*n.* **qui'etness; qui'etude** quietness.—**on the quiet** clandestinely: unobtrusively. [L. *quiētus,* quiet, calm.]

quietus *kwi-ē'təs, kwi-ā'tōōs, n.* an acquittance: discharge from office: discharge from life: extinction: silencing. [L. *quiētus est,* he is quiet]

quiff *kwif, n.* a lock of hair oiled and brushed down on the forehead or turned up and back from it. [Poss. **coif.**]

quill *kwil, n.* the hollow basal part of a feather: a large feather a porcupine's spine: a goose or other feather used as a pen: hence a pen generally: a thing made from a quill feather, as a toothpick, an angler's float, a plectrum: a weaver's bobbin of reed or other material: a musical pipe made from a reed or the like: a roll of curled bark, as cinnamon.—*v.t.* to goffer: to wind on a bobbin.—*adj.* **quilled** furnished with, or formed into quills: tubular.—*n* **quill'ing** a ribbon or strip gathered into flutings —**quill'-driver** (*used derogatorily*) a clerk: an assiduous writer; **quill'-driving; quill'-feather** a large stiff wing or tail feather; **quill'-pen.** [Origin obscure; cf. L.G. *quiele,* Ger. *Kiel.*]

quillet *kwil'it, n.* a subtlety in argument: a quibble [Perh. L. *quidlibet,* what you will.]

quilt *kwilt, n.* a bed-cover of two thicknesses with padding sewn in compartments: any material or piece of material so treated, esp. when worn under or instead of armour: a thick coverlet.—*v.t.* to pad, cover, or line with a quilt: to form into a quilt: to stitch in: to seam like a quilt.—*adj.* **quilt'ed.**—*ns.* **quilt'er; quilt'ing** the act of making a quilt: that which is quilted: a cloth for making quilts: a cloth with a pattern like a quilt. [O.Fr. *cuilte* (Fr. *couette*)—L. *culcita,* a cushion.]

quin *kwin, n.* short for **quintuplet.**

quinacrine *kwin'ə-krēn, n.* another name for **mepacrine.** [*quinine, acridine.*]

quinary *kwi'nər-i, adj.* fivefold: by fives: in fives: of the fifth order: based on five: with five variables.—*adj.* **qui'nate** in sets of five: with five leaflets arising at one point. [L. *quinī,* five by five.]

quince *kwins, n.* a golden, globose or pear-shaped, fragrant, acid fruit, good for jellies, marmalade, etc., or the tree or shrub (*Cydonia oblonga*), akin to pear and apple, that bears it: extended to the near-allied *Japanese quince* (see **japonica**). [Orig. pl. of *quine*—O.Fr. *coin* (Fr. *coing*)—L. *cotōneum*—Gr. *kydōnion*—*Kydōniā,* in Crete.]

quincentenary *kwin-sin-tēn'ər-i, -sin-ten'ər-i,* or *-sen'tinər-i, n.* and *adj.* quingentenary. [Irreg. formed—L. *quinque,* five, and **centenary.**]

quincunx *kwin'kungks, n.* an arrangement of five things at the corners and centre of a square, or of a great number of things (esp. trees) spaced in the same way.—*adj.* **quincuncial** (*-kun'shl*).—*adv.* **quincun'cially.** [L *quincunx*—*quinque,* five, *uncia,* a twelfth part.]

quingentenary *kwin-jen-tē'nər-i, -ten'ər-i,* or *-jen'tən-ər-i, n* a five-hundredth anniversary or its celebration.—Also *adj.* [L. *quingentī,* five hundred.]

quinine *kwin-ēn', kwin'ēn,* in U.S. *kwi'nin, n.* a colourless, inodorous, very bitter alkaloid got from cinchona bark, or one of its salts, used as an antipyretic and analgesic, formerly widely used to treat malaria —*n* **quin'idine** (*-i-dēn*) a crystalline alkaloid drug, isomeric with quinine, used to treat irregularities in the heart rhythm [Sp *quina*—Quechua *kina,* cinchona bark]

quinol *kwin'ol, n.* a reducing agent and photographic developer got by reduction of quinone.—*ns.* **quin'oline** (*-ō-lēn*) a pungent, colourless liquid first got from quinine; **quinone** (*kwin'ōn, kwin-ōn'*) a golden-yellow crystalline compound usually prepared by oxidising aniline: a reddish or colourless isomer of this: a general name for a benzene derivative in which two oxygen atoms replace two hydrogen. [As **quinine**.]

quinqu-, quinque- *kwin-kw(i)-*, in composition, five.—
n. **quinquagenarian** (*kwin-kwə-ji-nā'ri-ən*; L. *quīnquāgēnārius—quīnquāgēnī*, fifty each) one who is fifty years old, or between fifty and fifty-nine.—Also *adj.—n.* **quinquennium** (*kwin-kwen'i-əm*; L. *annus*, year) a period of five years:—*pl.* **quinquenn'ia.**—*adj.* **quinquenn'ial** occurring once in five years: lasting five years.—*n.* a fifth anniversary or its celebration.—*adv.* **quinquenn'ially.**—*n.* **quinquereme** (*kwin'kwi-rēm*; L. *rēmus*, an oar) an ancient ship with five sets of oars.—*adj.* **quinquevalent** (*kwin-kwev'ə-lənt* or *-kwi-vā'*) having a valency of five.—*n.* **quinquev'alence** (or *-vā'*). [L. *quīnque*, five.]

Quinquagesima *kwin-kwə-jes'i-mə, n.* Shrove Sunday (also **Quinquagesima Sunday**)—apparently as fifty days before Easter Sunday (both counted).—*adj.* **quinquages'imal** of the number fifty: of fifty days. [L. *quīnquāgēsimus, -a, -um,* fiftieth.]

quinque-, quinquennium, etc. See **quinqu-.**

quinsy *kwin'zi, n.* suppurative tonsillitis. [L.L. *quinancia*—Gr. *kynanchē.*]

quint *kwint, n.* an organ-stop a fifth above the foundation stops: (*kint*) a sequence of five cards in piquet. [Fr. *quinte*—L. *quīntus, -a, -um,* fifth.]

quint- *kwint-*, in composition, fifth. [L. *quīntus,* fifth.]

quinta *kin'tə, n.* a country house. [Sp. and Port.]

quintain *kwin'tin, -tən, n.* a post for tilting at, often with a turning cross-piece to strike the unskilful tilter: the sport of tilting at such a post. [O.Fr. *quintaine,* thought to be—L. *quīntāna via,* the road adjoining the fifth maniple in a camp.]

quintal *kwin'tl, n.* formerly, a hundredweight: now, 100 kilograms. [Fr. and Sp. *quintal*—Ar. *qintār*—L. *centum,* a hundred.]

quintan *kwin'tən, adj.* occurring every fourth (by inclusive reckoning fifth) day. [L. *quīntānus,* of the fifth.]

quinte *kēt, n.* the fifth of eight parrying or attacking positions in fencing. [Fr.]

quintessence *kwin-tes'əns,* or *kwin', n.* orig. a fifth entity, in addition to the four elements: the pure concentrated essence of anything: the most essential part, form, or embodiment of anything.—*adj.* **quintessential** (*-ti-sen'shl*). [Fr.,—L. *quīnta essentia,* fifth essence.]

quintet, quintette, quintett *kwin-tet', n.* a composition for five voices or instruments: a set of performers or instruments for such compositions: a group of five people or things. [It. *quintetto,* dim. of *quinto*—L. *quīntus,* fifth.]

quintillion *kwin-til'yən, n.* the fifth power of a million, represented by a unit and thirty ciphers: in U.S., the sixth power of one thousand—a unit with eighteen ciphers.—*n.* and *adj.* **quintill'ionth.** [Modelled on **million.**]

quintuple *kwin'tū-pl, adj.* fivefold: having five parts, members, or divisions.—*n.* five times as much.—*v.t* and *v.i.* to increase fivefold.—*n.* **quin'tuplet** (also *-tū'*) a set of five things: a group of five notes played in the time of four: one of five born at a birth. [L. *quīntus,* fifth, on the model of **quadruple.**]

quintuplicate *kwin-tū'pli-kāt, adj.* fivefold.—*n.* one of five corresponding things: fivefoldness.—*v t.* to make fivefold.—*n.* **quintuplica'tion.** [L. *quīntuplex, -icis—quīntus,* fifth, *plicāre,* to fold.]

quip *kwip, n.* a short, clever remark: a gibe —*v.i.* to utter quips.—*adj.* **quipp'ish.**—*n.* **quip'ster** one given to making clever remarks [Perh. from obs *quippy,* which may be—L. *quippe,* forsooth.]

quipu *kē'pōō, n.* a mnemonic contrivance of knotted cords used by the ancient Peruvians—depending on order, colour, and kind. [Quechua *quipu,* knot.]

quire *kwīr, n.* formerly, four sheets of paper or parchment folded together in eight leaves: later, the twentieth part of a ream, twenty-four sheets, each having a single fold.—*v.t.* to fold in quires. [O.Fr. *quaier* (Fr. *cahier*), prob. from L.L. *quaternum,* a set of four sheets—L. *quattuor,* four.]

quirk *kwûrk, n.* a trick or peculiarity of action, fashion or behaviour: a sudden turn, twist, jerk, or flourish: an acute sharp-edged groove alongside a moulding (*archit.*).—*n.* **quirk'iness.**—*adjs.* **quirk'ish; quirk'y.**

quirt *kwûrt, n* a Spanish-American braided hide riding-whip.—*v.t.* to strike with a quirt. [Mexican-Sp. *cuarta.*]

quisling *kwiz'ling, n.* one who aids the enemy: a native puppet prime minister set up by an occupying foreign power. [Vidkun *Quisling,* who played that part in Norway during German occupation (1940–45).]

quit *kwit, v.t.* repay: to release from obligation: to clear off: to discharge: to acquit: to depart from: to cease to occupy: to rid (*obs.* except *refl.*): to let go: to leave off: to behave, acquit (*refl.*).—*v.i.* to leave off: to depart:—*pr.p.* **quitt'ing;** *pa.p.* **quitt'ed, quit.**—*adj.* **quit** set free: clear: quits: acquitted: released from obligation.—*adj.* **quits** even: neither owing nor owed.—*ns.* **quitt'ance** release: discharge: acquittance: requital; **quitt'er** a shirker: one who gives up easily.—**quit'-claim** a deed of release.—*v.t.* to relinquish claim or title to: to release, discharge.—**quit'-rent** a rent in money or kind in lieu of services.—**cry quits** (formerly **quittance**) to declare oneself even with another, and so satisfied; **double or quits** see **double.** [O.Fr. *quiter*—L.L. *quiētāre,* to pay.]

quitch *kwich, n.* couch-grass.—Also **quitch'-grass.** [O.E. *cwīce,* cf. **couch-grass.**]

quite *kwīt, adv.* completely, wholly, entirely: enough fully to justify the use of the word or phrase qualified: fairly, somewhat. exactly, indeed, yes (*coll.*): often **quite so).**—**quite something** (*coll.*) something remarkable or excellent. [**quit.**]

quittance. See **quit.**

quiver[1] *kwiv'ər, n.* a case for arrows.—*n.* **quiv'erful** a large family (Psalms cxxvii 5) [O.Fr. *cuivre*; prob. Gmc. in origin; cf. O.H.G. *kohhar* (Ger *Kocher*) O.E. *cocer.*]

quiver[2] *kwiv'ər, v.t.* to shake with slight and tremulous motion: to tremble: to shiver.—*v.t* (of a bird) to cause (the wings) to move rapidly.—*ns.* **quiv'er, quiv'ering.**—*adv.* **quiv'eringly.**—*adj.* **quiv'erish.** [Perh. obs. *quiver,* nimble]

qui vive *kē vēv,* alert (in phrase **on the qui vive**). [From the French sentry's challenge, lit. (long) live who?—*qui,* who, *vive,* 3rd pers. sing. pres. subj. of *vivre,* to live—L. *vīvĕre.*]

quixotic *kwiks-ot'ik, adj.* like Don *Quixote,* the knight in the romance of Cervantes (1547–1616), extravagantly romantic in ideals or chivalrous in action: (of ideals, actions) absurdly generous.—*adv.* **quixot'ically.**—*ns.* **quix'otism; quix'otry.**

quiz *kwiz, n.* an odd-looking person: a piece of banter or quiet mockery: a hoax. one who practises any of these: a sportive catechism or general-knowledge test:—*pl.* **quizz'es.**—*v.t.* to poke fun at: to eye, often with an air of mockery: to catechise, interrogate.—*v i.* to practise derisive joking:—*pr.p.* **quizz'ing;** *pa.t.* and *pa.p.* **quizzed.**—*ns.* **quizz'er; quizz'ery.**—*adj.* **quizz'ical.**—*n.* **quizzical'ity.**—*adv.* **quizz'ically.**—**quiz'-master** question-master; **quizz'ing-glass** a monocle.

quod[1] *kwod,* neut. of L *quī,* which.—**quod erat demonstrandum** (*er'at dem-ən-stran'dəm, er-at'* *dēm-ōn stran'dōōm*), (abbrev. Q.E.D.) which was to be proved or demonstrated; **quod erat faciendum** (*fā-shē-en'dəm, fa-ki-en'dōōm*), (abbrev. Q.E.F.) which was to be done; **quod** (*pl.* **quae** *kwē, kwī*) **vide** (*vī'dē, vi', wi'de*) which see.

quod[2] *kwod, (slang) n.* prison.—*v.t.* to imprison.

quodlibet *kwod'li-bet, n.* a scholastic argument: a humorous medley of tunes. [L., what you please— *quod,* what, *libet,* it pleases.]

quoin *koin, n.* a wedge, esp. for locking type in a forme, or for raising a gun: a salient angle, esp. of a building: a corner-stone, esp. a dressed corner-stone: a keystone: a voussoir.—*v.t.* to wedge: to secure, or raise by wedging. [See **coin.**]

quoit *koit, kwoit, n.* a heavy flat ring for throwing as near as possible to a hob or pin: (in *pl.,* treated as *sing.*) the game played with quoits.—*v.i.* to play at quoits.— *v.t.* to throw as a quoit.—*n.* **quoit'er.**

quokka *kwok'ə, n.* a small marsupial, *Setonix brachyurus,* found in W. Australia. [Native name.]

quondam *kwon'dam, adj.* former. [L., formerly.]

Quonset hut® *kwon'set hut,* the U.S. equivalent of the Nissen hut.

quorum *kwō', kwō'rəm, n.* a minimum number of persons necessary for transaction of business in any body. [L. *quōrum,* of whom, from the wording of the commission, of whom we will that you, so-and-so, be one (two, etc.).]

quota *kwō'tə, n.* a proportional share, a part assigned: a regulated quantity of goods allowed by a government to be manufactured, exported, imported, etc.: a prescribed number of immigrants allowed into a country per year, students allowed to enrol for a course, fish allowed to be caught, etc.:—*pl.* **quo'tas.** [L. *quota (pars),* the how-manieth (part)—*quotus,* of what number—*quot,* how many.]

quote *kwōt, v.t.* to refer to: to cite: to adduce as authority, illustration, or example: to give the actual words of: to note, set down, mention, in writing or mentally: to give the current price of: to state the market price of (shares, etc.) on the Stock Exchange list: to enclose within quotation-marks.—*v.i.* to make quotations.—used as *interj.* to indicate that what follows immediately is a quotation.—*n.* a quotation: a quotation-mark.—*adj.* **quo'table** lending itself (or himself) to quotation: fit to quote.—*ns.* **quo't-ableness, quotabil'ity.**—*adv.* **quo'tably.**—*n.* **quota'-tion** act of quoting: that which is quoted: an estimated price submitted to a prospective purchaser: the current price of shares, etc., on the Stock Exchange list: a quadrat for filling blanks in type (orig. those between marginal references).—*n.* **quo'ter.**—*adj.* **quote'worthy.**—**quota'tion-mark** one of the marks (*print.* **quotes**) used to note the beginning and end of a quotation (see also **inverted commas** under **comma**); **quoted company** one whose shares are quoted on the Stock Exchange. [L.L. *quotāre,* to divide into chapters and verses—L. *quotus,* of what number— *quot,* how many.]

quoth *kwōth, (arch.) v.t.* (1st and 3rd pers. sing., past tense) said (followed by its subject).—*interj.* **quo'tha** forsooth, indeed (lit. quoth he). [O.E. *cwæth,* pret. of *cwethan,* to say; cf. **bequeath.**]

quotidian *kwot-id'i-ən, adj.* daily: everyday, common-place: of any activity of a living creature or a living part, that follows a regular recurrent pattern.—*n.* a fever or ague that recurs daily. [L. *quotīdiānus— quotīdiē,* daily—*quot,* how many, *diēs,* day.]

quotient *kwō'shənt, (math.) n.* the number of times one quantity is contained in another: a ratio, usu. multiplied by 100, used in giving a numerical value to ability, etc. (see **intelligence quotient**). [L. *quotiēns, quoties,* how often—*quot,* how many (with *t* from false appearance of being a participle).]

quo warranto *kwō wo-ran'tō,* a writ calling upon one to show by what warrant he holds or claims a franchise or office. [L. *quō warrantō* (abl.). by what warrant.]

Qurân, Qur'an *kōō-rän', n.* Same as **Koran.**

R

R, r är, n. the eighteenth letter ın our alphabet.—**R months** the time when oysters are in season (from the spelling of the names of the months from September to April); **the three R's** reading, wrıting, and arithmetic. [L. er.]

rabbet rab'ıt, n. a groove cut to receıve an edge.—v.t to groove: to join by a rabbet:—pr.p. **rabb'eting**; pa.t. and pa.p. **rabb'eted.**—**rabb'eting-machine'**, **-plane, -saw**; **rabb'et-joint.** [Fr. rabat—rabattre, to beat back.]

rabbi (with cap. when prefixed) rab'ī, n. a Jewish expounder or doctor of the law: the leader of a Jewish congregation:—pl. **rabb'is.**—n. **rabb'inate** the dignity or tenure of office of a rabbi: a body of rabbis.— adjs. **rabbin'ic, -al** pertaining to the rabbis or to theır opinions, learning, and language.—n. **Rabbin'ic** late Hebrew.—adv. **rabbin'ically.**—ns. **rabb'inism** the late Jewish belief which esteemed the oral equally with the written law; **rabb'inist, rabb'inite** one who adheres to the Talmud and traditions of the rabbis [Heb. rabbi, my great one—rabh, great, master.]

rabbit rab'ıt, n. the cony, a small burrowing animal of the hare family: its flesh (as food): its fur: a persistent but incurably **inferior** player at lawn-tennis or other game: a timid person.—v.i. to hunt rabbits: to talk at length and in a rambling fashion (coll.; often with on).—ns. **rabb'iter; rabb'itry** a place where rabbits are kept: the play of a rabbit in games.—adj. **rabb'ity.**—**rabb'it-hole; rabb'it-hutch; rabb'it-punch** a blow on the back of the neck; **rabb'it-warren** see **warren.**—**Welsh rabbit** melted cheese with or without ale, etc., on hot toast—now more usually **Welsh rarebit.** [M.E. rabet; poss. from O.N.Fr.]

rabble¹ rab'l, n. a disorderly assemblage or crowd: a mob: the lowest class of people.—**rabb'le-rous'er** one who stirs up the common people to discontent and violence, a demagogue; **rabb'le-rous'ing.** [Cf. Du. rabbelen, to gabble, L.G. rabbeln.]

rabble² rab'l, n. a device for stirring molten iron, etc. in a furnace. [Fr. râble—L. rutābulum, a poker.]

Rabelaisian rab-ə-lā'zı-ən, n. a follower, admirer, or student of François Rabelais (d. 1553 or 1554).—adj. of or like Rabelais: extravagantly humorous: robustly outspoken: (loosely) coarsely indecent.—n. **Rabelais'ianism.**

rabi rub'ē, n. the spring grain harvest in India, Pakistan, etc. [Ar. rabī', spring.]

rabid rab'id, adj. raging: fanatical: affected with rabies.—adv. **rab'idly.**—ns. **rabid'ity, rab'idness; rabies** (rā'bēz, -bi-ēz, or ra') the disease called hydrophobia, caused by a virus transmitted by the bite of an infected animal. [L. rabidus (adj.), rabiēs (n.)—rabēre, to rave.]

raccoon, racoon rə-koōn', n. an American animal (Procyon lotor, or other species) related to the bears: its fur. [From an American Indian name.]

race¹ rās, n. the descendants of a common ancestor: esp. those who inherit a common set of characteristics: such a set of descendants, narrower than a species: a breed: ancestry, lineage, stock· the condition of belonging by descent to a particular group: inherited dısposıtıon: a class or group, defined otherwise than by descent: raciness, piquancy —adj. **racial** (rā'shl, -shyəl, -shi-əl) of, relating to, race.—

ns **ra'cialism** race-hatred, rıvalry, or feeling: belief ın inherent superiority of some races over others, usu. with implication of a right to rule: discriminative treatment based on such belief; **ra'cialist.**—adv. **racily** (rās'i-li).—ns. **ra'ciness** quality of being racy; **rac'ism** racialism (q.v.); **rac'ist.**—adj. **ra'cy** havıng a distinctive flavour imparted by the soil, as wine: exciting to the mind by strongly characteristic thought or language: spirited: pungent: zestful: risqué.—**race'-ha'tred** animosity accompanying difference of race; **race relations** social relations between members of different races living in the same country or community; **race riot** a not caused by perceived discrimination on the grounds of race; **race'-su'icide** voluntary cessation of reproduction, leading to the extinction of the race [Fr ,—It. razza, of doubtful origin.]

race² rās, n. a fixed course, track, or path, over which anything runs: a channel bringing water to or from a wheel: a groove in which anything runs (as ball-bearings, a rope): a regular running over a fixed course, as of the sun: a rapid current: a competitive trial of speed in progression: (in pl.) a meeting for horse-racing: a competition in getting ahead of others figuratively.—v.i. to run swiftly: to contend in speed: to run wildly (as an engine, a propeller) when resistance is removed.—v.t. to cause (a horse, etc.) to race: to rush: to contend in a race with.—ns. **ra'cer; ra'cing.**—adj. **ra'cy.**—**race'-card** a programme for a race-meeting; **race'-course, -track** a course for running races over; **race'goer** an attender at race-meetings; **race'going; race'horse** horse bred for racing; **race'-meet'ing** see **meet¹; race'way** a mill-race: a track for running races over; **rac'ing-car.** [O.N. rās; O.E. rǽs.]

raceme ra-, rə-, rā-sēm', ras'ēm, n. an indefinıte inflorescence in which stalked flowers are borne on an unbranched main stalk: a similar group of sporangia. —ns. **racemate** (ras'i-māt) a racemic compound; **racemation** (ras-i-mā'shən) a cluster or bunch of grapes or of anything else.—adjs. **racemed'** (or ras', rās') in or having racemes; **racemic** (ra-sē'mik, -sem'ik) applied to an acid obtained from a certain kind of grape, an optically inactive form of tartaric acid: hence applied to similar compounds of dextrorotatory and laevorotatory enantiomorphs.—n. **racemisā'tion, -z-** a changing into a racemic form.—v.t. and v.i. **rac'emise, -ize.**—n. **rac'emism** the quality of being racemıc.—adj. **racemose** (ras'i-mōs) of the nature of or like a raceme: of, in, or having racemes: like a bunch of grapes. [L. racēmus, a bunch of grapes.]

rachis rā'kis, n. the spine: an axis, as of a feather, an inflorescence, a pinnate leaf:—pl. **ra'chises, rachides** (rak', rāk'i-dēz) [Gr rhachis, spine.]

rachitis ra-, rə-kī'tıs, n. rickets.—adj. **rachitic** (-kıt'ik) [Gr. rhachītis, ınflammatıon of the spine: adopted by Dr Gleeson in 1650 ın the belief that it was the etymon of **rickets.**]

Rachmanism rak'man-ızm, n. conduct of a landlord who charges extortionate rents for property in slum condition. [From the name of one such landlord exposed in 1963.]

racial, racism, raciness, racism, etc. See **race¹.**

rack¹ *rak, n.* an instrument for stretching, esp. an instrument of torture: hence an extreme pain, anxiety, or doubt: stress: a framework, grating, shelf, or the like, on or in which articles are disposed or set aside: a grating from which beasts may pull down fodder: a bar with teeth to work into those of a wheel, pinion, or endless screw.—*v.t.* to stretch forcibly or excessively: to strain: to wrest, overstrain, distort: to torture: to practice rapacity upon: to put in a rack: to move or adjust by rack and pinion.—*adj.* **racked** (also erroneously, **wracked**) tortured, tormented.—in composition, tortured, distressed by, as in *disease-racked*, etc.—*n.* **rack'er.**—*n.* and *adj.* **rack'ing.**— **rack'-rail** a cogged rail; **rack'-rail'way** a mountain railway with a rack in which a cog-wheel on the loco-motive works; **rack'-rent** a rent stretched to the utmost annual value of the things rented, exorbitant rent.—*v.t.* to subject to such rents.—**rack'-rent'er;** **rack and pinion** a means of turning rotatory into linear or linear into rotatory motion by a toothed wheel engaging in a rack; **rack one's brains** to strain one's memory, ingenuity, etc. [Prob M.Du. *recke* (Du. *rek, rak*) or L.G. *reck, recke, rack.*]

rack² *rak, n.* same as **wrack,** destruction.—**rack and ruin** a state of neglect and collapse. [**wrack¹,** or O.N. *rek,* wreckage.]

rack³ *rak, n.* flying cloud: driving mist: a track.—*v.i.* to drift, to drive. [App. O.N. *rek,* drifting wreckage, or some kindred form.]

rack⁴ *rak, v.t.* to draw off from the lees [Prov. *arracar*—*raca,* husks, dregs.]

rack⁵ *rak, n.* the neck and spine of a forequarter of a carcass (*dial.*). [Perh. O.E. *hracca,* occiput.]

rack⁶ *rak* (now *U.S.*) *n.* a horse's gait at which the legs at the same side move nearly together.—*v.i.* to go in that gait.—*n.* **rack'er.**

rack⁷ *rak, n.* aphetic for **arrack.**—**rack'-punch.**

racket¹ *rak'it, n.* a bat with usu. roughly elliptical head, of wood or metal strung with catgut or nylon, for playing tennis, badminton, etc.: a snowshoe of like design: (in *pl.*) a simplified derivative of the old game of tennis, similar to squash, played by two or four people in a four-walled court.—**rack'et-court, -ground;** **rack'et-press** a press for keeping a racket in shape; **rack'et-tail** a humming-bird with two long racket-shaped feathers.—*adj.* **rack'et-tailed.** [Fr. *raquette,* poss.—Ar. *rāhat,* coll. form of *rāha,* the palm of the hand.]

racket² *rak'it, n.* din: hubbub: noisy gaiety: fraudulent, violent, or otherwise unscrupulous money-making activities: strain of excitement.—*v.i.* to move about in a noisy, carefree manner:—*pr.p.* **rack'eting;** *pa.t.* and *pa.p.* **rack'eted.**—*n.* **racketeer'** one who extorts money or other advantage by threats or illegal interference.—*v.i.* to act as a racketeer.— *ns.* **racketeer'ing;** **rack'eter; rack'etry.**—*adj.* **rack'ety** noisy.—**stand the racket** to endure the strain: to pay expenses. [Prob. imit.]

racket³, rackett *rak'it, n.* an old instrument like the bassoon.

racon *rā'kon, n.* a radar beacon. [radar, beacon.]

raconteur *ra-kon-tûr', rä-kɔ̃-tœr, n.* a teller of anec-dotes:—*fem.* **raconteuse** (-*tœz*).—*n.* **raconteur'ing.** [Fr.]

racoon. See raccoon.

racquet. Same as **racket¹.**

racy. See **race¹,².**

rad¹ *rad, n.* short for **radical** (in politics)

rad² *rad, n.* a unit of dosage of any radiation, equal to 100 ergs of energy for one gram of mass of the mater-ial irradiated. [**rad(iation).**]

radar *rā'där, n.* the use of high-powered radio pulses, reflected or regenerated, for locating objects or determining one's own position: equipment for send-ing out and receiving such pulses.—**radar beacon** a fixed radio transmitter whose signals enable an aircraft, by means of its radar equipment, to determine its position and direction; **ra'dar-gun** a gun-like device used by police which, when pointed at a moving vehicle and 'fired', records (by means of radar) the speed of the vehicle; **ra'darscope** a cath-ode-ray oscilloscope on which radar signals can be seen; **radar trap** a device using radar which enables the police to identify motorists exceeding the speed limit over a particular section of the road (see also **speed trap).** [American codeword, from *radio detection* and *ranging,* appropriately a palindrome word.]

raddle *rad'l, n.* reddle or ruddle (red ochre).—*v.t.* to colour or mark with red ochre: to rouge coarsely.— *adj.* **radd'led** of a person, aged and worsened by de-bauchery. [See **ruddle.**]

radial *rā'di-ɔl, adj.* pertaining to a ray or radius: along, in the direction of, a radius or radii: having rays, spokes, or parts diverging from a centre: arranged like spokes or radii: near the radius of the arm.—*n.* a radiating part: a radial artery, nerve, engine, plate, tyre, etc.—*n.* **radialisation, -z-** (*rād-yɔl-ī-zā'shɔn*).— *v.t.* **ra'dialise, -ize** to arrange radially.—*n.* **radiality** (*-al'*) radial symmetry.—*adv.* **ra'dially** in the manner of radii or of rays.—**radial engine** one with its cylin-ders radially arranged; **radial symmetry** symmetry about several planes intersecting in a common axis; **radial velocity** the component of velocity along the observer's line of sight.—**radial-ply** tyre tyre in which layers or plies of fabric in the carcass are wrapped in a direction radial to the centre of the wheel. [L.L. *radiālis*—L. *radius.*]

radian *rā'di-ɔn, n.* a unit of circular measure, the angle subtended at the centre of a circle by an arc equal to the radius, nearly 57·3°. [L. *radius.*]

radiant *rā'di-ɔnt, rā'dyɔnt, adj.* emitting rays: issuing in rays: transmitted by radiation: glowing: shining: beaming with happy emotion.—*n.* that which emits radiations: a point from which rays emanate: the centre from which meteoric showers seem to proceed. —*ns.* **ra'diance, ra'diancy** the state of being radiant: a measure of the amount of electromagnetic radiation being transmitted from or to a point (on a surface).— *adv.* **ra'diantly.**—**radiant energy** energy given out as electromagnetic radiation; **radiant heat** heat trans-mitted by electromagnetic radiation. [L. *radiāns, -antis,* pr.p. of *radiāre,* to radiate—*radius.*]

radiate *rā'di-āt, v.i.* to emit rays: to shine: to issue in rays: to diverge from a point or points: to transmit wirelessly.—*v.t.* to send out in or by means of rays: to communicate by wireless.—*n.* **radia'tion** act of radi-ating: the emission and diffusion of rays: that which is radiated: energy transmitted in electromagnetic waves: radial arrangement.—*adjs.* **ra'diative, radi-a'tory.**—*n.* **ra'diator** that which radiates: apparatus for radiating heat, as for warming a room, or cooling an engine: a wireless transmitting aerial.—**radiation oncologist** see **radiologist** under **radio-; radiation sickness** an illness due to excessive absorption of radiation in the body, marked by diarrhoea, vomiting, internal bleeding, decrease in blood cells, loss of teeth and hair, reduction of sperm in the male, etc. [L. *radiāre,* to shine, *radiātus,* rayed—*radius.*]

radical *rad'i-kl, adj.* pertaining to, constituting, pro-ceeding from or going to the root: fundamental: origi-nal: intrinsic: thorough: primary: implanted by nature: proceeding from near the root (*bot.*): of or concerning the root of a word (*linguistics*): of or con-cerning the roots of numbers (*math.*): favouring thorough-going but constitutional social and political reform (usu. with *cap.*).—*n.* a root, in any sense: a group of atoms behaving like a single atom and passing unchanged from one compound to another (*chem.*; sometimes **rad'icle**): (*cap.*) an advocate of radical reform or member of the Radical party.—*n.* **radicalisa'tion**, **-z-**.—*v.t.* and *v.i.* **rad'icalise**, **-ize**.—*ns.* **Rad'icalism** the principles or spirit of a Radical.—*adv.* **rad'ically.**—*ns.* **rad'icalness**; **rad'icle** a little root: the part of a seed that becomes the root: a rhizoid: a radical (*chem.*).—**radical sign** the symbol √, indicating a square root. [L. *rādīx*, *-īcis*, a root.]

radices. See **radix**.

radii. See **radius**.

radio- *rā-di-ō-*, in composition (most terms can be spelt as one word, a hyphenated word, or two words), rays, radiation, radium, radius: radio, wireless: (of product or isotope) radioactive.—*n.* **ra'dio** a generic term applied to methods of signalling through space, without connecting wires, by means of electromagnetic waves generated by high-frequency alternating currents: a wireless receiving or transmitting set: a wireless message or broadcast:—*pl.* **ra'dios.**—*adj.* of, for, transmitted or transmitting by, electromagnetic waves.—*v.t.* and *v.i.* to communicate by wireless.—*adj.* **radioact'ive.**—*ns.* **radioactiv'ity** spontaneous disintegration, first observed in certain naturally occurring heavy elements (radium, actinium, uranium, thorium) with emission of α-rays, β-rays, and γ-rays: disintegration effected by high-energy bombardment; **radio altimeter** see **altimeter**; **radio astronomy** astronomical study by means of radar; study of radio waves generated in space; **ra'dio-beacon** apparatus that transmits signals for direction-finding; **radiobiol'ogy** the study of the effects of radiation on living tissue; **radiocar'bon** a radioactive isotope of carbon, *specif.* carbon-14 (**radiocarbon dating** a method of establishing the age of any organic material, e.g. wood, paper, by measuring content of carbon-14); **radiochem'istry** the chemistry of radioactive elements and compounds; **radio-com'pass** a radio direction-finding instrument; **radioel'ement** a radio-isotope; **radio frequency** a frequency suitable for radio transmission; **radiogoniom'eter** a radio direction-finder; **ra'diogram** an X-ray photograph, radiograph: a wireless telegram: (for **radio-gram'ophone**) a combined wireless receiver and gramophone; **ra'diograph** (*-gräf*) a recorded image, usu. a photograph, produced by X-rays: (formerly) the wireless telegraph; **radiog'rapher** a technician involved in radiology, e.g. in the taking of radiographs or in radiotherapy.—*adj.* **radiographic** (*-graf'ik*).—*ns.* **radiography** (*-og'rə-fi*) photography of interior of body or specimen by radiations other than light, as X-rays, etc.: (*formerly*) radiotelegraphy: study of radioactivity; **radio-i'sotope** a radioactive isotope of a stable element; **radioloca'tion** position-finding by radio signals: radar.—*adjs.* **radiolog'ic**, **radiolog'ical**.—*ns.* **radiol'ogist** a doctor specialising in the diagnostic use of X-rays and in other methods of imaging the internal structure of the body, now often called a **radiation oncologist**; **radiol'ogy** the study of radioactivity and radiation or their application to medicine, e.g. as X-rays, or as treatment for certain diseases; **radioluminesc'ence** luminous radiation arising from radiation from a radioactive material.—*adj.* **radiophonic** (*-fon'ik*) of music, produced electronically.—*n.sing.* **radiophon'ics.**—*adj.* **radiosen'sitive** quickly injured or changed by radiation.—*ns.* **ra'diosonde** (Fr. *sonde*, plummet, probe) apparatus for ascertaining atmospheric conditions at great heights, consisting of a hydrogen-filled balloon, radio transmitter(s), etc.; **ra'diotel'egram**, **ra'diotel'egraph**, **-teleg'raphy**, **ra'diotel'ephone**, **-teleph'ony** radio telegraph, tele-

phone etc.; **radio telescope** an apparatus for the reception and analysis and transmission in radio-astronomy of radio waves from and to outer space; **radiotherapeut'ics**, **-ther'apy** treatment of disease, esp. cancer, by radiation, as by X-rays, etc; **radio wave** an electromagnetic wave of radio frequency. [L. *rādius*, a rod, spoke, radius, ray.]

Radiolaria *rā-di-ō-lā'ri-ə*, *n.pl.* an order of marine Protozoa.—*adj.* **radiola'rian.**—Also *n.*—**radiolarian ooze** a deep-sea deposit in which the siliceous skeletons of Radiolaria predominate [L.L. *radiolus*, dim. of L. *rādius*, radius.]

radish *rad'ish*, *n.* a cruciferous plant, *Raphanus sativus* or other member of the genus: its pungent root, eaten as a salad. [Fr. *radis*—Prov. *raditz* or It. *radice*—L. *rādīx*, *-icis*, a root.]

radium *rā'di-əm*, *n.* a radioactive metallic element (Ra; at. numb. 88) discovered by the Curies in 1898, found in pitchblende and other minerals, remarkable for its active spontaneous disintegration.—**radium emanation** radon. [L. *rādius*, a ray.]

radius *rā'di-əs*, *n.* a straight line from the centre to the circumference of a circle or surface of a sphere (*geom.*): a radiating line: anything placed like a radius, as the spoke of a wheel: the outer bone (in supine position) of the forearm in man, or its homologue in other animals: a ray-flower or the ray-flowers of a head collectively: a distance from a centre, conceived as limiting an area or range:—*pl.* **radii** (*rā'di-ī*; L. *rā'di-ē*), **radiuses.**—*adj.* **ra'dial** (q.v.).—**radius vector** (*pl.* **radii vectō'res**) a straight line joining a fixed point and a variable point [L. *rādius*, a rod, spoke, ray.]

radix *rā'diks*, *n.* a source: a basis: the quantity on which a system of numeration, or of logarithms, etc., is based:—*pl.* **radices** (*rā'di-sez*, *rā-dē'kās*) [L. *rādīx*, *-icis*, root.]

radome *rā'dōm*, *n.* a protective covering for microwave antennae. [*radar dome*.]

radon *rā'don*, *n.* a gaseous radioactive element (Rn; at. numb. 86), the first disintegration product of radium—radium emanation. [**radium**, and **-on**.]

radula *rad'ū-lə*, *n* a mollusc's tongue or rasping ribbon:—*pl.* **rad'ulae** (*-lē*).—*adj.* **rad'ular**. [L. *rādula*, a scraper—*rādēre*.]

Raf *raf*, (*coll.*) *n.* the R.A.F. (Royal Air Force).

raffia *raf'i-ə*, *n.* the Raphia palm or its leaf-bast. [**Raphia**.]

raffish *raf'ish*, *adj.* rakish: flashy.—*adv.* **raff'ishly.**—*n.* **raff'ishness.** [Cf. **riff-raff**.]

raffle *raf'l*, *n.* a lottery for an article.—*v.t.* to dispose of by raffle.—*n.* **raff'ler**. [Fr *rafle*, a pair-royal.]

raft *räft*, *n.* a flat floating mass of logs or other material (ice, vegetation, etc.): a flat structure of logs, etc., for support or for conveyance on water: a wide layer of concrete to support a building on soft ground.—*v.t.* to transport on a raft: to form into a raft: to traverse by raft.—*v i.* to travel by raft: to form into a *raft.*—**rafts'man** one who works on a raft. [O.N. *raptr*, rafter]

rafter *räf'tər*, *n.* an inclined beam supporting a roof.—*v.t.* to furnish with rafters.—*adj.* **raft'ered** having (esp. visible) rafters.—*n.* **raft'ering**. [O.E *ræfter*, a beam.]

rag¹ *rag*, *n.* a worn, torn, or waste scrap of cloth: a tatter: a shred, scrap, or smallest portion: contemptuously or playfully, a flag, handkerchief, garment, newspaper: (in *pl.*) tattered clothing: ragtime, or a piece of ragtime music.—*adj.* of, for, or dealing in rags.—*v.t.* to perform in ragtime.—*adj.* **ragg'ed** shaggy: rough-edged: jagged: uneven in execution: torn or worn into rags: wearing ragged clothes.—*adv.* **ragg'edly.**—*n.* **ragg'edness.**—*adjs.* **ragg'edy**; **ragg'y**.

—**rag-and-bone′-man** one who collects or traffics in rags, bones, or other rubbish; **rag′-bag** a bag for rags and abandoned garments: a random or confused collection (*fig.*): a slattern; **rag′bolt** a bolt with barbs to prevent withdrawal; **rag′-book** a child's book mounted on cloth; **rag′-doll** a doll made of rags; **ragg′ed-Rob′in** a campion with deep-cleft petals; **ragged school** a voluntary school for destitute children (*hist.*); **ragged staff** (*her.*) a stick with branch stubs; **rag′-paper** paper made from rags; **rag′-picker** one who collects rags from bins, heaps, etc.; **rag′-tag** the rabble; **rag′time** a form of music of American Negro origin, highly syncopated in the melody: tune, song, or dance in ragtime; **rag′timer**; **rag trade** the trade concerned with designing, making and selling clothes; **rag′weed** ragwort; **rag′wheel** a toothed wheel; **rag′worm** a pearly white burrowing marine worm, used as bait by fishermen; **rag′wort** a common coarse yellow-headed composite weed of pastures.—**rag-tag and bobtail** riff-raff. [O.E. *ragg*, inferred from the adj. *raggig*, shaggy; O.N. *rögg*, shagginess, tuft.]

rag², **ragg** *rag*, *n.* a rough hard stone of various kinds, esp. one breaking in slabs: a large rough slate (3 ft. by 2).—**rag′stone**; **rag′work** undressed masonry in slabs. [Poss. from foregoing.]

rag³ *rag*, *v.t.* to rate: to banter: to assail or beset with questions, chaff, horseplay.—*v.i.* to wrangle: to indulge in a rag:—*pr.p.* **ragg′ing**; *pa.t.* and *pa.p.* **ragged** (*ragd*).—*n.* an outburst of organised horseplay, usually in defiance of authority: riotous festivity, esp. and orig. of undergraduates—now, in British universities, associated with the raising of money for charity.—*n.* **ragg′ing**.—*adj.* **ragg′y** (*slang*) irritated.—**rag day, rag week** in British universities the particular day or week during which money-making activities, processions, etc. for charity are organised.—**lose one's rag** (*coll.*) to lose one's temper. [Perh. shortened from **bullyrag**; perh. from **rag¹** as in *red rag*.]

raga *rä′gə*, *n.* a traditional Hindu musical form or mode: a piece composed in such a mode. [Sans. *rāga*, colour, tone (in music).]

ragamuffin *rag′ə-muf-in*, or *-muf′*, *n.* a ragged, disreputable boy or man. [Poss. **rag¹**.]

rage *rāj*, *n.* madness: overmastering passion of any kind, as desire or (esp.) anger: inspired frenzy: ardour: a fit of any of these: a mania or craze (for something): vogue: a thing in vogue: violence, stormy or furious activity.—*v.i.* to behave or speak with passion, esp. with furious anger: to be violent: to storm: to be prevalent and violent: to scold (with *at*).—*n.* **rā′ger**.—*adj.* **rā′ging**.—*adv.* **rā′gingly**.—**all the rage** quite the fashion. [Fr.,—L. *rabiēs*—*rabēre*, to rave.]

ragg, **ragged**(y), **raggee**, **raggy.** See **rag²**, **rag¹,³**, **ragi.**

ragi, raggee, raggy *rä′gē*, *rag′i*, *n.* a millet, much grown in India, Africa, etc. [Hind. (and Sans.) *rāgī*.]

raglan *rag′lən*, *n.* an overcoat with sleeve in one piece with the shoulder.—*adj.* of a sleeve, in one piece with the shoulder. [From Lord *Raglan* (1788–1855), commander in the Crimea.]

ragout *ra-gōō′*, *n.* a highly seasoned stew of meat and vegetables.—*v.t.* to make a ragout of. [Fr. *ragoût*— *ragoûter*, to restore the appetite.]

ragstone. See **rag².**

ragtime, ragweed, ragwheel, ragworm, ragwort. See **rag¹.**

raguly *rag′ū-li*, (*her.*) *adj.* with projections like oblique stubs of branches.—*Also* **rag′ūled.**

rah, 'rah *rä*, *interj.*, *n.*, *v.i.*, short form of **hurrah.**

raid *rād*, *n.* a sudden swift inroad, for assault or seizure: an air attack: an invasion unauthorised by government: an incursion of police: an onset or on-

slaught for the purpose of obtaining or suppressing something.—*v.t.* to make a raid on.—*v.i.* to go on a raid.—*n.* **raid′er.**—**raid the market** to derange prices artificially for future gain. [Scots form of **road** (revived by Scott)—O.E. *rād*, riding. See also **ride.**]

rail¹ *rāl*, *n.* a bar extending horizontally or at a slope between supports or on the ground, often to form a support, a fence, a guard, a track for wheels: the railway as a means of travel or transport: a horizontal member in framing or panelling (as in a door).—*v.t* to enclose or separate with rails: to furnish with rails: to send by railway.—*n.* **rail′ing** fencing: fencing materials: (often in *pl.*) a barrier or ornamental structure, usu. of upright iron rods secured by horizontal connections.—*adj.* **rail′less.**—**rail′-car** (*U.S.*) a railway carriage: a self-propelled railway carriage; **rail′card** any of various cards entitling its holder (e.g. a student, old age pensioner, etc.) to reduced train fares; **rail′-head** the furthest point reached by a railway under construction: the end of railway transport, **rail′man** a railway employee; **rail′road** (chiefly *U.S* and *Canada*) a railway.—*v.t.* (*coll.*) to force, push forward unduly, as a person into a particular course of action, a bill through parliament, etc. (orig. *U.S.*): to get rid of, esp. by sending to prison on a false charge —**rail′way** a track laid with rails for wheels to run on, esp. for locomotives with passengers and goods wagons: a system of such tracks with equipment and organisation.—*Also adj.*—**rail′way-carr′iage** a railway vehicle for passengers; **rail′way-cross′ing** an intersection of railway lines or of road and railway, esp. without a bridge.—**off the rails** disorganised: not functioning: mad: morally degenerate. [O.Fr. *reille* —L. *rēgula*, a ruler.]

rail² *rāl*, *v.i.* to scoff: to use vigorously or mockingly reproachful language: to banter: to revile (usu. with *at* or *against*).—*n.* **rail′er.**—*adj.* and *n.* **rail′ing.**— *adv.* **rail′ingly.**—*n.* **raillery** (*rāl′ər-i*) railing or mockery: banter: playful satire. [Fr. *railler.*]

rail³ *rāl*, *n.* any bird of the genus *Rallus*, esp. the water-rail, or other member of the family *Rallidae*, esp. the corncrake or land-rail. [O.Fr. *rasle* (Fr. *râle*).]

raiment *rā′mənt*, *n.* (*arch.* or *poet.*) clothing. [**arrayment.**]

rain *rān*, *n.* water from the clouds in drops: a shower: a fall of anything in the manner of rain: (in *pl.*) the rainy season.—*v.i.* to fall as or like rain: to send down rain.—*v.t.* to shower.—*n.* **rain′iness.**—*adjs.* **rain′less; rain′y.**—**rain′-bird** a bird, as the green woodpecker and various kinds of cuckoo, supposed to foretell rain; **rain′bow** the coloured bow caused by refraction and internal reflexion of light in raindrops: any similar array of colours.—*adj.* of, or coloured like, the rainbow.—*adj.* **rain′bowy.**—*adj.* **rain′bow-coloured.**—**rain′bow-trout** a finely marked and coloured Californian trout.—**rain′check** (*U.S.*) a ticket for future use given to spectators when a game or a sports meeting is cancelled or stopped because of bad weather (**take a raincheck (on)** (*coll.*, orig. *U.S*) to promise to accept an invitation at a later date); **rain′-cloud** nimbus, a dense dark sheet of cloud that may shed rain or snow; **rain′coat** a light overcoat proof against moderate rain; **rain′-doctor** a rainmaker; **rain′drop** a drop of rain.—*adj.* **rained off** of a sport, outdoor activity, etc., cancelled because of rain.—**rain′fall** a shower of rain: the amount (by depth of water) of rain that falls; **rain′-forest** tropical forest with very heavy rainfall; **rain′-gauge** an instrument for measuring rainfall; **rain′-maker** one who professes to bring rain.—*adj.* **rain′proof** more or less impervious to rain.—*v.t.* to make rainproof.—**rain′-shadow** an area sheltered by hills from the prevailing winds and having a lighter rainfall than the windward side of the hills; **rain'storm; rain'-wash** the washing away of earthy matters by rain: downward creep of superficial deposits soaked in rain: matter so transported; **rain'-water** water that falls or has lately fallen as rain.—**a rainy day** (*fig.*) a possible future time of need; **come rain or shine** whatever the weather or circumstances; **rain in** of rain, to penetrate a roof, tent, etc.; **right as rain** perfectly in order; **take a raincheck (on)** see **raincheck** above. [O.E. *regn*.]

raise *rāz*, *v.t.* to cause to rise: to make higher or greater: to lift: to advance: to elevate: to set up or upright: to rouse: to stir up: to rear, grow, or breed: to give rise to: to build, erect: to bring to life: to utter: to establish: to bring into consideration: to intensify: to call up: to cause to rise in view by approaching (*naut.*): to contact by radio: to levy, get together, collect: to cause to swell: to produce a nap on.—*n.* (*coll.*) an increase in wages or salary.—*adjs.* **rais(e)'able.**—*ns.* **rais'er; raising.—raised beach** (*geol.*) an old sea-margin above the present water-level.—**raise a hand** to hit, or generally treat badly; **raise an eyebrow, one's eyebrows** to look surprised (at); **raise a siege** to abandon, or put an end to, a siege; **raise Cain, the roof** (*coll.*) to make a lot of noise; **raise hell** (*coll.*) to make a lot of trouble (about); **raise money on** to get money by pawning or selling, esp. privately; **raise one's glass** to drink a health (to); **raise one's hat** to take one's hat off in salutation; **raise the wind** to get together the necessary money by any shift. [M.E. *reisen*—O.N. *reisa*, causative of *rīsa*, to rise; cf. **rise, rear**[3].]

raisin *rā'zn*, *n.* a dried grape. [Fr., grape—L. *racēmus*, a bunch of grapes.]

raison d'être *rā-zõ detr'*, (Fr.) reason for existence (purpose or cause).

raisonné *rā-zon-ā*, (Fr.) *adj.* logically set out, systematically arranged, and (usu.) provided with notes.

raj *rāj*, *n.* rule, sovereignty: government, esp. (with *cap.*) the British government of India, 1858–1947.— *n.* **ra'ja(h)** an Indian prince or king: a Malay chief.— *ns.* **ra'ja(h)ship; Rajput, -poot** (*rāj'pōōt*) a member of a race or class claiming descent from the original Hindu military and ruling caste. [Hind. *rāj, rājā, Rājpūt*—Sans. *rājan*, a king (cog. with L. *rēx*), *putra*, son.]

rake[1] *rāk*, *n.* a toothed bar on a handle, for scraping, gathering together, smoothing, etc.: a tool for various purposes, toothed, notched, or bladed and with long handle (e.g. croupier's implement for drawing in money): a wheeled field implement with long teeth for gathering hay, scraping up weeds, etc.: an extremely thin person or horse.—*v.t.* to scrape, smooth, clear, break up, draw, gather, remove, cover, uncover, search, ransack, with a rake or as if with a rake: to cover with ashes so as to keep smouldering: to graze, scrape: to pass over violently and swiftly: to enfilade: to take a view all over or quite through.—*v.i.* to work with or as if with a rake: to search minutely.—*n.* **rā'ker** one who rakes: a scavenger: a raking implement: in games, a long, fast, low-flying shot (perh. partly from· *dial. rake*, to range swiftly).—*n.* and *adj.* **rā'king.—rake'-off** pecuniary share, esp. unearned or illicit.—**rake up** to revive from oblivion (usu. something scandalous): to collect together. [O.E. *raca*.]

rake[2] *rāk*, *n.* a debauched or dissolute person, esp. a man of fashion.—*v.i.* to lead a rake's life: to make a practice of lechery.—*n.* **rā'kery** dissoluteness.—*adj.* **rā'kish.**—*adv.* **rā'kishly.**—*n.* **rā'kishness.** [rake-hell.]

rake[3] *rāk*, *n.* inclination from the vertical or horizon-

tal, e.g of a ship's funnel(s), a theatre stage: an angle, e.g. between the face of a cutting-tool and the surface on which it is working, or the wings and body of an aircraft.—*v.i.* to incline —*v t.* to slope: to cut aslant.—*n.* **rā'ker** a sloping shore, support —*adj.* **rā'kish** with raking masts: swift-looking: pirate-like: dashing: jaunty.—*adv.* **rā'kishly.**

rakee. See **raki.**

rakehell *rāk'hel*, *n.* an utterly debauched person.— See also **rake**[2]. [Prob. **rake**[1] and **Hell**: such as might be found by raking out hell.]

rakery. See **rake**[2].

raki *rak'ē*, *n.* a spirituous liquor used in the Levant and Greece.—Also **rak'ee.** [Turk *rāqī*.]

rakish. See **rake**[2,3].

râle, rale *ral*, (*path*) *n.* a sound from a diseased lung. [Fr.]

rallentando *ral-ən-tan'dō*, (*mus.*) *adj* and *adv.* becoming slower.—*n* a slowing:—*pl.* **rallentan'dos.** —Abbrev. **rall.** [It., pr.p. of *rallentare*, to slacken.]

rallier. See **rally**[1,2].

rally[1] *ral'i*, *v t* to reassemble: to gather to one's support: to bring together for united effort: to muster by an effort (as the faculties).—*v.i.* to come together, esp. from dispersal, or for renewed effort, or in support of a leader, friend, or cause: to recover: to recover in some degree lost health, power, vigour, value, etc.:—*pr.p.* **rall'ying;** *pa.p.* and *pa t.* **rall'ied.** —*n.* a reassembly for renewed effort: a gathering for a common purpose: a mass-meeting: a competition to test skill in driving, and ability to follow an unknown route, or to test quality of motor vehicles: a temporary or partial recovery: a quick exchange of blows in boxing: a series of to and fro strokes in deciding a point, as in tennis.—*n.* **rall'ier.—rall'ying-**cry a slogan to attract support for a cause, etc , **rall'ying-point.—rally round** to support, help someone in need. [O.Fr. *rallier*—pfx. *re-* and *allier*.]

rally[2] *ral'i*, *v t.* and *v t* to banter·—*pr.p.* **rall'ying;** *pa.t.* and *pa p.* **rall'ied.**—*n* **rall'ier.**—*adv* **rall'y-**ingly. [Fr. *railler*; cf **rail**[2].]

ram *ram*, *n.* a male sheep, a tup: Aries (*astrol.*): a battering-ram: a ship's beak for striking an enemy ship: a water-ram or hydraulic ram (see **hydraulic**): the monkey of a pile-driver: the striking head of a steam-hammer: a piston applying pressure: an act of ramming.—*v.t.* to thrust roughly, cram: to block up: to drive hard down: to strike, batter, pierce: to strike, dash into, violently:—*pr.p.* **ramm'ing;** *pa.t.* and *pa.p.* **rammed.**—*n.* **ramm'er.—ram'-jet (engine)** a simple form of aero-engine, consisting of forward air intake, combustion chamber, and rear expansion nozzle, in which thrust is generated by compression due solely to forward motion; **ram'rod** a rod for ramming down a charge or for cleaning a gun-barrel: a stern, inflexible person: a strict disciplinarian.—*adj.* rigid, inflexible: stern. [O.E. *ram, rom*.]

Ramadan, Ramadhan *ram-ə-dan'*, *n.* the Muslim month of fasting by day: the fast [Ar. *Ramadān*.]

ramal, ramate, etc See **ramus.**

Raman effect *räm'ən i-fekt'*, a change in frequency of light passing through a transparent medium—used in the study of molecules. [From Sir Chandrasekhara Raman (1888–1970), Indian physicist.]

ramble *ram'bl*, *v.i.* to wander: to walk for pleasure: to wander in mind or discourse: to be incoherent, or delirious: to straggle or trail, as a plant.—*n.* a roving about: an irregular excursion: a walk for pleasure.— *n.* **ram'bler** one who rambles: a trailing climbing plant, esp. a rose with small clustered flowers.—*n.* and *adj.* **ram'bling.—**adv. **ram'blingly.** [M.E. *romblen*; app conn. with **roam.**]

rambunctious *ram-bungk'shəs*, *adj.* difficult to control,

boisterous, exuberant.—*adv.* **rambunc'tiously.**—*n.*
rambunc'tiousness. [Perh. **rumbustious.**]
rambutan *ram-bōō'tən, n.* a lofty Malayan tree: its
hairy edible fruit. [Malay *rambūtan*—*rambut*,
hair.]
ramekin *ram'ə-kin, n.* a mixture of cheese, eggs, etc.,
baked in small moulds: a baking dish for one person.
[Fr. *ramequin*—obs. Flem. *rammeken*.]
rameous. See **ramus.**
ramie *ram'ē, n.* China grass, a plant of the nettle
family, long cultivated in China: its fibre, used for
cloth, bank-note paper, etc.: a garment thereof.
[Malay *rami*.]
ramify, etc. See under **ramus.**
rammer. See **ram.**
ramose. See under **ramus.**
ramp *ramp, v.i.* to rear: to slope from one level to
another: to range about wildly.—*v.t.* to provide with
a ramp: to hustle into paying a fictitious debt: to
swindle.—*n.* an inclined plane: a low hump made
across a road, e.g. to slow down traffic: the slope of a
wall-top or the like between two levels: an upwardly
concave bend in a handrail: a swindle: an exploitation
of a special situation to increase prices or the like.—
n. **rampáge'** turbulently or aggressively excited
behaviour or rushing about.—*v.i.* to storm: to rush
about wildly.—*adj.* **rampá'geous.**—*ns.* **rampá'geousness;** **ramp'ancy.**—*adj.* **ramp'ant** rearing: standing in profile, on the left hindleg (*her.*): unrestrained:
unchecked in growth or prevalence.—*adv.* **ramp'-
antly.**—*n.* **ramp'er.**—**on the rampage** storming
about, behaving wildly and violently in anger, exuberance, etc. [Fr. *ramper*, to creep, to clamber.]
rampart *ram'pärt, -pərt, n.* a flat-topped defensive
mound: that which defends.—*v.t.* to fortify or
surround with ramparts. [Fr. *rempart*—O.Fr.
rempar—*remparer*, to defend—L. pfx. *re-*, *ante*,
parāre, to prepare.]
rampion *ramp'yən, -i-ən, n.* a bell-flower (*Campanula
rapunculus*) whose root is eaten as a salad. [Cf. It.
raponzolo, Ger. *Rapunzel*, Fr. *raiponce*.]
ramrod. See **ram.**
ramshackle *ram'shak-l, adj.* tumbledown.
ramson *ram'zən, n.* (usu. in pl.) wild or broad-leaved
garlic. [O.E. *hramsa*, *hramse*, *hramsan* (pl.).]
ramus *rā'məs, n.* a branch of anything, esp. a nerve:—
pl. **rā'mi.**—*adjs* **rā'mal, rā'mous** of a branch;
rā'mate, ramose (*rə-mōs', rā'mōs*) branched.—*n.*
ramification (*ram-i-fi-kā'shən*) branching: arrangement of branches: a single branch or part of a complex
arrangement, or of a situation or problem, esp. a
consequence that must be taken into account.—*v.t.*
and *v.i.* **ram'ify** to divide into branches:—*pr.p.*
ram'ifying; *pa.t.* and *pa.p.* **rami'fied.**
ran *pa.t.* of **run.**
ranch *rän(t)sh, ran(t)sh, n.* a stock-farm, as in western
N. America, with its buildings and persons employed.
—*v.i.* to manage or work upon a ranch.—*ns.*
ranch'er, ranch'man. [From Amer. Sp.—Sp.
rancho, mess, mess-room.]
rancid *ran'sid, adj.* rank in smell or taste, as butter or
oil that is going bad.—*ns.* **rancid'ity, ran'cidness.**
[L. *rancidus*.]
rancour, U.S. **rancor,** *rang'kər, n.* harboured bitterness: deep-seated enmity: spite: virulence.—*adj.*
ran'corous.—*adv.* **ran'corously.** [O.Fr.,—L. *rancor, -ōris*, an old grudge—*rancēre*, to be rancid.]
rand *rand, n.* a border, margin: a ridge overlooking a
valley (*S. Afr. ront, rand*): the basic unit of the South
African decimal coinage, introduced 1961 as equivalent to ten shillings:—*pl.* **rand(s).**—**the Rand** the Wit-
watersrand goldfield. [O.E. and Du. *rand*, border.]
randan¹ *ran-dan'* or *ran', n.* a din, uproar: riotous

conduct: spree.
randan² *ran-dan'* or *ran', n.* a boat rowed by three, the
second with two oars.—Also **randan gig.**
randem *ran'dəm, n., adj.,* and *adv.* tandem with three
horses.
random *ran'dəm, adj.* haphazard, chance: uncontrolled: irregular: (of masonry) having stones of
irregular size and shape.—*v.t.* **ran'domise, -ize** to
arrange or set up so as to occur in a random manner
—*ns.* **randomisa'tion, -z-; ran'domiser, -z-.**—*advs.*
ran'domly, ran'domwise.—**random access** (*comput.*)
access to any data in a large store of information without affecting other data.—**at random** not following
any particular principle or order: haphazardly.
[O.Fr. *randon*—*randir*, to gallop.]
randy *ran'di, adj.* lustful
ranee. See **rani.**
rang *rang, pa.t.* of **ring².**
range *rānj, v.t.* to set in a row or rows: to assign a place
among others to: to classify: to arrange: to straighten,
level: to traverse freely or in all directions.—*v.i.* to lie
in a direction: to extend: to take or have a position in
a line, or alongside: to take sides: to lie evenly: to
move, have freedom of movement, occur, or vary,
within limits: to rove at large: to beat about, as for
game: to be inconstant: to have a range.—*n.* a row or
rank: a system of points in a straight line: anything
extending in line, as a chain of mountains, a row of
connected buildings: a stretch of open country, esp.
one used for grazing: line of lie: scope, compass:
movement, freedom of movement, or variation
between limits: space or distance between limits:
area, or distance within which anything moves, can
move, occurs, is possible, acts efficiently, or varies: a
place for practice in shooting: firing elevation of a
gun, etc. : an enclosed kitchen fireplace fitted with
appliances of various kinds.—*ns.* **ran'ger** a rover: a
forest or park officer: a member of a body of troops,
usu. mounted and employed in policing an area: a
soldier specially trained for raiding combat: (with
cap.) a member of a senior branch of the Girl Guide
organisation (also **Ranger Guide**): **rang'ership;
rang'iness.**—*adj.* **ran'gy** disposed or well able to
roam: roomy: long-legged and thin.—**range'finder** an
instrument for finding the distance of an object;
range, ranging, pole, rod a pole or rod used to mark
positions in surveying.—**range oneself** to side (with)
to take sides. [Fr. *ranger*, to range—*rang*, a rank.]
rani, ranee *rän'ē, fem.* of **raja.** [Hind. *rānī*—Sans.
rājñī, queen, fem. of *rājan*.]
rank¹ *rangk, n.* a row: a row of soldiers standing side by
side (opp. to *file*): any row thought of as so placed
(e.g. of squares along the player's side of a chessboard): (in *pl.*) soldiers, esp. private soldiers—often
(with *the*) private soldiers collectively: (in *pl.*) persons of ordinary grade: a row of cabs awaiting hire: a
cabstand: order, grade, or degree: an official position, esp. *mil.*: station: high standing.—*v.t.* to place
in a line: to assign to a particular class or grade: to
take rank over (*U.S.*).—*v.i.* to have a place in a rank,
grade, scale, or class.—*n.* **rank'er** one who serves or
has served as a private soldier: an officer who has
risen from the ranks.—*adj.* **rank'ing** with a high military, political, etc., position.—*n.* a position or grade.
—**pull rank** to use one's senior rank unfairly to get
one's way; **rank and file** common soldiers: ordinary
people: those in an organisation, etc. not involved in
its management. [O.Fr. *renc* (Fr. *rang*).]
rank² *rangk, adj.* coarsely overgrown: excessive (*law*):
out-and-out, arrant, utter: over-productive: offensively strong-scented or strong-tasted: gross: foul:
grossly obvious.—*adv.* **rank'ly.**—*n.* **rank'ness.**
[O.E. *ranc*, proud, strong.]

rankle *rangk'l*, *v.i.* to go on vexing, irritating, or embittering. [O.Fr. *rancler*, *raoncler*—L.L. *dra(cu)nculus*, an ulcer, dim. of L. *dracō*, dragon.]

ransack *ran'sak* (or *-sak'*), *v.t.* to search thoroughly: to plunder: to pillage.—*n.* **ran'sacker**. [O.N. *rann-saka—rann*, house, *sœkja*, to seek.]

ransom *ran'səm*, *n.* redemption from captivity: price of redemption or reclamation: expiation: an extortionate price.—*v.t.* to pay, demand, or accept ransom for: to redeem: to expiate.—*adj.* **ran'somable**.—*n.* **ran'somer**.—*adj.* **ran'somless**.—**a king's ransom** a very large sum of money; **hold to ransom** to retain until a ransom shall be paid: to hold up to gain a concession. [Fr. *rançon*—L. *redemptiō*, *-ōnis*, redemption.]

rant *rant*, *v.i.* to declaim bombastically: to storm, scold.—*v.t.* to utter declamatorily.—*n.* empty declamation: a tirade: a lively tune.—*ns.* **ran'ter** one who rants: an extravagant preacher; **ran'terism**.—*adv.* **rant'ingly**. [Obs. Du. *ranten*, to rave.]

rap¹ *rap*, *n.* a sharp blow: the sound of a knock: a crime or criminal charge (*slang*).—*v.t.* and *v.i.* to strike or knock sharply: to communicate by raps.—*v.t.* to censure, reprove: to utter sharply:—*pr.p.* **rapp'ing**; *pa.t.* and *pa.p.* **rapped**.—*n.* **rapp'er** one who raps: a door-knocker.—**beat the rap** (*U.S. slang*) to be acquitted of a crime: to avoid punishment; **take the rap** (*slang*) to take the blame or punishment, esp. in place of another. [Imit.]

rap² *rap*, *n.* an 18th-century Irish counterfeit halfpenny: as a type of worthlessness, a whit, esp. in *not worth a rap*.

rap³ *rap* (*coll.*) *n.* an informal talk, discussion, chat, etc.—*v.i.* to have a talk, discussion, etc.: to get along well, sympathise. [Perhaps from **rapport**.]

rapacious *rə-pā'shəs*, *adj.* grasping: greedy of gain: living by prey.—*adv.* **rapā'ciously**.—*ns.* **rapā'ciousness**; **rapacity** (*-pas'-*). [L. *rapāx*, *-ācis*—*rapĕre*, to seize and carry off.]

rape¹ *rāp*, *n.* seizure (*obs.*): unlawful sexual intercourse (usu. by force) with another person without that person's consent: violation, despoliation.—*v.t.* to seize and carry off (*obs.*): to commit rape upon: to ravish, violate.—*ns.* **rā'per; ra'pist**. [Prob. L. *rapĕre*, to snatch, confused with older *rap*, to snatch.]

rape² *rāp*, *n.* a plant akin to the turnip, cultivated for its herbage and oil-producing seeds: applied to various closely allied species or varieties.—**rape'-cake** refuse of rape-seed after the oil has been expressed; **rape'-oil**; **rape'-seed**. [L. *rāpa*, *rāpum*, a turnip.]

rape³ *rāp*, *n.* the refuse left after wine-making. [Fr. *râpe*.]

Raphia *rā'fi-ə*, *raf'i-ə*, *n.* a genus of handsome pinnately-leaved palms: (without *cap.*) raffia. [Malagasy.]

raphis *rā'fis*, **raphide** *rā'fīd*, *ns.* a needle-like crystal, usu. of calcium oxalate, occurring in plant cells:—*pl.* **raphides** (*raf'i-dez*, *rā'fīdz*). [Gr. *rhāphis*, *-idos*, a needle—*rhaptein*, to sew.]

rapid *rap'id*, *adj.* swift: quickly accomplished: steeply-sloping: requiring short exposure (*phot.*).—*n.* a very swift-flowing part of a river with steep descent and often broken water but no actual drop (usu. in *pl.*).—*n.* **rapidity** (*rə-pid'i-ti*).—*adv.* **rap'idly**.—*n.* **rap'idness**.—**rapid fire** the quick firing of guns, asking of questions, etc.—*adj.* **rap'id-fire**.—**rapid eye movement** (abbrev. **REM**) an observed manifestation of a phase of sleep during which dreams are particularly vivid. [L. *rapidus*—*rapĕre*, to seize.]

rapier *rā'pi-ər*, *n.* a long slender sword, suitable for thrusting. [Fr. *rapière*.]

rapine *rap'īn*, *-in*, *n.* plundering: ravishment. [L. *rapīna*—*rapĕre*, to seize.]

rapist. See **rape¹**.

rapparee *rap-ər-ē'*, *n.* a wild Irish plunderer, orig. of the late 17th. cent. [Ir. *rapaire*, half-pike, robber.]

rappee *ra-pē'*, *n.* a coarse, strong-flavoured snuff. [Fr. *râpé*, rasped, grated—*râper*, to rasp.]

rappel *rä-*, *rə-pel'*, *n.* call to arms by beat of drum: abseiling.—*v.i.* same as **abseil**:—*pr.p.* **rapelling;** *pa.t.* and *pa.p.* **rapelled'**. [Fr.]

rapper, rapping. See **rap¹**.

rapport *ra-pōr'*, *n* relation: connection: sympathy: emotional bond: spiritualistic touch. [Fr.]

rapporteur *ra-pōr-tœr'*, *n.* one whose task it is to carry out an investigation and/or draw up a report (for a committee, etc.). [Fr.—*rapporter*, to bring back.]

rapprochement *ra-prosh'mä*, *n.* a drawing together: establishment or renewal of cordial relations. [Fr.]

rapscallion *rap-skal'yən*, *n.* See **rascal**.

rapt *rapt*, *adj.* transported, enraptured, entranced: wholly engrossed. [L. *raptus*, pa.p. of *rapĕre*, to seize and carry off; partly also pa.p. of older *rap*, to snatch.]

raptor *rap'tər*, *n.* a bird of prey.—*adj.* **raptō'rial**. [L. *raptor*, *-ōris*, a plunderer—*rapĕre*, to seize.]

rapture *rap'chər*, *n.* a seizing and carrying away: extreme delight: transport: ecstasy.—*adj.* **rap'turous**.—*adv.* **rap'turously**. [rapt.]

rara avis *rā'ra ā'vis*, *rä'ra ä'wis*, (L.) a rare person or thing. [Lit., rare bird.]

rare¹ *rār*, *adj.* thin: not dense: sparse: seldom met with: uncommon: excellent: especially good: extraordinary.—*n.* **rarefac'tion** (*rār-i-*, *rar-i-*) rarefying.—*adjs.* **rarefac'tive**, **rar'efiable**.—*v.t.*, *v.i.* **rar'efy** to make, become less dense, refine:—*pr.p.* **rar'efying**; *pa.t.* and *pa.p.* **rar'efied**.—*adv.* **râre'ly** seldom: choicely: remarkably well.—*ns.* **râre'ness**; **rarity** (*râr'* or *rar'i-ti*) state of being rare: something valued for its scarcity: uncommonness.—**rare'bit** a now more common form of (*Welsh*) *rabbit*; **rare earth** an oxide of a **rare-earth element**, any of a group of metallic elements (some of them rare) closely similar in chemical properties and very difficult to separate: now more usu. a rare-earth element itself; **rare gas** inert gas. [Fr.,—L. *rārus*.]

rare² *rār*, *adj.* of meat, underdone. [older *rear*, lightly cooked, influenced by **rare¹**.]

rarebit. See **rare¹**.

raree-show *rār'ē-shō*, *n.* a show carried about in a box: a spectacle. [App. a foreign pron. of **rare show**.]

raring *rā'ring*, *adj.* eager (for), full of enthusiasm and sense of urgency, esp. in phrase **raring to go**. [rear².]

rarity. See **rare¹**.

rascal *räs'kl*, *n.* a knave, rogue, scamp: (playfully) a fellow.—*adj.* knavish.—*ns.* **ras'caldom** **ras'calism**; **rascality** (*-kal'-*); **rascallion** (*-kal'yən*), **rapscall'ion** a rascal: a low, mean wretch.—*adjs.* **ras'cal-like**, **ras'cally**. [O.Fr. *rascaille* (Fr. *racaille*), scum of the people.]

rase. See **raze**.

rash¹ *rash*, *adj.* over-hasty: wanting in caution.—*adv.* **rashly**.—*adv.* **rash'ly**.—*n.* **rash'ness**. [Cf. Dan. and Sw. *rask*.]

rash² *rash*, *n.* an eruption on the skin: a large number of instances at the same time or in the same place. [Perh. O.Fr. *rasche* (Fr. *rache*).]

rasher *rash'ər*, *n.* a thin slice of bacon. [Poss. from obs. *rash*, to slash.]

rasp¹ *räsp*, *n.* a coarse file: any similar surface: a mollusc's tongue: an insect's stridulating apparatus: a grating sound or feeling.—*v.t.* to grate as with a rasp: to grate upon: to utter gratingly.—*v.i.* to have a grating effect: to scrape, as on a fiddle.—*ns.*

rasp'atory a surgeon's rasp; **rasp'er** one who, or that which, rasps: in hunting, a difficult fence (coll.); **rasp'ing.**—adj. grating, harsh.—adv. **rasp'ingly.**—adj. **rasp'y.** [O.Fr. raspe (Fr. râpe); perh. Gmc.]

rasp² răsp, (now coll.) n. a raspberry.—n. **raspberry** (räz'bər-i) the fruit of Rubus idaeus: the plant producing it: extended to some kindred species: a sign of disapproval, esp. a noise produced by blowing hard with the tongue between the lips (slang).—adj. of, made with, or like raspberry. [Earlier raspis; origin unknown.]

rasse räs'(ə), n. a small civet. [Jav. rase.]

Rastafarian ras-tə-fär'i-ən, n. a member of a West Indian, esp. Jamaican, cult, who reject western culture and ideas and regard Haile Selassie, the former Emperor of Ethiopia, as divine.—Also **Ras'ta, Ras'taman.**—adjs. **Rastafa'rian, Rastafari** (-ä'ri). [From Haile Selassie's title and name, Ras Tafari.]

raster ras'tər, (television) n. a complete set of scanning lines appearing at the receiver as a rectangular patch of light on which the image is reproduced. [Ger., screen.—L. răstrum.]

rat¹ rat, n. any of the larger animals of the genus Mus (distinguished from mouse): extended to various kindred or superficially similar animals: a renegade, turn-coat (from the rat's alleged desertion of a doomed ship): a strike-breaker: one who works for less than recognised wages: a miserable or ill-looking specimen.—v.i. to hunt or catch rats: to desert or change sides for unworthy motives: (of a workman) to work as a rat:—pr.p. **ratt'ing;** pa.t. and pa.p. **ratt'ed.** —adj. **rat'proof.**—interj. **rats** (slang) expressing contemptuous incredulity, annoyance, etc.—ns. **ratt'er** a killer of rats, esp. a dog: one who rats; **ratt'ery** apostasy: a place where rats are kept or abound; **ratt'ing** apostasy: rat-hunting.—adjs. **ratt'ish; ratt'y** rat-like: rat-infested: angry, irritable (slang).— **rat'bag** (slang) a term of abuse: a despicable person; **rat'-catcher** a professional killer of rats; unconventional hunting garb; **rat'-catching; rat'-hole; rat'- hunting; rat'-kangaroo'** a marsupial about the size of a rabbit, akin to the kangaroo; **rat race** the scramble to get on in the world by fair means or foul; **rats'bane** poison for rats, esp. white arsenic: a name for many poisonous plants; **rat's'-tail, rat'-tail** anything like a rat's tail: a thin coherent dangling lock of hair: an excrescence on a horse's leg.—adj. **rat's'-tail, rat'- tail, rat'-tailed** having a tail like a rat: like a rat's tail: of a spoon, ridged along the back of the bowl.—**rat'- trap.**—**rat on** to inform against; **smell a rat** to have a suspicion that something is afoot. [O.E. ræt; cf. Ger. Ratte.]

rat² rat, v.t. (in imprecations) used for rot. [Cf. drat.]

rata rä'tə, n. a New Zealand tree (Metrosideros) of the myrtle genus, with hard wood. [Maori.]

ratable, rateable rä'tə-bl, adj. See rate¹.

ratafia rat-ə-fē'ə, n. a flavouring essence made with the essential oil of almonds: a cordial or liqueur flavoured with fruit-kernels: an almond biscuit or cake. [Fr.; ety. dub.]

ratan ra-tan', n. Same as rattan.

rat-a-tat rat-ə-tat'. Same as rat-tat.

ratatouille rat-ə-tōō'i, ra-ta-twē', n. a stew of tomatoes, aubergines, peppers and other vegetables [Fr.,—touiller, to stir.]

ratch rach, n. a ratchet: a ratchet-wheel.—n. **ratch'et** a pawl and/or ratchet-wheel.—**ratch'et-wheel** a wheel with inclined teeth with which a pawl engages. [Cf. Ger. Ratsche, Fr. rochet.]

rate¹ rät, n. price or cost: amount corresponding: ratio, esp. time-ratio, speed: amount determined according to a rule or basis: a standard: a class or rank, esp. of ships or of seamen: manner, mode: extent, degree: (often pl.) an amount levied by a local authority according to the assessed value of property: a clock's gain or loss in unit time.—v.t. to estimate: to value: to settle the relative rank, scale, or position of: to esteem, regard as: to deserve, be worthy of: to value for purpose of rate-paying.—v.i. to be placed in à certain class.—n. **rāt(e)abil'ity.**—adj. **rāt(e)'able.**—adv. **rāt(e)'ably.**—ns. **rāt'er** one who makes an estimate: (in composition) a ship, etc., of a given rate (as second-rater); **rāt'ing** a fixing of rates: classification according to grade: the class of any member of a crew: a sailor of such a class: the tonnage-class of a racing yacht; the proportion of viewers or listeners who are deemed to watch or listen to a particular programme or network.—**rat(e)able value** a value placed on a property, and used to assess the amount of rates payable to the local authority each year; **rate'-capping** the government's setting of a limit to local authority rate increases; **rāte'payer** one who pays a local rate. —**rate support grant** the money given by central government to local authorities to supplement the money raised by local rates. [O.Fr.,—L.L. (pro) ratā (parte), according to a calculated part—rērī, rătus, to think, judge.]

rate² rāt, v.t. to scold: to chide: to reprove. [M.E. raten; origin obscure.]

Ratel rä'təl, rà'təl, n. a badger-like genus (Mellivora) of Africa and India, akin to the gluttons: (without cap.) an animal of this genus. [Afrikaans.]

ratfink rat'fingk, (derog.) n. a mean, deceitful, despicable person.—Also adj. [rat¹, fink.]

rath räth, n. a prehistoric hill-fort. [Ir.]

rather rä'dhər, adv. more readily: more willingly: in preference: more than otherwise: more properly: somewhat, in some degree.—interj. ra'ther (some- times affectedly rà-dhûr') I should think so: yes, indeed. [Compar. of arch. rath, early; O.E. hrathor.]

ratify rat'i-fī, v.t. to approve and sanction, esp. by signature: to give validity or legality to:—pr.p. **rat'ifying;** pa.t. and pa.p. **rat'ified.**—ns. **ratifi- cā'tion; rat'ifier.** [Fr. ratifier—L. rătus, pa.p. of rērī (see rate¹), facĕre, to make.]

rating. See rate¹.

ratio rä'shi-ō, räsh'-yō, n. the relation of one thing to another of which the quotient is the measure: quotient: proportion: a portion, allowance (rare):— pl. **rā'tios.**—**inverse ratio** see inverse. [L. rătiō, -ōnis, reason—rērī, rătus, to think.]

ratiocinate rat- or rash-i-os'i-nät, v.i. to reason.—n. **ratiocinā'tion.**—adjs. **ratioc'inative, ratioc'inatory.** [L. ratiōcinārī, -ātus.]

ration ra'shən, sometimes rä', n. a fixed allowance or portion: (in pl.) food (coll.).—v.t. to put on an allowance: to supply with rations: to restrict the supply of to so much for each.—**ra'tion-book, -card** a book, card, of coupons or vouchers for rationed commodities. [Fr.,—L. ratiō, -ōnis.]

rational rash'ən-əl, adj. of the reason: endowed with reason: agreeable to reason: sane: intelligent: judicious: commensurable with natural numbers.—n. a rational being or quantity: (in pl.) rational dress, i.e. knickerbockers instead of skirts for women (hist.).—ns. **rationale** (rash-i-ō-nal', -yə-nal', -nal'i) underlying principle: a rational account: a theoretical explanation or solution; **rationalisation, -z-** (rash-nəl-ī-zā'shən).—v.t. **rat'ionalise, -ize** to make rational: to free from irrational quantities: to conform to reason: to reorganise scientifically: to interpret rationalistically: to substitute conscious reasoning for unconscious motivation in explaining: to organise (an industry) so as to achieve greater efficiency and economy.—*v i.* to think, or argue, rationally or rationalistically: to employ reason, rationalism, or rationalisation.—*ns.* **rat′ionalism** a system of belief regulated by reason, not authority: a disposition to apply to religious doctrines the same critical methods as to science and history, and to attribute all phenomena to natural rather than miraculous causes; **rat′ionalist.**—*adj.* **rationalist′ic.** —*adv.* **rationalist′ically.**—*n.* **rationality** (*rash-ən-al′i-ti*) quality of being rational: the possession or due exercise of reason: reasonableness—*adv.* **rat′ionally.**—**rational horizon** see horizon; **rational number** a number expressed as the ratio of two integers. [L. *ratiōnālis*, *-e*—*ratiō*.]

ratite *rat′īt*, *adj.* having a keel-less breastbone: of the **Ratitae** (*ra-ti′tē*), flightless birds—ostrich, rhea, emu, kiwi, etc. [L *ratis*, raft.]

ratlin, -line, -ling *rat′lin*, *n.* one of the small lines forming steps of the rigging of ships.

ratoon *rat-*, *rat-ōōn′*, *n.* a new shoot from the ground after cropping, esp. of sugar-cane or cotton.—*v.i.* to send up ratoons.—*v t.* to cut down so as to obtain ratoons [Sp. *retoño*, shoot.]

rattan, ratan *ra-tan′*, *n.* a climbing palm (*Calamus* or other) with very long thin stem: a cane made of it [Malay *rōtan*.]

rat-tat *rat′-tat′*, *n.* a knocking sound [Imit]

ratter, rattery, ratting, etc. See **rat¹**.

rattle *rat′l*, *v.i.* to make a quick succession or alternation of short hard sounds: to move along rapidly with a rattle: to chatter briskly and emptily—*v t.* to cause to rattle: to utter glibly, as by rote (often with *off*): to perform or push through to completion in a rapid, perfunctory, or noisy manner: to fluster, disconcert, irritate (*slang*)—*n* an instrument or toy for rattling: an instrument for making a whirring noise, formerly used by watchmen: a similar device used at merrymaking or other gatherings: a plant whose seeds rattle in the capsule—applied to two plants, **yellow-rattle** or **cock's-comb** and **red-rattle** or **marsh lousewort**: the rings of a rattlesnake's tail: the sound of rattling: a sound in the throat of a dying person.— *ns.* **ratt′ler** a rattlesnake (*coll.*): an excellent specimen of the kind (*coll.*); **ratt′ling.**—*adj.* smart, lively: strikingly good (*coll.*).—Also *adv.*— **ratt′lebag** a rattle or rattling apparatus; **ratt′le-brain, -head, -pate** a shallow, voluble, volatile person — *adjs* **ratt′le-brained, -headed, -pated.**—**ratt′lesnake** a venomous American viper with rattling horny rings on the tail; **ratt′le-trap** a rickety vehicle. [M E *ratelen*.]

ratty. See **rat¹**.

raucous *rö′kəs*, *adj.* hoarse, harsh.—*adv* **rau′cously.** —*n.* **rau′cousness.** [L *raucus*, hoarse]

raunchy *rön′chi*, *rän′chi*, (*slang*) *adj.* coarse, earthy: carelessly untidy, shabby —*n.* **raunch′iness.**

Rauwolfia *rö-wol′fi-ə*, *n.* a tropical genus of trees and shrubs, of which *R serpentina* and other species yield valuable drugs. [After the German botanist Leonhard *Rauwolf* (died *c.* 1600).]

ravage *rav′ij*, *v.t.* and *v.i* to lay waste: to destroy: to pillage.—*n.* devastation: ruin—*n.* **rav′ager.** [Fr. *ravager—ravir*, to carry off by force—L. *rapēre*.]

rave¹ *rāv*, *v.i.* to rage: to talk as if mad, delirious, or enraptured.—*v.t.* to utter wildly.—*n.* infatuation (*slang*): extravagant praise (*slang*)—*adj.* (*slang*) extravagantly enthusiastic: crazy.—*n.* **rā′ver** a person who raves: a lively, uninhibited person (*slang*)—*n.* and *adj.* **rā′ving.**—*adv.* **rā′vingly.**—**rave′-up** (*slang*) a lively celebration: a wild, uninhibited, thoroughly enjoyable party. [Perh. O.Fr. *raver*, which may be —L. *rabēre*, to rave.]

rave² *rāv*, *n.* a side piece of a wagon.

ravel *rav′l*, *v.t.* to entangle: to disentangle, untwist, unweave, unravel (usu. with *out*).—*v.i.* to become entangled:—*pr.p.* **rav′elling**; *pa t.* and *pa.p.* **rav′elled.**—*n.* a tangle: a broken thread.—*ns.* **rav′elling**; **rav′elment.** [App. Du. *ravelen*]

ravelin *rav′lin*, *n* a detached work with two embankments raised before the counterscarp [Fr.]

ravelment. See **ravel.**

raven¹ *rā′vn*, *n.* a large glossy black species of crow — *adj.* black as a raven. [O.E. *hræfn*; O N *hrafn*]

raven² *rav′in*, *v.t.* to devour hungrily or greedily —*v t* to prey rapaciously: to be intensely hungry: to hunger intensely (*for*).—*adjs.* **rav′enous, ravening** plundering: voracious: intensely hungry —*adv.* **rav′enously.**—*n* **rav′enousness.** [O Fr *ravine*, plunder— L. *rapīna*, plunder]

ravin *rav′in*, *n* rapine. preying [**raven²**.]

ravine *ra-vēn′*, *n* a deep, narrow gorge —*adj* **ravined′** scored with ravines: trenched [Fr ,—L *rapīna*, rapine, violence.]

ravioli *rav-i-ōl′ē*, *n* little edible pasta cases with savoury filling [It., *pl.* of *raviòlo*.]

ravish *rav′ish*, *v t* to seize or carry away by violence to abduct: to snatch away from sight or from the world· to rape to enrapture —*n* **rav′isher.**—*adj* **rav′ishing** delighting to rapture: transporting —*adv* **rav′ishingly.**—*n* **rav′ishment.** [Fr *ravir*, *ravissant* —L. *rapēre*, to seize and carry off]

raw *rö*, *adj* not altered from its natural state not cooked or dressed: unwrought. not prepared or manufactured: not refined: not corrected: not mixed: having the skin abraded or removed (also *fig*): crude· hard, harsh, cruel· untrained· red and inflamed· immature: inexperienced chilly and damp. naked — *n.* (with *the*) a skinned, sore, or sensitive place (usu with *on*): the raw state.—*adv* **raw′ish.**—*adv* **raw′ly.** —*n.* **raw′ness.**—*adjs* **raw′boned** with little flesh on the bones: gaunt, **raw′hide** of untanned leather —*n* a rope or whip of untanned leather.—**raw material** material (often in its natural state) that serves as the starting-point of a manufacturing or technical process: that out of which something is made, or makable, or may develop (*fig.*); **raw silk** natural untreated silk threads: fabric made from these —**a raw deal** harsh, inequitable treatment; **in the raw** in its natural state: naked. [O.E *hrēaw*]

ray¹ *rā*, *n.* a line along which light or other energy, or a stream of particles, is propagated: a narrow beam: a gleam of intellectual light: a radiating line or part. the radially extended fringing outer part of an inflorescence: a supporting spine in a fin —*v t* to radiate: to furnish with rays.—*v i* to radiate —*adjs* **rayed**; **ray′less.**—*n.* **ray′let** a small ray —**ray flower, floret** any of the small flowers radiating out from the margin of the flower head of certain composite plants; **ray′s fungus** a bacterium (*Actinomyces*) that forms radiating threads, some species pathogenic [O Fr *rais* (accus. *rai*)—L *radius*, a rod]

ray² *rā*, *n.* a skate, thornback, torpedo, or kindred flat-bodied elasmobranch fish [Fr. *raie*—L *raia*.]

ray³. Same as **re¹**.

raylet, etc. See **ray¹.**

rayon *rā′ən*, *n.* artificial silk (see silk). [Fr *rayon*, ray.]

raze, rase *rāz*, *v t.* to graze: to erase: to lay level with the ground.—*adj.* **razed, rased.** [Fr *raser*—L *rādēre*, *rāsum*, to scrape.]

razee *rā-zē′*, *n.* a ship cut down by reducing the number of decks. [Fr *rasé*, cut down.]

razor *rā′zər*, *n.* a keen-edged implement for shaving.— *adj.* (*fig.*) sharp, keen, precise —**rā′zor-back** a rorqual: a sharp-backed pig —*adj.* sharply ridged — **rā′zor-bill** a species of auk, with compressed bill;

ra´zor-blade; ra´zor-edge a very fine sharp edge, as that on which a balance swings. a critically balanced situation; **ra´zor-fish** a mollusc, with shell like a razor handle; **ra´zor-shell** its shell, or the animal itself, **ra´zor-strop.** [O Fr. *rasour*, see **raze²**.]

razz *raz, n.* raspberry in slang sense.—*v.t.* and *v i.* to jeer (at).

razzamatazz. See raz(z)mataz(z).

razzia *raz´ya, n.* a pillaging incursion [Fr ,—Algerian Ar. *ghâziah.*]

razzle-dazzle *raz´l-daz´l, (slang) n* a rowdy frolic or spree: dazzling show, confusion, etc —Also **razz´le.** [App. from **dazzle.**]

raz(z)mataz(z) *raz-mə-taz´,* **razzamatazz** *raz-ə-mataz´, ns.* to-do, hullabaloo: razzle-dazzle

re¹ *rā, (mus.) n* the second note of the scale in solfa notation—also anglicised in spelling as ray. [See **Aretinian.**]

re² *rē, (commercial jargon) prep.* concerning, with reference to. [L *in rē* (abl of *rēs,* thing), in the matter.]

re- *rē-, pfx.* again: again and in a different way—used so freely, esp. with verbs, that it is impossible to give a full list. [L.]

're *r,* a shortened form of **are.**

reach *rēch, v.t.* to stretch forth, hold out: to hand, pass: to succeed in touching or getting: to arrive at: to extend to: to attain to (*usu.* with *for* or *after*): to get at.—*v.i.* to stretch out the hand: to extend: to amount: to attain: to succeed in going or coming:—*pa.t.* and *pa.p.* **reached.**—*n.* act or power of reaching· extent of stretch: range, scope: a stretch or portion between defined limits, as of a stream between bends: the distance traversed between tacks (*naut.*).—*adj.* **reach´able.**—*n.* **reach´er.**—*p.adj.* **reach´ing.**—**reach´-me-down** ready-made.—*n.* (often in *pl.*) ready-made or second-hand attire. [O.E. *ræcan* (pa.t. *ræhte, rähte;* pa.p. *geræht*).]

react¹ *rē´akt´, v.t.* to act a second, etc., time.

react² *ri-akt´, v.i.* to return an impulse in the opposite direction: to act in return: to act with mutual effect: to act in resistance: to swing back in the opposite direction: to respond to a stimulus: to undergo chemical change produced by a reagent: loosely, to act, behave.—*ns.* **reac´tance** (*elect.*) the component of impedance due to inductance or capacitance; **re- ac´tant** (*chem.*) a substance taking part in a reaction; **reac´tion** action resisting other action: mutual action: an action or change in an opposite direction: backward tendency from revolution, reform, or progress: response to stimulus: the chemical action of a reagent: a physical or mental effect caused by medicines, drugs, etc.· a transformation within the nucleus of an atom: acidity or alkalinity. loosely, feeling or thought aroused by, in response to, a statement, situation, person, etc.—*adj.* **reac´tionary** of or favouring reaction, esp. against revolution, reform, etc.—*n* one who attempts to revert to past political conditions —*n.* and *adj.* **reac´tionist** reactionary.—*v.t.* **reac´tivate** to restore to an activated state.—*n* **reactiva´tion.**—*adj.* **reac´tive** of, pertaining to, reaction readily acted upon or responsive to stimulus. produced by emotional stress.—*adv.* **reac´tively.**—*ns.* **reac´tiveness, reactivity** (*rē-ak-tiv´i-ti*) **reactor** (*ri-ak´tər*) one who or that which undergoes a reaction: a device which introduces reactance into an electric circuit a container in which a chemical re-

action takes place: a nuclear reactor (see **nucleus**). [L.L. *reagère, -actum—agère,* to do.]

read *rēd, v.t.* to make out: to interpret: to look at and comprehend the meaning of written or printed words in: to understand as by interpretation of signs: to go over progressively with silent understanding of symbols or with utterance aloud of words or performance of notes: to accept or offer as that which the writer intended: to learn from written or printed matter: to find recorded. to observe the indication of: to register, indicate: to teach, lecture on: to study: to impute by inference (as to read a meaning into).—*v.i.* to perform the act of reading: to practice much reading: to study: to find mention: to give the reader an impression: to endure the test of reading: to deliver lectures: to have a certain wording:—*pa.t.* and *pa.p.* **read** (*red*).—*n* **read** (*rēd*) a spell of reading: reading-matter.—*adj.* **read** (*red*) versed in books: learned. —*ns.* **readabil´ity** (*rēd-*), **read´ableness.**—*adj.* **read´able** legible: easy to read: interesting without being of highest quality.—*adv* **read´ably.**—*ns.* **read´er** one who reads or reads much: one who reads prayers in church. a lecturer, esp. a higher grade of university lecturer: a proof-corrector: one who reads and reports on MSS. for a publisher: a reading-book, **read´ership.**—*adj.* **read´ing** addicted to reading.—*n.* perusal: study of books: public or formal recital, esp. of a bill before Parliament (see **first, second** and **third reading** below): the actual word or words that may be read in a passage of a text: the indication that can be read off from an instrument: matter for reading: an interpretation: a performer's conception of the meaning, rendering.—**read´ing-book** a book of exercises in reading; **read´ing-desk** a desk for holding a book or paper while it is read: a lectern; **read´ing-lamp** a lamp for reading by; **read´ing-room** a room for consultation, study, or investigation of books; papers, periodicals, etc , a proof-readers' room; **read´-out** output unit of a computer: data from it, printed, or registered on magnetic tape or punched paper tape: data from a radio transmitter.—**first, second** and **third reading** the three successive formal readings of a bill books before parliament, when (in Britain) it is introduced, discussed in general, and reported on by a committee; **read between the lines** to detect a meaning not expressed; **read into** to find (meanings) in a person's writing, words, behaviour, etc. which are not overtly stated and may not have been intended; **read off** to take as a reading from an instrument; **read out** to read aloud: to retrieve data from a computer, etc.: **read someone's mind** to guess accurately what someone is thinking; **read up** to amass knowledge of by reading. [O.E. *rædan* to discern, read—*ræd,* counsel.]

ready *red´i, adj.* prepared: willing: inclined: dexterous: prompt: handy: at hand: immediately available: direct.—*adv.* readily (in *compar.* and *superl.,* **read´ier, read´iest**).—*n.* (usu. with *the*) the position of a firearm ready to be fired: ready money (*slang*). time of, or for, making ready (*coll.*).—*v.t.* to make (*usu.* oneself) ready.—*adv.* **read´ily.**—*n.* **read´iness.** —**ready-, ready-to-** in composition, ready to, as in **read´y-mix, read´y-to-eat´, read´y-to-sew´ read´y-to- wear´**, etc.—*adj.* **read´y-made** made before sale, not made to order.—*n.* a ready-made article, esp. a garment.—**ready money** money ready at hand: cash — *adjs.* **read´y-money** paying, or for payment, in money

---

reaccus´tom *v t*

reacquaint´ *v.t.*

reacquaint´ance *n.*

reacquire´ *v.t.*

readapt´ *v.t.*

readapta´tion *n.*

readdress´ *v.t.*

readjust´ *v.t.*

readjust´ment *n.*

readmissa´ion *n.*

readmit´ *v.t.*

readmitt´ance *n.*

readopt´ *v.t*

readop´tion *n.*

read´vertise *v.t.* and *v.t.*

---

on the spot: **read'y-moneyed, -monied** having, or of the nature of, ready money.—**ready reckoner** a book of tables giving the value of so many things at so much each, and interest on any sum of money from a day upwards.—*adj.* **read'y-witted.**—**ready, steady, go!** words used by the starter of a race to the competitors [O.E. (ge)-*ræde*.]

reagent rē-ā'jənt, *n* a substance with characteristic reactions, used as a chemical test —*n.* **reā'gency.** [See **react.**]

real[1] rē'əl, ri', *adj.* actually existing: not counterfeit or assumed: true: genuine· sincere: authentic. per taining to things fixed, as lands or houses (*law*).—*adv.* (*coll·*, *U.S.*, *Scot·*) really, quite.—*adj.* **reall'-sable, -z-** (or rē').—*adj.* (or -li-).—*v.t.* rē'alise, -ize to make real, or as if real: to bring into being or act: to accomplish: to convert into real property or money. to obtain, as a possession: to feel strongly. to comprehend completely: to bring home to one's own experience: to provide the drawings for an animated cartoon.—*n.* rē'aliser, -z-.—*adj.* rē'alising, -z-.—*ns.* rē'alism the mediaeval doctrine that general terms stand for real existences—opp. to *nominalism*: the doctrine that in external perception the objects immediately known are real existences: the tendency to look to, to accept, or to represent things as they really are (often in their most ignoble aspect): literalness and precision of detail, with the effect of reality: the taking of a practical view in human problems; rē'alist.—*adj.* **realist'ic** pertaining to the realists or to realism: life-like.—*adv.* **realist'ically.**—*n.* **reality** (ri-al'i-ti, or rē-) the state or fact of being real: that which is real and not imaginary: truth: verity: the fixed permanent nature of real property (*law*).—*adv.* rē'ally in reality: actually· in truth —*ns.* rē'alness; **Realtor**©, rē'altor (*U.S.*), irregularly formed) an agent for the buying and selling of landed property, esp. one who is a member of the National Association of Real Estate Boards; rē'alty (*law*) land, with houses, trees, minerals, etc., thereon: the ownership of, or property in, lands—also **real estate.**—**real ale, beer** beer which continues to ferment and mature in the cask after brewing.—*adj.* **re'al-estate'** concerned with or dealing in property in land.—**real number** any rational or irrational number; **real presence** see **presence.**—*adj.* **real'time** (*comput.*) of or relating to a system in which the processing of data occurs as it is generated.—**for real** (*slang*) in reality: intended to be carried out or put into effect; **the real Mackay, McCoy** the genuine article, esp. good whisky (the expression has been variously explained). [L.L. *reālis* —L. *rēs*, a thing.]

real[2] rē'əl, (*obs.*) *adj.* royal.—**real tennis** royal tennis, or tennis properly so called, not lawn-tennis (also **court tennis**). [O.Fr.,—L. *rēgālis*, royal.]

real[3] rā-äl', rē'əl, *n.* a quarter of a peseta: a former Spanish coin, one-eighth of a dollar. [Sp.,—L. *rēgālis*, royal.]

realgar ri-al'gär, -gər, *n.* a bright red monoclinic mineral, arsenic monosulphide [Mediaeval L.—Ar. *rahj-al-ghār*, powder of the mine or cave.]

realign rē-ə-līn', *v.t.* to align afresh: to group or divide on a new basis.—*n.* **realign'ment.** [Pfx. re-.]

realise, etc. See **real**[1].

really. See **real**[1].

realm relm, *ns.* a kingdom: a domain, province, region.—*adj.* **realm'less.** [O.Fr. *realme*—L *rēgālis*, royal.]

realpolitik rä-äl'po-lē-tēk', *n.* practical politics based on the realities and necessities of life, rather than moral or ethical ideas. [Ger·]

realty. See **real**[1].

ream[1] rēm, *n.* 20 quires: (in *pl.*) a large quantity (*coll.*) —**printer's ream** 516 sheets of paper [Ar. *rizmah*, a bundle.]

ream[2] rēm, *v.t.* to enlarge the bore of.—*n.* **ream'er** a rotating instrument for enlarging, shaping, or finishing a bore —**ream'ing-bit.** [Apparently O.E. *rȳman*, to open up, to make room—*rūm*, room.]

reanimate rē-an'i-māt, *v t.* to restore to life: to infuse new life or spirit into.—*v.i.* to revive —*n.* **reanimā'tion.** [Pfx. re-.]

reap rēp, *v.t.* to cut down, as grain: to clear by cutting a crop: to derive as an advantage or reward. —*n* **reap'er** one who reaps: a reaping-machine.— **reap'ing-hook** a sickle; **reap'ing-machine.** [O.E. *rīpan* or *rīpan.*]

rear[1] rēr, *n.* the back or hindmost part or position, especially of an army or fleet: a position behind: the buttocks (*euph.*): a latrine (*slang*).—*adj.* placed behind: hinder.—*adjs.* **rear'most** last of all; **rear'ward** in or toward the rear.—*adv.* backward: at the back.—**rear-ad'miral** an officer next below a vice-admiral—orig. one in command of the rear; see **rear'-guard** (O.Fr. *rereguarde*) the rear of an army: a body of troops protecting it; **rear'-lamp, -light** a light carried at the back of a vehicle; **rear-view mirror** a mirror that shows what is behind a vehicle.—**bring up the rear** to come last (in a procession, etc.). [Aphetic for **arrear**; also partly from O.Fr. *rere* (Fr *arrière*).]

rear[2] rēr, *v.t.* to raise, cause or help to rise: to set up: to erect: to build up: to hold up: to bring up: to breed and foster.—*v.i.* to rise on the hind-legs. —*n.* **rear'er.** [O.E. *rǣran*, to raise, causative of *rīsan*, to rise.]

reason rē'zn, *n.* ground, support, or justification of an act or belief: a premise, esp. when placed after its conclusion: a motive or inducement: an underlying explanatory principle: a cause: the mind's power of drawing conclusions and determining right and truth: the exercise of this power: sanity: conformity to what is fairly to be expected or called for: moderation.— *v.i.* to exercise the faculty of reason: to deduce inferences from premises: to argue: to debate.—*v.t.* to examine or discuss: to debate: to think out: to set forth logically: to bring by reasoning.—*adj* **rea'sonable** endowed with reason: rational: acting according to reason: agreeable to reason: just: not excessive: not expensive: moderate.—*n.* **rea'sonableness.**— *adv·* **rea'sonably.**—*adj.* **rea'soned** argued out.—*ns.* **rea'soner**; **rea'soning.**—*adj.* **rea'sonless.**—**by reason of** on account of: in consequence of; **it stands to reason** it is obvious, logical; **listen to reason** listen to, and take heed of, the reasonable explanation, course of action, etc.; **pure reason** reason absolutely independent of experience; (**with**)**in reason** within the bounds of what is possible, sensible, etc. [Fr. *raison* —L. *ratiō, -ōnis—rērī, rātus*, to think.]

reassure *rē-ə-shōōr'*, *v.t.* to assure anew: to reinsure: to give confidence to: to confirm.—*ns.* **reassur'ance**; **reassur'er**.—*adj.* **reassur'ing**.—*adv.* **reassur'ingly**. [Pfx. re-.]

Réaumur *rā-ō-mūr*, *adj.* of a thermometer or thermometer scale, having the freezing-point of water marked 0° and boiling-point 80°. [From the French physicist, R. A. F. de *Réaumur* (1683–1757), who introduced the scale.]

reave, also (orig. *Scot.*) **reive** *rēv*, *v.t.* and *v.i.* to plunder: to rob:—*pa.t.* and *pa.p.* **reft**.—*n.* **reav'er**, **reiv'er**. [O.E. *rēafian*, to rob; cf. Ger. *rauben*, to rob.]

reback *rē-bak'*, *v.t.* to put a new back on. [Pfx. re-.]

rebarbative *ri-bärb'ə-tiv*, *adj.* repellent. [Fr. *rébarbatif—barbe*, beard.]

rebate[1] *ri-bāt'*, *v.t.* to reduce: to blunt: to repay a part of: to diminish by removal of a projection (*her.*).—*n.* (or *rē'*) discount: repayment or drawback. [Fr *rabattre*, to beat back—pfx. re- and *abattre*, to abate.]

rebate[2] *rē'bāt*, *rab'it*. Same as **rabbet**.

rebec. See rebeck.

rebeck, rebec *rē'bek*, *n.* a mediaeval instrument of the viol class shaped like a mandoline. [O.Fr. *rebec*—Ar. *rebāb*, *rabāb* (change of ending unexplained).]

rebel *reb'(ə)l*, *n.* one who rebels: one who resents and resists authority or grievous conditions: one who refuses to conform to the generally accepted modes of behaviour, dress, etc.—*adj.* rebellious.—*v.i.* (*ri-bel'*) to renounce the authority of the laws and government, or to take up arms and openly oppose them: to oppose any authority: to revolt: to offer opposition: to feel repugnance:—*pr.p.* **rebell'ing**; *pa.t.* and *pa.p.* **rebelled'**.—*adv.* **reb'el-like** (*Shak*).—*n.* **rebell'ion** (*-yən*) act of rebelling: revolt.—*adj.* **rebell'ious** engaged in rebellion: characteristic of a rebel or rebellion: inclined to rebel: refractory.—*adv.* **rebell'iously**.—*n.* **rebell'iousness**. [Fr. *rebelle*—L. *rebellis*, insurgent—pfx. re-, *bellum*, war.]

rebid *rē-bid'*, *v.t.* and *v.i.* to bid again, esp. (*bridge*) on the same suit as a previous bid.—*n.* a renewed bid, esp. on one's former suit. [Pfx. re-.]

rebind *rē'bīnd'*, *v.t.* to give a new binding to: to bind again:—*p. adj.* **rē'bound'**. [Pfx. re-.]

rebirth *rē-bûrth'*, *n.* reincarnation: revival of, e.g. an interest: spiritual renewal. [Pfx. re-.]

rebore *rē'bōr'*, *-bôr'*, *v.t.* to bore again (the cylinder of a car engine) so as to clear it.—Also *n.* [Pfx. re-.]

reborn *rē-bôrn'*, *p.adj.* born again q.v..

rebound[1]. See **rebind**.

rebound[2] *ri-bownd'*, *v.i.* to bound back from collision: to spring back (*lit.* and *fig.*): to re-echo: to recover quickly after a setback.—*n.* (*rē'*) act of rebounding. —**on the rebound** after bouncing: while reacting against a setback, disappointment, etc. [Fr. *rebondir*.]

rebuff *ri-buf'*, *n.* a sudden check: unexpected refusal: snub.—*v.t.* to check: to repulse: to snub. [O.Fr. *rebuffe*—It *ribuffo*, a reproof—It. *ri-* (=L. *re-*), back, *buffo*, puff.]

rebuke *ri-būk'*, *v.t.* to reprove sternly.—*n.* a reproach: stern reproof, reprimand.—*adj.* **rebūk'able**.—*n.* **rebūk'er**.—*adv.* **rebūk'ingly**. [A.Fr. *rebuker* (O.Fr. *rebucher*)—pfx. re-, *bucher*, to strike.]

rebus *rē'bəs*, *n.* an enigmatical representation of a word or name by pictures punningly representing parts of the word, as in a puzzle or a coat of arms:— *pl.* **re'buses**. [L. *rēbus*, by things, abl. pl. of *rēs*, thing.]

rebut *ri-but'*, *v.t.* to drive back: to repel: to meet in argument or proof: to refute:—*pr.p.* **rebutt'ing**; *pa.t.* and *pa.p.* **rebutt'ed**.—*adj.* **rebutt'able**.—*ns.* **rebutt'al**; **rebutt'er**. [O.Fr. *rebo(u)ter*, *rebuter*, to repulse.]

recal. See recall.

recalcitrance *ri-kal'si-trəns*, *n.* repugnance or opposition: refractoriness.—*adj.* **recal'citrant** refractory: obstinate in opposition. [L. *recalcitrāre*, to kick back—*calx*, *calcis*, the heel.]

recalesce *rē-kal-es'*, *v.t.* to show anew a state of glowing heat —*n.* **recales'cence** (*phys.*) the renewed glowing of iron at a certain stage of cooling from white-heat.—*adj.* **recales'cent**. [L. *re-*, again, *calēscēre*, to grow hot.]

recall (rarely **recal**) *ri-köl'*, *v.t.* to call back: to command to return: to bring back as by a summons: to remove from office by vote (*U.S.*): to revoke: to call back to mind.—*n.* act, power, or possibility of recalling or of revoking: a signal or order to return: a right of electors to dismiss an official by a vote (*U.S.*): remembrance of things learned or experienced, esp. in the phrase **total recall**, (power of) remembering accurately in full detail.—*adj.* **recall'able** capable of being recalled. [Pfx. re-.]

recant *ri-kant'*, *v.t.* to retract.—*v.i.* to revoke a former declaration: to unsay what has been said, esp. to declare one's renunciation of one's former religious belief.—*ns.* **recantā'tion** (*rē-*); **recant'er** (*ri-*). [L. *recantāre*, to revoke—*cantāre*, to sing, to charm.]

recap *rē-kap'*. Short for **recapitulate** and **recapitulation**.

recapitulate *rē-kə-pit'ū-lāt*, *v.t.* to go over again the chief points of: to go through in one's own life-history the stages of—*n* **recapitulā'tion** act of recapitulating: summing up: the reproduction, in the developmental stages of an individual embryo, of the evolutionary stages in the life-history of the race or type (*biol.*): the final repetition of the subjects in sonata form after development.—*adjs.* **recapit'ulative**; **recapit'ulatory**. [L. *recapitulāre*, *-ātum—re-*, again, *capitulum*, heading, chapter—*caput*, head.]

recapture *rē-kap'chər*, *v.t.* to capture back, as a prize from a captor: to recover by effort.—*n.* act of retaking: recovery.—*n.* **recap'turer**. [Pfx. re-.]

recast *rē-käst'*, *v.t.* to cast or mould anew: to reconstruct: to reassign parts in a theatrical production: to give (an actor) a different part:—*pa.t.* and *pa.p.* **recast'**.—*n.* (*rē'kast*, *rē-kast'*) shaping anew: that which has been shaped anew [Pfx. re-.]

recce *rek'i*, (*mil. slang*) *n.* reconnaissance.

recede *ri-sēd'*, *v i.* to go back, go farther off, become more distant: to go, draw, back (from): to grow less, decline: to bend or slope backward: to give up a claim, renounce a promise, etc.—*adj.* **reced'ing**. [L. *recēdēre*, *recēssum—re-*, back, *cēdēre*, to go, yield.]

re-cede, recede *rē'sēd'*, *v.t.* to cede again or back [Pfx re-.]

receipt *ri-sēt'*, *n.* receiving: place of receiving: a written acknowledgment of anything received: that which is received: a recipe, esp. in cookery (*arch.*).—*v.t.* to mark as paid: to give a receipt for (usu. *U.S.*).

rēassem'ble *v.t.* and *v.i.*
rēassem'bly *n.*
rēassert' *v.t.*
rēasser'tion, *n.*
rēassess', *v.t.*
rēassess'ment, *n.*

rēassign', *v.t.*
rēassign'ment, *n.*
rēattach' *v.t.* and *v.i.*
rēattach'ment *n.*
rēawake' *v.t.* and *v.i.*
rēawak'en *v.t.* and *v.i.*

rēawak'ening *n.*
rēbroad'cast *v.t.* and *n.*
rēbuild' *v.t.*
rēbur'ial *n.*
rēbur'y *v.t.*
rēbutt'on *v.t.*
rēcal'culate *v t.*

[O.Fr. *receite, recete* (Fr. *recette*)—L. *recepta*, fem. pa.p. of *recipère*, to receive, with *p* restored after L.]
receive *ri-sēv'*, *v.t.* to take, get, or catch, usu. more or less passively: to have given or delivered to one: to experience: to take in or on: to admit: to accept: to meet or welcome on entrance: to harbour: to await in resistance: to experience, or learn of, and react towards: to take into the body: to buy, deal in, (stolen goods): to be acted upon by, and transform, electrical signals.—*v.i.* to be a recipient: to participate in communion: to receive signals: to hold a reception of visitors.—*ns.* **receivabil'ity**, **receiv'ableness**.—*adj.* **receiv'able**.—*adj.* **received'** generally accepted.—*ns.* **receiv'er** one who receives: an officer who receives taxes: a person appointed by a court to manage property under litigation, receive money, etc.: one who receives stolen goods (*coll.*): a vessel for receiving the products of distillation, or for containing gases (*chem.*): an instrument by which electrical signals are transformed into audible or visual form, as a telephone receiver: a receiving-set; **receiv'ership** the state of being in the control of a receiver: the office or function of a receiver.—*n.* and *adj.* **receiv'ing.**—**Received (Standard) English** the English generally spoken by educated British people and considered the standard of the language; **Received Pronunciation** the particular pronunciation of British English which is generally regarded as being least regionally limited, most socially acceptable, and is considered the standard; **receiv'er-gen'eral** an officer who receives revenues; **receiv'ing-house** a depot: a house where letters, etc., are left for transmission; **receiv'ing-order** an order putting a receiver in temporary possession of a debtor's estate, pending bankruptcy proceedings; **receiv'ing-set** apparatus for receiving wireless communications.—**official receiver** an official appointed by the Department of Trade and Industry to manage the estate of a person, company, etc. declared bankrupt, until a trustee has been appointed. [A.Fr. *receivre* (Fr. *recevoir*)—L. *recipère*, *receptum*—*re-*, back, *capère*, to take.]

recency. See recent.
recension *ri-ken'shan*, *n.* a critical revision of a text: a text established by critical revision: a review. [L. *recēnsiō, -ōnis*—*re-*, again, and *cēnsēre*, to value, to assess.]
recent *rē'sant*, *adj.* of late origin or occurrence: fresh. modern: (*cap.*) of the present geological period—Post-Glacial.—*n.* **rē'cency**.—*adv.* **rē'cently**.—*n.* **rē'centness**. [L. *recēns, recentis.*]
receptacle *ri-sep'ta-kl*, *n.* that in which anything is or may be received or stored: the enlarged end of an axis bearing the parts of a flower or the crowded flowers of an inflorescence: in flowerless plants a structure bearing reproductive organs, spores, or gemmae.—*n.* **receptibil'ity** (*ri-*).—*adj.* **recept'ible**.—*ns.* **reception** (*ri-sep'shan*) the act, fact, or manner of receiving or of being received: taking in: act or manner of taking up signals: the quality of received radio or television signals: a formal receiving, as of guests: the part of a hotel, suite of offices, etc., where visitors, guests, etc. are received: a reception room: treatment on coming; **recep'tionist** one employed to receive callers, hotelguests, patients, customers, or the like, and make arrangements.—*adj.* **recep'tive** capable of receiving: quick to receive or take in esp. ideas: pertaining to reception or receptors.—*ns.* **recep'tiveness**, **receptivity** (*res-ep-tiv'i-ti*); **recep'tor** a receiver: an organ adapted for reception of stimuli.—**reception centre** a building, etc., where people are received for immediate assistance, as in the case of drug-addicts,

or victims of fire, etc.; **reception order** an order for the reception and detention of a person in a mental hospital; **reception room** a room for formal receptions: any public room in a house. [L. *recipère, receptum*, to receive.]

recess *rē-ses'*, *n.* a going back or withdrawing: remission of business: a break during a school day: part of a room formed by a receding of the wall: a niche or alcove: an indentation: a retired spot: a nook.—*v.t.* to make a recess in: to put into a recess.—*v.i.* to adjourn.—*adj.* **recessed'**.—*ns.* **recession** (*ri-sesh'an*) act of receding: withdrawal: the state of being set back: a temporary decline in trade; **recessional** (*ri-sesh'an-al*) hymn sung during recession or retirement of clergy and choir after a service.—*adjs.* **reces'sional**; **recessive** (*-ses'*) tending to recede: of an ancestral character, apparently suppressed in cross-bred offspring in favour of the alternative character in the other parent, though it may be transmitted to later generations (*genetics*; also *n.*): of accent, tending to move toward the beginning of the word.—*adv.* **reces'sively**.—*n.* **reces'siveness**.—**recessed arch** one arch within another. [See **recede.**]
recession[1] *rē-sesh'an*, *n.* a ceding again or back. [Pfx. **re-**.]
recession[2]. See recess.
réchauffé *rā-shō'fā*, *n.* a warmed-up dish: a fresh concoction of old material. [Fr.]
recherché *ra-sher'shā*, *adj* carefully chosen: particularly choice: rare or exotic. [Fr.]
recidivism *ri-sid'i-vizm*, *n.* the habit of relapsing into crime.—*n.* **recid'ivist**. [Fr. *récidivisme*—L. *recidivus*, falling back.]
recipe *res'i-pi*, *n.* directions for making something, esp. a food or drink: a method laid down for achieving a desired end:—*pl.* **rec'ipes**. [L. *recipe*, take, imper. of *recipère*.]
recipient *ri-sip'i-ant*, *adj.* receiving: receptive.—*n.* one who or that which receives.—*ns.* **recip'ience**, **recip'iency**. [L. *recipiēns, -entis*, pr.p. of *recipère*, to receive.]
reciprocal *ri-sip'rō-kl*, *adj.* acting in return: mutual: complementary: inverse: alternating: interchangeable: giving and receiving or given and received: expressing mutuality (*gram.*): reflexive.—*n.* that which is reciprocal: the multiplier that gives unity (*math.*).—*n.* **reciprocality** (*-kal'i-ti*).—*adv.* **recip'rocally**.—*v.t.* **recip'rocate** to give and receive mutually: to requite: to interchange: to alternate.—*v.i.* to move backward and forward: to make a return or interchange (*coll.*).—*n.* **reciproca'tion**.—*adj.* **recip'rocative**.—*ns.* **recip'rocator**; **reciprocity** (*res-i-pros'i-ti*) mutual relation: concession of mutual privileges or advantages, esp. mutual tariff concessions.—**recip'rocating-en'gine** an engine in which the piston moves to and fro in a straight line. [L. *reciprocus*.]
recite *ri-sīt'*, *v.t.* to repeat from memory: to declaim: to narrate: to give (the details of): to repeat to a teacher (*U.S.*).—*v.i.* to give a recitation: to repeat a lesson (*U.S.*).—*ns.* **recit'al** act of reciting: setting forth: enumeration: narration: a public performance of music, usu. by one performer, or one composer: that part of a deed which recites the circumstances (*law*); **recitation** (*res-i-tā'shan*) act of reciting: a piece for declaiming: the repeating or hearing of a prepared lesson (*U.S.*); **recitative** (*-ta-tēv'*) a style of song resembling speech in its succession of tones and freedom from melodic form: a passage to be sung in this manner.—*adj.* in the style of recitative.—*n.* **reciter** (*ri-sīt'ar*).—**recit'ing-note** the note on which,

in a Gregorian chant, the greater part of a verse is sung. [L. *recitāre—citāre, -ātum*, to call.]

reck *rek*, (usu. with a negative) *v.t.* to care about, heed: (used *impers.*) to concern.—*v.i.* (usu. with *of*) to care, concern oneself: (used *impers.*) to matter:—*pa.t.* and *pa.p.* **recked**.—*adj.* **reck'less** careless: heedless of consequences: rash.—*adv.* **reck'lessly**.—*n.* **reck'lessness**. [O.E. *reccan, rēcan*; cf. O.H.G *ruoh*, care, Ger. *ruchlos*, regardless.]

reckon *rek'n, -ən, v.t.* to count: to calculate (often with *up*): to include (in an account): to place or class: to estimate, judge to be: to think, believe, suppose, or expect.—*v.i.* to calculate: to judge: to go over or settle accounts (with): to concern oneself (with): to count or rely (on, upon).—*ns.* **reck'oner**; **reck'oning** counting: calculation, esp. of a ship's position: a bill: settlement of accounts: judgment. [O.E. *gerecenian*, to explain; Ger. *rechnen*.]

reclaim *ri-klām', v.t.* to win back: to win from evil, wildness, waste, submersion: (*rē-klām'*) to claim back.—*n.* recall: possibility of reform.—*adj.* **reclaim'able**.—*adv.* **reclaim'ably**.—*ns.* **reclaim'ant**; **reclaim'er**. [O.Fr. *reclamer*—L. *reclāmāre*.]

reclamation *rek-lə-mā'shən, n.* act of reclaiming: state of being reclaimed. [L. *reclāmātiō, -ōnis—reclāmāre—clāmāre*, to cry out.]

réclame *rā-klām, n.* art or practice by which publicity or notoriety is secured: publicity. [Fr.]

recline *ri-klīn', v.t.* to lay on the back: to incline or bend (properly backwards).—*v.i.* to lean in a recumbent position, on back or side.—*adjs.* **reclī'nable**; **reclinate** (*rek'li-nāt*) bent down or back.—*n.* **reclinā'tion** (*rek-li-*).—*adj.* **reclined'**.—*n.* **reclī'ner** someone or something that reclines, esp. a type of easy chair with a back that can be lowered towards a horizontal position.—*adj.* **reclī'ning**. [L. *reclināre, -ātum—clināre*, to bend.]

recluse *ri-klōōs', adj.* enclosed, as an anchorite: secluded: retired: solitary.—*n.* a religious devotee who lives shut up in a cell: one who lives retired from the world.—*n.* **reclusion** (*-klōō'zhən*).—*adj.* **reclu'sive** (*-siv*). [L. *reclūsus*, pa.p. of *reclūdere*, to open, in later Latin, shut away—*re-*, back, away, *claudēre*.]

recognise, -ize *rek'əg-nīz, v.t.* to know again: to identify as known or experienced before: to show sign of knowing (a person): to see, acknowledge, the fact of: to acknowledge (that): to acknowledge the validity of (a claim): to acknowledge the status or legality of (e.g. a government): to reward (meritorious conduct).—*adj.* **recognis'able, -z-** (or *rek'*).—*adv.* **recognis'ably, -z-** (or *rek'*).—*ns.* **recognisance, -z-** (*ri-kog'ni-zəns, ri-kon'*) a legal obligation entered into before a magistrate to do, or not to do, some particular act: money pledged for the performance of such an obligation; **recogniser, -z-** (*rek'əg-nīz-ər*, or *-nīz'ər*); **recognition** (*rek-əg-nish'ən*) act of recognising: state of being recognised: acknowledgment: acknowledgment of status: a sign, token, or indication of recognising.—*adjs.* **recognitive** (*ri-kog'*), **recog'nitory**. [L. *recognōscēre* and O.Fr. *reconoistre, reconoiss-*; see **cognition**.]

recoil *ri-koil' v.i.* to start back: to stagger back: to shrink in horror, etc.: to rebound: to kick, as a gun.—*n.* a starting or springing back: rebound: the kick of a gun: change in motion of a particle caused by ejection

of another particle, or (*sometimes*) by a collision (*nuc.*).—*n.* **recoil'er**.—*adj.* **recoil'less**. [Fr. *reculer—cul*—L. *cūlus*, the hinder parts.]

recollect¹ *rek-əl-ekt', v.t.* to recall to memory: to remember, esp. by an effort: to recall to the matter in hand, or to composure or resolution (usu. *refl.*).—*adj.* **recollect'ed**.—*adv.* **recollect'edly**.—*ns.* **recollect'edness; recollec'tion** (*rek-*) act or power of recollecting: a memory, reminiscence: a thing remembered.—*adj.* **recollec'tive**. [L. *recolligĕre*, to gather again or gather up—*colligĕre*; see **collect**.]

recollect², re-collect *rē'kol-ekt', v.t.* to gather together again. [Pfx. **re-** and **collect**.]

recombine *rē-kəm-bīn', v.t.* and *v.i.* to join together again.—*adj.* and *n.* **recombinant** (*ri-kom'bi-nənt*).—*n.* **recombinā'tion**.—**recombinant DNA** genetic material produced by the combining of DNA molecules from different organisms. [Pfx. **re-**.]

recommend *rek-ə-mend', v.t.* to commend or introduce as suitable for acceptance, favour, appointment, or choice: to make acceptable: to advise.—*adj.* **recommend'able**.—*adv.* **recommend'ably**.—*r* **recommendā'tion**.—*adj.* **recommend'atory**.—*n.* **recommend'er**. [Pfx. **re-**.]

recompense *rek'əm-pens, v.t.* to return an equivalent to or for: to repay.—*n.* (formerly **recompence**) return of an equivalent: that which is so returned: requital. [O.Fr. *recompenser*—L. *compēnsāre*, to compensate.]

reconcile *rek'ən-sīl, v.t.* to restore or bring back to friendship or union: to bring to agreement or contentment: to pacify: to make, or to prove consistent.—*n.* **rec'oncilability** (or *-sīl'*).—*adj.* **rec'oncilable** (or *-sīl'*).—*n.* **rec'oncilableness** (or *-sīl'*).—*adv.* **rec'oncilably** (or *-sīl'*).—*ns.* **rec'oncilement** (or *-sīl'*); **rec'onciler; reconcilā'tion** (*-sil-*).—*adj.* **reconciliatory** (*-sil'i-ə-tər-i*). [L. *reconciliāre, -ātum—conciliāre*, to call together.]

recondite *ri-kon'dīt, rek'ən-dīt, adj.* hidden: obscure: abstruse: profound. [L. *recondĕre, -itum*, to put away—*re-*, again, *condĕre*, to establish, store.]

recondition *rē-kən-dish'ən, v.t.* to repair and refit: to restore to original or sound condition. [Pfx. **re-**.]

reconnaissance *ri-kon'i-səns, n.* reconnoitring: a preliminary survey.

reconnoitre, in U.S. usu. **reconnoiter** *rek-ə-noi'tər, v.t.* to examine with a view to military operations or other purpose.—*v.i.* to make preliminary examination.—*n.* a reconnaissance.—*n.* **reconnoi'trer**. [Fr. *reconnoître* (now *reconnaître*)—L. *recognōscĕre*, to recognise.]

reconstitute *rē-kon'sti-tūt, v.t.* to constitute anew: to restore the constitution of (esp. dried foods).—*adj.* **reconstit'uent** (*-kən-*).—*n.* **reconstitū'tion**. [Pfx. **re-**.]

reconstruct *rē-kən-strukt', v.t.* to construct again: to rebuild: to remodel: to restore in imagination or theory.—*n.* **reconstruc'tion** the act of reconstructing: a thing reconstructed: reorganisation: a model representing a series of sections: a theoretical representation or view of something unknown.—*adj.* **reconstruc'tive**.—*n.* **reconstruc'tor**. [Pfx. **re-**.]

reconvert *rē-kən-vûrt', v.t.* to convert again to a former state, religion, etc.—*n.* **reconver'sion**. [Pfx. **re-**.]

record *ri-kord', v.t.* to set down in writing or other

permanent form: to register (on an instrument, scale, etc.): to trace a curve or other representation of: to perform before a recording instrument: to make a recording of (music, etc., person speaking, etc.): to mark, indicate: to bear witness to: to register (as a vote or verdict): to celebrate.—*v.i.* to make a record —*n.* record (*rek'örd*, formerly *ri-kord'*) a register: a formal writing of any fact or proceeding: a book of such writings: past history: a witness, a memorial: memory, remembrance: anything entered in the rolls of a court, esp. the formal statement or pleadings of parties in a litigation: a curve or other representation of phenomena made by an instrument upon a surface: a disc or cylinder on which sound is registered for reproduction by an instrument such as a gramophone: a performance or occurrence not recorded to have been surpassed: a list of a person's criminal convictions.—*adj.* not surpassed.—*adj.* record'able (*ri-*).— *ns.* record'er (*ri-*) one who records or registers, esp. the rolls, etc., of a city: a judge of a city or borough court of quarter-sessions: one who performs before a recording instrument: a recording apparatus: a fipple-flute, once called the 'English flute'; record'ership the office of recorder, or the time of holding it; record'ing a record of sound or images made, for later reproduction, e.g. on magnetic tape, film, or gramophone disc.—Also *adj.*—*n.* record'ist. —recorded delivery a service of the Post Office in which a record is kept of the collection and delivery of a letter, parcel, etc.; recording angel an angel supposed to keep a book in which every misdeed is recorded against the doer; Record Office a place where public records are kept; re'cord-player an instrument for playing gramophone records, run on batteries or mains.—beat or break a, the, record to outdo the highest achievement yet recorded; for the record (*coll.*) in order to get the facts straight; go on record as saying to be publicly known to say; court of record a court whose acts and proceedings are permanently recorded, and which has the authority to fine or imprison persons for contempt; off the record not for publication in the press, etc.; on record recorded in a document, etc.: publicly known; public records contemporary officially authenticated statements of acts and proceedings in public affairs, preserved in the public interest; set the record straight to put right a mistake or false impression. [O.Fr. *recorder*—L. *recordāri*, to call to mind, get by heart— *cor, cordis*, the heart.]

recount¹ *ri-kownt'*, *v.t.* to narrate the particulars of: to detail. [O.Fr. *reconter—conter*, to tell.]

recount², re-count *rē-kownt'*, *v.t*, *v.i.* to count over again.—*n.* (*rē'kownt*) a second or new counting (as of votes). [Pfx. re-.]

recoup *ri-kōōp'*, *v.t.* to deduct or keep back (from what is claimed by a counterclaim; *law*): to make good (a loss): to indemnify, compensate.—*n.* recoup'ment. [Fr. *recouper*—*couper*, to cut.]

recourse *ri-kōrs'*, *-kors'*, *n.* access: resort: a source of aid or protection: right to payment, esp. by the drawer or endorser of a bill of exchange not met by the acceptor.—have recourse to to go to for help, protection, etc.; without recourse a qualified endorsement of a bill or promissory note indicating that the endorser takes no responsibility for non-payment (*law, commerce*). [Fr. *recours*—L *recursus—re-*, back, *currĕre, cursum*, to run.]

re-cover, recover *rē-kuv'ər*, *v.t.* to cover again. [re-.]

recover *ri-kuv'ər*, *v.t.* to get or find again: to regain: to reclaim: to bring back: to retrieve: to restore: to rescue: to obtain as compensation: to obtain for

injury or debt.—*v.i.* to regain health or any former state: to get back into position.—*n.* return to a former position, as in rowing or exercise with a weapon: the position so resumed —*n.* recoverabil'ity.—*adj.* recov'erable.—*ns.* recov'erableness; recov'ery the act, fact, process, possibility, or power of recovering, or state of having recovered, in any sense. [O.Fr *recover*—L. *recuperāre*; see recuperate.]

recreant *rek'ri-ant*, (*arch.*) *adj.* craven: false.—*n.* a craven: a mean-spirited wretch: a renegade.—*n.* rec'-reance, rec'reancy.—*adv.* rec'reantly. [O.Fr., pr.p. of *recroire*, to yield in combat—L.L. *recrēdĕre*, to surrender—L. *crēdĕre*, to entrust.]

recreate *rē-krē-āt'*, *v.t.* to create again: (in the following senses *rek'ri-āt*) to reinvigorate: to amuse by sport or pastime.—*n.* recreation (*rē-krē-ā'shən*) the act of creating anew: a new creation: (in the following senses *rek-ri-ā'shən*), refreshment after toil, etc.: pleasurable occupation of leisure time: an amusement or sport.—*adjs.* recreā'tional (*rek-*), rē-creā'tive (and *rek'ri-ā-tiv*).—recreation ground (*rek-*) an open area for games, sports, etc. [Pfx. re-.]

recriminate *ri-krim'in-āt*, *v.i.* to charge an accuser.— *n.* recrimina'tion act of accusing in return: counter-charge.—*adj.* recrim'inative.—*n.* recrim'inator.— *adj.* recrim'inatory. [L. *crīminārī*, to accuse.]

recrudesce *rē-krōō-des'*, *v.i.* to break out afresh.—*ns.* recrudesc'ence, recrudesc'ency.—*adj.* recrudesc'ent. [L. *recrūdēscĕre—crūdus*, raw.]

recruit *ri-krōōt'*, *n.* a soldier or other newly enlisted.— *v.i.* to obtain fresh supplies: to recover in health, pocket, etc.: to enlist new soldiers.—*v.t.* to replenish: to restore: to reinvigorate: to enlist or raise. —*ns.* recruit'al; recruit'er.—*adj.* recruit'ing.—*n.* recruit'ment.—recruit'ing-ground a place where recruits may be obtained. [Obs. Fr. *recrute*, reinforcement, prob. pa.p. fem. of *recroître*—L. *recrēscĕre*, to grow again.]

recta, rectal, etc. See rectum.

rectangle *rek'tang-gl*, or *-tang'*, *n.* a four-sided plane figure with all its angles right angles.—*adjs.* rec'-tangled; rectang'ular of the form of a rectangle: at right angles: right-angled.—*n.* rectangular'ity.— *adv.* rectang'ularly.—rectangular hyperbola one whose asymptotes are at right angles [L.L. *rēct*(*i*)*angulum*—L. *angulus*, an angle.]

rect(i)- *rekt*(*i*)-, in composition, right: straight —*adjs.* rectilineal (*rek-ti-lin'i-əl*), rectilinear (*rek-ti-lin'i-ər*; L. *līnea*, a line) in a straight line or lines: straight: bounded by straight lines —*n.* rectilinearity (*-ar'i-ti*).—*adv.* rectilin'early. [L. *rēctus*, straight, right.]

recti. See rectus.

rectify *rek'ti-fī*, *v.t.* to set right: to correct: to redress: to adjust. to purify by distillation (*chem.*): to determine the length of (an arc): to change (an alternating current) to a direct current:—*pr.p.* rec'-tifying; *pa t.* and *pa.p.* rec'tified.—*adj.* rec'tifiable. —*ns.* rectifica'tion; rec'tifier apparatus for rectifying. [Fr. *rectifier*—L.L. *rēctificāre—facĕre*, to make.]

rectilineal, etc. See rect(i)-.

rectitude *rek'ti-tūd*, *n.* rightness: uprightness: integrity. [Fr.,—L.L. *rēctitūdō*—L *rēctus*, straight]

recto *rek'tō*, *n.* the right-hand page of an open book, the front page of a leaf—opp. to *verso*:—*pl.* rec'tos. [L. *rēctō* (*foliō*), on the right (leaf).]

recto-. See rectum.

rector *rek'tər*, *n.* in the Church of England, a clergy-man of a parish where the tithes would formerly have all come to him: an Episcopal clergyman with

recross' *v.t.* and *v.i.*

charge of a congregation in the U.S. or Scotland: the head-master of certain schools in Scotland: the chief elective officer of many Scottish (*Lord Rector*) and foreign universities: a college head: an ecclesiastic in charge of a congregation, a mission or a religious house, esp. the head of a Jesuit seminary (*R.C.*).—*ns.* **rec'torate** a rector's office or term of office.—*adj.* **rectorial** (-*tō'ri-əl*) of a rector.—*n.* an election of a Lord Rector.—*ns.* **rec'torship**; **rec'tory** the province or residence of a rector. [L. *rēctor*, -*ōris*—*regĕre*, *rĕctum*, to rule.]

rectrix *rek'triks*, *n.* a long tail-feather, used in steering:—*pl.* **rectrices** (*rek'tri-sēz*, *rek-tri'sēz*).—*adj.* **rectricial** (-*trish'l*). [L. *rēctrix*, -*īcis*, fem. of *rēctor*.]

rectum *rek'təm*, *n.* the terminal part of the large intestine:—*pl.* **rec'ta**, **rec'tums**.—*adj.* **rec'tal**.—*adv.* **rec'tally**.—In composition, **rec'to-**. [L. neut. of *rēctus*, straight.]

rectus *rek'təs*, *n.* a straight muscle:—*pl.* **rec'tī**. [L.]

recumbent *ri-kum'bənt*, *adj.* reclining.—*ns.* **recum'bence**, **recum'bency**.—*adv.* **recum'bently**. [L. *recumbĕre*—*cubāre*, to lie down.]

recuperate *ri-kū'pər-āt*, *v.t.* and *v.i.* to recover.—*adj.* **recu'perable** recoverable.—*n.* **recupera'tion**.—*adj.* **recu'perative** (-*ə-tiv*). [L. *recuperāre*, to recover.]

recur *ri-kûr'*, *v.i.* to come up or come round again, or at intervals: to come back into one's mind:—*pr.p.* **recurr'ing** (or -*kur'*); *pa.t.* and *pa.p.* **recurred'** (-*kûrd*).—*ns.* **recurr'ence**, **recurr'ency** (-*kur'*).—*adj.* **recurr'ent** (-*kur'*) returning at intervals: running back in the opposite direction or toward the place of origin. —*adv.* **recurr'ently**.—*n.* **recur'sion** (-*kûr'*; *rare*) a going back, return.—*adj.* (*math.*; of a formula) enabling a term in a sequence to be computed from one or more of the preceding terms.—*adj.* **recur'sive** (*math.*; of a definition) consisting of rules which allow values or meaning to be determined with certainty.—**recurring decimal** a decimal fraction in which after a certain point one figure (*repeating decimal*) or a group of figures (*circulating*) is repeated to infinity. [L. *recurrĕre*—*currĕre*, to run.]

recurve *ri-kûrv'*, *v.t.* and *v.i.* to bend back. [L. *recurvāre*; *rōstrum*, beak.]

recusant *rek'ū-zənt*, *n.* or *ri-kū'*) one (esp. a Roman Catholic) who refused to attend the Church of England when it was legally compulsory: a dissenter: one who refuses, esp. to submit to authority.—Also *adj.*—*ns.* **rec'usancy**, **rec'usance**. [L. *recūsāre*—*causa*, a cause.]

recycle *rē-sī'kl*, *v.t.* to pass again through a series of changes or treatment: loosely, to remake into something different: to cause (material) to be broken down by bacteria and then reconstitute it.—*adj.* **recy'clable**. [Pfx. **re-**.]

red *red*, *adj.* (*compar.* **redd'er**; *superl.* **redd'est**) of a colour like blood: extended traditionally to mean golden, and by custom to other colours more or less near red: having a red face (from shame, heat, embarrassment, etc.): revolutionary, or supposedly revolutionary.—*n.* the colour of blood: an object of this colour in a set of similar objects: a red pigment: red clothes: a revolutionary or one who favours sweeping changes, applied to socialist, communist, etc.—*v.t.* **redd'en** to make red.—*v.i.* to grow red: to blush.—*adj.* **redd'ish**.—*n.* **redd'ishness**.—*adj.* **redd'y**.—*adv.* **red'ly**.—*n.* **red'ness**.—**red admiral** a common butterfly (*Vanessa atalanta*) with reddish-banded wings; **red algae** one of the great divisions of seaweeds, the *Rhodophyceae*; **red biddy** a drink made of red wine and methylated spirit.—*adj.* **red'-blood'ed** having red blood: abounding in vitality, and usually in crudity.—**red'breast** the robin.—*adj.*

red'brick (**redbrick university** a general name given to a later English type of university, usu. one founded in the 19th or first half of the 20th. cent., contrasted with Oxford and Cambridge).—**red'-bud** the Judas-tree; **red cabbage** a purplish cabbage used for pickling; **red'-cap** a goldfinch: military policeman (*slang*): railway porter (*U.S.*); **red carpet** a strip of carpet put out for the highly favoured to walk on: treatment as a very important person.—*adj.* **red'-car'pet**; **red cedar** a name for various species of *Cedrela* and of juniper; **red cent** a cent (formerly made of copper) considered as a very small amount (*coll.*, esp. U.S.): a whit; **red'coat** (*obs.*) a British soldier; **red corpuscle** an erythrocyte, a blood cell which carries oxygen in combination with the pigment haemoglobin, and removes carbon dioxide; **Red Crescent** the Red Cross Society in Muslim countries; **Red Cross** a red cross on a white ground, the old national flag of England: the Swiss flag with colours reversed, the copyrighted symbol of an organisation (known as the **Red Cross**) for tending sick, wounded in war, etc.; **redcurr'ant** the small red berry of a shrub of the Gooseberry genus.—*adj.* **red'currant**.—**red deer** the common stag or hind, reddish-brown in summer; **Red Ensign** (*slang* **Red Duster**) red flag with Union Jack in canton; **red'eye** the rudd: poor quality whisky (*U.S.*); **red face** a blushing from discomfiture (*adj.* **red'-faced'**); **red'fish** a male salmon when, or just after, spawning: any of various red-fleshed fish; **red flag** a flag used as a signal of danger, defiance, no quarter: the banner of socialism or of revolution: a socialist's song; **red giant**, **dwarf** a red star of high, low, luminosity; **Red Guard** a member of a strict Maoist youth movement in China, esp. active in the cultural revolution of the late 1960s.—*adj.* **red'-haired**.—*adj.* and *adv.* **red'hand'ed** in the very act, or immediately after, as if with bloody hands.—**red'-hat** a cardinal: a cardinal's hat; **red'-head** a person with red hair.—*adj.* **red'-head'ed**.—**red'-heat** the temperature at which a thing is red-hot; **red herring** a herring cured and dried, of reddish appearance: a subject introduced to divert discussion or attention as a herring drawn across a track would throw hounds out.—*adj.* **red'-hot** heated to redness: extreme (*fig.*): (**red-hot poker** the plant Kniphofia).—**Red Indian** an American Indian; **red lead** an oxide of lead of a fine red colour, used in paint-making.—*adj.* **red'-letter** marked with red letters, as holidays or saints' days in old calendars: deserving to be so marked, special.—**red light** a rear-light: a danger-signal: a red lamp indicating a brothel. —*adj.* **red'-light** (*coll.*) of or relating to brothels, as in *red-light district*.—**red'-man**, **red man** a redskin, an American Indian; **red meat** dark-coloured meat, as beef and lamb; **red mullet** see **mullet**; **red'neck** (U.S.) a derog. term for a poor white farm labourer in the south-western states.—*adj.* ignorant, intolerant, narrow-minded.—**red pepper** see **pepper**; **red'poll** a name for two birds (*lesser* and *mealy redpoll*) akin to the linnet: a beast of a red breed of polled cattle.—*adj.* **red'-polled**.—**red rag** the tongue (*slang*): a cause of infuriation (as red is said to be to a bull); **red salmon** any of various types of salmon with red flesh, esp. the sockeye salmon; **red'-san'ders** a papilionaceous tree (*Pterocarpus santalinus*) of tropical Asia, with heavy dark-red heartwood, used as a dye, etc. (see also **sandalwood**); **red'shank** a sandpiper with red legs; **red shift** a shift of lines in the spectrum towards the red, usu. considered to occur because the source of light is receding (see under **dopplerite**); **red'-shirt** a follower of Garibaldi, from his garb: a revolutionary or anarchist; **red'skin** a Red Indian; **red snow** snow coloured by a microscopic red alga; **red spider (mite)** a spinning mite that infests leaves; **red**

squirrel the native English squirrel, now rare; **red'start** (O.E. *steort*, tail) a bird (*Ruticilla* or *Phoenicurus*) with a conspicuous chestnut-coloured tail: an American warbler, superficially similar; **red tape** the tape used in government offices: rigid formality of intricate official routine: bureaucracy.— *adj.* **red'-tape'.—red-tap'ism, red-tap'ist; red'-water** a cattle disease due to a protozoan parasite in the blood, transmitted by ticks; **red wine** wine coloured by (red) grape skins during fermentation; **red'wing** a thrush with reddish sides below the wings; **red'wood** a species of Sequoia with reddish wood much used commercially: any wood or tree yielding a red dye.— **in the red** overdrawn at the bank, in debt; **on red alert** in a state of readiness for an imminent crisis, e.g. war, natural disaster; **see red** to grow furious: to thirst for blood; **the Red Planet** Mars. [O.E. *rēad*.]

redact *ri-dakt'*, *v.t.* to edit, work into shape.—*ns.* **redac'tion; redac'tor.—***adj.* **redactō'rial** (*re-*, *rē-*). [L. *redigĕre*, *redactum*, to bring back.]

redan *ri-dan'*, (*fort.*) *n.* a fieldwork of two faces forming a salient. [O.Fr. *redan*—L. *re-*, *dēns*, *dentis*, a tooth.]

redargue *ri-dār'gū*, (*obs.* or *Scot.*) *v.t.* to refute: to confute. [L. *redarguĕre*—*re(d)-*, again, *arguĕre*, argue.]

redd *red*, (chiefly *Scot.*) *v.t.* to put in order, make tidy: to clear up.—*v.i.* to set things in order, tidy up (usu. with *up*):—*pr.p.* **redd'ing**; *pa.t.* and *pa.p.* **redd.**—*n.* an act of redding: refuse, rubbish.—*ns.* **redd'er; redd'ing.—redd'ing-up'** setting in order, tidying up. [Partly O.E. *hreddan*, to free, rescue; prob. influenced by O.E. *rǣdan*, to regulate.]

redden, etc. See **red**.

reddle. See **ruddle**.

rede *rēd*, (*arch.*) *n.* advice: resolution.—*adj.* **rede'less** (*arch.*) without counsel or wisdom. [O.E. *rǣd*, counsel.]

redeem *ri-dēm'*, *v.t.* to buy back: to compound for: to recover or free by payment: to free oneself from, by fulfilment: to ransom: to rescue, deliver, free: to get back: to reclaim: to pay the penalty of: to atone for: to compensate for: to put (time) to the best advantage.—*n.* **redeemabil'ity.—***adj.* **redeem'able.**—*n.* **redeem'ableness.—***adv.* **redeem'ably.**—*n.* **redeem'er.—***adjs.* **redeem'ing; redeem'less** not to be redeemed.—**the Redeemer** the Saviour, Jesus Christ. [L. *redimĕre* (perh. through Fr. *rédimer*)—*red-*, back, *emĕre*, to buy.]

redemption *ri-dem(p)'shən*, *n.* act of redeeming: atonement.—*adjs.* **redemp'tible; redemp'tive; redemp'tory.** [L. *redimĕre*, *redemptum*; cf. **redeem**.]

redeploy *rē-di-ploi'*, *v.t.* to transfer (e.g. military forces, supplies, industrial workers) from one area to another.—Also *v.i.*—*n.* **redeploy'ment.** [Pfx. **re-**.]

redingote *red'ing-gōt*, *n.* a long double-breasted (orig. man's, later woman's) overcoat. [Fr.,—Eng. **riding-coat**.]

redintegrate *red-in'ti-grāt*, *v.t.* to restore to wholeness: to re-establish.—*adj.* restored: renewed. —*n.* **redintegrā'tion.** [L. *redintegrāre*, *-ātum*—*red-*, again, *integrāre*, to make whole—*integer*.]

redivivus *red-i-vī'vəs*, *re-di-wē'woōs*, *adj.* resuscitated: come to life again. [L.,—*red-*, again, *vivus*, alive—*vivĕre*, to be alive.]

redolent *red'ə-lənt*, *adj.* fragrant: smelling (of, or

with): suggestive (of), imbued (with).—*ns.* **red'olence, red'olency.—***adv.* **red'olently.** [L. *redolēns*, *-entis*—*red-*, again, *olēre*, to emit smell.]

redouble *ri-dub'l*, *v.t.* and *v.i.* to double: to repeat: to increase: (*rē'dub'l*) to double after previous doubling.—*n.* (*rē'dub'l*) an act or fact or redoubling, as in bridge.—*n.* **redoub'lement** (*ri-*). [Pfx. **re-**.]

redoubt *ri-dowt'*, (*fort.*) *n.* a field-work enclosed on all sides, its ditch not flanked from the parapet: an inner last retreat. [Fr. *redoute*—It. *ridotto*—L. *reductus*, retired—*redūcĕre*; the *b* from confusion with next word.]

redoubtable *ri-dowt'ə-bl*, *adj.* formidable: valiant. [O.Fr. *redoutable*—*redouter*, to fear greatly—L. *re-*, back, *dubitāre*, to doubt.]

redound *ri-downd'*, *v.i.* to turn, recoil, be reflected, as a consequence (to one's credit, discredit, advantage, etc.): to conduce. [Fr. *rédonder*—L. *redundāre*—*red-*, back, *undāre*, to surge—*unda*, a wave.]

redox *rē'doks*, *adj.* of a type of chemical reaction in which one of the reagents is reduced, while another is oxidised. [Reduction and oxidation.]

redress *ri-dres'*, *v.t.* to set right: to readjust: to remedy: to compensate.—*n.* relief: reparation.—*n.* **redress'er** (*ri-*). [Fr. *redresser* (see **dress**); partly from pfx. **re-** and **dress**.]

re-dress *rē'dres'*, *v.t.* and *v.i.* to dress again: to dress in different clothes. [Pfx. **re-**.]

reduce *ri-dūs'*, *v.t.* to put back into a normal condition or place, as a dislocation or fracture (*surg.*): to change to another form: to express in other terms: to range in order or classification: to adapt, adjust: to put into (writing, practice; with *to*): to bring into a lower state: to lessen: to diminish in weight or girth: to weaken: to degrade (*mil.*): to impoverish: to subdue: to drive into (a condition; with *to*): to bring to the metallic state: to remove oxygen from, or combine with hydrogen, or lessen the positive valency of (an atom or ion) by adding electrons.—*v.i.* to resolve itself: to slim, or lessen weight or girth.—*ns.* **reduc'er** one who reduces: a means of reducing: a joint-piece for connecting pipes of varying diameter; **reducibil'ity.—***adj.* **reduc'ible** that may be reduced. —*n.* **reduc'ibleness.—***adj.* **reduc'ing.—***ns.* **reduc'tase** an enzyme which brings about the reduction of organic compounds; **reduction** (*-duk'shən*) act of reducing or state of being reduced: diminution: lowering of price: subjugation: changing of numbers or quantities from one denomination to another (*arith.*); **reduc'tionism** the belief that complex data and phenomena can be explained in terms of something simpler.—*n.* and *adj.* **reduc'tionist.—***adj.* **reduc'tive** bringing back (*arch.*): reducing.—*adv.* **reduc'tively.—reducing agent** a substance with a strong affinity for oxygen, or the like, serving to remove it from others.—**in reduced circumstances** (*euph.*) impoverished; **reduce to the ranks** to degrade, for misconduct, to the condition of a private soldier. [L. *redūcĕre*, *reductum*—*re-*, back, *dūcĕre*, to lead.]

reductio ad absurdum *ri-duk'shi-ō ad ab-sûr'dəm, re-dōōk'ti-ō ad ab-sōō r'dōōm*, reduction to absurdity: the proof of a proposition by proving the falsity of its contradictory: the application of a principle so strictly that it is carried to absurd lengths. [L.]

redundant *ri-dun'dənt*, *adj.* superfluous: of workers, no longer needed and therefore dismissed.—*ns.* **redun'dance, redun'dancy.—***adv.* **redun'dantly.**

[L. *redundāns*, *-antis*, pr.p. of *redundāre*, to overflow.]

reduplicate ri-dū'pli-kāt, *v.t.* to double: to repeat.—*v.i.* to double: to exhibit reduplication (*gram.*).—*adj.* doubled: showing reduplication (*gram.*): with edges turned outwards (*bot.*).—*n.* **reduplica'tion** a doubling: the doubling of the initial part, as in L. *fefelli*, perf. of *fallō* (*gram.*): the combination of two rhyming, alliterative, etc. words (the second sometimes a coinage for the purpose) to form one, as in *hurry-skurry*, *mishmash*.—*adj.* **redū'plicātive**. [L. *reduplicāre*, *-ātum—duplicāre*, to double.]

ree rē. See **ruff²**.

reebok rā'bok. *n.* a South African antelope. [Du.]

re-echo rē-ek'ō, *v.t.* to echo back: to repeat as if an echo.—*v.i.* to give back echoes: to resound.—*n.* a re-echoing. [Pfx. re-.]

reed rēd, *n.* a tall stiff marsh or water grass of various kinds: a thing made, or formerly made, of a reed or reeds—an arrow, a music pipe, the vibrating tongue of an organ-pipe or woodwind instrument (with or without the parts to which it is attached), a weaver's appliance for separating the warp threads and beating up the weft: thatching: a small reedlike moulding: a reed-instrument.—*v.t.* to thatch.—*ns.* **reed'iness**; **reed'ing** the milling on the edge of a coin: a reed moulding; **reed'ling** the bearded titmouse.—*adj.* **reed'y** abounding with reeds: resembling a reed sounding as a reed instrument.—**reed'-band** a band of reed-instruments; **reed'-bed**; **reed'-bird** the bobolink; **reed'-bunting** the blackheaded bunting; **reed'-grass** a reedlike grass of various kinds (as *Phalaris*, *Arundo*); **reed'-instrument** a woodwind with reed—as clarinet, oboe, bassoon; **reed'-organ** a keyboard instrument with free reeds, as the harmonium, the American organ; **reed'-pheas'ant** the bearded titmouse; **reed'-pipe** an organ-pipe whose tone is produced by the vibration of a reed, the pipe acting as resonator; **reed'stop** a set of reed-pipes controlled by a single organ-stop; **reed'-war'bler** a warbler that frequents marshy places and builds its nest on reeds.—**broken reed** (*fig.*) a person who is too weak or unreliable to be depended upon. [O.E. *hrēod*.]

reef¹ rēf, *n.* a chain of rocks at or near the surface of water: a shoal or bank: a gold-bearing lode or vein (orig. *Austr.*). [Du. *rif*—O.N. *rif*.]

reef² rēf, *n.* a portion of a sail that may be rolled or folded up.—*v.t.* to reduce the exposed surface of, as a sail: to gather up in a similar way.—*ns.* **reef'er** one who reefs: a midshipman (*slang*): a reefing-jacket (also **reef'er-jacket**): a cigarette containing marijuana (*coll.*); **reef'ing.**—**reef'ing-jack'et** a short thick double-breasted jacket; **reef'-knot** a flat knot used in tying reef-points, consisting of two loops passing symmetrically through each other; **reef'-point** a short rope on a reef-band to secure a reefed sail. [O.N. *rif*.]

reefer¹ rē'fər, (*slang*), *n.* a refrigerated railway car: a refrigerated ship. [refrigerator.]

reefer². See **reef².**

reek rēk, *n.* smoke: vapour: fume.—*v.i.* to emit smoke, fumes, or (esp. evil) smell: to exhale.—*adjs.* **reek'ing**; **reek'y.** [O.E. *rēc*.]

reel rēl, *n.* a cylinder, drum, spool, bobbin, or frame on which thread, fishing-line, wire, cables, photographic film, or the like may be wound: a length of material so wound: a lively dance, esp. Highland or Irish: a tune for it, usu. in 4–4, sometimes in 6–8 time.—*v.t.* to wind on a reel: to take off by or from a reel: to draw (in) by means of a reel.—*v.i.* to whirl: to seem to swirl or sway: to totter: to stagger: (of e.g. line of battle) to waver: to dance a reel.—*n.* **reel'er.**—*n.* and *adj.* **reel'ing.**—*adv.* **reel'ingly.**—**reel off** to utter rapidly and fluently; **Virginia reel** an American country-dance. [O.E. *hrēol*, but possibly partly of other origin.]

re-enter rē-en'tər, *v.t.* and *v.i.* to enter again or anew —*n.* **re-en'trance.**—*adj.* **re-en'trant** re-entering (opp. to *salient*): reflex (*math.*): returning upon itself at the ends (*elect.*).—*n.* a re-entering angle: a valley, depression, etc., running into a main feature: the concavity between two salients.—*n.* **re-en'try** entering again, esp., of a spacecraft, entering the earth's atmosphere again: resumption of possession: the reopening of an oil-well for further drilling: a card allowing a hand to take the lead again. [Pfx. re-.]

reeve¹ rēv, (*hist.*) *n.* a high official, chief magistrate of a district: a bailiff or steward. [O.E. *gerēfa*.]

reeve² rēv, *v.t.* to pass the end of a rope through: to pass through any hole: to thread one's way through: to fasten by reeving:—*pa.t.* and *pa.p.* **reeved, rove.**

reeve³ rēv, see **ruff².**

ref ref, (*coll.*) *n.* and *v.t.*, *v.i.* short for **referee**:—*pr.p.* **reff'ing**; *pa.t.* and *pa.p.* **reffed.**

refection ri-fek'shən, *n.* refreshment or relief: a meal. —*n.* **refectory** (ri-fek'tər-i; sometimes *ref'ik-*) a dining-hall, esp. monastic.—**refectory table** a long narrow dining-table supported on two shaped pillars each set in a base. [L. *reficĕre*, *refectum—facĕre*, to make.]

refer ri-fûr', *v.t.* to assign (to): to impute (to): to attribute (to): to bring into relation (to): to deliver, commit, or submit (to): to hand over for consideration (to): to direct for information, confirmation, testimonials, or whatever is required (to): to direct the attention of (to): to direct to sit an examination again, fail.—*v.i.* (with *to* in all cases) to have relation or application, to relate: to direct the attention: to turn for information, confirmation, etc.: to turn, apply, or have recourse: to make mention or allusion: —*pr.p.* **referr'ing**; *pa.t.* and *pa.p.* **referred'.**—*adjs.* **referable** (*ref'ər-ə-bl*, *ri-fûr'i-bl*), **referrable** (*-fûr'*) that may be referred or assigned.—*n.* **referee** (*ref-ə-rē'*; coll. shortening **ref**) one to whom anything is referred: an arbitrator, umpire, or judge.—*v.i.* to act as referee for.—*v.i.* to act as referee.—*n.* **ref'erence** the act of referring: a submitting for information or decision: the act of submitting a dispute for investigation or decision (*law*): relation: allusion: loosely, one who is referred to: loosely, a testimonial: a direction to a book or passage.—*v.t.* to make a reference to: to provide (a book, etc.) with references to other sources.—*n.* **referen'dum** the principle or practice of submitting a question directly to the vote of the entire electorate (*pl.* **-da, -dums**); **ref'erent** the object of reference or discussion: the first term in a proposition.

re-ed'ucate *v.t.*   re-enact' *v.t.*   re-erec'tion *n.*
re-educa'tion *n.*   re-enact'ment *n.*   re-estab'lish *v.t.*
re-elect' *v.t.*   re-engage' *v.t.* and *v.i.*   re-estab'lishment *n.*
re-elec'tion *n.*   re-engage'ment *n.*   re-examina'tion *n.*
re-embark' *v.t.* and *v.i.*   re-enlist' *v.t.* and *v.i.*   re-exam'ine *v.t.*
re-embarka'tion *n.*   re-enlist'ment *n.*   re-export' *v.t.*
re-emerge' *v.i.*   re-equip' *v.t.* and *v.i.*   re-ex'port *n.*
re-emer'gence *n.*   re-erect' *v.t.*   re-exporta'tion *n.*
                                        refash'ion *v.t.*

—*adj.* **referential.**—*adv.* **referen'tially.**—*n.* **referr'al** act or instance of referring or being referred, esp. to another person or organisation for, e.g. consideration, treatment, etc.—**reference book** a book to be consulted on occasion, not for consecutive reading; **ref'erence-mark** a character, as *, †, or a superscript figure, used to refer to notes; **referred pain** pain felt in a part of the body other than its source.—**terms of reference** a guiding statement defining the scope of an investigation or similar piece of work: loosely, the scope itself. [L. *referre*, to carry back—*ferre*, to carry.]

refill rē-fil', *v.t.* to fill again.—*n.* (rē' or -fil') a fresh fill: a duplicate for refilling purposes. [Pfx. **re-**.]

refine ri-fīn', *v.t.* to purify: to clarify: (*usu.* with *out*) to get rid of (impurities, etc.) by a purifying process: to free from coarseness, vulgarity, crudity: to make more cultured.—*v.i.* to become more fine, pure, subtle, or cultured: to improve by adding refinement or subtlety (with *on* or *upon*).—*adj.* **refined'.**—*adv.* **refin'edly.**—*ns.* **refin'edness; refine'ment** act or practice of refining: state of being refined: culture in feelings, taste, and manners: an improvement: a subtlety: an excessive nicety; **refin'er; refin'ery** a place for refining; **refin'ing.** [L. *re-*, denoting change of state, and **fine[1]**.]

refit rē-fit', *v.t.* to fit out afresh and repair.—*v.i.* to undergo refitting.—*ns.* **re'fit, refit'ment, refitt'ing.** [Pfx. **re-** and **fit[1]**.]

reflation rē-flā'shən, *n.* increase in the amount of currency, economic activity, etc. after deflation: a general increase, above what would normally be expected, in the spending of money.—*v.t.* (back-formation from *n.*) **reflate'.**—*adj.* **refla'tionary.** [Pfx. **re-** and *inflation.*]

reflect ri-flekt', *v.t.* to bend or send back or aside: to throw back after striking: to give an image of in the manner of a mirror: to express, reproduce: to cast, shed (e.g. credit, discredit) (*fig.*): to consider meditatively (that, how, etc.).—*v.i.* to bend or turn back or aside: to be mirrored: to meditate (on): to cast reproach or censure (on, upon): to bring harmful results.—*n.* **reflect'ance, reflecting factor** ratio of reflected radiation to incident radiation.—*adjs.* **reflect'ed; reflect'ing.**—*adv.* **reflect'ingly.**—*n.* **reflection,** also (now chiefly in scientific use) **reflexion** (ri-flek'shən) a turning, bending, or folding aside, back, or downwards: folding upon itself: rebound: change of direction when an electromagnetic wave or soundwave strikes on a surface and is thrown back: reflected light, colour, heat, etc.: an image in a mirror: the action of the mind by which it is conscious of its own operations: attentive consideration: contemplation: censure or reproach.—*adjs.* **reflec'tionless; reflect'ive** reflecting: reflected: meditative.—*adv.* **reflect'ively.**—*ns.* **reflect'iveness; reflectiv'ity** ability to reflect rays: reflectance; **reflect'or** a reflecting surface, instrument, or body: a reflecting telescope; **reflet** (ra-flē', -flā'; Fr.) an irridescent or metallic lustre.— *adj.* **reflex** (rē'fleks) bent or turned back: reflected: reciprocal: of an angle, more than 180°: turned back upon itself: involuntary, produced by or concerned with response from a nerve-centre to a stimulus from without: illuminated by light from another part of the same picture (*paint.*): using the same valve or valves for high- and low-frequency amplification (*radio*).— *n.* reflection: reflected light: a reflected image: an expression, manifestation, outward representation: a reflex action.—*v.t.* (-fleks') to bend back.—*adj.* **reflexed'** (*bot.*) bent abruptly backward or downward

—*n.* **reflexibil'ity.**—*adjs.* **reflex'ible; reflex'ive** (*gram.*) indicating that the action turns back upon the subject.—*advs.* **reflex'ively; reflex'ly** (or **rē'**).—*n.* **reflexol'ogy.**—*adj.* **reflexolog'ical.**—**reflecting factor** see **reflectance** above; **reflecting microscope** one using a system of mirrors instead of lenses; **reflecting telescope** one which has a concave mirror instead of a lens or lenses; **reflex arc** the simplest functional unit of the nervous system, by which an impulse produces a reflex action; **reflex camera** one in which the image is reflected on to a glass screen for composing and focusing. [L. *reflectĕre, reflexum—flectĕre,* to bend.]

reflet, reflex, etc. See **reflect.**

refluent ref'loō-ənt, (*rare*) *adj.* flowing back.—*ns.* **ref'-luence; reflux** (rē'fluks) the process of boiling a liquid in a flask with a condenser attached so that the vapour condenses and flows back into the flask, avoiding loss by evaporation (*chem.*; also *v.i., v.t.*). [L. *refluēns, -entis,* pr.p. of *refluĕre—fluĕre, fluxum,* to flow; *fluxus, -ūs,* a flow.]

re-form, also **reform** rē'förm', *v.t.* and *v.i.* to form again or anew.—*n.* **re'(-)forma'tion.**—*adj.* **rē'(-)formed'.** [Pfx. **re-**.]

reform ri-förm', *v.t.* to transform: to make better: to remove defects from: to bring to a better way of life. —*v.i.* to abandon evil ways.—*n.* amendment or transformation, esp. of a system or institution: an extension or better distribution of parliamentary representation.—*adj.* **reform'able** (-ri-).—*ns.* **reformabil'ity; reformation** (ref-ər-mā'shən) the act of reforming: amendment: improvement: (*cap.*) the religious revolution of the 16th century, which gave rise to the various evangelical or Protestant organisations of Christendom; **reforma'tionist.**—*adjs.* **reformative** (ri-förm'ə-tiv); **reform'atory** reforming: tending to produce reform.—*n.* (in U.K., formerly) an institution for reclaiming young delinquents.—*adj.* **reformed'.**—*ns.* **reform'er** one who reforms: one who advocates political reform: (*cap.*) one of those who took part in the Reformation of the 16th century; **reform'ism; reform'ist** a reformer: an advocate of reform, or of not very thorough-going reform.— **Reform Judaism** a form of Judaism, originating in the 19th cent., in which the Jewish Law is adapted so as to be relevant to contemporary life; **reform school** reformatory. [L. *refōrmāre, -ātum—förmāre,* to shape—*förma,* form.]

refract ri-frakt', *v.t.* (of a medium) to deflect (rays of light, sound, etc., passing into it from another medium).—*adjs.* **refract'able; refrac'ted; refract'-ing.**—*n.* **refrac'tion.**—*adj.* **refrac'tive.**—*ns.* **refractivity** (rē-frak-tiv'i-ti); **refractom'eter** an instrument for measuring refractive indices; **refrac'tor** (ri-) anything that refracts: a refracting telescope.—**refracting telescope** one in which the principal means of focusing the light is a lens or lenses; **refractive index** the ratio of the sine of the angle of incidence to that of the angle of refraction when a ray passes from one medium to another.—**angle of refraction** the angle between a refracted ray and the normal to the bounding surface; **double refraction** the separation of an incident ray of light into two refracted rays, polarised in perpendicular planes. [L. *refringĕre, refrāctum—frangĕre,* to break.]

refractory ri-frak'tər-i, *adj.* unruly: unmanageable: perverse: resistant to ordinary treatment, stimulus, etc.: esp. difficult of fusion: fire-resisting.—*n.* a substance that is able to resist high temperatures, etc., used in lining furnaces, etc.—*adv.* **refrac'torily.** —*n.* **refrac'toriness.** [L. *refrāctārius,* stubborn.]

reform'ulate *v.t.*

refrain¹ ri-frān', n. a burden, a line or phrase recurring, esp. at the end of a stanza: the music of such a burden. [O.Fr. refrain—refraindre—L. refringĕre —frangĕre, to break.]

refrain² ri-frān, v.i. to keep oneself from action, forbear: to abstain (from). [O.Fr. refrener—L.L refrēnāre—re-, back, frēnum, a bridle.]

refrangible ri-fran'ji-bl, adj. that may be refracted.— ns. refrangibil'ity, refran'gibleness. [See refract.]

refresh ri-fresh', v.t. to make fresh again: to freshen up: to give new vigour, life, liveliness, spirit, brightness, fresh appearance, coolness, moistness, etc., to.—v.i. to take refreshment, esp. drink (coll.). —refresh'er one who, or that which, refreshes: a cool drink (coll.): a fee paid to counsel for continuing his attention to a case, esp. when adjourned: a douceur to encourage further exertions (coll.): a subsequent course of training or instruction to maintain or reattain one's former standard, study new developments, etc. (also adj.).—adj. refresh'ing pleasantly cooling, inspiriting, reviving, invigorating.—adv. refresh'ingly.—ns. refresh'ment the act of refreshing: state of being refreshed: renewed strength or spirit: that which refreshes, as food or rest: (in pl.) drink or a light meal. [O.Fr. refrescher—re-, freis (fem. fresche), fresh.]

refrigerant ri-frij'ə-rant, adj. cooling.—n. a freezing or cooling agent.—v.t. refrig'erate to freeze: to make cold: to expose to great cold (as food for preservation).—v.i. to become cold.—n. refrigerā'tion.—adj. refrig'erative (-ra-tiv).—n. refrig'erator (-rā-tər) an apparatus or chamber for producing and maintaining a low temperature (contraction fridge, esp. when in domestic use).—adj. refrig'eratory (-rə-tər-i) cooling. —n. a water-filled vessel for condensing in distillation. [L. refrigerāre, -ātum—re-, denoting change of state, frigerāre—frigus, cold.]

refringent ri-frinj'ənt, (phys.) adj. refracting.—n. refring'ency. [L. refringĕre; see refract.]

reft reft, pa.t. and pa.p. of reave.

refuge ref'ūj, n. shelter or protection from danger or trouble: an asylum or retreat: a street island for pedestrians: recourse in difficulty.—ns. refugee (ref-ū-jē') one who flees for refuge to another country, esp. from religious or political persecution: a fugitive; refugium (ri-fū'ji-əm) a region that has retained earlier geographical, climatic, etc. conditions, and thus becomes a haven for older varieties of flora and fauna:—pl. refu'gia (-ji-ə).—house of refuge a shelter for the destitute. [Fr.,—L. refugium—fugĕre, to flee.]

refulgent ri-ful'jənt, adj. casting a flood of light: radiant: beaming.—ns. reful'gence, reful'gency. [L. refulgēns, -entis. pr.p. of refulgēre—re-, intens., fulgēre, to shine.]

refund¹ ri- or rē-fund', v.t. to repay.—v.t. to restore what was taken.—ns. refund (rē'fund); refund'er; refund'ment (ri-). [L. refundĕre—fundĕre, to pour.]

refund² rē-fund', v.t. to replace (an old issue) by a new: to borrow so as to pay off (an old loan). [Pfx. re-.]

refuse¹ ri-fūz', v.t. to decline to take or accept: to renounce: to decline to give or grant: of a horse, to decline to jump over: to fail to follow suit to (cards): to decline to meet in battle.—v.i. to make refusal.— adj. refus'able (ri-).—ns. refus'al the act of refusing: the option of taking or refusing; refus'er. [Fr. refuser—L. refūsum, pa.p. of refundĕre—fundĕre, to pour; cf. refund¹.]

refuse² ref'ūs, adj. rejected as worthless.—n. that which is rejected or left as worthless. [Fr. refus; see foregoing.]

refute ri-fūt', v.t. to disprove: loosely, to deny.—adj. refutable (ref'ūt-ə-bl, or ri-fūt').—adv. ref'utably (or ri-fūt').—ns. refu'tal, refutā'tion (ref-) act of refuting: that which disproves; refu'ter. [L. refūtāre, to drive back.]

regain ri- or rē-gān', v.t. to gain back: to get back to. —n. recovery.—adj. regain'able.—ns. regain'er; regain'ment. [Fr. regaigner (now regagner).]

regal rē'gl, adj. royal: kingly.—n. regality (ri-gal'i-ti) state of being regal: royalty.—adv. re'gally. [L. rēgālis—rēx, a king—regĕre, to rule.]

regale ri-gāl', v.t. to feast: to treat to (with with).—n. regale'ment. [Fr. régaler—It. regalare, perh.— gala, a piece of finery.]

regalia ri-gā'li-ə, rā-gā'li-a, n.pl. the insignia of royalty —crown, sceptre, etc.: loosely, insignia or special garb generally, as of the Freemasons. [L. rēgālis, royal, neut. sing. -e, pl. -ia.]

regality, etc. See regal.

regard ri-gärd', v.t. to look at: to observe: to heed: to consider: to esteem: to have respect or relation to.— n. orig., look: attention with interest: observation: estimation: esteem: kindly, affectionate, or respectful feeling: care: consideration: repute: respect: relation: reference: (in pl.) in messages of greeting, respectful good will.—adjs. regard'able; regard'ant looking backward (her.).—n. regard'er. —adj. regard'ful heedful: respectful.—adv. regard'fully.—n. regard'fulness.—prep. regard'ing concerning.—adj. and adv. regard'less without regard to consequences: careless (of).—adv. regard'lessly.—n. regard'lessness.—as regards with regard to, concerning; in regard of, to in reference to; in this regard in this respect; with regard to concerning: so far as relates to. [Fr. regarder—garder, to keep, watch.]

regatta ri-gat'ə, n. a yacht or boat race-meeting. [It. (Venetian) regata.]

regelation rē-ji-lā'shən, n. freezing together again (as of ice melted by pressure when the pressure is released).—v.t. and v.i. re'gelate. [Pfx. re- and L. gelāre, to freeze.]

regency rē'jən-si, n. the office, term of office, jurisdiction, or dominion of a regent: a body entrusted with vicarious government: specif., in French history, 1715-23, when Philip of Orleans was regent: in English history, 1810-20, when the Prince of Wales was Prince Regent.—adj. of, or in the style prevailing during, the French or English regency.—adj. regent ruling: invested with interim or vicarious sovereign authority.—n. a ruler: one invested with interim authority on behalf of another: a master or doctor who takes part in the regular duties of instruction and government in some universities.—n. re'gentship.— rē'gent-bird a bower-bird. [L. regēns, -entis, pr.p of regĕre, to rule.]

regenerate ri-jen'ər-āt, v.t. to produce anew: to renew spiritually (theol.): to put new life or energy into: to reform completely: to reproduce (a part of the body): to magnify the amplitude of an electrical output by relaying part of the power back into the input circuit (elect.).—v.i. to undergo regeneration, to be regenerated.—adj. (-it, -āt) regenerated, renewed: changed from a natural to a spiritual state.—adj. regen'erable.—ns. regen'eracy (-ə-si); regenerā'tion. —adj. regen'erative.—adv. regen'eratively.—n. regen'erator.—adj. regen'eratory (-ə-tər-i). [L.

reframe' v.t.

refreeze' v.t.

refu'el v.t.

refur'bish v.t.

refur'nish v.t. and v.i.

fāte; fär; mē; hûr (her); mīne; mōte; fôr; mūte; mōōn; fŏŏt; dhen (then); el'ə-mənt (element) *regenerāre, -ātum,* to bring forth again.—*re-,* again, *generāre,* to generate.]

regent. See **regency.**

reggae *reg'ā, rā'gā, n.* a simple, lively, strongly rhythmic rock music of the West Indies, imported into Britain by immigrants in the mid-1960s.

regicide *rej'i-sīd, n.* the killing or killer of a king.—*adj.* **regic'idal.** [L. *rēx, rēgis,* a king, on the analogy of **homicide, parricide,** etc.]

régie *rā-zhē,* (Fr.) *n.* a system of government monopoly, esp. in tobacco.

régime *rā-zhēm', n.* regimen: administration —Also **regime.** [Fr.,—L. *regimen.*]

regimen *rej'i-men, n.* government: system of government: course of treatment, as diet (*med.*). [L. *regimen, -inis—regĕre,* to rule.]

regiment *rej'mənt, rej'i-mənt, n.* rule (*arch.*): (often *rej'mənt*) a body of soldiers constituting the largest permanent unit, commanded by a colonel: a large number.—*v.t.* (*rej'i-ment, -ment'*) to form into a regiment or regiments: to systematise, classify: to subject to excessive control.—*adj.* **regimental** (*-t-ment'l*) of a regiment.—*n.* (in *pl.*) the uniform of a regiment.—*n.* **regimentation** (*-i-men-tā'shən*). [L.L. *regimentum*—L. *regĕre,* to rule.]

regina *ri-jī'nə, n.* queen: title of a reigning queen, abbrev. to R in signature. [L. *rēgīna.*]

region *rē'jən, n.* a tract of country: any area or district, esp. one characterised in some way: the larger of the two local government administrative units in Scotland (see also **district**): a realm: a portion or division, as of the body: a portion of space.—*adj.* **rē'gional.**—*n.* **regionalisā'tion, -z-** the dividing of England (in 1972) and Scotland (in 1973) into regions for local government administration.—*v.t.* **re'gionalise, -ize.** —*ns.* **rē'gionalism** regional patriotism; **rē'gionalist.** —*adv.* **rē'gionally.**—*adj.* **rē'gionary.**—**in the region of** near: about, approximately. [A.Fr. *regiun*—L. *rēgiō, -ōnis—regĕre,* to rule.]

régisseur *rā-zhē-sœr,* (Fr.) *n.* in a ballet company, a director.

register *rej'is-tər, n.* a written record or official list regularly kept: the book containing such a record: a recording or indicating apparatus, as a cash register: apparatus for regulating a draught: an organ stop or stop-knob: the set of pipes controlled by an organ stop: part of the compass of any instrument having a distinct quality of tone: the compass of an instrument or voice: the range of tones of a voice produced in a particular manner: the form of language used in certain situations e.g. legal, technical, journalistic: exact adjustment of position, as of colours in a picture, or letterpress on opposite sides of a leaf (*print.*): a device for storing small amounts of data (*comput.*).—*v.t.* to enter or cause to be entered in a register: to record: to indicate: to express: to represent by bodily expression: to adjust in register: to send by registered post.—*v.i.* to enter one's name (esp. as a hotel guest): to correspond in register: to make an impression, reach the consciousness (*coll.*). —*adj.* **reg'istered; reg'istrable.**—*ns.* **reg'istrar** (*-trar,* or *-trar'*) one who keeps a register or official record: one who makes an official record of births, deaths, and marriages registered locally: a hospital doctor in one of the intermediate grades; **reg'istrarship** office of a registrar; **registrā'tion; reg'istry** registration: an office or place where a register is kept —**register office** a record-office: a registry office (see below); **Reg'istrar-Gen'eral** an officer having the superintendence of the registration of all births, deaths, and

marriages; **registration number** the combination of letters and numbers shown on a motor vehicle's number plates, by which its ownership is registered; **registry office** a registrar's office, where births, etc., are recorded and civil marriages are celebrated.— **Registered General Nurse** (abbrev. **RGN**) one who has passed the examination of the General Nursing Council for Scotland; **ship's register** a document showing the ownership of a vessel. [O.Fr. *registre* or L.L. *registrum,* for L. pl. *regesta,* things recorded— *re-,* back, *gerĕre,* to carry.]

regius *rē'ji-əs, rā'gi-ōōs, adj.* royal, as **regius professor** one whose chair was founded by Henry VIII, or, in Scotland, by the Crown. [L. *rēgius—rēx,* king.]

reglet *reg'lit, n.* a flat, narrow moulding (*archit.*): a strip for spacing between lines (*print.*). [Fr. *réglet,* dim. of *règle*—L. *rēgula,* a rule.]

regnal *reg'nl, adj.* of a reign.—*adj.* **reg'nant** reigning (often after the noun, as **queen regnant** a reigning queen, not a *queen consort*): prevalent. [L. *rēgnālis* —*rēgnum,* a kingdom.

regorge *ri-, rē-gorj', v.t.* to disgorge, regurgitate.—*v.i.* to gush back. [Pfx. **re-** and **gorge;** or Fr. *regorger,* to overflow.]

regress *rē'gres, n.* passage back: return: reversion: backward movement: right or power of returning.—*v.i.* (*ri-gres'*) to go back: to return to a former place or state: to revert.—*n.* **regression** (*ri-gresh'ən*) act of regressing: reversion: return to an earlier stage of development, as in an adult's or adolescent's behaving like a child.— *adj.* **regressive** (*ri-gres'iv*).—*adv.* **regress'ively.**—*ns.* **regress'iveness** (*ri-*); **regressiv'ity** (*rē-*). [L. *regressus* —*regredī;* see **regrede.**]

regret *ri-gret', v.t.* to remember with sense of loss or feeling of having done amiss: to wish otherwise:— *pr.p.* **regrett'ing;** *pa.t.* and *pa.p.* **regrett'ed.**—*n.* sorrowful wish that something had been otherwise: sorrowful feeling of loss: compunction: an intimation of regret or refusal.—*adj.* **regret'ful.**—*adv.* **regret'fully.**—*adj.* **regrett'able** to be regretted.—*adv.* **regrett'ably** in a regrettable way: I'm sorry to say, unfortunately. [O.Fr. *regreter, regrater;* poss. conn. with *greet*[2].]

regular *reg'ū-lər, adj.* subject to a monastic rule (opp. to *secular*): governed by or according to rule, law, order, habit, custom, established practice, mode prescribed, or the ordinary course of things: placed, arranged, etc. at regular intervals in space or time: normal: habitual: constant: steady: uniform: periodical: duly qualified: inflected in the usual way, esp. of weak verbs (*gram.*): symmetrical: having all the sides and angles equal or all faces equal, equilateral, and equiangular, the same number meeting at every corner (*geom.*): also (of a pyramid) having a regular polygon for base and the other faces similar and equal isosceles triangles: permanent, professional, or standing (*mil.,* opp. to *militia, volunteer,* and *territorial*): thorough, out-and-out.—*n.* a member of a religious order who has taken the three ordinary vows: a soldier of the regular army: a regular customer.—*n.* **regularisā'tion, -z-.**—*v.t.* **reg'ularise, -ize** to make regular.—*n.* **regularity** (*-lar'i-ti*).—*adv.* **reg'ularly.**—*v.t.* **reg'ulate** to control: to adapt or adjust continuously: to adjust by rule.—*n.* **regulā'tion** act of regulating: state of being regulated: a rule or order prescribed.—*adj.* prescribed by regulation —*adj.* **reg'ulative.**—*n.* **reg'ulator** one who, or that which, regulates: a controlling device, esp. for the speed of a clock or watch.—*adj.* **reg'ulatory** (*-lə-tər-i*). [L. *rēgula,* a rule—*regĕre,* to rule.]

---

regrade' *v.t.*   **regroup'** *v.t.*   **regrowth'** *n.*
regrind' *v.t.*

regulus *reg'ū-las, n.* an impure metal, an intermediate product in smelting of ores: antimony.—*adj.* **reg'uline.** [L. *rēgulus*, dim. of *rēx*, a king.]

regurgitate *ri-, rē-gûr'ji-tāt, v.t.* to cast out again: to pour back: to bring back into the mouth after swallowing.—*v.i.* to gush back.—*adj.* **regur'gitant.**—*n.* **regurgita'tion.** [L.L. *regurgitāre, -ātum—re*, back, *gurges, gurgitis*, a gulf.]

rehabilitate *rē-(h)a-bil'i-tāt, v.t.* to reinstate, restore to former privileges, rights, rank, etc.: to clear the character of: to bring back into good condition, working order, prosperity: to make fit, after disablement, illness or imprisonment for earning a living or playing a part in the world: of buildings or housing areas, to rebuild, restore to good condition.—*n.* **rehabilita'tion.**—*adj.* **rehabil'itative.** [L.L. *rehabilitāre, -ātum*; see **habilitate**.]

rehash *rē-hash', n.* something made up of materials formerly used, esp. a restatement in different words of ideas already expressed by oneself or somone else. —Also *v.t.* [Pfx. re-, hash, n.]

rehear *rē-hēr', v.t.* to hear again: to try over again, as a lawsuit.—*n.* **rehear'ing.** [Pfx. re-.]

rehearse *ri-hûrs', v.t.* to repeat, say over: to enumerate: to recount, narrate in order: to perform privately for practice or trial: to practise beforehand: to train by rehearsal.—*v.i.* to take part in rehearsal.— *ns.* **rehears'al** the act of rehearsing: a performance for trial or practice; **rehears'er; rehears'ing.** [O.Fr. *rehercer, reherser—re-*, again, *hercer*, to harrow—*herce* (Fr. *herse*)—L. *hirpex, -icis*, a rake, a harrow.]

reheat *rē-hēt', v.t.* to heat again.—*n.* (*rē'hēt;* the use of) a device to inject fuel into the hot exhaust gases of a turbojet in order to obtain increased thrust.—*n.* **reheat'er.** [Pfx. re-.]

rehoboam *rē-(h)ō-bō'am, n.* a large liquor measure or vessel (esp. for champagne), the size of six normal bottles (approx. 156 fluid oz.). [*Rehoboam*, king of Israel.]

rehouse *rē-howz', v.t.* to provide with a new house or houses.—*n.* **rehous'ing.** [Pfx. re-.]

Reich *rīhh, n.* the German state: Germany as an empire (**First Reich** Holy Roman Empire, 962–1806; **Second Reich** under Hohenzollern emperors, 1871–1918), and as a dictatorship (**Third Reich** under Nazi régime, 1933–45).—*ns.* **reichsmark** (*-märk*) the German monetary unit 1924–48; **Reichstag-** (*-tähh*) the lower house of the parliament of Germany during the Second Reich and the Weimar Republic. [Ger., O.E. *rīce*, kingdom.]

reify *rē'i-fī, v.t.* to think of as a material thing: to materialise.—*n.* **reification** (*-fi-kā'shan*). [L. *rēs*, a thing.]

reign *rān, n.* rule, actual or nominal, of a monarch: predominating influence: time of reigning.—*v.i.* to be a monarch: to prevail. [O.Fr. *regne*—L. *rēgnum —regēre*, to rule.]

reimburse *rē-im-bûrs', v.t.* to repay: to pay an equivalent to for loss or expense.—*n.* **reimburse'ment.** [L.L. *imbursāre—in*, in, *bursa*, purse.]

rein[1] *rān, n.* the strap of a bridle or either half of it: any means of curbing or governing.—*v.t.* to furnish with reins: to govern with the rein: to restrain or control: to stop or check (with *in* or *up*).—*v.i.* to stop or slow up.—**draw rein** to pull up, stop riding; **give rein** (or a **free rein**) to to allow free play to; **keep a tight rein** (on) to control closely; **take the reins** to take control. [O.Fr. *rein, resne, rene* (Fr. *rêne*).]

rein[2]. See **reins**.

reincarnate *rē-in-kar'nāt, v.t.* to cause to be born again in another body or form: to embody again in flesh.— *adj.* reborn.—*ns.* **reincarna'tion;** **reincarna'tionism** belief in reincarnation of the soul; **reincarna'tionist.** [Pfx. re-.]

reindeer *rān'dēr, n.* a large heavy deer (*Rangifer*), wild and domesticated, of northern regions, antlered in both sexes, the American variety (or species) called the caribou:—*pl.* **rein'deer, rein'deers.**—**reindeer moss** a lichen, the winter food of the reindeer. [O.N. *hreinndýri*, or O.N. *hreinn* (O.E. *hrān*) and **deer**.]

reinforce *rē-in-fōrs', fôrs', v.t.* to strengthen with new force or support: to strengthen: to increase by addition.—*n.* **reinforce'ment** act of reinforcing: additional force or assistance, esp. of troops (commonly in *pl.*).—**reinforced concrete** concrete strengthened by embedded steel bars or mesh. [Alt., by 17th cent., of **renforce**.]

reins *rānz, n.pl.* (*rare* or *obs.* in *sing.*) the kidneys: the loins. [O.Fr. *reins*—L. *rēn, pl. rēnēs*.]

reinstate *rē-instāt', v.t.* to instate again: to restore to or re-establish in a former station or condition.—*ns.* **reinstāte'ment.** [Pfx. re-.]

reinsure *rē-in-shōōr', v.t.* to insure against the risk undertaken by underwriting an insurance: to insure again.—*ns.* **reinsur'ance; reinsur'er.** [Pfx. re-.]

reintegrate *rē-in'ti-grāt, v.t.* to integrate again: to redintegrate.—*n.* **reintegra'tion.**

reinvest *rē-in-vest', v.t.* to invest again.—*n.* **reinvest'ment.** [Pfx. re-.]

reinvigorate *rē-in-vig'ar-āt, v.t.* to put new vigour into. —*n.* **reinvigora'tion.** [Pfx. re-.]

reiterate *rē-it'ar-āt, v.t.* to repeat: to repeat again and again.—*n.* **reitera'tion** act of reiterating.—*adj.* **reit'erative.** [Pfx. re-.]

reive, reiver. Same as **reave, reaver.**

reject *ri-jekt', v.t.* to throw away: to discard: to refuse to accept, admit, or accede to: to refuse: to renounce: of the body, not to accept tissue, a transplanted organ, etc., from another source (*med.*).—*n.* (usu. *rē'*) one who or that which is rejected: an imperfect article, not accepted for export, normal sale, etc., and often offered for sale at a discount.—*adjs.* **rejec'table** or **-ible.**—*ns.* **rejec'tion; reject'or** (also *-er*). [L. *rejicĕre, rejectum—re-*, back, *jacĕre*, to throw.]

rejig *re-jig rē-jig', rejigger-jig'ar, vs.t.* to re-equip: to change or rearrange in a new or unexpected way that is sometimes regarded as unethical (*commerce*).—*n.* **re'jig, re'-jig.**

rejoice *ri-jois', v.t.* to gladden.—*v.i.* to feel joy (*arch.*): to exult: to make merry.—*adj.* **rejoice'ful.**—*ns.* **rejoic'er; rejoic'ing** act of being joyful: expression, subject, or experience of joy: (in *pl.*) festivities, celebrations, merry-makings.—*adv.* **rejoic'ingly.**—**rejoice in** to be happy because of: (*facet.*) to have. [O.Fr. *resjoir, resjoiss-* (Fr. *réjouir*)—L. *ue-, ex, gaudēre*, to rejoice.]

rejoin[1] *ri-join', (law)* to reply to a charge or pleading, esp. to a plaintiff's replication.—*v.t.* to say in reply, retort.—*n.* **rejoin'der** (*ri-*) the defendant's answer to a plaintiff's replication (*law*): an answer to a reply: an answer, esp. a sharp or clever one. [O.Fr. *rejoindre*.]

rejoin[2] *ri-, rē-join', v.t.* and *v.i.* to join again. [Pfx. re-.]

rejuvenate *ri-jōō'vi-nāt, v.t.* to make young again: to

---

reimport' *v.t.*
reinhab'it *v.t.*
reinsert' *v.t.*

reinser'tion *n.*
reinter'pret *n.*
reinterpreta'tion *n.*

reintroduce' *v.t.*
reintroduc'tion *n.*
reiss'uable *adj.*
reiss'ue *v.t.* and *n.*

---

restore to youthful condition or appearance or to activity.—*v.i.* to rejuvenesce.—*ns.* **rejuvena'tion; reju'venator.**—*v.i.* **rejuvenesce** (*-es'*) to grow young again: to recover youthful character: to undergo change in cell-contents to a different, usu. more active, character (*biol.*).—*v.t.* to rejuvenate.—*n.* **rejuvenesc'ence.**—*adj.* **rejuvenesc'ent.** [Pfx. **re-,** L. *juvenis,* young, *juvenēscĕre,* to become young.]

relapse *ri-laps',* v.i. to slide, sink, or fall back, esp. into evil or illness: to return to a former state or practice: to backslide: to fall away.—*n.* a falling back into a former bad state: the return of a disease after partial recovery.—*adj.* **relapsed'** having relapsed.—*n.* **relap'ser.**—*adj.* **relap'sing.**—**relapsing fever** an infectious disease characterised by recurrent attacks of fever with enlargement of the spleen, caused by a spirochaete transmitted by ticks and lice. [L. *relābī, relāpsus—lābī,* to slide.]

relate *ri-lāt',* v.t. to recount, narrate, tell: to refer, bring into connection or relation.—*v.i.* to date back in application (*law*): to have reference or relation: to connect: to get on well (with) (often with *to; coll.*).—*adj.* **relā'ted** narrated: connected: allied by kindred or marriage.—*ns.* **relā'tedness; relā'ter; relā'tion** act of relating: state or mode of being related: narrative or recital: statement: an information (*law*): way in which one thing is connected with another: a quality that can be predicated, not of a single thing, but only of two or more together (*philos.*): respect, reference: a relative by birth or marriage: (in *pl.*) mutual dealings: (in *pl.*) sexual intercourse (*euph.*).—*adj.* **relā'tional.**—*adv.* **relā'tionally.**—*adj.* **relā'tionless.**—*n.* **relā'tionship** state or mode of being related: relations: an emotional or sexual affair.—*adjs.* **relatival** (*rel-ə-tī'vl*) pertaining to relation, esp. grammatical relation; **rel'ative** (*-ə-tiv*) in or having relation: correlative: corresponding: having the same key-signature (*mus.*): relevant: comparative: not absolute or independent: relating, having reference (to): referring to an antecedent (*gram.*).—*n.* a relative word, esp. a relative pronoun: one who is related by blood or marriage.—*adv.* **rel'atively.**—*n.* **rel'ativeness.**—*v.t.* and *v.i.* **rel'ativise, -ize** to make or become relative.—*ns.* **rel'ativism** a doctrine of relativity: the view that accepted standards of right and good vary with environment and from person to person; **rel'ativist.**—*adj.* **relativis'tic** pertaining to relativity, or to relativism.—*ns.* **relativ'itist** one who studies or accepts relativity; **relativ'ity** state or fact of being relative: (in *pl.*) related aspects of pay, working conditions, etc., between different jobs or the same job in different areas: a principle which asserts that only relative, not absolute, motion can be detected in the universe (Einstein's **Special Theory of Relativity,** 1905, starts from two fundamental postulates: a. that all motion is relative, b. that the velocity of light is always constant relative to an observer; his **General Theory of Relativity,** 1916, which embraces the Special Theory deals with varying velocities, or accelerations—whereas the Special Theory dealt with constant relative velocity, or zero acceleration—and it is much concerned with gravitation); **relator** (*ri-lā'tər*) one who relates: a narrator: one who lays an information before the Attorney-General, enabling him to take action (*law*).—**relative aperture** in a camera, the ratio of the diameter of the lens to the focal length; **relative density** specific gravity (q.v.); **relative humidity** the ratio of the amount of water vapour in the air to the amount that would saturate it at the same temperature.—**relative atomic mass** same as **atomic weight; relative molecular mass** same as

molecular weight. [L. *relātus, -a, -um,* used as pa.p. of *referre,* to bring back—*re, ferre.*]

relative, etc. See **relate.**

relax *ri-laks',* v.t. and v.i. to loosen: to slacken: to make or become less close, tense, rigid, strict, or severe.—*adj.* and *n.* **relax'ant** (a substance) having the effect of relaxing.—*n.* **relaxā'tion** (*re-, rē-*) act of relaxing: state of being relaxed: partial remission (*law*): recreation.—*adj.* **relax'ative.**—*n.* **relax'in** a hormone which has a relaxing effect on the pelvic muscles, and is used to facilitate childbirth.—*adj.* **relax'ing** enervating. [L. *relaxāre, -ātum—laxus,* loose.]

relay¹ *ri-lā',* also *rē'lā, rē'lā',* n. a supply of horses, etc., to relieve others on a journey: a station for either of these: a relieving shift of men: a relay-race: an electrically-operated switch employed to effect changes in an independent circuit: any device by which a weak electric current or other small power is used to control a strong one: a relayed programme, or act or fact of relaying it.—*v.t.* to place in, relieve, control, supply, or transmit by relay: to rebroadcast (programme received from another station or source).—*v.i.* to obtain a relay: to operate a relay:—*pa.t.* and *pa.p.* **relayed.**—**re'lay-race'** a race between teams, each man running part of the total distance. [O.Fr. *relais,* relay of horses or dogs.]

relay² *rē-lā',* v.t. to lay again:—*pa.t.* and *pa.p.* **relaid'.** [Pfx. **re-.**]

release¹ *rē-lēs',* v.t. to grant a new lease of. [Pfx. **re-.**]

release² *ri-lēs',* v.t. to let loose: to set free: to let go: to relieve: to slacken: to undo: to remit: to surrender, convey, give up a right to (*law*): to make available, authorise sale, publication, exhibition, etc., of: to make available for public knowledge.—*n.* a setting free: discharge or acquittance: remission: the giving up of a claim, conveyance: a catch for holding and releasing: authorisation to make available on a certain date: a thing so made available.—*adj.* **releas'able.**—*ns.* **releasee'** one to whom an estate is released; **release'ment** release; **releas'er; releas'or** (*law*). [O.Fr. *relaissier*—L. *relaxāre,* to relax.]

relegate *rel'i-gāt,* v.t. to banish: to consign (to a, usu. unimportant, place or position): to remove to a lower class (*football*): to refer (to another, others) for decision or action.—*adj.* **rel'egable.**—*n.* **relegā'tion.** [L. *relēgāre, -ātum—re-,* away, *lēgāre,* to send.]

relent *ri-lent',* v.i. to soften, become less severe: to give way.—*n.* and *adj.* **relent'ing.**—*adj.* **relent'less** unrelenting: inexorable: merciless.—*adv.* **relent'lessly.**—*n.* **relent'lessness.** [L. *re-,* back, *lentus,* sticky, sluggish, pliant.]

relevant *rel'i-vənt, adj.* bearing upon, or applying to, the matter in hand, pertinent: related, proportional (to): sufficient legally.—*ns.* **rel'evance, rel'evancy.**—*adv.* **rel'evantly.** [L. *relevāns, -antis,* pr.p. of *relevāre,* to raise up, relieve; from the notion of helping; cf. **relieve.**]

reliable, reliant, etc. See **rely.**

relic *rel'ik, n.* that which is left after loss or decay of the rest: any personal memorial of a saint, held in reverence as an incentive to faith and piety (*R.C.*): a souvenir: a memorial of antiquity or object of historic interest: (of, e.g. a custom) a survival from the past. [Fr. *relique*—L. *reliquiae;* see **reliquiae.**]

relict *rel'ikt, n.* a survivor or surviving trace (*geol., zool.,* etc.): a widow (*arch.*).—*adj.* (*ri-likt'*) left behind: surviving: formed by removal of surrounding materials (*geol.*). [L. *relictus, -a, -um,* left, pa.p. of *relinquĕre,* to leave.]

relied. See **rely.**

relief ri-lēf', n. the lightening or removal of any burden, discomfort, evil, pressure, or stress: release from a post or duty: one who releases another by taking his place: that which relieves or mitigates: aid in danger, esp. deliverance from siege: assistance to the poor: fresh supply of provisions: a certain fine paid to the overlord by a feudal tenant's heir on coming into possession: anything that gives diversity: projection or standing out from the general surface, ground, or level: a sculpture or other work of art executed in relief: appearance of standing out solidly: distinctness by contrast, esp. in outline.—*adj.* providing relief in cases of overloading, distress, danger, difficulty.—*adj.* relief'less.—relief map a map in which the form of the country is shown by elevations and depressions of the material used, or by the illusion of such elevations and depressions. [Ó.Fr. *relef*—*relever*; see relieve, also rilievo.]

relieve ri-lēv', v.t. to bring, give, or afford relief to: to release: to release from duty by taking the place of: to ease (e.g. a burden): (*refl.*) to urinate or to defecate: to mitigate: to raise the siege of: to set off by contrast: to break the sameness of: to bring into relief.—*adj.* reliev'able.—*n.* reliev'er.—*adj.* reliev'ing.—relieve someone of to take from someone's possession, with or without someone's approval: to steal from someone: to free someone from (a necessity, restriction, etc.). [O.Fr. *relever*—L. *relevāre*, to lift, relieve—*levāre*, to raise—*levis*, light.]

relievo ri-lē'vō, also (from It.) rilievo rē-lyä'vō, (*art*) ns. relief: a work in relief: appearance of relief:—*pls.* relie'vos, rilie'vi (-vē). [It. *rilievo*.]

religieux rə-lē-zhyø, (Fr.) n. a monk or friar:—*fem.* religieuse (-zhyœz) a nun.

religion ri-lij'ən, n. belief in, recognition of, or an awakened sense of, a higher unseen controlling power or powers, with the emotion and morality connected therewith: rites or worship: any system of such belief or worship: devoted fidelity: monastic life.—*n.* relig'ioner a member of an order.—*v.t.* relig'ionise, -ize to imbue with religion.—*ns.* relig'ionism religiosity: bigotry; relig'ionist one attached to a religion: a bigot: one professionally engaged in religion.—*adjs.* relig'ionless; religiose (-lij'i-ōs, or -ōs') morbidly or sentimentally religious.—*n.* religiosity (-i-os'it-i) spurious or sentimental religion: religious feeling.—*adj.* relig'ious (-əs) of, concerned with, devoted to, or imbued with, religion: scrupulous: bound to a monastic life (*R.C.*): strict, very exact.—*n.* one bound by monastic vows.—*adv.* relig'iously.—*n.* relig'iousness. [L. *religiō, -ōnis*, n., *religiōsus*, adj., perh. conn. with *religāre*, to bind.]

religiose, etc. See religion.

reline rē-līn', v.t. to mark with new lines: to renew the lining of. [Pfx. re-.]

relinquish ri-ling'kwish, v.t. to give up: to let go.—*n.* relin'quishment. [O.Fr. *relinquir, relinquiss-*—L. *relinquĕre, relictum—re-, linquĕre*, to leave.]

relique rel'ik, ri-lēk', n. an old form of relic.—*n.* rel'iquary (-kwər-i) a receptacle for relics.—*adj.* of relics: residual. [Fr.]

reliquiae ri-lik'wi-ē, re-lik'wi-ī, n.pl. remains, esp. fossil remains. [L.—*relinquĕre*, to leave.]

relish rel'ish, n. a flavour: characteristic flavour: appetising flavour: zest-giving quality: an appetiser, condiment: zestful enjoyment: gusto.—*v.t.* to like the taste of: to enjoy: to appreciate discriminatingly.—*adj.* rel'ishable. [O.Fr. *reles, relais*, remainder—*relaisser*, to leave behind.]

relive rē-liv', v.t. and v.i. to live again.

relocate rē-lō-kāt', v.t. to locate again: to move (a firm, workers, etc.) to a different area or site.—*v.i.* to move one's place of business or residence.—*n.* reloca'tion. [Pfx. re-.]

reluctance ri-lukt'əns, n. unwillingness: magnetomotive force applied to whole or part of a magnetic circuit divided by the flux in it; reluc'tancy.—*adj.* reluc'tant unwilling: resisting.—*adv.* reluct'antly. [L. *reluctārī—re-*, against, *luctārī*, to struggle.]

rely ri-lī', v.i. to depend confidently (on, upon):—*pr.p.* rely'ing; *pa.t.* and *pa.p.* relied'.—*n.* reliabil'ity.—*adj.* reli'able to be relied on, trustworthy.—*n.* reli'ableness.—*adv.* reli'ably.—*n.* reli'ance trust: that in which one trusts.—*adj.* reli'ant. [O.Fr. *relier*—L. *religāre*, to bind back.]

rem rem, n. a unit of radiation dosage, the amount which has the same effect as one rad of X-radiation. [röntgen equivalent man or mammal.]

remade. See remake.

remain ri-mān', v.i. to stay or be left behind: to continue in the same place: to be left after or out of a greater number: to continue in one's possession, mind: to continue unchanged: to continue to be: to be still to be dealt with (often without subject *it*).—*n.* remain'der that which remains or is left behind after the removal of a part or after division: the residue, rest: an interest in an estate to come into effect after a certain other event happens (*legal*): right of next succession to a post or title: residue of an edition when the sale of a book has fallen off.—*v.t.* to sell (book) a. a remainder.—*n. pl.* or *n.sing.* remains' what is left. relics: a corpse: the literary productions of one dead [O.Fr. *remaindre*—L. *remanēre—re-*, back, *manēre*, to stay.]

remake rē-māk', v.t. to make anew.—*adj.* remade'.—*n.* remake' a thing (as a gutta golf-ball) made over again from the original materials: something made again, esp. (a new version of) a film. [Pfx. re-.]

remand ri-mänd', v.t. to send back (esp. a prisoner into custody or on bail to await further evidence).—*n.* act of remanding: recommittal.—remand home, centre in England, a place of detention for children and young persons on remand or awaiting trial: also for some undergoing punishment.—on remand having been remanded. [O.Fr. *remander*, or L.L. *remandāre—mandāre*, to order.]

remanent rem'ən-ənt, adj. remaining: of magnetism, remaining after removal of magnetising field.—*ns.* rem'anence, -ency. [L. *remanēns, -entis*, pr.p. of *remanēre*.]

remark¹ ri-märk', v.t. to notice: to comment (that), or say incidentally (that).—*v.i.* to comment, make an observation (often with *on, upon*).—*n.* noteworthiness: observation: comment: a distinguishing mark on an engraving or etching indicating an early state of the plate.—*adj.* remark'able noteworthy: unusual, singular, strange, distinguished.—*n.* remark'ableness.—*adv.* remark'ably.—*adj.* remarked' conspicuous: bearing a remark, as an etching.—*n.* remark'er. [O.Fr. *remarquer—re-*, intens., *marquer*, to mark.]

remark², re-mark rē-märk', v.t. to mark again. [re-.]

remeasure rē-mezh'ər, v.t. to measure anew.—*n.* remeas'urement. [Pfx. re-.]

remedy rem'i-di, n. any means of curing a disease, redressing, counteracting, or repairing any evil or loss: reparation: redress: range of tolerated variation in the weight of a coin.—*v.t.* to put right, repair, counteract:—*pr.p.* rem'edying; *pa.t.* and *pa.p.* rem'edied.—*adj.* reme'diable.—*adv.* reme'diably.—

relight' v.t. and v.i. remarr'iage n. remarr'y v.t. and v.i.
reload' v.t. and v.i.

fāte; fär; mē; hûr (her); mīne; mōte; för; mūte; mōōn; fōōt; dhen (then); el'ə-mənt (element) *adj.* **reme'dial** tending or intended to remedy: of or concerning the teaching of slow-learning children.— *adv.* **reme'dially.**—*adj.* **rem'ediless.**—*adv.* **rem'edilessly.**—*n.* **rem'edilessness.** [A.Fr. *remedie*, O.Fr. *remede*—L. *remedium.*]

remember *ri-mem'bər*, *v.t.* to keep in or recall to memory or mind: to bear in mind as one deserving of honour or gratitude, or as one to be rewarded, tipped, or prayed for: to regain one's good manners after a temporary lapse (*refl.*): to recall to the memory of another (often as a greeting).—*v.i.* to have the power or perform the act of memory.—*adj.* **remem'berable.** —*adv.* **remem'berably.**—*ns.* **remem'berer; remem'brance** memory: that which serves to bring to or keep in mind: a souvenir: the reach of memory: (in *pl.*) a message of friendly greeting; **remem'brancer** a recorder: an officer of exchequer responsible for collecting debts due to the Crown (**King's, Queen's Remembrancer**).—**Remembrance Sunday** the Sunday nearest to 11th November commemorating the fallen of the two World Wars (see **Armistice Day**). [O.Fr. *remembrer*—L. *re-*, again, *memor*, mindful.]

remex *rē'meks*, *n.* one of the large feathers of a bird's wing—primary or secondary:—*pl.* **remiges** (*rem'i-jēz*).—*adj.* **remigial** (*ri-mij'i-əl*). [L. *rēmex, -igis*, a rower.]

remind *ri-mīnd'*, *v.t.* to put in mind (of), to cause to remember.—*n.* **remind'er** that which reminds.—*adj.* **remind'ful** mindful: reminiscent, exciting memories. [Pfx. *re-* and **mind** *v.t.*]

reminiscence *rem-i-nis'əns*, *n.* recollection: an account of something remembered: the recurrence to the mind of the past.—*v.i.* **reminisce** (*-nis'*; back-formation) to recount reminiscences.—*adj.* **reminisc'ent** suggestive, remindful: addicted to reminiscences: pertaining to reminiscence.—Also *n.*—*adj.* **reminiscen'tial** (*-sen'shl*).—*adv.* **reminisc'ently.** [L. *reminīscēns, -entis*, pr.p. of *reminīscī*, to remember.]

remise *ri-mīz'*, *n.* surrender of a claim (*law*): (*rə-mēz'*) an effective second thrust after the first has missed (*fencing*): a coach-house (*obs.*).—*v.t.* (*ri-mīz'*) to surrender. [Fr *remis*, *remise—remettre*—L *remittēre*, to send back, remit, relax.]

remiss *ri-mis'*, *adj.* negligent: slack: lax: wanting in vigour.—*n.* **remissibil'ity.**—*adj.* **remiss'ible** that may be remitted.—*n.* **remission** (*ri-mish'ən*) act of remitting: abatement: relinquishment of a claim: the lessening of a term of imprisonment: pardon: forgiveness.—*adj.* **remiss'ive** remitting: forgiving.— *adv.* **remiss'ly.**—*n.* **remiss'ness.**—*adj.* **remiss'ory** of remission [L. *remittēre, remissum*; see **remit**.]

remit *ri-mit'*, *v.t.* to relax: to refrain from exacting or inflicting: to give up: to transfer: to transmit, as money, etc.: to refer to another court, authority, etc.: to refer for consideration: to send or put back.—*v.i* to abate: to relax: to desist:—*pr.p.* **remitt'ing;** *pa.t.* and *pa.p.* **remitt'ed.**—*n.* (*rē'mit, ri-mit'*) reference of a case or matter to another (*legal*): scope, terms of reference.—*ns.* **remit'ment; remitt'al** remission: reference to another court, etc., **remitt'ance** the sending of money, etc., to a distance: the sum or thing sent; **remittee** (*-ē'*) the person to whom a remittance is sent.—*adj.* **remitt'ent** (of an illness) remitting, becoming less severe, at intervals.—*adv.* **remitt'ently.**—*n.* **remitt'er, remitt'or** one who makes a remittance.—**remitt'ance-man** one dependent upon remittances from home. [L. *remittēre, remissum—re-*, back, *mittēre*, to send.]

remnant *rem'nənt*, *n.* a fragment or a small number surviving or remaining after destruction, defection, removal, sale, etc., of the greater part. esp. a remaining piece of cloth: a tag or quotation: a surviving trace. [**remanent.**]

remonetise, -ize *rē-mun'ə-tīz, -mon'*, *v.t.* to re-establish as legal tender.—*n.* **remonetisa'tion, -z-**. [Pfx. **re-**.]

remonstrance *ri-mon'strəns*, *n.* a strong or formal protest, expostulation.—*adj.* **remon'strant** remonstrating.—*n.* one who remonstrates.—*v.i.* **remon'strate** (sometimes *rem'*) to make a remonstrance.— *v.t.* to say in remonstrance.—*adv.* **remon'stratingly.** —*n.* **remonstra'tion** (*rem-ən-*).—*adjs.* **remon'strative, remon'stratory** (*-stra-tər-i*) expostulatory. —*n.* **remon'strator** (or *rem'*). [L. *re-*, again, *mōnstrāre*, to point out.]

remontant *ri-mon'tant, adj.* blooming more than once in the same season.—*n* a remontant plant, esp. a rose [Fr]

remora *rem'ə-rə, n.* the sucking-fish, formerly believed to stop ships by attaching its sucker. [L. *rēmōra*, delay, hindrance—*mora*, delay.]

remorse *ri-mòrs', n* the gnawing pain of conscience: compunction.—*adj.* **remorse'ful** penitent.—*adv.* **remorse'fully.**—*n.* **remorse'fulness.**—*adj* **remorse'less** without remorse. cruel: without respite.—*adv.* **remorse'lessly.**—*n.* **remorse'lessness.** [O.Fr. *remors* (Fr. *remords*)—L.L *remorsus*—L *remordēre, remorsum*, to bite again.]

remote *ri-mōt', adj.* far removed in place, time, chain of causation or relation, resemblance or relevance: widely separated: very indirect.—*adv.* **remote'ly.**— **remote control** control of a device from a distance by the making or breaking of an electric circuit or by means of radio waves [L *remōtus*, pa p of *removēre*; see **remove**.]

remoulade, rémoulade *rā-mōō-lad', n.* a sauce made with eggs, herbs, capers, etc., or sometimes with mayonnaise, and served with fish, salad, etc. [Fr. dial. *ramolas*, horseradish,—L. *armoracea*.]

remould *rē'mōld', n.* a used tyre which has had a new tread vulcanised to the casing and the walls coated with rubber.—Also *v.t.* [Pfx. **re-**.]

remount *rē-mownt', v.t* and *v.i.* to mount again.—*n.* a fresh horse, or supply of horses. [Pfx. **re-**.]

remove *ri-mōōv', v.t.* to put or take away: to transfer: to withdraw: to displace: to make away with—*v i* to go away: to change abode —*n.* removal: step or degree of remoteness or indirectness: in some schools, an intermediate class.—*n.* **removabil'ity.**—*adj.* **remov'able.**—*adv.* **remov'ably.**—*n.* **remov'al** the act of taking away: displacing: change of place: transference: going away: change of abode: a euphemism for murder —*adj.* **removed'** remote. distant by degrees, as in descent, relationship.—*ns.* **remov'edness; remov'er** one who or that which removes: one who conveys furniture from house to house [O.Fr. *removouvoir*— L. *removēre, remōtum—re-*, away, *movēre*, to move.]

remunerate *ri-mū'nə-rāt, v.t* to recompense: to pay for service rendered —*adj.* **remū'nerable.**—*n.* **remūnera'tion** recompense: reward: pay.—*adj* **remū'nerative** profitable.—*ns.* **remū'nerativeness; remū'nerātor.**— *adj.* **remū'neratory** (*-ə-tər-i*) giving a recompense. [L. *remunerārī* (late *-āre*), *-ātus—mūnus, -eris*, a gift]

renaissance *ri-nā'səns, ren'i-sans, -sàns', n.* a new birth: (*cap*) the revival of arts and letters, the transition from the Middle Ages to the modern world.— *adj* of the Renaissance —**Renaissance man** a man who typifies the renaissance ideal of wide-ranging culture and learning. [Fr ; cf. **renascence**.]

renal *rē'nl, adj* of the kidneys [L. *rēnālis—rēnēs* (sing. *rēn*, is rare), the kidneys]

---

renascent ri-nas'ənt, also -nās', adj coming into renewed life or vitality.—n. renasc'ence being born anew [L. renāscēns, pr p. of renāscī—nāscī, to be born.]

rend rend, v t to tear asunder with force to split to tear away.—v.i. to become torn.—pa.t. and pa.p rent. [O.E. rendan, to tear.]

render ren'dər, v.t. to give up. to give back, return, give in return: to make up. to deliver. to hand over. to give. to surrender: to yield. to tender or submit: to show forth: to represent or reproduce, esp artistically: to perform to translate. to perform or pay as a duty or service. to cause to be or become to melt. to extract, treat, or clarify by melting: to plaster with a first coat —adj. ren'derable.—ns. ren'derer; ren'dering; rendi'tion surrender rendering. a performance [O.Fr rendre—L L rendēre, app formed by influence of prendēre, to take—L reddēre —re-, back, dāre, to give]

rendezvous rä'dä-vōō, ron'di-, n appointed meeting-place: a meeting by appointment: a general resort.— pl. rendezvous (-vōōz).—v.i. to assemble at any appointed place. [Fr. rendez-vous, render yourselves —rendre, to render.]

rendition. See render.

renegade ren'i-gād, n one faithless to principle or party: a turncoat: esp a Christian turned Muslim — v.t. renegue, renege (ri-nēg', or -nāg') to renounce. to apostatise from.—v.i. to deny (often with on): to refuse (often with on): to revoke at cards —n. reneg'(u)er. [L.L. renegātus—L re-, negāre, to deny, partly Sp. renegado.]

renew ri-nū', v.i. to renovate: to revive: to begin again to repeat: to invigorate: to substitute new for. to restore: to regenerate. to extend the loan of.—v.i. to be made new: to begin again.—adj. renew'able.—ns renew'al; renew'edness; renew'er; renew'ing. [Pfx re-, and new, adj.]

reniform ren'i-förm, adj. kidney-shaped [L. rēnēs (sing. rēn), the kidneys, and förma, form. see renal.]

renin rē'nin, n. a protein enzyme secreted by the kidneys into the bloodstream, where it helps to maintain the blood pressure. [L. rēnēs (sing rēn), the kidneys.]

rennet ren'it, n. any means of curdling milk, esp a preparation of calf's stomach. [O.E rinnan, to run.]

rennin ren'in, n. an enzyme found in gastric juice, which causes coagulation of milk. [rennet.]

renounce ren'nowns', v.t. to disclaim: to disown. to reject publicly and finally: to recant: to abjure.—v t. to fail to follow suit at cards.—n. a failure to follow suit —ns. renounce'ment; renoun'cer. [O.Fr. renuncer —L. renuntiāre—re-, away, nuntiāre, -ātum, to announce.]

renovate ren'ō-vāt, v.t. to renew or make new again to make as if new: to regenerate.—ns. renovā'tion; ren'ovātor. [L. re-, again, novāre, -ātum, to make new—novus, new]

renown ri-nown', n. fame.—adj. renowned' famous [O.Fr. renoun (Fr. renom)—L re-, again, nōmen, a name.]

rent¹ rent, n an opening made by rending: a fissure — Also pa.t. and pa.p. of rend. [rend.]

rent² rent, n. periodical payment for use of another's property, esp. houses and lands: revenue.—v.t. to hold or occupy by paying rent. to let or hire out for a rent: to charge with rent —v.t. to be let at a rent —

adj rent'able.—ns rent'al a rent-roll. rent· annual value something rented or hired (U.S); rent'er a tenant who pays rent one who lets out property. a distributor of commercial films to cinemas.—rent· a(n)- (facet , also without hyphens) in composition, (as if) rented or hired, as in rent'-a-crowd, rent'-a-mob, rent'-an-army.—rental library (U S) a lending-library which takes fees for books borrowed, rent'-collector; rent'-day.—adj and adv rent'-free without payment of rent —rent'-restric'tion restriction of landlord's right to raise rent, rent'-roll a list of property and rents· total income from property —forrent (orig U S) to let [Fr rente—L reddita (pecūnia), money paid—reddēre, to pay]

renunciation ri-nun-si-ā'shən, n act of renouncing self-resignation —adjs renun'ciative (-shə-tiv, -syə-tiv, -si-ā-tiv), renun'ciatory (-shə-tər-i, -si-ə-tər-i) [L. renūntiāre, proclaim, see nuncio.]

reopen rē-ō'pn, v t. and v i. to open again. to begin again.—reopening clause in collective bargaining, a clause enabling any issue in a contract to be reconsidered before the contract expires (also reopener (clause)) [Pfx re-.]

reorient rē-ō', -o'ri-ənt, adj. rising again —v.t (-ent) to orient again —v.t reō'rientate to reorient.—n reōrienta'tion. [Pfx. re-.]

rep¹, repp rep, n a corded cloth [Fr. reps.]

rep² rep, n. a colloquial or slang abbreviation of repertory (theatrical), reputation (U.S.), representative.

repaid pa t and pa.p of repay.

repaint rē-pānt', v.t to paint anew —n. (rē'pānt) a repainted golf-ball —n. repaint'ing. [Pfx. re-.]

repair¹ ri-pār', v.i to betake oneself: to go: to resort —n resort· place of resort [O Fr. repairer, to return to a haunt—L.L. repatriāre, to return to one's country]

repair² ri-pār', v t. to mend to make amends for: to make good —n restoration after injury or decay· supply of loss: sound condition: condition in respect of soundness. part that has been mended, made sound.—adj repair'able capable of being mended.— ns repair'er; reparability (rep-ər-ə-bil'i-ti).—adj reparable (rep'ər-ə-bl) capable of being made good.— adv rep'arably.—n repara'tion repair· supply of what is wasted: amends: compensation.—adjs. reparative (ri-par'ə-tiv); repar'atory.—repair'man one who does repairs, esp. on something mechanical; repair'-shop. [O.Fr. reparer—L reparāre—parāre, to prepare]

repand ri-pand', (bot , zool.) adj slightly wavy [L repandus—re-, back, pandus, bent]

reparable, etc See repair².

repartee rep-ar-tē', n. a ready and witty retort: skill in making such retorts —v.t. and v i. to retort with ready wit [O.Fr. repartie—repartir—partir, to set out—L. partīrī, to divide.]

repass rē-pas', v.t. and v i. to pass again. to pass in the opposite direction.—n repassage (rē-pas'ij). [Pfx re-.]

repast ri-past', n. a meal [O Fr. repast (Fr. repas)-L.L repastus—L. pāscere, pastum, to feed.]

repatriate rē- or ri-pāt ri-āt, or -pat', v.t. to restore or send back someone to his country.—n. a repatriated person.—n repatriā'tion. [L.L repatriāre, -ātum, to return to one's country—L patria.]

repay rē-pā', ri-pā', v t. to pay back: to make return for to recompense. to pay or give in return.—v.i. to make repayment:—pr p. repay'ing; pa.t. and pa p

rēnegō'tiable adj.
rēnegō'tiate v.t
rēnegōtiā'tion n.
rēnum'ber v.t

rēocc'upy v t.
rēor'der v.t
rēoffend' v t

rēorganisā'tion, -z- n.
rēor'ganise, -ize v.t
rēpack' v.t and v.t.
rēpā'per v t

fāte, fär, mē; hūr (her); mine, mōte, for, mūte; mōōn, fōōt, dhen (then); el'ə-mənt (element)

repaid'.—*adj.* **repay'able** that is to be repaid: due.—*n.* **repay'ment.** [Pfx. **re-**.]

repeal *ri-pēl',* *v.t.* to revoke: to annul.—*n.* abrogation.—*adj.* **repeal'able.**—*n.* **repeal'er** one who repeals. [O.Fr. *rapeler*—pfx. *re-*, *apeler*, to appeal]

repeat *ri-pēt',* *v.t.* to say, do, perform, go over, again: to quote from memory: to say off: to recount: to say or do after another: to tell to others, divulge: to cause to recur: to reproduce.—*v.i.* to recur: to make repetition: to strike the last hour, quarter, etc., when required: to fire several shots without reloading: to rise so as to be tasted after swallowing: to vote (illegally) more than once (*U.S.*).—*n.* a repetition: a retracing of one's course: a passage repeated or marked for repetition (*mus.*): dots or other mark directing repetition: an order for more goods of the same kind: a radio or television programme broadcast for the second, third, etc., time.—*adj.* done or occurring as a repetition.—*adjs.* **repeat'able** able to be done again: fit to be told to others; **repeat'ed.**—*adv.* **repeat'edly** many times repeated: again and again.—*n.* **repeat'er** one who, or that which, repeats: a decimal fraction in which the same figure (or sometimes figures) is repeated to infinity: a watch or clock, or a firearm, that repeats: an instrument for automatically retransmitting a message (*teleg.*).—*n.* and *adj.* **repeat'ing.**—**repeat oneself** to say again what one has said already. [Fr. *répéter*—L. *repetĕre*, *repititum*—*re-*, again, *petĕre*, to seek.]

repechage *rep'ə-shäzh,* Fr. *rə-pesh-äzh,* (*rowing, fencing,* etc.) *adj.* pertaining to a supplementary competition in which second-bests in earlier eliminating competitions get a second chance to go on to the final. [Fr. *repêchage,* a fishing out again.]

repel *ri-pel',* *v.t.* to drive off or back: to repulse: to reject: to hold off: to provoke aversion in:—*pr.p.* **repell'ing;** *pa.t.* and *pa.p.* **repelled'.**—*ns.* **repell'ence, repell'ency.**—*adj.* **repell'ent** able or tending to repel: distasteful.—*n.* that which repels.—*adv.* **repell'ently.**—*n.* **repell'er.**—*adj.* **repell'ing.**—*adv.* **repell'ingly.** [L. *repellĕre*—*pellĕre*, to drive.]

repent[1] *ri-pent',* *v.i.* to regret or wish to have been otherwise, what one has done or left undone (with *of*): to change from past evil: to feel contrition.—*v.t.* (*refl.* or *impers.*) to affect with contrition or with regret (*arch.*): to regret, or feel contrition for (an action).—*n.* **repentance.**—*adj.* **repent'ant** experiencing or expressing repentance.—*adv.* **repent'antly.**—*n.* **repent'er.**—*adv.* **repent'ingly.** [O.Fr. *repentir*—L. *paenitēre,* to cause to repent.]

repent[2] *rē'pənt,* (*bot.*) *adj.* lying on the ground and rooting.—Also **rep'tant.** [L. *repēns, -entis,* pr.p. of *repĕre,* to creep.]

repercussion *rē-pər-kush'ən,* driving back: reverberation: reflection: a return stroke, reaction, or consequence.—*adj.* **repercussive** (*-kus'iv*). [L. *repercutĕre, -cussum*—*re-, per, quatĕre,* to strike.]

repertory *rep'ər-tər-i,* *n.* a stock of pieces that a person or company is prepared to perform.—Also *adj.*—*n.* **repertoire** (*rep'ər-twär;* Fr. *répertoire*) performer's or company's repertory.—**repertory theatre** a theatre with a repertoire of plays and a company of actors, called a **repertory company.** [L.L. *repertōrium*—L. *reperīre,* to find again—*parēre,* to bring forth.]

repetend *rep'i-tend, rep-i-tend',* *n.* the figure(s) that recur(s) in a recurring decimal number (*math.*): anything that recurs or is repeated. [L. *repetendum,* that which is to be repeated—L. *repetere,* to repeat.]

répétiteur *rā-pā-tē-tœr',* *n.* a coach, tutor who rehearses opera singers, etc. [Fr.; cf. **repeat.**]

repetition *rep-i-tish'ən,* *n.* act of repeating: recital from memory: a thing repeated: power of repeating a note promptly.—*adjs.* **repeti'tional, repeti'tionary, repetitious** (*-tish'as*); **repetitive** (*ri-pet'i-tiv*) iterative: overmuch given to repetition.—*advs.* **repeti'tiously, repet'itively.**—*ns.* **repeti'tiousness, repet'itiveness.** [L. *repetĕre;* see **repeat.**]

rephrase *rē-frāz',* *v.t.* to put in different words, usu. so as to make more understandable, acceptable, etc. [Pfx. **re-**.]

repine *ri-pīn',* *v.i.* to fret (with *at* or *against*): to feel discontent.—*n.* and *adj.* **repin'ing.** [App. from **pine**[2].]

replace *ri-* or *rē-plās',* *v.t.* to put back: to provide a substitute for: to take the place of, supplant.—*adj.* **replace'able.**—*ns.* **replace'ment** act of replacing: a person or thing that takes the place of another; **replac'er** a substitute.—**replaceable hydrogen** hydrogen atoms that can be replaced in an acid by metals to form salts. [Pfx. **re-**.]

replay *rē-plā',* *v.t.* to play again (a game, match, record, recording, etc.).—*n.* (*rē'plā*) a game, match, played again: a recording played again, esp. (also **action replay**) of a part of a broadcast game or match, often in slow motion. [Pfx. **re-**.]

replenish *ri-plen'ish,* *v.t.* to fill again: to fill completely: to stock abundantly: to people.—*ns.* **replen'isher; replen'ishment.** [O.Fr *replenir, -iss-,* from *replein,* full—L. *re-,* again, *plēnus,* full.]

replete *ri-plēt',* *adj.* full: filled to satiety: abounding (with *with*).—*ns.* **replete'ness, reple'tion.** [L. *replētus,* pa.p. of *replēre*—*plēre,* to fill.]

replevy *ri-plev'i,* *v.t.* to recover, or restore to the owner (goods distrained) upon pledge to try the right at law.—*adjs.* **replev'iable, replev'isable** (*-i-səb-l*).—*n.* **replev'in** replevying: a writ or action in such a case. [O.Fr. *replevir*—*plevir,* to pledge.]

replica *rep'li-kə,* *n.* a duplicate, properly one by the original artist: a facsimile. [It.,—L. *replicāre,* to repeat.]

replicate *rep'li-kāt,* *v.t.* to fold back: to repeat: to make a replica of.—*v.i.* of molecules of living material, to reproduce molecules identical with themselves.—*n.* (*mus.*) a tone one or more octaves from a given tone.—*adj.* folded back.—*n.* **replica'tion** the plaintiff's answer to the defendant's plea: doubling back: copy, reproduction. [L. *replicāre, -ātum,* to fold back—*plicāre,* to fold.]

reply *ri-plī',* *v.t.* to say in answer.—*v.i.* to answer: to respond in action, as by returning gun-fire: to echo: to answer a defendant's plea:—*pr.p.* **reply'ing;** *pa.t.* and *pa.p.* **replied'.**—*n.* an answer, response.—*n.* **repli'er.** [O.Fr. *replier*—L. *replicāre;* see **replicate.**]

repoint *rē-poynt',* *v.t.* to repair (stone or brickwork) by renewing the mortar, etc. [Pfx. **re-**.]

répondez s'il vous plaît *rā-pɔ̃-dā-sēl vōō ple,* or **R.S.V.P.** (Fr.) please answer (this invitation).

report *ri-pōrt', -pört',* *v.t.* to bring back, as an answer, news, or account of anything: to give an account of, esp. a formal, official, or requested account: to state in such an account: to relate: to circulate publicly: to transmit as having been said, done, or observed: to write down or take notes of, esp. for a newspaper or radio or television programme: to lay a charge against: (*refl.*) to make personal announcement of the presence and readiness of.—*v.i.* to make a statement: to write an account of occurrences: to make a formal report: to report oneself: to act as a reporter.—*n.* a statement of facts: a formal or official statement, as of results of an investigation or matter

---

repeo'ple *v.t.*
replan' *v.t.* and *v.i.*

replant' *v.t.*

repop'ulate *v.t.*

referred: a statement on a school pupil's work and behaviour or the like: an account of a matter of news, esp. the words of a speech: general talk: hearsay: explosive noise.—*adj.* **report'able.**—*n.* **report'age** journalistic reporting, style, or manner.—*adv.* **report'edly** according to report.—*n.* **report'er** one who reports, esp. for a newspaper or legal proceedings.— *n.* and *adj.* **report'ing.**—**reported speech** indirect speech; **report stage** the stage at which a parliamentary bill as amended in committee is reported to the House, before the third reading. [O.Fr. *reporter* —L. *reportāre*—re-, back, *portāre*, to carry.]

repose ri-pōz', *v.t.* to lay at rest: to give rest to, refresh by rest: to place, set (as confidence): to place in trust. —*v.i.* to rest: to be still: to rely (with *on, upon*).—*n.* rest: calm: restful feeling or effect.—*adj.* **repōsed'** calm: settled.—*adv.* **repō'sedly.**—*n.* **repōs'edness.**— *adj.* **repōse'ful.**—*adv.* **repōse'fully.** [Fr. *reposer*— L.L. *repausāre*; confused with the following.]

repository ri-poz'i-tə-ri, *n.* a place or receptacle in which anything is laid up: a collection or museum: a tomb: a storehouse, magazine, as of information: a place of accumulation: a confidant. [L. *repōnĕre*, *repositum*, to put back, lay aside—*pōnĕre*, to put; confused with foregoing.]

re-position, reposition rē-pəz-ish'ən, *v.t.* to put in a different position. [Pfx. re-.]

repossess rē-pəz-es', *v.t.* to regain possession of: to take back because payment has not been made: to put again in possession.—*n.* **repossession** (-esh'ən). [Pfx. re-.]

repoussé rə-pōō-sā, or -pōō', *adj.* raised in relief by hammering from behind or within.—*n.* repoussé work.—*n.* **repoussage** (-säzh'). [Fr.]

repp. Same as **rep**[1].

reprehend rep-ri-hend', *v.t.* to find fault with: to reprove.—*n.* **reprehend'er.**—*adj.* **reprehen'sible** blameworthy.—*adv.* **reprehen'sibly.**—*n.* **reprehen'sion.**—*adj.* **reprehen'sory.** [L. *repraehendĕre*, -*hēnsum*—re-, intens., *praehendĕre*, to lay hold of.]

represent rep-ri-zent', *v.t.* to use, or serve, as a symbol for: to stand for: to exhibit, depict, personate, show an image of, by imitative art: to act: to be a substitute, agent, deputy, member of parliament, or the like, for: to correspond or be in some way equivalent or analogous to: to serve as a sample of: to present earnestly to mind: to give out, allege (that).— *adj.* **represent'able** (*rep-ri*-).—*ns.* **representation** (-zən-tā'shən) act, state, or fact of representing or being represented: that which represents: an image: picture: dramatic performance: a presentation of a view of facts or arguments: a petition, expostulation: a body of representatives.—*adj.* **representā'tional** (*rep-ri-zən-*).—*ns.* **representā'tionalism, representā'-tionism** the doctrine that in the perception of the external world the immediate object represents another object beyond the sphere of consciousness; **representā'tionist.**—*adj.* **representative** (*rep-ri-zent'ə-tiv*) representing: exhibiting a likeness: typical.—*n.* a sample: a typical example or embodiment: one who represents another or others, as a deputy, delegate, ambassador, member of parliament, agent, successor, heir.—*adv.* **represent'atively.**—*ns.* **represent'ativeness; represent'er.—House of Representatives** the lower branch of the United States Congress, consisting of members chosen biennially by the people. [L. *repraesentāre*, -*ātum*—*praesentāre*, to place before.]

re-present rē-pri-zent', *v.t.* to present again.—*n.* **re'(-)presentā'tion.** [Pfx. re-.]

repress ri-pres', *v.t.* to restrain: to keep under: to put

down: to banish to the unconscious.—*adj.* **repress'-ible.**—*adv.* **repress'ibly.**—*n.* **repression** (-*presh'ən*). —*adj.* **repress'ive.**—*adv.* **repress'ively.**—*n.* **repress'or.** [L. *reprimĕre, repressum*—*premĕre*, to press.]

re-press rē'pres', *v.t.* to press again. [Pfx. re-.]

reprieve ri-prēv' *v.t.* to delay the execution of: to give a respite to.—*n.* a suspension of a criminal sentence, esp. a death sentence: interval of ease or relief. [Supposed to be from A.Fr. *repris*, pa.p. of *reprendre*, to take back (see **reprise**).]

reprimand rep'ri-mänd, -mànd, *n.* a severe reproof.— *v.t.* (also -*mänd'*, -*mand'*) to reprove severely, esp. publicly or officially. [Fr. *réprimande*—L. *reprimĕre, repressum*, to press back—*premĕre*, to press.]

reprint rē-print', *v.t.* to print again: to print a new impression of, esp. with little or no change.—*n.* **rē'-print** a later impression: printed matter used as copy.

reprise ri-prīz', *v.t.* to repeat.—*n.* resumption of an earlier subject (*mus.*; also *v.t.*).—*n.* **repris'al** seizure in retaliation: an act of retaliation. [Fr. *reprise*— *reprendre*—L. *repraehendĕre*.]

repro rep'rō, *n.* and *adj.* short for **reproduction**, esp. of modern copies of period styles of furniture (*pl.* **rep'ros**.)

reproach ri-prōch', *v.t.* to upbraid: to blame (oneself, etc., for, with): to reprove gently.—*n.* upbraiding: reproof: censure: disgrace: a source or matter of disgrace or shame.—*adj.* **reproach'able.**—*n.* **reproach'er.**—*adj.* **reproach'ful** reproving.—*adv.* **reproach'fully.**—*n.* **reproach'fulness.—above, beyond, reproach** excellent, too good to be criticised. [Fr. *reprocher*, perh. from L. *prope*, near; cf. **approach**; or from *reprobāre*; see **reprobate**.]

reprobate rep'rō-bāt, *adj.* given over to sin: depraved: unprincipled.—*n.* an abandoned or profligate person: one lost to shame.—*v.t.* to reject: to disapprove of: to censure.—*ns.* **rep'robacy** (*-bə-si*); **rep'robāter; reprobā'tion.** [L. *reprobāre*, -*ātum*, to reprove, contrary of *approbāre*—*probāre*, to prove.]

reprocess rē-prō'ses, *v.t.* to process again, esp. to remake used material into a new material or article. [Pfx. re-.]

reproduce rē-prō-dūs', *v.t.* to produce a copy of: to form anew: to propagate: to reconstruct in imagination.—*v.i.* to produce offspring: to prove suitable for copying in some way: to turn out (well, badly, etc.) when copied.—*n.* **reprodū'cer.**—*adj.* **reprodū'cible.** —*n.* **reproduction** (-*duk'shən*) the act of reproducing: the act of producing new organisms—the whole process whereby life is continued from generation to generation: regeneration: a copy, facsimile: a representation.—*adj.* **reproduc'tive.**—*adv.* **reproduc'-tively.**—*ns.* **reproduc'tiveness, reproductiv'ity.** [Pfx. re-.]

reprography ri-prog'rə-fi, *n.* the reproduction of graphic material, as by photocopying.—*n.* **reprog'ra-pher.**—*adj.* **reprograph'ic.** [Fr. *reprographie*.]

reproof ri-prōōf', *n.* a reproving: rebuke: censure: reprehension: (*rē-*) a second or new proof.—*v.t.* (*rē-*) to make waterproof again.—*n.* **reproval** (*ri-prōō'vl*) reproof.—*v.t.* **reprove'** to rebuke: to censure, condemn.—*ns.* **repro'ver; repro'ving.**—*adv.* **repro'-vingly.** [O.Fr. *reprover* (Fr. *réprouver*)—L. *reprobāre*; see **reprobate**.]

reptant rep'tənt, (*biol.*) *adj.* creeping. [L. *reptāre*, to creep.]

reptile rep'til, *adj.* creeping: like a reptile in nature.— *n.* any animal of the class **Reptilia** (-*til'i-ə*), vertebrates with scaly integument, cold blood, pulmonary respiration, and pentadactyl limbs (sometimes wanting): a creeping thing: a base, malignant, or treacherous person.—*adjs.* **reptilian** (-*til*'*i-ən*) [L.L. *reptilis*, -*e*—*repĕre*, to creep.]

republic *ri-pub'lik*, *n.* a form of government without a monarch, in which the supreme power is vested in the people and their elected representatives: a state or country so governed.—*adj.* **repub'lican** of or favouring a republic: (*cap.*) of the Republican party. —*n.* one who advocates a republican form of government: (*cap.*) in U.S., a member of the political party opposed to the *Democrats*, and favouring an extension of the powers of the national government.—*v.t.* **repub'licanise, -ize.**—*n.* **repub'licanism.** [L. *rēspublica*, commonwealth—*rēs*, affair, *publica* (fem.), public.]

repudiate *ri-pū'di-āt*, *v.t.* to cast off, disown: to refuse, or cease, to acknowledge (debt, authority, claim): to deny as unfounded (a charge, etc.).—*adj.* **repū'diable.**—*n.* **repūdiā'tion**—*adj.* **repū'diative.**—*n.* **repū'diator.** [L. *repudiāre*, -*ātum*—*repudium*, divorce—*re*-, away, and the root of *pudēre*, to be ashamed.]

repugnance, repugnancy *ri-pug'nans, -si, ns.* inconsistency: aversion.—*adj.* **repug'nant** inconsistent with (with *to*): (of things) incompatible: distasteful: disgusting. [L. *repugnāre*—*re*-, against, *pugnāre*, to fight.]

repulse *ri-puls'*, *v.t.* to drive back: to rebuff.—*n.* a driving back: a check: a refusal: a rebuff.—*n.* **repulsion** (-*pul'shən*) driving off: a repelling force, action, or influence.—*adj.* **repul'sive** that repulses or drives off: cold, reserved, forbidding: causing aversion and disgust.—*adv.* **repul'sively.**—*n.* **repul'siveness.** [L. *repulsus*, pa.p. of *repellĕre*—*re*-, back, *pellĕre*, to drive.]

repute *ri-pūt'*, *v.t.* to account, deem.—*n.* general opinion or impression: attributed character: widespread or high estimation: fame.—*adj.* **reputable** (*rep'ūt-a-bl*) in good repute: respectable: honourable: consistent with reputation.—*adv.* **rep'ūtably.**—*n.* **repūtā'tion** (*rep-*) repute: character generally ascribed: good report: fame: good name.—*adj.* **reputed** (*ri-pūt'id*) supposed, reckoned to be such: of repute.—*adv.* **repūt'edly** in common repute or estimation. [L. *reputāre*, -*ātum*—*putāre*, to reckon.]

request *ri-kwest'*, *n.* the asking of a favour: a petition: a favour asked for: the state of being sought after.— *v.t.* to ask as a favour: to ask politely: to ask for.—*n.* **request'er**—request stop a stop at which a bus, etc. will stop only if signalled to do so.—**on request** if, or when, requested. [O.Fr. *requeste* (Fr. *requête*)—L. *requisītum*, pa.p. of *requīrĕre*—*re*-, away, *quaerĕre*, to seek.]

requiem *rek'wi-əm, rē'kwi-əm, n.* a mass for the rest of the soul of the dead: music for it. [L., accus. of *requiēs* (*re*-, intens., *quiēs*, rest); first word of the introit.]

requiescat *re-kwi-es'kat, n.* a prayer for the rest of the soul of the dead.—**requiescat in pace** (*in pā'sē, pā'chā, pā'ke*) abbrev. R.I.P., may he (or she) rest in peace. [L., third pers. sing. subj. of *requiescĕre*.]

require *ri-kwīr'*, *v.t.* to demand, exact: to direct (a person to do something): to call for, necessitate.— *v.i.* to ask.—*adj.* **requir'able.**—*adj.* **required'** compulsory as part of a curriculum.—*ns.* **require'ment** a need: a thing needed: a necessary condition: a demand; **requir'er; requir'ing.** [L. *requīrĕre*; partly through O.Fr. *requerre*, later assimilated to L,]

requisite *rek'wi-zit, adj.* required: needful: indispen-

sable.—*n.* that which is required, necessary, or indispensable.—*ns.* **req'uisiteness; requisi'tion** the act of requiring: a formal demand or request: a formal call for the doing of something that is due: a demand for the supply of anything for military purposes: a written order for the supply of materials: the state of being in use or service.—*v.t.* to demand or take by requisition: to press into service.—*adj.* **requisi'tionary.**—*ns.* **requisi'tionist.** [L. *requisītus*, pa.p. of *requīrĕre*; see require.]

requite *ri-kwīt'*, *v.t.* to repay (an action): to avenge; to repay (a person, for):—*pa.t.* **requit'ed**; *pa.p.* **requit'ed.**—*adj.* **requi'table.**—*n.* **requi'tal** the act of requiting: payment in return: recompense.—*ns.* **requite'ment; requi'ter.** [Pfx. re-, and **quit.**]

reredos *rēr'dos, n.* a screen or panelling behind an altar or seat: a choir-screen. [O.Fr. *areredos*—*arere*, behind, *dos*, back.]

reread *rē-rēd'*, *v.t.* to read again:—*pa.t.* and *pa.p.* **re'read'** (-*red*). [Pfx. re-.]

rerun *rē'run'*, *v.t.* to run (a race, etc.) again: to broadcast (a series) again.—Also *n.* (*rē'run*). [Pfx. re-.]

resale *rē'sāl, rē-sāl'*, *n.* the selling again of an article.— **resale price maintenance** the setting of a fixed minimum price on an article by the manufacturer. [Pfx. re-.]

rescind *ri-sind'*, *v.t.* to annul, abrogate.—*n.* **rescission** (-*sizh'ən*) abrogation. [L. *rescindĕre*, *rescissum*— *re*-, back, *scindĕre*, to cut.]

rescore *rē'skōr', -skōr'*, *v.t.* to rewrite a musical score for different instruments, voices, etc. [Pfx. re-.]

rescript *rē'skript, n.* the official answer of a pope or an emperor to any legal question: an edict or decree: a rewriting.—Also *v.t.* [L. *rescriptum*—*re*-, *scrībĕre*, *scriptum*, to write.]

rescue *res'kū*, *v.t.* to free from danger, captivity, or evil plight: to deliver forcibly from legal custody: to recover by force:—*pr.p.* **res'cuing**; *pa.t.* and *pa.p.* **res'cued.**—*n.* the act of rescuing: deliverance from danger or evil: forcible recovery: forcible release from arrest or imprisonment: relief of a besieged place: a beach-rescue.—*adj.* **res'cuable.**—*n.* **res'cuer.** [O.Fr. *rescourre*—L. *re*-, *excutĕre*—*ex*, out, *quatĕre*, to shake.]

research *ri-sûrch'*, *n.* a careful search: investigation: systematic investigation towards increasing the sum of knowledge.—*v.i.* and *v.t.* to make researches (into or concerning).—*v.i.* **re-search** (*rē'*) to search again. —*n.* **research'er.** [Obs. Fr. *recerche* (mod. Fr. *recherche*); see **search.**]

resect *ri-sekt'*, *v.t.* to cut away part of, esp. the end of a bone.—*n.* **resection** (-*sek'shən*) cutting away, esp. bone (*surg.*): a positional fix of a point by sighting it from two or more known stations (*surveying*). [L. *resecāre*, -*sectum*, to cut off—*secāre*, to cut.]

Reseda *re'si-də, ri-sē'də, n.* the mignonette genus: (without *cap.*) a pale green colour.—Also *adj.* [L. *resēda*, said to be from *resēdā morbis*, assuage diseases, first words of a charm used in applying it as a poultice.]

resemble *ri-zem'bl*, *v.t.* to be like.—*n.* **resem'blance** likeness: appearance: an image.—*adj.* **resem'blant.** —*n.* **resem'bler.**—*adj.* **resem'bling.** [O.Fr. *resembler*—*re*-, again, *sembler*, to seem—L. *simulāre*, to make like.]

resent *ri-zent'*, *v.t.* to take, consider as an injury or affront.—*n.* **resent'er.**—*adj.* **resent'ful.**— *advs.* **resent'fully; resent'ingly.**—*n.* **resent'ment.**

---

republicā'tion *n.*   **resched'ule** *v.t.*   **reselect'ion** *n.*
repub'lish *v.t.*   **reseat'** *v.t.*   **resell'** *v.t.*:—*pa.t.* and *pa.p.* **resold'.**
repur'chase *v.t.* and *n.*   **reselect'** *v.t.*   **resent'ence** *v.t.*

For other sounds see detailed chart of pronunciation.

[O.Fr. *ressentir*—L. *re-*, in return, *sentīre*, to feel.]

reserpine ri-zûr'pin, -pēn, n. a drug got from *Rauwolfia serpentina* used against high blood pressure, and as a tranquilliser.

reserve ri-zûrv', v.t. to hold back: to save up, esp. for a future occasion or special purpose: to keep, retain: to preserve: to set apart: to book, engage.—n. the keeping of something reserved: state of being reserved: that which is reserved: a reserved store or stock: a tract of land reserved for a special purpose: a substitute kept in readiness (*sport*): (esp. in *pl.*) a military force kept out of action until occasion serves: (esp. in *pl.*) a force not usually serving but liable to be called up when required: (often *pl.*) resources of physical or spiritual nature available in abnormal circumstances: part of assets kept readily available for ordinary demands: artistic restraint: restrained manner: aloofness.—adj. kept in reserve: of the reserves.—adj. reserv'able.—n. reservā'tion (rez-) the act of reserving or keeping back: an expressed, or tacit, proviso, limiting condition, or exception: something withheld: a tract of public land reserved for some special purpose, as for Indians, schools, game, etc.: the pope's retention to himself of the right to nominate to a benefice: the booking of a seat, room, passage, etc.: a booked seat, room, etc.: the strip of grass, etc. between the two roads of a dual carriageway: a clause of a deed by which a person reserves for himself a right, interest, etc. in a property he is granting (*legal*).—adj. reserved' reticent: booked.—adv. reserv'edly.—ns. reservedness (ri-zûrvd'nis); reserv'ist a member of a reserve force.—reserve currency one ranking with gold in world banking transactions; reserved list a list of retired officers in the armed services who may be recalled for active service in the event of war; reserved occupation employment of national importance that exempts from service in the armed forces; reserve price the minimum price acceptable to the vendor of an article for sale or auction.—judgment reserved see under judge; without reserve frankly, fully, without reservation: without restrictions or stipulations regarding sale: without a reserve price. [O.Fr. *reserver*—L. *reservāre*—*re-*, back, *servāre*, to save.]

reservoir rez'ər-vwär, n. a store: a receptacle for fluids, esp. a basin, lake, or tank for storing water. [Fr.]

reset rē-set', v.t. to set again. [Pfx. re-.]

res gestae rēz jes'tē, rās ges'tī, (L.) exploits: tacts relevant to the case and admissible in evidence (*law*).

reshuffle rē-shuf'l, v.t. to shuffle again: to rearrange, esp. cabinet or government offices.—Also n. [Pfx. re-.]

reside ri-zīd', v.i. to dwell permanently: to be in residence: to abide: to inhere.—ns. residence (rez'i-dəns) act or duration of dwelling in a place: the act of living in the place required by regulations or performance of functions: a stay in a place: a dwelling-place: a dwelling-house, esp. one of some pretensions: that in which anything permanently inheres or has its seat; res'idency a residence: the official abode of a resident or governor of a protected state: an administrative district under a resident: a resident's post at a hospital, or the period during which it is held.—adj. res'ident dwelling in a place for some time: residing on one's own estate, or the place of one's duties, or the place required by certain conditions: not migratory: inherent.—n. one who resides: an animal that does not migrate: a doctor who works in, and usu. resides at, a hospital to gain experience in a particular field: a representative of a governor in a

protected state: the governor of a residency or administrative district.—adjs. residential (-den'shl) of, for, or connected with, residence: suitable for or occupied by houses, esp. of a better kind; residentiary (-den'shə-ri) resident: officially bound to reside: pertaining to or involving official residence.—n. one bound to reside, as a canon.—ns. residen'tiaryship; res'identship; resi'der. [L. *residēre*—*re-*, back, *sedēre*, to sit.]

residue rez'i-dū, n. that which is left, remainder: what is left of an estate after payment of debts, charges, and legacies.—adj. resid'ual remaining as residue or difference.—n. that which remains as a residue or as a difference.—adj. resid'uary of, or of the nature of, a residue, esp. of an estate.—n. residuum riz-id'ū-əm a residue:—pl. -ua. [L. *residuum*—*residēre*, to remain behind.]

resign ri-zīn', v.t. to yield up: to submit calmly: to relinquish: to entrust.—v.i. to give up office, employment, etc. (often with *from*).—n. resignation (rez-ig-nā'shən) act of giving up: state of being resigned or quietly submissive.—adj. resigned (ri-zīnd') calmly submissive.—adv. resignedly (ri-zīn'id-li).—ns. resign'edness; resign'er. [O.Fr. *resigner*—L. *resignāre*, -*ātum*, to unseal, annul.]

re-sign rē-sīn', v.t. to sign again. [Pfx. re-.]

resile ri-zīl', v.i. to recoil: to rebound: to recover form and position elastically: to draw back from a statement, agreement, course.—ns. resilience (ri-zil'i-əns) recoil: elasticity, physical or mental; resil'iency.—adj. resil'ient. [L. *resilīre*, to leap back—*salīre*, to leap.]

resin rez'in, n. any of a number of substances, products obtained from the sap of certain plants and trees (*natural resins*), used in plastics, etc.: any of a large number of substances made by polymerisation or condensation (*synthetic resins*) which, though not related chemically to natural resins, have some of their physical properties, very important in the plastics industry, etc.—v.t. to treat with resin: to rosin.—n. res'inate a salt of any of the acids occurring in natural resins.—adj. resinif'erous yielding resin.—n. resinifica'tion.—v.t. and v.i. res'inify to make or become a resin or resinous.—adj. res'inous. [Fr. *résine*—L. *resīna*.]

resipiscence res-i-pis'əns, n. recognition of error, change to a better frame of mind.—adj. resipisc'ent. [L. *resipiscentia*—*resipiscĕre*—*re-*, again, *sapĕre*, to be wise.]

resist ri-zist', v.t. to strive against, oppose: to withstand: to hinder the action of: to be little affected by.—v.i. to make opposition.—n. a protective coating, esp. one on parts of a textile to protect the blank areas of the design that is being printed.—Also adj.—n. resis'tance act or power of resisting: opposition: the body's ability to resist disease: (with *cap.*) an organisation of (armed) opposition to an occupying enemy force: the opposition of a body to the motion of another: that property of a substance in virtue of which the passage of an electric current through it is accompanied with a dissipation of energy: an electrical resistor; resis'tant one who, or that which, resists.—adj. making resistance: withstanding adverse conditions, as parasites, germs, antibiotics, corrosion.—n. one who, or that which, resists.—n. resistibil'ity.—adj. resis'tible.—advs. resis'tibly; resis'tingly.—adj. resis'tive.—adv. resis'tively.—n. resistiv'ity (rez-) capacity for resisting: (also specific resistance) a property of a conducting material expressed as resistance multiplied by cross-sectional area over length.—adj. resist'less (*arch.*) irresistible: unable to resist.—adv. resist'lessly.—ns.

resist'lessness; resist'or anything that resists: a piece of apparatus used to offer electric resistance.— resistance thermometer a device for measuring high temperatures by means of the variation in the electrical resistance of a wire as the temperature changes. —line of least resistance the easiest course of action. [L. *resistĕre*—*re*-, against, *sistĕre*, to make to stand.]

resit *rē-sit'*, *v.i.* and *v.t.* to sit (an examination) again after failing.—*n.* (*rē'*) an opportunity or act of resitting. [Pfx. re-.]

resoluble *rez'əl-ū-bl*, *adj.* that may be resolved, dissolved, analysed.—*adj.* resolute (*rez'əl-ōōt, -ūt*) having a fixed purpose: constant in pursuing a purpose: determined.—*adv.* res'olutely.—*ns.* res'oluteness; resolution (*rez-əl-ōō'shən, -ū-shən*) act of resolving: analysis: separation of components: melting: solution: the definition of a picture in TV or facsimile (measured by the number of lines used to scan the image of the picture): the smallest measurable difference, or separation, or time interval (*phys., electronics, nucleonics*): resolving power (q.v.): state of being resolved: fixed determination: that which is resolved: removal of or freedom from doubt: progression from discord to concord (*mus.*): a formal proposal put before a meeting, or its formal determination thereon: substitution of two short syllables for a long: the making visible of detail: the disappearance or dispersion of a tumour or inflammation.—*adj.* res'olutive.—*n.* resolvabil'ity.—*adj.* resolvable (*ri-zolv'*).—*v.t.* resolve' to separate into components: to make visible the details of: to analyse: to break up: to melt: to transform: to relax: to solve: to dissipate: to free from doubt or difficulty: to pass as a resolution: to determine: to disperse, as a tumour: to make (a discord) pass into a concord (*mus.*).—*v.i.* to undergo resolution: to come to a determination (often with *on* to indicate the course chosen).—*n.* resolution: fixed purpose: firmness of purpose.—*adj.* resolved' fixed in purpose.—*adv.* resolvedly (*ri-zol'vid-li*) resolutely.—*n.* resol'vedness.—*adj.* resol'vent having power to resolve.—*n.* that which causes or helps solution or resolution.—*n.* resol'ver.—resolving power the ability of telescope, microscope, etc., to distinguish very close, or very small, objects: the ability of a photographic emulsion to produce finely-detailed images. [L. *resolvĕre*, *resolūtum*—*re*-, intens., *solvĕre*, to loose.]

resolve, etc. See resoluble.

resonance *rez'ən-əns*, *n.* resounding: sonority: the sound heard in auscultation: sympathetic vibration: the ringing quality of the human voice when produced in such a way that sympathetic vibration is caused in the air-spaces in the head, chest and throat: (the state of a system in which) a large vibration (is) produced by a small stimulus of approx. the same frequency as that of the system (*phys., elect.*): increased probability of a nuclear reaction when the energy of an incident particle or photon is around a certain value appropriate to the energy level of the compound nucleus: a property of certain compounds, in which the most stable state of the molecule is a combination of theoretically possible bond arrangements or distributions of electrons (*chem.*).—*adj.* res'onant resounding, ringing: giving its characteristic vibration in sympathy with another body's vibration.—*adv.* res'onantly.— *v.i.* res'onate to resound: to vibrate sympathetically. —*n.* res'onātor a resonating body or device, as for increasing sonority or for analysing sound. [L. *resonāre*, *-ātum*—*re*-, back, *sonāre*, to sound.]

resorb *ri-sörb'*, *v.t.* to absorb back.—*adj.* resorb'ent. [L. *resorbēre*, to suck back.]

resorcin *ri-zor'sin*, *n.* a colourless phenol, C₆H₄(OH)₂, used in dyeing, photography, and medicine.—Also resor'cinol. [resin and orcin.]

resorption *ri-sorp'shən*, *n.* resorbing, esp. of a mineral by rock magma.—*adj.* resorp'tive. [See resorb.]

resort[1] *ri-zört'*, *v.i.* to betake oneself: to have recourse: to go or be habitually.—*n.* act of resorting: a place much frequented: a haunt: that which one has or may have recourse to.—*n.* resort'er a frequenter. —in the last resort as a last expedient. [O.Fr. *resortir* (Fr. *ressortir*), to rebound, retire—*sortir*, to go out; origin obscure.]

resort[2] *rē-sört'*, *v.t.* to sort anew. [Pfx. re-.]

resound *ri-zownd'*, *v.t.* to echo: to sound with reverberation: to spread (the praises of a person or thing).—*v.i.* to echo: to re-echo, reverberate: to sound sonorously.—*adj.* resound'ing echoing: thorough, decisive (*resounding victory*).—*adv.* resound'ingly. [Pfx. re-.]

resource *ri-sōrs'*, *-sörs*, *-z-*, *n.* source or possibility of help: an expedient: (*pl.*) money or means of raising money: means of support: means of occupying or amusing oneself: resourcefulness.—*adj.* resource'ful fertile in expedients: clever, ingenious: rich in resources.—*n.* resource'fulness.—*adj.* resource'less. [O.Fr. *ressource*—*resourdre*—L. *resurgĕre*, to rise again.]

respect *ri-spekt'*, *v.t.* to heed: to relate to, have reference to (*arch.*): to treat with consideration, refrain from violating: to feel or show esteem, deference, or honour to: to value.—*n.* a particular: reference: consideration: partiality or favour towards (with *of*): deferential esteem: (often in *pl.*) a greeting or message of esteem.—*n.* respectabil'ity.—*adj.* respec'table worthy of respect: considerable: passable: fairly well-to-do: decent and well-behaved: reputable: seemly: presentable.—*n.* respec'tableness.—*adv.* respec'tably.—*n.* respec'ter one who respects, esp. in *respecter of persons*, one who, something that, singles out individual(s) for unduly favourable treatment (usu. in *neg.*).—*adj.* respect'ful showing or feeling respect.—*adv.* respect'fully.—*n.* respect'fulness.— *prep.* respect'ing concerning: considering.—*adj.* respec'tive relative: particular or several, relating to each distributively.—*adv.* respec'tively.—respect of persons undue favour, as for wealth, etc.; in respect of in the matter of; with respect to with regard to. [L. *respicĕre*, *respectum*—*re*-, back, *specĕre*, to look.]

respire *ri-spīr'*, *v.i.* to breathe: to take breath.—*v.t.* to breathe: to exhale.—*adj.* respirable (*res'pər-ə-bl, ri-spīr'ə-bl*) fit for breathing.—*ns.* respiration (*res-pər-ā'shən*) breathing: the taking in of oxygen and giving out of carbon dioxide, with associated physiological processes: a breath; res'pirātor an appliance worn on the mouth or nose to filter or warm the air breathed: a gas-mask.—*adj.* respiratory (*res'pər-ə-tər-i, ri-spī'rə-tər-i*). [L. *respīrāre, -ātum* —*spīrāre*, to breathe.]

respite *res'pīt, -pit, n.* temporary cessation of something that is tiring or painful: postponement requested or granted: temporary suspension of the execution of a criminal (*law*).—*v.t.* to grant a respite to: to delay, put off: to grant postponement to. [M.E. *respit*—O.Fr. (Fr. *répit*)—L. *respectus, respicĕre*; see respect.]

resplendence, *ri-splend'əns*, resplendency *-ən-si, ns.* brilliance, shine: splendour.—*adj.* resplend'ent.— *adv.* resplend'ently. [L. *resplendēre*—*re*-, intens., and *splendēre*, to shine.]

respond *ri-spond'*, *v.i.* to answer: to utter liturgical responses: to act in answer: to react.—*n.* a response

---

rē-site' *v.t.*   rēsole' *v.t.*   rēspell' *v.t.*

to a versicle in liturgy: a half-pillar or half-pier attached to a wall to support an arch (answering to one at the other end of an arcade,' etc.).—*ns.* re-spond'ence, respond'ency correspondence.—*adj.* re-spond'ent answering: responsive.—*n.* one who answers: one who refutes objections: a defendant, esp. in a divorce suit.—*ns.* respond'er, respons'er, respons'or (*ris-*) one who, or that which, responds; response' an answer: an answer made by the congre-gation to the priest during divine service: a re-sponsory: a reaction, esp. sympathetic: the ratio of the output to the input level of a transmission system at any particular frequency (*electronics*).—*adj.* response'less.—*n.* responsibil'ity state of being responsible: a trust or charge for which one is respon-sible.—*adj.* respon'sible liable to be called to account as being in charge or control: answerable (*to* person, etc., *for* something): deserving the blame or credit of (with *for*): governed by a sense of responsibility: being a free moral agent: morally accountable for one's actions: trustworthy: able to pay: involving responsibility.—*adv.* respon'sibly.—*adj.* respon'sive ready to respond: answering.—*adv.* respon'sively.—*n.* respon'siveness.—*adj.* respon'sory making answer.—*n.* an anthem sung after a lesson: a liturgical response. [L. *respondēre, respōnsum*—*re-*, back, *spondēre,* to promise.]

rest[1] *rest, n.* repose, refreshing inactivity: intermission of, or freedom from, motion or disturbance: tran-quillity: repose of death: a place for resting: a prop or support (e.g. for a musket, a billiard cue, a violinist's chin): motionlessness: a pause in speaking or reading: an interval of silence in music, or a mark indicating it.—*v.i.* to repose: to be at ease: to be still: to be sup-ported (on): to lean (on): to have foundation in (with *on*): to remain: to be unemployed (*slang,* esp. *theat-rical*).—*v.t.* to give rest to: to place or hold in support (on): to base (on).—*n.* rest'er.—*adj.* rest'ful at rest: rest-giving: tranquil.—*adv.* rest'fully.—*n.* rest'ful-ness.—*n.* and *adj.* rest'ing.—*adj.* rest'less unresting, not resting, sleeping, or relaxing: never still: uneasily active: never-ceasing: allowing no rest.—*adv.* rest'-lessly.—*n.* rest'lessness.—rest'-cure treatment con-sisting of inactivity and quiet; rest'-home an estab-lishment for those who need special care and attention, e.g. invalids, old people, etc.; rest'-house a house of rest for travellers; rest mass (*phys.*) the mass of an object when it is at rest; rest'-room a room in a building other than a private house with lavatories, etc.—at rest stationary: in repose: free from disquiet; lay to rest to give burial to. [O.E. *rest, ræst;* conver-ging and merging in meaning with the following words.]

rest[2] *rest, n.* remainder: all others: reserve fund: a rally (*tennis,* etc.).—*v.i.* to remain (see also preceding word).—for the rest as regards other matters. [Fr. *reste*—L. *restāre,* to remain—*re-*, back, *stāre,* to stand.]

rest[3] *rest,* (*hist.*) *n.* a contrivance on a breastplate to prevent the spear from being driven back. [Aphetic for arrest.]

restaurant *rest'*(*ə-*)*-rā, -rong, -ront, -rənt, n.* a place where meals may be had.—*n.* restaurateur (*res-tar-ə-tûr', -tœr'*) the keeper of a restaurant.—res'-taurant-car a dining-car. [Fr.,—*restaurer,* to restore.]

rest-harrow *rest'-har-ō, n.* a papilionaceous plant (*Ononis*) with long, tough, woody roots. [rest[2], and harrow.]

restitution *res'ti-tū'shən, n.* a restoring, return: com-pensation.—*adj.* restitutive (*ri-stit'*, or *res'tit-*).—*n.* res'titūtor.—*adj.* restit'ūtory. [L. *restitŭere, -ūtum* —*re-*, *statuēre,* to make to stand.]

restive *res'tiv, adj.* obstinate, refractory: uneasy, as if ready to break from control.—*adv.* res'tively.—*n.* res'tiveness. [O.Fr. *restif*—L. *restāre,* to rest.]

restore *ri-stōr', -stôr, v.t.* to repair: to bring, put, or give back: to make good: to reinstate: to bring back to a (supposed) former state, or to a normal state: to reconstruct mentally, by inference or conjecture.—*adj.* restor'able.—*ns.* restor'ableness; restoration (*res-tō-rā'shən,* or *-tō-, -tə-, -to-*) act or process of restoring: a reinstatement of or in kingship (as the Restoration of the Stuarts, the Bourbons; *usu.* with *cap.*): renovations and reconstruction of a building, painting, etc.: a reconstructed thing or representa-tion.—*adj.* (with *cap.*) of the time of the Restoration of Charles II.—*ns.* restora'tionism (*theol.*) receiving of a sinner to divine favour: the final recovery of all men; restora'tionist.—*adj.* restorative (*ris-tor'ə-tiv, -tōr'*) tending to restore, esp. to strength and vigour.—*n.* a medicine that restores.—*adv.* restor'atively.—*n.* restor'er. [O.Fr. *restorer*—L. *restaurāre, -ātum.*]

restrain *ri-strān', v.t.* to hold back: to control: to subject to forcible repression.—*adjs.* restrain'able; restrained' controlled: self-controlled: showing re-straint.—*adv.* restrain'edly.—*ns.* restrain'edness; re-strain'er.—*n.* and *adj.* restrain'ing.—*n.* restraint' act of restraining: state of being restrained: restric-tion: forcible control: want of liberty: reserve.—re-straint of trade interference with free play of economic forces. [O.Fr. *restraindre, restrai(g)n-* — L. *restringĕre, restrictum*—*re-*, back, *stringĕre,* to draw tightly.]

restrict *ri-strikt', v.t.* to limit.—*adj.* restrict'ed.—*adv.* restrict'edly.—*ns.* restric'tion; restric'tionist.—Also *adj.*—*adj.* restric'tive tending to restrict: expressing restriction, as in relative clauses, phrases, etc., that limit the application of the verb to the subject, e.g. *people who like historic buildings should visit Edin-burgh.*—*adv.* restric'tively.—restricted area one from which the general public is excluded: one within which there is a speed limit; restrictive practice a trade practice that is against the public interest, as e.g. an agreement to sell only to certain buyers, or to keep up resale prices: used also of certain trade union practices, as the closed shop, demarcation. [L. re-*stringĕre, restrictum.*]

result *ri-zult', v.i.* to issue (with *in*): to follow as a consequence: to be the outcome.—*n.* consequence: outcome: outcome aimed at: quantity obtained by calculation: in games, the (usu. final) score.—*adj.* result'ant resulting.—*n.* a force compounded of two or more forces: a sum of vector quantities.—*adjs.* result'ing; result'less.—*n.* result'lessness. [L. re-*sultāre,* to leap back—*saltāre,* to leap.]

resume *ri-zūm', -zōōm', v.t.* to assume again: to take up again: to begin again.—*v.i.* to take possession again: to begin again in continuation.—*adj.* resum'able.—*ns.* résumé (*rā-zü-mā;* Fr. *pa.p.*) a summary; re-sumption (*ri-zump'shən,* or *-zum'*) act of resuming.—*adj.* resumptive (*-zump', -zum'*).—*adv.* resump'-tively. [L. *resūmĕre, -sūmptum*—*re-*, *sūmĕre,* to take.]

resupinate *ri-sōō'pin-āt, -sū', adj.* upside down by twisting (*bot.*).—*n.* resupina'tion. [L. *resupināre, -ātum,* and *resupīnus*—*re-*, back, *supīnus,* bent backward.]

rèspray' *v.t.* and *n.*   rèstate'ment *n.*   rèstruc'ture *v.t.*
rèstage' *v.t.*   rèstock' *v.t.*   rèstyle' *v.t.*
rèstate' *v.t.*   rèstring' *v.t.*   rèsubmit' *v.t.*

resurgent ri-sûrj'∂nt, adj. rising again.—n. **resur'-gence.**—v.t. **resurrect** (rez-∂r-ekt'; back-formation) to restore to life: to revive: to disinter.—v.i. to come to life again.—n. **resurrection** (-ek'sh∂n) a rising from the dead esp. (with cap.) that of Christ: resuscitation: revival: a thing resurrected.—adjs. **resurrec'tional; resurrec'tionary.**—v.t. **resurrec'tionlse, -ise.**—ns. **resurrec'tionlsm; resurrec'tionlst, resurrec'tion-man** one who stole bodies from the grave for dissection.—adj. **resurrect'lve.**—n. **resurrect'or.**—**resurrection plant** a plant that curls in a ball in drought and spreads again in moisture. [L. resurgĕre, resurrēc-tum—re-, surgĕre, to rise.]

resuscitate ri-sus'i-tāt, v.t. and v.i. to bring back to life or consciousness: to revive.—adjs. **resusc'itable; resusc'itant.**—n. one who, or that which, resuscitates.—n. **resuscitā'tion.**—adj. **resusc'itātive.**—n. **resusc'itātor.** [L. resuscitāre, -ātum—re-, sus-, sub-, from beneath, citāre, to put into quick motion.]

ret ret, v.t. to expose to moisture.—v.t. and v.i. to soak: to soften, spoil, or rot by soaking or exposure to moisture: to rot:—pr.p. **rett'ing;** pa.t. and pa.p. **rett'ed.**—n. **rett'ery** a place where flax is retted. [App. akin to **rot.**]

retable ri-tā'bl, n. a shelf or ornamental setting for panels, etc. behind an altar. [Fr. rétable—L.L. retrōtabulum.]

retail rē'tāl, n. sale to consumer, or in small quantities. —adj. in, of, engaged in, concerned with, such sale.—adv. by retail.—v.t. (ri-, rē-tāl') to sell by retail: to repeat in detail: to hand on by report.—ns. **retail'er; retail'ment.** [O.Fr. retail, piece cut off—tailler, to cut.]

retain ri-tān', v.t. to keep: to hold back: to continue to hold: to keep up: to employ or keep engaged, as by a fee paid: to keep in mind.—adj. **retain'able.**—ns. **retain'er** one who or that which retains: a dependent of a person of rank (hist.): a family servant of long standing: an authorisation: a retaining fee (in legal usage, **general** to secure a priority of claim on a counsel's services; **special** for a particular case); **retain'ership; retain'ment**—**retaining fee** the advance fee paid to a lawyer to defend a cause; **retaining wall** a wall to hold back solid material, as earth, or (loosely) water. [Fr. retenir—L. retinēre—re-, back, tenēre, to hold.]

retake rē-tāk', v.t. to take again: to take back, re-capture:—pa.t. **retook';** pa.p. **retā'ken.**—n. (rē') a second or repeated photographing or photograph, esp. for a motion picture.—ns. **retāk'er; retāk'ing.** [Pfx. **re-.**]

retaliate ri-tal'i-āt, v.t. to repay in kind (now usu. an injury).—v.i. to return like for like (esp. in hostility). —ns. **retaliā'tion** return of like for like: imposition of a tariff against countries that impose a tariff; **retalia'tionist.**—adj. **retal'iative.**—n. **retal'iātor.**—adj. **retal'iatory** (-āt-∂r-i, -∂t-∂r-i). [L. retāliāre, -ātum—re-, tāliō, -ōnis, like for like—tālis, such.]

retard ri-tärd', v.t. to slow: to keep back development or progress of: to delay: to delay the timing of (an ignition spark).—v.i. to slow down: to delay.—adj. **retar'dant** serving to delay or slow down a chemical reaction, as rusting.—Also n.—ns. **retardā'tion** (rē-), **retard'ment** slowing: delay: lag.—adjs. **retardātive** (ri-tard'∂-tiv); **retar'datory; retar'ded** delayed or slowed down: slow in development, esp. mental, or having made less than normal progress in learning.—ns. **retar'der** retardant: a substance that delays or prevents setting of cement. [L. retardāre, -ātum—re-, tardāre, to slow.]

retch rēch, also rech, v.i. to strain as if to vomit.—n. an act of retching. [O.E. hræcan—hrāca, a hawking.]

rete rē'tē, n. a network, as of blood-vessels or nerves. —adj. **retial** (rē'shi-∂l). [L. rēte, net.]

retention ri-ten'sh∂n, n. act or power of retaining: memory: custody: inability to void (med.).—n. **reten'tionlst** a person who advocates the retaining of a policy, etc., esp. that of capital punishment.—adj. **reten'tive** retaining: tenacious: retaining moisture.—adv. **reten'tively.**—ns. **reten'tiveness, retentiv'ity** (rē-). [L. retentiō, -ōnis; O.Fr. retentif; see **retain.**]

rethink rē-thingk', v.t. to consider again and come to a different decision about.—Also n. [Pfx. **re-.**]

retial. See **rete.**

retiarius rē-shi-ā'ri-∂s, rā-ti-ä'ri-ōōs, n. a gladiator armed with a net. [L. rētiārius—rēte, net.]

reticent ret'i-s∂nt, adj. reserved or sparing in communi-cation.—ns. **ret'icence, ret'icency.** [L. reticēns, -entis, pr.p. of reticēre—re-, tacēre, to be silent.]

reticle ret'i-kl, n. an attachment to an optical instru-ment consisting of a network of lines of reference.—adj. **reticular** (ri-tik'ū-l∂r) netted: netlike: re-ticulated: of the reticulum.—adv. **retic'ularly.**—v.t. **retic'ulate** to form into or mark with a network.—v.i. to form a network.—adj. netted: marked with net-work: net-veined.—adj. **retic'ulated** reticulate: (of masonry) of lozenge-shaped stones, or of squares placed diamond-wise.—adv. **retic'ulately.**—ns. **re-ticulā'tion; reticule** (ret'i-kūl) a reticle: a small bag carried by ladies; **retic'ulum** a network: the second stomach of a ruminant. [L. rēticulum, dim. of rēte, net.]

retiform rē'ti-förm, adj. having the form of a net. [L. rēte, net, fōrma, form.]

retina ret'i-n∂, n. the sensitive layer of the eye:—pl. **ret'inas, ret'inae** (-nē).—adj. **ret'inal.**—ns. **retini'tis** inflammation of the retina; **retinos'copist; retinos'-copy** examination of the eye by observing a shadow on the retina; **retinula** (ri-tin'ū-l∂) a cell playing the part of retina to an ommatidium:—pl. **retin'ulae** (-lē).—adj. **retin'ular.** [L.L. rētina, app.—L. rēte, net.]

retinal. See **retina.**

retinoscopy. See **retina.**

retinue ret'i-nū, formerly ri-tin'ū, n. a body of re-tainers: a suite or train. [Fr. retenue, fem. pa.p. of retenir; see **retain.**]

retire ri-tīr', v.i. to withdraw: to retreat: to recede: to withdraw from society, office, public or active life, business, profession, etc.: to go into seclusion or to bed.—v.t. to withdraw: to withdraw from currency: to cause to retire.—n. **reti'ral** giving up of office, business, etc.: withdrawal.—adj. **retired'** secluded: withdrawn from business or profession.—ns. **retired'-ness** (or ri-tī'rid-nis); **reti'ree** a person who retires from work; **retire'ment** act of retiring: state of being or having retired: solitude: a time or place of se-clusion.—adj. **retir'ing** reserved: unobtrusive: modest.—adv. **reti'ringly.**—n. **reti'ringness.**—**re-tired list** a list of officers who are relieved from active service but receive a certain amount of pay (**retired pay**). [Fr. retirer—re-, back, tirer, to draw.]

retook. See **retake.**

retool rē-tōōl', v.t. to re-equip with new tools (in a factory, etc.; also v.i.): to remake, refashion (chiefly U.S.). [Pfx. **re-.**]

retort ri-tört', v.t. to throw back: to return upon an assailant or opponent: to answer in retaliation or wittily: to purify or treat in a retort.—v.i. to make a sharp reply.—n. a ready and sharp or witty answer:

---

resurvey' v.t.
resur'vey n.

retell' v.t.:—pa.p. **retold'.**
retell'er n.

retie' v.t.

For other sounds see detailed chart of pronunciation.

the art or act of retorting: a vessel in which substances are placed for distillation, typically a flask with long bent-back neck.—*adj.* **retor'ted** turned back.—*ns.* **retor'ter; retortion** (-*tör'shən*).—*adj.* **retor'tive.** [L. *retorquēre, retortum*—*re*-, back, *torquēre*, to twist.]

retouch *rē-tuch'*, *v.t.* to touch again: to touch up, seek to improve by new touches.—*n.* an act of touching up, esp. of a photograph by pencil-work on the negative. —*n.* **retouch'er.** [Pfx. **re-**.]

retrace *ri-*, or *rē-trās'*, *v.t.* to trace back: to go back upon: to run over with the eye or in the memory: (*rē*-) to trace again: (*rē*-) to renew the outline of.—*adj.* **retrace'able** (*ri-*). [Fr. *retracer.*]

retract *ri-trakt'*, *v.t.* to withdraw: to revoke: to undo (the previous move) (*chess*).—*v.i.* to take back, or draw back from, what has been said or granted.—*adj.* **retrac'table** able to be retracted: that can be drawn up into the body or wings (*aero.*): that can be drawn up towards the body of a vehicle.—*n.* **retracta'tion** (*rē*-) revoking: recantation.—*adj.* **retrac'ted** drawn in: turned back.—*adj.* **retrac'tile** (*-tīl*) that may be drawn back, as a cat's claws.—*ns.* **retractility** (*rē-trak-til'i-ti*); **retraction** (*ri-trak'shən*) drawing back: retractation.—*adj.* **retrac'tive.**—*adv.* **retrac'tively.** —*n.* **retrac'tor** a device or instrument for holding parts back, esp. a surgical instrument for this purpose: a muscle that pulls in a part. [L. *retrahēre, retractum*—*re*-, back, *trahēre*, to draw.]

retral *rē'tral, ret'ral,* (*biol.*) *adj.* at or towards the rear. —*adv.* **re'trally.** [L. *retro*, backwards.]

retread *rē-tred'*, *v.t.* to tread again:—*pa.t.* **retrod'**; *pa.p.* **retrodd'en**: to remould (a tyre):—*pa.t.* and *pa.p.* **retread'ed.**—*n.* (*rē'tred*) a used tyre which has been given a new tread (also *fig.*). [Pfx. **re-**.]

re-treat, retreat *rē-trēt'*, *v.t.* to treat again. [Pfx. **re-**.]

retreat *ri-trēt'*, *n.* a withdrawal: an orderly withdrawal before an enemy, or from a position of danger or difficulty: a signal (by bugle or drum) for withdrawal or for retirement to quarters: seclusion for a time, e.g., for religious meditation: a time of such retirement: a place of privacy, seclusion, refuge, or quiet: an institution for treatment of the insane, drunkards, or others.—*v.i.* to draw back: to relinquish a position: to retire: to recede. [O.Fr. *retret, -e*, pa.p. of *retraire*—L. *retrahēre*, to draw back.]

retrench *ri-trench'*, *-trensh'*, *v.t.* to cut off, out, or down.—*v.i.* to cut down expenses.—*n.* **retrench'ment.** [O.Fr. *retrencher* (Fr. *retrancher*)—*re*-, off, *trencher*; see **trench**.]

retribution *ret-ri-bū'shən*, *n.* requital (now esp. of evil).—*adj.* **retrib'utive** (*ri*-) repaying: rewarding or punishing suitably.—*adv.* **retrib'utively.**—*n.* **retrib'utor.**—*adj.* **retrib'utory.** [L. *retribuēre, -ūtum,* to give back—*re*-, back, *tribuēre*, to give.]

retrieve *ri-trēv'*, *v.t.* to search for and fetch, as a dog does game: to recover, repossess: to rescue (from, out of): to save (time): to restore (honour, fortune): to make good (a loss, error): to return successfully (in tennis, etc.,) a shot, which is difficult to reach.—*v.i.* to find and fetch in game.—*adj.* **retriev'able.**—*n.* **retriev'ableness.**—*adv.* **retriev'ably.**—*ns.* **retriev'al** retrieving: the extraction of data from a file (*comput.*); **retriev'er** a dog (of a breed that can be) trained to find and fetch game that has been shot: one who retrieves.—*n.* and *adj.* **retriev'ing.** [O.Fr. *retroev-, retreuv-*, stressed stem of *retrover*—*re*-, again, *trouver*, to find.]

retro- *ret-rō-, rē-trō-,* *pfx.* backwards: behind. [L *retrō.*]

retroact *rē-trō-akt'*, or *ret'rō-*, *v.i.* to act backward, or

apply to the past (*law*): to react.—*n.* **retroac'tion.**—*adj.* **retroac'tive** applying to things past: operating backward.—*adv.* **retroac'tively.**—*n.* **retroactiv'ity.** [L. *retroagēre, -actum—agēre*, to do.]

retrocede *ret-rō-, rē-trō-sēd'*, *v.i.* to move back.—*v.t.* to grant back.—*adj.* **retrocē'dent.**—*n.* **retrocession** (*-sesh'ən*).—*adj.* **retroces'sive.** [L. *retrōcēdēre, -cēssum—cēdēre*, to go, yield; partly from **retro-** and **cede**, or Fr. *céder.*]

retrochoir *rē'trō-kwīr*, or *ret'rō-,* (*archit.*) *n.* an extension of a church behind the position of the high altar. [Pfx. **retro-**.]

retrod, retrodden. See **retread**.

retrofit *ret'rō-fit*, *v.t.* to modify (a house, aircraft, etc.) some time after construction by incorporating or substituting more up-to-date parts, etc.:—*pr.p.* **ret'rofitting**; *pa.t.* and *pa.p.* **ret'rofitted.**—*ns.* **ret'rofit; ret'rofitting.** [Pfx. **retro-**.]

retroflex *ret'rō-fleks,* or *rē'trō-, adj.* bent back (also **retroflect'ed, ret'roflexed**): cacuminal (*phon.*; also **ret'roflexed**).—*n.* **retroflexion, retroflection** (*-flek'-shən*). [L.L. *retroflexus—*L. *retro-*, back—L. *flectēre, flexum,* to bend.]

retrograde *ret'rō-grād* (or *rē'trō-*), *adj.* moving or directed backward or (*astron.*) from east to west, relatively to the fixed stars: inverse: habitually walking or swimming backwards: degenerating: reverting.—*n.* one who goes back or degenerates.—*v.i.* to go back or backwards: to have a retrograde movement (*astron.*).—*n.* **retrogradation** (*-grə-dā'shən*) retrogression (esp. *astron.*).—*v.i.* **retrogress'** to retrograde.—*n.* **retrogression** (*-gresh'ən*).—*adj.* **retrogress'ive.**—*adv.* **retrogress'ively.** [L. *retrōgradus,* going backward, *retrōgressus,* retrogression—*retrō-,* backward, *gradī, gressus,* to go.]

retroject *ret'rō-jekt,* *v.t.* to throw backwards (opp. to *project*).—*n.* **retrojec'tion.** [Pfx. **retro-** and **project**.]

retro-rocket *ret'rō-rok'it, rēt', n.* a rocket whose function is to slow down, fired in a direction opposite to that in which a body, e.g. a spacecraft, an artificial satellite, is travelling. [Pfx. **retro-**.]

retrorse *ri-trörs', adj.* turned back or downward.—*adv.* **retrorse'ly.** [L. *retrōrsus—retrōversus.*]

retrospect *ret'rō-spekt* (or *rē'trō-*), *n.* reference, regard: a backward view: a view or a looking back: a contemplation of the past.—*n.* **retrospec'tion.**—*adj.* **retrospec'tive** looking back: retroactive.—*n.* an exhibition, etc. presenting the life's work of an artist, etc.—*adv.* **retrospec'tively.** [L *retrōspicēre—*L. *specēre, spectum,* to look.]

retroussé *rə-trōōs'ā, adj.* turned up (esp. of the nose). [Fr. *retroussé,* turned up.]

retrovert *ret-rō-, rē-trō-vûrt', rē'trō-vûrt, v.t.* to turn back.—*n.* **retrover'sion.** [L. *retrōvertēre, -versum—vertēre,* to turn.]

retry *rē-trī', v.t.* to try again (judicially):—*pr.p.* **retry'ing**; *pa.t.* and *pa.p.* **retried'.**—*n.* **rētrī'al.** [Pfx. **re-**.]

retsina *ret-sēn'ə, n.* a Greek resin-flavoured wine. [Gr.]

retted, rettery, retting. See **ret**.

return *ri-tûrn', v.i.* to come or go back: to revert: to recur: to continue with change of direction (*archit.*). —*v.t.* to make a turn at an angle (*archit.*): to give, put, cast, bring, or send back: to report: to retort: to report officially: to report as appointed or elected: hence, to elect to parliament· to give in return: (in games) to lead back or hit back: to requite: to repay: to render: to yield. —*n.* the act of returning: a recurrence: reversion: continuation, or a continuing

---

stretch, at an angle, esp. a right angle (*archit.*, etc.): that which comes in exchange: proceeds, profit, yield: recompense: an answer: an answering performance: a thing returned, esp. an unsold newspaper: the rendering back of a writ by the sheriff, with his report (*law*): an official report or statement, e.g. of one's taxable income (*tax return*) or (esp. in *pl.*) of the votes cast in an election: hence, election to parliament: a return ticket.—*adj.* returning: for return: in return: at right angles.—*adjs.* **return'able**; **return'less.—return crease** see **crease¹**; **returning officer** the officer who presides at an election; **return match** a second match played by the same (sets of) players; **return ticket** a ticket entitling a passenger to travel to a place and back to his starting-point.—**by return (of post)** by the next post leaving in the opposite direction; **many happy returns (of the day)** a conventional expression of good wishes said to a person on his or her birthday. [Fr. *retourner*—*re-*, back, *tourner*, to turn.]

re-turn rē'tûrn', *v.t.* and *v.i.* to turn again or back. [Pfx. re-.]

retuse ri-tūs', *adj.* with the tip blunt and broadly notched. [L. *retūsus*—*retundĕre*, to blunt.]

reunion rē-ūn'yən, *n.* a union, or a meeting, after separation: a social gathering of friends or persons with something in common. [Fr. *réunion*—*re-*, again, *union*, union.]

reunite rē-ū-nīt', *v.t.* and *v.i.* to join after separation. [Pfx. re-.]

rev rev, *n.* a revolution in an internal-combustion engine.—*v.t.* to increase the speed of revolution in (often with *up*).—*v.i.* to revolve: to increase in speed of revolution:—*pr.p.* **revv'ing**; *pa.t.* and *pa.p.* **revved.** [revolution.]

revalorise, -ize rē-val'ər-īz, *v.t.* to give a new value to, esp. to restore the value of (currency).—*ns.* **rēvalorīsā'tion, -z-**; **rēvalūā'tion.—v.t. rēval'ue** to make a new valuation of: to give a new value to. [Pfx. re-.]

revamp rē-vamp', *v.t.* to renovate, revise, give a new appearance to.—Also *n.* [Pfx. re-.]

revanche ri-vänch', *n.* policy directed towards recovery of territory lost to an enemy.—*ns.* **revanch'ism**, **revanch'ist.**—Also *adj.* [Fr.; conn. with revenge (q.v.).]

reveal ri-vēl', *v.t.* to make known, as by divine agency or inspiration: to disclose: to allow to be seen.—*adj.* **reveal'able.—n.** **reveal'er.—n.** and *adj.* **reveal'ing.** [O.Fr. *reveler* (Fr. *révéler*)—L. *revēlāre*—*re-*, back, *vēlāre*, to veil—*vēlum*, a veil.]

reveal² ri-vēl', *n.* the side surface of a recess, or of the opening for a doorway or window between the frame and the outer surface of the wall. [O.Fr. *revaler*, to lower.]

reveille ri-val'i, *n.* the sound of the drum or bugle at daybreak to awaken soldiers. [Fr. *réveillez*, awake, imper. of *réveiller*—L. re-, *vigilāre*, to watch.]

revel rev'l, *v.i.* to feast or make merry in a riotous or noisy manner: to take intense delight, to luxuriate (with *in*):—*pr.p.* **rev'elling;** *pa.t.* and *pa.p.* **rev'elled.** —*n.* a riotous feast: merrymaking: a festival or (often in *pl.*) occasion of merrymaking, dancing, masking, etc.—*ns.* **rev'eller; rev'elling; rev'elry** revelling.— **Master of the Revels** an official organiser of entertainments. [O.Fr. *reveler*—L. *rebellāre*, to rebel.]

revelation rev-i-lā'shən, *n.* the act or experience of revealing: that which is revealed: a disclosure: an enlightening experience: divine or supernatural communication: **Revelation (of St John)** or, popularly, **Revelations** (*n.sing.*), the Apocalypse or last book of the New Testament.—*adj.* **revelā'tional.** —*n.* **revelā'tionist** a believer in divine revelation: the author of the Apocalypse.—*adj.* **rev'elatory.** [L. *revēlāre, -ātum*; see reveal¹.]

revenant rəv-nä', rev'ə-nənt, *n.* one who returns after a long absence, esp. from the dead: a ghost. [Fr., pr.p. of *revenir*, to come back.]

revenge ri-venj', *v.t.* to inflict injury in retribution for: (esp. *refl.*) to avenge.—*v.i.* to take vengeance.—*n.* (the act of inflicting) a malicious injury in return for injury received: the desire or opportunity of retaliation.—*adj.* **revenge'ful.**—*adv.* **revenge'fully.**—*n.* **revenge'fulness.**—*adj.* **revenge'less.**—*n.* **reveng'er.** —*n.* and *adj.* **reveng'ing.**—*adv.* **reveng'ingly.** [O.Fr. *revenger, revencher* (Fr. *revancher*)—L. *re-, vindicāre*, to lay claim to.]

revenue rev'in-ū *n.* receipts or return from any source: income: the income of a state: a government department concerned with it.—*adj.* **rev'enued.**—**rev'enuecutt'er** an armed vessel employed in preventing smuggling. [Fr. *revenue*, pa.p. (fem.) of *revenir*, to return.]

reverberate ri-vûr'bər-āt, *v.t.* to reflect: to echo: to heat in a reverberatory furnace.—*v.i.* to be reflected: to re-echo: to resound.—*adj.* **rever'berant** reverberating.—*n.* **reverberā'tion.**—*adj.* **rever'berative** (or *-āt-*).—*n.* **rever'berator.**—*adj.* **rever'beratory** (*-ət-ər-i*, or *-āt-*).—**reverberatory furnace** a furnace in which the flame is turned back over the substance to be heated. [L. *reverberāre, -ātum*—*re-*, back, *verberāre*, to beat—*verber*, a lash.]

revere ri-vēr', *v.t.* to regard with high respect: to venerate.—*adj.* **revēr'able.**—*n.* **reverence** (*rev'ər-əns*) high respect: veneration: a gesture or observance of respect.—*v.t.* to venerate.—*n.* **rev'erencer.**—*adj.* **rev'erend** worthy of reverence: (*cap.*; usu. written **Rev.**) a title prefixed to a clergyman's name.—*n.* a clergyman.—*adjs.* **rev'erent** feeling or showing reverence; **reverential** (*-en'shl*) respectful: submissive.— *advs.* **reveren'tially; rev'erently.**—*n.* **reverer** (*ri-vēr'ər*).—**His, Your, Reverence** (now Ir. or playful) a mode of referring to or addressing a clergyman; **Most Reverend** is used of an archbishop, **Right Reverend**, a bishop, or Moderator of the Church of Scotland, **Very Reverend**, a dean, a former Moderator, or (if a clergyman) a Scottish University principal; **Reverend Mother**, a Mother Superior of a convent; **saving (your) reverence**—an apology for introducing an unseemly word or subject. [O.Fr. *reverer* (Fr. *révérer*)—L. *reverērī*—*re-*, intens., *verērī*, feel awe.]

reverie rev'ə-ri, *n.* an undirected train of thoughts or fancies in meditation: mental abstraction: a piece of music expressing such a state of mind.—*n.* **rev'erist.** [Fr. *rêverie*—*rêver*, to dream.]

revers ri-vēr', *n.* any part of a garment that is turned back, as a lapel:—*pl.* **revers'** (pron. as *sing.*). [Fr., —L. *reversus.*]

reverse ri-vûrs', *v.t.* to turn the other way about, as upside down, outside in, etc.: to invert: to set moving backwards: to annul.—*v.i.* to move backwards or in the opposite direction: to set an engine, etc. moving backwards.—*n.* the contrary, opposite: the back, esp. of a coin or medal (opp. to *obverse*): a set-back, misfortune, defeat: an act of reversing: a backwards direction: reverse gear.—*adj.* contrary, opposite: turned about: acting in the contrary direction: of the

rē-type' *v.t.*
rēū'nify *v.t.*
rēūnificā'tion *n.*

rēuphol'ster *v.t.*
rēūs'able *adj.*

rēuse' (*-ūz'*), *v.t.*
rēuse' (*-ūs'*), *n.*

rear (*mil.*).—*n.* **rear'sal.**—*adj.* **reversed'.**—*adv.*
rever'sedly.—*adj.* **reverse'less** unalterable.—*adv.*
reverse'ly.—*ns.* **rever'ser; rever'si** (-*sē*) a game in
which a captured man is not removed from the board
but turned upside down to show the captor's colour;
reversibil'ity.—*adj.* **rever'sible** able to be reversed
(in any sense): allowing of restoration (of tissues,
etc.) to a normal state (*med.*): (of a garment or fabric)
having both sides well finished, so that either can be
used as the outer one.—*n.* a reversible garment.—*n.*
and *adj.* **rever'sing.**—*n.* **rever'sion** (-*shən*) the act or
fact of reverting or of returning: that which reverts or
returns: the return, or the future possession, of any
property after some particular event: the right to
succeed to possession or office: a sum payable upon
death: that which is left over, remains: return to
ancestral type (*biol.*).—*adj.* **rever'sional.**—*adv.*
rever'sionally.—*adj.* **rever'sionary.**—**reverse gear** a
gear combination which causes an engine, etc. to go in
reverse; **reversing light** a light on the back of a motor
vehicle which comes on when the vehicle is put into
reverse gear.—**reverse the charges** to charge a telephone call to the one who receives it instead of to the
caller. [L. *reversāre*, to turn round; partly through
Fr.]

revert *ri-vûrt'*, *v.t.* to turn back.—*v.i.* to return: to fall
back to a former state: to return to the original owner
or his heirs.—*adjs.* **rever'ted; rever'tible.** [L. *re-*,
vertère, to turn.]

revet *ri-vet'*, *v.t.* to face with masonry, etc:—*pr.p.* **revett'ing;** *pa.t.* and *pa.p.* **revett'ed.**—*n.* **revet'ment** a
retaining wall, facing. [Fr. *revêtir*, to reclothe.]

review *ri-vū'*, *n.* a viewing again (also **re-view** *rē'vū'*): a
looking back: a reconsideration: a survey: a revision:
a critical examination: a critique: a periodical with
critiques of books, etc.: a display and inspection of
troops or ships: the judicial revision of a higher court
(*law*).—*v.t.* to see, view, or examine again (also **review'**): to look back on or over: to examine critically:
to write a critique on: to inspect, as troops: to revise.
—*v.i.* to write reviews.—*adj.* **review'able.**—*ns.* **review'al; review'er** a writer of critiques.—**review body**
a committee set up to review (salaries, etc.); **review
copy** a copy of a book sent by the publisher to a
periodical for review. [Partly *pfx.* **re-** and **view;**
partly Fr. *revue*, pa.p. (fem.) of *revoir*.]

revile *ri-vīl'*, *v.t.* to assail with bitter abuse.—*v.i.* to
rail, use abusive language.—*ns.* **revile'ment** the act of
reviling: a reviling speech; **revil'er.**—*n.* and *adj.* **revil'ing.**—*adv.* **revil'ingly.** [O.Fr. *reviler*—L. *re-*,
vīlis, worthless.]

revise *ri-vīz'*, *v.t.* to examine and correct: to make a
new, improved version of: to study anew.—Also *v.i.*
—*n.* a further proof-sheet in which previous corrections have been given effect to.—*adj.* **revīs'able** liable
to revision.—*ns.* **revi'sal; revi'ser** (also **-or**); **revision**
(-*vizh'ən*) the act or product of revising.—*adjs.*
revi'sional, revi'sionary.—*ns.* **revi'sionism; revi'sionist** an advocate of revision (e.g. of established doctrines, etc.): a Communist favouring modification of
stricter orthodox Communism and evolution, rather
than revolution: opprobriously, a Communist who
does not hold to orthodox Communism.—*adj.* **revi'sory.**—**Revised Version** an English translation of
the Bible issued 1881–85 (Apocrypha 1895). [Fr.
reviser and L. *revīsēre*—*re-*, back, *vīsēre*, intens. of
vidēre, to see.]

revive *ri-vīv'*, *v.t.* and *v.i.* to bring back or come back to
life, vigour, being, activity, consciousness, memory,
good spirits, freshness, vogue, notice, currency, use,

the stage.—*n.* **revivabil'ity.**—*adj.* **revi'vable.**—*adv.*
revi'vably.—*ns.* **revi'val** the act or fact of reviving:
recovery from languor, neglect, depression, etc.: renewed performance, as of a play: a time of religious
awakening: a series of meetings to encourage this:
renewal: awakening; **revi'valism; revi'valist** one who
promotes religious revival: an itinerant preacher.—
adj. **revivalist'ic.**—*n.* **revi'ver** one who, or that which,
revives: a renovating preparation: a stimulant
(*slang*).—*n.* and *adj.* **revi'ving.**—*adv.* **revi'vingly.**—
n. **revi'vor** (*law*) the revival of a suit which was abated
by the death of a party or other cause.—**Gothic Revival** the resuscitation of Gothic architecture in and
before the 19th century; **Revival of Learning** the Renaissance. [L. *revīvěre*, to live again—*vīvěre*, to
live.]

revivify *ri-viv'i-fī*, *v.t.* to restore to life: to put new life
into: to reactivate:—*pr.p.* **reviv'ifying;** *pa.t.* and
pa.p. **reviv'ified.**—*n.* **revivifica'tion.** [L.L. *re-
vīvificāre*—*re-*, *vīvus*, alive, *facěre*, to make.]

revoke *ri-vōk'*, *v.t.* to annul: to retract.—*v.i.* to neglect
to follow suit at cards.—*n.* the act of revoking at
cards.—*adj.* **revocable** (*rev'ō-kə-bl*).—*ns.* **rev'oc-
ableness, revocabil'ity.**—*adv.* **rev'ocably.**—*n.* **revo-
ca'tion** the act of revoking.—*adj.* **rev'ocatory.** [L.
revocāre—*vocāre*, to call.]

revolt *ri-vōlt'*, *v.i.* to renounce allegiance: to rise in
opposition: to turn or rise in loathing, or repugnance.
—*v.t.* to inspire revulsion or repugnance in.—*n.* a
rebellion: secession.—*adj.* **revolt'ed** insurgent:
shocked, outraged.—*n.* **revolt'er.**—*adj.* **revolt'ing.**
—*adv.* **revolt'ingly.** [Fr. *révolter*—L. *re-*, *volūtāre*,
freq. of *volvěre*, *volūtum*, to turn.]

revolute. See **revolve.**

revolution *rev-əl-ōō'shən*, or -*ū'*, *n.* the act or condition
of revolving: movement in an orbit, as distinguished
from rotation: less commonly, rotation: a complete
turn by an object or figure, through four right angles,
about an axis: a cycle of phenomena or of time: recurrence in cycles: a great upheaval: a complete change,
e.g. in outlook, social habits or circumstances: a
radical change in government: a time of intensified
change in the earth's features (*geol.*).—*adj.* **revolu'-
tionary** of, favouring, or of the nature of, revolution,
esp. in government or conditions.—*n.* one who takes
part in, or favours, a revolution.—*v.t.* **revolu'tionise, -ize** to cause radical change, or a revolution, in.
—*ns.* **revolu'tionism; revolu'tionist.—Revolutionary
Calendar** calendar used in France from 1793 to 1805.
—**the American Revolution** the change from the condition of British colonies to national independence
effected by the thirteen states of the American Union
in 1776; **the French Revolution** the overthrow of the
old French monarchy and absolutism (1789); **the
Revolution** the expulsion of James II from the British
throne (1688–89), and establishment of constitutional government under William III and Mary.
[L.L. *revolūtiō*, -*ōnis*.]

revolve *ri-volv'*, *v.t.* and *v.i.* to ponder: to move about
a centre: to rotate.—*adj.* **revolute** (*rev'əl-ūt*, -*ōōt*;
bot.) rolled backward and usu. downward.—*n.* **revol'-
ver** a pistol with a rotating magazine.—*n.* and *adj.*
revol'ving.—revolving credit credit which is automatically renewed as the sum previously borrowed is
paid back, so allowing the borrower to make repeated
use of the credit so long as the agreed maximum sum
is not exceeded; **revolving door** a door consisting of
usu. four leaves fixed at right angles, rotating around
a central axis. [L. *revolvěre, revolūtum*—*volvěre*,
to roll.]

---

revictual (*rē-vit'l*), *v.t.* and *v.i.*:—*pr.p.* **revict'ualling;** *pa.t.* and *pa.p.* **revict'ualled.**
revis'it *v.t.* and *n.* **revit'alise, -ize** *v.t.*

revue ri-vū', n. a loosely constructed theatrical show, more or less topical and musical. [Fr., review.]

revulsion ri-vul'shən, n. diversion to another part, esp. by counter-irritation (med.): withdrawal: disgust: a sudden change, esp. of feeling.—adj. **revul'sive** (-siv). [L. revellĕre, revulsum, to pluck back— vellĕre, to pluck.]

revved, etc. See rev.

reward ri-wörd', n. that which is given in return for good (sometimes evil), or in recognition of merit, or for performance of a service.—v.t. to give or be a reward to or for.—adj. **reward'able**.—ns. **reward'ableness; reward'er**.—adjs. **reward'ful; reward'ing** profitable: yielding a result well worth while; **reward'less**. [O.Fr. rewarder, regarder—re-, again, warder, garder, to guard.]

reword rē-wûrd', v.t. to put into different words. [Pfx. re-.]

Rex reks, n. king: the title used by a reigning king, abbrev. to R in signature.

Reynard, reynard rān' or ren'ärd, -ərd, n. a fox, from the name given to the fox in the epic, Reynard the Fox. [M.Du. Reynaerd—O.H.G. Reginhart, lit strong in counsel.]

Reynolds number ren'əldz num'bər, (mech.) a number designating type of flow of a fluid in a system. [Osborne Reynolds (1842–1912), British physicist.]

rhabdomancy rab'də-man'si, n. divination by rod, esp. divining for water or ore.—n. **rhab'domantist**. [Gr. rhabdomanteia—rhabdos, rod, manteia, divination.]

Rhadamanthine rad-ə-man'thin, adj. rigorously just and severe, like Rhadamanthus (Gr. -os), a judge of the lower world.

Rhaeto-Romanic rē'tō-rō-man'ik, n. a general name for a group of Romance dialects spoken from southeastern Switzerland to Friuli.—Also **Rhae'tic, Rhae'to-Romance'**.—Also adjs. [Rhaetia, area of the Alps, and see **Romanic**.]

rhapsody raps'ə-di, n. an epic or instalment of an epic recited at one sitting (Gr. hist.): an ecstatic utterance of feeling: an irregular emotional piece of music.—n. **rhapsode** (raps'ōd) a reciter of Homeric or other epics.—adjs. **rhapsodic** (-od'ik); **rhapsod'ical** rhapsodic: unrestrainedly enthusiastic, rapt.—adv. **rhapsod'ically**.—v.t. **rhaps'odise, -ize** (-ə-dīz) to recite in rhapsodies.—v.i. to write or utter rhapsodies.—n **rhaps'odist** a rhapsode: one who rhapsodises. [Gr. rhapsōidiā, an epic, a rigmarole—rhaptein, to sew, ōidē, a song.]

rhatany rat'ə-ni, n. either of two South American caesalpiniaceous plants (species of Krameria): the astringent root of either plant. [Sp. ratania—Quechua rataña.]

rhea rē'ə, n. the South American ostrich. [Gr. Rhēā, wife and sister of Kronos.]

Rhenish ren'ish, rēn', adj. of the river Rhine.—n. Rhine wine.—n. **rhenium** (rē'ni-əm) a chemical element (symbol Re; at. numb. 75) discovered by X-ray spectroscopy in Germany in 1925. [L. Rhēnus, the Rhine.]

rheo- rē'ō-, rē-ō'-, in composition, current, flow.— adjs. **rheolog'ic, -al**.—ns. **rheol'ogist; rheol'ogy** the science of the deformation and flow of matter; **rhè'ostat** an instrument for varying an electric resistance. —adj. **rheotrop'ic**.—n. **rheot'ropism** (biol.) response to the stimulus of flowing water. [Gr. rheos, flow.]

rhesus rē'səs, n. a macaque, the bandar (Macacus rhesus, or Macaca mulatta), an Indian monkey.— Also **rhesus monkey**.—**Rhesus factor, Rh (-factor)** an usu. found in human red blood cells and in those of rhesus monkeys, **Rh-positive** persons being those who have the factor and **Rh-negative** those (a very much smaller number) who do not. [Gr. Rhēsos, a king of Thrace, arbitrarily applied.]

rhetor rē'tör, n. (Gr. hist.) a teacher of rhetoric or professional orator.—n. **rhetoric** (ret'ər-ik) the theory and practice of eloquence, whether spoken or written, the whole art of using language so as to persuade others: the art of literary expression: false, showy, artificial, or declamatory expression.—adjs. **rhetoric** (ri-tor'ik); **rhetor'ical** pertaining to rhetoric: oratorical: inflated, or insincere in style.—adv. **rhetor'ically**.—n. **rhetorician** (ret-ər-ish'ən) one who teaches the art of rhetoric: an orator: a user of rhetorical language.—**rhetorical question** a question in form, for rhetorical effect, not calling for an answer. [Gr. rhētōr.]

rheum room, n. a mucous discharge, esp. from the nose. —adj. **rheumatic** (rōō-mat'ik) of the nature of, pertaining to, apt to cause, or affected with, rheumatism. —n. one who suffers from rheumatism: (in pl.) rheumatic pains (coll.).—adv. **rheumat'ically**.—adj. **rheumat'icky**.—n. **rheumatism** (rōō'mə-tizm) a condition characterised by pain and stiffness in muscles and joints.—adjs. **rheum'atoid; rheumatolog'ical**.— ns. **rheumatol'ogist; rheumatol'ogy** the study of rheumatism.—adjs. **rheumed; rheum'y** of or like rheum: esp. of air, cold and damp.—**rheumatic fever** an acute disease characterised by fever, multiple arthritis, and liability of the heart to be inflamed, caused by a streptococcal infection; **rheumatoid arthritis** a disease characterised by inflammation and swelling of joints. [Gr. rheuma, -atos, flow— rheein, to flow.]

Rh(-factor). See **rhesus**.

rhin-, rīn-, rhino- rīn-ō- in composition, nose.—adj. **rhi'nal** of the nose.—n. **rhini'tis** inflammation of the mucous membrane of the nose.—adj. **rhinolog'ical**. —ns. **rhinol'ogist** a nose specialist; **rhinol'ogy** the study of the nose: nasal pathology.—adj. **rhinoplas'tic**.—ns. **rhi'noplasty** plastic surgery of the nose; **rhi'noscope** an instrument for examining the nose.— adj. **rhinoscop'ic**.—n. **rhinos'copy**. [Gr. rhīs, rhīnos, nose.]

Rhine rīn, n. a river of Europe.—**Rhine'stone** (also without cap.) a rock-crystal: a paste diamond; **Rhine'wine** wine made from grapes grown in the Rhine valley. [Ger. Rhein; Du. Rijn.]

rhinitis. See **rhin-**.

rhino[1] rī'nō, a contraction of **rhinoceros**:—pl. **rhinos**.

rhino[2] rī'nō, (slang) n. money. [Connection with **rhino, rhinoceros** obscure.]

rhinoceros rī-nos'ər-əs, rī-, n. a large ungulate of several species in Africa and southern Asia, constituting a family characterised by one or two horns on the nose:—pl. **rhinoc'eroses**.—adj. **rhinocerot'ic**. [Gr. rhīnokerōs, rhīs, rhīnos, nose, keras, horn.]

rhinological . . . rhinoscopy. See **rhin-**.

rhiz- rīz-, **rhizo-** rī-zō- in composition, root.—n. **rhi'zocarp** (Gr. karpos, fruit) a perennial herb: a plant fruiting underground.—adjs. **rhizocar'pic, rhizocar'pous**.—n. **rhi'zoid** a short hairlike organ in the lower plants, serving as a root.—adjs. **rhizoi'dal; rhizo'matous**.—ns. **rhizome** (Gr. rhizōma, a rootmass) a root-stock, an underground stem producing roots and leafy shoots; **rhizopod** a type of Protozoan. [Gr. rhiza, root.]

Rh-negative. See **rhesus**.

---

rewind' v.t.:—pa.t. and pa.p. **rewound'**.
rewire' v.t.
rework' v.t.

rewrap' v.t.
rewrite' v.t.:—pa.t. **rewrote'**; pa.p. **rewritt'en**.

re'write n.

rho *rō, n.* the seventeenth letter (P, ϱ) of the Greek alphabet, answering to R:—*pl.* **rhos.** [Gr. *rhō*.]

rhod- *rŏd-*, **rhodo-** *rŏ-dō* in composition, rose: rose-coloured.—*ns.* **rhō′damine** (*-mēn*; see **amine**) a dye-stuff, usually red, akin to fluorescein; **rhō′dium** a metallic element (Rh; at. numb. 45) of the platinum group, forming rose-coloured salts; **rhōdochro′site** (*-krō′sīt*; Gr. *rhodochrōs*, rose-coloured) manganese spar, a pink rhombohedral mineral, manganese carbonate; **Rhōdoden′dron** (or *rod-*; Gr. *dendron*, tree) a genus of trees and shrubs of the heath family, with leathery leaves and large showy slightly zygomorphic flowers, some species being called Alpine rose: (without *cap.*) a member of the genus; **rhō′dolite** a pink or purple garnet (gemstone); **rhō′donite** a rose-red anorthic pyroxene, manganese silicate; **rhōdop′sin** (Gr. *opsis*, sight) visual purple. [Gr. *rhodon*, rose.]

Rhode Island red *rōd ī′lənd red,* an American breed of domestic fowl.

Rhodian *rō′di-ən, n.* and *adj.* of Rhodes, an island and ancient city-state of the Aegean. [Gr. *Rhodos*.]

Rhodesian man *rō-dē′shyən man,* an extinct type of man represented by a skull found at Broken Hill, in Northern Rhodesia, in 1921.

rhodium . . . rhodopsin. See **rhod-**.

rhodora *rō-dō′rə, -dō′, n.* a handsome N. American species of Rhododendron, or separate kindred genus. [L. *rhodōra*, meadow-sweet.]

rhomb *rom(b), n.* an equilateral parallelogram (usu. excluding the square): a lozenge-shaped object: a rhombohedron (*crystal.*).—*adjs.* **rhombic** (*rom′bik*) shaped like a rhombus: orthorhombic (*crystal.*); **rhombohē′dral.**—*n.* **rhombohē′dron** (Gr. *hedrā*, seat) a crystal form of six rhombi:—*pl.* **rhombohē′dra, -hē′drons.**—*adj.* **rhom′boid** like a rhombus: nearly square, with the petiole at one of the acute angles (*bot.*).—*n.* a figure approaching a rhombus, a parallelogram, usu. one that is not a rhombus nor a rectangle.—*adj.* **rhomboid′al.**—*n.* **rhom′bus** a rhomb (*geom.*): an object shaped like a rhomb:—*pl.* **rhom′bi, rhom′buses.** [Gr. *rhombos*, bull-roarer, magic wheel, rhombus.]

Rh-positive. See **rhesus.**

rhubarb *rōō′bärb, -barb, n.* any species of the genus *Rheum,* of the dock family: the root-stock, or a cathartic got from it (chiefly from *R. officinale*): the leafstalks (chiefly of *R. rhaponticum*) cooked and used as if fruit: nonsense. [O.Fr. *reubarbe*—L.L. *rheubarbarum,* for *rhābarbarum*—Gr. *rhā,* rhubarb —*Rhā,* the Volga, and L. *barbarum* (neut.), foreign; influenced by *rheum,* Gr. *rheon.*]

rhumb *rum, n.* a loxodromic curve: any point of the compass.—**rhumb′-line, -course, -sailing.** [Fr. *rumb,* or Sp. or Port. *rumbo*—L. *rhombus*; see **rhomb.**]

rhumba. Same as **rumba.**

rhyme, rime *rīm, n.* in two (or more) words, identity of sound from the last stressed vowel to the end, the consonant or consonant group preceding not being the same in both (all) cases: extended to other correspondences in sound, as *head-rhyme* or *eye-rhyme* (q.q.v.): a word or group of words agreeing in this way with another: versification, verses, a poem or a short piece of verse, in which this correspondence occurs: a jingle.—*v.i.* to be in rhyme: to correspond in sound: to make or find a rhyme or rhymes: to make rhymes or verses.—*v.t.* to put into rhyme: to use or treat as a rhyme.—*adjs.* **rhymed, rimed** (*rīmd*); **rhyme′less.**—*ns.* **rhy′mer, ri′mer** a user of rhyme: a poet: an inferior poet: a minstrel; **rhyme′ster** a would-be poet; **rhym′ist** a versifier.—**rhyme′-roy′al** (app. a commendatory name) a seven-line stanza

borrowed by Chaucer from the French—its formula, *ababbcc*; **rhyme′-scheme** the pattern of rhymes in a stanza, etc.; **rhyming slang** a form of slang in which a word is replaced by another word, or part or all of a phrase, which rhymes with it.—**without rhyme or reason** without reasonable or sensible purpose or explanation. [O.Fr. *rime*—L. *rhythmus*—Gr. *rhythmos*; see **rhythm.**]

rhyolite *rī′ō-līt, n.* an acid igneous rock with a glassy groundmass and phenocrysts of quartz and alkali-feldspar.—*adj.* **rhyolitic** (*-lit′ik*). [Irregularly—Gr. *rhyax, -ākos,* a (lava) stream, *lithos,* a stone.]

rhythm *ridhm,* or *rithm, n.* regular recurrence, esp. of stress or of long and short sounds: a pattern of recurrence: an ability to sing, move, etc. rhythmically.—*adjs.* **rhythmed** (*ridhmd, rithmd*), **rhyth′mic, -al.**—*n.* **rhyth′mic** (also **rhyth′mics** *n.sing.*) the science or theory of rhythm.—*adv.* **rhyth′mically.**—*n.* **rhythmic′ity.**—*v.t.* **rhyth′mise, -ize** to subject to rhythm.—*v.i.* to act in or observe rhythm.—*n.* **rhyth′mist** one skilled in rhythm.—*adj.* **rhythm′less.**—**rhythm method** a method of birth control requiring the avoidance of sexual intercourse during the period in which conception is most likely to occur; **rhythm section** in a band, those instruments whose main function is to supply the rhythm (usu. percussion, guitar, double-bass and piano): the players of such instruments.—**rhythm and blues** a type of music combining the styles of rock and roll and the blues. [L. *rhythmus*—Gr. *rhythmos*—*rhein,* to flow; cf. **rhyme.**]

rhytidectomy *rī-ti-dek′tə-mi, n.* an operation for smoothing the skin of the face by removing wrinkles, a face-lift. [Gr. *rhytis,* a wrinkle, *ektomē,* cutting out.]

ria *rē′ə, (geol.) n.* a normal drowned valley. [Sp. *ría,* river-mouth.]

rial *rē′əl, rī-′əl, rē-′āl′, n.* the unit of currency in Iran, Oman and (also **riyal,** q.v.) Saudi Arabia and the Yemen Arab Republic. [Pers. *rial,* Ar. *riyal*; see **riyal.**]

rib¹ *rib, n.* one of the bones that curve round and forward from the backbone: a piece of meat containing one or more ribs: a curved member of the side of a ship running from keel to deck: a strengthening bar: a rodlike structure supporting or strengthening a membrane, etc., as the vein of a leaf, a member supporting the fabric of an umbrella: the shaft of a feather: one of the parallel supports of a bridge: a framing timber: a raised band: a prominence running in a line: a ridge: a ridge raised in knitting, by alternating plain and purl stitches, or a similar ridge raised in weaving: the pattern of ribs so formed (also **ribbing**): a moulding or projecting band on a ceiling.—*v.t.* to furnish, form, cover, or enclose with ribs:—*pr.p.* **ribb′ing;** *pa.t.* and *pa.p.* **ribbed.**—*adj.* **ribbed.**—*n.* **ribb′ing.**—*adjs.* **ribb′y;** **rib′less; rib′like.**—**rib′-bone; rib′cage** the enclosing wall of the chest formed by the ribs, etc.; **rib′-grass** the ribwort plantain.—**rib′-vaulting; rib′wort** (or **ribwort plantain**) a common weed (*Plantago lanceolata*) with narrow strongly ribbed leaves and short brown heads.—**false rib** one joined indirectly to the breast-bone or (**floating rib**) not at all; **true rib** one joined directly by its cartilage. [O.E. *ribb,* rib, *ribbe,* ribwort; Ger. *Rippe,* rib.]

rib² *rib, (slang) v.t.* to tease, ridicule, make fun of. [Perh. **rib¹**—the tickling of one's ribs causing laughter.]

ribald *rib′əld, n.* an obscene speaker or writer.—*adj.* licentious: foul-mouthed or derisive.—*n.* **rib′aldry** obscenity: coarse jesting. [O.Fr. *ribald, ribaut* (Fr. *ribaud*).]

riband *rib'ɔn(d)*, spelling of **ribbon,** used in derivatives and compounds (e.g. **blue riband,** q.v.), now rare except in heraldic and sporting use.

ribbon *rib'ɔn, n.* material woven in narrow bands or strips: a strip of such or other material: anything resembling such a strip, as a road, a stripe of colour: a torn strip, tatter, shred: a strip of inking cloth, as for a typewriter.—*adj.* made of ribbon: like a ribbon: having bands of different colours.—*adj.* **ribb'ony.**—*n.* **ribb'onry** ribbons collectively.—**ribb'on-building, -development** unplanned building, growth of towns, in long strips along the main roads; **ribb'on-fish** a long, slender, laterally compressed fish, esp. the oarfish; **ribbon microphone** a microphone in which the sound is picked up by a thin metallic strip; **ribb'on-seal** a banded North Pacific seal. [O.Fr. *riban*; origin obscure.]

ribose *rī'bōs, n.* a pentose, $C_5H_{10}O_5$.—*ns.* **riboflavin** (*rī-bō-flā'vin*; L. *flāvus,* yellow) a member of vitamin B complex, in yellowish-brown crystals, promoting growth in children; **ribonuclease** (*ri-bō-nū'kli-ās, -āz*) an enzyme in the pancreas, etc., the first enzyme to be synthesised (1969); **ribosome** (*rī'bō-sōm*) one of numerous particles in a cell on which proteins are assembled.—**ribonucleic acids** (*rī'bō-nū-klē'ik*) nucleic acids containing ribose, present in living cells, where they play an important part in the development of proteins.—abbrev. **RNA.** [From *arabinose,* a sugar, by transposition of letters.]

rice *rīs, n.* a grass (*Oryza sativa*) grown in warm climates: its grain, a valuable food.—*v.t.* (esp. *U.S.*) to form (soft food, esp. cooked potatoes), into strands by passing through a ricer, sieve, etc.—*ns.* **ric'er** a utensil for ricing food.—*adj.* **rice'y, ri'cy.**—**rice'-beer** a fermented drink made from rice; **rice'-bird** the bobolink (as a feeder on rice): the Java sparrow; **rice'-bis'cuit** a sweet biscuit made of flour mixed with rice; **rice'-flour; rice'-paper** sliced and flattened pith of an Asiatic tree of the Araliaceae: a similar material made from other plants, or from linen trimmings; **rice'-pudd'ing.** [O.Fr. *ris*—L. *oryza*—Gr. *oryza,* a word of Eastern origin.]

rich *rich, adj.* abounding in possessions: wealthy: abundantly furnished: having any ingredient or quality in great abundance: productive: fertile: deep in colour: full-toned: full-flavoured: abounding in fat, sugar, fruit, or seasonings: full: splendid and costly: sumptuous: elaborately decorated: pregnant with matter for laughter.—**-rich** in composition, abundantly furnished with a specified thing, as *oil-rich.*—*adv.* **rich'ly.**—*n.* **rich'ness.** [O.E. *rīce,* great, powerful; Ger. *reich,* Du. *rijk,* Goth. *reiks*; perh. reinforced by Fr. *riche,* rich.]

riches *rich'iz,* n. (now usu. treated as *pl.*) wealth. [O.Fr. *richesse—riche,* rich.]

Richter scale *rihht'ər skāl, n.* a seismological scale of measurement. [From its inventor, Dr Charles F. *Richter* (born 1900).]

rick[1] *rik, n.* a stack: a heap.—*v.t.* to stack.—*n.* **rick'er** an implement for shocking hay.—**rick'stand** a flooring for a stack; **rick'yard.** [O.E. *hrēac*; O.N. *hraukr.*]

rick[2] *rik, v.t.* to sprain or strain.—*n.* a sprain or strain. [App. a variant of **wrick.**]

ricker *rik'ər, n.* a spar or young tree-trunk. [Perh. Ger. *Rick,* pole.]

rickets *rik'its, n.sing.* a disease of children, characterised by softness of the bones caused by deficiency of vitamin D.—*adv.* **rick'etily** shakily.—*n.* **rick'etiness** unsteadiness.—*adj.* **rick'ety** affected with rickets: feeble, unstable: tottery, threatening to collapse. [Perh. M.E. *wrikken,* to twist; or Gr. *rhachitis* (see **rachitis**).]

Rickettsia *rik-et'si-ə, n.* a genus of micro-organisms found in lice and ticks and, when transferred to man by a bite, causing typhus and other serious diseases: (without *cap.*) a member of the genus Rickettsia.—*adj.* **rickett'sial.** [After Howard Taylor *Ricketts* (1871–1910), American pathologist.]

rick-rack, ric-rac *rik'rak, n.* a decorative braid in even zigzag form, or openwork made with it. [**rack**[1].]

ricksha, rickshaw *rik'shä, -shò, ns.* a small two-wheeled, hooded carriage drawn by a man or men, or powered by a man on a bicycle or motor-bicycle.—Also **jinrick'sha, jinrick'shaw.** [Jap. *jin,* man, *riki,* power, *sha,* carriage.]

ricochet *rik-ō-shā', -shet',* or *rik', n.* a glancing rebound or skip, as of a projectile flying low.—*v.i.* to glance: to skip along the ground:—*pr.p.* **ricocheting** (*-shā'ing, rik'*), **ricochetting** (*-shet'ing, rik'*); *pa.t.* and *pa.p.* **ricocheted** (*-shād', rik'*), **ricochetted** (*-shet'id, rik'*). [Fr.]

rictus *rik'təs, n.* the gape, esp. of a bird: unnatural gaping of the mouth.—*adj.* **ric'tal.** [L. *rictus, -ūs.*]

rid[1] *rid, v.t.* to free: to clear: to disencumber:—*pr.p.* **ridd'ing;** *pa.t.* and *pa.p.* **rid** or **ridd'ed.**—*n.* **ridd'ance** clearance: removal: disencumberment: deliverance.—**a good riddance** a welcome relief; **get rid of** to disencumber oneself of. [O.N. *rythja,* to clear; with senses converging upon **redd.**]

rid[2], **ridden.** See **ride.**

riddle[1] *rid'l, n.* an obscure description of something which the hearer is asked to name: a puzzling question: anything puzzling.—*v.t.* to solve: to puzzle.—*v.i.* to make riddles: to speak obscurely.—*ns.* **ridd'ler; ridd'ling.**—*adj.* enigmatic, obscure, puzzling.—*adv.* **ridd'lingly.** [O.E. *rædelse—rædan,* to guess, to read—*ræd,* counsel.]

riddle[2] *rid'l, n.* a large coarse sieve.—*v.t.* to separate with a riddle: to make full of holes like a riddle, as with shot.—*v.i.* to use a riddle: to sift.—*ns.* **ridd'ler; ridd'ling.** [O.E. *hriddel,* earlier *hridder.*]

ride *rīd, v.i.* to travel or be borne on the back of an animal, on a bicycle, or in a vehicle, boat, on a broomstick, the waves, etc.: to float buoyantly: to lie at anchor: to work up out of position: to admit of riding: to copulate (*vulg.*).—*v.t.* to traverse, trace, ford, or perform on horseback, on a bicycle, etc.: to sit on: to bestride: to sit on and control: to travel on: to control at will, or oppressively: to rest or turn on: to sustain, come through, esp. while riding at anchor: to give a ride to, or cause to ride: to convey by vehicle (*U.S.*): to copulate with (*vulg.*):—*pa.t.* **rōde,** arch. **rid;** *pa.p.* **ridd'en,** arch. **rid, rode.**—*n.* a journey on horseback, on a bicycle, or in a vehicle: a spell of riding: a road for horse-riding, esp. one through a wood: an act of copulation (*vulg.*): a partner (esp. female) in copulation (*vulg.*).—*n.* **ridabil'ity.**—*adj.* **ri'dable, ride'able.**—**-ridden** in composition, oppressed by the dominance or prevalence of a specified thing (e.g. **hag-ridden, cliché-ridden**).—*n.* **ri'der** one who rides or can ride: an object that rests on or astride of another: an added clause or corollary: a proposition that a pupil or candidate is asked to deduce from another.—*adjs.* **ri'dered; ri'derless.**—*n.* **ri'ding** a track, esp. a woodland track, for riding on: an exciseofficer's district: anchorage.—Also *adj.* **ri'ding-boot** a high boot.—*n.pl.* **ri'ding-breeches** breeches for riding, with loose-fitting thighs and tight-fitting legs. —**ri'ding-crop; ri'ding-habit** a woman's dress for riding, esp. one with a long skirt for riding sidesaddle; **ri'ding-hood** a hood formerly worn by women when riding; **ri'ding-light** a light hung out in the rigging at night when a vessel is riding at anchor; **ri'ding-school.**—**let (something) ride** to let (something) alone, not try to stop it; **ride down** to overtake by riding: to charge and overthrow or trample; **ride for a fall** to court disaster; **ride out** to keep afloat throughout (a storm): to survive, get safely through or past (a period of difficulty, etc.); **ride to hounds** to take part in fox-hunting; **ride up** to work up out of position; **take for a ride** to give (someone) a lift in a car with the object of murdering him in some remote place: to play a trick on, dupe. [O.E. *rīdan*; Du. *rijden*, Ger. *reiten*.]

rident rī'*dant*, *adj*. laughing or beamingly smiling. [L. *rīdēns*, -*entis*, pr.p. of *rīdēre*, to laugh.]

ridge rij, *n*. the earth thrown up by the plough between the furrows: a long narrow top or crest: the horizontal line of a roof-top: a narrow elevation: a hill-range.— *v.t.* and *v.i.* to form into ridges: to wrinkle.—*adj.* **ridged**.—*n*. **ridg'ing**.—*adj.* **ridg'y**.—**ridge'-piece**, **ridge'-pole** the timber forming the ridge of a roof; **ridge'-tile** a tile that bestrides the ridge of a roof; **ridge'way** a track along a hill-crest. [O.E. *hrycg*; O.N. *hryggr*, Ger. *Rücken*, back.]

ridicule rid'i-*kūl*, *n*. derision: mockery.—*v.t.* to laugh at: to expose to merriment: to deride: to mock.—*n*. **rid'iculer**.—*adj*. **ridic'ulous** deserving or exciting ridicule: absurd.—*adv*. **ridic'ulously**.—*n*. **ridic'u-lousness**. [L. *rīdiculus*—*rīdēre*, to laugh.]

Riding rī'*ding*, *n*. one of the three divisions of Yorkshire: extended to divisions elsewhere. [For *thriding*—O.N. *thrithi*, third.]

riding. See **ride**.

riel rē'*al*, *n*. the basic monetary unit of Kampuchea.

riem rēm, *n*. a raw-hide thong.—*n*. **riemple** (*rēm'pē*; dim. of *riem*) a long riem about the width of a shoe-lace, used as string, for the weaving of chair-backs and seats, etc. [Afrik.]

Riesling rēz'ling, *n*. a dry white table wine, named from a type of grape. [Ger.]

rieve, **riever**. Same as **reave**, **reaver**.

rife rīf, *adj*. prevalent: abounding: current.—Also *adv*.—*adv*. **rife'ly**.—*n*. **rife'ness**. [O.E. *rȳfe*, *rīfe*.]

riff rif, (*jazz*) *n*. a phrase or figure played repeatedly. [Perh. *refrain*.]

riffle[1] rif'*l*, *n*. a shallow section in a river where the water flows swiftly (*U.S.*).—*v.t.* to ruffle: to turn or stir lightly and rapidly (as the pages of a book), often in cursory search for something: to treat thus the pages of (a book): to shuffle by allowing the corner of a card from one part of the pack to fall alternately with that of a card in the other.—*v.i.* to form a riffle: to turn quickly the pages of a book (with *through*). [Cf. **ripple[1]**.]

riffle[2] rif'*l*, *n*. (e.g. in gold-washing) a groove or slat in a sluice to catch free particles of ore. [Cf. **rifle[2]**.]

riff-raff rif'-*raf*, *n*. the scum of the people: rubbish.— *adj*. rubbishy. [M.E. *rif and raf*—O.Fr. *rif et raf*.]

rifle[1] rī'*fl*, *v.t.* to plunder: to ransack.—*n*. **ri'fler**. [O.Fr. *rifler*.]

rifle[2] rī'*fl*, *v.t.* to groove spirally: (also *v.i.*) to shoot with a rifle.—*n*. a firearm with a spirally grooved barrel.—*n*. **ri'fling** the spiral grooving of a gun-bore.— **ri'fle-bird**, **ri'fleman-bird** an Australian bird of paradise; **ri'fle-green** a dark green, the colour of a rifleman's uniform (also *adj.*); **ri'fleman**; **ri'fle-pit** a pit to shelter riflemen; **ri'fle-range** the range of a rifle: a place for rifle practice; **ri'fle-shot**. [O.Fr. *rifler*, to scratch.]

rift rift, *n*. a cleft: a fissure.—*v.t.* and *v.i.* to cleave, split.—**rift valley** a valley formed by subsidence of a portion of the earth's crust between two faults. [Cf. Dan. and Norw. *rift*, a cleft.]

rig[1] rig, *v.t.* to fit with sails and tackling (*naut.*): to fit up or fit out: to equip: to set up, set in working order: to dress, clothe (now *coll.*):—*pr.p.* **rigg'ing**; *pa.t.* and *pa.p.* **rigged**.—*n*. the form and arrangement of masts,

sails, and tackling: an outfit: garb: general appearance: an articulated lorry (*coll.*): a well-boring plant, an oil-rig.—*n*. **rigg'er** one who rigs ships: one who attends to the rigging of aircraft: one who puts up and looks after scaffolding, etc., used for building operations: outrigger.— -**rigger** in composition, a ship rigged in manner indicated.—*n*. **rigg'ing** tackle: the system of cordage which supports a ship's masts and extends the sails: the system of wires and cords in an aircraft.—**rig out** to furnish with complete dress, etc; **rig up** to dress or equip: to put up quickly from available materials. [Perh. conn. with Norw. *rigga*, to bind.]

rig[2] rig, *n*. a frolic, prank, trick.—*v.t.* to manipulate unscrupulously or dishonestly: to set up fraudulently. —*n*. **rigg'ing** manipulating unscrupulously or dishonestly, as in price-rigging.—**run a rig** to play a prank.

rigadoon rig-*a*-*dōōn*', *n*. a lively jig-like dance for one couple, or its music. [Fr. *rigaudon*.]

rigg rig, *n*. the dogfish.

right rīt, *adj*. straight: direct: perpendicular: forming one-fourth of a revolution: with axis perpendicular to base: true: genuine: characteristic: truly judged or judging: appropriate: in accordance, or identical, with what is true and fitting: not mistaken: accurate: fit: sound: intended to be exposed (as a side, e.g. of cloth): morally justifiable: just: equitable: justly to be preferred or commended: at or towards that side at which in a majority of people is the better-developed hand (of a river, as referred to one going downstream: on the stage, from the point of view of an actor looking at the audience): for a part of the body, etc. on the right side: sitting at the president's right hand (in Continental assemblies): hence, conservative or inclined towards conservatism, right-wing.—*adv*. straight: straightway: quite: just, exactly: in a right manner: justly: correctly: very (*arch*. and *dial*. or in special phrases): to or on the right side.—*n*. that which is right or correct: rightness: fair treatment: equity: truth: justice: just or legal claim: what one has a just claim to: due: the right hand: the right side: a glove, shoe, etc., for the right hand, foot, etc.: the region on the right side: the right wing: the conservatives.—*v.t.* to set in order: to rectify: to redress: to vindicate: to avenge: to set right side up or erect.— *v.i.* to recover an erect position.—*interj*. expressing agreement, acquiescence, or readiness.—*adj*. **right'-able**.—*n*. **right'er** one who sets right or redresses wrong.—*adj*. **right'ful** having a just claim: according to justice: belonging by right.—*adv*. **right'fully**.—*ns*. **right'fulness**; **right'ing**; **right'ist** an adherent of the political right (conservatives).—Also *adj*.—*adj*. **right'less** without rights.—*adv*. **right'ly**.—*n*. **right'ness**.—*interj*. **righto'** (*pl*. **rightos'**), **right-oh'** (*coll.*) expressing acquiescence.—*adj*. and *adv*. **right'ward** towards the right: more right-wing.—*adv*. **right'wards**.—**right'-about'** the directly opposite quarter (in drill or dismissal; also **right-about-face**).— *adv*. to the right-about (face).—*v.i.* to turn right-about (face).—*adj*. **right'-and-left** having a right and a left side, part, etc.: on both sides: from both barrels. —*n*. a shot or a blow from each barrel or hand.—*adv*. on both sides: on all hands: towards one side, then the other: in all directions.—*adj*. **right-ang'led** having a right angle, one equal to a fourth of a revolution.— **right ascension** see **ascension**.—*adjs*. **right'-bank** on the right bank; **right'-hand** at the right side: towards the right: performed with the right hand: with thread or strands turning to the right: chiefly relied on (as *one's right-hand man*); **right'-hand'ed** using the right hand more easily than the left: with or for the right hand: with rotation towards the right, or clockwise.—

adv. towards the right.—**right'-hand'edness; right'-hand'er** a blow with the right hand: a right-handed person.—*n.* and *adj.* **Right Honourable** a title of distinction given to peers below the rank of marquis, to privy councillors, to present and past cabinet ministers, to certain Lord Mayors and Lord Provosts, etc.—*adj.* **right'-mind'ed** having a mind disposed towards what is right, just, or according to good sense: sane.—**right'-mind'edness; right'-of-way'** a track over which there is a **right of way** (see below): the strip of land occupied by a railway track, a road, etc. (*U.S.*):—*pl.* **right'-of-ways'** or **rights'-of-way'**.—*n.* and *adj.* **Right Reverend** see reverend.—**rights issue** (*commerce*) an issue of new shares which shareholders of a company may buy, usu. below the market price, in proportion to their current holdings.—*adj.* **right'-think'ing** of approved opinions.—**right whale** a whale of the typical genus Balaena, esp. the Greenland whale; **right wing** the political right: the wing on the right side of an army, football pitch, etc.—*adj.* **right'-wing** of or on the right wing: pertaining to the political right: (having opinions which are) conservative, opposed to socialism, etc.—**right'-wing'er.—all right see all; bill of rights** (often *caps.*) an accepted statement of the rights and privileges of the people or of individuals, which the government or state must not infringe (e.g. that embodied in the Bill of Rights, 1689, or in the U.S. Constitution); **by rights** rightfully: if all were right; **civil rights see civil; do someone right** to do someone justice; **have a right, no right** to be entitled or not entitled; **in one's own right** by absolute and personal right, not through another; **in one's right mind** quite sane; **in the right** right: maintaining a justifiable position; **put, set, to rights** to set in order; **right as a trivet, as rain see trivet, rain; right away** straightway: without delay; **right, left and centre** same as **left, right and centre; right of entry** a legal right to enter a place; **right off** without delay; **right of way** the right of the public to pass over a piece of ground (see also **right-of-way** above). [O.E. *riht* (n. and adj.), *rihte* (adv.), *rihten* (vb.).]

righteous rī'chəs, *adj.* just, upright.—*adv.* **right'-eously.**—*n.* **right'eousness.** [O.E. *rihtwīs—riht*, right, *wīs*, wise, prudent, or *wīse*, wise, manner.]

rigid rij'id, *adj.* stiff: unbending: unyielding: rigorous: strict: of an airship, having a rigid structure.—*v.t.* and *v.i.* **rigid'ify** to make or become rigid:—*pr.p.* **rigid'ifying;** *pa.t.* and *pa.p.* **rigid'ified.**—*n.* **rigid'ity.**—*adv.* **rig'idly.**—*n.* **rig'idness.** [L. *rigidus—rigēre,* to be stiff.]

riglin, rigling. See ridgel.

rigmarole rig'mə-rōl, *n.* a long rambling discourse: a long, complicated series of actions, instructions, etc., often rather pointless, boring or irritating. [From the **Ragman Rolls** in which Scottish nobles subscribed allegiance to Edward I.]

rigor rī'gör, rig'ör, *n.* a sense of chilliness with contraction of the skin, a preliminary symptom of many diseases (*med.*): a rigid irresponsive state caused by a sudden shock.—*ns.* **rigorism** (*rig'ər-izm*) extreme strictness: the doctrine that in doubtful cases the strict course should be followed; **rig'orist.**—*adj.* **rig'orous** rigidly strict or scrupulous: exact: unsparing: severe.—*adv.* **rig'orously.**—*ns.* **rig'or-ousness; rigour** (*rig'ər*) severity: unswerving enforcement of law, rule, or principle: strict exactitude: austerity: extreme strictness: severity of weather or climate.—**rigor mortis** (*mör'tis*) (L.) stiffening of the body after death. [L. *rigor—rigēre,* to be stiff.]

Rigveda rig-vā'də, -vē', *n.* the first of the four Vedas. [Sans. *ṛic,* a hymn, *veda,* knowledge.]

rile rīl, *v.t.* to annoy or irritate. [A form of roil.]

rilievo. See relievo.

rill ril, *n.* a very small brook: a runnel: a small trench: a narrow furrow on the moon or Mars (also **rille** from Ger. *Rille*). [Cf. Du. *ril,* Ger. (orig. L.G.) *Rille,* channel, furrow.]

rim rim, *n.* the outermost circular part of a wheel, not including the tire: an edge, border, brim, or margin, esp. when raised or more or less circular: an encircling band, mark, or line.—*v.t.* to form or furnish a rim to:—*pr.p.* **rimm'ing;** *pa.t.* and *pa.p.* **rimmed.**—*adjs.* **rim'less; rimmed.**—**rim'-brake** a brake acting on the rim of a wheel. [O.E. *rima* (found in compounds).]

rime rīm, *n.* hoar-frost or frozen dew: ice deposited by freezing of fog (*meteor.*).—*v.t.* to cover with rime.—*adj.* **rī'my.** [O.E. *hrīm.*]

rime[2]**, rimer,** etc. Same as **rhyme, rhymer,** etc.

rimu rē'mŏŏ, *n.* a coniferous tree of New Zealand, *Dacrydium cupressinum.* [Maori.]

rind rīnd, *n.* bark: peel: crust: outside.—*v.t.* to bark.—*adjs.* **rind'ed; rind'less; rind'y.** [O.E. *rinde;* Du. *rinde,* Ger. *Rinde.*]

rinderpest rin'dər-pest, *n.* a malignant and contagious disease of cattle. [Ger., cattle-plague.]

ring[1] ring, *n.* a circlet or small hoop, esp. one of metal, worn on the finger, in the ear, nose, or elsewhere: any object, mark, arrangement, group, or course of like form: an encircling band: a rim: an encircling cut in bark: a zone of wood added in a season's growth, as seen in sections: a mark of fungus growth in turf (**fairy ring**): a segment of a worm, caterpillar, etc.: a closed chain of atoms: a system of elements in which addition is associative and commutative and multiplication is associative and distributive with respect to addition (*math.*): a circular ripple: a circular earthwork or rampart: an arena: a space set apart for boxing, wrestling, circus performance, riding display of animals, or the like: an enclosure for bookmakers: pugilism: a combination or clique, esp. organised to control the market or for other self-seeking purpose: a system operated by some antique dealers who refrain from bidding against each other at an auction, so that one of their number may buy cheaply, and then share the profit made by subsequent resale.—*v.t.* to encircle: to put a ring on or in: to cut a ring in the bark of: to cut into rings: to go in rings round:—*pa.t.* and *pa.p.* **ringed.**—*adj.* **ringed.**—*n.* **ringer** (*ring'ər*) one who rings: a throw of a quoit that encircles the pin: a quoit so thrown: a person or thing of the highest excellence.—*n.* and *adj.* **ring'ing.**—*adj.* **ring'less.**—*n.* **ring'let** a long curl of hair.—*adj.* **ring'leted.**—*n.* **ring'ster** a member of a ring, esp. in a political or price-fixing sense.—*adv.* **ring'wise.**—*v.t.* **ring'-bark** to strip a ring of bark from.—**ring'-bolt** a bolt with a ring through a hole at one end; **ring'bone** a bony callus on a horse's pastern-bone: the condition caused by this; **ring circuit** (*elect.*) an electrical supply system in which a number of power-points are connected to the main supply by a series of wires, forming a closed circuit; **ring'-dove** the wood-pigeon, from the broken white ring or line on its neck; **ring'-fence** a fence continuously encircling an estate: a complete barrier: the compulsory separation, for tax purposes, of a company's business interests in North Sea oil from their other business interests; **ring'-finger** the third finger, esp. of the left hand, on which the wedding-ring is worn; **ring fort** (*archaeol.*) a dwelling-site of the Iron Age with a strong circular wall; **ring'leader** one who takes the lead in mischief; **ring main** (*elect.*) an electrical supply system in which the power-points and the mains are connected in a ring circuit; **ring'-master** one who has charge of performances in a circus-ring; **ring'-money** money in the form of rings.—*adj.* **ring'-necked** (*-nekt*) having the neck marked with a ring. —**ring'-ou'zel, -ou'sel see ouzel; ring'-plov'er** a ring-necked plover of various kinds; **ring pull** the tongue of metal and the ring attached to it, which one pulls from the top of a can of beer, lemonade, etc. to open it; **ring'-road** a road or boulevard encircling a town or its inner part; **ring'side** the side of the prize-ring; **ring'-snake** a common English snake, the grass-snake; **ring'-tail** the female or young male of the hen-harrier, from a rust-coloured ring on the tail-feathers: (without *hyphen*) a ringtailed cat (see **cacomistle**).—*adjs.* **ring'-tail, -tailed** (-tāld) having the tail marked with bars or rings of colour, as a lemur.—**ring'-taw** a game of marbles, with rings marked on the ground; **ring'-wall** an enclosing wall; **ring'way** a ring-road; **ring'worm** a skin disease characterised by ring-shaped patches, caused by fungi.—**a ringside seat**, view (*fig.*) (a position which allows one to have) a very clear view; **make, run, rings round** to be markedly superior to; **throw one's hat into the ring** (*coll.*) to offer oneself as a candidate or challenger: to issue a challenge, institute an attack. [O.E. *hring*.]

ring² *ring*, *v.i.* to give a metallic or bell-like sound: to sound aloud and clearly: to give a characteristic or particular sound: to resound, re-echo: to be filled with sound, or a sensation like sound, or report, or renown: to cause a bell or bells to sound, esp. as a summons or signal.—*v.t.* to cause to give a metallic or bell-like sound: to sound in the manner of a bell: to summon, usher, announce by a bell or bells: to call on the telephone: to re-echo, resound, proclaim:—*pa.t.* **rang**, now rarely **rung**; *pa.p.* **rung**.—*n.* a sounding of a bell: the characteristic sound or tone, as of a bell or a metal, or of a voice: a ringing sound: a set of bells.—*n.* **ring'er** one who, or that which, rings: a horse raced under the name of another horse, or an athlete or other contestant competing under a false name or otherwise disguised: (also **dead ringer**) a person or thing (almost) identical to some other person or thing (with *for*; *coll.*).—*n.* and *adj.* **ring'ing**.—*adv.* **ring'ingly**.—**ring a bell** to begin to arouse a memory; **ring down** or **up** (**the curtain**) to give the signal for lowering or raising it; **ring in, out** to usher in, out (esp. the year) with bell-ringing; **ring off** to end a telephone conversation by replacing the receiver; **ring out** to sound loudly, clearly, and suddenly; **ring the bell** to achieve a great success; **ring true** to sound genuine (like a tested coin); **ring up** to summon by bell, esp. to the telephone. [O.E. *hringan*; O.N. *hringja*; Ger. *ringen*; Dan. *ringe*.]

ringent *rin'jənt*, *adj.* gaping. [L. *ringēns, -entis*, pr.p. of *ringi*.]

ringhals *ring'hals*, *n.* a Southern African snake which spits or sprays its venom at its victims. [Afrik. *ring*, a ring, *hals*, a neck.]

rink *ringk*, *n.* a portion of a bowling-green, curling-pond, etc., allotted to one set of players: a division of a side playing on such a portion: a piece of ice pre-pared for skating: a building or floor for roller-skating or ice-skating. [Orig. Scots, tilting ground.]

rinse *rins*, *v.t.* to wash lightly by pouring, shaking, or dipping: to wash in clean water to remove soap traces.—*n.* an act of rinsing: liquid used for rinsing: a solu-tion used in hair-dressing, esp. one to tint the hair slightly and impermanently.—*adj.* **rins'able, rins'-ible**.—*ns.* **rins'er; rins'ing**. [O.Fr. *rinser* (Fr. *rincer*).]

riot *rī'ət*, *n.* wild revelry: debauchery: loose living: un-restrained squandering or indulgence: tumult: a great, usu. boisterous, success: a disturbance of the peace by a crowd (legally three or more): of colour, a striking display.—*v.i.* to take part or indulge in riot: to revel.—*ns.* **rī'oter; rī'oting**.—*adj.* **rī'otous**.—*adv.* **rī'otously**.—*n.* **rī'otousness**.—**Riot Act** a statute de-

signed to prevent riotous assemblies: a form of words read as a warning to rioters to disperse; **riot police** police specially equipped with shields, tear-gas gren-ades, etc. for dealing with rioting crowds.—**read the riot act** (*fig.*) to give vehement warning that some-thing must cease; **run riot** to act or grow without re-straint. [O.Fr. *riot, riotte*.]

rip¹ *rip*, *v.t.* to slash or tear open, apart, off, or out: to make by such an action: to reopen (with *up*): to cleave or saw with the grain: to strip (as a roof): to utter explosively (with *out*).—*v.i.* to part in rents: to break out violently: to rush, go forward unrestrainedly:—*pr.p.* **ripp'ing**; *pa.t.* and *pa.p.* **ripped**.—*n.* a rent: an unchecked rush.—**ripp'er** one who rips: a tool for ripping: a person or thing especially admirable (*slang*).—*adj.* **ripp'ing** (*slang*) excellent.—Also *adv.*—*adv.* **ripp'ingly**.—**rip'-cord** a cord for opening a balloon's gas-bag or enabling a parachute to open; **rip'-off** (*slang*) (*financial*) exploitation: a theft, stealing, cheating, etc.: a film, etc. that exploits the success of another by imitating it; **rip'-saw** a saw for cutting along the grain.—*adj.* **rip'-roaring** wild and noisy.—**rip'snorter** (*slang*) a fast and furious affair, or person: a gale.—*adj.* **rip'snorting**.—**let rip** to express oneself, or to act, violently or with abandon: to increase speed in greatly: (**let it rip**) to refrain from trying to check an action or process; **rip off** (*slang*) to steal: to steal from: to exploit, cheat, overcharge, etc. [Cf. Fris. *rippe*, Flem. *rippen*, Norw. *rippa*.]

rip² *rip*, *n.* an inferior horse: a disreputable person.

rip³ *rip*, *n.* stretch of broken water: disturbed state of the sea.—*n.* **rip'tide** tidal rip. [Perh. **rip¹**.]

riparian *rī-pā'ri-ən*, *adj.* of or inhabiting a river-bank.—*n.* an owner of land bordering a river.—*adj.* **ripā'-rial**. [L. *rīpārius*—*rīpa*, a river-bank.]

ripe *rīp*, *adj.* ready for harvest: arrived at perfection: fit for use: fully developed: ready: resembling ripe fruit: mature.—*adv.* **ripe'ly**.—*v.t.* and *v.i.* **rī'pen** to make or grow ripe or riper.—*n.* **ripe'ness**. [O.E. *rīpe*, ripe, *rīpian*, to ripen.]

ripieno *ri-pyā'nō*, (*mus.*) *adj.* supplementary.—*n.* a supplementary instrument or performer:—*pl.* **ripie'nos**. [It.]

riposte *ri-post'*, -*pōst'*, *n.* a quick return thrust after a parry: a retort.—*v.t.* and *v.i.* to answer with a riposte. [Fr.,—It. *risposta*, reply.]

ripper, ripping. See **rip¹**.

ripple¹ *rip'l*, *n.* light fretting of the surface of a liquid: a little wave: a similar appearance in anything: a sound as of rippling water.—*v.t.* to ruffle the surface of: to mark with ripples.—*v.i.* to move or run in ripples: to sound like ripples.—*n.* and *adj.* **ripp'ling**.—*adv.* **ripp'lingly**.—*adj.* **ripp'ly**.—**ripp'le-mark** an undulatory ridging produced in sediments by waves, currents, and wind, often preserved in sedimentary rocks.—*adj.* **ripp'le-marked**.

ripple² *rip'l*, *n.* a toothed implement for removing seeds, etc., from flax or hemp.—*v.t.* to clear of seeds by drawing through a ripple: to remove by a ripple.—*n.* **ripp'ler**. [Cf. L.G. and Du. *repel*, a ripple, hoe, Ger. *Riffel*.]

Rip Van Winkle *rip van wing'kl*, one very much behind the times, as was a character of that name in a story by Washington Irving: according to the story he returned home after having slept in the mountains for twenty years.

rise *rīz*, *v.i.* to get up: to become erect, stand up: to come back to life: to revolt (often with *up*): to close a session: to move upward: to come up to the surface: to fly up from the ground: to come above the horizon: to grow upward: to advance in rank, fortune, etc.: to swell: to increase: to increase in price: to become more acute in pitch: to be excited: to be cheered: to come into view, notice, or consciousness: to spring up: to take origin: to have source: to come into being: to extend upward: to tower: to slope up: to come to hand, chance to come: to respond as to provocation, or to a situation calling forth one's powers: to feel nausea:—*pa.t.* **rose** (*rōz*); *pa.p.* **risen** (*riz'n*).—*n.* rising: ascent: a coming up to the surface, as of a fish: the sport of making a butt of someone by deception: increase in height: vertical difference or amount of elevation or rising: increase of salary, price, etc.: an upward slope: a sharpening of pitch: origin: occasion: the riser of a step.—*ns.* **ris'er** one who rises, esp. from bed: that which rises: the upright portion of a step; **ris'ing** the action or process of the verb in any sense: a revolt.—*adj.* and *pr.p.* ascending: increasing: coming above the horizon: advancing: growing up: approaching the age of.—**give rise to** to cause, bring about; **on the rise** in process of rising, esp. in price; **rise and shine** a facetiously cheerful invitation to get out of bed briskly, esp. in the morning; **rise from the ranks** to work one's way up from private soldier to commissioned officer: to become a self-made man; **rise to it, the bait** (*fig.*, from fishing) to take the lure; **rise to the occasion** to prove equal to an emergency; **take a rise out of** to lure into reacting to provocation, or loosely, to make sport of; **take rise** to originate. [O.E. *rīsan*; O.N. *rísa*, Goth. *reisan*, Ger. *reisen*.]

risible *riz'i-bl*, *adj.* inclined to laugh: of laughter: ludicrous.—*n.* **risibil'ity**. [L. *rīsibilis—rīdēre*, *rīsum*, to laugh.]

risk, risk, *n.* hazard, danger, chance of loss or injury: the degree of probability of loss: a person, thing, or factor likely to cause loss or danger.—*v.t.* to expose to hazard: to incur the chance of unfortunate consequences by (doing something).—*n.* **risk'er**.—*adj.* **risk'ful**.—*adv.* **risk'ily**.—*n.* **risk'iness**.—*adjs.* **risk'y** dangerous, liable to mischance; **risqué** (*rēs'kā*; from the Fr. *pa.p.*) audaciously bordering on the unseemly.—**risk'-money** allowance to a cashier to compensate for ordinary errors.—**at risk** in a situation or circumstances where loss, injury, etc., are possible; **run a risk** to be in, get into, a risky situation; **run a, the, risk of** to risk (failing, etc.). [Fr. *risque*—It. *risco*.]

Risorgimento *ri-sōr-ji-men'tō*, *n.* the liberation and unification of Italy in the 19th century. [It.,—L. re- *surgēre*, to rise again.]

risotto *ri-zot'ō*, *n.* a dish of rice cooked in stock with meat, onions and other vegetables, and cheese:—*pl.* **risott'os**. [It.,—*riso*, rice.]

rissole *ris'ōl*, *rēs-ōl'*, *n.* a fried ball or cake of minced food. [Fr.]

ritardando *rē-tär-dan'dō*, *adj.* and *adv.* with diminishing speed.—*n.* a ritardando passage: a slowing down:—*pl.* **ritardan'dos**. [It.]

rite *rīt*, *n.* a ceremonial form or observance, esp. religious: a liturgy.—*adj.* **rite'less**.—**rite of passage** a term, for any of the ceremonies—such as those associated with birth, puberty, marriage, or death—which mark or ensure a person's transition from one status to another within his society. [L. *rītus*.]

ritenuto *rit-ə-nū'tō*, (*mus.*) *adj.* restrained—indicating a sudden slowing-down of tempo.—*n.* a ritenuto passage:—*pl.* **ritenū'tos**. [It., *pa.p.* of *ritenere*, to restrain, hold back.]

ritornello *rit-ör-nel'ō*, *n.* a short instrumental passage in a vocal work, e.g. a prelude or refrain:—*pl.* **ritornel'li** (*-lē*), **ritornell'os**. [It.]

ritual *rit'ū-əl*, *adj.* relating to, or of the nature of, rites. —*n.* the manner of performing divine service, or a book containing it: a body or code of ceremonies: an often repeated series of actions: the performance of rites: ceremonial.—*n.* **ritualisā'tion**, **-z-**.—*v i.* **rit'u-**

alise, -ize to practise or turn to ritualism.—*v.t.* to make ritualistic.—*ns.* **rit'ualism** attachment of importance to ritual, esp. with the implication of undue importance; **rit'ualist**.—*adj.* **ritualist'ic**.— *adv.* **ritualist'ically**.—*adv.* **rit'ually**.—**ritual murder** the killing of a human being as part of a tribal religious ceremony. [L. *rituālis—rītus*; see **rite**.]

ritzy *rit'zi*, (*slang*) *adj.* stylish, elegant, ostentatiously rich. [The *Ritz* hotels.]

rivage *riv'ij*, *rīv'ij*, (*poet.*) *n.* a bank, shore. [Fr.,— L. *rīpa*, a bank.]

rival *rī'vl*, *n.* one pursuing an object in competition with another: one who strives to equal or excel another: one for whom, or that for which, a claim to equality might be made.—*adj.* standing in competition: of like pretensions or comparable claims.—*v.t.* to stand in competition with: to try to gain the same object against: to try to equal or excel: to be worthy of comparison with:—*pr.p.* **rī'valling**; *pa.t.* and *pa.p.* **rī'valled**.—*adj.* **rī'valless**.—*ns.* **rī'valry** the state of being a rival: competition: emulation: the feeling of a rival; **rī'valship** emulation. [L. *rīvālis*, said to be from *rīvus*, river, as one who draws water from the same river.]

rive *rīv*, *v.t.* to tear asunder: to tear: to rend: to split.— *v.i.* to split:—*pa.t.* **rived**; *pa.p.* **riven** (*riv'n*), **rived** (*rīvd*). [O.N. *rīfa*.]

river *riv'ər*, *n.* a large stream of water flowing over the land: sometimes extended to a strait or inlet: a stream in general.—*adj.* of a river or rivers: dwelling or found in or near a river or rivers.—*adj.* **riv'erain** (*-ān*) of a river or its neighbourhood.—*n.* a riverside dweller.—*adjs.* **riv'ered** watered by rivers; **riv'erine** (*-īn*, *-ēn*) of, on, or dwelling in or near a river; **riv'erless**; **riv'erlike**; **riv'ery**.—**riv'er-bank**; **riv'er-basin** the whole region drained by a river with its affluents; **riv'er-bed** the channel in which a river flows; **riv'er-boat** a boat with a flat bottom or shallow draft; **riv'er-bottom** (*U.S.*) alluvial land along the margin of a river; **riv'er-head** the source of a river; **riv'er-horse** the hippopotamus; **riv'er-mouth**; **riv'erside** the bank or neighbourhood of a river.—*adj.* beside a river.— **riv'er-terr'ace** a terrace formed when a river eats away its old alluvium deposited when its flood-level was higher. [O.Fr. *rivere*—L. *rīpārius*, adj.—*rīpa*, bank.]

rivet *riv'it*, *n.* a bolt fastened by hammering the end.— *v.t.* to fasten with rivets: to fix immovably: to clinch or hammer out the end of:—*pr.p.* **riv'eting**; *pa.t.* and *pa.p.* **riv'eted**.—*ns.* **riv'eter**; **riv'eting**. [O.Fr. *rivet* —*river*, to clinch.]

riviera *riv-i-ā'rə*, *n.* a warm coastal district reminiscent of the Riviera in France and Italy on the Mediterranean Sea.

rivière *rē-vyer*, *riv-i-er'*, *n.* a necklace of diamonds or other precious stones, usu. in several strings. [Fr., river.]

rivulet *riv'ū-lit*, *n.* a small river. [L. *rīvulus*, dim. of *rīvus*, a stream.]

riyal *ri-yäl'*, *n.* the unit of currency in Dubai and Qatar, and (also spelt *rial*) in Saudi Arabia and the Yemen Arab Republic. [Ar.—Sp. *real*; see **real**[3].]

roach[1] *rōch*, *n.* a silvery freshwater fish of the carp family: applied to various American fishes.—**sound as a roach** perfectly sound. [O.Fr. *roche*.]

roach[2] *rōch*, *n.* a concave curve in the foot of a square sail.

roach[3] *rōch*, *n.* a cockroach (*U.S.*): (the butt of) a marijuana cigarette (*slang*; esp. *U.S.*).

road *rōd*, *n.* a track suitable for wheeled traffic, esp. for through communication (often in street-names): a highway: a way of approach: course: a mine-passage. (often in *pl.*) a roadstead: a railway (*U.S.*): journeying: wayfaring, tour.—*ns.* **road'ie** (*slang*) a member of the crew who transport, set up and dismantle equipment for musicians, esp. a pop group, on tour; **road'ster** a horse, cycle or car, suitable for ordinary use on the road.—**road'-bed** the foundation of a railway track: the material laid down to form a road; **road'block** an obstruction set up across a road, e.g. to prevent the escape of a fugitive; **road'-book** a guidebook to the roads of a district.—*adj.* **road'-borne**.— **road'-bridge** a bridge carrying a road; **road'-hog** a selfish or reckless motorist.—Also *v.i.*—*adj.* **road'-hoggish**.—**road'holding** the extent to which a motor vehicle holds the road when in motion; **road'house** a roadside public-house, etc., catering for motorists, etc.; **road'-maker**; **road'-making**; **road'man** one who keeps a road in repair; **road'-map**; **road'-mender**; **road'-mending**; **road'-metal** broken stones for roads; **road'-metalling**; **road'-roller** a heavy roller used on roads; **road'-runner** the chaparral cock; **road'-sense** aptitude for doing the right thing in driving; **road'show** a touring group of theatrical or musical performers: their performances; **road'side** the border of a road: wayside.—*adj.* by the side of a road.—**road sign** a sign along a road, motorway, etc. giving information on routes, speed limits, etc. to travellers; **road'stead** a place near a shore where ships may ride at anchor; **road'-train** in Australia, a number of linked trailers towed by a truck, for transporting cattle, etc.; **road'way** the way or part of a road or street used by horses and vehicles.—*n.pl.* **road works** the building or repairing of a road, or work involving the digging up, etc. of part of a road.—**road'worthiness**.—*adj.* **road'worthy** fit for the road.—**in, out of, the** (or **one's**) **road** in, out of, the way; **one for the road** a last alcoholic drink before setting off; **on the road** travelling, esp. as a commercial traveller or a tramp: on the way to some place; **road fund licence** a round certificate, usu. stuck on a vehicle's windscreen, showing that the vehicle excise duty (or *road fund licence fee*) payable on that vehicle has been paid; **road up** road surface being repaired; **take the road** to set off, depart; **take to the road** to become a tramp: to set off for, travel to, somewhere. [O.E. *rād*, a riding, raid; cf. **raid, ride**.]

roadster, roadstead. See **road**.

roam *rōm*, *v.i.* to rove about: to ramble.—*v.t.* to wander over: to range.—*n.* a wandering: a ramble.— *n.* **roam'er.** [M.E. *romen*; origin obscure.]

roan[1] *rōn*, *adj.* bay or dark, with spots of grey and white: of a mixed colour, with a decided shade of red. —*n.* a roan colour: a roan animal, esp. a horse. [O.Fr. *roan* (Fr. *rouan*).]

roan[2] *rōn*, *n.* grained sheepskin leather.—*adj.* of roan. [Poss. *Roan*, early form of *Rouen*.]

roan[3]. Same as **rone**.

roar *rōr*, *rör*, *v.i.* to make a full, loud, hoarse, low-pitched sound, as a lion, fire, wind, the sea, cannon: to bellow: to bawl: to guffaw: to take in breath with a loud noise, as a diseased horse: to rush forward with loud noise from the engine.—*v.t.* to utter vociferously: to shout (encouragement, abuse, etc.): to encourage by shouting (esp. with *on*).—*n.* a sound of roaring.—*ns.* **roar'er**; **roar'ing**.—*adj.* uttering or emitting roars: riotous: proceeding with very great activity or success.—*adv.* **roar'ingly**.—**roaring drunk** very drunk; **roaring forties** see **forty**; **the roaring game** curling. [O.E. *rārian*; partly from M.Du. *roer*, disturbance.]

roast *rōst*, *v.t.* to cook before a fire: to bake: to parch by heat: to heat strongly: to dissipate the volatile parts of (esp. sulphur) by heat: to criticise excessively: to banter (*slang*).—*v.i.* to undergo roasting.— *adj.* roasted.—*n.* a joint, esp. of beef, roasted or to be roasted: an operation of roasting.—*n.* **roas'ter** apparatus for roasting: a pig, etc., suitable for roasting: a very hot day.—*n.* and *adj.* **roast'ing**.— **roast'-beef**; **roast'-meat**.—**rule the roast** (mistakenly **roost**) to lord it, predominate. [O.Fr. *rostir* (Fr. *rôtir*); of Gmc. origin.]

rob *rob*, *v.t.* to deprive wrongfully and forcibly: to steal from: to plunder: to deprive.—*v.i.* to commit robbery:—*pr.p.* **robb'ing**; *pa.t.* and *pa.p.* **robbed**.— *ns.* **robb'er** one who robs; **robb'ery** theft from the person, aggravated by violence or intimidation: plundering.—**robb'er-crab** a large coconut-eating landcrab of the Indian Ocean.—**daylight robbery** glaring extortion, **rob Peter to pay Paul** to deprive one person in order to satisfy another. [O.Fr. *rober*, of Gmc. origin.]

robe *rōb*, *n.* a gown or loose outer garment: a gown or dress of office, dignity, or state: a rich dress: a woman's dress: a dressing-gown.—*v.t.* to dress: to invest in robes.—*v.i.* to assume official vestments.— *n.* **rob'ing**.—**robe-de-chambre** (*rob-də-shä-br'*; Fr.) a dressing-gown:—*pl.* **robes-de-chambre** (same pron.); **robe'-maker** a maker of official robes; **rob'ing-room** a room in which official robes may be put on.—**Mistress of the robes** the head of a department in a queen's household. [Fr. *robe*, orig. booty.]

robin *rob'in*, *n.* the redbreast or **robin redbreast** (*Erithacus rubecula*), a widely-spread singing bird with reddish-orange breast: extended to other birds as a red-breasted thrush of N. America—**Robin Goodfellow** a tricky English domestic spirit or brownie; **Robin Hood** a legendary mediaeval English outlaw who robbed the rich to give to the poor. [A form of *Robert*.]

Robinia *ro-bin'i-ə*, *n.* the locust or false acacia genus: (without *cap.*) a plant of this genus. [From the Paris gardener Jean Robin (1550–1629).]

roborant *rob'ər-ənt*, *n.* a strengthening drug or tonic.— Also *adj.* [L. *rōborāns, -antis*, pr p. of *rōborāre*, to strengthen, invigorate.]

robot *rō'bot*, *n.* a mechanical man. a more than humanly efficient automaton: esp. in S. Africa, an automatic traffic signal.—*adj.* **robot'ic**.—*n.sing.* **robot'ics** the branch of technology dealing with the design, construction and use of robots. [Czech *robota*, statute labour; from Karel Čapek's play *R.U.R.* (1920).]

robust *rō-bust'*, *adj.* stout, strong, and sturdy: constitutionally healthy. vigorous: thick-set: over-hearty. —*adv.* **robust'ly**.—*n.* **robust'ness**. [L. *rōbustus*— *rōbur*, strength, oak.]

roc *rok*, *n.* a fabulous bird, able to carry off an elephant. [Pers. *rukh*.]

rocaille *rō-kä'ē*, *n.* artificial rockwork or similar ornament: scroll ornament: rococo. [Fr.]

rocambole *rok'əm-bōl*, *n.* a plant close akin to garlic. [Fr.]

roche moutonnée *rosh' mōō-to-nā'*, *n.* a smooth, rounded hummocky rock-surface due to glaciation:— *pl.* **roches moutonnées** (same pron., or *-nāz*). [Fr. *roche*, a rock, *moutonnée*, a kind of wig.]

rochet *roch'it*, *n.* a close-fitting surplice-like vestment proper to bishops and abbots. [O.Fr., of Gmc. origin; cf. Ger. *Rock*, O.E. *rocc*.]

rock[1] *rok*, *n.* a large outstanding natural mass of stone: a natural mass of one or more minerals consolidated or loose (*geol.*): any variety or species of such an aggregate: a diamond or other precious stone (*slang*): a stone, pebble, lump of rock: a hard sweetmeat made in sticks: a sure foundation or support, anything immovable: a danger or obstacle.—*adj.* of rock: found on, in, or among rocks.—**rock'ery** a heap of soil and rock fragments in a garden, for growing rock-plants; **rock′iness**; **rock′ling** a small fish of the cod family with barbels on both jaws.—*adj.* **rock′y** full of rocks: like rocks.—**rock′-badger** the Cape hyrax; **rock′-bird** a puffin or other bird that nests or lives on rocks; **rock′-bottom** bedrock: the very bottom, esp. of poverty or despair.—*adj.* the lowest possible: to, at, the lowest possible level.—*adj.* **rock′-bound** hemmed in by rock: rocky.—**rock′-cake** a small hard bun with irregular top; **rock′-climber**; **rock′-climbing** mountaineering on rocky faces; **rock′-cork** mountain-cork; **rock′-crys′tal** colourless quartz, esp. when well crystallised; **rock′-dove** a pigeon that nests on rocks, source of the domestic varieties; **rock′-drill** a tool for boring rock; **rock′-garden** a rockery.—*adj.* **rock′s hewn** hewn out of rock.—**rock′-hopper** a crested penguin; **rock′-oil** petroleum; **rock′-pigeon** the rock-dove; **rock′-plant** a plant adapted to growing on or among rocks; **rock′-rabb′it** a hyrax; **rock′-rose** a plant of either of the genera *Cistus* and *Helianthemum*; **rock′-salm′on** dogfish or wolf-fish disguised for the market; **rock′-salt** salt as a mineral; **rock′-snake** a python.—*adj.* **rock′-sol′id** steady: dependable: firm: unwavering: unbeatable.—**rock′-tar′** petroleum; **rock′-tripe** an edible arctic lichen of various kinds; **rock wool** mineral wool; **rock′work** masonry in imitation of rock (*archit.*): rocks in rockery: rock-climbing.—**on the rocks** penniless: (of whisky, etc.) on ice; **the Rock Gibraltar**; **the Rockies** the Rocky Mountains. [O.Fr. *roke*—L.L. *rocca*.]

rock² *rok*, *v.t.* and *v.i.* to sway to and fro, tilt from side to side: to startle, stagger (*coll.*).—*n.* a rocking movement: (also **rock music**) a form of music with a strong beat, which developed from rock-and-roll.—*adj.* pertaining to rock music.—*n.* **rock′er** one who rocks: an apparatus that rocks: a curved support on which anything rocks: a rocking-chair: (*cap.*) a member of a teenage faction of the 1960s who wore leather jackets, rode motor bicycles, etc.: a mining cradle: a skate with curved blade.—*adv.* **rock′ily**.—*n.* **rock′iness**.—*n.* and *adj.* **rock′ing**.—*adj.* **rock′y** disposed to rock: shaky: unpleasant, unsatisfactory (*slang*).—**rock-and-roll** see **rock-′n′-roll**; **rocker switch** an electric light, etc. switch on a central pivot; **rock′ing-chair** a chair mounted on rockers; **rock′ing-horse** the figure of a horse mounted on rockers or on some other supports which allow the horse to rock; **rock′ing-stone** a finely poised boulder that can be made to rock; **rock′-′n′-roll′, rock′-and-roll′** a simple form of music deriving from jazz, country-and-western and blues music, with a strongly accented, two-beat rhythm: dancing thereto; **rock′-shaft** in engines, a shaft that oscillates instead of revolving.—**off one's rocker** out of one's right mind; **rock the boat** to make things difficult for one's colleagues, create trouble. [O.E. *roccian*.]

rocket¹ *rok′it*, *n.* a simple device, a cylinder full of inflammable material, projected through the air for signalling, carrying a line to a ship in distress, or for firework display: a missile projected by a rocket system: a system, or a vehicle, obtaining its thrust from a backward jet of hot gases, all the material for producing which is carried within the rocket: a severe reprimand (*slang*).—*v.i.* to move like a rocket: to fly straight up rapidly: of e.g. prices, to become higher very rapidly: to come to an important position with remarkable speed.—*ns.* **rocketeer′** a rocket technician or pilot: a specialist in rocketry, especially a designer; **rock′etry** the scientific study of rockets.—**rock′et-motor** a jet motor which uses an internally stored oxidiser instead of atmospheric oxygen, for combustion; **rock′et-range** a place for experimentation with rocket projectiles. [It. *rocchetta*, of Gmc. origin.]

rocket² *rok′it*, *n.* a salad plant (*Eruca sativa*) of Mediterranean countries. extended to other plants (**wall′-rocket** *Diplotaxis*; **yell′ow-rocket** winter-cress, *Barbarea*). [O.Fr. *roquette*—L. *ērūca*.]

rococo *rō-kō′kō, rō-kō-kō′*, *n.* a style of architecture, decoration, and furniture-making prevailing in Louis XV's time, marked by ornamental details unrelated to structure, and unsymmetrical and broken curves, a freer development of the baroque:—*pl.* **rococos**.—*adj.* in the style of rococo. [Fr., prob.—*rocaille* rockwork.]

rod *rod*, *n.* a long straight shoot: a slender stick: a slender bar of metal or other matter: a sceptre or similar emblem of authority: a stick as instrument of punishment: a stick or wand for magic, divination: a slender pole or structure carrying a fishing-line: a measuring stick: a pole or perch (5½ yards, or 16½ feet): a square pole (272½ sq. ft): a rod-shaped body of the retina sensitive to light: a revolver, a pistol (*U.S. slang*): a penis (*slang*).—*adjs.* **rod′less**; **rod′like**.—**rod′fisher**; **rod′fishing**; **rod′man, rods′man** one who holds, carries or uses a rod, esp. an angler. [O.E. *rodd*; cf. O.N. *rudda*, club.]

rode *rōd*, *pa.t.* of **ride**.

rodent *rō′dənt*, *adj.* gnawing: of the Rodentia.—*n.* a member of the Rodentia.—*n.pl.* **Rodentia** (*-den′shə, -shyə*) an order of mammals with prominent incisor teeth and no canines, as squirrels, beavers, rats.—*n.* **roden′ticide** a substance that kills rodents.—**rodent officer** an official rat-catcher. [L. *rōdēns, -entis*, pr.p. of *rōdĕre*, to gnaw.]

rodeo *rō′di-ō, rō-dā′ō*, *n.* a place where cattle are assembled: a round-up of cattle: an exhibition of cowboy skill: a contest suggestive of a cowboy rodeo involving, e.g. motor-bicycles:—*pl.* **ro′deos**. [Sp., —*rodear*, to go round—L. *rotāre*, to wheel.]

rodomontade *rod-ō-mon-tād′*, *n.* extravagant boasting, like that of *Rodomonte* in Ariosto's *Orlando Furioso*.—*v.i.* to bluster or brag.—*n.* **rodomontā′der**.

roe¹ *rō*, *n.* a mass of fish-eggs (also *hard roe*): sometimes milt (*soft roe*).—*adj.* **roed** containing roe.—*n.* **roe′stone** oolite. [M.E. *rowe*; cf. O.N. *hrogn*, M.H.G. *roge*, Ger. *Rogen*.]

roe² *rō*, *n.* a small species of deer.—**roe′buck** the male roe; **roe′-deer** a roe. [O.E. *rā, rāha*; Ger. *Reh*, Du. *ree*.]

roentgen. See **röntgen**.

rogation *rō-gā′shən*, *n.* an asking: supplication.—*adj.* **rogatory** (*rog′ə-tə-ri*).—**Rogation Days** the three days before Ascension Day, when supplications were recited in procession; **Rogation Sunday** that before Ascension Day; **Rogation Week** the week in which the Rogation Days occur. [L. *rogātiō, -ōnis*—*rogāre*, to ask.]

Roger *roj′ər*, *n.* a man's personal name: a word used in signalling and radio-communication for R, in the sense of received (and understood). [Fr., of Gmc. origin, equivalent to O.E. *Hrōthgār*.]

rogue *rōg*, *n.* a rascal: a mischievous person (often playfully or affectionately): a plant that falls short of a standard, or is of a different type from the rest of the crop: a variation from type: a horse that shirks: a savage elephant or other animal cast out or withdrawn from its herd.—*adj.* mischievous: disruptive. —*v.t.* to eliminate rogues from.—*n.* **roguery** (*rōg′ər-i*) rascally tricks: fraud: waggery.—*adj.* **roguish** (*rōg′ish*).—*adv.* **rog′uishly**.—*n.* **rog′uishness**.—**rogue′-el′ephant**; **rogues′ gallery** a police collection of photographs of criminals. [Cant.]

roil *roil*, *v.t.* to make turbid: to annoy, irritate.

roister *rois′tər*, *v.i.* to bluster, swagger: to revel noisily. —*n.* **rois′terer**.—*adj.* **rois′terous**. [O.Fr. *rustre*, a rough, rude fellow—O.Fr. *ruste*—L. *rusticus*, rustic.]

Roland rō'lənd, *n.* a hero of the Charlemagne legend: a worthy match (with allusion to a drawn contest between Roland and his comrade-in-arms, Oliver).—**a Roland for an Oliver** tit for tat: as good as one got.

role, rôle rōl, *n.* a part played by an actor: a function, part played in life or in any event.—*ns.* **role'-play, role's playing** the performing of imaginary roles, sometimes as a method of instruction, training or therapy. [Fr.]

roll rōl, *n.* a scroll: a sheet of paper, parchment, cloth, or other material bent spirally upon itself into a nearly cylindrical form: a document in such form: a register: a list, esp. of names: a spirally wound cake, or one of dough turned over to enclose other material: a small, individually-baked portion of bread formed into any of various shapes, that can be cut open and filled with other food: a revolving cylinder: a roller: a more or less cylindrical package, mass, or pad: a cylindrical moulding: a volute: a part turned over in a curve: an act of rolling: a swaying about an axis in the direction of motion: a continuous reverberatory or trilling sound: an undulation: a wavelike flow.—*v.i.* to move like a ball, a wheel, a wheeled vehicle, or a passenger in one: to perform revolutions: to sway on an axis in the direction of motion: to turn over or from side to side: to swagger: to wallow: to move in, on, or like waves: to flow: to undulate: to wander: to sound with a roll: to use a roller: to curl: to start: to get under way: to start operating: to make progress—*v.t.* to cause to roll: to turn on an axis: to move with a circular sweep (as the eyes): to wrap round on itself: to enwrap: to curl: to wind: to move upon wheels: to press, flatten, spread out, thin, or smooth with a roller or between rollers: to pour in waves.—*adjs.* **roll'able, rolled.**—*n.* **roll'er** one who or that which rolls: a revolving or rolling cylinder: a contrivance including a heavy cylinder or cylinders for flattening roads or turf: a long, coiled-up bandage (**roll'er-band'age**): a long heavy wave: a small solid wheel: a cylinder on which hair is wound to curl it: a kind of tumbler pigeon.—*n.* and *adj.* **roll'ing.**—**roll'-bar** a metal bar that strengthens the frame of a vehicle, lessening the danger to the vehicle's occupants if the vehicle overturns; **roll'-call** the calling of a list of names, to ascertain attendance; **roll'collar** a collar of a garment turned back in a curve; **rolled gold** metal coated with gold rolled very thin; **roll'er-bearing** a bearing consisting of two races between which a number of parallel or tapered rollers are located, usu. in a cage, suitable for heavier loads than ball-bearings; **roll'er-coast'er** a type of switchback railway at carnivals, etc., along which people ride in open cars at great speed; **roll'er-skate** a skate with wheels instead of a blade.—Also *v.i.*— **roll'er-skat'er**; **roll'er-skat'ing**; **roll'er-tow'el** a continuous towel on a roller; **roll'ing-mill** factory or machine for rolling metal into various shapes between rolls; **roll'ing-pin** a cylinder for rolling dough; **roll'ing-stock** the stock or store of engines and vehicles that run upon a railway; **rolling stone** see below.—*adjs.* **roll'-neck** of a jersey, etc., having a high neck which is made to be folded over loosely on itself; **roll'-on** of a deodorant, etc., contained in a bottle which has a rotating ball in its neck, by means of which the deodorant is applied.—*n.* a roll-on deodorant, etc.: a corset that fits on by stretching.— *adj.* **roll-on'-roll-off'** (of a ferry-boat or cargo boat, or service) designed to allow goods vehicles to embark and disembark without unloading, passenger traffic to drive straight on and off.—*adj.* **roll'-top** having a flexible cover of slats that rolls up.—**a rolling stone gathers no moss** a rover does not grow

rich; **be rolling in** to have large amounts of (e.g. money); **Master of the Rolls** the head of the Record Office; **heads will roll** severe punishments will be meted out, esp. loss of status or office; **roll along** to arrive by chance, or with a casual air; **rolled into one** combined in one person or thing; **roll in** to arrive in quantity; **roll on!** may (a specified event) come quickly!; **roll up** (*coll.*) to assemble, arrive. [O.Fr. *rolle* (n.), *roller* (vb.)—L. *rotula*, dim. of *rota*, a wheel.]

rollick rol'ik, *v.i.* to behave in a careless, swaggering, frolicsome manner.—*adj.* **roll'icking.**

rollmop rōl'mop, *n.* a fillet of herring rolled up, usu. enclosing a slice of onion, and pickled in spiced vinegar. [Ger. *Rollmops*—*rollen*, to roll, *Mops* a pug-dog.]

rollock. See **rowlock.**

roly-poly rōl'i-pōl'i, *n.* a pudding made of a sheet of dough, covered with jam or fruit, rolled up, and baked or steamed (also **roly-poly pudding**): a round, podgy person.—*adj.* round, podgy. [Prob. **roll.**]

rom rom, *n.* a gypsy man:—*pl.* **rom'a(s).** [Romany, man, husband.]

Romaic rō-mā'ik, *n.* and *adj.* modern Greek. [Mod. Gr. *Rhōmaikos*, Roman (i.e. of the Eastern Roman Empire)—*Rhōmē*, Rome.]

Roman rō'mən, *adj.* pertaining to Rome, esp. ancient Rome, its people, or the empire founded by them: pertaining to the Roman Catholic religion, papal: (without *cap.*) (of type) of the ordinary upright kind, as opp. to *italics*: (of numerals; see Roman Numerals in Appendices) written in letters (as IV, iv), opp. to *Arabic*: (of a nose) high-bridged.—*n.* a native or citizen of Rome: a Roman Catholic: Roman letter or type.—*adj.* **Romanic** (rō-man'ik) of Roman or Latin origin: Romance.—*n.* the Romance language or languages collectively.—*n.* **Romanisation, -z-** (rō-mə-nī-zā'shən).—*v.t.* **Ro'manise, -ize** to make Roman or Roman Catholic: to bring under Roman or Roman Catholic influence: to represent by the Roman alphabet.—*v.i.* to accept Roman or Roman Catholic ways, laws, doctrines, etc.—*ns.* **Ro'maniser, -z-**; **Ro'manism** Roman Catholicism; **Ro'manist** a Roman Catholic: one versed in Romance philology or Roman law or antiquities.—*adj.* Roman Catholic.—*adj.* **Romanist'ic.**—in composition, **Romano-** (rō-mā'nō-) Roman and (as **Roma'no-Brit'ish**).—**Roman candle** a firework discharging a succession of white or coloured stars.—*adj.* **Roman Catholic** recognising the spiritual supremacy of the Pope or Bishop of Rome. —*n.* a member of the Roman Catholic Church.— **Roman Catholicism** the doctrines and polity of the Roman Catholic Church collectively; **Roman Empire** the ancient empire of Rome, divided in the 4th century into the Eastern and Western Empires (see also Holy); **Roman law** the system of law developed by the ancient Romans—civil law. [L. *Rōmānus*— *Rōma*, Rome.]

roman à clef ro-mā-nä klā' (Fr.) (lit. *key novel*) a novel about real people under disguised names; **roman fleuve** (*flœv*'; lit. *river novel*) a novel in a series of self-contained narratives telling the story of a family, etc. over successive generations (also **saga novel**). [Fr.]

Romance rō-mäns', *n.* a general name for the vernaculars that developed out of popular Latin—French, Provençal, Italian, Spanish, Portuguese, Rumanian, Romansch, with their various dialects.—Also *adj.*— *n.* **romance** a tale of chivalry, orig. one in verse, written in one of these vernaculars: any fictitious and wonderful tale: a fictitious narrative in prose or verse which passes beyond the limits of ordinary life: romantic fiction as a literary genre: a romantic occurrence or series of occurrences: a love affair: romantic atmosphere or feeling: an imaginative lie: romanticism: a composition of romantic character (*mus.*).—*v.i.* to talk extravagantly or with an infusion of fiction: to lie.—*n.* **roman'cer.**—*n.* and *adj.* **roman'cing.** [L.L. *rōmānicē* (adv.), in (popular) Roman language.]

Romanes. See **Romany.**

Romanesque *rō-mən-esk'*, *adj.* of the transition from Roman to Gothic architecture, characterised by round arches and vaults.—*n.* the Romanesque style, art, or architecture. [Fr.]

Romanian. See **Rumanian.**

Romanise, Romanism, etc. See **Roman.**

Romansch, Romansh *rō-, mansh', -mänsh', n.* and *adj.* Rhaeto-Romanic: sometimes confined to the Upper Rhine dialects. [Romansch.]

romantic *rō-man'tik, adj.* pertaining to, of the nature of, inclining towards, romance: extravagant, wild: fantastic.—*n.* a romanticist.—*adv.* **roman'tically.**— *n.* **romanticisă'tion, -z-.**—*v.t.* **roman'ticise, -ize** (*-ti-sīz*) to make seem romantic.—*v.i.* to have or express romantic ideas.—*ns.* **roman'ticism** (*-sizm*) romantic quality, feeling, tendency, principles, or spirit; **roman'ticist.**—**Romantic Revival** the late 18th-century and early 19th-century revolt against classicism to a more picturesque, original, free, and imaginative style in literature and art. [Fr. *romantique*—O.Fr. *romant*, romance.]

Romany *rom'ə-ni, rōm', n.* a gypsy: (also **Romanes** *rom'ə-nes*) the Indic language of the gypsies (in pure form not now common in Britain).—*adj.* gypsy. [Gypsy,—*rom*, man.]

Rome *rōm, n.* the capital of the Roman Empire, now of Italy: often used for the Roman Catholic Church or Roman Catholicism.—*adj.* **Rōm'ish** Roman Catholic (*hostile*). [L. *Rōma.*]

Romeo *rō'mi-ō, n.* a young man very much in love: a Don Juan in the making:—*pl.* Rō'meos. [Shakespearean character.]

Romneya *rom'ni-ə, n.* a genus of shrubs, with large white poppy-like flowers with yellow centres: (without *cap.*) a plant of this genus. [Thomas *Romney* Robinson (1792–1882), British astronomer.]

romp *romp, v.i.* to frolic actively: to move along easily and quickly, esp. in winning a race.—*n.* one, esp. a girl, who romps: a tomboy: a vigorous frolic: a swift easy run.—*n.* **romp'er** one who romps: (usu. in *pl.*) a child's garb for play (also **romp'er-suit'**).—*adv.* **romp'ingly.**—**romp home** to win easily; **romp through** to do (something) quickly and easily. [ramp.]

rondavel *ron-dav'əl, ron', n.* in S. Africa, a round building, usu. with grass roof. [Afrik. *rondawel.*]

rondeau *ron'dō, rō-dō, n.* a form of poem characterised by closely-knit rhymes, consisting of thirteen lines, the burden repeating the first few words after the eighth and thirteenth lines:—*pl.* **ron'deaux** (*-dōz*).— *ns.* **ron'del** a verse-form of thirteen or fourteen lines on two rhymes, the seventh and thirteenth being identical with the first, and the eighth and (if present) the fourteenth with the second; **ron'do** (orig. It., from Fr.) a musical composition whose principal subject recurs in the same key in alternation with other subjects, often the last movement of a sonata: —*pl.* **ron'dos.** [Fr. *rondeau*, earlier *rondel*—*rond*, round.]

rone, roan *rōn, (Scot.) n.* a roof-gutter.

Roneo® *rō'ni-ō, n.* a duplicating machine:—*pl.* **Rō'neos.**—*v.t.* **rō'neo** to produce copies of by duplicating machine.

röntgen, roentgen *rœnt'yən, rent', ront', runt', also -gən,* (sometimes *cap.*), *adj.* of the German physicist Wilhelm Conrad *Röntgen* (1845–1923), discoverer of

the **röntgen rays** or X-rays (see **X**).—*n.* the international unit of dose of X-rays or gamma rays, defined in terms of the ionisation it produces in air under stated conditions.—*ns.* **röntgenog'raphy** photography by these rays; **röntgenol'ogy** the study of the rays.

roo *rōō, (Austr. coll.) n.* short form of kangaroo.

rood *rōōd, n.* Christ's cross: a cross or crucifix, esp. at the entrance to a church chancel: a rod, pole, or perch, linear or square (with variations in value; *locally*): the fourth part of an acre, or forty square poles.—**rood'-beam** a beam for supporting the rood; **rood'-loft** a gallery over the rood-screen; **rood'-screen** an ornamental partition separating choir from nave. [O.E. *rōd,* gallows, cross.]

roof *rōōf, n.* the top covering of a building or vehicle: a ceiling: the overhead surface, structure, or stratum of a vault, arch, cave, etc.: the upper covering of the mouth (the palate): a dwelling: a culmination: a high or highest plateau (as *the roof of the world*): an upper limit:—*pl.* **roofs.**—*v.t.* to cover with a roof: to shelter.—*adj.* **roofed.**—*ns.* **roof'er** one who makes or mends roofs; **roof'ing** materials for a roof: the roof itself.—*adjs.* **roof'less; roof'-like.**—**roof'-garden** a garden on a flat roof; **roof'-rack** a rack which may be fitted to the roof of a car, etc. to carry luggage, etc.; **roof'-top** the outside of a roof; **roof'-tree** the ridge-pole: the roof.—**have a roof over one's head** to have somewhere to live; **hit, go through the roof** to become very angry; **raise the roof** to make a great noise or commotion. [O.E. *hrōf.*]

rooinek *rō'i-nek, n.* an Afrikaans nickname for an Englishman. [Afrikaans, red neck—Du. *rood, nek,* from his complexion.]

rook¹ *rōōk, n.* a gregarious species of crow: a sharper.— *v.t.* to fleece.—*n.* **rook'ery** a breeding-place of rooks in a group of trees: a breeding-place of penguins, or seals, etc.—*adjs.* **rook'ish; rook'y.** [O.E. *hrōc.*]

rook² *rōōk, n.* a chessman whose move is in a vertical or horizontal line, its shape usu. being that of a tower with battlements. [O.Fr. *roc*—Pers. *rukh.*]

rookie *rōōk'i, (slang) n.* a raw beginner: a callow recruit. [App. from **recruit.**]

room *rōōm, rōōm, n.* space: necessary or available space: space unoccupied: opportunity, scope, or occasion: appointment, office: a compartment: a chamber: company in a room.—*v.t.* and *v.i.* (chiefly *U.S.*) to lodge: to share a room or rooms (with *with*). —*adj.* **roomed** having rooms.—*ns.* **room'er** (*U.S.*) a lodger, usu. taking meals elsewhere; **room'ful** as much or as many as a room will hold:—*pl.* **room'fuls.** —*adv.* **room'ily.**—*n.* **room'iness.**—*adj.* **room'y** having ample room: wide: spacious.—**room'ing-house** (*U.S.*) a house with furnished rooms to let; **room'-mate** a fellow-lodger: one who shares a room. —**room service** the serving of food, etc. to people in their room(s) in a hotel, etc.—**leave the room** esp. of children in school, to go to the toilet. [O.E. *rūm.*].

roost¹ *rōōst, n.* a perch or place for a sleeping bird: a henhouse: a sleeping-place: a set of fowls resting together.—*v.i.* to settle or sleep on a roost or perch: to perch: to go to rest for the night.—*n.* **roost'er** a domestic cock.—**come home to roost** to recoil upon oneself; **rule the roost** see **roast.** [O.E. *hrōst;* Du. *roest.*]

roost² *rōōst, (Orkney and Shetland) n.* a tidal race. [O.N. *rōst.*]

root¹ *rōōt, n.* ordinarily and popularly, the underground part of a plant, esp. when edible: that part of a higher plant which never bears leaves or reproductive organs, ordinarily underground and descending, and serving to absorb salts in solution, but often above-ground, often arising from other parts, often serving other functions, through morphologically comparable (*bot.*): the source, cause, basis, foundation, occasion of anything, as an ancestor, an element from which words are derived: an embedded or basal part, as of a tooth, a hair: a growing plant with its root: the factor of a quantity which, taken so many times, produces that quantity (*math.*): any value of the unknown quantity for which an equation is true (*math.*): the fundamental note on which a chord is built (*mus.*): (in *pl.*) one's ancestry, family origins: (in *pl.*) a feeling of belonging in a community, etc.—*v.i* to fix the root: to be firmly established: to develop a root.—*v.t.* to plant in the earth: to implant deeply: to fix by the root: to uproot (usu. with *up*): to remove entirely by uprooting, eradicate, extirpate (usu. with *out*).—*n.* root'age the act of striking root: the state of being rooted: a root-system.—*adj.* root'ed having roots: fixed by roots or as by roots: firmly established. —*adv.* root'edly.—*ns.* root'edness; root'er.—*adj.* root'less having no roots: belonging nowhere, constantly shifting about.—*n.* root'let.—*adj.* root'y.— *adj. and adv.* root'-and-branch' without leaving any part: thorough(ly), complete(ly).—root'-beer a drink made from roots of dandelion, sassafras, etc.; root'-cause fundamental cause; root'-climber a plant that climbs by means of roots, as ivy; root'-crop a crop of esculent roots; root'-hair a fine tubular outgrowth from a cell by which a young root absorbs water; root'stock rhizome, esp. if short, thick, and more or less erect (*bot.*); root'-sys'tem; root vegetable a vegetable which has an esculent root: the root itself. —strike, take, root to root to, to become established. [Late O.E. *rōt*—O.N. *rōt*; Dan. *rod*; Goth. *waurts*, O.E. *wyrt*.]

root², *rōōt, v.t.* to turn up with the snout.—*v.i.* to grub: poke about.—*v.i.* root'er.—*n.* and *adj.* root'ing.—*v.t.* and *v.i.* root'le to grub. [O.E. *wrōtan—wrōt*, a snout; see also root³.]

root³ *rōōt*, (orig. *U.S.*) *v.i.* to shout, to applaud, to support or encourage (a contestant, etc.) (with *for*). —*n.* root'er. [Prob. from root⁴.]

rope *rōp, n.* a stout twist of fibre, wire, etc., technically over 1 in. round: a string of pearls, onions, etc.: a glutinous stringy formation.—*v.t.* to fasten, bind, enclose, mark off, or (*U.S.* and *Austr.*) catch with a rope.—*v.i.* to form into a rope.—*adjs.* rop(e)'able (*Austr.*) of cattle or horses, wild, unmanageable: very angry; roped (*rōpt*).—*adv.* rōp'ily.—*n.* rōp'iness.— *n.* and *adj.* rōp'ing.—*adj.* rō'py stringy: glutinous: bad of its kind (*slang*).—rope'-dance a tight-rope performance; rope'-dancer; rope'-ladder a ladder of ropes; rope'-maker; rope'-making.—*v.t.* rope's-end' to beat with a rope's end.—*adj.* rope'-soled having a sole of rope.—rope'-trick a disappearing trick with a rope; rope'-walk a long narrow shed or alley for ropespinning; rope'-walker a tight-rope performer; rope'-way a means of transmission by ropes; rope'-yarn yarn for making ropes, or got by untwisting ropes; rop'ing-down' abseiling.—give someone (enough) rope (to hang himself) to allow a person full scope to defeat his own ends; know the ropes see know; rope in bring in, enlist (esp. one who has some reluctance); rope's end the end of a rope used for flogging; the rope capital punishment by hanging. [O.E. *rāp.*]

Roquefort rok'för, *n.* a cheese orig. made (of ewe's milk) at *Roquefort* in France.

roquet rō'kā, *n.* in croquet, a stroke by which the player's ball strikes an opponent's.—*v.t.* to strike by a roquet.—*v.i.* to play a roquet. [Prob. formed from croquet.]

ro-ro rō'rō *adj. n.* abbrev. for roll-on roll-off.

rorqual *rör'kwal, n.* any whale of the genus Balaenoptera (finback). [Fr.,—Norw. *røyrkval*—O.N., lit.

red whale]

Rorschach test *ror'shak test,* a test, designed to show intelligence, personality, and mental state, in which the subject interprets ink-blots of standard type. [Hermann *Rorschach,* Swiss psychiatrist.]

rorty *rör'ti,* (slang) *adj.* rowdy.—*ns.* rort (*Austr.*) a racket.

Rosa *rōz'ə, roz'ə, n.* the rose genus, giving name to the family Rosā'ceae.—*ns.* rosace (*rō-zās'*; from Fr.; *archit.*) a rosette: a rose-window.—*adj.* rosaceous (*rō-zā'shəs*) of the rose family: roselike.—*ns.* rosā'rian a rose-fancier; rosā'rium a rose-garden; rosary (*rō'zər-i*) a rose-garden or rose-bed (also rō'sery): a series of prayers: a string of beads used by Roman Catholics as a guide to devotions. [L. *rōsa,* rose; *rosārium,* rose-garden.]

rosaniline *rō-zan'i-lin, -lēn, -lin, n.* a base derived from aniline, with red salts used in dyeing [rose², aniline.]

rosarian, rosary. See Rosa.

rose¹, *pa.t.* of rise.

rose² *rōz, n.* the flower of any species of the genus Rosa —national emblem of England: a shrub bearing it, mostly prickly, with white, yellow, pink, orange, or red flowers, numerous stamens and carpels, achenes enclosed in the receptacle. extended to various flowers or plants, (see Christmas, guelder-rose, rock¹): a paragon: a rosette, esp. on a shoe: a rose-cut stone: a rose-window: a perforated nozzle: a ceiling fitting for an electric light: the typical colour of the rose—pink or light crimson: the pink glow of the cheeks in health.—*adj.* of, for, or like the rose or roses: rose-coloured.—*v.t.* to make like a rose, in colour or scent.—*adjs.* rō'seate (*-zi-it, -zi-āt*) rosy: of roses: unduly favourable or sanguine; rose'less; rose'like.—*n.* rō'sery a rose-garden (cf. rosary).— *adv.* rō'sily.—*n.* rōsiness.—*adj.* rō'sy of roses: roselike: rose-red: blooming: blushing: bright: hopeful: promising.—rose'-apple an E. Indian tree of the clove genus: its edible fruit; rose'-bay the oleander (rose-bay laurel, rose-laurel): any rhododendron: a willow-herb (rose-bay willow-herb); rose'-beetle the rose-chafer (the rose-bug; rose'-bowl an ornamental bowl for cut flowers; rose'-bud; rose'-bush; rose'-camp'ion a garden species of campion; rose'-chafer a beetle that eats roses.—*adj.* rose'-cheeked.—rose'-colour pink.—*adj.* rose'-col'oured pink: seeing or representing things in too favourable a light.—rose'-comb a fowl's low tubercled comb.—*adj.* rose'-cut cut in nearly hemispherical form, with flat base and many small facets rising to a low point above.—rose'-di'amond a rose-cut' diamond; rose'-en'gine an apparatus for engine-turning; rose'fish the bergylt; rose'-garden; rose'-hip the fruit of the rose.—*adj.* rose'-hued.—rose'-lau'rel oleander.—*adj.* rose'-lip'ped having red lips.—rose'-mall'ow hollyhock: hibiscus.—*adj.* rose'-pink rose-coloured: sentimental.— *n.* a pink colour: a pink pigment.—rose'-quartz a rose-coloured quartz.—*adj.* rose'-red.—rose'-root a stonecrop with rose-scented root; rose'-tree; rose'-wa'ter water distilled from rose-leaves.—*adj.* sentimental: superfine.—rose'-win'dow a round window with tracery of radiating compartments; rose'wood a valuable heavy dark-coloured wood of many trees, said to smell of roses when fresh-cut.—*adj.* rō'sy-cheeked.—rosy cross the emblem of the Rosicrucians. —*adj.* rō'sy-fing'ered Homer's favourite epithet (*rhododaktylos*) of the dawn.—bed of roses see bed; look, or see, through rose-coloured or rose-tinted spectacles to view matters over-optimistically; rose of Jericho a plant of N. Africa and Syria, that curls in a ball in drought; rose of Sharon (*Song of Solomon*) probably a narcissus: now applied to a species of hibiscus; **roses all the way, all roses** pleasant, happy: without difficulties, problems etc.; **under the rose** in confidence; **Wars of the Roses** a disastrous dynastic struggle in England (1455–85) between the Houses of Lancaster and York, from their emblems, the red and the white rose. [O.E. *rōse*—L. *rosa*, prob.—Gr. *rhŏdĕā*, a rose-bush, *rhodon*, rose.]

rosé *rō'zā*, *n.* a pinkish table wine in making which grape skins are removed early in fermentation. [Cf. **red wine**.] [Fr. lit., pink.]

roseate, etc. See **rose²**.

rosella *rō-zel'ə*, *n.* a handsome Australian parakeet, first observed at Rose Hill near Sydney. [For *rose-hiller*.]

rosemary *rōz'mə-ri*, *n.* a small fragrant pungent Mediterranean labiate shrub. [L. *rōs marīnus*, sea dew.]

roseola *rō-zē'ə-lə*, *n.* rose-coloured rash: German measles (also **rubella**). [Dim. from L. *roseus*, rosy.]

rosery. See **rose²**.

rosette *rō-zet'*, *n.* a knot of radiating loops of ribbon or the like in concentric arrangement, esp. worn as a badge or awarded as a prize: a close radiating group of leaves, usu. pressed to the ground: a rose-shaped ornament (*archit.*): any structure, arrangement, or figure or similar shape.—*adj.* **rosett'ed.** [Fr., dim. of *rose*.]

Rosh Hashanah *rosh hə-shā'nə*, the Jewish festival of New Year. [Heb., lit. head of the year.]

Rosicrucian *roz'* or *rōz'i-krōō'sh(y)ən*, *n.* a member of an alleged secret society whose members made pretensions to knowledge of the secrets of Nature, transmutation of metals, etc.—affirmed to have been founded (1459) by Christian *Rosenkreuz*: a member of one or other of various modern fraternities.—Also *adj.*—*n.* **Rosicru'cianism.** [Prob. a Latinisation of *Rosenkreuz*, rose cross, L. *rŏsa*, rose, *crux*, cross.]

rosily, rosiness. See **rose²**.

rosin *roz'in*, *n.* a resin obtained e.g. when turpentine is prepared from dead pine wood.—*v.t.* to rub with rosin.—*adj.* **ros'ined.**—*adj.* **ros'iny.** [**resin**.]

rosolio *rō-zō'lyō*, *n.* a sweet cordial made with raisins. [It. *rosolio*—L. *rōs sōlis*, dew of the sun.]

roster *rōs'ter* (or *ros'*), *n.* a list of employees, army personnel, etc. with assigned (turns of) duties: any roll of names (*coll.*).—*v.t.* to put in a roster.—*n.* **ros'-tering.** [Du. *rooster*, orig. gridiron (from the ruled lines)—*roosten*, to roast.]

rostrum *ros'trəm*, *rōs'trōōm*, *n.* a platform for public speaking, etc. (from the one called the *Rostra* in the Roman forum, adorned with the beaks (*rostra*) of captured ships): a beak or part resembling a beak (*biol.*).—*adjs.* **ros'tral; ros'trate, -d.** [L. *rōstrum*, beak—*rōdĕre*, *rōsum*, to gnaw.]

rosy. See **rose²**.

rot *rot*, *v.i.* to putrefy: to decay: to become corrupt: to suffer from wasting disease.—*v.t.* to cause to rot, to ret:—*pr.p.* **rott'ing;** *pa.t.* and *pa.p.* **rott'ed.**—*n.* decay: putrefaction: corruption: collapse, disintegration (often *fig.*): applied to various diseases of sheep, timber, etc.: worthless or rotten stuff (*slang*): bosh (*slang*).—*interj.* expressing contemptuous disagreement.—*n.* **rott'er** a thoroughly depraved or worthless person.—**rot'-gut** bad liquor. [O.E. *rotian*, pa.p. *rotod*; cf. **rotten**.]

rota *rō'tə*, *n.* a roster: a course, round, routine, cycle, of duty, etc.: (with *cap.*) the Roman Catholic supreme ecclesiastical tribunal.—*n.* **Rotarian** (*-tā'ri-ən*) a member of a Rotary club.—Also *adj.*—*n.* **Rota'rianism.**—*adj.* rotary (*rō'tər-i*) turning like a wheel: of the nature of rotation: working by rotation of a part: (with *cap.*) of an international system of clubs, formed to encourage service to and within the community, with a wheel as a badge.—*n.* **ro'tary** a rotary apparatus: (with *cap.*) a Rotary club: (with *cap.*) Rotarianism: a traffic roundabout (*U.S.*).—*adj.* **rotat'able.**—*v.t.* and *v.i.* **rotate'** to turn like a wheel: to put, take, go, or succeed in rotation.—*adj.* **rō'tate** wheel-shaped—with united petals in a plane with almost no tube.—*n.* **rota'tion** a turning round like a wheel: succession in definite order, as of crops: recurrent order: the conformal transformation (q.v.) in which a particular arrangement is rotated about a fixed point (*math.*, etc.).—*adjs.* **rota'tional; rotative** (*rō'tə-tiv*).—*n.* **rota'tor.**—*adj.* **rotatory** (*rō'tə-tər-i; rō-tāt'ər-i*) rotary.—*ns.* **rō'tavator®**, **rō'tovator®** (*rotary cultivator*) a motor-powered, hand-operated soil-tilling machine. [L. *rŏta*, a wheel, *rotāre*, *-ātum*, to run.]

rotch, rotche *roch*, *n.* the little auk.—Also **rotch'ie.** [Cf. Du. *rotje*, petrel.]

rote *rōt*, *n.* mechanical memory, repetition, or performance without regard to the meaning.—*v.t.* to fix by rote (according to others, to root): to discourse by rote. [L. *rŏta*, a wheel, and O.Fr. *rote*, road, have been conjectured.]

rotenone *rō'ti-nōn*, *n.* an insecticide and fish poison prepared from derris and other plants.

rotifer *rōt'if-ər*, *n.* a wheel-animalcule, or member of the **Rotif'era**, minute aquatic animals whose rings of waving cilia suggest a rotating wheel.—*adjs.* **rotif'eral, rotif'erous.** [L. *rŏta*, a wheel, *ferre*, to carry.]

rotisserie, rôtisserie *rō-tis'ə-ri*, *rō-tēs-rē*, *n.* a cooking apparatus incorporating a spit: a shop or restaurant in which meats are cooked by direct heat. [Fr., *cookshop—rôtir*, to roast.]

rotogravure *rō-tō-grə-vūr'*, *n.* a photogravure process using a rotary press: a print so produced. [L. *rŏta*, a wheel, Fr. *gravure*, engraving.]

rotor *rō'tər*, *n.* a rotating part, esp: of a dynamo, motor, or turbine: a revolving cylinder for propulsion of a ship: a revolving aerofoil. [For **rotator**.]

rotovator. See **rota**.

rotten *rot'n*, *adj.* putrefied: decaying: affected by rot: corrupt: unsound: disintegrating: deplorably bad (*slang*): miserably out of sorts (*slang*).—*adv.* **rott'-enly.**—*n.* **rott'enness.**—**rotten borough** a borough that still (till 1832) sent members to parliament though it had few or no inhabitants; **rott'enstone** a decomposed silicious limestone used for polishing metals. [O.N. *rotinn*; cf. **rot**.]

rotter, rotting, etc. See **rot**.

Rottweiler *rot'vīl-ər*, *n.* a large black German dog with smooth coat. [*Rottweil*, in S.W. Germany.]

rotund *rō-tund'*, *adj.* round: rounded: convexly protuberant.—*ns.* **rotund'a** a round (esp. domed) building or hall; **rotund'ity** roundness.—*adv.* **rotund'ly.** [L. *rotundus—rŏta*, a wheel.]

roturier *ro-tū-ryā*, *n.* a plebeian. [Fr., prob.—L.L. *ruptūra*, ground broken by the plough.]

rouble, ruble *roo'bl*, *n.* the Russian monetary unit, 100 kopecks. [Russ. *rubl'*.]

roucou *rōō-kōō'*, *n.* annatto. [Fr.,—Tupí *urucú*.]

roué *rōō'ā*, *n.* a profligate, rake, debauchee. [Fr. *roué*, broken on the wheel—pa.p. of *rouer—roue—* L. *rŏta*, a wheel.]

rouge *rōōzh*, *n.* a mixture of safflower and talc, or other powder used to redden the face: a polishing powder of hydrated ferric oxide.—*v.t.* to colour with rouge.—*v.i.* to use rouge.—**Rouge Croix** (*krwà*), **Rouge Dragon** two of the pursuivants of the Heralds' College; **rouge-et-noir** (*rōōzh-ē-nwàr*) a gambling card-game played on a table with two red and two black diamond marks on which stakes are laid. [Fr. *rouge*—L. *rubeus*, red.]

rough *ruf, adj.* uneven: rugged: unshaven: unpolished: crude: unelaborated: without attention to minute correctness: coarse: unrefined: ungentle: turbulent: unwell: aspirate.—*adv.* roughly: with roughness or risk of discomfort.—*n.* rough state: that which is rough: rough ground, esp. uncut grass, etc., beside a golf fairway: a hooligan, a rowdy: a crude preliminary sketch, etc.—*v.t.* to make rough: to ruffle: to shape roughly: to treat roughly.—*n.* **rough'age** refuse of grain or crops: bran, fibre, etc., in food: coarse food that promotes intestinal movement.—*v.t.* **rough'en** to make rough.—*v.i.* to become rough.—*adj.* **rough'ish.**—*adv.* **rough'ly.**—*n.* **rough'ness.**—*adjs.* **rough'-and-read'y** ready to hand or easily improvised, and serving the purpose well enough: willing and moderately efficient; **rough'-and-tumb'le** haphazard and scrambling.—Also *adv.*—*n.* a scuffle: haphazard struggling.—*v t.* **rough'cast** to shape roughly: to cover with roughcast.—*n.* plaster mixed with small stones, used to coat walls.—*adj.* coated with roughcast.—*adj.* **rough'-coat'ed.—rough dia- mond** see **diamond.**—*vs.t.* **rough'-draft, -draw** to draft roughly; **rough'-dry** to dry without smoothing. —*adjs.* **rough'-foot'ed** with feathered feet.—*vs.t.* **rough'-grind** to grind roughly; **rough'-hew** to hew to the first appearance of form.—**rough'-hew'er.**—*adj.* **rough'-hewn.—rough'-house, rough house** a disturbance: a brawl.—*v.i.* to brawl: to make a disturbance —*v.t.* to maltreat.—**rough justice** approximate justice, hastily assessed and carried out.—*adj.* **rough'-legged** with feathered or hairy legs.— **rough'neck** an unmannerly lout: a hooligan or tough: a member of an oil-rig crew employed to deal with equipment on the rig floor; **rough passage** a stormy sea voyage. a difficult, trying time; **rough'-rider** a rider of untrained horses: a horse-breaker.—*adj.* **rough'-shod** provided with horse-shoes fitted with projecting nails.—**rough shooting** shooting over moorland (mainly grouse).—*adj.* **rough'-spoken** rough in speech.—**rough'-stuff** coarse paint laid on after the priming, and before the finish: violent behaviour.—*adj.* **rough'-wrought.**—cut up rough see cut; **ride rough-shod over** to set at nought, domineer over without consideration; **rough in** to sketch in roughly; **rough it** to take whatever hardships come; **rough on** hard luck for: pressing hard upon; **rough out** to shape out roughly; **sleep rough** to sleep out-of-doors. [O.E. *rūh*, rough; Ger. *rauch, rauh*, Du. *ruig.*]

roulade *rōō-läd'*, *n.* a run, turn, etc., sung to one syllable (*mus.*): in cooking, a rolled slice, usu. of meat, usu. with a filling. [Fr.]

rouleau *rōō-lō'*, *n.* a roll or coil, often of ribbon: a cylindrical pile or column of coins, or other discs:— *pl.* **rouleaus, rouleaux** (*-lōz'*). [Fr.]

roulette *rōōl-et'*, *n.* a little roller: a game of chance in which a ball rolls from a rotating disc into one or other of a set of compartments answering to those on which the players place their stakes: a tool with a toothed disc for engraving rows of dots, for perforating paper, etc.: a cylinder for curling hair or wigs: the locus of a point carried by a curve rolling upon a fixed curve (*geom.*) [Fr.]

round *rownd, adj.* having a curved outline or surface: approaching a circular, globular, or cylindrical form: in a course returning upon itself: with horizontal swing: plump: pronounced with lips contracted to a circle: smooth and full-sounding: sonorous: finished-off: approximate, without regarding minor denominations: of a number. without fractions: full: not inconsiderable in amount: plain-spoken: candid: vigorous.—*adv.* about: on all sides: every way: in a ring: in a curve: in rotation: from one to another suc-

cessively: indirectly: circuitously: towards the opposite quarter: in the neighbourhood.—*prep.* about: around: on every side of: all over: to every side of in succession: past, beyond.—*n.* a round thing or part: a ring, circumference, circle, or globe: a whole slice of bread or toast: a cut of beef across the thigh-bone: a coil: a course returning upon itself: a dance in a ring, or its tune: a canon sung in unison: a cycle or recurring series of events or doings: a complete revolution or rotation: an accustomed walk: a prescribed circuit: a complete series of holes in golf: routine: a volley, as of firearms or applause: ammunition of one shot: a successive or simultaneous action of each member of a company or player in a game: a portion dealt around to each: a subdivision of a bout, as in boxing: a defined stage in a competition: roundness: the condition of being visible from all sides, not merely in relief (*sculp.*).—*v.t.* to make round: to go round: to finish off.—*v.i.* to become round: to go or turn round.— *adj.* **round'ed** (of a sound) round: finished, complete, developed to perfection.—*ns.* **round'edness;** **round'er** one who or that which rounds: one who goes the round: a complete circuit in rounders: (in *pl.*) a bat-and-ball game in which players run from station to station.—*n.* and *adj.* **round'ing.**—*adj.* **round'ish.** —*adv.* **round'ly.**—*n* **round'ness.**—*adj.* **round'about** circuitous: indirect: plump.—*n.* a circular revolving platform with handles, seats, etc., at playgrounds, etc.: a merry-go-round: a place where traffic circulates in one direction.—*adj.* **round'-arm** with nearly horizontal swing of the arm; **round dance** a dance in a ring: a dance in which couples revolve about each other.—*adjs.* **round'-eyed; round'-faced.** —**round game** a game, esp. a card-game, in which each plays for his own hand; **round'hand** a style of penmanship in which the letters are well rounded and free; **Round'head** a Puritan (from the close-cut hair; **round'-house** a lock-up (*obs.*): a cabin on the after part of the quarter-deck: an engine-house with a turntable (*U.S.*): (a boxing style using) a wild swinging punch (orig. *U.S.*); **round robin (Robin)** a paper with signatures in a circle, that no one may seem to be a ringleader: any letter, petition, etc., signed by many people: in sports, a tournament in which each player plays every other player.—*adj.* **round'-shoul'dered** with shoulders bending forward from the back.— **rounds'man** one who goes round esp. one sent by a shopkeeper to take orders and deliver goods: a policeman who acts as inspector (*U.S.*).—*adjs.* **round'-ta'ble** meeting on equal terms, like the inner circle of King Arthur's knights, who sat at a round table; **round'-the-clock'** lasting through the day and night (also *adv.*, without hyphens).—**round'-top** a mast-head platform; **round'-trip** a trip to a place and back again.—*adj* (*U.S.*) return.—**round'-up** a driving together or assembling, as of all the cattle on a ranch, a set of persons wanted by the police, a collection of facts or information, etc. (see also **round up** below); **round'-worm** a threadworm or nematode, a member of the Nematoda, unsegmented animals with long rounded body, mostly parasitic.—**bring, come, round** see **bring, come; get round to** to have the time or inclination to do (something) after delay; **go, make, the rounds** to go or be passed from place to place or person to person: to circulate: to patrol; **in round numbers, figures** to the nearest convenient large number, approximately; **in the round** capable of being viewed from all sides, not merely in relief: taking everything into consideration; **round about** an emphatic form of round: the other way about: approximately; **round down** to lower (a number) to the nearest convenient figure; **round off** to finish off neatly; **round on** to turn on, assail in speech; **round** out to fill out to roundness; **round the bend, twist** see **bend, twist; round the clock** see **round-the-clock** above; **round to** to turn the head of a ship to the wind; **round up** to ride round and collect: to gather in (wanted persons, facts, etc.): to raise (a number) to the nearest convenient figure (*n.* **round'-up**). [O.Fr. *rund* (Fr. *rond*)—L. *rotundus*—*rōta*, a wheel.]

roundel *rown'dl*, *n.* a disc: a rondel: a circular device. —*n.* **roun'delay** a song with a refrain: a dance in a ring. [O.Fr. *rondel*, *-le*, *rondelet*, dims. of *rond*, round.]

roup[1] *rowp*, (*Scot.*) *n.* sale by auction.—*v.t.* to sell by auction. [Scand.]

roup[2] *rōōp*, *n.* ar infectious disease of the respiratory passages of poultry.—*adj.* **roup'y**. [Perh. imit.]

rouse[1] *rowz*, *v.t.* to start, as from cover or lair: to stir up: to awaken: to excite: to haul in (as a cable).—*v.i.* to awake: to be excited to action.—*ns.* **rouse'about** (*Austr.*) an odd man on a station; **rous'er**.—*adj.* **rous'ing** awakening: stirring.—*adv.* **rous'ingly**.—*v.t.* **roust** to stir up: to rout out.—*n.* **roust'about** a wharf labourer (*U.S.*): one who does odd jobs (*U.S.*): a rouseabout (*U.S.* and *Austr.*): a general labourer employed in the maintenance of an oil-rig.

rouse[2] *rowz*, (*arch.*) *n.* a carousal: a bumper. [Prob. from **carouse**; poss. Scand. *rus*, drunkenness.]

roust, roustabout. See **rouse**.

rout[1] *rowt*, *n.* a rabble: a fashionable evening assembly (*arch.*): a defeated body: an utter defeat: disorderly flight: a gathering of three or more people for the purpose of committing an unlawful act (*legal*).—*v.t.* to defeat utterly: to put to disorderly flight. [O.Fr. *route*, from the pa.p. of L. *rumpĕre*, *ruptum*, to break.]

rout[2] *rowt*, *v.t.* to grub up: to scoop out: to turn out, fetch out: to rummage out: to bring to light.—*v.i.* to grub: to poke about.—*n.* **rout'er**. [An irreg. variant of **root**[2].]

route *rōōt* *n.* a way, course that is or may be traversed. —*v.t.* to fix the route of: to send by a particular route: —*pr.p.* **rout(e)'ing**; *pa.t.* and *pa.p.* **rout'ed.**—**route'-march** a long march of troops in training; **route'-step** an order of march in which soldiers are not required to keep step. [Fr.,—L. *rupta* (*via*), broken (way); see **rout**[1].]

routine *rōō-tēn'*, *n.* regular, unvarying, or mechanical course of action or round: the set series of movements gone through in a dancing, skating, or other performance: a comedian's, singer's, etc., act (*coll.*).—*adj.* keeping an unvarying round: forming part of a routine.—*adv.* **routine'ly**.—*ns.* **routi'nism**; **routi'nist**. [Fr.]

roux *rōō*, *n.* a thickening made of equal quantities of butter and flour cooked together. [Fr. (*beurre*) *roux*, brown (butter).]

rove[1] *rōv*, *v.t.* to wander over or through.—*v.i.* to wander about: to ramble: to change about inconstantly.—*n.* wandering.—*n.* **rō'ver** a pirate: a robber: a random or distant mark: a wanderer: an inconstant person: a croquet ball or player ready to peg out: (formerly) member of a senior branch of (Boy) Scout organisation (also **rover scout**).—*adj.* **rō'ving** wandering: not confined to a particular place, as *roving ambassador*, *commission*.—Also *n.*—*adv.* **rō'vingly**. [*Orig.*, in archery, to shoot at a random target; partly from Du. *rooven*, to rob; perh. partly from a Midland form of obs. Northern English *rave*, to wander.]

rove[2] *rōv*, *v.t.* to twist slightly in preparation for spinning.—*n.* a roved sliver.

rove[3] *rōv*, *pa.t.* and *pa.p.* of **reeve**[2].

rove[4] *rōv*, *n.* a metal plate or ring through which a rivet is put and clenched over. [O.N. *ró*.]

rove-beetle *rōv'-bē'tl*, *n.* the devil's coach-horse, or other beetle of the family Staphylinidae.

row[1] *rō*, *n.* a line or rank of persons or things, as seats, houses, turnips: a series in line, or in ordered succession: often in street-names, of a single or double line of houses.—**a hard row to hoe** a destiny fraught with hardship; **in a row** in unbroken sequence. [O.E. *rāw*; Ger. *Reihe*, Du. *rij*.]

row[2] *rō*, *v.t.* to propel with an oar: to transport by rowing: to achieve, render, perform, effect, compete in, by use of oars: to use, as an oar.—*v.i.* to work with the oar: to be moved by oars.—*n.* an act or spell of rowing: a journey in a rowing-boat.—*adj.* **row'able**. —*n.* **row'er.**—**row'boat** (*U.S.*); **row'ing-boat**. [O.E. *rōwan*.]

row[3] *row*, *n.* a noisy squabble: a brawl: a din, hubbub: a chiding.—*v.i.* to make a disturbance. [A late 18th-century word, poss. a back-formation from **rouse**[1].]

rowan *row'ən*, also *rō'ən*, *n.* the mountain-ash (*Sorbus*, or *Pyrus*, *aucuparia*), a tree of the rose family with pinnate leaves: its small red berry-like fruit.— **row'an-berry**; **row'an-tree**. [Cf. Norw. *raun*, Sw. *rönn*.]

rowdy *row'di*, *n.* orig. a lawless American backwoodsman: a noisy, turbulent person.—Also *adj.*— *adv.* **row'dily**.—*n.* **row'diness**.—*adj.* **row'dyish**.—*n.* **row'dyism**.

rowel *row'əl*, *n.* a little spiked wheel on a spur: a disc used as a seton for animals.—*v.t.* to prick with the rowel:—*pr.p.* **row'elling**; *pa.t.* and *pa.p.* **row'elled.**— **row'el-spur** a spur with a rowel. [Fr. *rouelle*—L.L. *rotella*, dim. of L. *rōta*, a wheel.]

rowen *row'ən*, *n.* aftermath. [From a Northern form of O.Fr. *regain*.]

rowlock *rol'ək*, *rul'*, *rōl'*, *n.* a contrivance serving as fulcrum for an oar.—Also **roll'ock**. [Prob. for **oar-lock**—O.E. *ārloc*.]

royal *roi'əl*, *adj.* of a king or queen: kingly: being a king or queen: of a reigning family: founded, chartered, or patronised by a king or queen: magnificent: of more than common size or excellence: of writing-paper, 19 by 24 in., of printing-paper, 20 by 25.—*n.* a royal person (*coll.*): a gold coin of various kinds: a sail immediately above the topgallant sail: a stag of twelve points.—*ns.* **roy'alism** attachment to monarchy; **roy'alist** an adherent of royalism: a cavalier during the English civil war: in American history, an adherent of the British government: in French history, a supporter of the Bourbons.—Also *adj.*— *adv.* **roy'ally**.—*n.* **roy'alty** kingship: the character, state, or office of a king: kingliness: members of royal families collectively: royal authority: a right or prerogative granted by a king or queen, esp. a right over minerals: a payment made by oil companies, etc., to the owners of the mineral rights in the area in which they operate: payment to an author, composer, etc., for every copy sold or every public performance.— **Royal Academy** an academy of fine arts in London, to which members and associates are elected; **royal assent** see **assent**; **royal blue** a bright, deep-coloured blue; **royal commission** (also with *caps*.) a body of persons nominated by the Crown to inquire into and report on some matter; **royal fern** (*Osmunda regalis*) the most striking of British ferns; **royal flush** see **flush**[4]; **royal icing** a kind of hard icing used esp. on rich fruit cakes; **royal jelly** the food of a developing queen-bee; **royal mast** the fourth and highest part of the mast, commonly made in one piece with the topgallant mast; **royal palm** a palm (*Oreodoxa regalis*) of the cabbage-palm genus; **royal standard** a banner bearing the British royal arms, flown wherever the monarch is present; **royal tennis** the earlier form of the game of tennis, distinguished from lawn tennis, and played in a wall court (also **real** or **court tennis**); **royal warrant** an official authorisation to supply goods to a royal household; **Royal We** (also without *caps.*) a monarch's use of the first person plural when speaking of himself or herself. [Fr.,—L. *rēgālis*, regal.]

rozzer *roz'ar*, (*slang*) *n.* a policeman.

rub[1] *rub*, *v.t.* to apply friction to: to move something with pressure along the surface of: to move with pressure along the surface of something: to clean, polish, or smooth by friction: to remove, erase, or obliterate by friction (usu. with *away*, *off*, *out*): to grind, sharpen, chafe, treat, by friction: to cause to pass by friction (with *in*, *through*, etc.).—*v.i.* to apply, or move with, friction: to meet an impediment (esp. of a bowl): to chafe: to admit of being rubbed:—*pr.p.* **rubb'ing;** *pa.t.* and *pa.p.* **rubbed.**—*n.* process or act of rubbing: an impediment, or a meeting with an impediment (*bowls*): an uneven place: a difficulty.— *n.* **rubb'er** one who, or that which, rubs or massages: an eraser: a thing for rubbing with, as a whetstone, etc. a rubbing part of a machine: caoutchouc, india-rubber, or a substitute: a piece of india-rubber, esp. for erasing: (in *pl.*) plimsolls: india-rubber overshoe (*U.S.*): condom.—*adj.* of, yielding, or concerned with, india-rubber.—*v.t.* **rubb'erise, -ize** to treat or coat with rubber.—*adj.* **rubb'ery.**—*n.* **rubb'ing** application of friction: an impression of an inscribed surface produced by rubbing heel-ball or plumbago upon paper laid over it.—**rubber band** a thin loop of rubber used to hold things together; **rubber goods** (*euph.*) condoms; **rubb'er-neck** one who cranes or twists his neck in curiosity.—*v.i.* (*U.S.*) to behave as a rubber-neck.—**rubber plant** any of various plants from whose sap rubber is made, esp. *Ficus elastica*, often grown as an ornamental pot-plant; **rubb'er-solu'tion** a solution of rubber in naphtha or carbon disulphide, for repairing pneumatic tyres; **rubb'er-stamp** stamp of rubber for making inked impressions. —*v.t.* to imprint with a rubber-stamp: to approve without exercise of judgment.—Also *adj.*— **rub'down** an act of rubbing down.—**rub along** to get along, to manage somehow (*coll.*) to be on more or less friendly terms (with); **rub down** to rub from head to foot: to remove (a surface) by rubbing in order to repaint, etc.; **rub in** to force into the pores by friction: to be unpleasantly insistent in emphasising; **rub off on (to)** (*fig.*) to pass to (someone, something, else) by close contact, association, etc.; **rub on (or of) the green** (*golf*) a chance outside interference with the ball (also *fig.*); **rub out** to erase: to murder (*slang*); **rub shoulders** to come into social contact (with); **rub someone's nose in it** (*coll.*) to remind someone insistently of a mistake, etc.; **rub the wrong way** to irritate by tactless handling, etc. **rub up** to polish: to freshen one's memory of.[Cf. L.G. *rubben*.]

rub[2]. See **rubber**[2].

rub-a-dub(-dub) *rub'a-dub(-dub')*, *n.* the sound of a drum. [Echoic.]

rubaiyat *rōō'bā-yat*, *n.* a Persian verse form consisting of four-line stanzas. [Arabic *ruba'īyāt*, pl. of *ruba'īyah*, quatrain.]

rubato *rōō-bā'tō*, (*mus.*) *adj.*, *adv.* and *n.* (in) modified or distorted rhythm:—*pl.* **ruba'ti** (*-tē*), **ruba'tos.** [It., pa.p. of *rubare*, to steal.]

rubber[1], **rubberise**, etc. See under **rub**[1].

rubber[2] *rub'ar*, *n.* formerly in bowls (also **rubbers,** *sing.* or *pl.*), now chiefly in bridge and whist, the winning of, or play for, the best of three games (sometimes five): vaguely, a spell of card-playing: used generally of a series of games in various sports, as cricket, tennis, etc.—Also **rub.**

rubbish *rub'ish*, *n.* waste matter: litter: trash: non-

sense.—Also *adj.*—*v.t.* to criticise, think of or talk about as rubbish.—*adjs.* **rubb'ishing; rubb'ishy** worthless: trashy.—**rubb'ish-heap.**

rubble *rub'l*, *n.* loose fragments of rock or ruined buildings: undressed irregular stones used in rough masonry and in filling in: masonry of such a kind.— *adj.* of rubble.—*adj.* **rubb'ly.**—**rubb'le-stone; rubb'le-work** coarse masonry.

rube *rōōb*, (*U.S. slang*) *n.* a country bumpkin: an uncouth, unsophisticated person. [*Reuben*.]

rubefy *rōō'bi-fī*, *v.t.* to redden.—*adj.* **rubefacient** (*-fā'shant*) reddening.—*n.* an external application that reddens the skin.—*n.* **rubefaction** (*-fak'shan*). [L. *rubefacĕre—rubeus*, red, *facĕre*, to make.]

rubella *rōō-bel'a*, *n.* German measles, an infectious disease with pink rash, like measles but milder.—*n.* **rubell'ite** a red tourmaline. [Dim. from L. *rubeus*, red.]

rubeola *rōō-bē'a-la*, *n.* measles. [Dim. from L. *rubeus*, red.]

Rubicon *rōōb'i-kon*, *-kan*, *n.* a stream of Central Italy, separating Caesar's province of Gallia Cisalpina from Italia proper—its crossing by Caesar (49 B.C.) being thus a virtual declaration of war against the republic: (without *cap.*) in piquet, the winning of a game before one's opponent scores 100.—*v.t.* (without *cap.*) to defeat in this way.—**cross the Rubicon** to take a decisive, irrevocable step. [L. *Rubicō*, *-ōnis*.]

rubicund *rōō'bi-kund*, *-kand*, *adj.* ruddy.—*n.* **rubicund'ity.** [L. *rubicundus—rubēre*, to be red.]

rubidium *rōō-bid'i-am*, *n.* a soft silvery-white metallic element (Rb; at. numb. 37). [L. *rubidus*, red (so called from two red lines in its spectrum).]

rubiginous *rōō-bij'i-nas*, *adj.* rusty-coloured.—Also **rubig'inose** (*-nōs*). [L. *rūbīgō* or *rōbīgō*, *-inis*, rust.]

ruble. See **rouble.**

rubric *rōō'brik*, *n.* a heading, guiding rule, entry, liturgical direction, orig. one in red: a thing definitely settled.—*adj.* **ru'brical.**—*adv.* **ru'brically.**—*v.t.* **ru'bricate** to mark with red: to write or print in red: to furnish with rubrics.—*ns.* **rubrica'tion; ru'bricator; rubrician** (*-brish'an*) one versed in liturgical rubrics. [L. *rubrīca*, red ochre, used in writing.—*ruber*, red.]

ruby *rōō'bi*, *n.* a highly-prized stone, a pure transparent red corundum: redness.—*adj.* red as a ruby.— *adjs.* **ru'by-coloured; ru'by-red'.**—**ru'by-wedding** a fortieth wedding anniversary. [O.Fr. *rubi* and *rubin* —L. *rubeus—ruber*, red.]

ruche *rōōsh*, *n.* a pleated frilling.—*v.t.* to trim with ruche.—*n.* **ruch'ing.** [Fr.; prob. Celt.]

ruck[1] *ruk*, *n.* a wrinkle, fold, or crease.—*v.t.* and *v.i.* to wrinkle (often with *up*).—*n.* **ruck'le** a pucker, crease. [O.N. *hrukka*, a wrinkle.]

ruck[2] *ruk*, *n.* a heap, stack, or rick, as of fuel, hay, etc.: a multitude: the common run: in Rugby, a gathering of players around the ball when it is on the ground.— *v.i.* in Rugby, to form a ruck. [Prob. Scand.]

ruckle. See **ruck**[1].

rucksack *rōōk'*, *ruk'sak*, *-zak*, *n.* a bag carried on the back by hikers, campers, etc. [Ger. dial. *ruck*, back, and Ger. *Sack*, bag.]

ruckus *ruk'as*, (*U.S.*) *n.* a disturbance. [Perh. a combination of **ruction** and **rumpus**.]

ruction *ruk'shan*, (*slang*) *n.* a disturbance: a rumpus. [Poss. for **insurrection**.]

Rudbeckia *rud-* or *rōōd-bek'i-a*, *n.* a N. American genus of composites, of the sunflower subfamily: (without *cap.*) a plant of this genus. [Swedish botanist *Rudbeck*.]

rudd *rud*, *n.* the red-eye, a fish close akin to the roach. [Prob. O.E. *rudu*, redness.]

rudder *rud'ar*, *n.* a steering apparatus: a flat structure hinged to the stern of a ship or boat for steering: a vertical control surface for steering an aeroplane to right or left: anything that steers: a principle, etc. that guides a person in life.—*adj.* **rudd′erless.—rudd′er-fish** the pilot-fish, or other fish that accompanies ships. [O.E. *rōthor*, oar.]

ruddle *rud′l, n.* red ochre.—*v.t.* to mark with ruddle: to rouge coarsely.—Also **radd′le, redd′le.** [O.E. *rudu,* redness.]

ruddock *rud′ək, n.* the redbreast. [O.E. *rudduc.*]

ruddy *rud′i, adj.* red: reddish: of the colour of the skin in high health: rosy, glowing, bright: (euphemistically) bloody:—*compar.* **rudd′ier,** *superl.* **rudd′iest.** —*v.t.* to make red:—*pr.p.* **rudd′ying;** *pa.t.* and *pa.p* **rudd′ied.—***adv.* **rudd′ily.—***n.* **rudd′iness.** [O.E. *rudig.*]

rude *rōōd, adj.* uncultured: unskilled: discourteously unmannerly: ungentle: harsh: crude: undeveloped. unwrought: coarse: rugged: rough: roughly or unskilfully fashioned: violent: robust.—*adv.* **rude′ly.—***ns.* **rude′ness;** *rud′ery (coll.).—adj.* **rud′ish.** [L. *rudis,* rough.]

ruderal *rōō′dər-əl, (bot.) n.* and *adj.* (a plant) growing in waste places or among rubbish. [L. *rūdus, -ĕris,* rubbish.]

rudiment *rōōd′i-mənt, n.* (usu. in *pl.*) a first principle or element: anything in a rude or first state: an organ in the first discernible stage: often applied to an organ that never develops beyond an early stage.—*adj.* **rudimental** (*-ment′l*) rudimentary.—*adv.* **rudimen′tarily.—***n.* **rudimen′tariness.—***adj.* **rudimen′-tary** of rudiments: elementary: in an early or arrested stage of development. [L. *rudīmentum—rudis,* rough, raw.]

rue[1] *rōō, n.* a strong-smelling shrubby Mediterranean plant (*Ruta graveolens*), with pinnately divided leaves and greenish-yellow flowers, punningly (see next word) symbolic of repentance: any other member of its genus. [Fr. *rue*—L. *rūta*—Gr. *rhytē*.]

rue[2] *rōō, n. (arch.)* repentance: regret: pity.—*v.t.* to repent of: to wish not to have been or happened:—*pr.p.* **rue′ing,** ru′ing; *pa.t.* and *pa.p.* **rued.—***adj* **rue′ful** sorrowful: mournful.—*adv.* **rue′fully.—***n.* **rue′fulness.** [O.E. *hrēow,* n., *hrēowan,* vb.]

rufescent *rōō-fes′ənt, adj.* inclining to redness. [L. *rūfescens, -entis,* pr.p. of *rūfescere,* to turn reddish—*rūfus,* reddish.]

ruff[1] *ruf, n.* a frill, usu. starched and plaited, worn round the neck, esp. in the reigns of Elizabeth and James; a beast's or bird's collar of long hair or feathers: a ruffed breed of domestic pigeons.—*adj.* **ruffed** (*ruft*) having a ruff. [Cf. **ruffle**[1].]

ruff[2] *ruf, n.* a kind of sandpiper, the male with an erectile ruff during the breeding season:—*fem.* **reeve, ree.** [Poss. **ruff**[1], but the fem. is a difficulty.]

ruff[3] *ruf, n.* an old card-game, slam, trump: an act of trumping.—*v.t.* and *v.i.* to trump. [Perh. conn. with O.Fr. *roffle,* It. *ronfa,* a card-game.]

ruff[4] *ruf, n.* a low vibrating beat of a drum.—*n.* **ruff′le** a ruff of drums. [Prob. imit.]

ruff[5], **ruffe** *ruf, n.* the pope, a small fresh-water fish of the perch family, with one dorsal fin. [Perh. rough.]

ruffian *ruf′i-ən, -yən, n.* a brutal, violent person: a bully.—*adj.* brutal: violent.—*adj.* **ruff′ianish.—***n.* **ruff′ianism.—***adj.* **ruff′ianly.—***adj.* **ruff′ian-like.** [O.Fr. *ruffian* (Fr. *rufien*).]

ruffle[1] *ruf′l, v.t.* to make uneven, disturb the smoothness of: to set up (as feathers): to disorder: to agitate: to turn the leaves of hastily: to disturb the equanimity of, to irritate, discompose.—*v.i.* to grow rough: to flutter.—*n.* a frill, esp. at the wrist or neck: a ruff: a rippled condition: annoyance: agitation.—*adj.* **ruff′-led.—***n.* and *adj.* **ruff′ling.** [Cf. L.G. *ruffelen.*]

ruffle[2] *ruf′l, (arch.) v.i.* to swagger.—*n.* **ruff′ler.**

ruffle[3]. See **ruff**[4].

ruffler. See **ruffle**[2].

rufous *rōō′fəs, adj.* reddish or brownish-red. [L. *rūfus,* akin to *ruber,* red.]

rug *rug, n.* a thick, heavy floor-mat: a thick covering or wrap, as for travelling.—**pull the rug (out) from under** (*fig.*) by a sudden action, argument, discovery, etc., to leave a person without support, defence, a standpoint, etc. [Cf. Norw. *rugga, rogga,* coarse coverlet, Sw. *rugg,* coarse hair.]

Rugby, rugby *rug′bi, n.* a form of football using an oval ball which (unlike *Association*) permits carrying the ball:—(*coll.*) **rugg′er.—Rugby (Union) football** the original form of the game, with 15 players; **Rugby League football** a modified form of the game subject to professional rules, with 13 players. [From *Rugby* school.]

rugged *rug′id, adj.* rough: uneven: uncouth: toilsome: sturdy and rough: massively irregular: robust, vigorous.—*adv.* **rugg′edly.—***n.* **rugg′edness.** [Prob. related to **rug**.]

rugger. See **Rugby.**

rugose *rōō′gōs, -gōs′, adj.* wrinkled: covered with sunken lines.—*adv.* **ru′gosely** (or *-gōs′*).—*n.* **rugosity** (*-gos′i-ti*). [L. *rūgōsus—rūga,* a wrinkle.]

ruin *rōō′in, rōō′in, n.* downfall: collapse: overthrow: complete destruction: wreck: loss of fortune or means: bankruptcy: undoing: seduction or departure from chastity of life: downfallen, collapsed, wrecked, or irretrievably damaged state (often in *pl.*): cause of ruin: broken-down remains, esp. of a building (often in *pl.*): devastation.—*v.t.* to reduce or bring to ruin. —*adj.* **ru′inable.—***n.* **ruina′tion** act of ruining: state of being ruined.—*adj.* **ru′ined.—***n.* **ru′iner.—***n.* and *adj.* **ru′ining.—***adj.* **ru′inous** fallen to ruins: decayed: bringing ruin.—*adv.* **ru′inously.—***n.* **ru′inousness.** [L. *ruina—ruĕre,* to tumble down.]

ruing. See **rue**[2].

rule *rōōl, n.* a straight-edged strip used as a guide in drawing straight lines or as a measuring-rod, or means of mechanical calculation: a type-high strip of metal for printing straight lines: a straight line printed or drawn on paper, etc.: a straight-edge used for securing a flat surface in plaster or cements: government: control: prevalence: that which is normal or usual: conformity to good or established usage: well-regulated condition: a principle: a standard: a code of regulations, as of a religious order: a regulation, whether imposed by authority or voluntarily adopted: an order of a court: a guiding principle: a method or process of achieving a result: a regulation that must not be transgressed: a maxim or formula that it is generally best, but not compulsory, to follow: (in *pl.*) an area around a prison in which privileged prisoners were allowed to live (*hist.*): the privilege of living there (*hist.*): (in *pl.*) Australian football (see **Australian** rules).—*v.t.* to draw with a ruler: to mark with (esp. parallel) straight lines: to govern: to control: to manage: to prevail upon: to determine or declare authoritatively to be: to determine, decree.— *v.i.* to exercise power (with *over*): to decide: to be prevalent: to stand or range in price.—*adjs.* **ru′lable** governable: allowable (*U.S.*); **rule′less** unruly: without rules.—*n.* **ru′ler** a strip or roller for ruling lines: one who rules.—*n.* **ru′lership.—***adj.* **ru′ling** predominant: prevailing: reigning: exercising authority. —*n.* a determination by a judge, esp. an oral decision: the act of making ruled lines.—*adj.* **rule-of-thumb′** according to rule of thumb (see below).—**as a rule** usually; **be ruled** take advice; **rule of the road** the regulations to be observed in traffic by land, water, or air; **rule of three** the method of finding the fourth term of a proportion when three are given; **rule of**

thumb any rough-and-ready practical method; **rule out** to exclude as a choice or possibility. [O.Fr. *reule* (Fr. *règle*)—L. *rēgula—regĕre* to rule.]

rum[1] *rum*, *n.* a spirit distilled from fermented sugar-cane juice or from molasses: intoxicating liquor generally *(U.S.).—adj.* **rumm'y.—rum'-butt'er** a mixture of butter and sugar with rum, etc.; **rum'-punch** punch made with rum; **rum'-runn'er** one who smuggles rum; **rum'-runn'ing; rum'-shop.—rum baba** baba au rhum (see **baba**). [Perh from its older name *rumbullion*.]

rum[2] *rum, adj.* queer, droll, odd *(slang).—advs.* **rum'ly; rumm'ily.—n. rumm'iness.—adj. rumm'y.** [Cant.]

Rumanian *rōō-mā'ni-ən*, **Romanian** *rō-, adjs.* pertaining to *Rumania* or its language.—*n.* a native or citizen of Rumania: the (Romance) language of Rumania. [Rumanian *România*—L. *Rōmānus*, Roman.]

rumba, rhumba *rōŏm'bə, rum'bə, n.* a violent Cuban Negro dance or a modification of it. [Sp.]

rumble[1] *rum'bl, v.i.* to make a low heavy grumbling or rolling noise: to move with such a noise.—*v.t.* to give forth, or to agitate or move, with such a sound.—*n.* a sound of rumbling: a seat for servants behind a carriage, or for extra passengers in a two-seater car (also **rumble seat**): a quarrel, disturbance, gang fight. —*n.* **rum'bler.—n.** and *adj.* **rum'bling.—adv. rum'-blingly.—rum'ble-tum'ble** a lumbering vehicle: a tumbling motion. [Cf. Du. *rommelen,* Ger. *rummeln.*]

rumble[2] *rum'bl, (slang) v.t.* to grasp: to see through, discover the truth about.

rumbustious *rum-bust'-yəs, (coll.) adj.* boisterous. [Prob. **robust.**]

rumen *rōō'men, n.* the paunch or first stomach of a ruminant:—*pl.* **ru'mina.** [L. *rūmen, -inis,* gullet.]

rumina. See **rumen.**

ruminant *rōō'min-ənt, n.* an animal that chews the cud. —*adj.* cud-chewing: meditative.—*adv.* **ru'minantly.** —*v.i.* **ru'minate** to chew the cud: to regurgitate for chewing: to meditate ((up)on).—*adv.* **ru'minatingly.** —*n.* **rumina'tion.—adj.** **ru'minative.—adv.** **ru'minatively.—n.** **ru'minator.** [L. *rūminăre, -ātum—rūmen, -inis,* the gullet.]

rummage *rum'ij, n.* a thorough search, as by customs officers: an overhauling search.—*v.t.* to ransack: to search.—*v.i.* to make a search.—*n.* **rumm'ager.— rummage sale** a sale at which buyers are allowed to rummage among the goods: also a sale of odds and ends or undesired goods. [Orig. stowage of casks— Fr. *arrumage* (now *arrimage*), stowage.]

rummer *rum'ər, n.* a large drinking-glass. [Du. *roemer*; Ger. *Römer.*]

rummy[1] See **rum**[1,2].

rummy[2] *rum'i, n.* a card-game in which cards are drawn from the stock and sequences, triplets, etc., are laid on the table.

rumour, in U.S. **rumor** *rōō'mər, n.* general talk, repute: hearsay: flying report: a current story.—*v.t.* to put about by report.—*n.* **ru'mourer.** [O.Fr.—L. *rūmor, -ōris,* a noise.]

rump *rump, n.* the hinder part of an animal's or bird's body: usu. contemptuously, a remnant.—*adj.* **rump'less.—rump steak** steak cut from the thigh near the rump.—**the Rump** the remnant of the long Parliament, after Pride's expulsion (1648), of about a hundred Presbyterian royalist members. [Scand.]

rumple *rum'pl, n.* a fold or wrinkle.—*v.t.* to crush out of shape: to make uneven. [Du. *rompel*; cf. O.E. *hrimpan,* to wrinkle.]

rumpus *rum'pəs, n.* an uproar: a disturbance.— **rumpus room** (orig. *U.S.*) a room in which children can play freely.

run *run, v.i.* to proceed by lifting one foot before the other is down: to go swiftly, at more than a walking pace: to proceed quickly: to betake oneself: to flee: to progress, esp. smoothly and quickly: to go about freely: to ride at a running pace: to roll: to revolve: to go with a gliding motion: to slip: to go on wheels: to travel, cover a distance: to make a short journey: to swim in shoals: to ascend a river for spawning: to ply: to have a definite sequence, as of notes, words: to proceed through a sequence of operations, work, or go, as a machine: to follow a course: to flow: to spread, diffuse: to emit or transmit a flow: to melt: to fuse: to have a course, stretch, or extent: to range: to average: to elapse: to tend: to be current: to be valid: to recur repeatedly or remain persistently (in the mind): to come undone, as by the dropping or breaking of a stitch: to compete in a race: to be a candidate *(U.S.).—v.t.* to cause to run: to chase, hunt: to drive forward: to thrust: to pierce: to drive: to pass quickly: to enter, promote, put forward (as a horse, candidate, or protégé): to render, by running or otherwise: to conduct, manage: to follow: to traverse: to cause to extend, form in a line: to sew slightly: to shoot along or down: to perform, achieve, or score by running, or as if by running: to flee or desert from: to incur: to risk and pass the hazard of: to smuggle: to have or keep current or running: to publish (a regular paper, magazine, etc.): to press or put to it, in competition or difficulty: to coagulate: to fuse: to emit, discharge, flow with:—*pr.p.* **runn'ing;** *pa.t.* **ran;** *pa.p.* **run.—n.** an act, spell, or manner of running: a journey, trip: distance, time or quantity run: a circuit of duty, as a delivery round, etc.: a continuous stretch, spell, series, or period: a shoal, migration, or migrating body: a roulade: a spell of being in general demand: a rush for payment, as upon a bank: a unit of scoring in cricket: a batsman's passage from one popping-crease to the other: a circuit in baseball: flow or discharge: course: prevalence: the ordinary or average kind, the generality: a track: a path made by animals: a range of feeding-ground: an enclosure for chickens, etc.: freedom of access to all parts: general direction: a ladder in knitting or knitted fabrics, esp. stockings.—*adj.* having been poured, smuggled, coagulated: having run.—*n.* **run'let** a runnel.—*adj.* **runn'able** of a stag, fit for hunting.—*n.* **runn'er** one who, or that which, runs or can run: a racer: a messenger: a rooting stem that runs along the ground: a rope to increase the power of a tackle: a smuggler: a Bow Street officer (*hist.*): a ring, or the like, through which anything slides or runs: the part on which a sledge, a skate, or a drawer slides: a strip of cloth as a table ornament: a revolving millstone: a climbing plant of the kidney-bean genus (*Phaseolus multiflorus*; **runner-bean, scarlet-runner**).— **runn'ing** racing: habitually going at a run: current: successive: continuous: flowing: discharging: cursive: done at or with a run: hasty.—*n.* action of the verb: the pace.—*adv.* **runn'ingly.—adj.** **runn'y** inclined to run or liquefy.—**run'about** a small light vehicle or aeroplane; **run'away** a fugitive: a horse that bolts: a flight.—*adj.* fleeing: done by or in flight: uncontrolled: overwhelming.—*adj.* **run'-down** in weakened health: (of a building, etc.) dilapidated.— *n.* (usu. **run'down**) a reduction in numbers: a statement bringing together all the main items, a summary (see also **run down** below).—*adj.* **run'flat** (of a tyre) able, after being punctured, to be safely driven on for a distance.—**run'-in** an approach: a quarrel, argument *(coll.*; see also **run in** below).—**runn'er-up'** the competitor next after the winner: one of a number of contestants coming close behind the winner:—*pl.* **runn'ers-up'; running battle** a battle between pursuers and pursued: a continuing skirmish; **runn'ing-board** a footboard along the side of a car; **running commentary** a commentary accompanying a text: a broadcast description of a game or other event in progress; **running dog** (*derog.*) in political jargon, a slavish follower; **runn'ing-knot** a knot that will form a noose on pulling; **running lights** the lights shown by vessels between sunset and sunrise; **running mate** a horse teamed with another, or making the pace for another: in U.S., the candidate for the less important of two associated offices, esp. the candidate for the vice-presidency considered in relation to the presidential candidate; **running repairs** minor repairs; **running stitch** a simple stitch usu. made in a line, in order to gather fabric, etc.; **running title, head** the title of a book, etc., continued from page to page on the upper margin; **run'-off'** a race held to resolve a dead heat or other uncertain result (also *fig.*): urination.—*adj.* run'-of-the-mill' constituting an ordinary fair sample, not selected: mediocre.—**run'-up** an approach (*lit.* and *fig.*; see also **run up** below); **run'way** a trail, track, or passageway: a firm strip of ground for aircraft to take off from and land on.—**give the runaround** (*slang*) to give a vague, indecisive, or deceptive reply to a question or meet a request with evasion; **get the runaround** (*slang*) to be treated thus; **in the long run** in the end or final result; **in, out of, the running** competing with, without, a fair chance of success; **make, take up, the running** to take the lead: to set the pace; **on the run** (*coll.*) pursued, esp. by the police; **run across** to come upon by accident; **run after** to pursue; **run along!** (*coll.*) off you go!; **run away with** to take away: to win (a prize, etc.) easily; **run down** to pursue to exhaustion or capture: to collide with and knock over or sink: to disparage: to become unwound or exhausted; **run dry** to cease to flow: to come to an end; **run for it** (*coll.*) to attempt to escape, run away from; **run hard, close** to press hard behind; **run in** to arrest and take to a lock-up: to bring (new machinery, car) into full working condition by a period of careful operation; **run in the blood, family** to be a hereditary character; **run into** to meet, come across: to extend into; **run into debt** to get into debt; **run it fine** to allow very little margin, as of time; **run off** to cause to flow out: to take impressions of, to print; **run off with** (*coll.*) to take away, steal; **run on** to talk on and on: to continue in the same line, and not in a new paragraph (*print.*); **run one's eyes over** to look at cursorily; **run out** to run short: to terminate, expire: to leak, let out liquid: to put out (a batsman running between the wickets and not yet in his ground): dismissed thus; **run out on** (*coll.*) to abandon, desert; **run over** to overflow: to go over cursorily: of a road vehicle, to knock down (a person or animal); **run short** to come to be short, lacking, or exhausted; **run through** to exhaust: to transfix: to read or perform quickly or cursorily but completely; **run to** to be sufficient for; **run to earth** to search out, find; **run together** to mingle or blend; **run to seed** see **seed**; **run up** to make or mend hastily: to build hurriedly: to string up, hang: to incur increasingly; **take a running jump** (*slang*) an expression of impatience, contempt, etc. [O.E. *rinnan, irnan, iernan*, to run; causative *rennan*, to curdle.]

runcible *run'si-bl, adj.* app. a nonsense-word of Edward Lear's, whose phrase *runcible spoon* has been applied to a sharp-edged, broad-pronged pickle-fork.

rune *rōōn, n.* a letter of the futhork or ancient Germanic alphabet: a secret, a mystic symbol.—*adj.* ru'nic of, pertaining to, written in, inscribed with runes. [O.E. and O.N. *rūn*, mystery, rune.]

rung[1] *rung, n.* a spoke: a cross-bar or rail: a ladder step. [O.E. *hrung*; Ger. *Runge*.]

rung[2] *rung.* See **ring[2]**.

runlet. See **run**.

runnable. See **run**.

runnel *run'l, n.* a little brook. [O.E. *rynel*, dim. of *ryne*, a stream—*rinnan*, to run.]

runner, running, runny. See **run**.

runt *runt, n.* a small, stunted, or old, ox or cow: a small pig, esp. the smallest of a litter: anything undersized: a large breed of domestic pigeon.

rupee *rōō-pē', n.* monetary unit of India, Pakistan, Bhutan, Nepal, Sri Lanka, Mauritius, the Seychelles and the Maldive Islands. [Urdu *rūpiyah*—Sans. *rūpya*, wrought silver.]

rupiah *rōō'pi-ə, n.* the standard unit of currency of Indonesia—*pl.* ru'piah, ru'piahs. [Hindi, rupee.]

rupture *rup'chər, n.* a breach, breaking, or bursting: the state of being broken: breach of harmony, relations, or negotiations: hernia, esp. abdominal.—*v.t.* and *v.i.* to break or burst. [L.L. *ruptūra*—L. *rumpĕre, ruptum*, to break.]

rural *rōō'rl, adj.* of the country.—*n.* ruralisa'tion, -z-.—*v.t.* ru'ralise, -ize to render rural.—*v.i.* to rusticate.—*ns.* ru'ralism; ru'ralist; rurality (*-al'i-ti*).—*adv.* ru'rally.—*n.* ru'ralness.—*adj.* ruridecanal (*rōō-ri-di-kā'nl*; sometimes *-dek'ən-l*) of a rural dean(ery).—**rural dean** see **dean[2]**. [L. *rūrālis—rūs, rūris*, the country.]

Ruritania *rōōr-i-tān'yə, n.* a fictitious land of historical romance (in S.E. Europe) discovered by Anthony Hope.—*n.* and *adj.* **Rurita'nian.**

Rusa *rōō'sə, n.* the genus of deer containing the sambar (without *cap.*) a sambar. [Malay *rūsa*.]

ruse *rōōz, n.* a trick, stratagem, artifice. [O.Fr. *ruse*—*ruser, reüser*, to get out of the way, double on one's tracks; see **rush[1]**.]

rush[1] *rush, v.i.* to move forward with haste, impetuosity, or rashness.—*v.t.* to force out of place: to hasten or hustle forward, or into any action: to move, transport, drive, push, in great haste: to capture, secure, by a rush: to overcharge (*coll.*).—*n.* a swift impetuous forward movement: a sudden simultaneous or general movement (as a *gold rush*): an onset: a stampede: a migratory movement or body: a run upon anything: an unedited print of a motion picture scene or series of scenes for immediate viewing by the film makers: rapidly increased activity: bustling activity: a feeling of euphoria experienced after the taking of a drug (*slang*): a sound of rushing.—*adj.* (*coll.*) done or needing to be done quickly.—*n.* rush'er.—**rush hour** one of the times during the day of maximum activity or traffic; **rush one's fences** to act precipitately. [A.Fr. *russcher*, O.Fr. *reusser, reüser, ruser* (Fr. *ruser*); see **ruse**.]

rush[2] *rush, n.* any plant of the grass-like marsh-growing genus Juncus: a stalk or round stalk-like leaf of such a plant: extended to various more or less similar plants (see **bulrush**): a type of something of no value or importance.—*adj.* of rush or rushes.—*n.* rush'iness.—*adjs.* rush'-like; rush'y; rush'-bottomed having a seat made with rushes, rush'light a candle or night-light having a wick of rush-pith: a small, feeble light. [O.E. *risce*.]

rusk *rusk, n.* a small cake like a piece of very hard toast. [Sp. *rosca*, a roll.]

russel *rus'l, n.* a ribbed cotton and woollen material.—**russ'el-cord** a kind of rep made of cotton and wool. [Poss. Flem. *Rijssel*, Lille.]

russet *rus'it, n.* a coarse homespun cloth: a reddish-brown colour: a reddish-brown variety of apple.—*adj.* made of russet: reddish-brown.—*adj.* russ'ety. [O.Fr. *rousset*—L. *russus*, red.]

Russian *rush'(y)ən, adj.* of Russia or its people.—*n.* a native or citizen of Russia: the Slavonic language of most Russians.—*ns.* **russ'ia** russia leather; **Russianisā'tion**, -z-.—*v.t.* **Russ'ianise, -ize** to give Russian characteristics to: to make Russian.—*ns.* **Russ'ianism; Russ'ianist; Russification** (*rus-i-fi-kā'shən*).—*v.t.* **Russ'ify** to Russianise.—*ns.* (*arch.*) **Russ'ky, Russ'ki** (*slang, usu. derog.*) Russian; **Russ'ophil(e)** one who favours Russian policy (also *adj.*); **Russoph'ilism; Russoph'ilist; Russ'ophobe** one who dreads or hates the Russians (also *adj.*); **Russophō'bia** the dread of Russian policy.—**russia** (or **Russia**) **leather** a fine brownish-red leather with a characteristic odour; **Russian boots** wide, calf-length leather boots; **Russian roulette** an act of bravado, specif. that of loading a revolver with one bullet, spinning the cylinder, and firing at one's own head.

rust *rust, n.* the reddish-brown coating on iron exposed to moisture: any similar coating or appearance: a plant disease characterised by a rusty appearance, caused by various fungi: a fungus causing such disease: injurious influence or consequence, esp. of mental inactivity or idleness: the colour of rust.—*v.i.* to become rusty: to affect with rust: to become dull or inefficient by inaction.—*v.t.* to make rusty: to impair by time and inactivity.—*adj.* **rust'ed.**—*adv.* **rust'ily.**—*n.* **rust'iness.**—*n.* and *adj.* **rust'ing.**—*adjs.* **rust'less** free from rust: proof against rust; **rust'y** covered with rust: impaired by inactivity, out of practice: rust-coloured: time-worn: rough: raucous: discoloured.—*adj.* **rust'-coloured.**—*adjs.* **rust'-proof; rust'-resistant.** [O.E. *rūst.*]

rustic *rus'tik, adj.* of, or characteristic of, the country or country-dwellers: country-dwelling: like countryfolk or their works: simple and plain: awkward: uncouth: unrefined: roughly made: made of rough branches: of masonry, with sunken or chamfered joints, sometimes with roughened face.—*n.* a peasant.—*adv.* **rus'tically.**—*v.t.* **rust'icate** to send into the country: to banish for a time from town or college: to build in rustic masonry.—*v.i.* to live in the country: to become rustic.—*ns.* **rusticā'tion; rust'icator.**—*v.t.* and *v.i.* **rus'ticise, -ize** (*-ti-sīz*).—*n.* **rusticity** (*-tis'i-ti*) rustic manner: simplicity: rudeness.—**rus'tic-work** rusticated masonry: summer-houses, etc., of rough branches. [L. *rūsticus—rūs,* the country.]

rustle *rus'l, v.i.* to make a soft, whispering sound, as of dry leaves: to go about with such a sound: to stir about, hustle (*U.S.*): to steal cattle (*U.S.*).—*v.t.* to cause to rustle: to get by rustling (*U.S.*).—*n.* a quick succession of small sounds, as that of dry leaves: a rustling: bustle (*U.S.*).—*n.* **rus'tler.**—*n.* and *adj.* **rus'tling.**—*adv.* **rus'tlingly.**—**rustle up** to arrange, gather together. [Imit.; cf. Flem. *ruysselen.*]

rusty. See **rust.**

rut[1] *rut, n.* a furrow made by wheels: a fixed course difficult to depart from.—*v.t.* to furrow with ruts: —*pr.p.* **rutt'ing;** *pa.t.* and *pa.p.* **rutt'ed.**—*adj.* **rutt'y.**—**in a rut** following a tedious routine from which it is difficult to escape.

rut[2] *rut, n.* sexual excitement in male deer: also in other animals.—*v.i.* to be in such a period of sexual excitement.—*n.* and *adj.* **rutt'ing.**—*adj.* **rutt'ish.** [O.Fr. *ruit, rut*—L. *rugītus—rugīre,* to roar.]

rutabaga *rōō-tə-bā'gə,* (*U.S.*) *n.* the Swedish turnip. [Sw. dial. *rotabagge.*]

ruth *rōōth, n.* pity: remorse: sorrow.—*adj.* **ruth'ful** pitiful, sorrowful.—*adv.* **ruth'fully.**—*adj.* **ruth'less** pitiless: unsparing.—*adv.* **ruth'lessly.**—*n.* **ruth'lessness.** [M.E. *ruthe, reuth;* see **rue**[2]; ending influenced by Scand., as O.N. *hryggth.*]

ruthenium *rōō-thē'ni-əm, n.* a metallic element (symbol Ru; at. numb. 44) of the platinum group, found in the Ural Mountains. [L.L. *Ruthenia,* Russia.]

rutherford *rudh'ər-fərd, n.* a unit of radioactive disintegration, equal to a million disintegrations a second—abbrev. **rd.**—*n.* **rutherford'ium** the U.S. name for the transuranic element (symbol Rf; at. numb. 104), called by the Russians kurchatovium. [After the physicist Baron *Rutherford* (1871–1937).]

ruthful, ruthless, etc. See **ruth.**

rutile *rōō'tīl, n.* a reddish-brown mineral of the tetragonal system, titanium oxide. [L. *rutilus,* reddish.]

rutty, etc. See **rut**[1].

rye[1] *rī, n.* a grass (*Secale,* esp. *S. cereale*) allied to wheat and barley: its grain, used for making bread: rye-whisky.—*adj.* of rye.—**rye'-bread; rye'-flour; rye'-grass** a pasture and fodder grass; **rye'-whis'ky** spirituous beverage made chiefly from rye. [O.E. *ryge.*]

ryot *rī'ət, n.* an Indian peasant. [Hind. *raiyat*—Ar. *ra'iyah,* a subject.]

fāte; fär; mē; hûr (her); *mīne; mōte; fôr; mūte; mōōn; fŏŏt; dhen* (then); *el'ə-mənt* (element)

S

S, s *es*, *n*. the nineteenth letter in our alphabet, a consonant, its usual sound a voiceless sibilant, but often voiced: any mark or object of the form of the letter.

's *z*, *s*, a sentence element used to form the possessive (e.g. *John's, the dog's, one's, the children's*): often also to form the plural of numbers or symbols (e.g. *3's*): a shortened form of **has, is**: a shortened form of **us** (pron. *s*; e.g. *let's go*).

sabadilla *sab-ə-dil'ə*, *n*. the seeds of a liliaceous plant, *Schoenocaulon*, yielding veratrine.—Also **cebadill'a, cevadill'a**. [Sp. *cebadilla*, dim. of *cebada*, barley.]

Sabaoth *sa-bā'oth*, *n.pl.* armies, used only in the Bible phrase, 'Lord of Sabaoth'. [Heb. *tsebāōth* (transliterated *sabaōth* in Gr.), pl. of *tsabā*, an army.]

Sabbath *sab'əth*, *n*. among the Jews, Saturday, set apart for rest from work: among most Christians, Sunday: a time of rest: (also **sabb'at**) a witches' midnight meeting.—*adj*. of or appropriate to the Sabbath.—*n*. **Sabbatā'rian** one who observes Saturday as Sabbath: one who believes in or practises observance, or strict observance, of the Sabbath (Saturday or Sunday).—Also *adj*.—*n*. **Sabbatā'rianism**.—*adjs*. **Sabb'-athless; sabbatic** (*səb-at'ik*), **-al** pertaining to, or resembling, the Sabbath: (**sabbat'ical**) on, or of, leave from one's work.—*n*. **sabbat'ical** a period of leave from one's work, esp. for teachers and lecturers.—*v.t.* **sabb'atise, -ize** to observe as a Sabbath.—*v.i.* to keep a Sabbath.—*n*. **sabb'atism**.—**Sabb'ath-breaker; Sabb'ath-breaking; Sabb'ath-day; sabbatical year** every seventh year, in which the Israelites allowed their fields and vineyards to lie fallow: a year off, for study, travel, etc. [Heb. *Shabbāth*.]

saber. American spelling of **sabre**.

sabin *sab'in*, *sā'bin*, (*phys.*) *n*. a unit of acoustic absorption. [From Wallace C. *Sabine* (1868–1919), U.S. physicist.]

Sabine *sā'bin*, *n*. one of an ancient people of central Italy, afterwards united with the Romans.—Also *adj*. [L. *Sabīnus*.]

sable¹ *sā'bl*, *n*. an arctic and subarctic marten: its lustrous dark brown fur: a paintbrush of its hair.—*adj*. of sable. [O.Fr.; prob. from Slav.]

sable² *sā'bl*, *n*. and *adj*. black: dark.—*n*. (in *pl*.) mourning garments.—**sable antelope** a large South African antelope, black above, white below.—*adj*. **sa'ble-coloured**. [Fr. *sable*; poss. the same as the foregoing.]

sabot *sab'ō*, *n*. a wooden shoe, as worn by the French peasantry.—*n*. **sab'otage** *-täzh'* malicious destruction: action taken to prevent the achievement of any aim.—Also *v.t.* and *v.i.*—*n*. **saboteur** (*-tœr'*) one who sabotages. [Fr. *sabot*.]

sabra *sä'bra*, *n*. a native-born Israeli, not an immigrant. [Mod. Hebrew *sābrāh*, type of cactus.]

sabre, in U.S. **saber**, *sā'bər*, *n*. a curved, cutting, cavalry sword: a light sword used in fencing.—*v.t.* to wound or kill with a sabre.—**sa'bre-cut**.—*v.i.* **sa'bre-ratt'le**.—**sa'bre-rattling** military bluster; **sa'bre-tooth** (in full **sabre-toothed tiger**) a fossil carnivore with extremely long upper canine teeth. [Fr. *sabre* —Ger. *Sabel* (now *Säbel*).]

sabretache *sab'ər-tash*, *n*. a flat bag slung from a cavalry officer's sword-belt. [Fr. *sabretache*—Ger. *Säbeltasche*—*Säbel*, sabre, *Tasche*, pocket.]

sac *sak*, (*biol.*) *n*. a pouch.—*adjs*. **sacc'ate** pouch-like: enclosed in a sac; **sacciform** (*sak'si-form*), **sacc'ûlar** sac-like; **sacc'ûlated** formed in a series of sac-like expansions: enclosed.—*ns*. **sacculâ'tion; sacc'ûle, sacc'ûlus** a small sac:—*pl*. **sacc'ules, sacc'uli**. [L. *saccus*, a bag; see **sack¹**.]

Saccharum *sak'ə-rəm*, *n*. the sugar-cane genus of grasses.—*ns*. **sacch'aride** a carbohydrate: a compound with sugar; **saccharim'eter** an instrument for testing concentration of sugar solutions; **saccharim'etry; sacch'arin, -ine** (*-in*, *-ēn*) an intensely sweet, white crystalline solid prepared from toluene: sickly sweetness.—*adj*. **sacch'arine** (*-in*, *-ēn*) sugary: of sickly sweetness.—*ns*. **saccharinity** (*-in'i-ti*); **saccharom'eter** a hydrometer or other instrument for measuring concentration of sugar solutions; **sacch'arose** (*-ōs*) any carbohydrate, esp. cane sugar. [L. *saccharum*—Gr. *sakcharon*, sugar, a word of Eastern origin.]

sacciform, saccular, etc. See **sac**.

sacerdotal *sas-ər-dō'tl*, *adj*. priestly.—*v.t.* **sacerdō'talise, -ize** to render sacerdotal.—*ns*. **sacerdō'talism** the spirit of the priesthood: devotion to priestly interests: priestcraft: attribution to a priesthood of special or supernatural powers: excessive influence of priests (*derog.*); **sacerdō'talist**.—*adv*. **sacerdō'tally**. [L. *sacerdōs, -ōtis*, a priest—*sacer*, sacred, *dāre*, to give.]

sachem *sā'chəm*, *n*. a North American Indian chief: a political leader (*U.S.*). [Algonquian.]

sachet *sa'shā*, *n*. a bag of perfume, or a bag for holding handkerchiefs, etc.: a small usu. plastic envelope, containing a liquid, cream, etc., such as shampoo. [Fr.]

sack¹ *sak*, *n*. a large bag of coarse material: a sackful: a varying measure of capacity: a woman's gown, loose at the back (*hist.*): a train hung from the shoulders of such a gown: a woman's loose-fitting waistless dress: (with **the**) dismissal (*coll.*): bed (*slang*).—*v.t.* to put into a sack: to dismiss (*coll.*).—*ns*. **sack'ful**:—*pl*. **sack'fuls; sack'ing** sackcloth.—**sack'cloth** cloth for sacks: coarse cloth, formerly worn in mourning or penance.—**sack'-race** one which each runner's legs are encased in a sack.—**in sackcloth and ashes** showing extreme regret, etc. (*facet.*). [O.E. *sacc*— L. *saccus*—Gr. *sakkos*; prob. Phoenician.]

sack² *sak*, *n*. the plundering or devastation of a town: pillage.—*v.t.* to plunder: to ravage. [Fr. *sac*; according to some the same as the foregoing (putting in a bag).]

sack³ *sak*, *n*. the old name of a Spanish wine, the favourite drink of Falstaff. [Fr. *sec*—L. *siccus*, dry.]

sackbut *sak'but*, *n*. an old instrument with a slide like the trombone. [Fr. *saquebute*, perh. O.Fr. *saquier*, to draw out, and *bouter*, to push.]

sacra, sacral. See **sacrum**.

sacral *sā'krəl*, *adj*. of or relating to sacred rites. [L. *sacrum*, a sacred object.]

sacrament *sak'rə-mənt*, *n*. a religious rite variously regarded as a channel or as a sign of grace—amongst Protestants generally *Baptism* and the *Lord's Supper* —amongst Roman Catholics, also *Confirmation, Penance, Holy Orders, Matrimony*, and *Extreme Unction*: the Lord's Supper specially: the bread or wine in the Lord's Supper: a symbol of something spiritual or secret: a sign, token, or pledge of a covenant.—*v.t.* to bind by an oath.—*adj.* **sacramental** (*-ment'l*).—*n.* (*R.C*) an act or object which may transmit or receive grace.—*ns.* **sacramen'talism; sacramen'talist** one who attaches importance to the spiritual nature of the sacraments.—*adv.* **sacramen'tally.**—**take the sacrament upon** or **to** to take communion in confirmation of (an oath). [L *sacrāmentum*, an oath, pledge—*sacrāre*, to consecrate—*sacer*, sacred.]

sacrarium *sä-krā'ri-əm*, L. *sa-kra'ri-ōōm*, *n.* the presbytery of a church:—*pl.* **sacra'ria.** [L. *sacrārium*— *sacer*, holy.]

sacred *sä'krid*, *adj.* consecrated: devoted: set apart or dedicated, esp. to God: holy: proceeding from God: religious: entitled to veneration: not to be violated.— *adv.* **sa'credly.**—*n.* **sa'credness.**—**Sacred College** the body of cardinals; **sacred cow** an institution, custom, etc., so venerated that it is above criticism (*coll.*), **Sacred Heart** (*R.C.*) the physical heart of Christ, adored with special devotion. [Pa.p. of obs. *sacre*— O.Fr. *sacrer*—L. *sacrāre*—*sacer*, sacred.]

sacrifice *sak'ri-fīs*, *n.* the offering of a slaughtered animal on an altar to a god: any offering to a god: Christ's offering of himself (*theol.*): the Mass (*R.C.*): destruction, surrender, or foregoing of anything valued for the sake of anything else, esp. a higher consideration: loss by selling cheap: a victim offered in sacrifice.—*v.t.* to offer up in sacrifice: to make a sacrifice of: to give up for a higher good or for mere advantage: to make a victim of: to allow to come to destruction or evil.—*v.i.* to offer sacrifice.— *n.* **sac'rificer.**—*adj.* **sacrificial** (*-fish'l*).—*adv.* **sacrifi'cially.** [L. *sacrificium*—*sacer*, sacred, *facĕre*, to make.]

sacrilege *sak'ri-lij*, *n.* a profanation of anything holy: the breaking into a place of worship and stealing therefrom (also *fig.*).—*adj.* **sacrilegious** (*-lij'əs*).— *adv.* **sacrile'giously.**—*ns.* **sacrile'giousness; sacrile'gist.** [Fr. *sacrilège*—L. *sacrilegium*—*sacer*, sacred, *legĕre*, to gather.]

sacring *sä'kring*, (*arch.*) *n.* consecration.—**sacring bell** in R.C. churches, a small bell rung to call attention to the more solemn parts of the service of the Mass. [See **sacred.**]

sacrist *sak'rist*, *sä'krist*, *n.* a sacristan.—*ns.* **sacristan** (*sak'*) an officer in a church who has care of the sacred vessels and other movables: a sexton; **sacristy** (*sak'*) an apartment in a church where the sacred utensils, vestments, etc., are kept: vestry. [L.L. *sacrista, sacristānus*, a sacristan, *sacristia*, a vestry—L. *sacer*.]

sacro-. See **sacrum.**

sacrosanct *sak'rō-sang(k)t*, *adj.* inviolable.—*n.* **sacrosanc'tity.** [L. *sacrōsanctus*—*sacer*, sacred, *sanctus*, pa.p. of *sancīre*, to hallow.]

sacrum *sä'krəm*, *sak'rəm*, *n.* a triangular bone composed of fused vertebrae wedged between two innominate bones, so as to form the keystone of the pelvic arch:—*pl.* **sa'cra.**—*adj.* **sa'cral—sa'crō-** in composition, sacrum, e.g. *adj.* **sacroil'iac** pertaining to the sacrum and ilium. [L. (*os*) *sacrum*, holy (bone), so called for unknown reason.]

sad *sad*, (*compar.* **sadd'er**, *superl.* **sadd'est**) *adj.* serious (*arch.*): grave: sober-minded: sorrowful: deplorable (often playfully): heavy, stiff: doughy: sober, dark-coloured.—*v.t.* **sadd'en** to make sad.— *v.i.* to grow sad.—*adj.* **sadd'ish.**—*adv.* **sad'ly** in a sad manner: unfortunately, sad to relate.—*n.* **sad'ness.**— *adjs.* **sad'-coloured; sad'-eyed, -faced, -hearted.** [O.E. *sæd*, sated; cf. Du. *zat*, Ger. *satt*; L. *sat, satis.*]

saddhu. See **sadhu.**

saddle *sad'l*, *n.* a seat for a rider: a pad for the back of a

draught animal: anything of like shape: a col: that part of the back on which the saddle is placed: a mark on that part: a butcher's cut including a part of the backbone with the ribs: the hinder part of a cock's back in a structure, e.g. a bridge, a support having a groove shaped to fit another part.—*v.t.* to put a saddle on: to encumber: to impose as a burden or encumbrance: (of a trainer) to be responsible for preparing and entering (a racehorse) for a race.—*adj* **sadd'leless.**—*ns.* **sadd'ler** a maker or seller of saddles: a soldier who has charge of cavalry saddles; **sadd'lery** the occupation of a saddler: his shop or stock-in-trade: a saddle-room.—**sadd'leback** a saddle-shaped hill, animal, etc.: a saddle-roof.—*adj.* (also **sadd'lebacked**) saddle-shaped: with a depression in the middle of the back: marked on the back: sloping from the middle to each side.—**sadd'le-bag** a bag carried at, or attached to, the saddle; **sadd'le-bow** (*-bō*) the arched front of a saddle; **sadd'le-cloth** a housing cloth placed under a saddle.—*adj.* **sadd'le-fast** firmly seated in the saddle.—**sadd'le-girth** a band that holds the saddle in its place; **sadd'le-horse** a riding horse; **sadd'le-roof** a tower roof with two gables.—*adj.* **sadd'le-sore** chafed with riding.— **saddle soap** a kind of soap used for cleaning and treating leather; **sadd'le-tree** the frame of a saddle.— **in the saddle** in control. [O.E. *sadol, sadel*; cf. Du *zadel*, Ger. *Sattel*.]

Sadducee *sad'ū-sē*, *n.* one of a Jewish priestly and aristocratic party of traditionalists, whose reactionary conservatism resisted the progressive views of the Pharisees, and who rejected, among various other beliefs, that of life after death.—*adj.* **Sadducean** (*-sē'ən*).—*ns.* **Sadd'uceeism, Sadd'ucism.** [Gr. *Saddoukaios*—Heb. *Tsadûqīm*, from *Zadok* the High Priest, the founder.]

sadhu, saddhu *sä'dōō*, *n.* a Hindu holy man, ascetic and mendicant. [Sans. *sādhu*,—*adj.*, straight, pious.]

sadism *sād'izm*, *n.* love of cruelty.—*n.* **sad'ist.**—*adj.* **sadistic** (*sə-dis'*).—*ns.* **sado-mas'ochism** obtaining pleasure by inflicting pain on oneself or another; **sado-mas'ochist.**—*adj.* **sado-masochist'ic.** [Comte (called Marquis) de *Sade* (1740–1814), who died insane, notoriously depicted this form of pleasure in his novels.]

saeter *set'ər*, *sät'*, *n.* in Norway, an upland meadow which provides summer pasture for cattle. [Norw.]

safari *sə-fä'rē*, *n.* an expedition for hunting in Africa: a long expedition involving difficulty and requiring planning.—**safari park** an enclosed park where wild animals (mostly non-native) are kept uncaged in the open on view to the public; **safari suit** a suit for men, boys, or women, typically of cotton and consisting of long square-cut **safari jacket** and long or short trousers. [Swahili.]

safe *sāf*, *adj.* unharmed: free from danger: secure: sound: certain: sure: reliable: cautious.—*n.* a chest or closet, safe against fire, thieves, etc.: a ventilated box or cupboard for meat, etc.—**safe'ly.**—*ns.* **safe'ness; safe'ty** the state or fact of being safe: a safeguard.— **safe'-blower; safe'-blowing** forcing of safes, using explosives; **safe'-breaker, -cracker; safe'-breaking, -cracking** illegal opening of safes; **safe'-con'duct** a permission to pass or travel with guarantee of freedom from molestation; **safe'-deposit, safe'ty-deposit** a safe storage for valuables, **safe'guard** keeping safe, protection: a contrivance, condition, or provision to secure safety.—*v.t.* to protect.—**safe house** (*coll.*) a place unknown to one's pursuers, where one can safely hide; **safe'-keeping** keeping in safety: safe custody; **safe period** that part of the menstrual cycle during which conception is most unlikely; **safe seat** a seat that the specified political party will certainly win in an election; **safe'ty-belt** a belt for fastening a workman, etc., to a fixed object while he carries out a dangerous operation: one fastening a passenger to his seat as a precaution against injury in a crash; **safe'ty-catch** any catch to secure safety, as in a miners' cage or a gun; **safety curtain** a fireproof theatre curtain; **safety factor** the ratio between the ultimate stress in a member, structure, or material, and the safe permissible stress in it; **safety film** photographic or cinematographic film with a non-flammable or slow-burning base of cellulose acetate or polyester; **safety fuse** a slow-burning fuse that can be lighted at a safe distance: a fuse inserted for safety in an electric circuit; **safety glass** a sandwich of plastic between sheets of glass: glass reinforced with wire, or toughened; **safety lamp** a miners' lamp that will not ignite inflammable gases; **safety lock** in firearms, a device for preventing accidental discharge; **safe'ty-match** a match that can be ignited only on a prepared surface; **safe'ty-net** a net stretched beneath an acrobat, etc., during a rehearsal or performance, in case he or she should fall: any precautionary measure (*fig.*); **safe'ty-pin** a pin in the form of a clasp with a guard covering its point: a pin for locking a piece of machinery, a grenade, a mine, etc.; **safety razor** a razor with protected blade; **safe'ty-valve** a valve that opens when the pressure becomes too great: any outlet that gives relief.—**err on the safe side** to choose the safer alternative; **safe and sound** secure and uninjured; **safe as houses** (*coll.*) very safe. [O.Fr. *sauf*—L. *salvus*.]

saffian *saf'i-ən, n.* leather tanned with sumach and dyed in bright colours. [Russ. *saf'yan.*]

safflower *saf'lowr, n.* a thistle-like composite (*Carthamus tinctorius*) cultivated in India: its dried petals, used for making a red dye and rouge.—**safflower oil** an oil produced from this plant and used in cooking, etc. [Cf. Du. *saffloer*, O.Fr. *saffleur.*]

saffron *saf'rən, n.* a species of crocus: its dried stigmas, used as a dye and flavouring: its colour, orange-yellow.—*adjs.* **saff'roned**; **saff'rony.**—*n.* **saf'ranin(e)** a coal-tar dye, giving various colours.—**saffron cake** a cake flavoured with saffron. [O.Fr. *safran* —Ar. *za'faran.*]

sag *sag, v.i.* to bend, sink, or hang down, esp. in the middle: to yield or give way as from weight or pressure: to droop: to move, drift, to leeward:—*pr.p.* **sagg'ing**; *pa.p.* and *pa.t.* **sagged.**—*n.* a droop.—*n.* and *adj.* **sagg'ing.** [Cf. Sw. *sacka*, to sink down.]

saga *sä'gə, n.* a prose tale of the deeds of Icelandic or Norwegian heroes in the old literature of Iceland: a body of legend about some subject: a long, detailed story (*coll.*).—**saga novel** see **roman fleuve**. [O.N. *saga*; cf. **saw³**.]

sagacious *sə-gā'shəs, adj.* keen in perception or thought: discerning and judicious: wise.—*adv.* **sagā'ciously.**—*ns.* **sagā'ciousness, sagacity** (*-gas'i-ti*). [L. *sagāx, -ācis.*]

sagamore *sag'ə-mōr, n.* an American Indian chief. [Penobscot *sagamo*; cf. **sachem.**]

sage¹ *sāj, n.* a garden labiate plant (*Salvia officinalis*) used as stuffing for goose, etc.—**sage'brush** a shrubby aromatic plant growing on dry American plains; **sage Derby** a kind of sage-cheese; **sage'-cheese** a cheese flavoured and mottled with sage leaves; **sage'-grouse** a large North American grouse that feeds on sage-brush; **sage'-green** greyish green, as sage leaves. [O.Fr. *sauge* (It. *salvia*)—L. *salvia—salvus*, safe.]

sage² *sāj, adj.* wise.—*n.* a man of great wisdom.—*adv.* **sage'ly.**—*n.* **sage'ness.** [Fr. *sage*, ult.—L. *sapēre*, to be wise.]

saggar, sagger *sag', ns.* a clay box in which pottery is packed for baking. [Perh. **safeguard.**]

sagged, sagging. See **sag.**

sagger. See **saggar.**

sagitta *sə-jit'ə, n.* a versed sine.—*adj.* **sagittal** (*saj'it-l*) arrow-shaped: pertaining or parallel to the sagittal suture.—*adv.* **sag'ittally.**—**sagittal suture** that between the two parietal bones of the skull. [L. *sagitta*, an arrow.]

sago *sā'gō, n.* a nutritive farinaceous substance produced from the pith of *Metroxylon* and other palms. —**sa'go-palm.** [Malay *sāgū.*]

saguaro *sa-(g)wä'rō, n.* the giant cactus:—*pl.* **sagua'ros.** [From an American Indian language.]

Saharan *sə-här'ən, adj.* of, resembling, or characteristic of, the Sahara desert.

sahib *sa'ib, n.* a term of respect given in India, Sir or Mr. [Ar *sāhib*, orig. friend.]

said *sed, pa.t.* and *pa.p.* of **say.**—*adj.* before-mentioned.—**saidst, saidest** see **say.**

saiga *si'gə, n* a west Asian antelope. [Russ.]

sail *sāl, n.* a sheet of canvas, framework of slats, or other structure, spread to catch the wind, so as to propel a ship, drive a windmill, etc.: any sail-like organ or object: sails collectively: a ship or ships: a trip in a vessel: an act or distance of sailing: a number sailing together: a condition of having sails set or filled.—*v.i.* to progress or travel by sail: to go by water: to set out on a voyage: to make excursions in sailing-craft: to glide or float smoothly along.—*v.t.* to navigate: to cause to sail, as a toy boat: to pass over or along in a ship: to fly through.—*adjs.* **sail'able** navigable; **sailed** having sails.—*ns.* **sail'er** a boat or ship that can sail; **sail'ing** travelling or journey by sails or on water: a ship's departure from port: the act or mode of directing a ship's course.—Also *adj.*—*adj.* **sail'less.**—*ns.* **sail'or** one who is employed in the management of a ship, esp. one who is not an officer: a mariner: a seaman: a navigator: one who is tolerant of the motion of a ship; **sail'oring** occupation as a sailor.—*adjs.* **sail'orless; sail'or-like, sail'orly.**—**sail'-board** a small, light, flat-hulled sailing-craft with a single mast; **sail'-boarding** the sport of sailing this (also called **windsurfing**); **sail'-boat** (esp. *U.S.*) a sailing-boat; **sail'-cloth** a strong cloth for sails; **sail'-fish** a fish that shows a large dorsal fin, esp. the basking shark; **sail'ing-boat** a boat moved by sails; **sail'ing-master** an officer in charge of navigation, esp. of a yacht; **sailing orders** instructions to the captain of a ship at setting forth on a voyage; **sail'ing-ship** a ship driven by sails; **sail'-maker; sail'or-hat** a lady's hat like a man's straw hat: a hat with a wide, upcurved brim; **sail'or-man** a seaman; **sail'or-suit** a child's outfit resembling that of a sailor; **sail'plane** a glider that can rise with an upward current—**full sail** with sails filled with the wind: with all sails set; **good, bad, sailor** a person who is unaffected, made ill, by the motion of a ship; **make sail** to spread more canvas; **put on sail** to set more sails in order to travel more quickly; **sail close to** (or **near**) **the wind** see **wind**; **set sail** to spread the sails: to set forth on a voyage (for); **shorten sail** to reduce its extent; **strike sail** to lower the sail or sails: **under sail** having the sails spread: moved by sails. [O.E. *segel*; cf. Du. *zeil*, Ger. *Segel.*]

sainfoin *sān'foin, n.* a leguminous fodder-plant.— Also **saint'foin.** [Fr. *sainfoin*, prob.—*sain*, wholesome, *foin*, hay—L. *sānum fēnum.*]

saint *sānt*, when prefixed to a name *sint, sn(t), adj.* (or *n.* in apposition) holy.—*n.* a holy person: one eminent for virtue: an Israelite, a Christian, or one of the blessed dead (*B.*): one canonised: a member of various religious bodies, esp. Puritans, as used of themselves or as a nickname.—*v.t.* to make a saint of: to hail as saint.—*n.* **saint'dom.**—*adj.* **saint'ed** made a saint, holy: gone to heaven.—*n.* **saint'hood.**—*adj.*

saint'like.—*n.* **saint'liness.**—*adj.* **saint'ly** of, like, characteristic of, or befitting a saint.—*n.* **saint'ship.** —**saint's day** a day set apart for the commemoration of a particular saint; **St Agnes's Eve** 20th January; **St Andrew's cross** a cross in the form of the letter X: a white saltire on a blue field, as borne on the banner of Scotland; **St Bernard's dog** or **(great) St Bernard** a breed of very large dogs, named after the hospice of the Great St Bernard, used, especially formerly, to rescue travellers lost in the snow; **St Elmo's fire** an electrical brush discharge forming a glow about a masthead, etc.; **St George's cross** a red cross on a white field; **St James's** the British court; **St John's wort** any Hypericum; **St Leger** a horse-race run at Doncaster, called from Col. *St Leger*; **St Stephen's Houses of Parliament**; **St Swithin's Day** 15th July; **St Vitus's dance** chorea. [Fr.,—L. *sanctus*, holy.]

saintfoin. See **sainfoin.**

Saintpaulia *sänt-pö'li-ə, n.* the genus to which the African violet (q.v.) belongs. [Baron Walter von *Saint Paul*, who discovered it.]

saith *seth*, (*arch.*) *3rd pers. sing. pres. indic.* of **say.**

sake[1] *sä'ki, sä'kē, n.* a Japanese alcoholic drink made from fermented rice.—Also **saké, saki.** [Jap.]

sake[2] *sāk, n.* a cause: account: regard: advantage: behalf: purpose: aim, object.—**for old sake's, times', sake** for the sake of old times, for auld lang syne; **for the sake of** in order to, for the purpose of. [O.E. *sacu*, strife, a lawsuit.]

saker *sä'kər, n.* a species of falcon (*Falco sacer*) used in hawking, esp. the female: an obsolete small cannon. —*n.* **sa'keret** the male saker. [Fr. *sacre*, prob.—Ar. *saqr*, confounded with L. *sacer*, sacred.]

saki[1] *sä'ki, -kē, n.* a South American monkey of the genus *Pithecia*, with long bushy non-prehensile tail. [Fr., for Tupí *sai*, or *saguin*.]

saki[2]. See **sake**[1].

sal[1] *säl, n.* a tree (*Shorea robusta*) of north India with teaklike wood. [Hind. *sāl*.]

sal[2] *sal*, (*chem.* and *pharmacy*) *n.* a salt.—**sal ammoniac** ammonium chloride; **sal volatile** (*vol-at'i-li*) ammonium carbonate, or a solution of it in alcohol and/or ammonia in water: smelling salts. [L. *sāl*.]

salaam *sä-läm', n.* a word and gesture of salutation in the East, chiefly among Muslims: obeisance: greeting.—*v.i.* to perform the salaam. [Ar. *salām*, peace; cf. Heb. *shālōm*.]

salable, salableness, salably. See **sale.**

salacious *sə-lā'shəs, adj.* lustful: lecherous: arousing lustful or lecherous feelings.—*adv.* **sala'ciously.**—*ns.* **sala'ciousness, salacity** (*-las'i-ti*). [L. *salāx, -ācis salīre*, to leap.]

salad *sal'əd, ns.* a cold dish of vegetables or herbs (either raw or pre-cooked), generally mixed: a plant grown for or used in salads: a confused mixture.— **salad cream** a type of bottled mayonnaise; **salad days** one's youth, esp. if carefree and showing inexperience; **salad dressing, oil** sauce, olive-oil, used in dressing salads; **salad herb, plant; salad plate.**— **fruit'-salad** see **fruit.** [Fr. *salade*—L. *sāl*, salt.]

salade. Same as **sallet.**

salamander *sal'ə-man-dər*, or *-man', n.* a member of a genus of tailed amphibians, closely related to the newts, harmless, but long dreaded as poisonous, once supposed able to live in fire or to put out fire: an elemental spirit believed by Paracelsists to live in fire: a poker used red-hot for kindling fires: a hot metal plate for browning meat, etc.—*adjs.* **salaman'drian; salaman'drine; salaman'droid** (also *n.*). [Fr. *salamandre*—L. *salamandra*—Gr. *salamandrā*; prob. of Eastern origin.]

salami *sə-lä'mi, sə-lä'mē, n.* a highly seasoned Italian sausage. [It., *pl.* of **salame.**]

salangane *sal'əng-gãn, n.* a swiftlet (*Collocalia*) that builds edible nests. [Tagálog *salangan*.]

salary *sal'ə-ri, n.* a periodical payment (usually at longer intervals than a week) for services other than mechanical.—*v.t.* to pay a salary to.—*n.* **salariat** (*sə-lä'ri-ət*) the salary-drawing class or body.—*adj.* **sal'aried.** [O.Fr. *salarie* (Fr. *salaire*)—L. *salārium*, salt-money, *sāl*, salt.]

salchow *sal'kov, n.* in ice-skating, a jump in which the skater takes off from the inside back edge of one skate, spins in the air and lands on the outside back edge of the other skate. [From Ulrich *Salchow*, 20th cent. Swedish skater.]

sale *sāl, n.* act of selling: the exchange of anything for money: power or opportunity of selling: demand: public offer of goods to be sold, esp. at reduced prices or by auction: the state of being offered to buyers.— *adj.* intended for selling: vendible.—*n.* **salabil'ity** (also **saleabil'ity**).—*adj.* **sal(e)'able** that may be sold: in good demand.—*n.* **sal(e)'ableness.**—*adv.* **sal(e)'ably.**—**sale'-cat'alogue; sale'-price** price asked at a special sale; **sale'-room** an auction-room; **sales'-clerk** (*U.S.*) one who sells in a store or shop; **sales'man** a man who sells goods, esp. in a shop (*fems.* **sales'woman, sales'girl, sales'lady**): a commercial traveller; **sales'manship** the art of selling: skill in presenting wares in the most attractive light or in persuading purchasers to buy; **sales'person; sales resistance** unwillingness to buy; **sales'-talk** boosting talk to effect a sale; **sales'-tax** a tax on the sale of goods and services, esp. one general in character and flat in rate.—**sale of work** a sale of things made by members of a church congregation or association so as to raise money; **sale or, and, return** an arrangement by which a retailer may return to the wholesaler any goods he does not sell. [Late O.E. *salu*, perh.— O.N. *sala*.]

salep *sal'ep, n.* dried Orchis tubers: a food or drug prepared from them. [Turk. *sālep*, from Ar.]

saleratus *sal-ə-rā'təs, (U.S.) n.* potassium or sodium bicarbonate, used in baking-powders. [L. *sāl aerātus*, aerated salt.]

Salesian *səl-ē'shən, adj.* of St Francis of *Sales* or his order, the Visitants.—*n.* a follower of St Francis: a member of his order.

salet. See **sallet.**

Salian *sä'li-ən, adj.* pertaining to a tribe of Franks on the lower Rhine.—*n.* one of this tribe.—*adj.* **Salic** (*sal'ik, sā'lik*).—**Salic law** a law among the Salian Franks limiting the succession of certain lands to males—held later to apply to the succession to the crown of France. [L. *Salii*, Salians.]

Salicaceae *sal-i-kā'si-ē, n.pl.* the family of willows and poplars.—*adj.* **salica'ceous** (*-shəs*).—*ns.* **sal'icet** (*-set*), **salicional** (*sal-ish'ə-nəl*) organ stops with tones like that of willow pipes; **sal'icin(e)** (*-sin*) a bitter crystalline glucoside got from willow-bark, etc.; **salicylate** (*sə-lis'i-lāt*) a salt of salicylic acid.—*adj.* **salicylic** (*sal-i-sil'ik*; Gr. *hýlē*, matter, material).— **salicylic acid** an acid originally prepared from salicin. [L. *salix, salicis*, a willow.]

salient *sä'li-ənt, adj.* leaping or springing: projecting outwards, as an angle: outstanding: striking.—*n.* an outward-pointing angle, esp. of a fortification or line of defences.—*ns.* **sa'lience; sa'liency.**—*n.pl.* **Salientia** (*-en'shyə*) the frog and toad order of Amphibia.—*adv.* **sa'liently.**—**salient point** first rudiment. [L. *saliēns, -entis*, pr.p. of *salīre*, to leap.]

saliferous *sə-lif'ər-əs, adj.* salt-bearing. [L. *sāl, salis*, salt, *ferre*, to bear.]

salina *sə-lē'nə*, or *-lī', n.* a salt lagoon, lake, marsh, or spring. [Sp.,—L. *salīna*—*sāl*, salt.]

saline *sā'līn, sa', sə-līn', adj.* salt: salty: of the nature of a salt: abounding in salt: of the salts of alkali metals and magnesium.—*n.* (*sə-līn'*, also *sā'lĭn*) a salina: a salt solution.—*ns.* **salinity** (*sə-lin'i-ti*); **salinometer** (*sal-i-nom'i-tər*) a hydrometer for measuring saltness of water. [L. *salīnus*, cf. **salina**.]

saliva *sə-lī'və*, *n.* spittle, a liquid secreted in the mouth to soften food and begin the process of digestion.— *adj.* **salivary** (*sal'i-vər-i*, *sə-lī'*) pertaining to, secreting, or conveying, saliva.—*v.t.* **sal'ivate** to produce or discharge saliva, esp. in excess.—*v.t.* to cause to secrete excess of saliva.—*n.* **saliva'tion** flow of saliva, esp. in excess. [L. *salīva*.]

Salk vaccine *so(l)k vak'sēn*, *-sin*, a vaccine developed by the American Dr Jonas E *Salk* and others, used against poliomyelitis.

sallee *sal'ē* (*Austr.*) *n.* Acacia of various kinds: a species of Eucalyptus. [From a native word.]

sallenders *sal'ən-dərz*, *n.* a skin disease affecting the hocks of horses. [Cf. Fr. *solandre*.]

sallet *sal'it*, *n.* a light helmet (esp. 15th century) with neck-guard.—Also **sal'et**, **salade** (*sa-läd'*). [Fr. *salade*.]

sallow[1] *sal'ō*, *n.* a willow, esp. the broader-leaved kinds.—*adj.* **sall'owy** abounding in sallows. [O.E. (Anglian) *salh*, late stem *salg-* (W.S. *sealh*, *sēales*).]

sallow[2] *sal'ō*, *adj.* esp. of a person's skin, of a pale yellowish colour.—*v.t.* to make sallow.—*adj.* **sall'owish.**—*n.* **sall'owness.** [O.E. *salo*, *salu*; cf. O.H.G. *salo*.]

sally[1] *sal'i*, *n.* an outrush: a sudden rushing forth of troops to attack besiegers: a going forth, excursion: outburst of fancy, wit, etc.—*v.i.* (*arch.* or *facet.*; usu. with *forth*) to rush out suddenly: to set forth, issue:— *pr.p.* **sall'ying**; *pa.t.* and *pa.p.* **sall'ied.**—**sall'yport** a gateway for making a sally from a fortified place: a large port for the escape of the crew from a fire-ship. [Fr. *saillie*—*saillir* (It. *salire*)—L. *salīre*, to leap.]

sally[2] *sal'i*, *n.* the raising of a bell by pull of the rope: the woolly grip of a bell rope. [Perh. from preceding.]

Sally Lunn *sal'i lun'*, a sweet tea-cake, usu. served hot with butter. [From a girl who sold them in the streets of Bath, *c.* 1797.]

sallyport. See **sally**[1].

salmagundi *sal-mə-gun'di*, *n.* a dish of minced meat with eggs, anchovies, vinegar, pepper, etc.: a medley, miscellany.—Also **salmagun'dy.** [Fr. *salmigondis*; origin obscure.]

salmi, salmis *sal'mē*, *n.* a ragout, esp. of game:—*pl.* **salmis** (*sal'mē*). [Fr.; perh. from preceding, or from It. *salame*, sausage.]

salmon *sam'ən*, *n.* a large, highly esteemed fish, with silvery sides, that ascends rivers to spawn: extended to many closely allied fishes, and to some that resemble it superficially in some respects: the flesh of any of these as food: the colour of salmon flesh, a pinkish orange:—*pl.* **salmon**; or **salmons** of kinds of salmon. —*adj.* salmon-coloured.—*adj.* and *n.* **sal'monoid.**— **salm'on-colour** an orange-pink.—*adj.* **salm'on-coloured.**—**salm'on-ladder** a series of steps to permit a salmon to pass upstream; **salm'on-leap** a waterfall ascended by salmon at a leap; **salmon pink**; **salm'on-trout'** a fish like the salmon, but smaller and thicker in proportion: in America applied to various kinds of trout. [O.Fr. *saumon*—L. *salmō*, *-ōnis*, from *salīre*, to leap.]

Salmonella *sal-mə-nel'ə*, *n.* a large genus of bacteria many of which are associated with poisoning by contaminated food: (without *cap.*) a member of the genus:—*pl.* **-as**, **-ae** (*-ē*).—*n.* **salmonellos'is** a disease caused by Salmonella bacteria. [Daniel E. *Salmon*, veterinarian.]

salmonoid. See **salmon.**

salon *sal-ɔ̄*, *-on*, *n.* a drawing-room: a reception-room: a periodic gathering of notable persons in the house of a society queen, literary hostess, etc.: a somewhat elegant shop or business establishment (e.g. *beauty salon*): a room or hall for the exhibiting of paintings, sculptures, etc.: (with *cap.*) a great annual exhibition of works by living artists in Paris. [Fr.]

saloon *sə-lōōn'*, *n.* a spacious hall for receptions, etc.: a large public room (for billiards, for dancing, for hairdressing, etc.): a large public cabin or dining-room for passengers: a saloon-car: a drinking-bar (*U.S.*).—*n.* **saloon'ist.**—**saloon'-bar'** a quieter and more comfortably furnished part of a public house than the public bar, usu. separated from it; **saloon'-car'** a motor-car with enclosed body; **saloon'-deck** an upper deck reserved for saloon-users. [Fr. *salon.*]

Salop *sal'əp*, *n.* Shropshire.—*adj.* **Salopian** (*-ō'pi-ən*) of Shropshire: of Shrewsbury School.—*n.* a native or inhabitant of Shropshire: one educated at Shrewsbury School [A.Fr. *Sloppesberie*—O.E. *Scrobbesbyrig.*]

salopette *sal'ə-pet*, *n.* a type of ski suit consisting of usu. quilted trousers extending to the shoulders and held up with shoulder-straps. [Fr.]

salpinx *sal'pingks*, *n.* the Eustachian tube: the Fallopian tube.—*n.* **salpingectomy** (*-pin-jek'tə-mi*) surgical removal of a Fallopian tube.—*n.* **salpingitis** (*-ji'tis*) inflammation of a Fallopian tube. [Gr. *salpinx*, *-ingos*, a trumpet.]

salse *sals*, *n.* a mud volcano. [*Salsa*, name of one near Modena.]

salsify *sal'si-fi*, *n.* a purple-flowered species of goat's-beard, cultivated for its root, tasting like oysters or asparagus—**black salsify** scorzonera. [Fr. *salsifis*, prob.—It. *sassefrica.*]

salt *solt*, *n.* chloride of sodium, occurring naturally as a mineral (rock-salt) and in solution in sea-water, brine-springs, etc.: smack, savour: piquancy: wit and good sense: saving or preserving quality: a salt-marsh or salting: an influx of salt water: a sailor, esp. an old sailor: a salt-cellar: a compound in which metal atoms or radicals replace one or more of the replaceable hydrogen atoms of an acid—generalised to include the acid itself: (in *pl.*) smelling-salts: Epsom salt or other salt or mixture of salts used in medicine, esp. as a purgative.—*adj.* containing salt: tasting of salt: seasoned or cured with salt: overflowed with salt water: growing in salt soil: inhabiting salt water: pungent.—*v.t.* to sprinkle, season, cure, impregnate with salt: to season: to acclimatise: to assign an excessive value to or in (*slang*): to add gold, ore, etc., to, in order to give a false appearance of riches (*mining slang*).—*adj.* **salt'ed.**—**salt'er** one who salts, or who makes or deals in salt: a drysalter.—*adv.* **salt'ily.**—*n.* **salt'iness; salt'ing** the act of preserving, seasoning, etc., with salt: a meadow flooded by the tides (suff. *-ing*, indicating a meadow in place-names).—*adj.* **salt'ish.**—*adv.* **salt'ishly.**—*n.* **salt'ishness.**—*adj.* **salt'less.**—*adv.* **salt'ly.**—*n.* **salt'ness.**—*adj.* **salt'y** saltish: piquant, racy, witty.—**salt'-bush** any Australian shrubby plant of the goosefoot family; **salt'-cat** a salt mixture given as a digestive to pigeons; **salt'-cellar** (O.Fr. *saliere*—L. *salārium*—*sāl*, salt) a table vessel for holding salt: a depression behind the collar-bone; **salt flat** a stretch of flat, salt-covered land formed by the evaporation of an area of salt water; **salt'-glaze** a glaze produced on pottery by volatilisation of common salt in the kiln; **salt'-lake** an inland lake of saline water; **salt'-lick** a place to which animals resort for salt; **salt'-marsh** land liable to be flooded with salt water; **salt'-mine** a mine of rock-salt; **salt'-pan** a large basin for obtaining salt by evaporation: a salt-work: a natural depression in which salt accumulates or has accumulated by evaporation; **salt'-spoon** a small spoon for taking salt at table.—*adj.* **salt'-water** of salt water.—**salt'-work(s)** a place where salt is made; **salt'-wort** a fleshy, prickly plant of sandy seashores, of the goosefoot family, or other plant of the genus.—**above, below, the salt** among those of high, or low, social class, the saltcellar marking the boundary when all dined together; **lay, put, cast salt on someone's tail** to find or catch someone, from the jocularly recommended method of catching a bird; **like a dose of salts** (*coll.*) very quickly; **rub salt in a wound, someone's wounds** to aggravate someone's sorrow, shame, regret, etc.; **salt away** to store away: to hoard; **salt down** to preserve with salt: hence, to lay by, store up; **salt of the earth** the choice few of the highest excellence (Matt. v 13); **take with a grain, pinch, of salt** to believe with some reserve; **worth one's salt** valuable, useful—*orig.* worth the value of the salt one consumes. [O.E. (Anglian) *salt* (W.S. *sealt*).]

saltant *sal'tant, sòl'tant, adj.* leaping.—*n.* **salta'tion** a leaping or jumping: an abrupt variation (*biol.*).—*adjs.* **saltato'rial, saltato'rious, sal'tatory**. [L. *saltāre*, -*ātum*, intens. of *salīre*, to leap.]

saltarello *sal-tə-rel'ō, n.* a lively dance with skips, for two dancers: its music, in triple time:—*pl.* **saltarell'os**. [It. *saltarello*, Sp. *saltarelo*—L. *saltāre*, to dance.]

saltern *sòlt'ərn, n.* a salt-works. [O.E. *s(e)altern—s(e)alt,* salt, *ærn,* house.]

saltigrade *sal'ti-grād, adj.* going by leaps.—*n.* a jumping spider. [L. *saltus,* -*ūs,* a leap, *gradī,* to go.]

saltimbanco *sal-tim-bangk'ō,* (*obs.*) *n.* a mountebank, a quack:—*pl.* **saltimbanc'os**. [It.]

saltimbocca *sal-tim-bok'ə, n.* an Italian dish containing veal and ham, with cheese or other ingredients. [It.]

saltire *sal', sòl'tīr, (her.) n.* an ordinary in the form of a St Andrew's cross. [O.Fr. *saultoir, sautoir*—L.L. *saltātōrium,* a stirrup.]

saltpetre (in U.S. **saltpeter**) *sòlt-pē'tər, n.* potassium nitrate.—**saltpe'tre-paper** touch-paper.—**Chile** or **cubic saltpetre** sodium nitrate; **Norway saltpetre** calcium nitrate. [O.Fr. *salpetre*—L.L. *salpetra,* prob. for L. *sāl petrae,* salt of stone.]

saltus *sal'təs,* (*logic*) *n.* a breach of continuity: a jump to conclusion. [L., a leap, pl. *saltūs.*]

salubrious *sə-lōō'bri-əs, -lū', adj.* healthful, healthgiving.—*adv.* **salu'briously.**—*ns.* **salu'briousness, salu'brity.** [L. *salūbris—salūs, salūtis,* health.]

saluki *sə-lōō'kē, -gē, n.* a silky-haired Persian or Arabian greyhound. [Ar. *seluqi.*]

salutary *sal'ū-tər-i, adj.* promoting health or safety: wholesome.—*adv.* **sal'ūtarily.**—*n.* **sal'ūtariness.** [L. *salūtāris—salūs,* health.]

salute *sal-ōōt', -ūt', v.t.* to greet with words or (now esp.) with a gesture or with a kiss: to greet: to hail: to honour formally by a discharge of cannon, striking of colours, etc.—*v.i.* to perform the act of saluting, esp. in the military manner.—*n.* the act or position of saluting: a greeting: a kiss: a complimentary discharge of cannon, dipping colours, presenting arms, etc.—*n.* **salutation** (*sal-ū-tā'shən*) the act or words of greeting: the Angelic Salutation (see **ave**).—*adj.* **salūta'tional.**—*n.* **salutatorian** (*sə-lōō-tə-tō'ri-ən, -tō'*) in American colleges, the graduand who pronounces the address of welcome.—*adv.* **salu'tatorily.**—*adj.* **salu'tatory.**—*n.* an address of welcome, esp. in American colleges.—*n.* **salu'ter.** [L. *salūtāre, -ātum* (vb.), and *salūs, salūtis* (n.), partly through Fr. *salut.*]

salvable, etc. See **salve**[1].

salvage *sal'vij, n.* compensation made by the owner to persons, other than the ship's company, for preserving ship or cargo from danger of loss: rescue of property from fire or other peril: the raising of sunken or wrecked ships' saving of waste material for utilisation: anything saved in any of these ways.—*v.t.* to save from danger of loss or destruction· to recover or save as salvage.—**sal'vage-corps** a body of men employed in salvage work. [L.L. *salvāgium—salvāre,* to save.]

salve[1] *salv, v.t.* to salvage (also *n.*).—*n.* **salvabil'ity.**—*adj.* **salv'able.**—*ns.* **salva'tion** the act of saving: the means of preservation from any serious evil: the saving of man from the power and penalty of sin, the conferring of eternal happiness (*theol.*); **Salva'tionism; Salva'tionist** a member of the Salvation Army.—**Salvation Army** an organisation for the spread of religion among the masses, founded by Wm. Booth in 1865 [L.L. *salvāre,* to save; partly back-formation from **salvage**.]

salve[2] *sav,* also *salv, n.* an ointment: a remedy: anything to soothe the feelings or conscience.—*v.t.* to anoint: to smear: to heal: to soothe.—*n.* and *adj.* **salv'ing.** [O.E. *s(e)alf,* ointment.]

salve[3] *sal'vi, n.* an antiphon beginning *Salve Regina* (*R.C.*). [L. *salvē,* imper. of *salvēre,* to be well.]

salver[1] *sal'vər, n.* a tray on which anything is presented. [Sp. *salva,* the precautionary tasting of food, as by a prince's taster, hence the tray on which it was presented to the prince—*salvar,* to save.]

salver[2]. See **salvor.**

Salvia *sal'vi-ə, n.* the sage genus: (without *cap.*) a plant of this genus [L. *salvia,* sage.]

salvo[1] *sal'vō, n.* a saving clause: an expedient for saving appearances, avoiding offence, etc.:—*pl.* **sal'vos.** [L. *salvō,* ablative of *salvus,* safe: (one's right, honour, etc.) being saved.]

salvo[2] *sal'vō, n.* a simultaneous discharge of artillery in salute or otherwise: a simultaneous discharge of bombs, etc.: a round of applause:—*pl.* **sal'vo(e)s.** [It. *salva,* salute—L. *salvē,* hail.]

sal volatile. See **sal**[2].

salvor, salver *sal'vər, n.* one who salvages.

samara *sam'ə-rə, sə-mä'rə, n.* a dry indehiscent, usually one-seeded fruit, with a wing. [L. *samara, samera,* elm seed.]

Samaritan *sə-mar'i-tən, adj.* of Samaria, in Palestine. —*n.* a native of Samaria, an adherent of the religion of Samaria, differing from Judaism in that only the Pentateuch is accepted as holy scripture: the Aramaic dialect of Samaria: one who charitably gives help in need (*good Samaritan;* Luke x. 30–37): a member of a voluntary organisation formed to help people who are distressed or despairing, esp. by talking to them on the telephone.—*n.* **Samar'itanism.** [L. *Samāritānus.*]

samarium *sə-mā'ri-əm, n.* a metallic element (Sm; at. numb. 62) observed spectroscopically in samarskite. —*n.* **samarskite** (*sə-mär'skīt*) a mineral containing uranium. [Named in honour of Col. *Samarski,* Russian engineer.]

samba *sam'bə, n.* a Brazilian Negro dance in duple time with syncopation: a ballroom development thereof: a tune for it.

sambar, sambur *sam'bər, n.* a large Indian deer. [Hindi *sābar.*]

Sam Browne *sam' brown',* a military officer's belt with shoulder strap. [Invented by General Sir Samuel James *Browne* (1824–1901).]

sambuca *sam-bū'kə, n.* an ancient musical instrument like a harp. [L. *sambūca*—Gr *sambȳkē,* prob. an Asiatic word; cf. Aramaic *sabbekā.*]

sambur. Same as **sambar.**

same *sām, adj.* identical (commonly with *as,* also with *with* or a relative): not different: unchanged:

unvaried: mentioned before.—*pron.* (*coll.*) the aforesaid, it, them, they, etc.—*n.* same'ness the being the same: tedious montony.—*adj.* sā'mey (*coll.*) (boringly) alike: monotonous.—all the same for all that; at the same time still, nevertheless; same here! (*coll.*) me too!; the same the same thing or person: the aforesaid: in the same way. [O.E. *same* (only in phrase *swā same*, likewise); Goth. *sama*; L. *similis*, like, Gr. *homos*.]

samel sam'l, *adj.* underburnt (as a brick). [App. O.E. pfx. *sam-*, half, *æled*, burned.]

samey. See same.

samfoo, samfu sam'fōō, *n.* an outfit worn by Chinese women, consisting of a jacket and trousers. [Cantonese.]

Samian sā'mɪ-ən, *adj.* of the Greek island of *Samos*.—*n.* a native of Samos.—Samian ware brick-red or black pottery, with lustrous glaze: a later imitation made in Roman Gaul, etc.

samisen sam'ɪ-sen, *n.* a Japanese guitar. [Jap.]

samite sam'īt, *n.* a kind of heavy silk fabric. [O.Fr. *samit*—L.L. *examitum*—Gr. *hexamiton*—*hex*, six, *mitos*, thread.]

samizdat sam'izdat, *n.* in the Soviet Union, the secret printing and distribution of government-banned literature.—Also *adj.* [Russ.]

samlet sam'lit, *n.* a young salmon. [salmon, suff. -let.]

Samnite sam'nīt, *n.* a member of an ancient Sabine people of central Italy.—Also *adj.* [L. *Samnīs*, *-ītis.*]

samovar sam'ō-vär, *-var'*, *n.* a Russian tea-urn, traditionally heated by charcoal in a tube that passes through it. [Russ. *samovar*, lit. self-boiler.]

Samoyed(e) sam-ō-yed', or sam', *n.* one of a Ugrian people of north-west Siberia: their language: (*samoi'ed*) a white-coated dog of a breed used by them.—Also *adj.*—*adj.* Samoyed'ic. [Russ. *Samoyed.*]

samp samp, (*U.S.*) *n.* a coarsely ground maize: porridge made from it. [From an American Indian word.]

sampan sam'pan, *n.* a Chinese boat.—Also san'pan. [Chin. *san*, three, *pan*, board.]

samphire sam'fīr, sampire -pīr, *ns.* a plant (*Crithmum maritimum*) of sea-cliffs, whose fleshy leaves are used in pickles: extended to other plants used in the same way. [Fr. (*herbe de*) *Saint Pierre*, Saint Peter('s herb).]

sample säm'pl, *n.* a specimen, a small portion to show the quality of the whole.—*adj.* serving as a sample.—*v.t.* to take, try, or offer a sample or samples of.—*ns.* sam'pler; sam'pling. [M.E. *essample*; see example.]

sampler sàm'plɔr, *n.* a test-piece of embroidery formerly expected from a girl, commonly including an alphabet, with figures, often names, etc. [O.Fr. *essemplaire*—L. *exemplar*; see exemplar.]

Samson sam'sn, *n.* an abnormally strong man (from the Hebrew champion of Judges xiii-xvi).—Samson('s) post a strong post in a ship.

samurai sam'ōō-rī, *-ū-rī*, (*Jap. hist*) *n.* a military retainer of a daimio: a member of the military caste:—*pl.* sam'urai. [Jap.,—*saburau*, to attend (one's lord).]

sanative san'ɔ-tiv, *adj.* healing.—*n.* sanatō'rium, (esp. U.S.) sanitā'rium, (imitation Latin) a hospital, esp. for consumptives or convalescents: a health station:—*pl.* -toriums, -toria.—*adj.* san'atory healing: of healing. [L. *sānāre*, *-ātum*, to heal.]

sanbenito san-be-nē'tō, *n.* a garment worn by Inquisition victims at public recantation or execution:—*pl.* sanbeni'tos. [Sp. *San Benito*, St Benedict, from its resemblance to St Benedict's scapular.]

sanctify sang(k)'tɪ-fī, *v.t.* to make, declare, regard as, or show to be sacred or holy: to set apart to sacred use: to free from sin or evil: to consecrate: to invest with a sacred character: to make efficient as the means of holiness: to sanction:—*pr.p.* sanc'tifying; *pa.t.* and *pa.p.* sanc'tified.—*n.* sanctifica'tion.—*adj.* sanc'tified made holy: sanctimonious.—*adv.* sanc'tifiedly (*-fī-id-li*).—*n.* sanc'tifier (*-fī-ɔr*) one who sanctifies: (usu. with *cap.*) the Holy Spirit.—*n.* and *adj.* sanc'tifying.—*adv.* sanc'tifyingly. [Fr *sanctifier*—L. *sanctificāre*—*sanctus*, holy, *facĕre*, to make.]

sanctimony sang(k)'tɪ-mən-i, *n.* outward or simulated holiness.—*adj.* sanctimonious (*-mō'ni-əs*): simulating holiness.—*adv.* sanctimō'niously.—*n.* sanctimō'niousness. [L. *sanctimōnia*—*sanctus*.]

sanction sang(k)'shən, *n.* motive for obedience to any moral or religious law (*ethics*): a penalty or reward expressly attached to non-observance or observance of a law or treaty (*law*): a military or economic measure taken by a country in order to persuade another to follow a certain course of action: the act of ratifying, or giving authority: confirmation: support: permission.—*v.t.* to give validity to: to authorise: to countenance. [L. *sanctiō*, *-ōnis*—*sancīre*, *sanctum*, to ratify.]

sanctitude sang(k)'tɪ-tūd, *n.* saintliness. [L *sanctitūdō*, *-inis.*]

sanctity sang(k)'tɪ-tɪ, *n.* the quality of being sacred or holy: purity: godliness: inviolability: saintship: (in *pl.*) holy feelings, obligations, or objects. [L. *sanctitās*, *-ātis*, sanctity.]

sanctuary sang(k)'tū-ɔr-i, *n.* a holy place: a place of worship: the most holy part of a temple, church, etc.: a place affording immunity from arrest: the privilege of refuge therein: a place of refuge: a nature, animal, or plant reserve. [L. *sanctuārium.*]

Sanctus sang(k)'təs, *n.* the hymn *Holy, holy, holy*, from Isa. vi: music for it.—sanc'tum a sacred place: a private room.—sanc'tum sancto'rum the Holy of Holies: any specially reserved retreat or room; sanctus bell a bell rung at the Sanctus: the sacring bell. [L. *sanctus*, *-a*, *-um*, holy.]

sand sand, *n.* a mass of rounded grains of rock, esp. quartz: (in *pl.*) a tract covered with this, as on a seabeach or desert: (in *pl.*) moments of time, from use in the hour-glass: firmness of character (*U.S. slang*).—*adj.* of sand.—*v.t.* to sprinkle, cover or mix with sand: to smooth or polish with abrasive material, esp. sandpaper.—*adj.* sand'ed sprinkled, covered, or mixed with sand: smoothed or polished with sandpaper, etc.—*ns.* sand'er; sand'iness; sand'ing.—*adjs.* sand'y consisting of, covered with, containing, like, sand: coloured like sand; sand'yish.—sand'bag a bag of sand or earth: a small bag of sand, etc., used as a cosh.—*v.t.* to furnish with sandbags: to assail with a sandbag:—*pa.p.* sand'bagged.—sand'bagger; sand's bank a bank of sand; sand'-bar a long sand-bank in a river or sea; sand'-bath a bath in sand: a vessel for heating without direct exposure to the source of heat; sand'-bed a layer of sand, esp. one used in founding or moulding; sand'-blast sand driven by a blast of air or steam for glass-engraving, finishing metal surfaces, cleaning stone and metal surfaces, etc.—Also *v.t.*—sand'-blasting.—*adj.* sand'-blind see separate entry.—sand'-box a box for sand for sprinkling, for golftees, or other purpose; sand'-boy a boy selling sand, proverbial for jollity; sand'-castle a model of a castle made by children at play on the sands or in a sand-pit; sand'-crack a crack in a hoof; sand'-dollar a flat seaurchin; sand'-dune; sand'-eel the launce; sand'-flag a fissile sandstone; sand'-flea the chigoe or jigger: a sand-hopper; sand'-fly a small biting midge: a small moth-like midge (*Phlebotomus*) that transmits **sand-fly fever**, a fever due to a viral infection; **sand'-glass** a glass instrument for measuring time by the running out of sand; **sand'-grain; sand'-grouse** any bird of the genera *Pterocles* and *Syrrhaptes*, with long pointed wings, once mistaken for grouse because of their feathered legs but now reckoned akin to pigeons, **sand'-hill** a hill of sand; **sand'-hog** (*U.S. slang*) one who works in compressed air; **sand'-hopper** an amphipod crustacean of the seashore that jumps by suddenly straightening its bent body; **sand'man** a fairy who supposedly throws sand into children's eyes towards bedtime; **sand'-martin** a martin that nests in sandy banks; **sand painting** the making of designs with coloured sand, as in various American Indian ceremonies; **sand'paper** paper or cloth coated with sand.—*v.t.* to smooth or polish with sandpaper.—**sand'piper** the name for a large number of ground-dwelling, wading birds intermediate between plovers and snipe, haunting sandy shores and river banks and uttering a clear piping note; **sand'-pit** a place from which sand is dug: a pit filled with sand for children's play; **sand'-pump** a pump for raising wet sand or mud; **sand'-shoe** a shoe for walking or playing on the sands, usually with canvas upper and rubber sole; **sand'-skipper** a sand-hopper; **sand'-spout** a moving pillar of sand; **sand'stone** a rock formed of compacted and more or less indurated sand; **sand'-storm** a storm of wind carrying along clouds of sand; **sand'-table** a tray for moulding sand on or for demonstration of military tactics: an inclined trough for separating heavier particles from a flow of liquid, as in ore-dressing, paper-making (also **sand'-trap**); **sand'-trap** a bunker: a sand-table; **sand'wort** any species of Arenaria; **sand'-yacht, sand'-yachting** see yacht. [O.E. *sand*.]

sandal *san'dl*, *n.* a sole bound to the foot by straps: an ornate shoe or slipper: a slipper-strap: a slight rubber overshoe.—*adj.* **san'dalled** wearing or fastened with sandals. [L. *sandalium*—Gr. *sandalion*, dim. of *sandalon*.]

sandal² *san'dl*, **sandalwood** *-wŏŏd*, *ns.* a compact and fine-grained very fragrant East Indian wood: the parasitic tree yielding it, *Santalum album* (**white sandalwood**), or other species: extended to other woods, as red-sanders, called **red sandalwood**. [L.L. *santalum*—Gr. *sandanon*,—Sans. *candana*, of Dravidian origin.]

sandarach, sandarac *san'dər-ak*, *n.* realgar: the resin (in full **gum sandarach, sandarac resin**) of the Moroccan **sandarach tree** (*Collitris quadrivalvis*; Coniferae) powdered to form pounce and used in making varnish. [L. *sandaraca*—Gr. *sandărăkě*, *-chě*.]

sand-blind *sand'blind*, *adj.* half-blind. [Prob. O.E. pfx. *sam*-, half, and **blind**, affected by **sand**.]

sanderling *san'dər-ling*, *n.* a sandpiper without a hind toe. [App. from **sand**.]

sanders *san'*, *săn'dərz*, **sanderswood** *-wŏŏd*, *ns.* sandalwood, esp. red sandalwood (**red-sanders**; see **red**). [O.Fr. *sandre*, variant of *sandal*, *santal*, sandalwood.]

sandwich *san(d)'wich*, *-wij*, *n.* any sort of food between two slices of bread, said to be named from the fourth Earl of *Sandwich* (1718–92), who ate a snack of this kind in order not to have to leave the gaming-table: anything in like arrangement.—*v.t.* to lay or place between two layers: to fit tightly or squeeze between two others or two of another kind. —*adj.* of a sandwich or sandwich course.—**sandwich course** an educational course consisting of alternating periods of academic and industrial work; **sand'wich-man** a man who perambulates the streets carrying two advertising boards (**sand'wich-boards**) hung over his shoulders, so that one is in front, the other behind.

sane *săn*, *adj.* sound in mind: rational.—*adv.* **sane'ly.**

—*n.* **sane'ness.** [L. *sănus*.]

sang *sang*, *pa.t.* of **sing**.

sangar, sungar *sung'gər*, *n.* a stone breastwork: a lookout post. [Pushtu *sangar*.]

sangaree *sang-gə-rē'*, *n.* a West Indian drink of wine, diluted, sweetened, spiced, etc.—Also **sangría** (*sang-grē'ə*) a similar Spanish drink. [Sp. *sangría*.]

sangfroid *săfrwä'*, *n.* coolness, self-possession. [Fr., cold blood.]

Sangraal, Sangrail, Sangreal *san(g)-grāl'*, *san(g)'grāl*, *ns.* the holy grail (see **grail**). [**saint, grail**.]

sangria. See **sangaree**.

sangui- *sang-gwi-*, in compounds, blood.—*n.* **sanguifica'tion** blood-making.—*v.i* **sang'uify** (*-fī*) to make blood.—*v.t.* to turn into blood.—*adv.* **sang'uinarily** (*-gwin-ə-ri-li*).—*n.* **sang'uinariness.**—*adjs.* **sang'uinary** bloody; **sanguine** (*sang'gwin*) blood-red: bloody: of the complexion or temperament in which blood was supposed to predominate over the other humours: hence ardent, confident and inclined to hopefulness: ruddy.—*n.* a blood-red colour: a red chalk: a drawing in red chalks.—*adv.* **sang'uinely.**—*n.* **sang'uineness.**—*adj.* **sanguin'eous** of or having blood: blood-red: bloody: full-blooded. —*n.* **sanguin'ity** sanguineness. [L. *sanguis*, *-inis*, blood; adjs. *sanguineus*, *sanguinārius*; partly through Fr *sanguin*.]

Sanhedrim, Sanhedrin *san'i-drim*, *-drin*, *-hed'*, *ns.* a Jewish council or court, esp. the supreme council and court at Jerusalem (*hist.*). [Heb. *sanhedrīn*—Gr. *synedrion*—*syn*, together, *hedrā*, a seat.]

sanicle *san'ik-l*, *n.* a woodland plant (in full **wood'-san'icle**; *Sanicula europaea*) with glossy leaves, head-like umbels, and hooked fruits: any plant of the genus: extended to various other plants. [O.Fr., perh. L. *sānāre*, to heal, from once-supposed power.]

sanies *sā'ni-ēz*, *n.* a thin discharge from wounds or sores.—*adj.* **sa'nious.** [L. *saniēs*.]

sanitary *san'i-tər-i*, *adj.* pertaining to, or concerned with the promotion of health, esp. connected with drainage and sewage disposal: conducive to health.— *n.* **sanita'rian** one who favours or studies sanitary measures.—Also *adj.*—*adv.* **san'itarily.**—*n.* **sanitā'rium** (sham Latin; esp. U.S.) a sanatorium:—*pl.* **-ia, -iums; sanita'tion** measures for the promotion of health, esp. drainage and sewage disposal; **sanita'tionist.**—*v.t.* **san'itise, -ize** to make sanitary: to clean up, make more acceptable by removing offensive elements, words, connotations, etc.—*n.* **sanitisa'tion, -z-.**—**sanitary engineer; sanitary engineering** the branch of civil engineering dealing with provision of pure water supply, disposal of waste, etc.; **sanitary inspector** see **public health inspector**; **sanitary towel** a pad of absorbent material for wearing during menstruation, etc. [Fr. *sanitaire*—L. *sănitās*, health.]

sanity *san'i-ti*, *n.* soundness of mind: rationality. [L: *sănitās*—*sănus*, healthy.]

sank *sangk*, *pa.t.* of **sink**.

sannyasi *sun-yä'si*, *n.* a Hindu religious hermit who lives by begging. [Hindi,—Sans. *samnyāsin*, casting aside.]

sanpan. See **sampan**.

sans *să*, *sanz*, *prep.* without.—**sansculotte** (*să-kü-lot*; Fr. *culotte*, knee-breeches) in the French Revolution, the nickname for a democrat (apparently as wearing long trousers instead of knee-breeches): hence generally (usu. in hostility) a strong republican, democrat, or revolutionary.—**sansculott'ism; sansculott'ist; sanserif** (*san-ser'if*; *print.*) a type without serifs.—Also *adj.*—**sans souci** (*sŏŏ-sē*) without care, worry. [Fr.]

sansa *san'sə*. Same as **zanze**.

sanserif. See **sans**.

Sanskrit, *sans'krit*, *n.* the ancient Indo-European literary language of India. —Also *adj.—adj.* **Sanskrit'ic.**—*n.* **Sans'kritist** one skilled in Sanskrit. [Sans. *saṁskṛta*, put together, perfected—*sam*, together, *karoti*, he makes, cog. with L. *creāre*, to create.]

Santa Claus *san'tə klöz'*, a fat rosy old fellow who brings children Christmas presents (also known as **Father Christmas**): an improbable source of improbable benefits. [Orig. U.S. modification of Du. dial. *Sante Klaas*, St Nicholas.]

Santolina *san-tō-lē'nə*, *n.* a genus of fragrant Mediterranean shrubs related to the camomile: (without *cap.*) a plant of the genus. [It. *santolina*,—L. *sanctus*, holy, *līnum*, flax.]

santonica *san-ton'i-kə*, *n.* the dried unexpanded flower-heads of a species of wormwood.—*n.* **san'tonin** (*-tən-*) an anthelmintic extracted from it. [Gr. *santonikon*, as found in the country of the *Santones* in Gaul.]

sap[1] *sap*, *n.* vital juice: juice generally: sapwood: a fool (*slang*).—*v.t.* to drain or withdraw the sap from.— *adjs.* **sap'ful** full of sap; **sap'less.**—*ns.* **sap'lessness; sap'ling** a young tree (also *adj.*): a young greyhound; **sapp'iness.**—*adj.* **sapp'y.**—**sap'-green** a green paint made from the juice of buckthorn berries: its colour (also *adj.*); **sap'wood** alburnum. [O.E. *sæp*.]

sap[2] *sap*, *n.* sapping: a trench (usually covered or zigzag) by which approach is made towards a hostile position.—*v.t.* to undermine.—*v.i.* to make a sap: to proceed insidiously:—*pr.p.* **sapp'ing;** *pa.p.* and *pa.t.* **sapped.**—*n.* **sapp'er** one who saps: a private in the Royal Engineers. [It. *zappa* and Fr. *sappe* (now *sape*); cf. L.L. *sappa*, a pick.]

sapajou *sap'ə-jōō*, *n.* a capuchin monkey. [Fr. from a Tupí name.]

sapan. Same as **sappan.**

sapele *sa-pē'lē*, *n.* a wood resembling mahogany, used for furniture: a tree of the genus *Entandrophragma* giving such wood. [W. African name.]

sapid *sap'id*, *adj.* having a decided taste: savoury: relishing, exhilarating.—*n.* **sapid'ity.** [L. *sapidus*— *sapĕre*, to taste.]

sapience *sā'pi-əns*, *n.* discernment: wisdom (often ironical): judgment.—*adjs.* **sā'pient; sapiential** (*-en'shl*).—*adv.* **sā'piently.** [L. *sapientia*—*sapĕre*, to be wise.]

sapling. See **sap**[1].

sapodilla *sap-ō-dil'ə*, *n.* a large evergreen tree of W. Indies, etc., *Achras sapota* (naseberry): its edible fruit (**sapodilla plum**): its durable timber. [Sp. *zapotilla.*]

saponaceous *sap-ō-*, or *sap-ə-nā'shəs*, *adj.* soapy: soaplike.—*adj.* **saponifiable** (*sap-on'i-fī'ə-bl*).—*n.* **saponificā'tion** the turning into or forming of soap: hydrolysis of esters.—*v.t.* and *v.i.* **sapon'ify:**—*pr.p.* **sapon'ifying;** *pa.t.* and *pa.p.* **sapon'ified.**—*n.* **saponin** (*sap'ə-nin*) a glucoside from soapwort, etc., that gives a soapy froth. [L. *sāpō, -ōnis*, soap, prob. from Gmc.]

sapor *sā'pōr*, *n.* taste.—*adj.* **sā'porous** (*-pər-əs*). [L. *sapor, -ōris.*]

sappan, sapan *sap'an, -ən, n.* brazil-wood (*Caesalpinia sappan*)—usu. **sap(p)'an-wood.** [Malay *sapang.*]

sapped, sapper, sapping. See **sap**[2].

sapphire *saf'īr*, *n.* a brilliant precious variety of corundum, generally of a beautiful blue: the blue colour of a sapphire.—*adj.* of sapphire: deep pure blue.— **sapph'ire-wing** a blue-winged humming-bird. [O. Fr. *safir*—L. *sapphīrus*—Gr. *sappheiros*, lapis lazuli.]

Sappho *saf'ō*, *n.* a great Greek lyric poetess (c. 600 B.C.) of Lesbos.—*adj.* **Sapph'ic.**—*n.* usu. in *pl.* (also without *cap.*) verses in a form said to have been invented by Sappho in stanzas of four lines each.—*ns.* **Sapph'ism** (also without *cap.*) lesbianism, of which she was accused; **sapph'ist** a lesbian. [Gr. *Sapphō.*]

sapr(o)- *sap-r(ō)-*, in composition, rotten, decayed.— **saprogenic, saprogenous** (*sap-rō-jen'ik* or *-ra-, sə-proj'i-nəs;* Gr. root of *gignesthai*, to produce) growing on decaying matter: causing or caused by putrefaction; **saprophagous** (*sap-rof'ə-gəs;* Gr. *phagein* (aor.), to eat) feeding on decaying organic matter.—*n.* **saprophyte** (*sap'rō-fīt* or *-rə-;* Gr. *phyton*, a plant) a plant that feeds upon decaying organic matter.—*adj.* **saprophytic** (*-fīt'ik*).—*adv.* **saprophyt'ically.**—*n.* **sap'rophytism.**—*adj.* **saprozō'ic** feeding on dead or decaying organic material. [Gr. *sapros*, rotten.]

sapsucker *sap'suk-ər, n.* a N. American woodpecker which feeds on the sap from trees. [**sap**[1], **suck.**]

saraband *sar'ə-band, n.* a slow Spanish dance, or dance-tune: a suite-movement in its rhythm, in 3–4 time strongly accented on the second beat (a dotted crotchet or minim). [Sp. *zarabanda.*]

Saracen *sar'ə-sən, n.* a Syrian or Arab nomad: a Muslim: an opponent of the Crusaders: a Moor or Berber.—Also *adj.* **Saracenic** (*-sen'ik*).— **Saracenic architecture** a general name for Muslim architecture; **Saracen's-stone** see **sarsen**. [O.E. *Saracene* (pl.)—L. *Saracēnus*—late Gr. *Sarakēnos.*]

sarangi *sä'rung-gē, n.* an Indian fiddle. [Hind.]

sarcasm *sär'kazm, n.* a bitter sneer: a satirical remark in scorn or contempt, often but not necessarily ironical: a jibe: the quality of such sayings.—*adj.* **sarcas'tic** containing or inclined to sarcasm (*coll.* shortening **sar'ky**).—*adv.* **sarcas'tically.** [L. *sarcasmus*—Gr. *sarkasmos*—*sarkazein*, to tear flesh like dogs, to speak bitterly—*sarx, sarkos*, flesh.]

sarcenet. See **sarsenet.**

sarco- *sär'kō, -kō'-*, in composition, flesh.—*ns.* **sarcocarp** (*sär'kō-kärp;* Gr. *karpos*, fruit; *bot.*) the fleshy pericarp of a stone fruit; **sar'coplasm** the protoplasmic substance separating the fibrils in muscle fibres.—*adjs.* **sarcoplas'mic; sarcous** (*sär'kəs*) of flesh or muscle. [Gr. *sarx, sarkos*, flesh.]

sarcode *sär'kōd, n.* protoplasm, esp. of Protozoa.— *adj.* **sar'cold** flesh-like.—*n.* short for sarcoidosis.—*n.* **sarcoidō'sis** a chronic disease of unknown cause characterised by the formation of nodules in the lymph nodes, lungs, skin, etc. [Gr. *sarkōdēs, sarkoeides—eidos*, form.]

sarcoma *sär-kō'mə, n.* a tumour derived from connective tissue:—*pl.* **sarcō'mata.**—*n.* **sarcomatō'sis** a condition characterised by the formation of sarcomas in many areas of the body.—*adj.* **sarcō'matous.** [Gr. *sarkōma—sarx*, flesh.]

sarcophagus *sar-kof'ə-gəs, n.* a limestone used by the Greeks for coffins, thought to consume the flesh of corpses: a stone coffin, esp. one with carvings: a tomb or cenotaph of similar form:—*pl.* **sarcoph'agi** (*-jī, -gī*), **sarcoph'aguses.** [Latinised from Gr. *sarkophagos—phagein* (aor.), to eat.]

sard *särd, n.* a deep-red chalcedony.—Also **sard'ius.** [L. *sarda, sardius*, and Gr. *sardion*, also *sardios* (*lithos*), the Sardian (stone)—*Sardeis*, Sardis, in Lydia.]

sardel *sär-del', **sardelle** -del'(ə), ns.* a small fish related to the sardine.

sardine *sär'dēn, sär-dēn', n.* a young pilchard, commonly tinned in oil: applied at various times and places to other fishes.—**packed like sardines** crowded closely together. [Fr. *sardine*—It. *sardina*—L. *sardina;* Gr. *sardīnos*, or *-ē*.]

Sardinian *sär-din'i-ən, -yən, adj.* of the island or former kingdom of *Sardinia* or of the inhabitants.—*n.* a native, citizen, or member of the people of Sardinia: their language or dialect of Italian.

sardius. See **sard.**

sardonic sär-don'ik, *adj.* scornful, heartless, or bitter, said of a forced unmirthful laugh: sneering.—*adv.* **sardon'ically.** [Fr. *sardonique*—L. *sardonius*—late Gr. *sardonios*, doubtfully referred to *sardonion*, a plant of Sardinia (Gr. *Sardō*) which was said to screw up the face of the eater.]

sardonyx sär'də-niks, *n.* an onyx with layers of cornelian or sard. [Gr. *sardonyx*—*Sardios*, Sardian, *onyx*, a nail.]

saree. See **sari.**

sargasso sär-gas'ō, *n.* gulf-weed (*Sargassum*): a floating mass or expanse of it, as the **Sargasso Sea** in the North Atlantic:—*pl.* **sargass'os.** [Port. *sargaço*.]

sarge. Coll. shortening of **sergeant.**

sari sär'ē, *n.* a Hindu woman's chief garment, a long cloth wrapped round the waist and passed over the shoulder and head.—Also **sar'ee.** [Hind. *sārī*.]

sark särk, (*Scot.*) *ns.* a shirt or chemise.—*n.* **sark'ing** a lining for a roof. [O.E. *serc*; O.N. *serkr*.]

sarky. See **sarcasm.**

Sarmatia sär-mä'shyə, -shi-ə, *n.* anciently a region reaching from the Vistula and Danube to the Volga and Caucasus: Poland (*poet.*).—*n.* and *adj.* **Sarmā'tian.**—*adj.* **Sarmatic** (*-mat'ik*).

sarment sär'mənt, *n.* a sarmentum: a long weak twig.—*adjs.* **sar'mentose** (or *-ōs'*), **sarmentous** (*-ment'əs*) having sarmenta or runners: creeping.—*n.* **sarmentum** (*-ment'əm*) a runner:—*pl.* **sarment'a.** [L. *sarmentum*, a twig—*sarpĕre*, to prune.]

sarong sä'rong, sə-rong', *n.* a Malay skirt-like garment for a man or woman: a cloth for making it. [Malay *särung*.]

saros sä'ros, sä'ros, *n.* a Babylonian cycle of 3600 years: an astronomical cycle of 6585 days and 8 hours, after which relative positions of the sun and moon recur. [Gr. *saros*—Babylonian *shāru*, 3600.]

sarrusophone sə-rus'ō-fōn, *n.* a reed instrument of brass, devised by a French bandmaster, *Sarrus.* [Gr. *phōnē*, voice.]

sarsaparilla sär-sə-pə-ril'ə, *n.* any tropical American Smilax: its dried root: a soft drink flavoured with this (*U.S.*): a medicinal preparation from it: extended to various plants or roots of like use. [Sp. *zarzaparilla* —*zarza*, bramble (from Basque), and a dim. of *parra*, vine.]

sarsen sär'sn, *n.* a sandstone boulder. [App. form of **Saracen.**]

sarsenet, sarcenet särs'nit, *-net*, *n.* a thin tissue of fine silk.—*adj.* of sarsenet. [A.Fr. *sarzinett*, probably *Sarzin*, Saracen.]

sartor sär'tōr, (*facet.*) *n.* a tailor.—*adj.* **sartorial** (*-tō'ri-əl*, *-tō'*) of or relating to a tailor, tailoring, dress, or the sartorius.—*adv.* **sarto'rially.**—*n.* **sarto'rius** a thigh muscle that crosses the leg, as when a tailor sits. [L. *sartor*, a patcher.]

sash¹ sash, *n.* a band or scarf, worn round the waist or over the shoulder.—*v.t.* to dress or adorn with a sash. [Ar. *shāsh.*]

sash² sash, *n.* a frame, esp. a sliding frame, for window panes.—*v.t.* to furnish with sashes.—**sash'-cord** a cord attaching a weight to the sash in order to balance it at any height; **sash'-window** a window with a sash or sashes, opp. to *casement window.* [Fr. *châssis.*]

sashay sa-shā', *v.i.* to walk, move, in a gliding or ostentatious way.—*n.* an excursion (esp. *fig.*). [Alteration of *chassé.*]

sasin sas'in, *n.* the common Indian antelope. [Nepalese.]

sasine sä'sin, (Scots law) *n.* the act of giving legal pos-

session of feudal property. [A variant of **seisin**, Law L. *sasina.*]

sasquatch sas'kwach, -kwoch, *n.* a large hairy manlike creature thought by some to inhabit parts of North America. [Indian name.]

sass sas, **sassy** sas'i. Same as **sauce, saucy.**

sassaby sə-sä'bi, *n.* the bastard hartebeest, a large S. African antelope. [Tswana *tsessébe.*]

sassafras sas'ə-fras, *n.* a tree of the laurel family common in N. America: the bark, esp. of its root, a powerful stimulant: an infusion of it: extended to various plants with similar properties.—**sassafras oil** a volatile aromatic oil distilled from sassafras. [Sp. *sasafrás.*]

Sassenach sas'ə-nahh, *n.* an Englishman. [Gael. *Sasunnach*—L. *Saxones*, Saxons.]

sassy. See **sass.**

sastruga. See **zastruga.**

sat sat, *pa.t.* and *pa.p.* of **sit.**

Satan sā'tən (old-fashioned *sat'ən*), *n.* the chief fallen angel: the chief evil spirit, adversary of God and tempter of men, the Devil.—*adjs.* **satanic** (sə-tan'ik), **-al.**—*adv.* **satan'ically.**—*n.* **sā'tanism** devilish disposition: Satan-worship.—*n.* and *adj.* **Sā'tanist.** [Gr. and L. *Satân, Satanâs*—Heb. *sâtân*, enemy—*sâtan*, to be adverse.]

satchel sach'l, *n.* a small bag, esp. with shoulder strap, as for school-books.—*adj.* **satch'elled.** [O.Fr. *sachel*—L. *saccellus*, dim. of *saccus*; see **sack¹, sac.**]

sate¹ sāt, *v.t.* to satisfy fully: to glut.—*adjs.* **sāt'ed**; **sate'less** insatiable.—*n.* **sāt'edness.** [Blend of M.E. *sade* (cf. **sad**) and L. *sat*, enough, or **satiate** shortened.]

sate² sat, also (in rhyme) *sāt*, an archaism for **sat.**

sateen sa-tēn', *n.* a glossy cotton or woollen fabric resembling satin.

satellite sat'ə-līt, *n.* an attendant: an obsequious follower: a body revolving about a planet, esp. now a man-made device used for communication, etc. (see **artificial satellite** below): a smaller companion to anything: a subordinate or dependent state, community, etc.—Also *adj.*—*adj.* **satellitic** (*-lit'ik*).—**satellite state, country** one which relies on and obeys the dictates of a larger, more powerful state; **satellite town** a town, often a garden city, limited in size, built near a great town to check overgrowth.—**artificial earth, satellite** any man-made body, including spacecraft, launched by rocket into space and put into orbit round the earth. [L. *satelles, satellitis*, an attendant.]

sati. Same as **suttee.**

satiate sā'shi-āt, *v.t.* to gratify fully: to glut.—*adj.* glutted.—*n.* **sātiabil'ity.**—*adj.* **sā'tiable.**—*ns.* **sātiā'tion; satiety** (sə-tī'ə-ti) the state of being satiated: surfeit. [L. *satiâre, -âtum*—*satis*, enough.]

satin sat'in, *n.* a closely woven silk with a lustrous and unbroken surface showing much of the warp.—*adj.* of, like satin.—*v.t.* to make satiny.—*n.* **satinet'**, **satinette'** a thin satin: a modification of satin with a slightly different weave: a cloth with a cotton warp and a woollen weft.—*adj.* **sat'iny** like satin.—**sat'in-bird** a satiny blue and black bower-bird; **sat'in-fin'ish** a satiny polish; **sat'in-paper** a fine, glossy writing-paper; **sat'in-stitch** an embroidery stitch, repeated in parallel lines, giving a satiny appearance; **sat'inwood** a beautiful, smooth, satiny ornamental wood from India: the tree (*Chloroxylon swietenia*) yielding it: extended to several more or less similar woods and trees. [Fr. *satin*, app.—L.L. *sēta*, silk (L. *saeta*, bristle).]

satire sat'īr, *n.* a literary composition, orig. in verse, essentially a criticism of folly or vice, which it holds up to ridicule or scorn—its chief instruments, irony, sarcasm, invective, wit, and humour: satirical writing as a genre: its spirit: the use of, or inclination to use, its methods: satirical denunciation or ridicule.—*adjs.* **satiric** (*sə-tir'ik*), **-al** pertaining to, or conveying, satire: sarcastic: abusive.—*adv.* **satir'ically.**—*n.* **satir'icalness.**—*v.t.* **satirise, -ize** (*sat'ər-īz*) to make the object of satire.—*v.i.* to write satire.—*n.* **sat'irist** a writer of satire [L. *satira, satura* (*lanx*), full (dish), a medley.]

satisfy *sat'is-fī, v.t.* to pay in full: to compensate or atone for: to give enough to: to be enough for: to supply fully: to fulfil the conditions of: to meet the requirements of: to content: to free from doubt: to convince.—*v.i.* to give content: to make payment or atonement:—*pr.p.* **sat'isfying;** *pa.t.* and *pa.p.* **sat'isfied.**—*n.* **satisfaction** (*-fak'shən*) the act of satisfying: the state of being satisfied, content: payment: quittance: gratification: comfort: that which satisfies: atonement (esp. that of Christ for mankind's sins): satisfying of honour, as by a duel: conviction.—*adv.* **satisfac'torily.**—*n.* **satisfac'toriness.**—*adjs.* **satisfac'tory** satisfying: giving contentment: such as might be wished: making amends or payment: atoning: convincing; **sat'isfiable; sat'isfied.**—*n.* **sat'isfier.**—*adj.* **sat'isfying.**—*adv.* **sat'isfyingly.** [O.Fr. *satisfier*—L. *satisfacĕre*—*satis,* enough, *facĕre,* to make.]

satori *sa-tō'rē, -tō', n.* sudden enlightenment—sought in Zen Buddhism. [Jap.,—*toshi,* be quick.]

satrap *sat'rap, -rəp, sā'trap, n.* a viceroy or governor of an ancient Persian province: a provincial governor, esp. if powerful or ostentatiously rich.—*adjs.* **sat'rapal, satrap'ic, -al.**—*n.* **sat'rapy** a satrap's province, office, or time of office. [Gr. *satrapēs,* from Old Pers. *khshathrapāvan-,* country-protector.]

Satsuma *sat'soo-mə, -soo', n.* a province of S.W. Japan.—**satsuma (orange)** a thin-skinned seedless type of mandarin orange, or its tree; **Satsuma ware** a yellowish pottery with gilding and enamel made in Satsuma from end of 16th century.

saturate *sat'ū-rāt, sa'chə-rāt, v.t.* to soak: to imbue: to charge to the fullest extent possible: to satisfy all the valencies of: to cover (a target area) completely with bombs dropped simultaneously.—*adj.* saturated: deep in colour, free from white.—*n.* a saturated compound (*chem.*).—*adjs.* **sat'urable; sat'urant** which saturates.—*n.* a saturating substance.—*adj.* **sat'urated** (of a solution) containing as much of a solute as can be dissolved at a particular temperature and pressure: containing no carbon-carbon double bonds in the molecule and consequently not susceptible to addition reactions (*chem.*).—*n.* **satura'tion.** —Also used as *adj.,* meaning of very great, or greatest possible, intensity (e.g. *saturation bombing*). —*n.* **sat'urator.—saturated fat** an animal fat (usu. solid, e.g. lard, butter) containing a high proportion of saturated fatty acids; **saturation point** the point at which saturation is reached: dewpoint: the limit in numbers that can be taken in, provided with a living, used, sold, etc.: the limit of emotional response, endurance, etc. [L. *saturāre, -ātum—satur,* full, akin to *satis,* enough.]

Saturday *sat'ər-di, n.* the seventh day of the week, dedicated by the Romans to Saturn, the Jewish Sabbath. [O.E. *Sæter-, Sætern(es)dæg,* Saturn's day.]

Saturn *sat'ərn, n.* the ancient Roman god of agriculture: commonly used for the Greek Kronos, with whom he came to be identified: the second in size and sixth in distance from the sun of the major planets, believed by the astrologers to induce a cold, melancholy, gloomy temperament: the metal lead (*alch.*). —*n.pl.* **Saturnä'lia** the festival of Saturn in mid-December, when slaves and masters exchanged garb and parts: hence (often as *sing.* without capital) an

orgy.—*adjs.* **saturnä'lian; Satur'nian** pertaining to Saturn, whose fabulous reign was called the golden age: happy: simple: of the planet Saturn.—*n.* one born under Saturn, or of saturnine temperament.— *adjs.* **satur'nic** affected with lead-poisoning; **sat'urnine** grave: gloomy: phlegmatic: caused or poisoned by lead.—*ns.* **sat'urnism** lead-poisoning. [L. *Sāturnus—serēre, sătum,* to sow.]

satyagraha *sut'ya-gru-ha,* or *-grä', n.* orig. Mahatma Gandhi's policy of passive resistance to British rule in India, now any non-violent campaign for reform. [Sans., reliance on truth.]

satyr *sat'ər, n.* a Greek god of the woodlands, with tail and long ears, represented by the Romans as part goat: a very lecherous person: any butterfly of the *Satyridae,* having dark wings with pale marking (also **sat'yrid**).—*n.* **satyrī'asis** morbid, overpowering sexual desire in men, corresponding to nymphomania in women.—*adj.* **satyric** (*sa-tir'ik*) of satyrs: having a chorus of satyrs. [L. *satyrus*—Gr. *satyros.*]

sauce *sós, n.* a dressing poured over food: anything that gives relish: vegetables eaten with meat (*U.S.*): stewed fruit (*U.S.*): pert or impertinent language or behaviour (*coll.*).—*v.t.* to add or give sauce to: to make piquant or pleasant: to be impertinent to.— *adv.* **sauc'ily.**—*n.* **sauc'iness.**—*adj.* **sauc'y** (*compar.* **sauc'ier;** *superl.* **sauc'iest**) tasting of sauce: pert: piquantly audacious, esp. arousing sexual desire: smart and trim (as of a ship): disdainful.—**sauce'-boat** a vessel for sauce; **sauce'pan** a handled and usu. lidded metal pan for boiling, stewing, etc.—orig. for sauces. [Fr. *sauce*—L. *salsa—sallĕre, salsum,* to salt—*sāl,* salt.]

saucer *sô'sər, n.* orig., a dish for salt or sauce: a shallow dish, esp. one placed under a tea or coffee cup: anything of like shape.—*n.* **sau'cerful:**—*pl.* **sau'cerfuls.** [O.Fr. *saussiere*—L.L. *salsārium*—L. *salsa,* sauce.]

sauerkraut *sow', zow'ər-krowt, n.* a German dish of cabbage allowed to ferment with salt, etc.—Also **sour'-crout.** [Ger., sour cabbage.]

sauna *so'nə, sow'nə, n.* (a building or room equipped for) a Finnish form of steam bath. [Finn.]

saunter *sôn'tər, v.i.* to wander about idly: to loiter: to lounge: to stroll.—*n.* a sauntering gait: a leisurely stroll.—*ns.* **saun'terer; saun'tering.**—*adv.* **saun'-teringly.**

saurian *sô'ri-ən, adj.* lizard-like.—*n.* a lizard.—*adj.* **saurischian** (*-is'ki-ən;* L. *ischium,* hip joint) of or belonging to the **Sauris'chia** (lit. "lizard-hipped"), an order of dinosaurs.—*n.* any dinosaur of the Saurischia.—*n.pl.* **Saurop'oda** (Gr. *pous, podos,* foot) a suborder of gigantic quadrupedal herbivorous dinosaurs, one of the two main groups of lizard-hipped dinosaurs.—*n.* **saur'opod.** [Gr. *saurā, sauros,* a lizard.]

saury *sô'ri, n.* a sharp-beaked fish (*Scombresox saurus*). [Perh. Gr. *sauros,* lizard.]

sausage *sos'ij, n.* chopped or minced meat with fat, cereal, etc. seasoned and stuffed into a tube of gut or the like or formed into the shape of a tube: anything of like shape.—**saus'age-dog** (*coll.*) a dachshund; **saus'age-meat** meat prepared for making sausages; **saus'age-roll** minced meat cooked in a roll of pastry —**not a sausage** (*coll.*) nothing at all. [Fr. *saucisse*— L.L. *salsīcia*—L. *salsus,* salted.]

sauté *sô'tā, adj.* fried lightly and quickly.—Also *v.t.*— *n.* a dish of sautéed food. [Fr.]

Sauterne(s) *sô-tûrn', -tern', n.* esteemed sweet white wine produced at *Sauternes* in the Gironde, France. **savable,** etc. See save.

savage *sav'ij, adj.* in a state of nature: wild: uncivilised: ferocious: furious.—*n.* an enraged horse or other animal: a human being in a wild or primitive state: a brutal, fierce, or cruel person.—*v.t.* to assail savagely, esp. with the teeth.—*v.i.* to play the savage.—*adv.* **sav'agely**.—*ns.* **sav'ageness**; **sav'agery** (-ri, -*ər-i*) fierceness: ferocity: uncivilised condition: wildness. [O.Fr. *salvage*—L. *silvāticus*, pertaining to the woods—*silva*, a wood.]

savanna, savannah *sə-van'ə*, *n.* a tract of level land, covered with low vegetation, treeless, or dotted with trees or patches of wood. [Sp. *zavana* (now *sabana*), said to be from Carib.]

savant *sa'vä, sä-vä'*, *n.* a learned man. [Fr. obs. pr.p. of *savoir*, to know.]

savate *sä-vät'*, *n.* boxing with the use of the feet. [Fr.]

save *sāv*, *v.t.* to bring safe out of evil: to rescue: to bring or keep out of danger: to protect: to preserve: to prevent or avoid the loss, expenditure, or performance of, or the gain of by an opponent: to reserve: to spare: to deliver from the power of sin and from its consequences: to husband: to hoard: to obviate, to prevent.—*v.i.* to act as a saviour: to be economical.—*prep.* except.—*conj.* were it not that: unless.—*n.* an act of saving, esp. in games.—*adj.* **sav'able**.—*n.* **sav'ableness**.—*adj.* **saved**.—*n.* **sa'ver**.—*adj.* **sa'ving** protecting: preserving: redeeming: securing salvation (*theol.*): frugal: making a reservation.—*prep.* excepting.—*n.* the action of the verb: that which is saved: (*pl.*) money laid aside for future use.—*adv.* **sa'vingly**.—*n.* **sa'vingness**.—**saving clause** a legal clause, or a statement, in which a reservation or condition is made; **saving grace** see **grace**; **savings bank** a bank established to encourage thrift by taking small deposits, investing under regulations for safety, and giving compound interest; **savings certificate** a certificate of having invested a small sum in government funds.—**save appearances** to keep up an appearance of wealth, comfort, consistency, harmony, propriety, etc; **save as you earn** (abbrev. SAYE) a government-operated savings scheme in which regular deductions are made from one's earnings; **save one's bacon, face, save the mark** see **bacon**, **face**, **mark**; **save up** to accumulate or hold for some purpose by refraining from spending or using. [Fr. *sauver*—L. *salvāre*—*salvus*, safe.]

saveloy *sav'ə-loi*, *n.* a highly seasoned sausage, orig. of brains. [Fr. *cervelat, cervelas*, a saveloy—L. *cerebellum*, dim. of *cerebrum*, the brain.]

savin *sav'in*, *n.* a species of juniper with very small leaves: its tops yielding an irritant volatile oil: extended to Virginian juniper ('red cedar') and other plants. [O.Fr. *sabine*—L. *sabīna* (*herba*), Sabine (herb).]

saviour *sā'vyər*, *n.* one who saves from evil: **Saviour** a title applied by Christians to Jesus Christ.

savoir-faire *sav-wär-fer'*, *n.* the faculty of knowing just what to do and how to do it: tact. [Fr.]

savoir-vivre *sav-wär-vē'vr'*, *n.* good breeding: knowledge of polite usages. [Fr.]

savory *sā'vər-i*, *n.* a labiate flavouring herb (*Satureia*, esp. *S. hortensis*, summer savory, or *S. montana*, winter savory). [App.—L. *satureia*.]

savour, also (*U.S.*) **savor**, *sā'vər*, *n.* taste: odour: flavour: relish.—*v.i.* to taste or smell in a particular way: to have a flavour: to smack.—*v.t.* to flavour, season: to taste, smell: to be conscious of: to relish: to perceive critically: to taste with conscious direction of the attention.—*adj.* **sā'voured**.—*adv.* **sā'vourily**.—*n.* **sā'vouriness**.—*adjs.* **sā'vourless**; **sā'voury** of good savour or relish: fragrant: having savour or relish: appetising: salty, piquant or spiced (opp. to *sweet*).—*n.* a savoury course or dish or small item of food. [O.Fr. *sav(o)ur* (Fr. *saveur*)—L. *sapor*—*sapēre*, to taste.]

Savoy *sə-voi'*, *n.* a district, formerly of the kingdom of Sardinia, now of S.E. France, giving name to a former palace and sanctuary and to a theatre in London: (without *cap.*) a winter cabbage with a large close head and wrinkled leaves—originally from *Savoy*.—*n.* **Savoyard** (*sav'oi-ärd*) a native or inhabitant of Savoy: a performer in the Gilbert and Sullivan operas produced at the Savoy theatre.—Also *adj.* [Fr *Savoie, Savoyard*.]

savvy *sav'i*, (*slang*) *v.t.* and *v i.* to know: to understand.—*n.* general ability: common sense: knowhow, skill. [Sp. *sabe*—*saber*, to know—L. *sapēre*, to be wise.]

saw[1] *sö, pa.t* of **see[2]**.

saw[2] *sö*, *n.* a toothed cutting instrument.—*v.t.* to cut with, or as with, or as, a saw: to play harshly or crudely (as a fiddler).—*v.i.* to use a saw: to make to and fro movements, as if with a saw:—*pa.t.* **sawed**; *pa.p.* **sawed** or (usu.) **sawn**.—*adj.* **sawed**.—*n.* and *adj.* **saw'ing**.—*adj.* **sawn**.—*n.* **saw'yer** one who saws timber, esp. at a sawpit: a stranded tree that bobs in a river (*U.S.*).—**saw'-blade**; **saw'-bones** (*slang*) a surgeon; **saw'dust** dust or small particles of wood, etc., detached in sawing.—*v.t.* to sprinkle with sawdust.—*adj.* **saw'dusty**.—**saw'-edge**.—*adj.* **saw'-edged** serrated.—**saw'-fish** a ray (*Pristis*) or (sometimes) a shark (*Pristiophorus*; **saw'-shark**) with a flattened bony beak toothed on the edges; **saw'-fly** a hymenopterous insect of various kinds with saw-like ovipositor; **saw'-frame** the frame in which a saw is set; **saw'-horse** a trestle for supporting wood that is being sawn; **saw'-mill** a mill for sawing timber.—*adj.* **sawn'-off** (or **sawed off**) shortened by cutting with a saw: short in stature (*slang*).—**saw'pit** a pit in which one sawyer stands while another stands above; **saw'-set** an instrument for turning saw-teeth to right and left; **saw'-tooth**.—Also *adj.*—*adj.* **saw'-toothed**.—**saw'wort** a name for various composites with serrate leaves (*Serratula, Saussurea*, etc.). [O.E. *saga*; Ger. *Sage*.]

saw[3] *sö*, *n.* a saying: a proverb. [O.E. *sagu*, from the root of *secgan*, to say, tell.]

sawder *sö'dər*, *v.t.* to flatter, blarney.—*n.* (in phrase *soft sawder*) flattery. [Prob. **solder**.]

sawn *sön*, *pa.p.* of **saw**.

sax[1] *saks*, *n.* a chopper for trimming slates. [O.E. *sæx* (W.S. *seax*), a knife.]

sax[2] *saks*, *n.* a coll. shortening of **saxophone**.

saxatile *sak'sə-tīl, -til*, *adj.* rock-dwelling. [L. *saxātilis*—*saxum*, a rock.]

Saxe *saks*, *adj.* made in, or characteristic of, Saxony (of china, etc): of a deep shade of light blue (**Saxe blue**, also **Saxon** or **Saxony blue**).—*n.* Saxon blue, a dye colour. [Fr. *Saxe*, Saxony.]

saxhorn *saks'hörn*, *n.* a brass wind-instrument having a long winding tube with bell opening, invented by Antoine or Adolphe *Sax* (1814–94).

saxicolous *sak-sik'ə-ləs*, *adj.* living or growing among rocks.—*adj.* **saxic'oline**. [L. *saxum*, a rock, *colēre*, to inhabit.]

saxifrage *sak'si-frij, -frāj*, *n.* any species of the genus *Saxifraga*, Alpine or rock plants with tufted foliage and small white, yellow or red flowers: extended to other plants.—*adj.* **saxifraga'ceous**. [L. *saxifraga*—*saxum*, a stone, *frangēre*, to break (from growing in clefts of rock).]

Saxon *saks'ən*, *n.* one of a N. German people that conquered most of Britain in the 5th and 6th centuries: the language of that people on the Continent (Old Saxon) or in Britain (Anglo-Saxon, Old English): a native, inhabitant, or citizen of Saxony in the later German sense (now in S. Germany).—*adj.* pertaining to the Saxons in any sense, their language, country, or architecture.—*v.t.* and *v.i.* **Sax'onise, -ize** to make or become Saxon.—*ns.* **Sax'onism** a Saxon or English idiom: a preference for native English words, institutions, etc.; **Sax'onist** a scholar in Old English; **sax'ony** a soft woollen yarn or cloth.—**Saxon architecture** a Romanesque style of building in England before the Norman Conquest, with characteristics of the woodwork of the period; **Saxon(y) blue** see **Saxe**; **Saxon Shore** (L *Litus Saxonicum*) in Roman times, the coast districts from Brighton to the Wash. [L *Saxōnēs* (pl.); of Ger. origin; perh. conn. O E. *sæx* (W.S. *seax*), O.H.G. *sahs*, knife, short sword.]

saxophone sak'sə-fōn, *n.* a jazz, military and dance band instrument with reed, (properly) metal tube, and about twenty finger-keys.—*n.* **saxophonist** (-sof'ən-ist). [*Sax*, the inventor (see **saxhorn**), Gr *phōnē*, the voice.]

say sā, *v.t.* to utter or set forth, as words or in words: to speak: to assert, affirm, state, declare: to tell: to go through in recitation or repetition —*v.i.* to make a statement: to speak: to declare, set forth in answer to a question:—*2nd sing. pr. ind.* **sayst** (*sāst*), **sayest** (*sā'ist*; both *arch.*); *3rd sing.* **says** (*sez, səz*), archaic **saith** (*seth*); *pr.p.* **say'ing**; *pa.p.* and *pa.t.* **said** (*sed*); *2nd sing.* **saidst** (*sedst*), also **said'est** (both *arch.*).—*n.* something said: a remark: a speech: what one wants to say: opportunity of speech: a voice, part, or influence in a decision.—*adj.* **say'able.**—*ns* **say'er**; **say'ing** something said: an expression: a maxim.— **say'-so** an authoritative saying: authority: a rumour: hearsay.—**I'll say!** (*coll.*) a response expressing wholehearted agreement, **I say** an exclamation calling attention or expressing surprise, protest, sudden joy, etc.; **it is said** or **they say** it is commonly reputed; **it says (that)** the text runs thus (*coll.*); **nothing to say for oneself** no defence of oneself to offer: no small-talk; **not to say** indeed one might go further and say; **say for example:** suppose: I say (*U.S.*): in verse an introduction to a rhetorical question; **says I, says you, he,** etc. (in *illit.* or jocular use) ungrammatical substitutes for said I, you, he, etc.; **says you** *interj* expressing incredulity; **sooth to say** in truth: if the truth must be told; **that is to say** in other words; **to say nothing of** not to mention; **to say the least at least:** without exaggeration; **what do you say to?** how about?: are you inclined towards?; **you, he can say that again** (*coll.*) you are, he is absolutely right, I agree entirely. [O.E. *secgan* (*sægde, gesægd*).]

scab *skab, n.* vaguely, a skin disease, esp. with scales or pustules, and esp. one caused by mites (as in *sheep scab*): a fungous disease of various kinds in potatoes, apples, etc.: a crust formed over a sore, or in any of these diseases: a scoundrel: a black-leg.—*v.i.* to develop a scab: to play the scab, act as a black-leg.— *adj.* **scabbed** (*skabd, skab'id*).—*n.* **scabb'iness.**—*adj.* **scabb'y.** [App. from an O.N equivalent of O.E. *scæb, sceabb* (see **shabby**) influenced by association with L. *scabiēs.*]

scabbard *skab'ərd, n.* a sheath, esp. for a sword.—*v.t.* to sheathe.—*adj.* **scabb'ardless.**—**scabb'ard-fish** a long narrow fish (*Lepidopus*) of the hairtail family. [M.E. *scauberc*, app.—A.Fr. *escaubers* (pl.), prob. Gmc.]

scabies *skā'bi-ēz, -bēz, n.* the itch. [L. *scābiēs—scabēre*, to scratch.]

scabious *skā'bi-əs, n.* a plant of the teasel family, long thought efficacious in treating scaly eruptions: a plant of the bell-flower family, of similar appearance [L. *scābiōsus—scābiēs*, the itch.]

scabrous *skā'brəs, adj.* rough: scurfy: beset with difficulties: bordering on the indecent.—*n.* **scā'brousness.** [L. *scābrōsus, scābridus—scāber*, rough]

scad *skad, n.* a fish (*Caranx*, or *Trachurus, trachurus*) with armoured and keeled lateral line, superficially like a coarse mackerel, also called *horse-mackerel*

[App. Cornish dial.; perh. **shad.**]

scad² *skad*, (esp. *U.S.*) *n* a large amount, a lot (usu. in *pl.*)

scaffold *skaf'əld, n.* a temporary erection for men at work on a building, and their tools and materials: a raised platform, as for performers, spectators, or executions: a framework: capital punishment.—*v.t* to furnish with a scaffold; **scaff'older; scaff'olding** a framework for painters, builders, etc., at work materials for scaffolds: a frame, framework [O.Fr. *escadafault* (Fr. *échafaud*)]

scā'lable. See **scale¹.**

scalar *skā'lər, adj.* having magnitude only, not direction —*n.* a scalar quantity [L. *scāla*, a ladder]

scal(l)awag. Same as **scallywag.**

scald¹ *skold, v t.* to injure with hot liquid: to cook or heat short of boiling: to treat with very hot water.— *v.t.* to be scalded: to be hot enough to scald.—*n.* a burn caused by hot liquid.—*n.* **scald'er.**—*n.* and *adj.* **scald'ing.** [O.Fr *escalder* (Fr. *échauder*)—L.L. *excaldāre*, to bathe in warm water—*ex,* from, *calidus,* warm, hot.]

scald², **scaldic.** Same as **skald, skaldic.**

scald³ *skōld, n* scurf on the head.—**scald'fish** the smooth sole; **scald'-head** a diseased scalp: scalp disease of various kinds [For *scalled,* scabby— O.N. *skalli,* bald head.]

scale¹ *skāl, n* a graduated series or order: a graduated measure: a system of definite tones used in music: a succession of these performed in ascending or descending order of pitch through one octave or more: the compass or range of a voice or instrument: a numeral system: a system or scheme of relative values or correspondences: the ratio of representation to object: relative extent.—*v.t.* to mount, as by a ladder: to climb: to change according to scale (often with *up* or *down*).—*adj.* **scal'able.**—*ns.* **scal'er** an instrument that counts very rapid pulses, by recording at the end of each group of specified numbers instead of after individual pulses; **scal'ing.** —**scal'ing-ladder** a ladder for scaling the walls of a fortress, etc.: a fireman's ladder.—**full-scale** see **full**; **on a large, small, scale** in a great, small, way; **on the scale of** in the ratio of; **to scale** in proportion to actual dimensions. [L. *scāla*, a ladder—*scandĕre*, to mount]

scale² *skāl, n.* a thin plate on a fish, reptile, etc.: a readily detached flake: a lamina: an overlapping plate in armour: a small, flat, detachable piece of cuticle: a reduced leaf or leaf-base: a small flat structure clothing a butterfly's or moth's wing: an encrustation: a film, as on iron being heated for forging.— *v t* to clear of scales· to peel off in thin layers.—*v.i.* to come off in thin layers or flakes —*adjs.* **scaled**; **scale'less; scale'like.**—*ns.* **scal'er** one who scales fish, boilers, etc.: an instrument for scaling, as for removing tartar from the teeth; **scal'iness; scal'ing.**—Also *adj* —*adj.* **scal'y** covered with scales: like scales: shabby: formed of scales: inclined to scale.—**scale'-arm'our** armour of overlapping scales; **scale'-board** a very thin slip of wood; **scale'-fern** a fern (*Ceterach officinarum*) whose back is densely covered with rusty-coloured scales; **scale'-insect** any insect of the *Coccidae*, in which the sedentary female fixes on a plant and secretes a waxy shield; **scale'-moss** a liverwort with small leaf-like structures, as *Jungermannia.* [M.E. *scāle*—O.Fr. *escale*, husk, chip of stone, of Gmc. origin.]

scale³ *skāl, n.* a balance pan: (usu in *pl.*) a balance: (in *pl*) Libra, a constellation and a sign of the zodiac.— *v.t.* to weigh: to weigh up.—*v.t.* to be weighed, as a jockey (often *scale in*). [A Northern form from O.N *skāl,* bowl, pan of balance; cf O.E. *scealu,* shell, cup, Du. *schaal*, Ger. *Schale*, and preceding word.]

scalene *skăl'ēn, skal-ēn'*, *adj.* (of a triangle) with three unequal sides: (of a cone or cylinder) with axis oblique to the base: denoting the muscles that connect the upper ribs to the cervical vertebrae, being obliquely situated and unequal-sided.

scallion *skal'yən, n.* the leek: an onion with defective bulb: a spring onion. [O.N.Fr. *escalogne*—L. *Ascalōnia* (*cēpa*), Ascalon (onion).]

scallop *skol'əp, skal'əp, n.* a bivalve (Pecten) having a sub-circular shell with radiating ridges and eared hinge-line: a valve of its shell: a dish or other object of like form: a shallow dish in which oysters, etc., are cooked, baked, and browned: hence, the cooked oysters, etc., themselves: a potato slice cooked in batter: one of a series of curves in the edge of anything: a scallop-shell as pilgrim badge: an escalope.—*v.t.* to cut into scallops or curves: to cook in a scallop with sauce and usu. breadcrumbs.—*v.i.* to gather, search for scallops.—*adj.* **scall'oped** having the edge or border cut into scallops or curves.—**scall'op-shell** the shell of a scallop, esp. that of a Mediterranean species, the badge of a pilgrim to the shrine of St James of Compostela.—Also **scollop.** [O.Fr. *escalope*; of Gmc. origin.]

scallywag, scallawag, scalawag *skal'i-wag, -ə-wag, ns.* an undersized animal of little value: a good-for-nothing.

scalp *skalp n.* the outer covering of the skull: the top or hairy part of the head: the skin on which the hair of the head grows: a piece of that skin torn off as a token of victory by the North American Indians: a bare rock or mountain-top.—*v.t.* to cut the scalp from: to buy cheap in order to resell quickly at a profit: of theatre, travel, or other tickets, to buy up and sell at other than official prices (*U.S.*): to destroy the political influence of (*U.S.*).—*n.* **scalp'er.**—*adj.* **scalp'less.**—**scalp'-lock** a long tuft of hair left unshaven as a challenge. [M.E. *scalp*; perh. Scand.]

scalpel *skal'pəl, n.* a small knife for dissecting or operating.—*n.* **scalp'er** an engraver's scauper.—*adj.* **scalp'riform** chisel-shaped. [L. *scalper*, dim. *scalpellum*, a knife.]

scaly. See **scale²**.

scammony *skam'ən-i, n.* Convolvulus scammonia, a twining Asian plant with arrow-shaped leaves: its dried root: a cathartic gum-resin obtained from its root or that of a substitute. [Gr. *skammōniā.*]

scamp¹ *skamp, n.* a rascal: a lively, tricky fellow.—*v.t.* **scamp'er** to run or skip about briskly.—*n.* an act of scampering.—*adj.* **scamp'ish.**—*adv.* **scamp'ishly.**—*n.* **scamp'ishness.** [O.Fr. *escamper* or It. *scampare*, to decamp.]

scamp² *skamp, v.t.* to do, execute, perfunctorily or without thoroughness.—*ns.* **scamp'er; scamp'ing.**—**scamp'-work.** [Poss. O.N. *skemma*, to shorten.]

scampi *skam'pi, n.pl.* crustaceans of the species *Nephrops norvegicus*, esp. (treated as *sing.*) when cooked and served as a dish. [Pl. of It. *scampo*, a shrimp.]

scan *skan, v.t.* to analyse metrically: to utter so as to bring out the metrical structure: to examine critically: to examine closely: to examine all parts of in systematic order: (in television) to pass a beam over every part of in turn: to make pictorial records of (part of) the body by various techniques, e.g. ultrasonics (*med.*): loosely, to cast an eye negligently over: to search out by swinging the beam (*radar*).—*v.i.* to agree with the rules of metre:—*pr.p.* **scann'ing;** *pa.t.* and *pa.p.* **scanned.**—*n.* a scanning.—*n.* **scann'er** one who scans or can scan: a perforated disc (also **scann'ing-disc**) used in television: the rotating aerial

by which the beam is made to scan (*radar*): an instrument which scans.—*n.* and *adj.* **scann'ing.**—*n.* **scan'sion** act, art, or mode of scanning verse: scanning in television. [L. *scandēre, scānsum*, to climb.]

scandal *skan'dl, n.* anything that brings discredit upon religion: injury to reputation: something said which is injurious to reputation: a false imputation: malicious gossip: slander: a disgraceful fact, thing, or person.—*n.* **scandalisā'tion, -z-.**—*v.t.* **scan'dalise, -ize** to give scandal or offence to: to shock.—*adj.* **scan'dalous** giving scandal or offence: calling forth condemnation: openly vile: defamatory.—*adv.* **scan'dalously.**—*n.* **scan'dalousness.**—**scan'dal-bearer** a propagator of malicious gossip; **scan'dalmonger** one who deals in defamatory reports; **scan'dalmongering.** [L. *scandalum*—Gr. *skandalon*, a stumbling-block.]

Scandinavian *skan-di-nā'vi-ən, adj.* of, or characteristic of, *Scandinavia*, the peninsula divided into Norway and Sweden, but, in a historical sense, applying also to Denmark and Iceland: North Germanic (*philol.*).—*n.* a native of Scandinavia: a member of the dominant Nordic race of Scandinavia.—*n.* **scan'dium** a metallic element (symbol Sc; at. numb. 21) discovered in 1879 in the Scandinavian mineral euxenite. [L. *Scandināvia* (from Gmc. word), and its shortened form *Scandia*.]

scanner, scansion. See **scan.**

scant *skant, adj.* not full or plentiful: scarcely sufficient: deficient: short, poorly supplied: sparing.—*adv.* barely: scantily.—*v.t.* to stint: to restrict: to reduce: to dispense sparingly: to treat inadequately.—*adv.* **scant'ily.**—*n.* **scant'iness.**—*adv.* **scant'ly.**—*n.* **scant'ness.**—*adj.* **scant'y** meagre: deficient: skimped: wanting in fullness: parsimonious. [O.N. *skamt*, neut. of *skammr*, short.]

scantling *skant'ling, n.* a measured size: a measurement: an allotted portion (*arch.*): dimensions of a cross-section: a sample or pattern: a narrow piece of timber. [O.Fr. *escantillon, eschantillon*, of uncertain etymology.]

scape¹ *skāp,* (*arch.*) n. an escape.—*v.t.* and *v.i.* (also **'scape**) to escape.—**scape'grace** a graceless, hare-brained fellow. [escape.]

scape² *skāp, n.* a flower-stalk rising from the ground, without foliage leaves (*bot.*): the basal part of an antenna (*entom.*): the shaft or stem of a feather: the shaft of a column (*archit.*). [L. *scāpus*, a shaft.]

scape³ *skāp, n.* a landscape or other picture of scenery. **— -scape** noun combining form indicating a type of scene or view, as *seascape, streetscape*. [landscape.]

scapegoat *skāp'gōt, n.* a goat on which, once a year, the Jewish high-priest laid symbolically the sins of the people, and which was then allowed to escape into the wilderness (Lev. xvi): one who is made to bear the misdeeds of another. [escape and goat.]

scaphoid *skaf'oid, adj.* boat-shaped.—*n.* **scaph'oid (bone)** a boat-shaped bone on the thumb side of the wrist joint. [Gr. *skaphē*, a boat, *eidos*, form.]

scapula *skap'ū-lə, n.* the shoulder-blade.—*adj.* **scap'ūlar** of the shoulder-blade or shoulder.—*n.* originally an ordinary working garb, now the mark of the monastic orders, a long strip of cloth with an opening for the head, worn hanging before and behind over the habit: two pieces of cloth tied together over the shoulders, worn by members of certain lay confraternities of the Roman Catholic Church: a supporting bandage worn over the shoulder: a shoulder feather —*adj.* and *n.* **scap'ūlary** scapular. [L. *scapulae*, the shoulder-blades.]

scar¹ *skär, n.* the mark left by a wound or sore: any mark or blemish: any mark, trace, or result of injury, material, moral or psychological, etc. (*fig.*): a mark at a place of former attachment, as of a leaf.—*v.t.* to mark with a scar.—*v.i.* to become scarred:—*pr.p* **scarr'ing**; *pa.t.* and *pa.p.* **scarred.**—*adjs.* **scar'less** without scars: unwounded; **scarred.**—*n* and *adj.* **scarr'ing.**—*adj.* **scarr'y.** [O.Fr. *escare*—L. *eschara* —Gr. *eschara*, a hearth, brazier, burn, scar.]

scar² *skär*, **scaur** *skor*, *ns.* a precipitous bare place on a hill-face: a cliff: a reef in the sea.—*adj.* **scarr'y.** [App. O.N. *sker*, *skera*, to cut.]

scarab *skar'ab*, *n.* a dung-beetle, esp. the sacred beetle of the ancient Egyptians: a gem cut in the form of a beetle.—*ns.* **scarabaeid** (*skar-ə-bē'id*) any beetle of the *Scarabaeidae*, a large family of beetles, some of them of great size (chafers, dung-beetles) [L. *scarabaeus*; cf. Gr. *kārabos*.]

scaramouch *skar'ə-mowch*, *n.* a bragging, cowardly buffoon. [Fr. *Scaramouche*—It. *Scaramuccia*, a stock character in Italian comedy.]

scarce *skärs*, *adj.* by no means plentiful: not often found: hard to get: short in supply —*adv.* scarcely: hardly ever.—*adv.* **scarce'ly** only just: not quite.— *ns.* **scarce'ness**; **scarc'ity** the state or fact of being scarce: shortness of supply, esp. of necessaries: dearth: deficiency.—**make oneself scarce** to leave quickly, unobtrusively, for reasons of prudence, tact, etc. [O.N.Fr. *escars* (Fr. *échars*), niggardly, from a L.L. substitute for L. *excerptus*, pa.p. of *excerpēre*— *ex*, out, *carpēre*, to pick.]

scare *skār*, *v.t.* to startle, to affright: to drive or keep off by frightening.—*v.i.* to become frightened.—*n.* a fright: a panic: a baseless public alarm.—*n.* **scar'er.**— *adj.* **scar'y**, **scarey** frightening: timorous.—**scare'-crow** anything set up to scare birds: a vain cause of terror: a person meanly clad; **scare'-head**, **-heading** a newspaper heading designed to raise a scare; **scare'monger** an alarmist, one who causes panic by initiating or encouraging rumours of trouble; **scare'mongering.**—**scare the (living) daylights out of**, **scare the pants off** (both *coll.*) to frighten considerably. [M.E. *skerre*—O.N. *skirra*, to avoid— *skiarr*, shy.]

scarf¹ *skärf*, *n.* a light, usually decorative piece of dress thrown loosely on the shoulders about the neck, or over the head, etc.: a military or official sash: a necktie: a muffler: a cravat:—*pl.* **scarfs**, **scarves.**— *adv.* **scarf'-wise.**—**scarf'-pin** an ornamental pin worn in a scarf; **scarf'-ring** an ornamental ring through which the ends of a scarf are drawn. [Perh. O.N.Fr. *escarpe* (Fr. *écharpe*), sash, sling.]

scarf² *skärf*, *n.* a joint between pieces placed end to end, cut so as to fit with overlapping like a continuous piece: an end so prepared: a longitudinal cut in a whale's carcase.—*v.t.* to join with a scarf-joint: to make a scarf in.—*n.* **scarf'ing.**—**scarf'-joint.** [Perh. Scand.]

scarfskin *skärf'skin*, *n.* the surface skin [Perh. **scarf¹**; perh. related to **scurf**.]

scarify *skar'i-fī*, *v.t.* to make a number of scratches or slight cuts in: to break up the surface of: to lacerate: to criticise severely:—*pr.p.* **scar'ifying**; *pa.t.* and *pa.p.* **scar'ified.**—*ns.* **scarification** (*-fi-kā'shən*); **scar'ificator** a surgical instrument for scarifying; **scar'ifier** an implement for breaking the surface of the soil or of a road. [L.L. *scarificāre*, *-ātum*—Gr. *skariphos*, an etching tool]

scarious *skā'ri-əs*, *adj.* thin, dry, stiff, and membranous (*bot.*).

scarlatina *skär-lə-tē'nə*, *n.* scarlet fever. [It. *scarlattina*.]

scarlet *skar'lit*, *n.* a brilliant red: a brilliant red cloth, garment, or garb, or its wearer.—*adj.* of the colour called scarlet: dressed in scarlet.—**scarlet fever** an infectious fever, usually marked by a sore throat and a scarlet rash; **scar'let-hat** a cardinal's (former)

hat; **scar'let-runn'er** a scarlet-flowered climber (*Phaseolus multiflorus*) of the kidney-bean genus, with edible beans; **scarlet woman** the woman referred to in Rev. xvii.—variously taken as pagan Rome, Papal Rome, or the world in its anti-Christian sense: a whore [O.Fr. *escarlate* (Fr. *écarlate*), thought to be from Pers. *saqalāt*, scarlet cloth.]

scarp *skärp*, *n* an escarp: an escarpment.—*v.t.* to cut into a scarp.—*adj.* **scarped.**—*n.* **scarp'ing.** [It. *scarpa*.]

scarper *skär'pər*, (*slang*) *v.i.* to run away, escape, leave without notice. [It *scappare*.]

scarred, **scarring**, **scarry.** See **scar¹·².**

scarves; **scary.** See **scarf**; **scare.**

scat¹ *skat*, *interj.* be off!—*v t.* to scare away.

scat² *skat*, *n.* singing a melody to nonsense syllables.— Also *v.t* and *v.i.* [Perh. imit.]

scathe *skādh n.* (*arch.*) hurt: injury —*v.t.* (*arch.*) to injure: to blast: to scorch with invective.—*adjs.* **scathe'less** without injury; **scath'ing.**—*adv.* **scath'ingly.** [O.N. *skathe*]

scatology *skat-ol'ə-ji*, *n.* study of excrement, esp. in order to assess diet: obscene literature: interest in the obscene.—*adjs.* **scatolog'ical**; **scatoph'agous** (Gr. *phagein* to eat) dung-eating.—*n.* **scatoph'agy.** [Gr. *skōr*, *skatos*, dung]

scatter *skat'ər*, *v.t.* to disperse. to throw loosely about: to strew: to sprinkle: to dispel: to reflect or disperse irregularly (waves or particles).—*v.i.* to disperse: to throw shot loosely.—*n.* a scattering: a sprinkling: dispersion: the extent of scattering.—*adj.* **scatt'ered** dispersed irregularly, widely, in all directions, or here and there: thrown about: distracted —*adv.* **scatt'eredly** (*-ərd-li*).—*ns.* **scatt'erer**; **scatt'ering** dispersion: that which is scattered: a small proportion occurring sporadically: the deflection of photons or particles as a result of collisions with other particles (*phys.*).—*adv.* **scatt'eringly.**—*adj.* **scatt'ery.**— **scatt'er-brain** one incapable of sustained attention or thought.—*adj.* **scatter'-brained.**—**scatter rugs**, cushions small rugs, cushions which can be placed anywhere in the room.—*adj.* **scatt'ershot** random, indiscriminate, wide-ranging, as shot from a gun.— **elastic, inelastic scattering** see **elastic, inelastic collision** under **collide.** [Origin obscure; *scatered* occurs in the *O.E. Chronicle*.]

scatty *skat'i*, (*coll.*) *adj.* slightly crazy and unpredictable in conduct.—*n.* **scatt'iness.** [Poss. *scatterbrain.*]

scauper *skö'pər*, *n.* a tool with semicircular face, used by engravers [**scalper.**]

scaur. Same as **scar².**

scavenger *skav'inj-ər*, *-inzh*, *n* one who cleans the streets: a person or apparatus that removes waste: an animal that feeds on garbage: one who deals or delights in filth —*v.i.* to act as scavenger.—*v.t.* **scav'enge** (back-formation) to cleanse.—*v.i.* to act as scavenger: to search (for useful items) among refuse.—*n.* the sweeping out of waste gases from an internal-combustion engine —*ns.* **scav'engering**; **scav'engery**; **scav'enging.** [Orig. *scavager*—A.Fr. *scawage*, inspection; prob. of Gmc origin.]

scena *shā'na*, *n.* an operatic scene: an elaborate dramatic recitative followed by an aria:—*pl.* **scene** (*shā'nā*). —*n.* **scenario** (*si-*, *se-*, *shā-na'ri-ō*) a skeleton of a dramatic work, film, etc., scene by scene: an outline of future development, or of a plan to be followed: *loosely*, any imagined or projected sequence of events, etc.:—*pl.* **scena'rios.** [It.,—L. *scēna*.]

scence. See **scena.**

scend, 'scend. See **send.**

scene *sēn*, *n.* the place of action in a play (hence in a story, an actual occurrence, etc): its representation on the stage: a painted slide, hanging, or other object, used for this purpose: a division of a play marked off by the fall of the curtain, by a change of place, or by the entry or exit of an important character: an episode: a dramatic or stagy incident, esp. an uncomfortable, untimely, or unseemly display of hot feelings: a landscape, picture of a place or action: a view, spectacle: the activity, publicity, etc., surrounding a particular business or profession, e.g. *the pop music scene* (*coll.*): area of interest or activity (*coll.*): situation, state of affairs (*slang*).—*v.t.* to set in a scene.—*n.* **scèn'ery** theatrical slides, hangings, etc., collectively: views of beautiful, picturesque, or impressive country.—*adj.* **scenic** (*sē'nik, sen'ik*) pertaining to scenery.—*adv.* **scen'ically.—scene dock, bay** the space where scenery is stored; **scene'-painter** one who paints scenery for theatres; **scene'-shifter** one who sets and removes the scenery in a theatre; **scenic railway** a railway on a small scale, running through artificial representations of picturesque scenery.—**behind the scenes** at the back of the visible stage: away from the public view (*lit.* and *fig.*): in a position to know what goes on; **come on the scene** to arrive; **set the scene** to describe the background to an event, etc. [L. *scēna*—Gr. *skēnē*, a tent, stage building.]

scent *sent, v.t.* to track, find, or discern by smell, or as if by smell: to perfume.—*v.i.* to give forth a smell: to sniff: to smell.—*n.* odour: sense of smell: a substance used for the sake of its smell: trail by smell: paper strewn by the pursued in hare and hounds.—*adjs.* **scent'ed** having a smell, fragrant: impregnated or sprinkled with perfumery.—*n.* and *adj.* **scent'ing.—** *adj.* **scent'less.— scent'-bag** a scent-gland: a sachet: a bag of strong-smelling stuff dragged over the ground for a drag-hunt; **scent'-bottle** a small bottle for holding perfume; **scent'-gland** a gland that secretes a substance of distinctive smell, for recognition, attraction, or defence; **scent'-organ** a scent-gland: a smelling organ.—**put, throw someone off the scent** to mislead someone. [Fr. *sentir*—L. *sentīre*, to perceive.]

scepsis, skepsis *skep'sis, n.* philosophic doubt. [Gr.; see next.]

sceptic, sometimes (and in U.S.) **skeptic,** *skep'tik, adj.* pertaining to the philosophical school of Pyrrho and his successors, who asserted nothing positively and doubted the possibility of knowledge.—*n.* a sceptic philosopher: one who withholds from prevailing doctrines, esp. in religion: one who inclines to disbelieve. —*adj.* **scep'tical** or of inclined to scepticism: (now often) doubtful, or inclined towards incredulity.— *adv.* **scep'tically.—** *n.* **scep'ticism** doubt: the doctrine that no facts can be certainly known: agnosticism: sceptical attitude towards Christianity: general disposition to doubt. [L. *scepticus*—Gr. *skeptikos,* thoughtful, *skeptesthai,* to consider.]

sceptre *sep'tar, n.* a staff or baton borne as an emblem of kingship.—*adjs.* **scep'tral** regal; **scep'tred** bearing a sceptre: regal; **scep'treless.** [L. *scēptrum*—Gr. *skēptron,* a staff—*skēptein,* to prop, stay.]

schadenfreude *shä'dən-froi-də, n.* pleasure in others' misfortunes. [Ger.,—*Schade,* hurt, *Freude,* joy.]

schappe *shap'ə, n.* a fabric of waste silk with gum, etc., partly removed by fermentation.—*v.t.* to subject to this process. [Swiss Ger.]

schapska. See **chapka.**

schedule *shed'ūl, sked'ūl, n.* a slip or scroll with writing: a list, inventory, or table: a supplementary, explanatory, or appended document: an appendix to a bill or act of parliament: a form for filling in particulars, or such a form filled in: a timetable, plan, programme, or scheme.—*v.t.* to set as in a schedule: to plan, appoint, arrange.—*adj.* **sched'uled** entered

in a schedule: planned, appointed, arranged (to happen at a specified time).—**scheduled castes** in India, the former untouchables; **scheduled territories** sterling area.—**behind schedule** not keeping up to an arranged programme: late; **on schedule** on time. [O.Fr. *cedule*—L.L. *sc(h)edula,* dim. of *scheda,* a strip of papyrus.]

scheelite *shē'līt, n.* native calcium tungstate. [From the Sw. chemist K. W. *Scheele* (1742–86).]

schema *skē'mə, n.* a scheme, plan: a diagrammatic outline or synopsis: the image of the thing with which the imagination aids the understanding in its procedure: a kind of standard which the mind forms from past experiences, and by which new experiences can be evaluated to a certain extent:—*pl.* **schě'mata.—** *adj.* **schematic** (*ski-mat'ik*) following, or involving, a particular plan or arrangement.—*adv.* **schemat'ically.—** *n.* **schematisa'tion,** *-z-.—v.t.* **schě'matise,** *-ize* to reduce to or represent by a scheme.—*ns.* **schě'matism** form or outline of a thing: arrangement, disposition in a scheme; **schě'matist** one who frames a scheme [Gr. *schēma, -atos,* form, from the reduced grade of the root of *echein,* to have (as in the fut. *schēsein*).]

scheme *skēm, n.* a diagram of positions, esp. (*astrol.*) of planets: a diagram: a table: a system: a plan of purposed action for achieving an end: a plan for building operations of various kinds, or the buildings, etc., constructed, or the area covered (e.g. *housing scheme, irrigation scheme*): a plan pursued secretly, insidiously, by intrigue, or for private ends: a project: a programme of action.—*v.t.* to plan: to lay schemes for.—*v.i.* to form a plan: to lay schemes.—*n.* **schě'mer.—** *n.* and *adj.* **schě'ming.** [schema.]

scherzo *sker'tsō, skûr', n.* a lively busy movement in triple time, usually with a trio, in a sonata or a symphony:—*pl.* **scher'zos, scher'zi** (*-ē*).—*adj.* and *adv.* **scherzan'do** with playfulness.—*n.* a scherzando passage or movement:—*pl.* **scherzan'dos, scherzan'di** (*-ē*). [It.,—Gmc.; cf. Ger. *Scherz,* jest]

Schick('s) test *shik(s) test,* a test for susceptibility to diphtheria, made by injecting the skin with a measured amount of diphtheria toxin. [From Bela *Schick* (1877–1967), American doctor.]

schiedam *skē'dam,* or *-dam', n.* Holland gin, chiefly made at Schiedam (*s'hhē-ddm'*), near Rotterdam.

schilling *shil'ing, n.* an Austrian coin (in use after 1925), the unit of the Austrian monetary system. [Ger.; cf. **shilling.**]

schipperke *skip'ar-kə, -ki,* also *ship', n.* a small tailless breed of dogs, orig. watchdogs on barges. [Du., little boatman.]

schism *sizm, skizm, n.* a breach, esp. in the unity of a church: promotion of such a breach: a body so formed.—*n.* **schismatic** (*siz-mat'ik, skiz-*) one who favours a schism or belongs to a schismatic body.— *adjs.* **schismat'ic,** *-al.—adv* **schismat'ically.—** *n.* **schismat'icalness.—great Eastern,** or **Greek schism** the separation of the Greek church from the Latin, finally completed in 1054; (**great**) **Western schism** the division in the Western church from 1378 to 1417, when there were antipopes under French influence at Avignon. [Gr. *schisma,* a split, rent, cleft, partly through O.Fr. (*s)cisme*]

schist *shist, n.* any crystalline foliated metamorphic rock, as mica-schist, hornblende-schist: sometimes extended to shaly rocks.—*adj* **schist'ose.** [Fr. *schiste*—Gr. *schistos,* split; pron. due to German influence.]

Schistosoma *shis-tə-sō'mə, skis-, n.* the Bilharzia genus.—*ns.* **schis'tosome** a member of the genus; **schistosomi'asis** the disease bilharzia. [Gr. *schistos,* split.]

schiz- *skiz-,* **schizo-** *skit'sō-, skid'zō-, skiz'ō-,* in composition, cleave, cloven.—*ns.* **Schizanthus** (*-an'thəs*; Gr. *anthos*, flower) a showy Chilean flowering plant of the *Solanaceae*; **schi'zocarp** (*-kärp*; Gr. *karpos*, fruit) a dry fruit that splits into several one-seeded portions.—*adjs.* **schizocar'pous**, **schizocar'pic**; **schizognathous** (*-og'nə-thəs*; Gr. *gnathos*, jaw) of some birds, having the bones of the palate separate; **schizoid** (*skit'soid*, *skid'zoid*; Gr. *eidos*, form) showing qualities of a schizophrenic personality, such as asocial behaviour, introversion, tendency to fantasy, but without definite mental disorder.—*n.* a schizoid person.—*adj.* **schizoid'al.**—*n.pl.* **Schizomycetes** (*-mi-sē'tēz*; Gr. *mykēs*, pl. *mykētēs*, a fungus) the bacteria:—*sing.* **schizomycete** (*-sēt'*).—*adjs.* **schizomycet'ic**, **schizomycet'ous.**—*ns.* **schizophrenia** (*-frē'ni-ə*; Gr. *phrēn*, mind) a psychosis marked by introversion, dissociation, inability to distinguish reality from unreality, delusions, etc.; **schizophrenic** (*-fren'ik*) a person suffering from schizophrenia (*coll.* shortening **schizo** *skit'sō*; *pl.* **schiz'os**).—Also *adj.*—*n.* **schizothymia** (*-thī'mi-ə*; Gr. *thymos*, mind, temper) manifestation of schizoid traits within normal limits.—*adj.* **schizothy'mic.** [Gr. *schizein*, to cleave.]

schlemiel, **schlemihl**, **shlemiel** *shlə-mēl'*, (*slang*) *n.* a clumsy person. [Yiddish.]

schlep *shlep*, (*slang*) *v.t.* to pull, drag (also **schlepp**):—*pr.p.* **schlepp'ing**; *pa.t.* and *pa.p.* **schlepped.**—*n.* a clumsy, stupid, incompetent person.—*adj.* **schlepp'y.** [Yiddish.]

schlieren *shlē'rən*, *n.pl.* streaks of different colour, structure, or composition in igneous rocks: streaks in a transparent fluid, caused by the differing refractive indices of fluid of varying density.—**schlieren photography** the technique of photographing a flow of air or other gas, the variations in refractive index according to density being made apparent under a special type of illumination. [Ger.]

schlimazel, **shlimazel** *shli-mà'zl*, (*U.S. slang*) *n.* a persistently unlucky person. [Yiddish; see **shemozzle**.]

schlock *shlok'*, (*U.S. slang*) *adj.* of inferior quality.—*n.* a thing or things of inferior quality. [Yiddish.]

schloss *shlos*, *n.* a castle, palace, manor house. [Ger.]

schmaltz *shmolts*, *shmälts*, *n.* mush: a production in music or other art that is very sentimental, or showy: sentimentality.—*adj.* **schmaltz'y** old-fashioned, old-style, outmoded: sentimental. [Yiddish—Ger. *Schmalz*, cooking fat, grease.]

schmuck *shmuk*, (orig. *U.S. slang*) *ns.* a stupid person. [Yiddish.]

schnapper *shnap'ər*. Same as **snapper** (Australian fish). [Germanised.]

schnapps, **schnaps** *shnaps*, *n.* Holland gin. [Ger. *Schnapps*, a dram.]

schnauzer *shnowt'sər*, *n.* a very old German breed of terrier. [Ger. *Schnauze*, snout.]

schnitzel *shnit'sl*, *n.* a veal cutlet. [Ger.]

schnorkel *shnór'kl*, *n.* a retractable tube or tubes containing pipes for discharging gases from, or for taking air into, a submerged submarine: a tube for bringing air to a submerged swimmer.—Anglicised as **snor'kel**, **snort.** [Ger., *Schnòrkel*, a spiral ornament.]

schnorrer *shnò'*, *shnô'*, *shno'rər*, (*U.S. slang*) *n.* a beggar.—*v.i.* **schnorr** (*shnòr*, *shnôr*) to beg, esp. in such a way as to make the giver feel in some way beholden [Yiddish.]

schnozzle *shnoz'əl*, (*slang*) *n.* nose. [Yiddish.]

scholar *skol'ər*, *n.* a pupil: a disciple: a student: (in times of less widespread education) one who could read and write, or an educated person: one whose learning (formerly esp. in Latin and Greek) is extensive and exact, or whose approach to learning is scrupulous and critical: generally a holder of a scholarship.—*adj.* **schol'ar-like** like or befitting a scholar.—*n.* **schol'arliness.**—*adj.* **schol'arly** of, natural to a scholar: having the learning of a scholar.—*n.* **schol'arship** scholarly learning: a foundation or grant for the maintenance of a pupil or student: the status and emoluments of such a pupil or student — **scholar's mate** in chess, a simple mate accomplished in four moves. [O.E. *scólere*, and (in part) O.Fr *escoler*, both from L.L. *scholāris*—*schola*; see **school**[1].]

scholastic *skol-*, *skəl-as'tik*, *adj.* pertaining to schools, universities, or to their staffs or teaching, or to schoolmen: subtle: pedantic.—*n.* a schoolman, one who adheres to the method or subtleties of the Mediaeval schools: a Jesuit who has taken first vows only: a university teacher (esp with implication of pedantry).—*adv.* **scholas'tically.**—*n.* **scholas'ticism** (*-sizm*) the aims, methods, and products of thought which constituted the main endeavour of the intellectual life of the Middle Ages: the method or subtleties of the schools of philosophy: the collected body of doctrines of the schoolmen [Gr *scholastikos*—*scholē*; see **school**[1].]

scholion *skō'li-on*, **scholium** *-əm*, *ns.* an explanatory note, such as certain ancient grammarians wrote on passages in manuscripts, often in *pl.* (Gr. and L.) **scho'lia.**—*n.* **scho'liast** a writer of scholia.—*adj.* **scholias'tic.** [Gr *schólion*, *schóliastēs*—*schōlē*; see **school**[1].]

school[1] *skōōl*, *n* a place for instruction: an institution for education, esp. primary or secondary, or for teaching of special subjects: a division of such an institution: a building or room used for that purpose: the work of a school: the time given to it: the body of pupils of a school: the disciples of a particular teacher: those who hold a common doctrine or follow a common tradition: a group of people meeting in order to play card games, usu. for money (*slang*): a method of instruction: the body of instructors and students in a faculty or department: a group of studies in which honours may be taken: (in Oxford, in *pl.*) the B.A. examinations.—*adj.* of school, schools, or the schools.—*v.t.* to educate in a school: to train, to drill: to instruct: to coach in a part to be played: to teach overbearingly: to discipline.—*adj.* **schooled** trained: experienced.—*n.* **school'ing** instruction or maintenance at school: tuition: training: discipline: school fees: reproof: reprimand.—*adj.* and *adv.* **school'ward.**—*adv.* **school'wards.**—**school age** the age at which children attend school.—*adj.* **school's age.**—**school'bag** a bag for carrying school-books; **school'-bell** a bell to announce time for school; **school'-board** formerly, an elected board of school managers for a parish, town, or district; **school'-book** a book used in school; **school'boy** a boy attending school.—Also *adj.*—*adj.* **school'boyish.**—**school's child**; **school'-dame** mistress of a dame's school; **school'-day** a day on which schools are open: (in *pl*) time of being a school pupil; **school'-divine'**; **school's divin'ity** scholastic or seminary theology; **school'fellow** one taught at the same school at the same time; **school'-friend** one who is or has been a friend at school; **school'girl** a girl attending school.—*adj.* **school'girlish.**—**school'house** a building used as a school: a house provided for a school-teacher (**school house** a headmaster's or headmistress's boarding-house: its boarders); **school'-inspec'tor** an official appointed to examine schools; **school'-leav'er** one who is leaving school because he has reached the statutory age, or the stage, for doing so.—*n.* and *adj* **school'-leav'ing.**—**school'-ma'am** a schoolmistress (*U.S.*): a prim pedantic woman (*coll.*); **school'man** a philosopher or theologian of mediaeval scholasticism, **school'-marm** (*coll.*) another form of **school-ma'am**.—*adj.* **school'-marmish.**—**school'master** the master or one of the masters of a school.—Also *v.t* and *v.t* —*n.* and *adj.* **school'mastering.**—*adjs.* **school'-masterish; school'masterly.**—**school'mastership; school'-mate** a school-friend: a schoolfellow; **school'-mistress; school'room** a school classroom: in a house, a room for receiving or preparing lessons in; **school'-ship** a training-ship; **school'-teach'er** one who teaches in a school, **school'-teach'ing; school'-term** a division of the school year; **school'-time** the time at which a school opens, or during which it remains open school-days; **school'-work; school year** the period of (more or less) continual teaching during the year comprising an academic unit during which a child or student remains in the same basic class, i e., in Britain, from autumn to early summer —**old school** see **old.** [O.E. *scól*—L *schóla*—Gr. *schölé*, leisure, a lecture, a school.]

school² *skōōl, n.* a shoal of fish, whales, or other swimming animals: a flock, troop, assemblage, esp. of birds.—*v.i.* to gather or go in schools.—*adj.* (or in composition) going in schools.—*n.* and *adj* **school'ing.** [Du. *school*; cf. **shoal¹**.]

schooner *skōōn'ər, n.* a swift-sailing vessel, generally two-masted, fore-and-aft rigged, or with top and topgallant sails on the foremast: a large beer glass (esp. *U.S.*, *Austr.*): also a large sherry glass.—*adj* **schoon'er-rigged.** [Early 18th-century (Massachusetts) *skooner, scooner*, said to be from a dial. Eng. word *scoon*, to skim.]

schorl *shörl, n* black tourmaline. [Ger. *Schorl.*]

schottische *sho-tēsh', shot'ish, n.* a dance, or dance-tune, similar to the polka. [Ger. (*der*) *schottische* (*Tanz*), (the) Scottish (dance); pronunciation sham French.]

schuss *shōōs, n.* in skiing, a straight slope on which it is possible to make a fast run: such a run.—*v.i.* to make such a run. [Ger.]

schwa, shwa *shvä, shwä, n* an indistinct vowel sound in phonetics, a neutral vowel (ə).—Cf. **sheva.** [Ger., —Heb. *schêwa.*]

scia-. For various words see under **skia-.**

sciamachy *sī-am'ə-ki,* **skiamachy** *ski-am'ə-ki, ns.* fighting with shadows: imaginary or useless fighting. [Gr. *skiamakhia.*]

sciatic *sī-at'ik, adj.* of, or in the region of, the hip.—*n* **sciat'ica** neuritis of the great sciatic nerve which passes down the back of the thigh. [L.L. *sciaticus*, fem. *-a*—Gr. *ischion*, hip-joint.]

science *sī'əns, n.* knowledge ascertained by observation and experiment, critically tested, systematised and brought under general principles: a department or branch of such knowledge or study: a skilled craft: trained skill.—*adjs.* **sciential** (*-en'shl*) of, having, or producing, science: scientific; **scientif'ic** (L. *facĕre*, to make) orig. (of a syllogism) demonstrative, producing knowledge: hence of, relating to, based on, devoted to, according to, used in, or versed in, science.—*adv.* **scientif'ically.**—*ns.* **sci'entism** the methods or mental attitudes of men of science: a belief that the methods used in studying natural sciences should be employed also in investigating all aspects of human behaviour and condition, e.g. in philosophy and social sciences; **sci'entist** a man of science, esp. natural science.—*adj.* **scientis'tic.**—*n.* **Scientol'ogy** a religious system which, it is claimed, improves the mental and physical well-being of its adherents by scientific means.—**science fiction** fiction dealing with life on the earth in future, with space travel, and with life on other planets, or the like.—**science park** a centre for industrial research, etc., attached to a univer-

sity, set up for the purpose of co-operation between the academic and the commercial world; **the (noble) science** the art of boxing. [L. *scientia—sciēns, -entis,* pr.p. of *scire,* to know.]

scienter *sī-en'tər, (legal) adv.* having knowledge, being aware wilfully [L.]

sci-fi *sī'-fī', coll.* abbrev for **science fiction.**

scilicet *sī'li-set, skē'li-ket, adv.* to wit, namely. [L. *scilicet—scire licet,* it is permitted to know.]

Scilla *sil'ə, n.* the squill genus of the lily family, including some bright blue spring flowers: (*without cap.*) any plant of this genus. [L.,—Gr. *skilla,* the officinal squill.]

Scillonian *si-lō'ni-ən, adj.* of, belonging to, concerning, the *Scilly* Isles, off the south-west coast of Britain —*n.* an inhabitant of these islands.

scimitar *sim'i-tər, n* a short, single-edged, curved sword, broadest at the point end, used by the Turks and Persians. [Poss. through Fr *cimeterre* or It. *scimitarra*—Pers. *shamshīr*; but doubtful.]

scintigraphy *sin-tig'rə-fi, n.* a diagnostic technique in which a pictorial record of the pattern of gamma ray emission after injection of isotope into the body gives a picture, of an internal organ.—*n* **scint'igram** a picture so produced. [*scintillation*]

scintilla *sin-til'ə, n.* a spark: a hint, trace.—*adj.* **scin'-tillant** sparkling —*v.i.* **scin'tillate** to sparkle: to talk wittily.—*v.t.* to emit in sparks. to sparkle with.—*ns.* **scintilla'tion** a flash of light produced in a phosphor by an ionising particle, e.g. an alpha particle, or a photon; **scin'tillator** an instrument for detecting radioactivity; **scintillom'eter** an instrument for detecting and measuring radioactivity; **scintill'oscope** an instrument which shows scintillations on a screen. —**scintillation counter** a scintillometer. [L., a spark.]

scio-. For various words see **skia-.**

sciolism *sī'ə-lizm, n* superficial pretensions to knowledge.—*n.* **sci'olist** a pretender to science.—*adjs.* **sciolis'tic; sci'olous.** [L. *sciolus,* dim. of *scius,* knowing—*scire,* to know.]

scion *sī'ən, n.* a detached piece of a plant capable of propagating, esp. by grafting: a young member of a family· a descendant, offshoot. [O.Fr *sion, cion.*]

scire facias *sī'ri fā'shi-as, skē're fa'ki-ās,* a writ requiring a person to appear and show cause why a record should not be enforced or annulled. [L. *scire faciās,* make him to know.]

scirocco. See **sirocco.**

scirrhus *skir'əs, sir'əs, (med.) n.* a hard swelling: a hard cancer —*adjs.* **scirr'hoid, scirr'hous.** [Latinised from Gr. *skirros, skiros,* a tumour.]

scissel *sis'l, n* metal clippings: scrap left when blanks have been cut out.—Also **sciss'il.** [O.Fr. *cisaille—ciseler—cisel,* a chisel, for the spelling cf. **scissors.**]

scissile *sis'il, adj.* capable of being cut: readily splitting.—*ns.* **scission** (*sish'ən, sizh'ən*) cutting: division: splitting: schism [L. *scissilis, scissio, -ōnis—scindĕre, scissum,* to cut, to split, cleave.]

scissors *siz'ərz, n.pl.* or (*rare*) *n.sing.* a cutting instrument with two blades pivoted to close together and overlap—smaller than shears: a position or movement like that of scissors: movement of the legs suggesting opening and closing of scissors (*gymnastics*): locking the legs round body or head of an opponent (*wrestling*): a style of high jump in which the leg nearest the bar leads throughout.—*v.t.* **sciss'or** to cut with scissors.—*adv.* **sciss'orwise.**—**sciss'or-bill** a skimmer; **sciss'ors-and-paste'** literary or journalistic matter collected from various sources with little or no original writing.—Also *adj.*—**sciss'or-tail** an American fly-catcher; **sciss'or-tooth** a carnassial tooth. [O.Fr. *cisoires*—L.L. *cisōrium,* a cutting instrument—*caedĕre, caesum*, to cut; the spelling *sc-* is due to erroneous association with *scindĕre, scissum*.]

Sciurus *sī-ū'rəs, n.* the squirrel genus, giving name to the fam. **Sciu'ridae.**—*adjs* **sciurine** (*sī-ūr'īn*, or *sī'*); **sciuroid** (*-ū'*). [L. *sciūrus*—Gr. *skiouros*—*skiā*, shadow, *ourā*, tail.]

sclera *sklēr'ə, n.* the sclerotic.—*adj.* **sclĕ'ral.**—*n.* **sclerenchyma** (*sklər-eng'ki-mə*; Gr. *enchyma*, in-filling) plant tissue with thick, lignified cell-walls: hard skeletal tissue, as in corals.—*adj.* **sclerenchymatous** (*skler-eng-kim'ə-təs*).—*ns.* **scleritis** (*sklər-ī'tis*) sclerotitis; **scleroder'm(i)a** hardness and rigidity of skin by substitution of fibrous tissue for subcutaneous fat. —*adjs.* **scleroder'mic, scleroder'mous** hard-skinned, **sclĕ'roid** (*bot.* and *zool.*) hard: hardened.—*ns.* **sclerō'ma** hardening: morbid hardening: formation of nodules in the nose, etc.; **sclerom'eter** an instrument for measuring the hardness of minerals; **sclerophyll** (*sklēr'ō-fil*) a hard, stiff leaf.—*adj.* **sclerophyll'ous.** —*ns.* **scleroph'ylly** possession of sclerophylls; **scleroprō'tein** insoluble protein forming the skeletal parts of tissues.—*v.t.* **sclerose** (*sklər-ōs'*, or *sklēr'*) to harden: to affect with sclerosis.—*v.i.* to become sclerosed.—*adj.* **sclerosed** (or *sklēr'*).—*n.* **sclerosis** (*sklər-ō'sis*) hardening: morbid hardening, as of arteries (*med.*): hardening of tissue by thickening or lignification (*bot.*).—*adj.* **sclerōt'ic** hard, firm, applied esp. to the outer membrane of the eye-ball: of sclerosis: sclerosed.—*n.* the outermost membrane of the eye-ball.—*n.* **sclerotī'tis** (*skler-, sklēr-*) inflammation of the sclerotic.—*n.* **sclerot'omy** (*med.*) incision into the sclerotic.—*adj.* **sclĕ'rous** hard or indurated: ossified or bony.—**disseminated** (or **multiple**) **sclerosis** see **disseminate**. [Gr. *sklēros*, hard.]

scoff¹ *skof, n.* mockery: a jibe, jeer: an object of derision.—*v.i.* to jeer (with *at*).—*n.* **scoff'er.**—*n.* and *adj.* **scoff'ing.**—*adv.* **scoff'ingly.** [Cf. obs. Dan. *skof,* jest, mockery, O.Fris. *schof.*]

scoff² *skof,* (*dial.* and *slang*) *v.t.* to devour: to plunder. —*v.i.* to feed quickly or greedily.—*n.* food: a meal. [App. Scot. *scaff*, food, reinforced from S. Africa by Du. *schoft,* a meal.]

scold *skōld, n.* a rude clamorous woman or other: a scolding.—*v.i.* to brawl: to vituperate: to find fault vehemently or at some length.—*v.t.* to chide: to rebuke.—*n.* **scold'er.**—*n.* and *adj.* **scold'ing.** [App. O.N. *skáld,* poet (through an intermediate sense, lampooner).]

scolex *skō'leks, n.* a tapeworm head:—*pl.* **scoleces** (*skō-lē'sēz*; erroneously **scō'lices**).—*adj.* **scōlecoid** (*-lē'koid*) like a scolex. [Gr. *skolēx, -ēkos,* a worm.]

scoliosis *skol-i-ō'sis, n.* lateral spinal curvature.—*adj.* **scoliotic** (*-ot'ik*). [Gr. *skoliōsis,* obliquity.]

scollop. Same as **scallop.**

Scomber *skom'bər, n.* the mackerel genus.—*adj.* **scom'-broid** of or like the mackerel family. [L. *scomber*— Gr. *skombros,* a mackerel.]

sconce¹ *skons, n.* a small fort or earthwork: a shelter. [Du. *schans.*]

sconce² *skons, n.* the head: the crown of the head: brains, wits.

sconce³ *skons,* (*Oxford*) *n.* a fine (paid in ale or otherwise): a two-handled mug used for the purpose (holding about a quart): a forfeit.—*v.t.* to fine.

sconce⁴ *skons, n.* a candlestick or lantern with a handle: a bracket candlestick: a street wall-lamp. [O.Fr. *esconse*—L.L. *absconsa,* a dark lantern—*abscondĕre,* to hide.]

scone *skon,* in the South of England often pronounced *skōn,* (*Scot.*) *n.* a flattish, usually round or quadrant-shaped plain cake of dough without much butter, with or without currants, baked on a girdle or in an oven.

[Perh. from Du. *schoon* (*brot*), fine (bread).]

scoop *skōōp, n.* a bailing-vessel: a concave shovel or lipped vessel for skimming or shovelling up loose material: an instrument for gouging out apple-cores, samples of cheese, etc.: anything of like shape: an act of scooping: a sweeping stroke: a scooped-out place: anything got by or as by scooping, a haul: the forestalling of other newspapers in obtaining a piece of news: an item of news so secured (also *adj.*) —*v.t.* to bail out: to lift, obtain, remove, hollow, or make with, or as if with, a scoop: to secure in advance of or to the exclusion of others.—*adj.* **scooped.**—*ns.* **scoop'er; scoop'ful;**—*pl.* **scoop'fuls; scoop'ing.**—*adj.* **scooped'-out.**—**scoop neck** a low rounded neckline; **scoop'-net** a long-handled dipping net: a net for scooping along the bottom. [Prob. partly M.L.G. or M.Du. *schôpe,* bailing-vessel, partly M.Du. *schoppe,* shovel.]

scoot¹ *skōōt v.i.,* to make off with celerity (*coll.*): to travel on a scooter (*coll.*)—*n.* an act of scooting.—*n.* **scoot'er** a child's toy, a wheeled footboard with steering handle, propelled by kicking the ground: a development thereof driven by a motor (also *motor-scooter*): a boat for sailing on ice and water (*U.S.*). [Prob. from O.N., akin to **shoot.**]

scopa *skō'pə, n.* a bee's pollen-brush:—*pl.* **sco'pae** (*-pē*).—*adj.* **scō'pate** tufted.—*n.* **scopula** (*skop'ū-lə*) a little tuft of hairs.—*adj.* **scop'ulate.** [L. *scōpae,* twigs, a broom.]

scope¹ *skōp, n.* point aimed at: aim: range: field or opportunity of activity: room for action: spaciousness: length of cable at which a vessel rides at liberty. [It. *scopo*—Gr. *skopos,* watcher, point watched, (*fig.*) aim—*skopeein,* to view.]

scope² *skōp, n.* short for **microscope, telescope, horoscope,** etc.

-scope *-skōp,* in composition, an instrument for viewing, examining, or detecting as in *telescope, oscilloscope, stethoscope.* [Gr. *skopeein,* to view.]

scopolamine *sko-pol'ə-mēn, n.* an alkaloid got from the genus **Scopolia** and other plants (see **hyoscine**) with sedative properties, used e.g. to prevent travel sickness and as a truth drug. [Named after *Scopoli* (1723–88), Italian naturalist; **amine.**]

scopula, scopulate. See **scopa.**

scorbutic, -al *skör-bū'tik, -əl, adjs.* of, like, of the nature of, or affected with, scurvy. [L.L. *scorbūticus,* poss. from M.L.G. *schorbuk.*]

scorch *skörch, v.t.* to burn slightly or superficially: to parch: to dry up, wither, or affect painfully or injuriously by heat or as if by heat: to wither with scorn, censure, etc.—*v.i.* to be burned on the surface: to be dried up: to cycle or drive furiously (*coll.*).—*n.* an act of scorching: an injury by scorching.—*adj.* **scorched.** —*n.* **scorch'er** one who, that which, scorches: a day of scorching heat (*coll.*).—*n., adj.,* and *adv.* **scorch'ing.** —*adv* **scorch'ingly.**—*n.* **scorch'ingness.**—**scorched earth** country devastated before evacuation so as to be useless to an advancing enemy; **scorched-earth policy.** [Perh. M.E. *skorken;* poss. affected by O.Fr. *escorcher,* to flay.]

scordato *skör-dä'tō,* (*mus.*) *adj.* put out of tune.—*n.* **scordatura** (*-tōō'rə*) a temporary departure from normal tuning. [It.]

score *skōr, skör, n.* a notch, gash, or scratch: an incised line: a boldly drawn line, as one marking a deletion: a line marking a boundary, starting-place, or defined position: an arrangement of music on a number of staves (perh. orig. with the bar divisions running continuously through all): a composition so distributed: a notch in a tally: an account of charges incurred (as in a tavern): a debt incurred: a reckoning, account: the total or record of points made in a game: an addition made thereto: a set of twenty (sometimes verging upon numeral *adj.*): applied also to an indefinitely large number.—*v.t.* to mark with or by scores: to record in or with a score: to make a score through as a mark of deletion (with *out*): to write in score: to distribute among the instruments of the orchestra: to make as a score: to add to a score: to achieve: to enumerate: to record.—*v.i.* to make a point: to achieve a success: of a man, to achieve sexual intercourse (*slang*): to obtain drugs (*slang*).—*ns.* scor'er one who, or that which, scores: one who keeps the marks in a game; scor'ing.—score'-board, scor'ing-board a board on which the score is exhibited, as at cricket; score'-card, scor'ing-card, score'-sheet a card, sheet, for recording the score in a game; score's draw (esp. *football*) a drawn result other than nil all —go off at score to make a spirited start; know the score to know the hard facts of the situation; on that score as regards that matter; pay off, settle, old scores to repay old grudges; score off, score points off (*coll.*) to achieve a success against, get the better of. [Late O.E. *scoru*—O.N. *skor, skora.*]

scoria *skō'*, *skö'ri-ə*, *n.* dross or slag from metal-smelting: a piece of lava with steam-holes:—*pl.* sco'riae (*-ri-ē*).—*adj.* scoriaceous (*-ri-ā'shəs*).—*n.* scorification reduction to scoria: assaying by fusing with lead and borax; sco'rifier a dish used in assaying.—*v.t.* sco'rify to reduce to scoria: to rid metals of (impurities) by forming scoria—*adj.* sco'rious. [L , —Gr. *skŏriā—skŏr,* dung.]

scorn *skorn, n.* hot or extreme contempt: the object of contempt.—*v.t.* to feel or express scorn for: to refuse with scorn.—*n.* scorn'er.—*adj.* scorn'ful.—*adv* scorn'fully.—*ns.* scorn'fulness; scorn'ing.—think scorn of (*arch.*) to disdain or think beneath one. [O.Fr. *escarn,* mockery; of Gmc. origin.]

scorper *skor'pər, n.* a gouging chisel. [For scauper.]

scorpioid *skòr'pi-oid, adj.* like a scorpion, or a scorpion's curled tail, esp. of an inflorescence in which the plane of each daughter axis is at right angles, to right and left alternately, with its parent axis, that of the whole coiled in bud. [Gr. *skorpios,* scorpion, *eidos,* form.]

scorpion *skor'pi-ən, n.* a member of the Arachnida with head and thorax united, pincers, four pairs of legs, and a segmented abdomen including a tail with a sting: a form of scourge (*B.*): an old engine for hurling missiles: (*cap.*) the constellation or the sign Scorpio (*astron.*).—*n.* Scor'pio (*-pi-ō*) a constellation: a sign of the zodiac (also without *cap.*; *pl.* -os).—*adj.* scorpion'ic.—scor'pion-fish any of the *Scorpaenidae* with spiny head and fins; scor'pion-fly an insect of the *Mecoptera* (from the male's upturned abdomen); scor'pion-grass forget-me-not; scor'pion-spider a whip-scorpion. [L. *scorpiō, -ōnis*—Gr. *skorpios.*]

scorzonera *skör-zō-nē'rə, n.* a plant like dandelion, with edible root—*black salsify.* [It.]

scot *skot, (hist.) n.* a payment, esp. a customary tax: a share of a reckoning.—*adj.* scot'-free' free from scot: untaxed: entirely free from expense, injury, etc.—scot and lot an old legal phrase embracing all parochial assessments for the poor, the church, lighting, cleansing, and watching. [O.E. *scot, sceot.*]

Scot *skot, n.* one of a Gaelic-speaking people of Ireland, afterwards also in Argyllshire (now part of Strathclyde) (*hist.*): (now) a Scotsman or Scotswoman of any race or language.—*n.* Scotland (*skot'lənd*) Ireland (*hist.*): now, the country forming the northern member of the United Kingdom.—*v.t* Scott'icise, -ize to render Scottish or into Scots.—*n* Scott'icism a Scottish idiom: Scottish feeling.—*v.t* Scot(t)ify to make Scottish:—*pr.p.* Scot(t)'ifying; *pa.t.* and *pa.p.* Scot(t)'ified.—*n.* Scot(t)ifica'tion.—

adj. Scottish (*skot'ish*; O.E. *Scottisc*) of Scotland, its people, or its English dialect.—*n.* Scots (see separate entry): (as *pl.*, *rare*) the Scots.—Scott'ishness; Scott'y, Scott'ie a nickname for a Scotsman: a Scotch terrier (*coll.*).—Scotland Yard earliest or (New Scotland Yard) two more recent headquarters (1890 and 1967) of the Metropolitan Police: hence the London Criminal Investigation Department.—Scottish Certificate of Education in secondary education in Scotland, a certificate obtainable at ordinary (Ordinary Grade) and higher (Higher Grade) levels, for proficiency in one or more subjects. [O E. *Scottas* (pl.)—L.L. *Scottus;* see also Scotch, Scotia, Scots.]

Scotch *skoch, adj* a form of Scottish or Scots, disliked by many Scotsmen applied esp. to products of Scotland: having the character popularly attributed to a Scotsman—an excessive leaning towards defence of oneself and one's property —*n.* Scotch whisky, or a glass of it: the Scottish (Northern English) dialect: (as *pl.*) the Scots.—*n.* Scotch'ness.—Scotch bluebell the harebell; Scotch broth broth made with pot-barley and plenty of various vegetables chopped small; Scotch catch or snap a short accented note followed by a longer; Scotch collops minced beef; Scotch egg a hard-boiled egg (often cut in two) enclosed in sausage-meat; Scotch fir Scots pine; Scotch'man a Scotsman; Scotch mist a fine rain; Scotch pebble an agate or similar stone; Scotch snap a Scotch catch (see above); Scotch tape® a transparent tape, adhering to paper, etc., when pressure is applied; Scotch terrier a rough-haired, prick-eared, strongly-built little dog (also Scottish terrier, Scottie, Scotty); Scotch verdict not proven; Scotch'woman. [From Scottish.]

scotch[1] *skoch, v.t.* to gash: to score: to maim, cripple for the time without killing: to frustrate: to quash.—*n.* a score on the ground (as for hop-scotch).

scotch[2] *skoch, n.* a strut, wedge, block, etc., to prevent turning or slipping, as of a wheel, gate, ladder.—*v.t.* to stop or block. [Perh. a form of scratch.]

scoter *skō'tər, n* northern sea-duck, usu. black or nearly

scotia *sko'ti-ə, -shi-ə, n.* a hollow moulding, esp at the base of a column [Gr. *skŏtiā—skotos,* darkness.]

Scotia *skō'sh(y)ə, n.* (*poet.*) Scotland.—*adj.* Scotic (*skot'ik*) of the ancient Scots of Ireland. [L.L *Scōtia, Scōticus.*]

Scotism *skō'tizm, n.* the metaphysical system of Johannes Duns *Scotus* (*c.* 1265–1308), the great assailant of the method of Aquinas in seeking in speculation instead of in practice the foundation of Christian theology.—*n.* Scō'tist a follower of Duns Scotus.—*adj.* Scotist'ic.

scoto- *skot-ō-,* in composition, dark.—*ns* scotodinia (*-din'i-ə;* Gr. *dīnos,* whirling) dizziness with headache and impairment of vision; scotoma (*-ōm'ə;* Gr. *skotōma,* dizziness) a blind spot due to disease of the retina or optic nerve.—*pl.* scotō'mata, scotō'mas.—*adj.* scotō'matous. [Gr. *skotos,* darkness.]

Scots *skots, adj.* Scottish (almost always used of money, measures, law, and language).—*n.* the dialect of Lowland Scotland.—Scots Greys a famous regiment of dragoons, established in 1683; Scots Guards a Scottish force which served the kings of France from 1418 to 1759: a well-known regiment of Guards in the British army; Scots'man; Scots pine (often called Scots fir) the only native British pine, *Pinus sylvestris;* Scots'woman. [Shortened form of Scots *Scottis,* Scottish.]

Scottish, etc See Scot.

scoundrel *skown'drəl, n.* a low mean blackguard: a man without principle.—*ns.* scoun'dreldom the world of scoundrels, scoun'drelism.—*adj.* scoun'drelly.

scour[1] *skowr, v.t.* to clean, polish, remove, or form by

hard rubbing: to scrub: to cleanse: to free from grease, dirt, or gum: to flush or cleanse by a current: to purge, esp. drastically: to clear out.—*n.* the action, place, or means of scouring: diarrhoea in cattle, etc. —*ns.* **scour'er; scour'ing** scrubbing: vigorous cleansing: erosion: purging: (often in *pl.*) matter removed or accumulated by scouring.—Also *adj.* [Prob. M.Du. or M.L.G. *schūren*—O.Fr. *escurer*— L. *ex cūrāre*, take care of.]

scour[2] *skowr, v.i.* to rush or scurry along: to range about, esp. in quest or pursuit.—*v.t.* to range over or traverse swiftly, vigorously, or in pursuit: to search thoroughly. [Poss. O.N. *skūr*, storm, shower; cf. **shower.**]

scourge *skûrj, n.* a whip: an instrument of divine punishment: a cause of widespread affliction.—*v.t.* to whip severely: to afflict.—*n.* **scourg'er.** [A.Fr. *escorge*—L. *excoriāre*, to flay—*corium*, leather (perh. as made of a strip of leather, perh. as a flaying instrument).]

scouse *skows, (coll.) n.* a native of Liverpool: the northern English dialect spoken in and around Liverpool. [Short for *lobscouse*, a stew or hash.]

scout[1] *skowt, n.* one sent out to bring in information: a spy: a member of the Scout Association (formerly **Boy Scout**): a patrolman on the roads: one who watches or attends at a little distance: a fielder, as in cricket: a person (usually term of approbation; *slang*): a person who seeks out new recruits, sales opportunities, etc.: a ship for reconnoitring: a small light aeroplane orig. intended for reconnaissance: a light armoured car for reconnaissance (now usu. **scout car**): a college servant at Oxford.—*v.i.* to act the scout: to reconnoitre (often with *about* or *around*).— *ns.* **scout'er** an adult working with instructors, etc., in the Scout Association; **scout'ing.**—**Scout Association** (formerly, the **Boy Scouts**) a world-wide movement for young people, intended to develop character and a sense of responsibility, founded (for boys) by Lord Baden-Powell in 1908; **scout's pace** alternately walking and running for a set number of paces; **scout'-master** the leader of a band of scouts: formerly, an adult in charge of a troop of Boy Scouts. [O.Fr. *escoute*—*escouter*—L. *auscultāre*, to listen.]

scout[2] *skowt, v.t.* to mock, flout: to dismiss or reject with disdain. [Cf. O.N. *skūta*, a taunt.]

scow *skow, n.* a flat-bottomed boat. [Du. *schouw.*]

scowl *skowl, v.i.* to contract the brows in a look of baleful malevolence: to look gloomy and threatening.—*n.* a scowling look.—*adj.* **scow'ling.**—*adv.* **scow'lingly.** [Cf. Dan. *skule*, to cast down the eyes, look sidelong.]

scrabble *skrab'l, v.i.* to scratch: to scrape: to scrawl: to scramble.—*n.* a scrawl: (® with *cap.*) a word-building game.—*n.* **scrabb'ler.** [Du. *schrabben*, to scratch, freq. *schrabbelen.*]

scrag *skrag, n.* a sheep's or (*slang*) human neck: the bony part of the neck: a lean person or animal.—*v.t.* to hang: to throttle: to wring the neck of: to tackle by the neck:—*pr.p.* **scrag'ging;** *pa.t.* and *pa.p.* **scragged.** —*adv.* **scragg'ily.**—*n.* **scragg'iness.**—*adj.* **scragg'y** lean, skinny, and gaunt.—**scrag'-end'** the scrag of a neck. [Prob. **crag**[2].]

scram *skram, (slang) v.i.* (esp. in the *imper.*) to be off: —*pr.p.* **scramm'ing;** *pa.t.* and *pa.p.* **scrammed.** [Perh. **scramble.**]

scramble *skram'bl, v.i.* to make one's way with disorderly struggling haste: to get along somehow: to clamber: to wriggle irregularly: to dash or struggle for what one can get before others: of an aircraft or its crew, to take off immediately, as in an emergency.— *v.t.* to put, make, get together, scramblingly: to jumble up (a message) so that it can be read only after

decoding: to beat (eggs) up and heat to thickness with milk, butter etc.: to make (a radiotelephone conversation) unintelligible by a device that alters frequencies: to order (an aircraft-crew) to take off immediately.—*n.* act of scrambling: a disorderly performance: a dash or struggle for what can be had: an emergency take-off by an aircraft: a form of motor or motor-cycle trial.—*n.* **scram'bler** one who, or that which, scrambles, esp. a telephone device.—*adj.* **scram'bling** confused and irregular.—*n.* the action of the verb scramble: participation in motor-cycle, etc. scrambles.—*adv.* **scram'blingly.**—**scrambled eggs** eggs cooked as described above: the gold braid on a military officer's cap (*slang*). [Cf. the dialect word *scramb*, to rake together with the hands.]

scrannel *skran'l, (arch.) adj.* thin: meagre: squeaking.

scrap[1] *skrap, n.* a small fragment: a piece of left-over food: a remnant: a punched-out picture, cutting, or the like, intended or suited for preservation in a scrap-book: residue after extraction of oil from blubber, fish, etc.: metal clippings or other waste: anything discarded as worn-out, out of date, or useless.—*adj.* consisting of scrap.—*v.t.* to consign to the scrap-heap: to discard:—*pr.p.* **scrapp'ing;** *pa.p.* and *pa.t.* **scrapped.**—*adv.* **scrapp'ily.**—*n.* **scrapp'iness.**— *adj.* **scrapp'y** fragmentary: disconnected: made up of scraps.—**scrap'-book** a blank book for pasting in scraps, cuttings, etc.; **scrap'-heap** a place where old iron is collected: rubbish-heap; **scrap'-iron, scrap'-metal** scraps of iron or other metal, of use only for remelting; **scrap'-man, scrap'-merchant** one who deals in scrap-metal; **scrap'-yard** a scrap-merchant's premises for the storing of scrap.—**not a scrap** not in the least; **throw on the scrap-heap** to reject as useless. [O.N. *skrap*, scraps; cf. **scrape.**]

scrap[2] *skrap, (slang) n.* a fight: scrimmage.—Also *v.i.* (*pr.p.* **scrapp'ing;** *pa.t.* and *pa.p.* **scrapped**).—*adj.* **scrapp'y** belligerent.

scrape *skrāp, v.t.* to press a sharp edge over: to move gratingly over: to smooth, clean, clear, reduce in thickness, abrade, remove, form, collect, bring, render, by such an action: to get together, collect by laborious effort (often *scrape together, scrape up*): to erase: contemptuously, to fiddle.—*v.i.* to graze: to scratch: to scratch the ground: to grate: to make a grating sound (as with the feet, in disapprobation): to draw back the foot in making obeisance: to fiddle: to save penuriously: to get with difficulty (with *through, along, home,* etc.).—*n.* an act, process, or spell of scraping: a grating sound: a scraped place in the ground: an abrasion: a backward movement of one foot accompanying a bow: a scraping or thin layer: a predicament that threatens disgrace or friction with authority.—*ns.* **scrāp'er** one who scrapes: a scraping instrument or machine; **scrāp'ie** a virus disease of sheep causing acute itching, the animals rubbing against trees, etc. to relieve it; **scrāp'ing** the action of the verb: its sound: a piece scraped off.—**scrap'er-board** a clay-surface board on which drawings can be made by scraping tints off as well as applying them: such a drawing: this method.—**bow and scrape** to be over-obsequious; **scrape acquaintance with** to contrive somehow to get on terms of acquaintance with; **scrape the bottom of the barrel** to utilise the very last of one's resources. [O.E. *scrapian* or O.N. *skrapa.*]

scraple. See under **scrape.**

scratch *skrach, v.t.* to draw a sharp point over the surface of: to hurt, mark, render, seek to allay discomfort in, by so doing: to dig or scrape with the claws: to write hurriedly: to erase or delete (usu. with *out*): to strike along a rough surface: to withdraw from a competition.—*v.i.* to use the nails or claws: to scrape: to make a grating or screechy noise: to retire from a contest or engagement: to get (along or through) somehow (*coll.*).—*n.* an act, mark, or sound of scratching: a slight wound: a scrawl: the line up to which boxers are led—hence test, trial, as in *come up to (the) scratch* (q.v. below): the starting-point for a competitor without handicap: one who starts from scratch: a fluke, esp. in billiards: (in *pl.*) a disease in horses with the appearance of scratches on the pastern.—*adj.* improvised: casual: hastily or casually got together: without handicap.—*n.* scratch'-er.—*adv.* scratch'ily.—*n.* scratch'iness.—*n.* and *adj.* scratch'ing.—*adv.* scratch'ingly.—*adjs.* scratch'less; scratch'y like scratches: uneven: ready or likely to scratch: grating or screechy: itchy.—scratch pad a note-pad; scratch test (*med.*) a test for allergy to a certain substance, made by introducing it to an area of skin that has been scratched; scratch'-wig a wig that covers only part of the head.—come up to (the) scratch (*fig.*) to reach an expected standard: to fulfil an obligation; start from scratch (*fig.*) to start at the beginning: to embark on (a task, career, etc.) without any advantages or without any preparatory work having been done; you scratch my back and I'll scratch yours (*coll.*) do me a favour and I'll do you one in return. [Poss. M.E. *cracchen*, to scratch, modified by dial. *scrat*, to scratch.]

scrawl *skröl*, *v.t.* and *v.i.* to make or write irregularly or hastily: to scribble.—*n.* irregular, hasty, or bad writing: a letter, etc., written thus.—*n.* scrawl'er.—*n.* and *adj.* scrawl'ing.—*adv.* scrawl'ingly.—*adj.* scrawl'y. [Perh. conn. with crawl or sprawl.]

scrawny *skrö'ni*, (orig. *U.S.*) *adj.* lean, meagre.

scray, scraye *skrā*, *n.* the tern. [Cf. W. *ysgräell*.]

scream *skrēm*, *v.t.* and *v.i.* to cry out in a loud shrill voice, as in fear or pain: to laugh shrilly and uncontrolledly: to shriek.—*v.i.* (of colours) to be acutely inharmonious (*coll.*): to be all too loudly evident (*coll.*).—*n.* a shrill, sudden cry, as in fear or pain: a shriek: a loud whistling sound: anything or anyone supposed to make one scream with laughter (*coll.*).—*n.* scream'er one who screams: a large spur-winged S. American bird (*horned screamer*; *crested screamer*) with loud harsh cry: a different S. American bird, the seriema (also called *crested screamer*): anything likely or intended to thrill with emotion, as a sensational headline (*slang*): an exclamation mark (*slang*).—*adj.* scream'ing.—*adv.* scream'ingly.—screaming farce one highly ludicrous. [Late O.E. *scrǽmen*.]

scree *skrē*, *n.* sloping mass of débris at the base of a cliff. [O.N. *skritha*, a landslip—*skrítha*, to slide.]

screech *skrēch*, *v.i.* to give forth a harsh, shrill, and sudden cry or noise.—*v.t.* to utter in such tones.—*n.* a harsh, shrill, and sudden cry: a strident creak: a screeching or screaming bird (as barn-owl, swift, missel-thrush).—*n.* screech'er.—*adj.* screech'y shrill and harsh, like a screech.—screech'-owl the barn-owl: a bringer of bad news. [M.E. *scrichen*; cf. scritch.]

screed *skrēd*, *n.* a long effusion, spoken or written: a band of plaster laid on the surface of a wall as a guide to the thickness of a coat of plaster to be applied subsequently (*building*): a layer of mortar finishing off the surface of a floor (also screed'ing): a strip of wood or metal temporarily inserted in a road surface to form a guide for the template for forming the final surface of the road (*civil engineering*).—*n.* screed'er. [O.E. *scréade*, shred.]

screen *skrēn*, *n.* a shield against danger, observation, wind, heat, light, or other outside influence: a piece of room furniture in the form of a folding framework or of a panel on a stand: a protection against wind on a vehicle: a sheltering row of trees: a body of troops or formation of ships intended as a cover: a wall masking a building: a partial partition cutting off part of a

room, a church choir, or side chapel: a coarse sifting apparatus: a net-ruled plate for half-tone photography: a mosaic of primary colours for colour photography: a white sheet or the like on which images may be projected: a screen grid.—*v.t.* to shelter or conceal: to sift coarsely: to sort out by, or subject to, tests of ability, desirability, etc.: to test for illness, etc.: to protect from stray electrical interference: to prevent from causing outside electrical interference: to project or exhibit on a screen or on the screen: to make a motion-picture of.—*v.i.* to show up on, or be suitable for, the screen.—*ns.* screen'er; screen'ing.—*n.pl.* screen'ings material eliminated by sifting.—screen grid an electrode placed between the control grid and anode in a valve, having an invariable potential to eliminate positive feedback and instability; screen'-play the written text for a film, with dialogue, stage-directions, and descriptions of characters and setting; screen printing, screen process see silk-screen printing; screen test one to determine whether an actor or actress is suitable for cinema work; screen'-writer a writer of screenplays.—screen off to hide behind, or separate by, a screen: to separate by sifting. [App. related in some way to O.Fr. *escran* (Fr. *écran*), which may be—O.H.G. *skirm*, *skerm* (Ger. *Schirm*).]

screw *skrōō*, *n.* a cylinder with a helical groove or (the *thread*) ridge, used as a fastening driven into wood, etc. by rotation (a *male screw*; for *female screw*, see female), as a mechanical power, and otherwise: anything of similar form: a screw-propeller or ship driven by one: a thumbscrew: a twisted cone of paper, or portion of a commodity contained in it: a turn of the screw: pressure (*fig.*): a twist: a spin imparted to a ball: a stingy fellow, an extortioner, a skinflint (*slang*): a prison officer (*slang*): a broken-winded horse: an act of sexual intercourse (*vulg.*): salary, wages (*coll.*).—*v.t.* to fasten, tighten, compress, force, adjust, extort by a screw, a screwing motion, or as if by a screw: to apply a screw to: to twist: to turn in the manner of a screw: to pucker: to summon up (courage, etc.; with *up*): to have sexual intercourse with (*vulg.*): to practise extortion upon: to cheat (*slang*): to disrupt, spoil (often with *up*; *coll.*): to burgle (*slang*).—*v.i.* to admit of screwing: to wind: to have sexual intercourse (*vulg.*).—*adj.* screwed (*slang*) tipsy.—*n.* screw'er.—*n.* and *adj.* screw'ing.—*adv.* screw'-wise.—*adj.* screwy eccentric, slightly mad.—screw'ball (*U.S.*) a ball in baseball that breaks contrary to its swerve: a crazy person, an eccentric.—Also *adj.*—screw'-bolt a bolt with a screw-thread; screw'-cap a lid that screws on to a container.—*adj.* screw'-down closed by screwing.—screw'driver an instrument for turning and driving screws; screw eye a screw formed into a loop for attaching rope, wire, etc.; screw jack a jack for lifting heavy weights, operated by a screw; screw'-pile a pile for sinking into the ground, ending in a screw; screw'-pine a plant of the genus Pandanus or its family—from the screw-like arrangement of the leaves; screw'-plate a plate of steel with holes for cutting screw-threads; screw'-press a press worked by a screw; screw'-propell'er a propeller with helical blades; screw'-steam'er a steamer driven by screw; screw'-thread the ridge of a screw; screw'top a bottle with a stopper that screws in or on, esp. a beer-bottle of the kind with its contents; screw'-wrench a tool for gripping screw-heads.—a screw loose something defective (esp. mentally); put on, turn, the screw to apply pressure progressively: to exact payment; put the screws on to coerce. [Earlier *scrue*; app. O.Fr. *escroue*, of obscure origin; prob. conn. with L.G. *schrûve*, Ger. *Schraube*.]

scribble[1] *skrib'l*, *v.t.* to scrawl: to write badly, carelessly, or worthlessly (in handwriting or substance).—*n.* careless writing: a scrawl.—*n.* **scribb'ler** a petty author; **scribb'ling.**—*adv.* **scribb'lingly.**—*adj.* **scribb'ly.**—**scribb'ling-book,** **-pad,** **-paper.** [A freq. of **scribe**, or L.L. *scrībillāre*—L. *scrībĕre*, to write.]

scribble² *skrib'l, v.t.* to card roughly.—*ns.* **scribb'ler** a carding machine: one who tends it; **scribb'ling.** [Prob. from L.G.]

scribe *skrīb, n.* an expounder and teacher of the Mosaic and traditional law (*B.*): a writer: a public or official writer: a clerk, amanuensis, secretary: a copyist: a penman: a pointed instrument to mark lines on wood, metal, etc—*v.t.* to mark, score with a scribe, etc.—*v.i.* to play the scribe.—*adj.* **scrī'bal.**—*ns.* **scrī'ber** a scribing tool, a scribe; **scrī'bing.** [L. *scrība*, a scribe, and *scrībĕre*, to write.]

scrim *skrim, n.* open fabric used in upholstery, book-binding, for curtains, etc.

scrimmage *skrim'ij,* **scrummage** *skrum'ij, ns.* a tussle: a scrum.—*v.i.* to take part in a scrimmage.—*ns.* **scrimm'ager, scrumm'ager.** [See **skirmish**.]

scrimp *skrimp, adj.* scanty: stinted.—*v.t.* to stint: to keep short.—*v.i.* to be sparing or niggardly.—*adj.* **scrimped.**—*adv.* **scrimp'ily.**—*n.* **scrimp'iness.**—*adj.* **scrimp'y** scanty. [Cf. Sw. and Dan. *skrumpen,* shrivelled, O.E. *scrimman,* to shrink.]

scrimshank. Same as **skrimshank.**

scrimshaw *skrim'shō, n.* a sailor's spare-time handicraft, as engraving fanciful designs on shells, whales' teeth, etc.: anything so executed.—*v.t.* and *v.i.* to work or decorate in this way.

scrip¹ *skrip, n.* a writing: a scrap of paper or of writing: (for *subscription*) a preliminary certificate, as for shares allotted: share certificates, or shares or stock collectively: paper money less than a dollar (*U.S. hist.*): a dollar bill, money (*U.S. slang*).—*n.* **scrip'oph'ily** the collecting of bond and share certificates. —**scrip issue** a bonus issue (q.v. at **bonus**). [**script,** **subscription;** partly perh. **scrap¹**.]

scrip² *skrip, n.* a small bag: a satchel: a pilgrim's pouch. [Cf. O.N. *skreppa,* a bag, and O.Fr. *escrep(p)e.*]

script *skript, n.* a writing: an original document (*law*): the actors', director's, etc., written copy of the text of a play: a text for broadcasting: handwriting, system or style of handwriting: scenario (*cinema*): handwriting in imitation of type: type in imitation of handwriting: a set of characters used in writing a language (as *Cyrillic script*).—*v.t.* to write a script for, or make a script from, esp. for broadcasting or the theatre or cinema.—**script'writer.** [L. *scriptum*—*scrībĕre,* to write.]

scriptorium *skrip-tō'ri-əm, -tō'ri-əm, n.* a writing-room, esp. in a monastery:—*pl.* **scripto'ria.**—*adj.* **scripto'rial.** [L. *scriptōrium*—*scrībĕre.*]

scripture *skrip'chər, n.* something written: (in *sing.* or *pl.*) sacred writings of a religion, esp. (*cap.*) the Bible. —Also *adj.*—*adj.* **scrip'tural** of, in, warranted by Scripture.—*ns.* **scrip'turalism** literal adherence to the Scriptures; **scrip'turalist.**—*adv.* **scrip'turally.** [L. *scriptūra*—*scrībĕre,* to write.]

scrivener *skriv'nər,* (*hist.*) *n.* a scribe: a copyist: one who draws up contracts, etc.: one who lays out money at interest for others.—*ns.* **scriv'enership; scriv'ening** writing.—**scrivener's palsy** writer's cramp. [O.Fr. *escrivain* (Fr. *écrivain*)—L.L. *scrībānus*—L. *scrība,* a scribe.]

scrobe *skrōb, n.* a groove.—*adj.* **scrobic'ulate** (*skrob-*) pitted. [L. *scrobis,* a ditch.]

scrofula *skrof'ū-lə, n.* tuberculosis, esp. of the lymphatic glands, called also king's evil.—*adj.* **scrof'ulous.** [L. *scrōfulae*—*scrōfa,* a sow (supposed to be liable to it).]

scroll *skrōl, n.* a roll of paper, parchment, etc.: a ribbon-like strip, partly coiled or curved, often bearing a motto: a writing in the form of a roll: a spiral ornament or part: a flourish to a signature, etc.—*v.t.* to set in a scroll.—*v.i.* to curl.—*adj.* **scrolled** formed into a scroll: ornamented with scrolls.—*ns.* **scroll'-ery, scroll'work** ornament in scrolls.—*adv.* **scroll'wise.**—**scroll'-saw** a saw for cutting scrolls. [Earlier *scrowl(e)*, perh. from O.Fr. *escroe* scrap of parchment.]

Scrooge *skrōōj, n.* a miser. [From Ebenezer Scrooge in Dickens's *Christmas Carol.*]

Scrophularia *skrof-ū-lā'ri-ə, n.* the figwort genus, giving name to the **Scrophulariaceae** (*-lar-i-ā'si-ē*), a family including foxglove, mullein, speedwell, eyebright: (without *cap.*) a plant of this genus.—*adj.* **scrophularia'ceous.** [L. *scrōfulae,* as reputedly cure for scrofula (q.v.).]

scrotum *skrō'təm, n.* the bag that contains the testicles. —*adj.* **scrō'tal.** [L. *scrōtum.*]

scrounge *skrownj,* (orig. *mil. slang*) *v.t.* to cadge.—*v.t.* to hunt around: to sponge.—*ns.* **scroung'er; scroung'ing.**

scrub¹ *skrub, v.t.* to rub hard: to wash by hard rubbing with a stiff brush: to purify (*gas-making*): to cancel (*slang*).—*v.i.* to use a scrubbing-brush: to drudge: to make a rapid to-and-fro movement as if scrubbing:—*pr.p.* **scrubb'ing;** *pa.t.* and *pa.p.* **scrubbed.**—*n.* an act of scrubbing: a worn or short-bristled brush or broom.—*ns.* **scrubb'er** one who scrubs: apparatus for freeing gas from tar, ammonia, and sulphuretted hydrogen: an unattractive woman (*slang*); **scrubb'ing**—**scrubb'ing-board** a washing-board; **scrubb'ing-brush** a brush with short stiff bristles for scrubbing floors, etc.—**scrub round** (*slang*) to cancel: to ignore intentionally; **scrub up** of a surgeon, to wash the hands and arms thoroughly before performing an operation. [Perh. obs. Du. *schrubben,* or a corresponding lost O.E. word.]

scrub² *skrub, n.* a stunted tree: stunted trees and shrubs collectively: brushwood: country covered with bushes or low trees, esp. the Australian evergreen dwarf forest or bush of Eucalyptus, Acacia, etc.: hence, a remote place, far from civilisation (*Austr. coll.*): an undersized or inferior animal, esp. one of indefinite breed: a player in a second or inferior team: a team of inferior players, or one with too few players: an insignificant or mean person: anything small or mean.—*adj.* mean: insignificant: undersized: (of a player) in a second or inferior team.—*adj.* **scrubb'y** stunted: covered with scrub: mean.—**scrub'land** an area covered with scrub; **scrub'-turkey, -fowl** a mound-bird; **scrub'-typhus** a typhus-like disease transmitted by a mite. [A variant of **shrub¹**.]

scruff¹ *skruf, n.* the nape of the neck. [Poss. O.N. *skopt, skoft,* the hair.]

scruff² *skruf, n.* scurf: an untidy, dirty person (*coll.*). —*n.* **scruff'iness.**—*adj.* **scruff'y** scurvy: untidy, dirty (*coll.*). [**scurf.**]

scrum *skrum, n.* a scrimmage: a closing-in of rival forwards round the ball on the ground, or in readiness for its being inserted (by the scrum-half) between the two compact pushing masses (*Rugby*).—*v.i.* to form a scrum:—*pr.p.* **scrumm'ing;** *pa.t.* and *pa.p.* **scrummed.**—**scrum'-half** (*Rugby*) a half-back whose duty it is to put the ball into the scrum and secure it as soon as it emerges therefrom. [Abbreviation of **scrummage**; see **scrimmage, skirmish**.]

scrummage. See scrimmage.

scrummy. See scrumptious.

scrumptious *skrump'shəs,* (*slang*) *adj.* delightful: delicious.—Also **scrumm'y.**—*adv.* **scrump'tiously.**

scrumpy *skrum'pi, n.* cider made from small, sweet apples. [*scrump,* a withered apple.]

For other sounds see detailed chart of pronunciation.

scrunch *skrunch, skrunsh,* variant of **crunch**.—*adj.*
scrunch'y.

scruple *skrōō'pl, n.* a small weight.—in apothecaries'
weight, 20 grains: a very small quantity (*arch.*): a
difficulty or consideration, usu. moral, obstructing
action, esp. one turning on a fine point or one that is
baseless: a doubt, disbelief, or difficulty: protest,
demur: scrupulousness.—*v.i.* to hesitate from a
scruple.—*v.t.* to have scruples about (followed by
infinitive).—*ns.* **scru'pler; scrupulosity** (-*pū-los'i-ti*).
—*adj.* **scru'pulous** directed by scruples: having
scruples, doubts, or objections: conscientious: cautious: exact.—*adv.* **scru'pulously.**—*n.* **scru'pulous-
ness.—make no scruple(s), make scruples, about**
(formerly **to, at**) to offer (no) moral objections to.
[L. *scrūpulus,* dim. of *scrūpus,* a sharp stone,
anxiety.]

scrutiny *skrōō'ti-ni, n.* close, careful, or minute investigation or examination: a searching look: official
examination of votes.—*ns.* **scruta'tor** a close
examiner: a scrutineer; **scrutineer'** one who makes a
scrutiny, esp. of votes.—*v.t.* and *v.i.* **scru'tinise, -ize**
to examine closely.—*n.* **scru'tiniser, -z-.**—*adj.*
scru'tinising.—*adv.* **scru'tinisingly.** [L. *scrūtinium,*
and *scrūtāri,* to search even to the rags—*scrūta,* rags,
trash.]

scry *skrī, v.i.* to practise crystal-gazing:—*pr.p.*
scry'ing; *pa.t.* and *pa.p.* **scried.** [Aphetic for
descry.]

scuba *skōō'bə, skū', n.* a device used by skin-divers.—
Also *adj.* [self-contained underwater breathing
apparatus.]

scud *skud, v.i.* to sweep along easily and swiftly: to
drive before the wind:—*pr.p.* **scudd'ing;** *pa.t.* and
pa.p. **scudd'ed.**—*n.* act of scudding: driving cloud,
shower or spray: a gust.—*n.* **scudd'er.** [Perh. Du. or
L.G.]

scuff *skuf, v.t.* and *v.i.* to shuffle: to brush, graze,
touch lightly: to abrade: to make or become shabby
by wear.—*v.i.* **scuff'le** to struggle confusedly: to
shuffle.—*n.* a confused struggle.—*n.* **scuff'ler.** [Cf.
Sw. *skuffa,* to shove.]

sculduggery, skulduggery *skul-dug'ə-ri,* underhand malpractices. [Perh. Scot. *sculduddery,*
unchastity.]

scull¹ *skul, n.* a short, light spoon-bladed oar for one
hand: an oar used over the stern: a small, light rowing-boat propelled by sculls: an act or spell of scul-
ling: (in *pl.*) a race between small, light rowing-boats
rowed by one person.—*v.t.* to propel with sculls, or
with one oar worked like a screw over the stern.—*v.i.*
to use sculls.—*ns.* **scull'er** one who sculls: a small
boat pulled by one man with a pair of sculls; **scull'ing.**
scull², **skull** *skul, n.* a shallow basket for fish, etc.
[Poss. O.N. *skjóla,* pail]

scullery *skul'ər-i, n.* a room for rough kitchen work, as
cleaning of utensils.—**scull'ery-maid.** [O.Fr. *es-
cuelerie—*L. *scutella,* a tray.]

scullion *skul'yən,* (*arch.*) *n.* a servant for drudgery: a
mean, contemptible person. [Poss. O.Fr. *escou-
illon,* a dish-clout; or from Fr. *souillon,* scullion,
influenced by **scullery.**]

sculp *skulp, v.t.* and *v.i.* to carve: to engrave. to
sculpture. [L. *sculpēre.*]

sculpin *skul'pin, n.* the dragonet: a large-headed,
spiny, useless fish (*U.S.*).

sculpsit *skulp'sit, skŏŏlp'sit,* (he) sculptured (this),
sometimes appended to the signature of the sculptor.
[L.]

sculpt *skulpt, v.t.* and *v.i.* to sculpture: to carve. [Fr.
*sculpter—*L. *sculpēre,* to carve.]

sculptor *skulp'tər, n.* an artist in carving: a statuary:—
fem. **sculp'tress.**—*adj.* **sculp'tural** (*-chər-əl*).—*adv.*

sculp'turally.—*n.* **sculp'ture** the act of carving, esp.
in stone: extended to clay-modelling or moulding for
casting: work, or a piece of work, in this kind: shaping
in relief: spines, ridges, etc., standing out from the
surface (*biol.*).—*v.t* to carve: to represent in
sculpture: to shape in relief: to mould, or form, so as
to have the appearance, or (*fig.*) other quality, of
sculpture: to modify the form of (the earth's surface).
—*adjs.* **sculp'tured** carved: engraved· (of features)
fine and regular: having elevations on the surface
(*bot., zool.*); **sculpturesque'.**—*n.* **sculp'turing.** [L.
sculptor, -ōris, sculptūra—sculpēre, sculptum, to
carve.]

scum *skum, n.* foam or froth: matter coming to or
floating on the surface: offscourings of the population, i.e. worthless people, or person.—*v.t.* to skim.
—*v.i.* to form, throw up a scum:—*pr.p.* **scumm'ing;**
pa.t. and *pa.p.* **scummed.**—*n.* **scumm'er** a skimming
instrument.—*n.pl.* **scumm'ings** skimmings.—*adj*
scumm'y. [Cf. Dan. *skum,* Ger. *Schaum,* foam.]

scumble *skum'bl, v.t.* to soften the effect of by a very
thin coat of opaque or semi-opaque colour, or by light
rubbing or by applying paint with a dry brush.—*n.*
colour so laid: the effect so produced.—*n.*
scum'bling. [Freq. of **scum.**]

scuncheon *skun'shən, n.* the inner part of a jamb.
[O.Fr. *escoinson.*]

scunner *skun'ər,* (*Scot.*) *v.i.* to take a loathing.—*v.t.* to
excite a loathing in: to disgust, nauseate.—*n.* a loathing: an object, or a manifestation, of loathing.—**take
a scunner to** to take a strong dislike to. [Perh. M.E.
scurn, to shrink.]

scup *skup, n.* the porgy. [Narraganset *mish-
cuppauog.*]

scupper¹ *skup'ər, n.* a hole to drain a ship's deck.

scupper² *skup'ər,* (*slang*) *v.t.* to slaughter: to do for: to
ruin: to sink (a ship). [Perh. conn. with above.]

scurf *skûrf, n.* small flakes or scales of dead skin, esp.
on the scalp: a crust of branny scales: an incrustation.
—*n.* **scurf'iness.**—*adj.* **scurf'y.** [O.E. *scurf,
sceorf.*]

scurrile(e) *skur'il,* (*arch.*) *adj.* indecently opprobrious
or jocular.—*n.* **scurril'ity.**—*adj.* **scurr'ilous** indecently abusive.—*adv.* **scurr'ilously.**—*n.* **scurr'ilousness.** [L. *scurrīlis—scurra,* a buffoon.]

scurry *skur'i, v.i.* to hurry briskly or flutteringly: to
scuttle.—*n.* flurried haste: a flurry. [Prob. from
hurry-scurry, reduplication of **hurry.**]

scurvy *skûr'vi, adj.* scurfy: shabby: vile, contemptible.
—*n.* a disease marked by bleeding and sponginess
of the gums, due to lack of fresh vegetables and
consequently of vitamin C.—*adv.* **scur'vily.**—*n.*
scur'viness.—**scur'vy-grass** a cruciferous plant (*Co-
chlearia officinalis*) used by sailors as an anti-scor-
butic. [**scurf;** the application to the disease helped
by similarity of sound; see **scorbutic.**]

'scuse *skūz, v.t.* aphetic for **excuse.**

scut *skut, n.* a short erect tail like a hare's.

scuta. See **scute.**

scutage *skū'tij,* (*hist.*) *n.* a tax on a knight's fee, esp.
one in lieu of personal service. [L.L *scūtāgium—*L.
scūtum, shield.]

scutal, scutate. See **scute.**

scutch *skuch, v.t.* to dress (e.g. flax) by beating.—*n.* a
tool for dressing flax.—*ns.* **scutch'er** a person, tool,
or part of a machine that scutches: the striking part of
a threshing-mill; **scutch'ing.—scutch-blade.** [Prob.
O.Fr. *escousser,* to shake off.]

scutcheon *skuch'ən, n.* an aphetic form of **escutcheon.**

scute *skūt, n.* a scutum: a dermal plate.—*adjs.* **scūt'al;**
scut'ate protected by scutes: shield-shaped;
scūt'iform.—*n.* **scūt'um** a scute: the second tergal
plate of a segment of an insect's thorax:—*pl.* **scūt'a.**

[L. *scūtum*, a shield.]

scutellum *skŭt-el'əm, n.* a scale of a bird's foot: the third tergal plate of a segment of an insect's thorax: a structure, supposed to be the cotyledon, by which a grass embryo absorbs the endosperm:—*pl.* **scutell'a.** —*adjs.* **scutell'ar;** **scut'ellate.**—*n.* **scutella'tion** scale arrangement. [L. *scutella*, a tray, dim. of *scutra*, a platter, confused in scientific use with *scūtulum*, dim. of *scūtum*, a shield.]

scutiform. See **scute.**

scutter *skut'ər, v.i.* to run hastily: to scurry.—*n.* a hasty run. [A variant of **scuttle**[3].]

scuttle[1] *skut'l, n.* a shallow basket: a vessel for holding coal.—*n.* **scutt'leful.** [O.E. *scutel*—L *scutella*, a trey.]

scuttle[2] *skut'l, n.* an opening in a ship's deck or side: its lid: a shuttered hole in a wall, roof, etc.: its shutter or trap-door.—*v.t.* to make a hole in, esp. in order to sink: to destroy, ruin.—**scutt'le-butt** a cask with a hole cut in it for drinking-water (also **scutt'le-cask**): rumour, gossip (*U.S.*). [O.Fr. *escoutille*, hatchway.]

scuttle[3] *skut'l, v.i.* to dash with haste.—*n.* an act of scuttling.—*n.* **scutt'ler.** [scud.]

scutum. See **scute.**

Scylla *sil'ə,* (*myth.*) *n.* a six-headed monster who sat over a dangerous rock opposite Charybdis [Gr *Skylla.*]

scyphus *sif'əs, n.* a large Greek drinking-cup (*ant.*): a cup-shaped structure:—*pl.* **scyph'i.**—*adj.* **scyph'-iform.** [Gr. *skyphos*, cup.]

scythe *sidh, n.* an instrument with a large curved blade for mowing: a blade attached to a war-chariot wheel. —*v.t.* and *v.i.* to mow with a scythe.—*adj.* **scythed** armed or cut with scythes.—*n.* **scyth'er.** [O.E. *sīthe.*]

Scythian *sith'i-ən, adj.* of Scythia, an ancient country N. and E. of the Black Sea, of its nomadic people or of their language.—*n.* a member of the people: the language of Scythia.

sea *sē, n.* the great mass of salt water covering the greater part of the earth's surface: the ocean: any great expanse of water: a great (esp. salt) lake—mainly in proper names: swell or roughness: a great wave: the tide: a wide expanse.—*adj.* **marine.**—*adj.* **sea'-like** like the sea.—*adv.* in the manner of the sea. —*adj., adv.* **sea'ward** towards the (open) sea.—*n.* seaward side, direction or position.—*adj., adv.* **sea'wardly.**—*adv.* **sea'wards.**—*sea'-air'* the air at sea or by the sea; **sea'-an'chor** a floating anchor used at sea to slow a boat down, or maintain its direction; **sea'-anem'one** a solitary soft-bodied polyp of the Zoantharia; **sea'-bank** the seashore: an embankment to keep out the sea; **sea'-ba'ther;** **sea'-ba'thing;** **sea'-beach** a strip of sand, gravel, etc., bordering the sea; **sea'-bear** the fur-seal; **sea'-beast.**—*adjs.* **sea'-beat,** **-en** lashed by the waves.—**sea'bed** the bottom of the sea; **sea'-bird; sea'board** the country bordering the sea.—Also *adj.*—**sea'-boots** long, waterproof boots worn by sailors.—*adjs.* **sea'borne** carried on the sea. —**sea'-bott'om** the floor of the sea; **sea'-breeze;** sea cabbage sea-kale; **sea'-calf** the common seal; **sea'-canā'ry** the white whale; **sea'-captain** the captain of a merchant ship; **sea'-change** a change effected by the sea (*Shak.*): a transformation; **sea'-chest** a seaman's trunk; **sea'-cliff; sea'-coal** (*arch.*) coal in the ordinary sense, not charcoal (possibly as first worked where exposed by the sea); **sea'coast; sea'-cock** a gurnard: a valve communicating with the sea through a vessel's hull; **sea'-cook** a ship's cook; **sea'craft** skill in navigation: seamanship: seagoing craft; **sea'-cu'cumber** a holothurian (as bêche-de-mer); **sea'-dev'll; sea'-dog** an old sailor; **sea'-ea'gle** erne or other *Haliaetus:* the eagle-ray; **sea'-el'ephant** the elephant-seal; **sea'farer** a traveller by sea, usu. a sailor; **sea'faring.**—Also *adj.* —**sea'-fight** a battle between ships at sea; **sea'-fish; sea'-fish'er; sea'-fish'ing; sea'-floor** the bottom of the sea; **sea'-fog** a fog coming from the sea; **sea'-folk; sea'food** food got from the sea, esp. shellfish; **sea'-front** the side of the land, of a town, or of a building that looks towards the sea: a promenade with its buildings fronting the sea; **sea'-gir'dle** tangle, esp. *Laminaria digitata.*—*adj.* **sea'-girt** surrounded by sea.—**sea'-god, -godd'ess.**—*adj.* **sea'-going** sailing on the deep sea: suitable for deep-sea voyage —**sea'-green** green like the sea.—Also *adj.* (see also **sea-green incorruptible** below).—**sea'gull** a gull, **sea'-holl'y** eryngo; **sea'horse** the fabulous hippocampus: Hippocampus or kindred fish; **sea'-ice'.**—*adj.* **sea'-island** (of cotton) of the kind grown on the islands off the coast of South Carolina.—**sea'-kale** a fleshy glaucous cruciferous seaside plant (*Crambe maritima*) cultivated for its blanched sprouts; **sea'-king** a viking chief; **sea'-lane** a navigable passage between islands, ships, icefloes, etc., **sea'-law** maritime law, esp. mediaeval customary law; **sea'-law'yer** a captious sailor; **sea'-legs** ability to walk on a ship's deck when it is pitching: resistance to seasickness; **sea'-leop'ard** a spotted seal of the southern seas; **sea'-lett'er, -brief** a document of description that used to be given to a ship at the port where she was fitted out: a document issued to a neutral merchant vessel in wartime, allowing it to pass freely (also **sea'-pass**); **sea'-lett'uce** a seaweed (*Ulva*) with flat translucent green fronds—green laver; **sea'-lev'el** the mean level of the surface of the sea.—**sea'-line** a coastline; **sea'-lion** a seal with external ears and with hind flippers turned forward; **sea'-loch** (*Scot.*) a lakelike arm of the sea; **sea'-lord** a naval member of the Board of Admiralty; **sea'man** a sailor: a man other than an officer or apprentice, employed aboard ship.—*adjs.* **sea'manlike** showing good seamanship; **sea'manly** characteristic of a seaman.—**sea'manship** the art of handling ships at sea; **sea'-mar'gin** the margin of the sea; **sea'-mew** any gull; **sea'-mile** a geographical or nautical mile; **sea'mon'ster; sea'-mount, sea'mount** a mountain under the sea of at least 3 000 ft; **sea'-nymph; sea'-ott'er** a N. Pacific animal (*Enhydris*) akin to the true otters: its silvery brown fur, now very rare; **sea'-pass** see **sea-letter** above; **sea'-pass'age** a journey by sea; **sea'-piece** a picture, poem, piece of music, etc., representing a scene at sea; **sea'-pink** thrift; **sea'plane** an aeroplane with floats instead of landing-wheels; **sea'port** a port or harbour on the sea: a place with such a harbour; **sea'-power** a nation strong at sea: naval strength; **sea'quake** a seismic disturbance at sea; **sea'-risk** hazard of injury or loss by sea; **sea'-road** a route followed by ships; **sea'-room** space to manoeuvre a ship safely; **sea'-ro'ver** a pirate (ship); **sea'-salt** salt got from sea-water; **sea'-sand; sea'scape** a picture, photograph, of the sea; **sea'-scor'pion** scorpion-fish; **Sea'-Scout** a member of a marine branch of the Scout Association; **sea'-scout'ing; sea'-serp'ent** an enormous mythical marine animal of serpent-like form; **sea'shell** a marine shell; **sea'shore'** the land immediately adjacent to the sea: the foreshore (*law*). —*adj.* **sea'sick'** sick owing to the rolling of a vessel at sea.—**sea'sick'ness; sea'side** the neighbourhood of the sea.—Also *adj.*—**sea'-slug** a nudibranch: a holothurian; **sea'-snail** any snail-like marine gasteropod; **sea'-squirt** an ascidian; **sea'-strand'; sea'-sur'geon** a tropical genus (*Acanthurus*) of spiny-finned fishes with a lancet-like spine ensheathed on each side of the tail; **sea'-swall'ow** a tern; **sea'-trout** the salmon-trout (*Salmo trutta*); **sea'-ur'chin** one of a class of Echinoderms with globular, ovoid, or heart-shaped, sometimes flattened body and shell of calcareous plates, without arms; **sea'-wall** a wall to keep out the sea; **sea'-wa'ter; sea'-wave; sea'-way** (often **sea'way**) a way by sea: progress through the waves: a heavy sea: a regular route taken by ocean traffic: an inland waterway on which ocean-going vessels can sail; **sea'weed** marine algae collectively: any marine alga; **sea'-wolf** the wolf-fish.—*adj.* **sea'-worn** worn by the sea or by seafaring.—**sea'worthiness.**—*adj.* **sea'-worthy** fit for sea: able to endure stormy weather.— **all at sea** out of one's reckoning: completely at a loss; **at full sea** at full tide; **at sea** away from land: on the ocean: astray; **follow the sea, go to sea** to become a sailor; **heavy sea** a sea in which the waves run high; **sea-green incorruptible** one honestly and unshakably devoted to an ideal or purpose, esp. in public life (orig. used by Carlyle of Robespierre); **short sea** a sea in which the waves are choppy, irregular, and interrupted; **the four seas** those bounding Great Britain; **Seven Seas** see **seven**. [O.E. *sǣ*; Du. *zee*, Ger. *See*, O.N. *sǣr*, Dan. *sö*.]

Seabee *sē'bē* (the letters *cb* phonetically represented), *n.* a member of a U.S. Navy construction battalion.

seal[1] *sēl*, *n.* a piece of wax, lead or other material, stamped with a device and attached as a means of authentication or attestation: a piece of wax, etc., stamped or not, used as a means of keeping closed a letter, etc.: the design stamped: an engraved stone or other stamp for impressing a device, or a trinket of like form: a confirming token: a usu. decorative label for affixing to Christmas mail, etc., often sold for charity: that which closes: an obligation to secrecy: an impression: a device to prevent passage of a gas: water in a gas-trap.—*v.t.* to set a seal to: to stamp: to fasten with a seal: to confirm: to ratify: to close up: to enclose: to settle irrevocably: to set apart.—*v.i.* to set one's seal to something.—*n.* **seal'ant** something that seals a place where there is a leak.—*adj.* **sealed.**—*ns.* **seal'er** a person or thing that seals: a substance used to coat a surface for protection, impermeability, etc.; **seal'ing.**—*adj.* **sealed'-beam'** of car headlights, consisting of a complete unit sealed within a vacuum.— **sealed book** something beyond one's knowledge or understanding; **seal'-engrav'ing** the art of engraving seals; **seal'ing-wax** formerly beeswax, now usually a composition of shellac, turpentine, vermilion or other colouring matter, etc., for sealing; **seal'-ring** a signet-ring.—**Great Seal** (also without *caps.*) the state seal of the United Kingdom; **Lord Privy Seal** formerly the keeper of the Privy Seal, now the senior cabinet minister without official duties; **Privy Seal** (also without *caps.*) formerly, the seal appended to documents that were to receive, or did not require, authorisation by the Great Seal, in Scotland used esp. to authenticate royal grants of personal rights; **seal off** to make it impossible for any thing, person, to leave or enter (e.g. an area); **set one's seal to, on** to give one's authority or assent to; **under seal** authenticated; **under sealed orders** under orders only to be opened at sea. [O.Fr. *seel*—L. *sigillum*, dim. of *signum*, a mark.]

seal[2] *sēl*, *n.* one of the paddle-footed Carnivora, usually excluding the walrus and often excluding the otaries: sealskin.—*adj.* of seal or sealskin.—*v.i.* to hunt seals.—*ns.* **seal'er** a seal-fisher; **seal'ery** sealfishery; **seal'ing.**—**seal'-fish'er** a hunter of seals: a sealing ship; **seal'-fish'ing; seal'-point** a variety of Siamese cat, with dark brown face, paws and tail; **seal'-rook'ery** a seals' breeding-place; **seal'skin** the prepared fur of the fur-seal, or an imitation (as of rabbit-skin, or of mohair): a garment made of this.— Also *adj.* [O.E. *seolh* (gen. *sēoles*); O.N. *selr*.]

Sealyham *sēl'i-əm*, *n.* (also without *cap.*; in full **Sealyham terrier**) a long-bodied, short-legged, hardcoated terrier, first bred at *Sealyham* in Pembrokeshire.

seam *sēm*, *n.* a line of junction between edges sewn together, or between other edges generally: the turned-up edges of such a line on the wrong side of the cloth: a crack: the mark of a cut: a wrinkle: a stratum, esp. if thin or valuable.—*v.t.* to join, furnish, or mark with seams.—*ns.* **seam'er** one who, or that which, seams: a ball delivered by seam bowling (*cricket*); **seam'iness.**—*adj.* **seam'less.**—*ns.* **seamster** (*sem'*), **seam'stress** see **sempster.**—*adj.* **seamy** (*sēm'i*) having a seam or seams: showing the disreputable side: sordid.—**seam allowance** in dressmaking, the margin allowed for the seams along the edge of the pieces of a garment; **seam bowler; seam bowling** (*cricket*) bowling in which the seam of the ball is used in delivery to make the ball swerve in flight or first to swerve and then to break in the opposite direction on pitching; **seam welding** resistance welding of overlapping sheets of metal using wheels or rollers as electrodes; **seam'y-side** the wrong side of a garment: hence (usu. **seamy side**) the disreputable side or aspect. [O.E. *sēam*—*sīwian*, to sew; Du. *zoom*, Ger. *Saum*.]

Seanad (Eireann) *shan'adh* (*e'ran*), the upper house of the legislature of the Republic of Ireland. [Ir., senate.]

séance *sā'äs*, *n.* a sitting, esp. of psychical researchers or Spiritualists. [Fr.,—L. *sedēre*, to sit.]

sear[1], **sere** *sēr*, *n.* the catch that holds a gun at cock or half-cock. [Cf. O.Fr. *serre*—L. *sera*, a bar.]

sear[2] *sēr*, *adj.* (usu. **sere**) dry and withered.—*v.i.* (rarely **sere**) to become sere.—*v.t.* to make sere: to dry up: to scorch: to brand: to cauterise: to render callous or insensible.—*n.* a mark of searing.—*adj.* **seared.**—*n.* **seared'ness.**—*n.* and *adj.* **sear'ing.**—*ns.* **sear'ness, sere'ness.**—**sear'ing-iron.**—**the sere, the** (so *Shak.*; not **and**) **yellow leaf** the autumn of life. [O.E. *sēar*, dry, *sēarian*, to dry up; L.G. *soor*, Du. *zoor*.]

search *sûrch*, *v.t.* to explore all over with a view to finding something: to examine closely: to examine for hidden articles by feeling all over: to ransack: to scrutinise: to probe: to put to the test: to seek out (usu. with *out*).—*v.i.* to make a search.—*n.* the act or power of searching: thorough examination: quest.— *adj.* **search'able.**—*n.* **search'er.**—*adj.* **search'ing** penetrating: thorough-going.—*adv.* **search'ingly.**—*n.* **search'ingness.**—**search'light** a lamp and reflector throwing a strong beam of light for picking out objects by night: the light so projected; **search'-par'ty** a party sent out in search of somebody or something; **search'-warr'ant** a warrant authorising the searching of a house, etc.—**right of search** the right of a belligerent to search neutral ships for contraband of war; **search me** (*slang*) I don't know. [O.Fr. *cerchier* (Fr. *chercher*)—L. *circāre*, to go about —*circus*, a circle.]

season *sē'zn*, *n.* one of the four divisions of the year: the usual, natural, legal, or appropriate time, or time of year, for anything: any particular time: time, esp. of some continuance, but not long.—*v.t.* to mature: to temper: to bring into suitable condition: to inure: to render savoury: to flavour: to imbue.—*v.i.* to become seasoned.—*adj.* **sea'sonable** in due season: timely.—*n.* **sea'sonableness.**—*adv.* **sea'sonably.**— *adj.* **sea'sonal** according to season.—*n.* **seasonal'ity** the quality of being seasonal.—*adv.* **sea'sonally.**— *adj.* **sea'soned.**—*ns.* **sea'soner; sea'soning** the process or act by which anything is seasoned: the process of acclimatisation: that which is added to food to give relish.—*adj.* **sea'sonless** without difference of seasons.—**season ticket** a ticket valid any number of times within a specified period.—**close season** see **close**; **in season** ripe, fit and ready for use: allowed to be killed: of a bitch, ready to mate: on heat: fit to be eaten; **in season and out of season** at all times; **out of season** inopportune: not in season.   [O.Fr. *seson* (Fr. *saison*)—L. *satiō*, -*ōnis*, a sowing.]

seat *sēt*, *n.* anything used or intended for sitting on: a chair, bench, saddle, etc.: part of a chair on which the body rests: a sitting: a mode of sitting: a place where one may sit, as in a theatre, church, etc.: a right to sit: a constituency: membership: that part of the body or of a garment on which one sits: that on which anything rests: site, situation: a place where anything is located, settled, or established: post of authority: a throne: a capital city: abode: mansion: sitting-room. —*v.t.* to place on a seat: to cause to sit down: to place in any situation, site, etc.: to establish: to fix: to assign a seat to: to furnish with a seat or seats: to fit accurately: to make baggy by sitting.—*v.i.* to become baggy by sitting.—*adj.* **seat'ed.**—*ns.* **seat'er** (in composition) a vehicle, sofa, etc., seated for so many; **seat'ing** the taking, provision, or arrangement of seats: a supporting surface: material for seats.—*adj.* **seat'less.**—**seat'-belt** a belt which can be fastened to hold a person firmly in his seat in car or aircraft, for safety; **seat earth** a bed of clay underlying a coal seam.—**lose one's seat** to fail to be re-elected to Parliament; **take a seat** to sit down; **take one's seat** to take up one's seat, esp. in Parliament.   [O.N. *sǣti*, seat; cf. O.E. *sǣt*, ambush.]

sebaceous, etc. See **sebum.**

sebum *sē'bəm*, *n.* the fatty secretion that lubricates the hair and skin.—*adj.* **sebaceous** (*si-bā'shəs*) tallowy: of, like, of the nature of, or secreting sebum.—*n.* **seborrhoea** (*seb-ə-rē'ə*) excessive discharge from the sebaceous glands.—*adj.* **seborrhoe'ic.**   [L. *sēbum*, suet.]

sec[1] *sek*, *adj.* dry, of wines.   [Fr.]

sec[2]. See **secant.**

secant *sē'kənt*, *sek'ənt*, *adj.* cutting.—*n.* a cutting line: a straight line which cuts a curve in two or more places (*geom.*): orig., a straight line from the centre of a circle through one end of an arc to the tangent from the other end (*trig.*): now, as a function of an angle, the ratio of the hypotenuse to the base of a right-angled triangle formed by dropping a perpendicular from a point on one side of the angle to the other (negative if the base is the side produced)—in trigonometrical notation written sec.   [L. *secāns*, -*antis*, pr.p. of *secāre*, to cut.]

sécateur *sek'ə-tûr*, *n.* (usu. in *pl.* and without accent) pruning-shears.   [Fr.]

secede *si-sēd'*, *v.i.* to withdraw, esp. from a party, religious body, federation, or the like.—*ns.* **sece'der** one who secedes: one of a body of Presbyterians who seceded from the Church of Scotland about 1733; **secession** (-*sesh'ən*) the act of seceding: a body of seceders.—Also *adj.*—*adj.* **secess'ional.**—*ns.* **secess'ionalism**; **secess'ionist** one who favours or joins in secession.—Also *adjs.*—**War of Secession** the American Civil War.   [L. *sēcēdĕre*, *sēcessum*, *sē*-, apart, *cēdĕre*, to go.]

sech *sesh*, *n.* a conventional abbreviation of *hyperbolic secant.*

seclude *si-klōōd'*, *v.i.* to shut off, esp. from association or influence.—*adj.* **seclud'ed** retired: withdrawn from observation or society.—*adv.* **seclud'edly.**—*n.* **seclusion** (*si-klōō'zhən*) the act of secluding: the state of being secluded: retirement: privacy: solitude.   [L. *sēclūdĕre*, -*clūsum*,—*sē*-, apart, *claudĕre*, to shut.]

second *sek'ənd*, *adj.* next after or below the first: other, alternate: additional: supplementary: another, as it were: inferior: subordinate: referring to the person or

persons addressed (*gram.*).—*adv.* next after the first: in the second place.—*n.* one who, or that which, is second or of the second class: a place in the second class: second gear: one who attends another in a duel or a prize fight: a supporter: the 60th part of a minute of time, or of angular measurement: the second person (*gram.*): the interval between successive tones of the diatonic scale (*mus.*): (in *pl.*) goods of a second quality: (in *pl.*) a second helping of food (*coll.*).—*v.t.* to follow: to act as second to: to back: to support after the mover of a nomination-or resolution: to transfer temporarily to some special employment (*si-kond'*; esp. *mil.*).—*adv.* **sec'ondarily.**—*n.* **sec'ondariness.**—*adj.* **sec'ondary** subordinate: subsidiary: of a second order: of a second stage: derivative: induced: of education, between primary and higher: of a feather, growing in the second joint of the wing: (*cap.*; *geol.*) Mesozoic.—*n.* a subordinate: a delegate or deputy: a satellite: that which is secondary, as a feather, coil, etc.—*n.* **sec'onder** one who seconds a motion, etc.—*adv.* **sec'ondly** in the second place.—*n.* **second'ment** temporary transfer to another position.—**Second Advent, Coming** a second coming of Christ; **secondary battery, cell** one on which the chemical action is reversible; **secondary coil** one carrying an induced current; **secondary colours** those produced by mixing two primary colours; **secondary electron** an electron in a beam of secondary emission; **secondary emission** emission of electrons from a surface or particle by bombardment with electrons, etc., from another source; **secondary growth** a cancer somewhere other than at the original site; **secondary modern** formerly, a type of secondary school offering a less academic, more technical education than a grammar school; **secondary picket; secondary picketing** the picketing by workers of a firm with which they are not directly in dispute but which has a trading connection with their own firm, in order to maximise the effects of a strike; **secondary school** a school for secondary education; **second ballot** a system of election whereby a second vote is taken, the candidate or candidates who received fewest votes in the first ballot being eliminated.—*n.* and *adj.* **sec'ond-best** next to the best (**come off second-best** to get the worst of a contest).—**second chamber** in a legislature of two houses, the house with fewer powers, usu. acting as a check on the other; **second childhood** mental weakness in extreme old age; **second class** the class next to the first.—*adj.* **sec'ond-class** (see also below).—**second cousin** one who has the same pair of great-grandparents, but different grandparents: loosely, a first cousin's child, or a parent's first cousin (properly first cousin once removed); **second-degree** see **degree**; **second floor** (see **floor** for British and U.S. senses).—*adj.* **sec'ond-floor'.**—**second growth** a new growth of a forest after cutting, fire, etc.; a second crop of grapes in a season. —*v.t.*, *v.i.* **sec'ond-guess'** (*coll.*, chiefly *U.S.*) to say with hindsight: to predict: to outdo in guessing.—*adj.* **sec'ond-hand'** derived from another: not original: already used by a previous owner: dealing in second-hand goods.—*n.* (*sek'*) a hand on a watch or clock that indicates seconds (see also **seconds-hand** below). —*adv.* indirectly, at second hand: after use by a previous owner.—**sec'ond-in-command'** the next under the commanding officer or other person in charge; **sec'ond-lieuten'ant** an army officer of lowest commissioned rank; **second man** a man assisting the driver of a train; **sec'ond-mark** the character ", used for seconds of arc or time or for inches; **second nature** a deeply ingrained habit.—*adj.* **sec'ond-rate** inferior: mediocre.—**second-rat'er**; **second self** a person with whom one has the closest possible ties, sharing beliefs, attitudes, feelings, ways of behaving;

sec'onds-hand a hand that marks seconds; **sec'ond-sight'** a gift of prophetic vision attributed to certain persons, esp. Highlanders; **second storey** the first floor.—*adj.* **sec'ond-strike'** (of a nuclear weapon) specially concealed so as to be ready to be used for striking back after a first attack by an enemy.—**second string** an alternative choice, course of action, etc.; **second thoughts** reconsideration.—*adj.* **second'-to-none'** supreme: unsurpassed.—**second wind** recovery of breath in prolonged exertion.—**at second hand** through an intermediate source, indirectly: by hearsay; **second-class citizen** a member of a group in the community not given the full rights and privileges enjoyed by the community as a whole; **second-class mail, post** mail sent at a cheaper rate either because of its character or because the sender is prepared to accept slower delivery. [Fr.,—L. *secundus*—*sequī, secūtus,* to follow.]

seconde *si-kond',* *sə-gɔd,* (*fencing*) *n.* a position in parrying. [Fr.]

secret *sē'krit, adj.* kept back from knowledge of others: guarded against discovery or observation: unrevealed: hidden: secluded: recondite, occult: preserving secrecy: admitted to confidence, privy.—*adv.* (*poet.*) secretly.—*n.* a fact, purpose, method, etc., that is kept undivulged: participation in knowledge of such a fact: anything unrevealed or unknown: secrecy: a piece of armour hidden by clothes: the key or principle that explains or enables: an inaudible prayer, esp. in the Mass.—*n.* **secrecy** (*sē'kri-si*) the state or fact of being secret: concealment: seclusion: confidence: power or habit of keeping secrets: the keeping of secrets: a secret.—*v.t.* **secrete** (*si-krēt'*) to hide: to appropriate secretly: to form and separate by the activity of living matter.—*n.* **secre'tion** the act of secreting: that which is secreted: a mass of mineral matter formed by inward growth in a cavity.—*adjs.* **secre'tional**; **sē'cretive** (also *si-krē'tiv*) given to secrecy: very reticent: indicative of secrecy.—*adv.* **secretively.**—*n.* **secretiveness.**—*adv.* **sē'cretly** in secret: in concealment: inaudibly (of prayers).—*n.* **sē'cretness.**—*adj.* **secre'tory** secreting.—**secret agent** one employed in secret service; **secret police** a police force which operates in secret, usu. dealing with matters of politics, national security, etc.; **Secret Service** a department of government service whose operations are not disclosed: its activities: (without *cap.*) espionage.—**in secret** with precautions against being known: in confidence, as a secret: secretly; **in the secret** admitted to, participating in, knowledge of the secret; **keep a secret** not to divulge a secret; **open secret** see **open**. [L. *sēcernĕre, sēcrētum*—*sē-,* apart, *cernĕre,* to separate.]

secretaire. See **secretary.**

secretary *sek'ri-tə-ri, n.* one employed to write or transact business for another or for a society, company, etc.: the minister at the head of certain departments of state: an ambassador's or minister's assistant.—*n.* **secretaire** (*sek'ri-tār, sək-rə-ter;* from Fr.) a secret repository: a writing desk, escritoire.—*adj.* **secretarial** (*-tār'i-əl*).—*ns.* **secretā'riat(e)** (*-ət*) secretaryship: a secretary's office: the administrative department of a council, organisation, legislative or executive body; **sec'retaryship** the office, duties, or art of a secretary.—**sec'retary-bird** a long-legged snake-eating African bird of prey (*Serpentarius*), said to be named from the tufts of feathers at the back of its head like pens stuck behind the ear; **sec'retary-gen'eral** the chief administrator of an organisation, e.g. the United Nations; **secretary hand** an old legal style of handwriting; **secretary type** a type in imitation of secretary hand.—**Secretary of State** a cabinet minister holding one of the more important folios: in

U.S., the foreign secretary. [M.E. *secretarie*—L.L. *sēcrētārius*—L. *sēcrētum;* see **secret.**]

secrete ... secretory. See **secret.**

sect *sekt, n.* a body of followers: a school of opinion, esp. in religion or philosophy: a subdivision of one of the main religious divisions of mankind: an organised denomination, used esp. by members of the greater churches to express their disapprobation of the lesser: a dissenting body: a party: a class of people.—*adjs.* **sectā'rial** distinguishing a sect (esp. in India); **sectā'rian** of a sect or sectary: narrow, exclusive: denominational.—*n.* one of a sect: one strongly imbued with the characteristics of a sect, esp. if bigoted.—*v.t.* **sectā'rianise, -ize.**—*ns.* **sectā'rianism; sectary** (*sekt'ər-i*) a follower, a votary: one of a sect: a dissenter. [L. *secta,* a school or following—*sequī, secūtus,* to follow, influenced by *secāre,* to cut.]

section *sek'shən, n.* the act of cutting: a division: a portion: one of the parts into which anything may be considered as divided or of which it may be built up: the line of intersection of two surfaces: the surface formed when a solid is cut by a plane: an exposure of rock in which the strata are cut across (*geol.*): a plan of anything represented as if cut by a plane or other surface: a thin slice for microscopic examination: in surgery, any process involving cutting: a one-mile square of American public lands: a subdivision of a company, platoon, battery, etc.: a number of men detailed for a special service: a district or region (*U.S.*): a frame for a honeycomb: a section-mark.—*v.t.* to divide into sections: to make a section of.—*adj.* **sec'tional.**—*n.* **sec'tionalism** a narrow-minded concern for the interests of a group, area, etc.: class spirit.—*adv.* **sec'tionally.**—*n.* **sec'tor** (*-tər*) a plane figure bounded by two radii and an arc: an object of like shape: an instrument of like shape for measuring angular distance (*astron.*): a length or section of a fortified line or army front: a mathematical instrument consisting of two graduated rules hinged together, originally with a graduated arc: a division, section, of (usu.) a nation's economic operations.—*v.t.* to divide into sectors.—*adjs.* **sec'toral; sectorial** (*-tō'ri-əl, -tō'*) sectoral: adapted for cutting.—*n.* a carnassial tooth.—**sec'tion-cutter** an instrument for making sections for microscopic work; **sec'tion-mark** the sign §, used to mark the beginning of a section of a book or as a reference mark. [L. *sectio*—*secāre, sectum,* to cut.]

secular *sek'ū-lər, adj.* pertaining to or coming or observed once in a lifetime, generation, century, age: appreciable only in the course of ages: pertaining to the present world, or to things not spiritual: civil, not ecclesiastical: lay: not concerned with religion: not bound by monastic rules (opp. to *regular*): of the secular clergy: lasting for a long time.—*n.* a layman: an ecclesiastic (as a parish priest) not bound by monastic rules.—*n.* **secūlarisā'tion, -z-.**—*v.t.* **sec'ularise, -ize** to make secular.—*ns.* **sec'ularism** the belief that the state, morals, education, etc., should be independent of religion.—*n.* and *adj.* **sec'ularist.**—*adj.* **secularist'ic.**—*n.* **secularity** (*-lar'-*).—*adv.* **sec'ularly.** —**secular arm** the civil power. [L. *saeculāris*— *saeculum,* a lifetime, generation.]

seculum. See **saeculum.**

secund *sē'kund,* also *sek'und, si-kund', adj.* (*bot.*) all turned to the same side. [L. *secundus,* following, second.]

secure *si-kūr', adj.* without care or anxiety: confident: over-confident: free from danger: safe: assured: affording safety: stable: firmly fixed or held: in police, etc., custody.—*v.t.* to make secure, safe, or certain: to make secure the possession of: to establish in security: to seize and guard: to get hold of: to con-

trive to get: to guarantee: to fasten.—*adj.* secûr'able.
—*adv.* secure'ly.—*ns.* secure'ment; secure'ness;
secûr'er; secûr'ity the state, feeling, or means of
being secure: protection from espionage: certainty: a
pledge: a guarantee: a right conferred on a creditor to
make him sure of recovery: (usu. in *pl.*) a bond or
certificate in evidence of debt or property.—*adj.* for
securing security.—**Security Council** a body of the
United Nations charged with the maintenance of
international peace and security; **security risk** a person considered from his political affiliations or lean-
ings to be unsafe for state service. [L. *secûrus—sē-*,
without, *cûra*, care.]

sedan si-dan', *n.* a covered chair for one, carried on two
poles (also **sedan'-chair**; *hist.*): a large closed motor-
car (*U.S.*), a saloon-car. [Poss. It. *sedere*, to sit.]

sedate si-dāt', *adj.* composed: staid.—*v.t.* to calm,
quieten, by means of sedatives.—*adv.* sedāte'ly.—*ns.*
sedāte'ness; sedā'tion the act of calming, or state of
being calmed, by means of sedatives.—*adj.* **sedative**
(*sed'ə-tiv*) calming: composing: allaying excitement
or pain.—*n.* a sedative medicine or agent. [L.
sedātus, pa.p. of *sedāre*, to still.]

sedentary sed'ən-tə-ri, *adj.* sitting much: requiring
much sitting: inactive: stationary: not migratory:
lying in wait, as a spider: attached to a substratum
(*zool.*).—*adv.* sed'entarily.—*n.* sed'entariness. [L.
sedentārius—sedēre, to sit.]

Seder sā'dər, *n.* the ceremonial meal and its rituals on
the first night or first two nights of the Passover.
[Heb., order.]

sederunt si-dē'runt, si-dā'rənt, sā-dā'rōōnt, *n.* in Scotland a sitting, as of a court: a list of persons present.
[L. *sedērunt*, there sat—*sedēre*, to sit.]

sedge sej, *n.* any species of a family distinguished from
grasses by its solid triangular stems and leaf-sheaths
without a slit: extended to iris and other plants.—*adj.*
sedg'y of, like, abounding with sedge.—**sedge'-**
warbler a common British warbler of watery places.
[O.E. *secg*; cf. L.G. *segge*.]

sedilia si-dil'i-ə, *n.pl.* seats (usu. three, often in niches)
for the officiating clergy, on the south side of the
chancel:—*sing.* **sedile** (*si-dī'li*, L. *se-dē'le*). [L.
sedīle, pl. *sedīlia*, seat.]

sediment sed'i-mənt, *n.* what settles at the bottom of a
liquid: dregs: a deposit.—*v.t.* to deposit as sediment:
to cause or allow to deposit sediment.—*adj.* **sedi-**
mentary (*-men'tər-i*).—*n.* **sedimentā'tion** deposition
of sediment.—**sedimentary rocks** those formed by
accumulation and deposition of fragmentary materials or organic remains. [L. *sedimentum—sedēre*, to
sit.]

sedition si-dish'ən, *n.* insurrection (*arch.*): public
tumult: (vaguely) any offence against the state short
of treason.—*adj.* sedi'tious.—*adv.* sedi'tiously.—*n.*
sedi'tiousness. [O.Fr.,—L. *sedītiō*, *-ōnis—sēd-*,
away, *īre*, *ītum*, to go.]

seduce si-dûs', *v.t.* to draw aside from party, belief,
allegiance, service, duty, etc.: to lead astray: to
entice: to corrupt: to induce to have sexual intercourse.—*ns.* sedûce'ment the act of seducing or
drawing aside: allurement; sedû'cer.—*n.* and *adj.*
sedû'cing.—*adv.* sedû'cingly.—*n.* **seduction** (*si-
duk'shən*) the act of seducing: allurement.—*adj.*
seduc'tive alluring.—*adv.* seduc'tively.—*ns.* seduc'-
tiveness; seduc'tress. [L. *sedûcĕre, sēductum—sē-*,
aside, *dûcĕre*, to lead.]

sedulous sed'û-ləs, *adj.* assiduous.—*ns.* **sedulity** (*si-
dû'li-ti*); sed'ulousness.—*adv.* sed'ulously. [L.
sēdulus—sē dolō, without deception, hence in
earnest.]

Sedum sē'dəm, *n.* the stonecrop genus: (without *cap.*) a
plant of the genus. [L. *sēdum*, house-leek.]

see[1] sē, *n.* the office of bishop of a particular diocese:
(wrongly according to some) a cathedral city, also a
diocese.—**Holy See** the papal court. [O.Fr. *se, sied*
—L. *sēdēs, -is—sedēre*, to sit.]

see[2] sē, *v.t.* to perceive by the sense seated in the eye:
to perceive mentally: to apprehend: to recognise: to
understand: to learn: to be aware by reading: to look
at: to judge, to deem: to refer to: to ascertain: to
make sure: to make sure of having: to wait upon,
escort: to call on: to receive as a visitor: to meet: to
consult: to experience: to meet and accept by staking
a similar sum.—*v.i.* to have power of vision: to see
things well enough: to look or inquire: to be attentive: to consider:—*pa.t.* saw; *pa.p.* seen.—*imper.*,
passing into *interj.*, see look: behold.—*n.* (*rare*) an act
of seeing.—*adj.* see'able.—*n.* see'ing sight: vision:
clear-sightedness: atmospheric conditions for good
observation (*astron.*).—*adj.* having sight, or insight:
observant: discerning.—*conj.* (also **seeing that**) since:
in view of the fact.—*n.* **seer** (*sē' ər*) one who sees: (*sēr*)
one who sees into the future.—*adj.* see'-through
transparent.—**have seen better days**, **one's best days**
to be now on the decline; **let me see** a phrase
employed to express reflection; **see about** to consider:
to do whatever is to be done about: to attend to; **see**
fit to think it appropriate (to); **see off** to accompany
(someone) at his departure: to reprimand (*slang*): to
get rid of (*coll.*); **see one's way clear** to (*coll.*) to feel
that one will be able to; **see out** to conduct to the
door: to see to the end: to outlast; **see over, round** to
be conducted all through; **see red** see **red**[1]; **see some-**
one right (*coll.*) to take care of someone, usu. in the
sense of giving them a tip or reward; **see the light** to
experience a religious conversion: to come round to
another's way of thinking, to come to understand and
agree with someone (usu. *facet.*); **see things** see thing;
see through to participate in to the end: to back up till
difficulties end: to understand the true nature of, esp.
when faults or bad intentions are concealed by a good
appearance; **see to** to look after: to make sure about;
see what I can do do what I can; **see you (later)**, **be**
seeing you (*coll.*) goodbye for now. [O.E. *sēon*;
Ger. *sehen*, Du. *zien*.]

seed sēd, *n.* that which is sown: a multicellular structure by which flowering plants reproduce, consisting
of embryo, stored food, and seed-coat, derived from
the fertilised ovule (*bot.*): a small hard fruit or part in
a fruit, a pip: a seed-like object or aggregate: semen:
spawn: the condition of having or proceeding to form
seed: sown land: grass and clover grown from seed: a
first principle: germ: a crystal introduced to start
crystallisation: offspring, descendants, race: a
tournament player who has been seeded (*coll.*).—*v.i.*
to produce seed: to run to seed.—*v.t.* to sow: to
sprinkle, powder, dust: to remove seeds from: in
lawn-tennis tournaments, etc., to arrange (the draw)
so that the best players do not meet in the early
rounds: to deal with (good players) in this way: to
disperse (freezing fog) by scattering small pellets of
dry ice above it (also **cloud seeding**).—*adj.* **seed'ed**
cleaned of seeds: having seeds: bearing seed: sown: of
a tournament player, who has been seeded.—*n.*
seed'er a seed-drill: an apparatus for removing seeds
from fruit: a seed-fish.—*adv.* seed'ily.—*n.* seed'iness.
—*n.* and *adj.* seed'ing.—*adjs.* seed'less; seed'-like.—
n. **seed'ling** a plant reared from the seed: a young
plant ready for planting out from a seedbed: a seed
oyster.—Also *adj.*—*adj.* **seed'y** abounding with seed:
having the flavour of seeds: not cleared of seeds: run
to seed: out of sorts: shabby.—**seed'bed** a piece of
ground for receiving seed: an environment, etc. that
fosters a particular thing (esp. something considered
undesirable); **seed'box** a plant capsule; **seed'cake** a

cake with caraway seeds; **seed'-coat** the covering derived from the ovule's integuments; **seed'-coral** coral in small irregular pieces; **seed'-corn** grain for sowing: assets likely to bring future profit; **seed'-drill** a machine for sowing seeds in rows; **seed'-fish** a fish about to spawn; **seed'-leaf** a cotyledon, leaf contained in a seed; **seed'lip** a sower's basket (O.E. *sædlēap-lēap*, basket); **seed'-lobe** a cotyledon; **seed money** money with which a project or enterprise is set up; **seed'-oyster** a very young oyster; **seed'-pearl** a very small pearl; **seed'-plot** a piece of nursery ground, a hot-bed; **seed'-potato** a potato tuber for planting; **seed'-shop; seeds'man** a dealer in seeds: a sower; **seed'-time** the season for sowing seeds; **seed'-vessel** a dry fruit: the ovary of a flower.—**go, run,** to **seed** to grow rapidly and untidily in preparation for seeding, instead of producing the vegetative growth desired by the grower: to disappoint expectation of development: to go to waste: (usu. **go**) to become unkempt, shabby; **sow the seed(s)** of to initiate. [O.E. *sǣd*.]

seek *sēk*, *v.t.* to look for: to try to find, get, or achieve: to ask for: to aim at: to resort to, betake oneself to: to advance against: to try.—*v.i.* to make search:—*pa.t.* and *pa.p.* **sought** (*sōt*).—*n.* **seek'er.—seek after** to go in quest of; **seek for** to look for; **seek out** to look for and find: to bring out from a hidden place; **sought after** in demand; **to seek** not to be found: wanting [O.E. *sēcan* (pa.t. *sōhte*, pa.p. *gesōht*); cf. Ger. *suchen*.]

seem *sēm*, *v.i.* to appear: to appear to the senses: to appear to be.—*ns.* **seem'er;** **seem'ing** appearance: semblance: a false appearance.—*adj.* apparent: ostensible.—*adv.* apparently: in appearance only (esp. in composition, as **seem'ing-sim'ple**.—*adv.* **seem'ingly** apparently: as it would appear.—*ns.* **seem'ingness; seem'liness.**—*adj.* **seem'ly** (*compar.* **seem'lier;** *superl.* **seem'liest**) becoming: suitable: decent: handsome.—**it seems** it appears: it would seem; **it would seem** it turns out: I have been told. [O.N. *sæma*, to beseem.]

seen. See **see**[2].

seep *sēp*, *v.i.* to ooze, percolate.—*n.* **seep'age.**—*adj.* **seep'y.**

seer[1] *sēr*, *n.* an Indian weight of widely ranging amount, officially about 2 lb. [Pers. *sīr*.]

seer[2]. See **see**[2].

seersucker *sēr'suk-ər*, *n.* a thin crinkly Indian linen (or cotton) fabric. [Pers. *shīr o shakkar*, lit. milk and sugar.]

seesaw *sē'sō'*, *sē'sō*, *n.* alternate up-and-down or backand-forth motion: repeated alternation: a plank balanced so that its ends may move up and down alternately: the sport of rising and sinking on it.—*adj.* going like a seesaw.—*adv.* in the manner of a seesaw —*v.i.* to play at seesaw: to move or go like a seesaw. —*v.t.* to make to go up and down. [Prob. a redup. of **saw**[2].]

seethe *sēdh*, *v.t.* to boil: to soak to a condition as if boiled.—*v.i.* to boil: to surge: to be agitated (by anger, excitement, etc.).—*pa.t.* **seethed;** *pa.p.* **seethed,** (arch.) **sodd'en.**—*n.* and *adj.* **seeth'ing.** [O.E. *sēothan* (pa.p. *soden*).]

segment *seg'mənt*, *n.* a part cut off: a portion: part of a circle, ellipse, etc., cut off by a straight line, or of a sphere, ellipsoid, etc., by a plane: a section: one of a linear series of similar portions, as of a somite or metamere of a jointed animal, or a joint of an appendage: a lobe of a leaf-blade not separate enough to be a leaflet.—*v.t.* and *v.i.* (also *-ment'*) to divide into segments.—*adj.* **segmental** (*-ment'l*).— *adv.* **segmen'tally.**—*adjs.* **seg'mentary, seg'mentate.** —*n.* **segmenta'tion.**—*adj.* **segment'ed** (or *seg'*). [L. *segmentum—secāre*, to cut.]

sego *sē'gō*, *n.* a showy liliaceous plant (*Calochortus*) of western U.S.:—*pl.* **sē'gos.** [Ute Indian name.]

segregate *seg'ri-gāt*, *v.t.* to set apart: to seclude: to isolate: to group apart.—*v.i.* to separate out in a group or groups or mass.—*adj.* set apart.—*n.* that which is segregated.—*adj.* **seg'regable.**—*n.* **segrega'tion** the act of segregating: the state of being segregated: separation of dominants and recessives in the second generation of a cross (*genetics*): the separation of hereditary factors from one another during spore formation: separation of one particular class of persons from another, as on grounds of race; **segregā'tionist** a believer in racial or other segregation.—*adj.* **seg'regative.** [L. *sēgregāre, -ātum—sē-*, apart, *grex, gregis*, a flock.]

segue *sā'gwā*, follows, usu. as a musical direction to proceed immediately with the next song, movement, etc., i.e. without a pause.—Also *n.*—*v.i.* to proceed immediately with the next movement, etc. (also *fig.*): —*pr.p.* **se'gueing;** *pa.t.* and *pa.p.* **se'gued.** [It.]

seguidilla *seg-i-dēl'ya*, *n.* a Spanish dance: a tune for it, in triple time. [Sp.]

sei *sā*, *n.* a kind of rorqual (*Balaenoptera borealis*)— also **sei whale.** [Norw. *sejhval*, sei whale.]

seicento *sā-chen'tō*, *n.* in Italian art, literature, etc., the seventeenth century. [It., abbrev of *mille seicento*, one thousand six hundred.]

seiche *sāsh*, *sesh*, *n.* a periodic fluctuation from side to side of the surface of lakes. [Swiss Fr.]

Seidlitz *sed'lits*, *adj.* applied to an aperient powder (or rather pair of powders), Rochelle salt and sodium bicarbonate mixed together, and tartaric acid— totally different from the mineral water of *Sedlitz* in Bohemia.

self *sāf*, *sif*, *n.* a long sand-dune lying parallel to the direction of the wind that forms it. [Ar. *saif*, sword.]

seignior *sā'*, *sē'nyər*, **seigneur** *sen-yœr*, *ns.* a title of address: a feudal lord, lord of a manor.—*ns.* **seign'iorage, seign'orage** a right, privilege, etc., claimed by an overlord: an overlord's royalty on minerals: a percentage on minted bullion.—*adjs.* **seignio'rial, seigneu'rial, seigno'ral** (*sān'*, *sen'*), **signo'rial** (*sin-*) manorial.—*ns.* **seign'iorship; seign'(i)ory** feudal lordship: the council of an Italian city-state (*hist.*): (also **seigneurie** *sen'yə-rē*) a domain.—**grand** (*grä*) **seigneur** a great lord: a man of aristocratic dignity and authority. [Fr. *seigneur*—L. *senior, -ōris*, compar. of *senex*, old. In L.L. *senior* is sometimes equivalent to *dominus*, lord.]

seine *sān*, or *sēn*, *n.* a large vertical fishing-net whose ends are brought together and hauled —*v.t.* and *v.i.* to catch or fish with a seine.—*ns.* **sein'er; sein'ing.**— **seine'-boat; seine'-fishing; seine'-net.** [O.E. *segne*—L. *sagēna*—Gr. *sagēnē*, a fishing-net.]

seise *sēz*, *v.t.* an old spelling of **seize**, still used legally in the sense of to put in possession.—*n.* **seis'in** possession (now, as freehold): an object handed over as a token of possession: *sasine* (*Scots law*)

seism-, seismo- *sīz-m(o,ō,ə)-*, in composition, earthquake.—*adjs.* **seis'mal, seis'mic, -al.**—*ns.* **seismicity** (*-mis'i-ti*) liability to or frequency of earthquakes; **seis'mism** earthquake phenomena; **seis'mogram** a seismograph record; **seis'mograph** an instrument for registering earthquakes; **seismog'rapher.**—*adjs.* **seismograph'ic, -al.**—*n.* **seismog'raphy** the study of earthquakes.—*adjs.* **seismolog'ic, -al.**—*ns.* **seismol'ogist; seismol'ogy** the science of earthquakes; **seismom'eter** an instrument for measuring earth-movements.—*adjs.* **seismomet'ric, -al.**—*ns.* **seismom'etry; seis'moscope** an instrument for detecting earthquakes.—*adj.* **seismoscop'ic.** [Gr. *seismos*, a shaking—*seiein*, to shake.]

seize, form., and still in legal sense, **seize** *sēz*, *v.t.* to put in legal possession: to fix: to take possession of: to grasp suddenly, eagerly, or forcibly: to take by force: to take prisoner: to apprehend: to lash or make fast. —*v.i.* to lay hold: to clutch: to jam or weld partially for want of lubrication.—*adj.* **seiz'able.**—*ns.* **seiz'er; seiz'in** seisin (see **seise**); **seiz'ing** the action of the verb: a cord to seize ropes with; **seizure** (*sē'zhər*) the act of seizing: capture: a sudden fit or attack of illness.—**seize, seise,** of to put in possession of; **seized, seised,** of in (legal) possession of: aware of; **seize up** to jam, seize. [O.Fr. *seisir, saisir*—L.L. *sacīre*, prob. Gmc.]

selachian *si-lā'ki-ən*, *n.* any fish of the shark class.—Also *adj.* [Gr. *selachos.*]

seldom *sel'dəm*, *adv.* rarely.—*adj.* infrequent.—*n.* **sel'domness.**—*adv.* **sel'dom-times.** [O.E. *seldum*, altered from *seldan.*]

select *si-lekt'*, *v.t.* to pick out from a number by preference.—*adj.* picked out: choice: exclusive.—*adj.* **selec'ted.**—*n.* **selec'tion** the act of selecting: a thing or collection of things selected: a horse selected as likely to win a race.—*adj.* **selec'tive** having or exercising power of selection: able to discriminate, e.g. between different frequencies: choosing, involving, etc., only certain things or people.—*adv.* **selec'tively.** —*ns.* **selectiv'ity** (*sel-*) ability to discriminate; **select'ness; select'or.**—*adj.* **selecto'rial.**—**select committee** a number of members of parliament chosen to report and advise on some matter; **selective weedkiller** a weedkiller that does not destroy garden plants. [L. *sēligĕre, sēlectum—sē-*, aside, *legĕre*, to choose.]

Selene *se-lē'nē*, *n.* the Greek moon-goddess.—*n.* **selenate** (*sel'i-nāt*) a salt of selenic acid.—*adjs.* **selenic** (*si-lē'nik, -len'ik*) of selenium in higher valency (**selenic acid**); **selē'nious, selē'nous** of selenium in lower valency (**selenious acid**).—*n.* **selenite** (*sel'i-nīt*) gypsum, esp. in transparent crystals (anciently supposed to wax and wane with the moon): a salt of selenious acid.—*adj.* **selenitic** (*sel-i-nit'ik*).—*n.* **selenium** (*si-lē'*) a non-metallic element (symbol Se; at. numb. 34) discovered in 1817.—*adj.* **selē'nodont** (Gr. *odous, odontos*, tooth) having crescentic ridges on the crowns of the molar teeth.—*ns.* **selē'nograph** a delineation of the moon; **selenographer** (*sel-in-og'rə-fər*) a student of selenography.—*adjs.* **selenographic** (*si-lē-nə-graf'ik*), **-al.**—*n.* **selenography** (*sel-i-nog'rə-fi*) the delineation or description of the moon: the study of the moon's physical features.—*adj.* **selēnolog'ical.**—*ns.* **selenol'ogist** a selenographer; **selenol'ogy** the scientific study of the moon.—**selenium cell** a photoelectric cell depending on the fact that light increases the electric conductivity of selenium. [Gr. *selēnē*, moon.]

self *self*, *pron.* (*commercial*, or *illit.*) oneself, myself, himself, etc.—*n.* a distinct person, personality, ego: a side of one's personality: identity: personality: what one is: self-interest: a self-coloured plant or animal: —*pl.* **selves** (*selvz*); of things in one colour, **selfs.**—*adj.* uniform in colour: made in one piece: made of the same material.—*n.* **self'hood** personal identity: existence as a person: personality.—*adj.* **self'ish** chiefly or wholly regarding one's own self: void of regard to others.—*adv.* **self'ishly.**—*n.* **self'ishness.** —*adj.* **self'less** having no regard to self.—*ns.* **self'lessness; self'ness** egotism: personality.—**one's self** see oneself; **second self** see second. [O.E. *self.*]

self- *self-*, in composition, acting upon the agent: by, of, in, in relation to, etc., oneself or itself: automatic. —**self'-aban'donment** disregard of self; **self'-abase'ment; self'-abnegā'tion** renunciation of one's own interest: self-denial.—*adj.* **self'-absorbed'**

wrapped up in one's own thoughts or affairs.—**self'-absorp'tion** the state of being self-absorbed: self-shielding (*phys.*); **self'-abuse'** self-deception (*Shak.*): revilement of oneself: masturbation; **self'-abus'er; self'-accusā'tion.**—*adjs.* **self'-act'ing** automatic; **self'-addressed'** addressed to oneself; **self'-adhē'sive** able to stick to a surface without the use of (additional) glue, etc.; **self'-adjust'ing** requiring no external adjustment; **self'-admin'istered.** —**self'-admirā'tion; self'-advance'ment; self'-advert'isement; self'-ad'vertiser; self'-aggrand'isement; self'-anal'ysis.**—*adj.* **self'-appoint'ed.** —**self'-apprecia'tion; self'-approbā'tion; self'-appro'val.**—*adjs.* **self'-approv'ing; self'-assert'ing, self'-assert'ive** given to asserting one's opinion or to putting oneself forward.—**self'-asser'tion; self'-assu'rance** assured self-confidence.—*adjs.* **self'-assured'; self'-aware'.—self'-aware'ness; self'-betray'al; self'-bind'er** a reaping-machine with automatic binding apparatus.—*adjs.* **self'-cat'ering** of a holiday, accommodation, etc., in which one cooks for oneself; **self'-cen'tred** centred in self: selfish; **self'-clean'ing; self'-clos'ing** shutting automatically.—**self'-cock'er** a firearm in which the hammer is raised by pulling the trigger.—*adj.* **self'-cock'ing.—self'-colour** uniform colour: natural colour.—*adj.* **self'-coloured.—self'-command'** self-control; **self'-complā'cence** satisfaction with oneself, or with one's own performances.—*adj.* **self'-complā'cent.—self'-conceit'** an over-high opinion of oneself, one's own abilities, etc.: vanity.—*adj.* **self'-conceit'ed.—self'-concern';** **self'-condemna'tion.**—*adjs.* **self'-condemned'** condemned by one's own actions or out of one's own mouth; **self'-condemn'ing; self'-confessed'** admitted, openly acknowledged (by oneself).—**self'-con'fidence** confidence in, or reliance on, one's own powers: self-reliance.—*adj.* **self'-con'fident.**—*adv.* **self'-con'fidently.—self'-congratulā'tion.**—*adjs.* **self'-congrat'ulatory** congratulating oneself; **self'-con'scious** conscious of one's own mind and its acts and states: conscious of being observed by others.—**self'-con'sciousness; self'-consist'ency** consistency of each part with the rest: consistency with one's principles.—*adjs.* **self'-consis'tent; self'-contained'** wrapped up in oneself, reserved: of a house, flat, room, etc., not approached by an entrance common to others: complete in itself.—**self'-contempt'; self'-contradic'tion** the act or fact of contradicting oneself: a statement whose terms are mutually contradictory.—*adj.* **self'-contradic'tory.** —**self'-control'** power of controlling oneself.—*adj.* **self'-convict'ed** convicted by one's own acts or words. —**self'-convic'tion.**—*adj.* **self'-correct'ing.—self'-crit'ical.—self'-crit'icism** critical examination and judgment of one's own works and thoughts; **self'-deceit'** self-deception; **self'-deceiv'er; self'-decep'tion** deceiving oneself.—*adj.* **self'-defeat'ing** that defeats its own purpose.—**self'-defence'** defending one's own person, rights, etc. (**art of self-defence** orig. boxing, now used more loosely); **self'-degradā'tion; self'-delu'sion** the delusion of oneself by oneself; **self'-deni'al** forbearing to gratify one's own appetites or desires.—*adj.* **self'-deny'ing.**—*adv.* **self'-deny'ingly.**—*adj.* **self'-destroy'ing.**—*v.t.* **self'-destruct'.** —**self'-destruc'tion** the destruction of anything by itself: suicide; **self'-determinā'tion** direction of the attention or will to an object: the power of a population to decide its own government and political relations or of an individual to live his own life; **self'-discipline; self'-dispar'agement; self'-distrust'; self'-doubt'; self'-dramatisā'tion, -izā'tion** presentation of oneself as if a character in a play: seeing in oneself an exaggerated dignity and intensity.—*adjs.*

self'-drive' of a motor vehicle, to be driven by the hirer; self'-driv'en driven by its own power; self'-ed'ucated educated by one's own efforts.—self'-effce'ment keeping oneself in the background out of sight: withdrawing from notice or rights.—adjs. self'-effac'ing; self'-elect'ive having the right to elect oneself or itself, as by co-option of new members.—self'-elec'tion.—adj. self'-employed' working independently in one's own business.—self's employ'ment; self'-esteem' good opinion of oneself: self-respect; self'-ev'idence.—adj. self'-ev'ident evident without proof.—self'-examina'tion a scrutiny into one's own state, conduct, etc.—adjs. self's ex'ecuting (legal) automatically coming into effect, not needing legislation to enforce; self'-explan'atory, self'-explain'ing obvious, bearing its meaning in its own face.—self'-express'ion the giving of expression to one's personality, as in art; self'-feed'er a device for supplying anything automatically, esp. a measured amount of foodstuff for cattle, etc.—adj. self-feed'ing.—self'-fertilisa'tion, -iza'tion.—adjs. self'-finan'cing; self'-flatt'ering.—self'-flatt'ery.—adjs. self'-fo'cusing; self'-forget'ful unselfishly forgetful of self.—adv. self'-forget'fully.—adj. self'-fulfill'ing.—self'-fulfil'ment.—adjs. self'-gen'erating; self'-glazed' glazed in one tint.—self'-glorifica'tion.—adj. self'-gov'erning.—self's gov'ernment autonomy: government without outside interference; self'-hate', self'-hat'red; self'-heal'ing spontaneous healing: healing oneself.—Also adj.—self'-help' doing things for oneself without help of others; self'-hypno'sis, self'-hyp'notism; self's im'age one's own idea of oneself; self'-immola'tion offering oneself up in sacrifice: suttee; self's import'ance an absurdly high sense of one's own importance: pomposity.—adj. self'-import'ant.—self'-improve'ment improvement, by oneself, of one's status, education, job, etc.—adjs. self's imposed' taken voluntarily on oneself; self'-induced' induced by oneself: produced by self-induction (elect.).—self'-induc'tance the property of an electric circuit whereby self-induction occurs; self's induc'tion the property of an electric circuit by which it resists any change in the current flowing in it; self's indul'gence undue gratification of one's appetites or desires.—adj. self'-indul'gent; self'-inflict'ed inflicted by oneself on oneself.—self'-in'terest private interest: regard to oneself; self'-justifica'tion.—adjs. self'-jus'tifying justifying oneself: automatically arranging the length of the lines of type (print.).—self'-knowl'edge knowledge of one's own nature.—adjs. self'-light'ing igniting automatically; exactly similar; self'-lim'ited (path.) running a definite course; self'-load'ing of a gun, automatically reloading itself; self'-lock'ing locking automatically.—self'-love' the love of oneself: tendency to seek one's own welfare or advantage.—adj. self'-made' risen to a high position from poverty or obscurity by one's own exertions.—self'-mas'tery self-command: self-control.—adjs. self'-op'erating; self'-opin'ionated obstinately adhering to one's own opinion; self'-perpet'uating.—self'-pit'y pity for oneself; self'-pollina'tion transfer of pollen to the stigma of the same flower (or sometimes the same plant or clone); self's por'trait a portrait of oneself done by oneself; self's por'traiture.—adj. self'-possessed' having self-possession.—self'-possess'ion collectedness of mind: calmness; self'-praise'; self'-preserva'tion care, action, or instinct for the preservation of one's own life.—adjs. self'-preser'vative, self'-preser'ving; self'-proclaimed'; self'-professed'; self'-prop'agating propagating itself when left to itself; self'-propelled'; self'-propell'ing carrying its own means

of propulsion.—self'-propul'sion; self'-protec'tion self-defence.—adjs. self'-protect'ing; self'-protec'tive; self'-rais'ing (of flour) already mixed with something that causes it to rise.—self'-realisa'tion, -z- attainment of such development as one's mental and moral nature is capable of; self'-regard' self-interest: self-respect.—adj. self'-reg'ulating regulating itself.—self'-reli'ance healthy confidence in one's own abilities.—adj. self'-reli'ant.—self'-renuncia'tion self-abnegation; self'-repress'ion restraint of expression of the self; self'-reproach' prickings of conscience; self'-respect' respect for oneself or one's own character.—adj. self'-respect'ing.—self'-restraint' a refraining from excess: self-control.—adj. self'-reveal'ing.—self'-revela'tion.—adj. self'-right'eous righteous in one's own estimation.—self'-right'eousness.—adj. self'-right'ing righting itself when capsized.—self'-rule'.—adj. self'-rul'ing.—self'-sac'rifice forgoing one's own good for the sake of others.—adjs. self'-sac'rificing; self'-same the very same.—self'-same'ness identity; self'-satisfac'tion satisfaction with oneself: complacence.—adjs. self'-sat'isfied; self'-seal'ing of envelopes, etc., that can be sealed by pressing two adhesive surfaces together: of tyres, that seal automatically when punctured.—self'-seed'er a plant that propagates itself by growing from its own seeds shed around it; self'-seek'er one who looks mainly to his own interests.—n. and adj. self'-seek'ing.—self'-ser'vice helping oneself, as in a restaurant, petrol station, etc.—Also adj.—adj. self'-ser'ving taking care of one's own interests above all others; self'-sown' sown naturally without man's agency.—self'-star'ter an automatic contrivance for starting a motor: a car fitted with one: a person with initiative.—adj. self's styled' called by oneself: pretended.—self'-suffi'ciency.—adjs. self'-suffi'cient requiring nothing from without: excessively confident in oneself; self's suffic'ing.—self'-support' support or maintenance without outside help: paying one's way.—adjs. self's support'ing; self'-taught.—self'-tor'ment; self'-treat'ment; self'-will' obstinacy.—adjs. self'-willed'; self'-wind'ing (of a watch) wound by the wearer's spontaneous movements.—self'-wor'ship. [O.E. self; Du. zelf, Ger. selbe, Goth. silba.]

-self -self, pl. -selves -selvz, a suff. forming reflexive and emphatic pronouns.—be oneself, himself, etc., to be in full possession of one's powers: to be (once more) at one's best; by oneself, etc., alone.

Seljuk sel-jōōk', n. a member of any of the Turkish dynasties (11th–13th cent.) decended from Seljūq.—adjs. Seljuk', Seljuk'ian.

sell sel, v.t. to give or give up for money or other equivalent: to betray: to impose upon, trick: to promote the sale of: to make acceptable: to cause someone to accept (e.g. an idea, plan): to convince of the value of something.—v.i. to make sales: to be sold, to be in demand for sale:—pa.t. and pa.p. sold.—n. (slang) a deception: let-down: an act of selling.—adj. sell'able.—n. sell'er one who sells: that which has a sale —sellers', seller's market one in which sellers control the price, demand exceeding supply; sell'ing-price the price at which a thing is sold; selling race, plate a race of which the winning horse must be put up for auction at a price previously fixed; sell'-out a betrayal: a show for which all seats are sold.—sell down the river to play false, betray; sell off to sell cheaply in order to dispose of (n. sell'-off); sell one's life dearly to do great injury to the enemy before one is killed; sell out to dispose entirely of: to betray; sell short to belittle, disparage: to sell (stocks, etc.) before one actually owns them, when intending to buy at a lower price; sell up to sell the goods of, for debt; **to sell** for sale. [O.E. *sellan*, to give, hand over.]

Sellotape® *sel'ə-tāp, n.* a brand of usu. transparent adhesive tape.—*v.t.* to stick with Sellotape.

seltzer *selt'sər, n.* a mineral water from Nieder-*Selters* near Wiesbaden in Germany, or an imitation.

selva *sel'və, n.* (usu. in *pl.* **selvas**) wet forest in the Amazon basin. [Sp., Port.—L. *silva*, wood.]

selvage, selvedge *sel'vij, n.* a differently finished edging of cloth: a border. [**self, edge**.]

selves *selvz, pl.* of **self**.

semantic *si-man'tik, adj.* relating to meaning, esp. of words.—*n. sing.* **seman'tics** the science of the meaning of words.—*n.pl.* (*loosely*) differences in, and shades of, meaning of words.—*adv.* **seman'tically**.—*ns.* **seman'ticist**; **sememe** (*se'mēm, sē'mēm*) the meaning of a morpheme. [Gr. *sēmantikos*, significant.]

semaphore *sem'ə-för, -för, n.* a signalling apparatus, an upright with arms that can be turned up or down—often the signaller's own body and arms with flags.—*v.t.* and *v.i.* to signal thus. [Fr. *sémaphore*—Gr. *sēma*, sign, signal, *-phoros*, bearing, bearer.]

semasiology *si-mā-zi-ol'ə-ji,* or *-si-, n.* the science of semantics. [Gr. *sēmāsia*, meaning.]

sematic *si-mat'ik,* (*biol.*) *adj.* serving for recognition, attraction, or warning. [Gr. *sēma*, sign]

semblance *sem'bləns, n.* likeness: appearance: outward show: apparition: image. [M.E.,—Fr. *sembler*, to seem, to resemble—L. *simulāre—similis*, like.]

semeiology *sem-i-, sēm-i-ol'ə-ji, n.* the study of symptoms: the study of signs and symbols (now usu. **semiology**).—*adj.* **semeiot'ic** pertaining to symptoms.—*n.sing.* **semeiot'ics** semeiology: semiotics. [Gr *sēmeion*, sign.]

sememe. See **semantic**.

semen *sē'men, n.* the liquid that carries spermatozoa. —See also **seminal**. [L. *sēmen, -inis*, seed.]

semester *si-mes'tər, n.* a university half-year course (in Germany, U.S., etc.). [L. *sēmēstris—sex*, six, *mēnsis*, a month.]

semi- *sem'i-, pfx.* half: (*loosely*) nearly, partly, incompletely.—*ns.* **sem'i** (coll. shortening) a semi-detached house.—*adj.* **sem'i-ann'ual** (chiefly *U.S.*) half-yearly.—*adv.* **sem'i-ann'ually**.—*adj.* **sem'i-automat'ic** partly automatic but requiring some tending by hand.—*n.* and *adj.* **sem'i-barbā'rian**.—*ns.* **sem'i-bar'barism**; **sem'ibrève** half a breve (2 minims or 4 crotchets); **sem'ibull** a pope's bull issued between election and coronation; **sem'ichōr'us** half, or part of, a chorus: a passage sung by it; **sem'icircle** half a circle, bounded by the diameter and half the circumference. —*adj.* **semicir'cular** (**semicircular canals** the curved tubes of the inner ear concerned with equilibrium).—*adv.* **semicir'cularly**.—*n.* **sem'icolon** the point (;) marking a division greater than the comma.—*adj.* **semiconduct'ing**.—*ns.* **semiconductiv'ity**; **semiconduct'or** formerly, any substance with electrical conductivity between that of metals and of non-conductors: now, any solid, non-conducting at low temperatures or in pure state, which is a conductor at high temperatures or when very slightly impure.—*adj.* **sem'icon'scious**.—*n.* **semicyl'inder** a longitudinal half-cylinder.—*adj.* **semidepō'nent** passive in form in the perfect tenses only.—Also *n.*—*adj.* **sem'idetached'** partly separated: joined by a party wall to one other house only.—*n.* **sem'i-diam'eter** half the diameter, esp. the angular diameter.—*adjs.* **semidiur'nal** accomplished in twelve hours: pertaining to half the time or half the arc traversed between rising and setting; **semi-divine'** half-divine: of, of the nature of, a demigod.—*ns.* **semidocument'ary** a cinemato-

graph film with an actual background but an invented plot; **sem'i-dome'** half a dome, esp. as formed by a vertical section.—*adjs.* **semidomes'ticated** partially domesticated: half-tame, **sem'i-doub'le** having only the outermost stamens converted into petals; **sem'i-dry'ing** of oils, thickening without completely drying on exposure.—*n.* **sem'i-ellipse'** half of an ellipse, bounded by a diameter, esp. the major axis.—*adjs.* **sem'i-ellip'tical**; **semifi'nal** in competitions, sports contests, etc., of the contest immediately before the final.—*n.* a last round but one.—*n.* **semifi'nalist** a competitor in a semifinal.—*adj.* **semiflu'id** nearly solid but able to flow to some extent.—Also *n.*—*adj.* **semiglob'ular**.—*n.* and *adj.* **semi-im'becile**.—*adjs.* **sem'i-independ'ent** not fully independent; **sem'i-liq'uid** half-liquid; **sem'i-lu'nar**, *-lu'nate* half-moon shaped.—*n.* **sem'ilune** (*-lōōn*) a half-moon-shaped object, body, or structure.—*adjs.* **sem'imen'strual** half-monthly; **sem'i-month'ly** (chiefly *U.S.*) half-monthly.—*n.* a half-monthly periodical.—*adjs.* **sem'i-nŭde** half-naked; **sem'i-offic'ial** partly official. —*adv.* **sem'i-offic'ially**.—*adjs.* **sem'i-opaque'** partly opaque; **sem'iovip'arous** producing imperfectly developed young; **semi-per'meable** permeable by a solvent but not by the dissolved substance.—*n.* **sem'i-plume** a feather with ordinary shaft but downy web. —*adj.* **semi-prec'ious** valuable, but not valuable enough to be reckoned a gemstone.—*n.* **sem'iquaver** half a quaver.—*adjs.* **sem'i-rig'id** of an airship, having a flexible gasbag and stiffened keel; **sem'i-skilled'**. — *n.* **sem'itone** half a tone—one of the lesser intervals of the musical scale as from B to C.—*adj.* **semiton'ic**. —*n.* **semitranspā'rency**.—*adjs.* **semitranspā'rent** imperfectly transparent; **semi-trop'ical** subtropical; **semi-tŭ'bular** like half of a tube divided longitudinally. —*n.* **sem'ivowel** a sound partaking of the nature of both a vowel and a consonant: a letter representing it, in English, chiefly *w* and *y*, and sometimes used of the liquid consonants *l* and *r*.—*adj.* **sem'i-week'ly** issued or happening twice a week.—Also *n.* and *adv.* [L. *sēmi-*, half; cf. Gr. *hēmi-*, O.E. *sam-*.]

seminal *sem'in-l, adj.* pertaining to, or of the nature of, seed or of semen: of or relating to the beginnings, first development, of an idea, study, etc.: generative: notably creative or influential in future development. —*adv.* **sem'inally**.—*adj* **seminif'erous** seed-bearing: producing or conveying semen. [L. *sēmen, -inis*, seed.]

seminar *sem'i-när, n.* (orig. *Ger.*) a group of advanced students working in a specific subject of study under a teacher: a class at which a group of students and a tutor discuss a particular topic: a discussion group on any particular subject.—*adjs.* **seminarial** (*-ā'ri-əl*); **semina'rian** of a seminary.—*ns.* **sem'inarist** (*-ər-ist*) a student in a seminary or in a seminar; **sem'inary** (*-ə-ri*) formerly, a pretentious name for a school (esp. for young ladies): a college, esp. for R.C. (in *U.S.* also other) theology. [L. *sēminārium*, a seed-plot— *sēmen*, seed.]

semiology *sem-i-ol'ə-ji,* (*linguistics*) *n.* the science of signs or signals in general: (*loosely*), semiotics.— Also **semeiology**.—*n.sing.* **semiot'ics** the theory of sign-systems in language.—*adj.* **semiot'ic**. [Gr. *semeion*, sign.]

Semite *sem'* or *sēm'īt, n.* a member of any of the peoples said (Gen. x) to be descended from Shem, or speaking a Semitic language.—*adj.* **Semitic** (*sem-, sim-, sam-it'ik*).—*n.* any Semitic language.—*ns.* **Sem'itism** a Semitic idiom or characteristic: Semitic ways of thought: the cause of the Semites, esp. the Jews; **Sem'itist** a Semitic scholar.—**Semitic languages** Assyrian, Aramaic, Hebrew, Phoenician, Arabic, Ethiopic, etc. [Gr. *Sēm*, Shem.]

semolina *sem-ə-lē'nə, -lī'nə, n.* the particles of fine, hard wheat that do not pass into flour in milling. [It. *semolino,* dim. of *semola,* bran—L. *simila,* fine flour.]

sempervivum *sem'pər-vīvəm* any plant of the *Crassulaceae,* including the house-leek and various ornamental plants. [L. *sempervivus,* everliving.]

sempiternal *sem-pi-tûr'nl, adj.* everlasting. [L *sempiternus—semper,* ever.]

semplice *sem'plē-che,* (*mus.*) *adj.* simple, without embellishments. [It.]

sempre *sem'pre,* (*mus.*) *adv.* always, throughout. [It.,—L. *semper,* always.]

sempster, seamster *sem'stər, n.* one who sews—orig *fem.,* now only *masc.:—fem.* **semp'stress, seam'stress.** [O.E. *sēamestre;* see **seam.**]

senary *sēn', sen'ər-i, adj.* of, involving, based on, six. *—n.* a set of six. [L. *sēnārius—sēnī,* six each—*sex,* six.]

senate *sen'it, n.* the governing body of ancient Rome: a legislative or deliberative body, esp. the upper house of a national or state legislature: a body of venerable or distinguished persons: the governing body of certain British universities (in Scotland, **Senā'tus Academ'icus**).—*n.* **senator** (*sen'ə-tər*) a member of a senate.—*adj.* **senatorial** (*sen-ə-tō'ri-əl, -tō'ri-əl*).—*adv.* **senato'rially.**—*n.* **sen'atorship.**—**sen'ate-house** the meeting-place of a senate.—**senā'tus consult'** (L. *senātūs consultum*) a decree of the senate. [L. *senātus—senex, senis,* an old man.]

send *send, v.t.* to cause, direct, or tell to go: to propel: to cause to be conveyed: to dispatch: to forward: to grant: orig. of jazz, to rouse (someone) to ecstasy.— *v.i.* to dispatch a message or messenger: to pitch into the trough of the sea (*naut.;* sometimes **scend, 'scend**):—*pa.t.* and *pa.p.* **sent;** *naut.* **send'ed.**—*n.* an impetus or impulse: a plunge.—*ns.* **send'er; send'ing** dispatching: pitching: transmission.—**send'-off** a demonstration at departing or starting a journey; **send'-up** a process of making fun of someone or something: a play, film, novel, etc., doing this.—**send down** to rusticate or expel; **send in** to submit (an entry) for a competition, etc.; **send for** to require by message to come or be brought; **send off** in football, etc., to order a player to leave the field and take no further part in the game, usu. after an infringement of the rules; **send on** to send in advance: to re-address and re-post (a letter or package); **send up** to make fun of: to sentence to imprisonment; **send word** to send an intimation. [O.E. *sendan.*]

sendal *sen'dəl, n.* a thin silk or linen. [O.Fr. *cendal,* prob.—Gr. *sindōn.*]

senescent *si-nes'ənt, adj.* verging on old age: ageing.— *n.* **senesc'ence.** [L. *senēscēns, -entis,* pr.p. *of senēscĕre,* to grow old—*senex,* old.]

seneschal *sen'i-shl, n.* a steward: a major-domo.—*n.* **sen'eschalship.** [O.Fr. (Fr. *sénéchal*), of Gmc. origin, lit. old servant.]

Señor *se-nyōr', -nyōr', Señora -a, Señorita -ē'ta, ns.* the Portuguese forms corresponding to the Spanish **Señor, Señora, Señorita.**

senile *sē'nīl, adj.* characteristic of or attendant on old age: showing the decay or imbecility of old age.—*n.* **senility** (*si-nil'i-ti*) old age: the imbecility of old age. [L. *senīlis—senex, senis,* old.]

senior *sēn'yər, adj.* elder: older or higher in standing: more advanced: first.—*n.* one who is senior: a fourth-year student (*U.S.*).—*ns.* **seniority** (*sē-ni-or'i-ti*) state or fact of being senior: priority by age, time of service, or standing.—**senior common room** see under **junior; senior service** the navy. [L. *senior, -ōris,* compar. of *senex,* old.]

senna *sen'ə, n.* a shrub (*Cassia,* of various species): its purgative dried leaflets.—**senna tea** an infusion of senna. [Ar. *sanā*]

sennight *sen'īt,* (*arch.*) *n.* a week. [**seven, night.**]

sennit *sen'it,* **sinnet** *sin'it, ns.* a flat braid of rope yarn.

Señor *se-nyōr', -nyòr', n.* a gentleman: in address, sir: prefixed to a name, Mr:—*fem.* **Señora** (*se-nyō'ra, -nyō'*) a lady: madam: as a title, Mrs.—*n.* **Señorita** (*sen-yō-rē'ta, -yō-*) a young lady: Miss. [Sp.,—L. *senior,* older.]

sense *sens, n.* faculty of receiving sensation, general or particular: immediate consciousness: inward feeling: impression: opinion: mental attitude: discernment: understanding: appreciation: feeling for what is appropriate: discerning feeling for things of some particular kind: (usu. in *pl.*) one's right wits: soundness of judgment: reasonableness: sensible or reasonable discourse: that which is reasonable: plain matter of fact: the realm of sensation and sensual appetite: meaning: interpretation: purport: gist: direction.—*adj.* pertaining to a sense or senses.—*v.t.* to have a sensation, feeling, or appreciation of: to appreciate, grasp, comprehend: to become aware (that): of computers, to detect (e.g. a hole, constituting a symbol, in punched card or tape).—*n.* **sensation** (*sen-sā'shən*) awareness of a physical experience, without any element derived from previous experiences: awareness by the senses generally: an effect on the senses: power of sensing: an emotion or general feeling: a thrill: a state, or matter, of general excited interest in the public, audience. etc.: melodramatic quality or method: enough to taste, as of liquor (*slang*).—*adj.* **sensā'tional.**—*ns.* **sensā'tionalism** the doctrine that our ideas originate solely in sensation: a striving after wild excitement and melodramatic effects; **sensā'tionalist.**—*adj.* **sensātionalist'ic.** —*adv.* **sensā'tionally.**—*ns.* **sensā'tionism; sensā'tionist, sensā'tion-monger** a dealer in the sensational.— *adj.* **sense'less** unconscious: deficient in good sense: meaningless.—*adv.* **sense'lessly.**—*ns.* **sense'lessness; sensibil'ity** sensitiveness, sensitivity: capacity of feeling or emotion: readiness and delicacy of emotional response: sentimentality: (often in *pl.*) feelings that can be hurt.—*adj.* **sen'sible** perceptible by sense: perceptible: appreciable: having power of sensation: conscious: sensitive: easily affected: aware: having or marked by good sense, judicious.—*n.* **sen'sibleness.** —*adv.* **sen'sibly** in a sensible manner: to a sensible or perceptible degree: so far as the senses show.—*n.* and *adj.* **sen'sing.**—*n.* **sensitisā'tion, -z-.**—*v.t.* **sen'sitise, -ize** to render sensitive, or more sensitive, or sensitive in a high degree.—*adj.* **sen'sitised.**—*n.* **sen'sitiser.**— *adj.* **sen'sitive** having power of sensation: feeling readily, acutely, or painfully: capable of receiving stimuli: reacting to outside influence: ready and delicate in reaction: sensitised: susceptible to the action of light (*phot.*): pertaining to, or depending on, sensation: of documents, etc., with secret or controversial contents.—*n.* one who or that which is sensitive, or abnormally or excessively sensitive.—*adv.* **sen'sitively.**—*ns.* **sen'sitiveness, sensitiv'ity** response to stimulation of the senses: heightened awareness of oneself and others within the context of personal and social relationships: abnormal responsiveness as to an allergen: degree of responsiveness to electric current, or radio waves, or to light: (of an instrument) readiness and delicacy in recording changes; **sensitom'eter** an instrument for measuring sensitivity, as of photographic films; **sen'sor** a device that detects a change in a physical stimulus and turns it into a signal which can be measured or recorded, or which operates a control.—**sensori-, senso-** in composition, sensory, as in *sensorineural, sensoparalysis.*—*adj.* **senso'rial** sensory.—*n.* **senso'rium** the seat of sensation in the

brain: the brain: the mind: the nervous system.—*adj.*
sen'sory of the sensorium: of sensation.—*adj.*
sen'sual (-*sū-əl*, -*shoo-əl*) of the senses, as distinct
from the mind: not intellectual or spiritual: carnal:
worldly: connected with gratification, esp. undue
gratification of bodily sense: voluptuous: lewd.—*n*
sensualisa'tion, -z-.—*v.t.* **sen'sualise**, **-ize** to make
sensual: to debase by carnal gratification.—*ns*
sen'sualism sensual indulgence: the doctrine that all
our knowledge is derived originally from sensation:
the regarding of the gratification of the senses as the
highest end; **sen'sualist** one given to sensualism or
sensual indulgence: a debauchee: a believer in the
doctrine of sensualism.—*adj.* **sensualist'ic**.—*n*
sensual'ity indulgence in sensual pleasures: lewdness.
—*adv.* **sen'sually**.—*ns.* **sen'sualness**; **sen'sum** sense-
datum—*adj.* **sen'suous** pertaining to sense (without
implication of lasciviousness or grossness): connected
with sensible objects: easily affected by the medium
of the senses.—*adv.* **sen'suously**.—*n.* **sen'suousness**.
—**sensa'tion-monger** see **sensationist** above; **sense's-
datum** what is received immediately through the
stimulation of a sense-organ, **sense'-organ** a structure
specially adapted for the reception of stimuli, as eye,
ear, nose; **sense'-percep'tion** perception by the
senses; **sensitive plant** a plant, esp. *Mimosa pudica*,
that shows more than usual irritability when touched
or shaken, by movements of leaves, etc.; **sensory
deprivation** the reduction to a minimum of all external stimulation reaching the body, a situation used in
psychological experiments, etc.—**five senses** the
senses of sight, hearing, smell, taste, and touch; **bring
someone to his senses** to make someone recognise the
facts: to let someone understand he must mend his
behaviour; **come to one's senses** to regain consciousness: to start behaving sensibly (again); **common
sense** see **common**; **in a sense** in a sense other than the
obvious one: in a way: after a fashion; **make sense** to
be understandable or sensible, rational; **make sense of**
to understand: to see the purpose in, or explanation
of, **sixth sense** an ability to perceive what lies beyond
the powers of the five senses; **take leave of one's
senses** to go mad, to start behaving unreasonably. [L.
sēnsus—sentīre, to feel.]

sent *sent*, *pa.t.* and *pa.p.* of **send**.

sentence *sen'təns*, *n.* opinion: a judgment, decision:
determination of punishment pronounced by a court
or a judge: a maxim: a number of words making a
complete grammatical structure, generally begun
with a capital letter and ended with a full-stop or its
equivalent: a group of two or more phrases forming a
musical unit.—*v t.* to pronounce judgment on: to
condemn.—*n.* **sen'tencer**.—*adj.* **sentential** (-*ten'shl*).
—*adv.* **senten'tially**.—*adj.* **senten'tious** full of
meaning: aphoristic, abounding in maxims.—*adv.*
senten'tiously.—*n.* **senten'tiousness**. [Fr.,—L *sententia—sentīre*, to feel.]

sentient *sen'sh(y)ənt*, *adj.* conscious: capable of sensation: aware: responsive to stimulus —*n.* that which is
sentient: a sentient being or mind.—*ns.* **sen'tience**,
sen'tiency. [L *sentiēns*, *-entis*, pr.p of *sentīre*, to
feel.]

sentiment *sen'ti-mənt*, *n.* a thought or body of thought
tinged with emotion: opinion: judgment: a thought
expressed in words: a maxim: a thought or wish propounded to be ratified by drinking: emotion: feeling
bound up with some object or ideal: regard to ideal
considerations: sensibility, refined feelings
consciously worked-up or partly insincere feeling.
sentimentality.—*adj.* **sentimental** (-*men'tl*) pertaining to, given to, characterised by, expressive of,
sentiment: given to, indulging in, expressive of,
sentimentality —*v.i* **sentimen'talise**, **-ize** to behave

sentimentally: to indulge in sentimentality —*v.t* to
make sentimental: to treat sentimentally.—*ns.*
sentimen'talism, **sentimentality** (-*mən-tal'i-ti*)
disposition to wallow in sentiment: self-conscious
working up of feeling: affectation of fine feeling:
sloppiness; **sentimen'talist**.—*adv.* **sentimen'tally**.
[L L. *sentimentum*—L *sentīre*, to feel.]

sentinel *sen'ti-nl*, *n.* one posted on guard, a sentry.
guard.—*adj.* acting as a sentinel —*v t* to watch over:
to post as a sentinel. to furnish with sentinels.—
sentinel crab a crab of the Indian Ocean with long
eye-stalks. [Fr *sentinelle*—It. *sentinella*, watch,
sentinel]

sentry *sen'tri*, *n.* a sentinel: a soldier on guard: watch,
guard.—**sen'try-box** a box to shelter a sentry; **sen'try-
go** a sentry's beat or duty.

Senussi *sen-oos'ē*, *n.* a member of a Muslim sect or
confraternity, chiefly in N E. Africa, founded by Sidi
Mohammed ben Ali es-Senussi (d. 1860):—*pl.*
Senussi.

senza *sen'tsa*, (*mus*) *prep.* without. [It.]

sepal *sep'l*, also *sēp'l*, *n.* a member of a flower calyx —
adjs. **sep'aline** (-*in*), **sep'aloid**, **sep'alous**. [Fr
sépale, invented by N J. de Necker (1790) from Gr
skepē, cover]

separate *sep'ə-rāt*, *v.t* to divide: to part: to sunder: to
sever: to disconnect: to disunite: to remove: to
isolate: to keep apart. to seclude: to set apart for a
purpose: to shut off from cohabitation, esp. by
judicial decree. to remove cream from by a separator
—*v.i.* to part: to withdraw: to secede: to come out of
combination or contact: to become disunited.—*adj.*
(*sep'ə-rit*, -*rāt*, *sep'rit*) separated: divided: apart from
another: distinct.—*n* an off-print: (in *pl.*) items of
dress, e.g. blouse, skirt, etc., worn together as an
outfit —*n.* **separability** (-*ə-bil't-ti*).—*adj.* **sep'arable**
that may be separated or disjoined.—*n.* **sep'arableness**.—*advs* **sep'arably**; **sep'arately**.—*ns.*
sep'arateness; **separa'tion** act of separating or
disjoining: state of being separate: disunion:
chemical analysis: cessation of cohabitation by agreement or judicial decree, without a formal dissolution
of the marriage tie; **separa'tionist**; **sep'aratism**
(-*ə-tizm*); **sep'aratist** one who withdraws or advocates
separation from an established church, federation,
organisation, etc.—*adj.* **sep'arative** (-*ə-tiv*) tending to
separate.—*n.* **sep'arator** one who, or that which,
separates: a machine for separating cream from milk
by whirling.—**separate development** segregation of
different racial groups, each supposed to progress in
its own way; **separate maintenance** a provision made
by a husband for his separated wife, **separation allowance** government allowance to a serviceman's wife
and dependents. [L *sēparāre*, -*ātum—sē-*, aside,
parāre, to put.]

Sephardim *si-fär'dēm*, -*dim*, *n.pl.* the Spanish and
Portuguese Jews —*adj.* **Sephar'dic**. [Heb.]

sepia *sē'pi-ə*, *n.* cuttlefish ink: a pigment made from it,
or an artificial imitation: its colour, a fine brown: a
sepia drawing.—*adj.* of the colour of sepia: done in
sepia. [L.,—Gr. *sēpiā*, cuttlefish.]

sepoy *sē'poi*, *n* an Indian soldier in European service
(*hist.*) [Urdu and Pers. *sipāhī*, horseman.]

seppuku *sep-oo'koo*, *n.* hara-kiri. [Jap]

seps *seps*, *n.* a very venomous snake known to the
Greeks. [Gr *sēps*]

sepsis *sep'sis*, *n.* putrefaction: invasion by pathogenic
bacteria —*pl* **sep'sēs**. [Gr *sēpsis*, putrefaction.]

sept[1] *sept*, *n* orig. in Ireland, a division of a tribe —
adj. **sept'al**. [Prob from **sect**, influenced by L *saeptum*; see next.]

sept[2] *sept*, (*arch.*) *n* an enclosure.—*adjs.* **sept'al** par-
titional, **sept'ate** partitioned.—*n.* **septa'tion** division

by partitions.—*n.* **sept'um** (*biol.*) a partition:—*pl.* **sept'a**. [L. *saeptum* (used in pl.), a fence, enclosure—*saepire*, to fence.]

sept-, septi-, septem- *sept-, -i-, -em-, -əm-*, in composition, seven.—*adj.* **septilateral** (*sep-ti-lat'ər-əl*; L. *latus, lateris*, a side) seven-sided.—*n.* **septillion** (*sep-til'yən*; modelled on **million**) the seventh power of a million: the eighth power of a thousand (*U.S.*). [L. *septem.*]

September *səp-, sep-tem'bər, n.* ninth, earlier seventh, month of the year.—*n.* **Septem'brist** a participator in the September massacres in Paris, 2nd to 7th Sept. 1792. [L. *September, -bris.*]

septenarius *sep-ti-nā'ri-əs, n.* a seven-foot verse.—*adj.* **septenary** (*sep-tē'nə-ri*, or *sep'tə-nə-ri*) numbering or based on seven.—*n.* a seven, set of seven (esp. years): a septenarius. [L. *septēnārius*, of seven.]

septennium *sep-ten'i-əm, n* seven years:—*pl.* **septenn'ia.**—*adj.* **septenn'ial.**—*adv.* **septenn'ially.** [L *septennis—annus*, a year.]

septet, septette, septett *sep-tet', n.* a composition for seven performers: a set of seven (esp. musicians). [Ger. *Septett*—L *septem*.]

sept-foil *set'foil, n.* tormentil: a figure divided by seven cusps. [Fr. *sept*, seven, O.Fr. *foil*—L. *folium*, a leaf.]

septic *sep'tik, adj.* putrefactive.—*n.* **septicaemia** (*sep-ti-sē'mi-ə*; Gr. *haima*, blood) presence of pathogenic bacteria in the blood.—*adv.* **sep'tically.**—*n.* **septicity** (*-tis'i-ti*).—**septic tank** a tank in which sewage is decomposed by anaerobic bacteria. [Gr. *sēptikos—sēpein*, to putrefy.]

septilateral, septillion. See **sept-.**

septimal *sep'ti-ml, adj.* relating to, based on, seven.—*n.* **septime** (*sep'tēm*) the seventh position in fencing. [L. *septimus*, seventh—*septem*, seven.]

septuagenarian *sep-tū-ə-ji-nā'ri-ən, n.* a person seventy years old, or between seventy and eighty.—*adj.* of that age. [L. *septuāgēnārius—septuāgēnī*, seventy each.]

Septuagesima *sep-tū-ə-jes'i-mə, n.* the third Sunday before Lent (also **Septuagesima Sunday**). [L. *septuāgēsimus, -a, -um*, seventieth.]

Septuagint *sep'tū-ə-jint, n.* the Greek Old Testament, traditionally attributed to 72 translators at Alexandria in the 3rd century B.C.—*adj.* **Septuagin'tal.** [L. *septuāgintā—septem*, seven.]

septum. See **sept²**.

septuple *sep'tū-pl*, also *-tū', -tōō-, -tōō', adj.* sevenfold.—*v.t.* to multiply sevenfold.—*n.* **sep'tuplet** one of seven at a birth. [L.L. *septuplus*—L. *septem*, seven.]

sepulchre *sep'əl-kər, n.* a tomb: a recess, usually in the north chancel wall, or a structure placed in it, to receive the reserved sacrament and the crucifix from Maundy Thursday or Good Friday till Easter (**Easter sepulchre**): burial.—*v.t.* (formerly sometimes *si-pul'kər*) to entomb: to enclose as a tomb.—*adjs.* **sepulchral** (*si-pul'krəl*) of, of the nature of, a sepulchre: as if of or from a sepulchre: funereal, gloomy, dismal: hollow-toned; **sepul'tural.**—*n.* **sep'ulture** burial.—**whited sepulchre** see **white.** [L. *sepulcrum, sepultūra—sepelīre, sepultum*, to bury.]

sequacious *si-kwā'shəs, adj.* ready to follow a leader or authority: compliant: pliant: observing logical sequence or consistency.—*ns.* **sequa'ciousness, sequacity** (*si-kwas'i-ti*). [L. *sequāx, sequācis—sequī*, to follow.]

sequel *sē'kwəl, n.* that which follows: consequences: upshot: a resumption of a story already complete in itself.—*n.* **sequela** (*si-kwē'lə*) morbid affection following a disease: often in *pl.* **seque'lae** (*-lē*). [L *sequēla—sequī*, to follow.]

sequence *sē'kwəns, n.* a state or fact of being sequent or consequent: succession: order of succession: a series of things following in order: a succession of quantities each derivable from its predecessor according to a law (*math.*): a set of three or more cards consecutive in value: successive repetition in higher or lower parts of the scale or in higher or lower keys (*mus.*): in cinematography, a division of a film: in liturgics, a hymn in rhythmical prose, sung after the gradual and before the gospel.—*adjs.* **sē'quent** following: consequent: successive: consecutive; **sequential** (*si-kwen'shl*) in, or having, a regular sequence: sequent: of data, stored one after another in a system (*comput.*).—*n.* **sequentiality** (*-shi-al'i-ti*).—*adv.* **sequen'tially.**—**sequence of tenses** the relation of tense in subordinate clauses to that in the principal. [L. *sequēns, -entis*, pr.p. of *sequī*, to follow.]

sequester *si-kwes'tər, v.t.* to set aside: to seclude: to set apart: to confiscate: to remove from someone's possession until a dispute can be settled, creditors satisfied, or the like: to hold the income of for the benefit of the next incumbent: to sequester the estate or benefice of: to remove or render ineffective (a metal ion) by adding a reagent that forms a complex with it (e.g. as a means of preventing or getting rid of precipitation in water).—*adj.* **seques'tered** retired, secluded.—*n.* **seques'trant** (*chem.*) a substance which removes an ion or renders it ineffective, by forming a complex with the ion.—*v.t.* **sequestrate** (*sek', sēk', or si-kwes'*) to sequester: to make bankrupt.—*ns.* **sequestrā'tion** (*sek-, sēk-*) act of sequestering: the action of a sequestrant (*chem.*); **seq'uestrator.** [L.L. *sequestrāre, -ātum*—L. *sequester*, a depositary—*secus*, apart.]

sequin *sē'kwin, n.* an old Italian gold coin: a spangle. [Fr.,—It. *zecchino—zecca*, the mint.]

Sequoia *si-kwoi'ə, n.* a genus of gigantic conifers, the Californian big tree and the redwood—sometimes called *Wellingtonia*: (without *cap.*) a tree of this genus. [After the Cherokee Indian scholar *Sequoiah*.]

sera. See **serum.**

sérac *sā-rak', sā'rak, n.* one of the cuboidal or pillar-like masses into which a glacier breaks on a steep incline. [Swiss Fr., originally a kind of cheese.]

seraglio *sə-, se-rä'li-ō, -lyō, n.* women's quarters in a Muslim house or palace: a harem: a collection of wives or concubines: a Turkish palace, esp. that of the sultans at Constantinople:—*pl.* **sera'glios.** [It. *serraglio*—L. *sera*, a door-bar, confused with Turk. *saray, serāī*, a palace.]

seral. See **sere²**.

serape *se-rä'pä, n.* a Mexican riding-blanket [Sp. *sarape.*]

seraph *ser'əf, n.* a six-winged celestial being (Isa. vi): an angel of the highest of the nine orders: a person of angelic character or mien:—*pl.* **ser'aphs, ser'aphim.**—*adj.* **seraphic** (*-af'*).—*adv.* **seraph'ically.** [Heb. *Serāphīm* (pl.).]

seraskier *ser-as-kēr', n.* a Turkish commander-in-chief or war minister.—*n.* **seraskier'ate** the office of seraskier. [Turk. pron of Pers. *ser'asker—ser*, head, Ar. *'asker*, army.]

Serb *sûrb*, **Serbian** *sûr'bi-ən, ns.* a native or citizen of Serbia (formerly a kingdom, now a republic of Yugoslavia): a member of the people principally inhabiting Serbia: the South Slav language of Serbia.—*adj.* of Serbia, its people, or their language.—*ns.* and *adjs.* **Serbo-Cro'at, Serbo-Croatian** (*-krō-ā'shən*) (of) the official language of Yugoslavia. [Serb. *Srb.*]

sere¹. See **sear²**.

sere² *sēr, n.* a series of plant communities following each other.—*adj.* **sēr'al.** [L. *seriēs*, series.]

fāte; fär; mē; hûr (her); *mīne; mōte; fŏr; mūte; mōōn; fŏŏt; dhen* (then); *el'ə-mənt* (element)

serein *sə-rē'*, *n.* fine rain from a cloudless sky. [Fr.,— L. *sērum*, evening, *sērus*, late.]

serenade *ser-i-nâd'*, *n.* a composition like a symphony, usually slighter and in more movements: a performance in the open air by night, esp. at a lady's window: a piece suitable for such performance.—*v.t.* to entertain with a serenade.—*v.i.* to perform a serenade.— *ns.* **serenä'der**; **serenata** (*-i-na'ta*) (a (symphonic) serenade: a pastoral cantata. [Fr. *sérénade*, and It. *serenata*—L. *serēnus*, bright clear sky: meaning influenced by L. *sērus*, late.]

serendipity *ser-ən-dip'i-ti*, *n.* the faculty of making happy chance finds.—*adj.* **serendip'itous.** [*Serendip*, a former name for Sri Lanka. Horace Walpole coined the word (1754) from the tale 'The Three Princes of Serendip'.]

serene *sə-rēn'*, *adj.* calm: unclouded: unruffled: an adjunct to the titles of some princes.—*n.* calm brightness: serene sky or sea.—*adv.* **serēne'ly.**—*ns.* **serēne'ness**; **serenity** (*-ren'i-ti*).—**all serene** (*slang*) everything as it should be: all right. [L. *serēnus*, clear.]

serf *sûrf*, *n.* a person in modified slavery, esp. one attached to the soil: a villein:—*pl.* **serfs.**—*ns.* **serf'dom, serf'hood.** [Fr.,—L. *servus*, a slave.]

serge *sûrj*, *n.* a strong twilled fabric, now usually of worsted.—*adj.* of serge. [Fr.,—L. *sērica*, silk.]

sergeant, serjeant *sär'jənt*, *n.* orig. a servant: (usu. with *g*) a non-commissioned officer next above a corporal: (with *g*) an officer of police: (usu. with *g*) alone or as a prefix, designating certain officials: (with *j*) formerly, a barrister of highest rank (in full **ser'jeant-at-law'**). —*ns.* **ser'gean(t)cy, ser'jean(t)cy** office or rank of sergeant, serjeant; **ser'geantship, ser'jeantship.**—**ser'- geant-** (or **ser'jeant-**) **at-arms'** an officer of a legislative body or the Court of Chancery, for making arrests, etc.; **ser'geant-fish** a fish with stripes, akin to the mackerels; **ser'geant-mā'jor** formerly, an officer of rank varying from major to major-general: now, the highest non-commissioned officer (**company ser-geant-major** the senior warrant-officer in a company; **regimental sergeant-major** a warrant officer on the staff of a battalion, regiment, etc.).—**Common Serjeant** in London, an assistant to the Recorder. [Fr. *sergent*—L. *serviēns*, *-entis*, pr.p. of *servīre*, to serve.]

serial, seriate, seriatim. See **series.**

Seric *ser'ik*, *adj.* Chinese: (without *cap.*) silken.—*adj.* **sericeous** (*sə-rish'əs*) silky: covered with soft silky hairs: with silky sheen.—*n.* **ser'iculture** silkworm breeding; **sericul'turist; ser'igraph** a print made by silk-screen process; **serig'rapher.**—*adj.* **serigraph'ic.** —*n.* **serig'raphy.** [Gr. *sērikos*—*Sēr*, a Chinese, a silkworm (pl. *Sēres*).]

sericulture. See **Seric.**

seriema *ser-i-ē'mə*, *-ā'mə*, *n.* the crested screamer. [Tupí.]

series *sē'rēz*, *-iz*, *n.* a set of things in line or in succession, or so thought of: a set of things having something in common, esp. of books in similar form issued by the same publishing house: a set of things differing progressively: the sum where each term of a sequence is added to the previous one (*math.*): a taxonomic group (of various rank): a geological formation: succession: sequence: linear or end-to-end arrangement: in music, a set of notes in a particular order, taken, instead of a traditional scale, as the basis of a composition:—*pl.* **se'ries.**—*adj.* **se'rial** forming a series: in series: in a row: in instalments: of publication in instalments: using series as the basis of composition (*mus.*): of supernumerary buds, one above another —*n.* a publication, esp. a story, in instalments: a motion picture, television or radio play appearing in instalments.—*v.t.* **se'rialise, -ize** to arrange in series: to publish serially.—*ns.* **serialisā'tion, -z-** publication in instalments. the use of notes and/or other elements of music in regular patterns; **se'rialism** serial technique, or use of it (*mus.*); **se'rialist** a writer of serials, or of serial music; **seriality** (*-al'i-ti*).—*adv.* **se'rially.** —*adj.* **se'riate** in rows.—*v.t.* to arrange in a series, or in order.—*adv.* **se'riately.**—*n.* **seriā'tion.**—*adv.* **seriā'tim** one after another.—**arithmetical series** a series progressing by constant difference; **geometrical series** a series progressing by constant ratio. [L. *seriēs*—*serēre*, *sertum*, to join.]

serif *ser'if*, *n.* the short cross-line at the end of a stroke in a letter.—Also **seriph.** [Origin obscure; poss. Du. *schreef*, stroke.]

serigraph, serigrapher, etc. See under **Seric.**

serin *ser'in*, *n.* a smaller species of canary.—*n.* **serinette'** a small barrel-organ for training songbirds. [Fr., canary.]

seringa *sə-ring'gə*, *n.* a Brazilian rubber-tree: mock-orange (*Philadelphus*). [Port.; see **syringa.**]

serious *sē'ri-əs*, *adj.* grave: staid: earnest: disinclined to lightness: in earnest: not to be taken lightly: approaching the critical or dangerous: concerned with weighty matters.—*adjs.* **se'riocom'ic, -al** partly serious and partly comic.—*adv.* **se'riously.**—*n.* **se'riousness.** [L.L. *sēriōsus*—L. *sērius*.]

seriph. See **serif.**

serjeant. See **sergeant.**

sermon *sûr'mən*, *n.* a discourse, esp. one delivered, or intended to be delivered, from the pulpit, on a Biblical text: a harangue.—*v.i.* **ser'monise, -ize** to compose sermons: to preach.—*v.t.* to preach to.—*n.* **ser'moniser, -z-.** [L. *sermō*, *sermōnis*, speech, prob. ult. from *serēre*, to join.]

sero- *sē'rō-*, in composition, serum.

serologist, etc. See **serum.**

serosa *si-rō'zə*, (*zool.*) *n.* the chorion: the serous membrane (see **serum**):—*pl.* **serō'sas, -sae** (*-zē*). [Modern L.; fem. of *serōsus*—*serum* (see **serum**).]

serosity, etc. See **serum.**

serotine *ser'ō-tīn*, *-tin*, *n.* a small reddish bat.—*adj.* late, in occurrence, development, flowering, etc.— *adj.* **serotinous** (*si-rot'i-nəs*).—*n.* **serotō'nin** a potent vasoconstrictor found particularly in brain and intestinal tissue and blood-platelets. [L. *sērōtinus*— *sērus*, late.]

serous, etc. See **serum.**

serow *ser'ō*, *n.* a Himalayan goat-antelope. [Lepcha (Tibeto-Burman language) *sa-ro*.]

serpent *sûr'pənt*, *n.* formerly, any reptile or creeping thing, esp. if venomous: now, a snake: a person treacherous or malicious: an obsolete wooden leathercovered bass wind instrument shaped like a writhing snake.—*adjs.* **serpentiform** (*-pent'*) snake-shaped; **ser'pentine** (*-tīn*) snakelike: winding: tortuous.—*n.* a soft, usually green mineral, occurring in winding veins and in masses, etc.: a rock (in full **ser'pentine-rock**), composed mainly of the mineral serpentine.—*v.t.* and *v.i.* to wind: to insinuate.—*adv.* **ser'pentinely.**—*adj.* and *adv.* **ser'pentlike.**— **ser'pent-eater** the secretary-bird; **ser'pent-liz'ard** the seps.—**the old serpent** Satan. [L. *serpēns*, *-entis*, pr.p. of *serpēre*, to creep; cf. Gr. *herpein*.]

serpigo *sər-pī'gō*, *n.* any spreading skin disease:—*pl.* **serpigines** (*-pij'in-ēz*); **serpi'goes.**—*adj.* **serpiginous** (*-pij'*). [L.L. *serpīgō*—L. *serpēre*, to creep.]

serpula *sûr'pū-lə*, *n.* a polychaete worm with twisted calcareous tube:—*pl.* **ser'pulae** (*-lē*). [L., a snake— *serpēre*, to creep.]

serr, serre. See **serried.**

serra *ser'ə*, *n.* a sawlike organ, edge, etc. (*zool.*, etc.): —*pl.* **serr'ae** (*-ē*); **serr'as.**—*ns.* **serradill'a** (Port.)

bird's-foot; **serr′an** a fish of the **Serranidae** (-ran′i-dē), akin to the perches.—*ns.* and *adjs.* **serranid** (*ser′ən-id*); **serr′anoid**.—*adjs.* **serr′ate**, **serra′ted** notched like a saw: with sharp forward-pointing teeth (*bot.*).—*v.t.* **serrate′** to notch.—*n.* **serra′tion** saw-edged condition: (usu. in *pl.*) a sawlike tooth.—*adjs.* **serr′ulate**, **-d** finely serrate.—*n.* **serrula′tion**. [L. and Port. (from L.) *serra*, a saw.]

serrate(d), etc. See **serra**.

serried *ser′id*, *adj.* close-set. [Fr. *serrer* or its pa.p *serré*—L. *sera*, bar, lock.]

serrulate, etc. See **serra**.

serum *sē′rəm*, *n.* a watery liquid, esp that which separates from coagulating blood: blood serum containing antibodies, taken from an animal that has been inoculated with bacteria or their toxins, used to immunise persons or animals: watery part of a plant fluid:—*pl.* **sē′rums**, **sē′ra**.—*adj.* **serolog′ical**.—*adv.* **serolog′ically**.—*ns.* **serol′ogist**; **serol′ogy** the study of serums and their properties; **seros′ity**.—*adj.* **sē′rous** pertaining to, like, of the nature of, serum.—**serous membrane** a thin membrane, moist with serum, lining a cavity and enveloping the viscera within; **serum hepatitis** a virus infection of the liver, usu. transmitted by transfusion of infected blood or use of contaminated instruments, esp. needles, consequently often occurring in drug addicts. [L. *sērum*, whey.]

serval *sûr′vl*, *n.* a large, long-legged, short-tailed African cat or tiger-cat. [Port. (*lobo*) *cerval*, lit. deer-wolf, transferred from another animal.]

servant *sûr′vənt*, *n.* one who is hired to perform service, especially personal or domestic service of a menial kind, or farm labour, for another or others: one who is in the service of the state, the public, a company, or other body: one who serves: in formal epistolary use, formerly in greeting and leave-taking, now in jocularity, applied in seeming humility to oneself: a slave.—*adj.* **ser′vantless**.—**ser′vant-girl**, **ser′vant-lass**, **ser′vant-maid**; **servants′ hall** a servants′ dining- and sitting-room.—**civil servant** one in the civil service (see **civil**). [Fr., pr.p. of *servir*—L. *servīre*, to serve.]

serve *sûrv*, *v.t.* to be a servant to: to be in the service of: to work for: to render service to: to perform service for or under: to perform the duties or do the work connected with: of a male animal, to copulate with: to attend as assistant: to be of use to or for: to avail: to suffice for: to satisfy: to further: to minister to: to attend to the requirements of: to supply: to furnish with materials: to help to food, etc.: to send or bring to table: to deal: to put into play by striking (*tennis*, etc.): to treat, behave towards: to be opportune to: to conform one's conduct to: to undergo, work out, go through: to bind (rope, etc.) with cord, etc.: to deliver or present formally, or give effect to (*law*).—*v.i.* to be a servant: to be in service or servitude: to render service: to be a member, or take part in the activities, of an armed force: to perform functions: to wait at table: to attend to customers: to act as server: to answer a purpose, be of use, do: to be opportune or favourable: to suffice.—*n.* service of a ball.—*ns.* **ser′ver** one who serves, esp. at meals, mass, or tennis: a salver: a fork, spoon, or other instrument for distributing or helping at table; **serv′ery** a room or rooms adjoining a dining-room, from which meals and liquors are served and in which utensils are kept.—*n.* and *adj.* **serv′ing**.—**serv′ing-man** (*arch.*) a man-servant.—**serve as** to act as: to take the place of; **serve one right** to be no more than one deserves; **serve one's time** to pass through an apprenticeship or a term of office; **serve out** to deal or distribute: to punish: to retaliate on; **serve the** (or **one's**) **turn** to suffice for one's immediate purpose or need; **serve time** to

undergo a term of imprisonment, etc.; **serve up** to bring to table [Fr. *servir*—L. *servīre*, to serve.]

service[1] *sûr′vis*, *n.* the condition or occupation of a servant or of one who serves: work: the act or mode of serving: employ: employment as a soldier, sailor, or airman, or in any public organisation or department: the personnel so employed: the force, organisation, or body employing it (in *pl.* usu. the fighting forces): that which is required of its members: that which is required of a feudal tenant: performance of a duty or function: actual participation in warfare· a performance of religious worship: a liturgical form or office or a musical setting of it: a good turn, good offices, benefit to another: duty or homage ceremonially offered, as in hand-drinking, correspondence, or greeting: use: hard usage: availability: disposal: supply, as of water, railway-trains, etc.: waiting at table: a set, as of dishes for a particular meal: supplementary activities for the advantage of customers· cord or other material for serving a rope.—*adj.* of the army, navy, or air force: (sometimes in *pl.*) of the army, navy and air force collectively: for the use of servants: of industry, etc., providing services rather than manufactured products.—*v.t.* to provide or perform service for (e.g. motor-cars).—*ns.* **serviceabil′ity**, **ser′viceableness**.—*adj.* **ser′viceable** able or willing to serve: advantageous: useful: capable of rendering long service, durable.—*adv.* **ser′viceably**. —*adj.* **ser′viceless**.—**ser′vice-book** a book of forms of religious service: a prayer-book; **ser′vice-court** in lawn-tennis, the area outside of which a served ball must not fall; **ser′vice-flat** a flat in which domestic service is provided, its cost being included in rent; **service hatch** one connecting dining room to kitchen, etc., through which dishes, etc., may be passed; **service industry** an industry which provides a service rather than a product, e.g. catering, entertainment, transport; **ser′vice-line** the boundary of the service-court, in lawn tennis 21 feet from the net; **ser′viceman**, **ser′vicewoman** a member of a fighting service; **ser′vice-pipe**, **-wire** a branch from a main to a building; **ser′vice-res′ervoir** a reservoir for supplying water to a particular area; **service road** a minor road parallel to a main road and serving local traffic without obstructing the main road; **service station** an establishment providing general services for motorists.—**active service** service of a soldier, etc., in the field (widely interpreted by the authorities); **at your service** at your disposal: also a mere phrase of civility; **civil service** see **civil**; **have seen service** to have fought in war: to have been put to long or hard use. [Fr.,—L. *servitum*.]

service[2] *sûr′vis*, *n.* a tree (*Sorbus domestica*) very like the rowan—also **sorb**.—**ser′vice-berry** its pear-shaped fruit: shadbush or its fruit (*U.S.*); **ser′vice-tree**.—**wild service** a tree of the same genus with sharp-lobed leaves. [O.E. *syrfe*—L. *sorbus*.]

serviette *sûr-vi-et′*, *n.* a table-napkin. [Fr.]

servile *sûr′vīl*, *adj.* pertaining to slaves or servants: slavish: meanly submissive: cringing: slavishly or unintelligently imitative.—*adv.* **ser′vilely**.—*n.* **servility** (-vil′i-ti) slavishness of manner or spirit: slavish deference [L. *servīlis*—*servus*, a slave.]

Servite *sûr′vīt*, *n.* a member of the mendicant order of Servants of the Virgin, founded at Florence in 1233.

servitor *sûr′vi-tər*, *n.* one who serves: a servant: a man-servant: a follower or adherent: formerly, in Oxford, an undergraduate partly supported by the college, his duty to wait on the fellows and gentlemen commoners at table.—*adj.* **servito′rial**.—*n.* **ser′vitorship**. [L.L. *servītor*, -ōris—L. *servīre*, to serve]

servitude *sûr′vi-tūd*, *n.* a state of being a slave: slavery: subjection: compulsory labour: subjection to irksome conditions: a burden on property obliging the owner to allow another person or thing an easement (*legal*). [L. *servitūdō*.]

servo *sûr′vō, adj.* of a system in which the main mechanism is set in operation by a subsidiary mechanism and is able to develop a force greater than the force communicated to it.—**ser′vo-control′** a reinforcing mechanism for the pilot's effort, usu. small auxiliary aerofoil; **ser′vo-mech′anism** a closed-cycle control system in which a small input power controls a larger output power in a strictly proportionate manner; **ser′vo-mo′tor** a motor using a servo-mechanism. [L. *servus*, a servant, slave.]

servus servorum Dei *sûr′vəs sûr-vō′rəm, -vò′rəm, dē′ī, ser′vŏŏs, ′wŏŏs, ser-vō′rōōm, -wō′, de′ē,* (L.) a servant of the servants of God (a title adopted by the popes).

sesame *ses′ə-mi, n.* a plant (*Sesamum indicum*) of the *Pedaliaceae*, yielding gingili-oil.—*adj.* **ses′amoid** shaped like a sesame seed.—*n.* a small rounded bone in the substance of a tendon.—**sesame seed**.—**open sesame** see **open**. [Gr. *sēsamē*, a dish of sesame (Gr. *sēsamon*).]

sesqui- *ses′kwi-*, in composition, in the ratio of one and a half to one.—*ns.* **sesquicenten′ary, sesquicentenn′ial** a hundred and fiftieth anniversary.—Also *adjs*.—*n.* **sesquiox′ide** an oxide with three atoms of oxygen to two of the other constituent.—*adjs.* **sesquip′edal, sesquipedā′lian** (L. *sēsquipedālis—pēs, pedis,* foot; of objects or words) a foot and a half long—of words, very long and pedantic.—*ns.* **sesquipedā′lianism, sesquipedality** (*-pi-dal′i-ti*).—*adj.* **sesquip′licate** (L. *sēsquiplex, -plicis*) of, or as, the square roots of the cubes.—*ns.* **sesquisul′phide** a compound with three atoms of sulphur to two. [L. *sēsqui—sēmisque—sēmis* (for *sēmi-as*), half a unit, *que*, and.]

sessile *ses′il, -il, adj.* stalkless: sedentary.—*adj.* **sess′ile-eyed**. [L. *sessilis*, low, squat—*sedēre, sessum,* to sit.]

session *sesh′ən, n.* an act of sitting: a seated position: a sitting, series of sittings, or time of sitting, as of a court or public body: the time between the meeting and prorogation of Parliament: a school year (sometimes a school day): in Scotland, etc., a division of the academic year: (in *pl.*) quarter-sessions: a period of time spent engaged in any one activity (*coll.*).—*adj.* **sess′ional**.—*adv.* **sess′ionally**.—**sess′ion-house′** a building where sessions are held (also **sess′ionshouse**).—**Court of Session** the supreme civil court of Scotland. [Fr.,—L. *sessiō, sessiōnis—sedēre, sessum,* to sit.]

sesterce *ses′tərs, n.* a Roman coin, the *sestertius*, worth 2¼ asses, later 4 asses. [L. *sestertius*, two and a half —*sēmis*, half, *tertius,* third.]

sestet, sestett, sestette *ses-tet′, n.* a group of six: the last six lines of a sonnet: a composition for six performers. [It. *sestetto—sesto*—L. *sextus*, sixth.]

sestina *ses-tē′nə, n.* an old verse-form of six six-lined stanzas having the same end-words in different orders, and a triplet introducing all of them. [It.,—L. *sextus*, sixth.]

set *set, v.t.* to seat: to place: to put: to fix: to put, place, or fix in position or required condition: to adjust to show the correct (or a specified) time, etc.: to apply: to cause to be: to plant: to stake: to put on eggs: to put under a hen: to dispose, array, arrange: to put to catch the wind: to spread, lay, cover, as a table: to compose, as type: to put in type: to embed: to frame: to mount: to beset or bestow about: to stud, dot, sprinkle, variegate: to form or represent, as in jewels: to cause to become solid, coagulated, rigid, fixed, or motionless: to begin to form (as fruit or seed): to regulate: to appoint: to ordain: to assign: to pre-

scribe: to propound: to present for imitation: to put upon a course, start off: to incite, direct: to put in opposition: to posit: to rate, value: to pitch, as a tune: to compose or fit music to: to sharpen, as a razor: to indicate by crouching: to arrange (hair) in a particular style when wet, so that it will remain in it when dry: to defeat (a bridge contract).—*v.i.* to sit (now *arch.* or *dial.*): to go down towards or below the horizon, to decline: to offer a stake: to become rigid, fixed, hard, solid, or permanent: to coagulate: of a bone, to knit: to begin to develop, as fruit: to have or take a course or direction: to begin to go: to dance in a facing position: of dogs, to point out game:—*pr.p.* **sett′ing**; *pa.t.* and *pa.p.* **set**.—*adj.* in any of the senses of the participle: prescribed: deliberate, intentional: prearranged: formal: settled: fixed: rigid: determined: regular: established: ready: of mature habit of body. —*n.* a group of persons or things, esp. such as associate, occur, or are used together or have something in common: a clique: a complete series, collection, or complement: a company performing a dance: a series of dance movements or figures: a complete apparatus, esp. for wireless or television receiving: an act, process, mode, or time of setting: a setting: a direction: a dog's indication of game: permanent effect of strain: hang of a garment: a set hair-style: a young plant-slip for planting: a set scene: any collection of objects, called 'elements', defined by specifying the elements (*math.*): habitual or temporary form, posture, carriage, position, or tendency: (for the following senses, **set** or **sett**) the number of a weaver's reed, determining the number of threads to the inch: the texture resulting: a square or a pattern of tartan: a paving-block of stone or wood: a tool for setting in various senses: a badger's burrow: a group of games in which the winning side wins six, with such additional games as may be required in the case of deuce (*tennis*).—*ns.* **set′ness**; **sett′er** one who or that which sets: a dog that sets: a dog of a breed derived from the spaniel and (probably) pointer; **sett′ing** surroundings: environment: a level of power, volume, etc., to which a machine or other device can be set: mounting of jewellery: the period of time in which a play, novel, etc., is set: adaptation to music: music composed for a song, etc.: a system of dividing pupils in mixed-ability classes into ability groups for certain subjects only.— **set′back** a check, reverse, or relapse; **set′-down** an unexpected rebuff: a snub; **set′-line** any of various kinds of fishing-line suspended between buoys, etc., and having shorter baited lines attached to it; **set′-off′** a claim set against another: a cross-claim which partly offsets the original claim: a counterbalance: an ornament: a contrast, foil: an offset (*archit., print.*); **set piece** a picture in fireworks: an elaborately prepared performance; **set′-screw** a screw used to prevent relative motion by exerting pressure with its point; **set speech** a studied oration; **set square** a right-angled triangular drawing instrument.—**sett′erforth′**; **sett′er-off′**; **sett′er-out′**; **sett′er-up′**; **set′-to′** a bout: a hot contest:—*pl.* **set′-tos′, set′-to′s′**; **set-up′** configuration, arrangement, structure, situation (see **set up** below).—**dead set** determined (on); **set about** to begin, take in hand: to attack; **set going** to put in motion; **set alight, set light to, set fire to, set on fire** to cause to break into flame and burn; **set apart** to put aside, or out of consideration; **set aside** to put away: to reject: to annul: to lay by; **set at naught** see **naught**; **set back** to check, reverse: to cost (in money; *slang*); **set by** to lay up: to put aside; **set down** to lay on the ground: to put in writing: to judge, esteem: to snub: to attribute, charge: to lay down authoritatively; **set eyes on** to see, catch sight of; **set fair** steadily fair (**set** fair to about to); **set fire to** see **set alight** above; **set forth** to exhibit, display: to expound, declare· to praise, recommend· to start on a journey; **set free** to release, put at liberty; **set hand to** to set to work on; **set in** to begin: to become prevalent; **set in hand** to undertake; **set little, much,** etc., by to regard, esteem little, much, etc.; **set off** to mark off, lay off: to start off: to send off: to show in relief or to advantage: to counterbalance: to make an offset, mark an opposite page; **set on** to incite to attack: to instigate: bent upon; **set one's face against** set face; **set one's hand to** to sign; **set one's heart on** see **heart**; **set oneself** to bend one's energies; **set oneself against** to oppose; **set on fire** see **set alight** above; **set on foot** to set agoing, to start; **set out** to mark off: to start, go forth: to begin wth an intention: to adorn: to expound: to display; **set sail** see **sail**; **set to** to affix: to apply oneself; **set up** to erect: to put up: to exalt: to arrange: to begin: to enable to begin: to place in view: to put in type: to begin a career: to make pretensions: to arrange matters so that another person is blamed (slang; n. set'-up); **set upon** (to) set on. [O.E. settan; settan is the weak causative of sittan, to sit; the noun is from the verb, but may be partly from O.E. set, seat, partly from O.Fr. sette—L. secta, sect.]

seta sē'ta, n. a bristle-like structure:—pl. **se'tae** (-tē).—adjs. **setaceous** (si-tā'shas), **setose** (sē'tōs, -tōs'). [L. saeta (sēta), bristle.]

seton sē'tn, n. a thread or the like passed through the skin as a counter-irritant and means of promoting drainage: an issue so obtained. [L.L. sētō, -ōnis, app.—L. sēta, saeta, bristle.]

sett. See set.

settee se-tē', n. a long seat with a back [Prob. settle.]

setter, setting. See under set.

settle set'l, n. a long high-backed bench.—v.t. to dispose in stability, rest, or comfort: to adjust: to lower: to compact, cause to subside: to regulate: to fix: to establish, set up, or install (e g. in residence, business, marriage, a parish): to colonise: to make clear: to determine: to decide: to put beyond doubt or dispute: to restore to good order: to quiet: to compose: to secure by gift or legal act: to create successive interests in, use or income going to one person while the corpus of the property remains another's: to make final payment of: to dispose of, put out of action.—v.i. to alight: to come to rest: to subside: to sink to the bottom (or form a scum): to dispose oneself: to take up permanent abode: to become stable: to fix one's habits (often with down): to grow calm or clear: to come to a decision or agreement: to adjust differences: to settle accounts (often with up).—adj. sett'led.—ns. sett'ledness; sett'lement act of settling: state of being settled: payment: arrangement: placing of a minister: a subsidence or sinking: a settled colony: a local community: an establishment of social workers aiming at benefit to the surrounding population: a settling of property, an instrument by which it is settled, or the property settled, esp. a marriage-settlement: residence in a parish or other claim for poor-relief in case of becoming destitute; sett'ler one who settles: a colonist: a decisive blow, argument, etc.; sett'ling; sett'lor (law) one who settles property on another.—sett'ling-day a date fixed by the stock exchange for completion of transactions.—settle for to agree to accept (usu. as a compromise); settle in to prepare to remain indoors for the night: to adapt to a new environment; settle with to come to an agreement with: to deal with. [O.E. setl, seat, setlan, to place; the vb. may be partly from, or influenced by, late O.E. sehtlian, to reconcile.]

setwall set'wol, n. valerian. [O.Fr. citoual—L.L. zedoāria—Ar. zedwār.]

seven sev'n, n. the cardinal number next above six. a symbol representing it (7, vii, etc): a set of that number of persons or things: a shoe or other article of a size denoted by that number. a card with seven pips: a score of seven points, tricks, etc : the seventh hour after midday or midnight: the age of seven years.—adj. of the number seven: seven years old.—adj. sev'enth last of seven: next after the sixth: equal to one of seven equal parts —n. a seventh part: a person or thing in seventh position· a tone or semitone less than an octave: a note at that interval.—adv. sev'enthly in the seventh place.—sev'en-a-side a speedy form of Rugby football played by seven men on each side instead of fifteen.—adj. sev'en-day for seven days.—adj. and adv. sev'enfold in seven divisions· seven times as much.—adj. sev'en-league taking seven leagues at a stride, as the ogre's boots acquired by Hop-o'-my-Thumb.—sev'enpence the value of seven pennies.—adj. sev'enpenny costing or worth sevenpence.—seven deadly sins pride, covetousness, lust, anger, gluttony, envy, and sloth; Seven Seas the Arctic, Antarctic, North and South Atlantic, North and South Pacific, and Indian Oceans; Seventh-day Adventists a sect that expect the second coming of Christ and observe Saturday as the Sabbath, seventh heaven see heaven; Seven Wonders of the World the Pyramids, the Hanging Gardens of Babylon, the Temple of Artemis at Ephesus, Phidias's statue of Zeus at Olympia, the Mausoleum at Halicarnassus, the Colossus of Rhodes, and the Pharos of Alexandria; Seven Years' War the struggle for Silesia between Frederick the Great and the Empress Maria Theresa (1756–63). [O.E. seofon.]

seventeen sev-n-tēn', or sev', n. and adj. seven and ten —adj. and n. sev'enteenth (or -tēnth').—adv. seventeenth'ly. [O.E. seofontiene—seofon, tien, ten.]

seventy sev'n-ti, n. and adj. seven times ten:—pl. sev'enties the numbers seventy to seventy-nine: the years so numbered in a life or any century: a range of temperature from seventy to just less than eighty degrees.—adj. sev'entieth last of seventy: next after the sixty-ninth: equal to one of seventy equal parts.—n. a seventieth part: a person or thing in seventieth position.—sev'enty-eight a seventy-eight-revolutions-per-minute gramophone record, standard before the introduction of long-playing microgroove records—usu. written 78. [O.E. (hund)seofontig.]

sever sev'ər, v.t. and v.i. to separate: to divide: to cleave.—adj. sev'erable.—n. sev'erance.—severance pay an allowance granted to an employee on the termination of his employment. [Fr sevrer, to wean—L. sēparāre, to separate.]

several sev'ər-l, adj. separate: belonging or pertaining distributively, not jointly: particular: various: more than one (usu. more than three), but not very many —pron. a few.—adv. sev'erally separately —n. sev'eralty separateness: individual ownership. [O.Fr.,—L. sēparāre, to separate.]

severe si-vēr', adj rigorous: very strict: unsparing: pressing hard: hard to endure: austerely restrained or simple.—adv. severe'ly.—ns. severe'ness; severity (si-ver'i-ti). [L. sevērus.]

severy sev'ə-ri, n. a compartment of vaulting. [O Fr. civoire—L. cibōrium; see ciborium.]

Sèvres sev'r', adj. made at Sèvres, near Paris.—n. Sèvres porcelain.

sew sō, v.t. to join, attach, enclose, or work upon with a needle and thread or with wire —v.i. to ply the needle:—pa.t. sewed (sōd); pa.p. sewn (sōn) or sewed.—ns. sew'er; sew'ing the act of sewing: that which is being sewn.—sew'ing-machine.—sew up to enclose or close up by sewing: to complete satisfactorily (slang): to tire out, bring to a standstill, nonplus, or make drunk (*slang*). [O.E. *siwian, seowian*.]

sewage *sōō'ij, sū', n.* refuse carried off by sewers.—
sewer (*sōō'ər, sū'ər*, a channel for receiving the discharge from house-drains and streets.—*v.t.* to provide with sewers.—*ns.* **sew'erage** system or provision of sewers: sewage; **sew'ering.**—**sew'age-farm** a place where sewage is treated so as to be used as manure; **sew'er-gas** the contaminated air of sewers; **sew'er-rat** the brown rat. [O.Fr. *essever*, to drain off—L. *ex, out, aqua*, water.]

sewellel *si-wel'əl, n.* an American rodent linking beavers and squirrels. [Chinook *shewallal*, a robe of its skin.]

sewen. See **sewin**.

sewer[1] *sū'ər, n.* an officer who superintends the service at table. [O.Fr. *asseour—asseoir*, to set down—L. *ad*, to, *sedēre*, to sit. Skeat makes it from M.E. *sew*, to set, serve, *sew*, pottage—O.E. *sēaw*, juice.]

sewer[2], **sewerage**. See **sewage**.

sewin, sewen *sū'in, n.* a Welsh sea-trout grilse.

sewn. See **sew**.

sex *seks, n.* that by which an animal or plant is male or female: the quality of being male or female: either of the divisions according to this, or its members collectively: the whole domain connected with this distinction: sexual intercourse.—Also *adj.*—*v.t.* to ascertain the sex of.—*adj.* **sexed** (*sekst*) having sex: being male or female: having sexual characteristics, feelings or desires to a specified degree (as in **over-, under-, highly-**, etc., **sexed**).—*ns.* **sex'iness; sex'ism** discrimination (orig. against women, now against women or men) on the grounds of sex.—*n.* and *adj.* **sex'ist.**—*adj.* **sex'less** of neither sex: without sex: without sexual feelings.—*n.* **sex'lessness.**—*ns.* **sexol'ogist; sexol'ogy** the study of (human) sexual behaviour and relationships; **sexploita'tion** the *exploitation* of sex for commercial gain in literature and the performing arts, esp. films.—*adj.* **sex'ual** of, by, having, characteristic of, sex, one sex or other, or organs of sex.—*ns.* **sex'ualism** emphasis on sex; **sex'ualist; sexual'ity.**—*adv.* **sex'ually.**—*adj.* **sex'y** over-concerned with sex: of a person, very attractive to the opposite sex: stimulating sexual instincts.—**sex'-appeal'** power of attracting, esp. of exciting desire in, the other sex; **sex'-cell** an egg-cell or sperm; **sex'-change** (esp. of humans) a changing of sex.—Also *adj.*—**sex'-chro'mosome** a chromosome that determines sex; **sex'-kitten** a young woman (mischievously) playing up her sex-appeal.—*adjs.* **sex'-lim'ited** developed only in one sex; **sex'-linked'** inherited along with sex, that is, by a factor located in the sex-chromosome.—**sex'pot** (*slang*) a person of very great or obvious physical attraction; **sex'-rever'-sal** change from male to female or female to male in the life of the individual; **sex shop** a shop selling items connected with sexual arousal, behaviour, etc.; **sexual intercourse** the uniting of sexual organs, involving the insertion of the male penis into the female vagina and the release of sperm; **sexual reproduction** the union of gametes or gametic nuclei preceding the formation of a new individual; **sexual system** the Linnaean system of plant classification according to sexual organisation; **sex(ual) therapist** one who deals with problems relating to sexual intercourse; **sex(ual) therapy**. [L. *sexus, -ūs*.]

sex-, seks-, sexi- -i-, in composition, six.—*adjs* **sex(i)va'lent** (or -*iv'ə-lənt*) of valency six; **sexpart'ite** parted in six: involving six participants, groups, etc. [L. *sex*, six.]

sexagenarian *sek-sə-ji-nā'ri-ən, n.* a person sixty years old, or between sixty and seventy.—*adj.* of that age. [L. *sexāgēnārius*, pertaining to sixty—*sexāgintā*, sixty.]

Sexagesima *sek-sə-jes'i-mə, n.* the second Sunday before Lent (also **Sexagesima Sunday**).—*adj.* **sexages'imal** pertaining to, based on, sixty.—*n.* a sexagesimal fraction.—*adv.* **sexages'imally**. [L. *sexāgēsimus, -a, -um*, sixtieth.]

sexcentenary *sek-sin-tēn'ər-i, -sin-ten'*, or -*sen'tin-ər-i, n.* a 600th anniversary.—Also *adj.*

sexennial *sek-sen'yəl, adj.* lasting six years: recurring every six years.—*adv.* **sexenn'ially**. [L. *sex*, six, *annus*, year.]

sext *sekst, n.* the office of the sixth hour, said at midday, afterwards earlier (*eccles.*).—*adj.* **sex'tan** recurring every fifth day. [L. *sextus*, sixth—*sex*, six.]

sextant *seks'tənt, n.* the sixth part of a circle or its circumference, a sector or an arc of 60°: an instrument with an arc of a sixth of a circle, for measuring angular distances. [L. *sextāns, -antis*, a sixth.]

sextet, sextett, sextette *seks-tet', n.* altered forms (partly through Ger.) of **sestet**.

sextillion *seks-til'yən, n.* the sixth power of a million: the seventh power of 1000 (*U.S.*). [For *sexillion*, after **billion**, etc.]

sextodecimo *seks-tō-des'i-mō, n.* a book or a size of book made by folding each sheet into sixteen leaves:—*pl.* **sextodec'imos**.—Also *adj.* [L. (*in*) *sextō decimō* (*in*) one-sixteenth.]

sexton *seks'tən, n.* an officer who rings a church bell, attends the clergyman, digs graves, etc.: a burying-beetle (also **sex'ton-bee'tle**). [**sacristan**.]

sextuple *seks'tū-pl, adj.* sixfold.—*n.* six times as much.—*v.t.* and *v.i.* to increase or multiply sixfold.—*n.* **sex'tuplet** one of six born at a birth. [L.L *sextuplus*.]

sexual, sexy, etc. See **sex**.

sez. Slang spelling of **says**.

sforzando *sför-tsän'dō, sforzato sför-tsä'tō*, (*mus.*) *adjs.* and *advs.* forced, with sudden emphasis.—Also *ns.*—*pls.* **sforzan'dos, -di** (-*dē*), **sforza'tos, -ti** (-*tē*). [It., pr.p. and pa.p. of *sforzare*, to force—L. *ex*, out, L.L. *fortia*, force.]

sfumato *sfoo-mä'tō*, (*paint.*) *n.* a misty, indistinct effect got by gradually blending together areas of different colour:—*pl.* **sfuma'tos**. [It., pa.p. of *sfumare*, to shade off,—ex, L. *fumare*, to smoke.]

sgian-dubh *skēn-doo'*. Same as **skene-dhu**.

sgraffito *zgräf-fē'tō, n.* decorative work in which different colours are got by removal of parts of outer layers of material laid on: pottery with such decoration:—*pl.* **sgraffi'ti** (-*tē*). [It.,—L. *ex-*, and It. *graffito*, q.v.]

sh *sh, interj.* hush:—*pl.* **sh's.**

shabby *shab'i, adj.* dingy, threadbare, or worn, as clothes: having a look of poverty: mean in look or conduct: low: paltry.—*adv.* **shabb'ily**.—*n.* **shabb'iness**.—*adj.* **shabb'y-genteel'** keeping up or affecting an appearance of gentility, though really very shabby.—*n.* **shabb'y-gentil'ity**. [Obs. or dial. *shab*, scab—O.E. *sceabb*.]

shabrack *shab'rak, n.* a trooper's housing or saddle-cloth. [Ger. *Schabracke*, prob.—Turk. *çäprāq*.]

shack *shak, n.* a roughly-built hut.—**shack up (with)** (*slang*) to live with someone, esp. though unmarried. [Amer.]

shackle *shak'l, n.* a prisoner's or slave's ankle-ring or wrist-ring, or the chain connecting a pair: a hobble: a staple-like link, closed with a pin: the curved movable part of a padlock: a coupling of various kinds: (in *pl.*) fetters, manacles: a hindrance.—*v.t.* to fetter: to couple: to hamper.—**shack'le-bolt** the pin of a shackle. [O.E. *sceacul*.]

shad *shad, n.* an anadromous fish akin to the herring: extended to various other fishes.—**shad'berry** the fruit of the **shad'bush**, a N. American rosaceous shrub flowering at shad spawning-time. [O.E. *sceadd*.]

shaddock *shad'ək*, *n*. an Oriental citrus fruit like a very large orange, esp. the larger pear-shaped variety, distinguished from the finer grapefruit: the tree that bears it. [Introduced to the W. Indies *c.* 1700 by Captain *Shaddock*.]

shade *shād*, *n*. partial or relative darkness: interception of light: obscurity: a shadow: a momentary expression of face: a shady place: (in *pl.*) the abode of the dead, Hades: shelter from light or heat: that which casts a shadow: a screen: a window-blind (*U.S.*): a cover to modify or direct light of a lamp: a projecting cover to protect the eyes from glare: (in *pl.*; *slang*) sunglasses: a variety or degree of colour: a hue mixed with black: the dark part of a picture: a slight difference or amount: the disembodied soul: a ghost. —*v.t.* to screen: to overshadow: to mark with gradations of colour or shadow: to soften down: to darken: to lower very slightly, as a price (*U.S.*).—*v.i.* to pass imperceptibly (*away*, *into*, etc.).—*adjs.* **sha'ded**; **shade'less.**—*adv.* **sha'dily.**—*ns.* **sha'diness**; **sha'ding** making a shade: the marking of shadows or shadow-like appearance: the effect of light and shade: fine gradations: nuances: toning down: slight lowering of prices.—*adj.* **sha'dy** having, or in, shade: sheltered from light or heat: not fit to bear the light, disreputable (*coll.*): mysterious, sinister.—**shade'-tree** a tree planted to give shade.—**in the shade** sheltered from strong light: overlooked, forgotten, in relative obscurity; **on the shady side of** over (a specified age); **put in the shade** to outdo completely; **shades of** (a specified person or thing)! an exclamation greeting something which reminds one in some way of the person or thing. [O.E. *sceadu*; see **shadow**.]

shadoof, shaduf *shā-dōōf'*, *n*. a contrivance for raising water by a bucket on a counterpoised pivoted rod. [Egyptian Ar. *shādūf*.]

shadow *shad'ō*, *n*. shade cast by the interception of light by an object: the dark figure so projected on a surface, mimicking the object: the dark part of a picture: a reflected image: a mere appearance: a ghost, spirit: an unreal thing: a representation: a person or thing wasted away almost to nothing: an inseparable companion: a spy or detective who follows one: shade: protective shade: darkness: gloom: affliction. —*adj.* unreal: feigned: existing only in skeleton: inactive but ready for the time when opportunity or need arises: denoting, in the main opposition party, a political counterpart to a member or section of the party in power.—*v.t.* to shade: to cloud or darken: to represent as by a shadow: to typify: to hide: to attend like a shadow, follow and watch.—*ns.* **shad'ower**; **shad'owiness**; **shad'owing.** —*adjs.* **shad'owless**; **shad'owy** shady: like a shadow: symbolic: secluded: unsubstantial.—**shad'ow-box'ing** sparring practice with an imaginary opponent: making a show of opposition or other action, as a cover for taking no effective steps; **shadow cabinet** a body of opposition leaders meeting from time to time and ready to take office; **shad'ow-fight** a fight between or with shadows or imaginary foes; **shad'ow-fig'ure** a silhouette; **shad'owgraph** an image produced by throwing a shadow on a screen; **shad'ow-play** one in which the spectators see only shadows on a screen.—**afraid of one's own shadow** extremely timid; **may your shadow never grow less** may you continue to prosper; **shadow of death** the darkness of death: the threatening approach of death. [O.E. *sceadwe*, gen., dat., and accus. of *sceadu* (**shade** representing the nom.)]

shaft *shäft*, *n*. anything long and straight: a stem: an arrow: a missile: the main, upright, straight, or cylindrical part of anything: the part of a cross below the

arms: the part of a column between the base and the capital: the rachis of a feather: the thill of a carriage on either side of the horse: a straight handle: a pole: a ray or beam of light: a rotating rod that transmits motion: a well-like excavation or passage: the penis (*vulg. slang*).—*adj.* **shaft'ed.**—*ns.* **shaft'er, shaft'-horse** a horse harnessed between shafts; **shaft'ing** a system of shafts.—*adj.* **shaft'less.** [O.E. *sceaft*.]

shag *shag*, *n*. a ragged mass of hair, or the like: a long coarse nap: a kind of tobacco cut into shreds: the green cormorant (app. from its crest), or other species: an act of sexual intercourse (*vulg. slang*).— *v.t.* and *v.i.* to have sexual intercourse (with) (*vulg. slang*):—*pr.p.* **shagg'ing**; *pa.t.* and *pa.p.* **shagged** (*shagd*).—*adj.* **shagged** (*shagd*) tired out (*coll.*).—*n.* **shagg'edness.**—*adv.* **shagg'ily.**—*n.* **shagg'iness.**—*adj.* **shagg'y** long, rough, and coarse: having long, rough, coarse hair, wool, vegetation, etc.: unkempt. —**shag'-bark** a kind of hickory tree.—**shaggy dog story** (from the shaggy dog featured in many) a whimsically extravagant story humorous from its length and the inconsequence of its ending. [O.E. *sceacga*.]

shagreen *shə-grēn'*, *n*. a granular leather from horse's or ass's skin: the skin of shark, ray, etc., covered with small nodules. [Fr. *chagrin*—Turk. *sagri*, horse's rump, shagreen.]

shah *shä*, *n*. the king of Persia (now Iran): also formerly of certain other Eastern countries. [Pers *shāh*.]

shake *shāk*, *v t.* to move with quick, short, to-and-fro movements: to brandish: to cause to tremble or to totter: to disturb the stability of: to cause to waver: to disturb: to put, send, render, cause to be, by shaking: to scatter or send down by shaking: to split.—*v.i.* to be agitated: to tremble: to shiver: to shake hands: to trill:—*pa.t.* **shook**; *pa.p.* **shāk'en.**—*n.* a shaking: tremulous motion: a damaging or weakening blow: a shaken-up drink: a trillo, rapid alternation of two notes a tone or semitone apart: a fissure: a moment (*coll.*).—*adjs.* **shak(e)able**; **shāk'en.**—*ns.* **shāk'er** one who shakes: a contrivance for shaking (e.g. drinks): a perforated container from which something is shaken (*cap.*) a name applied to members of various religious bodies, as the Quakers, etc.; **shāk'erism.**— *adv.* **shāk'ily.**—*n.* **shāk'iness.**—*n.* and *adj.* **shāk'ing.** —*adj.* **shāk'y** shaking or inclined to shake: loose: tremulous: precarious: uncertain: wavering: unsteady: full of cracks or clefts.—**shake'-down** a temporary bed (orig. made by shaking down straw): a trial run, operation, etc. to familiarise personnel with procedures and machinery (chiefly *U.S.*); **shake'-up** a disturbance or reorganisation (*coll.*).—**(no) great shakes** of (no) great account; **shake a leg** (*coll.*) to hurry up; **shake down** (*slang*) to extort money from: to go to bed (esp. in a temporary bed): to settle down; **shake hands (with)** to salute (someone) by grasping his or her hand and (often) moving it up and down; **shake, shiver, in one's shoes** to be extremely afraid, shiver with fear; **shake off** to get rid of; **shake out** to empty or cause to spread or unfold by shaking; **shake the head** to turn the head from side to side in token of reluctance, rejection, denial, disapproval, etc.; **shake up** to rouse, mix, disturb, loosen by shaking: to reorganise (*coll.*); **two shakes (of a lamb's tail**, etc.), a brace of shakes, etc. (*coll.*) a very short time. [O.E. *sc(e)acan*.]

Shakespearian, Shakespearean *shăk-spē'ri-ən*, *adj.* of or relating to *Shakespeare*, or his works.—*n.* a student of Shakespeare.

shako *shak'ō*, *n*. a nearly cylindrical military cap.:—*pl.* **shak'o(e)s.** [Hung. *csákó*.]

shale *shāl*, *n*. clay rock splitting readily into thin laminae along the bedding-planes.—*adj.* **shā'ly.**—**shale'-oil'** oil distilled from oil-shale. [Ger. *Schale*, lamina; or from the following word.]

shall *shal, shəl, v.t.* originally expressing debt or moral obligation, now used with the infinitive of a verb (without *to*) to form (in sense) a future tense, expressing in the first person mere futurity (as **will** in the second and third), in the second and third implying also promise, command, decree, or control on the part of the speaker (rules for use of *shall, will,* are often ignored): must, will have to, is to, etc. (2nd and 3rd persons, and interrogatively 1st): may be expected to, may chance to, may well (all persons): may in future contingency, may come to (all persons):—*inf.* obsolete; no *participles*; *2nd pers. sing.* (*arch.*) **shalt**; *3rd,* **shall**; *pa.t.* **should** (*shŏŏd, shəd*); *2nd pers.* (*arch.*) **shouldest, shouldst.** [O.E. *sculan,* pr.t. *sceal, scealt, sceal*; pa.t. *sceolde.*]

shalli. See **challis.**

shalloon *shə-lōōn', n.* a light woollen stuff for coat-linings, etc. [Perhaps made at *Châlons-sur-Marne.*]

shallop *shal'əp, n.* formerly, a heavy fore-and-aft-igged boat: a dinghy: a small or light boat. [Fr. *chaloupe.*]

shallot *shə-lot', n.* a garlic-flavoured species (*Allium ascalonicum*) of onion. [O.Fr. *eschalote,* variant of *escalogne.*]

shallow *shal'ō, adj.* of no great depth, concavity, profundity, penetration: superficial.—*adv.* at or to no great depth.—*n.* a shallow place: (used in plural with the) the shallow part.—*v.t.* to make shallow.—*v.i.* to grow shallow.—*n.* and *adj.* **shall'owing.**—*adv.* **shall'owly** simply, foolishly (*Shak.*): in a shallow manner.—*n.* **shall'owness.** [M.E. *schalowe,* perh. related to **shoal**².]

shalt *shalt, 2nd pers. sing.* of **shall.**

shaly. See **shale.**

sham *sham, n.* a counterfeit.—*adj.* pretended: false.—*v.t.* to pretend: to feign.—*v.i.* to make false pretences: to pretend to be (as *to sham dead, sick*):—*pr.p.* **shamm'ing**; *pa.t.* and *pa.p.* **shammed.**—*n.* **shamm'er.** [First found as slang, late 17th cent.]

shaman *shäm'an, -ən, n.* a doctor-priest working by magic, primarily of N. Asia:—*pl.* **sham'ans.**—Also *adj.*—*ns.* **Sham'anism** (also without *cap.*) the religion of N. Asia, based essentially on magic and sorcery; **sham'anist.**—*adj.* **shamanist'ic.** [Russ.,—Tungus.]

shamble *sham'bl, v.i.* to walk with an awkward, unsteady gait.—*n.* a shambling gait.—*n.* and *adj.* **sham'bling.** [Poss. from next word, in allusion to trestle-like legs.]

shambles *sham'blz, n. pl.* (sometimes treated as *sing.*) a flesh-market, hence, a slaughterhouse.—*n.sing.* a place of carnage (*fig.*): a mess, muddle (*coll.*).—*adj.* **shambol'ic** (*slang*) chaotic. [*shamble,* a stool, stall —O.E. *scamel* (Ger. *Schemel*), stool—L.L. *scamellum,* dim. of *scamnum,* a bench.]

shame *shām, n.* the humiliating feeling of having appeared to disadvantage in one's own eyes, or those of others, as by shortcoming, offence, or unseemly exposure, or a like feeling on behalf of anything one associates with oneself: susceptibility to such feeling: fear or scorn of incurring disgrace or dishonour: modesty: bashfulness: disgrace, ignominy: disgraceful wrong: cause or source of disgrace: a thing to be ashamed of: an instance, a case of hard, bad, luck (*coll.*).—*v.t.* to make ashamed: to cover with reproach: to disgrace: to put to shame by greater excellence: to drive or compel by shame.—*adjs.* **shamed** ashamed; **shame'ful** disgraceful.—*adv.* **shame'fully.**—*n.* **shame'fulness.**—*adj.* **shame'less** immodest: done without shame.—*adj.* **shame'lessly.** —*n.* **shame'lessness.**—*adj.* **shame'faced** very modest

or bashful: abashed.—*adv.* **shame'facedly** (*-fäst-li* or *fā'sid-li*).—**shame'facedness** modesty.—**for shame** an interjectional phrase, you should be ashamed; **put to shame** to disgrace, esp. by excelling; **shame on (you, them,** etc.)**!** (you, they, etc.) should be ashamed; **think shame** to be ashamed. [O.E. *sc(e)amu.*]

shammy *sham'i, n.* (in full **shamm'y-leath'er**) a soft leather, originally made from chamois-skin, now usually from sheepskin, by working in oil: a piece of it.—Also *adj.* [**chamois.**]

shampoo *sham-pōō', v.t.* to massage: to wash and rub (the scalp and hair): to clean (carpet, etc.) by rubbing with a special preparation:—*pa.t.* and *pa.p.* **shampooed', shampoo'd.**—*n.* an act or process of shampooing: a preparation for the purpose:—*pl.* **shampoos'.**—*n.* **shampoo'er.** [Hindi *cāpnā,* to squeeze.]

shamrock *sham'rok, n.* the national emblem of Ireland, a trifoliate leaf or plant. [Ir. *seamróg,* Gael. *seamrag,* dim. of *seamar,* trefoil.]

shandy *shan'di, n.* a mixture of beer and ginger beer or lemonade.

shanghai *shang-hī', v.t.* to drug or make drunk and ship as a sailor: to trick into performing an unpleasant task:—*pr.p.* **shanghai'ing**; *pa.t.* and *pa.p.* **shanghaied', shanghai'd.**—*n.* **shanghai'er.** [*Shanghai* in China.]

Shangri-la *shang'gri-lä, n.* an imaginary pass in the Himalayas, an earthly paradise, described in James Hilton's *Lost Horizon* (1933): hence, any remote or imaginary paradise.

shank *shangk, n.* the leg from knee to foot: the corresponding part in other vertebrates: the lower part of the foreleg, esp. as a cut of meat: a shaft, stem, straight or long part: the part of a shoe connecting sole with heel: the leg of a stocking: an act of shanking a golf-ball.—*v.i.* to be affected with disease of the footstalk: to strike with junction of the shaft (*golf*). —*adj.* **shanked** having a shank: affected with disease of the shank or footstalk.—**shank'-bone**—on Shanks's mare, nag, pony, etc., on foot. [O.E. *sc(e)anca,* leg.]

shanny *shan'i, n.* the smooth blenny.

shan't (sometimes **sha'n't**) *shänt,* (*coll.*) a contraction of **shall not.**

shantung *shan-tung', -tōōng', n.* a plain rough cloth of wild silk: a similar cotton or rayon fabric. [*Shantung* province in China.]

shanty¹ *shant'i, n.* a roughly built hut: a ramshackle dwelling: a low public-house.—**shanty town** a town, or an area of one, where housing is makeshift and ramshackle. [Perh. Fr. *chantier,* a timber-yard (in Canada a woodcutters' headquarters); perh. Ir. *sean tig,* old house.]

shanty² *shan'ti, n.* a song with chorus, sung by sailors while heaving at the capstan, or the like—also **chanty, chantie, chantey** (*shan'ti*).—*n.* **shant'yman** the solo-singer in shanties. [Said to be from Fr. *chantiez* (imper.), sing.]

shape *shāp, v.t.* to form: to fashion: to give form to: to body forth: to embody: to devise: to direct: to determine.—*v.i.* to take shape: to develop: to give promising signs: to become fit:—*pa.t.* **shaped**; *pa.p.* **shaped.**—*n.* form: figure: disposition in space: guise: form or condition: that which has form or figure: an apparition: a pattern: a mould (*cook.*): a jelly, pudding, etc., turned out of a mould.—*adjs.* **shap'able, shape'able; shaped.**—Also in composition, as *L-shaped.*—*adj.* **shape'less** of ill-defined or unsatisfactory shape.—*ns.* **shape'lessness; shape'liness.**—*adjs.* **shape'ly** well-proportioned.—*n.* **shap'er.**—*n.* and *adj.* **shap'ing.**—**in any shape or form** (often merely) at all; **in (good) shape** in good condition; **in**

the **shape of** in the guise of: of the nature of; **out of shape** deformed, disfigured: in poor physical condition, unfit; **shape one's course** to direct one's way; **shape up** to assume a shape: to develop, to be promising; **take shape** to assume a definite form or plan: to be embodied or worked out in practice. [O.E. *sceppan*.]

shard *shärd*, **sherd** *shûrd*, *ns.* a scrap, broken piece, esp. of pottery. [O.E. *sceard*, cleft, potsherd.]

share¹ *shār*, *n.* a part allotted, contributed, owned, taken: a division, section, portion: a fixed and indivisible section of the capital of a company.—*v.t.* to divide into shares: to apportion: to give or take a share of: to participate in: to have in common.—*v.i* to have, receive, or give a share.—*ns.* **shar'er**; **shar'ing.**—**share'-cap'ital** money derived from the sale of shares in a business, and used for carrying it on; **share'cropper** a tenant farmer who himself supplies only his labour, receiving seed, tools, etc., from his landlord and, with adjustment to allow for what he has already received, a share of the crop.—*v.i.* **share'crop.**—**share'holder** one who owns a share, esp. in a company; **share'holding; share'-out** a distribution in shares; **share'-pusher** one who seeks to sell shares otherwise than through recognised channels or by dubious advertisement, etc.—**go shares** to divide; **lion's share** see **lion**; **share and share alike** in equal shares. [O.E. *scearu*; cf. **shear**.]

share² *shār*, *n.* a ploughshare or corresponding part of another implement. [O.E. *scear*; cf. foregoing word, and **shear**.]

Sharia(t) *shə-rē'ə(t)*, *ns.* same as **Sheria(t)**.—Also without *cap.*

shark *shärk*, *n.* a general name for elasmobranchs other than skates, rays, and chimaeras—voracious fishes, with lateral gill-slits, and mouth on the under side: sometimes confined to the larger kinds, excluding the dogfishes: an extortioner: a swindler: a sharper.—**shark'skin** a heavy rayon material with dull finish: shagreen. [Ger. *Schurke*, scoundrel, Austrian Ger. *Schirk*, sturgeon, etc. have been suggested.]

sharp *shärp*, *adj.* cutting: piercing: penetrating: acute: having a thin edge or fine point: affecting the senses as if pointed or cutting: severe: harsh: keen: eager: alive to one's own interests: barely honest: of keen or quick perception: alert: fit, able: pungent, sarcastic: brisk: abrupt: having abrupt or acute corners, etc.: sudden in onset: clear-cut: unblurred: well-defined: stylish (*slang*): high in pitch, or too high.—*adv.* high or too high in pitch: punctually, precisely: sharply.—*n.* a note raised a semitone: the symbol for it: the key producing it: a long slender needle: (in *pl.*) hard parts of wheat.—*v.t.* and *v.i.* **sharp'en** to make or become sharp in any sense.—*ns.* **sharp'ener; sharp'er** a cheat.—*n.* and *adj.* **sharp'ing** cheating.—*adj.* **sharp'ish.**—*adv.* **sharp'ly.**—*n.* **sharp'ness.**—*adjs.* **sharp'-cut** well-defined: clear-cut; **sharp'-edged; sharp'-eyed; sharp'-ground** ground to a sharp edge; **sharp'-nosed** having a pointed nose: keen of scent; **sharp'-pointed.** —**sharp practice** unscrupulous dealing, verging on dishonesty.—*adjs.* **sharp'-set** hungry: keen in appetite for anything, esp. food or sexual indulgence: set with a sharp edge; **sharp'-shod** (of a horse) having spikes in the shoes to prevent slipping.— **sharp'shooter** a good marksman: a soldier set apart for work as a marksman; **sharp'shooting.**—*adjs* **sharp'-sight'ed** having acute sight: shrewd; **sharp'« tongued'** critical, sarcastic, harsh in speech; **sharp'« toothed'; sharp'-vis'aged** thin-faced; **sharp'-witt'ed** having an alert intelligence, wit or perception —**look sharp** be quick: hurry up; **sharp's the word** be brisk [O.E. *scearp*; O.N. *skarpr*, Ger. *scharf*.]

shaster *shas'tər*, **shastra** *shas'tra*, *ns.* a holy writing. [Sans. *śāstra—śās*, to teach.]

shat. See **shit.**

shatter *shat'ər*, *v.t.* to dash to pieces: to wreck.—*v.i.* to break into fragments.—*adj.* **shatt'ered** exhausted: extremely upset.—*adj.* **shatt'er-proof** proof against shattering. [Perh. L.G.]

shave *shāv*, *v.t.* to scrape or pare off a superficial slice, hair (esp. of the face), or other surface material from: to tonsure: to remove by scraping or paring: to pare closely: to graze the surface of: to plunder, fleece.— *v.i.* to remove hair with a razor—*pa.p.* **shāved** or *arch.* **shāv'en.**—*n* the act or process of shaving: a paring: a narrow miss or escape (esp. *close shave*): a paring or slicing tool.—*n.* **shave'ling** a tonsured cleric.—*adj.* **shā'ven** shaved: tonsured: close-cut: smoothed.—*ns.* **shā'ver** one who shaves: an electric razor: a chap, a youngster (*coll.*); **shā'ving** the act of scraping or using a razor: a thin slice, esp. a curled piece of wood planed off.—**shā'ving-brush** a brush for lathering the face; **shā'ving-soap** soap for lathering in preparation for shaving; **shā'ving-stick** a cylindrical piece of shaving-soap [O E. *sc(e)afan*.]

Shavian *shā'vi-ən*, *adj.* pertaining to the dramatist George Bernard Shaw (1856–1950).—*n.* a follower or admirer of Shaw.

shaw *sho*, *n.* the above-ground parts of a potato plant, turnip, etc. [Scots form of **show**.]

shawl *shöl*, *n.* a loose covering for the shoulders, etc.— *v.t.* to wrap in a shawl.—*n.* **shawl'ing.**—**shawl collar** a large rolled collar tapering from the neck to (near) the waistline; **shawl'-patt'ern** a pattern like that of an Eastern shawl such as those woven in Kashmir.— **Paisley shawl** see **paisley**. [Pers. *shāl*.]

shawm *shöm*, *ns.* a musical instrument of the oboe class, having a double reed and a flat circular piece against which the lips are rested. [O.Fr. *chalemie*, *-mel*—L. *calamus*, reed.]

Shawnee *shö-nē'*, *n.* an Indian of an Algonquin tribe now mostly in Oklahoma.—**shawnee'-wood** a species of Catalpa. [Shawnee *Shawunogi*.]

she *shē* (or when unemphatic *shi*), *nom.* (irregularly or ungrammatically *accus.* or *dat.*) *fem. pron. of the 3rd pers.* the female (or thing spoken of as female) named before, indicated, or understood (*pl.* **they**).—*n.* (*nom.*, *accus.*, and *dat.*) a female (*pl.* **shes**).—*adj.* female (esp. in composition, as **she'-ass'**, **she'-bear'**, **she'-dev'il**). [Prob. O.E. *sēo*, fem. of the def. art , which in the 12th cent. came to be used instead of the pron. *hēo*.]

shea *shē*, *shē'ə*, *n.* an African tree (**shea'-tree**, *Butyrospermum*) whose seeds (**shea'-nuts**) yield **shea'-butt'er**. [Mungo Park's spelling of Mandingo (W.Afr. language) *si*.]

sheading *shē'ding*, *n.* one of the six divisions or districts of the Isle of Man. [**shedding**.]

sheaf *shēf*, *n.* a bundle of things bound side by side, esp. stalks of corn: a bundle of arrows:—*pl* **sheaves** (*shēvz*)—*vs.t.* **sheaf, sheave** to bind in sheaves.— *vs.i.* to make sheaves—*adj.* **sheaved.** [O.E. *scēaf*.]

shear *shēr*, *v.t.* to cut, or clip, esp. with shears: to cut superfluous nap from: to achieve or make by cutting: to tonsure: to subject to a shear: to strip, fleece (also *fig*).—*v.i.* to separate: to cut: to penetrate:—*pa.t.* **sheared**, *arch.* and *poet.* **shore**; *pa.p.* **shorn**, also, less commonly in ordinary senses, but always of deformation and usually of metal-cutting, **sheared.**—*n.* a shearing or clipping. a strain, stress, or deformation in which parallel planes remain parallel, but move parallel to themselves.—*ns.* **shear'er** one who shears sheep; **shear'ing; shear'ling** a shear-hog.—*n.pl.* **shears** orig. scissors (also *Scot.*): now usu. a larger instrument of similar kind, with pivot or spring: a hoisting apparatus (see **sheers**).—**shear'-hog** a sheep between first and second shearings; **shear'-leg** see **sheer²**; **shear'-steel** steel suitable for making shears, etc.; **shear'water** one of a genus of oceanic birds that skim the water. [O.E. *sceran*.]

sheat-fish *shēt'-fish*, **sheath-fish** *shēth'*, *ns.* a gigantic fish (*Silurus glanis*, the European catfish) of European rivers: any kindred fish. [Ger. *Scheidfisch*.]

sheath *shēth*, *n.* a case for a sword or blade: a close-fitting (esp. tubular or long) covering: a clasping leaf-base, or similar protective structure: an insect's wing-case: a contraceptive device for men:—*pl.* **sheaths** (*shēdhz*).—*v.t.* **sheathe** (*shēdh*) to put into or cover with a sheath or casing.—*adj.* **sheathed** (*shēdhd*) having or enclosed in a sheath.—*n.* **sheath'ing** (-*dh*-) that which sheathes: casing: the covering of a ship's bottom.—*adj.* **sheath'less**.—**sheath'-bill** either of two Antarctic sea-birds (*Chionis*) having a white plumage and a horny sheath at the base of the bill; **sheath'-knife** a knife encased in a sheath.—**sheathe the sword** to end war. [O.E. *scēath, scǣth*.]

sheave¹ *shēv*, *n.* a grooved wheel, pulley-wheel. [Related to Scots *shive*, slice.]

sheave², sheaves, etc. See **sheaf**.

shebang *shi-bang'*, (*slang*, orig. U.S.) *n.* a vehicle: affair, matter, etc. [Perh. conn. with **shebeen**.]

shebeen *shi-bēn'*, *n.* an illicit liquor-shop. [Anglo-Ir.]

Shechinah *shi-ki'nə*, *n.* Same as **Shekinah**.

shed¹ *shed*, *v.t.* to part, separate: to cast off: to drop: to emit: to pour forth: to cast, throw (as light): to impart: to cause effusion of:—*pr.p.* **shedd'ing**; *pa.t.* and *pa.p.* **shed**.—*adj.* cast: spilt, emitted.—*ns.* **shedd'er** one who (or that which) sheds: a female salmon or the like after spawning; **shedd'ing**. [O.E. *scūdan, scēadan* (strong vb.), to separate.]

shed² *shed*, *n.* a structure, often open-fronted, for storing or shelter: an outhouse. [App. a variant of **shade**.]

she'd *shēd*, a contraction of **she had** or **she would**.

sheen *shēn*, *n.* shine: lustre: radiance: glistening attire. —*adj.* **sheen'y** lustrous: glistening. [O.E. *scēne* (W.S. *scīene, scȳne*), beautiful; influenced by **shine**.]

sheep *shēp*, *n.* a beardless woolly wild or domestic animal (*Ovis*) of the goat family: sheepskin: a sheepish person: one who is like a sheep, as in being a member of a flock (or congregation), in following an example, in being at the mercy of the wolf or the shearer, in tameness of spirit, etc.:—*pl.* **sheep**.—*adj.* **sheep'ish** like a sheep: embarrassed through having done something foolish or wrong.—*adv.* **sheep'ishly**. —*n.* **sheep'ishness**.—**sheep'-cote** an enclosure for sheep; **sheep'-dip** a disinfectant vermin-killing preparation used in washing sheep; **sheep'dog** a dog trained to watch sheep, or of a breed used for that purpose: a chaperon (*slang*).—*adj.* **sheep'-faced** sheepish, bashful.—**sheep'-farmer**; **sheep'fold**; **sheep'-hook** a shepherd's crook; **sheep'-pen**; **sheep's pox** a contagious eruptive disease of sheep, resembling smallpox; **sheep'-run** a tract of grazing country for sheep; **sheep's'-bit** (or **sheep's scabious**) a campanulaceous plant (*Jasione*) with blue heads resembling scabious; **sheep's'-eye** a wishful amorous look; **sheep's fescue** a temperate tufted pasture grass; **sheep'shank** a nautical knot for shortening a rope; **sheep's'-head** the head of a sheep, esp. as food (also *adj.*): an American fish allied to the porgie; **sheep's shearer**; **sheep'-shearing**; **sheep'skin** the skin of a sheep, with or without the fleece attached: leather or parchment prepared from it.—Also *adj.*—**sheep station** (*Austr.*) a large sheep farm; **sheep'-stealer**; **sheep'-stealing**; **sheep'-track**; **sheep'walk** a range of pasture for sheep; **sheep'-wash** a sheep-dip.—**black**

sheep the disreputable member of a family or group; **separate the sheep from the goats** to identify (esp. by some test) the superior members of any group. [O.E. *scēap*.]

sheer¹ *shēr*, *adj.* thin: pure: unmingled: mere, downright: plumb: unbroken: vertical or very nearly. —*adv.* clear: quite: plumb: vertically.—*adv.* **sheer'ly** completely, thoroughly, wholly, etc. [M.E *schēre*, perh. from a lost O.E. equivalent of O.N. *skærr*, bright.]

sheer² *shēr*, *v.i.* to deviate: to swerve.—*v.t.* to cause to deviate.—*n.* a deviation: an oblique position: the fore-and-aft upward curve of a ship's deck or sides.— *n.pl.* **sheers, shears** an apparatus for hoisting heavy weights, having legs or spars spread apart at their lower ends, and hoisting tackle at their joined tops.— **sheer'-leg, shear'-leg** one of the spars of sheers: (in *pl.*) sheers.—**sheer off** to move aside: to take oneself off. [Partly at least another spelling of **shear**; perh. partly from the L.G. or Du. equivalent, *scheren*, to cut, withdraw.]

sheet¹ *shēt*, *n.* a large wide expanse or thin piece: a large broad piece of cloth, esp. for a bed: a piece of paper, esp. large and broad: a section of a book printed upon one piece of paper, a signature: as much copy as will fill a sheet: a pamphlet, broadside, or newspaper.—*adj.* in the form of a sheet: printed on a sheet.—*v.t.* to wrap or cover with, or as with, a sheet: to furnish with sheets: to form into sheets.—*v.i.* to form or run in a sheet.—*adj.* **sheet'ed** wrapped or covered with a sheet, esp. a winding-sheet.—*n.* **sheet'ing** cloth for sheets: protective boarding or metal covering: formation into sheets.—**sheet'-copper, -iron, -lead, -metal, -rubber, -tin**, etc., copper, iron, etc., in thin sheets; **sheet'-glass** a kind of glass made in a cylinder and flattened out; **sheet'-lightning** the diffused appearance of distant lightning; **sheet music** music written or printed on (unbound) sheets. [O.E. *scēte* (W.S. *scīete*), *scēat*; cf. next word.]

sheet² *shēt*, *n.* a rope attached to the lower corner of a sail: (in *pl.*) the part of a boat between the thwarts and the stern or bow.—**sheet'-bend** a type of knot used esp. for joining ropes of different sizes.—**a sheet, or three sheets, in the wind** half-drunk, or drunk. [O.E. *scēata*, corner; akin to foregoing.]

sheet-anchor *shēt'angk'ər*, *n.* an anchor for an emergency: chief support: last refuge. [Formerly *shut-, shot-, shoot-anchor*; origin doubtful.]

sheikh, sheik *shāk, shēk*, *n.* an Arab chief.—*n.* **sheikh(h)'dom** a sheik's territory. [Ar. *shaikh—shākha*, to be old.]

sheila *shē'lə*, *n.* a young girl or a woman (*Austr.*). [From proper name.]

shekel *shek'l*, *n.* a Jewish weight (about 14 grams) and coin of this weight: the unit of currency of Israel: (in *pl.*) money (*slang*). [Heb. *sheqel—shāqal*, to weigh.]

Shekinah, Shechinah *shi-ki'nə*, *n.* the divine presence. [Heb. *shekīnāh—shākan*, to dwell.]

shelduck *shel'duk*, *n.* (*fem.* or generic) a large duck (*Tadorna*) with free hind-toe.—Also **sheld'duck**; (esp. *masc.*) **shel'drake**. [Prob. dial. *sheld* (cf. Du. *schillede*), variegation, and **duck, drake**.]

shelf *shelf*, *n.* a board fixed on a wall, in a bookcase, etc., for laying things on: a shelf-ful: a terrace: a ledge: a shoal: a sandbank:—*pl.* **shelves** (*shelvz*).—*n.* **shelf'-ful** enough to fill a shelf:—*pl.* **shelf'-fuls**.— **shelf'-cat'alogue** a library catalogue arranged by shelves; **shelf'-life** the length of time a product can be stored without deterioration occurring; **shelf'-mark** an indication on a book of its place in a library; **shelf'-room** space or accommodation on shelves.—**on the**

shelf shelved: laid aside from employment or prospect of marriage. [O.E. *scylf*, shelf, ledge, pinnacle, or L.G. *schelf*; perh. partly from some other source.]

shell *shel, n.* a hard outer covering, esp. of a shellfish, a tortoise, an egg, or a nut: a husk, pod, or rind: a shelled mollusc: an outer framework: a crust: a hollow sphere or the like: a mere outside, empty case, or lifeless relic: any frail structure: a frail boat: a conch trumpet: an explosive projectile shot from a cannon: in some schools, an intermediate class (from one that met in an apse at Westminster).—*adj.* of, with, or like shell or shells.—*v.t.* to separate from the shell: to case: to throw, fire, etc. shells at.—*v.i.* to peel, scale: to separate from the shell.—*n.* **shellac, shell-lac** (*shel-ak'*; also *shel'ak*) lac in thin plates, got by melting granules of lac, straining, and dropping.— *v.t.* to coat with shellac: (*shel-ak'*) to trounce (*U.S.*): —*pr.p.* **shellacking;** *pa.t.* and *pa.p.* **shellacked.**—*n.* **shellacking.**—*adj.* **shelled** having a shell: separated from the shell.—*ns.* **shell'er; shell'ful; shell'iness; shell'ing.**—*adjs.* **shell'-less; shell'y** of or like shell or shells: abounding in shells: having a shell.— **shell'back** an old sailor; **shell'-crater** a hole in the ground made by a bursting shell; **shell'-egg** one in the shell, in its natural state; **shell'fire** bombardment with shells; **shell'fish** a shelled aquatic invertebrate, esp. a mollusc or crustacean, or such animals collectively; **shell'-hole** a shell-crater; **shell'-jack'et** a tight, short undress military jacket.—*adj.* **shell'-like.**— **shell'-lime** lime made from seashells; **shell'-mon'ey** wampum.—*adj.* **shell'proof** able to resist shells or bombs.—**shell'shock** mental disturbance due to war experiences, once thought to be caused by the bursting of shells: mental disturbance due to similar violent, etc. experiences.—*adj.* **shell'shocked.**— **come out of one's shell** to cease to be shy and reticent; **shell out** (*slang*) to pay up: to disburse. [O.E. *scell* (W.S. *sciell*); Du. *schil*, O.N. *skel*.]

she'll *shēl,* a contraction of she shall or she will.

Shelta *shel'tə, n.* a secret jargon used by vagrants in Britain and Ireland. [*Shelru,* poss. a perversion of O.Irish *béulra,* language.]

shelter *shel'tər, n.* a shielding or screening structure, esp. against weather: (a place of) refuge, retreat, or temporary lodging in distress: asylum: screening: protection.—*v.t.* to screen: to shield: to afford asylum or lodging to: to harbour.—*v.i.* to take shelter.—*adj.* **shel'tered** affording shelter.—*n.* **shel'terer.**—*n.* and *adj.* **shel'tering.**—*adj.* **shel'terless.**—**sheltered housing** housing for the elderly or disabled consisting of separate units with a resident housekeeper or similar person to look after the tenants' well-being.

sheltie, shelty *shel'ti, n.* a Shetland pony or sheepdog. [Perh. O.N. *Hjalti,* Shetlander.]

shelve *shelv, v.t.* to furnish with shelves: to place on a shelf: to put aside, postpone.—*v.i.* to slope, incline. —*n.pl.* **shelves** *pl.* of **shelf.**—*n.* **shelv'ing** provision of, or material for, shelves: shelves collectively: the act of putting upon a shelf or setting aside: a slope.— *adj.* shallowing: sloping.—*adj.* **shel'vy** having sandbanks: overhanging. [See **shelf.**]

shemozzle *shi-moz'l,* (*slang*) *n.* a mess: a scrape: a rumpus. [Yiddish,—Ger. *schlimm,* bad, Heb. *mazzāl,* luck; cf. **schlimazel.**]

shenanigan *shi-nan'i-gən,* (*slang*; usu. in *pl.*) *n.* trickery: humbug.

she-oak *shē'-ōk,* (*Austr.*) *n.* a casuarina tree. [*she,* denoting inferior, and *oak,* from its grain.]

She'ol *shē'ōl, n.* the place of departed spirits. [Heb. *she'ōl.*]

shepherd *shep'ərd, n.* one who tends sheep (*fem.* **shep'-herdess:** a pastor.—*v.t.* to tend or guide as a shep-

herd: to watch over, protect the interests of, or one's own interests in.—*adj.* **shep'herdess.—shepherd('s) check, plaid, tartan** (cloth with) small black-and-white check; **shepherd's glass** scarlet pimpernel; **shepherd's pie** a dish of meat cooked with potatoes on the top; **shepherd's purse** a cruciferous weed with flat pods.—**the Good Shepherd** Jesus Christ. [O.E. *scēaphirde;* see **sheep, herd.**]

sherardise, -ize *sher'əd-īz, v.t.* to coat with zinc by heating with zinc-dust in absence of air. [From *Sherard* Cowper-Coles, the inventor of the process.]

Sheraton *sher'ə-tən, n.* a kind or style of furniture designed by Thomas *Sheraton* (1751–1806).—Also *adj.*

sherbet *shûr'bət, n.* a fruit-juice drink: an effervescent drink, or powder for making it: a kind of water-ice. [Turk. and Pers. *sherbet,* from Ar.]

sherd *shûrd, n.* See **shard.**

Sheria(t) *shə-rē'ə(t), ns.* the body of Islamic religious law.—Also without *cap.* [Turk. *sheri'at,* law.]

sherif, shereef *shə-rēf', n.* a descendant of Mohammed through his daughter Fatima: a prince, esp. the Sultan of Morocco: the chief magistrate of Mecca. [Ar. *sharīf,* noble, lofty.]

sheriff *sher'if, n.* the king's representative in a shire, with wide powers judicial and executive (*hist.*): now in England, the chief officer of the crown in the shire, county, with duties chiefly ministerial rather than judicial: in Scotland, the chief judge of the town or region: in the United States, the chief executive officer of the county, his principal duties to maintain peace and order, attend courts, guard prisoners, serve processes and execute judgments.—*ns.* **sher'iffalty** shrievalty; **sher'iffdom** the office, term of office, or territory under the jurisdiction of a sheriff; **sher'iffship.—sher'iff-clerk'** in Scotland, the registrar of the sheriff's court, who has charge of the records of the court:—*pl.* **sher'iff-clerks'; sher'iff-court'** the sheriff's court; **sher'iff-dep'ute** in Scotland, till the abolition of the heritable jurisdictions in 1748, a lawyer who acted as deputy for the sheriff: thereafter sometimes the sheriff himself:—*pl.* **sher'iff-dep'utes; sher'iff-prin'cipal** in Scotland, a sheriff properly so-called.—**high sheriff** an English sheriff proper: the chief executive officer of a district (*U.S.*); un'der-sheriff an English sheriff's deputy who performs the execution of writs. [O.E. *scīrgerēfa—scīr,* shire, *gerēfa,* reeve.]

Sherlock (Holmes) *shûr'lok (hōmz), n.* one who shows highly developed powers of observation and deduction, as did the detective, Sherlock Holmes, in the stories of Conan Doyle (1859–1930)—often used ironically.

Sherpa *shûr'pə, n.* one of an eastern Tibetan people living high on the south side of the Himalayas:—*pl.* **Sher'pa, Sher'pas.** [Tibetan *shar,* east, *pa,* inhabitant.]

sherry *sher'i, n.* a fortified wine grown in the neighbourhood of Jerez de la Frontera in Spain: a wine of like type.—**sherry-cobb'ler** a drink composed of sherry, lemon, sugar, ice, etc.; **sherry party** a gathering at which sherry is drunk. [*Xeres,* earlier form of Jerez.]

she's *shēz,* a contraction of she is or she has.

shetland *shet'lənd,* (usu. with *cap.*) *adj.* pertaining to the Shetland Islands off the N. coast of Scotland.— **Shetland pony** a small, hardy pony with a thick coat, originating in the Shetland Islands; **Shetland sheep** a breed of sheep of Shetland and formerly Aberdeenshire; **Shetland sheepdog** a breed of dog resembling and presumably bred from, the collie, though smaller in size and with a thicker coat; **Shetland wool** a fine loosely twisted wool obtained from Shetland sheep.

sheva *sha-vä'*, *n.* Hebrew point or sign (simple, or in compound forms) indicating absence of vowel or a neutral vowel.—Cf. **schwa.** [Heb. *shewâ.*]

shew *shō.* Same as **show**.—*pa.p.* **shewn** (*shōn*).—**shew'-bread** the twelve loaves offered weekly in the sanctuary by the Jews.

Shia(h) *shē'a*, *n.* a Muslim sect, or a member of it, recognising Ali, Mohammed's son-in-law, as his successor.—**Shiism** (*shē'izm*); **Shiite** (*shē'it*) a member of this sect.—Also *adj.*—*adj.* **Shiitic** (*-it'ik*). [Ar. *shī'a*, sect.]

shibboleth *shib'a-leth*, *n.* the Gileadite test-word for an Ephraimite, who could not pronounce *sh* (Judg. xii. 5–6; *B.*): any such test: a peculiarity of speech: the criterion or catchword of a group: a cant phrase. [Heb. *shibbōleth*, an ear of corn, or a stream.]

shied. See **shy**[1,3].

shiel, shēl, (*Scot.*) *n.* a hut: a shelter.—*n.* **shiel'ing,** a shepherd's summer hut: a summer grazing. [Prob. from a lost O.E. equivalent of O.N. *skáli*, hut.]

shield *shēld*, *n.* a broad plate carried to ward off weapons, esp. one with a straight top and tapering curved sides: a protective plate, screen, pad, or other guard: a protection: a shield-shaped escutcheon used for displaying arms: a shield-shaped piece of plate as a prize: any shield-shaped design or object:—*v.t.* to protect by shelter: to ward off.—*n.* **shiel'der.**—*adj.* **shield'less,**—**shield'-bearer; shield'-bug** insect with much developed scutellum.—*adj.* **shield'-shaped** usu., shaped like the conventional shield. [O.E. *sceld* (W.S. *scield*).]

shieling. See **shiel.**

shier, shies; shiest. See **shy**[1,2]; **shy**[1].

shift *shift*, *v.i.* to manage, get on, do as one can: to change: to change position: to fluctuate: to resort to expedients: to move: to go away: to move quickly (*coll.*): to undergo phonetic change.—*v.t.* to change: to change the position of: to remove: to dislodge: to transfer: to rid: to suit: to swallow (*slang*): to put off. —*n.* an expedient: an artifice: provision of things for use in rotation or substitution: a smock: a chemise: a loose dress roughly triangular or oblong: a set of persons taking turns (esp. in working) with another set: the time of working of such a set: a change: a change of position: a general or bodily displacement of a series (as of lines in the spectrum, consonant or vowel sounds, faulted strata): in violin-playing, any position of the left hand except that nearest the nut: a removal.—*adj.* **shift'ed.**—*n.* **shift'er.**—*adv.* **shift'ily.** —*ns.* **shift'iness; shift'ing.**—*adj.* moving about: unstable.—*adj.* **shift'less** without resource or expedient: inefficient: feckless.—*adv.* **shift'lessly.**—*n.* **shift'lessness.**—*adj.* **shift'y** full of, or ready with, shifts or expedients: evasive, tricky, suggesting trickery.—**shift'-key** a typewriter key used to bring a different set of letters (as capitals) into play; **shift'-work** (a system of) working in shifts; **shift'-worker; shift'-working.**—**make (a) shift** to contrive to do somehow; **shift about** to vacillate: to turn quite round to the opposite point; **shift for oneself** to depend on one's own resources; **shift one's ground** (usu. *fig.*) to change the position one has taken, e.g. in a discussion. [O.E. *sciftan*, to divide, allot; O.N. *skipta*.]

shigella *shig-el'a*, *n.* a rod-shaped bacterium of the genus **Shigella,** esp. one of the species which cause dysentery. [After K. *Shiga* (1870–1957), the Japanese bacteriologist who discovered it.]

shih tzu *shēd-zōō'*, *n.* a small dog of Tibetan and Chinese breed.

Shiism, Shiite, Shiitic. See **Shiah.**

shikar *shi-kär'*, *n.* hunting, sport.—*ns.* **shikar'ee, shikar'i** a hunter. [Urdu, from Pers. *shikār.*]

shillela(g)h *shi-lā'li, 'la*, *n.* an Irishman's oak or black-thorn cudgel, or any similar stout club, etc. [*Shillelagh*, an oak-wood in County Wicklow, or *sail*, willow, *éille* (*gen.*) thong.]

shilling *shil'ing*, *n.* a coin or its value, 12 old pence, 5 (new) pence or (Kenya, etc.) 100 cents.—*adj.* costing or offered for a shilling: also in compounds, as **two's-shilling, three'-shilling,** etc.—*n.* **shill'ingsworth** as much as can be purchased for a shilling.—**shill'ing-mark** a solidus sign.—**take the (king's, queen's) shilling** to enlist as a soldier by accepting a recruiting officer's shilling—discontinued in 1879. [O.E. *scilling.*]

shilly-shally *shil'i-shal'i*, *adv.* in silly hesitation.—*n.* vacillation: one who vacillates.—*v.i.* to vacillate.— **shill'y-shall'ier.** [A redup. of **shall I?**]

shily. See **shy**[1].

shim *shim*, *n.* a slip of metal, wood, etc., used to fill in space or to adjust parts.

shimmer *shim'ar*, *v.i.* to gleam tremulously, to glisten. —*ns.* **shimm'er, shimm'ering** a tremulous gleam.— *adj.* **shimm'ery.** [O.E. *scimerian–scimian*, to shine.]

shimmy *shim'i*, *n.* a shivering dance (also **shimm'y-shake**): a shaking of the hips: vibration in a motor-car or an aeroplane.—*v.i.* to dance the shimmy, or make similar movements: to vibrate. [App. from **chemise.**]

shin *shin*, *n.* the forepart of the leg below the knee: the lower part of a leg of beef.—*v.i.* to swarm, climb by gripping between the legs: to use one's legs, hasten along.—*v.t.* to kick on the shins.—**shin'-bone** the tibia; **shin'-plas'ter** (*U.S.*) a brown-paper patch for a sore on the shin: paper money of small value. [O.E. *scinu*, the shin.]

shindig *shin'dig*, (*slang*) *n.* a lively celebration or party: a row. [Cf. **shindy.**]

shindy *shin'di*, (*slang*) *n.* a row, rumpus.—**kick up a shindy** to make a disturbance. [Perh. **shinty.**]

shine *shin*, *v.i.* to give or reflect light: to beam with steady radiance: to glow: to be bright: to appear pre-eminent.—*v.t.* to cause to shine:—*pa.t.* and *pa.p.* **shone** (*shon*); in Biblical usage, and in the sense of polished, **shined.**—*n.* brightness: lustre: a dash, brilliant appearance: an act or process of polishing.—*adj.* **shine'less.**—*n.* **shin'er** one who or that which shines: a coin, esp. a sovereign (*slang*): a small glittering fish of various kinds: a black eye (*slang*).—*adj.* **shin'ing.**— *adv.* **shin'ingly.**—*n.* **shin'ingness.**—*adj.* **shin'y** clear, unclouded: glossy.—**take a shine to** (*coll.*) to fancy, take a liking to; **shine at** to be very good at; **take the shine out of** (*slang*) to outshine, eclipse: to take the brilliance or pleasure-giving quality out of. [O.E. *scinan.*]

shingle[1] *shing'gl*, *n.* a wooden slab (or substitute) used as a roofing-slate: these slabs collectively: a board: a small signboard or plate (*U.S.*): a mode of hair-cutting showing the form of the head at the back (from the overlap of the hairs).—*v.t.* to cover with shingles: to cut in the manner of a shingle.—*adj.* **shing'led.**— *ns.* **shing'ler; shing'ling.**—*adj.* **shing'le-roofed.** [L.L. *scindula*, a wooden tile—L. *scindĕre*, to split.]

shingle[2] *shing'gl*, *n.* coarse gravel: small water-worn pebbles found esp. on beaches: a bank or bed of gravel or stones.—*adj.* **shing'ly.**

shingles *shing'glz*, *n.pl.* the disease *Herpes zoster*, an eruption usually running along an intercostal nerve with acute inflammation of the nerve ganglia. [L. *cingulum*, a belt—*cingĕre*, to gird.]

Shinto *shin'tō*, *n.* the Japanese nature and hero cult, the indigenous religion of the country.—*ns.* **Shin'-toism; Shin'toist.** [Jap.,—Chin. *shin tao–shin*, god, *tao*, way, doctrine.]

shinty *shin'ti*, *n.* a game like hockey, of Scottish origin, played by teams of 12: the slim curved club (also **shin'ty-stick**) or leather-covered cork ball (or substitute) used therein.

shiny. See **shine**.

ship *ship*, *n.* a large vessel, esp. a three-masted square-rigged sailing vessel: a racing-boat: sometimes any floating craft: an aircraft: a ship's crew: a spaceship.—*v.t.* to put, receive, or take on board: to send or convey by ship: to send by land or air: to dispatch, send (off): to engage for service on board: to fix in position.—*v.i.* to embark: to engage for service on shipboard:—*pr.p.* **ship'ping;** *pa.t.* and *pa.p.* **shipped.** —*n.* **ship'ful;**—*adj.* **ship'less.**—*n.* **ship'ment** the act of putting on board: a consignment orig. by ship, now extended to other forms of transport.—*adj.* **shipped** furnished with a ship or ships (*Shak.*): embarked.— *ns.* **shipp'er** one who sends goods by ship; **ship'ping** ships collectively: accommodation on board ship: (the act of) putting aboard ship: transport by ship.— **ship'-bis'cuit** hard biscuit for use on shipboard; **ship'board** a ship's side, hence a ship; **ship'-broker** a broker for sale, insurance, etc., of ships; **ship'builder; ship'building;** **ship'-canal'** a canal large enough for ships; **ship('s')-car'penter** a carpenter employed on board ship or in a shipyard; **ship'-chand'ler** a dealer in supplies for ships; **ship'-chand'lery; ship'-fē'ver** typhus; **ship'lap** an arrangement of boards or plates in which the lower edge of one overlaps the upper edge of the next below it.—Also *v.t.* and *v.i.*—**ship'-load** the actual or possible load of a ship; **ship'-master** the captain of a ship; **ship'mate** a fellow sailor; **ship'-money** a tyrannical tax imposed by the king on seaports, revived without authorisation of parliament by Charles I in 1634–37; **ship'-of-the-line'** before steam navigation, a man-of-war large enough to take a place in a line of battle; **ship'-owner** the owner of, or owner of a share in, a ship or ships; **shipp'ing-art'icles** articles of agreement between the captain and his crew.—*adjs.* **ship'-rigged** having three masts with square sails and spreading yards; **ship'shape** in a seamanlike condition: trim, neat, proper.—**ship's husband** see husband; **ship's papers** documents that a ship is required to carry; **ship'-way** a sliding-way for launching ships: a support for ships under examination or repair: a ship-canal; **ship'-worm** a wormlike mollusc that makes shell-lined tunnels in wood; **ship'-wreck** the wreck or destruction (esp. by accident) of a ship: destruction, ruin, disaster.—*v.t.* to wreck: to make to suffer wreck.—**ship'wright** a wright or carpenter employed in shipbuilding; **ship'yard** a yard where ships are built or repaired.—**on shipboard** upon or within a ship; **ship a sea,** water to have a wave come aboard; **ship of the desert** the camel; **ship the oars** to put the oars in the rowlocks: to bring the oars into the boat; **ship water** see **ship a sea; take ship** to embark; **when one's ship comes home** (or in) when one becomes rich.   [O.E. *scip*.]

-ship *-ship*, in composition, denoting (1) a condition or state, as *friendship, fellowship;* (2) position, rank, status, as *lordship;* (3) a specified type of skill, as *craftsmanship, scholarship;* (4) the number of people who are (something), as *membership.*   [O.E. *-scipe,* conn. with **shape**.]

shiralee *shir'ə-lē,* (*Austr.*) *n.* a swagman's bundle.

shire *shir* (in composition *-shir, -shər*), *n.* a county: applied also to certain smaller districts as Richmondshire: a rural district having its own elected council (*Austr.*).—**shire'-horse** a large, strong draught-horse, once bred chiefly in the Midland shires.—**the Shires** (often *shērz*) those English counties whose names end in *-shire,* esp. (for hunting) Leicestershire, Rutlandshire (later Rutland), Northamptonshire, and part of Lincolnshire.   [O.E. *scir.*

office, authority.]

shirk *shûrk, v.t.* to evade: to slink out of facing or shouldering.—*v.i.* to go or act evasively.—*n.* one who shirks.—*n.* **shirk'er.**

Shirley poppy *shûr'li pop'i,* a variety of common poppy produced at Shirley, Croydon.

shirr *shûr, n.* a puckering or gathering.—*v.t.* to pucker, make gathers in: to bake (eggs broken into a dish).—*adj.* **shirred.**—*n.* **shirr'ing.**

shirt *shûrt, n.* a man's loose sleeved garment for the upper part of the body, typically with fitted collar and cuffs: a woman's blouse of similar form: an undershirt: a nightshirt.—*n.* **shirt'ing** cloth for shirts.— *adjs.* **shirt'less; shirt'y** (*slang*) ruffled in temper, annoyed.—**shirt'-band** the neckband of a shirt; **shirt'-butt'on; shirt dress** a straight dress with a shirt-type collar, resembling an elongated shirt: a shirtwaister (*U.S.*); **shirt'-frill'** a frill on the breast of the shirt; **shirt'-front'** the breast of a shirt: a dickey; **shirt'-pin** an ornamental pin fastening a shirt at the neck; **shirt'-sleeve; shirt'-stud; shirt'-tail** the flap at the back of a shirt; **shirt'waist** (*U.S.*) a woman's blouse; **shirt'waister** a tailored dress with shirtwaist top.—**Black Shirt** a fascist; **boiled shirt** a white shirt (with starched front); **Brown Shirt** a Nazi; **in one's shirt-sleeves** with one's jacket or jersey off; **keep one's shirt on** to keep calm; **lose one's shirt** to lose all one has; **put one's shirt on** to bet all one has on; **Red Shirt** a follower of Garibaldi.   [O.E. *scyrte.*]

shish kebab. See **kebab**.

shit, shite *shit, shīt,* (*vulg.*) *ns.* excrement: a contemptuous term for a person.—*vs t* to evacuate the bowels:—*pr p.* **shit(t)'ing;** *pa.t.* and *pa.p.* **shit, shat.** —*interjs.* expressing annoyance, disappointment, etc.   [O.E. *scitan,* to defecate.]

shiv. See **chiv**.

Shiva. See **Siva**.

shiver[1] *shiv'ər, n.* a splinter: a chip: a small fragment. —*v.t.* and *v.i.* to shatter.—*adj.* **shiv'ery** brittle.— **shiver my timbers** a stage sailor's oath.   [Early M.E. *scifre.*]

shiver[2] *shiv'ər, v.i.* to quiver: to make an involuntary muscular movement as with cold.—*v.t.* to cause to quiver.—*n.* a shivering movement or feeling.—*n.* and *adj.* **shiv'ering.**—*adv.* **shiv'eringly.**—*adj.* **shiv'ery** inclined to shiver or to cause shivers.—**shiver in one's shoes** see **shake; the shivers** (*coll.*) a shivering fit: the ague: a thrill of horror or fear.   [M.E. *chivere.*]

shivoo *shə-vōō', (Austr. coll.) n.* a (noisy) party. [From N. Eng. dial. *sheevo,* a shindy.]

shlemiel. See **schlemiel**.

shlimazel. See **schlimazel**.

shoal[1] *shōl, n.* a multitude of fishes, etc., swimming together: a flock, swarm, great assemblage.—*v.i.* to gather or go in shoals, swarm.—*adv.* **shoal'wise** in shoals.   [O.E. *scolu,* troop, cf. **school**[2].]

shoal[2] *shōl, adj.* shallow.—*n.* a shallow.—*v.i.* to grow shallow: to come to shallow water.—*v.t.* to find to be shallowing: to make shallow.—*n.* **shoal'ing.**—*adj.* **shoal'y** full of shallows.   [O.E. *sceald,* shallow.]

shoat *shōt, n.* a young hog.   [From M.E.]

shock[1] *shok, n.* a violent impact, orig. of charging warriors: a dashing together: a shaking or unsettling blow: a sudden shaking or jarring as if by a blow: a blow to the emotions or its cause: outrage at something regarded as improper: a convulsive excitation of nerves, as by electricity: the prostration of voluntary and involuntary functions caused by trauma, a surgical operation, or excessive sudden emotional disturbance: a stroke of paralysis (*coll.*).—*v.t.* to meet or assail with a shock: a shaking or impair by a shock: to give a shock to: to harrow or outrage the feelings of: to affect with abashed and horrified indignation.—*v.i.* to outrage others' feelings.—*adj.* **shocked**.—*n.* **shock'er** (*coll.*) a very sensational tale: any unpleasant, offensive, etc. person or thing.—*adj.* **shock'ing** giving a shock: revolting to the feelings, esp. to oversensitive modesty: execrable: deplorably bad.—*adv.* (*coll.*) deplorably.—*adv.* **shock'ingly.**—*n.* **shock'ingness.**—**shock'-absorber** a contrivance for damping shock, as in an aeroplane alighting or a car on a bad road.—*adj.* **shock'-proof** protected in some way from giving, or suffering the effects of, shock: unlikely to be upset, or to feel moral outrage; **shock tactics** orig. tactics of cavalry attacking in masses and depending for their effect on the force of impact: any action that seeks to achieve its object by means of suddenness and force; **shock therapy, treatment** the use of electric shocks in treatment of mental disorders: the use of violent measures to change one's way of thinking; **shock'-troops** troops trained or selected for attacks demanding exceptional physique and bravery; **shock wave** a wave of the same nature as a sound wave but of very great intensity, caused, e.g. by an atomic explosion, or by a body moving with supersonic velocity. [App. Fr. *choc* (n.), *choquer* (vb.), or perh. directly from a Gmc. source.]

shock² *shok, n.* a stook, or propped-up group of sheaves, commonly twelve.—*v.t.* to set up in shocks. —*n.* **shock'er.** [M.E. *schokke.*]

shock³ *shok, n* a mass of shaggy hair.—**shock'-head.**— *adjs.* **shock'-head, -ed.**

shod. See **shoe.**

shoddy *shod'i, n.* wool from shredded rags: cloth made of it, alone or mixed: anything inferior seeking to pass for better than it is.—*adj.* of shoddy: inferior and pretentious: cheap and nasty: sham.—*adv.* **shodd'ily.** —*n.* **shodd'iness.**

shoe *shoō, n.* a stiff outer covering for the foot, not coming above the ankle: a rim of iron nailed to a hoof. anything in form, position, or use like a shoe, as in a metal tip or ferrule, a piece attached where there is friction, a drag for a wheel, the touching part of a brake, the block by which an electric tractor collects current:—*pl.* **shoes** (*shoōz*); also, *arch.* and *dial.* **shoon** (*shoōn, Scot. shún, shin*).—*v.t.* to put shoes or a shoe on:—*pr.p.* **shoe'ing**; *pa.t.* and *pa.p.* **shod, shoed.**— *adj.* **shod** (*shod*).—*n.* **shoe'ing.**—*adj.* **shoe'less.**—*n.* **shoer** (*shoō'ər*) a horse-shoer.—**shoe'black** one who blacks shoes; **shoe'-brush; shoe'-buckle; shoe'horn,** an instrument for helping the heel into the shoe; **shoe'ing-smith; shoe'-lace** a string passed through eyelet holes to fasten a shoe; **shoe'-leather** leather for shoes: shoes or shoeing generally; **shoe'maker** one who makes (now often only sells or mends) shoes and boots; **shoe'making; shoe'-nail** a nail for fastening a horseshoe; **shoe'shine** (the act of) polishing shoes; **shoe'-shop; shoe'string** a shoe-lace (*U.S.*): a minimum of capital.—Also *adj.*—**shoe'-tree** a support, usually of wood or metal, inserted in a shoe when it is not being worn in order to preserve its shape.—**be in, step into, someone's or a dead man's, shoes** to be in, or succeed to, someone's place. [O.E. *scōh* (pl. *scōs*).]

shofar *shō'fär, n.* a kind of trumpet made from a ram's horn, blown in Jewish religious ceremonies and in ancient times as a call to battle, etc.:—*pl.* **shō'fars, shōfroth** (*-frōt'*). [Heb. *shôphār*, ram's horn.]

shogun *shō'goōn, -gōōn, n.* the commander-in-chief and real ruler of feudal Japan.—*adj.* **shō'gunal.**—*n.* **shō'gunate** the office, jurisdiction or state of a shogun. [Jap.,—*sho,* to lead, *gun,* army.]

shone *shon, pa.t.* and *pa.p.* of **shine.**

shoo *shoō, interj.* used to scare away fowls, etc.—*v.i.* to cry 'Shoo!'—*v.t.* to drive away by calling 'Shoo!' [Instinctive.]

shook¹ *shoōk, pa.t.* of **shake.**

shook² *shoōk, n.* a bundle of sheaves, a shock, stook. a set of cask staves and heads, or of parts for making a box, etc.]

shoon. See **shoe.**

shoot *shoōt, v.t.* to dart: to let fly with force: to discharge: to precipitate, launch forth: to tip out, dump: to cast: to kick or hit at goal (*games*): to score, for a hole or the round (*golf*): to thrust forward: to pull (one's shirt cuffs) forward so that they project from the sleeves of one's jacket: to slide along: to slide the bolt of: to put forth in growth: to pass rapidly through, under, or over: to hit, wound, or kill with a shot: to photograph, esp. for motion pictures. to variegate: to produce a play of colour in (usu. in *pa.p.*): to inject (esp. oneself) with (a drug) (*slang*). to play (a round of golf, game of pool, etc.)' to detonate.—*v.i* to dart forth or forward: of a cricket ball, to start forward rapidly near the ground: to send darting pains: to sprout· of vegetables, to bolt to elongate rapidly: to jut out far or suddenly: to begin, esp. to speak one's mind or to tell what one knows (*coll.*; usu. in *imper.*): to tower: to send forth a missile, etc.: to discharge a shot or weapon: to use a bow or gun in practice, competition, hunting, etc.:—*pa.t* and *pa.p.* **shot**; see also **shotten.**—*n* a shooting: a shooting match, party, expedition: the shooting of a film: new growth: a sprout: the stem and leaf parts of a plant: a dump: a chute (see **chute¹**).—*adj.* **shoot'able** that may be shot, or shot over.—*ns.* **shoot'er** a cricket ball that shoots (see above): a gun, etc (*coll.*); **shoot'ing** the action of the verb in any sense the killing of game with firearms over a certain area. the right to do so: the district so limited.—Also *adj.*— **shoot'ing-box, -lodge** a small house in the country for use in the shooting season; **shoot'ing-brake** a motorcar for the carriage both of passengers and of burden, an estate car; **shoot'ing-gall'ery** a long room used for practice or amusement with firearms; **shoot'ing-iron** (*slang*) a firearm, esp. a revolver; **shoot'ing-jack'et** a short coat for shooting in; **shoot'ing-range** a place for shooting at targets; **shoot'ing-star** a meteor; **shoot'- ing-stick** a printer's tool for driving quoins: a walking-stick with a head that opens out into a seat; **shooting war** actual war as distinct from cold war; **shoot'-out** a gunfight, esp. to the death or other decisive conclusion (also *fig.*).—**get shot of** (*slang*) to get rid of; **have shot one's bolt** see **bolt¹**; **shoot a line** (*slang*) to brag, exaggerate (*n.* **line'-shooter**); **shoot down** to kill, or to bring down (an aeroplane) by shooting: to rout in argument, **shoot down in flames** (*slang*) to reprimand severely; **shoot from the hip** (*coll.*) to speak bluntly or hastily, without preparation or without caring about the consequences; **shoot home** to hit the target; **shoot it out** to settle by military action, **shoot off** to discharge a gun: to begin: to rush away, **shoot up to** kill or injure by shooting: to grow very quickly; **the whole shoot, shooting-match** (*coll.*) the whole lot. [O.E. *scēotan*, in some senses merging with Fr. *chute, fall.*]

shop *shop, n.* a building or room in which goods are sold: a place where mechanics work, or where any kind of industry is pursued: a place of employment or activity, esp. a theatre: prison (*slang*): talk about one's own business.—*v.i.* to visit shops, esp. for the purpose of buying.—*v.t.* to imprison, or cause to be imprisoned (*slang*): to betray (someone), e.g. to inform against (him) to the police (*slang*; *n.* **shopp'er**). to give employment to:—*pr.p.* **shopp'ing**; *pa.p* **shopped.**—*ns.* **shop'ful; shopp'er** one who shops: a shopping bag, basket; **shopp'ing** visiting shops to buy or see goods: goods thus bought.—*adj.* for shopping. —*adj.* **shopp'y.**—**shop'-assist'ant** one who sells goods ın a shop; **shop'-bell** a bell that rıngs at the opening of a shop-door; **shop'-boy, -girl** a boy or girl employed ın a shop; **shop'breaker** one who breaks ınto a shop; **shop'breaking; shop'-door; shop-floor'** that part of a factory, etc. housing the production machinery and the maın part of the workforce: the people who work on the shop-floor.—*adj.* **shop'-floor.**—**shop'-front; shop'keeper** one who keeps a shop of his own; **shop'keeping; shop'-lift'er; shop'-lift'ing** stealing from a shop; **shop'man** one who serves in a shop: **shopping bag, basket** a receptacle for goods bought; **shopping centre** a place where there ıs a concentration of shops of dıfferent kınds; **shopping lıst** a list of items to be bought; **shopping precinct** see **precinct;** **shop's sign** ındıcatıon of trade and occupier's name over a shop.—*adj.* **shop'-soiled** somewhat tarnished by shop exposure.—**shop'-stew'ard** a representatıve of factory or workshop hands elected from theır own number; **shop'-walker** one who walks about in a shop to see customers attended to; **shop'-wın'dow** a wın-dow of a shop in whıch wares are dısplayed; **shop's woman.**—*adj* **shop'worn** shop-soiled.—**all over the shop** dispersed all around; **on the shop floor** among the workers ın a factory or workshop; **set up shop** to open a trading establıshment: to begın operations generally; **shop around** to compare prıces and qualıty of goods at varıous shops before makıng a purchase, **talk shop** to talk about one's own work or business; **the wrong shop** the wrong place to look for, e.g. sympathy or help. [O.E. *sceoppa*, a treasury.]

shoran *shor'an, n.* a system of aircraft navigation using the measurement of the tıme taken for two dıs-patched radar signals to return from known locations. [*Short range navigation.*]

shore¹ *shōr, shôr, n.* the land bordering on the sea or a great sheet of water: the foreshore.—*v.t.* to set on shore.—*adj.* **shore'less** havıng no shore, unlimited — *adj.* and *adv.* **shore'ward.**—*adv.* **shore'wards.**— **shore'-crab** a crab (*Carcınus maenas*) very common between tidemarks.—*adj.* **shore'-going** going, or for going, ashore: land-dwelling.—**shore'-leave** leave of absence to go ashore; **shore'lıne** the line of meeting of land and water: a rope connecting a net with the land; **shore'man** a dweller on the shore: a landsman; **shore's weed** a plant of lake-margıns of the plantain family.— **on shore** on the land: ashore. [M.E. *schore.*]

shore² *shōr, shôr, n.* a prop.—*v.t.* to prop (often with *up*).—*ns.* **shor'er; shor'ing** propping: a set of props. [Cf. Du. *schoor,* O.N. *skortha.*]

shore³ *shōr, shôr, pa.t.,* **shorn** *shorn, pa.p.* of **shear.**

short *shôrt, adj.* of little length, tallness, extent, or duration: in the early future (as *short day, date*): con-cise: curt: abrupt: snappish: crısp yet readily crumb-lıng: brittle: on the hither side: failing to go far enough or reach the standard: deficient: lacking: scanty, ın ınadequate supply: in want, ill supplied: in default: unable to meet engagements: pertaining to the sale of what one cannot supply: in accentual verse, loosely, unaccented (*pros.*): undiluted with water, neat (*coll.*)' of certaın fielding positions, rela-tively near the batsman (*cricket*).—*adv.* brıefly: abruptly: without leaving a stump: on this or the near sıde: see **sell short:** at a disadvantage (e.g. *taken short*).—*n.* that which ıs short: shortness, abbrevia-tion, summary: a short-cırcuit: (ın *pl.*) short trousers (i.e. thigh-length, as opposed to ankle-length): (ın *pl.*) undershorts (*U.S.*): (ın *pl.*) the bran and coarse part of meal, ın mixture: (ın *pl.*) short-dated secur-ities: a short film subordinate to a maın film ın a programme: a short alcoholıc drink (*coll*).—*v.t* to shortchange.—*n* and *v.t.* to short-circuit.—*n* **short'age** a lack, deficiency.—*v.t.* **short'en** to make shorter. to make to seem short or to fall short: to

draw in or back: to check: to make friable (by adding butter, lard, etc.).—*v.t.* to become shorter.—*ns.* **short'ener; short'ening** making or becomıng shorter: fat for making pastry.*short;* **short'ıe, short'y** (*coll.*) a very short person, garment, etc.—Also *adj.*—*adj.* **short'ısh.**—*adv.* **short'ly** soon: brıefly: curtly: a little: with shortness in that whıch ıs ındıcated.—*n.* **short'ness.**—**short'bread** a brittle crumbling cake of flour and butter; **short'cake** shortbread or other frıable cake: a lıght cake, prepared in layers with fruit between, served with cream (*U.S.*).—*v.t.* **short'change'** to give less than the correct change to: to deal dishonestly wıth (a person).—*adj.* **short's change'** pertaining to cheatıng.—**shortchan'ger; short'-cır'cuit** a new path of comparatıvely low resistance between two poınts of a cırcuit (*elect.*): a deviation of current by a path of low resıstance.—*v.t.* to establish a short-cırcuit in: to interconnect where there was obstruction between (*surg.*): to provıde with a short-cut.—*v.ı.* to cut off current by a short-cırcuit: to save a roundabout passage.—**short'comıng** an act of comıng or falling short: a neglect of, or failure ın, duty: a defect; **short commons** minimum rations; **short covering** (*Stock exchange*) the buying of securities, etc. to cover a short sale: the securities, etc. bought for this purpose.—*adj.* **short'-cut** cut short instead of ın long shreds.—*n* tobacco so cut: (also **short'cut, short cut**) a shorter way than the usual.—*adj.* **short-dāt'ed** having little time to run from its date, as a bill: of securities, redeemable in under five years.—**short'-dıvı'sıon** division without writing down the working out; **short'fall** the fact or amount of falling short; **short game** in golf, play on and around the green(s); **short'hand** a method of swift writing to keep pace with speaking: writing of such a kind.—Also *adj.*—*adj.* **short'-hand'ed** short of workers: with short hands.—**short'-horn** one of a breed of cattle having very short horns—*Durham* or *Teeswater;* **short'-leg** (*cricket*) the fielder or the field near (and in line with) the batsman on the leg side.— *adj.* **short'-lıfe** having a short duration, existence, etc. —**short lıst** (see also **leet¹**) a selected list of candi-dates for an office.—*v.t.* **short'-lıst** to include (some-one) in a short lıst.—*adj.* **short'-lıved** (or *-livd*) living or lasting only for a short time.—**short measure** less than the amount promised or paid for; **short odds** in betting, a nearly even chance, favourable odds in terms of risk, unfavourable in terms of potential gain. —*adj.* **short'-range** of or relating to a short distance or period of time.—**short score** a musical score with some of the parts omitted; **short selling** see **sell short** under **sell.**—*adj.* **short'-sight'ed** having clear sight only of near objects: lacking foresight.—*adv.* **short' sight'edly.**—**short'-sight'edness; short'-slip** (*cricket*) the fielder, or the field, near the batsman on the off side behind the wicket.—*adj.* **short'-spō'ken** curt in speech.—**short'sword** a sword with a short blade.— *adjs.* **short'-tem'pered** easily put into a rage; **short's term** extending over a short time: concerned with the immediate present and future as distinct from time further ahead.—**short-time'** (the condition of) working fewer than the normal number of hours per week.—*adj.* **short'-time.**—**short'-wave** of, or using wavelengths 50 metres or less; **short'-wınd'ed** soon becoming breathless.—**by a short head** by a distance less than the length of a horse's head: narrowly, barely; **caught, taken short** (*coll.*) having a sudden need to relieve oneself; **cut short** see **cut; fall short** see **fall; for short** as an abbreviation; **in short** in a few words; **in short supply** not available ın desired quan-tıty, scarce; **in the short run** over a brief period of time; **make short work of** to settle or dispose of promptly; **run short** see **run; short for** a shortened form of; **short of** less than: without going so far as: (also **short on**; *coll.*) having insufficient supplies of; **stop short** come to a sudden standstill; **take (up) short** to take by surprise or at a disadvantage: to interrupt curtly. [O.E. *sc(e)ort.*]

shot¹ *shot, pa.t.* and *pa.p.* of **shoot.—adj.** hit or killed by shooting: elongated by rapid growth: with warp and weft of different colours: showing play of colours: rid (with *of; coll.*).

shot² *shot, n.* act of shooting: a blast: an explosive charge: a photographic exposure, esp. for motion pictures: a unit in film-production: a stroke or the like in a game: an attempt: a spell: a turn: a guess: an aggressive remark: an injection (*coll.*): a dram (*coll.*): a marksman: a projectile, esp. one that is solid and spherical, without bursting charge: a cannon-ball: a weight for putting (*athletics*): a small pellet of which several are shot together: such pellets collectively: flight of a missile, or its distance: range, reach: a payment, esp. of a tavern reckoning: a contribution. *—v.t.* to load with shot:—*pr.p.* **shot'ting;** *pa.t.* and *pa.p.* **shot'ed.—adj. shot'ed.—shot'-blasting** the cleaning of metal, etc. by means of a stream of shot; **shot'gun** a smooth-bore gun for small shot, a fowling-piece.—*adj.* pertaining to a shotgun: involving coercion (e.g. *a shotgun merger, marriage*): **shot'-put** in athletics, the event of putting the shot; **shot'-tower** a tower where small shot is made by dropping molten lead into water.—**a shot in the arm** an injection in the arm (*med.*): a revivifying injection, as of money, new effort, fresh talent; **a shot across the bows** one thus directed so as to warn a ship off rather than damage it; **a shot in the dark** a random guess; **big shot** (*coll.*) a person of importance; **like a shot** instantly, quickly: eagerly, willingly. [O.E. *sc(e)ot, gesc(e)ot;* cf. **shoot.**]

shotten *shot'n, old* or *dial. pa.p.* of **shoot.—adj** (of a herring, etc.) having ejected the spawn: effete, exhausted.

should *shŏod, pa.t.* of **shall.** [O.E. *sceolde.*]

shoulder *shōl'dər, n.* the part about the junction of the body with the fore-limb: the upper joint of a foreleg cut for the table: part of a garment covering the shoulder: a bulge, protuberance, offshoot like the human shoulder: a curve like that between the shoulder and the neck or side: either edge of a road.— *v.t.* to thrust with the shoulder: to take upon the shoulder or in a position of rest against the shoulder: to undertake: to take responsibility for.—*v.i.* to jostle.—*adj.* **shoul'dered** having a shoulder or shoulders (**shouldered arch** a lintel on corbels).—*n.* and *adj.* **shoul'dering.—shoul'der-bag** a bag suspended from a strap worn over the shoulder; **shoul'der-belt** a belt that passes across the shoulder; **shoul'der-blade** the broad, flat, blade-like bone forming the back of the shoulder, the scapula; **shoul'der-bone** shoulder-blade; **shoul'der-gir'dle** the pectoral girdle. *—adv.* **shoul'der-height** as high as the shoulder.—*adj.* and *adv.* **shoul'der-high',** as high as the shoulder.— **shoul'der-joint; shoul'der-knot** a knot worn as an ornament on the shoulder; **shoul'der-mark** (*U.S.*) a badge of naval rank worn on the shoulder; **shoul'der-note** a note at the upper outside corner of a page; **shoulder pad** a pad inserted into the shoulder of a garment to raise and square it;—**shoul'der-strap** a strap worn on or over the shoulder esp. one suspending a garment, etc.: a narrow strap of cloth edged with gold lace worn on the shoulder with uniform to indicate rank (*U.S.*).—**put one's shoulder to the wheel** to set to work in earnest, as if to get a coach out of the mire; **shoulder-of-mutton sail** a triangular sail; **shoulder to shoulder** side by side: in unity; (**straight**) **from the shoulder** frank(ly) and forceful(ly). [O.E.

sculdor.]

shouldest, shouldst. See shall.

shouldn't *shŏod'ənt,* a contraction of **should not.**

shout *showt, n.* a loud cry: a call: a call for a round of drinks (*slang*): a turn to buy a round of drinks (*slang*) *—v.i.* to utter a shout: to speak in a raised, esp. angry, voice (with *at*): to stand drinks all round (*slang*).— *v.t.* to utter with a shout.—*n.* **shout'er.—***n.* and *adj.* **shout'ing.—*adv.* shout'ingly.—shouting match** (*coll.*) a quarrel or argument in which both sides loudly insult each other.—**all over bar the shouting** of a happening, contest, etc. as good as over, virtually finished or decided; **shout down** to make (another speaker) inaudible by shouting or talking loudly. [Ety. dub., poss., as **scout²,** conn. with O.N. *skuta,* a taunt.]

shove *shuv, v.t.* and *v.i.* to thrust: to push: to jostle.— *n.* a push, thrust.—*n.* **shov'er** one who shoves.— **shove'-half'penny** a similar game.—**shove off** to push (a boat) from the shore: to go away (*coll.*). [O.E. *scūfan.*]

shovel *shuv'l, n.* a broad spade-like tool for scooping, the blade usu. curved forward at the sides: a (part of) a machine having a similar shape or function: a scoop: a shovelful.—*v.t.* to move with, or as if with, a shovel: to gather in large quantities.—*v.i.* to use a shovel:— *pr.p.* **shov'elling;** *pa.t.* and *pa.p.* **shov'elled.—***ns.* **shov'elful** as much as a shovel will hold:—*pl.* **shov'elfuls; shov'eller** one who shovels: a duck with expanded bill (more commonly **shov'eler**).—**shov'el-hat** a hat with a broad brim, turned up at the sides, and projecting in front—affected by Anglican clergy; **shov'el-head** a shark with a flattish head, related to the hammerhead. [O.E. *scofl,* from *scūfan,* to shove.]

shovel-board *shuv'l-bōrd, -bŏrd,* **shuffle-board** *shuf', ns.* an old game in which a coin or other disc was driven along a table by the hand: a modern development played in America: a deck game played with wooden discs and cues: a table for the game. [App. **shove** and **board,** confused with **shovel** and **shuffle.**]

show (now rarely **shew**) *shō, v.t.* to present to view: to exhibit: to display: to set forth: to cause or allow to be seen or known: to prove: to manifest: to indicate: to usher or conduct (with *in, out, over, round, up,* etc.). *—v.i.* to appear: to come into sight: to be visible: to arrive, turn up (*slang*):—*pa.t.* **showed,** rarely **shewed** (*shŏd*); *pa.p.* **shown, shewn** (*shōn*), or **showed, shewed.—***n.* act of showing: display: exhibition: a sight or spectacle: an entertainment: parade: a demonstration: appearance: plausibility: pretence: a sign, indication: performance: in childbirth, a small discharge of blood and mucus at the start of labour.— *adj.* of the nature of, or connected with, a show: for show.—*n.* **shower** (*shō'ər*).—*adv.* **show'ily.—***ns.* **show'iness; show'ing** act of displaying, pointing out, etc.: appearance: a setting forth, representation.— *adj.* **show'y** cutting a dash: making a show: ostentatious: gaudy: flashy.—**show'-boat** a steamer serving as a travelling theatre; **show'bread see shew-bread; show business** the entertainment business, esp. the branch of the theatrical profession concerned with variety entertainments—also (*coll.*) **show'biz, show biz; show'card** a shopkeeper's advertising card; **show'case** a glass case for a museum, shop, etc.: any setting in which something or someone can be displayed to advantage.—**show'-down** in poker, putting one's cards face-up on the table: the name of a card-game similar to poker: an open disclosure of plans, means, etc.: an open clash; **show'girl** a girl who takes part in variety entertainments usu. as a dancer or singer; **show'ground** ground where a show is held; **show house** a house, usu. on a new housing estate, opened for public viewing as an example of the builders' work; **show'jumper; show'jumping** competition in which riders have to jump a succession of obstacles; **show'man** one who exhibits, or owns, a show: one who is skilled in publicly showing off things (e.g. his own merits).—*adj.* **show'manly.**— **show'manship** skilful display, or a talent for it; **show's off** one who behaves in an ostentatious manner in an effort to win admiration; **show'piece** something considered an especially fine specimen of its type, etc.: an exhibit, something on display, etc.; **show'place** a place visited or shown as a sight: a place where shows are exhibited; **show'room** a room where goods or samples are displayed; **show-stopper** see **stop the show** below; **show trial** one held purely for propaganda, the charges usu. being false, and the confession forcibly extracted.—**for show** for the sake of outward appearances: to attract notice; **give the show away** to let out a secret; **good, bad, show** well, not well, done: fortunate, unfortunate, occurrence or circumstances; **run the show** (*coll.*) to take, be in charge: to take over, dominate; **show a leg** (*coll.*) to get out of bed; **show fight** to show a readiness to resist; **show forth** to manifest, proclaim; **show off** to display or behave ostentatiously; **show of hands** a vote indicated by raising hands; **show up** to expose: to appear to advantage or disadvantage: to show clearly by contrast: to be present, arrive (*coll.*); **steal the show** to win the most applause: to attract the most publicity or admiration; **stop the show** to be applauded with so much enthusiasm as to interrupt the show, play, etc. (hence *n.* **show'-stopper** the act, line, etc. so applauded). [O.E. *scēawian,* to look.]

shower *show(˘ə)r, n.* a short fall, as of rain: a fall of drops of liquid: a fall, flight, or accession of many things together, as meteors, arrows, blows, volcanic dust or (esp. *U.S.*) wedding gifts: a party at which gifts are presented (*U.S.*): a shower-bath: fast particles in number arising from a high-energy particle: a disparaging term for a particular group of people (*slang*).—*v.t* and *v.i.* to drop in shower or showers: to sprinkle.—*v.i.* to take a shower-bath.—*adj.* **shower'- ful.**—*n.* **shower'iness.**—*n., adj.* **shower'ing.**—*adjs.* **shower'less; shower'y** marked by showers: raining by fits and starts.—**shower'-bath** a bath of water showered from above: the apparatus for the purpose. —*adj.* **shower'proof** impervious to showers.—*v.t.* to render showerproof. [O.E. *scūr;* O.N. *skūr,* Ger *Schauer.*]

shrank *shrangk, pa.t.* of **shrink.**

shrapnel *shrap'nl, n.* a shell filled with musketballs with a bursting-charge, invented by General *Shrapnel* (1761–1842): pieces scattered by the bursting of a shrapnel or other shell: any later improved version of the orig. shell.

shred *shred, n.* a scrap, fragment: a paring, esp. a curled paring: a ragged strip.—*v.t.* to cut,' cut off: to cut, tear or scrape into shreds.—*v.i.* to be reduced to shreds:—*pr.p.* **shredd'ing;** *pa.t.* and *pa.p.* **shredd'ed, shred.**—*adj.* **shredd'ed.**—*ns.* **shredd'er** a device or machine for shredding, e.g. vegetables, waste paper; **shredd'ing.**—*adjs.* **shredd'y; shred'less.** [O.E. *scrēade.*]

shrew *shrōō, n.* a small mouselike animal, formerly thought venomous: a brawling, troublesome person, now only a woman, a scold.—*adj.* **shrewd** severe, hard: uncomfortably near the mark: biting, keen: (now usually) showing keen practical judgment, astute.—*adv.* **shrewd'ly.**—*n.* **shrewd'ness.**—*adj.* **shrew'ish** of the nature of a shrew or scold: ill-natured.—*adv.* **shrew'ishly.**—*n.* **shrew'ishness.**— **shrew'mouse** a shrew:—*pl.* **shrew'mice.** [O.E. *scrēawa,* a shrewmouse.]

Shri. See Sri.

shriek *shrēk, v.t.* to utter a shriek.—*v.t.* to utter shriekingly.—*n.* a shrill outcry: a wild piercing scream.—*n.* **shriek'er.**—*n.* and *adj.* **shriek'ing.**—*adv.* **shriek'- ingly.** [Cf. **screak, screech.**]

shrieval *shrē'vl, adj.* pertaining to a sheriff.—*n.* **shriev'alty** office, term of office, or area of jurisdiction, of a sheriff. [**shrieve,** obs. form of **sheriff.**]

shrift *shrift, n.* absolution: confession.—**short shrift** short time for confession before execution: summary treatment of a person or a matter. [O.E *scrift— scrīfan,* to shrive.]

shrike *shrīk, n.* a butcher-bird, a passerine bird, of which some kinds impale small animals on thorns. [App. O.E. *scrīc,* perh. thrush.]

shrill *shril, adj.* high-pitched and piercing: keen.—*v.t.* and *v.i.* to sound or cry shrilly.—*n.* and *adj.* **shrill'ing.** —*n.* **shrill'ness.**—*adv.* **shril'ly.**—*adjs.* **shrill's tongued; shrill'-voiced.** [Cf. L.G. *schrell,* whence prob. Ger. *schrill.*]

shrimp *shrimp, n.* a small edible crustacean, esp. a decapod of *Crangon* or kindred genus: the colour of a shrimp, a bright pink: a very small person (*coll.*).— *v.i.* to fish for shrimps.—*n.* **shrimp'er.**—*n.* and *adj.* **shrimp'ing.**—**shrimp'-girl** a girl who sells shrimps; **shrimp'-net.**

shrine *shrīn, n.* orig. a chest or cabinet: a casket for relics or an erection over it: a place hallowed by its associations.—*v.t.* to enshrine.—*adj.* **shri'nal.** [O.E. *scrīn*—L. *scrīnium,* a case for papers—*scrībēre,* to write.]

shrink *shringk, v.i.* to contract: to shrivel: to give way: to draw back: to withdraw: to feel repugnance: to recoil.—*v.t.* to cause to contract: to withdraw: to fix by allowing to contract:—*pa.t.* **shrank,** old-fashioned **shrunk;** *pa.p.* **shrunk.**—*n.* act of shrinking: contraction: a psychiatrist, contracted from **head'shrinker** (*slang*).—*adj.* **shrink'able.**—*ns.* **shrink'age** a contraction into a less compass: extent of such diminution: in marketing, the loss of weight, size, values, etc. during shipping, preparation for sale, etc.; **shrink'er.**—*adv.* **shrink'ingly.**—*adjs.* **shrunk, shrunk'en** contracted, reduced, shrivelled.—**shrink'pack** a shrinkwrapped package.—*adjs.* **shrink'-proof, -resis'tant** that will not shrink on washing.—**shrink'-resis'tance.**—*v.t.* **shrink'wrap** to package (goods) in a clear plastic film that is subsequently shrunk (e.g. by heating) so that it fits tightly. [O.E. *scrincan, scranc, gescruncen.*]

shrive *shrīv, v.t.* to hear a confession from and give absolution to: to disburden by confession or otherwise.—*v.i.* to receive or make confession:—*pa.t.* **shrōve, shrived;** *pa.p.* **shriven** (*shriv'ən*), **shrived.**—*n.* **shri'ver** one who shrives: a confessor. [O.E. *scrīfan,* to write, to prescribe penance—L. *scrībēre.*]

shrivel *shriv'l, v.i.* and *v.t.* to contract into wrinkles:— *pr.p.* **shriv'elling;** *pa.t.* and *pa.p.* **shriv'elled.** [Cf. Sw. dial. *skryvla,* to wrinkle.]

shroff *shrof, n.* in the East, a banker, money-changer, or money-lender: an expert in detection of bad coin. —*v.t.* to examine with that view.—*v.i.* to practise money-changing. [Ar. *sarrāf.*]

shroud *shrowd, n.* a winding-sheet: a covering, screen, shelter, or shade: (in *pl.*) a set of ropes from the masthead to a ship's sides to support the mast.—*v.t.* to enclose in a shroud: to cover: to hide: to shelter.— *adj.* **shroud'ed.**—*n.* and *adj.* **shroud'ing.**—*adj.* **shroud'less.**—**shroud'-line** any one of the cords of a parachute by which the load is suspended from the canopy. [O.E. *scrūd.*]

shrove *shrōv, pa.t.* of **shrive.**

Shrove *shrōv, n.* (*obs.*) Shrovetide.—**Shrove'tide** the days preceding Ash Wednesday during which confessions were made for Lent; **Shrove Tuesday** the day before Ash Wednesday. [Related to O.E. *scrifan*, to shrive.]

shrub[1] *shrub*, *n.* a low woody plant, a bush, esp. one with little or no trunk.—*ns.* **shrubb'ery** a plantation of shrubs; **shrubb'iness.**—*adjs.* **shrubb'y** of, like, having the character of, a shrub: covered with shrubs; **shrub'less.** [O.E. *scrybb*, scrub.]

shrub[2] *shrub*, *n.* a drink of lemon or other juice with spirits, esp. rum, or (*U.S.*) of fruit juice (as raspberry) and vinegar. [Ar. *sharāb*, for *shurb*, drink.]

shrug *shrug*, *v.i.* to draw up the shoulders, a gesture expressive of doubt, indifference, etc.—*v.t.* to raise in a shrug:—*pr.p.* **shrugg'ing**; *pa.t.* and *pa.p.* **shrugged.**—*n.* an expressive drawing up of the shoulders.—**shrug off** to shake off: to show indifference to or unwillingness to tackle (e.g. responsibility, a difficulty.

shrunk, shrunken. See **shrink.**

shtick *shtik*, *n.* a familiar routine, line of chat, etc. adopted by, and associated with, a particular comedian, etc. [Yiddish *shtik*, piece, slice— M.H.G. *stücke*.]

shuck *shuk*, (*U.S.*) *n.* a husk, shell, or pod.—*v.t.* to remove the shuck from.—*ns.* **shuck'er; shuck'ing.**—*interj.* **shucks** (*slang*) expressive of disappointment, irritation or embarrassment.

shudder *shud'ər*, *v.i.* to shiver as from cold or horror. —*n.* a tremor as from cold or horror.—*n.* and *adj.* **shudd'ering.**—*adv.* **shudd'eringly.**—*adj.* **shudd'ery.** [Cf. Ger. (orig. L.G.) *schaudern*.]

shuffle *shuf'l*, *v.t.* to mix at random, as playing-cards: to jumble: to put (*out, in, off,* etc.) surreptitiously, evasively, scramblingly, or in confusion: to manipulate unfairly: to patch up: to shove (the feet) along without lifting clear: to perform with such motions.— *v.i.* to mix cards in a pack: to shift ground: to evade fair questions: to move by shoving the feet along: to shamble.—*n.* act of shuffling: a shuffling gait or dance: an evasion or artifice.—*n.* **shuff'ler.**—*n.* and *adj.* **shuff'ling.**—*adv.* **shuff'lingly.**—**shuffle off** to thrust aside, put off, wriggle out of. [Early modern; cf. **scuffle, shove, shovel.**]

shuffle-board. See **shovel-board.**

shun *shun*, *v.t.* to avoid:—*pr.p.* **shunn'ing**; *pa.t.* and *pa.p.* **shunned.** [O.E. *scunian*.]

shunt *shunt*, *v.t.* and *v.i.* to turn or move aside: to move to another track, esp. a side-track.—*v.t.* to bypass: to side-track: to shelve: to get rid of.—*v.i.* (*coll.*) to be off.—*n.* an act of shunting: a conductor diverting part of an electric current: a switch: an accident, mishap (*racing motorists' slang*).—*n.* **shunt'er.** —*n.* and *adj.* **shunt'ing.** [Perh. conn. with **shun.**]

shush *shush*, *v.t., v.i., interj.* (to) hush.

shut *shut*, *v.t.* to lock: to fasten: to bar: to stop or cover the opening of: to place so as to stop an opening: to forbid entrance into: to bring together the parts or outer parts of: to confine: to catch or pinch in a fastening.—*v.i.* to become closed: to admit of closing: to close in:—*pr.p.* **shutt'ing**; *pa.t.* and *pa.p.* **shut.**—*adj.* made fast: closed: rid (with *of; coll.*).—*n.* **shutt'er** one who, or that which, shuts: a close cover for a window: a device for regulating the opening of an aperture, as in photography, cinematography: a removable cover, gate, or piece of shuttering.—*v.t.* to close or fit with a shutter or shutters.—*adj.* **shutt'ered.**—*n.* **shutt'ering** closing and fitting with a shutter: material used as shutters: temporary support for concrete work.—**shut'-down** a temporary closing, as of a factory: the reduction of power in a nuclear reactor to the minimum; **shut'-eye** (*coll.*) sleep.—*adj.* **shut-in'** (or *shut'*) enclosed.—*n.* (*-in'; U.S.*) an invalid or cripple confined to his house.—*adj.* **shut'-out** intended to exclude, as (*bridge*) a bid to deter opponents from bidding.—**shut away** to keep hidden or repressed: to isolate: to confine; **shut down** to close down, or stop the operation of, often temporarily; **shut in** to enclose, to confine; **shut off** to exclude: to switch off; **shut out** to prevent from entering; **shut up** to close finally or completely: to confine: to cease speaking (*coll.*): to reduce to silence. [O.E. *scyttan*, to bar.]

shuttle *shut'l*, *n.* an instrument used for shooting the thread of the woof between the threads of the warp in weaving or through the loop of thread in a sewing-machine: anything that makes similar movements: rapid movement to and fro between two points: a shuttle service or the vehicle, craft, etc. used for this: a shuttlecock.—*v.t.* and *v.i.* to move shuttlewise: to move regularly between two points.—*adv.* **shutt'lewise** to and fro like a shuttle.—**shutt'lecock** a cork stuck with feathers to be driven to and fro with battledores or badminton rackets: the game played with battledores: something tossed to and fro repeatedly.—*v.t.* and *v.i.* to shuttle.—**shuttle diplomacy** shuttle-like travelling between two heads of states by an intermediary, in order to bring about agreement between them; **shuttle service** a train or other transport service moving constantly between two points. [O.E. *scytel*, dart; *scēotan*, to shoot; Dan. and Sw. *skyttel*.]

shwa. See **schwa.**

shy[1] *shī*, *adj.* shrinking from notice or approach: bashful: chary: disposed to avoidance (with *of*; also in composition, as in *workshy*): warily reluctant: (esp. in poker) short in payment:—*compar.* **shy'er** or **shī'er;** *superl.* **shy'est, shī'est.**—*v.i.* to recoil, to shrink (with *away, off*): to start aside, as a horse from fear:—*3rd pers. sing.* **shies;** *pr.p.* **shy'ing;** *pa.t.* and *pa.p.* **shied** (*shid*).—*n.* a sudden swerving aside:—*pl.* **shies.**—*n.* **shī'er, shy'er.**—*adj.* **shy'ish.**—*adv.* **shy'ly, shī'ly.**—*n.* **shy'ness.**—**fight shy of** to shrink from. [O.E. *scēoh*, timid.]

shy[2] *shī*, *v.t.* and *v.i.* to fling, toss:—*3rd pers. sing.* **shies;** *pr.p.* **shy'ing;** *pa.t.* and *pa.p.* **shied.**—*n.* a throw: a gibe: an attempt, shot: a thing to shy at:—*pl.* **shies.**—*n.* **shī'er, shy'er.**

Shylock *shī'lok*, *n.* a ruthless creditor, or a very grasping person. [From Shylock in *The Merchant of Venice*.]

shyster *shī'stər*, (*slang*) *n.* an unscrupulous or disreputable lawyer: an unscrupulous practitioner in any profession or business. [App. from **shy**[1].]

SI (**units**) *es ī* (*ū'nits*), the modern scientific system of units, used in the measurement of all physical quantities (see Appendices). [*Système International* (d'Unités).]

si *sē*, *n.* the seventh note of the scale, a later addition to the six Aretinian syllables, but superseded by *ti*. [Sancte Ioannes, the last line of the hymn which gave the Aretinian (q.v.) syllables.]

sial *sī'al*, *-əl*, *n.* the lighter partial outer shell of the earth, rich in silica and alumina.—*adj.* **sial'ic.**

siala- *sī'əl-ə-, sī-al'ə-,* **sialo-** *sī-al'ō-, -o'-*, in composition, saliva.—*adj.* **sial'ic** of, relating to, saliva.—*n.* **sialagogue** (*sī-al'ə-gog*; Gr. *agōgos*, leading) anything that stimulates flow of saliva.—Also *adj.*—*adj.* **sialagog'ic.** [Gr. *sialon*, saliva.]

sialic. See **sial** and **siala-.**

siamang *sē'ə-mang, syä'mang, n.* the largest of the gibbons, found in Sumatra and Malacca. [Malay.]

Siamese *sī-əm-ēz', adj.* of Siam (Thailand).—*n.* a native, or citizen, or the language of Siam: a Siamese cat.—**Siamese cat** a domestic fawn-coloured cat, with blue eyes and small head, prob. descended from the jungle cat of India, Africa, etc.; **Siamese twins** Chinese twins (1811–74), born in Siam, joined from

birth by a fleshy ligature: any set of twins thus joined
sib *sib, n.* a blood relation: a brother or sister.—*adj.*
akin: of canaries, inbred.—*n.* **sib'ling** a brother or
sister.—Also *adj.*—*n.* **sib'ship** a group of sibs.
[O.E. *sibb*, relationship, *gesibb*, related.]
sibilate *sib'i-lāt, v.t.* and *v.i.* to hiss.—*ns.* **sib'ilance**,
sib'ilancy.—*adj.* **sib'ilant** hissing.—*n.* a hissing consonant sound, as of *s* and *z.*—*n.* **sibila'tion.** [L.
sibilāre, -ātum, to hiss.]
sibling. See **sib.**
Sibyl *sib'il, n.* one of several ancient prophetesses
(*myth.*): (without *cap.*) a prophetess, sorceress, or
witch.—*adj.* **Sib'ylline** (*-īn*) —**Sibylline Books** prophetic books of the Cumaean Sibyl. [Gr. *Sibylla.*]
sic[1] *sik, sēk,* (L.) so, thus—printed within brackets in
quoted matter to show that the original is being
faithfully reproduced even though incorrect or apparently so.—**sic passim** (*pas'im*) so throughout.
sic[2]. Same as **sick**[2].
siccative *sik'ə-tiv, adj.* drying.—*n.* a drying agent. [L
siccus, dry.]
sice[1] *sīs, n.* the number six at dice. [O.Fr. *sis.*]
sice[2]. Same as **syce.**
Sicilian *si-sil'yən, adj.* of Sicily.—**Sicilian Vespers** the
massacre of the French in Sicily in 1282—beginning,
according to a late tradition, at the first stroke of the
vesper-bell.
sick[1] *sik, adj.* unwell, ill: diseased: vomiting or inclined
to vomit: pining: mortified: thoroughly wearied: out
of condition: sickly: of or for the sick: (of humour,
joke, comedy) gruesome, macabre, tending to exploit
topics not normally joked about, as illness, death,
etc.: disappointed (*coll.*).—*v.t.* (*coll.*) to vomit (with
up).—*v.t.* **sick'en** to make sick: to disgust: to make
weary of anything.—*v.i.* to become sick: to be disgusted.—*n.* **sick'ener.**—*n.* and *adj.* **sick'ening.**—*adv.*
sick'eningly.—*n.* **sick'ie** (*coll.*) a day's sick leave.—
adj. **sick'ish.**—*adv.* **sick'ishly.**—*ns.* **sick'ishness;**
sick'liness.—*adj.* **sick'ly** inclined to be ailing: feeble:
pallid: suggestive of sickness: mawkish: of sickness or
the sick.—*n.* **sick'ness.**—**sick'-bay** a compartment for
sick and wounded on a ship (also **sick'-berth**): an
infirmary at a boarding-school, etc ; **sick'-bed** a bed
on which someone lies sick; **sick'-ben'efit** a benefit
paid to one who is out of work by illness; **sick's
head'ache** headache with nausea; **sick'-leave** leave of
absence owing to sickness; **sick'-list** a list of sick.—
adjs. **sick'-listed** entered on the sick-list; **sick's
mak'ing** (*coll.*) sickening.—**sick'nurse** a nurse who
attends the sick; **sick'nurs'ing; sick'room** a room to
which one is confined by sickness.—**be sick** to vomit;
sick as a dog (*coll.*) vomiting profusely and unrestrainedly; **sicken for** to show early symptoms of;
sick of tired of; **sick to one's stomach** (*U.S.*) about to
vomit. [O.E. *sēoc*; Ger. *siech*, Du. *ziek.*]
sick[2] *sik, v.t.* to set upon, chase: to incite (e.g. dog) to
make an attack (on). [A variant of **seek.**]
sickle *sik'l, n.* a reaping-hook, an implement with a
curved blade and a short handle.—**sick'le-bill** a bird
of paradise, humming-bird, etc., with sickle-shaped
bill; **sick'le-feath'er** a cock's tail feather.—*adj.*
sick'le-shaped.—**sickle-cell(ed) anaemia** a severe
anaemia in which sickle-shaped red blood-cells appear in the blood. [O.E. *sicol, sicel,* perh.—L.
secula—secāre, to cut.]
side *sīd, n.* a line or surface forming part of a boundary,
esp. that which is longer: the part near such a boundary: a surface or part turned in some direction, esp.
one more or less upright, or one regarded as right or
left, not front or back, top or bottom: the part of the
body between armpit and hip: half of a carcase
divided along the medial plane: either of the extended surfaces of anything in the form of a sheet: a

page: a portion of space lying in this or that direction
from a boundary or a point: the father's or mother's
part of a genealogy: a department or division, as of a
school, a prison: an aspect: a direction: a region: a
neighbouring region: a border or bank: the slope of a
hill: the wall of a vessel or cavity: any party, team,
interest, or opinion opp. to another: part (as *on my
side,* for my part): a spin given to a billiard ball
causing it to swerve and regulating its angle of rebound: a pretentious air (*slang*).—*adj.* at or toward
the side: sidewise: subsidiary.—*v.i.* to take sides
(with *with*).—*adj.* **sid'ed** having sides: flattened on
one or more sides.—*adj.* **side'long** oblique: sloping:
sideways.—*adv.* in the direction of the side:
obliquely: on the side.—*n.* **sid'er** one who takes a
side.—*adj.* and *adv.* **side'ward.**—*adv.* **side'wards.**—
adjs., advs **side'way(s), side'wise** toward or on one
side.—*n.* **sid'ing** a short track for shunting or lying by.
—*n.* and *adj.* taking sides.—*v.t.* **si'dle** (prob. back-
formation from *sideling,* sideways) to go or edge
along sideways, esp. in a furtive or ingratiating manner.—**side'arms** weapons worn at the side; **side'-band**
(*wireless*) a band of frequencies not much above or
below the carrier frequency; **side'board** a piece of
dining-room furniture for holding plates, etc., often
with drawers and cupboards: (in *pl.*) side-whiskers;
side'burns short side-whiskers, a modification of the
rather more extensive growth pioneered by General
Burnside of America; **side'car** a jaunting-car: a small
car attached to the side of a motor-cycle usu. for the
carriage of a passenger: a kind of cocktail; **side'-chain**
a chain of atoms forming a branch attached to a ring;
side'-dish a supplementary dish; **side'-door** a door at
the side of a building or of a main door; **side'-drum** a
small double-headed drum with snares, slung from
the drummer's side or from a stand; **side'-effect, side
effect** a subsidiary effect: an effect, often undesirable, additional to the effect sought; **side'-face** profile; **side'-glance** a sidelong glance: a passing allusion;
side'-issue, side issue something subordinate, incidental, not important in comparison with main issue;
side'-kick (*slang*) partner, deputy: a special friend;
side'light light coming from the side: any incidental
illustration: a window, as opposed to a skylight: a
window above or at the side of a door: a light carried
on the side of a vessel or vehicle; **side'-line** a line
attached to the side of anything: a branch route or
track: a subsidiary trade or activity: (in *pl.*) (the area
just outside) the lines marking the edge of a football
pitch, etc., hence, a peripheral area to which
spectators or non-participants are confined.—*v.t.* to
remove (a player) from a team: to suspend from
normal operation or activity.—*adj.* and *adv.* **side'-on**
with side presented.—*adj.* **side'-road** by-road; **side'-sad-
dle** saddle for riding with both feet on one side (also
adv.); **side'-show** an exhibition subordinate to a larger
one: any subordinate or incidental doings; **side'-slip** a
skid: a lateral movement of an aircraft: a side-on
downward slide (*skiing*).—*v.i.* to slip sideways.—
sides'man a deputy churchwarden.—*adj.* **side'-split-
ting** extremely funny, making one laugh till one's
sides ache.—**side'-step** a step taken to one side: a step
attached to the side.—*v.i.* to step aside.—*v.t.* to
avoid, as by a step aside.—**side'-stroke** a stroke given
sideways: a stroke performed by a swimmer lying on
his side, **side'swipe** a blow dealt from the side, not
struck head-on: a criticism made in passing, incidentally to the main topic.—**side'-table** a table used
as a sideboard, or placed against the wall, or to the
side of the main table; **side'-track** a siding.—*v.t.* to
divert or turn aside: to shelve.—**side'-view** a view on
or from one side; **side'walk** (*U.S.*) pavement or foot-
walk.—**side'-whiskers** hair grown by a man down

either side of the face, in front of the ears; **side'winder** a rattlesnake of the southern U.S. that progresses by lateral looping motions: the name of an air-to-air missile directed at its target by means of a homing device. —**choose sides** to pick teams; **let the side down** to fail one's colleagues, associates, etc, by falling below their standard; **on the side** in addition to ordinary occupation, income, etc.; **on the short, long, tight,** etc., **side** rather too short, long, etc., than the contrary; **put on one side** to shelve; **put on side** to assume pretentious airs; **right, wrong side** the side intended to be turned outward or inward; **side by side** close together: abreast; **take sides** to range oneself with one party or other; **this side (of)** between here and .. short of. [O.E. *sīde*]

sidereal sī-dē'ri-əl, *adj.* of, like, or relative to the stars. —*n.* **sid'erostat** a mirror, or telescope with a mirror, for reflecting the rays of a star in a constant direction. —**sidereal day, time, year** day, time, year measured according to the time the earth takes to turn on its axis. [L. *sīdus*, *sīderis*, a star, constellation.]

siderite sid'ər-īt, *n.* a meteorite mainly of iron: ferrous carbonate, one of the ores of iron.—*adj.* **sideritic** (-*it'ik*).—*ns.* **sid'erolite** (Gr. *lithos*, stone) a meteorite, partly stony, partly of iron; **siderō'sis** lung disease caused by breathing in iron or other metal fragments [Gr. *sidēros*, iron.]

siderostat. See **sidereal.**

sidesman, siding, sidle, etc. See **side.**

siege sēj, *n.* investment or beleaguering of a town or fortress.—**siege'-artill'ery, siege'-gun** heavy artillery, gun, designed for use in sieges rather than in the field; **siege'craft** the art of the besieger; **siege'-works** a besieger's engineering works.—**state of siege** a condition of suspension of civil law or its subordination to military law. [O.Fr. *sege* (Fr. *siège*), seat—L. *sēdēs*, seat.]

siemens sē'menz, *n.* unit of electrical conductance (an SI additional unit), the equivalent of mho and reciprocal of ohm.

Sien(n)ese sē-e-nēz', *adj.* of Siena or its school of painting.—*n.* **sienna** (*sē-en'ə*) a fine pigment made from ferruginous ochreous earth—browny-yellow when *raw*, warm reddish-brown when *burnt* (i.e. roasted): its colour.

sierra si-er'ə, *n.* a mountain range.—*adj.* **sierr'an.** [Sp.,—L. *serra*, saw.]

siesta si-es'tə, *n.* a midday or afternoon nap. [Sp.,— L. *sexta* (*hōra*), sixth (hour).]

sieve siv, *n.* a vessel with meshed or perforated bottom for sifting—generally finer than a riddle.—*v.t.* and *v.i.* to sift.—**have a head, memory, like a sieve** to be very forgetful. [O.E. *sife.*]

sift sift, *v.t.* to separate as by passing through a sieve: to sprinkle as from a sieve: to examine closely and discriminatingly.—*v.i.* to use a sieve: to find passage as through a sieve.—*ns.* **sift'er; sift'ing** putting through a sieve: separating or sprinkling by a sieve: (in *pl.*) material separated by a sieve.—*adj.* **sift'ing.** —*adv.* **sift'ingly.** [O.E. *siftan—sife*, a sieve.]

sigh sī, *v.i.* to heave a sigh: to make a whispering sound.—*v.t.* to utter, regret, while away, bring, or render, with sighs.—*n.* a long, deep, audible respiration expressive of yearning, dejection, relief, etc.— *n.* **sigh'er**—*adjs.* **sigh'ful; sigh'ing.**—*adv.* **sigh'ingly.** —**sigh for** to yearn for. [Prob. a back-formation from the weak pa.t. of M.E. *siche*—O.E. (strong) *sīcan*; Sw. *sucka.*]

sight sīt, *n.* act, opportunity, or faculty of seeing: view: estimation: a beginning or coming to see: an instrumental observation: visual range: that which is seen: a spectacle: an object of especial interest: an unsightly, odd or ridiculous object: a guide to the eye on a gun or optical or other instrument: a sight-hole: a great many or a great deal (*slang*).—*v.t.* to catch sight of: to view: to take a sight of: to adjust the sights of.—*v.i.* to take a sight.—*adj.* **sight'ed** having sight, not blind: equipped with a sight: in composition, having sight of a particular kind, as *long-sighted*.—*n.* **sight'er** a sighting-shot.—*adj.* **sight'less** blind.—*adv.* **sight'-lessly.**—*ns.* **sight'lessness; sight'liness.**—*adjs.* **sight'ly** pleasing to look at: comely; **sight'worthy** worth looking at.—**sight'-hole** an aperture for looking through; **sight'-line** the line from the eye to the perceived object; **sight'-reader, -singer** one who can read or perform music at first sight of the notes; **sight'-reading, -singing.**—*v.i.*, *v.t.* **sight'-read.**—*v.i.* **sight'-sing.**—**sight'-screen** a screen placed behind the bowler at cricket.—*v.i.* **sight'see** to go about visiting sights, buildings, etc. of interest.—**sight'seeing; sight'seer** (*-sē-ər*).—**at sight** without previous view or study: as soon as seen: on presentation; **catch sight of** to get a glimpse of, begin to see; **keep sight of, keep in sight** to keep within seeing distance of: to remain in touch with; **lose sight of** to cease to see: to get out of touch with; **on sight** as soon as seen, at sight; **out of sight** not in a position to be seen or to see: out of range of vision; **put out of sight** to remove from view; **sight for sore eyes** a most welcome sight; **sight unseen** without having seen the object in question. [O.E. *sihth, gesiht.*]

sigla sig'lə, *n.pl.* abbreviations and signs, as in MSS, seals, etc. [L.]

sigma sig'mə, *n.* the eighteenth letter (Σ, early form C; σ, or when final, ς) of the Greek alphabet, answering to S.—*adjs.* **sig'mate** (*-māt*) shaped like Σ, C, or S; **sig'moid, -al,** C-shaped: S-shaped.—**sigmoid flexure** (*zool.*, etc.) a C-shaped or S-shaped bend: (also **sigmoid colon**) the convoluted part of the large intestine, between the descending colon and the rectum. [Gr. *sigma.*]

sign sīn, *n.* a gesture expressing a meaning: a signal: a mark with a meaning: a symbol: an emblem: a token: a portent: a miraculous token: an indication of positive or negative value, or that indicated: a device marking an inn, etc., instead of a street number: a board or panel giving a shopkeeper's name or trade, etc.: an indication: an outward evidence of disease, perceptible to an examining doctor, etc.: a trail or track (*U.S.*): a trace: a twelfth part (30°) of the zodiac, bearing the name of, but not now coincident with, a constellation.—*v.t.* to indicate, convey, communicate, direct, mark, by a sign or signs: to mark: to cross, make the sign of the cross over: to make the sign of: to attach a signature to: to write as a signature: to designate by signature: to engage by signature.—*v.i.* to make a sign: to sign one's name — *ns.* **signary** (*sig'nə-ri*) a system of symbols, as an alphabet or syllabary; **sign'er; signet** (*sig'nit*) a small seal: the impression of such a seal: a signet-ring: one of the royal seals for authenticating grants (for **Writer to the Signet** see under **write**).—**sign'board** a board bearing a notice or serving as a shop or inn sign, **sig'net-ring** a ring with a signet; **sign'-painter** one who paints signs for shops, etc.; **sign'post** a post for an inn sign. a finger-post or post supporting road-signs: an indication, clue.—*v.t.* to furnish with a signpost: to point out as a signpost does.—**sign'-writer** an expert in lettering for shop-signs, etc.; **sign'-writing.**—**sign away** to transfer by signing; **sign in, out** to sign one's name on coming in, going out; **sign off** to record departure from work: to stop work, etc: to discharge from employment: to leave off broadcasting: to signal that one does not intend to bid further (*bridge*); **sign of the cross** a gesture of tracing the form of a cross; **sign on** to engage (*v.t* or *v.i.*) for a job, etc., by signature (also **sign up**); **sign on the dotted line** to give one's consent, thereby binding oneself, to a proposed scheme, contract, etc. [Fr. *signe*—L. *signum*.]

signal *sig'nl*, *n*. an intimation, e.g. of warning, conveyed to a distance: a transmitted effect conveying a message: the apparatus used for the purpose: a piece of play intended to give information to one's partner (*cards*): an intimation of, or event taken as marking, the moment for action: an initial impulse.—*v.t.* to intimate, convey, or direct by signals: to signalise.—*v.i.* to make signals:—*pr.p.* **sig'nalling**; *pa.t.* and *pa.p.* **sig'nalled**.—*adj.* remarkable: notable.—*v.t.* **sig'nalise**, **-ize** to mark or distinguish signally.—*ns.* **sig'naller**; **sig'nalling**.—*adv.* **sig'nally** notably.— **sig'nal-box** a railway signalman's cabin; **sig'nalman** one who transmits signals: one who works railway signals. [Fr. *signal*—L. *signum*.]

signary; signatory. See **sign; signature.**

signature *sig'nə-chər*, *n*. a signing: a signed name: an indication of key, also of time, at the beginning of a line of music, or where a change occurs: a letter or numeral at the foot of a page to indicate sequence of sheets: a sheet so marked.—*n.* **sig'natory** one who has signed.—Also *adj.*—**sig'nature-tune'** a tune used to introduce, and hence associated with, a particular radio or television programme, group of performers, etc. [L.L. *signātūra*—L. *signāre*, *-ātum*, to sign.]

signet. See **sign.**

signify *sig'ni-fī*, *v.t.* to be a sign for: to mean: to denote: to betoken: to indicate or declare.—*v.i.* to be of consequence:—*pr.p.* **sig'nifying**; *pa.t.* and *pa.p.* **sig'nified**.—*adj.* **sig'nifiable**.—*n.* **signif'icance** (*-i-kəns*) meaning: import—also **signif'icancy**.—*adj.* **signif'icant** having a meaning: full of meaning: important, worthy of consideration: indicative.— *adv.* **signif'icantly**.—*n.* **significa'tion** meaning: that which is signified: importance.—*adj.* **signif'icative** (*-kə-tiv*) indicative: significant.—*adv.* **signif'icatively**.—*n.* **sig'nifier**.—**significant figures** (*arith.*) the figures 1 to 9, or ciphers occurring medially (the following numbers are expressed to three significant figures—3·15, 0·0127, 1·01). [L. *significāre*, *-ātum* —*signum*, a sign, *facĕre*, to make.]

Signor, Signior, *sē'nyōr,* **Signore** *-nyō'rā, -nyō',* *n*. an Italian word of address equivalent to Mr or sir: (without *cap.*) a gentleman.—*ns.* **Signora** (*sē-nyō'rā, -nyō'*) feminine of *Signor*, Mrs, madam: (without *cap.*) a lady; **Signorina** (*sē-nyō-rē'nā, -nyō-*) Miss: (without *cap.*) an unmarried lady; **signoria** (*-rē'ä; hist.*) the governing body of an Italian city-state.—*adj.* **signorial** see **seignior**.—*n.* **si'gnory** seignory: signoria. [It. *signor, signore.*]

sika *sē'ka, n*. a Japanese deer, small, spotted white in summer. [Jap. *shika*.]

sike, syke *sīk*, (*Scot.*) *n*. a rill or small ditch. [Northern,—O.E. *sīc*.]

Sikh *sēk, sik, n.* one of a North Indian monotheistic sect, founded by Nának (1469–1539), later a military confederacy: a Sikh soldier in the Indian army.—Also *adj.*—*n.* **Sikh'ism**. [Hind., disciple.]

silage *sī'lij, n*. fodder preserved by ensilage in a silo.— *v.t.* to put in silo. [**ensilage**, after **silo**.]

sild *sild, n*. a young herring. [Norw.]

silence *sī'lans, n*. absence of sound: abstention from sounding, speech, mention, or communication: a time of such absence or abstention: taciturnity.—*v.t.* to cause to be silent.—*interj.* be silent.—*adj.* **si'lenced**.—*n.* **si'lencer** one who or that which puts to silence: a device for reducing the sound of escaping gases by gradual expansion, used, e.g. for small-arms and internal combustion engines.—*adj.* **si'lent** noiseless: without sound: unaccompanied by sound: refraining from speech, mention, or divulging:

taciturn: not pronounced: inoperative.—*adv.* **si'lently**.—*n.* **si'lentness.**—**silent majority** those, in any country the bulk of the population, who are assumed to have sensible, moderate opinions though they do not trouble to express them publicly. [L. *silēre*, to be silent.]

silent, etc. See **silence.**

silenus *sī-lē'nas, n.* a woodland god or old satyr: **Silenus** their chief, foster-father of Bacchus, pot-bellied, bald, snub-nosed. [L. *Silēnus*—Gr. *Seilēnos*.]

silesia *sī-lē'zhə, n*. a thin, twilled cotton or linen used for lining clothes, etc., orig. made in *Silesia* (now part of Poland.).

silex *sī'leks, n.* silica. [L. *silex, silicis*, flint.]

silhouette *sil-ōō-et', n.* a shadow-outline filled in with black.—*v.t.* to represent or show in silhouette. [Étienne de *Silhouette* (1709–67), French minister of finance in 1759—reason disputed.]

silica *sil'i-kə, n.* silicon dioxide or silicic anhydride, occurring in nature as quartz, chalcedony, etc., and (amorphous and hydrated) as opal.—*adj.* composed of silica.—*n.* **sil'icate** a salt of silicic acid.—*adjs.* **siliceous, -ious** (*-ish'əs*) of, containing, silica; **silicic** (*-is'ik*) pertaining to, or obtained from, silica (**silicic acid** a general name for a group of acids containing silicon).—*n.* **sil'icide** (*-sīd*) a compound of silicon and another element.—*n.* **silicification** (*si-lis-i-fi-kā'shən*).—*adj.* **silicified** (*-lis'*).—*v.t.* **silic'ify** to render siliceous: to impregnate or cement with or replace by silica.—*v.i.* to become siliceous.—*ns.* **sil'icon** (*-kon, -kən*) a non-metallic element (Si; at. numb. 14), most abundant of all except oxygen, forming grey crystals or brown amorphous powder and having semiconducting properties; **sil'icone** any of a number of extremely stable organic derivatives of silicon, used in rubbers, lubricants, polishes, etc.; **silicosis** (*-kō'sis*) a disease caused by inhaling silica dust.—*n.* and *adj.* **silicot'ic.**—**silicon chip** see **chip**. [L. *silex, silicis*, flint.]

silicle, silicula, etc. See **siliqua.**

siliqua *sil'i-kwə, n.* a long pod of two carpels with a replum, characteristic of the Cruciferae.—Also **silique** (*-ēk'*).—*n.* **silicula** (*-ik'ū-lə*) a short pod of the same kind.—Also **sil'icle, sil'icule.**—*adjs.* **silic'ulose; sil'iquose.** [L. *siliqua*, pod, dim *silicula*.]

silk *silk, n.* a fibre produced by the larva of a silkworm moth, formed by the hardening of a liquid emitted from spinning-glands: a similar fibre from another insect or a spider: an imitation (**artificial silk**) made by forcing a viscous solution of modified cellulose through small holes: a thread, cloth, garment, or attire made from such fibres: the silk gown, or the rank, of a king's or queen's counsel.—*adj.* of or pertaining to silk.—*v.t.* to cover or clothe with silk.— *adj.* **silk'en** of, like, clad in, silk: glossy: soft and smooth: ingratiating: luxurious.—*v.t.* to make silken —*adv.* **silk'ily.**—*n.* **silk'iness.**—*adj.* **silk'y.**—**silk'-hat'** a top hat; **silk'worm** the moth (*Bombyx mori* or other) whose larva produces silk.—**silk-screen printing, process** a stencil process in which the colour applied is forced through silk or other fine-mesh cloth; **take silk** to become a K.C. or Q.C. [O.E. *seolc*—L. *sēricum*; see **Seric**.]

sill, cill *sil, n.* the timber, stone, etc., at the foot of an opening, as for a door, window, embrasure, port, dock-entrance, or the like: the bottom (of a title-page, a plough, a ledge): a bed of rock (*mining*): a sheet of intrusive rock more or less parallel to the bedding (*geol.*). [O.E. *syll*.]

sillabub. Same as **syllabub.**

silly *sil'i, adj.* feeble-minded: senseless: close-in (*cricket*; e.g. *silly mid-off*).—*n.* a silly person.—*adv.* **sill'ily.**—*n.* **sill'iness.**—**sill'y-bill'y** (*coll.*) a foolish person; **silly season** a season, usu. late summer, when newspapers fill up with trivial matter for want of more newsworthy material. [O.E. *sælig*.]

silo *sī'lō*, *n.* a pit or airtight chamber for storing grain, or for ensilage, or for storing other loose materials: a storage tower above ground, typically tall and cylindrical: an underground chamber housing a guided missile ready to be fired:—*pl.* **sī'los.**—*v.t.* to put, keep, in a silo:—*pa.p.* **sī'lo'd, sī'loed.** [Sp.,—L. *sīrus*—Gr. *siros, sīros, seiros,* a pit.]

silt *silt*, *n.* fine sediment.—*v.t.* to choke, block, cover, with silt (with *up*).—*v.i.* to become silted up.—*n.* **silta'tion.**—*adj.* **silt'y.** [M.E. *sylt.*]

Silurian *sil-ōō'ri-ən, -ū',* adj. of the *Sil'ūrēs,* a British tribe of S. Wales, etc.: applied by Murchison in 1835 to the geological system preceding the Devonian.—Also *n.*

silva *sil'və,* *n.* the assemblage of trees in a region:—*pl.* **sil'vas** or **sil'vae** (*-vē*).—*adj.* **sil'van** of woods: woodland: wooded.—*n.* a wood-god: a forest-dweller.—*adjs.* **silvat'ic, silves'trian** of the woods: woodland: rustic.—*n.* **silvicul'ture** forestry.—All these words are often found spelt with *y.* [L. *silva* (sometimes *sylva*), a wood.]

silver *sil'vər,* *n.* a white precious metal (Ag, for L. *argentum*; at. numb. 47): silver money: silver ware: cutlery, sometimes even when not of silver: a silver medal.—*adj.* of or like silver: silver-coloured: clear and ringing in tone.—*v.t.* to cover with silver: to make silvery.—*v.i.* to become silvery.—*ns.* **sil'veriness; sil'vering** coating with, or of, silver or quicksilver.—*v.t.* **silverise, -ize** to coat or treat with silver.—*adjs.* **sil'vern** made of silver: silvery; **sil'very** like silver: silver-coloured: light in tone.—**sil'ver-bath** (*phot.*) a solution of a silver salt, or a vessel for it, for sensitising plates; **sil'ver-bell** snowdrop-tree (*Halesia*); **sil'ver-fish** Lepisma, a bristletail; **sil'ver-foil'** silver-leaf; **sil'ver-fox'** an American fox with white-tipped black fur; **sil'ver-gilt** gilded silver. —Also *adj.*—**sil'ver-glance'** argentite; **silver iodide** a yellow powder that darkens when exposed to light, is used in photography, is scattered on clouds to cause rainfall, and has various medical uses; **silver jubilee** a twenty-fifth anniversary; **sil'ver-leaf** silver beaten into thin leaves: a disease of plum-trees; **silver medal** in athletics competitions, etc., the medal awarded as second prize; **silver nitrate** a poisonous colourless crystalline salt that turns grey or black in the presence of light or organic matter, and has uses in photography, as an antiseptic, etc.; **sil'ver-pap'er** fine white tissue-paper: silver-foil: (usu.) tinfoil; **sil'ver-plate'** utensils of silver: electroplate.—*adj.* **sil'ver-pla'ted.** —**sil'ver-point** the process or product of drawing with a silver-tipped pencil; **silver screen** the cinema screen. —**sil'verside** the top of a round of beef; **sil'versmith** a worker in silver.—*adj.* **sil'ver-tongued** plausible, eloquent.—**sil'ver-voiced.**—**silver wedding** the twenty-fifth wedding anniversary.—**born with a silver spoon in one's mouth** born to affluence. [O.E. *silfer, seolfor.*]

silvestrian, silviculture. See **silva.**

sima *sī'mə,* *n.* the part of the earth's crust underlying the sial. [From *silicon* and *magnesium.*]

simian *sim'i-ən,* adj. of the apes: apelike. [L. *sīmia,* ape.]

similar *sim'i-lər,* adj. (with *to*) like: resembling: exactly corresponding in shape, without regard to size (*geom.*).—*n.* **similarity** (*-lar'i-ti*).—*adv.* **sim'ilarly.** [Fr. *similaire*—L. *similis,* like.]

simile *sim'i-li,* (*rhet.*) *n.* (an) explicit likening of one thing to another:—*pl.* **sim'iles.**—*adj.* **sim'ilative** expressing similarity.—*n.* **simil'itude** likeness: semblance: comparison: parable. [L. neut. of *similis,* like.]

similor *sim'i-lōr,* *n.* a yellow alloy used for cheap jewellery. [Fr.,—L. *similis,* like, *aurum,* gold.]

simmer *sim'ər, v.i.* and *v.t.* to boil gently.—*v.i.* to be near boiling or breaking out.—*n.* a simmering state. —**simmer down** to calm down. [Earlier *simper.*]

simnel *sim'nl,* *n.* a sweet cake usu. covered with marzipan for Christmas, Easter, or Mothering Sunday.— Also **sim'nel-bread', -cake'.** [O.Fr. *simenel*—L. *simila,* fine flour.]

simony *sī'mən-i, sim'ən-i,* *n.* the buying or selling of a benefice.—*n.* **simō'niac** one guilty of simony.—*adjs.* **simoni'acal.**—*adv.* **simoni'acally.**—*n.* **sī'monist** one who practises or defends simony. [*Simon* Magus (Acts viii).]

simoom *si-mōōm',* *n.* a hot suffocating desert wind.— Also **simoon'.** [Ar. *samûm*—*samm,* to poison.]

simpatico *sim-pat'i-kō,* adj. sympathetic in the sense of congenial. [It.]

simper *sim'pər, v.i.* to smile in a silly, affected manner. —*n.* a silly or affected smile.—*adj.* **simp'ering.**—*adv.* **simp'eringly.** [Cf. Norw. *semper,* smart.]

simple *sim'pl,* adj. consisting of one thing or element: not complex or compound: not divided into leaflets (*bot.*): easy: plain: unornate: unpretentious: mean, sorry: mere, sheer: ordinary: unlearned or unskilled: of humble rank or origin: unaffected: artless: guileless: unsuspecting: credulous: weak in intellect: silly.—*n.* a simple person (also collectively) or thing: a medicine of one constituent: hence a medicinal herb.—*ns.* **sim'pleness; sim'pleton** a weak or foolish person, one easily imposed on (*coll.* short form **simp**); **simplicity** (*-plis'*); **simplifica'tion** the process, or an instance, of making simple or simpler.—*adj.* **sim'plificative.**—*n.* **sim'plifier.**—*v.t.* **sim'plify** to make simple, simpler, or less difficult:—*pr.p.* **sim'plifying;** *pa.t.* and *pa.p.* **sim'plified.**—*n.* **sim'plism** affected simplicity: oversimplification of a problem or situation.—*adj.* **simplis'tic** tending to oversimplify, making no allowances for problems and complexities: naïve.—*advs.* **simplis'tically; sim'ply** in a simple manner: considered by itself: alone: merely: without qualification: veritably: absolutely: really (*coll.*).—**simple fraction** a fraction that has whole numbers as numerator and denominator; **simple fracture** see **fracture; simple interest** interest calculated on the principal only.—*adj.* **simple-minded** lacking intelligence: foolish.—**sim'ple-mind'edness; simple sentence** a sentence with one predicate. [Fr. *simple,* and L. *simplus, simplex.*]

simpliste *sē-plēst, sim-plēst', sim'plist,* adj. simplistic, naïve. [Fr.]

simulacrum *sim-ū-lā'krəm,* *n.* an image: a semblance: —*pl.* **simula'cra, -crums.**—Also **sim'ulacre.** [L. *simulācrum.*]

simulate *sim'ū-lāt, v.t.* to feign: to have or assume a false appearance of: to mimic.—*adj.* **sim'ulated** (of a material, e.g. fur, leather, wood) not of such a material but made (usu. in an inferior material) to look like it: not genuine, feigned.—*n.* **simula'tion** feigning: mimicry: the making of working replicas or representations of machines or the re-creation of a situation, environment, etc. for demonstration or for analysis of problems.—*adj.* **sim'ulative.**—*n.* **sim'ulator** one who or that which simulates: a device used for simulating required conditions, etc., e.g. for training purposes.—*adj.* **sim'ulatory.**—**simulated pearl** a bead resembling a pearl. [L. *simulāre, -ātum;* cf. **similar, simultaneous.**]

simulcast *sim'əl-käst,* *n.* a programme broadcast simultaneously on radio and television: the transmission of such a programme.—Also *v.t.* [*simul*taneous and broad*cast.*]

simultaneous *sim-əl-tā'nyəs*, (U.S.) *sīm'ul-*, *adj.* being or happening at the same time: satisfied by the same roots (of equations) (*math.*).—*ns.* **simultaneity** (*-ə-nē'i-ti*), **simultā'neousness.**—*adv.* **simultā'neously.** [L. *simul*, at the same time.]

sin[1] *sin*, *n.* moral offence or shortcoming, esp. from the point of view of religion: condition of so offending: an offence generally: a shame, pity.—*v.i.* to commit sin. —*v.t.* to commit:—*pr.p.* **sinn'ing;** *pa.t.* and *pa.p.* **sinned.**—*adj.* **sin'ful** tainted with sin: wicked: involving sin: morally wrong.—*n.* **sin'fulness.**—*adj.* **sin'less.**—*adv.* **sin'lessly.**—*ns.* **sin'lessness; sinn'er.**—**sin bin** in ice-hockey, etc., an enclosure to which a player is sent for a statutory length of time when suspended from a game for unruly behaviour.—**sin'offering** a sacrifice in expiation of sin.—**live in sin** to cohabit in an unmarried state; **original sin** see **origin.** [O.E. *synn*.]

sin[2]. See **sine**[1].

Sinanthropus *sin-* or *sin-an'thrō-pəs* or *-thrō'*, *n.* Peking (fossil) man. [Gr. *Sīnai*, (the) Chinese, *anthrōpos*, man.]

sinapism *sin'ə-pizm*, *n.* a mustard plaster. [Gr. *sināpi*.]

since *sins*, *adv.* from that time on: after that time: past: ago.—*prep.* after: from the time of.—*conj.* from the time that: seeing that: because. [M.E. *sins, sithens*.]

sincere *sin-sēr'*, *adj.* pure, unmixed: unadulterated: unfeigned: genuine: free from pretence: the same in reality as in appearance.—*adv.* **sincere'ly.**—*ns.* **sincere'ness, sincerity** (*-ser'*). [Fr. *sincère*—L. *sincērus*, clean.]

sinciput *sing'si-put*, *n.* the forepart of the head or skull.—*adj.* **sincip'ital.** [L., —*sēmi-*, half, *caput*, head.]

sine[1] *sin*, (*math.*) *n.* orig. the perpendicular from one end of an arc to the diameter through the other: now (as a function of an angle) the ratio of the side opposite it (or its supplement) in a right-angled triangle to the hypotenuse.—*abbrev.* **sin.**—*adj.* **sinical** (*sin'i-kl*).—**sine curve** a curve showing the relationship between the size of an angle and its sine, a sinusoid; **sine wave** any oscillation whose graphical representation is a sine curve. [L. *sinus*, a bay.]

sine[2] *si'nē, si'ne*, (L.) *prep.* without.—**sine die** (*dī'ē, di'ā*) without a day (appointed)—of a meeting or other business, indefinitely adjourned; **sine dubio** (*dū'bi-ō, dōōb'i-ō*) without doubt; **sine prole** (*prō'lē, prō'le*) without issue; **sine qua non** (*kwā non, kwā nōn*) an indispensable condition.

sinecure *si'ni-kūr*, or *sin'*, *n.* a benefice without cure of souls: an office without work.—Also *adj.*—*ns.* **sin'ecurism; sin'ecurist.** [L. *sine*, without, *cūra*, care.]

sinew *sin'ū*, *n.* that which joins a muscle to a bone, a tendon: strength or that which it depends on (*fig.*).—*v.t.* to bind as by sinews: to strengthen.—*adjs.* **sin'ewed; sin'ewy.** [O.E. *sinu*, gen. *sinwe*.]

sinfonia *sin-fō-nē'ə*, *n.* a symphony: a symphony orchestra.—*n.* **sinfonietta** (*-nē-et'ə*) a simple, or light, little symphony: a small symphony orchestra.—**sinfonia concertante** (*kon-chər-tan'ti*) an orchestral work with parts for more than one solo instrument. [It.]

sing *sing*, *v.i.* to utter melodious sounds in musical succession in articulating words: to emit more or less songlike sounds: to compose poetry: to give a cantabile or lyrical effect: to ring (as the ears): to be capable of being sung: to confess, to turn informer, to squeal (*slang*, esp. U.S.).—*v.t.* to utter, perform by voice, musically: to chant: to celebrate: to proclaim, relate, in song or verse or in comparable manner: to bring, drive, render, pass, etc., by singing:—*pa.t.* **sang** or (now rarely) **sung;** *pa.p.* **sung.**—*adj.* **sing'-**

able.—*ns.* **sing'er** a person, bird, etc. that sings: one who sings as a profession: an informer (*slang*, esp. U.S.); **sing'ing.**—*adv.* **sing'ingly.**—**sing'ing-bird** a songbird; **sing'ing-master** a teacher of singing; **sing'song** a ballad: jingly verse: monotonous up-and-down intonation: an informal concert where the company sing: a meeting for community singing.—*adj.* of the nature of singsong.—*v.t.* and *v.i.* to sing, speak, utter, in a singsong way.—**sing along** (orig. U.S.) of an audience, to join in the familiar songs with the performer (with *with*; *n.* **sing'-along**); **sing another song** or **tune** to change to a humbler tone; **sing out** to call out distinctly: to inform, peach; **sing small** to assume a humble tone. [O.E. *singan*.]

singe *sinj*, *v.t.* to burn on the surface: to scorch: to remove by scorching.—*v.i.* to become scorched:—*pr.p.* **singe'ing;** *pa.t.* and *pa.p.* **singed.**—*n.* a burning on the surface: a slight burn. [O.E. *sen(c)gan*.]

Singhalese. Same as **Sinhalese.**

single *sing'gl*, *adj.* consisting of one only or one part: unique: one-fold: uncombined: unmarried: for one: man to man: of ale, weak, small: undivided: unbroken: of a flower, without development of stamens into petals or of ligulate instead of tubular florets: sincere: (of a travel ticket) valid for the outward journey only, not return.—*adv.* **singly.**—*n.* anything single: (usu. in *pl.*) an unmarried, unattached person: (in *pl.*) in tennis, etc., a game played by one against one: a hit for one run: a gramophone record with usu. only one tune, or other short recording, on each side.—*v.t.* to separate: to pick (out): to take aside.—*ns.* **sing'leness** (*-gl-nis*); **sing'let** (*-glit*) a thing that is single: an undershirt; **sing'leton** (*-gl-tən*) a single card of its suit in a hand: anything single.—*adv.* **sing'ly** (*-gli*) one by one: alone: by oneself.—*adj.* **sing'le-breast'ed** with one thickness over the breast and one row of buttons.—**single cream** cream with a low fat-content that will not thicken when beaten; **sing'le-deck'er** a vessel or vehicle, esp. a bus, with only one deck.—*adj.* **sing'le-figure.**—**single figures** a score, total, etc. of any number from 1 to 9; **single file** see **file.**—*adj., adv.* **sing'le-hand'ed** by oneself: unassisted: with or for one hand.—*adj.* **sing'le-heart'ed** sincere: without duplicity: dedicated, devoted in one's attitude.—*adj.* **sing'le-mind'ed** ingenuous: bent upon one sole purpose.—**sing'le-mind'edness; single parent** a mother or father bringing up children alone (hence **single-parent family**).—*adj.* **sing'le-phase** of an alternating electric current, requiring one outward and one return conductor for transmission.—**singles bar, club** one especially for unmarried or unattached people, where friendships can be formed; **sing'le-seat'er** a car, aeroplane, etc., seated for one. [O.Fr., —L. *singulī*, one by one.]

singletree *sing'gl-trē*, *n.* Same as **swingletree.**

singsong. See **sing.**

singular *sing'gū-lər*, *adj.* single: unique: proper: private: denoting or referring to one: pre-eminently good or efficacious: extraordinary: peculiar: strange: odd.—*adv.* **singularly.**—*n.* an individual person or thing: the singular number or a word in the singular number.—*n.* **singularisā'tion**, *-z-*.—*v.t.* **sing'ularise**, *-ize* to make singular: to signalise.—*n.* **singularity** (*-lar'i-ti*) fact or state of being singular: peculiarity: individuality: oddity: oneness: anything curious or remarkable.—*adv.* **sing'ularly** in a singular manner: peculiarly: strangely: singly. [L. *singulāris*.]

sinh *sinh, sīn-āch'*, *n.* a conventional abbreviation of hyperbolic sine.

Sinhalese *sin'hə-lēz, -lēz'*, **Singhalese, Cingalese** *sing'gəlēz, -lēz'*, also **Sinhala** *sin'hə-lə*, *adjs.* of Ceylon (Sri Lanka): of the most numerous of its peoples: or in their language, akin to Pali.—*ns.* a native or citizen of Ceylon: a member of the Sinhalese people: their language. [Sans. *Siṁala*, Ceylon.]

sinical *sin'i-kl*. See **sine¹**.

sinister *sin'is-tər, adj*. left: on the left side (in *her*. from the point of view of the bearer of the shield, not the beholder, and similarly sometimes in description of an illustration, etc.): underhand: inauspicious: suggestive of threatened evil: unlucky: malign.—*adv*. **sin'isterly.**—*adj*. **sin'istral** turning to the left: of a shell, coiled contrary to the normal way.—*n*. a left-handed person.—*n*. **sinistral'ity.** [L.]

sinistrorse *sin-is-trôrs', or sin', (biol.) adj*. rising spirally and turning to the right, i.e. crossing an outside observer's field of view from right to left upwards (like an ordinary spiral stair).—Also **sinistrors'al.** [L. *sinistrôrsus, sinistrôversus*, towards the left side —*sinister*, left, *vertěre, versum*, to turn.]

sink *singk, v.i*. to become submerged, wholly or partly: to subside: to fall slowly: to go down passively: to pass to a lower level or state: to penetrate: to be absorbed: to slope away, dip: to diminish: to collapse: to be withdrawn inwards.—*v.t*. to cause or allow to sink: in games, to cause to run into the hole (*coll.*): to excavate: to let in, insert: to abandon: to abolish: to merge: to pay: to lose under the horizon: to invest, esp. unprofitably or beyond easy recovery: to damn or ruin (esp. in imprecation):—*pa.t*. **sank**, now rarely **sunk;** *pa.p*. **sunk**, also **sunk'en**, *obs*. exc. as *adj*.—*n*. a receptacle or drain for filth or dirty water: a cesspool: a kitchen or scullery trough or basin with a drain, for washing dishes, etc.: a place where things are engulfed or where foul things gather: a depression in a surface: an area without surface drainage: a swallow-hole (*geol.*): a shaft: a natural or artificial means of absorbing or discharging heat, fluid, etc. (*phys.*, etc.).—*ns*. **sink'age** act or process of sinking: amount of sinking: a sunk area, depression: shrinkage; **sink'er** one who sinks: a weight for sinking anything, as a fishing-line.—*n*. and *adj*. **sink'ing.**—*adj*. **sink'y** yielding underfoot.—**sink'-hole** a hole for filth; **sink'ing-fund** a fund formed by setting aside income to accumulate at interest to pay off debt.—*adj*. **sink in** to be absorbed: to be understood; **sink unit** a fitting consisting of sink, draining board, with cupboards, etc., underneath. [O.E. *sincan* (intrans.).]

sinner, etc. See under **sin¹.**

Sino- *sin'ō-, sī'nō-, pfx*. Chinese. [Gr. *Sīnai*, Chinese (pl.).]

sinter *sin'tər, n*. a deposit from hot springs.—*v.t*. to heat a mixture of powdered metals, sometimes under pressure, to the melting-point of the metal in the mixture which has the lowest melting-point, the melted metal binding together the harder particles.—*v.i*. to coalesce under heat without liquefaction. [Ger. *Sinter.*]

sinus *sī'nəs, n*. an indentation: a notch: a cavity: an air-filled cavity in the bones of the skull, connecting with the nose: a narrow cavity through which pus is discharged:—*pl*. **sinuses.**—*adjs*. **sinuate** (*sin'ū-āt*), **-d** (*-id*) wavy-edged: winding.—*adv*. **sin'uately.**—*ns*. **sinua'tion** winding; **sinus'itis** (*sin-* or *sīn-əs-*) inflammation of a sinus of the skull communicating with the nose.—*adj*. **sinuose** (*sin'ū-ōs*) sinuous.—*n*. **sinuos'ity.**—*adj*. **sin'uous** wavy: winding: bending in a supple manner.—*adv*. **sin'uously.**—*n*. **sin'uousness.** [L. *sinus, -ūs*, a bend, fold, bay.]

Sioux *sōō, n*. an American Indian of a tribe now living in the Dakotas, Minnesota, and Montana:—*pl*. **Sioux** (*sōō, sōōz*).—Also *adj*. **Siou'an** pertaining to the Sioux, or to a larger group to which the Sioux belong: pertaining to the languages of this group.—*n*. the group of languages spoken by the Siouan peoples. [Fr. from a native word.]

sip *sip, v.t*. and *v.i*. to drink, or drink from, in small quantities by action of the lips:—*pr.p*. **sipp'ing;** *pa.t*. and *pa.p*. **sipped.**—*n*. the act of sipping: the quantity sipped at once.—*n*. **sipp'er.** [Cf. **sup;** O.E. *sypian*.]

sipe *sīp, n*. a tiny groove or slit in the tread of a tyre, aiding water dispersal and improving the tyre's grip. [From dial. *sipe*, to seep.]

siphon *sī'fən, n*. a bent tube or channel by which a liquid may be drawn off by atmospheric pressure: a tubular organ for intake and output of water, as in lamellibranchs: an aerated-water bottle that discharges by a siphon.—*v.t*. to convey, remove by means of (or as if by means of) a siphon (often with *off*).

sippet *sip'it, n*. a morsel, esp. of bread with soup.—*v.t*. and *v.i*. **sipp'le** to sip at leisure. [Cf. **sip, sup.**]

si quis *sī, sē kwis*, a public intimation. [L. *sī quis*, if anybody (wants, knows, has found, etc.).]

sir *sûr, n*. a word of respect (or disapprobation) used in addressing a man: a gentleman: (with *cap.*) prefixed to the Christian name of a knight or baronet (hence, a knight or baronet): (with *cap.*) a word of address to a man in a formal letter.—*v.t*. to address as 'sir':—*pr.p*. **sirr'ing;** *pa.t*. and *pa.p*. **sirred.** [O.Fr. *sire*, from L. *senior*, an elder.]

sire *sīr, n*. a term of address to a king (*arch.*): a father, esp. of a horse or other beast: an ancestor.—*v.t*. to beget, esp. of beasts. [See **sir.**]

Siren *sī'rən, n*. one of certain sea-nymphs, part woman, part bird, whose songs lured sailors to death (*Gr. myth.*): (without *cap.*) a fascinating woman, insidious and deceptive: a bewitching singer: a mermaid: (without *cap.*) a signalling or warning instrument that produces sound by the escape of air or steam through a rotating perforated plate.—Also *adj*.—*n.pl*. **Sire'nia** an order of aquatic mammals now represented by the dugong and the manatee.—*n*. and *adj*. **sire'nian.**—*adj*. **sirenic** (*-ren'*). [Gr. *Seirēn*.]

sirloin, surloin *sûr'loin, n*. the loin or upper part of a loin of beef. [From a by-form of Fr. *surlonge*—*sur*, over, and *longe* (cf. **loin**).]

sirocco *si-rok'ō, scirocco* *shi-, ns*. in Southern Italy, a hot, dry, dusty and gusty wind from North Africa, becoming moist further north: any oppressive south or south-east wind: a wind from the desert: a drying machine:—*pl*. **-os.**—Also **s(c)iroc** (*si-rok', sī'rok*). [It. *s(c)irocco*—Ar. *sharq*, east wind.]

sirrah *sir'ə, n*. sir, used in anger or contempt.—**sirree** (*sûr-ē'; U.S.*) a form of sir, sirrah, used for emphasis, esp. with *yes* or *no*. [An extension of **sir.**]

sirup. See **syrup.**

sirvente *sēr-vät', n*. a troubadour's lay. [Fr.]

sis, siss *sis (esp. U.S.) n*. a contracted form of **sister** (used in addressing a girl).—*n*. and *adj*. **siss'y** (orig. chiefly *U.S.*) cissy.

-sis *-sis, n. suff*. signifying action, process: condition caused by:—*pl*. **-ses** (*-sēz*). [Gr.]

sisal *sī'səl, sī'zəl, n*. (in full **sis'al-hemp'**, or **-grass'**) agave fibre. [First exported from *Sisal*, in Yucatán.]

siskin *sis'kin, n*. a yellowish-green finch. [Ger. dial. *sisschen*; app. Slav.]

siss, sissy. See **sis.**

sister *sis'tər, n*. a daughter of the same parents: a half-sister: formerly, a sister-in-law: a female fellow: a member of a sisterhood: a nun: a senior nurse, esp. one in charge of a ward.—*adj*. of the same origin: fellow: built on the same model.—*v.t*. to be a sister to: to call sister.—*adjs*. **sis'terless; sis'terly** kind or becoming a sister: kind: affectionate.—*ns*. **sis'terliness; sis'terhood** the act or state of being a sister: the relationship of sister: a society, esp a religious community, of women: a set or class of women.—**sis'terhook** one of a pair of hooks that close each other;

sis'ter-in-law a husband's or wife's sister, or a brother's wife: a husband or wife's brother's wife:—*pl.* **sis'ters-in-law**—*adj.* **sis'ter-like.** [App. O.N. *systir.*]

Sistine *sis'tīn, -tēn, -tin, adj.* of Pope *Sixtus,* esp. Sixtus IV (1471–84) or V (1585–90)—also **Six'tine.**—**Sistine Chapel** the Pope's chapel in the Vatican, built by Sixtus IV.

Sisyphean *sis-i-fē'an, adj.* relating to *Sisyphus,* king of Corinth, condemned in Tartarus to roll ceaselessly up a hill a huge stone which would roll back to the foot of the hill again each time he neared the top: endless, laborious and futile (*fig.*).

sit *sit, v.i.* to rest on the haunches: to perch, as birds: to brood: to have a seat, as in parliament: to be in session: to reside: to be a tenant: to be located, have station or (as the wind) direction: to pose, be a model: to undergo an examination, be a candidate: to weigh, bear, press: to be disposed in adjustment, hang, fit: to befit.—*v.t.* to seat: to have a seat on, ride: to undergo or be examined in:—*pr.p.* **sitt'ing;** *pa.t.* and *pa.p.* **sat,** (*arch.*) **sate** (*sat, sāt*).—*n.* a mode or spell of sitting.—*ns.* **sitt'er** one who sits: one who sits to an artist or with a medium: a baby-sitter: a sitting bird: an easy shot: an easy dupe (*slang*): anything difficult to fail in: a sitting-room (*slang*); **sitt'ing** the state of being seated or act of taking a seat: brooding on eggs: a clutch: a continuous meeting of a body: a spell of posing to an artist, etc.: a spell: a seat: a church seat.—*adj.* seated: brooding: in the course of a parliamentary session: befitting.—**sit'down** a spell of sitting.—*adj.* that one sits down to: (of a strike) in which workers down tools but remain in occupation of the plant, workshop, etc.—**sit'-in** the occupation of a building, etc. as an organised protest against some (supposed) injustice, etc. (also *adj.*); **sitt'ing-room** a room in which members of a family commonly sit: a space for sitting; **sitting target** an easy target or victim; **sitting tenant** the tenant currently occupying a property; **sit'-upon** (*coll.*) the buttocks.—**sit back** to take no active part, or no further active part; **sit by** to look on without taking any action; **sit down** to take a seat: to pause, rest: to begin a siege; **sit in** to act as a baby-sitter: to be present as a visitor, and (usu.) take part, as at a conference or discussion: to have or take part in a sit-in; **sit on** or **upon** to hold an official inquiry regarding: to repress, check (*slang*); **sit out** to sit apart without participating: to sit to the end of: to outstay; **sit tight** to maintain one's seat: to keep one's position quietly and unobtrusively; **sit up** to rise from a recumbent to a sitting position, or from a relaxed to an erect seat: to become alert or startled: to remain up instead of going to bed: to keep watch during the night. [O.E. *sittan.*]

sitar *si-tär', n.* a Hindu plucked-string instrument with a long neck.—Also **sittar'.** [Hind. *sitār.*]

sitcom *sit'kom,* (*coll.*) *n.* a situation comedy.

site *sīt, n.* situation, esp. of a building: ground occupied or set apart for a building, etc.—*v.t.* to locate. [L. *situs,* set—*sinēre.*]

sitology *sī-tol'a-ji,* **sitiology** *sit-i-, ns.* dietetics.—*n.* **sit(i)opho'bia** morbid aversion to food. [Gr. *sitos,* dim. *sītion,* grain, food.]

sitrep *sit'rep,* (*coll.*) *n.* a report on the current military position (also *fig.*). [*Situation report.*]

sittar. See **sitar.**

sitter, sitting, etc. See **sit.**

situate *sit'ū-it, adj.* (now *rare*) situated.—*v.t.* (*-āt*) to set, place, locate: to circumstance.—*adj.* **sit'uated** set, located: circumstanced.—*n.* **situa'tion** location: place: position: momentary state: condition: a set of circumstances, a juncture: a critical point in the action of a play or the development of the plot of a novel: office, employment.—*adj.* **situa'tional.**—**situation comedy** a comedy, now esp. in a television or radio series in which the same characters appear in each episode, which depends for its humour on the behaviour of the characters in particular, sometimes contrived, situations. [L.L. *situātus*—L. *situēre,* to place.]

sitz-bath *sits'-bäth, n.* a hip-bath. [Ger. *Sitzbad.*]

Siva *s(h)ē'va, s(h)i'va, n.* the third god of the Hindu triad, destroyer and reproducer.—Also **Shiva** (*shē'va, shi'va*).—*ns.* **S(h)i'vaism; S(h)i'vaite.** [Sans. *siva,* friendly, gracious.]

six *siks, n.* the cardinal numeral next above five: a symbol representing it (6, vi, etc.): a set of that number: an article of size denoted by it: a card with six pips: a score of six points, tricks, etc.: the sixth hour after midnight or after midday: a division of a Brownie Guide or Cub Scout pack: the age of six years.—*adj.* of the number six: six years old.—*n.* **six'er** anything counting for six (as a hit at cricket) or indicated by six: the leader of a Brownie Guide or Cub Scout six.—*adj.* and *adv.* **six'fold** in six divisions: six times as much.—*adj.* **sixth** last of six: next after the fifth: equal to one of six equal parts.—*n.* a sixth part: a person or thing in sixth position: an interval of five (conventionally called six) diatonic degrees (*mus.*): a combination of two tones that distance apart (*mus.*).—*adv.* **sixth'ly** in the sixth place.—*adjs.* **six'-day** of or for six days (i.e. usu. excluding Sunday); **six'-foot** measuring six feet.—**six'-foot'er** a person six feet high; **six'-gun** a six-shooter; **six'-pack** a pack which comprises six items sold as one unit, esp. a pack of six cans of beer; **six'pence** a coin worth six old pence: its value.—*adj.* **six'penny** costing or worth sixpence: cheap: worthless.—*n.* a sixpenny book.—*n.* and *adj.* **six'score.**—**six'-shooter** a six-chambered revolver.—**at sixes and sevens** in disorder; **hit, knock for six** to overcome completely: to take by surprise; **six (of one) and half a dozen (of the other)** equal, attributable to both parties equally: having alternatives which are considered equivalent, equally acceptable, etc.; **sixth form college** a school which provides the sixth form education for the pupils of an area; **the Six Counties** Northern Ireland. [O.E. *siex.*]

sixaine *siks-ān', n.* a stanza of six lines.—*n.* **sixte** (*sikst*) a parry with hand on guard opposite the right breast, sword point a little raised to the right. [Fr.]

sixteen *siks-tēn',* or *siks', n.* and *adj.* six and ten.—*n.* **sixteen'er** a verse of sixteen syllables.—*n.* (*pl. -mos*), *adj.* **sixteen'mo** sextodecimo.—*adj.* **sixteenth** (or *siks'*) last of sixteen: next after the fifteenth: equal to one of sixteen equal parts.—*n.* a sixteenth part: a person or thing in sixteenth position. [O.E. *siextēne* (*-tíene*); see **six, ten.**]

sixty *siks'ti, adj.* and *n.* six times ten:—*pl.* **six'ties** the numbers sixty to sixty-nine: the years so numbered in a life or century: a range of temperature from sixty to just less than seventy degrees.—*adj.* **six'tieth** last of sixty: next after the fifty-ninth: equal to one of sixty equal parts.—*n.* a sixtieth part: a person or thing in sixtieth position.—**sixty-four dollar question** (from a U.S. quiz game), the final and most difficult question one has to answer to win sixty-four dollars, having first won one dollar and placed this on oneself to win double on the second question, and so on until sixty-four dollars are at stake: hence, a hard question to answer, the supreme or crucial question.—Also **sixty-four thousand dollar question.** [O.E. *siextig.*]

size *sīz, n.* bigness: magnitude.—*v.t.* to arrange according to size: to measure.—*adj.* **siz'able** (or **size'-able**) of a fair size.—*ns.* **si'zar** (also **si'zer**) at Cambridge and Dublin, a student receiving an allowance from his college towards his expenses; **si′zarship**.— *adj.* (usu. in composition) **sized** having this or that size.—*ns.* **si′zer** a measurer: a gauge: a thing of considerable or great size (*slang*); **si′zing** sorting by size —**of a size** of the same size; **size up** to take mental measure of; **the size of it** (*coll.*) a description of the situation or state of affairs now obtaining. [**assize.**]

size² *siz*, *n.* a weak glue or gluey material.—*v.t.* to cover or treat with size.—*adj.* **sized.**—*ns.* **si′zer; si′ziness; si′zing** application of size, or material for the purpose.—*adj.* **si′zy.**

size³ *siz*. Same as **sice¹.**

sizel *siz′l*. Same as **scissel.**

sizzle *siz′l*, *v.i.* to make a hissing sound of frying.—*v.t.* and *v.i.* to fry, scorch, sear.—*n.* a hissing sound: extreme heat.—*ns.* **sizz′ler** a sizzling heat or day: a thing strikingly fierce or effective; **sizz′ling** a hissing. —*adj.* very hot: very striking. [Imit.]

sjambok *sham′bok*, *n.* a whip of dried hide.—*v.t.* to flog. [Afrik.—Malay *samboq*—Urdu *chābuk*.]

ska *skä*, *n.* a form of Jamaican music similar to reggae

skald, scald *sköld*, *n.* a poet: a Scandinavian bard.— *adj.* **skald′ic, scald′ic.** [O.N. *skäld*.]

skat *skät*, *n.* a three-handed card-game. [O Fr *escart*, laying aside.]

skate¹ *skät*, *n.* a sole or sandal mounted on a blade (for moving on ice): the blade itself: a boot with such a blade fixed to it: a roller-skate: a spell of skating.— *v.i.* to go on skates.—*ns.* **ska′ter; ska′ting.**— **skate′board** a narrow wooden board mounted on roller-skate wheels, on which one balances to ride; **skate′boarder; skate′boarding; ska′ting-rink.**—**get one's skates on** (*coll.*) to hurry; **skate around** (*fig.*) to avoid discussing or answering; **skate on thin ice** see **ice; skate over** (*fig.*) to hurry over lightly. [Du. *schaats*—O.N.Fr. *escache*, stilt—L.G. *schake*, shank.]

skate² *skät*, *n.* a kind of ray (*Raia batis*, or kindred species). [O.N. *skata*.]

skean. See **skene.**

skedaddle *ski-dad′l*, (*coll.*) *v.i.* to scamper off.—*n.* a scurrying off.

skeet *skēt*, *n.* a form of clay-pigeon shooting.

skeeter *skēt′ər*, (*U.S.*) *n* short for **mosquito.**

skein *skän*, *n.* a loosely tied coil or standard length of thread or yarn: a tangle: a web: the nuclear network (*biol.*): a flock of wild geese in flight. [O.Fr. *escaigne*.]

skeleton *skel′i-tn*, *n.* the hard parts of an animal: the bones: the veins of a leaf: a framework or outline of anything: a scheme reduced to its essential or indispensable elements: a set of persons reduced to its lowest strength: an emaciated person or animal.— Also *adj.*—*adj.* **skel′etal.**—*v.t.* **skel′etonise, -ize** to reduce to a skeleton.—**skeleton key** a key with its serrated edge or the shaped part of its bit filed down, so that it can open many locks.—**skeleton in the cupboard, closet, house,** etc. a hidden domestic sorrow or shame. [Gr. *skeleton* (*sōma*), dried (body)— *skellein*, to dry.]

skelp *skelp*, (*Scot.*) *v.t* to slap.—*v.i.* to move briskly along: to bound along.—*n.* a slap.—*adj.* **skelp′ing** very big or full: smacking: lusty.—*n.* a smacking.

skelter *skel′tər*, *v.i.* to scurry.—*n.* a scurry.

skene, skean *skēn*, *n.* an Irish or Highland dagger, knife, or short sword.—**skene′-dhu, skean′-dhu** (*-dōō′*) a dirk, dagger, stuck in the stocking. [Ir. and Gael. *sgian*, knife, *dhu*, black.]

skep *skep*, *n.* a basket: a beehive.—*v.t.* to hive:—*pr.p.* **skepp′ing;** *pa.t.* and *pa.p.* **skepped.**—*n.* **skep′ful.** [O.N. *skeppa*.]

skerry *sker′i*, *n.* a reef of rock. [O.N *sker*.]

sketch *skech*, *n.* a drawing, slight, rough, or without

detail, esp. as a study towards a more finished work: an outline or short account: a short and slightly constructed play, dramatic scene, musical entertainment, etc.: a short descriptive essay.—*v.t.* to make or give a sketch of: to outline, or give the principal points of.—*v.i.* to practise sketching.—*n.* **sketchabil′ity.**—*adj.* **sketch′able** worth sketching.— *n.* **sketch′er.**—*adv.* **sketch′ily.**—*n.* **sketch′iness.**— *adj.* **sketch′y** like a sketch: incomplete, slight: imperfect, inadequate.—**sketch′-book** a book of or for sketches (in drawing, literature or music). [Du. *schets*, prob.—It. *schizzo*—L. *schedium*, an extempore—Gr. *schedios*, offhand.]

skew *skū*, *adj.* oblique: of statistics or a curve representing them, not symmetrical about the mean.— *adv.* awry.—*n.* obliquity.—*v.t.* and *v.i.* to set, go, or look obliquely.—*adj.* **skewed** distorted: skew.—*adj.* and *adv.* **skew-whiff′** (*coll.*) crooked, awry. [App. O.N.Fr. *eskiu(w)er*—O.Fr. *eschuer*; see **eschew;** or M.Du. *schuwe*, to shun; cf. **shy.**]

skewbald *skū′böld*, *adj.* marked in white and another colour (not black).—*n.* a skewbald horse.]

skewer *skū′ər*, *n.* a long pin of wood or metal, esp. for meat.—*v.t.* to fasten or pierce with a skewer: to transfix.

ski *skē*, *n.* a long narrow runner orig. of wood, now also of metal, etc., fastened to the foot to enable the wearer to slide across snow, etc.:—*pl.* **ski** or **skis.**— *v.i.* to travel on skis:—*pr.p.* **ski′ing;** *pa.t.* and *pa.p.* **skied, ski′d.**—*adj.* **ski′able** (of surface) in condition for skiing on.—*ns.* **ski′er; ski′ing.**—**ski′-bob** a low bicycle on small skis instead of wheels; **ski′-bobbing, ski′-bobs; ski(-)joring** (*-jör′, -jor′*) the sport of being towed on skis by a horse or motor vehicle; **ski′-jump′ing; ski′-lift,** -tow devices for taking skiers uphill; **ski′-run** a slope for skiing on; **ski′-slope; ski′-stick** one of a pair of sticks, usu. pointed with a disc near the tip, used by skiers for balance or propulsion. [Norw.,—O.N. *skith*, snow-shoe, piece of split wood.]

skia- *ski′ə-, -a′-*, in composition, shadow.—Also **scia-** (*si′-*), **skio-, scio-.** [Gr. *skiä*, a shadow.]

skid *skid*, *n.* a support on which something rests, is brought to the desired level, or slides: a ship's wooden fender: a shoe or other device to check a wheel on a down-slope: an aeroplane runner: a skidding: a sideslip.—*v.i.* to slide along without revolving: to slip, esp sideways.—*v.t.* to check with a skid: to make to skid.—**skid′-lid** (*slang*) a crash helmet; **skid pad,** pan a piece of slippery ground on which motorists can learn to control a skidding car; **skid′pan** (*slang*) a drag for a wheel (also *fig.*); **skid road,** row (esp. *U.S.*) a squalid quarter where vagrants, chronic drunks, etc., live.—**put the skids on, under** (*slang*) to cause to hurry: to put a stop to, thwart; **the skids** (*fig.*; *coll.*) a downward path. [Prob. related to **ski.**]

skier¹. See **ski.**

skier², skiey. See under **sky.**

skiff *skif*, *n.* a small light boat. [Akin to **ship.**]

skiffle *skif′l*, *n.* a strongly accented jazz type of folk-music played by guitars, drums, and often unconventional instruments, etc., popular about 1957.

skijoring. See **ski.**

skill *skil*, *n.* expertness: a craft or accomplishment.— *adj.* **skil′ful.**—*adv.* **skil′fully.**—*n.* **skil′fulness.**— *adjs.* **skilled** expert. [O.N. *skil*, distinction, *skilja*, to separate]

skillet *skil′it*, *n.* a small, long-handled pan. [Origin doubtful.]

skilly *skil′i*, *n.* thin gruel.—Also **skilligalee′, skilligolee′.**

skim *skim*, *v.t.* to remove floating matter from the surface of: to take off by skimming (often with *off;*

also *fig.*): to glide lightly over: to read superficially and skippingly.—*v.i.* to pass over lightly: to glide along near the surface: to become coated over:—*pr.p.* **skimm'ing;** *pa.t.* and *pa.p.* **skimmed.**—*n.* the act of skimming: skim-milk.—*ns.* **skimm'er** one who or that which skims: a utensil for skimming milk: a sea-bird (*Rhyncops*) that skims the water; **skimm'ing.** —*adv.* **skimm'ingly.**—**skim'-milk** milk from which the cream has been skimmed. [App. related to **scum.**]

Skimmia *skim'i-ə, n.* an Asiatic genus of shrubs, cultivated for its holly-like leaves and drupes: (without *cap.*) a plant of this genus. [Jap. *shikimi.*]

skimp *skimp, v.t.* and *v.i.* to scrimp: to stint.—*adj.* scanty, spare.—*adv.* **skimp'ily.**—*adj.* **skimp'ing.**— *adv.* **skimp'ingly.**—*adj.* **skimp'y.** [Poss. **scamp** combined with **scrimp.**]

skin *skin, n.* the natural outer covering of an animal: a hide: a thin outer layer or covering: an integument: a membrane: a wine vessel made of an animal's skin.— *adj.* of skin.—*v.t.* to cover with a skin: to strip the skin from: to fleece.—*v.i.* to become covered with skin: to slip through or away:—*pr.p.* **skinn'ing;** *pa.t.* and *pa.p.* **skinned.**—*n.* **skin'ful** as much liquor as one can hold.—*adjs.* **skin'less; skinned** (usu. in composition). —*ns.* **skinn'er** one who prepares hides; **skinn'iness.**— *adj.* **skinn'y** of or like skin: emaciated.—*adj.* **skin'-deep** superficial.—**skin'-diver** orig., a naked pearl-diver: one involved in skin-diving; **skin'-diving** diving and swimming under water, with simple equipment, not wearing the traditional diver's helmet and suit, and not connected with a boat; **skin'flick** (*slang*) a film in which some of the characters appear in the nude and which usually includes scenes of sexual intercourse; **skin'flint** a very niggardly person; **skin'-game** a swindling trick; **skin'head** a member of certain gangs of young people wearing simple, severe, clothes, the boys having closely cropped hair; **skin test** a test made by applying a substance to, or introducing a substance beneath, a person's skin, to test for an allergy, immunity from a disease, etc.—*adj.* **skin'-tight** fitting close to the skin.—*n.* (in *pl.*) tights. —**by or with the skin of one's teeth** very narrowly; **get under someone's skin** to annoy someone: to interest someone seriously; **no skin off one's nose** (*coll.*) a matter about which one feels unconcerned or indifferent because it does not harm or inconvenience one, or because it may be to one's benefit; **save one's skin** to save one's life. [O.N. *skinn*; late O.E. *scinn.*]

skink *skingk, n.* an African lizard (Scincus) or kindred kind. [L. *scincus*—Gr. *skinkos.*]

skinny. See **skin.**

skint *skint,* (*slang*) *adj.* without money, hard up. [**skinned.**]

skio-. See **skia-.**

skip[1] *skip, v.i.* to spring or hop lightly: to make jumps over a twirling rope: to pass discontinuously.—*v.t.* to overleap: to omit: to cut, not go to (a class):—*pr.p.* **skipp'ing;** *pa.t.* and *pa.p.* **skipped.**—*n.* an act of skipping: a belt of inaudibility in wireless transmission: a college servant.—*n.* **skipp'er** one who skips: a dancer: a butterfly of the Hesperiidae, with short jerky flight: the saury.—*adj.* **skipp'ing** flighty, giddy.—*adv.* **skipp'ingly.**—**skip'jack** any of a number of species of fish that jump out of, or swim at the surface of, the water, such as the bonitos, and either of two species of tuna; **skipp'ing-rope; skip zone** an area round a broadcasting station where transmissions cannot be received.—**skip it!** (*coll.*) never mind, forget it! [Cf. O.N. *skopa,* to run.]

skip[2] *skip, n.* a box or truck for raising minerals from a mine: a large container for transporting building, etc., materials or refuse. [**skep.**]

skip[3] *skip, n.* the captain of a rink in bowls or curling.— *v.t.* and *v.i.* to act as a skip. [**skipper.**]

skipper *skip'ər, n.* a ship captain: the captain of an aeroplane: the captain of a team.—*v.t.* to act as skipper.—**skipper's daughters** white-topped waves. [Du. *schipper.*]

skippet *skip'it, n.* a flat box for protecting a seal (as of a document).

skirl *skirl, skûrl, (Scot.) v.t.* and *v.i.* to shriek or sing shrilly.—*v.i.* to make the sound of the bagpipes.—*n.* a shrill cry: the sound of the bagpipes. [Scand.]

skirmish *skûr'mish, n.* an irregular fight between small parties.—*v.i.* to fight slightly or irregularly.—*ns.* **skir'misher; skir'mishing.** [O.Fr. *escarmouche.*]

skirret *skir'it, n.* a water-parsnip with edible roots. [M.E. *skirwhit,* as if *skire white,* pure white, but perh. altered from O.Fr. *eschervis.*]

skirt *skûrt, n.* a garment, or part of a garment, generally a woman's, that hangs from the waist: the lower part of a gown, coat, or other garment: a saddle-flap: a midriff (of meat): a rim, border, margin: a part of, or attachment to, an object that suggests a skirt, e.g. the flap of material hanging down around the base of a hovercraft to contain the air-cushion, or a similar flap around a racing-car: a woman (*slang*; also **bit of skirt**).—*v.t.* to border: to pass along the edge of: to scour the outskirts of.—*v.i.* to be on or pass along the border: to leave the pack.—*adj.* **skirt'ed** wearing or having a skirt.—*n.* **skir'ting** material for skirts: skirting-board: (in *pl.*) dirty wool from the skirts of a fleece.—Also *adj.*—*adj.* **skirt'less.**—**skir'ting-board** the narrow board next to the floor round the walls of a room.—**divided skirt** trousers made to look like a skirt. [O.N. *skyrta,* a shirt, kirtle; cf. **shirt.**]

skit *skit, n.* a piece of banter or burlesque, esp. in dramatic or literary form: a humorous hit. [Perh. related to O.N. *skjóta,* to shoot.]

skitter *skit'ər, v.i.* to skim over the surface of water: to fish by drawing the bait over the surface. [Perh. from **skite** (see **skit**).]

skittish *skit'ish, adj.* unsteady: light-headed: frivolous: frisky: lively: volatile: changeable: wanton: coy. —*adv.* **skitt'ishly.**—*n.* **skitt'ishness.** [Perh. conn. with **skit.**]

skittle *skit'l, n.* a pin for the game of **skittles**, a form of ninepins in which a ball or cheese (see **cheese**[1]) is used.—*v.t.* to knock down.—**skitt'le-alley, -ball, -ground.**

skive[1] *skīv, v.t.* to pare, split.—*ns.* **skī'ver** split sheepskin leather; **skī'ving.** [O.N. *skifa.*]

skive[2] *skīv,* (*slang*) *v.t.* and *v.i.* (often with *off*) to evade (a duty, work, etc.).—Also *n.*—*n.* **skī'ver.**— *adj.* **skī'vy.**

skivvy *skiv'i,* (*slang*) *n.* a disrespectful word for a maidservant.

skoal *skōl, interj.* hail!: a friendly exclamation in salutation before drinking, etc. [O.N. *skål;* Norw. *skaal,* a bowl, Sw. *skål;* cf. **scale**[3,4].]

skol *skol.* Same as **skoal.**

skrimshank, scrimshank *skrim'shangk, (mil. slang) v.i.* to evade work or duty.—*n.* evasion of work.—*n.* **skrim'shanker.**

skry, skryer. Same as **scry, scryer.**

skua *skū'ə, n.* a genus (*Stercorarius*) of large predatory gulls. [O.N. *skúfr.*]

skulduddery, skulduggery. See **sculdudd(e)ry.**

skulk *skulk, v.i.* to sneak out of the way: to lurk: to malinger.—*ns.* **skulk, skulk'er** one who skulks.—*n.* and *adj.* **skulk'ing.**—*adv.* **skulk'ingly.**—**skulk'ing-place.** [Scand., as Dan. *skulke.*]

skull[1] *skul, n.* the bony case that encloses the brain: the sconce, noddle: a skullcap, esp. of metal: a crust of solidified metal on a ladle, etc.—**skull'cap** a close-fitting cap: a protective cap of metal for the top of the head: the top of the skull.—**skull and crossbones** see **crossbones** under **cross**. [M.E. *scolle*; perh. Scand.]

skull². Same as **scull²**.

skulpin. Same as **sculpin**.

skunk *skungk, n.* a small American musteline animal that emits an offensive fluid: its fur: a low fellow. [Algonkian *segonku*.]

skuttle. *Same as* **scuttle**.

sky *skī, n.* the apparent canopy over our heads: the heavens: the weather: the upper rows of pictures in a gallery: sky-blue.—*v.t.* to raise aloft: to hit high into the air: to hang above the line of sight.—*n.* **sky'er**, **ski'er** (*cricket*) a hit high into the air.—*adj.* **sky'ey** (or **ski'ey**) of the weather: of or like the sky.—*adj.* and *adv.* **sky'ward**.—*adv.* **sky'wards**.—*n.* and *adj.* **sky'-blue** light blue like the sky.—*adj.* **sky'-col'oured**.— **sky'-diver; sky'-diving, -jumping** jumping by parachute as a sport, using a special steerable parachute, and delaying opening it for a specified time.—*adj.* **sky'-high** very high.—Also *adv.*—*v.t.* **sky'jack** (*coll.*) to hijack (an aeroplane).—*ns.* **sky'jacker; sky'jacking.—sky'lark** the common lark.—*v.i.* to frolic boisterously.—*v.t.* to trick.—**sky'larking** running about the rigging of a ship in sport: frolicking; **sky'light** a window in a roof or ceiling: light from or in the sky: light through the bottom of an empty glass; **sky'line** the horizon: a silhouette or outline against the sky; **sky'man** a paratrooper.—**sky'-rock'et** a firework that bursts high in the sky.—*v.i.* to shoot up high: to rise high and fast.—**skysail** (*ski'sl*) a sail above the royal; **sky'scape** a view or a picture of the sky; **sky'scraper** a very lofty building: a triangular skysail: anything very high; **sky'way** a route for aircraft; **sky'-writing** tracing of words by smoke from an aircraft.—**the sky is the limit** (*coll.*) there are no restrictions on amount or extent (of something); **to the skies** (*coll.*) in a lavish or enthusiastic manner. [O.N. *skỳ*, cloud.]

Skye *skī, n.* (in full, **Skye terrier**) a small long-haired Scotch terrier. [From the island of *Skye*.]

slab¹ *slab, n.* a plane-sided plate: a large thick slice of cake, etc.: outer plank sawn from a log: a thin flat piece of stone, etc.—*v.t.* to cut slabs from: to form into slabs: to cover with slabs.—*adj.* **slabbed**.— **slab'stone** flagstone.

slab² *slab, adj.* semi-liquid, viscous.—*n.* mud.—*adj.* **slabb'iness.**—*adj.* **slabb'y** muddy. [Scand.; cf. Norw., Sw. *slabb*, wet filth.]

slabber *slab'ər, v.i.* to slaver, to drivel.—*v.t.* to beslobber: to gobble sloppily and grossly.—*n.* **slabb'erer.**— *adj.* **slabb'ery**. [Cf. L.G. and Du. *slabberen* and **slobber**.]

slack¹ *slak, adj.* lax or loose: not firmly extended or drawn out: not holding fast: remiss: not strict: not eager or diligent, inattentive: not busy: not violent or rapid, slow.—*adv.* in a slack manner: partially: insufficiently.—*n.* the slack part of a rope, belt, etc.: a time, occasion, or place of relaxed movement or activity: a slack-water haul of a net: (in *pl.*) long, loose trousers.—*vs.i.* **slack, slack'en** to become loose or less tight: to be remiss: to abate: to become slower: to fail or flag: to be inactive or lax.—*vs.t.* to make slack or less tight: to loosen: to slow, retard: to be remiss or dilatory in: to relax: to slake.—*n.* and *adj.* **slack'ening.**—*n.* **slack'er** an idler: one who is reprehensibly inactive: a shirker.—*adv.* **slack'ly.**—*n.* **slack'ness.**—*adj.* **slack'-hand'ed** remiss.—**slack'water** turn of the tide: a stretch of still or slow-moving water.—*adj.* pertaining to slack-water.—**slack off** to ease off; **slack up** to ease off: to slow. [O.E. *slæc* (*sleac*).]

slack² *slak, n.* coal-dross. [Cf. Ger. *Schlacke*.]

slag¹ *slag, n.* solid scum on melted metal: vitrified cinders: scoriaceous lava: a piece of slag.—*v.t.* and *v.i.* to form into slag.—*adj.* **slagg'y.—slag'-wool** fibre made from molten slag. [M.L.G. *slagge*.]

slag² *slag, (slang) n.* a slovenly or dissolute woman.

slag³ *slag, (slang) v.t.* to criticise, mock, deride.

slain *slān, pa.p.* of **slay**.

slàinte *slan'cha,* (Gael.) *interj.* good health!

slake¹ *slāk, v.t.* to quench: to extinguish: to deaden: to abate, mitigate, allay, reduce, moderate: to moisten: to hydrate (as lime): to refresh with moisture: to slacken.—*v.i.* to become slaked: to subside: to abate: to die down.—*adj.* **slake'less** that cannot be slaked. [O.E. *slacian, sleacian,* to grow slack—*slæc, sleac,* slack.]

slalom *sla'ləm, n.* a race in which tactical skill is required, esp. a downhill or zigzag ski-run among posts or trees or an obstacle race in canoes.—*v.i.* and *v.t.* (*fig.*) to move in a zigzag course. [Norw.]

slam¹ *slam, v.t.* or *v.i.* to shut or strike with violence and noise: to bang: to censure, criticise (*coll.*):—*pr.p.* **slamm'ing;** *pa.t.* and *pa.p.* **slammed.**—*n.* the act or sound of slamming: a harsh criticism (*coll.*).—*adv.* with a slam (also *fig.*).—*n.* **slamm'er** (*slang*) prison. [Cf. Norw. *slemma*.]

slam² *slam, n.* in whist, the winning of every trick: in bridge, the winning of every trick (*grand slam*) or of all but one (*small* or *little slam*).—*v.t.* to inflict a slam upon.

slander *slan', slan'dər, n.* a false or malicious report: injurious defamation by spoken words or by looks, signs, or gestures (distinct from *libel*): calumny.—*v.t.* to defame: to calumniate.—*n.* **slan'derer.**—*adj.* **slan'derous.**—*adv.* **slan'derously.**—*n.* **slan'derousness.** [O.Fr. *esclandre*—L. *scandalum*—Gr. *skandalon,* snare, scandal.]

slang *slang, n.* a jargon of thieves and disreputable persons: the jargon of any class, profession, or set: words and usages not accepted for dignified use.— Also *adj.*—*v.t.* to scold, vituperate.—*ns.* **slang'iness; slang'ing** a scolding.—Also *adj.*—*adj.* **slang'y.**— **slanging match** a bitter verbal quarrel, usu. involving an exchange of insults. [Of cant origin.]

slant *slant, slant, v.t.* and *v.i.* to slope: to turn, strike, fall, obliquely.—*v.t.* to bias in a certain direction in presentation.—*n.* a slope: obliquity: a sloping surface, line, ray, or movement: a divergence from a direct line: a jibe: a point of view, way of looking at a thing.—*adj.* sloping: oblique: inclined from a direct line.—*adj.* **slant'ed** biased, prejudiced.—*adj.* **slant'ing.**—*advs.* **slan'tingly, slant'ingways, slant'ly,** **slant'ways, slant'wise.**—*adj.* **slant'-eyed.** [M.E. **slent.**]

slap *slap, n.* a blow with the hand or anything flat: a snub, rebuke.—*v.t.* to give a slap to: to bring or send with a slap: to rebuke (also with *down*): to apply without much care or attention (usu. with *on*):—*pr.p.* **slapp'ing;** *pa.t.* and *pa.p.* **slapped.**—*adv.* with a slap: suddenly, violently: directly, straight.—*adv.* **slap'-bang** violently, all at once.—*adj.* dashing, violent.— *adv.* **slap'-dash** in a bold, careless way.—*adj.* offhand, rash.—*n.* roughcast: careless work.—*v.t.* to do in a hasty, imperfect manner: to roughcast.—*adj.* **slap'-happy** (*coll.*) recklessly or boisterously happy: slap-dash, happy-go-lucky: punch-drunk.—**slap'stick** (also **slapstick comedy**) knockabout low comedy or farce.—*adj.* **slap'-up** (*slang*) superlatively fine.—**slap and tickle** (*coll.*) amorous frolicking, with kissing, petting, etc.; **slap in the face** (*coll.*) an insult or rebuff; **slap on the back** (*coll.*) a mark of congratulations; **slap on the wrist** (*coll.*) a mild reprimand. [Allied to L.G. *slapp,* Ger. *Schlappe;* imit.]

slash *slash, v.t.* to cut by striking with violence and at random: to make long cuts in: to slit so as to show lining or material underneath: to lash: to criticise very harshly: to crack as a whip: to cut down, reduce drastically or suddenly (*coll.*).—*v.i.* to strike violently and at random with an edged instrument: to strike right and left.—*n.* a long cut: a cut at random: a cut in cloth to show colours underneath: a stripe on a non-commissioned officer's sleeve: an act of urination (*vulg.*).—*adj.* slashed cut with slashes: gashed.—*ns.* slash'er; slash'ing a slash or slashes.—*adj.* cutting mercilessly, unsparing: dashing: very big, slapping. [Perh. O.Fr. *esclachier*, to break; or conn. with lash.]

slat¹ *slat, v.t.* and *v.i.* to strike, beat: to flap.—*n.* a sudden sharp blow. [Poss. O.N. *sletta*, to slap, splash.]

slat² *slat, n.* a thin strip of wood, etc.—*adj.* slatt'ed having, or composed of, slats. [O.Fr. *esclat*.]

slate¹ *slāt, n.* a fine-grained easily-split rock, usu. a dull blue, grey, purple, or green: a slab of this material (or a substitute) for roofing, or for writing on: a preliminary list of candidates: slate-colour.—*adj.* of slate: slate-coloured, dull dark blue.—*v.t.* to cover with slate: to enter on a slate.—*adj.* slat'ed covered with slates.—*ns.* slat'er one who covers roofs with slates; slat'iness; slat'ing covering with slates; a covering of slates: materials for slating.—*adj.* slat'y of or like slate.—*adjs.* slate'-coloured dull bluish grey approaching black; slate'-grey, -grey of a light slate colour.—slate'-pencil a cut or turned stick of soft slate, compressed slate-powder, or pyrophyllite, for writing on slate.—a slate loose (*slang*) a slight mental derangement; clean slate see clean; on the slate (*coll.*) on credit; wipe the slate clean to allow a person to make a fresh start in a job, relationship, etc. by ignoring past mistakes, crimes, etc. [O.Fr. *esclate*; cf. slat².]

slate² *slāt, v.t.* to abuse: to review unsparingly: to reprimand.—*n.* slā'ting. [From the O.N. word answering to O.E. *slǣtan*, to bait.]

slattern *slat'ərn, n.* a slut, a dirty untidy woman.—*n.* slatt'ernliness.—*adj.* slatt'ernly sluttish.—Also *adv.* [App. slat¹.]

slaughter *slö'tər, n.* killing of animals, esp. for food: killing of great numbers: wanton or inexcusable killing, esp. of the helpless: carnage.—*v.t.* to make slaughter of.—*n.* slaugh'terer.—*adj.* slaugh'terous given to slaughter: destructive: murderous.—*adv.* slaugh'terously.—slaugh'terhouse a place where beasts are killed for the market; slaugh'terman a man employed in killing or butchering animals. [O.N. *slātr*, butchers' meat, whence *slātra*, to slaughter (cattle).]

Slav *slāv, n.* one whose language is Slavonic, i.e. belongs to that division of the Indo-European tongues that includes Russian, Polish, Wendish, Czech, Slovak, Serbian, Slovenian, and Bulgarian.—*adjs.* Slav, Slav'ic.—*n.* Sla'vism a Slavonic idiom used in another language: enthusiasm for Slavic ways or culture: anything characteristic of the Slavs.—*adj.* Slavonic (-*von'ik*) of the group of languages indicated above, or the peoples speaking them.—*n.* the parent language of the Slavs or any of its descendants. [Mediaeval L. *Sclavus*—Late Gr. *Sklabos*, from the stem of Slav *slovo*, word, *sloviti*, to speak; cf. Slovene.]

slave *slāv, n.* a person held as property: an abject: one who is submissive under domination: one who is submissively devoted: one whose will has lost power of resistance: one who works like a slave, a drudge: a mechanism controlled by another mechanism, e.g. in computing, by the central processor: a master-slave manipulator.—Also *adj.*—*v.i.* to work like a slave: to drudge.—*v.t.* to enslave: to treat as a slave.—*ns.*

slav'er a slave-trader: a ship employed in the slave-trade; slav'ery the state of being a slave: the institution of ownership of slaves: drudgery; slav'ey (*slang*) a domestic drudge, a maid of all work.—*adj.* slav'ish of or belonging to slaves: befitting a slave: servile: abject: servilely following or conforming: laborious.—*adv.* slav'ishly.—*n.* slav'ishness; slave'-driver one who superintends slaves at their work: a hard taskmaster; slave'-holder an owner of slaves; slave'-labour, slave'-owner, -owning; slave'-ship a ship used for transporting slaves; slave states those states of the American Union which maintained domestic slavery before the Civil War; slave'-trade, -traff'ic the buying and selling of slaves; slave'-trader, -traff'-icker. [O.Fr. (Fr.) *esclave*, orig. a Slav.]

slaver¹ *slav'ər, n.* spittle running from the mouth.—*v.i.* to let spittle run out of the mouth: to drivel: to fawn.—*v.t.* to beslobber.—*n.* slav'erer.—*adj.* slav'ering.—*adv.* slav'eringly.—*adj.* slav'ery slabbery. [Akin to slabber.]

slaver² See slave.

slavocracy, -crat. See slave.

Slavonic, See Slav.

slaw *slö, n.* cabbage salad. [Du. *sla—salade*.]

slay *slā, v.t.* and *v.i.* to kill:—*pa.t.* slew (*slōō*); *pa.p.* slain (*slān*).—*v.t.* (*coll.*) to amuse very much: to impress very much:—*pa.t.* slayed, sometimes slew; *pa.p.* slayed, rarely slain.—*n.* slay'er. [O.E. *slēan*, to strike, to kill.]

sleazy *slē'zi, adj.* flimsy: slatternly (*coll.*): squalid (*coll.*).—*adv.* sleaz'ily.—*n.* slea'ziness.

sled *sled, n.* a sledge, esp. a small sledge: a drag or wheelless structure for conveying goods, formerly for taking the condemned to execution.—*v.t.* to convey by sled.—*v.i.* to go on a sled:—*pr.p.* sledd'ing; *pa.t.* and *pa.p.* sledd'ed.—*n.* sledd'ing. [M.Du. or M.L.G. *sledde*; cf. sledge¹, sleigh, slide.]

sledge¹ *slej, n.* carriage with runners for sliding on snow: framework with wheels for dragging goods along: iron- or flint-studded board for threshing corn.—*v.t., v.i.* to convey, or to travel, by sledge.—*ns.* sledg'er; sledg'ing. [M.Du. *sleedse*; cf. sled.]

sledge² *slej, n.* a large heavy hammer.—Also sledge'-hammer. [O.E. *slecg—slēan*, to strike, slay.]

sleek *slēk, adj.* smooth: glossy: having an oily, plastered-down look: insinuating, plausible: slick: prosperous in appearance.—*v.t.* to make smooth or glossy: to calm or soothe.—*v.i.* to glide.—*adv.* smoothly, oilily.—*v.t.* sleek'en to sleek.—*ns.* sleek'er a slicker; sleek'ing.—*adv.* sleek'ly.—*n.* sleek'ness.—*adj.* sleek'y smooth: sly, untrustworthy. [A later form of slick.]

sleep *slēp, v.i.* to take rest by relaxation of consciousness: to slumber: to be motionless, inactive, or dormant: to appear still or restful: to be dead: to rest in the grave: to be numb.—*v.t.* to be in the state of (with *sleep*, etc., as cognate object): to render, make, put, by sleep: to afford sleeping accommodation for:—*pa.t.* and *pa.p.* slept (*slept*).—*n.* the state of being asleep: a spell of sleeping: dormancy: mucous matter which collects at the corners of the eyes (*coll.*).—*n.* sleep'er one who sleeps: a horizontal beam supporting and spreading a weight: a support for railway rails: a sleeping-car: a compartment or berth in a sleeping-coach: a Communist (or other) agent who spends a long time (often years) establishing himself as an inoffensive citizen preparing for the moment when he will be required to pass on a particular vital piece of information: a record, film, etc. which becomes popular after an initial period of not being so (*coll.*).—*adv.* sleep'ily.—*ns.* sleep'iness; sleep'ing state of abeyance.—*adj.* in a state of, occupied with, or for, sleeping: dormant.—*adj.* sleep'less without sleep:

unable to sleep.—*adv.* **sleep'lessly.**—*n.* **sleep'less-ness.**—*adj.* **sleep'y** inclined to sleep: drowsy: inducing or suggesting sleep.—**sleep'ing-bag** a bag for sleeping in, used by travellers, campers, etc.; **sleep'ing-berth; sleep'ing-car, -carr'iage, -coach** a railway-carriage with berths for sleeping in; **sleep'ing-draught** a drink to induce sleep; **sleep'ing-part'ner** one who has money invested in a business but takes no part in management; **sleep'ing-pill** one containing a sleep-inducing drug; **sleeping policeman** a low hump across a road intended to slow down traffic; **sleep'ing-sick'-ness** a deadly disease of tropical Africa, characterised by headache, great drowsiness, and exhaustion, caused by a trypanosome introduced by the bite of a tsetse-fly: sometimes erroneously applied to sleepy-sickness; **sleep'-walk'er** a somnambulist, **sleep'-walk'ing; sleep'y-head** a lazy, or sleepy-looking person; **sleep'y-sick'ness** encephalitis lethargica: formerly applied to sleeping-sickness.—**get to sleep** to manage to fall asleep; **go to sleep** to fall asleep, **in one's sleep** while asleep; **put to sleep** to anaesthetise: to kill (an animal) painlessly; **sleep around** to be sexually promiscuous; **sleep in** to oversleep: to sleep later than usual; **sleep off** to recover from by sleeping; **sleep on** to consider overnight, postpone a decision on; **sleep together** to have sexual relations with each other, **sleep with** to have sexual relations with. [O.E *slǣpan* (vb.), *slǣp* (n.).]

sleet *slēt, n.* rain mingled with snow or hail.—*v.i.* to hail or snow with rain mingled.—*n.* **sleet'iness.**—*adj.* **sleet'y.** [Prob. an unrecorded O.E. (Anglian) *slēt.*]

sleeve *slēv, n.* a covering for the arm: a tube into which a rod or other tube is inserted: a thin covering, container for a gramophone record: a wind-sock: a drogue.—*v.t.* to furnish with sleeves.—*adjs.* **sleeved** with sleeves: (in composition **-sleeved**) with sleeves of a stated type; **sleeve'less** without sleeves.—**sleeve'-board** a board for ironing sleeves; **sleeve'-nut** a double-nut for attaching the joint-ends of rods or tubes —**hang, pin,** (oneself, belief, etc.) **on a person's sleeve** to rely, or make depend, entirely upon him, her; **laugh in, or up, one's sleeve** to laugh privately or unperceived; **up one's sleeve** in secret reserve. [O.E (Anglian) *slēfe* (W.S. *sliefe*).]

sleigh *slā, n.* (esp. in *U.S.* and *Canada*) a sledge.—*v.i* to travel by sleigh.—*n.* **sleigh'ing.**—**sleigh'-bell** a small bell attached to a sleigh or its harness. [Du. *slee.*]

sleight *slīt, n.* cunning: dexterity: an artful trick: a juggling trick: trickery.—**sleight'-of-hand'** legerdemain. —Also *adj.* [O.N. *slægth*, cunning, *slǣgr*, sly.]

slender *slen'dər, adj.* thin or narrow: slim: slight.—*v.t.* and *v.i.* **slen'derise, -ize** to make or become slender. —*adv.* **slen'derly.**—*n.* **slen'derness.**

slept *slept, pa.t.* and *pa.p.* of **sleep.**

sleuth *slōōth, n.* a relentless tracker, a detective.—*v.t.* and *v.i.* to track. [O.N. *slōth*, track.]

slew¹ *slōō, pa.t.* of **slay.**

slew², **slue** *slōō, v.t.* and *v.i.* to turn about the axis: to swing round.—*n.* a turn, twist, swing round: a position so taken.—*adj.* **slewed, slued** (*slang*) tipsy [First recorded as a sailor's word: origin unknown.]

sley *slā, n* a weaver's reed [O.E. *slege*—*slēan*, to strike.]

slice *slīs, n.* a thin broad piece: a flat or broad-bladed instrument of various kinds, esp. a broad knife for serving fish: a slash: a sliced stroke (*golf*): a share (*coll.*): a representative section.—*v.t.* to cut into slices: to cut a slice from: to cut as a slice: in golf, to strike or play so as to send the ball curving to the right (left in left-hand play).—*v.i.* to slash: to cut in the manner of slicing: (of a boat) to move through the water in such a manner: to slice a stroke.—*n.* **sli'cer.**

—*n.* and *adj.* **sli'cing.** [O.Fr. *esclice*—O.H.G. *slīzan*, to split.]

slick *slik, adj.* sleek: smooth: smooth-tongued: glib: adroit: trim.—*adv.* smoothly: glibly: deftly: quickly: altogether.—*n.* a smooth place or surface: a slicker: a film of spilt oil: a glossy magazine —*v.t.* to polish, make glossy: to tidy up.—*ns.* **slick'er** a smoothing tool: a swindler: shifty person: a sophisticated city-dweller; **slick'ing.**—*adv.* **slick'ly.**—*n.* **slick'ness.** [M.E *sliken*—O.E. *slician*, (in composition) to smooth.]

slid. See **slide.**

slide *slīd, v.t.* to slip or glide: to pass along smoothly to glide in a standing position (without skates or snow-shoes) over ice or other slippery surface: to lapse: to pass quietly, smoothly, or gradually· to take its own course.—*v.t.* to thrust along glidingly: to slip: —*pa.t* and *pa p.* **slid.**—*n.* a slip: a polished slippery track (on ice): a chute or shoot: a slippery sloping surface in a park for children to slide down: a bed, groove, rail, etc., on or in which a thing slides: a sliding part, e.g. of a trombone: a sliding clasp: a slip for mounting objects for the microscope: a case (*dark slide*) for photographic plates or its sliding cover: a picture for projection on a screen: a sliding lid: a sledge· a runner: a sliding seat: a landslip: a gliding from one note to another (*mus.*). a falling in value.— *ns.* **slid'er** one who, or that which, slides.—*n.* and *adj* **slid'ing.**—*adv.* **slid'ingly.—slide'-rule** a mechanical calculating device consisting of two logarithmic graduated scales sliding one against the other; **slid'ing-keel** a centreboard; **sliding scale** a scale, e.g. of duties, varying according to variation in something else, e.g. prices: a slide-rule —**let slide** to take no action over. [O.E. *slīdan*, to slide.]

slight *slīt, adj.* flimsy: lacking solidity, massiveness, weight, significance: slim slender: trifling: small.— *adv.* slightly: slightingly, meanly.—*v.t* to ignore or overlook disrespectfully: to insult —*n.* contemptuous indifference: discourteous disregard: an affront by showing neglect or want of respect.—*adv.* **slight'-ingly.**—*adj.* **slight'ish.**—*adv.* **slight'ly.**—*n.* **slight'-ness.**—(**not**) **in the slightest** (not) at all. [Cf. O.E. *eorthslihtes*, close to the ground; O.L.G *slicht*, plain, Du. *slecht*, bad, Ger. *schlecht*, bad.]

silly *sli'li, adv.* See under **sly.**

slim *slim, adj* very thin· slender: slight: crafty:— *compar.* **slimm'er**, *superl.* **slimm'est.**—*v.t.* to make thin: to decrease (*fig.*).—*v.i.* to use means to become more slender:—*pr.p.* **slimm'ing**; *pa.t.* and *pa.p.* **slim-med.**—*adv.* **slim'ly.**—*ns.* **slimm'er; slimm'ing.**—*adj.* **slimm'ish.**—*n.* **slim'ness.**—*adj.* **slim'line** slim, or conducive to slimness (also *fig*).—**slimmers' disease** anorexia nervosa [Du. *slim*, crafty; reintroduced from Afrik.]

slime *slīm, n* ooze: very fine, thin, slippery, or gluey mud: bitumen: any viscous organic secretion, as mucus: moral filth: obsequiousness.—*v.t.* to smear or cover with slime.—*adv.* **slim'ily.**—*n.* **slim'iness.**— *adj.* **slim'y** viscous· covered with slime· disgusting: obsequiously servile. [O.E. *slīm.*]

sling¹ *sling, n.* a strap or pocket with a string attached to each end, for hurling a stone. a catapult: a ballista: a loop for hoisting, lowering, or carrying a weight: a hanging support for an injured arm or foot: an attached strap for carrying: a throw: a sweep or swing —*v.t.* to throw with a sling: to hang loosely. to move or swing by means of a rope: to hurl, toss, fling (*coll.*): to utter, to pass (*slang*).—*v.i.* to discharge stones from a sling: to bound along with swinging steps:—*pa.t.* and *pa.p.* **slung.**—*n. and adj.* **sling'er.—sling'-back** a sling-back shoe.—**sling-back(ed) shoe** one from which the back is absent except for a strap representing the top edge; **sling one's hook** (*slang*) to go away, remove oneself. [Prob. from several sources; cf. O.N. *slyngva*, to fling, O.E. *slingan*, to wind, twist, L.G. *sling*, noose.]

sling[2] *slung, n.* an American drink, spirits and water sweetened and flavoured. [Perh. foregoing in sense of toss off; poss. Ger. *schlingen*, to swallow.]

slink *slingk, v.i.* to go sneakingly:—*pa.t.* and *pa.p.* **slunk.**—*n.* a slinking gait.—*adj.* **slink'y** slinking: lean: sinuous: close-fitting. [O.E. *slincan.*]

slip[1] *slip, v.i.* to escape: to pass quietly, easily, unobtrusively, or stealthily. to glide. to get out of position accidentally: to slide, esp. accidentally: to lose one's former skill, grip, or control of the situation (*coll.*): to lose one's footing: to make a slight mistake from inadvertence rather than ignorance: to lapse morally.—*v.t.* to cause or allow to slide: to put with a sliding motion: to convey quietly or secretly: to let pass: to let slip: to cast: to disengage: to let loose: to escape from: to elude: to dislocate:—*pr.p.* **slipp'ing;** *pa.t.* and *pa.p.* **slipped.**—*n.* an act of slipping: a mistake from inadvertence: a slight error or transgression: an escape: an inclined plane, sloping down to the water: a slight dislocation: a landslip: a pillow-case: a garment easily slipped on, esp. one worn under a dress, a petticoat: a leash: any of three fielders (*first slip, second slip, third slip*) positioned on the off side somewhat behind the wicket-keeper (often in *pl.*) their position (*cricket*): a sledge-runner: (in *pl.*) the place at the side of the stage for slipping scenery from: the side of a theatre gallery.—*n.* **slipp'age** (the extent of) failure to reach a set target: act, instance or amount of slipping.—*n.* **slipp'er** a loose shoe easily slipped on: a skid for a wheel: a sledge-runner: one who slips.—*v.t.* to furnish with slippers: to beat with a slipper.—*adj.* **slipp'ered.**—*ns.* **slipp'eriness, slipp'iness.**—*adjs.* **slipp'ery, slipp'y** so smooth or slimy as to allow or cause slipping: elusive: evasive: apt to slip: unstable: uncertain.—**slip'-case** a box-like case for a book or set of books, open at one end to leave the spine(s) visible; **slip'-dock** a dock with a slipway; **slip'-knot** a knot that slips along a rope: a knot untied by pulling.—*adjs.* **slip'-on, slip's over** slipped on or over: slipped over the head without unbuttoning.—*ns.* a garment easily slipped on: one slipped over the head.—**slipp'erwort** calceolaria; **slip road** a local bypass: a road by which vehicles come off or on to a motorway.—*adj.* **slip'shod** shod with slippers, or with shoes down at the heel: slovenly: careless, carelessly executed.—**slip stitch** a concealed sewing stitch used on hems, facings, etc. in which only a few threads of the material forming the main body of the garment are caught up by the needle for each stitch; **slip stream, slip'stream** the stream of air driven back by an aircraft propeller or the stream of air behind any moving vehicle or other object; **slip's up** (*coll.*) an error or failure; **slip'way** a pier in a dock or shipyard that slopes down into the water.—**give someone the slip** to escape stealthily from someone; **let slip** to reveal accidentally: to miss (an opportunity); **look slippy** (*coll.*, esp. *imper.*) to be quick, hurry; **slip off** to fall off: to take off quickly: go away quietly; **slip of the tongue** or **pen** a word, etc. said, or written, in error when something else was intended; **slip on** to put on loosely or in haste; **slip the cable** to let it go overboard instead of waiting to weigh the anchor: to die; **slip up** to make a mistake, to fail (*coll.*). [Perh. L.G. or Du. *slippen*; but O.E. has *slipor*, slippery, *slÿpescôh*, slipper.]

slip[2] *slip, n.* a scion, cutting: a scion, descendant: a young or slender person: anything slender or narrow: a small piece of paper, etc., for a memorandum, or for indexing, etc. [Perh. M.Du. or M.L.G. *slippe*, strip.]

slip[3] *slip, n.* a creamy paste for coating and decorating pottery.—**slip'ware** pottery decorated with slip. [O.E. *slipa, slypa,* slime, paste.]

slippage, slipper, slippery, etc. See **slip**[1].

slipslop *slip'slop, n.* sloppy stuff: twaddle.

slit *slit, v.t.* to cut lengthwise: to split: to cut into strips:—*pr.p.* **slitt'ing;** *pa.t.* and *pa.p.* **slit.**—*n.* a long cut: a narrow opening.—*adj.* cut lengthwise: cut open: having a slit.—*n.* **slitt'er.**—**slit'-pocket** an overcoat pocket with a slit to give access to a pocket within; **slit'-trench** (*mil.*) a narrow trench for one or more people. [M.E. *slitten,* app. related to O.E. *slitan.*]

slither *slidh'ər, v.i.* to slide, esp. interruptedly.—*adj.* slippery.—*n.* a scree.—*adj.* **slith'ery** slippery. [Old word **slidder.**]

sliver *sliv'ər,* or *slī'vər, v.t.* to split, to tear off lengthwise, to slice.—*n.* a piece cut or rent off, a slice, splinter: a continuous strand of loose untwisted wool or other fibre. [O.E. (*tō*-)*slīfan,* to cleave.]

slivovitz *sliv'ə-vitz, n.* a dry plum brandy.—Also **slivovic(a), slivowitz.** [Serbo-Croatian *sljivovica* —*sl(j)iva,* plum.]

slob *slob, n.* mud: ooze: mud-flat: a sloven: a boor (*slang*): a person of wealth but no refinement (*slang*). —*adj.* **slobb'y.** [Ir. *slab.*]

slobber *slob'ər, v.t.* and *v.i.* to slabber.—*adj.* **slobb'ery.** [Cf. Du. *slobberen,* to eat or work in a slovenly way; **slabber, slubber.**]

sloe *slō, n.* the blackthorn fruit or bush.—*adj.* of blackthorn wood: made with sloes: black.— **sloe'bush.**—*adj.* **sloe'-eyed** dark-eyed, slant-eyed, or both. [O.E. *slā, slāg, slāh.*]

slog *slog, v.t.* and *v.i.* to hit hard.—*v.i.* to work or walk doggedly:—*pr.p.* **slogg'ing;** *pa.t.* and *pa.p.* **slogged.** —*n.* a hard blow (generally with little regard to direction): a strenuous spell of work: something which requires strenuous, esp. protracted, effort.—*n.* **slogg'er.**

slogan *slō'gən, n.* a clan war-cry: a party catchword: an advertising catch-phrase.—*v.i.* **slo'ganise, -ize** to utter or repeat slogans, esp. as a substitute for reasoned discussion.—*n.* **slo'ganising, -z-.** [Earlier **slog(h)orne, sloggorne;** said to be from Gael. *sluagh,* army, *gairm,* cry.]

sloop *sloop, n.* a light boat: a one-masted cutter-rigged vessel, differing from a cutter in having a fixed bowsprit and proportionally smaller sails: (also **sloop'-of-war**) formerly a vessel, of whatever rig, between a corvette and a gun vessel, under a commander, carrying from ten to eighteen guns. [Du. *sloep.*]

slop[1] *slop, n.* slush: spilled liquid: a puddle: (in *pl.*) liquid refuse: (in *pl.*) weak or insipid liquor or semi-liquid food: (in *pl.*) gush, wishy-washy sentiment.— *v.t.* and *v.i.* to spill: to splash with slops: to slobber.— *v.t.* to wash away.—*v.i.* to walk in slush:—*pr.p.* **slopp'-ing;** *pa.t.* and *pa.p.* **slopped.**—*adv.* **slopp'ily.**—*n.* **slopp'iness.**—*adj.* **slopp'y** wet: muddy: wishy-washy, watery: slipshod (of work or language): sentimental: maudlin.—**slop'-basin, -bowl** a basin for slops at table; **slop'-pail** a pail for removing bedroom slops.— **slop out** (of a prisoner) to take away and empty out one's slops, to take slops from (a cell). [O.E. (*cū*-)*sloppe,* (cow-)droppings (cowslip)—*slūpan,* to slip.]

slop[2] *slop, n.* a loose garment—gown, cassock, smock-frock, etc.: (in *pl.*) wide baggy trousers or breeches: the wide part of these: (in *pl.*) ready-made clothing: (in *pl.*) clothes and bedding issued to seamen.— **Sloppy Joe** a large, loose sweater; **slop'-shop** a shop for ready-made clothes; **slop'work** the making of slop-clothing: cheap inferior work. [Cf. O.E.

oferslop, loose outer garment; M.Du. *slop*; O.N. *sloppr*.]

slope *slōp*, *n*. an incline: an inclined surface: an inclined position: an inclination, upward or downward slant.—*v.t.* to form with a slope, or obliquely: to put in a sloping position: to turn downwards, bow.—*v.i.* to have or take a sloping position or direction: to move down a slope: to decamp, disappear (*slang*).—*adj.* **slop'ing.**—*adv.* **slop'ingly.**—*adj.* **slop'y** sloping. —**at the slope** (of a rifle) on the shoulder with the barrel sloping back and up; **slope arms** to place or hold in this position; **slope off** (*slang*) to go away, esp. suddenly or furtively. [Aphetic from *aslope*, on the slope.]

sloppy. See **slop**[1,2].

slosh *slosh*, *n*. slush: a watery mess: a heavy blow (*slang*).—*v.i.* to flounder or splash in slush: to hit (*slang*).—*v.t.* to splash: to smite, beat (*slang*).—*adjs.* **sloshed** (*coll.*) intoxicated; **slosh'y.** [**slush.**]

slot[1] *slot*, *n*. a bar or bolt: a crosspiece that holds other parts together. [L.G. or Du. *slot*, lock.]

slot[2] *slot*, *n*. a long narrow depression or opening, as one to receive a coin, an armature winding, or part of a mechanism, or opening into the conduit of an electric or cable tramway or railway: a slit: a (usu. regular) place or position in e.g. a radio or television programme: a niche in an organisation.—*v.t.* to make a slot in, furnish with a slot: to pass through a slot: to put into a slot: to fit into a small space (*lit.* or *fig.*; with *in* or *into*).—*v.i.* (with *in* or *into*) to fit into a slot in something: to fit into a story, etc. (*fig.*).—*pr.p.* **slott'ing;** *pa.t.* and *pa.p.* **slott'ed.**—*n.* **slott'er** a person or machine that cuts slots.—**slot'-machine'**, **-me'ter** one operated by inserting a coin in a slot. [O.Fr. *esclot*.]

sloth *slōth*, or *sloth*, *n*. laziness, sluggishness: a sluggish arboreal tropical American edentate.—*v.t.* and *v.i.* to pass, spend (time) in sloth.—*adj.* **sloth'ful** given to sloth: inactive: lazy.—*adv.* **sloth'fully.**—*n.* **sloth'fulness.**—**sloth'-bear** a black Indian bear, with prolonged snout and lips. [M.E. *slawthe*, altered from O.E. *slǣwth*—*slāw*, slow.]

slouch *slowch*, *n*. an awkward lubberly clown: an inefficient person (*U.S. slang*): a droop: a stoop: a loose, ungainly stooping gait.—*adj.* drooping.—*v.i.* to go or bear oneself slouchingly: to droop.—*v.t.* to turn down the brim of.—*n.* **slouch'er.**—*adjs.* **slouch'ing; slouch'y.** [Cf. O.N. *slōka*, a slouching fellow.]

slough[1] *slow*, *n*. a hollow filled with mud: a marsh.— **the Slough of Despond** (the state of) extreme despondency, great depression. [O.E. *sloh*.]

slough[2] *sluf*, *n*. a cast skin: a coating: dead tissue in a sore.—*v.i.* to come away as a slough (with *off*): to cast the skin: to develop a slough.—*v.t.* to cast off, as a slough.—*adj.* **slough'y.** [M.E. *sloh*; origin uncertain.]

Slovak *slō'vak*, *slō-vak'*, *n*. a member of a Slavonic people living E. of the Czechs: their language.—Also *adj.*—*adjs.* **Slovakian** (*-vak'*, *-väk'*), **Slovak'ish.** [Slovak *Slovák*.]

sloven *sluv'n*, *n*. a person, esp. a man, carelessly or dirtily dressed or slipshod in work.—*n.* **slov'enliness.** —*adj.* and *adv.* **slov'enly.** [Cf. O.Du. *slof; sloef*, L.G. *sluf*, slow, indolent.]

Slovene *slō-vēn'*, *slō'*, *n*. a member of a branch of the Southern Slavs found chiefly in Slovenia, the northernmost constituent republic of Yugoslavia, and adjoining areas.—Also *adj.*—*n.* and *adj.* **Slové'nian.** [O.Slav. *Slovēne*.]

slow *slō*, *adj.* not swift: late: behind in time: not hasty: not ready: not progressive: dull: for slow-moving traffic: (of business) slack: (of an oven, etc.) heating gently, cooking slowly: which lessens the speed of the ball, players, etc. (*sport*): acting, etc. slowly.—*n.* anything that is slow.—*adv.* slowly (also in compounds).—*v.t.* to delay, retard, slacken the speed of. —*v.i.* to slacken in speed.—*adj.* **slow'ish.**—*n.* **slow'ing** a lessening of speed.—*adv.* **slow'ly.**—*n.* **slow'ness.**—**slow'coach** a laggard: a sluggish person; **slow-down** see **slow down** below.—**slow'-match** a slowly burning rope for firing explosives.—*adjs.* **slow'-mo'tion** much slower than normal or (*cinematograph*) actual motion; **slow'-mov'ing; slow'-paced.**—**slow'poke** (esp. *U.S.*) an irritatingly slow person.—**go slow, go-slow, go slow with** see **go'**; **slow down, up** to slow (*n.* **slow'-down**). [O.E. *slāw*.]

slow-worm *slō'wûrm*, *n*. the blindworm, a harmless snakelike legless lizard. [O.E. *slāwyrm*, prob. from root of *slēan*, to strike, *wyrm*, worm, assimilated to **slow.**]

slub[1], **slubb** *slub*, *v.t.* to twist after carding to prepare for spinning.—*n.* a roving.—*ns.* **slubb'er; slubb'ing.**

slub[2] *slub*, *n*. a lump in yarn.—*adj.* lumpy.—*adjs.* **slubbed, slubb'y.**

slubber *slub'ər*, *v.t.* to smear, soil, daub.—*v.i.* to wallow. [Du. *slobberen*, to lap, L.G. *slubbern*.]

sludge *sluj*, *n*. soft mud or mire: half-melted snow: a slimy precipitate, as from sewage.—*adj.* **sludg'y** miry: muddy. [Cf. **slush.**]

slue. Same as **slew**[2].

slug[1] *slug*, *n*. a heavy, lazy fellow: a land-mollusc with shell rudimentary or absent: a sea-slug: anything slow-moving.—*n.* **slugg'ard** one habitually inactive. —Also *adj.*—*adj.* **slugg'ish** habitually lazy: slothful: slow: inert.—*adv.* **slugg'ishly.**—*n.* **slugg'ishness.** [Cf. Norw. dial. *slugg*, a heavy body, *sluggje*, a slow heavy person, Sw. dial. *slogga*, to be sluggish.]

slug[2] *slug*, *n*. a lump of crude ore (*mining*): a lump of metal, esp. one for firing from a gun: a bullet: a solid line of type cast by a composing machine (*print.*): the gravitational unit of mass, approx. 32·174 pounds (= 14·5939 kg) in the **slug-foot-second** system (47·88 kg in slug-metre-second reckoning): a quantity of liquor that can be swallowed in one gulp. [Perh. conn. with foregoing or following.]

slug[3] *slug*, *v.t.* and *v.i.* to slog: to fling heavily.—Also *n.*—*n.* **slugg'er.** [Cf. **slog.**]

sluggard, sluggish, etc. See **slug**[1].

sluice *slōōs*, *n*. a structure with a gate for stopping or regulating flow of water: a floodgate or water-gate: a regulated outlet or inlet: a drain, channel: a trough for washing gold from sand, etc.: a sluicing.—*v.t.* to let out or drain by a sluice: to wet or drench copiously: to wash in or by a sluice: to flush or swill by flinging water: to dash.—*adj.* **sluic'y** streaming as from a sluice: sluice-like: soaking.—**sluice'-gate.** [O.Fr. *escluse* (Fr. *écluse*)—L.L. *exclūsa* (*aqua*), a sluice, i.e. (water) shut out, pa.p. of L. *exclūdĕre*, to shut out.]

slum *slum*, *n*. an overcrowded squalid neighbourhood. —*v.i.* (also *v.t.* with *it*) to adopt a lower standard of social behaviour, a less sophisticated level of cultural or intellectual activity, etc. than is or would be normal for oneself.—*ns.* **slumm'er; slumm'ing.**— *adj.* **slumm'y.** [Cant.]

slumber *slum'bər*, *v.i.* to sleep, esp. lightly: to be negligent or inactive.—*v.t.* to pass in slumber.—*n.* light sleep: repose.—*n.* **slum'berer.**—*n.* and *adj.* **slum'bering.** [M.E. *slūmeren*—O.E. *slūma*, slumber.]

slump *slump*, *v.i.* to fall or sink suddenly into water or mud: to fail or fall through helplessly: (of prices, trade, etc.) to fall suddenly or heavily: to flop, clump: to plump.—*n.* a sinking into slush, etc.: the sound so made: a sudden or serious fall of prices, business, etc. —opp. to *boom.* [Cf. Norw. *slumpe*, to slump, plump, L.G. *schlump*, marshy place.]

slung slung, pa.t. and pa.p. of **sling**[1].

slunk slungk, pa.t. and pa.p. of **slink**.

slur slûr, n. an aspersion, stain, imputation of blame: disparagement: discredit to one's reputation: a slight: a blur: a running together resulting in indistinctness in writing or speech: a smooth or legato effect (mus.): a curved line indicating that notes are to be sung to one syllable, played with one bow, or with a smooth gliding effect.—v.t. to disparage, asperse: to glide over slyly so as to mask or to avert attention: to blur: to sound indistinctly: to sing or play legato: to go through perfunctorily:—pr.p. **slurr'ing**; pa.t. and pa.p. **slurred**.—adj. **slurred**.—n. slurr'y (slur'i) a thin paste or semi-fluid mixture.

slurp slûrp, v.t. to drink (liquid) or eat (semi-liquid food) noisily.—v.i. to flow with, or produce, a slurp or slurps.—n. the noise produced by, or similar to that produced by, slurping food or drink. [Du. slurpen, slorpen, to sip audibly, gulp.]

slurry. See slur.

slush slush, n. liquid mud: melting snow: worthless sentimental drivel or gush.—adj. **slush'y.**—**slush fund, money** (slang, orig. U.S.) a fund of money used, usu. corruptly, in political campaigning and propaganda, bribery, undeclared commissions, etc. [Cf. slosh.]

slut slut, n. a dirty, untidy woman.—adj. **slutt'ish.**—adv. **slutt'ishly.**—ns. **slutt'ishness, slutt'ery.** [Cf. Ger. dial. schlutt(e).]

sly slī, adj. skilful in doing anything so as to be unobserved: cunning: wily: secretive: surreptitious: done with artful dexterity: with hidden meaning:—compar. **sly'er**; superl. **sly'est.**—adj. **sly'ish.**—adv. **sly'ly** (or **slī'ly**).—n. **sly'ness.**—**on the sly** surreptitiously. [O.N. slægr; cf. **sleight**.]

slype slīp, n. a passage between walls: esp. a covered passage from a cloister between transept and chapter-house. [Perh. **slip**[2].]

smack[1] smak, n. taste: a distinctive or distinguishable flavour: a trace, tinge.—v.i. to savour (of): to have a suggestion or trace (of) (fig.). [O.E. smæc.]

smack[2] smak, n. a small decked or half-decked coaster or fishing-vessel, usu. rigged as cutter, sloop, or yawl. [Du. smak.]

smack[3] smak, v.t. to strike smartly, to slap loudly: to kiss roughly and noisily: to make a sharp noise with, as the lips by separation: to taste with relish or with smacking sound.—v.i. to make such a sound.—n. a sharp sound: a crack: a slap: a hearty kiss.—adv. sharply, straight.—n. **smack'er** (slang) a £1 (note): a dollar (bill): a kiss.—n. and adj. **smack'ing.** [Prob. imit.; Du. or L.G. smakken, to smite, Ger. schmatzen, to smack.]

small smöl, adj. slender: narrow: fine in grain, texture, gauge, etc.: little in size, extent, quantity, value, power, importance, or degree: unimposing, humble: petty: dilute: short of full standard: operating on no great scale: soft or gentle in sound: minor.—n. a small thing, portion or piece: the narrow part (as of the back, the leg): (in pl.) underclothes.—adv. in a low tone: gently: in small pieces: on a small scale.—v.t. and v.i. to make or become small.—n. **small'ness.**—**small ads** classified advertisements; **small'-arm** (commonly in pl.) a weapon that can be carried by a man; **small beer** see beer.—adj. **small'-bore'** (of a firearm) having a barrel with a small bore, of a calibre not more than ·22 inch.—**small capitals** (coll. **small caps**) capital letters of the height of lower case.—**smallest room** (euph.) a lavatory, esp. in a house; **small'holder; small'holding** a holding of land smaller than an ordinary farm: esp. one provided by a local authority: the working of such.—n.pl. **small'-hours**

hours immediately after midnight.—**small letter** (usu. in pl.) a lower-case letter.—adj. **small'-mind'ed** petty.—n.pl. **small'-pipes** the Northumberland bagpipe.—**small'pox** (orig. pl.) a contagious, febrile disease, characterised by pock eruptions; **small screen** television (adj. **small'-screen**); **small'-sword** a light thrusting sword for fencing or duelling; **small'-talk** light or trifling conversation.—adj. **small'-time** (slang) unimportant.—**small wonder** (it is) a matter little to be wondered at.—**feel small** to feel insignificant; **in a small way** with little capital or stock: unostentatiously; **in small** on a small scale; **look small** to look silly: to be snubbed; **the small print** (place where) important information (is) given inconspicuously. [O.E. smæl.]

smallage smol'ij, n. wild celery. [**small**, Fr. ache—L. apium, parsley.]

smarm smarm, **smalm** smäm, vs.t. to fawn ingratiatingly and fulsomely: to be unctuous.—adv. **smarm'-ily, smalm'ily.**—n. **smarm'iness, smalm'iness.**—adj. **smarm'y, smalm'y.**

smart smärt, v.i. to feel a smart (also fig.): to be punished.—v.t. to cause to smart.—n. prolonged stinging pain.—adj. sharp and stinging: brisk: acute, witty: pert, vivacious: trim, spruce, fine: fashionable: keen, quick, and efficient in business.—adv. smartly.—v.t. **smart'en** to make smart, to brighten (with up.).—adv. **smart'ly.**—ns. **smart'ness; smart'y, smart'ie** a would-be smart fellow.—**smart Al'ick, Al'ec(k), alec** a would-be clever person.—Also adj. (with hyphen).—**smart'-money** money staked or invested by experienced gamblers or investors: the people staking or investing the money; **smart'ypants** (coll.; pl. the same) a smarty.—**look smart** to be quick. [O.E. smeortan.]

smash smash, v.t. to shatter violently: to ruin: to strike overhand with great force (lawn tennis, etc.): to dash violently.—v.i. to fly into pieces: to be ruined, to fail: to dash violently: to smash a tennis ball, etc.—n. an act or occasion of smashing, destruction, ruin, bankruptcy.—ns. **smash'er** one who smashes: anything great or extraordinary (slang): a person of dazzling charm (slang); **smash'ing.**—adj. crushing: dashing: strikingly good (slang).—adj. **smash-and-grab'** effected by smashing a shop-window and grabbing goods.—**smash'-hit'** (slang) overwhelming success, **smash'-up** a serious smash. [Imit.]

smatter smat'ər, n. a smattering.—n. **smatt'ering** a scrappy, superficial knowledge. [M.E. smateren, to rattle, to chatter.]

smear smēr, n. a rub with, mark or patch of, anything sticky or oily: the matter so applied, esp. to a slide for microscopic study: a fine glaze for pottery: a slur.—v.t. to anoint: to overspread with anything sticky or oily: to apply as a smear: to rub smearily: to defame.—adv. **smear'ily.**—n. **smear'iness.**—adj. **smear'y** sticky: greasy: ready to smear: showing smears.—**smear campaign** a series of verbal or written attacks intended to defame or discredit; **smear'-dab** see lemon[2]; **smear test** a test involving the microscopic study of a smear, as for example a cervical smear (q.v.). [O.E. smeru, fat, grease.]

smectic smek'tik, (chem.) adj. said of a mesomorphic substance whose atoms or molecules are oriented in parallel planes. [L. smecticus, cleansing,—Gr. smēktikos, detergent, (from the soapy consistency of a smectic substance).]

smegma smeg'mə, n. a sebaceous secretion, esp. that under the prepuce. [Gr. smēgma, -atos, soap.]

smell smel, n. the sense by which gases, vapours, substances very finely divided, are perceived, located in the higher animals in the mucous membrane of the nose: the specific sensation excited by such a substance: a pleasant scent or (often) an unpleasant one: the property of exciting it: an act or instance of exercising the sense: a smack, savour, property of suggesting, intimation (*fig.*).—*v.i.* to affect the sense of smell: to have odour (esp. unpleasant), or an odour (of): to have or use the sense of smell: to have a savour, give a suggestion (of something, *fig.*).—*v.t.* to perceive, detect, find, by smell (often with *out*): to take a smell at:—*pa.t.* and *pa.p.* **smelled** or **smelt**.—*ns.* **smell'er; smell'iness.**—*n.* and *adj.* **smell'ing.**—*adjs.* **smell'-less; smell'y** having a bad smell.—**smell'-ing-bottle** a bottle of smelling-salts or the like; **smell'-ing-salts** a preparation of ammonium carbonate with lavender, etc., used as a stimulant in faintness, etc.; **smell'-trap** a drain-trap.—**smell at** (formerly **to, of**) to sniff at, take a smell at; **smell of** to have the smell of: to savour of; **smell out** to find out by prying. [Very early M.E. *smel*, prob. O.E. but not recorded.]

smelt[1] *smelt*, *n.* a fish of or akin to the salmon family, with cucumber-like smell. [O.E. *smelt*.]

smelt[2] *smelt*, *v.t.* to melt in order to separate metal from ore.—*ns.* **smel'ter; smel'ting.** [Prob. M.L.G. or M.Du. *smelten*.]

smew *smū*, *n.* a small species of merganser.

smidgen, smidgeon, smidgin *smij'ən, -in*, (*coll.*) *n.* a very small amount.

Smilax *smī'laks*, *n.* a genus of the lily family, mostly climbers with net-veined leaves, some yielding sarsaparilla: (without *cap.*) a southern African twining plant of the asparagus family, with bright green foliage, much used by florists as decoration. [Gr. *smilax*.]

smile *smīl*, *v.i.* to express amusement, slight contempt, favour, pleasure, etc., by a slight drawing up of the corners of the lips: to look joyous: to be favourable.—*v.t.* to render, drive, express, by smiling: to give (a smile).—*n.* an act of smiling: the expression of the features in smiling: favour.—*n.* **smil'er.**—*n.* and *adj.* **smil'ing.**—*adv.* **smil'ingly.**—**smile at** to show amusement at, disregard of; **smile on** to show favour to, be propitious to. [M.E. *smilen*; poss. from L.G.]

smirch *smûrch*, *v.t.* to besmear, dirty: to sully.—*n.* a stain. [Earlier *smorch*, supposed to be from O.Fr. *esmorcher*, to hurt, influenced by *smear*.]

smirk *smûrk*, *v.i.* to smile affectedly, smugly, or foolishly: to look affectedly soft.—*n.* an affected, smug, or foolish smile.—*adjs.* **smirk** trim, spruce; **smirk'y** simpering. [O.E. *smercian*.]

smite *smīt*, *v.t.* to strike: to beat: to kill: to overthrow in battle: to affect with feeling: to afflict.—*v.i.* to strike: to meet forcibly:—*pa.t.* **smôte;** *pa.p.* **smitt'en.**—*n.* **smi'ter.** [O.E. *smitan*, to smear.]

smith *smith*, *n.* one who forges with the hammer: a worker in metals: one who makes anything.—*v.t.* to forge: to fashion.—*v.t.* to do smith's work.—*ns.* **smith'ery** a smithy: smith's work, smithing; **smithy** (*smidh'i*) a smith's workshop.—*v.t.* and *v.i.* to smith. —**smith'craft.** [O.E. *smith*.]

smithers *smidh'ərz*, *n.pl.* shivers, small fragments.— Also **smithereens'** (with Irish dim. suffix).

smithy. See **smith.**

smitten *smit'n*, *pa.p.* of **smite.**

smock *smok*, *n.* a smock-frock: a loose, protective garment, usu. of coarse cloth, worn by artists, etc.—*v.t.* to clothe in a smock or smock-frock: to decorate with smocking.—*n.* **smock'ing** honeycombing, as on the yoke and cuffs of a smock.—**smock'-frock** an outer garment of coarse white linen formerly worn by farmworkers in the south of England. [O.E. *smoc*.]

smog *smog*, *n.* smoky fog.—*adj.* **smogg'y.**

smoke *smōk*, *n.* the gases, vapours, and fine particles that come off from a burning body: solid particles suspended in a gas: fumes: vapour: fog: a cloud or column of smoke: that which may be smoked—tobacco, a cigarette, or cigar (*coll.*): a spell of smoking: tear gas (*coll.*).—*v.i.* to exhale or emit smoke, vapour, dust, etc.: to reek: to send smoke in a wrong direction: to take into the mouth and puff out the smoke of tobacco or the like: to lend itself to, admit of, smoking.—*v.t.* to dry, scent, preserve, fumigate, suffocate, blacken, taint, drive, render by smoke: to take in and emit the smoke from.—*adjs.* **smok'able** fit to be smoked; **smoked; smoke'less** emitting no smoke: containing little or no smoke.—*adv* **smoke'lessly.**—*ns* **smoke'lessness; smok'er** one who smokes tobacco: a smoking-carriage or compartment: one who smoke-dries meat: a smoking-concert.—*adv.* **smok'ily.**—*n.* **smok'iness.**—*n.* and *adj.* **smok'ing.**—*adj.* **smok'y** giving out smoke: like smoke: coloured like or by smoke: filled, or subject to be filled, with smoke: tarnished or noisome with smoke.—*n.* (*Scot.*) a smoked haddock.—**smoke'-ball** a shell emitting smoke as a screen or to drive out an enemy; **smoke'-bomb** a bomb that emits smoke on bursting; **smoke'-bush, -tree** a sumach with light feathery or cloudlike panicles.—*adj.* **smoke'-dried.**—*v.t.* **smoke'-dry** to cure or dry by means of smoke.—**smoke'-helmet** a head-covering for firemen or others who work in dense smoke; **smoke'-hole** a fumarole: a hole for escape of smoke; **smoke'-house** a building where meat or fish is cured by smoking, or where smoked meats are stored; **smokeless zone** (*coll.*) a smoke control area.—*adj.* **smoke'proof** impervious to smoke.—**smoke'-room; smoke'-screen** a cloud of smoke raised to conceal movements (also *fig.*); **smoke signal** (often in *pl.*) a signal or message conveyed by means of patterns of smoke (also *fig.*); **smoke'-stack** a ship's funnel: a chimney; **smoke-tree** see **smoke-bush; smoke tunnel** a wind tunnel into which smoke is put at certain points in order to make wind effects visible; **smoking cap, jacket** a light ornamental cap or jacket formerly worn by smokers; **smoking carriage, compartment, room** a railway-carriage, compartment, room, set apart for smokers.—**end, go up, in smoke** (of e.g. hopes) to vanish: (of e.g. plan) to come to nothing; **smoke control area** one in which the emission of smoke from chimneys is prohibited; **smoke out** to discover: to drive out of a hiding place by smoke or fire. [O.E. *smoca* (n.), *smocian* (vb.).]

smolt *smōlt*, *n* a young river salmon when it is bluish along the upper half of the body and silvery along the sides. [Orig. Scot.]

smooch *smōōch*, (*coll.*), *v.i.* to kiss, pet. [Origin uncertain; poss. related to dial. *smouch*, to kiss.]

smooth *smōōdh*, *adj.* having an even surface: without roughness: evenly spread: glossy: hairless: of even consistency: slippery: gently flowing: easy: bland: fair-spoken: classy or elegant (*slang*).—*adv.* **smoothly.**—*v.t.* **smooth**, rarely **smoothe**, to make smooth: to free from obstruction, difficulty, harshness: to remove by smoothing (often with *away*): often *fig.*): to calm, soothe: to blandish: to make (difficulties or problems) seem less serious or less important (often with *over*).—*v.i.* to become smooth.—*n.* a smooth place or part: an act of smoothing.—*v.t.* **smooth'en** to make smooth.—*ns.* **smooth'er** one who, or that which, smooths; **smooth'ie** (*slang*) a plausible or smooth-spoken person: a person elegant or suave in manner or appearance, esp. insincerely or excessively so.—*n.* and *adj.* **smooth'ing.**—*adv.* **smooth'ly.** —*n.* **smooth'ness.**—*adj.* **smooth'-bore** not rifled (also **smooth'-bored**).—*n.* a gun with a smooth-bored barrel.—*adj.* **smooth'-coated** not shaggy-haired.— **smooth dab** see **lemon**[2].—*adj.* **smooth'-faced** having a smooth face or surface: pleasant-looking: beardless: unwrinkled: plausible.—**smoothing iron** a flatiron;

smoothing plane a small fine plane used for finishing.
—*adj.* **smooth'-leaved.**—**smooth muscle** unstriated muscular tissue (e.g in the walls of the intestines) whose action is slow rhythmic contraction and relaxation, independent of the will.—*adjs.* **smooth'-spoken, smooth'-tongued** conciliatory, plausible, flattering, or soft in speech. [O.E. *smōth* (usu. *smēthe*).]

smørbrød *smȫr'brōō, smor', smœr'brȫ,* (*Norw.*), **smørrebrød** *smœr'ə-brœdh, smȫr'ə-brȫd,* (*Dan.*) *ns.* lit., bread and butter: hors d'œuvres served on slices of buttered bread.

smörgåsbord *smȫr'gas-bord,* Sw. *smœr'gȫs-bōōrd, n.* a Swedish-style table assortment of hors d'œuvres and many other dishes to which one helps oneself. [Sw.]

smorzando *smört-san'dō* (It. *zmort san'dō*), **smorzato** *-sà'tō, adjs.* and *advs.* with a gradual fading away: growing slower and softer. [It.; ger. and pa.p. of *smorzare,* to tone down, extinguish.]

smote *smōt, pa.t.* of **smite.**

smother *smudh'ər, v.t.* to suffocate by excluding the air, esp. by a thick covering: to stifle: to envelop closely: to cover up thickly: to suppress: to conceal.—*v.i.* to be suffocated or suppressed: to smoulder.—*n.* smoke: thick floating dust: a smouldering fire or condition: a welter: suffocation.—*adj.* **smoth'ered.**—*ns.* **smoth'erer; smoth'eriness.**—*n.* and *adj.* **smoth'ering.** —*adv.* **smoth'eringly.**—*adj.* **smoth'ery** tending to smother: stifling.—**smothered mate** (*chess*) checkmate by a knight, the king having been prevented from moving by the positions of his own forces. [M.E. *smorther*—O.E. *smorian,* to smother.]

smoulder *smōl'dər, v.i.* to burn slowly or without flame: to linger on in a suppressed or hidden state.—*n.* smouldering fire.—*n.* and *adj.* **smoul'dering.** [M.E. *smolder;* origin obscure.]

smudge[1] *smuj, n.* a smear: a blur: a rubbed blot.—*v.t.* to smear: to blur: to soil: to daub.—*n.* **smudg'er.**—*adv.* **smudg'ily.**—*n.* **smudg'iness.**—*adj.* **smudg'y.**

smudge[2] *smuj, n.* a choking smoke.—*v.t.* to fumigate with smoke.—*adj.* **smud'gy** smoky.

smug *smug, adj.* neat, prim, spruce: smooth: sleek: affectedly smart: offensively self-complacent.—*n.* a smug person.—*adv.* **smug'ly.**—*n.* **smug'ness.**—*adj.* **smug'-faced.** [Connection with L.G. *smuk,* trim, presents difficulty.]

smuggle *smug'l, v.t.* to import or export illegally or without paying duty: to convey secretly.—*adj.* **smug'led.**—*n.* **smug'ler** one who smuggles: a vessel used in smuggling.—*n.* and *adj.* **smugg'ling.** [L.G. *smuggeln;* Ger. *schmuggeln.*]

smut *smut, n.* soot: worthless or bad coal: a flake or spot of dirt, soot, etc.: a black spot: a disease of plants, esp. cereals, giving an appearance of soot: the fungus causing it: obscene discourse.—*v.t.* to soil, spot, or affect with smut: to become smutty.—*adj.* **smutt'ed.**—*adv.* **smutt'ily**—*n.* **smutt'iness.**—*adj.* **smutt'y** stained with smut: affected with smut: obscene, filthy. [Cf. L.G. *schmutt;* Ger. *Schmutz,* dirt.]

smutch *smutch, v.t.* to smut: to sully.—*n.* a dirty mark: soot: grime: a stain.

snack *snak, n.* a light repast.—*v.i.* to take a snack.— **snack'-bar, snack'-counter** a place where light meals can be bought. [Cf. M.Du. *snacken,* to snap; **snatch.**]

snaffle *snaf'l, n.* a jointed bit (less severe than the curb).—*v.t.* to put a snaffle on: to control by the snaffle: (the following meanings *slang*) to arrest: to capture: to purloin: to get possession of.—**snaff'le-bit; snaff'le-bridle; snaff'le-rein.** [Ety. dub.; cf. Du. *snavel,* Ger. *Schnabel,* beak, mouth.]

snafu *sna-fōō', (U.S. slang) n.* chaos.—*adj.* chaotic. [situation normal—all fouled (or fucked) up.]

snag *snag, n.* a stump, as of a branch or tooth: a jag: a short tine: an embedded tree, dangerous for boats: hence a catch, a hidden obstacle or drawback: a caught thread in a stocking.—*v.t.* to catch on a snag: to tear on a snag: to hack so as to form snags: to clear of snags:—*pr.p.* **snag'ging;** *pa.t.* and *pa.p.* **snagged.**—*adjs.* **snagged, snag'gy.** [Cf. O.N. *snagi,* peg.]

snail *snāl, n.* any terrestrial or air-breathing gasteropod mollusc with well-developed coiled shell: extended to other shelled gasteropods: a sluggish person or animal: a snail-wheel.—*adj.* and *adv.* **snail'-like.**—*adj.* **snail'y.**—*adj.* **snail'-paced.**—**snail'-shell.** —**snail's pace** a very slow speed; **snail'-wheel** a cam that controls the striking of a clock. [O.E. *snegl, snægl, snæl.*]

snake *snāk, n.* a serpent, or member of the Ophidia, a class of elongated limbless (or all but limbless) scaly carnivorous reptiles, often venomous, with forked tongue, no eyelids or external ears, teeth fused to the bones that bear them: an ungrateful or treacherous person (in allusion to Aesop): a wretch, drudge: anything snakelike in form or movement: the band (narrower than the **tunnel** allowed by the IMF on the world market) within which the relative values of certain EEC currencies are allowed to float.—*v.i.* to wind: to creep.—*adj.* **snake'like.**—*advs.* **snake'wise** in the manner of a snake; **snāk'ily.**—*n.* **snāk'iness.**— *adj.* **snāk'y.**—**snake'bird** the darter: the wryneck; **snake'bite** the bite of a venomous snake; **snake'-charmer** one who handles snakes and sets them to perform rhythmical movements; **snake'-pit** (*fig.*) a mental hospital: a place, or circumstances, characterised by disordered emotions and relationships.—**snake in the grass** (*fig.*) one who injures furtively: a lurking danger; **snakes and ladders** a board game played with counters and dice in which 'ladders' afford short cuts to the finish, but 'snakes' oblige one to descend to nearer the starting-point. [O.E. *snaca.*]

snap *snap, v.i.* to make a bite (often with *at*): to speak tartly in sudden irritation: to grasp (with *at*): to shut suddenly, as by a spring: to make a sharp noise: to go with a sharp noise: to break suddenly.—*v.t.* to bite suddenly: to seize, secure promptly (usu. with *up*): to answer or interrupt sharply (often with *up*): to shut with a sharp sound: to cause to make a sharp sound: to send or put with a sharp sound: to utter snappishly (sometimes with *out*): to break suddenly: to take an instantaneous photograph of, esp. with a hand-camera:—*pr.p.* **snapp'ing;** *pa.t.* and *pa.p.* **snapped.**— *n.* an act, instance, or noise of snapping: a small catch or lock: a crack: a gingerbread biscuit: a crisp, incisive quality in style: lively energy: an easy and profitable place or task: a sharper, a cheat: a riveter's or glassmoulder's tool: a snapshot: a sudden cold spell (also **cold snap**): a type of card game.—*adj.* sudden, unexpected: offhand: (of decision, judgment) taking, made, on the spur of the moment without deep consideration of all possibilities: snapping shut.—*adj.* with a snap.—*n.* **snapp'er** an animal that snaps: one who snaps or snaps up: a snapping-turtle: any fish of the family Lutianidae, akin to the basses: (also **schnapper**) a highly esteemed food-fish of Australian and New Zealand waters.—*adv.* **snapp'ily.**—*n.* and *adj.* **snapp'ing.**—*adv* **snapp'ingly.**—*adj.* **snapp'ish** inclined to snap: quick and tart.—*adj.* **snapp'y** snappish: snapping: having the quality of snap: instantaneous.—**snap'dragon** a plant (*Antirrhinum*) of the figwort family whose flower when pinched and released snaps like a dragon; **snap'-link** a link with a side opening closed by a spring; **snapp'ing-tur'tle** a large American fiercely snapping fresh-water tortoise; **snap'shot** a hasty shot: a photograph taken quickly and informally, with simple equipment.— **look snappy, make it snappy** (coll.) to hurry; **snap into it** to get going quickly; **snap someone's head, nose, off** to answer irritably and rudely; **snap out of it** (coll.) to give it (e.g. a mood, habit) up at once; **snap up** to take or purchase eagerly and quickly. [Prob. Du. snappen, to snap; Ger. schnappen.]

snare snãr, n. a running noose for trapping: a trap: an allurement, temptation, entanglement, moral danger: a loop for removing tumours, etc.: a string stretched across the lower head of a side-drum.—v.t. to catch, entangle, entrap, in a snare: to remove with a snare.—ns. snar'er; snar'ing.—adj. snar'y.— **snare'-drum** a side-drum. [O.E. sneare or O.N. snara; prob. partly from Du. snaar or L.G. snare.]

snarl[1] snãrl, v.i. to make a surly resentful noise with show of teeth: to speak in a surly manner.—v.t. to utter snarlingly.—n. an ill-natured growling sound: a snarling.—n. snarl'er.—n. and adj. snarl'ing.—adj. snarl'y. [Old word snar; cf. Dutch snarren.]

snarl[2] snãrl, n. a knot: a tangle: a knot in wood.—v.t. to tangle: to raise with a snarling-iron.—v.i. to tangle.—adj. snarled.—ns. snarl'er; snarl'ing.— **snarl'ing-iron, -tool** a curved tool for raised work in hollow metalware.—**snarl up** (used esp. in pa.p. and p.adj. forms) to make muddled or tangled and thus stop operating, moving, etc. smoothly (n. snarl'-up). [snare.]

snatch snach, v.t. to seize suddenly: to pluck away quickly: to grab: to take as opportunity occurs.—v.i. to make a snap or seizure.—n. a seizure or attempt to seize: a grab: a short spell: a fragment, as of song, verse: in weight-lifting, a type of lift in which the weight is raised from the floor to an overhead position in one movement.—n. snatch'er.—advs. snatch'ily, snatch'ingly.—adj. snatch'y irregular.—snatch squad a group of policemen, etc. who force a sudden quick passage into e.g. a disorderly or rioting crowd in order to arrest troublemakers or ringleaders.— **snatch at** to try to snatch or seize. [M.E. snacchen; poss. related to snack.]

snazzy snaz'i, (slang) adj. very attractive or fashionable: flashy.

sneak snēk, v.i. to go furtively or meanly, slink, skulk: to cringe: to behave meanly: to tell tales.—v.t. to pass furtively to steal (slang).—n. a sneaking fellow: one who sneaks away: a sneaking thief: a tell-tale: a ball bowled along the ground (cricket).—n. sneak'er one who, or that which, sneaks: a soft-soled shoe: a sand-shoe.—adv. sneak'ily.—n. sneak'iness.—adj. sneak'ing mean, crouching: secret, underhand, not openly avowed: lurking under other feelings.—adv. sneak'ingly.—adjs. sneak'ish befitting a sneak; sneak'y sneaking: cunning.—sneak'-raid a bombing or other raid made under conditions of concealment; **sneak'-thief** a thief who steals through open doors or windows without breaking in. [Connection with O.E. snican, to crawl, is obscure.]

sneck snek, (Scot. and Northern) n. a latch: a doorcatch.—v.t. to fasten with a sneck. [Cf. snack, snatch.]

sneer snēr, v.i. to show cynical contempt by the expression of the face, as by drawing up the lip (sometimes with at): to express such contempt in other ways.— v.t. to utter sneeringly: to render, drive, by sneering. —n. a sneering expression: an act of sneering.—n. sneer'er.—n. and adj. sneer'ing.—adv. sneer'ingly.— adj. sneer'y. [Perh. related to Fris. sneere, to scorn.]

sneeze snēz, v.i. to make a sudden, involuntary and audible expiration through the nose and mouth, due to irritation of the inner nasal membrane.—n. an act of sneezing.—ns. sneez'er; sneez'ing.—adj. sneez'y.

—**sneeze'wort** a species of yarrow (Achillaea ptarmica) once used as a substitute for snuff: white hellebore.—**not to be sneezed at** not to be despised. [M.E. snesen, fnesen—O.E. fnēsan, to sneeze.]

snell snel, n. a short piece of hair, gut, etc., attaching a hook to a line.—v.t. to attach (a hook) to a line.

snib snib, (Scot.) n. a small bolt: a catch for a windowsash.—v.t. to fasten with a snib. [Cf. L.G. snibbe, beak.]

snick[1] snik, v.t. to cut out, snip, nick: to deflect slightly by a touch of the bat (cricket).—n. a small cut: a glancing stroke in cricket.

snick[2] snik, n., v.t., and v.i. click. [Imit.]

snicker snik'ər, v.i. to snigger: to nicker, neigh.—v.t. to say gigglingly.—n. a giggle. [Imit.; cf. snigger.]

snide snīd, adj. sham: counterfeit: base: mean: dishonest: derogatory in an insinuating way: showing malice.—Also n.—adv. snide'ly.—n. snide'ness.

sniff snif, v.t. to draw in with the breath through the nose: to smell: to suspect or detect by smell or as if by smell.—v.t. to draw in air sharply and audibly through the nose: to draw up mucus or tears escaping into the nose: to smell tentatively: to express disapprobation with reticence by a slight sound in the nose: to snuffle.—n. an act or a sound of sniffing: a smell: a small quantity inhaled by the nose.—n. sniff'er.— adv. sniff'ily.—n. sniff'iness.—n. and adj. sniff'ing. —v.i. sniff'le to snuffle slightly, to sniff.—n. an act of sniffling: the sound made by sniffling: (often in pl. with the) a slight cold: (often in pl. with the) liquid mucus running out of or blocking the nose.—n. sniff'ler one who sniffles.—adj. sniff'y inclined to be disdainful.—vs.i. sniff to sniff, snivel: to blow out steam, etc.; sniff'er to sniff.—n. a sniff: (in pl.) stoppage of the nasal passages in catarrh, the sniffles: a dram (slang).—adj. sniff'y (slang) having a tempting smell: inclined to sniff in disdain.—sniffer dog a dog trained to smell out drugs or explosives; **sniff'ing-valve** an air-valve of a cylinder, etc.—**not to be sniffed at** not to be despised. [Imit.; cf. snuff[1].]

snigger snig'ər, v.i. to laugh in a half-suppressed way, often offensively.—v.t. to say with a snigger.—n. a half-suppressed laugh.—n. snigg'erer.—n., adj. snigg'ering.—adv. snigg'eringly. [Imit.]

snip snip, v.t. to cut as with scissors:—pr.p. snipp'ing; pa.t. and pa.p. snipped.—n. a small cut, as with scissors: a small shred: a small, slender or despicable person: a small piece: a notch, slit, or slash: the sound of a stroke of scissors: a white or light patch or stripe on a horse, esp. on the nose: a certainty: a bargain.— ns. snipp'er; snipp'et a little piece snipped off: a scrap, as of literature, news; snipp'etiness.—adj. snipp'ety trivial, fragmentary.—n. snipp'ing a clipping.—adj. snipp'y fragmentary: stingy: snappish.— n.pl. snips hand-shears for sheetmetal. [L.G. or Du. snippen; Ger. dial. schnippen.]

snipe snip, n. a bird akin to the woodcock, with a long straight flexible bill, or other of its genus or family: a sniping shot:—pl. usu. snipe of the bird, snipes of species of the bird, and in other senses.—v.i. to shoot snipe, go snipe-shooting: to shoot at single men from cover: to attack, criticise, esp. from a position of security (fig.; often with at).—v.t. to pick off by riflefire from (usu. distant) cover.—ns. snip'er; snip'ing. [Prob. Scand.; the O.E. word is snite.]

snipper, snippet. See snip.

snitch snich, (slang) n. the nose: a fillip on the nose: an informer.—v.i. to inform, peach.—v.t. (coll.) to pilfer.—n. snitch'er an informer: a handcuff.

snivel sniv'l, n. mucus of the nose: a sniff: a hypocritical snuffle: cant.—v.i. to run at the nose: to sniff: to snuffle: to whimper: to cry, as a child.—v.t. to utter with snivelling:—pr.p. sniv'elling; pa.t. and

pa.p. **sniv'elled.**—*n.* **sniv'eller.**—*adjs.* **sniv'elling;**
sniv'elly. [O.E. *snofl*, mucus.]

snob snob, *n.* one who makes himself ridiculous or
odious by the value he sets on social standing or rank,
by his fear of being ranked too low, and by his
different behaviour towards different classes.—*n.*
snobb'ery snobbishness: snobbish behaviour.—*adj.*
snobb'ish.—*adv.* **snobb'ishly.**—*ns.* **snobb'ishness;**
snobb'ism.—*adj.* **snobb'y.** [Orig. slang.]

snoek. See **snook**[1].

snog snog, (slang) *v.i.* to embrace, kiss, indulge in love-
making.—Also *n.*

snood snōōd, *n.* a fillet for the hair, once in Scotland the
badge of virginity: revived in the sense of a conspicuous net supporting the back-hair: the hair-line, gut,
etc., by which a fish-hook is fixed to the line.—*v.t.* to
bind, dress, fasten, with a snood. [O.E. *snōd*.]

snook[1] snōōk, *n.* one of several fishes—a garfish, or (in
S. Africa and now elsewhere also **snoek** snōōk) the
barracouta (*Thyrsites atun*). [Du. *snoek*, pike.]

snook[2] snōōk, *n.* the gesture of putting the
thumb to the nose, to express derision, defiance, etc.
—Also **snooks.**—**cock a snook** to make that gesture
(also *fig.*).

snooker snōōk'ər, *n.* a variety of the game of pool,
played with 15 red balls, 1 white cue ball and 6 balls of
other colours, the object being to pocket the non-
white balls in a certain order and gain more points in
so doing than one's opponent: a situation in snooker
where the path between the cue ball and the ball to be
played is blocked, forcing an indirect shot to be
played.—*v.t.* to render a direct stroke impossible for:
to get the better of, the plans of, (a person), by
making it difficult or impossible for him to act as he
intended because of an obstacle one has put in his way
(*fig.*).

snoop snōōp, (slang) *v.i.* to go about sneakingly, to pry.
—Also *n.*—*n.* **snoop'er.** [Du. *snoepen*, to eat,
steal.]

snoot snōōt, *n.* an expression of contempt.—*n.* **snoot'-**
ful enough alcohol to make one drunk.—*adj.* **snoot'y**
haughtily supercilious. [Cf. Du. *snuit*, snout, face.]

snooze snōōz, *v.i.* to doze.—*n.* a nap.—*n.* **snooz'er.**

snoozle snōō'zl, *v.i.* to nuzzle.—*v.t.* to thrust nuzzl-
ingly. [Cf. **snooze**, **nuzzle**.]

snore snōr, snör, *v.i.* to breathe roughly and hoarsely
in sleep with vibration of uvula and soft palate or of
the vocal chords: to snort.—*v.t.* to pass in snoring: to
render by snoring.—*n.* a noisy breathing of this kind.
—*ns.* **snor'er;** **snor'ing.** [Imit.; cf. **snort**.]

snorkel snör'kl, an anglicised form of **schnorkel**.—*n.*
snor'kelling swimming with a snorkel.

snort snört, *v.i.* to force the air with violence and noise
through the nostrils, as horses.—*v.t.* to express by or
utter with a snort: to force out, as by a snort.—*n.* an
act or sound of snorting: a quick drink (slang).—*n.*
snort'er one who snorts: anything characterised by
extreme force, esp. a gale (coll.).—*n.* and *adj.* **snort'-**
ing.—*adv.* **snort'ingly.**—*adj.* **snort'y** snorting: inclined to snort (coll.): contemptuous and ready to
take offence. [Imit.]

snot snot, *n.* mucus of the nose: a mean fellow.—*v.i.*
snott'er to breathe through an obstruction in the nostrils: to sob, snuffle, blubber.—*adv.* **snott'ily.**—*n.*
snott'iness.—*adj.* **snott'y** like, or foul with, snot:
superciliously stand-offish, with nose in air: mean, of
no importance.—*adj.* **snott'y-nosed.** [O.E. *gesnot*,
snỹtan, to blow the nose; allied to **snout**.]

snout snowt, *n.* the projecting nose of a beast, as of a
swine: any similar projection: a cigar or cigarette
(slang): a police informer (slang).—*v.t.* to furnish
with a snout.—*adjs.* **snout'ed;** **snout'y** like a snout:
snouted: haughtily supercilious (see **snooty**). [M.E.

snūte, prob. from unrecorded O.E.; cf. **snot**.]

snow[1] snō, *n.* atmospheric vapour frozen in crystalline
form, whether in single crystals or aggregated in
flakes: a snowfall: any similar substance, as carbonic
acid snow (frozen carbon dioxide): snowlike specks
on the screen caused by electrical interference (*TV*):
cocaine, morphine, heroin (slang).—*adj.* of snow.—
v.i. to shower snow: to fall as snow or like snow.—*v.t.*
to shower like snow: to strew as with snow: to whiten,
whiten the hair of (*fig.*): (with *up*, *under*) to bury,
block, shut in, overwhelm, with snow or as if
with snow.—*adv.* **snow'ily.**—*n.* **snow'iness.**—*adjs.*
snow'less; snow'like; snow'y abounding or covered
with snow: white, like snow: pure.—**snow'ball** a ball
made of snow pressed hard together: (also **snowball-**
tree) a sterile *Viburnum opulus* : a round white pudding, cake, or sweetmeat: something that grows like a
snowball rolled in snow, esp. a distribution of begging
letters, each recipient being asked to send out so
many copies.—*v.t.* to throw snowballs at.—*v.i.* to
throw snowballs: to grow greater ever more quickly.
—**snow'-bird** any finch of the N. American genus
Junco, white underneath, familiar in winter: applied
to various other birds that appear in winter.—*adj.*
snow'-blind.—**snow'-blind'ness** amblyopia caused by
the reflection of light from snow; **snow'-blink** a reflection from fields of snow, like ice-blink; **snow'-**
blower a snow-clearing machine which takes in the
snow in front of it and blows it to the side of the road;
snow'-boot a boot or overshoe for walking in snow.—
adj. **snow'-bound** shut in, prevented from travelling,
by snow.—**snow'-bunting** a black-and-white (in
summer partly tawny) bunting of the Arctic regions, a
winter visitor in Britain; **snow'cap** a cap of snow as on
the polar regions or a mountain-top.—*adj.* **snow'-**
capped.—**snow'drift** a bank of snow drifted together
by the wind; **snow'drop** a drooping white flower of
early spring, or the plant that bears it; **snow'fall** a
quiet fall of snow: the amount falling in a given time;
snow'-field a wide range of snow, esp. where permanent; **snow'-finch** an Alpine bird like the snow-
bunting; **snow'flake** a feathery clump of snow
crystals.—*n.pl.* **snow'-goggles** goggles to guard
against snow-blindness.—**snow'-goose** a white Arctic
American goose; **snow'-guard** a board to keep snow
from sliding off a roof; **snow-in-summ'er** a white-
flowered garden mouse-ear chickweed; **snow leopard**
the ounce (*Panthera uncia*), an animal related to the
leopard, found in the mountainous regions of Central
Asia; **snow'line** the limit of perpetual snow;
snow'man a great snowball made in human form: the
abominable snowman (see **abominate**); **snow'mobile**
a motorised sleigh or a tractor-like vehicle capable of
travelling over snow; **snow'-plough** an implement for
clearing snow from roads and railways: a skiing position in which the skis form a V, with the tips touching;
snow'-shoe a long broad framework strapped to the
foot for walking on snow.—*n.pl.* **snow'-spec'tacles**
spectacles worn as a protection against the glare of
snow.—**snow'storm.**—*adj.* **snow'-white** as white as
snow.—**snowy owl** a great white owl of northern regions.—**not a snowball's chance (in hell, in an oven)**
(coll.) no chance at all; **snowed under** overwhelmed with rapid accumulation of; **snowed in, up**
blocked or isolated by snow. [O.E. *snāw*.]

snub snub, *v.t.* to rebuke: to take up, cut short, rebuff,
in a humiliating or mortifying manner: to check: to
bring to a sudden stop: to cut or break short: to make
snub:—*pr.p.* **snubb'ing;** *pa.t.* and *pa.p.* **snubbed.**—*n.*
an act of snubbing: a check: a snub nose: a stub, snag,
knob.—*adj.* flat, broad, and turned up.—*n.* and *adj.*
snubb'ing.—*adv.* **snubb'ingly.**—*adjs.* **snubb'ish,**
snubb'y inclined to snub or check: somewhat snub.—

snub nose a short turned-up nose.—*adj.* **snub'-nosed.** [O.N. *snubba*, to chide, snub]

snudge *snuj, v.i.* to save in a miserly way.—*n.* a mean stingy fellow.

snuff[1] *snuf, v.i.* to draw in air violently and noisily through the nose: to sniff: to smell at anything doubtfully: to take snuff.—*v.t.* to draw into the nose: to smell, to examine, suspect, or detect by smelling. —*n.* a powdered preparation of tobacco or other substance for snuffing: a pinch of snuff or act of snuffing: a sniff: resentment, huff.—*ns.* **snuff'er** one who snuffs; **snuff'iness.**—*n.* and *adj.* **snuff'ing.**—*adj.* **snuff'y** like, smelling of, soiled with or showing traces of, snuff: touchy, huffy.—**snuff'box** a box for snuff; **snuff'-colour, -brown** a yellowish or greyish brown, slightly paler than bistre.—*adj.* **snuff'-coloured.**—**snuff'-mill** a factory or a hand-mill for grinding tobacco into snuff: a snuff-mull; **snuff'-mull** a snuff box; **up to snuff** knowing, not likely to be taken in: up to scratch, in good order. [M.Du. *snuffen.*]

snuff[2] *snuf, n.* a sooty ill-smelling knob on a wick: a worthless or offensive residue.—*v.t.* to remove the snuff from: to make brighter: to put out as with snuffers (with *out*; also *fig.*).—*n.* **snuff'er** (in later use **snuffers, or pair of snuffers**) an instrument like a pair of scissors for removing snuffs from the wicks of candles, or of oil-lamps: one with a cap-shaped part for extinguishing candles: an attendant, esp. in a theatre, who snuffed candles.—**snuff it, snuff out** (*slang*) to die. [M.E. *snoffe*; conn. with foregoing and with L.G. *snuppen*, Ger. *schnappen*, obscure.]

snuffle *snuf'l, v.i.* to breathe hard or in an obstructed manner through the nose: to sniff: to speak through the nose.—*v.t.* to sniff: to say or utter nasally.—*n.* an act or sound of snuffling: a snuffling tone: cant: (in *pl.*) an obstructed condition of the nose.—*n.* **snuff'-ler** (*snuf'lər, snuf'l-ər*).—*n.* and *adj.* **snuffling** (*snuf'ling, snuf'l-ing*). [Freq. of **snuff**[2]; cf. **snivel** and Du. *snuffelen*, Ger. *schnüffeln.*]

snug *snug, adj.* lying close and warm: comfortable: sheltered: not exposed to view or notice: in good order: compact: fitting close.—*n.* a snuggery.—*v.i.* to lie close.—*v.t.* to make snug: to stow away snugly: —*pr.p.* **snugg'ing;** *pa.t.* and *pa.p.* **snugged.**—*n.* **snugg'ery** a snug room or place, esp. a bar-parlour. —*v.i.* **snugg'le** to nestle.—*v.t.* to hug close: to wrap close.—*adv.* **snug'ly.**—*n.* **snug'ness.**

so[1] *sō, adv.* merging in *conj.* or *interj.* in this, that, or such manner, degree, or condition: to such an extent: likewise: accordingly: well: therefore: in due course, thereupon, thereafter: as: soever: thus: for like reason: in a high degree: as has been stated: provided: in case: in order (*coll.*): be it: that will do: very good. —**so'-and-so** this or that person or thing: such-and-such a person or thing: used to replace a descriptive oath (*coll.*; also *adj.*).—*adj.* **so'-called** styled thus—usu. implying doubt or denial of the meaning or implications of the following term, or a wish to disassociate oneself from the implications of the term.—**so many** such-and-such a number of; **so much** such-and-such an amount (of): that amount of: an equal amount.—**and so forth,** and **so on** and more of the same or the like: and the rest of it; **just so** exactly right, impeccable; **quite so;** or **so** or thereabouts; **quite so** just as you have said, exactly; **so as** in such a manner as or that: in order (with *to*) (*coll.*): if only, on condition that; **so far** to that, or to such an, extent, degree, or point; **so long!, so long as** see long; **so much as** as much as: even; **so much** for that disposes of: that is the end of: no more of; **so much so** to such an extent (that); **so so** see **so-so; so that** with the purpose that: with the result

that: if only; **so then** thus then it is, therefore; **so to say** or **speak** if one may use that expression; **so what** see **what.** [O.E. *swā.*]

so[2] *sō.* See **sol**[1].

soak *sōk, v.t.* to steep in a liquid: to drench: to saturate: to draw through the pores.—*v.i.* to be steeped in a liquid: to pass through pores: to drink to excess, to guzzle: to soften by heating.—*n.* the process or act of soaking: a drenching: a marshy place: a hard drinker, a carouse.—*ns.* **soak'age** soaking: liquid that has percolated; **soak'er.**—*n.* and *adj.* **soak'ing.**—*adv.* **soak'ingly.**—**soak'away** a depression into which water percolates. [M.E. *soke*—O.E. *socian,* a weak vb. related to *sūcan,* to suck.]

soap *sōp, n.* an alkaline salt of a higher fatty acid: esp. such a compound of sodium (*hard soap*) or potassium (*soft soap*), used in washing: smooth words, flattery (*slang*).—*v.t.* to rub with soap: to flatter.—*adv.* **soap'ily.**—*n.* **soap'iness.**—*adjs.* **soap'less; soap'y.**—**soap'box** a box for packing soap: a wayside orator's improvised platform; **soap'-bubb'le** a globe of air enclosed in a film of soap-suds; **soap'-dish.**—*n.pl.* **soap flakes.**—**soap opera** a sentimental, melodramatic serial broadcast on radio or television, written around the lives of the members of a family or other small group, and chiefly concerned with the emotional involvement of the characters (also *fig.*; orig. American and often sponsored by soap manufacturers); **soap powder; soap'stone** steatite, or French chalk, a compact kind of talc with soapy feel. —*n.pl.* **soap'-suds** soapy water, esp. when frothy.— **soap'-work(s)** a soap factory; **soap'wort** a tall herb of the pink family, whose roots and leaves contain saponin. [O.E. *sāpe.*]

soar *sōr, sōr, v.i.* to mount high in the air: to fly aloft: to rise to a great height: to glide or skim high in the air: to glide in a rising current: to increase rapidly in number or amount.—*v.t.* to reach, traverse, or accomplish in upward flight.—*n.* and *adj.* **soar'ing.**— *adv.* **soar'ingly.** [Fr. *essorer,* to expose to air, raise into air—L. *ex,* out, *aura,* air.]

sob *sob, v.i.* to catch the breath convulsively in distress or other emotion: to make a similar sound: to weep noisily.—*v.t.* to utter with sobs: to bring by sobbing: —*pr.p.* **sobb'ing;** *pa.t.* and *pa.p.* **sobbed.**—*n.* a convulsive catch of the breath: any similar sound.—*n.* and *adj.* **sobb'ing.**—*adv.* **sobb'ingly.**—**sob'-story** a pitiful tale told to arouse sympathy; **sob'-stuff** cheap and extravagant pathos, to stir tears: maudlin films or scenes. [Imit.]

sobeit *sō-bē'it, conj.* provided. [**so be it.**]

sober *sō'bər, adj.* not drunk: temperate, esp. in use of intoxicants: moderate: restrained: without excess or extravagance: serious: sedate: quiet in colour: sombre.—*v.t.* to make sober (often with *up*).—*v.i.* to become sober (often with *up*).—*adj.* **so'bering** making sober: causing to become serious, grave or thoughtful.—*adv.* **so'berly.**—*ns.* **so'berness; sobriety** (*sō- or sa-brī'i-ti*) the state or habit of being sober: calmness: gravity. [Fr. *sobre*—L. *sōbrius—sē-,* apart, not, *ēbrius,* drunk.]

sobole *sō'bōl, soboles sob'ō-lēz, (bot.) ns.* a creeping underground stem producing roots and buds:—*pl.* **sob'ōles.** [L. *sobolēs, subolēs,* a shoot—*sub,* under, and the root of *alĕre,* to nourish, sustain.]

sobriquet *sō'brē-kā, n.* a nickname.—Also **soubriquet** (*sōō').* [Fr. *sobriquet,* earlier *soubriquet,* a chuck under the chin.]

soc *sok, (law) n.* the right of holding a local court.—*ns.* **soc'age, socc'age** tenure of lands by service fixed and determinate in quality; **soc'ager, soc'man, soke'man** a tenant by socage. [O.E. *sōcn,* inquiry, jurisdiction.]

so-called *sō'kōld, adj.* See under **so**[1].

For other sounds see detailed chart of pronunciation.

soccer sok'ər, (coll.) n. association football.
sociable sō'shə-bl, adj. inclined to society: companionable: favourable to social intercourse: friendly, fond of others' company.—ns. **sociabil'ity**, **so'ciableness**. —adv. **so'ciably**.—adj. **social** (sō'shl) pertaining to life in an organised community: pertaining to welfare in such: growing or living in communities: pertaining to, or characterised by, friendly association: convivial: gregarious, sociable: pertaining to fashionable circles.—n. an informal party or gathering or club, church, etc.—n. **socialisa'tion**, **-z-** the act or process of socialising: the process by which infants and young children become aware of society and their relationships with others.—v.t. **so'cialise**, **-ize** to render social: to put on a socialistic footing.—v.i. (coll.) to behave in a sociable manner, e.g. at parties, etc.—ns. **so'cialism** the theory, principle, or scheme of social organisation which places means of production and distribution in the hands of the community; **so'cialist** an adherent of socialism.—Also adj.—adj. **socialist'ic**.—adv. **socialist'ically** in a socialistic manner.— ns. **so'cialite** (coll.) one who has a place in fashionable society; **sociality** (sō-shi-al'i-ti) the quality or fact of being social: social relations, association, or intercourse: sociability.—adv. **so'cially**.—n. **so'cialness**.—adjs. **so'ciative** expressing association; **soci'etal** (-sī') pertaining to society, social.—adv. **soci'etally** by society.—n. **soci'ety** fellowship, companionship: company: association: a community: the body of mankind, the fashionable world generally: a corporate body: any organised association —adj. of fashionable society.—**social anthropology** the branch of anthropology which deals with the culture, customs and social structure of, esp. primitive, societies; **social climber** (often derog.) a person who tries to become accepted into a social stratum higher than that to which he belongs by a deliberate policy of getting to know and associating with people belonging to that higher stratum; **social contract** the voluntary agreement between individuals upon which an organised society, its rights, functions, and the relationships within it are founded; **social democracy** the practices and policies of socialists who believe that socialism can and should be achieved by democratic means; **social democrat** a supporter of social democracy: (with caps.) a member or supporter of a Social Democratic party.—adj. **social democratic**.— **social insurance** state insurance by compulsory contributions against sickness, unemployment, and old age; **social science** the scientific study of human society and behaviour, including such disciplines (the social sciences) as anthropology, sociology, economics, political science and history; **social security** security against sickness, unemployment, old age, provided by a social insurance scheme; **social service** welfare work (also in pl.): (in pl.) the public bodies carrying out such work; **social work** any of various forms of welfare work intended to promote the well-being of the poor, the aged, the handicapped, etc.; **social worker**.—**the alternative society** a better, more humane, form of society as envisaged by those who refuse to follow the ways of society as it is today; **the Society of Jesus** see Jesuit. [L. socius, a companion.]
socio- sō'sɪ-ō-, sō'shi-ō-, -sɪ-o'-, -shi-o'-, in composition, social, of or pertaining to society, as sociocultural, socioeconomic, sociopolitical.—ns **sociobiol'ogist; sociobiol'ogy** a scientific discipline combining biology and the social sciences which attempts to establish that social behaviour and organisation in humans and animals has a genetic basis and is to be explained in terms of evolution and genetics, **sociolinguist.**—adj. **sociolinguis'tic** of or pertaining

to sociolinguistics: pertaining to language as it functions as a social tool.—n.sing. **sociolinguis'tics** the study of language as it functions in society and is affected by social and cultural factors.—adjs. **sociolog'ic, -al** pertaining to sociology: dealing solely with environmental factors in considering a human problem: social.—ns. **sociol'ogist; sociol'ogy** the study of the structure and functioning of human society.—adj. **sociomet'ric.**—ns. **sociom'etry** the measurement of social phenomena: the study of personal interrelationships within a social group; **so'ciopath.**—adj. **sociopath'ic.**—n. **sociop'athy** any of several personality disorders resulting in asocial or antisocial behaviour. [L. socius, a companion.]
sock¹ sok, n. a short stocking.—**pull up one's socks** to brace oneself for doing better; **put a sock in it** (slang; usu. imper.) to become silent, stop talking, etc. [O.E. socc—L. soccus.]
sock² sok, (dial. and slang) v.t. to thrust hard: to strike hard: to drub.—n. a violent blow, esp. with the fist.— **sock it to** (slang) to speak, behave, etc. in a vigorous manner towards.
socket sok'it, n. a hollow into which something is inserted, as the receptacle of the eye, of a bone, of a tooth, of the shaft of an iron golf-club: the hollow of a candlestick.—v.t. to provide with or place in a socket: to strike with the socket:—pr.p. **sock'eting**; pa.t. and pa.p. **sock'eted.**—adj. **sock'eted.** [O.Fr. soket, dim. of soc.]
sockeye sok'ī, n. the blueback salmon. [Amer. Ind. sukai, the fish of fishes, the native name on the Fraser River.]
socle sō'kl, sok'l, (archit.) n. a plain face or plinth at the foot of a wall, column, etc. [Fr.,—It. zoccolo—L. socculus, dim. of soccus, a shoe.]
Socratic, -al sō-krat'ik, -i-kl, so-, adjs. pertaining to Socrates, the celebrated Greek philosopher (d. 399 B.C.), to his philosophy, or to his method of teaching, by a series of simple questions revealing to his interlocutors their own ignorance.
sod¹ sod, n. a turf, usu. one cut in rectangular shape: sward.—adj. of sod.—v.t to cover with sod.—adj. **sodd'y** covered with sod: turfy. [M.L.G. sode; Ger. Sode.]
sod² sod, (vulg.) n. a term of abuse, affection, etc.— interj. (vulg.) a term expressing annoyance, etc. (sometimes behaving as a verb with it, him, etc. as object).—adj. **sodd'ing.**—**sod off** (vulg.) to go away; **Sod's law** (facet.) the law that states that the most inconvenient thing is the most likely to happen. [Abbrev. of **sodomite.**]
soda sō'da, n. sodium oxide (Na₂O): sodium hydroxide (caustic soda): sodium carbonate, the soda of commerce (in powder form, anhydrous, soda-ash; in crystals, with water of crystallisation, washing-soda): sodium bicarbonate (baking-soda): soda-water (coll.): a drink made of soda-water with flavouring, ice-cream, etc. (U.S.).—adj. of or containing soda or sodium.—adj. **sodaic** (sō-dā'ik) containing, pertaining to, soda.—n. **so'dium** a bluish-white alkaline metal (symbol Na; at. numb. 11), the base of soda.— **so'da-fountain** an apparatus for supplying counter for serving, sodas, ice-cream, etc.; **so'da-lime** a mixture of caustic soda and quicklime; **so'da-scone** a scone made with baking-soda; **so'da-siph'on** a siphon which dispenses soda-water; **so'da-wa'ter** water (now commonly without sodium bicarbonate) charged with carbon dioxide; **sodium amytal** (am'ɪ-tal; ® with caps.; also **amytal sodium**) a salt (C₁₁H₁₇O₃N₂Na) used as a sedative and hypnotic; **sodium lamp** a street lamp using sodium vapour and giving yellow light [It. and L.L. soda.]
sodality sō-dal'ɪ-ti, n. a fellowship or fraternity. [L

sodālitās—sodālis, a comrade.]

sodden sod'n, former pa.p. of **seethe**.—adj. soaked thoroughly: boggy: doughy, not well baked: bloated, saturated with drink.

sodium. See **soda.**

Sodom sod'əm, n. one of the 'cities of the plain' (see Gen. xviii, xix): any place of utter depravity (fig.).— v.t. sod'omise, -ize to practise sodomy upon.—n. **Sod'omite** (-īt) an inhabitant of Sodom: (without cap.) one who practises sodomy.—adjs. **sodomitic** (-it'ik), -al.—n. sod'omy anal intercourse or copulation with an animal, imputed to the inhabitants of Sodom.

soever sō-ev'ər, adv. generally used to extend or render indefinite the sense of who, what, where, how, etc.

sofa sō'fə, n. a long upholstered seat with back and arms.—**sō'fa-bed** a piece of furniture serving as a sofa by day, a bed at night. [Ar. suffoh.]

soffit sof'it, n. a ceiling, now generally restricted to the ornamented underside of a stair, entablature, archway, etc. [It. soffitto—L. suffixus, pa.p. of suffigēre, to fasten beneath—sub, under, figēre, to fix.]

soft soft, söft, adj. easily yielding to pressure: easily cut: easily scratched (min.): malleable: yielding: not rigorous enough: not loud: not glaring: diffused: weak in muscle or mind: out of training: smooth: pleasing or soothing to the senses: tender: mild: sympathetic: gentle: effeminate: unable to endure rough treatment or hardship: (relatively) unprotected: gently moving: easy: free from calcium and magnesium salts, as water: bituminous, of coal: pronounced with a somewhat sibilant sound, not guttural or explosive: voiced or sonant: of drinks, nonalcoholic: apt to fall in price: of drugs, not habit-forming in an obvious degree: of rays, radiation, not highly penetrating.—adv. softly: gently: quietly.— v.t. **soften** (sof'n) to make soft or softer: to mitigate: to tone down, make less glaring or smoother.—v.i. to grow soft or softer.—ns. **softener** (sof'nər); **softening** (sof'ning); **soft'ie** a softy.—adv. **soft'ly.**—ns. soft'ness; soft'y a silly person, a weak fool: one who is soft-hearted or sentimental.—**soft'back** a paperback. —Also adj.—**soft'ball** an American game similar to baseball, played on a smaller diamond with a soft ball.—adjs. **soft'-billed; soft'-bod'led.**—v.t. soft'-**boil**'.—adjs. **soft'-boiled** boiled not long enough to be quite solid: soft-hearted (coll.); **soft'-cen'tred.**—**soft commodities** foodstuffs, coffee, cotton, etc., as opposed to metals.—adj. **soft'-core** not explicit, blatant or graphic.—**soft currency** one unstable in value in the international money-market through fluctuation in its gold backing.—adjs. **soft'-finned** without fin-spines; **soft'-foot'ed** softly treading.—ns. pl. **soft furnishings** curtains, coverings, rugs, etc.; **soft'-goods** cloth, and cloth articles, as opp. to hardware, etc.— adj. **soft'-heart'ed** kind, generous: tender-hearted.— **soft line** a flexible or lenient attitude, policy, etc.; **soft loan** one without conditions attached.—adjs. **soft'ly-soft'ly** cautious, careful, delicate; **soft'-nosed** of a bullet, with a tip that expands on striking.—**soft option** an alternative that is easy to carry out, undergo, etc.; **soft palate** the back part of the palate; **soft pedal** a pedal for reducing tone in the piano, esp. by causing the hammer to strike only one string (una corda).—v.t. and v.i. **soft'-ped'al** to play with the soft pedal down: to subdue, tone down, avoid emphasising or alluding to (slang).—**soft porn(ography)** mild, soft-core pornography; **soft sell** selling or sale by preliminary softening up or other indirect method: mild persuasion, or mildly persuasive tactics.—adjs. **soft'-sell; soft'-shell,** -ed having a soft shell: moderate in policy or principles; **soft'-shoe** characteristic of or pertaining to a form of tap-dancing done

in soft-soled shoes.—**soft soap** a kind of soap containing potash: flattery: blarney.—v.t. **soft'-soap** to rub or cover with soft soap: to flatter for some end.— adj. **soft'-spo'ken** having a mild or gentle voice: affable: suave: plausible in speech.—**soft spot** see spot; **soft touch** see touch; **soft underbelly** the vulnerable part; **soft'ware** computer programmes, esp. general ones for routine operations (compare hardware): computer program (or analogous) accessories (other than the actual parts of a computer, etc.): material recorded in microform; **soft'wood** timber of a conifer (also adj.).—**go soft on** to be lenient with; **softening of the brain** a softening of brain tissues: marked deterioration of mental faculties (coll.); **soften up** to lessen resistance in (coll.): to wear down by continuous shelling and bombing. [O.E. sōfte, sēfte.]

sog sog, n. a soft wet place.—v.t. and v.i. to soak.— adj. **sogged.**—adv. **sogg'ily.**—n. **sogg'iness.**—n. and adj. **sogg'ing.**—adj. **sogg'y** soaked: soft or heavy with moisture: boggy: soppy: sultry: spiritless.

soh. See sol[1].

soi-disant swä-dē-zä, adj. self-styled, pretended, would-be. [Fr.]

soigné, fem. **soignée** swa-nyā, adj. well groomed. [Fr.]

soil[1] soil, n. the ground: the mould in which plants grow: the mixture of disintegrated rock and organic material which nourishes plants: country.—adj. having soil.—adj. **soil'-bound** attached to the soil.— **soil science** the study of the composition and uses of soil. [O.Fr. soel, suel, sueil—L. solum, ground.]

soil[2] soil, n. dung: filth: sewage: a spot or stain.—v.t. to make dirty: to stain: to manure.—v.i. to take a soil: to tarnish.—adj. **soiled.**—n. and adj. **soil'ing.**—**soil'** pipe an upright discharge-pipe which receives the general refuse from water-closets, etc., in a building. [O.Fr. soil, souil wallowing-place.]

soil[3] soil, v.t. to feed on fresh-cut green food: to purge by so doing: to fatten. [O.Fr. saouler—saol, saoul —L. satullus—satur, full; or from soil[2].]

soirée swär'ā, swör'ā, n. an evening party: an evening social meeting with tea, etc. [Fr.,—soir, evening— L. sērus, late.]

soixante-neuf swa-sät-nœf, (Fr.) n. a sexual position in which both partners simultaneously orally stimulate each other's genitalia. [Lit. sixty-nine, from the position adopted.]

sojourn sō', so', su'jərn, sometimes -jûrn', v.t. to stay for a day: to dwell for a time.—n. a temporary residence.—ns. **so'journer; so'journing, so'journment.** [O.Fr. sojourner—L. sub, under, diurnus, of a day—diēs, a day.]

sokeman. See under soc.

sol[1] sol, n. the fifth note of the scale in sol-fa notation. —Also so, soh (sō). [See Aretinian.]

sol[2] sol, n. a colloidal suspension in a liquid.—n. **sola'tion** liquefaction of a gel. [For solution.]

sola sō'lə, n. the hat-plant or spongewood, an Indian plant: its pithlike stems.—adj. of sola.—**sola** (often solar) **hat, helmet** a topi of sola.— Also **sō'lah,** (corr.) **sōl'ar.** [Hindi śolā.]

solace sol'is, -əs, n. consolation, comfort in distress: pleasure, amusement: a source of comfort or pleasure.—v.t. to comfort in distress: to console: to allay.—v.t. to take comfort.—n. **sol'acement.** [O.Fr. solas—L. sōlātium—sōlārī, -ātus, to comfort in distress.]

solah. See sola[2].

solan sō'lən, n. the gannet.—Also **soland (goose), solan goose.** [O.N. súla.]

solar[1] sō'lər, adj. of, from, like, or pertaining to the sun: measured by the sun: influenced by the sun:

For other sounds see detailed chart of pronunciation.

powered by energy from the sun's rays: with branches radiating like the sun's rays.—*ns.* **solarimeter** (-im'it-ər) a device for measuring solar radiation; **sōlarīsā'tion**, -z- the act, process, or effect of solarising: the reversal of an image by over-exposure (*phot.*).—*v.t.* **sō'larīse, -īze** to expose to sunlight or affect by such exposure, esp. excessive or injurious exposure.—*v.i.* to be so affected.—*n.* **solā'rium** a sundial: a place for sunning or sunbathing.—**solar battery** a battery of solar cells; **solar cell** a photoelectric cell converting the energy of sunlight into electric power; **solar day, time, year** see day, time, year; **solar energy** energy got from the sun's rays, esp. when used for home-heating, etc.; **solar panel** a panel of solar cells; **solar plexus** (*anat.*) a network of nerves behind the stomach (so called from its radiating nerves); **solar power** solar energy (*adj.* **sō'lar-powered**); **solar prominences** large prominent or protruding parts of the great volumes of heated gas surrounding the sun; **solar system** the sun with its attendant bodies—major and minor planets, meteors, comets, satellites; **solar wind** charged particles from the sun travelling at about one and a half million kilometres an hour. [L. *sōlāris*, solar, *sōlārium*, a sundial—*sōl*, the sun.]

solar² *sō'lər.* See **sole**.

solation. See **sol²**.

solatium *sō-lā'shi-əm, sō-lā'ti-ōōm, n.* compensation for disappointment, inconvenience, wounded feelings. [L. *sōlātium*.]

sold *sōld, pa.t.* and *pa.p.* of **sell²**.—**sold on** keen on.

solder *sōl'dər*, also *sol', sod', sōd', sŏd', n.* a fusible alloy for uniting metals.—*v.t.* to make fast with solder: to join: to mend, patch up.—*v.i.* to adhere.—*ns.* **sol'derer**; **sol'dering.**—**sol'dering-bolt, -iron** a tool with pointed or wedge-shaped copper bit for use in soldering. [O.Fr. *soudre, souldure—souder, soulder*, to consolidate—L. *solidāre*, to make solid.]

soldier *sōl'jər, sōld'yər, n.* a man engaged in military service: a private: a man of military skill: an ant, or white ant, of a specialised fighting caste: a scarlet, pugnacious, or armoured animal of various kinds (beetle, fish, etc.): a diligent worker for a cause: a brick set upright in a wall.—*v.i.* to serve as a soldier. —*n.* **sol'diering.**—*adj.* **sol'dier-like** having the appearance of a soldier: soldierly.—*adv.* in the manner of a soldier.—*n.* **sol'dierliness.**—*adj.* **sol'dierly** befitting a soldier: having the qualities of or befitting a soldier.—*ns.* **sol'diership** the state or quality of being a soldier: military qualities: martial skill; **sol'diery** soldiers collectively: a military body or class: soldiership.—**sol'dier-crab** a hermit crab.—**old soldier** see old; **soldier of fortune** one ready to serve anywhere for pay or his own advancement; **soldier on** to continue doggedly in face of difficulty or discouragement. [O.Fr. *soldier*—L. *solidus*, a piece of money, the pay of a soldier.]

sole¹ *sōl, n.* the underside of the foot: the bottom of a boot or shoe: the under-surface of a golf-club head: the bottom, under-structure, floor, or under-surface of various things.—*v.t.* to put a sole on.—**sole'-plate** a bed-plate or similar object. [O.E. and O.Fr. *sole*—L. *solea*, sole, sandal—*solum*, bottom.]

sole² *sōl, n.* an elliptical flat fish (*Solea*) with small twisted mouth and teeth on the underside only. [Fr. *sole*—L. *solea*.]

sole³ *sōl, adj.* alone: only: without husband or wife: without another: solitary: consisting of one person: exclusive: uniform.—*advs.* **sole**; **sole'ly** alone: only: singly.—*n.* **sole'ness.** [Fr.,—L. *sōlus*, alone.]

solecism *sol'i-sizm, n.* a breach of syntax: any absurdity, impropriety, or incongruity.—*n.* **sol'ecist.**— *adjs.* **solecist'ic, -al.**—*adv.* **solecist'ically.** [Gr.

soloikismos, said to come from the corruption of the Attic dialect among the Athenian colonists (*oikizein*, to colonise) of *Soloi* in Cilicia.]

solemn *sol'əm, adj.* attended with or marked by special (esp. religious) ceremonies, pomp, or gravity: attended with an appeal to God, as an oath: grave: in serious earnestness: with formal dignity: awed: awe-inspiring: stately: pompous: glum: sombre.—*v.t.* **solemnify** (*sə-lem'ni-fi*) to make solemn.—*n.* **solemnisation,** -z- (*sol-əm-nī-zā'shən*).—*v.t.* **sol'emnise, -ize** (-nīz) to perform religiously or solemnly: to celebrate with rites: to make solemn.—*ns.* **sol'emniser**, -z-; **solemnity** (-lem'ni-ti) a solemn ceremony: high seriousness: affected gravity.—*adv.* **sol'emnly.**—*n.* **sol'emnness.**—**solemn mass** high mass. [O.Fr. *solempne, solemne* (Fr. *solennel*)—L. *sollemnis, sōlennis*, doubtfully referred to *sollus*, all, every, *annus*, a year.]

solenoid *sō'lə-noid, n.* a cylindrical coil of wire, acting as a magnet when an electric current passes through it, converting electrical energy to mechanical energy. —*adj.* **solenoid'al.** [Gr. *sōlēn*, a pipe]

soleus *sō'li-əs, n.* the flat muscle of the leg beneath the gastrocnemius. [Mod. L.,—L. *soles*, sole.]

sol-fa *sol'fä', (mus.) n.* a system of syllables (*do* or *ut, re, mi, fa, sol* or *so, la, si* or *ti*) representing and sung to the notes of the scale.—*adj.* belonging to the system.—*v.t.* and *v.i.* to sing to sol-fa syllables:— *pr.p.* **sol-faing** (-fä'ing); *pa.t.* and *pa.p.* **sol-faed, -fa'd** (-fäd').—*ns.* **sol-fa'ism** singing by syllables: solmisation; **sol-fa'ist** a teacher, practiser, or advocate of solmisation; **solfeggio** (-fed'jō; It.) an exercise in sol-fa syllables:—*pl.* **solfeggi** (-fed'jē).—**tonic sol-fa** see under **tone¹.** [**sol¹; fa.**]

solfatara *sol-fä-tä'rə, n.* a volcanic vent emitting only gases, esp. one emitting acid gases (hydrochloric acid and sulphur dioxide):—*pl.* **solfata'ras.**—*adj.* **solfata'ric.** [From the *Solfatara* (lit. sulphur-mine, sulphur-hole) near Naples—It. *solfo*, sulphur.]

solfeggio. See **sol-fa**.

soli. See **solo**.

solicit *sō-lis'it, v.t.* to petition: to importune: to seek after: to call for, require: to invite to immorality: to conduct, manage.—*v.i.* to petition: to act as solicitor: (of prostitutes) to make advances: (of beggars) to importune for alms.—*ns.* **solic'itant** one who solicits (also *adj.*); **solicita'tion** a soliciting: an earnest request: an invitation; **solic'iting** any action of the verb, esp. (of prostitutes) the making of advances; **solic'itor** one who asks earnestly: a lawyer who prepares deeds, manages cases, instructs counsel in the superior courts, and acts as an advocate in the inferior courts; **solic'itorship.**—*adj.* **solic'itous** soliciting or earnestly asking or desiring: very desirous: anxious: careful.—*adv.* **solic'itously.**—*ns.* **solic'itousness, solic'itude** the state of being solicitous: anxiety or uneasiness of mind: trouble.—**Solic'itor-Gen'eral** in England, the law-officer of the crown next in rank to the Attorney-General—in Scotland, to the Lord-Advocate. [L. *sōlicitāre, sollicitāre—sō-, sollicitus —sollus*, whole, *citus*, aroused.]

solid *sol'id, adj.* resisting change of shape, having the particles firmly cohering (opp. to *fluid*): distinguished from *liquid* and *gaseous*): hard: compact: full of matter: not hollow: strong: having or pertaining to three dimensions: substantial: worthy of credit: weighty: of uniform undivided substance: financially sound, wealthy: reliable: sensible: unanimous: unbroken: unvaried.—*n.* a substance, body, or figure that is solid: a solid mass or part.—*n.* **solidarity** (-dar'i-ti) oneness of interests, aims, etc.—*adj.* **sol'idary** (-dər-i) marked by solidarity: jointly responsible: joint and several.—*adj.* **solidifiable** (sə-lid'i-fī-ə-bl).—*n.*

solidifica'tion.—v.t. solid'ify to make solid or compact.—v.i. to grow solid:—pr.p. solid'ifying; pa.t. and pa.p. solid'ified.—n. solid'ity the state of being solid: fulness of matter: strength or firmness, moral or physical: soundness: volume.—adv. sol'idly.—ns. sol'idness sol'idus: a sign (/) denoting the former English shilling, representing old lengthened form of s (£ s. d. = librae, solidi, denarii, pounds, shillings, pence), used also for other purposes, as in writing fractions:—pl. solidi (-dī).—adjs. sol'id-hoofed with uncloven hoofs; sol'id-state of, consisting of, or relating to solid substances: of, consisting of or relating to semiconductor materials (and their electrical properties).—solid-state physics branch of physics which covers all properties of solid materials, now esp. electrical conduction in crystals of semiconductors, and superconductivity and photoconductivity; solid with packed tight with: on a firm footing of understanding with: supporting fully. [L. solidus, -a, -um, solid.]

solidungulate sol-id-ung'gū-lāt, adj. with uncloven hoofs. [L. solidus, solid, ungula, a hoof.]

solidus. See solid.

soliloquy so-, sō-, sə-lil'ə-kwi, n. a talking to oneself: a speech of this nature made by a character in a play, etc.—v.i. solil'oquise, -ize to speak to oneself: to utter a soliloquy in a play, etc. [L. sōliloquium—sōlus, alone, loquī, to speak.]

solipsism sol'ip-sizm, n. the theory that self-existence is the only certainty, absolute egoism—the extreme form of subjective idealism.—n. and adj. sol'ipsist.—adj. solipsis'tic. [L. sōlus, alone, ipse, self.]

solitaire sol-i-tār', n. a recluse: a game played by one person with a board and balls, pegs, etc.: patience (the card game) (U.S.): a diamond, etc., set by itself. —solitaire'-board a board with cups, holes, etc. for playing solitaire. [Fr., see next.]

solitary sol'i-tər-i, adj. alone: single: separate: living alone, not social or gregarious: without company: remote from society: retired, secluded: lonely: growing single (bot.).—n. one who lives alone: a hermit: solitary confinement (coll.).—adv. sol'itarily.—n. sol'itariness.—solitary confinement imprisonment in a cell by oneself. [L. sōlitārius—sōlus, alone.]

solitude sol'i-tūd, n. solitariness: absence of company. —adj. solitud'inous. [L. sōlitūdō—sōlus.]

solmisation, -ization sol-mi-zā'shən, n. sol-faing: a recital of the notes of the gamut. [sol¹, mi.]

solo sō'lō, n. a piece or passage for one voice or instrument, accompanied or unaccompanied: any performance in which no other person or instrument participates: a motor-bicycle without side-car: a card game (solo whist) based on whist, in which various declarations are made and the declarer may or may not have a partner:—pl. sō'lōs, soli (sō'lē).—adj. performed, or for performances, as a solo: performing a solo: for one.—adv. alone.—v.i. to fly solo: to play (a) solo.—n. sō'loist. [It.,—L. sōlus, alone.]

Solomon sol'ə-mən, n. a person of unusual wisdom, from Solomon, king of Israel (see 1 Kings iii. 5–15).—adjs. Solomonian (-mō'ni-ən), Solomonic (-mon'ik).—Sol'omon's-seal any species of Polygonatum, a genus of the lily family, with small dangling greenish flowers (perh. from the scars on the rootstock): a symbol formed of two triangles interlaced or superposed, forming a six-pointed star.

so-long, so long sō-long', (coll. or slang) interj. goodbye. [Prob. so¹ and long; poss. salaam.]

solstice sol'stis, n. the time when the sun reaches its maximum distance from the equator (summer solstice when it touches the tropic of Cancer, about 21st June; the winter solstice when it touches that of Capricorn, about 21st December): the turning-point then reached.—adj. solstitial (-stish'l) pertaining to, or happening at, a solstice, esp. at the summer solstice [Fr.,—L. sōlstitium—sōl, the sun, sistēre, stātum, to make to stand—stāre.]

soluble sol'ū-bl, adj. capable of being solved, dissolved, or resolved.—n. solubilisa'tion, -z-.—v.t. sol'ubilise, -ize to render soluble: to make more soluble.—ns. solubil'ity (a measure of) the ability of a substance to dissolve; sol'ute a dissolved substance. —adj. (sol' or -ūt') loose: free: not adhering: dissolved.—n. solution (səl-, sol-ōō'shən, -ū'shən) the act of solving or dissolving: the condition of being dissolved: the preparation resulting therefrom: the separating of parts: abnormal separation: an explanation: the removal of a doubt: the solving of a problem: the payment of a debt, or similar discharge of an obligation. [L. solvēre, solūtum, to loosen.]

solve solv, v.t. to unbind: to dissolve: to settle: to clear up or explain: to find an answer to or a way out of.—n. solvabil'ity.—adj. sol'vable capable of being solved.—ns. sol'vate a definite combination of solute and solvent; sol'vency.—adj. sol'vent able to solve or dissolve: able to pay all debts.—n. anything that dissolves another: that component of a solution which is present in excess, or whose physical state is the same as that of the solution.—n. sol'ver one who solves.—solvent abuse self-intoxication by inhaling the fumes given off by various solvents—adhesives, petrol, etc. [L. solvēre, to loosen, prob. from sē-, sě-, aside, luěre, to loosen.]

soma¹, Soma sō'mə, n. a plant (perhaps an asclepiad), or its intoxicating juice, used in ancient Indian religious ceremonies, and personified as a god. [Sans. soma (Avestan haoma, juice).]

soma² sō'mə, n. the body: the body of an animal or plant excluding the germ-cells.—n. somascope (sō'mə-skōp; Gr. skopeein, to view) an instrument using ultrasonic waves converted into a television image to show the character of diseased internal tissues of the body.—adj. somatic (-mat'ik).—adv. somat'ically.—somat'otype a type consisting of a physical build paired with a particular temperament.—v.t. to place with regard to somatotype.—n. so'mite a body-segment. [Gr. sōma, body.]

sombre som'bər, adj. dark and gloomy: melancholy, dismal.—v.t. and v.i. to make or become sombre.—adv. som'brely.—n. som'breness. [Fr. sombre (cf. Sp. sombra, shade)—perh. L. sub, under, umbra, a shade.]

sombrero som-brā'rō, n. a broad-brimmed hat:—pl. sombre'ros. [Sp., hat—sombra, shade.]

some sum, indef. pron. one, an indefinite part of the whole number or quantity: (a) certain (undetermined) one(s).—adj. one or other: in an indefinite number or quantity: a little: not a little: considerable: a certain: certain unspecified: several: a few: in approximate number, length, etc., more or less: remarkable, outstanding, of note (coll., esp. U.S.; also ironical).—adv. very much (U.S.).—n. (or pron.) some'body some person: a person of importance:—pl. some'bodies.—advs. some'day at an unspecified time in the future; some'how in some way or other.—n. (or pron.) some'one (also some one) somebody.—adv. some'place somewhere.—n. (or pron.) some'thing a thing undefined: a thing of some account: a portion.—adv. in some degree.—Also used as substitute for any word (n., adj., vb.) or component of any word forgotten or avoided.—adv. some'time at a time not fixed: at one time or other: formerly.—adj. former: late.—adv. some'times at times: now and then.—n. some'what an unfixed quantity or degree: something.—adv. in some degree.—adv. some'where in or to some place.—

someone else some other person; **someone else's** some other person's. [O.E. *sum*.]

-some[1] *-sum, -səm, suff.* (1) forming adjectives with the meaning full of, e.g. *gladsome, wholesome*: (2) forming nouns denoting a group with a certain number of members, e.g. *twosome, threesome*. [O.E. *-sum*; Ger. *-sam*; cf. **same**.]

-some[2] *-sōm, suff.* forming nouns denoting a body, e.g. *chromosome*. [Gr. *soma*, body.]

somersault *sum'ər-sölt, n.* a leap or other movement in which one turns heels over head.—*v.i.* to turn a somersault. [O.Fr. *sombre saut* (Fr. *soubresaut*)— L. *suprā*, over, *saltus, -ūs*, a leap—*salīre*, to leap.]

somite. See under **soma**[2].

somnambulance *som-nam'bū-ləns, n.* (L. *ambulāre*, to walk) sleep-walking.—*adj.* and *n.* **somnam'bulant**.—*adjs.* **somnam'bular, -y**.—*v.i.* **somnam'bulate** to walk in one's sleep.—*ns.* **somnambūlā'tion**; **somnam'bulātor, somnam'būle** a sleep-walker.—*adjs.* **somnif'erous** (L. *ferre*, to bring), **somnif'ic** (L. *facĕre*, to make) sleep-bringing.—*ns.* **somnil'oquence, somnil'oquism, somnil'oquy** (L. *loquī*, to talk) talking in one's sleep.—*v.i.* **somnil'oquise, -ize**.—*ns.* **somnil'oquist**; **som'nolence, -ency** sleepiness.—*adj.* **som'nolent.** [L. *somnus*, sleep, *somnium*, a dream.]

son *sun, n.* a male child or offspring: a descendant, or one so regarded or treated: a disciple: a native or inhabitant: the produce of anything: a familiar (sometimes patronising) mode of address to a boy or to a male younger than oneself.—*ns.* **sonn'y** a little son: a familiar mode of address to a boy; **son'ship** the state or character of a son.—**son'-in-law** a daughter's husband: formerly, a stepson:—*pl.* **sons'-in-law**.— **son of a gun** see **gun**; **son of man** a man: applied to Jesus Christ or the Messiah; **son of the manse** a minister's son; **the Son** the second person in the Trinity, Jesus Christ. [O.E. *sunu*.]

sonant *sō'nənt, adj.* voiced: syllabic.—*n.* a voiced sound: a syllabic consonant.—*ns.* **so'nance** a sounding; **so'nancy** sonant character. [L. *sonāns, -antis*, pr.p. of *sonāre*, to sound.]

Sonar *sō'när, n.* the American equivalent of Asdic: (without *cap.*) natural equipment that provides echo location in bats and some marine animals: (without *cap.*) echo-sounding equipment in general. [*sound navigation and ranging*.]

sonata *sō-, sə-, so-nä'tə, n.* orig., an instrumental composition: a composition usually of three or more movements designed chiefly for a solo instrument.— *n.* **sonatina** (*son-ə-tē'nə*) a short sonata.—**sonata form** the form usual in the first movement of a sonata or symphony. [It., fem. pa.p. of *sonare*—L. *sonāre*, to sound.]

sondage *sō-däzh, n.* a trial bore or excavation. [Fr.]

sonde *sond, n.* any device for obtaining information about atmospheric and weather conditions at high altitudes. [Fr.]

son et lumière *son ā lüm'yər*, a dramatic spectacle presented after dark, involving lighting effects on natural features of the country or on a chosen building and an appropriate theme illustrated by spoken words and by music. [Fr.]

song *song, n.* that which is sung: a short poem or ballad suitable for singing or set to music: the melody to which it is sung: an instrumental composition of like form and character: singing: the melodious outburst of a bird: any characteristic sound: a poem, or poetry in general: a theme of song: a habitual utterance, manner, or attitude towards anything: a fuss: a mere trifle.—*adjs.* **song'ful** abounding in song: melodious: song-like: like singing: ready to break into song; **song'less** without song or power of song; **song'-like**.— *n.* **song'ster** a singer:—*fem.* **song'stress**.—**song'bird** a

bird that sings: any one of the Oscines; **song'book** a book of songs; **song'craft** the art of making songs; **song'-cycle** a sequence of songs connected in subject; **song'smith** a composer; **song'-thrush** the mavis or throstle (see also **thrush**[1]); **song'writer** one who composes music and/or words for (esp. popular) songs.—**make a song (and dance) about** to make overmuch of: to make an unnecessary fuss about; **Song of Songs** or **Song of Solomon** Canticles, a book of the O.T. long attributed to Solomon. [O.E. *sang—singan*, to sing.]

sonic *son'ik, adj.* pertaining to or using sound-waves: travelling at about the speed of sound.—*n.sing.* **son'ics** the study of the technological application of sounds, esp. supersonic waves.—**sonic bang, boom** (*aero.*) a loud double report caused by shock-waves projected outward and backward from the leading and trailing edges of an aircraft travelling at supersonic speed; **sonic barrier** the sound barrier; **sonic mine** an acoustic mine. [L. *sonus*, sound.]

sonnet *son'it, n.* a short poem of fourteen lines of ten or eleven syllables, rhymed according to one or other of certain definite schemes, forming an octave and a sestet, properly expressing two successive phases of one thought. [It. *sonetto*, dim. of *suono*—L. *sonus*, sound.]

sonny. See **son**.

sono- *son'ō-*, in composition, sonic.

sonofabitch *sun'əv-ə-bich', (slang; esp. U.S.) n.* son of a bitch, an opprobrious term of address or of description, or vulgar exclamation:—*pl.* **sons of bitches**.

sonorous *so-, sə-nō'rəs, so'nə-rəs, adj.* sounding, esp. loudly, deeply, impressively, etc.: full-sounding: sounding or ringing when struck.—*ns.* **son'orant** a frictionless continuant or nasal (*l, r, m, n, ng*) capable of fulfilling a vocalic or consonantal function: the consonants represented by *w, y*, having consonantal or vocalic articulations; **sonority** (*sō-, sə-nor'i-ti*) sonorousness: type, quality, etc. of sound.—*adv.* **sono'rously** (or *so'*).—*n.* **sono'rousness** (or *so'*) sonorous quality or character. [L. *sonōrus—sonor, -ōris*, a sound—*sonāre*, to sound.]

sook. Same as **souk**.

soon *sōōn, adv.* immediately or in a short time: without delay: early: readily: willingly:—*compar.* **soon'er**.— **no sooner . . . than** immediately; **sooner or later** eventually. [O.E. *sōna*.]

soot *sŏŏt, n.* a black deposit from imperfect combustion of carbonaceous matter: a smut.—*v.t.* to cover, smear, dirty, clog, or treat with soot.—*adv.* **soot'ily**. —*n.* **soot'iness**.—*adjs.* **soot'less**; **soot'y** of, foul with, or like, soot. [O.E. *sōt*.]

sooth *sōōth, n.* truth, reality.—*adj.* true: truthful.— *adv.* in truth: indeed.—*v.i.* **sooth'say** to foretell: to divine.—**sooth'sayer** one who foretells, a diviner or prognosticator; **sooth'saying**. [O.E. *sōth*, truth, true.]

soothe *sōōdh, v.t.* to calm, comfort, compose, tranquillise: to appease: to allay, soften.—*v.i.* to have a tranquillising effect.—*n.* **sooth'er**.—*n.* and *adj.* **sooth'ing**.—*adv.* **sooth'ingly**. [O.E. *(ge)sōthian*, to confirm as true—*sōth*, true.]

sootily, sootiness, sooty. See **soot**.

sop *sop, n.* bread or other food dipped or soaked in liquid: a puddle: a soaking: a propitiatory gift or concession (from the drugged sop the Sibyl gave to Cerberus to gain passage for Aeneas to Hades, *Aen.* vi. 420).—*v.t.* to steep in liquor: to take up by absorption (with *up*): to soak.—*v.i.* to soak in, percolate: to be soaked:—*pr.p.* **sopp'ing**; *pa.t.* and *pa.p.* **sopped**. —*adv.* **sopp'ily**.—*n.* **sopp'iness**—*n.*, adj., and *adv.* **sopp'ing**.—*adj.* **sopp'y** drenched: thoroughly wet: sloppily sentimental. [O.E. *sopp* (n.), *soppian* (vb.); prob. conn. with *sūpan*, to sup.]

soph *sof*, *n.* a short form of **sophomore**.

sophia *sof'i-ə*, *n.* wisdom: divine wisdom.—*adjs.* **soph'ic, -al**.—*ns.* **soph'ism** a specious fallacy; **soph'ist** one of a class of public teachers of rhetoric, philosophy, etc., in ancient Greece: a captious or intentionally fallacious reasoner.—*adjs.* **sophis'tic, -al** pertaining to, or of the nature of, a sophist or sophistry: fallaciously subtle.—*adv.* **sophis'tically**.—*v.t.* **sophis'ticate** to adulterate: to falsify: to make sophistic(al): to give a fashionable air of worldly wisdom to: to make (e.g., a machine) highly complex and efficient.—*v.i.* to practise sophistry.—*adjs.* **sophis'ticate, sophis'ticāted** adulterated: falsified: worldly-wise: devoid or deprived of natural simplicity, complex: very refined and subtle: with qualities produced by special knowledge and skill: with the most up-to-date devices.—*ns.* **sophis'ticate** a sophisticated person; **sophisticā'tion**; **sophis'ticātor**; **soph'istry** (an instance of) specious but fallacious reasoning: the art of reasoning speciously. [Gr. *sophiā*, wisdom, *sophisma*, skill.]

sophomore *sof'ə-mōr, -mor*, (esp. *U.S.*) *n.* a second-year student.—Also *adj.*—*adjs.* **sophomoric** (*-mor'*), **-al** of a sophomore: bombastic. [Prob. from *sophom* (obs. form of *sophism*) and *-or*, as if from *sophos*, wise, *mōros*, foolish.]

sopor *sō'por*, (*path.*) *n.* unnaturally deep sleep.—*adj.* **soporif'ic** inducing sleep.—*n.* a sleep-bringing agent. [L. *sopor, -ōris*, deep sleep, *facēre*, to make.]

sopped, sopping, soppy. See **sop**.

soprano *sō-, sə-prä'nō*, *n.* the highest variety of voice, treble: a singer with such a voice: a part for such a voice:—*pl.* **sopra'nos, sopra'ni** (*nē*).—*adj.* of, or possessing, a treble voice or a part for it: in a group of instruments of the same type but of different sizes, that with the range close to the range of a soprano voice.—*adj.* **sopranino** (*sō-prə-nē'nō*) (of an instrument) higher than the corresponding soprano.—Also *n.*:—*pl.* **soprani'nos, -ni'ni** (*-nē*).—*n.* **sopra'nist** a soprano singer. [It., from *sopra*—L. *suprā* or *super*, above.]

sorb[1] *sorb*, *n.* the service-tree, the wild service-tree, or (sometimes) the rowan-tree: its fruit (also **sorb's apple**).—*n.* **sor'bate** a salt of sorbic acid.—**sorbic acid** an acid obtained from the rowan-berry, used in food preservation; **sorb'itol** (*-i-tol*) a white crystalline substance ($C_6H_8(OH)_6$) derived from (and used as a substitute for) sugar. [L. *sorbus* (the tree), *sorbum* (the fruit).]

sorb[2] *sorb*, *v.t.* to absorb or adsorb.—*adj.* **sorbefacient** (*-i-fā'shənt*) promoting absorption.—Also *n.*—*n.* and *adj.* **sor'bent**. [L. *sorbēre*, to suck in, *faciēns, -entis*, pr.p. of *facēre*, to make.]

sorbate. See **sorb**[1].

sorbet *sòr'bət, sor'bā*, *n.* sherbet: water-ice. [Fr.,—It. *sorbetto*; cf. **sherbet**.]

sorbic acid, sorbitol. See **sorb**[1].

sorbo (rubber) *sòr'bō* (*rub'ər*), *n.* a spongy type of rubber:—*pl.* **sor'bos, sorbo rubbers**. [From **absorb**.]

sorcery *sor'sə-ri*, *n.* divination by the assistance of evil spirits: enchantment: magic: witchcraft.—*n.* **sor'cerer**:—*fem.* **sor'ceress**.—*adj.* **sor'cerous**. [O.Fr. *sorcerie*—L. *sors, sortis*, lot.]

sordamente. See **sordo**.

sordes *sôr'dēz*, *n. sing.* or *pl.* filth: a crust on the teeth and lips in fevers.—*adj.* **sor'did** dirty: squalid: mean: meanly avaricious: mercenary: of low or unworthy ideals.—*adv.* **sor'didly**.—*ns.* **sor'didness**; **sor'dor** dirt: sordidness. [L. *sordēs* (pl.), dirt, *sordidus*, dirty.]

sordo *sòr'dō*, (*mus.*) *adj.* muted, damped:—*fem.*

sor'da.—*adv.* **sordamente** (*-dà-men'tā*) gently, softly.—*n.* **sordino** (*-dē'nō*) a mute or damper to soften or deaden the sound of an instrument:—*pl.* **sordini** (*-nē*).—Also **sordine** (*-dēn'*; Fr. *sourdine*).—**con sordino** with mute; **senza sordino** without mute. [It.,—L. *surdus*, deaf, noiseless.]

sore *sōr, sor*, *n.* a painful or tender injured or diseased spot: an ulcer or boil: grief: an affliction.—*adj.* wounded: tender: readily sensitive to pain: irritable: touchy: painful: afflicted: vexed: irritated: causing pain: painful to contemplate: grievous: bringing sorrow or regret: aggrieved (*coll.*).—*adv.* painfully: grievously: severely: distressingly: in distress: hard: eagerly: very much.—*adv.* **sore'ly**.—*n.* **sore'ness**.—**sore point** a subject provoking bitter argument.—**a sore thumb** something obtrusive, too painful or too awkward to be ignored; **stick out like a sore thumb** (*coll.*) to be very obvious, noticeable, etc. [O.E. *sār.*]

Sorghum *sor'gəm*, *n.* a tropical Old World genus of grasses near akin to sugar-cane, including durra and Kaffir corn: (without *cap.*) any grass of this genus: (without *cap.*) molasses made from its juice (*U.S.*).—*n.* **sor'go, sor'gho** a variety of durra from which sugar is prepared (sweet **sorghum**, or Chinese sugar-cane): —*pl.* **sor'g(h)os**. [It. *sorgo*, prob. from an East Ind. word, or poss. from (unattested) vulg. L. *Syricum* (*grānum*), Syrian (grain)]

sorites *sō-rī'tēz, so-, n.* a string of propositions in which the predicate of one is the subject of the next (or the same in reverse order): a sophistical puzzle on the model of 'How many grains make a heap?'.—*adjs.* **sorit'ic, -al.** [Gr. *sōreitēs*—*sōros*, a heap.]

Soroptimist *sor-opt'i-mist, adj.* of an international organisation of women's clubs.—*n.* a member of one of these clubs. [L. *soror*, sister, and **optimist**.]

sororal *sor-ō'rəl, -o', sororial -ri-əl, adjs.* sisterly: of, of the nature of, a sister.—*n.* **sororicide** (*-or'i-sīd*; L. *caedēre*, to kill) the killing or killer of a sister.—*n.* **sorority** (*sor-or'i-ti*) a sisterhood: a women's academic society (*U.S.*). [L. *soror*, sister.]

sorosis *so-, sə-, so-rō'sis, n.* a fleshy fruit formed from a crowd of flowers, as the pineapple. [Gr. *sōros*, a heap.]

sorption *sorp'shən, n.* absorption and/or adsorption.

sorrel[1] *sor'l*, *n.* any of the acid-tasting species of the dock genus: applied also to other plants. [O.Fr. *sorele, surele—sur*, sou—O.H.G. *sûr*, sour.]

sorrel[2] *sor'l, adj.* reddish-brown or light chestnut.—*n.* a reddish-brown colour: a sorrel horse. [O.Fr. *sorel* —*sor* (Fr. *saur, saure*), sorrel; poss. L.G.]

sorrow *sor'ō*, *n.* pain of mind: grief, sadness: affliction: lamentation: one sorrowed for.—*v.t.* and *v.i.* to grieve.—*n.* **sorr'ower**.—*adj.* **sorr'owful** full of sorrow: causing, showing, or expressing sorrow: sad: dejected.—*adv.* **sorr'owfully**.—*n.* **sorr'owfulness**.—*n.* and *adj.* **sorr'owing**. [O E. *sorg, sorh.*]

sorry *sor'i, adj* regretful: expressing pity, sympathy, etc.: (often merely formally) apologetic: distressing: poor, miserable, wretchedly bad, contemptible, worthless:—*compar* **sorr'ier**; *superl.* **sorr'iest**.—*interj.* of (often slight) apology.—*n.* **sorr'iness**.—*adj.* **sorr'yish**. [O.E. *sārig*, wounded—*sār*, pain; influenced in meaning by **sorrow**, but not connected in origin.]

sort *sòrt*, *n.* a class, kind, or species: quality or rank: one, a specimen or instance, of a kind (often ungrammatically in the singular with *these* or *those*, to denote examples of this or that kind): something of the nature but not quite worthy of the name: a letter, figure, or other character in a fount of type: manner.—*v.t.* to separate into lots or classes: to group, classify, arrange: to pick out: to select: to set in accord: to geld: to castigate, punish: to deal effectively with (esp. in a vague threat) (*coll.*).—*adj.* **sort'able** capable of being sorted: assorted.—*ns.* **sort'er** one who (or that which) separates and arranges, as letters; **sort'ilege** (*-i-lij*; L. *sortilegus*, a diviner) divination; **sortil'eger**; **sortil'egy**.—*n.* and *adj.* **sort'ing**.—**after a sort** to some extent; **a good sort** a decent fellow; **in a sort** in a manner; **in some sort** in a way: as it were; **of a sort, of sorts** inferior; **out of sorts** out of order, slightly unwell; **sort of** (*coll.*, used adverbially and parenthetically) as it were: to an extent: rather; **sort out** to classify, separate, arrange, etc.: to deal with, punish, etc. [L. *sors, sortis*, a lot, *sortīrī*. to draw lots; partly through O.Fr.]

sortie *sór'ti*, *n.* a sally of besieged to attack the besiegers: a raiding excursion.—*v.i.* to sally. [Fr., *sortir*, to go out, to issue; origin doubtful.]

sortilege, etc. See **sort.**

S O S *es-ō-es'*, *n.* an appeal for help or rescue.—*v.i.* to make such an appeal. [Arbitrary code signal.]

so-so (or **so so**) *sō'sō*, *adj.* neither very good nor very bad: tolerable: indifferent.—Also *adv.* [**so**[1].]

sostenuto *sos-te-nōō'tō, -nä'*, (*mus.*) *adj.* sustained.— *adv.* with full time allowed for each note. [It.]

sot *sot, n.* one stupefied by drinking: a habitual drunkard.—*adj.* **sott'ed** besotted.—*n.* **sott'ing.**—*adj.* **sott'ish** like a sot: foolish: stupid with drink. [O.Fr. *sot.*]

soterial *sō-tē'ri-əl, adj.* pertaining to salvation.—*adj.* **sōtēriolog'ical**.—*n.* **sōtēriol'ogy** the doctrine of salvation. [Gr. *sōtēria*, salvation—*sōtēr*, a saviour.]

Sotho *sōō'tōō, sō'tō, n.* See **Basuto.**

sotto voce *sot'tō vō'che, adv.* in an undertone, aside. [It., below the voice.]

sou *sōō, n.* a French five-centime piece. [Fr.,—L. *solidus.*]

soubise *sōō-bēz', n.* an onion sauce (**soubise sauce**). [Fr., after the French Marshal Prince de *Soubise* (1715–87).]

soubrette *sōō-bret', n.* a pert, coquettish, intriguing maid-servant in comedy: a singer of light songs of similar character: a maid-servant, lady's maid. [Fr., —Prov. *soubreto* (fem.), coy.]

soubriquet. See **sobriquet.**

souchong *sōō-shong', -chong', n.* a fine sort of black tea. [Chin. *hsiao*, small, *chung*, sort.]

Soudan(ese). See **Sudan.**

souffle *sōō'fl, n.* a murmuring in auscultation. [Fr.]

soufflé *sōō'flä, n.* a light dish, properly one with white of egg whisked into a froth.—*adj.* prepared thus. [Fr., pa.p. of *souffler*—L. *sufflāre*, to blow.]

sough[1] *sow, suf, v.i.* to sigh, as the wind.—*v.t.* to whine out: to sigh out: to hum.—*n.* a sighing of the wind: a deep sigh: a vague rumour: a whining tone of voice. [O.E. *swōgan*, to rustle.]

sough[2] *suf, n.* a drain, sewer. [Cf. Flem. dial. *zoeg*, a small ditch.]

sought *sót, pa.t.* and *pa.p.* of **seek.**

souk *sōōk, n.* among Eastern Muslim people, a marketplace.—Also **suk(h), suq.** [Ar. *sūq.*]

soul *sōl, n.* that which thinks, feels, desires, etc.: a spirit, embodied or disembodied: innermost being or nature: moral and emotional nature, power, or sensibility: nobleness of spirit or its sincere expression: a complete embodiment or exemplification: the essential part: an indwelling or animating principle: the moving spirit, inspirer, leader: a person: (also **soul music**) the popular music of American Negroes, typically emotional and earthy, a blend of blues, jazz, gospel and pop elements.—*adj.* of or relating to soul music: of or characteristic of American Negroes or their food, music, culture, etc.—*adjs.* **souled** having a soul, esp., in compounds, of this or that kind; **soul'ful** having or expressive of deep or elevated feeling, sincere or affected.—*adv.* **soul'fully.**—*n.* **soul'-fulness.**—*adj.* **soul'less** without a soul: lacking animation or nobleness of mind: mean, without spirit.— *adv.* **soul'lessly** in a soulless manner.—*n.* **soul'-lessness.**—**soul** brother, **sister** a fellow Negro, Negress.—*adj.* **soul'-destroying** (of a task, situation, etc.) extremely monotonous, unrewarding, etc.— **soul food** (*U.S.*) food traditionally eaten by American Negroes; **soul mate** a person to whom one is deeply emotionally or spiritually attached; **soul'-search'ing** a critical examination of one's actions, motives, etc.— Also *adj.*—**by, upon my soul!** an exclamation of surprise, etc. [O.E. *sāwol.*]

sound[1] *sownd, adj.* safe: whole: uninjured, unimpaired: in good condition: healthy: wholesome: deep (as sleep): solid: thorough (as a beating): wellfounded: well-grounded: trustworthy: of the right way of thinking: orthodox.—*adv.* soundly, completely fast, as in sleep.—*adv.* **sound'ly.**—*n.* **sound'ness.**— **sound as a bell** see **bell.** [O.E. *gesund.*]

sound[2] *sownd, n.* a strait: a fish's swimming bladder. [O.E. *sund*, swimming.]

sound[3] *sownd, n.* the sensation of hearing: a transmitted disturbance perceived or perceptible by the ear: mere noise, without meaning or sense: a report, rumour: hearing-distance.—*v.i.* to give out a sound: to resound: to be audible: to be sounded: to give an impression on hearing: to call, as by trumpet.—*v.t.* to cause to make a sound: to produce, utter, make, the sound of: to utter audibly: to pronounce: to announce, publish, proclaim, celebrate, signal, direct, by sound: to examine by percussion and listening.— *ns.* **sound'er** that which sounds: a telegraph-receiving instrument in which Morse signals are translated into sound signals; **sound'ing** emission of sound: a signal by trumpet, bell or the like, as for the rise of the curtain: examination by percussion.—*adj.* making a sound: sonorous: resounding: having a magnified sound.—*adv.* **sound'ingly.**—*adj.* **sound'less.**—*adv.* **sound'lessly.**—**sound'-bar** a bass-bar; **sound barrier** (*aero.*) a difficulty met about the speed of sound when power required to increase speed rises steeply; **sound'-board** a thin resonating plate of wood or metal in a musical instrument: in an organ, the apparatus that conveys the air from the windchest to the appropriate pipes; **sound effects** sounds other than dialogue or music used in films, radio and television; **sound'-film** a cinematograph film with sychronised soundtrack; **sound'-hole** an *f*-shaped hole in the belly of a violin, etc.; **sound'ing-board** a structure for carrying a speaker's voice towards the audience: a sound-board: any person, object or institution used to test the acceptability or effectiveness of an idea, plan, etc.— *adj.* **sound'proof** impenetrable by sound.—*v.t.* to render soundproof.—**sound'proofing; sound'-ranging** the calculation of position by timing the arrival of sound waves from (three or more) known positions; **sound spectrogram** a record produced by a **sound spectrograph**, an electronic instrument which makes a graphic representation of the qualities of a sound as frequency, intensity, etc.; **sound spectrography; sound'-track** on a cinematograph film, the magnetic tape on which sounds are recorded: a recording of the sound (esp. musical) accompaniment to a film; **sound'-wave** a longitudinal disturbance propagated through air or other medium.—**sound off** (**about, on**) to speak loudly and freely, esp. in complaint: to boast. [M.E. *soun*—A.Fr.—L. *sonus*; for *d* cf. **pound**[2].]

sound[4] *sownd, v.t.* to measure the depth of: to probe: to try to discover the inclinations, thoughts, etc., of (often with *out*).—*v.i.* to take soundings: to dive deep, as a whale.—*n.* a probe for examining the bladder, etc.—*ns.* **sound′er** one who sounds: apparatus for taking soundings; **sound′ing** the action of that which or one who sounds: an ascertained depth: (in *pl.*) waters in which an ordinary sounding-line will reach the bottom.—**sound′ing-lead** the weight at the end of a sounding-line; **sound′ing-line** a line with a plummet at the end for soundings; **sounding rocket** a rocket devised to gather high-altitude meteorological data and to radio it back to earth. [O.E. *sund-* (in compounds), cf. **sound²**; or perh. O.Fr. *sonder*, to sound, which may be from Gmc.]

soup *sōōp, n.* the nutritious liquid obtained by boiling meat or vegetables in stock: *loosely*, anything resembling soup in consistency, etc.: a photographic developer (*slang*).—*adj.* **soup′y.**—*adj.* **soup′ed-up** (*slang*) of e.g. an engine, having had the power increased.—**soup′-kitchen** a place for supplying soup to the poor; **soup′-plate** a large deep plate; **soup′spoon.**—**in the soup** in difficulties or trouble; **soup up** (*slang*) to increase the power of. [O.Fr. *soupe*; cf. **sop.**]

soupçon *sōōp-sõ, n.* a hardly perceptible quantity. [Fr., suspicion.]

sour *sowr, adj.* having an acid taste or smell: turned, rancid, or fermented: rank: cold and wet: embittered, crabbed, or peevish: disagreeable: inharmonious (*lit.*, *fig.*): bad, unsuccessful: containing sulphur compounds.—*v.t.* to make sour: to treat with dilute acid.—*v.i.* to become sour.—*n.* an acid drink, as a gin or whisky cocktail that contains lemon or lime-juice: an acid solution used in bleaching, curing skins, etc.—*n.* **sour′ing** turning or becoming sour: vinegar: the crab-apple: treatment with dilute acid in bleaching.—*adj.* **sour′ish.**—*advs.* **sour′ishly; sour′ly.**—*n.* **sour′-ness.**—**sour′-crout** see **sauerkraut; sour′dough** leaven: a piece of dough reserved to leaven a new batch: in Canada and Alaska, an old-timer.—*adj.* **sour′-eyed** morose-looking.—**sour′puss** (*slang*) a sour-tempered person. [O.E. *sûr.*]

source *sōrs, sõrs, n.* a spring: the head of a stream: an origin: a rise: an originating cause: that from which anything rises or originates: a book or document serving as authority for history, or furnishing matter or inspiration for an author: any person, publication, etc. providing information.—**source′-book** a book of original documents for historic study. [O.Fr. *sorse*, from *sourdre*—L. *surgĕre*, to rise.]

sousaphone *sōō′zǝ-fōn, n.* a large tuba-like brass wind instrument invented by the American bandmaster and composer J. P. *Sousa* (1854–1932).

souse *sows, n.* pickled meat, esp. pig's feet or ears: pickling liquid: a plunge in pickling or other liquid: a ducking: a drenching: a wash: a sluicing with water: a getting drunk (*slang*).—*v.t.* to pickle: to marinade and cook in spiced wine or vinegar: to plunge, immerse, duck: to drench, soak: to make drunk.—*v.i.* to be drenched: to wash thoroughly: to get drunk.—*adj.* **soused** pickled: very wet: drunk (*slang*).—*n.* and *adj.* **sous′ing.** [Partly O.Fr. *sous, souce*—O.H.G. *sulza*, from the root of **salt;** partly imit.]

souslik. Same as **suslik.**

soutache *sōō-täsh′, n.* a narrow braid. [Fr.]

soutane *sōō-tän′, n.* a cassock. [Fr.,—It. *sottana*—L. *subtus*, beneath.]

souterrain *sōō-te-rē, sōō′tǝ-rān, n.* an underground chamber: an earth-house. [Fr.]

south *sowth, adv.* in the direction contrary to north.— *n.* the point of the horizon, the region, or the part, in that direction: the south wind: (*cap.*; with *the*) the Southern States of the U.S.—*adj.* lying towards the south: forming the part, or that one of two, that is towards the south: blowing from the south: (of a pole

of a magnet, usu.) south-seeking.—*adj.* and *adv.* **southerly** (*sudh′*) towards or (of wind) from the south.—*adj.* **southern** (*sudh′*) of the south: in the south or in the direction toward it: (of wind) from the south: (*cap.*) of, from or pertaining to the South.—*n.* a southerner.—*n.* **southerner** (*sudh′*) a native or inhabitant of the south: (*cap.*) an inhabitant of the U.S. South.—*adjs.* (*superl.*), **southernmost** (*sudh′*); **south′most.**—*adj., adv.,* and *n.* **southward** (*sowth′wǝrd; naut. sudh′ǝrd*).—*adj.* and *adv.* **south-wardly.**—*adv.* **south′wards.**—*adjs.* **south-bound** (*sowth′*) bound for the south; **south′-country.**—*adj.* and *adv.* **south-east′** (or *sowth′*) midway between south and east.—*n.* the direction midway: the region lying in, the wind blowing from, that direction. —**south-east′er** a strong wind from the south-east.—*adj.* and *adv.* **south-east′erly** towards or (of wind) from the south-east.—*adj.* **south-east′ern** belonging to, or being in, the south-east, or in that direction.—*adj.* and *adv.* **south-east′ward** towards the south-east.—*n.* the region to the south-east.— *adj.* and *adv.* **south-east′wardly.**—*adj.* **south-east′wards.**—**Southern Cross** a conspicuous southern constellation with four bright stars placed crosswise; **southernwood** (*sudh′*) an aromatic plant of southern Europe, of the wormwood genus (Artemisia); **southland** (*sowth′*), the south (also *adj.*); **south′lander.**—*adj.* **south′paw** left-handed: in boxing, leading with the right hand.—*n.* a left-handed person, esp. in sport: a boxer who leads with his right hand.—**south pole** the end of the earth's axis in Antarctica: its projection on the celestial sphere: (usually) the south-seeking pole of a magnet (logically the north-seeking); **South Sea** the Pacific ocean.—*adj.* **south-seeking** (*sowth′*) turning towards the earth's magnetic south pole.—*ns., adjs.* and *advs.* **south-south-east′, south-south-west′** in a direction midway between south and south-east or south-west.—*adj.* and *adv.* **south-west** (*sowth′* or *sow′*, or *-west′*) midway between south and west.—*n.* the direction between south and west: the region lying that way: the wind blowing from that direction.—**south-sou′-west′er** a gale from the south-west: a waterproof hat with flap at the back of the neck.—*adjs.* **south′-west′erly** toward or (of wind) from the south-west; **south′-west′ern** belonging to, or lying in, the south-west or in that direction.—*adj, adv.,* and *n.* **south-west′ward.**—*adj.* and *adv.* **south-west′wardly.**—*adv.* **south-west′wards.**—**south by east, south by west** one compass point east, west of south. [O.E. *sûth.*]

Southdown *sowth′down, adj.* pertaining to the *South Downs* in Hampshire and Sussex, the famous breed of sheep so named.—*n.* a sheep of this breed.

southerly, southern, etc., See **south.**

souvenir *sōō′vǝ-nēr,* or *-nēr′, n.* a memento: a keepsake. [Fr. *souvenir*—L. *subvenīre*, to come up, to come to mind—*sub,* under *venīre,* to come.]

sovereign *sov′rin, -rǝn, n.* a supreme ruler or head: a monarch: a gold coin from Henry VII to Charles I worth 22s. 6d. to 10s., from 1817 a pound.—*adj.* supreme: excelling all others: having supreme power residing in itself, himself or herself: of sovereignty: (of contempt) utmost: highly efficacious.—*adv.* **sov′ereignly** supremely: as a sovereign.—*n.* **sov′ereignty** pre-eminence: supreme and independent power: the territory of a sovereign or of a sovereign state. [O.Fr. *sovrain* and It. *sovrano*—L. *super,* above.]

soviet *sõ′vi-ǝt, so′, n.* a council, esp. one of those forming since 1917 the machinery of local and national government in Russia (the Union of Soviet Socialist Republics)—the local councils elected by workers, peasants, and soldiers, the higher councils consisting of deputies from the lower.—*adj.* (*cap.*) of the U.S.S.R.—*adj.* soviet'ic.—*v.t.* so'vietise, -ize to transform to the soviet model.—*n.* so'vietism the principles and practices of a soviet government, specif. communism: a characteristic mannerism indicative of soviet ideology.—*n.* Sovietol'ogist one who has made a special study of the theory and practice of government in the U.S.S.R. and of current affairs there.—the Soviet the U.S.S.R. [Russ. *sovet*, council.]

sow¹ *sow*, *n.* a female pig: a female badger, etc.: a term of reproach for a fat, lazy, greedy, or sluttish person, esp. a woman: a main channel for molten iron, leading to *pigs*: metal solidified there.—sow'-thistle a thistle-like genus of plants (*Sonchus*) with milky juice and yellow flowers. [O.E. *sū*, *sugu*.]

sow² *sō*, *v.t.* to scatter or put in the ground, as seed: to plant by strewing: to scatter seed over: to spread, strew, disseminate.—*v.i.* to scatter seed for growth: —*pa.t.* sowed (*sōd*); *pa.p.* sown (*sōn*) or sowed.—*ns.* sow'er; sow'ing.—sow the seeds of to initiate, implant. [O.E. *sāwan*.]

sox *soks*, *n.pl.* a slang spelling of socks.

soy *soi*, soya *sō'yə*, *soi'ə*, *ns.* a thick, dark, salty sauce made from fermented soy beans and wheat flour (also soy, soya sauce): the soy bean, rich in oil and protein: the eastern Asiatic plant producing it.—*adj.* made from soy beans or soy flour.—soy bean; soya bean; soy, soya flour. [Jap. *shō-yu*, coll. *soy*, Du. *soya*, *soja*—Chin. *shi-yu*, salt bean oil.]

sozzled *soz'ld*, (*coll.*) *adj.* drunk.

spa *spä*, formerly *spō*, *n.* a mineral spring: a mineral water resort.—spa'-well. [*Spa* in Belgium.]

space *späs*, *n.* that in which material bodies have extension: a portion of extension: room: intervening distance: an interval: an open or empty place: regions remote from the earth: an interval between lines or words: a type used for making such an interval: an interval between the lines of the stave: a portion, extent, or interval of time: a short time: opportunity, leisure.—*v.t.* to make, arrange, or increase intervals between.—*ns.* spac'er one who, or that which, spaces: an instrument for reversing a telegraphic current: a space-bar; spacing (*spā'ing*) a space or spatial arrangement: the existence or arrangement of spaces, or of objects in spaces.—*adjs.* spacial (*spā'shl*) spatial; spacious (*spā'shəs*) extensive: ample: roomy: wide.—*adv.* spa'ciously.—*n.* spa'ciousness.—space age the present time when exploration of, and ability to travel in, space up to the limit of and beyond the earth's atmosphere are increasing; space'-bar a bar for making spaces in typewriting; space'craft a vehicle, manned or unmanned, designed for putting into space, orbiting the earth, or reaching other planets; space'-heater a device which warms the air in a room or similar enclosed area; Space Invaders® an electronic game played on a machine with a screen, involving 'shooting' at graphic representations of supposed invaders from outer space; space'-lattice an arrangement of points in three-dimensional space at the intersections of equally spaced parallel lines—such as the arrangement of atoms in a crystal disclosed by X-ray spectroscopy; space'man, -woman a traveller in space; space'-platform, space'-station a platform in space planned as an observatory and/or a landing-stage in space travel; space probe a spacecraft designed to obtain, and usu. transmit, information about the environment into which it is sent; space'-ship a spacecraft; space shuttle a spacecraft designed to transport men and materials to and from space-stations; space'-suit a suit devised for use in space-travel; space'-time' normal three-dimensional space plus dimension of time, modified by gravity in re-

lativity theory; space-time continuum physical space or reality, regarded as having four dimensions (length, breadth, height and time) in which an event can be represented as a point fixed by four co-ordinates; space'-travel; space'-traveller; space vehicle see vehicle.—space out to set wide apart or wider apart; spaced out (*slang*) in a dazed or stupefied state (as if) caused by the taking of drugs. [Fr. *espace*—L. *spatium*.]

spade¹ *spād*, *n.* a broad-bladed digging tool: a whaler's knife: a spade's depth.—*v.t.* to dig or remove with a spade.—*n.* spade'ful as much as a spade will hold:—*pl.* spade'fuls.—spade'work preparatory drudgery.—call a spade a spade to speak out plainly without euphemism. [O.E. *spadu*, *spædu*.]

spade² *spād*, *n.* a playing-card with black leaf-shaped (on Spanish cards sword-shaped) pips: (*offensive*) a Negro or other coloured person. [Sp. *espada*, sword—L. *spatha*—Gr. *spathē*, a broad blade.]

spadger *spaj'ər*, (*slang*) *n.* a sparrow. [Form of sparrow.]

spadix *spā'diks*, (*bot.*) *n.* a fleshy spike of flowers:—*pl.* spadices (-*di'sēz*).—*adjs.* spadiceous (*spa-dish'əs*) having, like, of the nature of, a spadix: coloured like a date: shaped like a palm-branch. [Gr. *spādix*, -*ikos*, a torn-off (palm) branch, in L. date-coloured, bay.]

spaghetti *spā-*, *spə-get'i*, *n.* an edible, cord-like paste intermediate between macaroni and vermicelli.—spaghetti (alla) bolognese (*al-a bol-o-nyä'zi*) spaghetti served with a meat and tomato sauce; spaghetti western an internationally-financed western, typically filmed in Europe by an Italian producer, characterised by a violent and melodramatic content and a baroque style. [It., pl. of *spaghetto*, dim. of *spago*, a cord.]

spahi *spā'hē*, *n.* formerly a Turkish, now a French Algerian cavalryman.—Also spa'hee. [Turk. (from Pers.) *sipāhi*; cf. sepoy.]

spake *spāk*. See speak.

spall *spöl*, *v.t.* and *v.i.* to split, splinter, to chip.—*n.* a chip or splinter, esp. of stone.—*v.t.* and *v.i.* spalt to splinter.—*adj.* brittle.—*n.* spalla'tion a nuclear reaction in which bombardment by high-energy particles produces a large number of disintegration particles not entirely identifiable. [Cf. M.E. *spalden*, to split; Ger. *spalten*.]

spalpeen *spal-pēn'*, *n.* a rascal, a mischievous fellow: a boy. [Ir. *spailpín*, a (migratory) labourer.]

Spam® *spam*, *n.* a type of luncheon-meat made from pork, spices, etc. [Spiced ham.]

span¹ *span*, *n.* the space from the end of the thumb to the end of the little finger when the fingers are extended: nine inches: the distance from wing-tip to wing-tip in an aeroplane: the distance between abutments, piers, supports, etc., or the portion of a structure (e.g. a bridge) between: the total spread or stretch: a stretch of time, esp. of life.—*v.t.* to measure by spans: to measure: to arch over: to stretch over: to bridge: to encompass:—*pr.p.* spann'ing; *pa.t.* and *pa.p.* spanned.—*adj.* span'-long of the length of a span.—span'-roof a roof with equal slopes. [O.E. *spann*.]

span² *span*, *n.* a pair of horses: a team of oxen. [Du. and L.G. *span*.]

span³ *span*, *adj.* fresh, short for span'-new' quite new, new as a fresh-cut chip.—spick and span see spick¹. [O.N. *spān-nŷr*—*spān*, chip (cf. spoon²), *nŷr*, new.]

span⁴ *span*. See spin.

spanaemia *span-ē'mi-ə*, *n.* deficiency of red corpuscles in the blood.—*adj.* spanae'mic. [Gr. *spanos*, lacking, *haima*, blood.]

spandrel, spandril *span'drəl*, *n.* the space between the curve of an arch and the enclosing mouldings, string-course, or the like [Poss conn. with **expand.**]

spangle *spang'gl, n.* a small, thin, glittering plate of metal: a sparkling speck, flake, or spot.—*v t* to adorn with spangles —*v.i.* to glitter —*adj.* **spang'led.** —*n.* and *adj.* **spang'ling.**—*adj.* **spang'ly.** [O.E *spang,* clasp.]

Spaniard *span'yərd, n.* a native or citizen of *Spain*: a Spanish ship *(arch.).* [M.E. *Spaignarde*—O.Fr *Espaignart.*]

spaniel *span'yəl, n.* a kind of dog, usu. liver-and-white, or black-and-white, with large pendent ears: one who fawns.—*adj.* like a spaniel: fawning, mean. [O.Fr. *espaigneul* (Fr. *épagneul*)—Sp. *Español,* Spanish]

Spanish *span'ish, adj.* of or pertaining to *Spain.*—*n.* the language of Spain.—**Spanish Main** (i.e. mainland) the mainland coast of the Caribbean Sea: often popularly the Caribbean Sea itself. [*Spain,* with vowel-shortening.]

spank¹ *spangk, v.t.* and *v.i.* to move or drive with speed or spirit.—*n.* **spank'er** one who walks with long vigorous strides: a fast-going horse: any person or thing particularly striking or dashing: a fore-and-aft sail on the aftermost mast.—*adj* **spank'ing** spirited, going freely: striking, beyond expectation: very large.—*adv.* **spank'ingly.** [Poss. back-formation from **spanking.**]

spank² *spangk, v.t.* to strike with the flat of the hand, to smack.—*n.* a loud slap, esp. on the buttocks.—*n.* **spank'ing.** [Prob. imit.]

spanner *span'ər, n.* a wrench for nuts, screws, etc.— **throw a spanner in the works** to cause confusion or difficulty, upset plans. [Ger. *Spanner—spannen,* to stretch; cf. **span².**]

spar¹ *spär, n.* a rafter: a pole: a bar or rail (chiefly *Scot.*): a general term for masts, yards, booms, gaffs, etc.—*v.t.* to fasten with a spar: to fasten: to shut: to fit with spars.—**spar deck** a light upper deck. [O.E. *gesparrian,* to bar; Du. *spar* (n.) *sperren* (vb.); O.N. *sparri*; Ger. *sperren* (vb.).]

spar² *spär, n.* any bright non-metallic mineral, with a good cleavage (esp. in compounds, as *calc-spar, fluorspar, feldspar*; also *Iceland spar*): a crystal or fragment thereof: an ornament made of it.—*adj.* **sparry** *(spär'i)* of or like spar. [M.L.G. *spar,* related to O.E. *spærstān,* gypsum.]

spar³ *spar, v.i.* (of game-cocks) to fight with spurs: to box, or make the actions of boxing: to dispute:—*pr.p.* **spar'ring;** *pa.t* and *pa.p.* **sparred.**—*n.* a boxing-match or demonstration: a cock-fight: a dispute.—*ns.* **spar'er; spar'ring.**—**sparring partner** one with whom a boxer practises: a friend with whom one enjoys lively arguments [Perh. O.Fr. *esparer* (Fr. *éparer*), to kick out; prob. Gmc.]

sparable *spar'ə-bl, n.* a small headless nail used by shoemakers [*sparrow-bill.*]

spare *spär, v.t.* to do without: to part with voluntarily: to afford: to abstain from using: to refrain from: to forbear to hurt, injure, punish, kill, end: to treat mercifully: to relieve or save from: to avoid: to avoid incurring.—*adj.* sparing: frugal: scanty: lean: not in actual use: not required: kept or available for others or for such purposes as may occur.—*adv.* sparely.—*n.* sparing: a spare room: a spare man: a spare part: a duplicate kept or carried for emergencies: in skittles or ten-pin bowling, overturning all the pins with the first two balls—i.e. with a ball to spare (a *double spare,* with first ball only): the score for so doing.—*adv.* **spare'ly.**—*ns.* **spare'ness; spär'er.**—*adj.* **spär'ing.**—*adv.* **spär'ingly.**—**spare part** a part for a machine ready to replace an identical part if it becomes faulty **(spare-part surgery** surgery involving the replacement of organs, by transplants or artificial devices); **spare rib** a piece of pork consisting of ribs

with a little meat adhering to them; **spare room** a bedroom for visitors; **spare time** leisure time *(adj.* **spare'-time); spare tyre** an extra tyre for a motor-vehicle, carried in case of a puncture: a roll of fat around the midriff *(coll.).*—**go spare** *(slang)* to become furious or frenzied; **to spare** over and above what is required [O.E. *sparian,* to spare, *spær,* sparing.]

sparge *spärj, v.t* to sprinkle. [L. *spargĕre,* to sprinkle.]

spark *spärk, n* a glowing or glittering particle: anything of like appearance or character, as easily extinguished, ready to cause explosion, burning hot: a flash: an electric discharge across a gap: anything active or vivid: a gay sprightly person.—*v.i.* to emit sparks: to sparkle —*v t.* to send forth as sparks: to send sparks through.—*n.sing.* **sparks** a ship's wireless operator *(naut slang):* an electrician *(slang).*— **spark'-coil** an induction coil: a connection of high-resistance used to prevent sparking in electrical apparatus; **spark'ing-plug, spark'-plug** in an internal-combustion engine, a plug carrying wires between which an electric spark passes to fire the explosive mixture of gases.—**make sparks fly** to cause anger, irritation; **spark (off)** to cause to begin, kindle, animate. [O.E. *spærca, spearca.*]

sparkle *spärk'l, n.* a little spark: glitter: scintillation: emission of sparks: appearance of effervescence (as of carbon dioxide in wine): vivacity: spirited animation: coruscation of wit.—*v.i.* to emit sparks: to glitter: to effervesce with glittering bubbles: to be bright, animated, vivacious, or witty.—*v.t.* to cause to sparkle: to throw out as, in, or like sparks.—*n.* **spark'ler** that which sparkles: a diamond or other gem *(slang):* a small firework which can be held in the hand.—*n.* and *adj.* **spark'ling.**—*adv.* **spark'lingly.** [Dim. and freq. of **spark.**]

sparrer, sparring, etc. See **spar³.**

sparrow *spar'ō, n.* any member of a family of small finch-like birds: extended to many other, usually brown, birds, as the hedge-sparrow.—**sparr'ow-hawk** a member of a genus *(Accipiter)* of long-legged, short-winged falcons, like the goshawks, but smaller. [O.E. *spearwa.*]

sparrow-grass *spar'ō-gräs, n.* a corruption of **asparagus.**

sparry. See **spar².**

sparse *spars, adj.* thinly scattered: scanty.—Also *adv.* —*adv.* **sparse'ly.**—*ns.* **sparse'ness; spars'ity.** [L *sparsus,* pa.p. of *spargĕre,* to scatter.]

Sparta *spär'tə, n.* a city of Greece, capital of ancient Laconia.—*n.* **Spar'tan** a citizen or native of Sparta or Laconia: one displaying Spartan qualities.—*adj.* of Sparta: Laconian: characteristic of Sparta—simple, hardy, rigorous, frugal, laconic, militaristic, despising culture.—*adv.* **Spar'tanly.** [Gr. *Spartē* (Doric *Spartā*).]

spasm *spazm, n.* a violent involuntary muscular contraction: a sudden convulsive action, movement, or emotion.—*adjs.* **spasm'ic; spasmod'ic, -al** relating to, or consisting in, spasms: convulsive: intermittent — *adv.* **spasmod'ically.**—*adj.* **spas'tic** of the nature of spasm: characterised or affected by spasms: spasmodic: awkward, clumsy, useless *(slang).*—*n.* one affected with spastic paralysis —*adv.* **spas'tically.**—*n.* **spasticity** *(-tis'i-ti)* tendency to spasm.—**spastic paralysis** permanent muscle constriction or involuntary jerky muscle movement caused by injury to the muscle-controlling part of the brain. [Gr. *spasma, -atos,* and *spasmos, -ou,* convulsion; adjs. *spasmōdēs, spastikos—spaein,* to draw, convulse]

spat¹ *spat, pa.t* and *pa.p* of **spit².**

spat² *spat, n.* a large drop, as of rain: a splash, spattering: a petty quarrel.—*v.t. (rare)* to slap, to strike lightly.—*v.i.* to engage in a petty quarrel. [Prob. imit.]

spat³ *spat, n.* a short gaiter:—a fairing covering an aircraft wheel. [**spatterdash.**]

spatchcock *spach'kok, n.* a fowl killed and cooked at once: a fowl slit lengthways, opened out, and cooked (usu. grilled) flat.—*v.t.* to treat in this way: to interpolate. [Prob. **dispatch** and **cock¹**; cf. **spitchcock.**]

spate *spāt, (orig. Scot.) n.* a flood: a sudden rush or increased quantity.—**in spate** (of a river) in a swollen, fast-flowing condition.

spathe *spādh, (bot.) n.* a sheathing bract, usu. a conspicuous one enclosing a spadix.—*adjs.* **spathaceous** (*spa-thā'shas*), **spathed** (*spādhd*) having a spathe. [Gr. *spathē*, a broad blade.]

spathic *spath'ik, adj.* of the nature of, or like, spar: lamellar. [Ger. *Spat(h)*, spar.]

spatial, spacial *spā'shl, adj.* relating to space.—*n.* **spatiality** (*spā-shi-al'i-ti*).—*adv.* **spā'tially.**—*adj.* **spatiotemp'oral** of space-time or space and time together. [L. *spatium*, space.]

spatter *spat'ar, v.t.* to throw out or scatter upon: to scatter about: to sprinkle, esp. with mud or liquid.— *v.i.* to fly or fall in drops: to let drops fall or fly about. —*n.* a spattering: what is spattered.—**spatt'erdash** a long gaiter or legging. [Cf. Du. and L.G. *spatten.*]

spatula *spat'ū-la, n.* a broad blunt blade or flattened spoon.—*adjs.* **spat'ular; spat'ulate** shaped like a spatula: broad and rounded at the tip and tapering at the base.—*n.* **spat'ule** a spatula. [L. *spatula, spathula*, dim. of *spatha*—Gr. *spathē*, a broad blade.]

spavin *spav'in, n.* see **bone-spavin.** [O.Fr. *espa(r)vain.*]

spawn *spön, n.* a mass of eggs laid in water: fry: brood: contemptuously, offspring: mushroom mycelium.— *v.t.* to produce as spawn: contemptuously, to generate, esp. in mass.—*v.i.* to produce or deposit spawn: to teem: to come forth as or like spawn.—*n.* **spawn'er** one who spawns: a female fish, esp. at spawning-time.—*n.* and *adj.* **spawn'ing.**—**spawn'ing-bed, -ground** a bed or place in the bottom of a stream on which fish deposit their spawn. [O.Fr. *espandre*, to shed—L. *expandēre*, to spread out.]

spay *spā, v.t.* to remove or destroy the ovaries of. [A.Fr. *espeier—espee* (Fr. *épée*), sword.]

speak *spēk, v.i.* to utter words: to talk: to discourse: to make a speech: to sound: to give tongue: to give expression, information, or intimation by any means.— *v.t.* to pronounce: to utter: to express: to use as a language, talk in: to bring or render by speaking:— *pa.t.* **spoke**, or *(arch.)* **spake**; *pa.p.* **spō'ken.**—**speak** *(coll.)* in composition, a particular jargon or style of language, such as *techno-speak, doublespeak*, etc.— *adj.* **speak'able** able or fit to be spoken or expressed in speech.—*ns.* **speak'er** one who speaks: the president (orig. the mouthpiece) of a legislative body, as the House of Commons: a loudspeaker; **speak'ership; speak'ing** the act of expressing ideas in words: discourse.—*adj.* uttering or transmitting speech: seeming to speak, lifelike.—*adv.* **speak'ingly.**— **speak'-eas'y** *(U.S.)* an illicit liquor-shop, shebeen; **speaking clock** a British telephone service which states the exact time when dialled; **speaking terms** see term; **speak'ing-tube** a tube for speaking through to another room.—**so to speak** as one might put it, as it were; **speak for** to speak on behalf of or in favour of: to be a proof of: to witness to: to bespeak; engage; **speak out** to speak boldly, freely, unreservedly, or so as to be easily heard; **speak the same language** see language; **speak to** to reprove: to attest, testify to: to discuss; **speak up** to speak so as to be easily heard: to

state one's opinions boldly; **to speak of** worth mentioning; **to speak to** so as to have conversation with. [Late O.E. *specan* (for *sprecan*).]

spear *spēr, n.* a long weapon made of a pole with a pointed head: a barbed fork for catching fish: anything sharp or piercing: a spiky shoot or blade: a reed. —*v.t.* to pierce with a spear.—*adjs.* speared armed with the spear; **spear'y.**—**spear'fish** a kind of swordfish; **spear gun** an underwater sporting gun which fires spears; **spear'head** the head of a spear: the front of an attack.—Also *v.t.*—**spear'man** a man armed with a spear; **spear'mint** a common gardenmint; **spear'-point; spear'-thistle** a common thistle (*Cnicus lanceolatus* or *Cirsium lanceolatum*). [O.E. *spere*; with some senses from **spire¹.**]

spec¹ *spek, n.* a coll. shortening of **speculation.**—**on spec** as a gamble, on the chance of achieving something.

spec² *spek, n.* a coll. shortening of **specification.**

speccy *spek'i, (coll.) n.* and *adj.* (one who is) bespectacled. [Cf. **specs, spectacle.**]

special *spesh'l, adj.* particular: peculiar: distinctive: exceptional: additional to ordinary: detailed: intimate: designed for a particular purpose: confined or mainly applied to a particular subject.—*n.* any special or particular person or thing: any person or thing set apart for a particular duty—a constable, a railway-train, etc.: a particular dish offered in a restaurant, often at a lower price, etc.: a newspaper extra, a dispatch from a special correspondent.—*n.* **specialisa'tion, -z-.**—*v.t.* **spec'ialise, -ize** to make special or specific: to differentiate: to adapt to conditions: to specify: to narrow and intensify: to become or be a specialist in (with *in*).—*v.i.* to become or be a specialist: to become differentiated: to be adapted to special conditions.—*ns.* **spec'ialiser, -z-; spec'ialism** (devotion to) some particular study or pursuit; **spec'ialist** one who devotes himself to a special subject.—*adj.* **specialist'ic.**—*n.* **speciality** (*spesh-i-al'i-ti*), **specialty** (*spesh'al-ti*) the particular characteristic skill, use, etc. of a person or thing: a special occupation or object of attention.—*adv.* **specially** (*spesh'a-li*).—**Special Branch** a British police department which deals with political security; **special constable** see constable; **special correspondent** a person employed to send reports to a particular newspaper, agency, etc.; **special delivery** the delivery of mail by special messenger outside normal delivery times, **special licence, offer, pleading, verdict** see licence, etc.; **special school** a school designed for the teaching of children with particular needs, esp the mentally or physically handicapped.—**Special Drawing Rights** (also without *caps.*; abbrev. **SDR(s)**) a reserve of International Monetary Fund assets which members of the fund may draw on in proportion to their IMF contributions; **Special Theory of Relativity** see relate. [L. *speciālis—speciēs*, species.]

speciate, -ation. See species.

species *spē'shēz, -shiz, -shi-ēz, n.* a eucharistic element: a group of individuals having common characteristics, specialised from others of the same *genus (log.)*: a group of closely allied mutually fertile individuals showing constant differences from allied groups, placed under a genus (*biol.*): a kind, sort:— *pl.* **spē'cies.**—*n.* **specia'tion** formation of new biological species.—*ns.* **specie** (*spē'shē, -shi-ē*; orig. the L. abl. as in the phrase *in specie*, in kind) formerly, payment or requital in the same kind: now, coined money; **speciesism** (*spē'shēz-izm*) the assumption that man is superior to all other species of animals and that he is therefore justified in exploiting them to his own advantage. [L. *speciēs*, pl. *-ēs*, appearance, kind, species—*specēre*, to look at.]

specify *spes'i-fī, v.t.* to mention particularly: to make specific: to set down as requisite:—*pr.p.* **spec'ifying;** *pa.t.* and *pa.p.* **spec'ified.**—*adjs.* **spec'ifiable** (or *fī'*); **specific** (*spi-sif'ik*) constituting or determining a species: pertaining to a species: peculiar to a species: of special application or origin: specifying: precise: of a parasite, restricted to one particular host: of a stain, colouring certain structures or tissues only: of a physical constant, being the ratio per unit volume, area, (or especially) mass, etc.—*n.* a remedy or medicine for a particular disease or part of the body: anything that is specific.—*adj.* **specif'ical.**—*adv.* **specif'ically.** —*v.t.* **specif'icate** to specify.—*ns.* **specifica'tion** (*spes-*) making, becoming, or being specific: the act of specifying: any point or particular specified: a detailed description of requirements, etc.: the description of his invention presented by an applicant for a patent; **specificity** (*spes-i-fis'i-ti*).—*adj.* **spec'ified.**—**specific gravity** the weight of any given substance as compared with the weight of an equal bulk or volume of water or other standard substance at the same, or at standard, temperature and pressure; **specific heat (capacity)** the number of heat-units necessary to raise the unit of mass of a given substance one degree in temperature. [O.Fr. *specifier*—L.L. *specificāre*—L. *speciēs*, kind, *facĕre*, to make.]

specimen *spes'i-min, n.* an object or portion serving as a sample, esp. for purposes of study or collection: a remarkable type: derogatorily, a person (*coll.*). [L. *specimen*—*specĕre*, to see.]

specious *spē'shəs, adj.* looking well at first sight: fair-showing: plausibly deceptive.—*ns.* **speciosity** (*-shi-os'i-ti*), **spe'ciousness.**—*adv.* **spe'ciously.** [L. *speciōsus,* showy—*speciēs,* form—*specĕre,* to look at.]

speck[1] *spek, n.* a small spot: a particle.—*adjs.* **speck'less; speck'y.** [O.E. *specca.*]

speck[2] *spek, n.* fat: bacon: blubber. [Ger. *Speck,* Du. *spek,* fat; cf. O.E. *spic,* fat bacon.]

speckle *spek'l, n.* a little spot, esp. of colour.—*v.t.* to mark with speckles.—*adj.* **speck'led.** [**speck**[1].]

specs, also **specks,** *speks, n.pl.* a colloquial shortening of **spectacles.**

spectacle *spek'tə-kl, n.* a sight: a show, pageant, exhibition: (in *pl.*) a pair of lenses mounted in frames with side-pieces to grip the temples: (in *pl.*) a marking resembling spectacles.—*adjs.* **spec'tacled; spectacular** (*-tak'ū-lər*) of the nature of, or marked by, display: sensational, very impressive.—*n.* a theatrical show, esp. on television, or any display, that is large-scale and elaborate.—*n.* **spectacularity** (*-lar'i-ti*).—*adv.* **spectac'ularly.** [L. *spectāculum*—*spectāre, -ātum,* intens. of *specĕre,* to look at.]

spectator *spek-tā'tər, n.* one who looks on:—*fem.* **spectā'tress, spectā'trix.**—*v.i.* **spectate'** (*back-formation*) to look on.—*adj.* **spectatorial** (*-tə-tō'ri-əl, -to'*).—*n.* **spectā'torship** the action, office, or quality of a spectator.—**spectator sport** a sport that has great appeal for spectators. [L. *spectātor*—*spectāre,* to look.]

spectra, spectral, etc. See **spectrum.**

spectre, in U.S. **specter,** *spek'tər, n.* an apparition: a ghost.—*adj.* **spec'tral** relating to, or like, a spectre.— *n.* **spectral'ity** the state of being spectral: a spectral object.—*adv.* **spec'trally.**—*n.* **spectrol'ogy** the study of ghosts. [Fr. *spectre*—L. *spectrum*—*specĕre,* to look at.]

spectro- *spek'trō, -tro',* in composition, spectre, spectrum (qq.v.).

spectrum *spek'trəm, n.* an after-image: the range of colour produced by a prism or diffraction-grating: any analogous range of radiations in order of wavelength:

range of frequencies of sound or a sound: range of opinions, activities, etc. (*fig.*):—*pl.* **spec'tra.**—*adj.* **spec'tral** relating to, or like, a spectrum.—*ns.* **spectral'ity; spec'trogram** a photograph of a spectrum: a sound spectrogram (q.v.); **spec'trograph** a spectroscope designed for use over a wide range of frequencies (well beyond visible spectrum) and recording the spectrum photographically.—*adjs.* **spectrograph'ic, -al.**—*ns.* **spectrog'raphy; spectrol'ogy** the science of the spectrum or spectrum analysis; **spectrom'eter** an instrument for measuring refractive indices: one used for measurement of wavelength or energy distribution in a heterogeneous beam of radiation; **spectrom'etry; spec'troscope** a general term for an instrument (*spectrograph, spectrometer,* etc.) used in spectroscopy, the basic features of which are a slit and collimator for producing a parallel beam of radiation, a prism or grating for 'dispersing' different wavelengths through differing angles of deviation, and a telescope, camera or counter tube for observing the dispersed radiation—*adjs.* **spectroscop'ic, -al.**—*adv.* **spectroscop'ically.**—*ns.* **spectroscopist** (*spek-tros'kə-pist,* or *spek'trə-skop-ist*); **spectros'copy** (or *spek'*) the study of spectra.—**spectrum analysis** determination of chemical composition by observing the spectrum of light or X-rays coming from or through the substance. [L. *spectrum,* an appearance —*specĕre,* to look at.]

specular *spek'ū-lər, adj.* mirror-like: having a speculum: by reflection: visual: giving a wide view. [L. *speculāris*—*speculum,* a mirror, and *specula,* a watch-tower.]

speculate *spek'ū-lāt, v.t.* to reflect: to theorise: to make conjectures or guesses: to take risk in hope of gain, esp. in buying and selling.—*n.* **specula'tion** act of speculating or its result: theorising: conjecture: mere guesswork: a more or less risky investment of money for the sake of unusually large profits.—*adj.* **spec'ulative** of the nature of, based on, given to, speculation or theory.—*adv.* **spec'ulatively.**—*ns.* **spec'ulativeness; spec'ulator** one who speculates in any sense.—*adj.* **spec'ulatory** exercising speculation [L. *speculātus,* pa.p. of *speculārī*—*specula,* a lookout —*specĕre,* to look at.]

speculum *spek'ū-ləm, n.* a mirror: a reflector, usu. of polished metal: an instrument with which to view cavities of the body (*med.*): a bright patch on a wing, esp. a duck's:—*pl.* **spec'ula.**—**speculum metal** an alloy of copper and tin, with or without other ingredients, which can be highly polished and used for mirrors, lamp reflectors, etc. [L. *speculum,* a mirror—*specĕre,* to look at.]

sped *sped, pa.t.* and *p> p.* of **speed.**

speech *spēch, n.* that which is spoken: language: the power of speaking: manner of speaking: a continuous spoken utterance: a discourse, oration: talk: colloquy: mention: parole (q.v.) (*linguistics*): the sounding of a musical instrument.—*v.i.* **speech'ify** to make speeches, harangue (implying contempt).— *adj.* **speech'less** destitute or deprived of the power of speech.—*adv.* **speech'lessly.**—*n.* **speech'lessness.**— **speech community** a community based on a common language or dialect; **speech day** the public day at the close of a school year, or on which prizes won during the previous year are presented; **speech'-maker** one accustomed to speak in public; **speech therapy** treatment of speech defects; **speech'-train'ing** training in clear speech. [Late O.E. *spēc, spæc,* O.E. *sprēc, spræc.*]

speed *spēd, n.* quickness, swiftness, dispatch: the rate at which a distance is covered: the time taken for a photographic film to accept an image: amphetamine (*slang*).—*v.i.* to move quickly: to hurry: to drive at high, or at dangerously, unduly, or illegally high, speed.—*v.t.* to give or bring success to (*arch.*): to send swiftly: to push forward: to haste: to betake with speed: to urge to high speed: to set or regulate the speed of:—*pa.t.* and *pa.p.* sped (also speed'ed).—*n.* speed'er one who, or that which, speeds or promotes speed.—*adv.* speed'ily.—*ns.* speed'iness quickness; speed'ing success: promotion, furtherance: progressive increase of speed (often with *up*): motoring at excessive speed.—Also *adj.*—*adj.* speed'less.—*ns.* speedom'eter a device indicating the speed at which a vehicle is travelling (coll. shortening speed'o, *pl.* speed'os); speed'ster a speedboat: a fast (sports) car: one who speeds.—*adj.* speed'y swift: prompt: soon achieved.—speed'-boat a very swift motor-boat; speed'-boating; speed'-cop (*slang*) a policeman who watches out for motorists who are exceeding a speed-limit; speed'-limit the maximum speed at which motor vehicles may be driven legally on certain roads; speed merchant one who drives a motor vehicle exceedingly fast (*slang*); speed trap a section of road over which the police (often using radar) check the speed of passing vehicles and identify drivers exceeding the limit (see also radar trap); speed'-up an acceleration, esp. in work; speed'way a road for fast traffic: a motor-cycle racing track: the sport of motor-cycle racing; speed'well any species of the genus Veronica, typically blue-flowered, posterior petals united; posterior sepal wanting.—speed up to quicken the rate of working. [O.E. *spēd.*]

speiss spīs, *n.* a mass of arsenides and commonly antimonides, a first product in smelting certain ores. [Ger. *Speise.*]

spelean, spelean spi-lē'ən, *adj.* cave-dwelling.—*adj.* spel(a)eological (spē-li-ə-loj'i-kl, spel-).—*ns.* spel(a)eol'ogist; spel(a)eol'ogy the scientific study of caves: exploration of caves. [Gr. *spēlaion,* cave.]

spellikin. See spill².

spell¹ spel, *n.* a magic formula: a magic influence: enchantment: entrancement.—*v.t.* to say a spell over: to bind with a spell: to enchant.—*v.t.* spell'bind (*back-formation*).—spell'binder an orator, usu. political or evangelical, who holds his audience spellbound: any person or thing that entrances.—*adj.* spell'bound bound by a spell: entranced. [O.E. *spell,* narrative, *spellian,* to speak, announce.]

spell² spel, *v.t.* to read laboriously, letter by letter: to name or set down in order the letters of: to constitute or represent orthographically: to import, amount to (*fig.*).—*v.i.* to spell words, esp. correctly:—*pa.t.* and *pa.p.* spelled, spelt.—*n.* a mode of spelling.—spell'ing-bee a spelling competition; spell'ing-book a book for teaching to spell; spelling pronunciation (*linguistics*) a pronunciation of a word that, as a side-effect of literacy, closely represents its spelling, superseding the traditional pronunciation, e.g. forehead as fōr'hed (orig. for'id).—spell (it) out to be extremely specific in explaining something. [O.Fr. *espeller* (Fr. *épeler*), of Gmc. origin; cf. foregoing.]

spell³ spel, *v.t.* to take the place of at work: to relieve, give a rest to: to take a turn at.—*v.i.* to take turns: to rest:—*pr.p.* spell'ing; *pa.t.* and *pa.p.* spelled.—*n.* a shift: a turn at work: a bout, turn: a short time: a stretch of time: a rest: a fit of irritation, illness, etc. [O.E. *spelian,* to act for another.]

spellikin, spellican. See spill².

spelt¹ spelt, *n.* an inferior species of wheat grown in the mountainous parts of Europe. [O.E. *spelt.*]

spelt². See spell².

spelter spel'tər, *n.* zinc, esp. impure zinc. [Cf. L.G. *spialter.*]

spencer¹ spens'ər, *n.* a kind of wig: a short double-breasted overcoat: a woman's short under-garment,

formerly over-jacket. [After various persons of the name.]

spencer² spens'ər, *n.* in ships and barques, a fore-and-aft sail abaft the fore and main masts. [Perh. the name Spencer, as foregoing.]

spend spend, *v.t.* to expend: to pay out: to give, bestow, employ, for any purpose: to shed: to consume: to use up: to exhaust: to waste: to pass, as time.—*v.i.* to make expense:—*pa.t.* and *pa.p.* spent.—*adj.* spen'dable.—*ns.* spen'der; spen'ding.—*adj.* spent used up: exhausted: of fish, exhausted by spawning.—spending money pocket money; spend'thrift one who spends the savings of thrift: a prodigal.—*adj.* excessively lavish; spent force a person or thing whose former strength, usefulness, etc. is exhausted.—spend a penny see penny. [O.E. *spendan*—L. *expendēre* or *dispendēre,* to weigh out.]

sperm spûrm, *n.* seed or semen: generative substance: a male gamete or germ-cell: a sperm-whale: sperm-oil: spermaceti.—sperm in composition, seed.—adjective combining forms -spermal, -spermous.—For some compounds beginning sperma-, spermo- see spermato- (spûr'mə-tō-) below.—*ns.* sper'maduct, sper'miduct a duct conveying spermatozoa; sperma'rium (*pl.* sperma'ria), sper'mary the male germ-gland.—*adjs.* spermat'ic, -al of, pertaining to, conveying sperm: generative.—*ns.* spermat'ic a spermatic vessel; sper'matid a cell that develops directly into a spermatozoon; sper'matoblast (Gr. *blastos,* a shoot) a spermatid.—*adj.* spermatoblas'tic.—*ns.* sper'matocyte (Gr. *kytos,* vessel) a sperm mother-cell or its predecessor; spermatogenesis (-jen'), spermatogeny (-ə-toj'i-ni) sperm-formation.—*adjs.* spermatogenet'ic, spermatogen'ic, spermatog'enous.—*ns.* spermatogonium (-gō'ni-əm) one of the cells that by repeated division form the spermatocytes; sper'matophore a case enclosing the spermatozoa.—*n.pl.* Spermatoph'yta (also Spermaph'yta, Spermoph'yta; Gr. *phyton,* plant) the flowering plants as one of the four phyla of the vegetable kingdom.—*n.* spermat'ophyte (sperm'aphyte, etc.).—*adjs.* spermatophytic (-fit'ik; also sperma-, spermo-); spermatozö'al, spermatozö'an, spermatozö'ic.—*ns.* spermatozö'id, spermatozö'on (Gr. *zōion,* animal; *pl.* -zō'a) a male germ-cell.—*adj.* sper'mic spermatic.—*n.* sper'micide any substance which kills spermatozoa.—*adj.* spermici'dal.—For some compounds in spermo- see spermato- above.—*adj.* sper'mous spermatic.—sperm bank a store of semen for use in artificial insemination; sperm'-cell a male gamete; sperm'-oil oil from the sperm-whale; sperm'-whale the cachalot, a whale from which spermaceti is obtained. [Gr. *sperma, -atos,* seed, semen—*speirein,* to sow.]

spermaceti spûr-mə-set'i, *n.* a waxy matter obtained mixed with oil from the head of the sperm-whale and others.—Also *adj.* [L. *sperma cēti* (gen. of *cētus,* a whale—Gr. *kētos*), whale's sperm, from a wrong notion of its origin.]

spermarium, spermatic, etc. See sperm.

spew, spū, *v.t.* to vomit.—*v.i.* to vomit: to ooze, run.—*n.* vomited matter.—*n.* spew'er. [O.E. *spiwan,* spiowan, to spit.]

Sphagnum sfag'nəm, *n.* a genus of mosses—peat or bog-moss, formerly useful as wound-dressings. [Gr. *sphagnos,* a name for various plants.]

sphalerite sfal'ər-īt, *n.* zinc-blende. [Gr. *sphaleros,* deceptive, from its resemblance to galena.]

sphene sfēn, *n.* titanite.—*adj.* sphe'nic wedge-like.—*n.pl.* Spheniscformes (sfē-nis-i-för'mēz) the penguin order of birds.—*n.* Sphe'nodon (Gr. *odous, odontos,* a tooth) genus, also known as Hatteria, to which the tuatara (q.v.) belongs: (without *cap.*) an animal of this genus.—*adj.* **sphē'noid** wedge-shaped, applied to a set of bones at the base of the skull.—*n.* a sphenoid bone: a wedge-shaped crystal form of four triangular faces.—*adj.* **sphenoid'al**. [Gr. *sphēn*, *sphēnos*, a wedge.]

sphere *sfēr*, *n.* a solid figure bounded by a surface of which all points are equidistant from a centre: its bounding surface: the apparent sphere of the heavens, upon which the stars are seen in projection: any one of the concentric spherical shells which were once supposed to carry the planets in their revolutions: a circle of society, orig. of the higher ranks (as if a planetary sphere): domain, scope, range: a field of activity: condition of life: a world, mode of being: a ball: a spherical object, esp. a planet.—*adjs.* **sphēr'al**; **sphered**; **sphere'less**; **spheric** (*sfer'ik*), -al of a sphere or spheres: having the form of a sphere.— *n.* **spherical'ity**.—*adv.* **spher'ically**.—*ns.* **spher'icalness**, **sphericity** (*-is'i-ti*) state or quality of being spherical.—*n.* **sphē'roid** a body or figure nearly spherical, but not quite so.—*adj.* **sphēroi'dal**.—*ns.* **sphēroid'icity**; **sphēroni'eter** an instrument for measuring curvature of surfaces.—*adj.* **spherūlar** (*sfer'*). —*ns.* **spher'ūle** a little sphere.—**spherical aberration** loss of image definition which occurs when light strikes a lens or mirror with a spherical surface.— **music, harmony, of the spheres** the music, inaudible to mortal ears, produced according to Pythagoras by the motions of the celestial spheres in accordance with the laws of harmony. [Gr. *sphairă*.]

sphincter *sfingk'tər*, (*anat.*) *n.* a ring-like muscle whose contraction narrows or shuts an orifice.—*adjs.* **sphinc'teral**, **sphincterial** (*-tē'ri-əl*), **sphincteric** (*-ter'ik*). [Gr. *sphinktēr—sphingein*, to bind tight.]

Sphinx, sphinx *sfingks*, *n.* a monster of Greek mythology, with the head of a woman and the body of a lioness, that proposed riddles to travellers, and strangled those who could not solve them: any similar monster or representation of one: an enigmatic or inscrutable person:—*pl.* **sphinx'es**, **sphinges** (*sfin'jēz*). [Gr.,—*sphingein*, to draw tight.]

sphragistic *sfrə-jist'ik*, *adj.* pertaining to seals and signets.—*n. sing.* **sphragist'ics** the study of seals. [Gr. *sphrāgistikos—sphrāgis*, a seal.]

sphygmus *sfig'məs*, *n.* the pulse.—*ns.* **sphyg'mogram** a sphygmograph record; **sphyg'mograph** an instrument for recording pulse-beat; **sphygmog'raphy**; **sphygmomanom'eter**, **sphygmom'eter** an instrument for measuring arterial blood-pressure. [Latinised from Gr. *sphygmos*, pulse.]

spic *spik*, (esp. *U.S. derog.*) *n.* a person from a Spanish-speaking American country, or of Mexican, S. American, etc., origin.—Also **spi(c)k**.

spica *spī'kə*, *n.* a spiral bandage with reversed turns suggesting an ear of barley.—*adjs.* **spi'cate**, **-d** in, having, or forming a spike: spikelike; **spic'ūlar** of the nature of or like a spicule; **spic'ūlate** having spicules. —*n.* **spic'ūle** a minute needle-like body, crystal, splinter, or process: one of the spike-like forms seen forming and re-forming on the edge of the sun, caused by ejections of hot gas several thousand miles above its surface. [L. *spīca*, an ear of corn.]

spiccato *spik-kä'tō*, *adj.* and *adv.* half staccato.—*n.* spiccato playing or passage:—*pl.* **spicca'tos**. [It.]

spice *spīs*, *n.* an aromatic and pungent vegetable substance used as a condiment and for seasoning food —pepper, nutmeg, ginger, cinnamon, etc.: such substances collectively or generally: a characteristic smack, flavour: anything that adds piquancy or interest: an aromatic odour: a touch, tincture (*fig.*).—*v.t.* to season with spice: to tincture, vary, or diversify.— *adj.* **spiced** impregnated with a spicy odour: seasoned with spice.—*adv.* **spic'ily**.—*n.* **spic'iness**.—*adj.* **spic'y**

producing or abounding with spices: fragrant: pungent: piquant, pointed: racy: risqué: showy.—**spice's box** a box, often ornamental, for keeping spices; **spice'-bush** an aromatic American shrub (*Lindera*) of the laurel family; **spice'-cake** a spiced cake. [O.Fr. *espice* (Fr. *épice*)—L.L. *speciēs*, kinds of goods, spices —L. *speciēs*, a kind.]

spick[1] *spik*, *n.* a nail, a spike.—*adj.* tidy, fresh.—**spick and span** trim and speckless, like a spike new cut and a chip new split; **spick and span new** brand-new. [**spike**[2].]

spick[2]. See **spic**.

spicule, etc. See under **spica**.

spider *spī'dər*, *n.* an arachnid of the order Araneida, the body divided into two distinct parts: a frying-pan, properly one with feet: any of various spider-like radiating structures, instruments, tools, etc.: a rest for a cue in billiards: an arrangement of elastic straps with hooks attached, used to fasten luggage, etc., on to the roof-rack of a car or on to a motor-bicycle, etc. —*adjs.* **spi'der-like**; **spi'dery** spider-like: abounding in spiders.—**spi'der-line** a thread of silk spun by a spider: any fine thread in an optical instrument, for measurement, position-marking, etc.; **spi'der-man** an erector of steel building structures; **spi'der-monkey** an American monkey with long slender legs and tail; **spider plant** any of various spiky-leaved plants used ornamentally, especially one which grows new shoots on trailing stems: spider-wort; **spi'der-stitch** a stitch in lace or netting in which threads are carried diagonally and parallel to each other; **spi'der-web** the snare spun by a spider; **spi'der-wheel** in embroidery, a circular pattern with radiating lines; **spi'der-work** lace worked by spider-stitch. [O.E. *spīthra— spinnan*, to spin.]

spiegeleisen *spē'gl-ī-zn*, *n.* a white cast-iron containing manganese, largely used in the manufacture of steel by the Bessemer process. [Ger.,—*Spiegel*—L. *speculum*, a mirror, Ger. *Eisen*, iron.]

spiel *spēl*, *shpēl*, *n.* a (esp. plausible) story or line of talk.—*v.i.* to talk glibly, tell the tale.—Also *v.t.*—*n.* **spiel'er** a person with a glib, persuasive line of talk: a swindler: a card sharper: a gambling den. [Ger. *spielen*, to play.]

spiffing *spif'ing*, (*coll.*) *adj.* excellent.

spiflicate, spifflicate *spif'li-kāt*, (*slang*) *v.t.* to do for: to quell: to confound: to handle roughly.—*n.* **spif(f)lica'tion**.

spignel *spig'nl*, *n.* baldmoney (*Meum*).

spigot *spig'ət*, *n.* a vent-peg or peg controlling a faucet. [Prov. *espigot*—L. *spīculum*.]

spik. See **spic**.

spike[1] *spīk*, *n.* an ear of corn: an inflorescence in which sessile flowers or spikelets are arranged on a long axis (*bot.*): a kind of lavender (**spike'-lav'ender**).—*n.* **spike'let** in grasses, etc., a small crowded spike, itself forming part of a greater inflorescence.—**spike'-oil** the oil of spike-lavender. [L. *spīca*, an ear of corn.]

spike[2] *spīk*, *n.* a hard thin pointed object: a large nail: a sharp metal projection, e.g. one of those forming a row along the top of a railing, etc.: a sharp-pointed metal rod set upright on a base, on which to impale documents requiring attention, etc.: (in *pl.*) spiked shoes, worn to prevent slipping.—*v.t.* to fasten, set, or pierce with a spike or spikes: to make useless (as a gun), orig. by driving a spike into the vent: to frustrate, put a stop to: to make (a drink) stronger by adding spirits or other alcohol (*coll.*).—*adj.* **spiked**. —*adv.* **spik'ily**.—*n.* **spik'iness**.—*adj.* **spik'y** having, furnished with, spikes: having a sharp point.—**spike heel** a very narrow metal heel on a woman's shoe; **spike'-nail** a large small-headed nail. [O.E. *spīcing*, a spike-nail; poss. from L. *spīca*, an ear of corn.]

spikenard *spīk'närd, n.* an aromatic oil or balsam yielded by an Indian plant (*Nardostachys*) or a substitute: the plant itself. [L. *spīca nardi.*]

spile *spīl, n.* a plug: a spigot: a pile for a foundation: a stake, or post for fencing.—*v.t.* to pierce and provide with a spile. [Cf. L.G. *spile*, Du. *spijl*, Ger. *Speil*.]

spilikin. See spill².

spill¹ *spil, v.t.* to allow to run out of a vessel: to shed: to waste: to throw from a vehicle or the saddle (*coll.*): to empty from the belly of a sail or empty of wind for reefing.—*v.i.* to overflow: to be shed: to be allowed to fall, be lost, or wasted:—*pa.t.* and *pa.p.* **spilled, spilt.**—*n.* a fall, a throw: a spilling.—*ns.* **spill'age** the act of spilling: that which is spilt; **spill'er; spill'ing; spilth** spilling: anything spilt or poured out lavishly: excess.—**spill'over** an overflow (also *fig.*).—**spill over** to overflow (also *fig.*); **spill the beans** to cause embarrassment by letting out a secret. [O.E. *spillan.*]

spill² *spil, n.* a spile: a thin strip of wood or paper for lighting a candle, a pipe, etc.—*n.* **spill'ikin** a small slip of wood, ivory, etc., to be picked out from a heap without disturbing the others in the game of **spil'likins.**—Also **spilikin, spel(l)ikin, spellican.**

spilt *spilt, pa.t.* and *pa.p.* of **spill¹.**—Also *adj.*

spilth. See spill¹.

spin *spin, v.t.* to draw out and twist into threads: to draw out a thread as spiders do: to form by spinning: to draw out: to make to last (usu. with *out*): to send hurtling: to twirl, set revolving rapidly: to fish with a swivel or spoon-bait.—*v.i.* to practise the art or trade or perform the act of spinning: to rotate rapidly: to whirl: to hurtle: to go swiftly, esp. on wheels: to spirt: to stream vigorously: to lengthen out, last (usu. with *out*): to fish with rotating bait:—*pr.p.* **spinn'ing;** *pa.t.* **spun,** *arch.* **span;** *pa.p.* **spun.**—*n.* act or result of spinning: a rotatory motion: a cycle ride: a short trip in a motor-car: a spurt at high speed: a spiral descent (*lit.* and *fig.*): confused excitement.—*ns.* **spinn'er** one who spins: a spinneret: a spinning-machine: a ball with imparted spin, causing it to swerve or break (*cricket*): a spin-bowler: an artificial fly that revolves in the water (*fishing*); **spinn'eret** a spinning organ in spiders, etc.: a plate with holes from which filaments of plastic material are expressed (also **spinnerette**).—*n.* and *adj.* **spinn'ing.**—**spin'-bowl'ing** in cricket, a style of bowling in which the ball is give a twisting motion by the bowler's wrist or fingers, in order to make its speed and direction, as it rises after striking the ground, unpredictable; **spin'-bowl'er; spin'-dri'er, spin'-dry'er** a device that dries washed clothes without wringing, to a point ready for ironing, by forcing the water out of them under pressure of centrifugal force in a rapidly revolving drum.—*v.t.* **spin'-dry.**—**spinn'ing-jenn'y** a machine by which a number of threads can be spun at once; **spinn'ing-mill** a factory where thread is spun; **spinning mule** an early form of spinning machine; **spinn'ing-wheel** a machine for spinning yarn, consisting of a wheel driven by the hand or by a treadle, which drives one or two spindles; **spin'-off** a by-product that proves profitable on its own account.—Also *adj.*—**spin stabilisation** the stabilising of the flight of a projected bullet, space rocket, etc., by giving it a spinning motion.—**flat spin** a state of panic; **spin a yarn** to tell a story; **spin out** to prolong, protract. [O.E. *spinnan.*]

spina. See spine.

spinach *spin'ij, -ich, n.* a plant of the goosefoot family: its young leaves used as a vegetable: extended to various other plants. [O.Fr. *espinage, espinache;* of doubtful origin, poss.—L. *spīna*, poss. Ar. *isfināj.*]

spinal, spinate. See spine.

spindle *spin'dl, n.* the pin by which thread is twisted: a pin on which anything turns: the fusee of a watch: anything very slender: a spindle-shaped structure formed in mitosis (*biol.*).—*adj.* **spin'dly** disproportionally long and slender.—*adjs.* **spin'dle-legged, -shanked** having long slender legs, like spindles.—*ns.pl.* **spin'dle-legs, -shanks** long slim legs: hence (as a *sing.*) an overlong and slender person.—**spin'dle-oil** very light and fluid lubricating oil —*adj.* **spin'dle-shaped** shaped like a spindle, thickest in the middle and tapering to both ends.—**spin'dle-tree** a shrub (*Euonymus europaeus*) of the *Celastraceae*, whose hard-grained wood was used for making spindles. [O.E. *spinel—spinnan*, to spin.]

spindrift *spin'drift, n.* the spray blown from the crests of waves. [See spoon¹.]

spine *spīn, n.* a thorn, esp. one formed by a modified branch or leaf: a long sharp process of a leaf: a thin, pointed spike, esp. in fishes: the spinal column: any ridge extending lengthways: heartwood: the back of a book —*adjs.* **spi'nal** of the backbone; **spi'nate, spined** having a spine or spines; **spine'less** having no spine: weak: vacillating: lacking courage, esp. moral courage.—*adv.* **spine'lessly.**—*ns.* **spine'lessness; spinesc'ence.**—*adjs.* **spinesc'ent** tapering or developing into a spine: tending to become spinous: somewhat spiny.—*n.* **spi'niness.**—*adjs.* **spi'nose** (or *-nōs'*) full of spines: thorny; **spi'nous** spinose: like a thorn or spine in appearance (*anat.*, etc.).—*ns.* **spinule** (*spin'* or *spīn'*) a minute spine.—*adjs.* **spin'ūlate, spin'ūlose, spin'ūlous; spi'ny** full of spines: thorny: troublesome: perplexed.—**spina bifida** (*spī'nə bif'i-də, bī'*) condition in which (a) vertebra(e) fail(s) to unite perfectly at the embryo stage, exposing the spinal cord; **spinal anaesthesia** injection of an anaesthetic into the spinal canal, producing loss of sensation but not unconsciousness; **spinal canal** a passage running through the spinal column, containing the spinal cord; **spinal column** in vertebrates, the articulated series of vertebrae extending from the skull to the tip of the tail, forming the axis of the skeleton and enclosing the spinal cord; **spinal c(h)ord** the main neural axis in vertebrates; **spine'-chiller** a frightening story, thought, happening.—*adj.* **spine'-chilling.** [L. *spīna*, a thorn.]

spinel *spi-nel'* (or *spin'əl*), *n.* a mineral, magnesium aluminate or other member of a group of aluminates, ferrates, and chromates, crystallising in octahedra.—**spinel ruby** ruby-spinel, a precious variety of typical spinel formerly confounded with ruby. [It. *spinella*.]

spinescence, etc. See spine.

spinet(te) *spin'it*, or *spi-net'*, *n.* an instrument like a small harpsichord.—Also **spinnet.** [It. *spinetta*, poss. from maker G. *Spinetti* (fl. 1500).]

spinnaker *spin'ə-kər, n.* triangular sail carried on the side opposite to the mainsail by vessels sailing before the wind: large sail carried by racing yachts. [Prob. **spin,** not *Sphinx* (yacht that carried a spinnaker).]

spinner, spinneret, etc. See spin.

spinnet. See spinet(te).

spinney, spinny *spin'i, n.* a small clump of trees or copse:—*pl.* **spinn'eys, spinn'ies.** [O.Fr. *espinei*—L. *spīnētum*, a thorn-hedge, thicket—*spīna*, thorn.]

spino- *spi-nō-,* in composition, spine.

spinode *spī'nōd*, (*geom.*) *n.* a cusp or stationary point of a curve. [L. *spīna*, thorn, *nōdus*, knot.]

spinose, spinous, etc. See spine.

spinster *spin'stər, n.* an unmarried woman: an old maid.—**spin'sterhood.**—*adjs.* **spinsterial** (*-stē'ri-əl*), **spinstē'rian,** **spin'sterish,** **spin'sterly.**—*ns.* **spin'stership; spin'stress** a woman who spins: a spinster. [**spin,** and suffix **-ster.**]

spinule, spiny, etc. See under spine.

spiracle *spīr'ə-kl, n.* a breathing-hole: a vent, orifice, passage.—*n.* **spirac'ulum:**—*pl.* **spirac'ula.** [L. *spīrāculum—spīrāre,* to breathe.]

Spiraea *spī-rē'ə, n.* the meadow-sweet genus of the rose family: (without *cap.*) a plant or shrub of the genus.— Also **Spirē'a, spirē'a** (esp. *U.S.*). [Gr. *speiraiā,* meadow-sweet, or privet—*speira,* a coil (from its coiled fruits).]

spiral. See **spire².**

spirant *spī'rənt, (phon.) adj.* fricative, open, produced by narrowing without stopping the air-passage.—*n.* a spirant consonant (including or excluding nasals, liquids, and semi-vowels).—*n.* **spirā'tion** breathing. [L. *spīrāre,* to breathe.]

spirated. See **spire².**

spire¹ *spīr, n.* a tapering or conical body, esp. a tree-top: a flower-spike: a tall slender architectural structure tapering to a point. [O.E. *spīr,* shoot, sprout.]

spire² *spīr, n.* a coil: a spiral: the spiral part of a shell, excluding the body-whorl.—*v.i.* to wind, mount, or proceed in spirals.—*adj.* **spir'al** winding like the thread of a screw: with parts arranged in spirals (*bot.*).—*n.* a spiral line, course, or object: a curve (usu. plane), the locus of a point whose distance from a fixed point varies according to some 'rule as the radius vector revolves (*math.*): a helix: a gradual but continuous rise or fall, as of prices.—*v.i.* to go in a spiral.—*v.t.* to make spiral.—*n.* **spirality** (*-al'i-ti*).— *adv.* **spir'ally.**—*adj.* **spir'ated** spirally twisted.—*n.* **spir'ochaete** (*-kēt;* Gr. *chaitē,* hair, mane) a spirally coiled bacterium, cause of syphilis and other diseases. —*adjs.* **spi'roid** with the form of, or like, a spiral; **spir'y** spirally coiled.—**spiral galaxy** (*astron.*) one of a large class of galaxies, with two spiral arms emerging from a bright central ellipsoidal nucleus about which they rotate. [Gr. *speira,* a coil, a tore.]

spirit *spir'it, n.* vital principle: the principle of thought: the soul: a disembodied soul: a ghost: an incorporeal being: enthusiasm: actuating emotion, disposition, frame of mind: a leading, independent, or lively person: animation: verve: courage: mettle: real meaning: essence, chief quality: (in *pl.*) cheerful or exuberant vivacity: (in *pl.*) state of mind, mood: (in *pl.*) spirituous liquor: (the following also in *pl.,* sometimes with vb. in *sing.*) a distilled liquid: an aqueous solution of ethyl alcohol: a solution in alcohol.—*v.t.* to give spirit to: to inspirit, encourage, cheer: to convey away secretly, to kidnap (often with *away, off*).—*adj.* **spir'ited** full of spirit, life, or fire: animated: possessed by a spirit.—*adv.* **spir'itedly.**— *ns.* **spir'iting** the action of one who spirits in any sense: the offices of a spirit or sprite; **spir'itism** spiritualism: animism; **spir'itist.**—*adjs.* **spiritist'ic; spir'itless** without spirit, cheerfulness, or courage: dejected: dead.—*adv.* **spir'itlessly.**—*adjs.* **spir'itous** of the nature of spirit, pure: ardent, spirituous; **spir'itual** of, of the nature of, relating to, spirit, a spirit, spirits, the mind, the·higher faculties, the soul: highly refined in thought and feeling, habitually or naturally looking to things of the spirit: incorporeal: ecclesiastical, religious.—*n.* that which is spiritual: an American Negro religious song.—*n.* **spiritualisa'tion,** *-z-.*—*v.t.* **spir'itualise, -ize** to make spiritual: to imbue with spirituality: to refine: to free from sensuality: to give a spiritual meaning to.—*ns.* **spir'itualiser, -z-; spir'itualism** a being spiritual: the interpretation of a varied series of abnormal phenomena as for the most part caused by spiritual beings acting upon specially sensitive persons or mediums (also **spiritism**); **spir'itualist** one who has a regard only to spiritual things: (with *cap.*) one who holds the doctrine of spiritualism or spiritism.—*adj.* **spiritualist'ic.**—*n.* **spirituality** (*-al'i-ti*) state of being

spiritual: that which is spiritual.—*adv.* **spir'itually.**— *ns.* **spir'itualness** the state or quality of being spiritual; **spirituos'ity** spirituous character: immateriality.—*adj.* **spir'ituous** containing, of the nature of, a volatile principle (*arch.*): alcoholic.—*ns.* **spir'ituousness.—spirit duplicator** one that uses a solution of alcohol in the copying process; **spir'it-gum** a preparation used by actors for attaching false beards, etc.; **spir'it-lamp** lamp burning methylated or other spirit to give heat; **spir'it-level** a glass tube nearly filled with, usu., alcohol, showing perfect levelness when the bubble is central; **spirit master** the master sheet used in a spirit duplicator; **spir'it-varnish** shellac or other resin in a volatile solvent, usu. alcohol; **spir'it-world** the world of disembodied spirits.—(**Holy**) **Spirit** see **holy; in spirits** cheerfully vivacious; **out of spirits** depressed; **spirit(s) of ammonia** sal volatile; **spirit(s) of salt** hydrochloric acid in water; **spirit(s) of wine** alcohol. [L. *spīritus,* a breath—*spīrāre,* to breathe.]

spirochaete, etc. See **spire².**

spirograph *spī'rō-gräf, n.* an instrument for recording breathing movements. [L. *spīrāre,* to breathe.]

spiroid. See **spire².**

spirt *spûrt, v.i.* to shoot out forcibly, or in a fine strong jet.—*v.t.* to squirt in a fine strong jet.—*n.* a sudden fine jet. [Origin uncertain; cf. Ger. dial. *spirzen,* to spit; **spurt.**]

spirtle. Same as **spurtle.**

spiry. See under **spire².**

spit¹ *spit, n.* a broach for roasting meat: jocularly, a sword: a long narrow tongue of land or sand running into the sea: a wire or spindle holding a spool in a shuttle.—*v.t.* to transfix: to string on a rod or wire: —*pr.p.* **spitt'ing;** *pa.t.* and *pa.p.* **spitt'ed.**—*adj.* **spitt'ed.** [O.E. *spitu.*]

spit² *spit, v.t.* to throw out from the mouth: to eject with violence: to utter with hate, scorn or violence: to spawn.—*v.i.* to throw out saliva from the mouth: to rain in scattered drops: to make a spitting sound: to sputter:—*pr.p.* **spitt'ing;** *pa.t.* and *pa.p.* **.spat.**—*n.* saliva, spume: a light fall of rain or snow: an exact replica (*slang;* usu. *dead* or *very spit,* from the phrase *as like him as if he had spit him out of his mouth*).— *ns.* **spitt'er; spitt'ing.**—Also *adj.*—*ns.* **spitt'le** spit, saliva; **spittoon'** a vessel for spitting in.—**spit'fire** that which emits fire, e.g. a volcano, cannon: (with *cap.*) a type of fighting aeroplane used in World War II: a hot-tempered person; **spitting image** (form of *dual. spitten image*—for *spit and image*) the exact likeness of (see above).—**spit and polish** cleaning up of uniform and equipment, esp. to excess; **spit (it) out** to speak out, tell (it). [Northern O.E. *spittan.*]

spit³ *spit, v.t.* and *v.i.* to dig: to plant with a spade.—*n.* a spade's depth: a spadeful. [O.E. *spittan,* or (M.)Du. and (M.)L.G. *spit.*]

spitchcock *spich'kok, n.* an eel split and broiled.—*v.t.* to split and broil, as an eel. [Orig. unknown; cf. **spatchcock.**]

spite *spīt, n.* grudge: lasting ill-will: hatred.—*v.i.* to vex: to thwart: to hate.—*adj.* **spite'ful** full of spite: desirous to vex or injure: malignant.—*adv.* **spite'-fully.**—*n.* **spite'fulness.—in spite of** in opposition to all efforts of, in defiance of, in contempt of: notwithstanding; **spite (of)** despite. [**despite.**]

spitter. See **spit².**

spittle, spittoon. See under **spit².**

spitz *spits, n.* a Pomeranian dog: a group of breeds of dog generally having long hair, pointed ears and a tightly curled tail, incl. husky, samoyed, Pomeranian, etc. [Ger.]

spiv *spiv, (slang) n.* a flashy black-market hawker: one who makes money by dubious means: an idler.—*adj.*

spivv'y. [Perh. conn. with **spiff.**]

splanchnic *splangk'nik, adj.* visceral, intestinal. [Gr. *splanchnon*, pl. *splanchna*, entrails.]

splash *splash, v.t.* to spatter, as with water or mud: to throw about brokenly, as liquid: to dash liquid on or over: to effect by or with splashing: to variegate as if by splashing: to display, print very prominently.—*v.i.* to dabble: to dash liquid about: to move, go, with throwing about of broken liquid: to fly about dispersedly.—*n.* the dispersion of liquid suddenly disturbed, as by throwing something into it or by throwing it about: liquid thrown on anything: a spot formed by or as if by throwing liquid: a little sodawater: ostentation, publicity, display: a sensation, excitement, dash.—*n.* and *adj.* **splash'ing.**—*adj.* **splash'y** splashing: with splashing: wet and muddy: full of puddles: ostentatious, showy.—**splash'-back** a piece of glass, plastic, etc., or area of tiles covering the part of a wall behind a wash-basin to protect against splashing; **splash'-board** a mudguard: a dashboard; **splash'down** (moment of) the landing of a manned spacecraft on the sea.—*adj.* **splash'proof.**— **splash down** of spacecraft, to land on the sea on completion of mission; **splash out (on)** (*coll.*) to spend a lot of money (on). [**plash³.**]

splat¹ *splat, n.* a thin strip forming the upright middle part of a chair-back. [Obs. *plat*, a flat part.]

splat² *splat, n.* the sound made by a soft, wet object striking a surface.—*adv.* with this sound. [Onomatopoeic.]

splatter *splat'ǝr, v.t.* and *v.i.* to spatter: to splash: to sputter.—*n.* a splash: a spattering. [Cf. **spatter.**]

splay *splā, v.t.* and *v.i.* to slope, slant, or bevel (*archit.*): to spread out.—*n.* a slant or bevel, as of the side of a doorway, window, or the like.—*adj.* having a splay: turned outwards.—**splay foot** a flat foot turned outward.—*adjs.* **splay'-foot, -ed.** [**display.**]

spleen *splēn, n.* a soft, pulpy, blood-modifying organ close to the stomach, once thought the seat of anger and melancholy: hence, spite: ill-humour: melancholy.—*n.* **splenec'tomy** (*splin-*; Gr. *ek*, out, *tomē,* a cutting) excision of the spleen.—*adj.* **splenetic** (*splin-et'ik*) of the spleen: affected with spleen: peevish: melancholy.—*n.* a splenetic person.—*adj.* **splen-et'ical.**—*adv.* **splenet'ically.**—*adj.* **splenic** (*splē'nik, splen'*) of the spleen.—*n.* **spleni'tis** (*splin-*) inflammation of the spleen. [L. *splēn*—Gr. *splēn.*]

splendid *splen'did, adj.* brilliant, resplendent: magnificent: excellent (*coll.*).—*adv.* **splen'didly.**—*n.* **splen'didness.**—*adjs.* **splendif'erous** (now only *coll.*); **splen'd(o)rous.**—*n.* **splen'dour,** U.S. **splendor,** (*-dǝr*) brilliance: magnificence. [L. *splendēre,* to shine, *splendidus, splendor.*]

splenectomy, splenetic, etc. See **spleen.**

splenial *splē'ni-ǝl, adj.* of the splenius.—*n.* **splē'nius** a large thick muscle on the back of the neck. [Gr. *splēnion,* pad, compress.]

splenic, etc. See **spleen.**

splice *splīs, v.t.* to unite by interweaving the strands: to join together by overlapping: to unite, esp. (*slang*; also *v.i.*) in matrimony.—*n.* the act of splicing: a joint made by splicing: the part of the handle of a cricket-bat or the like that fits into the blade.—**splice the mainbrace** (*nautical slang*) to serve out an allowance of spirits: to fall to drinking. [Du. (now dial.) *splissen.*]

spline *splin, n.* a key to make wheel and shaft revolve together: a thin strip or slat.—*v.t.* to put splines on. [Orig. E. Anglian.]

splint *splint, n.* a strip, slip of wood, lath: a splinter: a contrivance for holding a broken bone, or the like, in position: a bony enlargement on a horse's leg between knee and fetlock: splint-coal.—*v.t.* to put in

splints.—*n.* **splint'er** a piece of wood, metal, etc., split off, esp. a needle-like piece: a slender strip of wood, esp. one used as a torch.—*v.t.* and *v.i.* to split into splinters.—*adj.* **splint'ery** made of, or like, splinters: apt to splinter.—**splint'-coal** a hard coal of uneven fracture that does not cake; **splint'er-bar** the cross-bar of a coach, supporting the springs; **splint'er-bone** the fibula; **splinter group** a party or group formed by a breakaway from a larger body.—*adj.* **splint'er-proof** proof against the splinters of bursting shells or bombs, or against splintering. [M.Du. *splinte* (Du. *splint*) or (M.)L.G. *splinte, splente.*]

split *split, v.t.* to break in pieces, wreck: to rend: to cleave lengthwise: to divide: to disunite: to divulge (*coll.*).—*v.i.* to be dashed to pieces (often with *up*): to suffer shipwreck: to divide or part asunder (often with *up*): to divulge secrets (*coll.*): to divide one's votes instead of plumping: to burst with laughter: to go at full speed: to break off relations (with) (*slang*; often with *up*):—*pr.p.* **splitt'ing;** *pa.t.* and *pa.p.* **split.** —*n.* a crack or rent lengthwise: a schism: a half-bottle of aerated water, etc., a half-glass of spirits: (in *pl.*) the acrobatic feat of going down to the floor with the legs spread out laterally or one forward and one back: a division, share-out (usu. of money, stolen goods, etc.) (*coll.*): a sweet dish, usu. of sliced-open fruit and cream, etc.—*adj.* having been split: having a split or break.—*n.* **splitt'er** one who, or that which, splits: one who splits hairs in argument, classification, etc.: a splitting headache (*coll.*).—*adj.* **splitt'ing** rending: cleaving: ear-splitting: of a headache, very severe: very rapid.—**split infinitive** an infinitive with an adverb between 'to' and the verb.—*adj.* **split'-lev'el** on more than one level.—**split pea** a dried pea deprived of its seed-coat and thus broken across at the embryo; **split personality** a tendency towards schizophrenia; **split pin** a pin made of a doubled piece of metal formed into a ring at the head to give tension and usu. inserted in a hole in a bolt to hold a nut, etc., firmly; **split ring** a ring formed as if split spirally, as for keeping keys together; **split screen** a cinematic technique of showing different scènes simultaneously on separate parts of the screen.—*adj.* **split'-screen.**— **split second** a fraction of a second.—*adj.* **split'-second** timed to a fraction of a second.—**full split** at full speed; **split on** (*coll.*) to betray, give (a person) away; **split one's sides** to laugh immoderately; **split the difference** to divide equally the sum of matter in dispute, to take the mean. [Du. *splitten.*]

splodge. See **splotch.**

splosh *splosh, n., v.i., v.t.* a usu. humorous variant of **splash.**

splotch *sploch,* **splodge** *sploj, ns.* a big or heavy splash, spot, or stain.—*vs.t.* to mark with splotches or splodges.—*vs.i.* to trudge flounderingly or splashily.—*adjs.* **splotch'y, splodg'y.** [Perh. conn. with O.E. *splott,* spot.]

splurge *splûrj, n.* any boisterous display.—*v.i.* to make such a display: to spend a lot of money (on).—*adj.* **splur'gy.** [Imit.]

splutter *splut'ǝr, v.i.* to eject drops: to scatter ink upon a paper, as a bad pen: to scatter liquid with spitting noises: to articulate confusedly as in rage.—*v.t.* to utter splutteringly.—*n.* an act or noise of spluttering. —*n.* **splutt'erer.**—*n.* and *adj.* **splutt'ering.**—*adv.* **splutt'eringly.**—*adj.* **splutt'ery.** [Prob. imit.; cf. **sputter.**]

Spode *spōd, n.* (also without *cap.*) a porcelain made with addition of bone-ash by Josiah *Spode* (1754–1827) at Stoke.—Also *adj.*

spoil *spoil, n.* (often in *pl.*) plunder, booty: acquisitions, prizes: spoliation: pillage: material cast out in excavation: a thing spoiled in making (*rare*).—*v.t.* to despoil: to strip: to deprive: to corrupt: to mar: to impair: to make useless: to treat over-indulgently: to harm the character so.—*v.i.* to practise spoliation: to go bad: to deteriorate:—*pa.t.* and *pa.p.* **spoiled** or (only in sense of damage) **spoilt.**—*n.* **spoil'age** waste by spoiling: material so wasted.—*adj.* **spoiled.**—*n.* **spoil'er** any thing or person that spoils: an aerodynamic device fitted to the wings of an aircraft to reduce lift and assist descent: a similar device fitted to motor-vehicles, esp. racing cars, to lessen drag and reduce the tendency to become unstable through a lifting effect at high speeds.—**spoil'-sport** one who stops or interferes with sport or other people's pleasure: a meddler; **spoilt paper** in a ballot, a voting paper marked, esp. deliberately, in such a way as to be invalid.—**spoiling for** (a fight, etc.) more than ripe or ready for: intent on. [O.Fr. *espoille*—L. *spolium*, spoil.]

spoke[1] *spōk, pa.t.* of speak.

spoke[2] *spōk, n.* one of the radiating bars of a wheel.—*adv.* **spoke'wise.**—**spoke'shave** a two-handled planing tool for curved work.—**put a spoke in someone's wheel** to thwart someone. [O.E. *spāca.*]

spoken *spōk'n, pa.p.* of **speak.**—in composition, of speech, speaking, as **fair'-spoken, plain'-spoken.**—**spo'ken for** chosen, reserved.

spokesman *spōks'mən, n.* one who speaks for another, or for others:—*pl.* **spokes'men:**—*fem.* **spokes'-woman; spokes'person.** [speak, man.]

spoliate *spō'li-āt, v.t.* and *v.i.* to despoil, to plunder.—*n.* **spōliā'tion.**—*adj.* **spō'liative** serving to take away or diminish.—*n.* **spō'liator.**—*adj.* **spō'liatory** (*-ə-tər-i*). [L. *spoliāre, -ātum—spolium,* spoil.]

spondee *spon'dē, n.* a foot of two long syllables.—*adjs.* **spondaic** (*-dā'ik*), **spondā'ical.** [L. *spondēus* (*pēs*)—Gr. *spondeios* (*pous*), (a foot) used in the slow solemn hymns sung at a *spondē* or drink-offering.]

spondyl *spon'dil, n.* a vertebra.—*n.* **spondyll'tis** inflammation of a vertebra. [Gr. *sp(h)ondylos,* a vertebra.]

sponge *spunj, n.* any member of the phylum Porifera, sessile aquatic animals with a single cavity in the body, with numerous pores: the fibrous skeleton of such an animal, remarkable for its power of sucking up water: a piece of such a skeleton, or a substitute, used for washing, obliterating, absorbing, etc.: a swab for a cannon: any sponge-like substance, as leavened dough, a cake or pudding, swampy ground: a hanger-on or parasite (*coll.*): a drunkard (*coll.*): an application of a sponge: the life or behaviour of a sponger upon others (*coll.*).—*v.t.* to wipe, wipe out, soak up, remove, with a sponge: to drain, as if by squeezing a sponge: to gain by the art of the parasite.—*v.i.* to suck in, as a sponge: to fish for sponges: to live on others parasitically (often with *on* or *off*).—*adj.* **spongeous** (*spun'jəs*) spongy.—*n.* **spong'er** one who uses a sponge: a sponge-fisher: a sponge-fishing boat: an apparatus for sponging cloth: a sponge or parasite.—*adv.* **spon'gily** in a spongy way, or manner.—*n.* **spon'giness.**—*adj.* **spongy** (*spun'ji*) absorptive: porous: wet and soft: drunken.—**sponge'-bag** a waterproof bag for carrying a sponge; **sponge'-bath** an application of water to the body by or from a sponge, as for a sick or bedridden person; **sponge'-cake** a very light sweet cake of flour, eggs, and sugar; **sponge'-cloth** a cotton cloth of open texture; **sponge'-finger** a finger-shaped sponge-cake; **sponge'-fisher; sponge'-fishing; sponge'-rubber** rubber processed into sponge-like form; **sponge'wood** sola.—**sponge down** to clean or wipe with a sponge (*n.* **sponge'-down); throw up the sponge** to acknowledge defeat by throwing into the air the sponge with which a boxer is rubbed down between rounds: to give up any

struggle. [O.E. *sponge, spunge,* and O.Fr. *esponge*—L. *spongia*—Gr. *spongiā.*]

sponsal *spon'sl, adj.* spousal.—*ns.* **spon'sion** the act of becoming surety for another; **spon'sor** one who promises solemnly for another: a surety: a godfather or godmother: a promoter: one who pays for radio or television broadcast introducing advertisement.—Also *v.t.*—*adj.* **sponso'rial.**—*n.* **spon'sorship.** [L. *spondēre, spōnsum,* promise.]

sponson *spon'sn, n.* an outward expansion from a ship's deck: a short projecting length of plane: a wing-section giving extra lift: an air-filled tank on the side of a canoe to give buoyancy: a structure to give a seaplane steadiness on the water.

sponsor. See sponsal.

spontaneous *spon-tā'nyəs, -ni-əs, adj.* of one's free will: acting by its own impulse or natural law: produced of itself: impulsive: unpremeditated.—*ns.* **spontaneity** (*-tə-nē'i-ti*), **spontā'neousness.**—*adv.* **spontā'neously.**—**spontaneous combustion** catching fire by causes at work within, esp. slow oxidation of a mass of matter. [L. *spontāneus—sponte,* of one's own accord.]

spoof *spoōf,* (*slang*) *n.* a hoaxing game invented and named by Arthur Roberts (1852–1933), comedian: a card game: a parody, take-off.—*adj.* bogus.—*v.t.* and *v.i.* to hoax: to parody.—*ns.* **spoof'er; spoof'ery.**

spook *spoōk, n.* a ghost: a spy, an undercover agent (*slang,* orig. *U.S.*).—*v.i.* to play the spook.—*v.t.* to frighten, startle.—*adv.* **spook'ily.**—*n.* **spook'iness.**—*adjs.* **spook'ish, spook'y.** [App. L.G.]

spool *spoōl, n.* a cylinder, bobbin, or reel for winding yarn, etc., upon.—*v.t.* and *v.i.* to wind on spools.—*n.* **spool'er.** [L.G. *spōle;* Du. *spoel,* or O.N.Fr. *espole.*]

spoon[1] *spoōn, v.i.* to scud before the wind.—*n.* **spoon'-drift** light spray borne on a gale.—Also **spin'drift.**

spoon[2] *spoōn, n.* an instrument with a shallow bowl and a handle: anything of like shape, as an oar: (a stroke with) a wooden-headed golf-club with face slightly hollowed: a spoon-bait: a simpleton: a maudlin love-maker: mawkish love-making.—*v.t.* to transfer with, or as if with, a spoon: to shove, scoop, or hit softly up into the air, instead of striking cleanly and definitely: to dally sentimentally with: to catch with a spoon-bait.—*v.i.* to make love sentimentally: to fish with a spoon-bait.—*n.* **spoon'ful** as much as fills a spoon: a small quantity:—*pl.* **spoon'fuls.**—*adj.* **spoon'y, spoon'ey** silly: foolishly and demonstratively fond.—*n.* one who is spoony.—**spoon'-bait, -hook** a lure on a swivel, used in trolling for fish; **spoon'bill** any bird of a family akin to the ibises, with long, flat, broad bill, spoon-shaped at the tip.—*adj.* **spoon'-fed** fed with a spoon: artificially fostered (*fig.*): taught by doled-out doses of cut-and-dried information.—*v.t.* **spoon'-feed.—born with a silver spoon in one's mouth** see **silver; spoons** on silly in manifestation of love for. [O.E. *spōn,* sliver, chip, shaving.]

spoonerism *spoō'nər-izm, n.* a transposition of initial sounds of spoken words—e.g. 'shoving leopard' for 'loving shepherd'. [Rev. W. A. *Spooner* (1844–1930), a noted perpetrator of transpositions of this kind.]

spoor *spoōr, n.* track, esp. of a hunted animal. [Du. *spoor,* a track.]

sporadic *spor-ad'ik, adj.* scattered: occurring here and there or now and then: occurring casually.—*adv.* **sporad'ically.** [Gr. *sporadikos—sporas, sporados,* scattered—*speirein,* to sow.]

spore *spōr, spör, n.* a unicellular asexual reproductive body: sometimes extended to other reproductive bodies.—*ns.* **sporan'glum** (*pl.* **sporan'gia**) a spore-case, sac in which spores are produced.—Also

spore'-case; spor'ophyte (Gr. *phyton*, plant) the spore-bearing or asexual generation in the life-cycle of a plant.—*adj.* **sporophytic** (*-fit'ik*).—*n.pl.* **Sporozŏ'a** a parasitic group of Protozoa reproducing by spores, including the causal organisms of malaria and pébrine.—*ns.* **sporozŏ'ite** (Gr. *zōion*, an animal) in Protozoa, an infective stage developed within a spore; **sporŭlā'tion** formation of spores: breaking up into spores. [Gr. *sporā*, a seed—*speirein*, to sow.]

sporran *spor'ən, n.* an ornamental pouch worn in front of the kilt by the Highlanders of Scotland. [Gael. *sporan.*]

sport *spört, spört, v.i.* to make merry: to practise field diversions: to trifle: to deviate from the normal.— *v.t.* to wear, use, exhibit, set up, publicly or ostentatiously: to wager.—*n.* recreation: pastime: dalliance, amorous behaviour: play: a game, esp. one involving bodily exercise: mirth: jest: contemptuous mirth: a plaything (esp. *fig.*): a laughing-stock: field diversion: success or gratification in shooting, fishing, or the like: a sportsman: a person of sportsmanlike character, a good fellow: an animal or plant that varies singularly and spontaneously from the normal type: (in *pl.*) a meeting for races and the like.—*adj.* **sports** suitable for sport.—*adv.* **sport'ily.**—*n.* **sport'iness.**—*adj.* **sport'ing** relating to, engaging in, or fond of sports: willing to take a chance: sportsmanlike: in the U.K., pertaining to one of the two major classes of dogs recognised by the Kennel Club (the other being *non-sporting*), comprising hounds, gun dogs, and terriers: in the U.S., pertaining to one of the six recognised groups of breeds, essentially comprising the gun dogs (as opposed to hounds, terriers, etc.).—*adv.* **sport'ingly.**—*adjs.* **sport'ive** inclined to sport: playful: merry: amorous, wanton; **sport'y** (*coll.*) sportsmanlike.—**sporting chance** as good a chance of winning or being successful as of losing or failing; **sports car** a low car, usu. for two, capable of attaining high speed; **sports jacket** a man's jacket, usu. tweed, for casual wear; **sports'man** one who practises, or is skilled in, sport: one who shows fairness and good humour in sport.—*adj.* **sports'manlike.**—**sports'manship; sports shirt** a man's casual shirt; **sports'wear; sports'woman.** [Aphetic for **disport.**]

sporulation. See **spore.**

spot *spot, n.* a mark made by a drop of wet matter: a blot: a small discoloured or differently coloured place: a locality, place or limited area, precise place: an eruption on the skin: a moral flaw: one of the marked points on a billiard-table, from which balls are played: a relatively dark place on the sun: a small quantity of anything (*coll.*): a spotlight: a place on e.g. a television or radio programme: a turn, performance, esp. a short one.—*v.t.* to mark with spots: to tarnish, as reputation: to pick out, detect, locate, identify (*coll.*): to place on a spot, as in billiards.— *v.i.* to become spotted:—*pr.p.* **spott'ing;** *pa.t.* and *pa.p.* **spott'ed.**—*adj.* on the spot, random (see **spot check** below): of monetary transactions, to be paid immediately, usu. in cash: involving payment in cash only.—*adj.* **spot'less** without a spot: untainted: pure. —*adv.* **spot'lessly.**—*n.* **spot'lessness.**—*adj.* **spott'ed.** —*ns.* **spott'edness; spott'er** one who spots or detects; **spott'ing.**—*adj.* **spott'y.**—**-spotting** in composition, noting, identifying, as in *trainspotting*.—**-spot** verb combining form.—**-spotter** noun combining form.— **spot cash** money down; **spot'-check** a check on the spot without warning: a check of random samples to serve in place of a general check; **spot'light** (apparatus for projecting) a circle of light on an actor or a small part of a stage (also *fig.*): an adjustable, focused-beam car lamp additional to fixed lights.—

v.t. to turn the spotlight on: to draw attention to (*fig.*).—*adj.* **spot-on'** (*coll.*) on the target: accurate. —**spotted dick** a pudding or loaf with currants; **spotted dog** a Dalmatian dog: a spotted dick.—*v.t.* **spot'-weld** to join metal with single circular welds.— *n.* a weld of this kind.—**spot'-welder.—in a spot** in a difficult situation; **knock (the) spots off** to surpass easily; **on the spot** at the very place: there and then: straightway: alert, equal to the occasion: in difficulty or danger (e.g. *put on the spot*, orig. to doom to be murdered) (*adj.* **on-the-spot'**); **soft spot** (*coll.*) affectionate feeling; **tight spot** (*coll.*) a dangerous or difficult situation; **weak spot** (*coll.*) weakness: an area in which one is not knowledgeable. [Cf. obs. Du., L.G., *spot*, O.N. *spotti.*]

spouse *spows, spowz, n.* a husband or wife.—*adj.* **spous'al** nuptial: matrimonial.—*n.* usually in *pl.*, nuptials: marriage. [O.Fr. *spus, -e, espous, -e* (Fr. *époux*, fem. *épouse*)—L. *spŏnsus*, pa.p. of *spondēre*, to promise.]

spout *spowt, v.t.* to throw out in a jet: to declaim.—*v.t.* to issue in a jet: to blow as a whale: to declaim (*derog.*).—*n.* a projecting lip or tube for discharging liquid from a vessel, a roof, etc.: a gush, discharge, or jet: an undivided waterfall: a waterspout: the blowing, or the blow-hole, of a whale: a shoot.—*ns.* **spout'er** one who, or that which, spouts: a declaimer: a spouting oil-well: a spouting whale: a whaling ship. —**spout'-hole** a blow-hole.—**up the spout** (*slang*) pawned: failed, gone wrong: pregnant. [M.E. *spouten.*]

sprag *sprag, n.* a mine prop: a bar inserted to stop a wheel: a device to prevent a vehicle from running backwards.—*v.t.* to prop, or to stop, by a sprag:— *pr.p.* **spragg'ing;** *pa.t.* and *pa.p.* **spragged.**

sprain *sprān, v.t.* to overstrain the muscles of.—*n.* a wrenching of a joint with tearing or stretching of ligaments. [Connection with O.Fr. *espreindre*, to squeeze out, is disputed.]

sprang *sprang, pa.t.* of **spring.**

sprat *sprat, n.* a fish like the herring, but much smaller. —**a sprat to catch a mackerel, herring, whale** a small risk taken in order to make a great gain. [O.E. *sprot.*]

sprawl *spröl, v.i.* to lie or crawl with limbs flung about: to straggle.—*v.t.* to spread stragglingly.—*n.* a sprawling posture, movement, or mass.—*n.* **sprawl'er.**— *adjs.* **sprawl'ing, sprawl'y.** [O.E. *sprēawlian*, to move convulsively.]

spray[1] *sprā, n.* a cloud of small flying drops: an application or dispersion of such a cloud: an apparatus or a preparation for so dispersing.—*v.t.* to sprinkle in or with fine mist-like jets.—*n.* **spray'er.**—*adj.* **spray'ey.** —*adj.* **spray'-dried'.—spray drying** the rapid drying of a liquid by spraying it into a flow of hot gas; **spray'gun** a device for applying paint, etc., by spraying.— *adj.* **spray'-on'** applied in a spray, usu. by an aerosol. [M.Du. *sprayen.*]

spray[2] *sprā, n.* a shoot or twig, esp. one spreading out in branches or flowers: an ornament, casting, etc., of similar form.—*v.i.* to spread or branch in a spray.— *adj.* **spray'ey** branching. [Poss. conn. with **sprig** or with O.E. *spræc*, twig.]

spread *spred, v.t.* to cause to extend more widely or more thinly: to scatter abroad or in all directions: to stretch: to extend, esp. over a surface: to apply (a soft substance) by smoothing it over a surface: to open out so as to cover a wider surface: to overlay: to set with provisions, as a table.—*v.i.* to extend or expand: to be extended or stretched: to become bigger or fatter: to open out: to go further apart: to unfold: to admit of spreading: to be propagated or circulated:—*pa.t.* and *pa.p.* **spread.**—*n.* extent: compass: reach: expanse:

an expanded surface the act or degree of spreading: an expansion. the process of becoming bigger or fatter: that which is spread out, a feast: anything for spreading on bread: a cover, esp. a bedcover: a ranch (*U.S.*): a double page, i.e. two facing pages (*print.*).—*adj.* extended: flat and shallow (as a gem).—*n* spread'er.—*n* and *adj.* spread'ing.—*adv.* spread'ingly.—spread'-ea'gle a heraldic eagle with the wings and legs stretched out: a skating figure.—*v.t.* to tie up with outstretched limbs: to spread out: to outrun.—*v.i.* to cut, do, or make, spreadeagles: to lie, fall, etc., with outstretched limbs.—spread one's wings to try one's powers or capabilities: to increase the area of one's activities. [O.E. *sprǣdan*.]

sprechgesang *shprehh'gə-zang,* (*music*) *n.* a style of vocalisation between singing and speaking, originated by Arnold Schoenberg.—*n.* sprech'stimme (*-shtim-ə*) music using this form of vocalisation [Ger., speaking-song, speaking-voice.]

spree *sprē, n.* a merry frolic: a drunken bout.—*v.i.* to carouse. [Orig. slang.]

sprig *sprig, n.* a small shoot or twig: a scion, a young person: an ornament like a spray: a headless or almost headless nail: a sprig-like object, ornament, or design, esp. embroidered or applied.—*v.t.* to embroider with representations of twigs: to nail with sprigs: —*pr.p.* sprigg'ing; *pa.t.* and *pa.p.* sprigged.

spright *sprīt, n.* an unhistorical spelling of sprite, obs. except perhaps in the sense of impish person.—*n.* spright'liness.—*adj.* spright'ly vivacious: animated: lively: brisk.

spring *spring, v i.* to move suddenly, as by elastic force: to bound: to start up suddenly: to break forth. to appear: to issue: to come into being: to take origin: to sprout: to branch off: to give way, split, burst, explode, warp, or start.—*v.t.* to cause to spring up: to start: to release the elastic force of: to let off, allow to spring: to cause to explode: to make known suddenly (with *on* or *upon*): to open, as a leak: to crack, as a mast: to bend by force, strain: to leap over: to set together with bevel-joints: to attach or fit with springs: to procure the escape of a (prisoner) from jail (*slang*):—*pa.t.* sprang; *pa.p.* sprung.—*n.* a leap: a sudden movement: a recoil or rebound: elasticity: an elastic contrivance usu. for setting in motion or for reducing shocks: a source of action or life: rise: beginning: cause or origin: a source: an outflow of water from the earth: (often with *cap.*) the season when plants spring up and grow—in North temperate regions roughly February or March to April or May, astronomically from the spring equinox to the summer solstice: high water: spring tide: a split, bend, warp, etc., esp. a crack in a mast.—*adj.* of the season of spring: sown, appearing, or used in spring: having or worked by a spring.—*n.* spring'er one who or that which springs: a kind of spaniel.—*adv.* spring'ily.—*ns.* spring'iness; spring'ing the act of leaping, sprouting, starting, rising, or issuing: a place of branching: providing with springs.—*adj.* leaping: arising: dawning: sprouting: with the freshness of youth: resilient: starting.—*adjs.* spring'less; spring'like; spring'y elastic: resilient: abounding with springs.—See also sprung.—spring'-bal'ance an instrument for weighing by the elasticity of a spiral spring; spring'-bed a spring-mattress.—*adj.* spring'-blad'ed of a knife, having a blade that springs out on pressure of a button.—spring'board a springy board for jumping or diving from: anything which serves as a starting-point, or from which one can launch ideas, projects, etc.; spring'bok (from Du.) a S. African antelope (also spring'buck): (with *cap.*) a S.A. international sportsman (from emblems of sporting teams, orig. 1906 rugby team; shortened to **Bok**):

hence also any South African, esp. when overseas; spring'-box the frame of a sofa, etc., in which the springs are set; spring'-carr'iage; spring'-cart one mounted upon springs; spring chicken a young chicken, usu. between two and ten months old, particularly tender when cooked (chiefly *U.S.*): a young, lively, sometimes naïve, person.—*v.t.* and *n.* spring'-clean'.—spring'-clean'ing a thorough house-cleaning, usu. in spring; spring'-clip a spring-loaded clip; spring fever (*facet.*) spring lassitude; spring'-halt a jerking lameness in which a horse suddenly twitches up his leg or legs; spring'-lig'ament a ligament of the sole of the foot.—*adj* spring'-load'ed having or operated by a spring.—spring'-lock a lock that fastens by a spring: one that opens when a spring is touched; spring'-matt'ress a mattress of spiral springs in a frame; spring onion a type of onion, its small bulb and long leaves being eaten raw in salads; spring roll a deep-fried savoury pancake enclosing a mixture of vegetables, pork, prawns, etc., orig. Chinese; spring'tide springtime; spring'-tide', spring tide a tide of maximum amplitude after new and full moon, when sun and moon pull together; spring'time the season of spring.—spring a leak to begin to leak; spring a mine to cause it to explode. [O.E. *springan.*]

springe *sprinj, n.* a snare with noose and spring: a gin. —*v.t.* to catch in a springe:—*pr.p.* spring'ing; *pa.t.* and *pa.p.* springed (*sprinjd*). [Earlier *sprenge*, from a probable O.E. *sprencg.*]

sprinkle *spring'kl, v.t.* to scatter in small drops or particles: to scatter on: to baptise with a few drops of water: to strew, dot, diversify.—*v.i.* to scatter in drops.—*n.* an aspersorium or utensil for sprinkling.— *ns.* sprin'kle, sprin'kling the act of one who sprinkles: a small quantity sprinkled (also *fig.*): in bookbinding, mottling of edges by scattering a few drops of colour; sprin'kler any thing or person that sprinkles: any of various devices for scattering water in drops, e.g. over growing plants, as fire-extinguishers, etc. (sprinkler system a system of such fire-extinguishers which operate automatically on a sudden rise in temperature). [Freq. from O.E. *sprengan*, the causative of *springan*, to spring.]

sprint *sprint, n* a short run, row, cycle or race at full speed.—*v.i.* to run at full speed.—*ns.* sprin'ter; sprin'ting. [Cf. O.N. *spretta*, Sw. *spritta.*]

sprit *sprit, (naut.) n.* a spar set diagonally to extend a fore-and-aft sail.—spritsail (*sprit'sl*) a sail extended by a sprit. [O.E. *sprēot*, pole.]

sprite *sprit, n.* goblin, elf, imp, impish or implike person [O.Fr. *esprit*; cf. spirit, spright.]

sprocket *sprok'it, n.* a tooth on the rim of a wheel or capstan for engaging the chain: a toothed cylinder for driving a cinematograph film: a sprocket-wheel: a piece of wood used to build a roof out over eaves.— sprock'et-wheel a wheel with sprockets

sprog *sprog, n.* a recruit (*R.A.F. slang*): a child, infant (*coll.*). [Poss. a reversed portmanteau form of frog spawn or a recruit's confusion of sprocket and cog².]

sprout *sprowt, n.* a new growth: a young shoot: a side bud, as in Brussels sprouts (see Brussels): a scion, descendant: sprouting condition.—*v.i.* to shoot: to push out new shoots.—*v.t.* to put forth as a sprout or bud: to cause to sprout. [O.E. *sprūtan* (found in compounds).]

spruce[1] *sprōos, adj.* smart: neat, dapper: over-fastidious, finical.—*adv.* sprucely.—*v.t.* to smarten. —*v.i.* to become spruce or smart (often with *up*).— *adv.* spruce'ly.—*n.* spruce'ness. [Prob. from next word, from the vogue of 'spruce leather' (obtained from Pruce or Prussia) in the 16th century.]

spruce[2] *sprōo s, n.* any conifer of the genus Picea, with long shoots only, four-angled needles, and pendulous cones (also **spruce fir**): its wood.—*adj.* of spruce or its wood. [From *obs. Pruce*, Prussia.]

sprue[1] *sprōō, n.* a passage by which molten metal runs into a mould: the metal that solidifies in it—**dead-head.**

sprue[2] *sprōō, n.* a tropical disease affecting mouth, throat, and digestion. [Du. *spruw.*]

sprung *sprung, pa.t.* and *pa.p.* of **spring.**—*adj.* strained: split: loosed: furnished with springs.— **sprung rhythm** a poetic rhythm close to the natural rhythm of speech, with mixed feet, and frequent single stressed syllables.

spry *sprī, adj.* nimble: agile:—*compar.* **spry'er;** *superl.* **spry'est.**—*adv.* **spry'ly.**—*n.* **spry'ness.**

spud *spud, n.* a small narrow digging tool: a stumpy person or thing: a potato (*slang*).—*v.t.* and *v.i.* to dig with a spud.—**spud'-bashing** (*slang*) peeling potatoes.—**spud (in)** to start the drilling of an oil-well.

spume *spūm, n.* foam: scum.—*v.i.* to foam.—*v.t.* to throw up or off as foam or scum.—*adj.* **spū'my.** [L. *spūma*—*spuēre*, to spew.]

spun *spun, pa.t.* and *pa.p.* of **spin,** and *adj.*—*adj.* **spun'-out** unduly lengthened.—**spun silk** a fabric made from waste silk fibres, sometimes mixed with cotton; **spun sugar** sugar spun into fine fluffy threads, as in candy floss; **spun'-yarn** rope-yarn twisted into a cord.

spunk *spungk, n.* spirit, mettle, courage.—*adj.* **spunk'y** spirited: fiery-tempered. [Cf. Ir. *sponc,* tinder, sponge—L. *spongia,* a sponge—Gr. *spongiā.*]

spur *spûr, n.* a goading instrument on a rider's heel: incitement, stimulus: a hard sharp projection: a claw-like projection at the back of a cock's or other bird's leg: an artificial substitute for this on a game-cock: a short, usu. flowering or fruit-bearing, branch: a great lateral root: anything that projects in the shape of a spur, as an extension from an electrical circuit: a lateral branch, as of a hill range: a siding or branch line of a railway: a strut: a structure to deflect the current from a bank.—*v.t.* to apply the spur to: to urge on: to provide with a spur or spurs: to prune into spurs.—*v.i.* to press forward with the spur: to hasten: to kick out: —*pr.p.* **spurr'ing;** *pa.t.* and *pa.p.* **spurred.**—*adjs.* **spur'less; spurred** having or wearing spurs or a spur: in the form of a spur: urged: affected with ergot, as rye.—*n.* and *adj.* **spurr'ing.**—*adj.* **spurr'y** like, of the nature of, having, a spur.—**spur'-gear, -gear'ing** a system of spur-wheels; **spur'-wheel** a cog-wheel.— *adj.* **spur'-winged** with a horny spur on the pinion of the wing.—**on the spur of the moment** without premeditation; **set spurs to** to apply the spur and ride off quickly; **win one's spurs** to earn knighthood: to gain distinction by achievement. [O.E. *spura, spora.*]

spurge *spûrj, n.* any species of Euphorbia, a genus of very varied habit, with milky, generally poisonous, juice, and an inflorescence (cyathium) of flowers so reduced as to simulate a single flower.—**spurge'-lau'rel** a European evergreen shrub (*Daphne laureola*) with yellowish-green flowers, thick leaves, and poisonous berries. [O.Fr. *espurge* (Fr. *épurge*)—L. *expurgāre,* to purge—*ex,* off, *purgāre,* to clear.]

spurious *spūr'i-əs, adj.* bastard: illegitimate: not genuine: false: sham: forged: simulating but essentially different.—*n.* **spurios'ity.**—*adv.* **spūr'iously.**—*n.* **spūr'iousness.** [L. *spurius,* false.]

spurn *spûrn, v.t.* to reject with contempt.—*n.* and *adj.* **spurn'ing.** [O.E. *spornan, spurnan,* related to **spur.**]

spurrey, sometimes **spurry,** *spur'i, n.* any plant of the genus Spergula: applied to kindred plants. [Du. *spurrie.*]

spurry. See spur.

spurt *spûrt, v.t.* to spout, or send out in a sudden stream or jet.—*v.i.* to gush out suddenly in a small stream: to flow out forcibly or at intervals: to make a sudden short intense effort.—*n.* a sudden or violent gush: a jet: a short spell, esp. of intensified effort, speed, etc. [Variant of **spirt.**]

spurtle *spûr'tl, (Scot.) n.* a porridge-stick.

sputa. See sputum.

sputnik *spoot'nik, n.* a man-made earth satellite. [After the Russian *Sputnik* ('travelling companion') 1, the first such satellite, put in orbit in 1957.]

sputter *sput'ər, v.t.* to spit or throw out moisture in scattered drops: to speak rapidly and indistinctly, to jabber: to make a noise of sputtering.—*v.t.* to spit out or throw out in or with small drops: to utter hastily and indistinctly: to remove atoms from a cathode by positive ion bombardment—the unchanged atoms being deposited on a surface, and the process being used for coating glass, plastic, another metal, etc., with a thin film of metal.—*n.* sputtering: matter sputtered out.—*n.* **sputt'erer.**—*n.* and *adj.* **sputt'ering.**— *adj.* **sputt'ery.** [Imit.; cf. Du. *sputteren,* and **spit**[2].]

sputum *spū'təm, n.* matter spat out:—*pl.* **spū'ta.** [L. *spūtum*—*spuēre,* to spit.]

spy *spī, n.* a secret agent employed to watch others or to collect information, esp. of a military nature: a spying: a look:—*pl.* **spies.**—*v.t.* to watch, observe, investigate, or ascertain secretly (often with *out*): to descry, make out: to discover.—*v.i.* to play the spy:— *pr.p.* **spy'ing;** *pa.t.* and *pa.p.* **spied;** *3rd pers. pres. indic.* **spies.**—*n.* and *adj.* **spy'ing.**—**spy'glass** a small hand-telescope; **spy'-hole** a peep-hole; **spy'master** a person who controls and coordinates the activities of undercover agents. [O.Fr. *espie* (n.), *espier* (vb.); see **espy.**]

squab *skwob, adj.* fat, clumsy: unfledged, newly hatched.—*n.* a young pigeon or rook: a fledgling: a short stumpy person. [Poss. Scand.; cf. Sw. dial. *sqvabb,* loose flesh, *sqvabbig,* flabby.]

squabble *skwob'l, v.i.* to dispute in a noisy manner: to wrangle.—*n.* a noisy, petty quarrel: a brawl.—*n.* **squabb'ler.** [Cf. Sw. dial. *sqvabbel.*]

squacco *skwak'ō, n.* a small crested heron:—*pl.* **squacc'os.** [It. dial. *sguacco.*]

squad *skwod, n.* a small group of soldiers drilled or working together: any working party: a set or group. —*n.* **squadd'y** (*mil. coll.*) a private, an ordinary soldier.—**squad car** a police car. [Fr. *escouade.*]

squadron *skwod'rən, n.* a detachment, body, group: a division of a cavalry regiment under a major or captain: a section of a fleet under a flag-officer: a group of aeroplanes forming a unit under one command.—*v.t.* to form into squadrons.—*adjs.* **squad'ronal; squad'roned.**—**squad'ron-lead'er** an air-force officer answering in rank to a lieutenant-commander or major. [It. *squadrone*—*squadra,* square.]

squail *skwāl, n.* counter for playing squails: (in *pl.*) a parlour-game in which small discs are snapped from the edge of the table to a centre mark. [Cf. obs. *skail, skayle,* a ninepin.]

squalid *skwol'id, adj.* filthy, foul: neglected, uncared-for, unkempt: sordid and dingy: poverty-stricken.— *n.* **squalid'ity.**—*adv.* **squal'idly.**—*ns.* **squal'idness; squal'or** the state of being squalid: dirtiness: filthiness [L. *squālidus,* stiff, rough, dirty, *squālor,* -*ōris.*]

squall *skwol, v.i.* to cry out violently: to yell: to sing loudly and unmusically: of wind, to blow in a squall. —*v.t.* to sing or utter loudly and unmusically.—*n.* a loud cry or yell: a short violent wind.—*n.* **squall'er.**— *n.* and *adj.* **squall'ing.**—*adj.* **squall'y** abounding or disturbed with squalls or gusts of wind: gusty, blustering: threatening a squall. [Prob. imit.]

squalor. See **squalid**.

squama *skwā'mə, skwä'mə, n.* a scale: a scalelike structure:—*pl.* **squa'mae** (*-mē, -mī*).—*adjs.* **squa'mose, squa'mous** scaly. [L. *squāma*, a scale.]

squander *skwon'dər, v.t.* to spend lavishly or wastefully.—*n.* a squandering.—*adj.* **squan'dered.**—*n.* **squan'derer.**—*n.* and *adj.* **squan'dering.**

square *skwār, n.* an equilateral rectangle: an object, piece, space, figure, of approximately that shape, as a window-pane, paving-stone, space on a chessboard: an open space, commonly but not necessarily of that shape, in a town, along with its surrounding buildings: the product of a quantity multiplied by itself: an instrument for drawing or testing right angles: a carpenter's measure: squareness: due proportion: order: honesty, equity, fairness: a person of narrow, traditional outlook and opinions, esp. in musical taste (*slang*).—*adj.* having or approaching the form of a square: relatively broad, thick-set: right-angled: in football, etc., in a line, position, etc., across the pitch: equal to a quantity multiplied by itself: measuring an area in two dimensions: exact, suitable, fitting: true, equitable, fair, honest: even, leaving no balance, equal in score: directly opposed: complete, unequivocal: solid, full, satisfying: (of taste in music, etc.), traditional and orthodox (*slang*): bourgeois in attitude (*slang*).—*v.t.* to make square or rectangular, esp. in cross-section: to make nearly cubical: to form into squares: to construct or determine a square equal to: to multiply by itself: to reduce to any given measure or standard, to adjust, regulate: to bring into accord, reconcile: to place at right angles with the mast or keel (*naut.*): to make equal: to pay: to bribe. —*v.i.* to suit, fit: to accord or agree: to take an attitude of offence and defence, as a boxer (often with *up to*—see below): to make the score or account even. —*adv.* at right angles: solidly: directly: evenly: fairly, honestly.—*adj.* **squared.**—*adv.* **square'ly.** —*n.* **square'ness.**—*adv.* **square'wise.**—*n.* and *adj.* **squar'ing.**—*adj.* **squar'ish.**—**square'-bashing** parade-ground drill (*mil. slang*).—*adj.* **square'-built** of a form suggesting squareness: broad in proportion to height.—**square'-dance** a folk-dance done by a group of couples in a square formation; **square'-danc'ing; square deal** (*coll.*) a fair and honest arrangement, transaction, etc.; **square foot, inch, mile** an area equal to that of a square whose side measures a foot, etc.; **square knot** a reef-knot; **square'-leg** (*cricket*) a fielder to the left of, and in line with, the batsman; **square meal** a full, satisfying meal; **square number** a number the square root of which is an integer.—*adj.* **square'-rigged** having the chief sails square, and extended by yards suspended by the middle at right angles to the masts—opp. to *fore-and-aft*.—**square'-rigg'er** a square-rigged ship; **square root** that quantity which being multiplied into itself produces the quantity in question; **square'-sail** (*-sl*) a four-sided sail extended by yards suspended by the middle generally at right angles to the mast.—*adjs.* **square'-shoul'dered** with broad, straight shoulders; **square'-toed'** ending square at the toes.—**back to square one** back to the original position with the problem, etc., unchanged; **on the square** honestly; **square up** (*coll.*) to settle (a bill, account, etc.); **square up to** to face up to and tackle; **squaring the circle** (**quadrature of the circle**) finding a square of the same area as a circle—for hundreds of years this was attempted by Euclidian means (i.e. with straightedge and compass) until in 1882 it was proved impossible: any impossible task. [O.Fr. *esquarre* (Fr. *équerre*)—L. *ex* and *quadra*, a square.]

squarrose *skwar'ōs, skwor'ōs, -ōs', adj.* rough with projecting or deflexed scales, bracts, etc.: standing out straight or deflexed. [L. *squarrōsus*, scurfy.]

squash[1] *skwosh, v.t.* to press into pulp: to crush flat: to squeeze: to put down, suppress: to snub.—*v.i.* to form a soft mass as from a fall: to crowd: to squelch: to become crushed or pulpy.—*n.* anything soft and unripe or easily crushed: a crushed mass: a drink made from fruit juice: a crushed condition: a close crowd: a squeezing: a soft rubber ball for playing squash: a game for two or four players played with a small rubber ball, which is struck with a racket against the walls of an enclosed court (also **squash rackets, racquets**).—*adv.* with a squash.—*n.* **squash'er.**—*n.* **squash'iness.**—*adj.* **squash'y** pulpy: squelching: sopping. [O.Fr. *esquacer* (Fr. *écacher*), to crush—L. *ex, quassāre*; see **quash**.]

squash[2] *skwosh, n.* the gourd of several species of Cucurbita: the plant bearing it. [Narragansett *askutasquash*.]

squat *skwot, v.i.* to sit down upon the hams or heels: to sit close, as an animal: to settle on land or in unoccupied buildings without title.—*v.t.* to cause to squat: —*pr.p.* **squatt'ing;** *pa.t.* and *pa.p.* **squatt'ed.**—*adj.* crouching: short and thick, dumpy.—*n.* the act of squatting: a building in which people squat (*coll.*).— *ns.* **squat'ness; squatt'er** one who squats: a large landowner (*Austr.*); **squatt'iness.**—*adj.* **squatt'y** short and thick. [O.Fr. *esquatir*, to crush.]

squaw *skwò, n.* an American Indian woman, esp. a wife.—**squaw'man** a white man with an Indian wife. [Massachusett *squa*.]

squawk *skwok, n.* a croaky call or cry: a complaint, protest (*slang*).—*v.i.* to utter a squawk.—*v.t.* to utter with a squawk.—*n.* **squawk'er.**—*n.* and *adj.* **squawk'ing.**—*adj.* **squawk'y.** [Imit.]

squeak *skwēk, v.i.* to give forth a high-pitched nasalsounding note or cry: to inform or confess (*slang*).— *v.t.* to utter, sing, render, squeakily.—*n.* a squeaky sound: a narrow escape or bare chance.—*ns.* **squeak'er** one who squeaks: a young bird: an informer: a squeaking toy.—*adv.* **squeak'ily.**—*n.* **squeak'iness.** —*n.* and *adj.* **squeak'ing.**—*adj.* **squeak'y.**— **a narrow squeak** a narrow escape. [Imit.]

squeal *skwēl, v.i.* to utter a high-pitched cry: to cry out in pain: to complain: to turn informer (*slang*).—*v.t.* to utter, sing, render, express, with squealing.—*n.* a high sustained cry.—*n.* **squeal'er** one who squeals: an informer (*slang*).—*n.* and *adj.* **squeal'ing.** [Imit.]

squeamish *skwēm'ish, adj.* sick: easily nauseated: qualmish: easily shocked, disgusted, or offended: fastidious: coy: reluctant from scruples or compunction.—*adv.* **squeam'ishly.**—*n.* **squeam'ishness.** [M.E. *scoymous*—A.Fr. *escoymous.*]

squeegee *skwē'jē, -jē', n.* an implement with edge of rubber, leather, etc., for clearing water or mud from decks, floors, windows, etc.: a photographer's roller or brush for squeezing out moisture.—*v.t.* to clear, press, or smooth with a squeegee. [App. **squeeze**.]

squeeze *skwēz, v.t.* to crush, press hard, compress: to grasp tightly: to embrace: to force by pressing: to effect, render, or put by pressing: to crush the juice or liquid from: to force to discard winning cards: to fleece, extort from.—*v.i.* to press: to crowd: to crush: to force a way: to yield to pressure.—*n.* the act of squeezing: pressure: a restriction or time of restriction (usually financial or commercial): a crowded assembly: an embrace: a close grasp: a few drops got by squeezing.—*adj.* **squeez'able.**—*n.* **squeez'er** one who squeezes: an instrument, machine, or part, for squeezing.—*n.* and *adj.* **squeez'ing.**—*adj.* **squeez'y** confined, cramped, contracted.—**squeeze'-box** (*slang*) a concertina.

squelch *skwelch, skwelsh, n.* the gurgling and sucking sound of walking in wet mud: a heavy blow on, or fall of, a soft body: its sound: a pulpy mass: a disconcerting or quashing retort or rebuff.—*v.i.* to make, or walk with, the sound of a squelch.—*v.t.* to crush under heel: to put down, suppress, snub, crush.—*n.* **squelch'er** one who squelches: an overwhelming blow, retort, etc.—*n.* and *adj.* **squelch'ing.**—*adj.* **squelch'y.** [Imit.]

squib *skwib, n.* a firework, consisting of a paper tube fitted with explosive powder, which burns noisily and explodes: a petty lampoon.—**damp squib** an idea, plan, etc. that fails to work successfully or to impress. [Perh. imit.]

squid *skwid, n.* any ten-armed cephalopod, esp. Loligo: a bait or lure of, or in imitation of, a squid: an anti-submarine mortar:—*pl.* **squid, squids.**

squiff(y) *skwif('i), (coll.) adjs.* tipsy.

squiggle *skwig'l, v.i.* to squirm, wriggle: to make wriggly lines.—*n.* a twist, wriggle, wriggly line.—*adj.* **squigg'ly.** [Imit., or poss. from *squirm* and *wriggle.*]

squill *skwil, n.* any plant of the liliaceous genus Scilla. [L. *squilla, scilla,* sea-onion, shrimp—Gr. *skilla,* sea-onion.]

squint *skwint, adv.* asquint, obliquely.—*adj.* looking obliquely: looking askance: squinting: strabismic: oblique: indirect.—*v.i.* to look obliquely: to have the eyes focusing in different directions, either by purposely crossing them, or by strabismus: to have a side reference or allusion: to hint disapprobation: to glance aside or casually: to glance.—*v.t.* to cause to squint: to direct or divert obliquely.—*n.* the act or habit of squinting: strabismus: an oblique look: a glance: a peep: an oblique reference, hint, tendency, or aim.—*n.* **squint'er.**—*n.* and *adj.* **squint'ing.**—*adv.* **squint'ingly.**—**squint'-eye(s)** one who squints.—*adj.* **squint'-eyed.** [Cf. Du. *schuinte,* slant.]

squire *skwīr, n.* an esquire, an aspirant to knighthood attending a knight: one who escorts or attends a lady: an English or Irish landed gentleman, esp. of old family: in some parts of Britain, a form of sometimes ironically respectful address.—*v.t.* to escort or attend. [esquire.]

squirm *skwûrm, v.i.* to writhe, go writhing.—*n.* a wriggle.—*adj.* **squirm'y.** [Prob. imit.]

squirrel *skwir'ǝl, n.* a nimble, bushy-tailed arboreal rodent (Sciurus or kindred genus): the pelt of such an animal: a person who hoards things (*fig.*).—*adj.* made of the pelt of a squirrel.—*v.t.* to hoard (usu. with *away*).—**squirr'el-cage** a cage with a treadmill for a squirrel: in an induction motor, a rotor whose winding suggests this; **squirr'el-monkey** a small golden-haired South American monkey. [O.Fr. *escurel*—L.L. *scurellus,* dim. of L. *sciūrus*—Gr. *skiouros*—*skiā,* shade, *ourā,* tail.]

squirt *skwûrt, v.t.* to throw out in a jet.—*v.i.* to spirt. —*n.* an instrument for squirting: a jet: an unimportant and irritatingly pretentious person (*slang*).—*n.* **squirt'er.**—*n.* and *adj.* **squirt'ing.** [Cf. L.G. *swirtjen, swürtjen.*]

squish *skwish, v.i.* to make a squelching or squirting sound.—*n.* the sound of squishing: bosh (*slang*).—*adj.* **squish'y.**—**squish lip system** a type of diesel engine combustion chamber designed to lessen fumes and noise pollution.

squit *skwit, (slang) n.* a contemptible person: nonsense. [Cf. **squirt.**]

squitch *skwich, n.* quitch-grass.

Sri, Shri *shrē,* in India a title of great respect given to a man, now generally used as the equivalent of *Mr.* [Sans. *śrī,* majesty, holiness.]

'st *st,* a shortened form of **hast.**

stab *stab, v.t.* to wound or pierce by driving in a pointed weapon: to give a sharp pain (also *fig.*).—*v.i.* to thrust or pierce with a pointed weapon:—*pr.p.* **stabb'ing;** *pa.t.* and *pa.p.* **stabbed.**—*n.* an act of stabbing: a wound with a pointed weapon.—*n.* **stabb'er.**—*n.* and *adj.* **stabb'ing.**—*adv.* **stabb'ingly.**—**have a stab at** (*coll.*) to have a go at, attempt; **stab in the back** (*lit.* and *fig.*) to injure in a treacherous manner. [Perh. variant of **stub.**]

stabile, stabilise, etc, **stability.** See **stable**[1].

stable[1] *stā'bl, adj.* standing firm: firmly established: durable: firm in purpose or character: constant: not ready to change: not radioactive.—*adj.* **stā'bile** (*-bīl, -bil*) not moving: not fluctuating: not decomposing readily, e.g. under moderate heat.—*n.* an abstract art construction differing from a mobile in having no movement.—*n.* **stabilisation, -z-** (*stab-, stāb-i-lī-zā'shǝn,* or *-li-*).—*v.t.* **stabilise, -ize** (*stab', stāb'*) to render stable or steady: to fix: to fix the value of: to establish, maintain, or regulate the equilibrium of.—*ns.* **stab'iliser, -z-** anything that stabilises: an additional plane or other device for giving stability to an aircraft: a gyroscope or other means of steadying a ship: a substance that retards chemical action; **stability** (*stabil'i-ti*) the state of being stable: steadiness: fixity: the power of recovering equilibrium: the fixing by vow of a monk or nun to one convent for life; **stā'bleness**—*adv.* **stā'bly.**—**stable equilibrium** the condition in which a body will return to its old position after a slight displacement. [Fr., —L. *stabilis*—*stāre,* to stand.]

stable[2] *stā'bl, n.* a building for horses, or sometimes other animals: a set of horses kept together: a horse-keeping establishment, organisation, or staff (as a horse-keeping establishment often *pl.* in form but treated as *sing.*): a number of skilled trained persons, esp. young men, who work together under one head or one manager.—*v.t.* to put or keep in a stable.—*n.* **stā'bling** the act of putting into a stable: accommodation for horses, cattle, cycles, etc.—**sta'ble-boy, -man** one who works at a stable; **stable lad** a person (male or female) whose job is to look after the horses at a racing-stable; **sta'blemate** a horse from the same stable as another: anything manufactured, originated, produced, etc., in the same place as another (e.g. different models of the same car), or a person from the same club, etc. as another (*fig.*). [O.Fr. *estable* (Fr. *étable*)—L. *stabulum*—*stāre,* to stand.]

staccato *sta-kä'tō, stäk-kä'tō, (mus.) adj.* and *adv.* with each note detached.—*n.* a staccato performance, manner, or passage:—*pl.* **stacca'tos.** [It., pa.p. of *staccare,* for *distaccare,* to separate.]

stack[1] *stak, n.* a large built-up pile of hay, corn, wood, etc.: a group or cluster of chimneys or flues: the chimney or funnel of a steamer, steam-engine, etc.: an isolated pillar of rock, often rising from the sea: a set of compactly arranged bookcases for storing books not on the open shelves of a library: a temporary storage area for data in a computer memory: an ordered, built-up pile: a standard quantity of gambler's chips bought at one time: aircraft waiting to land and circling at definite heights according to instructions: a large amount (*slang*).—*v.t.* to pile into a stack: to shuffle (cards) for cheating: to arrange (aircraft waiting to land) in a stack (see above).—*adj.* **stacked** piled in a stack: of shoe-heels, made of horizontal layers of leather: (also **well'-stacked'**) of a woman, having a large bust (*slang*).—*n.* **stack'ing.**—**stack'-room** in a library, a room where books are stored in stacks.—**stack against, in favour of** to arrange (circumstances) to the disadvantage, advantage, of (**have the cards stacked against, in favour of** to be faced with circumstances arranged in this way); **stack up** to pile or load high. [O.N. *stakkr*, a stack of hay.]

staddle *stad'l, n.* a support, esp. for a stack of hay, etc.: a stump left for coppice.—**stadd'le-stone'** a low mushroom-shaped arrangement of a conical and flat, circular stone, used as a support for a hay stack. [O.E. *stathol*, foundation.]

stadholder. See **stadtholder**.

stadium *stā'di-əm, n.* a Greek measure of length, 600 Greek, or 606⅔ English feet: a race-course, sports-ground:—*pl.* **stā'dia**. [Latinised from Gr. *stadion*.]

stadtholder, stadholder *stat', stät', stad', städ'hōl-dər, ns.* the head of the Dutch republic (*hist.*). [Du. *stadhouder*, lit. stead-holder—*stad*, place (now only town), *houder*, holder; spelling influenced by Ger. *Stadt*, town.]

staff *stäf, n.* a stick carried in the hand: a prop: a long piece of wood: a pole: a flagstaff: a long handle: a stick or ensign of authority: a token authorising an engine-driver to proceed: a set of lines and spaces on which music is written or printed: a stanza: in a watch or clock, the spindle of a balance-wheel (these have *pl.* **staffs** or **staves** *stāvz*; see also **stave**): a body of officers who help a commanding officer, or perform special duties: a body of persons employed in an establishment, usu. on management, administration, clerical, etc., work as distinct from manual: the body of teachers or lecturers in a school, college, university, etc. (these three meanings have *pl.* **staffs** *stäfs*).—*adj.* (or in composition) belonging or attached to the staff: applied also to officers of a higher grade.—*v.t.* to provide with a staff.—*n.* **staff'er** a member of the permanent staff of a business, etc., usu. as opposed to temporary or casual employees.—**staff's coll'ege** a college that trains officers for staff appointments; **staff'-corps** a body of officers and men assisting a commanding officer and his staff: formerly a body that supplied officers to the Indian army; **staff's duty** the occupation of an officer who serves on a staff, having been detached from his regiment; **staff's notation** musical notation in which a staff is used, as opposed to the tonic sol-fa system; **staff nurse** a nurse immediately below a sister in rank; **staff'-off'icer** an officer serving on a staff; **staff'room** a room for the use of the staff, as of a school; **staff'-ser'geant** a non-commissioned officer serving on a regimental staff.—**staff of life** staple food, esp. bread. [O.E. *stæf*.]

stag *stag, n.* a male deer, esp. a red deer over four years old: a male of various kinds (cock, turkey-cock, etc.): a man who goes to dances, etc., unaccompanied by a woman.—*adj.* male: of or for males.—**stag'-beet'le** any beetle of the family *Lucanidae*, from the large antler-like mandibles of the males; **stag'hound** the buck-hound: the Scottish deer-hound; **stag'-hunt**; **stag'-party** a party of men only, esp. one held for a man about to be married. [O.E. *stagga*, stag.]

stage *stāj, n.* a tier, shelf, floor, storey: a tiered structure for plants: a scaffold: an elevated platform, esp. for acting on: the theatre: theatrical representation: the theatrical calling: any field of action, scene: a place of rest on a journey or road: the portion of a journey between two such places: in a microscope, etc., the support for an object to be examined: a subdivision of a geological series or formation: a point reached in, or a section of, life, development, or any process: a stagecoach: one of the sections in a step-rocket: one of the elements in a complex piece of electronic equipment.—*adj.* pertaining to the stage: as conventionally represented on the stage (e.g. *a stage rustic*).—*v.t.* to represent or put on the stage: to contrive dramatically, organise and bring off.—*adj.* **staged** in storeys or tiers: put on the stage.—*ns.* **sta'ger** one who has had much experience in anything,

an old hand (*old stager*): a stage-horse; **sta'ging** scaffolding: putting on the stage: the jettisoning of any of the stages of a rocket.—*adj.* **sta'gy** (also **sta'gey**) savouring of the stage: artificially histrionic.—**stage'box'** a box over the proscenium; **stage'coach** formerly, a coach that ran regularly with passengers from stage to stage; **stage'coaching; stage'coachman; stage'-craft** skill in the technicalities of the theatre; **stage'-direc'tion** in a copy of a play, an instruction to the actor to do this or that; **stage'-door** the actors' entrance to a theatre; **stage'-driver** one who drives a stage; **stage'-effect'** theatrical effect; **stage'-fe'ver** a passion to go on the stage; **stage'-fright** nervousness before an audience, esp. for the first time (also *fig.*); **stage'-hand** a workman employed about the stage; **stage'-horse** a stagecoach horse.—*v.t.* **stage'-man'age** (back-formation) used *lit.*: also *fig.*, to arrange (an event) effectively as if it were a stage scene.—**stage's man'ager** one who superintends the production of plays, with general charge behind the curtain; **stage'-name** a name assumed professionally by an actor or actress—*n.pl.* **stage rights** legal rights to perform a play.—*adj.* **stage'-struck** sorely smitten with stage-fever.—**stage'-wag'on** a wagon for conveying goods and passengers at fixed times; **stage'-whis'per** an audible utterance conventionally understood by the audience to represent a whisper: a loud whisper meant to be heard by people other than the person addressed; **sta'ging-area, -base** a point for the assembly of troops en route for an operation; **sta'ging-post** a regular point of call on an air-route.—**stage left, right** at the left or right of the stage, facing the audience. [O.Fr. *estage* (Fr. *étage*), a storey of a house—inferred L.L. *staticus*—L. *stāre*, to stand.]

stagger *stag'ər, v.i.* to reel: to go reeling or tottering: to waver.—*v.t.* to cause to reel: to give a shock to: to cause to waver: to nonplus, confound: to dispose alternately or variously: to arrange so that one thing or part is ahead of another.—*n.* a staggering: a wavering: a staggered arrangement: (in *pl.*, often treated as *sing.*) giddiness, also any of various kinds of disease causing horses, etc., to stagger.—*adj.* **stagg'ered**.—*n.* **stagg'erer**.—*n.* and *adj.* **stagg'ering**.—*adv.* **stagg'eringly**. [Earlier *stacker*—O.N. *stakra*, freq. of *staka*, to push.]

stagnant *stag'nənt, adj.* still, standing, without current: foul, unwholesome, or dull from stillness: inert.—*n.* **stag'nancy**.—*adv.* **stag'nantly**.—*v.i.* **stag'nate** (or *-nāt'*) to be stagnant.—*n.* **stagna'tion**. [L. *stagnāre, -ātum—stagnum*, pond.]

staid *stād, adj.* steady: sober: grave: sedate.—*adv.* **staid'ly**.—*n.* **staid'ness**. [For stayed—**stay**.]

stain *stān, v.t.* to impart a new colour to: to tinge: to tarnish: to impregnate with a substance that colours some parts to as to show composition and structure: to bring reproach on.—*v.i.* to take or impart a stain.—*n.* a dye or colouring-matter: discoloration: a spot: taint of guilt: pollution: a cause of reproach: shame.—*adj.* **stained**.—*n.* **stain'er**.—*n.* and *adj.* **stain'ing**.—*adj.* **stain'less** free from stain: not liable to stain, rust, or tarnish.—*adv.* **stain'lessly**.—*n.* **stain'lessness**.—**stained glass** glass painted with certain pigments fused into its surface; **stainless steel** a steel that will not rust, containing 8 to 25 per cent. of chromium. [From vb. *distain*, to stain, sully, ult.—L. *dis-*, neg., and *tingĕre*, to colour.]

stair *stār, n.* a series of steps (in Scotland, the whole series from floor to floor, elsewhere, usu. in *pl.*, a flight from landing to landing): one such step.—**stair'-case** the structure enclosing a stair: stairs with banisters, etc.; **stair'foot** the level place at the foot of stairs; **stair'head** the level place at the top of stairs; **stair'-rod** a rod for holding a staircarpet in place;

stair'-tower, -turret one enclosing a winding stair; **stair'way** a staircase: a passage by stairs; **stair'-well** the well of a staircase —**below stairs** in the basement: among the servants [O.E *stæger–stīgan*, to ascend.]

stake[1] *stāk, n.* a stick or pole pointed at one end: a post: a post to which one condemned to be burned was tied: hence, death or martyrdom by burning.— *v.t.* to fasten to or with, to protect, shut, support, furnish, pierce, with a stake or stakes: to mark the bounds of with stakes (often with *off* or *out*) —**stake a claim (for, to)** to intimate one's right to or desire to possess; **stake out** (*coll.*) to place (a person, etc.) under surveillance [O.E *staca,* stake]

stake[2] *stāk, v.t.* to deposit as a wager: to risk, hazard —*n.* anything pledged as a wager: a prize: anything to gain or lose: an interest, concern: the condition of being at hazard: a grubstake: (in *pl.*) a race for money staked or contributed.—**at stake** hazarded: in danger. at issue. [Perh. M.Du. *staken,* to place.]

stalactite *stal'ək-tīt* (also *sta-lak'tīt*), *n.* an icicle-like pendant of calcium carbonate, formed by evaporation of water percolating through limestone, as on a cave roof: the material it is composed of: anything of similar form.—*adjs.* **stalactitic** (*-tit'ik*), **-al.**—*adv.* **stalactit'ically.**—*n.* **stal'agmite** (also *-ag'*) an upward-growing conical formation on the floor, formed by the drip from the roof or from a stalactite.—*adjs.* **stalagmitic** (*-mit'ik*), **-al.** [Gr. *stalaktos, stalagma, stalagmos,* a dropping—*stalassein,* to drip.]

stalag *stal'ag, shtä'läg, shtä'lähh, n.* a German camp for prisoners of war (non-commissioned officers and men). [Ger. *Stamm,* base, *Lager,* camp.]

stalagmite. See under **stalactite.**

stale[1] *stāl, adj.* no longer fresh: past the best: out of condition by over-training or overstudy: impaired by lapse of time: tainted: vapid or tasteless from age — *adv.* **stale'ly.**—*n.* **stale'ness.** [Perh from the root *sta-,* as in **stand.**]

stale[2] *stāl, n.* urine, now esp. of horses.—*v.i.* to urinate. [Cf Du. *stalle,* Ger. *Stall,* O.Fr vb *estaler.*]

stale[3] *stāl,* (now *rare* or *obs.*) *n.* and *v.t* stalemate.— **stale'mate** an unsatisfactory draw resulting when a player not actually in check has no possible legal move (*chess*): an inglorious deadlock.—*v.t.* to subject to a stalemate. [Cf. A.Fr *estale,* perh.— Eng. **stall.**]

Stalinism *stä'lin-izm, n.* the rigorous rule of the Russian Communist dictator Josef *Stalin* (1879–1953), esp. in its concentration of all power and authority in the Communist world in Russia.

stalk[1] *stök, n.* the stem of a plant: a slender connecting part: a shaft: a tall chimney.—*v.t.* to remove the stalk from.—*adjs.* **stalked** having a stalk; **stalk'less;** **stalk'y** running to stalk: like a stalk. [Dim. from the root of O.E. *stela, stalu,* stalk.]

stalk[2] *stök, v.i.* to stride stiffly or haughtily: to go after game keeping under cover.—*v.t.* to approach under cover: to stalk over or through (a tract of country, etc.).—*n.* an act of stalking: a stalking gait.—*n.* **stalk'er.**—*n.* and *adj.* **stalk'ing.**—**stalk'ing-horse** a horse or substitute behind which a sportsman hides while stalking game: anything put forward to mask plans or efforts [O.E. (*bi*)*stealcian,* freq. of **steal.**]

stall[1] *stöl, n* a standing-place: a stable, cowshed, or the like: a compartment for one animal: a bench, table, booth, or stand for display or sale of goods, or used as a working-place: a church-seat with arms, usu. one of those lining the choir or chancel on both sides, reserved for cathedral clergy, for choir, for monks, or for knights of an order: an office entitling one to such a seat: a doorless pew: an individual armed seat in a

theatre, etc , esp an orchestra stall: a working place in a mine: a covering for a finger (as in *fingerstall*): an instance of stalling in aircraft or engine: a standstill —*v t.* to put or keep in a stall: to induct, install: to bring to a standstill: to cause (an aeroplane) to fly in such a way that the angle between the aerofoils and the direction of motion is greater than that at which there is maximum lift and so lose control: to stop (an engine) by sudden braking, overloading, etc : to mire.—*v.i* to come to a standstill: of aircraft or engine, to be stalled.—**stall starting gate, starting stall** or **gate** a group of stalls into which horses are shut for the start of a race [O E. *stall, steall.*]

stall[2] *stol, n.* a ruse, trick: a decoy, esp one who diverts attention from a criminal action —*v.t* to delay or obstruct to stave off (with *off*) —*v t* to hang back, play for time: to be obstructive, evasive or deceptive. [Old word *stale,* a decoy.]

stallion *stal'yən, n.* an uncastrated male horse, esp one kept for breeding. [O.Fr. *estalon* (Fr. *étalon*)— O.H.G *stal,* stall]

stalwart *stol'wərt, adj.* stout, strong, sturdy: determined in partisanship.—*n.* a resolute person.— *adv.* **stal'wartly.**—*n.* **stal'wartness.** [Orig. Sc vts form of *stalworth*—O.E. *stælwierthe,* serviceable - *stæl,* place (*stathol,* foundation), *wierthe,* worth.]

stamen *stä'mən, n.* the pollen-producing part of a flower, consisting of anther and filament:—*pl.* **stä'mens,** and see also **stamina** below—*adj.* **stä'mened** having stamens.—*n.pl.* **stamina** (*stam'*) stamens (*rare*).—*n.sing.* native or constitutional strength: staying power: mainstay.—*adjs.* **stam'inal** of stamens or stamina; **stam'inate** having stamens but no carpels. [L. *stämen* (pl *stämina*), a warp thread (upright in an old loom)—*stäre,* to stand.]

stammer *stam'ər, v.i.* to falter in speaking: to speak with involuntary hesitations, to stutter.—*v.t.* to utter falteringly or with a stutter —*n* involuntary hesitation in speech, a stutter: a faltering mode of utterance.—*n* **stamm'erer.**—*n.* and *adj.* **stamm'ering.**—*adv.* **stamm'eringly.** [O.E *stamerian.*]

stamp *stamp, v.t.* to bray, pound, crush: to bring the foot forcibly down upon: to trample: to strike flatwise with the sole (or other part) of: to impress, imprint, or cut with a downward blow, as with a die or cutter: to mint, make, shape by such a blow: to fix or mark deeply: to impress with a mark attesting official approval, ratification, payment, etc.: to affix an adhesive stamp to: to attest, declare, prove to be: to characterise.—*v.t.* to bring the foot down forcibly and noisily: to walk with a heavy tread —*n.* the act of stamping: an impression: a stamped device, mark, imprint: an adhesive paper used as a substitute for stamping: attestation: authorisation: cast, form, character: distinguishing mark, imprint, sign, evidence: an instrument or machine for stamping.— *n.* **stamp'er.**—*n.* and *adj.* **stamp'ing.**—**Stamp Act** an act of parliament imposing or regulating stamp-duties, esp that of 1765 imposing them on the American colonies; **stamp'-album** a book for keeping a collection of postage-stamps in; **stamp'-collector** a receiver of stamp-duties· one who makes a hobby of collecting postage-stamps; **stamp'-duty** a tax imposed on the paper on which legal documents are written; **stamp-hinge** see **hinge;** **stamp'ing-ground** an animal's usual resort: a person's habitual place of resort; **stamp'-, stamp'ing-mill** a crushing-mill for ores —**stamp out** to put out by tramping: to extirpate· to make by stamping from a sheet with a cutter [M.E *stampen,* from an inferred O E *stampian.*]

stampede *stam-pēd', n.* a sudden rush of a panic-stricken herd: any impulsive action of a multitude.—

v.i to rush in a stampede —*v.t* to send rushing in a stampede. [Sp. *estampida*, crash—*estampar*, to stamp.]

stance *stans, n.* a mode of standing, as in golf. [Fr. *stance* (now meaning 'stanza')—It. *stanza*, a stopping-place, station—L. *stāre*, to stand.]

stanch, staunch *stanch, stansh, stonch, stonsh, v.t* to stop the flowing of, as blood: to quench, allay.—*n.* a styptic: a floodgate —*n* **stanch'er; stanch'ing.**—*adj.* **stanch'less** that cannot be quenched or stopped. [O.Fr. *estancher* (Fr. *étancher*)—L.L. *stancāre*, to stanch.]

stanchion *stān'shən, stan'shən, n.* an upright iron bar of a window or screen. an upright beam used as a support (*naut.*).—*v.t.* to fasten by means of or to a stanchion. [O.Fr. *estançon—estance*, prop—L. *stāre*, to stand.]

stand *stand, v.i.* to be, become, or remain upright, erect, rigid, or still: to be on, or rise to. one's feet: to be steadfast: to have or take a position: to be or remain: to be set or situated: to be set down: to have a direction: to hold good: to endure, continue to exist: to scruple, demur: to insist punctiliously: to be a representative, representation, or symbol: to be a candidate.—*v.t.* to withstand: to tolerate: to endure: to sustain: to suffer, undergo: to abide by: to be at the expense of, offer and pay for: to station, cause to stand: to set erect or in position:—*pa.t.* and *pa.p.* **stood.**—*n.* an act, manner, or place of standing: a taking up of a position for resistance: resistance: the partnership of any two batsmen at the wicket, the period of time of the partnership, or the runs made during it (*cricket*). a standing position: a standstill: a stoppage: a loss, a nonplus: a post, station: a place under cover for awaiting game: a place for vehicles awaiting hire: an erection for spectators: a stop on tour to give one or more performances, or the place where it is made (*theat.*): a platform: a witness-box (*U.S.*): a base or structure for setting things on: a piece of furniture for hanging things from: a standing growth or crop.—*n.* **stan'der.**—*adj.* **stand'ing** established: settled: permanent: fixed: stagnant: erect: having a base: done as one stands: from a standing position, without preliminary movement (e.g. *standing jump, start*).—*n.* the action of one who or that which stands: duration: continuance: place to stand in: position or grade in a profession, university, in society: a right or capacity to sue or maintain an action.—**stand'-by** that which, or one whom, one relies on or readily resorts to: something, someone, available for use in an emergency (see also **on stand-by** below).—*adj.* (of an airline passenger, ticket, fare, etc.) occupying, for, an aircraft seat not booked in advance but taken as available. usu. with some price-reduction, at the time of departure.—**stand'-in'** a substitute; **standing committee** one permanently established to deal with a particular matter; **stand'ing-ground** a place, basis, or principle to stand on; **standing joke** a subject that raises a laugh whenever it is mentioned; **standing order** an instruction from a customer to his bank to make regular payments from his account: an order placed with a shopkeeper, etc. for the regular supply of a newspaper or other goods: a military order with long-term application: (in *pl.*) regulations for procedure adopted by a legislative assembly (also **standing rules**); **stand'ing-room** room for standing, without a seat; **stand'ing-stone** (*archaeol.*) a great stone set erect in the ground; **stand'-off** a Rugby half-back who stands away from the scrum as a link between scrum-half and the three-quarters (also **stand-off half**).—*adj.* **stand-off'ish** inclined to hold aloof, keep others at arm's-length.—**stand'-pipe** an open vertical pipe connected to a

pipeline, to ensure that the pressure head at that point cannot exceed the length of the pipe: one used to obtain water for an attached hose, **stand'point** a viewpoint; **stand'still** a complete stop.—*adj* stationary: unmoving: forbidding or refraining from movement.—**stand'-to** a precautionary parade or taking of posts.—*adj.* **stand'-up** erect: done or taken in a standing position: of a fight, in earnest: delivering, or consisting of, a comic monologue without feed or other support.—**it stands to reason** it is only logical to assume; **make a stand** to halt and offer resistance; **one-night stand** see **one**; **on stand-by** in readiness to help in an emergency; **stand by** to support: to adhere to, abide by: to be at hand: to hold oneself in readiness; **stand down** to leave the witness box: to go off duty: to withdraw from a contest or from a controlling position; **stand fast** to be unmoved; **stand for** to be a candidate for: to represent, symbolise: to champion: to put up with, endure (*coll.*); **stand in** to become a party: to have an understanding, be in league: to deputise, act as a substitute (for); **stand off** to keep at a distance: to direct the course from: to suspend temporarily from employment; **stand on** to continue on the same tack or course: to insist on: to set store by (see **ceremony**): to behove: to found upon; **stand one's ground** to maintain one's position; **stand one's hand, stand sam** (*coll.*), **stand shot, stand treat** to treat the company, esp. to drinks; **stand on one's own feet** to manage one's own affairs without help; **stand out** to project, to be prominent: not to comply, to refuse to yield; **stand over** to keep (someone who is working, etc.) under close supervision: to postpone or be postponed; **stand to** to fall to, set to work: to back up: to uphold: to take up position in readiness for orders; **stand to gain, win,** etc. to be in a position to gain, win, etc.; **stand up** to get to one's feet: to take position for a dance: to be clad (with *in*): to fail to keep an appointment with (*coll.*); **stand up for** to support or attempt to defend; **stand upon** to stand on; **stand up to** to meet (an opponent, etc.) face to face, to show resistance to: to fulfil (an obligation, etc.) fairly: to withstand (hard wear, etc.); **stand well** to be in favour; **stand with** to be consistent. [O.E. *standan*.]

standard *stand'ərd, n.* a flag or military symbolic figure on a pole, marking a rallying-point: a rallying-point (also *fig.*): a long tapering flag notched and rounded at the end, bearing heraldic symbols and fixed in the ground (*her.*): a flag generally: a cavalry regimental flag: a standard-bearer: that which stands or is fixed: an upright post, pillar, stick: a standing shrub or tree not trained on an espalier or a wall: a tree left growing amidst coppice: an exemplar or substance chosen to be or afford a unit: a basis of measurement: a criterion: an established or accepted model: an accepted authoritative statement of a church's creed: a definite level of excellence or adequacy required, aimed at, or possible.—*adj.* serving as or conforming to a standard: of enduring value: growing as a standard: standing upright.—*n.* **standardisā'tion, -z-.**—*v.t.* **stand'ardise, -ize** to make, or keep, of uniform size, shape, etc.—*n.* **stand'ardiser, -z-.**—**stand'ard-bearer** one who carries a standard or banner: an outstanding leader; **standard deviation** the root of the average of the squares of the differences from their mean of a number of observations; **standard English** the form of English taught in schools, etc., and used, esp. in formal situations, by the majority of educated English-speakers; **standard error** standard deviation: standard deviation divided by the root of the number of observations; **standard lamp** a lamp on a tall support; **standard solution** a solution of known concentration, used for purposes of comparison.—

(international) standard book number a number allotted to a book by agreement of (international) publishers which shows area, publisher and individual title. [O.Fr. *estandart*; prob. conn. either with **extend** or **stand**, and in any case influenced by or partly from **stander**.]

stang *stang, n.* a stake, pole. [O.N. *stöng.*]

stanhope *stan'əp, -hōp, n.* a light open one-seated carriage first made for Fitzroy *Stanhope* (1787–1864).

Stanislavski method, system *stan-ı-släv'skı, -slaf',* method acting (q.v.). [K. *Stanislavskı* (1863–1938), Russian actor and director.]

stank *stangk, pa.t.* of **stink.**

stann- *stan-,* in composition, tin.—*n.* **stann'ary** (*-ə-ri*) a tin-mining district (esp. the **Stannaries** in Cornwall and Devon).—Also *adj.*—**Stannary Parliament** the ancient parliament of tinners, comprising twenty-four representatives (**stannators**) for all Cornwall. [L. *stannum,* tın.]

stanza *stan'zə n.* a group of lines of verse forming a definite pattern: a pattern so composed. [It. *stanza* —L. *stāre,* to stand.]

stapedectomy, stapedial. See **stapes.**

stapes *stā'pēz, n.* the stirrup-shaped innermost ossicle of the ear.—*n.* **stapedectomy** (*stap-i-dek'tə-mi*) the surgical excision of this bone.—*adj.* **stapedial** (*stə-pē'di-əl*). [L.L. *stapēs, -edıs,* a stirrup.]

staph. See **Staphyloccus** under **staphyle.**

staphyle *staf'i-lē, n.* the uvula.—*n.* **Staphylococc'us** (Gr. *kokkos,* a grain) a pus-causing bacterium found in clustered masses (*coll.* shortening **staph**).—*adj.* **staphylococc'al.** [Gr. *staphylē,* a bunch of grapes, a swollen uvula.]

staple¹ *stā'pl, n.* a settled mart or market: a leading commodity: a main element (as of diet, reading, conversation): unmanufactured wool or other raw material: textile fibre, or its length and quality.—*adj.* constituting a staple: leading, main.—*v.t.* to grade according to staple.—*n.* **stā'pler** a merchant of a staple: one who grades and deals in wool. [O.Fr. *estaple*—L.G. *stapel,* heap, mart.]

staple² *stā'pl, n.* a U-shaped rod or wire for driving into a wall, post, etc., as a fastening: a similarly-shaped piece of wire that is driven through sheets of paper and compressed, to fasten them together: the curved bar, etc. that passes through the slot of a hasp, receives a bolt, etc.: the metallic tube to which the reed is fastened in the oboe, etc.—*v.t.* to fasten with a staple.—*n.* **stā'pler** an instrument for (dispensing and) inserting staples into papers, etc.—**stā'pling-machine** a machine that stitches paper with wire [O.E. *stapol,* post, support; cf. foregoing.]

star *stär, n.* any of those heavenly bodies visible by night that are really gaseous masses generating heat and light, whose places are relatively fixed (**fixed stars**): more loosely, these and the planets, comets, meteors and even, less commonly, the sun, moon and earth: a planet as a supposed influence, hence (usu. in *pl.*) one's luck: an object or figure with pointed rays, most commonly five: an asterisk: a starfish: a radial meeting of ways: a star-shaped badge of rank or honour: a white mark on a beast's forehead: a pre-eminent or exceptionally brilliant person: a leading performer, or one supposed to draw the public.—*adj.* of stars: marked by a star: leading, pre-eminent, brilliant.—*v.t.* to make a star of: to have a (specified person) as a star performer: to mark with a star: to shatter or crack in a radiating form: to set with stars: to bespangle.—*v.i.* to shine, as a star: to attract attention: to appear as a star performer:—*pr.p.* **starr'ing**; *pa.t.* and *pa.p.* **starred.**—*n.* **star'dom** the state of being, status of, a star performer esp. of stage or screen.—*adj.* **star'less.**—*n.* **star'let** a kind of starfish

(*Asterına*): a little star: a young film actress, esp. one hailed as a future star.—*adj.* and *adv.* **star'like.**—*adj.* **starred** adorned or studded with stars: influenced by or having a star: decorated or marked with a star: turned into a star: star-shaped: radially cracked, fissured.—*n.* **starr'iness.**—*n., adj.* **starr'ing.**—*adj.* **starr'y** abounding or adorned with stars: consisting of, or proceeding from, the stars: like, or shining like, the stars.—**star billing** prominent display of the name of a performer, etc. on posters, etc.—*adj.* **star's bright'** bright as a star or with stars.—**star'fish** any member of the Asteroidea, a class of echinoderms with five arms merging in a disc.—*v.i.* **star'-gaze.**— **star'-gazer** an astrologer: an astronomer: one who gazes at the sky, or in abstraction. a dreamer or wool-gatherer: a fish with upward-looking eyes (Uranoscopus or other).—**star'light** light from the stars.— *adj.* of or with starlight: lighted by the stars: bright as a star.—*adj.* **star'lit** lighted by the stars.—**star'-map** a map showing the positions of stars; **star'-nose** (or **star-nosed mole**) a North American mole with star-shaped nose-tip.—*adjs.* **starr'y-eyed** out of touch with reality: innocently idealistic: radiantly happy; **star'-shaped** shaped like a conventional star, with pointed rays.—**star'-shell** a shell that explodes high in the air, lighting up the scene; **star'shine** starlight; **star sign** a sign of the zodiac.—*adj.* **star'-spang'led** spangled or studded with stars (**Star-spangled Banner** the Stars and Stripes: an American national hymn).— **star'spot** an area of relative darkness on the surface of a star; **star'-stone** a sapphire, ruby, or other stone showing asterism.—*adj.* **star'-studded** covered with stars: of the cast of a film, play, etc., having a high proportion of leading performers.—**star'-turn** the chief item in an entertainment: a pre-eminent performer; **star'-wheel** a spur-wheel with V-shaped teeth; **star'wort** any plant of the genus Aster: stitchwort: a water-plant (**water-starwort** Callitriche).— *adj.*—**see stars** (*coll.*) to see spots of light, as result e.g. of blow on the head: to be in a dazed condition; **star-of-Bethlehem** a plant (Ornithogalum) of the lily family with starlike flowers; **Star of David** the Jewish religious symbol—Solomon's-seal (see second meaning of this); **Stars and Stripes** the flag of the United States of America, with thirteen stripes alternately red and white, and a blue field containing as many stars as there are states. [O.E. *steorra.*]

starboard *star'bə(r)d, -börd, -bord, n.* the right-hand side of a ship.—*adj.* and *adv.* of, to, towards, or on, the right.—*v.t.* to turn to the right—opp. to *port.* [O.E. *stēorbord*—*stēor,* steering, *bord.* board, side of a ship (ancient Gmc. ships being steered by a paddle at the right side).]

starch *starch, n.* the principal reserve food-material stored in plants, chemically a carbohydrate, ($C_6H_{10}O_5)_x$, used in the laundry as a stiffener: stiffness, formality.—*adj.* of starch: stiff, rigid, formal.—*v.t.* to stiffen or stick with starch.—*adj.* **starched.**—*ns.* **starched'ness** (or *-id-*); **starch'er.**— *adv.* **starch'ily.**—*n.* **starch'iness.**—*adj.* **starch'y** of or like starch: stiff: precise.—*adj.* **starch'-reduced** of bread, etc. for the use of slimmers, containing less than the usual amount of starch. [O.E. *stercan,* to stiffen, inferred from *stercedferhth,* stiff-spirited; cf. **stark.**]

Star Chamber *stär chām'bər,* a court (abolished 1641) with a civil and criminal jurisdiction, which met in the old council chamber at Westminster and was empowered to act without a jury and to use torture: generally, an over-zealous inquiry or investigation. [Prob. named from the gilt *stars* on the ceiling, not from the Jewish bonds (*starrs*) kept in it.]

stare *stär, v.i.* to look with a fixed gaze: to glare: to be insistently or obtrusively conspicuous (with indirect obj. as to *stare one in the face*).—*v.t.* to render by staring.—*n.* a fixed look.—*n.*, *adj.*, and *adv.* **star'ing.** [O.E. *starian.*]

stark *stärk, adj.* stern: harsh: unyielding: sheer: out-and-out: stark-naked (q.v.).—*adv.* utterly.—*adj.* **starkers** see **stark-naked.**—*adv.* **stark'ly.**—*n.* **stark'ness.** [O.E. *stearc*, hard, strong.]

stark-naked *stärk'-nā'kid, adj.* utterly naked: quite bare—shortened to **stark** or (*coll.*) **stark'ers.** [M.E. *stert-naked*—O.E. *steort*, tail, *nacod*, naked; influenced by foregoing.]

starling¹ *star'ling, n.* a bird with black, brown-spotted, iridescent plumage, a good mimic: any other member of its genus, Sturnus. [O.E. *stærling*, dim. of *stær*, see **stare**².]

starling² *stär'ling, n.* piling protecting a bridge pier. [Prob. for *staddling* from **staddle.**]

starr *stär, n.* a Jewish deed or bond, e.g. of acquittance of debt. [Heb. *sh'tār*, a writing.]

starry, etc. See **star.**

start *stärt, v.i.* to shoot, dart, move suddenly forth, or out: to spring up or forward: to strain forward: to break away: to make a sudden involuntary movement as of surprise or becoming aware: to spring open, out of place, or loose: to begin to move: of a car, engine, etc., to begin to work, to fire: to set forth on a journey, race, career.—*v.t.* to begin: to set going: to set on foot: to set up: to drive from lair or hiding-place: to cause or undergo displacement or loosening of: to pour out or shoot.—*n.* a sudden movement: a sudden involuntary motion of the body: a startled feeling: a spurt: an outburst or fit: a beginning of movement, esp. of a journey, race, or career: a beginning: a setting in motion: a help in or opportunity of beginning: an advantage in being early or ahead: the extent of such an advantage in time or distance.—*n.* **start'er** one who starts, esp. in a race: one who gives the signal for starting: a dog that starts game: an apparatus or device for starting a machine, as that (also called **self-starter**) for starting an internal-combustion engine: anything used to begin a process: (also in *pl.*) the first course of a meal (see also **for starters** below).—**starting block** (usu. in *pl.*) a device for helping a sprinter make a quick start to a race, consisting of a framework with blocks of wood or metal attached, on which the sprinter braces his feet; **starting gate, stall** see **stall**¹; **start'ing-point** the point from which anything starts, or from which motion begins; **start'ing-post** the post or barrier from which the competitors start in a race; **start'ing-price** odds on a horse when the race begins.—**for a start** in the first place, as a preliminary consideration; **for starters** (*coll.*) as the first course of a meal: in the first place, for a start; **start in** to begin; **start out** to begin: to begin a journey; **start up** to rise suddenly: to come suddenly into notice or being: to set in motion. [M.E. *sterten.*]

startle *stärt'l, v.i.* to start: to undergo a start: to feel sudden alarm.—*v.t.* to surprise as with fright: to cause to undergo a start: to take aback: to awake, excite.—*n.* sudden alarm or surprise.—*adj.* **start'led.** —*n.* and *adj.* **start'ling.** [M.E. *stertle*—O.E. *steartlian*, to stumble, struggle, kick, or formed afresh from **start.**]

start-naked. Earlier (now *dial.*) form of **stark-naked.**

starve *stärv, v.i.* to die, now only of hunger or (chiefly *Scot.* and *Northern*) cold: to suffer extreme hunger (or cold): to be in want.—*v.t.* to cause to starve: to afflict with hunger (or cold): to deprive of food: to force, subdue, cure, by want of food: to deprive of anything needful.—*n.* **starvā'tion.**—*adj.* **starved.**—*n.* **starve'ling** a lean, hungry, weak, or pining person, animal, or plant.—Also *adj.*—*n.* and *adj.* **starv'ing.**

[O.E. *steorfan*, to die.]

stash *stash,* (*coll.*) *v.t.* to stow in hiding (often with away).—*n.* a secret store, or its hiding-place.

stasis (also **-stasis** in composition) *stā'sis, stas'is,* (chiefly *med.*) *n.* stoppage, arrest, esp. of growth, of blood-circulation or bleeding, or of the contents of the bowels: (maintenance of) a state of equilibrium or constant state. [Gr. *stasis*, stoppage, stationariness.]

-stat *-stat,* in composition, used to designate a regulating device that causes something to remain constant or stationary, as in *barostat, hygrostat, thermostat.* [Gr. *-statēs*, causing to stand—*histanai*, to cause to stand.]

statant *stā'tant,* (*her.*) *adj.* standing on four feet. [L. *stāre*, to stand.]

state *stāt, n.* condition: a perturbed condition of mind (*coll.*): mode of existence: circumstances at any time: a phase or stage: status: station in life: high station: pomp, display, ceremonial dignity: an estate, order, or class in society or the body politic: hence (in *pl.*) the legislature (*hist.*): public welfare: constitution: the civil power: the organisation of the body politic, or of one of the constituent members of a federation: the territory of such a state: high politics: a statement, report (now chiefly *mil.*).—*adj.* of, belonging to, relating to, the state or a federal state: public: ceremonial: pompous: affectedly solemn and mysterious: magnificent.—*v.t.* to set forth: to express the details of: to set down fully and formally: to assert, affirm: to specify.—*adjs.* **stāt'al** of a federal state; **stāt'ed** settled: established: declared.—*n.* **state'hood** the status of a state.—*adj.* **state'less** without nationality.—*adv.* **state'lily.**—*n.* **state'liness.**—*adj.* **state'ly** showing state or dignity: majestic, greatly impressive. —*adv.* majestically: loftily.—*ns.* **state'ment** the act of stating: that which is stated: a formal account, declaration of facts, etc.: a financial record, e.g. one issued regularly by a bank to a customer, stating his personal balance and detailing debits and credits; **stāt'ism** (the belief in) state control of economic and social affairs.—*n.*, *adj.* **stāt'ist** (see also separate entry).—*adj.* **state'-aid'ed** receiving contributions from the state.—**state'-cabin** a stateroom on a ship; **state'craft** the art of managing state affairs; **State Department** in the U.S., the government department dealing with foreign affairs; **stately home** a large, fine old house in private ownership but usu. open to the public; **state'-paper** an official paper or document relating to affairs of state; **state religion** a religion recognised by the state as the national religion; **state'room** a room of state: a private cabin or railway compartment; **state school** one controlled by a public authority, and financed by taxation; **States'-Gen'eral** the representative body of the three orders (nobility, clergy, burghers) of the French kingdom (*hist.*): the Dutch parliament.—*adj.*, *adv.* **State'side** (*coll.*; also without *cap.*) of, in, towards or to the U.S.— **states'man** one skilled in government: one who takes an important part in governing the state, esp. with wisdom and broad-mindedness:—*fem.* **states'woman.**—*adjs.* **states'manlike, states'manly** befitting a statesman.—*n.* **states'manship.**—**lie in state** of a corpse, to be laid out in a place of honour before being buried; **State Enrolled Nurse** (abbrev. **SEN**) a nurse who has passed a particular examination of the General Nursing Council of England and Wales or the General Nursing Council of Scotland (see also **State Registered Nurse** below); **state of affairs** a situation, set of circumstances; **state of the art** the level or position at a given time, esp. the present, of generally accepted and available knowledge, technical achievement, etc. in a particular field, etc. (*adj.* **state'-of-the-art'**); **State Registered Nurse** (abbrev. **SRN**) in England and Wales, a nurse who has passed a more advanced examination of the General Nursing Council of England and Wales than a **State Enrolled Nurse** (for Scotland, see **Registered General Nurse** under **register**); **the States** the United States; **turn State's evidence** see **evidence**. [L. *status, -ūs—stāre, statum*, to stand; partly through O.Fr. (see **estate**.)]

stater *stā'tər, n.* an ancient Greek standard coin of various kinds. [Gr. *statēr*, orig. a pound weight— *histanai*, to set, establish, weigh.]

static, -al *stat'ik, -əl, adjs.* pertaining to statics: pertaining to bodies, forces, charges, etc., in equilibrium: stationary: stable: resting: acting by mere weight: pertaining to sense of bodily equilibrium.—*n.* (**static**) atmospheric disturbances in wireless reception: white specks or flashes on a television picture: crackling on a long-playing plastic record: static electricity.—*adv.* **stat'ically**.—*n.sing.* **stat'ics** the science of forces in equilibrium.—**static electricity** electrical charges that are stationary, not moving along in a current. [Gr. *statikos*, bringing to a standstill— *histanai*, to cause to stand.]

station *stā'shən, n.* a standing still: a mode of standing: position: a chosen fixed point: a standing-place: a fixed stopping-place, esp. one on a railway with associated buildings and structures: a place set apart and equipped for some particular purpose: a local office, headquarters, or depot: a habitat: an assigned place or post: an assigned region for naval duty: a place in India where officials and officers reside: an Australian stock-farm: position in life (esp. a high position) or in the scale of nature: a holy place visited as one of a series, esp. one of (usu. fourteen) representations of stages in Christ's way to Calvary, disposed around a church interior or elsewhere (*R.C.*).—*adj.* of a station.—*v.t.* to assign a station to: to set: to appoint to a post, place, or office.—*adj.* **sta'tionary** still: unmoving: fixed: settled: permanently located: continuously resident.—*n.* **sta'tioner** a dealer in writing-materials and the like.— *adj.* **sta'tionery** belonging to a stationer.—*n.* the goods sold by a stationer.—**sta'tion-hand** (*Austr.*) a man employed on a station; **sta'tion-house** a lock-up at a police station: a police station (*U.S.*); **sta'tion-master, -manager** one in charge of railway station; **sta'tion-wagon** a motor vehicle usable by adjustment for either passengers or light hauling. [L. *statiō, -ōnis—stāre*, to stand.]

statism. See **state.**

statist *stā'tist, n.* an advocate of statism (q.v. under **state**): a statistician.—*adj.* **statistic** (*sta-tist'ik*) statistical: relating to status.—*n.* a statistician: (in *pl.*) tabulated numerical facts, orig. those relating to a state, or (with *sing.* verb) the classification, tabulation, and study of such facts: one such fact.—*adj.* **statist'ical** of, concerned with, of the nature of, statistics.—*adv.* **statist'ically**.—*n.* **statistician** (*stat-is-tish'ən*) one skilled in statistics: a compiler or student of statistics. [It. *statista* and Ger. *Statistik* —L. *status*, state.]

stative *stā'tiv, adj.* indicating a state, as opposed to an action, etc. (*linguistics*). [L. *statīvus—stāre*, to stand.]

stato- *stat'ō-*, in composition, standing.—**stat'oscope** a sensitive barometer for detecting minute differences. [Gr. *statos*, set, placed.]

stator *stā'tər, n.* a stationary part within which a part rotates. [L. *stātor*, stander.]

statue *stat'ū, n.* a representation (usu. near or above life-size) of human or animal form in the round.—*adj.* **stat'uary** of or suitable for sculpture: sculptured:

statuesque.—*n.* sculpture: a sculptor.—*adjs.* **stat'ued** furnished with statues: sculptured; **statuesque** (*-esk'*) like a statue.—*adv.* **statuesque'ly**.—*ns.* **statuesque'ness; statuette'** a small statue, figurine. [L. *statua—statuēre*, to cause to stand—*stāre*.]

stature *sta'chər, stat'yər, n.* body height: eminence.— *adj.* **stat'ured** having a stature. [L. *statūra*.]

status *stā'təs, n.* state: condition: standing: position, rank, importance, in society or in any group.—**status symbol** a possession or a privilege considered to mark a person out as having a high position in his social group. [L. *stātus*.]

status quo *stā'təs, stat'ōōs, kwō*, (L.) the state in which: the existing condition.

statute *stat'ūt, n.* a law expressly enacted by the legislature: a written law: the act of a corporation or its founder, intended as a permanent rule or law: a bond or other proceeding based on a statute: a hiring-fair. —*adj.* **stat'utory** enacted by statute: depending on statute for its authority.—**stat'ute-book** a record of statutes or enacted laws; **stat'ute-law** law in the form of statutes; **statute mile** see **mile**.—**statute of limitations** a statute prescribing the period of time within which proceedings must be taken to enforce a right or bring a legal action. [L. *statūtum*, that which is set up—*statuēre*.]

staunch¹ *stönch, stönsh, adj.* watertight: stout and firm: firm in principle, pursuit, or support: trusty, hearty, constant, zealous.—*adv.* **staunch'ly**.—*n.* **staunch'ness**. [O.Fr. *estanche*.]

staunch² (*v.t.*). See **stanch**.

stave *stāv, n.* one of the pieces of which a cask or tub is made: a staff, rod, bar, shaft: a staff (*mus.*): a stanza, verse of a song.—*v.t.* to break a stave or the staves of: to break: to burst inward (often with *in*): to delay (e.g. the evil day; with *off*): to ward (off), keep back: to put together, or repair, with staves: to break up:— *pa.t.* and *pa.p.* **staved** or **stove**. [By-form of **staff**.]

staves *stāvz,* plural of **staff** and of **stave.**

stavesacre *stāvz'ā-kər, n.* a tall larkspur whose seeds were formerly used against lice. [O.Fr. *stavesaigre* —L.L. *staphisagria*—Gr. *staphis*, raisins, *agrios*, wild.]

stay *stā, n.* a rope supporting a mast: a guy: a support: a prop: a connecting piece or brace to resist tension: (in *pl.*) a stiff corset (often **pair of stays**): a stopping, bringing or coming to a standstill: a suspension of legal proceeding: delay: a sojourn: duration: staying-power.—*v.t.* to support or incline with a stay or stays: to support: to prop: to abide: to endure: to endure to the end: to stop: to detain: to hold, restrain, check the action of: to allay: to hold back.—*v.i.* to stop: to remain: to tarry: to wait: to be kept waiting: to sojourn: to dwell (*Scot.*):—*pa.t.* and *pa.p.* **stayed**.— *adj.* **stayed** wearing stays.—*n.* **stay'er** one who, or that which, remains, stops, holds, or supports: a person or animal of good lasting or staying qualities for a race.—*n.* and *adj.* **stay'ing**.—*adj.* **stay'-at-home** keeping much at home: untravelled.—*n.* a stay-at-home person.—**stay'ing-power** ability to go on long without flagging; **stay'-maker** a maker of corsets; **staysail** (*stā'sl*) a sail extended on a stay.—**come to stay** to become permanent or established; **stay on** to remain, tarry after the normal time for departing; **stay out** to outstay: to stay to the end of; **stay over** (*coll.*) to remain overnight; **stay put** not to move from the place or position in which one has been put; **stay the course** to endure to the end of the race (*lit.* and *fig.*). [Partly O.E. *stæg*, stay (rope); partly O.Fr. *estayer*, to prop, from the same Gmc. root, partly O.Fr. *ester*—L. *stāre*, to stand.]

stead *sted, n.* a place (now chiefly in compounds and idiomatic phrases): esp. the place which another had or might have: service, avail, advantage.—*v.t.* to avail, help, serve (*arch.*):—*pa.t.* and *pa.p.* **stead'ed**, **stead** (*sted*).—*adj.* **stead'fast** firmly fixed or established: firm: constant: resolute: steady.—*adv.* **stead'-fastly.**—*n.* **stead'fastness.**—*adv.* **stead'ily.**—*ns.* **stead'iness**; **stead'ing** farm-buildings with or without the farmhouse.—*adj.* **stead'y** (*compar.* **stead'ier**, *superl.* **stead'iest**) firm in standing or in place: fixed: stable: constant: resolute: consistent: regular: uniform: sober, industrious.—*v.t.* to make steady: to make or keep firm:—*pr.p.* **stead'ying**; *pa.t.* and *pa.p.* **stead'ied.**—*n.* a rest or support, as for the hand, a tool, or a piece of work: a regular boyfriend or girlfriend (*coll.*).—*interj.* be careful!: keep calm!: hold the present course (*naut.*).—*adj.* **stead'y-going** having, showing steady habits or action.—**steady state** (*astron.*) the theory that the universe is in a steady state showing no overall change.—**go steady** (*coll.*) (esp. of a boy and girl not yet engaged to be married) to have a steady relationship, to go about regularly together; **stand one in good stead** to prove of good service to one; **steady on!** keep calm!: don't be so foolish, hasty, etc. [O.E. *stede*, place; *stedefæst*, steadfast.]

steak *stāk, n.* any of several cuts of beef graded for frying, braising, stewing, etc.: a slice of meat (esp. hindquarters of beef) or fish.—**steak'house** a restaurant specialising in fried or grilled beefsteaks. [O.N. *steik*; *steikja*, to roast on a spit.]

steal *stēl, v.t.* to take by theft, esp. secretly: to take, gain or win by address, by contrivance, unexpectedly, insidiously, gradually, or furtively.—*v.i.* to practise theft: to take feloniously: to pass quietly, unobtrusively, gradually, or surreptitiously:—*pa.t.* **stole**; *pa.p.* **stō'len.**—*n.* (*coll.*) an act of stealing, a theft: something acquired by theft: a bargain, a snip.—*n.* **steal'er.**—*n.* and *adj.* **steal'ing.**—*adv.* **steal'ingly.**— **steal a march** on see **march**[2]; **steal someone's thunder** to make use of another's invention against him: to rob someone of the opportunity of achieving a sensational effect by forestalling him; **steal the show** to show. [O.E. *stelan.*]

stealth *stelth, n.* secret procedure or manner: furtiveness.—*adv.* **stealth'ily.**—*n.* **stealth'iness.**—*adj.* **stealth'y** acted or acting with stealth: furtive. [steal.]

steam *stēm, n.* water in the form of gas or vapour or of a mist or film of liquid drops: steam-power: a spell of travel by steam-power: energy, force, spirit (*fig.*).— *adj.* of, for, using, worked by, steam.—*v.i.* to rise or pass off in steam or vapour: to emit or generate steam, vapour, or smell: (of windows, etc.) to become dimmed with condensed vapour (often with *up*): to move by means of steam-power.—*v.t.* to expose to steam: to cook by means of steam: to dim with vapour.—*adj.* **steamed.**—*n.* **steam'er** one who steams: apparatus for steaming: a steamship: a motor-car, a road-locomotive, fire-engine, etc., worked by steam.—*adv.* **steam'ily.**—*n.* **steam'iness.** —*n.*, *adj.*, and *adv.* **steam'y** of, like, full of, covered with, as if covered with, emitting, steam or vapour.—**steam bath** a steam-filled compartment, e.g. one at a Turkish bath, etc. in which to refresh oneself by sweating, etc., or one in a laboratory for sterilising equipment; **steam'boat**, **steam'ship**, **steam'-vessel** a vessel driven by steam; **steam'-boiler** a boiler for generating steam; **steam's chamber**, **-chest**, **-dome** a chamber above a steam-boiler serving as a reservoir for steam.—*adj.* **steam's driv'en.**—**steam'-engine** any engine worked by steam; **steam'-gauge** a pressure gauge for steam; **steam's hamm'er** a vertical hammer worked by steam; **steam iron** an electric iron having a compartment in which

water is heated to provide steam to damp material; **steam'-jack'et** a hollow casing supplied with steam; **steam'-navvy**, **-shovel** an excavator driven by steam; **steam'-pack'et** a steam-vessel plying between certain ports; **steam'-power** the force or agency of steam when applied to machinery; **steam'-roll'er** a steam-engine with a heavy roller for wheels, used in road-mending, etc.: any weighty crushing force (*fig.*).— *v.t.* (*coll.*) to crush (objections, etc.): to force (e.g. legislation through parliament, etc.).—**steam'-tur'bine** an engine in which expanding steam acts on blades attached to a drum.—**full steam ahead** forward at the greatest speed possible: with maximum effort; **get up steam** to build up steam pressure: to collect one's forces: to become excited; **let off steam** to release steam into the atmosphere: to work off energy: to give vent to anger or annoyance; **steamed up** of windows, etc., dimmed with condensed vapour: indignant (*slang*); **steam open** to open (esp. envelopes) by softening gum by exposure to steam; **under one's own steam** by one's own unaided efforts. [O.E. *stēam.*]

stear-, steat- *stē'ər-, -ar', -ət-, -at'*, in composition, suet, fat.—*n.* **stearate** (*stē'ər-āt*) a salt of stearic acid. —*adj.* **stearic** (*stē-ar'ik*) of or from stearin (**stearic acid** a fatty acid $C_{17}H_{35}COOH$).—*n.* **ste'arin** glyceryl ester of stearic acid: a mixture of stearic and palmitic acids (also **ste'arine**): the solid part of a fat.—*adj.* **ste'arine** made of stearin(e), as candles.—*n.* **steatite** (*stē'ə-tīt*) soapstone.—*adj.* **steatitic** (*-tit'ik*).—*ns.* **steatopygia** (*stē-ə-tō-pī'ji-ə, -pij'i-ə*) an accumulation of fat on the buttocks; **steatō'sis** fatty degeneration. [Gr. *stēar*, *stēatos*, suet.]

steed *stēd, n.* a horse, esp. a spirited horse. [O.E. *stēda*, stud-horse, stallion.]

steel *stēl, n.* iron containing a little carbon with or without other things: a cutting tool or weapon, an instrument, object, or part made of steel, as a steel knife-sharpener, a piece of steel: extreme hardness, staying power, trustworthiness (*fig.*).—*adj.* of or like steel.—*v.t.* to cover or edge with steel: to harden: to nerve: to make obdurate.—*adj.* **steeled** made of, covered, protected, provided or edged with, steel: hardened: nerved.—*ns.* **steel'iness**; **steel'ing.**—*adj.* **steel'y** of or like steel.—**steel band** a West Indian band, using steel drums, etc.—*n.* and *adj.* **steel'-blue** blue like a reflection from steel.—**steel drum** a percussion instrument made from the top of an oil drum, hammered out into a bowl-like shape and faceted so as to produce different notes; **steel'-engrav'ing** engraving on steel plates: an impression or print so got; **steel erector** a spider-man.—*n.* and *adj.* **steel's grey'**, **-gray'** bluish-grey like steel.—**steel'-plate** a plate of steel: one on which a design is engraved: a print from it.—*adj.* **steel'-plat'ed** plated with steel.— **steel'-wool** steel shavings used for cleaning and polishing; **steel'work** work executed in steel: (often in *pl.* form) a factory where steel is made; **steel'worker.** [O.E. *stýle.*]

steelyard *stēl'yärd, n.* a weighing machine consisting of a lever with a short arm for the thing weighed and a long graduated arm on which a single weight moves.

steenbok *stān', stēn'bok, n.* a small S. African antelope.—See also **steinbock**. [Du.—*steen*, stone, *bok*, buck.]

steep[1] *stēp, adj.* rising or descending with great inclination: precipitous: headlong: difficult: excessive, exorbitant.—*n.* a precipitous place.—*v.t.* and *v.t.* **steep'en** to make or become steeper.—*adj.* **steep'ish.** —*adv.* **steep'ly.**—*n.* **steep'ness.** [O.E. *stēap*; cf. **stoop**[1].]

steep[2] *stēp, v.t.* to soak: to wet thoroughly: to saturate: to imbue.—*v.i.* to undergo soaking or thorough wetting.—*n.* a soaking process: a liquid for steeping anything in.—*n.* **steep'er.** [M.E. *stepen.*]

steeple *stēp'l, n.* a church or other tower with or without, including or excluding, a spire: a structure surmounted by a spire: the spire alone.—*adj.* **steep'led** having a steeple or steeples or appearance of steeples.—**steep'lechase** orig. an impromptu horse-race with some visible church-steeple as goal: a horse-race across-country: one over a course with obstacles to be jumped: a foot-race of like kind.—*v.i.* to ride or run in a steeplechase.—**steep'lechaser; steep'le-chasing; steep'lejack** one who repairs steeples and chimney-stalks. [O.E. *stēpel, stȳpel, stīpel,* from root of **steep¹.**]

steer¹ *stēr, n.* a young ox, esp. a castrated one from two to four years old. [O.E. *stēor.*]

steer² *stēr, v.t.* to direct with, or as with, the helm: to guide: to govern.—*v.i.* to direct a ship, cycle, etc., in its course: to be directed, take or follow a course in answer to the helm.—*ns.* **steer'age** act or practice of steering: the effect of a rudder on the ship: part of a passenger ship with lowest fares (also *adj.*); **steer'er; steer'ing.**—**steer'age-way** sufficient movement of a vessel to enable it to be controlled by the helm; **steering column** in a motor vehicle the shaft on which the steering-wheel is mounted; **steering committee** a group who decide what measures shall be brought forward and when; **steer'ing-gear** the mechanism that transmits motion from the steering-wheel; **steer'ing-wheel** the wheel whereby a ship's rudder is turned, or a motor-car, etc., guided; **steers'man** one who steers. —**steer clear of** to avoid. [O.E. *stēoran, stȳran,* to steer.]

steeve *stēv, n.* angular elevation, esp. of a bowsprit.— *v.t.* and *v.i.* to incline to the horizon.

stegosaur *steg'ə-sör, n.* any of several quadrupedal, herbivorous dinosaurs of the Jurassic period, characterised by armour of various sorts.—*adj.* **stegosaur'-ian.**—**Stegosaur'us** a member of this class, having two lines of kite-shaped plates along the backbone. [Gr. *steganos,* covered, watertight, *stegos,* roof.]

stein *stēn, stīn, shtīn, n.* a large beer mug, often earthenware and frequently with a hinged lid [Ger.]

steinbock *stīn'bok, n.* the Alpine ibex: also used for **steenbok.** [Ger. *Stein,* stone, *Bock,* buck.]

stele *stē'lē, n.* an upright stone slab or tablet: (*stē'lē, stēl*) the central cylinder in stems and roots of the higher plants (*bot.*):—*pl.* **stē'lae.**—*adjs.* **stē'lar, stē'lene.** [Gr. *stēlē*—root of *histanai,* to set, stand.]

stellar *stel'ər, adj.* of the stars: of the nature of a star: starry.—*adjs.* **stell'ate** star-shaped: with branches radiating from a point: with sides that intersect one another, giving a starlike effect, as in the pentagram; **stell'ated** stellate: starred.—*adv.* **stell'ately.**—*adjs.* **stellif'erous** having or bearing stars or starlike marks or forms; **stell'ified; stell'iform** star-shaped.—*v.t.* **stell'ify** to turn into a star: to set among the stars.—*n.* **stell'ifying.**—*adjs.* **stell'ular, stell'ulate** like a little star. [L. *stēlla,* a star.]

stelliferous, etc. See stellar.

stem¹ *stem, n.* the leaf-bearing axis of a plant: a stalk: anything stalk-like, as the slender vertical part of a written musical note, of a wine-glass, the winding shaft of a watch: an upright stroke of a letter: the main line (or sometimes a branch) of a family: a race or family: the base of a word, to which inflectional suffixes are added (*philol.*): a curved timber at the prow of a ship: the forepart of a ship.—*v.t.* to provide with a stem: to deprive of stalk or stem: to make way against, breast.—*v.i.* to grow a stem: to spring, take rise.—*adjs.* **stem'less; stemmed.**—**from stem to stern** from one end of a vessel to the other: completely,

throughout. [O.E. *stefn, stemn.*]

stem² *stem, v.t.* to stop, check: to dam: to tamp: to staunch: in skiing, to slow down by pushing the heels apart:—*pr.p.* **stemm'ing;** *pa.t.* and *pa.p.* **stemmed.**— *n.* in skiing, the process of stemming, used in turning. [O.N. *stemma.*]

stembuck *stem'buk,* **stembok** -*bok,* for **steenbok.**

stemma *stem'ə, n.* a garland: a scroll: a pedigree, family tree:—*pl.* **stemm'ata.**—*adj.* **stemm'atous.** [Gr. *stemma,* usu. in pl. *stemmata.*]

sten. See sten gun.

stench *stench, -sh, n.* stink.—*v.t.* to cause to stink.— *adj.* **stench'y.**—**stench'-trap** a device to prevent rise of gases in drains. [O.E. *stenc,* smell (good or bad).]

stencil *sten's(i)l, v.t.* and *v.i.* to paint by brushing over a perforated plate: to make a stencil for producing copies of typewriting or writing:—*pr.p.* **sten'cilling;** *pa.t.* and *pa.p.* **sten'cilled.**—*n.* the plate or the colouring-matter so used: the design or lettering so produced: a piece of waxed paper, etc., on which letters are cut by typewriter or stylus so that ink will pass through.—*adj.* **sten'cilled.**—*ns.* **sten'ciller; sten'-cilling.**—**sten'cil-plate.** [O.Fr. *estinceller,* to spangle—*estincelle*—L. *scintilla,* a spark.]

sten (also **Sten**) **gun** *sten gun,* a small automatic gun. [Shepherd and Turpin, the designers, and Enfield, as in **bren gun.**]

steno- *sten-ō-, -ə-,* in composition, contracted.—*n.* **sten'ograph** a shorthand character or report: a machine for writing shorthand, operated by keyboard.—*v.t.* to write in shorthand.—*n.* **stenog'raph-er.**—*adjs.* **stenograph'ic, -al.**—*adv.* **stenograph'-ically.**—*ns.* **stenog'raphist; stenog'raphy** the art, or any method, of writing very quickly: shorthand.— *adj.* **stenosed** (*sti-nōst'*) morbidly contracted.— *n.* **steno'sis** constriction, narrowing of a tube or passage: constipation.—*adj.* **stenotic** (*sti-not'ik*).—*ns.* **sten'otype** a phonetic typewriter or its use; **sten'otyper, sten'otypist; sten'otypy.** [Gr. *stenos,* narrow.]

Stentor *stent'ör, n.* a very loud-voiced Greek at Troy (*Iliad*), hence (also without *cap.*) a loud-voiced person.—*adj.* **stento'rian.** [Gr. *Stentōr.*]

step *step, n.* a pace: a movement of the leg in walking, running, or dancing: the distance so covered: a footstep: a footfall: a footprint: gait: a small space: a short walk or journey: a degree of a scale: a stage upward or downward: one tread of a stair: a rung of a ladder: a doorstep: something to put the foot on in mounting or dismounting: a stage in discontinuous or stairwise rise or fall: a move towards an end or in a course of proceeding: coincidence in speed and phase: a support for the end of a mast, pivot, or the like: (in *pl.*) walk, direction taken in walking: (in *pl.*) a step-ladder (often a **pair of steps**): (in *pl.*) a flight of stairs. —*v.i.* to advance, retire, mount, or descend by taking a step or steps: to pace: to walk: to walk slowly or gravely: to walk a short distance.—*v.t.* to perform by stepping: to measure by pacing: to arrange or shape stepwise: to set, as a foot (now *U.S.*):—*pr.p.* **stepp'-ing;** *pa.t.* and *pa.p.* **stepped.**—*n.* **stepp'er.**—*adv.* **step'wise** in the manner of steps.—**step'-down** a decrease in rate, quantity, output, etc.—*adj.* reducing voltage: decreasing by stages.—**step'-ladder** a ladder with flat treads and a hinged prop; **stepp'ing-stone** a stone rising above water or mud to afford a passage: a means to gradual progress (*fig.*); **step'-up** an increase in rate, quantity, output, etc.—*adj.* increasing or changing by steps: raising voltage.—**break step** to change the sequence of right and left foot, so as to get out of step; **keep step** to continue in step; **in step** with simultaneous putting forward of the right (or left) feet in marching, etc.: (*fig.*) in conformity or agreement (with others); **out of step** not in step; **step by step** gradually, little by little; **step down** to withdraw, retire, resign, from a position of authority, etc.: to decrease the voltage of: to reduce the rate of; **step in** to enter easily or unexpectedly (also **step into**): to intervene; **step on it** (*slang*; see **gas, juice**) to hurry; **step out** to go out a little way: to increase the length of the step and so the speed: to have a gay social life; **step out of line** to depart from the usual, or accepted, course of action; **step up** to come forward: to build up into steps: to raise by a step or steps: to increase the voltage of: to increase the rate of, as production; **take steps** to take action. [O.E. (Mercian) *steppe* (W.S. *stæpe*).]

step- *step-*, *pfx.* indicating affinity by another marriage or mating.—*ns.* **step'child, -daughter, -son** a wife's or husband's but not one's own child, daughter, son; **step'mother** a father's wife not one's own mother; **step'father** a mother's husband not one's own father; **step'-parent; step'brother, -sister** the son, daughter, of a stepfather or stepmother. [O.E. *stéop-* (as in *stéopmódor*), orig. meaning orphan.]

Stephanotis *stef-ə-nō'tis, n.* a genus of asclepiads of Madagascar, etc., cultivated for their scented flowers: (without *cap.*) any plant of this genus. [Gr. *stephanótis*, fit for a wreath—*stephanos*, a crown, wreath.]

steppe *step, n.* a dry, grassy, generally treeless and uncultivated and sometimes salt plain, as in the south-east of Europe and in Asia. [Russ. *step'*.]

steradian *sti-rā'di-ən, n.* a unit of measurement for solid angles, the angle subtended at the centre of a sphere by an area on its surface numerically equal to the square of the radius. [Gr. *stereos*, solid, and **radian**.]

stercoraceous *stûrk-ə-rā'shəs, adj.* of, of the nature of, dung.—*adj.* **sterc'oral** stercoraceous.—*v.t.* **sterc'orate** to manure. [L. *stercus, -oris*, dung.]

stere *stēr, n.* a timber measure, a cubic metre—about 35·315 cubic feet.—Also in compounds, as **decastere** (*dek'ə-*) 10 steres, **decistere** (*des'i-*) a tenth of a stere. [Fr. *stère*—Gr. *stereos*, solid.]

stereo- *stēr'i-ō-, ster'i-ō-,* in composition solid, hard, three-dimensional.—*n.* **ster'eo** stereophonic reproduction of sound: a piece of stereophonic equipment, such as a record-player, tape-recorder, etc.: a unit comprising such pieces:—*pl.* **ster'eos.**—*adj.* stereophonic.—*n., adj., v.t.,* and *v.i.* a contr. of **stereotype, stereoscope, stereoscopic.**—*ns.* **stereochem'istry** the study of the spatial arrangement of atoms in molecules; **ster'eogram** a picture or diagram suggestive of solidity: a stereographic double picture: a radiogram for reproducing stereophonic records; **ster'eograph** a stereogram (in picture senses).—*adjs.* **stereograph'ic, -al.**—*ns.* **stereog'raphy;** **stereol'somer** an isomer differing only in spatial arrangement of atoms.—*adj.* **stereoisomer'ic.**—*ns.* **stereoisom'erism; stereom'eter** an instrument for measuring specific gravity or for measuring solids.—*adjs.* **stereomet'ric, -al.**—*adv.* **stereomet'rically.**—*n.* **stereom'etry.**—*adj.* **stereophon'ic** giving the effect of sound from different directions in three-dimensional space.—*adv.* **stereophon'ically** by stereophony.—*ns.* **stereoph'ony** stereophonic reproduction of sound; **ster'eoscope** an instrument by which the images of two pictures differing slightly in point of view are seen one by each eye and so give an effect of solidity.—*adjs.* **stereoscop'ic, -al.**—*adv.* **stereoscop'ically.**—*ns.* **stereos'copist; stereos'copy.**—*adjs.* **stereoson'ic** stereophonic; **stereospecif'ic** relating to, or (of atoms) having, a fixed spatial arrangement.—*n.* **ster'eotype** a solid metallic plate for printing, cast from a mould (made of papier-mâché or other material) of movable types: the art, method, or process of

making such plates: a fixed conventionalised representation.—*adj.* pertaining to, or done with, stereotypes.—*v.t.* to make a stereotype of: to print with stereotypes.—*adj.* **ster'eotyped** transferred as letterpress from set-up movable type to a mould, and thence to a metal plate: fixed, unchangeable, as opinions: conventionalised.—*n.* **ster'eotyper.**—*adj.* **stereotyp'ic.**—*ns.* **ster'eotyping; ster'eotypy** the producing of stereotype plates: the repetition of senseless movements, actions or words in cases of insanity, etc. (*med.*).—*adj.* **steric** (*ster'ik*) relating to spatial arrangement of atoms. [Gr. *stereos*, solid.]

steric. See **stereo-**.

sterile *ster'il (U.S. -il), adj.* unfruitful: barren: not producing, or unable to produce, offspring, fruit, seeds, or spores: of a flower, without pistils: sterilised: destitute of ideas or results.—*n.* **sterilisation, -z-** (*ster-i-li-zā'shən*).—*v.t.* **ster'ilise, -ize** to cause to be fruitless: to deprive of power of reproduction: to destroy micro-organisms in.—*ns.* **ster'iliser, -z-** one who, or that which sterilises: apparatus for destroying germs; **steril'ity** quality of being sterile: unfruitfulness, barrenness, in regard to reproduction. [L. *sterilis*, barren.]

sterling *stûr'ling, n.* English, Scottish, or British money of standard value.—*adj.* of sterling or standard English money: genuine: of authority: of thoroughly good character: (of silver) of standard quality, i.e. containing at least 92·5 per cent silver (usu. alloyed with copper).—**sterling area** a group of countries with currencies tied to sterling. [Prob. a coin with a star—O.E. *steorra*, star—some early Norman pennies being so marked.]

stern[1] *stûrn, adj.* severe: austere: rigorous: unrelenting.—*adv.* **stern'ly.**—*n.* **stern'ness.** [O.E. *styrne.*]

stern[2] *stûrn, n.* the hind-part of a vessel: the rump or tail.—*adjs.* **sterned** having a stern (in compounds); **stern'most** farthest astern.—*advs.* **stern'ward** (also *adj.*), **-s.**—**stern'port** a port or opening in the stern of a ship; **stern'-post** the aftermost timber of a ship, supporting the rudder; **stern'-sheet** (usu. in *pl.*) the part of a boat between the stern and the rowers; **stern'way** the backward motion of a vessel; **stern'-wheel'er** (*U.S.*) a small vessel with one large paddle-wheel at the stern. [O.N. *stjörn*, a steering, or lost O.E. equivalent.]

sternum *stûr'nəm, n.* the breast-bone: the under part of a somite in arthropods.—*adj.* **ster'nal.**—*ns.* **ster'nebra** (modelled on *vertebra*) a segment of the breast-bone; **ster'nite** the ventral plate of a segment in arthropods.—*adj.* **sternit'ic.** [Latinised from Gr. *sternon*, chest.]

sternutation *stûr-nū-tā'shən, n.* sneezing.—*adjs.* **sternū'tative, sternū'tatory** that causes sneezing.—*n.* a substance that causes sneezing.—Also **ster'nūtātor.** [L. *sternūtāre*, intens. of *sternuère*, to sneeze.]

sterol *ster'ol, ster', n.* a solid higher alcohol such as cholesterol, ergosterol.—*n.* **ster'oid** (or *ster'*) any of a class of compounds including the sterols, bile acids, adrenal hormones, etc. [See **cholesterol.**]

stertorous *stûr'tər-əs, adj.* with snoring sound.—*adv.* **ster'torously.**—*n.* **ster'torousness.** [L. *stertĕre*, to snore.]

stet *stet, v.t.* to restore after marking for deletion:—*pr.p.* **stett'ing;** *pa.t.* and *pa.p.* **stett'ed.** [L., let it stand, 3rd sing. pres. subj. of *stāre*, to stand; written on a proofsheet with dots under the words to be retained.]

stethoscope *steth'ə-skōp, n.* an instrument for auscultation.—*adjs.* **stethoscopic** (*-skop'ik*).—*adv.* **stethoscop'ically.**—*ns.* **stethoscopist** (*-os'kə-pist*); **stethos'copy.** [Gr. *stēthos*, chest, *skopeein*, to look at, examine.]

Stetson *stet'sn*, *n.* a broad-brimmed felt hat. [Maker's name.]

stevedore *stēv'ə-dōr, -dör, n.* one who loads and unloads shipping vessels.—*v.t.* and *v.i.* to load and unload (cargo, a ship). [Sp. *estibador*, packer—*estibar*, to stow—L. *stīpāre*, to press.]

stew[1] *stū, n.* a room for hot-air baths: a hot bath: an overheated or sweaty state: mental agitation: worry: a dish of stewed food, esp. meat with vegetables.— *v.t.* to bathe in hot air or water: to bathe in sweat: to keep in a swelter or narrow confinement: to simmer or boil slowly with some moisture: to over-infuse.— *v.i.* to swelter: to undergo stewing: to be in a state of worry or agitation.—*adj.* **stewed** having been stewed: drunk (*coll.*).—*n.* **stew'er.**—*n.* and *adj.* **stew'ing.**— *adj.* **stew'y** like a stew: sweltering.—**stew'pan, stew'- pot** one used for stewing.—**in a stew** in a state of worry, agitation; **let someone stew in his own juice** to leave someone alone and await developments, let someone reap the consequences of his own actions. [O.Fr. *estuve* (Fr. *étuve*), stove; prob. conn. with **stove**[1].]

stew[2] *stū, n.* a fish-pond: a fish-tank: an artificial oyster-bed.—**stew'pond.** [O.Fr. *estui* (Fr. *étui*).]

steward *stū'ərd, n.* one who manages the domestic concerns of a family or institution: one who superintends another's affairs, esp. an estate or farm: the manager of the provision department or attendant on passengers in a ship, aircraft, etc.: a college caterer: one who helps in arrangements, marshalling, etc., at races, a dance, a wedding, an entertainment: an overseer: a foreman: the treasurer of a congregation, guild, society, etc.:—*fem.* **stew'ardess.**—*ns.* **stew'ardship, stew'ardry** office of a steward: management. [O.E. *stig-weard—stig*, hall ('sty'), *weard*, ward, keeper.]

sthenic *sthen'ik, adj.* strong, robust: morbidly active. [Gr. *sthenos*, strength.]

stibium *stib'i-əm, n.* antimony.—*adj.* **stib'ial.**—*ns.* **stib'ine** (*-ēn, -in*) antimony hydride, a poisonous gas; **stib'nite** native antimony trisulphide. [L.,—Gr. *stibi, stimmi*—Egypt. *stm* (Copt. *stēm*).]

stich *stik, n.* a line of verse or section of prose of comparable length.—*adj.* **stich'ic** of or pertaining to stichs.—*ns.* **stichol'ogy** metrical theory; **stichom'etry** measurement by lines: division into lines.—**stichous** in composition, having a certain number of lines or rows, e.g. *distichous*. [Gr. *stichos*, a row—*steichein*, to march.]

stick[1] *stik, v.t.* to pierce, transfix: to stab: to spear: to thrust: to fasten by piercing: to insert: to set in position: to set or cover with things fastened on: to cause to adhere: to endure (esp. with *it*) (*coll.*): to function successfully (*coll.*): to bring to a standstill or nonplus: to leave someone (with) (something unpleasant) (*coll.*).—*v.i.* to be fixed by insertion: to jut, protrude: to adhere: to become or remain fixed: to remain: to be detained by an impediment: to jam: to fail to proceed or advance: to scruple: to hold fast, keep resolutely (with *to*):—*pa.t.* **stuck;** *pa.p.* **stuck.** —*n.* a hitch: adhesiveness.—*n.* **stick'er** one who or that which sticks: a piercing weapon: a person or thing difficult to get rid of: a gummed label or poster.— *adv.* **stick'ily** in a gluey, muggy, etc., way.—*n.* **stick'iness.**—*n.* and *adj.* **stick'ing.**—*adj.* **stick'y** adhesive: tenacious: gluey: muggy: difficult (*coll.*): unpleasant (*coll.*).—*v.t.* to make sticky.—**stick'ing-place, -point** the point at which a thing sticks or stays firmly: the point beyond which a thing cannot proceed; **stick'ing-plaster** an adhesive plaster for closing wounds; **stick'-in-the-mud** an old fogy.—Also *adj.*— **stick'up** a hold-up; **sticky end** an unpleasant end, disaster.—*adj.* **stick'y-fing'ered** (*coll.*) prone to pilfering.—**sticky wicket** a difficult situation to cope

with.—*adj.* **stuck'-up'** self-importantly aloof.—**get stuck in(to)** to deal with, consume, attack in a vigorous, aggressive, eager, etc. manner; **stick around** (*coll.*) to remain in the vicinity; **stick at** to hesitate or scruple at (often with *nothing*): to persist at; **stick by** to be firm in supporting, to adhere closely to; **stick 'em up** hold up your hands (or be shot); **stick in one's throat** to be difficult, or against one's conscience, for one to countenance; **stick out** to project: to be obvious: to continue to resist; **stick out for** to insist upon; **stick to** to persevere in holding to; **stick together** to be allies: to support each other; **stick up** to stand up: to waylay and plunder; **stick up for** to speak or act in defence of; **stick with** to remain with: to force (a person) to cope with (something unpleasant)— often in passive, i.e. **be stuck with; stuck for** unable to proceed because of the lack of; **stuck on** enamoured of. [O.E. *stician*; cf. **stick**[2], **stitch**.]

stick[2] *stik, n.* a rod of wood, esp. for walking with or for beating: a twig: anything shaped like a rod of wood: a timber tree or trunk: a piece of firewood: a tally: an instrument for beating a percussion instrument: an instrument for playing hockey or other game: a bow for a fiddle, or the wooden part of it: a person of stiff manner: one lacking enterprise: a rod: a control-rod of an aeroplane: a group of bombs, or of paratroops, released at one time from an aeroplane: a piece of furniture (usu. in *pl.*): a support for a candle: (in *pl.*) hurdles in steeple-chasing: blame, criticism (*slang*).—*adj.* in the form of a stick: made of sticks.— *v.t.* to furnish or set with sticks:—*pa.t., pa.p.* **sticked.** —**stick'-in'sect** twig-like insect.—**big stick** force, coercion; **give someone stick** (*slang*) to censure, punish someone; **in a cleft stick** in a dilemma; **right or wrong end of the stick** a true or mistaken understanding of the situation; **the sticks** rural areas, the backwoods. [O.E. *sticca*.]

stickle *stik'l, v.i.* to contend, stand up (with *for*): to be scrupulous or obstinately punctilious.—*n.* **stick'ler** a punctilious and pertinacious insister or contender, esp. for something trifling. [Prob. M.E. *stightle*— O.E. *stihtan*, to set in order.]

stickleback *stik'l-bak, n.* a small spiny-backed riverfish. [O.E. *sticel*, sting, prick, and **back**.]

stiff *stif, adj.* not easily bent: rigid: wanting in suppleness: moved or moving with difficulty or friction: dead: approaching solidity: thick, viscous, not fluid: dense, difficult to mould or cut: resistant: difficult: toilsome: pertinacious: stubborn: formidable: strong: firm, high, or inclining to rise (in price, etc.): excessive: not natural and easy: constrained: formal: certain (not to run, to win, to lose; *slang*): excessively bored (with a pun on *board*).—*adv.* stiffly: stark: very, extremely (*coll.*).—*n.* (*slang*) one who, that which, is stiff: a corpse.—*v.t.* and *v.i.* **stiff'en** to make or become stiff or stiffer.—*n.* **stiff'ener** one who, or that which stiffens: a strong alcoholic drink (*coll.*).— *n.* and *adj.* **stiff'ening.**—*adj.* **stiff'ish.**—*adv.* **stiff'ly.** —*n.* **stiff'ness.**—**stiff'-neck** a drawing down of the head towards the shoulder, often due to cold or draught.—*adj.* **stiff'-necked** obstinate: haughty: formal and unnatural.—**stiff upper lip** see **lip; stiff with** (*coll.*) full of, crowded with. [O.E. *stīf*, stiff.]

stifle[1] *stī'fl, v.t.* to stop the breath of by foul air or other means: to make breathing difficult for: to suffocate, smother: to choke down: to suppress: to repress: to make stifling.—*v.i.* to suffocate.—*n.* a stifling atmosphere, smell, or condition.—*adj.* **sti'fled.** —*n.* **sti'fler.**—*n.* and *adj.* **sti'fling** (*-fling*).—*adv.* **sti'flingly.**

stifle[2] *stī'fl, n.* the joint of a horse, dog, etc., answering to the human knee.—**sti'fle-bone** the knee-cap; **sti'fle-joint.**

stigma *stig'mə, n.* a brand: a mark of infamy: a disgrace or reproach attached to any one: any special mark: a spot: a bleeding spot: a scar: a spot sensitive to light: the part of a carpel that receives pollen (*bot.*): (in *pl.*) the marks of Christ's wounds or marks resembling them, claimed to have been impressed on the bodies of certain persons, as Francis of Assisi in 1224:—*pl.* **stig'mata;** also (esp. *bot.* or *fig.*) **stig'mas.**—*adj.* **stigmatic** (*-mat'ik*) of, pertaining to, of the nature of, a stigma: marked or branded with a stigma: giving infamy or reproach: not astigmatic.—*n.* one who has received the stigmata.—*adj.* **stigmat'ical.**—*adv.* **stigmat'ically.**—*n.* **stigmatisa'tion,** *-z-* act of stigmatising: production of stigmata or of bleeding spots upon the body, as by hypnotism.—*v.t.* **stig'matise, -ize** to mark with a stigma or the stigmata: to brand, denounce, describe condemnatorily (with *as*).—*ns.* **stig'matism** impression of the stigmata: anastigmatism; **stig'matist** one impressed with the stigmata. [Gr. *stigma, -atos,* tattoo-mark, brand, *stigmē,* a point.]

stilb, *n.* the CGS unit of intrinsic brightness, one candela/cm^2.—*n.* **stilbene** (*stil'bēn*) a crystalline hydrocarbon, used in dye-manufacture. [Gr. *stilbein,* to shine.]

stilboestrol, U.S. **stilbestrol,** *stil-bēs'trəl, n.* a synthetic oestrogen. [Gr. *stilbos,* glistening and **oestrus.**]

stile[1] *stīl, n.* a step, or set of steps, for climbing over a wall or fence. [O.E. *stigel.*]

stile[2] *stīl, n.* an upright member in framing or panelling. [Perh. Du. *stijl,* pillar, doorpost.]

stiletto *sti-let'ō, n.* a dagger with a narrow blade: a pointed instrument for making eyelet-holes: a stiletto heel:—*pl.* **stilett'os.**—*v.t.* to stab with a stiletto:—*pr.p.* **stilett'oing;** *pa.t.* and *pa.p.* **stilett'oed.**—stiletto **heel** a high, thin heel on a woman's shoe. [It., dim. of *stilo,* a dagger—L. *stilus,* a style.]

still[1] *stil, adj.* motionless: inactive: silent: calm: quiet: not sparkling or effervescing.—*v.t.* to quiet: to silence: to appease: to restrain.—*v.i.* to become still. —*adv.* motionlessly: inactively: quietly: up to the present time or time in question: as before: yet, even (usu. with a comparative): even so, even then: nevertheless, for all that.—*n.* calm: quiet: an ordinary photograph, not a cinematographic one.—*n.* **still'er.** —*n.* and *adj.* **still'ing.**—*n.* **still'ness.**—*adj.* **still'y** (*poet.*) still: quiet: calm.—*adv.* **stil'ly** (*arch.*) silently: gently.—**still'-birth** birth of the already dead: anything born without life.—*adj.* **still'-born** dead when born (also *fig.*).—**still'-life** the class of pictures representing inanimate objects: a picture of this class:—*pl.* **still'-lifes.**—Also *adj.*—**still and all** (*coll.*) nevertheless. [O.E. *stille,* quiet, calm, stable.]

still[2] *stil, n.* an apparatus for distillation.—**still'-room** an apartment where liquors, preserves, and the like are kept, and where tea, etc., is prepared for the table: a housekeeper's pantry; **still'-room-maid.** [Aphetic for **distil.**]

stillage *stil'ij, n.* a frame, stand, or stool for keeping things off the floor: a box-like container for transporting goods. [Prob. Du. *stellage, stelling–stellen,* to place.]

stilt *stilt, n.* a thin wooden prop with a foot-rest enabling one to walk above the ground: a tall support: a very long-legged wading bird (*Himantopus candidus* or other species) akin to the avocets (also **stilt'-bird, -plov'er**).—*v.t.* to raise on stilts or as if on stilts.—*adj.* **stilt'ed** elevated as if on stilts: stiff and pompous.—*adv.* **stilt'edly.**—*ns* **stilt'edness; stilt'er; stilt'iness; stilt'ing.** [M.E. *stilte.*]

Stilton *stil'tən, n.* a rich white, often blue-veined, cheese first sold chiefly at *Stilton* in Cambridgeshire.

stimulus *stim'ū-ləs, n.* an action, influence, or agency that produces a response in a living organism: anything that rouses to action or increased action:—*pl.* **stim'uli.**—*adj.* **stim'ulable** responsive to stimulus.— *n.* **stim'ulancy.**—*adj.* **stim'ulant** stimulating: increasing or exciting vital action.—*n.* anything that stimulates or excites: a stimulating drug: alcoholic liquor. —*v.t.* **stim'ulate** to incite: to instigate: to excite: to produce increased action in (*physiol.*).—*v.i.* to act as a stimulant.—*adj.* **stim'ulating.**—*n.* **stimula'tion.**— *adj.* **stim'ulative** tending to stimulate.—*n.* that which stimulates or excites.—*n.* **stim'ulator** one who stimulates: an instrument for applying a stimulus. [L. *stimulus,* a goad.]

sting *sting, n.* in some plants and animals a weapon (hair, modified ovipositor, fin-ray, tooth, etc.) that pierces and injects poison: the act of inserting a sting: the pain or the wound caused: any sharp, tingling, or irritating pain or its cause (also *fig.*): stinging power: pungency: a goad: an incitement.—*v.t.* to pierce, wound, pain, or incite with or as if with a sting: to cause or allow anything to sting: to rob, cheat, or involve in expense (*slang*).—*v.i.* to have or use a power of stinging: to have a stinging feeling:—*pa.t.* and *pa.p.* **stung.**—*adj.* **stinged** having a sting.—*n.* **sting'er.**—*n.* and *adj.* **sting'ing.**—*adv.* **sting'ingly.**— *adjs.* **sting'less; sting'y** (*coll.*).—**sting'-ray** (*U.S.* and *Austr.* **stingaree** *sting'gə-rē, -ə-rē,* or *-rē'*) a ray (Trygon, etc.) with a formidable barbed dorsal spine on its tail.—**take the sting out of** (*coll.*) to soften the pain of (*lit.* and *fig.*). [O.E. *sting,* puncture, *stingan,* to pierce.]

stingy[1] *stin'ji, adj.* niggardly.—*adv.* **stin'gily.**—*n.* **stin'giness.** [Prob. **sting.**]

stingy[2]. See **sting.**

stink *stingk, v.i.* to give out a strong, offensive smell: to be offensive, have a bad reputation, suggest or imply evil or dishonesty (*fig.*).—*v.t.* to impart a bad smell to: to drive by an ill smell:—*pa.t.* **stank, stunk;** *pa.p.* **stunk.**—*n.* an offensive smell.—*n.* **stink'er** one who, or that which, stinks: a disagreeable person or thing (*coll.*): a petrel of offensive smell.—*adj.* **stink'ing** which stinks (*lit.* and *fig.*).—*adv.* very, extremely (*coll.*).—Also *n.*—*adv.* **stink'ingly.**— **stink'-bomb** a usu. small bomb-like container which releases ill-smelling gases when exploded; **stink'horn** a stinking fungus, *Phallus impudicus;* **stink'-wood** the ill-smelling wood of various trees, esp. *Ocotea bullata* of S. Africa.—**like stink** (*coll.*) very much, to a great extent: intensely; **raise a stink** to complain: to cause trouble, esp. disagreeable publicity; **stink out** (*coll.*) to drive out by a bad smell: to fill (a room, etc.) with a bad smell. [O.E. *stincan,* to smell (well or ill).]

stint[1] *stint, v.t.* to restrain (*arch.* or *dial.*): to check (*arch.*): to limit: to apportion (esp. pasturage): to be niggardly with or towards: to allot stingily.—*n.* restraint, restriction: proportion allotted, fixed amount: allowance: a set task: a (conventional) day's work.—*adj.* **stint'ed.**—*adv.* **stint'edly.**—*ns.* **stint'edness; stint'er.**—*n.* and *adj.* **stint'ing.**—*adv.* **stint'ingly.** [O E. *styntan,* to dull—*stunt,* stupid.]

stint[2] *stint, n.* the dunlin or other small sandpiper.

stipe *stīp, n.* a stalk, esp. of a fungal fruit-body, a fern-leaf, or an ovary.—Also **stipes** (*stī'pēz*); *pl.* **stipites** *stip'i-tēz*).—*adj.* **stipitate** (*stip'*). [L. *stīpes, -itis,* post, stock.]

stipel *stī'pl, n.* a stipule-like appendage at the base of a leaflet.—*adj.* **stipellate** (*stī'pəl-āt, stip-el'āt*) having stipels. [Dim. from **stipule.**]

stipend *stī'pənd, n* a soldier's pay: a salary, esp. a

Scottish parish minister's: a periodical allowance.—
adj. **stipendiary** (*stī-*, *sti-pen'di-ə-ri*) receiving
stipend.—*n.* one who performs services for a salary,
esp. a paid magistrate [L. *stīpendium—stips*,
payment, dole, *pendĕre*, to weigh.]
stipites, stipitate. See **stipe.**
stipple *stip'l*, *v.t.* to engrave, paint, draw, etc., in dots
or separate touches.—*n.* painting, engraving, etc., in
this way: the effect so produced.—*adj.* **stipp'led.**—
ns. **stipp'ler; stipp'ling.** [Du. *stippelen*, dim. of
stippen, to dot.]
stipulate *stip'ū-lāt*, *v.t.* to set or require as a condition
or essential part of an agreement: to guarantee (*rare*).
—*v.i.* to make stipulations.—*ns.* **stipulā'tion** act of
stipulating: a contract: a condition of agreement: a
requiring of such a condition; **stip'ulator.**—*adj.* **stip'-**
ulatory (*-ə-tər-i*). [L. *stipulārī, -ātus*, prob.—Old L.
stipulus, firm, conn. *stīpāre*, press firm.]
stipule *stip'ūl*, *n.* a paired, usu. leafy, appendage at a
leaf-base.—*adjs.* **stipulā'ceous, stip'ular, -y; stip'u-**
lāte, stip'uled. [L. *stipula*, straw, stalk, dim. of
stīpes; new meaning assigned by Linnaeus.]
stir [1] *stûr v.t.* to set in motion: to move around: to move
(something, esp. in liquid or powder form) around by
continuous or repeated, usu. circular, movements of
a spoon or other implement through it, e.g. in order
to mix its constituents: to disturb: to rouse: to move
to activity: to excite.—*v.i.* to make a movement: to
begin to move: to be able to be stirred: to go about: to
be active or excited: (esp. in *pr.p.*) to be out of bed: to
go forth: to cause trouble or dissension (*coll.*):—*pr.p.*
stirr'ing; *pa.t.* and *pa.p.* **stirred.**—*n.* movement:
slight movement: activity: commotion: sensation: an
act of stirring.—*adjs.* **stir'less** without stir; **stirred.**—
n. **stirr'er.**—*n.* and *adj.* **stirr'ing.**—*adv.* **stirr'ingly.**
—*v.t.* and *v.i.* **stir'-fry'** to fry (food) rapidly while
stirring it in the pan.—**stir up** to excite: to incite: to
arouse: to mix by stirring. [O.E. *styrian.*]
stir [2] *stûr n.* (*slang*) *n.* prison. [Perh. O.E. *stēor, stȳr,*
punishment, or various Romany words.]
stirk *stûrk, n.* a yearling or young ox or cow. [O.E.
stirc, calf.]
stirps *stûrps, n.* family, race: a permanent variety:
pedigree:—*pl.* **stirpes** (*stûr'pēz*). [L. *stirps, stirpis.*]
stirrup *stir'əp, n.* a support for a rider's foot: a foot-
rest, clamp, support, of more or less similar shape:
the stirrup-bone: a rope secured to a yard, having a
thimble in its lower end for reeving a foot-rope
(*naut.*).—**stirr'up-bone** the stapes; **stirr'up-cup** a cup
taken on horseback on departing, or arriving;
stirr'up-pump a portable pump held in position by
the foot in a rest. [O.E. *stigrāp—stīgan,* to mount,
rāp, rope.]
stitch *stich, n.* a sharp pricking pain, now esp. in the
intercostal muscles: a complete movement of the
needle in sewing, knitting, surgery, or the like: a loop
or portion of thread, etc., so used: a mode of stitching: the least scrap of clothing, sails, etc.—*v.t.* to
join, adorn, or enclose, with stitches.—*v.i.* to sew.—
adj. **stitched.**—*ns.* **stitch'er; stitch'wort** any plant of
the chickweed genus (*Stellaria*), once thought good
for stitches in the side.—**in stitches** in pained helplessness with laughter. [O.E. *stice,* prick; cf. **stick** [1].]
stoa *stō'ə, n.* a portico or covered colonnade:—*pl.*
stō'as, stō'ae, stō'ai (*-ī*). [Gr. *stŏā.*]
stoat *stōt, n.* a small carnivorous mammal of the weasel
family with black-tipped tail, called ermine in its
white northern winter coat. [M.E. *stote.*]
stochastic *stə-kas'tik, adj.* random. [Gr. *sto-*
chastikos, skilful in aiming.]
stock *stok, n.* a trunk or main stem: the perennial part
of a herbaceous plant: the rooted trunk that receives
a graft: a log: a post: a block: a stump: an upright

beam: anything fixed, solid and senseless: the
wooden part of a gun: a handle: stock-gillyflower (see
below): a stiff band worn as a cravat: (in *pl.*) a device
for holding a delinquent by the ankles, and often
wrists: (in *pl.*) a framework on which a ship is built: a
box or trough: source: race: kindred: family: a fund:
capital of a company, divisible into shares: repute,
estimation (*fig.*): shares of a public debt: (in *pl.*) public funds: supply, store, equipment: a repertoire of
plays done by a stock company (see below): the
animals kept on a farm: supply of goods for sale: the
undealt part of a pack of cards or set of dominoes: raw
material: liquor from simmered meat, bones, etc.—
v.t. to store: to keep for sale: to put in the stocks: to
fit with a stock: to supply or furnish with stock (e.g. a
river with fish): to root up.—*adj.* concerned with
stock or stocks: kept in stock: conventionally used,
standard: hence banal, trite: used for breeding purposes.—*adv.* **stock'ily.**—*ns.* **stock'iness; stock'ist** one
who keeps a commodity in stock.—*adjs.* **stock'less;**
stock'y thickset, strong-stemmed: solid.—**stock'-**
breeder one who raises livestock; **stock'-breeding;**
stock'broker a stock exchange member who buys and
sells stocks or shares for clients (**stockbroker belt** the
area outside a city, esp. that to the south of London,
in which wealthy businessmen live); **stock'broking;**
stock company (*U.S.*) a permanent repertory company attached to a theatre; **stock'-dove** a dove like a
small wood-pigeon; **stock exchange** a building for the
buying and selling of stocks and shares: an association
of persons transacting such business: (with *caps.*) the
institution in London where such business is done;
stock'-farmer a farmer who rears livestock; **stock'-**
gill'yflower, now usu. **stock,** a favourite cruciferous
garden plant (*Matthiola incana*; from its half-shrubby
character); **stock'holder** one who holds stocks in the
public funds, or in a company: a person who owns
livestock (*Austr.*); **stock'-in-trade** all the goods a
shopkeeper has for sale: standard equipment or
devices necessary for a particular trade or profession:
a person's basic intellectual and emotional resources
(often implying inadequacy or triteness); **stock'-**
jobber a stock exchange member who deals only with
other members (in some special group of securities): a
stockbroker (*U.S.*): an unscrupulous speculator;
stock'-jobbery, -jobbing; stock'-list a list of stocks
and current prices regularly issued; **stock'man** (esp.
Austr.) man in charge of farm-stock; **stock'-market** a
stock exchange: stock exchange business; **stock'pile**
heap of road-metal, ore, etc.: reserve supply.—Also
v.t.—**stock'piling** accumulating reserves, as of raw
materials; **stock'-pot** the pot in which the stock for
soup is kept; **stock'-room** a store-room.—*adj.* and
adv. **stock'-still'** utterly still (as a post or stock).—
stock'taking inventorying and valuation of stock;
stock'-whip a herdsman's whip with short handle and
long lash; **stock'yard** a large yard with pens, stables,
etc., where cattle are kept for slaughter, market, etc.
—**in, out of stock** available, not available, for sale; **on**
the stocks in preparation; **stock-car racing** motor
racing in which modified standard models of cars are
used, not cars built as racers; **take stock** (**of**) to make
an inventory of goods on hand: to make an estimate
of; **take stock in** to trust to, attach importance to.
[O.E. *stocc,* a stick.]
stockade *stok-ād', n.* a barrier of stakes.—*v.t.* to
defend with a stockade. [Fr. *estacade*—Sp. *esta-*
cada; cf. **stake** [1].]
stockfish *stok'fish, n.* unsalted dried hake, cod, etc.,
commonly beaten with a stick before cooking.
[Prob. Du. *stokvisch.*]
stocking *stok'ing, n.* a close covering for the foot and
lower leg: distinctive colouring or feathering of an

animal's leg.—*n.* **stockinet'**, **-ette'**, **stockingette'** an elastic knitted fabric for undergarments, etc.—*adj* **stock'inged** wearing stockings (but usu. not shoes).— **stock'ing-fill'er** a small present for a Christmas stocking; **stock'ing-mask'** a nylon stocking pulled over the head to distort and so disguise the features; **stock'ing-sole'**; **stock'ing-stitch** a style of knitting in which a row of plain stitch alternates with a row of purl.—**in one's stocking-feet**, **-soles** with stockings but no shoes. [**stock.**]

stodge *stoj*, *v.t.* to stuff, cram, gorge.—*n.* cloggy stuff: heavy, often uninteresting, food.—*adv.* **stodg'ily.**— *n.* **stodg'iness.**—*adj.* **stodg'y** heavy and cloggy solemnly dull. [Perh. imit.]

stoep *stoo̅p*, (*S.Afr.*) *n.* a platform along the front, and sometimes the sides, of a house: a verandah.—U.S **stoop.** [Du.; cf. **step.**]

Stoic *sto̅'ik*, *n.* a disciple of the philosopher Zeno (d. c. 261 B C.), who taught in the *Stoa Poikilē* (Painted Porch) at Athens.—*adjs.* **Sto̅'ic**, **-al** pertaining to the Stoics, or to their opinions: (without *cap.*) indifferent to pleasure or pain.—*adv.* **sto̅'ically.**— *ns.* **sto̅'icalness**; **sto̅'icism** (*-sizm*) the philosophy of the Stoics: indifference to pleasure or pain: limitation of wants: austere impassivity. [Gr. *Stōikos—stōā*, a porch.]

stoich(e)iology *stoi-kī-ol'ə-ji*, *n.* the branch of biology that deals with the elements comprising animal tissues.—*adj.* **stoich(e)iolog'ical.**—*n* **stoich(e)iometry** (*stoi-kī-om'i-tri*) the branch of chemistry that deals with the numerical proportions in which substances react.—*adj.* **stoich(e)iomet'ric.** [Gr. *stoicheion*, an element.]

stoke *stōk*, *v.t.* to feed with fuel.—*v.i.* to act as stoker. —*n.* **stok'er** one who, or that which, feeds a furnace with fuel.—**stoke'hold** a ship's furnace chamber: a stoke-hole; **stoke'-hole** the space about the mouth of a furnace.—**stoke up** to fuel a fire or furnace (also *fig.*): to make a good meal (*fig.*). [Du. *stoker*, stoker—*stoken*, to stoke.]

stokes *stōks*, *n.* the CGS unit of kinematic viscosity — Also (esp. *U.S.*) **stoke.** [Sir G. *Stokes* (1819–1903), British physicist.]

STOL *stol*, *n.* a system by which aircraft land and take off over a short distance: an aircraft operating by this system.—See also **VTOL.** [short *take-off* and *landing.*]

stole¹ *stōl*, *pa.t.* of **steal.**

stole² *stōl*, *n.* a narrow vestment worn on the shoulders, hanging down in front: a woman's outer garment of similar form. [O.E. *stole*—L *stōla*, a Roman matron's long robe—Gr. *stolē.*]

stolen *stōl'ən*, *pa.p.* of **steal.**—Also *adj.*

stolid *stol'id*, *adj.* impassive: blockish: unemotional. —*ns.* **stolid'ity**, **stol'idness.**—*adv.* **stol'idly.** [L *stolidus.*]

stolon *stō'lən*, *n.* a shoot from the base of a plant, rooting and budding at the nodes: a stemlike structure or outgrowth (*zool.*).—*adj.* **stōlonif'erous** producing stolons. [L. *stolō*, *-ōnis*, twig, sucker.]

stoma *stō'mə*, *n.* a mouthlike opening, esp. one by which gases pass through the epidermis of green parts of a plant:—*pl.* **stō'mata.**—*adjs.* **stomatal** (*stōm'*, *stom'ə-tl*), **stomat'ic.**—*ns.* **stomati'tis** inflammation of the mucous membrane of the mouth; **stomatol'ogy** study of the mouth.—**-stomous** in composition, with a particular kind of mouth. [Gr. *stōma*, *-atos*, mouth.]

stomach *stum'ək*, *n.* the strong muscular bag into which food passes when swallowed, and where it is principally digested: the cavity in any animal for the digestion of its food: loosely or euphemistically, the belly: appetite, relish for food, inclination generally:

disposition, spirit, courage, pride, spleen.—*v.t.* to brook or put up with· to digest —*adj.* of the stomach.—*adjs.* **stom'achal; stom'ached.**—*ns* **stom'acher** (*-chər*, *-kər*) a covering or ornament for the chest, esp. one worn under the lacing of a bodice; **stom'achful** as much as the stomach will hold (*pl.* **stom'achfuls**).—*adj.* **stomachic** (*stəm-ak'ik*) of the stomach: good for the stomach —*n* a stomachic medicine.—**stom'ach-ache**; **stom'ach-pump** a syringe with a flexible tube for withdrawing fluids from the stomach, or injecting them into it. [O Fr. *estomac*, L. *stomachus*, Gr. *stomachos*, throat, later stomach —*stoma*, a mouth.]

stomatal, etc. See **stoma.**

stomp *stomp*, *v.i* to stamp (*coll.*): to dance (*coll.*).— *n.* an early jazz composition with heavily accented rhythm: a lively dance with foot stamping: a stamp (*coll.*) [Variant of **stamp.**]

-stomy *-stəm-i*, in composition, used in naming a surgical operation to form a new opening into an organ. [Gr. *stoma*, a mouth.]

stone *stōn*, *n.* a detached piece of rock, usu small: the matter of which rocks consist: a gem: a tombstone: a printer's table for imposing: a concretion: a diseased state characterised by formation of a concretion in the body: (now *slang*) a testicle. a hard fruit kernel: (with *pl.* **stone**) a standard weight of 14 lb avoirdupois.—*adj.* of stone: of the colour of stone: of stoneware.—*v.t.* to pelt with stones· to free from stones: to lay or wall with stones —*adjs.* **stoned** having, containing, or freed from, a stone or stones: very drunk, or very high on drugs (*slang*); **stone'less.** —*n.* **ston'er** one who stones: one who weighs, or a horse that carries, so many stone.—*adv.* **ston'ily.**—*n.* **ston'iness.**—*adj.* **ston'y** of or like stone: abounding with stones: hard: pitiless: obdurate: stony-broke.— **Stone Age** a stage of culture before the general use of metal, divided into the Old Stone Age (Palaeolithic) and the New (Neolithic) —*adj.* **stone'-blind** completely blind.—**stone'chat** a little black, ruddy and white bird of furzy places, with a note like the clicking of two stones.—*adj* **stone'-cold** cold as a stone.—*n* and *adj.* **stone'-colour** grey —*adj.* **stone'-coloured.**—**stone'crop** any plant of the wall-pepper genus (*Sedum*); **stone'-cur'lew** a large plover, the thick-knee, **stone'-cutter** one who hews stone· a machine for dressing stone, **stone'-cutting.**—*adjs* **stone'-dead**, **stone'-deaf** dead, deaf, as a stone.— **stone'fish** a poisonous tropical fish of the Scorpaenidae, which resembles a stone on the seabed; **stone'-fly** an insect (*Perla*) whose larvae live under stones in streams; **stone'-fruit** a fruit with a stone.— *adj.* **stone'ground** of flour, ground between millstones.—**stone'-ma'son** a mason who works with stone; **stone('s)'-throw** the distance a stone may be thrown; **stonewall'** parliamentary obstruction (*Austr.*): defensive play in cricket.—*v.t.* to obstruct: to block: to offer wall-like resistance.—**stonewall'er; stonewall'ing; stone'ware** a coarse kind of potter's ware baked hard and glazed: a high-fired, vitrified, non-porous ceramic material or objects made of it, **stone'work** work in stone —*adjs.* **stony-broke'** (*slang*) penniless, or nearly so; **ston'y-heart'ed** hardhearted.—**leave no stone unturned** to do everything that can be done in order to secure the effect desired; **stone me!, stone the crows!** (*slang*) expressions of astonishment [O.E. *stān.*]

stonker *stong'kər* (*slang*), *v.t.* to kill, destroy, overthrow, thwart.—*n* **stonk** (*stongk*; *mil. slang*; backformation) intense bombardment.

stood *stood*, *pa.t.*, *pa.p.* of **stand.**

stooge *stoo̅j*, (*slang*) *n.* a performer speaking from the auditorium: an actor's feeder: a stage butt: a subordinate or drudge: a scapegoat.—Also *v.i.*

stook *stŏŏk*, *n.* a shock of sheaves, set up in the field.—*v.t.* to set up in stooks.—*n.* **stook'er.** [Cf. L.G. *stuke*, bundle.]

stool *stŏŏl*, *n.* a seat without a back: a low support for the feet or knees: a seat used in evacuating the bowels: defecation: faeces: a stand: a stump from which sprouts shoot up: a growth of shoots: a piece of wood to which a bird is fastened as a decoy.—*v.i.* to evacuate the bowels: to put forth shoots: to lure wildfowl with a stool.—**stool'ball** an old game resembling cricket; **stool'-pigeon** a decoy-pigeon: a decoy: a police informer (shortened form **stool'ie**; *slang*).—**fall between two stools** to lose both possibilities by hesitating between them, or trying for both. [O.E. *stōl.*]

stoop *stŏŏp*, *v.i.* to bend the body forward: to lean forward: to submit: to descend from rank or dignity: to condescend: to lower oneself by unworthy behaviour: to swoop down, as a bird of prey.—*v.t.* to bend, incline, lower, or direct downward.—*n.* a bending of the body: inclination forward: descent: condescension: a swoop.—*adj.* **stooped** having a stoop, bent.—*n.* **stoop'er.**—*adj.* **stoop'ing.**—*adv.* **stoop'ingly.** [O.E. *stūpian.*]

stoop². See stoup.

stoop³. American spelling of **stoep**.

stop *stop*, *v.t.* to snuff, block, plug, choke, close up (often with *up*): to obstruct: to render impassable: to hinder or prevent the passage of: to bring to a standstill: to bring down, hit with a shot: to cause to cease: to counter: to restrain: to withhold: to hinder: to prevent: to cease from, leave off, discontinue: to limit the vibrating length of, esp. by pressure of a finger (*mus.*): to punctuate: to adjust the aperture of, with a diaphragm.—*v.i.* to come to a standstill, halt: to cease: to desist: to come to an end: to stay, tarry, sojourn (*coll.*):—*pr.p.* **stopp'ing;** *pa.t.* and *pa.p.* **stopped.**—*n.* act of stopping: state of being stopped: cessation: a halt: a pause: a halting-place: hindrance: obstacle: interruption: a contrivance that limits motion: a card that interrupts the run of play: a diaphragm: the stopping of an instrument or string: a fret on a lute or guitar: a finger-hole, a key for covering it, or other means of altering pitch or tone: a set of organ pipes of uniform tone quality: a knob operating a lever for bringing them into use: a sound requiring complete closure of the breath passage, a mute (*phon.*; also **stop'-consonant**): a punctuation mark.—*adj.* **stop'less.**—*n.* **stopp'age** act of stopping: state of being stopped: stopping of work, as for a strike: obstruction: an amount stopped off pay.—*adj.* **stopped.**—*n.* **stopp'er** one who stops: that which stops: a plug.—*v.t.* to close or secure with a stopper.—*n.* **stopp'ing** the action of one who or that which stops in any sense (**double stopping** simultaneous stopping of and playing on two strings): stuffing or filling material, esp. for teeth.—**stop'-bath** a substance in which a photographic negative or print is immersed in order to halt the action of the developer; **stop'-cock** a short pipe opened and stopped by turning a key or handle: loosely, the key or handle; **stop'-gap** a temporary expedient or substitute.—Also *adj.*—*adj.* **stop'-go'** (of policy) alternately discouraging and encouraging forward movement.—**stop'-off, stop'-o'ver** a break of journey; **stopp'ing-out** use in places of a protective covering against acids in etching, against light in photography; **stopp'ing-place; stop'-press** late news inserted in a news-paper after printing has begun: a space for it.—Also *adj.*—**stop'-watch** an accurate watch readily started and stopped, used in timing a race, etc.—**pull out all the stops** to express with as much emotion as possible: to act with great energy; **stop off, stop over, stop in,** U.S. **stop by,** to break one's journey, pay a visit to (usu. with *at*). [O.E. *stoppian*, found in the compound *forstoppian*, to stop up—L. *stuppa*, tow—Gr. *styppē*.]

stope *stŏp*, *n.* a step-like excavation in mining.—*v.t.* to excavate, or extract in this way.—*n.* **stop'ing.** [Perh. conn. with **step**.]

storable, storage. See **store.**

storax *stō'raks*, *stŏ'*, *n.* the resin of *Styrax officinalis*, once used in medicine: now that of *Liquidambar orientale* (*liquid storax*). [L. *stŏrax*—Gr. *stŷrax*.]

store *stōr*, *stŏr*, *n.* a hoard: a stock laid up: sufficiency or abundance: keeping: a storehouse: a shop: a co-operative shop or one with many departments or branches: value, esteem: a computer memory unit, in which programme and data are stored: (in *pl.*) supplies of provisions, ammunition, etc., for an army, ship, etc.—*adj.* of a store: sold in a shop, ready-made.—*v.t.* to stock, furnish, supply: to lay up, keep in reserve: to deposit in a repository: to give storage to: to put (data) into a computer memory.—*adj.* **stor'able.**—*ns.* **stor'age** placing, accommodation, reservation, or safe-keeping, in store: reservation in the form of potential energy: the keeping of information in a computer memory unit: charge for keeping goods in store; **stor'er.—storage battery** an accumulator; **storage capacity** the maximum amount of information that can be held in a computer store; **storage heater** an electric heater which stores up heat during the off-peak periods; **store'house** a house for storing goods of any kind: a repository: a treasury; **store'keeper** a man in charge of stores: a shopkeeper (chiefly *U.S.*); **store'room** a room in which stores are kept: space for storing.—**in store** in hoard for future use, ready for supply: in reserve, awaiting; **set store by** to value greatly. [O.Fr. *estor*, *estoire*—L. *instaurāre*, to provide.]

storey (also now less frequently **story**) *stō'ri*, *stŏ'*, *n.* all that part of a building on the same floor: a tier:—*pl.* **stor'eys.**—*adj.* **stor'eyed** (**stor'ied**) having storeys.—**first storey** the ground floor; **second storey** the first floor, etc. [Prob. same word orig. as **story¹**.]

storiated. See **story¹**.

storied. See under **story¹** and **storey.**

stork *stŏrk*, *n.* a large white and black wading bird (*Ciconia alba*) with a great red bill and red legs: the bringer of babies (*facet.*): any member of its genus or of its family (akin to the ibises).—**stork's'-bill** a genus (*Erodium*) of the geranium family, with beaked fruit: also applied to Pelargonium. [O.E. *storc.*]

storm *stŏrm*, *n.* a violent commotion of the atmosphere: a tempest: a wind just short of a hurricane: any intense meteorological phenomenon: a violent commotion or outbreak of any kind: a paroxysm: a violent assault (*mil.*): calamity (*fig.*).—*v.i.* to be stormy: to rage: to rush violently or in attack: to upbraid passionately.—*v.t.* to take or try to take by assault.—*adv.* **storm'ily.**—*n.* **storm'iness.**—*n.* and *adj.* **storm'ing.**—*adjs.* **storm'less; storm'y** having many storms: agitated with furious winds: boisterous: violent: passionate.—*adj.* **storm'bound** delayed, cut off, confined to port by storms.—**storm'-centre** the position of lowest pressure in a cyclonic storm: any focus of controversy or strife; **storm'-cloud; storm'-cock** the missel-thrush; **storm'-cone** a cone, drum, hoisted as a storm-signal; **storm'-lantern** a lantern with flame protected from wind and weather; **storm'-pet'rel** or (popularly) **storm'y-pet'rel** see **petrel.**—*adj.* **storm'proof** proof against storms or storming.—**storm'-trooper.**—*n.pl.* **storm'-troops** shock-troops: a body formed in Germany by Adolf Hitler, disbanded 1934.—**storm'-warning; storm'-window** a window raised above the roof, slated above and at the sides: an additional outer casement.—**a storm in a teacup** (or other small vessel) a great commotion in a narrow sphere, or about a trifle; **take by storm** to take by assault: to captivate totally and instantly (*fig.*). [O.E. *storm*.]

Storting, Storthing *stōr'ting, stōr', n.* the legislative assembly of Norway. [Norw. *stor*, great, *ting* (O.N. *thing*), assembly.]

story[1] *stō'ri, stō', n.* legend: a narrative of incidents in their sequence: a fictitious narrative: a tale: an anecdote: the plot of a novel or drama: a theme: an account, report, statement, allegation: a news article: a lie, a fib.—*v.t.* to tell or describe historically, to relate: to adorn with scenes from history. —*adjs.* **sto'riated** decorated with elaborate ornamental designs; **sto'ried** told or celebrated in a story: having a history: adorned with scenes from history.— **sto'ry-book** a book of tales true or fictitious.—*adj.* rather luckier or happier than in real life.—**story line** the main plot of a novel, film, television series, etc., or line along which the plot is to develop; **sto'ry-teller** one who relates tales: a liar; **sto'ry-telling.—the same old story** an often-repeated event or situation; **the story goes** it is generally said. [A.Fr. *estorie*—L. *historia*.]

story[2]. See **storey**.

stoup, stoop *stōōp n.* a drinking vessel (*arch.*); a holy-water vessel. [Cf. O.N. *staup* and Du. *stoop*; O.E. *stēap*.]

stout *stowt, adj.* resolute: dauntless: vigorous: enduring: robust: strong: thick: fat.—*adv.* stoutly.—*n.* extra-strong porter.—*adj.* **stout'ish.**—*adv.* **stout'ly.** —*n.* **stout'ness.**—*adj.* **stout'-heart'ed.**—*adv.* **stout's heart'edly.**—**stout'-heart'edness.** [O.Fr. *estout*, bold—Du. *stout*.]

stove[1] *stōv, n.* a closed heating or cooking apparatus: a fire-grate: a kiln or oven for various manufacturing operations: a drying room.—*v.t.* to put, keep, heat, or dry in a stove.—**stove enamel** a type of heat-proof enamel produced by heating an enamelled article in a stove; **stove'pipe** a metal pipe for carrying smoke and gases from a stove: a tall silk hat (*U.S.*; in full **stovepipe hat**). [O.E. *stofa*.]

stove[2] *stōv, pa.t.* and *pa.p.* of **stave.**

stow *stō, v.t.* to place, put, lodge: to put away: to store: to desist from (*stow it*, stop it; *slang*): to pack: to have room for: to arrange.—*v.i.* (with *away*) to hide as a stowaway.—*ns.* **stow'age** act or manner of stowing: a place for stowing things: money paid for stowing goods: things stowed; **stow'er; stow'ing.—stow'away** one who hides in a ship, etc., to get a passage.—*adj.* travelling as a stowaway: that can be packed up and stored, carried, etc. [O.E. *stōw*, place.]

strabism *strā'bizm,* **strabismus** *stra-biz'mas, ns.* a muscular defect of the eye, preventing parallel vision: a squint.—*adjs.* **strabis'mal, strabis'mic, -al.** [Gr. *strābos* and *strabismos*, squinting.]

strad. See **Stradivarius.**

straddle *strad'l, v.i.* to part the legs wide: to sit, stand, or walk with legs far apart: to seem favourable to both sides.—*v.t.* to bestride: to set far apart: to overshoot and then shoot short of, in order to get the range.—*n.* act of straddling: an attempt to fill a noncommittal position: a stock transaction in which the buyer obtains the privilege of either a *put* or a *call*: a style of high jump in which the legs straddle the bar while the body is parallel to it.—*adv.* astride. [Freq. of **stride.**]

Stradivarius *strad-i-vā'ri-as,* or *-vā',* **Stradivari** *-vā' rē,* (*coll.*) **strad,** *ns.* a stringed instrument, usu. a violin, made by Antonio *Stradivari* (1644-1737) of Cremona.

strafe, straff *sträf* (in U.S. *sträf*), (originally war slang

of 1914) *v.t.* to punish: to bombard: to rake with machine-gun fire from low-flying aeroplanes.—*n.* an attack. [Ger. *strafen*, to punish.]

straggle *strag'l, v.i.* to wander from one's company or course: to be absent without leave: to stretch dispersedly or sprawlingly: to grow irregularly and untidily.—*n.* **stragg'ler.**—*n.* and *adj.* **stragg'ling.**— *adv.* **stragg'lingly.**—*adj.* **stragg'ly** straggling: irregularly spread out.

straight *strāt, adj.* uncurved: in a right line: direct: upright: flat, horizontal: in good order: accurate: frank and honourable: respectably conducted: balanced, even, square: settled: downright: normal: conventional in tastes, opinions, etc. (*slang*): heterosexual (*slang*): in sequence (*poker*): in succession (*tennis*): of a theatrical part, not comic: undiluted, neat: uninterrupted: consistent.—*n.* a straight condition: good behaviour: a straight line, part, course, flight, esp. the last part of a racecourse: a heterosexual person (*slang*).—*adv.* in a straight line: directly: all the way: immediately: upright: outspokenly: honestly.—*v.t.* and *v.i.* **straight'en** to make or become straight.—*n.* **straight'ener.**—*adj.* **straight'ish.**—*adv.* **straight'ly** in a straight line or manner: straightway.—*n.* **straight'ness.**—*adv.* **straight'way** (*arch.*) directly: immediately: without loss of time.—**straight angle** two right angles; **straight'edge** a strip or stick for testing straightness or drawing straight lines; **straight fight** esp. in politics, a contest in which only two persons or sides take part. —*adj.* **straightfor'ward** going forward in a straight course: without digression: without evasion: honest: frank.—*adv.* straightforwardly.—*adv.* **straightfor'wardly.**—**straightfor'wardness.**—**straight man** an actor who acts as stooge to a comedian.—*adj.* **straight'-out** (*U.S.*) out-and-out.—**straight play** one without music: a serious drama as opposed to a comedy.—**go straight** to give up criminal activities; **keep a straight bat** (*fig.*) to behave honourably; **keep a straight face** to refrain from smiling; **straight away, off** immediately; **straighten out** to disentangle, resolve; **the straight and narrow** (path) the virtuous way of life. [O.E. *streht*, pa.p. of *streccan*; see **stretch.**]

strain[1] *strān, v.t.* to stretch: to draw tight: to draw with force: to exert to the utmost: to injure by overtasking: to force unnaturally, unduly, or amiss: to change in form or bulk by subjecting to a stress: to press to oneself, embrace: to squeeze, press: to grip, grasp tightly: to compress: to restrain: to squeeze out, express: to filter (esp. coarsely).—*v.i.* to make violent efforts: to tug: to retch: to have difficulty in swallowing or accepting (with *at*): to make efforts at evacuation: to percolate, filter.—*n.* the act of straining: a violent effort: an injury by straining, esp. a wrenching of the muscles: any change of form or bulk under stress: pitch, height: a section of a melody: a melody: emotional tone, key, manner.—*adj.* **strained** having been strained: tense, forced or unnatural.—*adv.* **strain'edly** (or *strānd'li*).—*n.* **strain'er** one who, or that which, strains: a sieve, colander, etc.—*n.* and *adj.* **strain'ing.** [O.Fr. *estraindre*—L. *stringĕre*, to stretch tight.]

strain[2] *strān, n.* breed, race, stock, line of descent: natural, esp. inherited, tendency or element in one's character. [App. O.E. (*ge*)*strēon*, gain, getting, begetting.]

strait *strāt, adj.* (*rare*) close: narrow.—*n.* a narrow part, place, or passage, esp. (often in *pl.*) by water: (usu. in *pl.*) difficulty, distress, hardship.—*v.t.* **strait'**-**en** to distress: to put into difficulties.—*adj.* **strait'-ened.—strait'-jacket, -waist'coat** a garment for restraint of the violently insane: anything which inhibits freedom of movement or initiative (*fig.*).—*v.t.* and *v.i.* **strait'-lace**.—*adj.* **strait'-laced'** narrow in principles of behaviour: prudish. [O.Fr. *estreit* (Fr. *étroit*)—L. *strictus*, pa.p. of *stringĕre*, to draw tight.]

strake *strāk*, *n.* a strip: one breadth of plank or plate in a ship, from stem to stern: a section of a cart-wheel rim. [Akin to **stretch**.]

stramonium *stra-mō′ni-əm*, *n.* the thorn-apple: a drug like belladonna got from its seeds and leaves. [Mod. L., poss. from a Tatar word.]

strand[1] *strand*, *n.* a sea or lake margin (*poet.*).—*v.t.* and *v.i.* to run aground.—*adj.* **strand'ed** driven on shore: left helpless without further resource. [O.E. *strand*.]

strand[2] *strand*, *n.* a yarn, thread, fibre, or wire twisted or plaited with others to form a rope, cord, or the like: a thread, filament: a tress.—*v.t.* to form of strands.

strange *strānj*, *adj.* alien: from elsewhere: not of one's own place, family, or circle: not one's own: not formerly known or experienced: unfamiliar: interestingly unusual: odd: like a stranger: distant or reserved: unacquainted, unversed.—*adv.* **strange'ly**.—*ns.* **strange'ness** the quality of being strange: a quantum number which represents unexplained delay in strong interactions between certain elementary particles; **strān'ger** a foreigner: one whose home is elsewhere: one unknown or little known: a visitor: a non-member: an outsider: a person not concerned: one without knowledge, experience, or familiarity (with *to*).—**strange particles** K-mesons and hyperons, which have a non-zero strangeness (q.v.) number. [O.Fr. *estrange* (Fr. *étrange*)—L. *extrāneus*—*extrā*, beyond.]

strangle *strang′gl*, *v.t.* to kill by compressing the throat: to choke: to constrict: to choke back, suppress, stifle.—*ns.* **strang'lement**; **strang'ler**.—*n.pl.* **strang'les** a contagious disease of horses.—**strang'lehold** a choking hold in wrestling: a strong repressive influence. [O.Fr. *estrangler* (Fr. *étrangler*)—L. *strangulāre*; see next word.]

strangulate *strang′gū-lāt*, *v.t.* to strangle: to compress so as to suppress or suspend function.—*adj.* **strang'ulated** strangled: constricted, much narrowed.—*n.* **strangulā'tion**. [L. *strangulāre*, *-ātum*—Gr. *strangalaein*, to strangle, *strangos*, twisted.]

strangury *strang′gū-ri*, *n.* painful retention of, or difficulty in discharging, urine. [L. *strangūria*—Gr. *strangouriā*—*stranx*, a drop, trickle, *ouron*, urine.]

strap *strap*, *n.* a narrow strip, usu. of leather: a thong: a metal band or plate for holding things in position: a looped band: a string or long cluster: anything strap-shaped: an application of the strap in punishment.—*v.t.* to beat or bind with a strap: to make suffer from scarcity, esp. of money.—*v.i.* to work vigorously: to admit of or suffer strapping:—*pr.p.* **strapp'ing**; *pa.t.* and *pa.p.* **strapped**.—*adj.* **strap'less** without a strap or straps, esp. (of woman's dress) without shoulder-straps.—*ns.* **strapp'er** one who works with straps: a tall robust person; **strapp'ing** fastening with a strap: materials for straps: strengthening bands: a thrashing.—*adj.* tall and robust.—*adj.* **strapp'y** having (many) straps (used esp. of clothing and footwear).—**strap'-hanger** standing passenger in a train, bus, etc., who holds on to a strap for safety; **strap'-work** (*archit.*) ornamentation of crossed and interlaced fillets.—**strapped for** (*slang*) short of. [Northern form of **strop**.]

strata *strä′tə*, *strä′*, *pl.* of **stratum**.

stratagem *strat′ə-jəm*, *n.* a plan for deceiving an enemy or gaining an advantage: any artifice generally. [Fr. *stratagème*—L.—Gr. *stratēgēma*, a piece of generalship, trick; see next word.]

strategy *strat′i-ji*, *n.* generalship, or the art of conducting a campaign and manoeuvring an army: artifice or finesse generally.—*adjs.* **strategic** (*strat-ēj′ik*, *arch. -ej′ik*), **-al** pertaining to, dictated by, of value for, strategy.—*n.sing.* **strate'gics** strategy.—*adv.* **strateg'ically**.—*n.* **strat'egist** one skilled in strategy.—**strategic position** a position that gives its holder a decisive advantage. [Gr. *stratēgia*—*stratēgos*, a general—*stratos*, an army, *agein*, to lead.]

strath *strath*, *n.* in the Highlands of Scotland, a broad valley. [Gael. *srath*, a valley—L. *strāta*, a street.]

strathspey *strath-spā′*, *n.* a Scottish dance, allied to and danced alternately with the reel: a tune for it, differing from the reel in being slower. [*Strathspey*, the valley of the *Spey*.]

stratify, etc. See under **stratum**.

stratum *strä′təm*, *strä′*, *n.* a layer: a bed of sedimentary rock: a layer of cells in living tissue: a region determined by height or depth: a level of society:—*pl.* **stra'ta**.—*n.* **stratifica'tion** (*strat-*).—*adjs.* **strat'ified**; **strat'iform** layered: forming a layer.—*v.t.* **strat'ify** to deposit or form in layers:—*pr.p.* **strat'ifying**; *pa.t.* and *pa.p.* **strat'ified**.—*ns.* **stratig'rapher**, **stratig'raphist**.—*adjs.* **stratigraph'ic**, **-al**.—*adv.* **stratigraph'ically**.—*n.* **stratig'raphy** the geological study of strata and their succession: stratigraphical features.—*adj.* **stra'tose** in layers.—*n.* **stratosphere** (*strat′* or *strāt′ō-sfēr*) a region of the atmosphere beginning about 4½ to 10 miles up, in which temperature does not fall as altitude increases.—*adjs.* **stratospheric** (*-sfer′ik*); **stra'tous** of stratus.—*n.* **stra'tus** a wide-extended horizontal sheet of low cloud.—**stra'to-cū'mulus** a cloud in large globular or rolled masses, not rain-bringing. [L. *strātum*, *-ī*, *strātus*, *-ūs*, something spread, a bedcover, horse-cloth—*sternĕre*, *strātum*, to spread.]

straw *strö*, *n.* the stalk of corn: dried stalks, etc., of corn, or of peas or buckwheat, etc. (*collec.*): a tube for sucking up a beverage: a trifle, a whit.—*adj.* of straw: of the colour of straw.—*adj.* **straw'y** of or like straw.—**straw'board** a thick cardboard, made of straw; **straw boss** (*U.S.*) an assistant, temporary, or unofficial, foreman.—*n.* and *adj.* **straw'-colour** delicate yellow.—*adj.* **straw'-coloured**.—**straw'-hat**; **straw man** a man of straw (see **man**); **straw poll** an unofficial vote taken to get some idea of the general trend of opinion.—**catch, clutch, grasp at a straw** (or **at straws**) to resort to an inadequate remedy in desperation; **man of straw** see **man**; **straw in the wind** a sign of possible future developments. [O.E. *strēaw*.]

strawberry *strö′bə-ri*, *-bri*, *n.* the fruit (botanically the enlarged receptacle) of any species of the rosaceous genus *Fragaria*: the plant bearing it.—*adj.* of the colour (pinkish-red) or flavour of strawberries.—**strawberry blonde** a woman with reddish-yellow hair; **straw'berry-mark** a reddish birthmark; **straw'berry-tom'a'to** the Cape gooseberry; **straw'berry-tree** *Arbutus unedo*, a small tree (wild at Killarney) of the heath family, with red berries. [O.E. *strēawberige*, possibly from the chaffy appearance of the achenes.]

stray *strā*, *v.i.* to wander: to wander away, esp. from control, or from the right way: to get lost.—*n.* a domestic animal that has strayed or is lost: a straggler: a waif: anything occurring casually, isolatedly, out of place.—*adj.* gone astray: casual: isolated.—*adj.* strayed wandering, gone astray.—*n.* **stray'er**.—*n.* and *adj.* **stray'ing**. [O.Fr. *estraier*, to wander—L. *extrā*, beyond, *vagārī*, to wander.]

streak *strēk*, *n.* an irregular stripe: the colour of a mineral in powder, seen in a scratch: a scratch: a strain, vein, interfused or pervading character: a line of bacteria, etc. (placed) on a culture medium: the line or course as of a flash of lightning: a rush, swift dash: a course, succession, as of luck.—*v.t.* to mark with streaks.—*v.i.* to become streaked: to rush past: to run naked, or in a state of indecent undress, in public (*coll.*).—*adj.* **streaked** streaky, striped.—*n.* **streak'er.**—*adv.* **streak'ily.**—*ns.* **streak'iness**; **streak'ing.**—*adj.* **streak'y** marked with streaks, striped: fat and lean in alternate layers: uneven in quality.—**like a streak** like (a flash of) lightning. [O.E. *strica*, a stroke, line, mark.]

stream *strēm, n.* a running water: a river or brook, esp. a rivulet: a flow or moving succession of anything: a large number or quantity coming continuously: a division of pupils on the roll of a school consisting of those of roughly equal ability or similar bent, or those following a particular course of study: any similar division of people: a current: a drift: a tendency.—*v.i.* to flow, issue, or stretch, in a stream: to pour out abundantly: to float out, trail: to wash for ore.—*v.t.* to discharge in a stream: to wave, fly: to wash for ore: to divide (pupils, etc.) into streams.—*n.* **stream'er** a pennon, ribbon, plume, or the like streaming or flowing in the wind: a luminous beam or band of light, as of the aurora: one who washes detritus for gold or tin: a headline: a narrow roll of coloured paper.— *adj.* **stream'ered.**—*n.* **stream'iness**—*n.* and *adj.* **stream'ing.**—*adv.* **stream'ingly.**—*adj.* **stream'y** abounding in streams: flowing in a stream.—**stream'- line** a line followed by a streaming fluid: the natural course of air-streams.—*v.t.* to make streamlined.— *adj.* **stream'lined** having boundaries following streamlines so as to offer minimum resistance: a term of commendation with a variety of meanings, as efficient, without waste of effort, up-to-the-minute, of superior type, graceful, etc. (*slang*).—**stream of consciousness** the continuous succession of thoughts, emotions, and feelings, both vague and well-defined, that forms an individual's conscious experience. [O.E. *strēam.*]

street *strēt, n.* a paved road, esp. Roman (*ant.*): a road lined with houses, broader than a lane, including or excluding the houses and the footways: those who live in a street or are on the street.—*adj.* of or characteristic of the street, esp. in densely populated cities, or to the people who frequent them, esp. the poor, the homeless, prostitutes, petty criminals, etc. (also in compounds).—**street'-car** (*U.S.*) a tram-car; **street cries** the slogans of hawkers; **street'-door** the door that opens on the street; **street'lamp, street'light; street'-sweep'er** one who, or that which, sweeps the streets clean; **street'-walker** any one who walks in the streets, esp. a whore.—*n.* and *adj.* **street'-walking.**— **street'way** the roadway.—*adj.* **street'wise** familiar with the ways, needs, etc. of the people who live and work on the city streets, e.g. the poor, the homeless, the petty criminals, etc.—**not in the same street as** much inferior to; **on the street** (*slang*) homeless, destitute; **on the streets** (*slang*) practising prostitution; **streets ahead of** far superior to; **streets apart** very different; **up one's street** (*fig.*) in the region in which one's tastes, knowledge, abilities, lie. [O.E. *strēt*—L. *strāta* (*via*), a paved (way), from *sternĕre*, *strātum*, to spread.]

Strelitzia *strel-it'si-a, n.* a S. African genus of the banana family, with large showy flowers: (without *cap.*) a plant of the genus. [From Queen Charlotte, wife of George III, of the house of Mecklenburg-Strelitz.]

strength *strength, n.* the quality, condition, or degree of being strong: the power of action or resistance: the ability to withstand great pressure or force: force: vigour: a strong place, stronghold: a beneficial characteristic: numbers: a military force: the number on the muster-roll, or the normal number.—*v.t.* **strength'en** to make strong or stronger: to confirm. —*v.i.* to become stronger.—*n.* **strength'ener.**— *n.* and *adj.* **strength'ening.**—*adjs.* **strength'ful; strength'less** without strength.—**go from strength to strength** to move successfully forward, through frequent triumphs or achievements; **on** or **upon the strength of** in reliance upon: founding upon. [O.E. *strengthu—strang*, strong.]

strenuous *stren'ū-as, adj.* active: vigorous: urgent. zealous: necessitating exertion.—*ns.* **strenuity** (*stri-nū'i-ti*); **strenuosity** (*stren-ū-os'i-ti*) strenuousness: a straining after effect.—*adv.* **stren'uously.**—*n* **stren'uousness.** [L. *strēnuus*.]

strep. See strepto-.

strepto- *strep'tō-*, in composition, bent, flexible, twisted.—*adjs.* **streptococcal** (*-kok'l*), **streptococcic** (*-kok'sik*).—*ns.* **Streptococcus** (*-kok'as*) a genus of bacteria forming bent chains, certain species of which can cause scarlet fever, pneumonia, etc.: (without *cap.*) any bacterium of this genus (*coll.* shortening **strep**):—*pl.* **streptococ'ci** (*-sī*); **streptomycin** (*-mī'sin*) an antibiotic got from fission fungi. [Gr. *streptos*, twisted, flexible.]

stress *stres, n.* strain: a constraining influence: physical, emotional or mental pressure: force: the system of forces applied to a body: the insistent assigning of weight or importance: emphasis: relative force of utterance.—*v.t.* to apply stress to: to lay stress on: to emphasise.—*adjs.* **stressed; stress'ful; stress'less.** [Aphetic for **distress.**]

stretch *strech, v.t.* to extend (in space or time): to draw out: to expand, make longer or wider by tension: to spread out: to reach out: to exaggerate, strain, or carry further than is right: to lay at full length: to lay out: to place so as to reach from point to point or across a space: to hang (*slang*).—*v.i.* to be drawn out: to reach: to be extensible without breaking: to straighten and extend fully one's body and limbs: to exaggerate.—*n.* the act of stretching: the state of being stretched: reach: extension: utmost extent: strain: undue straining: exaggeration: extensibility: a single spell: a continuous journey: an area, expanse: a straight part of a course: a term of imprisonment (*slang*).—*adj.* capable of being stretched.—*adj.* **stretched.**—*n.* **stretch'er** one who stretches: anything used for stretching e.g. gloves, hats, etc.: a frame for stretching a painter's canvas: a frame for carrying the sick or wounded: a cross-bar or horizontal member: a brick, etc., placed with its length in the direction of the wall.—*v.t.* to transport (a sick or wounded person) by stretcher.—*adj.* **stretch'less** no longer liable to stretch; **stretch'y** able, apt, or inclined to stretch.—**stretch'er-bearer** one who carries injured from the field.—**at a stretch** continuously, without interruption: with difficulty; **stretch one's legs** to take a walk, esp. for exercise. [O.E. *streccan.*]

stretto *stret'ō, n.* part of a fugue in which subject and answer are brought closely together: (also **strett'a:**— *pl.* **strett'e** -*tā*) a passage, esp. a coda, in quicker time: —*pl.* **strett'i** (-*ē*). [It., contracted.]

strew *strōō v.t.* to scatter loosely: to cover dispersedly:—*pa.t.* strewed; *pa.p.* strewed, strewn. —*n.* an assemblage of things strewn.—*ns.* **strew'age; strew'er; strew'ing.** [O.E. *strewian, streowian.*]

strewth *strōō th, interj.* a vulg. minced oath (for *God's truth*).

stria *strī'a, strē'a, n.* a fine streak, furrow, or threadlike line, usu. parallel to others: one of the fillets between the flutes of columns, etc. (*archit.*):— *pl.* **stri'ae** (*strī'ē, strē'ī*).—*v.t.* **stri'ate** to mark with striae.—*adjs.* **stri'ate, -d.**—*ns.* **striā'tion; stri'ature** mode of striation. [L. *stria*, a furrow, flute of a column.]

stricken *strik'n, pa.p.* of **strike**, and *adj.*, struck, now chiefly poet. in U.K. or in special senses and phrases: wounded in the chase: afflicted.

strickle *strik'l, n.* an instrument for levelling the top of a measure of grain or shaping the surface of a mould: a tool for sharpening scythes. [O.E. *stricel.*]

strict *strikt, adj.* restricted: exact: rigorous: allowing no laxity: austere: observing exact rules, regular: severe: exactly observed: thoroughgoing.—*adj.* **strict'ish.**—*adv.* **strict'ly.**—*ns.* **strict'ness; strict'ure** a binding: a closure: tightness: abnormal narrowing of a passage (*med.*): a (now only adverse) remark or criticism.—*adj.* **strict'ured** morbidly narrowed. [L. *strictus*, pa.p. of *stringĕre*, to draw tight.]

stridden. See **stride**.

stride *strīd, v.i.* to walk with long steps: to take a long step: to straddle.—*v.t.* to stride over: to bestride:— *pa.t.* **strōde;** *pa.p.* **stridd'en** (*strid'n*).—*n.* a long step: a striding gait: the length of a long step.—*adv.* **stride'ways** astride.—**be into, get into, hit one's stride** to achieve one's normal or expected level of efficiency, degree of success, etc ; **make great strides** to make rapid progress; **take in one's stride** to accomplish without undue effort or difficulty. [O.E. *strīdan*, to stride.]

stridence *strī'dəns, -cy -dən-si, ns.* harshness of tone.— *adj.* **stri'dent** loud and grating.—*adv.* **stri'dently.**— *n.* **stri'dor** a harsh shrill sound: a harsh whistling sound of obstructed breathing (*med.*).—*adj.* **stridūlant** (*strid'*) stridulating: pertaining to stridor. —*adv.* **strid'ulantly.**—*v.i.* **strid'ūlate** to make a chirping or scraping sound, like a grasshopper.—*ns.* **stridūlā'tion** the act of stridulating; **strid'ūlātor** an insect that makes a sound by scraping: the organ it uses.—*adjs.* **strid'ūlatory; strid'ūlous.** [L. *stridēre* and *strīdēre*, to creak.]

strife *strīf, n.* contention: a contest: variance: striving. [O.Fr. *estrif;* see **strive**.]

striga *strī'gə, n.* a stria: a bristle:—*pl.* **strigae** (*strī'jē*). —*adjs.* **stri'gate; stri'gose** (or -*gōs'*). [L. *striga*, a swath, a furrow, a flute of a column.]

strigil *strij'il, n.* a flesh-scraper: in bees, a mechanism for cleaning the antennae. [L. *strigilis.*]

strigose. See **striga**.

strike *strīk, v.t.* to draw, describe, give direction to (as a line, path): to delete, cancel: to constitute (orig. by cutting down a list): to mark off: to lower (as a sail, flag, tent): to take down the tents of (*strike camp*): to dismantle: to remove: to leave off or refuse to continue: to deal, deliver, or inflict: to give a blow to or with: to hit, smite: to come into forcible contact with: to impinge on: to bring forcibly into contact: to impel: to put, send, move, render, or produce by a blow or stroke: to render as if by a blow: to sound by percussion or otherwise: to announce by a bell: to dash: to pierce: to stamp: to coin: to print: to impress: to impress favourably: to thrust in or down, cause to penetrate: to visit, afflict: to assail, affect: to affect strongly or suddenly: to arrive at, estimate, compute, fix, settle (as a balance, an average, prices): to make (a compact or agreement), to ratify: to come upon: to reach: to achieve: to occur to: to assume: to hook by a quick turn of the wrist: to cause to strike.—*v.i.* to make one's way: to set out: to take a direction or course: to dart, shoot, pass quickly: to penetrate: to jerk the line suddenly in order to impale the hook in the mouth of a fish: to put forth roots: to chance, alight, come by chance: to interpose: to deal or aim a blow, perform a stroke: to sound or be sounded or

announced by a bell: to hit out: to seize the bait: to strike something, as a rock, sail, flag: to touch: to run aground: to admit of striking: to go on strike:—*pa.t.* **struck;** *pa.p.* **struck,** *arch.* **strick'en** (q.v.).—*n.* a stroke, striking: an attack, esp. by aircraft: a raid: the direction of a horizontal line at right angles to the dip of a bed (*geol.*): a find (as of oil), stroke of luck: a cessation of work, or other obstructive refusal to act normally, as a means of putting pressure on employers, etc.: the part that receives the bolt of a lock: in tenpin bowling, the knocking down of all the pins with the first ball bowled, or the score resulting from this: a ball missed by the batter, or a similar event counting equivalently against him (*baseball*): the position of facing the bowling (*cricket*).—*ns.* **strik'er** one who, that which, strikes: a batsman (*baseball*): a forward, attacker (*football*): the batsman facing the bowling (*cricket*); **strik'ing.**—*adj.* that strikes or can strike: impressive, arresting, noticeable.—*adv.* **strik'ingly.**—*n.* **strik'ingness.**— *adj.* **strike'-bound** closed or similarly affected because of a strike.—**strike'-breaker** one who works during a strike or who does the work of a striker esp. if brought in with a view to defeating the strike; **strike'-breaking; strike'-pay** an allowance paid by a trade union to members on strike; **strik'ing-circle** (*hockey*) the area in front of goal from within which the ball must be hit in order to score.—**be struck off** of doctors, lawyers, etc., to have one's name removed from the professional register because of misconduct; **on strike** taking part in a strike: of a batsman, facing the bowling (*cricket*); **strike a match** to light it by friction or a grazing stroke; **strike at** to attempt to strike, aim a blow at; **strike back** to return a blow; **strike down** to fell: to make ill or cause to die; **strike home** to strike right to the point aimed at; **strike it rich** (*coll.*) to make a sudden large financial gain, e.g. through discovering a mineral deposit, etc.; **strike off** to erase from an account, to deduct: to remove (from a roll, register, etc.): to print: to separate by a blow; **strike oil** to find petroleum when boring for it: to make a lucky hit; **strike out** to efface: to bring into light: to direct one's course boldly outwards: to dismiss or be dismissed by means of three strikes (*baseball*; *n.* **strike'out**); **strike through** to delete with a stroke of the pen; **strike up** to begin to beat, sing, or play: to begin (as an acquaintance); **struck on** inclined to be enamoured of; **take strike** (*cricket*) of a batsman, to prepare to face the bowling. [O.E. *strican*, to stroke, go, move.]

Strine *strīn, n.* Australian speech. [Alleged pron. of *Australian.*]

string *string, n.* a small cord or a piece of it: cord of any size: a piece of anything for tying: anything of like character, as a tendon, nerve, fibre: a leash: a shoelace (*U.S.*): a stretched piece of catgut, silk, wire, or other material in a musical instrument: (in *pl.*) the stringed instruments played by a bow in an orchestra or other combination: (in *pl.*) their players: anything on which things are threaded: a set of things threaded together or arranged as if threaded: a train, succession, file, or series: a drove, number, of horses, camels, etc.: a long bunch: a sloping joist supporting the steps in wooden stairs: a string-course: (in *pl.*) awkward conditions or limitations.—*adj.* of, like or for string or strings.—*v.t.* to fit or furnish with a string or strings: tie up: to hang: to extend like a string: to put on or in a string: to take the strings or stringy parts off: to hoax, humbug (*slang*).—*v.i.* to stretch out into a long line: to form into strings:—*pa.t.* and *pa.p.* **strung.**—*adj.* **stringed** (*stringd*) having strings: of stringed instruments.—*n.* **stringer** (*string'ər*) one who, or that which, strings: a horizontal member in a framework: a journalist employed part-time by a newspaper or news agency to cover a particular (esp. remote) town or area.—*adv.* **string′ily** in a stringy fashion.—*ns.* **string′iness; string′ing.**—*adjs.* **string′less; string′y** consisting of, or abounding in, strings or small threads: fibrous: capable of being drawn into strings: like string or a stringed instrument.—**string′-band** a band of stringed instruments: **string bass** a double-bass; **string′-bean** (*U.S.*) the French bean; **string′-board** a board facing the well-hole of a staircase, and receiving or covering the ends of the steps; **string′-course** a projecting horizontal course or line of mouldings running quite along the face of a building; **string′-piece** a long, heavy, usu. horizontal timber: the string of a staircase; **string quartet** a musical ensemble of two violins, a viola and a cello: music for such an ensemble; **string′-tie** a narrow necktie of uniform width; **string vest** a vest made of a net-like fabric; **string′y-bark** one of a class of Australian gum-trees with very fibrous bark.—**no strings (attached)** with no conditions or limitations; **on a string** under complete control: kept in suspense; **pull (the) strings** to use influence behind the scenes, as if working puppets (*n.* **string′-pulling**); **string along** (*v.t.*) to string, fool: to give someone false expectations; (*v.i.*) to go along together, co-operate; **string up to hang**; **strung up** nervously tensed. [O.E. *streng.*]

stringent *strin′jənt, adj.* tight: binding: rigorous: characterised by difficulty in finding money.—*n.* **strin′gency.**—*adj.* and *adv.* **stringendo** (*-jen′dō*; It.; *mus.*) hastening the time.—*adv.* **strin′gently.** —*n.* **strin′gentness.** [L. *stringēns, -entis,* pr.p. of *stringĕre,* to draw together.]

stringhalt *string′hölt, n.* a catching up of a horse's legs, usu. of one or both hind-legs.—Also **spring′-halt.** [App. **string** (sinew) and **halt²**.]

strip *strip, v.t.* to pull, peel, or tear off: to divest: to undress: to reduce to the ranks: to deprive of a covering: to skin, to peel, to husk: to lay bare: to expose: to deprive: to clear, empty: to dismantle: to clear of fruit, leaves, stems, or any other part: to press out the last milk from, or obtain in this way: to cut in strips: to put strips on: to remove a constituent from a substance by boiling, distillation, etc. (*chem.*).—*v.i.* to undress: to perform a strip-tease: to lose the thread, as a screw: to come off:—*pr.p.* **stripp′ing;** *pa.t.* and *pa.p.* **stripped.**—*n.* a long narrow piece: a long thin piece of rolled metal, as steel strip: a narrow space in a newspaper in which a story is told in pictures (also **strip cartoon**): light garb for running, football, etc.: a strip-tease: an airstrip.—*n.* **stripp′er** one who or that which strips: a strip-tease artist.—*n.pl.* **stripp′ings** the last milk drawn at a milking.—**strip club** one which regularly features strip-tease artists; **strip lighting** lighting by means of long fluorescent tubes; **strip mill** a mill where steel is rolled into strips; **strip′-mine** an opencast mine; **strip′-tease** an act of undressing slowly and seductively, esp. in a place of entertainment.—**strip down** to dismantle, remove parts from; **strip off** to take one's clothes off. [O.E. *strӯpan.*]

stripe *strip, n.* a blow, esp. with a lash: a band of colour: a chevron on a sleeve, indicating rank: a striped cloth or pattern: a stripe: a strain: a kind, particular sort (*U.S.*).—*v.t.* to make stripes upon: to mark with stripes: to lash.—*adjs.* **striped** having stripes of different colours: marked with stripes; **strip′ey** stripy.—*ns.* **strip′iness; strip′ing.**—*adj.* **strip′y** stripe-like: having stripes. [Perh. different words; cf. Ger. *Streif,* stripe, Du. *strippen,* to whip]

stripling *strip′ling, n.* a youth: one yet growing. [Dim. of **strip.**]

strive *strīv, v.i.* to contend: to be in conflict: to struggle: to endeavour earnestly: to make one's way with effort:—*pa.t.* **strove** (*strōv*); *pa.p.* **striven** (*striv′n*).—*n.* **striv′er.**—*n.* and *adj.* **striv′ing.**—*adv.* **striv′ingly.** [O.Fr. *estriver;* poss. Gmc.]

strobic *strob′ik, adj.* like a spinning-top: spinning or seeming to spin.—*n.* **strobe** (*strōb*) the process of viewing vibrations with a stroboscope: a stroboscope. —*n.* **stroboscope** (*strob′, strōb′ə-skōp*) an optical toy giving an illusion of motion from a series of pictures seen momentarily in succession: an instrument for studying rotating machinery or other periodic phenomena by means of a flashing lamp which can be synchronised with the frequency of the periodic phenomena so that they appear to be stationary.— *adj.* **stroboscopic** (*strob-, strōb-ə-skop′ik*).—**stroboscopic** (more commonly **strobe**) **lighting** periodically flashing light, or the equipment used to produce it. [Gr. *strobos,* a whirling—*strephein,* to twist.]

strobila *stro-bī′lə, n.* in the life-cycle of jellyfishes, a chain of segments, cone within cone, that separate to become hydrozoans: a chain of segments forming the body of a tapeworm:—*pl.* **strobi′lae** (*-lē*).—*ns.* **strobile** (*strob′* or *strōb′il, -il*) a strobila: a strobilus; **strobi′lus** a close group of leaves with their sporangia, a cone: a scaly spike of female flowers, as in the hop: —*pl.* **strobi′li** (*-lī*). [Gr. *strobilē,* a conical plug of lint, *strobilos,* a spinning-top, whirl, pine-cone— *strobos* (see foregoing).]

stroboscope, etc. See **strobic.**

strode *strōd, pa.t.* of **stride.**

stroganoff *strog′ən-of, adj.* of meat, cut thinly and cooked with onions, mushrooms and seasoning in a sour cream sauce.—*n.* (often **beef,** etc. **stroganoff**) a dish cooked in this way. [After Count Paul Stroganoff, 19th-cent. Russ. diplomat.]

stroke¹ *strōk, n.* an act or mode of striking: a hit or attempt at hitting: a blow: a striking by lightning: a reverse: an attack of apoplexy or of paralysis: the striking of a clock or its sound: a dash or line: a touch of pen, pencil, brush, etc.: a beat, pulse: a sudden movement or occurrence: a particular named style or manner of swimming: a single complete movement in a repeated series, as in swimming, rowing, pumping, action of an engine: a stroke-oar: a single action towards an end: an effective action, feat, achievement. —*v.t.* to put a stroke through or on: to cross (commonly with *out*).—*v.i.* to row stroke: to make a stroke, as in swimming.—**stroke′-oar** the aftmost oar in a boat: its rower, whose stroke leads the rest; **stroke play** scoring in golf by counting the total number of strokes played (rather than the number of holes won).—**off one's stroke** operating less effectively or successfully than usual; **on the stroke (of)** punctually (at). [O.E. (inferred) *strāc.*]

stroke² *strōk, v.t.* to rub gently in one direction: to rub gently in kindness or affection: to put by such a movement: to strike, move (a ball, etc.) smoothly.— *n.* an act of stroking.—*ns.* **strok′er; strok′ing.** [O.E. *strācian—strāc,* stroke (n.).]

stroll *strōl, v.i.* to wander as a vagrant or itinerant: to walk leisurely.—*n.* a leisurely walk.—*n.* **stroll′er** one who strolls: an itinerant: a push-chair.—*n.* and *adj.* **stroll′ing.**—**strolling player** an itinerant actor. [Perh. Ger. *strolchen—Strolch,* vagrant.]

stroma *strō′mə, n.* a supporting framework of connective tissue (*zool.*): a dense mass of hyphae in which a fungus fructification may develop (*bot.*): the denser part of a blood-corpuscle, chloroplast, etc.:—*pl.* **strom′ata.**—*adjs.* **strōmatic** (*-mat′ik*), **strō′matous.** [Gr. *strōma,* a bed, mattress.]

strong *strong, adj.* powerful: forcible: forceful: fast-moving: vigorous: hale: robust: of great staying power: firm: resistant: difficult to overcome: stead-fast: excelling: efficient: of great tenacity of will and effective in execution: able: well-skilled or versed: competent: rich in resources or means to power: well provided: numerous: numbering so many: of vigorous growth: stiff, coarse, and abundant, indicating strength: without ambiguity, obscurity, or under-statement: intemperate, offensive and unseemly: gross: violent: grievous: having great effect: intense: ardent and convinced: performed with strength: powerfully, or unpleasantly powerfully, affecting the senses: rank: vivid: marked: stressed, emphasised: bold in definition: in high concentration: showing the characteristic properties in high degree: (of prices, markets) steady or tending to rise: of Germanic verbs, showing ablaut variation in conjugation (*gram.*):—*compar.* **stronger** (*strong'gər*); *superl.* **strong'est** (-*gist*).—*adj.* **strongish** (*strong'gish*).— *adv.* **strong'ly.—strong'arm** one who uses violence. —*adj.* by, having, or using, physical force.—*v.t.* to treat violently, show violence towards;—**strong'-box** a safe or strongly made coffer for valuables; **strong drink** alcoholic liquor; **strong head** power to with-stand alcohol or any dizzying influence; **strong'hold** a fastness or fortified refuge: a fortress: a place where anything is in great strength; **strong interaction** one produced by short-range forces, involving baryons or mesons, and completed in about 10^{-23} seconds; **strong language** swearing: plain, emphatic language; **strong'man** one who performs feats of strength: one who wields political, economic, etc. power; **strong meat** anything tending to arouse fear, repulsion, etc. —*adj.* **strong'-mind'ed** resolute, determined, having a vigorous mind.—**strong'-mind'edness; strong'point** (*mil.*) a favourably situated and well-fortified defen-sive position; **strong point** that in which one excels, one's forte; **strong'room** a room constructed for safe-keeping of valuables or prisoners. [O.E. *strang*, *strong.*]

strontium *stron'sh(i-)əm, stron'ti-əm, n.* an element (symbol Sr; at. numb. 38), a yellow metal.—*ns.* **stron'tia** its oxide; **stron'tianite** its carbonate, a min-eral first found in 1790 near *Strontian* (*stron-tē'ən*) in Argyllshire.—**strontium-90** a radioactive isotope of strontium, an important element in nuclear fall-out.

strop *strop, n.* a strip of leather, etc., for sharpening razors: a rope or band round a dead-eye (*naut.*).—*v.t.* to sharpen on a strop:—*pr.p.* **stropp'ing;** *pa.t.* and *pa.p.* **stropped.** [Older form of **strap**—O.E. *strop*, prob.—L. *struppus*, a thong.]

Strophanthus *strof-, strŏf-an'thəs, n.* an African and Asiatic genus of the periwinkle family, yielding arrow-poison: (without *cap.*) a plant of the genus, or its dried seeds used in medicine.—*n.* **strophan'thin** a very poisonous glucoside in its seeds. [Gr. *strophos*, twisted band, *anthos,* flower.]

strophe *strof'i, strŏf'i, n.* in a Greek play, the song sung by the chorus as it moved towards one side, answered by an exact counterpart, the *antistrophe*, as it returned: part of any ode thus answered: (*loosely*) a stanza.—*adj.* **stroph'ic.** [Gr. *strŏphē*, a turn.]

stroppy *strop'i,* (*slang*) *adj.* quarrelsome, bad-tem-pered: rowdy, obstreperous. [Perh. **obstreperous.**]

strove *strōv, pa.t.* of **strive.**

strow *strō, strŏō.* Same as **strew:**—*pa.t.* **strowed;** *pa.p.* **strown.**

struck. See **strike.**

structure *struk'chər, n.* the manner of putting to-gether: construction: the arrangement of parts: the manner of organisation: a thing constructed: an organic form.—*v.t.* to organise, build up: to construct a framework for.—*adj.* **struc'tural.**—*n.* **struc'tur-alism** the belief in and study of unconscious, under-

lying patterns in thought, behaviour, social organis-ation, etc.; **struc'turalist.**—*Also* *adj.*—*adv.* **struc'turally.**—*adjs.* **struc'tured** having a certain structure: having a definite structure or organisation; **struc'tureless.—structural formula** a chemical formula showing the arrangement of atoms in the molecule and the bonds between them; **structural linguistics** the study of language in terms of the inter-relations of its basic units; **structural steel** a strong mild steel suitable for construction work; **structural unemployment** unemployment due to changes in the structure of society or of a particular industry. [L. *structūra—struĕre, structum* to build.]

strudel *s(h)trŏō'dl, n.* very thin pastry enclosing fruit, or cheese, etc. [Ger., eddy, whirlpool.]

struggle *strug'l, v.i.* to strive vigorously in resistance, contention, or coping with difficulties: to make great efforts or exertions: to contend strenuously: to make way with difficulty.—*n.* a bout or course of strug-gling: strife: a hard contest with difficulties.—*n.* **strugg'ler.**—*n.* and *adj.* **strugg'ling.**—*adv.* **strugg'-lingly.** [M.E. *strogelen.*]

strum *strum, v.t.* and *v.i.* to play in a haphazard unskil-ful way: to sound the strings of a guitar, etc. with a sweep of the hand: to play in this way (rather than plucking individual strings):—*pr.p.* **strumm'ing;** *pa.t.* and *pa.p.* **strummed.**—*n.* a strumming. [Cf. **thrum.**]

struma *strŏō'mə, n.* scrofula: a scrofulous tumour: goitre: a cushion-like swelling (*bot.*):—*pl.* **stru'mae** (-*mē,* -*mī*).—*adjs.* **strumatic** (*strŏō-mat'ik*), **strumose** (*strŏō' mōs*), **stru'mous.** [L. *strūma,* a scrofulous tumour.]

strumpet *strum'pit, n.* a whore.

strung *strung, pa.t.* and *pa.p.* of **string.**

strut [1] *strut, v.i.* to walk stiffly in vanity or self-importance: to walk in an ostentatious, swaggering manner:—*pr.p.* **strutt'ing;** *pa.t.* and *pa.p.* **strutt'ed.** —*n.* a strutting gait.—*n.* **strutt'er.**—*n.* and *adj.* **strutt'ing.**—*adv.* **strutt'ingly.** [O.E. *strūtian* or some kindred form.]

strut [2] *strut, n.* a rod or member that resists pressure: a prop.—*v.t.* to support as, or with, a strut or struts. [Cf. L.G. *strutt,* rigid, and foregoing.]

Struthio *strŏō'thi-ō, n.* the African ostrich genus.— *adjs.* **stru'thioid, stru'thious.** [L.,—Gr. *strouthiōn,* an ostrich.]

strychnine *strik'nēn, n.* a very poisonous alkaloid ($C_{21}H_{22}N_2O_2$) got from nux vomica seeds.—*adj.* **strych'nic.**—*ns.* **strych'ninism, strych'nism** strych-nine poisoning. [Gr. *strychnos,* nightshade (of vari-ous kinds).]

stub *stub, n.* a stump: (also **stub'-nail**) a short thick nail: a counterfoil: a short piece left after the larger part has been used (as a cigarette, pencil, etc.): some-thing blunt and stunted.—*v.t.* to grub up: to remove stubs from: to wear or cut to a stub: to wound with a stub: to strike as against a stub: to extinguish by press-ing the end on something (often with *out*):—*pr.p.* **stubb'ing;** *pa.t.* and *pa.p.* **stubbed.**—*adj.* **stubbed** cut or worn to a stub: cleared of stubs: stumpy: blunt.— *n* **stubb'iness.**—*adj.* **stubb'y** abounding with stubs: short, thick, and strong. [O.E. *stubb, stybb.*]

stubble *stub'l, n.* a stump of reaped corn: such stumps collectively: straw: an ill-shaven beard.—*adjs.* **stubb'led** stubbly, **stubb'ly** like or covered with stubble. [O.Fr. *estuble*—L.L *stupula*—from L. *stipula;* see **stipule.**]

stubborn *stub'ərn, adj.* obstinate: unreasonably or troublesomely obstinate: hard to work or treat.— *adv.* **stubb'ornly.**—*n.* **stubb'ornness.**

stubby. See **stub.**

stucco *stuk'ō, n* a plaster used for coating walls,

making casts, etc.: work done in stucco (*pl* stucc'ŏs) —*v.t.* to face or overlay with stucco: to form in stucco:—*pa.t.* and *pa.p.* stucc'oed, stucc'ŏ'd. [It. *stucco*; from O.H.G. *stucchi*, crust, coating.]

stuck. See stick¹.

stud¹ *stud*, *n.* a horse-breeding establishment: the animals kept there: stud-horse: a sexually potent or active man (*slang*).—*adj.* kept for breeding: of a stud. —stud'-book a record of horses' (or other animals') pedigrees; stud'-farm a horse-breeding farm; stud'-horse a stallion kept for breeding; stud poker a variety of the game of poker.—at stud, out to stud being used for breeding purposes. [O.E. *stŏd*.]

stud² *stud*, *n.* a spur, stump, or short branch: an upright in a timber framework or partition: a cross-piece strengthening a link in a chain: one of several rounded projections on the soles of certain types of footwear improving the grip: a projecting boss, knob, or pin: a large-headed nail: a type of fastener consisting of two interlocking discs.—*v.t.* to adorn, set, or secure with studs: to set at intervals:—*pr.p.* studd'ing; *pa.t.* and *pa.p.* studd'ed.—*adj.* studd'ed.—*n.* studd'ing. [O.E. *studu*, post.]

studding-sail *stun'sl*, *n.* a narrow sail set at the outer edges of a square sail when wind is light.—Also stun'sail.

student *stū'dənt*, *n.* one who studies: one devoted to books or to any study: one who is enrolled for a course of instruction in a college or university: an undergraduate.—*adj.* studied (*stud'id*) well considered: deliberately contrived, designed: over-elaborated with loss of spontaneity: well prepared by study: deep read: versed.—*adv.* stud'iedly.—*ns.* stud'iedness; stud'ier; studio (*stū'di-ō*) an artist's workroom: a workshop for photography, cinematography, radio or television broadcasting, the making of gramophone records, etc.:—*pl.* stu'dios.—*adj.* studious (*stū'di-əs*) devoted to or assiduous in study: heedful: studied: deliberate.—*adv.* stu'diously.—*n.* stu'diousness.— *v.t.* study (*stud'i*) to apply the mind to in order to acquire knowledge or skill· to make one's object, seek to achieve: to be solicitous about: to scrutinise: to take into consideration: to think out.—*v.i.* to apply the mind closely to books, nature, acquisition of learning or of skill: to take an educational course: to rack one's mind: to muse, meditate, reflect:—*pr.p.* stud'ying; *pa.t.* and *pa.p.* stud'ied.—*n.* an object of endeavour, solicitude, or mental application: (in *pl.*) related objects of mental application or departments of knowledge: a state of doubtful consideration: attentive and detailed examination: a scrutiny: reverie: application of the mind to the acquisition of knowledge or skill: a department of knowledge: a preliminary essay towards a work of art: an exercise in art: a musical composition affording an exercise in technique: a presentation in literature or art of the results of study: a room devoted to study, actually or ostensibly.—studio couch a couch, that can be converted into a bed. [L. *studēre* (pr.p. *studēns, -entis*), to be zealous, *studium*, zeal, study.]

studio, study, etc. See student.

stuff *stuf*, *n.* matter: substance: essence: material: a preparation used or commodity dealt in in some particular industry or trade: cloth, esp. woollen: a medicinal mixture: goods: luggage: provision.—*v.t.* to line: to be a filling for: to fill very full: to thrust in: to crowd: to cram: to obstruct, clog: to cause to bulge out by filling: to fill with seasoning, as a fowl: to fill the skin of, so as to reproduce the living form: (of a man) to have sexual intercourse with (*vulg.*).—*v.i.* to feed gluttonously: to practise taxidermy.—*adj.* stuffed provisioned: well stored: filled: filled out with stuffing: clogged in nose or throat, etc. (often with

up).—*n.* stuff'er.—*adv.* stuff'ily.—*ns.* stuff'iness; stuff'ing that which is used to stuff or fill anything— straw, sawdust, feathers, hair, etc.: savoury ingredients put into meat, poultry, etc., in cooking.— *adj.* stuff'y badly ventilated, musty: stifling: stodgy (*slang*): strait-laced: stuffed up.—stuffed shirt a pompous, unbendingly correct person, esp if of little real importance.—and stuff and that sort of thing or rubbish; bit of stuff (*slang*) girl, woman; do one's stuff to do what is expected of one; get stuffed! (*vulg. slang*) *interj.* expressing anger, derision, contemptuous dismissal, etc.; hot stuff (*coll.*) denoting a very attractive, effective, etc. person or thing; knock the stuffing out of to reduce (an opponent) to helplessness; know one's stuff to have a thorough knowledge of the field in which one is concerned; stuff it, them, you, etc. (*vulg. slang*) *interj.* expressing disgust, scorn, frustration, etc ; that's the stuff! excellent!; (a drop of) the hard stuff (some) strongly alcoholic drink, esp. whisky [O.Fr. *estoffe*, stuff—L. *stuppa* —Gr. *styppē*, tow.]

stultify *stul'ti-fī*, *v.t.* to dull the mind: to cause to appear foolish or ridiculous: to destroy the force of, as by self-contradiction:—*pr.p.* stul'tifying; *pa.t.* and *pa.p.* stul'tified.—*ns.* stultifica'tion; stul'tifier. [L. *stultus*, foolish.]

stum *stum*, *n.* must, grape-juice unfermented: new wine used to revive dead or vapid wine.—*v.t.* to renew or doctor with stum:—*pr.p.* stumm'ing; *pa.t.* and *pa.p.* stummed. [Du. *stom*, must—*stom*, mute]

stumble *stum'bl*, *v.i.* to take a false step, come near to falling in walking: to walk unsteadily: to err: to lapse into wrongdoing: to light by chance or error (with *across* or *on*).—*n.* a trip: a false step: a lapse: a blunder.—*n.* stum'bler.—*adv.* stum'blingly.—stum'-bling-block an obstacle: a cause of perplexity or error. [M.E. *stomble*, stumble.]

stumer *stū'mər*, (*slang*) *n.* a counterfeit coin or note: a forged or worthless cheque: a sham: a dud: a failure.

stump *stump*, *n.* the part of a felled or fallen tree left in the ground: a tree-stump used as a platform: hence, a campaign of stump-oratory: a short thick remaining basal part, esp. of anything that projects: a leg (*facet.*): a stumping walk or its sound: a pencil of soft material for softening hard lines, blending, etc.: one of the three sticks forming (with the bails) a wicket (*cricket*) —*v.t.* to reduce to a stump: to remove stumps from: (of the wicket-keeper; sometimes with *out*) to dismiss by breaking the wicket when the striker is out of his ground (*cricket*): to nonplus, foil, defeat: to soften or tone with a stump: to walk over or strike heavily and stiffly: to traverse making stump-speeches.—*v.i* to walk stiffly and heavily, as if on wooden legs: to make stump-speeches.—*n.* stump'er. —*adv.* stump'ily.—*n.* stump'iness.—*n.sing.* stumps (*cricket*) the end of play.—*adj.* stump'y short and thick.—stump'-orator one who speaks from an improvised platform: in U.S. a political public speaker in general; stump'-oratory; stump'-speech. —draw stumps (*cricket*) to end play; on the stump engaged in a (political) speech-making tour, campaign; stir one's stumps to move, be active; stump up to pay up, fork out. [Cf. M.L.G. *stump*.]

stun *stun*, *v.t.* to render unconscious as by a blow: to stupefy, daze, as with din or sudden emotion.—*pr.p.* stunn'ing; *pa.t.* and *pa.p.* stunned.—*n.* a shock, stupefying blow: stunned condition.—*adj.* of a weapon, designed to stun rather than kill.—*ns.* stunn'er one who, or that which, stuns: a person or thing supremely excellent (*slang*): a very attractive person (*slang*); stunn'ing stupefaction.—*adj.* stupefying, dazing· supremely excellent (*slang*):

very attractive (*slang*).—*adv.* **stunn'ingly.** [O.Fr. *estoner*, to astonish; cf. O.E. *stunian*, to make a din.]

stung *stung, pa.t.* and *pa.p.* of **sting.**

stunk *stungk, pa.t.* and *pa.p.* of **stink.**

stunsail *stun'sl.* See **studding-sail.**

stunt[1] *stunt, v.t.* to make stupid or senseless: to stun with amazement, fear, etc.:—*pr.p.* **stū'pefying;** *pa.t.* and *pa.p.* **stū'pefied.**—*adj.* **stupefacient** (-*fā'shənt*) stupefying.—*n.* a stupefying drug.—*n.* **stupefaction** (-*fak'shən*) the act of stupefying: the state of being stupefied: extreme astonishment.—*adjs.* **stupefac'tive** stupefying; **stu'pefied.**—*n.* **stu'pefier.**—*adj.* **stu'pefying.** [L. *stupēre*, to be struck senseless, *facēre*, to make.]

stunt[1] *stunt, v.t.* to hinder from growth, to dwarf, check.—*n.* a check in growth: a stunted animal.—*adj.* **stunt'ed** dwarfed.—*n.* **stunt'edness.** [O.E. *stunt*, dull, stupid: O.N. *stuttr*, short.]

stunt[2] *stunt, n.* a difficult, often showy, performance, enterprise, or turn: a craze or campaign.—Also *adj.*—*v.i.* to perform stunts.—**stunt'man** one paid to perform dangerous and showy feats (esp. a stand-in for a film actor).

stupa *stōō'pə, n.* a Buddhist dome-shaped memorial shrine. [Sans. *stūpa.*]

stupe *stūp, n.* a medicated piece of tow or cloth used in fomentation.—*v.t.* to treat with a stupe. [L. *stūpa* for *stuppa*—Gr. *styppē*, tow.]

stupefy *stū'pi-fī, v.t.* to make stupid or senseless: to stun with amazement, fear, etc.:—*pr.p.* **stū'pefying;** *pa.t.* and *pa.p.* **stū'pefied.**—*adj.* **stupefacient** (-*fā'shənt*) stupefying.—*n.* a stupefying drug.—*n.* **stupefaction** (-*fak'shən*) the act of stupefying: the state of being stupefied: extreme astonishment.—*adjs.* **stupefac'tive** stupefying; **stu'pefied.**—*n.* **stu'pefier.**—*adj.* **stu'pefying.** [L. *stupēre*, to be struck senseless, *facēre*, to make.]

stupendous *stū-pen'dəs, adj.* astounding: astoundingly huge: often used as a coll. term of approbation or admiration.—*adv.* **stupen'dously.**—*n.* **stupen'dousness.** [L. *stupendus*, gerundive of *stupēre*, to be stunned.]

stupid *stū'pid, adj.* stupefied: senseless: insensible: deficient or dull in understanding: showing lack of reason or judgment: foolish: dull: boring.—*ns.* **stupid'ity,** **stu'pidness.**—*adv.* **stu'pidly.** [L. *stupidus.*]

stupor *stū'pər, n.* torpor: lethargy: stupefaction.—*adj.* **stu'porous.** [L. *stupor, -ōris—stupēre.*]

sturdy *stûr'di, adj.* orig., giddy: obstinate: resolute: robust: stout.—*adv.* **stur'dily.**—*n.* **stur'diness.** [O.Fr. *estourdi*, stunned, giddy.]

sturgeon *stûr'jən, n.* any member of a genus (*Acipenser*) of large fishes with cartilaginous skull, long snout, and rows of bony shields on the skin, yielding caviar. [A.Fr. *sturgeon*, of Gmc. origin.]

stutter *stut'ər, v.i.* and *v.t.* to speak, say, or pronounce with spasmodic repetition of (esp. initial) sounds: to stammer.—*n.* a speech impediment characterised by spasmodic repetition of (esp. initial) sounds.—*n.* **stutt'erer.**—*n.* and *adj.* **stutt'ering.**—*adv.* **stutt'eringly.** [A freq. of obs. *stut*, to stutter.]

sty[1], **stye** *stī, n.* a small inflamed swelling on the eyelid. [Obs. or dial. *stian, styan*—O.E. *stīgan*, to rise.]

sty[2] *stī, n.* a pen for swine: any place extremely filthy: any place of gross debauchery:—*pl.* **sties.**—*v.t.* and *v.i.* to lodge in a sty:—*pr.p.* **sty'ing;** *pa.t.* and *pa.p.* **stied.** [O.E. *stig*, pen, hall.]

Stygian *stij'i-ən, -yən, adj.* of the Styx, one of the rivers of Hades: hellish: infernal: black as the Styx. [Gr. *Styx.*]

style *stīl, n.* a pointed instrument for writing on wax tablets: a similar instrument or tool of various kinds: a slender process of various kinds (*biol.*): the slender part of the gynaeceum, bearing the stigma (*bot.*): a hand, pointer, index: the manner of writing, mode of expressing thought in language or of expression, execution, action or bearing generally: the distinctive manner peculiar to an author or other: the particular custom or form observed, as by a printing-house in optional matters: designation: manner: form: fashion: an air of fashion or consequence: a kind,

type: a mode of reckoning dates—*Old Style*, according to the Julian calendar, as in Britain till 1752, Russia till 1917; *New Style*, according to the Gregorian calendar, adopted in Britain by omitting eleven days, 3rd to 13th September 1752.—*v.t.* to designate: to arrange, dictate, the fashion or style of.—*-style adj.* and *adv.* combining form denoting in the style of, resembling.—*adjs.* **sty'lar; sty'late** having a style or a persistent style; **style'less.**—*n.* **sty'let** a probe: a wire in a catheter: a bristle-like process.—*adjs.* **styllf'erous** bearing a style; **sty'liform** like a style or a bristle.—*v.t.* **stylïsa'tion, -z-.**—*v.t.* **sty'lïse, -ïze** to conventionalise.—*adj.* **sty'lïsh** displaying style: fashionable: showy: imposingly smart: pretending to style.—*adv.* **sty'lïshly.**—*ns.* **sty'lïshness; sty'lïst** one with a distinctive and fine (esp. literary, etc.) style: one who arranges a style, esp. in hairdressing.—*adj.* **stylïst'ic.**—Also *n.*—*adv.* **stylïst'ically.**—*n.sing.* **stylïs'tics** the science of the variations in language, including the effective values of different words, forms, and sounds, that constitute style in the literary and also the wider sense.—*adj.* **sty'loïd** like a style or bristle: forming a slender process.—*n.* a spiny process of the temporal bone.—*n.* **sty'lus** a style: the cutter used in making gramophone records: a gramophone needle:—*pl.* **sty'lï** (-*lī*), **sty'luses.—style's book** a book of forms for deeds, etc., or rules for printers and editors.—**in style** in a grand manner. [L. *stilus*, a writing instrument, literary composition or style, confused with Gr. *stylos*, a column.]

stylite *stī'līt, n.* an anchorite living on the top of a pillar. [Gr. *stylītēs—stylos*, a pillar.]

stylobate *stī'lō-bāt, n.* the substructure of a row of columns. [Gr. *stylobatēs—stylos*, a column, *batēs*, one who treads, from the root of *bainein*, to go.]

stylography *stī-log'ra-fi, n.* a mode of writing with a style.—*n.* **styl'ograph** (*stī'lə-gräf*) a stylographic pen, from which ink is liberated by pressure on a needlepoint.—*adj.* **stylographic** (-*graf'ik*). [Gr. *stylos*, a style, *graphein*, to write.]

styloid. See **style.**

stylus. See **style.**

stymie *stī'mi, n.* a situation on the putting-green in which an opponent's ball blocks the way to the hole (*golf*).—Also *fig.*—*v.t.* to put in such a situation (also **lay someone a stymie**): to frustrate, thwart, prevent, stop.

styptic *stip'tik, adj.* drawing together: astringent: checking bleeding.—*n.* a styptic agent.—**styptic pencil** a healing agent for minor cuts. [Gr. *styptikos—styphein*, to contract.]

Styrax *stī'raks, n.* a genus of plants abounding in resinous and aromatic substances, as benzoin: (without *cap.*) any plant of this genus.—*n.* **sty'rene** an unsaturated hydrocarbon obtained from essential oils and coal-tar, forming thermoplastics on polymerisation. [Gr. *styrax*; cf. **storax.**]

Styx *stiks.* See **Stygian.**

suable *sū'* or *sōō'ə-bl, adj.* that may be sued.—*n* **suabil'ity.**

suave *swäv* (formerly *swāv*), *adj.* smooth, bland.—*adv.* **suave'ly.**—*n.* **suavity** (*swav'i-ti*). [Fr.,—L. *suāvis*, sweet.]

sub- *sub-, sab-, pfx.* (1) under, below; (2) subordinate, subsidiary; (3) part of, a subdivision of; (4) almost, nearly, slightly, imperfectly, bordering on; (5) secretly; (6) (*chem.*) in smaller proportion.—*n.* **sub** (*coll.*) a subordinate: a subeditor: a subway: a subscription (also **subs**): a subscriber: a substitute: a submarine: subsistence money, hence a loan, an advance payment.—*v.i.* (*coll.*) to act as a sub: to work as a substitute: to work as a newspaper subeditor.—*v.t.* (*coll.*) to subedit:—*pr.p.* **subb'ing;**

pa.t. and *pa.p.* **subbed.** [L. *sub*, under, near; in composition also in some degree, secretly.]

subah *sōō'bà, n.* a province of the Mogul empire: a subahdar.—*ns.* **suba(h)dar'** the governor of a subah: an Indian captain. [Urdu.]

subalpine *sub-al'pīn, adj.* bordering on the alpine: at the foot of the Alps. [Pfx. **sub-** (4), (1).]

subaltern *sub'əl-tərn, adj.* ranked successively: subordinate: (of officers) under the rank of captain: particular (*log.*): being at once a genus and a species of a higher genus (*log.*).—*n.* a subordinate: a subaltern officer: a proposition differing from another in quantity alone (both being affirmative or both negative, but one universal, the other particular) (*log.*).—*ns.* **subalternation** (*sub-öl-tər-nā'shən*) the relation between a universal and particular of the same quality; **subalter'nity** subordinate position. [L. *subalternus*—*sub*, under, *alter*, another.]

subaquatic *sub-ə-kwat'ik, adj.* under water (also **subā'-queous**): partially aquatic (*zool.* and *bot.*).—*adj.* **suba'qua** of underwater sport. [Pfx. **sub-** (1), (4).]

subatom *sub-at'əm, n.* a constituent part of an atom —*adj.* **subatom'ic** relating to particles constituting the atom and changes within the atom.—*n.sing.* **subatom'ics** the study of these particles and changes. [Pfx. **sub-** (3).]

subclavian *sub-klā'vi-ən,* **subclavicular** *-klə-vik'-ū-lər, adjs.* under the clavicle. [Pfx. **sub-** (1), **clavicle.**]

subclinical *sub-klin'i-kəl, adj.* of a slightness not detectable by usual clinical methods. [Pfx. **sub-** (4).]

subconscious *sub-kon'shəs, adj.* dimly conscious: away from the focus of attention: not conscious but of like nature to the conscious.—*n.* the subconscious mind or activities.—*adv.* **subcon'sciously.**—*n.* **subcon'sciousness.** [Pfx. **sub-** (4).]

subcontinent *sub-kon'ti-nənt, n.* a great portion of a continent with a character of its own (a term formerly applied to South Africa, later to India): a land-mass hardly great enough to be called a continent.—*adj.* **subcontinent'al** almost continental: underlying a continent. [Pfx. **sub-** (2), (4), (1).]

subcontract *sub-kon'trakt, n.* a contract subordinate to another contract, as for the subletting of work.—*v.i.* **subcontract'** to make a subcontract.—*v.t.* to make a subcontract for.—*n.* **subcontract'or.** [Pfx. **sub-** (2).]

subcontrary *sub-kon'trə-ri, adj.* (of a particular proposition in relation to another differing only in quality) such that at least one must be true (*log.*).—*n.* a subcontrary proposition. [Pfx. **sub-** (4).]

subcritical *sub-krit'i-kl, adj.* of insufficient mass to sustain a chain reaction (*phys*): below the critical temperature for hardening metals. [Pfx. **sub-** (1).]

subculture *sub'kul'chər, n.* a culture (as of bacteria) derived from a previous one: a social, ethnic or economic group with a particular character of its own within a culture or society.—*adj.* **sub'cul'tural.** [Pfx. **sub-** (2), (3).]

subdeacon *sub-dē'kən, n.* a member of the order of the ministry next below that of deacon, preparing the vessels, etc., at the eucharist [Pfx **sub-** (2).]

subdivide *sub'di-vīd', v t.* and *v.i.* to divide into smaller divisions: to divide again —*n.* **subdivid'er.**—*adj.* **subdivisible** (*-viz'*).—*n.* **subdivision** (*-vizh'ən*).—*adjs.* **subdivis'ional; subdivi'sive.** [Pfx. **sub-** (3).]

subdominant *sub'dom'i-nənt, n.* (*mus.*) the tone next below the dominant. [Pfx. **sub-** (1), (4)]

subdue *sub-dū', v.t.* to overcome: to overpower: to subject: to make submissive: to allay: to reduce: to quieten: to tone down.—*adj.* **subdu'able.**—*n.* **subdu'al** subjugation: an overcoming.—*adj.* **subdued'** toned down: quiet: passive. [O.Fr. *souduire*—L. *subdūcere*; *sub*, and *dūcere, ductum*, to lead, take.]

subedit *sub-ed'it, v.t* to select and dispose matter for (a newspaper): also, to assist in editing.—*n.* **subed'itor.**—*adj.* **subeditorial** (*-tōr', -tor'*).—*n.* **subed'itorship.** [Pfx. **sub-** (2).]

suber *sū'bər,* (*bot.*) *n.* cork.—*n.* **su'berate** a salt of suberic acid.—*adjs.* **subē'reous, suberic** (*-ber'ik*) of cork (**suberic acid** an acid, $HOOC \cdot (CH_2)_6 \cdot COOH$, got by action of nitric acid on cork).—*ns.* **su'berin** the chemical basis of cork; **suberisā'tion, -z-.**—*v.t.* **su'berise, -ize** to convert into cork.—*adjs.* **su'berose, su'berous** corky. [L. *sūber, -eris,* the cork oak.]

subfamily *sub'fam'i-li, n.* a primary division of a family, of one or more genera. [Pfx. **sub-** (3).]

subfloor *sub'flōr, -flōr, n.* a rough floor forming the foundation for the finished floor. [Pfx. **sub-** (1).]

subfusc, subfusk *sub-fusk', adj.* dusky: sombre.—*n.* formal academic dress at Oxford University. [L. *subfuscus*—*sub, fuscus,* tawny.]

subgenus *sub-jē'nəs, n.* a primary division of a genus: —*pl.* **subgenera** (*-jen'ə-rə*), **subge'nuses.**—*adj.* **subgener'ic.**—*adv.* **subgener'ically.** [Pfx. **sub-** (3).]

subhuman *sub-hū'mən, adj.* less than human: below but near the human. [Pfx. **sub-** (4).]

subirrigation *sub-ir-i-gā'shən, n.* irrigation by underground pipes: irrigation from beneath. [Pfx. **sub-** (1).]

subito *sōō'bi-tō,* (*mus.*) *adv.* suddenly: immediately. [It.]

subjacent *sub-jā'sənt, adj.* underlying. [L. *subjacēns, -entis*—*sub, jacēre,* to lie.]

subject *sub'jikt, adj.* (often with *to*) under rule, government, jurisdiction, or control: owing allegiance: under obligation: subordinate: subservient: dependent: liable: prone, disposed: dependent upon condition or contingency.—*adv.* conditionally (with *to*).—*n.* one who is subject: one who is under, or owes allegiance to, a sovereign, a state, etc.: a citizen: a thing over which a legal right is exercised: that in which attributes inhere: a thing existing independently: the mind regarded as the thinking power (opp. to the *object* about which it thinks): that of which something is predicated, or the term denoting it (*log.*): that part of a sentence or clause denoting that of which something is said (*gram.*): a topic: a matter of discourse, thought, or study: a department of study: a theme: that on which any operation is

---

subabdom'inal *adj.* sub- (1).	**sub'breed** *n.* sub- (3).	**subcutā'neously** *adv.* sub- (1).
suba'cid *adj.* sub- (4).	**subcat'egory** *n.* sub- (3).	**sub'dean'** *n.* sub- (2).
subacid'ity *n.* sub- (4).	**subcau'dal** *adj.* sub- (1).	**sub'dean'ery** *n.* sub- (2).
subacid'ulous *adj.* sub- (4).	**subcent'ral** *adj.* sub- (1), (4).	**subdis'trict** *n.* sub- (3).
subā'gency *n.* sub- (2).	**sub'class** *n.* sub- (3).	**subē'qual** *adj.* sub- (4).
subā'gent *n.* sub- (2).	**sub'clause** *n.* sub- (2).	**subequato'rial** *adj.* sub- (4).
subang'ular *adj.* sub- (4).	**subcommiss'ion(er)** *ns.* sub- (2), (3).	**subfer'tile** *adj.* sub- (4).
subantarc'tic *adj.* sub- (4).	**subcommitt'ee** *n* sub- (2), (3).	**subfertil'ity** *n.* sub- (4).
subarc'tic *adj.* sub- (4).	**subcontig'uous** *adj.* sub- (4).	**subglā'cial** *adj.* sub- (1).
subar'id *adj.* sub- (4).	**subcontin'uous** *adj.* sub- (4).	**sub'group** *n.* sub- (3).
subbase'ment *n.* sub- (1).	**subcrā'nial** *adj.* sub- (1).	**sub-head', -head'ing** *ns.* sub- (3)
sub'branch *n.* sub- (2).	**subcutā'neous** *adj.* sub- (1).	

performed: that which is treated or handled: matter for any action or operation: a ground: a sufferer from disease, a patient: a person peculiarly sensitive to hypnotic influence: that which it is the object of the artist to express a theme or phrase upon which a movement of music is built.—*v.t.* **subject** (*sab-jekt'*) to make subject: to make liable: to subordinate: to submit: to subdue: to lay open.—*adj.* **subject'ed** made subject.—*n.* **subjec'tion.**—*adj.* **subject'ive** (also *sub'*) relating to the subject: derived from, expressive of, existing in, one's own consciousness: introspective.—*adv.* **subject'ively.**—*ns.* **subject'-iveness; subjectivisā'tion, -z-.**—*v.t.* **subject'ivise, -ize.**—*ns.* **subject'ivism** a philosophical doctrine which refers all knowledge to, and founds it upon, subjective states; **subject'ivist.**—*adj.* **subjectivist'ic.** —*adv.* **subjectivist'ically.**—*ns.* **subjectiv'ity; subj'ectship** the state of being subject.—**subj'ject-cat'alogue** a catalogue of books arranged according to subjects dealt with; **subj'ject-heading; subj'ject-matter** the subject, theme, topic. [L. *subjectus,* thrown under—*sub,* under, *jacĕre,* to throw.]

subjoin *sub-join',* v.t. to add at the end or afterwards. [Pfx. **sub-,** in addition, **join.**]

sub judice *sub joo'di-sē, ū'di-ke,* under consideration. [L.]

subjugate *sub'joo-gāt,* v.t. to bring under the yoke: to bring under power or domination: to conquer.—*ns.* **subjugā'tion; subj'jugator.** [L. *subjugāre, -ātum—sub, jugum,* a yoke]

subjunctive *sab-jungk'tiv,* adj. added to something, expressing condition, hypothesis, or contingency (*gram.*).—*n.* the subjunctive mood: a subjunctive form: a verb in the subjunctive mood.—*adv.* **subjunct'ively.** [L. *subjunctīvus—sub, jungĕre,* to join.]

subkingdom *sub'king-dam,* n. a subordinate kingdom: a phylum (*biol.*). [Pfx. **sub-** (2).]

sublease *sub'lēs,* n. an underlease or lease by a tenant to another.—*v.t.* and *v.i.* **sublease'.**—*ns.* **sublessee'** the holder of a sublease: **subless'or** one who grants a sublease. [Pfx **sub-** (2).]

sublet *sub-let',* v.t. and v.i. to underlet or lease as by one himself a tenant to another:—*pa.t.* and *pa.p.* **sublet'.**—*n.* a subletting.—*ns.* **sublett'er; sublett'-ing.** [Pfx. **sub-** (2).]

sublieutenant *sub-lə-ten'ant,* n. in the navy formerly *mate,* or *passed midshipman,* an officer ranking with an army lieutenant [Pfx. **sub-** (2).]

sublime *sab-līm',* adj. exalted: lofty: majestic: supreme: of the highest or noblest nature: awakening feelings of awe and veneration.—*n.* that which is sublime: the lofty or grand in thought or style: the supreme degree.—*v.t.* to raise aloft: to exalt: to transmute into something higher: to subject to, or obtain by, sublimation: to deposit as a sublimate: to purify as by sublimation.—*v.i.* to undergo sublimation.—*adj.* **sublim'able.**—*v.t.* **sublimate** (*sub'lim-āt*) to elevate: to sublime: to purify by sublimation: to transmute into something higher: to direct unconsciously the sexual impulse into some non-sexual activity: to direct into a higher channel.—*n.* a product of sublimation, esp. corrosive sublimate.—*adj.* sublimed or sublimated.—*adj.* **sub'limated.**—*n.* **sublimā'tion** the change from solid to vapour without passing through the liquid state—usu. with subsequent change back to solid: purification by this process: elevation: ecstasy: the acme, height: transmutation into something higher: the unconscious

diversion towards higher aims of the energy attaching to an instinct (often sexual instinct).—*adj.* **sublimed** (*sab-līmd'*).—*adv.* **sublime'ly.**—*n.* **sublime'ness.**—*n* and *adj.* **sublīm'ing.**—*n.* **sublimity** (*sab-lim'*). [L *sublimis,* in a high position, exalted—*sublimāre, -ātum,* to exalt.]

subliminal *sub-lim'in-al,* adj. beneath the threshold of consciousness, subconscious.—**subliminal advertising** advertising in the cinema, etc., directed to the subconscious, shown too rapidly and briefly to make a conscious impression [L. *sub,* under, *līmen, -inis,* threshold.]

sublunar *sub-loon'ar, adj* under the moon. earthly: of this world.—Also **sublu'nary.** [Pfx. **sub-** (1).]

submachine-gun *sub-ma-shēn'-gun, n.* a light machine-gun, usu. one fired from the shoulder. [Pfx. **sub-** (4).]

submarginal *sub-mar'ji-nal, adj* near the margin [Pfx. **sub-** (4).]

submarine *sub'ma-rēn, adj.* under the sea: under the surface of the sea.—*n.* a submersible vessel, esp. for warfare.—*n* **submarin'er** (or *-mar'in-*) a member of the crew of a submarine. [Pfx. **sub-** (1).]

submaxillary *sub-maks'i-la-ri,* or *-il'ə-, adj.* of or under the lower jaw. [Pfx. **sub-** (1).]

submediant *sub-mē'di-ant, (mus.) n.* the sixth above the tonic. [Pfx. **sub-** (1).]

submerge *sab-mûrj',* v.t. to put under the surface of liquid: to sink: to cover over with liquid: to overwhelm: to conceal, suppress.—*v.i.* to sink under the surface of liquid—*adj.* **submerged'** sunk: entirely under the surface of liquid: growing under water, submersed: obscured, concealed: swamped.—*n.* **submerg'ence** submersion.—*v.t.* **submerse** (*-mûrs'*) to submerge.—*n* **submers'ibility.**—*adj.* **submers'-ible** capable of being submerged at will.—*n.* a submersible boat.—*n.* **submer'sion** (*-shən*) the act of submerging: the state or fact of being submerged. [L *submergĕre, -mersum—sub, mergĕre,* to plunge.]

submit *sab-mit',* v.t. to yield, resign: to subordinate: to subject: to refer for decision, consideration, sanction, arbitration, etc : to put forward in respectful contention: to lodge.—*v.i.* to yield: to surrender: to be resigned: to consent:—*pr.p.* **submitt'ing;** *pa.t.* and *pa.p.* **submitt'ed.**—*adj.* **submiss'ible.**—*n.* **submission** (*-mish'ən*) an act of submitting: a reference, or agreement to refer, to arbitration. a view submitted: resignedness: submissiveness. a surrender.—*adj.* **submiss'ive** willing or ready to submit: yielding.—*adv.* **submiss'ively.**—*n.* **submiss'iveness.**—*adj.* **submitt'-ed.**—*n* **submitt'er.**—*n.* and *adj.* **submitt'ing.** [L. *sub,* beneath, and *mittĕre, missum,* to send.]

submultiple *sub-mul'ti-pl,* n. an aliquot part. [L.L. *submultiplus.*]

subnormal *sub-nor'mal, adj* less than normal, esp medically, of a person with a low range of intelligence.—*n.* **subnormal'ity.** [Pfx **sub-** (4), (1).]

suborbital *sub-or'bi-tal, adj.* below the orbit of the eye: of less than a complete orbit. [Pfx. **sub-** (1).]

subordinate *sub-or'di-nāt, -nit, adj.* lower in order, rank, nature, power, etc.: dependent: under orders of another: lower in a series of successive divisions: underlying.—*n.* a person or thing that is subordinate or ranked lower. one who works under another.—*v.t.* to place in a lower order: to consider of less value: to subject.—*adv.* **subor'dinately.**—*ns.* **subor'din-ateness; subordinā'tion.**—*adj.* **subor'dinative.**—**subordinate clause** (*gram.*) a clause which cannot function as a separate sentence in its own right, but

---

sublibrā'rian *n.* **sub-** (2).
subling'ual adj. **sub-** (1).
submicroscop'ic adj. **sub-** (4).

submin'iature adj. **sub-** (4).
sub'office *n.* **sub-** (2), (3).

subor'der *n.* **sub-** (3).
subor'dinal adj. **sub-** (4).

performs an adjectival, adverbial or nominal function; **subordinating conjunction** (*gram.*) a conjunction which introduces a subordinate clause. [L.L. *subordinātus—sub-, ordināre*, to ordain.]

suborn *sab-ōrn'*, *v.t.* to bribe or procure to commit perjury or other unlawful or wrongful act.—*ns.* **suborna'tion** (*sub-ör-*); **suborn'er** (*sab-*). [L. *sub-*, in sense of secret, *ornāre*, to equip.]

subplot *sub'plot*, *n.* a subordinate plot, as in a play. [Pfx. **sub-** (2).]

subpoena *sub-* or *sə-pē'nə*, *n.* a writ commanding attendance in court under a penalty.—*v.t.* to serve with such a writ:—*pa.t.* and *pa.p.* **subpoe'na'd, -naed**. [L.]

subreption *sub-rep'shən*, *n.* procuring an advantage by concealing the truth (distinguished from *obreption*). [L. *subreptiō, -ōnis—sub-*, secretly, *rapēre*, to snatch; cf. **surreptitious**.]

subrogate *sub'rō-gāt*, or *-rə-*, *v.t.* to substitute: to put in place of another, as successor to his rights (*legal*).—*n.* **subroga'tion**. [See **surrogate**.]

sub rosa *sub rō'zə*, *soōb ro'zā*, (L.) under the rose: privately.

subroutine *sub'roō-tēn'*, *n.* a part of a computer program, complete in itself, which performs a specific task, e.g. calculation of a square root, and which can be called into use at any time throughout the running of the main program. [Pfx. **sub-** (2).]

subs. See **sub-**.

subscribe *sab-skrīb'*, *v.t.* to sign (orig. and esp. at the bottom): to profess to be (by signing): to declare assent to: to make a signed promise of payment for: to contribute.—*v.i.* (usu. with *to*) to sign one's name: to assent: to contribute money: to put one's name down as a purchaser or donor: to make periodical payments by arrangement.—*adjs.* **subscrib'able; subscribed'**.—*n.* **subscrib'er**.—*n.* and *adj.* **subscrib'ing**.—*adj.* and *n.* **subscript** (*sub'skript*) (a character) written beneath, esp. the iota under a Greek long vowel, in α, η, ω.—*n.* **subscrip'tion** an act of subscribing: that which is subscribed: a signature: assent: a raising of money from subscribers: a method of sale to subscribers: a contribution to a fund, society, etc.: a membership fee.—*adj.* **subscrip'tive**.—**subscriber trunk dialling** a dialling system in which subscribers in exchanges in many countries of the world can dial each other directly:—abbrev. **S.T.D.** [L. *subscrībere—sub, scrībere*, to write.]

subsellium *sub-sel'i-əm*, *n.* a misericord:—*pl.* **subsell'ia**. [L., a low bench—*sub, sella*, seat.]

subsequent *sub'si-kwənt*, *adj.* following or coming after.—Also *adv.* (with *to*) after.—*n.* **sub'sequence**.—*adv.* **sub'sequently**. [L. *subsequēns, -entis*, pr.p. of *subsequī—sub*, under, after, *sequī*, to follow.]

subserve *sub-sûrv'*, *v.t.* to help forward.—*ns.* **subser'vience, subser'viency**.—*adj.* **subser'vient** serving to promote: subject: obsequious.—*adv.* **subser'viently**. [L. *subservīre—sub*, under, *servīre*, to serve.]

subset *sub'set*, (*math.*) *n.* a set contained within a larger set. [Pfx. **sub-** (3).]

subshrub *sub'shrub*, *n.* a low-growing shrub.—*adj.* **subshrubb'y**. [Pfx. **sub-** (4).]

subside *sab-sīd'*, *v.i.* to settle, sink down: to fall into a state of quiet.—*n.* **subsidence** (*sub'si-dəns*; often *sab-sī'dəns*) the process of subsiding, settling, or sinking. [L. *subsīdēre—sub*, down, *sīdēre*, to settle.]

subsidy *sub'si-di*, *n.* aid in money: a special parliamentary grant of money to the king (*hist.*): a grant of public money in aid of some enterprise, industry, etc., or to keep down the price of a commodity, or from one state to another.—*adv.* **subsid'iarily**.—*adj.* **subsid'iary** furnishing a subsidy, help, or additional supplies: aiding: subordinate.—*n.* one who, or that which, aids or supplies: an assistant: a subordinate: a subsidiary company.—*v.t.* **sub'sidise, -ize** to furnish with a subsidy, grant, or regular allowance: to purchase the aid of, to buy over.—**subsidiary company** one of which another company holds most of the shares; **subsidiary troops** mercenaries. [L. *subsidium*, orig. troops stationed behind in reserve, aid—*sub*, under, *sīdēre*, to settle.]

subsist *sab-sist'*, *v.i.* to have existence (often with *in*): to remain, continue: to inhere: to have the means of living (often with *on*).—*n.* **subsist'ence** the state of being subsistent: real being: the means of supporting life: livelihood.—*adj.* (used e.g. of allowance, wage) providing the bare necessities of living.—*adj.* **subsist'ent**.—**subsistence farming** farming in which the land-yield will support the farmer, but leave little or nothing to be sold; **subsistence level** the level of income which will purchase bare necessities only; **subsistence money, allowance** part of wages paid in advance for immediate needs. [L. *subsistere*, to stand still—*sub*, under, *sistere*, to stand.]

subsoil *sub'soil*, *n.* broken-up rock underlying the soil.—*v.t.* to turn up or loosen the subsoil of. [Pfx. **sub-** (1).]

subsonic *sub-son'ik*, *adj.* of speed, less than that of sound. [Pfx. **sub-** (4).]

substance *sub'stəns*, *n.* that in which qualities or attributes exist, the existence to which qualities belong: that which constitutes anything what it is: the principal part: gist: subject-matter: body: matter: kind of matter, esp. one of definite chemical nature: wealth, property: solidity, body: solid worth: foundation, ground.—*adj.* **substantial** (*sab-stan'shl*) of or having substance: being a substance: essential: actually existing: real, material: solid and stable: solidly based: durable: enduring: firm, stout, strong: considerable in amount: well-to-do: of sound worth.—*v.t.* **substan'tialise, -ize** to give reality to.—*ns.* **substan'tialism** the theory that there is a real existence or substratum underlying phenomena; **substan'tialist; substantiality** (*-shi-al'i-ti*).—*adv.* **substan'tially**.—*n.* **substan'tialness**.—*v.t.* **substan'tiate** (*-shi-āt, -si-āt*) to prove or confirm.—*n.* **substantia'tion**.—*adj.* **substantival** (*sub-stan-tī'vl*) of, of the nature of, a substantive.—*adv.* **substantiv'ally**.—*adj.* **sub'stantive** (*-tiv*) relating to substance: expressing existence: real: of real, independent importance: substantival: (of dyes) taking effect without a mordant: definite and permanent: considerable in amount.—*n.* (*gram.*) a noun.—*adv.* **sub'stantively**.—*n.* **sub'stantiveness**.—*v.t.* **sub'stantivise, -ize** (or *-stan'*) to turn into a noun.—*n.* **substantiv'ity** substantiality: affinity for a dyestuff.—**in substance** in general: in the most important aspects. [L. *substantia*, substance, essence, property—*sub*, under, *stāre*, to stand.]

substation *sub'stā-shən*, *n.* a subordinate station, esp. a switching, transforming, or converting electrical station intermediate between the generating station and the low-tension distribution network. [Pfx. **sub-** (2).]

---

subphy'lum *n.* sub- (3).
sub-post'-office *n.* sub- (3).
subpre'fect *n.* sub- (2).
subprē'fecture *n.* sub- (2).
subprin'cipal *n.* sub- (2).

sub'prior (*fem.* subpri'oress) *n.* sub- (2).
subre'gion *n.* sub- (3).
subrē'gional *adj.* sub- (3).
sub'sec'tion *n.* sub- (3).
subser'ies *n.* sub- (3).

sub'species *n.* sub- (3).
subspecif'ic *adj.* sub- (3).
subspecif'ically *adv.* sub- (3).
substan'dard *n.* sub- (1).

For other sounds see detailed chart of pronunciation.

substitute *sub'sti-tūt*, *n.* a deputy: one put in place of another: a thing used instead of another.—*v.t.* to put in place of another: to use instead of something else (often with **for**).—*v.i.* (orig. *U.S.*) to act as substitute.—*n.* **substit'uent** something that may be, is, substituted, esp. an atom or group replacing another in a molecule.—*adj.* **sub'stituted.**—*n.* **substitū'tion** the act of substituting: the condition of being a substitute: the substituting of one atom or radical for another without breaking up the molecule (*chem.*).—*adjs.* **substitū'tional, substitū'tionary.**—*adv.* **substitū'tionally.**—*adj.* **sub'stitutive.**—*adv.* **sub'stitutively.** [L. *substituēre, -ūtum*—*sub*, under, *statuēre*, to set.]

substrata, substrate, etc. See **substratum.**

substratosphere *sub-strat'ō-sfēr*, *n.* the region of the atmosphere below the stratosphere and over 3½ miles above the earth. [Pfx. **sub-** (4).]

substratum *sub-strā'tam, -strä'*, *n.* the substance in which qualities inhere: a basis, foundation, ground: the material in which a plant grows or on which an animal moves or rests: an underlying layer:—*pl.* **substra'ta.**—*adjs.* **substrā'tal, substrā'tive.**—*n.* **sub'strate** a substratum: a base: the substance on which an enzyme acts: the substances used by a plant in respiration (*bot.*). [L. *substernēre, -strātum*—*sub*, *sternēre*, to spread.]

substruct *sub-strukt'*, *v.t.* to build beneath, lay as a foundation.—*n.* **substruc'tion.**—*adj.* **substruc'tural.**—*n.* **sub'structure** an understructure: a foundation. [Pfx. **sub-** (1).]

subsume *sub-sūm'*, *v.t.* to take in under a more general term or proposition: to include in something larger: to take over (*officialese*).—*n.* **subsumption** (*sab-sump'shan*).—*adj.* **subsump'tive.** [L. *sub*, under, *sūmēre*, to take.]

subtemperate *sub'tem'par-it, -āt*, *adj.* slightly colder than temperate, cold-temperate. [Pfx. **sub-** (4).]

subtend *sab-tend'*, *v.t.* to be opposite to (*geom.*): to have in the axil (*bot.*). [L. *sub*, under, *tendēre*, *tentum* or *tēnsum*, to stretch.]

subter- *sub'tar-*, in composition, under.—*n.* **subterfuge** (*sub'tar-fūj*; L. *fugēre*, to take flight) an evasive device, esp. in discussion. [L. *subter*, under.]

subterranean *sub-ta-rā'ni-an*, *adj.* underground: operating underground: hidden, working, etc., in secret.—*adj.* **subterres'trial** existing underground. L. *sub*, under, *terra*, the earth.]

subtil, subtile, etc. See **subtle.**

subtitle *sub'tī-tl*, *n.* an additional or second title, as to a book: descriptive reading matter in a cinematograph film, esp. a printed translation at the foot of the screen of dialogue that is in a language foreign to the viewers.—*v.t.* to provide with a subtitle. [Pfx. **sub-** (2).]

subtle, also (*arch.*) **subtil, subtile,** all pronounced *sut'l*, *adj.* fine, delicate, thin: tenuous: elusive: showing or calling for fine discrimination: nice! overrefined or overrefining: abstruse: ingenious: crafty: insidious.—*n.* **subtilisā'tion, -z-** (*sut-*).—*v.t.* **subtilise, -ize** (*sut'*) to rarefy, refine: to make subtle. —*v.i.* to refine, use subtlety.—*ns.* **subt'leness,** also **subt'il(e)ness, subtlety,** also **subtil(e)ty, subtility** (*sub-til'i-ti*), the state or quality of being subtle: a subtle trick or refinement—*adv.* **subt'ly,** also **subt'il(e)ly.** [O.Fr. *soutil* and its source L. *subtīlis* —*sub*, under, *tēla*, a web.]

subtonic *sub-ton'ik*, (*mus.*) *n.* the note next below the

tonic, the leading note. [Pfx. **sub-** (1).]

subtopia *sub-tō'pi-a*, (*derog.*) *n.* a region where the city has sprawled into the country.—*adj.* **subto'pian.** [L. *sub*, under, Gr. *topos*, a place; modelled on **Utopia.**]

subtract *sab-trakt'*, *v.t.* to withdraw, remove: to take from another quantity so as to find the difference (*math.*).—*n.* **subtrac'tion** withdrawal, removal: the operation of finding the difference between two quantities by taking one from the other (*math.*).— *adj.* **subtract'ive.**—*ns.* **subtract'or** a light-filter to eliminate a particular colour; **subtrahend** (*sub'tra-hend*) that which is to be subtracted. [L. *sub-*, in sense of away, *trahēre, tractum*, to draw, gerundive *trahendus*, requiring to be drawn.]

subulate *sū'bū-lāt*, *adj.* awl-shaped. [L. *sūbula*, an awl.]

suburb *sub'arb*, *n.* a district adjoining a town: (in *pl.*) the outskirts of a town: outskirts generally.—*adj.* **suburban** (*sab-ûr'ban*) situated or living in the suburbs: typical of the suburbs: without the good qualities either of town or country: provincial, narrow in outlook.—*n.* one living in a suburb.—*n.* **suburbanisā'tion, -z-.**—*v.t.* **subur'banise, -ize** to make suburban.—*ns.* **subur'banism** the state of being suburban; **subur'banite** one who lives in the suburbs; **subur'bia** the suburban world. [L. *suburbium*—*sub*, under, near, urbs, a city.]

subvention *sab-ven'shan*, *n.* a grant of money in aid.— *adj.* **subven'tionary.** [L. *subventiō, -ōnis*, a coming to help—*sub*, *venīre*, *ventum*, to come.]

subvert *sab-vûrt'*, *v.t.* to overthrow: to overturn: to pervert.—*n.* **subver'sion** overthrow: ruin.—*adj.* **subver'sive** tending to overthrow.—*n.* a subversive person, esp. politically.—*n.* **subvert'er.** [L. *sub*, under, *vertēre*, *versum*, to turn.]

subway *sub'wā*, *n.* a tunnel for foot-passengers: an underground passage for water-pipes, gas-pipes, sewers, etc.: (esp. *U.S.*) an underground railway. [Pfx. **sub-** (1).]

subzero *sub-zē'rō*, *adj.* less than zero, esp. of temperature. [Pfx. **sub-** (1).]

succedaneum *suk-si-dā'ni-am*, *n.* a substitute.—*adj.* **succedā'neous** (esp. *med.*) serving as a substitute. [L., neut. of *succēdāneus—succēdēre*, to come after.]

succeed *sak-sēd'*, *v.t.* to come after: to follow up or in order: to follow: to take the place of, esp. in office, title, or possession.—*v.i.* to follow in order: to take the place of another (often with *to*): to turn out well: to prosper: to obtain one's wish or accomplish what is attempted: to avail, be successful (with *in*).—*ns.* **succeed'er** one who is successful: a successor.—*adj.* **succeed'ing.**—*n.* **success** (*sak-ses'*) fortune (good or bad): prosperous progress, achievement, or termination: prosperity: attainment of wealth, influence or acclaim: a successful person, book, affair, etc.—*adj.* **success'ful** resulting in success: achieving, having achieved, or having, the desired effect or termination: prosperous.—*adv.* **success'fully** with success. —*ns.* **success'fulness; succession** (*-sesh'an*) a coming after or following: a coming into another's place: a sequence in time or place: law, recognised mode, right, order, or turn, of succeeding one to another: in Roman and Scots law, the taking of property by one person in place of another: heirs collectively.—*adj.* **success'ional.**—*adv.* **success'ionally.**—*adjs.* **success'ionless; successive** (*sak-ses'iv*) coming in succession or in order.—*adv.* **success'ively.**—*n.* **success'iveness.**

sub'ten'ancy *n.* sub- (2).
sub'ten'ant *n.* sub- (2).
subter'minal *adj.* sub- (4).
sub'tot'al *n., v.t.* sub- (3)

subtriang'ular *adj.* sub- (4).
subtrop'ic, -al *adjs.* sub- (4).
subtrop'ics *n.pl.* sub- (4).
sub'type *n.* sub- (3).

subu'nit *n.* sub- (3).
subvari'ety *n.* sub- (3).
sub'war'den *n* sub- (2).

—*adj.* **success′less.**—*adv.* **success′lessly.**—*ns.* **success′lessness; success′or** one who, or that which, succeeds or comes after: sometimes, one appointed to succeed; **success′orship.**—**succession** duty a tax imposed on succession to property; **success story** (the record of) a person's rise to prosperity, fame, etc.—**in succession** following one another, one after another. [L. *succēdĕre*, *-cēssum—sub-*, in sense of near, next after, *cēdĕre*, to go.]

succentor *sək-sent′ər*, *n.* a subordinate cantor: bass soloist in a choir. [L. *succentor—succinĕre—sub*, under, *canĕre*, to sing.]

succès *sük-se*, (Fr.) *n.* success.—**succès d'estime** (*des-tēm*) a success of esteem or approval (if not of profit); **succès fou** (*fōō*) success with wild enthusiasm; **succès de scandale** (*də skä-dal*) success of a book, dramatic entertainment, due not to merit but to its connection with or reference to a topical scandal.

success, etc. See **succeed.**

succinate. See **succinum.**

succinct *sək-*, *suk-singkt′*, *adj.* concise.—*adv.* **succinct′ly.**—*n.* **succinct′ness.** [L. *succinctus—sub*, up, *cingĕre*, to gird.]

succinum *suk′sin-əm*, *n.* amber.—*n.* **suc′cinate** a salt of succinic acid.—*adj.* **succin′ic** of, relating to, or got from, amber.—**succinic acid** an acid got from resins, etc. [L. *succinum*, amber.]

succotash *suk′ō-tash*, *n.* a stew of green Indian corn and beans and sometimes pork. [Narragansett *msiquatash*.]

Succoth. See **Sukkoth.**

succour, U.S. **succor,** *suk′ər*, *v.t.* to aid in distress: to relieve.—*n.* aid: relief.—*adj.* **succ′ourable.**—*n.* **succ′ourer.**—*adj.* **succ′ourless.** [A.Fr. *socorre—*, *succurrēre*, to run to help—*sub*, up, *currĕre*, to run.]

succubus *suk′ū-bəs*, **succuba***-bə*, *ns.* a devil supposed to assume a female body and consort with men in their sleep:—*pl.* **succ′ubuses, succ′ubæ, succ′ubi, succ′ubae** (*-bē*). [L. *succuba*, a whore—*sub*, under, *cubāre*, to lie.]

succulent *suk′ū-lənt*, *adj.* juicy: sappy: juicy and fleshy, or (loosely) merely fleshy (*bot.*).—*n.* a succulent plant.—*ns.* **succ′ulence, succ′ulency.**—*adv.* **succ′ulently.** [L. *sūculentus—sūcus*, juice.]

succumb *sə-kum′*, *v.i.* to lie down under or sink under pressure, difficulty, temptation, etc. (often with *to*): to die. [L. *sub*, under, *cumbĕre*, to lie down.]

succursal *suk-ûr′sl*, *adj.* subsidiary (usu. *ecclesiastical*): branch. [Fr.,—L. *succurrēre*, to succour.]

such *such*, *adj.* of that kind, the like kind, or the same kind (often followed by *as* or by a clause beginning with *that*): so characterised: of what kind: what (exclamatorily): so great: before-mentioned: some particular but unspecified.—*adv.* so (preceding the indefinite article if any).—*pron.* such a person, persons, thing, or things: the before-mentioned: that.—*adj.* **such′like** of such a kind.—*pron.* suchlike persons or things (or person or thing).—*adj.* **such′-and-such** this or that, some, some or other (before the indefinite article if any).—*pron.* such-and-such a person.—**as such** as it is described: in a particular capacity; **such as** for example; **such as it is** being what it is (and no better); **such that** in such a way, to such an extent, etc., that. [O.E. *swilc*; cog. with Goth. *swaleiks*.]

suck *suk*, *v.t.* to draw in with the mouth: to draw something (esp. milk) from with the mouth: to apply to or hold in the mouth and perform the movements of sucking: to draw by suction: to render by suction: to absorb: to draw in: to extract: to imbibe: to drain.—*v.i.* to draw with the mouth: to draw the breast: to draw by suction: to make a noise of sucking: to draw in air as a dry pump: to draw in.—*n.* act or spell of sucking: milk drawn from the breast: suction.—*adj.*

sucked.—*n.* **suck′er** one who, or that which, sucks: a sucking-pig, new-born whale, or other unweaned animal: a sucking-fish: an adhesive organ: a device that adheres, draws water, etc., by suction, as a pump piston: a toy consisting of a leather disc and a string, for lifting stones, etc.: a sucking organ: a shoot rising from underground and developing into a new plant: a new shoot: a gullible person, one taken advantage of (*coll.*).—*v.t.* to strip off superfluous shoots from.—*v.i.* to develop suckers.—*adj.* **suck′ered** having suckers.—*n.* and *adj.* **suck′ing.**—**suck′ing-fish** remora or other fish with an adhesive disc; **suck′ing-pig** a young milk-fed pig.—**suck in** to engulf; **sucks (to you)!** a derisive expression; **suck up to** (*slang*) to toady to. [O.E. *sūcan, sūgan*.]

suckle *suk′l*, *v.t.* to give suck to, as a mammal feeding its young.—*n.* **suck′ling** an unweaned child or animal: the act of giving suck. [**suck.**]

sucre *sōō′krä*, *n.* the monetary unit of Ecuador. [Named after Antonio José de *Sucre* (1795-1830).]

sucrose *sōō′, sū′krōs*, *n.* cane-sugar from any source.—*n.* **su′crase** same as **invertase.** [Fr. *sucre*, sugar.]

suction *suk′shən*, *n.* the act or power of sucking or of drawing or adhesion by reducing pressure of air.—*adj.* **sucto′rial** adapted for sucking.—**suction pump** a pump for raising fluids by suction. [L. *sūgĕre*, *suctum*; related to **suck.**]

sud. See **suds.**

Sudan *sōō-dan′*, *n.* a region of Africa, south of the Sahara and Libyan deserts: a republic of N.E. Africa. —*n.* **Sudanese** (*-ēz′* or *sōō′*) a native or inhabitant of (the) Sudan:—*pl.* **Sudanese.**—*adj.* of or pertaining to (the) Sudan or its inhabitants.—*n.* **Sudan′ic** a group of languages spoken in the Sudan.—*adj.* of or relating to these languages: (also without *cap.*) of or relating to the Sudan.—Also **Soudan**(**ese**).

sudate *sū′dāt, sōō′*, (*rare*) *v.i.* to sweat.—*ns.* **suda′rium,** a cloth for wiping sweat, esp. the veil or handkerchief of St. Veronica, believed to have retained miraculously the image of Christ's face; **suda′tion** sweating: sweat: a watery exudation from plants; **sudatorium** (*-də-tō′ri-əm, -tō′*) a sweating-room.—*adj.* **su′datory** (*-tə-ri*) of sweat: inducing sweating. [L. *sūdāre, -ātum*, to sweat.]

sudd *sud*, *n.* a mass of floating vegetable matter obstructing the White Nile: a temporary dam. [Ar. *sudd*, obstruction.]

sudden *sud′n*, *adj.* without warning or apparent preparation: unexpected: hasty: abrupt: swift in action or production.—*adv.* **sudd′enly.**—*n.* **sudd′enness.**—**sudden death** (*sport*) an extended period to settle a tied contest, play terminating the moment one of the contestants scores.—**(all) of a sudden,** all at once. [A.Fr. *sodain*—L. *subitāneus*.]

sudor *sū′dōr, sōō′, -dər*, (*med.*) *n.* sweat.—*adj.* **sudorif′erous** provoking or secreting sweat; **sudorif′ic** causing sweat.—*n.* a diaphoretic. [L. *sūdor, -ōris*, sweat.]

suds *sudz*, *n.pl.* froth of soapy water (rarely in *sing. sud*).—*adj.* **sud′sy.** [Prob. conn. with **seethe.**]

sue *sū, sōō*, *v.t.* to prosecute at law: to petition for, apply for.—*v.i.* to make legal claim: to make application: to entreat:—*pr.p.* **su′ing;** *pa.t.* and *pa.p.* **sued.**—*n.* and *adj.* **su′ing.**—**sue out** to petition for and take out. [O.Fr. *suir* (Fr. *suivre*)—L. *sequi, secūtus*, to follow.]

suede, suède *swād*, *n.* undressed kid.—Also *adj.*—*n.* **suedette′** a fabric made to resemble suede. [Fr. (*gants de*) *Suède*, (gloves of) Sweden.]

suet *sū′it, sōō′*, *n.* a solid fatty tissue, accumulating about the kidneys and omentum of the ox, sheep, etc.—*adj.* **su′ety** (also **su′etty**).—**suet pudding** a boiled pudding, savoury or sweet, made with suet. [O.Fr. *seu*—L. *sēbum*, fat.]

suffer *suf'ər, v.t.* to undergo: to endure: to be affected by: to permit *(arch.)*.—*v.i.* to feel pain or punishment: to sustain loss: to be injured: to die: to be executed or martyred: to be the object of an action.—*adj.* **suff'erable.**—*n.* **suff'erableness.**—*adv.* **suff'erably.**—*ns.* **suff'erance** suffering: endurance: forbearance: tacit assent: toleration; **suff'erer.**—*n.* and *adj.* **suff'ering.**—**on sufferance** tolerated, but not encouraged. [L. *sufferre*—*sub*, under, *ferre*, to bear.]

suffice *sə-fīs', v.i.* to be enough: to be competent or adequate.—*v.t.* to satisfy.—*n.* **sufficiency** *(sə-fish'ən-si)*; state of being sufficient: competence: a sufficient quantity: means enough for a comfortable living, a competency: conceit.—*adj.* **suffic'ient** sufficing: competent *(arch.)*: adequate: effective.—*n.* *(coll.)* a sufficient quantity, enough.—*adv.* **suffic'iently.**—*adj.* **suffic'ing.**—**suffice it** be it enough. [Through Fr.—L. *sufficĕre*, to suffice—*sub, facĕre,* to make.]

suffix *suf'iks, n.* a syllable or other addition at the end of a word: an index placed after and below a symbol, as *n* in *x*ₙ *(math.)*.—*v.t.* **suffix'** (also *suf'iks*) to add as a suffix. [L. *suffixus*—*sub*, under, *figĕre*, to fix.]

suffocate *suf'ə-kāt, v.t.* and *v.i.* to choke by stopping of the breath: to stifle.—*n.* and *adj.* **suff'ocating.**—*adv.* **suff'ocatingly.**—*n.* **suffoca'tion.** [L. *suffōcāre*—*sub*, under, *faucēs*, the throat.]

Suffolk punch. See **punch**[1].

suffragan *suf'rə-gən, n.* an assistant, a coadjutor-bishop: any bishop in relation to his metropolitan.—Also *adj.*—*n.* **suff'raganship.** [L.L. *suffrāgāneus,* assistant, supporting.—L. *suffrāgium,* a vote.]

suffrage *suf'rij, n.* a prayer, esp. for the dead, or in a litany: a vote: supporting opinion: power of voting.—*ns.* **suffragette** *(suf'rə-jet')* a woman seeking by violent methods (or otherwise) to obtain votes for women; **suff'ragist** a believer in the right (e.g. of women) to vote; **suff'ragism.** [L. *suffrāgium,* a vote.]

suffuse *sə-fūz', v.t.* to pour over: to overspread or cover, as with a liquid, a tint.—*n.* **suffu'sion** *(-zhən)*. [L. *sub*, underneath, *fundĕre, fūsum,* to pour.]

Sufi *sōō'fē, n.* a pantheistic Muslim mystic:—*pl.* **Su'fis.**—*n.* **Su'f(i)ism.**—*adjs.* **Su'fic, Suf(i)ist'ic.** [Ar. *çūfī,* lit. man of wool—*çuf,* wool.]

sugar *shōōg'ər, n.* a sweet substance *(sucrose, cane-sugar)*, obtained chiefly from cane and beet: extended to any member of the same class of carbohydrates: a term of endearment *(coll.)*.—*adj.* of sugar.—*v.t.* to sprinkle, coat, or mix with sugar.—*adj.* **sug'ared** sweetened or coated with sugar: sugary.—*ns.* **sug'ariness; sug'aring** sweetening with sugar: coating trees with sugar as a method of collecting insects: formation of sugar from maple sap *(sugaring off, U.S.)*.—*adjs.* **sug'arless; sug'ary** like sugar in taste or appearance: abounding in sugar: offensively or cloyingly sweet.—**sugar basin,** bowl a small basin for holding sugar at table; **sug'ar-beet** any variety of common beet, esp. variety *Rapa,* grown for sugar; **sug'ar-can'dy** sugar in large crystals; **sug'ar-cane** a woody grass *(Saccharum officinarum)* from which sugar is chiefly obtained.—*adj.* **sug'ar-coat'ed** coated with sugar.—**sug'ar-cube, -lump** a small square block of sugar; **sug'ar-daddy** an elderly man lavishing money on a young woman or young women; **sug'ar-gum** a eucalyptus with sweetish foliage; **sug'ar-house** a sugar factory; **sug'ar-loaf** a loaf or mass of sugar: a hill or other object of like form; **sug'ar-ma'ple** a N. American maple *(Acer saccharum* or kindred species) from whose sap sugar is made; **sugar pea** see **mange-tout;** **sug'ar-plum** a small round boiled sweet: a compliment or other gratification; **sug'ar-refi'ner;**

sug'ar-refi'nery; sug'ar-refi'ning; sugar sifter a container for sugar with a perforated top; **sugar soap** an alkaline cleansing or stripping preparation for paint surfaces; **sugar tongs** small tongs for lifting lumps of sugar at table.—**sugar of lead** lead acetate, sweet and poisonous, used as a mordant for dyeing and printing textiles, and as a drier for paints and varnishes; **sugar the pill** to compensate somewhat for an unpleasant prospect, unwelcome imposition, etc. [O.Fr. (Fr.) *sucre*—Ar. *sukkar;* the *g* unexplained; cf. **Saccharum.**]

suggest *sə-jest', v.t.* to introduce indirectly to the thoughts: to call up in the mind: to put forward, as a plan, hypothesis, thought, etc.: to give an impression of.—*v.i.* to make suggestions.—*ns.* **suggest'er; suggestibil'ity.**—*adj.* **suggest'ible** capable of being suggested, or of being influenced by suggestion, esp. hypnotic.—*ns.* **suggest'ion** *(-yən)* process or act of suggesting: hint: proposal: indecent proposal: incitement, temptation: communication of belief or impulse to a hypnotised person.—*adj.* **suggest'ive** containing a hint: fitted to suggest: pertaining to hypnotic suggestion: tending to awake indecent imaginations *(coll. euphemism)*.—*adv.* **suggest'ively.**—*n.* **suggest'iveness.** [L. *suggerĕre, -gestum, sub,* under, *gerĕre,* to carry.]

sui *sōō'ī, sōō'ē, sōō'ē,* (L.) of himself, herself, itself.—**sui generis** *(jen'ər-is, ge'ne-ris)* of its own kind, the only one of its kind.—**sui juris** *(jōōr'is, ūr')* having full legal capacity to act: (in Roman law) having the rights of a freeman.

suicide *sū'i-sīd, sōō', n.* one who kills himself intentionally: self-murder: a self-inflicted disaster.—*adj.* **suici'dal.**—*adv.* **suici'dally.**—**suicide pact** an agreement between people to kill themselves together.—**commit suicide** to kill oneself. [L. *sui,* of himself, *caedĕre,* to kill.]

suint *swint, n.* dried perspiration in wool. [Fr.]

suit *sūt, sōōt, n.* process or act of suing: an action at law: courtship: a petition: a series: a sequence: a set: a set of cards of the same denomination, in the pack or in one hand: a number of things of the same kind or made to be used together, as clothes or armour.—*v.t.* to provide, furnish: to fall in with the requirements of: to fit: to become, look attractive on: to please.—*v.i.* to agree: to be convenient.—*n.* **suitabil'ity.**—*adj.* **suit'able** that suits: fitting: accordant: adequate.—*n.* **suit'ableness.**—*adv.* **suit'ably.**—*adj.* **suit'ed** dressed, clothed.—*ns.* **suit'ing** (sometimes in *pl.*) cloth suitable for making suits; **suit'or** one who sues: a petitioner: a wooer.—**suit'-case** an easily portable oblong travelling-bag for carrying suits or clothes.—**follow suit** to play a card of the suit led: to do the same; **strong suit** one's forte; **suit yourself** do what you like. [Fr. *suite;* cf. **sue, suite.**]

suite *swēt, n.* a train of followers or attendants: a set, as of furniture or rooms: a sequence of instrumental movements, usu. dance-tunes, in related keys. [Fr., —a L.L. form of L. *secūta,* fem. pa.p. of *sequī,* to follow.]

suitor. See **suit.**

suk(h). See **souk.**

sukiyaki *s(ōō)-kē-(y)ä'kē, n.* thinly-sliced beef, vegetables, soya sauce, etc., cooked quickly together, often at table. [Jap.]

Sukkoth *suk'əth, suk'ət, sōō'kəs,* **Sukkot** *suk'ət, ns.* the Jewish Feast of Tabernacles.—Also **Succoth.** [Heb., hut, tent.]

sulcus *sul'kəs, n.* a groove, furrow, fissure: a fissure between two convolutions of the brain:—*pl.* **sul'ci** *(-sī)*.—*adjs.* **sul'cate, -d** furrowed, grooved: with parallel longitudinal furrows. [L. *sulcus,* a furrow.]

sulfate, sulfur, etc. U.S. spellings of sulphate, sulphur, etc.

sulk *sulk*, *v.i.* to be sullen.—*n.* one who sulks: (usu. in *pl.*) a fit of sulking.—*adv.* sulk'ily.—*n.* sulk'iness.—*adj.* sulk'y sullen: inclined to sulk. [Prob. from the root in O.E. *āseolcan*, to slack, be slow.]

sullage *sul'ij*, *n.* filth: refuse, sewage: scum: scoria: silt. [Perh. conn. with sully.]

sullen *sul'ən*, *adj.* gloomily angry and silent: malignant, baleful: dark: dull.—*adv.* sullenly.—*n.* (usu. in *pl.*) a fit of sullenness, the sulks.—*adv.* sull'enly.—*n.* sull'enness. [App. through O.Fr. deriv. from L *sōlus*, alone.]

sully *sul'i*, *v.t.* to soil: to spot: to tarnish.—*pr.p.* sull'ying; *pa.t.* and *pa.p.* sull'ied. [O.E. *sylian*, to defile—*sol*, mud; or from O.Fr. *souiller*, to soil.]

sulphur *sul'far*, sulfur (q.v.) *n.* a yellow non-metallic element (S; at. numb. 16) and mineral, very brittle, fusible, and inflammable.—*adj.* of sulphur.—*v.t.* to treat or fumigate with sulphur.—*adj.* sul'pha of a class of synthetic antibacterial drugs, the sulphonamides.—*ns.* sulphadi'azine a sulphonamide used against pneumonia, etc.; sulphanil'amide a sulphonamide used against bacteria; sul'phate a salt of sulphuric acid.—*v.t.* to form a deposit of lead sulphate on: to treat or impregnate with sulphur or a sulphate.—*v.i.* to become sulphated.—*ns.* sul'phide a compound of an element or radical with sulphur: a salt of hydrosulphuric acid; sul'phite a salt of sulphurous acid.—*pfx.* sul'pho- sulphur.—*ns.* sulphon'amide an amide of a sulphonic acid, any of a group of drugs with antibacterial action; sul'phone any of a class of substances consisting of two organic radicals combined with SO_2.—*adj.* sulphon'ic.—*v.t.* sul'phurate to combine with, or subject to the action of, sulphur.—*ns.* sulphūrā'tion; sulphūrā'tor.—*adjs.* sulphū'reous sulphury: sulphur-yellow; sul'phuretted combined with sulphur; sulphū'ric containing sulphur in higher valency—opp. to *sulphurous*.—*v.t.* sul'phurise, -ize to sulphurate.—*adjs.* sul'phurous (-*für*-, or -*fər*-) pertaining to, resembling, or containing sulphur: containing sulphur in lower valency (*chem.*; -*für*'); sulphury (*sul'fər-i*) like sulphur.—sul'phur-bottom the blue whale (from the yellowish spots underneath); sulphur dioxide SO_2, a suffocating gas discharged into the atmosphere in waste from industrial processes, used in manufacture of sulphuric acid, and in bleaching, preserving, etc.; sulphuretted hydrogen (*arch.*) hydrogen sulphide, H_2S; sulphuric acid oil of vitriol, H_2SO_4; sulphurous acid H_2SO_3; sul'phur-root, sul'phurwort an umbelliferous plant akin to parsnip, with yellow flower and juice. [L. *sulphur*, *sulfur*, *sulpur*, *-uris*.]

sultan *sul'tən*, *n.* a Muslim ruler, esp. the Ottoman emperor: the purple coot: a small white (orig. Turkish) variety of hen.—*ns.* sultana (*sul-* or *səl-tä'na*) a lady of a sultan's harem: a king's mistress: a concubine: a small, pale, seedless raisin; sul'tanate.—*adj.* sultanic (*sul-tan'ik*).—*n.* sul'tanship. [Ar. *sultân*.]

sultry *sul'tri*, *adj.* close and oppressive: hot with anger: passionate, voluptuous: (of language) lurid, verging on the indecent.—*adv.* sul'trily.—*n.* sul'triness. [swelter.]

sum *sum*, *n.* total: whole: aggregate: result of addition: amount: a quantity of money: a problem in addition, hence in arithmetic generally: chief points: substance or result: summary: height, culmination, completion.—*v.t.* (often with *up*) to add: to make up the total of: to be an epitome of, exemplify in little: to summarise: to reckon up, form an estimate of.—*v.i.* (with *up*) to summarise or make a summing-up:—*pr.p.* summ'ing; *pa.t.* and *pa.p.* summed.—*n.* summation see summa.

—*adjs.* sum'less; summed.—*n.* summ'er.—*n.* and *adj.* summ'ing.—summ'ing-up' a recapitulation or review of the leading points, a judge's summary survey of the evidence given to a jury before it withdraws to consider its verdict; sum total complete or final sum.—in sum in short: to sum up; sum and substance the gist: the essence. [O.Fr. *summe*—L. *summa*—*summus*, highest.]

sumac, sumach *sōō'*, *shōō'*, *sū'mak*, *n.* any tree or shrub of the genus *Rhus*: the leaves and shoots used in dyeing. [Fr. *sumac* or L.L. *sumach*—Ar. *summāq*.]

Sumerian *sōō-mēr'i-ən*, *adj.* of or relating to the ancient civilisation, people, language, etc. of the region of *Sumer* in southern Babylonia.—*n.* a native of Sumer: the language.

summa *sum'ə*, *n.* a treatise giving a summary of a whole subject.—*adv.* summ'arily.—*n.* summ'ariness.—*v.t.* summ'arise, -ize to present in a summary or briefly.—*ns.* summ'arist one who summarises.—*adj.* summ'ary condensed: brief: compendious: done by a short method: without unnecessary formalities or delay, without further application to the court.—*n.* an abstract, abridgment, or compendium.—*n.* summā'tion process of finding the sum: addition: a summing-up, summary.—*adjs.* summā'tional; summ'ative additive.—summary offence (*legal*) one which is tried by a magistrate. [L. *summa*, sum, *summārium* a summary.]

summer[1] *sum'ər*, *n.* the warmest season of the year: a spell of warm weather (see Indian summer): a year of age or time.—*adj.* of, for, occurring in, summer.—*v.i.* to pass the summer.—*v.t.* to keep through the summer.—*n.* summ'ering.—*adjs.* summ'erlike; summ'ery like summer: suitable for summer.—summ'er-house a structure in a garden for sitting in: a summer residence; summer pudding a pudding made of fruit and bread; summer school a course of study held during the summer; summ'ertide the summer season; summ'ertime the summer season: summer time time adopted from 1916 for daylight-saving purposes—one hour in advance of Greenwich time.—*adj.* summ'er-weight of clothes, light enough to be worn in summer. [O.E. *sumer*, *sumor*; Du. *zomer*, Ger. *Sommer*.]

summer[2] *sum'ər*, *n.* a great horizontal beam or lintel (also summ'er-tree). [See sumpter.]

summersault, summerset. Same as somersault, somerset.

summit *sum'it*, *n.* the highest point or degree: the top: a summit conference.—*adj.* summ'itless.—summit conference, talks a conference between heads of states; sometimes extended to mean a conference between heads of lesser organisations; summ'it-level the highest level. [O.Fr. *sommette*, *somet* (Fr *sommet*), dim. of *som*—L. *summum*, highest.]

summon *sum'ən*, *v.t.* to call up, forth, or together: to call upon to appear or to do something: to rouse to exertion.—*adj.* summ'onable.—*n. sing.* summ'ons a summoning or an authoritative call: a call to appear, esp. in court:—*pl.* summ'onses.—*v.t.* to serve with a summons. [O.Fr. *somoner*—L. *summonēre*—*sub*-, secretly, *monēre*, to warn: sense partly from O.E. *somnian*, to assemble.]

summum bonum *sum'əm bō'nəm*, *sōōm'ōōm bo'nōōm*, (L.) the chief good.

sumo *sōō'mō*, *n.* a traditional Japanese sport, a form of wrestling:—*pl.* su'mos. [Jap. *sumō*.]

sump *sump*, *n.* a hole or depression that receives liquid, as for molten metal, for sea-water at a saltwork, drainage-water in a mine, oil in an engine. [Du. *somp*; Ger. *Sumpf*.]

sumpter *sum(p)'tər*, *n.* a pack-horse.—sump'ter-

horse. [O.Fr. *sommetier*, a pack-horse driver—Gr. *sagma*, a pack-saddle, *sattein*, to pack.]

sumptuary *sum(p)′tū-ər-i, adj.* pertaining to or regulating expense.—*n.* **sumptūos′ity** sumptuousness.—*adj.* **sump′tŏous** costly: magnificently luxurious.—*adv.* **sump′tŏously.**—*n.* **sump′tŏousness.** [L. *sŭmptus*, cost—*sūmĕre, sŭmptum*, to take.]

sun *sun, n.* the body which is the gravitational centre and source of light and heat to our planetary system (often with *cap.*): the central body of a system: a great luminary: a climate: sunshine: a year (*poet.*): a day (*poet.*).—*v.t.* to expose to the sun's rays:—*pr.p.* **sunn′ing;** *pa.t.* and *pa.p.* **sunned.**—*adj.* **sun′less.**—*n.* **sun′lessness.**—*adj.* **sun′like.**—*adv.* **sunn′ily.**—*n.* **sunn′iness.**—*adj.* **sunn′y** of, from, like or lighted, coloured or warmed by the sun: genial: cheerful.—*adj.* and *adv.* **sun′ward** towards the sun.—*adv.* **sun′wards; sun′wise** in the direction of the sun's apparent revolution.—*adj.* **sun′-and-plan′et** geared so that one wheel moves round another.—**sun′-bath, -bathe** exposure of the body to the sun's rays.—*v.i.* **sun′bathe**—*n.* **sun′bather (-bādh-); sun′bathing.**—*adj.* **sun′-baked** baked or dried by the heat of the sun.—**sun′beam** a shaft of sunlight; **sun′-bear** the Malayan bear: sometimes the Himalayan bear; **sun′bed** a sun-lamp in the form of a bed, upon which one lies in order to obtain an artificial suntan; **sun′-bird** any of a family of small tropical birds akin to honey-eaters, superficially like humming-birds; **sun′-blind** an outside shade or awning for a window; **sun′-bonnet** a light bonnet projecting beyond the face to protect from the sun; **sun′bow** an iris formed by the sun, esp. in the spray of a cataract; **sun′burn** reddening (often excessive) or browning of the skin by the sun.—*v.t.* to become so browned.—*adjs.* **sun′burned, sun′burnt.**—**sun′burst** a strong outburst of sunlight: a jewel or ornament resembling the rayed sun.—*adj.* **sun′-cured** cured in the sun.—**sun dance** a N. American Indian ceremonial dance, performed in honour of the sun; **sun′-deck** the upper deck of a passenger ship; **sun′-dew** an insectivorous bog-plant (*Drosera*); **sun′dial** a device for telling the time by a shadow cast by the sun; **sun′-disc** a winged disc, symbol of the sun-god; **sun′-dog** a mock sun or parhelion; **sun′down** sunset; **sun′-downer** in Australia, a loafer who arrives at a station in time for a meal and lodging, but too late for work: a drink after sunset; **sun′-dress** a low-cut dress, leaving the arms, shoulders and back exposed to the sun.—*adjs.* **sun′-dried** dried in the sun; **sun′fast** (*U.S.*) of fabric colour, not fading in the sunlight.—**sun′-fish** a fish of nearly circular profile, as the opah, or any member of the family *Molidae*; **sun′flower** a composite plant (Helianthus) or its large head with yellow rays, fabled to turn toward the sun: applied to various more or less similar kinds; **sun′glass** a burning-glass: (in *pl.*) dark-lensed spectacles used against strong light; **sun′god** a god personifying or concerned with the sun; **sun′hat,** (*arch.*) **sun′-helmet** a hat with shady brim; **sun′-lamp** a lamp that gives out ultraviolet rays curatively or to induce artificial suntan: a lamp producing a very bright light, used in film-making; **sun′light** the light of the sun.—*adj.* **sun′lit** lighted up by the sun.—**sun′-lounge,** *U.S.* **sun′-parlor,** a room with large windows, or a glass wall, to admit the maximum sunlight; **sun′-myth** a solar myth; **sunny side** a pleasant or cheerful part or point of view: an age less than one specified, as *on the sunny side of fifty* (see also below).—*adj.* **sun′proof.**—**sun′rise** rising or first appearance of the sun above the horizon: the time or colour-effects of this rising; **sun′set** the setting or going down of the sun: the time or phenomenon of going down; **sun′-shade** a parasol: an awning; **sun′shine** bright sunlight: brightness: prosperity: geniality.—*adjs.* **sun′shine** sunshiny: fairweather; **sun′shiny.**—**sun′shine-roof, sun′-roof** a carroof that can be slid open; **sun′spot** a relatively dark patch on the surface of the sun; **sun′stroke** a nervous disease caused by great heat; **sun′suit** a child's outfit for playing in the sun, leaving most of the body exposed; **sun′tan** a browning of the skin as a result of exposure to the sun.—*adj. v.t.*—*adj.* **sun′tanned.**—**sun′trap** a sheltered, sunny place; **sun′-up** sunrise; **sun′-visor.**—**a place in the sun** a place or opportunity for good living or attaining prosperity; **between sun and sun, from sun to sun** between sunrise and sunset; **catch the sun** to be sunburnt; **take the sun** to ascertain the sun's meridian altitude: to walk or laze in the sun; **under the sun** on earth. [O.E. *sunne.*]

sundae *sun′dā, -di, n.* an ice-cream with syrup or crushed fruit: a mixed nougat or confection. [Perh. Sunday.]

Sunday *sun′di, n.* the first day of the week, anciently dedicated to the sun, now regarded as the Sabbath by most Christians.—*adj.* of, for, occurring on, Sunday.—**Sunday best** one's best clothes; **Sunday painters** people who paint seriously but in their spare time; **Sunday school** a school for religious (orig. general) instruction on Sunday.—**a month of Sundays** a long time; **the Sundays** the Sunday newspapers. [O.E. *sunnan dæg.*]

sunder *sun′dər, v.t.* and *v.i.* (*arch., poet.*) to separate: to part.—**in sunder** (*B.*) asunder. [O.E. *syndrian,* to separate, *sundor,* separate.]

sundry *sun′dri, adj.* separate: more than one or two: several: divers.—*n.pl.* **sun′dries** sundry things: different small things.—**all and sundry** all collectively and individually. [O.E. *syndrig.*]

sung *sung.* See sing.

sunk *sungk,* **sunken** *sungk′n.* See sink.

Sunna *sŏŏn′ə, sun′ə, n.* Muslim traditional teaching.—*n.* **Sunn′i (-ē)** an orthodox Muslim.—Also **Sunn′ite.**

sunny, sunward(s), sunwise. See sun.

Suomi *swö′mē, n.* the Finnish language.—*n.pl.* the Finns.—*adjs.* **Suo′mic, Suo′mish.**

sup *sup, v.t.* to take into the mouth, as a liquid: to eat with a spoon.—*v.i.* to eat the evening meal (*arch.*): to sip:—*pr.p.* **supp′ing;** *pa.t.* and *pa p.* **supped.**—*n.* a small mouthful, as of a liquid. [O.E. *sŭpan;* partly from O.Fr. *soper, souper* (Fr *souper*), to take supper.]

super- *sōō′, sū′pər,* in composition, above, beyond, in addition, in excess, very.—*n.* **su′per** a colloquial shortening of **supernumerary** (esp. a supernumerary actor), and of **superintendent.**—*adj.* coll. shortening of **superfine:** very good or very delightful.—*v.i.* **superabound′** to be more, very, or excessively abundant.—*n.* **superabun′dance.**—*adj.* **superabund′ant.**—*adv.* **superabund′antly.**—*adj.* **superacute′** abnormally or excessively acute.—*v.t* **superadd′** to add over and above.—*n.* **superaddi′tion.**—*v.t.* **super′cal′ender** to give a high polish to by calendering.—*adj.* **supercal′endered.**—*n.* **supercar′go** a person in a ship placed in charge of the cargo and superintending all commercial transactions of the voyage:—*pl.* **supercar′goes.**—*n.* **supercar′goship.**—*v.t.* **super′charge′** to fill to excess: to charge above the normal: to add pressure to.—*ns.* **su′percharger** a device for increasing the pressure in an internal combustion engine; **su′perclass** a biological category between a division and a class; **superclus′ter** (*astron.*) a large cluster of galaxies.—*adj.* **supercolum′nar** (*archit.*) above a column or colonnade: with one colonnade above another.—*ns.* **supercolumniā′tion; superconductiv′ity** complete loss of electrical resistivity shown by certain pure metals and alloys at temperatures approaching absolute zero.—*adjs.* **superconduc'ting; superconduc'tive.**—*ns.* **superconduc'tor; supercon'tinent** any of the vast land-masses from which the continents were orig. formed.—*v.t.* **supercool'** to cool below normal freezing-point without freezing.—*adj.* **supercrit'ical** capable of sustaining a chain reaction such that the rate of reaction increases.—*ns.* **super-e'go** (*psych.*) the strong unconscious inhibitory mechanism which criticises the ego and causes it pain and distress when it accepts unworthy impulses from the id; **supereleva'tion** excess in height: the difference in height between the opposite sides of a road or railway on a curve; **superem'inence** eminence in a superior degree: excellence beyond others.—*adj.* **superem'inent.**—*adv.* **superem'inently.**—*adj.* **super-exc'ellence** excellence above others, or in an uncommon degree.—*adj.* **superexc'ellent.**—*n.* **su'perfamily** a group between a suborder and a family.—*adjs.* **superfatt'ed** (of soap) having an excess of fat, so that there is no free alkali; **su'perfine** of specially fine size or quality (short form **super**): over-nice.—*n.* **su'perfineness.**—*adj.* **superflu'id.**—*ns.* **superfluid'ity** a phenomenon observed in a form of helium in which internal friction is negligible; **supergi'ant** a very bright star of enormous size and low density, such as Betelgeuse and Antares; **su'pergrass** (*slang*) a police informer who has given information leading to the arrest of a great number of criminals.—*v.t.* **superheat'** to heat to excess: to heat (steam, etc.) above the temperature of saturation: to heat above normal boiling-point without vaporisation.—*n.* state of being superheated: amount of superheating.—*n.* **superheat'er.**—*adj.* **superhet'erodyne** heterodyne with beats above audible frequency (*coll.* **superhet'**).—*n.* a superheterodyne receiver.—*n.* **superhigh'way** (*U.S.*) a wide road for fast motor-traffic.—*adj.* **superhu'man** above man: above the capacity of man: more or higher than human.—*adv.* **superhu'manly.**—*v.t.* **superimpose'** to set on the top of something else: to place one over another: to establish in superaddition.—*adj.* **superimposed'.**—*ns.* **superimposi'tion; superincum'bence.**—*adj.* **superincum'bent** resting on the top: overlying: overhanging.—*v.t.* **superinduce'** to bring in over and above, or in supersession of, something else: to superadd.—*ns.* **superinduce'ment, superinduc'tion.**—*v.t.* **superintend'** to have or exercise oversight or charge of: to control, manage.—*v.i.* to exercise supervision.—*ns.* **superinten'dence; superinten'dency** office or district of a superintendent.—*adj.* **superinten'dent** superintending.—*n.* one who superintends: the head of a school, institution, etc.: a police officer above an inspector.—*ns.* **superinten'dentship; su'per-jet** a supersonic jet aircraft.—*adjs.* **superlu'nar, superlu'nary** above the moon: not of this world.—*ns.* **su'perman** a being of higher type than man: ideal man: a dominating man; **su'permarket** (orig. *U.S.*) a large, mainly self-service, retail store selling food and other domestic goods (also **su'permart**).—*adjs.* **supermun'dane** above the world; **supernat'ural** above or beyond nature: not according to the course of nature: miraculous: spiritual.—*n.* that which is supernatural.—*v.t.* **supernat'uralise, -ize** to bring into the supernatural sphere.—*ns.* **supernat'uralism** the belief in the influence of the supernatural in the world; **supernat'uralist.**—*adv.* **supernat'urally.**—*n.* **su'pernature** the supernatural.—*adj.* **supernor'mal** beyond what is normal: in greater number, amount, concentration, etc., than the normal.—*n.* **superord'er** a category between an order and a subclass or sometimes class (*biol.*).—*adj.* **superord'inate** superior in rank.—*n.* a superior in rank.—*n.* **superphos'phate** an acid phosphate: now

usu. a mixture of calcium sulphate and calcium acid phosphate used as a manure.—*adj.* **superphys'ical** beyond, or of higher order than, the physical.—*v.t.* **superpose'** to bring, or suppose to be brought, into coincidence: to place vertically over or on something else.—*adj.* **superposed'.**—*ns.* **superposi'tion; su'per-power** a very powerful state, often applied to the U.S. and the U.S.S.R.—*v.t.* **supersat'urate** to saturate beyond the normal point.—*n.* **supersatura'tion.**—*adj.* **supersen'sitive** excessively sensitive.—*ns.* **supersen'sitiveness; su'perstar** an extremely popular and successful star of the cinema, popular music, etc.; **su'perstore** a large supermarket, which usu. sells many different goods in addition to food; **super-stra'tum** (or *-strā'*) overlying stratum.—*adj.* **superstruct'ural.**—*n.* **su'perstructure** an upper structure or part of a structure.—*adjs.* **supersubstan'tial** transcending substance, esp. material substance; **supersubt'le** over-subtle: extremely subtle.—*ns.* **su'pertanker** a very large tanker, with a minimum capacity of 75 000 tons; **su'pertax** an extra or additional tax on large incomes (term not in official use).—*adjs.* **superterra'nean** living or situated on the earth's surface; **superterres'trial** supermundane.—*n.* **superton'ic** the tone next above the tonic. [L. *super*, above.]

superable *sū'pər-ə-bl, sōō'*, *adj.* that can be overcome. —*adv.* **su'perably.**

superannuate *sōō-, sū-pər-an'ū-āt*, *v.t.* to set aside or cause to retire on account of age: to pension off.—*adj.* superannuated.—*n.* a superannuated person.—*adjs.* **superann'uable; superann'ūated.**—*n.* **superannūa'tion** the act or state of superannuating: a pension: a regular contribution paid by an employee towards a pension. [L. *super*, above; *annus*, year.]

superb *sōō-, sū-pûrb'*, *adj.* magnificent: gorgeous: triumphantly effective: supremely excellent (*coll.*). —*adv.* **superb'ly.**—*n.* **superb'ness.** [L. *superbus*, proud.]

supercalender ... to ... **supercharger.** See **super-**.

superciliary *sōō', sū'pər-sil'i-ər-i, adj.* of, on, or near the eyebrow: marked above the eye.—*adj.* **super-cil'ious** disdainfully superior in manner.—*adv.* **super-cil'iously.**—*n.* **supercil'iousness.** [L. *supercilium*, eyebrow, superciliousness—*super*, above, *cilium*, eyelid.]

superclass ... to ... **supereminently.** See **super-**.

supererogation *sōō-, sū-pər-er-ō-gā'shən, n.* doing more than is required.—*adj.* **supererogatory** (*-ə-rog'ə-tar-i*).—**works of supererogation** (*R.C.*) works which, not absolutely required of each individual for salvation, may be done for the sake of greater perfection—affording the church a store of surplus merit, to eke out the deficient merit of others. [L. *super*, above, *ērogāre, -ātum*, to pay out.]

superexcellence ... to ... **superfatted.** See **super-**.

superfetation *sōō-, sū-pər-fē-tā'shən, n.* fertilisation of an ovum in one already for some time pregnant. [L. *superfētāre*—pfx. *super-*, over, *fētus*, a fetus.]

superficies *sōō-, sū-pər-fish'i-ēz, n.* a surface, that which has length and breadth but no thickness (*geom.*): a surface layer: external features, appearance:—*pl.* **superfic'ies.**—*adj.* **superficial** (*-fish'l*) of, on, or near the surface: not going much deeper than the surface (*derog.*).—*n.* that which is superficial.—*n.* **superficiality** (*-fish-i-al'i-ti*).—*adv.* **superfic'ially.** —*n.* **superfic'ialness.** [L. *superficiēs*—*super, faciēs*, face.]

superfine ... to ... **superfluidity.** See **super-**.

superfluous *sōō-, sū-pûr'floo-əs, adj.* above what is enough: redundant: unnecessary.—*n.* **superfluity** (*-flōō'*) state of being superfluous: a thing that is superfluous: superabundance.—*adv.* **super'-**

fluously.—*n.* **super'fluousness** superfluity. [L. *superfluus*, overflowing—*super*, *fluĕre*, to flow.]

superfoetation. Same as **superfetation.**

supergiant . . . to . . . **superintendentship.** See **super-.**

superior *sōō'-*, *sū-pē'ri-ər*, *adj.* upper: higher in nature, place, rank, or excellence: better (with *to*): surpassing others: beyond the influence, rising above (with *to*): supercilious or uppish: very worthy and highly respectable: set above the level of the line (*print.*): of an ovary, inserted on the receptacle above the other parts (*bot.*).—*n.* one superior to others: the head of a religious house, order, etc.—*n.* **superiority** (*-or'i-ti*) quality or state of being superior: pre-eminence: advantage.—**superiority complex** (*psych.*) overvaluation of one's worth, often affected to cover a sense of inferiority; **superior planets** those more distant from the sun than is the earth. [L., compar. of *superus*, on high—*super*, above.]

superjacent *sōō-*, *sū-pər-jā'sənt*, *adj.* lying above. [L. *super*, *jacēns*, *-entis*, pr.p. of *jacēre*, to lie.]

superlative *sōō-*, *sū-pûr'lə-tiv*, *adj.* raised above others or to the highest degree: superior to all others: most eminent: expressing the highest degree (*gram.*).—*n.* the superlative or highest degree (*gram.*): an adjective or adverb in the superlative degree: any word or phrase of exaggeration.—*adv.* **super'latively.**—*n.* **super'lativeness.** [L. *superlātīvus*—*super*, *lātus*, carried.]

superlunar . . . to . . . **supermundane.** See **super-.**

supernal *sōō-*, *sū-pûr'nl*, (*poet.*) *adj.* on high: celestial: of a higher world: exalted: topmost.—*adv.* **super'nally.** [L. *supernus*—*super*.]

supernatant *sōō-*, *sū-pər-nā'tant*, *adj.* floating or swimming above, esp. of an upper layer of liquid. [L. *supernatāns*, *-antis*—*super*, *natāre*, swim, float.]

supernatural . . . to . . . **supernormal.** See **super-.**

supernova *sōō-*, *sū-pər-nō'və*, *n.* very brilliant nova resulting from an explosion which blows the star's material into space, leaving an expanding cloud of gas:—*pl.* **supernō'vae** (*-vē*), **supernō'vas.** [L. *super-*, above, and **nova.**]

supernumerary *sōō-*, *sū-pər-nū'mər-ər-i*, *adj.* over and above the stated, usual, normal, or necessary number.—*n.* a supernumerary person or thing: an actor without speaking parts. [L.L. *supernumerārius*—L. *super*, *numerus*, number.]

superorder . . . to . . . **supersaturation.** See **super-.**

superscribe *sōō-*, *sū-pər-skrīb'*, *v.t.* to write or engrave above, on the top or on the outside of something: to address (as a letter): to sign at the top.—*adj.* **su'perscript** (*-skript*) written above: superior (*print.*).—*n.* a superior character (*print.*).—*n.* **superscrip'tion** act of superscribing: that which is superscribed. [L. *super*, above, *scrībēre*, *scrīptum*, to write.]

supersede *sōō-*, *sū-pər-sēd'*, *v.t.* to set aside in favour of another: to come or put in the room of, to replace.—*ns.* **superse'dence**; **superse'der**; **superse'dure**; **supersession** (*-sesh'ən*). [L. *supersedēre*, to sit above, refrain from—*super*, above, *sedēre*, *sessum*, to sit.]

supersensitive. See **super-.**

supersonic *sōō-*, *sū-pər-son'ik*, *adj.* too high-pitched for human hearing (ultrasonic): (capable of) (travelling) faster than the speed of sound. [L. *super*, above, *sonus*, sound.]

superstar. See **super-.**

superstition *sōō-*, *sū-pər-stish'ən*, *n.* false worship or religion: an ignorant and irrational belief in supernatural agency, omens, divination, sorcery, etc.: a deep-rooted but unfounded general belief.—*adj.* **superstit'ious.**—*adv.* **superstit'iously.**—*n.* **superstit'iousness.** [L. *superstitiō*, *-ōnis.*]

superstore . . . to . . . **supertonic.** See **super-.**

supervene *sōō-*, *sū-pər-vēn'*, *v.i.* to come in addition, or

closely after.—*n.* **supervention** (*-ven'shən*). [L. *super*, above, *venīre*, *ventum*, to come.]

supervise *sōō'*, *sū'pər-vīz*, or *-vīz'*, *v.i.* to superintend. —Also *v.t.*—*ns.* **supervision** (*-vizh'ən*) act of supervising: inspection: control; **supervisor** (*-vī'zər*; also *sōō'*, *sū'*) one who supervises: an overseer: an inspector; **supervi'sorship.**—*adj.* **supervi'sory** pertaining to, or having, supervision. [L. *super*, over, *vidēre*, *vīsum*, to see.]

supine *sōō'*, *sū'pīn*, or *-pīn'*, *adj.* lying on the back: leaning backward, inclined, sloping: negligently inert: indolent: passive.—*n.* a Latin verbal noun in *-tum* or *-tū*, possibly as formed from the stem of the passive participle.—*v.t.* **su'pinate** (*-pin-āt*) to bring (the hand) palm upward or forward.—*ns.* **supinā'tion; su'pinator** a muscle that supinates the hand. —*adv.* **supine'ly.**—*n.* **supine'ness.** [L. *supīnus*, supine; related to *sub*, under, *super*, over.]

supper *sup'ər*, *n.* a meal taken at the close of the day.— *v.t.* to furnish with supper.—*adj.* **supp'erless.**—*n.* **supp'ertime.** [O.Fr. *soper* (Fr. *souper*).]

supping. See **sup.**

supplant *sə-plänt'*, *v.t.* to oust: to supersede: to dispossess and take the place of.—*ns.* **supplantation** (*sup-lan-tā'shən*); **supplant'er.** [L. *supplantāre*, to trip up—*sub*, under, *planta*, the sole.]

supple *sup'l*, *adj.* pliant: lithe: yielding.—*n.* **supp'leness.**—*adv.* **supp'ly.**—**supple jack** a woody liane of many kinds: a pliant cane. [Fr. *souple*—L. *supplex*, bending the knees—*sub*, under, *plicāre*, to fold.]

supplement *sup'li-mənt*, *n.* that which supplies a deficiency or fills a need: that which completes or brings closer to completion: any addition by which defects are made good: a special part of a periodical publication accompanying an ordinary part: the quantity by which an angle or an arc falls short of 180° or a semicircle.—*v.t.* **supplement** (*-ment'*; also *sup'li-mant*) to supply or fill up: to add to.—*adjs.* **supplement'al**, **supplement'ary** added to supply what is wanting: additional.—Also *ns.—advs.* **supplement'ally**, **supplement'arily.**—*ns.* **supplementā'tion; supplement'er; supple'tion** the adding of a word to supply a missing form of a conjugation, etc., as *went* for the past tense of *to go* (*gram.*).—**supplementary benefit** in Britain, a state allowance paid each week to those with low incomes in order to bring them up to a certain established level. [L. *supplēmentum*, a filling up, *supplēre*, to fill up.]

supplicant *sup'li-ənt*, *adj.* supplicating: asking earnestly: entreating.—*n.* a humble petitioner.—*n.* **supp'liance** supplication.—*adv.* **supp'liantly.** [Fr. *suppliant*, pr.p. of *supplier*—L. *supplicāre.*]

supplier. See **supply[1].**

supplicant *sup'li-kənt*, *adj.* supplicating: asking submissively.—*n.* one who supplicates or entreats earnestly.—*v.t.* and *v.i.* **supp'licate** to entreat earnestly: to petition: to pray.—*adj.* **supp'licating.**—*adv.* **supp'licatingly.**—*n.* **supplicā'tion.**—*adj.* **supp'licatory** containing supplication or entreaty: humble. [L. *supplicāre*, *-ātum*—*supplex*; see **supple.**]

supply[1] *sə-plī'*, *v.t.* to make good: to satisfy: to provide, furnish: to fill, occupy (as a substitute):—*pr.p.* **supply'ing;** *pa.t.* and *pa.p.* **supplied'.**—*n.* act of supplying: that which is supplied or which supplies a want: amount provided or in hand: available amount of a commodity: amount of food or money provided (used generally in *pl.*): a parliamentary grant for expenses of government: a person who takes another's duty temporarily, a substitute.—*n.* **suppli'er** one who supplies.—**supply-side economics** (an economic policy based on) the cutting of taxes in order to stimulate production, in the belief that supply creates demand. [O.Fr. *suppleier; supplier* (Fr. *suppléer*)—L. *supplère*, to fill up.]

supply². See **supple**.

support *sə-pōrt', -pört', v.t.* to bear the weight of: to hold up: to endure: to sustain: to maintain: to corroborate: to make good: to uphold: to back up: to represent in acting: to supply with means of living: to nourish.—*n.* act or fact of supporting or upholding: that which, or one who, supports, sustains, or maintains: maintenance: backing: a prop: an actor playing a subordinate part with a star.—*adj.* **support'able** capable of being held up, borne, sustained, or maintained.—*n.* support'ableness.—*adv.* support'ably.—*n.* support'er one who, or that which, supports: an adherent: one who attends matches and watches with interest the fortunes of a team: a figure on each side of the escutcheon (*her.*).—*n.* and *adj.* support'ing.—*adjs.* support'ive; support'less.—support hose, stockings elasticated stockings; supporting film, programme a film, films, acts, etc., accompanying the main film, or star performance in a variety show [L. *supportāre*—*sub*, up, *portāre*, to bear.]

suppose *sə-pōz', v.t.* to incline to believe: to conceive, imagine, guess: to assume provisionally or for argument's sake: to imply, presuppose: (esp. in *pass.*) to expect in accordance with rules or conventions.—*adj.* suppo'sable.—*adv.* suppo'sably.—*adj.* supposed' believed to be: assumed: conjectured.—*adv.* suppo'sedly according to supposition.—*ns.* suppo'ser; suppo'sing.—suppose if: what if; supposing (*coll.*) if: what if, how about. [Fr. *supposer*—pfx. *sup-* (*sub-*), *poser*; see pose¹.]

supposition *sup-ə-zi'shən, n.* an act of supposing: that which is supposed: assumption: presumption, opinion.—*adj.* supposi'tional hypothetical: conjectural: supposed.—*adv.* supposi'tionally.—*adjs.* supposititious (-*zi'shəs*) suppositional; supposititious (*sə-poz-i-tish'əs*) put by trick in the place of another: spurious.—*adv.* supposi'titiously.—*ns.* supposi'tiousness; suppos'itory a medicated plug for administration by the rectum or other canal. [L. *suppōnĕre, -positum*, to set under, substitute—*sub, pōnĕre*, to put.]

suppress *sə-pres', v.t.* to crush, put down: to subdue: to hold back, keep from publication, circulation, divulgation, expression, development: to check, stop, restrain: to hold in: to moderate: to leave out.—*n.* suppress'ant a substance, as a drug, that suppresses rather than eliminates.—Also *adj.*—*adj.* suppressed'.—*adv.* suppress'edly.—*adj.* suppress'ible.—*n.* suppression (-*presh'*) act of suppressing: stoppage: concealment.—*adj.* suppress'ive.—*n.* suppress'or. [L. *supprimĕre, suppressum*—*sub*, under, *premĕre*, to press.]

suppurate *sup'ū-rāt, v.i.* to gather pus or matter.—*n.* suppurā'tion.—*adj.* supp'urative. [L. *sub*, under, *pūs, pūris*, pus.]

supra- *soo'prə-, sū'prə-*, in composition, above.—*adjs.* supramun'dane above the world; supranat'ional overriding national sovereignty: in, belonging to, more than one nation; supra-or'bital above the orbit of the eye; supraré'nal above the kidneys (suprarenal capsules, glands the adrenal glands; suprarenal extract an extract from these used in the treatment of haemorrhage, Addison's disease, etc.); supraseg-men'tal (*phon.*) representing or continuing through two or more speech sounds. [L. *suprā*, above.]

supreme *sū-, soo-prēm'*, poet. also *sū', soo', adj.* highest: greatest: most excellent.—*n.* the highest point: the highest authority.—*ns.* suprem'acism (belief in) the supremacy of one particular group of people; suprem'acist; supremacy (-*prem'ə-si*) state of

being supreme: supreme position or power.—*adv.* supremely (-*prēm'*).—*n.* supreme'ness.—supreme sacrifice the giving up of one's life; Supreme Soviet the legislature of the U.S.S.R., consisting of two bodies, the Council of the Union and the Council of Nationalities. [L. *suprēmus*, superl. of *superus*, high—*super*, above.]

suprême, supreme *sū-prem, sū-, soo-prēm', n.* a rich cream sauce: a dish of meat served in this sauce. [Fr.]

supremo *sū-, soo-prä'mō, n.* a supreme head:—*pl.* supre'mos. [Sp.,—L. *suprēmus*, highest.]

suq. See **souk**.

sur- *sûr-, pfx.* over, above, beyond. [Fr.,—L. *super*.]

sura, surah *soo'rə, n.* a chapter of the Koran. [Ar. *sūra, sūrah*, step.]

surah *sū', soo'rə, n.* a soft twilled silk or artificial fabric.—Also *adj.* [Poss. from *Surat*.]

sural *sū'rl, adj.* pertaining to the calf of the leg. [L. *sūra*, the calf.]

surat *soo-rat'*, or *soo', n.* coarse uncoloured cotton. [*Surat*, in India.]

surbase *sûr'bās, n.* a cornice or series of mouldings above the base of a pedestal, etc. [Pfx. sur-.]

surcease *sûr-sēs', (arch.) v.i.* to cease —*v.t.* to desist from: to end.—*n.* cessation. [O.Fr. *sursis*, pa.p. of *surseoir*—L. *supersedēre*, to refrain from.]

surcharge *sûr-charj', v.t.* to overload: to saturate: to print over the original printing: to disallow: to exact a surcharge from.—*n.* sur'charge (or -*charj'*): an extra charge: an excessive load: an amount not passed by an auditor, which must be refunded: a new valuation or cancel-mark printed on or over a stamp.—*adj.* surcharged'.—*ns.* surcharge'ment; surcharg'er. [Pfx. sur-.]

surcingle *sûr'sing-gl, n.* a girth or strap for holding a saddle on an animal's back. [O.Fr. *surcengle*—L. *super, cingulum*, a belt.]

surcoat *sûr'kōt, n.* a mediaeval outer garment, usu. sleeveless, often with heraldic devices, worn over armour or ordinary dress. [O.Fr. *surcote, surcot*—*sur*, over, *cote*, garment.]

surculus *sûr'kū-ləs, (bot.) n.* a sucker.—*adj.* sur'culose having or producing suckers. [L. *sūrculus*, a twig.]

surd *sûrd, adj.* that cannot be expressed in rational numbers (*math.*): voiceless (*phon.*).—*n.* an irrational quantity (*math.*): a voiceless consonant (*phon.*). [L. *surdus*, deaf.]

sure *shoor, adj.* secure: safe: fit to be depended on: unerring: stable: certain: assured: confident beyond doubt: without other possibility.—*interj.* (*coll.*) certainly, undoubtedly, yes.—*advs.* sure (now chiefly *Ir.* or *U.S.*, except in comp. and in conventional phrases), surely firmly: confidently: safely: certainly: assuredly: as it would seem (often ironically).—*ns.* sure'ness; sure'ty certainty: safeguard: legal security against loss: one who becomes bound for another: a sponsor; sure'tyship.—*adjs.* sure'-fire (*coll.*) infallible; sure'footed not liable to stumble.—*adv.* surefoot'edly.—*n.* surefoot'edness.—sure thing a certainty, certain success: (as *interj.*) certainly, beyond doubt.—be sure do not omit; for sure certainly: of a certainty; make sure see make; stand surety for to act as guarantor for; sure enough no doubt: in very fact: accordingly: there's no denying; to be sure certainly: I admit. [O.Fr. *sur, seur* (Fr. *sûr*)—L. *sēcūrus*; see secure.]

surf *sûrf, n.* surging water or waves rushing up a sloping beach: sea-foam.—*v.i.* to bathe in or ride on surf.—*ns.* surf'er; surf'ing riding breaking waves on a surf-board, etc.—*adj.* surf'y.—surf'-bird an American Pacific shore-bird akin to sandpipers; surf'board a board on which a bather allows himself to be carried inshore by the surf; **surf'boarding**; **surf'-boat** a boat for use in surf; **surf'-riding** riding on a surf-board.

surface *sûr'fis*, *n*. the outer boundary or face of anything: the outside or upper layer: that which has length and breadth but no thickness (*geom.*): area: outer appearance, character or texture.—*adj*. of, on, or near a surface.—*v.t.* to put a surface, or some kind of surface or finish, upon.—*v.i.* to rise to the surface: to regain consciousness (*coll.*).—*adj.* **sur'faced** having this or that kind of surface.—*ns.* **sur'facer**; **sur'facing**.—*adj.* **sur'face-ac'tive** able to alter the surface tension of liquids (see also **surfactant**) — **sur'face-craft** a floating, not submersible, craft; **sur'face-mail** mail sent otherwise than by air; **surface noise** the noise produced by the friction of a stylus on a record; **surface structure** (*linguistics*) the formal structure of sentences, esp. when analysed into their constituent parts; **surface tension** that property in virtue of which a liquid surface behaves like a stretched elastic membrane; **surface worker** a person engaged in any of the ancillary jobs in a coal-mine not done underground.—*adj.* **sur'face-to-air'** of a missile, etc., travelling from a base on the ground to a target in the air.—Also *adv.*—*adj.* and *adv.* **sur'face-to-sur'face.**—**sur'face-vessel; sur'face-water** drainage-water. [Fr., from *sur*—L. *super*, and *face*—L. *faciēs*, face.]

surfactant *sər-fak'tənt*, *n*. a substance, e.g. a detergent, which has the effect of altering the interfacial tension of water and other liquids or solids. [*surface-active agent*.]

surfeit *sûr'fit*, *n*. overfulness: excess: sickness or satiety caused by overeating or overdrinking.—*v.t.* to feed or fill to satiety or disgust.—*adj.* **sur'feited.** [O.Fr. *surfait*, excess—L. *super*, above, *facēre*, to make.]

surge *sûrj*, *n*. an uprush, boiling or tumultuous movement of liquid: a sudden increase of power: a great wave: a swell.—*v.i.* to well up: to heave tumultuously: to slip back: to jerk.—*n.* and *adj.* **sur'ging.** [L. *surgēre*, to rise.]

surgeon *sûr'jən*, *n.* one who treats injuries or diseases by manual operations: an army or naval doctor: a ship's doctor.—*n.* **sur'gery** the art and practice of a surgeon: a doctor's or dentist's consulting-room: a doctor's or dentist's time of consultation: a set, usu. regular, time when a member of parliament is available to his constituents for consultation.—*adj.* **sur'gical.**—*adv.* **sur'gically.**—**sur'geon-fish** a seasurgeon; **surgeon general** the senior officer in the medical branch of the service (*mil.*): head of the public health service (*U.S.*); **surgeon's knot** a knot like a reef-knot but with a double turn in the first part (used in ligaturing a cut artery); **surgical boot, shoe** a boot, shoe designed to correct deformities of the foot; **surgical spirit** methylated spirit with small amounts of castor oil and oil of wintergreen. [A.Fr. *surgien*.]

suricate *sū'*, *soo'ri-kāt*, *n.* a S. African animal of the civet family.

surly *sûr'li*, *adj.* morose: gruff and grumpy: rough and gloomy: refractory.—*adv.* **sur'lily.**—*n.* **sur'liness.** [From **sir** and **like**[1].]

surmise *sər-mīz'*, *n.* suspicion: conjecture.—*v.t.* to imagine: to suspect: to conjecture, guess.—*adj.* **surmis'able.**—*n.* **surmis'er.**—*n.* and *adj.* **surmis'ing.** [O.Fr.,—*surmettre*, to accuse—L. *super*, upon, *mittēre*, to send.]

surmount *sər-mownt'*, *v.t.* to mount above: to be on or go to the top of: to surpass: to get the better of.—*adjs.* **surmount'able; surmount'ed.**—*n.* **surmount'er.** —*n.* and *adj.* **surmount'ing.** [O.Fr. *surmunter* (Fr.

surmonter)—L.L. *supermontāre*]

surmullet *sər-mul'it*, *n.* a species of red mullet. [Fr. *surmulet*]

surname *sûr'nām*, *n.* a family name.—*v.t.* to name by a surname. [On the analogy of Fr. *surnom*, from Eng. **name.**]

surpass *sər-pas'*, *v.t.* to go or be beyond: to exceed: to excel.—*adjs.* **surpass'able; surpass'ing** passing beyond others: excellent in a high degree.—Also (*poet.*) *adv.*—*adv.* **surpass'ingly.** [Fr *surpasser*—*sur-*, *passer*, to pass.]

surplice *sûr'plis*, *n.* a white linen vestment worn over the cassock—*adj.* **sur'pliced** wearing a surplice [Fr. *surplis*—L.L. *superpellicium*, an over-garment— *pellis*, skin.]

surplus *sûr'pləs*, *n.* that which is left over: remainder: excess over what is required: excess of revenue over expenditure.—Also *adj*—*n.* **sur'plusage** surplus: superfluity. [Fr.,—L.L. *superplūs*—*super*, *plūs*, more.]

surprise *sər-prīz'*, *n.* a taking unawares: a sudden capture owing to unpreparedness: the emotion caused by anything sudden or contrary to expectation: astonishment: anything that causes or is intended to cause this emotion.—Also *adj.*—*v.t.* to come upon suddenly or unawares: to capture by an unexpected assault: to lead unawares, to betray (with *into*): to strike with wonder or astonishment: to confuse.—*v.i.* (*formal*) to cause surprise.—*n.* **surpris'al** act of surprising.—*adj* **surprised'**—*adv.* **surpris'edly.**—*n.* **surpris'er.**—*n.* and *adj.* **surpris'ing.**—*adv.* **surpris'ingly.**—*n.* **surpris'ingness.**—(much, greatly, etc.) **to one's surprise** causing one great surprise. [O.Fr. (Fr.) fem. pa.p. of *surprendre*—L. *super*, *prehendēre*, to catch.]

surra *soo'rə*, *n.* a trypanosome disease of horses, etc., in Eastern Asia. [Marathi *sūra*, wheezing.]

surrealism *sər-ē'ə-lizm*, *n.* a movement in French art and literature, from about 1919 on, that aimed at drawing upon the subconscious and escaping the control of reason or any preconceptions.—*adj.* **surre'al.** —*adj.* and *n.* **surre'alist.**—*adj.* **surrealist'ic.**—*adv.* **surrealist'ically.** [Fr. *surréalisme*—*sur*, above, and *réalisme*, realism.]

surrebut *sur-i-but'*, *v.i.* to reply to a defendant's rebutter.—*ns.* **surrebutt'al** a plaintiff's evidence in response to a defendant's rebuttal; **surrebutt'er** the plaintiff's reply to a defendant's rebutter. [Pfx. **sur-.**]

surrejoin *sur-i-join'*, *v.t.* and *v.i.* to reply to a defendant's rejoinder.—*n.* **surrejoind'er** a plaintiff's reply to a defendant's rejoinder. [Pfx. **sur-.**]

surrender *sə-ren'dər*, *v.t.* to deliver over: to relinquish: to yield up: to resign.—*v.i.* to yield oneself up: to yield.—*n.* act of surrendering.—*n.* **surren'derer.**— **surrender value** the amount to be paid to an insured person who surrenders his policy. [A.Fr. *surrender*, O.Fr. *surrendre*—*sur-*, *rendre*; see **render.**]

surreptitious *sur-əp-tish'əs*, *adj.* done by stealth or fraud: stealthy.—*adv.* **surrepti'tiously.** [See **subreption.**]

surrey *sur'i*, (*U.S.*) *n.* a light four-wheeled vehicle for four, usu. with two seats. [Developed from a vehicle used in *Surrey*.]

surrogate *sur'ō-gāt*, *n.* a substitute: a deputy, esp. of an ecclesiastical judge: one who grants marriage licences: a judge of probate (*U.S.*): a person or thing standing, for another person or thing, or a person who fills the role of another in one's emotional life.—*ns.* **surr'ogacy; surr'ogateship; surrogā'tion** subrogation.—**surrogate mother** a woman who bears a baby for another, esp. childless, couple, after either (artificial) insemination by the male, or implantation of an embryo from the female [L. *surrogāre, -ātum—sub*, in the place of, *rogāre*, to ask.]

surround *sə-rownd'*, *v.t.* to go or extend all around: to encompass, environ: to invest: to make a circuit of.—*n.* an act of surrounding (esp. hunted animals): a border, esp. the floor or floor-covering around a carpet.—*adj.* **surround'ing.**—*n.* (in *pl.*) environment, things round about. [O.Fr. *suronder*—L. *superundāre*, to overflow—*super*, *unda*, wave.]

surtax *sûr'taks*, *n.* an additional tax: tax payable on incomes above a certain high level (term not in official use in this sense).—*v.t.* to tax additionally: to charge surtax. [Pfx. **sur-**.]

surtout *sər-tōō', -tōōt'*, (*hist.*) *n.* an overcoat: a close-bodied frock-coat. [Fr.,—L.L *supertōtus*, an outer garment—L. *super*, *tōtus*, all.]

surveillance *sər-vā'ləns*, *n.* vigilant supervision: spy-like watching —*n.* **surveill'ant.** [Fr.,—*surveiller*—*sur, veiller*, to watch—L. *vigilāre*.]

survey *sər-vā'*, *v.t.* to view comprehensively and extensively: to examine in detail: to examine the structure of a building: to obtain by measurements data for mapping.—*ns.* **sur'vey** a general view, or a statement of its results: an inspection: collection of data for mapping: an organisation or body of men for that purpose; **survey'ing; survey'or** one who surveys buildings: an overseer: a measurer of land: an inspector (of roads, of weights and measures, of customs duties, etc.); **survey'orship.** [O.Fr. *surveoir*—L. *super*, over, *vidēre*, to see.]

survive *sər-vīv'*, *v.t.* to live beyond: to outlive.—*v.t.* to remain alive.—*n.* **survi'val** a surviving or living after: anything that continues to exist after others of its kind have disappeared, or after the time to which it naturally belongs.—*adj.* (esp. of standard equipment) designed to help one to survive exposure or other dangerous condition.—*adj.* **survi'ving.**—*n.* **survi'vor.**—**survival of the fittest** the longer average life of the fit in the struggle for existence, and the consequent transmission of favourable variations in greater proportion to later generations. [Fr *survivre*—L. *super*, beyond, *vīvēre*, to live.]

sus *sus*, (*slang*) *n.* suspicious behaviour.—*v.i.* (*slang*) to arrest for suspicious behaviour:—*pa.t., pa.p.* **sussed.**—Also **suss.**—**sus(s) out** (*slang*) to investigate: to find out, discover. [suspect, suspicion.]

susceptible *sə-sep'ti-bl*, *adj.* (usu. with *to*) capable, admitting: capable of receiving: impressionable: easily affected by emotion (esp. amatory).—*ns.* **susceptibil'ity, suscep'tibleness.**—*adv.* **suscep'tibly.** [L. *suscipēre, susceptum*, to take up—*sus-* (*subs-*), up, *capēre*, to take.]

sushi *sōō'shi*, *n.* a Japanese dish of cold rice and fish, vegetables, etc., and a vinegar sauce. [Jap.]

suspect *səs-pekt'*, *v.t.* to mistrust: to imagine to be guilty: to doubt: to be ready to believe, but without sufficient evidence: to incline to believe the existence, presence, or agency of: to have an inkling of: to conjecture.—*v.i.* to imagine guilt, to be suspicious.—*n.* (*sus'pekt*) a person suspected.—*adj.* suspected.—*adj.* **suspect'ed.** [L. *suspicēre, suspectum*, to look at secretly or askance—*su-* (*sub-*), *specēre*, to look.]

suspend *səs-pend'*, *v.t.* to hang: to make to depend: to sustain from falling: to put or hold in a state of suspense or suspension: to make to stop for a time: to defer: to debar from any privilege, office, emolument, etc., for a time: to hold in an indeterminate state.—*adj.* **suspen'ded.**—*ns.* **suspend'er** one who, or that which, suspends: a strap to support a sock or stocking: (in *pl.*) braces (*U.S.*); **suspense'** tense uncertainty: indecision.—*adj.* **suspense'ful.**—*n.* **suspen'sion** (*-shən*) act of suspending: interruption: delay: temporary privation of office or privilege: a condi-

tional withholding: a mixture of a fluid with dense particles which are prevented from settling by viscosity and impact of molecules (*chem.*): in a motor vehicle or railway carriage, the system of springs, etc., supporting the chassis on the axles.—*adj.* **suspen'sive.**—*adv* **suspen'sively.**—*adj.* **suspen'sory** suspending: having the power or effect of delaying or staying.—**suspended animation** temporary cessation of the outward signs and of some of the functions of life; **suspended sentence** a legal sentence not served unless another crime is committed; **suspen'der-belt** a woman's undergarment with stocking suspenders; **suspense account** an account in which items are entered which cannot at once be placed in an ordinary account; **suspension bridge** a bridge with roadway supported by chains passing over elevated piers. [L. *suspendēre, -pēnsum*—pfx. *sus-* (*subs-*), *pendēre*, to hang.]

suspicion *səs-pish'ən*, *n.* act of suspecting: state of being suspected: the imagining of something without evidence or on slender evidence: inkling: mistrust: a slight quantity:—*adjs.* **suspi'cionless; suspi'cious** full of suspicion: showing suspicion: inclined to suspect: giving ground for suspicion: liable to suspicion, doubtful.—*adv.* **suspi'ciously.**—*n.* **suspi'ciousness.**—**above, beyond suspicion** too honest, virtuous, etc., to be suspected of a crime or fault; **on suspicion (of)** suspected (of); **under suspicion** suspected. [L. *suspiciō, -ōnis*; see suspect.]

suspire *səs-pīr'*, (*arch.* or *poet.*) *v.i.* to sigh: to breathe. [L. *suspīrāre—su-* (*sub-*), *spīrāre*, to breathe.]

suss. See **sus.**

sustain *səs-tān'*, *v.t.* to hold up: to bear: to support: to provide for: to maintain: to sanction: to keep going: to keep up: to support the life of: to prolong.—*adjs.* **sustain'able; sustained'.**—*adv.* **sustain'edly.**—*n.* **sustain'er** one who, or that which, sustains: the main motor in a rocket.—*n.* and *adj.* **sustain'ing.**—*ns.* **sustain'ment; sustenance** (*sus'ti-nəns*) that which sustains: maintenance: nourishment; **sustenta'tion** sustenance.—**sustaining pedal** a pedal on a piano which sustains the note(s) played by allowing the strings to continue vibrating. [L. *sustinēre*—pfx. *sus-* (*subs-*), *tenēre*, to hold.]

susurrus *sū-, sōō-sur'əs*, (*poet.*) *n.* a murmuring: a whisper: a rustling.—*adj.* **susurr'ant.**—*n.* **susurra'tion.** [L. *susurrus.*]

sutler *sut'lər*, (*hist.*) *n.* one who sells liquor or provisions to soldiers in camp or garrison. [Du. *zoetelaar* (earlier *soeteler*).]

sutra *sōōt'rə*, *n.* in Sanskrit literature, an aphoristic rule or book of aphorisms on ritual, grammar, metre, philosophy, etc.: in Buddhist sacred literature, a group of writings including the sermons of Buddha and other doctrinal works. [Sans. *sūtra*, thread.]

suttee, satī *sut'ē, sut-ē'*, *n.* an Indian widow who burned herself on her husband's pyre: the custom of so doing.—*n.* **suttee'ism.** [Sans. *satī*, a true wife.]

suture *sū', sōō'chər, -tūr, n* a seam: a stitching: the stitching of a wound: a junction or meeting of margins, esp. of bones.—*v t.* to stitch up.—*adj.* **su'tural.** —*adv.* **su'turally.**—*adj.* **su'tured.** [L. *sūtūra*, a seam—*suēre*, to sew.]

suzerain *sōō'zə-rān*, or *sū'*, *n.* a feudal lord: a state having supremacy over another.—*n.* **su'zerainty** position or power of a suzerain. [Fr., formed in imitation of *souverain* from *sus-*, over.]

svelte *svelt, adj.* lissom, lithe. [Fr.]

swab *swob, n* a mop for cleaning or drying floors or decks: a sponge or the like for cleaning the bore of a fire-arm: a bit of cotton-wool or the like for mopping up blood or discharges, applying antiseptics, cleaning a patient's mouth, or taking a specimen of secretion for examination: a specimen so taken: a lubber or clumsy fellow (*slang*).—*v.t.* to mop with a swab:—*pr.p.* **swabb'ing;** *pa.t.* and *pa.p.* **swabbed.**—*n.* **swabb'er.** [Du. *zwabber*, swabber.]

swaddle *swod'l, v.t.* to swathe: to bandage: to bind tight with clothes, as an infant.—*n.* swaddling-clothes: a bandage.—**swadd'ling-band, swadd'ling-cloth** a cloth for swaddling an infant:—*pl.* **swadd'ling-clothes** (*B.*). [O.E. *swæthel, swethel*, bandage; cf. **swathe.**]

swaddy *swod'i, n.* a soldier, esp. a militiaman. [Perh. Scand., or from **squad, squaddy.**]

swag *swag, v.i.* to sway: to sag:—*pr.p.* **swagg'ing;** *pa.t.* and *pa.p.* **swagged.**—*n.* a swagging: a festoon: a bundle, esp. a tramp's bundle: baggage, esp. in the Australian bush: plunder (*slang*).—*v.i.* **swagg'er** to walk with a blustering or overweening air of superiority and self-confidence: to brag noisily or ostentatiously: to bully.—*n.* a swaggering gait, manner, mien, or behaviour.—*adj.* (*slang*) ostentatiously fashionable: smart.—*n.* **swagg'erer.**—*n.* and *adj.* **swagg'ering.**—*adv.* **swagg'eringly.**—*n.* **swagg'ie** (*Austr. slang*) a swagman.—**swagg'er-cane, swagg'er-stick** a short military cane: **swagg'er-coat** a coat which hangs loosely from the shoulder; **swag'man** (*Austr.*) one who carries his swag about with him in his search for work. [Related to **sway;** prob. Scand.]

swage *swāj, n.* any of several tools including a tool in two grooved parts, for shaping metal.—*v.t.* to shape with a swage: to reduce the cross-section of a rod or tube, e.g. by forcing it through a tapered aperture between two grooved dies.—**swage block** a block with various holes, grooves, etc., for use in metal-working. [O.Fr. *souage*.]

Swahili *swä-hē'li, n.* the people of Zanzibar and the opposite coast: one of them: loosely, their language (*Kiswahili*), a Bantu tongue modified by Arabic, spoken in Kenya, Tanzania and other parts of East Africa. [Ar. *sawāhil*, pl. *sāhil*, coast, with suffix.]

swain *swān*, (*arch., poet.*), often *ironical*) n. a young man: a peasant: rustic: a lover. [O.N. *sveinn*, young man, servant; O.E. *swān*.]

swallow[1] *swol'ō, n.* a long-winged migratory bird (*Hirundo rustica*) that catches insects on the wing: any bird of its genus or family: extended to various unrelated birds of similar form or habits.—**swall'ow-dive** a dive during which one's arms are outstretched to the sides.—Also *v.i.*—**swall'ow-tail** a forked tail: a long-tailed dress coat: a butterfly with prolongations of the hind wings.—*adj.* **swall'ow-tailed** with forked and pointed tail. [O.E. *swalwe, swealwe*.]

swallow[2] *swol'ō, v.t.* to receive through the gullet into the stomach: to engulf (often with *up*): to take in: to accept, sit down under (as an affront): to believe credulously.—*v.i.* to perform the action of swallowing something.—*n.* an act of swallowing: a gulp: a quantity swallowed at once.—*n.* **swall'ower.**—**swall'ow-hole** a funnel or fissure through which water passes underground esp. in limestone.—**swallow one's pride** to humble oneself. [O.E. *swelgan* (vb.) *geswelg* (n.).]

swam *swam, pa.t.* of **swim.**

swami *swä'mē, n.* a Hindu idol: a Hindu religious instructor, esp. as a form of address. [Hindi *svāmī*, lord, master.]

swamp *swomp, n.* a tract of wet, spongy land: low ground filled with water.—*v.t.* to sink or involve in, or as in, a swamp: to cause to fill with water, as a boat: to overwhelm, inundate.—*v.i.* to become swamped.—*adj.* of, of the nature of, swamp: living or growing in swamps.—*adj.* **swamp'y.**—**swamp boat** a flat-bottomed boat with a raised aeroplane engine for travelling over swamps; **swamp cypress** a deciduous conifer of swamps in Southern U.S.; **swamp fever** a

viral disease of horses; **swamp'land.** [Perh. from L.G.; prob. akin to O.E. *swamm*, mushroom.]

swan *swon, n.* any species of *Cygnus*, a genus of large, graceful, stately, long-necked birds of the duck family.—*adj.* **swan'like.**—*n.* **swann'ery** a place where swans are kept or bred.—**swan'herd** one who tends swans; **swan'-maid'en** in Germanic folklore, a maiden who can become a swan by putting on her feather-garment; **swan'-mark** the notch made on the swan's upper mandible; **swan'-neck** an S-shaped bend or piece; **swans'-down, swans'down** the under-plumage of a swan: a soft woollen or mixed cloth: a thick cotton with a soft nap on one side; **swan'-shot** a shot of large size; **swan'-song** the fabled song of a swan just before its death: a writer's or musician's last work: last work of any kind: final appearance; **swan'-upp'ing** an annual expedition up the Thames for the marking of young swans belonging to the Dyers' and Vintners' Companies (those belonging to the crown being unmarked).—**swan about, around** (*slang*) to move about aimlessly or gracefully. [O.E. *swan*.]

swank *swangk, n.* (*slang*) ostentation: pretentiousness.—*v.i.* (*slang*) to show off.—*n.* **swank'er.**—*adj.* **swank'y** ostentatiously smart. [Cf. O.E. *swancor*, pliant.]

swap, swop *swop, v.t.* to give in exchange: to barter.—*v.i.* to barter:—*pr.p.* **swapp'ing, swopp'ing;** *pa.t.* and *pa.p.* **swapped, swopped.**—*n.* an exchange.—*n.* **swapp'er, swopp'er.**—*n.* **swapp'ing, swopp'ing.**—**swap'-shop** a shop, meeting, etc., where goods are exchanged for other goods or services rather than money. [M.E. *swappen*, to hit.]

swaraj *swä-räj', (Ind.)* n. self-government, independence, home-rule.—*ns.* **swaraj'ism** formerly, the policy of Indian political independence; **swaraj'ist.** [Sans. *svarājya—sva*, own, *rājya*, rule.]

sward *swörd*, (usu. *poet.*) n. the grassy surface of land: green turf.—*v.t.* to cover with sward. [O.E. *sweard*, skin, rind.]

swarf *swörf, n.* grit from an axle, etc.: stone or metal grindings, filings, turnings, etc. [O.N. *svarf*, file-dust.]

swarm[1] *swörm, n.* a body of bees going off to found a new community: a throng of insects or other small animals: a throng.—*v.i.* to go off in a swarm: to occur or come in swarms: to abound, teem. [O.E. *swearm*; Ger. *Schwarm*.]

swarm[2] *swörm, v.t.* and *v.i.* to climb by clasping with arms and legs.

swart *swört*, **swarth** *swörth*, (*arch.* or *dial.*) *adjs.* black: dusky.—*n.* **swarthiness** (*swör'dhi-nis*).—*adj.* **swarthy** (*swör'dhi*) blackish: dark-skinned.—*n.* **swart'ness.** [O.E. *sweart*.]

swash[1] *swosh, n.* a wash of liquid: swaggering (*arch.*).—*v.t.* and *v.i.* to splash.—**swash'buckler** one who clashes a sword on a buckler, hence a bully, a blusterer: a dare-devil.—*adj.* **swash'buckling** of, resembling a swashbuckler: adventurous, exciting. [Imit.]

swash[2] *swosh, n.* a piece of turner's work with mouldings oblique to the axis: a flourish on a letter.—Also *adj.*—**swash letters** Italic capitals with top and bottom flourishes; **swash plate** a disc set obliquely on a revolving axis.

swastika *swos'ti-ka, swas', n.* an ancient and worldwide symbol, a cross with arms bent at a right angle, esp. clockwise, emblematic of the sun, good luck, or Naziism. [Sans. *svastika—svasti*, well-being—*su*, good, *asti*, he is.]

swat *swot, v.t.* to hit smartly or heavily.—*n.* a sharp or heavy blow: a swatter.—*n.* **swatt'er** an instrument consisting of a flexible shaft with flap-like head, with which to swat flies. [squat.]

swatch *swoch, n.* a sample, esp. of cloth.

swath *swōth, swoth, n.* a band of mown ground or of grass or corn cut by the scythe or mowing-machine: a broad band: the sweep of a scythe or mowing-machine.—Also **swathe** (*swādh*) [O.E. *swæth* and *swathu*, track; Du. *zwade.*]

swathe *swādh, v.t.* to bind round, envelop: to bandage. —*n* a bandage: a wrapping —*n.pl.* **swath'ing-clothes** swaddling-clothes. [O.E. *swathian.*]

sway *swā, v.t.* to incline about or from side to side: to cause to incline: to divert: to influence by power or moral force: to govern.—*v.i.* to swing: to oscillate: to swerve: to incline to one side: to rule: to have preponderating weight or influence.—*n.* a sweep: a swing: a swerve: directing force or influence: preponderance: rule.—*n.* **sway'er.**—*n.* and *adj.* **sway'ing.**—*adj.* **sway'back** (of a horse) having a hollow back.—*n.* a nervous disease of lambs causing difficulty in walking or standing.—**hold sway (over)** to have power, authority (over). [Perh. from a lost O.E. word, or the corresponding O.N. *sveigja*, to bend, swing.]

swear *swār, v.i.* to take or utter an oath: to utter imprecations.—*v.t.* to assert, promise, confirm, on oath: to assert loudly or boldly: to administer an oath to: to put on oath: to bind by oath: to admit to office by an oath: to bring, put, render, by swearing:—*pa.t.* **swōre;** *pa.p.* **swōrn.**—*n.* an oath or a curse, or bad language generally.—*n.* **swear'er.**—*n.* and *adj.* **swear'ing.**—*adj.* **sworn** attested: bound by oath: having taken an oath: devoted, inveterate, confirmed, as if by oath.—**swear'-word** a word that is considered bad language.—**swear at** to hurl oaths and curses at; **swear by** to invoke as witness to an oath: to put complete confidence in; **swear in** to inaugurate by oath; **swear off** to renounce, promise to give up; **swear to** to affirm or identify on oath. [O.E. *swerian*; Du. *zweren*, Ger. *schwören.*]

sweat *swet, n.* the moisture excreted by the skin: moisture exuding or seeming to exude from anything: a state, fit, or process of exuding sweat: exercise or treatment inducing sweat: labour: drudgery: fidgety anxiety.—*v i.* to give out sweat or moisture: to toil, drudge for poor wages: to suffer penalty, smart: to exude: to become coated with moisture: to worry, be anxious.—*v.t.* to give forth as, or like, sweat: to cause to sweat: to squeeze money or extortionate interest from: to exact the utmost from: to compel to hard work for mean wages: to unite by partial fusion of metal surfaces:—*pa.t.* and *pa.p.* **sweat'ed** (or **sweat**) —*adj.* **sweat'ed.**—*ns.* **sweat'er** one who sweats: a jersey, orig. one for reducing weight by sweating, now for leisure wear, etc.· one who sweats workers; **sweat'iness.**—*n.* and *adj.* **sweat'ing.**—*adj.* **sweat'y.**— **sweat band** the leather or similar band inside a man's hat: a similar band worn to absorb perspiration from the forehead. an absorbent wristlet worn by e.g. tennis players to prevent sweat running down to their hands; **sweated labour** hard work obtained by exploitation; **sweater-girl** (*coll.*) a woman with a well-developed bust, usually wearing a tight-fitting sweater; **sweat gland** any of the glands producing sweat; **sweating sickness** an epidemic disorder (usu. fatal) which ravaged Europe and esp. England in the 15th and 16th centuries—a violent inflammatory fever, with a fetid perspiration over the whole body; **sweat'-shirt** a short- or long-sleeved knitted cotton sweater; **sweat shop** a factory or shop using sweated labour; **sweat suit** a loose-fitting suit consisting of sweater and trousers, usu. close-fitting at wrist and ankle, worn by athletes, etc.—**in a cold sweat** in a state of terror or anxiety; **sweat blood** to work or worry extremely hard; **sweat it out** (*slang*) to endure, live through a time of danger, etc. [O.E. *swætan* to sweat.]

Swede *swēd, n.* a native or citizen of *Sweden*: (without *cap.*) a Swedish turnip—a buff-flowered, glaucous-leaved kind.—*adj.* **Swēd'ish.**—*n.* the Scandinavian language of Sweden.

sweep *swēp, v.i.* to pass swiftly or forcibly, esp. with a swinging movement or in a curve: to move with trailing or flowing drapery, hence with pomp, indignation, etc.: to extend in a long curve: to range systematically or searchingly.—*v.t.* to pass something brushingly over: to pass brushingly: to wipe, clean, move, or remove with a broom: to carry along or off with a long brushing stroke or force: to wipe out or remove at a stroke (often with *away, up*): to perform with a sweeping movement: to trail with a curving movement: to drag as with a net or rope: to describe, generate, or swing through, as a curve, angle, or area: —*pa.t.* and *pa.p.* **swept.**—*n.* act of sweeping: a swinging movement, swing: onrush: impetus: a clearance: range, compass: a curved stair: a curved carriageway before a building: a sweepstake· a long oar: a chimney-sweeper: a blackguard (*slung*): sweepback. —*ns.* **sweep'er** a person who, or thing which sweeps: in association football, a player in front of the goalkeeper who assists the defence; **sweep'ing** the action of the verb in any sense: (usu. in *pl.*) things collected by sweeping, rubbish.—*adj.* performing the action of sweeping in any sense: of wide scope, wholesale, indiscriminate.—*adv.* **sweep'ingly.**—*n.* **sweep'ingness.** —*adj.* **sweep'y.**—**sweep'back** the angle at which an aeroplane wing is set back relatively to the axis.—*adj.* **swept'-back.**—**sweep'-net, -seine** a long net paid out in a curve and dragged ashore: an insect net with a handle; **sweep'stake(s)** a method of gambling by which participators' stakes are pooled, numbers, horses, etc., assigned by lot, and prize(s) awarded accordingly on decision of event: such a prize, race, etc.—**make a clean sweep (of)** to clear out completely: to win all the awards, prizes, etc.; **sweep the board** see **board.** [Prob. from a lost O.E. word related to *swāpan*, to sweep.]

sweet *swēt, adj.* having one of the fundamental varieties of taste, that of sugar, honey, ripe fruits: sugary· grateful to the taste, senses, or feelings: fragrant: clear and tuneful: smoothly running: easy, free from harshness, benign: fresh, not salt: fresh, not tainted: amiable: mild, soft, gentle: delightful, charming (*coll.*): all right, satisfactory (*Austr. coll.*): dear, beloved (*arch.*): more or less enamoured (with *on*, or *upon*; *coll.*).—*adv.* sweetly —*n.* that which is sweet: a sweet dish (pudding, fruit, etc.) as a course: a sweetmeat, confection: a beloved person.—*v.t.* **sweet'en** to make sweet: to mitigate something unpleasant: to pacify, make (a person) agreeable (often with *up*).—*ns* **sweet'ener** one who or that which sweetens: a bribe (*slang*); **sweet'ening; sweet'ing** a sweet apple: a darling (*arch.*).—*adj.* **sweet'ish.**—*n.* **sweet'ishness.**—*adv.* **sweet'ly.**—*ns.* **sweet'ness; sweet'y, sweet'ie** a sweetmeat, confection: a sweetheart (*coll.*).—*adjs.* **sweet'-and-sour'** cooked with sugar and vinegar or lemon juice, soy sauce, etc.— **sweet'-bay** the laurel (*Laurus nobilis*): a kind of magnolia (*U.S.*); **sweet'bread** the pancreas, or sometimes the thymus, esp. as food; **sweet'-brier, -briar** a wild rose with fragrant foliage (*Rosa rubiginosa*); **sweet chestnut** see **chestnut**; **sweet'-Cic'ely** an aromatic umbelliferous plant, *Myrrhis odorata*; **sweet'-corn** a sweet variety of maize; **sweet'-flag** an aromatic araceous pond-plant, *Acorus calamus*; **sweet'-gale** bog-myrtle, a low-growing aromatic shrub found in bogs; **sweet'heart** a lover or beloved.—*v.t* and *v.i.* to court.—**sweet'le-pie** (*coll.*) a term of endearment.— *adj.* **sweet'meal** of biscuits, made of whole meal and sweetened.—**sweet'meat** a confection made wholly or chiefly of sugar: any sweet food (*obs.*); **sweet′pea′** a S. European papilionaceous garden plant (*Lathyrus odoratus*) with bright-coloured fragrant flowers; **sweet pepper** see **pepper**; **sweet′-potā′to** batata, a tropical and sub-tropical twining plant (*Ipomoea batatas*) of the convolvulus family, with large sweetish edible tubers.—*adjs.* **sweet′-sa′voured**; **sweet′-scent′ed** having a sweet smell.—**sweet′-sop** a tropical American evergreen (*Anona squamosa*): its pulpy fruit; **sweet talk** flattery, persuasion.—*v.t.* **sweet′-talk** (*coll.*) to coax, flatter, persuade.—*adjs.* **sweet′-tem′pered** having a mild, amiable disposition; **sweet′-toothed′** fond of sweet things.—**sweet′-will′iam** *Dianthus barbatus*, a garden pink with bearded petals.—**a sweet tooth** a fondness for sweet things; **sweetness and light** an appearance of mildness, reasonableness, etc. [O.E. *swēte*.]

swell *swel*, *v.i.* to expand: to increase in volume: to be inflated: to bulge out: to grow louder: to rise into waves: to heave: to well up: to rise and fall in loudness: to be elated or dilated with emotion: to give a feeling of expansion or welling up.—*v.t.* to augment: to expand: to dilate: to fill full: to louden: to elate:—*pa.t.* **swelled**; *pa.p.* **swelled, swollen** (*swōl′ən*).—*n.* act, power, habit, or condition of swelling: a heaving: a bulge: an enlargement: a loudening: a device in an organ for increasing tone: a crescendo followed by a diminuendo: rising ground: a dandy, a bigwig, an adept (*slang*).—*adj.* (*slang*) a vague word of commendation.—*adj.* and *n.* **swell′ing**.—*adv.* **swell′ingly**.—**swelled head** conceit, esp. in one carried away by success.—*adj.* **swelled′-head′ed**, also **swell′-head′ed, swoll′en-headed** conceited. [O.E. *swellan*; Ger. *schwellen*.]

swelter *swelt′ər*, *v.i.* to endure great heat: to sweat copiously.—*n.* a sweltering: a sweating.—*n.* and *adj.* **swelt′ering**. [O.E. *sweltan*, to die.]

swept *swept*, *pa.t.* and *pa.p.* of **sweep**.

swerve *swûrv*, *v.i.* to turn aside: to deviate.—*v.t.* to deflect: to cause a ball to swerve in the air.—*n.* a turning aside: a deviation: a deflection.—*adj.* **swerve′less**.—*n.* **swerv′er**.—*n.* and *adj.* **swerv′ing.** [M.E.; the O.E. *sweorfan*, to rub, file, scour, is not known to have had this sense.]

swift *swift*, *adj.* fleet: rapid: speedy: prompt.—*adv.* swiftly.—*n.* a bird (*Apus*, or *Cypselus*, *apus*) superficially like a swallow but structurally nearer the humming-birds and goatsuckers: any bird of its genus or family: the common newt: a reel for winding yarn: the main cylinder of a carding-machine.—*n.* **swift′let** a bird (*Collocalia*) akin to the swift, the builder of edible nests.—*adv.* **swift′ly**.—*n.* **swift′ness**.—*adjs.* **swift′-foot, -ed; swift′-winged.** [O.E. *swift*, from same root as **swoop.**]

swig *swig*, *n.* a deep draught.—*v.t.* to take a swig or swigs of or from.—*v.i.* to drink, take swigs:—*pr.p.* **swig′ging**; *pa.t.* and *pa.p.* **swigged**.—*n.* **swig′ger.**

swill *swil*, *v.t.* or *v.i.* to rinse: to dash water over: to wash: to drink greedily or largely.—*n.* a large draught of liquor: hog-wash.—*n.* **swill′er**.—*n.* and *adj.* **swill′ing.** [O.E. *swilian*, to wash.]

swim *swim*, *v.i.* to propel oneself in water (or other liquid): to float: to come to the surface: to travel or be conveyed by water: to be suffused: to be immersed or steeped: to glide smoothly: to be dizzy.—*v.t.* to pass by swimming: to make to swim or float:—*pr.p.* **swimm′ing**; *pa.t.* **swam** (*swam*); *pa.p.* **swum**.—*n.* an act, performance, or spell of swimming: a place where many fishes swim: the general movement or current of affairs.—*adj.* **swimm′able** capable of being swum.—*ns.* **swimm′er; swimm′eret** a crustacean's abdominal appendage used in swimming.—*n.* and *adj.* **swimm′ing**.—*adv.* **swimm′ingly** smoothly,

successfully (*coll.*).—**swimm′ing-bath; swimming costume** swimsuit; **swimm′ing-pool; swim′suit; swim′wear** garments worn for swimming.—**in the swim** in the main current (of affairs, business, etc.); **swim with, against, the stream, tide** to conform to, go against, normal behaviour, opinions, etc. [O.E. *swimman*.]

swindle *swin′dl*, *v.t.* and *v.i.* to cheat.—*n.* a fraud: anything not really what it appears to be.—*n.* **swin′dler** a cheat.—*n.* and *adj.* **swin′dling.** [Ger. *Schwindler*, a giddy-minded person, swindler—*schwindeln*, to be giddy.]

swine *swin*, *n.* a pig: a term of strong abuse:—*pl.* **swine**.—*n.* **swin′ery** a place where pigs are kept: swinishness.—*adj.* **swin′ish** of or like swine: beastly.—*adv.* **swin′ishly**.—*n.* **swin′ishness.**—**swine′-fe′ver** hog-cholera, a highly contagious disease of swine due to a virus; **swine′herd** one who herds swine. [O.E. *swin*, a pig.]

swing *swing*, *v.i.* to sway or wave to and fro, as a body hanging freely: to amuse oneself on a swing: to oscillate: to hang: to be hanged: to sweep, wheel, sway: to swerve: to move forward with swaying gait: to turn round as a ship: to attract, excite, be perfectly appropriate to place or mood (*slang*): of a person, to be thoroughly responsive (to jazz, etc.) or up-to-date (*slang*).—*v.t.* to cause to swing: to set swinging: to control: to sway: to hurl, whirl: to brandish: to move in a sweep: to perform as swing-music: to influence the result of (e.g. a doubtful election) in favour of an individual or party: to arrange, fix (*slang*):—*pa.t.* **swung**; *pa.p.* **swung**.—*n.* act, manner, or spell of swinging: oscillating, waving, sweeping: motion to and fro: the sweep or compass of a swinging body: the sweep of a golf-club, bat, or the like: sway: scope, free indulgence: impetus: vigorous sweeping rhythm: jazz music with impromptu complications as played in the 1930s and 1940s: a suspended seat or carriage for the amusement of swinging: a reversal of fortune: the movement of voters from one party to another as compared with the previous election.—*ns.* **swing′er** (*swing′ər*) a person or thing that swings: a ball bowled so as to swerve in the air (*cricket*): a lively and up-to-date person (*slang*); **swinging** (*swing′ing*) the act of moving to and fro in suspension, esp. as a pastime.—*adj.* swaying: turning: with a swing: having a free easy motion: fully alive to the most recent trends, up-to-date, lively, daring (*coll.*).—*adv.* **swing′ingly**.—*n.* **swingom′eter** a device which shows the direction and extent of the current swing of the counted votes in an election.—**swing′boat** a boat-shaped swinging carriage for fairs, etc.; **swing′-bridge** a bridge that may be opened by swinging it to one side; **swing′-door** a door (usu. one of a pair) that opens either way and swings to of itself; **swing′-music** big-band jazz with strong rhythm and improvisations; **swing′-wing′** (*aircraft*) (aircraft) having wings that can be set at right angles or swept back.—**in full swing** in mid-career: in fully active operation; **swing the lead** see **lead**[2]. [O.E. *swingan*; Ger. *schwingen*.]

swinge *swinj*, (*arch.*) *v.t.* to beat: to lash:—*pr.p.* **swinge′ing**.—*adj.* **swinge′ing** great, huge, thumping.—*adv.* **swinge′ingly.** [M.E. *swenge*—O.E. *swengan*, to shake, causative of *swingan*, to swing.]

swingle *swing′gl*, *n.* a scutching tool: the swipple of a flail.—*v.t.* to scutch.—*n.* **swing′ling**.—**swing′letree** a whippletree. [Cf. O.E. *swingell*, stroke, scourge, rod.]

swingometer. See swing.

swinish. See swine.

swipe *swip*, *n.* a sweeping stroke.—*v.t.* to strike with a swipe: to purloin (*coll.*).—*v.i.* to make a swipe. [O.E. *swipian*, to beat.]

swipple *swip'l, n.* a swingle or striking part of a flail. [Cf. **swipe, sweep.**]

swirl *swûrl, n.* an eddy: a whirl: a curl.—*v.t.* to whirl: to wind.—*v.i.* to eddy: to whirl: to spin.—*adj.* **swirl'y.** [Orig. Scot.; cf. Norw. dial. *svirla.*]

swish[1] *swish, n.* the sound of twigs sweeping through the air or of fabric rustling along the ground.—*v.i.* to go with a swish.—*adv.* with a swish.—*n.* and *adj.* **swish'ing.**—*adj.* **swish'y.** [Imit.]

swish[2] *swish,* (*slang*) *adj.* smart.

Swiss *swis, adj.* of Switzerland.—*n.* a native or citizen of Switzerland: the German dialect spoken by most Swiss:—*pl.* **Swiss.**—*n.* **Swit'zer** a Swiss.—**Swiss chard** see **chard; Swiss Guards** the Pope's bodyguard; **Swiss roll** a thin cake rolled up with jam.

switch *swich n.* a long flexible twig: a tapering riding-whip: a rod, cane: a tress, usu. false: a changeover: a device for making, breaking, or changing an electric circuit: a turn of a switch.—*v.t.* to strike with a switch: to whisk, jerk, lash: to divert: to turn (off, on, or to another circuit).—*v.i.* to use a switch: to turn aside: to change over.—*n.* **switch'ing.**—*adj.* **switch'y.** —**switch'back** orig. a zigzag mountain railway on which the train shunted back at each stage: an up-and-down track on which cars rise by the momentum gained in coming down: an up-and-down road; **switch'blade** a flick-knife; **switch'board** a board or frame bearing apparatus for making or breaking an electric current or circuit: a board for connecting telephones; **switch'man** a pointsman; **switch'-over** action of the verb: a changeover.—**switched** on aware of and responsive to all that is most up to date (*coll.*); under the influence of drugs (*coll.*). [Earlier *swits, switz;* prob. from Du. or L.G.]

swither *swidh'ər,* (*Scot.*) *v.i.* to be undecided.—*n.* indecision: flurry. [Poss. O.E. *swethrian,* to subside.]

Switzer. See **Swiss.**

swivel *swiv'l, n.* a ring or link that turns round on a pin or neck: a swivel-gun.—*v.t.* and *v.i.* to turn on a pin or pivot:—*pr.p.* **swiv'elling;** *pa.t.* and *pa.p.* **swiv'elled.** —**swiv'el-chair** a chair with a seat that swivels round; **swiv'el-eye** a squint-eye. [O.E. *swifan,* to move quickly, to turn round.]

swiz *swiz,* **swizzle** *swiz'l,* (*slang*) *ns.* fraud: great disappointment. [Poss. **swindle.**]

swizzle *swiz'l, v.i.* to drink to excess.—*n.* a mixed or compounded drink containing rum or other spirit.— **swizzle'-stick** a stick or whisk used to mix a swizzle.

swollen *swōl'ən, swōln, pa.p.* of **swell,** and *adj.*

swoon *swōōn, n.* a fainting fit.—*v.i.* to faint: to be languorous.—*n.* and *adj.* **swoon'ing.**—*adv.* **swoon'-ingly.** [Prob. from M.E. *iswowen,* in a swoon.]

swoop *swōōp, v.i.* to come down with a sweeping rush: to rush suddenly.—*n.* an act of swooping: a sudden onslaught.—**at one fell swoop** by one terrible blow: by one complete decisive action: suddenly. [App. O.E. *swāpan,* to sweep.]

swop. See **swap.**

swoosh *swōōsh, n.* a noise of or resembling a rush of air, water, etc.—*v.i.* to make this noise. [Prob. imit., or from **swish**[1], **swoop.**]

sword *sōrd, sôrd, n.* a weapon with a long blade, sharp upon one or both edges, for cutting or thrusting: a blade or flat rod resembling a sword: destruction or death by the sword or by war: war: military force: the emblem of vengeance or justice, or of authority and power.—*adjs.* **sword'less; sword'-like.**—**sword'-arm** the arm that wields the sword; **sword'-bay'onet** a bayonet shaped somewhat like a sword, and used as one; **sword'-bearer** a public officer who carries the sword of state; **sword'-belt** a belt from which the sword is hung; **sword'-bill** a S. American humming-

bird with a bill longer than its body; **sword'-blade; sword'-cane, -stick** a cane or stick containing a sword; **sword'-cut; sword'-dance** a dance performed sword in hand or among or over swords; **sword'fish** a large fish with upper jaw compressed and prolonged as a stabbing weapon; **sword'-grass** a name for many plants with sword-shaped leaves; **sword'-guard** the part of a sword-hilt that protects the bearer's hand; **sword'-knot** a ribbon tied to the hilt of a sword; **sword'play** fencing.—*adj.* **sword'-shaped.**—**swords'man** a man skilled in the use of a sword; **swords'manship; sword'-swallower** a performer who seems to swallow swords; **sword'-tail** a small Central American freshwater fish with sword-like tail-lobe.—**cross swords with** see **cross; put to the sword** (of armies, etc.; *hist.*) to kill (prisoners, etc.) by the sword. [O.E. *sweord.*]

swore, sworn. See **swear.**

swot *swot,* (*slang*) *v.t.* and *v.i.* to study hard:—*pr.p.* **swott'ing;** *pa.t.* and *pa.p.* **swott'ed.**—*n.* hard study: one who swots.—*ns.* **swott'er; swott'ing.** [**sweat.**]

swum *swum, pa.p.* of **swim.**

swung *swung, pa.t.* and *pa.p.* of **swing.**

sy-. See **syn-.**

Sybarite *sib'ə-rīt, n.* an inhabitant of *Sybaris,* a Greek city in ancient Italy, on the Gulf of Tarentum, noted for luxury: one devoted to luxury.—Also *adj.—adjs.* **Sybaritic** (*-rit'ik*), **-al, Sybarit'ish.**—*n.* **Sy'baritism.** —All words also without *cap.*

sybil. Same as **sibyl.**

sycamore *sik'ə-mōr, -mor, n.* a kind of fig-tree (now often **sycomore** or **sycomore fig**): in England, the great maple (*Acer pseudo-platanus*) called in Scotland the plane: in U.S., any true plane. [Gr. *sȳkomoros—sȳkon,* a fig, *moron,* black mulberry.]

syce, sice *sīs,* (*India*) *n.* a groom, mounted attendant: a chauffeur. [Ar. *sā'is.*]

sycomore. See **sycamore.**

syconium *sī-kō'ni-əm, n.* a multiple fruit in which the true fruits (the pips) are enclosed in a hollow fleshy receptacle—the fig. [Gr. *sȳkon,* a fig.]

sycophant *sik'ō-fant, n.* a servile flatterer.—*n.* **syc'o-phancy.**—*adj.* **sycophantic** (*-fant'ik*).—*adv.* **syco-phant'ically.**—*adj.* **syc'ophantish** (or *-fant'*).—*adv.* **syc'ophantishly.** [Gr. *sȳkophantēs,* an informer— *sȳkon,* a fig, *phainein,* to show; variously explained.]

sycosis *sī-kō'sis, n.* inflammation of the hair follicles, esp. of the beard. [Gr. *sȳkōsis,* a fig-shaped ulcer— *sȳkon,* a fig.]

syenite *sī'an-īt, n.* a coarse-grained rock composed of orthoclase and usu. hornblende.—*adj.* **syenitic** (*-it'ik*). [L. *syēnītēs* (*lapis*), a hornblende granite found at Aswan (Gr. *Syēnē*).]

syke. See **sike.**

syl-. See **syn-.**

syllable *sil'ə-bl, n.* a word or part of a word uttered by a single effort of the voice.—*v.t.* to express by syllables, to utter articulately.—*n.* **syll'abary** a set of characters representing syllables.—*adj.* **syllabic** (*sil-ab'ik*), of or constituting a syllable or syllables: syllable by syllable.—*adv.* **syllab'ically.**—*ns.* **syllabic-a'tion** syllabification; **syllabicity** (*-is'i-ti*); **syllab'ics** verse patterned not by stresses but by syllables; **syllabifica'tion** pronunciation as a syllable: division into syllables.—*vs.t.* **syllab'ify** to divide into syllables; **syll'abise, -ize** to form or divide into syllables. —*adj.* **syll'abled** having (in compounds, so-many) syllables.—**syllabic verse,** metre syllabics.—**in words of one syllable** (*coll.*) very simply, bluntly. [L. *syllaba*—Gr. *syllabē—syn,* with, *lab-,* root of *lambanein,* to take; *-le* as in principle, participle.]

syllabub, sillabub *sil'ə-bub, n.* a dish of cream curdled (as with wine), flavoured and frothed up.

syllabus *sil'ə-bəs, n.* an abstract or programme, as of a series of lectures or a course of studies: a catalogue of doctrinal positions or practices condemned by the R.C. Church (1864, 1907):—*pl.* **syll'abuses, syll'abi** (-*bī*). [L.,—Gr. *sillybē*, a book-label.]

syllepsis *sil-ep'sis, n.* a figure in rhetoric by which a word does duty in a sentence in the same syntactical relation to two or more words but has a different sense in relation to each:—*pl.* **syllep'ses** (-*sēz*).—*adj.* **syllep'tic.**—*adv.* **syllep'tically.** [Gr. *syllēpsis*, a taking together—*syn*, together, and the root of *lambanein*, to take.]

syllogism *sil'ō-jizm, -ə-jizm, n.* a logical argument in three propositions, two premises and a conclusion that follows necessarily from them: deductive reasoning.—*n.* **syllogisation**, **-z-** (-*jī-zā'shən*).—*v.i.* **syll'ogise, -ize** to reason by syllogisms.—*v.t.* to deduce syllogistically.—*n.* **syll'ogiser, -z-.**—*adj.* **syllogistic** (-*jist'ik*).—*adv.* **syllogist'ically.** [Gr. *syllogismos*—*syn*, together, *logos*, reason.]

sylph *silf, n.* a spirit of the air: a slim person: a kind of humming-bird.—*adj.* **sylph'-like.** [Coined by Paracelsus.]

sylva, sylvan, sylviculture. See **silva.**

symbiosis *sim-bi-ō'sis, n.* a mutually beneficial partnership between organisms of different kinds: esp. such an association where one lives within the other. —*n.* **sym'biont** (-*bi-ont*) an organism living in symbiosis.—*adj.* **symbiotic** (-*bi-ot'ik*).—*adv.* **symbiot'ically.** [Gr. *syn*, together, *bios*, livelihood.]

symbol *sim'b(ə)l, n.* an emblem: that which by custom or convention represents something else: a type: a creed, or a typical religious rite (*theol.*).—*adjs.* **symbolic** (-*bol'ik*), **-al.**—*adv.* **symbol'ically.**—*ns.* **symbol'icalness; symbolisa'tion, -z-.**—*v.t.* **sym'bolise, -ize** to be symbolical of: to represent by symbols.—*n.* **sym'bolism** representation by symbols or signs: a system of symbols: use of symbols: use of symbols in literature or art: (often with *cap.*) a late 19th-cent. movement in art and poetry that treated the actual as an expression of something underlying.—*n.* and *adj.* **sym'bolist.**—*adjs.* **symbolist'ic, -al.**—*n.* **symbol'ogy** (for **symbolol'ogy**) the study or use of symbols.— **symbolic logic** a branch of logic which uses symbols instead of terms, propositions, etc., in order to clarify reasoning. [Gr. *symbolon*, a token—*syn*, together, *ballein*, to throw.]

symmetry *sim'i-tri, n.* exact correspondence of parts on either side of a straight line or plane, or about a centre or axis: balance or due proportion: beauty of form: disposition of parts.—*adjs.* **symmet'ric, -al** having symmetry.—*adv.* **symmet'rically.**—*n.* **symmet'ricalness.** [Gr. *symmetriā*—*syn*, together, *metron*, a measure.]

sympathectomy *sim-pəth-ek'tə-mi, n.* excision of part of a sympathetic nerve. [From **sympathetic**, and Gr. *ektomē*, excision.]

sympathy *sim'pə-thi, n.* community of feeling: power of entering into another's feelings or mind: harmonious understanding: compassion, pity: affinity or correlation whereby one thing responds to the action of another or to action upon another: agreement: (often in *pl.*) a feeling of agreement or support, or an expression of this.—*adj.* **sympathet'ic** feeling, inclined to, expressing, sympathy: in sympathy: acting or done in sympathy: induced by sympathy (as sounds in a resonating body): congenial: compassionate: of the sympathetic nervous system (see below).—*adv.* **sympathet'ically.**—*v.i.* **sym'pathise, -ize** to be in sympathy: to feel with or for another: to be compassionate: to be in accord, correspond.—*n.* **sym'pathiser, -z-.**—**sympathetic ink** see **ink; sympathetic magic** magic depending upon a supposed sympathy, e.g. between a person and his name or portrait; **sym-**

pathetic nervous system a system of nerves supplying the involuntary muscles and glands, esp. those originating from the cervical, thoracic, and lumbar regions of the spinal cord; sometimes also including those from the brain and the sacral region (the **parasympathetic nervous system**); **sympathetic sympathy, strike** a strike in support of other workers, not in furtherance of the strikers' own claims.—**in sympathy** (**with**) in agreement (with), in support (of). [Gr. *sympatheia*—*syn*, with, *pathos*, suffering.]

sympetalous *sim-pet'ə-ləs, adj.* having the petals united. [Gr. *syn*, together, *petalon*. lead.]

symphony *sim'fə-ni, n.* harmony, esp. of sound: an orchestral composition on a great scale in sonata form (*mus.*): a symphony orchestra.—*adj.* **symphonic** (*sim-fon'ik*).—*n.* **sym'phonist** a composer or performer of symphonies.—**symphonic poem** a large orchestral composition in programme music with the movements run together; **symphony orchestra** a large orchestra comprising strings, woodwind, brass and percussion, capable of performing symphonies. [Gr. *symphōniā*, harmony, orchestra—*syn*, together, *phōnē*, a sound.]

symphysis *sim'fi-sis, n.* the union or growing together of parts, concrescence: union of bones by fusion, cartilage, or ligament: a place of junction of parts.— *adj.* **symphyseal, -ial** (*sim-fiz'i-əl*). [Gr. *symphysis* —*syn*, with, *phyein*, to grow.]

sympodium *sim-pō'di-əm, (bot.) n.* a stem composed of a succession of branches each supplanting and seeming to continue its parent branch:—*pl.* **sympo'dia.**—*adj.* **sympo'dial.**—*adv.* **sympo'dially.** [Gr *syn*, together, *pous, podos,* foot.]

symposium *sim-pō'zi-əm, n.* a drinking party (*hist.*): a meeting for philosophic conversation: a conference: a collection of views on one topic:—*pl.* **sympo'sia.**— *adjs.* **sympō'siac, sympō'sial.** [Latinised from Gr. *symposion*—*syn*, together, *posis*, drinking.]

symptom *sim(p)'təm, n.* a subjective indication of a disease, i.e. something perceived by the patient, not outwardly visible: a characteristic sign or indication of the existence of a state.—*adjs.* **symptomat'ic, -al.** —*adv.* **symptomat'ically.**—*v.t.* **symp'tomatise, -ize** to be a symptom of.—*n.* **symptomatol'ogy** the study of symptoms: the symptoms of a patient or a disease taken as a whole. [Gr. *symptōma, symptōsis*—*syn*, with, and root of *piptein*, to fall.]

syn-, sy-, syl-, sym- *pfxs.* together, with. [Gr. *syn*, with.]

synaeresis *sin-ē'rə-sis, n.* the running together of two vowels into one or into a diphthong: the spontaneous expulsion of liquid from a gel:—*pl.* **synae'reses.** [Gr. *syn*, together, *hairesis*, taking—*haireein*, to take.]

synaesthesia *sin-ēs-thē'zi-ə, -zhyə, n.* sensation produced at a point different from the point of stimulation: a sensation of another kind suggested by one experienced (e.g. in colour-hearing).— *adj.* **synaesthet'ic.** [Gr. *syn*, together, *aisthēsis*, sensation.]

synagogue *sin'ə-gog, n.* an assembly of Jews for worship: a Jewish place of worship.—*adjs.* **syn'agogal** (-*gō-gl*), **synagog'ical** (-*gog'*, -*goj'i-kl*). [Gr. *synagōgē*—*syn*, together, *agōgē*, a bringing—*agein*, to lead.]

synallagmatic *sin-a-lag-mat'ik, adj.* mutually or reciprocally obligatory. [Gr. *synallagmatikos*— *synallagma*, a covenant—*syn*, together, *allagma*, exchange.]

synantherous *sin-an'thər-əs, adj.* with anthers united. [Gr. *syn*, and **anther.**]

synanthesis *sin-an-thē'sis, (bot.) n.* simultaneous ripening of stamens and stigmas.—*adjs.* **synanthet'ic;**

synan'thic showing synanthy; **synan'thous** synanthic: flowering and leafing simultaneously.—*n.* **synan'thy** abnormal fusion of flowers. [Gr. *syn*, together, *anthēsis*, flowering, *anthos*, a flower.]

synapsis *sin-aps'is*, *n.* the pairing of chromosomes of paternal and maternal origin before the reducing division: a synapse:—*pl.* **synaps'es** (*-ēz*).—*n.* **synapse'** (also *sin'*, *sīn'*) an interlacing or enveloping connection of a nerve-cell with another. [Gr. *synapsis*, contact, junction—*syn*, together, *haptein*, to fasten; *synaptē* (*euchē*, a prayer), joined together.]

synarthrosis *sin-ər-thrō'sis*, *n.* immovable articulation: —*pl.* **-ses** (*-sēz*).—*adj.* **synarthrō'dial**.—*adv.* **synarthrō'dially**. [Gr. *synarthrōsis*—*syn*, together, *arthron*, a joint; also *arthrōdiā*, a flattish joint.]

sync. See **synch**.

syncarp *sin'kärp*, (*bot.*) *n.* a compound fruit formed from two or more carpels, of one or more than one flower.—*adj.* **syncarpous** (*sin-kär'pəs*) of or having united carpels.—*n.* **syn'carpy**. [Gr. *syn*, together, *karpos*, a fruit.]

synch, sync *singk*, *n.*, *v.i.*, *v.t.* short for **synchronisation, synchronise**.—**out of sync(h)** not synchronised: having different and jarring rhythms: (*loosely*), ill-matched (*with with*).

synchondrosis *sing-kon-drō'sis*, *n.* connection of bones by cartilage:—*pl.* **-ses** (*-sēz*). [Gr. *synchondrōsis*—*syn*, with, *chondros*, a cartilage.]

synchromesh *sing'krō-mesh*, *adj.* of a gear in which the speeds of the driving and driven members are automatically synchronised before coupling, so as to avoid shock and noise in gear-changing.—*n.* such a gear. [*synchronised mesh*.]

synchronal *sing'krə-nl*, *adj.* coinciding in time.—*adj.* **synchronic** (*-kron'*) synchronous: concerned with the study of a subject (*esp.* linguistics) at a particular period, without considering the past or the future— *opp.* to *diachronic*.—*adv.* **synchron'ically**.—*ns.* **synchronicity** (*-is'i-ti*); **synchronisā'tion, -z-**.—*v.i.* **syn'chronise, -ize** to coincide or agree in time.—*v.t.* to cause to coincide or agree in time: to time together or to a standard: to represent or identify as contemporary: to make (the sound-track of a film) exactly simultaneous with the picture.—*ns.* **synch'roniser, -z-; synch'ronism** coincidence in time: simultaneity: keeping time together: exhibition of contemporary history in one scheme: the bringing together in one picture of different parts of a story.—*adjs.* **synchronis'tic, -al**.—*adv.* **synchronis'tically**.—*adj.* **synch'ronous** simultaneous: contemporary: keeping time together.—*adv.* **synch'ronously**.—*ns.* **synch'ronousness; synch'rony** simultaneity.—**synchronous motor** an electric motor whose speed is exactly proportional to the frequency of the supply current; **synchronous orbit** geostationary orbit. [Gr. *syn*, together, *chronos*, time.]

syncline *sin'klīn*, (*geol.*) *n.* a fold in which the beds dip downwards towards the axis.—*adj.* **synclin'al**.—*n.* a syncline. [Gr. *syn*, together, *klīnein*, to cause to lean.]

syncope *sing'kə-pi*, *n.* a fainting fit caused by a sudden fall of blood pressure in the brain (*med.*).—*adj.* **sync'opal** of syncope.—*v.t.* **sync'opate** to shorten by cutting out the middle (of a word): to alter the rhythm of temporarily by transferring the accent to a normally unaccented beat (*mus.*).—*adj.* **sync'opated**. —*ns.* **syncopā'tion; sync'opātor**.—*adj.* **syncopic** (*sing-kop'ik*). [Gr. *synkopē*, a cutting up, cutting short—*syn*, together, *koptein*, to cut off.]

syncretism *sing'kri-tizm*, or *sin'*, *n.* reconciliation of, or attempt to reconcile, different systems of belief: fusion or blending of religions, as by identification of gods, taking over of observances, or selection of whatever seems best in each: illogical compromise in religion: the fusion of orig. distinct inflectional forms of a word.—*adj.* **syncretic** (*sin-krē'tik*, or *sing-*).— *v.t.* and *v.i.* **syncretise, -ize** (*sing'kri-tīz*).—*n.* **syn'cretist**.—*adj.* **syncretis'tic**. [Gr. *synkrētismos*, a confederation (*orig. app.* of *Cretan* communities).]

syncytium *sin-sish'i-əm*, (*biol.*) *n.* a multinucleate cell: a tissue without distinguishable cell-walls.—*adj.* **syncyt'ial**. [Gr. *syn*, together, *kytos*, a vessel.]

syndactyl *sin-dak'til*, *adj.* with fused digits.—*n.* **syndac'tylism**.—*adj.* **syndac'tylous**.—*n.* **syndac'tyly**. [Gr. *syn*, *daktylos*, finger, toe.]

syndesis *sin'di-sis*, *n.* a binding: synapsis (*biol.*).—*adjs.* **syndetic** (*-det'ik*), **-al** connective: of a construction in which clauses are connected by conjunctions (*gram.*). —*adv.* **syndet'ically**. [Gr. *syndesis*—*syn*, *deein*, to bind.]

syndesmosis *sin-des-mō'sis*, *n.* the connection of bones by ligaments:—*pl.* **-es** (*-ēz*).—*adj.* **syndesmotic** (*-mot'ik*). [Gr. *syndesmos*—*syn*, *desmos*, a bond.]

syndetic, etc. See **syndesis**.

syndic *sin'dik*, *n.* at various times and places a magistrate or mayor: a member of a committee of the Senate of Cambridge University: one chosen to transact business for others, *esp.* the accredited legal representative of a corporation, society, or company. —*adj.* **syn'dical**.—*ns.* **syn'dicalism** a development of trade-unionism which originated in France, aiming at putting the means of production in the hands of unions of workers; **syn'dicalist**.—Also *adj.*—*adj.* **syndicalist'ic**.—*n.* **syn'dicate** a body of syndics: a council: a body of men chosen to watch the interests of a company, or to manage a bankrupt's property: a combination of persons for some common purpose or interest: an association of businessmen or companies to undertake a project requiring a large amount of capital: an association of criminals who organise and control illegal operations: a combined group of newspapers.—*v.t.* to control, effect, or publish by means of a syndicate: to sell (as an article) for simultaneous publication in a number of newspapers or periodicals: to join in a syndicate.—*ns.* **syndicā'tion; syn'dicātor**. [Gr. *syndikos*—*syn*, with, *dikē*, justice.]

syndrome *sin'drōm*, *sin'drə-mi*, *-mē*, or *sin'drō-mi*, *-mē*, *n.* concurrence, *esp.* of symptoms: a characteristic pattern or group of symptoms: a pattern or group of actions, feelings, observed happenings, etc., characteristic of a particular problem or condition.— *adj.* **syndromic** (*-drom'ik*). [Gr. *syndromē*.]

synecdoche *sin-ek'də-kē*, *-ki*, (*rhet.*) *n.* the figure of putting part for the whole, or the whole for part.— *adjs.* **synecdochic** (*-dok'*), **-al**.—*adv.* **synecdoch'ically**. [Gr. *synekdochē*—*syn*, together, *ek-dechesthai*, to receive.]

synecology *sin-ē-kol'ə-ji*, *n.* the ecological study of communities of plants or animals.—*adjs.* **synecolog'ic, -al**.—*adv.* **synecolog'ically**. [Gr. *syn*, together, and *ecology*.]

syneresis. Same as **synaeresis**.

synergy *sin'ər-ji*, *n.* combined or co-ordinated action. —*adjs.* **synergetic** (*-jet'ik*), **syner'gic** working together.—*ns.* **synergism** (*sin'* or *-ûr'*) increased effect of two substances, as drugs, obtained by using them together; **syn'ergist** (or *-ûr'*) a substance which increases the effect of another (e.g. pesticide): a muscle, etc., that acts with another.—*adj.* **syner'gistic**. [Gr. *synergiā*, co-operation—*syn*, together, *ergon*, work.]

synesis *sin'ə-sis*, *n* syntax having regard to meaning rather than grammatical form. [Gr., sense.]

syngamy *sing'gə-mi*, *n.* union of gametes.—*adjs.* **syngamic** (*sin-gam'ik*), **syngamous** (*sing'gə-məs*). [Gr. *syn*, together, *gamos*, marriage.]

syngenesis *sin-jen'i-sis*, *n.* reproduction by fusion of male and female elements, the offspring being derived from both parents.—*adj.* **syngenetic** (*-net'ik*). [Gr. *syn*, together, *genesis*, formation, generation.]

synizesis *sin-i-zē'sis*, *n.* the union into one syllable of two vowels without forming a recognised diphthong. [Gr. *synizēsis*, a collapse—*syn*, with, together, and *hizein*, to seat, to sit down.]

synod *sin'əd*, *n.* a meeting: an ecclesiastical council: a Presbyterian church court intermediate between presbytery and the General Assembly: the supreme court of the former United Presbyterian Church.—*adjs.* **syn'odal** of, of the nature of, or done in a synod; **synodic** (*-od'ik*), **-al** synodal: pertaining to conjunction (*astron.*): from conjunction to conjunction.—*adv.* **synod'ically.—synodic period** (*astron.*) the time between two successive conjunctions of a heavenly body with the sun.—**General Synod of the Church of England** governing body giving the laity more say in the decisions of the Church. [Gr. *synodos*, a meeting, conjunction—*syn*, together, *hodos*, a way.]

synonym *sin'ə-nim*, *n.* a word having the same meaning with another.—*adjs.* **synonym'ic**, **-al** of synonyms.—*ns.* **synonym'ity** the fact or quality of being synonymous.—*adj.* **synon'ymous** having the same meaning.—*adv.* **synon'ymously.—***ns.* **synon'ymousness; synon'ymy** rhetorical use of synonyms: a setting forth of synonyms: a list of synonyms. [Gr. *synōnymon*—*syn*, with, *onoma*, a name.]

synopsis *sin-op'sis*, *n.* a general view: a summary:—*pl.* **synop'ses.—***adjs.* **synop'tic**, **-al** affording or taking a general view of the whole.—*adv.* **synop'tically.—***n.* **synop'tist** one of the writers of the Synoptic Gospels. —*adj.* **synoptis'tic.—Synoptic Gospels** those of Matthew, Mark, and Luke, which readily admit of being brought under one combined view. [Gr *synopsis*—*syn*, with, together, *opsis*, a view.]

synovia *sin-ō'vi-ə*, *n.* an unctuous fluid in the joints.— *adj.* **syno'vial.—***n.* **synovi'tis** inflammation of a synovial membrane.—**synovial membrane** a membrane of connective tissue that lines tendon sheaths and capsular ligaments and secretes synovia. [App. an arbitrary coinage of Paracelsus.]

syntactic, syntagma, etc. See **syntax.**

syntan *sin'tan*, *n.* a synthetic *tan*ning agent.

syntax *sin'taks*, *n.* grammatical structure in sentences: one of the classes in some R.C. schools.—*adjs.* **syntac'tic**, **-al.—***adv.* **syntac'tically.—***n.* **syntag'ma** a systematic body, system, or group: a word or words constituting a syntactic unit:—*pl.* **syntag'mata.** [Gr. *syntaxis*—*syn*, together—*tassein*, to put in order.]

syntenosis *sin-tə-nō'sis*, *n.* the connection of bones by tendons:—*pl.* **-oses** (*-ō'sēz*). [Gr. *syn*, with, *tenōn*, a sinew.]

synthesis *sin'thi-sis*, *n.* building up: putting together: making a whole out of parts: the combination of separate elements of thought into a whole: reasoning from principles to a conclusion—opp. to *analysis*:— *pl.* **syn'theses** (*sēz*).—*v.t.* **syn'thesise, -ize** to put together in synthesis: to form by synthesis.—*ns.* **syn'thesiser, -z-** one who, or that which, synthesises: a computerised instrument for generating sounds, often beyond the range of conventional instruments, used esp. in making electronic music.—*n.* **syn'thesist** one who makes a synthesis.—*adjs.* **synthetic** (*-thet'*), **-al** pertaining to, consisting in, or formed by, synthesis: artificially produced but of like nature with, not a mere substitute for, the natural product: not sincere, sham (*coll.*).—*n.* **synthet'ic** a synthetic substance.—*adv.* **synthet'ically.—***v.t.* **syn'thetise, -ize** to synthesise.—*ns.* **syn'thetiser, -z-, syn'thetist.** —**synthetic languages** those that use inflectional

forms instead of word order, prepositions, etc., to express syntactical relationships. [Gr. *synthesis—syn*, with, together, *thesis*, a placing.]

syphilis *sif'i-lis*, *n.* a contagious venereal disease due to infection with a micro-organism *Spirochaeta pallida* (*Treponema pallidum*).—*adj.* **syphilit'ic.—***n.* a person suffering from syphilis.—*adj.* **syph'iloid** like syphilis. [Title of Fracastoro's Latin poem (1530), whose hero *Syphilus* is infected.]

syphon, syren. Same as **siphon, siren.**

Syriac *sir'i-ak*, *n.* the ancient Aramaic dialect of *Syria.* —Also *adj.*—*adj.* **Syr'ian** relating to Syria.—*n.* native or citizen of Syria.

syringa, syringe, etc. See **syrinx.**

syrinx *sir'ingks*, *n.* Pan-pipes: the vocal organ of birds: a rock-cut tunnel, as in Egyptian tombs:—*pl.* **syringes** (*-in'jēz*) or **syr'inxes.—***ns.* **syringa** (*-ing'gə*) orig. and still popularly the mock-orange: the lilac; **syr'inge** (*-inj* or *si-rinj'*) an instrument for injecting or extracting fluids.—*v.t.* and *v.i.* to clean, spray, or inject with a syringe.—*adj.* **syringeal** (*-in'ji-əl*).—*n.* **syringomyelia** (*si-ring-gō-mī-ē'li-ə*; Gr. *myelos*, marrow) a chronic, progressive disease of the spinal cord, causing paralysis and loss of sensitivity to pain and temperature. [Gr. *syrinx*, *-ingos*, Pan-pipes, gallery.]

syrup *sir'əp*, *n.* a saturated solution of sugar boiled to prevent fermentation: any thick sweet liquid: a sugar-flavoured liquid medicine: cloying sweetness (*fig.*; *coll.*).—Also (esp. *U.S.*) **sir'up.—***adj.* **syr'upy.— golden syrup** the uncrystallisable part finally separated in manufacture of crystallised sugar. [Fr. *sirop* —Ar. *sharāb*; cf. **shrub²**, **sherbet.**]

syssarcosis *sis-är-kō'sis*, *n.* the connection of one bone with another by intervening muscle:—*pl.* **-oses** (*-ō'sēz*). [Gr. *syn*, together, *sarx*, flesh.]

systaltic *sis-tal'tik*, *adj.* alternately contracting and dilating, pulsatory. [Gr. *systaltikos*, depressing; cf. **systole.**]

system *sis'tim*, *-təm*, *n.* anything formed of parts placed together or adjusted into a regular and connected whole: a set of things considered as a connected whole: a group of heavenly bodies moving mainly under the influence of their mutual attraction: a set of bodily organs of like composition or concurring in function: the bodily organism: one of the great divisions of the geological strata: a body of doctrine: a theory of the universe: a full and connected view of some department of knowledge: an explanatory hypothesis: a scheme of classification: a manner of crystallisation: a plan: a method: a method of organisation: methodicalness: (with *the*, often with *cap.*) society seen as a soulless and monolithic organisation thwarting individual effort.—*adjs.* **systemat'ic**, **-al** pertaining to, or consisting of, for the purpose of, observing, or according to system: methodical: habitual: intentional.—*adv.* **systemat'ically.—***n.* **systematician** (*-ə-tish'ən*).—*n.sing.* **systemat'ics** the science of classification: the study of classification of living things in accordance with their natural relationships.—*ns.* **systematisa'tion, -z-, systematisa'tion, -z-.—***vs.t.* **sys'tematise, -ize, sys'temise, -ize** to reduce to a system.—*n.* **sys'tematiser, -z-; sys'tematism; sys'tematist.—***adjs.* **sys'temed; systemic** (*-tem'ik*) pertaining to the bodily system or to a system of bodily organs: affecting the body as a whole: (of a pesticide, etc.) spreading through all the tissues, without harming the plant but making it toxic to the insect, etc.; **sys'temless** without system: not exhibiting organic structure.—**system building** building using standardised factory-produced components.— *adj.* **sys'tem-built'.—systems analysis; systems analyst** one who analyses the operation of a scientific, industrial, etc., procedure, usu. with a computer, in order to plan more efficient methods and use of equipment. [Gr. *systēma—sy-, syn-*, together, and the root of *histanai*, to set.]

systole *sis'to-lē, -ta-lē, n.* rhythmical contraction, esp. of the heart—opp. to *diastole.—adj.* **systolic** (*-tol'ik*). [Gr. *systolē—syn*, together, *stellein*, to place.]

syzygy *siz'i-ji, n.* conjunction or opposition: the period of new or full moon:—*pl.* **syz'ygies.**—*adj.* **syzyg'ial.** [Gr. *syzygiā*, union, coupling—*sy-, syn-*, with, together, and *zygon*, a yoke.]

For other sounds see detailed chart of pronunciation.

T

T, t *tē, n.* the twentieth letter in our alphabet, eighteenth in the Roman, its usual sound a voiceless stop produced with the tip of the tongue in contact with teeth, gums, or palate: an object or mark in the form of the letter (also **tee**).—**T′-band′age** a bandage composed of two strips fashioned in the shape of the letter T; **T′-bar** a metal bar with cross-section in the shape of the letter T: a type of ski-lift (also **T′-bar lift**); **T′-bone** a bone shaped like a T, esp in a sirloin steak; **T′-junction** a road junction in the shape of a T; **T′-shirt** see **tee**[1]; **T′-square** a T-shaped ruler —**to a T** with perfect exactness.

′t a shortened form of **it.**

ta *tä, interj.* (hypocoristic or affected) thank you.

tab[1] *tab, n.* a small tag, flap, or strap, forming an appendage: a loop for hanging up by: reckoning, tally, check.—*adj.* **tabbed.**—*v.t.* to fix a tab to:—*pr.p.* **tabb′ing;** *pa.t.* and *pa.p* **tabbed.**—**pick up the tab** (*coll.*) to pay the bill.

tab[2] *tab, n.* short for **tablet.**

tab[3] *tab, n.* short for (typewriter) **tabulator.**—*v.t.* short for **tabulate.**

tabard *tab′ərd, n.* a mediaeval peasant's overcoat: a knight's sleeveless or short-sleeved coat: now, a herald's coat: a woman's outer garment, a sleeveless tunic. [O.Fr. *tabart.*]

tabaret *tab′ə-ret, n.* an upholsterer's silk stuff, with alternate stripes of watered and satin surface.

Tabasco® *tə-bas′kō, n.* a hot pepper sauce [*Tabasco* state in Mexico.]

tabefaction, tabefy. See **tabes.**

tabby *tab′i, n.* a coarse waved or watered silk: a tabby-cat.—*adj.* brindled.—**tabb′y-cat** a brindled cat, esp. a greyish or brownish cat with dark stripes: hence (or from *Tabitha*) a female cat. [Fr. *tabis,* app. from '*Attābiy,* a quarter in Baghdad where it was made.]

tabernacle *tab′ər-na-kl, n.* a tent or movable hut: the tent carried by the Jews through the desert and used as a temple: a place of worship, esp. temporary or dissenting: a receptacle for the vessel containing the pyx (*R.C.*): a canopied niche or seat: a canopy: a socket for a mast.—*adjs.* **tab′ernacled; tabernacular** (*-nak′ū-lər*). [L. *tabernāculum,* dim. of *taberna,* a hut.]

tabes *tā′bēz, n.* wasting away.—*n.* **tabefaction** (*tab-i-fak′shən*) wasting away, emaciation.—*v.t.* and *v.i.* **tab′efy.**—*n.* **tabescence** (*tab-es′əns*) wasting: shrivelling.—*adjs.* **tabesc′ent; tabetic** (*-bet′ik*), **tab′id.** [L. *tābēs, -is.*]

tabla *tab′lə, -la, n.* an Indian percussion instrument, a pair of small drums played with the hands. [Hind.]

tablature *tab′lə-chər, n.* a tablet: a painting, picture, pictorial representation or work: an old notation for lute music with a line for each string and letters or figures to indicate the stopping, used with modifications for other instruments. [L. *tabula,* a board.]

table *tā′bl, n.* a slab or board: a layer: a flat surface· a panel: a string-course: a slab with or for an inscription: a slab inscribed with laws: hence, in *pl.,* a code of law (as the **Twelve Tables** of ancient Rome): a board for a game, e.g. chess: a broad flat surface on a cut gem: an article of furniture consisting of a flat top on legs, pillar, or trestles, for use at meals, work, play, for holding things, etc.· supply of food, enter-

tainment: the company at a table: a board or committee: a condensed statement: a syllabus or index: a compact scheme of numerical information: hence, in *pl.,* a collection of these for reference —*adj.* of, for, like, or pertaining to a table, or meals.—*v.t.* to tabulate: to lay on the table: to pay down: to put forward (a bill, order, etc) for discussion in parliament: to postpone discussion of (a bill, etc.) for some time or indefinitely (*U.S.*).—*adj.* **tabled** (*tā′bld*) flat-topped: having a smooth sloping surface of dressed stone: having a table or tables.—*n.* **ta′bleful** as many as a table will hold.—**ta′ble-cloth** a cloth for covering a table, esp. at meals; **ta′ble-cover** a cloth for covering a table, esp. at other than meal-times.—*adj.* **ta′ble-cut** (of gems) cut with a flat top.—**table-d'hôte** (*ta-bl′-dōt*; Fr., host's table) a meal at a fixed price; **ta′bleland** an extensive region of elevated land with a flat or undulating surface: a plateau; **table licence** a licence to serve alcoholic drinks with meals only; **ta′ble-lin′en** linen table-cloths, napkins, etc.; **table manners** social behaviour during meals; **ta′ble-mat** a mat placed under dishes on a table; **table salt** fine salt suitable for use at table; **ta′ble-skitt′les** a game in which a suspended ball is swung to knock down pegs set up on a board; **ta′ble-spoon** one of the largest spoons used at table; **ta′ble-spoon′ful** as much as will fill a table-spoon:—*pl.* **ta′ble-spoon′fuls; ta′ble-talk** familiar conversation, as at table, during and after meals; **ta′ble-tenn′is** a game like lawn-tennis played on a table using celluloid or similar balls; **ta′ble-top** the top of a table: a flat top.—*adj.* **ta′ble-topped.**—**ta′ble-turn′ing** movements of tables (or other objects) attributed by spiritualists to the agency of spirits—by the sceptical to collective involuntary muscular action; **ta′ble-ware** dishes, spoons, knives, forks, etc., for table use, **table wine** an unfortified wine usually drunk with a meal.—**at table** at a meal; **lay on the table** to table (a bill, etc.); see **table** *v.t.,* above); **turn the tables** to bring about a complete reversal of circumstances; **under the table** not above board: hopelessly drunk. [Partly O.E. *tabule, tabele,* partly O.Fr. (and Fr.) *table,* both—L. *tabula,* a board.]

tableau *tab′lō, n.* a picture or vivid pictorial impression: a suddenly created situation that takes all aback:—*pl.* **tableaux** (*tab′lōz*).—**tableau** (**vivant**) a 'living picture', a motionless representation by living persons in costume:—*pl.* **tableaux** (**vivants**) (*tà-blō-vē-vä*). [Fr. dim. of *table.*]

tablet *tab′lit, n.* a small slab: a slab or stiff sheet for making notes on: a panel, esp. inscribed or for inscription: a brittle confection of sugar and condensed milk, made in slabs (*Scot.*): a small flat cake of any solid material, often medicinal [O.Fr. *tablete,* dim. of *table.*]

tabloid *tab′loid, n.* anything in a concentrated form, a summary: a newspaper of small format, measuring approx. 30 × 40 centimetres (about 12 × 16 inches), usu rather informal in style and with many photographs —*adj.* of, in the form of, tabloids: concentrated. [From *Tabloid,* trademark for a medicine in tablet form]

taboo, tabu *tə-boo′, adj.* subject to taboo: forbidden —*n.* a Polynesian (or other) system of prohibitions

---

fāte; fär; mē; hûr (her); *mīne; mōte, for; mūte; moon; foot, dhen* (then), *el′ə-mənt* (element) connected with things considered holy or unclean: any one of these prohibitions: any recognised or general prohibition, interdict, restraint, ban, exclusion, ostracism.—*v.t.* to forbid approach to or use of: to place under taboo:—*pr.p.* **taboo'ing**; *pa.t.* and *pa.p.* **tabooed'**. [Tongan *tabu* (pron. *tä'bōō*), holy, unclean.]

tabor, tabour *tā'bər, n.* a small drum like a tambourine without jingles, usually played with one stick.—*ns.* **tā'borer** one who beats the tabor; **tabouret**, *U.S.* **taboret** (*tab'ə-ret, tä-bōō-rä*) a stool, orig. drum-shaped. [O.Fr. *tabour*; an Oriental word.]

tabu. Same as **taboo**.

tabula *tab'ū-lə, n.* a writing-tablet: a flattened structure:—*pl.* **tab'ulae** (*-lē*; L. *-lī*).—*adj.* **tab'ular** of, in the form of, like, according to, a table: horizontally flattened.—*n.* **tabularisā'tion**, *-z-.*—*v.t.* **tab'ularise, -ize** to tabulate.—*adv.* **tab'ularly**.—*v.t.* **tab'ulate** to reduce to the form of a table or synopsis.—*ns.* **tabulā'tion**; **tab'ulator** a person who, or a machine which, tabulates data: a device in a typewriter which sets and then finds automatically the margins needed in tabular work: a machine which prints very rapidly data from punched cards, etc., on to continuous paper (*comput.*).—*adj.* **tab'ulatory** (*-lə-tə-ri*).—**tabula rasa** (*tab'ū-lə rä'zə, tab'ŏŏ-la rä'sa*) a smoothed or blank tablet: a mind not yet influenced by outside impressions and experience. [L. *tabula*, table.]

tacamahac *tak'ə-mə-hak, n.* a gum-resin yielded by several tropical trees: an American species of poplar, or its resin. [From Nahuatl.]

tace *tā'sē, ta'kā, imper.* be silent.—**tacet** (*tā'set, ta'ket; mus.*) is silent. [L. *tacē, imper., tacet,* 3rd pers. sing. pres. indic., of *tacēre,* to be silent.]

tach- *tak-,* **tache-, tachy-** *tak'i-,* in composition, speed, speedy.—*ns.* **tacheom'eter, tachymeter** (*-im'*) a surveying instrument for rapid measurement of distances.—*adjs.* **tacheomet'rical, tachymet'rical**.—*ns.* **tacheom'etry, tachym'etry; tachis'toscope** an instrument which flashes images, sentences, etc., on a screen for very brief, exactly timed, periods, now used esp. to increase reading speed.—*adj.* **tachistoscop'ic**.—*ns.* **tach'ogram** a record, made by a tachograph; **tach'ograph** a recording tachometer: a tachograph: an instrument fitted to commercial vehicles to record mileage, speed, number and location of stops, etc.; **tachom'eter** a device showing speed of rotation: an instrument for measuring the velocity of machines or currents.—*adj.* **tachomet'rical**.—*ns.* **tachom'etry; tachycar'dia** abnormal rapidity of heart-beat; **tach'ygraph, tachyg'rapher, -phist**.—*adjs.* **tachygraph'ic, -ical**.—*ns.* **tachyg'raphy** shorthand, esp. ancient Greek and Roman; **tachyon** (*tak'i-on*) a theoretical particle moving faster than light. [Gr. *tachys,* gen. *-eos,* swift, *tachos,* swiftness.]

tache *tash,* (*coll.*) *n.* short for **moustache**.

tachism(e) *tash'izm, n.* a mid-20th-century movement in abstract painting characterised by a clotted laying on of pigment.—*n.* and *adj.* **tach'ist(e)**. [Fr. *tache,* blob (of paint).]

tachogram, etc. See under **tach-**.

tacit *tas'it, adj.* unspoken: silent.—*adv.* **tac'itly**.—*n.* **tac'itness**.—*adj.* **tac'iturn** disinclined to speak.—*n.* **taciturn'ity**.—*adv.* **tac'iturnly**. [L. *tacitus, taciturnus.*]

tack[1] *tak, n.* a short, sharp nail with a broad head: a long temporary stitch: a fastening strip: a rope or other fastening for the lower windward corner of a sail: the corner itself: an act of tacking: an alternate course in zigzag: course of action: a change of policy, a strategical move: something tacked on: stickiness. —*v.t.* to attach or fasten, esp. in a slight manner, as

by tacks or long stitches: to change the course of by a tack.—*v i.* to change the course or tack of a ship by shifting the position of the sails: to zig-zag: to shift one's position, to veer.—*adj.* **tacked**.—*ns.* **tack'er; tack'iness; tack'ing** proceeding by tacks: fastening: fastening by tacks.—*adj.* **tack'y** sticky.—**tack hammer** a light hammer for driving tacks.—**on the right (wrong) tack** following the right (wrong) course of action, train of thought, etc [O.Fr. *taque,* doublet of *tache.*]

tack[2] *tak, n.* food generally, fare, esp. of the bread kind, as *hard tack* (ship's biscuit), *soft tack* (loaves).

tack[3] *tak, n.* riding harness, saddles, bridles, etc. [tackle.]

tacker. See **tack[1]**.

tackle *tak'l, n.* the ropes, rigging, etc., of a ship: tools, gear, weapons, equipment (for sports, etc.): ropes, etc., for raising heavy weights: a pulley: an act of tackling (*football*).—*v.t.* to harness: to seize or take hold of: to grapple with: to come to grips with: to begin to deal in earnest with: to confront, encounter, challenge.—*v.t.* and *v.i.* (*Rugby football*) to seize and stop or (*association football*) intercept (a player) in an effort to get the ball away from him.—*ns.* **tack'ler; tack'ling** furniture or apparatus belonging to the masts, yards, etc., of a ship: harness for drawing a carriage: tackle or instruments. [Cf. L.G. *takel.*]

tacky[1] *tak'i,* (*slang*) *adj.* (orig. *U.S*) shabby: sleazy: vulgar.—*n.* **tack'iness**.

tacky[2]. See **tack[1]**.

taco *tä'kō, n.* in Mexican cooking, a very thin rolled pancake with a meat filling, usu. fried crisp:—*pl.* **ta'cos.** [Mex. Sp.]

tact *takt, n.* adroitness in managing the feelings of persons dealt with: nice perception in seeing and doing exactly what is best in the circumstances.—*adj.* **tact'ful**.—*adv.* **tact'fully**.—*adj.* **tact'ile** (*-īl*) perceptible by touch: pertaining to the sense of touch: concerned in perception by touch: suggestive of touch.—*n.* **tactil'ity**.—*adj.* **tact'less**.—*adv.* **tact'lessly**.—*n.* **tact'lessness**. [L. *tactus, -ūs—tangĕre, tactum,* to touch.]

tactic, -al *tak'tik, -əl, adjs.* relating to taxis, or to tactics: (**tactical**) skilful, adroit, calculated.—*n.* **tac'tic** a system, or a piece, of tactics.—*adv.* **tac'tically**.—*n.* **tactician** (*-tish'ən*) one skilled in tactics.—*n.sing.* **tac'tics** the science or art of manoeuvring in presence of the enemy—*n.pl.* purposeful procedure. [Gr. *taktikos,* fit for arranging, *taktos,* ordered, verbal adj. of *tassein,* to arrange.]

tadpole *tad'pōl, n.* the larva of a toad or frog [O.E. *tāde,* toad, and **poll** (head).]

taedium. Now *obs.,* same as **tedium**.—**taedium vitae** (*tē'di-əm vī'tē, tī'di-ŏŏm wē'tī,* L.) weariness of life.

tael *tāl, n.* Chinese *liang* or ounce, about 1⅓ oz. (38 g.): a money of account (not normally a coin) in China, orig. a tael weight of pure silver. [Port.,—Malay *tail,* weight.]

ta'en *tān,* a contraction of **taken**.

taenia *tē'ni-ə, n.* a ribbon or fillet: the fillet above the architrave of the Doric order: a ribbon-like structure: (with *cap.*) the tapeworm genus: a member of the genus:—*pl.* **tae'niae** (*-ni-ē*), **-s**.—*ns.* **taen'iacide** (*-sīd*) a substance that destroys tapeworms; **taen'iasis** infestation with tapeworm.—*adjs.* **tae'niate, tae'nioid** like a ribbon or a tapeworm. [L.,—Gr. *tainiā,* a band.]

tafferel, taffrail *taf'ril, n.* the upper part of a ship's stern timbers. [Du. *tafereel,* a panel—*tafel,* a table —L. *tabula,* a table.]

taffeta *taf'i-tə, n.* a thin glossy silk-stuff: loosely applied to various similar or mixed fabrics.—*adj.* of taffeta. [Through Fr. or L.L from Pers. *tāftah,* woven—*tāftan,* to twist.]

For other sounds see detailed chart of pronunciation.

taffrail. See **tafferel.**

Taffy *taf'i*, (*slang*) *n.* a Welshman. [Imit. of Welsh pron. of *Davy*.]

tafia *taf'i-ə*, *n.* a variety of rum. [Perh. a W. Indian name, but cf. Malay *tāfiā*.]

tag¹ *tag*, *n.* a tab: a tie-on label: the point of a lace: any small thing tacked or attached to another: a loose or flapping end: the tip of a tail: a trite quotation (esp. Latin): a moral to a story: a refrain.—*v.t.* to put a tag or tags on: to attach as a tag: to tack, fasten, append: to remove tags from: to dog or follow closely.—*v.i.* to make tags, to string words or ideas together: to go behind as a follower (with *on* or *along*):—*pr.p.* **tagg'ing;** *pa.t.* and *pa.p.* **tagged.**—*n.* **tagg'er.**—**tag's end** the fag-end; **tagged atom** a radioactive isotopic atom of a tracer element.—**tag along (with)** to follow.

tag² *tag*, *n.* the game of tig.—*v.t.* to tig.

Tagálog *tä-gä'log*, *n.* a people of the Philippine Islands: their language.—Also *adj.*

Tagetes *tä-jē'tēz*, *n.* a Mexican and S. American genus of composites with yellow and orange flowers: (without *cap.*) a plant of this genus:—*pl.* **tagē'tes.** [L. *Tagēs*, an Etruscan god.]

tagliatelle *tä-lya-tel'ā*, *tal-yə-tel'i*, *n.* pasta made in long thin strips. [It.]

tahina *tə-hē'nə*, **tahini** *-nē*, *ns.* a paste made of crushed sesame seeds.

tahr *tār*, *n.* a beardless Himalayan wild goat [App. confused with Nepali *thār*; see **thar.**]

tahsil *tä(hh)-sēl'*, *n.* in India, a division for revenue and certain other purposes.—*n.* **tahsildar'** an officer of a tahsil. [Hindi *taḥsīl*—Ar.]

t'ai chi (ch'uan) *tī'jē'(chwän')*, a Chinese system of exercise and self-defence in which good use of coordination and balance allows effort to be minimised. [Chin., great art of boxing.]

taiga *tī'gə*, *n.* marshy pine forest. [Russ. *taigá*.]

tail¹ *tāl*, *n.* the posterior extremity of an animal, usually a slender prolongation beyond the anus: a bird's train of feathers: a fish's caudal fin: anything of like appearance, position, etc.: the back, lower, hinder, latter, or inferior part or prolongation of anything (often opp. to the *head*): the stem of a note in music: a downward extension of a letter: a retinue, suite: a queue: a train: anything long and trailing or hanging: (usu. in *pl.*) the reverse of a coin: (often in *pl.*) the skirts of a garment: (in *pl.*) a tail-coat: one who follows another and keeps constant watch on him (*coll.*): the buttocks (*coll.*): female genitalia (*slang*): sexual intercourse (*slang*): a woman (*slang*; also **piece, bit, of tail**).—*v.t.* to furnish with a tail: to be a tail to: to remove the tail or stalk from: to grip by the tail: to join end to end: to dog, shadow.—*v.i.* to straggle: to taper (often with *off* or *away*): to lessen or deteriorate slowly (with *off* or *away*).—*adj.* **tailed.**—*n.* **tail'ing** inner covered end of a projecting brick or stone in a wall: (in *pl.*) refuse, dregs.—*adj.* **tail'less** having no tail.—**tail'back** a line of traffic stretching back from anything obstructing or slowing down traffic flow; **tail'-board** a movable board at the hinder end of a cart, wagon or lorry; **tail'-coat** a man's formal coat, cutaway at the front and with narrow tails at the back; **tail'-end** the fag-end; **tail'-end'er** (*coll.*) one coming at the end; **tail'-feath'er** one of the rectrices or rudder-feathers of a bird's tail: a feather of the back forming a train, as in the peacock; **tail'-gate** lower gate of a lock: a tail-board: a door at the back of a car that opens upwards on hinges at the top; **tail'-light** a light carried at the back of a train, a tram, or other vehicle; **tail'piece** a piece at the tail or end: an engraving, design, etc., occupying the bottom of a page, as at the end of a chapter: a strip of ebony, etc., to which the ends of the strings are attached in a

fiddle; **tail'-pipe** the suction-pipe in a pump; **tail'plane** a horizontal aerofoil on the tail of an aircraft; **tail'race** the channel in which water runs away below a mill-wheel; **tail'skid** a support under the tail of an aeroplane on the ground: in a motor vehicle, a skid starting with the rear wheels; **tail'-spin** a spiral dive of an aeroplane: a state of great agitation and uncertainty how to act (*fig.*); **tail wind** a wind blowing in the same direction as one is travelling.—**on someone's tail** following someone very closely; **tail-end Charlie** (*coll.*) a tail-ender; **tail off** to become gradually less or fewer; **turn tail** to turn (and run away); **with the tail between the legs** like a beaten cur.

tail² *tāl*, (*law*) *n.* limitation of inheritance to certain heirs.—*adj.* limited. [Fr. *taille*, cutting.]

tailor *tāl'ər*, *n.* one whose business is to cut out and make outer garments, esp. for men (*fem.* **tail'oress**).—*v.i.* to work as a tailor.—*v.t.* to make clothes for: to fit with clothes: to fashion by tailor's work: to make or adapt so as to fit a special need exactly (*fig.*).—*n.* **tail'oring.**—**tail'or-bird** an Asian warbler (*Orthotomus sutorius* or kindred) that sews leaves together to form a nest.—*adj.* **tail'or-made** made by a tailor, esp. of plain, close-fitting garments for women: exactly adapted (for a purpose).—*n.* a tailor-made garment. [A.Fr. *taillour* (Fr. *tailleur*)—L.L *tāliātor*, *-ōris*—*tāliāre*, to cut.]

taint *tānt*, *n.* a tincture of some evil quality: a stain: a blemish: pollution: infection: a latent or incipient defect or corruption.—*v.t.* to affect or imbue with anything objectionable: to contaminate: to infect: to impart a scent to.—*v.i.* to become infected or corrupted: to go bad: to weaken, wilt, wither.—*adjs.* **taint'ed; taint'less.**—*adv.* **taint'lessly.** [Partly aphetic for **attaint**; partly O.Fr. *taint* (Fr. *teint*)—L. *tinctus*, *-ūs*—*tingĕre*, *tinctum*, to wet, dye.]

'taint *tānt*, slang or illit. contraction of **it is not.**

taipan *tī'pan*, *n.* a large venomous Australian snake, *Oxyuranus scutellatus*. [Aboriginal name.]

taisch, taish *tīsh*, *n.* in the Scottish Highlands, an apparition or voice of one about to die: second-sight. [Gael. *taibhis*, *taibhse*, apparition.]

taj *täj*, *n.* a crown: a dervish's tall conical cap.—**Taj Mahal** (*mə-häl'*) the magnificent mausoleum at Agra erected by Shah Jehan for his wife Mumtáz-i-Mahal (d. 1629). [Ar. and Pers. *tāj*, crown.]

takahe(a) *tä'kə-hā*, *n.* a notornis (q.v.). [Maori.]

take *tāk*, *v.t.* to lay hold of: to get into one's possession: to seize: to catch: to capture: to captivate: to receive or come to have willingly or by an act of one's own: to appropriate: to assume, adopt: to accept: to receive: to admit: to have normally assigned to one: to find out, come upon, surprise, detect: to swallow or inhale: to apply to oneself: to obtain: to engage, secure: to have recourse to: to attend a course in: to call for, necessitate, use up: to remove: to cause to go: to subtract: to convey: to escort: to detract: to derive: to understand: to apprehend: (with *it*) to assume, suppose: to mistake: to conceive: to accept as true: to tolerate: to observe or measure: to ascertain something from: to execute, perform: to set down: to portray: to photograph: to charge oneself with: to asseverate: to strike: to come upon and affect.—*v.t.* to have the intended effect: to be effective, to work: to please the public: to betake oneself, begin: to bite (as a fish): to make a capture or acquisition: to admit of being taken: to become, fall, e.g. ill (*coll.*):—*pa.t.* **took;** *pa.p.* **tä'ken.**—*n.* an act of taking: a capture: quantity taken on one occasion: the amount of money taken, e.g. from a business enterprise, admission charges, etc.: the filming of one scene (*cinematogra-*

phy).—*adjs.* **take'able** (or **tā'kable**); **tā'ken**.—*ns.* **tā'ker**; **tā'king** action of the verb in any sense: (usu. in *pl.*) that which is taken, receipts.—*adj.* captivating: alluring: infectious, catching.—*adv.* **tā'kingly**.—*adj.* **take'-away** (of cooked food) sold for consumption away from the place of sale: (of a restaurant) selling such food.—*n.* such a restaurant.—**take'-in'** a deception, fraud, or disappointment of hopes; **take'-off** a burlesque mimicking: a drawback: place, act, or mode of leaving the ground for a jump, dive, or flight (also *fig.*).—*adj.* **take'-out** (*U.S.*) take-away.—*n.* (*bridge*) a conventional bid asking one's partner to bid a different suit.—**take'over** acquirement of control of a business by purchase of a majority of its shares.—Also *adj.*—**take'-up** the fact, or an instance, of taking up (i.e. using, accepting).—Also *adj.*—**on the take** engaged in small-scale dishonest profit-making; **take after** to follow in resemblance; **take against** to take a dislike to: to oppose; **take back** to retract; **take down** to reduce: to lower: to go above in class: to demolish, pull down: to take to pieces: to report or write down to dictation: (**a peg**) to humiliate in some degree; **take effect** to come off, succeed: to come into force; **take five** (or **ten**) to take a short break of five (or ten) minutes; **take for** to suppose to be, esp. wrongly; **take heed** to be careful; **take-home pay** pay after deduction of tax, etc.; **take in** to enclose: to comprise: to annex: to subdue: to receive: to conduct to the dining-room: to subscribe for: to tighten: to furl: to grasp, realise: to accept as true: to cheat; **take in hand** to undertake; **take into one's head** to be seized with a notion; **take in vain** to use with unbecoming levity; **take it** (*coll.*) to endure punishment or misfortune without giving way; **take it or leave it** to accept something with all its disadvantages, or else do without it; **take it out of** to exact the utmost from: to exhaust the strength or energy of; **take it out on** to make (an innocent person or object) suffer for one's anger or frustration: to vent one's ill-temper, anger, etc., on; **take notice** to observe: to show that observation is made; **take off** to remove: to swallow: to mimic: to leave the ground for a jump or flight: to begin a rapid improvement or expansion; **take on** to receive aboard: to undertake: to assume: to take into employment: to grieve (*coll.*): to accept a challenge from: (of ideas, etc.) to gain acceptance; **take someone up on** to accept someone's offer or challenge with respect to: to put a person's statement to the test; **take out** to remove from within: to extract: to go out with: to obtain on application; **take over** to receive by transfer: to convey across: to assume control of; **takeover bid; takeover bidder; take to** to betake oneself to: to adapt oneself to: to become fond of; **take to pieces** to separate into component parts; **take to task** to call to account, reprove; **take up** to lift, to raise: to pick up for use: to absorb: to accept: to interrupt sharply: to arrest: to adopt the practice, study, etc., of, begin to go in for: to begin to patronise, seek to advance: to resume: to take in hand: to engross, occupy or fill fully: (usu. in passive) to interest, please (with *about* or *with*; *dial.*): to borrow: to secure, fasten; **take upon oneself** to assume: to presume: to take responsibility for: to undertake; **take up with** to begin to associate with, form a connection with. [Late O.E. *tacan* (pa.t. *tōc*) to touch, take—O.N. *taka* (pa.t. *tōk*; pa.p. *tekinn*).]

takin *tā'kin*, *tä-kēn'*, *n.* a large ungulate (*Budorcas taxicolor*) akin to the goats and antelopes. [Tibetan.]

talapoin *tal'ə-poin*, *n.* a Buddhist monk, esp. of Pegu, in Burma: a small green W. African guenon monkey. [Port. *talapão*—Old Peguan *tala pôi*, my lord.]

talar, talaria. See under **talus**[1].

talc *talk*, *n.* a very soft, pliable, greasy, silvery-white mineral, acid magnesium silicate: talcum powder.—*adjs.* **talck'y**, **talc'ose**, **talc'ous**.—*n.* **talc'um** talc.—**talcum powder** purified powdered talc, usu. perfumed, applied to the skin to absorb moisture. [Fr. *talc* or L.L. *talcum*—Ar. *talq*—Pers. *talk*.]

tale *tāl*, *n.* an act of telling: a narrative, story: a false story: a mere story: (in *pl.*) things told idly or to get others into trouble.—**tale'bearer** one who maliciously tells tales or gives information; **tale'bearing**.—Also *adj.*—**tale'-teller** a teller of stories, narrator: a talebearer.—**old wives' tale** a marvellous story for the credulous; **tell one's** (or **its**) **own tale** to speak for oneself or itself; **tell tales** to play the informer; **tell tales out of school** to reveal confidential matters. [O.E. *talu*, story, number.]

talent *tal'ənt*, *n.* an ancient unit of weight and of money: hence (from the parable, Matt. xxv. 14–30) faculty: any natural or special gift: special aptitude: eminent ability short of genius: persons of special ability: young girls or young men, esp. attractive, handsome, etc. (*coll.*): disposition.—*adjs.* **tal'ented** possessing talent or aptitude; **tal'entless**.—**talent scout, spotter** one whose business is to discover and recruit talented people, esp. on behalf of the entertainment industry. [L. *talentum*—Gr. *talanton*, a balance, a talent.]

tales *tā'lēz*, (orig. *pl.*) *n.* the filling up, from those who are present, of a deficiency in the number of jurymen. [From the phrase '*tālēs* de circumstantibus', such of the bystanders: *tālēs*, pl. of L. *tālis*, such.]

tali. See **talus**[1].

talion *tal'i-ən*, *n.* like for like: retaliation. [L. *tāliō*, *-ōnis*, like punishment—*tālis*, such.]

talipes *tal'i-pēz*, *n.* club-foot.—*adj.* **tal'iped** (*-ped*) having a club-foot.—Also *n.* [L. *tālus*, ankle, *pēs*, foot.]

talipot, talipat *tal'i-pot*, *-pat*, *-put*, *ns.* an E. Asian fan-palm (*Corypha*). [Sinh. *talapata*—Sans. *tālī*, palmyra palm, *pattra*, leaf.]

talisman *tal'is-mən*, or *-iz-*, *n.* an object supposed to be indued with magical powers: an amulet, charm:—*pl.* **tal'ismans**.—*adjs.* **talismanic** (*-man'ik*), **-al.** [Ar. *tilsam*—Gr. *telesma*, payment, certificate, later completion, rite, consecrated object—*teleein*, to complete, fulfil, consecrate.]

talk *tok*, *v.i.* to speak, esp. informally or idly: to converse.—*v.t.* to utter: to speak about: to speak in: to bring or render by talking.—*n.* conversation: rumour: discussion: gossip: mention of possibility or proposal: a general theme: utterance: a short informal address. —*adj.* **talk'ative** given to much talking.—*adv.* **talk'atively**.—*ns.* **talk'ativeness**; **talk'er**; **talk'ie** (commonly in *pl.*) a talking film, cinematograph picture accompanied by sound.—*n.* and *adj.* **talk'ing**.—**talk'-back** a two-way radio system; **talking book** a recording of a reading of a book, esp. for use by the blind; **talk'ing-point** a matter of or for talk; **talking shop** (*coll.*) a meeting or a place for discussion, as opposed to decision or action; **talk'ing-to** a reproof; **talk-show** see **chat-show**.—**now you're talking** (*coll.*) now you are saying something important or to the point; **talk back** to reply impudently; **talk big** to talk boastfully; **talk down** to argue down: to talk as to inferiors in intellect or education: to bring (an aircraft) to a landing by radioed instructions from the ground; **talk-down system; talking of** apropos of, now that mention has been made of; **talk into** to persuade; **talk out** to defeat (a parliamentary bill or motion) by going on speaking until it is too late to vote on it: to resolve (a difference of opinion) by thorough discussion; **talk over** to persuade, convince: to discuss, consider together; **talk round** to talk of all sorts of related matters without coming to the point: to bring to one's way of thinking by persuasive talk; **talk shop** see shop; **talk tall** to boast; **talk to** to address: to rebuke; **talk turkey** see **turkey**; **talk up** to speak boldly: to praise or boost: to make much of. [M.E. *talken*, freq. of **tell**.]

tall *töl*, *adj.* high in stature: long, esp. in a vertical direction: lofty: (usu. of a person) of a stated height, as *six feet tall*: great, remarkable: grandiloquent: hardly to be believed.—*n.* **tall′ness**.—**tall′boy** a high chest of drawers, one portion superimposed on another; **tall order** see **order**.—**a tall man of his hands** a deft worker: a sturdy fighter; **talk, walk, tall** see **talk, walk**. [App. O.E. *getæl*, prompt.]

tallage *tal′ij*, *n.* a tax levied by a feudal lord on his tenants (*hist.*): an aid, toll, or rate. [O.Fr. *taillage* —*tailler* to cut, to tax.]

tallith *tal′ith*, *n.* the Jewish prayer shawl. [Heb. *tallūth*.]

tallow *tal′ō*, *n.* fat, grease: rendered fat, esp. of ox and sheep: any coarse, hard fat.—*adj.* of, for, or like tallow.—*v.t.* to grease with tallow: to produce tallow.—*adjs.* **tall′owish**; **tall′owy**.—**tall′ow-can′dle** a candle made of tallow. [M.E. *talgh*.]

tally *tal′i*, *n.* a stick notched to mark numbers or keep accounts: half of such a stick split across the notches, serving as receipt or record: anything that answers to a counterpart: a score or account, esp. one kept by notches or marks: credit, tick: a mark made in scoring an account: a distinguishing mark: a label: a tag: a number taken as a unit in computation: a full number: —*pl.* **tall′ies**.—*v.t.* to notch or mark as a tally: to count by tally: to reckon: to match, adapt.—*v.i.* to correspond, match, agree: to deal on credit:—*pr.p.* **tall′ying**; *pa.t.* and *pa.p.* **tall′ied**.—**tally clerk** a checker of ship's cargoes against a list; **tall′yman** one who keeps a tallyshop: a salesman for a tallyshop: one who keeps a score or record:—*fem.* **tall′ywo′man**; **tall′yshop** shop where goods are sold to be paid by instalments, the seller having one account-book which tallies with the buyer's; **tall′y-sys′tem**, **-trade** mode of dealing on credit for payment by instalments. [A.Fr. *tallie*—L. *tālea*, a stick.]

tally-ho *tal-i-hō′*, *interj.* the huntsman's cry betokening that a fox has been sighted.—*n.* cry of tally-ho: a four-in-hand coach:—*pl.* **tally-hos′**.—*v.i.* to call tally-ho. [Cf. Fr. *taïaut*.]

Talmud *tal′mood*, -mud, *n.* the fundamental code of Jewish civil and canon law, the *Mishnah* and the *Gemara*.—*adjs.* **Talmud′ic**, **-al**.—*n.* **Tal′mudist** one learned in the Talmud.—*adj.* **Talmudist′ic**. [Heb. *talmūd*, instruction—*lāmad*, to learn.]

talon *tal′ən*, *n.* a hooked claw or finger: an ogee moulding: the part of the bolt of a lock that the key presses on when it is turned: cards remaining after the deal, the stock.—*adj.* **tal′oned**. [Fr. *talon*—L.L. *tālō*, *-ōnis*—L. *tālus*, the heel.]

talus[1] *tā′los*, *n.* the ankle-bone:—*pl.* **tā′li**.—*n.* **tā′lar** a robe reaching the ankles:—*n.pl.* **talaria** (*ta-lā′ri-ə*) winged sandals, or wings on the ankles, as of Hermes. [L. *tālus*, ankle.]

talus[2] *tā′los*, *n.* the sloping part of a work (*fort.*): a scree (*geol.*). [Fr.,—L.L. *talutium*, a slope.]

tam. See **Tam o' Shanter**.

tamale *tä-mäl′i*, *n.* a highly seasoned Mexican dish of crushed maize, with meat.—Also (more correctly) **tamal′**. [Sp. *tamal* (pl. *tamales*),—Nahuatl *tamalli*.]

tamandua *tä-män′dū-a*, -dwä′, *n.* a S. American ant-eater smaller than the ant-bear. [Port. *tamanduá*—Sp. *tamándoa*—Tupí *tamanduá*.]

tamarack *tam′ə-rak*, *n.* the American or black larch. [Amer. Ind.]

tamari *ta-mä′ri*, *n.* a concentrated sauce made of soya beans and salt. [Jap.]

tamarin *tam′ə-rin*, *n.* a small S. American squirrel-monkey (Midas). [Fr., from Carıb.]

tamarind *tam′ə-rind*, *n.* a large tropical caesalpiniaceous tree (*Tamarindus indica*): its pod, filled with a pleasant, acidulous, sweet, reddish-black pulp. [Ar. *tamr-Hindī*, date of India.]

tamarisk *tam′ər-isk*, *n.* a genus (**Tam′arix**) giving name to a family (**Tamarica′ceæ**) of xerophytic plants, one species a naturalised shrub of S. English seashores. [L. *tamariscus*, *tamarix*.]

tambour *tam′bōōr*, *n.* a drum: a frame for embroidery: a rich gold and silver embroidery: embroidery done on a tambour: palisading to defend a gate, etc.: a flexible top (as of a desk) or front (as of a cabinet) made of narrow strips of wood fixed closely together on canvas, the whole sliding in grooves.—*v.t.* to embroider on a tambour.—*v.i.* to do tambour-work. —*ns.* **tambour′a** an Eastern instrument like a guitar; **tambourin** (*tä-bōō-rě*) a Provençal dance or dance-tune with drone bass; **tambourine** (*tam-ba-rēn′*) a shallow single-headed drum with jingles, played on with the hand. [Fr. *tambour*, drum; Pers. *tanbūr*, Ar. *tunbūr*, tamboura.]

tame *tām*, *adj.* having lost native wildness and shyness: cultivated: domesticated: gentle: spiritless: without vigour: dull, flat, uninspiring.—*v.t.* to reduce to a domestic state: to make gentle: to subdue: to reclaim.—*n.* **tamabil′ity**, **tameabil′ity**.—*adjs.* **tam′-able**, **tame′able**; **tame′less**.—*n.* **tame′lessness**.—*adv.* **tame′ly**.—*ns.* **tame′ness**; **tam′er**; **tam′ing**. [O.E. *tam*.]

Tamil *tam′il*, *n.* a Dravidian language of south-east India and north, east, and central Sri Lanka: one of the people speaking it.—*adjs.* **Tam′il**, **Tamil′ian**, **Tamil′ic**.

tammy *tam′i*, *n.* a Tam o' Shanter.

Tam o' Shanter *tam-ō-shan′tar*, *n.* the hero of Burns's poem so entitled: a cap with broad circular flat top— *coll.* **tam**, **tamm′y**.

tamp *tamp*, *v.t.* to stop up (a shot hole) with earth, etc., after the explosive has been introduced: to ram down so as to consolidate (as ballast on a railway track): to pack round.—*ns.* **tamp′er** one who, or that which, tamps: an instrument for pressing down tobacco in a pipe: a casting round the core of a nuclear weapon to delay expansion and act as a neutron reflector; **tamp′ing** the act of filling up a hole for blasting: the material used; **tamp′ion**, **tomp′ion** a plug: a protective plug placed in the muzzle of a gun when not in use; **tamp′on** a plug of cotton or other material inserted into a wound or orifice to control haemorrhage, etc.—*v.t.* to plug.—*ns.* **tamponade′**, **tam′ponage** surgical use of a tampon. [Fr. *tampon*.]

tamper[1] *tam′par*, *v.i.* (usu. with *with*) to work, machinate, practise: to have secret or corrupt dealings: to interfere unwarrantably: to meddle.—*ns.* **tam′perer**; **tam′pering**. [A by-form of **temper**.]

tamper[2], **tampon**, etc. See **tamp**.

tam-tam *tum′-tum*, *tam′-tam*, *n.* a gong, esp one used in an orchestra: esp. formerly, a tom-tom. [**tom-tom**.]

tan[1] *tan*, *n.* oak bark or other material used for tanning: a tawny brown colour.—*adj.* tawny.—*v.t.* to convert into leather by steeping in vegetable solutions containing tannin, or mineral salts, or synthesised chemicals: to treat with tan or tannin: to make brown or tawny: to beat (*coll.*).—*v.t* to become tanned:—*pr.p.* **tann′ing**; *pa.t.* and *pa.p* tanned.—*adj.* **tann′able**.—*ns.* **tann′age** tanning: that which is tanned; **tann′ate** a salt of tannic acid.—*adj.* **tanned**.—*ns.* **tann′er**; **tann′ery** a place for tanning.—*adj.* **tann′ic**

(tannic acid tannin).—*ns.* tann'in a colourless amorphous substance got from gall-nuts, sumach, and many barks, used in tanning and dyeing; tann'ing the art or act of tanning or converting skins and hides into leather.—*adj.* tan'-coloured.—tan'-pit, -vat a vat in which hides are steeped with tan. [O.E. *tannian* (found in pa.p. *getanned*), *tannere*, tanner; also O.Fr. *tan*—Bret. *tann*, oak.]

tan² *tan*, (*trig.*) *n.* a conventional abbrev. of tangent.

tanager *tan'ə-jər*, *n.* any bird of the S. American family Thraupidae, closely allied to the finches, the males having brightly-coloured plumage. [Tupí *tangará*.]

tandem *tan'dəm*, *adv.* in the position of horses harnessed singly one before the other.—*n.* a team (usu. two) so harnessed: a vehicle with such a team: a bicycle, tricycle, etc., for two, one before the other: generally, an arrangement of two things, one placed before the other.—Also *adj.*—*adv* tan'demwise.—in tandem with one behind the other: together or in conjunction. [Punning application of L. *tandem*, at length.]

tandoori *tan-, tun-dōōr'i*, *n.* a type of Indian cooking in which meat and vegetables are baked in a clay oven. —Also *adj.* [Hind. *tandoor*, a clay oven.]

tang tang, *n.* a projecting piece or shank: a point, sting, spike: part of a tool that goes into the haft: a prong: a barb: biting, characteristic, or extraneous flavour, after-taste, or smell: a smack, tinge: pungency.— *adjs.* tanged (*tangd*) with a tang: barbed; tangy (*tang'i*) having a fresh or sharp taste or smell (also *fig.*). [O.N. *tange*, point, tang.]

tanga *tang'gə*, *n.* a brief string-like bikini.

tangelo *tan'ji-lō*, *n.* a hybrid between *Tang*erine orange and pomelo:—*pl.* tan'gelos. [Portmanteau word.]

tangent *tan'jənt*, *adj.* touching without intersecting.— *n.* a line that touches a curve: (as a function of an angle) the ratio of the side of a right-angled triangle opposite the given angle to the side opposite the other acute angle (*trig.*) (the tangent of an obtuse angle is equal numerically to that of its supplement, but has the negative sign.)—*abbrev.* tan: the striking-pin of a clavichord.—*n.* tan'gency (-*jən-si*) fact of being tangent: a contact or touching.—*adj.* tangential (-*jen'shəl*) of a tangent: in the direction of a tangent: peripheral, irrelevant (*fig.*).—*n.* tangentiality (*tan-jen-shi-al'i-ti*).—*adv.* tangen'tially in the direction of a tangent.—at a tangent in the direction of the tangent: in continuation in the momentary direction instead of following the general course. [L. *tangēns*, -*entis*, pr.p. of *tangĕre*, to touch.]

Tangerine *tan'jə-rēn*, or -*rēn'*, *adj.* of Tangier on the Morocco coast: (without *cap.*) tangerine-coloured.— *n.* a native of Tangier: (without *cap.*) a mandarin or Tangerine orange—a small, flattish, loose-skinned variety: (without *cap.*) the colour of this fruit, a reddish orange.

tangible *tan'ji-bl*, *adj.* perceptible by the touch: capable of being possessed or realised: material, corporeal.—*n.* (usu. *pl.*) a tangible thing or asset, i.e. physical property as opposed to goodwill.—*ns.* tangibil'ity; tan'gibleness.—*adv.* tan'gibly. [L. *tangibilis*—*tangĕre*, to touch.]

tangle¹ *tang'gl*, *v.t.* to form into, involve in, or cover with, a confused interwoven mass: to entangle: to hamper or trap (*coll.*).—*v.i.* to become tangled: to become involved in conflict or argument (with) (*coll.*): (with *with*) to embrace (*coll.*).—*n.* a tangled mass or condition: a perplexity, complication: involved relations, conflict, argument.—*adj.* tang'led. —*ns.* tang'lement; tang'ler.—*adj.* tang'lesome.—*n.* and *adj.* tang'ling.—*adv.* tang'lingly.—*adj.* tangled: inclined to tangle. [App. from earlier *tagle*.]

tangle² *tang'gl*, *n.* coarse seaweed, esp. the edible Laminaria.—*adj.* tang'ly. [App. conn. with O.N. *thöngull*, Laminaria stalk.]

tango *tang'go*, *n.* a ballroom dance or dance-tune in 4-4 time, of Argentinian origin, characterised by long steps and pauses:—*pl.* tan'gos.—*v.i.* to dance the tango:—*pa.t.* and *pa.p.* tang'oed.—*n.* tang'oist. [Sp., a S. American Negro festival or dance.]

tangram *tan'gram*, *n.* a Chinese toy, a square cut into seven pieces that will fit in various forms.

tangy. See tang.

tanh *tansh, than*, a conventional abbreviation for hyperbolic tangent.

tanist *tan'ist*, *n.* a Celtic chief's heir elect.—*n.* tan'istry the system of succession by a previously elected member of the family. [Ir. *tánaiste*, Gael. *tànaiste*, heir, successor.]

tank *tangk*, *n.* a large basin or cistern: a reservoir of water, oil, etc.: an armoured, enclosed, armed vehicle moving on caterpillar wheels: a receptacle for developing solutions (*phot.*): a prison or prison cell (*U.S. slang*).—*v.t.* to store in a tank: to plunge into a tank: to defeat (*slang*).—*v.i.* to drink heavily (with *up*): to refuel (often with *up*; *coll.*).—*n.* tank'age storing in tanks: charge for such storage: the capacity of a tank or tanks.—*adj.* tanked (*slang*; often with *up*) drunk.—*ns.* tank'er a ship or heavy vehicle that carries liquids, esp. oil in bulk: an aircraft that refuels others; tank'ful:—*pl.* tank'fuls; tank'ing (*slang*) a defeat.—tank'-car, -wag'on a railway wagon for carrying oil or other liquid in a large tank; tank'-engine a locomotive that carries its water and coal in itself (without a tender); tank farm an area with tanks for storing oil; tank'-far'mer; tank top a sleeveless pullover, usu. with a low round neckline, worn over a shirt, etc. [Port. *tanque*—L. *stagnum*, a pool.]

tanka *tang'kə*, *n.* a Japanese poem of five lines. [Jap *tan*, short, *ka*, verse.]

tankard *tangk'ərd*, *n.* a large mug-like vessel [Cf M. Du. *tanckaert*.]

tannable, tannage. See under tan¹.

tannate, tanned. See under tan¹.

tanner¹ *tan'ər*, (*slang*) *n.* a sixpence.

tanner², tannic, tannin. See under tan¹.

Tannoy® *tan'oi*, *n.* a sound-reproducing and amplifying system.

tanrec. See tenrec.

tansy *tan'zi*, *n.* a bitter, aromatic roadside composite plant (*Tanacetum vulgare*) with small heads of tubular yellow flowers. [O.Fr. *tanasie*, through L.L. from Gr. *athanasiā*, immortality.]

Tantalus *tan'tə-ləs*, *n.* a son of Zeus punished in Tartarus for revealing secrets of the gods by having to stand in water that ebbed when he would drink, overhung by grapes that drew back when he reached for them.—*n.* tan'talate a salt of tantalic acid.—*adjs.* Tantalean (-*tā'*), Tanta'lian, Tantalic (-*tal'ik*) of Tantalus; tantal'ic of tantalum (tantalic acid HTaO₃).—*n.* tantalisā'tion, -z-.—*v.t.* tan'talise, -ize to torment by presenting something to excite desire but keeping it out of reach.—*n.* tan'taliser, -z-.—*n.* and *adj.* tan'talising, -z-.—*adv.* tan'talisingly, -z-.— *ns.* tan'talism the punishment of Tantalus: a tormenting; tan'talite (*min.*) a black mineral, iron tantalate; tan'talum a metallic element (Ta; at. numb. 73) so named from its inability to absorb water.

tantamount *tan'tə-mownt*, *adj.* amounting to as much or to the same: equivalent: equal in value or meaning. [A.Fr. *tant amunter*, to amount to as much.]

tantara *tan-tä'rä*, *n.* a blast of trumpet or horn.—Also tantara'ra. [Imit.]

tantivy *tan-tiv'ı*, *adv.* at full gallop. headlong.—*n.* a hunting cry.—*interj.* expressive of the sound of the hunting-horn [Imit]

tant mieux *tã myø*, (Fr.) so much the better.

tant pis *tã pē*, (Fr.) so much the worse.

Tantra *tan'-*, *tun'trə*, *n.* any of a number of Hindu and Buddhist writings giving religious teaching and ritual instructions (including the use of incantations, diagrams, etc.): the teaching of the Tantras.—*adj.* **Tan'-tric.**—*ns.* **Tan'trism** the teaching of the Tantras; **Tan'-trist.** [Sans *tantra*, thread, fundamental doctrine.]

tantrum *tan'trəm*, *n.* a capricious fit of ill-temper without adequate cause.

taoiseach *tē'shohh*, *n.* the prime minister of the Republic of Ireland. [Ir., chief, leader.]

Taoism *tä'ō-izm*, *tow'*, *dow'*, *n.* the philosophical system supposedly founded by the Chinese philosopher Lao-tzu (perh. b. 604 B.C.): a religious system combining Taoist philosophy with magic and superstition and the worship of many gods.—*n.* and *adj.* **Ta'oist.**—*adj.* **Taoist'ic.**

tap¹ *tap*, *n.* a gentle knock or its sound: a protective piece on a shoe heel: a metal piece attached to the sole and heel of a shoe for tap-dancing: tap-dancing. —*v.t.* and *v.i.* to knock gently.—*v.t.* to furnish or repair with a tap:—*pr.p.* **tapp'ing;** *pa.t.* and *pa.p* **tapped.**—*n.* **tapp'er.**—*n.* and *adj.* **tapp'ing.—tap' dance** (also *v.ı.*); **tap'-danc'er; tap'-danc'ing** dancing characterised by rhythmical striking of dancer's tapped shoes on the floor; **tap'-shoe** a tapped shoe for tap-dancing. [O.Fr. *taper.*]

tap² *tap*, *n.* a peg or stopper: a hole or short pipe with a valve for running off a fluid: a screw for cutting an internal thread: a receiver secretly attached to a telephone wire: an instance of tapping a telephone wire. —*v.t.* to pierce, so as to let out fluid: to broach: to draw off: to draw upon, esp. for the first time (*fig.*): secretly to attach a receiver to a telephone wire in order to overhear a conversation: to get money from (*slang*): to furnish with a tap, or with a screw-thread: —*pr.p.* **tapp'ing;** *pa.t.* and *pa.p.* **tapped.**—*ns.* **tapp'er; tapp'ing** the act or art of drawing out or running off a fluid; **tap'ster** one who draws liquor, a barman.—**tap'-house** a tavern; **tap'room** a room where beer is served from the tap or cask; **tap'root** a strong main root striking down vertically; **tap'-wa'ter** water from a household tap.—**on tap** kept in cask— opp. to *bottled*: continuously and readily available (*fig.*). [O.E. *tæppa*, tap.]

tape *tãp*, *n.* material woven in narrow bands: a strip of such material, used for tying up, connecting, etc.: a ribbon of paper printed by a recording instrument, as in telegraphy: a tape-measure: magnetic tape: a tape-recording.—*v.t.* to furnish, fasten, bind, measure with a tape: to get the range or measure of: to tape-record.—*n.* **tã'per.—tape deck** a machine for recording sound on tape and replaying it through a separate amplifier; **tape'line, -meas'ure** a flexible measuring strip of tape, steel, or other material; **tape'-machine** a telegraphic instrument by which messages received are automatically printed on a tape.—*v.t.* **tape'-record'** to record sound using a tape-recorder.—**tape'-recorder** an instrument for recording sound on magnetic tape and subsequently reproducing it; **tape'-recording** a magnetic tape on which sound has been recorded: the sound so recorded; **tape'script** a tape-recorded reading of a complete text; **tape'worm** a ribbon-shaped segmented parasitic worm, esp. of Taenia or kindred genus.—**breast the tape** in winning a foot-race, to touch or break with the breast the line stretched across the track at the winning-post; **have (something or someone) taped** to have a thorough understanding

of. [O.E. *tæppe*, tape, fillet.]

taper *tã'pər*, *n.* a long, thin waxed wick or spill: lengthwise diminution in width: gradual leaving off.—*v.t.* to become gradually smaller towards one end: to diminish slowly in size, quantity or importance (with *off*). —*v.t.* to make to taper.—*adj.* **tã'pered** tapering: lighted by tapers.—*n.* **tã'perer** one who bears a taper —*n.* and *adj.* **tã'pering.—*adv.* **tã'peringly.**—*n.* **tã'perness.**—*adv.* **tã'perwise.** [O.E. *tapor.*]

tapestry *tap'ıs-trı*, *n.* an ornamental textile used for the covering of walls and furniture, and for curtains, made by passing coloured threads among fixed warp threads: a machine-made imitation of this.—*adj.* of tapestry.—*adj.* **tap'estried.** [Fr. *tapısserie—tapıs*, a carpet—L.L. *tapētium*—Gr. *tapētıon*, dim. of *tapēs*, -*ētos*, prob. of Iranian origin.]

tapioca *tap-ı-ō'kə*, *n.* a farinaceous substance got by heating cassava: extended to a kind of sago and a preparation of potato starch: a pudding made from tapioca. [Tupí-Guaraní *tıpyoca.*]

tapir *tã'pər*, *n.* a large odd-toed ungulate with short flexible proboscis, of which several species are found in S. America, Malacca, etc. [Tupí *tapira.*]

tappet *tap'it*, *n.* a projection that transmits motion from one part of a machine to another by tapping.— **tapp'et-loom, -mō'tion, -ring, -rod,** etc. [**tap¹.**]

tar *tär*, *n.* a dark, viscous mixture got by destructive distillation of wood, coal, peat, etc.: a natural bituminous substance of like appearance (*mineral tar*): a sailor (perh. for **tarpaulin**).—*v.t.* to smear, coat, treat, with tar:—*pr.p.* **tarr'ing;** *pa.t.* and *pa.p.* **tar-red.**—*n.* **tarriness** (*tär'i-nıs*).—*n.* and *adj.* **tarr'ing.**— *adj.* **tarr'y** (*tär'ı*) of, like, covered or soiled with, tar. —**tar'brush** a brush for applying tar; **tarmacad'am** (also **tar'mac, Tarmac®** in *U.S.*) a road surfacing of broken stone covered or mixed with tar: (**tar'mac**) the runways of an aerodrome; **tar'-pa'per** heavy paper treated with tar, used as a building material; **tar'-sand** a deposit of sand or sandstone saturated with bitumen, from which petroleum can be extracted.—*v.t.* **tar'-seal** to seal the surface of (a road) by covering with tarmacadam.—**tar and feather** to smear with tar and then cover with feathers; **tarred with the same brush** or **stick** with the same defects; **touch of the tar-brush** (*derog.*) a certain amount of e.g. Negro blood resulting in darkish skin. [O.E. *teru, teoro.*]

taradiddle. See tarradiddle.

taramasalata *tar-ə-mə-sə-lä'tə*, (*cook.*) *n.* a Greek dish, a pink creamy paste made of grey mullet or smoked cod's roe with olive oil and garlic. [Mod. Gr., *taramas,* preserved roe, *salata,* salad.]

tarantara. See taratantara.

tarantas(s) *ta-ran-täs'*, *n.* a four-wheeled Russian vehicle mounted on poles. [Russ. *tarantas*]

tarantella *tar'ən-tel'ə*, *n.* a lively Neapolitan dance: a tune for it.—*ns.* **tar'antism** an epidemic dancing mania; **tarantôla** (*-an'*) a large venomous South European spider long supposed to cause tarantism in South Italy: in America applied to large venomous spiders of the bird-catching family: in Australia applied to several large harmless spiders. [It. *tarantella, tarantola*—Gr. *Taras, -antos,* Tarentum, Taranto.]

tarantism, tarantula. See tarantella.

taratantara *tär-ä-tan'tä-rä,* or *-tan-ta'rä, n.* the sound of a trumpet.—Also *interj., adj., adv., v.t.,* and *v.i.*— Also **taran'tara.** [Imit.]

Taraxacum *ta-raks'ə-kəm, n.* the dandelion genus (without *cap.*) its root and rootstock, a tonic laxative. [App. from Ar. *tarakhshaqôq*—Pers. *talkh chakôk,* assimilated to Gr. *taraxis,* disturbance.]

tarboosh, tarboush, tarbush *tär-bōōsh', n.* a fez [Ar.

tarbūsh.]

tardigrade *tär'di-grād, adj.* slow-paced: of, or pertaining to, the Tardigrada.—*n.* a member of the Tardigrada.—*n.pl.* **Tardigra'da** formerly the sloths: now, a class of arthropods. [L. *tardus*, slow, *gradī*, to step.]

tardy *tär'di, adj.* slow: sluggish: behindhand: too long delayed: late.—*adv.* **tar'dily.**—*n.* **tar'diness.** [Fr. *tardif—tard*—L. *tardus*, slow.]

tare[1] *tär, n.* a vetch of various kinds, esp. of the lentil-like group: a weed, prob. darnel (*B.*).

tare[2] *tär, n.* the weight of a vessel, wrapping, or container, which subtracted from the gross weight gives the net weight: the weight of an empty vehicle, without cargo, passengers, etc.—*v.t.* to ascertain or allow for the tare of. [Fr.,—Sp. *tara*—Ar. *tarhah*, thrown away.]

targe *tärj, n.* a shield, esp. a light shield. [O.Fr. *targe*—O.N. *targe*, shield.]

target *tär'git, n.* a small buckler or round shield: a shield-like or other mark to shoot at for practice or competition: a surface on which electrons impinge: an object aimed at (also *fig.*): a butt: a result to be aimed at: a shooting score: a neck and breast of lamb.—*adj.* chosen as a target, aimed at.—*v.t.* to aim: to aim at.—*adjs.* **tar'getable** which can be aimed, or aimed at; **tar'geted** selected as a target, aimed at.—**target area** an area containing a target, or which is a target, e.g. of missiles; **target practice** repeated shooting at a target to improve one's aim.—**on target on the** correct course for a target: on schedule. [O.Fr. *targuete*; cf. **targe.**]

tariff *tar'if, n.* a list or set of customs duties: a list of charges.—*v.t.* to set a tariff on.—**tariff wall** a barrier to the flow of imports made by high rates of customs duties. [It. *tariffa*—Ar. *ta'rīf*, explanation—'*arafa*, to explain.]

tarlatan *tär'lə-tən, n.* an open, transparent muslin. [Fr. *tarlatane.*]

tarmac(adam). See **tar.**

tarn *tärn, n.* a small mountain lake. [O.N. *tjörn.*]

tarnal *tär'nl,* **tarnation** *tär-nā'shən,* (*U.S. slang*) *adjs.* and *advs.* softened forms of **eternal** and **damnation,** app. influenced by each other.

tarnish *tär'nish, v.t.* to dull, discolour, diminish the lustre of, by exposure to the air, etc.: to sully.—*v.i.* to become dull: to lose lustre.—*n.* loss of lustre: a surface discoloration on metal or mineral: a film of oxide, sulphide, etc.—*adjs.* **tar'nishable; tar'nished.** —*n.* **tar'nisher.** [Fr. *ternir, terniss- —terne,* dull, wan; poss. Gmc.]

taro *tä'rō, n.* a plant (*Colocasia*) of the arum family, widely cultivated for its edible rootstock in the islands of the Pacific:—*pl.* **ta'ros.** [Polynesian.]

tarot *tar'ō, n.* a card of Italian origin with picture, used in card games and also in fortune-telling.[1] [Fr. *tarot* —It. *tarocco.*]

tarpan *tär'pan, n.* a small extinct wild horse of the steppes of S. European Russia. [Tatar.]

tarpaulin *tär-pö'lin, n.* strong linen or hempen cloth waterproofed with tar or otherwise: a sheet of it. [App. **tar** and **palling—pall**[1].]

tarpon *tär'pən, n.* a gigantic fish (*Megalops*) akin to the herring, angled for on the Florida and Gulf coasts.

tar(r)adiddle *tar-ə-did'l, n.* a fib, a lie: nonsense. [App. founded on **diddle.**]

tarragon *tar'ə-gən, n.* an aromatic Artemisia used for flavouring vinegar, sauces, etc. [Ar. *tarkhūn,* perh. —Gr. *drakōn,* a dragon.]

tarry[1] *tär'i.* See **tar.**

tarry[2] *tar'i, v.i.* to linger: to loiter: to delay: to stay behind: to sojourn: to wait:—*pr.p.* **tarr'ying;** *pa.t.* and *pa.p.* **tarr'ied.**—*n.* **tarr'ier** one who tarries or

delays.

tarsal. See **tarsus.**

tarsier. See under **tarsus.**

tarsus *tär'səs, n.* the part of the foot to which the leg is articulated:—*pl.* **tar'si.**—*adj.* **tar'sal** relating to the tarsus or ankle.—*n.* a bone of the tarsus.—*n.* **tar'sier** (*-si-ər*) a spectral-looking lemuroid of the East Indies with long tarsal bones.—*adj.* **tar'sioid** like the tarsier: of the tarsier family. [Gr. *tarsos,* the flat of the foot.]

tart[1] *tärt, adj.* sharp: biting: acidulous.—*adj.* **tart'ish.** —*adv.* **tart'ly.**—*n.* **tart'ness.** [O.E. *teart.*]

tart[2] *tärt, n.* a dish of pastry distinguished from a pie either by being uncovered or by containing sweet not savoury materials: a girl (*slang*; often disrespectful): a prostitute (*slang*).—*ns.* **tartine** (*-ēn;* Fr.) a slice of bread with butter or jam; **tart'let** a small tart.—*adj.* **tart'y** (*slang*).—**tart up** (*coll.*) to make more showy or striking, esp. in an inartistic way: to smarten up (*adj.* **tart'ed-up'**). [O.Fr. *tarte.*]

Tartan® *tär'tən, n.* a material used to lay tracks for athletic events, usable in all weathers.

tartan *tär'tən, n.* a woollen (or other) checked stuff: a distinctive checked pattern, as of a Highland clan.— *adj.* of tartan: checked in tartan: Scottish, esp. referring to self-consciously Scottish artefacts or attitudes (*derog.*).—*adj.* **tar'taned** clad in tartan.

tartar *tär'tər, n.* recrystallised and partially purified argol, chiefly acid potassium tartrate (with calcium tartrate, etc.): a deposit of calcium phosphate and other matter on the teeth.—*adjs.* **tartareous** (*-tā'ri-əs*) of or like tartar; **tartaric** (*tär-tar'ik*) of or got from tartar (**tartaric acid,** $C_4H_6O_6$, prepared from argol).—*v.t.* **tar'tarise, -ize** to treat, mix, or combine with tartar.—*ns.* **tar'trate** a salt of tartaric acid; **tar'trazine** (*-zēn*) a yellow dye used in textiles, food and drugs.—**cream of tartar** purified argol. [L.L. *tartarum,* perh. from Ar.]

Tartar *tär'tər, n.* a Tatar: (without *cap.*) a formidable, rough, unmanageable person: (without *cap.*) one who unexpectedly turns the tables on his assailant.—Also *adj.*—*n.* and *adj.* **Tartarian** (*-tā'ri-ən*) Tartar, Tatar. —*adjs.* **Tartaric** (*-tar'ik*) of the Tartars; **Tar'tarly** like a Tartar: ferocious. [See **Tatar.**]

tartareous. See **tartar.**

tartar(e) (sauce) *tär'tər, tär-tär' (sōs), n.* a mayonnaise dressing with chopped pickles, olives, capers, etc., added, usu. served with fish. [Fr. *sauce tartare.*]

tartaric, tartarise. See **tartar.**

tartine. See **tart**[2].

tartrate, tartrazine. See **tartar.**

tarwhine *tär'(h)wīn, n.* an Australian sea-bream.

Tarzan *tär'zan, n.* a man of great strength and agility. [From the hero of stories by Edgar Rice Burroughs (d. 1950) about a man brought up by apes.]

tash *tash,* (*coll.*) *n.* short for **moustache.**

tasimeter *ta-sim'i-tər, n.* an instrument for measuring changes in pressure, etc., by variations in electrical conductivity. [Gr. *tasis,* a stretch, *metron,* measure.]

task *täsk, task, n.* a piece or amount of (esp. burdensome, difficult or unpleasant) work set or undertaken.—*v.t.* to burden with severe work: to employ fully.—**task'-force, task'-group** a group formed by selection from different branches of the armed services to carry out a specific task: a similar group within the police force: a working party (q.v.) for a civilian purpose; **task'master** one who allots tasks esp. involving hard work:—*fem.* **task'mistress.** [O.Fr. *tasque* (Fr. *tâche*)—L.L. *tasca, taxa*—L. *taxāre,* to rate.]

Tasmanian *tas-, taz-mā'ni-ən, adj.* of Tasmania, discovered in 1642 by Abel Janszoon *Tasman.*—*n.* a native or citizen of Tasmania.—**Tasmanian devil** a ferocious Tasmanian dasyure; **Tasmanian wolf** (or **tiger**) a striped wolf-like dasyure of Tasmania, now virtually extinct.

tass *tas*, *n.* a drinking-cup: a small drink.—*n.* **tass'ie** (*Scot.*) a small cup. [Fr. *tasse*—Ar. *tâss*, cup.]

tassel *tas'l*, *n.* an ornamental hanging tuft of threads: an inflorescence of like appearance, esp. of maize.—*v.t.* to furnish with tassels.—*v.i.* to form tassels, flower:—*pr.p.* **tass'elling**; *pa.t.* and *pa.p.* **tass'elled**.—*adj.* **tass'elled**.—*n.* **tass'elling**.—*adj.* **tass'elly**. [O.Fr. *tassel*.]

tassie. See **tass.**

taste *tāst*, *v.t.* to try, or to perceive, by the sense seated in the tongue and palate: to try by eating a little: to eat a little of: to partake of: to experience, perceive. —*v.i.* to try or perceive by the mouth: to have a flavour: to act as taster: to have experience.—*n.* the act of tasting: the particular sensation caused by a substance on the tongue: the sense by which we perceive the flavour of a thing: the quality or flavour of anything: a small portion: an experience: discernment of, accordance with, what is socially right: the faculty by which the mind perceives the beautiful: nice perception: choice, predilection, liking.—*adjs.* **tāst'able; tāst'ed** having a taste; **taste'ful** full of taste: having a pleasant or a high relish: showing good taste. —*adv.* **taste'fully.**—*n.* **taste'fulness.**—*adj.* **taste'less** without taste: without good taste: insipid.—*adv.* **taste'lessly.**—*ns.* **taste'lessness; tāst'er** one skilful in distinguishing flavours by the taste: one employed to test the innocuousness of food by tasting it before serving it to his master: any implement or device used to obtain samples for tasting.—*adv.* **tāst'ily.**—*n.* **tāst'ing.**—*adj.* **tāst'y** savoury: tasteful (*coll.*).—**taste'-bud, -bulb** a group of cells on the tongue sensitive to taste.—**good taste** intuitive feeling for what is aesthetically or socially right; **to one's taste** to one's liking. [O.Fr. *taster* (Fr. *tâter*), as if from a L.L. freq. of L. *taxāre*, to touch, handle, estimate—*tangĕre*, to touch.]

tat¹, tatt *tat*, *v.t.* to make by tatting.—*v.i.* to make tatting.—*n.* **tatt'ing** knotted lace edging made by hand with a shuttle from sewing-thread: the making of it.

tat² *tat*, *n.* East Indian hempen matting. [Hindi *ṭāṭ*.]

tat³ *tat*, *n.* a tap—*v.t.* to touch, tap: to flog

tat⁴. See **tatt¹.**

ta-ta *ta-tä'*, (*childish* and *coll.*) *interj.* good-bye.

Tatar *tä'tər*, *n.* orig. a member of any of certain tribes in Chinese Tartary: extended to any of the Mongol, Turkish, and other warriors who swept over Asia and Europe: loosely, one of the mixed inhabitants of Tartary, Siberia, and the Russian steppes: a speaker of a Turkic language.—Also *adj.*—*adjs.* **Tatarian** (*tä-tä'ri-ən*), **Tataric** (*-tar'ik*) of the Tatars: of the Turkic group of languages. [Turk. and Pers. *Tatar*; association with Gr. *Tartaros*, hell, seems to have suggested the form **Tartar.**]

tater *tä'tər*, *n.* a colloquial form of **potato.**

tatler. See **tattle.**

tatou *ta'tŏŏ*, or *-tŏŏ'*, *n.* an armadillo, esp. the giant armadillo. [Tupí *tatú*.]

tatt¹ *tat*, *n.* a rag, esp. an old one: pretentious odds and ends of little real value, e.g. in an antique shop—more often **tat** (also *fig.*).—*v.t.* to touch up.—*adv.* **tatt'ily.**—*n.* **tatt'iness.**—*adj.* **tatt'y** (of clothes or ornament) fussy: precious, and often bogus: cheap, of poor quality: untidy: shabby. [**tatter.**]

tatt². See **tat¹.**

tatter *tat'ər*, *n.* a torn shred: a loose hanging rag.—*v.t.* to tear to tatters.—*v.i.* to fall into tatters.—*n.* **tatterdemā'lion** (or *-mal'yən*) a ragged fellow.—*adjs.* **tatt'-**

ered; tatt'ery ragged   [Cf. Icel. *toturr.*]

Tattersall's *tat'ər-sölz*, *n.* a famous London horsemart and haunt of racing-men—founded 1766 by Richard *Tattersall* (1724–95): a sweepstake or lottery agency with headquarters at Melbourne, Australia (*coll.* Tatts).

tatting. See **tat¹.**

tattle *tat'l*, *n.* trifling talk: chatter.—*v.i.* to talk idly or triflingly: to tell tales or secrets.—*v.t.* to tell or utter in tattle.—*n.* **tatt'ler** (formerly **tat'ler**) one given to tattling.—*n.* and *adj.* **tatt'ling** chattering: tale-telling.—*adv.* **tatt'lingly.**—**tatt'le-tale** (chiefly *U.S.*) a tell-tale. [Used by Caxton to translate M.Du *tatelen*; imit]

tattoo¹ *tə-tŏŏ'*, *n.* a beat of drum or other signal calling soldiers to quarters: a drumming: a military fête by night. [Du. *taptoe—tap*, tap (of a barrel), *toe*, to, in the sense of shut]

tattoo² *tə-tŏŏ'*, *n.* a design marked on the skin by pricking in colouring matter.—*v.t.* to mark in this way:—*pa.t.* and *pa.p.* **tattooed'.**—*ns.* **tattoo'er, tattoo'ist.** [Tahitian *ta'tau*, Marquesan *ta'tu*.]

Tatts. See **Tattersall's.**

tatty. See **tatt¹.**

tau *tow*, *n.* the nineteenth letter (T, τ) of the Greek alphabet, answering to T: a tau-cross.—**tau'-cross** St Anthony's cross, in the form of a T. [Gr. *tau*, of Semitic origin.]

taught *töt*, *pa.t.* and *pa.p.* of **teach.**

taunt *tönt*, *v.t.* to reproach stingingly: to censure sarcastically.—*v.i.* to jibe.—*n.* a biting jibe.—*n.* **taunt'er.**—*n.* and *adj.* **taunt'ing.**—*adj.* **taunt'ingly.** [Poss. O Fr. *tanter*—L. *tentāre*, to tempt; or Fr. *tant pour tant*, tit for tat.]

taupe *töp*, *n.* and *adj.* (of) a brownish-grey colour. [Fr., mole,—L. *talpa.*]

Taurus *tö'rəs* (or L. *tow'rōōs*), *n.* the Bull, a sign of the zodiac and a constellation formerly coinciding with it. —*adjs.* **tau'rean, tau'ric** of a bull; **tau'riform** having the form of a bull; **tau'rine** (or *-in*) of a bull: bull-like. —*n.* **tauromachy** (*-om'ə-ki*) bull-fighting: a bull-fight. [L. *taurus* and Gr. *tauros.*]

taut *töt*, *adj.* tightly drawn: tense: in good condition.—*v.t* and *v i.* **taut'en** to tighten.—*n.* **taut'ness.** [Prob. conn. with **tow¹, tight.**]

taut- *tot-*, **tauto-** *töt'ō-, töt-o'-* in composition, the same.—*adjs.* **tautologic** (*-loj'*), **-al.**—*adv.* **tautolog'ically.**—*v.i.* **tautol'ogise, -ize** to use tautology.—*ns.* **tautol'ogism; tautol'ogist.**—*adj.* **tautol'ogous** (*-ə-gəs*) tautological.—*ns.* **tautol'ogy** use of words that (esp. needlessly or pointlessly) say the same thing; **taut'omer** a readily interconvertible isomer.—*adj.* **tautomer'ic.**—*n* **tautom'erism.**—**taut'onym** a binomial name in which the specific name repeats the generic.—*adjs.* **tauton'ymous; tautophon'ical.**—*n.* **tautoph'ony** repetition of a sound. [Gr. *tauto*, for *to auto*, the same]

tautog *tö-tog'*, *n.* a labroid fish of the North American Atlantic coast. [Narragansett *tautauog.*]

tavern *tav'ərn*, *n.* a public-house.—*ns.* **taverna** (*-ûr'nə*) a type of guest-house with bar in Greece, popular as holiday accommodation; **tav'erner** a publican [O.Fr. (Fr.) *taverne*—L. *taberna*, shed, stall, tavern, from root of *tabula*, a board.]

taw¹ *tö*, *n.* a large or choice marble: a game at marbles: the line shot from at marbles.

taw² *tö*, *v.t.* to prepare and dress, esp. skins for white leather.—*ns.* **taw'er** a maker of white leather; **taw'ery** a place where skins are dressed; **taw'ing.** [O.E. *tawian*, to prepare.]

tawdry *tö'dri*, *adj.* showy without taste or worth: gaudily adorned.—*n.* trumpery.—*adv.* **taw'drily.**—*n.* **taw'driness.** [From *St Audrey.*]

tawery. See taw².

tawny tō'ni, *adj.* and *n.* yellowish brown.—*n.* taw'ni-ness.—tawny eagle a tawny-coloured eagle of Africa and Asia, *Aquila rapax*; tawny owl a tawny-coloured European owl, *Strix aluco*. [Fr. *tanné*, pa.p. of *tanner*, to tan.]

taws, tawse tōz, (esp. *Scot.*) *n.sing.* or *n.pl.* a leather strap, usu. cut into fingers at the end, for corporal punishment. [Poss. pl. of taw², n.]

tax taks, *v.t.* to lay a tax on: to burden: to accuse, censure (usu. with *with*): to assess: to examine (accounts) in order to allow or disallow items.—*n.* a contribution exacted by the state: anything imposed, exacted, or burdensome.—*n.* taxabil'ity.—*adj.* tax'-able.—*adv.* tax'ably.—*n.* taxâ'tion.—*adjs.* tax'ative taxing: of taxing; taxed.—*ns.* tax'er (also tax'or); tax'ing imposition of taxes.—tax avoidance legal evasion of payment of tax; tax'-collect'or.—*adj.* tax'-deduct'ible of expenses, etc., able to be deducted from one's income before it is assessed for tax.—tax evasion illegal evasion of payment of tax; tax exile a person living abroad so as not to pay high taxes—*adj.* and *adv.* tax'-free without payment of tax.—tax'-gath'erer; tax haven a country or state where taxes are low; tax'-payer one who pays tax or taxes; tax return a yearly statement of one's income, from which the amount due in tax is calculated; tax shelter a financial arrangement made in order to pay the minimum taxation.—*adj.* tax'-shel'tered or produced by a tax shelter: of or involving investments legally exempt from tax. [Fr. *taxe*, a tax—L. *taxāre*, to handle, value, charge.]

taxi tak'si, *n.* a taxicab: loosely, any motor-car on hire: —*pl.* tax'is, tax'ies.—*v.i.* to travel by taxi: of an aeroplane, to run along the ground, at low speed under its own power:—*pr.p.* tax'ying; *pa.t.* and *pa.p.* tax'ied; *3rd pers. pres. indtc.* tax'ies.—tax'icab a motor-cab furnished with a taximeter; tax'i-driver; tax'iman a taxi-driver. [Abbrev. of taximeter.]

taxidermy taks'i-dûr-mi, *n.* the art of preparing, stuffing, and mounting skins.—*adjs* taxider'mal, taxider'mic.—*v.t.* tax'idermise, -ize.—*n.* tax'idermist. [Gr. *taxis*, arrangement, *derma*, a skin.]

taximeter tak'si-mē-tər, tak-sim'i-tər, *n.* an instrument attached to a cab for indicating (distance travelled and) fare due. [Fr. *taxe*, price, Gr. *metron*, measure.]

taxis tak'sis, *n.* arrangement: movement of a whole organism in response to stimulus (*biol.*).—*n.* tax'on a biological category (e.g. *species*) or its name: —*pl.* tax'a.—*n.* taxon'omer a taxonomist—*adjs.* taxonom'ic, -al.—*adv.* taxonom'ically.—*ns.* taxon'omist; taxon'omy classification or its principles: classification of plants or animals (now including study of means by which formation of species, etc., takes place). [Gr.,—*tassein*, to arrange.]

taxor. See tax.

tazza tat'sə, *n.* a shallow cup mounted on a foot: a saucer-shaped bowl. [It., cup.]

tch-. For some words see ch-.

tchick chik, ch', *n.* a sound made by pressing the tongue against the roof of the mouth and then drawing back one side, as in urging a horse on. [Imit.]

te. See ti.

tea tē, *n.* a tree, *Thea sinensis*, close akin to Camellia, cultivated in China, Assam, etc.: its dried and prepared leaves, buds, and shoots: an infusion of the leaves in boiling water: extended to various substitutes: any vegetable infusion as a beverage: an afternoon meal or light refreshment at which tea is generally served.—tea'-bag a bag containing tea-

leaves for infusion; tea biscuit any of various kinds of sweetish biscuits, often eaten with tea, tea'-bread light spongy bread or buns to be eaten with tea; tea'-break a break for tea during the working day; tea'-caddy, tea'-can'ister an air-tight box or jar for holding tea; tea'-cake a light cake to be eaten with tea; tea ceremony in Japan, the ceremonial making and serving of tea; tea'-chest a chest or case in which tea is packed; tea'-cloth a small table-cloth: a cloth used in washing up after tea; tea'-cosy a thick cover for a tea-pot to keep the tea hot; tea'cup a cup used in drinking tea; tea'cupful:—*pl.* tea'cupfuls; tea'-drinker; tea'-house a house in China, Japan, or other eastern countries where tea, etc. is served; tea'-kettle a kettle for boiling water for tea; tea'-leaf a leaf of tea: (usu. in *pl.*) a small piece of such a leaf, esp. when it has been used in making tea: (*slang*) a thief; tea'-party a social gathering at which tea is served: the persons present; tea'-plant; tea'-planta'tion; tea'-planter a cultivator of the teaplant; tea'pot a spouted vessel for pouring out tea; tea'-room a room or restaurant where tea and light refreshments are served; tea'-rose a rose supposed to smell of tea; tea'-ser'vice, -set a set of utensils for a tea-table; tea'-shop a shop where tea is sold: a restaurant in which teas are served; tea'spoon a small spoon used with the teacup; tea'spoonful:—*pl.* tea'spoonfuls; tea'-table a table at which tea is drunk: the company at tea; tea'-taster an expert who judges tea by tasting it; tea'-tasting.—*n.pl.* tea'-things the tea-pot, cups, etc —tea'(-)time the hour of the meal called tea.—Also *adj.*—tea'-towel a cloth for drying crockery, etc.; tea'-tray a tray for carrying tea-things; tea'-tree the common tea plant or shrub: a name of Australian plants (*Melaleuca, Leptospermum*) furnishing substitutes for tea; tea'-trolley a small tiered table on wheels used for serving afternoon tea, etc.; tea'-urn a large closed urn with a tap, often also a heating device, for making tea in quantity —another cup of tea a very different thing; black tea that which has been fermented between rolling and firing (heating with charcoal in a sieve); (usu. not) for all the tea in China (not) for anything whatever; green tea that which is fired immediately after rolling; high tea tea with meat, eggs, fish, or the like; one's cup of tea (*slang*) what is to one's taste or appeals to one; Russian tea tea with lemon and no milk usually served in a glass. [South Chinese *te*, the common form being *ch'a* or *ts'a*.]

teach tēch, *v.t.* to show: to direct: to impart knowledge or art to: to guide the studies of: to impart the knowledge or art of: to accustom: to counsel.—*v.i.* to practise giving instructions:—*pa.t.* and *pa.p.* taught (tōt). —*n.* teachabil'ity.—*adj.* teach'able capable of being taught: apt or willing to learn.—*ns.* teach'ableness; teach'er one whose profession is, or whose talent is the ability to impart knowledge, practical skill, or understanding; teach'ership; teach'ing the act, practice, or profession of giving instruction: doctrine: instruction.—*adj.* occupied with giving instruction: instructive.—teach'-in a long public debate consisting of a succession of speeches by well-informed persons holding different views on a matter of general importance, usu. with discussion, etc.; teaching aid any object or device used by a teacher to help explain, illustrate, etc., a subject; teaching hospital a hospital in which medical students are trained; teaching machine any mechanical device capable of presenting an instructional programme.—that'll teach you, him, etc. (*coll.*) that (unpleasant experience) will teach you, him, etc. to behave better, be more careful, etc. next time. [O.E. *tǣcan*, to show, teach.]

teak tēk, *n.* a tree (*Tectona grandis*) of India, Malaya, etc.: its hard and durable wood. [Malayalam *tēkka*.]

teal *tēl*, *n.* any of several kinds of small freshwater duck, esp. of the genus *Anas*:—*pl.* **teals, teal.** [M.E. *tēle*, prob. from O E.]

team *tēm*, *n.* a set of animals harnessed together: a set of persons working or playing in combination: a side: a stock of animals.—*v.t.* to yoke: to join in order to make a team or co-operative effort: to match (clothes, etc.).—*v.i.* to drive a team.—*adj.* **teamed** harnessed in a team.—*ns.* **team'er** a teamster; **team'ing** driving a team: work apportioned to a team; **team'ster** one who drives a team: a truck-driver (*U.S.*).—*adv.* **team'wise** harnessed together.— **team'-mate** a fellow member of a team; **team'-spirit** the spirit of self-suppression in co-operation; **teamwork** work done by organised division of labour: co-operation, pulling together, regard to success of the whole rather than personal exploits.—**team up with** to join forces with. [O.E. *tēam*, child-bearing, brood, team.]

teapoy *tē'poi*, *n.* a small table or tripod: (by confusion with **tea**) a tea-caddy. [Hind. *tīn*, *tīr*-, three, Pers. *pāi*, foot.]

tear[1] *tēr*, *n.* a drop of liquid secreted by the lachrymal gland: an exuding drop: a blob, bead, pear-shaped drop: a small flaw or cavity as in glass.—*adj.* **tear'ful** lachrymose: brimming with, ready to shed, or shedding, tears.—*adv.* **tear'fully.**—*n.* **tear'fulness.**— **tear'-drop** a tear; **tear'-duct** the lachrymal duct; **tear'-gas** a gas or volatile substance that blinds temporarily by provoking tears; **tear'-gland** the lachrymal gland; **tear'-jer'ker** an extravagantly sentimental song, book, film, etc., inviting pity, grief, sorrow.—*adj.* **tear'-stained** stained with tears.—**in tears** weeping. [O.E. *tēar*.]

tear[2] *tār*, *v.t.* to draw asunder or separate with violence: to rend: to lacerate: to cause pain, bitterness, etc., to: to make or render by tearing.—*v.i.* to move or act with violence: to rush, move very quickly: to rage: to become torn:—*pa.t.* **tore** (*tor*, *tōr*), *pa.p.* **torn** (*törn*, *tôrn*).—*n.* tearing: a rent: a rush (*slang*): a spree.—*n.* **tear'er** one who, or that which, tears: a boisterous person (*slang*).—*adj.* **tear'ing** great, terrible, rushing.—*adj.* **tear'away** impetuous, reckless: pertaining to a tearaway.—*n.* a reckless and (now also) violent young person.—**tear'-sheet** a page that can be torn out for reference —**tear a strip off** (*slang*) to reprimand; **tear into** to attack, either physically or with criticism, etc.; **tear oneself away** to go off with great unwillingness; **tear one's hair** to pull the hair in a frenzy of grief or rage (also *fig.*); **tear up** to remove from a fixed state by violence: to pull to pieces. [O.E. *teran*.]

tease *tēz*, *v.t.* to open out the fibres of: to comb or card, as wool: to backcomb the hair: to vex with importunity, jests, etc.: to plague, irritate, esp. playfully or pleasantly: to tantalise: to banter.—*n.* one who teases: an act of teasing.—*n.* **teas'er.**—*n.* and *adj* **teas'ing.**—*adv.* **teas'ingly.** [O.E. *tǣsan*, to card.]

teasel *tēz'l*, *n.* any species of Dipsacus, esp. *D. fullonum*: its head with hooked bracts used in raising a nap on cloth: an artificial substitute for its head.—*v.t* to raise a nap on with the teasel:—*pr.p.* **teas'el(l)ing;** *pa.t.* and *pa.p.* **teas'el(l)ed.**—*ns.* **teas'el(l)er;** **teas'el(l)ing.**—Also **teazel, teazle,** etc. [O.E. *tǣsel* —*tǣsan*; see **tease.**]

teat *tēt*, *n.* the small protuberance through which the mammalian young suck the milk: a similar protuberance through which milk is sucked from a baby's feeding-bottle: a nipple.—*adj.* **teat'ed** having a teat or teats. [O.E. *titt*, *tit*.]

teazel, teazle see **teasel.**

tebbad *teb'ad*, *n* a sandstorm [Cf Pers. *tab*, fever, *bād*, wind.]

'tec *tek*, *n.* a slang abbrev. for **detective.**

technetium *tek-nē'shi-əm*, *n.* the chemical element of atomic number 43 (Tc), the first element to be artificially made [Gr *technētos*, artificial—*technē*, art.]

technic *tek'nik*, *adj.* technical.—*n.* technology: (often in *pl* form) technicality, technique —*adj.* **tech'nical** pertaining to art, esp. a useful art or applied science: industrial: belonging to, or in the language of, a particular art, department of knowledge or skill, profession: so called in strict legal or technical language.—*n.* **technical'ity.**—*adv.* **tech'nically.**—*ns.* **tech'nicalness; technician** (-*nish'ən*), **tech'nicist** (-*nisist*) one skilled in a practical art: a person who does the practical work in a laboratory, etc.; **Tech'nicolor**® a process of colour photography in motion-pictures —*adj.* **tech'nicolour** (modelled on above) in bright, artificial colours: cheaply romantic.—*n.sing.* **tech'nics** technology: the study of industry.—*n.* **technique** (*tek-nēk'*) method of performance, manipulation, esp. everything concerned with the mechanical part of an artistic performance; **techno-** in composition, craft, art, e.g. *technography*: technical, technological, e.g. *technophobia*, *technomania*.—*ns.* **technoc'racy** government or management by technical experts: a state, etc., so governed: a body of technical experts in governing position; **tech'nocrat** a member of a technocracy: a believer in technocracy.—*adjs.* **technocrat'ic; technolog'ical.**—*adv.* **technolog'ically.**—*ns.* **technol'ogist; technol'ogy** the practice of any or all of the applied sciences that have practical value and/or industrial use: technical method(s) in a particular field of industry or art: technical means and skills characteristic of a particular civilisation, group, or period.—**technical college** a college of further education that specialises in technical subjects, as industrial skills, secretarial work, etc.; **technical knockout** a boxer's defeat on the referee's decision that, though not actually knocked out, he is unable to continue the fight. [Gr. *technē*, art, adj. *technikos*.]

techy. See **tetchy.**

tectonic *tek-ton'ik*, *adj.* pertaining to building: structural.—*n sing.* **tecton'ics** building as an art: structural geology: (*n.pl.*) the constructive arts: (*n.pl.*) structural features.—*adv.* **tecton'ically.** [Gr. *tektōn*, a builder.]

tectrix *tek'triks*, *n.* a feather covering the quill-bases on a bird's wings and tail (also called **covert**):—*pl.* **tectrices** (-*trī'sēz*).—*adj.* **tectricial** (-*trish'l*). [L. *tēctrīx*, *-īcis*, fem. of *tēctor*, *-ōris*, a coverer, plasterer —*tegēre*, to cover.]

ted *ted*, *v.t.* to spread as new-mown grass, for drying:— *pr.p.* **tedd'ing;** *pa.t.* and *pa.p.* **tedd'ed.**—*n.* **tedd'er.** [Prob. from a lost O E *teddan*.]

Ted *ted*, *n.* a Teddy boy.—**Teddy boy** an unruly adolescent, orig. in the 1950s, affecting a dandyish garb reminiscent of Edward VII's time. [**Edward.**]

teddy *ted'i*, **teddy-bear** (-*bār'*) *ns.* a woolly toy bear. [From Theodore (*Teddy*) Roosevelt, a famous hunter and President of U.S.A. (1901–1909).]

Te Deum *tē dē'əm*, L. *tā de'ŏŏm*, *n.* a famous Latin hymn of the Western Church: a musical setting of it. [From its first words, *Tē Deum laudāmus*, thee, God, we praise.]

tedium *tē'di-əm*; *n.* wearisomeness, esp. owing to length: irksomeness: boredom.—*n.* **tedios'ity.**—*adj* **te'dious.**—*adv.* **te'diously.**—*n.* **te'diousness.** [L *taedium*—*taedēre*, to weary.]

tee[1] *tē*, *n.* the twentieth letter of the alphabet (T, t.): an object or mark of that shape.—**tee'-shirt** a slip-on shirt usu. with short sleeves, no collar and no buttons; **tee'-square** see T.

tee² *tē, n.* the mark aimed at (*quoits, curling*, etc): the peg or other elevation from which the ball is first played at each hole (*golf*): the strip of ground (also **tee'ing-ground**) where this is done.—*v.t.* and *v ι.* to place (the golf-ball) on the tee:—*pr.p* **tee'ing;** *pa.t.* and *pa.p.* **teed, tee'd.—tee up** or **off** to start (play); **to a tee** exactly.

teehee *tē'hē', interj.* expressing derision or merriment. —*n.* a laugh.—*v.i.* to titter. [Imit.]

teem¹ *tēm, v.i.* to bear or be fruitful: to be pregnant: to be full, abound.—*adjs.* **teem'ful; teem'ing; teem'less** barren. [O.E. *tīeman—tēam*; see **team.**]

teem² *tēm, v.t.* to pour, empty.—*v.i.* to pour: to flow copiously. [O.N. *tœma,* to empty.]

teen *tēn, n.* any number or year of age, etc., from thir*teen* to nine*teen* (usu. ιn *pl.*).—*adjs.* **teen'age** in the teens: appropriate to one in the teens; **teen'aged.— teen'ager; tee'ny-bopper** (*slang*) a young teenager, esp. a girl, who follows enthusiastically the latest trends in pop-music, clothes, etc. [O.E. suffix -*tīene* —*tīen,* ten.]

teeny *tē'ni, adj.* a form of tiny.—Also (*dim.*, often *facet.*) **teen'sy, teen'tsy, teen'ty, teen'y-ween'y.**

teepee. See tepee.

teeter *tē'tar, n.* see-saw.—*v.t., v.i.* to see-saw: to move unsteadily. [titter².]

teeth *tēth, pl.* of **tooth:** (legislative) power to make a government recommendation effective (*fig.*).—*v.i.* **teethe** (*tēdh*) to develop or cut teeth.—*n.* and *adj.* **teething** (*tēdh'ing*).—**teething ring** a ring of plastic, bone, etc., for a baby to chew when teething; **teething troubles** pain and irritation caused by the cutting of teeth: mechanical difficulties encountered on first using a new machine or in the early stages of any undertaking. [O.E. pl. *tēth.*]

teetotal *tē-tō'tl, adj.* abstaining totally from intoxicating drinks.—*ns.* **teetō'talism; teetō'taller** a total abstainer from intoxicating drinks.—*adv.* **teetō'tally.** [Said to be from a stammering pronunciation of total.]

teetotum *tē-tō'tam,* (*arch.*) *n.* a small top inscribed with letters, or a gambling game decided by the letter that came uppermost, T standing for L. *tōtum,* all, i.e. take all the stakes.

Teflon® *tef'lon, n.* a trademark for polytetrafluoroethylene as used e.g. to coat the inside of cooking pans to render them non-stick.

teg, tegg *teg, n.* a sheep in its second year. [Perh. Scand.]

tegmen *teg'man, n.* a covering: the inner coat of the testa (*bot.*): the leathery fore-wing in Orthoptera:— *pl.* **teg'mina.**—*adj.* **tegmental** (*-ment'əl*).—*ns.* **teg'ment'um** a leaf specialising as a scale protecting a bud; **teg'ūment** a covering: an integument.—*adjs.* **tegūment'al, tegūment'ary.** [L. *tĕgmen, tĕgmentum, tegumentum—tegĕre,* to cover.]

tegula *teg'ū-lə, n.* a flat roofing-tile:—*pl.* **teg'ūlae** (*-lē*).—*adj.* **teg'ūlar.**—*adv.* **teg'ūlarly.**—*adj.* **teg'ūlāted** composed of plates overlapping like tiles. [L. *tegula,* a tile—*tegĕre,* to cover.]

tegument, etc. See **tegmen.**

te igitur *tē' ij'i-tar,* L. *tā ig'i-tōōr,* the first paragraph of the canon of the mass: a service-book on which oaths were taken. [L. *tē igitur,* thee therefore (the first words).]

tektite *tek'tīt, n.* a type of small glassy stone, of uncertain and perh. extra-terrestrial origin, found in certain areas of the earth. [Gr. *tēktos,* molten.]

tel. See **tel(l).**

tel-. See **tele-.**

telaesthesia, U.S. **telesthesia,** *tel-ēs-thē'zι-ə, -zhi-ə,*

-zhə, or -*is-, n.* an abnormal impression of sense received from a distance —*adj.* **tel(a)esthetic** (*-thet'ik*). [**tele-** (1), Gr. *aisthēsiā,* sensation.]

telamon *tel'ə-mən,* (*archit.*) *n.* a man's figure as a pillar: —*pl.* **telamones** (*-mō'nēz*). [Gr mythological hero, *Telamōn—tlēnai,* to endure, bear.]

telangiectasis *tel-an-ji-ek'tə-sis, n.* dilatation of the small arteries or capillaries.—*adj.* **telangiectatic** (*-ek-tat'ik*). [Gr. *telos,* end, *angeιon,* a vessel, *ektasis,* extension.]

tele- *tel-i,* (also **tel-**), in composition, (1) far, distant; (2) television. [Gr. *tēle,* far.]

tele-ad *tel'i-ad, n.* a classified advertisement submitted to a newspaper, etc , by telephone. [**tele-** (1), advertisement.]

telecast *tel'i-kast, n.* a televιsion broad*cast* —Also *v.t.* —*n.* **tel'ecaster.**

telecommunication *tel-i-kə-mū-ni-kā'shən,* ṅ. communication of information, in verbal, written, coded, or pictorial form, by telephone, telegraph, cable, radio, television: (in *pl.*) the science of such communication. [**tele-** (1), **communication.**]

telecontrol *tel-i-kon-trōl', n.* control of mechanical devιces remotely, either by radio (as ships and aircraft), by sound waves, or by beams of light. [**tele-** (1), **control.**]

teledu *tel'ə-dōō, n.* the stinking badger of Java. [Javanese.]

telefilm *tel'i-film, n.* a regular sound-film made specially for subsequent television transmission. [**tele-** (2), **film.**]

telegenic *tel-i-jen'ik, adj.* visually suitable for television. [**tele-** (2), modelled on **photogenic.**]

telegnosis *tel-i(g)-nō'sis, n.* the knowledge of events taking place far away, not obtained in any normal way. [**tele-** (1), Gr. *gnōsis,* knowing.]

telegony *ti-leg'ə-ni, n.* the (imaginary) transmitted influence of a previous mate on the offspring of a female by a later mate [**tele-** (1), Gr. *gonos,* begetting.]

telegram *tel'i-gram, n.* a message sent by telegraph.— *adjs.* **telegrammat'ic, telegramm'ic** of or like a telegram. [**tele-** (1), Gr. *gramma,* that which is written —*graphein,* to write.]

telegraph *tel'i-graf, n.* a combination of apparatus for transmitting information to a distance, now almost exclusively by electrical impulses: often taken as the name of a newspaper.—*v.t.* to convey or announce by telegraph: to signal: to give a premature indication of something to come.—*v ι.* to signal: to send a telegram.—*ns.* **telegrapher** (*ti-leg'rə-far;* now chiefly *U.S.*) a telegraphist; **tel'egraphese'** the jargon or contracted idiom used in telegrams.—*adj.* **telegraphic** (*-graf'ik*).—*adv* **telegraph'ically.**—*ns.* **teleg'raphist** one who works a telegraph; **teleg'raphy** the science or art of constructing or using telegraphs.—**tel'egraph-plant** an Indian papilionaceous plant (*Desmodium gyrans*) whose leaflets move like semaphore arms; **tel'egraph-pole** a pole supporting telegraph-wires; **tel'egraph-wire** a wire for carrying telegraphic messages. [**tele-** (1), Gr. *graphein,* to write.]

telekinesis *tel-i-ki-nē'sis, -ki-, n.* the production of motion at a distance by means beyond the range of the senses.—*adj.* **telekinetic** (*-net'ik*). [**tele-** (1), Gr. *kinēsis,* movement.]

telemark *tel'i-märk, n.* a sudden turn on the outer skι, first practised at *Telemark* in Norway.—*v.i.* to execute a telemark.

telemessage *tel'i-mes-ij, n.* a message sent by telex or telephone, superseding the telegram. [**tele-**(1)]

telemeter *ti-lem'i-tar, n.* an instrument for measuring distances: a photographer's rangefinder. an instrument for measuring an electrical or other quantity and signalling the measurement to a distant point (also **radiotelemeter**).—*v.t.* to record and signal by telemeter.—*adj.* **telemetric** (*tel-i-met'rik*).—*n.* **telem'etry**. [tele- (1), Gr. *metron*, measure.]

teleology *tel-i-ol'ə-ji*, *n.* the doctrine of the final causes of things: interpretation in terms of purpose.—*adjs.* **teleologic** (*-ə-loj'ik*), **-al.**—*adv.* **teleolog'ically.**—*ns.* **teleol'ogism; teleol'ogist.** [Gr. *telos*, end, purpose, *logos*, a discourse.]

telepathy *ti-lep'ə-thi*, *n.* communication between mind and mind otherwise than through the known channels of the senses.—*n.* **telepath** (*tel'i-path*) one who practises telepathy.—*v.t.* and *v.i.* to communicate by telepathy.—*adj.* **telepath'ic.**—*adv.* **telepath'ically.**—*v.t.* **telep'athise, -ize** to affect or act upon through telepathy.—*v.i.* to practise telepathy.—*n.* **telep'athist** one who believes in or practises telepathy. [tele- (1), Gr. *pathos*, feeling.]

telephone *tel'i-fōn*, *n.* an instrument for reproducing sound at a distance, esp. by means of electricity.— Also *adj.*—*v.t.* and *v.i.* to communicate by telephone.—*n.* **tel'ephoner.**—*adj.* **telephonic** (*-fon'ik*).—*adv.* **telephon'ically.**—*ns.* **telephonist** (*ti-lef'ə-nist*) one who works a telephone; **teleph'ony** telephonic communication.—**telephone box, booth, kiosk** a usu. enclosed place with a telephone for public use. [tele- (1), Gr. *phōnē*, a sound.]

telephotography *tel-i-fō-tog'rə-fi*, *n.* a photography of distant objects by means of suitable lenses.—*n.* **telepho'tograph** (*tel-i-fō'tō-gräf*).—*adj.* **telephotographic** (*-graf'ik*), abbrev. **telepho'to.**—**telephoto lens** a lens of long focal length for obtaining large images of distant objects. [tele- (1), photography.]

teleprinter *tel-i-print'ər*, *n.* a telegraph transmitter with typewriter keyboard. [tele- (1), printer.]

teleprompter *tel-i-promp'tər*, *n.* a device by which a television speaker sees a projection of what he is to say invisible to the audience. [tele- (2).]

telerecording *tel-i-ri-kör'ding*, *n.* recording for broadcasting by television: a television transmission from a recording. [tele- (2), recording.]

telescope *tel'i-skōp*, *n.* an optical instrument for viewing objects at a distance.—*v.t.* to drive or slide one into another like the movable joints of a telescope: to compress, shorten, make smaller, etc. (*lit.* and *fig.*).—*v.i.* to fit, slide, shorten, etc. in such a way.—*adjs.* **telescopic** (*-skop'ik*), **-al** of, performed by, or like a telescope: seen only by a telescope: sliding, or arranged, like the joints of a telescope: capable of retraction and protrusion.—*adv.* **telescop'ically.**—*ns.* **telescopist** (*ti-les'kə-pist*) one who uses the telescope; **teles'copy** the art of constructing or of using the telescope.—**telescope, telescopic sight** a telescope on a gun used as a sight. [tele- (1), Gr. *skopeein*, to see.]

telesthesia. See telaesthesia.

telestich *tel-es'tik, tel'es-tik*, *n.* a poem or block of words whose final letters spell a name or word. [Gr. *telos*, end, *stichos*, row.]

teletext *tel'i-tekst*, *n.* written data, such as business news, etc., transmitted by television companies in the form of coded pulses which can be decoded by a special adaptor for viewing on a conventional television. [tele- (2), text.]

telethon *tel'ə-thon*, (orig. *U.S.*) *n.* a very long television programme, esp. one seeking support for e.g. a political candidate, or a charity. [*tele*vision mara*thon*.]

Teletype® *tel'i-tīp*, *n.* a printing telegraph apparatus.—**Teletype'setter**® a telegraphic machine which delivers its message as a perforated roll that can be used to actuate a type-setting machine; **teletype'writer** (*U.S.*) a teleprinter. [tele- (1), Gr. *typos*; see **type.**]

television *tel-i-vizh'ən*, *n.* the viewing of distant objects or events by electrical transmission: the electrical transmission of these: a television set.— Abbrev. **TV.**—Also *adj.*—*v.t.* and *v.i.* **tel'eview** to view by television.—*n.* **tel'eviewer** a television watcher.—*v.t.* and *v.i.* **tel'evise** (*tel'i-vīz*) to transmit by television.—*adjs.* **televi'sional, televi'sionary** of, relating to, television.—*n.* **televi'sor** a receiver for television.—*adj.* **televi'sual** televisional: telegenic.— **television set** a television receiver; **TV game** an electronic game, played on a television set. [tele- (1), vision.]

telewriter *tel-i-rī'tər*, *n.* telegraph instrument that reproduces writing. [tele- (1), writer.]

telex *tel'eks*, *n.* a Post Office service whereby subscribers hire the use of teleprinters: a teleprinter used in this service: a message transferred by this service. —*v.t.* to send (someone) (a message) by telex. [*tele*typewriter exchange.]

telic. See telos.

tell(l) *tel*, *n.* in Arab lands, a hill, ancient mound. [Ar. *tall.*]

tell *tel*, *v.t.* to count: to count out: to utter: to narrate: to disclose: to inform: to discern: to explain: to order, direct, instruct.—*v.t.* to give an account: to have an effect (on): to have weight: to make an effective story: to play the informer:—*pa.t.* and *pa.p.* **told.**— *adj.* **tell'able** capable of being told: fit to tell.—*ns.* **tell'er** one who tells or counts: one who counts votes: a clerk whose duty it is to receive and pay money, esp. in a bank; **tell'ership.**—*adj.* **tell'ing** effective.—*n.* numbering: narration: direction, orders.—*adv.* **tell'ingly.**—**tell'ing-off** a rating, chiding; **tell'-tale, tell'tale** one who tells the private concerns or misdeeds of others: anything revealing or betraying: an indicator.—*adj* blabbing: revealing, betraying: indicating.—**take a telling** to do as one is bid without having to be told again; **tell me another** you'll have to tell me a more credible story; **tell off** to count off: to detach on some special duty: to rate, chide; **tell on** (*coll.*) to betray, give away secrets about; **you're telling me** (*interj.*; *slang*) I know that only too well. [O.E. *tellan.*]

Tellus *tel'əs*, *n.* the Roman earth-goddess: the earth.— *n.* **tell'ūrate** a salt of telluric acid.—*adjs.* **tell'ūretted** combined with tellurium; **tellū'rian** terrestrial.—*n.* an inhabitant of the earth. a tellurion.—*adj.* **tellū'ric** of or from the earth: of tellurium in higher valency (**telluric acid** H_2TeO_4).—*ns.* **tell'ūride** a compound of tellurium with another element or radical; **tellū'rion, -an** an apparatus representing the earth and sun, demonstrating the occurrence of day, night, the seasons, etc.—*v.t.* **tell'ūrise, -ize** to combine with tellurium.—*ns.* **tell'ūrite** native oxide of tellurium (*min.*): a salt of tellurous acid (*chem.*); **tellū'rium** the element (Te) of atomic number 52; **tellūrom'eter** an electronic instrument used to measure survey lines by measurement of the time required for a radar signal to echo back.—*adj.* **tell'ūrous** of tellurium in lower valency (**tellurous acid** H_2TeO_3). [L. *Tellūs, -ūris.*]

telly *tel'i*, (*slang*) *n.* television.

telos *tel'os*, *n.* aim, purpose, ultimate end.—*adj.* **tel'ic** expressing purpose: purposive. [Gr. *telos*, end, purpose.]

telpher *tel'fər*, *adj.* pertaining to a system of telpherage.—*n* a car or carrier in such a system.—*ns.* **tel'pherage** any system of automatic electric transport: an electric ropeway or cableway system: overhead traction in general. [Gr. *tēle*, far, *phoros*, bearing—*pherein*, to bear.]

telson *tel'sən*, *n.* the hindermost part of a crustacean or arachnid. [Gr. *telson*, a headland in ploughing.]

Telugu *tel'ŏŏ-gŏŏ, n.* a Dravidian language of south-east India: one of the people speaking it:—*pl.* **Tel'ugus, Tel'ugu.**—Also *adj.*

temerity *ti-mer'i-ti, n.* rashness: unreasonable contempt for danger. [L. *temeritās, -ātis,* and *temerārius—temere,* by chance, rashly.]

temp *temp,* (*coll.*) *n.* a temporarily-employed secretarial worker.—*v.i.* to work as a temp. [temporary.]

temper *tem'par, v.t.* to mix in due proportion: to modify by blending or mixture: to moderate: to soften: loosely, esp. formerly, to harden (steel) by heating to red heat and quenching: properly, to heat again, less strongly, and cool in air: to adjust: to tune. —*v.i.* to become tempered.—*n.* due mixture or balance of different or contrary qualities: state of a metal as to hardness, etc.: constitution of the body: temperament: disposition: habitual or actual frame of mind: mood: composure: self-control: uncontrolled anger: a fit of ill-humour or rage.—*n.* **tem'-pera** (*paint.*; orig. It.) a painting medium in which the pigment is mixed with egg yolk.—*adj.* **tem'perable** capable of being tempered.—*n.* **tem'perament** proportioned mixture: internal constitution or state: disposition: high excitability, nervous instability, and sensitiveness (*coll.*): a system of compromise in tuning (*mus.*).—*adj.* **temperament'al.**—*adv.* **temperament'ally.**—*n.* **tem'perance** moderation, esp. in the indulgence of the natural appetites and passions —in a narrower sense, moderation in the use of alcoholic liquors, and even entire abstinence from them. —*adj.* advocating or consistent with temperance in or abstinence from alcoholic drinks.—*adj.* **tem'perate** moderate: self-restrained, esp. in appetites and passions: abstemious: moderate in temperature.—*adv.* **tem'perately.**—*n.* **tem'perateness.**—*adj.* **tem'perative** having moderating influence.—*n.* **tem'perature** tempering: tempered condition: mixture: constitution: proportion: degree of hotness: condition determining interchange of heat between bodies: a body temperature above normal (*coll.*).—*adj.* **tem'pered** having a certain specified disposition or temper: brought to a certain temper, as steel: tuned or adjusted to some mean, or to equal, temperament (*mus.*).—*adv.* **tem'peredly.**—*n.* **tem'perer.**—*n.* and *adj.* **tem'pering.**—**temperate zones** the parts of the earth of moderate temperature between the tropics and the polar circles.—**bad temper** an angry humour: an inclination to irascibility; **equal temperament** a compromise in tuning by which the octave is divided into twelve equal intervals; **good temper** an unruffled humour: good-nature; **keep one's temper** to restrain oneself from showing, or losing, one's temper; **lose one's temper** to break out in anger; **out of temper** in an irritable mood: angry; **temperature-humidity index** an index measuring temperature and humidity with regard to human discomfort. [L. *temperāre,* to temper, restrain, compound, moderate, partly through O.E. *temprian.*]

tempest *tem'pist, n.* a violent wind storm: a violent commotion or agitation (*fig.*).—*adj.* **tempestuous** (*-pest'*).—*adv.* **tempest'uously.**—*n.* **tempest'u-ousness.** [O.Fr. *tempeste*—a L.L. form of L. *tempestās,* a season, tempest—*tempus,* time.]

templ. See **tempo.**

Templar. See **temple**[1].

template, templet *tem'plit, n.* a mould shaped to a required outline from which to execute moulding: a thin plate cut to the shape required, by which a surface of an article being made is marked out: any model from which others form, are produced, etc. [L. *templum,* a small timber.]

temple[1] *tem'pl, n.* a building or place dedicated to, or regarded as the house of, a god: a place of worship: (*cap.*) the headquarters of the Knights Templars in Jerusalem: (*cap.*) in London, two inns of court.—*adj.* **tem'plar** of a temple.—*n.* **Tem'plar** a member of a religious and military order (**Knights Templar(s)**) founded in 1119 for the protection of the Holy Sepulchre and pilgrims going thither: a student or lawyer living in the Temple, London.—*adj.* **tem'pled.** [L. *templum.*]

temple[2] *tem'pl, n.* the flat portion of either side of the head above the cheekbone. [O.Fr.,—L. *tempus, -oris.*]

templet. See **template.**

tempo *tem'pō,* (*mus.*) *n.* time: speed and rhythm:—*pl.* **tem'pos, tem'pi** (*-pē*). [It.]

temporal[1] *tem'par-l, adj.* pertaining to time: pertaining to time in this life or world—opp. to *eternal:* worldly, secular, or civil—opp. to *spiritual, sacred* or *ecclesiastical:* pertaining to tense (*gram.*).—*n.* **temporality** (*-al'i-ti*) state or fact of being temporal: what pertains to temporal welfare: (usu. *pl.*) secular possessions, revenues of an ecclesiastic.—*adv.* **tem'porally.**—*adj.* **tempora'neous** temporal.—*adv.* **tem'porarily.**—*n.* **tem'porariness.**—*adj.* **tem'porary** for a time only: transient.—*n.* a person employed temporarily (see also temp).—*n.* **temporisa'tion, -z-.** —*v.i.* **tem'porise, -ize** to comply with the time or occasion: to yield to circumstances: to behave so as to gain time.—*n.* **tem'poriser, -z-.**—*n.* and *adj.* **tem'porising, -z-.**—*adv.* **tem'porisingly, -z-.** [L. *tempus, -oris,* time.]

temporal[2] *tem'par-l, adj.* of or at the temple (of the head).—*n.* a bone, muscle, or scale in that position. [L. *tempus, -oris;* see **temple**[2].]

temporaneous, temporary, etc. See **temporal**[1].

tempt *tem(p)t, v.t.* to put to trial: to test: to try or tend to persuade, esp. to evil: to entice.—*adj.* **temp'table.** —*n.* **tempta'tion** act of tempting: state of being tempted: that which tempts enticement to evil: trial; **temp'ter** one who tempts, esp. the devil:—*fem.* **temp'tress.**—*n.* **temp'ting** action of the verb.—*adj.* attractive, enticing.—*adv.* **temp'tingly.**—*n.* **temp'-tingness.** [O.Fr. *tempter*—L. *tentāre,* an intens. of *tendĕre,* to stretch.]

ten *ten, n.* the cardinal number next above nine: a symbol representing it (x, etc.): a set of that number of things or persons: an article of a size denoted by 10: a card with ten pips: a score of ten points, tricks, etc.: the tenth hour after midday or midnight: the age of ten years.—*adj.* of the number ten: ten years old.— *adj.* and *adv.* **ten'fold** in ten divisions: ten times as much.—*n.* **tenn'er** (*slang*) a ten-pound note: a ten-dollar bill: ten years.—*adj.* **tenth** the last of ten: next after the ninth: equal to one of ten equal parts.—*n.* a tenth part: a tenth part of the annual profit of a church living: a person or thing in tenth position.— *adv.* **tenth'ly.**—*adj.* **ten'-foot** measuring ten feet.— **ten'pence** an amount in money equal to ten pennies; **ten-pence, -penny piece** in Britain, a coin worth 10 pence (also **ten'penny-piece**').—*adj.* **tenpin bowling, ten'pins** an American game like skittles.—**ten-gallon hat** (*U.S.*) cowboy's broad-brimmed hat; **ten minute rule** a parliamentary procedure by which a member makes a short speech (usu. lasting ten minutes) introducing a bill. [O.E. (Anglian) *tēn, tēne* (W.S. *tien, tiene*).]

tenable *ten'a-bl adj.* capable of being retained, kept, or defended.—*ns.* **tenabil'ity, ten'ableness.** [Fr. *tenable—tenir,* to hold.]

tenace *ten'ās, -is, n.* the combination in one hand of the cards next above and next below the other side's best in the suit. [Sp. *tenaza,* pincers.]

tenacious *ti-nā'shas, adj.* retaining or holding fast:

sticking stiffly: tough: stubborn.—*adv.* **tenā'ciously.**
—*ns.* **tenā'ciousness, tenacity** (*-nas'i-ti*). [L. *tenâx,
-âcis—tenēre,* to hold.]

tenaculum *te-nak'ū-ləm, n.* a surgical hook or forceps.
[L. *tenâculum,* holder, pincers.]

tenant *ten'ənt, n.* one who has, on certain conditions,
temporary possession of any place: an occupant.—
v.t. to hold as a tenant: to occupy.—*n.* **ten'ancy** possession by private ownership: a temporary occupation
or holding of land or property by a tenant: time of
such holding.—*adj.* **ten'antable** fit to be tenanted: in
a state of repair suitable for a tenant; **ten'antless.**—
ns. **ten'antry** the state or time of being a tenant: a set
or body of tenants; **ten'antship.—tenant farmer** a
farmer who rents a farm. [Fr. *tenant,* pr.p. of *tenir*
—L. *tenēre,* to hold.]

tench *tench, -sh, n.* a freshwater fish (*Tinca tinca*) of
the carp family. [O.Fr. *tenche* (Fr. *tanche*)—L.
tinca.]

tend¹ *tend, v.t.* to attend to: to mind: to watch over or
stand by and perform services for or connected with:
to minister to, wait upon.—*adj.* **ten'ded.**—*n.* **ten'der**
one who tends: a small craft that attends a larger: a
carriage attached to a locomotive to carry fuel and
water. [Aphetic for **attend.**]

tend² *tend, v.i.* to stretch, aim at, move, or incline in
some direction: to be directed to any end or purpose:
to be apt.—*n.* **ten'dency** a trend, drift, inclination:
proneness.—*adjs.* **tendential** (*-den'shl*), **tenden'-
tious, tenden'cious** purposely tending: with an object:
biased.—*adv.* **tenden'tiously.**—*n.* **tenden'tiousness.**
[L. *tendĕre* and Fr. *tendre,* to stretch.]

tender¹. See under **tend¹.**

tender² *ten'dər, v.t.* to offer for acceptance, esp. to
offer in payment: to proffer.—*v.i.* to make a tender.
—*n.* an offer or proposal, esp. of some service: the
paper containing it: the thing offered.—*ns.* **ten'derer;
ten'dering.** [Fr. *tendre,* to stretch, reach out.]

tender³ *ten'dər, adj.* soft, delicate: easily chewed, not
tough: easily impressed or injured: not hardy: gentle:
sensitive, esp. to pain: requiring gentle handling:
easily moved to pity, love, etc.: careful not to hurt:
considerate, careful (with *of*): expressive, or of the
nature, of the softer passions: compassionate, loving,
affectionate.—*v.t.* **ten'derise, -ize** to break down the
connective tissue of (meat) by pounding or by applying a chemical or marinade.—*n.* **ten'deriser, -z-** a
pounding instrument or a substance that tenderises
meat.—*adv.* **ten'derly.**—*n.* **ten'derness.—ten'der-
foot** one not yet hardened to life in the prairie, min-
ing-camp, etc.: a newcomer: a greenhorn:—*pl.*
ten'derfeet.—*adj.* **ten'der-heart'ed** full of feeling.—
adv. **ten'der-heart'edly.—ten'der-heart'edness.—
ten'der-loin** the tenderest part of the loin of beef,
pork, etc., close to the lumbar vertebrae. [Fr.
tendre—L. *tener.*]

tendon *ten'dən, n.* a cord, band, or sheet of fibrous
tissue attaching a muscle to a bone or other structure.
—*adj.* **ten'dinous.** [L.L. *tendō, -inis* or *-ōnis,* app.—
Gr. *tenōn, -ontos,* sinew, tendon.]

tendril *ten'dril, n.* a plant's coiling threadlike climbing
organ (leaf, leaflet, or shoot).—*adjs.* **ten'drillar,
ten'drillous; ten'drilled.**

tenebrae *ten'i-brē, n.pl.* (*R.C.*; also with *cap.*) matins
and lauds in Holy Week with gradual extinction of
lights.—*adj.* **teneb'rious** dark—*ns.* **ten'ebrism** the
naturalist school of painting of Caravaggio affecting
dark colouring; **ten'ebrist; teneb'rity.**—*adjs.* **ten'e-
brose, ten'ebrous** dark.—*n.* **tenebros'ity.** [L. *tenebrae,* darkness.]

tenement *ten'i-mənt, n.* a holding, by any tenure: anything held, or that may be held, by a tenant: one of a
set of apartments in one building, each occupied by a

separate family: a building divided into dwellings for
a number of families (*Scot.*).—*adjs.* **tenemental**
(*-ment'l*); **tenement'ary.** [L.L. *tenementum*—L.
tenēre, to hold.]

tenesmus *ti-nes'məs, n.* painful and ineffectual
straining to relieve the bowels. [Latinised from Gr.
teinesmos—teinein, to strain.]

tenet *ten'et* (also *tē'nit*) *n.* any opinion, principle, or
doctrine which a person holds or maintains as true.
[L. *tenet,* (he) holds—*tenēre,* to hold.]

tenfold, tenner. See **ten.**

tennis *ten'is, n.* an ancient game played with ball, rackets (orig. palms of the hands), and net, in a specially
constructed building or enclosed court (distinguished
from lawn-tennis as **close, court, real,** or **royal**
tennis): now usu. lawn-tennis.—**tenn'is-ball; tenn'is-
court; tennis elbow** inflammation of the bursa of the
elbow, caused by over-exercise; **tenn'is-match;
tenn'is-player; tenn'is-racket; tenn'is-shoe.** [Prob.
Fr. *tenez,* (A.Fr. *tenetz*) imper. of *tenir,* to take,
receive.]

tenon *ten'ən,* a projection at the end of a piece of wood,
etc., inserted into the socket or mortise of another, to
hold the two together.—*v.t.* to fix or fit with a tenon.
—*n.* **ten'oner.—ten'on-saw** a thin back-saw for
tenons, etc. [Fr. *tenon—tenir,* to hold—L. *tenēre.*]

tenor *ten'ər, n.* continuity of state: general run or
course: purport: the higher of the two kinds of voices
usu. belonging to adult males (app. because the
melody was assigned to it): an instrument, e.g. the
viola, of corresponding compass: one who sings
tenor.—Also *adj.*—**ten'or-clef** the C clef placed on
the fourth line. [L. *tenor—tenēre,* to hold.]

tenpence, etc. See **ten.**

tenrec *ten'rek,* **tanrec** *tan'rek, ns.* a large Madagascan
insectivore (*Centetes*). [Malagasy *t(r)àndraka.*]

tense¹ *tens, n.* time in grammar, the form of a verb to
indicate the time of the action. [O.Fr. *tens* (Fr.
temps)—L. *tempus,* time.]

tense² *tens, adj.* stretched tight: strained: rigid: pronounced with the tongue tightened or narrowed.—
v.t. and *v.i.* to make or become tense.—*adv.* **tense'ly.**
—*ns.* **tense'ness** state of being tense; **tensibil'ity.**—
adjs. **tens'ible** capable of being stretched; **tens'ile** (*il;*
in U.S. *-il, -əl*) tensible: in relation to stretching.—*ns.*
tensility (*-il'i-ti*); **tension'etry** the branch of physics
relating to tension, tensile strength, etc.; **tension**
(*ten'shən*) stretching: a pulling strain: stretched or
strained state: strain generally: electromotive force:
a state of barely suppressed emotion, as excitement,
suspense, anxiety, or hostility: a feeling of strain with
resultant symptoms (*psych.*): strained relations
(between persons): opposition (between conflicting
ideas or forces); **tens'ity** tenseness.—*adj.* **tens'ive**
giving the sensation of tenseness or stiffness.—*n.*
tens'or a muscle that tightens a part: a mathematical
or physical entity represented by components which
depend in a special way on the choice of a coordinate
system.—**tensile strength** the strength of a material
when being stretched, expressed as the greatest stress
it can resist before breaking. [L. *tēnsus,* pa.p. of
tendĕre, to stretch.]

tent *tent, n.* a portable lodge or shelter, commonly of
canvas stretched on poles.—*v.i.* to camp in a tent.—
v.t. to canopy: to lodge in tents.—*n.* **tent'age** tents
collectively: material for making tents.—*adj.* **tent'ed**
covered with tents: formed like a tent: dwelling in
tents.—*ns.* **tent'er** one who lives in a tent; **tent'ful** as
many as a tent will hold; **tent'ing.—tent'-maker;
tent'-peg, -pin** a strong notched peg driven into the
ground to fasten a tent; **tent'-pole** a pole to support a
tent. [Fr. *tente*—L. *tendĕre, tentum,* to stretch.]

tentacle *tent'ə-kl, n.* a slender flexible organ for feeling, grasping, etc.: a gland-tipped insect-capturing process in sundew.—Also **tentaculum** (-ak'ū-ləm; *pl.* **tentac'ula**).—*adjs.* **ten'tacled; tentac'ular; tentac'ulate**. [L. *tentāre*, to feel.]

tentation *ten-tā'shən, n.* a method of adjusting by a succession of trials.—*adj.* **tentative** (*ten'tə-tiv*) done or made provisionally and experimentally.—*adv.* **ten'tatively**. [L. *tentāre*, to try.]

tenter[1] *ten'tər, n.* a frame for stretching cloth: a tenter-hook: a hook.—*v.t.* to stretch on hooks.—**ten'terhook** a sharp, hooked nail as on a tenter: a hook.—**on tenter-hooks** in impatient suspense. [App. conn. with Fr. *tenture*, hangings, and L. *tendēre*, to stretch.]

tenter[2]. See tent.

tenth. See ten.

tenue *tə-nū, n.* bearing, carriage: manner of dress. [Fr.]

tenuity *ten-ū'-ti, n.* thinness. slenderness: rarity.—*adj.* **ten'uous** thin: slender: rarefied.—*adv.* **ten'uously.**—*n.* **ten'uousness**. [L. *tenuis*, thin; cf. *tendēre*, to stretch.]

tenure *ten'yər, n.* holding, occupation: time of holding: the holding of an appointment in a university or college for an assured length of time: conditions on which property is held: a tenant's rights, duties, etc. —*adj.* **tenūr'ial**. [A.Fr. *tenure*—*tenir*, to hold.]

tenuto *te-nōō'tō,* (*mus.*) *adj.* sustained. [It., pa.p. of *tenere*, to hold.]

teocalli *tā, tē-ō-kal'(y)i, n.* a Mexican pyramid temple. [Nahuatl,—*teotl*, god, *calli*, house.]

tepee, teepee *tē'pē, ti-pē', n.* an American Indian tent formed of skins, etc., stretched over a frame of converging poles. [Sioux *tipī*, dwelling.]

tepid *tep'id, adj.* moderately warm: lukewarm.—*ns.* **tepid'ity, tep'idness** lukewarmness. [L. *tepidus*—*tepēre*, to be warm.]

tequila, tequilla *tə-kē'lə, n.* Mexican intoxicating drink made from an agave. [From district of Mexico.]

ter- *tûr-,* in composition, thrice.—*adj.* **tercentenary** (*tûr'sən-tē'nə-ri,* or *-ten'ə-ri,* or *tûr-sen'ti-nə-ri*) of three hundred (usu. years).—*n.* a 300th anniversary. —*adj.* **tercentennial** (*tûr-sen-ten'yəl*) of 300 years.— *n.* a 300th anniversary.—*adj.* **tervalent** (*tûr'və-lənt, tər-vā'lənt*) trivalent. [L.]

tera- *ter'ə-, pfx.* ten to the twelfth power, formerly **megamega-**, as in *terawatt.*

teras *ter'əs,* (*med.*) *n.* a monstrosity:—*pl.* **ter'ata.**—*n.* **ter'atism** a monster: an abnormal person or animal, esp. as a foetus.—*adj.* **teratogenic** (*ter-ə-tō-jen'ik*) producing monsters: causing abnormal growth (in a foetus.).—*ns.* **terat'ogen** an agent that raises the incidence of congenital malformations; **teratogeny** (*-toj'i-ni*) the production of monsters.—*adjs.* **ter'atoid** monstrous; **teratolog'ic, -al.**—*ns.* **teratol'ogist** (*teratol'ogy* the study of malformations or abnormal growths, animal or vegetable; **teratō'ma** a tumour, containing tissue from all three layers of an embryo:—*pl.* **teratō'mata**. [Gr. *teras, -atos,* a monster.]

terbium *tûr'bi-əm, n.* a rare metal (symbol Tb; at. numb. 65) found in certain yttrium minerals.—*adj.* **ter'bic**. [From *Ytterby;* see **yttrium**.]

tercel *tûrs'əl,* **tiercel** *tēr'səl, ns.* a male hawk. [O.Fr. *tercel*—L. *tertius,* third, perh. as being one-third smaller than the female, or as supposed to hatch from the last egg of three.]

tercentenary, tercentennial. See **ter-**.

tercet *tûr'sit, n.* a group of three lines in verse. [It. *terzetto.*]

terebene *ter'i-bēn, n.* a light-yellow disinfectant liquid, used as a solvent for paint.—*n.* **ter'ebinth** the turpentine-tree (*Pistacia terebinthus;* family Anacardiaceae).—*adj.* **terebinth'ine** of or relating to the

terebinth: of, relating to, resembling turpentine. [Gr. *terebinthos.*]

Teredo *te-rē'dō, n.* the ship-worm genus of molluscs: (without *cap.*) a mollusc of the genus:—*pl.* **terē'dos, -dines** (*-din-ēz*). [L. *terēdō, ınıs*—Gr. *terēdōn, -onos,* a boring worm—root of *teirein,* to wear away.]

terete *tə-rēt', ter'ēt,* (*biol.*) *adj.* smooth and cylindrical. [L. *terēs, terētis,* smooth, *terēre,* to rub.]

tergum *tûr'gəm, n.* the back: the back or back plate of a somite.—*adj.* **ter'gal.**—*v.i.* **ter'giversate** (*-ji-;* L. *versārī,* to turn) to turn one's back: to desert: to shuffle, shift, use evasions.—*ns.* **tergiversā'tion; ter'giversātor**. [L. *tergum,* the back.]

term *tûrm, n.* an end: the normal time of child-birth: any limited period: the time for which anything lasts: a division of the academic or school year: a period of sittings: (in *pl.*) conditions, stipulations: (in *pl.*) charge, fee: a quantity added to or subtracted from others in an expression (*alg.*): an item in a series: that which may be a subject or predicate of a proposition: a word used in a specially understood or defined sense: an expression generally: a bust in continuity with its pedestal.—*v.t.* to call, designate.—*adj.* **term'less** endless: unconditional.—*adj.* and *adv.* **term'ly.**—*n.* a publication appearing once a term.— *n.* **term'or** one who holds an estate for a term of years or for life.—**term'-time.**—**bring to terms** to compel to the acceptance of conditions; **come to terms** to come to an agreement: to submit; **come to terms with** (*fig*) to find a way of living with (some personal trouble or difficulty); **in terms of** having or using as unit: in the language peculiar to; **on speaking terms** friendly enough to speak to each other: well enough acquainted to speak; **on terms** in friendly relations: on an equal footing. [Fr. *terme*—L. *terminus,* a boundary.]

termagant *tûr'mə-gənt, n.* a boisterous brawler or bully, esp. a woman.—*adj.* boisterous: brawling.—*n.* **ter'magancy.**—*adv.* **ter'magantly**. [M.E. *Termagan* or *Tervagant,* a supposed Muslim idol, represented in old plays as of a violent character.]

Terminus *tûr'min'əs, n.* the Roman god of boundaries: (the following meanings without *cap.*) a boundary stone: an end-point, esp. of a route, railway or electric circuit: a railway station at such a point:—*pl.* **ter'mini** (*-i*).—*n.* **terminabil'ity.**—*adj.* **ter'minable** that may come or be brought to an end.—*n.* **ter'minableness.**—*adv.* **ter'minably.**—*adj.* **ter'minal** of, at, forming, or marking, an end, boundary, or terminus: final: suffering from a terminal illness: of a term: occurring every term.—*n.* an end: an ending: a rail, air, or other terminus: the storage base and distribution centre at the head of e.g. an oil pipe-line: a free end in an open electric circuit: a device linked to a computer and at a distance from it, by which the computer can be operated (also **terminal unit**).—*adv.* **ter'minally.**—*v.t.* and *v.i.* (often with *with* or *in*) **ter'minate.**—*n.* **termina'tion** ending.—*adjs.* **termina'tional; ter'minative** tending to terminate or determine: expressive of completion: definitive: absolute.—*adv.* **ter'minatively.**—*n.* **ter'minātor.**— *adjs.* **ter'minatory; terminolog'ical.**—*adv.* **terminolog'ically.**—*n.* **terminol'ogy** nomenclature: the set of terms used in any art, science, etc.—**terminal illness** a fatal disease in its final stages; **terminal unit** see **terminal** above; **terminal velocity** speed of object on impact with a target: the greatest speed attained by an object falling or fired through a fluid; **terminological inexactitude** (*facet.*) a lie [L. *Terminus, terminus.*]

terminus *tûr'min-əs, ter'min-ōōs,* (L.) *n.* the end, limit. —**terminus ad quem** (*ad kwem*) the limit to which: destination; **terminus a quo** (*ā kwō*) the limit from which starting-point.

termite tûr'mīt, n. a so-called white-ant, a pale-coloured insect only superficially like an ant.—ns. **termitarium** (tûr-mi-tā'ri-əm), **ter'mitary** (-tər-i-) a nest or mound of termites. [L. termes, termitis, a wood-worm.]

termly, termor. See term.

tern[1] tûrn, n. a long-winged aquatic bird allied to the gulls. [Cf. O.N. therna; O.E. stearn, tearn.]

tern[2] tûrn, n. a three, set of three.—adjs. **ter'nal** threefold; **ter'nary** in threes: of three components: based on three: of a third order.—adj. **ter'nate** with three leaflets (bot.): grouped in threes.—adv. **ter'nately.** [L. ternī, three each—trēs, three.]

terne tûrn, n. an alloy, chiefly of lead and tin, known as **terne metal:** sheet-iron or steel coated with this alloy (also **terne plate**).—v.t. **terne** to cover with terne metal. [Fr. terne, dull.]

terotechnology ter'ō-tek-nol'ə-ji, n. the application of managerial, financial, engineering and other skills to extend the operational life of, and increase the efficiency of, equipment and machinery. [Gr. tereo, to watch, observe, and technology.]

terpene tûr'pēn, n. any one of a group of hydrocarbons with a composition $C_{10}H_{16}$.—n. **terpin'eol** a terpene alcohol used extensively as a perfume base. [turpentine.]

Terpsichore tərp-sik'ə-rē, n. the Muse of choral song and dance.—adj. **terpsichoŕe'an** relating to dancing. [Gr. Terpsichorē—terpsis, delight—terpein, to enjoy, choros, dance.]

terra ter'ə, n. the Latin and Italian word for earth: any area of higher land on the moon's surface:—pl. **terr'ae** (-ē).—n. **terrā'rium** a vivarium for land animals or, usu. in the form of a large, often sealed, bottle or the like, for plants:—pl. **-iums, -ia.**—**terra alba** (al'bə) any of various white, earth-like substances such as gypsum, kaolin, pipeclay, etc.; **terr'acotta** a composition of clay and sand used for statues, etc., and, esp. formerly, as building material for facings, etc.: an object of art made of it: its colour, a brownish red.—Also adj.—**terr'a-fir'ma** properly, mainland: (coll. and erroneously) dry land.

terrace ter'is, n. a raised level bank or walk: a level stretch along the side or top of a slope: ground or a structure that rises stepwise: a balcony: a connected row of houses, properly one overlooking a slope: the open areas rising in tiers around a football stadium, where spectators stand.—v.t. to form into a terrace.—adj. **terr'aced** in terraces.—n. **terr'acing.**—**terrace(d) house** one of the houses forming a terrace. [Fr. terrasse—It. terrazza—L.L. terrācea, an earthen mound—L. terra, the earth.]

terracotta. See terra.

terrain ter'ān, or -ān', n. ground, a tract, regarded as a field of view or of operations, or as having some sort of unity or prevailing character. [Fr., from a L.L. form of terrēnum, terrene.]

Terramycin® ter-ə-mī'sin, n. an antibiotic effective against a wide range of bacteria. [L. terra, the earth, and Gr. mykēs, fungus.]

terrapin ter'ə-pin, n. an American freshwater or brackish-water tortoise of many kinds: extended to European water tortoises. [Of Algonquin origin.]

terrazzo te-rat'sō, -raz'ō, n. a mosaic covering for concrete floors consisting of marble or other chips set in cement and then polished:—pl. **terrazz'os.** [It., terrace, balcony.]

terrene ti-rēn', ter'ēn, adj. of the earth: earthly: mundane: earthy: terrestrial.—n. a region, terrain. [L. terrēnus—terra, the earth.]

terreplein ter', tär'plān, n. the top of a rampart, or space behind the parapet. [Fr.,—L. terra, earth, plēnus, full.]

terrestrial ti-res'tri-əl, adj. of, or existing on, the earth: earthly: living or growing on land or on the ground: representing the earth.—n. a dweller on earth.—adv. **terres'trially.** [L. terrestris—terra, the earth.]

terret ter'it, n. a ring or loop through which driving reins pass. [O.Fr. toret, dim. of tor, tour, a round.]

terrible ter'i-bl, adj. fitted to excite terror or awe: awful: dreadful: very bad: very notable, exceeding (coll.).—n. **terr'ibleness**—adv. **terr'ibly** in a terrible manner: very (coll.). [L. terribilis—terrēre, to frighten.]

terricolous ter-ik'ə-ləs, adj. living in or on the soil. [L. terricola, a dweller upon earth—terra, earth, colēre, to inhabit.]

terrier ter'i-ər, n. a small dog of various breeds, orig. one that would follow burrowing animals underground. [O.Fr.,—L.L. terrārius (adj.)—terra, land.]

terrify ter'i-fī, v.t. to cause terror in: to frighten greatly:—pr.p. **terr'ifying;** pa.t. and pa.p. **terr'ified.**—adj. **terrif'ic** creating or causing terror: fitted to terrify: dreadful: prodigious (coll.): (loosely) very good, enjoyable, attractive, etc. (coll.).—adv. **terrif'ically.** [L. terrificāre—terrēre, to terrify, facēre, to make.]

terrigenous te-rij'i-nəs, adj. earth-born: derived from the land. [L. terrigenus—terra, earth, genēre (gignēre), to produce.]

terrine te-rēn', n. a casserole, etc., orig. of earthenware: a dish of meat or fish, etc., cooked in it. [Fr.; see tureen.]

territory ter'i-tər-i, n. possessions in land: the whole, or a portion, of the land belonging to a state: part of a confederation with an organised government but not yet admitted to statehood: a dependency: a region: a jurisdiction: a field of activity (lit. and fig.): domain: an area that an animal or bird treats as its own.—adj. **territo'rial,**—n. a soldier in the Territorial Army.—v.t. **territo'rialise, -ize** to make a territory of: to make territorial: to put on a territorial basis.—n. **territorial'ity.**—adv. **territo'rially.**—adj. **terr'itoried** possessed of territory.—**Territorial Army** the name (1920–67, and from 1980) of the voluntary military force organised on a territorial basis; **territorial imperative** the instinct, in vertebrate animals, to occupy and defend a particular area; **territorial waters** that part of the sea reckoned as part of the adjacent state—orig. within three-mile limit. [L. territōrium, domain of a town.]

terror ter'ər, n. extreme fear: a time of, or government by, terrorism: an object of dread: one who makes himself a nuisance (coll.).—n. **terrorisā'tion, -z-.**—v.t. **terr'orise, -ize** to terrify: to govern by terror.—ns. **terr'oriser, -z-; terr'orism** an organised system of intimidation, esp. for political ends; **terr'orist.**—adj. **terr'or-stricken** smitten with terror.—**King of Terrors** death; **Reign of Terror,** or **the Terror,** the period in the first French Revolution when thousands went to the guillotine. [L. terror—terrēre, to frighten.]

terry ter'i, n. a pile fabric with uncut looped pile: one of the loops.—Also adj.

terse tûrs, adj. compact or concise.—adv. **terse'ly.**—ns. **terse'ness; tersion** (tûr'shən) wiping. [L. tersus—tergēre, tersum, to rub clean.]

tertial tûr'shl, adj. of the third rank among flight-feathers of a wing.—n. a tertiary flight-feather.—adj. **ter'tian** (-shən) occurring every other day (i.e. on the third day, reckoning both first and last days).—n. a fever with paroxysms every other day.—adj. **ter'tiary** (-shər-i) of the third degree, order, or formation: tertial (ornith.): (with cap.) of the third great division of the geological record and time, including Eocene, Oligocene, Miocene, Pliocene: ranking above secondary (esp. of education).—*n.* the Tertiary period: a tertiary feather: that which is tertiary.—**tertiary college** a college, esp. one with vocational courses, for the teaching of sixth-form level students. [L. *tertiālis, tertiānus, tertiārius*—*tertius*, third.]

tertium quid (L.) *tûr'sh(y)əm kwid, ter'ti-ŏōm*, a third something related to two specific known things.

tervalent. See ter-.

Terylene® *ter'i-lēn, n.* a synthetic fabric of polyester fibres, light, strong and crease-resistant.

tesla *tes'lə, n.* the unit of magnetic flux density, equal to 1 weber per sq. metre.—**tesla coil** (*elect.*) a simple source of high voltage oscillations for rough testing of vacuums and gas (by discharge colour) in vacuum systems. [N. *Tesla*, U.S. inventor.]

tessella *tes-el'ə, n.* a little tessera:—*pl.* **tessell'ae** (*-ē, -i*).—*adj.* **tess'ellar.**—*v.t.* **tessellate** (*tes'i-lāt*) to pave with tesserae: to mark like a mosaic.—*v.i.* (of a number of identical shapes) to fit together exactly, leaving no spaces.—*adj.* marked out in little squarish areas.—*adj.* **tess'ellated.**—*n.* **tessellā'tion.** [L. *tessella*, dim. of *tessera*; see next.]

tessera *tes'ə-rə, n* one of the small pieces of which a mosaic is made:—*pl.* **tess'erae** (*-ē;* L. *-ī*).—*adj.* **tess'eral** of tesserae: cubic, isometric (*crystal.*). [L. *tessera*, a die, small cube—Gr. *tessares, tesseres, -a*, four.]

tessitura *tes-i-tōō'rə, n.* the ordinary compass of a voice. [It., texture.]

test[1] *test, n.* any critical trial: a means of trial: anything used to distinguish or detect substances, a reagent (*chem.*): a trial of fitness for an examination: an oath or other evidence of religious belief required as a condition of office or exercise of rights: a test-match.—*v.t.* to put to proof: to try or examine critically.—*n.* **test'a** a hard shell: a seed-coat, derived from the ovule integuments.—*adjs.* **test'able; testaceous** (*-ā'shəs*) of or having a hard shell: brick-red.—*ns* **testee'; test'er.**—*n.* and *adj.* **test'ing.**—**test ban** the banning, by mutual agreement between nations, of the testing of any or all nuclear weapons; **test'-bed** an iron framework on which a machine is placed for testing: anything with a like purpose (also *fig.*), **test'-case** a law case that may settle similar questions in the future; **test'-drive** a trial drive of a motor-vehicle, usu. with a view to purchasing the vehicle if it is satisfactory.—Also *v.t.*—**test'-flight** a trial flight of a new aeroplane.—*vs.t.* **test'-fly; test'-market** to offer for sale in order to test demand for, success of, etc., a product.—**test'-match** an international cricket match forming one of a series; **test'-paper** paper saturated with some substance that changes colour when exposed to certain chemicals: a paper or questions to test fitness for a more serious examination;**test pilot** one whose work is testing new aircraft by flying them, **test'-tube** a glass cylinder closed at one end, used in chemistry, bacteriology, etc.—**test-tube baby** esp. formerly, a child born as as the result of artificial insemination, now usu. one born from an ovum implanted in the womb after fertilisation in a laboratory. [O.Fr. *test* and *teste*—L. *testa*, an earthen pot, a potsherd, a shell.]

test[2] *test, v.t.* to attest legally and date.—*ns.* **test'acy** (*-ə-si*) the state of being testate, **testā'mur** a certificate of having passed an examination.—*adj* **test'āte** having made and left a will.—*ns.* **testā'tion** a witnessing, a giving by will; **testā'tor** one who leaves a will:—*fem.* **testā'trix.** [L. *testārī*, to testify, witness, pa.p. (neut.) *testātum;* 1st pers. pl *testāmur*]

testament *tes'tə-mənt, n.* that which testifies, or in

which an attestation is made: the solemn declaration in writing of one's will: a will: (with *cap.*) either of the main divisions (**Old** and **New**) of the Bible.—*adjs.* **testamental** (*-ment'*), **testamen'tary** pertaining to a testament or will: bequeathed or done by will.—*adv* **testamen'tarily.** [L. *testāmentum.*]

testamur, testate, etc. See test[2].

testee. See test[1].

tester[1] *tes'tər, n.* a canopy or its support, or both, esp. over a bed. [O.Fr. *testre*, the vertical part of a bed behind the head, and *testiere*, a head-covering—*teste* (Fr. *tête*), head—L. *testa*, an earthen pot, the skull.]

tester[2]. See test[1].

testicle *tes'ti-kl, n.* a male reproductive gland.—*adjs.* **testic'ular** of or like a testicle; **testic'ulate, -d** like a testicle.—*n* **tes'tis** a testicle: a rounded body like it:—*pl.* **tes'tes** (*-ēz*). [L. *testis* and its dim. *testiculus.*]

testify *tes'ti-fī, v.i.* to bear witness: to make a solemn declaration: to protest or declare a charge (with *against*).—*v.t.* to bear witness to: to affirm or declare solemnly or on oath: to proclaim, declare:—*pr.p.* **tes'-tifying;** *pa.t.* and *pa.p.* **tes'tified.**—*ns.* **testificā'tion** the act of testifying or of bearing witness; **testif'icātor.**—*adjs.* **testif'icatory; tes'tified.**—*n.* **tes'tifier.** [L. *testificārī*—*testis*, a witness, *facēre*, to make.]

testimony *tes'ti-mən-i, n.* evidence: declaration to prove some fact: proof.—*adj.* **testi'mōnial** of, affording, of the nature of, testimony.—*n.* a written attestation: a writing or certificate bearing testimony to one's character or abilities: a gift or memorial as a token of respect.—*v.t.* **testimō'nialise, -ize** to present with a testimonial. [L. *testimōnium*—*testārī*, to witness.]

testis. See testicle.

testosterone *tes-tos'tər-ōn, n.* the chief male sex hormone, a steroid secreted by the testes.

testudo *tes-tū'dō, n.* a wheeled shelter used by Roman besiegers: a similar shelter made by joining shields:—*pl.* **testū'dōs, testū'dinēs.**—*adjs.* **testū'dinal, testū'dinary, testūdin'eous** like a tortoise, tortoise-shell, or a testudo. [L. *testūdō, -inis*, tortoise.]

testy *tes'ti, adj* irritable.—*adv* **tes'tily.**—*n.* **tes'tiness.** [O.Fr. *testif*, headstrong—*teste* (Fr. *tête*), head—L. *testa*, pot.]

tetanus *tet'ə-nəs, n.* a disease marked by painful spasms of the muscles of the jaw and other parts: the state of prolonged contraction of a muscle under quickly repeated stimuli.—*adjs.* **tet'anal, tet'anoid, tetanic** (*ti-tan'ik*).—*n.* **tet'any** heightened excitability of the motor nerves with painful muscular cramps. [L.,—Gr. *tetanos*—*teinein*, to stretch.]

tetchy, techy *tech'i, adj.* irritable.—*adv.* **tetch'ily.**—*n.* **tetch'iness.**

tête *tet,* (Fr.) *n.* a head.—**tête-à-tête** (*a-tet*) a private confidential interview: a sofa for two face to face:—*pl* **tête-à-têtes, têtes-à-têtes.**—*adj.* confidential, secret —*adv.* in private conversation: face to face.

tether *tedh'ər, n.* a rope or chain for confining a beast within certain limits —*v.t.* to confine with a tether: to restrain within certain limits.—**at the end of one's tether** desperate, having no further strength, resources, etc. [App. O.N. *tjŏthr.*]

tetra- *tet'rə-*, **tetr-**, in composition, four.—*adj* **tetraba'sic** capable of reacting with four equivalents of an acid: (of acids) having four replaceable hydrogen atoms.—*ns.* **tetrachlo'ride** any compound with four chlorine atoms per molecule; **tetrachlor(o)-eth'ylene** C_2Cl_4, a liquid used in dry-cleaning, as a solvent, etc.; **tet'rachord** (*-kōrd*) a four-stringed instrument: a series of four sounds, forming a scale of two tones and a half.—*adj.* **tetracyclic** (*-sī'klik*) of, in, or with four whorls or rings.—*ns.* **tetracy'cline** a crystalline antibiotic used to treat a wide range of infections, esp. of the respiratory and urinary tracts; **tetrad** (*tet'rad*) a group of four: an atom, radical, or element having a combining power of four (*chem.*).— *adjs.* **tet'rad, tetrad'ic; tetraethyl** (*-eth'il*) having four ethyl groups, as **tetraethyl lead** or **lead tetraethyl**, Pb(C₂H₅)₄, used in motor spirit as an anti-knock agent.—*n.* **tet'ragon** (*-gən, -gon*) a plane figure of four angles.—*adj.* **tetragonal** (*-rag'ə-nəl*) having the form of a tetragon; referable to three axes at right angles, two of them equal (*crystal.*).—*ns.* **tetragram** (*-gram*) a word or inscription of four letters: the **tetragrammaton; tetragramm'aton** the name YaH-WeH, JeHoVaH, etc., as written with four Hebrew letters, regarded as a mystic symbol: any other sacred word of four letters, as the Latin *Deus.*—*adj.* **tetrahe'dral.**—*n.* **tetrahedron** (*-hē'drən*) a solid figure or body with four plane faces.—*adj.* **tetram'eral** four-parted.—*n.* **tetram'erism** division into four parts.—*adj.* **tetram'erous** having four parts, or parts in fours.—*n.* **tetrameter** (*te-tram'i-tər*) a verse of four measures.—Also *adj.*—*ns.* **tetraplē'gia** quadriplegia; **tetrapod** (*-pod*) a four-footed animal. —*adjs.* **tetrap'teran, tetrapterous** (*te-trap'tə-ran, -ras*) four-winged.—*ns.* **tetrarch** (*tet'rärk*, or *tē'trärk*) under the Romans, the ruler of the fourth part of a province: a subordinate prince: the commander of a subdivision of a Greek phalanx; **tet'rarchy** the office, rank, time of office, or jurisdiction of a tetrarch: the fourth part of a province (also **tet'rarchate**); **tet'rastich** (*-stik*) a stanza or set of four lines.—*adjs.* **tetrastichal** (*ti-tras'ti-kl*), **tetrastichic** (*tet-rə-stik'ik*) of, of the nature of, tetrastichs; **tetras'tichous** in four rows; **tetratom'ic** having, or composed of, four atoms to a molecule; **tetravalent** (*te-trav'ə-lənt, tet-rə-vā'lənt*) quadrivalent.—*ns.* **tetrode** (*tet'rōd*) a thermionic valve with four electrodes; **tetrox'ide** an oxide with four atoms of oxygen in the molecule; **tetryl** (*tet'ril*) a yellow crystalline explosive compound used as a detonator. [Gr. *tetra-, tettares, tessares,* four.]

tetrabasic ... to ... **tetrahedron.** See **tetra-**.
tetralogy *te-tral'ə-ji, n.* a group of four dramas, usu. three tragic and one satyric: any series of four related dramatic or operatic works or stories. [Gr. *tetralogia—logos,* discourse.]
tetrameral ... to ... **tetrameter.** See **tetra-**.
tetraploid *tet'rə-ploid, adj.* having four times the haploid (twice the normal) number of chromosomes.—*n.* **tet'raploidy** the condition of being tetraploid. [Gr. *tetraploos,* fourfold, *eidos,* form.]
tetrapod ... to ... **tetryl.** See **tetra-**.
Teuton *tū'tən, n.* any speaker of a Germanic language: (*popularly*) a German.—*adj.* **Teutonic** (*-ton'ik*) Germanic—of the linguistic family that includes English, German, Dutch, and the Scandinavian languages: (*popularly*) German in the narrower sense.—*n.* the parent language of the Teutons, primitive Germanic. [L. *Teutonēs,* from the root of O.E. *thēod,* people, nation.]
text *tekst, n.* the actual words of a book, poem, etc., in their original form or any form they have been transmitted in or transmuted into: a book of such words: words set to music: the main body of matter in a book, distinguished from notes, commentary, or other subsidiary matter: matter commented on: a short passage from the Bible taken as the ostensible subject of a sermon, quoted in authority, displayed as a motto, etc.: a theme.—*adj.* **textile** (*-il,* in U.S. *-il*) woven: capable of being woven.—*n.* a woven fabric.—*adj.* **tex'tual** pertaining to, or contained in, the text: serving for a text.—*ns.* **text'ualism** (too) strict adherence to a text, esp. that of the Bible: textual criticism, esp.

of the Bible; **text'ualist** one learned in the text, esp. of the Bible: a literal interpreter: a quoter of texts.— *adv.* **text'ually.**—*adj.* **text'ural** pertaining to, in the matter of, texture.—*adv.* **textur'ally.**—*n.* **text'ure** anything woven, a web: manner of weaving or connecting: disposition of the parts of a body: structural impression resulting from the manner of combining or interrelating the parts of a whole, as in music, art, etc.: the quality conveyed to the touch, esp. by woven fabrics.—*v.t.* to give (specified) texture to, texturise: to weave.—*adjs.* **text'ured; text'ureless.**—*v.t.* **text'urise, -ize** to give a particular texture to.—*adj.* **text'-book, text'book** (of an operation, example, etc.) exactly as planned, in perfect accordance with theory or calculation.—*n.* a book containing the main principles of a subject.—**textual criticism** critical study directed towards determining the true reading of a text.—**texturised vegetable protein** a vegetable substance, usu. made from soya beans, prepared to resemble meat in appearance and taste. [L. *texēre, textum,* to weave.]

Thai *tī, tä'ē, adj.* of Thailand.—*n.* a native of (also **Thai'lander**) or the language of Thailand, country of Asia known before 1939 and between 1945 and 1949 as Siam.
thalamus *thal'ə-mas, n.* an inner room, chamber: the receptacle of a flower: part of the mid-brain where the optic nerve emerges:—*pl.* **thal'ami.**—*adj.* **thal'amic** (or *thal-am'ik*) of the thalamus. [Gr. *thalamos,* an inner room, bedroom.]
thalassian *tha-las'i-ən, adj.* marine.—*n.* a sea turtle.— *n.* **thalassaemia, thalassemia** (*thal-ə-sē'mi-ə*) a hereditary disorder of the blood causing anaemia, sometimes fatal in children.—*adjs.* **thalassae'mic, thalassē'mic; thalass'ic** marine: of the seas. [Gr. *thalassa, thalatta,* sea.]
thaler *tä'lər, n.* an obsolete German silver coin. [Ger.; cf. **dollar.**]
Thalia *thə-lī'ə, n.* the Muse of comedy and pastoral poetry: one of the Graces.—*adj.* **thali'an.** [Gr. *Thaleia, Thaliā—thallein,* to bloom.]
thalidomide *thə-lid'ə-mīd, tha-, n.* a non-barbiturate sedative drug, withdrawn in 1961 because found to cause malformation in the foetus if taken during pregnancy.—**thalidomide baby** an infant showing the teratogenic effects of thalidomide.
thallium *thal'i-əm, n.* a highly toxic lead-like metal (Tl; at. numb. 81) discovered in 1861.—*adjs.* **thall'ic** of trivalent thallium; **thall'ous** of univalent thallium. [Gr. *thallos,* a young shoot, from the bright green line in its spectrum.]
thallus *thal'əs, n.* a plant body not differentiated into leaf, stem, and root:—*pl.* **thall'uses, thall'i.**—*adjs.* **thall'iform; thall'ine; thall'oid.**—*n.pl.* **Thallophy'ta** the lowest main division of the vegetable kingdom—bacteria, fungi, algae.—*n.* **thall'ophyte** a member of the Thallophyta. [Gr. *thallos,* a young shoot.]
thalweg *täl'vähh, -veg, n.* the longitudinal profile of the bottom of a river-bed. [Ger.,—*Thal* (now *Tal*), valley, *Weg,* way.]
than *dhan, dhən, conj.* used after a comparative, actual or felt, to introduce that which is in the lower degree. —*prep.* in comparison with. [O.E. *thonne, thanne, thænne,* than, orig. then.]
thanage. See **thane.**
thanatism *than'ə-tizm, n.* belief that the soul dies with the body.—*n.* **than'atist.**—*adj.* **than'atoid** apparently dead: deathly: deadly.—*ns.* **thanatol'ogy** the scientific study of death; **thanatophō'bia** a morbid dread of death; **thanatop'sis** a view of, or reflection upon, death; **thanatō'sis** gangrene. [Gr. *thanatos,* death.]
thane *thān, n.* in Old English times a king's

companion, a noble of lower rank than eorl or ealdorman: a hereditary (not military) tenant of the
crown (*Scot. hist.*).—*ns.* thā′nage, thane′dom,
thane′hood, thane′ship.—See also thegn. [O.E.
thegn, servant, follower, courtier, nobleman.]

thank *thangk, n.* (usu. in *pl.*) gratitude: an expression
of gratitude.—*v.t.* to express gratitude to:
(*ironically*) to blame.—*n.* thank′er.—*adj.* thank′ful
grateful: gladly relieved.—*adv.* thank′fully grate-
fully, with a thankful feeling: one feels thankful (that).—*n.* thank′fulness.—*adj.* thank′less
unthankful: not expressing thanks for favours:
not gaining even thanks.—*adv.* thank′lessly.—*n.*
thank′lessness.—thanks′giver; thanks′giving the
act of giving thanks: a public acknowledgment of divine
goodness and mercy: (with *cap.*) a day (**Thanksgiving
Day**) set apart for this, esp. in the U.S.A. fourth
Thursday of November.—have (only) oneself to
thank for to be the cause of (one's own misfortune);
I'll thank you, him, etc. to used, usu. in anger, to
introduce a request or command; no thanks to not
owing to, implying that gratitude is far from being
due; thanks, thank you elliptical forms of thanks be
to you, I thank you, or the like; thanks be thank God;
thanks to owing to; thank you for nothing an expression implying that no gratitude is due at all. [O.E.
thanc, thonc.]

thar *t′här, tär, n.* properly the serow: by confusion
applied to the tahr. [Nepali (Indic language of
Nepal) *thär.*]

that *dhat, demons* pron. and *demons. adj.* (*pl.* those)
pointing out a person or thing: the former: the more
distant: not this but the other: the one to be indicated
or defined.—*rel. pron.* (*sing.* and *pl.*; *dhat, dhat*)
who, whom, or which (esp. when defining or limiting,
not merely linking on an addition).—*adv.* (*dhat; coll.*
with a *neg.*, or *dial.*) to that extent.—*conj.* (*dhat,
dhat*) used to introduce a noun clause, an adverbial
clause of purpose, reason, or consequence, or an expression of a wish in the subjunctive.—*adv.* that′-
away (*U.S. dial.*, or *facet.*) in that direction.—*n.*
that′ness the quality of being a definite thing, that.—
and all that and all the rest of that sort of thing—a
summary way of dismissing what is vaguely thought
of; (and) that's that (and) that is the end of that matter: no more of that; at that at that point: moreover:
nevertheless; (just) like that straight off. [O.E.
thæt, neut. demons. pron.]

thatch *thach, v.t.* to cover, or roof, with straw, reeds,
heather, palm-leaves, or the like.—*v.i.* to do
thatching.—*n.* a covering or covering material of the
kind: thick hair.—*adj.* thatched.—*ns.* thatch′er;
thatch′ing the act or art of covering with thatch:
materials used for thatching.—Also *adj.* [O.E.
thæc, covering, thatch, and *theccan,* to cover.]

thauma- *thö′mə-,* thaumat- *-mət-,* in composition,
wonder, miracle.—*ns.* thaumatogeny (*-toj′*) the doctrine of the miraculous origination of life; thau′mat-
rope an optical toy that combines pictures by persistence of images in the eye; thaumaturge (*tho′mə-tûrj*)
a wonder-worker.—*adjs.* thaumatur′gic, -al.—*n.pl.*
thaumatur′gics wonderful, esp. magical, performances: feats of legerdemain.—*ns.* thaumatur′gism;
thaumatur′gist. [Gr. *thauma, -atos,* wonder,
thaumatourgos (*-ergon,* work), a wonder-worker.]

thaw *tho, v.i.* to melt or grow liquid, as ice: to become
so warm as to melt ice: to become less cold, stiff, or
reserved in manner (*fig.*).—*v.t.* to cause to melt.—*n.*
the melting of ice or snow by heat: the change of
weather that causes it.—Also *fig.*—*n.* thaw′er.—*n.*
and *adj.* thaw′ing.—thaw out to return from frozen to
normal condition. [O.E. *thawian.*]

the[1] *dhē* (emphatic), *dhə* (usu.), *dhı, dhē* (before

vowels), *demons. adj.* called the definite article, used
to denote a particular person or thing: also to denote
a species. [O.E. *the* (supplanting *se*), masc. of *thæt,*
that.]

the[2] *dhə, adv.* (with comparatives) by how much: by so
much. [O.E. *thȳ,* by that, by that much, the instrumental case of the def. art.]

Thea *thē′ə, n.* the tea genus of plants. [From the root
of tea, but taken as if from Gr. *theä,* goddess.]

theanthropic *thē-an-throp′ik, adj.* at once divine and
human: embodying deity in human forms.—*ns.* the-
an′thropism, thean′thropy the ascribing of human
qualities to deity, or divine qualities to man: a doctrine of union of the divine and human; thean′thropist.
[Gr. *theos,* a god, *anthropos,* man.]

thearchy *thē′ärk-i, n.* a theocracy: a body of divine
rulers.—*adj.* thear′chic. [Gr. *theos,* a god, *archein,*
to rule.]

theatre (*U.S.* theater) *thē′ə-tər, n.* a structure, orig. in
the open air, for drama or other spectacle: a cinema
(*U.S.* and *Austr.*): any place backed by a curving
hillside or rising by steps like seats of a theatre: a
building or room which is adapted for anatomical or
surgical demonstrations, etc.: a scene of action, field
of operations. (with *the*) the social unit comprising
actors, producers, etc., or its characteristic environment and conditions: (with *the*) plays or a specified
group of plays, collectively.—*adjs.* the′atral; theatric
(*-at′*), -al relating or suitable to, or savouring of, the
stage: stagy: histrionic: aiming at or producing
dramatic effects.—*ns.* theat′ricalism, theatrical′ity
staginess, artificiality.—*adv.* theat′rically.—*n.*
theat′ricalness.—*n.pl.* theat′ricals dramatic performances: theatrical affairs, properties, or persons.
—*ns.* theat′ricism theatricality, affectation, staginess; theat′rics the staging of plays, etc., or the art
of doing this: histrionics.—the′atre-go′er one who
habitually goes to the theatre; the′atre-in-the-round′
a theatre with central, or arena, stage and audience
on all sides: the style of staging plays in such a
theatre.—theatre of cruelty a branch of drama, intended to induce in the audience a feeling of suffering
and an awareness of evil; theatre of the absurd a
branch of drama dealing with fantastic deliberately
unreal situations, in reaction against the tragedy and
irrationality of life. [Gr. *theätron—theaesthai,* to
see.]

Thebes *thēbz, n.* a city of ancient Boeotia (Greece): a
city of ancient Egypt.—*n.* the′baine (*-bä-ēn, -ba-ēn*)
an alkaloid ($C_{19}H_{21}NO_3$) got from opium.—*adj.*
The′ban of Thebes.—*n.* a native of Thebes: a
Boeotian. [Gr. *Thēbai,* Thebes.]

theca *thē′kə, n.* a sheath, case, or sac: a spore-case. a
lobe or loculus of an anther:—*pl.* the′cae (*-sē*).—
adjs. the′cal of a theca; the′cate having a theca.
[Latinised from Gr. *thēkē,* case, sheath.]

thee *dhē, pron., dat.* and *accus.* of thou.—*v.t.* to use
thee in speaking to. [O.E. *thē, the.*]

theft *theft, n.* act of thieving: a thing stolen. [O.E.
theofth, thiefth—theof, thief]

thegn *thän,* (*hist.*) *n.* the older form of thane.

theine *thē′in, -in, n.* caffeine.—*ns.* the′ic one who
drinks overmuch tea or who suffers from theism;
the′ism a morbid state resulting from overmuch tea-
drinking. [**Thea.**]

their *dhār, dhər, pron.* (*gen. pl.*) or *poss. adj.* of or
belonging to them.—*pron.* theirs (a double genitive)
used predicatively or absolutely. [O.N. *theirra,*
superseding O.E. *thæra,* gen. pl. of the def. art.]

theism[1] *thē′izm, n.* belief in the existence of God with
or without a belief in a special revelation.—*n.* the′ist.
—*adjs.* theist′ic, -al. [Gr. *theos,* God.]

theism[2]. See theine.

them *dhem, dhəm, pron., dat.* and *accus.* of **they.—demons. adj.** (*dial.* or *coll.*; *dhem*) those.—**them and us** (*coll.*) any of various pairs of groups in society, such as management and workforce, considered to be in opposition to each other. [O.N. *theim* or O.E. (Anglian) *thæm* (dat.).]

theme *thēm, n.* a subject set or proposed for discussion, or spoken or written about: a thesis, a brief essay or exercise: the stem of a word without its inflexions: subject, a short melody developed with variations or otherwise (*mus.*).—*n.* **thē'ma** (or *them'ə*) a theme:—*pl.* **them'ata.**—*adj.* **thematic** (*thi-mat'ik*) of, or relating to a theme.—*adv.* **themat'ically.**—**theme song** a melody that is repeated often in a musical drama, film, or radio or television series, and is associated with a certain character, idea, emotion, etc.: a person's characteristic, often repeated, complaint, etc. [Gr. *thēma, -atos*—root of *tithēnai*, to place, set.]

themselves *dhəm-selvz', pron., pl.* of **himself, herself, itself.** [**them, self.**]

then *dhen, dhən, adv.* at that time: afterward: immediately: at another time: further, again: on the other hand, at the same time: for that reason, therefore: in that case.—*adj.* being at that time.—*n.* that time.—*adv.* **thenabout(s)** about that time.—**by then** by that time; **then and there** at once and on the spot. [O.E. *thonne, thanne, thænne.*]

thenar *thē'när, n.* the palm: the ball of the thumb: the sole.—Also *adj.* [Gr. *thēnär, -äros.*]

thence *dhens, adv.* from that place: from those premises: from that time: from that cause.—*advs.* **thence'forth, thencefor'ward** from that time forward: from that place onward. [M.E. *thennes—thenne* (O.E. *thanon*, thence).]

theo- *thē'ō-, -o-,* or *-o'-,* in composition, god.—*In the following article, strict alphabetical order is not followed; in most cases, the abstract noun in -y precedes adjectives, etc., dependent on it.*—**theo-brō'mine** (*-mēn, -mĭn, -min*) an alkaloid got from the chocolate nut; **theocracy** (*thē-ok'rə-si*) that constitution of a state in which God, or a god, is regarded as the sole sovereign, and the laws of the realm as divine commands rather than human ordinances—the priesthood necessarily becoming the officers of the invisible ruler: the state thus governed; **theocrat** (*thē'ō-krat*) a divine or deified ruler.—*adjs.* **theocrat'ic, -al.**—*adv.* **theocrat'ically.**—*ns.* **theocrasy** (*thē-ok'rə-si,* or *thē'ō-krā'si*) a mixture of religions: the identification or equating of one god with another or others: a mystic intimacy with deity reached through profound contemplation; **theodicy** (*thē-od'i-si*) a vindication of the justice of God in establishing a world in which evil exists.—*n.* and *adj.* **theodicē'an.**—*n.* **theogony** (*thē-og'ə-ni*) the birth and genealogy of the gods.—*adjs.* **theogonic** (*thē-ə-gon'ik*), **-al.**—*ns.* **theog'onist** a writer on theogony; **theology** (*thē-ol'ə-ji*) the study of God, religion and revelation: a system of theological doctrine; **theologian** (*thē-ə-lō'jyən*) one well versed in theology: a divine, a professor of or writer on divinity.—*adjs.* **theologic** (*thē-ə-loj'ik*), **-al.**—*adv.* **theolog'ically.**—*v.t.* **theol'ogise, -ize** to render theological.—*v.i.* to discourse, speculate, etc., on theology.—*ns.* **theol'ogiser, -z-; theomachy** (*thē-om'ə-ki*) war among or against the gods, as by the Titans and giants: opposition to the divine will; **theom'achist; theomancy** (*thē'ō-man-si*) divination by means of oracles, or of persons inspired immediately by some divinity.—*adj.* **theoman'tic.**—*ns.* **theomania** (*-mā'ni-ə*) religious madness: belief that one is a god; **theomā'niac.**—*adj.* **theomorphic** (*-mör'fik*) having the form or likeness of a god: in the image of God.—*n.* **theophany** (*thē-of'ə-ni*) a manifestation or appearance of deity to

man.—*adj.* **theophanic** (*thē-ō-fan'ik*).—*ns* **theosophy** (*thē-os'ə-fi*) divine wisdom: immediate divine illumination or inspiration claimed to be possessed by specially gifted men, along with abnormal control over natural forces: the system of doctrine expounded by the Theosophical Society; **theosoph** (*thē'ə-sof*), **theos'opher, theos'ophist.**—*adjs.* **theosoph'ic, -al.**—*adv.* **theosoph'ically.**—**Theosophical Society** a religious body founded by Mme. Blavatsky and others in 1875, whose doctrines include belief in karma and reincarnation. [Gr. *theos,* a god.]

theodolite *thē-od'ə-līt, n.* a surveying instrument for measuring horizontal and vertical angles.

theophylline *thē-ō-fil'ēn, -ĭn, -in, n.* an isomer of theobromine found in tea. [**Thea,** and Gr. *phyllon,* leaf.]

theorem *thē'ə-ram, n.* a demonstrable or established but not self-evident principle: a proposition to be proved.—*adjs.* **theoremat'ic, -al.**—*adv.* **theorem at'ically.**—*n.* **theorematist** (*-rem'ə-tist*).—*adjs.* **theoret'ic, -al** pertaining, according, or given to theory: not practical: speculative.—*n.* (usu. in *pl.*) the speculative parts of a science.—*adv.* **theoret'ically.**—*ns.* **theoretician** (*-et-ish'ən*) one who is concerned chiefly with the theoretical aspect of a subject; **the'oric, the'orique** (*Shak.*) theory, speculation.—*v.i.* **the'orise, -ize** to form a theory: to form opinions solely by theories: to speculate.—*ns.* **the'oriser, -z-; the'orist** a theoriser: one given to theory and speculation: one who is expert in the abstract principles of a subject; **the'ory** an explanation or system of anything: an exposition of the abstract principles of a science or art: speculation as opposed to practice. [Gr. *theōrēma, -atos,* spectacle, speculation, theorem, *theōriā,* view, theory—*theōreein,* to be a spectator, to view.]

therapeutic *ther-ə-pū'tik, adj.* pertaining to the healing art: curative.—*adv.* **therapeu'tically.**—*n. sing* **therapeu'tics** that part of medicine concerned with the treatment and cure of diseases.—*ns.* **therapeu'tist** one versed in therapeutics; **ther'apist; ther'apy** therapeutics: treatment used to combat a disease or an abnormal condition: curative power. [Gr. *therapeutēs,* servant, worshipper, medical attendant—*therapeuein,* to take care of, to heal, *therapeiā,* service, treatment.]

there *dher, dhär, adv.* in that place: at that point: to that place: with regard to that: (also *dhr*) used without any meaning of its own to allow the subject to follow the predicate, and also in corresponding interrogative sentences, etc.: used without any meaning to draw or attract attention.—*n.* that place.—*interj.* expressing reassurance, finality, accompanying a blow, etc.—*advs.* **there'about, -s** (also *-bowts'*) about or near that place: near that number, quantity, degree, or time; **thereaft'er** after or according to that: accordingly; **thereat'** at that place or occurrence: on that account; **thereby'** beside that: about that amount: by that means: in consequence of that; **therefor'** for that; **therefore** (*dher'fər*) for that reason: consequently; **therefrom'** from that; **therein'** in or into that or it; **thereinaft'er, thereinbefore'** later, earlier, in the same document; **therein'to** into that place, thing, matter, etc.; **thereof'** of that: from that: **thereon'** on that; **thereto', thereun'to** to that: in addition; **there'tofore** before that time; **thereun'der** under that; **thereupon'** upon that: immediately; **therewith'** with that: thereupon; **there'withal** with that: immediately after: in addition.—**so there** an expression of triumph, defiance, derision, finality, etc.; **there and then** forthwith; **there or thereabouts** somewhere near. [O.E. *thær;* akin to **the, that,** etc.]

therio-, theri, thero- *thēr', -i-, -ō-,* in composition, beast, mammal.—*adj.* **therianthrop'ic** combining human and animal forms.—*n.* **therian'thropism** the representation or worship of therianthropic forms or gods.—*ns.* **theriol'atry** animal-worship; **ther'iomorph** an animal form in art.—*adj.* **theriomorph'ic** beastlike: of theriomorphism.—*n.* **theriomorph'ism** belief in gods of the form of beasts.—*adjs.* **theriomor'phous** beastlike: mammal-like; **ther'oid** beastlike.—*n.* **therol'ogy** the study of mammals. [Gr. *thēr*, and *thērion*, a wild beast.]

therm *thûrm, n.* 100,000 British thermal units (used as a unit in reckoning payment for gas).—*n.pl.* **thermae** (*-ē*) hot springs or baths.—*adj.* **therm'al** pertaining to heat: warm.—*n.* an ascending current of warm air — *adv.* **therm'ally.**—*adjs.* **therm'ic, -al** of heat.—*adv* **therm'ically.**—*n.* **therm'ion** an electrically charged particle emitted by an incandescent body.—*adj.* **thermion'ic** (**thermionic valve** or **tube** a vacuum tube containing a heated cathode from which electrons are emitted, an anode for collecting some or all of these electrons and, generally, additional electrodes for controlling their flow to the anode).—*n.sing.* **thermion'ics** the science of thermions—*ns.* **thermi'stor** (*thermal resistor*) a semi-conductor, a mixture of certain oxides with finely divided copper, of which the resistance is very sensitive to change of temperature; **therm'ite** (**Thermit®**) a mixture of aluminium powder with oxide of metal (esp. iron), which when ignited evolves great heat, used for local heating and welding.—*adj.* **thermochem'ical.**—*ns.* **thermochem'ist; thermochem'istry** the study of heat changes accompanying chemical action; **therm'o-couple** a pair of metals in contact giving a thermoelectric current.—*adj.* **thermodynam'ic.**—*n.sing.* **thermodynam'ics** the science of heat as a mechanical agent.—*adj.* **thermo-elec'tric.**—*ns.* **thermo-electric'ity** electricity developed by the unequal heating of bodies, esp. between a junction of metals and another part of a circuit; **thermogenesis** (*-jen'*) production of heat, esp. in the body by physiological processes.—*adjs.* **thermogenet'ic, thermogen'ic.** —*ns.* **therm'ogram** a thermograph record of temperature; **therm'ograph** a self-registering thermometer: the photographic apparatus used in thermography.—*adj.* **thermograph'ic.**—*n.* **thermog'raphy** any process of writing, photographing, etc. involving the use of heat.—*adj.* **thermola'bile** readily decomposed by heat.—*ns.* **thermol'ogy** the science of heat; **thermoluminesc'ence** release of light by irradiated material upon subsequent heating; **thermol'ysis** dissociation or dissolution by heat: loss of body heat. —*adj.* **thermolyt'ic.**—*n.* **thermometer** (*-om'i-tar*) an instrument for measuring temperature depending on any of several properties of a substance that vary linearly with change of temperature.—*adjs.* **thermometric** (*-ə-met'rik*), **-al.**—*adv.* **thermomet'rically.**—*ns.* **thermomet'rograph** a self-registering thermometer; **thermom'etry.**—*adjs.* **thermonuc'lear** used of the fusion of nuclei as seen in **thermonuclear reaction,** a power reaction produced by the fusion of nuclei at extremely high temperatures, as in the hydrogen bomb: pertaining to the use of such reactions as a source of power or force; **therm'ophil(e)** (*-fīl*), **thermophil'ic, thermoph'ilous** requiring, or thriving best in, a high temperature.—*n.* **therm'opile** (*-pīl*) an apparatus for the direct conversion of heat into electrical energy.—*adj.* **thermoplast'ic** plastic when heated.—*n.* any resin that can be melted and cooled repeatedly without appreciable change in properties.—*n.* **therm'os** (orig. trademark for) a brand of vacuum flask (also **thermos flask**).—*adj.* **thermosett'ing** setting, after melting and moulding with change of properties.—*n.* **therm'osphere** the region of the earth's atmosphere above the mesosphere, in which the temperature rises steadily with height.—*adj.* **thermosta'ble** not readily decomposed by heating.—*n.* **therm'ostat** a device for keeping temperature steady.—*adj.* **thermostat'ic.**—*adv.* **thermostat'ically.**—*adjs.* **thermotact'ic, thermotax'ic** of or showing thermotaxis.—*n.* **thermotax'is** a taxis towards a position of higher or lower temperature.—*adj.* **thermotrop'ic.**—*n.* **thermot'ropism** (Gr. *tropos,* turning) orientation determined by temperature differences.—**thermal reactor** a nuclear reactor in which fission is induced mainly by low-energy neutrons, **thermal shock** stress, often resulting in fracture, resulting when a body is subjected to sudden changes in temperature; **thermal springs** natural springs of hot water; **thermal underwear** underwear made for exceptional warmth; **thermic lance** a cutting instrument consisting of a steel tube containing metal rods which, with the help of oxygen, are raised to an intense heat [Gr. *thermos,* hot, *thermē,* heat, *thermotēs,* heat.]

thero-. See **thero-.**

thesaurus *thi-so'ras, n.* a treasury: a storehouse of knowledge, esp. of words, quotations, etc., a dictionary. [L.,—Gr. *thēsauros.*]

these *dhēz, demons. adj.* and *demons. pron., pl.* of **this.** [O.E. *thǣs,* a by-form of *thǣs,* pl. of *thēs, thēos, this,* this; cf. **those.**]

thesis *thē'sis, thes'is, n.* a position or that which is set down or advanced for argument: a subject for a scholastic exercise, esp. one presented for a doctorate: an essay on a theme:—*pl.* **theses** (*thē'sēz*). [Gr. *thesis,* from the root of *tithenai,* to put, set]

Thespian *thes'pi-ən,* (also without *cap.*) *adj.* pertaining to tragedy: tragic.—*n.* a tragic actor: an actor [Gr. *Thespis,* founder of Greek tragedy.]

theta *thē'tə, thā'tə, n.* the eighth (orig. ninth) letter of the Greek alphabet (Θ, θ) transliterated *th* [Gr. *thēta*; Semitic.]

theurgy *thē'ər-ji, n* magic by the agency of good spirits: miraculous divine action —*adjs.* **theur'gic, -al.**—*n.* **the'urgist.** [Gr. *theourgiā—theos,* a god, *ergon,* work.]

thew *thū,* (used chiefly in *pl.* **thews, thewes**) *n.* manner: moral quality: bodily quality, muscle or strength — *adjs.* **thewed** muscular; **thew'y** muscular, strong. [O.E *thēaw,* manner.]

they *dhā, pron., nom. pl.,* used as *pl* of **he, she, it:** often used as a *sing.* (with *pl vb.*) of common gender, he or she, people in general, some.—**they'd** a contraction of **they had** or **they would; they'll** a contraction of **they will** or **they shall; they're** a contraction of **they are; they've** a contraction of **they have.** [M.E *thei—*O.N. *theirr,* which supplanted *hi* (O.E. *hīe*).]

thiamine, thiamin *thī'ə-mēn, -min, n* vitamin B₁. [Gr. *theion,* sulphur, and **amine.**]

thick *thik, adj.* having a great (or specified) distance in measurement from surface to surface in lesser dimension: deep: dense: viscous: close set or packed: crowded: intimate, in close confidence (*fig*): abundant: frequent, in quick succession: abundingly covered or occupied: foggy: opaque: dull: stupid: gross: husky, muffled: indistinctly articulate: excessive, approaching the intolerable (*slang*).—*n.* the thickest part of anything: the midst —*adv* **thickly,** closely: frequently: fast: to a great (or specified) depth.—*v.t.* and *v.i.* **thick'en** to make or become thick or thicker.—*ns.* **thick'ener; thick'ening** a' making or becoming thicker: a thickened place. material added to something to thicken it.—Also *adj.* —*n.* **thick'et** a dense mass of trees or shrubs.—*adjs.* **thick'eted; thick'ety**—*adj.* **thick'ish** somewhat thick. —*adv.* **thick'ly.**—*n.* **thick'ness** a quality or degree of being thick: the space between outer surfaces: a layer.—**thick ear** a bruised, swollen ear, usually a result of a blow administered as punishment; **thick'head** a blockhead: any bird of an Australian family akin to fly-catchers and shrikes.—*adj.* **thick'•head'ed** having a thick head or skull: stupid.—**thick'•knee** the stone-curlew, a large plover with thickened knees.—*adj.* **thick'set** closely set or planted: having a short thick body.—*n.* a thicket.—*adjs.* **thick'-skinned'** having a thick skin: insensitive: indifferent to criticism or insult.—**thick'-skull'ed** having a thick skull: doltish; **thick'-witt'ed** doltish.—**a bit thick** more than one can reasonably be expected to put up with; **as thick as thieves** very friendly; **lay it on thick** to praise extravagantly: to exaggerate; **through thick and thin** in spite of all obstacles: without any wavering. [O.E. *thicce*.]

thief *thēf, n.* one who takes unlawfully what is not his own, esp. by stealth:—*pl.* **thieves** (*thēvz*). [O.E. *thēof.*]

thieve *thēv, v.i.* to practise theft: to steal.—*n.* **thiev'ery** the practice of thieving: what is thieved.—*n.* and *adj.* **thiev'ing.**—*adj.* **thiev'ish** given to, or like, theft: thief-like: furtive.—*adv.* **thiev'ishly.**—*n.* **thiev'ish-ness.** [O.E. *thēofian,* to thieve, and *thēof,* thief.]

thigh *thī, n.* the thick fleshy part of the leg from the knee to the trunk.—**thigh'-bone** the bone of the leg between the hip-joint and the knee, the femur. [O.E. *thēoh* (Anglian *thēh*).]

thill *thil, n.* the shaft of a vehicle. [Poss. O.E *thille,* board, plank.]

thimble *thim'bl, n.* a cover for the finger, used in sewing: an object of similar form: a metal ring with a grooved or concave outer edge fitted into a rope ring, etc. to prevent chafing (*naut.*).—*n.* **thim'bleful** as much as a thimble will hold: a small quantity:—*pl* **thim'blefuls.**—**thim'ble-case; thim'ble-rig** a sleight-of-hand trick in which the performer conceals, or pretends to conceal, a pea or small ball under one of three thimble-like cups; **thimb'le-rigger; thim'ble-rigging.** [O.E. *thȳmel,* thumb-stall—*thūma,* thumb.]

thin *thin, adj.* (*compar.* **thinn'er;** *superl.* **thinn'est**) having little thickness: slim: lean: freely mobile: watery: dilute: of little density: rarefied: sparse: slight: flimsy: wanting in body or solidity: meagre: poor.—*n.* that which is thin.—*adv.* thinly.—*v.t.* to make thin or thinner: to make less close or crowded (with *away, out,* etc.).—*v.i.* to grow or become thin or thinner:—*pr.p.* **thinn'ing;** *pa.t.* and *pa.p.* **thinned.** —*adv.* **thin'ly.**—*ns.* **thinn'er** a person or thing that thins, esp. (often in *pl.*, sometimes treated as *n.sing.*) a diluent for paint; **thin'ness; thinn'ing.**—*adj.* **thinn'-ish** somewhat thin.—*adj.* **thin'-skinned'** having thin skin: sensitive: irritable.—**a thin time** a time of hardship, misery, etc.; **into, out of, thin air** into, out of, nothing or nothingness; **thin on the ground** present in very small, inadequate, quality or numbers; **thin on top** balding. [O.E. *thynne.*]

thine *dhīn, pron., gen.* of **thou',** used predicatively or absolutely, belonging to thee: thy people: that which belongs to thee: adjectivally, esp. before a vowel or *h,* thy. [O.E. *thīn.*]

thing *thing, n.* an assembly, parliament, court, council (*hist.*): a matter, affair, problem, point: a circumstance: a fact: an event, happening, action: an entity: that which exists or can be thought of: an inanimate object: a living creature (esp. in pity, tolerant affection, kindly reproach): a possession: that which is wanted or is appropriate (*coll.*): a slight obsession or phobia (*coll.*): (in *pl.*) clothes: (in *pl.*) utensils, esp. for the table: (in *pl.*) personal belongings.—*ns.* **thing'amy, thing'ummy, thing'umbob, thing'umajig**

(*coll.*)' what-d'you-call-him (-her, -it): what's-his-name, etc.—used when one cannot or will not recall the name.—*adj.* **thing'y** real: actual: objective· matter-of-fact.—*n.* **thingumajig.—thing'-in-itself'** a noumenon, the Ger. *Ding an sich.*—**a good thing** a fortunate circumstance; **and things** and other (similar) things, **a stupid, wise,** etc , **thing to do** a stupid, wise, etc., action; **be all things to all men** to meet each on his, her, own ground, accommodate oneself to his, her, circumstances and outlook: (loosely, in a bad sense) to keep changing one's opinions, etc., so as to suit one's company; **be on to a good thing** (*coll.*) to be in a particularly profitable position, job, etc., **do one's (own) thing** (*coll.*) to behave as is natural to, characteristic of, oneself: to do something in which one specialises; **do the handsome thing** by to treat generously; **for one thing ... for another (thing)** expressions used in enumerating reasons; **have a good thing going** (*slang*) to be established in a particularly profitable position, etc., **hear things** to hear imaginary noises, voices, etc.; **know a thing or two** to be shrewd; **make a good thing of it** to reap a good advantage from; **make a thing of** to make an issue, point of controversy, of: to fuss about; **no such thing** something very different: no, not at all; **not a thing** nothing; **not quite the thing** not in very good health (see also **the thing**); **one of those things** a happening one cannot account for or do anything to prevent; **see things** to see something that is not really there; **the (done) thing** that which is conventional, fashionable, approved, right, or desirable. [O.E. and O.N. *thing,* parliament, object, etc.]

think *thingk, v.i.* to exercise the mind (often with *about, of,* or *arch.* on, *upon*): to revolve ideas in the mind: to judge: to be of opinion. to consider: to aspire or form designs (with *of* or *about*):—*v.t.* to form, conceive, or revolve in the mind: to have as a thought: to imagine: to judge: to believe or consider: to expect: to purpose, design: to bring by thinking—*pa.t.* and *pa.p.* **thought** (*thot*).—*n.* (*coll.*) a spell of thinking: a thought.—*adj.* **think'able** capable of being thought: conceivably possible.—*n.* **think'er.**—*n.* and *adj.* **think'ing.**—*adv.* **think'ingly.—think'•tank** (*coll.*) a person or a group of people, usu. expert in some field, regarded as a source of ideas and solutions to problems.—**have another think coming** to be wrong in what one thinks (about future events or actions); **I don't think** I disbelieve: a warning that what was said was ironical (*coll.*); **I shouldn't, wouldn't, think of** I would not under any conditions; **just, to think of it** an expression of surprise, disapproval, longing, etc.; **put on one's thinking-cap** to devote some time to thinking about some problem; **think again** to change one's opinion (of necessity); **think aloud** to utter one's thoughts unintentionally; **think back** to to bring to one's mind the memory of (a past event, etc.); **think better of** to change one's mind concerning on reflection; **think for** to expect; **think little of** to have a poor opinion of—opp. to **think much,** or well, **of; think nothing of** not to consider difficult, exceptional, etc.; **think nothing of** it does not matter, is not important; **think out** to devise, project completely: to solve by a process of thought; **think over** to reconsider at leisure; **think through** to solve by a process of thought: to project and consider all the possible consequences, problems, etc. relating to (some course of action); **think twice** (often with *about*) to hesitate (before doing something): to decide not to do; **think up** to find by thinking, devise, concoct. [O.E. *thencan.*]

thio- *thī'ō-,* in composition, sulphur, indicating in chemistry a compound theoretically derived from another by substituting an atom or more of sulphur for oxygen, as *thiosulphate.*—*ns.* **thiocy'anate** a salt of **thiocyan'ic acid**, HSCN; **thi'ol** (or -ōl) mercaptan; **thiopent'one**, (U.S.) **thiopent'al**, see **Pentothal**. [Gr. theion, sulphur.]

third thûrd, adj. the last of three: next after the second: equal to one of three equal parts.—n. a third part. a person or thing in third position: an interval of two (conventionally called three) diatonic degrees (mus.): a note at that interval.—adv. in the third place.—v.t. to divide by three: to support after the seconder.—n. **third'ing** a third part.—adv. **third'ly** in the third place.—adj. **third'-class**.—adv. **third'-class'**.—adj. **third'-hand'**.—**third man** (cricket) a fielder on the offside between point and slip.—adjs. **third'-party** of a person other than the principals (as insured and insurer); **third'-rate** of the third order: of poor quality.—**Third World** the developing countries not aligned politically with the large power blocks. [O.E. thridda.]

thirl thûrl, (dial.) n. a hole: an opening.—v.t. to pierce: to thrill [O.E. thyrel, hole—thurh, through.]

thirst thûrst, n. the uneasiness caused by want of drink: vehement desire for drink: eager desire for anything. —v.i. to feel thirst.—n. **thirst'er**.—adj. **thirst'ful**.— adv. **thirst'ily**.—n. **thirst'iness**.—adjs. **thirst'less**; **thirst'y** suffering from thirst: dry: parched: vehemently desiring. [O.E. thurst (n.), thyrstan (vb.).]

thirteen thûr'tēn, or -tēn', adj. and n. three and ten.— adj. **thir'teenth** (or -tēnth') last of thirteen: next after the twelfth: equal to one of thirteen equal parts.—n. a thirteenth part: a person or thing in thirteenth position.—adv. **thirteenth'ly**. [O.E. thrēotīene, -tēne-threo, three.]

thirty thûr'ti, adj. and n. three times ten.—n.pl. **thir'ties** the numbers from thirty to thirty-nine: the years so numbered in life or any century: a range of temperatures from thirty to just under forty degrees.— adj. **thir'tieth** last of thirty: next after the twenty-ninth: equal to one of thirty equal parts.—n. a thirtieth part: a person or thing in thirtieth position.— adj., adv. **thir'tyfold**.—adjs. **thir'tyish** somewhere about the age of thirty; **thirty-two'mo** (for tricesimo secundo, 32mo) in sheets folded to give 32 leaves (64 pages).—n. a book so constructed:—pl. -mos. [O.E. thrītig—threo, three, -tig, suff. denoting ten.]

this dhis, sing. demons. pron. or adj. denoting a person or thing near, topical, just mentioned, or about to be mentioned: (up to and including) the present moment: sometimes used almost with the force of an indef. art.:—pl. **these**.—n. **this'ness** the quality of being this, not something else.—**this and that** or **this, that and the other** various minor unspecified objects, actions, etc. [O.E., neut. of thes, thēos, this.]

thistle this'l, n. a prickly composite plant—the national emblem of Scotland.—adj. **this'tly** like a thistle: overgrown with thistles.—**this'tle-down** the tufted feathery parachutes of thistle seeds. [O.E. thistel.]

thither dhidh'ər adv. to that place: to that end or result.—adv. on the far side.—advs. **thith'erward**, -s toward that place. [O.E. thider.]

thixotropy thiks-ot'rə-pi, n. the property of showing a temporary reduction in viscosity when shaken or stirred.—adj. **thixotropic** (trop'ik) of, or showing, thixotropy: (of paints) non-drip. [Gr thixis, action of touching, tropos, a turn.]

tho'. Same as **though**.

thole¹ thōl, n. a pin in the side of a boat to keep the oar in place: a peg.—**thole'-pin** a peg, thole. [O.E. thol.]

thole² thōl, (now Scot.) v.t. and v.i. to endure [O.E. tholian, to suffer.]

tholus thō'ləs, n. a round building, dome, cupola, or tomb:—pl. **thō'li** (-lī).—Also **tholos** (thol'os; pl thol'oi). [Gr. tholos.]

Thomism tō'mizm, n. the doctrines of Thomas Aquinas (b. prob. 1225; d. 1274).—n. and adj. **Thō'mist**.—adjs. **Thōmist'ic, -al**.

thong thong, n. a strap; a strip: the lash of a whip or crop.—adj. **thonged** having a thong or thongs. [O.E. thwang.]

thorax thō'raks, tho', n. the part of the body between the head and abdomen, in man the chest, in insects the division that bears legs and wings.—pl. **tho'raxes**, **-races** (-sēz)—adj **thoracic** (-ras').—**thoracic duct** the main trunk of the vessels conveying lymph in the body. [Gr. thōrāx -ākos.]

thorium thō'ri-əm, thō', n. a radioactive metal (Th; at. numb. 90) resembling aluminium.—n. **thoron** (thō'ron, tho') the radioactive gas given off by the decomposition of thorium. [Thor, the god.]

thorn thôrn, n. a sharp hard part (leaf, stem, or root) of a plant: an animal spine: anything prickly: a spiny plant: hawthorn: the Old English and Old Norse letter þ (th).—v.t. to set with thorns: to prick.—adj. **thorned**.—n. **thorn'iness**.—adjs. **thorn'less; thorn'y** full of thorns: prickly: troublesome: harassing.— **thorn'-apple** a poisonous plant of the potato family, with a prickly capsule; **thorn'back** a ray with nail-like crooked spines in its back. **thorn'-bush** any thorny shrub, esp. hawthorn; **thorn'-hedge** a hedge of hawthorn; **thorn'tree** a thorny tree, esp. a hawthorn.— **thorn in the flesh** any cause of constant irritation [O.E. thorn.]

thoron. See **thorium**.

thorough thur'ə, adj. passing or carried through, or to the end: complete: entire: out-and-out: assiduous and scrupulous in completing work.—adv. **thor'oughly**.—n. **thor'oughness.—thor'ough-bass** (mus.) a bass part all through a piece, usu. with figures to indicate the chords.—adj. **thor'oughbred** thoroughly or completely bred or trained: bred from a dam and sire of the best blood, as a horse, and having the qualities supposed to depend thereon: pure-bred' (with cap.) pertaining to the Thoroughbred breed of horses.—n. an animal, esp. a horse, of pure blood: (with cap.) a race-horse of a breed descended from any of three Arabian stallions of the early 18th cent.—**thor'oughfare** a passage or way through: a road open at both ends: a public way or street: right of passing through.—adj. **thor'oughgoing** going through or to the end: going all lengths: complete: out-and-out. [The longer form of **through**.]

thorp, thorpe thorp, (arch.) n. a hamlet: a village. [O.E. thorp, throp.]

those dhōz, demons. pron. and adj., pl. of **that**. [O.E. thās, pl. of thes, this.]

thou¹ dhow, pron. of the second person sing., the person addressed (now generally used only in solemn address). [O.E. thū.]

thou² thow, a coll. short form of **thousand(th)**.

though dhō, conj. admitting: allowing: even if: notwithstanding that.—adv. nevertheless: however.—**as though** as if. [O.N. thauh, thō.]

thought¹ thôt. See under **think**. [O.E. thōhte, pa.t., (ge)thōht, pa.p.]

thought² thôt, n. thinking: mind: consciousness: reasoning: deliberation: that which one thinks: notion: idea: fancy: consideration: opinion: meditation: design: care: considerateness: purpose: intention.—adj. **thought'ful** full of thought: employed in meditation: attentive: considerate: expressive of or favourable to meditation.—adv. **thought'fully**.—n. **thought'fulness**.—adj. **thought'less** unthinking: incapable of thinking: carefree: careless. inattentive:

inconsiderate.—*adv.* **thought'lessly.**—*n.* **thought'-lessness.**—**thought'-pro'cess** train of thought: manner of thinking; **thought'-reader; thought'-reading** discerning what is passing in another's mind by any means other than the ordinary and obvious; **thought'-trans'ference** telepathy; **thought'-wave** a wave-like progress of a thought among a crowd or a public: a sudden accession of thought in the mind: an impulse in some hypothetical medium assumed to explain telepathy.—**on second thoughts** on reconsideration; **take thought** to bethink oneself: to conceive a purpose. [O.E *(ge)thōht.*]

thousand *thow'zənd, n.* and *adj.* ten hundred: often used vaguely or hyperbolically.—*adj., adv.,* and *n.* (a) **thou'sandfold** a thousand times as much.—*adj.* **thou'sandth** last of a thousand, or in an equivalent position in a greater number: equal to one of a thousand equal parts.—*n.* a thousandth part: a person or thing in thousandth position.—**one in (of) a thousand** anything exceedingly rare or excellent. [O.E. *thūsend.*]

thrall *thröl, n.* a slave, serf: slavery, servitude.—*v.t.* to enslave.—*n.* **thral'dom** (also **thrall'dom**) slavery: bondage. [O.E. *thrǣl*—O.N. *thræll.*]

thrash *thrash, v.t.* to thresh: (with *out*) to discuss exhaustively, or arrive at by debate: to beat soundly: to defeat thoroughly.—*v.i.* to lash out, lay about one.—*n.* an act of threshing or thrashing: a party (*coll.*).—*n.* **thrash'er** a thresher: a thresher-shark: one who thrashes.—*n.* and *adj.* **thrash'ing** threshing: beating. [Orig. a dialect form of **thresh.**]

thrasher[1] *thrash'ər,* thresher *thresh'ər, ns.* any of several American birds akin to the mocking-bird. [Perh. Eng. dial. *thresher,* thrush.]

thrasher[2]. See **thrash.**

thraw *thrö,* a Scots form of **throw** with some old senses preserved; also of **throe,** with senses overlapping **throw.**—*adj.* **thrawn** twisted: wry: cross-grained, perverse.

thread *thred, n.* a very thin line of any substance, esp. linen or cotton, twisted or drawn out: a filament: a fibre: the prominent spiral part of a screw: a continuous connecting element in a story, argument, etc.—*v.t.* to pass a thread through: to string on a thread: to pass or pierce through, as a narrow way: to furnish with a thread.—*adj.* made of linen or cotton thread.—*ns.* **thread'er; thread'iness.**—*adj.* **thread'y** like thread: slender: containing or consisting of thread.—*adj.* **thread'bare** worn to the bare thread: having the nap worn off: hackneyed: used till its novelty or interest is gone.—**thread mark** a coloured thread incorporated in bank-notes to make counterfeiting difficult; **thread'-worm** any member of the *Nematoda,* more or less thread-like worms, many parasitic: esp. *Oxyuris vermicularis,* parasitic in the human rectum.—**thread of life** the thread imagined to be spun and cut by the Fates. [O.E. *thrǣd.*]

threat *thret, n.* a declaration or indication of an intention to inflict, punish, or hurt: an appearance of impending evil: a source of danger (to).—*v.t.* **threat'en** to offer a threat of, or against: to intimidate by threats: to seem to impend over: to indicate danger of, or to.—*v.i.* to use threats: to portend evil.—*adj.* **threat'ened.**—*n.* **threat'ener.**—*n.* **threat'ening.**—*adj.* menacing. portending danger or evil: (of sky) heavily clouded over.—*adv.* **threat'eningly.**—*adj.* **threat'ful** menacing. [O.E. *thrēat* (n.), *thrēatian, thrēatnian* (vbs.).]

three *thrē, n.* two and one: a set of three: a symbol for three: a card with three pips: a score of three points, strokes, etc.: an article of a size denoted by three: the third hour after midnight or midday: the age of three years.—*adj.* of the number three: three years old.—

ns. **three'ness** the state of being three; **three'some** a company of three persons: a game or dance for three.—*adj.* for three: triple.—**three balls** the pawnbroker's sign.—*adj.* **three'-card** played with three cards (see also **three-card trick** below).—**three cheers** three shouts of 'hurrah', to show approbation, etc. (also *fig.*).—*adjs.* **three'-colour** involving or using three colours as primary; **three'-cor'nered** triangular in form or section: having three competitors or three members; **three'-deck.**—**three'-deck'er** a ship with three decks or guns on three decks: a sandwich, with three layers of bread.—*adjs.* **three'-dimen'sional** having, or seeming to have, three dimensions: giving the effect of being seen or heard in an environment of three dimensions—usu. **3-D:** (of, e.g. a literary work) developed in detail and thus realistic.—**three'-dimen-sional'ity.**—*adj.* and *adv.* **three'fold** in three divisions: three times as much.—*n.* **three'foldness.**—*adjs.* **three'-foot** measuring or having three feet; **three'-four** (*mus.*) with three crotchets to the bar; **three'-hand'ed** having three hands: played by three players; **three'-legged** (*-legd, -leg'id*) having three legs: of a race, run by pairs of runners, each with a leg tied to his partner's; **three'-part** composed in three parts or for three voices.—**threepence** (*threp', thrip', thrup'əns*) money, or a coin, of the value of three old pence.—*adj.* **threepenny** (*threp', thrip', thrup'ni* or *-ə-ni*) sold or offered at threepence: of little worth: mean, vulgar.—*n.* a coin of the value of threepence (also **threepenny bit, piece**).—*adjs.* **three'-piece** comprising three parts, three matching pieces, etc., **three'-ply** having three layers or strands.—*adj.* and *adv.* **three-quar'ter** to the amount of three-fourths: (*adj.*) being three-quarters of the normal size or length (used of beds, coats, etc.).—*n.* a three-quarter back.—*n.* and *adj.* **three'score** sixty.—*adjs.* **three'-sid'ed** having three sides; **three'-way** giving connection in three directions from a centre.—**three-card trick** a card-sharper's ploy in which the victim is invited to wager on which of three cards, turned face-down and deftly manipulated, is the queen (also *find the lady*); **three-colour process** the method of producing colour pictures from three primary originals—yellow, red, blue—prepared by photography; **three-mile limit** by international law, the outer limit of the territorial waters around a state; **three-point landing** (*aero.*) a landing with all three wheels touching the ground at the same moment—a perfect landing; **three-point turn** the process of turning a vehicle round to face in the opposite direction by moving it forward, reversing, then moving forward again, turning the steering-wheel appropriately; **three-quarter back** a player between half-backs and full-back; **three-ring circus** a circus with three rings in which simultaneous separate performances are given: a showy or extravagant event (*fig.*). [O.E. *thrēo,* fem. and neut. of *thrī.*]

thremmatology *threm-ə-tol'ə-ji, n.* the science of breeding domestic animals and plants. [Gr. *thremma, -atos,* a nurseling, *logos,* discourse.]

threnody *thrēn', thren'ə-di, n.* an ode or song of lamentation.—Also **thren'ode** (*-ōd*).—*adjs* **threnō'dial, threnodic** (*-od'*).—*n.* **thren'odist.** [Gr. *thrēnōidiā, thrēnos,* a lament, *ōidē,* song.]

thresh *thresh, v.t.* to beat out, subject to beating out, by trampling, flail, or machinery: to thrash —*v.t.* to thresh corn: to thrash —*n.* an act of threshing.—*ns.* **thresh'el** a flail· a flail-like weapon, a spiked ball; **thresh'er** one who threshes: a flail: a threshing-machine or a beating part of it: a large long-tailed shark (also **thresh'er-shark**).—*n.* and *adj.* **thresh'ing.**—**thresh'ing-floor** a surface on which grain is threshed, **thresh'ing-machine, -mill** one for threshing corn. [O.E. *therscan*; cf. Ger. *derschen*, to thresh; see **thrash.**]

thresher. See thrasher[1], thresh.

threshold *thresh'ōld*, *n.* the sill of a house door: the place or point of entering: the outset: the limit of consciousness: the point at which a stimulus begins to bring a response, as in *threshold of pain*, etc.: the smallest dose of radiation which will produce a specified result.—*adj.* at or constituting a threshold. [O.E. *therscold*, *therscwald*, *threscold*, app.—*therscan*, to thrash, thresh, in its older sense of trample, tread.]

threw *thrōō*, *pa.t.* of **throw.**

thrice *thrīs*, *adv.* three times: three times as much. [M.E. *thriēs*—O.E. *thrīwa*, *thrīga*, thrice—*thrī*, three, with adverbial gen. ending *-es*.]

thrift *thrift*, *n.* the state of thriving: frugality: economy: sea-pink, a seaside and alpine plant.—*adv.* **thrift'ily.**—*n.* **thrift'iness.**—*adj.* **thrift'less** not thrifty: extravagant: not thriving.—*adv.* **thrift'lessly.** —*n.* **thrift'lessness.**—*adj.* **thrift'y** showing thrift or economy: thriving by frugality: prosperous, in good condition (*U.S.*):—*compar.* **thrift'ier**, *superl.* **thrift'iest.** [**thrive.**]

thrill *thril*, *v.t.* to pierce: to affect with a strong glow or tingle of sense or emotion, now esp. a feeling of extreme pleasure.—*v.t.* to pierce, as something sharp: to pass tinglingly: to quiver: to feel a sharp, shivering sensation.—*n.* a tingle: a shivering feeling or emotion.—*n.* **thrill'er** a sensational or exciting story, esp. one about crime and detection.—*adj.* **thrill'ing.**—*adv.* **thrill'ingly.**—*n.* **thrill'ingness.**—*adj.* **thrill'y.** [O.E. *thyrlian*, to bore—*thyrel*, a hole.]

Thrips *thrips*, *n.* a genus of minute black insects, common in flowers: (without *cap.*) an insect of the genus, or of any of the genera of the order (*erron.* **thrip**) popularly extended to leaf-hoppers, and to other small insects:—*pl.* **thrips, thrip'ses.** [Gr *thrips*, *thripos*, a wood-worm.]

thrive *thrīv*, *v.i.* to grow healthily and vigorously: to get on, do well: to prosper: to increase in goods: to be successful: to flourish:—*pa.t.* **thrōve**, also **thrived;** *pa.p.* **thriven** (*thriv'n*).—*n.* and *adj.* **thri'ving.** [O.N. *thrifa*, to grasp.]

thro', thro. Same as **through.**

throat *thrōt*, *n.* the passage from mouth to stomach: the forepart of the neck, in which are the gullet and windpipe: voice: a narrow entrance, aperture or passage: the narrow part, as of a vase.—*adj.* **throat'ed** with a throat.—*adv.* **throat'ily.**—*n.* **throat'iness.**— *adj.* **throat'y** sounding as from the throat: hoarse: croaking: deep or full-throated: somewhat sore-throated: full or loose-skinned about the throat.— **throat microphone** one held directly against the speaker's throat and actuated by vibrations of the larynx.—**cut the, one's, throat** usu., to cut the jugular vein: to pursue some course ruinous to one's interests; **sore throat** an inflamed and uncomfortable condition of the tonsils and neighbouring parts; **stick in one's throat** to be more than one can bear, manage; **thrust, ram, down someone's throat** to assert or force upon someone insistently without listening to an answer. [O.E. *throte*; cf. **throttle.**]

throb *throb*, *vi.* to beat strongly, as the heart or pulse: —*pr.p.* **throbb'ing;** *pa.t.* and *pa.p.* **throbbed.**—*n.* a beat or strong pulsation.—*n.* and *adj.* **throbb'ing.**— *adv.* **throbb'ingly.** [M.E. *throbben.*]

throe *thrō*, *n.* a spasm: a paroxysm: a pang, esp. a birth-pang.—**in the throes** in travail: in the struggle (of), struggling (with): in the thick (of). [M.E. *thrahes*, *throwes*, *thrawes.*]

thrombus *throm'bas*, *n.* a clot of blood in a living

vessel:—*pl.* **throm'bi**—*ns.* **throm'bin** an enzyme that causes clotting; **throm'bocyte** a platelet; **thrombo-em'bolism** an embolism caused by an embolus carried by the bloodstream from its point of origin causing a blockage elsewhere; **thrombo-phlebi'tis** phlebitis with formation of a thrombus.— *v.t.* **thrombose** (*-bōs'*) to cause thrombosis in.—*n.* **thrombō'sis** clotting in a vessel during life:—*pl.* **-ō'sēs.**—*adj.* **thrombot'ic.** [Gr. *thrombos*, clot.]

throne *thrōn*, *n.* a king's, pope's, or bishop's chair of state: kingship.—*v.t.* to enthrone.—*adjs.* **throned; throne'less.—throne'-room.** [Gr. *thronos*, a seat.]

throng *throng*, *n.* a crowd: a great multitude: crowding.—*v.t.* and *v.i.* to crowd: to press.—*adjs.* **thronged** packed, crowded; **throng'ful** thronged.—*n.* and *adj.* **throng'ing.** [O.E. *gethrang—thringan*, to press.]

throstle *thros'l*, *n.* the song-thrush (see **thrush**[1]): a machine for drawing, twisting, and winding fibres (from its sound). [O.E. *throstle.*]

throttle *throt'l*, *n.* the throat or windpipe: a throttle-valve: a throttle-lever.—*v.t.* to choke by pressure on the windpipe: to strangle (also *fig.*): to check the flow of: to cut down the supply of steam, or of gas and air, to or in.—*n.* **thrott'ler.**—*n.* and *adj.* **thrott'ling.**— **thrott'le-lever** a lever that opens and closes a throttle-valve; **thrott'le-valve** a valve regulating the supply of steam or of gas and air in an engine.—**at full throttle** at full speed; **throttle down** to slow down by closing the throttle. [App. dim. of **throat.**]

through *thrōō*, *prep.* from end to end, side to side, or boundary to boundary of, by way of the interior: from place to place within: everywhere within: by way of: along the passage of: clear of: among: from beginning to end of: up to and including, to or until the end of (*U.S.*): by means of: in consequence of.—*adv.* from one end or side to the other: from beginning to end: all the way: clear: into a position of having passed: in connection or communication all the way.—*adj.* passing, or serving for passage, all the way without interruption.—*prep.* **throughout'** in, into, through, during, the whole of.—*adv.* in every part: everywhere.— **through'-put** the amount of material, etc. put through a process; **through'-traff'ic** the traffic between two centres at a distance from each other: traffic passing straight through an area, as opposed to that travelling within the area; **through'way**, (*U.S.*) **thru'way**, an expressway —**be through** (*U.S.*) to have done (with): to be at an end: to have no more to do (with); **through and through** through the whole thickness: completely: in every point. [O.E. *thurh.*]

throve *thrōv*, *pa.t* of **thrive.**

throw *thrō*, *v t.* to wind or twist together, as yarn: to form on a wheel, as pottery: to turn, with a lathe: to move (a switch) so as to connect, disconnect: to cast, hurl, fling through the air: to project: to emit: to make a cast of dice amounting to: to dislodge from the saddle: to cast down in wrestling: to defeat, get the better of, or discomfit: to give birth to: to produce: to render suddenly: to cause to be in some place or condition, esp. with suddenness: to put: to execute, perform: to lose (a contest) deliberately, esp. in return for a bribe (*coll.*): to bemuse, perplex, disconcert.—*v.i.* to cast or hurl: to cast dice:—*pa.t.* **threw** (*thrōō*); *pa.p.* **thrown** (*thrōn*) —*n* a deflection: amplitude of movement: an act of throwing: a cast, esp. of dice or a fishing-line: the distance to which anything may be thrown: the vertical displacement of a fault (*geol.*): a small woollen wrap or rug: a turn, article, etc. (*coll.*).—*n.* **throw'er.**—*n.* and *adj* **throw'ing.**—*adj.* **thrown** twisted: cast, flung.— **throw'-away** an advertisement brochure or handbill freely distributed to the public (*U.S.*): a contest without serious competition: a line, or a joke, that an actor purposely delivers without emphasis, often for the sake of realism.—*adj.* of manner or technique, casual, without attempt at dramatic effect: ridiculously cheap, as if being thrown away: discarded or not recovered after use.—**throw′-back** a reversion (e.g. to an earlier developmental type): a set-back; **throw′-in** an act of throwing in: a throw to put the ball back into play (*football, basketball, etc.*); **throw′-out** an act of throwing out: a rejected thing.—**throw a fit** (*coll.*) to have a fit, behave wildly; **throw a party** (*coll.*) to give a party; **throw away** to reject, toss aside: to squander: to fail to take advantage of: to bestow unworthily; **throw back** to retort, to refuse: to revert to some ancestral character; **throw down** to demolish; **throw in** to interject: to throw the ball in: to add as an extra; **throw in the towel, throw in one's hand** to give up, surrender; **throw off** to divest oneself of: to disengage or release oneself from: to utter or compose offhand; **throw on** to put on hastily; **throw oneself at** to make a determined and obvious attempt to captivate; **throw oneself into** to engage heartily in; **throw oneself on**, or **upon** to assail: to entrust oneself to the power of; **throw open** to cause to swing wide open: to make freely accessible; **throw out** to cast out: to reject: to expel: to emit: to utter: to cause to project: to disconcert: to distance, leave behind; **throw over** to discard or desert; **throw together** to put together in a hurry: to bring into contact by chance; **throw up** to erect hastily: to show prominently: to give up, to resign: to vomit; **throw up (something) against** someone to reproach someone with (something). [O.E. *thrāwan*, to turn, to twist.]

thru. A U.S. spelling of **through**, alone or in compounds.

thrum[1] *thrum, n.* the end of a weaver's thread: any loose thread or fringe: bits of coarse yarn.—*adj.* made of or having thrums.—*v.t.* to furnish, cover, or fringe with thrums:—*pr.p.* **thrumm′ing**; *pa.t.* and *pa.p.* **thrummed.**—*adj.* **thrumm′y** made of, or like, thrums. [O.E. *thrum* (found in composition).]

thrum[2] *thrum, v.t.* and *v.i.* to strum: to hum, drone, repeat in sing-song: to drum with the fingers:—*pr.p.* **thrumm′ing**; *pa.t.* and *pa.p.* **thrummed.**—*n.* a strumming.—*n.* **thrumm′er.**—*n.* and *adj.* **thrumm′ing.**—*adv.* **thrumm′ingly.**

thrush[1] *thrush, n.* any member of the subfamily Turdinae (fam. *Muscicapidae*) of songbirds, esp. those of the genus Turdus, particularly those species having a spotted breast, e.g. the song-thrush (*Turdus philomelos*) and missel-thrush (*T. viscivorus*): applied to other birds more or less similar. [O.E. *thrysce*.]

thrush[2] *thrush, n.* an inflammation in a horse's frog: a disease, usu. of infants, chiefly affecting the mouth and throat.

thrust *thrust, v.t.* and *v.i.* to push: to force: to stab, pierce: to intrude:—*pa.t.* and *pa.p.* **thrust.**—*n.* a push: a pushing force: the force that drives an aircraft forward and its measurement: the horizontal force on the abutment of an arch: a stab.—*n.* **thrust′er.**—*n.* and *adj.* **thrust′ing.** [O.N. *thrȳsta*, to press.]

thruway. A U.S. spelling of **throughway.**

thud *thud, n.* a dull sound as of a heavy body falling soft.—*v.i.* to make a thud.—*v.t.* to beat. [Perh. O.E. *thyddan*, to strike.]

thug *thug, n.* a member of a religious fraternity that murdered stealthily by strangling or poisoning (*India*): a cut-throat: a ruffian.—*ns.* **thuggee′**; **thugg′ism** the practice and superstition of the thugs; **thugg′ery** thuggism: ruffianly or violent behaviour. [Hindi *thag*, cheat.]

Thule *thū′lē, n.* an island six days N. of Orkney discovered by Pytheas (4th cent. B C), variously

identified as Shetland, Iceland, Norway, Jutland: hence (usu. *ultima Thule*) the extreme limit.—*ns.* **thu′lia** thulium oxide; **thu′lium** a metallic element (Tm; at. numb. 69). [L. *Thūlē*—Gr. *Thoulē*.]

thumb *thum, n.* the short, thick digit on the side of the human hand: the part of a glove that covers it: in other animals the corresponding digit, or that of the hind foot, esp. when opposable: a thumb's breadth, an inch.—*v.t.* to handle awkwardly: to play, spread, press, touch, wear, or smudge with the thumb: to read assiduously: to turn the pages (of a book) rapidly with the thumb: to signal to with the thumb: to hit (in the eye) with the thumb (*boxing*).—*adj.* **thumbed** having thumbs: marked by the thumb, worn.—**thumb′-hole** a hole to insert the thumb in; **thumb′-index** one arranged as indentations on the outer margins of the pages of books; **thumb′nail** the nail of the thumb: a sketch (**thumb′nail sketch**) as small as a thumbnail.—*adj.* brief, concise.—**thumb′piece** a piece that is pressed by the thumb or receives the thumb; **thumb′print** an impression of the markings of the thumb, taken as a means of identification; **thumb′-screw** an old instrument of torture for compressing the thumb by means of a screw; **thumb′-tack** (*U.S.*) a drawing-pin.—**be all (fingers and) thumbs, one's fingers are all thumbs, have one's fingers all thumbs** to be awkward and fumbling; **bite one's thumb** to make a sign threatening revenge; **rule of thumb** a rough-and-ready practical manner, found by experience to be convenient; **thumb a lift, ride** (*coll.*) to beg a lift from passing motorists by signalling from the side of the road with the thumb; **thumb one's nose** to cock a snook (*lit.* and *fig.*) (see snook[2]); **thumbs down** a sign indicating disapproval, disallowance, failure, etc. (also *fig.*); **thumbs up** a sign indicating approval, success, hope of, or wishes for, success etc. (also *fig.*); **under one's thumb** under one's domination. [O.E. *thūma.*]

thump *thump, n.* a dull heavy blow or its sound.—*v.t.* and *v.i.* to beat with a dull heavy blow: to make such a sound.—*v.t.* to trounce.—*n.* **thump′er** one who, or that which, thumps: anything very big, a big lie, etc. (*coll.*).—*adj.* **thump′ing** (*coll.*) unusually big. [Prob. imit.]

thunder *thun′dər, n.* the deep rumbling sound after a flash of lightning: any loud noise: a thunderbolt: vehement denunciation.—*v.i.* to make thunder: to sound as thunder: to inveigh or denounce with vehemence.—*v.t.* to give out with noise or violent denunciation: to deal like thunder.—*ns.* **thun′derer**; **thun′dering.**—*adj.* discharging thunder: unusually big, tremendous (*coll.*).—Also *n.* and *adv.*—*adv.* **thun′deringly.**—*adjs.* **thun′derless**; **thun′derous** like, threatening, or suggesting thunder.—*adv.* **thun′derously.**—*adj.* **thun′dery** indicative of thunder, or attended by it.—**thun′derbolt** a missile of the thunder-god: a popularly imagined material body seen as lightning: anything sudden and overwhelming: a fulmination: a violent and irresistible destroyer or hero; **thun′der-clap** a sudden crash of thunder; **thun′der-cloud** a cloud charged with electricity: a black or livid threatening appearance; **thun′der-god** a god that wields thunder; **thun′der-shower** a shower accompanied with thunder, or a short heavy shower from a thunder-cloud; **thun′der-storm** continued discharges of electricity from the clouds, producing lightning and thunder, generally with heavy rain.—*adj.* **thun′der-struck** (also **-stricken**) struck by lightning: struck dumb with astonishment.—**steal someone's thunder** see steal[1]. [O.E. *thunor*, thunder, *Thunor*, the thunder-god, Thor.]

thurible *thū′ri-bl, n* a censer. [L. *t(h)ūs, t(h)ūris,* frankincense—Gr. *thyos*, a sacrifice.]

Thursday *thûrz'di*, *n*. the fifth day of the week, originally sacred to Thunor, the English thunder-god. [O.E. *Thunres dæg*, Thunor's day.]

thus *dhus*, *adv*. in this or that manner: to this degree or extent: accordingly, therefore. [O.E. *thus*.]

thwack *thwak*, *v.t*. to whack.—*n*. a whack.—*n*. **thwack'er**.—*n*. and *adj*. **thwack'ing**. [Perh. **whack**, or O.E. *thaccian*, to smack.]

thwart *thwôrt*, *adv*. crosswise: from side to side.—*adj*. crosswise, transverse: cross, adverse: cross, perverse, cross-grained.—*prep*. across, athwart.—*v.t*. to cross' to cross the path of: to obstruct: to oppose: to frustrate.—*n*. frustration: hindrance: a rower's bench.—*adj*. **thwar'ted** frustrated.—*adv*. **thwar'tedly**.—*n*. **thwar'ter**.—*n*. and *adj*. **thwar'ting**. [O.N. *thvert*, neut. of *thverr*, perverse.]

thy *dhi*, *poss. pron*. or *adj*. of thee. [**thine**.]

thylacine *thī'la-sēn*, *-sin*, *-sin*, *n*. the so-called Tasmanian wolf (q.v.). [Gr. *thȳlakos*, pouch.]

thyme *tīm*, *n*. any member of the labiate genus Thymus, low half-shrubby plants, esp. the fragrant garden thyme (*T. vulgaris*) and wild thyme (*T. serpyllum*).—*n*. **thymol** (*thī'mol*) an antiseptic phenol obtained from oil of thyme by distillation.—*adj*. **thymy** (*tīm'i*) like, smelling of, or abounding in, thyme.—**lemon thyme** a species of thyme (*T. citriodorus*) with a lemony flavour and scent; **oil of thyme** a fragrant essential oil got from garden and other thymes. [Fr. *thym*—L. *thȳmum*—Gr. *thȳmon*.]

thymus *thī'mas*, *n*. a ductless gland near the root of the neck, vestigial in adult man.—Also *adj*.—*ns*. **thymec'tomy** surgical removal of the thymus; **thymine** (*thī'mēn*) one of the four bases in deoxyribonucleic acids. [Gr. *thymos*, thymus gland.]

thymy. See **thyme**.

thyratron *thī'ra-tron*, *n*. a gas-filled valve with heated cathode, able to carry very high currents—orig. a trademark for one containing mercury vapour.—*n*. **thyristor** (*thī-ris'tar*) a thyratron-like semiconductor device.

thyroid *thī'roid*, *adj*. shield-shaped: pertaining to the thyroid gland or the thyroid cartilage.—*n*. the thyroid gland, a ductless gland in the neck whose overactivity may lead to exophthalmic goitre, and defect to cretinism: the principal cartilage of the larynx, forming Adam's apple.—*ns*. **thyroidi'tis** inflammation of the thyroid gland; **thyrotrō'pin**, **thyrotrō'phin** a hormone, produced in the anterior lobe of the pituitary gland, which stimulates the thyroid gland; **thyrox'in(e)** an iodine compound, the active principle of the thyroid gland. [Gr. *thȳreoeidēs*, shield-shaped, the thyroid cartilage—*thȳreos*, a (door-shaped) shield—*thȳrā*, a door, *eidos*, form.]

thyrsus *thûr'sas*, *n*. the wand of Bacchus, a staff wreathed with ivy: a dense panicle broadest in the middle (*bot*.): esp. one whose lateral branches are cymose:—*pl*. **thyr'si** (*-sī*).—*n*. **thyrse** (*thûrs*) a thyrsus.—*adjs*. **thyr'soid**, **-al** having the form of a thyrsus. [Gr. *thyrsos*.]

thyself *dhī-self'*, *pron*. emphatic for, or usually along with, thou or thee: reflexive for thee. [**thee** (altered to **thy**), and **self**.]

ti *tē*, (*mus*.) *n*. in the tonic sol-fa system a substitute for *si*, to avoid the initial sound of *so* (*sol*).—Also, in anglicised spelling, **te**.

tiara *ti-ä'ra*, *n*. the lofty ornamental head-dress of the ancient Persians: the Jewish high-priest's mitre: the pope's triple crown: a jewelled head-ornament.—*adj*. **tia'ra'd**, **tia'raed** wearing a tiara. [Gr. *tiārā*.]

Tibet *ti-bet'*, *n*. a country W. of China.—*adj*. **Tibet'an** (or *tib'*) of Tibet.—*n*. the language of Tibet: a native of Tibet.

tibia *tib'i-a*, *n*. the shinbone, the thicker of the two bones of the leg below the knee in humans: the corresponding bone in other vertebrates: the fourth joint of an insect's leg:—*pl*. **tib'ias**, **tib'iae** (*-i-ē*).—*adj*. **tib'ial**. [L. *tībia*, shinbone, flute.]

tic *tik*, *n*. a convulsive motion of certain muscles, esp. of the face: an involuntary habitual response (*fig*.).—**tic'-douloureux** (*-dol-a-roō'*, Fr. *tēk doō-loō-rœ*) an affection of the fifth cranial nerve with paroxysms of pain in face and forehead. [Fr.]

tich *tich*, (*coll*.) *n*. a very small person: often used (with *cap*.) as a nickname.—*adj*. **tich'y**. [From the music-hall artist Harry Relph, known as Little *Tich*.]

tick¹ *tik*, *n*. any of the larger blood-sucking acarids: applied also to similar bloodsucking Diptera.—**tick fever** any disease transmitted by ticks. [O.E. *ticia* (perh. for *tīca* or *ticca*).]

tick² *tik*, *n*. the cover of a mattress: ticking.—*ns*. **tick'en**, **tick'ing** the cloth of which ticks are made. [L. *thēca*—Gr. *thēkē*, a case; see **theca**.]

tick³ *tik*, *n*. the sound of a watch, clock, etc.: a beat: a moment: a speck: a small mark, often an angular line, used to indicate or mark off as checked or dealt with.—*v.i*. to make a sound as of a clock: to beat.—*v.t*. to mark with a tick (sometimes with *off*): to dot: to measure, record, give out, by ticks (sometimes with *out*).—*adj*. **ticked** speckled.—*ns*. **tick'er** anything that ticks, esp. a telegraph instrument that prints signals on a tape, or (*slang*) a watch: the heart (*slang*).—*n*. and *adj*. **tick'ing**.—**tick'er-tape** paper ribbon on which a ticker prints: anything similar, such as a streamer; **tick'ing-off'** a reprimand; **tick-tack-toe'** (*U.S*.) noughts and crosses; **tick'-tick'** a ticking: (**tick'-tick**) a child's word for a watch; **tick'-tock'** a ticking, as of a big clock: a tapping: (**tick'-tock**) a child's word for a clock.—**in two ticks** in a moment; **make** (**someone** or **something**) **tick** (*coll*.) to cause to operate or function: to be the driving-force behind: to cause to behave, think, etc. in a certain way; **tick away** (of time, life, etc.) to pass away with the regularity of the ticking of a clock; **tick off** (*slang*) to reprimand; **tick over** of an engine, to run gently, disconnected from the transmission: of a person, to lead an inactive, uneventful existence: to function, operate. [M.E. *tek*.]

tick⁴ *tik* (*slang*) *n*. credit. [**ticket**.]

ticket *tik'it*, *n*. a card, slip, or (*formerly*) placard bearing a notice or serving as a token of any right or debt, as for admission, penalty for some offence (esp. motoring), etc.: a certificate (*slang*): discharge from the army (*slang*): a list of candidates put forward by a party for election (*U.S*.): any or all of the principles associated with a particular political party, esp. as a basis for its election to government.—*v.t*. to label: to designate.—**tick'et-collec'tor**; **tick'et-day** the day before settling day on the Stock Exchange; **tick'et-holder** a person possessing a ticket, e.g. for a concert; **tick'et-office** a place where tickets are sold; **tick'et-punch** an instrument for punching holes in tickets.—**straight ticket** all the nominees of a political party, and no others; **the ticket** (*slang*) exactly the right thing or the thing to be done; **ticket of leave** (formerly) a licence to be at large before expiry of sentence; **ticket-of-leave man**. [O.Fr. *estiquet(te)*—*estiquer*, to stick—O.L.G. *stekan*; cf. **stick**.]

tickety-boo, **tickettyboo** *tik'it-i-boō'*, (*coll*.) *adj*. fine, satisfactory.

tickle *tik'l*, *v.t*. to excite with a pleasant thrill: to affect with a disturbing feeling of a light touch, usually uncomfortable and tending to excite laughter: to amuse: to please: to perplex: to touch lightly: to beat.—*v.i*. to be the seat of a tickling or itching feeling.—*n*. an act or feeling of tickling: a slight touch.—*n*. **tick'ler**.

For other sounds see detailed chart of pronunciation.

—*n.* and *adj.* **tick'ling.**—*adj.* **tick'lish** easily tickled: unstable: precarious: easily affected: nice: critical.—*adv.* **tick'lishly.**—*n.* **tick'lishness.**—*adj.* **tick'ly** tickling: ticklish.—**tickle pink, to death** to please or amuse very much. [Perh a freq. of **tick.**]

tick-tack-toe. See **tick³.**

tidal. See **tide.**

tidbit. Same as **titbit.**

tiddle *tid'l,* *v.i.* to potter, trifle.

tiddler *tid'lər,* *n.* a small fish, e.g a minnow or a stickleback: anything very small.

tiddly¹ *tid'li,* (slang) *n.* drink.—*adj.* slightly drunk.—Also **tidd'ley.** [Earlier **titley.**]

tiddly² *tid'li,* (coll. or dial) *adj.* small, tiny —Also **tidd'ley.** [Perhaps a childish form of **little.**]

tiddlywink *tid'li-wingk,* *n.* any of the discs used in **tiddlywinks,** a game in which small discs are flipped into a cup by pressing the edge of the small disc with a bigger one.

tide *tid,* *n.* a time: season: festival: opportunity: trend: ebb and flow, esp. of the sea twice daily: a time of ebbing, of flowing, of both, or of suitable state for work.—*v.t.* (esp. *fig.*) to carry as the tide: to effect by means of the tide.—*v.i.* to run like a tide.—*adjs.* **tid'al** or, depending on, regulated by, the tide: flowing and ebbing; **tide'less.**—**tidal wave** a great wave caused by the tide: improperly, a great wave started by an earthquake and running on with its own velocity; **tide'mark** a line on the shore made by the tide: a mark of the limit of washing; **tide'-rip** disturbed sea due to currents: a tidal wave; **tide'-table** a table of times of high-tide; **tide'-water** water brought by the tide: river water affected by the tide (*U S.*); seaboard (*U.S.*); **tide'-way** a track followed by the tide: a channel through which there is a strong current or tide.—**tide over** to carry over, or surmount, difficulties, for the time at least. [O.E *tid.*]

tidings *ti'dingz,* *n.pl.* news. [Late O E. *tidung*—O.E. *tidan,* to tide, happen, or—O.N. *tithindi,* events, tidings.]

tidy *ti'di,* *adj.* fairly good or big (coll.): trim: orderly: neat.—*n.* a cover for a chair-back: a receptacle for odd scraps.—*v.t* to make tidy: to clear away for the sake of tidiness:—*pr p.* **ti'dying;** *pa.t.* and *pa.p.* **ti'died.**—*adv.* **ti'dily.**—*n* **ti'diness.** [**tide;** cf Ger *zeitig.*]

tie *ti,* *v.t.* to bind: to fasten: to knot: to make as a knot: to restrict, restrain: to unite: to mark with a curved line indicating sustentation not repetition (*mus.*): to perform or mark in this way (*mus.*): to limit: to oblige: to subject to bonds.—*v.t.* to be equal in votes or score:—*pr.p.* **ty'ing;** *pa.t.* and *pa.p.* **tied** (*tid*).—*n.* a knot, bow, etc.· a bond: a string, ribbon, etc., for tying: a necktie: a railway sleeper (*U.S.*): a restraint: an obligation: a mode of tying: an equality in score or votes: a match in any stage of a tournament in which the losers are eliminated: a curved line drawn over notes of the same pitch to be performed as one, sustained not repeated (*mus.*).—*adjs.* **tied** having been tied: having a tie as a result: of a public-house or garage, denoting one whose tenant is bound to get his supplies from one particular brewer or distiller, or oil and petrol producer: of a house, cottage, etc., denoting one whose tenant may occupy the premises only as long as he is employed by the owner; **tie'less.**—*n* **ti'er** one who ties.—**tie'-beam** a beam connecting the lower ends of rafters to prevent moving apart; **tie'-break** in tennis, a number of points played at the end of a tied set to decide the winner; **tie'-breaker** a tie-break: any game(s), question(s) or competition(s) intended to break a tie and decide a winner; **tie'-clip** an ornamental clip which attaches one's tie to one's shirt; **tie'-dye'ing** a method of hand-

dyeing textiles in which parts of the material are bound or knotted so as to resist the dye.—Also **tie'-and-dye';** **tie'-in** a connection: something, esp. a book, which ties in with something else, e.g. a film; **tie'-pin** an ornamental pin stuck in a necktie; **tie'-up** a standstill: an entanglement: a connection: a business association.—**tie down** to fix: to bind by conditions, etc.; **tie in, up, with** to agree with: to be closely associated with: to be linked with, as for example a book containing the story of, or a story concerning the characters in, a popular film or TV series; **tie up** to parcel up: to tie so as to remain up· to tether: to moor: to secure against squandering, alienation, etc., re-strict the use of, by conditions. [O.E. *teah,* band, string, *tigan,* to tie.]

tier *ter,* *n.* a row, rank, or layer, esp one of several placed one above another.—*v.t.* to pile in tiers. [O.Fr. *tire,* sequence.]

tierce *ters,* *n.* one-third of a pipe: a cask or vessel of that capacity. (*tûrs*) a sequence of three cards of the same suit: a third (*mus.*): the note two octaves and a third above a given note (*mus.*). [O.Fr. *tiers,* **tierce** —L *tertia* (*pars*).]

tiercel. See **tercel.**

tiff *tif,* *n.* a display of irritation, a huff: a slight quarrel.—*v t.* to be in a huff: to squabble. [Prob. imit.]

tiffany *tif'ə-ni,* *n.* a silk-like gauze.—*adj.* of tiffany: transparent. [Gr. *theophaneia,* theophany, or *dia-phaneia,* transparency]

tiffin *tif'in,* (India) *n.* lunch, a light repast.

tig *tig,* *n.* a touch: a twitch: a game in which one who is 'it' seeks to touch another —*v.t.* to touch, esp. in the game of tig. [Poss. a form of **tick³.**]

tiger *ti'gər,* *n.* a fierce striped Asiatic beast, one of the two largest cats (*Felis tigris*): a ferocious or bloodthirsty person: a formidable opponent or competitor (slang):—*fem.* **ti'gress.**—*adj.* **ti'gerish** (**ti'grish**) like a tiger in disposition.—*n.* **ti'gerism** swagger.—*adjs.* **ti'gerly; ti'gery, ti'grine** (-*grin*), **ti'-groid** like a tiger.—**ti'ger-cat** a general name for a middle-sized striped or spotted wild cat—margay, oc-elot, serval, etc.; **ti'ger-lil'y** a lily with black-spotted orange flowers; **ti'ger-moth** any one of a family of moths with long and usually brightly coloured wings; **ti'ger-shark** a voracious striped shark of the Indian Ocean; **ti'ger-snake** the most deadly of Australian snakes (*Notechis scutatus*), brown with black cross-bands. [Fr. *tigre*—L. *tigris*—Gr. *tigris,* prob from Zend.]

tight *tit,* *adj.* close: compact: close-fitting: too close-fitting: cramped. allowing little space, time, or opportunity, for deviation from plan: (of situation) difficult or dangerous: (of contest) close: (of style) concise: taut, not slack: (of, e.g. control) very firm, strict: precise: under control: firmly fixed: impervious, not leaky, proof: trim: neat: snug: competent: hampered or characterised by want of money: (of money) scarce, hard to obtain: unwilling to part with money: intoxicated.—*adv.* tightly: soundly.—*v.t* and *v.i* **tight'en** (often with *up*) to make or grow tight or tighter.—*n.* **tight'ener** one who, or that which, tightens.—*adj.* **tight'ish.**—*adv.* **tight'ishly.**—*adv* **tight'ly.**—*n.* **tight'ness.**—*n.pl.* **tights** close-fitting breeches: a close-fitting garment covering the lower part of the body and the legs.—*adjs.* **tight'-fisted** stingy; **tight'-knit', tight'ly-knit'** close-knit: closely integrated: tightly organised; **tight'-lipped** uncommunicative.—**tight'-rope** a taut rope on which feats of balancing and acrobatics are performed: a middle course between dangerous or undesirable alternatives (*fig.*); **tight'wad** a skin-flint, miser.—**a tight corner, spot** a difficult situation; **run a tight ship** to be in control of an efficient, well-run organisation or group. [Earlier *thight*, app. from an older form of O.N. *thēttr*.]

tigon *tī'gon, n.* the offspring of a tiger and a lioness.— Also **tig'lon.** [*tiger*, *lion*.]

tike. Same as **tyke.**

tiki *tī'ki, tē'kē, n.* an image, often in the form of a small greenstone ornament, representing an ancestor—in some Polynesian cultures, worn as an amulet. [Maori.]

tilde *til'dä, -di, -də, tild, n.* the diacritical sign over *n* in Spanish to indicate the sound *ny*—thus *ñ* (as in *cañon*): used in Portuguese over *a* and *o* to indicate nasalisation. [Sp.,—L. *titulus*, a title.]

tile *tīl, n.* a slab of baked clay (or a substitute) for covering roofs, floors, etc.: a tube of baked clay used in drains: a piece for playing mah-jongg: tiling.—*v.t.* to cover with tiles: to drain by means of tiles.—*adj.* **tiled** covered with tiles.—*ns.* **ti'ler; til'ery** a place where tiles are made; **til'ing.—have a tile loose** (*slang*) to be a little mad; **on the tiles** on the loose. [O.E. *tigele*—L. *tēgula*—*tegēre*, to cover.]

till *til, n.* a money-drawer or receptacle in or behind a counter. [Cf. M.E. *tillen*, to draw, O.E. *fortyllan*, to draw aside, seduce.]

till *til, prep.* to the time of.—*conj.* to the time when. [O.E. (Northumbrian) *til*—O.N. *til*.]

till *til, v.t.* to work, cultivate.—*adj.* **till'able** arable. —*ns.* **till'age** the act or practice of tilling: husbandry: a place tilled; **till'er; till'ing.** [O.E. *tilian*, to aim at, till—*till*, limit.]

till *til, n.* a stiff impervious clay: boulder-clay (*geol.*): shale (*mining*).

tiller *til'ər, n.* the handle or lever for turning a rudder. —**till'er-chain, -rope** the chain or rope connecting the tiller with the steering-wheel. [M.E. *tillen*, to draw or O.Fr. *telier*, cross-bow stock—L.L. *tēlārium*, a weaver's beam—L. *tēla*, a web.]

tiller *til'ər, n.* a sapling: a shoot from a tree stool: a sucker from the base of a stem.—*v.i.* to form tillers. [O.E. *telgor*, shoot, twig.]

tiller. See **till**.

tilt *tilt, v.i.* to pitch, as a ship: to lean, heel over: to slope: to slant, esp. in a vertical plane: to joust, ride and thrust with a spear: to charge, attack (with *at*): to criticise (with *at*): to thrust.—*v.t.* to incline: to tip out: to send by tilting: to forge with a tilt-hammer.— *n.* an act of tilting: a condition of being tilted: a slope: a joust, a course with a lance: an encounter: a duel: a thrust.—*ns.* **tilt'er; tilt'ing.—tilt'-hammer** a heavy pivoted hammer lifted by a cam.—**full tilt** at full speed in a headlong course. [O.E. *tealt*, tottering.]

tilth *tilth, n.* cultivation: cultivated land: the depth of soil turned up in cultivation. [From **till**.]

timbal, tymbal *tim'bl, n.* a kettledrum.—*n.* **timbale** (*tē-bal, tam'bal, tim'bl*) a dish of meat, fish, etc. cooked in a cup-shaped mould or shell: a mould of pastry. [Fr. *timbale*.]

timber *tim'bər, n.* wood suitable for building or carpentry, whether growing or cut: material generally: a beam, or large piece of wood in a framework, as of a house, ship, etc.: familiarly, a wooden object or part: a wooden leg: wood (*dial.*): woodland, forest-land (*U.S.*).—*adj.* of timber: wooden.—*v.t.* to furnish with timber or beams.—*interj.* a warning given when a tree being felled is about to fall.—*adj.* **tim'bered** built: constructed: built of wood: furnished with timber: wooded.—*n.* **tim'bering** timber collectively: work in timber.—**tim'ber-line** the upper limit of timber-trees on the mountains, etc.; **tim'ber-tree** a tree suitable for timber; **tim'ber-wolf** an American variety of the common wolf, the grey wolf; **tim'ber-yard** a yard or place where timber is stored or sold. [O.E. *timber*, building, wood, *timbrian*, to build.]

timbre *tēbr', tim'bər, tam'bər, n.* the quality of a sound, tone-colour, distinguished from pitch and loudness. [O.Fr., bell—L. *tympanum*, a drum.]

timbrel *tim'brəl, n.* an ancient Oriental tabor or tambourine. [O.Fr. *timbre*—L. *tympanum*, drum.]

time *tīm, n.* a concept arising from change experienced and observed: a quantity measured by the angle through which the earth turns on its axis: (with *cap.*) any of the clock-settings used as standard times in the various time zones, as *Pacific Time, Central European Time*, etc.; a moment at which, or stretch of duration in which, things happen: season: the due, appointed, usual time: the hour of death or of parturition: spell: a period: the actual time of being something or somewhere, as of apprenticeship, residence, sentence, student days, life, etc.: the duration of the world: leisure or opportunity long enough for a purpose: a spell of exciting, usually pleasurable, experience: the time, or shortest time, of performance, as a race: rhythm, tempo: rate of speed: an occasion: an occasion regarded as one of a recurring series: one of a number of multiplied instances: generalised as an indication of multiplication (*so many times* = multiplied by so much): (the rate of) payment for work by the hour, day, etc.: a reckoning of time: an interval: past time: an allotted period, esp. its completion, as in boxing rounds, permitted drinking hours, etc.: the call, bell, whistle, buzzer, or other signal announcing this: (in *pl.*) the contemporary conditions: (in *pl.* with *cap.*) often the name of a newspaper: (*cap.*) a personification of time, a bald-headed old man with a forelock, a beard, a scythe, often an hour-glass.—*v.t.* to arrange, fix, choose, a time for: to mark, adjust, or observe the rhythm or time of: to ascertain the time of: to regulate as to time.—*v.i.* to keep or beat time. —*adj.* of time: reckoned by time: timed: for a future time.—*interj.* indicating that time is up, or that action is now permitted.—*adjs.* **timed; time'less** independent of time: unconnected with the passage of time: eternal.—*adv.* **time'lessly.**—*ns.* **time'lessness; time'liness.**—*adj.* **time'ly** in good time, early: seasonable: well-timed.—*adv.* early, soon: in due time or good time.—*adj.* **tim(e)ous** (*tīm'əs*; chiefly *Scot.*) in good time: seasonable.—*adv.* **tim(e)'ously** in good time.—*ns.* **tim'er** one who or that which times anything: a clock-like device which sets something off or switches something on or off at a given time: (in composition) one who belongs to, works for, etc., such-and-such a time; **tim'ing** fixing, choosing, adjusting, ascertaining, or recording of times: (the co-ordination of) departure and arrival times: co-ordination in time.—**time'-bomb** a bomb that explodes by a time-fuse; **time'-card** a card for use with a time-clock; **time'-clock** a clock-like apparatus which stamps on cards the time of arrival and departure of e.g. office or factory workers.—*adjs.* **time'-consum'ing** requiring much time: wasting time; **time'-hon'oured** honoured on account of antiquity.—**time'-keeper** a clock, watch, or other instrument that measures time: one who keeps account of workmen's hours: one who beats or observes time; **time'-lag** the interval of delay between two connected phenomena. —*adj.* **time'-lapse** of or relating to **time-lapse photography**, a method of recording and condensing long or slow processes by taking a large number of photographs at regular intervals, the resulting film being projected at normal speed.—**time'-lim'it** a time within which something is to be done; **time'-machine** a hypothetical machine by which one may travel through time; **time'-out'** a short break during a sporting contest for rest, discussion of tactics, etc.: any similar short suspension of activity; **time'piece** a piece of machinery for keeping time, esp. one that does not strike but is bigger than a watch.—*n.* and *adj.* **time'-saving.**—**time'scale** the time envisaged for the carrying-out of (the stages of) a project: a statement of the times of appearance, completion, etc. of a series of events, stages, etc.; **time'-server** one who serves or meanly suits his opinions to the times or those in authority for the time; **time'-service.**—*n.* and *adj.* **time'-serving.**—**time'-sharing** the optimum utilisation of a computer and its peripheral devices whereby the differential processing-time of each machine is allowed for, and is used accordingly: a scheme by which a person buys the right to use a holiday home for the same specified period of time each year for a specified number of years; **time'-sheet** a record of the time worked by a person; **time'-signal** an intimation of the exact time given by wireless or otherwise from an observatory; **time'-signature** (*mus.*) an indication of measure at the beginning of a line or wherever there is a change; **time'-switch** one working automatically at a set time; **time'table** a table of times, as of classes, etc.—*v.t.* to put on a timetable: to plan, divide into sessions, etc., according to a timetable.—*adj.* **time'-worn** worn or decayed by time.—**time zone** one of 24 longitudinal divisions of the globe, each 15° wide, having a standard time throughout its area: a similar zone adapted to a particular country.—**against time** with the aim or necessity of finishing by a certain time; **ahead of time** earlier than expected; **ahead of one's time** having ideas, etc. too advanced or progressive to be acceptable at the time; **all in good time** in due course: soon enough; **at one time** formerly: simultaneously; **at the same time** simultaneously: notwithstanding; **at the time** at the time stated or under consideration; **at times** at distant intervals: occasionally; **before one's time** ahead of one's time; **behind time** late; **behind the times** not abreast of changes; **between times** in the intervals; **common time** time with two beats or a multiple of two beats to a measure; **do time** to serve a sentence of imprisonment; **for a time** during a time: temporarily; **for the time being** at the present time or the actual time in question; **from time to time** now and then; **gain time** to provide oneself with more time to do something (e.g. by delaying something else); **half the time** as often as not, frequently; **have a good time** to enjoy oneself; **have a time of it** (*coll.*) to experience problems, difficulties, etc.; **have little, no, time for** to have little, no, interest in or patience with; **in good time** quite early enough: with some time to spare; **in one's time** at some past time in one's life, esp. when one was at one's peak; **in one's own (good) time** at a time, rate, etc. of one's own choosing; **in one's own time** in one's spare time, when not at work; **in time** after a lapse of time: early enough: keeping rhythm; **keep time** to run accurately, as a clock (also **keep good time**): to move or perform in the same rhythm: to record times of workmen, etc.; **know the time of day** to know the state of affairs: to know what one is about, or the best way of doing something; **local time** time reckoned from the local meridian; **lose time** to fall behindhand: to let time pass without full advantage; **make time** to regain advantage of lost time: to find an opportunity; **not before time** rather tardily: none too soon; **no time (at all)** a very short time; **on, upon, a time** once: at a time in the past (usu. imaginary); **on time** up to time: punctually; **out of time** not keeping rhythm: too late (*law*); **solar time** time reckoned by the sun; **standard time** a system of time adopted for a wide area instead of local time—usually Greenwich mean time or a time differing from it by a whole number of hours; **take one's time** (*coll.*) not to hurry, dawdle; **take Time by the forelock** to seize an opportunity before it is too late; **take time off**

(*U.S. out*) to find time to do something, for an activity; **the time of one's life** a very enjoyable time; **time after time** repeatedly; **time and again** repeatedly; **time and motion study** an investigation of the motions performed and time taken in industrial, etc., work with a view to increased production; **time of day** the time by the clock· the point of time reached: a greeting, salutation; **time out of mind** during the whole time within human memory, from time immemorial; **time was** there once was a time (when); **time-zone disease, fatigue** jet lag; **triple time** three beats, or three times three beats, to a measure; **up to time** punctual, punctually: not later than the due time. [O.E. *tīma*.]

timid *tim'id, adj.* inclined to fear: wanting courage: faint-hearted.—*n.* **timid'ity.**—*adv.* **tim'idly.**—*n.* **tim'idness.**—*adj.* **tim'orous** (*-ər-əs*) timid.—*adv.* **tim'orously.**—*n.* **tim'orousness.** [L. *timidus*, timid, *timor, -ōris*, fear—*timēre*, to fear.]

timing. See **time.**

timocracy *tī-mok'rə-si, n.* a form of government in which property is a qualification for office: one in which ambition or desire of honour is a ruling principle.—*adjs.* **timocratic** (*-ŏ-krat'ik*), * **-al.** [Gr. *tīmokratiā—tīmē*, honour, *krateein*, to rule.]

timorous, etc. See **timid.**

timothy *tim'ə-thi, n.* (in full **timothy-grass**) cat's-tail grass (*Phleum pratense*) much valued for feeding cattle. [*Timothy* Hanson, who promoted its cultivation in America about 1720.]

timous. Same as **timeous** (see **time**).

timpano *timp'ə-nō, n.* an orchestral kettledrum:—*pl.* **tim'pani** (*-nē*), often shortened to **timps** (*coll.*).—*n.* **timp'anist.** [It.; see **tympanum.**]

tin *tin, n.* a silvery-white, easily fusible, malleable metal (symbol Sn for L. *stannum*; at. numb. 50): a vessel of tin or tin-plate, a can, etc.: a tinful.—*adj.* made of tin or tin-plate or (*coll.*) of corrugated iron.—*v.t.* to coat or overlay with tin or tinfoil: to cover thinly with solder before soldering: to pack in tins:—*pr.p.* **tinn'ing;** *pa.t.* and *pa.p.* **tinned.**—*n.* **tin'ful:**—*pl.* **tin'fuls.**—*adj.* **tinned.**—*ns.* **tinn'er** a tinsmith: a tin-miner: a canner; **tinn'ing.**—*adj.* **tinn'y** like tin, esp. in sound.—*n.* (also **tinn'ie**) a mug of tin-plate.—**tin'-can;** **tin'foil** tin or (now) tin-lead alloy (or aluminium) in thin sheets, as for wrapping; **tin hat** (*slang*), a military steel helmet; **tin lizzie** (*coll.*) an old or decrepit motor-car; **tin'-opener** an instrument for cutting open tins of food, etc.; **tin'-plate** thin sheet-iron or steel coated with tin.—Also *adj.*—**tin'pot** a pot of or for tin or tin-plate.—*adj.* paltry, rubbishy.—**tin'smith** a worker in tin; **tin'stone** cassiterite; **tin'ware** articles made of tin; **tin whistle** a cheap six-holed metal flageolet.—**put the tin hat, lid, on** to finish off, bring to an end, suppress; **Tin Pan Alley** the realm of popular music production. [O.E. *tin.*]

tinamou *tin'ə-mōō, n.* a South American partridge-like bird (*Tinamus*). [Fr.,—Galibi (Indian language of Fr. Guiana) *tinamu.*]

tinct *tingkt, n.* a tint: a tinge.—*adj.* **tinctŏ'rial** of dyeing.—*n.* **tinct'ure** a tinge or shade of colour: a colouring matter: a metal, colour, or fur (*her.*): a quality or slight taste added to anything: an alcoholic solution of a drug (*med.*).—*v.t.* to tinge: to imbue. [L. *tingĕre, tinctum,* to dye; cf. **tint, tinge.**]

tinder *tin'dər, n.* dry inflammable matter, esp. that used for kindling fire from a spark.—*adj.* **tin'dery** irascible.—**tin'der-box** a box for tinder, and usu flint and steel. [O.E. *tynder.*]

tine *tīn, n.* a spike as of a fork, harrow, or deer's horn.—*adj.* **tined.** [O.E. *tind.*]

tinea *tin'i-ə, n.* ringworm: any of several skin diseases caused by fungi. [L. *tinea,* moth, bookworm, etc.]

ting *ting, v.t.* and *v.i.* to ring.—*n.* the sound of a small bell.—*n.* **ting'-a-ling** a tinkling.—Also *adv.* [Imit.]

tinge *tinj, v.t.* to tint or colour: to suffuse: to impart a slight modification to:—*pr.p.* **ting'ing.**—*n.* a slight colouring or modification. [L. *tingĕre, tinctum*; conn. with Gr. *tengein*, to wet, to stain.]

tingle *tung'gl, v.i.* to feel or be the seat of a thrilling sensation: to thrill: to throb: to ring: to vibrate.—*v.t.* to cause to tingle: to ring.—*n.* a tingling sensation.—*n.* **ting'ler** a stinging blow.—*n.* and *adj.* **ting'ling.**—*adjs.* **ting'lish** thrilling; **ting'ly** tingling. [M.E. *tinglen*, a variant of *tinklen*.]

tinier, etc. See **tiny.**

tink *tingk, n.* a clear high-pitched short bell-like sound.—*v.t.* and *v.i.* to sound in this way.—*n.* **tink'er** a mender of kettles, pans, etc.: a botcher or bungler: a slight, temporary, or unskilful patching-up.—*v.t.* to do tinker's work: (often with *with*) to botch, potter, patch up, adjust or deal with in trivial ways.—*n.* **tink'ering.**—*v.i.* **tink'le** to make small, sharp sounds: to jingle: to clink repeatedly or continuously: to go with tinkling sounds: to tingle.—*v.t.* to cause to tinkle: to ring: to make empty sounds or mere sound. —*n.* a sound of tinkling.—*n.* **tink'ler** a small bell.—*n.* and *adj.* **tink'ling.**—*adv.* **tink'lingly.**—*adj.* **tink'ly.**— **give someone a tinkle** to call someone on the telephone; **not give a tinker's curse, damn** not to care. [M.E. *tinken*, to tink, *tinkere*, tinker (perh. unconnected).]

tinnie, tinny. See **tin.**

tinnitus *ti-nī'tas, n.* a ringing or other noise in the ears. [L. *tinnītus, -ūs*, a jingling—*tinnīre*, to ring.]

tinsel *tin'sl, n.* thin glittering metallic sheets or spangles: anything showy, but of little value.—*adj.* of or like tinsel: gaudy.—*v.t.* to adorn with, or as with, tinsel: to make glittering or gaudy:—*pr.p.* **tin'selling;** *pa.t* and *pa.p.* **tin'selled.**—*adj.* **tin'selly** like tinsel, gaudy, showy. [O.Fr. *estincelle*—L. *scintilla*, a spark.]

tint *tint, n.* a slight tinge distinct from the principal colour: a hue mixed with white: a series of parallel lines in engraving, producing a uniform shading.— *v.t.* to colour slightly: to tinge.—*v.i.* to take on a tint. —*ns.* **tint'er** one who, or that which, tints; **tint'iness;** **tint'ing.** [L. *tinctus*; cf. **tinct, tinge.**]

tintinnabulate *tin-tin-ab'ū-lāt, v.i.* to ring.—*adjs.* **tintinnab'ulant, tintinnab'ular, tintinnab'ulary.**—*n.* **tintinnabulā'tion** bell-ringing.—*adj.* **tintinnab'ulous.**—*n.* **tintinnab'ulum** a bell: a bell-rattle:—*pl.* **tintinnab'ula.** [L. *tintinnabulum*, a bell—*tintinnāre*, to jingle, reduplicated from *tinnīre*, to jingle.]

tiny *tī'ni, adj.* very small:—*compar.* **ti'nier,** *superl.* **ti'niest.**—*n.* **ti'niness.**

tip[1] *tip, n.* a slender extremity: the furthest part.—*v.t.* to put a tip to: to be the tip of: to remove the tip from: —*pr.p.* **tipp'ing;** *pa.t.* and *pa.p.* **tipped.**—*adj.* **tipped.** —*n.* **tipp'ing.**—**on the tip of one's tongue** almost, but not yet quite, remembered: on the very point of being spoken. [Cf. O.N. *typpa*, to tip.]

tip[2] *tip, v.t.* to strike lightly but definitely: to hit glancingly:—*pr.p.* **tipp'ing;** *pa.t* and *pa.p.* **tipped.**—*n.* a tap. [Cf. Du. and Ger. *tippen*, Sw. *tippa*, to tip.]

tip[3] *tip, v.t.* to give, hand, pass, convey: to give a tip to: to indicate.—*v.i.* to give tips:—*pr.p.* **tipp'ing;** *pa.p.* and *pa.t.* **tipped.**—*n.* a gratuity: a hint or piece of special information supposed to be useful in betting, examinations, etc.: a trick or dodge.—*ns.* **tipp'er;** **tipp'ing; tip'ster** one whose business it is to furnish tips.—**tip'-off** a hint, warning, secret information (e.g. about a crime).—**tip off** to give a tip-off to; **tip someone the wink** to convey a secret hint. [Orig. rogues' cant.]

tip[4] *tip, v.t.* to cast down: to upset: to tilt: to shoot,

dump, empty out, by tilting: to toss off.—*v.i.* to topple over: to tilt:—*pr.p.* **tipp'ing;** *pa.p.* and *pa.t.* **tipped.**—*n.* a tilt: a place for tipping rubbish, coal, etc.: a dump.—*ns.* **tipp'er** one who, or that which, tips: a lorry or truck, the main part of which can be tipped up for unloading (also *adj.*); **tipp'ing.**—*adj.* **tip'-up** constructed so as to allow of being tilted.—**tip one's hat** to raise, tilt, or touch the brim of, one's hat as a polite greeting, esp. to a woman; **tip the balance** or **scale(s)** to make more, or less, favourable to someone: to be the deciding factor in a result; **tip the scale(s)** to depress one end of the scales: to weigh (with *at*). [M.E. *type*; origin obscure.]

tippet *tip'it, n.* a long band of cloth or fur e.g. on a hanging part of a garment (*hist.*): a shoulder cape, esp. of fur: an animal's ruff of hair or feathers. [Prob. **tip[1]**.]

tipple *tip'l, v.t.* and *v.i.* to drink constantly in small quantities: to booze.—*n.* liquor tippled.—*n.* **tipp'ler.** [Cf. Norw. dial. *tipla*, to drip slowly.]

tipstaff *tip'stäf, n.* a staff tipped with metal: an officer who carries it, a sheriff's officer:—*pl.* **tip'staffs, tip'staves** (*-stävz*). [**tip[1], staff.**]

tipster. See **tip[3].**

tipsy *tip'si, adj.* partially intoxicated.—*v.t.* **tip'sify** to fuddle.—*adv.* **tip'sily.**—*n.* **tip'siness.**—**tip'sy-cake** a cake made of pastry and almonds, with wine. [Prob. **tip[4]**.]

tiptoe *tip'tō, n.* the end of the toe or toes, more often merely the toes.—*adv.* on tiptoe, literally or figuratively, through excitement, expectation, etc.—*v.i.* to walk on tiptoe, to go lightly and stealthily:—*pr.p.* **tip'toeing;** *pa.t.* and *pa.p.* **tip'toed.** [**tip[1], toe.**]

tiptop *tip'top', n.* the extreme top: the height of excellence.—*adj.* of the highest excellence.—Also *adv.* [**tip[1], top[1].**]

tirade *ti-rād', tī-rād', tē-rād', n.* a long vehement harangue: a string of invective. [Fr.,—It. *tirata*—*tirare*, to pull.]

tire[1] *tīr, n.* a metal hoop to bind a wheel: an *obs.* or *U.S.* spelling of **tyre.**—*v.t.* to put a tire on.—*adj.* **tired; tire'less.**—*n.* **tir'ing.** [Prob. **attire.**]

tire[2] *tīr, v.i.* to weary: to become fatigued: to have interest or patience exhausted or worn down.—*v.t.* to weary: to fatigue: to bore: to wear out.—*adj.* **tired** fatigued: wearied, bored (with *of*): showing deterioration through time or usage—e.g. limp, grubby, played out.—*n.* **tired'ness.**—*adj.* **tire'less** untiring.— *adv.* **tire'lessly.**—*n.* **tire'lessness.**—*adj.* **tire'some** fatiguing: wearisome: boring: tedious: loosely, irritating, troublesome, irksome.—*adv.* **tire'somely.**—*n.* **tire'someness.**—*adj.* **tir'ing.** [App. O.E. *tīorian*, to be tired.]

tiro *tī'rō* (also **tyro**) *n.* a beginner: a novice:—*pl.* **ti'ros,** also **ty'roes, ti'roes.** [L. *tīrō* (L.L. *tȳrō*), *-ōnis,* a recruit.]

'tis *tiz,* a contraction of **it is.**

tisane *ti-zan', n.* a medicinal decoction. [See **ptisan.**]

'tisn't *tiz'nt,* a contraction of **it is not.**

tissue *tish'ōō, -ū, tis'ū, n.* anything woven, esp. a rich or gauzy fabric: an aggregate of similar cells (*biol.*): a fabric, mass, or agglomeration, as of lies, nonsense: tissue-paper: soft, absorbent paper: a handkerchief made of soft, absorbent paper.—*v.t.* to weave or interweave, esp. with gold or silver thread: to clothe, cover, adorn, with tissue.—**tissue culture** the growing of detached pieces of tissue, plant or animal, in nutritive fluids: a piece so grown; **tiss'ue-pa'per** a thin, soft, semitransparent paper; **tiss'ue-typ'ing** the determination of body tissue types, e.g. to ensure compatibility between the donor and the recipient in transplant surgery. [Fr. *tissu*, woven, pa.p. of *tître* (O.Fr. *tistre*)—L. *texĕre*, to weave.]

tit¹ *tit, n.* a variant of **teat**: (usu. in *pl.*) a female breast (*vulg.*): a contemptible person (*vulg.*).

tit² *tit, n.* (*dial.*) a tap.—**tit for tat** a tip for a tap, retaliation: a hat—usu. shortened to **tit'fer** (*cockney rhyming slang*).

tit³ *tit, n.* a titmouse (q.v.). [Icel. *tittr*, titmouse.]

Titan *tī'tən, n.* a son or daughter (**Ti'taness**) or other descendant of Uranus and Gaea: one of the elder gods and goddesses overthrown by Zeus: Hyperion: Helios, the sun-god: Saturn's greatest satellite (*astron.*): (without *cap.*) anything gigantic: (without *cap.*) a man of great intellect but not the highest inspiration.—*adjs.* **Titanesque** (*-esk'*); **Tita'nian**; **Titanic, titanic** (*tī-* or *ti-tan'ik*). [Gr. *Tītān.*]

titanium *tī-tā'ni-əm, n.* a metallic element (Ti; at. numb. 22).—strong, light and corrosion-resistant.— *n.* **titanate** (*tī'tən-āt*) a salt of titanic acid.—*adjs.* **titanic** (*-tan'ik*) of quadrivalent titanium (**titanic acid** H_2TiO_3); **titanif'erous** containing titanium.—*n.* **ti'tanite** a brown, green, or yellow monoclinic mineral, calcium silicate and titanate.—*adj.* **ti'tanous** of trivalent titanium.—**titanium white** titanium dioxide used as pigment. [Gr. *Tītān*, Titan, on the analogy of *uranium.*]

titbit *tit'bit, n.* a choice delicacy or item.—Also, esp. *U.S.*, **tid'bit.**

titch. Another spelling of **tich.**

titer. See under **titrate.**

titfer *tit'fər.* See **tit².**

tithe *tīdh, n.* a tenth part, an indefinitely small part: the tenth of the produce of land and stock allotted originally for church purposes: any levy of one-tenth. —*v.t.* to take a tithe of or from: to pay a tithe on.— *adj.* **tith'able** subject to the payment of tithes.—*adj.* **tithed.**—*ns.* **tith'er** one who collects tithes; **tith'ing** a tithe: exaction or payment of tithes.—**tithe'-barn** a barn for storing the parson's tithe in corn.—*adj.* **tithe'-free** exempt from paying tithes. [O.E. *tēotha*, tenth.]

titi *tē'tē, n.* a small South American monkey (*Callicebus*).

Titian, titian *tish'ən, -yən, n.* a red-yellow colour used by the Venetian painter *Titian* (Tiziano Vecellio, c. 1490–1576).

titillate *tit'il-lāt, v.t.* to tickle: to stimulate gently.— *ns.* **titilla'tion; tit'illātor.** [L. *titillāre, -ātum.*]

titivate, tittivate *tit'i-vāt, tidivate tid', (slang) vs.i.* and *vs.t.* to smarten up, by dress or otherwise.—*ns.* **tit(t)iva'tion, tidiva'tion.** [Poss. coined from **tidy.**]

titlark *tit'lärk, n.* a pipit, esp. the meadow-pipit [**tit³** and **lark¹**.]

title *tī'tl, n.* an inscription or descriptive placard: a chapter-heading: the name of a book, poem, tale, picture, etc.: a title-page: a book or publication, as an item in a catalogue (*publishers' jargon*): an appellation of rank or distinction: a right to possession: a championship (*sport*).—*v.t.* to designate: to give or attach a title to.—*adjs.* **ti'tled** having a title; **ti'tleless** untitled.—**ti'tle-deed** a document that proves right to possession; **ti'tle-holder** a person holding a title, esp. a championship in some sport; **ti'tle-page** the page of a book containing its title; **ti'tle-role** the part in a play which gives its name to it. [O.E. *titul* or *titul* and O.Fr. *title* (Fr. *titre*)—L. *titulus.*]

titmouse *tit'mows, n.* a tit, any of various kinds of little active acrobatic bird of Parus or kindred genus:—*pl.* **titmice** (*tit'mīs*). [**tit³**, and M.E. *mose*, titmouse— O.E. *māse.*]

titrate *tī'trāt, tī-trāt', v.t.* to subject to titration.—*ns.* **titra'tion** measurement of the strength of a solution by finding how much of another solution of known strength is required to complete a chemical reaction; **titre** (*U.S. 'titer; tī'tər, tē'*) the concentration of a

substance in a solution as determined by titration. [Fr. *titre*, standard.]

titter¹ *tit'ər, v.i.* to giggle, snicker, or laugh restrainedly.—*n.* a stifled laugh.—*n.* **titt'erer.**—*n.* and *adj.* **titt'ering.** [Cf. Sw. dial. *tittra.*]

titter² *tit'ər, v.i.* to totter, sway. [O.N. *titra*, to shake.]

tittivate. See **titivate.**

tittle *tit'l, n.* a dot, stroke, accent, vowel-point, contraction or punctuation mark: the smallest part. [O.Fr. *title*—L. *titulus*, a title.]

tittle² *tit'l, (dial) v.t.* and *v.t.* to whisper: to tattle.— **titt'le-tatt'le** idle, empty talk.—*v.i.* to prate idly.— **titt'le-tatt'ler; titt'le-tatt'ling.**

tittup, titup *tit'əp, v.i.* to prance, skip about gaily.—*n.* a light springy step, a canter.—*adj.* **titt'upy, tit'upy** gay, lively: unsteady. [Imit.]

titty *tit'i, n.* a teat: the breast. [Dim. of **tit¹**, teat.]

titubate *tit'ū-bāt, v.t.* to stagger, stumble.—*n.* **titt'ūbancy** staggering.—*adj.* **tit'ūbant.**—*n.* **titūba'tion.** [L. *titubāre, -ātum*, to stagger.]

titule *tit'ūl, n.* and *v.t.* Same as **title.**—*adj.* **tit'ūlar** pertaining to title: in name or title only: nominal: having the title without the duties of an office.—*n.* a titled person: one who enjoys the bare title of an office, without actual possession: a person invested with a title: that from which a church takes its name (*patron* if a saint or angel; *R.C.*).—*n.* **titularity** (*-ar'i-ti*).—*adv.* **tit'ularly.**—*adj.* **tit'ulary** titular.— *n.* one holding a title. [L. *titulus.*]

titup. See **tittup.**

tizzy *tiz'i, n.* a state of agitation, nervousness, confusion, or dither over little (*slang*; also **tizz**).

T.N.T. Abbrev. for **trinitrotoluene**, see **trinitro-.**

to *tōō, tŏŏ, tə, prep.* serving as sign of the infinitive (which is sometimes understood) and forming a substitute for the dative case: in the direction of: as far as: all the way in the direction of: until: into the condition of: towards: beside: near: at: in contact with, close against: before: for: of: with the object or result of: against: in accordance, comparison, or relation with: in honour of, or expressing good wishes for: along with in addition.—*adv.* in one direction, forward: in or into position, contact, closed or harnessed condition.—**to and fro** alternately this way and that; **toing and froing** going backwards and forwards in an agitated way, or without achieving anything: also *fig.* [O.E. *tō.*]

toad *tōd, n.* a toothless tailless amphibian that walks or crawls instead of jumping like the frog, esp. one of *Bufo* or kindred genus: a hateful or contemptible person or animal.—*n.* **toad'y** a sycophant.—*v.t.* to fawn as a sycophant:—*pr.p.* **toad'ying**; *pa.t.* and *pa.p.* **toad'ied.**—*adj.* **toad'yish.**—*n.* **toad'yism.**—**toad'fish** a toadlike fish of many kinds; **toad'flax** any species of Linaria, a genus closely allied to snapdragon with flax-like leaves; **toad'-in-the-hole** a dish of sausage-meat cooked in batter; **toad'-stone** a basalt lava or tuff ; **toad'stool** any mushroom-like fungus, often excluding the edible mushroom. [O.E. *tāde, tādige, tādie.*]

toast *tōst, v.t.* to dry and parch: to brown (as bread): to half-melt (as cheese): to warm or heat by rays: to drink to.—*v.i.* to drink toasts: to undergo, or be suitable for, toasting.—*n.* bread toasted: the person or thing drunk to, esp. the lady most admired for the moment: a proposal of health.—*adj.* **toast'ed.**—*ns.* **toast'er** one who toasts: a toasting-fork: an electric apparatus for making toast; **toast'ing.**—**toast'ing-fork, -iron** a long-handled fork for toasting bread; **toast'master** the announcer of toasts, introducer of speakers, at a dinner; **toast'mistress; toast'-rack** a stand with partitions for slices of toast.—**on toast**

served on a slice of toast: at one's mercy. [O.Fr. *toster*—L. *tostus*, roasted, pa.p. of *torrēre*.]

tobacco *tə-bak'ō*, *n.* an American plant, *Nicotiana tabacum*, or other species of the genus: its prepared leaves used for smoking, chewing, or snuffing:—*pl.* **tobacc'o(e)s.**—*n.* **tobacc'onist** a seller or manufacturer of tobacco.—**tobacc'o-pipe** a pipe for smoking tobacco; **tobacc'o-plant**; **tobacc'o-pouch** a pouch for holding tobacco. [Sp. *tabaco*, from Haitian.]

to-be *tōō-*, *tə-bē'*, *n.* the future.—*adj.* (now usu. following and attached to the word it modifies) future.

toboggan *tə-bog'ən*, *n.* a flat sledge turned up in front. —*v.i.* to slide, coast, travel, on, or as if on, a toboggan.—*ns.* **tobogg'aner**; **tobogg'aning**; **tobogg'anist.** [Micmac *tobākun*.]

Toby *tō'bi*, *n.* a beer-mug or similar object shaped like a man with a three-cornered hat (also **To'by-jug**; also without *cap.*): Punch's dog.

toccata *to-kä'tə*, (*mus.*) *n.* primarily a work intended to display the performer's touch, or in which he seems to try the touch of an instrument in a series of runs and chords before breaking into a fugue: loosely, a sort of fantasia or overture. [It.,—*toccare*, to touch.]

toc emma *tok em'ə*, (*mil. slang*) a trench mortar.—**Toc H** (*āch*) a society for handing on the spirit of comradeship of the 1st World War, from its first meetings at Talbot House, at Poperinghe in Belgium. [Formerly signallers' names of the initial letters T, M and T, H.]

Tocharian, Tokharian *to-kä'ri-ən*, or -*kä'*, **Tocha'rish, Tokha'rish** -*rish*, *ns.* an extinct Indo-European language, akin to Latin and Celtic, preserved in MSS discovered in the 20th century in Chinese Turkestan [Gr. *Tocharoi*, a people guessed to be its speakers on the strength of the Uigar (language of Chinese Turkestan) name *Tochri*.]

tocher *tohh'ər*, (*Scot.*) *n.* a dowry. [Ir. *tochar*, Gael. *tochradh.*]

tocology, tokology *tok-ol'ə-ji*, *n.* obstetrics.—*n.* **tocoph'erol** vitamin E, whose deficiency causes sterility in some species. [Gr. *tokos*, birth, offspring, *logos*, discourse, *pherein*, to bring.]

tocsin *tok'sin*, *n.* an alarm-bell, or the ringing of it. [Fr. *tocsin*—Prov. *tocasenh*—*tocar*, to touch, strike, *senh*—L *signum*, sign (L.L. bell).]

tod *tod*, in phrase **on one's tod**, alone. [Rhyming slang *on one's Tod Sloan.*]

today, to-day *tōō-*, *tə-dā'*, *n.* this or the present day.— *adv.* on the present day: nowadays [O.E. *tōdæg(e)*.]

toddle *tod'l*, *v.i.* to walk with short feeble steps, as a child: to saunter: to go, depart (*facet.*) —*n.* a toddling gait: an aimless stroll: a toddling child —*n.*—**todd'ler** one who toddles, esp. a child.—*adj* **todd'ling.** [Orig. Northern dial.]

toddy *tod'i*, *n.* fermented palm juice: a mixture of spirits, sugar, and hot water. [Hindi *tārī—tār*, a palm-tree, prob. of Dravidian origin.]

to-do *tə-*, *tōō-dōō'*, *n.* a bustle: a stir: a commotion:— *pl.* **to-dos'.**

toe *tō*, *n.* one of the five small members at the point of the foot: the front of a hoof: the corresponding part of a shoe, sock, golf-club head, etc.: the lowest part of the front of anything, esp. if it projects.—*v.t.* to stand with the toes against: to kick: to strike with the toe of a club: to perform with the toe: to furnish with a toe, as a stocking.—*v i.* to place the toes:—*pr.p* **toe'ing**; *pa.t.* and *pa.p.* **toed.**—*adj.* **toed** (*tōd*) having toes.—**toe'cap** a cap covering the toe of a shoe; **toe's hold** a place to fix the toes in: a small established position: a hold in which the toes are held and the foot is bent back or twisted (*wrestling*); **toe'-nail** a nail on a

human or animal toe: an obliquely driven nail; **toe'piece.**—**big** or **great toe** largest of the toes, **little toe** smallest of the toes; **on one's toes** poised for a quick start, alert, eager, **toe the line** to stand with toes against a marked line, as in starting a race: to conform; **tread on the toes of (someone)** to offend (someone). [O.E. *tā* (*pl. tān*)]

toe-rag *tō'rag*, (*slang*) *n* a beggar, tramp: generally, a ruffian or rascal.—Also **toe-ragg'er.**

toff *tof*, (*slang*) *n.* a person of the upper classes: a swell: a good sort —*adj* **toff'ish.**—*n* **toff'ishness.** [Perh. **tuft.**]

toffee, toffy *tof'i*, *n.* a hard-baked sweetmeat, made of sugar and butter.—**toff'ee-app'le** a toffee-coated apple on a stick.—*adj.* **toff'ee-nose(d)** (*slang*) supercilious, conceited.—**for toffee** (*coll.*) at all, as in *he can't dance for toffee*, etc.

toft *toft*, *n.* a homestead (*hist.*): a hillock (*dial*) [Late O.E. *toft*—O.N *topt*, *tupt*, *toft*.]

tog[1] *tog*, (*slang*) *n.* a garment—generally in *pl.*—*v.t.* to dress—*pr.p.* **togg'ing**; *pa.t.* and *pa.p* **togged.**—**tog** up to dress esp in one's best clothes [Prob. ultimately L. *tōga*, a robe.]

tog[2] *tog*, *n.* a unit of measurement of thermal insulation as a property of textile fabrics.—**tog rating, value** the amount of thermal insulation provided by a fabric, measured in togs. [App. an invention— perh. conn. with *tog*[1].]

toga *tō'gə*, *n.* the mantle or outer garment of a Roman citizen, a long piece of cloth wound round and draped over the body.—*adjs* **tō'ga'd, tō'gaed, tō'gate, -d.** [L. *tōga*.]

together *tə-*, *tōō-gedh'ər*, *adv.* in or to the same place: at the same time: in or into connection, company, or concert.—*adj.* (*slang*, chiefly *U.S.*) well-organised, mentally composed, emotionally stable, etc —*n* **togeth'erness** unity: closeness: a sense of unity or community with other people.—**get, put it (all) together** (*slang*, chiefly *U S.*) to perform something successfully, get something right: to become well-organised, stable, etc : to establish a good relationship (with). [O.E. *tōgædere*—*tō*, to, *geador*, together.]

toggle *tog'l*, *n* a cross-piece on a rope, chain, rod, etc , to prevent slipping through a hole, or to allow twisting: a short bar acting as a button, passed through a loop for fastening: an appliance for transmitting force at right angles to its direction.—*v t.* to hold or furnish with a toggle: to fix fast.—**togg'lejoint** an elbow or knee joint: a mechanism consisting of two levers hinged together, force applied to straighten the hinge producing a considerable force along the levers; **togg'le-switch** in telecommunications and electronics, a switch which, in a circuit having two stable or quasi-stable states, produces a transition from one to the other [App conn with **tug** and **tow**[1].]

toheroa *tō-ə-rō'ə*, *n.* an edible shellfish found at low tide buried in sandy beaches. [Maori.]

toil[1] *toil*, *v i.* to struggle hard: to labour hard. to make one's way by strong effort —*n* a struggle: hard labour.—*adj.* **toiled.**—*n.* **toil'er.**—*adj.* **toil'ful.**—*n* and *adj.* **toil'ing.**—*adjs* **toil'less**; **toil'some** involving toil: toiling· owing to toil —*adv.* **toil'somely.**—*n* **toil'someness.**—*adj* **toil'-worn** worn with toil [A.Fr *toiler* (Fr *touillier*) said to be—L. *tudiculāre*, to stir.]

toil[2] *toil*, (usu in *pl* , often *fig.*) *n* a net: a snare.—*ns* **toile** (*twal*) a thin dress material; **toilet** (*toil'it*) a dressing-table with a mirror: the articles used in dressing: the mode or process of dressing. the whole dress and appearance of a person, any particular costume: a dressing-room, bathroom, or lavatory; **toil'etry** any article or preparation used in washing and dressing oneself:—*pl.* **toil′etries; toil′et-paper** paper for the lavatory; **toil′et-roll** a roll of toilet-paper; **toil′et-soap** soap for personal use; **toilet tissue** soft, absorbent toilet-paper; **toilet training** the training of children to control bladder and bowels and to use the lavatory; **toilet water** a lightly perfumed liquid similar to Cologne. [Fr *toile*, dim. *toilette*—L. *tēla*, web.]

toing and froing. See **to**.

tokamak *tō′kə-mak, n.* a tyre-shaped device for producing thermonuclear power in which plasma is held in place by a complex magnetic field generated by internal electric currents.—Also *adj.* [Russ.]

Tokay *tō-kā′, n.* a sweetish and heavy wine with an aromatic flavour, produced at *Tokay* in Hungary: the grape that yields it.

token *tō′kn, n.* a sign: a symbol: a portent: an indication: an evidence: an authenticating sign, word, or object: a keepsake: a coin or voucher, issued privately, redeemable in current money or goods (as *gift, record, token*).—*adj.* serving as a symbol: hence, being a mere show or semblance, as *token force, token resistance.*—*v.t.* to betoken.—*n.* **tō′kenism** the practice of doing something once to give an impression of doing it regularly, e.g. employing one coloured person to avoid a charge of racialism.— **to′ken-money** money current for more than its intrinsic value as metal: private tokens.—**by the same token** further in corroboration, or merely by the way. [O.E. *tācen*.]

Tokharian, Tokharish. See **Tocharian.**

tokology. See **tocology.**

tolbooth. See **toll¹.**

tolbutamide *tol-būt′əm-īd, n.* a drug taken by mouth in the treatment of diabetes.

told *tōld, pa.t.* and *pa.p.* of **tell.**

tole *tōl, n.* painted or japanned tinware, popular in the 18th and 19th cents. [Fr. *tôle*, sheet metal, from a dial. word for table.]

Toledo *tō-lē′dō, n.* a sword-blade made at *Toledo* (*-lā′*) in Spain.—*pl.* **Tolē′dos.**

tolerate *tol′ə-rāt, v.t.* to endure: to endure with patience or impunity: to allow, allow to exist.—*n.* **tolerabil′ity.**—*adj.* **tol′erable** endurable: passable: fair.—*adv.* **tol′erably.**—*n.* **tol′erance** the ability to endure: the disposition or willingness to tolerate or allow: the permissible range of variation.—*adj.* **tol′erant** tolerating: enduring: capable of enduring (e.g. unfavourable conditions, a parasite, a drug) without showing serious effects (*biol.* and *med.*): indulgent: favouring toleration.—*adv.* **tol′erantly.**— *ns.* **tolera′tion** the act of tolerating: the allowance of what is not approved: the liberty given to a minority to hold and express their own political or religious opinions; **tolera′tionist; tol′erātor.**—**tolerance dose** the maximum dose which can be permitted to a specific tissue during radiotherapy involving irradiation of any other adjacent tissue. [L. *tolerāre, -ātum—tollĕre*, to lift up.]

toll¹ *tōl, n.* a tax for the liberty of using a bridge or road, selling goods in a market, etc.: the cost in damage, injury, or lives (as *toll of the road*).—*v.i.* to take or pay toll.—*v.t.* to take toll of: to take as toll.— **tolbooth, tollbooth** (*tōl′* or *tol′bōōth, -bōōdh*) an office where tolls are collected: a town-hall: a prison: often a combination of these; **toll′-bar** a movable bar across a road, etc., to stop passengers liable to toll; **toll′bridge, -gate** a bridge, gate, where toll is taken; **toll′-call** a short-distance telephone trunk-call: a trunk call (*U.S.*, etc.); **toll′-gath′erer.**—*adj.* and *adv.* **toll′-free′.**—**toll′-house; toll′man** the man who collects toll: a toll-gatherer.—**take toll of** to inflict loss, hardship, pain, etc., on. [O.E. *toll.*]

toll² *tōl, v.i.* to sound, as a large bell, esp. with a measured sound.—*v.t.* to cause to sound, as a bell: to sound, strike, signal, announce, summon, send, by tolling: to toll for the death of.—*n.* the sound of a bell tolling.—*n.* **toll′er.**

Tolu *tō-lōō′, n.* (in full **balsam of Tolu**) a balsam yielded by the South American papilionaceous tree *Myroxylon toluifera* (also without *cap.*).—*ns.* **toluene** (*tol′ū-ēn*), **tol′uol** methyl benzene, a colourless flammable liquid ($C_6H_5·CH_3$) used as a solvent and in the manufacture of other organic chemicals —*adj.* **tolū′ic.**—*n* **tolū′idine** (*-i-dēn*) an amine ($C_6H_4·CH_3NH_2$) derived from toluene, used in making dyes. [From Santiago de *Tolú* in Colombia.]

Tom *tom, n.* short for *Thomas:* (without *cap.*) a male, esp. a cat.—**Tom′-and-Jerr′y** hot rum and eggs, spiced and sweetened; **tom′-cat; Tom Collins** a cocktail of gin, lime-juice, soda, etc.—**Tom, Dick, and Harry** anybody: people in general; **Tom Thumb** a famous dwarf in English folklore, hence any very-small person.

tomahawk *tom′ə-hok, n.* a North American Indian war-axe.—*v.t.* to assail or kill with a tomahawk: to hack, cut up, or slate. [Virginian Indian *tamahāk.*]

tomato *tə-mä′tō* (*U.S.* *-mā′*), *n. Lycopersicum esculentum* or *Solanum lycopersicum,* a South American plant close akin to the potato: its red or yellow pulpy edible fruit:—*pl.* **toma′toes.** [Sp. *tomate*—Mex. *tomatl.*]

tomb *tōōm, n.* a grave: a vault for the disposal of dead bodies: a sepulchral monument.—*v.t.* to entomb: to bury.—**tomb′stone** a memorial stone over a tomb. [O.Fr. (Fr.) *tombe*—L. *tumba*—Gr. *tymbos.*]

tombac, tombak *tom′bak, n.* an alloy of copper with a little zinc: an alloy of copper and arsenic. [Fr. *tombac*—Malay *tambaga,* copper.]

tombola *tom-bō′lə, tom′, n.* a kind of lottery (at a fête, etc.): a type of bingo, played esp. in the Services. [It.,—*tombolare,* to tumble.]

tomboy *tom′boi, n.* a high-spirited romping girl: a girl with boyish looks, dress, habits, etc. [**Tom** and **boy.**]

tome *tōm, n.* a big book or volume. [Fr.,—L. *tomus* —Gr. *tomos—temnein,* to cut.]

tomentum *tō-men′tam, n.* a matted cottony pubescence.—*adjs.* **tomentose** (*tō-mən-tōs′, tō-men′tōs*), **tomen′tous.** [L.]

tomfool *tom′fōōl′, n.* a great fool: a buffoon: a trifling fellow.—*adj.* extremely foolish.—*v.i.* to play the fool.—*n.* **tomfool′ery** foolish trifling or jesting: buffoonery: trifles, ornaments.—*adj.* **tom′foolish.** [**Tom.**]

tommy *tom′i, n.* (sometimes with *cap.*) a private in the British army.—**Tommy Atkins** a generic name for the private in the British army; **tomm′y-gun** a light machine-gun (after its American inventor, General J. T. *Thompson*); **tomm′y-rot** absolute nonsense. [From the name **Thomas.**]

tomography *tō-mog′rə-fi, n.* radiography of a layer in the body by moving the X-ray tube and photoplate in such a way that only the chosen plane appears in clear detail.—*ns.* **tom′ogram** a radiogram produced by tomography; **tom′ograph** a machine for making tomograms.—*adj.* **tomograph′ic.** [Gr. *tomos,* slice, *graphein,* to draw.]

tomorrow, to-morrow *tə-, tōō-mor′ō, n.* the day after today: the future.—*adv.* on the day after today: in the future. [O.E. *tō morgen.*]

tompion. Same as **tampion** (see **tamp**).

tomtit *tom′tit′, n.* the blue or other tit. [**Tom,** **tit³.**]

tom-tom *tom′-tom, n.* an Indian drum: any primitive drum or substitute: (esp. formerly) a Chinese gong, tam-tam.—*v.i.* to beat thereon.

-tomy *-tə-mı,* in composition used to denote surgical incision into an organ. [Gr. *-tomia,* the operation of cutting—*tomē,* a cut—*temnein,* to cut.]

ton *tun, n.* a measure of capacity, varying with the substance measured—timber, wheat, etc. (see **tonnage**): a weight = 20 cwt = 2240 lb = 1016 kg (2400 lb was formerly a *long ton*): in U.S. usually = 2000 lb = 907·2 kg (*short*) or 2240 lb (*long*): 100 units of various kinds. £100 (*coll.*): a score, total, etc. of 100 (*coll.*). 100 runs (*cricket; coll.*): 100 m.p.h. (preceded by *a* or *the; slang*): a great weight (*coll.*): (in *pl.*) many, a great amount (*coll.*).— **-tonn'er** in composition, a vehicle, vessel, etc. weighing a specified number of tons or having a specified amount of tonnage: a load of a specified number of tons.—*adj* **ton'-up** orig. of a motor-cyclist, having done a ton: noisy and reckless: travelling at 100 m.p.h.—**metric ton** see **tonne**. [O.E. *tunne,* a vat, tub; see **tun**.]

tonal, tonality. See **tone**.

tondo *ton'dō, n.* a circular painting or circular carving in relief:—*pl.* **ton'di** (*-dē*), **ton'dos**.—*n* **tondi'no** (*-dē'nō*) a circular or semicircular moulding (*archit.*). a small tondo:—*pl.* **tondi'ni** (*-nē*), **tondi'nos**. [It., short for *rotondo,* round,—L. *rotundus.*]

tone *tōn, n* the character of a sound: quality of sound accent: intonation: vocal inflexion, rise or fall in pitch: a sound of definite pitch: a major second, one of the larger intervals between successive notes in the scale, as C and D: vocal expression: bodily firmness, elasticity, or tension, esp. in muscles: the prevailing character or spirit: mood: temper· harmony or general effect of colours: depth or brilliance of colour: a tint or shade.—*v.t.* to give tone or the desired tone to.—*v.i.* to take a tone: to harmonise (with *in*).—*adjs.* **tōn'al** of tone: according to key; **tōnal'itive** of tonality.—*n.* **tōnal'ity** a relation in key: a key: a rendering of colour relations.—*adjs.* **toned** having a tone (in compounds): braced up: treated to give tone: slightly tinted; **tone'less** soundless: expressionless: dull: relaxed: listless.—*adv.* **tone'lessly.**—*ns* **tone'lessness; toneme** (*tō'nēm*) in a tone language, a phoneme consisting of a particular intonation.—*adjs.* **tonēm'ic; tonetic** (*-et'*) of or relating to linguistic tones, tone languages or intonation.—*adv.* **tonet'ically.**—*adj.* **tonic** (*ton'ik*) relating to tones· producing tension: giving tone and vigour to the system (*med.*): giving or increasing strength.—*n.* a tonic medicine: a keynote (*mus.*): tonic water: any person or thing that enlivens, invigorates, etc.—*ns* **tonicity** (*ton-is'i-ti*) the property or condition of having tone: mode of reaction to stimulus: the healthy state of muscular fibres when at rest; **tōn'us** tone: a tonic spasm.—*adj.* **tōn'(e)y** (*slang*) high-toned: fashionable.—**tone'-arm** part of a gramophone, the arm that carries an electric pick-up; **tone control** a manual control in a radio set which adjusts the relative amplitude of high, medium, and low frequencies.—*adj.* **tone'-deaf** unable to appreciate or distinguish differences in musical pitch.—**tone language** a language (e.g. Chinese) in which difference of intonation distinguishes words of different meaning that would otherwise sound the same; **tone poem** a piece of programme music, not divided into movements, conveying or translating a poetic idea or literary theme; **tone row** in serial music, the basic set of notes in the chosen order; **tonic sol-fa** (*mus.*) a system of notation and teaching devised by Sarah Glover (1785-1867) and developed by John Curwen, using sol-fa syllables (modified) and their initial letters for the notes of the scale with *doh* (*do*) for the tonic, and dividing the bar by colons, dots, and inverted commas; **tonic spasm** a prolonged uniform muscular spasm; **tonic water** aerated quinine water

—**tone down** to give a lower tone to· to moderate· to soften, to harmonise the colours of as to light and shade, as a painting; **tone up** to heighten: to intensify· to make healthier, more vigorous. [Gr. *tonos,* pitch, tension, partly through Fr *ton* and L *tonus*]

tong *tong, n.* a Chinese guild, association, or secret society [Chin *t'ang*]

tonga-bean. See **tonka-bean.**

tongs *tongz, n.pl* a gripping and lifting instrument, consisting of two legs joined by a pivot, hinge, or spring [O E *tang, tange*]

tongue *tung, n.* the fleshy organ in the mouth, used in tasting, swallowing, and speech: the tongue of an ox, etc., as food. the power of speech the manner of speaking· speech: discourse· voice: utterance· a language: anything like a tongue in shape: a point of land: a bell clapper: a flap in the opening of a shoe or boot: any narrow projection —*v t* to utter: to articulate: to lick: to touch with the tongue: to furnish with a tongue: to produce or play by tonguing (*mus.*) —*v.i* to give tongue: to stick out: to practise tonguing (*mus.*).—*adjs.* **tongued** having a tongue; **tongue'less** having no tongue —*ns.* **tongue'let** a little tongue; **tongu'ing** articulation to separate the notes in playing wind instruments.—*adj.* and *adv.* **tongue'-in-cheek** ironical(ly) or whimsical(ly), not sincere(ly) or serious(ly) —**tongue'-lashing** a severe verbal reprimand.—*adjs.* **tongue'-tacked, -tied** impeded by a short fraenum: unable to speak out —**tongue'-twister** a formula or sequence of words difficult to pronounce without blundering.—**give tongue** to give utterance; **lose one's tongue** to become speechless from emotion; **on the tip of one's tongue** see **tip'**; **speaking in tongues, gift of tongues** glossolalia; **with (one's) tongue in (one's) cheek** tongue-in-cheek (*adv.*) [O.E *tunge;* L *lingua* (from *dingua*).]

tonic, tonicity. See **tone.**

tonight, to-night *ta-, tōō-nīt', n.* this night: the night of the present day.—*adv* on this night or the night of today. [O.E. *tō niht*]

tonka-bean *tong'ka-bēn', n.* the coumarin-scented seed of a large papilionaceous tree (*Dipteryx*) of Guiana, used for flavouring snuff, etc —Also **tonga-** (*tong'ga-*) **bean.** [Said to be the Guiana Negroes' name.]

tonnage *tun'ıj, n.* a tax of so much a *tun* on imported wines (sometimes **tunnage;** *hist.*): a charge or payment by the *ton*: the carrying capacity of a ship in *tons* (orig. in *tuns* of wine); *register ton* = 100 cu. feet, *freight ton* = 40 cu. feet, of space for cargo: the total amount of shipping so measured: a duty on ships, estimated in tons.—**gross tonnage** the total space capable of carrying cargo in a ship, measured in register tons; **net register tonnage** gross tonnage less deducted spaces (those spaces required in running the ship). [See **ton, tun.**]

tonne *tun, n.* the preferred name for a **metric ton,** equal to 1000 kilograms (0·984 ton). [Fr.]

-tonner. See **ton.**

tonometer *tōn-om'ə-tər, n.* a device for determining the frequencies of tones (*mus.*): an instrument for measuring fluid pressure within the eyeball, or blood pressure: an instrument for measuring vapour pressure [Gr. *tonos,* pitch, tension, *metron,* measure.]

tonsil *ton'sl, -sil, n.* either of two glands at the root of the tongue.—*adj* **ton'sillar.**—*n.* **tonsillec'tomy** surgical removal of a tonsil —*adj* **tonsillit'ic.**—*ns.* **tonsilli'tis** inflammation of the tonsils; **tonsillot'omy** complete or partial removal of a tonsil.—Also **tonsilitis,** etc. [L. *tōnsillae* (pl.).]

tonsor *ton'sər, n.* a barber.—*adj.* **tonso'rial.**—*n.* **ton'sure** (*-shər*) the act or mode of clipping the hair, or of shaving the head: in the R.C. and Eastern Churches, the shaving or cutting of part of the hair of the head on entering the priesthood or a monastic order: the shaven part.—*adj.* **ton'sured** having the crown of the head shaven, as a priest: shaven: bald: clipped. [L. *tŏnsor,* barber, *tŏnsūra,* a shearing—*tondēre, tŏnsum,* to clip.]

tontine *ton'tēn, ton-tēn',* n. a scheme of life annuity, increasing as the subscribers die.—Also *adj.*—*n.* **tontin'er.** [Lorenzo *Tonti,* its inventor (1653).]

tonus, tony. See **tone.**

Tony *tō'ni,* n. in U.S., an award for meritorious work in the theatre. [After U.S. actress *Antoinette Perry.*]

too *tōō, adv.* as well, in addition, also, likewise (never at the beginning of a sentence in English usage): undesirably in excess: so much as to be incompatible with a condition.—**too much** more than is reasonable, tolerable, etc.: also used as an interjection expressing approval, amazement, etc. (*slang,* chiefly *U.S.*). [Stressed form of **to.**]

took *tōōk, pa.t.* of **take.**

tool *tōōl,* n. a working instrument, esp. one used by hand: the cutting part of a machine-tool: a weapon, esp. a gun (*slang*): one who is used as the mere instrument of another: (esp. in *pl.*) anything necessary to the pursuit of a particular activity.—*v.t.* to shape or finish with a tool: to mark with a tool, esp. to ornament or imprint designs upon (a book cover), or to chisel the face of (stone): to supply with tools, esp. with machine tools for a particular purpose (also **tool up**).—*n.* **tool'ing** workmanship done with a tool.— **tool'bag, tool'box** a bag, box for carrying and storing tools; **tool'kit** a set of tools; **tool'maker** a worker who makes or repairs tools, esp. machine-tools; **tool'pusher** the supervisor of drilling operations at an oilwell; **tool'room** that part of a factory occupied by toolmakers; **tool'-shed.** [O.E. *tōl.*]

toon[1] *tōōn,* n. an Indian tree of the mahogany family, with red wood and astringent bark. [Hind. *tūn.*]

toon[2], **toun** *tōōn,* (*Scot.*) n. same as **town.**

toot *tōōt, v.i.* to make short sounds, as on a flute or horn.—*v.t.* to blow, as a horn, etc.—*n.* a blast as of a horn.—*n.* **toot'er** one who toots, or his instrument. [Prob. imit.]

tooth *tōōth,* n. one of the hard bone-like bodies set in the jaws, used for biting and chewing: a hard projection of similar use in invertebrates: a tooth-like projection, prong, cog, jag, as on a leaf-margin, comb, saw, or wheel:—*pl.* **teeth** (*tēth*) q.v.—*v.t.* to furnish with teeth: to cut into teeth.—*v.i.* of cog-wheels, to interlock.—*adjs.* **toothed** (*tōōtht,* also *tōōdhd*) having teeth: dentate; **tooth'ful** full of teeth: toothsome.— *n.* a small drink of spirits, etc.—*adjs.* **tooth'less** lacking teeth: powerless or ineffective; **tooth'some** palatable, tasty: attractive, pleasant, agreeable.—*n.* **tooth'someness.**—*adj.* **tooth'y** with prominent teeth: toothsome.—**tooth'ache** an ache or pain in a tooth; **tooth'brush** a brush for cleaning the teeth; **toothbrush moustache** a small stiff moustache; **tooth'paste, -pow'der** a paste, powder, used with a toothbrush; **tooth'pick** an instrument for picking shreds of food from between the teeth; **tooth'wort** a pale fleshy plant (*Lathraea squamaria*), parasitic on tree-roots, with tooth-like scale-leaves.—**a colt's tooth** an addiction to youthful pleasures; **armed to the teeth** armed as completely as possible, from top to toe; **a sweet tooth** a taste for sweet things; **cast, throw,** in someone's teeth to fling at someone as a taunt or reproach; **get one's teeth into** to tackle, deal with, vigorously, eagerly, etc.; **in, to, someone's teeth** to someone's face: in direct affront; **in the teeth of** in direct opposition to; **long in the tooth** elderly, like a horse whose

gums are receding; **take the teeth out of** to render harmless or powerless; **tooth and nail** with all possible vigour and fury. [O.E. *tōth* (pl. *tēth*).]

tootle *tōōt'l, v.i.* to make feeble sounds, as on the flute: to go casually along, esp. by car.—*n.* a soft sound on the flute, etc.: a casual trip, a drive. [Freq. of **toot.**]

tootsie, tootsy (-wootsy) *tōōt'si* (-*wōōt'si*), *ns.* jocular or childish words for a foot or toe. [Perh. a childish pron. of **foot.**]

top[1] *top,* n. the highest or uppermost part or place: the upper end or surface: topspin: a circus tent (*slang*; **the big top** the main tent): (esp. in *pl.*) the part of a root vegetable that is above the ground: (in *pl.*) in oilrefining, the first part of a volatile mixture to come off in the distillation process.—*adj.* highest: best: most important, able, etc.—*v.t.* to cover on the top: to tip: to rise above: to surpass: to rise to the top of: to surmount: to be on or at the top of: to take off the top of: to hit (the ball) on the upper half (*golf*): to kill (*slang*).—*v.i.* to finish up, round off (with *off* or *up*): —*pr.p.* **topp'ing;** *pa.t.* and *pa.p.* **topped.**—*adj.* **top'less** without a top: (of female garb) leaving the breasts uncovered.—*n.* **top'lessness.**—*adjs.* **top'most** (-*mōst, -mast*) uppermost: highest; **topped.**—*ns.* **topp'er** one who, or that which, tops in any sense: one who excels (*coll.*): a top hat (*coll.*); **topp'ing** the act of one who tops: (the action of) that which tops: (*pl.*) pieces cut from the top: a sauce or dressing to go over food.—*adj.* surpassing, pre-eminent.—*adv.* **topp'ingly.**—**top'-boot** a long-legged boot with a showy band of leather round the top; **top'coat** an overcoat; **top dog** the winner, leader or dominant person; **top drawer** the highest level, esp. of society (*out of the top drawer,* belonging to this social rank).—*adj.* **top'draw'er.**—*v.t.* **top'-dress.**—**top'-dress'ing** surface dressing of manure: the application of it: any superficial covering or treatment (*fig.*).—*adjs.* **top'-flight** excellent, superior, of the highest class; **top-gallant** (*tə-, top-gal'ənt*) above the topmast and topsail and below the royal mast (also *n.*).—**top'-hat'** a tall cylindrical hat of silk plush.—*adjs.* **top'-heav'y** having the upper part too heavy or large for the lower (often *fig* , e.g. of an organisation with too many administrative staff): tipsy; **top'-hole'** (*slang*) tiptop (also *interj.*).— **top'knot** a crest, tuft of hair, often a piece of added hair, or knot of ribbons, etc., on the top of the head: a small fish (of several species) akin to the turbot.— *adjs.* **top'knotted; top'-level** at the highest level; **top'line** important enough to be mentioned in a headline —**top-lin'er** one who is top-line: a principal performer, star —*adjs.* **top'loftical, top'lofty** (*facet.*) high and mighty: stuck-up.—**top'loftiness; top'mast** (-*mast, -mast*) the second mast, or that immediately above the lower mast —*adjs.* **top'-notch'** (*slang*) topping; **top'-priority** very urgent.—**top'sail** (-*sl, -sāl*) a sail across the topmast; **top secret** profoundly secret and of the highest importance; **top'side** the upper part: the outer part of a round of beef: (also in *pl.*) the part of the outer surface of a vessel above the water-line; **top'-soil** the upper part or surface of the soil; **top'spin** spin imparted to a ball by hitting it sharply on the upper half with a forward and upward stroke to make it travel higher, further, or more quickly.—**at the top of one's voice** at one's loudest; **go over the top** to go over the front of a trench and attack the enemy: to take sudden action after hesitation: to exceed the bounds of reason, decorum, etc.; **(in the) top flight** in the highest class; **off the top of one's head** without previous thought or preparation; **on top of the world** near the North Pole: on a high mountain: revelling in existence; **over the top** (*coll.*) too far, to an excess; **(the) tops** (*slang*) the very best; **top out** to finish (a building) by putting on the top or highest course (*n.* topp'ing-out); **top the bill** to be the most important attraction in a programme of entertainment, etc.; **top up** to fill p, e.g. with fuel oil, alcoholic beverage: to bring (e.g. a wage) up to a generally accepted or satisfactory level (*ns.* top'-up, topp'ing-up). [O.E. *top.*]

top² *top, n.* a toy that can be set spinning on its pointed base (also **spinning top**).—*ns.* top'maker; top'making.—**sleep like a top** to sleep very soundly. [App. late O.E. *top* (but the meaning is doubtful).]

topaz *tō'paz, n.* a precious stone, silicate of aluminium and fluorine, yellowish, bluish or colourless.—*adj.* tō'pazine.—*n.* topaz'olite a yellow garnet.—**oriental topaz** a yellow corundum. [Gr. *topazos,* a green gem.]

tope¹ *tōp, v.i.* to drink hard.—*n.* tō'per a drunkard. [Poss. Fr. *toper,* to accept a wager.]

tope² *tōp, n.* a small species of shark. [Said to be Cornish.]

topee. See **topi.**

tophus *tō'fus, n.* a gouty deposit:—*pl.* tō'phi (-fī).—*adj.* topha'ceous. [L. *tōphus, tōfus,* porous stone, tufa.]

topi¹, **topee** *tō-pē', tō'pē, n.* a hat, esp. a sola hat, pith-helmet, worn esp. in India.—**to'pi-wall'ah** a European in India. [Hindi *ṭopī,* hat (perh. from Port. *topo,* top).]

topi² *tō'pi, n.* a large African antelope with curved horns and long muzzle. [App. from a native word.]

topiary *tō'pi-ə-ri, n.* a branch of gardening, the clipping of trees into imitative and fantastic shapes.—Also *adj.*—*adj.* topiā'rian.—*n.* tō'piarist. [L. *topiārius*—*topia* (pl.), landscape, landscape gardening—Gr. *topos,* a place.]

topic *top'ik, n.* a general consideration suitable for argument: a subject of discourse or argument: a matter.—*adj.* top'ical local: relating to a topic or subject: relating to matters of interest of the day.—*n.* topical'ity the quality of being topical: an item or matter possessing that quality.—*adv.* top'ically. [Gr. *topikos,* pertaining to place or to commonplaces, *ta topika,* the general principles of argument—*topos,* a place.]

topography *top-og'rə-fi, n.* the detailed study, description, or features of a limited area.—*n.* topog'rapher.—*adjs.* topographic (*top-ə-graf'ik*), -al.—*adv.* topograph'ically. [Gr. *topographia*—*topos,* a place, *graphein,* to describe.]

topology *top-ol'ə-ji, n.* the topographical study of a particular place: topographical anatomy: a branch of geometry concerned with those properties of a figure which remain unchanged even when the figure is bent, stretched, etc.: the study of those properties of sets of points (e.g. geometrical figures) that are invariant under one-to-one continuous transformations (*math.*).—*adjs.* topolog'ic(al).—*adv.* topolog'ically.—*n.* topol'ogist. [Gr. *topos,* a place, *logos,* a discourse.]

toponymy *top-on'i-mi, n.* the study of place-names (also *n.sing.* toponym'ics): the nomenclature of regions of the body.—*n.* toponym (*top'ə-nim*) a place-name.—*adjs.* topon'ymal, toponymic (-ə-nim'ik), -al. [Gr. *topos,* place, *onyma* (*onoma*), name.]

topped, topping, etc. See **top¹.**

topple *top'l, v.i.* to overbalance and fall headlong: to threaten to fall from top-heaviness.—*v.t.* to cause to topple. [top¹.]

topsyturvy *top'si-tûr'vi, adv.* bottom upwards.—*adj.* turned upside down.—*n.* confusion.—*adv.* topsytur'vily. [top, and the obs. *terve,* to turn.]

toque *tōk, n.* a 16th-century form of cap or turban: a woman's close-fitting brimless or nearly brimless hat. [Fr.]

tor, torr *tör, n.* a hill, a rocky height. [O.E *torr,* tor —L. *turris,* tower, or perh. from Celtic.]

Torah *tō', tō'rə, n.* the Mosaic Law: the book of the law, the Pentateuch. [Heb. *Tōrāh.*]

torc. See **torque.**

torch *törch, n.* a stick of inflammable material carried or stuck up to give light: a large candle: a portable electric lamp: an appliance producing a hot flame for welding, burning, etc.: a source of enlightenment (*fig.*).—*v.t.* to light with torches.—*n.* torchère (*torsher*'; from Fr.) a tall ornamental candlestick or lampstand.—torch'-bear'er one who carries a torch: a leading, prominent figure in a cause, etc. (*fig.*); torch'light; torch'-singer; torch'-song a popular song of the 1930s giving lugubrious expression to the pangs of unrequited love.—**carry the torch (for)** to suffer unrequited love (for). [Fr. *torche*—L. *torquēre, tortum,* to twist.]

tore¹ *tör, tōr, pa.t.* of **tear².**

tore². See **torus.**

toreador *tor'i-ə-dör, n.* a bullfighter, esp. on horseback.—*n.* torero (*tor-ā'rō*) a bullfighter on foot:—*pl.* tore'ros. [Sp.]

tori, toric. See **torus.**

torii *tor'ē-ē, n.* a Japanese Shinto temple gateway. [Jap.]

torment *tör'ment, n.* torture: anguish: a source of distress.—*v.t.* torment (-ment') to torture: to put to extreme pain: to distress: to afflict: to pester: to harass: to agitate, stir violently: to distort, force violently.—*adj.* tormen'ted.—*adv.* tormen'tedly.—*n.* tor'mentil a four-petalled Potentilla with an astringent woody root, growing on heaths.—*n.* and *adj.* torment'ing.—*adv.* tormen'tingly.—*n.* tormen'tor. [L. *tormentum*—*torquēre,* to twist.]

torn *törn, törn, adj.* and *pa.p.* of **tear².—that's torn it!** (*coll.*) an expression of annoyance indicating that something has spoilt one's plans, etc.

tornado *tör-nā'dō, n.* orig. a violent tropical Atlantic thunderstorm: a very violent whirling wind-storm affecting a narrow strip of country: loosely a hurricane:—*pl.* torna'does.—*adj.* tornadic (-*nad'ik*). [Prob Sp. *tronada,* thunderstorm, altered as if from Sp. *tornada,* turning.]

torold, -al. See under **torus.**

torpedo *tör-pē'dō, n.* a member of the genus **Torpedo** of cartilaginous fishes with organs on the head that give an electric shock, related to the skates and rays: a self-propelled submarine weapon of offence (usually cigar-shaped), carrying an explosive charge which goes off when it hits a ship or other object: a bomb, cartridge, case of explosives, or detonator of various kinds, used in warfare, as a fog-signal, firework, etc.:—*pl.* torpe'does.—*v.t* to attack, strike, destroy, by torpedo: to wreck (e.g. a plan) —*ns.* torpe'do; torpe'doist.—torpe'do-boat a small swift warship discharging torpedoes; torpe'do-tube a kind of gun from which torpedoes are discharged. [L. *torpēdō, -inis,* numbness, the torpedo (fish)—*torpēre,* to be stiff.]

torpid *tör'pid, adj.* numb: lethargic: having lost the power of motion and feeling: sluggish: dormant.—*n.* torpid'ity.—*adv.* tor'pidly.—*ns.* tor'pidness; tor'pitude; tor'por numbness: inactivity: dullness: stupidity. [L. *torpidus, torpefacēre, torpēscere, torpor*—*torpēre,* to be numb.]

torque *tork, n.* the measure of the turning effect of a tangential force: a force or system of forces causing or tending to cause rotation or torsion: a necklace in the form of a twisted band (also **torc**).—**torque'-converter** (*mech.*) a device which acts as an infinitely variable gear; **torque'-meter.** [L. *torquēre,* to twist; *torquēs, -is,* a necklace; *torquātus,* wearing a torquēs.]

torr¹. See **tor.**

torr² *tor, n.* a unit used in expressing very low pressures, 1/760 of a standard atmosphere [E *Torricelli,* see **Torricellian.**]

torrefy *tor'i-fi, v.t* to scorch to parch:—*pr.p.* **torr'efying;** *pa.t.* and *pa.p.* **torr'efied.**—*n.* torre-fac'tion. [L. *torrēre,* to parch, roast, *facēre,* to make.]

torrent *tor'ənt, n.* a rushing stream: an abounding, strong or turbulent flow.—*adj.* rushing in a stream.—*adj.* **torrential** (-en'shl). [L. *torrēns, -entis,* boiling, pr.p. of *torrēre,* to dry.]

Torricellian *tor-i-chel'i-ən, adj.* pertaining to the Italian mathematician *Torricelli* (1608–47) who discovered in 1643 the principle of the barometer.—**Torricellian tube** the barometer; **Torricellian vacuum** the vacuum in the barometer.

torrid *tor'id, adj.* scorching or parching: violently hot: dried with heat: intensely passionate, emotional, etc.—*ns.* **torrid'ity, torr'idness.**—**torrid zone** the belt round the earth between the tropics. [L. *torridus—torrēre,* to parch, roast.]

torse *tôrs, n.* a heraldic wreath. [Fr.,—L *torquēre,* to twist.]

torsion *tor'shən, n.* twisting: a twist: the strain produced by twisting: the force with which a thread or wire tends to return when twisted.—*adjs.* **tor'sional; tor'sive** twisted spirally.—**tor'sion-bal'ance** an instrument for measuring very minute forces by a horizontal needle suspended by a very fine filament; **torsion bar** a metal bar which absorbs force by twisting, used esp. in vehicle suspension. [L. *torsio, -ōnis—torquēre, tortum,* to twist.]

torsk *tôrsk, n.* a North Atlantic fish (*Brosmius brosme*) of the cod family. [Sw., Norw., Dan. *torsk*—O.N. *thorskr.*]

torso *tôr'sō, n.* the trunk of a statue or body, without head or limbs:—*pl.* **tor'sos.** [It., stalk, core, torso—L. *thyrsus*—Gr *thyrsos.*]

tort *tôrt, n.* any wrong, not arising out of contract, for which there is a remedy by compensation or damages (*Eng. law*). [Fr.,—L.L. *tortum*—L. *torquēre, tortum,* to twist.]

torte *tôr'tə, tôrt, n* a rich sweet cake or pastry, Austrian in origin, often garnished or filled with fruit, nuts, cream, chocolate, etc. [Ger., perh.—L.L. *torta,* a round loaf.]

torticollis *tôr-ti-kol'is, (path.) n.* wry-neck. [L.L.,—L. *tortus,* twisted, *collum,* neck.]

tortilla *tôr-tē(l)'ya, -yə, n.* a Mexican round flat maize cake. [Sp., dim. of *torta,* cake.]

tortoise *tôr'təs, n.* any land or freshwater (rarely marine) chelonian (now, in Britain, usu. restricted to land forms): a testudo (*mil.*).—**tortoise-shell** (*tôr'tə-shel*) the shell of a tortoise: a translucent mottled material, the horny plates (esp. of the back) of the hawk's bill turtle: a similar synthetic material: a tortoise-shell butterfly or cat.—*adj.* made of, or mottled like, tortoise-shell.—**tortoise-shell butterfly** a butterfly with orange or reddish wings marked with black and yellow, edged with blue, etc.; **tortoise-shell cat** a domestic cat (nearly always female) mottled in yellow and black. [L.L. *tortuca.*]

Tortrix *tor'triks, n.* genus of small moths whose caterpillars commonly live in rolled-up leaves: (without *cap.*) any moth of this genus:—*pl.* **tortrices** (-trī'sēz).—*n.* **tortri'cid** any moth of the family.—Also *adj.* [Invented L., twister.]

tortuous *tôr'tū-əs, adj* full of windings: far from straightforward (*fig.*).—*n.* **tortuos'ity.**—*adv.* **tor'-tuously.**—*n.* **tor'tuousness.** [L. *tortuōsus—torquēre, tortum,* to twist.]

torture *tôr'chər, n.* a putting to the rack or severe pain

to extort a confession, or as a punishment: extreme pain: anguish.—*v.t.* to put to torture: to subject to extreme pain: to exact by torture: to distort violently—*n.* **tor'turer.**—*n.* and *adj.* **tor'turing.**—*adv.* **tor'-turingly.**—*adj.* **tor'turous** causing torture or violent distortion. [Fr.,—L *tortūra,* torment—*torquēre.*]

torus *tô', tô'rəs, n.* a large moulding, semicircular or nearly in section, common at the base of a column: a figure generated by the revolution of a circle or other conic section about a straight line in its own plane: the receptacle of a flower: a ring-shaped discharge-tube:—*pl.* **to'ri.**—*n.* **tore** (*tôr, tōr; archit.* and *geom.*) a torus.—*adjs.* **toric** (*tor', tōr', tor'*) of, or having the form of, a torus or a part of a torus; **toroid** (*tor', tôr', tor'*) shaped like a torus.—*n* a coil or transformer of that shape.—*adj.* **toroid'al.** [L. *tōrus,* a bulge, swelling, bed, torus moulding.]

Tory *tô', tô'ri, n.* a Conservative in politics: a bigoted or extreme Conservative.—*n* **Tô'ryism** the principles of the Tories. [Ir. *toirdhe,* a pursuer.]

tosh *tosh, (slang) n.* bosh, twaddle.

toss *tos, v.t.* to fling, jerk: to fling up, or about, or to and fro: to agitate.—*v.i* to be tossed: to be in violent commotion: to tumble about: to fling: to toss up a coin.—*n.* an act of throwing upward: a throwing up or back of the head: a toss-up.—*n* **toss'er.**—*n.* and *adj.* **toss'ing.**—**toss'-up'** the throwing up of a coin to decide anything: an even chance or hazard.—**argue the toss** to dispute a decision; **toss off** to perform, produce quickly, cursorily: to drink off: to remark casually: to masturbate (*slang*); **toss up** to throw a coin in order to decide.

tot¹ *tot, n.* anything little, esp. a child, a drinking-cup, or a dram.—*n.* **tott'ie, tott'y** (*dim.*).—*adj.* (*dial.*) very small. [Cf. Icel. *tottr,* a dwarf.]

tot² *tot, v.t.* and *v.i.* to add up or total (also **tot up**):—*pr.p.* **tott'ing;** *pa.t.* and *pa.p.* **tott'ed.**—*n.* **tott'ing-up'.** [total.]

total *tō'tl, adj.* whole: complete: including all: co-ordinating everything towards one end.—*n.* the whole: the entire amount.—*v.t.* to bring to a total, add up: to amount to:—*pr.p.* **tō'talling;** *pa.t.* and *pa.p.* **tō'talled.**—*ns.* **totalisā'tion, -z-; tō'talisātor, -z-, tō'taliser, -z-,** (familiarly shortened to **tote** *tōt*), a system of betting in which the total amount staked (minus tax, etc.) is divided among the winners in proportion to the size of their stake: an automatic betting-machine, the *pari mutuel.*—*v.t.* **tō'talise, -ize** to find the sum of: to bring to a total.—*v.i.* to use a totalisator.—*adj.* **totalitarian** (*tō-tal-i-tā'ri-ən*) belonging to a form of government that includes control of everything under one authority, and allows no opposition.—Also *n.*—*ns.* **totalitā'rianism; totality** (*tō-tal'i-ti*) condition or fact of being total: an entirety: completeness: the whole.—*adv.* **tō'tally.**—**total allergy syndrome** a collection of symptoms claimed to be caused by various allergies to modern substances and conditions; **total internal reflection** (*phys.*) the complete reflection of a light ray at the boundary of a medium with a lower refractive index. [L.L. *tōtālis*—L. *tōtus,* whole.]

tote¹ *tōt, (orig. U.S.) v.t.* to carry.—**tote bag** a large bag for shopping, etc.

tote². See **total.**

totem *tō'təm, n.* any species of living or inanimate thing regarded by a class or kin within a local tribe with superstitious respect as an outward symbol of an existing intimate unseen relation.—*adj.* **totemic** (-*tem'ik*).—*ns.* **tō'temism** the use of totems as the foundation of a social system of obligation and restriction; **tō'temist** one designated by a totem.—*adj.* **totemist'ic.**—**totem pole** a pole carved and painted with totemic symbols, set up by Indians in the north-west of North America [From Algonquin.]

tother, t'other *tudh'ər, pron.* and *adj* the other [that other.]

totter *tot'ər, v.i.* to sway. to waver· to rock· to threaten to fall: to reel· to stagger: to be on the verge of ruin — *n.* a tottering movement.—*n.* **tott'erer.**—*n* and *adj* **tott'ering.**—*adv.* **tott'eringly.**—*adj.* **tott'ery** shaky [Cf. Norw dial. *tutra, totra,* to quiver]

tottie, totty. See tot¹.

totting. See tot².

toucan *tōō'kən, -kan, -kan', n* any member of the *Rhamphastidae,* large South American fruit-eating birds, with an immense beak [Fr.,—Tupí *tucana*]

touch *tuch, v t.* to come or be in contact with: to cause to be in contact: to meet without cutting, or meet tangentially (*geom.*). to get at· to reach as far as to attain: to equal, rival, or compare with. to make a light application to: to begin to eat, eat a little of: to affect, esp injuriously: to impress: to affect with emotion, esp pity: to have to do with: to concern: to hit, wound, or injure to strike home to: to mark or modify by light strokes· to tinge: to test as with a touchstone: to receive, draw, pocket to extract money from (*for* so much): to make some reference to, say something about —*v t* to be or come in contact: to verge. to make some mention or reference (with *on, upon*): to have reference —*n.* the act, condition, impression, sense, or mode of touching: a feeling: a slight application, modification, stroke: a small quantity· a slight affection of illness: a tinge: a trace: a smack: ability, skill: a trait: a little: a slight hit, wound, blemish, reproach: the manner or nicety of producing tone on (now esp.) a keyed instrument: the instrument's response: a characteristic manner: a stroke of art: the relation of communication, sympathy, harmony: communication, contact: a game in which one has to pursue and touch others· a test, as of touchstone: either side of the field outside the bounds (*football,* etc.): a sum got by theft or by touching (*slang*): that which will find buyers at such and such a price (*slang*).—*adj.* **touch'able** capable of being touched: fit to be touched.—*n.* **touch'ableness.**—*adj.* **touched** having been touched: slightly unsound mentally.—*n.* **touch'er.**—*adv* **touch'ily.**—*n.* **touch'iness.**—*n.* **touch'ing.**—*adj.* affecting: moving: pathetic.—*prep.* concerning.—*adv.* **touch'ingly.**—*n.* **touch'ingness.**—*adjs.* **touch'less** without a sense of touch: intangible; touchy over-sensitive: irascible.— **touch'-and-go'** a narrow escape· a critical or precariously balanced situation —*adj.* precarious: offhand.—**touch'-down** in Rugby and American football, touching of the ball to the ground by a player behind the goal-line: of aircraft, the act of alighting; **touch'-hole** the small hole of a cannon through which the fire is communicated to the charge; **touch'-judge** an official who marks when and where the ball goes into touch (*Rugby football*); **touch'-line** the side boundary in football, etc ; **touch'-mark** the maker's official stamp on pewter; **touch'-me-not** the plant balsam (from its explosive fruit): a forbidden topic — *adj* stand-offish.—**touch'-paper** paper steeped in saltpetre for firing a train; **touch'stone** a highly siliceous, usually black or other stone for testing gold or silver by streak, as black marble· any criterion.—*adj.* **touch'-tone** of telephones, having push buttons (rather than a dial) that cause distinct tones to sound at the exchange —*v.t.* and *v.i* **touch'-type** to type without looking at the keys of the typewriter.—**touch'-typist; touch'wood** decayed wood that can be used as tinder —**an easy, a soft touch** (*coll*) a person or institution easily persuaded, esp to lend money; **in, out of, touch** in, out of, communication or direct relations; **touch down** of aircraft, to alight, **touch off** to trigger (also *fig.*); **touch up** to

improve by a series of small touches: to lash lightly, stimulate; **touch wood,** (*U S*) **knock (on) wood** to touch something wooden as a superstitious guard against ill-fortune (also used as interjections, to accompany the gesture or independently). [O.Fr *tuchier* (Fr. *toucher*)]

touché *tōō'shā, tōō-shā', interj.* claiming or acknowledging hit in fencing, or a point scored in argument, etc [Fr , touched, scored against.]

tough *tuf, adj.* stiff and dense· tenacious. hard to cut, chew, break up or penetrate. resistant: viscous, sticky· capable of, or requiring, strenuous effort and endurance: unyielding: robust: laborious: refractory: criminal, ruffianly: unlucky (*coll.*).—*n* a rough: a criminal, hooligan (also **tough guy**).—*interj* (*coll*) tough luck —*v.t.* or *v.i* **tough'en** to make or become tough —*n.* **tough'ener.**—*n.* and *adj.* **tough'ening.**— *n.* **tough'ie** (*coll.*) a tough person, problem, etc — *adj* **tough'ish** rather tough —*adv* **tough'ly.**—*n.* **tough'ness.**—*adj.* **tough'-mind'ed** hard-headed, unsentimental, determined.—**get tough with** (*coll.*) to deal with (more) severely, sternly. [O.E *tōh.*]

toupee *tōō-pē', -pā',* or *tōō', n* a tuft, lock, fringe, or patch, esp. of false hair: a wig. [Fr. *toupet.*]

tour *tōōr, n.* a round: a prolonged journey from place to place, e.g. for pleasure, or to give entertainment as a performer, or to give lectures, play matches, etc.: a pleasure trip or outing: a shift or turn of work: a period of military service in a particular place (also **tour of duty**).—*v.i.* to make a tour, go on tour.—*v.t.* to make a tour through or of: to tour with (a play).— *n.* **tour'er** a touring-car: a tourist.—*n* and *adj.* **tour'ing.**—*ns.* **tour'ism** the activities of tourists and those who cater for them; **tour'ist** one who makes a tour, esp. a sight-seeing traveller or a sportsman.— *adjs.* **touris'tic; tour'isty** (*derog.*) designed for, or full of, tourists.—**tour'ing-car** a long motor-car, suitable for touring; **tourist class** the cheapest class of accommodation on a boat or aeroplane; **tour operator** a person or firm organising (esp. packagetour) holidays. [Fr.; see **turn.**]

touraco *tōō'ra-kō,* or *-kō', n.* an African bird (*Turacus*) of the plantain-eater family, with a horny shield on the forehead and remarkable pigments in its feathers: —*pl* **touracos.** [Supposed to be a W. African name.]

tour de force *tōōr də fors,* (Fr.) a feat of strength or skill.

tourmaline *tōōr'mə-lēn, n.* a beautiful mineral of complex and varying composition, usually black or blackish [Fr.,—Sinh. *tòramalli,* carnelian.]

tournament *tōōr'nə-mənt, n.* a military sport of the Middle Ages in which combatants engaged in single combat or in troops, mainly on horseback, with spear and sword: a military and athletic display: a series of games to determine a winner or winning team by elimination.—*n* **tourney** (*tōōr', tûr', tör'ni*) a tournament —*v.i.* to ride in a tournament —*n* **tour'neyer.** [O.Fr *tournoiement, tornoi—torner*— L *tornāre,* to turn.]

tournedos *tōōr'nə-dō, n.* a small beef fillet served with some kind of garnish.—*pl* **tour'nedos** (*-dōz*). [Fr.]

tourney, tourneyer. See **tournament.**

tourniquet *tōōr'ni-ket, -kā, n* any appliance for compressing an artery [Fr ,—L *tornāre,* to turn.]

touse, touze, towse, towze *towz, v t* to haul, to pull about: to dishevel, rumple, tumble —*v.i* to tease each other: to be toused: to tussle: to rummage.—*n.* a tousing.—*n.* **tous'er,** towse'er one who touses: (*cap.*) a common name for a big dog.—*n* and *adj* **tous'ing.**— *v.t.* **tousle, touzle** (*towz'l*) to disarrange, to tumble: to dishevel —*v t* to tease to touse things.—*n* a tousled mass.—*adj.* **tousy, towsy** (*towz'i*) shaggy, unkempt, tousled: rough

tout[1] *towt, v.i.* to look out for custom in an obtrusive, aggressive or brazen way.—*v.t.* to advertise, praise or recommend strongly.—*n.* one who touts: a low fellow who hangs about racing-stables, etc., to pick up profitable information.—*n.* **tout'er**.

tout[2] *tōō*, (Fr.) *adj.* all: every: whole.—*adv.* quite: entirely.—**tout à fait** (*tōō ta fe*) entirely; **tout de suite** (*tōōt swet*) at once, immediately; **tout le monde** (*lə m5d*) all the world, everybody.

touze, touzle. See **touse.**

tovarish *to-vä'rish, n.* comrade. [Russ. *tovarıshch.*]

tow[1] *tō* (*Scot.*), *v.t.* to pull with a rope, primarily by water: to pull along.—*n.* the condition of being towed: an act of towing: that which is towed.—*ns.* **tow'age** an act of towing: a fee for towing; **tow'er.**—*n.* and *adj.* **tow'ing.**—**tow'bar** a metal bar or frame used for towing trailers, etc.; **tow'line, -rope** a line used in towing; **tow'path, tow'ing-path** a path for horses towing barges.—**have, take, in tow** to tow (another vehicle, vessel, etc.): to take along with one, be accompanied by: to have, assume, charge of; **on tow** (of vehicles), **under tow** (of vessels) being towed. [O.E. *togian,* to drag.]

tow[2] *tō, n.* prepared fibres of flax, hemp, or jute: esp separated shorter fibres.—*adj.* of or like tow.—*adj.* **tow'y.**—**tow'-head** a person with light-coloured or tousled hair.—*adj.* **tow'-headed.** [O.E. *tow-* (in compounds).]

toward *tō'ərd, tōrd, adj.* (*arch.*) or (*dial.*) approaching: favourable: ready to do or learn: on the left or near side.—*adv.* in the direction facing one, inward.— *prep.* (now more commonly **towards**) (*tə-, tōō-wōrd'(z), tword(z), tōrd(z), tōrd(z)*) in the direction of: with a tendency to: for, as a help to: near, a little short of. [O.E. *tōweard,* adj., adv., prep.—*tō,* to, suff. *-weard, -ward.*]

towel *tow'əl, n.* a cloth for drying.—*v.t.* to rub with a towel: to thrash:—*pr.p.* **tow'elling**; *pa.t.* and *pa.p.* **tow'elled.**—*n.* **tow'elling** a rubbing with a towel: an absorbent cloth for towels, sometimes used for dressing-gowns, curtains, etc.: a thrashing.—**tow'el-rail** a rod for hanging towels on. [O.Fr. *toaille,* from Germanic.]

tower *towr, tow'ər, n.* a lofty building, standing alone or forming part of another: a fortress: a lofty or vertical flight.—*v.i.* to rise into the air: to be lofty: to stand on high.—*adjs.* **tow'ered; tow'ering** very high, elevated: very violent; **tow'erless; tow'ery** having towers: lofty.—**tower block** a tall residential or office building.—**tower of strength** a stable, reliable person; **tower over** to be considerably taller than: to be markedly superior to. [O.Fr. *tur*—L. *turris,* a tower.]

towhee *tow'hē, tō'hē, n.* an American finch. [Imit.]

town *town, n.* a populous place bigger or less rural than a village: a municipal or political division of a county (*U.S.*): the principal town of a district: an urban community: the people of a town: the business or shopping centre: urban communities generically.—*adj.* of a town: urban.—*n.* **townee', tow'nie** a townsman, not a member of the university or a country dweller.—*ns.* **town'ship** a village, a community or local division: a thirty-six square mile block of public land (*U.S.*): a site for a town (*Austr.*): a small settlement (*Austr.*): the territory or district of a town: the corporation of a town: a subdivision of a county or province (*U.S.*): an administrative district (*U.S.*): an urban settlement of black and coloured Africans (*S.Afr.*); **town'y** a townsman.—**town clerk** a secretary and legal adviser of a town; **town council** the governing body in a town; **town councillor; town'-crī'er** one who makes public proclamations in a town; **town'-dweller; town hall** a public hall for the official business of a town;

town'house a house or building for transacting the public business of a town; **town house** a house in town belonging to the owner of another in the country: a fashionable, esp. terraced, house in a town, etc.; **town'-plann'ing** deliberate designing in the building and extension of towns to avoid the evils of fortuitous and speculative building; **town'scape** a portion of a town which the eye can view at once: a picture of it: the design or building of (part of) a town.—Also *v.t., v.i.*—**town'scaping; towns'folk** the people of a town; **towns'man** an inhabitant or fellow-inhabitant of a town:—*fem.* **towns'woman; towns'people** townsfolk —**go to town** (*coll.*) to act, behave, perform enthusiastically, with thoroughness, without restraint; **on the town** out to amuse oneself in town; **take to town** (*slang*) to mystify, bewilder; **town and gown** the general community and the members of the university [O.E. *tūn,* an enclosure, town.]

towse, towsy. See **touse.**

towy. See **tow**[2].

towze. See **touse.**

toxic *toks'ik, adj.* of poison: poisonous: poisoned: due to poison.—*adj.* **tox'ical.**—*adv.* **tox'ically.**—*adj* **tox'icant** poisonous.—*n.* a poisonous substance.—*ns.* **toxicā'tion, toxicity** (*-is'-*) toxic quality, **tox'in** a ptomaine: a specific poison of organic origin, **tox'oid** a toxin that has been treated to remove its toxic properties without destroying its ability to stimulate formation of antibodies.—*n.* **toxaemia** (*-ē'mi-ə*) blood poisoning —*adjs.* **toxaem'ic; toxicolog'ical.**— *ns.* **toxicol'ogist; toxicol'ogy** the science of poisons; **toxocara** (*tok-sə-kar'ə*) a parasitic worm found in the intestines of dogs and known to cause disease (**toxocari'asis**) and eye damage in humans [Gr. *toxon,* a bow, *toxikos,* for the bow, *toxikon,* arrow-poison.]

toxophilite *toks-of'i-līt, n.* a lover of archery: an archer —*adj.* **toxophilit'ic.**—*n.* **toxoph'ily** love of archery: archery. [Gr. *toxon,* a bow, *phileein,* to love.]

toy *toi, n.* a plaything: a trifle: a thing only for amusement or look: a dwarf breed.—*adj.* made in imitation as a plaything.—*v.i.* to trifle: to sport: to dally amorously.—*n.* **toy'er.**—*n.* and *adj.* **toy'ing.**—**toy. dog** a very small pet dog; **toy'man, -woman** a seller of toys; **toy'shop** a shop where toys are sold. [Poss. Du. *tuig,* tools.]

tra-. See **trans-.**

trabeate, -d *trab', trāb'i-āt, -id, adjs.* built of horizontal beams, not arches and vaults.—*ns.* **trabeā'tion** an entablature: a combination of beams in a structure; **trabecula** (*trə-bek'ū-lə*) a cell, row of cells, band, or rodlike structure running across a cavity or forming an internal support to an organ:—*pl.* **trabec'ulae** (*-lē*).—*adjs.* **trabec'ular; trabec'ulate, -d.** [L. *trabs, trabis,* beam; dim. *trabecula.*]

trace[1] *trās, n.* a beaten path (*U.S.*): a track: a footprint: an indication, mark of what is or has been: a mental or neural change caused by learning: a small quantity that can just be detected: a tracing: a line marked by a recording instrument.—*v.i.* to be traceable, date back.—*v.t.* to traverse: to track: to follow step by step: to detect: to discover the whereabouts of: to follow or mark the outline of, esp. mechanically or on a translucent paper: to outline, delineate, or write: to produce as tracery: to cover with tracery.— *n.* **traceabil'ity.**—*adj.* **trace'able** that may be traced. —*n.* **trace'ableness.**—*adv.* **trace'ably.**—*adj.* **trace'-less.**—*adv.* **trace'lessly.**—*ns.* **trā'cer** one who traces: an instrument for tracing: a probe for tracing a nerve, etc.: a device by which a projectile leaves a smoke-trail: a projectile equipped with it: a chemical substance used to mark the course followed by a process.—*adj.* **trā'ceried.**—*ns.* **trā'cery** ornamentation in flowing outline: ornamental open-work in Gothic architecture; **trā'cing** the act of one who traces: a drawing copied mechanically or on translucent paper laid over the original: an instrumental record.—**trace element** a substance (as zinc, copper, molybdenum, etc.) whose presence in the soil in minute quantities is necessary for plant and animal growth; **tracer bullet; tracer element** (*physiol.*, etc.) an isotope, often a radio-isotope, used for experiments in which its particular properties enable its position to be kept under observation; **tracer shell; tra'cing-paper** translucent paper for tracing on. [Fr. *trace*—L. *tractus*, pa.p. of *trahēre*, to draw.]

trace[2] *trās*, *n.* (usu. in *pl.*) a rope, chain, or strap attached to an animal's collar, for drawing a vehicle: a short piece of wire, gut or nylon connecting the hook to the fishing line. [O.Fr. *trays*, *trais*, pl. of *trait*, draught; cf. **trait.**]

trachea *tra-kē'ə*, *U.S. trā'*, *n.* the windpipe: the air-tube in air-breathing arthropods:—*pl.* **trachē'ae** (*-ē*).—*adjs.* **trachē'al; trā'cheate, -d** having a trachea.—*ns.* **tracheitis** (*trak-i-ī'tis*) inflammation of the trachea, **tracheos'copy** inspection of the trachea; **tracheos'tomy** surgical formation of an opening into the trachea; **tracheot'omy** cutting into the trachea. [Mediaeval L. *trāchēa* for L. *trāchīa*—Gr. *trācheia* (*artēriā*), rough (artery).]

trachoma *tra-kō'mə*, *n.* a disease of the eye, with hard pustules on the inner surface of the eyelids [Gr. *trāchōma*.]

trachyte *trak'īt*, *n.* a fine-grained intermediate igneous rock. [Gr. *trāchys*, rough.]

tracing. See under **trace**[1].

track *trak*, *n.* a mark left: a beaten path: a made path: a sequence, path of thoughts or actions: the predetermined line of travel of an aircraft: a course, usu. oval-shaped, on which races are run: a railway line, the rails and the space between: the groove cut in a gramophone record by the recording instrument: one out of several items recorded on a disc or tape: one of several areas or paths on magnetic recording equipment receiving information from a single input channel: the endless band on which the wheels of a caterpillar vehicle run (*adj.* **tracked** equipped with such metal bands): the distance between a pair of wheels measured as the distance between their respective points of contact with the ground.—*v t* to follow the track of: to find by so doing: to traverse: to beat, tread (a path, etc.): to follow the movement of (satellite, spacecraft, etc.) by radar, etc , and record its positions.—*v.i.* to follow a trail: to make one's way (*coll.*): to run in alignment, esp. (of gramophone needles) to follow the grooves: to move a camera in a defined path while taking a shot (**tracking shot**) —*ns.* **track'age** provision of railway tracks; **track'er; track'ing** the action of the verb.—*adj.* **track'less** without a path: untrodden: leaving no trace: running without rails.—**track event** in a sports competition, a race of any kind; **track record** a record of past performance orig. that of an athlete, now generally that of any individual, company, etc.; **track shoe** a lightweight spiked running shoe worn by athletes; **track suit** a warm one worn by athletes before and after, e.g. a race, or when in training; **track'way** a beaten track: an ancient road.—**across the tracks, the wrong side of the tracks** a slum or other socially disadvantageous area; **in one's tracks** just where one stands; **keep track of** keep oneself informed about; **make tracks** to make off: to go quickly; **off the beaten track** away from frequented roads: out of the usual (*fig*); **track down** to find after intensive search; **tracker dog** one used for tracking, especially in police searches.

[Fr. *trac*; prob. Gmc.]

tract *trakt*, *n.* a stretch or extent of space or time: a region, area: a tractate: a pamphlet or leaflet, esp. political or (now) religious: a region of the body occupied by a particular system (e g *the digestive tract*).—*n.* **tractabil'ity.**—*adj.* **tract'able** easily drawn, managed or taught: docile.—*ns.* **tract'ableness; tractā'rian** a writer of tracts, esp (*cap.*) of the *Tracts for the Times* (Oxford, 1833–41—Pusey, Newman, Keble, Hurrell Froude, etc.).—Also *adj.*—*ns.* **Tractā'rianism** the system of religious opinion promulgated in these, its main aim to assert the authority and dignity of the Anglican Church—the Oxford movement; **tract'ate** a treatise, a tract; **tractā'tor** a tractarian.—*adj.* **tract'ile** (*-īl*) ductile, capable of being drawn out.—*ns.* **tractility** (*-il'*); **traction** (*trak'shən*) the act of drawing or state of being drawn: the pulling on a muscle, organ, etc , by means, e.g. of weights, to correct an abnormal condition (*med.*): the propulsion of vehicles.—*adjs.* **trac'tional; tract'ive** pulling.—*n.* **tract'or** a traction-engine: a vehicle that propels itself or hauls other vehicles or agricultural implements: the short front section of an articulated lorry, containing the engine and driver's cab: a motorised plough.—**trac'tion-engine** a locomotive for hauling on roads, fields, etc. [L. *tractus, -ūs*, a dragging, draught, tract, *tractus, tractātus*, pa.ps. of *trahēre, tractāre*, to draw.]

trad *trad*, *adj.* a shortened form of *traditional*, esp in *traditional jazz*, a rhythmically monotonous style of jazz which originated in New Orleans round about the beginning of the 20th century.—Also *n.*

trade *trād*, *n.* a practice: an occupation, way of livelihood, esp. skilled but not learned: shopkeeping: commerce: buying and selling: a craft: men engaged in the same occupation: customers: commodities, esp. for barter: a deal: (in *pl*) the trade-winds.—*v.i.* to resort, esp for commerce: to ply: to have dealings or intercourse: to engage in commerce: to deal: to traffic: to buy and sell: to reckon, count, presume (with *on*), esp. unscrupulously.—*v.t.* to exchange (esp commercially), to barter.—*n.* **trād'er.**—*n* and *adj.* **trād'ing.**—**trade cycle** the recurring series of conditions in trade from prosperity to depression and back to prosperity; **trade discount** a discount offered to others in the same trade; **trade gap** the amount by which a country's visible imports exceed its visible exports in value; **trade'-in** that which is given in part payment; **trade journal** a periodical containing information and comment on a particular trade, **trade'mark** any name or distinctive device warranting goods for sale as the production of any individual or firm, **trade'name** a name serving as a trademark. a name in use in the trade; **trade'-off** the giving up of one thing in return for another, usu. as an act of compromise (also *v.* **trade off**); **trade plate** a temporary number plate attached to a vehicle by dealers, etc prior to its being registered; **trade price** the price at which goods are sold to members of the same trade, or by wholesale to retail dealers, **trade route** a route followed by caravans or trading ships; **trade secret** a secret and successful formula, process, technique, etc. known only to one manufacturer; **trades'-folk, -people** shopkeepers: mechanics' craftsmen: people employed in trade; **trades'man** a shopkeeper a craftsman: a mechanic—*fem* **trades'woman.**—*adj* **trades'manlike.**—**trade union** an organised association of workers of an industry for the protection of their common interests; **trade unionism; trade unionist; trades union** an association of trade unions, as the **Trades Union Congress (T.U.C.); trade wind** a wind blowing toward the thermal equator and deflected westward by the eastward rotation of the earth,

trading estate an industrial estate; **trading post** a store, etc. established in an esp. remote, thinly-populated or hostile area; **trading stamp** a stamp given to a purchaser of goods who, when he has accumulated a specified number, may exchange them without payment for articles provided by the trading stamp firm.—**trade down (up)** to deal in lower grade, cheaper (higher grade, dearer) goods; **trade in** to give in part payment. [Prob. L.G. *trade*; akin to **tread**.]

Tradescantia *trad-is-kan'shi-ə, n.* the spider-wort genus: (without *cap.*) any plant of this genus. [After the English gardener, naturalist, and traveller John Tradescant (*c.* 1567–1637).]

tradition *trə-dish'ən, n.* a handing over (*law*): oral transmission from generation to generation, esp. (often with *cap.*) of certain Christian, Judaic and Islamic doctrines and customs: a tale, belief or practice thus handed down: a long-established belief or custom: anything bound up with or continuing in the life of a family, community, etc.: the continuous development of a body of, e.g. literature, music.— *adjs.* **tradi'tional, tradi'tionary.**—*ns.* **tradi'-tionalism; tradi'tionalist; traditional'ity.**—*advs.* **tradi'tionally, tradi'tionarily.**—*ns.* **tradi'tioner, tradi'tionist** one who adheres to tradition.—**traditional jazz** see **trad.** [L. *trāditiō,* -*ōnis, trāditor,* -*ōris*—*trādēre,* to give up—*trāns,* over, *dāre,* to give.]

traduce *trə-dūs',* in U.S. -*dōōs', v.t.* to calumniate: to defame.—*ns.* **traduce'ment; tradū'cer.** [L. *trādūcere, trāductum*—*trāns,* across, *dūcere,* to bring.]

traffic *traf'ik, n.* commerce, trade: immoral or illegal trading: dealing: transportation of goods and persons on a railway, on an air route, etc.: vehicles, pedestrians, etc. (collectively), using a throughfare: a passing to and fro.—*v.i.* to trade: to trade immorally or illegally:—*pr.p.* **traff'icking;** *pa.t.* and *pa.p.* **traff'-icked.**—*ns.* **traff'icātor** formerly, a movable pointer by means of which the driver of a vehicle gave warning of a change of direction; **traff'icker.**—*n.* and *adj.* **traff'icking.**—**traffic island** a raised section in the centre of a road to separate lanes, guide traffic, etc.; **traffic jam** congestion, and resultant stoppage, of traffic, e.g. at a busy junction; **traff'ic-lights',** **-sig'nals** coloured lights to regulate street traffic at crossings; **traffic warden** an official controlling road traffic, esp. the parking of vehicles.

tragacanth *trag'ə-kanth, n.* a gum (also **gum traga-canth**) got from several spiny shrubs of the genus Astragalus: the plant yielding it. [Gr. *tragakantha*—*tragos,* goat, *akantha,* thorn.]

tragedy *traj'i-di, n.* a species of drama in which the action and language are elevated, and the ending usually sad, esp. involving the fall of a great man: the art of such drama: any sad story or turn of events: anything with death or killing in it (*journalism*).—*ns.* **tragedian** (*trə-jē'di-ən*) a writer or (usually) an actor of tragedy; **tragedienne** (*trə-jē-di-en'*) an actress of tragic rôles.—*adjs.* **tragic** (*traj'ik*), **-al** pertaining to, of the nature of, tragedy.—*adv.* **trag'ically.**—*n.* **trag'icalness.**—**trag'i-com'edy** a play (or story) in which grave and comic scenes or themes are blended: a comedy that threatens to be a tragedy.—*adjs.* **trag'i-com'ic, -al.**—*adv.* **trag'i-com'ically.** [L *tragoedia*—Gr. *tragōidiā,* tragedy, app. lit. goat-song.]

tragi. See **tragus.**

tragopan *trag'ō-pan, n.* a brilliant Asiatic horned pheasant. [Gr. *trugopān,* hornbill—*tragos,* goat, *Pān,* the god Pan.]

tragus *trā'gas, n.* a small prominence at the entrance of the external ear:—*pl.* **trā'gi** (*-jī*). [Gr. *tragos,* goat, tragus.]

trail *trāl, v.t.* to draw along or near the surface: to drag wearily: to drag along: to carry horizontally: to track, follow: to lag behind.—*v.i.* to be drawn out in length: to hang, float, or drag loosely behind: to sprawl over the ground or a support: to straggle: to lag: to be losing in a game or competition: to move with slow sweeping motion or with dragging drapery: to drag oneself along.—*n.* anything drawn out in length or trailed: a train, tail: a track, as of game: a beaten path in the wilds: a path, route: an act or manner of trailing.—*n.* **trail'er** one who trails: a tracker: a creeping plant: an esp. two-wheeled conveyance, towed or dragged by a car, bicycle, or tractor: a house on wheels, a caravan (*U.S.*): a short film advertising a forthcoming entertainment on television or in the cinema.—**trail'-blazer** a pioneer: a person or thing that leads the way in anything.—*adj.* and *n.* **trail'-blazing.**—**trailing edge** the rear edge; **trail'-net** a drag-net.—**trail away, off** esp. of a sound, to become fainter.

train¹ *trān, v.t.* to instruct and discipline: to cause to grow in the desired manner: to prepare for performance by instruction, practice, diet, exercise, or otherwise: to bring up: to direct, aim (as a gun or telescope).—*v.i.* to prepare oneself by instruction, exercise, diet, or otherwise: to be under drill: to travel by rail.—*n.* that which is dragged along or follows: a tail: tail-feathers or trailing back-feathers: the part of a dress that trails: a retinue: a series: a sequence: a number of things in a string: a process: a line of combustible material to fire a charge: a set of wheels acting on each other, for transmitting motion. —*adj.* **train'able.**—*adj.* **trained** having received training: having a train.—*ns.* **trainee'** one who is under training; **trainee'ship** the period of being a trainee: the position of, or maintenance provided for, a trainee; **train'er** one who prepares men for athletic feats, horses for a race, or the like: any machine or device used in training, esp. an aeroplane with duplicated controls for training pilots; **train'ing** practical education in any profession, art, or handicraft: a course of diet and exercise for developing physical strength, endurance, or dexterity.—**train'-bearer** one who holds up a train, as of a robe, or gown; **train'ing-ship** a ship in which boys are trained for the sea; **train'-spotter** one who collects locomotive numbers as a hobby; **train'-spotting.—in train** in progress; **in training** undergoing training: physically fit. [Mainly O.Fr. *trainer, trahiner* (Fr. *traîner*), to drag (nouns *train, traîne*); partly with overlap of meanings, from O.Fr. *traîne,* guile.]

train² *trān, n.* (usu. **train'-oil'**) whale-oil extracted from the blubber by boiling. [Du. *traen* (now *traan*), tear, exudation.]

traipse, trapes *trāps, v.i.* to trail: to trudge.—*n.* a trudge.—*n.* and *adj.* **traips'ing, trapes'ing.**

trait *trā,* or *trāt, n.* a stroke, touch: a characteristic. [Fr.,—L. *trahere, tractum,* to draw.]

traitor *trā'tar, n.* a betrayer: one who commits treason (*fem.* **trait'ress**)—Also *adj.*—*ns.* **trai'torhood, trait'orism, trai'torship.**—*adj.* **trait'orous.**—*adv.* **trait'orously.**—*n.* **trait'orousness.** [Fr. *traître*—L. *trāditor*—*trādēre,* to give up.]

traject *trə-jekt', v.t.* to transmit.—*n.* **trajectory** (*traj'ik-tar-i,* or *trə-jekt'ər-i*) the curve described by a body under the action of given forces. [L. *trājicēre, -jectum*—*trāns,* across, *jacēre,* to throw.]

tram *tram, n.* a barrow or car shaft: a tramway: a tramway-car.—Also *adj.*—**tram'-car** a tramway-car; **tram'-conductor; tram'-line** a line of tramway: (in *pl.*) the lines marking the sides of a tennis or badminton court and the lines parallel to them inside the court; **tram'way** a track or system of tracks with sunken rails along a road; **tram'way-car** a carriage for conveying passengers on a tramway. [Cf. L.G *traam*, beam, shaft, etc.]

trammel *tram'l*, *n.* a net whose inner fine-meshed layer is carried by the fish through the coarse-meshed outer layer, and encloses it in a pocket: anything that confines.—*v.t.* to shackle: to confine: to impede: to entangle:—*pr.p.* **tramm'elling**; *pa.t.* and *pa p.* **tramm'elled.**—*n.* **tramm'eller.**—**tramm'el-net'** a trammel. [O.Fr. *tramail*, a net—L.L. *tramacula*, from L. *trēs*, three, *macula*, a mesh.]

tramontane *tra-mon'tān*, *adj.* beyond the mountains (the Alps from Rome): foreign: uncivilised.—*n.* a dweller beyond the mountains: a foreigner: a barbarian.—*n.* **tramontana** (*trà-mon-ta'na*) in Italy, a north wind. [It. *tramontana*—L. *trāns*, beyond, *mōns, montis*, a mountain.]

tramp *tramp*, *v.t.* to tread, esp. heavily or noisily: to walk: to go on a walking tour or long walk: to go about as a vagrant.—*v.t.* to traverse on foot: to trample.—*n.* a foot-journey: the sound of heavy footsteps: a vagrant: a cargo-boat with no fixed route: a prostitute, an immoral woman (*slang*).—*adv.* with tramping noise.—*n.* **tramp'er.** [M.E. *trampen*.]

trample *tramp'l*, *v t.* to tread roughly under foot· to treat with pride, to insult.—*v.i.* to tread roughly or in contempt: to tread forcibly and rapidly.—*n* a trampling—*ns.* **tramp'ler; tramp'ling.**—Also *adj.* [Freq. of **tramp.**]

trampolin(e) *tram'pə-lin*, *-lēn*, *ns.* a framework holding a piece of canvas, stretched and attached by springs, for acrobats, gymnasts, diving learners, etc , to jump, somersault, etc. on.—*n.* **tram'polinist.** [It. *trampolino*, springboard.]

tran-. See **trans-.**

trance *trans*, *n.* a dazed, abstracted, ecstatic or exalted state: a deep sleeplike state, profound and prolonged. [Fr. *transe*—*transir*—L. *trānsīre*, to go across, in L.L. to die.]

tranche *trāsh*, *n* a slice: a block, portion, esp of an issue of shares. [Fr.]

trannie, tranny. See **transistor.**

tranquil *trangk'wil*, *adj.* calm: peaceful.—*n.* **tranquillisā'tion**, *-z-.*—*v.t.* **tranq'uillise, -ize** to make tranquil.—*n.* **tranquilli'ser**, *-z-* that which tranquillises: a sedative drug.—*adv.* **tranquilli'singly**, *-z-.*—*n.* **tranquill'ity.**—*adv.* **tran'quilly.** [L. *tranquillus.*]

trans- *tranz-, trānz-, trənz-, trans-, trans-, trəns-, pfx.* across, beyond, through.—Also **tran-, tra-.** [L. *trāns*, across, beyond.]

transact *tranz-akt', tranz-, trənz-, -s-, v.t.* to conduct, negotiate: to perform.—*ns.* **transac'tion** the act of transacting: a piece of business performed: (*pl.*) the reports or publications of certain learned societies; **transac'tor.** [L. *trānsactum*, pa.p. of *trānsigĕre—agĕre*, to carry on.]

transalpine *tranz-al'pīn, tranz-, adj.* beyond the Alps (orig. from Rome): crossing the Alps. [L. *trāns-alpīnus—Alpae*, Alps.]

transatlantic *tranz-ət-lan'tik, tranz-, adj.* beyond the *Atlantic* Ocean: crossing the Atlantic. [Pfx. **trans-.**]

transceiver *tran-sē'vər, trān-, n.* a piece of radio equipment (e.g. a walkie-talkie) whose circuitry permits both transmission and reception. [*transmitter* and *receiver.*]

transcend *tran-send', tran-, v.t.* to rise above: to surmount: to surpass: to exceed: to pass or lie beyond the limit of.—*ns.* **transcend'ence, transcend'ency.**—*adjs.* **transcend'ent** transcending: superior or supreme in excellence: surpassing others: beyond human knowledge: abstrusely speculative, fantastic; **transcenden'tal** transcending: supereminent, sur-

passing others: concerned with what is independent of experience: vague.—*v.t.* **transcenden'talise, -ize.**—*ns.* **transcenden'talism** the investigation of what is *a priori* in human knowledge, or independent of experience: the American reaction against Puritan prejudices, humdrum orthodoxy, old-fashioned metaphysics, materialistic philistinism, and materialism—best associated with the name of R. W. Emerson (1803–82); **transcenden'talist.**—*advs.* **transcenden'tally; transcend'ently.**—*n.* **transcend'entness.**—**transcendental meditation** a system of meditation designed to promote spiritual well-being and a relaxed state of consciousness through silent repetition of a mantra. [L. *trānscendĕre—scandĕre*, to climb.]

transcontinental *tranz-kont-i-nent'l, trānz-, adj* extending or passing across, or belonging to the farther side of, a *continent*. [Pfx **trans-.**]

transcribe *tran-skrīb', trān-, v.t* to write over from one book into another: to copy: to transliterate: to arrange (a composition) for an instrument, voice, or combination other than that for which it was composed (*mus.*): to record for future broadcasting or the like: to broadcast a transcription of: to transfer (information) from one type of storage system to another (*comput.*).—*ns.* **transcrib'er; transcript** (*tran'skript, tran'*) a written or printed copy, esp. a legal or official copy of (sometimes secret) proceedings, testimony, etc.; **transcrip'tion** the act or result of transcribing.—*adjs.* **transcrip'tional; transcrip'tive.**—*adv.* **transcrip'tively.** [L. *trānscrībĕre, -scrīptum.*]

transducer *trans-dū'sər, trāns-, -z-,* in U.S. *-dōos', n.* a device that transfers power from one system to another in the same or in different form. [L. *trānsdūcĕre, -ductum*, to lead across.]

transept *tran'sept, tran-, n.* part of a church at right angles to the nave, or of another building to the body: either wing of such a part where it runs right across.—*adj.* **transept'al** of a transept. [L. *saeptum* (used in pl.) fence, enclosure.]

transfer *trans-fûr', trans-, v.t.* to carry or bring over: to convey from one place, person, ownership, object, group, football club, etc , to another: to change over: to convey (as a design) to another surface.—*v.i* to change over:—*pr.p.* **transferr'ing**; *pa.t.* and *pa.p.* **transferred'.**—*ns* **trans'fer** the act of transferring: conveyance from one person, place, etc., to another: that which is transferred or is to be transferred (as a picture); **transferabil'ity** (also **transferrabil'ity, transferribil'ity).**—*adj.* **trans'ferable** (also **transfer'able, transferr'able, transferr'ible** (*-fûr'*)).—*ns.* **transferee'** the person to whom a thing is transferred: one who is transferred; **trans'ference** the act of transferring or conveying: unconscious transferring of one's hopes, desires, fears, etc., from one person or object to another (*psych.*); **trans'feror** (*law*), **transferr'er** (*general*), one who transfers.—**transferable vote** a vote which, if the candidate voted for should be out of the running, is to be transferred to another as second (third, etc.) choice; **transfer list** a list of footballers available for transfer to another club. [L. *trānsferre—ferre*, to carry.]

transfigure *trans-fig'ər, trans-, v.t.* to change the appearance of: to glorify.—*ns.* **transfiguration** (*-ə-* or *-ū-rā'shən*) a transformation or glorification in appearance: (with *cap*) the Christian festival of the transfiguration of Christ (Matt. xvii. 2); **transfig'urement.** [L. *trānsfigūrāre—figūra*, form.]

transfix *trans-fiks', trāns-, v.t* to pierce through: to paralyse with sudden emotion.—*n.* **transfixion** (*-fik'shən*). [L. *trānsfigĕre, -fixum—figĕre*, to fix.]

transform *trans-form', trans-, v.t* to change the shape of: to change to another form, appearance, substance, character: to change the form of (an algebraic expression or geometrical figure).—*v.i.* to be changed in form or substance.—*n.* (*trans'*) an expression or figure derived from another (*math.*).—*adj.* **transform'able.**—*ns.* **transforma'tion** change of form, constitution, or substance: metamorphosis: (also **transformational rule**) any of a number of grammatical rules converting the deep structure of a sentence into its surface structure (*linguistics*): reflection, rotation, translation, or dilatation (*geom.*).—*adjs.* **transforma'tional; transform'ative; transformed'.**—*n.* **transform'er** one who, that which, transforms: an apparatus for obtaining an electric current from another of a different voltage.—*n.* and *adj.* **transform'ing.**—**transformational grammar** a method of studying or describing a language by stating which elements or structures can be derived from or related to others by transformation: a grammatical description which includes transformational rules. [L. *trānsfōrmāre—fōrma*, form.]

transfuse *trans-fūz', trāns-, v.t.* to pour out into another vessel: to transfer to another's veins: to cause to pass, enter, or diffuse through.—*n.* **transfū'ser.**—*adj.* **transfū'sible.**—*ns.* **transfū'sion** (-*zhən*) transfusing, esp. of blood; **transfū'sionist.**—*adj.* **transfū'sive** (-*siv*) tending or having power to transfuse.—*adv.* **transfū'sively.** [L. *trānsfundēre—fundēre, fūsum*, to pour.]

transgress *trans-gres', trāns-, -z-, v.i.* to overstep, exceed: to infringe.—*v.i.* to offend by violating a law: to sin.—*n.* **transgression** (-*gresh'ən*) an overstepping: an infringement: sin.—*adjs.* **transgress'ional; transgressive** (-*gres'iv*).—*n.* **transgress'or.** [L. *trānsgredī, -gressum—gradī, gressum*, to step.]

tranship, transship *tran(s)-ship', trān(s)-, trən(s)-, v.t.* to transfer from one ship or other conveyance to another.—*v.i.* to change ship, etc.—*ns.* **tran(s)ship'ment; tran(s)shipp'er; tran(s)shipp'ing.** [Pfx. **tran(s)-.**]

transhume *trans-(h)ūm', trans-, -z-, v.t.* and *v.t.* to transfer or pass from summer to winter or from winter to summer pastures.—*n.* **transhu'mance.**—*adj.* **transhu'mant.** [Sp. *trashumar*—L. *trāns, humus*, ground.]

transient *tran'zi-ənt, trān', -si-, adj.* passing: of short duration: making, or for persons making, only a short stay.—*n.* a temporary resident, worker, etc.—*ns.* **tran'sience, tran'siency.**—*adv.* **tran'siently.**—*n.* **tran'sientness.** [L. *trānsiēns, -euntis*—pr.p. of *trānsīre*, to cross—*īre, itum*, to go.]

transistor *tranz-ist'ər, trānz-, -s-, n.* a three-electrode semiconductor device, able to perform many functions of multi-electrode valves.—*n.* **transistorisa'tion, -z-.**—*v.t.* **transistorise, -ize** to fit with a transistor.—**transistor (radio)** a small portable radio (*slang* shortenings **trann'ie, trann'y**). [*transfer* and *resistor*.]

transit *tran'zit, trān', -sit, n.* the conveyance or passage of things or people over, across, or through' the passage of a heavenly body over the meridian.—*v.t.* to pass across: to reverse.—*n.* **transition** (-*sizh'ən, -zish'ən, sish'ən*) passage from one place, state, stage, style or subject to another: a change of key (*mus.*): in archit., esp. the passage from Romanesque or Norman to Gothic.—*adj.* **transitional.**—*adjs.* **transi'tional, transi'tionary.**—*adv.* **transi'tionally.**—*adj.* **trans'i-tive** passing over: having the power of passing: taking a direct object (*gram.*).—*adv.* **trans'itively.**—*n.* **trans'itiveness.**—*adv.* **trans'itorily.**—*n.* **trans'itoriness.**—*adj.* **trans'itory** lasting or appearing for a short time.—**transit camp** a camp where e.g. refugees, immigrants, soldiers, etc. are temporarily accommodated before travelling on to a further desti-

nation; **trans'sit-instrument** a telescope mounted in the meridian and turned on a fixed east and west axis, **tran'sit-theodolite** one whose telescope can be reversed.—**in transit** of goods, etc., in the process of being transported from one place to another [L. *trānsitus, -ūs, trānsitiō, -ōnis—īre, itum*, to go.]

translate *trans-lāt', trans-, trans-, -z-, v.t.* to remove to another place: to remove to heaven, especially without death: to render into another language: to interpret, put in plainer terms, explain: to transform: to perform a translation on (*mech., math.*).—*v.t.* to practise translation: to admit of translation.—*adj.* **transla'table.**—*n.* **transla'tion** the act of translating. removal to another place: rendering into another language: a version: motion, change of place, such that every point moves in the same direction at the same speed: similar change of place of a geometrical figure. —*adj.* **transla'tional.**—*n.* **transla'tor.** [L. *trāns-lātum*, used as supine of *trānsferre*; see *transfer*.]

transliterate *tranz-lit'ə-rāt, trānz-, -s-, v t.* to write in letters of another alphabet, etc.—*ns.* **transliter-a'tion; translit'erātor.** [L. *littera*, letter.]

translocation *tranz-lō-kā'shən, trānz-, -s-, n.* transference from place to place, esp. of materials within the body of a plant: the transfer of a portion of a chromosome to another part of the same chromosome or to a different chromosome (*genetics*).—*v.t.* **translocate'.** [L. *locus*, place.]

translucent *tranz-lōō'sənt, trānz-, -s-, -lū', adj.* shining through: imperfectly transparent: clear.—*ns.* **translu'cence, translu'cency.**—*adv.* **translu'cently.** [L. *trānslūcēns, -entis—lūcēre,* to shine—*lūx, lūcis,* light.]

translunar *tranz-lōō'nər, trānz-, -s-, adj.* pertaining to the region beyond the moon's orbit round the earth —*adj* **translun'ary** (or *tranz'*) beyond the moon: visionary. [Pfx **trans-.**]

transmigrate *tranz'mī-grāt, trānz', -s-, -grāt', v.t.* to remove to another place of abode: of the soul, to pass into another body.—*ns.* **transmigra'tion; transmi-grā'tionism** belief in the transmigration of souls; **transmigra'tionist.** [L. *trānsmigrāre, -ātum—mi-grāre*, to migrate.]

transmissible, transmission, etc See *transmit.*

transmit *tranz-mit', trānz-, -s-, v.t.* to send on: to pass on: to hand on: to communicate: to send out or broadcast: to transfer: to allow the passage of, act as a medium for (heat, energy, light, sound, etc).—*v.t.* to send out a radio signal, etc.:—*pr.p.* **transmitt'ing;** *pa.t* and *pa.p.* **transmitt'ed.**—*n.* **transmissibil'ity.**—*adj* **transmiss'ible.**—*n* **transmission** (*mish'ən*) the process of transmitting or being transmitted: that which is transmitted: a programme, message, etc sent out by radio, etc.: the system of interdependent parts in a motor vehicle, by which power is transferred from the engine to the wheels.—*adjs.* **trans-miss'ional; transmiss'ive** having the quality of transmitting or of being transmitted.—*ns.* **transmiss'iv'ity; transmitt'al; transmitt'er** one who or that which transmits: apparatus for sending forth anything, as signals, messages, etc. [L *trānsmittēre, missum—mittēre, missum,* to send.]

transmogrify *tranz-mog'ri-fī, trānz-, -s-, (coll., facet.) v.t.* to transform, transmute.—*n.* **transmogri-fica'tion.**

transmontane *tranz-mon'tān, trānz-, -s-, adj.* another form of **tramontane.**

transmute *tranz-mūt', trānz-, -s-, v.t.* to change to another form or substance.—*n.* **transmūtabil'ity.**—*adj.* **transmū'table.**—*n.* **transmū'tableness.**—*adv* **transmū'tably.**—*ns.* **transmūta'tion** a changing into a different form, nature, or substance, esp. that of one chemical element into another; **transmū'ter.** [L.

trānsmūtāre—mūtāre, to change.]

transnational *tranz-nash'nəl, trănz-, -s-, adj.* transcending national boundaries, concerning more than one nation. [Pfx. **trans-**.]

transoceanic *tranz-ō-shı-an'ik, trănz-, -s-, adj.* across or crossing the ocean. [Pfx. **trans-**.]

transom *tran'səm, n.* a cross-piece: a cross-beam: a structure dividing a window horizontally: a lintel: a small window over the lintel of a door or window [App. L. *trānstrum*, a cross-beam.]

transparent *trans-pār'ənt, trăns-, trans-, -z-, -par', adj.* able to be seen through: easily detected, understood: obvious, evident: ingenuous.—*n.* **transpar'ency** the quality of being transparent: that which is transparent: a picture, photograph, design, device visible, or to be viewed, by transmitted light.—*adv.* **transpar'ently.**—*n.* **transpar'entness.** [L.L. *trānspārēns, -entis*—L. *părēre*, to appear.]

transpire *tran-spīr', trăn-, v.t.* to give off as vapour: to emit through the skin.—*v.i.* to exhale: to give off water-vapour (as plants) or waste material through the skin (as animals): to become known, come to light: (*loosely*) to happen.—*adj.* **transpīr'able.**—*n.* **transpiration** (*tran-spi-rā'shən*).—*adj.* **transpīr'atory.** [L. *spīrāre*, to breathe.]

transplant *trans-plant', trăns-, -z-, v.t.* to remove (a plant) from the ground where it grows and plant in another place: to graft upon another animal or another part of the same: to remove and establish elsewhere.—*v.i.* to bear transplanting.—*n.* **trans'plant** a part or organ removed from its normal position and grafted into another position in the same individual or into another position in the same planting.—*adj.* **transplan'table.**—*ns.* **transplantā'tion; transplan'ter; transplan'ting.** [L. *trānsplantāre—plantāre*, to plant.]

transponder *tranz-pon'dər, trănz-, -s-, n.* a radio or radar device which, on receiving a signal, transmits a signal of its own. [*transmitter responder*.]

transport *trans-pōrt', -pört', trăns-, -z-, v.t.* to carry, convey, remove: to send overseas, as a convict: to carry away by strong emotion: to throw into an ecstasy.—*ns.* **trans'port** carriage, conveyance, of goods or people from one place to another: the management of, arrangements for, such conveyance: means of conveyance for getting from place to place: ecstasy: one who has been transported or sentenced to transportation; **transportabil'ity.**—*adj.* **transport'able.**—*n.* **transportā'tion** removal: removal of offenders beyond seas: conveyance of goods or people: means of transport.—*adj.* **transport'ed.**—*adv.* **transport'edly.**—*ns.* **transport'edness; transport'er** someone or something that transports, esp. a large vehicle for carrying heavy goods.—*n.* and *adj.* **transport'ing.**—*adv.* **transport'ingly.**—*adj.* **transport'ive** tending or having power to transport.— **transport café** a roadside café catering mainly for long-distance lorry drivers. [L. *trānsportāre—portāre*, to carry.]

transpose *trans-pōz', trăns-, -z-, v.t.* to transfer: to turn, alter: to change the order of, interchange: to write, perform, or render in another key (*mus.*).— *adj.* **transpōs'able.**—*ns.* **transpōs'al** a change of place or order; **transpōs'er.**—*n.* and *adj.* **transpōs'ing.**—*n.* **transposition** (*-pō-, -pa-zish'ən*).—*adjs.* **transposi'tional; transposi'tive** (*-poz'*).—**transposing instrument** one for which music is written in a different key from the actual sounds. [Fr. *transposer*; see **pose.**]

transsexual, trans-sexual *trans-seks'ū-al, trăns-, n.* a person anatomically of one sex but having an abnormally strong desire to belong to the opposite sex: one who has had medical and surgical treatment so that they resemble those of the opposite sex.—

Also *adj.*—*n.* **transsex'ualism.** [Pfx **trans-.**]

trans-ship, transship. Same as **tranship.**

transubstantiate *tran-səb-stan'shi-āt, trăn-, -zəb-, v.t.* to change to another substance.—*ns.* **transubstantiā'tion** a change into another substance: the doctrine that, in the consecration of the elements of the eucharist, the whole substance of the bread and wine is converted into Christ's body and blood; **transubstantiā'tion(al)ist, transubstan'tiātor** one who believes in transubstantiation. [L. *substantia*, substance.]

transude *tran-sūd', trăn-, -zūd', v.i.* and *v t* to ooze out.—*ns.* **tran'sūdate** a substance that transudes; **transūdā'tion.** [L. *sūdāre*, to sweat.]

transuranic *trans-ū-ran'ik, trans-, -z-, adj.* of greater atomic number than *uranium.*—Also **transurā'nian, transurā'nium.** [Pfx. **trans-.**]

transverse *tranz'vûrs, tranz', -vûrs', adj.* set, sent, lying, etc. crosswise.—*adj.* crosswise—*n.* anything set crosswise.—*adj.* **transvers'al** transverse.—*n.* a line cutting a set of lines.—*n.* **transversal'ity.**—*advs* **transvers'ally; transverse'ly.**—*n.* **transver'sion.**— **transverse wave** (*phys.*) a wave motion in which the disturbance of the medium occurs at right angles to the direction of wave propagation. [L. *trānsversus —vertere, versum*, to turn.]

transvest *tranz-vest', trănz-, v.t.* and *v.i.* to dress oneself in the clothes of another, esp. of the opposite sex. —*n.* and *adj.* **transvestite** (*-vest'īt*), (one) given to this.—*ns.* **transvest'ism; transvest'itism.** [Pfx. **trans-,** and L. *vestis—vestīre, vestītum*, to dress.]

trap¹ *trap, n.* a snare, device for catching: a hidden danger: a pitfall: a trap-door: a bend in a pipe to stop foul gases: a light carriage: a contrivance for throwing up or releasing a ball or clay pigeons: the mouth (*slang*): a bunker or other hazard (*golf*): (in *pl.*) drums or other percussion instruments (*jazz*).—*v.t.* to catch in a trap: to provide with traps: to control (a ball) so that it stops dead (*football*).—*v.i.* to act as a trapper:—*pr.p.* **trapp'ing;** *pa.t.* and *pa.p.* **trapped.**— *n.* **trapp'er** one who traps animals for their fur.—*n.* and *adj.* **trapp'ing.**—**trap'-door** a door set in a floor, stage or ceiling, esp. flush with its surface; **trap'-shooting** clay pigeon shooting. [O.E *trappe—træppe, treppe.*]

trap² *trap, n.* a dark fine-grained igneous rock (lying often in steps or terraces).—**trap'-rock.** [Sw. *trapp —trappa*, a stair.]

trap³ *trap, n.* (in *pl.*) personal luggage.—*n.pl.* **trapp'ings** gay, colourful clothes: ornaments, esp. those put on horses: characteristic accompaniments, adornments, paraphernalia (of office, etc.). [App. conn. with Fr. *drap*, cloth.]

trapes. See traipse.

trapezium *trə-pē'zi-əm, n.* orig., any quadrilateral that is not a parallelogram: one with no sides parallel (*U.S.*): one with one (and only one) pair of parallel sides (*Brit.*):—*pl.* **trapē'zia, -ziums.**—*n.* **trapēze** (*trə-pēz'*) a swing-like apparatus used by acrobats, consisting of one or more cross-bars suspended between two ropes—*adjs.* **trapē'zial** pertaining to a trapezium; **trapē'ziform** having the form of a trapezium.—*ns.* **trapē'zius** (also **trapezius muscle**) (either of two triangular halves of) a large, flat, quadrilateral-shaped muscle across the back of the shoulders; **trapezoid** (*trap'i-zoid*, also *trə-pē'zoid*) a quadrilateral with no sides parallel: one with two sides parallel (*U.S.*).—*adj.* **trapezoid'al.** [Latinised from Gr. *trapezion*, dim. of *trapeza*, a table; lit. four-legged.]

Trappist *trap'ist, n.* a Cistercian of the reformed rule established by De Rancé (1626–1700), abbot of La *Trappe* in Normandy—austere and silent.—Also *adj*

trash *trash, n.* broken twigs, hedge-cuttings: scraps: anything worthless: rubbish: nonsense: worthless people.—*v.t.* to free from trash: to lop the tops from.—*adv.* **trash'ily.**—*n.* **trash'iness.**—*adj.* **trash'y** like trash: worthless.—**trash'-can** (*U.S.*) a receptacle for refuse. [Prob. Scand.]

trass *tras, n.* an earthy volcanic tuff used as a hydraulic cement. [Du. *tras.*]

trattoria *trät-tō-rē'ə, n.* an Italian restaurant. [It.]

trauma *trö'mə, trow'mə, n.* a wound: an injury: an emotional shock that may be the origin of a neurosis (*psych.*): the state or condition caused by a physical or emotional shock:—*pl.* **trau'mas, trau'mata.**—*adj.* **traumatic** (*-mat'ik*) relating to, resulting from, or causing, wounds: of, causing, a lasting emotional shock: (*loosely*) frightening, unpleasant.—*adv.* **traumat'ically.**—*v.t.* **trau'matise, -ize** to inflict a mental or physical trauma on. [Gr. *trauma, -atos,* a wound.]

travail *trav'āl, -əl, n.* excessive labour: toil: labour in childbirth.—*v.i.* to labour: to suffer the pains of childbirth. [O.Fr. (Fr.) *travail.*]

travel *trav'l, v.i.* to journey: to go: to go round soliciting orders: to move along a course: to go with impetus: to be capable of withstanding a journey: to move —*v.t.* to journey over or through:—*pr.p.* **trav'elling;** *pa.t.* and *pa.p.* **trav'elled.**—*n.* journeying.—*adj.* **trav'elled** having made journeys: experienced: frequented.—*n.* **trav'eller** one who travels or has travelled: one of the travelling people: one who travels for a mercantile house: a piece of mechanism that moves on a gantry, etc.—*n.* and *adj.* **trav'elling.**—*n.* **travelogue** (*trav'ə-log*) a talk, lecture, article, or film on travel.—**travel agency** an agency which provides information, brochures, tickets, etc., relating to travel; **travel agent; traveller's cheque** a cheque which can be cashed at any foreign branch or specified agent of the bank issuing it; **trav'eller's-joy** *Clematis vitalba,* sometimes called old man's beard; **travelling folk, people** the name by which itinerant people often call themselves, in preference to the derogatory names gipsies or tinkers.—*adj.* **trav'el-sick** suffering from travel sickness.—**travel sickness** nausea experienced, as a result of motion, by a passenger in a car, ship, aircraft, etc. [**travail.**]

traverse *trav'ûrs, adj.* cross: oblique.—*n.* a crossing or passage across: a passage across the face of a rock in mountaineering: a survey by measuring straight lines from point to point and the angles between: anything set or lying across: an obstruction: a screened-off compartment: a denial or contradiction.—*v.t.* (or *-vûrs'*) to cross: to pass through, across, or over: to move about over: to pass over by traverse: to survey by traverse: to oppose: to thwart: to dispute: to deny, contradict: to turn sideways.—*v.i.* to make a traverse: to move to the side: to direct a gun to the right or left.—*adjs.* **trav'ersable; trav'ersed** crossed, passed over.—*n.* **trav'erser.**—*n.* and *adj.* **trav'ersing.** [Fr. *travers, traverse, traverser*—L. *trāns, vertēre, versum,* to turn.]

travertine *trav'ər-tīn, -tēn, -tin, n.* a pale limestone deposited from solution, e.g. from springs.—Also **travertin.** [It. *travertino*—L. *tīburtīnus* (*lapis*), stone of Tibur.]

travesty *trav'is-ti, n.* disguise, esp. of a man as a woman or vice versa: burlesque: ridiculously inadequate representation (of).—*v.t.* to disguise: to burlesque. [Fr. *travesti,* pa.p. of *travestir,* to disguise—L. *trāns, vestīre,* to clothe.]

travois *trä-voi'* (*pl.* **travois** *trä-voiz'*), *n.* a North American Indian drag, a pair of trailing poles attached to each side of the saddle, joined by a board

or net. [Canadian Fr. pron. of Fr. *travail.*]

trawl *tröl, n.* an open-mouthed bag-net for dragging along the sea-bed: a trawl-line (q.v.): an act of trawling.—*v.t.* and *v.i.* to catch or fish with a trawl.—*v.i.* to look for something (e.g. a suitable person for a post, etc.) by gathering suggestions from various sources (with *for;* strictly, a meaning developed from **troll**[2]).—*ns.* **traw'ler** one who trawls: a trawling vessel; **traw'ling.**—**trawl'-line** a buoyed line with baited hooks at intervals; **trawl'-net.** [Cf. **trail**[1] and M.Du. *traghel,* drag-net.]

tray *trā, n.* a flat low-rimmed vessel used for carrying articles (as crockery, etc.).—*n.* **tray'ful:**—*pl* **tray'fuls.**—**tray'-cloth** a cloth for covering a tray. [O.E. *trīg, trēg,* board.]

treacherous *trech'ər-əs, adj.* ready to betray: not to be trusted: misleadingly inviting in appearance.—*adv.* **treach'erously.**—*ns.* **treach'erousness; treach'ery** betrayal: readiness to betray: falseness: treason. [O.Fr. *trecheor,* deceiver—*trechier,* to trick.]

treacle *trē'kl, n.* the dark, viscous uncrystallisable syrup obtained in refining sugar (also called **black treacle**): also molasses, the drainings of crude sugar: blandishments, esp. when suggestive of the cloying and nauseating taste and thickness of treacle: intolerable sentimentality.—*n.* **trea'cliness.**—*adj.* **trea'cly** of, or like, treacle: thick and sweet: unctuously blandishing: intolerably sentimental. [O.Fr. *triacle*—Gr. *thēriakē* (*antidotos,* an antidote to the bites) of beasts—*thērion,* a wild beast.]

tread *tred, v.i.* to set the foot down: to step: to walk: to trample: to copulate, as a cock.—*v.t.* to walk on: to press with the foot, as in threshing, pressing grapes: to trample: to render by treading: to perform by treading: to copulate with as a cock-bird:—*pa.t.* **trod;** *pa.p.* **trodd'en, trod.**—*n.* a footprint: a track: the act or manner of treading: a step or tramp: the part that touches the ground, as of a shoe, a wheel.—*ns.* **tread'er; tread'ing; tread'le, tredd'le** a foot-lever for working a machine: a pedal.—*v.i.* to work a treadle.—*ns.* **tread'ler; tread'ling.**—**tread'mill** a cylinder turned by treading on boards on its outside, as formerly by prisoners: a mill so worked: routine drudgery (*fig.*); **tread'-wheel** a wheel or cylinder turned by treading outside or inside: a treadmill.—**tread water** to float upright by an action as if of climbing a ladder. [O.E. *tredan.*]

treason *trē'zn, n.* betraying of the government or an attempt to overthrow it: treachery: disloyalty.—*adj.* **trea'sonable** pertaining to, consisting of, or involving treason.—*adv.* **trea'sonably.**—*adj.* **trea'sonous.**—**high treason** offences against the state. [A.Fr. *tresun,* O.Fr. *traïson* (Fr. *trahison*)—*traïr* (*trahir*)—L. *tradēre,* to betray.]

treasure *trezh'ər, n.* wealth stored up: riches: anything much valued.—*v.t.* to hoard up: to collect for future use: to value greatly: to store, enrich.—*ns.* **treas'urer** one who has the care of a treasure or treasury: one who has charge of collected funds; **treas'urership; treas'ury** place where treasure is deposited: (often with *cap.*) a department of a government which has charge of the finances.—**treas'ure-chest** a box for keeping articles of value; **treas'ure-house** a house for holding treasures: a treasury: a store of valuable things; **treasure hunt** a hunt for treasure: a game in which competitors attempt to win a prize by being first to complete a course indicated by clues which have to be solved; **treas'ure-trove** ownerless objects of intrinsic or historical value found hidden (in England gold and silver only), property of the crown. [O.Fr. *tresor* (Fr. *trésor*)—L. *thēsaurus*—Gr. *thē-sauros.*]

treat *trēt, v.t.* to deal with: to handle: to discuss: to behave towards: to deal with the case of: to deal with (disease) by applying remedies: to subject to a process: to stand a drink or other gratification to.—*v.i.* to negotiate: to deal (with *of*).—*n.* a free entertainment, pleasure excursion, or feast: a turn or act of providing and paying: a source of great gratification. —*adj.* **treat'able** able to be treated.—*ns.* **treat'er;** **treat'ing; treat'ise** (-*iz*, -*is*) is a written composition, esp. one treating a subject formally or systematically; **treat'ment** the act or manner of treating: management: behaviour to anyone: way of applying remedies; **treat'y** negotiation: a formal agreement, esp. between states.—**Dutch treat** see **Dutch; stand treat** see **stand; the (full) treatment** (*coll.*) the appropriate method (in every detail) of dealing, whether ceremoniously or punitively, with a particular type of person, case, etc. [O.Fr. *traitier*—L. *tractāre*, to manage—*trahĕre, tractum,* to draw.]

treble *treb'l, adj.* triple: threefold: in the treble (*mus.*): high-pitched.—*n.* that which is triple: three times as much: the highest part, soprano (*mus.*): a treble singer, voice, instrument, string, sound, etc.: the narrow inner ring on a dartboard, or a hit on this: a bet involving three horse-races, the stake and winnings from the first being bet on the second, and those from the second on the third.—*v.t.* to make three times as much.—*v.i.* to become threefold.—*n.* **treb'leness.**—*adv.* **treb'ly.**—**treble chance** a mode of competing in football pools in which, in a selection of matches made from a list, the aim is to pick all draws; **treble clef** the G clef on the second line. [O.Fr.,— L. *triplus*; see **triple.**]

trebuchet *treb'ū-shet, trā-bū-shā', n.* a mediaeval military engine for launching stones, etc. [O.Fr.]

trecento *trā-chen'tō, n.* and *adj.* 14th-century (in Italian art, etc.).—*n.* **trecen'tist.** [It., three (for thirteen) hundred.]

treddle. Same as **treadle. **See **tread.**

tree *trē, n.* a large plant with a single branched woody trunk (sometimes loosely applied): timber: a wooden structure or part of various kinds: a gallows: a cross for crucifixion: a branching figure or structure, as a pedigree, a branching stand for rings, etc. (*ring-tree, mug-tree*).—*v.t.* to drive into a tree, to corner (also *fig.*).—*adj.* in composition, inhabiting, frequenting, growing on trees: taking the form of a tree.—*adj.* **tree'less.**—**tree'-creeper** a little bird (*Certhia*) that runs up tree-trunks in search of insects; **tree'-fern** a fern with a tall woody trunk; **tree'-frog** an arboreal amphibian, esp. one of the family *Hylidae,* nearer to toads than to frogs; **tree'-kangaroo'** a tree-climbing kangaroo (*Dendrolagus*); **tree'-line** same as **timberline.**—*adj.* **tree'-lined** (of roads, etc.) having trees along either side.—**treenail, trenail** (*trē'nāl, tren'l*) a long wooden pin or nail to fasten the planks of a ship to the timbers; **tree'-shrew** any insectivore of the East Indian family Tupaiidae, squirrel-like animals akin to shrews; **tree'-snake** a tree-dwelling snake; **tree'-surgeon** one who preserves diseased trees by filling cavities, amputating damaged branches, etc.; **tree'-surgery; tree'top** the top of a tree; **tree'-trunk.—at the top of the tree** in the highest position in e.g. a profession; **family tree** pedigree; **up a tree** in difficulties. [O.E. *trēow, trēo.*]

tref *trāf,* **trefa** *trā'fə, adjs.* in the Jewish religion, forbidden as food, not kosher. [Heb. *terēphāh,* torn flesh—*taraph,* to tear.]

trefoil *trē'foil, n.* a three-lobed form, ornament, or aperture, as in tracery or heraldry: a leaf of three leaflets: a trifoliate plant, esp. of the clover genus (Trifolium). [A.Fr. *trifoil*—L. *trifolium*— *trēs,* three, *folium,* a leaf.]

trek *trek, v.t.* to drag.—*v.i.* to journey by ox-wagon: to

migrate: to tramp and camp, dragging one's equipment: to make a long hard journey, usu. on foot:— *pr.p.* **trekk'ing;** *pa.t.* and *pa.p.* **trekked.**—*n.* a journey or stage: a migration.—*n.* **trekk'er.** [Du. *trekken,* to draw.]

trellis *trel'is, n.* a structure of cross-barred or lattice work.—*v.t.* to provide with a trellis: to train on a trellis.—*adj.* **trell'ised.**—**trell'is-work** lattice-work. [O.Fr. *treliz*—L. *trilix, -īcis,* woven with triple thread.]

trema *trē'mə, n.* an orifice: a diaeresis.—*n.* **trematode** (*trem'ə-tōd*) any member of the **Tremato'da,** a class of parasitic worms with adhesive suckers.—*n.* and *adj.* **trem'atoid.** [Gr. *trēma, -atos,* a hole.]

tremble *trem'bl, v.i.* to shake, as from fear, cold, or weakness: to quiver: to vibrate: to pass tremulously. —*v.t.* to set trembling.—*n.* the act of trembling: tremulousness: a tremulous state: (in *pl.*) a morbid trembling.—*ns.* **trem'blement; trem'bler.**—*n.* and *adj.* **trem'bling.**—*adv.* **trem'blingly.**—*adj.* **trem'bly** tremulous.—**trembling poplar** the aspen. [O.Fr. (Fr.) *trembler*—L. *tremulus,* trembling—*tremĕre,* to shake.]

tremendous *tri-men'dəs, adj.* awe-inspiring: huge (*coll.*): prodigious, extraordinary, very good (*slang*). —*adv.* **tremen'dously.**—*n.* **tremen'dousness.** [L. *tremendus,* to be trembled at.]

tremolo *trem'ō-lō,* (*mus.*) *n.* a tremulous effect as by a rapid succession of interruptions or of up and down bows: a device in an organ or electronic instrument for producing this:—*pl.* **trem'olos.**—Also *adj.* [It. *tremolo, tremolando, tremolante.*]

tremor *trem'ər, n.* a quiver: a thrill: an agitation: a vibration.—*adj.* **trem'orless.** [L. *tremor, -ōris.*]

tremulous *trem'ū-ləs, adj.* trembling: quivering.—*adj.* **trem'ulant** tremulous.—*adv.* **trem'ulously.**—*n.* **trem'ulousness.** [L. *tremulus,* trembling, and L.L. *tremulāre, -ātum,* to tremble.]

trenail. See under **tree.**

trench *trench, trensh, n.* a long narrow cut in the earth, often used in warfare as a cover for troops.—*v.i.* to make trenches: to dig deep with spade or plough: to encroach: to border, verge.—*v.t.* to cut: to make trenches in: to put in a trench: to furnish with a trench: to entrench.—*adj.* **trench'ant** cutting: incisive, forthright.—*adv.* **trench'antly.**—*n.* **trench'er.** —**trench'-coat** a waterproof coat with belt, for man or woman; **trench'-feet'** a diseased condition of the feet owing to exposure to cold and wet in trench warfare; **trench'-fe'ver** a disease causing pain in joints and muscles, prevalent among soldiers living in trenches, transmitted by lice; **trench'-mor'tar** a small smooth-bore gun, throwing large shells short distances, useful in trench warfare; **trench warfare** warfare in which each side entrenches itself in lines facing the enemy. [O.Fr. *trenche,* cut), *trencher* to cut, prob.—L. *truncāre.*]

trencher *tren'chər, -shər, n.* a plate or platter: a board. —**tren'cher-cap** a college-cap, mortar-board; **tren'cher-man** a hearty eater. [A.Fr. *trenchour* (Fr. *tranchoir*)—*trencher,* to cut.]

trend *trend, v.i.* to have a tendency or prevailing direction.—*n.* general tendency.—*adj.* **tren'dy** (*coll.*) in the forefront of fashion in any sphere.—*n.* (*derog.*) a trendy person.—*n.* **trend'setter** one who helps to give a new direction to fashion.—*adj.* **trend'setting.** [O.E. *trendan.*]

trente-et-quarante *trät-ā-ka-rät, n.* the card-game rouge-et-noir. [Fr., thirty and forty.]

trepan *tri-pan', n.* a cylindrical saw: a tool for boring shafts.—*v.t.* to remove a piece of the skull from: to cut a cylindrical disc from: to cut an annular groove in.—*ns.* **trepanation** (*trep-ə-nā'shən*); **trepann'er.**—

n. and adj. trepann'ing. [Fr. *trépan*—L.L. *trepanum*—Gr. *trypanon*—*trypaein*, to bore.]

trepang *tri-pang'*, *n.* sea-slug, a holothurian eaten by the Chinese. [Malay *tripang*.]

trephine *tri-fēn'*, *-fīn'*, *n.* an improved trepan.—*v.t* to perforate with the trephine. [Earlier *trafine*—L. *très fīnēs*, three ends, with a suggestion of **trepan.**]

trepidation *trep-i-dā'shən*, *n.* trembling: alarmed agitation.—*adjs.* **trep'id** quaking; **trep'idant**; **trepid'atory.** [L. *trepidāre*, *-ātum*, to hurry with alarm—*trepidus*, restless.]

trespass *tres'pas*, *v.i.* to interfere with another's person or property: to enter unlawfully upon another's land: to encroach (on): to intrude (with *on*): to sin.—*n.* act of trespassing: any injury to another's person or property: a sin.—*n.* **tres'passer.** [O.Fr. *trespasser*—L. *trāns*, *passus*, a step.]

tress *tres*, *n.* a plait or braid of the hair of the head: a long lock.—*v.t.* to form into tresses.—*adjs.* **tressed** braided: in tresses: having tresses; **tress'y** having or like tresses. [Fr. *tresse*—L.L. *tricia*, perh. Gr. *tricha*, threefold—*treis*, three.]

trestle *tres'l*, *n.* a support composed of a horizontal beam on sloping legs: a braced framework.—**trest'le-table** one of boards laid on trestles; **trest'lework** a braced framework. [O.Fr. *trestel*—L *trānstrum*, cross-beam.]

trevally *tri-val'i*, *n.* an Australian horse-mackerel (Caranx) of various species.

trews *trōōz*, *n.pl.* (orig. *sing.*) trousers, esp. of tartan cloth. [Ir. *trius*, Gael. *triubhas*.]

trey *trā*, *n.* the three in cards and dice: a set of three [O.Fr. *treis*, *trei*—L. *trēs*, three.]

tri- *trī-*, *tri-* in composition, three, threefold. [L. *très*, *tria*, and Gr. *treis*, *tria*.]

triable. See try.

triacid *trī-as'id*, *adj.* having three replaceable hydrogen atoms: capable of replacing three hydrogen atoms of an acid. [**tri-**.]

triact *trī'akt*, *adj.* three-rayed.—*adjs.* **triact'inal** (*-i-nəl* or *-ī'nəl*), **triact'ine** (*-in*). [**tri-** and Gr. *aktīs*, *-īnos*, ray.]

triad *trī'ad*, *-əd*, *n.* a group, set, or union of three: in Welsh literature, a group of three sayings, stories, etc., about related subjects: a chord of three notes, esp. the common chord (*mus.*): an atom, element, or radical with a combining power of three (*chem.*): any of many Chinese secret societies, some now associated with criminal activities, esp. heroin trading.—*adjs.* **trī'ad, triad'ic.** [L. *trias*—Gr. *trias*, *triados*—*treis*, three.]

triage. See try.

trial *trī'əl*, *n.* a trying: examination by a test: examination by a court to determine a question of law or fact, esp. the guilt or innocence of a prisoner: (often in *pl.*) examination, sometimes merely formal, of a candidate: a testing journey, as of motor-cars, motorcycles: a trial match: suffering: temptation: attempt: a piece used as a test: a troublesome thing, a nuisance. —*adj.* done, taken, etc., for the sake of trial.—**trial balance** (*book-k*) in the double-entry system, a statement drawn up of the credit and debit totals to demonstrate that they are equal; **trial marriage** for a couple intending matrimony, a period of living together with a view to testing their compatibility; **trial run** a test drive in a motor vehicle to ascertain its efficiency: any introductory test, rehearsal, etc.—**by trial and error** by trying out several methods and discarding those which prove unsuccessful; **on trial** undergoing proceedings in a court of law: on probation, as an experiment; **stand trial** to undergo trial in a court of law; **trial of strength** a contest to find out who is the stronger (or strongest). [A.Fr *trial*—

trier, to try.]

triangle *trī'ang-gl* (also *-ang'*), *n.* a plane figure with three angles and three sides (*math.*): part of the surface of a sphere bounded by three arcs of great circles (*spherical triangle*): any mark or thing of that shape: a musical instrument of percussion, formed of a steel rod bent in triangle-form, open at one angle.—*adjs.* **trī'angled; triang'ūlar** having three angles: of a number, capable of being represented by dots in a triangle, as 1, 3, 6, 10, etc.: involving three persons or parties.—*n* **triangūlar'ity.**—*adv.* **triang'ūlarly.**—*v.t.* **triang'ūlate** to survey by means of a series of triangles —*adj.* with, marked with, made up of, triangles: triangular.—*adv.* **triang'ūlately.**—*n.* **triangūla'tion** the act or process of triangulating, e.g. for map-making: the series of triangles so used.—**the eternal triangle** an emotional situation involving two men and a woman or two women and a man. [L. *triangulum*—*angulus*, an angle.]

Trias *trī'as*, (*geol.*) *n.* the oldest Mesozoic or Secondary system.—*adj.* **Triassic** (*trī-as'ik*). [Gr. *trias*, triad, from its threefold division in Germany.]

triatomic *trī-ə-tom'ik*, *adj.* consisting of three atoms: having three replaceable atoms or groups: trivalent. [**tri-**.]

tribade *trib'ad*, *n.* a woman homosexual.—*ns.* **trib'adism, trib'ady.** [Fr. through L. *tribas*, *-adis*—Gr. *tribas*, *-ados*—*tribein*, to rub.]

tribal, etc. See tribe.

tribasic *trī-bā'sik*, *adj.* capable of reacting with three equivalents of an acid: (of acids) having three replaceable hydrogen atoms. [**tri-, base.**]

tribe *trīb*, *n.* a division of a nation or people for political purposes: a set of peoples theoretically of common descent: an aggregate of families, forming a community: a race: a breed: a class or set of people: (*loosely*) a classificatory division.—*adj.* **trī'bal.**—*n.* **trī'balism** the existence of tribes as a social phenomenon: (loyalty to) the conventions, etc. of one's tribe; **trī'balist.**—*adj.* **trī'balistic.**—*adv.* **trī'bally.**—*adj.* **tribe'less.**—*ns.* **tribes'man, tribes'woman.**—*n.pl.* **tribes'people.** [L. *tribus*, *-ūs*, one of the divisions of the ancient Roman people.]

tribo- *trī'bo-*, *trib'*, *-ō-*, in composition, rubbing, friction.—*ns.* **tribo-electric'ity** generation of electric charges by friction; **tribol'ogy** the study of friction, wear, lubrication, etc. between surfaces moving in contact with one another; **tribol'ogist; triboluminescence** (*-es'əns*) emission of light caused by friction. —*adj.* **triboluminès'cent.**—*n.* **tribom'eter** apparatus for measuring sliding friction. [Gr. *tribein*, to rub.]

tribrach *trī'brak*, *n.* a foot of three short syllables.—*adj.* **tribrach'ic.** [Gr. *tribrachys*—*brachys*, short.]

tribulation *trib-ū-lā'shən*, *n.* severe affliction. [L *tribulāre*, *-ātum*, to afflict.]

tribune *trib'ūn*, *n.* a magistrate elected by the Roman plebeians to defend their rights: a champion of popular rights: in this and the following sense, sometimes used as the title of a newspaper: a platform for speaking from: a raised area or stand: bishop's stall or throne.—*n.* **tribunal** (*trib-*, *trīb-ū'nl*) a judgment-seat: a court of justice or arbitration: a body appointed to adjudicate in some matter or to enquire into some disputed question.—*adj.* of, of the nature of, or authorised by, a tribunal.—*ns* **trib'unāte**, **trib'uneship** the office of tribune. [L. *tribūnus*, tribune, *tribūnal*, tribunal—*tribus*, a tribe.]

tribute *trib'ūt*, *n.* a payment in acknowledgment of subjection: an act, gift, words, or other expression of subjection: (*loosely*) a testimony, a credit (to).—*adj.* **trib'utary** paying tribute: contributing: paid in tribute.—*n.* a payer of tribute: a stream that runs into another. [L. *tribūtum*—*tribuěre*, to assign.]

trice *trīs*, (*naut.*) *v.t.* to haul.—*n.* a moment (as if the time of a single tug). [M Du *trisen* (Du *trijsen*), to hoist.]

triceps *trī'seps*, *adj* three-headed.—*n* a muscle with three separately arising heads, esp. the muscle at the back of the upper arm that straightens the elbow [L. *trīceps*, *-cipitis—caput*, head.]

triceratops *trī-ser'ə-tops*, *n.* a quadrupedal, herbivorous dinosaur of the Cretaceous period, having a horn over each eye and one on its nose. [tri- and Gr. *keras*, *-atos*, horn, *ōps*, face.]

trich- *trik-*, tricho- *-ō-*, *-o'-*, in composition, hair [Gr. *thrix*, gen *trichos*.]

trichiasis *trik-ī'ə-sis*, *n.* turning in of hairs around an orifice, esp. of eyelashes so that they rub against the eye. [L.L.—Gr *thrix*, *trichos*, hair.]

Trichina *trik'i-nə*, *tri-kī'nə*, Trichinella *trik-i-nel'ə*, *ns.* a genus of nematode worms parasitic in rat, pig, and man· (without *cap.*) a worm of the genus·—*pl.* -ae (*-ē*), *-as.—ns.* trichiniasis (*trik-i-nī'ə-sis*), trichinō'sis a disease caused by trichinae, trichinisā'tion, -ization infestation with trichinae.—*adjs.* trich'inised, *-z-*, trich'inosed (*-nōst*) infested with trichinae; trichinot'ic, trich'inous pertaining to trichinosis [Gr *trichinos*, of hair—*thrix*, *trichos*, hair.]

trichlor(o)- *tri-klōr'(ō)-*, *-klor'*, in composition, having three atoms of chlorine, esp replacing hydrogen.—*n* trichlor(o)ethylene (*tri-klōr(-ō)-eth'i-lēn*, *-klor*) an acetylene derivative, used as a solvent, in paint manufacture, and as an analgesic and anaesthetic (*coll.* trike *trīk*).

tricho-. See trich-.

trichoid *trik'oid*, *adj.* hairlike. [Gr. *trichoeidēs*.]

trichology *trik-ol'ə-ji*, *n.* the scientific study of hair and its disorders.—*adj.* tricholog'ical.—*n* trichol'ogist one versed in trichology. [Gr. *thrix*, *trichos*, a hair.]

trichomonad *trik-ə-mon'ad*, *n.* a parasitic protozoon of the genus Trichomonas (*tri-kom'* or *-kə-mon'*) —*n.* trichomoni'asis (*-mon-ī'*) a sexually-transmitted disease caused by trichomonads. [Gr. *trichos*, hair, *monas*, *-ados*, a unit.]

Trichoptera *trik-op'tər-ə*, *n.pl.* an order of insects with hairy wings, the caddis-flies.—*adj* trichop'terous. [tricho- and Gr. *pteron*, wing.]

trichosis *trik-ō'sis*, *n.* arrangement, distribution, or morbid condition of hair. [Gr. *trichōsis*, hairiness.]

trichotomous *trī-kot'ə-məs*, *adj.* divided into three· forking in threes —*v.t.* and *v.i.* trichot'omise, -ize to divide in three or threes.—*adv.* trichot'omously.—*n* trichot'omy trichotomous division or forking. [Gr *tricha*, threefold—*treis*, three, *tomē*, a cutting— *temnein*, to cut.]

trichroic *trī-krō'ik*, *adj.* having or exhibiting three colours, esp when viewed in different directions —*n* tri'chroism. [Gr. *trichroos*, three-coloured.]

trichromatic *trī-krō-mat'ik*, *adj.* characterised by three colours. having three fundamental colour-sensations.—*n.* trichro'mat one who has normal colour vision.—*adjs.* tri'chrome trichromatic; trichrō'mic trichromatic.—*n.* trichrō'matism. [Gr. *trichrōmatos—chrōma*, colour.]

trick *trik*, *n.* an artifice: a deceitful device. a deception: a prank: a performance aimed at astonishing, puzzling, or amusing: an expedient· a knack: a characteristic habit, mannerism, trait: a spell or turn, esp. at the helm: a round of play at cards: the cards so played and taken by the winner, forming a unit in scoring: a trinket, toy.—*v.t.* to deceive, to cheat. to beguile: to dress or decorate fancily (with *out*).—*adj.* of the nature of, for the purpose or performance of, a trick.—*ns.* trick'er; trick'ery the act or practice of playing tricks: artifice: stratagem: imposition.—*adv.* trick'ily.—*n* trick'iness.—*n.* and *adj.* trick'ing.—

adj. trick'ish tricky.—*adv.* trick'ishly.—*ns.* trick'ishness; trick'siness.—*adj.* trick'some.—*ns.* trick'ster a cheat: one who practises trickery; trick'stering playing the trickster.—*adjs.* tricks'y pranked up: capricious: sportive: mischievous: tricky, trick'y addicted to trickery: clever in tricks: ticklish: difficult to handle: complicated.—trick cyclist an acrobat who performs tricks on a unicycle or cycle: a psychiatrist (*slang*).—do the trick to bring something about; how's tricks? (*slang*) how are you?; up to (one's) tricks misbehaving. [O.Fr. *trique*, Northern form of *triche*, deceit]

trickle *trik'l*, *v.i* to run in drops or in a small irregular stream —*v.t.* to emit in a trickle.—*n.* a succession of drops —*n.* and *adj.* trick'ling.—*adj* trick'ly trickling. [M.E. *triklen*, prob. for *striklen*, freq. of strike.]

triclinic *trī-klin'ik*, (*min.*) *adj.* referred to three unequal axes obliquely inclined to each other. [Gr *treis*, three, *klinein*, to bend.]

triclinium *trī-klin'i-əm*, (*Rom. ant.*) *n.* a couch running round three sides of a table for reclining on at meals: a dining-room. [L *triclīnium—Gr triklīnion—Gr. treis*, three, *klinē*, a couch.]

tricolour, tricolor *trī'kul-ər*, *adj* three-coloured.—*n.* (*tri'*) a three-coloured flag, esp. that of France (*trē-kol-or*).—*adj* tri'coloured. [L *tricolor* and Fr. *tricolore*.]

tricorn, tricorne *trī'korn*, *adj.* three-horned. threecornered—*n.* a three-cornered hat. [L *tricornis*, three-horned—*cornū*, a horn.]

tricot *trē'kō*, *n.* a hand-knitted woollen fabric, or imitation. a soft, slightly-ribbed cloth for women's garments [Fr *tricot*, knitting]

tricuspid, -ate *trī-kus'pid*, *-āt*, *adjs.* with three cusps or points. [L. *tricuspis*, *-idis—cuspis*, a point.]

tricycle *trī'si-kl*, *n.* a three-wheeled cycle: a light three-wheeled car for the use of a disabled person.— Coll. shortening trike (*trīk*).—*vs.i.* to ride a tricycle. —*n.* tri'cycler.—*adj.* tricyclic (*trī-sī'klik*) having three whorls or rings: of a chemical compound, having three rings in its molecular structure, some compounds of this type being used as anti-depressant drugs —*ns.* tri'cycling (*-si-*); tri'cyclist. [tri- and Gr. *kyklos*, circle, wheel.]

trident *trī'dənt*, *n.* a three-pronged spear, esp that of the sea-god Poseidon or Neptune. anything of like shape.—*adjs.* tri'dent, tridental (*-dent'*), trident'āte three-pronged, tridented (*trī-dent'id*) three-pronged: (*trī'dənt-id*) having a trident. [L. *tridēns*, *-dentis— dēns*, tooth.]

Tridentine *trī-*, *tri-dent'īn*, *adj.* of Trent in Southern Tirol, or the Council (1545–63) held there.—*n.* a native of Trent: one who accepts the degrees of the Council, an orthodox Roman Catholic. [L. *Tridentum*, Trent.]

tridimensional *tri-di-men'shən-əl*, *adj.* having three dimensions. [tri-.]

tried, tries, trier see try.

triecious, See trioecious.

triennial *trī-en'yəl*, *adj.* continuing three years: happening every third year.—*adv.* trienn'ially. [L. *triennis—annus*, a year.]

trifacial *trī-fā'shl*, *adj.* threefold and pertaining to the face —trifacial nerve the trigeminal nerve. [tri- and L. *faciēs*, face]

trifid *trif'id*, *trī'fid*, *adj.* cleft into three parts (*bot.*, etc.): (of a spoon) having a three-pointed decorative top to its handle. [L. *findēre*, to cleave.]

trifle *trī'fl*, *n.* anything of little importance or value: a small amount: a light confection of whipped cream or white of egg, sponge-cake, wine, etc.—*v.i.* (often with *with*) to busy oneself idly: to play, toy: to behave without seriousness or respect: to meddle irresponsibly: to sport: to dally.—*v.t.* to spend or pass idly.—*n.* **tri'fler.**—*adj.* **tri'fling** of small value, importance, or amount: trivial.—*adv.* **tri'flingly.**—*n.* **tri'flingness.**—**a trifle** slightly. [O.Fr. *trufle*, mockery, deception.]

trifocal *trī-fō'kəl, adj.* of a spectacle lens, giving separately near, intermediate, and far vision—*n.pl* **trifo'cals** spectacles with such lenses. [**tri-**.]

trifoliate *trī-fō'li-āt, adj.* with three leaves or leaflets.—*n.* **Trifo'lium** the clover or trefoil genus: (without *cap.*) any plant of this genus. [L. *trifolium—folium*, leaf.]

triforium *trī-fō'ri-əm, -fo', (archit.) n.* a gallery, storey, or arcade over an aisle:—*pl* **trifo'ria.** [L.L]

triform *trī'form, adj.* having a triple form—also **tri'formed.** [L. *trifōrmis—fōrma*, form]

trifurcate *trī'fər-kāt,* or *-fûr', adj.* three-forked.—*v i* to divide into three branches.—*adj.* **tri'furcated** (or *-fûr').*—*n.* **trifurca'tion.** [L. *trifurcus—furca*, a fork.]

trig[1] *trig, adj.* trim, neat (chiefly *Scot.*): tight, sound.—*v.t.* to make trig: to block, hold back with a wedge —*n.* a block or wedge to stop a wheel.—*adv.* **trig'ly.** —*n.* **trig'ness.** [O.N. *tryggr*, faithful, secure.]

trig[2] *trig, n.* an abbreviation of **trigonometry, trigonometric(al).**

trigeminal *trī-jem'i-nl, adj* threefold: three-branched.—**trigeminal nerve** a facial nerve having three branches, supplying the eye, nose, skin, scalp and muscles of mastication (also called **trifacial nerve**).—**trigeminal neuralgia** another term for **tic-douloureux.** [L. *trigeminus*, born three at a birth—*geminus*, born at the same birth.]

trigger *trig'ər, n* a lever that releases a catch so as to fire a gun or set a mechanism going: anything that starts a train of actions.—*v.t.* (often with *off*) to set in action.—*adj.* **trigg'er-happy** over-ready to shoot (*lit.* and *fig.*): irresponsibly willing to take the risk of beginning a fight or a war. [Du. *trekker—trekken,* to pull.]

triglyceride *trī-glis'ər-īd, n.* any of a group of commonly occurring fats, those fatty acid esters of glycerol in which all three hydroxyl groups have had their hydrogen atoms replaced by acid radicals. [**tri-**.]

triglyph *trī'glif, n.* a three-grooved tablet in the Doric frieze.—*adj.* **triglyph'ic.** [Gr. *triglyphos—glyph-ein,* to carve.]

trigon *trī'gon, n* a triangle: a set of three signs 120° apart, the zodiac being divided into four trigons—watery, earthly, airy, fiery (*astrol.*).—*adjs.* **trigonal** (*trig'ə-nl*) of a trigon: triangular: trigonous; **trigonic** (*trī-gon'ik*) of a trigon: triangular; **trigonous** (*trig'ə-nəs*) triangular in section, or nearly so. [Gr. *trigōnon—gōniā,* an angle.]

trigonometry *trig-ə-nom'i-tri, n.* the branch of mathematics that treats of the relations between the sides and angles of triangles.—*adjs.* **trigonometric** (*-nə-met'rik*), **-al**.—*adv.* **trigonomet'rically.**—**trigonometrical point** (*geog.*, etc.) in triangulation, a fixed point whose position as vertex of a triangle is calculated astronomically (often shortened to **trig point**). [Gr. *trigōnon,* a triangle, *metron,* a measure.]

trigraph *trī'graf, n.* a combination of three letters for one sound. [**tri-** and Gr. *graphē,* a writing.]

trihedral *trī-hed'rəl, -hēd', (geom.,* etc.) *adj.* having three faces.—*n.* a trihedral figure, formed by three planes meeting at a point.—Also **trihed'ron** (or *-hēd'*). [**tri-** and Gr. *hedrā,* a seat.]

trike. See **trichloroethylene** and **tricycle.**

trilateral *trī-lat'ər-al, adj.* three-sided: of, having,

three parties or participants. [**tri-** and L. *latus, lateris,* side.]

trilby *tril'bi, n.* a soft felt hat.—Also **trilby hat.** [From George du Maurier's novel, *Trilby* (1894).]

trilinear *trī-lin'i-ər, adj.* consisting of, having, or referred to three lines.—*adj.* **trilin'eate** marked with three lines. [**tri-** and L. *līnea,* line.]

trilingual *trī-ling'gwəl, adj* in or using three languages, esp. native or habitual languages [**tri-** and L. *lingua,* tongue.]

trilith *trī'lith, n.* a form of megalithic monument consisting of two upright stones supporting another lying crosswise.—Also **trilithon** (*trī', trī'*) —*adj.* **trilith'ic.** [**tri-** and Gr *lithos,* stone.]

trill *tril, n* a tremulous sound: a run or roulade of bird-song: a consonant-sound produced by vibration. —*v.t.* and *v.i.* to play sing, pronounce, sound, with a trill [It. *trillo;* imit.]

trillion *tril'yən, n* the cube of a million: the cube of ten thousand (*U.S ,* and before 1948 in France).—*n.* and *adj.* **trill'ionth.** [Fr.,—**tri-**, after **million.**]

Trillium *tril'i-əm, n.* a three-leaved genus of the lily family: (without *cap.*) any plant of this genus [L. *trēs,* three.]

trilobe *trī'lōb, n* something that has three lobes.—Also *adj.*—*adjs.* **trilobate(d)** (*trī'* or *-lō'*), **tri'lobed** having three lobes.—*n.* **trilobite** (*trī'lō-bīt* or *tril'ə-bīt*) any fossil arthropod of a Palaeozoic order (**Trilobi'ta**), with broad head-shield and body longitudinally furrowed into three lobes —*adj.* **trilobitic** (*-bit'ik*). [**tri-** and Gr. *lobos,* lobe.]

trilogy *tril'ə-ji, n.* a group of three tragedies. any similar group, as of novels: a triad. [Gr. *trilogiā—logos,* discourse.]

trim *trim, v.t* to put in due condition. to fit out: to make ready for sailing: to adjust the balance of (a boat or aircraft): to dress, arrange: to set in order: to decorate (clothes, etc) as with ribbons, lace, contrasting edging, etc.: to make tidy or neat: to clip into shape: to make compact: to reduce the size of, by removing excess: to rebuke sharply: to thrash: to adjust the inclination of a plane to the horizontal —*v i* to balance: to adjust one's behaviour as expediency dictates:—*pr.p.* **trimm'ing;** *pa t* and *pa.p* **trimmed.**—*adj.* in good order: neat: tidy: well-kept: clean-cut: slim.—*adv* trimly.—*n.* condition for sailing or flight: balance: condition, order: a fit, trim condition· humour, disposition, temper, way: array: fittings: the colour-scheme and chrome parts on the outside of a motor-vehicle, or the upholstery, door-handles, etc. inside it: decorative additions to clothes, e.g contrasting edging, etc.: an act of trimming: window-dressing (*U.S*): parts trimmed off: adjustment of an aircraft's controls to achieve stability in a desired condition of flight —*adv.* **trim'ly.**—*ns.* **trimm'er** one who or that which trims: one who fluctuates between parties, adjusting his opinions, etc. to match his changing loyalties: a scold: anything trouncing or redoubtable: a small horizontal beam on a floor into which the ends of joists are framed. a trimming tab; **trimm'ing** making trim: balancing: clipping: (usu. in *pl.*) ornamental additions: (in *pl.*) accessories: (in *pl.*) sauces and other accompaniments for a dish: (in *pl.*) fittings: (in *pl.*) parts trimmed off.—*adj.* that trims.—*adv* **trimm'ingly.**—*n.* **trim'ness.**—**trimming tab, trim tab** a tab or aerofoil on an aircraft or boat, that can be adjusted in mid-passage to trim the craft.—**trim one's sails** to rule one's conduct, principles, etc., to accord with prevailing circumstances. [O.E. *trymman, trymian,* to strengthen, set in order—*trum,* firm.]

trimaran *trī'ma-ran, n.* a boat with three hulls. [**tri-** and cata*maran.*]

trimer *trī'mər*, (*chem.*) *n.* a substance in which molecules are formed from three molecules of a monomer.—*adjs.* **trimer'ic** (*chem.*) having the same empirical formula but a relative molecular mass three times as great; **trim'erous** (*bot.*) having three parts, or parts in three. [**tri-** and Gr. *meros*, part.]

trimester *tri-mes'tər*, *n.* three months: an academic term.—*adj.* **trimes'trial.** [L. *trimēstris*, of three months—*mēnsis*, a month.]

trimeter *trim'i-tər*, *n.* a verse of three measures.—*adjs.* **trim'eter**, **trimetric**, **-al** (*trī-met'rik*, *-l*). [Gr. *trimetros—metron*, measure.]

trimonthly *trī-munth'li*, *adj.* every three months. [**tri-.**]

trimorphism *trī-mor'fizm*, *n.* occurrence of three forms in the same species (*biol.*): the property of crystallising in three forms (*chem.*).—*adjs.* **trimor'phic**, **trimor'phous.** [**tri-** and Gr. *morphē*, form.]

trine *trīn*, *adj.* threefold: 120° apart (*astrol.*): hence, benign (*astrol.*).—*n.* a triad: the aspect of two planets, as seen from the earth, distant from each other one-third of the zodiac or 120°: a triplet.—*adjs.* **trinal** (*trī'nl*), **tri'nary.** [L. *trīnus—trēs*, *tria*, three.]

trinitro- *trī-nī'trō-*, in composition, having three nitro-groups (NO₂), esp. replacing hydrogen.—*ns.* **trinit-rotol'uene** or **-tol'uol** a high explosive (familiarly T.N.T.), a trinitro-derivative of toluene. [**tri-.**]

trinity *trin'i-ti*, *n.* threefoldness: three in one: a triad: esp. (with *cap.*) the triune God of orthodox Christians (Father, Son, Holy Ghost): (with *cap.*) any symbolical representation of the persons of the Trinity: (with *cap.*) Trinity Sunday: (with *cap.*) Trinity term.—*adj.* **Trinitā'rian** of, in relation to, believing in, the Trinity.—*n.* one who holds the doctrine of the Trinity.—*n.* **Trinitā'rianism**—**Trinity Sunday** the Sunday after Whitsuntide; **Trinity term** the university term beginning after Trinity Sunday. [L. *trinitās*, *-ātis*—*trīnus*, threefold.]

trinket *tring'kit*, *n.* a small ornament or piece of jewellery: any paltry object.—*ns.* **trink'eting**; **trink'etry** trinkets collectively. [Poss. O.Fr. *trenquet*, small knife.]

trinomial *trī-nō'mi-əl*, *adj.* consisting of three words: of three terms connected by the sign plus or minus.—*n.* a trinomial name or expression.—*ns.* **trino'mialism** the system of naming by three words (for genus, species, and subspecies); **trino'mialist.** [After **binomial.**]

trio *trē'ō*, *n.* a set of three: a composition for, or combination of, three performers (*mus.*): division of a minuet, scherzo, or march:—*pl.* **tri'os.** [It.]

triode *trī'ōd*, *adj.* with three electrodes.—*n.* a three-electrode valve. [**tri-** and Gr. *hodos*, a path, way.]

trioecious, **triecious** *trī-ē'shəs*, *adj.* having male, female, and hermaphrodite flowers on different plants. [**tri-** and Gr. *oikos*, house.]

triolet *trī'ō-lit*, *trē'ō-lā*, *-let*, *n.* an eight-lined poem rhymed *ab aa abab*, lines 4 and 7 repeating 1, and 8 repeating 2. [Fr.]

trioxide *trī-oks'īd*, *n.* a compound with three atoms of oxygen. [**tri-.**]

trip *trip*, *v.i.* to move with short, light steps or skips: to stumble: to catch one's foot: to make a slip in chastity, accuracy, etc.: to tip up: to make an excursion: to experience the hallucinatory effects of LSD or similar drug (also **trip out**; *slang*).—*v.t.* to cause to stumble or fall by catching the foot (often with *up*): to catch in a fault: to dance trippingly: to trip or dance upon: to release by striking: to tilt up:—*pr.p.* **tripp'-ing**; *pa.t.* and *pa.p.* **tripped.**—*n.* a light, short step or skip: a catching of the foot: a stumble: a slip, lapse: a single journey or run, one way or to and fro: a pleasure excursion, jaunt: a specially arranged run at

a cheap fare: a company of excursionists: a striking part that releases a catch: a hallucinatory experience under the influence of a drug such as LSD (*slang*): any stimulating experience (good or bad) (*slang*).—*n.* **tripp'er** one who trips: an excursionist, esp. of the disturbing kind: a device that when struck, passed over, etc., operates a switch.—*n.* and *adj.* **tripp'ing.**—*adv.* **tripp'ingly.**—**trip'-hammer** a tilt-hammer; **trip'-wire** a wire which releases some mechanism when pulled, e.g. by being tripped over. [O.Fr. *triper*; of Gmc. origin.]

tripartite *trī-pär'tīt*, *adj.* in three parts: cleft in three nearly to the base (*bot.*): relating to three parties.—*n.* **tripartition** (*-tish'ən*). [L. *tripartītus—partīrī*, to divide—*pars*, a part.]

tripe *trīp*, *n.* entrails (*arch.*): parts of the compound stomach of a ruminant, prepared as food: rubbish, poor stuff (*coll.*): claptrap (*coll.*).—**tripe'man**, **-wife**, **-woman** a dresser or seller of tripe; **tripe'-shop.** [O.Fr. (Fr.) *tripe*.]

triphibious *trī-fib'i-əs*, *adj.* using or taking place in the three elements, land, water, air. [**tri-**, and **-phibious**, after **amphibious.**]

triphthong *trif'thong*, *n.* a combination of three vowel sounds in one syllable: (*loosely*) a trigraph.—*adj.* **triphthongal** (*-thong'gl*). [**tri-** and Gr. *phthongos*, sound.]

tripinnate *trī-pin'āt*, *-it*, *adj.* pinnate with the pinnae themselves pinnate, and their pinnae again pinnate. [**tri-.**]

triplane *trī'plān*, *n.* an aeroplane with three sets of main planes, one above another. [**tri-.**]

triple *trip'l*, *adj.* threefold: consisting of three: three times as much.—*n.* a quantity three times as much.—*v.t.* and *v.i.* to treble.—*ns.* **trip'leness**; **trip'let** three of a kind, or three united: three lines rhyming together: a group of three notes occupying the time of two, indicated by a slur and the figure 3 (*mus.*): one of three born at a birth.—*adj.* **trip'licate** threefold: made thrice as much: as the cubes of the quantities.—*n.* a third copy or thing corresponding to two others of the same kind: the triplicate ratio.—*v.t.* to make threefold.—*ns.* **triplica'tion** the act of triplicating; **trip'ling** a making triple.—*adv.* **triply** (*trip'li*).—**triple jump** an athletic event, based on a hop, skip and jump, in which a competitor tries to cover the longest possible distance; **triple point** the temperature and pressure at which solid, liquid, and gaseous phases of a substance can co-exist, esp. triple point of water, 273·16K; **triple time** time or rhythm of three beats, or of three times three beats, in a bar; **Triplex® glass** a combination of glass and mica in three layers. [Fr.,—L. *triplus*—Gr. *triploos* (*triploos*); and L. *triplex*.]

triploid *trip'loid*, *adj.* having three times the haploid number of chromosomes.—*n.* **trip'loidy.** [Gr. *triploos*, triple.]

triply. See **triple.**

tripod *trī'pod*, *trip'od*, *n.* anything on three feet or legs, esp. a stand for an instrument.—*adj.* three-legged.—*adj.* **tripodal** (*trip'əd-əl*).—*n.* **tripody** (*trip'ə-di*) a verse or group of three feet. [Gr. *tripous*, *tripodos—pous*, *podos*, foot.]

tripoli *trip'ə-li*, *n.* diatomite. [Orig. brought from *Tripoli* in Africa.]

tripos *trī'pos*, *n.* a Cambridge honours examination: the list of successful candidates in it. [Prob. traceable to a B.A., known as Mr *Tripos*.]

tripper, **tripping**, etc. See **trip.**

triptane *trip'tān*, *n.* trimethyl butane, a powerful aviation fuel. [trimethyl *butane*, with *b* altered to *p*.]

triptych *trip'tik*, *n.* a set of three tablets, painted panels, etc., hinged together.—*n.* **triptyque** (*trēp-tēk*;

Fr.) an international pass for a motor-car. [Gr. *triptychos*, threefold—*ptyx*, *ptychos*, a fold—*ptyssein*, to fold.]

triquetra *trī-kwet'rə*, *n.* an ornament consisting of three interlaced arcs, common in early art in northern Europe.—*pl.* **triquet'ra**. [L. *triquetrus*, *-a*, *-um*, triangular—*trēs*, three.]

trireme *trī'rēm*, *n.* an ancient galley—esp. a war-galley —with three sets of rowers. [L. *trirēmis*—*rēmus*, an oar.]

trisect *trī-sekt'*, *v.t.* to cut or divide into three (usu. equal) parts.—*ns.* **trisec'tion** (*-shən*); **trisect'or** one who trisects: a line that trisects. [**tri-** and L. *secāre*, *sectum*, to cut.]

trishaw *trī'shó*, *n.* a three-wheeled light vehicle pedalled by a driver behind the passenger seat. [**tri-**, *rickshaw*.]

triskele *tris'kēl*, *n.* a figure consisting of three radiating curves or legs, as in the arms of the Isle of Man.— Also **triskelion** (*tris-kel'i-on*):—*pl.* **triskel'ia**. [**tri-** and Gr. *skelos*, a leg.]

trismus *triz'məs*, *n.* tetanic spasm of the muscles of mastication, causing difficulty in opening the mouth. [Latinised from Gr. *trismos*, a creaking, grating— *trizein*, to grate, gnash.]

trist, triste *trist*, (*arch.*) *adj.* sorrowful: dismal. [Fr. *triste*—L. *tristis*, sad.]

trisyllable *tri-sil'ə-bl*, also *trī-*, *n.* a word of three syllables.—*adjs.* **trisyllabic** (*-ab'ik*), **-al.**—*adv.* **trisyllab'ically.** [**tri-**.]

trite *trīt*, *adj.* worn: worn-out: well-trodden: used till novelty and interest are' lost: hackneyed.—*adv.* **trite'ly.**—*n.* **trite'ness.** [L. *trītus*, rubbed, pa.p. of *terĕre*, to rub.]

tritheism *trī'thē-izm*, *n.* belief in three Gods: belief that the Father, Son, and Holy Ghost are actually different beings.—*n.* **tri'theist.**—*adjs.* **tritheis'tic**, **-al.** [**tri-** and Gr. *theos*, a god.]

tritiate. See tritium.

Triticum *trit'i-kəm*, *n.* the wheat genus of grasses.—*n.* **trit'icale** a hybrid cereal grass, a cross between wheat and rye, grown as a food crop [L. *trīticum*, wheat— *terĕre*, *trītum*, to rub.]

tritium *trish'i-əm*, *trit'*, *n.* an isotope of hydrogen of triple mass.—*v.t.* **tritiate** (*trit'i-āt*) to replace normal hydrogen atoms by tritium.—*ns.* **tritia'tion; triton** (*trī'tən*) the nucleus of tritium. [Gr. *tritos*, third.]

Triton *trī'tən*, *n.* a minor Greek sea-god, son of Poseidon and Amphitrite, represented with a dolphin's tail, sometimes horse's foreleps, blowing a conch: a genus of large gasteropods with shells that can be used like conchs: the larger of the two satellites of the planet Neptune. [Gr. *Trītōn*, *-ōnos*.]

triton. See tritium.

tritone *trī'tōn*, (*mus.*) *n.* an augmented fourth, an interval of three whole tones. [Gr. *trītónos*—*tonos*, tone.]

triturate *trit'ū-rāt*, *v.t.* to rub or grind to a fine powder —*n.* the fine powder thus obtained.—*ns.* **tritura'tion; trit'urātor** [L.L. *trītūrāre*, *-ātum*—L. *terĕre*, to rub.]

triumph *trī'əmf*, *n.* in ancient Rome, a solemn procession in honour of a victorious general: a pageant: exultation for success: complete or signal victory or achievement.—*v.i.* to celebrate a victory with pomp: to rejoice for victory: to obtain victory, prevail (often with *over*): to exult (often with *over*).—*adjs.* **triumphal** (*trī-umf'l*) pertaining to triumph: used in celebrating victory; **triumph'ant** celebrating or having achieved a triumph: exultant.—*adv.* **triumph'antly.**—*n.* **tri'umpher.**—*n.* and *adj.* **tri'umphing.**— **triumphal arch** an arch erected in connection with the triumph of a Roman general: any decorative arch in

public rejoicings, etc. [L. *triumphus*; akin to Gr. *thriambos*, a hymn to Bacchus.]

triumvir *trī-um'vər*, *trē-ōōm'vir*, *n.* one of three men in the same office or government: one of three sharing supreme power:—*pl.* **trium'viri, trium'virs.**—*adj.* **trium'viral.**—*n.* **trium'virate** an association of three men in office or government, or for any political ends —esp. that of Pompey, Crassus, and Caesar (60 B C), and that of Octavian (Augustus), Mark Antony, and Lepidus (43 B C): any trio or triad. [L. *triumvir*, from the gen. pl. *trium virōrum*, of three men.]

triune *trī'ūn*, *adj.* three in one.—*n.* a trinity in unity.— *n.* **triū'nity.** [L. *trēs*, *tria*, three, *ūnus*, one.]

trivalent *trī-vā'lənt*, *triv'ə-lant*, *adj.* having a valency of three.—*ns.* **triva'lence** (or *triv'əl-*), **triva'lency** (or *triv'əl-*). [**tri-** and **-valent.**]

trivet *triv'it*, *n.* a tripod, esp. one for a pot or kettle: a bracket with three projections for fixing on the top bar of a grate: a three-legged pot: a usu. metal plate placed in a pressure cooker to raise the food to be cooked off the bottom of the vessel.—**right as a trivet** perfectly right (from its stability). [O.E. *trefet*, app. —L. *tripēs*, *tripedis*—*pēs*, a foot.]

trivia *trī'vi-ə*, *n.pl.* trifles, trivialities, unimportant details.—*adj.* **trivial** (*triv'i-əl*) of the trivium: to be found anywhere: of little importance: trifling: vernacular (*biol.*): specific, opp. to generic (of a name; *biol.*): with value zero (*math.*).—*n.* **trivialisa'tion**, **-z-.**—*v.t.* **triv'ialise, -ize** to make trivial, unimportant. —*ns.* **triv'ialism** a trivial matter or remark; **triviality** (*-al'i-ti*) the state or quality of being trivial: that which is trivial, a trifle.—*adv.* **triv'ially.**—*ns.* **triv'ialness; triv'ium** in mediaeval schools the group of liberal arts first studied—grammar, rhetoric, and logic. [L. *trivium*, a place where three ways meet— *trēs*, three, *via*, a way.]

tri-weekly *trī-wēk'li*, *adj.* occurring or appearing once in three weeks or three times a week.—*adv.* once in three weeks: three times a week —*n.* a periodical appearing three times a week. [**tri-**.]

-trix *-triks*, *suff* denoting a feminine agent:—*pl.* **-trixes, -trices** (*-trī-sēz*, *-tri-siz*) [L]

trocar *trō'kar*, *n.* a surgical perforator used with a cannula. sometimes a cannula. [Fr. *trocart—trois*, three, *carre*, side.]

trochaic. See trochee.

trochal. See trochus.

trochanter *trō-kan'tər*, *n.* a rough eminence on the thigh-bone for insertion of muscles: the second segment of an insect's leg —*adj* **trochanteric** (*-ter'ik*) [Gr *trochantēr—trechein*, to run]

troche. See trochus.

trochee *trō'kē*, (*pros.*) *n* a foot of two syllables, a long followed by a short in English, etc , a stressed followed by an unstressed.—*adj.* **trochaic** (*-kā'ik*).— *n.* a trochaic verse. [Gr. *trochaios* (*pous*, foot), running, tripping—*trochos*, a running—*trechein*, to run]

trochlea *trok'li-ə*, (*zool.*) *n.* any pulley-like structure, esp. a foramen through which a tendon passes —*adj.* **troch'lear.**—**trochlear** nerve the fourth cranial nerve. [L. *trochlea*—Gr. *trochiliā*, a pulley.]

trochoid, etc. See trochus.

trochus *trō'kəs*, *n* a wheel or hoop (*Gr. ant.*): the inner ring of cilia in a rotifer.—*adj.* **tro'chal** wheel-like.— *n.* **troche** (*trōk*, *trōsh*, *trōch*) a round medicinal tablet.—*n.* **troch'oid** the curve traced by a fixed point, not on the circumference, in the plane of a rolling circle —*adj* wheel-like: trochoidal —*adj* **trochoid'al** of the nature of a trochoid. [Gr. *trochos*, a wheel—*trechein*, to run]

trod, trodden. See tread.

troglodyte *trog'lə-dīt*, *n.* a cave-dweller —Also *adj.*— *n.* **Troglodytes** (*-lod'i-tēz*) the wren genus.—*adjs*

troglodytic (-dit'ik), **-al** cave-dwelling.—*n.* **trog'-lodytism** (-dit-izm). [Gr. *tróglodýtēs—tróglē*, a hole, *dýein*, to get into.]

trogon *trō'gon*, *n.* any member of a family (**Trogon'idae**) of tropical and esp. South American birds with brilliant plumage, including the quetzal. [App. Gr. *trōgōn*, nibbling.]

troika *troi'kǝ*, *n.* a Russian vehicle for three horses abreast: a team of three horses abreast: a team of three men, etc., acting equally as leaders. [Russ.,—*troe*, a set of three.]

troilism *troi'lizm*, *n.* sexual activity between three people (of two sexes).

Trojan *trō'jǝn*, *adj.* of Troy.—*n.* a citizen or inhabitant of Troy: a doughty, trusty, or hard-working person.—**Trojan horse** the gigantic wooden horse inside which the Greeks entered Troy a person, organisation, placed within a country, group, etc., with the purpose of destroying it. [L. *Trōjānus—Trōja*, Troy.]

troll[1] *trōl*, *n.* in Scandinavian mythology, a goblin or supernatural dwarf (earlier giant). [O.N.]

troll[2] *trōl*, *v.t.* to fish for, or in, with a spinning or otherwise moving bait: to convey by trolley.—*v.i.* to sing a catch: to fish with revolving or trailing lure (see also **trawl**): to travel by trolley.—*n.* a moving round, repetition: a round song: trolling: a lure for trolling. —*ns.* **troll'er**; **trolley** (*trol'i*) a costermonger's cart: a bogie· a pulley, receptacle, or car travelling on an overhead wire or rail: a trolley-wheel: a tram-car (*U.S.*).—*n.* and *adj.* **troll'ing** (*trōl'*).—**troll'ey-bus'** a bus that receives power by a trolley-wheel from an overhead wire; **troll'ey-car'** (*U.S.*) a tram-car so driven; **troll'ey-man** a man who works a trolley or on a trolley; **troll'ey-ta'ble** a tiered trolley for a dining-room; **troll'ey-wheel** a grooved wheel by which a bus, tram-car, etc., obtains current from an overhead wire; **troll'ing-bait**, **-spoon** a metallic revolving lure used in trolling. [Cf. O.Fr. *troller* (Fr. *trôler*), to quest, Ger. *trollen*, to roll.]

trollop *trol'ǝp*, *n.* a slatternly woman: a strumpet.—*adjs.* **troll'oping**, **troll'opish**, **troll'opy**. [Perh. **troll**[2].]

trombone *trom-bōn'*, *n.* a brass musical wind instrument, consisting of a tube bent twice on itself, with a slide.—*n.* **trombōn'ist**. [It.; augm. of *tromba*, trumpet.]

trommel *trom'ǝl*, *n.* a revolving cylindrical sieve for cleaning or sizing minerals. [Ger. *Trommel*, drum.]

trompe, tromp *tromp*, *n.* an apparatus for producing a blast of air in a furnace by falling water. [Fr.]

trompe l'œil *trɔ̃p lœ-y'*, (Fr.) lit. 'something that deceives the eye': appearance of reality achieved by use of minute, often trivial, details or of other effects in painting, architecture, etc.

-tron *-tron*, *suff.* signifying agent, instrument, particularly (1) thermionic valve, e.g. *klystron*, (2) elementary particle, e.g. *positron*, (3) particle accelerator, e.g. *cyclotron*. [Gr.]

tronc *trongk*, Fr. *trɔ̃*, *n.* a collection of tips to be divided out later, e.g. among waiters: the system by which this is done. [Fr., collecting box.]

troop *trōōp*, *n.* a body of soldiers: (in *pl.*) military forces: a band of people: a flock, herd, swarm of animals: (esp. in *pl.*) a great number: a division of a cavalry squadron: a group of (Boy) Scout patrols: a troupe.—*v.i.* to pass in a body or in rapid succession: to be off, pack.—*v.t.* to cause to troop: to receive and carry ceremonially along the ranks (as *troop the colour* or *colours*).—*n.* **troop'er** a private soldier: a mounted policeman (*U.S.* and *Austr.*): a cavalry horse: a troop-ship.—**troop'-carrier** a motor vehicle, ship or aeroplane for carrying troops; **troop'-ship** a ship for transporting troops. [Fr. *troupe*—L.L. *troppus*; poss. Gmc.]

tropaeolum *trop-ē'ǝ-lǝm*, *n.* the Indian cress and canary-creeper genus, South American trailing or climbing plants constituting a family **Tropaeolá'ceae**, akin to the geraniums—misnamed nasturtium. [Gr. *tropaion*, a trophy (from the shield-shaped leaves and helmet-like flowers).]

trope *trōp*, *n.* a figure of speech, properly one in which a word or expression is used in other than its literal sense. [Gr. *tropos*, a turn—*trepein*, to turn.]

-trope *-trōp*, in composition, a tendency towards or affinity for, as in *heliotrope*.—**tropic** adjective combining form. [Gr. *tropos*, a turn]

troph-, tropho- *trof-*, *-ō-*, *-o'-*, *traf-*, **-troph-**, **-trophy**, *-traf(-i)* in composition, nutrition.—*adj.* **troph'ic** relating to nutrition.—*n.* **troph'oblast** the outer layer of epiblast in a mammalian ovum.—*adj.* **tropho-blast'ic**.—*ns.* **trophol'ogy** the study of nutrition; **troph'oplasm** protoplasm which is mainly concerned with nutrition; **trophozō'ite** in Protozoa, the trophic phase of the adult. [Gr. *trophē*, food, *trophos*, a feeder; *trephein*, to feed.]

trophy *trō'fi*, *n.* a memorial of victory, orig. arms or other spoils set up on the spot: displayed spoils, as skulls and antlers: a piece of plate or suchlike awarded as a prize: a memorial of success, glory, etc.: an ornamental group of weapons, flags, etc., or a representation of it.—*adj.* **trō'phied**. [Fr. *trophée* —L. *trophaeum*—Gr. *tropaion—tropē*, a turning—*trepein*, to turn.]

tropic *trop'ik*, *n.* an imaginary circle on the celestial sphere about 23° 28' N. (*tropic of Cancer*) or S. (*of Capricorn*) of the equator, where the sun turns on reaching its greatest declination north or south: a corresponding circle on the terrestrial globe: (*pl.*) the part of the earth between the tropics of Cancer and Capricorn: a turning-point or limit.—*adj.* of, relating to, the sun's turning: of the tropics: of, of the nature of, a tropism.—*adj.* **trop'ical** of, relating to, a tropic or the tropics: found in, characteristic of, the tropics: fervidly hot: luxuriant: of a trope, figurative.—*adv.* **trop'ically**.—*ns.* **trōp'ism** (*biol.*) orientation in response to stimulus: a general term for heliotropism, geotropism, etc.; **tropist** (*trōp'*) a user of tropes: one who understands the Bible as figurative.—*adjs.* **tropistic** (*trop-ist'ik*) of tropism; **tropolog'ic**, **-al**.—*adv.* **tropolog'ically**.—*ns.* **tropol'ogy** figurative language: a moral interpretation of the Bible; **trop'opause** the boundary between troposphere and stratosphere; **trop'osphere** the lowest layer of the atmosphere in which temperature falls as height increases.—*adj.* **trophosphēr'ic**. [Gr. *tropos*, a turning.]

troppo *trop'ō*, (It.) *adj.* and *adv.* in music, too much: excessively.

trot *trot*, *n.* a pace between walking and running (in a horse with legs moving together diagonally): an act or spell of trotting: continual activity in moving about: a toddling child: in angling, a trotline.—*v.i.* to go, ride, or drive at a trot: to jog: to bustle about.—*v.t.* to cause to trot: to conduct around: to bring out for exhibition: to trot upon: to execute at a trot:—*pr.p.* **trott'ing**; *pa.t.* and *pa.p.* **trott'ed**.—*ns.* **trott'er** one that trots: a horse trained to trot in harness racing: a foot, esp. of a sheep or pig; **trott'ing** the action of the verb: harness racing.—**trot'line** in angling, a long line across a waterway to which shorter lines with baited hooks are attached.—**on the trot** (*coll.*) in succession, without a break: busy, bustling about; **the trots** (*slang*) diarrhoea; **trot out** to exhibit the paces of: to bring forward, produce for show. [O.Fr. *trot* (n.) *troter* (vb.); perh. Gmc.]

Trot *trot*, (*derog.*) *n.* and *adj.* coll. for **Trotskyist**, **Trotskyite**.

troth *trŏth, troth,* (*arch*) *n.* a variant of **truth:** faith, fidelity.—*interj.* in truth —*adjs* **troth'ful; troth'less.** —**troth'-plight** a plighting of troth, betrothal.

Trotskyism *trot'skɪ-ɪzm, n* the form of Communism associated with Leon *Trotsky* (pseudonym of Lev Davidovich Bronstein, 1879–1940), who advocated world-wide revolution —*ns.* **Trot'skyist, Trot'skyite.** —Also *adjs.*

troubadour *trōō' bə-dōō ɪ, -dôr,-dor, n.* one of a class of lyric poets of chivalric love, who first appeared in Provence, and flourished from the 11th to the 13th century [Fr ,—Prov *trobador—trobar* (Fr. *trouver*) to find.]

trouble *trub'l, v.t.* to agitate. to disturb: to muddy to make turbid: to molest: to afflict: to annoy: to busy or engage overmuch to put to inconvenience.—*v ɪ* to take pains: to put oneself to inconvenience: to be troublesome.—*n.* disturbance: affliction: distress. a scrape: travail. anything amiss: disease· uneasiness· exertion: the taking of pains. a cause of trouble — *adj.* **troub'led** (-*ld*) —*adv.* **troub'ledly.**—*n.* **troub'ler.**—*adj.* **troub'lesome** causing or giving trouble or inconvenience: vexatious: importunate.— *adv.* **troub'lesomely.**—*n.* **troub'lesomeness.**—*n.* and *adj.* **troub'ling.**—*adj* **troub'lous** (*arch. or poet.*) full of trouble or disorder: agitated: tumultuous: disturbing.—*adv.* **troub'lously.**—**troub'lemaker** one who disturbs the peace and (usu.) incites others to do so, **troub'leshooter** an expert detector and mender of any trouble, mechanical or other.—*n.* and *adj.* **troub'leshooting.—trouble spot** a place where trouble, esp. social or political unrest, often occurs. —**ask, look, for trouble** to behave in such a way as to bring trouble on oneself; **I'll trouble you** to please; **in trouble** (*euph.*) pregnant (when unmarried); **trouble someone for** to ask someone to provide, pass, etc. [O.Fr *trubler* (Fr. *troubler*) from a L.L. freq. of L. *turbāre,* to disturb—*turba,* a crowd.]

trough *trof, n.* a long, narrow vessel for watering or feeding animals: a vessel for kneading, brewing, washing, tanning, or various domestic and industrial purposes: a channel, gutter, or conduit: a long narrow depression: a hollow between wave-crests: a low point (*fig.*).—**troughing and peaking ranging between low and high points or levels** [O.E. *trog.*]

trounce *trowns, v.t.* to punish, beat, rebuke or censure severely.—*ns.* **trounc'er; trounc'ing.**

troupe *trōōp, n.* a company, esp. of performers.—*v.ɪ* to travel about as a member of a theatrical troupe.— *n.* **troup'er** a member of a theatrical troupe: an experienced actor: an experienced person (*fig.*). [Fr See **troop.**]

trousers *trow'zərz, n.pl.* long breeches: a garment worn on the lower part of the body with a loose tubular branch for each leg: any other garment of similar form. (The sing. is used to form compounds, as **trous'er-butt'on, -clip, -leg', -pock'et, -stretch'er,** etc.)—*adj.* **trou'sered** wearing trousers.—*n* **trou'sering** (usu. in *pl*) material for trousers.— **trouser suit** a women's suit, consisting of a jacket and trousers.—**(caught) with one's trousers down** (taken) unawares; **wear the trousers** of a wife, to be the dominant partner in a marriage. [See **trews.**]

trousseau *trōō'sō, n.* a bride's outfit'—*pl.* **trou'sseaux, trou'sseaus** (-*sōz*) [Fr., dim. of *trousse,* bundle]

trout *trowt, n.* a freshwater fish (*Salmo fario*) of the salmon genus, much sought after by anglers· extended to various fishes related or superficially like· an unpleasant, interfering old person, usu. a woman: —*pl.* **trout** (rarely **trouts**).—*adj.* **trout'-coloured** speckled like a trout.—**trout'-farm** a place where trout are reared artificially; **trout'-rod** a fishing-rod for trout; **trout'-stream** a stream in which trout are

caught [O.E *truht*—L *tructa, tructus*—Gr *trōk-tēs,* a sea-fish with sharp teeth—*trōgein,* to gnaw, nibble]

trouvère *trōō-ver', trouveur* *trōō -vœr', ns* one of the mediaeval narrative or epic poets of northern France [Fr]

trove. See **treasure.**

trow *trō,* (*arch.*) *v t* to trust: to believe [O E *trēowan* (*trēowian, trūwian*)]

trowel *trow'əl, n* a flat or scoop-shaped tool with a short handle, for plastering, gardening, etc —*v t* to dress, apply, move, with or as if with a trowel.—*pr p.* **trow'elling;** *pa t* and *pa.p.* **trow'elled.**—*n.* **trow'eller.—lay it on with a trowel** to spread something thickly: to say grossly flattering things [O Fr *truelle*—L L *truella* (L *trulla,* dim of *trua,* a ladle)]

troy *troi, n.* a system of weights used for precious stones and metals, the pound (no longer in legal use) of 5760 grains being divided into 12 ounces of 20 pennyweight (also *adj*)—Also called **troy weight.** [*Troyes,* in France.]

truant *trōō'ənt, n.* one who, idly or without excuse, absents himself from school (also *fig*).—Also *adj —v.ɪ* to play truant —*ns* **tru'ancy, tru'antry, tru'antship.—play truant** to stay from school without leave or good reason. [O Fr. *truant* (Fr *truand*), prob from Celtic.]

truce *trōōs, n.* a suspension of hostilities: a respite — *adjs.* **truce'less; trucial** (*trōō'shl, -syəl, -shɪ-əl*) bound by a truce.—**truce'-break'er.—Trucial States** a group of Arab sheikdoms, on the S. coast of the Persian Gulf, in treaty with Britain. [M.E. *trewes, treowes,* pl. of *trewe*—O.E. *trēow,* truth, pledge, treaty; cf. **true.**]

truck[1] *truk, v.t.* to exchange: to barter: to pay in goods.—*v.ɪ.* to traffic: to have dealings or intercourse· to barter: to bargain.—*n.* exchange of goods: barter: payment in goods: dealings, intercourse: a small job, chore: small goods (*coll.*): rubbish (*coll.*): fresh vegetables, market-garden produce (*U.S.*).— *ns.* **truck'age** barter; **truck'er** one who trucks: a market-gardener (*U.S.*); **truck'ing.—truck'-farm** (*U.S.*) a market-garden; **truck'-farmer; truck'· farming; truck'-shop** (*hist.*) a shop operated by employers in which their workmen are obliged to buy goods; **truck system** the practice of paying workmen in goods instead of money, forbidden by the Truck Acts, 1831, etc.—**have no truck with** to have nothing to do with [O.Fr *troquer,* to truck]

truck[2] *truk, n.* an open railway wagon for goods: a trolley: a bogie: a lorry.—*v.i.* to drive a truck (chiefly *U.S.*).—*v t.* to convey by truck: to put on a truck.— *ns.* **truck'age** carriage by truck: charge for carriage by truck: supply of trucks; **truck'er, truck'man** (chiefly *U.S*) a lorry driver; **truck'ing.—truck'-load.** [L *trochus,* a wheel—Gr. *trochos—trechein,* to run.]

truckle *truk'l, n.* a truckle-bed.—*v.i.* to sleep in a truckle-bed· to behave with servility (usu. with *to*).— *n.* **truck'ler.**—*n* and *adj* **truck'ling.—truck'le-bed** a low bed that may be wheeled under another. [Gr *trochileiā, -iā,* etc , a pulley—*trochos,* a wheel]

truculent *truk'-, trōōk'ū-lənt, adj.* aggressive and discourteous.—*ns.* **truc'ulence, truc'ulency.**—*adv* **truc'ulently.** [L *truculentus—trux,* wild, fierce]

trudge *truj, v ɪ* to walk with labour or effort: to plod doggedly.—*v t* to plod wearily or doggedly along, over, etc —*n* a heavy or weary walk· a trudger —*n* **trudg'er.**—*n* and *adj* **trudg'ing.**

trudgen *truj'ən, n* a swimming stroke in which each hand alternately is raised above the surface, thrust forward, and pulled back through the water [John *Trudgen,* who popularised the stroke in England.]

true *trŏŏ, adj.* faithful: constant: trusty: genuine: properly so called· typical: conformable: accurately adjusted or in tune straight or flat: agreeing with fact: actual: absolute: corrected: accurate. exact: right: rightful: honest: sincere: truthful —*adv.* truly: faithfully honestly in accurate adjustment: dead in tune. after the ancestral type —*v.t.* to adjust accurately.—*n* that which is true, truth: accurate adjustment.—*n.* true'ness.—*adv.* tru'ly.—**true bill** a bill of indictment endorsed, after investigation, by a grand jury, as containing a case for the court.—*adj* , *n.* true blue, true'-blue· see blue¹.—*adjs.* true'-born of genuine birth. pure-bred· true to the qualities of the breed: legitimate; true'-heart'ed sincere: faithful.— **true'-heart'edness; true'-love** one truly or really beloved: a sweetheart· a faithful lover: a true-love-knot: herb-Paris.—Also *adj* —**true'-love-knot, true'-lov'er's-knot** an ornamental or symbolic knot or interlaced design, as a two-looped bow or a knot with two interlaced loops.—**true time** the time according to the position of the sun, as opposed to mean time — out of true not straight, not properly balanced, adjusted, or calibrated. [O.E. *trēowe*.]

truffle *truf'l, trŏŏf'l, n.* any fungus of the genus Tuber or the family Tuberaceae: its underground edible fructification: a rich confection, made with chocolate, butter, etc , usu. shaped into balls.—*adj.* truff'led cooked, stuffed, dressed, with truffles.— **truff'le-dog, -pig** one trained to find truffles. [O.Fr. *truffle* (Fr. *truffe*), poss.—L. *tūber*, lump, swelling.]

truism *trŏŏ'izm, n.* a self-evident truth: a commonplace or trite statement.—*adj.* truist'ic. [true.]

truly. See true.

trumeau *trŏŏ-mō', n.* a piece of wall or pillar between two openings:—*pl.* trumeaux (*-mōz'*). [Fr.]

trump¹ *trump,* (arch. or poet.) *n.* a trumpet: a blast. [O.Fr. *trompe.*]

trump² *trump, n.* a card of a suit that takes any card of any other suit: an old card-game like whist.—Also *adj.—v.t.* to play a trump card upon instead of following suit: to take in this way (also *fig.*).—*v.i.* to play trumps on another suit.—**trump'-card** the card turned up to determine the trump suit: any card of that suit: a means of triumph (*fig.*): a victorious expedient (*fig*).—**no'-trumps** a declaration in bridge whereby no suit is more powerful than the rest.—*adj.* **no'-trump.—turn up trumps** (*fig.*) to behave in a very helpful or generous way, esp. unexpectedly. [triumph.]

trump³ *trump, v.t.* to concoct and put forward unscrupulously (with *up*).—*adj.* **trumped'-up.** [trump², affected by, or partly from, trumpery.]

trumpery *trum'pər-ı, n.* showy and worthless stuff: rubbish: ritual foolery.—Also *adj.* [Fr. *tromper*, to deceive.]

trumpet *trum'pit, n.* an orchestral, military, and signalling wind instrument of powerful and brilliant tone, in its present form a narrow tube bent twice upon itself, with cupped mouthpiece and flaring bell, giving, by action of the lips and breath-pressure, harmonics of its fundamental, the scale filled up by use of crooks, slides, or valves: applied to other instruments more or less like: a trumpet-shaped object, as a flared bell or horn: a sound of, or as if of, a trumpet: a trumpeter.—*v.t* to sound or play on a trumpet or with trumpet-like sound: to proclaim, celebrate, summon, denounce, expel, etc., by trumpet.—*v.t.* to sound a trumpet: to make a sound like a trumpet:— *pr.p.* **trum'peting;** *pa.t.* and *pa.p.* **trum'peted.—***adj.* **trum'peted** sounded on a trumpet: loudly extolled: having a trumpet: funnel-shaped.—*n.* **trum'peter.—** *n.* and *adj.* **trum'peting.—trum'pet-call** a conventional phrase or passage played on the trumpet as a

signal: any call to action; **trumpeter swan** an American swan. the largest of the world's swans; **trum'pet-flower** a name for various plants with large trumpet-shaped flowers, **trum'pet-ma'jor** a headtrumpeter in a regiment.—*adj.* **trum'pet-shaped** like the bell of a trumpet.—**blow one's own trumpet** to sound one's own praises. [Fr *trompette*, dim. of *trompe*, trump]

truncal. See trunk.

truncate *trungk-āt', v.t.* to cut short· to lop —*adjs* **trunc'ate, -d** appearing as if squared off at the tip ending in a transverse line or plane, esp one parallel to the base —*adv* **trun'cately.**—*n.* **trunca'tion.** [L. *truncāre, -ātum—truncus;* cf. **trunk.**]

truncheon *trun'shən, -chən, n.* a short staff: a cudgel (*arch.*, except that of a policeman): a staff of authority —*v.t* to beat with a truncheon —*adj.* **trun'-cheoned** furnished with a truncheon. [O.Fr *tronchon* (Fr. *tronçon*)—*tronc;* see **trunk.**]

trundle *trun'dl, n.* a little wheel, castor: a roller.—*v t* and *v t* to wheel, esp. heavily or clumsily: to roll. to bowl along.—**trun'dle-bed** a truckle-bed [O.E *trendel.*]

trunk *trungk, n.* the stem of a tree: the body of an animal apart from head and limbs. the body generally: a main line of road, railway, telephone, etc.· the main body of anything: the shaft of a column: the body of a pedestal: a chest or box, esp for travelling· a box-like channel, trough, shaft, conduit, or chute: a tube: a proboscis: same as **bus** (*comput*): (in *pl.*) pants worn for sports, swimming, etc : the boot, luggage compartment of an automobile (*U.S*).—*adjs.* **trunc'al** pertaining to the trunk: principal; trunked having a trunk.—*ns.* **trunk'ful** as much as will fill a trunk:—*pl.* **trunk'fuls; trunk'ing** casing.—**trunk'-call'** a long-distance telephone call, involving connection between two centres; **trunk dialling** the dialling of trunk telephone calls directly, connections not being made by an operator; **trunk'-line** the main line of a railway, canal, gas or oil pipeline, etc.; **trunk'-road** a main road, esp. one administered by central authority. [Fr. *tronc* and L. *truncus*, a stock, a torso —*truncus*, maimed; with associations of Fr. *trompe*, a trump, a proboscis.]

trunnion *trun'yən, n.* either of a pair of side projections on which anything (as formerly a big gun) is pivoted to move in a vertical plane [Fr *trognon*, stump.]

truss *trus, n.* a bundle, esp. of hay or straw, or a block cut from a stack: a framed structure for supporting a weight: a tuft of flowers or fruit at the top of the main stalk or stem: a corbel (*archit.*): a surgical appliance for retaining a reduced hernia.—*v.t* to bundle up: to fix for cooking, as with a skewer: to furnish with a truss.—*adj.* **trussed.**—*ns.* **truss'er; truss'ing.** [Fr. *trousse* (n.), *trousser* (vb.).]

trust *trust, n.* worthiness of being relied on: fidelity: confidence in the truth of anything: confident expectation: a resting on the integrity, friendship, etc., of another: faith: hope: credit (esp. sale on credit or on promise to pay): ground of confidence: that which is given or received in confidence: charge· responsibility: anything felt to impose moral obligations: an arrangement by which property is handed to or vested in a person, to use and dispose of it for the benefit of another: an estate so managed for another: an arrangement for the control of several companies under one direction, to cheapen expenses, regulate production, beat down competition, and so obtain a maximum return.—*adj.* held in trust.—*v.t.* to place trust in: to believe: to expect confidently: to hope: to give credit to: to commit to trust —*v.i.* to have trust: to rely (with *to*).—*ns.* **trustee'** one to whom anything is entrusted: one to whom the management of a property is committed in trust for the benefit of others; **trustee'ship** the state of being or action of a trustee: a trust territory; **trust'er.**—*adj.* **trust'ful** trusting.—*adv.* **trust'fully.**—*n.* **trust'fulness.**—*adv.* **trust'ily.**—*n.* **trust'iness.**—*adj.* **trust'ing** confiding. —*adv.* **trust'ingly.**—*adj.* **trust'less** not to be trusted: distrustful.—*n.* **trust'lessness.**—*adv.* **trust'worth-ily.**—*n.* **trust'worthiness.**—*adjs.* **trust'worthy** worthy of trust or confidence: trusty; **trust'y** to be trusted: deserving confidence: faithful: honest: strong: firm: —*compar.* **trust'ier,** *superl.* **trust'iest.**—*n.* one who can be trusted: a well-behaved prisoner, often granted special privileges.—**trust, trustee, account** a savings account, the balance of which can be left to a beneficiary; **trust company, corporation** a commercial enterprise formed to act as a trustee; **trust fund** a fund of money, etc., held in trust; **trust territory** a territory ruled by an administering country under supervision of the Trusteeship Council of the United Nations (also **trusteeship**).—**breach of trust** a violation of duty by a trustee, etc.; **in trust** as a charge, for safe-keeping, for management as a trustee; **investment trust** an organisation which invests its stockholders' money and distributes the net return among them; **on trust** on credit: (accepted) without question; **unit trust** type of investment trust in which given amounts of different securities form a unit, choice of a number of differently constituted units being available. [O.N. *traust*, trust.]

truth *trōōth*, *n.* faithfulness: constancy: veracity: agreement with reality: fact of being true: actuality: accuracy of adjustment or conformity: in the fine arts, a faithful adherence to nature: that which is true or according to the facts of the case. the true state of things, or facts: a true statement: an established fact: true belief: known facts, knowledge.—*adj.* **truth'ful** habitually or actually telling what one believes to be true: put forward in good faith as what one believes to be true: conveying the truth.—*adv.* **truth'fully.**—*n.* **truth'fulness.**—**truth drug, truth serum** any of various drugs, which make subjects under questioning less wary in their replies; **truth'-teller.**—*adj.* **truth's telling.**—**truth table** a Boolean logic table in which the binary digits 0 and 1 are assigned values either 'true' or 'false'; **truth'-value** in logic, the truth or falsity of a statement.—**God's truth** a thing or statement absolutely true; **in truth** truly, in fact; **tell the truth** to speak truthfully, not to lie. [O.E. *trēowth* —*trēowe, triewe*, true.]

try *trī*, *v.t.* to test: to use, treat, resort to, experimentally: to put to the test: to strain: to annoy, irritate, afflict: to examine critically: to examine and decide the truth, justice, guilt or innocence, of, as a judge: to conduct in court, as a lawyer (*U.S.*): to attempt, endeavour, essay (*usu.* with *to*).—*v.i.* to make an effort:—*3rd pers. pr.t.* **tries;** *pr.p.* **try'ing;** *pa.t.* and *pa.p.* **tried** (*trīd*).—*n.* a trial: effort: in Rugby football, the score of three points (Rugby League) or four points (Rugby Union) gained by a player who succeeds in placing the ball with his hand over the goal line: in American football, an attempt to gain further points after scoring a touchdown.—*adj.* **tri'-able** subject to legal trial: that can be tried.—*ns.* **tri'age** sorting out; **tri'al** see separate article.—*adj.* **tried** (*trīd*) proved good by test.—*ns.* **tri'er** one who tries in any sense—also **try'er** in the sense of one who is assiduous in trying to win; **try'ing.**—*adj.* making trial or proof: adapted to try: searching, severe: testing: distressing: causing strain.—*adv.* **try'ingly.**— **try'-on** an act of trying on a garment: an attempt at imposition by audacity (*slang*); **try'-out** a test performance; **trysail** (*trī'sl*) a reduced sail used by small craft, instead of the mainsail, in a storm: a small fore-

and-aft sail set with a boom and gaff.—**try and** (*coll.*) try to; **try for** make an attempt to reach or gain; **try it on** to attempt to do something risky or audacious to see how far one can go unscathed; **try on** to put on for trial, as a garment; **try out** to test. [O.Fr. *trier*, to pick out.]

trypanosome *trip'ən-ə-sōm*, *n.* a protozoon (**Try-panosō'ma** of various species, fam. **Trypano-somat'idae**) parasitic in the blood of vertebrates.— *adj.* **trypanocidal** (*-sī'dl*).—*ns.* **tryp'anocide** (*-sīd*) a drug that kills trypanosomes; **trypanosomiasis** (*-sō-mī'ə-sis*) disease caused by a trypanosome, esp. sleeping-sickness. [Gr. *trȳpanon*, a borer— *trȳpaein*, to bore, *sōma*, body.]

trypsin *trip'sin*, *n.* a digestive ferment secreted by the pancreas.—*adj.* **tryp'tic.**—*n.* **tryptophan(e)** (*trip'tō-fan, -fān*) an amino-acid obtained e.g. by the cleavage of casein (a protein found in milk) by pancreatic enzymes. [Gr. *tripsis*, rubbing (as first got by rubbing down the pancreas with glycerine), or *trȳein*, to wear out, modelled on **pepsin**.]

trysail. See **try**.

tryst *trīst*, (chiefly *Scot.*) *n.* an appointment to meet: appointed place of meeting. [O.Fr. *triste*, a hunter's station.]

tsar, also czar, rarely tzar, *zär, tsar*, (*hist.*) *n.* the title of the emperors of Russia and of the kings of Bulgaria: a great potentate or despot.—*ns.* **tsar'dom,** **czar'dom; tsar'evi(t)ch, czar'evi(t)ch** (Russ. *tsär-ye'vĕch*) a son of a tsar; **tsarev'na, czarev'na** a daughter of a tsar: a wife of a tsarevitch; **tsarina, czarina** (*-ē'nə*; not a Russian form), **czarit'za, tsarit'sa** a Russian empress; **tsar'ism, czar'ism** the government of the Russian tsars: absolutism; **tsar'ist, czar'ist** an upholder of tsarism; **tsesar'evi(t)ch, cesar'-evi(t)ch, -wi(t)ch** (Russ. *-ye'vĕch*) the eldest son of a tsar: heir to the tsardom; **tsesarev'na, cesarev'na** the wife of a tsar's eldest son. [Russ. *tsar'*, etc.—L. *Caesar*, Caesar.]

tsetse *tset'si*, *n. Glossina morsitans*, or other species of the African genus Glossina, small flies that transmit trypanosome parasites and cause sleeping-sickness, nagana (**tsetse-fly disease**), etc.—Also **tset'se-fly.** [Tswana.]

T-shirt. See **tee¹**.

tsigane. See **tzigany**.

tsunami *tsōō-nä'mē*, *n.* a very swiftly travelling sea wave that attains great height. [Jap. *tsu*, harbour, *nami*, wave.]

Tswana (*t*)*swä'nə*, *n.* a Negro people of southern Africa: a member of this people: their language, of the Bantu family:—*pl.* **Tswan'a(s).**—Also *adj.*

Tuareg *twä'reg*, *n.* a nomadic Berber of the Sahara: the language of the Tuaregs. [Ar. *tawāriq*.]

tuatara *tōō-a-ta'rə*, **tuatera** *-tä'rə*, *ns.* a New Zealand lizard-like reptile. [Maori, spine on the back.]

tub *tub*, *n.* an open wooden vessel made of staves and hoops: a small cask: anything like a tub: a tubful: a clumsy ship or boat: a bath: a bucket, box, or vehicle for bringing up coal from the mine.—*v.t.* to set, bathe, treat, in a tub.—*v.i.* to take a bath.—*ns.* **tubb'er; tubb'iness.**—*adj.* **tubb'y** plump, round like a tub.—*n.* **tub'ful** as much as a tub will hold: —*pl.* **tub'fuls.**—**tub'-thump'er** a declamatory or ranting preacher or public speaker; **tub'-thump'ing.** [Cf. L.G. *tubbe*.]

tuba *tū'bə, tōō'bə*, *n.* a straight trumpet (*Rom. ant.*): the low-pitched brass instrument of the saxhorn class: a powerful organ reed-stop. [L. and It. *tuba*.]

tube *tūb*, *n.* a pipe: any long hollow body: a collapsible cylinder from which material in the form of paste or viscous liquid can be squeezed out: a thermionic valve: underground railway in tube-shaped tunnel:

any vessel in a plant or animal body: a television set (*slang*): a can or bottle of beer (*Austr. slang*).—*v.t.* to furnish with, enclose in, a tube.—*v.t.* to travel by tube.—*n.* tub'age insertion of a tube.—*adjs.* tub'al, tub'ar; tu'bate tubular.—*n.* tubec'tomy surgical cutting or removal of the Fallopian tubes.—*adj.* tubed (*tūbd*).—*n.* tube'ful.—*adjs.* tube'less; tub'iform shaped like a tube.—*n.* tub'ing the act of making or supplying tubes: tubes collectively: material for tubes.—*adj.* tub'ular having the form of a tube: made of or with tubes: having a sound like that made by the passage of air through a tube.—*v.t.* tub'ulate to form into a tube: to furnish with a tube.—*adj.* tubular.—*adj.* tub'ulated.—*ns.* tubula'tion; tub'ulature; tub'ule a small tube.—tube'-foot in echinoderms, a tube protruding through a pore, used in locomotion and respiration; tube'-skirt a very tight skirt; tube'-worm a worm that makes a tube to dwell in; tubular bells an orchestral musical instrument in the percussion section, consisting of a number of metal tubes suspended in a frame, giving the sound of bells when struck. [Fr.,—L. *tubus*, a pipe.]

tuber *tū'bər, n.* a lump: a rounded swelling: a swelling, usually underground, in a plant where reserves are stored up—of stem nature (as in the potato, Jerusalem artichoke, etc.), or of root nature (as in the dahlia).—*adjs.* tuberif'erous; tu'beriform; tuberose (*tū'bə-rōs, -rōz*) tuberous.—*n.* (*tū'bə-rōs, -rōz*; often, by false association with tube and rose, *tūb'rōz*) a Mexican amaryllid (*Polianthes tuberosa*) grown for its fragrant creamy-white flowers, propagated by tubers.—*n.* tuberosity (*-ros'i-ti*).—*adj.* tub'erous having tubers: of the nature of, or like, a tuber: knobbed.—tuberous root a fleshy root resembling a tuber but not having buds or eyes. [L. *tūber*, a swelling, from root of L. *tumēre*, to swell.]

tubercle *tū'bər-kl, n.* a small tuber, protuberance, or swelling: a nodule: a nodule or morbid growth in the lung or elsewhere, in cases of tuberculosis.—*adjs.* tu'bercled having tubercles; tubercular (*-bûr'*) nodular: having tubercles: affected by, suffering from, tuberculosis; tuber'culate, -d having, covered with, tubercles.—*ns.* tuberculā'tion; tu'bercule a tubercle; tuber'culin a preparation from a culture of tubercle bacillus used for testing for tuberculosis; tubercuḷisā'tion.—*v.t.* tuber'culise, -ize to infect with tuberculosis.—*n.* tuberculō'sis consumption or phthisis, a disease caused by the tubercle bacillus (*Bacillus tuberculosis*), characterised by development of tubercles.—*adj.* tuber'culous of, affected by, tuberculosis.—*n.* tuber'culum a tubercle.—*adj.* tuber'culin-test'ed (of milk) from cows that have been tested for and certified free from tuberculous infection. [L. *tūberculum*, dim. of *tūber*.]

tuberose. See under tuber.

tubiform, tubing, tubular, etc. See tube.

tuck *tuk, v.t.* to draw or thrust in or together! to stuff, cram: to fold under: to gather or gird up (often with *up*): to contract (with *up*): to enclose by pressing clothes closely around or under: to put tucks in: to put, stow, away: to eat (with *in*; *slang*).—*v.t.* to make an onslaught upon food (usu. with *in* or *into*).—*n.* an act of tucking: a pleat or fold, now one stitched down: eatables, esp. delicacies (*slang*).—*n.* tuck'er a piece of cloth tucked or drawn over the bosom: food (*Austr. slang*).—*v.t.* (*U.S. slang*) to tire exceedingly (often with *out*).—tuck'-box a box of or for tuck, at a boarding school; tuck'-in' (*slang*) a hearty feed.—*adj.* contrived for tucking in an edge.—tuck'-shop (orig. *schoolboys'*, etc. *slang*) a confectioner's or a pastrycook's shop: now esp. such a shop or anything similar on school premises. [O.E. *tūcian*, to disturb, afflict.]

Tudor *tū'dər, adj.* pertaining to the Welsh family of Tudor, the time when it held the English throne (1485–1603), or the style of architecture that prevailed then.—*adj.* Tudoresque'.—Tudor rose a red and white rose (combining Lancaster and York) adopted as a badge by Henry VII.

Tuesday *tūz'di, n.* the third day of the week. [O.E. *Tiwes dæg*, the day of *Tiw* (the God of war).]

tufa *tōō'fə, tū'fə, n.* calc-sinter (often *calcareous tufa*).—*adj.* tufa'ceous. [It. *tufa*, a variant of *tufo*—L. *tōfus*, a soft stone.]

tuff *tuf, tōōf, n.* a rock composed of fine volcanic fragments and dust.—*adj.* tuffa'ceous. [Fr. *tuf, tuffe*—It. *tufo*; see tufa.]

tuft *tuft, n.* a bunched cluster: a clump: a crest: a separate lock of hair: one of the cut or uncut loops of wool, etc., forming the pile of a carpet or rug: a gold tassel formerly worn on a nobleman's cap in the English universities.—*v.t.* to separate into tufts: to make or adorn with tufts.—*adj.* tuft'ed having or made of tufts: having many short crowded branches all arising at or near the same level (*bot.*): (of birds) with a tuft or crest of feathers on the head.—*n.* tuft'ing.—*adj.* tuft'y. [Supposed to be—O.Fr. *tuffe* (Fr. *touffe*)—L. *tūfa*, crest—Gmc.]

tug *tug, v.t.* to pull forcibly: to haul: to tow: to drag.—*v.t.* to pull forcibly: to strive: to toil:—*pr.p.* tugg'ing; *pa.t.* and *pa.p.* tugged.—*n.* a forcible or jerking pull: a hard struggle: a rope or chain for pulling: a tugboat: an aeroplane towing a glider.—*n.* tugg'er one who tugs.—*n.* and *adj.* tugg'ing.—*adv.* tugg'ingly.—tug'-boat a towing vessel; tug-of-love' a dispute over the guardianship of a child, e.g. between divorced parents, or natural and foster parents, tug-of-war' a laborious contest: a contest in which opposing teams tug at a rope and strive to pull one another over a line. [M.E. *toggen*, intens. from root of O.E. *tēon*; cf. tow[1].]

tui *tōō'ē, n.* the parson-bird. [Maori.]

tuition *tū-ish'ən, n.* teaching, instruction.—*adjs.* tui'tional, tui'tionary. [L. *tuitiō, -ōnis—tuērī, tuitus*, to watch over.]

tular(a)emia *tōō-lə-rē'mi-ə, n.* a disease of rodents caused by a bacterium (*Bacterium tularense*, or *Pasteurella tularensis*) transmitted to man either by insects or directly, causing fever, etc.—*adj.* tular(a)e'mic. [*Tulare* county, California, where it was first discovered, and Gr *haima*, blood.]

tulip *tū'lip, n.* any plant or flower of the bulbous liliaceous genus Tu'lipa, with showy, usually solitary, flowers.—tu'lip-tree a North American timber tree (Liriodendron), of the Magnolia family, with tuliplike flowers, tu'lip-wood its wood [O.Fr. *tulipe, tulippe, tulipan*—Turk. *tulbend*, turban]

tulle *tōōl, tāl, tul, n.* a delicate thin silk network fabric. [Fr.; from *Tulle*, in the department of Corrèze]

tum. See tummy.

tumble *tum'bl, v.i.* to roll, wallow, toss about: to perform as a dancer or acrobat: to turn over in flight or fall: to fall headlong, floundering, or revolving: to collapse, fall in a heap: to rush confusedly and hastily: to come by chance (usu. with *on*): to comprehend (often with *to*; *slang*).—*v.t.* to send tumbling or headlong: to overthrow: to bundle from one place to another: to jumble: to throw about: to disorder, rumple.—*n.* act of tumbling: a fall: a somersault: a tumbled condition or mass.—*ns.* tum'bler one who tumbles: an acrobat: a large drinking-glass or tall cup, formerly one that could not stand: a tumblerful: a revolving barrel or cage: part of a lock that holds the bolt in place, till it is moved by the key: part of a firearm lock that receives the thrust of the mainspring and forces the hammer forward: a machine which dries (clothes, etc.) by tumbling them in a strong current of hot air (also **tum'ble-, tum'bler-dri'er**): a machine consisting of a revolving drum in which (gem)stones are polished (also **tum'bling-barrel, -box**); **tum'blerful** as much as will fill a tumbler:—*pl.* **tum'blerfuls.**—*n.* and *adj.* **tum'bling.**—*adj.* **tum'bledown** dilapidated, threatening to fall.— **tum'bler-switch** a switch that is turned over to put electric current off or on; **tum'ble-weed** a type of plant that snaps off above the root, curls into a ball, and rolls about in the wind.—**tumble over** to toss about carelessly, to upset: to fall over. [Freq. from O.E *tumbian*]

tumbrel, tumbril *tum'brəl, -bril, ns* a two-wheeled military cart (*arch.*): a dung-cart: the name given to the carts that conveyed victims to the guillotine during the French Revolution. [O.Fr. *tomberel* (Fr. *tombereau*)—*tomber*, to fall.]

tumefy *tū'mi-fī, v.t.* and *v.i.* to swell:—*pr.p.* **tu'mefying**; *pa.t.* and *pa.p.* **tu'mefied.**—*adj.* **tumefacient** (*tū-mi-fā'shənt*).—*ns.* **tumefac'tion**; **tumescence** (*tū-mes'əns*) a tendency to swell: a swelling.—*adjs.* **tumesc'ent**; **tu'mid** swollen or enlarged: inflated: bombastic.—*adv.* **tu'midly.**—*n.* **tu'midness.**—*adjs.* **tumorigen'ic, tumorgen'ic** causing or producing tumours.—*ns* **tumorigenic'ity, tumorgenic'ity.**—*adj.* **tu'morous.**—*n.* **tumour, tumor** (*tū'mər*) swelling: a morbid swelling or enlargement, now esp. a new growth of cells in the body without inflammation. [L. *tumefacere, tumēscere, tumidus, tumor—tumēre*, to swell, *facēre*, to make.]

tummy *tum'i, n.* a childish form of **stomach.**—Also **tum.**—**tumm'y-button** a childish term for navel.

tumour, etc. See **tumefy.**

tump *tump, (U.S.) v.t.* to drag.—**tump'-line** a strap across the forehead or chest for carrying burdens or hauling. [Prob. from an Indian word.]

tumuli. See **tumulus.**

tumult *tū'mult, -məlt, n.* violent commotion, usu. with uproar: a riot: a state of violent and confused emotion.—*adj* **tumult'uous** full of tumult: disorderly: agitated. noisy.—*adv* **tumult'uously.**—*n.* **tumult'uousness.** [L. *tumultus, -ūs—tumēre,* to swell.]

tumulus *tū'mū-ləs, n.* a burial mound, a barrow:—*pl.* **tu'muli** (*-lī, -lē*). [L.,—*tumēre,* to swell.]

tun *tun, n.* a large cask: an obsolete liquid measure— 216 gallons of ale, 252 of wine.—*v.t.* to put in a tun.— *ns.* **tunn'age** see **tonnage; tunn'ing.** [O.E. *tunne*; cf. **ton.**]

tuna[1] *tōō'nə, tū'nə, n.* a prickly-pear, plant or fruit [Haitian.]

tuna[2] *tōō'nə, tū'nə, n.* a kind of large sea-fish of the mackerel family: its flesh as food:—*pl.* **tu'na, tu'nas.** —Also **tuna-fish, tunn'y(-fish).** [Sp.,—L. *tunnus*— Gr. *thynnos.*]

tunable. See **tune.**

tundra *tōōn'-, tun'drə, n.* an Arctic plain with permanently frozen subsoil, and lichens, mosses, and dwarfed vegetation. [Lapp.]

tune *tūn, n.* tone: a melody or air: melodiousness: accurate adjustment in pitch or frequency: harmonious adjustment (*fig.*): frame of mind, temper.—*v.t.* to adjust the tones of: to put in condition for producing tones in tune: to put in smooth working order: to synchronise: to adjust (a radio receiver) so as to produce the optimum response to an incoming signal: to put in accord, bring to a desired state.—*adj.* **tun'-able** tuneful: in tune.—Also **tune'able.**—*n.* **tun'-ableness.**—*adv.* **tun'ably.**—*adjs.* **tuned** (*tūnd*); **tune'ful** full of tune: melodious: musical.—*adv.* **tune'fully.**—*n.* **tune'fulness.**—*adj.* **tune'less** without

tune: not melodious or tuneful: unmusical.—*ns.* **tun'er** one who tunes instruments, engines, etc.: an apparatus for receiving radio signals: a knob, dial, etc. by which a radio or television receiver is adjusted to different wavelengths; **tun'ing.**—**tuner amplifier** a piece of hi-fi equipment incorporating a radio receiver and an amplifier which can also be used with a record-player or tape deck; **tune'smith** (*facet.*) a songwriter or composer of light music; **tun'ing-fork** a two-pronged instrument giving a sound of known pitch or vibration.—**change one's tune, sing another tune** to alter one's attitude, or way of talking; **in tune** true in pitch: in accord (*fig.*); **out of tune** not true in pitch: not agreeing (*fig.*); **to the tune of** to the amount of; **tune in** to adjust a wireless receiver for reception (often with *to*); **tune up** to put instruments into tune for beginning: of engines, etc., to (be) put into smooth working order: to begin to perform, strike up [A form of **tone.**]

tung-oil *tung'-oil, n.* wood-oil obtained from seeds of the tung'-tree or Chinese varnish tree (*Aleurites fordii* or other species). [Chin. *yu-t'ung*, tung-oil.]

tungsten *tung'stən, n.* an element (symbol W; at numb. 74), a rare metal also known as wolfram, used for making lamp filaments and high-speed steel [Sw., lit. heavy stone—*tung*, heavy, *sten*, stone.]

Tungus *tōōng'gŏŏs, tōōng-gŏŏs', -gŏŏz', n.* a member of an Eastern Siberian people and race, of the type usually called Mongol:—*pl.* **Tungus, Tunguses:** their language.—Also *adj.*—*n.* **Tungus'ic** the family of Ural-Altaic languages that includes Tungus and Manchu.—*adj* of or relating to (speakers of) these languages (also **Tungus'ian**) [Russ *Tunguz*; Chin *Tung-hu.*]

tunic *tū'nik, n.* a Roman shirt-like undergarment: applied also to various similar garments, usually a sort of belted coat and gown, or blouse: a close-fitting soldier's or policeman's jacket: a tunicle: an investing layer, membrane, or integument (*biol.*).—*adjs.* **tu'nicate, -d** (*bot.* and *zool.*) having a tunic: formed in concentric coats; **tu'nicked.**—*n.* **tu'nicle** a little tunic: an ecclesiastical vestment worn by a subdeacon or a bishop at mass. [L. *tunica*]

tunnage. See **tun, ton.**

tunnel *tun'l, n.* a passage cut underground: any tubular passage: an animal's burrow, in earth, wood, etc.: a flue, chimney.—*v.t* to make a passage or passages through: to hollow out.—*v i.* to make a tunnel:—*pr.p.* **tunn'elling;***pa.t.* and*pa.p.* **tunn'elled.**—*n.* **tunn'-eller.**—*n.* and *adj.* **tunn'elling.**—**tunn'el-net** a funnel-shaped net; **tunnel vision** a medical condition in which one is unable to see objects other than those straight ahead single-minded concentration on one's own pursuits or viewpoints to the total exclusion of those of others. [O Fr. *ton(n)el* (Fr *tonneau*) cask, and *tonnelle*, vault, tunnel-net, dims. of *tonne*, cask.]

tunny *tun'i, n.* a tuna, esp. *Thunnus thynnus* [L. *tunnus*—Gr. *thynnos.*]

tup *tup, n.* a ram: a paving rammer: a pile-driving monkey: the striking-face of a steam-hammer—*v t.* to copulate with (a ewe)

tupelo *tōō'pə-lō, n.* an American gum-tree (*Nyssa*):— *pl.* **tu'pelos.** [From an Indian name.]

Tupí, Tupi *tōō-pē', tōō'pē, n.* a S. American Indian of a group of peoples inhabiting the Atlantic coast and the Amazon basin: their language, serving as a lingua franca.—Also *adj.*—*adj.* **Tupi'an.**

tupik *tū'pik, n.* an Eskimo skin tent [Eskimo]

tuppence, tuppeny. Coll. for **twopence, -penny.**

tuque *tūk, n.* a Canadian cap made by tucking in one tapered end of a long cylindrical bag, closed at both ends. [Fr. *toque.*]

turaco. Same as **touraco.**

turban *tûr′bən n.* a head-covering worn by people of certain Eastern nations, consisting of a cap with a sash wound round it: a ladies' headdress of similar appearance.—*adj.* **tur′baned** wearing a turban. [Turk. *tulbend*—Pers. *dulband*; cf. **tulip**.]

turbid *tûr′bid, adj.* disordered: muddy: thick.—*ns.* **turbidim′eter** a device for determining the surface area of a powder by measuring the light-scattering properties of a fluid suspension; **turbid′ity.**—*adv.* **tur′bidly.**—*n.* **tur′bidness.** [L. *turbidus*—*turba*, tumult.]

turbine *tûr′bin* (sometimes -*bin*), *n.* a rotary motor in which a wheel or drum with curved vanes is driven by reaction or impact or both by a fluid (water in the **water-turbine**, steam in the **steam-turbine**, expanding hot air in the **gas-turbine**) admitted to it and allowed to escape.—*adjs.* **tur′binal** turbinate; **tur′binate, -d** shaped like a top or inverted cone: spirally coiled: scroll-like; **tur′bined** having, driven by, a turbine or turbines.—*n.* **Tur′bo** a tropical genus of turbinate wide-mouthed gasteropods, large specimens often used as ornaments: (without *cap.*) a member of this genus:—*pl.* **turbines** (*tûr′bi-nēz*).—turbo- in composition, having, connected to, driven by, a turbine.—**tur′bocar** a car propelled by a turbocharged engine.—*adj.* **tur′bocharged.**—**tur′bocharger** a turbine operated by the exhaust gases of an engine, thereby boosting its power; **tur′bocharging.** —*adj.* **turbo-elec′tric** using a form of electric drive in which turbine-driven generators supply electric power to motors coupled to propeller, axle shafts, etc.—**tur′bofan** a gas-turbine aero-engine in which part of the power developed is used to drive a fan which blows air out with the exhaust and so increases thrust (also **turbofan engine**); **tur′bo-gen′erator** a generator of electric power, driven by a steam-turbine; **tur′bo-jet′** (an aeroplane powered by) an internal-combustion aero-engine in which the gas energy produced by a turbine-driven compressor is directed through a nozzle to produce thrust; **tur′boprop** a jet-engine in which the turbine is coupled to a propeller; **tur′bo-su′percharger** an aero-engine supercharger operated by a turbine driven by the exhaust gases of the engine. [L. *turbō, -inis*, a whirl, a spinning-top.]

turbit *tûr′bit, n.* a domestic pigeon having white body, coloured wings, and short beak.

Turbo, turbo-. See **turbine**.

turbot *tûr′bət, n.* a large, highly-esteemed flatfish (*Psetta maxima*) with bony tubercles: extended to various more or less similar fishes. [O.Fr. *turbot*.]

turbulent *tûr′bū-lənt, adj.* tumultuous, violently disturbed: in violent commotion: producing commotion: stormy: of fluid, showing turbulence: insubordinate, unruly: having an exciting, disturbing effect.—*n.* **tur′bulence** disturbed state: unruly character or action: irregular eddying motion of particles in a fluid: irregular movement of large volumes of air (also **atmospheric turbulence**).—*adv.* **tur′bulently.** [L. *turbulentus*—*turba*, a turmoil.]

turd *tûrd, n.* a lump of dung: a despicable person (*vulg.*). [O.E. *tord.*]

tureen *tə-rēn′, tū-rēn′, n.* a large dish for holding soup, vegetables, etc., at table. [Fr. *terrine*—L. *terra*, earth.]

turf *tûrf, n.* the surface of land matted with the roots of grass, etc.: a cake of turf cut off: a sod: peat: horse-racing, the race-course, the racing world:—*pl.* **turfs**, sometimes **turves.**—*v.t.* to cover with turf.—*adj.* **turfed.**—*ns.* **tur′finess; tur′fing; tur′fite** (*slang*) one devoted to horse-racing (also **turf′man;** chiefly *U.S.*).—*adj.* **tur′fy** of, like, or abounding in, turf: pertaining to horse-racing.—**turf′-account′ant** a euphemism for bookmaker.—**turf out** to throw out

forcibly [O.E. *turf.*]

turgescence *tûr′-jes′əns, n.* the act or process of swelling up: swollenness: distension of cells and tissues with water.—*adjs.* **turgesc′ent** swelling: growing big; **tur′gid** swollen: extended beyond the natural size: dilated: inflated: pompous: bombastic.—*ns* **turgid′ity, tur′gidness.**—*adv.* **tur′gidly.**—*n.* **turgor** (*tûr′gòr*) the state of being full, the normal condition of the capillaries: balance of osmotic pressure and elasticity of cell-wall (*bot.*). [L. *turgēre*, to swell.]

Turing machine *tū′ring mə-shēn′,* a hypothetical computer, able to perform an infinite number of calculations. [First described by A M. *Turing* (1912–54), British mathematician.]

turion *tū′ri-ən, n.* an underground bud, growing upward into a new stem [L. *turiō, -ōnis,* a shoot.]

Turk *tûrk, n.* a native or citizen of *Turkey*: a Muslim of the former Ottoman empire: any speaker of a Turkic language; an unmanageable unruly person: a Turkish horse: a Turkish ship.—*adj.* Turkish.—*adj.* **Turki** (*tōōr′kē*) of the Turkish distinguished from the Tatar branch of Turko-Tatar languages.—*n.* a Turki speaker or language.—*adjs.* and *ns.* **Turk′ic, Turko-Ta′tar** (of) that branch of the Ural-Altaic languages to which Turkish belongs.—*adj.* **Turk′ish** of Turkey, the Turks, or their language: Turkic.—*n.* the language of the Turks.—**Turkey** red a fine durable red dye, obtained from madder, but now mostly chemically; **Turkish bath** a kind of hot-air bath, the patient being sweated, rubbed down, massaged, and gradually cooled; **Turkish delight** a gelatinous sweetmeat, orig. Turkish; **Turk's cap (lily)** the lily *Lilium martagon,* from the appearance of the rolled-back petals of the nodding flower; **Turk's head** a kind of knot.—**turn Turk** to become Muslim. to be completely reversed.

turkey *tûrk′i, n.* formerly, a guinea-fowl (thought to have come from *Turkey*): now, an American genus (*Meleagris*) of the pheasant family: a domestic breed of that genus: its flesh as food (in *U.S.* also a substitute) extended to various big birds, as bustard, ibis, brush turkey: a play, film, etc. that is a complete failure (*slang,* chiefly *U.S.*).—**turkey buzzard, vulture** an American vulture; **turk′ey-cock** a male turkey: a strutting, pompous, vain blusterer; **turk′ey-hen** a female turkey; **turk′ey-trot′** a kind of ragtime dance.—**talk turkey** (*U S.*) to talk bluntly: to talk business.

Turki. See **Turk.**

turmeric *tûr′mər-ik, n.* a plant (*Curcuma longa*) of the ginger family: its rootstock, or a powder made from it, used in making curry-powder and as a dye —**turmeric paper** a chemical test-paper impregnated with turmeric, changed from yellow to brown by alkali [Cf. Fr. *terre-mérite*—as if from L *terra merita,* deserved earth; origin unknown.]

turmoil *tûr′moil, n.* commotion: disquiet: tumult.

turn *tûrn, v.i.* to revolve: to rotate, to spin, whirl: to move round: to hinge: to depend: to issue: to change or reverse direction or tendency: to return: to deviate: to direct oneself, face (with *to, towards*): to betake oneself: to direct one's attention: to change sides, religion, mode of life: to change: to be transformed, converted (often with *into*): to become: to result, prove or lead in the issue: to be shaped on the lathe: to sour: to change colour: to become giddy: to be nauseated: to bend back, become turned —*v.t.* to rotate: to move round: to change the direction of: to deflect: to bend: to bend back the edge of: to reverse: to pass round or beyond: to perform by turning: to wind: to set outside-in, or remake in that form: to set upside-down: to direct: to point: to apply: to send, drive, set: to pour or tumble out to employ in circulation, pass through one's hands: to translate: to change: to make sour: to nauseate: to make giddy: to transfer, hand over: to convert, make: to make the subject of (with *to* or *into*): to render: to put by turning: to form in a lathe: to shape: to round off, fashion: to pass, become (a certain age, hour, etc.).— *n.* act, occasion, or place of turning: new direction or tendency: a twist: a winding: a complete revolution: a bend: a single traversing of a beat or course: a short walk (or ride or drive): a fit of illness or emotion, esp. an emotional shock, jar, or feeling of faintness: an embellishment in which the principal note is preceded by that next above and followed by that next below (or vice versa in the **inverted turn**), the whole ending (and sometimes beginning) with the principal note (*mus.*): turning-point: a culmination: a time or moment of change: a crisis: a spell: a recurring opportunity or spell in rotation or alternation: rotation: a trick: a performer's act or the performer: a shift: a bout: fashion: manner: cast of mind: aptitude: bent: occasion, exigency: a vicissitude: a characteristic quality or effect: act of kindness or malice.—*adj.* **turned** fashioned: wrought in a lathe: beyond the age: reversed: outside-in: soured.—*ns.* **turn′er** one who, or that which, turns: one who uses a lathe; **turn′ing** rotation: reversal: a bend: the act of making a turn: winding: deviation: a place where a road strikes off: a shaping, esp. the art of shaping wood, metal, etc., into forms having a curved (generally circular or oval) transverse section, and also of engraving figures composed of curved lines upon a smooth surface, by means of a turning-lathe: (in *pl.*) a shaving from the lathe: in pottery, the shaping of a vase: conversion, transformation.—**turn′about** a turning to face the opposite way (also *fig.*; also **turn′(a)round**); **turnaround** see **turnabout** and **turnround**; **turn′buckle** a coupling with screw-threads for adjusting tension; **turn′coat** a renegade to his principles or party; **turn′cock** valve which by turning regulates flow of water: an official who turns off and on the water for the mains, etc.—*adj.* **turn′-down** folded down.—*n.* a turn-down part: a turn-down collar: a turning down, rejection; **turning circle** the smallest possible circle in which a vehicle can turn round; **turn′ing-lathe**; **turn′ing-point** the point at which anything turns in its course: a maximum or minimum point on a graph: a critical point; **turn′key** an under-jailer: (a contract for) a job in which the contractor is to complete the entire operation, leaving the building, plant, etc., ready for use (also *adj.*); **turnkey system** (*comput.*) a computer system complete with hardware and software, usu. designed, installed, tested and maintained by the supplier; **turn′off, turn′-off** a smaller road leading from a main one; **turn′-out** a getting out of bed: a coming on duty: a call to come on duty: a muster or assembly: output: get-up; **turn′over** a turning over: a transference: a part folded over: a small pie made by folding over the crust: the total amount of money changing hands in a business: the number of employees starting or finishing employment at a particular place of work over a given period: the money value of total sales over a period.—*adj.* folded over, or made to fold over.— **turn′pike** a spiked barrier (*hist.*): a turnstile (*obs.*): a toll-gate: a turnpike-road: a motorway on which tolls are paid (*U.S.*); **turn′pike-road** a road on which there are or were tollgates: a main road; **turn′round**, **turn′around** a turning round: the whole process of docking, unloading, taking on cargo, passengers, or both, and setting sail again; **turn′spit** one who turns a spit: a dog employed to drive a wheel by which roasting-spits were turned: a spit; **turn′stile** a revolving frame that allows one person to pass at a time;

turn′stone a bird (Arenaria), intermediate between the true plovers and sandpipers, that turns over pebbles on the beach in search of food; **turn′table** a rotating table, platform, or disc, or pair of rings, one rotating within another, as for turning a locomotive, carrying a gramophone record, cementing a microscope slide, turning a camera, etc.; **turn′-up** (or *tûrn-up′*) a disturbance: a thing or part that is turned up, esp. the cuff at the bottom of a trouser-leg: an unexpected or fortuitous result or occurrence: a piece of good luck.—*adj.* turned up.—**a good (bad) turn** a helpful service (disservice); **at every turn** everywhere: incessantly; **(take) a turn for the better**, worse (to make) an improvement, deterioration; **by turns** one after another: at intervals; **in turn** one after another, in succession; **in one's turn** when it is one's occasion, opportunity, duty, etc.; **not to turn a hair** to be quite undisturbed or unaffected; **on the turn** at the turning-point, changing: on the point of turning sour; **take a turn** to go for a stroll: to have a go (*coll.*); **take one's turn**, **take turns** to participate in rotation; **to a turn** exactly, perfectly (as if of the spit); **turn about** to face round to the opposite quarter: to spin, rotate; **turn about**, **turn and turn about** alternately: in rotation; **turn a deaf ear** to to ignore; **turn again** to turn back: to revert; **turn against** to use to the injury of: to render hostile to: to rebel against; **turn around one's (little) finger** to be able to persuade to anything; **turn aside** to avert: to deviate: to avert the face; **turn away** to dismiss from service, to discharge: to avert, to turn or look in another direction: to deviate, to depart: to refuse admittance to; **turn back** to cause to retreat: to return: to fold back; **turn down** to bend, double, or fold down: to invert: to lower, as a light, volume on a radio, etc.: to reject; **turn in** to bend inward: to enter: to register (a score): to surrender, hand over voluntarily: to go to bed (*coll.*); **turn in on oneself** to become introverted; **turn into** to become by a process of change; **turn it up**, **in** stop (saying) it (*imper.*, *coll.*); **turn loose** to set at liberty; **turn off** to deviate: to dismiss: to divert: to shut or switch off: to make (someone) lose interest in or enthusiasm (for) (*slang*); **turn of speed** a burst of speed; **turn of the century**, **year** the period of the end of one century, year, and the beginning of the next; **turn on** to set running (as water): to set in operation by switching on (also *fig.*): to depend on: to turn towards and assail: to give (a person) a sense of heightened awareness and vitality as do psychedelic drugs (*slang*): to rouse the interest of, excite (*slang*); **turn one's hand to** to apply oneself to; **turn someone's head** or **brain** to make someone giddy: to infatuate with success; **turn out** to bend outwards: to drive out, to expel: to remove the contents of: to dress, groom, take care of the appearance of: to produce and put forth: to prove in the result: to muster: to switch off (a light): to get out of bed (*coll.*): to go out of doors (*coll.*); **turn over** to roll over: to set the other way up: to change sides: to hand over, pass on: to handle or do business to the amount of: to examine by turning the pages: to ponder: to rob (*slang*); **turn round** of a ship, aircraft, etc., to arrive, unload, reload and leave again; **turn the other cheek** to accept harm, violence, etc , without defending oneself; **turn the scale** to decide, determine; **turn the stomach** to nauseate; **turn to** to have recourse to: to point to: to result in: to change or be changed into: to set to work; **turn up** to point upwards: to fold upwards: to come, or bring, to light: to appear by chance: to set face up to invert: to grub up: to disturb: to make brighter, as a light, radio volume, etc. (as if by turning a knob): to refer to, look up; **turn-up for the book** a totally unexpected occurrence; **turn upon** to cast back upon, retort: to hinge on. [O.E. *turnian, tyrnan*, and perh. partly O.Fr. *torner* (Fr. *tourner*); all from L. *tornāre*, to turn in a lathe—*tornus*, a turner's wheel—Gr. *tornos*, lathe, compasses.]

turnip *tûr'nip, n.* the swollen edible root of *Brassica rapa* or (*Swedish turnip*) of *B. rutabaga*, cruciferous biennials: the root as food: the plant producing it: extended to more or less similar roots and plants.— **tur'nip-lan'tern** a lantern made by scooping out the flesh of a turnip. [See **neep**; the first part may be from **turn** or Fr. *tour*, implying roundness.]

turpentine *tûr'pən-tīn, n.* a balsam, orig. that of the terebinth tree (*Chian turpentine*), now generally of conifers: popularly, oil of turpentine: a tree that yields turpentine, esp. the terebinth.—*v.t.* to treat or smear with turpentine.—**tur'pentine-tree** the terebinth-tree.—**oil** (or **spirit**) **of turpentine** (*coll. turps*) an oil distilled from turpentine. [O.Fr. *terbentine*—L. *terebinthina* (*rēsīna*), terebinth (resin); see **terebinth**.]

turpeth *tûr'pəth, n.* an Oriental plant of the Convolvulus family, or its cathartic root. [L.L *turpethum, turbithum*—Pers. and Ar. *turbed, turbid*.]

turpitude *tûr'pi-tūd, n.* baseness: depravity: vileness [L. *turpitūdō—turpis*, base.]

turps. See **turpentine**.

turquoise *tûr'kwâz, -k(w)oiz, n.* a massive opaque sky-blue to pale green mineral, a hydrous basic aluminium phosphate, found in Persia: blue colour of the stone. [O.Fr. *turkeis*, Turkish, as first brought through *Turkey* or from *Turkestan*.]

turret *tur'it, n.* a small tower, usu. attached to a building, often containing a winding stair: a tower, often revolving, carrying a gun: part of a lathe that holds the cutting tool.—*adj.* **turr'eted** having turrets: formed like a tower or a long spiral.—**turret lathe** a lathe having a number of tools carried on a turret mounted on a saddle which slides on the lathe bed. [O.Fr. *tourete*, dim. of *tur*; see **tower**.]

turriculate, -d *tur-ik'ū-lāt, -id, adjs.* turreted: formed in a long spiral. [L. *turris*, a tower; dim. *turricula*.]

turtle[1] *tûr'tl, (arch.) n.* a turtle-dove: a constant or demonstrative lover.—**tur'tle-dove** any dove of the genus *Turtur* or *Streptopelia*, a favourite cage-bird, a type of conjugal affection and constancy. [O.E. *turtla, turtle*—L. *turtur*.]

turtle[2] *tûr'tl, n.* any marine chelonian: sometimes a freshwater chelonian: esp. in U.S. a terrestrial chelonian: the edible flesh of a turtle, esp. the green turtle: turtle-soup.—**tur'tleback** anything arched like a turtle's back, esp. a structure over a ship's bows or stern; **tur'tle-neck** (a garment having) a high close-fitting neckline.—*adj.* **tur'tle-necked**.—**tur'tle-shell** the shell of the hawk's-bill turtle, commonly called tortoise-shell; **tur'tle-soup** a soup made from the flesh, fat, and gelatinous tissue of the female green turtle (*Chelone mydas*).—**mock turtle** a soup made of calf's head or other meat in lieu of turtle meat; **turn turtle** to render a turtle helpless by turning it on its back: to turn bottom up. [Fr. *tortue*, tortoise, from L.L. *tortuca*.]

turves. See **turf**.

Tuscan *tus'kən, adj.* of *Tuscany* in Italy: Doric as modified by the Romans, with unfluted columns, and without triglyphs (*archit*).—*n.* classical Italian as spoken in Tuscany: a native of Tuscany: an ancient Etruscan. [L. *Tuscānus*, Etruscan.]

tusche *tŏŏsh, n.* a substance used in lithography for drawing the design which then does not take up the printing medium. [Ger. *tuschen*, to touch up (with paint, etc.).]

tusk *tusk, n.* a long, protruding tooth: a tush: a sharp projection.—*v.t.* to pierce with the tusks.—*adjs.*

tusked, tusk'y.—*n.* **tusk'er** a boar, elephant, etc., with tusks.—*adj.* **tusk'less.**—**tusk'-shell** the mollusc Dentalium or its shell. [O.E. *tūx* (*tūsc*).]

tusser, tussore *tus'ər, n.* a fawn-coloured silk from wild Indian silkworms: its colour: a dress made of it. [Hind. *tasar*, shuttle—Sans. *tasara*, silkworm.]

tussis *tus'is, (med.) n.,* a cough.—*adjs.* **tuss'al, tuss'-ive.** [L.]

tussle *tus'l, n.* a sharp struggle.—*v.i.* to struggle. [Freq. of **touse**; cf. **tousle**.]

tussock *tus'ək, n.* a tuft: a bunchy clump of grass, rushes, etc.: tussock-grass.—*adj.* **tuss'ocky.**—**tuss'ock-grass** a large grass (*Poa flabellata*) of the Falkland Islands, forming great tufts.

tussore. Same as **tusser**.

tut *tut, interj.* an exclamation of rebuke, mild disapprobation, impatience, etc.—*v.i.* to say 'tut':—*pr.p* **tutt'ing;** *pa.t.* and *pa.p.* **tutt'ed.**—Also **tut'-tut'.**

tutee. See **tutor**.

tutelage *tū'ti-lij, n.* guardianship: state of being under a guardian: tuition.—*adjs.* **tu'telar, tu'telary** protecting: having the charge of a person or place.—*ns.* a guardian spirit, god, or saint. [L. *tūtēla,* guard—*tūtārī,* to guard—*tuērī,* to look to.]

tutor *tū'tər, n.* a guardian: a private instructor: a coach: one who helps a boy or girl with lessons: a college officer who has supervision of an undergraduate: a college teacher who instructs by conference with a small group of students: an instruction-book.—*v.t.* to act as tutor to: to instruct: to coach: to control: to discipline.—*ns.* **tutee'** a person who is tutored; **tu'torage** tutorship: tutoring: charge for tutoring; **tu'toress** a female tutor.—*adj.* **tutorial** (*tū-tō'ri-əl, -tō*) of a tutor.—*n.* a conference or sitting with a college tutor.—*adv.* **tuto'rially.**—*n.* **tu'toring.**—*v.t.* and *v.i.* **tu'torise, -ize.**—*ns.* **tu'torism; tu'torship** [L. *tūtor, -ōris,* a guardian—*tuērī,* to look to.]

tutsan *tut'sən, n.* a species of St John's wort (*Hypericum androsaemum*) once regarded as a panacea. [O.Fr. *toutesaine, tout*—L. *tōtus,* all, *sain*—L. *sānus,* sound.]

tutti *tŏŏt'(t)ē, (mus.) pl. adj.* all (performers).—*n.* a passage for the whole orchestra or choir, or its rendering. [It., pl. of *tutto*—L. *tōtus,* all.]

tutti-frutti *tŏŏt'(t)ē-frŏŏt'(t)ē, n.* a confection, esp. ice-cream, flavoured with different kinds of fruit. [It., all fruits.]

tut-tut *tut'-tut.* Same as **tut**.

tutty *tut'i, n.* crude zinc oxide. [O.Fr. *tutie*—L.L. *tutia*—Ar. *tūtiyā*.]

tutu *tŏŏ'tŏŏ, n.* a ballet dancer's short, stiff, spreading skirt. [Fr.]

tu-whit tu-whoo *tŏŏ-(h)wit' tŏŏ-(h)wŏŏ',* an owl's hoot.

tuxedo *tuk-sē'dō,* (orig. *U.S.*) *n.* a dinner-jacket:—*pl.* **tuxe'dos, -does.** [From a fashionable club at *Tuxedo* Park, N.Y.]

tuyère. See **twyer**.

twaddle *twod'l, n.* senseless or prosy commonplace talk.—*v.i.* to talk twaddle.—*n.* **twadd'ler.**—*n.* and *adj.* **twadd'ling.**—*adj.* **twadd'ly.** [Perh. **twattle**.]

twain *twān, (arch.) adj.* two.—*n.* a couple, pair.—**in twain** asunder. [O.E. *twēgen* (masc.), two.]

twang *twang, n.* the sound of a plucked string: a nasal tone: a local intonation (*coll.*).—*v.t.* and *v.i.* to sound with a twang.—*n.* and *adj.* **twang'ing.**—*adv.* **twang'ingly.**—*adj.* **twangy** (*twang'i*). [Imit.]

'twas *twoz, twaz,* a contraction of **it was**.

twat *twot, twat, n.* (*vulgarly*) the vulva: a coarse general term of reproach (*slang*).

twattle *twot'l, n.* chatter: babble: twaddle.—*v.t.* and *v.i.* to babble.—*n.* **twatt'ler.**—*n.* and *adj.* **twatt'ling.** [Perh. conn. with **tattle**.]

For other sounds see detailed chart of pronunciation.

tway *twā*, *adj.* and *n.* a form of **twain**, or of **two** (*Scot.*).
—**tway'-blade** an orchid (*Listera*) with small green flowers and one pair of leaves.

tweak *twēk*, *v.t.* to twitch, to pull: to pull or twist with sudden jerks.—*n.* a sharp pinch or twitch. [App. conn. with **twitch**¹.]

twee *twē*, (*coll.*) *adj.* small and sweet: sentimentally pretty. [*tweet* for 'sweet', and later *tiny* and *wee*.]

tweed *twēd*, *n.* a rough woollen cloth much used for men's suits: (in *pl.*) clothes of tweed. [Said to be from a misreading of **tweel**, the cloth being made in the Tweed basin; or perhaps a shortening of *tweeled* (*twilled*).]

tweedle *twē'dl*, *v.i.* to play casually, strum, tootle.—*ns.* **tweedledee'**, **tweedledum'** a fiddler (in conjunction as types of the almost indistinguishable; orig. the proverbial names of two rival musicians). [Prob. imit.]

tweel *twēl*, *n.* a Scots form of **twill**.

'tween. A contraction of **between**.

tweet *twēt*, **tweet'-tweet'** *ns.* the note of a small bird.—*vs.t.* and *vs.i.* to pipe as a small bird.—*n.* **tweet'er** a loudspeaker used in high-fidelity sound reproduction for the higher frequencies. [Imit.]

tweezers *twēz'ərz*, *n.pl.* small pincers for pulling out hairs, etc. [Obs. *tweeze*, a surgeon's case of instruments—Fr. *étui*.]

twelfth *twelfth*, *adj.* last of twelve: immediately following the eleventh in order, position, etc.: equal to one of twelve equal parts.—*n.* a twelfth part: a person or thing in twelfth position: a tone eleven (conventionally twelve) diatonic degrees above or below a given tone (*mus.*).—*adv.* **twelfth'ly** in the twelfth place.—**Twelfth'-day** the twelfth day after Christmas, Epiphany, 6th Jan.; **twelfth man** (*cricket*) a player selected beyond the necessary eleven to play if required as a substitute; **Twelfth'-night** the evening of 6th Jan.: also the evening of 5th Jan.—**the (glorious) Twelfth** 12th Aug., opening day of the grouse-shooting season. [O.E. *twelfta—twelf*.]

twelve *twelv*, *n.* the cardinal number next above eleven: a symbol representing that number: a set of that number of things or persons: an article of a size denoted by 12: a score of twelve points: the hour of midday or midnight: the age of twelve years.—*adj.* and *adv.* **twelve'fold.**—*ns.* **twelve'mo** (*pl.* -mos) duodecimo, written 12mo; **twelve'month** a year.—*adj.* **twelve'-tone** (or -**note**) pertaining to music based on a pattern formed from the twelve notes of the chromatic scale, esp. as developed by Arnold Schönberg (1874–1951) and his pupils (**twelve-tone, -note, row** the basic pattern of notes; see also **series, serial**).—**the Twelve** the twelve apostles. [O.E. *twelf*, prob. two left; see **eleven**.]

twenty *twen'ti*, *adj.* twice ten: nineteen and one.—*n.* the number next above nineteen: a score.—*n.pl.* **twen'ties** the numbers twenty to twenty-nine: the years so numbered in life or any century: a range of temperatures from twenty to just less than twenty-nine degrees.—*adj.* **twen'tieth** next after the nineteenth: last of twenty: equal to one of twenty equal parts.—*n.* a twentieth part: a person or thing in twentieth position.—*n., adj.,* and *adv.* **twen'tyfold** twenty times as many or much.—*adj.* **twen'tyish** about twenty.—**twenty-pence, -penny piece** in Britain, a coin worth 20 pence.—*adj.* **twen'ty-twen'ty** of human vision, normal. [O.E. *twēntig*, prob.—*twēgen*, twain, and suff. -*tig*, ten.]

'twere. A contraction of **it were.**

twerp *twûrp*, (*slang*) *n.* a contemptible person, either stupid or a cad, or both.

twi-, twy- *twī*, *pfx.* two: double.—*adjs.* **twi'-, twy'fold** twofold; **twi'-, twy'forked** bifurcate. [O.E. pfx. *twi-*.]

twibill *twi'bil*, *n.* a double-headed axe. [O.E. *twibill* —pfx. *twi-*, **bill**¹.]

twice *twīs*, *adv.* two times: doubly: for a second time. —**twice over** twice (emphatically). [Late O.E. *twiges—twiga*, *twiwa*, *tuwa*, twice, with adverbial gen. ending.]

twiddle *twid'l*, *v.t.* to twirl idly: to finger idly, play with: to rotate.—*v.i.* to twirl: to trifle with something.—*n.* a twirl: a curly mark, ornament.—*n.* **twidd'ler.**—*n., adj.* **twidd'ling.**—*adj.* **twidd'ly.**— **twiddle one's thumbs** to-rotate the thumbs around each other: to be idle (*fig.*). [Prob. suggested by **twirl, twist,** and **fiddle.**]

twig¹ *twig*, *n.* a small shoot or branch: a divining-rod. —*adj.* made of twigs.—*adj.* **twigg'y.** [O.E. *twig*.]

twig² *twig*, (*coll.*) *v.t.* and *v.i.* to observe: to understand. [Poss. Ir. *tuigim*, discern; cf Gael. *tuig*, understand.]

twilight *twī'līt*, *n.* the faint light after sunset and before sunrise: dim light or partial darkness: a period of decay following a period of success, vigour, greatness, etc. (*fig.*).—*adj.* of twilight: faintly illuminated: obscure, indefinite: partial, transitional. —*adjs.* **twi'lighted**, **twi'lit**.—**twilight sleep** partial anaesthesia in childbirth by the use of drugs; **twilight zone** a dilapidated, decaying area of a city or town typically situated between the main business and commercial area and the suburbs: any area or state transitional or indefinite in character. [Pfx. *twi-*, **light**.]

'twill. A contraction of **it will.**

twill *twil*, or (*Scot.*) **tweel**, *twēl*, *ns.* a woven fabric showing diagonal lines, the weft yarns having been worked over one and under two or more warp yarns: the appearance so produced.—*v.t.* to weave with a twill.—**cavalry twill** a strong woollen twill used esp for trousers. [O.E. *twilic.*]

twin *twin*, *n.* one of two born at a birth: one very like, or closely associated with, another: a counterpart: a combination of two crystals symmetrically united.— *adj.* twofold, double: born two at a birth: forming one, or composed, of two like parts or counterparts: very like another.—*v.t.* to couple, or to produce, like a twin or twins.—*v.i.* to be born at the same birth: to bring forth two at once: to be paired or suited:—*pr.p.* **twinn'ing**; *pa.p.* **twinned**.—*adj.* **twinned** produced at one birth: constituting a twin.—*ns.* **twinn'ing**; **twin'ship** the condition or relation of a twin or twins. —**twin bed** one of a matching pair of single beds; **twin'-broth'er** a brother born at the same birth; **twin'-set** a cardigan and jumper made more or less to match; **twin'-sist'er** a sister born at the same birth; **twin town** a town paired with another foreign town of similar size for the purpose of social, cultural and commercial exchanges.—**the Twins** Gemini. [O.E. *getwinn* (n.), twin, *twinn* (adj.), double; cf. pfx. **twi-**.]

twine *twīn*, *n.* a twisted cord: string or strong thread: a coil: a twist: a twisted stem or the like: an act of twisting or clasping.—*v.t.* to wind: to coil: to wreathe: to twist: to twist together: to encircle: to make by twisting.—*v.i.* to wind: to coil: to twist: to make turns: to rise or grow in spirals.—*adj.* **twined**.— *n.* **twi'ner** one who, or that which, twines: a twining plant.—*n.* and *adj.* **twi'ning**.—*adv.* **twi'ningly**.—*adj.* **twi'ny**.—**twining plant** one that climbs by twining its stem round a support. [O.E. *twīn*, double or twisted thread, linen thread.]

twinge *twinj*, *v.t.* to tweak or pinch: to affect with a momentary pain.—*v.i.* to feel or give a momentary pain.—*n.* a tweak, a pinch: a sudden short shooting pain: a brief pang. [O.E. *twengan*, to pinch.]

twinkle *twing'kl*, *v.i.* to blink: to quiver the eyelid: to shine by flashes: to glitter: to sparkle: to flicker, vibrate.—*v.t.* to guide by twinkling.—*n.* a blink: a wink: a glitter: a quiver: a flicker: a sparkle: a twinkling.—*ns.* **twink'ler; twink'ling** a quick motion of the eye: the time occupied by a wink: an instant. the scintillation of the fixed stars.—*adj.* scintillating: quivering. [O.E. *twinclian*.]

twirl *twûrl, v t* and *v.i.* to spin: to whirl: to twist: to coil.—*n* a twist: a spin: a whirl: a whorl: a curly figure.—*n* **twirl'er.**—*adj.* **twirl'y.**

twirp. An alternative spelling of **twerp.**

twist *twist, v.t.* to twine: to unite or form by winding together: to form from several threads: to wind spirally: to form into a spiral: to wring: to wrest: to distort: to force, pull out of natural shape, position, etc.: to entangle: to impart a spin to: to force round: to pervert, warp.—*v.i.* to twine: to coil: to move spirally or tortuously: to turn aside: to revolve: to writhe —*n.* that which is twisted or formed by twisting: a cord: a strand: thread: silk thread: warp yarn: a twisted part: torsion: an act or manner of twisting: a contortion: a wrench: a wresting: a turning aside: a spin, screw, or break: a distortion: a perverted bent or set: an unexpected event or change of direction (*lit.* and *fig.*): a tangle: a twisted roll of tobacco or bread: a small curled piece of lemon, etc. flavouring a drink: a spiral ornament in the stem of a glass.—*adjs.* **twist'-able; twist'ed.**—*n.* **twist'er** one who, or that which, twists: a sophistical, slippery, shuffling, or dishonest person: a ball sent with a twist: a tornado (*U.S coll.*). —*n.* and *adj.* **twist'ing.**—*adj.* **twist'y.**—**twist drill** a drill for metal having one or more deep helical grooves round the body.—**round the twist** (*coll*) crazy, mad; **the twist** a dance which became popular in 1962, in which the dancer constantly twists the body; **twist someone's arm** to persuade someone, esp. forcefully. [O.E. *twist*, rope.]

twit[1] *twit, v.t.* to upbraid: to taunt:—*pr.p.* **twitt'ing;** *pa.t.* and *pa.p.* **twitt'ed.**—*n.* a reproach.—*n.* and *adj.* **twitt'ing.** [O.E. *ætwitan*, to reproach.]

twit[2] *twit,* (*slang*) *n.* a fool.

twitch[1] *twich, v.t.* to jerk: to pluck: to snatch: to steal: to pinch or twinge.—*v.i.* to jerk: to move spasmodically.—*n.* a sudden, quick pull: a spasmodic contraction of the muscles: a twinge.—*n.* **twitch'er.** —*n.* and *adj.* **twitch'ing.**—*adj.* **twitch'y** which twitches: on edge, nervous (*coll.*). [Related to O.E. *twiccian*, to pluck.]

twitch[2] *twich,* **twitch'-grass.** Forms of **quitch, quitch-grass** (see **couch-grass**).

twite *twīt, n.* the mountain linnet, *Acanthis flavirostris*, a N. European finch with streaked brown plumage. [From its note.]

twitter *twit'ǝr, n.* a tremulous feeble chirping: a flutter of the nerves.—*v.i.* to make a succession of small tremulous noises.—*v.t.* to chirp out.—*ns.* **twitt'erer.** —*n.* and *adj.* **twitt'ering.**—*adv.* **twitt'eringly.**—*adj.* **twitt'ery.** [imit.]

twitting. See **twit**[1].

'twixt. Abbreviation for **betwixt.**

two *tōō, n.* the sum of one and one: a symbol representing two: a pair: a deuce, card with two pips: a score of two points, strokes, etc.: an article of a size denoted by two: the second hour after midnight or midday: the age of two years.—*adj.* of the number two: two years old.—*n.* **two'er** anything that counts as, or for, two, or scores two.—*adj.* and *adv.* **two'fold** in two divisions: twice as much.—*ns.* **two'foldness; two'ness** the state of being two: duality; **two'some** a company of two: a tête-à-tête.—*adj.* **two'-bit** paltry.—**two'-by-four'** (a piece of) timber measuring four inches by two inches in cross-section (somewhat less when dressed) —*adjs*

two'-digit in double figures; **two'-dimen'sional.**— **two'-dimensional'ity** the property of having length and breadth but no depth.—*adjs.* **two'-edged** having two cutting edges: capable of being turned against the user; **two'-eyed'** having two eyes; **two'-faced** having two faces: double-dealing, false; **two'-fisted** clumsy: capable of fighting with both fists; **two'-foot** measuring, or with, two feet; **two'-footed** having two feet: capable of kicking and controlling the ball equally well with either foot (*football*, etc.).—*adjs.* **two'-four'** (*mus.*) with two crotchets to the bar; **two'-hand'ed** with or for two hands: for two persons: ambidextrous.—**two-hand'er** anything designed for, written for or requiring both hands or two people.— *adj* **two'-head'ed** having two heads: directed by two authorities; **two'-horse** for two horses (**two-horse race** any contest in which only two of the participants have a genuine chance of winning).—**twopence** (*tup'ǝns*), or (decimalised currency) **two pence** (*tōō pens*), the sum of two pennies: a coin worth two pence.—**twopence piece, -penny piece** in Britain, a coin worth 2 pence (also **two'penny-piece**).—*adjs.* **twopenny** (*tup'ni*) sold, offered at, or worth, twopence: cheap, worthless; **twopenny-halfpenny** (*tup'ni-hāp'ni*), **twopence-halfpenny** paltry, petty.—*ns.* **two-penn'yworth, two-penn'orth** (*tōō-pen'ǝrth*), also (chiefly *Scot.*) **twopenceworth** (*tup'*), **two'-piece** anything consisting of two separate parts, pieces or members.—Also *adj.*—*adjs.* **two'-ply** having two layers, or consisting of two strands: woven double; **two'-roomed.**—*n.* and *adj.* **two'-score** forty.—**two'-seater** a vehicle or aeroplane seated for two.—*adj.* **two'-sid'ed** having two surfaces, aspects, or parties: facing two ways: double-faced: having the two sides different.—**two-sid'edness; two'-step** a gliding dance in duple time: a tune for it.—*adjs.* **two'-stor'eyed, -stor'ey; two'stroke** consisting of two piston strokes, as an engine cycle: relating to, or designed for, such an engine.—*v.t.* **two'-time'** to deceive: to double-cross.—**two'-tim'er** one who deceives or double-crosses.—*adjs.* **two'-tim'ing; two'-tone** having two colours or two shades of the same colour.—**two'-up** an Australian game in which two coins are tossed and bets made on both falling heads up or both tails up.— *adj.* **two'-way** permitting passage along either of two ways esp. in opposite directions: able to receive and send signals (*radio*): of communication between two persons, groups, etc., in which both participate equally: involving shared responsibility: able to be used in two ways.—**in two** asunder, so as to form two pieces; **in two twos, two ticks** (*slang*) in a moment; **two or three** a few. [O.E. *twā*, fem. and neut., two (masc. *twēgen*).]

twy- pfx. See **twi-.**

twyer, tuyère *twēr,* also *twir, twē-yer', ns.* a nozzle for a blast of air. [Fr. *tuyère*.]

Tyburn *tī'bǝrn, n.* the historic place of execution in London.

Tyche *tī'kē,* (*Gr. myth.*) *n.* the goddess of fortune.—*n.* **ty'chism** a theory that accepts pure chance. [Gr. *tychē*, chance.]

tycoon *tī-kōōn', n.* the title by which the Shoguns of Japan were known to foreigners: a business magnate. [Jap *taikun*, great prince—Old Chin *t'ai*, great, *kiun*, prince.]

tying *tī'ing, pr.p.* of **tie.**

tyke, tike *tīk,* (chiefly *Northern*) *n.* a dog: a cur: a rough-mannered fellow: a Yorkshireman [O.N. *tik*, bitch.]

Tylopoda *tī-lop'ǝ-dǝ, n.pl.* a section of the ungulates with padded toes—camels and llamas.—*n.* and *adj.* **ty'lopod.** [Gr *tylos*, a knob, callus, *pous, podos*, a foot.]

tymbal. Same as **timbal.**

tympan *tim'pan, n.* any instrument of the drum kind (*arch.*): a tympanum: a frame covered with parchment or cloth, on which sheets are placed for printing (*print.*): material placed between the platen and the paper to give an even impression (*print.*).—*adjs.* **tym'panal** (*anat., zool.*) of the tympanum; **tympanic** (*-pan'ik*) of or like a drum or tympanum: tympanitic.—*n.* a bone of the ear, supporting the drum-membrane.—*adj.* **tympaniform** (or *-pan'*) drum-shaped: drum-like.—*ns.* **tym'panist** a drummer (**tim'panist** one who plays the timpani); **tympani'tes** flatulent distension of the belly.—*adj.* **tympanitic** (*-it'ik*) of, affected with, tympanites.—*ns.* **tympani'tis** inflammation of the membrane of the ear; **tym'pano** (*pl. -i -ē*) a variant of **timpano**; **tym'panum** a drum: a drumhead: the middle ear: the membrane separating it from the outer ear—the drum: in insects a vibratory membrane in various parts of the body, serving as an eardrum: the recessed face of a pediment (*archit.*): a space between a lintel and an arch over it (*archit.*): a wheel for scooping up water:—*pl.* **tym'pana.** [L. *tympanum*—Gr. *tympanon, typanon,* a kettledrum—*typtein,* to strike.]

Tynwald *tin'wold, n.* the parliament of the Isle of Man. [O.N. *thing-völlr—thing,* assembly, *völlr,* field.]

type *tīp, n.* a mark or stamp: the device on a coin or medal: a distinguishing mark: insignia: a designation: an emblem: a foreshadowing: a model or pattern: a kind: the general character of a class: that which well exemplifies the characteristics of a group: a person of well-marked characteristics (*loosely* and *derogatorily*) a person: the actual specimen on which the description of a new species or genus is based (type **specimen**): a rectangular piece of metal or of wood on one end of which is cast or engraved a character, sign, etc., used in printing: printing types collectively, letter: print: lettering.—*adj.* serving as a type.—*v.t.* to prefigure, foreshadow: to symbolise: to be the type of: to determine the type of (*med.*): to exemplify: to typewrite.—*v.i.* to typewrite.—*adjs.* **ty'pal; typic** (*tip'*) typical; **typ'ical** pertaining to, or constituting, a type: emblematic: figurative: characteristic: representative.—*n.* **typical'ity.**—*adv.* **typ'ically.**—*ns.* **typ'icalness; typifica'tion; typ'ifier.**—*v.t.* **typify** (*tip'*) to make or be a type of:—*pr.p.* **typ'ifying;** *pa.t.* and *pa.p.* **typ'ified.**—*ns.* **typing** (*tīp'ing*); **typist** (*tīp'ist*) one who uses a typewriter: one whose occupation is typewriting; **typog'rapher** (*coll.* shortening **typo** (*ī'pō*)—*pl.* **ty'pos**) a compositor; a person engaged in or skilled in typography: a typographical error.—*adjs.* **typograph'ic, -al.**—*adv.* **typograph'ically.**—*ns.* **typog'raphist** one versed in the history or art of printing; **typog'raphy** the art or style of printing.—*adj.* **typolog'ical.**—*ns.* **typol'ogist; typol'ogy** the study of types and their succession in biology, archæology, etc.: the doctrine that things in the New Testament are foreshadowed symbolically in the Old.—*v.t.* **type'cast** to cast (someone) in a rôle that accords with what he is by nature: to cast continually for the same kind of part. —*p.adj.* **type'cast.**—**type'-face** the printing surface of a type: the manner in which it is cut: a complete range of type cut in a particular style; **type'-genus** the genus that gives name to its family; **type'-met'al** metal used for making types: an alloy of lead with antimony and tin, and sometimes copper; **type'script** typewritten matter or copy: type in imitation of handwriting or of typewriting.—*adj.* **typewritten.**—**type'setter** a

compositor: a machine for setting type; **type'setting; type'-species** a species taken as the one to which the generic name is primarily attached.—*v.t.* and *v.i.* **type'write** to print or copy with a typewriter.—**type'writer** a machine, usu. with a keyboard, for printing as a substitute for handwriting: a typist (*rare*); **type'writing.**—*adj.* **type'written.** [L. *typus*—Gr. *typos,* blow, mark, stamp, model; *typtein,* to strike.]

-type *-tīp, suff.* of the same type as: resembling. [type.]

typhlitis *tif-lī'tis, n.* inflammation of the blind-gut.— *adj.* **typhlitic** (*-lit'ik*). [Gr. *typhlos,* blind.]

typhoid *tī'foid, adj.* like typhus.—*n.* (for **typhoid fever**) enteric fever, long confounded with typhus, on account of the characteristic rash of rose-coloured spots.—*adj.* **typhoid'al.** [Gr. *typhōdēs,* delirious—*typhos,* a fever, *eidos,* likeness; cf. **typhus.**]

typhoon *tī-fōōn', n.* a violent cyclonic storm of the China seas and West Pacific area. [Gr. *typhōn,* a whirlwind; but partly also from Port. *tufāo*—Ar., Pers., Hind. *tūfān,* a hurricane, and partly from Chin. *t'ai fung,* a great wind.]

typhus *tī'fas, n.* a dangerous fever transmitted by lice and marked by the eruption of red spots.—*adjs.* **ty'phoid** (q.v.); **ty'phous.** [Latinised from Gr. *typhos,* fever, stupor, delusion.]

typical, typify, typist, typography, etc. See under **type.**

tyrant *tī'rant, n.* in the orig. Greek sense, an absolute ruler, or one whose power has not been constitutionally arrived at: now usu. a ruler who uses his power arbitrarily and oppressively: an oppressor: a bully.—*n.* **tyr'anness** a female tyrant.—*adjs.* **tyrannic** (*ti-ran'ik;* sometimes *tī-*), **-al.**—*adv.* **tyrann'ically.**—*n.* **tyrann'icalness.**—*adj.* **tyrannici'dal.**— **tyrann'icide** the killing or the killer of a tyrant.—*v.i.* **tyrannise, -ize** (*tir'*) to act as a tyrant: esp. to rule with oppressive severity.—*v.t.* to act the tyrant to.—*n.* **tyrannosaur(us)** (*-ran'a-sōr, -sōr'as*) a large bipedal carnivorous dinosaur common during the Cretaceous period.—*adj.* **tyrannous** (*tir'*) despotic: domineering: overpowering: oppressive.—*adv.* **tyr'annously.**—*n.* **tyranny** (*tir'*) absolute or illegally established power: the government or authority of a tyrant: absolute power cruelly administered: oppression: cruelty: harshness. [Gr. *tyrannos,* partly through O.Fr. *tirant* (Fr. *tyran*) and L. *tyrannus.*]

tyre *tīr, n.* a variant spelling of **tire**[1]: a rubber band, cushion, or tube round a wheel-rim.—*adjs.* **tyred;** **tyre'less.—tubeless tyre** a pneumatic tyre that has no inner tube, and, being self-sealing, deflates only slowly when punctured. [See **tire**[1].]

Tyrian *tir'i-an, adj.* of Tyre: red or purple, like the dye formerly prepared at the ancient Mediterranean port of Tyre.—*n.* a native of Tyre.

tyro. See **tiro.**

Tyrolese *tir-a-lēz', adj.* relating to the mountainous west Austrian province of Tyrol (Tirol), or to its people.—*n.* a native of Tyrol.—*n.* and *adj.* **Tyrolê'an** (or *tir-ō'li-an*).

tyrosine *tī'rō-sēn, n.* an amino-acid formed by decomposition of proteins, first got from cheese. [Gr. *tyros,* cheese.]

tzar. See **tsar.**

tzigany *tsig'ä-ni, -a-ni, -ny', n.* a Hungarian gypsy.— Also *adj.*—Also **tzigane** (*tsi-gän'*). [Hung. *cigány,* gypsy.]

U

U, u *ū*, *n.* the twenty-first letter in our alphabet —*adj* (*cap.*; of words, phrases, customs, etc) ordinarily used by, found in, the upper classes.—*adj* **non'-U** not so used or found (U for *upper* class).—**U'-boat** a German submarine (Ger. *Unterseeboot*), **U'-bolt, U'-trap, U'-tube** a bolt, drain-trap, tube, bent like the letter U.—*adj.* **U'-shaped.**—**U'-turn** a turn made by a vehicle which reverses its direction of travel, crossing into the oncoming traffic on the other side of the road: any reversal of direction (*fig.*).

ubiety *ū-bī'i-ti*, *n.* the state of being in a definite place, whereness: location [L. *ubi*, where.]

ubiquity *ū-bik'wi-ti*, *n.* existence everywhere at the same time: omnipresence.—*adj.* **ubiq'uitous** to be found everywhere.—*adv.* **ubiq'uitously.** [L. *ubīque*, everywhere—*ubi*, where.]

udder *ud'ər*, *n.* the organ containing the mammary glands of the cow, mare, etc.: a dug or teat.—*adj* **udd'ered.** [O.E. *ūder*.]

udometer *ū-dom'i-tər*, *n.* a name for a rain-gauge —*adj.* **udomet'ric.** [Through Fr.—L *ūdus*, wet, Gr *metron*, a measure.]

ufology *ōō-fol'ə-ji*, *n.* the study of unidentified *flying objects*, such as flying saucers.—*n.* **ufol'ogist.** [Formed from initials U F O and -*logy*.]

ugh *uhh*, *ug*, *ōōh*, *ûh*, *interj.* an exclamation of repugnance.—*n* used as a representation of a cough or grunt.

ugli *ug'li*, *n.* a cross between the grapefruit and the tangerine, or its fruit [*ugly*; from the fruit's unprepossessing appearance]

ugly *ug'li*, *adj.* offensive to the sight or other sense, or to refined taste or moral feeling: ill-natured: threatening: disquieting: suggesting suspicion of evil —*n* **ugliftca'tion.**—*v.t* **ug'lify** to make ugly —*adv.* **ug'lily.**—*n.* **ug'liness.**—**ugly duckling** a despised member of a family or group who later proves the most successful [O N. *uggligr*, frightful, *uggr*, fear.]

Ugrian *ū'gri-ən*, *ōō'*, *adj* of that division of the Finno-Ugrian languages and peoples that includes the Magyars, Ostyaks, and Voguls.—Also *n.*—*adjs* **U'gric; U'gro-Finn'ic** Finno-Ugrian.

uhlan *ōō'län*, *ū'*, *n.* a light cavalryman in semi-oriental uniform: a Prussian lancer. [Ger. *Uhlan*—Polish *ulan*, orig a light Tatar horseman—Turk *oğlān*, a young man]

uhuru *ōō-hōō'rōō*, *n.* freedom (e.g. from slavery): national independence. [Swahili—*huru*, free]

uitlander *œ'*, *ā'it-land-ər* (chiefly *hist.*) *n.* a foreigner (orig. a British person in the Transvaal or Orange Free State). [Du. equivalent of **outlander**.]

ukase *ū-kāz'*, -*kās'*, *n.* an edict with force of law in Tsarist Russia: an edict issued by the Supreme Soviet: any arbitrary decree. [Russ. *ukaz*.]

ukelele. A common spelling of **ukulele.**

Ukrainian *ū-krān'i-ən*, *n.* a native or citizen of (the) *Ukraine*, a republic of the U.S.S.R., a rich agricultural region in S.W. Russia: its language.—Also *adj.*

ukulele *ū-kə-lā'li*, *ōō-kōō-lä'lä*, *n.* a small, usually four-stringed, guitar. [Hawaiian, jumping flea.]

ulcer *ul'sər*, *n.* an open sore discharging pus: a continuing source of evil, pain or corruption, an unsound element (*fig.*).—*v.i.* **ul'cerate** to form an ulcer.—*v.t.* to cause an ulcer in: to affect with insidious corruption.—*n* **ulcera'tion.**—*adjs.* **ul'cerative; ul'cered; ul'cerous.**—*adv* **ul'cerously.**—*n* **ul'cerousness.** [L *ulcus, ulcĕris*]

ulema *ōō'li-mə*, *n* the body of professional theologians, expounders of the law, in a Muslim country: a member of such a body. [Ar *'ulema*, pl. of *'ālim*, learned]

uliginous *ū-lij'i-nəs*, *adj* slimy: oozy: swampy: growing in swampy places [L. *ūlīginōsus—ūlīgō*, -*inis*, moisture.]

ulitis *ū-lī'tis*, *n.* inflammation of the gums. [Gr. *oula*, gums, -*itis*.]

ullage *ul'ij*, *n.* the quantity a vessel lacks of being full, or sometimes the amount left in the vessel: loss by evaporation or leakage: dregs (*slang*) [A.Fr. *ulliage*, O.Fr. *eullage—œiller*, to fill up.]

ulna *ul'nə*, *n.* the inner and larger of the two bones of the forearm:—*pl* **ul'nae** (-*nē*) —*adj.* **ul'nar.** [L. *ulna*, elbow, arm.]

ulosis *ū-lō'sis*, *n.* the formation of a scar [Gr *oulōsis —oulē*, a scar]

ulotrichous *ū-lot'ri-kəs*, *adj* woolly-haired —*n* **ulot'-richy** (-*ki*) woolly-hairedness [Gr. *oulos*, woolly, *thrix, trichos*, hair]

ulster *ul'stər*, *n* a long loose overcoat.—*adj.* **ul'stered** wearing an ulster. [First made in *Ulster*, Ireland]

ult. See **ultimate.**

ulterior *ul-tē'ri-ər*, *adj.* on the further side· beyond: in the future: remoter· (of e.g. a motive) beyond what is avowed or apparent —*adv.* **ultē'riorly.** [L *ulterior* —*ultrā* (adv and prep), *uls* (prep), beyond.]

ultima *ul'ti-mə*, *n.* the last syllable of a word [L , fem of *ultimus*, last.]

ultimate *ul'ti-māt*, -*mit*, *adj.* furthest· last· final· fundamental: maximum· most important· limiting.—*n* a final point: a fundamental.—*n* **ul'timacy** (-*mə-si*).—*adv* **ul'timately.**—*n* **ultimā'tum** final terms: a last offer or demand: a last word:—*pl.* **ultimā'ta.**—*adj.* **ul'timo** (*abbrev.* **ult.**) in the last (month) —*n* **ultimogeniture** (-*jen'*) succession of the youngest —**the ultimate deterrent** the hydrogen bomb [L. *ultimus*, last.]

ultra- *ul'trə-*, *pfx* (1) beyond in place, position (as **ultra-Neptunian** beyond the planet Neptune). (2) beyond the limit, range, etc., of (as **ultra-microscopic**): (3) beyond the ordinary, or excessive(ly) (as **ul'tra-Conserv'ative, ul'tra-Conserv'atism, ul'tra-fash'ionable, ul'tra-mod'ern, ul'tra-Prot'estant**) —*adj* **ul'tra** extreme, esp in royalism, fashion, or religious or political opinion —*n* an extremist —*ns*. **ultraism** (*ul'trə-izm*) (an) extreme principle(s), opinion(s), or measure(s): *adj.* **ul'traist.** [L. *ultrā*, beyond]

ultracentrifuge *ul-trə-sen'tri-fūj*, *n.* a very fast-running type of centrifuge. [Pfx **ultra-** (2)]

ultrafiche *ul'trə-fēsh*, *n.* a sheet of microfilm the same size as a microfiche but with a greater number of microcopied records on it. [Pfx. **ultra-** (3)]

ultra-high *ul-trə-hī'*, *adj* very high —**ultra-high frequency** see **frequency.** [Pfx **ultra-** (3).]

ultraism, ultraist. See **ultra-.**

ultramarine *ul-trə-mə-rēn'*, *adj.* overseas: from overseas: deep blue —*n.* a deep blue pigment, orig made from lapis-lazuli brought from beyond the sea: its colour. [L. *ultrā*, beyond, *marīnus*, marine.]

ultramicro- *ul-trə-mī-krō-*, *pfx.* smaller than, dealing with smaller quantities than, **micro-**, e.g. *n.* **ultramicrochem'istry** chemistry dealing with minute quantities.

ultramicroscope *ul-trə-mī'krə-skōp*, *n.* a microscope with strong illumination from the side, whereby the presence of ultramicroscopic objects can be observed through the scattering of light from them.—*adj.* **ultramicroscopic** (*-skop'ik*) too small to be visible under the ordinary microscope: pertaining to ultramicroscopy.—*n.* **ultramicroscopy** (*-kros'kə-pi*). [Pfx. **ultra-** (2).]

ultramontane *ul-trə-mon'tān*, *adj.* beyond the mountains (i.e. the Alps): extreme in favouring the Pope's supremacy.—*ns.* **ultramon'tanism** (*-tən-izm*); **ultramon'tanist**. [L. *ultra*, beyond, *montānus—mōns*, *montis*, a mountain.]

ultramundane *ul-trə-mun'dān*, *adj.* beyond the world, or beyond the limits of our system. [Pfx. **ultra-** (1).]

ultrashort *ul'trə-shört'*, *adj.* (of electromagnetic waves) of less than ten metres' wavelength. [Pfx. **ultra-** (3).]

ultrasonic *ul-trə-son'ik*, *adj.* pertaining to, or (of an instrument or process) using, vibrations of the same nature as audible sound waves but of greater frequency.—*n.sing.* **ultrason'ics** the study of such vibrations, used medically for diagnostic and therapeutic purposes.—*n.* **ultrasonography** (*-sən-og'rə-fi*) the directing of ultrasonic waves through body tissues to detect abnormalities. [Pfx. **ultra-** (2).]

ultrasound *ul'trə-sownd'*, *n.* sound vibrations too rapid to be audible, useful esp. in medical diagnosis. [Pfx. **ultra-** (2).]

ultrastructure *ul'trə-struk'chər*, *n.* the ultimate structure of protoplasm at a lower level than can be examined microscopically. [Pfx. **ultra-** (2).]

ultraviolet *ul-trə-vī'ə-lit*, *adj.* beyond the violet end of the visible spectrum: pertaining to, or using, radiations of wavelengths less than those of visible light. [Pfx. **ultra-** (1).]

ultra vires *ul'trə vī'rēz*, *ōōl'trä wē'räs*, (L.) beyond one's powers or authority.

ululate *ūl'ū-lāt*, also *ul'*, *v.i.* to hoot or screech.—*adj.* **ul'ulant**.—*n.* **ulula'tion** howling, wailing. [L. *ŭlŭlāre*, *-ātum*, to hoot.]

um *əm*, *um*, *interj.* expressing hesitation in speech.

umbel *um'bəl*, *n.* a flat-topped inflorescence in which the flower stalks all spring from about the same point in an axis.—*adjs.* **um'bellate**, **-d** constituting an umbel: having umbels.—*adv.* **um'bellately**.—*n.* **umbellifer** (*um-bel'i-fər*) any plant of the Umbelliferae.—*n.pl.* **Umbellif'erae** the carrot and hemlock family of plants with umbels, schizocarpic fruit, leaves with sheathing bases.—*adj.* **umbellif'erous**. [L. *umbella*, a sunshade, dim. of *umbra*, a shade.]

umber *um'bər*, *n.* a brown earthy mineral (hydrated oxides of iron and manganese) used as a pigment.—*v.t.* to colour with umber.—*adj.* brown like umber.—*adjs.* **um'bered**, **um'bery**. [It. *terra d'ombra*, shadow earth, or poss. Umbrian earth.]

umbilicus *um-bil'i-kəs*, *um-bi-lī'kəs*, *n.* the navel: a depression at the base of a shell: a small depression.—*adjs.* **umbilical** (*-bil'*; sometimes *-bi-lī'*) relating to the umbilicus or the umbilical cord; **umbil'icate** navel-like: having a depression like a navel.—**umbilical cord** a long flexible tube connecting the foetus to the placenta: an electrical cable or other servicing line attached to a rocket vehicle or spacecraft during preparations for launch: the lifeline of an astronaut outside his vehicle in space by which he receives air

and communicates with the vehicle: any similar connection of fundamental importance. [L. *umbilīcus*, the navel.]

umbles *um'blz*, *n.pl.* entrails (liver, heart, etc.), esp. of a deer.—Also **hum'bles.**—**um'ble-pie'** also **hum'ble-pie'** a pie made from the umbles of a deer. [O.Fr. *nombles*, from *lomble*, loin.]

umbo *um'bō*, *n.* the boss of a shield: a knob: the protuberant solid part of a bivalve shell: a knob on a toadstool cap:—*pl.* **umbō'nes**, **um'bos.**—*adjs.* **um'bonal** (*-bən-əl*); **um'bonate** (*bot.*) having a central boss.—*n.* **umbona'tion**. [L. *umbō*, *-ōnis*.]

umbra *um'brə*, *n.* a shadow: the darker part of the shadow or dark inner cone projected in an eclipse (*astron.*): the darker part of a spot.—*adjs.* **um'bral** of an umbra; **umbratile** (*um'brə-til*, *-til*), **umbratilous** (*-brat'i-ləs*) shadowy: shaded: shade-giving: indoor: secluded; **umbrif'erous** shade-giving; **umbrose** (*-brōs'*) shade-giving: dusky; **um'brous** shaded. [L. *umbra*, shade, shadow, dim. *umbrāculum*, adj. *umbrātilis*.]

umbrage *um'brij*, *n.* shade, shadow: that which casts a shade: suspicion of injury: offence.—*adj.* **umbra'geous** shady or forming a shade. [Fr. *ombrage*—L. *umbrāticum* (neut. adj.)—*umbra*, a shadow.]

umbral . . . umbratilous. See umbra.

umbrella *um-brel'ə*, *n.* a portable shelter against sun, rain, etc., now usu. a canopy with a sliding framework of ribs on a stick: anything of similar form: a protection (*fig.*): a general cover (*fig.*): a cover of fighter aircraft for ground forces (*mil.*).—*adjs.* **umbrella** covering many or a variety of things; **umbrell'aed**, **umbrell'a'd** with an umbrella.—**umbrell'a-fir** a Japanese conifer with radiating tufts of needles; **umbrell'a-stand** a rack or receptacle for closed umbrellas and walking-sticks; **umbrell'a-tree** a tree of any kind with leaves or branches arranged umbrella-wise, esp. a small magnolia. [It. *ombrella*, *ombrello*—*ombra*, a shade—L. *umbra*.]

Umbrian *um'bri-ən*, *adj.* of *Umbria*, in central Italy.—*n.* a native thereof: an Indo-European language akin to Oscan.

umbriferous, **umbrose**, **umbrous**. See umbra.

umiak, **oomia(c)k**, **oomiac** *ōō'mi-ak*, *ōō'm'yak*, *n.* an open skin boat. [Eskimo.]

umlaut *ōōm'lowt*, *n.* a vowel-change brought about by a vowel or semivowel (esp. *i*, *j*) in the following syllable: (*loosely*) the two dots placed over a letter representing an umlauted vowel in German. [Ger.,—*um*, around, *Laut*, sound.]

umpire *um'pīr*, *n.* a third person called in to decide a dispute or a deadlock: an arbitrator: an impartial person chosen to supervise the game, enforce the rules, and decide disputes (*cricket*, etc.).—Also *v.i.* and *v.t.* [M.E. *noumpere*, *oumper*—O.Fr. *nomper—non*, not, *per*, pair, peer, equal.]

umpteen *um(p)'tēn*, **umpty** *um(p)'ti*, (*slang*) *adjs.* an indefinitely large number.—*adjs.* **ump'teenth**, **ump'tieth** latest or last of many. [*Umpty* in Morse, a dash, from its sound on a telegraph key.]

un, **'un** *un*, *ən*, (*dial.*) *pron.* for **one**: also for **him**. [O.E. accus. *hine*.]

There is hardly a limit to words with prefix un-, *and only a selection is given below. Words from un-abashed to unzoned are listed continuously, either in the text or at the foot of the page, and words beginning with un- in which un- is not a prefix follow after these.*

un- *un-*, *pfx.* (1) meaning 'not' (in many cases, the resultant word is more than a mere negation; it has a positive force; e.g. **unkind** usu. means 'cruel' rather than just 'not kind'): (2) indicating a reversal of process, removal, or deprivation: (3) merely emphasising reversal or deprivation already expressed by the simple word, as in **unloose**. (Partly O.E. *un-*, neg.; cf. Ger. *un-*, L. *in-*, Gr. *an-*, *a-*; partly O.E. *on-* (or *un-*), the unstressed form of *and-*; cf. Ger. *ent-*, Gr. *anti*, against).—*adjs.* **unaba'ted** not made less in degree; **una'ble** not able: not having sufficient strength, power, or skill (to do); **unaccent'ed** without accent or stress in pronunciation: not marked with an accent; **unaccomm'odated** unprovided; **unaccomm'odating** not compliant; **unaccom'panied** not accompanied, escorted, or attended: having no instrumental accompaniment (*mus.*); **unaccom'plished** not achieved: lacking accomplishments; **unaccount'able** difficult or impossible to explain: not answerable (to a higher authority): (of a person) puzzling in character.—*adv.* **unaccount'ably** inexplicably.—*adjs.* **unaccount'ed-for** unexplained: not included in an account; **unaccus'tomed** not customary: not habituated.—*n.* **unaccus'tomedness.**—*adjs.* **unacknowl'edged** not acknowledged, recognised, confessed, or noticed; **unacquaint'ed** not on a footing of acquaintance: ignorant of (with *with*): uninformed; **unact'ed** not performed; **unadop'ted** not adopted (**unadopted road** a road for the repairing, maintenance, etc., of which the Local Authority is not responsible); **unadul'terāte, -d** unmixed, pure, genuine; **unadvised'** not advised: without advice: not prudent or discreet: ill-judged.—*adv.* **unadvis'edly.**—*n.* **unadvis'edness.**—*adj.* **unaffect'ed** not affected or influenced: untouched by emotion: without affection: not assumed: plain: real: sincere.—*adv.* **unaffect'edly.**—*n.* **unaffect'edness.**—*adjs.* **unallied'** not akin: without allies; **unalloyed'** not alloyed or mixed, pure (*lit.* and *fig.*); **un-Amer'ican** not in accordance with American character, ideas, feeling, or traditions: disloyal, against American interests; **unan'swerable** impossible to answer: not to be refuted, conclusive.—*adv.* **unan'swerably.**—*adjs.* **unan'swered** not answered: unrequited; **unapproach'able** out of reach, inaccessible: stand-offish: in-

accessible to advances or intimacy: beyond rivalry.—*n.* **unapproach'ableness.**—*adv.* **unapproach'ably.**—*adjs.* **unappro'priated** not taken possession of: not applied to some purpose: not granted to any person, corporation, etc.; **unapt'** unfitted: unsuitable: not readily inclined or accustomed (to): lacking in aptitude, slow.—*adv.* **unapt'ly.**—*n.* **unapt'ness.**—*adjs.* **unarmed'** without weapons: defenceless: unprotected: unaided or without accessory apparatus: without arms or similar limbs or appendages; **unasked'** not asked: not asked for: uninvited; **unassum'ing** making no assumption: unpretentious, modest.—*adv.* **unassum'ingly.**—*n.* **unassum'ingness.**—*adjs.* **unattached'** not attached: not belonging to a club, party, college, diocese, department, regiment, etc.: not married or about to be; **unattend'ed** not accompanied or attended; **unavail'able** not available; **unavail'ing** of no avail or effect, useless.—*n.* **unavoidabil'ity.**—*adj.* **unavoid'able** not to be avoided: inevitable.—*n.* **unavoid'ableness.**—*adv.* **unavoid'ably.**—*adj.* **unaware'** not aware.—*n.* **unaware'ness.**—*adv.* **unawares'** without being, or making, aware: without being perceived: unexpectedly.

Words with prefix un- (*continued*)
   adj. **unbacked'** without a back: without backing or backers: unaided.—*n.* **unbal'ance** want of balance.—*v.t.* to throw off balance: to derange.—*adjs.* **unbal'anced** not in a state of equipoise: without mental balance, erratic or deranged: (of e.g. a view, judgment) not giving due weight to all features of the situation: not adjusted so as to show balance of debtor and creditor (*book-k.*); **unbanked** not deposited in, provided with, or having, a bank.—*v.t.* **unbar'** to remove a bar from or of: to unfasten.—*adj.* **unbear'able** intolerable.—*n.* **unbear'ableness.**—*adv.* **unbear'ably.**—*adj.* **unbecom'ing** unsuitable: not suited to the wearer, or not showing her, him to advantage: (of behaviour, etc.) not befitting, unseemly (with *to*, *in*).—*adv.* **unbecom'ingly.**—*n.*

---

unabashed' *adj.* un- (1).
unabbrev'iated *adj.* un- (1).
unabridged' *adj.* un- (1).
unabsolved' *adj.* un- (1).
unacadem'ic *adj.* un- (1).
unaccen'tuated *adj.* un- (1).
unaccept'able *adj.* un- (1).
unaccept'ableness *n.* un- (1).
unaccred'ited *adj.* un- (1).
unachiev'able *adj.* un- (1).
unadapt'able *adj.* un- (1).
unadapt'ed *adj.* un- (1).
unaddressed' *adj.* un- (1).
unadjust'ed *adj.* un- (1).
unadorned' *adj.* un- (1).
unadvent'urous *adj.* un- (1).
unafraid' *adj.* un- (1).
unaid'ed *adj.* un- (1).
unaimed' *adj.* un- (1).
unaired' *adj.* un- (1).
unalike' *adj.* un- (1).
unallott'ed *adj.* un- (1).
unallow'able *adj.* un- (1).
unal'terable *adj.* un- (1).
unal'terably *adv.* un- (1).
unal'tered *adj.* un- (1).
unambig'uous *adj.* un- (1).
unambig'uously *adv.* un- (1).
unambi'tious *adj.* un- (1).
unambi'tiously *adv.* un- (1).

unamend'ed *adj.* un- (1).
unamused' *adj.* un- (1).
unamū'sing *adj.* un- (1).
unamū'singly *adv.* un- (1).
unanalys'able -*z- adj.* un- (1).
unan'alysed, -z- *adj.* un- (1).
unanalyt'ic, -al *adjs.* un- (1).
unanch'ored *adj.* un- (1).
unann'otated *adj.* un- (1).
unannounced' *adj.* un- (1).
unappar'ent *adj.* un- (1).
unapp'etising, -z- *adj.* un- (1).
unapp'licable *adj.* un- (1).
unapplied' *adj.* un- (1).
unappre'ciated *adj.* un- (1).
unappre'ciative *adj.* un- (1).
unar'guable *adj.* un- (1).
unartifi'cial *adj.* un- (1).
unartifi'cially *adv.* un- (1).
unascend'ed *adj.* un- (1).
unascertain'able *adj.* un- (1).
unascertained' *adj.* un- (1).
unashamed' *adj.* un- (1).
unasham'edly *adv.* un- (1).
unas'pirated *adj.* un- (1).
unassail'able *adj.* un- (1).
unasser'tive *adj.* un- (1).
unassigned' *adj.* un- (1).
unassim'ilated *adj.* un- (1).
unassist'ed *adj.* un- (1).

unassist'edly *adv.* un- (1).
unassist'ing *adj.* un- (1).
unasso'ciated *adj.* un- (1).
unassuaged' *adj.* un- (1).
unatōned' *adj.* un- (1).
unattain'able *adj.* un- (1).
unattain'ableness *n.* un- (1).
unattain'ably *adv.* un- (1).
unattained' *adj.* un- (1).
unattend'ing *adj.* un- (1).
unattest'ed *adj.* un- (1).
unattired' *adj.* un- (1).
unattract'ive *adj.* un- (1).
unattract'ively *adv.* un- (1).
unattract'iveness *n.* un- (1).
unauthen'tic *adj.* un- (1).
**unau'thorised, -z- adj.* un- (1).
unauthor'itative *adj.* un- (1).
unavowed' *adj.* un- (1).
unavow'edly *adv.* un- (1).
unawāk'ened *adj.* un- (1).
unawed' *adj.* un- (1).
unbait'ed *adj.* un- (1).
unband'ed *adj.* un- (1).
unbarred' *adj.* un- (1).
unbathed' *adj.* un- (1).
unbāthed' *adj.* un- (1).
unbeat'able *adj.* un- (1).
unbeat'en *adj.* un- (1).
unbefitt'ing *adj.* un- (1)

Words beginning with pfx. **un-** *are listed first* (pp. 1079 ff.); *other UN- words follow* (pp. 1092 ff.)

For other sounds see detailed chart of pronunciation.

unbecom'ingness.—*adjs.* unbegot'; unbegott'en not yet begotten: existing independent of any generating cause; unbeknown', unbeknownst' (*coll.*) unknown. —*advs.* unobserved, without being known.—*n.* un'belief (or -*lēf'*) disbelief, or withholding of belief, esp. in accepted religion.—*adj.* unbeliev'able incredible: (*loosely*) astonishing, remarkable.—*adv.* unbeliev'ably.—*n.* unbeliev'er one who does not believe, esp. in the prevailing religion: a habitually incredulous person.—*adj.* unbeliev'ing.—*adv.* unbeliev'ingly.—*v.t.* unbelt' to ungird.—*adj.* unbelt'ed without a belt: freed from a belt.—*v.t.* unbend' to relax from a bending tension, as a bow: to straighten: to undo, unfasten (*naut.*).—*v.i.* to become relaxed: to behave with freedom from stiffness, to be affable. —*adjs.* unbend'ed; unbend'ing not bending: unyielding: resolute.—*n.* a relaxing.—*adv.* unbend'ingly.— *n.* unbend'ingness.—*adjs.* unbent' not bent: relaxed: not overcome; unbi'ased (sometimes unbi'assed).— *adv.* unbi'as(s)edly.—*adj.* unbidd'en not bid or commanded: uninvited: spontaneous.—*v.t.* unbind' to remove a band from: to loose: to set free.—*n.* unbind'ing the removal of a band or bond: a loosing: a setting free.—*adj.* loosening: not binding.—*adj.* unblink'ing without blinking: not wavering: not showing emotion, esp. fear.—*adv.* unblink'ingly.— *adj.* unblush'ing not blushing: without shame: impudent.—*adv.* unblush'ingly.—*v.t.* unbolt' to draw back a bolt from.—*adjs.* unbolt'ed unfastened by withdrawing a bolt: not fastened by bolts: not separated by bolting or sifting: coarse; unborn' not yet born: non-existent.—*v.t.* unbo'som to pour out, tell freely (what is in the mind): (*refl.*) to confide freely (also *v.i.*).—*adjs.* unbound' not bound: loose: without binding (also *pa.t.* and *pa.p.* of unbind, freed from bonds); unbound'ed not limited: boundless: having no check or control.—*adv.* unbound'edly.—*n.* unbound'edness.—*adj.* unbowed' not bowed or bent: not vanquished or overcome, free.—*v.t.* unbri'dle to free from the bridle: to free from (usu. politic) restraint.—*adj.* unbri'dled not bridled: unrestrained.— *n.* unbri'dledness.—*adjs.* un-Brit'ish not in accordance with British character or traditions; unbrō'ken not broken: (of a record) not surpassed: uninterrupted: not thrown into disorder: not variegated: not infringed.—*adv.* unbrō'kenly.—*n.* unbrō'kenness.— *v.t.* unbuck'le to unfasten the buckle(s) of: to unfasten.—*v.i.* to undo the buckle(s) of a garment, etc : to unbend (*fig.*).—*v.i.* and *v.t.* unbun'dle to price and sell separately the constituents of a larger package of products or services.—*n.* unbun'dling.—*v.t.* unbur'den to free from a burden: to discharge, cast off, as a burden: (*refl.*) to tell one's secrets or anxieties freely. —*adj.* unbur'dened not burdened: relieved of a burden.—*v.t.* unbutt'on to loose the buttons of.— *v.i.* to loose one's buttons: to unbend and tell one's thoughts.—*adj.* unbutt'oned without a button: with buttons loosed: in a relaxed confidential state.

Words with prefix un- (*continued*).

adj. uncalled'-for (or uncalled for) not required, unnecessary: unprovoked: offensively or aggressively gratuitous.—*adv.* uncann'ily.—*n.* uncann'iness.— *adj.* uncann'y weird, supernatural: (of e.g. skill) much greater than one would expect from an ordinary human being.—*v.t.* uncap' to remove a cap from.— *v.i.* to take off one's cap.—*adjs.* uncared'-for (uncared for) neglected: showing signs of neglect; uncar'ing without anxiety, concern, or caution; unceas'ing ceaseless: never-ending.—*adv* unceas'ingly.—*adjs.* unceremō'nious informal: off-hand.— *adv.* unceremō'niously.—*n.* unceremō'niousness.— *adj.* uncer'tain not certain (of, about): not definitely known or decided: subject to doubt or question (in no uncertain terms unambiguously): not to be depended upon: subject to vicissitude: hesitant, lacking confidence.—*adv.* uncer'tainly.—*ns.* uncer'tainness; uncer'tainty (uncertainty principle the principle that it is not possible to measure accurately at the same time both position and velocity).—*v.t.* unchain' to release

---

unbefriend'ed *adj.* un- (1).
unbeloved' (or -*luv'id*), *adj.* un- (1).
unbestowed' *adj.* un- (1).
unbetrayed' *adj.* un- (1).
unbett'ered *adj.* un- (1).
unblām'able *adj.* un- (1).
unblām'ably *adv.* un- (1).
unblāmed' *adj.* un- (1).
unbleached' *adj.* un- (1).
unblem'ished *adj.* un- (1).
unblend'ed *adj.* un- (1).
unblock' *v.t.* un- (2).
unblood'ed *adj.* un- (1).
unblood'ied *adj.* un- (1).
unblunt'ed *adj.* un- (1).
unbranched' *adj.* un- (1).
unbreached' *adj.* un- (1).
unbreak'able *adj.* un- (1).
unbrīb'able *adj.* un- (1).
unbridged' *adj.* un- (1).
unbroth'erly *adj.* un- (1).
unbudg'eted *adj.* un- (1).
unburned', unburnt' (or *un'*), *adjs.* un- (1).
unbus'inesslike *adj.* un- (1).
unbutt'ered *adj.* un- (1).
uncage' *v.t.* un- (2).
uncal'culated *adj.* un- (1).
uncal'culating *adj.* un- (1).
uncan'did *adj.* un- (1).

uncan'didly *adv.* un- (1).
uncan'didness *n.* un- (1).
uncan'onised, -z- *adj.* un- (1).
uncapsīz'able *adj.* un- (1).
uncar'peted *adj.* un- (1).
uncart' *v.t.* un- (2).
uncashed' *adj.* un- (1).
uncat'alogued *adj.* un- (1).
uncaught' *adj.* un- (1).
uncel'ebrated *adj.* un- (1).
uncen'sored *adj.* un- (1).
uncen'sured *adj.* un- (1).
uncertif'icated *adj.* un- (1).
unchall'engeable *adj.* un- (1).
unchall'engeably *adv.* un- (1).
unchall'enged *adj.* un- (1).
unchange'able *adj.* un- (1).
unchange'ableness *n.* un- (1).
unchange'ably *adv.* un- (1).
unchanged' *adj.* un- (1).
unchang'ing *adj.* un- (1).
unchang'ingly *adv.* un- (1).
unchap'eroned *adj.* un- (1).
uncharacterist'ic *adj.* un- (1).
unchar'itable *adj.* un- (1).
unchar'itableness *n.* un- (1).
unchar'itably *adv.* un- (1).
unchaste' *adj.* un- (1).
unchastised', -z- *adj.* un- (1).
uncheered' *adj.* un- (1).

uncheer'ful *adj.* un- (1).
uncheer'fully *adv.* un- (1).
uncheer'fulness *n.* un- (1).
unchewed' *adj.* un- (1).
unchiv'alrous *adj.* un- (1).
unchō'sen *adj.* un- (1).
unchron'icled *adj.* un- (1).
unclaimed' *adj.* un- (1).
unclear' *adj.* un- (1).
uncleared' *adj.* un- (1).
unclear'ly *adv.* un- (1).
unclear'ness *n.* un- (1).
unclench' *v.t.* and *v.t.* un- (2).
unclutt'ered *adj.* un- (1).
uncollect'ed *adj* un- (1).
uncol'oured *adj.* un- (1).
uncombed' *adj.* un- (1).
uncommer'cial *adj.* un- (1).
uncommū'nicable *adj.* un- (1).
uncommū'nicated *adj.* un- (1).
uncommū'nicative *adj.* un- (1).
uncommū'nicativeness *n.* un- (1).
uncommū'ted *adj.* un- (1).
uncompact'ed *adj.* un- (1).
uncompas'sionate *adj.* un- (1).
uncompelled' *adj.* un- (1).
uncom'pensated *adj.* un- (1).
uncompet'itive *adj.* un- (1).
uncomplain'ing *adj.* un- (1).
uncomplain'ingly *adv.* un- (1).

Words beginning with pfx. un- *are listed first* (pp. 1079 ff.); *other* UN- *words follow* (pp. 1092 ff.).

from a chain: to remove a chain from: to let loose.— *adjs.* **unchained'; uncharged'** not charged; **unchart'ed** (*lit.* and *fig.*) not mapped in detail: not shown in a chart; **unchart'ered** not holding a charter: unauthorised; **unchecked'** not checked or verified: not restrained; **unchris'tian** against the spirit of Christianity: uncharitable: unreasonable, outrageous (*coll.*).—*adv.* **unchris'tianly.**—*adjs.* **uncir'cumcised** not circumcised: gentile: unpurified (*fig.*); **unciv'il** discourteous: unseemly; **unciv'ilised, -z-** not civilised: away from civilised communities.—*adv.* **unciv'illy.**— *v.t.* **unclasp'** to loose from a clasp: to relax from clasping: to open.—*adjs.* **unclass'ified** not classified: of a road, minor, not classified as a motorway, A-road or B-road: not on the security list; **unclean** (*-klēn'*) not clean: foul: ceremonially impure: lewd; **uncleaned'** not cleaned.—*n.* **uncleanliness** (*-klen'*).—*adj.* **uncleanly** (*-klen'*).—*adv.* (*-klēn'*).—*n.* **uncleanness** (*-klēn'nis*).—*adj.* **uncleansed** (*-klenzd'*).—*v.t.* **unclog'** to free from a clog or obstruction.—*adj.* **unclogged'** not clogged.—*v.t.* and *v.i.* **unclose** (*un-klōz'*) to open.—*adjs.* **unclose** (*un-klōs'*) not close, **unclosed** (*un-klōzd'*) not closed: unenclosed: opened.—*v.t.* **unclothe'** to take the clothes off: to divest of covering.—*adj.* **unclothed'.**—*v.t.* and *v.i* **uncloud'** to clear of clouds or obscurity.—*adjs.* **uncloud'ed** free from clouds, obscurity or gloom: calm; **uncom'fortable** feeling, involving, or causing discomfort or disquiet.—*n.* **uncom'fortableness.**— *adv.* **uncom'fortably.**—*adjs.* **uncommitt'ed** not pledged to support any party, policy or action: impartial: not committed; **uncomm'on** not common: unusual: remarkable: great: strange.—*adv.* **uncommm'only** rarely (esp. *not uncommonly*, frequently): in an unusually great degree.—*n.* **uncomm'onness.**— *adjs.* **uncom'plicated** straightforward, not made difficult by the variety of factors involved: (of a person) simple in character and outlook; **uncompliment'ary** not at all complimentary, derogatory; **uncompound'ed** not compounded, unmixed; **uncom'promising**

refusing to compromise: unyielding: out-and-out.— *adv.* **uncom'promisingly.**—*ns.* **uncom'promisingness; unconcern'** want of concern or anxiety: indifference. —*adj.* **unconcerned'** not concerned, not involved (in): impartial: uninterested: indifferent: untroubled, carelessly secure.—*adv.* **unconcern'edly.**— *adj.* **uncondi'tional** not conditional: absolute, unlimited.—*adv.* **uncondi'tionally.**—*n.* **uncondi'- tionalness.**—*adjs.* **uncondi'tioned** not subject to condition or limitation: infinite, absolute, unknowable (of a person, response) not conditioned by learning or experience: not put into the required state; **uncon'- scionable** (of a person) unscrupulous' not conformable to conscience: outrageous, inordinate.—*adv* **uncon'scionably.**—*adj.* **uncon'scious** without consciousness: unaware (of): not self-conscious—*n.* (with **the**) the deepest, inaccessible level of the psyche in which are present in dynamic state repressed impulses and memories.—*adv.* **uncon'sciously.**—*n.* **uncon'sciousness.**—**unconsid'ered** not esteemed: done without considering; **unconstrain'able; unconstrained'.**—*adv.* **unconstrain'edly.**—*adjs.* **uncontrôll'able** not capable of being controlled; **unconven'- tional** not conventional: free in one's ways—*n* **unconventional'ity.**—*adjs.* **uncool'** (*coll., derog.*) not sophisticated or smart, old-fashioned; **unco- or'dinated** not co-ordinated: having clumsy movements, as if muscles were not co-ordinated.—*v t* **uncoup'le** to loose from being coupled: to disjoin — *adj.* **uncouth** (*un-kōōth'*) strange and wild or unattractive' awkward, ungraceful, uncultured, esp in manners or language.—*adv* **uncouth'ly.**—*n.* **uncouth'- ness.**—*v.t* **uncov'er** to remove the cover of: to lay open: to expose: to drive out of cover.—*v.t.* to take off the hat.—*adjs.* **uncov'ered; uncrit'ical** not critical, without discrimination: not in accordance with the principles of criticism.—*adv.* **uncrit'ically.**— *v.t.* **uncross'** to change, move, from a crossed position.—*adjs.* **uncrossed'** not crossed—not passed over, marked with a cross, thwarted, etc.; **uncrowned'** not

uncomplè'ted *adj.* un- (1).	**uncorrect'ed** *adj.* un- (1).	**undestroyed'** *adj.* un- (1).
uncompli'ant *adj.* un- (1).	**uncorrob'orated** *adj.* un- (1).	**undetect'ed** *adj.* un- (1).
uncomply'ing *adj.* un- (1).	**uncount'able** *adj.* un- (1).	**undě'viating** *adj.* un- (1)
uncomprehend'ed *adj.* un- (1).	**uncount'ed** *adj.* un- (1).	**undě'viatingly** *adv.* un- (1)
uncomprehend'ing *adj.* un- (1).	**uncropped'** *adj.* un- (1).	**undiagnosed'** *adj.* un- (1).
unconcealed' *adj.* un- (1).	**uncrow'ded** *adj.* un- (1).	**undigest'ed** *adj.* un- (1).
uncongé'nial *adj.* un- (1).	**uncrush'able** *adj.* un- (1).	**undilut'ed** *adj.* un- (1).
unconnect'ed *adj.* un- (1).	**uncrys'tallised, -z-** *adj.* un- (1)	**undimin'ished** *adj.* un- (1).
unconq'uerable *adj.* un- (1).	**uncult'ivable** *adj.* un- (1).	**undimmed'** *adj.* un- (1).
unconq'uerably *adv.* un- (1).	**uncult'ivated** *adj.* un- (1).	**undiplomat'ic** *adj.* un- (1).
unconq'uered *adj.* un- (1).	**uncured'** *adj.* un- (1).	**undirect'ed** *adj.* un- (1).
unconscien'tious *adj.* un- (1).	**undam'** *v.t.* un- (2).	**undisclosed'** *adj.* un- (1).
unconscien'tiously *adv.* un- (1).	**undam'aged** *adj.* un- (1)	**undiscour'aged** *adj* un- (1).
unconsol'idated *adj.* un- (1).	**undammed'** *adj.* un- (1, 2).	**undiscov'erable** *adj.* un- (1).
unconstitū'tional *adj.* un- (1).	**undamned'** *adj.* un- (1).	**undiscov'erably** *adv.* un- (1).
unconstitūtional'ity *n.* un- (1).	**undamped'** *adj.* un- (1).	**undiscov'ered** *adj.* un- (1).
unconstitū'tionally *adv.* un- (1).	**undeclared'** *adj.* un- (1).	**undismayed'** *adj.* un- (1).
unconsumed' *adj.* un- (1).	**undefeat'ed** *adj.* un- (1).	**undisor'dered** *adj.* un- (1).
uncon'summated *adj.* un- (1).	**undefend'ed** *adj.* un- (1).	**undispŭt'ed** *adj.* un- (1).
uncontam'inated *adj.* un- (1).	**undefiled'** *adj.* un- (1).	**undispŭt'edly** *adv.* un- (1).
uncontrived' *adj.* un- (1).	**undelib'erate** *adj.* un- (1).	**undissolved'** *adj.* un- (1).
uncontrover'sial *adj.* un- (1).	**undeliv'ered** *adj.* un- (1)	**undissol'ving** *adj.* un- (1).
unconvert'ed *adj.* un- (1).	**undelud'ed** *adj.* un- (1).	**undistilled'** *adj.* un- (1).
unconvict'ed *adj.* un- (1).	**undemand'ing** *adj.* un- (1).	**undistort'ed** *adj.* un- (1).
unconvinced' *adj.* un- (1).	**undemocrat'ic** *adj.* un- (1).	**undisturbed'** *adj.* un- (1).
unconvinc'ing *adj.* un- (1).	**undemon'strative** *adj.* un- (1).	**undivers'ified** *adj.* un- (1).
uncooked' *adj.* un- (1).	**undemon'strativeness** *n.* un- (1).	**undivorced'** *adj.* un- (1).
unco-op'erative *adj.* un- (1).	**undepressed'** *adj.* un- (1).	**undivulged'** *adj.* un- (1).
unco-op'eratively *adv.* un- (1).	**undeprived'** *adj.* un- (1).	**undoc'umented** *adj.* un- (1).
uncork' *v.t.* un- (2).	**undespoiled'** *adj.* un- (1)	**undrained'** *adj* un- (1).

Words beginning with pfx. **un-** *are listed first* (pp. 1079 ff.); *other UN- words follow* (pp. 1092 ff)

For other sounds see detailed chart of pronunciation

crowned: possessing kingly power without the actual title (**uncrowned king, queen** (*facet.*) a man, woman having supreme influence, or commanding the highest respect, within a particular group); **uncul'tured** not cultured: not cultivated.—*v.t.* and *v.t.* **uncurl'** to take or come out of curl, twist, roll.—*adjs.* **uncurled'** not curled: unrolled, uncoiled; **uncut'** not cut: not shaped by cutting: not abridged: of a book, with margins not cut down by the binder.

Words with prefix **un-** (*continued*).

adjs. **undat'ed** with no date marked or assigned, **undaunt'ed** not daunted: bold, intrepid.—*adv.* **undaunt'edly.**—*n.* **undaunt'edness.**—*adj.* **undeceiv'able** incapable of being deceived.—*v.t.* **undeceive'** to free from a mistaken belief, reveal the truth to.—*adjs.* **undeceived'** not deceived: set free from a delusion; **undecid'ed** not decided or settled: uncertain, irresolute.—*adv.* **undecid'edly.**—*adjs.* **undefined'** not defined: indefinite; **undeni'able** not to be denied, indisputable: not to be refused: obviously true or excellent.—*adv.* **undeni'ably** assuredly, one cannot deny it.—*adj.* **undeserved'** not deserved.—*adv.* **undeser'vedly.**—*adj.* **undeser'ving.**—*adv.* **undeser'vingly.**—*n.* **undesirabil'ity.**—*adj.* **undesir'able** not to be wished for.—*n.* an undesirable or objectionable person or thing.—*n.* **undesir'ableness.**—*adv.* **undesir'ably.**—*adjs.* **undesired'; undesir'ing; undesir'ous; undeter'mined** not settled, not fixed: not ascertained: not limited; **undeterred'** not discouraged or prevented (from); **undevel'oped** not developed: of land, not built on or used for public works.—*v.t.* **undid'.** *pa.t.* of **undo.**—*adjs.* **undifferen'tiated** not differentiated; **undig'nified; undiscerned'** unobserved, unperceived.—*adv.* **undiscern'edly.**—*adj.* **undiscern'ible.**—*adv.* **undiscern'ibly.**—*adjs.* **undiscern'ing** showing lack of discernment or discrimination; **undischarged'** not paid or settled: (of e.g. obligation) not carried out: not released from debt or other liability: (of gun) not fired; **undisc'iplinable.**—*n.* **undisc'ip-**

line lack of discipline.—*adjs.* **undisc'iplined** untrained: unruly; **undisguised'** not disguised: frank, open.—*adv.* **undisguis'edly.**—*adjs.* **undisting'uished** not distinguished or observed: not marked out by conspicuous qualities, not famous: not having an air of distinction; **undisting'uishing** not discriminating; **undistrib'uted** not distributed (**undistributed middle** the fallacy of reasoning without distributing the middle term, i.e without making it universal, in at least one premise); **undivid'ed** not divided: (of one's attention to something) wholly concentrated, not distracted.—*v.t.* **undo** (*un-dōō'*) to reverse the doing of: to cancel, annul: to bring to nothing: to unfasten by unbolting, etc.: to open: to unbutton, untie, etc.: to unravel.—*v.i* to come undone:—*pa.t.* **undid'**; *pa.p* **undone** (*un-dun'*).—*ns.* **undoer; undo'ing** the reversal of what has been done: unfastening: opening: ruin or cause of ruin.—*adjs.* **undomes'ticated** not domesticated: not tamed: emancipated from mere domestic interests; **undone** (*un-dun'*) not done: annulled: brought to naught: unfastened (**come undone** to become unfastened, detached): opened: ruined; **undoubt'ed** not doubted: unquestioned: certainly genuine or such as is represented.—*adv.* **undoubt'edly** without doubt, certainly.—*adjs.* **undreamed', undreamt'** (also with *-of*) not imagined even in a dream.—*v.t.* **undress'** to remove the clothes or dressing from.—*v.i.* to take off one's clothes.—*n.* (*un'*) scanty or incomplete dress: ordinary, informal dress: uniform for ordinary occasions.—Also *adj.*—*adj.* **undressed'** not dressed—not set in order, or made trim, or treated or prepared for use, etc.: divested of clothes (**get undressed** to take one's clothes off).—*n.* **undress'ing.**—*adj.* **undue'** not due or owing: unjustifiable: inappropriate: excessive.—*adv.* **undu'ly** unjustifiably: more than is right or reasonable, excessively.—*adjs.* **undyed'** not dyed; **undy'ing** not dying, immortal: unceasing.—*adv.* **undy'ingly.**

Words with prefix **un-** (*continued*).

adj. **unearned'** not earned by work: (**unearned in-**

Words beginning with pfx. **un-** *are listed first* (pp. 1079 ff.); *other UN- words follow* (pp. 1092 ff.).

fāte; fär; mē; hûr (her); mīne; mōte; fôr; mūte; mōōn; fŏŏt; dhen (then); el'ə-mənt (element)

come income, e.g. dividends, that is not remuneration for work done: (of something pleasant or unpleasant) unmerited.—*v.t.* **unearth'** to dig up, disinter: to bring out of obscurity, bring to light.—*adj.* **unearthed'** not connected to earth electrically: dug up, brought to light, etc.—*n.* **unearth'liness.**—*adj.* **unearth'ly** celestial: weird, ghostly: unconscionable, absurd (esp. of an early hour).—*n.* **unease'** lack of ease: discomfort: apprehension.—*adv.* **uneas'ily.**—*n.* **uneas'iness.**—*adjs.* **uneas'y** not at ease: disquieted: apprehensive: showing troubled restlessness (*lit.* and *fig.*): uncomfortable; **uneconom'ic** not in accordance with sound economics; **uneconom'ical** not economical; **uned'ifying** not instructing or uplifting morally or aesthetically: morally degrading or degraded; **uned'ited** never edited, never before published; **unemo'tional.**—*adv.* **unemo'tionally.**—*adjs.* **unemploy'able; unemployed'** out of work: not put to use or profit: for or pertaining to those who are out of work.—*n.* the number of people out of work in a given period.—*n.* **unemploy'ment** (**unemployment benefit** a weekly payment supplied under the national insurance scheme to a person who is unemployed).—*adj.* **unend'ing** endless: everlasting: never ceasing, incessant.—*adv.* **unen'dingly.**—*adjs.* **un-Eng'lish** not English in character; **unen'viable** not to be envied.—*adv.* **unen'viably.**—*adjs.* **unen'vied; unen'vious; unen'vying; une'qual** not equal: not equal (to): varying, not uniform; **une'qualled** without an equal.—*adv.* **une'qually.**—*adj.* **unequiv'ocal** unambiguous: explicit: clear and emphatic.—*adv.* **unequiv'ocally.** —**unerr'ing** making no error, infallible: not, or never, missing the mark (*lit.* and *fig.*).—*adv.* **unerr'ingly.**—*n.* **unerr'ingness.**—*adj.* **unexam'pled** unprecedented, without like or parallel; **unexcep'tionable** not liable to objection or criticism, exactly right, excellent.—*n.* **unexcep'tionableness.**—*adv.* **unexcep'tionably.**—*adj.* **unexcep'tional** not admitting, or forming, an exception: unexceptionable.—*adv.* **unexcep'tionally.**

Words with prefix **un-** *(continued).*

adj. **unfail'ing** never failing or giving out: infallible: constant: inexhaustible.—*adv.* **unfail'ingly.**—*adj.* **unfair'** not fair, ugly: inequitable, unjust: involving deception or fraud and leading to undue advantage over business rival(s).—*adv.* **unfair'ly.**—*n.* **unfair'ness.**—*adj.* **unfaith'ful** not of the approved religion: not faithful, violating trust: breaking faith with one's husband, wife or lover, usu. by having sexual intercourse with someone else: not true to the original.— *adv.* **unfaith'fully.**—*n.* **unfaith'fulness.**—*adj.* **unfash'ionable** not fashionable.—*adv.* **unfash'ionably.**— *v.t.* **unfasten** (*un-fäs'n*) to release from a fastening.— *v.i.* to become loose or open.—*adjs.* **unfas'tened** released from fastening: not fastened; **unfa'thered** without a father or acknowledged father: deprived of a father; **unfa'therly** unbefitting a father; **unfath'omable** not able to be fathomed (*lit.* and *fig.*).—*n.* **unfath'omableness.**—*adv.* **unfath'omably.**—*adjs.* **unfath'omed** not sounded, of unknown depth: of unascertained meaning (*fig.*); **unfeel'ing** without feeling: without kind or sympathetic feelings: hardhearted.—*adv.* **unfeel'ingly.**—*n.* **unfeel'ingness.**— *v.t.* **unfett'er** to free from fetters.—*adjs.* **unfett'ered** unrestrained; **unfin'ished; unfit'** not fit: not in fit condition: not meeting required standards.—*adv.* **unfit'ly** unsuitably, inappropriately.—*n.* **unfit'ness.** —*adj.* **unfitt'ed** not provided (with): without fittings: not made to fit, or tested for fit: not adapted, qualified, or able.—*n.* **unfitt'edness.**—*adj.* **unfitt'ing** unsuitable.—*adv.* **unfitt'ingly.**—*v.t.* **unfix'** to unfasten, detach: to unsettle (*fig.*).—*adjs.* **unfixed'**; **unflapp'able** (*coll.*) imperturbable, never agitated or alarmed.—*n.* **unflappabil'ity.**—*adj.* **unfledged'** not yet fledged: undeveloped: of early youth.—*v.t.* **unfold'** to open the folds of: to spread out: to tell: to disclose, make known: to reveal, display.—*v.i.* to open out, spread open to the view (*lit.* and *fig.*).— *adj.* **unfold'ed** not folded: opened out from folds.—*n.* **unfold'er.**—*n.* and *adj.* **unfold'ing** opening out from

unflatt'eringly *adv.* un- (1).	**ungath'ered** *adj.* un- (1).	**unheed'edly** *adv.* un- (1).
unflā'voured *adj.* un- (1).	**ungauged'** *adj.* un- (1).	**unheed'ful** *adj.* un- (1).
unflinch'ing *adj.* un- (1).	**ungen'erous** *adj.* un- (1).	**unheed'fully** *adv.* un- (1).
unflinch'ingly *adv.* un- (1).	**ungen'erously** *adv.* un- (1).	**unheed'ing** *adj.* un- (1).
unflus'tered *adj.* un- (1).	**unglazed'** *adj.* un- (1).	**unheed'ingly** *adv.* un- (1).
unfō'cus(s)ed *adj.* un- (1).	**unglossed'** *adj.* un- (1).	**unheed'y** *adj.* un- (1).
unforesee'able *adj.* un- (1).	**unglove'** *v.t.* un- (2).	**unhelped'** *adj.* un- (1).
unforeseen' *adj.* un- (1).	**ungloved'** *adj.* un- (1).	**unhelp'ful** *adj.* un- (1).
unforetold' *adj.* un- (1).	**unglue'** *v.t., v.i.* un- (2).	**unher'alded** *adj.* un- (1).
unforewarned' *adj.* un- (1).	**ungrace'ful** *adj.* un- (1).	**unherō'ic, -al** *adjs.* un- (1).
unforgett'able *adj.* un- (1).	**ungrace'fully** *adv.* un- (1).	**unherō'ically** *adv.* un- (1).
unforgett'ably *adv.* un- (1).	**ungrace'fulness** *n.* un- (1).	**unhind'ered** *adj.* un- (1).
unforgiv'able *adj.* un- (1).	**ungrammat'ic, -al** *adjs.* un- (1).	**unhired'** *adj.* un- (1).
unforgiv'ing *adj.* un- (1).	**ungrammat'ically** *adv.* un- (1).	**unhitch'** *v.t.* un- (2).
unfor'midable *adj.* un- (1).	**ungroomed'** *adj.* un- (1).	**unhon'oured** *adj.* un- (1).
unform'ulated *adj.* un- (1).	**unguid'ed** *adj.* un- (1).	**unhook'** *v.t.* un- (2).
unforthcom'ing *adj.* un- (1).	**unhack'neyed** *adj.* un- (1).	**unhurr'ied** *adj.* un- (1).
unfor'tified *adj.* un- (1).	**unhall'owed** *adj.* un- (1).	**unhurr'iedly** *adv.* un- (1).
unfos'tered *adj.* un- (1).	**unhamp'ered** *adj.* un- (1).	**unhurt'** *adj.* un- (1):
unfranked' *adj.* un- (1).	**unhar'dened** *adj.* un- (1).	**unhygien'ic** *adj.* un- (1).
unfrequen'ted *adj.* un- (1).	**unharmed'** *adj.* un- (1).	**unhy'phenated** *adj.* un- (1).
unfright'ened *adj.* un- (1).	**unharm'ful** *adj.* un- (1).	**unidentifi'able** *adj.* un- (1).
unfrō'zen *adj.* un- (1).	**unharm'fully** *adv.* un- (1).	**unident'ified** *adj.* un- (1).
unfruit'ful *adj.* un- (1).	**unharmo'nious** *adj.* un- (1).	**unidiomat'ic** *adj.* un- (1).
unfruit'fully *adv.* un- (1).	**unhar'vested** *adj.* un- (1).	**unidiomat'ically** *adv.* un- (1).
unfū'elled *adj.* un- (1).	**unhast'y** *adj.* un- (1).	**unillu'minated** *adj.* un- (1).
unfulfilled' *adj.* un- (1).	**unhaunt'ed** *adj.* un- (1).	**unillu'minating** *adj.* un- (1).
unfunn'y *adj.* un- (1).	**unheat'ed** *adj.* un- (1).	**unill'ustrated** *adj.* un- (1).
ungall'ant *adj.* un- (1).	**unhedged'** *adj.* un- (1).	**unimpaired'** *adj.* un- (1).
ungall'antly *adv.* un- (1).	**unheed'ed** *adj.* un- (1).	**unimpēd'ed** *adj.* un- (1).

Words beginning with pfx. **un-** *are listed first (pp. 1079 ff.); other* **UN-** *words follow (pp. 1092 ff.).*

For other sounds see detailed chart of pronunciation.

folds: disclosing.—*adjs.* **unforced'**; **unfor'ested** not wooded; deforested; **unforgott'en**; **unformed'** unmade, uncreated: formless, unshaped: immature, undeveloped; **unfor'tunate** unlucky: regrettable: of ill omen.—*n.* an unfortunate person.—*adv.* **unfor'-tunately** in an unlucky way: by bad luck: I'm sorry to say.—*n.* **unfor'tunateness.**—*adjs.* **unfought'**; **un-found'ed** not founded: without foundation, baseless. —*v.t.* and *v.i.* **unfreeze'** to thaw: to (allow to) progress, move, etc. after a temporary restriction or stoppage: to free (prices, wages, funds) from the control imposed by a standstill order.—*adj.* **unfriend'ed** not provided with or supported by friends.—*n.* **unfriend'liness.**—*adj.* **unfriend'ly** ill-disposed: somewhat hostile.—*v.t.* **unfrock'** to strip of a frock or gown: to depose from priesthood: to remove from a comparable position in another sphere of activity.—*adjs.* **unfrocked'.**—*v.t.* **unfurl'** to release from being furled: to unfold, display.—*v.i.* to spread open.—*adj.* **unfur'nished** not furnished: unsupplied.

Words with prefix un- (*continued*).

n. **ungain'liness.**—*adj.* **ungain'ly** awkward, clumsy, uncouth.—*adv.* **awkwardly.**—*n.* **ungen'tlemanliness.** —*adjs.* **ungen'tlemanly** unbecoming a gentleman; **ungetat'able**, **unget-at'-able** (*coll.*) inaccessible.— *v.t.* **ungird'** to free from a girdle or band: to undo the fastening of and take off.—*adj.* **ungirt'** (or **ungird'ed**) not girt: freed from the girdle: not tightened up, not strengthened for action (*fig.*).—*n.* **ungod'liness.**— *adjs.* **ungod'ly** not godly: outrageous, unconscionable (*coll.*); **ungov'ernable** uncontrollable: unruly.—*adv.* **ungov'ernably**; **ungov'erned**; **ungra'cious** without grace: wanting in courtesy, affability or urbanity.—*adv.* **ungra'ciously.**—*n.* **ungra'ciousness.** —*adjs.* **ungrad'ed** not classified in grades; **ungrate'ful** not feeling gratitude: disagreeable, irksome: not repaying one's labour, thankless.—*adv.* **ungrate'fully.**—*n.* **ungrate'fulness.**—*v.t.* **unguard'**

to render, or leave, unguarded.—*adj.* **unguard'ed** without guard: unprotected: unscreened: incautious: inadvertent.—*adv.* **unguard'edly.**—*n.* **unguard'-edness.**—*v.t.* **ungum'** to free from gum or gummed condition.—*adj.* **ungummed'** not gummed: freed from gum or gumming: (**come ungummed** of a plan, to go amiss; *slang*).

Words with prefix un- (*continued*).

v.t. **unhand'** to take the hands off: to let go.—*adv.* **unhand'ily** awkwardly.—*n.* **unhand'iness.**—*adj.* **unhand'y** not skilful, awkward: not convenient.— *adv.* **unhapp'ily** in an unhappy manner: unfortunately, regrettably, I'm sorry to say: unsuccessfully.—*n.* **unhapp'iness.**—*adj.* **unhapp'y** bringing misfortune: not fortunate: miserable: infelicitous, inapt.—*v.t.* **unhar'ness** to take the armour or the harness off.—*adj.* **unhatched'** not out of the egg: not developed: not shaded.—*adv.* **unheal'thily.**—*n.* **unheal'thiness.**—*adjs.* **unheal'thy** not healthy: morbid: unfavourable to health: dangerous (*slang*); **unheard'** not heard: not granted a hearing: not heard of, unknown to fame; **unheard'-of**; **unhes'itating** not hesitating or doubting: prompt: ready.—*adv.* **unhes'itatingly.**—*v.t.* **unhinge'** to take from the hinges: to derange.—*adj.* **unhinged'.**—*adjs.* **unhistor'ic**, **-al** not mentioned in history: not in accordance with history: not having actually existed or happened —*adv.* **unhō'lily.**—*n.* **unhō'liness.**—*adjs.* **unhō'ly** not holy: very wicked: unconscionable, outrageous, unearthly (*coll.*); **unhoped'-for** beyond what was expected with hope; **unhope'ful.**—*adv.* **unhope'fully.**— *vs.t.* **unhorse'** to dislodge or throw from a horse; **unhouse'** to deprive of or drive from a house or shelter.—*adjs.* **unhoused'** houseless: deprived of a house; **unhung'** not hung: without hangings: unhanged.

Words with prefix un- (*continued*).

adjs. **unidēalist'ic**; **unimag'inable.**—*n.* **unimag'in-**

Words beginning with pfx. **un-** *are listed first* (pp. 1079 ff.); *other* UN- *words follow* (pp. 1092 ff.).

fāte; fär; mē; hûr (her); mīne; mōte; fôr; mūte; mōōn; fōōt; dhen (then), el'ə-mənt (element) ableness.—*adv.* unimag'inably.—*adj.* unimag'inative not imaginative, prosaic —*adv.* unimag'inatively.— *n.* unimag'inativeness.—*adjs.* unimag'ined; unim- peach'able not to be impeached: not liable to be accused: free from fault: blameless; unimpos'ing unimpressive; unimproved' not made better: not cultivated, cleared, or built upon: not put to use; un- inform'ative; uninformed' not having received in- formation: untaught: not imbued with life or activity; unin'terested not personally concerned: not taking an interest; unin'teresting.—*adv.* unin'terestingly.

Words with prefix un- *(continued).*

v.t. unjoint' to disjoint.—*adjs.* unjoint'ed disjoint- ed, incoherent: without joints; unkempt' uncombed: unpolished, rough; unkept' not kept: untended, unkind' wanting in kindness: cruel; unkin'dled not kindled.—*n.* unkind'liness want of kindliness.—*adj.* unkind'ly unnatural: not kind.—*adv.* in an unkindly manner: cruelly.—*n.* unkind'ness want of kindness or affection: cruelty: ill-feeling.—*v.t.* unknit (*un-nit'*) to undo the knitting of: to untie: to smooth out from a frown: to relax.—*adj.* loose, unfirmed.—*v.t.* unknot (*un-not'*) to free from knots: to untie.—*adjs.* unknowable (*un-nō'ə-bl*) incapable of being known; unknow'ing ignorant, unaware: unwitting.—*adv.* unknow'ingly.—*adj.* unknown (*un-nōn'*) not known. —*n.* an unknown person or quantity: (with *the*) that which is unknown.

Words with prefix un- *(continued).*

adjs. unla'boured showing no traces of labour: un- restrained, easy.—*v.t.* unlace' to free from being laced: to undo the lacing of.—*adj.* unla'den not laden.—*v.t.* unlatch' to lift the latch of.—*adj.* unlaw'- ful forbidden by law: illegitimate: illicit: acting illegally —*adv.* unlaw'fully.—*n.* unlaw'fulness.— *v.t.* unlearn' to undo the process of learning: to rid one's mind of, eliminate habit(s) of.—*adj.* unlearned (*-lûr'nd*) having no learning: (*-lûrnd'*) not learnt, got

up, acquired: eliminated by unlearning —*adj* and *pa.p.* unlearnt (*-lûrnt'*) not learnt· eliminated by unlearning.—*v.t.* unleash' to free from a leash, let go —*adjs.* unled' not led, without guidance; unlett'ered unlearned: illiterate· without lettering; unli'censed without a licence: unauthorised —*adj.* and *adv* (tending to become a *prep*) unlike' not like.—*adj* unlik(e)'able not likeable.—*ns.* unlike'lihood, unlike'liness improbability.—*adj.* unlike'ly not likely: improbable.—*adv* in an unlikely manner, improbably.—*n.* unlike'ness want of resemblance.— *v.t.* unlim'ber to remove (a gun) from its limber ready for use.—*adj* unlined' without lines or lining —*v.t.* unlink' to undo the linking or links of —*v i.* to be- come unlinked.—*adjs.* unlinked' not linked; unlist'- ed not entered in a list: (of a telephone number) not listed in a directory, ex-directory (*U S*); unlived'·in not lived in.—*v.t.* unload' to take the load or charge from: to discharge: to disburden: to remove as a load to get rid of: to dump.—*v.i.* to discharge freight — *adj.* unload'ed not loaded: discharged.—*ns.* unload'er; unload'ing.—*v.t.* unlock' to undo the locking of: to free from being locked up: to let loose: to open, make accessible, or disclose —*v.i* to become unlocked —*adjs.* unlocked'; unlooked'-for unexpected.—*vs.t.* unloose' to loosen, unfasten, de- tach (also, more usu., unloos'en): to set free —*adjs.* unlord'ly; unlov'able (also unlove'able).—*adjs.* unloved'; unlov'ing.—*adv.* unlov'ingly.—*n.* unlov'- ingness.—*adv.* unluck'ily in an unlucky way by bad luck: I'm sorry to say, unfortunately —*n.* unluck'- iness.—*adj.* unluck'y unfortunate: ill-omened· bring- ing ill-luck

Words with prefix un- *(continued)*

adjs. unmade' not made: self-existent: subjected to unmaking; unmaid'enly unbecoming a maiden: not like a maiden; unmailed' not sent by post (mail[2]); unmā'kable.—*v.t.* unmake' to undo the making of· to undo, ruin.—*n.* unmā'king.—*v.t* unman'· to deprive

unmilled' *adj* un- (1).	unobjec'tionably *adv* un- (1).	unpar'doning *adj* un- (1)
unministė'rial *adj.* un- (1).	unobnox'ious *adj.* un- (1)	unpas'teurised, -z- *adj.* un- (1)
unmirac'ulous *adj.* un- (1).	unobscured *adj* un- (1).	unpas'toral *adj* un- (1)
unmissed' *adj.* un- (1).	unobstruc'ted *adj.* un- (1).	unpā'tented *adj* un- (1)
unmistāk'able *adj.* un- (1).	unobstruc'tive *adj.* un- (1).	unpathed (*-padhd'*) *adj* un- (1)
unmistāk'ably *adv.* un- (1).	unobtain'able *adj.* un- (1).	unpatriot'ic *adj* un- (1)
unmixed' *adj.* un- (1).	unobtained' *adj* un- (1).	unpatriot'ically *adv* un- (1).
unmod'ernised, -z- *adj.* un- (1).	unobtru'sive *adj.* un- (1).	unpat'ronised, -z- *adj.* un- (1).
unmod'ifiable *adj.* un- (1).	unobtru'sively *adv.* un- (1).	unpeace'able *adj* un- (1)
unmod'ified *adj.* un- (1).	unobtru'siveness *n.* un- (1).	unpeace'ful *adj* un- (1)
unmod'ulated *adj.* un- (1).	unob'vious *adj.* un- (1)	unpeace'fully *adv* un- (1)
unmois'tened *adj.* un- (1).	unocc'upied *adj.* un- (1).	unpeg' *v t* un- (2)
unmolest'ed *adj.* un- (1).	unoff'ered *adj.* un- (1).	unperceiv'able *adj* un- (1)
unmoth'erly *adj.* un- (1).	unoiled' *adj* un- (1).	unperceiv'ably *adv* un- (1)
unmourned' *adj.* un- (1).	unopposed' *adj.* un- (1).	unperceived' *adj* un- (1)
unmown' *adj.* un- (1).	unoppress'ive *adj.* un- (1).	unperceiv'edly *adv* un- (1)
unmur'muring *adj.* un- (1).	unordained' *adj.* un- (1).	unpercep'tive *adj* un- (1)
unmūs'ical *adj.* un- (1).	unor'ganised, -z- *adj.* un- (1).	unper'forated *adj* un- (1)
unmūs'ically *adv.* un- (1).	unor'namented (or *-ment'*) *adj.* un- (1)	unperformed' *adj* un- (1)
unmū'tilated *adj.* un- (1).	unor'thodox *adj.* un- (1).	unperfumed' (or *-pūr'*) *adj.* un- (1)
unneed'ed *adj.* un- (1).	unor'thodoxy *n.* un- (1).	unper'ilous *adj* un- (1)
unneed'ful *adj.* un- (1).	unostentā'tious *adj.* un- (1).	unper'ishable *adj* un- (1)
unneed'fully *adv.* un- (1).	unox'idised, -z- *adj.* un- (1).	unper'ishing *adj* un- (1)
unnō'ted *adj.* un- (1).	unpac'ified *adj.* un- (1).	unper'jured *adj* un- (1)
unnō'ticeable *adj.* un- (1).	unpaid' *adj.* un- (1).	unperplexed' *adj.* un- (1)
unnō'ticed *adj.* un- (1).	unpam'pered *adj.* un- (1).	unper'secuted *adj* un- (1)
unnō'ticing *adj.* un- (1).	unpar'donable *adj.* un- (1).	unpersuad'able *adj.* un- (1).
unnour'ished *adj.* un- (1).	unpar'donableness *n.* un- (1).	unpersuad'ed *adj.* un- (1)
unnour'ishing *adj.* un- (1).	unpar'donably *adv.* un- (1).	unperturbed' *adj.* un- (1)
unobjec'tionable *adj.* un- (1).	unpar'doned *adj.* un- (1).	unphilosoph'ic, -al *adjs.* un- (1)

Words beginning with pfx. un- *are listed first (pp. 1079 ff.); other* UN- *words follow (pp. 1092 ff)*

For other sounds see detailed chart of pronunciation.

of the nature, attributes or powers of humanity, manhood, or maleness: to deprive of fortitude: to deprive of men.—*adv.* **unman'fully.**—*adj.* **unman'like.**—*n.* **unman'liness.**—*adjs.* **unman'ly** not becoming a man: unworthy of a noble mind: base: cowardly; **unmanned'** without a crew: without a garrison: without inhabitants: deprived of fortitude; **unmann'ered** unmannerly: free from mannerism.—*n.* **unmann'erliness.**—*adj.* **unmann'erly** not mannerly: ill-bred.—*adv.* in an unmannerly manner.—*adjs.* **unmanufac'tured** in a raw state; **unmanured'** not manured; **unmarked'** bearing no mark: not noticed; **unmar'ketable** not suitable for the market, not saleable; **unmarred'** not married; **unmarr'iageable; unmarr'ied** not married, usu. never having been married: freed from marriage.—*v.t.* **unmask'** to take a mask or a disguise from: to discover the identity of (e.g. a thief) (*fig.*): to reveal the place of (a gun, battery) by firing: to expose, show up.—*v.i.* to put off a mask.—*adj.* **unmasked'** not wearing a mask: undisguised: divested of mask or disguise: revealed (of e.g. identity); **unmatch'able; unmatched'** matchless: not accompanied by a match or like; **unmean'ing** meaningless: purposeless: expressionless; **unmeant** (*un-ment'*); **unmeas'urable** immeasurable: too great to measure: inordinate: not susceptible of measurement; **unmeas'ured; unmechan'ic, -al; unmech'anised, -z-** not mechanised; **unmed'itated** not meditated, unpremeditated; **unmen'tionable** not fit to be mentioned.—*n.pl.* **unmen'tionables** underclothing.—*adjs.* **unmer'ciful** merciless: excessively and unpleasantly great; **unmer'ited** unmerited; **unmind'ed** unheeded; **unmind'ful** not keeping in mind, regardless (of).—*adv.* **unmind'fully.**—*n.* **unmind'fulness.**—*adj.* **unmit'igable** that cannot be mitigated.—*adv.* **unmit'igably.**—*adjs.* **unmit'igated** not mitigated: unqualified, out-and-out; **unmo'dish** unfashionable; **unmon'eyed** (**unmon'ied**) without money: not rich.—*v.t.* **unmoor'** to loose from moorings.—*v.i.* to cast off moorings.—*adjs.* **unmor'al** having no relation to morality: amoral; **unmoralis'ing, -z-.**—*n.* **unmoral'ity** detachment from questions of morality.—*adjs.* **unmo'tivated** having no motive: lacking incentive; **unmould'ed** not moulded.—*v.t.* **unmount'** to remove from mountings or mount: to dismount.—*v.i.* to dismount.—*adjs.* **unmount'ed** not mounted; **unmov'able** (also **unmove'able**) immovable: not movable.—*adv.* **unmov(e)'ably.**—*adj.* **unmoved'** not moved, firm: not touched by emotion, calm.—*v.t.* **unmuzz'le** to take a muzzle off.—*adj.* **unmuzz'led.**

Words with prefix un- (*continued*).
v.t. **unnail'** (*un-nāl'*) to free from nails or from being nailed.—*adjs.* **unnam(e)able** (*un-nā'mə-bl*) impossible to name: not to be named; **unnamed** (*un-nāmd'*); **unnatural** (*un-nat'ū-rəl*) not according to nature: without natural affection: monstrous, heinous: (of a sexual act, vice, etc.) considered not only immoral but also unacceptably indecent or abnormal (e.g. buggery, sodomy).—*v.t.* **unnat'uralise, -ize** to make unnatural: to divest of nationality.—*adj.* **unnat'uralised, -z-** not naturalised.—*adv.* **unnat'urally** in an unnatural way (esp. *not unnaturally* of course, naturally).—*n.* **unnat'uralness.**—*adjs.* **unnavigable** (*un-nav'*) not navigable; **unnav'igated.**—*adv.* **unnecessarily** (*un-nes'*).—*n.* **unnec'essariness.**—*adjs.* **unnec'essary** not necessary; **unneigh'bourly** not neighbourly, friendly, or social.—*adv.* in an unneighbourly manner.—*v.t.* **unnerve** (*un-nûrv'*) to deprive of nerve, strength, or vigour: to weaken.—*adjs.* **unnerved'; unnerv'ing; unnumbered** (*un-num'bərd*) not counted, too many to be numbered: not marked or provided with a number; **unnurtured** (*un-nûr'chərd*) not nurtured or educated: ill-bred.

Words with prefix un- (*continued*).
adjs. **unobe'dient** disobedient; **unobserv'able.**—*n.* **unobser'vance** failure to observe (rules, etc.): failure to notice: lack of observing power: inattention.—

Words beginning with pfx. un- are listed first (pp. 1079 ff); other UN- words follow (pp. 1092 ff.).

adjs. **unobser'vant; unobserved'.**—*adv.* **unob-serv'edly.**—*adjs.* **unobser'ving; unoffend'ed; unof-fend'ing; unoffi'cial** not official.—*adv.* **unoffi'cially.** —*adj.* **unoffi'cious** not officious.—*adv.* **unoften** (*un-of'n*; *rare*) seldom (usu. as *not unoften*).—*adjs.* **uno'pened** not opened: of a book, not having the leaves cut apart; **unor'dered** disordered: unarranged, not ordered or commanded; **unor'derly** not orderly; **unor'dinary** not ordinary; **unorig'inal** not original.— *n.* **unoriginality** (*-al'*).—*adjs.* **unowed'** not owed or due; **unowned'** unavowed, unacknowledged: ownerless.

Words with prefix **un-** *(continued).*

v.t. **unpack'** to undo the packing of: to take out of a pack: to open.—*v.i.* to do unpacking.—*adj.* **unpacked'** subjected to unpacking: (*un'pakt'*) not packed.—*ns.* **unpack'er; unpack'ing.**—*adjs.* **unpaint'-ed** not painted; **unpaired'** not paired: not forming one of a pair; **unpal'atable** unpleasant to taste, distaste-ful, disagreeable (*lit.* and *fig.*).—*adv.* **unpal'atably.** —*adjs.* **unpan'elled** not panelled; **unpa'pered** not papered; **unpar'allel** not parallel; **unpar'alleled** with-out parallel or equal; **unpared'** (of fruit) not having the skin removed: (of nails) not cut; **unparent'al** not befitting a parent; **unparl'iament'ary** contrary to the usages of Parliament: not such as may be spoken, or (of language) used, in Parliament; **unpass'ionate, unpass'ioned** without passions: calm: dispassionate; **unpaved'** without pavement; **unpavil'ioned** without a canopy; **unpay'able; unpeeled'** not peeled; **unpeered'** unequalled.—*v.t.* **unpen'** to let out from a pen.—*adj.* **unpenned'** unwritten: unconfined: let loose.—*v.t.* **unpeo'ple** to empty of people.—*adj.* **unpeo'pled** uninhabited: without servants: depopulated.—*n.* **un'per'son** an individual whose existence is officially denied, ignored, or deleted from record, e.g. one who has been politically superseded.—*adj.* **unpervert'ed** not perverted.—*v.t.* **unpick'** to pick loose, undo by picking.—*adjs.* **unpick'able** impossible to pick: able

to be unpicked; **unpicked'** not gathered: not selected: not having had unwanted material removed by pick-ing: picked loose.—*v.t.* **unpin'** to free from pins or pinning: to unfasten the dress of by removing pins.— *adjs.* **unplaced'** not assigned to or set in a place: not inducted to a church: not appointed to an office: not among the first three in a race; **unpleas'ant** not pleasant: disagreeable.—*adv.* **unpleas'antly.**—*n.* **un-pleas'antness** the state or quality of being unpleasant, disagreeableness: a disagreeable incident: disagree-ment involving open hostility.—*adjs.* **unpleased';** **unpleas'ing** not pleasing: displeasing.—*adv.* **unpleas'-ingly.**—*adj.* **unpleas'urable.**—*adv.* **unpleas'urably.** —*adjs.* **unplumbed'** unsounded: unfathomed; **un-point'ed** not pointed: without point or points: with joints uncemented; **unpoi'soned** not poisoned; **unpol-led'** not polled: not having voted; **unpor'tioned** with-out a portion; **unpossessed'** not possessed: not in pos-session; **unpost'ed** not posted, in any sense: not posted up: without a post; **unpo'table** undrinkable, unfit to drink; **unprac'tised** having little or no prac-tice or experience, inexpert: not carried out in prac-tice.—*n.* **unprac'tisedness.**—*adjs.* **unpraised'** not praised; **unpraise'worthy; unprec'edented** (*-pres'*, or *-prēs'*) not warranted by judicial, etc., precedent: of which there has been no previous instance.—*adv.* **unprec'edentedly.**—*n.* **unpredictabil'ity.**—*adj.* **unpredict'able** that cannot be foretold: (of a person, thing) liable to behave in a way that cannot be predicted.—*adjs.* **unpreferred'** without preferment or advancement; **unpremed'itable** not to be fore-seen; **unpremed'itated** not studied or purposed beforehand.—*adv.* **unpremed'itatedly.**—*ns.* **unpre-med'itatedness; unpremedita'tion.**—*v.t.* **unpre-pare'** to make unprepared.—*adj.* **unprepared'** not prepared or ready: not prepared for death: without preparation.—*adv.* **unprepa'redly.**—*n.* **unprepa'red-ness.**—*adjs.* **unprepossessed'** not prepossessed or pre-judiced; **unprepossess'ing** not predisposing others in one's favour, unpleasing; **unpresent'able** not fit to be

unqual'ified *adj.* un- (1).
unqual'ifiedly *adv.* un- (1).
unquanti'fied *adj.* un- (1).
unquelled' *adj.* un- (1).
unquench'able *adj.* un- (1).
unquench'ably *adv.* un- (1).
unquenched' *adj.* un- (1).
unran'somed *adj.* un- (1).
unrat'ified *adj.* un- (1).
unreach'able *adj.* un- (1).
unreached' *adj.* un- (1).
unrebuked' *adj.* un- (1).
unreceipt'ed *adj.* un- (1).
unreceived' *adj.* un- (1).
unrecep'tive *adj.* un- (1).
unrecip'rocated *adj.* un- (1).
unreclaim'able *adj.* un- (1).
unreclaimed' *adj.* un- (1).
unrec'ognisable, -z- (or *-nīz'*) *adj.* un- (1).
unrec'ognisably, -z- (or *-nīz'*) *adv.* un- (1).
unrec'ognised, -z- *adj.* un- (1).
unrecollect'ed *adj.* un- (1).
unrecommend'able *adj.* un- (1).
unrecommend'ed *adj.* un- (1).
unrec'ompensed *adj.* un- (1).
unrec'oncilable (or *-sīl'*) *adj.* un- (1).
unreconcil'ableness *n.* un- (1).
unrec'oncilably (or *-sīl'*) *adv.* un- (1).

unrec'onciled (or *-sīld'*) *adj.* un- (1).
unrecord'ed *adj.* un- (1).
unrecov'erable *adj.* un- (1).
unrecov'erably *adv.* un- (1).
unrecov'ered *adj.* un- (1).
unrect'ified *adj.* un- (1).
unreduced' *adj.* un- (1).
unrefined' *adj.* un- (1).
unreflect'ed *adj.* un- (1).
unreflect'ing *adj.* un- (1).
unreflect'ingly *adv.* un- (1).
unreflect'ive *adj.* un- (1).
unreform'able *adj.* un- (1).
unreformed' *adj.* un- (1).
unrefreshed' *adj.* un- (1).
unrefresh'ing *adj.* un- (1).
unreg'imented *adj.* un- (1).
unreg'istered *adj.* un- (1).
unreg'ulated *adj.* un- (1).
unrehearsed' *adj.* un- (1).
unrelāt'ed *adj.* un- (1).
unrelieved' *adj.* un- (1).
unrel'ished *adj.* un- (1).
unremark'able *adj.* un- (1).
unremarked' *adj.* un- (1).
unrem'edied *adj.* un- (1).
unremem'bered *adj.* un- (1).
unremūn'erative *adj.* un- (1).
unrenewed' *adj.* un- (1).
unrenowned' *adj.* un- (1).

unrepaid' *adj.* un- (1).
unrepair' *n.* un- (1).
unrepair'able *adj.* un- (1).
unrepaired' *adj.* un- (1).
unrepeal'able *adj.* un- (1).
unrepealed' *adj.* un- (1).
unrepelled' *adj.* un- (1).
unrepen'tance *n.* un- (1).
unrepen'tant *adj.* un- (1).
unrepen'ting *adj.* un- (1).
unrepen'tingly *adv.* un- (1).
unreplen'ished *adj.* un- (1).
unreport'able *adj.* un- (1).
unreport'ed *adj.* un- (1).
unrepresent'ative *adj.* un- (1).
unrepresent'ed *adj.* un- (1).
unrepriev'able *adj.* un- (1).
unreprieved' *adj.* un- (1).
unrep'rimanded *adj.* un- (1).
unreproach'ful *adj.* un- (1).
unreprodūc'ible *adj.* un- (1)
unrequit'ed *adj.* un- (1).
unrescind'ed *adj.* un- (1).
unresent'ed *adj.* un- (1).
unresent'ful *adj.* un- (1).
unrespon'sive *adj.* un- (1).
unrespon'sively *adv.* un- (1).
unrespon'siveness *n.* un- (1).
unrestored' *adj.* un- (1).
unrestrain'able *adj.* un- (1).

Words beginning with pfx. **un-** *are listed first* (pp. 1079 ff.); *other* **UN-** *words follow* (pp. 1092 ff.).

For other sounds see detailed chart of pronunciation.

seen; **unpretend'ing** not pretending or making pretence: modest; **unpreven'table; unpriced'** having no fixed or stated price: beyond price, priceless; **unpriest'ly** unbecoming, unlike, not of the nature of, a priest; **unprin'cipled** without good principles: not based on or in accordance with principles: not restrained by conscience: profligate; **unprint'able** not fit to be printed; **unprint'ed; unproce'dural** not in accordance with established or accepted procedures; **unprofessed'; unprofess'ional** not of a profession or the profession in question: beyond the limits of one's profession: unbecoming to a member of a particular profession.—*adv.* **unprofess'ionally.**— *adj.* **unprof'ited** without profit or advantage; **unpropor'tionable** out of due proportion.—*adv.* **unpropor'tionably.**—*adj.* **unpropor'tionate** out of due proportion.—*adv.* **unpropor'tionately.**—*adjs.* **unpropor'tioned** not proportioned.—**unprotest'ed** not objected to or protested against; **unprovi'ded** not furnished, provided, or provided for (also **unprovi'ded-for**); **unprovoked'** not provoked: uncalled for.—*adv.* **unprovŏ'kedly.**—*adj.* **unprovŏ'king.**—*v.t.* **unpurse'** to relax (the lips) from pursing: to disburse.—*adj.* **unputdown'able** (*coll.*) of a book, too absorbing to be set aside, compelling one to read to the end without interruption.

Words with prefix un- (*continued*).

adj. **unques'tionable** not to be questioned, certain, beyond doubt.—*adv.* **unques'tionably** in such a way as to be unquestionable: certainly, without doubt.— *adjs.* **unques'tioned** not called in question: not subjected to questioning: not examined; **unques'tioning; unqui'et** disturbed: restless: uneasy.—*n.* disquiet, inquietude.—*adj.* **unquŏt'able** unsuitable or unfit for quotation.—*v.i.* **unquote'** to close a quotation: to mark the end of a quoted passage with superscript comma(s).—used as *interj.* to indicate that a quotation is finished.—*adj.* **unracked'** not drawn off from the lees: not stretched on the rack: not strained.

—*v.t.* **unrav'el** to disentangle: to unknit.—*v.i.* to become disentangled.—*adj.* **unrav'elled.**—*ns.* **unrav'eller; unrav'elling; unrav'elment.**—*adjs.* **unread** (*un-rĕd'*) not informed by reading: not perused; **unreadable** (*un-rēd'a-bl*) indecipherable: too dull or ill-written to be read.—*n.* **unread'ableness.**—*adv.* **unreadily** (*-red'*).—*n.* **unread'iness.**—*adjs.* **unread'y** not ready, prepared, or prompt: hesitating, holding back; **unrĕ'al.**—*n.* **unrĕ'alism.**—*adj.* **unrealist'ic.**— *n.* **unreal'ity** want of reality or existence: an unreal thing.—*adv.* **unrĕ'ally.**—*n.* **unrea'son** lack of reason or reasonableness' nonsense.—*adj.* **unrea'sonable** not agreeable to reason: exceeding the bounds of reason, immoderate: not influenced by reason.—*n.* **unrea'sonableness.**—*adv.* **unrea'sonably.**—*adjs.* **unrea'soned** not argued out; **unrea'soning** not reasoning: showing lack of reason, irrational.—*adv* **unrea'soningly.**—*adjs.* **unrecall'able; unrecalled'; unreconstruct'ed** not reconstructed; **unredeem'able; unredeemed'** not redeemed, esp. spiritually or from pawn: without compensatory quality or circumstance, hence unmitigated, unrelieved; **unredressed'** not redressed.—*n.* **unregen'eracy.**—*adjs.* **unregen'erate** not regenerate: unrepentant, refusing to be reformed; **unregen'erated.**—*v.t.* **unrein'** to relax the rein of, give rein to —*adjs.* **unreined'** unchecked; **unrelen'ting.**—*adv.* **unrelen'tingly.**—*ns.* **unrelen'tingness; unreliabil'ity** (see note at rely).— *adj.* **unreli'able** not to be relied upon.—*n* **unreli'-ableness.**—*adjs.* **unrelig'ious** not connected with religion: not religious without being necessarily contrary or hostile to religion: irreligious; **unremitt'ed.** —*adv.* **unremitt'edly.**—*adj.* **unremitt'ent.**—*adv.* **unremitt'ently.**—*adj.* **unremitt'ing** not remitting or relaxing: continued: incessant.—*adv.* **unremitt'ingly.** —*n.* **unremitt'ingness.**—*adj.* **unremorse'ful** feeling no remorse.—*adv.* **unremorse'fully.**—*adjs.* **unremov'able** not removovable; **unremoved'** not removed; **unrepeat'able** not repeatable: indecent, gross: that cannot be done, etc. again; **unrepeat'ed;**

Words beginning with pfx. un- *are listed first* (pp. 1079 ff.); *other* UN- *words follow* (pp. 1092 ff.).

unrestrained' *adj.* un- (1).	unroman'tically *adv.* un- (1).	unscientif'ically *adv.* un- (1).
unrestrain'edly *adv.* un- (1).	unround'ed *adj.* un- (1).	unscorched' *adj.* un- (1).
unrestraint' *n.* un- (1).	unrubbed' *adj.* un- (1).	unscoured' *adj.* un- (1).
unrestric'ted *adj.* un- (1).	unrum'pled *adj.* un- (1).	unscratched' *adj* un- (1).
unretard'ed *adj.* un- (1).	unsafe' *adj.* un- (1).	unscru'pulous *adj.* un- (1).
unreten'ive *adj.* un- (1).	unsafe'ly *adv* un- (1).	unscru'pulously *adv* un- (1)
unretouched' *adj.* un- (1).	unsafe'ness *n.* un- (1).	unscru'pulousness *n* un- (1)
unreturned' *adj.* un- (1).	unsafe'ty *n.* un- (1).	unscru'tinised, -z- *adj.* un- (1).
unreturn'able *adj.* un- (1).	unsal(e)abil'ity *n.* un- (1).	unsea'worthy *adj.* un- (1).
unreturn'ing *adj.* un- (1).	unsal(e)'able *adj.* un- (1).	unsec'onded *adj.* un- (1)
unrevealed' *adj.* un- (1).	unsal'aried *adj* un- (1).	unsecured' *adj.* un- (1)
unreveal'ing *adj.* un- (1).	unsalt'ed *adj.* un- (1).	unsegment'ed *adj* un- (1)
unrevenged' *adj.* un- (1).	unsanc'tioned *adj.* un- (1).	unseg'regated *adj.* un- (1).
unrevised' *adj.* un- (1).	unsăt'ed *adj* un- (1).	unsensa'tional *adj.* un- (1).
unrevoked' *adj.* un- (1).	unsă'tiating *adj.* un- (1).	unsens'itive *adj.* un- (1).
unrewar'ded *adj.* un- (1).	unsatir'ical *adj.* un- (1).	unsent'enced *adj.* un- (1).
unrewar'ding *adj.* un- (1).	unsatisfac'torily *adv.* un- (1).	unsentiment'al *adj.* un- (1).
unrhymed' *adj.* un- (1).	unsatisfac'toriness *n.* un- (1).	unsep'arated *adj.* un- (1).
unrhyth'mical *adj.* un- (1).	unsatisfac'tory *adj.* un- (1).	unser'viceable *adj.* un- (1)
unrhyth'mically *adv.* un- (1).	unsat'isfiable *adj.* un- (1).	unsev'ered *adj* un- (1)
unribbed' *adj.* un- (1).	unsat'isfied *adj.* un- (1).	unshă'ded *adj* un- (1)
unridd'en *adj.* un- (1).	unsat'isfying *adj.* un- (1).	unshak(e)'able *adj* un- (1)
unrid(e)'able *adj.* un- (1).	unsat'urated *adj.* un- (1).	unshak(e)'ably *adv* un- (1)
unri'fled *adj.* un- (1).	unsaved' *adj.* un- (1).	unshăk'en *adj.* un- (1).
unripe' *adj.* un- (1).	unscarred' *adj.* un- (1)	unshăk'enly *adv.* un- (1).
unri'pened *adj.* un- (1).	unscent'ed *adj.* un- (1)	unshared' *adj* un- (1)
unripe'ness *n.* un- (1).	unsched'uled *adj.* un- (1).	unsharp'ened *adj* un- (1).
unris'en *adj.* un- (1).	unschol'arly *adj.* un- (1).	unshaved' *adj.* un- (1)
unri'valled *adj.* un- (1).	unschooled' *adj* un- (1)	unshă'ven *adj.* un- (1).
unroman'tic, -al *adjs.* un- (1).	unscientif'ic *adj.* un- (1).	unshel'tered *adj* un- (1).

unreprov'able; unreproved' (or -prōō'vid) not re-
proved; unreprov'ing; unrequired' unasked: un-
asked-for: unnecessary.—n. unreserve' absence of
reserve.—adj. unreserved' not reserved: without
reserve or reservation: unrestricted, unqualified.—
adv. unreser'vedly.—n. unreser'vedness.—adjs.
unresist'ed; unresist'ing.—adv. unresis'tingly.—
adjs. unresolv'able; unresolved' not resolved,
determined, settled, or solved: irresolute: undecided:
not separated into its constituent parts.—n. unresol'-
vedness irresolution.—adj. unrespect'ed.—n. unrest'
want of rest: disquiet: disturbance: discontent verging on insurrection.—adj. unrest'ful not restful:
uneasy: full of unrest.—n. unrest'fulness.—adj. unrest'ing.—adv. unrest'ingly.—n. unrest'ingness.—
adjs. unrev'erend not reverend; unrev'erent not reverent.—v.t. unridd'le to read the riddle of: to solve.
—adj. unrigh'teous.—adv. unrigh'teously.—n.
unrigh'teousness.—adj. unright'ful.—adv. unright'-
fully.—n. unright'fulness.—v.t. unrip' to rip up or
open: to strip, lay bare: to disclose.—adj. unripped'
not ripped: ripped up or open.—vs.t. unriv'et to loose
from being riveted: to detach (fig.); unrobe' to strip
of a robe, to undress.—v.i. to take off a robe, esp. of
state.—v.t. unroll' to open out from a rolled state.—
v.i. to become unrolled.—v.t. unroof' to strip the
roof from.—adj. unroofed' not roofed: stripped of its
roof.—v.t. unruff'le to restore or recover from ruff-
ling.—adj. unruff'led smooth: calm: not disturbed or
flustered.—ns. unrule' anarchy; unrul'iness.—adj.
unrul'y ungovernable: unmanageable: turbulent:
stormy.

Words with prefix un- (*continued*).

v.t. unsadd'le to take the saddle from: to dislodge
from the saddle.—adjs. unsadd'led; unsaid' not said
(see also unsay); unsailed' unnavigated; unsaint'ly;
unsanc'tified.—adv. unsa'vourily.—n. unsa'vouriness.—adj. unsa'voury not savoury, tasteless: of ill
savour: offensive.—v.t. unsay' to retract:—pa.t. and

pa.p. unsaid'.—adjs. unsay'able that cannot be said;
unscal'able that cannot be climbed.—v.t. unscale' to
remove scales from.—adjs. unscaled' unclimbed:
cleared of scales: scaleless; unscathed' not harmed,
not injured.—v.t. unscram'ble to decode from a
scrambled state, or to restore to natural sound: to
restore (something in which categories have been
deliberately jumbled) to a system of classification
and separation.—adj. unscreened' not screened:
unsifted.—v.t. unscrew' to loose from a state of being
screwed: to open, loose, or detach by screwing.—v.i.
to admit of unscrewing: to come unscrewed.—adjs.
unscrip'ted not using a script: unrehearsed: of comments, moves, etc., not planned, not in the script
(radio, TV); unscrip'tural not in accordance with, or
not warranted by, the Bible; unscru'pled unscrupulous: not scrupled at.—v.t. unseal' to remove or
break the seal of: to free from sealing or closure: to
open.—adjs. unsealed' not sealed: freed from a seal:
opened; unsea'sonable not in season: ill-timed.—n.
unsea'sonableness.—adv. unsea'sonably.—adj. unsea'soned not seasoned.—v.t. unseat' to oust,
remove, or throw from a seat, esp. on horseback or in
Parliament.—adjs. unseat'ed not seated: ousted,
thrown, removed from a seat; unsee'able invisible;
unseed'ed not seeded: in lawn-tennis tournaments,
etc., not placed in the draw of top players; unsee'ing
not seeing: unobservant: without insight or understanding.—n. unseem'liness.—adj. unseem'ly not
seemly, becoming, or decent: ill-looking.—adv. in an
unseemly manner.—adj. unseen' not seen: invisible.
—n. an unprepared passage for translation.—adjs.
unseiz'able; unseized' not seized: not taken or put in
possession.—adv. unsel'dom misused to mean
seldom (as in not unseldom, frequently).—adj.
unselfcon'scious.—adv. unselfcon'sciously.—n. unselfcon'sciousness.—adj. unself'ish.—adv. unself'-
ishly.—n. unself'ishness.—v.t. unsett'le to change
from being settled: to make uncertain, unstable, or
restless: to unfix.—v.i. to become unsettled.—adj.

---

unshield'ed adj. un- (1).	unsol'id adj. un- (1).	unsti'fled adj. un- (1).
unshift'ing adj. un- (1).	unsoured' adj. un- (1).	unstint'ing adj. un- (1).
unshock'able adj. un- (1).	unsown' adj. un- (1).	unstoop'ing adj. un- (1).
unshocked' adj. un- (1).	unspe'cialised, -z- adj. un- (1).	unstrapped' adj. un- (1).
unshorn' adj. un- (1).	unspecif'ic adj. un- (1).	unstrength'ened adj. un- (1).
unshot' adj. un- (1).	unspec'ified adj. un- (1).	unstressed' adj. un- (1).
unshown' adj. un- (1).	unspectac'ular adj. un- (1).	unstruc'tured pa.p., adj. un- (1).
unshrink'able adj. un- (1).	unspilled' adj. un- (1).	unstuffed' adj. un- (1).
unshrink'ing adj. un- (1).	unspilt' adj. un- (1).	unsubdu'able adj. un- (1).
unshrink'ingly adv. un- (1).	unspoiled' adj. un- (1).	unsubdued' adj. un- (1).
unshriv'en adj. un- (1).	unspoilt' adj. un- (1).	unsub'limated adj. un- (1).
unsigh'ing adj. un- (1).	unspo'ken adj. un- (1).	unsubmerged' adj. un- (1).
unsigned' adj. un- (1).	unsport'ing adj. un- (1).	unsubmis'sive adj. un- (1).
unsink'able adj. un- (1).	unsports'manlike adj. un- (1).	unsubmitt'ing adj. un- (1).
unskil'ful adj. un- (1).	unspott'ed adj. un- (1).	unsubscribed' adj. un- (1).
unskil'fully adv. un- (1).	unsprink'led adj. un- (1).	unsub'sidised, -z- adj. un- (1).
unskil'fulness n. un- (1).	unspun' adj. un- (1).	unsubstan'tiated adj. un- (1).
unskilled' adj. un- (1).	unsta'ble adj. un- (1).	unsubt'le adj. un- (1).
unslaked' adj. un- (1).	unsta'bleness n. un- (1).	unsucked' adj. un- (1).
unsleep'ing adj. un- (1).	unstaid' adj. un- (1).	unsull'ied adj. un- (1).
unslipp'ing adj. un- (1).	unstaid'ness n. un- (1).	unsumm'oned adj. un- (1).
unslung' adj. un- (1).	unstain'able adj. un- (1).	unsu'pervised adj. un- (1).
unsmart' adj. un- (1).	unstained' adj. un- (1).	unsupplied' adj. un- (1).
unsmil'ing adj. un- (1).	unstamped' adj. un- (1).	unsuppressed' adj. un- (1).
unsmil'ingly adv. un- (1).	unstates'manlike adj. un- (1).	unsurpass'able adj. un- (1).
unsoftened (-sof'(ə)nd) adj. un- (1).	unstead'fast adj. un- (1).	unsurpass'ably adv. un- (1).
unsoiled' adj. un- (1).	unstead'fastly adv. un- (1).	unsurpassed' adj. un- (1).
unsold' adj. un- (1).	unstead'fastness n. un- (1).	unsuscept'ible adj. un- (1).
unsolic'ited adj. un- (1).	unster'ile adj. un- (1).	unsustain'able adj. un- (1).
unsolic'itous adj. un- (1).	unster'ilised, -z- adj. un- (1).	unsustained' adj. un- (1).

Words beginning with pfx. un- *are listed first (pp. 1079 ff.); other UN- words follow (pp. 1092 ff.).*

For other sounds see detailed chart of pronunciation.

unsett'led not settled, fixed, or determined: changeable: not having the dregs deposited: not yet inhabited and cultivated: turbulent, lawless.—*n.* and *adj.* unsett'ling.—*v.t.* unsew' to undo the stitching of (a garment, etc.).— *adjs.* unsewn' (also unsewed') not sewn; unsexed'; unsex'ual.—*v.t.* unshack'le to loose from shackles: to remove a shackle from.—*adjs.* unshack'led; unshamed' not ashamed: not put to shame; unshape'ly.—*v.t.* unsheathe' to draw from the sheath: to uncover.—*adjs.* unsheathed' drawn from the sheath: not sheathed; unshed' not shed.—*v.t.* unshell' to shell, remove the shell from.—*adj.* unshod' shoeless: with shoe or shoes removed.—*vs.t.* unshoe' to strip of a shoe or shoes; unshutt'er to open or remove the shutters of.—*adjs.* unsift'ed not sifted: not critically examined: inexperienced; unsight'ed not seen: (of gun, etc.) having no sights: fired without use of sights.—*n.* unsight'liness.—*adj.* unsight'ly displeasing to the eye: ugly.—*adjs.* unsis'terly;unsized' not fitted, adjusted, or sorted in respect of size: not treated with size; unskinned' skinned: not skinned.—*vs.t.* unsling' to free from slings or from being slung:—*pa.t.* and *pa.p.* unslung'; unsluice' to let flow: to open the sluice of.—*v.t.* unsnarl' to disentangle.—*adj.* unsoaped' not soaped: unwashed.—*n.* unsociabil'ity.—*adj.* unsö'ciable disinclined to associate with others.—*n.* unsö'ciableness.—*adv.* unsö'ciably.—*adjs.* unsö'cial not social: not regarding or conducing to the good of society: not sociable: (of hours of work) not falling within the normal working day; unsö'cialised, -z- not socialised, not aware of one's function in, or lacking attributes for living in, society.—*adv.* unsö'cially.—*vs.t.* unsock'et to take out of the socket; unsolder (*un-sod'ər*, or *-sol'*, *-sō'*, *-sōl'*) to separate from being soldered.—*adjs.* unsol'emn not solemn: informal; unsolv'able impossible to solve; unsolved' not solved; unsophis'ticated genuine, unadulterated: unfalsified: free from artificiality: ingenuous: inexperienced in evil.—*ns.* unsophis'ticatedness; un-

sophistica'tion.—*adjs.* unsort'ed not sorted or arranged: ill-chosen: unfitting, unsuitable, unsought' not sought or solicited; unsound' not sound; unsound'-ed not sounded, pronounced, or made to sound: unfathomed, unplumbed.—*adv.* unsound'ly.—*n.* unsound'ness.—*adjs.* unspared' not spared: unstinted; unspar'ing not sparing, liberal, profuse: unmerciful.—*adv.* unspar'ingly.—*n.* unspar'ingness.—*adj.* unspeak'able unutterable: inexpressible, esp. in badness.—*adv.* unspeak'ably.—*adjs.* unspeak'ing; unspent' not spent; unspir'ited; unspir'itual.—*adv.* unspir'itually.—*adj.* unsprung' not sprung: without springs.—*v.t.* unstack' to remove from a stack.—*adjs.* unstaunch'able; unstaunched' (or *un'*).—*v.t.* unstarch' to free from starch.—*adjs.* unstarched' not starched; unstat'ed not stated.—*adv.* unstead'ily.—*n.* unstead'iness.—*adj.* unstead'y.—*v.t.* to make unsteady.—*adj.* unstick' to free from sticking.—*v.i.* to come off from the surface:—*pa.t.* and *pa.p.* unstuck'.—*adj.* unstuck', loosened from sticking: (come unstuck of a plan, to go amiss; *slang*).—*vs.t.* unstitch' to take out the stitches of; unstop' to free from being stopped: to draw out the stop of.—*adj.* unstopp'able not able to be stopped.—*adv.* unstopp'-ably.—*adj.* unstopped' not stopped: of a consonant, open: without a pause at the end of the line.—*vs.t.* unstopp'er to take the stopper from; unstow' to empty of contents: to take out of stowage.—*adj.* unstrained' not strained or purified by straining: not subjected to strain: not forced, natural.—*v.t.* unstrap' to undo the straps of.—*adj.* unstreamed' (of schoolchildren) not divided into classes according to ability.—*v.t.* unstring' to take the strings from: to loose the strings of: to take from a string: to put out of tone: to disorganise.—*v.t.* to loose the strings of one's purse.—*adjs.* unstringed' not stringed, not provided with strings; unstrung' with strings removed or slacked: not strung: relaxed: disorganised: unnerved; unstuck see unstick; unstud'ied not studied: not having studied: without premeditation: unlaboured:

---

unsustain'ing *adj.* un- (1).
unsweet'ened *adj.* un- (1).
unswept' *adj.* un- (1).
unswer'ving *adj.* un- (1).
unswer'vingly *adv.* un- (1).
unsympathet'ic *adj.* un- (1).
unsympathet'ically *adv.* un- (1).
unsym'pathising, -z- *adj.* un- (1).
unsystemat'ic, -al *adjs.* un- (1).
unsystemat'ically *adv.* un- (1).
unsys'tematised, -z- *adj.* un- (1).
untä'ken *adj.* un- (1).
untal'ented *adj.* un- (1).
untalked'-of *adj.* un- (1).
untanned' *adj.* un- (1).
untapped' *adj.* un- (1).
untar'nished *adj.* un- (1).
untarred' *adj.* un- (1).
untaste'ful *adj.* un- (1).
untemp'ted *adj.* un- (1).
untenabil'ity *n.* un- (1).
untend'ed *adj.* un- (1).
unter'minated *adj.* un- (1).
unterres'trial *adj.* un- (1).
untest'ed *adj.* un- (1).
unthanked' *adj.* un- (1).
unthank'ful *adj.* un- (1).
unthick'ened *adj.* un- (1).
unthreat'ened *adj.* un- (1).

unti'dily *adv.* un- (1).
unti'diness *n.* un- (1).
unti'dy *adj.* un- (1)
unti'dy *v.t.* un- (2).
untilled' *adj.* un- (1).
untinged' *adj* un- (1).
untir'ing *adj.* un- (1).
untir'ingly *adv.* un- (1).
untoll'ing *adj.* un- (1).
untorn' *adj.* un- (1).
untrained' *adj.* un- (1).
untramm'elled *adj.* un- (1).
untramp'led *adj.* un- (1).
untrans'ferable (or *-fer'*) *adj.* un- (1).
untransformed' *adj.* un- (1).
untransla'table *adj.* un- (1).
untransmiss'ible *adj.* un- (1).
untransmitt'ed *adj.* un- (1).
untransmü'table *adj.* un- (1).
untransmū'ted *adj.* un- (1).
untrav'elled *adj.* un- (1).
untrav'ersed *adj.* un- (1).
untrem'bling *adj.* un- (1).
untrem'blingly *adv.* un- (1).
untrem'ulous *adj.* un- (1).
unty'ing *n.* un- (2).
untyp'ical *adj.* un- (1).
unurged' *adj.* un- (1).
unü'sable *adj.* un- (1).
unü'sably *adv.* un- (1).

unü'tilised, -z- *adj.* un- (1).
unvac'cinated *adj.* un- (1).
unvan'quishable *adj.* un- (1).
unvan'quished *adj.* un- (1).
unvä'riable *adj.* un- (1).
unvä'ried *adj.* un- (1).
unvä'riegated *adj.* un- (1).
unvä'rying *adj.* un- (1).
unvent'ilated *adj.* un- (1).
unver'ifiable *adj.* un- (1).
unverifiabil'ity *n.* un- (1).
unver'ified *adj.* un- (1).
unvi'able *adj.* un- (1).
unviewed' *adj.* un- (1).
unvi'olated *adj.* un- (1).
unwaked' *adj.* un- (1).
unwäk'ened *adj.* un- (1).
unwalled' *adj.* un- (1).
unwant'ed *adj* un- (1).
unwar'like *adj.* un- (1).
unwarmed' *adj.* un- (1).
unwarned' *adj.* un- (1).
unwarped' *adj.* un- (1).
unwarr'antable *adj.* un- (1).
unwarr'antably *adv.* un- (1).
unwarr'anted *adj.* un- (1).
unwarr'antedly *adv* un- (1).
unwast'ed *adj.* un- (1).
unwäst'ing *adj.* un- (1).
unwatched' *adj.* un- (1).

Words beginning with pfx un- *are listed first* (pp 1079 ff.); *other* UN- *words follow* (pp. 1092 ff.).

fāte; fär; mē; hûr (her); mīne; mōte; för, mūte; mōōn; fōōt; dhen (then); el'ə-mənt (element) spontaneous: natural, easy; **un'stuffy** (*fig.*) not stodgy or straight-laced; **unsubstan'tial** not substantial, real, corporeal, solid, or strong; **unsuccess'ful.**—*adv.* **unsuccess'fully.**—*ns.* **unsuccess'fulness; unsuitabil'ity.**—*adj.* **unsuit'able.**—*n.* **unsuit'ableness.**—*adv.* **unsuit'ably.**—*adjs.* **unsuit'ed** not suited or adapted; **unsuit'ing; unsung'** not sung: not celebrated in song; **unsupport'ed.**—*adv.* **unsupport'edly.**—*adjs.* **unsure** (*un-shōōr'*) insecure: precarious: uncertain: doubtful: not assured: untrustworthy; **unsuspec'ted** not suspected: not known or supposed to exist.—*adv.* **unsuspec'tedly.**—*n.* **unsuspec'tedness.**—*adj.* **unsuspec'ting.**—*adv.* **unsuspec'tingly.**—*n.* **unsuspec'tingness.**—*adj.* **unsus'picious.**—*adv.* **unsuspi'ciously.**—*n.* **unsuspi'ciousness.**—*adj.* **unswayed'** uninfluenced: not swung; **unsworn'** not confirmed, or not bound, by oath; **unsymmet'rical.**—*adv.* **unsymmet'rically.**—*n.* **unsymm'etry** asymmetry.

Words with prefix un- (*continued*).

vs.t. **untack'** to detach from tacking; **untack'le** to strip of tackle: to free from tackle: to unharness.— *adj.* **untaint'ed** not tainted: unblemished: not attainted.—*n.* **untaint'edness.**—*adjs.* **untaint'ing; untām'able** (also **untame'able**).—*n.* **untam(e)'ableness.**—*adv.* **untam(e)'ably.**—*adjs.* **untame'** not tame; **untamed'.**—*v.t.* **untang'le** to disentangle. —*adjs.* **untang'led; untaught'** uninstructed: not taught or communicated by teaching: spontaneous, native, inborn; **untaxed'** not taxed: not charged with any fault; **unteach'able** not teachable; **untem'pered** not tempered: not regulated; **unten'able** (or **-tē'**) not tenable, not defensible.—*n.* **unten'ableness.**—*v.t.* **unteth'er** to release from a tether. —*adjs.* **unteth'ered** not tethered; **unthatched'** not thatched; **unthawed'** not thawed.—*v.t.* and *v.i.* **unthink'** to think to the contrary, reverse in thought. —*n.* **unthinksbil'ity.**—*adjs.* **unthink'able** that cannot be thought: outside the realm of thought: beyond the power of thought: inconceivable: unimaginable: utterly impossible (often of things impending but too painful to think about); **unthink'ing** not thinking: thoughtless.—*adv.* **unthink'ingly.**—*n.* **unthink'ingness.**—*adj.* **unthought'ful.**—*adv.* **unthought'fully.**—*n.* **unthought'fulness.**—*adj.* **unthought'-of.** —*v.t.* **unthread'** to take a thread from: to unweave: to loosen: to find one's way through.—*adj.* **unthread'ed** not threaded.—*adv.* **unthrift'ily.**—*n.* **unthrift'iness.**—*adj.* **unthrift'y** not thrifty: wasteful: prodigal: not thriving: unprofitable.—*v.t.* **untie'** to loose from being tied: to unbind.—*v.i.* to come loose. —*adj.* **untied'** not tied: loosed.—*v.t.* **untile'** to strip of tiles.—*adj.* **untiled'** not tiled: stripped of tiles.—*n.* **untime'liness.**—*adj.* **untime'ly** not timely: before the time, premature: immature: unseasonable, ill-timed: inopportune.—*adv.* at an unsuitable time: too early, prematurely: unseasonably: inopportunely.—*adj.*

untime'ous (*untī'məs*) untimely.—*adv.* **untime'ously.** —*adjs.* **untinned'** not tinned; **unti'tled** having no title: deprived of title; **untold'** (or **un'**) not counted: innumerable: not narrated: not communicated: not informed; **untouch'able** impossible to touch: not to be equalled or touched.—*n.* one whose excellence in some respect cannot be rivalled: (*esp.* formerly) a Hindu of very low caste, a member of one of the scheduled castes.—*adjs.* **untouched'** not touched: intact: unrivalled; **untoward** (*un-tō'ərd, -tə-wörd'*) not easily guided: froward: awkward: inconvenient: unlucky: unfavourable: unfitting.—*n.* **unto'wardliness, untoward'liness.**—*adv.* **unto'wardly, untoward'ly.**—*adj.* **untoward.**—*n.* **unto'wardness, untoward'ness.**—*v.t.* **untrace'** to loose from traces.— *adjs.* **untrace'able** impossible to trace; **untraced'; untreat'able** that cannot be treated; **untreat'ed; untried'** not tried, tested, attempted, experienced, subjected to trial in court; **untrimmed'** not trimmed; **untrod', untrodd'en** not trodden upon: unfrequented; **untroub'led** not troubled or disturbed: not turbid; **untrue'** not true: false: not faithful: dishonest: inexact: not in accordance with a standard.— *ns.* **untrue'ness; untru'ism** an untrue platitude.— *adv.* **untru'ly** falsely.—*v.t.* **untruss'** to unpack: to unfasten: to untie (*esp.* points of clothes): to untie the points of.—*adv.* **untrust'worthily.**—*n.* **untrust'worthiness.**—*adjs.* **untrust'worthy** not worthy of trust; **untrust'y** not trusty, not deserving trust.—*n.* **untruth'** unfaithfulness: falseness: falsity: that which is untrue: a lie.—*adj.* **untruth'ful** not truthful.—*adv.* **untruth'fully.**—*n.* **untruth'fulness.**—*v.t.* **untuck'** to unfold or undo from being tucked up or in: to take out tucks from.—*adjs.* **untucked'** not tucked; **untūn'able** (also **untune'able**) harsh.—*n.* **untūn'ableness.**—*adv.* **untūn'ably.**—*adjs.* **untuned'** not tuned: put out of tune; **untune'ful.**—*adv.* **untune'fully.**—*n.* **untune'fulness.**—*adjs.* **unturned'** not turned; **untū'tored** untaught: uninstructed.—*vs.t.* and *vs.i.* **untwine'** to untwist: to separate by untwisting; **untwist'** to twist backwards so as to open out: to straighten out from a twist.—*adj.* **untwist'ed** not twisted: subjected to untwisting.—*n.* **untwist'ing.**

Words with prefix un- (*continued*).

adjs. **unused** (*un-ūzd'*) not used: (also *un-ūst'*) unaccustomed; **unuseful** (*-ūs'*).—*adv.* **unuse'fully.**—*n.* **unuse'fulness.**—*adj.* **unūs'ual.**—*adv.* **unūs'ually** more than usually: in an unusual way.—*n.* **unūs'ualness.**—*adj.* **unutt'erable** beyond utterance, inexpressible: not to be uttered.—*n.* an unutterable thing.—*adv.* **unutt'erably.**—*adjs.* **unutt'ered; unval'uable** not valuable, of little worth; **unval'ued** not prized or highly esteemed: without having a value assigned; **unvar'nished** not varnished: not artfully embellished or sophisticated.—*v.t.* **unveil'** to remove or set aside a veil from: to open to public view by ceremonial removal of a covering: to disclose, reveal.

unwatch'ful *adj.* **un-** (1).	**unwea'ryingly** *adv.* **un-** (1).	**unwit'nessed** *adj.* **un-** (1).
unwatch'fulness *n.* **un-** (1).	**unwebbed'** *adj.* **un-** (1).	**unwon'** *adj.* **un-** (1).
unwā'vering *adj.* **un-** (1).	**unwed'** *adj.* **un-** (1).	**unwood'ed** *adj.* **un-** (1).
unwā'veringly *adv.* **un-** (1).	**unwedd'ed** *adj.* **un-** (1).	**unwooed'** *adj.* **un-** (1).
unweakened (**-wēk'**) *adj.* **un-** (1).	**unweed'ed** *adj.* **un-** (1).	**unworn'** *adj.* **un-** (1).
unweaned' *adj.* **un-** (1).	**unwel'come** *adj.* **un-** (1).	**unworr'ied** *adj.* **un-** (1).
unwearable (**-wār'**) *adj.* **un-** (1).	**unwell'** *adj.* **un-** (1).	**unwoundable** (**-wōō nd'**) *adj.* **un-** (1).
unwea'riably *adv.* **un-** (1).	**unwhipped'** *adj.* **un-** (1).	**unwound'ed** *adj.* **un-** (1).
unwea'ried *adj.* **un-** (1).	**unwinged'** *adj.* **un-** (1).	**unwō'ven** *adj.* **un-** (1).
unwea'riedly *adv.* **un-** (1).	**unwiped'** *adj.* **un-** (1).	**unwrung'** *adj.* **un-** (1).
unwea'ry *adj.* **un-** (1).	**unwith'ered** *adj.* **un-** (1).	**unzip'** *v.t.* **un-** (2).
unwea'rying *adj.* **un-** (1).		

Words beginning with pfx. **un-** *are listed first* (pp. 1079 ff.); *other* UN- *words follow* (pp. 1092 ff.).

For other sounds see detailed chart of pronunciation.

—*v.i.* to remove one's veil: to become unveiled, to reveal oneself.—*adj.* **unveiled'** without a veil: with veil set aside or removed: unconcealed and undisguised.—*ns.* **unveil'er; unveil'ing** the ceremonial removal of a covering; **unverac'ity**.—*adj.* **unversed'** not experienced or skilled: not put in verse.—*adj.* **unvir'tuous**.—*adv.* **unvir'tuously**.—*v.t.* **unvoice'** to change to, or utter with, a voiceless sound.—*adj.* **unvoiced'** not given voice to: without voice.—*n.* **unvoic'ing**.

Words with prefix un- (*continued*).

    adv. **unwā'rily**.—*n.* **unwā'riness**.—*adjs.* **unwā'ry** not wary; **unwashed' (the great unwashed** see **great**).—*n.* **unweal'** affliction, ill.—*adj.* **unweath'ered** not worn by the weather or atmospheric agencies.—*v.t.* **unweave'** to undo from being woven.—*adjs.* **unweighed'** not weighed: not pondered: unguarded; **unwept'** not wept for; **unwhole'some** not wholesome: unsound: tainted in health, taste or morals.—*adv.* **unwhole'somely.**—**unwhole'someness**.—*adv.* **unwiel'dily.**—**unwiel'diness**.—*adjs.* **unwiel'dy** difficult to wield or move, from bulk or weakness: heavily awkward: unmanageable.—*adjs.* **unwilled'** not willed: involuntary; **unwill'ing** reluctant: done reluctantly.—*adv.* **unwill'ingly**.—*n.* **unwill'ingness**.—*v.t.* **unwind** (*un-wīnd'*) to undo the winding of: to free from being wound: to wind down or off: to slacken: to relax (*coll.*).—*v.i.* to become unwound: to relax (*coll.*):—*pa.t.* and *pa.p.* **unwound** (*un-wownd'*).—*adj.* not wound: released from being wound.—*n.* and *adj.* **unwind'ing** uncoiling.—*adj.* not winding.—*v.t.* **unwire'** to take the wire from.—*n.* **unwis'dom** lack of wisdom: foolishness: injudiciousness.—*adj.* **unwise'** not wise: injudicious: foolish.—*adv.* **unwise'ly**.—*n.* **unwise'ness**.—*adjs.* **unwished'-for** not wished for; **unwitt'ing** without knowing: unaware: not cognisant: unintentional.—*adv.* **unwitt'ingly**.—*n.* **unwitt'ingness**.—*adjs.* **unwitt'y** foolish: unskilled: without wit; **unwo'manly** not befitting or becoming a woman: not such as a woman is expected to be.—*adv.* in an unwomanly manner.—*adj.* **unwont'ed** unaccustomed: unusual.—*adv.* **unwont'edly**.—*adjs.* **unwork'able** not workable: impracticable; **unwork'ing; unwork'manlike** not like or worthy of a good workman.—*n.* **unworld'liness**.—*adj.* **unworld'ly** not of this world: spiritual: above worldly or self-interested motives.—*adv.* **unwor'thily**.—*n.* **unwor'thiness**.—*adjs.* **unwor'thy** not worthy: worthless: unbecoming: discreditable: undeserved; **unwound** see **unwind**.—*v.t.* **unwrap** (*un-rap'*) to remove wrappings from: to unroll, unwind.—*v.i.* to become unwrapped.—*v.t.* and *v.i.* **unwrink'le** to smooth out from a wrinkled state.—*adj.* **unwrink'led** not wrinkled, smooth; **unwritt'en** not written or reduced to writing, oral: (of a rule, law, etc.) traditional, generally accepted: containing no writing; **unwrought** (*un-röt'*) not done or worked: not fashioned, formed, composed, or worked up: not mined: not tilled: undone, brought back to an original state; **unyiel'ding** not yielding: stiff: obstinate.—*adv.* **unyiel'dingly**.—*n.* **unyiel'dingness**.—*v.t.* **unyoke'** to loose from a yoke or harness: to disjoin.—*v.i.* to unyoke an animal: to cease work.—*adjs.* **unyoked'** not yoked or harnessed: freed from yoke or harness; **unzoned'** not in zones: ungirt.

una corda *ün'ə kör'də, ōon'ä kòr'dä,* (It.; *mus.*) one string (soft pedal).

unanimous *ū-nan'i-məs, adj.* of one mind: without a dissentient.—*n.* **unanimity** (*ū-nan-im'i-ti*) agreement without a dissentient.—*adv.* **unan'imously**. [L. *ūnanimus—ūnus,* one, *animus,* mind.]

unau *ū'nö, ōo'now, n.* the two-toed sloth. [Fr., from Tupí.]

una voce *ün'ə vō'sē, ōon'a wō'ke,* (L.) with one voice.
uncate. See **uncus**.
uncial *un'shəl, -si-əl, adj.* of a form of writing in (usu. large) somewhat rounded characters used in ancient manuscripts.—*n.* an uncial letter: uncial writing: MS written in uncials. [L. *unciālis—uncia,* a twelfth.]
unciform, uncinate, etc. See **uncus**.
uncle *ung'kl, n.* the brother of one's father or mother, or an aunt's husband, or a great-uncle (used with *cap.* as a title either before a man's first name, or independently): a pawnbroker (*slang*): (with *cap.*) a title sometimes used by children for male friends of their parents.—*v.t.* to address as uncle.—**Uncle Sam** the United States or its people; **Uncle Tom** (*U.S. derog.*) an American Negro whose co-operative attitude to white people is thought to show disloyalty to the Negro cause (based on the hero of Harriet Beecher-Stowe's *Uncle Tom's Cabin*.). [O.Fr. *uncle* (Fr. *oncle*)—L. *avunculus,* a maternal uncle.]
uncouth. See **un-**.
unction *ungk'shən, n.* an anointing: that which is used for anointing: ointment: that quality in language which raises emotion or devotion: warmth of address: religious glibness: divine or santifying grace: gusto.—*n.* **unctûos'ity** unctuousness.—*adj.* **unc'tûous** oily: greasy: full of unction: offensively suave and smug.—*adv.* **unc'tûously**.—*n.* **unc'tûousness**.—**extreme unction** (*R.C. Church*) the sacrament of anointing a person with consecrated oil in his last hours. [L. *unctiō, -ōnis,* unction, besmearing, *ūnctum,* fat.]
uncus *ung'kəs, n.* a hook or hook-like process:—*pl.* **unci** (*un'sī*).—*adjs.* **unc'ate** hooked; **unciform** (*un'si-fōrm*) hook-shaped; **un'cinate, -d** unciform: hooked at the end. [L. *uncus* and *uncinus,* hook.]
undé, unde. See **undee**.
undecimal *un-des'i-məl, adj.* based on the number eleven. [L. *undecim,* eleven—*ūnus,* one, *decem,* ten.]
undee, undée, undé, unde *un'dā,* (*her.*) *adj.* wavy. [Fr. *ondé*.]
under *un'dər, prep.* beneath: below: in or to a position lower than that of, especially vertically lower: at the foot of: within, on the covered side of: short of: in or into subjection, subordination, obligation, liability, etc., to: in course of: in the state of: (of cultivated land) supporting a specified crop: by the authority or attestation of: in accordance with: in the aspect of: referred to the class, heading, name, etc., of: in the reign or administration of.—*adv.* in or to a lower (esp. vertically lower) position: in or into a lower degree or condition: in or into subjection: in or into a covered, submerged, or hidden state: below: under par (*golf*).—*adj.* lower: subordinate: falling short.—*n.* an **derling** a contemptuous word for a subordinate: a weakling.—*adj.* **un'dermost** lowest: inmost.—*adv.* in or to the undermost place.—**under the counter** see **count²**. [O.E. *under*.]
under- *un-dər-,* in composition, (1) below, beneath; (2) lower in position (*lit.*); (3) lower in rank, or subordinate; (4a) too little in quantity, too small, insufficient; (4b) in too small a degree, insufficiently; (5) not coming, or not allowed to come, to the surface or into the open.—*v.i.* **underachieve'** to achieve less than one's potential or less than expected, esp. academically.—*ns.* **underachiev'er; underachieve'ment**.—*v.t.* and *v.i.* **underact'** to make too little of in acting: to play, for the sake of effect, with little emphasis.—*adj.* **un'der-age** (when) not of full, or the required, age: immature.—*n.* **underā'gent** a subordinate agent.—*adj.* and *adv.* **un'derarm** placed or held under the arm: with the arm below the shoulder.—*adj.* **unassuming**.—*n.* **un'derbelly** the under surface of a

body or of something suggesting a body: soft underbelly (q.v.).—*v.t.* **underbid'** to offer at a price lower than that of: to outbid: to bid less than the value of (*bridge*).—*v.i.* to bid unduly low.—*n.* (*bridge*) a bid too low to be valid, or less than the hand is worth.—*ns.* **underbidd'er** one who underbids: the next below the highest bidder; **un'derblanket** a blanket of a warm material placed under, rather than over, a person in bed; **un'derbrush** undergrowth or brushwood or shrubs.—*v.t.* **underbuild'** to build under in support, underpin: to build too little upon or in.—*n.* **un'derbush** underbrush.—*v.t.* **underbuy'** to buy at less than the price paid by, or the value of.—*n.* **un'dercarriage** the supporting framework under the body of a carriage or wagon: the landing-gear of an aircraft, or its main part.—*v.t.* **undercharge'** to charge too little, or too little for.—*adj.* **underclad'** not wearing clothes enough.—*ns.* **un'derclay** a bed of clay underlying a coal-seam representing the soil in which the plants grew; **un'dercliff** a terrace of material that has fallen from a cliff.—*n.pl.* **un'derclothes** and *n.sing.* **un'derclothing** clothes worn under others, esp. those next to the skin.—*v.t.* **underclub'** (*golf*) to hit with a club which has too great loft to achieve the desired distance.—Also *v.i.*—*n.* **un'dercoat** a coat worn under another: an underlayer of fur or hair, or of paint.—*adj.* **un'dercover** working, done, in secret: (under cover of hidden by, using as concealment).—*ns.* **un'dercovert** a covert of undergrowth; **un'dercroft** (cf. Du. *krocht*, crypt), a crypt, vault; an **undercurrent** a current under the surface (*lit.* and *fig.*).—*adj.* running below or unseen.—*v.t.* **undercut'** to cut under: to cut away under the surface, so as to leave part overhanging: to undermine: to strike with a heavy blow upward: to underbid: to go beyond in lowering prices.—*adj.* made so as to cut from the underside: effected by undercutting: having the parts in relief cut under.—*n.* (*un'*) the act or effect of cutting under: a blow dealt upward: the tender-loin, or fillet, or underside of a sirloin.—*v.t.* **underdevel'op.**—*adj.* **underdevel'oped** insufficiently developed: of a country, with resources inadequately used, having a low standard of living, and backward in education.—*n.* **underdevel'opment.**—*v.t.* **underdo'** to do, perform, act, or esp. cook, insufficiently or inadequately:—*pa.t.* **underdid'**; *pa.p.* **underdone'.**—*ns.* **underdo'er; un'derdog** the dog that gets the worst of it in a fight: anyone in adversity: a person dominated, or being or likely to be beaten, by another.—*adj.* **underdone'** done less than is requisite: insufficiently or slightly cooked.—*vs.t.* **un'derdraw** to draw or describe with moderation or reticence or short of the truth.—*ns.* **un'derdrawing** an outline drawing on a canvas, etc., done before paint is applied; **un'derdress** underclothing: a dress or part of a dress worn or showing under another.—*v.t.* and *v.i.* **underdress'** to dress too plainly or simply.—*adj.* **underdressed'.**—*ns.* **un'derdrive** a gear which transmits to the driving shaft a speed less than engine speed; **underemploy'ment** making too little use (of): the condition of having too large a part of the labour force employed: partial employment, or employment on work requiring less skill than the worker has.—*v.t.* **underes'timate** to estimate or value too low.—*n.* an estimate that falls short of the truth or true quantity.—*n* **underestima'tion.**—*v.t.* **underexpose'** to expose too

little, esp. (*phot.*) to light.—*ns.* **underexpos'ure;** **un'derfelt** an older term for underlay, usu. of felt; **un'derflow** undercurrent.—*adv.* **underfoot'** beneath one's feet.—*adj.* (*un'*) downtrodden.—*ns.* **un'derfur** short fur hidden by longer hairs; **un'dergarment** any article of clothing worn under another, esp. that worn next to the skin, underclothing.—*adj.* **un'derglaze** applied or done before glazing.—*n.* **undergrad'uate** a student who has not taken any degree (*coll.* contraction **un'dergrad**).—*adj.* pertaining to such.—*adj.* **un'derground** under the surface of the ground: secret: characterised by avant-gardism and experimentation, rejection of current trends or norms, appeal to a minority, anti-establishment tendencies, etc.—*n.* the underworld: an underground place: an underground railway: underlying ground: low ground: a secret resistance movement, or body of people: a group whose activities are partly concerned with resisting things they disapprove of in social, artistic, and political life.—*adv.* **underground'** beneath the surface of the earth: secretly.—*n.* **un'dergrowth** low plants growing under taller, esp. shrubs under trees: stunted growth.—*adv.* **underhand'** surreptitiously: with the hand below the elbow or shoulder.—*adj.* **un'derhand** surreptitious, secret: not straightforward: delivered underhand.—*n.* an underhand ball: (with *the*) a subordinate position.—*adj.* and *adv.* **underhan'ded** short of hands.—*adv.* **underhan'dedly.**—*n.* **underhan'dedness.**—*adj.* **underhung'** (or *un'*) (of a lower jaw) protruding: having a protruding lower jaw: running on rollers on a rail below.—*n.* **under-jaw'** the lower jaw.—*adjs.* **underlaid** see **underlay; underlain** see **underlie.**—*v.t.* **underlay'** to support or furnish with something laid under: to lay under:—*pa.t.* and *pa.p.* **underlaid'.**—*n.* (*un'*) something laid under, e.g. felt or rubber to help preserve carpet.—*n.* **underlay'er** one who underlays: (*un'*) a lower layer, substratum.—*vs.t.* **underlie'** to lie beneath (*lit.* and *fig.*): to undergo: to be subject or liable to:—*pr.p.* **underly'ing**; *pa.t.* **underlay'**; *pa.p.* **underlain'; underline'** to draw a line under: to stress. —*n.* (*un'*) a caption, legend.—*ns.* **un'derling** see **under; un'derlip** a lower lip.—*adj.* **underly'ing** lying beneath (*lit.* and *fig.*): fundamental: present though not immediately obvious.—*adjs.* **undermanned'** having too small a staff, crew, etc.; **undermen'tioned** mentioned underneath or hereafter.—*v.t.* **undermine'** to dig beneath (e.g. a wall) in order that it may fall: to wash away, remove by burrowing, etc., the ground from under: to weaken gradually or insidiously (*fig.*): to intrigue against: to tamper with the fidelity of.—*ns.* **undermi'ner; undermi'ning; un'dernote** a note added below.—*v.t.* to note below. —*adj.* **undernour'ished** living on less food than is necessary for satisfactory health and growth (also *fig.*).—*n.* **undernour'ishment.**—*n.pl.* **un'derpants** an undergarment worn by men and boys, covering the buttocks and sometimes the legs.—**un'derpass** a road passing under another road, a railway, etc.—*v.i.* **underperform'** to do less well than expected, possible, etc.—*v.t.* **underpin'** to support by building underneath, or to prop up (also *fig.*): to corroborate. —*n.* **underpinn'ing.**—*v.t.* **underplay'** to play a low card while holding up a higher.—*v.t.* to play down, understate.—*v.t.* and *v.i.* to underact.—*n.* (*un'*) the act of so doing.—*n.* **un'derplot** a subordinate plot in a

Words beginning with pfx. **un-** *are listed first* (pp. 1079 ff.); *other UN- words follow* (pp. 1092 ff.).

play or tale: a secret scheme, a trick.—*adj.* **under-priced'** having too low a price.—*v.t.* **underprize'** to value too little.—*adj.* **under-priv'ileged** not enjoying normal social and economic rights.—Also *n.*—*v.t* and *v.i.* **under-produce'.**—*n.* **under-produc'tion** too little production: production short of demand.—*vs.t.* **underquote'** to offer at a price lower than; **underrate'** to rate too low.—*n.* (*un'*) a price less than the worth. —*n.* **under-representá'tion** too little representation: less representation than one is entitled to.—*adjs.* **under-represent'ed; un'der-ripe'** not quite ripe.— *v.t.* **underscore'** to underline.—*n.* **un'derscrub** brushwood.—*v.t.* **underseal'** to coat exposed parts of underside of (a motor vehicle) with corrosion-resisting substance.—Also *n.* (*un'*).—*ns.* **underseal'ing; un'der-sec'retary** a secretary immediately under the principal secretary; **under-sec'retaryship.**—*v.t.* **undersell'** to sell below the price charged by: to sell too cheap.—*adj.* **undersexed'** having less than normal interest in sexual relations or activity.—*v.* **un'der-shirt** a man's collarless undergarment usu. of woven cotton, which may or may not have sleeves.—*v.t.* **undershoot'** to fail to reach by falling short (also *fig.*). —*n.* (*aero.*) a falling short of the mark in landing.— *ns.* **un'dershrub** a shrubby plant, or a low shrub; **un'derside** the lower surface.—*v.t.* **undersign'** to sign below.—*adjs.* **un'dersigned** (or *-sīnd'*) whose signature is appended; **un'dersized** below the usual or desired size.—*n.* **un'derskirt** a petticoat: a foundation for a dress or skirt.—*adj.* **underslung'** suspended, or supported, from above, or hung so as to extend below a part which, in another arrangement, it might be wholly above.—*v.i.* and *v.t.* **underspend'** to spend less than one could or should (of e.g. a budget) —*adj.* **understaffed'** having too few members of staff. —*v.t.* **understate'** to state more moderately than truth would allow or require: to state or describe, or to use artistically, without emphasis.—*adj.* **under-stat'ed** effective through simplicity, without embellishment or dramatic emphasis.—*ns.* **understate'-ment** (or *un'*); **un'dersteer** a tendency in a motor-car to follow a wider curve than the turning applied by the steering wheel should cause it to follow.—Also *v.i.*—*vs.t.* **understock'** to supply with an insufficient amount of stock; **understood** see **understand.**—*n.* **un'derstratum** an underlayer:—*pl.* **un'derstrata.**— *v.t.* **un'derstudy** to study (a part), or to study the part of (an actor or other person) in order to take over in an emergency, or in due course.—Also *v.i.*—*n.* one who understudies.—*n.* **un'derthrust** (*geol.*) a fault in which one mass of rock is moved under another relatively static layer.—*adj.* **undertimed'** (of a photograph) underexposed.—*ns.* **un'dertint** a subdued tint: a tint showing through; **un'dertone** a subdued tone of voice, sound, colour, etc.: a tone felt as if pervading, underlying, or perceptible through others, including (*fig.*) an emotional tone: a difference tone (q.v.): a low state of body.—*adj.* **un'dertoned** in an undertone: (*-tōnd'*) wanting in tone.—*ns.* **un'dertow** (*-tō*) an undercurrent opposed to the surface current: the recoil or back-draught of a wave; **un'der-trick** a trick short of the number declared; **undervalu'ation.** —*v.t.* **underval'ue** to value below the real worth: to reduce the value of: to esteem too lightly.—*n.* (*un'*) a value or price under the real worth.—*ns.* **underval'uer; un'dervest** an undershirt, or a similar garment for a woman; **un'derwater** underground water:

undertow.—*adj.* existing, acting, carried out, etc., below the surface of the water: below the water-line. —Also *adv.*—*ns.* **un'derwear** underclothing; **un'der-weight** shortness of weight: short weight.—*adj.* short in weight.—*n.* **un'derwood** undergrowth: a coppice. —*v.t.* **underwork'** to employ too little in work: to work for less than the wage of.—*v.i.* to do less work than is desirable.—*n.* (*un'*) a substructure: underhand, inferior, or subordinate work.—*ns.* **un'derworker; un'der-work'man; un'derworld** the world beneath the heavens: the world or a region, beneath the earth: the place of departed souls: the part of the world below the horizon: the antipodes: a submerged, hidden, or secret region or sphere of life, esp. one given to crime, profligacy, or intrigue.—*v t.* **un'derwrite** to write (something) beneath: to subscribe to (a statement, etc.): to accept the risk of insuring: to guarantee to take, or find others to take (certain shares, under certain conditions): to write too little about: (*refl.*) to write below the level of which one is capable.—*v.i.* to practise as an underwriter.—*ns.* **un'derwriter** one who practises insurance business, esp. in ships; **un'derwriting.**

underachieve ... to ... **underglaze.** See **under-.** **undergo** *un-dar-gō'*, *v.t.* to be subjected to: to endure or suffer: to pass through, experience. [Late O.E. *undergân—gân*, to go.]

undergraduate ... to ... **undermining.** See **under-.** **underneath** *un-dar-nēth'*, *adv.* and *prep.* beneath, below in position (*lit.* and *fig.*).—*n.* the under part or side. [O.E. *underneothan.*]

undernote ... to ... **understaffed.** See **under-.** **understand** *un-dar-stand'*, *v.t.* to comprehend: to grasp with the mind: to be able to follow the working, logic, meaning, etc., of: to take the meaning of (a sign, person): to realise: to have a sympathetic, usu. tacit, perception of the character, aims, etc., of (a person): to know the meaning of: to be expert in: to have knowledge or information (that), to have been informed: to assume, take to be true: to interpret (as), take to mean: to imply: to support.—*v.t.* to have understanding: to comprehend—*pa.t.* and *pa.p.* **understood'.**—*adj.* **understand'able.**—*n.* **understand'ing** the act of comprehending: the power to understand: intellect: an informal agreement: an understood condition (e.g. *on the understanding that*): sympathetic or amicable agreement of minds. —*adj.* intelligent: discerning: sympathetic.—*adv.* **understand'ingly.**—*adj.* **understood'** (often *gram.*) implied but not expressed.—**understand each other** or **one another** to have reached an agreement, sometimes collusive. [O.E. *understandan—under, standan*, to stand.]

understate ... to ... **understudy.** See **under-.** **undertake** *un-dar-tāk'*, *v.t.* to pledge oneself (that): to take upon oneself: to take upon oneself (to deal with, manage, or look after): to set about, engage in: to engage in contest with.—*v.i.* to promise: to become a surety (for): to conduct funerals (*coll.*):—*pa.t.* **undertook'**; *pa.p.* **undertâ'ken.**—*adj.* **undertâ'kable.** —*ns.* **un'dertaker** one who takes in hand an enterprise, task, or encounter: one who manages funerals; **un'dertaking** that which is undertaken: any business or project engaged in: a task one sets oneself: the business of conducting funerals.—Also *adj.* [12th cent. *undertaken*, to entrap—O.E. *under*, late O.E *tacan*; see **take.**]

---

underpow'ered *adj.* under- (4b).   **undersea'** *adv.* under- (1).   **underutilisa'tion, -z-** *n.* under- (4a).
underprepared' *adj.* under- (4b).   **underuse** (*-ūz'*) *v.t.* under- (4b).   **underû'tilise, -ize** *n.* under- (4b).
un'dersea *adj.* under- (1).   **underuse** (*-ūs'*) *n.* under- (4a).

Words beginning with pfx. **un-** *are listed first* (pp. 1079 ff.); *other UN- words follow* (pp. 1092 ff.).

underthrust ... to .. **underwrought**. See **under-**.

undies un'diz, (coll.) n.pl. women's underclothing. [under.]

undulate un'dū-lāt, v.t. and v.i. to move like or in waves: to make or be wavy: to vibrate.—adj. **wavy**: with wavy margin, surface, or markings.—Also **un'dulated**.—n. **un'dulancy**.—adj. **un'dulant** undulating: rising and falling.—adv. un'dulately.—adj. **un'dulating**.—adv. **un'dulatingly**.—ns. **undula'tion** an undulating, a wavelike motion or form: waviness: a wave; **undula'tionist** one who holds the undulatory theory of light.—adj. **un'dulatory** of the nature of undulation: undulating: wavy: referring light to waves in a medium.—**undulant fever** a remittent fever with swelling of the joints and enlarged spleen, caused by a bacterium (Brucella) transmitted by goat's (or cow's) milk. [L. undulātus, undulated —unda, a wave.]

unguent ung'gwənt, n. ointment. [L. unguentum—unguēre, to anoint.]

unguis ung'gwis, n. a claw or nail:—pl. **ung'ues** (-gwēz).—adjs. **ung'ual** (-gwəl) of or bearing a claw; **unguiculate** (ung-gwik'ū-lāt), -d clawed, **unguiform** (ung'gwi-förm). [L. unguis, a nail.]

ungula ung'gū-lə, n. a hoof (zool.): a section of a cylinder, cone, etc., cut off by a plane oblique to the base (geom.):—pl. **ung'ulae** (-lē).—adj. **ung'ulate** hoofed. —n. a hoofed animal, a member of the order **Ungula'ta**, hoofed digitigrade mammals. [L. ungula, claw, hoof—unguis, nail.]

uni ū'ni, n. a coll. shortening of **university**.

uni- ū-ni-, in composition, one.—adj. **uniax'ial** having one axis, esp. (crystal.) one optic axis or (biol.) one main line of growth or unbranched axis.—adv. **uniax'ially**.—adjs. **unicam'eral** (L. camera, vault; see **chamber**) having or consisting of but one chamber; **unicell'ular** of or having but one cell.—n. **ū'nicorn** (L. cornū, a horn) a fabulous animal mentioned by ancient Greek and Roman authors as a native of India, with a body like a horse and one straight horn: (cap.) one of the Scottish pursuivants.—adj. **one-horned**.—n. **ū'nicycle** an acrobat's one-wheeled cycle.—adjs. **unidirec'tional** mainly or wholly in one direction; **uniflor'ous** (L. flōs, flōris, a flower) one-flowered; **unifo'liolate** (L. foliolum, dim. of folium, leaf; bot.) having a single leaflet, but compound in structure; **unilat'eral** (L. latus, lateris, side) one-sided: on one side: affecting, involving, etc. only one person, group, etc. out of several.—ns. **unilat'eralism**; **unilat'eralist** one who favours unilateral action, esp. in abandoning or reducing production of nuclear weapons; **unilateral'ity**.—adv. **unilat'erally**.—adjs. **uniling'ual** (L. lingua, tongue) of, in, using, one tongue, language; **unilo'bar**, **unilobed'** having one lobe; **unilob'ular** having one lobule; **uninu'clear** with a single nucleus; **uninu'cleate**; **unip'arous** (L. parĕre, to bring forth) producing one at a birth; **unipar'tite** not divided into parts; **uniper'sonal** existing as only one person; **unipo'lar** of, from, or using one pole: of a nerve cell, having one process only.—n. **unipolar'ity**.—adj. **unisē'rial** in one series or row.—adv. **unisē'rially**.—adj. **unisē'riate** uniserial.—adv. **unisē'riately**.—adjs. **ū'nisex** of a style, esp. in clothes, adopted by both sexes: applicable to, usable by, etc. persons of either sex; **unisex'ual** of one sex only.—n. **unisexual'ity**.—adv. **unisex'ually**.—n. **ū'nison** (or -zən; L. sonus, sound, sonāre, to sound) identity of pitch: loosely, pitch differing by one or more octaves: a sound of the same pitch: complete agreement.—adj. in unison.—n. **unis'onance**.—adjs. **unis'onant**; **unis'onous**.—ns. **univā'lence** (or -iv'əl-), **univā'lency** (or -iv'əl-).—adj. **univā'lent** (chem.) having a valency of one, capable of combining with one atom of hydrogen or its equivalent.—adj. and n. (pertaining to) one of the single chromosomes which separate in the first meiotic division.—adj. **ū'nivalve** having one valve or shell only.—n. a shell of one valve only: a mollusc whose shell is composed of a single piece.—adjs. **unival'vular**; **univā'riant** having one degree of freedom; **univā'riate** (of a distribution) having one variate only. [L. ūnus, one.]

Uniat ū'ni-ət, n. a member of any community of Christians, esp. in eastern Europe and Asia, that acknowledges the papal supremacy but which is allowed to retain its own customs and practices with regard to all else—clerical matrimony, communion in both kinds, church discipline, rites and liturgy.—Also **U'niate** (-āt, -ət). [Russ. uniyat—uniya, union— L.L. ūniō, -ōnis—L. ūnus, one.]

uniaxial ... to ... **unifoliolate**. See **uni-**.

uniform ū'ni-form, adj. alike: alike all over, throughout, or at all times: unvarying: of a military or other uniform.—n. a distinctive garb for members of a body: a suit of it.—v.t. to make uniform: to clothe in uniform.—adj. **ū'niformed** wearing uniform.—n. **uniform'ity** the state or fact of being uniform: agreement with a pattern or rule: sameness: likeness between parts.—adv. **ū'niformly**.—n. **ū'niformness**. [L. ūniformis—ūnus, one, fōrma, form]

unify ū'ni-fī, v.t. to make into one: to consolidate.— adj. **ū'nifiable**.—n. **unifica'tion**.—adj. **ū'nified**.—n. **ū'nifier**.—n. and adj. **ū'nifying**.—**unified field** an ultimate basis on which the physicist seeks to bring within a single theory the workings of all natural phenomena. [L.L. unificāre—L. ūnus, one, facĕre, to make.]

unilateral ... to ... **uninucleate**. See **uni-**.

union ūn'yən, n. a uniting: the state of being united: the state of wedlock: a united whole: combination: a growing together in healing: general concord: the incorporation of states in a federation or in a single state: a single state (or sometimes a federation) thus formed: an association or league, esp. a trade union: a student's club: a connecting part for pipes, etc.: a device emblematic of union borne in the canton of a flag: the same device used separately as a flag, as the Union Jack: a textile fabric of more than one kind of fibre: the set formed from all the elements present in two (or more) sets.—n. **unionisa'tion**, **-z-**.—v.t. **ūn'ionise**, **-ize** to recruit into a trade union: to organise the workforce of into a trade union.—ns. **ūn'ionism** (also cap.), **ūn'ionist** an advocate or supporter of or believer in union or trade unions: a member of a trade union: (cap.) an opponent of Irish Home Rule, esp. a Liberal Unionist (see **Liberal**)— hence a Conservative: (cap.) a supporter of the federal union of the United States, esp at the time of the Civil War.—Also adj.—**union flag** a flag symbolising union, esp. the national flag of the United Kingdom, consisting of a union of the crosses of St George, St Andrew, and St Patrick, commonly called the **Union Jack**.—**the Union** the legislative incorporation of England and Scotland in 1707, or of Ireland with both in 1801: the American Union or United States: the Union of South Africa (1910). [Fr. union—L.L. ūniō, -ōnis—L. ūnus, one.]

unionised[1]. See **un-**.

unionised[2]. Pa.t. and pa.p. of **unionise** (see under **union**).

uniparous ... to ... **unipolarity**. See **uni-**.

unique ū-nēk', adj. sole: without a like: often used loosely for unusual, pre-eminent: found solely in, belonging solely to, etc. (with to).—n. anything that is unique.—adv. **unique'ly**.—n. **unique'ness**. [Fr.,—L. ūnicus—ūnus.]

uniserial ... to ... **unisonous.** See **uni-**.

unit *ū'nit*, *n.* one: a single thing or person: a single element, section, or item, regarded as the lowest subdivision of a whole: a group of persons forming a subdivision of a larger body: a distinct part within a piece of electrically powered equipment which has its own specific function: a single complete domestic fixture combining what are sometimes separate parts: the least whole number: anything taken as one: a quantity by reference to which others are measured. —*adj.* of the character or value of a unit: individual. —*n.* **Unitā'rian** one who asserts the unity of the Godhead as opposed to the Trinity, ascribes divinity to God the father only, and who believes in freedom of, and tolerance of the differences in, religious beliefs, etc.: a member of a particular body holding such doctrines: a monotheist generally: (without *cap.*) a holder of some belief based on unity or union.—Also *adj.*—*n.* **Unitā'rianism** (also without *cap.*).—*adj.* **ū'nitary** pertaining to unity or to a unit: of the nature of a unit: integral: based on unity.—**unit furniture** furniture which may be bought as single items rather than as sets or suites; u**'nitholder** one holding a unit of securities in a unit trust; **unit-pack'aging** a method of packaging (pills, etc.) in which the items are individually encased; **unit price; unit-pri'cing** a method of pricing foodstuffs, etc. by showing the cost per agreed unit, e.g. kilogram, pound, as well as, or instead of, the overall price of the item; **unit trust** see **trust**.—**unit of account** a monetary unit not necessarily corresponding to any actual denomination of currency and in certain cases of variable value, used as a basis of exchange or comparison or as a unit in accounting. [For **unity**.]

unite *ū-nīt'*, *v.t.* to make one: to join into one: to join: to combine: to clasp: to marry: to have in combination: to make to agree or adhere.—*v.i.* to become one: to combine: to join: to grow or act together.— *adj.* **unī'ted.**—*adv.* **unī'tedly.**—*ns.* **unī'tedness;** **unī'ter.**—*n. and adj.* **unī'ting.**—*n.* **unition** (*ū-nish'ən*) conjunction.—*adj.* **unitive** (*ū'ni-tiv*) harmonising, uniting.—**United Kingdom (of Great Britain and Ireland; from 1922 Northern Ireland)** the official title adopted in 1801 for the kingdom consisting of England and Wales, Scotland, and Ireland; **United Nations** an association of states that in 1945 undertook many of the functions of the dissolved League of Nations; **United States** a federal union of states, esp. that of (north) America. [L. *ūnītus*, pa.p. of *ūnīre*, to unite—*ūnus*, one.]

unity *ū'ni-ti*, *n.* oneness: the number one: the state or fact of being one or at one: that which has oneness: a single whole: the arrangement of all the parts to one purpose or effect.—**the unities** (of *place, time,* and *action*) the three canons of the classical drama—that the scenes should be at the same place, that all the events should be such as might happen within a single day, and that nothing should be admitted not directly relevant to the development of the plot. [L. *ūnitās*, *-ātis*—*ūnus*, one.]

univalence ... to ... **univariate.** See **uni-**.

universe *ū'ni-vûrs*, *n.* all that is: the whole system of things: the cosmos: a system of stars such as the galactic system: the world.—*adj.* **univers'al** of the universe: comprehending, affecting, or for use by, the whole world or all people: without exception: comprising all the particulars: all-round: unlimited: capable of being applied to a great variety of uses.— *n.* that which is universal: a universal proposition: a general term: a universal concept.—*n.* **universalisā'tion**, *-z-*.—*v.t.* **univer'salise**, *-ize-*.—*ns.* **Univer'salism** the doctrine or belief of universal salvation, or the ultimate salvation of all mankind, and even of the fallen angels; **Univer'salist** a believer in Universalism.—Also *adj.*—*adj.* **universalis'tic.**—*n.* **universality** (*-sal'*) the state or quality of being universal.—*adv.* **univer'sally.**—*n.* **univer'salness.**—**universal joint** one capable of turning all ways. [L. *ūniversum*, neut. sing. of *ūniversus*, whole, *ūnus*, one, *vertĕre*, *versus*, to turn.]

university *ū-ni-vûr'si-ti*, *n.* an institution of higher learning with power to grant degrees, its body of teachers, students, graduates, etc., its college or colleges, or its buildings.—*adj.* **universitā'rian.** [L. *ūniversitās* *-ātis*, a whole, in L.L. a corporation; see foregoing.]

univocal *ū-niv'ə-kl* or *ū-ni-vō'kl*, *adj.* of one voice: having one meaning only: unmistakable: unambiguous.—*adv.* **univocally.** [L. *ūnivocus*—*ūnus*, one, *vōx*, *vōcis*, a voice.]

unless *un-les'*, *ən-les'*, *conj.* (tending to pass into a *prep.*) if not. [Earlier followed by *than* or *that*: on *lesse than*, on a less condition than.]

uno animo *ū'nō*, *ōō'nō*, *an'i-mō*, *adv.* with one mind. [L.]

until *un-til'*, *ən-til'*, *prep.* and *conj.* till. [Pfx. *und-*, as far as; **till**.]

unto *un'tōō*, *-tōō*, (*arch.* or *formal*) *prep.* to. [Pfx. *und-*, as far as; **to**.]

up *up*, *adv.* in, to, toward a higher place, level, or state: aloft: on high: towards a centre (as a capital, great town, university): in residence, at school or college: northward: to windward: in or to a more erect position or more advanced stage of erection: out of bed: on horseback: in an excited state: in revolt: with (increased) vigour, intensity, or loudness: afoot: amiss: into prominence, notice, consideration: forward for sale: in or into court: into custody, keeping, possession: away in a receptacle, place of storage or lodging (as a sheath, purse, stable): ahead in scoring: into closed or compact state, together: to a total: in, near, towards arrival, overtaking, or being abreast: as far as: all the way: to a standstill: at an end: to a finish: thoroughly, completely, fully: well informed, versed.—Also elliptically passing into a verb or interjection by omission of *go*, *come*, *put*, etc., often followed by *with*.—*adj.* placed, going, or directed up: top: risen: (of time) ended: having gained (so many) more holes than an opponent (*golf*):—*compar.* **upp'er;** *superls.* **up'most**, **upp'ermost** see below.—*prep.* in an ascent along, through, or by: to or in a higher position on: to or in an inner or more remote part of: along against the current: along.—*n.* a rise: a high place: a success, spell of prosperity: one who is in prosperity.—*v.t.* to drive upstream (as swans for owner marking): to lift or haul up: to raise, increase.—*v.i.* (*coll.*) to set up: to move up: to intervene boldly, start into activity or speech:—*pr.p.* **upp'ing;** *pa.t.* and *pa.p.* **upped** (*upt*).—*adjs.* **up'most** uppermost; **upp'er** (see above) higher: superior: higher in rank.—*n.* the part of a boot or shoe above the sole and welt: an upper tooth: a drug producing a stimulant or euphoric effect, or a pep pill containing such a drug (*slang*).—*adj.* **upp'ermost** (see above) highest: first to come into the mind.—*adv.* in the highest place, first.—*n.* **upp'ing** the action of **up** *v.t.* (q.v.).—*adj.* **upp'ish** assuming, pretentious, snobbish.—*adv.* **upp'ishly.**—*n.* **upp'ishness.**—*adj.* **upp'ity** uppish: difficult to control, resistant to persuasion.—*advs.* **up'ward** (*-wərd*), **upwards** from lower to higher: from outlet towards source: from modern to more ancient: in the upper part (**up'ward**, **upwards**, of more than; **and upwards** and higher, and more).—*prep.* **up'ward** upwards along.— *adj.* **up'ward** directed upward: ascending: placed high.—*adv.* **up'wardly.**—*n.* **up'wardness** a rising

tendency: a state of being high.—*adjs.* up'-**and-com'ing** alert and pushful: likely to succeed (in a career, etc.); up'-**and-down'** (see also **up and down** below) undulating: going or working both, or alternately, up and down; up'-**and-o'ver** (of a door, etc.) raised to a horizontal position when opened.—Also up'-**o'ver**.
—up'-**and-un'der** (*Rugby*) a movement in which the ball is kicked high and forwards, and the players rush to try to catch it; up'**beat** an unaccented beat, at which the conductor raises his baton.—*adj.* (*coll.*) cheerful: optimistic.—up'-**bow** a movement of the bow from point towards nut over the strings; up'-**current**, -**draught** a rising current of air; up'**land** inland, hilly, or high-lying country: upper or high land, as opp. to meadows, river-sides, etc. (*U.S.*).—*adj.* high-lying: remote: inland: rural: of the uplands.—up'**lander**.—up'-**line** a railway line for upgoing trains (i.e. those going to, not from, e.g. a city).—*adjs.* upp'er**brack'et** in an upper grouping in a list, etc.; upp'er**case'** (*print.*) lit. kept in an upper case, capital as opposed to small (of letters).—**upper class(es)** the people of the highest social rank (*adj.* upp'er-**class'**); **upper crust** the top of a loaf: the aristocracy, or the upper class(es) in any society (*adj.* upp'er-**crust'**); **upper cut** an upward short-arm blow; **upper hand** mastery, advantage; **upper house** in a bicameral legislature, the house that is the more restricted in membership, e.g. House of Lords, Senate of U.S. and other countries; up'**side** the upper side.—*adv.* on the upper side.—*adv.* up'**side-down'**, **upside down** with the upper part undermost: in or into, complete confusion.—*adj.* turned upside down.—*adv.* up'**sides** (**with**) on a par (with): beside.—up'**swing** an upward swing: an economic recovery; up'-**train** a railway train proceeding towards the chief terminus; up'**trend**.—**be up in** to have a knowledge of; **it is all up (with)** there is no hope (for); (**on**) **the up and up (in)** a state of continuous progress towards ever greater success: honest, on the level; **something is up** something is amiss, something unusual or unexpected is happening or has happened; **up against** face to face with, confronted with (**up against it** in almost desperate straits); **up and doing** bestirring oneself; **up and down** to and fro: here and there through or about: throughout: vertically: out-and-out; **up for** available for or undergoing (some process): standing as a candidate for; **up front** at the front: to the forefront: foremost; **ups and downs** undulations: vicissitudes; **up to** as far up as: into the immediate neighbourhood or presence of: immersed or embedded as far as: about, meditating or engaged in doing (*coll.*): capable of and ready for (*coll.*): incumbent upon (orig. *U.S.*); **up to date** to the present time or time in question: containing all recent facts, statistics, etc.: knowing the latest developments of fashion, usage, etc. (*adj.* up'**to-date'**); **up top** (*coll.*) in the head, in respect of intelligence; **up to the minute**, **moment** right up to the present time (*adjs.* up-**to-the-minute'**, -**moment'** very up-to-date); **up town** into town: in or to the residential part of a town (*U.S.*); **up with** abreast of: even with: to take off, swallow: put, get, etc. up (see under **up**), often as an exclamation of approbation and partisanship; **up yours** (*vulg. slang*) an expression of strong refusal, defiance, contempt, etc.; **what's up (with you**, etc.)? what's the matter, trouble? [O.E. *ūp*, *upp*, up, *uppe*, above, *uppian*, to rise.]
up- in composition, has meanings of *adv.*, *prep.* (and

adj.; see previous article) **up.**—*v.i.* up-**anch'or** to weigh anchor.—*vs.t.* up**bear'** to raise aloft: to hold up: to sustain; up**braid** see separate article.—*n.* up'**break** a break-up: an outbreak.—*v.t.* (-**brāk'**) to break up or open.—*v.i.* to break out.—*n.* up'**bringing** bringing up.—*v.t.* up**build'** to build up.—*ns.* up**build'ing** (or up') building up: development: edification; up'**burst** a bursting upwards.—*v.t.* and *v.i.* (-**bûrst'**).—*adj.* up**burst'ing**.—*n.* up'**cast** an upward throw: an upthrow: material thrown up: an upward current of air from a mine: a shaft carrying it (up'**cast-shaft**).—*adj.* thrown or turned upward.—*n.* up'**country** the interior, inland part.—*adj.* (-**kun'**) of or in the interior.—*adv.* in or to the interior.—*v.t.* up**date'** to bring up to date —*n.* (*up'*) the act of bringing up to date: that which is brought up to date —*v.t.* up-**end'** to set on end: to affect or alter greatly, turn upside down.—*v i.* to rise on end.—*n.* up'**flow** an upward flowing.—*v.i.* (-**flō'**) to stream up.—*n.* up'**grade** an upward slope or course.—*adj.* and *adv.* up-**hill**.—*v.t.* (-**grād'**) to raise in status, quality, value, etc —*ns.* up'**growth** the process of growing up, development: that which grows up: a structure that has grown upward; up**heav'al** a heaving up: the bodily elevation of tracts of country: a profound, thorough, or revolutionary change or movement.—*vs.t.* up**heave'**; up**held** see up**hold**.—*adj.* up'**hill** ascending: difficult.—Also *n.*—Also *adv.* (-**hil'**).—*v.t.* up**hold'** to hold up: to sustain: to countenance: to defend: to keep in repair or good condition: to maintain, warrant:—*pa.t* and *pa.p.* up**held'**.—*n.* up**hold'er** a support or supporter.—*n.* and *adj.* up**hold'ing**.—*n.* up'**keep** maintenance.—*v.t.* up**lift'** to lift up, raise: to elevate: to raise to a higher moral or spiritual level: to elate: to collect (e g. a parcel), draw (money) (*Scot.*). to increase (e.g an interim dividend) (*commerce*) — *n.* up'**lift** a lifting up, raising: upheaval: elevation, esp. moral or spiritual, or the feeling thereof: an increase (*commerce*).—*n.* and *adj.* up**lift'ing**.—*adv.* up**lift'ingly**.—*adj.* up'**lying** upland, elevated.—*ns.* up'**make** the action or mode of making up: constitution (especially mental or moral): proofs arranged in page form; up'**maker**; up'**making** filling-up, esp between bilge-ways and ship's bottom before launching: arrangement of lines into columns or pages (*print.*).—*adj* up-**mar'ket** of (buying, selling, or using) commodities relatively high in price, quality or prestige.—Also *adv.*—*v.t.* to make (more) up-market.—*preps.* up**o'** (*a-pō'*; from *up of*; *arch.* or *dial.*) upon; up**on** (*a-pon'*, *a-pǝn*) on.—*v.t.* up**raise'** to raise or lift up: to exalt. up**raised'**.—*v.t.* up**rate'** to upgrade: to increase the rate or size of.—*adj.* up'**right** (also up'**rīt'**, up-**rīt'**) right or straight up: in an erect position (**upright piano** one with the strings in a vertical plane): of habitual rectitude: honest: just.—*n.* up'**right** an upright post, stone, stroke, or the like: a vertical member of a structure: an upright piano: verticality: a basket-maker's tool.—*v.t.* to set erect or right side up.—*adv.* (up'**rīt**, up'**rīt'**, up-**rīt'**) vertically: honestly.—*adv.* up'**rightly** in an upright manner: honestly: vertically.—*ns.* up'**rightness; uprise'** (or *up'*) rising.—*v.i.* (-**rīz'**) to rise up, arise:—*pa.t.* up**rose'**; *pa.p.* up**ris'en**.—*n.* up**ris'ing** (or *up'*) a rising up: a violent revolt against a ruling power.—*adj.* which rises up or is rising up.—*n.* up'**roar** see separate entry.—*v.t.* up**root'** to pull up by the roots: to destroy (*fig.*): to remove forcibly and completely (from e.g.

upcurved' *adj.*

upgoing (-gō' or *up'*) *n.*

up'river *adj.*

up'rush *n.*

up'sweep *n.*

up'swept *adj.*

uptilt'ed *adj.*

Words made with **up** *adj. are listed first (p. 1096), then those with* **up-** *pfx.* (pp. 1097 ff.); *other UP- words follow* (p. 1098).

For other sounds see detailed chart of pronunciation.

native land).—*ns.* **uproot'al** uprooting; **uproot'er; uproot'ing.**—*v.i.* **uprose'** *pa.t.* of **uprise.**—*v.t.* **upset'** to overturn, capsize: to spill or tip out: to interfere with, defeat (a plan): to disconcert: to distress: to disorder (a bodily process or organ): to affect temporarily the health of (a person).—*v.i.* to be upset:—*pa.t.* and *pa.p.* **upset'.**—*n.* (**up'set'**) an overturn or derangement.—*adj.* (**up'set**) of a price, the lowest that will be accepted, at which bidding is started.—**upsett'er.**—*adj.* **upsett'ing** causing upset.—*n.* overturning: overthrow.—*n.* **up'shot** the final shot (*archery*): the outcome, final result: the conclusion of an argument: the substance, general effect.—*adv.* **up'stage** towards the back of the stage. —*adj.* towards the back of the stage: stand-offish, superior (*slang*).—*v.t.* (**up-stāj'**) to treat in a supercilious manner: to move upstage so that (another actor) has to turn his back to the audience, and thus to put him at a disadvantage: to divert interest or attention away from (someone or something).—*adv.* **up'stairs'** in or toward a higher storey, or (*fig.*) position. —*adj.* **up'stairs(s)** of or in an upper storey or flat.—*n.* **upstairs'** the part of a building about the ground floor.—*adj.* **upstand'ing** erect: on one's feet (*Scot.*): straight and well-built: honest and downright.—*n.* **up'start** one who has suddenly risen to wealth, importance, or power, a parvenu.—*adj.* newly or suddenly come into being: characteristic of a parvenu: pretentious and vulgar: new-fangled.—*v.i.* **upstart'** to start up.—*adj.* **up'state'** (*U.S.*) pertaining to a part of a state away from, and usu. to the north of, the principal city of the state.—Also *adv.*—*adv.* **up'stream'** against the current.—*adj.* (**up'**) further up the stream: going against the current.—*v.i.* (**-strēm'**) to stream up.—*n.* **up'stroke** an upward stroke: an upward line in writing.—*v.i.* **upsurge'** to surge up.—*n.* (**up'**) a surging up.—*ns.* **upsur'gence; up'take** the act of lifting up: a pipe or flue with upward current: the act of taking up: mental apprehension (orig. *Scot.*).— *v.t.* (**-tāk'**) to take up.—*v.t.* **uptear'** to pull up or out by the roots, from the base, etc.—*adj.* **up'-tem'po** played or sung at a fast tempo.—*v.t.* **upthrow'** to throw up.—*n.* (**up'**) an upheaval, uplift: the amount of vertical displacement of the relatively raised strata at a fault.—*v.t.* **upthrust'** to thrust upward.—*n.* (**up'**).—*adj.* **uptight'** (*coll.*) tense, in a nervy state: angry, irritated: conventional, strait-laced.—*adj.* and *adv.* **up'town'** in or toward the upper part or (*U.S.*) the residential quarters of a town.—*ns.* **up'trend** upward tendency; **up'turn** an upheaval: a disturbance: a movement upward, a rise: an upturned part.—*adj.* **up'turned.**—*n.* and *adj.* **upturn'ing.**—*v.t.* **upval'ue** to increase the value of.—*adv.* **upwind** (**up-wind'**), **up-wind'** against the wind.
upaithric *ū-pī'thrik*, *adj.* from the same root as, and identical in meaning with, **hypaethral** (q.v.).
Upanis(h)ad *ōō-pan'i-shad*, *ōō-pä'ni-shäd*, *n.* any of a number of Sanskrit theosophic or philosophical treatises. [Sans. *upa*, near, *ni-ad*, a sitting down.]
upbraid *up-brād'*, *v.t.* to reproach or chide.—*v.i.* to utter reproaches.—*n.* and *adj.* **upbraid'ing.** [O.E. *ūpbregdan.*]
upholster *up-hōl'stər*, *v.t.* to furnish with stuffing, springs, covers, etc.: to cushion, be a cover to: to provide with curtains, carpets, etc.—*v.i.* to do upholstery.—*ns.* **uphol'sterer** one who makes or deals in furniture, beds, curtains, etc.:—*fem.* **uphol'stress; uphol'stery** upholsterer's work or goods. [Back formation from *upholsterer*—**upholder.**]
uphroe *ū'frō.* Same as **euphroe.**
upmost. See **up.**
upo', upon. See **up-.**
upper, uppermost. See **up.**

uproar *up'rōr*, *-rōr*, *n.* insurrection, commotion and tumult (now *rare*): loud outcry, clamour.—*adj.* **uproar'ious.**—*adv.* **uproar'iously.**—*n.* **uproar'iousness.** [Du. *oproer*—*op*, up, *roeren*, to stir; modified by association with **roar.**]
ups-a-daisy *ups'ə-dā'zi*, *interj.* of encouragement in lifting a child or helping to climb.
upsilon. See **ypsilon.**
upsy-daisy. Same as **ups-a-daisy.**
uracil. See **urea.**
uraemia *ū-rē'mi-ə*, *n.* retention of waste materials in the blood.—*adj.* **urae'mic.**—Also **urē'mia, urē'mic.** [Gr. *ouron*, urine, *haima*, blood.]
Ural *ū'rəl*, *n.* a river and mountain range of Russia.— *adjs.* **Uralian** a (*ū-rā'li-ən*) of the Ural Mountains: pertaining to Uralic (also *n.*).—*n.* **Uralic** (*ū-*) a language group comprising Finno-Ugric and the Samoyed languages.—*adj.* **Uralian.**—*adj.* **Ural-Altaic** (*-al-tā'ik*) of the Ural and Altai Mountains: applied to a family of languages—Finno-Ugrian, Turko-Tatar, Mongolian, Manchu, Tungus, etc., and their speakers.
urali. Same as **wourali.**
uranalysis. See under **urine.**
Urania *ū-rā'ni-ə*, *n.* the Muse of astronomy: a name for Aphrodite.—*adjs.* **Uranian** (also without *cap.*; *ū-rā'ni-ən*) heavenly: of the heavens: astronomical: of Urania or of Uranus, god or planet; **uranic** (*ū-ran'ik*) of uranium in higher valency: celestial.—*n.* **uranide** (*ū'rən-īd*) a transuranium element.—*ns.* **uranium** (*ū-rā'ni-əm*) a radioactive metal (U; at. numb. 92) named by Klaproth, 1789, after the recently discovered planet; **uranography** (*ū-rən-og'rə-fi*) descriptive astronomy, esp. of the constellations; **uranom'etry** astronomical measurement.—*adj.* **ū'ranous** of uranium in lower valency.—*n.* **Uranus** (*ū'rə-nəs* or *ū-rā'*) an old Greek god, father of Kronos (Saturn) and the Titans: a planet discovered in 1781 by Herschel. [Gr. *ouranos*, heaven.]
urari. Same as **wourali.**
urate *ū'rāt.* See **uric.**
urban *ûr'bən*, *adj.* of or belonging to a city.—*adj.* **urbane** (*ûr-bān'*) pertaining to, or influenced by, a city: civilised: refined: courteous: smooth-mannered. —*adv.* **urbane'ly.**—*n.* **urbanisā'tion**, **-z-.**—*v.t.* **ur'banise, -ize** to make (a district) town-like, as opposed to rural, in character.—*adj.* **urbanist'ic** pertaining to the planning and development of towns.— *ns.* **urbanity** (*-ban'i-ti*) the quality of being urbane: also townishness, town-life; **urbanol'ogist** one who studies urban conditions; **urbanol'ogy.**—**urban district** a thickly-populated district, a subdivision of a country, administered by an **Urban District Council; urban guerrilla** one who is engaged in terrorist activities in towns and cities; **urban renewal** (esp. *U.S.*) the clearing and/or redevelopment of slums or the like. [L. *urbānus*—*urbs*, a city.]
urchin *ûr'chin*, *n.* a hedgehog: a sea-urchin: a mischievous child, esp. a boy: a child.—*adj.* like, of the nature of, due to, an urchin. [O.Fr. *herichon*, *heriçon* (Fr. *hérisson*)—L. *ēricius*, a hedgehog.]
urd *ûrd*, *n.* an Indian plant of the bean family (*Phaseolus mungo*), or its edible blackish seed.— Also **urd bean, black gram.** [Hindi.]
Urdu *ōōr'dōō*, *ōōr-dōō'*, *n.* and *adj.* Hindustani: a form of it with many Persian and Arabic words, the official literary language of Pakistan. [Hind. *urdū*, camp (language); cf. **horde.**]
urea *ū-rē'ə*, by some *ū'*, *n.* carbamide, $CO(NH_2)_2$, a substance found in mammalian urine, the chief form in which nitrogenous waste is carried off.—*n.* **ûr'acil** a base in ribonucleic acid.—*adj.* **urē'al** (or *ū'ri-əl*).— **urea resins** thermosetting resins made by heating urea

and aldehyde, usu. formaldehyde [Gr. *ouron*, urine.]

uremia, uremic. Same as **uraemia, uraemic.**

Urena *ū-rē'nə*, *n.* a tropical genus of the mallow family, yielding a jute substitute: (without *cap.*) any plant of the genus. [Malayalam *uren.*]

urent *ū'rənt*, *adj.* burning, stinging. [L. *ūrēns, -entis*, pr.p. of *ūrēre*, to burn.]

uresis *ū-rē'sis*, *n.* urination. [Gr. *ourēsis*]

ureter *ū-rē'tər*, *n.* a duct that conveys urine from the kidneys to the bladder or cloaca.—*adjs.* **urē'teral**, **ureteric** (*ū-ri-ter'ik*).—*n.* **urēteri'tis** inflammation of a ureter. [Gr. *ourētēr, -ēros—ouron*, urine.]

urethan(e) *ū'ri-than*, *-thān*, or *-than'*, *-thān'*, *ns.* an anaesthetic, $NH_2 \cdot COOC_2H_5$, prepared from urea and ethyl alcohol.

urethra *ū-rē'thrə*, *n.* the canal by which the urine is discharged from the bladder:—*pl.* **-as, -ae** (*-ē*).—*adjs.* **urē'thral**; **urēthrit'ic.**—*n.* **urēthri'tis** inflammation of the urethra. [Gr. *ourēthrā—ouron*, urine.]

uretic *ū-ret'ik*, *adj.* pertaining to, or occurring in, urine. [Gr. *ourētikos—ouron*, urine.]

urge *ûrj*, *v.t.* to put forward (an argument, etc.; or in argument, with *that*): to incite: to allege earnestly: to advise strongly: to drive, impel.—*v.t.* to press: to be urgent or insistent: to push on.—*n.* an impulse: a prompting.—*n.* **ur'gency.**—*adj.* **ur'gent** urging: pressing: calling for immediate attention.—*adv.* **ur'gently.** [L. *urgēre*.]

urial, oorial *ōō'ri-əl*, *n.* a Himalayan wild sheep [Punjabi *hureāl*.]

uric *ū'rik*, *adj.* of, or got from, or present in, urine.—*n.* **ū'rate** a salt of uric acid.—**uric acid** an acid, $C_5H_4O_3N_4$, present in urine and blood. [Gr. *ouron*, urine.]

urine *ū'rin*, *n.* the excretory product, usually amber liquid, of the kidneys, chief means of voiding nitrogenous waste.—*ns.* **ū'rinal** (or *-rī'*) a vessel for urine, esp. for an incontinent or bed-ridden person: a room or building having fixed receptacle(s) for use in urination; **urinal'ysis** analysis of urine, e.g. to detect disease.—Also **uranal'ysis.**—*adj.* **ū'rinary** pertaining to, or like, urine.—*n.* a reservoir for urine.—*v.i* **ū'rinate** to discharge urine.—*n.* **urinā'tion.**—*adj.* **urinogen'ital** pertaining jointly to urinary and genital functions or organs.—*ns.* **urinol'ogy, urinos'copy**, etc., barbarous forms for **urology**, etc.—*adj.* **ū'rinous** like, of the nature of, urine. [L. *ūrīna*.]

urn *ûrn*, *n.* a vase with rounded body, usually a narrowed mouth and often a foot: esp. such a vase for ashes of the dead: hence any respository for the dead: a monumental imitation of a burial-urn: a vessel for water: a closed vessel with a tap and now usu. with heating device inside, for making tea or coffee in quantity: a moss-capsule: an urn-shaped body.— **urn'field** a late Bronze Age cemetery of cinerary urns. [L. *urna*.]

uro-¹ *ū-rō-, -ro-*, in composition, urine.—*adjs.* **urogen'ital** urinogenital; **urograph'ic.**—*ns.* **urog'raphy** radiological examination of the urinary tract; **ū'rolith** a calculus in the urine or the urinary tract; **urolithi'asis** the formation of uroliths: the condition caused by uroliths.—*adjs.* **urolog'ic(al).**—*ns.* **urol'ogist; urol'ogy** the branch of medicine dealing with diseases and abnormalities of the urinary tract and their treatment; **uros'copy** diagnostic examination of urine; **urō'sis** disease of the urinary organs [Gr. *ouron*, urine; cf L. *ūrīna*.]

uro-² *ū-rō-, -ro-*, in composition, tail: posterior part — *n.pl.* **Urodē'la** (Gr. *dēlos*, clear, plain) the (permanently) tailed Amphibia.—*ns.* and *adjs* **urodē'lan, ū'rodele.**—*adj.* **urosthen'ic** (Gr. *sthenos*, strength) having a tail developed for propulsion —*n*

ū'rostyle (Gr. *stȳlos*, column) a prolongation of the last vertebra. [Gr. *ourā*, tail.]

Ursa *ûr'sə*, *n.* the Latin name of two constellations, *Ursa Major* and *Ursa Minor*, the Great and the Little Bear.—*adj.* **ur'sine** of a bear: bear-like.—*n* **Ur'sus** the bear genus. [L. *ursus, ursa*, bear.]

Urtica *ûr-tī'kə*, commonly *ûr'ti-kə*, *n.* the nettle genus (without *cap.*) a plant of the nettle genus.—*n* **urtica'ria** nettle-rash [L. *urtīca*, a nettle—*ūrēre*, to burn.]

us *us*, *pron.* the objective (dative and accusative) case of **we**.—Also in editorial and royal use as a singular. [O.E. *ūs*.]

usage *ū'zij, -sij*, *n.* use. act or mode of using: treatment: practice: custom: the normal or acceptable speech patterns, vocabulary, etc of a language or dialect.—*n* **ū'sance** time allowed for payment of foreign bills of exchange. [O.Fr.,—L *ūsus*, use.]

use¹ *ūz*, *v t* to put to some purpose: to avail oneself of: to treat or behave towards: to make use of (a person; see following article).—*v.t.* to be accustomed (to; used chiefly in the past tense, pronounced in this sense *ūst*, **use(d)n't** *ūs'nt*, for *used not*).—*adjs.* **ū'sable; used** (*ūzd*) already made use of: second-hand.—*n.* **ū'ser** one who uses. a right established by long use (*law*).—*adj.* **used'-up'** exhausted.—*adj.* **u'ser-friend'ly** (*comput*) easy for those having little skill or training to use.—**use up** to consume: to exhaust: to tire out. [Fr. *user*—L.L. *ūsāre*—L. *ūtī, ūsus*, to use.]

use² *ūs*, *n.* the act of using: the state or fact of being used: an advantageous purpose to which a thing can be applied: the fact of serving a purpose: usefulness: employment causing wear: a need to use (with *for*): the manner of using: the power of using (e.g. tongue, limb): the habit of using: custom: the profit derived from property: (in *pl.*) a form of equitable ownership peculiar to English law by which one person enjoys the profit of lands, etc., the legal title to which is vested in another in trust.—*adj.* **use'ful** advantageous, serviceable (**useful**, or **applied**, **arts** those arts with a utilitarian purpose, e.g. weaving, pottery, as opposed to the fine arts (see **art**)).—*adv.* **use'fully.**— *n.* **use'fulness.**—*adj.* **use'less** having no use: not answering any good purpose or the end proposed.— *adv.* **use'lessly.**—*n.* **use'lessness.**—**have no use for** to have no liking for; **in use** in employment or practice; **make use of** to use, employ: to take the help, etc., of (a person) in obtaining an end with no intention of repaying him; **of no use** useless; **of use** useful; **out of use** not used or employed; **use and wont** the customary practice. [L. *ūsus*—*ūtī*, to use.]

usher *ush'ər*, *n.* a door-keeper: one who escorts persons to seats in a hall, etc.: an officer who introduces strangers or walks before a person of rank:—*fem.* **ush'eress, usherette'** (esp. in a theatre or cinema).— *v.t* to conduct: to show (in, out): to introduce, lead up to (now usu. with *in*).—*ns* **ush'ering; ush'ership.** [A.Fr. *usser*, O.Fr. *ussier* (Fr. *huissier*)—L. *ostiārius*, a door-keeper—*ostium*, a door.]

usual *ū'zhōō-əl*, *adj.* occurring in ordinary use: common: customary.—*n* (*coll*) normal health: one's habitual drink, etc.—*adv* **ū'sually.**—*n.* **ū'sualness.**—**as usual** as is or was usual, **the usual** (*coll*) menstruation [L *ūsuālis—ūsus*, use.]

usucapion *ū-zū-kā'pi-ən*, **usucaption** *-kap'shən*, (*Rom. law*) *ns* the acquisition of property by long possession and enjoyment.—*n* **usuca'pient** one who claims or holds by usucapion —*v t* **ū'sucapt** (*-kapt*) to acquire so.—*adj* **usucapt'ible.** [L *ūsūcapēre—ūsus*, use, *capēre, captum*, to take]

usufruct *ū'zū-frukt*, *n* the use and profit, but not the property, of a thing —*v t* to hold in usufruct —*adj.*

usufruc'tuary.—*n.* one who has usufruct. [L.L. *ūsūfrūctus*—L. *ūsus* (*et*) *frūctus*, use and fruit.]

usurer, etc. See **usury**.

usurp *ū-zûrp'*, *v.t.* to take possession of by force, without right, or unjustly: to assume (the authority, place, etc., of someone, or something, else): to take possession of (the mind): to take or borrow (a name or a word).—*v.i.* to practise usurpation: to encroach (on).—*n.* **usurpa'tion.**—*adj.* **usur'patory.**—*adj.* **usurped'.**—*n.* **usur'per.**—*n.* and *adj.* **usur'ping.** [Fr. *usurper* and L. *ūsūrpāre*, perh. from *ūsus*, use, *rapēre*, to seize.]

usury *ū'zha-ri*, *n.* the taking of (now only iniquitous or illegal) interest on a loan.—*n.* **ū'surer** a moneylender (now for excessive interest):—*fem.* **ū'suress.**—*adj.* **usū'rious.**—*adv.* **usū'riously.**—*n.* **usū'riousness.** [L.L. *ūsūria*, L. *ūsūra*—*ūtī*, *ūsus*, to use.]

usus loquendi *ūz'as lo-kwen'dī*, *ōōs'ōōs lo-kwen'dē*, (L.) current usage of speech.

ut[1] *ōōt*, *ut*, *n.* a syllable representing the first note of the scale, now generally superseded by *do*. [See Aretinian, gamut.]

ut[2] *ut*, *ōōt*, (L.) *adv.*, *conj.* as.—**ut infra** (*in'fra*, *ēn'frā*) as below; **ut supra** (*sū'pra*, *sōō'prā*, *sōō'*) as above.

utensil *ū-ten'sil*, formerly *ū'*, *n.* any useful or ceremonial tool or vessel. [O.Fr. *utensile*—L. *ūtēnsilis*, fit for use—*ūtī*, to use.]

uterus *ū'tər-as*, *n.* the womb:—*pl.* **ū'teri.**—*n.* **uterec'tomy** hysterectomy.—*adj.* **ū'terine** (*-īn*) of, in, or for the uterus: of the same mother by a different father.—*ns.* **uteri'tis** inflammation of the womb. [L.]

utile *ū'til*, *adj.* (with *to*) useful, profitable. [M.E.—O.Fr.—L. *ūtilis*, useful—*ūtī*, to use.]

utilise, **-ize** *ū'ti-līz*, *v.t.* to make use of, turn to use.— *adj.* **ū'tilisable**, **-z-**.—*ns.* **utilisā'tion**, **-z-**; **ū'tiliser**, **-z-**; **util'ity** usefulness: the power to satisfy the wants of people in general (*philos.*): a useful thing: a public utility, public service (esp. *U.S.*): (usu. in *pl.*) stock or bond of public utility.—*adj.* produced or supplied primarily for usefulness: provided in order that the public may be supplied in spite of rise of prices: (of a breed of dog) originally bred to be useful, to serve a practical purpose.—**utility room** a room, esp. in a private house, where things required for the work of running the house are kept. [Fr. *utiliser*, *utilité*—L. *ūtilis*, useful—*ūtī*, to use.]

utilitarian *ū-til-i-tā'ri-ən*, *adj.* consisting in, based upon, or pertaining to, utility or to utilitarianism: concerned with, looking to, usefulness alone, without regard to, or without caring about, beauty, pleasantness, etc.—*n.* one who holds utilitarianism: one who looks to usefulness alone.—*v.t.* **utilitā'rianise**, **-ize** to make to serve a utilitarian purpose.—*n.* **utilitā'rianism** the ethical theory which finds the basis of moral distinctions in the utility of actions, i.e. their fitness to produce happiness. [Jeremy Bentham's coinage from **utility**.]

utility. See **utilise**.

uti possidetis *ū'tī pos-i-dē'tis*, L. *ōō'tē pos-i-dā'tis*, in international law, the principle under which belligerents keep the territory or property they possess at the close of hostilities unless otherwise agreed. [L., as you possess.]

utmost *ut'mōst*, *-mast*, *adj.* outmost: last: in the greatest degree, extreme.—*n.* the limit: the extreme: the most or greatest possible. [O.E. *ūtemest*, with double superlative suffix *-m-est* from *ūte*, out.]

Utopia *ū-tō'pi-ə*, *n.* an imaginary state described in Sir Thomas More's Latin political romance or satire *Utopia* (1516): (often without *cap.*) any imaginary state of ideal perfection.—*adj.* **Utō'pian** (also without *cap.*).—*n.* an inhabitant of Utopia: one who imagines or believes in a Utopia: (often without *cap.*) one who advocates impracticable reforms or who expects an impossible state of perfection in society.—*n.* **utō'pianism.** [Gr. *ou*, not, *topos*, a place.]

utricle *ū'tri-kl*, *n.* a little bag, bladder, or cell: a bladder-like envelope of some fruits: a chamber in the inner ear.—*adj.* **utric'ūlar** like or having a utricle. [L. *ūtriculus*, a small bag, dim. of *ūter*, *ūtris*, a bag, a bottle.]

utter[1] *ut'ər*, *adj.* extreme: total: out-and-out:— *superl.* **utt'erest.**—*adv.* **utt'erly.**—*adj.* and *n.* **utt'ermost** utmost.—*n.* **utt'erness.**—**utter barrister** an ordinary barrister, not a king's or queen's counsel or a serjeant-at-law. [O.E. *ūtor*, outer— *ūt*, out.]

utter[2] *ut'ər*, *v.t.* to put (money) in circulation: to (try to) pass off (a forged document, etc.) as genuine or put (counterfeit money) into circulation: to offer for sale (*obs.*): to put out, emit, esp. with force (*lit.* and *fig.*: *arch.*): to speak, pronounce, give voice to. —*v.i.* (*coll.*) to make a remark or express an opinion.—*adj.* **utt'erable.**—*ns.* **utt'erableness**; **utt'erance** an act of uttering: a manner of speaking: the expression in speech, or in other sound, of a thought or emotion (e.g. **give utterance to**): a stretch of speech in some way isolated from, or independent of, what precedes and follows it (*linguistics*); **utt'erer**; **utt'ering** circulation.—*adj.* **utt'erless** that cannot be uttered in words. [M.E. *uttren*—O.E. *ūt*, out; and M.Du. *uteren*, to announce.]

uva *ū'və*, *n.* a grape: a grape-like berry, one formed from a superior ovary. [L. *ūva*.]

uvula *ū'vū-lə*, *n.* the fleshy conical body suspended from the palate over the back part of the tongue:— *pl.* **ū'vulas**, **-lae** (*lē*).—*adj.* **ū'vular** of, produced by vibration of, the uvula. [Dim. from L. *ūva*, grape.]

uxorial *uk-sō'ri-əl*, *-sō'*, *-zō'*, *-zō'*, *adj.* of a wife.—*n.* **uxo'ricide** (*-sīd*) a wife-killer: wife-killing.—*adj.* **uxo'rious** excessively or submissively fond of a wife. [L. *uxor*, *-ōris*, a wife.]

Uzbeg *uz'beg*, **Uzbek** *-bek*, *ns.* a member of a Turkic people of Turkestan: their language.—*Also adjs.*

V

V, v *vē, n.* the twenty-second letter of our alphabet, representing a voiced labiodental sound: an object or mark shaped like the letter —**V'-bomb** (Ger *Vergeltungswaffe*, retaliation weapon) a self-propelled long-range projectile, as a rocket or a flying bomb, made by the Germans in World War II; **V'-day** Victory day—*specif.* 8th May 1945, when Germany surrendered unconditionally; **V'-neck** the neck of a garment cut to a point below.—*adjs.* **V'-necked; V'-shaped.**—**V'-sign** a sign made with the index and middle fingers in the form of a V, with palm turned outwards in token of victory, with palm inwards as a sign of contempt or derision.

vac *vak, n.* a colloquial shortening of **vacation.**

vacant *vā'kənt, adj.* empty: unoccupied: of or at leisure: thoughtless: inane.—*n.* **vā'cancy** emptiness: leisure: idleness: inanity: empty space: a gap: a situation unoccupied.—*adv.* **vā'cantly.**—*v.t.* **vacate** (*və-kāt', U.S. vā'kāt*) to make or leave empty: to quit. —*n.* **vacā'tion** a vacating: a voiding: holidays, esp. of schools, colleges, law-courts.—*v.i.* (esp. *U.S*) to take a holiday.—*n.* **vacā'tionist** a holiday-maker.—*adj.* **vacā'tionless.**—**vacant possession** (of property) (the state of being ready for) occupation immediately after purchase, the previous owner or occupier already having left. [L *vacāre, -ātum*, to be empty, pr.p. *vacāns, -antis.*]

vaccine *vak'sēn, -sin, n.* cowpox virus or lymph containing it: any preparation used to confer immunity to a disease by inoculation —*adj.* **vac'cinal** (*-sin-*).—*v.t.* **vac'cinate** to inoculate with vaccine.—*ns.* **vaccinā'tion; vac'cinātor.**—*adj.* **vac'cinatory.**—*n.* **vac'cin'ia** cowpox. [L. *vaccīnus—vacca*, a cow.]

vacillate *vas'i-lāt, v.i.* to sway to and fro: to waver: to be unsteady —*adj* **vac'illāting.**—*adv.* **vac'illatingly.** —*n.* **vacillā'tion, -ātum**] [L *vacillāre, -ātum*]

vacuum *vak'ū-əm, n.* theoretically, an entirely (in practice, a very nearly completely) empty space (*pl.* **vac'ūums, vac'ūa**): a vacuum-cleaner (*coll.; pl.* **vac'ūums**).—*v.t.* and *v.i.* to clean with a vacuum-cleaner.—*adj.* pertaining to a vacuum: containing a vacuum∙ in which a vacuum is used to carry out a specific operation —*n.* **vacū'ity** emptiness: space unoccupied: idleness, listlessness∙ vacancy of mind.— *adj* **vac'ūolar** of a vacuole.—*ns.* **vacūolā'tion; vac'ūole** a very small cavity, esp. in protoplasm.— *adj.* **vac'ūous** empty∙ exhausted of air, etc : mentally vacant —*adv.* ∙ **vac'ūously.**—*n.* **vac'ūousness.**— **vacuum brake** a brake in the working of which suction by vacuum(s) supplements the pressure applied by the operator, esp. a braking system of this type applied simultaneously throughout a train.—*v.t.* and *v.i* **vac'ūum-clean'.**—**vacuum cleaner** an apparatus for removing dust by suction; **vacuum flask** a flask for keeping liquids hot or cold by aid of a vacuum lining —*adj.* **vac'ūum-packed'** sealed in a container from which most of the air has been removed.—**vacuum pump** a general term for apparatus which displaces gas against a pressure; **vacuum tube** a sealed glass tube in which a vacuum has been made, e.g. a thermionic valve. [L *vacuus*, neut. *vacuum*, empty.]

vade-mecum *vā'di-mē'kəm, va', mä'koŏm, n.* a handbook, pocket-companion. [L. *vāde*, go (imper of *vādēre*), *mēcum*, with me.]

vagabond *vag'ə-bond, adj.* roving: without settled home: unsettled.—*n.* one who wanders without settled habitation. an idle wanderer: a vagrant: (often playfully or vaguely) a scamp, a rascal.—*n.* **vag'abondism.** [Fr. *vagabond* and L. *vagābundus— vagāri*, to wander.]

vagal. See **vagus.**

vagary *vā'gə-rı, və-gā'rı, n.* a devious excursion: a digression or rambling: a freakish prank: a caprice:— *pl.* **vagaries.** [App. L. *vagārī*, to wander.]

vagi. See **vagus.**

vagina *və-jī'nə, n.* a sheathing leaf-base: a female genital passage:—*pl.* **vagi'nae** (*-nē*), **-nas.**—*adjs.* **vagi'nal** (or *vaj'i-nəl*); **vag'inate, -d** sheathed: having a sheath. —*ns.* **vaginis'mus** spasmodic contraction of the vagina; **vagini'tis** inflammation of the vagina. [L. *vāgīna,* sheath.]

vagrant *vā'grənt, adj.* wandering: without settled dwelling: unsettled: uncertain, erratic.—*n.* one who has no settled home. a tramp.—*n.* **vā'grancy.** [Perh. A.Fr. *wakerant* of Gmc. origin (cf. **walk**), assimilated to L *vagārī,* to wander.]

vague *vāg, adj.* lacking precision or sharpness of definition: indistinct: blurred: lacking in character and purpose, or addicted to haziness of thought.—*adv.* **vague'ly.**—*n.* **vague'ness.** [L. *vagus,* wandering— *vagārī,* to wander.]

vagus *vā'gus, n.* the tenth cranial nerve, concerned in regulating heart beat, rhythm of breathing, etc :—*pl.* **vā'gi** (*-jī*).—*adj.* **vā'gal** (*-gəl*). [L., wandering.]

vail[1] *vāl, (arch.) v.t* to lower, let down: to doff in salutation or submission.—*v.i.* to lift one's hat: to yield. [O Fr *valer,* or Fr. *avaler,* to descend.]

vail[2] *vāl, (arch.) n* (usu. in *pl.*) a tip, perquisite, dole, or bribe [O.Fr *valour,* vail, to be worth.]

vain *vān, adj.* without real worth: futile. unavailing: thoughtless: empty-minded: pettily self-complacent: valuing oneself inordinately on some trivial personal distinction conceited —*adv* **vain'ly.**—*n* **vain'ness** vanity.—*adj.* **vainglorious** (*-glo', -glō'*) given to, or proceeding from, vainglory.—*adv.* **vainglo'riously.**— **vainglo'riousness; vain'glo'ry** vain or empty glory in one's own performances: idle boastfulness.—**in vain** fruitlessly: to no end; **take in vain** to utter with levity. [Fr. *vain*—L *vānus,* empty.]

vair *vār, n.* a kind of squirrel fur, bluish-grey and white [O.Fr.,—L. *varius,* variegated]

Vaisya *vīs'ya, vīsh', **Vaishya** vīsh'ya, ns.* a member of the third caste among the Hindus. [Sans. *vaiçya— viç,* settler.]

valance *val'əns, n.* a hanging border of drapery —*adj.* **val'anced** furnished with a valance [Poss. A.Fr. *valer,* to descend.]

vale[1] *vāl, n.* a valley (chiefly *poet.*): the world (as in *vale of tears, earthly vale*).—**vale of years** old age. [Fr. *val*—L. *vallis,* a vale]

valediction *val-i-dik'shən, n.* a bidding farewell: a farewell —*adj.* **valedic'tory** saying farewell: farewell: taking leave —*n* (*U S.*) a farewell oration spoken by a graduand. [L. *valē,* farewell, *dīcĕre, dictum,* to say.]

valence *vā'ləns, n.* valency (*chem.*): chemical bond (*chem.*).—*n.* **vā'lency** combining power: its degree as

For other sounds see detailed chart of pronunciation.

measured by the number of hydrogen (or equivalent) atoms with which an atom can combine, or by the charge on an ion.—-**valent** (or -və-lənt) in composition, having a stated valency, as in *trivalent*.— **valency electrons** those of the outermost shell of the atom, largely responsible for its chemical and physical properties. [L. *valēre*, to be strong.]

Valenciennes *val-ən-sēnz'*, *-si-en'*, *va-lä-syen'*, *n.* a kind of lace made at *Valenciennes* in France.

-valent. See valence.

Valentine *val'ən-tīn, n.* the name of several saints on whose day, 14th February, the birds were fabled to choose their mates: (without *cap.*) a person chosen that day in mock betrothal: (without *cap.*) an amatory or grotesque missive or a gift sent that day

valerian *və-lē'rı-ən, n.* the plant all-heal (*Valeriana officinalis*) or other plant of the genus, akin to the teasels: its rhizome and roots which have medicinal properties.—**valeric** (-*er'ik*) **acid** a fatty acid. [Perh. from someone called *Valerius*, or from L. *valēre*, to be strong.]

valet *val'it* (or *val'ā*), *n.* a man-servant who attends to clothes and toilet.—*v.t.* (*val'it*) to serve or attend to as valet.—*n.* val'eting.—**valet de chambre** (*val'ā də shäbr'*) an attendant: a footman. [Fr.]

valeta. Same as veleta.

valetudinarian *val-i-tū-di-nā'ri-ən, adj.* sickly: weak: anxious and fanciful about one's own health.—*n.* a valetudinarian person.—*n.* **valetūdinā'rianism.**—*adj.* and *n.* **valetūd'inary** (*-ə-ri*) valetudinarian. [L. *valētūdinārius*—*valētūdō*, state of health—*valēre*, to be strong.]

valgus *val'gəs, n.* the condition of being bow-legged or (sometimes) knock-kneed. [L., bow-legged.]

Valhalla *val-hal'ə, n.* the palace of bliss for the souls of slain heroes (*Scand. myth.*). [O.N. *Valhöll*—*valr*, the slain, *holl*, hall.]

valiant *val'yənt, adj.* brave: actively courageous: heroic.—*ns.* val'iance, val'iancy valour: a deed of valour.—*adv.* val'iantly. [Fr. *vaillant*—L. *valēre*, to be strong.]

valid *val'id, adj.* sound: legally adequate, or efficacious: fulfilling all the necessary conditions: in logic, well based, applicable.—*v.t.* val'idate to make valid: to ratify: to confirm, substantiate.—*ns.* valida'tion the act of validating: the checking of the correctness of input data (*comput.*); valid'ity.—*adv.* val'idly.—*n.* val'idness. [L. *validus*—*valēre*, to be strong.]

valine *vā'lēn, val', n.* an amino-acid, $C_5H_{11}NO_2$, essential to health and growth in humans and vertebrate animals. [From *valeric* acid.]

valise *və-lēz'*, (*U.S.*) *-ēs'*, (now rare except *U.S.*) *n.* a travelling bag for hand or saddle: a kit-bag. [Fr.]

Valium® *val'i-əm, n.* a proprietary name for diazepam, a tranquilliser.

Valkyrie *val'kir-i, val-kīr'i, -kir'i, -kēr'i, (Scand. myth.) n.* any one of the minor goddesses who conducted the slain from the battlefield to Valhalla:—*pl.* **Valkyries.** [O.N. *Valkyrja*—*valr*, the slain, and the root of *kjōsa*, to choose.]

valley *val'i, n.* an elongated hollow between hills: a stretch of country watered by a river: a trough between ridges: the hollow of an M-shaped roof:—*pl.* val'leys. [O.Fr. *valee* (Fr. *vallée*)—*val*—L. *vallis*, a valley.]

vallum *val'əm, n.* a rampart: a wall of sods, earth, or other material, esp. of that thrown up from a ditch. [L.]

valonia, vallonia, valonea *və-lō'ni-ə, n.* a tanning material, acorns of a Levantine oak (valonia oak) or similar species. [It. *vallonea*—Gr. *balanos*, an acorn.]

valour *val'ər, n.* intrepidity: courage: bravery.—*n.* **valorisa'tion**, *-z-* fixing of price.—*v.t.* val'orise, -ize to fix the price of.—*adj.* val'orous intrepid: courageous. —*adv.* val'orously. [O.Fr. *valour*—L.L *valor*, *-ōris*—L. *valēre*, to be strong.]

valse *vals, n.*, *v.i.* and *v.t.* waltz. [Fr.]

value *val'ū, n.* worth: a fair equivalent: intrinsic worth or goodness: recognition of such worth: that which renders anything useful or estimable: the degree of this quality: relative worth: high worth: esteem: efficacy: excellence: price: precise meaning: relative duration (*mus.*): relation with reference to light and shade (*paint.*): the special determination of a quantity (*math.*): the exact amount of a variable quantity in a particular case: the sound represented by a written symbol (*phon.*): (in *pl'*) moral principles, standards, etc.—*v.t.* to estimate the worth of: to rate at a price: to esteem: to prize.—*adj.* val'uable having value or worth: of high value.—*n.* a thing of value, a choice article—often in *pl.*—*n.* val'uableness.—*adv.* val'uably.—*v.t.* val'uate to appraise.—*n.* valua'tion estimation of value.—*adj.* valua'tional.—*n.* val'uator an appraiser.—*adjs.* val'ued that has a value assigned: priced: highly esteemed: prized; val'ueless.—*n.* val'uer one who estimates values, a valuator: one who sets a high value.—**valuation roll** a list of properties and their assessed values for local taxation purposes; **value judgment** a personal estimate of merit in a particular respect.—**value-added tax** a tax on the rise in value of a product due to the manufacturing and marketing processes. [O.Fr. *value*, fem. pa.p. of *valoir*, to be worth—L. *valēre*.]

valuta *vä-lū'tə, -lōō', n.* the comparative value of a currency: a standard of money. [It.]

valve *valv, n.* a single piece forming part or the whole of a shell: one of the parts of a dry fruit separating in dehiscence: a structure or device that regulates flow or passage or allows it in one direction only: a rectifier (*elect.*): loosely, a thermionic valve used in wireless apparatus as rectifier, amplifier, oscillator or otherwise.—*adjs.* val'val; val'var; val'vate with or having a valve or valves: meeting at the edges without overlapping (*bot.*); valved; valve'less. [L. *valva*, a folding-door.]

vamoose *və-mōōs', vamose -mōs', (slang) vs.i.* to make off.—*vs.t.* to leave. [Sp. *vamos*, let us go.]

vamp¹ *vamp, n.* the part of a boot or shoe covering the front of the foot: anything patched up: a simple and uninspired improvised accompaniment.—*v.t.* to provide with a vamp: to repair with a new vamp: to patch up: to give a new face to: to improvise inartistically (*mus.*).—*v.i.* to improvise crude accompaniments.— *n.* vam'per.—*n.* and *adj.* vamp'ing. [O.Fr. *avanpié* —*avan*, before, *pié*—L. *pēs, pedis*, foot.]

vamp². See vampire.

vampire *vam'pīr, n.* in eastern European folklore, a dead person that leaves the grave to prey upon the living: a blood-sucker, a relentless extortionate parasite or blackmailer: an adventuress who allures and exploits men (abbrev. **vamp**): a vampire-bat.—*v.t.* to prey upon.—*n.* vamp see above.—*v.t.* to allure.— *adj.* vampir'ic.—*v.i.* vam'pirise, -ize to play the vampire.—*v.t.* (*lit* and *fig.*) to suck the blood of.—*n.* vam'pirism belief in human vampires: the actions of a vampire.—*adj.* vamp'ish.—vamp'ire-bat' a blood-sucking Central and South American bat (as Desmodus, Diphylla): applied to various bats wrongly supposed to be blood-suckers (as Vampyrus). [Some Slav. languages have *vampir*.]

van¹ *van, n.* a shortened form of **vanguard** (*lit.*, or *fig.* as in *in the van of modern fashion*).

van² *van, n.* a winnowing basket or shovel: a shovel for testing ore: a test of ore by washing on a shovel: a wing: a windmill sail.—*v.t.* to winnow or test with a van.—*n.* vann'er one who vans: an ore-separator.—*n.* and *adj.* vann'ing. [Southern form of fan; perh. in part directly from L. *vannus* or O.Fr. *van.*]

van³ *van, n.* a large covered wagon: a light vehicle, whether covered or not, used in transporting goods: a railway carriage or compartment for luggage, the guard, etc.—*v.t.* and *v.i.* to send, convey, confine, travel, or tour in a van:—*pr.p.* vann'ing; *pa.t.* and *pa.p.* vanned. [An abbreviated form of caravan.]

vanadium *və-nā'di-əm, n.* a silvery metallic element (V; at. numb. 23). [Named by a Swedish chemist Sefström from O.N. *Vana-dís*, the goddess Freyja.]

Van Allen radiation belts *van al'ən rā-di-ā'shən belts,* zones of intense particle radiation surrounding the earth at a distance of above 1200 miles (1930 km) from it. [J. A. *Van Allen,* American physicist, b. 1914.]

Vandal *van'dəl, n.* one of a fierce people from northeastern Germany who overran Gaul, Spain, and North Africa, sacked Rome in 455, destroyed churches, etc.: (usu. without *cap.*) one who destroys what is beautiful: (without *cap.*) one who wantonly damages property.—*adjs.* Van'dal; Vandal'ic.—*v.t.* van'dalise, -ize to inflict wilful and senseless damage on (property, etc.).—*n.* Van'dalism (or van'-).

Vandyke *van-dīk',* or *van'-, n.* a painting by the great Flemish artist Anthony *Van Dyck* (1599–1641): (in the following, usu. without *cap.*) a deeply cut collar similar to those seen in his portraits (also called Vandyke collar): a point of a deep-cut edging: a short pointed beard (also called Vandyke beard).—*v.t.* and *v.i.* to notch or zig-zag.—*adj.* vandyked'.—van'dyke brown a deep brown used by Van Dyck: a mixture of lampblack or other material and ochre.

vane *vān, n.* a flag: a weathercock or revolving plate, or a streamer, serving to show how the wind blows: a blade of a windmill, propeller, revolving fan, or the like: a fin on a bomb or a paravane: a sight on an observing or surveying instrument: the web of a feather.—*adjs.* vaned having a vane or vanes; vane'less. [Southern form of obs. *fane,* a flag.]

vang *vang, n.* a guy-rope to steady a gaff. [A form of fang.]

vanguard *van'gärd, n.* the foremost of an army, etc.: the forefront: those who lead the way or anticipate progress. [Fr. *avant-garde—avant,* before, *garde,* guard.]

vanilla *və-nil'ə, n.* a flavouring substance got from the pods of *Vanilla planifolia,* a Mexican climbing orchid, and other species: the plant yielding it.—*n.* vanill'in its aromatic principle ($C_8H_8O_3$). [Sp. *vainilla—vaina—*L. *vāgīnā,* a sheath.]

vanish *van'ish, v.i.* to disappear: to fade out: to cease to exist: to become zero.—*v.t.* to cause to disappear.—*n.* a vanishing: a glide with which a sound ends.—*n.* van'isher.—*n.* and *adj.* van'ishing.—*n.* van'ishment.—vanishing cream cosmetic cream that, when rubbed over the skin, virtually disappears; vanishing point the point at which parallel lines seen in perspective converge: the verge of disappearance of anything. [Aphetic for evanish.]

Vanitory® *van'i-tər-i, n.* a unit consisting of a wash-hand basin and a dressing-table.—Also Vanitory unit.—Sometimes without *cap.*

vanity *van'i-ti, n.* the quality of being vain: that which is vain.—van'ity-bag, -box, -case one containing a mirror and cosmetic appliances.—vanity unit a Vanitory unit or the like. [Fr. *vanité—*L. *vānitās, -ātis;* see vain.]

vanner, vanning, etc. See van², van³.

vanquish *vangk'wish, v.t.* to conquer: to overcome.—*v.i.* to be victor.—*adj.* vanq'uishable.—*ns.*

vanq'uisher; vanq'uishment. [A.Fr. *venquir, venquiss-* (Fr. *vaincre)—*L. *vincĕre,* to conquer.]

vantage *van'tij, n.* advantage.—van'tage-ground, -point a favourable or commanding position. [A.Fr. *vantage;* cf. advantage.]

vapid *vap'id, adj.* insipid: dull: flat.—*n.* vapid'ity.—*adv.* vap'idly.—*n.* vap'idness. [L. *vapidus.*]

vaporetto *vä-pə-ret'ō,* It. *va-po-ret'tō, n.* a small steamship that plies the canals in Venice:—*pl.* vaporett'os, -i (-ē). [It.,—*vapore,* a steamboat.]

vapour, or (esp. *U.S.*) vapor, *vā'pər, n.* a substance in the form of a mist, fume, or smoke, esp. one coming off from a solid or liquid: a gas below its critical temperature, liquefiable by pressure: water in the atmosphere: (in *pl.*) exhalations supposed to arise in the stomach or elsewhere in the body, affecting the health (*old med.*): (in *pl.,* usu. with *the*) low spirits, boredom, nervous disorder: anything insubstantial, vain, or transitory: a fanciful notion: bluster.—*v.i.* to pass off in vapour: to evaporate: to brag: to emit vapour: to bluster.—*v.t.* to make to pass into vapour: to steam: to affect with the vapours: to boast: to drive by bluster.—*n.* vaporim'eter an instrument for measuring vapour pressure or vapour.—*adj.* vaporis'able, -z-.—*n.* vaporisa'tion, -z-.—*v.t.* va'porise, -ize to convert into vapour: to spray.—*v.i.* to become vapour.—*ns.* vaporis'er, -z- an apparatus for discharging liquid in a fine spray; vaporos'ity.—*adj.* va'porous, of, in the form of, like, or full of vapour: vain: affected with the vapours: insubstantial: flimsy: vainly fanciful.—*adv.* va'porously.—*n.* va'porousness.—*adj.* va'poured full of vapours: affected with the vapours.—*n.* and *adj.* va'pouring.—*adj.* va'pourish vapoury.—*n.* va'pourishness.—*adj.* va'poury full of vapour: affected with the vapours.—vapour density the density of a gas or vapour relative to that of hydrogen at the same temperature and pressure; vapour trail a white trail of condensed vapour left in the sky from the exhaust of an aircraft. [L. *vapor, -ōris.*]

vaquero *vä-kā'rō, n.* a herdsman:—*pl.* vaque'ros. [Sp.,—L. *vacca,* a cow.]

varactor *var-ak'tər, n.* a two-electrode semi-conductor device in which capacitance varies with voltage.

variable *vā'ri-ə-bl, adj.* that may be varied: changeable: tending or liable to change or vary: showing variations: unsteady: quantitatively indeterminate (*math.*): changing in brightness (*astron.*).—*n.* a quantity subject to continual increase or decrease (*math.*): a quantity which may have an infinite number of values in the same expression (*math.*): a shifting wind: a variable star.—*ns.* variabil'ity; va'riableness.—*adv.* va'riably.—*ns.* va'riance variation: deviation: alteration: discrepancy: disagreement: dispute: the average of the squares of the deviations of a number of observations from the mean; va'riant a different form of the same thing (esp. a word): a different reading: a specimen slightly differing from the type.—*adj.* changeful: varying: diversified: different: diverging from type.—*n.* va'riate any one of the observed values of a quantity: a variant: the variable quantity which is being studied (*statistics*).—*v.t.* and *v.i.* to change, vary.—*n.* varia'tion a varying: a change: continuous change: difference in structure or character among offspring of the same parents or among members of a related group: departure from the mean or usual character: the extent to which a thing varies: a variant: declination of the compass: an inequality in the moon's motion discovered by Tycho Brahe: a change in the elements of an orbit by the disturbing force of another body: transformation of a theme by means of figures in counterpoint, florid treatment, changes in tempo, key, and the like (*mus.*): a solo dance (*ballet*).—*adj.* varia'tional pertaining to variation.—*n.* **varia'tionist** a composer of variations: one who attaches importance to variation. —*adj.* **va'riative** variational.—**variable costs** costs which, unlike fixed costs (q.v.) vary with the level of production; **variable gear** see **gear; variable-geometry aeroplane** an aeroplane of varying wing, swept-back for flight, but at right angles for take-off and landing, so removing need for long runways and high landing-speeds.—**at variance** in disagreement or dissension [Partly through O.Fr., from L *variāre, -ātum*, to vary—*varius*; see **vary.**]

varicella *var-i-sel'ə, n.* chickenpox. [Irreg. dim. of **variola.**]

varices, varicocele, varicose. See under **varix.**

varicoloured *vā'ri-kul'ərd, adj.* diversified in colour. [L. *varius*, various, *color*, colour.]

varied. See **vary.**

variegate *vā'ri-(ə-)gāt, v.t.* to diversify, esp. with colours in patches.—*adj.* **va'riegated.**—*ns.* **variega'tion; va'riegator.** [L. *variegātus—varius*; see **vary.**]

variety *və-rī'ə-ti, n.* the quality of being various: diversity: difference: many-sidedness, versatility: a varied set: a kind differing in minor characters: a race not sufficiently distinct to be counted a species: music-hall entertainment, a succession of varied turns:—*pl.* **vari'eties.**—*adj.* of, for, performing in, music-hall entertainment. [L. *varietās, -ātis—varius*, various.]

variform. See **various.**

variola *və-rī'ə-la, n.* smallpox: sheep-pox.—*adjs.* **vari'olar; variolous** (*və-rī'ō-ləs*) of, pertaining to, suffering from, smallpox. [L.L. *variola*, pustule, pox —L. *varius*, various, spotted.]

variometer, variorum. See **various.**

various *vā'ri-əs, adj.* varied, different: several: unlike each other: changeable: uncertain: variegated.—*adj.* **va'riform** of various forms.—*n.* **variom'eter** (Gr. *metron*, measure) an instrument for comparing magnetic forces: a variable inductance of two connected coils, one rotating within the other: an instrument that indicates by a needle the rate of climb and descent (*aero.*).—*adj.* **vario'rum** with the notes of various commentators or editors (L. *cum notis variōrum*): with the readings of various manuscripts or editions.—*n.* a variorum edition: a succession of changes (*jocular*).—*adv.* **va'riously.**—*n.* **va'riousness.** [L. *varius*; see **vary.**]

varistor *və-ris'tər, n.* a two-electrode semi-conductor used to short-circuit transient high voltages in delicate electronic devices. [*variable* resistor.]

varix *vā'riks* (L. *va', wa'riks), n.* an abnormally dilated, lengthened, and tortuous vein, artery, or lymphatic vessel: dilatation: a ridge marking a former position of the mouth of a shell:—*pl.* **varices** (*va', vā'ri-sēz*; L. *va'rikās, wa'*).—*n.* **varicocele** (*var'i-kō-sēl*; Gr. *kēlē*, tumour) an enlargement of the veins of the spermatic cord or those of the scrotum.—*adj.* **var'icose** of the nature of, like, pertaining to, affected by, a varix or varices: abnormally dilated or enlarged permanently, as a vein: dilated.—*ns.* **varicosity** (*var-i-kos'i-ti*) the state of being varicose: a distended place; **varicot'omy** the surgical removal of a varix or a varicose vein. [L. *varix, -icis*, a varicose vein.]

varlet *vär'lit, n.* an attendant (*arch.*): a knave (*arch.*). [O.Fr. *varlet*; cf. **valet.**]

varmint, varment *var'mint, n.* old variants (now *dial* or *slang*) of **vermin:** a noxious or troublesome animal or person.

varna *vûr'nə, vär'nə, n.* any of the four great Hindu castes. [Sans., class.]

varnish *vär'nish, n.* a resinous solution that dries to give a glossy coat to a surface: a gloss or glaze: a specious show: an application of varnish.—*v.t.* to

coat with varnish: to give a fair show to.—*ns.* **var'nisher; var'nishing.** [Fr. *vernis*; prob.—Mediaeval L. *veronix*, sandarac.]

varsity *vär'si-ti, (coll.) n.* and *adj.* university.

varus *vā'rəs, n.* (for *tālipēs vārus*) in-turned club-foot [L. *vārus*, bent, knock-kneed.]

varve *värv, (geol.) n.* a seasonal layer of clay deposited in still water, of service in fixing Ice Age chronology. [Sw. *varv*, layer.]

vary *vā'ri, v.t.* to make different: to diversify, modify: to alter or embellish (a melody) preserving its identity (*mus.*): to change to something else: to make of different kinds.—*v.i.* to alter or be altered. to be or become different: to change in succession: to deviate: to disagree: to be subject to continuous increase or decrease (*math.*):—*pr.p.* **va'rying;** *pa.t* and *pa.p.* **va'ried.**—*n.* a change.—*adj.* **va'ried.**—*n* and *adj.* **va'rying.** For **variance, variation,** etc., see **variable.** [M.E.—(O.) Fr. *varier* or L. *variāre*—L. *varius*, various.]

vas *vas* (L *vas, wàs), n.* a vessel, tube, duct, carrying liquid:—*pl.* **vasa** (*vā'sə;* L. *va'sa, wā'.*—**vas(o)**-(*vas(-ō)*) in composition, vas: vas deferens.—*adj.* **vā'sal.**—*n.* **vasec'tomy** (Gr. *ek*, out, *tomē*, a cut) excision of the vas deferens, or part of it, esp. in order to produce sterility.—*adj.* **vas'iform** tubular: vase-shaped.—*ns.* **vasoconstric'tion** narrowing of a blood-vessel; **vasoconstric'tor** a nerve or drug that causes vasoconstriction.—*adj* **vasoconstric'tory.**—*ns.* **vasodilatā'tion** expansion of a blood-vessel; **vasodilā'tor** a nerve or drug that causes vasodilatation.—*adjs.* **vasodil(at)ā'tory; vasomō'tor** causing constriction or expansion of blood-vessels.—**vas def'erens** a spermatic duct:—*pl.* **vā'sa deferen'tia** (*-shyə*). [L. *vās, vāsis*, vessel.]

vasculum *vas'kū-ləm, n.* a botanist's collecting case:—*pl.* **vas'culums, vas'cula.**—*adj.* **vas'cular** relating to, composed of, or provided with conducting vessels.—**vascular bundle** a strand of conducting tissue in the higher plants, composed of xylem, phloem, and cambium. [L. *vāsculum*, dim. of *vās*, a vessel.]

vase *väz, (U S.) vāz, n.* a vessel, usually tall, round in section, and ornamental, anciently used for domestic purposes. [Fr.,—L. *vās.*]

vasectomy. See **vas.**

Vaseline® *vaz'* or *vas'i-lēn, n.* a name applied to products of a certain firm, consisting in large part, but not solely, of petroleum jelly (*paraffinum molle*) and preparations thereof.—Also *v.t.* [Ger. *Wasser*, water, and Gr. *elaion*, oil.]

vasiform, vasomotor, etc. See **vas.**

vassal *vas'əl, n.* one who holds land from, and renders homage to, a superior. a dependant, retainer: a slave. —*adj.* in the relation or state of a vassal: subordinate. servile: of a vassal.—*v.t.* to subject —*n.* **vass'alage** the state of being a vassal: dependence. [Fr.,—L.L *vassallus*, servant—Celtic.]

vast *väst, adj.* boundless: huge: exceedingly great —*n* an immense tract, boundless or empty expanse of space or time.—*adv.* **vast'ly.**—*n.* **vast'ness.** [L *vastus*, waste, desolate, huge; cf. **waste.**]

vat *vat, n.* a large vessel or tank, esp. for fermentation, dyeing, or tanning: dyeing liquor.—*v.t.* to put in a vat. [O.E. *fæt.*]

vatic *vat'ik, adj.* prophetic: oracular: inspired. [L. *vātēs*, a prophet.]

Vatican *vat'i-kən, n.* an assemblage of buildings on the Vatican Hill in Rome, including one of the pope's palaces: the papal authority.—*ns.* **Vat'icanism** the system of theology and ecclesiastical government based on absolute papal authority, ultramontanism; **Vat'icanist** one who upholds such a system.—**Vatican City** a small area on the Vatican Hill set up as an independent papal state in 1929; **Vatican Council** the council that met in St Peter's (1869) and proclaimed papal infallibility (1870), or the similar council (**Vatican II**) held between 1962 and 1965. [L. *Môns Vâticânus*, the Vatican Hill.]

vaudeville *vō'də-vil, vōd'vil, n.* originally a popular song with topical allusions: a play interspersed with dances and songs incidentally introduced and usually comic: variety entertainment.—Also *adj.*—*n.* **vaudevill'ian** one who performs in or writes material for vaudeville.—Also *adj.* [From *vau* (*val*) *de Vire*, the valley of the Vire, in Normandy, where they were composed in the 15th century.]

vault[1] *vōlt,* earlier *vot, n.* an arched roof or ceiling: a chamber with an arched roof or ceiling, esp. underground: a cellar: a wine-cellar: hence (in *pl.*) a publichouse: a burial-chamber: a cavern: anything vault-like.—*v.t.* to shape as a vault: to roof with an arch: to form vaults in.—*v.i.* to curve in a vault.—*n.* **vaul'tage** a range of vaults: vaulted work.—*adj.* **vaul'ted** arched: concave overhead: covered with an arch or vault.—*n.* **vaul'ting** vaulted work. [O.Fr. *vaute, vaulte, voute, volte* (Fr. *voûte*)—L. *volvère, volûtum,* to roll.]

vault[2] *vōlt,* earlier *vōt, v.i.* to leap, esp. by resting on the hand or a pole.—*v.t.* to vault over or upon.—*n.* an act of vaulting.—*n.* **vault'er.**—*n.* and *adj.* **vault'ing.** —**vault'ing-horse** a wooden horse for gymnastic exercise. [App. O.Fr. *volter,* to leap.]

vaunt *vönt* (also *U.S. vänt), v.i.* to boast: to behave boastfully or exultingly.—*v.t.* to boast: to boast of.— *n.* a boast: boastful demeanour.—*adj.* **vaunt'ed.**—*n.* and *adj.* **vaunt'ing.**—*adv.* **vaunt'ingly.** [O.Fr. *vanter*—L.L. *vānitāre*—L. *vānitās,* vanity—*vānus,* vain; partly aphetic for obs. *avaunt,* to boast.]

vavasour *vav'ə-sōōr, n.* one who held his lands of a tenant in chief.—*n.* **vav'asory** the tenure or the lands of a vavasour. [O.Fr., app.—L.L. *vassus vassōrum,* vassal of vassals—*vassus,* vassal.]

've *v.* A shortened form of **have.**

veal *vēl, n.* calf's flesh as food.—*adj.* of veal. [O.Fr. *veël* (Prov. *vedel*)—L. *vitellus,* dim. of *vitulus;* cf. Gr. *italos,* a calf.]

vector *vek'tər, n.* a directed quantity, as a straight line in space, involving both its direction and magnitude (*math.*): a carrier of disease or infection: the course of an aircraft, missile, etc.—*v.t.* to direct, esp. from the ground, (an aircraft in flight) to the required destination.—*adj.* **vecto'rial.** [L. *vector, -ōris,* bearer, carrier—*vehĕre, vectum,* to convey.]

Veda *vā'də,* or *vē', n.* any one of, or all of, four ancient holy books of the Hindus:—*pl.* **Vedas.**—*n.* **Vedan'ta** a system of Hindu philosophy based on the Vedas.— *adjs.* **Vedan'tic, Ve'dic.**—*ns.* **Ve'dism; Ve'dist** one learned in the Vedas. [Sans. *veda,* knowledge; cf. **wit,** L. *vidēre,* to see, Gr. *oida,* I know; Sans. *Vedânta*—*anta,* end.]

vedalia *vi-dā'li-ə, n.* an orig. Australian ladybird, *Rodolia cardinalis,* introduced elsewhere to control insect pests.

Vedda *ved'ə, n.* (a member of) an aboriginal people of Sri Lanka.—*adj.* **Vedd'oid** of, pertaining to, or resembling, the Veddas: of a S. Asian race, dark-skinned and curly-haired, to which the Veddas belong.— Also *n.*

vedette *vi-det', n.* a mounted sentry stationed to watch an enemy: a small vessel (**vedette'-boat**) for like purpose. [Fr.,—It. *vedetta*—*vedere*—L. *vidēre,* to see.]

Vedic, Vedism, Vedist. See **Veda.**

vee *vē, n.* the twenty-second letter of the alphabet (V, v): a mark or object of that shape.—in composition (also **V-** (q.v.)), shaped like the letter V.

veer *vēr, v.i.* to change direction, esp. (of the wind) clockwise: to change course, esp. away from the wind: to come round or shift round in mental attitude.—*v.t.* to turn, shift: to turn away from the wind. —*n.* a shifting round.—*n.* and *adj.* **veer'ing.** [Fr. *virer.*]

veg *vej, n.* a coll. contraction of **vegetable(s).**

Vegan *vē'gən, n.* (often without *cap.*) one of a sect of vegetarians using no animal produce at all.—Also *adj.*—*n.* **Ve'ganism** (also without *cap.*).

vegetable *vej'i-tə-bl, n.* an organism belonging to the great division distinguished from animals by being unable to deal with solid food, commonly but not necessarily fixed in position—a plant: a plant or part of one used for food, other than those received fruits: a person whose capabilities are so low, esp. because of damage to the brain, that he is scarcely human: a dull, uninteresting person.—*adj.* of, for, derived from, composed of, of the nature of, vegetables.—*adj.* **veg'etal** vegetable: vegetative: of a level of life below the sensitive.—*n.* **vegetarian** (-*tā'ri-ən*) one who lives wholly on vegetable food, with or without dairy products, honey, and eggs.—Also *adj.*—*n.* **vegetā'rianism** the theory or practice of a vegetarian. —*v.i.* **veg'etate** to grow or live as, or like, a vegetable: to increase vegetatively: to live an inactive, almost purely physical, or dull life.—*n.* and *adj.* **veg'etating.** —*n.* **vegetā'tion** the process of vegetating: vegetable growth: growing plants in mass.—*adj.* **veg'etative** growing, as plants: producing growth in plants: concerned with the life of the individual rather than of the race (*biol.*): by means of vegetative organs, not special reproductive structures (*biol.*): pertaining to unconscious or involuntary bodily functions as resembling the process of vegetable growth (*biol.*): without intellectual activity, unprogressive.—*adv.* **veg'etatively.**—*n.* **veg'etativeness.**—**vegetable kingdom** that division of natural objects which consists of vegetables or plants; **vegetable marrow** a variety of pumpkin cooked as a vegetable; **vegetative nervous system** the nervous system regulating involuntary bodily activity, as the secretion of the glands, the beating of the heart, etc. [L. *vegetābilis,* animating, *vegetāre,* to quicken, *vegetus,* lively; cf. **vigour.**]

vehement *vē'(h)ə-mənt, adj.* forcible: impetuous: very strong or urgent.—*ns.* **ve'hemence, ve'hemency.**— *adv.* **ve'hemently.** [L. *vehemēns, -entis.*]

vehicle *vē'i-kl, n.* a means of conveyance or transmission: a medium: a substance with which a medicine, a pigment, etc., is mixed for administration or application: a structure in or on which persons or things are transported, esp. by land: (**space vehicle**) a structure for carrying burdens through air or space or (also **launch vehicle**) a rocket used to launch a spacecraft. —*adj.* **vehicular** (*vi-hik'û-lər*)—**vehicle-actuated signals** see **pad**[2]. [L. *vehiculum*—*vehĕre,* to carry.]

veil *vāl, n.* a curtain: a covering: a covering for the head, face, or both, for protection, concealment, or ceremonial reason: a nun's or novice's head-covering: a piece of gauzy drapery worn on the head by a bride: a gauzy face-covering worn by ladies: a disguise or concealment: an obstruction of tone in singing: a velum.—*v.t.* to cover with a veil: to cover: to conceal, disguise, or obscure.—*adj.* **velled.**—*n.* **veil'ing** the act of concealing with a veil: a veil: material for making veils.—Also *adj.*—**draw a veil** over to conceal discreetly: to refrain from mentioning; **take the veil** to become a nun. [O.Fr. *veile* (Fr. *voile*)—L. *vēlum,* a curtain, veil, sail.]

vein *vān, n.* one of the vessels or tubes that convey the blood back to the heart: loosely, any blood vessel: one of the horny tubes forming the framework of an insect's wing: a vascular bundle forming a rib, esp. a small rib, in a leaf: a small intrusion, or a seam of a different mineral running through a rock: a fissure or cavity: a streak in wood, stone, etc.: a streak running through one's nature, a strain of character or ability: (a recurrent characteristic streak in) manner, style: a mood or humour.—*v.t.* to form veins or the appearance of veins in.—*adj.* **veined** having veins: streaked, variegated.—*n.* **vein'ing** formation or disposition of veins: streaking.—*adjs.* **vein'ous** full of veins.— **vein'y** veined: veinous. [Fr. *veine*—L. *vēna*. See **vena**.]

vela, velar, velate, etc. See **velum**.

velatura *vel-ə-too͞o′rə, n.* a method of glazing a painting by rubbing with the hand. [It.]

Velcro® *vel′krō, n.* a type of fastening for clothes, etc consisting of two strips of specially treated nylon fabric which when pressed together form a secure fastening.

veld, also (outside S. Africa) **veldt,** *felt, velt, n.* in South Africa, open, unforested, or thinly-forested grass-country. [Du. *veld* (formerly *veldt*), field.]

veld(-)schoen (older form of **veld′skoen).** *Same as* **velskoen.**

veleta *və-lē′tə, n.* a dance or dance-tune in slow waltz time.—Also **valē′ta.** [Sp., weather-cock.]

vell *vel, n.* the fourth stomach of a calf, used in making rennet.

velleity *ve-lē′i-ti, n.* volition in its lowest from: mere inclination. [L.L. *velleitās,* irregularly formed from L. *velle,* to wish.]

vellum *vel′əm, n.* a finer kind of parchment: a manuscript, etc. printed on vellum.—*adj.* made of, printed on, etc. vellum. [O.Fr. *velin*—*vel,* calf.]

veloce *vā-lō′chä, (mus.) adj.* and *adv.* with great rapidity. [It.]

velocipede *vi-los′i-pēd, n.* an early form of bicycle [Fr. *vélocipède*—L. *vēlōx, -ōcis,* swift, *pēs, pedis,* foot.]

velocity *vi-los′i-ti, n.* rate of motion (distance per unit of time) in stated direction: loosely, speed. [L. *vēlōcitās, -ātis*—*vēlōx,* swift.]

velodrome *vel′ə-drōm, n.* a building containing a cycle-racing track. [Fr. *vélodrome.*]

velour(s) *və-loo͞o′r, n.* a woollen stuff with velvet-like pile.—Also *adj.* [Fr. *velours.*]

velouté (sauce) *və-loo͞o-tā′ (sōs), n.* a smooth white sauce made with stock. [Fr., velvety.]

velskoen *fel′skoo͞on, (S.Afr.) n.* a shoe made of rawhide. [Du. *vel,* skin, *schoen,* shoe.]

velum *vel′əm* (L. *vā′, wā′lŏŏm), n.* a veil, integument, or membrane: the membrane joining the rim of a young toadstool with the stalk: the pendulous soft palate: a ciliated disc, a locomotor organ in some molluscan larvae:—*pl.* **vē′la.**—*adj.* **vē′lar** of the velum: produced by the back of the tongue brought close to, or in contact with, the soft palate (*phon.*).— *n.* a velar consonant, back consonant.—*adj.* **velar′ic** pertaining to a velar.—*n.* **velarisā′tion, -z-.**—*v.t.* **ve′larise, -ize** to pronounce a (non-velar sound) with the back of the tongue brought close to the soft palate, esp. through the influences of a vowel sound.— *adj.* **ve′larised, -z-.**—*adjs.* **vē′late, -d** having a velum. [L. *vēlum,* veil, sail.]

velvet *vel′vit, n.* a silk fabric with soft close short pile: an imitation with silk pile: any of various other velvety fabrics: the velvet-like covering of a growing antler: a velvety surface or skin.—*adj.* made of velvet: soft like velvet.—*adj.* **vel′veted** clad in velvet. —*n.* **velveteen′** a cotton, or mixed cotton and silk, imitation of velvet; **vel′vetiness; vel′veting** velvet material.—*adj.* **vel′vety** soft and smooth like velvet: deep and soft in colouring.—**vel′vet-pa′per** flock paper; **vel′vet-pile** material with a soft nap.—**on**

velvet in a safe or advantageous position: secure against losing, whatever happens; **the velvet glove** gentleness, concealing strength (see **iron hand** at **iron**). [L.L. *velvettum,* conn. with L. *villus,* a tuft.]

vena *vē′nə,* (L. *vā′, wā′na), n.* vein:—*pl.* **ve′nae.**—*adj.* **vē′nal** venous.—*ns.* **venation** (*vi-nā′shən*) arrangement of veins or nervures: the veins themselves considered together; **venepunc′ture, veni-** the puncturing of a vein, esp. with a hypodermic needle; **venesec′tion** the opening of a vein so as to let blood as a remedial measure.—*adj.* **venose** (*vē′nōs, -nōs′*) veiny: veined with noticeable veins.—*n.* **venosity** (*vē-nos′i-ti*) the state or quality of being venous, or of having or being like venous blood —*adj.* **vē′nous** pertaining to, or contained in, veins: of blood, deprived of oxygen and, in man, dark red in colour: veined.—*n.* **venule** (*ven′ūl*) a branch of a vein in an insect's wing: any of the small-calibre blood vessels into which the capillaries empty and which unite to form veins [L. *vēna;* see **vein**.]

venal[1] *vē′nl, adj.* for sale: to be bought or bought over: corruptly mercenary.—*n.* **venality** (*-nal′i-ti*).—*adv* **vē′nally.** [L. *vēnālis*—*vēnum,* goods for sale.]

venal[2]. See **vena**.

venatic, -al *vi-nat′ik, -əl, adjs.* pertaining to hunting. [L. *vēnārī,* to hunt]

venation. See **vena**.

vend *vend, v.t.* to sell or offer for sale, deal in, esp in a small way: to utter (perh. for vent).—*n.* a sale: the amount sold.—*ns.* **vendee′** a buyer; **ven′der, -dor** a seller; **vendibil′ity.**—*adj.* **vend′ible** that may be sold, offered for sale, or readily sold.—*n.* a thing for sale: a possible object of trade.—**vending machine** a slot-machine dispensing goods. [Fr. *vendre* or L. *vendēre,* to sell.]

vendace *ven′das, n.* a whitefish found in the Castle Loch and Mill Loch at Lochmaben: another species in Derwentwater and Bassenthwaite Lake. [Possibly O.Fr. *vendese, vendoise,* dace.]

vendee. See **vend**.

vendetta *ven-det′ə, n* a blood-feud: any similarly prolonged, violent, etc. feud or quarrel. [It.,—L. *vindicta,* revenge—*vindicāre,* to claim.]

vendible, vendor, etc. See **vend**.

veneer *və-nēr′, v.t.* to overlay or face with a thin sheet of fine wood or other substance: to disguise with superficial refinement.—*n.* a thin slice for veneering: a specious superficial show.—*ns.* **veneer′er; veneer′ing.** [Formerly *fineer*—Ger. *furniren*— O.Fr. *fornir* (Fr. *fournir*), It. *fornire,* to furnish.]

venepuncture. See **vena**.

venerate *ven′ə-rāt, v.t.* to revere.—*adj.* **ven′erable** worthy of reverence: hallowed by associations or age: aged-looking: an honorific prefix to the name of an archdeacon, or one in process of canonisation.—*n.* **ven′erableness.**—*adv.* **ven′erably.**—*ns.* **venerā′tion** the act of venerating: the state of being venerated: awed respect; **ven′erātor.** [L. *venerārī, -ātus.*]

venery *ven′ə-ri, n.* sexual indulgence.—*adj.* **venereal** (*vi-nē′ri-əl*) pertaining to sexual desire or intercourse: transmitted by sexual intercourse: pertaining to or affected by venereal disease.—*ns.* **venereol′ogist;** **venereology** (*vi-nē-ri-ol′ə-ji*) the study of venereal diseases.—**venereal disease** any of various contagious diseases characteristically transmitted by sexual intercourse. [L. *venereus*—*Venus, Veneris,* the goddess of love.]

venesection. See **vena**.

Venetian *vi-nē′sh(y)ən, adj.* of Venice.—*n.* a native or inhabitant of Venice: a Venetian blind.—*adj.* **Vene′tianed** having Venetian blinds or shutters.— **Venetian blind** a window-blind of horizontal slats adjustable to let in or keep out light.

vengeance *ven'jəns, n.* the infliction of injury in punishment or revenge: retribution.—*adj.* **venge'ful** vindictive, revengeful: retributive.—*adv.* **venge'fully.**—*n.* **venge'fulness.—with a vengeance** orig., with a curse: violently, thoroughly, exceedingly (*coll.*) [O.Fr. *venger*—L *vindicāre.*]

venial *vē'ni-əl, adj.* pardonable: excusable.—*n.* **veniality** (*-al'ı-tı*).—**venial sin** sin other than mortal. [L *veniālis,* pardonable—*venia,* pardon.]

venin. See **venom.**

venipuncture. See **vena.**

venison *ven'(i-)zn,* or (esp. in Scotland) *-i-sən, n.* a beast of the chase, esp. a deer (*Shak.*): its flesh as food: now deer's flesh. [A.Fr. *venison* (Fr. *venaison*)—L. *vēnātiō, -ōnis,* hunting—*vēnārī,* to hunt.]

Venite *vi-nī'ti* (L. *ve-, we-nē'te*), *n* the 95th Psalm, beginning *Venite exultēmus.*

Venn diagram *ven dī'ə-gram,* (*math.*) a diagram in which sets and their relationships are represented, by circles or other figures. [John Venn (1834–1923), mathematician.]

venom *ven'əm, n.* poison, esp. snake-poison: spite (*fig.*).—*n.* **ven'in** any of various toxic substances in venom.—*adjs.* **ven'omed** venomous: charged with poison, envenomed; **ven'omous** poisonous: having power to poison, esp. by bite or sting: malignant, full of spite.—*adv.* **ven'omously.**—*n.* **ven'omousness.** [O.Fr. *venim* (Fr. *venin*)—L. *venēnum,* poison.]

venose, venosity, venous. See under **vena.**

vent[1] *vent, n.* a slit in a garment, now in the back of a coat. [Fr. *fente*—L. *findĕre,* to split.]

vent[2] *vent, n.* an opening: an aperture: an air-hole or passage: a touch-hole: an outlet: a volcanic orifice: an animal's or bird's anus: issue: emission: discharge: escape: passage into notice: publication: utterance: expression: the opening in a parachute canopy through which air escapes at a controlled rate.—*v.t.* to give a vent or opening to: to let out, as at a vent: to allow to escape: to publish: to utter: to discharge: to emit: to pour forth.—*v.i.* to have or find an outlet: to take breath or rise for breath.—*adj.* **vent'ed.**—*n.* and *adj* **vent'ing.**—**vent'-hole** a hole for admission or escape of air, fumes, etc., or to admit light; **vent'-peg, -plug** a plug for stopping the vent of a barrel; **vent'-pipe** an escape-pipe, as for steam or foul gases.—**give vent to** to allow to escape or break out: to give, usu. violent, expression to (an emotion). [Fr.,—L. *ventus,* wind; partly Fr. *éventer,* to expose to air; associated with foregoing and following words.]

venter *ven'tər, n.* the belly, abdomen: a swelling or protuberance: a medial swelling: a shallow concave surface of a bone: the upper side or surface of a leaf, etc.—*adj.* **ven'tral** of the belly: on the upper side or towards the axis (*bot.*): on the side normally turned towards the ground—opp. to *dorsal* (*zool.*).—*n.* a ventral fin.—*adv* **ven'trally.**—*n.* **ven'tricle** a cavity in the body: esp. a cavity in the brain, or a contractile chamber of the heart.—*adjs.* **ven'tricose, ven'tricous** bellying: swollen in the middle or at one side, or all round at the base: big-bellied; **ventric'ōlar** of, of the nature of, a ventricle: abdominal.—*ns.* **ven'tricule, ventric'ŏlus** a ventricle.—**ventral fins** the posterior paired fins. [L. *venter, -tris,* dim. *ventriculus.*]

ventil *ven'til, n.* a valve for giving sounds intermediate between the open harmonics in wind instruments: a valve in an organ for controlling the wind supply to various stops. [Ger.,—L.L. *ventile,* shutter, sluice —*ventus,* wind.]

ventilate *ven'ti-lāt, v.t.* to fan, winnow, blow upon: to open or expose to the free passage of air: to provide with duct(s) for circulating air or for escape of air: to cause (blood) to take up oxygen, by supply of air: to

supply air to (lungs): to expose to examination and discussion, to make public.—*adj.* **ven'tilable.**—*n.* **ventila'tion.**—*adj.* **ven'tilative.**—*n.* **ven'tilator** one who ventilates: a contrivance for introducing fresh air: a machine which ventilates the lungs of a person whose respiratory system is not functioning adequately (also **ventilator machine**). [L. *ventilāre, -ātum,* to fan, wave, agitate—*ventus,* wind.]

venting. See **vent**[2].

ventral, ventricle, etc. See under **venter.**

ventriloquism *ven-tril'ə-kwizm, n.* the art of speaking so as to give the illusion that the sound comes from some other source.—*adj.* **ventriloquial** (*-lō'kwi-əl*). —*adv.* **ventrilo'quially.**—*v.i.* **ventril'oquise, -ize** to practise ventriloquism.—*n.* **ventril'oquist.**—*adjs.* **ventriloquis'tic, ventril'oquous.**—*n.* **ventril'oquy** ventriloquism. [L *ventriloquus,* one who speaks by a spirit in the belly—*venter,* the belly, *loquī,* to speak.]

venture *ven'chər, n.* that which is put to hazard (esp. goods sent by sea at the sender's risk): an undertaking whose issue is uncertain or dangerous: an attempt: a thing put forward as an attempt.—*v.t.* to send on a venture: to expose to hazard: to risk: to take the risk of: to dare to put forward.—*v i.* to make a venture: to run a risk: to dare.—*n.* **ven'turer.**—*adj.* **ven'turesome** inclined to take risks: involving the taking of risk: risky.—*n.* and *adj.* **ven'turing.**—*adj.* **ven'turous** adventurous: daring.—*adv.* **ven'turously.**—*n.* **ven'turousness.**—**Venture Scout** a member of senior branch of the Scout organisation, formerly called Rover (Scout). [For a(d)**venture.**]

venturi (**tube**), also **Venturi**, *ven-tōōr'ē* (*tūb*) a tube or duct, wasp-waisted and expanding at the ends, used in measuring flow rate of fluids, as a means of accelerating air flow, or to provide a suction source for vacuum-operated instruments [G.B. *Venturi* (1746–1822), Italian physicist]

venue *ven'ū, n.* a hit in fencing: the place where an action is laid (*law*): the district from which a jury comes to try a question of fact: in England, usually the county where a crime is alleged to have been committed: a scene of action: a meeting-place, esp. for a sport. [O Fr. *venue,* arrival—*venir*—L. *venīre,* to come.]

venule. See **vena.**

Venus *vē'nəs, n.* the goddess of love (*Roman myth.*): the most brilliant of the planets, second in order from the sun.—*ns.* and *adjs.* **Venusian** (*ven-ōō'si-ən, -shi-ən, -shən, ven-ū'*), less commonly **Venutian** (*ven-ōō'shi-ən, -shən, ven-ū'*) (an inhabitant) of the planet Venus.—**Venus's comb** an umbelliferous plant with long-beaked fruits set like comb teeth; **Venus's flower-basket** a beautiful glass sponge; **Venus's fly-trap, Venus Fly Trap** see **Dionaea; Venus's girdle** a ribbon-like ctenophoran (*Cestus*); **Venus's looking-glass** a garden plant with small bright flowers; **mount of Venus** the elevation at the base of the thumb: (*mons Veneris*) a fatty elevation on the human female pubic symphysis. [L., orig. personified from *venus, -eris,* desire.]

veracious *və-rā'shəs, adj.* truthful.—*adv.* **verā'ciously.** —*n.* **veracity** (*-ras'i-ti*) truthfulness [L. *vērāx, -ācis* —*vērus,* true.]

veranda, verandah *və-ran'də, n.* a roofed gallery, terrace, or open portico along the front or side of a building. [Hindi *varandā,* app.—Port. *varanda,* a balcony.]

Veratrum *və-rā'trəm, n.* the white hellebore genus: (without *cap.*) a plant of this genus.—*ns.* **veratria(e)** (*ver'ə-trin, -trēn*) an alkaloid or mixture of alkaloids got from white hellebore rhizomes, sabadilla, etc. [L. *vērātrum,* hellebore.]

verb *vûrb, n. (gram.)* the part of speech which asserts or predicates something.—*adj.* **ver'bal** of, pertaining to, derived from, a verb or verbs: of, in, of the nature of, in the matter of, or concerned with, words, or words rather than things: word for word: oral.—*n.* a word, esp. a noun, derived from a verb: an oral statement, esp. an arrested suspect's confession of guilt, made to the police, or claimed by them to have been made *(slang).—n.* **verbalisā'tion,** **-z-.—***v.t.* **ver'balise, -ize** to turn into a verb: to put in words.— *v.i.* to use many words.—*ns.* **ver'balism** an expression: wording: undue attention to words alone: literalism; **ver'balist** one skilled in words: a literalist: one who looks to words alone; **verbal'ity** the quality of being verbal or merely verbal: mere words.—*adv.* **ver'bally.**—*n.* **ver'biage** superfluity of words.—*adjs.* **verb'less; verbose'** using or containing more words than are desirable: wordy.—*adv.* **verbose'ly.**—*ns.* **verbose'ness, verbosity** *(-bos').*—**verbal inspiration** dictation of every word of a book (usu. the Bible) by God; **verbal noun** a form of a verb, e.g. infinitive or gerund, functioning as a noun. [L. *verbum,* word.]
verbatim *vər-bā'tim, -ba'tim, adv.* word for word (also *adj.*).—**verbatim et litteratim** *(-ā'tim, -a'tim)* word for word and letter for letter. [L.]
verbiage, verbose, etc. See **verb.**
verdant *vûr-dənt, adj.* green: fresh green or grass-green: green, unsophisticated, raw and gullible.—*n.* **ver'dancy.**—*adv.* **ver'dantly.**—*ns.* **ver'derer, -or** *(hist.)* a forest officer who had charge of the vert and venison; **ver'dure** fresh greenness: greenery.—*adjs.* **ver'dured** clad with verdure; **ver'dureless;** **ver'durous.** [O.Fr. *verd* (Fr. *vert*)—L. *viridis,* green.]
verd-antique *vûrd-an-tēk' (obs. Fr.),* or **verde-antico** *ver'dä-än-tē'kō* (It.) *ns.* a breccia of serpentine containing calcite, etc.—**oriental verd-antique** a green porphyry. [Antique green; Fr. now *vert.*]
verderer, verderor. See **verdant.**
verdict *vûr'dikt, n.* the finding of a jury on a trial: judicial decision or decision generally.—**open verdict** see **open; special verdict** a verdict in which specific facts are found and put on the record. [O.Fr. *verdit* and L.L. *vērēdictum*—L. *vērē,* truly, *dictum,* said.]
verdigris *vûr'di-grēs, n.* basic cupric acetate: popularly, the green coating of basic cupric carbonate that forms in the atmosphere on copper, brass, or bronze. [O.Fr. *verd de Grèce,* green of Greece.]
verdure, etc. See **verdant.**
Verey light. See **Very light.**
verge[1] *vûrj, n.* a rod: a rodlike part: the axis of a clock pallet: a watch with a verge: an intromittent organ: a wand or staff of office: extent of jurisdiction (esp. of the lord-steward of the royal household): a precinct: a pale: a range: scope: jurisdiction: a limit, boundary: a rim: the brink, extreme edge: the horizon: the edge of a roof projecting beyond the gable: a grass edging. —*v.t.* to edge.—*v.i.* to border, be on the edge (with *on;* also *fig.*): to act as verger.—*ns.* **ver'ger** one who looks after the interior of a church building, etc.: attendant in a church; **ver'gership.**—**on the verge of** *(fig.)* on the point of: on the brink of. [L. *virga,* a rod; the area of jurisdiction of the holder of the office symbolised by the rod, hence, limit, boundary.]
verge[2] *vûrj, v.i.* to incline: to tend downward: to tend: to pass gradually, merge. [L. *vergĕre,* to bend.]
verglas *ver'glä, n.* a film of ice on rock. [Fr., (*verre,* glass, *glace,* ice) from O.Fr.]
veridical *vi-rid'i-kl, adj.* truth-telling: coinciding with fact: (of a dream or vision) corresponding exactly with what has happened or with what happens later: seemingly true to fact.—*n.* **veridicality** *(-kal'i-ti).* [L. *vēridicus*—*vērus,* true, *dicĕre,* to say.]
verier, veriest. See **very.**

verify *ver'i-fī, v.t.* to testify: to assert or prove to be true: to ascertain, confirm, or test the truth or accuracy of:—*pr.p.* **ver'ifying;** *pa.t.* and *pa.p.* **ver'ified.** —*n.* **verifiabil'ity.**—*adj.* **ver'ifiable.**—*n.* **verificā'tion.**—*adj.* **ver'ificatory.**—*n.* **ver'ifier.** [L. *vērus,* true, *facĕre,* to make.]
verily. See **very.**
verisimilar *ver-i-sim'i-lər, adj.* truth-like.—*n.* **verisimil'itude.** [L. *vērisimilis*—*vērus,* true, *similis,* like.]
verism *ver', vēr'izm, n.* use of everyday contemporary material, including what is ugly or sordid, in the arts, esp. in early 20th-cent. Italian opera (It. *verismo vā-rēs'mō*): the theory supporting this.—*adj.* and *n.* **ver'ist.**—*adj.* **verist'ic.** [L. *vērus,* true.].
vérité. See **cinéma vérité** under **cinema.**
verity *ver'i-ti, n.* truth: a truth: truthfulness: sincerity: faithfulness:—*pl.* **ver'ities.**—*adj.* **ver'itable** true: genuine: real, actual: truly so to be called.—*adv.* **ver'itably.** [L. *vēritās, -ātis*—*vērus,* true.]
verjuice *vûr'jōōs, n.* juice of unripe fruit.—*adj.* sour.— *adj.* **ver'juiced** soured. [Fr. *verjus*—*vert* (L. *viridis*), green, and *jus,* juice (L. *jūs,* broth).]
verkrampte *fər-kram(p)'tə, n.* and *adj.* in S. Africa, (a person) of rigidly conservative political attitudes, esp. towards black and coloured people. [Afrik., restricted.]
verligte *fər-lihh'tə, n.* and *adj.* in S. Africa, (a person) of enlightened and liberal political attitudes, esp. towards black and coloured people. [Afrik., enlightened.]
vermeil *vûr'mil, -māl, n.* and *adj.* bright red, scarlet, vermilion: silver-gilt or gilt bronze. [O.Fr. and Fr., —L. *vermiculus,* a little worm, kermes, dim. of *vermis,* worm; cf. **vermilion.**]
vermes *vûr'mēz, n.pl.* worms.—*adj.* **ver'micidal** (L. *caedēre,* to kill).—*n.* **ver'micide** a worm-killing agent. —*adjs.* **vermic'olar** of, like, of the nature of, caused by, a worm: vermiculated: peristaltic; **vermic'olate, -d** worm-eaten: marked, inlaid, rusticated, with curving lines in the appearance of worm-tracks or worms. —*ns.* **vermiculā'tion** any wormlike appearance or action, esp. the movement of the intestines; **vermic'olite** an altered mica that curls before the blowpipe flame and expands greatly at high-temperature, forming a water-absorbent substance used in seed-planting, and also used as insulating material. —*adjs.* **vermic'olous** wormy; **ver'miform** having the form of a worm; **vermifugal** *(-mif'ū-gl)* expelling worms.—*n.* **ver'mifuge** *(-mi-fūj)* a drug that expels worms.—**vermiform appendix** see **appendix** at **append.** [L. *vermis,* a worm.]
vermicelli *vûr-mi-sel'i,* or *-chel'i, n.* a very slender macaroni: (more usu. **chocolate vermicelli**) short thin pieces of chocolate used for decoration of cakes, sweets, etc.—Also *adj.* [It., pl. of *vermicello,* dim. of *verme*—L. *vermis,* worm.]
vermicidal, vermiculite, etc, **vermiform, vermifugal,** etc. See **vermes.**
vermilion *vər-mil'yən, n.* a bright-red pigment, mercuric sulphide: its bright scarlet colour.—*adj.* bright scarlet.—*v.t.* to colour vermilion. [O.Fr. *vermillon* --*vermeil;* see **vermeil.**]
vermin *vûr'min, n.* a collective name for obnoxious insects, troublesome animals, animals destructive to game, odious, despicable people: any one species or individual of these.—*adjs.* **ver'minous, ver'miny** infested with vermin: like vermin. [Fr. *vermin*—L. *vermis,* a worm.]
vermouth *vûr'məth, vär'-, vûr'mōōt, n.* a drink with white wine base, flavoured with wormwood or other aromatic herbs. [Fr.—Ger. *Wermut(h),* wormwood.]

vernacular *vər-nak'ū-lər, adj.* (of language) indigenous, native, spoken by the people of the country or of one's own country: of, in, or using the vernacular language: of the jargon or idiom of a particular group: (of other things) native, local, endemic, esp. of architecture or general style of building.—*n.* a native language or dialect: a class jargon: profane language (*facet.*).—*n.* **vernac'ularism** a vernacular expression or idiom: the use of the vernacular; **vernac'ularist** a user of the vernacular. [L. *vernāculus—verna*, a home-born slave.]

vernal *vûr'nəl, adj.* of, happening or appearing in spring: springlike.—*n.* **vernalisā'tion**, *-z-.—v.t.* **ver'nalise, -ize** to make springlike: to freshen: to hasten the development of (seeds or seedlings) by treating them in various ways before planting, e.g. by subjecting them to a low temperature.—*n.* **vernā'tion** arrangement of leaves in the vegetative bud (rarely that of the individual leaf). [L. *vērnālis*, vernal, *vērnāre*, to sprout—*vēr*, spring.]

vernicle *vûr'ni-kl, n.* a sudarium with the face of Christ, held to have been miraculously impressed on it when St *Veronica* wiped his face: any representation of this: a medal or badge bearing it, worn by pilgrims who had been at Rome.

vernier *vûr'ni-ər, n.* a short scale sliding on a graduated scale to give fractional readings, invented by the Burgundian P. *Vernier* (*c.* 1580–1637): a small auxiliary device that enables a piece of apparatus to be adjusted very accurately (e.g a **vernier condenser** a condenser of small capacitance connected in parallel with one of larger capacitance): a small rocket engine used to make the movement of a booster rocket, or of a ballistic missile, more precisely as required.—Also *adj.*

veronica *və-ron'i-kə, n.* a vernicle. [St *Veronica.*]
véronique *vā-ro-nēk', (Fr.) adj.* (used after the noun) served with white grapes, e.g. *sole véronique.*

verruca *ve-rōō'kə, n.* a wart: a wartlike outgrowth:—*pl.* **verru'cae** (*-sē*; L. *-kī*), **verru'cas.**—*adjs.* **verru'ciform** (*-si-förm*) wartlike; **verrucose'** (or *ver'*, or *-rōō'*), **verru'cous** (or *ver'*) warty [L. *verrūca*, a wart.]

vers *ver*, (Fr.) *n.* verse.—*n.* **verslibrist** (*ver-lē'brist*) a writer of free verse.—**vers d'occasion** (*dok-az-yō*) occasional verse, produced for a particular event; **vers libre** (*lē'br'*) free verse. [Fr.]

versal *vûr'səl, n.* an ornamental letter at the beginning of a section, e.g. in an illuminated manuscript. [**verse, -al.**]

versant *vûr'sənt, n.* the general slope of surface of a country. [Fr. *versant—verser*, to turn over—L. *versāre.*]

versatile *vûr'sə-tīl, adj.* turning freely: dangling as an anther attached by the middle of the back (*bot.*): capable of free movement, reversible, as a toe (*zool.*): turning easily from one thing to another: of many-sided ability: capable of many uses.—*adv.* **ver'-satilely.**—*ns.* **ver'satileness,** **versatility** (*-til'i-ti*). [L. *versātilis—versāre,* freq. of *vertĕre,* to turn.]

verse *vûrs, n.* a line of metre: metrical composition, form, or work: versification: a stanza: a short division of a chapter, esp. of the Bible: a portion of an anthem to be performed by a single voice to each part: a versicle.—*v.t.* and *v.i.* to versify.—*ns.* **ver'set** a very short organ interlude or prelude: a versicle: a little scrap of verse; **ver'sicle** a little verse: in liturgy, the verse said by the officiant.—*adj.* **versic'ular** of or in verse.—*ns.* **versificā'tion** the making of verse: manner of construction of verse: a turning into verse or its product; **ver'sificātor,** **ver'sifier** a maker of verses.—*v.i.* **ver'sify** to make verses.—*v.t.* to tell in verse: to turn into verse:—*pr.p.* **ver'sifying;** *pa.t.* and *pa.p.* **ver'sified.**—*n.* **ver'sing** the composing of verse.—**free**

verse see **free.** [O.E. *fers*, reinforced by Fr. *vers*, both—L. *versus, vorsus, -ūs,* a line, row, verse—*vertĕre,* to turn.]

versed[1] *vûrst, adj.* thoroughly acquainted, skilled (with *in*).—*v.t.* **verse** to make conversant (with *in*) [L. *versātus,* pa.p. of *versārī,* to busy oneself.]
versed[2] *vûrst,* (*math.*) *adj.* lit. turned, reversed.—*n.* **versine** (*vûr'sīn*), contr. **versin,** the versed sine, one minus the cosine. [L. *versus,* pa.p. of *vertĕre,* to turn.]

verset, versicle, etc. See **verse.**

versicoloured *vûr'si-kul-ərd, adj.* diversely or changeably coloured. [L. *versicolor, -ōris—vertĕre, versum,* to change, *color,* colour.]

versicular, versification, etc See **verse.**
versin(e). See **versed[2].**

version *vûr'shən, n* a turning: translation: a particular form in which something is embodied, as a particular way of telling a story: a variant.—*adj.* **ver'sional.** [L. *versiō, -ōnis—vertĕre, versum,* to turn.]

verslibrist. See **vers.**

verso *vûr'sō, n.* a left-hand page of an open book: the reverse of a coin or medal:—*pl* **ver'sos.** [L *versō* (*foliō*), turned leaf (abl.)]

versus *vûr'səs,* (*law, games*) *prep.* against—abbreviated *v* and *vs.* [L.]

vert *vûrt, n.* in forest law, every green leaf or plant having green leaves that may serve as cover for deer: green colour (*her.*). [Fr *vert*—L. *viridis,* green.]

vertebra *vûr'ti-brə, n* a joint of the backbone:—*pl.* **ver'tebrae** (*-brē, -brī*).—*adj.* **ver'tebral.**—*adv.* **ver'tebrally.**—*n.pl.* **Vertebrā'ta** the backboned animals.—*adj.* **ver'tebrate** backboned: of the Vertebrata: articulated.—*n.* a backboned animal.—*adj.* **ver'tebrated** having a backbone: articulated like a backbone.—*n* **vertebrā'tion** vertebral structure: division into vertebrae or vertebra-like segments: backbone (*fig*).—**vertebral column** spinal column [L., *—vertĕre,* to turn]

vertex *vûr'teks, n.* the top or summit: the zenith (*astron.*): the crown of the head (*anat.*): the point opposite the base (*geom*): the meeting-point of the lines bounding an angle: the intersection of a curve with its axis—*pl* **ver'tices** (*-ti-sēz*).—*adj* **ver'tical** (*-ti-kl*) of or at the vertex: perpendicular to the plane of the horizon: in the direction of the axis (*bot*): comprising the various stages in the production of the same goods: in strata: (of mechanism) in which one part is above another.—*n.* a vertical line or position.—*n.* **verticality** (*-kal'i-ti*).—*adv* **ver'tically.**—*ns.* **ver'ticalness;** **verticity** (*-tis'i-ti*) power of turning — **vertical angles** opposite angles formed by intersecting lines; **vertical circle** a great circle of the heavens passing through the zenith and the nadir; **vertical take-off** (*aero.*) immediate take-off without preliminary run —Also as *adj.* [L. *vertex, -icis,* eddy, summit—*vertĕre,* to turn.]

verticil *vûr'ti-sil,* (*bot.*) *n.* a whorl.—*adjs.* **verti'cillate, -d** whorled. [L. *verticillus,* dim of *vertex.*]

vertigo *var-tī'gō,* often *vûr'ti-gō,* L. *ver-tē', wer-, n.* giddiness: dizziness: a whirling:—*pl.* **vertigos, vertigoes** or **vertigines** (*-tij'i-nēz*).—*adj.* **vertiginous** (*-tij'*) dizzy: giddy: whirling: dizzying.—*adv.* **vertig'inously.**—*n.* **vertig'inousness.** [L *vertīgō, -inis—vertĕre,* to turn.]

vertu *var-tōō', n.* an erroneous form of **virtu.**

vervain *vûr'vān, n.* a wild verbena, long believed to have great magical and medicinal powers. [O.Fr. *verveine*—L. *verbēna.*]

verve *vûrv, n.* enthusiasm that animates a poet or artist: gusto: spirit: animation: energy. [Fr.]

vervet *vûr'vit, n.* an African monkey. [Fr.]

very *ver'i, adj.* true: so called in the true or full sense of the word,—that and nothing less, even or exactly that: veritable: actual: mere: precise: extreme:—used, chiefly formerly, in *compar*. **ver'ier**, and also (oftener) in *superl*. **ver'iest**, most truly so called, merest.—*adv*. in high degree: utterly: quite: truly: precisely.—*adv*. **ver'ily** truly: of a certainty: really.— **the very thing** precisely what is wanted or needed. [Older *verray*, *veray*—A.Fr. *ver(r)ai* (Fr. *vrai*), from a derivative of L. *vērus*, true.]

Very light *ver'i līt*, a signalling or illuminating coloured flare fired from a pistol.—Also **Verey**. [Edward W. *Very*, inventor, 1877.]

vesica *vi-sī'kə*, *ves'ı-* (*anat*.) *n*. a bladder, sac, esp. the urinary bladder:—*pl*. **vesicae** (*vi-sī'sē*, *ves'ı-*).—*adjs*. **vesical** (*ves'i-kl*) of or pertaining to a vesica; **ves'icant** blistering.—*n*. anything that causes blisters.—*v.t*. and *v.i*. **ves'icate** to blister.—*n*. **vesicā'tion**.—*n*. and *adj*. **ves'icatory** (or *-ik'*) vesicant.—*ns* **ves'icle** a small globule, bladder, sac, blister, cavity, or swelling: a primary cavity of the vertebrate brain; **vesic'ula** a vesicle.—*adjs*. **vesic'ular**; **vesic'ulate**, **-d**.—*n*. **vesiculā'tion** formation of vesicles. [L. *vēsica*, bladder, blister.]

vesper *ves'pər*, *n*. evening: (usu. *pl*.) the last but one of the seven canonical hours: (usu. *pl*.) evensong, evening service generally: a vesper-bell.—**ves'per bell** the bell that summons to vespers. [L. *vesper*.]

vessel *ves'l*, *n*. a utensil for holding something: a craft or structure (usually bigger than a boat) for transport by water: a conducting tube for body-fluids in animals, for water in plants.—**the weaker vessel** a woman (1 Pet. iii. 7). [O.Fr. *vessel* (Fr. *vaisseau*)— L. *vāscellum*, dim. of *vās*, *vāsis*, a vessel.]

vest *vest*, *n*. a waistcoat (chiefly *U.S.*): an undershirt: an additional facing to the front of a bodice.—*v.t*. to clothe: to robe: to drape: to put vestments on: to invest: to settle, secure, or put in fixed right of possession (*law*): to endow (*law*).—*v.i*. to descend, devolve, or to take effect, as a right.—*adj*. **vest'ed** clad: robed: wearing vestments: not contingent or suspended, hence (*law*) already acquired.—*n*. **vest'ing** the act or fact of clothing, investing, securing legally, etc.: material for waistcoats.—**vested interest** a particular interest in the continuance of an existing system, institution, etc., for personal reasons, often financial: (in *pl*.) interests already established: (in *pl*.) the class of persons who have acquired rights or powers in any sphere of a country's activities; **vest'-pocket** a waistcoat-pocket.—*adj*. small enough to go into one (also *fig*.). [L. *vestis*.]

Vesta *ves'tə*, *n*. the Roman goddess of the hearth and household: (without *cap*.) a wax-stemmed match: a short match with wooden stem:—*pl*. **ves'tas**.—*adj*. **ves'tal** (often with *cap*.) pertaining or consecrated to Vesta: of or like the Vestal virgins: virgin: chaste.—*n*. (often with *cap*.) one of the Roman patrician virgins consecrated to Vesta: a woman dedicated to celibacy: a nun: a virgin: a woman of spotless chastity. [L.]

vestibule *ves'ti-būl*, *n*. an entrance-hall: a cavity serving as entrance to another, esp. that of the inner ear (*anat*.).—*v.t*. to furnish with a vestibule.—*adj*. **vestib'ular**.—*n*. **vestib'ulum** a vestibule. [L. *vestibulum*.]

vestige *ves'tij*, *n*. a footprint: a trace: a surviving trace of what has almost disappeared: a reduced and functionless structure, organ, etc., representing what was once useful and developed (*biol*.; also **vestig'ium**:— *pl*. **vestig'ia**).—*adj*. **vestig'ial**. [L. *vestīgium*, footprint.]

vestment *vest'mənt*, *n*. a garment: a ceremonial garment, esp. one worn in religious ceremonies: a covering. [L. *vestimentum*—*vestīre*, to clothe.]

vestry *ves'tri*, *n*. a room in which vestments are kept

and parochial meetings held: a small room attached to a church: a meeting for church affairs: a robing-room: a cloakroom: apparel.—*adj*. **ves'tral**.— **ves'try-clerk** an officer chosen by the vestry to keep the parish accounts and books; **ves'tryman** a member of a vestry; **ves'try-room** a vestry: meeting-place of a vestry. [Prob. through O.Fr.—L. *vestiārium*— *vestis*, a garment.]

vesture *ves'chər*, *n*. garb (*arch*.). [O.Fr.,—L.L *vestītūra*—*vestis*, garment.]

vet *vet*, *n* (*coll*.) a veterinary surgeon.—*v.t*. to treat, or examine, medically (animal; also, *facet*., person): to examine, (e.g. a writing) thoroughly and critically (and pass as sound or correct):—*pr.p*. **vett'ing**; *pa.t*. and *pa.p*. **vett'ed**.

vetch *vech*, *n*. the tare or other species of the genus *Vicia*: extended to some kindred plants.—*n*. **vetch'ling** any plant of the sweet-pea genus (Lathyrus).—**bitter vetch** various species of *Vicia* and Lathyrus; **milk vetch** Astragalus. [O.N.Fr. *veche* (Fr. *vesce*)—L. *vicia*.]

veteran *vet'ə-rən*, *n*. one who has seen long service: an old and experienced soldier: one old or long experienced in any activity.—*adj*. old, experienced: long exercised, esp. in military life.—**veteran car** an old motor-car, specif. one made before 1905. [L. *veterānus*—*vetus*, *veteris*, old.]

veterinary *vet'ə-rin-ər-i*, *adj*. concerned with diseases of animals.—*n*. one skilled in the diseases of domestic animals.—Also **veterinā'rian**, **veterinary surgeon**. [L. *veterinārius*—*veterinae*, cattle, beasts of burden.]

veto *vē'tō*, *n*. any authoritative prohibition: the power of rejecting or forbidding: the right to reject or forbid a proposed measure:—*pl*. **vetoes** (*vē'tōz*).—*v.t*. to reject by a veto: to withhold assent to: to forbid. [L. *vetō*, I forbid.]

vex *veks*, *v.t*. to harass: to distress: to annoy: to tease: to trouble, agitate, disturb: to discuss to excess.—*n*. **vexā'tion** a vexing: state or feeling of being vexed: a source of grief or annoyance.—*adj*. **vexā'tious** vexing: wantonly troublesome: (of a law action) brought on insufficient grounds, with the intention merely of annoying the defendant.—*adv*. **vexā'tiously**.—*n*. **vexātiousness**.—*n*. and *adj*. **vex'ing**.—**vexed question** a matter greatly debated. [Fr. *vexer*—L. *vexāre*, to shake, annoy.]

vexillum *vek-sil'əm*, *n*. the series of barbs on the sides of the shaft of a feather:—*pl*. **vexill'a**.—*ns*. **vexillol'ogist**; **vexillol'ogy** the study of flags. [L., a flag.]

vezir. See **vizier**.

via[1], **viâ** *vī'ə*, *vē'* (L. *vē'a*, *wē'*), *prep*. by way of. [L. *viā*, abl of *via*, way.]

via[2] *vī'ə*, *vē'ə*, *vē'ə*, *wē'*, (L.) *n*. a way, road.—**via dolorosa** (*dol-ə-rō'sə*, *do-lō-rō'sa*) the way to Calvary (lit. mournful way).

viable *vī'ə-bl*, *adj*. capable of living, surviving, germinating, or hatching: (of plan, project) of such a kind that it has a prospect of success.—*n*. **viabil'ity**. [Fr., —*vie*—L. *vīta*, life.]

viaduct *vī'ə-dukt*, *n*. a structure carrying a road or railway over a valley, etc. [After **aqueduct**—L. *via*, a way.]

vial *vī'əl*, *n*. same as **phial**: a spirit-level.

viand *vī'ənd*, *n*. an article of food: (usu. in *pl*.) food. [Fr. *viande*—L. *vīvenda*, food necessary for life— *vīvēre*, to live.]

viaticum *vī-at'ik-əm* (L. *vē-*, *wē-ä'ti-kŏŏm*), *n*. money, provisions, etc., for a journey: the eucharist given to persons in danger of death (*R.C. Church*). [L. *viāticum*—*via*, way.]

vibes *vībz*, (*coll*.) *n.pl*. feelings, sensations, etc., experienced or communicated (shortening of **vibrations**).—*n.sing*. or *pl*., also *n*. **vibe** (*vīb*), coll.

shortenings of **vibraphone**.—*n.* **vi'bist** (*coll.*).

vibex *vī'beks, n.* a streak due to extravasation of blood:—*pl.* **vibices** (*vī-, vī-bī'sēz*). [L. *vībīces*, weals.]

vibra-. Variant of **vibro-**.

vibrancy, vibrant. See **vibrate**.

vibraphone *vī'brə-fōn, n.* an instrument having metal bars under which are electrically-operated resonators, played by striking the bars with small hammers.—*n.* **vi'braphonist**. [L. *vibrāre*, to shake, Gr. *phōnē*, voice.]

vibrate *vī'brāt, -brāt', v.i.* to shake: to tremble: to oscillate: to swing: to change to and fro, esp. rapidly: to resound, ring: to tingle, thrill.—*v.t.* to cause to vibrate: to give off in vibrations.—*n.* **vibrancy** (*vī'brən-si*).—*adjs.* **vī'brant** vibrating: thrilling: resonant; **vi'bratile** (*-brə-tīl*, in U.S. *-til, -təl*) vibratory: having or capable of vibratory motion.—*ns.* **vibratility** (*-til'i-ti*); **vibrā'tion** a vibrating: state of being vibrated: tremulousness: quivering motion: a whole period or movement to and fro of anything vibrating: sometimes a half period or movement one way: (in *pl.*) feelings communicated from person to person (*coll.*): (in *pl.*) feelings aroused in one by a person, place, etc. (*coll.*).—*adjs.* **vibrā'tional; vibrā'tionless; vī'brative** (*-brə-tiv*) vibrating: consisting in vibrations: causing vibrations.—*n.* **vi'brātor** that which vibrates: a vibrating part in many appliances: a vibrating tool: a type of dildo that can be made to vibrate mechanically.—*adj.* **vibratory** (*vī'brə-tər-i*) of, of the nature of, causing, or capable of, vibration. [L. *vibrāre, -ātum*, to tremble.]

vibrato *vē-brä'tō,* or *vi-, n.* a throbbing effect, without perceptible change of pitch, in singing and in stringed and wind instrument playing, obtained by varying breath pressure or by the shaking movement of the finger on a string:—*pl.* **vibra'tos**. [It.]

vibrissa *vī-bris'ə, n.* a tactile bristle, as a cat's whisker: a vaneless rictal feather: a bristle, hair, as in the nostril:—*pl.* **vibriss'ae** (*-ē*). [L., a hair in the nostril.]

vibro- *vī-brō-, -bro-,* in composition, vibration.—*ns.* **vi'brograph, vibrom'eter** an instrument for recording vibrations. [L. *vibrāre, -ātum*, to tremble, to shake.]

vicar *vik'ər, n.* one who holds authority as the delegate or substitute of another: a deputy or substitute: a parson of a parish who receives only the smaller tithes or a salary (*Ch. of Eng.*): a bishop's deputy (*R.C.*).—*ns.* **vic'arage** the benefice or residence of a vicar; **vic'arate** vicariate.—*adjs.* **vicarial** (*vī-, vi-kā'ri-əl*) delegated: of a vicar or vicars; **vica'riate** delegated.—*n.* office, authority, time of office, or sphere of a vicar, in any sense.—*adj.* **vica'rious** filling the place of another: exercised, performed or suffered by one person or thing instead of another: (*loosely*) not experienced personally but imagined through the experience of others.—*adv.* **vica'riously**.—*ns.* **vica'riousness; vic'arship** (the time of) office of a vicar.—**vic'ar-apostol'ic** a titular bishop appointed to a country where there are no sees: one exercising authority in a vacant see or during the bishop's incapacity; **vicarious sacrifice** the suffering and death of Christ held by orthodox Christians to be accepted by God in lieu of the punishment to which guilty man is liable.—**Vicar of Christ** (*R.C.*) the pope, as representative of Christ on earth. [L. *vicārius*, substituted; see **vice-**.]

vice¹ (in U.S. **vise**) *vīs, n.* a tool for gripping an object that is being worked on. [Fr. *vis*, screw—L. *vītis*, a vine.]

vice² *vīs, n.* a blemish or fault: immorality: depravity: an immoral habit: a bad trick or habit as in a horse.—*adj.* **vicious** (*vish'əs*) addicted to vice or bad habits: immoral: depraved: bad: faulty: malignant, spiteful:

ill-tempered: foul, impure, morbid: impaired, nullified by a flaw.—*adv.* **vic'iously**.—*n.* **vic'iousness.**—**vice squad** a police squad whose task is to see that the laws dealing with gambling, prostitution, etc., are observed; **vicious circle** reasoning in a circle, seeking to prove a proposition by means of a conclusion drawn from it: a process in which an evil is aggravated by its own consequences. [Fr.,—L. *vitium*, a blemish; L.L. *viciōsus* for L. *vitiōsus*, faulty, vicious.]

vice³ *vī'si, vī'sē, vīs, prep.* in place of: in succession to.—**vice versa** (*vûr'sə*) the other way round. [L. *vice*, abl. (nom. not used), turn, place, alteration.]

vice- *vīs-,* in composition, in place of.—**vice'-ad'miral** a navy officer ranking next under an admiral; **vice's ad'miralty** the office or jurisdiction of a vice-admiral; **vice'-chair'man** a deputy chairman: a croupier; **vice's chair'manship; vice'-cham'berlain** the Lord Chamberlain's deputy and assistant, **vice'-chan'cellor** one acting for a chancellor: in certain British universities, the head of administration, the chancellor being titular head only; **vice'-chan'cellorship; vice'-con'sul** a consul's deputy: one who acts as consul in a less important district, **vice'-con'sulate; vice'-con'sulship; vicegerency** (*-jer'* or *-jēr'ən-si*)—*adj.* **vicegerent** (*-jer', -jēr';* L. *vicem gerēns, -entis,* wielding office) acting in place of another, having delegated authority.—*n.* one ruling or acting in place of a superior.—**vice'-gov'ernor** deputy governor; **vice's pres'idency; vice'-pres'ident** a president's deputy or assistant: an officer next below the president.—*adj.* **vice'-presiden'tial.**—**vice'-princ'ipal** assistant principal.—*adj.* **vice-re'gal** of a viceroy.—**vicere'gent** properly, a substitute for a regent: often blunderingly for vicegerent; **vicereine** (*vīs'ren', -rān'*) a viceroy's wife; **vice'roy** a governor acting in the name of the sovereign; **vice'roy'alty, vice'royship**. [**vice³**.]

vicenary *vis'i-nər-i, adj.* based on the number twenty. [L. *vīcēnārius—vīcēnī,* twenty each—*vīgintī,* twenty.]

vicennial *vī-sen'yəl, adj.* lasting, or coming at the end of, twenty years [L. *vicennium—vīciēs,* twenty times, *annus,* a year.]

vicesimal, etc. See **vigesimal**.

Vichyite *vē'shē-īt, vish'i-īt, n.* an adherent of the French Government (1940–42) ruling the unoccupied part of France from *Vichy,* and collaborating with the Germans.—Also *adj.*—*n.* **vichyssoise'** a cream soup usu. served chilled, with ingredients such as potatoes and leeks.—**Vichy (water)** mineral water from Vichy springs, containing sodium bicarbonate, etc., or a natural or artificial water resembling it.

vicinity *vi-sin'it-i, n.* neighbourhood: nearness. [L. *vīcīnus,* neighbour—*vīcus,* street, village, district.]

vicious. See under **vice²**.

vicissitude *vi-sis'i-tūd, n.* change: alternation: mutation: change of fortune—*adj.* **vicissitu'dinous.** [L. *vicissitūdō, -inis;* see **vice³**.]

victim *vik'tim, n.* a living being offered as a sacrifice: one subjected to death, suffering, or ill-treatment: a prey: a sufferer.—*n.* **victimisā'tion, -z-.**—*v.t.* **vic'timise, -ize** to make a victim of: to treat oppressively in revenge: to cheat.—*n.* **vic'timiser, -z-.** [L. *victima,* a beast for sacrifice.]

victor *vik'tər, n.* a winner in contest.—*adj.* **victo'rious** (*-tō', -to'*) having gained a victory: winning in contest: of, with, marking victory.—*adv.* **victo'riously**—*ns.* **victo'riousness; victory** (*vik'tər-i*) a contest gained: success against an opponent. [L. *victor, -ōris—vincĕre, victum,* to conquer.]

victoria *vik-tō'ri-ə, -tō', n.* (also with *cap.*) a large red plum (also **victoria plum**).—*adj.* **Victo'rian** of, contemporary with, typical of, the reign (1837–1901) of Queen Victoria: strict but somewhat conventional in morals, inclining to prudery and solemnity.—*n.* a contemporary of Queen Victoria: a person of Victorian morality or outlook.—*n.pl.* **Victoriana** (*vık-tō-ri-ā'nə*, *-tö-*, or *-ā'nə*; also without *cap.*) bric-à-brac and other characteristic possessions or creations of the Victorian age.—*n.* **Victo'rianism**.—**Victoria Cross** a bronze Maltese cross, a decoration for conspicuous bravery on the field, founded by Queen Victoria (1856).

victual *vit'l*, *n.* (commonly in *pl.*) food, esp. human food.—*v.t.* to supply or store with provision.—*v.i.* to lay in victuals:—*pr.p.* **victualling** (*vit'l-ing*); *pa.t.* and *pa.p.* **victualled** (*vit'ld*).—*ns.* **vict'uallage** provisions, **victualler** (*vit'l-ər*) a purveyor of provisions. [O.Fr. *vitaille*—L.L. *victuālia*—L. *victuālis*, relating to living—*vivĕre*, *victum*, to live.]

vicuña *vi-kōō'nyə*, *n.* a wild species of the llama genus: cloth of its wool, or an imitation. [Sp., from Quechua.]

vide *vī'dē*, *vē'*, *wē'dā*, (L.) see.—**vide infra** (*in'frə*, *ēn'frä*) see below; **vide supra** (*sū'prə*, *sōō'prä*) see above.

videlicet *vi-del'i-sıt*, *vi-*, *wi-dā'li-ket*, L. to wit, namely; usu. abbrev. **viz.**

video *vid'i-ō*, *n.* a video recorder:—*pl.* **vid'eos**.—*adj.* pertaining to the bandwidth and spectrum position of the signal arising from TV scanning, or to the signal, or to the resultant image, or to television: using, used for, relating to, etc., the system of video recording.—*v.t.* and *v.i.* to make a video recording (of):—*pr.p.* **vid'eoing**, *pa.p.* **vid'eoed**.—**vid'eotex** a system used to display pages of information on a television screen, as teletext or viewdata (q.v.).—**video camera** a camera which records its (moving) film on to videotape, **vid'eocassette'** a cassette containing videotape, **vid'eodisc** a disc on which television picture and sound can be recorded and played back; **video frequency** that in the range required for a video signal; **video game** an electronically-operated game played by means of a visual display unit; **video nasty** a video film which includes horrific or gruesome scenes of violence, sexual outrage, or other atrocities; **vid'eophone**, also **vid'eotel'ephone**, a telephone with accompanying means of transmitting a picture of each speaker; **video recorder** a machine for recording and playing back television broadcasts or films made on videotape, using videotape or videodiscs; **video (tape) recording** recording both television picture and sound on magnetic tape (**videotape**) so that the programme can be rebroadcast or replayed on a television set; **video tube** a television tube. [L. *vidēre*, to see]

vidimus *vī'dı-məs* (L. *vē'*, *wē'di-mōōs*), *n.* an attested copy: an inspection, as of accounts, etc. [L *vidimus*, we have seen—*vidēre*, to see.]

vie *vī*, *v.i.* to contend in rivalry:—*pr.p.* **vy'ing**; *pa.t.* and *pa.p.* **vied** (*vīd*). [Fr. *envier*—L. *invītāre*, to challenge, invite.]

Viennese *vē-e-nēz'*, *adj.* of Vienna, the capital of Austria.—*n. sing.* and *pl.* an inhabitant (*pl.* inhabitants) of Vienna.—**vienna** (or **Vienna**) **loaf** a long, round-ended loaf of white bread; **vienna steak** a meat rissole.

Vietnamese *vē-et-nəm-ēz'*, *n.* a native or inhabitant, or the language, of Vietnam:—*pl.* as *sing.*—Also *adj.*

vieux jeu *vyø zhø*, (Fr., lit. old game or joke), a subject that has lost all novelty.

view *vū*, *n.* an act, possibility or opportunity of looking: range or field of sight: whole extent seen: a prospect, wide or distant extent seen: that which is seen: inspection: appearance: aspect: the picture of a scene: general survey of a subject: mode of thinking of something: opinion: intention, purpose: expectation.—*v.t.* to see: to look at: to look at on television to observe: to consider: to examine intellectually.—

v.i. to watch television.—*adj.* **view'able** able to be seen: sufficiently interesting to be looked at or watched.—*ns.* **view'er** one who views: a television watcher: an apparatus used to project film for purposes of editing and cutting: device with magnifying lens, etc., for viewing transparencies; **view'iness** character of being viewy, **view'ing**.—**view'data** a communications system by which information can be received and requested via a telephone line and presented through a television or video display, **view'finder** a camera attachment or part for determining the field of view; **view'phone** another name for **videophone**; **view'point** point of view: standpoint. a selected position for admiring scenery.—**in view** in sight: in mind: as an aim or prospect, **in view of** in a position to see or to be seen by: having regard to, **on view** open to general inspection; **take a dim view of** to regard unfavourably; **with a view to** having in mind: with a design of. [Fr. *vue*—*vu*, pa.p. of *voir*—L. *vidēre*, to see.]

vigesimal *vi-jes'i-məl*, *adj.* based on the number twenty (more rarely **vicesimal** *vi-ses'i-məl*). [L. *vigēsimus* (*vicēsimus*), twentieth—*vigintī*, twenty.]

vigil *vij'il*, *n.* watching, esp. by night, esp. for religious exercises: the eve of a holy day: a religious service by night: a keeping awake, wakefulness.—*n.* **vig'ilance** watchfulness: wakefulness.—*adj.* **vig'ilant** watchful.—*ns.* **vigilante** (*-an'ti*; originally *U.S.* from Sp.) a member of an organisation to look after the interests, threatened in some way, of a group: a member of a vigilance committee, **vigilan'tism**.—*adv.* **vig'ilantly**.—**vigilance committee** (*U S.*) an unauthorised body which, in the absence or inefficiency of regular government, exercises powers of arrest, punishment, etc. [L. *vigilia*—*vigil*, awake, watchful; cf. *vigēre*, to be lively.]

vignette *vēn-yet'*, *n.* orig. a design of vine-leaves and tendrils: a small embellishment without a border, in what would have been a blank space, esp. on a title-page or as a headpiece or tailpiece: a photographic portrait shading off around the head: the illustration on a bank-note: a character sketch, a word-picture.—*v t.* to make a vignette of —*ns* vignett'er; vignett'ist. [Fr.,—*vigne*—L. *vinea*, a vine, a vineyard.]

vigour, *U.S* **vigor**, *vig'ər*, *n.* active strength: vital power: forcefulness: activity: energy.—*adj.* **vig'orous**.—*adv.* **vig'orously**.—*n.* **vig'orousness**. [A Fr *vigour* (Fr. *vigueur*), and L *vigor*, *-ōris*—*vigēre*, to be strong.]

vihara *vē-hä'rə*, *n* a Buddhist or Jain precinct, temple, or monastery. [Sans. *vihāra*.]

viking *vī'king*, *n.* (also with *cap.*) any of the Scandinavian adventurers who raided, traded with, and settled in, many parts of Europe between the eighth and eleventh centuries: any aggressive sea-raider, a pirate.—*n.* **vī'kingism**. [O.N. *vīkingr*, prob.—O.E. *wīcing*, pirate.]

vile *vīl*, *adj.* worthless: mean: paltry: base: detestable loathsome: foul: depraved: very bad.—*adv.* **vile'ly**.—*ns.* **vile'ness**; **vilifica'tion** (*vıl-*) act of vilifying: defamatory speech: abuse, **vilifier** (*vil'*).—*v.t.* vilify (*vıl'*) to make vile. to disparage: to defame.—*pr.p.* **vil'ifying**; *pa.t.* and *pa.p.* **vil'ified**. [O.Fr. *vil* and L *vilis*, worthless.]

villa *vil'ə*, *n.* orig., a country house or farmhouse with subsidiary buildings. a country seat, in Italy often a castle: a detached house of some size: a superior middle-class dwelling-house. [L. *villa*, a country house, partly through O.Fr *ville*, farm, village, etc. (Fr., town), and It. *villa*, country house.]

village *vil'ij*, *n.* a manor, a parish, or an outlying part of a parish: an assemblage of houses smaller than a town: the people of a village.—*adj.* of, dwelling in, a village.—*n.* vill'ager an inhabitant of a village. [Fr. *village*, L. *villāticus*.]

villain *vil'ən, n.* a villein (*orig.*): a violent, malevolent or unscrupulous evil-doer: playfully, a wretch: the wicked enemy of the hero or heroine in a story or play: a criminal (*slang*).—*adj.* low-born: base: villainous.—*ns.* vill'ainage, vill'anage villeinage; vill'ainess a she-villain.—*adj.* vill'ainous (or vill'anous) of the nature of, like, or suited to a villain: detestable, vile.—*adv.* vill'ainously (vill'anously).—*ns.* vill'ainy (vill'any) the act of a villain: extreme wickedness: an atrocious crime. [O.Fr. *villain*—L.L. *villānus*—L. *villa*, a country house.]

-ville *-vil,* (*slang*) in composition, a supposed world, milieu, etc., frequented by a specified type of person, characterised by a specified quality, etc., as in *squaresville, dullsville.* [The suffix *-ville* in names of towns, esp. in U.S.—Fr. *ville*, town.]

villeggiatura *vi-lej-ə-tōō'rə, n.* country retirement or holiday. [It.]

villein *vil'ən, -in,* (*hist.*) *n.* orig. app. a free villager: later (13th cent.) a serf, free in relation to all but his lord, and not absolutely a slave.—*n.* vill'e(i)nage a villein's tenure or status. [A.Fr.; cf. villain.]

villus *vil'əs, n.* a long soft hair: a hair-like process:—*pl.* vill'i (-*ī*).—*adjs.* vill'iform having the form of villi; vill'ose, vill'ous covered with or formed of villi: like the pile of velvet.—*n.* villos'ity. [L. *villus*, wool.]

vim *vim,* (*slang*) *n.* energy, vigour. [App. L. *vim*, accus. of *vis*, force.]

vimana *vi-män'ə, n.* the central shrine of an Indian temple with pyramidal roof: a temple gate. [Sans. *vimāna*, lit. a marking out.]

vin *vē,* (Fr.) *n.* wine.—vin blanc (*blä*) white wine; vin ordinaire (*ȯr-dēn-er*) inexpensive table wine for ordinary use; vin rosé rosé (*q.v.*).

vina *vē'nə, n.* an Indian stringed instrument with fretted finger-board over two gourds. [Sans. *vīṇā.*]

vinaigrette *vin-ā-gret', n.* a box or bottle for aromatic vinegar or smelling-salts: a mixture of oil, vinegar and seasoning used as a salad dressing. [Fr.,—*vinaigre*, vinegar.]

vincible *vin'si-bl, adj.* that may be overcome.—*n.* vincibil'ity. [L. *vincibilis*—*vincĕre, victum,* to conquer.]

vincristine *vin-kris'tēn, n.* an alkaloid substance derived from the tropical periwinkle, *Vinca rosea,* used in the treatment of certain types of blood cancer. [L. *vinca,* and *crista,* fold.]

vinculum *ving'kū-ləm, n.* a bond: a horizontal line placed above, equivalent to brackets (*math.*): a tendinous band (*anat.*):—*pl.* vinc'ula. [L.,—*vincīre*, to bind.]

vindicate *vin'di-kāt, v.t.* to justify: to clear from criticism, etc.: to defend with success: to make good a claim to: to lay claim to: to maintain.—*n.* vindicability (-*kə-bil'i-ti*).—*adj.* vin'dicable.—*n.* vindicā'tion act of vindicating: defence: justification: support.—*adj.* vin'dicative (or *vin-dik'ə-tiv*) vindicating: tending to vindicate.—*n.* vin'dicator one who vindicates.—*adv.* vin'dicatorily.—*adj.* vin'dicatory (-*ə-tər-i,* or *-ā-tər-i*) serving or tending to vindicate: punitive: retributive: avenging. [L. *vindicāre, -ātum.*]

vindictive *vin-dik'tiv, adj.* revengeful: pursuing revenge: punitive (as in *vindictive damages*): retributive (as in *vindictive justice*).—*adv.* vindic'tively.—*n.* vindic'tiveness. [L. *vindicta*, revenge; see vindicate.]

vine *vīn, n.* a woody climbing plant (*Vitis vinifera* or other of the genus) that produces grapes: a climbing or trailing stem or plant (*hort.*).—*n.* vi'ner a vine-grower; vinery (*vī'nə-ri*) a hot-house for rearing vines.—*adj.* vinicul'tural (*vīn-, vin-*).—*ns.* vin'icul-

ture cultivation of the vine for wine-making, and often also the making of the wine; vinicul'turist; vinifica'tion (*vin-*) the process of converting grape-juice, etc., into wine; vinol'ogist (*vīn-, vin-*); vinol'ogy scientific study of vines, esp. grapevine; vinos'ity vinous character: characteristic qualities of a particular wine: addiction to wine.—*adjs.* vi'nous pertaining to wine: like wine: wine-coloured: caused by or indicative of wine; vi'ny pertaining to, like, consisting of, or bearing vines: entwining.—*n.* vine'-dresser one who trims and cultivates vines; vine fruit the fruit of the vine in any form, i.e. as grape or raisin, etc.; vine'-stock the stock on which a vine of another kind is grafted; vineyard (*vin'yərd, -yārd*) a plantation of vines. [O.Fr. *vine, vigne*—L. *vīnea*, a vineyard, a vine—*vīnum*, wine.]

vinegar *vin'i-gər, n.* a condiment and pickling medium, a dilute impure acetic acid, made from beer, weak wine, etc.—*v.t.* to apply vinegar to.—*adjs.* vin'egarish sourish; vin'egary like or flavoured with vinegar: sour (also *fig.*). [Fr. *vinaigre*—*vin* (L. *vīnum*), wine, *aigre*, sour (L. *ācer*, keen, sharp, pungent).]

vingt-et-un *vē-tā-œ̃, n.* a card game, its object to have a total of pips in one's hand nearest to, but not exceeding, twenty-one. [Fr. *vingt-et-un*, twenty-one.]

viniculture. See vine.

vino *vē'nō,* (*slang*) *n.* wine.—*pl.* vi'nos. [It. and Sp.]

vinology, vinous, etc. See vine.

vintage *vint'ij, n.* the gathering of grapes and preparation for wine-making: a season's yield of grapes or wine: the time of gathering grapes: wine, esp. of a good year: the product of a particular period: a period of origin.—*adj.* pertaining to the grape vintage: of wine, of a specified year and of good quality: generally, e.g. of a play by an author or of a period, among the (best and) most characteristic: out of date and no longer admired.—vintage car an old-fashioned car (specif. built between 1919 and 1930); vintage year one in which a particular product (usu. wine) reaches an exceptionally high standard. [A.Fr. *vintage*, O.Fr. (Fr.) *vendange*—L. *vindēmia*—*vīnum*, wine, grapes, *dēmĕre*, to remove—*dē*, out of or away, *emĕre*, to take; modified by influence of vintner.]

vintner *vint'nər, n.* a wine-seller.—*n.* vint'ry a wine-store: a wine-shop. [O.Fr. *vinetier*—L.L. *vīnetārius* —L. *vīnum*, wine.]

viny. See vine.

vinyl *vīn'il, n.* an organic radical CH₂CH—.—vinyl resins, plastics thermoplastic resins, polymers or co-polymers of vinyl compounds, e.g. co-polymers of vinyl chloride CH₂CHCl, and vinyl acetate CH₃COOCH:CH₂.

viol *vī'əl, n.* any member of a class of instruments, forerunners of the violin class, represented now by the double-bass.—*ns.* viola (*vi-ō'lə*) a tenor fiddle, slightly bigger than the violin, tuned a fifth lower; violer (*vī'ə-lər*) a viol player: a fiddler; violin (*vī-ə-lin'*, or *vī'*) a musical instrument with four strings (E, A, D, G) played with a bow: a violinist; vi'olinist (or *-lin'*) a player on the violin; violist (*vī'əl-ist*) a player on the viol: (*vē-ō'list*) a player on the viola; violoncellist (*vē-, vī-ə-lən-chel'ist*) a cello-player; violoncello *o* a bass instrument of the violin class, commonly called cello:—*pl.* violoncell'os. [Partly old word *vielle*; partly Fr. *viole* and It. *viola,* dim. *violino,* augmentative *violone,* and its dim. *violoncello;* origin doubtful; cf. L.L. *vitula,* and fiddle.]

Viola *vī'ə-lə, n.* the violet and pansy genus of plants: (without *cap.*) any plant of this genus. [L. *viola.*]

violate *vī'ə-lāt, v.t.* to fail to observe duly: to abuse: to ravish: to profane.—*adj.* violated: defiled.—*adj.*

vi'olable that may be violated.—*adv.* **vi'olably.**—*n.* **viola'tion.**—*adj.* **vi'olative** causing, tending to, or involving violation.—*n.* **vi'olator.** [L. *violāre, -ātum—vīs*, strength.]

violent *vī'ə-lənt, adj.* intensely forcible: impetuous and unrestrained in action: overmasteringly vehement: due to violence: wrested: expressing violence.—*n.* **vi'olence** the state or quality of being violent: excessive, unrestrained, or unjustifiable force: outrage: profanation: injury: rape.—*adv.* **vi'olently.** [L. *violentus* or *violēns, -entis—vīs*.]

violer. See **viol.**

violet *vī'ə-lit, n.* any plant or flower of the genus Viola: extended to unrelated plants: a bluish purple.—*adj.* bluish purple.—**shrinking violet** (*facet.*) a shy, hesitant person. [Fr. *violette*—L. *viola*.]

violin, violist, violoncello, etc. See **viol.**

viper *vī'pər, n.* the adder: any member of its genus (**Vi'pera**) or family (**Viperidae** *vī-per'i-dē*): extended to some other snakes, as the pit-vipers, horned vipers: an ungrateful or treacherous, malignant person (*fig.*).—*adjs.* **vi'perish** venomous: spiteful: like a viper; **vi'perous** having the qualities of a viper: venomous: malignant.—*adv.* **vi'perously.—viper's bugloss** a stiff bristly plant (*Echium*) of dry places with intensely blue flowers, once thought a remedy or prophylactic for snake-bite [L. *vīpera—vīvus*, living, *parēre*, to bring forth.]

virago *vi-rä'gō, vi-rā'gō, n.* a heroic or manlike woman: an amazon: a scold: a termagant:—*pl.* **vira'goes, -gos.** [L. *virāgō, -inis—vir*, a man.]

viral. See **virus.**

virement *vē-rə-mä, vīr'mənt, n.* authorised transference of a surplus to balance a deficit under another head. [Fr.]

virescent *vir-es'ənt, vīr-, adj.* turning green: inclining to green: fresh: green: abnormally green.—*n.* **viresc'ence.** [L. *virēns, -entis*, pr.p. of *virēre*, to be green; *virēscēns*, pr.p. of *virēscĕre*, to become green.]

Vireo *vir'i-ō, n.* a genus of American singing birds, the greenlets, giving name to the family **Vireonidae** (*-on'i-dē*): (without *cap.*) a bird of this family:—*pl.* **vir'eos.** [L. *vireō, -ōnis*, perh. greenfinch.]

virga *vûr'gə, n.* (also *n.pl.*) trails of water, drops, or ice particles coming from a cloud but not reaching the ground as precipitation. [L., a twig, streak in the sky.]

virgin *vûr'jin, n.* a maiden: one (esp. a woman) who has had no sexual intercourse: a madonna, a figure of the Virgin: Virgo, a sign, and a constellation, of the zodiac.—*adj.* in a state of virginity: of a virgin: maidenly: pure: chaste: undefiled: in the original condition—unattained, untouched, unexploited, never scaled, felled, captured, wrought, used, etc.—*adj.* **vir'ginal** of or appropriate to a virgin or virginity: in a state of virginity: like a virgin.—*adv.* **vir'ginally.**—*ns.* **vir'ginhood, virgin'ity** state or fact of ,being a virgin.—*adj.* **vir'ginly** pure.—*adv.* **chastely.**—*n.* **Vir'go** (*-gō*, L. *vir'gō, wir'*) the Virgin, in the zodiac. —**virgin birth, generation** parthenogenesis: (**Virgin Birth**) (the doctrine of) the birth of Christ, His mother being a virgin.—**virgo intacta** (*in-tak'tə*, L. *-ta*) a woman or girl who has not had sexual intercourse.—**the (Blessed) Virgin** Mary the mother of Christ; **the Virgin Queen** Elizabeth I of England. [Partly through Fr.,—L. *virgō, -inis*.]

virginal[1] *vûr'jin-əl, n.* (often in *pl.*, also *pair of virginals*) an old keyboard instrument, a spinet, esp. a box-shaped spinet. [Perh. as played by young ladies; *see above*.]

virginal[2], **virginhood,** etc. See **virgin.**

Virginia *vər-jin'yə, n.* a tobacco grown and manufactured in *Virginia*.—*adj.* **Virgin'ian.**—*n.* a native or

citizen of Virginia.—**Virginia creeper** an American climbing-plant near akin to the vine, bright red in autumn. [After Elizabeth, the *virgin* queen.]

virginity, Virgo, etc. See **virgin.**

virgule *vûr'gūl, n.* a slanting line, an old form of comma.—*adj.* **vir'gulate** shaped like a rod. [Fr.,— L. *virgula*, dim. of *virga*, a twig, rod.]

viricide. See **virus.**

virid *vir'id, adj.* green.—*n.* **viridesc'ence.**—*adj.* **viridesc'ent** greenish. [L. *viridis*, green—*virēre*, to be green.]

virile *vir'īl,* sometimes *vīr'*; also *-il, adj.* having qualities of a mature male human being: robustly masculine: manly: of a man, sexually potent.—*n.* **viril'ity** the state or quality of being a man: the power of a mature male: the power of procreation: manhood: masculinity: vigour, energy. [L. *virīlis—vir*, a man.]

virology, virose, etc. See under **virus.**

virtu *vûr-tōō', n.* a love of the fine arts: taste for curiosities: objects of art or antiquity.—*adj.* **virtuose** (*-tū-ōs'*), **virtuo'sic** exhibiting the qualities of a virtuoso.—*ns.* **virtuosity** (*-os'*) the character of a virtuoso: exceptional technical skill in music or other fine art: interest in or knowledge of articles of virtu; **virtuoso** (*vir-tōō-ō'sō, vûr-tū-ō'sō, -zō*) one skilled or interested in works of art, antiquities, curiosities, and the like: a musician (or other artist) of the highest technical skill:—*pl.* **virtuō'sos, virtuō'si** (*-sē*):—*fem.* **virtuō'sa,** *pl.* **virtuō'se** (*-sä*); **virtuō'soship.** [It. *virtù* —L. *virtūs, -ūtis; see* **virtue.**]

virtual, virtue. See **virtu.**

virtue *vûr'tū, n.* excellence: worth: moral excellence: the practice of duty: a good quality, esp. moral: sexual purity: (*loosely*) virginity: inherent power: efficacy: one of the orders of the celestial hierarchy.— *adj.* **vir'tual** in effect, though not in fact: not such in fact but capable of being considered as such for some purposes.—*n.* **virtual'ity** essential nature: potentiality.—*adv.* **vir'tually** in effect, though not in fact: (*loosely*) almost, nearly.—*adjs.* **vir'tueless;** **vir'tuous** having virtue: morally good: blameless: righteous: practising duty: according to the moral law: chaste.—*adv.* **vir'tuously.—*n.* **vir'tuousness.** by, in, virtue of** through the power, force, or efficacy of: because of: on account of; **make a virtue of necessity** to do as if from sense of duty (or with a sense of duty called in for the occasion) something one must needs do. [O.Fr. *vertu* and L. *virtus*, bravery, moral excellence—*vir*, a man.]

virtuose, -osic, etc. See **virtu.**

virulent *vir'ū-lənt,* or *-ōō-, adj.* highly poisonous or malignant: venomous: acrimonious.—*ns.* **vir'ulence, vir'ulency.**—*adv.* **vir'ulently.** [L. *virulentus— virus, see* **virus.**]

virus *vī'rəs, n.* venom: contagious or poisonous matter (as of ulcers, etc.): the transmitted cause of infection: a pathogenic agent, a combination of chemicals, but capable of increasing rapidly inside a living cell: any corrupting influence.—*adj.* **vi'ral** pertaining to or caused by a virus.—*ns.* **vi'ricide** (or *vir'*) a substance that destroys or eliminates a virus.—*adj.* **virolog'ical.** —*ns.* **virol'ogy** the study of virus, viruses and virus diseases; **virol'ogist.**—*n.* **viro'sis** a disease caused by a virus.—**virus disease** a disease caused by a virus. [L. *vīrus*, venom.]

vis *vis, vēs, wēs,* (L.) *n.* force, power.—**vis major** (*mä'jər, ma'yor*) superior force.

visa *vē'zə, n.* an authenticating endorsement on a passport, etc.—*v.t.* to put a visa on.—*pa.t.* and *pa.p.* **vi'saed.** [L. *visa,* pa.p. fem. of *vidēre,* to see.]

visage *viz'ij, n.* the face.—*adj.* **vis'aged.**—*n.* **visagiste** (*vē-zazh-ēst*) an expert in facial make-up. [Fr *visage*—L. *vīsus,* look.]

vis-à-vis *vē-za-vē, adv.* face-to-face —*prep.* face-to-face with: in relation to, with regard to.—*n.* an opposite number. [Fr. *vis*, face (—L. *vīsus*, look), *à*, to.]

viscacha *vis-kaʹcha, n.* a S. American burrowing rodent of heavy build —Also **vizcaʹcha, biscaʹcha, bizcaʹ-cha.** [Sp.,—Quechua *huiscacha*.]

viscera, visceral, viscerate, visceri-, viscero-, etc. See **viscus.**

viscid *visʹid, adj.* semi-fluid, sticky, glutinous, viscous: of a surface, clammy and covered with a sticky secretion (*bot.*).—*n.* **viscidʹity.** [L.L. *viscidus*—L. *viscum*, see **viscous.**]

visco-, visco(si)meter, etc. See **viscous.**

viscose *visʹkōs, n.* the sodium salt of cellulose xanthate, used in the manufacture of **viscose rayon.** [See **viscous.**]

viscount *vīʹkownt, n.* an officer who acted as administrative deputy to an earl, a sheriff (*hist*). (esp. with *cap.*) a similar official in Jersey: a title of nobility next below an earl (first granted in 1440): the son or young brother of a count:—*fem.* **viscountess** (*vīʹkownt-es*) the wife of a viscount: a woman holding a viscounty in her own right.—*ns.* **viʹscountcy, viʹscountship** a viscounty; **viʹscounty** the jurisdiction of, or territory under, a viscount (*hist.*): the rank or dignity of a viscount. [O.Fr. *visconte* (Fr. *vicomte*)—vis- (L. *vice*, in place of), *conte*, count, after L.L *vicecomes*—L *comes*, a companion.]

viscous *visʹkəs, adj.* resistant, or highly resistant, to flow owing to forces acting between the molecules: tenacious: sticky: viscid.—*n.* **visʹcousness,** —**visʹcō-** in composition, viscous, viscosity.—*n.* **viscomʹeter** an instrument for measuring viscosity.—*adjs.* **viscometʹric, -al.**—*n.* **viscomʹetry.**—Also **viscosimʹeter, viscosimetʹric, -al, viscosimʹetry.**—*n.* **viscosʹity.**—**viscous flow** a type of fluid flow in which there is a continuous steady motion of the particles, the motion at a fixed point always remaining constant; **viscous water** water thickened by addition of chemicals, used in fighting forest fires. [L.L. *viscōsus*, sticky—L *viscum*, bird-lime, mistletoe.]

viscus *visʹkəs,* (*med., zool.*) *n.* any one of the organs situated within the chest and the abdomen—heart, lungs, liver, etc.:—*pl.* **viscera** (*visʹər-ə*; in common use, esp. the abdominal organs).—*adj.* **visʹceral.**—*v.t.* **visʹcerate** to disembowel.—**visʹcerō-** in composition, of or pertaining to the viscera or to a viscus.—Also **visʹceri-.** [L. *viscus*, pl. *viscera.*]

vise. U.S. spelling of **vice¹.**

visible *vizʹi-bl, adj.* that may be seen: in sight: obvious: (of supplies of a commodity) actually in store, known to be available: relating to goods rather than services (*econ.*): ready or willing to receive a visitor or visitors. —*n.* a visible thing (often in *pl.*).—*ns.* **visibilʹity** the state or quality of being visible, or perceivable by the eye: the clearness of the atmosphere: clarity and range of vision in the atmospheric conditions, seeing: a visible thing (usu. in *pl.*); **visʹibleness.**—*adv.* **visʹibly.**—**visible means** means or resources which are apparent to or ascertainable by others; **visible radiation** electromagnetic radiation which can be detected by the eye, light. [Through O.Fr. or direct from L. *visibilis*—*vidēre*; see **vision.**]

Visigoth *vizʹi-goth, n.* one of the Western Goths, as distinguished from the Ostrogoths or Eastern Goths; they formed settlements in the south of France and in Spain, and their kingdom in the latter lasted into the 8th century.—*adj.* **Visigothʹic.** [L.L. *Visigothī*—Gmc. word meaning perh. noble Goths, perh. west Goths.]

vision *vizhʹən, n.* the act of seeing: the faculty of sight: anything seen: television, esp. as opposed to sound radio: a look, glance: a vivid concept or mental pic-ture: hence, a person or scene of great beauty (sometimes ironically): a pleasing imaginative plan for, or anticipation of, future events: an apparition: a revelation, esp. divine, in sleep or a trance (sometimes without article): the act or power of perceiving imaginative mental images: imaginative perception foresight: mystical awareness of the supernatural.—*v.t.* to see as a vision, to imagine: to present, or to call up, as in a vision.—*adj.* **visʹional** of, pertaining to, a vision, derived from a vision: visionary, not real: pertaining to sight —*adv.* **visʹionally.**—*n.* **visʹionariness.** —*adj.* **visʹionary** capable of seeing visions: apt to see visions: given to reverie or fantasy: out of touch with reality, unpractical: of the nature of, or seen in, a vision, visional: fanciful, not real: impracticable: characterised by visions or fantasy: pertaining to physical or mental vision —*n.* one who sees visions one who forms impracticable schemes.—*adj.* **visʹioned** inspired so as to see visions: seen in a vision: produced by, or associated with, a vision: **visʹionless** destitute of vision —**vision mixer** one who blends or combines different camera shots in television or films. [Fr.,—L. *visiō, visiōnis*—*vidēre, vīsum,* to see.]

visit *vizʹit, v.t.* (of God or a human being) to come to, or to go to see, in order to succour: to go to with intention of injuring: to go to see professionally: to pay a call upon, or to be in the habit of doing so: to go to stay with: to make a stay in, as migratory birds: to go to for sight-seeing, pleasure, or religious purposes: to examine, inspect, esp officially. to punish (a person) (with *with*; *arch.*): to inflict (punishment, etc.) (with *on*): (of an idea) to take temporary hold on the mind of: to afflict, trouble, as with disease (*arch.*).—*v.i.* to be in the habit of seeing or meeting each other at home: to make a visit or visits.—*n.* an act of visiting: a short stay: a sight-seeing excursion: an official or a professional call.—*adjs.* **visʹitable** subject to official visitation: attractive to visitors; **visʹitant** paying visits, visiting.—*n.* one who visits: one who is a guest in the house of another: a supernatural visitor: a migratory bird.—*n.* **visitāʹtion** the act of visiting: a long and wearisome visit: a formal visit by a superior, esp. ecclesiastical: an examination by authority: a visit of God, or of a good (or evil) supernatural being: a dispensation of divine favour or displeasure: a sore affliction: the operation of a destructive power, or an instance of it: an influence acting on the mind: an unusual and extensive irruption of a species of animals into a region.—*adjs.* **visitāʹtional, visʹitative.** —*n.* **visʹitator** an official visitor.—*adj.* **visitatōʹrial.** —*ns.* **visitee'** the person to whom a visit is paid; **visʹiting** the act, or an instance, of paying a visit: a visitation, in the senses of divine dispensation, heavy affliction, or influence operating on the mind.—*adj.* that visits: often opp. to *resident*: pertaining to visiting.—*n.* **visʹitor** one who visits, calls on, or makes a stay with a person: a person authorised to visit for purposes of inspection or supervision:—*fem.* **visʹitress.**—*adj.* **visitōʹrial.**—**visʹiting-card** a small card bearing the name and address, or title, left in paying visits, and sometimes sent as an act of courtesy or in token of sympathy; **visitors' book** a book in which visitors write their names and sometimes comments.—**visit with** (*U.S.*) to visit: to be a guest with. [Fr. *visiter*—L. *visitāre*, freq. of *visēre*, to go to see, visit—*vidēre*, to see.]

visor *vizʹər, n.* a part of a helmet covering the face, or the upper part of the face, movable, and perforated to allow of seeing and breathing: a mask: a disguise, feigning appearance: a hood placed over a signal light: the peak of a cap: a movable flap on a motor-car windscreen, used as a shade against the sun.—Also

viz'or.—*v.t.* to disguise, or cover with, a visor.—Also **viz'or.**—*adj.* **vis'ored, viz'ored** having a visor: wearing a visor: masked. [A.Fr. *viser* (Fr. *visière*)—*vis*, countenance.]

vista *vis'ta, n.* a view or prospect, esp. through, or as through, an avenue: an avenue or other long narrow opening or passage: the trees, etc., that form the avenue: a mental view or vision extending far into the past or future, or into any subject engaging the thoughts. [It. *vista*, sight, view—L *vidēre, vīsum*, to see.]

visual *vizh'ū-əl, viz'ū-əl, adj.* of, pertaining to, sight: concerned with seeing, or (*fig.*) with mental vision: attained by, or received through, sight: of the nature of, or conveying, a mental vision: visible, having visibility: optic, as in **visual axis** (see **optic axis** under **optic**).—*n.* a visible: a rough sketch of the layout of an advertisement: (often in *pl.*) a drawing, piece of film, etc., as distinct from the words or sound accompanying it.—*n.* **visualisā'tion**, **-z-**.—*v.t.* **vis'ualise**, **-ize** to make visible, externalise to the eye: to call up a clear visual image of.—*v.t.* to call up a clear visual image: to become visible (*med.*).—*ns.* **vis'ualiser**, **-z-**; **vis'ualist** a visualiser.—*adv.* **vis'ually**.—**visual aid** a picture, photograph, film, diagram, etc., used as an aid to teaching; **visual arts** painting, sculpture, films, etc. as opposed to literature, music, etc.—**visual display unit** (*comput.*; *abbrev* **VDU**) a cathode ray tube which displays data, entered by keyboard or light pen, from a computer's memory. [L.L. *visuālis*—*vīsus*, sight.]

visuo- in composition, sight. [L. *vīsus*.]

vital *vī'tl, adj.* being a manifestation of organic life: supporting, or necessary to, life: life-giving, invigorating: characteristic of life, or of living things: animate, living: full of life: lively, energetic: pertaining to life, birth, and death: due to a living agency: fatal to life: essential, or (loosely) highly important.—*n.* **vitalisā'tion**, **-z-**.—*v.t.* **vi'talise**, **-ize** to give life to: to stimulate activity in: to give vigour to: to make lifelike.—*n.* **vi'taliser**, **-z-**.—*adj.* **vi'talising**, **-z-**.—*ns.* **vi'talism** the doctrine that there is a vital principle (q.v.); **vi'talist** one who holds this doctrine.—*adj.* **vitalis'tic**.—*n.* **vitality** (*-tal'*) the state or quality of being vital: the principle of life, power of living: the state of being alive: the quality of being fully or intensely alive: the capacity to endure and flourish: animation, liveliness: a living or vital thing or quality:—*pl.* **vital'ities**.—*adv.* **vi'tally**.—*n.pl.* **vi'tals** (rarely in *sing.*) the interior organs essential for life: the part of any whole necessary for its existence.—**vital force** the force on which the phenomena of life in animals and plants depend—distinct from chemical and mechanical forces operating in them; **vital functions** the bodily functions that are essential to life, as the circulation of the blood; **vital principle** that principle—the *anima mundi*—which, according to the doctrine of vitalism, gives life to all nature: a principle that directs all the actions and functions of living bodies; **vital spark**, **flame** the principle of life in man: hence, life or a trace of life; **vital statistics** statistics dealing with the facts of population—births, deaths, etc.: a woman's bust, waist and hip measurements (*facet.*). [L. *vitālis*—*vīta*, life.]

vitamin *vit'ə-min, vīt', n.* any of numerous organic substances, 'accessory food factors', present in minute quantities in nutritive foods and essential for the health of the animal organism.—*v.t.* **vi'taminise**, **-ize** to add vitamins to (a food). [Coined in 1906 from L. *vīta*, life, and (inappropriately) **amine**.]

vite *vēt*, (*mus.*) *adv.* quickly. [Fr.]

vitellus *vi-, vī-tel'əs, n.* the yolk of an egg:—*pl.* **vitelli'i**.

—*adj.* **vit'ellary** pertaining to the vitellus: yellow like the yolk of an egg.—*n.* **vitell'icle** a yolk-sac.—*adj.* **vitelligenous** (*-ij'*) producing yolk.—*ns.* **vitell'in** a phosphoprotein present in yolks of eggs; **vitell'ine** a vitellus—*adj.* vitellary. [L., a yolk; a transferred use of *vitellus*—*vitulus*, a calf.]

vitiate *vish'i-āt, v.t.* to render faulty or defective: to spoil: to make impure: to deprave, corrupt, pervert, debase: to make ineffectual or invalid or inconclusive.—*adj.* **vi'tiable**.—*ns.* **vitiā'tion**; **vi'tiator**; **vitios'ity** the state or quality of being vicious, or (*Scots law*) faulty. [L *vitiāre, -ātum*—*vitium*; see **vice**[2].]

viticulture, etc. See **Vitis**.

vitiligo *vit-i-lī'gō, -ə-lē'gō, n.* a skin abnormality in which irregular patches of the skin lose colour and turn white. [L. *vitilīgo*, a skin eruption.]

vitiosity. See **vitiate**.

Vitis *vī'tis, n* the grapevine genus of woody climbing plants.—*ns* **vit'iculture** cultivation of the vine; **viticul'turist.** [L. *vītis*, a vine—*viēre*, to twist.]

vitrage *vē-trazh, vit'rij, n.* (used also adjectivally) a kind of thin curtain for windows or glazed doors. [Fr., glass window.]

vitrail *vit'rāl, vē-tra'ē, n* stained glass:—*pl.* **vitraux** (*vē-trō', vit'*).—*adj.* **vitrailled** (*vit'rāld*).—*n.* **vit'raillist** a maker of glass, esp. stained glass. [Fr.]

vitreous *vit'ri-əs, adj.* glassy: pertaining to, consisting of, or like glass: glass green in colour: resembling glass in absence of crystalline structure, in lustre, etc. (*geol.*).—*ns.* **vitreos'ity, vit'reousness; vitresc'ence.** —*adjs.* **vitresc'ent** tending to become glass, capable of being turned into glass; **vitresc'ible**.—*ns.* **vitrescibil'ity; vit'reum** the vitreous humour of the eye.—*adj* **vit'ric**—*ns* **vitrifac'tion, vitrifica'tion** the act, process, or operation of vitrifying, or converting into glass: the state of being vitrified: a vitrified substance; **vitrifac'ture** the manufacture of glass.—*adjs.* **vit'rifiable; vit'rified; vit'riform** having the form or appearance of glass —*v.t.* and *v.i.* **vit'rify** to make into, or to become, glass or a glassy substance.—*n.* **vit'rine** (*-rēn, -rin*) a glass display case used to protect delicate articles, exhibit specimens, etc.—**vitreous humour** the jelly-like substance filling the posterior chamber of the eye of a vertebrate, between the lens and the retina. [L. *vitrum*, glass.]

vitriol *vit'ri-əl, n* oil of vitriol (q v): a hydrous sulphate of a metal, as *blue, green,* and *white vitriol,* respectively that of copper (cupric), iron (ferrous), and zinc: rancorous, caustic criticism, etc. (*fig.*).—*v.t.* **vit'riolate** to convert into, or to treat with, vitriol.—*n.* **vitriolā'tion.**—*adj.* **vitriolic** (*-ol'*) pertaining to, or having the qualities of, vitriol: biting, scathing, expressing intense ill-will.—*n.* **vitriolisā'tion, -z-.**—*v.t.* **vit'riolise, -ize** to vitriolate: to injure with vitriol.—**elixir of vitriol** aromatic sulphuric acid (i.e. sulphuric acid mixed with certain other substances for use in medicine); **oil of vitriol** concentrated sulphuric acid—because formerly prepared from green vitriol. [Fr.,—L.L. *vitriolum*—L. *vitreus,* of glass.]

vitro- *vit'rō-,* in composition, glass. [L. *vitrum,* glass.]

vitro-di-trina *vit'rō-di-trē'nä, n.* a Venetian white glass in which fine threads of cane form a lace-like pattern. [It., glass of lace.]

vitta *vit'ə, n.* a fillet or band for the head: a strap or sash: a stripe of colour (*bot.* and *zool.*): a thin, elongated cavity containing oil, found in the pericarps of some fruits (*bot.*):—*pl.* **vitt'ae** (*-ē*).—*adj.* **vitt'ate** having vittae: striped lengthwise. [L.]

vittle(s) *vit'l(z).* A variant (esp. *dial.*) form of **victual(s).**

vitular *vit'ū-lər, adj.* pertaining to a calf or to calving.

—*adj.* **vituline** (*vit'ū-līn*) pertaining to a calf or to veal. [L. *vitulus*, a calf.]

vituperate *vi-tū'po-rāt*, or *vī-*, *v.t.* to assail with abusive reproaches, revile.—*v.t.* to use abusive language.—*n.* **vitūpera'tion** the act of vituperating: censure: railing, abuse.—*adj.* **vitū'perative** (*-rat-* or *-rāt-*) containing vituperation: uttering, or prone to utter, abuse.— *adv.* **vitū'peratively.**—*n.* **vitū'perātor.**—*adj.* **vitū'peratory** vituperative. [L. *vituperāre*, *-ātum*—*vitium*, a fault, *parāre*, to set in order, prepare.]

Vitus.—St Vitus's dance. See chorea.

viva[1] *vē'va*, (It.; Sp.) *interj.* long live.

viva[2]. See viva voce.

vivace *vē-vä'che*, (*mus.*) *adj.* lively:—*superl.* **vivacis'simo.** [It.]

vivacious *vi-vā'shos*, or *vī-*, *adj.* lively, full of vitality: sprightly, sportive.—*adv.* **viva'ciously.**—*ns.* **vivā'-ciousness, vivac'ity** the state of being vivacious: vigour: animation: liveliness or sprightliness of temper or behaviour. [L. *vīvāx*, *vīvācis*—*vīvēre*, to live.]

vivamente. See vivo.

vivarium *vī-vā'ri-əm*, *n.* an artificial enclosure for keeping or raising living animals, as a park, a fish-pond: a glass-sided box, etc.:—*pl.* **vivā'ria, -iums.**— Also **vi'vary.** [L. *vīvārium*—*vīvus*, alive—*vīvēre*, to live.]

vivat *vī'vat*, *vē'vat*, *wē'wat*, (L.) *interj.* long live.

viva voce *vī'və vō'sē*, *vē'va*, *wē'wä vō'*, *wō'ke*, *adv. phrase* by the living voice: by oral testimony.—*n.* (usu. **viva alone**) an oral examination.—*v.t.* (usu. **viva**) to examine orally. [L.]

vive *vēv*, (Fr.) *interj.* long live.

vives *vīvz*, *n.sing.* a disease of horses, swelling of the submaxillary glands. [O.Fr. *avives*, *vives*—Sp. *avivas*—Ar. *addhība*—*al*, the, *dhība*, she-wolf.]

vivi- *vi'vi-*, in composition, alive, living.—*adj.* **viviparous** (*vī-vip'ə-rəs*, or *vi-*; L. *parēre*, to produce) producing living young that have reached an advanced stage of development—opp. to *oviparous*: germinating from a seed still on the parent plant (*bot.*): producing bulbils or young plants in the flower clusters, etc. (*bot.*).—*ns.* **vivip'arism** viviparous reproduction; **viviparity** (*viv-i-par'i-ti*), **vivip'arousness** the quality of being viviparous.—*adv.* **vivip'arously.** —*ns.* **vivip'ary** viviparity in plants; **vivisection** (*-sek'shən*; L. *sectiō*—*secāre*, to cut) the act or practice, or an instance, of making surgical operations on living animals for the purposes of physiological research or demonstration: merciless and minute examination or criticism (*fig.*).—*v.t.* **vivisect'** to practise vivisection on.—Also *v.i.*—*adj.* **vivisec'tional.**— *n.* **vivisec'tionist** one who practises or defends vivisection.—*adj.* **vivisec'tive** practising vivisection.—*n.* **vivisec'tor** one who practises vivisection. [L. *vīvus.*]

vivid *viv'id*, *adj.* full of life, vigorous: lively, intense: very bright: presenting a clear and striking picture: forming brilliant mental images.—*adv.* **viv'idly.**—*ns.* **viv'idness, vivid'ity.**—*adj.* **vivif'ic** vivifying.—*ns.* **vivifica'tion; viv'ifier.**—*v.t.* **viv'ify** to endue with life: to make vivid: to assimilate, convert into living tissue. [L. *vīvidus*—*vīvēre*, to live.]

viviparous, vivisection, etc. See vivi-.

vivo *vē'vō*, (*mus.*) *adj.* lively.—*adv.* **vivamente** (*vē-va-men'tā*) in a lively manner. [It.]

vixen *vik'sn*, *n.* a she-fox: an ill-tempered woman.— *adjs.* **vix'en, vix'enish, vix'enly** ill-tempered, snarling. [South. dial. form of *fixen*—O.E. *fyxen*, fem. of *fox*.]

viz. See videlicet.

vizcacha. See viscacha.

vizier, vizir *vi-zēr'*, *viz'yər*, *viz'i-ər*, *n.* a minister or councillor of state in various Muslim states.—Also **visier', vezir', wizier'.**—*ns.* **vizier'ate, vizir'ate,**

vizier'ship, vizir'ship the office of a vizier.—*adj.* **vizier'ial, vizir'ial.**—**Grand Vizier** in pre-Republican Turkey, the prime minister, and at one time also commander of the army. [Ar. *wazīr*, a porter—*wazara*, to bear a burden.]

vizor. Same as visor.

vizsla *viz'lə*, *n.* a Hungarian breed of hunting dog with smooth red or rust-coloured coat. [*Vizsla*, a town in Hungary.]

Vlach *vlak*, *n.* one of a non-Slav people of south-eastern Europe, found chiefly in Rumania, a Wala-chian. [O.Slav. *Vlachŭ*—O.H.G. *walh*, a foreigner, esp. a Slav or a Latin.]

vocable *vō'kə-bl*, *n.* that which is sounded with the voice—a word, or a single sound of a word.—*adj.* capable of being uttered.—*adj.* **vocabular** (*vō-*, *və-kab'*) of or concerning words.—*n.* **vocab'ulary** a list of words explained in alphabetical order: a dictionary: any list of words: the words of a language: the words known to and used by, e.g. a particular person: the words used in a (particular) science or art: the signs or symbols used in any non-verbal type of communication, e.g. in computer technology. a collection of forms used in an art or by a particular practitioner of an art.—*adj.* **vō'cal** having a voice: uttered by the voice: oral: sung, or for singing—opp. to *instrumental*: giving forth sound: resounding: talkative: eloquent: concerned in the production of speech: of or pertaining to a vowel: having a vowel function: voiced.—*n.* (often in *pl.*) singing, or that which is sung, esp. in a piece of popular music.—*adj.* **vocal'ic** containing (esp. many) vowels: of, pertaining to, or of the nature of, a vowel or vowels.—*n.* **vocalisā'-tion, -z-.**—*v.t.* **vō'calise, -ize** to form into voice, to articulate: to sing: to give expression to: to make vocal, endow with power of expression: to convert into a vowel: to utter with voice (*phon.*).—*v.i* to sing: to sing on a vowel or vowels.—*ns.* **vō'caliser, -z-; vō'calism** exercise of the vocal organs: the art of using the voice in singing: a vocal sound: system of vowels; **vō'calist** a singer—esp. opp. to *instrumentalist*; **vōcal'ity, vō'calness.**—*adv.* **vō'cally.**—**vocal c(h)ords** in air-breathing vertebrates, folds of the lining membrane of the larynx, by the vibration of the edges of which, under the influence of the breath, the voice is produced; **vocal music** music produced by the human voice alone, as opp. to *instrumental music*; **vocal score** a musical score showing the singing parts in full. [L. *vocābulum* and *vōcālis*—*vōx, vōcis*, voice.]

vocal, etc. See under vocable.

vocation *vō-kā'shən*, *n.* a calling, summons (*rare*): a calling by God to his service in special work or in a special position, or to a state of salvation: a fitness for God's or other specified work: a way of living or sphere of activity to which one has been called by God, or for which one has a special fitness: one's occupation, business, or profession.—*adj.* **vocā'-tional** pertaining to, concerned with, or in preparation for, a trade or occupation.—*n.* **vocā'tionalism** the giving of an important place in education to vocational training.—*adv.* **vocā'tionally.**—*adj.* **vocative** (*vok'ə-tiv*) pertaining to the act of calling: applied to the grammatical case used in direct personal address. —*n.* the case of a word when a person or thing is addressed: a word in that case. [L. *vocātiō, -ōnis*, and *vocātīvus*—*vocāre*, to call.]

voces. See vox.

vociferate *vō-sif'ə-rāt*, *v.i.* to cry with a loud voice, to bawl.—*v.t.* to utter in a loud voice.—*n.* **vocifera'tion** the act of vociferating: a violent or loud outcry.—*adj.* **vocif'erous** making a loud outcry: noisy.—*adv.* **vocif'-erously.**—*n.* **vocif'erousness.** [L.,—*vōx, vōcis*, voice, *ferre*, to carry.]

vodka *vod'kə, n.* a Russian spirit, properly distilled from rye, but sometimes from potatoes, etc. [Russ., dim. of *voda*, water.]

vogue *vōg, n.* popularity: a place in popular favour, or the period of it: the mode or fashion at any particular time.—*adj.* in vogue, fashionable.—*adjs.* **vog'uey**, **vog'uish**.—**vogue word** a word much used at a particular time. [Fr. *vogue* (orig. the course of a rowing vessel)—*voguer*, to row—It. *vogare*.]

voice *vois, n.* sound produced by the vocal organs of living beings, esp. of human beings in speech or song: sound given out by anything: the faculty or power of speech or song: the ability to sing, esp. well: a mode of utterance: the quality and range of musical sounds produced by a singer: a singer: a part for a singer, or one of the parts in an instrumental composition: utterance, expression: one who speaks: sound uttered with resonance of the vocal cords *(phon.)*: a mode of inflecting verbs to indicate whether that represented by the subject acts or is acted upon, or acts so as to affect itself *(gram.*; see **active, passive**).—*v.t.* to give utterance or expression to: to regulate the tone of *(mus.)*: to write the voice parts of: to utter with vibration of the vocal cords *(phon.)*.—*adjs.* **voiced** endowed with voice: having a voice of a specified kind: uttered with voice *(phon.)*; **voice'less** having no voice: speechless, silent: unspoken: failing to, or unable to, express one's opinion or desire, or to make this felt: having no vote: not voiced *(phon.)*.—*ns.* **voice'lessness**; **voic'er**; **voic'ing** the regulation of the tone of organ pipes, ensuring proper power, pitch, and quality.—**voice'-box** the larynx; **voice'-over** the background voice of an unseen narrator in a film, etc.; **voice'-print** an electronically recorded visual representation of speech indicating frequency, amplitude and duration.—**give voice to** to express; **in voice** in good condition for singing or speaking; **with one voice** unanimously. [A.Fr. *voiz*, *voice* (Fr. *voix*) —L. *vōx*, *vōcis*.]

void *void, adj.* containing nothing, empty, deserted: unoccupied, unutilised: having no holder, vacant: devoid, destitute, free (with *of*): ineffectual, useless: not binding in law, null, invalid.—*n.* an empty space: (with *the*) the expanse of space: emptiness: an emotional lack strongly felt *(fig.)*: an unfilled space *(archit.)*: the total absence of cards of a particular suit *(bridge,* etc.).—*v.t.* to make vacant, to empty, clear: to send out, discharge, emit: to make of no effect, to nullify.—*adj.* **void'able** that may be voided: that may be either voided or confirmed *(law)*.—*ns.* **void'ance** the act of voiding or emptying: the state of being void: of a benefice, the fact or state of being vacant; **void'ing** the act of voiding: that which is voided (often in *pl.*); **void'ness**. [O.Fr. *voide*, empty— popular L. *vocitus*—*vocitāre*, to empty—*vocuus*, for L. *vacuus*.]

voile *voil, n.* any of several kinds of thin semi-transparent material. [Fr., veil.]

voir dire *vwär dēr (law)*, an oath administered to a witness. [O.Fr. *voir*, true, truth, *dire*, to say.]

voix céleste *vwä sä-lest*, in an organ, a labial stop with a soft, tremulous sound. [Fr., heavenly voice.]

volant *vō'lənt, adj.* flying: passing lightly through the air: flying or pertaining to flight *(zool.)*: nimble: represented as flying *(her.)*.—*adjs.* **volante** *(vō-län'tā; mus.)* moving lightly and rapidly; **volatile** *(vol'ə-tīl,* in U.S. *-til, -tal)* capable of flying: moving lightly and rapidly about: evaporating very quickly: flighty, apt to change: explosive: not retaining information after the power supply is cut off *(comput.)*. —*n.* a creature capable of flying: a volatile substance. —*ns.* **vol'atileness**, **volatility** *(-til'-)*.—*adj.* **vol'atilisable**, **-z-**.—*n.* **volatilisa'tion**, **-z-**.—*v.t.* and *v.i.*

vol'atilise, **-ize** (or *-at'*) to make or become volatile. —*v.t.* to cause to evaporate: to make light, unsubstantial, delicate *(fig.)*.—*adj.* **vol'itant** flying: flitting: fluttering: moving about: able to fly.—*n.* **volita'tion** flight: power of flying.—*adjs.* **volita'tional**; **volitō'rial** having the power of flight.—**volatile oils** see **essential oils**. [L. *volāre*, to fly, *volitāre*, to flit, flutter.]

volante. See **volant**.

volatile, etc. See **volant**.

vol-au-vent *vol-ō-vä, n.* a kind of pie of light puff pastry filled with meat, or fish, etc [Fr., lit. flight in the wind]

volcano *vol-kā'nō, n.* a centre of eruption of subterranean matter, typically a more or less conical hill or mountain, built of ash and lava, with a central crater and pipe: a state of affairs, emotional condition, etc., suggestive of a volcano because an upheaval or outburst seems imminent *(fig.)*: a form of firework:—*pl.* **volcan'oes**.—*adj.* **volcanic** *(vol-kan'ik)* pertaining to, of the nature of, produced or caused by, a volcano: characterised by the presence of volcanoes.—*adv.* **volcan'ically**.—*ns.* **volcanicity** *(-kə-nis'i-ti)* vulcanicity; **volcanisa'tion**, **-z-**.—*v.t.* **vol'canise**, **-ize** to subject to the action of volcanic heat.—*adj.* **vol'canised**, **-z-**.—*ns.* **volcanism**, **volcanist** see **vulcanism**, **vulcanist**.—*adj.* **volcanolog'ical**.—*ns.* **volcanol'ogist** a vulcanologist, one who studies volcanoes and volcanic phenomena; **volcanol'ogy** vulcanology.—**volcanic glass** rock without a crystalline structure, as obsidian, pumice, etc., produced by rapid cooling of molten lava; **volcanic mud, sand** volcanic ash which has been deposited under water and sorted and stratified; **volcanic rocks** those formed by volcanic agency. [It. *volcano*—L. *Volcānus*, *Vulcānus*, god of fire.]

vole[1] *vōl, n.* in certain card games, (the winning of) all the tricks in one deal.—*v.i.* to win all the tricks in one deal.—**go the vole** to risk all for great gain: to try everything. [Fr.,—L. *volāre* to fly.]

vole[2] *vōl, n.* any of numerous blunt-nosed, short-eared, mouselike or ratlike rodents, including the so-called water-rat and some field-mice. [For *volemouse,* i.e. field-mouse, of Scand. origin.]

volente Deo *və-len'tē dē'ō, vō-, wō-len'tā dā'ō,* or *de'ō,* (L.) God willing.

volet *vol'ā, n.* one of the wings of a triptych picture. [O.Fr. (mod. Fr., a shutter)—L. *volāre,* to fly.]

volitant, volitation. See **volant**.

volition *vō-lish'ən, n.* the act of willing or choosing: the exercise of the will, or the result of this: the power of determining.—*adjs.* **voli'tional**, **voli'tionary**.—*adv.* **voli'tionally**.—*adjs.* **voli'tionless**; **vōl'itive** of, pertaining to, the will: originating in the will: willed, deliberate: expressing a wish *(gram.)*.—*n.* a desiderative verb, etc. [Fr.,—L.L. *volitiō*—L. *volō,* pres. indic. of *velle,* to will, be willing.]

Völkerwanderung *fœlk-ər-vàn'dər-ŏong,* (Ger.) *n.* the migration of Germanic and other peoples, chiefly in the 4th to 6th centuries.

volley *vol'i, n.* a flight of missiles: the discharge of many missile-throwing weapons (e.g. small arms) at once: a round fired by every gun in a battery: an outburst of many, e.g. words, at once *(fig.)*: in tennis, cricket, etc., a return of the ball before it reaches the ground—a **half-volley** is a return by striking the ball immediately after it bounces: a ball so returned:—*pl.* **voll'eys**.—*v.t.* to discharge in a volley: to return (a ball) before it bounces: to fire a volley or volleys at.— *v.t.* to fly, be discharged, in a volley: to sound, produce sounds, like a volley: to roll, move, be emitted, like a volley: to make a volley at tennis, etc.—*adj.* **voll'eyed**.—**voll'ey-ball** a game in which a large ball is volleyed by the hand over a high net. [Fr. *volée*, a flight—L. *volāre*, to fly.]

volpino *vol-pē'nō*, *n.* a small Italian dog with long, straight hair and fox-like appearance:—*pl.* **volpin'os.** [It.,—*volpe*—L. *vulpēs*, fox.]

volplane *vol'plän*, *v.i.* to glide down to earth in an aeroplane with the engine shut off.—*n.* a descent of this kind. [Fr. *vol plané*—*vol*, flight, *plané*, pa.p. of *planer*, to glide.]

volt[1], **volte** *volt*, *n.* a sudden movement or leap to avoid a thrust (*fencing*): a gait of a horse going sideways round a centre: a track made by a horse executing this movement.—*n.* **vol'tage.** [Fr. *volte* —It. *volta*—L. *volvĕre, volūtum*, to turn.]

volt[2] *völt*, *n.* the MKSA and SI unit of electromotive force, electric potential, or potential difference, the difference of potential between two points in a conductor carrying a current of one ampere when the power dissipated between them is one watt.—**volta-** (*vol'ta-*) used in composition for *voltaic*, as in **vol'ta-electric'ity, vol'ta-elec'tric.**—*n.* **voltage** (*volt'*, *völt'*) electromotive force in volts: power, intensity (*fig.*). —*adj.* **voltaic** (*vol-tā'ik*) pertaining to Alessandro *Volta*, who constructed the first electrical battery, a **voltaic pile**, and established the science of current electricity: of electricity, generated by chemical action: used in producing such electricity: of, pertaining to, caused by, voltaic electricity.—*ns.* **voltameter** (*vol-tam'i-tǝr*) an instrument for measuring an electric current by means of the amount of metal deposited, or gas liberated, from an electrolyte in a given time by the passage of the current; **völt'meter** an instrument for measuring electromotive force directly, calibrated in volts.—**voltaic cell** a primary cell. [Alessandro *Volta*, Italian scientist (1745–1827).]

voltage[1,2]; **voltaic.** See volt[1,2]; volt[2].

voltameter; **volte.** See volt[2]; volt[1].

volte-face *volt-fäs*, *n.* a turning round: a sudden and complete change in opinion or in views expressed (*fig.*). [Fr.]

voluble *vol'ū-bl*, *adj.* fluent in speech: too fluent or glib: twining (*bot.*).—*ns.* **volubil'ity, vol'ubleness.**—*adv.* **vol'ubly.** [L. *volūbilis*—*volvĕre, volutum*, to roll.]

volume *vol'ūm*, *n.* a roll or scroll, which was the form of ancient books: a book, whether complete in itself or part of a larger work: a quantity: bulk: cubical content: dimensions: fullness of tone: loudness, or the control for adjusting it on a radio, etc.—*adj.* of, concerned with, large volumes or amounts.—*adjs.* **volu'minal** pertaining to cubical content; **volu'minous** consisting of many coils, windings, folds: bulky, filling much space: in many volumes: capable of filling many volumes: having written much, as an author.—*adv.* **volu'minously.**—*ns.* **volu'minousness, voluminos'ity.**—**volumetric analysis** the estimation of the amount of a particular constituent present in a compound by determining the quantity of a standard solution required to satisfy a reaction in a known quantity of the compound.—**speak, express,** etc., **volumes** to mean much, to be very significant. [Fr., —L. *volūmen, -inis*, a roll—*volvĕre, volūtum*, to roll.]

voluntary *vol'ǝn-tǝr-i*, *adj.* acting by choice, able to will: proceeding from the will: spontaneous, free: done or made without compulsion or legal obligation: designed, intentional: freely given, or supported by contributions freely given: free from state control: subject to the will: of or pertaining to voluntaryism. —*n.* one who does anything of his own free-will: a volunteer (*obs.*): a piece of music played at will: a voluntary or extempore composition of any kind: a piece of music played before, during, or after a church service: an unwarranted fall from a horse: an upholder of voluntaryism.—*adv.* **vol'untarily.**—*ns.* **vol'untariness; vol'untarism** the philosophical doctrine that the will dominates the intellect: voluntaryism; **vol'untarist.**—*adjs.* **voluntaris'tic; vol'untātive** voluntary.—**voluntary muscle** a muscle, or muscular tissue, that is controlled by the will; **voluntary school** in England, a school supported by voluntary subscriptions, in many cases controlled by a religious body. [L. *voluntārius*—*voluntās*, choice—*volō*, pres. indic. of *velle*, to will.]

volunteer *vol-ǝn-tēr'*, *n.* one who enters any service, esp. military, of his own free choice: a soldier belonging to any body other than the regular army: one who acts of his own free will, esp. (*law*) in a transaction, without either legal obligation to do so or promise of remuneration: one to whom property is transferred without his giving valuable consideration. —*adj.* consisting of, or pertaining to, volunteers: giving voluntary service: given voluntarily: of a plant or plants, growing spontaneously.—*v.t.* to offer voluntarily to give, supply, perform: to give (information) unasked.—*v.i.* to enter into any service of one's own free-will or without being asked. [Fr. *volontaire*—L. *voluntārius.*]

voluptuary *vǝ-lup'tū-ǝr-i*, *n.* one excessively given to bodily enjoyments or luxury, a sensualist.—*adj.* promoting, or characterised by, sensual pleasure.—*adj.* **voluptuous** (*vǝ-lup'tū-ǝs*) full of, or suggestive of, pleasure, esp. sensuous: pertaining to, consisting of, derived from, or ministering to, sensual pleasure: shapely and sexually attractive: given to excess of pleasure, esp. sensual.—*adv.* **volup'tuously.**—*ns.* **volup'tuousness, voluptuos'ity.** [L. *voluptuārius*— *voluptās*, pleasure.]

volute *vǝ-, vo-lūt'*, -*lōot'*, *n.* a spiral scroll used esp. in Ionic capitals: a spiral form: a thing or part having such a shape: any marine shell of the genus *Voluta* or kindred genera, allied to the whelks, or the animal itself: a whorl of a spiral shell.—*adj.* rolled up in any direction, having a spiral form.—*adj.* **volu'ted** in spiral form: having a volute or volutes.—*n.* **volu'tion** a revolving movement: a convolution: a whorl.—*adj.* **vol'ūtoid** like a volute. [L. *volvĕre, volūtum*, to roll.]

volvulus *vol'vū-lǝs*, *n.* twisting of an abdominal viscus causing internal obstruction. [Formed from L *volvĕre*.]

vomer *vō'mǝr*, *n.* a bone of the skull in most vertebrates—in man, a thin flat bone, shaped like a wedge or ploughshare, forming part of the middle partition of the nose.—*adj.* **vomerine** (*vō'* or *vo'*).—**vo'mero-** used in composition, as **vomeronas'al**, pertaining to the vomer and the nasal cavity. [L. *vōmer*, a ploughshare.]

vomit *vom'it*, *v.i.* to throw up the contents of the stomach by the mouth, to spew: of an emetic, to cause vomiting: to issue with violence.—*v.t.* to spew: to throw out with violence: to cause to vomit:—*pr.p.* **vom'iting;** *pa.t.* and *pa.p.* **vom'ited.**—*n.* the act of vomiting: matter ejected from the stomach: vile persons or things (*fig.*): something that excites vomiting, an emetic.—*n.* **vom'iting.**—*adj.* **vom'itive** causing to vomit.—*n.* an emetic. [L. *vomĕre, -itum*, to throw up.]

voodoo, voudou *vōō'dōō*, or -*dōō'*, *n.* superstitious beliefs and practices of African origin found among Negroes of the West Indies and southern United States, formerly including serpent-worship, human sacrifice and cannibalism, but now confined to sorcery: any form of magic-working: a Negro sorcerer or witch.—*adj.* of, pertaining to, carrying out, voodoo practices.—*v.t.* to bewitch by voodoo charms.—*ns.* **voo'dooism** (or -*dōō'*) voodoo superstitions; **voo'-dooist** (or -*dōō'*).—*adj.* **voodooist'ic**. [West African *vodu*, a spirit.]

voortrekker *fōr-trek'ər*, *fōōr'*, or *vōr-*, *n.* (usu. with *cap.*) one of the Dutch farmers from Cape Colony who took part in the Great Trek into the Transvaal in 1836 and following years: (without *cap.*) a pioneer. [Cape Du.,—Du. *voor-*, before, and **trek.**]

voracious *və-rā'shəs*, *vō-*, *vō-*, *adj.* eating greedily or in large quantities: taking in, engulfing, much (*fig.*): very eager, or insatiable (*fig.*): characterised by greediness (*lit.* and *fig.*).—*adv.* **vora'ciously.**—*ns.* **voracity** (-*ras'*), **vora'ciousness.** [L. *vorāx, vorācis —vorāre,* to devour.]

vortex *vōr'teks, n.* a whirling motion of a fluid forming a cavity in the centre, a whirlpool, an eddy, a whirlwind: a pursuit, way of life, situation, etc., that engulfs one irresistibly or remorselessly, taking up all one's attention or energies (*fig.*):—*pl.* **vor'tices** (-*ti-sēz*), **vor'texes.**—*adj.* **vor'tical** of or pertaining to a vortex: whirling.—*adv.* **vor'tically.**—*ns.* **vor'ticism** (-*tis-izm*) a British movement in painting, a development from futurism, blending cubism and expressionism, and emphasising the complications of machinery that characterise modern life; **vor'ticist** one who supports vorticism.—*adjs.* **vor'ticose, vortic'ular, vortiginous** (-*ij'*) vortical. [L. *vortex, vertex, -icis—vortĕre, vertĕre,* to turn]

votary *vō'tə-ri, n.* one devoted as by a vow to some service, worship, or way of life: one enthusiastically addicted to a pursuit, study, etc.: a devoted worshipper or adherent:—*fem.* **vō'taress.**—*n.* **vō'tarist** a votary.—*adj.* **vōt'ive** given, erected, etc., by vow: undertaken or observed in fulfilment of a vow: consisting of, or expressing, a vow or a wish. [L L. *vōtārius*—L. *vovēre, vōtum,* to vow.]

vote *vōt, n.* an expression of a wish or opinion in an authorised formal way: collective opinion, decision by a majority: votes or voters of a certain class collectively: a voter· the right to vote: that by which a choice is expressed, as a ballot: the total number of votes cast.—*v.i.* to express choice, esp. at an election, by vote: to declare oneself in favour of, or against (with *for, against*), esp. by vote.—*v.t.* to determine by vote: to grant by vote: to bring about (a specified result or change) by vote: to declare by general consent (*coll.*): to pronounce, adjudge to be (*coll.*): to propose, suggest (*coll.*): to present for voting: to record the votes of.—*adj.* **vote'less.**—*n* **vō'ter.**— **split one's vote(s)** to divide one's votes among two or more candidates; **split the vote** to injure a cause by influencing a body of possible supporters to vote in some other way (*n.* **vote'-splitt'ing**); **vote Conservative, Labour,** etc., to give one's vote, on a particular occasion or habitually, to the Conservative, Labour, etc., candidate or party; **vote down** to defeat or suppress by vote, or otherwise; **vote in** to elect; **vote of no confidence** the legal method of forcing the resignation of a government or governing body; **vote with one's feet** to indicate one's dissatisfaction with a situation or conditions by leaving. [L. *vōtum,* a wish—*vovēre, vōtum,* to vow.]

votive. See **votary.**

vouch *vowch, v.t.* to assert or guarantee to be true: to support by evidence: to testify (that)—*v.i.* to bear witness, or be surety (with *for*).—*n.* an assertion: an attestation.—*n.* **vouch'er** (partly A.Fr. *voucher,* infin.; partly suff. *-er*) a piece of evidence, or a written document serving as proof: a paper which confirms the truth of anything, as a receipt, a certificate of correctness: a ticket, etc., substituting, or exchangeable, for cash or goods: one who vouches or

gives witness: a mechanical contrivance used in shops for automatically registering the amount of money drawn. [O.Fr. *voucher, vocher,* to call to defend— L. *vocāre,* to call.]

vouchsafe *vowch-sāf', v.t* to condescend, be graciously willing to tell, etc.—*v i.* to condescend:—*pr.p.* **vouchsaf'ing;** *pa.t.* and *pa p.* **vouchsafed'.**—*n.* **vouchsafe'ment.** [Orig. two words, **vouch, safe.**]

voudou. See **voodoo.**

voussoir *vōō-swär', n.* one of the wedge-like stones that form part of an arch.—*v.t* to form with voussoirs [Fr., through L.L., from L. *volūtus—volvēre,* to roll.]

vow *vow, n* a voluntary promise made to God, or to a saint, or to a god or gods: a binding undertaking or resolve: a solemn or formal promise of fidelity or affection: a firm assertion: an earnest wish or prayer. —*v.t.* to give, dedicate, by solemn promise: to promise or threaten solemnly: to maintain solemnly —*v.i.* to make vows.—*adj.* **vowed** devoted, confirmed, undertaken, etc., by vow, or as by vow.— **baptismal vows** the promises made at baptism by the person baptised, or by the sponsors or parents in his name; **simple vow** a more limited, less permanent vow than a solemn vow; **solemn vow** such a vow as the Church takes under her special charge, solemnly accepts, as those of poverty, obedience, and chastity, involving complete and irrevocable surrender [O.Fr. *vou* (Fr. *vœu*)—L. *vōtum—vovēre,* to vow.]

vowel *vow'əl, n.* a speech-sound produced by the unimpeded passage of the breath (modified by the vocal cords into voice) through the mouth, different vowel sounds being made by altering the form and position of the tongue and the lips: a letter (as *a, e, i, o, u*) used alone or in combination to represent a vowel sound —*adj.* vocal: of, representing, of the nature of, a vowel —*adj* **vow'elless** without vowels. [Fr. *voyelle*—L. *vōcālis—vōx, vōcis,* voice.]

vox *voks,* (L. *vōks, wōks*), *n.* voice:—*pl.* **voces** (*vō'sēz, -kēs, wō'*).—**vox angelica** (*an-jel'i-kə, an-gel'i-ka*), **vox caelestis** (*sē-les'tis, kī-*) voix céleste, **vox humana** (*hū-mä'nə, hōō-mä'na*) in organ-building, a reed-stop producing tones resembling those of the human voice; **vox populi, vox Dei** (*pop'ū-lī, dē'ī, po'pōō-lē, de'ē* or *dä'ē*) the voice of the people is the voice of God, hence **vox populi** (often shortened to **vox pop**) public or popular opinion. [L. *vōx.*]

voyage *voi'ij, n.* a passage by water or by air to some place at a considerable distance: a round trip: a cruise: an account of such a journey —*v i.* to make a voyage, cruise, journey.—*v.t.* to traverse, pass over. —*adj.* **voy'ageable** navigable.—*n.* **voy'ager.** [O.Fr. *veage, voiage,* etc.—L. *viāticum;* see **viaticum.**]

voyeur *vwa-yœr', n.* one who derives gratification from surreptitiously watching sexual acts or objects: a peeping Tom: one who takes a morbid interest in sordid sights.—*n.* **voy'eurism**—*adj* **voyeuris'tic.** [Fr., one who sees.]

vraisemblance *vrä-, vre-sä-bläs', n.* verisimilitude: a picture. [Fr. *vrai,* true, *semblance,* appearance.]

vroom *vrōōm, vrŏŏm,* (*coll.*) *n* power, drive, energy, etc.—*v.i.* to travel speedily. [Imit.]

VTOL *vē'tol, n.* a system enabling aircraft to land and take off vertically: an aircraft operating by this system. [*Vertical take-off* and *landing.*]

Vulcan *vul'kən, n.* the god of fire and metal-working (*Roman myth.*): (without *cap.*) a blacksmith or an iron-worker.—*adj.* **vulcanic** (-*kan'ik*) volcanic.—*n.* **vulcanicity** (-*is'i-ti*) volcanic action or phenomena.— *adj.* **vulcanī'sable, -z-.**—*n.* **vulcanīsā'tion, -z-.**—*v.t.* **vul'canise, -ize** to treat (rubber, etc.) with sulphur or sulphur compounds, etc. to improve its strength or otherwise modify its properties.—*v.i.* to admit such treatment.—*n.* **vul'canism** volcanic activity (also **vol'canism**); **vul'canist**, **vol'canist** a vulcanologist; **vul'canite** the harder of the two kinds of vulcanised rubber, the softer kind being called *soft rubber*: a general name for any igneous rock of fine grain-size.—*adj.* **vulcanolog'ical.**—*ns.* **vulcanol'ogist**; **vulcanol'ogy** the scientific study of volcanoes and volcanic phenomena. [L. *Vulcānus.*]

vulgar *vul'gər, adj.* pertaining to the common people: plebeian: vernacular: public: common, usual, customary: common to all: prevalent: commonplace: low: unrefined: coarse: lacking in taste, manners, delicacy, etc.: spiritually paltry, ignoble, debased, or pretentious.—*n.* the common people: one of the unrefined, of the uneducated, or of those not in good society: the common language of a country.—*n.* **vulgā'rian** a vulgar person: a rich unrefined person.—Also *adj.*—*n.* **vulgarisā'tion, -z-.**—*v.t.* **vul'garise, -ize** to make common or ordinary: to make unrefined or coarse.—*ns.* **vul'garism** a vulgar phrase: coarseness: an instance of this; **vulgarity** (-gar').—*adv.* **vul'garly.**—**vulgar fraction** a fraction written in the common way (one number above another, separated by a line), as opposed to a *decimal fraction*; **vulgar tongue** the vernacular. [L. *vulgāris—vulgus,* the people.]

Vulgate *vul'gāt,* or *-git, n.* an ancient Latin version of the Scriptures, made by St Jerome and others in the 4th century, and later twice revised—so called from its common use in the R.C. church: (without *cap.*) a comparable accepted text of any other book or author.—*adj.* of or pertaining to the Vulgate:

(without *cap.*; of speech, etc.) commonly used or accepted. [L. *vulgāta (editio),* popular edition (of the Bible); see **vulgar.**]

vulgus *vul'gəs, n.* the common people. [L.; see **vulgar.**]

vulnerable *vul'nər-ə-bl, adj.* capable of being wounded: liable to injury, or hurt to feelings: open to successful attack: capable of being persuaded or tempted: in contract bridge, of a side that has won a game towards the rubber, liable to increased penalties (or premiums) accordingly.—*ns.* **vulnerabil'ity, vul'nerableness.**—*adj.* **vul'nerary** pertaining to wounds: useful in healing wounds.—*n.* anything useful in curing wounds. [L. *vulnerāre,* to wound—*vulnus, vulneris,* a wound.]

Vulpes *vul'pēz, n.* the genus including the common fox.—*adj.* **vulpine** (*vul'pin, -pīn*) of, pertaining to, or like a fox: cunning. [L. *vulpēs,* a fox.]

vulture *vul'chər, n.* any of a number of large rapacious birds of prey, feeding largely on carrion, regarded as belonging to two families: one who or that which resembles a vulture.—Also *adj.*—*adjs.* **vul'turine, vul'turish, vul'turous** of, pertaining to, or like a vulture: rapacious. [O.Fr. *voutour, voltour,* etc. (Fr. *vautour*)—L. *vulturius—vultur.*]

vulva *vul'və, n.* the external organ of generation of the female mammal, or the orifice of it.—*adjs.* **vul'val, vul'var, vul'vate; vul'viform** oval: like a cleft with projecting edges.—*n.* **vulvi'tis** inflammation of the vulva.—**vul'vo-** used in composition, as **vul'vo-û'terine,** pertaining to the vulva and the uterus. [L. *vulva, volva,* wrapping, womb.]

vying *vī'ing, pr.p.* of **vie.**

W

W, w *dub'l-ū, n.* the twenty-third letter of our alphabet, a doubled u or v used to express the voiced consonantal sound heard, e.g. in Eng. *way, weak, warrant.* In mod. Eng. *w* is found as a consonant and also as the second component in certain vowel and diphthong digraphs, i.e. those in *law, few, now.* The unvoiced form of the consonant is written *wh* (corresponding to O.E. *hw*), as in *what, when,* but many English people substitute the voiced sound in pronouncing words spelt *wh,* and Northern speakers insist upon sounding *hw. W* is no longer pronounced in *write, two,* etc.

Waac *wak, n.* the Women's Army Auxiliary Corps (founded 1917), or a member of it, now **WRAC.**—*n.* **Waaf** *(waf)* the Women's Auxiliary Air Force (1939), or a member, now **WRAF.** [From the initial letters.]

wacke *wak'ə, n.* an old name for a decomposed basalt. [Ger ,—O.H.G.·*wagge,* a pebble.]

wacky *wak'ı, (slang) adj.* crazy.—*n* **wack'iness.**

wad *wod, n* a pad of loose material thrust in to aid packing, etc.: formerly a little mass of paper, tow, or the like, now a disc of felt or paper, to keep the charge in a gun: a bundle.as of hay: a roll or bundle, as of bank notes. a compact mass, often small.—*v.t.* to form into a mass: to pad, stuff out: to stuff a wad into—*pr.p.* **wadd'ing;** *pa t.* and *pa.p.* **wadd'ed.**—*n.* **wadd'ing** a wad, or the materials for wads: sheets of carded cotton for stuffing garments, etc.: cottonwool.

waddle *wod'l, v.i.* to take short steps and sway from side to side in walking, as a duck does· to move in a way suggestive of this.—*n* the act of waddling. a clumsy, rocking gait.—*adj* **wadd'ling.** [Freq of **wade.**]

waddy *wod'ı, n* a native Australian wooden club used in warfare —*v.t.* to strike with a waddy. [Perh. from Eng. **wood.**]

wade *wād, v.i.* to walk through a substance that yields with difficulty to the feet, as water: to go (through) with difficulty or labour *(fig.).*—*v.t.* to cross by wading: to cause to cross thus.—*n.* the act of wading.—*n.* **wā'der** one who wades: a bird that wades in search of food, e.g. the snipe, sandpiper, etc.: a high waterproof boot.—*n.* and *adj.* **wā'ding.**—**wade in** to make a very vigorous attack; **wade into** to tackle, as a job, energetically: to make a vigorous attack on *(lit* and *fig.).* [O.E. *wadan,* to go.]

wadi, wady *wod'i, n.* the dry bed of a torrent: a river-valley. [Ar. *wādī.*]

wafer *wā'fər, n.* a very thin crisp cake or biscuit baked in **wafer-irons** or **-tongs,** formerly eaten with wine: a similar biscuit eaten with ice-cream, etc.: a thin round cake of unleavened bread, used in the Eucharist: a thin leaf of coloured paste for sealing letters, etc.: a thin cake of paste used to form a wrapping for powders *(med.):* a thin slice of anything.—*v.i.* to close, fasten, stick (as on a wall), with a wafer.—*adj.* **wā'fery** like a wafer. [O.N.Fr. *waufre*—M.L.G. *wafel,* cake of wax.]

waffle[2] *wof'l, n.* a kind of cake made from batter, baked in an iron utensil of hinged halves called a **waff'le-i'ron.** [Du. *wafel,* wafer.]

waffle[2] *wof'l, (slang) v.i.* to talk incessantly or nonsensically: to waver, vacillate.—Also *n.*

waft *wäft, woft, waft, v.t.* to bear, convey, transport, propel, safely or lightly, on the surface of or through a fluid medium, as air or water *(poet.;* also *fig.).*—*v.i.* to float, sail, pass through the air.—*n.* a scent, or sound, or puff or smoke or vapour carried by the air: a rush of air (also *fig.*): an act of wafting, or of waving: a waving movement: a flag or substitute hoisted as a signal at different positions at the after-part of a ship: the act of displaying such a signal.—*ns.* **waft'er;** **waft'ing.** [From obs. *wafter,* a convoying vessel, prob.—L.G. or Du. *wachter,* guard.]

wag *wag, v.i.* to move, or be moved, from side to side, or to shake to and fro: to oscillate: to move, or to move one's limbs: of tongue, chin, beard, etc., to move in light, gossiping or indiscreet talk.—*v.t.* to move, shake, wave, to and fro or up and down: to move, stir a limb, etc.: to move in chatter or indiscreet talk: to move so as to express reproof or derision, etc.:—*pr.p.* **wagg'ing;** *pa.t.* and *pa.p.* **wagged.**—*n.* a shake: an act of wagging: a droll, mischievous fellow, a habitual joker, a wit.—*n.* **wagg'ery** mischievous merriment or jesting: an instance of such.—*adj.* **wagg'ish** droll, mischievous, etc.—*adv.* **wagg'ishly.**—*n.* **wagg'ishness.** [M.E. *waggen,* from same root as O E. *wagian,* to shake.]

wage *wāj, v.t.* to engage in, to carry on, esp. war —*n.* payment for services, esp. not professional, or *(fig.)* reward (both often **wages** *pl* in form, but sometimes construed as *sing*).—*n.* **wā'ger** something staked on an issue: a bet: that on which bets are laid.—*v.t.* to hazard on the issue of anything.—*v i* to lay a wager. —*n.* **wā'gerer.**—**wage'-earn'er** one who works for wages: one who earns the money that supports, or money that helps to support, the household; **wage'** **earn'ing; wage'-freeze** a fixing of wages at a certain level for some time ahead; **wage'-packet** a small envelope in which a worker's wages are issued: *(loosely)* wages. [M.E. *wagen*—O.N.Fr. *wagier* (O.Fr. *gagier*), to pledge (through popular L from a Gmc. word).]

waggle *wag'l, v.i.* and *v.t.* to wag, esp. in an unsteady manner.—Also *n.*—*adj* **wagg'ly.** [Freq. of **wag.**]

waggon, etc. See **wagon.**

wag-'n-bietjie. See under **wait.**

Wagnerian *väg-nē'ri-ən, adj.* pertaining to or characterised by the ideas or style of Richard *Wagner* (1813–83), German composer of music-dramas.—*n.* a follower or admirer of Richard Wagner.—*adj.* **Wagneresque'.**—*ns.* **Wag'nerism, Wagne'rianism** the art theory of Richard Wagner, its main object being the freeing of opera from traditional and conventional forms, and its one canon, dramatic fitness; **Wag'nerist, Wag'nerite** an adherent of Wagner's musical methods.

wagon, waggon *wag'ən, n.* a four-wheeled vehicle, esp. one for carrying heavy goods: an open railway truck or a closed railway van.—*ns.* **wag'onage** conveyance by wagon, or money paid for it; **wag'oner, wagg'oner** one who drives a wagon; **wagonette'** a kind of carriage with one or two seats crosswise in front, and two back seats arranged lengthwise and facing inwards; **wag'onful.**—**wag'on-load** the load carried by a wagon: a great amount; **wag'on-train** a collection or service of army vehicles for the conveyance of ammunition, provisions, the sick, etc.: a train of usu. horse-drawn wagons used by pioneer settlers to travel into new territory.—**on (off) the wagon** (*slang*) abstaining (no longer abstaining) from alcohol. [Du. *wagen*.]

wagon-lit *vä-gɔ̃-lē'*, *n.* a sleeping-carriage on a continental train:—*pl.* **wagons-lit** (pron. as *sing.*; sometimes **wagon-lits**). [Fr. *wagon* (—Eng. **wagon**) *lit*, bed.]

wagtail *wag'tāl*, *n.* any bird of the *Motacilla* and *Dendronanthus*, so named from their constant wagging of the tail: applied also to other birds.

Wahabi, Wahabee *wä-hä'bē*, *n.* one of a sect of Muslims founded in about 1760 by Abd-el-*Wahhab* (1691–1787), whose aim was to restore primitivé Islam.—Also **Waha'b(i)ite**.—*n.* **Waha'bi(i)sm** the doctrine and practices of the Wahabis.

wahine *wä-hē'ne*, *n.* a Maori woman. [Maori.]

wahoo *wa-hoo'*, *n.* a large fast-moving marine food and game fish, akin to the mackerel.

waif *wäf*, *n.* a piece of property found ownerless, as a strayed animal, or goods cast up by the tide (also *fig.*): a homeless wanderer: a neglected ownerless child.—**waifs and strays** homeless, destitute persons. [O.Fr. *waif*; prob.—Scand.]

wail *wāl*, *v.i.* to lament or sorrow audibly, esp. with prolonged high-pitched mournful cries.—*v.t.* to bemoan: to grieve over.—*n.* the action of wailing: a cry of woe: an animal cry or mechanical sound suggesting this.—*n.* **wail'er.**—*adj.* **wail'ful** sorrowful: expressing woe.—*n.* and *adj.* **wail'ing.**—*adv.* **wail'ingly.**—**Wailing Wall** a wall in Jerusalem, a remnant of the temple dating back to before the destruction of the city in 66 A.D., where Jews traditionally pray on Fridays. [M.E. *weilen, wailen.*]

wain *wän*, *n.* a wagon, esp. for hay or other agricultural produce (now usu. *poet.*).—**wain'wright** one who makes wagons. [O.E. *wægen, wæn—wegen*, to carry.]

wainscot *wän'skot, -skǝt*, or *wen'*, *n.* fine oak for panelling, etc.: woodwork, esp. panelled, on an interior wall: the lower part of an interior wall when lined with material different from that on the upper part.—*v.t.* to line with, or as if with, boards or panels:—*pr.p.* **wain'scoting, wain'scotting**; *pa.t.* and *pa.p.* **wain'scoted, wain'scotted.**—*n.* **wain'scoting, wain'scotting** the act of lining with boards or panels: materials for making a wainscot: wainscots collectively. [Orig. perh. wood used for a partition in a wagon—Du. *wagen-schot—wagen*, wagon, *schot*, partition.]

waist *wäst*, *n.* the smallest part of the human trunk, between the ribs and the hips: a narrow middle part of an insect: the part of a garment that lies round the waist of the body: the narrow middle part, as of a musical instrument: the middle part of a ship.—*adj.* **waist'ed** having a waist, often of specified type.—**waist'band** part of a garment that fits the waist: a belt or sash; **waist'coat** (*wäs', wäst'kōt*) a garment, plain or ornamental, reaching to or below the waist, and now sleeveless, intended to show partly, worn by men at different periods under doublet, coat, jacket, etc. a woman's similar garment or front.—*adjs.* **waist's deep, -high** as deep, high, as to reach up to the waist. —**waist'line** a line thought of as marking the waist, but not fixed by anatomy in women's fashions: the measurement of a waist. [M.E. *wast*, from presumed O.E. *wæst*, growth, size.]

wait *wät*, *v.i.* to be, remain, in expectation or readiness (with *for*): to be, remain, in a place in readiness (also **wait about, around**): to delay action: to be delayed: to be in attendance, or in readiness to carry out orders: to bring food to the table and clear away used dishes.

—*n.* an ambush—now used only in such phrases as *to lie in wait, to lay wait*: the act of waiting or of expecting: a delay: (in *pl.*) persons who welcome in Christmas by playing or singing out-of-doors at night. —*ns.* **wait'er** one who waits, esp. at table in a hotel dining-room, etc.; **wait'ing** the act of waiting: attendance.—Also *adj.*—*n.* **wait'ress** a female waiter.— **wait'-a-bit** (also often *adj.*) a name given to various plants, esp. S. African (*Afrik.* **wag-'n-bietjie** *vuhh'ǝ(n)-bē-kē*) with thorns that catch the clothing of the passer-by; **wait'ing-list, wait'-list** a list of people waiting, as candidates awaiting a vacancy, etc.; **wait'ing-room** a room for the use of persons waiting.—**lie in wait** to be in hiding ready to attack or surprise (*lit.* and *fig.*); **play a waiting game** (*lit.* and *fig.*) to avoid action as far as possible in the hope of having an opportunity later to use one's energies with maximum effect; **wait on** to wait for (*dial.*): to wait upon; **wait upon, on** to attend upon; **wait up** to stay out of bed waiting (with *for*); **wait upon, on** to attend and serve. [O.N.Fr. *waitier* (O.Fr. *guaitier*, Fr. *guetter*), to watch, attend; of Gmc. origin.]

waive *wāv*, *v.t.* to give up voluntarily, as a claim or a contention (*law*): to refrain from claiming, demanding, taking, or enforcing: to forgo: to defer, postpone.—*n.* **wai'ver** the act, or an act, of waiving, or a written statement formally indicating this. [A.Fr. *weyver*—O.Fr. *guesver*, to abandon; from same root as **waif**.]

wake¹ *wāk*, *v.i.* to be, or to remain, awake, or active or vigilant: to keep watch or vigil, or to pass the night in prayer: to hold a wake: to awake, be roused from, or as from, sleep, from indifference, etc. (often with *up*): to become animated or lively: to be stirred up, aroused.—*v.t.* to rouse from sleep: to keep vigil over: to excite, stir up: to disturb with noise: to animate: to reanimate, revive:—*pa.t.* **waked** (*wākt*) or **woke** (*wōk*); *pa.p.* **waked, wo'ken.**—*n.* the feast of the dedication of a church, formerly kept by watching all night: a festival: a watch or vigil beside a corpse, sometimes with revelry.—*adj.* **wake'ful** not asleep: unable, or indisposed, to sleep: vigilant: waking.— *adv.* **wake'fully.**—*n.* **wake'fulness.**—*v.i.* **wa'ken** to be, or become, awake: to become active or lively.— *v.t.* to rouse from sleep, unconsciousness, inaction: to excite, stir up, evoke.—*adj.* **wa'kened.**—*n.* **wa'kener.** —*adj.* **wa'kening.**—*n.* the act of one who wakens.— *ns.* **wa'ker** one who wakes; **wa'king.**—*adj.* that wakes, keeps watch, or is vigilant: that rouses or becomes awake: passed, or experienced, in the waking state.—**wake'-robin** the cuckoo-pint, *Arum maculatum*: the spotted orchis, *Orchis maculata*: applied to various other flowers, esp. in U.S., to any of the genus *Trillium*, **waking hours** the period of the day during which one is normally awake.—**wake(n) to, wake up to** to become conscious of, alive to. [A combination of an O.E. strong verb *wacan*, to be born, to awake, and an O.E. weak verb *wacian*, to be awake, to watch; cf. **watch**.]

wake² *wāk*, *n.* the streak of smooth-looking or foamy water left in the track of a ship: disturbed air behind a flying body: the rear of, area passed through by, someone or something.—**in the wake of** (*fig.*) close behind: immediately after (usu. implying consequence). [Of Scand. origin.]

Waldenses *wol-den'sēz*, *n.pl.* a Christian community of austere morality and devotion to the simplicity of the Gospel, orig. followers of Peter *Waldo*, a merchant of Lyons and preacher in the second half of the 12th century.—*adj.* and *n.* **Walden'sian.**

wale *wāl*, *n.* same as **weal²**: a ridge on the surface of cloth: (in *pl.*) planks all along the outer timbers on a ship's side.—*v.t.* to mark with wales: to make or furnish with, or secure with, wales. [O.E. *walu*.]

walk *wök, v.i.* of a biped, to move along leisurely on foot with alternate steps, the walker always having at least one foot on the ground: of a quadruped, to move along in such a way that there are always at least two feet on the ground: to pace: to journey on foot: to ramble, go on foot for pleasure, etc.: to move: to behave in a certain way, follow a certain course: to move off, depart, withdraw: to conduct oneself, behave.—*v.t.* to pass through or upon, perambulate, traverse: to follow, trace out, on foot: to measure, wear out, etc. by walking: to cause to walk, or to move as if walking: to lead or accompany by walking. —*n.* the action, or an act, of walking: a spell of walking, especially for pleasure: a perambulation in procession: a gait: that in or through which one walks: a possible or suitable route or course for walking: a path or place for walking: a tree-bordered avenue: a distance walked, or a distance as measured by the time taken to walk it: conduct: a course of life, sphere of action: a hawker's district or round.—*adj.* walk'-able.—*ns.* walk'er one who walks or takes part in walking-races: any device which helps esp. babies and elderly people to walk; walk'ing the verbal noun of walk: pedestrianism: the sport of walking-races: the condition of a surface from the point of view of one who walks on it.—*adj.* that walks, or that moves as if walking: that oscillates: used in or for walking: performed by walking: worked by a person or animal who walks.—*adv.* walk'about on the move, as in *go walkabout*, esp. temporarily back into the bush (of Australian aborigines), or meeting the public on foot (of royalty, politicians, etc.).—*n.* a wandering, a journey: a walk by royalty, etc. in order to meet the public.—walk'ie-talk'ie, walk'y-talk'y a portable radiotelephone transmitting and receiving set.—*adj.* walk'-in of a cupboard, etc., big enough to walk into and move around in.—walk'ing-orders, -papers, -ticket (*slang*) dismissal; walk'ing-part one in which the actor has nothing to say; walk'ing-race a race in which competitors must walk rather than run; walk'-ing-stick, -cane, -staff a stick, cane, or staff used in walking; walk'ing-stick, -straw, -twig a stick-insect; walk'ing-toad a natterjack; walk'-on a walking-part. —*adj.* walk'-on of an air-service or aeroplane, for which one does not have to purchase a ticket in advance, the seats being non-bookable: pertaining to a walking-part.—walk'-out the act of walking out, usually to indicate disapproval: a sudden industrial strike; walk'-over a race where only one competitor appears, and has merely to cover the course to win: an easy or unopposed victory; walk'way a road, path, etc., constructed for pedestrians only.—charity walk, sponsored walk an organised walk in aid of charity, each participator having obtained from a sponsor or sponsors an agreement to contribute according to distance covered; walk a tight-rope to follow a narrow and difficult route beset with dangers, as if on a tight-rope; walk away from to outdistance or undo easily; walk away with to win with ease; walk into (*coll.*) to beat: to storm at: to eat heartily of: to collide or meet with unexpectedly; walk it (*coll.*) to succeed, win easily; walk off to leave: to depart: to get rid of by walking, as disagreeable feelings or effects; walk off with to take surreptitiously or feloniously: to win easily; walk on to walk ahead: to continue to walk: to have a walking-part; walk on air to be exultant or light-hearted; walk out to leave, esp. as a gesture of disapproval: to strike; walk out on (*coll.*) to desert, leave in the lurch; walk over to cross, or traverse: to win an uncontested race: to have an easy victory or easy success (*coll.*): to disregard the rights or feelings of (*coll.*); walk tall (*coll.*) to be

proud, have self-respect; walk the plank see plank; walk the streets to wander about in search of work, or simply aimlessly: to be a prostitute. [M.E. *walken, walkien,* to walk—O.E. *wealcan,* to roll, revolve, *wealcian,* to roll up, curl.]

wall *wöl, n.* an erection of brick, stone, etc., for security or to enclose a space such as a piece of land: the side of a building or of a room: (in *pl.*) fortifications: any bounding surface suggestive of a wall, e.g. the membranous covering or lining of an organ of the body or of a plant or animal cell: a barrier (*fig.*). —*v.t.* to enclose with, or as with, a wall: to fortify with, or as with, walls: to divide as by a wall.—wall- in composition, growing on, living in, for hanging on, or otherwise associated with, a wall.—*adj.* walled enclosed with a wall: fortified.—*ns.* wall'er one who builds walls; wall'ing walls collectively: materials for walls.—*adj.* wall'-less.—wall bars horizontal bars fixed to a wall, used by gymnasts; wall'-board building-board; wall'covering wallpaper, or anything used in the same way; wall-eye see separate entry; wall'e facing a facing for a wall; wall'flower one of the Cruciferae, with fragrant flowers, yellow when wild, found on old walls: any other plant of the same genus (*Cherianthus* or *Cheirinia*): a person who remains a spectator at a dance, usu. a woman who cannot obtain partners (*coll.*); wall'-gill'yflower a wallflower; wall'-paint'ing the decoration of walls with ornamental painted designs: a work of art painted on a wall; wall'paper paper, usually coloured or decorated, for pasting on the walls of a room; wall pass (*football*) a one-two; wall'-plate a horizontal piece of timber or of rolled steel on a wall, etc., to bear the ends of joists, etc.; Wall Street a street in New York, the chief financial centre in the United States: hence, American financial interests.—*adj.* wall'-to-wall' of carpets, etc., covering the entire floor: covering, crowding the entire room, space, etc. (*fig.; coll.*).—wall unit a piece of furniture attached to or standing against a wall.—go to the wall to be hard pressed: to be forced to give way: to fail, go under: to give precedence to something else; hang by the wall to remain unused; turn one's face to the wall to resign oneself to death or despair; up the wall (*coll.*) mad, distracted; wall up to block with a wall: to entomb in a wall; with one's back to the wall in desperate straits: at bay. [O.E. *wall* (W.S. *weall*)— L. *vallum,* a rampart.]

walla. See wallah.

wallaby *wol'ab-i, n.* any of a number of small kangaroos.—the Wallabies the Australian national Rugby Union football team. [Native Austr. *wolabá.*]

Wallace's line *wol'is-iz līn,* a line passing through the East Indian group of islands between Bali and Lombok, roughly separating the very different faunas of the Oriental region and the Australian region, or rather a transitional region. [Alfred Russel *Wallace* (1823–1913), naturalist.]

wallah *wol'a, -ə, n.* (often in combination) one employed in, or concerned with, a specific type of work: one who occupies an eminent position in an organisation, etc.—Also wall'a. [Hindi *-wälä,* properly an adjectival suffix.]

wallaroo *wol-ə-rōō', n.* any of various large kangaroos (*Macropus*). [Native Austr. *wolarū.*]

wallet *wol'it, n.* a bag for carrying necessaries on a journey: a pocket-book, a small case for holding money, papers, etc. [M.E. *walet,* poss.—*watel,* a bag of woven material.]

wall-eye *wöl'ī, n.* an eye in which the iris is pale, or the white part is very large or noticeable (e.g. as the result of a squint): the disease of the eye called glaucoma.—*adj* **wall'-eyed** very light grey in the eyes, or in one eye: having a divergent squint: having a staring or a blank expression or (*fig.*) appearance. [O.N. *vagleygr*, perh. conn. with mod. Icel *vagl*, a film over the eye.]

Walloon *wol-ōōn'*, *adj.* of or pertaining to a people living chiefly in southern Belgium and adjacent parts of eastern France, or to their language.—*n.* a man or woman of this people: their language, a dialect of French [Fr. *Wallon*; of Gmc. origin.]

wallop *wol'əp*, *v.i* to move quickly but clumsily, noisily, and with effort: to flounder.—*v.t.* (*coll.*) to beat soundly, thrash: to strike with force.—*n.* a plunging movement (*coll.*): a heavy blow (*coll*): physical or financial power (*coll.*): beer (*slang*)—*adv.* with a wallop: heavily or noisily —*ns.* **wall'oper** one who or that which wallops: something extremely large or big (*coll*); **wall'oping**.—*adj.* that wallops: extremely large or big, bouncing, whopping (*coll.*). [O.N Fr. *waloper* (Fr. *galoper*); cf **gallop.**]

wallow *wol'ō*, *v.i.* to roll about in mud, etc., as an animal does (implying enjoyment): to immerse or indulge oneself (in emotion, etc.): to flounder: in a bad sense, to live in filth or gross vice: to surge, heave, blow, well up, etc —*n.* the act of wallowing: the place, or the filth, an animal wallows in: a hollow or depression suggestive of a wallowing-place.—*ns* **wall'ower**; **wall'owing.**—*adj.* that wallows: very rich (*slang*) [O.E *wealwian*—L *volvēre.*]

walnut *wol'nut*, *n.* a genus (Juglans) of beautiful trees, some yielding valuable furniture wood: their wood· the nut of the Common or English Walnut.—*adj.* made from walnutwood: light brown in colour.— **wal'nut-juice** juice from the husk of walnuts used to stain the skin, **wal'nutwood.** [O.E. *walhhnutu*— *w(e)alh*, foreigner, *hnutu*, a nut.]

Walpurgis night *val-pûr'gis nīt*, or *-pōōr'*, the eve of the first of May, when witches, according to German popular superstition, rode on broomsticks and he-goats to hold revel with their master the devil, esp. on the Brocken in the Harz Mountains. [So called because May 1st is the day of St *Walpurga*, abbess of Heidenheim, who died about 778.]

walrus *wol'rəs*, *wol'rʌs*, *n̄.* an aquatic, web-footed, carnivorous animal, allied to the seals, having the upper canine teeth developed into enormous tusks — **walrus moustache** one with long drooping ends [Du *walrus*, *walros*, lit whale horse; of Scand origin.]

waltz *wolts*, *wòls*, *n.* orig. a German dance performed by couples with a rapid whirling motion: a slower circling dance, also in triple time: the music for such. a piece of instrumental music in 3–4 time (**concert waltz**).—*v.i.* to dance a waltz: to move trippingly, to whirl (*slang*; also *v t.*): to walk quickly and arrogantly or determinedly (*coll.*; also *v.t.*).—*ns.* **waltz'er**; **waltz'ing.**—**waltz into** to storm at; **waltz Matilda** see **Matilda.** [Ger. *Walzer—walzen*, to roll, dance.]

wampum *wom'pəm*, *wòm'pəm*, *n.* a shortened form of the N. American Indian (Algonquian) name for beads made from shells, used as money, etc.— **wam'pumpeag** (-*pēg*) the word of which wampum is an abbreviation—lit. white string of beads

wan *won*, *adj.* wanting colour: pale and sickly: faint — *adv.* **wan'ly.**—*n.* **wan'ness.**—*adj.* **wann'ish** somewhat wan. [O.E. *wann*, dark, lurid.]

wand *wond*, *n.* orig. something slender and supple, as a twig, or a thin stem or branch, or a young shoot of a willow used in basketmaking (now *poet.* and *dial.*): a rod of authority, a caduceus, a rod used by a fairy, a magician, a conjurer, a conductor, or a diviner: a measuring rod. [O.N. *vöndr*, a shoot of a tree; Dan. *vaand.*]

wander *won'dər*, *v.i.* to ramble or move with no definite object, or with no fixed course, or by a round-about way (*lit.* and *fig.*): to go astray, deviate from the right path or course, the subject of discussion, the object of attention, etc (*lit.* and *fig.*): to lose one's way (*coll*): to be incoherent in talk, disordered in mind, or delirious.—*v.t* to traverse: to lead astray, or to bewilder (*coll.*).—*n.* a ramble, stroll.—*adj.* **wan'dered** astray: incoherent: bewildered.—*n.* **wan'derer.**—*adj.* and *n.* **wan'dering.**—*adv* **wan'der-ingly.**—**Wandering Jew** a legendary Jew in folklore esp. of north-western Europe who cannot die but must wander till the Day of Judgment, for an insult offered to Christ on the way to the Crucifixion; **wandering Jew** any of several trailing or creeping plants; **wandering sailor** a name given to various other similar plants; **wanderlust** (*won'dər-lust*; *van'dər-lōōst*) an urge to travel or to move from place to place. [O.E. *wandrian*]

wanderoo *won-də-rōō'*, *n.* usu. applied to the lion-tailed macaque, a native of the Malabar coast of India: properly, a langur of Sri Lanka [Sinhalese *wanderu*, monkey.]

wane *wān*, *v.i.* to decrease in size, esp. of the moon— opp. to *wax*: to decline in power, prosperity, intensity, brightness, etc.· to draw to a close.—*n.* gradual decrease or decline (esp in phrases, as on the **wane, in wane, in the, her, its wane**), or the time when this is taking place: a defective edge or corner on a plank of wood.—*adjs.* **waned** diminished: dying or dead; **wan'ey, wan'y.**—*adj.* and *n.* **wan'ing.** [O.E. *wanian, wonian*, to lessen—*wana, wona* deficient, lacking.]

wangle *wang'gl*, (*coll.*) *v.t* to obtain or accomplish by craft: to manipulate.—*v t.* to use tricky methods to attain one's ends.—*n.* an exercise of such methods.— *ns.* **wang'ler; wang'ling.**

wanigan *won'i-gən*, *n* in a lumber camp, a chest for supplies, or a kind of houseboat for loggers and their supplies: also the pay-office. [Algonquian.]

wank *wangk*, (*vulg. slang*) *v.i* (of men) to masturbate —*n.* an act or instance of masturbation.—*n.* **wank'er** one who masturbates: a worthless, contemptible person.

Wankel engine *wang'kəl en'jin*, a rotary automobile engine having an approximately triangular central rotor turning in a close-fitting oval-shaped chamber rather than conventional pistons and cylinders. [F. *Wankel* (b. 1902), German engineer who invented it.]

wannish. See **wan.**

want *wont*, *n* the state or fact of being without or of having an insufficient quantity· absence or deficiency of necessities: poverty: a lack, deficiency: (in *pl.*) requirements or desires.—*v.t.* to be destitute of or deficient in: to lack, be without: to feel need of, desire: to require, need: to fall short (of something) by (a specified amount).—*v.i.* to be in need or destitution: to lack (with *for*)—*adj.* **want'ed** lacking: needed: desired: searched for, esp. by the police.—*n.* **want'er.**—*adj.* **want'ing** absent, missing, lacking: deficient (with *in*)· below the desired or expected standard (in the phrase **found wanting**).—Also *n.*—*prep.* without, lacking, less.—**want ad** (chiefly *U.S.*) a small advertisement, esp in a newspaper, specifying goods, property, employment, etc. required by the advertiser. [O.N. *vant*, neut. of *vanr*, lacking, and O.N. *vanta*, to lack.]

wanton *won'tən*, *adj.* thoughtlessly cruel: lascivious: immoral, licentious, lewd: unprovoked, unjust, merciless: of animals and inanimate things, frisky, gay, moving freely or capriciously (*poet.*): growing luxuriantly (*poet.*): unrestrained, prodigal.—*n.* a lewd person, esp. female: a trifler.—*v i.* to frolic: to play lasciviously, or amorously: to trifle: to indulge oneself: to grow luxuriantly.—*adv.* **wan'tonly.**—*n.* **wan'-tonness.** [M.E. *wantowen*—pfx. *wan-* (prob. akin to **wane**), O.E. *togen*, pa.p. of *tēon*, to draw, lead, educate.]

wapens(c)haw. See **wappens(c)haw.**

wapentake *wop'n-tāk*, (esp. *hist.*) *n.* a name given in Yorkshire and certain other shires to a territorial division of the county similar to the *hundred* of southern counties. [Late O.E. *wǣpen(ge)tæc*, O.N. *vápnatak*, lit. weapon-taking, assent at a meeting being signified by brandishing a weapon.]

wapins(c)haw. See **wappens(c)haw.**

wapiti *wop'i-ti, n.* a species (*Cervus canadensis*) of deer of large size, native to N. America. [Algonquian.]

wappens(c)haw *wop'n-shō, wap', n.* in Scottish usage, a periodical gathering of the people within an area for the purpose of seeing that each man was armed in accordance with his rank, and ready to take the field when required (*hist.*): a rifle-shooting competition (in *S.Afr.* equivalent to Du. *wapenschouwing*).—Also **wappens(c)haw, wapins(c)haw, weapon-s(c)haw.**—*ns.* **wapp'ens(c)hawing** (app. an older form than wappenshaw), **weap'on-s(c)hawing.** [See **weapon, show.**]

war *wōr, n.* a state of conflict: a contest between states, or between parties within a state (**civil war**) carried on by arms: any long-continued struggle, often against or between impersonal forces (*fig.*): fighting (*poet.*): open hostility: a contest, conflict.—*v.i.* to make war: to carry on war: to contend:—*pr.p.* **warr'ing;** *pa.t.* and *pa.p.* **warred.**—*adj.* of, characteristic of, resulting from, or relating to war.—*adj.* **war'like** of or pertaining to war: martial, military: fond of war: bellicose.—*ns.* **war'likeness; warr'ior** a skilled fighting man (*poet.*), except when used of one at an early stage of civilisation): a redoubtable person.—**war baby** a baby born during a war, esp. a serviceman's illegitimate child: any discreditable or troublesome result of war; **war bonnet** a head-dress, often with long trailing chains of feathers, worn by members of certain N. American Indian tribes; **war bride** a soldier's bride, met as a result of wartime movements or postings; **war chest** funds set aside to pay for a war, political campaign, etc.; **war cloud** a cloud of smoke and dust over a battlefield: a sign that war is threatening or impending (*fig.*); **war correspondent** a journalist or other person assigned to a seat of war so as to give first-hand reports of events; **war crime** one connected with war, esp. one that violates the code of war; **war cry** a cry used in battle for encouragement or as a signal: a slogan (*fig.*); **war dance** a dance engaged in by some savage tribes before going to war: a dance imitating the actions of a battle; **war'fare** (from **fare**, *n.*) an engaging in, waging, or carrying on of war: an armed contest: conflict or struggle of any kind (*fig.*).—*adj.* and *n.* **war'faring.**—**war'-game** a mock or imaginary battle or military exercise used to train personnel in tactics: a game, esp. with detailed rules and using models, in which players enact historical or imaginary battles, etc.; **war'-god, -godd'ess** a deity who presides over war, assigning victory or defeat, etc.; **war'head, war's head** the section of a torpedo or other missile containing the explosive material; **war'-horse** a charger, a horse used in battle: an old warrior in any field of conflict, or any standard, familiar, rather hackneyed piece of music, etc. (*fig.*); **war'lord** a commander or commander-in-chief, esp. where and when the military power is great—now usu. derogatory; **war memorial** a monument erected to the memory of those (esp. from a particular locality) who died in a

war; **war'monger** one who encourages war, esp. for personal gain; **war'mongering; war neurosis** a better term for shellshock; **war paint** paint applied to the face and person by savages, indicating that they are going to war: full-dress, or finery, esp. a woman's make-up (*coll.*); **war'path** among the Red Indians, the path followed on a military expedition: the expedition itself: in **on the warpath** (*fig.*) engaged in conflict, in a mood for battle; **war'plane** any aircraft designed or intended for use in warfare; **war'ship** an armed vessel for use in war; **war'time** a period during which a war is being fought.—*adj.* of or pertaining to, characteristic of, a time of war.—**war'-whoop** a cry uttered on going into battle; **war widow** a woman whose husband has been killed in war.—**carry the war into the enemy's camp, country** to take the offensive boldly (*lit.* and *fig.*); **cold war** an intense, remorseless struggle for the upper hand by all means short of actual fighting; **declare war (on, against)** to announce formally that one is about to begin hostilities: to set oneself to get rid of (*fig.*); **go to war** to resort to armed conflict; **have been in the wars** (*fig.*) to show signs of having been knocked about; **make, wage, war** to carry on hostilities; **private war** warfare between persons in their individual capacity, as by duelling, family feuds, etc.; **total war** with every weapon at the combatant's disposal, sticking at nothing and sparing no-one; **war of nerves** systematic attempts to undermine morale by means of threats, rumours and counter-rumours, etc. [Late O.E. *werre*—O.N.Fr. *werre* (O.Fr. and Fr. *guerre*)—O.H.G. *werra*, quarrel.]

waratah *wor'ə-ta, n.* any of a genus of Australian shrubs with showy flowers. [Native name.]

warble[1] *wor'bl, v.i.* to sing in a quavering way, or with variations (sometimes used disparagingly): to sing sweetly as birds do: to make, or to be produced as, a sweet quavering sound.—*v.t.* to sing in a vibratory manner, or sweetly: to express, or to extol, in poetry or song: to cause to vibrate or sound musically.—*n.* the action, or an act, of warbling: a quavering modulation of the voice: a song.—*n.* **war'bler** one that warbles: a songster: a singing-bird: any bird of the family *Sylviidae*—willow-wren, reed-warbler, whitethroat, blackcap, etc.: any of numerous small, brightly-coloured American birds of a different family, *Parulidae*.—*n.* and *adj.* **war'bling.**—*adv.* **war'blingly.** [O.N.Fr. *werbler*; of Gmc. origin.]

warble[2] *wor'bl, n.* a small hard swelling on a horse's back, caused by the galling of the saddle, etc.: a swelling caused by a warble-fly or a botfly.—**war'ble-fly** any of several flies of the same family as botflies whose larvae cause painful swellings that spoil the hides of horses, cattle, etc.

ward *wörd, v.t.* to parry or keep away (now usually **ward off**).—*n.* an act of watching or guarding: the state of being guarded: a look-out, watch: care, protection: guardianship: custody: a person, as a minor, under a guardian: a means of guarding, as a bolt, bar: a part of a lock of special configuration to prevent its being turned by any except a particular key, or the part of the key of corresponding configuration: an administrative, electoral, etc. division of a town, etc : a division or department of a prison: a room with several beds in a hospital, etc.: the patients in a ward collectively.—*ns.* **ward'en** one who guards or keeps people, animals or things (esp. buildings): a title of certain officers of the crown: a member of certain governing bodies: a superintendent: the head of certain institutions, as schools, colleges, hostels, etc.: one appointed for duties among the civil population in cases of fire or air-raids or to control traffic circulation and parking of motor vehicles; **ward'er** one who guards or keeps: one in charge of prisoners in a jail (*fem.* **ward'ress**)—now officially a 'prison officer'.— *n.* and *adj.* **ward'ing.**—*n.* **ward'ship** the office of, or the state of being under, a guardian: protection, custody (*fig.*): the state of being in guardianship (*fig.*).—**ward'robe** a room or a piece of furniture for containing clothes or theatrical costumes: one's stock of wearing apparel: a department of a royal or noble household having charge of robes, wearing apparel, jewels, etc.; **wardrobe mistress** one who looks after the theatrical costumes of a company or of an individual actor or actress; **wardrobe trunk** a trunk in which clothing may be hung as in a wardrobe; **ward'-room** the mess-room of the officers of a warship: the officers collectively. [O.E. *weardian*.]

-ward(s) -*ward*(z), -*word*(z), *suffs.* forming adjs. and advs. with the sense of motion towards. [O.E. -*weard* (gen. -*weardes*), cog. with Ger. -*wärts*; conn. with O.E. *weorthan*, to become, L. *vertĕre*, to turn.]

warden. See **ward.**

ware[1] *wār, n.* (now usu. in *pl.*) articles of merchandise collectively: pottery, articles of fine workmanship: in composition, with defining word, articles of the same type or material, as *hardware, earthenware.*—*n.* **ware'house** a building or room for storing goods: a shop.—*v.t.* (-*howz*) to deposit in a warehouse, esp. a bonded warehouse: to store up (*fig.*).—*n.* **ware'-housing** the act of depositing goods in a warehouse.—**ware'houseman** a man who keeps, or is employed in, a warehouse or a wholesale store. [O.E. *waru.*]

ware[2] *wār, v.i.* and *v.t.* (*arch.*; usu. in *imper.*) to beware, beware of.—*adv.* **wār'ily.**—*n.* **wāre'iness.**—*adj.* **wār'y** guarding against deception or danger: cautious: circumspect.—**be wary of** to show caution in regard to. [O.E. *wær;* see **aware.**]

warehouse, etc. See **ware**[1].

warfare. See **war.**

warfarin *wör'fɔ-rin, n.* a crystalline insoluble substance ($C_{19}H_{16}O_4$) used as a rodenticide and (in the form of its sodium salt) as a medical anticoagulant. [Wisconsin Alumni Research Foundation (the patent owners) and cou*marin.*]

warily, wariness, etc. See **ware**[2].

warlock *wör'lok, n.* a wizard: a magician (*Scot.*): a demon. [O.E. *wǣrloga,* a breaker of an agreement— *wēr,* a compact, *lēogan,* to lie.]

warlord. See **war.**

warm *wörm, adj.* having moderate heat: hot: imparting heat or a sensation of heat: retaining heat: affecting one, pleasantly or unpleasantly, as heat does (*fig.*): strenuous: harassing: characterised by danger or difficulty: passionate: angry: excited: ardent, enthusiastic: lively, glowing: affectionate: amorous: of a colour, containing red or, sometimes, yellow: esp. in a game, close to discovery or attainment: of a scent or trail, fresh.—*v.t.* to make warmer: to interest: to excite: to impart brightness or suggestion of life to: to beat (*coll.*).—*v.i.* to become warm or ardent.—*n.* a warm area, environment (*coll.*): an act or instance of warming up or being warmed up (*coll.*).—*adv.* warmly.—*adj.* **warmed.**— *ns.* **warm'er; warm'ing** the action of making or becoming warm.—*adv.* **warm'ly.**—*ns.* **warm'ness; warmth.**—*adjs.* **warm'-blood'ed** having bodily temperature constantly maintained at a point usu. above the environmental temperature: ardent, passionate; **warmed'-o'ver** (*U.S.*), **-up'** heated anew.—**warm front** (*meteor.*) the advancing front of a mass of warm air.—*adj.* **warm'-heart'ed** affectionate: hearty: sympathetic: generous.—**warm'-heart'edness; warm'ing-pan** a covered pan, with a long handle, for holding live coals to warm a bed; **warm'-up** a practice exercise before an event: a preliminary entertain-

ment, etc. intended to increase the excitement or enthusiasm of the audience.—**warm up** to make or become warm: to heat, as cooked food: to become animated, interested, or eager: to limber up prior to any athletic event, contest, etc. [O.E. *wearm.*]

warn *wörn, v.t.* to give notice of danger or evil to: to notify in advance: to caution (with *against*): to bid, instruct, to go or to keep away (with *off, away,* etc.; *lit* and *fig.*): to admonish.—*v.i.* to give warning— specif., of a clock about to strike.—*ns.* **warn'er; warn'ing** a caution against danger, etc.: something that gives this: previous notice: notice to quit, etc.: an admonition: the sound just before a clock strikes.— Also *adj.*—*adv.* **warn'ingly.**—**warning coloration** conspicuous coloration on an animal to deter potential attackers. [O.E. *warnian, warenian, wearnian,* to caution, and perh. in part *wiernan,* to refuse, forbid.]

warp *worp, v.t.* to twist out of shape: to turn from the right course: to distort: to pervert, as the mind or character: to misinterpret, give a deliberately false meaning to: to arrange, as threads, so as to form a warp: to move, as a vessel, by hauling on ropes attached to posts on a wharf, etc.: to improve (land) by flooding so that it is covered by a deposit of alluvial mud.—*v.i.* to be twisted out of shape: to become perverted or distorted (*fig.*).—*n.* the state or fact of being warped: the permanent distortion of a timber, etc.: a mental twist or bias (*fig.*): the threads stretched out lengthwise in a loom to be crossed by a woof (also *fig.*): a rope used in towing, one end being fastened to a fixed object: alluvial sediment.—*adj.* **warped.**—*ns.* **war'per; war'ping.** [O.E. *weorpan, werpan.*]

warragal *wor'ɔ-gal, n.* the Australian wild dog, the dingo: a wild Australian horse: an Australian aboriginal.—*adj.* wild, savage.—Also **warr'igal.** [Native word.]

warrant *wor'ɔnt, v.t.* to secure, guarantee the possession of, to: to guarantee to be as specified or alleged: to attest, guarantee, the truth of—(*coll.*) equivalent to 'to be sure, be convinced', 'to be bound' (in phrases **I (I'll) warrant you**): to authorise: to justify, be adequate grounds for.—*n.* one who or that which vouches, a guaranty: a pledge, assurance: a proof: that which authorises: a writ for arresting a person or for carrying a judgment into execution: in the services, an official certificate inferior to a commission: authorisation: justification: a writing authorising the payment of money.—*adj.* **warr'ant-able** that may be permitted: justifiable.—*adv.* **warr'-antably.**—*adj.* **warr'anted.**—*ns.* **warrantee'** one to whom a warranty is given; **warr'anter** one who authorises or guarantees: a warrantor; **warr'anting; warr'antor** (*law*) one who gives warranty: a warranter; **warr'anty** (*law*) an act of warranting: an undertaking or assurance expressed or implied in certain contracts: a guarantee: authorisation: justification: evidence.—**warr'ant-off'icer** in the services, an officer holding a warrant.—**general warrant** a warrant for the arrest of suspected persons, no specific individual being named or described in it. [O.Fr. *warantir* (*guarantir*); cf. Gmc. origin.]

warren *wor'ɔn, n.* a piece of ground kept for breeding game, esp. hares, rabbits, partridges, etc.: a series of interconnected rabbit burrows: the rabbits living there: a densely-populated slum dwelling or district: a maze of narrow passages. [A.Fr. *warenne* (O.Fr. *garenne*), of Gmc. origin.]

warrigal. See **warragal.**

warrior, warship. See under **war.**

wart *wört, n.* a small, hard excrescence on the skin: a small protuberance.—*adjs.* **wart'ed; wart'less;**

wart'y like a wart: overgrown with warts.—wart'-hog any of a genus of wild hogs found in Africa, with large wart-like excrescences on their cheeks.—warts and all with no blemishes or shortcomings concealed. [O.E. *wearte*; prob. allied to L. *verrūca*.]

wartime. See **war.**

wary. See **ware**[2].

was *woz*, used as the *1st* and *3rd pers. sing.* of the *pa.t.* of the verb **to be.** [O.E. *wæs—wesan*, to be.]

wash *wosh*, *v.t.* to cleanse, or to free from impurities, etc., with water or other liquid: to wet, moisten: to have the property of cleansing: (of an animal) to clean by licking: to flow over, past, against: to sweep along, down, etc.: to form or erode by flowing over: to cover with a thin coat of metal or paint: in mining, to separate from earth by means of water.—*v.i.* to clean oneself, clothes, etc., with water: to wash clothes, etc., as one's employment: to stand cleaning (with *well, badly,* etc.): to be swept or carried by water: to stand the test, bear investigation (*coll.*).— *n.* a washing: the process of washing: a collection of articles for washing: that with which anything is washed: a lotion: the break of waves on the shore: the sound of water breaking, lapping, etc.: the rough water left behind by a boat, etc., or the disturbed air behind an aerofoil, etc. (also *fig.*): the shallow part of a river or arm of the sea: a marsh or fen: erosion by flowing water: alluvial matter: a liquor of fermented malt prior to distillation: waste liquor, refuse of food, etc.: a watery mixture: a thin, tasteless drink: a broad but thin layer of colour put on with a long sweep of the brush: a thin coat of paint, metal, etc.: the blade of an oar: in mining, the material from which valuable minerals may be extracted by washing.—*adj.* wash'able.—*ns.* wash'er one who washes: a washing-machine: a ring, usu. flat, of metal, rubber, etc., to keep joints or nuts secure, etc. (perh. a different word); wash'iness the state of being watery: feebleness; wash'ing the act of cleansing, wetting, or coating, with liquid: clothes, or other articles, washed, or to be washed: a thin coating: the action of breaking, lapping, etc.: (usu. in *pl.*) liquid that has been used to wash something, or matter separated or carried away by water or other liquid.—*adj.* that washes: used for washing: washable.—*adj.* wash'y watery, moist: thin, feeble.—*adj.* wash'-and-wear' of garments, easily washed, quick-drying, and requiring no ironing.—wash'-basin, -bowl, wash'hand basin a bowl to wash face, hands, etc., in; wash'-board a corrugated board for rubbing clothes on in washing (also wash'ing-board), also used as a percussion instrument in certain types of music: a thin plank on a boat's gunwale to prevent the sea from breaking over; wash'-cloth a piece of cloth used in washing; wash'-day a day (or the regular day) when one washes one's clothes and linen (also wash'ing-day); wash'-drawing one made with washes.—*adjs.* washed'-out' deprived of colour, as by washing: deprived of energy or animation (*coll.*); washed'-up' deprived of energy or animation (*coll.*): done for, at the end of one's resources (*slang*): finished (with *with*; *slang*).— wash'erman a man who washes clothes, esp. for a living:—*fem.* wash'erwoman; wash'-house, wash'ing-house a house or room for washing clothes in; wash'ing-line a clothes-line; wash'ing-machine a machine for washing clothes; wash'ing-powder a powdered preparation used in washing clothes; wash'ing-soda see **soda**; wash'ing-up' cleaning up, esp. of dishes and cutlery after a meal: collectively, the items of crockery, etc. to be washed after use (washing-up machine a dish-washer); wash'-out a complete failure (*coll.*): a useless person (*coll.*); wash'room a room containing lavatories and facilities for washing: a lavatory

(chiefly *U.S.*); wash'-stand a piece of furniture for holding ewer, basin, and other requisites for washing the person.—come out in the wash (of a stain, etc.) to disappear on washing: to become intelligible, work out satisfactorily (*coll.*); wash away to obliterate; wash down (of liquid) to carry downward: to wash from top to bottom: to help the swallowing or digestion of (a solid food); wash one's hands of see **hand**; wash out to remove by washing: to wash free from dirt, soap, etc.: to disappear or become fainter as a result of washing: to cancel (*coll.*): to exhaust (*coll.*; esp. in *pass.*); wash up to wash one's hands and face (esp. *U.S.*): to wash the dishes and cutlery after a meal: to sweep up on to the shore: to spoil, finish (*coll.*; esp. in *pass.*). [O.E. *wæscan, wascan.*]

wasp *wosp*, *n.* any of a large number of insects belonging to the order *Hymenoptera* and constituting many families, including the *Vespidae*, to which the common wasp (*Vespa vulgaris*) and the European hornet (*Vespa crabro*) belong: a petulant and spiteful person.—*adj.* was'pish like a wasp: having a slender waist, like a wasp: quick to resent an injury: spiteful, virulent.—*adv.* was'pishly.—*n.* was'pishness.—*adj.* was'py waspish.—wasp('s) nest the nest of a wasp: a place very full of enemies or of angry people, or circumstances in which one is assailed indignantly from all sides (*fig.*).—*adj.* wasp'-waist'ed very slender waisted: laced tightly. [O.E. *wæsp, wæps*; cf. L. *vespa.*]

wassail *wos'(ā)l, was'l, n.* the salutation uttered in drinking a person's health (*hist.*): a liquor in which such healths were drunk, esp ale with roasted apples, sugar, nutmeg, and toast (*hist.*): a festive occasion: revelry: a drinking-bout: a drinking or festive song.— *v.i.* to hold a wassail or merry drinking-meeting: to sing good wishes, carols, etc., from house to house at Christmas.—*ns.* wass'ailer one who wassails: a reveller; wass'ailing; wass'ailry. [O.N. *ves heill*, 'be in health'.]

Wassermann('s) reaction, test *väs'ər-man(z) rē-ak'shən, test,* a test of the blood serum, or of the cerebrospinal fluid, to determine whether the person from whom it is drawn is suffering from syphilis [A. von *Wassermann* (1866–1925), German bacteriologist.]

waste *wāst, adj.* uncultivated, and at most sparsely inhabited: desolate. lying unused: unproductive: empty, unoccupied: refuse, rejected, superfluous.— *v.t.* to devastate: to consume, wear out, impair gradually: to cause to decline, shrink physically, to enfeeble: to spend, use, occupy, unprofitably: to use, bestow, where due appreciation is lacking (often in passive): to fail to take advantage of: to turn to waste material.—*v.i.* to be diminished, used up, or impaired by degrees: to lose strength or flesh or weight (often waste away): to be used to no, or little, purpose or affect: to use, consume, spend too lavishly.—*n.* an uncultivated, unproductive, or devastated region: a vast expanse, as of ocean or air: an act or process of wasting: too lavish, or useless, expenditure, or an example of it: squandering: superfluous, refuse, or rejected. material: gradual decay: destruction: loss. —*n.* wâst'age loss by use or natural decay, etc.: (esp. in the phrase natural wastage) loss of employees through retirement, voluntary resignation, etc. rather than forced dismissal: useless or unprofitable spending: loss, or amount of loss, through this.—*adj.* waste'ful characterised by, or addicted to, over-lavishness.—*adv.* waste'fully.—*ns.* waste'fulness; wâst'er one who or that which wastes: a spendthrift: a good-for-nothing (*coll.*): an inferior article, esp. one spoilt in the making: an animal that is not thriving, or that is not suitable for breeding purposes; wâst'ing.—

adj. that is undergoing waste: destroying, devastating: enfeebling.—*n.* **wāst'rel** a waster, esp. a profligate: a neglected child.—*adj.* waste, refuse: of an animal, feeble: going to waste: spendthrift.—**waste'= bas'ket, waste'paper-bas'ket** a basket for holding useless scraps of paper, etc.; **waste'land** a desolate, barren area (*lit.* and *fig.*); **waste paper** used paper no longer required for its original purpose; **waste'-pipe** a pipe for carrying off waste or surplus water; **waste product** material produced in a process that is discarded on the completion of that process; **wasting asset** any asset (esp. a natural resource, such as a mine) whose value decreases with its depletion and which cannot be replaced or renewed.—**go to waste** to be wasted; **lay waste** see **lay²**. [O.Fr. *wast* (*guast*)—L. *vāstus*, waste.]

wat *wät, n.* a Thai Buddhist temple or monastery. [Sans. *vāṭa*, enclosed ground.]

watch *woch, n.* a division of the night, of fixed length (*hist.*): the act or state of remaining on the alert or of observing vigilantly: the lookout: close observation: the act of guarding: surveillance: one who watches: a watchman, or a body of watchmen: a period, usu. of four hours (but see **dog-watch**) of duty on deck: the part of the ship's officers and crew who are on duty at the same time: a sailor's or fireman's turn or period of duty: a small timepiece for carrying in the pocket, on the wrist, etc.—*v.i.* to remain awake: to keep vigil: to be on the alert: to look out (with *for*): to look with attention: to keep guard: to keep guard over (with *over*).—*v.t.* to keep in view, to follow the motions of with the eyes (*lit.* and *fig.*): to look at, observe, attentively: to have in keeping: to guard: to tend: to beware of danger to or from, to be on the alert to guard or guard against (*coll.*): to be on the alert to take advantage of, as an opportunity.—*n.* **watch'er.** —*adj.* **watch'ful** habitually on the alert or cautious: watching or observing carefully: characterised by vigilance: requiring vigilance, or in which one must be on the alert.—*adv.* **watch'fully.**—*n.* **watch'fulness.** —**watch'case** the outer case of a watch; **watch'-chain** a chain for securing a watch to one's clothing; **watch'= committ'ee** a committee of a local governing body exercising supervision over police services, etc., **watch'-dog** a dog kept to guard premises and property: any person or organisation closely monitoring governmental or commercial operations, etc. to guard against inefficiency and illegality (*fig.*); **watch'-glass** a glass covering for the face of a watch: a small curved glass dish used in laboratories to hold small quantities of a solution, etc.; **watching brief** instructions to a counsel to watch a legal case; **watch'maker** one who makes or repairs watches; **watch'making; watch'man** a man who watches or guards, now usu. a building, formerly the streets of a city, at night; **watch'-night** a service lasting until midnight held by various denominations on Christmas Eve or New Year's Eve; **watch'-strap** a strap for fastening a watch round the wrist; **watch'-tower** a tower on which a sentinel is placed to look out for the approach of danger; **watch'word** any signal: a maxim, rallying-cry.—**Black Watch** the 42nd and 73rd Regiments, now the 1st and 2nd Battalions of the Black Watch or Royal Highland Regiment; **on the watch** vigilant, looking out (for danger, etc.); **watch one's step** to step with care: to act warily, be careful not to arouse opposition, give offence, etc. (*fig.*; *coll.*); **watch out** (*coll.*; orig. *U.S.*) to look out, be careful; **watch over** to guard, take care of. [O.E. *wæcce* (n.), *wæccan, wacian* (vb.); cog. with *wacan*, to wake.]

water *wö'tər, n.* in a state of purity, at ordinary temperatures, a clear transparent colourless liquid, perfectly neutral in its reaction, and devoid of taste or smell: extended to the same substance (H_2O) in solid or gaseous state (ice, steam): any body of this (in varying degrees of impurity), as the ocean, a lake, river, etc.: the surface of a body of water: one of the four elements recognised by early natural philosophers: a quantity of the liquid used in any one stage of a washing operation: a liquid resembling or containing water: mineral water: tears: saliva: (usu. in *pl.*) the amniotic fluid, filling the space between the embryo and the amnion: urine: sweat: rain: transparency, lustre, as of a diamond: class, quality, excellence (esp. in the phrase **of the first water**): (in *pl.*) waves, moving water, a body of water.—*v.t.* to wet, overflow, irrigate, supply, dilute with water: to wet and press so as to give a wavy appearance to.— *v.i.* to fill with, or shed, water: of the mouth, to secrete saliva at the sight or thought of food, or (*fig.*) in anticipation of anything delightful: of an animal, to drink: to take in water.—*adj.* pertaining to, or used in, the storage or distribution of water: worked by water: used, living, or operating, on or in water: by way of or across water: made with, or formed by, water.—*adj.* **wa'tered** soaken in or with, sprinkled, supplied with, water: having a supply of water in the form of a river, rivers, etc.: periodically flooded: diluted: marked with a wavy pattern by watering.— *ns.* **wa'terer** a vessel for watering with; **wa'teriness; wa'tering** the act of one who, or that which, waters: dilution with water: the art or process of giving a wavy, ornamental appearance: such an appearance. —*adjs.* **wa'terless** of or pertaining to water: full of water: moist: consisting of, or containing, water: like water: thin or transparent: tasteless: weak, vapid: associated with, or controlling, the sea, the tides, rain, etc.—**wa'ter-bag** a bag for holding water: a camel's reticulum; **wa'ter-bail'iff** an official whose duty it is to enforce byelaws relating to fishing, or to prevent poaching in protected waters; **wa'ter= barr'el, -cask** a barrel, cask, for holding water; **wa'ter-bath** a bath composed of water: a vessel of water in which other vessels can be immersed in chemical work; **Wa'ter-bearer** Aquarius; **wa'ter-bed** a bed whose mattress is a large water-filled plastic bag: a rubber mattress filled with water, sometimes used to prevent bed-sores; **wa'ter-beetle** any of a large number of beetles living on or in water, having fringed legs by means of which they swim easily; **wa'ter-bis'cuit** a thin plain biscuit made with water; **wa'ter-blis'ter** one containing watery fluid, not blood or pus; **wa'ter-boat'man** any of a number of aquatic hemipterous insects having one pair of legs suggestive of sculls.—*adj.* **wa'ter-borne** floating on water: conveyed by water, esp. in a boat: transmitted by means of water, as a disease.—**wa'ter-bott'le** a skin or leather bag, or a glass, rubber, etc., bottle for containing water; **wa'ter-brash** pyrosis, a sudden gush into the mouth of acid fluids from the stomach, accompanied by a burning sensation (heartburn) in the gullet; **wa'ter-breather** any animal that breathes by means of gills.—*adj.* **wa'ter-breathing.**—**wa'ter= buck** any of several antelopes, esp. *Cobus ellipsiprymnus*; **wa'ter-buffalo** the common domestic buffalo (Bubalus) of India, etc.; **wa'ter-bug** any of a large variety of hemipterous insects, including waterboatmen, etc , found in or beside ponds, etc.; **wa'ter= butt** a large barrel for rain-water, usu. kept out of doors; **wa'ter-cannon** a high-pressure hose pipe, used to disperse crowds; **Wa'ter-carrier** Aquarius; **wa'ter= chestnut** a water-plant (*Trapa natans*, or other species) or its edible seed: a Chinese sedge, *Eleocharis tuberosa*, or its edible tuber; **wa'ter-chute** (*-shōōt, -shōōt*) an artificial cascade or slope leading to water, down which people (sometimes in boats or toboggans) slide for sport; **wa'ter-clock** a clock which is made to go by the fall of water; **wa'ter-closet** (abbrev. **W.C.**) a closet used as a lavatory, the discharges being carried off by water; **wa'ter-colour** a pigment diluted with water and gum (or other substance), instead of oil: a painting in such a colour or colours;—*v.t.* **wa'ter-cool** to cool by means of water, esp. circulating water.—*adj.* **wa'ter-cooled.**—**wa'tercooler** a machine for cooling by means of water or for keeping water cool.—*adj.* and *n.* **wa'ter-cooling.**—**wa'tercourse** a channel through which water flows or has flowed: an artificial water-channel: a stream, river; **wa'ter-craft** a boat: boats collectively: skill in swimming, etc., or in managing boats; **wa'tercress** a perennial cress (*Nasturtium officinale*) growing in watery places, used as a salad; **wa'ter-culture** a method of cultivation, often an experimental means of determining the mineral requirements of a plant, the plant being grown with its roots dipping into solutions of known composition; **wa'ter-cure** medical treatment by means of water; **wa'ter-diviner** one who, usu. with the help of a divining-rod, detects, or tries to detect, the presence of underground water; **wa'ter-drinker** a drinker of water: a teetotaller.—*adj.* **wa'tered-down** much diluted (*lit* and *fig.*)—**wa'terfall** a fall or perpendicular descent of a body of water, a cataract or cascade; **wa'ter-flea** the common name for any of numerous minute aquatic crustaceans; **wa'ter-fowl** a fowl that frequents water: swimming game-birds collectively; **wa'terfront** the buildings or part of a town along the edge of and facing the sea, a river etc.; **wa'ter-gas** a mixed gas obtained by passing steam (**blue water-gas**) or steam and air (**semi-water-gas**) over incandescent coke, or other source of carbon; **wa'ter-gate** a floodgate: a gate admitting to a river or other body of water; **Wa'tergate** a U.S. political scandal involving the attempted break-in at the Democratic Party headquarters (the *Watergate* building, Washington D.C.) in 1972 by agents employed by President Richard Nixon's re-election organisation, and the subsequent attempted cover-up by senior White House officials who had approved the break-in; the term has since been extended to describe any similar misuse of power by politicians or other public figures, or any widespread public scandal; **wa'ter-gauge, -gage** an instrument for measuring the quantity or height of water; **wa'ter-glass** a concentrated and viscous solution of sodium or potassium silicate in water, used as adhesive, protective covering, etc., and, esp. formerly, for preserving eggs; **wa'ter-hammer** the noise made by the sudden stoppage of moving water in a pipe: the concussion so caused; **wa'ter-hen** any of a number of ralline birds, esp. *Gallinula chloropus*—also called the moorhen; **wa'ter-hole** a pool in which water has collected, as a spring in a desert or a pool in the dried-up course of a river; **wa'ter-hyacinth** a tropical floating aquatic plant (*Eichhornia crassipes*); **wa'ter-ice** sweetened fruit juice or a substitute diluted with water, frozen and served with meals as a kind of ice cream; **wa'tering-can, -pot** a vessel used for watering plants; **wa'tering-hole** a water-hole, where animals go to drink: a place where humans seek (esp. alcoholic) refreshment (*coll.*); **wa'tering-place** a place where water may be obtained: a place to which people resort to drink mineral water, or for bathing, etc.; **wa'tering-trough** a trough in which horses and cattle drink: a trough between the rails containing water to be scooped up by locomotives; **wa'ter-jacket** a casing containing water placed round, e.g. the cylinder-block of an internal-combustion engine, to keep it cool; **wa'ter-jet;**

wa'ter-jump a place where a jump across a stream, pool, ditch, etc., has to be made, as in a steeplechase; **wa'ter-level** the level formed by the surface of still water; **wa'terlily** a name commonly given to the different species of Nymphaea and Nuphar, and also to other members of the family Nymphaeaceae—the three British species are the white waterlily (*Nymphaea alba*), and the yellow waterlilies (*Nuphar luteum* and *Nuphar minimum*—the latter being rare), **wa'ter-line** any of several lines on a ship to which it is submerged under different conditions of loading: the water-level.—*v.t.* **wa'ter-log** to make unmanageable by flooding with water, as a boat: to saturate with water so as to make heavy or inert, or unfit for use, or to impede life or growth (also *fig.*).—*adj.* **wa'terlogged.**—**wa'ter-main** a large subterranean pipe supplying water; **wa'terman** a man who plies a boat for hire, a boatman, a ferryman: a good oarsman; **wa'termark** the line of the greatest height to which water has risen: a tidemark: a ship's water-line: a distinguishing mark in paper, a design visible by transmitted light.—*v.t.* to mark with a watermark: to impress as a watermark.—**wa'ter-meadow** a meadow kept fertile by flooding from a stream; **wa'ter-melon** a plant (*Citrullus vulgaris*) of the cucumber family, of African origin, having a pulpy, pleasantly flavoured fruit: the fruit itself; **wa'ter-me'ter** an instrument for measuring the quantity of water passing through a particular outlet; **wa'ter-mil'foil** see **milfoil; wa'termill** a mill driven by water; **wa'ter-moc'assin** a poisonous snake of the southern United States; **wa'ter-nymph** a naiad; **wa'ter-pipe** a pipe for conveying water: a hookah; **wa'ter-pistol** a weapon or toy for throwing a jet of water or other liquid; **wa'ter-plant** a plant that grows in water; **wa'ter-plantain** a plant (*Alisma plantago*) having plantain-like leaves: any other plant of the same genus; **wa'ter-po'lo** an aquatic ball-game played by swimmers, seven a side: also, a similar game played by contestants in canoes; **wa'ter-power** the power of water, employed to move machinery, etc.: a flow or fall of water which may be so used —*adj.* **wa'terproof** coated, e.g. with rubber, so as to be impervious to water: so constructed that water cannot enter.—*n* a material or an outer garment made impervious to water.—*v.t.* and *v.i.* to make, become, or be, impervious to water, esp. by coating with a solution.—**wa'terproofing** the act of making any substance impervious to water: the material with which this is done; **wa'ter-pump** a pump for raising water; **wa'ter-rail** the common rail (*Rallus aquaticus*) of Europe, **wa'ter-rat** the popular name of the water-vole: the American musk-rat; **wa'ter-rate** a rate or tax for the supply of water; **wa'ter-reactor** a water-cooled nuclear reactor.—*adjs.* **wa'ter-repell'ent, wa'ter-resis'tant** resistant to penetration by water. treated with a substance which is resistant to water.—**wa'tershed** the line separating two river-basins: a drainage or a catchment area (*erron*): a slope or structure down which water flows: a crucial point or dividing line between two phases, conditions etc.—*adj.* **wa'terside** on the brink of water, shore of a sea, lake, etc —*n.* the edge of a sea, lake, etc., a shore.—*v t* **wa'ter-ski.**—*n.* a type of ski used in water-skiing.—**wa'ter-skiing** the sport of being towed at speed on skis behind a motor-boat; **wa'ter-snake** a snake frequenting the water; **wa'ter-softener** a device or substance for removing the causes of hardness in water; **wa'ter-soldier** an aquatic plant (*Stratiotes aloides*) common in lakes and ditches in the east of England; **wa'ter-splash** a shallow stream running across a road; **wa'ter-spout** a pipe, etc , from which water spouts: the spout of water: torrential rain: a disturbance like a very small tornado, a revolving column of cloud, mist, spray; **wa'ter-sprite** a spirit inhabiting the water; **wa'ter-supply** the obtaining and distribution of water, as to a community: amount of water thus distributed; **wa'ter-table** a moulding or other projection in the wall of a building to throw off the water. the level below which fissures and pores in the strata are saturated with water (*geol.*); **wa'ter-tap** a tap or cock used for letting out water; **wa'ter-thrush** *Seiurus motacilla* or *S. noveboracensis*, N American warblers with brownish backs and striped underparts, living near water.—*adj.* **wa'tertight** so tight as not to admit water or let it escape: such that no flaw, weakness, or source of misinterpretation, can be found in it (*fig.*); **wa'tertightness; water torture** torture using water, esp. dripping it slowly onto the victim's forehead; **wa'ter-tower** a tower containing tanks in which water is stored so that it may be delivered at sufficient pressure for distribution to an area; **water vapour** water in gaseous form, esp. when evaporation has occurred at a temperature below boiling-point, **wa'ter-vole** *Arvicola amphibius*, a large British vole commonly known as the water-rat, **wa'ter-wag'tail** a wagtail, esp the pied wagtail, **wa'terway** any channel for water: a stretch of navigable water: a route over, or by, water; **wa'ter-weed** any plant with very small flowers and leaves growing in ponds, etc.; **wa'ter-wheel** a wheel moved by water an engine for raising water; **wa'ter-wings** a wing-like inflated device for keeping one afloat in water; **wa'terwork** (usu. in *pl.*) any apparatus or plant by which water is supplied, as to a town, etc.: used humorously of shedding tears, euphemistically of the human urinary system.—*adj.* **wa'ter-worn** worn by the action of water.—**above water** out of difficulties, esp. financial; **deep water or waters** water too deep for safety: difficulty or distress (*fig.*); **hold water** to be correct or well-grounded, to bear examination; **keep one's head above water** (*fig.*) to keep solvent; **like water** copiously: extravagantly, recklessly; **make a hole in the water** (*slang*) to drown oneself; **make the mouth water** to arouse a delightful feeling of anticipation or desire, **make water** (of a boat) to leak, take in water; **make, pass, water** to micturate, **oil on troubled waters** anything that allays or assuages, from the effect of pouring oil on rough water; **pour, throw cold water on, over** to discourage by one's unwillingness or indifference; **still waters run deep** a quiet exterior often conceals strong emotions, resolution, cunning, etc.; **under water** below the surface; **water down** (*lit.* and *fig.*) to make less strong; **water of crystallisation, hydration** the water present in hydrated compounds, which, when crystallised from solution in water, retain a definite amount of water; **water of life** spiritual refreshment: whisky, brandy, etc.; **water on the brain** hydrocephalus, **water on the knee** an accumulation of serous fluid in the knee-joint. [O.E. *wæter.*]

Waterloo *wò-tər-lōō'*, or *wo'*, *n.* a final defeat [*Waterloo*, near Brussels, where Napoleon was finally defeated in 1815.]

watertight, waterway, watery. See **water.**

watt *wot*, *n.* the practical and M.K.S. unit of power, equal to a rate of working of one joule per second.— *n.* **watt'age** an amount of power expressed in watts — **watt'-hour'** a common unit of electrical energy, being the work done by one watt acting for one hour, **watt'meter** an instrument containing a series (*current*) and a shunt (*voltage*) coil whose combined torque produces a deflection of the needle that is a direct measure of the circuit power in watts. [James *Watt* (1736–1819).]

wattle *wot'l*, *n.* (collective *sing.* or in *pl*) material for fences, roofs, etc., in the form of rods, branches, etc ,

either interwoven to form a network or loose any of various Australian acacias: (perh a different word) the coloured fleshy excrescence under the throat of some birds, or a similar excrescence or process on any part of the head of a bird, fish, etc.—*v.t.* to bind with wattle or twigs: to form by plaiting twigs.—*adj.* **watt'led.**—*n.* **watt'ling** the act of making wattles by interweaving twigs, etc.: wattle-work, or the material for it.—**watt'le-work** wickerwork.—**wattle and daub** wattle-work plastered with mud and used as a building material [O E *watul, watel.*]

waul, wawl *wol*, *v.t.* to cry as a cat or a newly-born baby.—Also *n.*—*n.* and *adj* **waul'ing, wawl'ing.** [Imit]

wave *wāv*, *n.* a ridge on the surface of a liquid, esp. of the sea: a surge, consisting of vibrating particles of liquid, moving across the surface of a body of liquid such as the sea (*transverse wave*)—the vibrations of the individual particles being at right angles to the line of advance. a unit disturbance in any travelling system of vibrating particles as a light-wave (*transverse wave*) or a sound-wave (*longitudinal wave*—the vibrations of the particles being in the direction of advance): an undulating or vibratory motion (e.g. as a signal), or sound: curved inequality of surface: a line or streak like a wave: an undulation: an undulating succession of curves in hair, or one of these: a movement of the raised hand expressing greeting, farewell etc.: a swelling up or increase, normally followed by a subsidence or decline (*fig.*).—*v.i.* to move like a wave: to move backwards and forwards: to flutter, as a signal. to make a signal in this way: to move the raised hand in greeting, farewell, etc : to undulate.— *v.t.* to move backwards and forwards: to brandish: to waft or beckon. to express by a wave: to direct, signal an instruction to, by a wave. to raise into inequalities of surface. to give an undulating appearance to.— *adjs.* **waved** showing a wave-like form or outline: undulating: of hair, artificially made to undulate: moved to and fro; **wave'less.**—*n.* **wave'let** a little wave.—*adj.* **wave'like.**—*v.i.* **wāv'er** to move to and fro: to shake, be unsteady, be in danger of falling: to falter, show signs of giving way: to vacillate: to vary, change —*n* **wāv'erer**—*n* and *adj.* **wāv'ering.**—*adv.* **wāv'eringly** in a wavering or irresolute manner.—*n.* **wāv'eringness.**—*adjs.* **wāv'erous, wāv'ery** unsteady. —*ns* **wave'son** goods floating on the sea after a shipwreck; **wāv'iness** the state or quality of being wavy.— *n.* and *adj.* **wāv'ing.**—*adj.* **wāv'y** full of, or rising in, waves: playing to and fro: undulating.—**wave'band** a range of wavelengths occupied by transmission of a particular type; **wave energy, wave power** energy or power derived, by means of some device, from the movement of sea waves; **wave'form, wave'shape** a graph showing variation of amplitude of electrical signal, or other wave, against time; **wave'front** in a propagating vibratory disturbance, the continuous locus of points which are in the same phase of vibration; **wave'guide** (*electronics*) a hollow metal conductor, usu. rectangular, within which very high-frequency energy can be transmitted efficiently; **wave'length** the distance between two successive similar points on an alternating wave, e.g. between successive maxima or between successive minima. the distance, measured radially from the source, between two successive points in free space at which an electromagnetic wave has the same phase; **wave mechanics** the part of quantum mechanics dealing with the wave aspect of the behaviour of radiations; **wave'meter** an instrument for measuring wavelengths, directly or indirectly; **wave'-mo'tion** undulatory movement: motion in waves, or according to the same laws, **wave number** in an electromagnetic wave, the reciprocal of the wavelength, i.e. the number of waves in unit distance; **Wavy Navy** the Royal Naval Volunteer Reserve, so called from the undulating gold braid on officers' sleeves.—**make waves** to create a disturbance, make trouble; **on the same wavelength as** in tune with, having the same attitude of mind, background knowledge, etc.; **wave aside** to dismiss (a suggestion, etc.) as irrelevant or unimportant; **wave down** to signal to stop by waving [O.E. *wafian*, to wave.]

wawl. See **waul.**

wax[1] *waks*, *n.* any of a class of substances of plant or animal origin, usu. consisting of esters of monohydric alcohols, e.g. beeswax, $C_{30}H_{61}O \cdot CO \cdot C_{15}H_{31}$: any of certain hydrocarbons of mineral origin: any substance like a wax in some respect, as that in the ear: a substance used to seal letters: that used by shoemakers to rub their thread: a person easily influenced (*fig.*).—*v.t.* to smear, rub, with wax.— *adj.* **wax'en** made of wax: like wax: easily impressed, penetrated, effaced —*ns.* **wax'er** one who or that which waxes; **wax'lness; wax'ing.**—*adj.* **wax'y** resembling wax in texture or appearance: soft: impressible. impressionable (*fig.*): pallid, pasty.—**wax'berry** (the fruit of) the wax-myrtle; **wax'bill** any of various small seed-eating birds of the weaver-finch family with coloured bills like sealing-wax; **wax'-cloth** cloth covered with a coating of wax, used for table-covers, etc.: a popular name for all oil floorcloths; **wax's flower** any of several plants, as of the genus *Hoya* of Australasia; **wax'-light** a candle or taper made of wax; **wax'-myrtle** U.S. candleberry tree; **wax'-palm** either of two S. American palms yielding wax; **wax's paper** paper spread with a thin coating of white wax and other materials; **wax pocket** in bees, a ventral abdominal pouch which secretes wax; **wax'-tree** a tree from which wax is obtained, as a Japanese sumac (*Rhus succedanea*), the wax-myrtle, etc ; **wax'wing** (a member of) a genus of passerine birds (Bombycilla) with small red horny appendages, resembling the red sealing-wax, on their wings; **wax'work** work made of wax, esp. figures or models formed of wax; **wax'-worker**.—*n.sing.* **wax'works** an exhibition of wax figures. [O.E. *weax*]

wax[2] *waks*, *v.i.* to grow or increase, esp. of the moon, as opp to *wane*: to pass into another state, become, as *wax lyrical* (*fig.*). [O.E. *weaxan*.]

wax[3] *waks*, (*coll.*) *n.* a passion, fit of anger.—*adj.* **wax'y** (*coll.*) irate, incensed.

way[1] *wā*, *n.* passage: a road, street, track: direction of motion: the correct or desired route or path: length of space, distance (also in *pl.* (*coll.*, esp. *U.S.*)): distinct: room or opportunity to advance: freedom of action, scope: manner (of life)· condition, state: advance in life: normal, habitual, course or conduct: (in *pl.*) characteristic conduct, idiosyncrasies: manner, style: method: means: course: respect: will: progress or motion through the water, headway (*naut.*): (in *pl.*) the machined surfaces of the top of a lathe bed on which the carriage slides, shears: (in *pl.*) the framework of timbers on which a ship slides when being launched.—**way'-bill** a list of passengers and goods carried by a public vehicle: a list of places to be visited on a journey: a document giving details regarding goods sent by rail; **way'farer** a traveller, esp. on foot.—*n.* and *adj.* **way'faring.**—**way'faring-tree** the *Viburnum lantana*, a large shrub common in hedges.—*v.t.* **waylay'** to lie in ambush for: to attack or seize in the way: to lie in wait for in order to converse with (*fig.*).—**waylay'er; way'-leave** permission to pass over another's ground or property; **way's maker** a pioneer: a precursor; **way'mark** a guide-post: something which serves as a guide to a traveller; **way's**

post a guide-post; **way'slde** the border of a way, path, or highway.—*adj.* growing or lying near the wayside. —**way'-station** (*U.S.*) an intermediate station between principal stations; **way'-traffic** local traffic, as distinguished from through or express traffic; **way'-train** (*U.S.*) a train stopping at most of the stations on a line.—*adj.* **way'worn** worn-out by travel.—**be by way of** to be supposed, alleged (inaccurately) to be, do; **by the way** incidentally: while travelling: beside one's path; **by way of** travelling through, via: as if for the purpose of: in character of, as a substitute for; **come one's way** to come in the same direction: to come within one's experience or reach, to become attainable (*fig.*); **get one's (own) way** to get what one wants; **go; go out of the, one's, way** to give oneself trouble: to make a special point (of doing something); **go the way of all the earth, of all flesh** to die; **have a way** with to be good at dealing with or managing (people, etc.); **have a way with one** to have a fascinating personality or persuasive manner; **have it both ways** (usu. with a *neg.*) to benefit from two actions, situations, arguments, etc., each of which excludes the possibility, validity, etc. of the other; **have it one's (own) way** to do, think, etc. as one pleases, with no regard for others' advice or opinions; **have one's way** to carry one's point, get what one wants; **in a bad way** in a serious condition: very upset; **in a fair way** to likely to succeed in; **in a small, big** (or **large**) **way** on a petty, or a large or grandiose, scale; **in a way** to some extent: from one point of view; **in his,** etc., **(own) way** as far as his, etc., individual merits go, leaving aside the disadvantageous aspects; **in no way** not at all; **in the way** on the way: in the path (*lit.* and *fig.*): impending, obstructing; **lead the way** to act as a guide in any movement; **look the other way** to look away, sometimes deliberately in order not to see someone or something (also *fig.*); **lose the, one's, way** to become lost; **make one's way** to push oneself forward (*lit.* and *fig.*); **make way** to give place: to advance; **one way and another** considering various aspects; **on the, one's, way** moving towards a destination or event: in progress; **on the way out** becoming unpopular, unfashionable, etc.; **out of the way** so as not to hinder or obstruct; **the Way** the Christian Religion (Acts ix. 2, etc.); **under way** in motion, as a vessel; **ways and means** resources: methods e.g. of raising money for the carrying on of government. [O.E. *weg*.]

way[2], **'way** *wā*, *adv* , a shortened form of **away**, far: at a considerable distance or interval of time.—*adj.* **way-out'** (*slang*) lost in what one is doing: excellent, unusual, very satisfying, far-out, eccentric.

wayward *wā'ward*, *adj.* wilful: capricious: irregular.— *adv.* **way'wardly.**—*n.* **way'wardness.** [For **away-ward**—**away**, and suff. **-ward**.]

wazir *wā-zēr'*, *n.* a vizier. [Ar. *wazīr*.]

we *wē*, *pron. pl.* of I: I and others: used for I by monarchs: also used by editors, etc. [O.E. *wē*.]

weak *wēk*, *adj.* wanting strength: not able to sustain a great weight: easily overcome: frail: wanting health: feeble of mind: wanting moral or mental force: impressible, easily led: lacking artistic force: unconvincing: inconclusive: having little of the important ingredient: of a verb, inflected by regular syllabic addition instead of by change of main vowel: of a sound or accent, having little force: of a verse line, having the accent on a normally unstressed syllable: tending downward in price.—*v.t.* **weak'en** to make weaker: to reduce in strength or spirit.—*v.i.* to grow weak or weaker: to become less resolute or determined, show signs of giving in.—*ns.* **weak'ener;** **weak'lness;** **weak'ling** a weak or feeble creature.— *adv.* **weak'ly.**—*adj.* sickly: not robust: feeble.—*n.*

weak'ness the state of being weak: a liking or fondness for.—**weaker sex** women; **weak force, interaction,** a force involved in radioactive decay, supposed to be one of four forces governing the universe.—*adjs.* **weak'-head'ed** having a feeble intellect: easily affected by alcoholic liquor; **weak'-heart'ed** of weak spirit: soft-hearted; **weak'-kneed** having weak knees: weak in will; **weak'-mind'ed** having feeble intelligence: having, or showing, lack of resolution: too easily convinced or persuaded.—**weak's mind'edness; weak moment** a moment of weakness; **weak side, point** that side or point in which a person is most easily influenced or most liable to temptation. [O.N. *veikr*; allied to O.E. *wāc*, pliant—*wīcan*, to yield.]

weal¹ *wēl*, *n.* a sound or prosperous state: welfare.—**the public, general,** or **common, weal** the well-being, interest, and prosperity of the country. [O E. *wela, weola*, wealth, bliss; allied to **well²**.]

weal² *wēl*, *n.* a raised streak left by a blow with a lash, etc. [See **wale**.]

weald *wēld*, (*poet.*) *n* open country or wooded country.—**the Weald** a district, once forested, between the North and South Downs. [O.E. (W S.) *weald*, a forest, wold; cf. **wold**.]

wealth *welth*, *n.* valuable possessions of any kind: riches: an abundance (*fig.*).—*adv.* **wealth'ily.**—*n.* **wealth'iness.**—*adj.* **wealth'y** rich: prosperous. [M.E. *welthe—wele*—O.E. *wela*; see **weal**.]

wean¹ *wān*, (*Scot.*) *n.* a child. [**wee one.**]

wean² *wēn*, *v.t.* to accustom to nourishment other than the mother's milk. to reconcile to the want of anything (with *from*): to estrange the affections of from any object or habit.—*adj* **wean'ling** newly weaned (also *fig.*).—*n.* a child or animal newly weaned. [O.E. *wenian*, to accustom.]

weapon *wep'n*, *n.* any instrument of offence or defence.—*adjs.* **weap'oned; weap'onless** having no weapons.—*n* **weap'onry** weapons collectively: armament. [O.E. *wǣpen*.]

weapon-s(c)haw. See **wappens(c)haw.**

wear¹ *wār*, *v.t.* to be dressed in: to carry on the body: to arrange, as clothes, in a specified way: to display, show of a ship, to fly (a flag): to consume, waste, damage, by use, time, exposure: to make by friction: to exhaust, to weary: to tolerate, accept, or believe—*v.i.* to be wasted by use or time: to consume slowly: to last under use: to resist the ravages of age: to stand the test of time.—*pa.t.* **wore** (*wor, wōr*); *pa.p.* **worn** (*wŏrn, wōrn*).—*n.* the act of wearing: lessening or injury by use or friction: durability: fitness for wearing: articles worn (usu. in composition, as *menswear*): fashion.—*n.* **wearabil'ity.**—*adj.* **wear'able** fit to be worn: good for wearing.—*n.* **wear'er.**—*adj.* **wear'ing** made or designed for wear: consuming: exhausting.—*n.* the process of wasting by attrition or time: the action of carrying on the body, or displaying, or flying: durability: passing.—**the worse for wear** worn, showing signs of wear: showing signs of exhaustion, intoxication, etc.; **wear and tear** damage by wear or use; **wear away** to impair, consume, by wear: to decay or fade out: to pass off; **wear down** (*fig.*) to diminish, or overcome, gradually by persistence; **wear off** to rub off by friction: to diminish by decay: to pass away by degrees; **wear out** to impair by use: to render, become, useless by decay: to consume tediously: to harass; **wear thin** to become thin, threadbare, through use. [O.E. *werian*, to wear.]

wear² *wār*, (*naut.*) *v.t.* and *v.i.* to bring, or be brought, to another course by turning the helm to windward:—*pa.t.* and *pa.p.* **wore.** [Prob. **veer.**]

weary *wē'ri*, *adj.* having the strength or patience exhausted: very tired: causing weariness: tiresome,

tedious.—*v.t.* to make weary: to reduce the strength or patience of: to harass.—*v.i.* to become weary or impatient: to long (with *for*; *Scot.*).—*adj.* **wea'ried** tired.—*adv.* **wea'rily.**—*n.* **wea'riness.**—*adj.* **wea'risome** causing weariness: tedious.—*adv.* **wea'risomely.** [O.E. *wērig*, weary.]

weasand *wē'zənd*, *n.* the gullet· the windpipe: the throat. [O.E. *wǣsand.*]

weasel *wē'zl*, *n.* a small carnivore (*Mustela nivalis*) with long slender body, active, furtive, and bloodthirsty, eating frogs, birds, mice, etc.: any of various related species: a person resembling a weasel, esp. in bad qualities.—*v.i.* to equivocate: to extricate oneself from, circumvent (an obligation, etc.), esp. indefensibly (with *out of, round*, etc.).—*n.* **wea'sel-(l)er.**—*adj.* **wea'selly.**—**weasel word** a word that makes a statement evasive or misleading.—**weasel out** to evade obligation. [O.E. *wesle*.]

weather *wedh'ər*, *n.* atmospheric conditions as to heat or cold, wetness, cloudiness, etc.: type or vicissitude of atmospheric conditions or of fortune.—*v.t.* to affect by exposing to the air: to sail to the windward of: to come safely through (*lit.* and *fig.*): to slope, as a roof.—*v.i.* to become discoloured, disintegrated, etc., by exposure.—*adj.* (*naut.*) toward the wind, windward —*adj.* **weath'ered** having the surface altered in colour, form, texture, or composition by the action of the elements (*geol.*): seasoned by exposure to weather: made slightly sloping so as to throw off water (*archit.*).—*n.* **weath'ering** the action of the elements in altering the form, colour, texture, or composition of rocks (*geol.*): seasoning by weather: a slight inclination given to the top of a cornice or moulding, to prevent water from lodging on it (*archit.*): the act of passing to windward of (*naut.*).—*adj.* **weath'er-beaten** damaged or worn away by, or seasoned by, the weather.—**weath'er-board** a board shaped so as to shed water from a building.—*v.t.* to fit with such planks or boards.—**weath'er-boarding** thin boards placed overlapping to keep out rain: exterior covering of a wall or roof.—*adj.* **weath'er-bound** detained by bad weather.—**weath'er-box, -house** a toy constructed on the principle of a barometer, consisting of a house with the figures of a man and wife who come out alternately as the weather is respectively bad or good; **weath'er-chart** a weather-map, chart; **weath'ercock** a vane (often in the form of a cock) to show the direction of the wind: one who changes his opinions, allegiance, etc., easily and often; **weath'er-eye** the eye considered as the means by which one forecasts the weather (also *fig.*); **weather forecast** a forecast of the weather based on meteorological observations; **weath'er-glass** a glass or instrument that indicates the changes of the weather: a barometer; **weather-house** see **weather-box; weath'erman** one who prepares weather forecasts or who delivers such forecasts on radio or television.—**weath'er-map** a map indicating meteorological conditions over a large tract of country.—*adj.* **weath'er-proof** proof against rough weather.—*v.t.* to make weather-proof.—**weather report** loosely, a weather forecast; **weath'er-ship** a ship engaged on meteorological work; **weath'er-station** a station where phenomena of weather are observed; **weath'er-strip** a thin piece of some material used to keep out wind and cold; **weath'er-symbol** a conventional sign indicating a meteorological phenomenon; **weath'er-vane** a weathercock; **weather window** a period of time in which the weather is suitable for a particular purpose, e.g. oil-drilling (also *fig.*).—*adj.* **weath'er-wise** skilful in foreseeing the changes of the weather (*lit.* and *fig.*).—*adv.* with regard to weather conditions.—*adj.* **weath'er-worn** worn away or damaged by wind, storms, etc.—**keep one's weather eye open** to be alert: to keep a sharp lookout; **make heavy weather of** to find excessive difficulty in; **under the weather** indisposed, seedy: drunk; **weather out** to hold out against till the end; **weather the storm** to come safely through a period of difficulty, etc. [O.E. *weder*.]

weave[1] *wēv, v.t.* to make by crossing threads, strands, etc., above and below one another: to interlace, as in a loom to form cloth: to work into a fabric, story, etc.: to depict by weaving: to unite, work into a whole: to construct, contrive.—*v.i.* to practise weaving:—*pa.t.* **wōve**, *rarely* **weaved;** *pa.p.* **wōv'en;** *cf.* **wove.**—*n.* the texture of a woven fabric.—*ns.* **weav'er** one who weaves: any bird of a passerine family (*Ploceidae*) resembling the finches, so called from their remarkable woven nests; **weav'ing** the act or art of forming a web or cloth by the intersecting of two distinct sets of fibres, threads, or yarns—those passing longitudinally from end to end of the web forming the *warp*, those crossing and intersecting the warp at right angles forming the *weft.*—**weav'er-bird** a weaver or, less commonly, a weaver-finch; **weav'er-finch** any member of a family of small finch-like birds (*Estrildidae*) which includes the waxbills. [O.E. *wefan*.]

weave[2] *wēv, v.i.* to move to and fro: to wind in and out: to move back or forward with sinuous movements of the body (*boxing*).—*n.* and *adj.* **weav'ing.**—**get weaving** (*slang*) to get busy, get on the move. [M.E. *weve*.]

web *web, n.* that which is woven: a whole piece of cloth as woven in the loom: a kind of cloth or weave: a thin metal plate or sheet: in paper-making, an endless wire-cloth working on rollers: a large sheet or roll of paper: any connective tissue (*anat.*): the fine texture spun by the spider, etc., as a snare: the skin between the toes of water-fowl, etc.: anything like a cloth web in complication or a spider's web in flimsiness or in power to entangle: a plot, snare.—*v.t.* to envelop, or to connect, with a web.—*adj.* **webbed** having a web: having the toes or fingers united by a web of skin.—*n.* **webb'ing** a narrow woven fabric of hemp, used for belts, etc., for various purposes in upholstery: the webs of webbed hands or feet.—*adj.* **webb'y.**—*adj.* **web'-fing'ered.**—**web'-foot** a foot the toes of which are united with a web or membrane.—*adj.* **web'-foot'ed.**—**web offset** a method of offset printing using a reel of paper.—*adj.* **web'-toed.**—**web'wheel** a wheel in which the rim, spokes and centre are formed from one single piece of material: a wheel with a web or plate instead of spokes. [O.E. *webb*; from root of **weave**[1].]

weber *vā'bər, wē'bər, n.* the M.K.S. unit of magnetic flux. [Wilhelm *Weber*, German physicist (1804–91).]

wed *wed v.t.* to marry: to join in marriage: to unite closely.—*v.i.* to marry:—*pr.p.* **wedd'ing;** *pa.t.* **wedd'ed** or, *dial.*, **wed;** *pa.p.* **wedd'ed** or, *dial.* and *poet.*, **wed.**—*adj.* **wedd'ed** married: of or pertaining to marriage: closely joined; persistently devoted.—*n.* **wedd'ing** marriage: marriage ceremony.—**wedd'ing-breakfast** a meal served after a wedding; **wedd'ing-cake** a highly decorated cake served at a wedding, and also divided among absent friends; **wedd'ing-day** the day of marriage: its anniversary; **wedd'ing-dress** a bride's dress; **wedd'ing-march** music in march time played as the bride's party enters the church and at the close of a marriage ceremony; **wedd'ing-ring** a plain, usu. gold, ring given by the groom to the bride at a wedding: any more or less similar ring given by the bride to the groom.—**silver, golden, diamond wedding (anniversary)** the celebrations of the 25th,

50th, and 60th anniversaries of a wedding. [O.E. *weddian*, to promise, to marry (Ger. *wetten*, to wager)—*wedd*, a pledge.]

we'd *wēd,* a contraction of **we had** or **we would.**

wedge *wej, n.* a piece of wood or metal, thick at one end and sloping to a thin edge at the other, used in splitting, fixing tightly, etc.: anything shaped more or less like a wedge, as:—a formation of troops, the flying formation of geese and other wildfowl, a large piece, e.g. of cake, a stroke in cuneiform characters: an iron-headed golf-club with much loft used for approaching: a stroke with such a club: a shoe in which the heel and sole together form a wedge and there is no gap under the instep (also **wedge-heeled shoe**).—*v.t.* to cleave with a wedge: to force or drive with a wedge: to thrust in tightly: to crowd closely: to fasten or fix with a wedge or wedges: to make into a wedge.—*v.i.* to force one's way like a wedge: to become fixed or jammed by, or as if by, a wedge: to make a stroke with a wedge (*golf*).—*adj.* **wedged.**—*adj.* **wedge'-shaped** shaped like a wedge.—**the thin**, or **small, end of the wedge** a small beginning that is bound to be followed by a large or significant development. [O.E. *wecg*.]

Wedgwood® *wej'wŏŏd, n.* superior pottery, including that lightly glazed with cameo reliefs in white, made by Josiah *Wedgwood* (1730–95) and his successors.

wedlock *wed'lok, n.* matrimony: the married state, esp. in the phrase **born in,** or **out of, wedlock,** i.e. legitimate or illegitimate. [O.E. *wedlāc—wedd,* a pledge, and suff. *-lāc* implying action of some kind.]

Wednesday *wenz'di, wed'nz-di, n.* the fourth day of the week. [O.E. *Wōdnes dæg,* Woden's day.]

wee[1] *wē,* (*Scot.*) *adj.* tiny. [M.E. *we, wei,* a bit, time, or space, as in phrase *a little wei.*]

wee[2] *wē, interj.* imitating the squeal of a young pig.—Also *v.i.* and *n.*

wee[3] *wē.* Same as **wee-wee.**

weed[1] *wēd, n.* any useless plant of small growth: any plant growing where it is not wanted by man: any wild herb: anything useless, troublesome, or obnoxious: a worthless, contemptible fellow: (often with *the*) tobacco, or a cigar or cigarette (*coll.*): marijuana (*slang*).—*v.t.* to free from weeds: to remove, uproot (weeds, etc.) (often with *out*): to identify and remove (something or someone inferior, unwanted, *etc.*) from a group or collection (*usu.* with *out*).—*v.i.* to remove weeds.—*adj.* **weed'ed.**—*ns.* **weed'er;** **weed'iness; weed'ing** the action of the verb to weed: what is weeded out.—*adjs.* **weed'less; weed'y** weedlike: full of weeds: lanky, ungainly: of worthless, insipid, etc. character.—*adj.* **weed'-grown** overgrown with weeds.—**weed'killer** anything, esp. a chemical preparation, for killing weeds. [O.E. *wēod,* a herb.]

weed[2] *wēd, n.* a garment, or (as collective *sing.*) clothing (*arch.*): (in *pl.*) a widow's mourning apparel. [O.E. *wǣd, wēde,* clothing.]

week *wēk, n.* the space of seven days, esp. from Sunday to Saturday (inclusive): the working days of the week: (in *pl.*) an indefinite period.—*adj.* **week'ly** coming, happening, or done, once a week.—*adv.* once a week: every week.—*n.* a publication appearing once a week.—**week'day** any day of the week except Sunday, and now usu. also excluding Saturday; **week'-end, week'end** (or *-end'*) the non-working period from Friday evening to Sunday evening (a **long week-end** usu. incorporating Friday and Monday or yet more liberally extended).—*v.i.* to spend a week-end holiday.—**week-end'er; week-end'ing; week'night** the evening or night of a weekday.—**a week, two weeks,** etc. **today** one week, two weeks, etc. from today; **Great Week, Holy Week, Passion Week** the week preceding Easter Sunday; **this day week** a week from today; **week about** in alternate periods of seven days; **week in, week out** continuously without a break. [O.E. *wice*.]

ween *wēn*, (*arch.* or *obs.*) *v.t.* to think or fancy: to believe: to expect. [O.E. *wēnan*.]

weeny *wē'ni*, (*coll.* esp. *childish*) *adj.* very small, tiny. [*wee* and *tiny* or *teeny*.]

weep *wēp*, *v.i.* to express grief by shedding tears: to wail or lament: to drip, rain: to ooze in drops: to leak: to exude: to be pendent, as a weeping-willow.—*v.t.* to lament: to pour forth: to express while, or by, weeping: to exude:—*pa t.* and *pa.p.* **wept.**—*ns.* **weep'er; weep'ie, weep'y** (*slang*) a highly emotional film, play or book.—*n.* and *adj.* **weep'ing.**—*adv.* **weep'ingly.**—*adj.* weep'y tearful (*coll.*).—**weep'ing-willow** an ornamental Chinese willow (*Salix babylonica*), with pendent branches. [O.E. *wēpan*; allied to *wēp*, clamour.]

weever *wē'vər*, *n.* a genus of fishes (Trachinus), of which two species are British, with sharp dorsal spines capable of inflicting serious wounds. [Prob. O.Fr. *wivre*, serpent, weever—L. *vipera*.]

weevil *wēv'l*, *n.* a popular name for a large number of beetles with the anterior part of the head prolonged into a beak or proboscis, which, either in the larval or the adult form, damage fruit, nuts, grain, or trees: any insect injurious to stored grain.—*adjs.* **weev'illed, weev'lled, weev'illy, weev'ily** infested by weevils. [O.E. *wifel*.]

wee-wee *wē'wē*, (*coll.*, esp. *childish*) *n.* the act of urinating: urine.—Also *v.i.*

weft *weft*, *n.* the threads woven into and crossing the warp: the thread carried by the shuttle (also **woof**): a web: a film, cloud. [O.E. *weft, wefta*; allied to *wefan*; see **weave**[1].]

weigh[1] *wā*, *v.t.* to compare with by, or as if by, the balance (with *against*): to find the heaviness of: to be equal to in heaviness: to counterbalance: to raise, as a ship's anchor: to apportion: to hold in the hand(s) in order to, or as if to, estimate the weight: to estimate the value of: to ponder in the mind, consider carefully: to consider worthy of notice—*v.i.* to have weight: to be considered of importance: to press heavily: to weigh anchor.—*adjs.* **weigh'able** capable of being weighed; **weighed** experienced: considered, balanced.—*ns.* **weigh'er; weigh'ing; weight** the heaviness of a thing, esp. as determined by weighing: quantity as determined in this way: the force with which a body is attracted to the earth, measured by the product of the mass and the acceleration: a mass of metal adjusted to a standard and used for finding weight: a method of estimating, or a unit of, weight: the amount something ought to weigh: a standard amount that a boxer, etc., should weigh: a heavy object: anything heavy or oppressive: a ponderous mass: pressure: importance: power: impressiveness: the frequency of an item in a frequency distribution or a number indicating this.—*v.t.* to make more heavy (*lit.* and *fig.*): to attach weights to: to hold down in this way: to increase the weight of, as fabrics, by adding chemicals: to assign a handicap weight to (a horse; also *fig.*): to oppress, burden: to attach numbers indicating their relative frequency to (items in a frequency distribution).—*adv.* **weigh'tily.**—*ns.* **weigh'tiness; weight'ing** a weighting allowance.—*adj.* **weight'less.**—*n.* **weight'lessness** the condition of a freely falling body at the beginning of the fall when its inertia exactly balances the gravitational force, or that of a space traveller and his unpowered space craft in orbit beyond the earth's atmosphere.—*adj.* **weigh'ty** heavy: important: having much influence: being the fruit of judicious consideration and hence worthy of attention.—**weigh'bridge** a machine for weighing vehicles with their loads; **weigh'ing-machine** a machine or apparatus for weighing; **weigh-out** see **weigh out**; **weighting allowance** a salary differential to balance the higher cost of living in a particular area; **weight'-lifter; weight'-lifting** a sport in which competitors lift and hold above their heads (or attempt to) a barbell made increasingly heavy as the competition progresses; **weight'-watcher** a person, esp. female, who is attempting to reduce weight by careful dieting, esp. one who attends meetings of an association of like people.—**throw one's weight about** to over-exercise one's authority: to domineer; **weigh down** to force down: to depress (*fig.*): to preponderate over, outweigh; **weigh in** to ascertain one's weight before a boxing match or other sports competition, or after a horse-race (*n.* **weigh'-in**): to join in a project (*slang*); **weigh in with** (*fig.*) to produce (a new argument, etc.) in a discussion; **weigh out** to weigh and dispense in portions accordingly: to ascertain one's weight before a horse-race (*n.* **weigh'-out**); **weigh up** to force up (*lit.* and *fig.*): to consider carefully and assess the quality of, as a person (*coll.*); **weigh with** (*fig.*) to appear important to, to influence. [O.E. *wegan*, to carry.]

weigh[2] *wā*, *n.* a variant of **way** in the phrase 'under way', through confusion with the phrase 'to weigh anchor'.

weight. See **weigh**[1].

weir *wēr*, *n.* a dam across a river: a fence of stakes set in a stream for catching fish. [O.E. *wer*, an enclosure, allied to *werian*, to protect.]

weird *wērd*, (*arch.* and *Scot.*), *n.* fate: (*cap.*; in *pl.*) the Fates.—*adj.* concerned with, controlling, fate: unearthly, uncanny: peculiar, odd (*coll.*).—*ns.* **weird'ie, weird'o** (*pl.* **weird'os**) an eccentric: someone unconventional in dress, etc.—*adv.* **weird'ly.**—*n.* **weird'ness.**—**the Weird Sisters** the Fates: the Fates of Scandinavian mythology: the witches in *Macbeth*. [O.E. *wyrd*, fate; allied to *weorthan*, to become.]

Weismannism *vīs'man-izm*, *n.* the doctrine in biology of August Weismann (1834–1914), whose central teaching is that acquired characters are not transmitted.

weka *we', wā', or *wē'kə*, *n.* any of the flightless rails (Ocydromus) of New Zealand. [Maori, imit.]

welch *welsh*, an old form of **welsh**.

welcome *wel'kəm*, *adj.* received with gladness: admitted willingly: causing gladness: free (to): free to take or enjoy.—*n.* the act of welcoming: a kindly reception: a reception.—*v.t.* to greet: to receive with kindness or pleasure: to accept or undergo gladly.—*interj.* expressing pleasure, as to a guest on his arrival.—*ns.* **wel'comeness; wel'comer.**—**he's, you're,** etc. **welcome** it is (or was) no trouble, no thanks are needed; **make someone welcome** to welcome someone, make him feel welcome; **outstay one's welcome** to stay too long; **wear out one's welcome** to stay too long or visit too often. [O.E. *wilcuma*—*wil-*(*willa*, will, pleasure), and *cuma*, guest, with later alteration suggesting a connection with **well**[2] and **come**, prob. under the influence of e.g. O.Fr. *bien venuz*; cf. O.N. *velkominn*.]

weld[1] *weld*, *n.* a scentless species of mignonette, also known as dyer's rocket, yielding a yellow dye: the dye itself. [Cf. Ger. *Wau*.]

weld[2] *weld*, *v.t.* to join (two pieces of metal) by raising the temperature at the joint by means of external heat or (**resistance welding**) of a heavy electric current or (**arc welding**) of an electric arc and then applying pressure, or (**cold welding**) by pressure alone: to join closely.—*v.i.* to undergo welding: to be capable of being welded.—*n.* a welded joint.—*n.* **weldabil'ity.** —*adj.* **weld'able.**—*n.* **weld'er, weld'or.**—*n.* and *adj.*

weld'ing.—*adj.* **weld'less** having no welds.—*n.* **weld'-ment** the action or process of welding: a welded assembly. [Same as obs. or dial. verb **weld**, meaning melt, weld.]

welfare *wel'fār, n.* the state of faring or doing well. freedom from calamity, etc.: enjoyment of health, etc.: prosperity: welfare work.—*ns.* **wel'farism** the social policies characteristic of a welfare state; **wel'farist.**—**welfare state** a state in which socialist principles have been put into effect with the purpose of ensuring the welfare of all who live in it; **welfare work** efforts to improve conditions of living for a class, as the very poor, or a group, as employees or workers; hence **welfare worker.** [**well²**, **fare**.]

welkin *wel'kin, n.* the sky or region of clouds. [O.E *wolcnu*, pl. of *wolcen*, cloud, air, sky.]

well¹ *wel, n.* a spring: a mineral spring: a source (*fig.*): a lined shaft sunk in the earth whence a supply of water, oil, etc., is obtained: an enclosure in a ship's hold round the pumps: the vertical opening enclosed between the outer ends of the flights in a winding stair: a lift-shaft: a cavity.—*v.i.* to issue forth, as water from the earth (*lit.* and *fig.*).—*v.t.* to pour forth.—*n* **well'ing** an outpouring.—**well'-head** the source of a spring: a fountain-head (*fig.*): the top of a well, or a structure built over it; **well'-hole** a hole for a well of any kind: the shaft of a well: a shaft for machinery; **well'-house, well'-room** a room built over a well; **well'-sinker** one who digs wells; **well'-sinking; well'-spring** a fountain.—**well over** to overflow [O.E. *wella*; cf. *weallan*, to boil.]

well² *wel* (*compar.* **bett'er;** *superl.* **best**), *adj* (usu. predicative) good in condition: in health: fortunate: comfortable: satisfactory.—*adv.* rightly: skilfully: thoroughly: intimately: favourably, successfully: abundantly: with some degree of luxury: with reason or propriety: conveniently: to a considerable extent: clearly: easily: very possibly: very, esp. in combination: so be it (as a sign of assent).—*interj.* expressing surprise, hesitation, resignation, etc , or introducing resumed narrative.—*adjs.* **well'-acquaint'ed** having intimate personal knowledge; **well'-advised'** prudent; **well'-aimed'; well'-appoint'ed** well-equipped.—**well'-appoint'edness.**—*adjs.* **well'-bal'anced** having the parts properly adjusted for smooth working: sane and sensible; **well'-behaved'** behaving or acting in accordance with propriety or with requirements.—**well'-be'ing** welfare.—*adjs.* **well'-beloved'** (*-luvd'* or *-luv'id*) very dear; **well'-born'** born of a good family, not of mean birth, **well'-bred'** educated to polished manners: of good stock; **well'-built'** (of a building, buildings, a person, a garment, etc.) of strong or well-proportioned make or form, **well'-chos'en** (now esp. of words in a speech) carefully chosen; **well'-connec'ted** having friends or relatives in positions of importance or in the upper social strata; **well'-defined'** clearly and precisely determined; **well'-devel'oped** having developed to an advanced, elaborate, good, desirable, etc. state, **well'-direct'ed** skilfully aimed (*lit.* and *fig.*); **well'-disposed'** well-placed or well-arranged: inclined to be friendly: favourable; **well'-dressed'** wearing stylish clothes; **well'-earned'** thoroughly deserved; **well'-ed'ucated** having a good education; **well'-fa'voured** good-looking; **well'-fed'** plump: given nutritious food; **well'-formed'** shapely, well-proportioned: correct according to the established rules of grammar (*linguistics*); **well'-found'** adequately provided, fully equipped; **well'-found'ed** built on secure foundations: based on solid evidence or sound reasoning; **well'-groomed'** well-dressed; **well'-ground'ed** firmly founded; **well'-heeled'** prosperous, rich; **well'-hung'** hung skilfully: of meat, hung long enough to mature;

well'-informed' having sound and sufficient information on a particular subject: full of varied information; **well'-inten'tioned** having, or arising from, good intentions or purpose; **well'-judged'** correctly calculated, judicious; **well'-judg'ing; well'-known'** fully known: celebrated: notorious; **well'-made'; well'-mann'ered** polite; **well'-marked'** obvious, decided; **well'-mean'ing** well-intentioned; **well'-meant'** rightly, kindly, intended.—*adv.* **well'-nigh** nearly, almost.—*adjs.* **well'-off'** in good circumstances; **well'-oiled'** (*slang*) drunk; **well'-ord'ered** correctly governed: properly arranged; **well'-placed'** in a good position (for some purpose): in a position senior enough or intimate enough to gain information, etc.; **well'-preserved'** in good condition, not decayed: looking youthful or younger than one's age; **well'-propor'tioned** having correct or pleasing proportions; **well'-read'** (*-red'*) of wide reading; **well'-reg'ulated** well-ordered; **well'-respect'ed** highly esteemed; **well'-round'ed** suitably curved: symmetrical: well constructed and complete; **well'-set'** properly arranged, or well placed: fitly put together: firmly fixed: strongly built; **well'-set-up'** (*coll.*) well-built, shapely; **well'-spent'** spent usefully or profitably; **well'-spo'ken** spoken well or fittingly: ready, graceful, or courteous in speech; **well'-thought'-of** esteemed; **well'-thought-out'** reasoned soundly and arranged with skill; **well'-thumbed'** showing marks of much handling; **well'-timed'** opportune: keeping accurate time; **well'-to-do'**, prosperous, well-off; **well'-trodd'en** frequently followed or walked along (usu. *fig.*); **well'-turned'** accurately rounded: shapely: felicitously expressed; **well'-uphol'stered** (*facet.*; of a person) plump, fat.—**well'-wisher.**—*adj.* and *n.* **well'-wishing.**—*adjs.* **well'-won'** gained honestly or by hard endeavour; **well'-worked-out'** thoroughly or logically planned or developed; **well'-worn'** much worn: trite.—**all very well** an ironic phrase used to introduce an objection to what has gone before; **as well as** in addition to: no less than; **very well** a phrase signifying assent, sometimes ironic; **well and good** a phrase signifying acceptance of facts or a situation, **well and truly** completely, thoroughly; **well away** progressing rapidly: far away: drunk (*slang*); **well done** an expression of praise: (of meat) well, thoroughly, cooked; **well enough** in a moderate but sufficient degree; **well in** (*coll.*) having a good relationship: prosperous (*Austr.*); **well now, well then** phrases used to preface questions, conclusions, comments, or requests for such, or other remarks; **well up in** (*coll.*) well versed in, well acquainted with; **well, well** an expression of surprise; **wish someone well** to wish someone success or good fortune. [O.E. *wel.*]

we'll *wēl*, a contraction of **we will** or **we shall.**

wellie. See **welly.**

Wellingtonia *wel-ing-tō'ni-ə, n.* a synonym of Sequoia. [Named after the Duke of *Wellington* (1769–1852).]

wellingtons *wel'ing-tənz, n.pl.* a kind of riding-boots covering the knee in front, but cut away behind. rubber boots loosely covering the calves: (in *sing.*) one of a pair of wellingtons.—Also **wellington boot.** [As previous word.]

welly, wellie *wel'i,* (*coll.*) *n.* a wellington of the loose rubber kind.—Also **well'y-, well'ie-boot'.**

Welsh *welsh, adj.* pertaining to *Wales* or its inhabitants.—*n.pl.* the inhabitants of Wales.—*n.sing.* their language.—**Welsh dresser** a dresser usu. with open shelves above cupboards and drawers; **Welsh harp** a large harp with three rows of strings, two tuned in unison and in the diatonic scale, the third in the sharps and flats of the chromatic; **Welsh'man** a native of Wales; **Welsh rabbit, Welsh rarebit** see **rabbit;**

Welsh'woman. [O.E. (Angl. and Kentish) *welisc—wealh*, foreigner; Anglo-Saxons' name for Britons, etc.]

welsh *welsh*, *v.i.* to run off from a race-course without settling or paying one's bets: to dodge fulfilling an obligation.—*v.t.* to cheat in such a way.—Also **welch**. —*n.* **welsh'er**, **welch'er**.

welt *welt*, *n.* a band or strip fastened to an edge to give strength or for ornament: a narrow strip of leather used in one method of sewing the upper to the sole of a shoe: a weal: a lash, blow.—*v.t.* to furnish with a welt: to lash, beat.

welter *wel'tar*, *v.i.* to be, or lie, soaked, as in blood (*poet.*): to be sunk (in) (*lit.* and *fig.*): to roll, toss, about in the waves: to roll, surge, as the sea (*poet.*).—*n.* a state of turmoil or confusion: confusion, agitation: a surging mass.—*adj.* **wel'tering**. [M.Du. *welteren*; cf. O.E. *gewæltan*, to roll.]

welter-weight *wel'tar-wāt*, *n.* a boxer over 61 kg (9 st 9 lb), amateur 63·5 kg (10 st), and not over 66 kg (10 st 7 lb), amateur 67 kg (10 st 8 lb): a wrestler over 68 kg (10 st 10 lb) and not over 74 kg (11 st 8 lb).

wen[1] *wen*, *n.* a sebaceous cyst.—*adjs.* **wenn'ish**, **wenn'y** wen-like. [O.E. *wen(n)*, a swelling, a wart.]

wen[2] *wen*, *n.* a rune (**⊳**), having the value of modern English *w*, adopted (as **⊳⊳**) into the O.E. alphabet. [O.E., orig. *wynn*, joy (of which *w* is the initial letter).]

wench *wench*, *-sh*, *n.* a damsel, girl: a working-girl, a maid-servant: a whore (*obs.* or *arch.*).—*v.i.* to frequent the company of whores: to associate innocently with women.—*n.* **wench'er** one who indulges in lewdness. [O.E. *wencel*, a child.]

wend *wend*, *v.t.* to turn to the opposite tack (*naut.*).—*v.i.* to make one's way (*arch.*; also *fig.*):—*pa.t.* and *pa.p.* **wend'ed**, (*obs.*) **went** (now used as *pa.t.* of **go**).—**wend one's way** to make one's way, follow the road, esp. in a leisurely fashion. [O.E. *wendan*, a common Gmc. verb.]

Wend *wend*, *n.* one of a branch of the Slavs which once occupied the north and east of Germany: one of the Slavic population of Lusatia (part of Brandenburg, Saxony and Silesia) who still speak the Wendish tongue.—*adjs.* **Wend'ic**, **Wend'ish**.—*ns.* the Wendish language. [Ger. *Wende*.]

Wendy House® *wen'di hows*, a structure of cloth or the like, decorated to simulate a little house, stretched over a rigid frame, usu. erected indoors for children to play in. [From the house built for *Wendy* in J. M. Barrie's *Peter Pan*.]

wennish, **wenny**. See **wen[1]**.

Wensleydale *wenz'li-dāl*, *n.* a breed of long-woolled sheep: a variety of cheese. [*Wensleydale* in North Riding of Yorks.]

went *went*, properly *pa.t.* of **wend**, but now used as *pa.t.* of **go**.

wentletrap *wen'tl-trap*, *n.* any member of a genus (Scalaria) of gasteropod molluscs, having a spiral shell with many deep whorls, crossed by elevated ribs. [Du. *wenteltrap*, a winding staircase, a spiral shell.]

wept *wept*, *pa.t.* and *pa.p.* of **weep**.

were *wûr*, *v.i.* the *pl.* of **was**, used as *pa.t.* (*pl.*) and *pa.subj.* (*sing.* and *pl.*) of **be**. [O.E. *wǣron*, subj. *wǣre*.]

we're *wēr*, a contraction of **we are**.

werewolf *wēr'wŏŏlf*, *wûr'wŏŏlf*, *n.* a person supposed to be able to change himself for a time into a wolf. [O.E. *werwulf—wer*, man, *wulf*, a wolf.]

wergild *wûr'gild*, **weregild** *wēr'gild*, *ns.* among Teutonic peoples, a fine by which homicide and other heinous crimes against the person were expiated. [O.E. *wergield*, from *wer*, man, *gield—gieldan*, to pay.]

wert *wûrt*, used as the *2nd pers. sing.* of the past indicative (for **wast**) and subjunctive of **be**. [**were**, and suff. *-t*.]

Wesleyan *wez'*, *wes'li-an*, *adj.* pertaining to Wesleyanism.—*n.* an adherent of Wesleyanism.—*n.* **Wes'leyanism** the system of doctrine and church polity of the Wesleyan Methodists—Arminian Methodism. [Named after John *Wesley* (1703–91).]

west *west*, *n.* the quarter where the sun sets: one of the four chief points of the compass: the direction faced when one stands with one's back to the high altar of a church: the regions in the west of any country, esp. (*Amer.*) those beyond the Appalachian Mts. (**Middle West**) or beyond the Mississippi or the Rocky Mountains (**Far West**).—*adj.* situated towards, or (of wind) coming from, the west: opposite the high altar of a church.—*adv.* towards the west.—*v.i.* to move towards the west.—*v.i.* **west'er** to turn westward: to change into the west.—*n.* and *adj.* **west'ering**.—*adj.* **west'erly** lying or moving towards the west: from the west —*adv.* towards the west: from the west.—*n.* a westerly wind.—*adj.* **west'ern** situated in the west: belonging to the west: moving towards, or (of wind) coming from, the west.—*n.* an inhabitant of a western region or country: a film or novel whose scene is the western United States, esp. the former Wild West.—*n.* **west'erner** a person belonging to the west.—*v.t.* and *v.i.* **west'ernise**, **-ize** to make or become like the people of Europe and America in customs, or like their institutions, practices, ideas.—*ns.* **westernisā'tion**, **-z-**; **west'ernism** idiom or other characteristic of a western people.—*adj.* **west'ernmost** furthest to the west.—*n.* **west'ing** space or distance westward: departure westward: direction or course towards the west.—*adj.* **west'most** most westerly.—*adj.* and *adv.* **west'ward** towards the west.—*advs.* **west'wardly**, **west'wards** towards the west.—*adv.* **west'-about** towards the west.—**West Bank** the Jordanian territory to the west of the river Jordan and the Dead Sea, annexed by Israel in 1967.—*adj.* **west'bound**.—**west's by-north'** (*-south'*) 11¼ degrees north (south) from due west; **West Country** the south-western part of England; **West End** the fashionable quarter in the west of London: a similar district in other large towns; **Western Church** the Latin Church, as distinguished from the Eastern or Greek Church; **west's north** (or **south**)**-west'** 22½ degrees north (south) from the west; **West Saxon** a southern dialect of Old English, the chief literary dialect before the Norman Conquest.—**go west** to go to America: to go to the western states or western frontier: to die, or to be destroyed or completely dissipated; **the West Europe** or Europe and America; **Wild West** the western United States in the days of the first settlers, chiefly cattlemen and goldminers, before the establishment of law and order. [O.E.]

Westminster *west'min-star*, *n.* used for Parliament—from the London borough where the Houses of Parliament are situated.

wet *wet*, *adj.* containing, soaked with, covered with, water or other liquid: rainy: bringing or foreboding moisture: tearful: grown in damp soil: using liquid: given to drinking, or tipsy (*slang*): allowing the sale of intoxicating liquors. ineffectual, or crazy (*slang*).—*n.* water, moisture, wetness: the rain: an act of wetting: a weak, ineffectual, wavering person (*coll.*).—*v.t.* to make wet: to soak with water: to celebrate by drinking (*slang*):—*pr.p.* **wett'ing**; *pa.t.* and *pa.p.* **wet**, or **wett'ed**.—*n.* **wet'ness**.—*adj.* **wett'ish** somewhat wet.—**wet'back** (*U.S.*) one illegally entering the U.S.A. from Mexico by wading or swimming the Rio Grande; **wet blanket** see **blanket**; **wet'-cell** a cell with a liquid electrolyte; **wet dream** an erotic dream with ejaculation of semen.—*adj.* **wet'-fly** (of angling) with the fly underwater.—**wet'land** (also in *pl.*) marshy land.—*adj.* **wet'-look** made of a glossy material, usu. PVC, which gives the appearance of being wet.— **wet'-nurse** a nurse who suckles a child for its mother; **wet pack** (the wrapping of a person in) blankets or the like dampened with warm or cold water as a medical treatment; **wet'-rot** a form of decay in timber, caused by certain fungi which develop in wood which is alternately wet and dry; **wet suit** a suit for wearing in cold water, which allows water to pass through but retains body heat; **wetting (out) agent** a substance that promotes wetting, e.g. a substance, such as an acid, oil, or hydrocarbon, added to a heterogeneous mixture to facilitate the absorption or adhesion between the constitutents.—**wet behind the ears** very young, immature, gullible; **wet bulb thermometer** a psychrometer; **wet one's whistle** (*coll.*) see under **whistle**; **wet the bed** to urinate accidentally in bed. [O.E. *wǣt* (noun and adj.), *wǣtan* (verb).]

wether *wedh'ər, n.* a castrated ram. [O.E.]

we've *wēv*, a contraction of **we have**.

whack (*h*)*wak*, (*coll.*) *v.t.* to strike hard and smartly: to put or take with violence: to beat decisively: to parcel out, share.—*v.i.* to strike: to settle accounts.— *n.* a blow: a share: an attempt.—*adj.* **whacked** (*coll.*) exhausted.—*n.* **whack'er** (*coll.*) something big of its kind: a blatant lie.—*adj.* **whack'ing** (*coll.*) very large, astounding.—*n.* a beating (*lit.* and *fig.*).—*interj.* **whack'ö** (*coll.*) an expression of pleasure or enthusiasm:—*pl.* **whack'o(e)s.** [From the sound made.]

whacky. Same as **wacky.**

whale[1] (*h*)*wāl, n.* any of an order of cetaceous mammals, including the *toothed* whales, such as the sperm whales and the dolphins, and the *whalebone* whales, such as the right whales and the rorquals, in which the teeth are only embryonic: something very large of its kind (*slang*).—*v.i.* to catch whales.—*ns.* **whal'er** a whale-boat: a whale-man; **whal'ery** whaling.—*adj.* **whal'ing** connected with whale-catching.—*n* the business of catching whales.—**whale'-back** a kind of steamboat used on the Great Lakes, to carry grain, etc., having rounded upper deck, etc.: a mound shaped like the back of a whale; **whale'-boat** a long, narrow boat sharp at both ends once used in the pursuit of whales: a similar boat carried on a large vessel as a life-boat; **whale'bone** a light flexible substance consisting of the baleen plates of whales: an article made of this.—*adj.* made of whalebone.—**whale'-fisher; whale'-fishery; whale'-fishing; whale'-man** a person or ship employed in whale-fishing; **whale'-oil** oil got from the blubber of a whale; **whale'-shark** a huge but harmless shark of tropical seas.—**bull, cow, whale** an adult male, female, whale. [O.E. *hwæl.*]

whale[2] (*h*)*wāl,* (*slang*) *v.t.* to thrash: to strike violently.—*n.* **whal'ing** a thrashing. [Perh. **wale.**]

wham (*h*)*wam, n.* a resounding noise caused by a hard blow.—*v.i.* to hit with a wham:—*pr.p.* **whamm'ing;** *pa.t.* and *pa.p.* **whammed.**—*v.t.* to (cause to) hit with a wham.—Also used as *adv.* and *interj.* [Imit.]

whang (*h*)*wang, n.* a resounding noise: a blow.—*v.i.* to make, or hit with, the sound of a blow, explosion, etc. —*v.t.* to (cause to) hit with a whang.—Also used as *adv.* and *interj.* [Imit.]

whangee (*h*)*wang-ē', n.* any of several grasses of a genus (Phyllostachys) allied to the bamboos, found in China and Japan: a cane made from the stem of one. [Prob. Chin. *huang,* yellow, *li,* bamboo.]

whare (*h*)*wor'i, hwär'ā, fär'ā,* (*New Zealand*) *n* a house. [Maori.]

wharf (*h*)*wörf, n.* a landing-stage, built esp. along the shore, for loading or unloading vessels:—*pl.* **wharfs,**

wharves.—*v.t.* to place on, or bring to, a wharf.—*ns.* **wharf'age** the dues paid for using a wharf: accommodation at a wharf; **wharf'ing** material for making a wharf: wharfs; **wharfinger** ((*h*)*wörf'in-jər*) one who has the care of, or owns, a wharf. [Late O.E. *hwearf,* bank, shore.]

what (*h*)*wot, interrog. pron.* neuter of **who:** used to form a question regarding identity, selection from an indefinite number, nature, value, etc.—also used elliptically (as for *what did you say, do you think? what is it?*).—Also *interrog. adj.*—*rel. pron.* and *adj.* that which: such . . . as: any (thing) whatever.—*indef. pron.* (or *n.*) something.—*adv.* in what way, how? to what degree?.—*interj.* used in summoning, calling attention, expressing surprise, disapprobation, or protest, etc.—*n.* **what'ness** of a thing is: essence.—*ns.* **what'-d'you** (or ye)-**call**(-**it,** -'**em,** etc.) a word substituted for the name of a thing (or person) in forgetfulness or contempt.—*prons.* **whatev'er, whate'er'** anything which: no matter what: what? (*coll.*).—*adjs.* any or all that, no matter what.—*ns.* **what's'-his-(her-, its-)name, what'sit,** *U.S.* **what'sis** (*coll.*) that person, or thing, indicated or understood (often used when the name of the person, etc. has been forgotten).—*adj.* and *pron.* **whatsoev'er** whatever.—*n.* **what'-you-may-call-it** same as **what-d'you-call-it.**—**and what all** and so on, and suchlike things; **know what it is** to know what is involved in an action or experience: to have experienced, suffered, it; **or whatever** or whatever else arises, etc.; **so what?** what of it?; **what about** an expression used to make a suggestion, ask for an opinion, etc.; **what else?** could anything else be the case?; **what for . . .** for what reason, or intended for what purpose (*dial.*; in standard English **what . . . for**): punishment, esp. a whipping (*slang*); **what have you** (*coll.*) what not: anything else of the kind; **what ho** a loud hail, summons; **what if** what would it matter if?. what would happen if? **what . . . like?** a common form of request for a description or opinion of something or someone, as *what is she like?, what does this look, sound, like?*; **what next?** what is to be done next?: what will happen next? (often said in despair or trepidation); **what not** elliptical for 'what may I not say?' implying the presence or existence of many other things; **what of** what comes of, follows from?: what do you think of?; **what of it?** does it matter? (usu. implying that one thinks that it does not); **what then?** what would come of it?, what would be the consequence?; **what's what** the true position of affairs: the proper, conventional, or profitable way to behave or proceed; **what with** by reason of. [O.E. *hwæt,* neut. of *hwā,* who.]

whatnot (*h*)*wot'not, n.* a light piece of furniture with shelves for bric-à-brac, etc.: anything, no matter what: a nondescript article. [**what, not.**]

whatsis, etc. See under **what.**

whaup (*h*)*wöp,* (*Scot.*) *n.* a curlew. [Primarily imit.]

wheat (*h*)*wēt, n.* any cereal grass of the genus Triticum, or its grain, furnishing a white or brown flour for bread, etc.—known as *bearded,* or *beardless* or *bald,* according to the presence or the absence of the awns or beard; and as *winter* or *spring* (also *summer*) according to whether it is a type normally sown in autumn or spring.—*adj.* **wheat'en** made of wheat: whole-meal.—**wheat'-berry, wheat'-corn** the grain of wheat; **wheat'-bird** the chaffinch; **wheat'-crop; wheat'-ear** an ear of wheat; **wheat'-field; wheat'-germ** the vitamin-rich germ or embryo of wheat, part of a grain of wheat; **wheat'-meal** meal made of wheat, esp. whole-meal; **wheat'sheaf** a sheaf of wheat. [O.E. *hwǣte;* allied to **white;** named from its colour.]

wheatear (*h*)*wēt'ēr, n.* a bird akin to the chats, a

common summer visitant of Britain. [Prob. corr. of **white arse**.]

Wheatstone('s) bridge (h)*wēt′stən*(*z*) *brij*, an apparatus for measuring electrical resistance, much used, but not invented, by Sir Charles *Wheatstone* (1802–75).

whee (h)*wē*, *interj.* an expression of delight, exuberance, etc.

wheedle (h)*wēd′l*, *v.t.* and *v.i.* to entice by soft words, flatter, cajole: to obtain by coaxing (with *out of*): to cheat by cajolery (with *out of*).—*n.* **wheed′ler**.—*adj.* **wheed′lesome** coaxing.—*n.* **wheed′ling**. [Perh. from O.E. *wǣdlian*, (orig.) to be in want, to beg.]

wheel (h)*wēl*, *n.* a circular frame turning on an axle: an old instrument of torture: a steering-wheel: a potter's wheel: a spinning-wheel: a rotating firework: the wheel attributed to Fortune personified, the emblem of mutability: hence, the course of events: a disc: a circular design: a circular motion: (in *pl.*) the parts of a machine, esp. fig.—*v.t.* to cause to turn or revolve, esp. round an axis or pivot, as a body of troops: to cause to move in a circular course: to put a wheel or wheels on: to form, or treat, on the wheel: to convey on wheels: to propel on wheels.—*v.i.* to turn round or on an axis: to change direction: to move in a circle: to reel, be giddy: to roll forward: to travel in a wheeled vehicle: to ride a bicycle or tricycle (*coll.*): to be provided with wheels on which to be propelled.—*adj.* **wheeled** having wheels: moving on wheels.—*ns.* **wheel′er** one who wheels: a cyclist (*coll.*): in composition, that which wheels, or has such-and-such a kind of or so-many wheels; **wheel′ie** (*coll.*) a manoeuvre involving travelling for a short distance with the front wheel(s) off the ground; **wheel′ing** the act of moving or conveying on wheels: a turning or circular movement.—*adj.* **wheel′y** like a wheel.—**wheel′-animal**, **-animalcule** a rotifer; **wheel′barrow** a barrow with one wheel in front and two handles and legs behind: loosely, any other hand-cart; **wheel′base** the distance between the front and rear axles of a vehicle: the area enclosed by lines joining the points at which the wheels of a locomotive, etc., touch the rails on the ground, or the length of this area; **wheel′-chair** a chair moving on wheels, esp. an invalid's chair.—**wheel′er-deal′er**; **wheel′er-deal′ing** (*coll.*; *orig. U.S.*) shrewd dealing or bargaining in business, politics, etc. to one's maximum advantage and often with little regard for others; **wheel′-house** a shelter in which a ship's steering-wheel is placed; **wheel′-lock** formerly, a lock for firing a gun by means of a small steel wheel; **wheel′-spin** rotation of the wheels without forward or backward movement of the vehicle; **wheel′-window** a circular window with radiating tracery; **wheel′wright** a wright who makes wheels and wheel-carriages.—**at the wheel** driving a vehicle, or steering a boat (also *fig.*); **big wheel** a person of importance or self-importance; **go on wheels** (*fig.*) to move swiftly, smoothly, and hence pleasantly; **left, right, wheel** (a command to perform) a swing to the left, or right; **potter's wheel** a horizontal revolving disc on which clay vessels are shaped; **wheel and axle** one of the mechanical powers, in its primitive form a cylindrical axle, on which a wheel, concentric with the axle, is firmly fastened, the power being applied to the wheel, and the weight attached to the axle; **wheel and deal** (*coll.*; *orig. U.S.*) to engage in wheeler-dealing; **wheeling and dealing** (*coll.*; *orig. U.S.*) same as **wheeler-dealing**; **wheels within wheels** said of a situation in which a complication of influences is at work. [O.E. *hwēol*.]

wheeze (h)*wēz*, *v.i.* to breathe with a hissing sound: to breathe audibly or with difficulty.—*v.t.* to utter with such a sound.—*n.* the act, or sound, of wheezing: a gag (*theatrical slang*): a standard joke (*slang*): a cunning plan (*coll.*).—*adv.* **wheez′ily**.—*ns.* **wheez′iness; wheez′ing**.—*adj.* **wheez′y**. [Prob. O.N. *hvæsa*, to hiss.]

whelk[1] *wilk*, (h)*welk*, *n.* a popular name for a number of marine gasteropods, esp. applied to species of the genus *Buccinum* common on the coasts of northern seas. [Wrong form of **welk**—O.E. *wiloc*, *weoluc*.]

whelk[2] (h)*welk*, *n.* by confusion with **wale**, the mark of a stripe on the body, a wrinkle or protuberance. [Late O.E. (W.S.) *hwylca*—*hwelian*, to suppurate.]

whelm (h)*welm*, *v.t.* to overturn, overthrow: to submerge: to overpower: to overburden: to ruin, destroy: to pass over in such a way as to submerge it. [M.E. *whelmen*, to turn over.]

whelp (h)*welp*, *n.* the young of the dog kind and of lions, etc.—a puppy, a cub, etc.: (*contemptuously*) a young man: a ridge running longitudinally on the barrel or drum of a capstan or windlass to control the cable: a sprocket on a wheel.—*v.i.* and *v.t.* to bring forth (young). [O.E. *hwelp*; O.N. *hvelpr*.]

when (h)*wen*, *adv.* (*interrog.* and *rel.*) and *conj.* at what time? at which time: at or after the time that: upon or after which: while: although: at which (or *rel. pron.*).—*n.* the time: which time.—*conjs.* **when′as′** (*arch.*) when: in as much as: whereas; **whenev′er**, **whene′er′** at every time when; **whensoev′er** at what time soever.—say when tell me when to stop. [O.E. *hwanne*; from the stem of interrog. pron. *hwā*, who.]

whence (h)*wens*, *adv.* and *conj.* (also *from whence*) from what place: from which things: wherefore.—*conjs.* **whencesoev′er**, **whencev′er** from what place, cause, or source soever. [M.E. *whennes*, *whannes*.]

where (h)*wār*, *adv.* (*interrog.* and *rel.*) and *conj.* at or to which place: at what place? to what place? from what source (*lit.* and *fig.*): to a, or the, place in which (*arch.*): in what circumstances or condition: at what point (*fig.*): whereas: wherever: in, at, or to which (or *rel. pron.*).—*n.* the, or a, place: which place.—*n.* **where′ness** the state of having place or position: position, situation.—*adv.* and *conj.* **whereabout′** about which, about where: near what?—also **where′abouts**.—*n.* **where′about**, now usu. *pl.* **where′abouts**, one's situation, esp. approx.—*advs.* and *conjs.* **whereas′** when in fact: but on the contrary: taking into consideration, in view of, the fact that; **whereat′** at which: at what?; **whereby′** by which; **wherefor′** for which; **where′fore** (-*for*) for which, or what, reason: why?—*n.* the cause.—*advs.* and *conjs.* **wherefrom′** whence; **wherein′** in which place or respect: in what?; **whereof′** of which: of what?; **whereon′** on which: on what?; **whereone′er′**, **wheresoev′er** in or to what place soever: whencesoever (*arch.*); **whereto′** to which: to what?; **whereupon′** upon or in consequence of which; **where′er′**, **wherev′er** at whatever place; **wherewith′**, **wherewithal′** with which? with what.—*n.* (usu. **wherewithal**) the means.—*from where* whence: from the, or a, place where; **see, look**, etc., **where** behold; **tell someone where to get off** (*coll.*) to tell someone that his behaviour is unacceptable and will not be tolerated; **where it is** (*coll.*) the real situation, point, or explanation; **where it's at** (*slang*) (the scene of) whatever is considered to be the most important, exciting, with-it, etc.; **where you are** what you are saying or getting at. [O.E. *hwǣr*, *hwār*; from stem of **who**; cf. **there**.]

wherry (h)*wer′i*, *n.* a shallow, light boat, sharp at both ends for speed: a kind of barge:—*pl.* **wherr′ies**.

whet (h)*wet*, *v.t.* to sharpen by rubbing: to make keen: to excite:—*pr.p.* **whett′ing**; *pa.t.* and *pa.p.* **whett′ed**.—*n.* the act of sharpening: sharpness: an incitement or stimulus: something that sharpens the appetite: an appetiser.—*n.* **whett′er**.—**whet′stone** a stone for sharpening edged instruments: a stimulant. [O.E. *hwettan*, cog. with *hwæt*, sharp.]

whether (*h*)*wedh'ər conj.* introducing the first of two alternative words, phrases, or clauses, the second being introduced by *or*, or (in the case of clauses) sometimes by *or whether*: introducing a single dependent question.—**whether or no** (sometimes **not**) whether so or not so: in any case, in any event. [O.E. *hwæther*, from stem of *hwā*, who.]

whew *hū*, (*h*)*wū, interj.* expressing wonder or dismay. —*n.* a whistling sound, esp. one noting astonishment —*v.i.* to utter such a sound. [Imit.]

whey (*h*)*wā, n.* the watery part of milk, separated from the curd, esp. in making cheese.—*adj.* of or containing whey: like whey: whey-coloured.—**whey'-face** a pale or white face.—*adj.* **whey'-faced** pale, esp. with terror. [O.E. *hwæg.*]

which (*h*)*wich, interrog. pron.* what one of a number?. —Also used adjectivally.—*rel. pron.* who, whom (*obs.*): now used chiefly of things, ideas, etc., not persons: that: often having as antecedent a circumstance or statement, being equivalent to 'and that' or 'but that'.—*prons.* and *adjs.* **whichev'er**, **whichsoev'er** every one which: any one, no matter which.—**which is which?** which is the one, which is the other? [O.E. *hwilc, hwelc*, from the stem of *hwā*, who, and *lic* (from a word meaning body, form), like; cf. **such** and **each.**]

whicker (*h*)*wik'ər*, (*dial.*) *v.i.* to neigh: to bleat: to snigger, titter. [Imit.]

whidah(-bird). See **widow-bird.**

whiff (*h*)*wif, n.* a sudden puff of air or smoke from the mouth: a slight inhalation: a puff of smell: a slight blast: a small amount, esp. of something causing or associated with a transient sensation (*fig.*): a cigarette (*slang*): a jiffy (*coll.*).—*v.t.* to throw out in whiffs: to puff: to drive or convey by, or as if by, a whiff: to inhale, smell.—*v.i.* to go out or off in a whiff: to move with, or as with, a puff of air: to blow slightly: to smell.—*v.i.* **whiff'le** to blow in puffs: to move as if blown by a puff: to talk idly: to make a slight whistling sound: to veer: to vacillate: to prevaricate.—Also *v.t.*—*n.* **whiff'ler.**—*n.* and *adj.* **whiff'ling.**—*adj.* **whiff'y.** [Prob. partly M.E. *weffe*; imit.]

whiffletree (*h*)*wif'l-trē, n.* Same as **whippletree.**

Whig (*h*)*wig, n.* a name applied to members of one of the great English political parties—applied in the late 17th century to those upholding popular rights and opposed to the King; after 1830 almost superseded by 'Liberal': a Scottish Presbyterian, first so called in the middle of the 17th century: one of those who in the colonial period were opposed to British rule (*U.S.*): one of the party formed from the survivors of the old National Republican party and other elements, first so called in 1834—it fell to pieces in the 1850's (*U.S.*). —*adj.* of, pertaining to, or composed of, Whigs—also **Whigg'ish.**—*adv.* **Whigg'ishly.**—*ns.* **Whigg'ery**, **Whigg'ism, Whigg'ishness** Whig principles. [Prob. short for **whiggamore.**]

whiggamore (*h*)*wig'ə-mōr*, -*mōr, n.* one of the 7000 Western Covenanters who marched on Edinburgh in 1648, sealing the doom of Charles I: a Scottish Presbyterian, a Whig. [Origin disputed; most prob. *whig*, to urge forward, *mere*, mare.]

while (*h*)*wīl, n.* a space of time: time and trouble spent. —*conj.* (also **whilst**) during the time that: at the same time that: as long as: although: notwithstanding the admitted fact that.—*v.t.* to pass without irksomeness (with *away*).—*conj.* **whiles** (*B.*) while, at the same time that.—*adv.* (*Scot.*) at times (orig. gen. of O.E. *hwīl*).—*adv.* **whi'lom** (*arch.*) formerly, once.—*adj.* former (orig. dat. pl. of O.E. *hwīl*, time).—**all the while** during all the time (that); (every) **once in a while** now and then. [O.E. *hwīl.*]

whim (*h*)*wim, n.* a caprice: a fancy: a vertical rope drum revolved by a horse, used for hoisting from shallow shafts.—*adjs.* **whimm'y** full of whims; **whim'sical** (-*zi-*) full of whim: odd, fantastical: delicately fanciful: (*loosely*) expressing gently humorous tolerance.—*ns.* **whimsical'ity, whim'sicalness.**—*adv.* **whim'sically.**—*n.* **whim'sy, whim'sey** a whim, freak: whimsical behaviour: delicate, or affectedly delicate, fantasy.—*adj.* full of whims, changeable.—*adv.* **whim'sily.**—*n.* **whim'siness.** [Cf. O.N. *hvima*, to have the eyes wandering.]

whimbrel (*h*)*wim'brəl, n.* a species of small curlew.— Also **wim'brel.** [Prob. imit. of bird's cry; dim. suff. -*rel.*]

whimmy. See **whim.**

whimper (*h*)*wim'pər, v.i.* to cry feebly, brokenly, and querulously or whiningly: to make a plaintive sound.—*v.t.* to express or utter in a whimper.—*n.* a peevish cry.—*n.* **whim'perer.**—*n.* and *adj.* **whim'pering.**—*adv.* **whim'peringly.** [Imit.; cf. Ger. *wimmern.*]

whimsical, whimsy etc. See **whim.**

whin[1] (*h*)*win, n.* gorse, furze.—*adj.* **whinn'y** abounding in whins.—**whin'chat** a bird that frequents whins, similar to the stonechat. [Prob. Scand.]

whin[2]. See **whinstone.**

whine (*h*)*wīn, v.i.* to utter a plaintive cry: to complain in an unmanly way.—*v.t.* to express or utter in a whine: to cause to make a whining noise.—*n.* a plaintive cry: an affected nasal tone of utterance.—*ns.* **whi'ner; whi'niness; whi'ning.**—*adv.* **whi'ningly.**—*adj.* **whi'ny.** [O.E. *hwīnan*, to whine.]

whinge (*h*)*wēnj*, (*h*)*winj*, (*dial.*) *v.i.* to whine: to cry fretfully: to complain peevishly (also *Austr.*).—*adj.* and *n.* **whinge'ing.**—*n.* **whing'er.** [O.E. *hwinsian*, from root of *hwīnan*; see **whine.**]

whinny[1] (*h*)*win'i, v.i.* to neigh:—*pr.p.* **whinn'ying**; *pa.t.* and *pa.p.* **whinn'ied.**—*n.* a neigh. [Imit.]

whinny[2]. See **whin**[1].

whinstone (*h*)*win'stōn*, -*stən, n.* any hard and compact kind of rock, usually basalt or the like: a piece of this. —Also **whin.** [*whin* (origin obscure), and **stone.**]

whiny. See **whine.**

whip (*h*)*wip, n.* a lash with a handle for punishing or driving: a stroke administered as by a whip: a whipping motion: a driver, coachman: one who enforces the attendance and discipline of a political party: a call made on members of parliament to be in their places against an important division (called, according to number of times message is underlined as indication of urgency, **three-line whip**, etc.): a whipper-in, the person who manages the hounds: a simple form of hoisting apparatus, a small tackle consisting of a single rope and block: a preparation of whipped cream, eggs, etc.: a whipping or overcasting: an appeal for contributions (usu. **whip'-round**): a long twig or slender branch.—*v.t.* to strike with a lash: to drive, or make to move, with lashes: to punish with lashes, or (*loosely*) by spanking: to strike in a manner suggesting a lash: to lash with sarcasm: to defeat, outdo (*coll.*): to stiffen (e.g. cream, white of egg) or make (eggs, etc.) frothy, by rapid agitation with a whisk or similar utensil: to keep together, as a party: to move quickly, snatch (with *up, away, out*, etc.): to rouse (with *up*).—*v.i.* to move nimbly: to move in the manner of a whiplash:—*pr.p.* **whipp'ing**; *pa.t.* and *pa.p.* **whipped, whipt.**—*ns.* **whipp'er; whipp'ing.**—*adj.* **whipp'y** whip-like: pliant: supple.—**whip'cord** cord for making whips: a fabric with a bold steep warp twill, used chiefly for dresses, suitings, and coatings: a whip-like seaweed, as *Chorda filum* or *Chordaria flagelliformis*.—*adjs.* **whip'cord; whip'cordy** like whipcord.—*v.t.* **whip'-graft** to graft by fitting a tongue cut on the scion to a slit cut slopingly in the stock.—Also *n.*—*ns.* **whip'-grafting; whip'-hand** the hand that holds the whip: the advantage; **whip'lash** the lash of a whip: something resembling the lash of a whip (also *fig.*): a whiplash injury.—*v.i.* to move like a whiplash.—**whipp'er-in** one who keeps the hounds from wandering; **whipp'ersnapper** a little or young insignificant but pretentious or irritating person; **whipp'ing-boy** a boy formerly educated along with a prince and punished for the royal pupil's faults: one on whom falls the odium or punishments of the shortcomings of others; **whipp'ing-cream** cream with enough butterfat in it to allow it to be beaten stiff; **whipp'ing-post** a post to which offenders are tied to be whipped: the punishment itself; **whipp'ing-top** (or **whip'-top**) a top kept spinning by means of a whip; **whip-round** see whip; **whip'-saw** a narrow saw for dividing timber lengthwise, usu. set in a frame and often worked by two persons.—*v.t.* to cut with a whip-saw: to have the advantage of at every point (*slang*).—**whip'-scorpion** any arachnid of the order Pedipalpida, slightly resembling true scorpions but being without sting and having usu. a whip-like appendage at the rear of the body; **whip'-snake** any of various snakes resembling a whiplash; **whip'-stock** the rod or handle of a whip.—*adjs.* **whip'-tail, -tailed** having a long, slender tail.—**whip into shape** to get (esp. a person) into a desired state or condition, esp. by force or rigorous training; **whiplash injury** a neck injury caused by the sudden jerking backwards and then forwards of the head, common in motor-vehicle accidents in which the vehicle is hit from behind. [M.E. *whippen.*]

whippet (*h*)*wip'it, n.* a breed developed from a cross between a greyhound and spaniel or terrier: a racing-dog. [Partly whip, and partly obs. *whippet,* to move briskly.]

whippletree (*h*)*wip'l-trē, n.* the cross-piece of a carriage, plough, etc., which is made so as to swing on a pivot and to which the traces of a harnessed animal are fixed. [From whip.]

whip-poor-will (*h*)*wip-pōōr-wil', or -pər-, n.* a species of goatsucker, a native of N. America. [Imitative of its call.]

whippy, etc. See whip.

whirr(r) (*h*)*hwûr, n.* a sound from rapid whirling or vibratory motion.—Also *adv.*—*v.i.* to whirl round with a buzzing noise: to fly, move, with such a sound.—*v.t.* to hurry away with, or as if with, a whirring or whizzing sound:—*pr.p.* **whirr'ing;** *pa.t.* and *pa.p.* **whirred.**—*n.* **whirr'ing.** [Imit.]

whirl (*h*)*wûrl, n.* a turning with rapidity: anything that revolves, esp. rapidly: a great or confusing degree, as of activity or emotion: commotion, agitation: a whorl.—*v.i.* to revolve rapidly: to move rapidly, esp. in an agitated manner: to turn swiftly round or aside. —*v.t.* to turn round rapidly: to carry, or move, away rapidly, as on wheels: to throw violently.—*n.* **whirl'er.**—*n.* and *adj.* **whirl'ing.**—**whirl'igig** (*-gig*) a toy that is spun or whirled rapidly round: a merry-go-round: anything that revolves rapidly (*lit.* and *fig.*): an ancient instrument of punishment, consisting of a pivoted wooden cage in which the prisoner was spun round: any water-beetle of the family Gyrinidae, esp. *Gyrinus natator* (also **whirligig beetle**); **whirl'pool** a circular current in a river or sea, produced by opposing tides, winds, or currents: an eddy; **whirl'wind** a small rotating wind-storm, which may extend upwards to a height of many hundred feet—a miniature cyclone; **whir'lybird** (*slang*) a helicopter.—**give something a whirl** (*coll.*) to try something out. [M.E. *whirlen*—O.N. *hvirfla,* freq. of *hverfa,* to turn round.]

whirr. See whir(r).

whish (*h*)*wish, v.i.* to move with the whizzing sound of rapid motion: to say 'whish'.—*interj.* asking for silence—hush!—Also **whisht.**—*n.* **whisht** silence: a whisper.—*v.i.* to keep silent.

whisk (*h*)*wisk, v.t.* to move quickly and lightly: to sweep rapidly: to beat up with a quick, light movement.—*v.i.* to move nimbly and rapidly.—*n.* a rapid sweeping motion: a small bunch of anything used for a brush: a small instrument for beating or whisking, esp. eggs.—*n.* **whis'ker** he who, or that which, whisks: formerly, hair on the upper lip, now usu. hair on the side of the face, side-whiskers (esp in *pl.*): a long bristle on the face of a cat, etc.: a hair's breadth, a very small amount (*fig.*): a very thin, strong fibre or filament made by growing a crystal, e.g. of silicon carbide, silicon nitride or sapphire.—*adjs.* **whis'kered, whis'kery** having whiskers; **whis'king** moving briskly. [Scand., earliest uses Scot.]

whisky (*Ir.* and *U.S.* **whiskey**) (*h*)*wis'ki, n.* as legally defined, a spirit obtained by distillation from a mash of cereal grains saccharified by the diastase of malt: formerly applied also to a spirit obtained from potatoes, beetroot, or any starch-yielding material: a glass of any of such spirits.—*adj.* **whis'keyfied, whis'kified** intoxicated.—**whisk(e)y sour** a sour having whisky as its chief ingredient. [Gael. *uis-gebeatha*—*uisge,* water, *beatha,* life.]

whisky-john (*h*)*wis'ki-jon, n.* the grey or Canada jay—Also **whis'ky-jack.** [From Amer. Indian name of similar sound.]

whisper (*h*)*wis'pər, v.i.* to speak with a low sound: to speak in a whisper: to speak covertly, spread rumours: to plot secretly: to make a sound like soft speech.—*v.t.* to utter in a low voice or under the breath, or covertly, or by way of gossip.—*n.* a low hissing voice or sound: a sound uttered with breath not voice: voiceless speech with narrowed glottis (*phon.*): a hissing or rustling sound: cautious or timorous speaking: a secret hint: a rumour.—*n.* **whis'perer.**—*n.* and *adj.* **whis'pering.**—*adv.* **whis'peringly** in a whisper or low voice.—*adj.* **whis'pery.**—**whispering campaign** an attack by means of furtively spread rumours; **whis'pering-gallery, -dome** a gallery or dome so constructed that a whisper or slight sound is carried to an unusual distance. [O.E. *hwisprian.*]

whist[1] (*h*)*wist, interj.* hush: silence: be still—*v.t.* to become silent. [Imit.]

whist[2] (*h*)*wist, n.* a card game played by two against two.—**whist'-drive** a progressive whist party; **whist'-player.** [Earlier whisk; perh. assimilated to **whist**[1], because of the silence during play.]

whistle (*h*)*wis'l, v.i.* to make a shrill sound by forcing the breath through the contracted lips or the teeth: to make such a sound in derision, etc.: of a bird, to pipe, sing: to make a like sound with an instrument: to sound shrill: to make a call or signal by whistling: to whizz through the air.—*v.t.* to perform or utter by whistling: to call or bring by a whistle: to send with a whistling sound.—*n.* an act of whistling: the sound made in whistling, or one like it: a small wind instrument giving a high-pitched sound by air impinging on a sharp edge: an instrument sounded by escaping steam, etc., as on steam locomotives: a summons: the throat (*slang*).—*ns.* **whis'tler; whis'tling.**—*adv.* **whis'tlingly.**—**whis'tle-blower** (*slang*) one who blows the whistle on someone or something; **whis'tle-blowing** (*slang*); **whis'tle-stop** (*coll.*) a small town or railway-station, where trains stop only by signal (**whistle-stop speech** an electioneering speech made on tour (orig. at railway stations); **whistle-stop tour** orig. such an electioneering tour, now any rapid tour involving brief stops at many places).—*v.i.* of a political candidate, to make an electioneering tour with many brief personal appearances.—**whistling swan** an American swan with a musical whistling call. —**blow the whistle** (*slang*) to expose, give information (usu. to the authorities) about, illegal or underhand practices: to declare (something) illegal, underhand or otherwise unacceptable; **boatswain's whistle** (also **pipe, call**) a whistle of special shape used by a boatswain or boatswain's-mate to summon sailors to various duties; **wet one's whistle** (*coll.*) to take a drink of liquor, **whistle down the wind** to talk to no purpose; **whistle for** to summon by whistling: to ask for in vain (*coll.*); **whistle in the dark** to do something to quell one's fear. [O.E. *hwistlian.*]

whit (*h*)wit, *n.* the smallest particle imaginable. a bit [By-form of **wight**.]

white (*h*)wīt, *adj.* of the colour of pure snow: snowy: of the light complexion characteristic of Europeans: that absorbs the minimum and reflects the maximum of light rays: pale, pallid: bloodless· colourless: pure· unblemished: innocent: purified from sin: bright. light-coloured or golden, as wine: clothed in white· auspicious, favourable: reliable, honest: (of a witch) not malevolent, using her power for good purposes. —*n.* the colour of snow: anything white, as a white man, a white butterfly, the centre of a target, the albuminous part of an egg, a pigment.—*v.t.* to make white.—*v.t.* **whit'en** to make white: to bleach: to free from guilt, or to make to appear guiltless.—*v.i.* to become or turn white.—*ns.* **whit'ener**; **white'ness**; **whit'ening** act or process of making or becoming white: a substance used to make white, whiting; **whites** white attire; **Whit'ey** (also without *cap.*; *coll.*, often *derog.*) a white man: white men as a race, **whit'ing** a small sea-fish allied to the cod, so-called from its white colour: ground chalk free from stony matter and other impurities, extensively used as a size, colour, etc.—(also **white'ning, Spanish white** and—the finest quality—**Paris white**).—*adjs* **whit'ish** somewhat white, **whit'y** whitish.—**white admiral** any of a genus of butterflies, of the same family as the red admiral, having white bands on the wings; **white ant** a termite; **white'bait** the fry of various species of herring, etc.; **white'beam** a small tree (*Sorbus*, or *Pyrus, aria*) with leaves white and downy on the underside; **white bread** bread made from flour which has been refined by boulting; **white'cap** the male redstart, or other bird with light-coloured head: a crested wave —*adj.* **white'-collar** pertaining to, or designating, the class of workers, as clerks, etc., who are not engaged in manual labour.—**white corpuscle** a leucocyte, one of the colourless amoeba-like cells occurring in suspension in the blood plasma of many animals, in lymph, etc.; **whited sepulchre** one professedly righteous but inwardly wicked, a hypocrite (Matt. xxiii. 27); **White Dwarf** (also without *caps.*) the name given to a small class of stars outside the normal spectral sequence, because their luminosities are extremely low for their spectral type; **white elephant** see **elephant**; **White Ensign** a flag with a white field and St George's cross, with the Union Jack in the canton, now flown by the Royal Navy and the Royal Yacht Squadron; **white'-eye** any bird of the genus *Zosterops* or of related genera of the fam. *Zosteropidae*, most species of which have a conspicuous ring of minute white feathers round the eye; **white'-face** white make-up, esp. as worn by a traditional type of clown. —*adj.* **white'-faced** having a face pale with fear or from illness: wearing white make-up, e.g. as a clown: of animals, having the face, or part of it, white.— **white feather** see under **feather**; **white'fish** a general name for such fish as the whiting, haddock, men-

haden, etc.; **white flag** an emblem of truce or surrender; **white'-fly** any of several insect pests belonging to the family *Aleurodidae*; **White Friar** (also without *caps.*) one of the Carmelite order of friars, so called from their white dress; **white gold** gold alloyed with nickel or palladium to give it a white colour.—*n.pl* **white goods** household linen: refrigerators, washing machines, freezers and the like, usu. painted with white enamel.—**white heat** the degree of heat at which bodies become white: an intense state, as of emotion, activity, etc.; **white hole** a suggested source of the matter and energy observed flowing into the universe (cf. **black hole**); **white hope** a person on whom hopes for success, honour, etc. are grounded (*often* **great white hope**); **white horse** a white-topped wave: a figure of a horse on a hillside, formed by removing the turf from the underlying chalk—the most famous being in Berkshire, at Uffington.—*adj.* **white'-hot'**.—**White House** the official residence, in Washington, of the President of the U.S.A.; **white lead** basic lead carbonate used in painting white; **white'-leg** an ailment of women after parturition— also called milk-leg; **white lie** see **lie**; **white light** light containing all wavelengths in the visible range at the same intensity—the term is used, however, to cover a wide range of intensity distribution in the spectrum; **white line** a longitudinal line, either continuous or broken, on a highway to separate lanes of traffic — *adj.* **white'-livered** having a pale look (once thought to be caused by a white liver): cowardly —**white man** one of the white race: one assumed to deal fairly with others (*coll.*); **white meat** the flesh of poultry, rabbits, calves, etc.: the lighter parts of the cooked flesh of poultry (e.g. the breast), as opposed to the darker meat of the leg; **white metal** a tin-base alloy with over 50 per cent. of tin: sometimes, an alloy in which lead is the principal metal; **white noise** a mixture of sound waves covering a wide frequency range; **white'-out** a phenomenon in snow regions in fog or overcast conditions in which earth and sky merge in a single whiteness; **white paper** a statement, printed on white paper, issued by government for the information of parliament; **white'-pudding** an oatmeal and suet pudding in a sausage skin; **white race** one of the main divisions of mankind, distinguished generally by light complexion and certain types of hair and skull— also known as Caucasian; **white sale** a sale of linen goods at reduced prices; **white sauce** a sauce made with roux, liquid such as milk or a chicken or veal stock, and such flavouring as desired, **white slave** a girl procured for prostitution purposes (esp. when exported)—whence **white slaver, white slavery** and **white slave traffic**; **white spirit** a petroleum distillate used as a substitute for turpentine in mixing paints, and in paint and varnish manufacture; **white'thorn** the common hawthorn; **white'throat** either of two warblers of the same genus (Sylvia) as the blackcap, having white throat feathers: a species of American sparrow: any of several species of humming-bird; **white tie** a white bow tie, part of formal evening dress: hence, formal evening dress (also *adj.*); **white'ware** articles made of white porcelain, pottery, or other ceramic material; **white'wash** a liquid, as lime and water, or whiting, size and water, used for coating walls: a wash for the skin: false colouring: an act of whitewashing.—*v.t.* to cover with whitewash: to give a fair appearance to: to attempt to clear (a stained reputation), to attempt to cover up (a misdemeanour, esp. by one in an official position): to beat (an opponent) so decisively in a game that he fails to score at all (*coll.*).—**white'washer** one who whitewashes; **white'-water** shoal water near the shore, breakers: the foaming water in rapids, etc.;

white whale the beluga; **white wine** yellowish-coloured or uncoloured (as opp. to *red*) wine; **white'wood** a name applied to a large number of trees or their timber—the American tulip-tree, whitewood cedar (*Tecoma*, or *Tabebuia, leucoxylon*; Bignoniaceae), etc.; **whit'ing-pout** see pout².—**white man's burden** (*Kipling*) his alleged obligation to govern backward coloured peoples; **white of (an) egg** the albumen, the pellucid viscous fluid surrounding the yolk; **white of the eye** that part of the ball of the eye which surrounds the iris or coloured part; **white out** to omit or cover up (secret or sensitive material in a report, transcript, etc.) so leaving areas of blank paper on the page(s). [O.E. *hwīt*.]

Whitehall (*h*)*wīt'hōl, n.* a street with government offices, in London: the British government or its policy.

whither (*h*)*widh'ər, adv.* and *conj.* to what place?: to which place: (used relatively) to which: to what: whithersoever.—*adv.* **whithersoev'er** to whatever place. [O.E. *hwider*, allied to **who**.]

whiting. See **white**.

whitlow (*h*)*wit'lō, n.* a painful inflammation of a finger or toe, esp. near the nail. [Perh. a corr. of *whick-flaw*, quick-flaw (cf. **quick** and **flaw**) or of *whitflaw*,—**white** and **flaw**.]

Whit-Monday (*h*)*wit'-mun'dā, n.* the Monday following Whitsunday.

Whitsun (*h*)*wit'sn, adj.* pertaining to, or observed at, Whitsuntide.—*n.* Whitsuntide.—**Whit'sunday** the seventh Sunday after Easter, commemorating the day of Pentecost, when the converts in the primitive Church wore white robes; **Whit'suntide** the season of Pentecost, comprising **Whit'sun-week, Whit'-week**, the week beginning with Whitsunday. [**white, Sunday**.]

whittle (*h*)*wit'l, v.t.* to pare or cut with a knife: to shape with a knife: to diminish gradually (often with *down*): to lessen the force or scope of (often with *down*).—*v.i.* to cut wood aimlessly.—**whittle away, whittle away at** to whittle, whittle down (usu. *fig.*). [M.E. *thwitel*—O.E. *thwītan*, to cut.]

whizz, whiz (*h*)*wiz, v.i.* to make a hissing sound, like an arrow or ball flying through the air: to move rapidly.—*v.t.* to cause to whizz:—*pr.p.* **whizz'ing;** *pa.t.* and *pa.p.* **whizzed.**—*n.* a hissing sound: a bargain, agreement (*slang*).—Also *adv.*—*ns.* **whizz'er; whizz'ing.** —*adv.* **whizz'ingly.**—**whizz'-bang** (*slang*) a light shell of high velocity which is heard arriving before the sound of a gun's report: a firework suggestive of this; **whizz(z)'-kid** (*slang*) one who achieves success rapidly and at a relatively early age, because of high intelligence, progressive ideas, pushfulness, etc. [Imit.; cf. **wheeze, hiss**.]

who *hōō, rel.* and *interrog. pron.* what person: which person: he who, the person who: whoever: of what name, standing, etc. (objective case **whom**; possessive case **whose**.—*prons.* **whoev'er, whosoev'er** every one who: whatever person (objective case **whom'ever, whomsoev'er;** possessive case **whosev'er, whosesoev'er**).—**know who's who** to know the position and influence of everyone; **who but he** who else?, he only. [O.E. *hwā*.]

whoa (*h*)*wō, interj.* stop.

who-dun-it, whodunnit *hōō-dun'it,* (*coll.*) *n.* a story concerned with the elucidation of a crime mystery. [**who, done** (vulg. pa.t. of **do**), **it**.]

whole *hōl, adj.* sound in health (*arch.*; *B.*): uninjured: restored to health: healed: not broken: undamaged: not broken up, or ground, or deprived of any part: containing the total amount, number, etc.: complete: of a sister or brother, full-blooded.—*n.* the entire thing: a system or combination of parts.—*adv.* **wholly.**—*n.* **whole'ness.**—*adj.* **whole'some** healthy in body, taste, morals: indicating health: conducive to bodily or spiritual health.—*adv.* **whole'somely.**—*ns.* **whole'someness; whol'ism** same as **holism**.—*adj.* **wholist'ic.**—*adv.* **wholly** (*hōl'li, hō'li*) completely, altogether.—**whole'food** food, unprocessed or processed as little as possible, produced without any artificial fertilisers, pesticides, etc.—*adj.* **whole'-heart'ed** hearty, generous, zealous and sincere.—*adv.* **whole'-heart'edly.**—*adj.* **whole'-hog** (*slang*) out-and-out, complete.—**whole'-meal** meal made from entire grains of wheat (also *adj.*); **whole note** (*U.S.*) a semibreve; **whole number** a unit, or a number composed of units, an integral number; **whole'sale** sale of goods, usually by the whole piece or large quantity, to a retailer.—*adj.* buying and selling, or concerned with buying and selling, thus: extensive and indiscriminate.—*adv.* by wholesale: extensively and indiscriminately.—**whole'saler** one who sells by wholesale.—*adj.* **whole'-wheat** whole-meal.—**go the whole hog** to do a thing thoroughly or completely: to commit oneself to anything unreservedly; **the whole** all the: the complete; **upon, on, the whole** generally speaking: all things considered. [O.E. *hāl*, healthy.]

whom, whomever, whomsoever. See **who.**

whoop (*h*)*wōōp, hōōp,* sometimes **hoop** *hōōp, n.* a loud eager cry: a N. American Indian war-cry: (*hōōp*) the long noisy inspiration heard in whooping-cough.—*v.i.* to give a loud cry of triumph, eagerness, scorn, etc.: to hoot.—*v.t.* to cheer, or insult, with shouts: to summon, or to urge on, by whooping.—*ns.* **whoop'er** one who whoops: a whooping swan or whooping crane (also **hoop'er**); **whoop'ing.**—**whoop'ing-cough, hoop'ing-cough** an infectious and epidemic disease, mostly attacking children, characterised by periodic spasms of the larynx that end in a long crowing inspiration; **whooping crane** an American crane (*Grus americana*), on the brink of extinction; **whooping swan** a swan (*Cygnus cygnus cygnus*) with a whooping call, common in N. Europe and Asia.—**whoop it up** (*coll.*) to indulge in noisy, boisterous entertainments or celebrations. [O.Fr. *houper*, to shout.]

whoopee (*h*)*wōōp'ē, interj.* an exclamation of delight.—Also *n.*—**make whoopee** (*coll.*) to indulge in hilarious amusements or dissipation. [**whoop.**]

whoops *wōōps.* Same as **oops.**

whoosh, woosh (*h*)*wōōsh, n.* the sound of, or like that made by, something large passing rapidly through the air.—*v.i.* to make such a sound: to do something with, or as if with, such a sound (also *v.t.*).—Also *adv.* [From the sound.]

whop (*h*)*wop,* (*coll.* or *dial.*) *v.t.* to whip, thrash: to defeat or surpass: to throw or pull suddenly or violently.—*v.i.* to strike, or to move, quickly: to flop down:—*pr.p.* **whopp'ing;** *pa.t.* and *pa.p.* **whopped.**—*n.* a blow: a bump: the noise made by either of these —*n.* **whopp'er** one who whops: anything very large, esp. a monstrous lie.—*adj.* **whopp'ing** very large.—*n.* thrashing. [Prob. partly imitative.]

whore *hōr, hor, n.* a prostitute: any unchaste woman.—*v.i.* to be, or to have to do with, a whore or whores. —*adj.* **whō'rish.**—*adv.* **whō'rishly.**—*n.* **whō'rishness.** —**whore'house** a brothel; **whore'monger** a lecher: a pander; **whore'son** (*-sən*) son of a whore: a bastard: a term of coarse contempt or familiarity.—*adj.* mean, scurvy. [Late O.E. *hōre,* prob.—O.N *hōra,* adulteress.]

whorl (*h*)*wörl,* (*h*)*wûrl, n.* a group of similar members arising from the same level on a stem, and forming a circle around it: a single turn in a spiral shell: a convolution—e.g. in the ear.—*adj.* **whorled** having whorls: arranged in the form of a whorl or whorls. [Late M.E. *wharwyl,* etc., variants of **whirl.**]

For other sounds see detailed chart of pronunciation.

whortleberry (h)wör´tl-ber-i, -bar-i, n. a widely-spread heath plant with a dark blue edible berry, called also the bilberry—in Scotland, blaeberry: extended to certain other plants of the same genus (Vaccinium). [Variant of dial. *hurtleberry*.]

whose *hōōz*, pron. the possessive case of who (q.v.) and also which.—**whosesoever´, whosoever** see who.

why (h)wī, adv. and conj. for what cause or reason, on which account?: therefore: (used relatively) on account of which.—*interj.* expressing sudden realisation, or protest, or marking resumption after a question or a slight pause.—*adv.* **whyev´er** (coll.) for whatever reason.—**for why** (arch. and dial.) for what reason: because; **the why and wherefore** the whole reason. [O.E. hwī, hwȳ, instrumental case of hwā, who, and *hwæt*, what.]

whydah (-bird). See **widow-bird**.

wick¹ wik, n. a village or town (dial.): as suffix (-ik, -wik, also -wich -ij, -ich, -wich) in Berwick, Greenwich, etc. [O.E. wīc, prob. an old Gmc. borrowing from L. vīcus, a village.]

wick² wik, n. the twisted threads of cotton or other substance in a candle, lamp, or lighter, which draw up the inflammable liquid to the flame.—**get on someone's wick** (coll.) to irritate someone. [O.E. wēoce, wēoc.]

wicked wik´id, adj. evil in principle or practice: sinful: ungodly: (of an animal) vicious: cruel: mischievous, spiteful: very bad, harmful, or offensive: roguish (coll.).—n. (with the) wicked persons collectively.—*adv.* wick´edly.—n. wick´edness.—**the wicked one** the devil. [M.E. wicked, wikked, prob.—wicke, wikke, wicked—O.E. wicca, wizard.]

wicker wik´ər, n. a small pliant twig or osier: wickerwork.—*adj.* made of twigs or osiers: encased in wickerwork. wick´ered made of wicker: covered with wickerwork.—**wick´erwork** basketwork of any kind. [M.E. wiker, of Scand. origin.]

wicket wik´it, n. a small gate: a small door in or near a larger one: an opening or a window with a grille, as at a ticket-office, bank, etc. (U.S.): (the following meanings all *cricket*) the upright arrangements of three stumps with two bails on top which the batsman defends against the bowling: a stump: the pitch, esp. in respect of its condition: a batsman's stay at the wicket, or his joint stay there with another: a batsman's innings.—wick´et-door, -gate a wicket; **wick´et-keeper** in cricket, the fieldsman who stands immediately behind the striker's wicket.—get, take, etc., a wicket to bowl a batsman, or have him put out in any way as a result of one's bowling; **keep wicket** to be wicket-keeper; **over, round, the wicket** (of bowling) delivered with the hand nearer, farther away from, the wicket. [O.N.Fr. wiket (Fr. guichet); of Gmc. origin.]

wide wīd, adj. extending far: having a considerable distance between the sides: broad: of a specified breadth: roomy: expanded: opened as far as possible: far apart: far from the point aimed at: very different: of large scope, comprehending or considering much (fig.): astute, wily (slang): lax in morals (slang): lax, reverse of narrow (phon.).—n. wideness: in cricket, a ball bowled out of reach of the batsman: a penalty run allowed for this.—*adv.* (now usu. far and wide) to a great distance, over a large region: far from the point aimed at, the subject under discussion, the truth, etc.: far to one side (with of): so that there is a large space or distance between.— -wide in composition, extending throughout a specified area, etc. as nationwide, countrywide.—*adv.* wide´ly.—v.t. and v.i. wi´den to make or grow wide or wider.—ns. wi´dener; wide´ness; width (width) breadth.—*adjs.* wide´-angle (phot.) pertaining to a lens having an angle of view of 60° or more and a short focal length; **wide´-awake´** fully awake: on the alert: keen and knowing (coll.).—n. (wīd´ə-wāk) a low wide-brimmed soft felt hat.—**wide´-boy** (slang) an astute or wily person, esp. one prone to sharp practice.—*adjs.* wide´-bod´y of aircraft, having a wide fuselage; **wide´-eyed** showing great surprise: naive, credulous; **wide´-open** opened wide: open to attack (coll.): lax in enforcing laws and regulations (U.S.); **wide´-rang´ing** covering a wide range of topics, interests, cases, etc.; **wide´spread** extended or extending widely: found, operative, etc., in many places.—**to the wide** completely: utterly; **wide of the mark** far out, astray from the truth. [O.E. wīd.]

widgeon. See **wigeon**.

widget wij´it, n. a gadget, a thingumajig.

widow wid´ō, n. a woman who has lost her husband by death and has not married again: an extra hand in some card games: a short last line at the end of a paragraph which stands at the top of a page or column of print (print.).—v.t. to bereave of a husband (or wife): to strip of anything valued.—ns. wid´ower a man whose wife is dead; **wid´owerhood; wid´owhood** the state of being a widow, or (rarely) of being a widower.—**wid´ow-bird** any of a group of African birds belonging to, or related to, the weaver-finch family, having much black in the plumage, called also **whidah** (-bird), **whydah** (-bird) ((h)wī´da, (h)wī´) in the belief that they were named from *Whydah* (Ouidah) in Dahomey: any of various birds of a related family (Ploceidae); **widow's cruse** a source of supply that never fails (1 Kings xvii. 10–16); **widow's mite** a small offering generously given (Mark xii. 42; see also **mite**); **widow's peak** a point of hair over the forehead, like the cusped front of a widow's cap in former days.—**golf, etc. widow** a woman whose husband frequently goes off to play golf (or whatever). [O.E. widewe.]

width. See **wide**.

wield wēld, v.t. to control, manage: to use with skill.—*adj.* wield´able capable of being wielded.—ns. wield´er; wield´iness.—*adj.* wield´y easy to wield: manageable. [O.E. weldan (not recorded; W.S. wealdan).]

Wiener schnitzel vē´nər shnit´səl, (Ger.) a veal cutlet dressed with bread-crumbs and eggs. [Ger., Viennese cutlet.]

wife wīf, n. a woman: a married woman: the woman to whom one is married:—pl. **wives**.—n. wife´hood the state of being a wife.—*adjs.* wife´less without a wife; **wife´-like; wife´ly.**—**wife´-swapping** (coll.) a form of sexual activity in which married couples exchange partners temporarily. [O.E. wīf.]

wig¹ wig, n. an artificial covering of hair for the head worn to conceal baldness, or for fashion's sake, as in the full-dress full-bottomed wig of Queen Anne's time, still worn by the Speaker and by judges, and the smaller tie-wig, still represented by the judge's undress wig and the barrister's or advocate's frizzed wig: a judge (slang).—*adjs.* wigged wearing a wig; **wig´less** without a wig. [Short for periwig.]

wig² wig, (coll.) v.t. to scold:—pr.p. wigg´ing; pa.t. and pa.p. wigged.—n. wigg´ing (coll.) a scolding. [wig¹.]

wigeon, (now rarely) **widgeon,** wij´ən, n. any of various ducks of the genus *Anas* which have the bill shorter than the head, the legs short, feet rather small, wings long and pointed, and the tail wedge-shaped: in the U.K., specif. A. penelope.

wiggle wig´l, v.i. and v.t. to waggle, wriggle.—n. a wiggling motion.—Also v.i., v.t. and n. wigg´le-wagg´le.—n. wigg´ler one who wriggles.—*adj.* wigg´ly wriggly: much or irregularly waved. [Freq.

of verb from which is derived dial. *wig*, to wag.]

wight *wit, n.* a creature or a person (*arch., dial.,* or ironically). [O.E. *wiht*, a creature, thing; cf. **whit**.]

wigwag *wig'wag, v.i.* to twist about: to signal by means of flags.—*n.* the act of wigwagging: a level-crossing signal which gives its indication by swinging about a fixed axis.—*adj.* twisting.—*adv.* to and fro. [Dial. *wig* (from same root as **wiggle**) and **wag**.]

wigwam *wig'wom, -wam, n.* an American Indian dome-shaped hut, made by laying bark, skins, etc. over a framework of sticks: any similar construction, such as a tepee. [Eng. corr. of Algonquian word.]

wild *wild, adj.* being in a state of nature, not tamed or cultivated: of an undomesticated or uncultivated kind: uncivilised: uninhabited: desolate: tempestuous: violent: fierce: passionate: unrestrained: licentious: agitated: shy: distracted: very angry: very enthusiastic, eager, keen: strong and irrational: fantastic: crazy: disordered: unconsidered: wide of the mark: fresh and natural: (of a playing-card) having any value desired.—Also *adv.*—*n.* (also in *pl.*) an uncultivated region: a wilderness or desert (also *fig.*): an empty region of air or water (*poet.*).—*n.* **wild'ing** that which grows wild or without cultivation: a wild crab-apple: a garden plant self-sown, an escape.—*adj.* **wild'ish** somewhat wild.—*adv.* **wild'ly.**—*n.* **wild'ness.**—**wild card** a person allowed to compete in a sports event despite his lacking the stipulated qualifications, etc.: (the offering of) such a chance to compete; **wild'cat** an undomesticated species of cat (*Felis sylvestris*) native to Europe: any of various small wild animals of the cat family: a quick-tempered, fierce person: a speculative or unsound financial scheme (*U.S.*): one who takes part in such a scheme (*U.S.*): an exploratory well (*U.S.*).—*adj.* (of business, scheme, etc.) haphazard, reckless, unsound financially: (of a strike), unauthorised by union officials: (of an oil-well) exploratory (*U.S.*).—*v.t.* and *v.i.* (*U.S.*) to drill an experimental well in an area of unknown productivity in search of oil, gas, ore, etc.—**wild'catter** (*U.S.*); **wild'-cherry** any uncultivated tree bearing cherries, as the gean (*Prunus avium*), or its fruit; **wild'-dog** any wild species of the dog genus or family, as the dingo, etc.; **wild duck** any duck excepting the domesticated duck: specif., the mallard; **wild'fire** a sweeping, destructive fire: a composition of inflammable materials: **(like wildfire** extremely fast); **wild'-fowl** the birds of the duck tribe: game-birds; **wild'-fowler; wild'-fowling** the pursuit of wild-fowl; **wild'-land** land completely uncultivated; **wild'life** wild animals, birds, etc. regarded collectively (**wildlife park** a safari park); **wild man** a man of extreme or radical views in politics; **wild'-water** the foaming water in rapids, etc.; **wild'-wood** wild uncultivated, or unfrequented, wood.—Also *adj.*—**run wild** to take to loose living: to live or grow in freedom from constraint or control: to revert to the wild or uncultivated state; **sow one's wild oats** see **oat**; **wild-goose chase** see **chase.** [O.E. *wilde*; common Gmc. word.]

wildebeest *vild'i-bāst, wild'i-bēst, vild'ə-bēst,* (*S.Afr.*) *n.* a gnu. [Du. *wilde*, wild, *beest*, ox.]

wilderness *wil'dar-nəs, n.* a region uncultivated and uninhabited: a pathless or desolate tract of any kind: a large confused or confusing assemblage.—*v.t.* **wil'der** (prob. formed from *wilderness*; *poet.*) to cause to stray: to bewilder.—*v.i.* to wander wildly or widely.—*adjs.* **wil'dered; wil'dering.**—*n.* **wil'derment.**—**crying in the wilderness** see **cry; in the (political) wilderness** not in office: not having any office, being passed over or refused office. [M.E., —*wilderne*, wild, wilderness—O.E. *wilddēoren*—*wild*, wild, *dēor*, animal.]

wilding. See **wild.**

wile *wil, n.* a trick: deceit: a pleasing artifice: (in *pl.*) cajolery.—*v.t.* to beguile, inveigle: to coax, cajole.—*adj.* **wile'ful** full of wiles.—*adv.* **wil'ily.**—*n.* **wil'iness.**—*adj.* **wil'y** full of craft or cunning: using tricks or stratagem. [O.E. *wil, wile*; cf. **guile**.]

wilful. See under **will.**

wilily, wiliness. See **wile.**

will *wil, n.* the power or faculty of choosing or determining: the act of using this power: volition: choice or determination: pleasure: inclination: lust: command: arbitrary disposal: feeling towards, as in **good-** or **ill-will** (see **good, ill**): the disposition of one's effects at death: the written document containing this.—*v.t.* to decree: to seek to force, influence (oneself or another to perform a specified action) by silent exertion of the will: to dispose of by will, to bequeath: —in the foregoing senses, *pa.t.* and *pa.p.* **willed;** *3rd pers.* **wills:** used with the infinitive of a verb to form (in sense) a future tense, expressing in the second and third person simple futurity (as **shall** in the first), or custom, or persistent habit, 'and in the first person promise or determination on the part of the speaker: also, in third person, can: to be likely to:—in these senses, *pa.t.* **would** (*wŏŏd*); no *pa.p.*; *3rd pers.* **will.**—*v.i.* to exercise choice, choose, decree: to be willing. —*adj.* **wil'ful** governed only by one's will, obstinate: done intentionally.—*adv.* **wil'fully.**—*n.* **wil'fulness.** —*adj.* **willed** having a will: voluntary: given, or disposed of, by will: brought under another's will, as in hypnotism: in combination, having a will of a particular kind, as **weak-willed, strong-willed,** etc.—*n.* **will'er** one who wills.—*adj.* **will'ing** not reluctant: eager: ready and prompt to act: voluntary: chosen: of or pertaining to the will.—*adv.* **will'ingly.**—*n.* **will'ingness.**—*adj.* **will'ing-heart'ed** heartily consenting. —**will power** the ability to control one's actions, emotions, impulses, etc.—**at will** when or as one chooses; **a will of one's own** a strong, self-assertive will; **have one's will** to obtain what one desires; **with a will** heartily and energetically. [O.E. *willa*, will, *willan, wyllan* (pa.t. *wolde, walde*), to wish.]

willet *wil'it, n.* a N. American bird of the snipe family. [Imit.]

willie. See **willy.**

willies *wil'iz,* (*slang*) *n.pl.* the creeps.

williwaw *wil'i-wo, n.* a gust of cold wind blowing seawards from a mountainous coast, e.g. in the Straits of Magellan: a sudden squall (also *fig.*).

will-o'-the-wisp *wil'-ō-thə-wisp', n.* the *ignis fatuus*: any elusive and deceptive person or thing:—*pl.* **wills-** or **-wisps.** [Orig. *Will-with-the-wisp*—*Will*, abbrev. of William, and **wisp** (q.v.).]

willow *wil'ō, n.* any tree or shrub of the genus *Salix*, having slender, pliant branches: any of several plants resembling it: the wood of the willow: a cricket-bat. —*adjs.* **will'owed** abounding with, or grown with, willows; **will'owish** like a willow: of the colour of willow leaves: slender and supple; **will'owy** abounding in willows: flexible: slender and graceful.— **will'ow-herb** a perennial herb (*Epilobium* or *Chamaenerion*) of the evening primrose family (including rose-bay, bay-willow, French or Persian willow) with willow-like leaves and seeds; **willow pattern** a blue design of Chinese character but English origin used on china from the late 18th cent. onwards. [O.E. *welig.*]

willy, willie *wil'i, n.* hypocoristic for the penis.

willy-nilly *wil'i-nil'i, adv.* willing or unwilling: compulsorily.—*adj.* having no choice: vacillating (*erron.*). [**will** and obs. *nill*—O.E. *ne*, not, *willan*, to wish.]

willy-willy *wil'i-wil'i,* (*Austr.*) *n.* a cyclone.

For other sounds see detailed chart of pronunciation.

wilt[1] *wilt, v.i.* to droop, become limp: to lose energy: to lose self-confidence or courage (*fig.*).—*n* the act of wilting: any of various diseases that cause wilting of plants. [Orig. dial.]

wilt[2] *wilt,* (*arch.*) *2nd pers. sing.* of **will.**

Wilton *wil'tən, n.* (in full **Wilton carpet**) a carpet having a cut pile, long made at *Wilton,* in Wilts.

wily. See **wile.**

wimble *wim'bl, n* an instrument for boring holes, turned by a handle.—*v.t.* to bore through with a wimble [Through O Norm Fr., from M.Du. *wimpel.*]

wimbrel. See **whimbrel.**

wimp *wimp,* (*slang*) *n* an ineffectual person.

wimple *wim'pl, n.* a veil folded round the head, neck and cheeks (still part of a nun's dress): a fold, wrinkle, ripple.—*v.t.* to wrap in, or hide with, a wimple: to enwrap, enfold: to lay in folds.—*v.i.* to meander: to ripple. [O.E. *wimpel,* neck-covering.]

Wimpy® *wim'pi, n.* a kind of hamburger.

win *win, v.t.* to get by labour: to gain in contest: to secure: to achieve, effect: to reach: to be the victor in: to induce: to gain influence over: to obtain the favour of: to mine (an ore): to open up (a new portion of a coal-seam).—*v.i.* to gain the victory: to get oneself (into a desired place, state, etc.):—*pr.p.* **winn'ing;** *pa.t.* and *pa.p* **won** (*wun*).—*n.* (*coll.*) a victory, success.—*adj.* **winn'able.**—*ns.* **winn'er** one who wins: something very good or successful (*slang*); **winn'ing** the act of one who wins: (usu. in *pl*) that which is won.—*adj.* that wins: of or pertaining to the act of winning: attractive, prepossessing: persuasive.—*adv* **winn'ingly.**—*n.* **winn'ingness.**—**winning gallery** in real tennis, the gallery furthest away from the net at either end of the court, any shot played into this winning a point; **winn'ing-post** the goal of a race-course.—**win by a (short) head** to win very narrowly; **win in a canter** to win easily; **win, or gain, one's spurs** to earn one's knighthood by valour on the field, hence to gain recognition or reputation by merit of any kind; **win out** to get out: to be successful (*coll.*; also **win through**); **win over** to bring over to one's opinion or party. [O.E. *winnan,* to struggle, to suffer.]

wince *wins, v.i.* to shrink or start back: to make an involuntary movement, e.g. in pain: to be affected acutely, as by a sarcasm.—*n.* an involuntary start back or shrinking.—*n.* **win'cer.**—*n.* and *adj.* **win'cing.** [Cf. O.Fr. *guinchir, ganchir,* to wince—a Gmc. word.]

wincey *win'si, n.* a cloth, plain or twilled, usu. with a linen or cotton warp and woollen filling.—*n.* **winceyette'** a plain cotton cloth of light weight, raised slightly on both sides. [Orig. Scot.]

winch *winch, winsh, n.* a reel or roller: the crank of a wheel or axle: a powerful type of hauling or hoisting machine.—*v.t.* to haul, hoist, etc. using such a machine (with *up, in,* etc.).—**winch'man** one who operates a winch or takes part in winching operations, e.g. aboard a helicopter. [O.E. *wince,* from a Gmc. and Indo-European root.]

Winchester (**rifle**)® *win'chəs-tər* (*rī'fl*), orig. a tradename for a repeating rifle made by Oliver F. *Winchester,* American manufacturer: now a tradename for fire-arms, etc., produced by the makers of the rifle.

wind[1] *wind, n.* air in motion: a current of air, usually horizontal, either natural or produced by artificial means: any of the directions from which the wind may blow: breath: power of breathing: flatulence: conceit: empty, insignificant words: the wind instruments in an orchestra: their players: air impregnated with scent of game: a hint or suggestion, as of something secret.—*v.t.* to perceive by the scent: to expose to

wind: to drive, punch hard, so as to put out of breath: to allow to recover wind.—*ns.* **wind'age** the difference between the size of the bore of a gun and that of the ball or shell: the influence of the wind in deflecting a missile, the amount of deflection due to wind, or the allowance made for it: air friction on a moving, esp. revolving, part of a machine; **wind'er** (*slang*) a blow that takes one's breath away.—*adv.* **wind'ily.**—*n.* **wind'iness.**—*adj.* **wind'less** without wind.—*adv* and *adj.* **wind'ward** towards or on the side the wind blows from.—Also *n.*—*adv.* **wind'wards.**—*adj.* **wind'y** like, characterised by, exposed to, the wind: suffering from, producing, or produced by, flatulence: suggestive of wind, as insubstantial, changeable, boastful, conceited, wordy (*fig.*): frightened, nervous (*coll.*).—**wind'-bag** the bellows of a bagpipe: a person of mere words, an excessively talkative person (*slang*); **wind'-break** a protection against the force of the wind, such as a fence or line of trees; **wind'burn** inflammation of the skin due to over-exposure to the wind; **wind'cheater** a close-knitted pullover: an anorak; **wind'-chest** the box or reservoir that supplies compressed air to the pipes or reeds of an organ; **wind'-cone** (*aero.*) a sleeve floating from the top of a mast, its angle with the ground giving a rough conception of the velocity of the wind, and its angle in a horizontal plane the wind direction; **wind'fall** fruit blown off a tree by the wind: any unexpected money or other advantage; **windfall tax** a tax levied on windfall profits, profits arising, esp. suddenly and unexpectedly, as a result of events not directly connected with the company, etc. concerned, such as changes in currency exchange rates.—*adj.* **wind'fallen** blown down by wind.—**wind'-flower** an anemone, esp. the wood-anemone; **wind'-gauge** an instrument for measuring the velocity of the wind: a gauge for measuring pressure of wind in an organ: appliance fixed to a rifle by means of which the force of the wind is ascertained so that allowance may be made for it in sighting; **wind'-hover** (*hov', huv'ər*) the kestrel; **wind'-instrument** a musical instrument sounded by means of wind, esp. by the breath; **wind'jammer** a large sailing vessel; **wind'mill** a mill in which the motive-power is the wind acting on a set of vanes or sails: a wind-driven set of vanes used to pump water, etc.; **wind'pipe** the passage for the breath between the mouth and lungs, the trachea; **wind power** wind considered as an energy source, e.g. for the generation of electricity by means of windmills, etc.; **wind'rose** a rosette-like diagram showing the relative frequency and strength of winds in a locality for given periods of the year; **wind'row** a row of hay, etc., set up for drying; **wind'screen** a shelter against wind, esp. a transparent screen on motor-cars, etc.; **wind'shield** (*U.S.*) a windscreen; **wind'-side** the side next the wind; **wind'-sleeve, -sock** a wind-cone; **wind'surfing** (also called **sailboarding**) the sport of sailing on a sailboard, a sailing-craft consisting usu. of a surfboard fitted with a single, flexible mast, the sail being controlled by a hand-held boom.—*adjs.* **wind'swept** exposed to, or swept by, the wind; **wind'-tight** air-tight.—**wind'-tunnel** an experimental apparatus for producing a uniform steady air-stream past a model for aerodynamic investigation work.—**cast, fling, throw, to the winds** to scatter, throw away, recklessly: to abandon (restraint, prudence, caution, discretion, etc.); **get one's wind** to recover one's breath; **get the wind up** (*slang*) to become nervous, apprehensive, agitated; **get wind of** to get a hint or intimation of; **how the wind blows or lies** the state of the wind: the position of affairs; **in the wind** astir, afoot; **in the wind's eye, in the teeth of the wind** right against the wind; **like the wind** rapidly; **put the wind** up someone (*slang*) to make someone apprehensive or agitated, **sail close to the wind** to keep the boat's head so near to the wind as to fill but not shake the sails: to be in danger of transgressing an approved limit; **second wind** power of respiration recovered after breathlessness: the energy necessary for a renewal of effort (*fig*); **take the wind out of someone's sails** (*fig.*) to deprive someone of an advantage, to frustrate, discomfit someone; **tilt at windmills** to struggle with imaginary opposition, as Don Quixote, who charged at a windmill thinking it was an enemy; **wind(s) of change** a pervasive influence bringing change. [O E]

wind² *wind*, *v.t.* to turn, to twist, to coil: to encircle: to screw the mechanism of, as a time-piece: to make, direct, as one's way, or to traverse, by turning and twisting: to haul or hoist, as by a winch —*v i.* to turn round something: to twist: to move, go, by turns and twists, or (*fig*) deviously:—*pr.p.* **wind'ing;** *pa.t.* and *pa.p.* **wound** (*wownd*); chiefly *naut.* **wind'ed.**—*n.* a turn, coil, or twist: a turning: a twisted condition.—*n.* **wind'er** one who winds: an instrument for winding: a clock or watch key: an electrically driven winding-engine for hoisting a cage or cages up a vertical mine-shaft: a twisting plant: a triangular step at the turn of a stair or in a spiral staircase.—*adj.* and *n.* **wind'ing.**—*adv.* **wind'ingly.**—**wind'ing-sheet** a sheet for enwrapping a corpse; **wind'-up** the close, finish.—**wind down** to relax, become quiet after a period of activity: to lose strength: to reduce the strength or scope of; **wind up** to bring, or come, to a conclusion: to adjust for final settlement: to terminate the activities of, liquidate (a commercial firm, etc.): to excite very much (esp. in *pa.p.* **wound up** excited; *fig.*): to coil completely: to wind the spring or the mechanism of tightly: to tighten: to hoist, as by a winch. [O.E. *windan*.]

windage. See **wind¹**.

windlass *wind'las*, *n.* any of various modifications of the wheel and axle employing a revolving cylinder, used for hauling or hoisting.—*v.i.* to use a windlass.—*v.t.* to hoist by means of such. [O.N. *vindáss—vinda*, to wind, *áss*, pole.]

windlestraw *win'dl-strō*, *n.* a thin, dry stalk of grass: any of various long-stalked species of grass, as rye-grass. [O.E. *windelstrēaw—windel*, a woven basket, *strēaw*, straw.]

window *win'dō*, *n.* an opening in the wall of a building, etc., for air and light: the frame in the opening: the space immediately behind the opening: a window-pane: any opening suggesting a window: a weather-window (q.v.): in various technical uses designating a part that is clear, free of a particular type of obstruction, etc.—*v.t.* to furnish with windows.—*adjs.* **win'-dowed** having a window or windows, or openings or holes resembling these; **win'dowless** having no windows.—**win'dow-box** a box for growing plants in on a window-sill; **win'dow-dressing** the arranging of goods in a shop window: the art of doing so effectively: (the art of) presenting a cause, situation, etc., in a favourable light; **window envelope** an envelope with a transparent panel through which the address of the recipient on the enclosed letter can be read; **win'dow-frame** a frame that surrounds a window, **win'dow-ledge** a window-sill; **win'dow-pane** a sheet of glass set in a window; **win'dow-sash** a frame in which panes of glass are set; **win'dow-seat** a seat in the recess of a window; **win'dow-shopping** gazing in shop windows rather than making actual purchases; **win'dow-sill** the sill of a window opening. [M.E *windowe, windoge—O.N *vindauga—vindr*, wind, *auga*, eye]

Windsor *win'zər*, *adj.* pertaining to *Windsor*, in Berkshire, as in **Windsor chair**, a chair with a solid wooden seat that has sockets into which the legs and the (usu slender, spindle-shaped) uprights of the back are fitted; **Windsor knot** a type of wide, triangular knot used in tying a tie; **Wind'sor-soap** a kind of perfumed toilet-soap (usu. brown).

wine *win*, *n.* the fermented juice of grapes: a liquor made from other fruits: a rich red colour.—Also *adj.*—*v.t.* to supply with wine: to treat with wine.—*v.i.* to take wine, especially at a wine-party.—*adj.* **wi'n(e)y** like wine: intoxicated.—*ns.* **wi'nery** (chiefly *U S.*) a place where wine is prepared, **wino** (*wi'nō; coll.*) an alcoholic addicted to wine:—*pl.* **wi'nos.**—**wine'-bibber** a continual drinker of wine: a drunkard; **wine'-bibbing;** **wine'-cellar** a cellar for storing wine —*adj* **wine'-coloured** of the colour of red wine.—**wine'-cooler** a receptacle for cooling wine in bottles about to be served at table; **wine'-glass** a small glass used in drinking wine; **wine'-glassful; wine'-grower** one who cultivates a vineyard and makes wine.—*n.* and *adj.* **wine'-growing.—wine lake** a surplus of wine bought up by an economic community to prevent a fall in prices; **wine'-list; wine'-merchant** a dealer in wine, esp. wholesale; **wine'-party** a drinking-party; **wine'-press** a machine in which grapes are pressed in the manufacture of wine; **wine'-taster** one whose business it is to sample wines; **wine'-tasting** (a gathering for) sampling wines; **wine'-vault(s)** a vaulted wine-cellar: a place where wine is tasted or drunk.—**Adam's wine** water. [O.E. *win* from L. *vinum*.]

wing *wing*, *n.* the organ of a bird, insect, or other creature, by which it flies: an animal organ resembling a wing: flight: means of flying: anything resembling a wing: a fan or vane: (usu. in *pl.*) a sail: any side-piece, on a building, etc.: the side of a stage: side scenery: a plane of an aeroplane: the mudguard of a motor vehicle: a side-piece on the back of an armchair: a section of a political party: (a player on) either the extreme left or extreme right of the forward line in football, etc.: either edge of a football, etc. pitch, along which such a player moves: a group of three squadrons in the Royal Air Force: (in *pl.*) a qualified pilot's badge: formerly, the badge of any member of an air-crew other than the pilot: means or power of rapid movement (*fig.*): protection (*fig.*).—*v.t.* to furnish, or transport, with wings: to lend speed to: to supply with side-pieces: to bear in flight, to waft: to effect on wings: to traverse by flying: to wound in the wing: to wound in the arm or shoulder.—*v.i.* to soar on the wing: to go with speed.—*adj.* **winged** (*wingd* or *wing'id*) furnished with wings: (*wingd*) of a fruit or seed, having a flattened appendage: (*wingd*) wounded in the wing, shoulder, or arm: swift: lofty, sublime: (in **winged words**) spoken, uttered, flying from one person to another.—*n.* **wing'er** one who plays in a position on the wing in football, etc.—*adj.* **wing'less** without wings.—*n.* **wing'let** a small wing: a wing-like appendage.—*adj.* **wing'y** having, resembling, or soaring on, wings: lofty.—**wing'beat** a beat or flap of a bird's or insect's wing; **wing'-case** the horny case or cover over the wings of some insects, as the beetles; **wing collar** a man's stiff collar, worn upright with the points turned down; **wing'-commander** a Royal Air Force officer corresponding in rank to a naval commander or to a lieutenant-colonel.—*adj.* **wing'-footed** having wings attached to the feet (*myth*, etc.): fast-moving, swift (*poet.*) —**wing forward** one of the two outside men of the second row of the scrum, a flanker (*Rugby football*); **wing'-loading** (*aero.*) the maximum flying weight of an aeroplane divided by the total area of the main planes; **wing mirror** a rear-view mirror projecting from the wing, or more generally, the side of a vehicle; **wing nut** a butterfly-nut (q.v.); **wing'span,**

wing'-spread the distance from tip to tip of a bird's extended wings, or of the wings of an aircraft.—in the wings (coll.) waiting in reserve; lend wings to to give speed to; make, take, wing to begin flight: to depart; on, upon, the wing flying: in motion: departing; under someone's wing under someone's protection. [O.N. vængr, a wing.]

wingding wing'ding, (chiefly Amer.) n. a wild party: a drug-addict's seizure: a pretended seizure.

winge winj, (dial.). Non-Scottish (esp. Austr.) variant of whinge.

wink wingk, v.i. to move the eyelids, or an eyelid, quickly: to give a hint, or convey amused understanding, by a sign of this kind: to blink: to seem not to see: to connive (usu. with at): to flicker, twinkle.—v.t. to close and open quickly: to flicker: to express by flash-lights.—n. the act of winking: a hint, as by winking: a blink: a closing of the eyes for sleep: a short spell of sleep: a very small time or distance.—ns. wink'er one who winks: (in pl.) direction indicators on a motor vehicle, consisting of flashing lights (coll.); wink'ing the act of giving a wink.—adv. wink'ingly.—easy as winking very easily indeed; forty winks (coll.) a short nap. [O.E. wincian.]

winkle wing'kl, n. a periwinkle (see periwinkle²): the penis (slang or hypocoristic).—wink'le-pickers shoes with long pointed toes, esp. popular in the early 1960s.—winkle out (fig.) to force out gradually and with difficulty (perh. derived from Ger. Winkel, corner).

winnable, winner, winning, winningly. See win.

winnow win'ō, v.t. to separate the chaff from by wind: to fan: to sift: to separate: to blow upon.—v.i. to separate chaff from grain: to fly: to blow in gusts.—n. a fan for winnowing.—ns. winn'ower; winn'owing. [O.E. windwian, to winnow—wind; see wind¹.]

wino. See wine.

winsome win'səm, adj. cheerful: pleasant: attractive.—adv. win'somely.—n. win'someness. [O.E. wynsum, pleasant—wyn, joy—and -sum (see suff. -some).]

winter win'tər, n. the cold season of the year—in northern temperate regions, from November or December to January or February; astronomically, from the winter solstice to the vernal equinox: a year (usu. in pl.): any season of cheerlessness.—adj. wintry: suitable for wear or use in winter: sown in autumn, as winter wheat, winter barley, winter crop, etc.—v.i. to pass the winter.—v.t. to feed and keep through winter.—adj. win'tered exposed to winter.—v.t. win'terise, -ize to make suitable for use under wintry conditions.—n. win'triness.—adj. win'try, win'tery resembling, or suitable to, winter: stormy: cheerless.—win'ter aconite see aconite; win'ter-cherry any species of Physalis, esp. Physalis alkekengi: its edible fruit; win'ter-cress a cruciferous plant (Barbarea) formerly cultivated for winter salad; win'ter-garden an ornamental garden of evergreens, etc., or a conservatory with flowers, for winter: (in pl., with cap.) used sometimes as the name of a theatre, concert-hall, etc.; win'tergreen a plant of genus Pyrola, also of Chimaphila: a plant of genus Gaultheria, whose oil is an aromatic stimulant, used in flavouring confectionery and in medicine (chick'weed-win'tergreen either of two plants—Trientalis europaea or Trientalis americana—belonging to the Primulaceae, having white starlike flowers); winter quarters the quarters of an army during winter: a winter residence; winter sports open-air sports practised on snow and ice, as skiing, etc.—adj. win'ter-weight of clothes, heavy enough or thick enough to be suitable for cold weather.—nuclear winter the period of extreme winter-like conditions

thought by some scientists to be likely to follow a nuclear war. [O.E.]

wintry. See winter.

winy. See wine.

wipe wīp, v.t. to clean or dry by rubbing: to clear away (with away, off, out, up): to draw across something in order to, or as if to, clean it: to clear (magnetic tape) of its content (also fig.).—n. the act of cleaning by rubbing: a blow: a handkerchief (slang).—ns. wi'per one who wipes, esp. one who is employed in certain industrial jobs: that which wipes or is used for wiping: a moving arm or other conducting device for making a selected contact out of a number of possible connections (elect.): a moving arm, usu. electrically operated, for removing raindrops, etc., from the windscreen of a motor vehicle; wi'ping the act of one who wipes: a thrashing.—wipe out to obliterate, annihilate or abolish: to fall from a surfboard, skis, etc. (slang). [O.E. wīpian.]

wire wīr, n. a thread or rope of metal: a piece of wire, or (in pl.) a group or network of wires, used for some purpose: the metal thread used in telegraphy, etc.: a metallic string of a musical instrument: a telegram (coll.): a fence made of wire.—adj. formed of, pertaining to, or using, wire: running on wire.—v.t. to bind, support, protect, snare, or furnish, with wire: to supply, as a building, with wires necessary for carrying an electric current: to send, or to inform, by telegraph.—v.i. to telegraph.—adjs. wired; wire'less without a wire or wires: of or pertaining to telegraphy or telephony without wires.—n. wireless telegraphy or telephony, radio: a receiving or transmitting set used for this purpose: a message or broadcast so transmitted: broadcast programmes: broadcasting generally.—v.t. and v.i. to communicate by radio.—n. wi'rer one who wires, or who uses wire, e.g. to snare animals.—adv. wi'rily.—ns. wi'riness; wi'ring the action of the verb: the complex of wires in an electrical system or installation.—adj. wi'ry made of, or like, wire: flexible and strong: of a person, strong and able to endure.—wire brush a brush with wire bristles, for cleaning rust off metal, dirt off suede shoes, etc.; wired'-glass glass in which a wire mesh has been incorporated during rolling as a resistance against fire and explosion blast.—v.t. wire'draw to draw into wire by pulling through successively smaller holes in a hard steel dieblock.—wire'drawer; wire'drawing; wire gauge any system for designating the diameter of wires by means of a set of numbers: the diameter of a particular piece of wire; wire'-gauze a kind of stiff close fabric made of fine wire; wire'-grass a kind of fine meadow-grass (Poa compressa): any of various other grasses with wiry stems.—adj. wire'-haired having a coat of rather rough, hard hair.—wireless station a station for wireless transmission; wireless telegraphy, telephony signalling through space, without the use of conducting wires between transmitter and receiver, by means of electromagnetic waves generated by high-frequency alternating currents; wire nail a common type of nail, round or elliptical in cross-section, cut from steel wire; wire'-nett'ing a texture of galvanised wire woven in the form of a net; wire'-puller one who exercises an influence felt but not seen: an intriguer; wire'-pulling; wire'-rope a rope of twisted wire.—v.t. wire'tap to tap (a telephone).—wire wool a mass of very fine wire for scouring; wire'work the making of wire, or of objects of wire: articles, or fabric, made of wire; wire'worker; wire'working; wire'-worm a name given to the larvae of click-beetles, from their slenderness and uncommon hardness.—give (someone) the wire (chiefly mil.) to give advance information; pull the wires to be a wire-puller (q.v.); wire away or in to act or work with vigour; **wire-haired terrier** a type of wire-haired fox-terrier; **wire into** to eat vigorously and assiduously. [O.E. *wīr*.]

wisdom. See under **wise¹**.

wise¹ *wīz, adj.* having knowledge: learned: able to make good use of knowledge: judging rightly: discreet: skilful: dictated by wisdom: containing wisdom: pious, godly.—*n.* **wisdom** (*wiz'dəm*) the quality of being wise: judgment: the ability to make right use of knowledge: a wise discourse, saying or teaching (*arch.*): learning (*hist.*): skilfulness, speculation, spiritual perception (*B.*).—*adv.* **wise'ly.**—*n.* **wise'ness.**—**wis'dom-tooth** any of four double back teeth cut after childhood, usually from the late teens; **wise'crack** a lively, pungent retort or comment.—*v.i.* to make such.—*adj.* **wise'cracking** making, or addicted to making, wisecracks.—**wise guy** a conceited, over-confident person: a smart alec.—**never, none, the wiser** still in ignorance; **put someone wise** (*slang*) to put someone in possession of information, make aware; **the Wise Men (of the East), Three Wise Men** the three Magi (in some traditions kings) who according to Matt. II came to worship the baby Jesus at Bethlehem; **wise to** (*slang*) aware of; **wise up** (*slang*) to make or become aware, in possession of information. [O.E. *wīs*; from root of **wit**.]

wise² *wīz, (arch.) n.* way, manner, now chiefly in the phrases **in any wise, in no wise** in any way, in no way, and as a *suff.*, meaning in the manner of, e.g. **likewise, otherwise** or (*coll.*) in the matter of, e.g. **moneywise, business-wise.** [O.E. *wīse*; akin to **wise¹** and **wit.**]

wiseacre *wīz'ā-kər,* n. one who unduly assumes an air of superior wisdom: a wise guy: a simpleton quite unconscious of being such. [M.Du. *wijssegger*—O.H.G. *wīzago,* a prophet.]

wisent *wē'zənt, vē', n.* another name for the European bison. [Ger.]

wish *wish, v.i.* to have a desire: to long: to be inclined: to express a desire, esp. as part of a superstitious ritual.—*v.t.* to desire or long for: to express a desire for: to ask: to invoke: to bid: to foist, palm off (with *on, on to; coll.*).—*n.* desire, longing: a thing desired: an expression of desire: (usu. in *pl.*) an expression of desire for good fortune for another.—*n.* **wish'er.**—*adj.* **wish'ful** having a wish or desire: eager.—*adv.* **wish'fully.**—*n.* **wish'fulness.**—*n.* and *adj.* **wish'ing.**—**wish fulfilment** (*psych.*) the satisfaction of a desire in dreams, day-dreams, etc.; **wishful thinking** (*psych.*) a type of thinking in which the individual substitutes the fantasy of the fulfilment of the wish for the actual achievement: a belief that a particular thing will happen, or is so, engendered by desire that it should happen, or be so: loosely, thinking about and wishing for an event or turn of fortune that may not take place; **wish'ing-bone, wish'bone** the V-shaped bone formed by the fused clavicles in a bird's breast, pulled apart in playful divination, the longer part indicating the first to be married or fulfilment of a wish; **wish'ing-stone, -tree, -well,** etc., a stone, tree, well, etc., supposed to have the power of making a wish expressed at it come 'true.—**wish someone further** (*slang*) to wish someone was in some other place, not present; **wish someone joy of something** (usu. *iron.*) to hope that the possession of something will be of benefit to someone. [O.E. *wȳscan,* to wish.]

wish-wash *wish'-wosh, (coll.) n.* anything wishy-washy.—*adj.* **wish'y-wash'y** thin and weak: diluted: feeble: of poor quality. [Formed from **wash.**]

wisp *wisp, n.* a small bundle of straw or hay: a tuft, a shred: a thin strand or band: a small broom: a twisted bunch used as a torch: the will-o'-the-wisp.—*adj.*

wis'py wisp-like, light and fine in texture: flimsy, insubstantial.

wist *wist.* See **wit¹.**

Wistaria *wis-tā'ri-ə, n.* a genus of papilionaceous plants, some of the species among the most magnificent ornamental climbers known in English gardens, named from the American anatomist Caspar *Wistar* (1761–1818)—also **Wiste'ria** (without *cap.*) any plant of this genus.

wistful *wist'fŏŏl, -fl, adj.* longing: yearning with little hope: pensive.—*adv.* **wist'fully.**—*n.* **wist'fulness.**

wit¹ *wit, v.t.* and *v.i.* (*arch.:* except in legal use) to know: to be aware (with *of*): to recognise, discern: to know how:—*infin.* **wit;** *pr.t.* 1st pers. sing. **wot;** 2nd **wost** (*wott'est*); 3rd **wot** (*wots, wott'eth*); *pr.p.* **witt'ing;** *pa.p.* **wist.**—*n.* **witt'ing** (*obs.* and *dial.*) knowledge: information.—*adj.* cognisant: conscious: deliberate.—*adv.* **witt'ingly** knowingly: by design.—**to wit** that is to say, namely. [O.E. *witan,* to know (pres. tense *wāt, wāst, wāt,* pl. *witon;* pa.t. *wiste,* or *wisse,* pl. *wiston,* pa.p. *wist*).]

wit² *wit, n.* the understanding (*arch.*): imagination or invention (*arch.*): ingenuity: intelligence, sense (in phrase **have the wit to**): a mental faculty (chiefly in *pl.*): the power of combining ideas with a pointed verbal effect: the product of this power: humour, wittiness: a person endowed with wit.—*adj.* **wit'less** lacking wit, wisdom, sense: out of one's mind: stupid, unintelligent: unaware, unconscious.—*adv.* **wit'lessly.**—*ns.* **wit'lessness;** **wit'ling** one who has little wit: a pretender to wit.—*adj.* **witt'ed** having wit or understanding (usu. in composition, as *quick-witted*).—*n.* **witticism** (*wit'i-sizm*) a witty remark: a sentence or phrase affectedly witty: (*formerly*) a jibe.—*adv.* **witt'ily.**—*n.* **witt'iness.**—*adj.* **witt'y** possessed of wit: amusing, droll: sarcastic.—**at one's wits' end** utterly perplexed; **have one's wits about one** to be alert and resourceful; **live by one's wits** to gain a livelihood by ingenious expedients rather than by honest labour; **the five wits** the five senses. [O.E. (*ge*)*wit*—**wit¹.**]

witan *wit'an, n.pl.* members of the witenagemot: the witenagemot.—*n.* **witenagemot** (*wit'ən-ə-gə-mōt';* popularly *-nag'*) the supreme council of England in Anglo-Saxon times, composed of the bishops, the ealdormen of shires, and a number of the king's friends and dependents. [Pl. of O.E. *wita,* a man of knowledge (*witena,* gen. pl.); *gemōt,* meeting.]

witch¹ *wich, n.* a woman regarded as having supernatural or magical power and knowledge usu. through compact with the devil or a minor evil spirit: a hag, crone: a fascinating woman (*coll.*).—*v.t.* to bewitch: to effect, change, transport, etc., by means of witchcraft: to fascinate.—*v.i.* to practise witchcraft or fascination.—*ns.* **witch'ery** witchcraft: fascination; **witch'ing** sorcery: enchantment.—*adj.* suited to witchcraft: weird: fascinating.—*adv.* **witch'ingly.**—**witch'craft** the craft or practice of witches: the black art, sorcery: supernatural power; **witch'-doctor** in tribal societies, a magician who detects witches and counteracts evil magical influences: one who professes to heal by means of magic; **witch'es'-broom** a dense tuft of poorly developed branches formed on a woody plant attacked by a parasite (chiefly fungi and mites); **witch hunt** (orig. *U.S.*) the searching out of political opponents for exposure on grounds of alleged disloyalty to the state, etc.: also applied to any similar non-political search. [M.E. *wicche* (both masc. and fem.)—O.E. *wicca* (masc.), *wicce* (fem.), wizard, witch, and verb *wiccian.*]

witch² *wich, n.* any of several trees with pliant branches, as the wych-elm, the rowan, etc.—**witch'alder** any of a genus of N. American shrubs related to the witch-hazel—not an alder; **witch'-elm** the wych-elm; **witch'-hazel** any of a number of trees, as the wych-elm, or a N. American shrub (*Hamamelis virginica*) from whose bark is made a supposed remedy for bruises, etc.—a distillate of the bark dissolved in alcohol. [O.E. *wice*; allied to *wīcan*, to give way.]

witchetty *wich'i-ti*, *n*. any of the edible grubs of species of certain moths (*Cossus*).—Also **witchetty grub**. [Austr. native name.]

witenagemot. See **witan**.

with *widh*, *with*, *prep*. denoting nearness, agreement, or connection: by, beside: among: on the side of: in the company of: in the possession or care of: containing: supplemented by: possessing: characterised by: in the same direction as: at the time of: at the same time as: immediately after: in competition or contest against: in respect of, in the regard of: by, by means of, through: because of: in spite of: using: from (as in *to part with*).—*adv*. **withal** (*widh-ôl'*) with all or the rest: besides: therewith: thereupon: nevertheless, for all that.—*prep*. an emphatic form of *with*, used after its object.—**be with someone** to understand someone; **feel, be, or think, with** to feel as, or be of the same opinion as, the other person specified; **in with** (*coll*.) friendly with; **with it** (*slang*) following current trends in popular taste; **with that** thereupon. [O.E. *with*, against; O.N. *vith*, Ger. *wider*. It ousted the O.E. *mid*, with (Ger. *mit*).]

withdraw *widh-drö'*, or *with-*, *v.t*. to draw back or away: to take back or away: to take from deposit or investment, as money: to remove (with *from*): to recall, retract.—*v.i*. to retire: to go away: to take back what one has said, or to recall a motion one has proposed:—*pa.t*. **withdrew** (-*drōō'*);*pa.p*. **withdrawn'**.—*ns*. **withdraw'al**; **withdraw'er**.—*adj*. **withdrawn'** (of place) secluded: remote: (of a person or his manner) detached: uncommunicative: introverted.—**withdrawal symptom** any of a number of symptoms, such as pain, nausea, sweating, caused by depriving a person of a drug to which he is addicted; **withdraw'ing-room** a room used to retire into: a drawing-room. [Pfx. *with-*, against, back, and **draw**.]

withe *widh*, *with*, or *widh*, *n*. a flexible twig, esp. of willow: a band of twisted twigs.—*v.t*. to bind with a withe or withes.—*adj*. **with'y** made of withes: like withes, flexible: wiry and agile. [O.E. *withthe*; cf **withy**.]

wither *widh'ər*, *v.i*. to fade or become dry: to lose freshness: to languish, decline: to decay, waste.—*v.t*. to cause to dry up, fade, or decay: to cause to feel very unimportant or despicable.—*adj*. **with'ered**.—*ns*. **with'eredness**; **with'ering**.—*adj*. fading, becoming dry, etc., or causing to do so: blasting, blighting, scorching (*fig*.): snubbing.—*adv*. **with'eringly**. [M.E. *wederen*, to expose to weather.]

withers *widh'ərz*, *n.pl*. the ridge between the shoulderbones of a horse. [O.E. *wither*, against, an extension of *with*, against.]

withershins *widh'ər-shinz*, (*Scot*.) *adv*. in the contrary direction, contrary to the course of the sun: in the wrong way. [L.G. *weddersins*; cf. O.E. *wither*, against, L.G. *sind*, direction.]

withhold *widh-hôld'*, or *with-*, *v.t*. to hold back, restrain: to keep back: to refuse to give:—*pa.t*. and *pa.p*. **withheld'** (*arch. pa.p*. **withhold'en**).—*ns*. **withhold'er**; **withhold'ment**. [Pfx. *with-*, against, and **hold**.]

within *widh-in'*, or *with-*, *prep*. in or to the inner part of (*arch*.): inside: in the limits of: not going beyond: entered from: into.—*adv*. in the inner part: inwardly: in the mind, soul, heart: behind the scenes: indoors: in or to an inner room (*arch*.): herein.—**within reach**

in a position from which it can be obtained, or attained, without much difficulty, effort, or loss of time. [O.E. *withinnan*—*with*, against, with, *innan*, in.]

without *widh-owt'*, or *with-*, *prep*. outside, or out of (*arch*.): outside the limits of (*arch*.): beyond (*arch*.): not with: in absence of: not having: not using: with no help from: free from.—*adv*. on the outside: outwardly: outside, not members of, a particular group or society: out of doors (*arch*.).—*conj*. (*arch*. or *dial*.) unless, except.—**from without** from the outside; **without distinction** indiscriminately. [O.E. *withūtan*—*with*, against, *ūtan*, outside.]

withstand *widh-stand'*, or *with-*, *v.t*. to stand, maintain one's position, against: to oppose or resist:—*pa.t*. and *pa.p*. **withstood'**.—*n*. **withstand'er**. [O.E. *withstandan*—*with*, against; see **stand**.]

withy *widh'i*, *n*. the osier willow: any willow: a flexible twig or branch, esp. one used for binding. [O.E. *wīthig*, willow; cf. **withe**.]

witling. See **wit**[2].

witness *wit'nis*, *n*. knowledge brought in proof: testimony of a fact: that which furnishes proof: one who sees or has personal knowledge of a thing: one who gives evidence: one who or that which attests.—*v.t*. to have direct knowledge of: (*loosely*) to see: to be the scene of: to give testimony to: to attest: to act as legal witness of.—*v.i*. to give evidence.—*n*. **wit'nesser.**—**wit'ness-box** the enclosure in which a witness stands when giving evidence in a court of law.—**bear witness** to give, or be, evidence (esp. with *to*). [O.E. (*ge*)*witnes*—(*ge*)*wit*; see **wit**[2].]

witter *wit'ər*, *v.i*. to talk or mutter peevishly or ineffectually (esp. with *on*).

witticism. See **wit**[2].

witting, witty, etc. See **wit**[1,2].

wive *wīv*, *v.t*. to take for a wife: to provide with a wife.—*v.i*. to marry a wife. [O.E. *wīfian*—*wīf*, wife.]

wivern *wī'vərn*, (*her*.) *n*. a fictitious monster, winged and two-legged, allied to the dragon and the griffin. [O.N.Fr. *wivre*, a viper—L *vīpera*.]

wives *wīvz*, *pl*. of **wife**.

wizard *wiz'ərd*, *n*. one, usu. a man, who practises witchcraft or magic: one who works wonders.—*adj*. with magical powers: wonderful, delightful (*slang*).—*n*. **wiz'ardry** sorcery [M.E. *wysar*(*d*)—*wys*, wise, and noun suff. -*ard*.]

wizen *wiz'n*, *adj*. dried up, thin, shrivelled (now usu. **wiz'ened**).—*v.i*. and *v.t*. to become, or to make, dry and shrivelled. [O.E. *wisnian*, to wither.]

woad *wōd*, *n*. a genus (Isatis) of cruciferous plants, mostly Mediterranean—**dyer's woad** (*Isatis tinctoria*) yielding a good and very permanent dye, largely superseded by indigo: a blue dye. [O.E. *wād*.]

wobbegong *wob'i-gong*, *n*. a carpet shark. [Austr. native word.]

wobble *wob'l*, *v.i*. to move unsteadily or uncertainly from side to side: to move along thus: to quiver: to quaver (*coll*.): to vacillate.—Also *v.t*.—*n*. an unsteady, unequal motion or movement.—*ns*. **wobb'ler**; **wobb'liness**; **wobb'ling**.—*adj*. **wobb'ly** shaky: inclined to wobble.—**wobb'le-board** a sheet of hardboard shaken to obtain certain sound-effects. [L.G. *wabbeln*.]

Woden *wō'dən*, *n*. the chief god of the ancient Germanic peoples. [O.E. *Wōden*; cf. **Odin**.]

wodge *woj*, (*coll*.) *n*. a large or roughly-cut portion: a lump. [**wedge**.]

woe *wō*, *n*. grief (*arch*.): misery: (often in *pl*.) a misfortune or calamity: an exclamation of grief.—*adjs*. **woe'ful, woe'some** sorrowful or afflicted: bringing misery or calamity: deplorable: wretched, paltry.—*adv*. **woe'fully**.—*n*. **woe'fulness**.—*adj*. **woe'begone**

beset with woe: dismal-looking, suggesting misery.—
woe is me (*arch.*) unhappy that I am! cursed am I; **woe
unto** calamity will befall: may calamity befall.
[O.E. (interj.) *wā*; cf. **wall**.]

wog *wog*, *n.* an offensive name for an Arab, an Egyptian, etc.: a foreigner generally, usu. coloured.
[Perh. from **(golly)wog**.]

woggle *wog'l*, *n.* the ring a Scout threads his neckerchief through.

wok *wok*, *n.* a hemispherical frying-pan used in Chinese cookery. [Chin.]

woke, woken. See **wake**¹.

wold *wōld*, *n.* an open tract of country, now chiefly upland country. [O.E. (Angl.) *wald*, forest, applied orig. to wooded parts of the country; cf. **weald**.]

wolf *wōōlf*, *n.* the common name of certain gregarious and rapacious species of the genus Canis—including the common wolf (*Canis lupus*), the grey or timber wolf, and the coyote: anything very ravenous: a greedy and cunning person: a dissonance heard in a keyed instrument tuned by unequal temperament (*mus.*): an extraneous non-harmonic note made by the bow on a string of a violin, etc. (*mus.*): a man who pursues women (*coll.*):—*pl.* **wolves** (*wōōlvz*).—*v.i.* to hunt for wolves (also **wolve** *wōōlv*).—*v.t.* (often with *down* or *up*; *coll.*) to devour ravenously.—*ns.*
wolf'er, wolv'er one who hunts wolves; **wolf'ing,
wolv'ing** the hunting of wolves for their skins.—*adjs.*
wolf'ish, wolv'ish like a wolf: rapacious: ravenous.—
adv. **wolf'ishly, wolv'ishly.**—**Wolf Cub** one who belonged to the Wolf Cubs, a junior division of the Boy Scouts organisation (now Cub Scouts); **wolf'-dog** a dog of large breed formerly used in hunting wolves: a cross between a wolf and a domestic dog; **wolf'-fish** any genus of fierce and voracious salt-water fishes—called also sea-wolf; **wolf'-hound** a wolf-dog, esp. of large size, as the Russian wolf-hound; **wolf'-pack** a pack of wolves; **wolf's'-bane, wolfs'bane** an aconite, esp. *Aconitum lycoctonum*; **wolf'-spi'der** any spider of the genus (Lycosa) to which the true tarantula belongs, or of the family Lycosidae; **wolf'-whistle** a two-note whistle uttered in admiration, typically by a man at the sight of a woman.—**cry wolf** to give a false alarm—from the story of the boy who cried 'Wolf' when there was none, and was not believed when there was one; **keep the wolf from the door** to keep away poverty or hunger; **throw, fling to the wolves** to abandon to certain destruction; **wolf in sheep's clothing** someone who behind a kindly and inoffensive exterior is dangerous and unscrupulous. [O.E. *wulf*.]

wolfram *wōōlf'rəm*, *n.* (also **wolf'ramite**) a native compound of tungstate of iron and manganese: tungsten. [Ger.]

Wolof *wō'lof*, *n.* a tribe living near the Senegal River in western Africa: a member of the tribe: its language.—Also *adj.*

wolve, wolver. See **wolf.**

wolverene, wolverine *wōōl-və-rēn'*, *n.* the American glutton: its fur. . [Extension of **wolf.**]

wolves, wolvish. See **wolf.**

woman *wōōm'ən*, *n.* an adult female of the human race: a wife (now *dial.*): a mistress: the female sex, women collectively: a female attendant: a charwoman or daily domestic help (*coll.*):—*pl.* **women** (*wim'ən*).—Also *adj.*—*n.* **wom'anhood** the state, character, or qualities of a woman: womenkind.—*v.t.*, *v.i.*
wom'anise, -ize to make, become, effeminate: (*v.i.*, *derog.*) of a man, to pursue women with a view to amorous adventures.—*n.* **wom'aniser, -z-.**—*adj.* **wom'anish** effeminate: feminine.—*adv.*
wom'anishly.—*ns.* **wom'anishness; wom'ankind**

(also **wom'enkind, wom'enfolk, -folks**) a group of women taken together, as the women of a family, or the female sex.—*adj.* and *adv.* **wom'an-like.**—*n.*
wom'anliness.—*adj.* **wom'anly** like or becoming a woman: feminine.—*adv.* in the manner of a woman.
—**wom'an-hater** a man who hates women, a misogynist; **wom'an-suffrage, women's suffrage** possession of the electoral franchise by women; **women's liberation** a movement of active feminists forming part of the women's movement (*coll.* contr. **women's lib**); **women's liberationist** (*coll.* contr. **women's libber**); **women's movement** the movement amongst women to try to achieve equality with men, with regard to e.g. job opportunities, pay, legal status, etc., **women's rights** equal rights with men thus sought by women; **wom'enswear** clothes for women.—**kept woman** a mistress; **woman of the town** a whore; **woman of the world** a woman of fashion, or of worldly wisdom: a woman who knows and makes allowance for, or accepts, the ways of the world; **Women's Royal Voluntary Service** (from its formation in 1938 until 1966 the **Women's Voluntary Service**) a nationwide service assisting government departments, local authorities and other voluntary bodies in organising and carrying out welfare and emergency work for the community. [O.E. *wimman—wifman—wif*, a woman, *man*, man, human being.]

womb *wōōm*, *n.* the uterus, the organ in which the young of mammals are developed and kept till birth: the place where anything is produced: any deep cavity.—**womb'-leasing** the contracting of surrogate mothers (q.v.) to bear children for childless couples. [O.E. *wamb, womb*.]

wombat *wom'bat, -bət, n.* an animal of a genus (*Phascolomys*) of Australian marsupial mammals of the same order as opossums. [Native name.]

women. See **woman.**

womera. Same as **woomera.**

won *wun*, *pa.t.* and *pa.p.* of **win.**

wonder *wun'dər*, *n.* the state of mind produced by something new, unexpected, or extraordinary: the quality of being strange or unexpected: a strange, astonishing, admirable, thing or happening: a prodigy: a miracle.—*v.i.* to feel wonder: to be amazed (with *at*): to speculate: to feel doubt.—*v.t.* to speculate, to ask oneself (with noun clause or direct quotation).—*n.* **won'derer.**—*adj.* **won'derful** exciting wonder: strange: expressing vague commendation, admirable, extremely good (*coll.*).—*adv.*
(*arch.* or *dial.*) wonderfully.—*adv.* **won'derfully.**—
n. **won'derfulness.**—*n.* and *adj.* **won'dering.**—*adv.*
won'deringly.—*n.* **won'derment** surprise: an expression of wonder: a wonderful thing: quality of being wonderful.—*adjs.* **won'derous, won'drous** such as may excite wonder.—Also *adv.*—*adv.* **won'drously.**
—*n.* **won'drousness.**—**won'derland** a land of wonders.—*adjs.* **won'der-struck, -strick'en** struck with wonder or astonishment.—**won'der-work** a prodigy, miracle; **won'der-worker; won'der-working.**—**nine days' wonder** something that astonishes everybody for the moment; **no wonder, small wonder** it isn't surprising; **seven wonders of the world** see seven. [O.E. *wundor*.]

wondrous. See **wonder.**

wonky *wongk'i*, (*coll.*) *adj.* unsound: shaky: amiss: awry. [Perh. O.E. *wancol*, unstable.]

wont *wōnt*, *adj.* used or accustomed.—*n.* habit.—*v.i.* to be accustomed.—*adj.* **wont'ed** accustomed, habituated (*U.S.*): usual (*arch.*). [Orig. pa.p. of obs. *won*, to be accustomed.]

won't *wōnt*, will not. [Contr. of M.E. *wol not.*]

woo *wōō*, *v.t.* to try to win the affection of: to court: to solicit eagerly: to seek to gain.—Also *v.i.*:—*pa.t.* and *pa.p.* **wooed** (*wōōd*).—*n.* **woo'er.**—*n.* and *adj.* **woo'ing.**—*adv.* **woo'ingly.** [O.E. *wōgian*, to woo.]

wood *wōōd, n.* a collection of growing trees (often in *pl.*): wooded country: the hard part of the substance of trees and shrubs, xylem: trees cut or sawed, timber: a kind of timber or wood: firewood: the cask or barrel, as distinguished from the bottle: a wooden-headed golf-club: a bowl (*bowls*).—*v.t.* to cover with trees: to supply or load with wood.—*v.i.* to take in a supply of wood.—*adjs.* **wood'ed** supplied with wood: covered with trees; **wood'en** made of, or like, wood: of a golf-club, with head made of wood: hard: dull, insensible: heavy, stupid: lacking animation or grace of manner or execution: clumsy.—*adv.* **wood'enly.**—*ns.* **wood'enness** wooden quality: want of spirit or expression; **wood'iness** the state or quality of being woody.—*adj.* **wood'less** without wood.—*n.* **wood'lessness.**—*adjs.* **wood'sy** (-*zi*; *U.S.*) pertaining to, or characteristic of, woods; **wood'y** abounding with woods: situated in a wood: pertaining to wood: consisting wholly or largely of wood: ligneous: like wood in texture, or smell, or taste, etc.—**wood's alcohol** wood-spirit; **wood'-anemone** any anemone growing in woods, esp. *Anemone nemorosa*, which has a single whorl of leaves and a white flower; **wood's ash** (often in *pl.*) ash obtained by burning wood or plants—a source of potassium salts; **wood'bine, wood'bind** the honeysuckle: applied also to other climbers, such as some kinds of ivy, the Virginia-creeper, etc.; **wood'block** a die cut in relief on wood and ready to furnish ink impressions: a woodcut; **wood'-carver; wood'-carving** the process of carving in wood: an object, or part of one, so ornamented or made; **wood'cock** a genus (Scolopax) of birds allied to the snipes, but of a more bulky body, and with shorter and stronger legs; **wood'craft** skill in the chase and everything pertaining to life in the woods: forestry generally: skill in working or carving wood; **wood'cut** a design for printing incised into the surface of a block of wood cut plank-wise, i.e. along the grain: an impression taken from this; **wood'-cutter** one who cuts wood: one who makes woodcuts; **wood'-cutting; wood'-engraver** one who makes wood-engravings: any of certain beetles that make a pattern of furrows in the wood of trees; **wood'-engraving** a design for printing, incised into the surface of a block of hard wood cut across the grain: an impression taken from this: the art of cutting such designs; **wood'en-head** a blockhead, stupid person.—*adj.* **wood'en-head'ed** having a head of wood: stupid.—**wood'en-head'edness; wooden leg** an artificial leg made of wood, **wooden spoon** a booby prize; **wood'-fibre** a thick-walled, elongated, dead element found in wood—developed by the elongation and lignification of the wall of a single cell; **wood'-flour, wood'-meal** a fine powder, made from sawdust and wood waste, used as a filler in many industries, in the manufacture of guncotton and dynamite, and as an absorbent in surgical dressings, **wood'-grouse** the capercailzie; **wood'land** land covered with wood (also *adj.*); **wood'lander** an inhabitant of woodland; **wood'-lark** a species of lark that perches on trees but sings chiefly on the wing; **wood'louse** (*pl.* **wood'lice**) any of numerous crustaceans of family *Oniscidae*, found in damp places, under stones and bark, in woodwork, among moss, etc.; **wood'man** a man who cuts down trees: a forest officer: a huntsman; **wood'mouse** a type of fieldmouse, *Apodemus sylvaticus*, with large ears and a long tail; **wood'-nightshade** *Solanum dulcamara*, bitter-sweet; **wood'-nymph** a nymph of the woods; **wood'-paper** paper made from wood-pulp; **wood'pecker** any of a family (*Picidae*) or birds in the order Picariae, remarkable for modification of the

skull and bill enabling the latter to be used to drill holes, and for the long flexible tongue, used to extract insects from crevices; **wood'-pigeon** the ring-dove, a common species of pigeon (*Columba palumbus*) living in woods; **wood'-pile** a pile of wood, esp. firewood; **wood'-pulp** wood mechanically or chemically pulped for paper-making; **wood'ruff** a genus of plants with whorled leaves and a funnel-shaped corolla, esp. *sweet woodruff* which has small white flowers and a pleasant scent; **wood'-screw** a screw for fastening pieces of wood or wood and metal; **wood'shed** a shed for storing firewood; **woods'-man** a woodman; **wood'-sorrel** any plant of the genus Oxalis, esp. *Oxalis acetosella*, with trifoliate leaves and white or rose-tinted flowers, which yields potassium binoxalate, $KHC_2O_4 \cdot H_2O$; **wood'-spirit** methyl alcohol, methanol; **wood'-tar** a product of destructive distillation of wood, containing paraffins, naphthalene, phenols; **wood'-warbler** a yellowish-green European warbler, *Phylloscopus sibilatrix*: any bird of the genera *Dendroica, Vermivora*, etc. of the American family *Parulidae*; **wood'wind** a wind-instrument, formerly usu. of wood, some now of metal (e.g. silver) or other material—flute, oboe, bassoon, clarinet, etc.: (used collectively) the section of an orchestra comprising these; **wood'work** a part of any structure made of wood: carpentry: goalposts, etc. (*football*, etc.; *coll*); **wood'-worm** a larva that bores in wood; **wood'y-night'shade** same as **wood-nightshade.**—**knock (on) wood** see **touch wood** under **touch; not see the wood for the trees** to fail to grasp the whole because of the superabundance of, or one's over-concentration on, detail, **out of the wood(s)** out of difficulty or danger; **something nasty in the woodshed** (*facet*) an unpleasant or shocking experience in one's past [O.E *wudu*.]

woodchuck *wōōd'chuk, n.* a N. American species of marmot (*Marmota* or *Arctomys monax*) [Corr. of an Amer Indian name.]

wooer, wooing, etc See **woo.**

woof *wōōf, n.* weft: thread for a weft: texture [M.E *oof*, with *w* added by association with **warp,** etc.]

woofer *wōōf'ər, n.* a large loudspeaker used to reproduce low-frequency sounds only —Cf. **tweeter.** [Imit. of a dog's bark.]

wool *wōōl, n.* a modification of hair in which the fibres are shorter, curled, and possess an imbricated surface —the covering of sheep, etc.: short, thick human hair: any light, fleecy substance like wool: any substance with a fibrous texture, resembling wool, e.g. steel-wool: thread or yarn made from animal wool: fabric woven or knitted from it —*adjs.* **woolled** (*wōōld*) bearing wool; **wooll'en** made of, or pertaining to, wool: clad in, or covered with, wool.—*n.* cloth made of wool.—*n.* **wooll'iness.**—*adj.* **wooll'y** consisting of, or like, wool: clothed with wool: lacking in clearness, firmness or definition (*fig.*).—*n.* a garment of wool, esp a knitted one:—*pl.* **wooll'ies.**—*n.* **wool'sey** (-*zi*) a fabric of cotton and wool.—**wool's ball** a ball of wool, such as is sometimes found in a sheep's stomach.—*adj.* **wool'-bearing** bearing or yielding wool.—**wool'-card, wool'-comb** a machine for wool-carding, **wool'-combing** separating the fibres of wool preparatory to spinning; **wool'-carder, wool'-comber; wool'-clip** crop of wool; **wool'fat** lanolin; **wool'fell** the skin with the wool still on it; **wool's gath'ering** absent-minded dreaming.—*adj.* dreamy. absent-minded.—**wooll'en-mill** a mill where wool is spun and woven into material; **wooll'y-bear** the hairy caterpillar of a number of moths, including the tiger-moths.—*adjs.* **wooll'y-haired, -head'ed** having the hair like wool.—**wool'man** a dealer in wool; **wool's mill** a woollen-mill; **wool'-oil** any oil obtained from wool-fat: an oil used to oil wool before spinning; **wool'-pack** the package in which wool was formerly done up for sale: a bundle weighing 240 lb; **wool'sack** the seat of the Lord Chancellor in the House of Lords, being a large square sack of wool covered with scarlet: the office of Lord Chancellor; **wool'sorter** one who sorts wool according to quality, etc.; **wool'-staple** the fibre or pile of wool: a market where wool was sold; **wool'-stapler** a dealer in wool: a woolsorter. —**pull, draw, the wool over someone's eyes** to hoodwink, deceive, someone. [O.E. *wull*.]

woollen, woolly, woolsey. See **wool**.

woomera *woom'ər-ə*, **womera** *wom'*, **woomerang** *woom'ər-ang*, *ns.* a throw-stick. [Austr. native.]

woorali, woorara. See **wourali**.

woosh. See **whoosh**.

woozy *woo'zi*, *adj.* fuddled (with drink, drugs, etc.): dazed, dizzy: blurred, woolly, vague.—*adv.* **wooz'ily**. —*n.* **wooz'iness**.

wop *wop*, *n.* a derogatory term for an Italian, or other foreigner of olive complexion. [It. (dial.) *guappo*— Sp. *guapo*, bold, handsome.]

Worcester(shire) sauce *woos'tər(-shər) sôs*, a pungent sauce orig. made in Worcestershire.

word *wûrd*, *n.* a unit of spoken language: a written sign representing such an utterance: (in *pl.*) language: a saying: a brief conversation: a rumour: a hint: a signal or sign: a message: a promise: a declaration: a password: a watch-word: a war-cry: a set of bits stored and transferred as a single unit of meaning (*comput.*): (in *pl.*) verbal contention.—*v.t.* to express in words.—*n.* **word'age** words generally, esp. text as opposed to pictures, etc.: verbiage, wordiness: quantity of words, length of text: choice of words, wording.— *adj.* **word'ed** expressed in words.—*adv.* **word'ily**. *ns.* **word'iness**; **word'ing** the act of expressing in words: choice of words, phrasing.—*adjs.* **word'less** unspoken: silent; **word'y** using, or containing, too many words: conducted in words.—*adj.* **word'-blind**. —**word'-blindness** the lack, or loss, of the ability to read, a non-technical name for both **alexia** and **dyslexia**; **word'book** a book with a collection of words: a dictionary, or vocabulary; **word'-building** the formation of words from letters or from root words and affixes; **word'-lore** information about the history, use, etc., of words; **word'-painter**; **word'-painting** the act or art of describing vividly in words.—*adj.* **word'-per'fect** having memorised (words to be repeated, recited, etc.) exactly.—**word'-picture** a description in words that presents an object, scene, etc., to the mind as if in a picture; **word play** puns, etc.; **word processing**; **word processor** any of several types of machine that perform electronically the tasks of typing, datarecording, dictating, transcribing, etc., some incorporating screens for visual display; **word salad** (*psych.*) a confused outpouring of speech, most often occurring in cases of schizophrenia; **word'smith** an accomplished user of words (sometimes *iron.*): a coiner of words; **word'-square** a square grid composed of a set of words that read the same down as they do across.—**a good word** a recommendation, favourable mention, praise; **a word in one's ear** a confidential conversation; **break one's word** to fail to fulfil a promise; **by word of mouth** orally, through the spoken word (*adj.* **word'-of-mouth**'); **eat one's words** to retract, apologise, usu. under compulsion; **have a word with** to have some conversation with; **have words (with)** to quarrel, dispute (with); **in a word, in one word** in short, to sum up; **in so many words** explicitly: bluntly; **my word** mild interj. expressing surprise, annoyance, *etc.*; **not the word for it** not a strong enough word to express or describe it; **of few, or many, words** taciturn, or verbose; **put words into**

someone's mouth to attribute, or supply, to someone, words that he did not, or does not intend to, use; **take someone at his word** to accept statements as being literally true; **take the words out of someone's mouth** to say exactly what someone was about to say himself; **the last word** the closing remark in an argument, esp. if having an appearance of conclusiveness: the conclusive statement: the ultimate authority: (also **latest word**) the most up-to-date, or the most finished, example; **the Word** the Scriptures: the gospel message: the second person in the Trinity; **word for word** literally, verbatim. [O.E.]

wore *wôr*, *wōr*, *pa.t. of* **wear**[1,2].

work *wûrk*, *n.* effort directed to an end: employment: that on which one works: the product of work, anything made or done: materials for work: needlework: a deed: doings: the result of action: any production of art, as a literary composition: a book: manner of working, workmanship: (in *pl.*) a factory, workshop (as *adj.*, of a racing-car, entered officially in a race by the manufacturer): the act of producing an effect by means of a force (F) whose point of application moves through a distance (s) in its own line of action— measured by the product of the force and the distance (W = Fs; *phys.*): (in *pl.*) walls, trenches, etc. (*fort.*): (usu. in *pl.*) an action in its moral aspect, esp. as tending to justification (*theol.*): (in *pl.*) mechanism, e.g. of a watch.—*v.i.* to make efforts to achieve or attain anything: to be occupied in business or labour: to move, make one's way, slowly and laboriously: to move, become, etc., in a manner not intended or desired: to be in action: to operate, function: to produce effects: to behave in the desired way when worked: to prove practicable: to ferment: to be agitated, move convulsively: to strain, labour.—*v.t.* to make by labour: to bring into any state by action: to effect or strive to effect: to carry on operations in: to keep in operation: to keep employed: to put in motion: to influence: to affect powerfully: to provoke, excite: to prepare for use by manipulation: to fashion, make: to embroider: to make (as one's way) by effort: to solve: to make use of, make profit through (*coll.*): to influence, cajole, or trick (*coll.*): —*pa.t.* and *pa.p.* **worked** or **wrought** (see separate article).—*ns.* **workabil'ity**, **work'ableness**.—*adjs.* **work'able** that may be worked, esp. practicable; **workaholic** (*-ə-hol'ik*) addicted to work, coined facetiously in imitation of *alcoholic*.—Also *n.*—*adj.* **worked** that has been treated or fashioned in some way: embroidered: ornamented.—*n.* **work'er** one who works: a toiler: one employed in manual work: in social insects, one of a caste of sterile individuals that do all the work of the colony.—*adj.* **work'ful** industrious.—*n.* **work'ing** the act or process of shaping, making, effecting, solving, fermenting, etc.: an exposition of the process of calculation: manner of operating or functioning: contortion due to agitation: slow and laborious progress: (in *pl.*) the parts of a mine, etc., where work is, or has been, carried on.— *adj.* active: operational: labouring: having a job or employment: relating to labour, a job or employment.—*adj.* **work'less** having no job, unemployed — Also *n.pl.*—*adj.* **work'aday** suitable for a work day: toiling: dull, prosaic.—**work'-bag, -basket** a bag, basket, for holding materials for work, esp. needlework; **work'book** a book of exercises, often with spaces for the answers, to accompany another book; **work'-box** a box for holding instruments or materials for work; **work'-day** a day for work, a week-day.—*adj.* pertaining to a work-day.—**worker priest** a priest in the Roman Catholic Church who also works full-time or part-time in a secular job in order to understand better the problems of lay people; **work ethic** the general attitude of a group towards work, esp. one (**Protestant work ethic**) which places a high moral value on (hard) work; **work'-fellow** one who is engaged in the same work with another; **work'folk, work'folks** work-people; **work'force** the number of workers engaged in a particular industry, factory, etc.: the total number of workers potentially available; **work'horse** a horse used in a labouring capacity rather than for recreation, racing, etc.: a person or machine heavily depended on to do arduous work; **work'house** (*hist.*) a house where any work or manufacture is carried on: a house of shelter for the poor, who are given work to do; **working breakfast, lunch**, etc. one arranged as an alternative to a formal meeting, for the discussion of diplomatic or other business; **work'ing-class** that of manual workers (often in *pl.*; also *adj.*); **work'ing-day** a day on which work is done: the period of actual work each day; **work'ing-drawing** a drawing of the details of a building by which the builders are guided in their work; **working hours** the period of the day during which work is normally done, and offices, shops, etc. are open; **working majority** a majority sufficient to enable the party in office to carry on without accidental defeats; **working man, woman** a worker, esp. a manual one; **work'ing-model** a model of a machine that can do, on a smaller scale, the same work as the machine; **working paper** one produced as a basis for discussion, to report on progress made, etc., rather than as a final statement; **work(ing) party** a group of persons who carry out a specially assigned task: a group appointed to investigate a subject, as methods of attaining maximum efficiency in an industry; **working week** that part of the week in which work is normally done—esp. Monday to Friday: any week in which such work is done, as opposed e.g. to holidays; **work'load** the amount of work assigned to an individual, machine, etc. for completion within a certain time; **work'man** a man who works, esp. manually: a skilful artificer.—*adjs.* **work'man-like** like a workman: becoming a skilful workman: well performed; **work'manly** becoming a skilful workman.—**work'manship** the skill of a workman: manner of making: that which is made or produced by one's hands (also *fig.*); **work'-mate** workfellow: a companion at work; **work'-people** people engaged in manual labour, workers; **work'place** the office, factory, etc. where one works; **work'room** a room for working in; **works committee, council** a body on which both employer and employees meet to handle labour relations within a business; **work'shop** a room or shop where work is done: a group of people working on a creative or experimental project: such a project.—*adj.* **work'-shy** hating, avoiding work, lazy (also used as *n.*).—**work study** a time and motion study; **work'-table** a table on which work is done, esp., formerly, a small table used by ladies at their needlework; **work'top** a surface designed to be used for working on, fitted e.g. along the top of kitchen units, etc.; **work'wear** overalls or other clothing for work, issued to factory-workers, etc.—**give someone the works** (*slang*) to give someone the full punitive, coercive, ceremonious, etc. treatment considered appropriate to his case; **have one's work cut out** to have one's work prescribed: to be faced with a difficult task; **Ministry** (previously **Office**) **of Works** formerly, the body which has the management and control of public works and buildings, of which the expenses are defrayed from public money; **out of work** without employment (*adj.* and *n.pl.* **out'-of-work'** unemployed (people)); **place of work** one's workplace (q.v.); **public works** building, etc., operations financed by the state; **set to work** to employ in, or to engage energetically in, a piece of work; **the**

works (*coll.*) the lot, everything; **work at** to apply oneself to; **work for, against** to exert oneself in support of, in opposition to; **work in** to intermix: to introduce carefully and deliberately (*fig.*): to make to penetrate: of workers, to continue at work, esp. by occupying the premises and taking over the running of the business, as a protest against proposed factory closure, dismissal, etc. (*n.* **work'-in**); **work into** to make way gradually into: to insinuate: to change, alter, into; **work of art** a production in one of the fine arts (also *fig.*); **work off** to separate and throw off: to get rid of gradually; **work on, upon** to act or operate upon: to influence, or try to do so; **work one's passage** to earn one's passage by services on board (also *fig.*); **work out** to effect by continued labour: to expiate: to exhaust: to solve or calculate: to develop in detail, elaborate: to come out by degrees: to turn out in the end: to reach a final (satisfactory) result: of an athlete, etc., to train, exercise (*n.* **work'-out**); **work over** to do, work at, thoroughly or elaborately: to examine in detail: to beat up, thrash (*n.* **work'(ing)-over**) (*slang*); **work the oracle** (*slang*) to achieve the desired result by manipulation, intrigue, wire-pulling, favour, etc.: to raise money; **work to rule** of workers, to observe all the regulations scrupulously for the express purpose of slowing down work, as a form of industrial action (*n.* **work'-to-rule'**); **work up** to excite, rouse: to create by slow degrees: to expand, elaborate: to use up, as material: to make one's, its, way gradually upwards: to reach, achieve, by effort and gradually; **work with** (*fig.*) to strive to influence by appeals, etc. [O.E. *weorc*.]

world *wûrld, n.* the earth: the earth and its inhabitants: the universe: the system of things: the present state of existence: any analogous state: any planet or heavenly body: public life or society: a sphere of interest or activity: environment: the public: the materialistically minded: mundane interests: a secular life: a very large extent of country, as the 'New World': very much or a great deal, as 'a world of good': a large quantity: time, as in 'world without end'.—*ns.* **world'liness**; **world'ling** one who is devoted to worldly pursuits and temporal possessions.—*adj.* **world'ly** pertaining to the world, esp. as distinguished from the world to come: devoted to this life and its enjoyments: bent on gain.—**World Bank** the popular name of the International Bank for Reconstruction and Development, an agency of the United Nations set up in 1945 to make loans to poorer countries; **world'-beater** (*coll.*) a person, product, enterprise, etc. that is supreme in its class.—*adj.* **world'-beating.**—**World Court** the popular name of the Permanent Court of International Justice at the Hague; **world language** a language either widely used internationally or designed for international use.—*adj.* **world'ly-mind'ed** having the mind set on the present world.—*n.* **world'ly-mind'edness.**—*adj.* **world'ly-wise'** having the wisdom of those experienced in, and affected by, the ways of the world.—**world power** a state, group of states, etc., strong enough to make its influence felt in world politics; **World Series** (*baseball*) a set of championship matches played annually in the U.S.; **World War** a war of world-wide scope, esp. the Great War of 1914–1918 (First World War, World War I), 1939–45 (Second World War, World War II).—*adjs.* **world'-wearied, -weary** tired of the world, bored with life.—*adj. and adv.* **world'wide** (extending) over, or (found) everywhere in, the world.—**all the world** everybody: everything; **all the world and his wife** (*coll.*) everybody: an ill-assorted assembly; **best, worst, of both worlds** the advantage, disadvantage, of both alternatives in a choice; **carry the world before one** to pass through every obstacle to success; **dead to the world** (*coll.*) deeply asleep: in a drunken stupor; **for all the world** precisely, entirely; **in the world** an intensive phrase, usu. following an interrogative pronoun or adverb; **next world** life after death; **on top of the world** (*coll.*) in a state of great elation or happiness; **out of this world** wonderful, delightful, good beyond all experience; **the New World** the western hemisphere, the Americas; **the Old World** the eastern hemisphere, comprising Europe, Africa, and Asia; **the other world** the non-material sphere, the spiritual world; **the whole world** the sum of what is contained in the world; **the world's end** the most distant point possible; **think the world of** to be very fond of; **world without end** eternally (*adj.* world'-without-end'). [O.E. *woruld, world, weorold,* orig. meaning age or life of man—*wer,* man, and the root of **old.**]

worm *wûrm, n.* a snake, a dragon (*arch.*): loosely used for any elongate invertebrate lacking appendages, as an earthworm or marine worm (Chaetopoda), a flat-worm (Platyhelminthes), a round-worm (Nematoda): a grub: a maggot: anything spiral: the thread of a screw: anything that corrupts, gnaws, or torments: a mean, grovelling creature: (in *pl.*) any intestinal disease arising from the presence of parasitic worms.—*v.i.* to seek for or catch worms: to move, make one's way, like a worm, to squirm: to work slowly or secretly.—*v.t.* to treat for, rid of, worms: to work (oneself) slowly or secretly (*refl.*): to elicit by slow and indirect means.—*adj.* **wormed** bored, injured by worms.—*ns.* **worm'er; worm'ery** a place, apparatus, etc. in which worms are bred, e.g. as fishing-bait.—*adj.* **worm'y** like a worm: grovelling: containing a worm: abounding in worms: pertaining to worms.—**worm'-cast** a little spiral heap of earth voided by an earthworm or lugworm as it burrows.—*adjs.* **worm'-eaten** eaten into by worms: old: wornout; **worm'-eating** living habitually on worms.—**worm'-gear** a gear connecting shafts whose axes are at right angles but do not intersect, consisting of a core carrying a single- or multi-start helical thread of special form (the *worm*), meshing in sliding contact with a concave face gear-wheel (the *worm-wheel*); **worm'-gearing; worm'-hole** the hole made by a wood-worm, earthworm, etc.—*adj.* **worm'-holed** perforated by worm-holes.—**worm'-powder** a vermifuge; **worm'-seed** any of a number of plants acting, or reputed to act, as anthelmintics, as species of Artemisia (e.g. *Artemisia santonica*), *Erysimum cheiranthoides* etc.: the drug santonica; **worm'-tube** the twisted shell or tube produced by several marine worms; **worm'-wheel** see **worm'-gear.** [O.E. *wyrm,* dragon, snake, creeping animal.]

wormwood *wûrm'wood, n.* the bitter plant *Artemisia absinthium,* formerly used as a vermifuge, with which absinthe is flavoured: bitterness.—cf. **absinthe.** [O.E. *wermōd,* wormwood; influenced by **worm** and **wood.**]

worn *wōrn, wörn, pa.p.* of **wear**[1].—*adj.* that has been worn: showing effects of wear, or (*fig.*) of work, worry, illness, age, etc.: of land, exhausted: hackneyed, trite.—*adj.* **worn'-out** much injured or rendered useless by wear: wearied: past, gone.

worrit *wur'it, v.t., v.i.,* and *n.* Dial. form of **worry.**

worry *wur'i, v.t.* to tear with the teeth: to harass: to pester: to tease: to cause to be anxious: to make, get, etc., by persistent methods.—*v.i.* to trouble oneself: to be unduly anxious: to fret:—*pa.t.* and *pa.p.* **worr'ied.**—*n.* the act of worrying: trouble, perplexity: over-anxiety: a cause of this: the act of injuring by biting and shaking.—*ns.* **worr'ier; worr'iment** (*coll.*) worry, anxiety.—*adj.* **worr'isome** inclined to worry: causing trouble.—*n.* and *adj.* **worr'ying.**—

adv. **worr'yingly.**—**worry beads** a string of beads providing an object for the hands to play with, thus relieving mental tension—esp. popular in Greece.—**I should worry!** it is nothing for me to worry about. [O.E. *wyrgan,* found in compound *āwyrgan,* to harm.]

worse *wûrs, adj.* (used as *compar.* of **bad, ill**) bad or evil in a greater degree: less well than before.—*adv.* badly in a higher degree: less well: with more severity.—*v.i.* and *v.t.* **wors'en** to grow, or make, worse.—*n.* **worse'ness.**—*adj.* and *adv.* **wors'er** a redundant comparative of *worse.*—**for better or for worse** whatever may befall of good fortune or bad; **for the worse** to a worse state; **none the worse** for not harmed by; **the worse for** harmed or impaired by; **worse off** poorer. [O.E. *wyrsa.*]

worship *wûr'ship, n.* adoration paid, as to a god: religious service: profound admiration and affection: the act of revering or adoring: (with *cap.*; preceded by *Your, His,* etc.) a title of honour in addressing or referring to certain magistrates, etc.—*v.t.* to pay divine honours to: to adore or idolise.—*v.i.* to perform acts of adoration: to take part in religious service:—*pr.p.* **wor'shipping;** *pa.t.* and *pa.p.* **wor'-shipped.**—*adjs.* **wor'shipable** capable of being worshipped; **wor'shipful** worthy of worship or honour: used as a term of respect: worshipping, adoring.—*adv.* **wor'shipfully.**—*n.* **wor'shipper.**—**house,** or **place, of worship** a church or chapel, synagogue, mosque, temple. [O.E. *weorthscipe—weorth, wurth,* worth, suff. *-scipe, -ship.*]

worst *wûrst, adj.* (used as *superl.* of **bad, ill**) bad or evil in the highest degree.—*adv.* in the highest degree of badness.—*n.* the highest degree of badness: the most evil state or effect: the least good part.—*v.t.* to get the advantage over in a contest: to defeat.—**do one's worst** to do one's utmost in evil or mischief; **get the worst of it** to be defeated in a contest; **if the worst comes to the worst** if the worst, or least desirable, possibility occurs: if all else fails. [O.E. *wyrst, wyrrest,* from the same source as **worse.**]

worsted[1] *wŏŏst'id,* or *wŏŏrst'id, n.* orig., a fine wool fabric: twisted thread or yarn spun out of long, combed wool: smooth, closely-woven material made from this.—*adj.* made of worsted yarn. [*Worstead,* village near Norwich, England.]

worsted[2] *wûrst'id, pa.t.* and *pa.p.* of **worst.**

wort[1] *wûrt, n.* any herb or vegetable (now *rare* except in composition). [O.E. *wyrt,* a root, herb.]

wort[2] *wûrt, n.* malt unfermented or in the act of fermentation: such liquor boiled with hops: malt extract used as a medium for the culture of micro-organisms. [O.E. *wyrt;* allied to **wort**[1].]

worth *wûrth, n.* value: price: that quality which renders a thing valuable: moral excellence: merit: importance.—*adj.* equal in value to: having a certain value: worth while: having possessions to the value of: deserving of.—*adv.* **worth'ily** (*-dh-*).—*n.* **worth'i-ness** (*-dh-*).—*adj.* **worth'less** (*-th-*) having no value, virtue, excellence, etc.: useless.—*adv.* **worth'lessly.**—*n.* **worth'lessness.**—*adj.* **worth'y** (*-dh-*) having worth: valuable: estimable (used patronisingly): deserving: deserving of: suited to, in keeping with: of sufficient merit.—*n.* a man of eminent worth: a notability, esp. local (sometimes ironical):—*pl.* **wor'thies.**—*adj.* **worthwhile'** such as to repay trouble and time spent on it (predicatively **worth while;** see **while**): good: estimable.—**for all one is worth** with all one's might or energy; **for what it is worth** a phrase implying that the speaker is doubtful of the truth of what he has reported or unwilling to be responsible for its accuracy; **worth it** worth while. [O.E. *weorth, wurth,* value.]

For other sounds see detailed chart of pronunciation.

wot, wotteth, etc. See **wit**[1].

wotcher *wot'chər,* (*slang*) *interj.* a greeting, developed from *arch.* **what cheer?** how are you?

would *wŏŏd pa.t.* of **will**[1].—*adj.* **would'-be** aspiring, or merely professing, to be: meant to be.

Woulfe-bottle *wŏŏlf'-bot'l, n.* a form of usu. three-necked bottle used for purifying gases, or dissolving them in suitable solvents—from the London chemist Peter *Woulfe* (c. 1727–1803).

wound[1] *wownd, pa.t.* and *pa.p.* of **wind**[2].

wound[2] *wŏŏnd, n.* any division of soft parts produced by external mechanical force—whether incised, punctured, lacerated, or poisoned: any cut, bruise, hurt, or injury (also *fig.*).—*v.t.* to make a wound in (*lit.* and *fig.*), to injure.—*adj.* **wound'able** capable of being wounded.—*n.* **wound'er.**—*n.* and *adj.* **wound'-ing.**—**wound'wort** any of several plants of popular repute as vulneraries, as the kidney-vetch, a number of plants of genus Stachys. [O.E. *wund.*]

wourali, woorali *wŏŏ-rä'li,* **woora'ra** (*-rä'rə*), **oura'li, oura'ri** (*-rä'ri*), **ura'li** (*ŏŏ-*), **ura'ri** *ns.* the plant yielding curare (q.v.). [Carib. variants of *kurari;* see **curare.**]

wove, woven *pa.t.* and *pa.p.* of **weave.**—**wove paper** paper that shows in its fabric the marks of a fine wire gauze sieve or mould.

wow *wow, interj.* an exclamation of wonder, tinged with other emotions as aversion, sorrow, or admiration, pleasure.—*v.t.* (*slang*) to impress (an audience, etc.) considerably, to amaze, bowl over.—*n.* a bark: a howl: rhythmic or arrhythmic changes in reproduced sound, fundamentally arising from fluctuation in speed of either reproducer or recorder: anything thrillingly good, successful, or according to one's wishes (*slang*).—*n.* **wow'ser** (*-zər;* perh. not connected with wow; esp. *Austr. slang*) a puritanical person who tries to interfere with the pleasures of others, a spoil-sport. [Imit.]

wrack[1] *rak, n.* destruction, devastation.—Cf. **rack**[2]. [O.E. *wræc—wrecan,* to drive.]

wrack[2] *rak, n.* wreckage: any of the *Fucaceae,* the bladder-wrack family of seaweeds. [M.Du. or M.L.G. *wrak;* cf. **wreck**[1].]

wraith *rāth, n.* a spectre: an apparition, esp. of a living person: a thin, pale person (*fig.*). [Orig. Scot.; perh. O.N. *vörthr,* a guardian.]

wrangle *rang'gl, v.i.* to argue, debate, dispute (*arch.*): to dispute noisily or peevishly.—*v.t.* to obtain, persuade, spend, tire, in or by wrangling: to debate.—*n.* a noisy dispute: the action of disputing, esp. noisily. —*ns.* **wrang'ler** one who disputes, esp. angrily: in the University of Cambridge, one of those who attained the first class in the examinations for mathematical honours: a herdsman, esp. of horses (*Western U.S.*); **wrang'lership.**—*adj.* **wrang'lesome** given to wrangling.—*n.* and *adj.* **wrang'ling.** [M.E. *wranglen,* a freq. verb allied to **wring.**]

wrap *rap, v.t.* to roll or fold together: to fold, lap, round something: to enfold, envelop (*lit.* and *fig.*): to embrace: to hide, obscure: to cover by folding or winding something round (often with *up*).—*v.i.* to wind, twine: (with *up*) to put on wraps: to dress warmly:—*pr.p.* **wrapp'ing;** *pa.t.* and *pa.p.* **wrapped.** —*n.* a protective covering, for a person or thing, now esp. an outdoor garment: a single turn or fold round: (*in pl.; coll.*) secrecy, concealment.—*ns.* **wrapp'er** one who, or that which, wraps: a loose paper book cover: a paper band, as on a newspaper for the post; **wrapp'ing** (also **wrapp'ing-paper**) coarse paper for parcels, etc.—**wrap'(a)round, wrap'over** (**skirt, blouse,** etc.) one designed so as to be wrapped round the body and secured with one edge overlapping the other, rather than fastened by a zip, row of buttons, etc.—**keep under wraps** (*coll.*) to keep secret, conceal; **take the wraps off** (*coll.*) to reveal, disclose; **wrapped up in** bound up in: comprised in: engrossed in, devoted to; **wrap up** (*slang*) to settle completely: to have completely in hand: (as *interj.*) be quiet! [M.E. *wrappen,* also *wlappen.*]

wrasse *ras, n.* a genus (Labrus) of bony fishes including many species on European and N. African coasts. [Cornish *wrach.*]

wrath *rōth, roth, n.* violent anger: an instance, or fit, of this: holy indignation: violence or severity (*fig.*).— *adj.* **wrath'ful** very angry: springing from, or expressing, or characterised by, wrath.—*adv.* **wrath'-fully.**—*n.* **wrath'fulness.** [O.E. *wræththu—wrāth,* adj.]

wreak *rēk, v.t.* to give expression, vent, free play to: to find expression, outlet, for (*refl.*): to bestow: to inflict: to effect or bring about.—*n.* **wreak'er.** [O.E. *wrecan.*]

wreath *rēth, n.* a circlet of interwoven materials, esp. flowers, etc.: a single twist or coil in a helical object: a drift or curl of vapour or smoke:—*pl.* **wreaths** (*rēdhz*).—*v.t.* **wreathe** (*rēdh*) to form by twisting: to twist together: to form into a wreath: to twine about or encircle: to encircle, decorate, etc. with a wreath or wreaths.—*v.i.* to be interwoven: to twine: to twist: to form coils.—*adj.* **wreathed** (or *rēdh'id*). [O.E. *writha;* allied to *writhan,* to writhe.]

wreck *rek, n.* destruction: the act of wrecking or destroying: the destruction of a ship: a badly damaged ship: shipwrecked property: anything found underwater and brought ashore: the remains of anything ruined: a person ruined mentally or physically.—*v.t.* to destroy or disable: to involve in a wreck: to cast up, as on the shore: to ruin.—*v.i.* to suffer wreck or ruin. —*ns.* **wreck'age** the act of wrecking: wrecked material: a person, or persons, whose life is, or lives are, ruined; **wreck'er** a person who purposely causes a wreck or who plunders wreckage: one who criminally ruins anything: a person who (or machine which) demolishes or destroys: a person or ship employed in recovering disabled vessels or their cargo: a person, vehicle or train employed in removing wreckage: a person who is employed in demolishing buildings, etc.—*n.* and *adj.* **wreck'ing.** [A.Fr. *wrec, wrek,* etc., of Scand. origin; allied to **wreak.**]

wren *ren, n.* a member of a genus (Troglodytes) of small birds, having the wings very short and rounded, and the tail short and carried erect, or of any of several related genera, together forming the family Troglodytidae: specif. in the U.K., *T. troglodytes:* extended to various very small birds. [O.E. *wrenna, wrænna.*]

Wren *ren, n.* a member of the W.R.N.S.

wrench *rench, rensh, v.t.* to wring or pull with a twist: to force by violence: to sprain: to distort.—*v.i.* to perform, or to undergo, a violent wrenching.—*n.* an act or instance of wrenching: a violent twist: a sprain: an instrument for turning nuts, etc.: emotional pain at parting or change. [O.E. *wrencan,* to deceive, twist, *wrenc,* deceit, twisting.]

wrest *rest, v.t.* to turn, twist: to twist, extract, or take away, by force or unlawfully: to get by toil: to twist from truth or from its natural meaning: to misinterpret: to pervert.—*n.* the act of wresting: violent pulling and twisting: distortion: an instrument, like a wrench, for tuning the piano, etc.—*n.* **wrest'er.** [O.E. *wræstan.*]

wrestle *res'l, v.i.* to contend by grappling and trying to throw another down: to struggle: to strive: to apply oneself keenly: to pray earnestly: to writhe, wriggle: to proceed with great effort (*lit.* and *fig.*).—*v.t.* to contend with in wrestling: to push with a wriggling or wrestling motion: (with *out*) to go through, carry out, with a great struggle.—*n.* the act, or a bout, of wrestling: a struggle.—*ns.* wrest'ler; wrest'ling the action of the verb to wrestle: a sport or exercise in which two persons struggle to throw and pin each other to the ground, governed by certain fixed rules. [O.E. *wræstlian*; allied to *wræstan*, to wrest.]

wretch *rech, n.* a most miserable, unfortunate or pitiable person: a worthless, or despicable, person: a being, creature (in pity, sometimes admiration).—*adj.* wretch'ed (*-id*) very miserable: unfortunate, pitiable: distressingly bad: despicable: worthless.—*adv.* wretch'edly.—*n.* wretch'edness. [O.E. *wrecca*, an outcast—*wrecan*; see wreak.]

wrick *rik, v.t.* to twist, sprain, strain.—*n.* a sprain, strain. [Allied to L.G. *wrikken*, to turn.]

wrier, wriest. See wry.

wriggle *rig'l, v.i.* and *v.t.* to twist to and fro: to move, advance, sinuously (*lit.* and *fig.*): to use evasive tricks.—*n.* the act or motion of wriggling: a sinuous marking or bend.—*ns.* wrigg'ler; wrigg'ling. [L.G. *wriggeln*.]

wright *rīt n.* a maker or repairer (chiefly used in compounds, as shipwright, etc.). [O.E. *wyrhta, wryhta*, allied to *wyrht*, a work—*wyrcan*, to work.]

wring *ring, v.t.* to twist: to expel moisture from by hand twisting or by roller pressure: to force out by twisting: to force out: to clasp and shake fervently: to clasp convulsively, as the hands (in grief or agitation): to distress, afflict: to extort: to subject to extortion: to distort.—*v.i.* to writhe: to twist:—*pa.t.* and *pa.p.* wrung.—*n.* an act or instance of wringing: a cider-, wine-, or cheese-press.—*ns.* wring'er one who writes-: a machine for forcing water from wet clothes (also wring'ing-machine); wring'ing.—*adj.* wring'ing-wet so wet that water can be wrung out.—wring from to extort from; wring out to squeeze out by twisting: to remove from liquid and twist so as to expel the drops. [O.E. *wringan*, to twist.]

wrinkle[1] *ring'kl,* (*coll.*) *n.* a tip, valuable hint. [Perh from O.E. *wrenc*, a trick; perh. same as wrinkle[2].]

wrinkle[2] *ring'kl, n.* a small crease or furrow on a surface: a crease or ridge in the skin (esp. as a result of ageing):an unevenness.—*v.t.* to contract into wrinkles or furrows: to make rough.—*v.i.* to shrink into ridges.—*adjs.* wrink'led; wrink'ly full of wrinkles: liable to be wrinkled.

wrist *rist, n.* the joint by which the hand is united to the arm, the carpus: the part of the body where that joint is, or the part of a garment covering it: a corresponding part of an animal: a wrist-pin.—*n.* wrist'let a band or strap for the wrist: a bracelet: a watch for wearing on the wrist (also wrist'-watch, or wrist'let-watch): a handcuff (*slang*).—*adj.* wrist'y making extensive use of the wrist(s), as in a golf shot, etc.—wrist'band a band or part of a sleeve covering the wrist; wrist'-pin a pin joining the end of a connecting rod to the end of a piston-rod.—a slap, smack on the wrist (*coll.*) a small (and often, by implication, ineffectual) punishment. [O.E.]

writ[1] *rit, arch. pa.t.* and *pa.p.* of write.—writ large written in large letters, hence (*fig.*) on a large scale, or very obvious.

writ[2] *rit, n.* a legal or formal document: a written document by which one is summoned or required to do something (*law*).—Holy Writ the Scriptures; serve a writ on to deliver a summons to. [O.E. (*ge*)*wrīt*.]

write *rīt, v.t.* to form (letters or words) with a pen, pencil, or other implement on a (usu. paper) surface: to express in writing: to compose: to draw, engrave, etc.: to record: to decree or foretell: to indicate (a quality, condition, etc.) clearly: to communicate, or to communicate with, by letter.—*v.i.* to perform, or

to practise, the act of writing: to be employed as a clerk: to compose, as articles, novels, etc.: to work as an author: to compose, or to send, a letter: to communicate with a person by letter:—*pr.p.* writ'ing; *pa.t.* wrōte, (*arch.*) writ (*rit*); *pa.p.* written (*rit'n*), (*arch.*) writ.—*ns.* writ'er one who writes: a professional scribe or clerk: an ordinary legal practitioner in a Scottish country town: an author: his works: one who paints lettering for signs: a seller (of options) (*Stock exchange*); writ'ership the office of a writer; writ'ing the act of one who writes: that which is written: (often *pl.*) a literary production, or composition: handwriting, penmanship: the state of being written.—*adj.* writt'en reduced to, expressed in, writing—opp. to *oral.*—*adj.* write'-in (*U.S.*) of or relating to a candidate not listed in the ballot paper, but whose name is written in by the voter.—*n.* such a candidate or vote.—write'-off a car so badly damaged that the cost of repair would exceed the car's value: a total loss: see also write off below; writ'ing-book a book of paper for practising penmanship; writ'ing-case a portable case containing materials for writing; writ'ing-desk a desk with a sloping top for writing on; writ'ing-paper paper finished with a smooth surface, for writing on; writ'ing-table a table fitted or used for writing on; written law statute law as distinguished from common law.—*adj.* writt'en-off (of a car) damaged beyond reasonable repair: completely ruined: see also write off below.—write down to put down in written characters: to write in disparagement of: to write so as to be intelligible or attractive to people of lower intelligence or inferior taste: to reduce the book value of an asset (*n.* write'-down); write (in) for to apply for: to send away for; write off to cancel, esp., in book-keeping, to take (e.g a bad debt) off the books: to regard, accept, as an irredeemable loss: to destroy, damage irredeemably, (a car, etc.) (*n.* write'-off; *adj.* writt'en-off); write out to transcribe: to write in full: to exhaust one's mental resources by too much writing (*refl.*): to remove a character or scene from the script of a film, broadcast, etc.; Writer to the Signet a member of an ancient society of solicitors in Scotland who have the exclusive privilege of preparing crown writs; write up to put a full description of in writing: to write a report or review of: to write in praise of, esp. to praise above its merits: to bring the writing of up to date: to increase the book value of an asset (*n.* write'-up); writing (also, esp. *U.S.*, handwriting) on the wall a happening or sign foreshowing downfall and disaster (Dan. v. 5 ff.). [O.E. *wrītan*, orig. meaning to scratch.]

writhe *rīdh, v t.* to twist: to coil: to wreathe: to twist violently: to contort.—*v.i.* to twist, esp. in pain.—*n.* and *adj* writh'ing.—*adv.* writh'ingly. [O.E. *writhan*, to twist; cf. wreath, wrest, wrist.]

wrong *rong, adj.* not according to rule: incorrect: erroneous: not in accordance with moral law: wicked: not that (thing) which is required, intended, advisable, or suitable: amiss, unsatisfactory: not working properly, out of order: mistaken, misinformed: under, inner, reverse.—*n.* whatever is not right or just: any injury done to another: damage, harm (*rare*): wrong-doing: the state or position of being or doing wrong.—*adv.* not correctly: not in the right way: astray.—*v.t.* to do wrong to: to deprive of some right: to defraud: to impute fault to unjustly: to dishonour.—*n.* wrong'er one who wrongs.—*adj.* wrong'ful wrong: unjust: unlawful: not legitimate.—*adv.* wrong'fully.—*n.* wrong'fulness.—*adv.* wrong'ly.—*n.* wrong'ness.—wrong'-do'er an offender, transgressor; wrong'-do'ing evil or wicked action or conduct.—*v.t.* wrong'-foot' to cause to be (physically or mentally) off balance, or at a disadvantage.—*adj.* **wrong'-head'ed** obstinate and perverse, adhering stubbornly to wrong principles or policy.—*adv.* **wrong'-head'edly.**—**wrong'-head'edness.**—**get on the wrong side of someone** to arouse dislike or antagonism in someone; **get out of bed on the wrong side** to arise in the morning in an ill temper; **go wrong** to fail to work properly: to make a mistake or mistakes: to stray from virtue; **in the wrong** holding an erroneous view or unjust position: guilty of error or injustice; **private wrong** a violation of the civil or personal rights of an individual; **public wrong** a crime which affects the community; **put in the wrong** to cause to appear in error, guilty of injustice, etc. [O.E. *wrang*, a wrong.]

wrote *rōt, pa.t.* of **write.**

wroth *rōth, roth, adj.* wrathful: in commotion, stormy. [O.E. *wrāth,* angry.]

wrought *rōt, pa.t.* and *pa.p.* of **work,** now used chiefly in certain senses:—e.g. fashioned: ornamented: manufactured: beaten into shape, shaped by tools (as metal).—**wrought'-iron** malleable iron, iron containing only a very small amount of other elements, but containing slag in the form of particles elongated in one direction, more rust-resistant than steel and welding more easily.—*adj.* **wrought'-up** in an agitated condition, over-excited. [O.E. *worhte, geworht,* pa.t. and pa.p. of *wyrcan, wircan,* to work.]

wrung *rung, pa.t.* and *pa.p.* of **wring.**

wry *ri, adj.* twisted or turned to one side: not in the right direction: expressing displeasure or irony (*fig.*): perverse, distorted (*fig.*):—*compar.* **wry'er** or **wri'er;** *superl.* **wry'est** or **wri'est.**—*v.t.* to give a twist to: to

pervert.—*adv.* wryly.—*adv.* **wry'ly.**—*n.* **wry'ness.**—**wry'bill** a New Zealand bird allied to the plovers with bill bent sideways; **wry'-neck** a twisted position of the head on the neck due to disease of the cervical vertebrae or to affections (esp. rheumatic) of the muscles of the neck; **wry'neck** a member of a genus of small birds (Jynx) allied to the woodpecker, which twist round their heads strangely when surprised.—**make a wry face** or **mouth** to pucker up the face, or mouth, as in tasting anything bitter or astringent, or in sign of disgust or pain. [O.E. *wrīgian,* to strive, move, turn.]

wunderkind *vōōn' dər-kint, n.* a child prodigy: one who shows great talent, attains great success, etc. at an early (or comparatively early) age:—*pl.* **wun'derkinder** (*-kin-dər*). [Ger., lit. wonder child.]

wunner. See **oner** under **one.**

wurst *vōōrst, wûrst, n.* a large German sausage of several types. [Ger., lit. something rolled.]

wuther *wudh' ər,* (*dial.*) *v.i.* to move swiftly or with force: to make a sullen roaring, as the wind: to throw or beat violently.—*n.* a blow or blast, or the sound of these: a tremble.—*adj.* **wuth'ering.** [From O.N.]

wyandotte *wī'an-dot, n.* a useful breed of the domestic fowl, of American origin. [From the N. American tribe so called.]

wych-elm *wich'elm, n.* a common wild elm, also called Scotch elm or witch-hazel.—**wych'-hazel** same as **witch-hazel.** [**witch**[2] and **elm.**]

wye *wī, n.* the letter Y (q.v.) or anything shaped like it.

wynd *wind,* (*Scot.*) *n.* a lane, narrow alley in a town. [Same as **wind**[2].]

wyvern. Same as **wivern.**

fāte; fär; mē; hûr (her); mīne; mōte; fōr; mūte; mōōn; fōōt; dhen (then); el'ə-mənt (element)

X

X, x *eks, n.* the twenty-fourth letter in our alphabet; as Roman numeral X stands for ten; X (see also **chi**) as an abbreviation represents the word Christ—**Xian, Xmas;** *x* in algebra is the first of the unknown quantities.—**X'-chromosome** a chromosome associated with sex-determination, usually occurring paired in the female zygote and cell, and alone in the male zygote and cell; **X'-particle** a meson; **X'-rays** electromagnetic rays of very short wavelength which can penetrate matter opaque to light-rays, produced when cathode rays impinge on matter—discovered by Röntgen in 1895.—*adj.* **X'-ray.**—*n.* a photograph taken by X-rays.—*v.t.* to photograph or treat by, or otherwise expose to, X-rays.—**X-ray telescope** a telescope designed to investigate the emission of X-rays from stars; **X-ray therapy** the use of X-rays for medical treatment; **X-ray tube** an evacuated tube in which X-rays are emitted from a metal target placed obliquely opposite to an incandescent cathode whose rays impinge on the target.

xanth- *zanth-,* **xantho-** *zan'thō-, -tho'-,* in composition, yellow.—*ns.* **xanthein** *(zan'thē-in)* a soluble yellow colouring matter of flowers; **xanthene** *(zan'thēn)* a white crystalline compound of carbon, hydrogen, and oxygen, from which are derived **xanthene dyestuffs.**—*adj.* **xan'thic** of a yellow tint, esp. as a description of flowers: pertaining to xanthin or xanthine: designating **xanthic acid,** any of a series of compounds of an alcohol with carbon disulphide. —*ns.* **xan'thin** a name given to the insoluble yellow colouring matter of various flowers: also to a principle in madder: (usu. **xan'thine**) a white substance, closely allied to uric acid, found in muscle tissue, the liver and other organs, urine, etc., leaving a lemon-yellow residue when evaporated with nitric acid.—*n.* **xanthochroia** *(-thō-kroi'ə)* yellowness of the skin.— *adjs.* **xanthochrō'ic,** **xanthochroid** *(-kroid;* also used as *n.*).—*n.* **xanthochroism** *(-thok'rō-izm)* a condition in which all pigments other than yellows disappear, as in goldfish, or normal colouring is replaced by yellow. —*adj.* **xanthochroous** *(-thok'rō-əs)* xanthochroic.— *ns.* **xanthochrō'mia** any yellowish discoloration, esp. of the cerebrospinal fluid; **xanthoma** *(zan-thō'mə)* a yellow tumour composed of fibrous tissue and of cells containing cholesterol ester, occurring on the skin (e.g. in diabetes) or on the sheaths of tendons, or in any tissue of the body.—*adj.* **xanthom'atous.**—*ns* **xanthophyll** *(zan'thō-fil)* $C_{40}H_{56}O_2$, one of the two yellow pigments present in the normal chlorophyll mixture of green plants; **xanthop'sia** the condition in which objects appear yellow to the observer, as in jaundice or after taking santonin; **xanthop'terin(e)** *(-in)* a yellow pigment obtained from the wings of yellow butterflies and the urine of mammals.—*adj.* **xanthous** *(zan'thəs)* yellow. [Gr. *xanthos,* yellow.]

xebec *zē'bek, n.* a small three-masted vessel much used by the former corsairs of Algiers. [Fr. *chebec,* influenced by Sp. form; perh. from Turkish or Arabic.]

xen- *zen-, zēn-,* **xeno-** *zen-ō-, zi-no'-,* in composition, strange, foreign, guest.—*n.* **xenogamy** *(zen-og'ə-mi;* Gr. *gamos,* marriage; *bot.)* cross-fertilisation.—*adj.* **xenogenous** *(zi-noj'-i-nəs)* due to outside cause.—*ns.* **xen'ograft** a graft from a member of a different species; **xen'olith** a fragment of rock of extraneous origin which has been incorporated in magma.—*adj.* **xenomorphic** *(-mōr'fik;* Gr. *morphē,* form) crystalline in internal structure but not in outward form.— *ns.* **xenon** *(zen', zēn'on)* a zero-valent element (Xe; at. numb. 54), a heavy gas present in the atmosphere in proportion of $1:17 \times 10^7$ by volume, and also a fission product; **xen'ophile** one who likes foreigners or things foreign; **xen'ophobe** *(-fōb;* Gr. *phobos,* fear) one who fears or hates foreigners or things foreign; **xenophobia** *(-fō'bi-ə),* **xenoph'oby** fear or hatred of things foreign; **Xen'opus** a genus of African aquatic frogs.—**xenon lamp** a high-pressure lamp, containing traces of xenon, used in film projectors, high-speed photography, etc. [Gr. *xenos,* (n.) guest, host, stranger, (adj.) strange, foreign.]

xer- *zēr-,* **xero-** *zē-rō-,* in composition, dry.—*ns.* **xerasia** *(zi-rā'si-ə)* a morbid dryness of the hair; **xeroderma** *(zē-rō-dûr'mə;* Gr. *derma,* skin), **xeroder'mia** a disease characterised by abnormal dryness of the skin and by overgrowth of its horny layer.—*adjs.* **xerodermat'ic,** **xeroder'matous,** **xeroder'mic.**—*ns.* **xerog'raphy** a non-chemical photographic process in which the plate is sensitised electrically and developed by dusting with electrically-charged fine powder; **xeroma** *(-rō')* xerophthalmia.—*adj.* **xerophilous** *(-of'il-əs;* Gr. *philos,* loving) of a plant, tolerant of a droughty habitat.—*ns.* **xeroph'ily** adaptation to dry conditions; **xerophthalmia** *(-of-thal'mi-ə;* Gr. *ophthalmos,* eye) a dry lustreless condition of the conjunctiva due to deficiency of vitamin A in the diet; **xē'rophyte** *(-fit;* Gr. *phyton,* plant) a plant able to inhabit places where the water supply is scanty, or where conditions, e.g. excess of salts, make it difficult to take in water.—*adj.* **xerophytic** *(-fit')* able to withstand drought.—*ns.* **xerō'sis** abnormal dryness, as of the skin, mouth, eyes, etc.; **xerostoma** *(-os'tom-ə;* Gr. *stoma,* mouth), **xerostō'mia** excessive dryness of the mouth due to insufficiency of the secretions; **xerotes** *(zē'rō-tēz)* a dry habit of body.—*adj.* **xerotic** *(-rot')* of bodily tissues, abnormally dry.—*n.* **Xerox®** a registered trademark used inter alia in respect of copying machines operating a xerographic method of reproduction: a copy so produced.—*v.t.* to produce a copy by this method. [Gr. *xēros,* dry.]

Xhosa *kō'sə, -zə, n.* a group of Bantu-speaking tribes from the Cape district of South Africa: a member of one of these tribes: the language of these tribes.— *adj.* **Xho'san.**

xi *zī, ksī, ksē, n.* the fourteenth letter of the Greek alphabet (Ξ, ξ).

Xian. See under **X.**

xiph-, **xipho-** *zif-, zif-ō-, -ō-,* in composition, sword.— *adjs.* **xiph'oid** sword-shaped; **xiphoid'al.** [Gr. *xiphos,* a sword.]

Xmas *eks'məs, kris'məs, n.* short for **Christmas** (see also **X**).

X-rays. See under **X.**

xylem *zī'lam, n.* woody tissue concerned in the conduction of aqueous solutions, and with mechanical support.—*ns.* **xy'lene** $C_6H_4(CH_3)_2$, any of three dimethyl-benzenes, occurring in coal-tar but not separable by fractional distillation; **xy'lenol** $(CH_3)_2 \cdot C_6H_3 \cdot OH$, any of six monohydric phenols

For other sounds see detailed chart of pronunciation.

derived from xylenes.—*adj.* **xy'lic** pertaining to xylem: designating any of six acids, derivatives of xylene.—*n.* **xy'locarp** a hard and woody fruit, as a coconut.—*adj.* **xylocarp'ous**.—*ns.* **xylography** (*zī-log'rə-fi*) the art of engraving on wood; **xyl'ograph** an impression or print from a wood block: an impression of the grain of wood for surface decoration; **xylog'rapher**.—*adjs.* **xylograph'ic, -al; xy'loid** woody, ligneous.—*ns.* **xy'lol** (L. *oleum*, oil) xylene; **xylol'ogy** the study of the structure of wood.—*adj.* **xylon'ic** designating an acid obtained by oxidising xylose.—*n.* **Xy'lonite®** a non-thermosetting plastic of the nitrocellulose type.—*adjs.* **xylophagous** (*-lof'ə-gəs*) wood-

eating; **xyloph'ilous** fond of wood, living upon wood. —*n.* **xy'lophone** (Gr. *phōnē*, voice) a musical instrument consisting of a graduated series of wooden bars, which are rested on straw, etc., and are struck by wooden hammers: an instrument used to measure the elastic properties of wood.—*adj.* **xylophon'ic**.—*ns.* **xyloph'onist; xylopyrog'raphy** designs on wood made with a hot poker; **xy'lose** a pentose found in many plants, also known as wood-sugar ($C_5H_{10}O_5$); **xy'lyl** (*-lil*) any of the univalent radicals, C_8H_9, of the xylenes or their derivatives. [Gr. *xylon*, wood.]

xyster *zis'tər, n.* a surgeon's instrument for scraping bones. [Gr. *xystēr*, a graving tool.]

fāte; fär; mē; hûr (her); *mīne; mōte; för; mūte; mōōn; fōōt; dhen* (then); *el'ə-mənt* (element)

Y

Y, y *wī, n.* the twenty-fifth letter of our alphabet. Early printers used y as a substitute for thorn (þ), which their founts lacked: hence it came to be so used in MSS. and inscriptions, as *yat* or *y*[t] for *that*, *ye* for *the*; cf. **ye**[2]. **Y'-chromosome** one of a pair of chromosomes associated with sex-determination (the other being the **X-chromosome**); **Y'-level** a type of engineers' level whose essential characteristic is the support of the telescope, namely, Y-shaped rests in which it may be rotated, or reversed end-for-end.— Also **wye'-level.**

-y[1] *-i, suff.* forming adjectives with the senses 'characterised by', 'full of', 'having the quality of', 'inclined to', as *icy, sandy, slangy, shiny.* [O.E. *-ig.*]

-y[2] *-i, suff.* forming nouns denoting (1) a diminutive, or a term of affection, as *doggy, daddy;* (2) a person or thing having a certain specified characteristic, as *fatty.* [Orig. Scot. **-ie** in names, etc.]

-y[3] *-i, suff.* forming nouns denoting a quality, state, action or entity, as *fury, jealousy, subsidy, society.* [O.Fr. *-te,*—L. *-ia.*]

yacht *yot, n.* orig. a light fast-sailing vessel: a sailing, steam, etc., vessel elegantly fitted up for pleasure-trips or racing.—*v.i.* to sail or race in a yacht.— **yacht'er** one engaged in sailing a yacht.—*n. and adj.* **yacht'ing.**—*adj.* **yacht'-built** built on the model of a yacht.—**yacht'-club** a club of yachtsmen; **yachts'-man, -woman** one who keeps or sails a yacht; **yachts'-manship** the art of sailing a yacht.—**land'-, sand'-yacht** a wheeled boat with sails, for running on land, usu. sea-beaches; **land'-, sand'-yachting.** [Du. *jacht,* from *jagen,* to chase.]

yack, or **yak** *yak,* in full **yackety-yak** *yak'i-ti-yak'*, *(slang) ns.* persistent, often idle or stupid talk.—*vs.i.* to talk persistently, esp. in a foolish or gossiping manner.—Also **ya(c)k'ety-ya(c)k'**, **yak'ity-yak'.** [Imit.]

yah[1] *yā.* Variant of **yea.**

yah[2] *yä, interj.* an exclamation of derision, contemptuous defiance (also **yah'-boo'**) or disgust.

Yahweh *yä'wā, n.* Jehovah (q.v.).—*n.* **Yah'wist** Jehovist.—Also **Yah've(h), Yah'vist.**

yak[1] *yak, n.* a species of ox found in Tibet, and domesticated there, covered all over with a thick coat of long silky hair, that of the lower parts hanging down almost to the ground. [Tibetan.]

yak[2], **yakety-yak,** etc. See **yack.**

Yakut *yä-kōōt', n.* a member of a mixed Turkish race in Siberia, in the Lena district: their Turkic language.

Yale[©] **lock** *yäl lok,* a trademark for certain kinds of lock. [Linus *Yale* (1821–68), American locksmith.]

yam *yam, n.* a large tuberous root like the potato, growing in tropical countries: any plant of the genus Dioscorea, some species of which yield these tubers: a sweet-potato *(Southern U.S.).* [Port. *inhame.*]

yammer *yam'ər, (dial.* and *coll.) v.i.* to lament, wail: to whine: to make an outcry: to express yearning.—Also *n.—n. and adj.* **yamm'ering.** [O.E. *geom(e)rian—geomor,* sad; influenced in M.E. by Du. *jammeren.*]

yamulka. Same as **yarmulka.**

Yang. See **Yin.**

yank *yangk, v.t. (coll.)* to carry, move, pull with a jerk. —*v.i.* to pull or jerk vigorously *(coll.)*: to move actively *(fig.).—n.* a strong jerk *(coll.).*

Yankee *yang'ki, n.* in America, a citizen of the New England States, or an inhabitant of the northern United States, as opposed to the southern: in British usage, generally an inhabitant of the United States.— Also *adj.*—Also **Yank** *(coll.).*—**Yank'ee-Doo'dle** a Yankee (from a popular song). [Prob. *Janke,* a diminutive of Du. *Jan,* John.]

yaourt. See **yoghurt.**

yap *yap, v.i.* to bark sharply or constantly (as a small dog): to speak constantly, esp. in a noisy or foolish manner *(coll.)*: to scold *(coll.).—n.* a yelp: a cur: incessant, foolish chatter *(coll.).—ns.* **yapp'er,** **yap'ster** a dog. [Imit.]

yapp *yap, n.* a limp leather binding in which the cover overlaps the edges of the book. [*Yapp,* a bookseller.]

yapper, yapster. See **yap.**

yard[1] *yärd, n.* in English speaking countries, a measure of 3 feet or 36 inches and equivalent to 0·9144 metre: a piece of material this length: a long beam on a mast for spreading square sails.—*n.* **yard'age** the aggregate number of yards: the length, area, or volume measured or estimated in linear, square, or cubic yards: the cutting of coal at so much a yard.—**yard's-arm** either half of a ship's yard (right or left) from the centre to the end; **yard'stick** a stick 3 feet long: any standard of measurement *(fig.).*—**by the yard** sold or measured in yard lengths: in large quantities *(fig.);* **yard of ale,** etc., a tall slender glass for ale, etc., or its contents. [O.E. *gyrd, gierd,* a rod, measure.]

yard[2] *yärd, n.* an enclosed place, esp. near a building, often in composition, as 'backyard,' 'courtyard,' 'farmyard,' 'prison-yard,' or where any special work is carried on, as 'brickyard,' 'wood-yard,' 'dockyard,' 'railway-yard': a garden.—**the Yard** New Scotland Yard, the London Metropolitan Police headquarters. [O.E. *geard,* fence, dwelling, enclosure.]

yardang *yär'dang, n.* a ridge formed by wind erosion from sand, silt, etc., usually lying parallel to the prevailing wind direction. [Turk. abl. of *yar,* steep bank, precipice.]

yarmulka, yarmulke *yär'məl-kə, n.* the skullcap worn by Jewish males, esp. during prayers or ceremonial occasions. [Yiddish,—Pol. *yarmulka,* small cap.]

yarn *yärn, n.* spun thread: one of the threads of a rope, or these collectively: a sailor's story, spun out to some length, and often having incredible elements: a story generally *(coll.).—v.i.* to tell stories. [O.E. *gearn,* thread.]

yarrow *yar'ō, n.* a strong-scented plant, *Achillea millefolium,* or similar species of milfoil. [O.E. *gearwe.*]

yashmak *yash'mak,* or *-mak', n.* the double veil worn by Muslim women in public, the eyes only being uncovered. [Ar. *yashmaq.*]

yatag(h)an *yat'ə-gan, n.* a long Turkish dagger, without guard, usu. curved. [Turk. *yātāghan.*]

yaw *yö, v.i.* of a ship, to deviate temporarily from, to turn out of the line of, its course: to move unsteadily or zigzag *(fig.)*: to deviate in a horizontal direction from the line of flight *(aero.).—v.t.* to cause to deviate from course, zigzag, etc.—*n.* a deviation from the course: the angular motion of an aircraft in a horizontal plane about the normally vertical axis. [Origin uncertain; cf. O.N. *jaga,* to move to and fro, as a door on its hinges.]

For other sounds see detailed chart of pronunciation.

yawey. See **yaws.**

yawl[1] *yōl, v.i.* to howl.—*n.* a howl. [Variant of **yowl.**]

yawl[2] *yōl, n.* a ship's small boat, generally with four or six oars: a small fishing-boat: a small sailing-boat with jigger and curtailed mainboom. [Du. *jol.*]

yawn *yón, v.i.* to take a deep involuntary breath from drowsiness, boredom, etc.: to gape: to be wide open, as a chasm.—*v.t.* to render, to make, or to effect, by yawning: to utter with a yawn.—*n.* an involuntary deep breath from weariness or boredom: a chasm, opening: a boring event, person, etc. (*coll.*).—*adj.* **yawn'ing** gaping, opening wide: drowsy.—*n.* the action of the verb to yawn.—*adv.* **yawn'ingly.**— *adj.* **yawn'y.** [O.E. *gānian,* to yawn, and *geonian, ginian* (in composition, *gīnan,* pa.t. *gān*), to gape widely.]

yawp *yóp,* (chiefly *U.S.*) *v.i.* to utter or cry harshly or hoarsely and noisily: to yelp, bark.—*n.* such a harsh, etc. cry.—*n.* **yawp'er.** [Imit.; cf. **yap, yelp.**]

yaws *yoz, n.* a tropical epidemic and contagious disease of the skin—also known as framboesia, button scurvy, verruga Peruviana, buba or boba, etc.—*adj.* **yaw'(e)y** pertaining to yaws. [Origin uncertain; perh. Amer. Indian.]

Y-chromosome. See under **Y.**

ye[1] *yē, yi, pron.* the second person pl. (sometimes sing.) pronoun, now *arch., B., dial., poet.*; cf. **you.** Formerly, as in the A.V. of the English Bible, *ye* was always used as a nominative, and **you** as a dative or accusative; later *ye* was sometimes used for all these cases. [M.E. *ye,* nom.; *your,* gen.; *you, yow,* dat. and accus. pl.—O.E. *gē,* nom. ye; *ēower,* gen.; *ēow,* dat. and accus.]

ye[2] *thē, thi, demons. adj.* archaic script for 'the', arising from the thorn letter, þ. See **Y.**

yea *yā, adv.* yes: verily: indeed more than that.—*n.* an affirmative vote or voter. [O.E. *gēa*; cf. **yes.**]

yeah *ye, yä,* (*coll.*) *adv.* yes.

year *yēr, yûr, n.* a period of time determined by the revolution of the earth in its orbit: the time taken by any specified planet to revolve round the sun: the period beginning with 1st January and ending with 31st December, consisting of 365 days, except in a **leap year,** when one day is added to February, making the number 366—the present **legal, civil** or **calendar year:** a space of twelve calendar months, or a period within each twelve-month space characterised by a particular activity, etc.: students etc. as a group at the same stage of their education: (in *pl.*) a period of life, esp. age or old age: (in *pl.*) a very long time:—*pl.* **years** (collective *pl.*, used adjectively with numeral prefixed, **year,** e.g. *a three year period*).—*n.* **year'ling** an animal a year old: a bond maturing after one year (*finance*).—*adj.* a year old: maturing after one year (*finance*).—*adj.* **year'ly** happening every year: lasting a year: for a year.—*adv.* once a year: from year to year.—**year'-book** a book published annually, reviewing the events of the past year.—*adjs.* **year'long** lasting a year: **year'-round** existing, lasting, open, etc. throughout the year.—**anomalistic year** the earth's time of passage from perihelion to perihelion —365 days, 6 hours, 13 minutes, 49 seconds; **astronomical year** the time of one complete mean apparent circuit of the ecliptic by the sun—365 days, 5 hours, 48 minutes, 46 seconds—called also the **equinoctial, natural, solar,** or **tropical year;** ecclesiastical year the year as arranged in the ecclesiastical calendar, with the saints' days, festivals, etc.; **embolismic year** a year of thirteen lunar months (384 days) occurring in a lunisolar calendar such as that of the Jews; **financial year, fiscal year** see **finance, fisc;** **Hebrew year** a lunisolar year, of 12, or 13, months of 29 or 30 days (in every cycle of nineteen years the 6th, 8th, 11th, 14th, 17th, and 19th having thirteen months instead of twelve); **Julian year** the year according to the Julian calendar (introduced by Julius Caesar, modified by Augustus, superseded by the Gregorian calendar), a period of 365¼ days, longer than an astronomical year by about 11 minutes (see style); **leap-year** see above, **legal, civil,** or **calendar, year** the year by which dates are reckoned; it has begun on different dates at different periods, and for six centuries before 1752 it began in England on 25th March; since then (earlier in Scotland) it has begun on 1st January; **lunar year** a period of twelve lunar months or 354 days; **sidereal year** the period required by the sun to move from a given star to the same star again—having a mean value of 365 days, 6 hours, 9 minutes, 9·6 seconds; **the year dot** see **dot; year in, year out** (happening, done, etc.) every year: with monotonous regularity; **Year of Grace,** or of **our Lord** a formula used in stating any particular year since Christ's birth. [O.E. *gēar.*]

yearn *yûrn, v.i.* to feel earnest desire: to express longing, as in sound or appearance.—*n.* a yearning.—*n.* and *adj.* **yearn'ing.**—*adv.* **yearn'ingly.** [O.E. *geornan* (W.S. *giernan*), to desire.]

yeast *yēst, n.* a substance used in brewing, baking, etc., consisting of minute fungi, which produce zymase, and hence induce the alcoholic fermentation of carbohydrates: leaven (*fig.*).—*v.i.* (*lit.* and *fig.*) to ferment, or be covered with froth.—*n.* **yeast'iness.**— *adj.* **yeast'y** like yeast: frothy, foamy: insubstantial. —**yeast'-plant** any of a group of tiny, one-celled fungi (Saccharomyces) that produce alcoholic fermentation in saccharine fluids; **yeast'-powder** dry powdered yeast used in baking: baking-powder. [O.E. *gist, gyst.*]

yell *yel, v.i.* to howl or cry out with a sharp noise: to scream from pain or terror.—*v.t.* to utter with a yell. —*n.* a sharp outcry: a particular cry affected by an American college: something or someone very funny (*slang*).—*n.* **yell'ing.** [O.E. (Angl.) *gellan;* Ger. *gellen;* conn. with O.E. *galan,* to sing.]

yellow *yel'ō, adj.* of the colour of sulphur or of the primrose: of the colour of gold: of Mongolic race: of mixed black and white race: cowardly, base (*coll.*): sensational (*coll.*).—*n.* the colour of the rainbow between the orange and the green: any dye or pigment producing such a colour: a yolk: a plant disease in which the foliage yellows: (in *pl.*) jaundice in horses, etc.—*v.t.* and *v.i.* to make, or become, yellow.—*adj.* **yell'owish** somewhat yellow.—*ns.* **yell'owishness; yell'owness** the quality or state of being yellow.—*adj.* **yell'owy** yellowish.—*adjs.* **yell'ow-backed, -bellied, -billed, -breasted, -covered, -crowned, -eyed, -footed, -fronted, -headed, -horned, -legged, -necked, -ringed, -rumped, -shouldered, -spotted,** etc.—**yell'ow-bell'y** (*slang*) a coward (*adj.* **yell'ow-bell'ied**); **yell'ow-bird** any of various birds of a yellow colour—the golden oriole, etc.; **yell'ow-boy** (*slang*) a gold coin: a mulatto or dark quadroon (*fem.* **yell'ow-girl**); **yell'ow-bunting** the yellow-hammer; **yellow fever** an acute disease occurring in tropical America and West Africa, caused by infection with a virus transmitted to man by the bite of a mosquito *Aëdes aegypti,* characterised by high fever, acute nephritis, jaundice, and haemorrhages; **yellow flag** a flag of a yellow colour, displayed by a vessel in quarantine or over a military hospital or ambulance; **yell'ow-hammer, -ammer** a finch (*Emberiza citrinella*), so named from its yellow colour—also called yellow-bunting; **Yellow Jack** (*slang*) yellow fever; **yellow line** a yellow line on a road indicating parking restrictions; **yell'ow-metal** a brass consisting of sixty parts copper and forty parts zinc; **yellow pages** that part of a telephone directory, printed on yellow paper, which classifies participating subscribers alphabetically according to trades, professions, services, etc.; **yellow peril** the danger that the yellow races may crush the white and overrun the world; **yellow press** newspapers abounding in exaggerated, sensational articles; **yell'ow-rattle** see **rattle**; **yell'ow-snow** snow sometimes observed in the Alps and in the Antarctic regions, coloured yellow by the growth on it of certain algae; **yell'ow-spot** the macula lutea, the small area at the centre of the retina in vertebrates at which vision is most distinct.—**a yellow streak** a tendency to dastardly behaviour; **yellow brick road** a path to fame, wealth, etc. [O.E. *geolu*.]

yelp *yelp, v.i.* to utter a sharp cry or bark.—*n.* a sharp, quick cry or bark.—*n.* **yelp'er**.—*n.* and *adj.* **yelp'ing**. [O.E. *gielpan*, to boast, exult.]

yen[1] *yen, n.* the Japanese monetary unit:—*pl.* yen. [Jap.,—Chin. *yüan*, round, a dollar.]

yen[2] *yen, (coll.) n.* an intense desire, longing, urge.—*v.i.* to desire, yearn. [Chin. *yeen*, craving, addiction.]

yeoman *yō'mən, n.* a gentleman serving in a royal or noble household, ranking between a sergeant and a groom (*hist.*): after the fifteenth century, one of a class of small farmers, commonly freeholders, the next grade below gentlemen (often serving as foot soldiers; *hist.*): a man of small estate, any small farmer or countryman above the grade of labourer: an assistant to an official: a member of the yeomanry cavalry or of the yeomen of the guard: a petty officer on a war vessel whose duties are clerical:—*pl.* **yeo'men**.—*adj.* **yeo'manly** of yeoman's rank: humble and honest: staunch: brave.—*adv.* staunchly, bravely.—*n.* **yeo'manry** the collective body of smaller freeholders: a cavalry volunteer force in Great Britain formed during the wars of the French Revolution, later mechanised as part of the Territorials.—**Yeomen of the Guard** a veteran company of picked soldiers, employed in conjunction with the gentlemen-at-arms, on special occasions, as the sovereign's bodyguard—constituted a corps in 1485 by Henry VII, and still wearing the costume of that period. [M.E. *yoman, yeman*; perh. for *young man*.]

yep *yep,* (esp. *U.S.*) dial. and coll. variant of **yes**.

yerba *yûr'bə, n.* a herb, esp. (also **yerba mate, yerba de maté**) Paraguay tea or maté (q.v.). [Sp.,—L. *herba*.]

yes *yes, adv.* ay: a word of affirmation or consent: used to indicate that the speaker is present, or (often said interrogatively) to signal someone to speak or act: formerly, on the contrary: yea.—*n.* a vote or answer of yes: one who votes or answers yes:—*pl.* **yes(s)'es**, **yes's**.—**yes'-man** (*coll.*) one who agrees with everything that is said to him: an obedient follower with no initiative. [O.E. *gēse, gīse—gēa, gē*, yea, and *sī*, let it be.]

yester *yes'tər* (*dial.* and *arch.* **yes'tern**), *adj.* relating to yesterday: last.—*adv.* **yestreen'** (contr. of **yestereven**; *Scot.* and *poet.*) yesterday evening.—*n.* **yes'terday** the day last past: (often in *pl.*) the (recent) past.—*adv.* on the day last past: formerly: in the (recent) past.—**yesteryear'** (orig. *D. G. Rossetti*) last year, or the past in general. [O.E. *geostran, giestran* (always followed by *dæg*, etc.).]

yet *yet, adv.* in addition, besides: up to the present time: still: hitherto: at the same time: even: before the affair is finished.—*conj.* nevertheless: however.—**as yet** up to the time under consideration. [O.E. *giet, gieta*.]

yeti *yet'i, n.* the abominable snowman. [Native Tibetan name.]

yew *ū, n.* any tree of genus Taxus—family Taxaceae, itself a division of the group Coniferae—widely diffused over the northern parts of the world, with narrow lanceolate or linear leaves, esp. *Taxus baccata* (in Europe long planted in graveyards) which yields an elastic wood good for bows: its wood: a bow made of its wood· yew twigs regarded as emblematic of grief —yew'-tree. [O.E. *īw, ēow*.]

Yiddish *yid'ish, n.* a language spoken by Jews, based on ancient or provincial German with Hebrew and Slavonic additions, usu. written in the Hebrew alphabet.—*ns.* **Yid** (*offensive*), **Yidd'isher** a Jew. [Ger. *jüdisch*, Jewish.]

yield *yēld, v.t.* to grant, accord: to admit, concede: to give out: to furnish, afford: to produce: to deliver, surrender, relinquish, resign.—*v.i.* to submit: to cease fighting or contesting: to give way under pressure: to give place.—*n.* an amount yielded: a product: the return of a financial investment, usually calculated with reference to the cost and dividend.—*adj.* **yield'able** that may be yielded: inclined to yield.—*ns.* **yield'ableness; yield'er.**—*adj.* **yield'ing** giving, or inclined to give, way: compliant.—*n.* a giving way: compliance.—*adv.* **yield'ingly.**—*n.* **yield'ingness.**—**yield point** in the case of iron and annealed steels, the stress at which a substantial amount of plastic deformation takes place suddenly. [O.E. (W.S.) *gieldan*, to pay.]

Yin, Yang *yin, yang, ns.* the two opposing principles of Chinese philosophy and religion influencing destiny, the former negative, feminine and dark, the latter positive, masculine and light. [Chin. *yin*, dark, *yang*, bright.]

yip *yip, v.t.* to give a short, sudden cry—esp. of a dog. —Also *n.* [Imit.]

yippee *yip-ē', interj.* expressing delight, exultation, etc.

yippy *yip'i, n.* one of a group of young people with ideals based on those of the hippies. [From the Youth International Party of 1968.]

-yl *-il, suff.* forming nouns denoting a radical, as carbonyl, carboxyl, etc. [Gr. *hȳlē*, matter.]

ylang-ylang *ē'lang-ē'lang, n.* a tree of the Malay Archipelago and Peninsula, the Philippines, etc., or an essence (also **ylang-ylang oil**) distilled from its flowers. [Tagálog.]

Y-level. See Y.

yo *yō, interj.* calling for, or accompanying, effort, etc.: —*pl.* yos.—*interjs.* **yo-(hō-)hō'** calling for attention: same as yo-heave-ho; **yo-heave'-hō'** formerly, a sailors' chant while hauling on ropes.

yob *yob,* (*slang*) *n.* a raw recruit: a teenage loafer: a lout.—Also **yobb'o**:—*pl.* **yobb'os.** [Back-slang for **boy**.]

yodel, yodle *yō'dl, v.t.* and *v.i.* to sing or shout, changing frequently from the ordinary voice to falsetto and back again after the manner of the mountaineers of the Tirol.—*n.* a song or phrase sung, or a cry made, in this fashion.—Also **jodel** (*yō'dl*).—*n.* **yō'deller, yō'dler.** [Ger. dial. *jodeln.*]

yoga *yō'gə, n.* a system of Hindu philosophy showing the means of emancipation of the soul from further migrations and union with the supreme being: any of a number of systems of physical and mental discipline by means of which such emancipation is attained: yogic exercises.—*ns.* **yō'gi** (*-gē*), **yō'gin** a Hindu ascetic who practises the yoga system, consisting in the withdrawal of the senses from external objects, long continuance in unnatural postures, etc.—*adj.* **yō'gic.**—*n.* **yō'gism.**—**hatha yoga** (*hath'ə, hut'ə*; Sans. *hatha*, force) a form of yoga (the most common in the Western Hemisphere) stressing the importance of physical exercises and positions and breathing-control in promoting physical and mental well-being. [Sans., union.]

yoghourt, yoghurt yog'ərt, yō'gərt, n. a semi-liquid food made from fermented milk.—Also **yaourt** (yä'ōōrt). [Turk. yŏghurt.]

yogi(n), etc. See **yoga.**

yoicks yoiks, interj. an old fox-hunting cry.—vs.i. or vs.t. **yoick(s)** to make, or urge on by, this cry.

yoke yōk, n. that which joins together: the frame of wood joining draught oxen at the necks: any similar frame, as one for carrying pails: a part of a garment that fits the shoulders (or the hips): a mark of servitude: slavery: an oppressive burden: a bond of union: a pair or couple, as of oxen.—v.t. to put a yoke on: to join together: to attach a draught-animal to: to enslave.—v.i. to be joined: to go together. [O.E. geoc.]

yokel yō'kl, n. a country bumpkin.—adj. yō'kelish.

yolk[1] yōk, n. the yellow part of the egg of a bird or reptile: the nutritive non-living material contained in an ovum.—adjs. **yolked, yolk'y** like yolk.—**yolk'-sac** (zool.) the yolk-containing sac which is attached to the embryo by the **yolk'-stalk,** a short stalk by means of which yolk substance may pass into the alimentary canal of the embryo. [O.E. geolca, geoleca—geolu, yellow.]

yolk[2] yōk, n. wool-oil.—adj. yolk'y.—Cf. suint. [O.E. ēowocig, yolky.]

Yom Kippur yŏm kip'ōōr, the Day of Atonement, a Jewish fast day.—**Yom Tob** or **Tov** (tōb, tōv) any religious festival. [Heb. yōm, day, kippūr, atonement, tōbh, good.]

yomp yomp, (esp. mil. coll.) v.i. to carry heavy equipment on foot over difficult terrain. [Poss. imit.]

yon yon, (now poet. or dial.) adj. that: those: yonder. —Also pron. that: the thing you know of.—adv. yonder.—prep. yond (Scot. usu. yont) to, or in, a position beyond.—adj. and pron. yon.—adv. yonder. —adv. yon'der to, or at, a distance within view.—adj. that, those, at a distance within view (or so conceived).—pron. that one, yon.—hither and yon(d) (dial.) hither and thither; hither, or here, and yonder hither and thither; the yonder the farther, more distant. [O.E. geon (adj., pron.), geond (prep., adv.), and M.E. yonder.]

yoni yō'nē, n. a representation of the female genitals, the symbol under which the Hindu deity Sakti is worshipped. [Sans.]

yonks yongks, (coll.) n. ages, a long time.

yont. See **yon.**

yoo-hoo yōō'-hōō, interj. a call to attract someone's attention.

yore yōr, yōr, n. time long ago or long past.—Also adj. —of yore in times past. [O.E. gēara, formerly; app. connected with gēar, a year.]

yorker yōrk'ər, (cricket) n. a ball pitched to a point directly under the bat.—v.t. **yerk** to bowl (or attempt to bowl) someone out with a yorker. [Prob. from Yorkshire, but history quite unknown.]

Yorkish yōrk'ish, adj. pertaining to the county or city of York: adhering to the House of York in the Wars of the Roses.—n. **York'ist** one of this party.—Also adj. —adj. **York'shire** of or from the county of Yorkshire: —abbrev. **Yorks.**—n. one of a breed of animal, esp. pigs, originating in Yorkshire.—**Yorkshire pudding** a pudding made of unsweetened batter, and baked along with meat or in meat dripping—orig. under the spit so as to catch the drippings; **Yorkshire terrier** a small long-haired kind of terrier.

Yoruba yo'rŏŏ-ba, yŏ', n. sing. and pl. a linguistic group of coastal West Africa: a member of the group: the language of the group.—adjs. **Yo'ruba,**

Yo'ruban.

you ū, pron. the commonly used second person pronoun (all cases), orig. plural (cf. **thou**), now standard for both singular and plural: (indef. pron.) anyone: the personality (or something in tune with the personality) of the person addressed (coll.).—**you-all'** (U.S.) you (esp. in pl.); **you'-know-what', you'-know-who** some unspecified but well-understood or well-known thing or person. [O.E. ēow (perh. through a later form eōw), orig. only dat. and accus.; cf. **ye**[1].] **you'd** yōōd, yōōd, a contraction of you had or you would. **you'll** yōōl, yōōl, a contraction of you will or you shall.

young yung, adj. not long born: in early life: in the first part of growth: youthful: vigorous: relating to youth: junior, the younger of two persons having the same name.—n. the offspring of animals: (with the) those who are young.—adj. **youngish** (yung'(g)ish) somewhat young.—n. **young'ling** a young person or animal.—adj. youthful, young.—ns. **young'ness; young'ster** a young person, esp. a young man: a child (coll.).—**young blood** fresh accession of strength, personnel, ideas, etc.; **Young England** during the corn-laws struggle (1842–45), a little band of young Tory politicians, who hated Free Trade and Radicalism, and professed a sentimental attachment to earlier forms of social life in England; **Young England, America,** etc., the rising generation in England, America, etc.; **young lady,** man a girl- or boyfriend, sweetheart; **young person** in Factory Acts, etc., a person who is under eighteen years of age but no longer a child: someone aged fourteen and over, but under seventeen (law); **Young Turk** one of a body of Turkish reformers who brought about the revolution of 1908: (also without caps.) a progressive, rebellious, impetuous, etc. member of an organisation.—**with young** pregnant. [O.E. geong.]

youngberry yung'ber-i, -bar-i, n. a large reddish-black fruit, a cross between a variety of blackberry and a variety of dew-berry. [B. M. Young, an American fruitgrower, and berry.]

younker yung'kər, n. a young person. [Old Du. jonckher (Du. jonker), from jong heer, young master or lord.]

your yor, ūr, pron. (gen. pl.) or poss. adj. of or belonging to you: used to denote a person of a class well known—the ordinary (implying some contempt; coll.): of or relating to an unspecified person or people in general.—prons. **yourn** (dial.) yours; **yours** (a double genitive) used predicatively or absolutely: short for 'your letter'.—**you and yours** you and your family or property; **yours faithfully, sincerely, truly,** etc., **yours to command,** etc., forms used conventionally in letters just before the signature: also sometimes used by a speaker to mean himself (coll.). [O.E. ēower, gen. of gē, ye.]

you're yōr, ūr, a contraction of you are.

yourself ūr-self', yōr-, pron. the emphatic form of **you:** in your real character: having command of your faculties; sane: in good form: the reflexive form of **you** (objective):—pl. **yourselves'.**

yourt. See **yurt.**

youth yōōth, n. the state of being young: early life, the period immediately succeeding childhood: an early period of existence: a young person, esp. a young man (pl. **youths** yōōdhz): young persons collectively.—adj. **youth'ful** pertaining to youth or early life: young: suitable to youth: fresh: buoyant, vigorous.—adv. **youth'fully.**—n. **youth'fulness.**—**youth club** a place or organisation providing leisure activities for young people; **youth hostel** a hostel where hikers, etc., who are members of an organisation find inexpensive and simple accommodation.—v.i. to stay in youth hostels.—**youth hosteller; youth leader** a social worker who works with the youth of a particular community or area. [O.E. *geoguth—geong*, young.]

you've *yōōv, yŏŏv*, a contraction of **you have**.

yow(e) *yow*, (*dial.*) *n*. variant of **ewe**.

yowl *yowl*, *v.i.* to cry mournfully, as a dog: to yell, bawl.—*n*. a distressed cry.—*n*. **yowl'ing** a howling. [M.E. *youlen*.]

yo-yo *yō'-yō*, *n*. a toy consisting of a reel attached to, and manoeuvred by, a string which winds and unwinds round it: any person or thing resembling a yo-yo in movement or ease of manipulation.—Also *adj*. [Orig. a trademark.]

ypsilon *ip-sī'lon, -sĕ'*, or *ip'si-*, *n*. the twentieth letter of the Greek alphabet (Υ, υ).—Also **upsilon** (*ŭp-sī'lon, ŭp'si-, up'si-*).

ytterbium *i-tûr'bi-əm*, *n*. a metallic element (Yb; at. numb. 70) a member of the rare-earth group.—*n*. **ytter'bia** ytterbium oxide (Yb₂O₃). [*Ytterby*, a Swedish quarry.]

yttrium *it'ri-əm*, *n*. a metallic element (Y; at. numb. 39) in the third group of the periodic system, usu. classed with the rare-earths.—*n*. **ytt'ria** its oxide, a yellowish-white powder.—*adjs*. **ytt'ric**, **ytt'rious**; **yttrif'erous**. [From *Ytterby*; see **ytterbium**.]

yu *yü*, *ü*, *n*. precious jade (nephrite or jadeite).—Also **yu'-stone**. [Chin. *yü, yü-shih*.]

yuan *yü-än*, *n*. the monetary unit of the People's Republic of China:—*pl*. **yuan**. [Chin. *yüan*.]

yuca (also **yucca**), *yuk'ə*, *n*. cassava.—*n*. **Yucc'a** (sometimes **Yuc'a**) a genus of plants of the family Liliaceae, natives of Mexico, New Mexico, etc., some (as *Yuca gloriosa*, the Spanish dagger) cultivated in gardens on account of the singularity and splendour of their appearance: (without *cap*.) any plant of this genus. [Of Carib origin.]

yucky, yukky *yuk'i*, (*slang*) *adj*. dirty, unpleasant.—*n*. **yuck, yuk** messiness, etc.—*interj*. expressing distaste, disgust. [Imit.]

yuga *yōō'gə*, *n*. one of the Hindu ages of the world.—Also **yug**. [Sans.]

Yugo-Slav, Yugoslav *yōō'gŏ-släv*, or *-släv'*, *n*. a native, citizen, or inhabitant of Yugoslavia, one of the southern group of Slavs consisting of Serbs, Croats, and Slovenes: the Slavonic language (Serbo-Croatian) dominant in Yugoslavia.—Also *adj*.—*adjs*. and *ns*. **Yugoslav'ian, Yugoslav'ic**.—Also **Jugo-Slav, Jugoslav**, etc. [Serbo-Croatian *jugo- —jug*, the south, and **Slav**.]

yuk, yukky. See **yucky**.

yulan *yōō'lan*, *n*. a Chinese magnolia, with large white flowers. [Chin.]

Yule *yōōl*, *n*. the season or feast of Christmas.—**Yule log** the block of wood cut down in the forest, then dragged to the house, and set alight in celebration of Christmas; **Yule'tide** the time or season of Yule or Christmas.—Also **yule**, **yule'tide**. [O.E. *gēol*, **Yule**.]

yum-yum *yum'-yum'*, (*coll.*) *interj*. expressing delighted or pleasant anticipation, esp. of delicious food.—*interj*. **yumm'y** yum-yum.—*adj*. delicious, attractive, etc. [Imit.]

yup *yup*, *yəp*. Same as **yep**.

yurt, yourt *yōōrt*, *n*. a light tent of skins, etc., used by nomads in Siberia. [From Russ.]

For other sounds see detailed chart of pronunciation.

Z

Z, z *zed, n.* the twenty-sixth and last letter in our alphabet: used as a contraction-mark (=;) in *viz., oz.,* etc.

zabaglione *zä-bäl-yō'ni, n.* a frothy custard made from egg yolks, marsala and sugar.—Also **zabalone** (-*bə-yō'ni*). [It.]

zaffre, zaffer *zaf'ər, n.* the impure oxide (used as a pigment) obtained by partially roasting cobalt ore previously mixed with two or three times its weight of fine sand. [Fr. *zafre*, of Ar. origin.]

Zairean *zä-ē'ri-ən, adj.* of or relating to Zaire, a republic of central Africa.—*n.* a native of Zaire.

zakuska *zä-kōōs'ka, n.* an hors-d'œuvre: a snack:—*pl.* **zakuski** (-*kě*). [Russ.]

zambo *zam'bō, n.* the offspring of a Negro man and an American Indian woman: anyone of mixed Negro and Indian blood:—*pl.* **zam'bos.** [Sp.]

Zamia *zā'mi-ə, n.* a genus of palm-like trees or low shrubs of the family *Cycadaceae* some species of which yield an edible starchy pith: (without *cap.*) a plant of this genus. [Named through misreading in Pliny *azaniae nuces*, pine cones that open on the tree —Gr. *azanein, azainein,* to dry.]

zanella *zə-nel'ə, n.* a mixed twilled fabric for covering umbrellas.

Zantedeschia *zan-ti-des'ki-ə, n.* a genus of plants of the Araceae, including *Zantedeschia aethiopica,* known as calla lily. [Francesco *Zantedeschi,* Italian botanist.]

zany *zā'ni, n.* an assistant clown or buffoon (*hist.*): a simpleton (*dial.*): one who plays the fool (*coll.*).—*adj.* of, or pertaining to, a zany: crazy, clownish (*coll.*).—*v.t.* to play the zany to.—*n.* **zā'nyism** the condition or habits of a buffoon. [Fr. *zani*—It. *zanni,* a corr. of *Giovanni,* John.]

Zanzibari *zan-zib-är'i, n.* a native of Zanzibar.

zap *zap,* (*coll.*) *v.t.* to hit, strike, destroy, kill, etc. (*lit* and *fig.*): to cause to move quickly.—*v.i.* to go speedily or suddenly.—*n.* vitality, force.—*interj.* expressing suddenness.—*adj.* **zapp'y** (*slang*) showy, punchy, speedy, or otherwise impressive.—**zap (it) up** to make (things) livelier. [Imit.]

zapateado *thä-pä-te-ddh'ō, n.* a lively Spanish dance, for a solo performer, with much clicking and stamping of the heels:—*pl.* **zapatead'os.** [Sp.]

zapotilla *zap-ō-til'ə, n.* Same as **sapodilla.**

zarape *sä-rä'pe, n.* Same as **serape.**

Zarathustrian *zar-ə-thōōs'tri-ən, adj.* and *n.* Zoroastrian.—*ns.* **Zarathus'trianism, Zarathus'trism** Zoroastrianism.—*adj.* and *n.* **Zarathus'tric** Zoroastrian.

zareba *zə-rē'bä, n.* in the Sudan, a stockade, thornhedge, etc., against wild animals or enemies: a fortified camp generally.—Also **zaree'ba, zari'ba, zere'ba, zeri'ba.** [Ar. *zarībah,* pen or enclosure for cattle.]

zarf *zärf, n.* an ornamental holder for a hot coffee-cup. —Also **zurf.** [Ar. *zarf,* a vessel.]

zarzuela *thär-thōō-ā'lä, -thwä', n.* a Spanish kind of operetta or vaudeville—named from the royal residence of La Zarzuela.

zastruga *zas-trōō'gä, n.* one of a series of long parallel snow-ridges on open wind-swept regions of snow:— *pl.* -**gi** (*gě*).—Also **sastru'ga.** [Russ.]

zax. Variant of **sax**[1].

Zea *zē'ə, n.* a genus of cereals having monoecious flowers; the only species is *Zea mays,* maize or Indian corn. (without *cap.*) the fresh styles and stigmas of this plant, formerly used as a diuretic. [Gr. *zeä* or *zeia,* one-seeded wheat.]

zeal *zēl, n.* strong feeling, as love, anger, etc., or passionate ardour (*B.*): intense (sometimes fanatical) enthusiasm: activity arising from warm support or enthusiasm.—*ns.* **zealot** (*zel'ət*) an enthusiast: a fanatic: (with *cap.*) one of a militant Jewish sect vigorously opposing the Roman domination of Palestine until the ruin of Jerusalem in 70 A.D.; **zealotism** (*zel'*) the character of a zealot; **zealotry** (*zel'*).—*adj.* **zealous** (*zel'*) full of zeal: warmly engaged in, or ardent in support of, anything: devoted.—*adv.* **zealously** (*zel'*).—*n.* **zealousness** (*zel'*). [O.Fr. *zele*—L. *zēlus* —Gr. *zēlos—zeein,* to boil.]

zebec, zebeck. Variants of **xebec.**

zebra *zē'brə, ze'brə, n.* any of a group of striped animals of the genus Equus—all of which are peculiar to the African continent: any animal, fish, plant or mineral having stripes reminiscent of a zebra's.— **zebra crossing** a stripe-marked street crossing where pedestrians have priority; **ze'bra-finch** an Australian weaver-bird striped black and grey; **ze'bra-par(r)'akeet** the budgerigar; **ze'bra-wood** the hard and beautifully striped wood of a Guiana tree, *Connarus guianensis*: the tree itself: applied also to various other trees or their wood. [African.]

zebu *zē'bū, n.* a humped domestic ox (*Bos indicus*) very nearly allied to the common ox, diffused over India, China, the east coast of Africa, etc. [Fr. *zébu,* the name taken by Buffon from the exhibitors of one at a French fair in 1752.]

zebub *zē'bub, n.* the zimb. [Ar. (dial.) *zubâb,* a fly.]

zed *zed,* in U.S. **zee** *zē, ns.* the twenty-sixth letter of the alphabet (Z, z): a bar of metal of form similar to the letter Z. [Fr. *zède*—L. and Gr. *zēta.*]

zedoary *zed'ō-ə-ri, n.* certain species of curcuma, natives of India, China, etc., whose rootstocks are aromatic, bitter, and pungent [Through mediaeval L.—Ar. *zedwâr.*]

zee *zē.* See **zed.**

Zeeman effect *zā'man if-ekt'* the splitting of a spectral line into several symmetrically disposed components which occurs when the source of light is placed in a strong magnetic field. [Named from Dutch physicist Pieter Zeeman (1865–1943).]

zeitgeist *tsīt'gīst, n.* the spirit of the age. [Ger.]

zeloso *zel-ō'sō, (mus.) adv.* with fervour. [It.]

zelotypia *zel-ō-tip'i-ə, n.* jealousy: morbid zeal in the prosecution of any project or cause. [Gr. *zēlotypiä,* jealousy—*zēlos,* zeal, *typtein,* to strike.]

Zen *zen, n.* a Japanese Buddhist sect which holds that the truth is not in scriptures but in man's own heart if he will but strive to find it by meditation and self-mastery. [Jap.—Chin. *ch'an*—Pali *jhāna,* Sans. *dhyāna,* religious contemplation.]

zenana *ze-nä'nə, n.* in India and Iran, apartments in which women are secluded, corresponding to the harem in Arabic-speaking Muslim lands.—**zenana mission** a mission to women of the zenanas, necessarily conducted by women. [Pers. *zanāna—zan,* a woman.]

Zend *zend, n.* the Avesta or Zend-Avesta: Avestan, the ancient East-Iranian Indo-European language in which the Zend-Avesta was long orally preserved and at last written—closely related to the Vedic Sanskrit.
—**Zend-Aves'ta** (properly meaning the Avesta with the commentary on it), the ancient sacred writings of the Parsees, including works of widely differing character and age, collected into their present canon under Shah-puhar or Shah-pur II (309–338 A.D.). [Pers. *zend, zand*, commentary.]

zendik *zen'dik, n.* an unbeliever in revealed religion in the East: one who practises magic. [Ar. *zendîq.*]

zenith *zen'ith*, U.S. *zên', n.* the point on the celestial sphere vertically above the observer's head, one of the two poles of the horizon, the other being the nadir: the greatest height (*lit.* and *fig.*).—*adj.* **zen'-ithal.**—**zenithal projection** a type of projection in which the plane of projection is tangential to the sphere.—**zen'ith-dis'tance** the angular distance of a heavenly body from the zenith. [O.Fr. *cenit(h)*, ultimately from Ar. *samt*, short for *samt-ar-ras*, lit. way, direction, of the head.]

zeolite *zê'ō-lît, n.* any of a large group of alumino-silicates of sodium, potassium, calcium, and barium, containing very loosely held water.—*adjs.* **zeolitic** (-*lit'*); **zeolit'iform.** [Gr. *zeein*, to boil (in allusion to the fact that many intumesce under the blowpipe), *lithos*, a stone.]

zephyr *zef'ər, n.* the west wind: a soft, gentle breeze: thin light worsted or woollen yarn: a shawl, jersey, or other garment made of such: any of various types of light-weight material, as a gingham, a flannel with a silk warp, a thin woollen cloth, etc.: anything very light and fine of its kind: (*cap.*) the god of the west wind. [Gr. *Zephyros*; akin to *zophos*, darkness, the west.]

zeppelin *zep'əl-in, n.* a dirigible, cigar-shaped airship of the type designed by Count Zeppelin (*c.* 1900).

zereba, zeriba. Same as **zareba.**

zero *zê'rō, n.* a cipher: nothing: the point from which the reckoning begins on scales, such as those of the barometer, etc.: the lowest point (*fig.*): zero hour:—*pl.* **zê'ros.**—*v.t.* to set at, adjust to, zero.—*adj.* having no measurable size, amount, etc.: not any (*coll.*).—*adj.* **zê'roth** denoting a term in a series regarded as preceding the 'first' term.—**zero hour** the exact time (hour, minute, and second) fixed for launching an attack or beginning an operation; **zero option** a proposal, originally made by President Reagan of the United States, to limit or abandon the deployment of (medium range) nuclear missiles if the opposing side does likewise.—*adjs.* **ze'ro-ra'ted** of goods on which the purchaser pays no value-added tax but on which the seller can claim back any value-added tax already paid by him.—**absolute zero** see **absolute; zero-base(d) budgeting** a system in which the budget of an organisation, department, etc. is drawn up anew each year without reference to any previous budget; **zero in (on)** (*slang*) to direct oneself straight towards a target: to focus one's attention or energies on, as if on a target: to aim for, move towards. [Fr. *zéro*—Ar. *sifr*; cf. **cipher.**]

zest *zest, n.* orange or lemon peel, or the oil squeezed from it, used as a flavouring: anything that gives a relish: piquancy: relish: enthusiasm.—*adj.* **zest'ful.** —*adv.* **zest'fully.**—*n.* **zest'fulness.**—*adj.* **zest'y.** [Fr. *zeste*, orig. the woody thick skin quartering a walnut; origin obscure.]

zeta *zê'tə, n.* the Greek z (Z, ζ).

zetetic *zē-tet'ik, adj.* proceeding by inquiry.—*n.* a search, investigation: a seeker, the name taken by some of the Pyrrhonists. [Gr. *zētētikos—zēteein,* to seek.]

zeugma *zûg'mə, n.* a figure of speech by which an adjective or verb is applied to two nouns, though strictly appropriate to only one of them.—*adj.* **zeug-mat'ic.** [Gr.,—*zeugnynai*, to yoke.]

zho *zhō, n.* one, esp. the male, of a kind of hybrid domestic cattle in parts of the Himalayas—said to be a cross between the male yak and the common horned cow.—Also **zo, dso** and **dzo** (*dzō*).—*ns.* **zhomo** (*zhō'mō*) the female of this cross.—Also **dsō'mo; zō'bō** the male of this cross.—Also **zō'bu, dsō'bō.**—Pl. in all cases *-s.* [Tibetan *mdzo.*]

zibel(l)ine *zib'ə-lin, -lîn, adj.* pertaining to the sable.—*n.* the fur of the sable: (*zib'ə-lēn*) a soft woollen material with a lustrous pile. [Fr.,—It. *zibellino*, prob. from Slav.; cf. **sable.**]

zibet *zib'it, n.* an Asiatic civet. [It. *zibetto*—Ar. *zabād*; cf **civet.**]

ziganka *zi-gang'kə, n.* a Russian country-dance: the music for such, usu. quick, with a drone bass. [Russ. *tsyganka*, a gypsy woman.]

ziggurat *zig'ŏŏ-rat, n.* a Babylonian temple-tower, pyramidal in general shape, consisting of a number of storeys each successive one of which was smaller than that below it. [Assyrian *ziqquratu*, a pinnacle, top of a mountain.]

zigzag *zig'zag, n.* a short, sharp turning: a line, road, fence, moulding, with sharp angles to right and left alternately.—*adj.* having short, sharp alternate turns: bent from side to side alternately.—*v.t.* to form with short, alternate turns.—*v.i.* to move forward making an alternation of short, sharp turns:—*pr.p.* **zig'zagging;** *pa.t.* and *pa.p.* **zig'zagged.**—*adv.* with frequent sharp turns.—also **zig'zaggy.**—*n.* **zig-zag'gery** angular crookedness.—*adj.* **zig'zaggy** zig-zag. [Fr. *zigzag*; Ger. *Zickzack.*]

zilch *zilch,* (*slang*) *n.* zero, nothing.

zillah, zila *zil'a, n.* an administrative district in India. [Ar. *dila* (in Hindi pronunciation, *zila*), a rib, thence a side, a district.]

zillion *zil'yən,* (*coll.*) *n.* an extremely large but unspecified number, many millions—analogous in formation and use to *million, billion.*

zimb *zimb, n.* an Ethiopian dipterous insect, like the tsetse, hurtful to cattle. [Amharic, a fly.]

Zimbabwean *zim-bä'bwi-ən, adj.* of or pertaining to the Republic of Zimbabwe (formerly Rhodesia) in southern Africa.—*n.* a native of Zimbabwe.

Zimmer® *zim'ər, n.* a metal frame held in front of one walking.—Also without *cap.* [Name of original manufacturer.]

zinc *zingk, n.* a bluish-white metallic element (Zn; at. numb. 30), resistant to atmospheric corrosion, it is a constituent of several alloys (e.g. brass) and is used in galvanising, battery electrodes, etc.—Also *adj.*—*v.t.* to coat with zinc:—*pr.p.* **zincing** (*zingk'ing*), **zinck'ing, zink'ing;** *pa.t.* and *pa.p.* **zinced** (*zingkt*), **zincked, zinked.**—*adj.* **zincif'erous** (*zingk-*), **zin-kif'erous** containing or producing zinc.—*ns.* **zincite** (*zingk'ît*) a native oxide of zinc, brittle, translucent, deep red; **zinc(k)ifica'tion, zinkifica'tion** the process of coating or impregnating an object with zinc.—*v.t.* **zinc(k)'ify, zink'ify** to cover or impregnate with zinc. —*adj.* **zinc(k)'y, zink'y** pertaining to, containing, or looking like, zinc.—*ns.* **zinco** (*zing'kō*) a line block executed in zinc, i.e. the normal line block:—*pl.* **zinc'os; zinc'ograph** a plate or picture produced by zincography; **zincographer** (*-kog'rə-fər*).—*adjs.* **zincograph'ic, -al.**—*n.* **zincography** (*-kog'rə-fî*) an engraving process in which zinc is covered with wax and etched: any process in which designs for printing are made on zinc plates.—*adj.* **zinc'oid** like zinc.—*adj.* **zinc'ous** pertaining to, or like, zinc.—**zinc'-blende** sphalerite, native sulphide of zinc; **zinc'-colic** a colic caused by the slow poison of zinc oxide; **zinc ointment** a mixture of zinc oxide and suitable ointment base (wool fat, petroleum jelly, etc.); **zinc oxide** a whitish solid, much used as a paint pigment in the rubber and other industries, and also medicinally, as an antiseptic and astringent (also called **flowers of zinc**); **zinc white** zinc oxide used as a pigment; **zinc'-worker**. [Ger. *Zink*.]

zing *zing*, *n*. a short shrill humming sound, as made by a bullet or vibrating string: zest, spirit, vitality, etc. (*coll*.).—*v.i.* to move very swiftly, esp. with a high-pitched hum.—*adj.* **zing'y** (*coll.*) full of zest, etc. [Imit.]

zingy. See **zing.**

Zinjanthropus. See **nutcracker man** at **nut.**

zinked, zinkify, etc. See **zinc.**

Zinnia *zin'i-ə*, *n*. a genus of American composite plants: (without *cap*.) any plant of this genus. [From J. G. *Zinn*, botanist (1727–59).]

Zion *zī'ən*, *n*. Jerusalem: the Israelitish theocracy: the Christian Church: heaven.—*ns.* **Zi'onism** the movement which secured national privileges and territory in Palestine for the Jews and which now helps to maintain and develop the state of Israel; **Zi'onist** a supporter of Zionism. [Heb. *tsīyōn*, orig. the name of a part of one of the hills of Jerusalem.]

zip *zip*, *n*. the ping or sound of a bullet striking an object or whizzing through the air: a whizzing sound: a zip-fastener: energy, vigour (*coll*.).—*v.i.* and *v.t.* to whizz: to fasten with a zip: to be full of, act with, proceed with, or (usu. **zip up**) infuse with, life and energy (*coll*.).—*n.* **zipp'er** a zip-fastener.—*adj.* **zipp'y** (*coll.*) quick, energetic, lively.—**zip-fastener** (*zip-fäs'nər*) a fastening device for clothes, etc., on which two sets of teeth can be opened or interlocked by pulling a slide. [Imit.]

zip code *zip cōd*, (*U.S.*) the postal code. [*zone improvement plan*.]

zircon *zûr'kən*, *n*. a tetragonal mineral, zirconium silicate, of which jacinth and jargoon are varieties.—*ns.* **zircall'oy** an alloy of zirconium with tin, chromium and nickel, widely used (esp. in the nuclear power industry) for its heat- and corrosion-resistant properties; **zirco'nia** oxide of zirconium.—*adj.* **zirconic** (-*kon'*) of zirconium.—*n.* **zirco'nium** a metallic element (Zr; at. numb. 40), highly resistant to corrosion.—**cubic zirconia** a synthetic stone used as a diamond substitute, produced from zirconia heated with any of various stabilising metallic oxides. [Ar. *zarqūn*—Pers. *zargūn*, gold-coloured; cf. **jargoon.**]

zither *zidh'*, *zith'ər*, *n*. a stringed instrument having a wooden frame and flat sounding-board with from twenty-nine to forty-two metal strings, placed on a table or on the knees, the strings being played by a plectrum on the right thumb.—Also **zith'ern.** [Ger.]

Zizania *zi-* or *zī-zā'ni-ə*, *n*. a genus of tall aquatic grasses, known as **wild, water, Indian,** or **Canada rice** (ordinary cultivated rice is of genus *Oryza*). [Gr. *zizanion*, darnel.]

zloty *zlot'i*, *zwot'ŭ*, *n*. the monetary unit of Poland.—*pl.* **zloty, zlotys.** [Pol. *zloty*, lit. golden.]

zo. See **zho.**

zoa. See **zoon** under **zoo-.**

zoanthropy *zō-an'thrə-pi*, *n*. a form of mental delusion in which a man believes himself to be a beast.—*adj.* **zoanthropic** (-*throp'*). [Gr. *zōion*, animal, *anthrōpos*, man.]

zobo, zobu. See **zho.**

zodiac *zō'di-ak*, *n*. an imaginary belt in the heavens, about 18° wide, through which the ecliptic passes centrally, and which forms the background of the motions of the sun, moon, and planets; it is divided into

twelve equal parts of 30° called **signs of the zodiac,** named from the constellations that once corresponded to them but do so no longer. The constellations, with the appropriate symbols of the corresponding signs, are as follows: Aries (*Ram*),♈; Taurus (*Bull*),♉; Gemini (*Twins*),♊; Cancer (*Crab*),♋; Leo (*Lion*),♌; Virgo (*Virgin*),♍; Libra (*Balance*), ♎; Scorpio (*Scorpion*),♏; Sagittarius (*Archer*),♐; Capricornus(*Goat*),♑;Aquarius(*Water-bearer*),♒; Pisces (*Fishes*),♓: a year (*obs*.): a set of twelve, or a recurrent series or course (*fig*.).—*adj.* **zodi'acal.**—**zodiacal light** a faint illumination of the sky, lenticular in form and elongated in the direction of the ecliptic on either side of the sun, fading away at about 90° from it; best seen after sunset or before sunrise in the tropics. [Fr. *zodiaque*—L. *zōdiacus*—Gr. *zōidiakos*, of figures—*zōidion*, a small carved or painted figure—*zōion*, an animal.]

zoechrome. See **zoetrope.**

zoetic *zō-et'ik*, *adj*. pertaining to life, vital. [Gr. *zōē*, life.]

zoetrope *zō'i-trōp*, *n*. the 'wheel of life', an instrument in which figures on the inside of a rotating cylinder are made visible through slots and provide an illusion of animated motion: (also **zō'echrome**) any of several early processes for colour cinematography, using rapidly repeated images of the selected colours in sequence on a screen, the synthesis arising from persistence of vision in the eye.—*adj.* **zoetropic** (-*trop'ik*). [Gr. *zōē*, life, *tropos*, a turning—*trepein*, to turn, *chrōma*, colour.]

zoic *zō'ik*, *adj*. pertaining to animals: of rocks, containing evidences of life, in the form of fossils. [Gr. *zōikos*, of animals—*zōion*, an animal.]

Zöllner's lines *tsæl'nərz linz*, rows of parallel lines appearing to be not parallel through the optical effect of oblique intersecting lines.—Also **Zöllner's illusion, pattern.** [J. K. F. *Zöllner* (1834–82), German physicist.]

Zollverein *tsol'fər-īn*, *n*. a customs union: a union of the German states, under the leadership of Prussia, to enable them to act as one state in their commercial relations with other countries (*hist*.). [Ger., *Zoll*, duty, *Verein*, union.]

zombi, zombie *zom'bi*, *n*. orig. in Africa, the deity of the python: in American voodooism, the snake deity: a corpse reanimated by sorcery: the power supposed to enter such a body: a stupid or useless person: a very slow-moving, lethargic person.—*n.* **zom'biism** belief in a zombi, or practice of rites associated with it. [W. African *zumbi*, fetish.]

zona(e), zonal, zonary, etc. See under **zone.**

zone *zōn*, *n*. a girdle, a belt, an encircling stripe of different colour or substance: one of the five great belts into which the surface of the earth is divided by the tropics and arctic and antarctic circles: any continuous tract with particular characteristics: a region: a group of strata characterised by a distinctive fauna or flora, and bearing the name of one fossil, called the **zonal index** (*geol*.): a set of crystal faces all parallel to the same line (the **zonal, zone, axis**): that part of the surface of a sphere between two parallel planes, intersecting the sphere (*math*.).—*v.t.* to encircle, as with a zone: to mark with zones, divide into, or assign to, zones.—*n.* **zō'na** (*pl.* **zō'nae -ē**) a girdle: a zone: an area, patch, strip, or band (*zool*.): herpes zoster.—*adj.* **zō'nal,** **zō'nary** like a zone: arranged in zones: pertaining to a zone; **zō'nate(d)** marked with zones, belted.—*n.* **zonā'tion** (*bot*.) the formation of bands differentiated by colour or other characteristics, or the arrangement of such bands: the occurrence of vegetation in well-marked bands, each band having its characteristic dominant species.—*adjs.* **zoned**

wearing a zone: having zones; **zone′less.**—*n.* **zō′ning** division into zones: assignment according to zones.— **zona pellucida** the transparent outer layer of an ovum; **zonal defence** (*football*, etc.) a method of defending in which a player patrols a particular area of the field rather than marking a specific opponent; **zone′-ticket** a railway ticket available for a time between any stations of a group. [L. *zōna*—Gr. *zōnē*, a girdle—*zōnnynai*, to gird.]

zonked *zongkt*, (*slang*) *adj.* utterly exhausted: intoxicated: under the influence of drugs.

zoo- *zō-ō-*, *zō-o′-*, *zō- zō-*, in composition, esp. in zool. terms, etc., animal.—*n.* **zoo** (*zōō*) orig., the Zoological Gardens, London: now any similar collection of animals.—*adj.* **zooblotic** (*zō-ō-bī-ot′ik*) parasitic on, or living in association with, an animal.—*n.* **zooblast** (*zō′ō-blast*; Gr. *blastos*, a germ) an animal cell.—*adj.* **zoochem′ical.**—*n.* **zoochem′istry** the chemistry of the animal body.—*adj.* **zoogamous** (*zō-og′ə-mas*; Gr. *gamos*, marriage) pertaining to zoogamy.—*ns.* **zoog′amy** sexual reproduction of animals; **zoogeny** (*zō-oj′ə-ni*; Gr. *-geneia*, suff. denoting production) the doctrine, or the process, of the origination of living beings—also **zoogony** (*-og′*).—*adjs.* **zoogenic** (*-jen′*), **zoog′enous** produced from animals.—*n.* **zoogeog′rapher.**—*adjs.* **zoogeograph′ic,** **-al.**—*ns.* **zoogeog′raphy** the science of the distribution of animals on the surface of the globe.—*adj.* **zoog′enous** (*zool.*) viviparous.—*ns.* **zoog′ony** zoogeny; **zoog′rapher,** **zoog′raphist** one who pursues zoog′raphy, the study or description of animals and their habits, or, the painting of animals.—*adjs.* **zoograph′ic,** **-al.**—*ns.* **zooid** (*zō′oid*; Gr. *eidos*, form) earlier, a free-moving cell, as a sperm-cell: in alternation of generations, an individual of an asexually-produced form: usu., an individual forming part of a colonial organism; **zool′ater** (Gr. *latreiā*, worship) one who worships animals; **zoolatrī′a, zool′atry** worship of animals.—*adj.* **zool′atrous.**—*n.* **zoolite** (*zō′ō-līt*; Gr. *lithos*, a stone) a fossil animal.—Also **zō′olith.**—*adjs.* **zoolith′ic, zoolit′ic; zoological** (*zō-ō-loj′i-kl*, or *zōō-ō-*; **zoological garden**, park a garden or park where living wild animals are kept, studied and exhibited).—*adv.* **zoolog′ically.**—*ns.* **zool′ogist** (*zō-*, or *zōō-*) one versed in **zoology** (*zō-ol′ə-ji*, or *zōō-ol′*), the science of animal life included along with botany in the science of biology; **zoomancy** (*zō′ō-man-si*; Gr. *manteiā*, divination) divination by observation of animals.—*adjs.* **zōōman′tic; zoomet′ric.**—*ns.* **zoometry** (*-om′ə-tri*; Gr. *metron*, a measure) comparative measurement of the parts of animals; **zō′omorph** (*-mörf*; Gr. *morphē*, form) in art, a representation of an animal form: an image or symbol of a god, etc., who is conceived as having an animal form.—*adj.* **zoomor′phic** pertaining to zoomorphism: representing animals in art.—*ns.* **zoomor′phism** the representation, or the conception, of a god or a man in an animal form.—Also **zoomor′phy; zō′on** a morphological individual, the total product of a fertilised ovum, or the group of zooids constituting a compound animal:—*pl.* **zō′a, zō′ons.**—*adjs.* **zō′onal** like a zoon; **zoon′ic** relating to animals.—*ns.* **zoon′omist; zoonomy** (*zō-on′ə-mi*; Gr. *nomos*, law) animal physiology.—Also **zoonō′mia; zoopathol′ogy** the study of disease in animals; **zoopathy** (*zō-op′ə-thi*; Gr. *pathos*, suffering) animal pathology.—*n.pl.* **Zoophaga** (*zō-of′ə-gə*; Gr. *phagein*, to eat) the carnivorous animals collectively.—*n.* **zooph′agan** a carnivorous animal.—*adj.* **zooph′agous** of or relating to the Zoophaga: feeding on animals.—*ns.* **zō′ophile** (*-fīl*; Gr. *philos*, loving) a zoophilous plant; **zoophil′ia, zooph′ilism, zooph′ily** love of animals: erotic fondness for animals; **zoophilist** (*zō-of′il-ist*) a

lover of animals: one who has zoophilia.—*adj.* **zooph′ilous** loving animals: experiencing zoophilia: pollinated by animals other than insects (*bot.*): of insects, feeding on animals (*zool.*).—*n.* **zō′ophyte** (*-fīt*) (now old-fashioned) any of numerous invertebrates resembling plants, as sponges, corals, sea-anemones, etc., esp. hydroid colonies of a branched form.—*adjs.* **zoophytic** (*-fit′*), **-al; zooph′ytoid; zoophytolog′ical** (*-fīt-*).—*ns.* **zoophytol′ogist; zoophytol′ogy; zooplank′ton** floating and drifting animal life; **zō′osperm** (Gr. *sperma*, seed) a spermatozoid: a zoospore.— Also **zoosper′mium.**—*adj.* **zoospermat′ic.**—*ns.* **zoosporan′gium** (*bot.*) a sporangium in which zoospores are formed; **zō′ospore** (Gr. *sporos*, a seed) an asexual reproductive cell that can swim by means of flagella. —*adjs.* **zoospor′ic; zoos′porous.**—*ns.* **zō′otaxy** (Gr. *taxis*, arrangement) the science of the classification of animals, systematic zoology; **zootechnics** (*-tek′niks*; Gr. *technē*, art), **zō′otechny** the science of the breeding and domestication of animals; **zoother′apy** (Gr. *therapeiā*, treatment) veterinary therapeutics; **zō′othome** (Gr. *thōmos*, heap) a group of zooids, as a mass of coral; **zootox′in** a toxin produced by an animal, as a snake; **zō′otrope** a zoetrope. [Gr. *zōion*, animal.]

zoom *zōōm*, *v.i.* to make a loud, deep, persistent buzzing noise: to move with this sound: to move very quickly: to use the stored energy of the forward motion of an aircraft in order to gain height (*aero.*): to soar (*fig.*): to change focus rapidly, as with a zoom lens.—*v.t.* to cause to zoom.—*n.* the act of zooming: a zooming noise.—**zoom lens** a lens of variable focal length used, e.g., for bringing television, cinematograph, or cine-camera pictures from distance to close-up without moving the camera: a similar lens used in still cameras and in microscopes. [Imit.]

zoot suit *zōōt sūt*, *sōōt*, a flashy type of man's suit with padded shoulders, fitted waist, knee-length coat, and trousers narrow at the ankles (introduced late 1940s). —*n.* **zoot′suiter** one who wears a zoot suit. [Origin unknown; prob. rhyming with **suit.**]

zoppo *tsop′pō*, (*mus.*) *adj.* with syncopation. [It.]

zoril, zorille, zorillo, *zorino.* See **zorro.**

Zoroastrianism *zōr-*, *zor-ō-as′tri-ən-izm*, *n.* an ancient religion founded or reformed by *Zoroaster*—the Greek pronunciation of *Zarathustra*—set forth in the Zend-Avesta, and still adhered to by the Guebres in Iran and Parsees in India.—*n.* and *adj.* **Zoroas′trian.** [L. *Zōroastrēs*—Gr.]

zorro *sor′ō*, *n.* a S. American fox or fox-like wild dog: —*pl.* **zorr′os.**—*ns.* **zoril, zorille** (*zor′il*, *-il′*) an African skunk-like musteline animal (*Zorilla*); **zorillo** (*sor-ē′yō*, *zor-il′ō*) a S. American skunk:—*pl.* **zorill′os; zorino** (*zor-ēn′ō*) a euphemism for a skunk fur used to make garments:—*pl.* **zorin′os.** [Sp. *zorro*, *zorra*, fox, *zorilla* (Fr. *zorille*) skunk.]

zoster *zos′tər*, *n.* an ancient Greek waist-belt for men: herpes zoster or shingles. [Gr. *zōstēr*, a girdle.]

Zouave *zōō-äv′*, *zwav*, *n.* one of a body of French infantry of great dash, orig. Algerians, wearing a quasi-Moorish dress: any of a number of volunteer regiments modelling themselves on the Zouaves who fought on the side of the North in the American Civil War: a woman's short embroidered jacket. [From the *Zouaoua*, an Algerian tribe.]

zounds *zowndz*, *zōōndz*, (*arch.*) *interj.* an exclamation of anger and astonishment. [A corr. of *God's wounds.*]

zucchetto *tsoō-ket′ō*, *n.* the skullcap of an ecclesiastic, covering the tonsure:—*pl.* **zucchett′os.**—Also **zuchett′a, -o** (*pl.* **-os**). [It. dim. of *zucca*, a gourd.]

zucchini *zōō-kē′nē*, (*U.S.* and *Austr.*) *n.* a courgette:— *pl.* **zucchi′ni, zucchi′nis.** [It.]

For other sounds see detailed chart of pronunciation.

zugzwang *tsōōhh'tsvāng*, *n.* in chess, a blockade position in which any move is disadvantageous to the blockaded player. [Ger.]

Zulu *zōō'lōō*, *n.* a branch of the great Bantu family, belonging to S. Africa, conspicuous for physical development: a member thereof: the language of the Zulus.—*adj.* pertaining to the Zulus, their language, etc. [Native name.]

Zuñi *zōō'nyē*, *sōō'nyē*, *n.* one of a tribe of Pueblo Indians living in large communal houses near the Zuñi river in New Mexico.—*adj.* and *n.* Zu'ñian.

zurf. Same as zerf.

Zwieback *tsvē'bäk*, or *tswē'*, *n.* biscuit rusk, or a sweet spiced bread toasted. [Ger.]

Zwinglian *zwing'gli-ən*, *tsving'li-ən*, *adj.* pertaining to the Swiss reformer Huldreich Zwingli (1484–1531), or his doctrines, esp. his divergence from Luther in the doctrine of the Eucharist.—*n.* a follower of Zwingli.—*ns.* Zwing'lianism; Zwing'lianist.

zwitterion *tsvit'ər-ī-ən*, *n.* an ion carrying both a positive and a negative charge. [Ger. *Zwitter*, a hybrid, and ion.]

zygo- *zī'gō-*, *zig'ō*, *zyg- zīg-, zig-,* in composition, yoke, union or presence of two similar things.—*adj.* **zy'gal** pertaining to a zygon: formed like a letter H.— *n.* **zygapophysis** (*-pof'i-sis*; Gr. *apophysis*, process) one of the yoke-pieces or articulations of the vertebrae:—*pl.* **zygapoph'yses.**—*adj.* **zygobranchiate** (*-brangk'i-āt*; Gr. *branchia*, gills) having paired, symmetrically placed, gills: belonging to the **Zygobranchia'ta**, a division of the Gastropoda.—*ns.* and *adjs.* **zy'gobranch, zygobranch'iate.**—*adjs.* **zygodactyl** (*-dak'til*; Gr. *daktylos*, toe) having two toes before and behind, as parrots.—Also **zygodactyl'ic, zygodac'tylous.**—*n.* **zygodac'tylism.**—*adjs.* **zygomor'phic, zygomorphous** (*mōr'fəs*; Gr. *morphē* form) yoke-shaped—of flowers symmetrical about one plane only.—*ns.* **zygomor'phism, zy'gomorphy; zy'gophyte** (*-fīt*; Gr. *phyton*, a plant) a plant in which reproduction takes place by means of zygospores.— *adjs.* **zygopleural** (*-plōō'rəl*; Gr. *pleurā*, side) bilaterally symmetrical; **zy'gose** pertaining to zygosis. —*ns.* **zygosis** (*-gōsis*; *biol.*) conjugation; **zy'gospore** (Gr. *sporā*, a seed) a spore produced by the union of buds from two adjacent hyphae in the process of conjugation by which some fungi multiply.—Also **zy'gosperm.**—*n.* **zy'gote** (Gr. *zygōtos*, yoked; *bot.* and *zool.*) the product of the union of two gametes: by extension, the individual developing from that product.—*adj.* **zygotic** (*-got'*). [Gr. *zygon*, yoke.]

zyme *zīm*, *n.* a ferment: a disease-germ.—*n.* **zy'mase** any of a group of enzymes inducing the alcoholic fermentation of carbohydrates.—*adj.* **zy'mic** relating to fermentation.—**zym(o)-** in composition, relating to fermentation.—*n.* **zy'mogen** a non-catalytic substance formed by plants and animals as a stage in the development of an enzyme.—*adjs.* **zymogen'ic; zy'moid** like a ferment; **zymolog'ic, -al** pertaining to zymology.—*ns.* **zymol'ogist** one skilled in zymology; **zymol'ogy** the science of fermentation; **zymol'ysis** the action of enzymes.—*adj.* **zymolit'ic.**—*ns.* **zymom'eter, zymosim'eter** an instrument for measuring the degree of fermentation; **zymō'sis** fermentation: the morbid process, thought to be analogous to fermentation, constituting a zymotic disease.—*adj.* **zymot'ic** pertaining to fermentation: of the nature of, pertaining to, or causing, an infectious disease.—*n.* an infectious disease.—*adv.* **zymot'ically.** [Gr. *zȳmē*, leaven, *zȳmōsis*, fermentation.]

zymurgy *zī'mûr-ji*, *n.* the department of technological chemistry that treats of wine-making, brewing, distilling, and similar processes involving fermentation. [Gr. *zȳmē*, leaven, *ergon*, work.]

fāte; fär; mē; hûr (her); *mīne; mōte; fōr; mūte; mōōn; fōōt; dhen* (then); *el'ə-mənt* (element)

List of abbreviations and symbols

A Associate ... See note (2) above; Amateur; Academician; argon; ampere; angstrom; atomic (in A-bomb); denoting the first, or a high, class (as in A-road); advanced (in A-level); Austria (IVR).

Å Ångström.

a are (metric measure); accepted; acre; active; afternoon; *annus* year; *ante* before.

ā, āā in prescriptions, *ana* (Gr.), i.e. of each a like quantity.

AA Automobile Association; Alcoholics Anonymous; anti-aircraft.

AAA Amateur Athletic Association; American Automobile Association.

AAM air-to-air missile.

A and M (Hymns) Ancient and Modern.

AAQMG Assistant Adjutant and Quartermaster General.

AAS *Academiae Americanae Socius* Fellow of the American Academy.

AB able-bodied seaman; *Artium Baccalaureus* Bachelor of Arts.

ABA Amateur Boxing Association.

Abb. Abbess; Abbot; Abbey.

abbr., abbrev. abbreviated; abbreviation.

ABC Associated British Cinemas; American Broadcasting Corporation.

abd abdicated; abridged.

ABFM American Board of Foreign Missions.

ab init. *ab initio* from the beginning.

abl. ablative.

ABM anti-ballistic missile.

Abp Archbishop.

abr. abridged; abridgment.

ABS Associate of the Building Societies Institute; Association of Broadcasting Staff.

abs., absol. absolute(ly).

abs. re. *absente reo* the accused being absent.

ABTA Association of British Travel Agents.

AC aircraft(s)man; Aero Club; Alpine Club; *ante Christum* before Christ; (or ac) alternating current (*elect.*).

Ac actinium.

a/c account.

ACA Associate of the Institute of Chartered Accountants.

ACAS Advisory, Conciliation and Arbitration Service.

acc. (or acct., a/c) account; accountant; (or accus.) accusative; according.

ACGB Arts Council of Great Britain.

ACP African, Caribbean and Pacific.

ACT Australian Capital Territory.

act. active; acting.

ACTT Association of Cinematographic Television and Allied Technicians.

ACW aircraft(s)woman.

AD *anno Domini* in the year of the Lord.

ad (or advt) advertisement; after date; *ante diem* before the day.

ADC aide-de-camp; (or AD and C) advise duration and charge.

ad fin. *ad finem* at, towards, or to, the end.

ad inf. *ad infinitum* to infinity.

ad init. *ad initium* at or to the beginning.

ad int. *ad interim* in the meantime.

adj. adjective; adjourned; adjustment.

Adjt. Adjutant.

Adjt.-Gen. Adjutant-General.

ad lib. *ad libitum* at pleasure.

ad loc. *ad locum* at the place.

Adm. Admiral.

admin. administration.

ADP automatic data processing.

adv. advent; adverb; *adversus* against; advocate; advisory.

ad val. *ad valorem* according to value.

advt advertisement.

ae., aet. *aetatis* of his age, aged (so many years).

AEA Atomic Energy Authority (UK).

AEB Associated Examining Board.

AEC Atomic Energy Commission (US).

AEI Associated Electrical Industries.

AERE Atomic Energy Research Establishment.

AEU Amalgamated Engineering Union.

AF Associate Fellow ... See note (2) above; Admiral of the Fleet; audio frequency.

AFA Amateur Football Association.

AFC Air Force Cross.

AFG Afghanistan (IVR).

AFL-CIO American Federation of Labor and Congress of Industrial Organizations.

AFM Air Force Medal.

AG Adjutant-General; (or A-G) Attorney-General; *Aktiengesellschaft* (Ger.) joint stock company.

Ag *argentum* silver.

agm annual general meeting.

AGR advanced gas-cooled reactor.

agr., agric. agriculture.

Agt Agent.

AH *anno Hegirae* in the year of Hegira—i.e. from the flight of Mohammed (AD 622, 13 Sept.).

Ah ampere hour.

AHA Area Health Authority.

ahl *ad hunc locum* at this place.

AHS *anno humanae salutis* in the year of human salvation.

ahv *ad hanc vocem* at this word.

AI artificial insemination.

AID artificial insemination by donor; Agency for International Development (US).

AIDS See *acquire* in Dict.

AIH artificial insemination by husband.

AL Albania (IVR).

Al aluminium.

Al(a). Alabama.

Alas. Alaska.

Alta. Alberta.

Alcan Aluminium Company of Canada.

Ald. Alderman.

alg. algebra.

ALGOL, Algol Algorithmic language.

alt. alternate; altitude; alto.

Alta. Alberta.

AM Associate Member ... See note (2) above; *Artium Magister* Master of Arts; (or **am**) *ante meridiem* before noon; *Anno Mundi* in the year of the world; *Ave Maria* Hail Mary; amplitude modulation.

Am americium.

Am., Amer. America; American.

AMC American Motors Corporation.

AMDG *ad majorem Dei gloriam* to the greater glory of God.

AMMA Assistant Masters' and Mistresses' Association.

ammo ammunition.

amp. ampere.

amt amount; air mail transfer.

amu atomic mass unit.

an. *anno* in the year; anonymous; *ante* before.

anal. analysis; analogy.

anat. anatomy.

anc. ancient(ly).

Ang. *Anglice* in English.

anme *anonyme* (Fr.) limited liability.

anon. anonymous.

ans. answer.

antiq. antiquities; antiquarian.

Anzac (a soldier serving with the) Australian-New Zealand Army Corps.

Anzus (the alliance between) Australia, New Zealand and the United States.

AO Army Order.

AOB any other business.

AOCB any other competent business.

AOC-in-C Air Officer Commanding-in-Chief.

AOF Ancient Order of Foresters.

aor. aorist.

AP Associated Press.

APEX Association of Professional, Executive, Clerical and Computer Staff.

apo. apogee.

Apoc. Apocalypse; Apocrypha(l).

app. appendix; apparent(ly); apprentice.

appro. approval; approbation.

approx. approximate(ly).

APR annual percentage rate.

Apr. April.

APRC *anno post Romam conditam* in the year after the founding of Rome (753 BC).

APT Advanced Passenger Train.

AQ achievement quotient.

aq. *aqua* water.

Ar argon.

Ar., Arab. Arabic.

ar *anno regni* in the year of the reign.

ar., arr. arrive(s); arrival.

ARA Associate of the Royal Academy.

ARAMCO Arabian-American Oil Company.

ARC Agricultural Research Council.

arccos inverse cosine.

arch. archaic; architecture.

archaeol. archaeology.

Archd. Archdeacon; Archduke.

archit. architecture.

arcsin inverse sine.

arctan inverse tangent.

arg. *argentum* silver.

arith. arithmetic(al).

Ariz. Arizona.

Ark. Arkansas.

ARP Air Raid Precautions.

ARR *anno regni regis* or *reginae* in the year of the king's or the queen's reign.

arr. arranged; arrive(s); arrival.

art. article; artificial; (or arty.) artillery.

AS Anglo-Saxon; *anno salutis* in the year of salvation; Assistant Secretary.

As arsenic.

ASA Amateur Swimming Association; American Standards Association.

asap as soon as possible.

ASC American Society of Cinematographers.

Asda Associated Dairies.

Asdic an acronym from Allied (or Anti-) Submarine Detection and Investigation Committee, used for a particular device for locating submerged objects.

ASE Amalgamated Society of Engineers; Association for Science Education.

Asean Association of South-East Asian Nations.

ASF Associate of the Institute of Shipping and Forwarding Agents.

ASH Action on Smoking and Health.

ASLEF Associated Society of Locomotive Engineers and Firemen.

ASM air-to-surface missile.

Ass., Assoc. Association.

Asst Assistant.

AST Atlantic Standard Time.

ASTMS Association of Scientific, Technical and Managerial Staffs.

astr., astron. astronomy.

astrol. astrology.

AT Alternative Technology.

At astatine.

ATA Air Transport Auxiliary.

ATC Air Training Corps; air traffic control; automatic train control.

atm. atmosphere.

at. no., at. numb. atomic number.

Att. Attic (Greek); Attorney.

Att.-Gen. Attorney-General.

attrib. attribute(d); attributive(ly).

Atty Attorney.

ATV Associated Television.

at. wt atomic weight.

AU (or **ÅU**) Ångström unit (now usu. Ångström; abbrev. Å); astronomical unit.

Au *aurum* gold.

AUC *anno urbis conditae* or *ab urbe condita* in the year from the building of the city—Rome (753 BC).

AUEW Amalgamated Union of Engineering Workers.

Aufl. *Auflage* (Ger.) edition.

Aug. August.

aug. augmentative.

AUS Australia, including Papua, New Guinea (IVR).

AUT Association of University Teachers.

aut., auto. automatic.

Auth. Ver., AV Authorised Version.

AV audio-visual.

av *annos vixit* lived (so many) years.

av. (or ave) avenue; average.

AVM Air Vice-Marshal.

avoir., avdp. avoirdupois.

AWOL absent, or absence, without official leave.

AWRE Atomic Weapons Research Establishment.

ax. axiom.

az. azimuth.

B Baron; British; Bachelor; boron; bel; black (on lead pencils); Belgium (IVR).

B magnetic flux density.

2B, 3B. Same as BB, BBB (on lead pencils).

b born; book; bowled.

b breadth.

BA *Baccalaureus Artium* Bachelor of Arts; British America; British Association (for the Advancement of Science); British Academy; Buenos Aires; British Airways; Booksellers' Association (of Great Britain and Ireland).

Ba barium.

BAA British Airports Authority.

BABS beam, or blind, approach beacon system.

BAC British Aircraft Corporation.

Bach. Bachelor.

BACIE British Association for Commercial and Industrial Education.

BAgr(lc) Bachelor of Agriculture.

BAI *Baccalaureus in Arte Ingeniaria* Bachelor of Engineering.

bal. balance.

BALPA British Airline Pilots' Association.

B and B bed and breakfast.

B and FBS British and Foreign Bible Society.

BAOR British Army of the Rhine.

Bap., Bapt. Baptist.

bap., bapt. baptised.

Ber. Barrister.

bar. baritone.

BArch Bachelor of Architecture.

Bart Baronet.

Bart's St Bartholomew's Hospital, London.

BASF *Badische Anilin und Soda-Fabrik* (German chemical company).

BAT British-American Tobacco Company.

bat., batt. battalion; battery.

BB Boys' Brigade; double, or very, black (on lead pencils).

bb books.

BBB triple black, blacker than **BB** (on lead pencils).

BBBC British Boxing Board of Control.

BBC British Broadcasting Corporation (orig. Company).

BBFC British Board of Film Censors.

BC Before Christ; Board of Control; British Columbia; Battery Commander.

BCAL British Caledonian (Airways).

BCC British Council of Churches.

bcg bacillus of Calmette and Guérin, an attenuated strain of the tubercle bacillus, used for inoculation.

BCh *Baccalaureus Chirurgiae* Bachelor of Surgery.

BCL Bachelor of Civil Law.

BCom(m) Bachelor of Commerce.

BCS British Computer Society.

BD Bachelor of Divinity.

bd bound.

BDA British Dental Association.

Bde Brigade.

BDH British Drug Houses.

BDI *Bundesverband der Deutschen Industrie* (Ger.) Federation of German Industry.

BDS Bachelor of Dental Surgery.

bds boards.

BE Bachelor of Engineering; Board of Education.

Be beryllium.

be bill of exchange.

BEAB British Electrical Approvals Board.

BEAMA British Electrical and Allied Manufacturers' Association.

BEd Bachelor of Education.

Beds Bedfordshire.

BEF British Expeditionary Force.

bef. before.

Belg. Belgian; Belgium; Belgic.

BEM British Empire Medal.

Benelux a name for Belgium, the Netherlands and Luxembourg.

BEng Bachelor of Engineering.

Berks Berkshire.

B ès L *Bachelier ès Lettres* (Fr.) Bachelor of Letters.

B ès S *Bachelier ès Sciences* (Fr.) Bachelor of Sciences.

bet. between.

BeV billion electron-volt(s) (in USA, where billion means 1000 million, same as GeV).

bf brought forward; bloody fool.

BFPO British Forces Post Office.

BG Bulgaria (IVR).

bhp brake horse-power.

BHS British Home Stores.

Bi bismuth.

Bib. Bible.

Bibl. Biblical.

bibl. bibliotheca (=a library, book-collection, or catalogue).

biblio., bibliog. bibliography.

BICC British Insulated Callender's Cables.

BIM British Institute of Management.

biog. biography.

biol. biology.

BIPM *Bureau International des Poids et Mesures* (Fr.) International Bureau of Weights and Measures.

BIR British Institute of Radiology.

BIS Bank for International Settlements.

bis. bissextile (=having a day added, as a leap year.).

Bk berkelium.

bk book; bank; bark.

bkg banking.

bkt basket.

BL Bachelor of Law; Bachelor of Letters; British Legion; British Leyland; British Library.

bl barrel; bale; bill of lading.

bldg building.

BLESMA British Limbless Ex-Servicemen's Association.

BLit(t) *Baccalaureus Lit(t)erarum* Bachelor of Literature or Letters.

BLLD British Library Lending Division.

BLMC British Leyland Motor Corporation.

BLRD British Library Reference Division.

Blvd Boulevard.

BM Bachelor of Medicine; British Museum; *Beatae Memoriae* of blessed memory; Brigade Major.

BMA British Medical Association.

BMEWS ballistic missile early warning system.

BMJ British Medical Journal.

BML British Museum Library.

BMus Bachelor of Music.

BMW *Bayerische Motoren Werke* (Ger.) Bavarian motor works.

Bn Baron.

bn battalion.

BNEC British National Export Council.

BNFL British Nuclear Fuels Limited.

BNOC British National Oil Corporation.

b.o. branch office; buyer's option; (or B.O.) body odour.

BOA British Optical Association.

BOC British Oxygen Company.

BOCM British Oil and Cake Mills.

Bol. Bolivia.

bor. borough.

BOSS Bureau of State Security (South Africa).

bot. botany; bought; bottle.

Boul. Boulevard.

BP British Pharmacopoeia; British Petroleum; Baden Powell; be prepared.

Bp Bishop.

bp boiling-point; bills of parcels; bills payable; (or b.pl.) birthplace; *bonum publicum* the public good.

BPC British Printing Corporation; British Pharmaceutical Codex.

BPharm Bachelor of Pharmacy.

BPhil *Baccalaureus Philosophiae* Bachelor of Philosophy.

BQ *Bene quiescat* may he (or she) rest well.

BR British Rail; Brazil (IVR).

Br bromine.
Br. Brother.
br bank rate.
br. branch; brig; brown; bridge.
Braz. Brazil; Brazilian.
BRCS British Red Cross Society.
BRD *Bundesrepublik Deutschland* (Ger.) German Federal Republic.
b. rec. bills receivable.
Bret. Breton.
Brig. Brigadier.
Brig.-Gen. Brigadier-General.
Brit. Britain; Britannia; British; Briton.
Bro. Brother.
Bros. Brothers.
BRS British Road Services.
BS Bachelor of Science or of Surgery; Blessed Sacrament; Balance Sheet; (or **bs**) Bill of Sale; British Shipbuilders.
BSA Building Societies Association; Birmingham Small Arms.
BSAC British Sub Aqua Club.
BSC British Steel Corporation; British Sugar Corporation.
BSc Bachelor of Science.
BSI British Standards Institution; Building Societies Institute.
BSM British School of Motoring.
BS(S) British Standards (Specification).
BST British Summer Time; British Standard Time.
Bt Baronet.
BTA British Tourist Authority.
Btu British thermal unit.
bu. bushel(s).
Bucks Buckinghamshire.
Bulg. Bulgaria; Bulgarian.
BUNAC British Universities North America Club.
BUPA British United Provident Association.
bus., bush. bushel(s).
BV *Beata Virgo* Blessed Virgin; *Bene vale* farewell.
BVM The Blessed Virgin Mary.
BVM(&)S Bachelor of Veterinary Medicine and Surgery.

C carbon; coulomb; Conservative.
C symbol for electrical capacitance.
°C degree(s) Celsius, centigrade.
c centi-; *caput* chapter; cent; centime; *circa* about; caught.
¢ cent(s).
© copyright.
CA Chartered Accountant (Scotland); County Alderman.
Ca calcium.
ca *circa* about; cases.
CAA Civil Aviation Authority.
CAB Civil Aeronautics Board (USA); Citizens' Advice Bureau.
cad cash against documents.
CAI computer-aided instruction.
CAL computer-assisted learning.
cal calorie.
Cal., Calif. California.
Cam., Camb. Cambridge.
Cambs Cambridgeshire.
CAMRA Campaign for Real Ale.
CAN customs assigned number.
Can. Canada; Canadian; Canon; Canto.
C and A Clemens and August (clothing stores).
C and G City and Guilds (of London Institute).
C & W country and western music.
Cant. Canterbury; Canticles.
Cantab. *Cantabrigiensis* of Cambridge.

Cantuar. *Cantuaria* Canterbury; *Cantuariensis* of Canterbury.
CAP Common Agricultural Policy.
cap. capital; *caput* chapter; *capitulum* head, chapter; *capiat* let him (or her) take.
caps capitals (in printing).
Capt. Captain.
CAR Central African Republic.
Car. *Carolus* Charles.
car. carat.
CARD Campaign Against Racial Discrimination.
Card. Cardinal.
Cards Cardiganshire.
CARE Co-operative for American Relief to Everywhere.
carp. carpentry.
CASE Confederation for the Advancement of State Education.
CAT College of Advanced Technology; computer-aided typesetting; see **compute** in Dict.
cat. catechism; catalogue.
Cath. Catholic.
cath. cathedral.
CB Companion of the Order of the Bath; confined (or confinement) to barracks; Citizens' Band (radio).
Cb columbium (now niobium).
CBC Canadian Broadcasting Corporation.
CBE Commander of the Order of the British Empire.
CBI Confederation of British Industry.
CBM Californian Business Machines.
CBS Confraternity of the Blessed Sacrament; Columbia Broadcasting System.
CC County Council; Cricket Club; closed circuit (transmission).
cc cubic-centimetre(s); *capita* chapters.
CCA current cost accounting.
CCCP See USSR.
CCF Combined Cadet Force.
CCPR Central Council of Physical Recreation.
CCS Corporation of Certified Secretaries.
CD *Corps Diplomatique* (Fr.) Diplomatic Corps; Civil Defence; contagious disease(s).
Cd cadmium.
cd candela.
CDN Canada (IVR).
Cdr Commander.
CDSO Companion of the Distinguished Service Order.
CDV Civil Defence Volunteers.
CE Civil Engineer; Council of Europe.
Ce cerium.
CEDO Centre for Education Development Overseas (formerly CREDO).
CEGB Central Electricity Generating Board.
CEI Council of Engineering Institutions.
cel. celebrated.
Celt. Celtic.
cen. central; century.
CEng Chartered Engineer.
cent. *centum* a hundred; century; central.
CENTO Central Treaty Organisation.
CERN *Conseil Européen pour la Recherche Nucléaire* (Fr.) European Organisation for Nuclear Research.
cert. certainty; (or **certif.**) certificate; certificated; certify.
CET Central European Time.
cet. par. *ceteris paribus* other things being equal.
CF Chaplain to the Forces.
Cf californium.
cf calf (book-binding).
cf. *confer* compare.
cfi (and) **i** cost, freight, and insurance.
cg centigram(me)(s).
c.g. centre of gravity.

CG(L)I City and Guilds (of London) Institute.

CGPM *Conférence Générale des Poids et Mesures* (Fr.) General Conference of Weights and Measures.

CGS (or **cgs**) centimetre-gramme-second (unit or system); Chief of the General Staff.

CGT capital gains tax; *Confédération Générale du Travail* (Fr.) General Confederation of Labour.

CH Companion of Honour; *Confederatio Helvetica* Switzerland (also IVR).

Ch. Chief; China; Church; Champion.

ch central heating.

ch. chaldron; chapter; child.

Chamb. Chamberlain.

Chanc. Chancellor; Chancery.

Chap. Chaplain; Chapter.

Chas Charles.

ChB *Chirurgiae Baccalaureus* Bachelor of Surgery.

chem. chemistry; chemical.

Ch. Hist. Church History.

Chin. China; Chinese.

Ch.J. Chief-Justice.

ChM *Chirurgiae Magister* Master of Surgery.

choc. chocolate.

Chr. Christ; Christian.

chron. chronicle; chronology; chronological.

CI Channel Islands.

Ci curie.

CIA Central Intelligence Agency (USA).

Cia *Compagnia* (It.) Company.

CID Criminal Investigation Department; Council of Industrial Design.

CIE *Córas Iompair Éireann* (Ir.) Transport Organisation of Ireland.

Cie *Compagnie* (Fr.) Company.

cif cost, insurance, freight.

CIGS Chief of Imperial General Staff (now CGS).

CII Chartered Insurance Institute.

CIM Commission on Industry and Manpower.

C-in-C Commander-in-Chief.

CIPM *Comité International des Poids et Mesures* (Fr.) International Committee of Weights and Measures.

CIR Commission on Industrial Relations.

cir., circ. *circa, circiter, circum* about.

circs. circumstances.

CIS Chartered Institute of Secretaries.

CIT Chartered Institute of Transport.

cit. citation; citizen.

civ. civil; civilian.

CJ Chief-Justice.

Cl chlorine.

cl centilitre(s); *cum laude* with praise.

cl. class; clause.

class. classical; classification.

CLit Companion of Literature.

CLR computer language recorder.

CLT computer language translator.

CM Certificated Master; Corresponding Member; Common Metre; *Chirurgiae Magister* Master of Surgery.

Cm curium.

cm centimetre(s).

CMG Companion of the Order of St Michael and St George.

CMI computer-managed instruction.

Cmnd Command Paper.

CMRST Committee on Manpower Resources for Science and Technology.

CMS Church Missionary Society.

CNAA Council for National Academic Awards.

CND Campaign for Nuclear Disarmament.

CNR Canadian National Railway.

CNS central nervous system.

CO conscientious objector; Colonial Office (before Aug. 1966); Commonwealth Office (from Aug. 1966; see also FCO); Commanding Officer; Criminal Office; Crown Office.

Co cobalt.

Co. Company; County.

c/o care of.

coad. coadjutor.

COBOL, Cobol a computer language.

Cod. Codex.

c.o.d. cash (or collect) on delivery.

co-ed. co-educational.

C of A Certificate of Airworthiness.

C of E Church of England; Council of Europe.

C of I Church of Ireland.

C of S Church of Scotland; Chief of Staff.

cog. cognate.

c.o.g. centre of gravity.

COGB Certified Official Government Business.

COHSE Confederation of Health Service Employees.

COI Central Office of Information.

COL computer-oriented language.

Col. Colonel; Colorado.

col. column.

coll. college; colleague; collector; colloquial.

collat. collateral(ly).

colloq. colloquial(ly).

Colo. Colorado.

COM computer output microfilm.

Com. Commander; Commodore; Committee; Commissioner; Commonwealth; Communist.

com. common; comedy; commerce; committee; commune.

Comdr Commander.

Comdt Commandant.

COMECON Council for Mutual Economic Aid, or Assistance (Communist Nations).

comm. commentary; commander; communication.

Commr Commissioner.

commn commission.

Commy Commissary; Communist.

comp. comparative; compositor; compare; compound; compounded.

compar. comparative; comparison.

COMSAT Communications Satellite (USA).

Com. Ver. Common Version.

Con. Consul.

con, *contra* against; *conju(n)x* consort; conclusion; conversation; convenience.

conc. concentrated; concentration.

Cong. Congress; Congregation(al).

conj. conjunction; conjunctive.

Conn. Connecticut.

conn. connection; connected; connotation.

cons. consonant.

con. sec. conic section.

Consols Consolidated Funds.

cont., contd continued.

contr. contracted; contraction.

contr. bon. mor. *contra bonos mores* contrary to good manners or morals.

conv. conventional.

co-op. co-operative.

Cop., Copt. Coptic.

Cor. Corinthians; Coroner.

Cor. Mem. Corresponding Member.

Corn. Cornish; Cornwall.

corol., coroll. corollary.

Corp. Corporation; Corporal.

corr. corrupted; corruption; correspond.

Cor.Sec. Corresponding Secretary.

CoS Chief of Staff.

cos cosine.

cosec cosecant.

cosech hyperbolic cosecant.

cosh hyperbolic cosine.

cot cotangent.

coth hyperbolic cotangent.

CP Clerk of the Peace; Common Pleas; Carriage Paid; College of Preceptors; Communist Party; Cape Province (S. Africa).

cp candle-power.

cp. compare.

CPA Chartered Patent Agent.

CPAC Consumer Protection Advisory Committee.

CPAG Child Poverty Action Group.

CPC Clerk of the Privy Council.

CPI consumer price index.

Cpl Corporal.

cpp current purchasing power.

CPR Canadian Pacific Railway.

CPS *Custos Privati Sigilli* Keeper of the Privy Seal.

CPSA Civil and Public Services Association.

CPU central processing unit.

CR *Carolus rex* King Charles; *civis romanus* a Roman citizen; *Custos Rotulorum* Keeper of the Rolls.

Cr chromium.

cr. credit; creditor; crown.

CRAC Careers Research and Advisory Centre.

CRE Commission for Racial Equality.

cres., crese. crescendo; crescent.

crim. con. criminal conversation (i.e. adultery).

CRMP Corps of Royal Military Police.

CRO cathode-ray oscillograph; Commonwealth Relations Office (until 1966); Criminal Records Office.

CRT cathode-ray tube.

CS Court of Session; Clerk to the Signet; Civil Service; Christian Science; Chemical Society; orthobenzylidene malononitrile, an irritant 'gas' synthesised (1928) by Corson and Stoughton; Czechoslovakia (IVR).

Cs caesium.

c/s cycles per second (hertz).

CSE Certificate of Secondary Education.

CSEU Confederation of Shipbuilding and Engineering Unions.

CSIRO Commonwealth Scientific and Industrial Research Organisation.

CSO community service order.

CSP Council for Scientific Policy; Chartered Society of Physiotherapists.

CST Central Standard Time.

CSU Civil Service Union.

CSV community service volunteer.

CSYS Certificate of Sixth Year Studies.

Ct. Connecticut.

ct cent; carat.

CTC Cyclists' Touring Club.

CTOL conventional take-off and landing.

CTT capital transfer tax.

Cu *cuprum* copper.

cu., cub. cubic.

CUP Cambridge University Press.

cur., curt current (this month).

cusec cubic feet per second.

cv *curriculum vitae* (see Dict.), or *cursus vitae* course, progress, of life.

cva cerebrovascular accident (see Dict.).

CVO Commander of the (Royal) Victorian Order.

cwo cash with order.

cwr continuous welded rail.

CWS Co-operative Wholesale Society.

cwt hundred-weight(s)—c (*centum* a hundred), wt (weight).

D deuterium; Federal Republic of Germany (IVR).

3-D three-dimensional (see dimension in Dict.)

d day; diameter; *dele* delete; dead; died; deserted; degree; *denarius* or *denarii* a penny or pence (before 1971): duke.

DA District Attorney; Diploma of Art.

D(A)AG Deputy (Assistant) Adjutant-General.

Dan. Daniel; Danish.

D and C. dilatation and curettage (an operation which cleans out a body-cavity, esp. the womb).

DATEC data and telecommunications.

dau. daughter.

dB decibel.

DBE Dame Commander of the Order of the British Empire.

DC *Da capo* (It.) return to the beginning (*mus.*); District of Columbia; (or **dc**) direct current (*elect.*): District Commissioner.

DCL Doctor of Civil Law; Distillers Company Limited.

DCM Distinguished Conduct Medal.

DCMG Dame Commander of the Order of St Michael and St George.

DCS Deputy Clerk of Session.

DCVO Dame Commander of the (Royal) Victorian Order.

DD *Divinitatis Doctor* Doctor of Divinity.

dd, D/D days after date; day's date.

D-day. See Dict.

DDD *dat, dicat, dedicat* gives, devotes, and dedicates; *dono dedit dedicavit* gave and dedicated as a gift.

DDR *Deutsche Demokratische Republik* (Ger.) German Democratic Republic (also IVR).

DDS Doctor of Dental Surgery.

DDT dichlorodiphenyltrichloroethane, an insecticide.

DE Department of Employment.

DEA Department of Economic Affairs.

Dec. December.

dec. deceased.

dec., decl. declaration; declension.

DEd Doctor of Education.

def. definition; (or **deft**) defendant.

deg. degree(s).

Del. Delaware.

del. delegate; (or **delt**) *delineavit* drew it.

demon., demons. demonstrative.

DEng Doctor of Engineering.

dent. dental; dentist; dentistry.

DEP Department of Employment and Productivity.

Dep., Dept., dep., dept department; deputy.

dep. deposed; depart(s); departure.

der., deriv. derivation; derived.

derv See Dict.

DES Department of Education and Science.

DesRCA Designer of the Royal College of Art.

DEW distant early warning.

DF Defender of the Faith; Dean of the Faculty.

DFC Distinguished Flying Cross.

DFM Distinguished Flying Medal.

dft defendant; draft.

DG *Dei gratia* by the grace of God.

dg decigram(me)(s).

d.h. *das heisst* (Ger.) that is to say.

DHSS Department of Health and Social Services (formerly Security).

dial. dialect.

diam. diameter.

DIC Diploma of the Imperial College.

dict. dictator; dictionary.

diff. different; difference.

DIG Disabled Income Group.

DIH Diploma in Industrial Health.

dil. dilute.

DIN *Deutsche Industrie Normen* (Ger.) German Industrial Standards.

DIng *Doctor Ingeniariae* Doctor of Engineering.

Dip. Diploma, as e.g. **Dip. Ed.,** Diploma in Education, **Dip. Tech.,** Diploma in Technology.

Dir. Director.

dis. discontinued.

disc. discount; discoverer.

diss. dissertation.

dist. distance; distinguish; district; distilled.

div. divide; division; divine; divorced.

DIY do-it-yourself.

DJ dee-jay, disc-jockey.

DK Denmark (IVR).

DL Deputy Lieutenant.

dl decilitre(s).

DLit(t) *Doctor litterarum* or *litteraturae* Doctor of Letters or Literature.

DM Deutsche Mark (Federal German currency).

dm decimetre(s).

DMus Doctor of Music.

DMZ demilitarised zone.

DNA deoxyribonucleic acids (see Dict.)

DNB Dictionary of National Biography.

Dnr dinar (Yugoslav currency).

do *ditto* (It.) the same (aforesaid).

DOA dead on arrival.

d.o.b. date of birth.

DOC District Officer Commanding.

DOE Department of the Environment.

DOG Directory of Opportunities for Graduates.

DOM *Deo optimo maximo* to God, best and greatest; *Dominus Omnium Magister* God the master of all; dirty old man.

Dom. *Dominus* Lord; Dominion.

dom. domestic.

DOMS Diploma in Ophthalmic Medicine and Surgery.

Dor. Doric.

doz. dozen.

DP Displaced Person; data processing; duly performed (the work of the class).

DPH Diploma in Public Health.

DPh, DPhil *Doctor Philosophiae* Doctor of Philosophy.

DPM Diploma in Psychological Medicine.

dpm disintegrations per minute.

DPP Director of Public Prosecutions.

dpt department.

Dr Doctor; debtor; Drummer; Driver; drachma (Greek currency).

dr dead reckoning.

dr. dram; drawer.

DS *Dal segno* (It.) from the sign (*mus.*); disseminated sclerosis.

ds, D/S. days after sight.

DSC Distinguished Service Cross.

DSc *Doctor Scientiae* Doctor of Science.

DSM Distinguished Service Medal.

DSO Distinguished Service Order.

dsp *decessit sine prole* died without issue.

DT data transmission; (or **dt, DT's, dt's**) delirium tremens.

DTh *Doctor Theologiae* Doctor of Theology.

DTI Department of Trade and Industry.

DV *Deo volente* God willing.

dvp *decessit vita patris* died in father's lifetime.

dwt pennyweight—**d** (*denarius* a penny), wt (weight).

Dy dysprosium.

dyn dyne; dynamo; dynamometer.

E East; English; Spain (IVR).

E energy.

E and OE errors and omissions excepted.

eaon except as otherwise noted.

Ebor. *Eboracum* York; *Eboracensis* of York.

EBU European Broadcasting Union.

EC East Central; Established Church.

ECE Economic Commission for Europe.

ECG electrocardiogram (-graph).

ECG(D) Export Credits Guarantee (Department).

ECO English Chamber Orchestra.

ECSC European Coal and Steel Community.

ECT electroconvulsive therapy.

ECU English Church Union.

Ed. Editor.

ed., edit. edited; edition.

EdB Bachelor of Education.

EDC European Defence Community.

EDF European Development Fund.

Edin. Edinburgh.

edit. edited; edition.

EDP electronic data processing.

EDS English Dialect Society.

EE errors excepted.

EEC European Economic Community.

EEG electroencephalogram (-graph).

EET Eastern European Time.

EETS Early English Text Society.

EFL English as a foreign language.

EFTA European Free Trade Association.

e.g., eg, ex. gr. *exempli gratia* for example.

EGU English Golf Union.

EI East Indies.

EIS Educational Institute of Scotland.

ejusd. *ejusdem* of the same.

El Al Israeli airline (lit. 'towards the sky').

ELDO European Launcher Development Organisation.

elec., elect. electric; electricity.

ELT English language teaching.

EMA European Monetary Agreement.

EMF European Monetary Fund.

emf electromotive force.

EMI EMI Limited (formerly Electrical and Musical Industries Limited).

Emp. Emperor, Empress.

EMS European Monetary System.

emu electromagnetic unit.

ENE east-north-east.

Eng. England; English.

eng. engineer; engraver; engraving.

Ens. Ensign.

ENSA Entertainments National Services Association.

ENT Ear, Nose and Throat.

Env. Ext. Envoy Extraordinary.

EOC Equal Opportunities Commission.

eod every other day.

EP extended play (record): electroplated.

Ep. Epistle.

EPA European Productivity Agency.

EPNS electroplated nickel silver; English Place-Name Society.

EPU European Payments Union.

ER *Elisabeth Regina* Elizabeth, Queen.

Er erbium.

ER(I) *Edwardus Rex (Imperator)* Edward, King (and Emperor).

ERNIE electronic random number indicator equipment (computer).

Es einsteinium.

ESA European Space Agency.

Esc. escudo (Portuguese currency).

ESE east-south-east.

ESL English as a second language.

ESN educationally subnormal.

ESP extra-sensory perception.

esp., espec. especially.

Esq., Esqr. Esquire.

ESRO European Space Research Organisation.

ESSO Standard Oil.

EST Eastern Standard Time; electric shock treatment.

est. established; estimated.

ESU English-Speaking Union.

ET Arab Republic of Egypt (IVR).

ETA estimated time of arrival.

et al. *et alii, aliae,* or *alia* and others; *et alibi* and elsewhere.

etc., &c. *et ceteri* or *cetera* and the others, and so forth.

ETD estimated time of departure.

et seq. or **sq.** (sing.), *et sequens* et **sqq.** (pl.) *et sequentes* or *sequentia* and the following.

ETU Electrical Trades Union.

ety., etym. etymology; etymological.

EU Evangelical Union.

Eu europium.

Euratom *European Atomic* Energy Community.

eV electron-volt.

ex. examined; example: exception; excursus; executive; export.

Exc. Exellency.

exc. except; exception.

ex. div. *extra dividendum* without dividend.

ex. gr. *exempli gratia* for the sake of example.

ex lib. *ex libris* from the books (of)—as on bookplates.

exp. export; exponential.

exr executor.

exrx executrix.

ext. extension; externally; extinct; extra; extract.

F Fellow . . . See note (2) p 1171; Fahrenheit; farad; fluorine; France (IVR).

F force.

f following; farthing; feminine; fathom; foot; forte; folio.

f frequency.

FA Football Association; Faculty of Actuaries.

Fa. Florida.

fam. familiar; family.

FAO Food and Agriculture Organisation.

FAS Fellow of the Society of Arts; Fellow of the Antiquarian Society.

fas free alongside ship.

FBA Fellow of the British Academy.

FBI Federal Bureau of Investigation.

FCA Fellow of the Institute of Chartered Accountants.

FCO Foreign and Commonwealth Office (**FO** and **CO** combined in 1968).

fcp, fcap foolscap.

FD *Fidei Defensor* Defender of the Faith.

Fe *ferrum* iron.

Feb. February.

fec. *fecit* did it, or made it (sing.).

fem. feminine.

FET field-effect transistor.

feud. feudal.

ff *fecerunt* did it, or made it (pl.); folios; following (pl.).

ff fortissimo.

FH fire hydrant.

FIAT *Fabbrica Italiana Automobile Torino* (It.) Italian Motor Works in Turin.

Fid. Def. *Fidei Defensor* Defender of the Faith.

FIDO Fog Investigation and Dispersal Operation; Film Industry Defence Organisation.

fi. fa. *fieri facias* that you cause to be made (a writ of execution).

FIFA *Fédération Internationale de Football Association* (Fr.) International Association Football Federation.

FIFO first in, first out.

fig. figure; figurative(ly).

FIS Family Income Supplement.

fl. *floruit* flourished; florin.

Flor., Fla. Florida.

fl. oz. fluid ounce(s).

FM frequency modulation; Field-Marshal.

Fm fermium.

fm fathom.

FO Foreign Office (see **FCO**); Field Officer; Flying Officer.

fo., fol. folio.

fob free on board.

FOC father of the chapel.

foc free of charge.

FOE Friends of Europe; Friends of the Earth.

for free on rail.

FORTRAN, Fortran Formula Translation, the name of a type of scientific computer language.

FP fireplug; former pupil; Free Presbyterian.

fp forte-piano; freezing-point.

FPA Family Planning Association.

FPS foot-pound-second.

Fr francium; franc.

Fr. Father; France; French; Friar; Friday.

fr. fragment; franc; frequently.

frat. fraternise; fraternity.

FRCP Fellow of the Royal College of Physicians (**Edin.,** of Edinburgh; **Lond.,** of London; **Irel.,** of Ireland).

FRCPS Glasg. Fellow of the Royal College of Physicians and Surgeons of Glasgow.

FRCS Fellow of the Royal College of Surgeons (**Ed.,** of Edinburgh; **Eng.,** of England; **Irel.,** of Ireland).

F(R)FPSG (formerly) Fellow of the (Royal) Faculty of Physicans and Surgeons of Glasgow (now **FRCPS Glasg.**).

FRG Federal Republic of Germany.

FRPS Fellow of the Royal Photographic Society.

FRS Fellow of the Royal Society (**E,** of Edinburgh).

FSF Fellow of the Institute of Shipping and Forwarding Agents.

FT Financial Times.

ft foot, feet; fort.

fth, fthm fathom.

fur. furlong(s).

fut. future.

fz sforzando

G Gauss; giga-.

G constant of gravitation, the factor linking force with mass and distance.

g gram(me).

g acceleration of gravity (see gravity in Dict.).

GA General Assembly.

Ga gallium.

Ga. Georgia.

Gael. Gaelic.

gal., gall. gallon(s).

G. and S. Gilbert and Sullivan.

GATT General Agreement on Tariffs and Trade.

gaz. gazette; gazetteer.

GB Great Britain (also IVR).

GBE (Knight or Dame) Grand Cross of the British Empire.

gbh grievous bodily harm.

GBS George Bernard Shaw.

GC George Cross.

GCA ground control(led) approach system or control apparatus.

GCB (Knight) Grand Cross of the Bath.

GCE General Certificate of Education.

GCH (Knight) Grand Cross of Hanover.

GCHQ Government Communications Headquarters.

GCM General Court-martial; (or gcm) greatest common measure.

GCMG (Knight) Grand Cross of the Order of St Michael and St George.

GCVO (Knight or Dame) Grand Cross of the (Royal) Victorian Order.

Gd gadolinium.
Gdns gardens.
GDP gross domestic product.
GDR German Democratic Republic.
Ge germanium.
GEC General Electric Company.
Gen. Genesis; (or Gend) General.
gen. gender; genitive; genus.
gent. gentleman.
Geo. Georgia; George.
geog. geography.
geol. geology:
geom. geometry.
Ger. German.
ger. gerund.
GeV giga-electron-volt (the equivalent of a thousand million electron-volts, same value in Europe as BeV in USA).
GHQ General Headquarters.
GI government (or general) issue (US Army); hence, common soldier.
Gib. Gibraltar.
GIGO garbage in, garbage out.
Gk Greek.
GKN Guest, Keen and Nettlefold.
Gl glucinum (now beryllium).
Glam. Glamorganshire.
GLC Greater London Council.
Gld guilder (Dutch currency).
GLORIA Geological Long Range Asdic.
Glos. Gloucestershire.
GM George Medal; (or G-M) Geiger-Müller counter; General Motors.
gm gram(me).
GmbH Gesellschaft mit beschränkter Haftung (Ger.) limited liability company.
GMC General Medical Council.
GMT Greenwich Mean Time.
GMWU General and Municipal Workers Union.
GNP gross national product.
GOC General Officer Commanding.
Gov. Governor; (or Govt) Government.
GP General Practitioner; Gallup Poll; Gloria Patri glory to the Father.
GPI general paralysis of the insane.
GPO General Post Office.
GR Greece (IVR).
Gr. Greek.
gr. grain; grammar; grouse; gunner.
GR(I) Georgius Rex (Imperator) George, King (and Emperor).
GS General Staff; General Service; Geological Society.
gs guineas.
GSM gram(me)s per square metre.
GSO General Staff Officer.
GSP Good Service Pension.
GT gran turismo used of a fast motor-car built for touring in style.
gua. guinea.
GUM Gosudarstvenni Universalni Magazin (Russ.) State Universal Store.
GUS Great Universal Stores.

H hydrogen; henry; hydrant; hospital; hard (on lead pencils); Hungary (IVR).
2H. Same as HH (on lead pencils).
h hour.
h height.
HA Heavy Artillery.
Ha hahnium.
ha hectare; hoc anno this year.
HAC Honourable Artillery Company; high-alumina cement.

h and c hot and cold (water laid on).
Hants Hampshire (Hantshaving, orig. name of county).
HB hard black (on lead pencils).
hbar hectobar.
HBM His (or Her) Britannic Majesty.
HC Heralds' College; House of Commons; Holy Communion.
HCF (or Hon CF) Honorary Chaplain to the Forces; (or hcf) highest common factor.
HCM His (or Her) Catholic Majesty.
HE His Excellency; His Eminence; High Explosive; Horizontal Equivalent.
He helium.
Heb., Hebr. Hebrew; Hebrews.
HEH His (or Her) Exalted Highness.
her. heraldry; heres heir.
Herts Hertfordshire.
HF high frequency.
Hf hafnium.
hf half; hf-bd half-bound; hf-cf half-calf; hf-mor half-morocco.
HG His (or Her) Grace.
Hg hydrargyrum mercury.
HGV heavy goods vehicle.
HH His (or Her) Highness; very hard (on lead pencils).
HIDB Highlands and Islands Development Board.
HI-FI, hi-fi high fidelity.
HIH His (or Her) Imperial Highness.
HIM His (or Her) Imperial Majesty.
HIS hic iacet sepultus here lies buried.
hist. historian; history.
HJ(S) hic jacet (sepultus) here lies (buried).
HK House of Keys (Isle of Man); Hong Kong (also IVR).
hl hectolitre(s).
HM His (or Her) Majesty.
HMA Headmasters' Association.
HMAS His (or Her) Majesty's Australian Ship.
HMC His (or Her) Majesty's Customs.
HMCS His (or Her) Majesty's Canadian Ship.
HMG His (or Her) Majesty's Government.
HMI His (or Her) Majesty's Inspector, Inspectorate.
HMP hoc monumentum posuit erected this monument.
HMS His (or Her) Majesty's Ship or Service.
HMSO His (or Her) Majesty's Stationery Office.
HMV His Master's Voice (gramophone company).
HNC Higher National Certificate.
HND Higher National Diploma.
Ho holmium.
ho. house.
Hon. Honourable; Honorary.
Hons Honours.
Hon. Sec. Honorary Secretary.
hor. horizon; horology.
hort., hortic. horticulture; horticultural.
HP hire-purchase; High Priest; half-pay; (or hp) horse-power.
HQ headquarters.
HR House of Representatives; Home Rule.
Hr Herr.
hr hour.
HRE Holy Roman Emperor or Empire.
HRH His (or Her) Royal Highness.
HRIP hic requiescit in pace here rests in peace.
HS hic situs here is laid.
HSE Health and Safety Executive; hic sepultus (or situs) est here is buried (or laid).
HSH His (or Her) Serene Highness.
HSS Historiae Societatis Socius Fellow of the Historical Society.
HT high tension.
HTV Harlech Television.
Hunts Huntingdonshire.

HWM   high water mark.
Hz   hertz (cycles per second).

I   iodine; Island, Isle; Italy (IVR).
I   electric current.
IA   Institute of Actuaries.
Ia.   Iowa.
IAAF   International Amateur Athletic Federation.
IAEA   International Atomic Energy Agency.
IAM   Institute of Advanced Motorists.
IAS   Indian Administrative Service.
IATA   International Air Transport Association.
IB   Institute of Bankers.
IBA   Independent Broadcasting Authority.
Ib., Ibid.   *ibidem* in the same place.
IBM   International Business Machines (computer manufacturers).
IBRD   International Bank for Reconstruction and Development (World Bank).
IC   integrated circuit.
I/c   in charge.
ICA   Institute of Contemporary Arts.
ICAO   International Civil Aviation Organisation.
ICBM   intercontinental ballistic missile.
ICE   Institution of Civil Engineers; internal combustion engine.
ICFC   Industrial and Commercial Finance Corporation.
IChemE   Institution of Chemical Engineers.
ICI   Imperial Chemical Industries.
ICJ   International Court of Justice.
ICL   International Computers Limited.
ICS   Indian Civil Service (in Republic of India, IAS).
ICWA   Institute of Cost and Works Accountants.
ID   Intelligence Department; identification; infectious diseases.
Id.   Idaho.
id.   *idem* the same.
IDA   International Development Association.
IDN   *in Dei nomine* in the name of God.
IDV   International Distillers and Vintners.
i.e., ie   *id est* that is.
IEC   International Electrotechnical Commission.
IEE   Institution of Electrical Engineers.
IF   intermediate frequency.
IFC   International Finance Corporation.
IHC, IHS   for the Greek capitals IHC (H, capital eta (= E) and C, a form of sigma (= S)), first two and last letters of *Iesous* Jesus, often misread as *Jesus Hominum Salvator* Jesus Saviour of Men.
ihp   indicated horse-power.
IL   Institute of Linguists; Israel (IVR).
ILC   irreversible letter of credit.
ILEA   Inner London Education Authority.
Ill.   Illinois.
ill.   illustration; illustrated.
ILN   Illustrated London News.
ILO   International Labour Organisation or (its secretariat) International Labour Office.
ILP   Independent Labour Party.
IMechE   Institution of Mechanical Engineers.
IMF   International Monetary Fund.
imit.   imitative.
IMM   Institution of Mining and Metallurgy.
Imp.   Imperial; *Imperator* Emperor.
imp.   (or *imperf.*) imperfect; (or *imper.*) imperative; *imprimatur* let it be printed; (or *impers.*) impersonal.
IMunE   Institution of Municipal Engineers.
In   indium.
in   inch(es).
inc.   including; incorporated.
incl.   including; included.
IND   Same as IDN; India (IVR).
Ind.   Indiana; Independent.

ind., indic.   indicative.
indecl.   indeclinable.
indef.   indefinite.
indiv.   individual.
Ind. Ter.   Indian Territory.
inf.   *infra* below; infantry; infinitive.
infra dig.   *infra dignitatem* beneath one's dignity.
init.   *initio* in the beginning.
in lim.   *in limine* on the threshold, at the outset.
in loc.   *in loco* in its place.
in loc. cit.   *in loco citato* in the place cited.
in pr.   *in principio* in the beginning.
INRI   *Jesus Nazarenus Rex Judaeorum* Jesus of Nazareth King of the Jews.
Inst.   Institute.
inst.   instant—the present month; institute.
Inst. P.   Institute of Physics.
int.   interest; interior; interpreter; international; integral.
Interpol   See Dict.
interrog.   interrogation; interrogative(ly).
in trans.   *in transitu* in transit.
intrans.   intransitive.
intro., introd.   introduction.
inv.   *invenit* designed it; invented; invoice.
IOB   Institute of Building.
IOC   International Olympic Committee.
IoJ   Institute of Journalists.
IOM   Isle of Man.
IOU   I owe you.
IOW   Isle of Wight.
IPA   Institute of Practitioners in Advertising; International Publishers' Association; International Phonetic Alphabet.
IPC   International Publishing Corporation.
IPCS   Institution of Professional Civil Servants.
IQ   Intelligence Quotient.
iq   *idem quod* the same as.
IQS   Institute of Quantity Surveyors.
IR   Iran (IVR).
Ir   iridium.
Ir.   Irish.
IRA   Irish Republican Army.
IRB   Irish Republican Brotherhood.
IRBM   intermediate range ballistic missile.
Irel.   Ireland.
IRL   Ireland (IVR).
IRQ   Iraq (IVR).
ISBN   International Standard Book Number.
ISCh   Incorporated Society of Chiropodists.
ISD   international subscriber dialling.
is(l).   island.
ISO   Imperial Service Order; International Organisation for Standardisation.
ISS   International Social Service.
ISSN   International Standard Serial Number.
ISTC   Iron and Steel Trades Confederation.
IT   Information Technology.
It.   Italian; Italian vermouth.
ITA   Independent Television Authority (now IBA).
ita   initial teaching alphabet.
ital.   italic; Italian.
ITN   Independent Television News.
ITO   International Trade Organisation.
ITT   International Telephone and Telegraph Corporation.
ITU   International Telecommunications Union.
ITV   Independent Television.
IU   international unit.
IU(C)D   intra-uterine (contraceptive) device.
IUPAC   International Union of Pure and Applied Chemistry.
IUPAP   International Union of Pure and Applied Physics.

IVR International Vehicle Registration.
IW Isle of Wight.

J joule; Japan (IVR).
J. Judge; Justice.
JAL Japan Air Lines.
Jan. January.
Jas James.
JC *Juris Consultus* Jurisconsult; Jesus Christ; Justice Clerk.
JCD *Juris Civilis Doctor* Doctor of Civil Law.
JCR junior common room.
JFK John Fitzgerald Kennedy.
JHS Same as IHC.
JMB Joint Matriculation Board.
Josh. Joshua.
JP Justice of the Peace.
Jr. Jun., Jun Junior.
JUD *Juris Utriusque Doctor* Doctor both of Canon and of Civil Law.
Jul. July.
Jun. June; Junior.
junc. junction.
jurisp. jurisprudence.

K Kelvin (thermometer scale); kelvin; *kalium* potassium.
k kilo-.
Kan. Kansas.
KB Knight of the Bath; Knight Bachelor; King's Bench.
KBE Knight Commander of the Order of the British Empire.
KC King's Counsel; King's College; Kennel Club.
KCB Knight Commander of the Bath.
KCMG Knight Commander of the Order of St Michael and St George.
KCVO Knight Commander of the (Royal) Victorian Order.
Ken. Kentucky.
KG Knight of the Order of the Garter.
kg kilogram(me)(s)..
KGB *Komitet Gosudarstvennoi Bezopasnosti* (Russ.) Committee of State Security.
KGCB Knight of the Grand Cross of the Bath.
kilo kilogram(me); kilometre.
k.k. *kaiserlich-königlich* (Ger.) Imperial-Royal.
KKK Ku Klux Klan.
KL Kuala Lumpur.
KLH Knight of the Legion of Honour.
KLM *Koninklijke Luchtvaart Maatschappij* (Du.) Royal Dutch Airlines.
KM Knight of Malta.
km kilometre(s).
kn knot (nautical, etc., measure).
KO, ko knock out; kick off.
K of L Knight of Labour.
kpg, kph kilometres per gallon, hour.
Kr krypton.
kr kreutzer; krone.
Ks. Kansas.
KT Knight of the Thistle.
Kt Knight.
Kt Bach. Knight Bachelor.
kW kilowatt.
kWh kilowatt-hour.
Ky. Kentucky.

L Lake; Latin; Liberal; lumen; learner (driver); *libra* pound; Luxembourg (IVR).
L symbol for inductance; luminance.
l litre (the abbreviation, though the accepted one, is undesirable as liable to be misread); latitude; league; left; long; (or lb) *libra* pound.

l length.
LA Law Agent; Literate in Arts; Los Angeles; Library Association.
La lanthanum.
La. Louisiana.
Lab. Labour.
lab. laboratory.
LAC Licentiate of the Apothecaries' Company.
LAMDA London Academy of Music and Dramatic Art.
Lancs Lancashire.
lang. language.
LAR Libya (IVR).
LASER light amplification by stimulated emission of radiation.
Lat. Latin.
lat. latitude.
lb *libra* pound.
lb, lbw leg before wicket.
LBC London Broadcasting Company.
lc lower-case (in printing); *loco citato* in the place cited; left centre; letter of credit.
LCD liquid crystal display.
LCh, LChir *Licentiatus Chirurgiae* Licentiate in Surgery.
LCJ Lord Chief-Justice.
LCM, lcm least common multiple.
Ld Lord.
Ldp, Lp Lordship.
LDS Licentiate in Dental Surgery.
LDV Local Defence Volunteers (later Home Guard).
LEA Local Education Authority.
LEAP Life Education for the Autistic Person.
lect. lecture.
LED light emitting diode.
leg. legal; legate; legislature.
Leics Leicestershire.
LEPRA Leprosy Relief Assocation.
lex. lexicon.
LF low frequency.
LGU Ladies Golf Union.
lh left hand.
LHD *Litterarum Humaniorum Doctor* Doctor of Letters.
LI Long Island; Light Infantry.
Li lithium.
Lib. Liberal.
lib. *liber* book.
lib. cat. library catalogue.
Lieut. Lieutenant.
LIFO last in, first out.
LILO last in, last out.
Lincs Lincolnshire.
liq. liquid.
lit. literal(ly); literature.
lith., litho., lithog. lithograph; lithography.
Lit. Hum. *litterae humaniores* humane letters, the humanities.
Lit(t)D *Litterarum Doctor* Doctor of Letters.
LJ Lord Justice.
LLB *Legum Baccalaureus* Bachelor of Laws.
LLCM Licentiate of the London College of Music.
LLD *Legum Doctor* Doctor of Laws.
LLM *Legum Magister* Master of Laws.
LM long metre.
lm lumen.
ln natural logarithm.
LNG liquefied natural gas.
LOB Location of Offices Bureau.
loc. cit. *loco citato* at the place quoted.
L of C line of communication.
log logarithm.
lon., long. longitude.

Lond. London.
Londinense *London Rhodesian* (industrial conglomerate).
loq. *loquitur* speaks.
LP long-playing (record); Lord Provost; low pressure; Labour Party.
LPG liquefied petroleum gas.
LPO London Philharmonic Orchestra.
Lr lawrencium; lira (Italian currency).
LRAM Licentiate of the Royal Academy of Music.
LRCP Licentiate of the Royal College of Physicians (Edin., of Edinburgh; Lond., of London; Irel., of Ireland).
LRCS Licentiate of the Royal College of Surgeons (Ed., of Edinburgh; Eng., of England; Irel., of Ireland).
LSA Licentiate of the Society of Apothecaries.
LSD lysergic acid diethylamide (a hallucinatory drug).
L.S.D. *librae, solidi, denarii* pounds, shillings, pence.
LSE London School of Economics.
LSO London Symphony Orchestra.
LT low tension.
Lt. Lieutenant.
LTA Lawn Tennis Association.
Lt.-Col. Lieutenant-Colonel.
Ltd limited liability.
Lt.-Gen. Lieutenant-General.
LTh Licentiate in Theology.
Lu lutetium.
LV luncheon voucher.
LWM low water mark.
LWT London Weekend Television.
lx lux.

M Member ... See note (2) p 1171; mega-.
M, m *mille* a thousand.
M. *Monsieur* (Fr.) Mr (pl. MM.).
m milli-; metre; mile; married; masculine; *meridiem* noon.
m mass.
3M Minnesota Mining and Manufacturing Company.
MA *Magister Artium* Master of Arts.
mach. machinery.
MAFF Ministry of Agriculture, Fisheries and Food.
mag. magazine; magnetic.
Maj. Major.
MAL Malaysia (IVR).
Man., Manit. Manitoba.
Man. Dir. Managing Director.
M & B ® a trademark of May & Baker Ltd. (used e.g. for sulphonamides prepared by this firm and, esp. formerly, others).
M & S Marks & Spencer.
Mar. March.
marg. margin; marginal; margarine.
Marq. Marquis.
mas., masc. masculine.
MASER microwave amplification by stimulated emission of radiation.
Mass. Massachusetts.
math., maths mathematics.
Matt. Matthew.
max. maximum.
mb millibar.
MB *Medicinae Baccalaureus* Bachelor of Medicine; mark of the Beast.
MBE Member of the Order of the British Empire.
MC Member of Congress; Master of Ceremonies; Military Cross.
MCC Marylebone Cricket Club; Member of the County Council.
MCh *Magister Chirurgiae* Master of Surgery.
MCP male chauvinist pig.
Mc/s megacycles per second (megahertz).
MD *Medicinae Doctor* Doctor of Medicine; mentally

deficient; Managing Director.
Md mendelevium.
Md. Maryland.
Mdlle, Mlle *Mademoiselle* (Fr.) Miss.
Mdm Madam.
MDS Master of Dental Surgery.
ME Methodist Episcopal; Mining or Mechanical Engineer; Most Excellent; Middle English.
Me. Maine.
mech. mechanic; mechanical.
med. medical; medicine; mediaeval; *medius, -a, -um* middle.
Mem. Member.
mem. memorandum; *memento* remember.
memo. memorandum.
MEP Member of the European Parliament.
Messrs *Messieurs* (Fr.) Sirs, Gentlemen; used as pl. of Mr.
met., meteor. meteorology.
metal., metall. metallurgy.
meth(s). methylated spirits.
MeV mega-electron-volt(s).
MEX Mexico (IVR).
Mex. Mexico; Mexican.
MEZ *Mitteleuropäische Zeit* (Ger.) Central European Time.
mf mezzo-forte.
mfd manufactured.
MFH Master of Foxhounds.
mfrs manufacturers.
MG machine-gun; Morris Garage.
Mg magnesium.
mg milligram(me)(s).
Mgr Monseigneur, Monsignor.
MHG Middle High German.
MHR Member of the House of Representatives.
MHz megahertz.
MI Military Intelligence; MI5 Security Services, MI6 Secret Intelligence Service (initials based on wartime Military Intelligence departments).
MI. Mississippi.
Mich. Michigan.
MICR magnetic ink character recognition.
MIDAS Missile Defence Alarm System.
Middx Middlesex.
mil., milit. military.
Min. Ministry.
min. mineralogy; minimum; minute.
Minn. Minnesota.
MIRV Multiple Independently Targeted Re-entry Vehicle (type of missile).
misc. miscellaneous; miscellany.
Miss. Mississippi.
MIT Massachusetts Institute of Technology.
MJ megajoule(s).
MJI Member of the Institute of Journalists.
MK (on cars) mark.
Mkk markka (Finnish currency).
MKS metre-kilogram-second unit, or system.
MKSA metre-kilogram-second-ampere unit, or system.
ml millilitre(s).
MLA Member of Legislative Assembly; Modern Language Association.
MLC Member of Legislative Council; Meat and Livestock Commission.
MLitt *Magister Litterarum* Master of Letters or Literature.
Mlle *Mademoiselle* (Fr.) Miss;—pl. **Mlles** *Mesdemoiselles*.
MLR minimum lending rate.
MM (Their) Majesties; Martyrs; Military Medal.
MM. *Messieurs* (Fr.) Gentlemen, Sirs.
mm millimetre(s).

Mme *Madame* (Fr.) Mrs;—pl. Mmes *Mesdames*.
MN Merchant Navy.
Mn manganese.
MO Medical Officer.
Mo molybdenum.
Mo. Missouri.
mo. month.
MOD Ministry of Defence.
mod. modern; moderate.
mod. con. modern convenience.
MOH Medical Officer of Health.
mol mole (unit).
mol. wt molecular weight.
Mon. Monmouthshire; Monday.
Monsig. Monsignor.
Mont. Montana; Montgomeryshire.
mos months.
MOS(T) metal oxide silicon (transistors).
MOT Ministry of Transport (now Transport Industries).
MP Member of Parliament; Military Police; Metropolitan Police; Municipal Police (US); mounted police.
mp mezzo-piano; melting-point.
mpg, mph miles per gallon, hour.
MPharm Master of Pharmacy.
MPS Member of the Pharmaceutical Society; Member of the Philological Society.
MR Master of the Rolls.
Mr Mister; Master.
MRA Moral Rearmament.
MRC Medical Research Council.
MRCA multirole combat aircraft.
MRCP Member of the Royal College of Physicians.
MRG Minority Rights Group.
Mrs Mistress (fem. of Mr, Mister).
MS manuscript; Master of Surgery; *Memoriae Sacrum* Sacred to the Memory; milestone; multiple sclerosis.
Ms. See Dict.
ms millisecond(s); (or M/S) months (after)
MSC Manpower Services Commission.
MSc Master of Science.
MSF medium standard frequency.
msl mean sea-level.
MSS manuscripts.
MST mountain standard time.
MSW Medical Social Worker.
MT Mechanical Transport; mean time.
Mt, mt mount.
MTh Master of Theology.
mth month.
Mts, mts mountains.
mus. music; museum.
MusB(ac) Bachelor of Music.
MusD(oc) Doctor of Music.
MusM Master of Music.
mv merchant vessel; motor vessel; muzzle velocity.
MVO Member of the Royal Victorian Order.
MW medium wave.
Mx Middlesex.
myth. mythology.

N nitrogen; newton; neper; North, Northern; Norway (IVR).
n name; noun; *natus* born; neuter; noon; nano-.
Na *natrium* sodium.
NAAFI Navy, Army, and Air-Force Institute(s) (providing canteens for the armed forces).
NACRO National Association for the Care and Resettlement of Offenders.
NALGO National and Local Government Officers' Association.
N and Q Notes and Queries.

NASA National Aeronautics and Space Administration (USA).
Nat. National.
nat. *natus* born.
nat. hist. natural history.
NATO North Atlantic Treaty Organisation.
nat. ord. natural order.
Nat. Phil. natural philosophy.
Nat. Sci. Natural Science(s).
NATSOPA National Society of Operative Printers, Graphical and Media Personnel.
NATTKE National Association of Television, Theatrical, and Kinematographic Employees.
Nat. West. National Westminster Bank.
naut. nautical.
nav. naval; navigation.
NAVAR combined navigation and radar system.
Nazi *Nazionale Sozialisten* (Ger.) German National Socialist Party.
NB New Brunswick; North Britain; North British; North bag (in postal sorting); (or nb) *nota bene* note well, or take notice.
Nb niobium.
NBC National Broadcasting Company (USA).
nbg no bloody good.
NBL National Book League.
NBS National Bureau of Standards (USA).
NC New Church; numerical control.
N.C. North Carolina.
NCB National Coal Board.
NCCL National Council for Civil Liberties.
NCO non-commissioned officer.
NCR National Cash Register Company.
ncv no commercial value.
Nd neodymium.
N.D., N.Dak. North Dakota.
nd no date, pot dated.
NDPS National Data Processing Service.
NE north-east; New England.
Ne neon.
NEB New English Bible; National Enterprise Board.
Neb., Nebr. Nebraska.
NEC National Executive Committee.
NED New English Dictionary (now OED).
NEDC National Economic Development Council (Neddy).
NEDO National Economic Development Office.
neg. negative.
NEI *non est inventus* has not been found.
nem. con *nemine contradicente* no one contradicting.
nem. diss. *nemine dissentiente* no one dissenting.
NERC Natural Environment Research Council.
Neth. Netherlands.
neut. neuter.
Nev. Nevada.
New M. New Mexico.
NF Norman French; Northern French; National Front.
N.F., Nfd Newfoundland.
NFER National Foundation for Educational Research.
NFS National Fire Service.
NFU National Farmers' Union.
NFWI National Federation of Women's Institutes.
NGA National Graphical Association.
N.H. New Hampshire.
NHBRC National House-Builders' Registration Council (or Certificate).
NHI National Health Insurance.
NHS National Health Service.
NI Northern Ireland; national insurance.
Ni nickel.
NIRC National Industrial Relations Court.
N.J. New Jersey.

NKVD *Narodny Komitet Vnutrennikh Del* (Russ.) People's Committee of Internal Affairs.
NL Netherlands (IVR).
NLRB National Labor Relations Board (USA).
N.M., N. Mex. New Mexico.
a mile international nautical mile.
NNE north-north-east.
NNI noise and number index.
NNW north-north-west.
N.O. New Orleans; natural order.
No nobelium.
no (or No) *numero* (in) number; not out.
nom., nomin. nominative.
Non-Coll. Non-Collegiate.
non-com. non-commissioned.
Noncon. Nonconformist.
non obst. *non obstante* notwithstanding.
non pros. *non prosequitur* does not prosecute.
non seq. *non sequitur* it does not follow (see Dict.).
non-U not upper class.
NOP National Opinion Poll.
nop not otherwise provided.
Northants Northamptonshire.
Northumb. Northumberland.
Nos, nos numbers.
Notts Nottinghamshire.
Nov. November.
NP Notary Public; New Providence; (or np) new paragraph.
Np neptunium.
np no place (of publication).
NPFA National Playing Fields Association.
NPG National Portrait Gallery.
NPL National Physical Laboratory.
nr near.
NRA National Rifle Association.
NS New Style; Nova Scotia.
ns nanosecond(s); not specified.
NSB National Savings Bank.
NSPCC National Society for Prevention of Cruelty to Children.
NSRA National Small-bore Rifle Association.
NSW New South Wales.
NT New Testament; Northern Territory; National Trust.
ntp normal temperature and pressure.
NTS National Trust for Scotland.
NU name unknown.
NUBE National Union of Bank Employees.
NUGMW National Union of General and Municipal Workers.
NUI National University of Ireland.
NUJ National Union of Journalists.
NUM National Union of Mineworkers.
Num., Numb. Numbers.
NUPE National Union of Public Employees.
NUR National Union of Railwaymen.
NUS National Union of Students; National Union of Seamen.
NUT National Union of Teachers.
NV New Version.
NV(A)LA National Viewers' and Listeners' Association.
nvd no value declared.
NW north-west.
NWT North-west Territory (Canada).
NY New York (city or state).
NYC New York City.
NYO National Youth Orchestra.
NZ New Zealand (also IVR).

O oxygen.
O. Ohio.

o/a on account of.
O&C Oxford and Cambridge (Schools Examination Board).
OAP Old Age Pension or Pensioner.
OAPEC Organisation of Arab Petroleum-Exporting Countries.
OAS on active service; Organisation of American States.
OAU Organisation of African Unity.
ob. *obiit* died.
obdt obedient.
OBE Officer of the Order of the British Empire.
obj. object; objective.
obl. oblique; oblong.
obs. obsolete; observation.
o/c overcharge.
OC Officer Commanding.
OCF Officiating Chaplain to the Forces.
OCR optical character recognition or reader.
Oct. October.
oct. octavo.
OCTU Officer Cadet Training Unit.
OD Ordnance Datum or Data.
OE Old English.
OECD Organisation for Economic Co-operation and Development.
OED Oxford English Dictionary.
OF Old French; Oddfellow.
off. official; officinal.
OFT Office of Fair Trading.
OHMS On His (or Her) Majesty's Service.
OK See Dict.
Okla. Oklahoma.
OM Order of Merit; Old Measurement.
ONC ordinary national certificate.
OND ordinary national diploma.
ono or near(est) offer.
Ont. Ontario.
Op. Opera; Opus.
op out of print.
op. opposite; operation.
op. cit. *opere citato* in the work cited.
OPEC Organisation of Petroleum-Exporting Countries.
opp. opposed; opposite.
Ops Operations; Operations Officer; Operations room.
opt. optative; *optime* very well indeed.
OR other ranks; operations research.
Or., Ore., Oreg. Oregon.
ord. ordained; order; ordinary; ordnance.
orig. origin; orginal(ly).
OS Old Style; Ordinary Seaman; outsize; Ordnance Survey.
Os osmium.
osp *obiit sine prole* died without issue.
OT Old Testament; occupational therapy.
OTC Officers' Training Corps.
OU Open University.
OUP Oxford University Press.
Oxbridge *Oxf*ord and *Cam*bridge.
Oxf. Oxford.
OXFAM Oxford Committee for *Fam*ine Relief.
Oxon. *Oxon*ia Oxford; *Oxon*iensis of Oxford.
oz ounce(s) (15th cent. It. *ōz*, abbreviation of *onza*).

P phosphorus; parking; President; Prince; pedal; Portugal (IVR).
P power.
p new penny; new pence; piano; pico-; page.
p. participle.
PA Press Association; Publishers Association; personal assistant; Public Address (system).
Pa protactinium; pascal.

Pa., Penn. Pennsylvania.
pa. past.
p.a. (or pa) per annum; participial adjective.
paint. painting.
Pal. Palestine.
pam. pamphlet.
Pan. Panama.
Pan Am Pan-American (World Airways Incorporated).
P and O Peninsular and Oriental (Steamship Navigation Co.).
pa.p. past participle.
par. paragraph; parallel; parish.
pass. passive.
pa.t. past tense.
Pat. Off. Patent Office.
PAYE Pay As You Earn (Income Tax).
PB Pharmacopoeia Britannica; Plymouth Brethren.
Pb *plumbum* lead.
PBX private branch exchange.
PC Police Constable; Privy Councillor; *Patres Conscripti* Conscript Fathers.
pc postcard.
pce piece.
PCM pulse code modulation.
PCS Principal Clerk of Session.
Pd palladium.
pd paid.
PDI pre-delivery inspection.
PDSA People's Dispensary for Sick Animals.
PE Protestant Episcopal; physical education.
p/e price-earnings ratio.
PEC photoelectric cell.
ped. pedal,
PEI Prince Edward Island.
PEN Poets, Playwrights, Editors, Essayists, and Novelists.
Pen. Peninsula.
Penn., Pa. Pennsylvania.
PEP Political and Economic Planning.
per. period; person.
per an. per annum.
per cent See Dict.
perf. perfect.
perh. perhaps.
per pro. *per procurationem* by the agency (of).
Pers. Persian.
pers. person; personal.
Pes. peseta (Spanish currency).
PF Procurator Fiscal; Patriotic Front.
Pf pfennig (German currency).
pf piano-forte.
PG paying guest.
Pg. Portugal; Portuguese.
PGA Professional Golfers' Association.
pH pH value (see Dict.).
phar., pharm pharmaceutical; pharmacopoeia; pharmacy.
PhB *Philosophiae Baccalaureus* Bachelor of Philosophy.
PhD *Philosophiae Doctor* Doctor of Philosophy.
Phil. Philadelphia; philology; philological; philosophy; philosophical.
phon., phonet. phonetics.
phonog. phonography.
phot. photography.
phr. phrase.
phys. physiology; physics; physician.
PIA Pakistan International Airlines.
PIB Prices and Incomes Board.
pinx. *pinxit* painted it.
PL Poet Laureate; Public Library.
pl. plural.
PLA Port of London Authority.

PLC, plc Public Limited Company.
PLO Palestine Liberation Organisation.
PLP Parliamentary Labour Party.
PLR public lending right.
plu., plur. plural.
plup. pluperfect.
PM Past Master; (or pm) *post meridiem* after noon; Postmaster; (or pm) *post mortem* after death; Prime Minister; Provost-Marshal.
Pm promethium.
pm premium.
PMG Postmaster-General; Paymaster-General.
PMO Principal Medical Officer.
Pmr Paymaster.
PMRAFNS Princess Mary's Royal Air Force Nursing Service.
pn promissory note.
PNdB perceived noise decibel.
PO Post Office; Petty Officer; Pilot Officer.
Po polonium.
po postal order.
po. pole.
pod pay on delivery.
Pol. Econ. Political Economy.
POO post-office order.
pop. population; popular.
pos., posit. positive.
POUNC Post Office Users' National Council.
POW prisoner of war.
PP parish priest; present pupil; past President.
pp pages; *per procurationem* by proxy (also *per pro* for and on behalf of); pianissimo.
p.p. past participle.
ppc picture post-card.
PPE Philosophy, Politics and Economics.
PPI Plan Position Indicator.
PPS *post postscriptum* a later additional postscript; Parliamentary Private Secretary.
PQ Province of Quebec.
PR prize ring; Puerto Rico; proportional representation; *Populus Romanus* the Roman people; public relations.
Pr praseodymium.
Pr. Prince; priest; Provençal.
pr. pair; per; present; price.
Preb. Prebend; Prebendary.
pref. preface.
prep. preparation; preparatory; preposition.
Pres. President.
pret. preterite.
Prin. Principal.
PRN *pro re nata* for special occasion arising.
PRO Public Relations Officer; Public Record Office.
pro. professional; prostitute; probationary.
prob. probably.
Prof. Professor.
PROP Preservation of the Rights of Prisoners.
prop. proper(ly); proposition; property.
Prot. Protestant.
pro tem. *pro tempore* for the time being.
Prov. Proverbs; Provincial; Provost.
prox. *proximo (mense)* next (month).
prox. acc. *proxime accessit* next (in order of merit) to the winner.
Pru. Prudential Assurance Company.
PS *post scriptum* written after (something), a postscript; Philological Society; Pharmaceutical Society.
Ps., Psa. Psalm(s).
PSA pleasant Sunday afternoon; Property Services Agency; Public Services Authority.
PSBR public sector borrowing requirement.
psc passed staff college.
pseud. pseudonym.

PST   Pacific Standard Time.
PSV   public service vehicle.
PT   physical training; pupil teacher; purchase tax.
Pt   platinum.
pt   part; pint(s); post-town.
PTA   Parent/Teacher Association.
Pte   private (military).
PTO   please turn over.
pty.   proprietary.
PU   pick-up.
Pu   plutonium.
pulv.   *pulvis* powder (*pharm.*).
PVC   polyvinyl chloride (a type of plastic).
pw   per week.
PWD   Public Works Department.
pwt   pennyweight.
pxt   *pinxit* painted.

Q   symbol for electric charge; quality.(-value).
Q., Qu.   query, question; (or Que.) Quebec; Queensland.
q   *quadrans* farthing; query; quintal.
QAB   Queen Anne's Bounty.
QARANC   Queen Alexandra's Royal Army Nursing Corps.
QARNNS   Queen Alexandra's Royal Naval Nursing Service.
QB   Queen's Bench.
QC   Queen's Counsel; Queen's College.
qd   *quasi dicat* as if he would say.
qe   *quod est* which is.
QE2   Queen Elizabeth the Second (liner).
QED   *quod erat demonstrandum* which was to be demonstrated.
QEF   *quod erat faciendum* which was to be done.
QEH   Queen Elizabeth Hall.
QEI   *quod erat inveniendum* which was to be found.
qid   *quater in die* four times a day.
ql   *quantum libet* as much as you please.
QM   Quartermaster.
qm   *quomodo* in what manner, how.
QMG   Quartermaster-General.
QMS   Quartermaster-Sergeant.
QPR   Queen's Park Rangers Football Club.
qq   quartos.
qqv   *quae vide* which (pl.) see (sing. qv).
qr   quarter.
qs, quant. suff.   *quantum sufficit* a sufficient quantity.
QSO   quasi-stellar object (quasar).
qt   quantity; quart(s).
q.t.   quiet.
qto   quarto.
qty   quantity.
Qu.   Queen; question.
qu., quar.   quart; quarter(ly).
quango   See Dict.
qv   *quod vide* which (sing.) see (pl. qqv); *quantum vis* as much as you will.

R   *rex, regina* King, Queen; rand (S. African currency); Röntgen unit; (or Réau) Réaumur's thermometric scale; Romania (IVR).
R   symbol for electric resistance.
®   registered trade mark.
r   right; radius; *recipe* take.
RA   Royal Academy or Academician; Royal Artillery; Rear Admiral; Argentina (IVR).
Ra   radium.
RAAF   Royal Australian Air Force.
RAC   Royal Automobile Club; Royal Armoured Corps.
Rad.   Radical.
rad   radian.
rad.   *radix* root.
RADA   Royal Academy of Dramatic Art.

RADC   Royal Army Dental Corps.
RAEC   Royal Army Educational Corps.
RAeS   Royal Aeronautical Society.
RAF   Royal Air Force.
RAM   Royal Academy of Music.
r.a.m.   relative atomic mass.
RAMC   Royal Army Medical Corps.
RAN   Royal Australian Navy.
R and A   Royal and Ancient (Golf Club) St Andrews.
R and B   rhythm and blues (type of popular music).
R and D   research and development.
RAOC   Royal Army Ordnance Corps.
RAPC   Royal Army Pay Corps.
RAS   Royal Astronomical Society; Royal Asiatic Society.
RAVC   Royal Army Veterinary Corps.
Rb   rubidium.
RBA   Royal Society of British Artists.
RBS   Royal Society of British Sculptors.
RC   Roman Catholic; Red Cross; Royal College of Art.
RCA   Royal Canadian Academy; Radio Corporation of America.
RCAF   Royal Canadian Air Force.
RCM   Royal College of Music; Regimental Court-martial.
RCMP   Royal Canadian Mounted Police.
RCN   Royal Canadian Navy.
RCOG   Royal College of Obstetricians and Gynaecologists.
RCP   Royal College of Physicians.
RCS   Royal College of Surgeons; Royal Corps of Signals; Royal College of Science.
RCT   Royal Corps of Transport.
RCVS   Royal College of Veterinary Surgeons.
RD   Rural Dean; Naval Reserve Decoration; refer to drawer.
Rd   Road; rand (S. African currency).
RDC   Rural District Council.
RDS   Royal Dublin Society.
RE   Royal Engineers; Royal Society of Etchers and Engravers; Royal Exchange.
Re   rhenium.
Réau   Réaumur's thermometric scale.
rec.   *recipe* take.
recd   received.
REconS   Royal Economic Society.
ref.   referee; reference.
Ref. Ch.   Reformed Church.
Reg. Prof.   Regius Professor.
regt   regiment.
rel.   relating; relation; relative.
rel. d.   relative density.
REME   Royal Electrical and Mechanical Engineers.
rep.   representative; republic; report; reporter.
rept   receipt; report.
retd   retired; returned.
Rev.   revise(d); revision; (or Revd) Reverend.
rev   revolution.
Rev. Ver.   Revised Version.
RF   *République française* (Fr.) French Republic; radio frequency.
Rf   rutherfordium.
RFC   Rugby Football Club.
RFU   Rugby Football Union.
RGG   Royal Grenadier Guards.
RGN   Registered General Nurse.
RGS   Royal Geographical Society.
Rgt   Regiment.
RH   Royal Highness.
Rh   rhodium; rhesus (see Dict.).
rh   right hand.
RHA   Royal Horse Artillery; Royal Hibernian Academy; Road Haulage Association.

rhet. rhetoric.

RHF Royal Highland Fusiliers.

RHG Royal Horse Guards.

RHistS Royal Historical Society.

RHM Rank Hovis McDougall.

RHS Royal Humane Society; Royal Horticultural Society; Royal Historical Society; Royal Highland Show.

RI Royal Institute of Painters in Water Colours; Rhode Island; religious instruction; Indonesia (IVR).

RIA Royal Irish Academy.

RIAM Royal Irish Academy of Music.

RIBA Royal Institute of British Architects.

RIC Royal Irish Constabulary; Royal Institute of Chemistry.

RICS Royal Institution of Chartered Surveyors.

RIGB Royal Institution of Great Britain.

RIP *requiescat in pace* may he (or she) rest in peace.

RIPHH Royal Institute of Public Health and Hygiene.

RJET remote job entry terminal.

RL Lebanon (IVR).

RLO returned letter office.

RLS Robert Louis Stevenson.

Rly, rly railway.

RM Royal Mail; Royal Marines.

RMA Royal Military Academy, Sandhurst; Royal Marine Artillery.

RMetS Royal Meteorological Society.

RMO Resident Medical Officer.

RMP (Corps of) Royal Military Police.

RMS Royal Mail Steamer; Royal Microscopical Society.

RN Royal Navy.

Rn . radon.

RNA ribonucleic acids (see Dict.).

RNAS Royal Naval Air Service(s).

RNIB Royal National Institute for the Blind.

RNLI Royal National Lifeboat Institution.

RNR Royal Naval Reserve.

RNVR Royal Naval Volunteer Reserve.

RNZAF Royal New Zealand Air Force.

RNZN Royal New Zealand Navy.

ro *recto* on the right-hand page.

ROC Royal Observer Corps.

ROI Royal Institute of Oil Painters.

Rom. Romans.

rom. roman (in printing).

Ro-Ro roll-on-roll-off.

ROSPA see RSPA.

RP Reformed Presbyterian; Regius Professor; Received Pronunciation; Royal Society of Portrait Painters.

RPA radiation protection adviser.

RPI retail price index.

RPM retail price maintenance.

rpm, rps revolutions per minute, second.

RPO Royal Philharmonic Orchestra.

RPS Royal Photographic Society.

RR Right Reverend.

RRE Radar Research Establishment.

RRP recommended retail price.

RS Royal Society.

Rs Rupees.

RSA Royal Society of Antiquaries; Royal Society of Arts; Royal Scottish Academy or Academician; Republic of South Africa.

RSE Royal Society of Edinburgh.

RSFSR Russian Soviet Federated Socialist Republic.

RSG Regional Seats of Government.

RSL Royal Society of Literature.

RSM Regimental Sergeant-Major; Royal Society of Medicine; Royal School of Music.

RSO railway sub-office; railway sorting office; rural

sub-office; radiological safety officer; Resident Surgical Officer.

RSPA, Rospa Royal Society for the Prevention of Accidents.

RSPB Royal Society for the Protection of Birds.

RSPCA Royal Society for the Prevention of Cruelty to Animals.

RSS (or **SRS**) *Regiae Societatis Socius* Fellow of the Royal Society; Royal Statistical Society.

RSV Revised Standard Version.

RSVP *répondez s'il vous plaît* (Fr.) reply, if you please.

RT radiotelephone, -phony.

RTE *Radio Telefis Éireann* (Ir.) Irish Television.

Rt Hon. Right Honourable.

RTO Railway Transportation (or Traffic) Officer.

Rt Rev. Right Reverend.

RTZ Rio Tinto Zinc Corporation Limited.

RU Rugby Union.

Ru ruthenium.

RUC Royal Ulster Constabulary.

R-unit Röntgen unit—unit of measurement of X-ray radiation.

RV Revised Version.

RWS Royal Society of Painters in Water Colours.

Ry, ry railway.

RYA Royal Yachting Association.

RYS Royal Yacht Squadron.

RZS Royal Zoological Society (E, of Edinburgh).

S sulphur; square; stokes; siemens; South; Sabbath; Saint; society; sun; Sweden (IVR).

s second(s).

$ dollar.

SA South Africa; South America; South Australia; Salvation Army; sex-appeal; *Société anonyme* (Fr.) limited liability company; Society of Arts; Society of Antiquaries (Scot., of Scotland).

sa *secundum artem* according to art; *sine anno* without date.

sae stamped addressed envelope.

SALT Strategic Arms Limitation Talks.

SAM surface-to-air missile.

SARAH Search and Rescue and Homing.

SAS *Societatis Antiquariorum Socius* Fellow of the Society of Antiquaries; Scandinavian Airlines System; Special Air Service.

Sask. Saskatchewan.

Sat. Saturday.

S.A.T.B. soprano, alto, tenor, bass.

SAYE save as you earn.

Sb *stibium* antimony.

SBN Standard Book Number.

SC *senatus consultum* a decree of the Roman senate; Special Constable; Supreme Court; Staff College; Staff Corps.

S.C. South Carolina.

Sc scandium.

sc *scilicet* namely; *sculpsit* (he) sculptured (this); (or s. caps, sm. caps) small capitals (in printing).

s/c self-contained.

ScB *Scientiae Baccalaureus* Bachelor of Science.

ScD *Scientiae Doctor* Doctor of Science.

SCE Scottish Certificate of Education.

SCF Save the Children Fund.

Sch. schilling (Austrian currency); school.

sci.fa. *scire facias* that you cause to know.

sci. fi. science fiction.

scil., sciz, *scilicet* namely (cf. **viz**).

SCL Student of Civil Law.

SCM Student Christian Movement; State Certified Midwife.

Scot. Scotland; Scottish.

SCR senior common room.

Script. Scripture.

SCUBA self-contained underwater breathing apparatus.

sculp., sculpt. *sculpsit* (he) sculptured (this); sculpture; sculptor.

S.D., S.Dak. South Dakota.

sd *sine die* without a day (fixed).

SDA Scottish Development Agency.

SDC single data converter.

SDLP Social and Democratic Labour Party.

SDP social, domestic and pleasure; Social Democratic Party.

SDR special drawing rights.

SE south-east; Society of Engineers.

Se selenium.

SEAC South-East Asia Command.

SEATO South-East Asia Treaty Organisation.

Sec., Secy Secretary.

sec secant.

sec. *secundum* in accordance with; second; section.

sech hyperbolic secant.

sec. leg. *secundum legem* according to law.

sec. reg. *secundum regulam* according to rule.

sect. section.

SED Scottish Education Department.

Sem. seminary; Semitic.

SEN State Enrolled Nurse.

Sen. Senator; senior.

Sep., Sept. September; Septuagint.

seq. *sequens* following (pl. **seqq.,** *sequentes* or *sequentia*).

Serg., Sergt Sergeant.

Sess. Session.

SF science fiction; Sinn Fein; signal frequency; Finland (IVR).

SFA Scottish Football Association; Sweet Fanny Adams (= nothing at all).

sfz sforzando.

SG Solicitor-General.

sg specific gravity.

SGHWR steam-generating heavy water reactor.

SGP Singapore (IVR).

SHAEF Supreme Headquarters of the Allied Expeditionary Force.

SHAPE Supreme Headquarters Allied Powers Europe.

shv *sub hoc verbo* or *sub hac voce* under this word.

SI Système International (d'Unités).

Si silicon.

sig. signature.

sin sine.

sing. singular.

sinh hyperbolic sine.

SIPRI Stockholm International Peace Research Institute.

SIS Secret Intelligence Service.

SJ Society of Jesus.

SL Solicitor at Law; Sergeant-at-Law; (or S Lat.) South latitude.

SLADE Society of Lithographic Artists, Designers, Engravers and Process Workers.

sld sailed.

slp *sine legitima prole* without lawful issue.

SM Short Metre; Sergeant-Major.

Sm samarium.

Smith. Inst. Smithsonian Institution.

SMLondSoc *Societatis Medicae Londiniensis Socius* Member of the London Medical Society.

SMM *Sancta Mater Maria* Holy Mother Mary.

SMMT Society of Motor Manufacturers and Traders.

SMO Senior Medical Officer.

SMP School Mathematics Project.

smp *sine mascula prole* without male issue.

Sn *stannum* tin.

sn *secundum naturam* according to nature.

SNCF *Société Nationale des Chemins de Fer français* (Fr.) French national railways.

SNO Scottish National Orchestra.

SNP Scottish National Party.

SO Staff Officer; Signal Officer; standing order; special order.

so seller's option.

s.o.b. son of a bitch.

Soc. Society.

SOGAT Society of Graphical and Allied Trades.

Sol., Solr Solicitor.

sol. solution.

Sol.-Gen. Solicitor-General.

sop. soprano.

SOS See Dict.

sp *sine prole* without issue.

sp. spelling; species (pl. **spp.**).

SPCK Society for Promoting Christian Knowledge.

SPG Special Patrol Group.

sp.gr. specific gravity (now relative density).

SPQR *Senatus Populusque Romanus* the Senate and People of Rome.

SPR Society for Psychical Research.

sps *sine prole superstite* without surviving issue.

spt seaport.

SPUC Society for the Protection of the Unborn Child.

sp.vol. specific volume.

sq. (or **Sq.**) square; *sequens* following (in pl. **sqq.,** *sequentes* or *sequentia*).

sqn squadron.

SR Southern Region.

Sr senior; Sir; Señor; strontium.

sr steradian.

SRC Science Research Council; Student Representative Council.

SRCh State Registered Chiropodist.

SRI *Sacrum Romanum Imperium* Holy Roman Empire.

SRN State Registered Nurse.

SRS (or **RSS**) *Societatis Regiae Socius* Fellow of the Royal Society.

SRU Scottish Rugby Union.

SS Saints; *Schutzstaffel* (Ger.) Hitler's bodyguard.

ss steamship; screw steamer.

SSAFA Soldiers', Sailors' and Airmen's Families Association.

SSC Solicitor before the Supreme Court (Scotland); *Societas Sanctae Crucis* Society of the Holy Cross.

SSD *Sanctissimus Dominus* Most Holy Lord (the Pope).

SSE south-south-east.

SSM surface-to-surface missile.

SSN Standard Serial Number.

SSRC Social Science Research Council.

SST supersonic transport.

SSW south-south-west.

St Saint; Strait; Street.

st. stone (weight).

Staffs Staffordshire.

STD subscriber trunk dialling.

std standard.

Ste *Sainte* (Fr.) fem. of Saint.

ster., stereo stereophonic; stereotype.

ster., stg sterling.

STOL short take-off and landing.

STP *Sanctae Theologiae Professor* Professor of Theology.

stp standard temperature and pressure.

str steamer.

str. strong.

STS Scottish Text Society.

STUC Scottish Trades Union Congress.

STV Scottish Television; Single Transferable Vote.

SU strontium unit—unit of measurement of strontium radiation; Scripture Union; Soviet Union (also IVR).

sub. subject.

subj. subject; subjunctive.

subst. substitute; substantive.

suf., suff. suffix.

sup. superfine; superior; (or **superl.**) superlative; supreme; *supra* above; supine; supplement.

superl. superlative.

supp., suppl. supplement.

Supr. Supreme.

Supt Superintendent.

Surg. surgeon; surgery.

sv *sub voce* under that heading; *sub verbo* under the word.

SW south-west; small women('s); short wave.

SWALK sealed with a loving kiss.

SWG standard wire gauge.

syn. synonym.

T tritium; tesla.

t tonne (cf. **l**, litre).

t time.

TA Territorial Army.

Ta tantalum.

tal. qual. *talis qualis* just as they come, average quality.

tan tangent.

tanh hyperbolic tangent.

TASS *Telegrafnoye Agentsvo Sovietskovo Soyuza* (Russ.) telegraph agency of the Soviet Union; Technical, Administrative and Supervisory Section (of AUEW).

Tb terbium.

TB tuberculosis.

Tc technetium.

TCCB Test and County Cricket Board.

TCD Trinity College Dublin; Twentieth Century Dictionary.

TCL Trinity College of Music, London.

TCP trichlorophenylmethyliodosalicyl (a proprietary germicide).

TD Territorial Decoration; *Teachta Dála* (Ir.) member of the Dáil.

Te tellurium.

tech. technical; technology.

TEFL teaching English as a foreign language.

tel. telephone.

tel., teleg. telegram; telegraph.

temp. temporal; *tempore* in the time of; temperature; temporary.

Ten., Tenn. Tennessee.

ten. tenor.

Ter., Terr. Territory; terrace.

term. termination.

TES Times Educational Supplement.

TESL teaching English as a second language.

Test. Testament.

Teut. Teutonic.

Tex. Texas.

Text. Rec. *textus receptus* the revised text.

TF Territorial Force.

tf till forbidden.

TFR Territorial Force Reserve.

TGWU Transport and General Workers' Union.

Th thorium.

Th. Thursday.

ThD Doctor of Theology.

theat. theatrical.

theol. theology; theologian.

THES Times Higher Educational Supplement.

THF Trust Houses Forte.

ThL Theological Licentiate.

Tho., Thos Thomas.

TI Tube Investments.

Ti titanium.

tid *ter in die* thrice a day.

TIF *Transports Internationaux par Chemin de Fer* (Fr.) International Rail Transport.

TIR *Transports Internationaux Routiers* (Fr.) International Road Transport.

TIROS Television and Infrared Observation Satellite.

Tl thallium.

TLS Times Literary Supplement.

TM transcendental meditation.

Tm thulium.

TN trade name.

TNT trinitrotoluene.

TO turn over; Telegraph-office; Transport Officer.

Toc H Talbot House.

TPI Town Planning Institute.

tpr teleprinter.

TR Turkey (IVR).

tr. transpose; transactions; translator; trustee.

trans. transitive; translated; translation.

TRH Their Royal Highnesses.

trig. trigonometry.

Trin. Trinity.

TSB Trustee Savings Bank.

TSO town sub-office.

TT teetotal; Tourist Trophy; tuberculin tested.

Tu., Tues. Tuesday.

TUC Trades Union Congress.

TV television.

TVA Tennessee Valley Authority.

TVP texturised vegetable protein.

TWA Trans-World Airlines.

TWI Training within Industry.

typ., typo. typographer; typography.

U uranium; Unionist; upper-class (see Dict. under U); Uruguay (IVR).

UAR United Arab Republic.

UCAR Union of Central African Republics.

UCATT Union of Construction, Allied Trades and Technicians.

UCCA Universities Central Council on Admissions.

UDA Ulster Defence Association.

UDC Urban District Council; Universal Decimal Classification.

UDI Unilateral Declaration of Independence.

UDR Ulster Defence Regiment.

UDT United Dominions Trust.

UEFA Union of European Football Associations.

UF United Free Church (of Scotland).

UFO unidentified flying object.

UGC University Grants Committee.

UHF ultra high frequency.

UJD *Utriusque Juris Doctor* Doctor of both Laws (Canon and Civil).

UK United Kingdom.

UKAEA United Kingdom Atomic Energy Authority.

ULCC ultra large crude carriers.

ult., ulto *ultimo* in the last (month); ultimate(ly).

UMIST University of Manchester Institute of Science and Technology.

UN United Nations.

UNA United Nations Association.

UNCTAD, Unctad United Nations Commission for Trade and Development.

UNEP United Nations Environment Programme.

UNESCO United Nations Educational, Scientific and Cultural Organisation.

UNICEF United Nations International Children's Emergency Fund—now United Nations Children's Fund.

UNIDO United Nations Industrial Development Organisation.

Unit. Unitarian.

Univ. University; Universalist.
UNO United Nations Organisation.
UNRRA United Nations Relief and Rehabilitation Administration.
UP United Presbyterian; United Press.
UPU Universal Postal Union.
UPW Union of Post Office Workers.
Uru. Uruguay.
US United States; United Service(s); Under-secretary.
us *ut supra* as above.
USA United States of America (also IVR); United States Army.
USAF United States Air Force.
USCL United Society for Christian Literature.
USDAW Union of Shop, Distributive and Allied Workers.
USIS United States Information Service.
USN United States Navy.
USPG United Society for the Propagation of the Gospel.
USS United States Ship or Steamer.
USSR (also CCCP (Russ.)) Union of Soviet Socialist Republics.
usu. usually.
USW ultrasonic waves; ultrashort waves.
usw *und so weiter* (Ger.) and so forth.
UT Universal Time.
Ut. Utah.
ut dict. *ut dictum* as said.
ut sup. *ut supra* as above.
UU Ulster Unionist.
uv ultraviolet.
UVF Ulster Volunteer Force.
UWIST University of Wales Institute of Science and Technology.

V vanadium; volt.
V symbol for electric potential difference.
v velocity; *versus* against; *vide* see; verb; verse; volume.
VA Royal Order of Victoria and Albert; Vicar Apostolic; volt-ampere(s).
Va. Virginia.
vac. vacuum; vacation.
VAD Voluntary Aid Detachment.
val. value.
V and A Victoria and Albert Museum.
var. variant; variety; variable.
var. lect. *varia lectio* variant reading.
VAT Value-added Tax.
Vat. Vatican.
vb verb.
VC Victoria Cross; Vice-Chancellor; Vice-Consul.
VCR video cassette recorder.
VD Venereal Disease(s); Volunteer (Officers') Decoration.
vd various dates; vapour density.
VDC Volunteer Defence Corps.
VDQS *Vins délimités de qualité supérieure* (Fr.) wines of superior quality from approved vineyards.
VDU visual display unit.
VE Victory in Europe (1945).
veg. vegetable(s).
Ven. Venerable.
VERA versatile reactor assembly; vision electronic recording apparatus.
verb. sap. *verbum sapienti*, or **verb. sat.**, *verbum sat(is)* a word to the wise is enough.
Vet., Veter. Veterinary.
Vet. Surg. Veterinary Surgeon.
VF voice frequency; video frequency.
VG Vicar-General; (or vg) very good.
vg *verbi gratia* for example.
VHF very high frequency.

v.i. verb intransitive.
Vic. Vicar; Vicarage.
Vict. Victoria; Victoria University.
vid. *vide* see.
vil(l). village.
VIP Very Important Person.
VIR *Victoria Imperatrix Regina*. See VRI.
Vis., Visc. Viscount.
viz *videlicet* namely (z = mediaeval Latin symbol of contraction).
VJ Victory over Japan (1945).
vl *varia lectio* variant reading (pl. vvll).
VLCC very large crude carrier.
VLF very low frequency.
vo *verso* on the left-hand page.
voc. vocative.
vocab. vocabulary.
vol. volunteer; volume.
VP Vice-President.
VR *Victoria Regina* Queen Victoria.
VRD Volunteer Reserve Decoration.
VRI *Victoria Regina et Imperatrix* Victoria, Queen and Empress.
VRQ verbal reasoning quotient.
VS Veterinary Surgeon; *volti subito* turn quickly.
VSO Voluntary Service Overseas.
VSOP very special old pale.
Vt Vermont.
v.t. verb transitive.
VTO(L) vertical take-off (and landing).
VTR video tape recorder.
Vul., Vulg. Vulgate.
vul., vulg. vulgar.
vvll See vl.
VW *Volkswagen* (Ger.) people's car.
vy various years.

W *wolframium* tungsten; watt; West; Welsh; women('s).
w weak.
WA West Africa; Western Australia.
WAAC Women's Army Auxiliary Corps (now WRAC).
WAAF Women's Auxiliary Air Force (earlier and later WRAF).
Wash. Washington.
WASP White Anglo-Saxon Protestant.
Wb weber.
WBA West Bromwich Albion Football Club; World Boxing Association of America.
WBC World Boxing Council.
WC water-closet; Western Central; Wesleyan Chapel.
WCC World Council of Churches.
W/Cdr Wing-Commander.
WCT World Championship Tennis.
WEA Workers' Educational Association.
Wed. Wednesday.
wef with effect from.
WEU Western European Union.
wf wrong fount (in printing).
WFTU World Federation of Trade Unions.
wg wire gauge.
WHO World Health Organisation.
WI West Indies; Women's Institute.
Wilts Wiltshire.
Wis. Wisconsin.
wk week.
WLF Women's Liberal Federation.
Wm William.
WMO World Meteorological Organisation.
WNP Welsh Nationalist Party.
WNW west-north-west.
WO War Office (1964 absorbed in Ministry of Defence); Warrant Officer; walk-over.
Worcs Worcestershire.

Wp, Wpfl Worshipful.
WP Warsaw Pact.
wp weather permitting.
wpb wastepaper basket.
wpm words per minute.
WR Western Region.
WRAC Women's Royal Army Corps.
WRAF Women's Royal Air Force.
WRI Women's Rural Institute.
WRNS Women's Royal Naval Service.
WRVS Women's Royal Voluntary Service (previously WVS).
WS Writer to the Signet.
WSW west-south-west.
wt weight.
W.Va. West Virginia.
WVS Women's Voluntary Service (now WRVS).
WWF World Wildlife Fund.
Wy., Wyo. Wyoming.

X, Xt Christ. (*X* = Gr. *Ch*)
x ex (L. without), as in x.d., ex dividend.
Xe. xenon.
Xm., Xmas Christmas.
Xn, Xtian Christian.

Y yttrium; yen (Japanese currency).
y year; yard.
Yb ytterbium.
yd yard.
ye the (the y not being a y but representing the old letter thorn, þ).
Yeo. Yeomanry.
YHA Youth Hostels Association.
YMCA Young Men's Christian Association.
Yn yen (Japanese currency).
Yorks. Yorkshire.
yr your; younger; year.
yt that (y as in ye above).
YTV Yorkshire Television.
YU Yugoslavia (IVR).
YWCA Young Women's Christian Association.

ZA South Africa (IVR).
zB *zum Beispiel* (Ger.) for example.
Zn zinc.
ZPG zero population growth.
Zr zirconium.
ZST Zone Standard Time.

Some useful conversion tables

The following tables may be used for conversion from British to metric (SI) units and vice versa.

in to cm		cm to in	ft to m		m to ft	miles to km		km to miles
2·54	1	0·3937	0·3048	1	3·28084	1·60934	1	0·62137
5·08	2	0·7874	0·6096	2	6·562	3·219	2	1·243
7·62	3	1·1811	0·9144	3	9·843	4·828	3	1·864
10·16	4	1·5748	1·2192	4	13·123	6·437	4	2·485
12·70	5	1·9685	1·5240	5	16·404	8·047	5	3·107
15·24	6	2·3622	1·8288	6	19·685	9·656	6	3·728
17·78	7	2·7559	2·1336	7	22·966	11·265	7	4·350
20·32	8	3·1496	2·4384	8	26·247	12·875	8	4·971
22·86	9	3·5433	2·7432	9	29·528	14·484	9	5·592

sq in to sq cm		sq cm to sq in	sq ft to sq m		sq m to sq ft	sq miles to sq km		sq km to sq miles
6·4516	1	0·155	0·0929	1	10·764	2·58999	1	0·3861
12·903	2	0·310	0·1858	2	21·528	5·18	2	0·772
19·355	3	0·465	0·2787	3	32·292	7·77	3	1·158
25·806	4	0·620	0·3716	4	43·056	10·36	4	1·544
32·258	5	0·775	0·4645	5	53·820	12·95	5	1·931
38·710	6	0·930	0·5574	6	64·583	15·54	6	2·317
45·161	7	1·085	0·6503	7	75·347	18·13	7	2·703
51·613	8	1·240	0·7432	8	86·111	20·72	8	3·089
58·064	9	1·395	0·8361	9	96·875	23·31	9	3·475

fl oz to cm³		cm³ to fl oz	imp gal to litre		litre to imp gal	oz to g		g to oz
28·4131	1	0·03519	4·54596	1	0·21997	28·3495	1	0·03527
56·826	2	0·0704	9·092	2	0·4400	56·6990	2	0·07054
85·239	3	0·1056	13·638	3	0·6599	85·0485	3	0·10581
113·652	4	0·1408	18·184	4	0·8799	113·3980	4	0·14108
142·065	5	0·1760	22·730	5	1·0999	141·7475	5	0·17635
170·478	6	0·2111	27·276	6	1·3199	170·0970	6	0·21162
198·891	7	0·2463	31·822	7	1·5398	198·4465	7	0·24689
227·304	8	0·2815	36·368	8	1·7598	226·7960	8	0·28216
255·717	9	0·3167	40·914	9	1·9798	255·1455	9	0·31743

lb to kg		kg to lb	ton to tonne		tonne to ton	lbf to newton		newton to lbf
0·45359	1	2·20462	1·0160	1	0·984205	4·4482	1	0·2248
0·907	2	4·409	2·032	2	1·9684	8·896	2	0·4496
1·361	3	6·614	3·048	3	2·9526	13·345	3	0·6744
1·814	4	8·818	4·064	4	3·9368	17·793	4	0·8992
2·268	5	11·023	5·080	5	4·9210	22·241	5	1·1240
2·722	6	13·228	6·096	6	5·9052	26·689	6	1·3489
3·175	7	15·432	7·112	7	6·8894	31·138	7	1·5737
3·629	8	17·637	8·128	8	7·8736	35·586	8	1·7985
4·082	9	19·842	9·144	9	8·8578	40·034	9	2·0233

Examples of use of tables

Reading from line 7 of the first table:

$$7 \text{ in} = 17·78 \text{ cm and } 7 \text{ cm} = 2·7559 \text{ in.}$$

Values above 9 may be obtained by decimal point adjustment and addition. Taking an example based on the third table:

To convert 573 miles to km	500 miles =	804·7 km
	70 miles =	112·65 km
	3 miles =	4·828 km
	573 miles =	922·178 km

Such results should be treated as approximations. In the example given the conversion of 500 miles is correct only to the nearest 0·1 km, therefore the final sum can be correct only to the same degree; hence the conversion of 573 miles from the table is correctly stated as '922·2 km to the nearest 0·1 km'. The precise figure for 573 miles is 922·154 112 km.

Temperature conversion table

°F to °C	°C	°C to °F
− 17·78	0	32·0
− 12·22	10	50·0
− 6·67	20	68·0
− 1·11	30	86·0
4·44	40	104·0
10·00	50	122·0
15·56	60	140·0
21·11	70	158·0
26·68	80	176·0
32·24	90	194·0
37·80	100	212·0

SI metric units of measurement

The Système International d'Unités has been internationally adopted as a coherent system of units for the measurement of all physical quantities.

Base units

Seven independent quantities have been chosen which are measured in the *base units* of the system (Table 2)

Derived units

To measure any other quantity, a *derived unit* is formed by multiplying or dividing any two or more base units, or powers of them, together; e.g. speed is measured in metres per second, where the metre and the second are base units. The more frequently used derived units have been given names of their own for convenience; e.g power is measured in watts, where one watt is derived from one kilogram multiplied by one metre squared divided by one second cubed.

Abbreviations

Each unit name has an agreed abbreviation (column 3 in Table 2). To abbreviate a unit compounded from more than one unit name, the abbreviations of the constituent units are written with a small space between them; e.g a newton metre is abbreviated N m. Where a unit is raised to a power, the conventional algebraic indices are used; e.g. a metre squared, or square metre, is abbreviated m^2.

Division of units

The word *per* indicates division by all succeeding units. To abbreviate units which are to be divided, negative indices are preferred, but a solidus (/) may be used; e.g metre per second is abbreviated $m\,s^{-1}$ or m/s, kilogram per metre cubed is $kg\,m^{-3}$ or kg/m³.

Multiples and Submultiples

To avoid the use of many zeroes in either very large or very small numbers, prefixes indicating multiplication or division by some power of a thousand (Table 1) can be added to a unit, e.g. mega-: multiply by a million, so a megawatt (1 MW) is a million watts; milli- divide by a thousand, so a milliwatt (1 mW) is a thousandth of a watt.

TABLE 1

prefix	abbrev.	factor	prefix	abbrev.	factor
exa-	E	10^{18} = million million million	*deci-	d	10^{-1} = tenth
peta-	P	10^{15} = thousand million million	*centi-	c	10^{-2} = hundredth
tera-	T	10^{12} = million million	milli-	m	10^{-3} = thousandth
giga-	G	10^{9} = thousand million	micro-	μ	10^{-6} = millionth
mega-	M	10^{6} = million	nano-	n	10^{-9} = thousand millionth
kilo-	k	10^{3} = thousand	pico-	p	10^{-12} = million millionth
*hecto-	h	10^{2} = hundred	femto-	f	10^{-15} = thousand million millionth
*deca-	da	10 = ten	atto-	a	10^{-18} = million million millionth
*deka-/					

* These prefixes are used only exceptionally where kilo- or milli- would be impractical; thus a centimetre ($\frac{1}{100}$ metre) is accepted as an everyday unit of convenient size, but it is not a preferred SI unit.

TABLE 2

Equivalents are given to four significant figures' accuracy, except where they are exact as indicated by bold figures.

Quantity	SI unit	abbreviation and derivation	equivalent in British units	SI equivalent of one British unit
Base units				
Length	metre	m	3·281 feet	0·3048 m
Mass*	kilogram	kg	2 205 pounds	0·453 592 37 kg
Time	second	s	—	—
Temperature interval	kelvin	K	$\frac{5}{9}$ °Fahrenheit	$\frac{5}{9}$ K
Current, electric	ampere	A	—	—
Amount of substance	mole	mol	—	—
Luminous intensity	candela	cd	0·9833 candle	1·017 cd
Some derived and additional units				
Length	kilometre	km	0·6214 mile	1·609 km
	centimetre	cm	0·3937 inch	2·54 cm
*Mass	tonne, metric ton	$t = Mg$	0·9842 ton	1·016 t
Area	metre squared	m^2	10·76 ft^2	0·092 90 m^2
	hectare	$ha = 10\,000\ m^2$	2·471 acres	0·4047 ha
Volume	metre cubed	m^3	1·308 yd^3	0·7646 m^3
	litre	$l = dm^3$	0·2200 gal (UK)	4·546 litres
*Weight; Force	newton	$N = kg\ m\ s^{-2}$	0·2248 lbf	4·448 N
Energy; Work; Heat	joule	$J = m\ N$ $= kg\ m^2\ s^{-2}$	$\left\{\begin{array}{l} 0\text{·}2388\ \text{calorie} \\ 0\text{·}7376\ \text{ft lbf} \\ 1\ kJ = 0\text{·}9478\ \text{Btu} \end{array}\right.$	4·1868 J 1·356 J 1·055 kJ
Power	watt	$W = J\ s^{-1}$ $= kg\ m^2\ s^{-3}$	0·001 341 hp	745·7 W
Velocity; Speed	metre per second	$m\ s^{-1}$	3·281 ft/s	0·3048 $m\ s^{-1}$
	kilometre per hour	$km\ h^{-1}$	0·6214 mile/h	1·609 $km\ h^{-1}$
Pressure; Stress	pascal	$Pa = N\ m^{-2}$	1 kPa = 0·1450 lbf/in^2	6·895 kPa
	bar	$bar = 10^5\ Pa$	14·50 lbf/in^2	0·068 95 bar
Frequency	hertz	$Hz = s^{-1}$	1 c/s	1 Hz
Angle	radian	rad	57° 18'	$\frac{\pi}{180}$ rad
Solid angle	steradian	sr	—	—
Temperature, absolute	degree Celsius or Centigrade	°C	$(\frac{9}{5}\ t°C + 32)$ °F	$\frac{5}{9}$ (t °F − 32) °C
	kelvin	K	$\frac{9}{5}$ degree Rankine	$\frac{5}{9}$ K
Potential difference; Electromotive force	volt	$V = kg\ m^2\ s^{-3}\ A^{-1} = W\ A^{-1}$		
Resistance Reactance Impedance $\Big\}$ electrical	ohm	$\Omega = kg\ m^2\ s^{-3}\ A^{-2} = V\ A^{-1}$		
Capacitance, electrical	farad	$F = kg^{-1}\ m^{-2}\ s^4\ A^2 = A\ s\ V^{-1}$		
Inductance, magnetic	henry	$H = kg\ m^2\ s^{-2}\ A^{-2} = V\ s\ A^{-1}$		

* The mass of a body is the quantity of matter in it; its weight is the force with which the earth attracts it, and is directly proportional to its mass. The use of the term 'weight', where 'mass' is strictly intended, is acceptable in non-technical usage when referring to objects within the earth's atmosphere

Mathematical symbols

$+$	plus	$\propto$	varies directly as
$-$	minus	∞	infinity
$\pm$	plus or minus	i or j	imaginary square root of -1

$+$ plus

$-$ minus

$\pm$ plus or minus

$\times$ multiply by

$\div$ divide by

$=$ is equal to

$\equiv$ is identically equal to

$\left.\begin{array}{l}\approx\\\simeq\\\fallingdotseq\end{array}\right\}$ is approximately equal to

$\neq$ is not equal to

$>$ is greater than

$\gg$ is much greater than

$\ngtr$ is not greater than

$<$ is less than

$\ll$ is much less than

$\nless$ is not less than

$\geqslant$ is greater than or equal to

$\leqslant$ is less than or equal to

$\cap$ intersection

$\cup$ union

$\in$ is member of set

$\subset$ is a subset of

$\exists$ there exists

$\forall$ for all values of

$\cdot$ denotes an operation

$\Leftrightarrow$ is equivalent to; if and only if

$\Rightarrow$ implies

$\left.\begin{array}{l}\{\}\\\varnothing\end{array}\right\}$ empty set

$\{x, y\}$ the set whose members are x and y

E universal set

N the set of natural numbers

W the set of whole numbers

Z the set of integers

Q the set of rational numbers

R the set of real numbers

C the set of complex numbers

$\rightarrow$ maps to

$\therefore$ therefore

$\because$ because

$\angle$ angle

$\parallel$ parallel

$\perp$ perpendicular

x^n $x.x.x \ldots$ to n factors

x^{-n} $\dfrac{1}{x^n}$

$\sqrt{x}$ the square root of x

$x^{\frac{1}{n}}, \sqrt[n]{x}$, the nth root of x

$x^0 = 1$

$x \rightarrow a$ x approaches the limit a

$x!, \lfloor x$ factorial x

$\propto$ varies directly as

∞ infinity

i or j imaginary square root of -1

$\left.\begin{array}{l}\omega, \omega^2\\h, h^2\end{array}\right\}$ the complex cube roots of 1, $\frac{1}{2}(-1 \pm \sqrt{3i})$

π pi; the ratio of the circumference of a circle to its diameter, 3·14159...

e, ε (1) the base of natural logarithms, 2·718 28 ..
(2) the eccentricity of a conic section

$\log_n x$ log x to the base n

$\left.\begin{array}{l}\log_{10} x\\\lg x\end{array}\right\}$ log x to the base 10, i.e. common logarithm

$\log_e x, \ln x$ log x to the base e, i.e. natural or Napierian (q.v.) logarithm

M modulus of common logarithms
$\log_{10} e = 0.4343\ldots$
$(\log_{10} x = \log_e x \times 0.4343)$

$\sin \theta = y/r$

$\cos \theta = x/r$

$\tan \theta = y/x$

$\sec \theta = r/x$

$\operatorname{cosec} \theta = r/y$

$\cot \theta = x/y$

$\left.\begin{array}{l}\sin^{-1} x\\\arcsin x\end{array}\right\}$ the principal value of the angle whose sine is x

Similarly $\cos^{-1} x$, arccos x, etc.

sh x, sinh x (hyperbolic sine of x) $\frac{1}{2}(e^x - e^{-x})$

ch x, cosh x $\frac{1}{2}(e^x + e^{-x})$

th x, tanh x sh x/ch x

sech x, cosech x, coth x 1/ch x, 1/sh x, 1/th x

Σ the sum of the terms

Π the product of the terms

$|x|$ the absolute value of x

$\bar{x}$ the mean value of x

$\begin{vmatrix} a_1 & b_1 & c_1 \\ a_2 & b_2 & c_2 \\ a_3 & b_3 & c_3 \end{vmatrix}$ a determinant representing $a_1 b_2 c_3 - a_1 b_3 c_2 + a_3 b_1 c_2 - a_2 b_1 c_3 + a_2 b_3 c_1 - a_3 b_2 c_1$

$f(x), F(x), \phi(x)$, etc function of x

Δ finite difference or increment

$\Delta x, \delta x$ the increment of x

$\dfrac{dy}{dx}, D_x y$ the derivative of y with respect to x

$F'(x)$ stands for $\dfrac{d(F(x))}{dx}$

$\dfrac{d^n y}{dx^n}$ the nth derivative of y with respect to x

$\dfrac{\partial y}{\partial u}$ the partial derivative of y with respect to u, where y is a function of u and another variable (or variables)

∇ $\dfrac{\partial}{\partial x} + \dfrac{\partial}{\partial y} + \dfrac{\partial}{\partial z}$ vector derivative

∇^n nth vector derivative

$\int$ integral

Roman numerals

I	=	1	L	=	50
II	=	2	LI	=	51
III	=	3	LII, etc.	=	52, etc.
IV (or IIII, e.g. on clocks)	=	4	LX	=	60
V	=	5	LXI	=	61
VI	=	6	LXII, etc.	=	62, etc.
VII	=	7	LXX	=	70
VIII	=	8	LXXI	=	71
IX	=	9	LXXII, etc.	=	72, etc.
X	=	10	LXXX	=	80
XI	=	11	LXXXI	=	81
XII	=	12	LXXXII, etc.	=	82, etc.
XIII	=	13	XC	=	90
XIV	=	14	XCI	=	91
XV	=	15	XCII, etc.	=	92, etc.
XVI	=	16			
XVII	=	17	C	=	100
XVIII	=	18	CC	=	200
XIX	=	19	CCC	=	300
XX	=	20	CCCC or CD	=	400
XXI	=	21	D	=	500
XXII, etc.	=	22, etc.	DC	=	600
XXX	=	30	DCC	=	700
XXXI	=	31	DCCC	=	800
XXXII, etc.	=	32, etc.	CM (or DCCCC)	=	900
XL	=	40			
XLI	=	41	M	=	1000
XLII, etc.	=	42, etc.	MM	=	2000

The Greek alphabet

A	α	alpha	=	a		N	ν	nū	=	n
B	β	bēta	=	b		Ξ	ξ	xī	=	x (*ks*)
Γ	γ	gamma	=	g		O	o	omīcron	=	o
Δ	δ	delta	=	d		Π	π	pī	=	p
E	ε	epsīlon	=	e		P	ρ	rhō	=	r
Z	ζ	zēta	=	z		Σ	σ ς	sigma	=	s
H	η	ēta	=	ē		T	τ	tau	=	t
Θ	θ ϑ	thēta	=	th (*th*)		Υ	υ	ūpsīlon	=	u (*yōō*, *ŏŏ*, *ü*)
								(often transcribed *y*)		
I	ι	iōta	=	i		Φ	φ	phī	=	ph (*f*)
K	κ	kappa	=	k		X	χ	chī	=	kh (*hh*)
								(often transcribed *ch*, as in Latin)		
Λ	λ	lambda	=	l		Ψ	ψ	psī	=	ps
M	μ	mū	=	m		Ω	ω	ōmega	=	ō

The Greek alphabet, apart from its use as the official script in Greek-speaking areas, is of world-wide importance as a source of symbols used in all branches of science and mathematics. The equivalents in our alphabet given above are intended as a guide to transliteration and as an indication of the anglicised pronunciation of ancient Greek. We have not attempted to describe modern Greek pronunciation. See also Dict. under **digamma**.

Some geographical facts

Countries and capitals of the world

Country	Capital	Country	Capital
Afghanistan	Kabul	France	Paris
Albania	Tirana	French Guiana	Cayenne
Algeria	Algiers	French Polynesia	Papeete
Andorra	Andorra La Vella		
Angola	Luanda	Gabon	Libreville
Antigua	St John's	Gambia	Banjul
Argentina	Buenos Aires	Federal Republic of	
Australia	Canberra	Germany (West)	Bonn
Austria	Vienna	German Democratic	
		Republic (East)	East Berlin
Bahamas	Nassau	Ghana	Accra
Bahrain	Manama	Gibraltar	Gibraltar
Bangladesh	Dacca	Greece	Athens
Barbados	Bridgetown	Grenada	St George's
Belgium	Brussels	Guadeloupe	Pointe à Pitre
Belize	Belmopan	Guam	Agaña
Benin	Porto Novo	Guatemala	Guatemala City
Bermuda	Hamilton	Guinea	Conakry
Bhutan	Thimbu	Guinea-Bissau	Bissau
Bolivia	La Paz	Guyana	Georgetown
Botswana	Gaborone		
Brazil	Brasilia	Haiti	Port au Prince
Brunei	Bandar Seri Begawan	Honduras	Tegucigalpa
Bulgaria	Sofia	Hungary	Budapest
Burma	Rangoon		
Burundi	Bujumbura	Iceland	Reykjavik
		India	Delhi
Cambodia see		Indonesia	Jakarta
Kampuchea		Iran	Tehran
Cameroon	Yaoundé	Iraq	Baghdad
Canada	Ottawa	Irish Republic	Dublin
Cape Verde Islands	Praia	Israel	Jerusalem
Cayman Islands	George Town	Italy	Rome
Central African Republic	Bangui	Ivory Coast	Abidjan
Chad	Ndjaména		
Chile	Santiago	Jamaica	Kingston
China	Peking	Japan	Tokyo
Colombia	Bogotá	Jordan	Amman
Comoros	Moroni		
Congo	Brazzaville	Kampuchea (Cambodia)	Phnom Penh
Costa Rica	San José	Kenya	Nairobi
Cuba	Havana	Kiribati Republic	Tarawa
Cyprus	Nicosia	North Korea	Pyongyang
Czechoslovakia	Prague	Korea	Seoul
		Kuwait	Kuwait
Denmark	Copenhagen		
Djibouti	Djibouti	Laos	Vientiane
Dominica	Roseau	Lebanon	Beirut
Dominican Republic	Santo Domingo	Lesotho	Maseru
		Liberia	Monrovia
Ecuador	Quito	Libya	Tripoli
Egypt	Cairo	Liechtenstein	Vaduz
El Salvador	San Salvador	Luxemb(o)urg	Luxemb(o)urg
Equatorial Guinea	Malabo		
Ethiopia	Addis Ababa	Madagascar	Antananarivo
		Malawi	Lilongwe
Falkland Islands	Stanley	Malaysia	Kuala Lumpur
Fiji	Suva	Maldive Islands	Malé
Finland	Helsinki	Mali	Bamako

Country	Capital	Country	Capital
Malta	Valletta		
Martinique	Fort de France	Singapore	Singapore
Mauritania	Nouakchott	Solomon Islands	Honiara
Mauritius	Port Louis	Somalia	Mogadishu
Mexico	Mexico City	South Africa	Cape Town
Mongolia	Ulan Bator		(legislative)
Montserrat	Plymouth		Pretoria
Morocco	Rabat		(administrative)
Mozambique	Maputo	South West Africa see	
		Namibia	
Namibia (South West		Spain	Madrid
Africa)	Windhoek	Sri Lanka	Colombo
Nepal	Kathmandu	Sudan	Khartoum
Netherlands	Amsterdam*	Surinam	Paramaribo
		Swaziland	Mbabane

* Amsterdam is the official capital;
The Hague is the seat of government

Country	Capital	Country	Capital
		Sweden	Stockholm
		Switzerland	Berne
Netherlands Antilles	Willemstad	Syria	Damascus
New Caledonia	Noumea		
New Hebrides see		Taiwan	Taipei
Vanuatu		Tanzania	Dar-es-Salaam
New Zealand	Wellington	Thailand	Bangkok
Nicaragua	Managua	Togo	Nuku'alofa
Niger	Niamey	Trinidad and Tobago	Port of Spain
Nigeria	Lagos	Tunisia	Tunis
Norway	Oslo	Turkey	Ankara
		Turks and Caicos Islands	Grand Turk
Oman	Muscat	Tuvalu	Funafuti
Pakistan	Islamabad	Uganda	Kampala
Panama	Panama City	United Arab Emirates	Abu Dhabi
Papua New Guinea	Port Moresby	United Kingdom	
Paraguay	Asunción	England	London
Peru	Lima	Northern Ireland	Belfast
Philippine Islands	Manila	Scotland	Edinburgh
Poland	Warsaw	Wales	Cardiff
Portugal	Lisbon	United States of America	Washington D.C.
Puerto Rico	San Juan	Upper Volta	Ouagadougou
		Uruguay	Montevideo
Qatar	Doha	USSR	Moscow
Romania	Bucharest	Vanuatu (New Hebrides)	Vila
Rwanda	Kigali	Venezuela	Caracas
		Vietnam	Hanoi
St Helena	Jamestown	Virgin Islands (U.K.)	Road Town
St Kitts-Nevis-Anguilla	Basseterre	Virgin Islands (U.S.)	Charlotte Amalie
St Lucia	Castries		
St Vincent	Kingstown	Yemen Arab Republic	Sana'a
American Samoa	Pago Pago	(North Yemen)	
Western Samoa	Apia	Yemen People's	Aden
San Marino	San Marino	Democratic Republic	
São Tomé e Príncipe	São Tomé	(South Yemen)	
Saudi Arabia	Riyadh (royal)	Yugoslavia	Belgrade
	Jeddah		
	(administrative)	Zaire	Kinshasa
Senegal	Dakar	Zambia	Lusaka
Seychelles	Victoria	Zimbabwe	Harare (formerly
Sierra Leone	Freetown		Salisbury)

Counties and regions of the United Kingdom

Common written abbreviations of the English counties are given in brackets after each county. The form *Salop* is also used in speech. There are no commonly used abbreviations for Welsh and Northern Irish counties or Scottish regions.

England

Avon
Bedfordshire (Beds.)
Berkshire (Berks.)
Buckinghamshire (Bucks.)
Cambridgeshire (Cambs.)
Cheshire (Ches.)
Cleveland
Cornwall (Corn.)
Cumbria
Derbyshire (Derbys.)
Devon
Dorset (Dors.)
Durham (Dur.)
Essex
Gloucestershire (Glos.)

Hampshire (Hants.)
Hereford and Worcester
Hertfordshire (Herts.)
Humberside
Isle of Wight (I. of W.)
Kent
Lancashire (Lancs.)
Leicestershire (Leics.)
Lincolnshire (Lincs.)
County of London
County of Manchester
Merseyside
Norfolk (Norf.)
Northamptonshire (Northants.)
Northumberland (Northd.)

North Yorkshire (North Yorks.)
Nottinghamshire (Notts.)
Oxfordshire (Oxon.)
Shropshire (Salop)
Somerset (Som.)
South Yorkshire (South Yorks.)
Staffordshire (Staffs.)
Suffolk (Suff.)
Surrey
Sussex
Tyne and Wear
Warwickshire (Warwicks.)
West Midlands
West Yorkshire (West Yorks.)
Wiltshire (Wilts.)

Wales

Clwyd
Dyfed
Gwent

Gwynedd
Mid Glamorgan
Powys

South Glamorgan
West Glamorgan

Northern Ireland

Antrim
Armagh

Down
Fermanagh

Londonderry
Tyrone

Scotland

Borders
Central
Dumfries and Galloway
Fife

Grampian
Highland
Lothian
Orkney

Shetland
Strathclyde
Tayside
Western Isles

States of the United States of America

Alabama
Alaska
Arizona
Arkansas
California
Colorado
Connecticut
Delaware
(District of Columbia)
Florida
Georgia
Hawaii
Idaho
Illinois
Indiana
Iowa
Kansas

Kentucky
Louisiana
Maine
Maryland
Massachusetts
Michigan
Minnesota
Mississippi
Missouri
Montana
Nebraska
Nevada
New Hampshire
New Jersey
New Mexico
New York
North Carolina

North Dakota
Ohio
Oklahoma
Oregon
Pennsylvania
Rhode Island
South Carolina
South Dakota
Tennessee
Texas
Utah
Vermont
Virginia
Washington
West Virginia
Wisconsin
Wyoming

Clothing and Shoe Sizes

The following tables show equivalent sizes of clothes and shoes according to the British, American, and continental European measurement systems. The equivalents are only approximate.

Shoes

British	3	3½	4	4½	5	5½	6	6½	7
American	4½	5	5½	6	6½	7	7½	8	8½
Continental	36	36	37	38	38	39	39	40	41

British		7½	8	8½	9	9½	10	10½	11
American		8½	9½	9½	10½	10½	11½	11½	12
Continental		42	42	43	43	44	44	45	46

Men's Shirts

British	14	14½	15	15½	16	16½	17	17½
American	14	14½	15	15½	16	16½	17	17½
Continental	35/36	37	38	39/40	41	42	43	44

Women's dresses

British	8	10	12	14	16	18	20	22
American	6	8	10	12	14	16	18	20
Continental	36	38	40	42	44	46	48	50

Inch/centimetre equivalents

Inch	12	13	14	15	16	17	18	19	20	21
Cm	30	33	35	38	41	43	45	48	51	53

Inch	22	23	24	25	26	27	28	29	30	32
Cm	55	58	61	63	66	69	71	74	76	81

Inch	34	36	38	40	42	44	46	48	50
Cm	85	91	97	102	107	112	117	122	125

ISO paper sizes

The A series is used for standard book printing and stationery, the B series for posters, wall charts, etc. The dimensions given are of trimmed sizes.

A series	mm	inches
A0	841 × 1189	33·11 × 46·81
A1	594 × 841	23·39 × 33·11
A2	420 × 594	16·54 × 23·39
A3	297 × 420	11·69 × 16·54
A4	210 × 297	8·27 × 11·69
A5	148 × 210	5·83 × 8·27
A6	105 × 148	4·13 × 5·83
A7	74 × 105	2·91 × 4·13
A8	52 × 74	2·05 × 2·91
A9	37 × 52	1·46 × 2·05
A10	26 × 37	1·02 × 1·46

B series		
B0	1000 × 1414	39·37 × 55·67
B1	707 × 1000	27·83 × 39·37
B2	500 × 707	19·68 × 27·83
B3	353 × 500	13·90 × 19·68
B4	250 × 353	9·84 × 13·90
B5	176 × 250	6·93 × 9·84
B6	125 × 176	4·92 × 6·93
B7	88 × 125	3·46 × 4·92
B8	62 × 88	2·44 × 3·46
B9	44 × 62	1·73 × 2·44
B10	31 × 44	1·22 × 1·73